Tolley™

Tax Direct

GW00602788

Instant access to the latest tax news and developments online...

Tax Direct is the ultimate online service that provides you with instant access to the most [...] information and the latest news, cases and legislative developments.

Tax Direct comprises two complementary modules:

Tax Direct News

Providing up-to-the-minute tax news, this unrivalled service features the latest tax cases, legislative developments and official guidance, as well as commentary and views from the respected Tolley tax journals and newsletters. Further resources include: updated tax office addresses; a Finance Bill tracking service; rates and allowances; exchange rates; indexation factors; and a Points of Practice page.
Tax Direct News is easy to use, with a range of invaluable tools:

- Hypertext links from all new developments to relevant reference materials
- A customisable email alerter service
- A fast and intelligent search facility
- The ability to personalise the page to feature the news of importance to you.

Tax Direct Library

Featuring a vast range of works from Tolley, **Tax Direct Library** contains all the tax information your practice needs. With expert commentary and guidance from authoritative works such as Simon's and De Voil, regularly updated legislation in the Yellow and Orange, a tax case library with reports and digests of all important tax cases and the complete set of Tolley Annuals, **Tax Direct Library** is the ultimate online service for tax professionals. Furthermore, its intuitive search facilities, clear navigation tools and hypertext links make it a user-friendly and time-saving business tool.

Tax Direct Full Service

Combine both the News and Library modules for a complete set of up-to-date tax information.

Tax Direct can be accessed through an ordinary web browser such as Internet explorer (version 3 or higher) or Netscape Navigator (version 3 or higher) with all the timesaving search facilities these powerful tools provide. The service can therefore be easily installed and accessed through your company intranet system.

Tax Direct Full Service: Single User: £1835 + VAT
Tax Direct News Service: Single User £340 + VAT Product code: TNCD
Tax Direct Library: Single User £1495 + VAT Product Code: TRSD

Yellow Tax Handbook
2002–03

42nd Edition

PART I

The legislation relating to—
income tax
corporation tax
capital gains tax
for the year

2002–03

CONSULTANT EDITOR
MALCOLM GAMMIE QC FTII ATT
of One Essex Court
Past President, The Chartered Institute of Taxation

Members of the LexisNexis Group worldwide

United Kingdom	LexisNexis Butterworths Tolley, a Division of Reed Elsevier (UK) Ltd, Halsbury House, 35 Chancery Lane, LONDON, WC2A 1EL, and 4 Hill Street, EDINBURGH EH2 3JZ
Argentina	LexisNexis Argentina, BUENOS AIRES
Australia	LexisNexis Butterworths, CHATSWOOD, New South Wales
Austria	LexisNexis Verlag ARD Orac GmbH & Co KG, VIENNA
Canada	LexisNexis Butterworths, MARKHAM, Ontario
Chile	LexisNexis Chile Ltda, SANTIAGO DE CHILE
Czech Republic	Nakladatelství Orac sro, PRAGUE
France	Editions du Juris-Classeur SA, PARIS
Hong Kong	LexisNexis Butterworths, HONG KONG
Hungary	HVG-Orac, BUDAPEST
India	LexisNexis Butterworths, NEW DELHI
Ireland	Butterworths (Ireland) Ltd, DUBLIN
Italy	Giuffrè Editore, MILAN
Malaysia	Malayan Law Journal Sdn Bhd, KUALA LUMPUR
New Zealand	LexisNexis Butterworths, WELLINGTON
Poland	Wydawnictwo Prawnicze LexisNexis, WARSAW
Singapore	LexisNexis Butterworths, SINGAPORE
South Africa	Butterworths SA, DURBAN
Switzerland	Stämpfli Verlag AG, BERNE
USA	LexisNexis, DAYTON, Ohio

A CIP Catalogue record for this book is available from the British Library.

1st Edition   September 1962

42nd Edition   August 2002

ISBN   0 406 950350 (Parts I and II); 0 406 955468 (Part I)

Visit us at our website: http://www.butterworths.com; **or email on:** yellowandorange@butterworths.com

Typeset, printed and bound in Great Britain by William Clowes Limited, Beccles and London.

CONTENTS

i

FINANCE ACT 2002—KEY DATES

17 April 2002 **Budget Day**
24 July 2002 **Finance Act 2002 passed**

PREFACE

The march of new tax legislation, tax regulation, departmental guidance and tax cases is relentless. Practitioners, with some justification, can feel battered from all sides by the volume of material that emerges each year, not just within the UK but, nowadays, for both direct and indirect taxes, from Europe. At times it seems a small miracle to find amidst the torrent at least one statutory provision that remains unamended and unaffected by new developments.

This year has proved no exception. The current editions of the Yellow and Orange Tax Handbooks incorporate the additions and amendments that have been made to all the main taxes by the 500 pages of the Finance Act 2002. They include the secondary legislation and departmental guidance and refer to the new cases that have emerged since the 2001-02 editions.

The scope of the change in some areas is significant. The 2002 Act provides a comprehensive new tax regime for intellectual property, goodwill and intangible assets—a field of taxation previously governed by provisions that originated more than 150 years ago at the inception of the income tax. Youth, however, is no guarantee against change. The Act contains substantial amendments to the foreign exchange and loan relationships legislation, both of which were first enacted within the last ten years. The length of legislative provision is also not a guide to its significance: thus the four lines reducing the starting rate of corporation tax to zero has a considerable impact on the choice of business form.

The prospect of a new Income Tax (Earnings and Pensions) Act and a new regime modernising stamp duty for land transactions already promises that the process of change will continue in 2003. Given the amount of material, the days are long gone since the Tax Handbooks were of a size and weight that could easily be transported. Nevertheless, the aim of the Tax Handbooks remains to provide in a manageable and accessible form the best guidance available for users to track current tax legislation and to chart a course through it for those whom they advise. We hope that we have achieved this objective in 2002-03 but we are always looking for ways to refine and improve the Tax Handbooks and to that end I am always pleased to receive comments and suggestions from users on the layout and content of the Tax Handbooks.

PUBLISHERS' NOTE

Tax legislation

The Yellow and Orange Tax Handbooks are indispensable to the practitioner who needs to refer to the tax legislation as currently in force. Each year the legislation is augmented and amended by one or more Finance Acts and lesser amendments are made from time to time by a variety of other statutes. An increasing amount of the detailed regulation of taxes is contained in statutory instruments—orders or regulations—which are also amended frequently. The Handbooks are normally published annually. They contain the text of the relevant statutes and statutory instruments as amended together with current texts of extra-statutory concessions, statements of practice, published official interpretations and decisions, selected press releases and internal guidance where available.

The Yellow Tax Handbook (Parts I & II) covers income tax, corporation tax, capital gains tax, inheritance tax, national insurance contributions, tax credits and petroleum revenue tax. Its companion volume, the Orange Tax Handbook, covers value added tax, stamp duties, insurance premium tax, landfill tax, aggregates levy and climate change levy.

This edition of the Yellow Tax Handbook contains texts in the version applicable to the year 2002–03 as known at the date when the Finance Act 2002 was passed. It does not take account of any changes made after that date.

Organisation

The text of the Handbook is arranged in the following order—Part I: UK statutes relating to income tax, corporation tax, and capital gains tax including FA 2002 and Part II: statutory instruments, EC legislation, concessions, statements of practice, official interpretations and decisions, selected press releases, miscellaneous non-statutory material, followed by separate sections for inheritance tax, national insurance contributions, tax credits, petroleum revenue tax, and destination tables for consolidation statutes. National insurance contributions and tax credits material, which were formerly in the Orange Tax Handbook, now appear in Part II of Yellow. This is due to the transfer of functions from the DSS to the Inland Revenue in relation to NIC matters. It also reflects practitioners' needs, particularly those dealing with PAYE who want to see income tax and NICs together. Inheritance tax and petroleum revenue tax have also been moved from the Orange Tax Handbook to Part II of this handbook as they are direct taxes and therefore more appropriately positioned here.

Within each category, items are printed in chronological order. To enable individual items to be located quickly, an item reference is printed in bold type in the outside top corner of each page.

Amendments and modifications

Amendments to existing legislation which take effect for the current year are made in the text of the amended legislation. An **Amendment** note under the amended text indicates the authority for the amendment and, where appropriate, the timing of its commencement. All relevant provisions of the Finance Act 2002 are reproduced in full but otherwise the text of provisions which merely amend other Acts is generally omitted and replaced by a note indicating the legislation amended.

Sometimes the effect of a provision is modified by a later Act or statutory instrument but the scope of the modification is limited in some way so that the original provision remains generally unaffected. In this case, the original provision is printed without modification but a **Cross reference** to the later Act or statutory instrument is provided, see below.

Prospective amendments

The Handbook sets out the text of the legislation as it applies for the current tax year. Amendments which are stated to come into effect on a specified date after the end of that year are therefore strictly outside the scope of the current edition and are not made in the text of the Act affected. However, a **Prospective amendment** note is provided to indicate the existence of the amendment and the provision making the prospective amendment is retained in full in successive editions of the Handbook until the amendment becomes effective.

Retrospective amendments

For the tax legislation as it applied in an earlier year, reference should be made to the appropriate earlier edition of the Yellow Tax Handbook. Care must be taken, however, to ensure that amendments made retrospectively are not overlooked. A list of provisions affected by amendments made retrospectively by the Finance Act 2002 is provided at the front of this edition. Similar lists are provided for amendments made by each year's Finance Act(s) in the corresponding earlier editions.

Repealed legislation

Generally, repealed legislation is omitted. Exceptionally, where it may be necessary to refer to the repealed text in dealing with tax liabilities for the current year, the text is retained and is printed in italics.

Defined terms

Where a word or phrase used in the main Acts has been defined elsewhere, a cross-reference to the definition is provided in a **Definitions** note below the text.

Cross references

The notes under each section or Schedule paragraph include references to commentary in *Simon's Direct Tax Service* and to other relevant statutory provisions, statutory instruments, tax cases, published Revenue practice and other published or unpublished official and professional bodies' views. These are presented under the following headings—

Commentary—refers to paragraph number for commentary relating to the provision in *Simon's Direct Tax Service*.

Concession; Statement of Practice; Revenue interpretation; Revenue decision—refer to published official practice separately reproduced in this Handbook.

Revenue & other press releases—refer to published or unpublished official and professional bodies' views reproduced in this Handbook or *BDO Stoy Hayward Yellow Tax Guide* or elsewhere.

Revenue Internal Guidance—refers to published Revenue views expressed in the Revenue Internal Guidance Manuals not reproduced in this Handbook.

Cross reference—refers to provisions in the same or another Act or statutory instrument.

Simon's Tax Cases—provides references to the most significant cases reported in *Simon's Tax Cases* and *Simon's Tax Cases Special Commissioners' Decisions*. Cases decided on the previous corresponding statutory provision are marked by an asterisk.

Note—introduces other references not within any of the above categories.

July 2002

MEANING OF "THE TAXES ACTS"

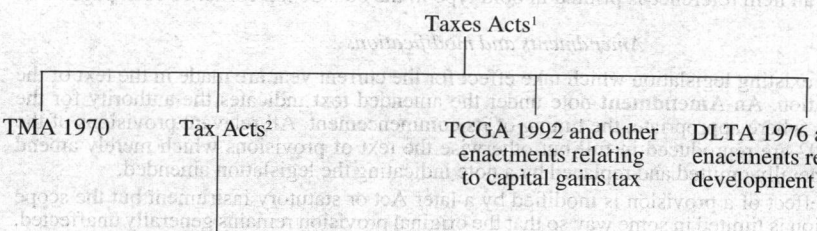

Taxes Acts[1]

TMA 1970   Tax Acts[2]   TCGA 1992 and other enactments relating to capital gains tax   DLTA 1976 and other enactments relating to development land tax[5]

TA 1988 and other provisions of the Income Tax Acts[3]   TA 1988 and other provisions of the Corporation Tax Acts[4]

[1] Defined in TMA 1970 s 118(1).
[2] Defined in TA 1988 s 831(2).
[3] Defined in TA 1988 s 831(1)(b).
[4] Defined in TA 1988 s 831(1)(a).
[5] Repealed with effect generally from 19 March 1985 by FA 1985 s 93, Sch 25 Pt I and Sch 27 Pt X.

ABBREVIATIONS

The following abbreviations are used in this book—

AEA 1925	Administration of Estates Act 1925
ACT	Advance Corporation Tax
APRT	Advanced petroleum revenue tax
art	article(s)
BES	Business Expansion Scheme
CAA	Capital Allowances Act
CCAB	Consultative Committee of Accountancy Bodies
C&E	Customs & Excise
CGT	Capital gains tax
CGTA 1979	Capital Gains Tax Act 1979
Ch	Chapter of statute
col	column(s)
Comrs	Commissioners
CPA 1947	Crown Proceedings Act 1947
CRT	Composite rate tax
CSPSSA 2000	Child Support, Pensions and Social Security Act 2000
CT	Corporation tax
CTD	Certificates of tax deposit
CTT	Capital transfer tax
CTTA 1984	Capital Transfer Tax Act 1984
Dir	EC Directive
DLT	Development land tax
DLTA 1976	Development Land Tax Act 1976
DSS	Department of Social Security
DTI	Department of Trade and Industry
DTR	Double taxation relief
EC	European Community/Communities
edn	edition
EEC	European Economic Community
EEIG	European Economic Interest Grouping
EIS	Enterprise Investment Scheme
ESC	Extra-statutory concession
ESOT	Employee share ownership trust
et seq	(et sequens) and the following
EU	European Union
FA	Finance Act
FII	Franked investment income
FIMBRA	Financial Intermediaries, Managers and Brokers Regulatory Association
F(No 2)A	Finance (No 2) Act
FSA	Friendly Societies Act
FYA	first-year allowance
HA 1988	Housing Act 1988
HL	House of Lords
HM	Her Majesty
HMSO	Her Majesty's Stationery Office
IA	Interpretation Act
IA 1986	Insolvency Act 1986
ICAEW	Institute of Chartered Accountants in England & Wales
IHT	Inheritance tax
IHTA 1984	Inheritance Tax Act 1984
IR	Inland Revenue
IR Comrs	Commissioners of Inland Revenue
IRRA 1890	Inland Revenue Regulation Act 1890
IT	Income tax
LAUTRO	Life Assurance and Unit Trust Regulatory Organisation
LIFFE	London International Financial Futures and Options Exchange
MIRAS	Mortgage interest relief at source

NB	(nota bene) note well
NHA 1980	National Heritage Act 1980
NI	National insurance
NIC	National insurance contributions
OJ	Official Journal of the European Communities
OTA	Oil Taxation Act
para	paragraph(s)
PAYE	Pay as you earn
PCTA 1968	Provisional Collection of Taxes Act 1968
PEP	Personal equity plan
PR	Press release
PRP	Profit-related pay
PRT	Petroleum revenue tax
PSO	Pension Schemes Office
Pt	Part(s)
QCB	Qualifying corporate bond
r	Rule(s)
RD	Revenue decision
reg	regulations
RI	Revenue Interpretation
s	section(s)
SAYE	Save as you earn
Sch	Schedule
SSA	Social Security Act
SSAA 1992	Social Security Administration Act 1992
SS(C)A	Social Security (Contributions) Act
SSCBA 1992	Social Security Contributions and Benefits Act 1992
SSCPA 1992	Social Security (Consequential Provisions) Act 1992
SS(No 2)A	Social Security (No 2) Act
SSHBA	Social Security and Housing Benefits Act
SS(MP)A	Social Security (Miscellaneous Provisions) Act
SSPA 1975	Social Security Pensions Act 1975
SSPA 1991	Statutory Sick Pay Act 1991
SI	Statutory Instrument
SP	Statement of Practice
SSAP	Statement of Standard Accounting Practice
sub-para	sub-paragraph(s)
sub-s	sub-section(s)
TA	Income and Corporation Taxes Act
TCGA 1992	Taxation of Chargeable Gains Act 1992
TCA 1999	Tax Credits Act 1999
TESSA	Tax-exempt special savings account
TMA 1970	Taxes Management Act 1970
TR	Technical release
TSBA	Trustee Savings Banks Act
UCITS	Undertakings for Collective Investment in Transferable Securities
UK	United Kingdom
VAT	Value added tax
VATA 1994	Value Added Tax Act 1994
VCT	Venture capital trust
vol	volume(s)
WDA	writing down allowance

RETROSPECTIVE LEGISLATION

Subscribers are advised to retain Handbooks for earlier years to use when dealing with tax for those years. Each Handbook shows the legislation operative for the corresponding year so far as it was known at the time of the passing of the Finance Act of that year. In view of the increasing practice of passing tax legislation with retrospective effect, it is necessary when dealing with past years to consider whether the provisions have been affected or amended by subsequent legislation.

The following is a list of the legislation affected by the retrospective provisions in FA 2002. The "Effective date" column shows only the operative dates. Reference must be made to the provisions mentioned in the third column to ascertain under what conditions those dates operate.

Note—The following abbreviation is used in the Table below: DATHHE = "deemed always to have had effect".

Provision affected	Subject matter	Retrospective enactment	Effective date
		FA 2002	
TA 1988			
ss 200, 200ZA	Parliamentary visits to EU candidate countries	s 41	1 April 2002
s 473	Computation of profits: mark to market basis: roll-over of securities held as circulating capital	s 67(1), (2)	1 August 2001
s 546B	Special provision in respect of certain TA 1988 s 546 excesses	s 87(8)-(10)	6 April 2001
s 577A(1)	Expenditure involving crime	s 68	1 April 2002
s 587B	Gifts of shares, securities and real property to charity	s 97	1 April 2002
s 587C	Supplementary provision for gifts of real property	s 97(5)	1 April 2002
s 747	Imputation of chargeable profits and creditable tax of CFCs	s 90	1 April 2002
Sch 5AA	Guaranteed returns on transactions involving futures and options	s 78	26 July 2001
TCGA 1992			
s 179A	Companies leaving groups: reallocation within group of gain and loss accruing under TCGA 1992 s 179	s 42	1 April 2002
s 179B	Companies leaving groups: roll-over of degrouping charge on business assets	s 43	1 April 2002
s 192A	Disposals by companies with substantial shareholdings	s 44	1 April 2002
FA 1994			
s 153	Qualifying payments	s 70	26 July 2001
s 168A	Qualifying contracts for unallowable purposes	s 69	26 July 2001
FA 1996			
s 88A	Loan relationships: accounting method where rate of interest is reset	s 71	19 December 2001
s 92(1)-(1D)	Loan relationships: convertible securities etc	s 72	26 July 2001
s 92(1E)–(1G)	Disapplication of s 92 where issuing company is a connected company	s 73	19 December 2001
s 92A	Debtor relationships	s 74	26 July 2001
s 93	Asset-linked loan relationships	s 75	26 July 2001

Provision affected	Subject matter	Retrospective enactment	Effective date
s 93A	Relationships linked on the value of chargeable assets: guaranteed returns	s 76	26 July 2001
s 93B	Loan relationships ceasing to be within FA 1996 s 93	s 77	26 July 2001
Sch 13 para 3A	Issue price etc of securities issued in accordance with qualifying earn-out right	s 104(2)	DATHHE
Sch 13 para 9A	Securities issued to connected persons etc at a price in excess of market value: transfer to connected person	s 104(3)	26 March 2002
FA 2000			
Sch 20 paras 1, 5, 8, 12	R&D relief for SMEs	s 56, Sch 15	1 April 2002

STATUTES

CONTENTS

CONTENTS

INLAND REVENUE REGULATION ACT 1890

(53 & 54 Vict. c 21)

ARRANGEMENT OF SECTIONS

Commissioners and Officers

An Act to consolidate certain enactments relating to the Regulation of the Inland Revenue.

[25th July 1890]

Commissioners and Officers

1 Appointment of Commissioners

(1) It shall be lawful for Her Majesty the Queen to appoint persons to be Commissioners for the collection and management of inland revenue, and the Commissioners shall hold office during Her Majesty's pleasure.

(2) The Commissioners shall have all necessary powers for carrying into execution every Act of Parliament relating to inland revenue, and shall in the exercise of their duty be subject to the authority, direction, and control of the Treasury, and shall obey all orders and instructions which have been or may be issued to them in that behalf by the Treasury.

Commentary—*Simon's Direct Tax Service* A2.302.
Simon's Tax Cases—*IRC v National Federation of Self-Employed and Small Businesses Ltd* [1981] STC 260; *IRC v Nuttall* [1990] STC 194.
Cross references—See TMA 1970 s 1(1) (income tax, corporation tax, and capital gains tax to be under care and management of Commissioners of Inland Revenue ("the Board")).
TMA 1970 s 6, Sch 1 ("declaration").
TMA 1970 s 29 ("assessments").

2 Quorum of Commissioners

The Commissioners may act by any two or more of their number, and by that number shall constitute a board of commissioners, and may do and order and direct and permit to be done throughout the United Kingdom or in any part thereof all acts, matters, and things relating to inland revenue.

Provided that where by any Act of Parliament or otherwise anything has been or is hereafter expressly directed or authorised to be done by one of the Commissioners, it shall be valid if done by one Commissioner.

Commentary—*Simon's Direct Tax Service* **A2.302.**

3 Offices

The Commissioners shall have their chief office in London and shall also keep offices in such other places as they deem necessary, and those offices shall be kept open on the prescribed days and during the prescribed hours.

Commentary—*Simon's Direct Tax Service* **A2.303.**

4 Appointment of collectors, officers, and other persons

(1) The Commissioners shall, unless the Treasury otherwise direct, appoint such collectors, officers, and other persons for collecting, receiving, managing, and accounting for inland revenue as are not required by law to be appointed by any other authority.

(2) All such appointments shall continue in force notwithstanding the death of any Commissioner, or his ceasing to hold office, and the persons holding the same shall have full power to execute the duties of their respective offices and to enforce, in the execution thereof, all laws, regulations, penalties, and forfeitures relating to inland revenue in every part of the United Kingdom.

(3) The Commissioners may suspend, reduce, discharge, or restore as they see cause, any such collector, officer, or person.

(4) Where a collector, officer, or person is authorised to receive or collect or have in his custody or possession any money arising from inland revenue, the Commissioners may require him to give security to their satisfaction.

Commentary—*Simon's Direct Tax Service* **A2.701.**
Cross references—See TMA 1970 s 1 (Board's appointment of inspectors and collectors of taxes).
Tax Credits Act 1999 s 5(4) (the reference to collecting, receiving, managing and accounting for inland revenue in sub-s (1) above includes a reference to paying and managing the working families' tax credit and disabled person's tax credit).

[4A Exercise of functions of Commissioners

Any function conferred by or under any enactment, including any future enactment, on the Commissioners may be exercised by any officer of the Commissioners acting under their authority:

Provided that this section shall not apply to the making of any statutory instrument.][1]

Simon's Tax Cases—*R v IRC, ex p Taylor* [1988] STC 832.
Cross reference—See TMA 1970 s 20C(2) (disapplication of this section in respect of Board's power to approve an application for warrant to obtain documents).
Amendments—[1] This section inserted by FA 1969 Sch 20 para 11(1), (2).

6 Accountant-General

Every person appointed to the office of Accountant-General ...[1] shall hold his office during the pleasure of the Treasury.

Amendments—[1] Words repealed by the Public Accounts and Charges Act 1891, s 1(1) and Sch.

9 Salaries and superannuation allowances not assignable or subject to be taken in execution

Save as provided by any law in relation to the commutation of a pension or the estate of a bankrupt, the remuneration payable to any person for being or having been a Commissioner, collector, officer, or person employed in relation to inland revenue, shall not before payment thereof to or for the use of that person be capable of assignment or liable to be taken under legal process.

Commentary—*Simon's Direct Tax Service* **A2.801.**

11 Obstruction of officers

If any person by himself or by any person in his employ obstructs, molests, or hinders—

    (a) an officer or any person employed in relation to inland revenue in the execution of his duty, or of any of the powers or authorities by law given to the officer or person; or

    (b) any person acting in the aid of an officer or any person so employed;

he shall for every such offence incur a fine of [level 3 on the standard scale][1].

Commentary—*Simon's Direct Tax Service* **A2.801.**
Amendments—[1] Words substituted by virtue of the Criminal Justice Act 1982 ss 38, 46. Standard scale is defined in the Interpretation Act 1978 Sch 1 and the Criminal Justice Act 1982 s 37.

12 Unlawful assumption of character of officer

If any person not being an officer takes or assumes the name, designation, or character of an officer for the purpose of thereby obtaining admission into any house or other place, or of doing or procuring to be done any act which he would not be entitled to do or procure to be done of his own authority, or for any other unlawful purpose, he shall be guilty of a misdemeanour, and shall in addition to any other punishment to which he may be liable for the offence, be liable, on summary conviction, to be imprisoned with or without hard labour, for any term not exceeding three months.

Note—By the Criminal Justice Act 1948 s 1(2), hard labour was abolished and enactments conferring power to sentence to imprisonment with hard labour are to be construed as conferring power to sentence to imprisonment.

Accounts

13 Commissioners to keep accounts

(1) The Commissioners shall collect and cause to be collected every part of inland revenue, and all money under their care and management, and shall keep distinct accounts thereof at their chief office.

(2) There shall be set forth in such accounts the amounts respectively charged, collected, and received, and remaining in arrears of each part of inland revenue, and of the several payments made or allowed by the Commissioners in respect of each such part and of the expenses of the collection and management of the said revenue, and of all other payments and expenses made or incurred on any other account whatsoever.

Commentary—*Simon's Direct Tax Service* **A3.201.**
Simon's Tax Cases—s 13, *IRC v Nuttall* [1990] STC 194.
s 13(1), *IRC v National Federation of Self-Employed and Small Businesses Ltd* [1981] STC 260.
Cross-references—See Tax Credits Act 1999 s 5(5) (duties of the Board under this section include a duty to set forth in the accounts amounts of payments, expenses and amounts received in respect of the working families' tax credit and the disabled person's tax credit).

Legal Proceedings

24 Rules as to evidence in certain cases

(1) All regulations, minutes, and notices purporting to be signed by a secretary or assistant secretary of the Commissioners and by their order shall, until the contrary is proved, be deemed to have been so signed and to have been made and issued by the Commissioners, and may be proved by the production of a copy thereof purporting to have been so signed.

(2) In any proceeding the letter or instructions under which a collector or officer or person employed in relation to inland revenue has acted shall be sufficient evidence of any order issued by the Treasury or by the Commissioners, and mentioned or referred to therein.

(3) Evidence of a person being reputed to be or having acted as a Commissioner, or collector, or officer, or person employed in relation to inland revenue, shall, unless the contrary is proved, be sufficient evidence of his appointment or authority to act as such.

[(4) Any notice or other document purporting to be issued in exercise of any function conferred on the Commissioners shall, until the contrary is proved, be deemed to be so issued.][1]

Commentary—*Simon's Direct Tax Service* **A2.801, A3.808.**
Simon's Tax Cases—*B & S Displays Ltd v Special Comrs* [1978] STC 331; *R v IRC, ex p Taylor* [1988] STC 832.
Amendments—[1] Sub-s (4) inserted by FA 1969 Sch 20 para 11(1), (3).

27 Officers may conduct proceedings before justices

Any officer or person employed or authorised by the Commissioners or the Solicitor of inland revenue in that behalf may, although he is not a solicitor, advocate, or writer to the signet, prosecute, conduct, or defend any information, complaint, or other proceeding to be heard or determined by any justice of the peace in the United Kingdom or by any sheriff in Scotland where the proceeding relates to inland revenue or to any fine, penalty, or other matter under the care and management of the Commissioners.

[Any person who has been admitted as a solicitor, and is employed or authorised by the Commissioners or the Solicitor of Inland Revenue, may appear in, conduct, defend, and address the Court in any legal proceedings in a county court in England or Ireland where the proceeding relates to inland revenue, or to any matter under the care or management of the Commissioners of Inland Revenue.][1]

Amendments—[1] Words added by FA 1896 s 38.

Fines, Penalties, and Forfeitures

32 Power to reward informers

The Commissioners may at their discretion reward any person who informs them of any offence against any Act relating to inland revenue or assists in the recovery of any fine or penalty, provided that a reward exceeding fifty pounds shall not be paid in any case without the consent of the Treasury.

Commentary—*Simon's Direct Tax Service* **A3.817.**

34 Expenses of prosecutions

All costs, charges, and expenses payable by the Commissioners in respect of proceedings for the recovery of any fine, penalty, or forfeiture incurred under any Act relating to inland revenue, and all sums of money allowed as rewards, shall be deemed to be charges of collection and management, and shall be paid out of money provided by Parliament for that purpose.

35 Power to mitigate fines and stay proceedings

(1) The Commissioners may in their discretion mitigate any fine or penalty incurred under this Act or any other Act relating to inland revenue, or stay or compound any proceedings for recovery thereof, ...[1] and may also after judgment further mitigate or entirely remit any such fine or penalty... [2]

(2) The Treasury may mitigate or remit any such fine or penalty either before or after judgment ...[3]

Cross references—See TMA 1970 s 102 (power of Board to mitigate penalties).
IHTA 1984 s 260 (proceedings for fines etc do not apply to inheritance tax or CTT).
Amendments—[1] Words repealed by the Customs and Excise Act 1952 Sch 12 Part I.
[2] Words repealed by ITMA 1964 s 17(4), (5), Sch 6 Part II.
[3] Words repealed by the Customs and Excise Act 1952 s 320(1), Sch 12 Part I.

36 Recovery of fines imposed by this Act

All fines imposed by this Act may be proceeded for and recovered in the same manner and in the case of summary proceedings with the like power of appeal, as any fine or penalty under any Act relating to the excise.

Cross references—See TMA 1970 s 100 (procedure for recovery of penalties).

Construction

37 Meaning of certain expressions in past Acts, etc

(1) ...[1]

(2) Where in any Act, or in any bond, security, deed, or other instrument or writing, reference is made to the ... [1], "Commissioners of Stamps and Taxes", "Commissioners of Stamps", or "Commissioners for the Affairs of Taxes", or any officer or person appointed by those Commissioners respectively, the Act, bond, security, deed, or other instrument or writing shall be construed as referring to the Commissioners and officers and persons appointed by them, or acting under their orders and directions.

Amendments—[1] Sub-s (1) and words in sub-s (2) repealed by the Customs and Excise Act 1952 s 320 and Sch 12 Part I.

38 General definitions in Revenue Acts

(1) In this Act ...[1] expressions referring to England shall be construed as applying also to Wales.

(2) ...[2]

Amendments—[1] Words repealed by the Interpretation Act 1978 ss 25(1), 26, and Sch 3.
[2] Sub-s (2) repealed by the Statute Law (Repeals) Act 1978.

39 Definitions

In this Act, unless the context otherwise requires,—

"Inland Revenue" means the revenue of the United Kingdom collected or imposed as stamp duties, taxes, ...[1], and placed under the care and management of the Commissioners, and any part thereof:

"Commissioner" means Commissioner of Inland Revenue:

"Accountant General" means Accountant and Comptroller General of Inland Revenue: ...[2]

"Collector" means Collector of Inland Revenue:

"Officer" means Officer of Inland Revenue: ...[3]

"Prescribed" means prescribed by the Commissioners:

"High Court" means, as respects Scotland, the Court of Session sitting as the Court of Exchequer.

Simon's Tax Cases—*IRC v National Federation of Self-Employed and Small Businesses Ltd* [1981] STC 260.
Amendments—[1] Words from the definition of "Inland Revenue" repealed by the Customs and Excise Act 1952 Sch 12 Part I.
[2] Words repealed by the Public Accounts and Charges Act 1891 s 1 and Sch.
[3] Words repealed by the Statute Law (Repeals) Act 1974.

Repeal: Commencement: Short Title

42 Short title

This Act may be cited as the Inland Revenue Regulation Act 1890.

FINANCE (NO 2) ACT 1931

(21 & 22 Geo. 5 c 49)

22 Provisions in cases where Treasury has power to borrow money

(1) Any securities issued by the Treasury under any Act may be issued with the condition that—

(*a*) so long as the securities are in the beneficial ownership of persons who are not ordinarily resident in the United Kingdom, the interest thereon shall be exempt from income tax; and

(*b*) so long as the securities are in the beneficial ownership of persons who are neither domiciled nor ordinarily resident in the United Kingdom, neither the capital thereof nor the interest thereon shall be liable to any taxation present or future.

(2) ...[1]

Commentary—*Simon's Direct Tax Service* **I10.321.**
Simon's Tax Cases—s 22(1), *Von Ernst & Cie SA v IRC* [1980] STC 111.
Cross references—See FA 1940 s 60(1) (extension of the Treasury's powers under this section).
Amendments—[1] Sub-s (2) repealed by Income Tax Act 1952 s 527 and Sch 25 Pt I.

FINANCE ACT 1940

(3 & 4 Geo. 6 c 29)

60 Extension of power of Treasury to attach exemptions from taxation to securities

(1) The power of the Treasury under section twenty-two of the Finance (No 2) Act 1931 to issue securities with the condition as to exemption from taxation specified in that section shall extend to the issuing of securities with that condition so modified, whether as to the extent of the exemption or the cases in which the exemption is to operate, as the Treasury may specify in the terms of the issue.

(2) ...[1]

Amendments—[1] Sub-s (2) repealed by Income Tax Act 1952 s 527 Sch 25 Pt I.

CROWN PROCEEDINGS ACT 1947

(10 & 11 Geo. 6 c 44)

ARRANGEMENT OF SECTIONS

An Act to amend the law relating to the civil liabilities and rights of the Crown and to civil proceedings by and against the Crown, to amend the law relating to the civil liabilities of persons other than the Crown in certain cases involving the affairs or property of the Crown, and for purposes connected with the matters aforesaid.   [31st July 1947]

Cross references—See TMA 1970 s 100 (procedure for recovery of penalties).
TMA 1970 s 100D (penalty proceedings before court where not instituted under this Act).

PART I
SUBSTANTIVE LAW

1 Right to sue the Crown

Where any person has a claim against the Crown after the commencement of this Act, and, if this Act had not been passed, the claim might have been enforced, subject to the grant of His Majesty's fiat, by petition of right, or might have been enforced by a proceeding provided by any statutory provision repealed by this Act, then, subject to the provisions of this Act, the claim may be enforced as of right, and without the fiat of His Majesty, by proceedings taken against the Crown for that purpose in accordance with the provisions of this Act.

Modifications—For the expression "commencement of this Act" in relation to Northern Ireland there shall be substituted a
reference to 1 January 1950 (see the Crown Proceedings (Northern Ireland) Order, SI 1981/233, art 3).
See also SI 1981/233, art 30, for modifications of this section in respect of its application to Northern Ireland.

PART II
JURISDICTION AND PROCEDURE

Cross references—See Tax Credits Act 1999 Sch 4 para 5(4) (proceedings brought within Tax Credits Act 1999 Sch 4 para 5 are treated as civil proceedings by the Crown within the meaning of Part II of this Act).

The High Court

13 Civil proceedings in the High Court

Subject to the provisions of this Act, all such proceedings by or against the Crown as are mentioned in the First Schedule to this Act are hereby abolished, and all civil proceedings by or against the Crown in the High Court shall be instituted and proceeded with in accordance with rules of court and not otherwise.

In this section the expression "rules of court" means, in relation to any claim against the Crown in the High Court which falls within the jurisdiction of that court as a prize court, rules of court made under section three of the Prize Courts Act 1894.

Commentary—*Simon's Direct Tax Service* **A3.1402.**
Modifications—See the Crown Proceedings (Northern Ireland) Order, SI 1981/233, arts 8, 30, for modifications of this section in respect of its application to Northern Ireland.

County Courts

15 Civil proceedings in the county court

(1) Subject to the provisions of this Act, and to any enactment limiting the jurisdiction of a county court (whether by reference to the subject matter of the proceedings to be brought or the amount sought to be recovered in the proceedings or otherwise) any civil proceedings against the Crown may be instituted in a county court.

(2) Any proceedings by or against the Crown in a county court shall be instituted and proceeded with in accordance with county court rules and not otherwise.

Modifications—See the Crown Proceedings (Northern Ireland) Order, SI 1981/233, arts 10, 30, for modifications of this section in respect of its application to Northern Ireland.

General

16 Interpleader

The Crown may obtain relief by way of interpleader proceedings, and may be made a party to such proceedings, in the same manner in which a subject may obtain relief by way of such proceedings or be made a party thereto, and may be made a party to such proceedings notwithstanding that the application for relief is made by a sheriff or other like officer; and all rules of court and county court rules relating to interpleader proceedings shall, subject to the provisions of this Act, have effect accordingly.

Commentary—*Simon's Direct Tax Service* **A3.1403.**
Modifications—The whole section is substituted as it applies to the Crown in right of the Government of Northern Ireland by the Crown Proceedings (Northern Ireland) Order, the Crown Proceedings (Northern Ireland) Order, SI 1981/233, art 11.

17 Parties to proceedings

(1) The [Minister for the Civil Service][1] shall publish a list specifying the several Government departments which are authorised departments for the purposes of this Act, and the name and address for service of the person who is, or is acting for the purposes of this Act as, the solicitor for each such department, and may from time to time amend or vary the said list.

Any document purporting to be a copy of a list published under this section and purporting to be printed under the superintendence or the authority of His Majesty's Stationery Office shall in any legal proceedings be received as evidence for the purpose of establishing what departments are authorised departments for the purposes of this Act, and what person is, or is acting for the purposes of this Act as, the solicitor for any such department.

(2) Civil proceedings by the Crown may be instituted either by an authorised Government department in its own name, whether that department was or was not at the commencement of this Act authorised to sue, or by the Attorney General.

(3) Civil proceedings against the Crown shall be instituted against the appropriate authorised Government department, or, if none of the authorised Government departments is appropriate or the person instituting the proceedings has any reasonable doubt whether any and if so which of those departments is appropriate, against the Attorney General.

(4) Where any civil proceedings against the Crown are instituted against the Attorney General, an application may at any stage of the proceedings be made to the court by or on behalf of the Attorney General to have such of the authorised Government departments as may be specified in the application substituted for him as defendant to the proceedings; and where any such proceedings are brought against an authorised Government department, an application may at any stage of the proceedings be

made to the court on behalf of that department to have the Attorney General or such of the authorised Government departments as may be specified in the application substituted for the applicant as the defendant to the proceedings.

Upon any such application the court may if it thinks fit make an order granting the application on such terms as the court thinks just; and on such an order being made the proceedings shall continue as if they had been commenced against the department specified in that behalf in the order, or, as the case may require, against the Attorney General.

(5) No proceedings instituted in accordance with this Part of this Act by or against the Attorney General or an authorised Government department shall abate or be affected by any change in the person holding the office of Attorney General or in the person or body of persons constituting the department.

Commentary—*Simon's Direct Tax Service* **A3.1404.**
Modifications—See the Crown Proceedings (Northern Ireland) Order, SI 1981/233, arts 13, 30, for modifications of this section in respect of its application to Northern Ireland.
Amendments—¹ Words substituted by the Minister for the Civil Service Order, SI 1968/1656, art 3(2).

18 Service of documents

All documents required to be served on the Crown for the purpose of or in connection with any civil proceedings by or against the Crown shall, if those proceedings are by or against an authorised Government department, be served on the solicitor, if any, for that department, or the persons if any, acting for the purposes of this Act as solicitor for that department, or if there is no such solicitor and no person so acting, or if the proceedings are brought by or against the Attorney General, on the Solicitor for the affairs of His Majesty's Treasury.

Commentary—*Simon's Direct Tax Service* **A3.1404.**
Modifications—See the Crown Proceedings (Northern Ireland) Order, SI 1981/233, arts 13, 30, for modifications of this section in respect of its application to Northern Ireland.

19 Venue and related matters

(1) In any case in which civil proceedings against the Crown in the High Court are instituted by the issue of a writ out of a district registry the Crown may enter an appearance either in the district registry or in the central office of the High Court, and if an appearance is entered in the central office all steps in relation to the proceedings up to trial shall be taken at the Royal Courts of Justice.

(2) The trial of any civil proceedings by or against the Crown in the High Court shall be held at the Royal Courts of Justice unless the court, with the consent of the Crown, otherwise directs.

Where the Crown refuses its consent to a direction under this subsection the court may take account of the refusal in exercising its powers in regard to the award of costs.

(3) Nothing in this section shall prejudice the right of the Crown to demand a local venue for the trial of any proceedings in which the Attorney General has waived his right to a trial at bar.

20 Removal and transfer of proceedings

(1) If in a case where proceedings are instituted against the Crown in a county court an application in that behalf is made by the Crown to the High Court, and there is produced to the court a certificate of the Attorney General to the effect that the proceedings may involve an important question of law, or may be decisive of other cases arising out of the same matter, or are for other reasons more fit to be tried in the High Court, the proceedings shall be removed into the High Court.

Where any proceedings have been removed into the High Court on the production of such a certificate as aforesaid, and it appears to the court by whom the proceedings are tried that the removal has occasioned additional expense to the person by whom the proceedings are brought, the court may take account of the additional expense so occasioned in exercising its powers in regard to the award of costs.

(2) Without prejudice to the rights of the Crown under the preceding provisions of this section, all rules of law and enactments relating to the removal or transfer of proceedings from a county court to the High Court, or the transfer of proceedings from the High Court to a county court, shall apply in relation to proceedings against the Crown:
...¹

Amendments—¹ Sub-s (2) proviso repealed by the Supreme Court Act 1981 Sch 7.

21 Nature of relief

(1) In any civil proceedings by or against the Crown the court shall, subject to the provisions of this Act, have power to make all such orders as it has power to make in proceedings between subjects, and otherwise to give such appropriate relief as the case may require:

Provided that:—

   (*a*) where in any proceedings against the Crown any such relief is sought as might in proceedings between subjects be granted by way of injunction or specific performance, the court shall not grant an injunction or make an order for specific performance, but may in lieu thereof make an order declaratory of the rights of the parties; and

(*b*) in any proceedings against the Crown for the recovery of land or other property the court shall not make an order for the recovery of the land or the delivery of the property, but may in lieu thereof make an order declaring that the plaintiff is entitled as against the Crown to the land or property or to the possession thereof.

(2) The court shall not in any civil proceedings grant any injunction or make any order against an officer of the Crown if the effect of granting the injunction or making the order would be to give any relief against the Crown which could not have been obtained in proceedings against the Crown.

22 Appeals and stay of execution

Subject to the provisions of this Act, all enactments, rules of court and county court rules relating to appeals and stay of execution shall, with any necessary modifications, apply to civil proceedings by or against the Crown as they apply to proceedings between subjects.

23 Scope of Part II

(1) Subject to the provisions of this section, any reference in this Part of this Act to civil proceedings by the Crown shall be construed as a reference to the following proceedings only:

(*a*) proceedings for the enforcement or vindication of any right or the obtaining of any relief which, if this Act had not been passed, might have been enforced or vindicated or obtained by any such proceedings as are mentioned in paragraph 1 of the First Schedule to this Act;

(*b*) proceedings for the enforcement or vindication of any right or the obtaining of any relief which, if this Act had not been passed, might have been enforced or vindicated or obtained by an action at the suit of any Government department or any officer of the Crown as such;

(*c*) all such proceedings as the Crown is entitled to bring by virtue of this Act;

and the expression ''civil proceedings by or against the Crown'' shall be construed accordingly.

(2) Subject to the provisions of this section, any reference in this Part of this Act to civil proceedings against the Crown shall be construed as a reference to the following proceedings only:

(*a*) proceedings for the enforcement or vindication of any right or the obtaining of any relief which, if this Act had not been passed, might have been enforced or vindicated or obtained by any such proceedings as are mentioned in paragraph 2 of the First Schedule to this Act;

(*b*) proceedings for the enforcement or vindication of any right or the obtaining of any relief which, if this Act had not been passed, might have been enforced or vindicated or obtained by an action against the Attorney-General, any Government department, or any officer of the Crown as such; and

(*c*) all such proceedings as any person is entitled to bring against the Crown by virtue of this Act;

and the expression ''civil proceedings by or against the Crown'' shall be construed accordingly.

(3) Notwithstanding anything in the preceding provisions of this section, the provisions of this Part of this Act shall not have effect with respect to any of the following proceedings, that is to say:—

(*a*) proceedings brought by the Attorney General on the relation of some other person;

(*b*) proceedings by or against the Public Trustee;

(*c*) proceedings by or against the Charity Commissioners;

(*d*) ...¹

(*e*) ...²

(*f*) proceedings by or against the Registrar of the Land Registry or any officers of that registry.

(4) Subject to the provisions of any Order in Council made under the provisions hereinafter contained, this part of this Act shall not affect proceedings initiated in any court other than the High Court or a county court.

Modifications—See the Crown Proceedings (Northern Ireland) Order, SI 1981/233, arts 13, 30, 33, for modifications of this section in respect of its application to Northern Ireland.
Amendments—¹ Sub-s (3)(*d*) repealed by the Charities Act 1960 s 48(2), Sch 7 Part I.
² Sub-s (3)(*e*) repealed by the Education Act 1973 Sch 2 Part III.

PART III

JUDGMENTS AND EXECUTION

24 Interest on debts, damages and costs

(1) Section seventeen of the Judgments Act 1838 (which provides that a judgment debt shall carry interest) [and section 44A of the Administration of Justice Act 1970 (which enables the court to order an appropriate rate for a judgment debt expressed in a currency other than sterling)]⁴ shall apply to judgment debts due from or to the Crown.

(2) Where any costs are awarded to or against the Crown in the High Court, interest shall be payable upon those costs unless the court otherwise orders, and any interest so payable shall be at the same rate as that at which interest is payable upon judgment debts due from or to the Crown.

(3) [Section 35A of the Supreme Court Act 1981 and [section 69 of the County Courts Act 1984]² (which respectively empower the High Court and county courts to award interest on debts and damages) and section 3 of the Law Reform (Miscellaneous Provisions) Act 1934 (which empowers other courts of record to do so)]¹ shall apply to judgments given in proceedings by and against the Crown.

(4) ...³

Commentary—*Simon's Direct Tax Service* A3.1204, 1407.
Modifications—For references to the "commencement of this Act" in relation to Northern Ireland there shall be substituted references to 1 January 1950 (the Crown Proceedings (Northern Ireland) Order, SI 1981/233, art 3).
See also SI 1981/233, arts 19, 30, for modification of this section in respect of its application to Northern Ireland.
Amendments—¹ Words in sub-s (3) substituted by the Administration of Justice Act 1982 s 76 and Sch 1 Part III.
² Words in sub-s (3) substituted by the County Courts Act 1984 s 148(1), Sch 2 para 21.
³ Sub-s (4) repealed by the Statute Law (Repeals) Act 1993 s 1(1), Sch 1 Pt I.
⁴ Words in sub-s (1) inserted by the Private International Law (Miscellaneous Provisions) Act 1995 s 4(1) with effect as from a day to be appointed.

25 Satisfaction of orders against the Crown

(1) Where in any civil proceedings by or against the Crown, or in any proceedings on the Crown side of the King's Bench Division, or in connection with any arbitration to which the Crown is a party, any order (including an order for costs) is made by any court in favour of any person against the Crown or against a Government department or against an officer of the Crown as such, the proper officer of the court shall, on an application in that behalf made by or on behalf of that person at any time after the expiration of twenty-one days from the date of the order or, in case the order provides for the payment of costs and the costs require to be taxed, at any time after the costs have been taxed whichever is the later, issue to that person a certificate in the prescribed form containing particulars of the order:

Provided that, if the court so directs, a separate certificate shall be issued with respect to the costs (if any) ordered to be paid to the applicant.

(2) A copy of any certificate issued under this section may be served by the person in whose favour the order is made upon the person for the time being named in the record as the solicitor, or as the person acting as solicitor, for the Crown or for the Government department or officer concerned.

(3) If the order provides for the payment of any money by way of damages or otherwise, or of any costs, the certificate shall state the amount so payable, and the appropriate Government department shall, subject as hereinafter provided, pay to the person entitled or to his solicitor the amount appearing by the certificate to be due to him together with the interest, if any, lawfully due thereon:

Provided that the court by which any such order as aforesaid is made or any court to which an appeal against the order lies may direct that, pending an appeal or otherwise payment of the whole of any amount so payable, or any part thereof, shall be suspended, and if the certificate has not been issued may order any such directions to be inserted therein.

(4) Save as aforesaid no execution or attachment or process in the nature thereof shall be issued out of any court for enforcing payment by the Crown of any such money or costs as aforesaid, and no person shall be individually liable under any order for the payment by the Crown, or any Government department, or any officer of the Crown as such, of any such money or costs.

(5) ...¹

Modifications—For references to the "commencement of this Act" in relation to Northern Ireland there shall be substituted references to 1 January 1950 (the Crown Proceedings (Northern Ireland) Order, SI 1981/233, art 3).
See SI 1981/233, arts 20, 30, for other modifications of this section in respect of its application to Northern Ireland.
Amendments—¹ Sub-s (5) repealed by the Statute Law (Repeals) Act 1993 s 1(1), Sch 1 Pt I.

26 Execution by the Crown

(1) Subject to the provisions of this Act, any order made in favour of the Crown against any person in any civil proceedings to which the Crown is a party may be enforced in the same manner as an order made in an action between subjects, and not otherwise.
...²

(2) Sections four and five of the Debtors Act, 1869 (which provide respectively for the abolition of imprisonment for debt, and for saving the power of committal in case of small debts), shall apply to sums of money payable and debts due to the Crown:

Provided that for the purpose of the application of the said section four to any sum of money payable or debt due to the Crown, the section shall have effect as if there were included among the exceptions therein mentioned default in payment of any sum payable in respect of death duties ...¹.

(3) Nothing in this section shall affect any procedure which immediately before the commencement of this Act was available for enforcing an order made in favour of the Crown in proceedings brought by the Crown for the recovery of any fine or penalty, or the forfeiture or condemnation of any goods, or the forfeiture of any ship or any share in a ship.

Commentary—*Simon's Direct Tax Service* A3.1408.
Modifications—For references to the "commencement of this Act" in relation to Northern Ireland there shall be substituted references to 1 January 1950 (the Crown Proceedings (Northern Ireland) Order, SI 1981/233, art 3).
See also SI 1981/233, arts 21, 29, 30, for modification of this section in respect of its application to Northern Ireland.

Amendments—¹ Words in sub-s (2) proviso repealed by FA 1972 ss 54(8), 134 and Sch 28 Part II.
² Words in sub-s (1) repealed by the Statute Law (Repeals) Act 1993 s 1(1), Sch 1 Pt I.

PART IV

MISCELLANEOUS AND SUPPLEMENTAL

Miscellaneous

28 Discovery

(1) Subject to and in accordance with rules of court and county court rules:—

(*a*) in any civil proceedings in the High Court or a county court to which the Crown is a party, the Crown may be required by the court to make discovery of documents and produce documents for inspection; and

(*b*) in any such proceedings as aforesaid, the Crown may be required by the court to answer interrogatories:

Provided that this section shall be without prejudice to any rule of law which authorises or requires the withholding of any document or the refusal to answer any question on the ground that the disclosure of the document or the answering of the question would be injurious to the public interest.

Any order of the court made under the powers conferred by paragraph (*b*) or this subsection shall direct by what officer of the Crown the interrogatories are to be answered.

(2) Without prejudice to the proviso to the preceding subsection, any rules made for the purpose of this section shall be such as to secure that the existence of a document will not be disclosed if, in the opinion of a Minister of the Crown, it would be injurious to the public interest to disclose the existence thereof.

Commentary—*Simon's Direct Tax Service* **A3.1105.**
Modifications—See the Crown Proceedings (Northern Ireland) Order, SI 1981/233, art 30, for modifications of this section in respect of its application to Northern Ireland.

33 Abolition of certain writs

No writ of extent or of diem clausit extremum shall issue after the commencement of this Act.

Modifications—For references to the "commencement of this Act" in relation to Northern Ireland there shall be substituted references to 1 January 1950 (the Crown Proceedings (Northern Ireland) Order, SI 1981/233, art 3).

Supplemental

35 Rules of court and county court rules

(1) Any power to make rules of court or county court rules shall include power to make rules for the purpose of giving effect to the provisions of this Act, and any such rules may contain provisions to have effect in relation to any proceedings by or against the Crown in substitution for or by way of addition to any of the provisions of the rules applying to proceedings between subjects.

(2) Provision shall be made by rules of court and county court rules with respect to the following matters:

(*a*) for providing for service of process, or notice thereof, in the case of proceedings by the Crown against persons, whether British subjects or not, who are not resident in the United Kingdom;

(*b*) for securing that where any civil proceedings are brought against the Crown in accordance with the provisions of this Act the plaintiff shall, before the Crown is required to take any step in the proceedings, provide the Crown with such information as the Crown may reasonably require as to the circumstances in which it is alleged that the liability of the Crown has arisen and as to the departments and officers of the Crown concerned;

(*c*) for providing that in the case of proceedings against the Crown the plaintiff shall not enter judgment against the Crown in default of appearance or pleading without the leave of the court to be obtained on an application of which notice has been given to the Crown;

(*d*) for excepting proceedings brought against the Crown from the operation of any rule of court providing for summary judgment without trial, and for enabling any such proceedings to be put in proper cases into any special list which may be kept for the trial of short causes in which leave to defend is given under any such rule of court as aforesaid;

(*e*) for authorising the Crown to deliver interrogatories without the leave of a court in any proceedings for the enforcement of any right for the enforcement of which proceedings by way of English information might have been taken if this Act had not been passed, so, however, that the Crown shall not be entitled to deliver any third or subsequent interrogatories without the leave of the court;

(*f*) for enabling evidence to be taken on commission in proceedings by or against the Crown;

(*g*) for providing:

(i) that a person shall not be entitled to avail himself of any set-off or counter-claim in any proceedings by the Crown for the recovery of taxes, duties or penalties, or to avail himself in proceedings of any other nature by the Crown of any set-off or counterclaim arising out of a right or claim to repayment in respect of any taxes, duties or penalties;

(ii) that a person shall not be entitled without the leave of the court to avail himself of any set-off or counterclaim in any proceedings by the Crown if either the subject matter of the set-off or counterclaim does not relate to the Government department in the name of which the proceedings are brought or the proceedings are brought in the name of the Attorney General;

(iii) that the Crown, when sued in the name of a Government department, shall not, without the leave of the court, be entitled to avail itself of any set-off or counterclaim if the subject matter thereof does not relate to that department; and

(iv) that the Crown, when sued in the name of the Attorney General, shall not be entitled to avail itself of any set-off or counterclaim without the leave of the court.

(3) Provision may be made by rules of court for regulating any appeals to the High Court, whether by way of case stated or otherwise, under enactments relating to the revenue, and any rules made under this subsection may revoke any enactments or rules in force immediately before the commencement of this Act so far as they regulate any such appeals, and may make provision for any matters for which provision was made by any enactments or rules so in force.

Commentary—*Simon's Direct Tax Service* A3.1409.
Cross references—See CPA 1947 s 50 (modification of this section in its application to Scotland).
TMA 1970 s 69 (treatment of interest charged on overdue tax for the purposes of sub-s (2)(*b*), (*g*)(i) of this section).
Modifications—For references to the "commencement of this Act" in relation to Northern Ireland there shall be substituted references to 1 January 1950 (the Crown Proceedings (Northern Ireland) Order, SI 1981/233, art 3)..
See also SI 1981/233, arts 24, 30, for modifications of this section in respect of its application to Northern Ireland.

38 Interpretation

(1) Any reference in this Act to the provisions of this Act shall, unless the context otherwise requires, include a reference to rules of court or county court rules made for the purposes of this Act.

(2) In this Act, except in so far as the context otherwise requires or it is otherwise expressly provided, the following expressions have the meanings hereby respectively assigned to them, that is to say:

"Agent", when used in relation to the Crown, includes an independent contractor employed by the Crown;

"Civil proceedings" includes proceedings in the High Court or the county court for the recovery of fines or penalties, but does not include proceedings on the Crown side of the King's Bench Division;

...

"Officer", in relation to the Crown, includes any servant of His Majesty, and accordingly (but without prejudice to the generality of the foregoing provision) includes a Minister of the Crown [and a Member of the Scottish Executive];

"Order" includes a judgment, decree, rule, award or declaration;

"Prescribed" means prescribed by rules of court or county court rules, as the case may be;

"Proceedings against the Crown" includes a claim by way of set-off or counterclaim raised in proceedings by the Crown.

...

(3) Any reference in this Act to His Majesty in His private capacity shall be construed as including a reference to His Majesty in right of His Duchy of Lancaster and to the Duke of Cornwall.

(4) Any reference in Parts III or IV of this Act to civil proceedings by or against the Crown, or to civil proceedings to which the Crown is a party, shall be construed as including a reference to civil proceedings to which the Attorney General, or any Government department, or any officer of the Crown as such is a party:

Provided that the Crown shall not for the purposes of Parts III and IV of this Act be deemed to be a party to any proceedings by reason only that they are brought by the Attorney General upon the relation of some other person.

(5) ...[1]

(6) Reference in this Act to any enactment shall be construed as references to that enactment as amended by or under any other enactment, including this Act.

Note—Words omitted from this section are not relevant to this Handbook.
Cross references—See CPA 1947 s 51(2) (modification of this section in its application to Scotland).
Modifications—See the Crown Proceedings (Northern Ireland) Order, SI 1981/233, arts 26, 29, 30, for modifications of this section in respect of its application to Northern Ireland.
Amendments—[1] Sub-s (5) repealed by the Armed Forces Act 1981 s 28(2), Sch 5 Pt I.
[2] Words in definition "Officer" inserted by the Scotland Act 1998 Sch 8 para 7(2)(*c*) with effect from 20 May 1999.

40 Savings

(2) Except as therein otherwise expressly provided, nothing in this Act shall:

(*b*) authorise proceedings to be taken against the Crown under or in accordance with this Act in respect of any alleged liability of the Crown arising otherwise than in respect of His Majesty's Government in the United Kingdom [or the Scottish Administration][1], or affect proceedings against the Crown in respect of any such alleged liability as aforesaid; or (*g*) affect any right of the Crown to demand trial at bar or to control or otherwise intervene in proceedings affecting its rights, property or profits:

and, without prejudice to the general effect of the foregoing provisions Part III of this Act shall not apply to the Crown except in right of His Majesty's Government in the United Kingdom [or the Scottish Administration][1].

(5) This Act shall not operate to limit the discretion of the court to grant relief by way of mandamus in cases in which such relief might have been granted before the commencement of this Act, notwithstanding that by reason of the provisions of this Act some other and further remedy is available.

Note—Words omitted from this section are not relevant to this Handbook.
Commentary—*Simon's Direct Tax Service* **A3.908.**
Modifications—For references to the "commencement of this Act" in relation to Northern Ireland there shall be substituted references to 1 January 1950 (the Crown Proceedings (Northern Ireland) Order, SI 1981/233, art 3).
See also SI 1981/233, art 27, for modifications of this section as it applies to Northern Ireland.
Amendments—[1] Words in sub-s (2) inserted by the Scotland Act 1998 Sch 8 para 7(3)(*a*) with effect from 20 May 1999.

PART V

APPLICATION TO SCOTLAND

Modifications—Part V excepted in the application of this Act to Northern Ireland by the Crown Proceedings (Northern Ireland) Order, SI 1981/233, art 28.

41 Application of Act to Scotland

The provisions of this part of this Act shall have effect for the purpose of the application of this Act to Scotland.

42 Exclusion of certain provisions

Section one, Part II (except section thirteen so far as relating to proceedings mentioned in the First Schedule) and section twenty-one, Part III (except section twenty-six) and section twenty-eight of this Act shall not apply to Scotland.

Note—The parenthesis after the words "First Schedule" in the official text appears to be misplaced. It should presumably be printed after the words "section twenty-one".

43 Interpretation for purposes of application to Scotland

In the application of this Act to Scotland:

(*a*) for any reference to the High Court (except a reference to that Court as a prize court) there shall be substituted a reference to the Court of Session; for any reference to the county court there shall be substituted a reference to the sheriff court; the expression "plaintiff" means pursuer; the expression "defendant" means defender; the expression "county court rules" means Act of Sederunt applying to the sheriff court; and the expression "injunction" means interdict;

(*b*) ...

44 Proceedings against the Crown in the sheriff court

Subject to the provisions of this Act and to any enactment limiting the jurisdiction of the sheriff court (whether by reference to the subject matter of the proceedings or otherwise) civil proceedings against the Crown may be instituted in the sheriff court in like manner as if the proceedings were against a subject:

Provided that where in any proceedings against the Crown in the sheriff court a certificate by the [appropriate Law Officer][1] is produced to the effect that the proceedings may involve an important question of law, or may be decisive of other cases, or are for other reasons more fit for trial in the Court of Session, the proceedings shall be remitted to the Court of Session, and where any proceedings have been so remitted to the Court of Session, and it appears to that Court that the remit has occasioned additional expense to the pursuer, the Court shall take account of the additional expense so occasioned in deciding any question as to expenses. [In this proviso, "the appropriate Law Officer" means—

(*a*) the Lord Advocate, where the proceedings are against any part of the Scottish Administration, and

(*b*) the Advocate General for Scotland, in any other case.][1]

Amendments—[1] Words inserted by the Scotland Act 1998 Sch 8 para 7(4) with effect from 20 May 1999.

45 Satisfaction of orders granted against the Crown in Scotland

(1) Where in any civil proceedings by or against the Crown or to which the Crown has been made a party, any order (including an award of expenses) is made by any court in favour of any person against the Crown or against a Government department or against an officer of the Crown as such, the clerk of court shall, on an application in that behalf made by or on behalf of that person at any

time after the expiration of twenty-one days from the date of the order, or, in a case where there is an award of expenses and the expenses require to be taxed, at any time after taxation whichever is the later, issue to that person a certified copy of the order of the court.

(2) A copy of any such order may be served by the person in whose favour the order is made upon the person for the time being named in the record as the solicitor, or the person acting as solicitor, for the Crown or for the Government department or officer concerned.

(3) If the order decerns for the payment of any money by way of damages or otherwise or of any expenses, the appropriate Government department shall, subject as hereinafter provided, pay to the person entitled or to his solicitor the amount appearing from the order to be due to him together with the interest, if any, lawfully due thereon:

Provided that the court by which any such order as aforesaid is made or any court to which an appeal against the order lies may direct that pending an appeal or otherwise payment of the whole of any amount so payable, or any part thereof, shall be suspended.

(4) No such order as aforesaid shall warrant any diligence or execution against any person to enforce payment of any such money or expenses as aforesaid, and no person shall be individually liable under any order for the payment by the Crown, or any Government department or any officer of the Crown as such, of any such money or expenses.

47 Recovery of documents in possession of Crown

Subject to and in accordance with Acts of Sederunt applying to the Court of Session and the sheriff court, commission and diligence for the recovery of documents in the possession of the Crown may be granted in any action whether or not the Crown is a party thereto, in like manner in all respects as if the documents were in the possession of a subject:

Provided that—

(i) this subsection shall be without prejudice to any rule or law which authorises or requires the withholding of any document on the ground that its disclosure would be injurious to the public interest; and
(ii) the existence of a document shall not be disclosed if, in the opinion of a Minister of the Crown, it would be injurious to the public interest to disclose the existence thereof.

Commentary—*Simon's Direct Tax Service* **A3.1105.**

50 Application to Scotland of s 35

Section thirty-five of this Act shall have effect as if for subsection (2) thereof there were substituted the following subsection:—

"(2) The following provisions shall apply as regards proceedings in the Court of Session or the sheriff court—

(*a*) where decree in absence has been granted against the Crown the decree shall not be operative without the leave of the court obtained on an application of which notice has been given to the Crown;
(*b*) a person shall not be entitled to avail himself of any set-off or counterclaim in any proceedings by the Crown for the recovery of taxes, duties or penalties, or to avail himself in proceedings of any other nature by the Crown of any set-off or counterclaim arising out of a right or claim to repayment in respect of any taxes, duties or penalties;
(*c*) a person shall not be entitled without the leave of the court to avail himself of any set-off or counterclaim in any proceedings by the Crown if the subject matter of the set-off or counterclaim does not relate to the Government department on whose behalf the proceedings are brought;
(*d*) the Crown [in right of Her Majesty's Government in the United Kingdom][1], in any proceedings against a Government department, or against the [Advocate General for Scotland][2] on behalf of a Government department,

[(i) shall not be entitled to avail itself of any set-off or counterclaim if the subject matter thereof relates to the Scottish Administration, and
(ii)][1] shall not, without the leave of the court, be entitled to avail itself of any set-off or counterclaim if the subject matter thereof does not relate to that department.

[(*e*) a part of the Scottish Administration, in any proceedings against that part or against the Lord Advocate on its behalf, shall not be entitled to avail itself of any set-off or counterclaim if the subject matter thereof relates to another part of the Scottish Administration or to the Crown in right of Her Majesty's Government in the United Kingdom.][1]''

Cross references—See TMA 1970 s 69 (treatment of interest charged on overdue tax for the purpose of CPA 1947 s 35(2)(*b*), (*g*)(i)).
Amendments—[1] Words inserted by the Scotland Act 1998 Sch 8 para 7(5)(*a*)(i), (iii), (*b*) with effect from 20 May 1999.
[1] Words substituted by the Scotland Act 1998 Sch 8 para 7(5)(*a*)(i), (ii) with effect from 20 May 1999.

51 Application to Scotland of ss 36 and 38

(1) ...[1]

(2) Section thirty-eight of this Act shall have effect as if in subsection (4) thereof:

(i) there were included a reference to this Part of this Act;

(ii) for the reference to the Attorney General there were substituted a reference to the Lord Advocate [or the Advocate General for Scotland];

(iii) the proviso were omitted.

Amendments—[1] Sub-s (1) repealed by the Statute Law Repeals Act 1993, s 1(1) Sch 1 Pt I.
[2] Words inserted by the Scotland Act 1998 Sch 8 para 7(6) with effect from 20 May 1999.

PART VI
EXTENT, COMMENCEMENT, SHORT TITLE, ETC

52 Extent of Act

Subject to the provisions hereinafter contained with respect to Northern Ireland, this Act shall not affect the law enforced in courts elsewhere than in England and Scotland, or the procedure in any such courts.

Modifications—Section 52 excepted in the application of this Act to Northern Ireland by the Crown Proceedings (Northern Ireland) Order, SI 1981/233, art 28.

53 Provisions as to Northern Ireland

(1) His Majesty may by Order in Council provide for extending this Act to Northern Ireland with such additions, exceptions and modifications as appear to His Majesty to be expedient.

(2) An Order in Council under this section may provide for amending the law both in its application to the Crown in right of His Majesty's Government in the United Kingdom and in its application to the Crown in right of His Majesty's Government in Northern Ireland.

(3) An Order in Council under this section may provide for amending the law—

(a) with respect to the right of the Crown to sue in a county court in Northern Ireland; and

(b) with respect to the award of costs to or against the Crown in Northern Ireland.

(4) An Order in Council under this section may be varied or revoked by a further Order in Council made thereunder.

(5) An Order in Council under this section may include such provisions as appear to His Majesty to be incidental to or consequential on any provisions contained in such an Order by virtue of the preceding provisions of this section.

(6) ...[1]

(7) An Order in Council under this section shall be laid before Parliament as soon as may be after it is made, and, if either House of Parliament, within the next twenty-eight days on which that House has sat after such an Order is laid before it, resolves that the Order be annulled, the Order shall thereupon cease to have effect except as respects things previously done or omitted to be done, without prejudice, however, to the making of a new Order ...[2].

Amendments—[1] Sub-s (6) repealed by the Northern Ireland Constitution Act 1973 s 41(1)(a) and Sch 6 Part I.
[2] Words in sub-s (7) repealed by the Statute Law Revision Act 1953 s 1, Sch 1.

54 Short title and commencement

(1) This Act may be cited as the Crown Proceedings Act 1947.

(2) ...[1]

Note—The Act was brought into force on 1 January 1948, by the Crown Proceedings Act 1947 (Commencement) Order, SR & O 1947/2527.
Amendments—[1] Sub-s (2) repealed by the Statute Law Revision Act 1950.

FIRST SCHEDULE
PROCEEDINGS ABOLISHED BY THIS ACT

Section 23

1—(1) Latin informations and English informations.

(2) Writs of capias ad respondendum, writs of subpoena ad respondendum, and writs of appraisement.

(3) Writs of scire facias.

(4) Proceedings for the determination of any issue upon a writ of extent or of diem clausit extremum.

(5) Writs of summons under Part V of the Crown Suits Act, 1865.

2—(1) Proceedings against His Majesty by way of petition of right, including proceedings by way of petition of right intituled in the Admiralty Division under section fifty-two of the Naval Prize Act, 1864.

(2) Proceedings against His Majesty by way of monstrans de droit.

Note—The heading "Section 23" appears to be a misprint for "Section 13".
Modifications—See the Crown Proceedings (Northern Ireland) Order, SI 1981/233, art 29, for modifications of this section in respect of its application to Northern Ireland.

PROVISIONAL COLLECTION OF TAXES ACT 1968

(1968 Chapter 2)

ARRANGEMENT OF SECTIONS

An Act to consolidate the Provisional Collection of Taxes Act 1913 and certain other enactments relating to the provisional collection of taxes or matters connected therewith.

[1st February 1968]

1 Temporary statutory effect of House of Commons resolutions affecting income tax, ...

(1) This section applies only to income tax, [corporation tax ...⁹]⁴ ...

[(1A) ...] ²,³

(2) Subject to that, and to the provisions of subsections (4) to (8) below, where the House of Commons passes a resolution which—

(a) provides for the renewal for a further period of any tax in force or imposed during the previous financial year (whether at the same or a different rate, and whether with or without modifications) or for the variation or abolition of any existing tax, and

(b) contains a declaration that it is expedient in the public interest that the resolution should have statutory effect under the provisions of this Act,

the resolution shall, for the period specified in the next following subsection, have statutory effect as if contained in an Act of Parliament and, where the resolution provides for the renewal of a tax, all enactments which were in force with reference to that tax as last imposed by Act of Parliament shall during that period have full force and effect with respect to the tax as renewed by the resolution.

In this section references to the renewal of a tax include references to its reimposition, and references to the abolition of a tax include references to its repeal.

(3) The said period is—

(a) in the case of a resolution passed in [November or December]⁵ in any year, one expiring with [5th May in the next calendar year]⁶;

[(aa) in the case of a resolution passed in February or March in any year, one expiring with 5th August in the same calendar year; and]⁸

(b) in the case of any other resolution, one expiring at the end of four months after the date on which it is expressed to take effect or, if no such date is expressed, after the date on which it is passed.

(4) A resolution shall cease to have statutory effect under this section unless within the next [thirty]⁷ days on which the House of Commons sits after the day on which the resolution is passed—

(a) a Bill renewing, varying or, as the case may be, abolishing the tax is read a second time by the House, or

(b) a Bill is amended by the House [in Committee or on Report, or by any Standing Committee of the House]¹ so as to include provision for the renewal, variation or, as the case may be, abolition of the tax.

(5) A resolution shall also cease to have statutory effect under this section if—

(a) the provisions giving effect to it are rejected during the passage of the Bill containing them through the House, or

(b) an Act comes into operation renewing, varying or, as the case may be, abolishing the tax, or

(c) Parliament is dissolved or prorogued.

(6) Where, in the case of a resolution providing for the renewal or variation of a tax, the resolution ceases to have statutory effect by virtue of subsection (4) or (5) above, or the period specified in subsection (3) above terminates, before an Act comes into operation renewing or varying the tax, any money paid in pursuance of the resolution shall be repaid or made good, and any deduction made in pursuance of the resolution shall be deemed to be an unauthorised deduction.

(7) Where any tax as renewed or varied by a resolution is modified by the Act renewing or varying the tax, any money paid in pursuance of the resolution which would not have been payable under the new conditions affecting the tax shall be repaid or made good, and any deduction made in pursuance of the resolution shall, so far as it would not have been authorised under the new conditions affecting the tax, be deemed to be an unauthorised deduction.

(8) When during any session a resolution has had statutory effect under this section, statutory effect shall not be again given under this section in the same session to the same resolution or to a resolution having the same effect.

Commentary—*Simon's Direct Tax Service* **A1.104.**
Note—Words omitted from the heading and sub-s (1) are not relevant for the purposes of this work.
Amendments—¹ Words in sub-s (4)(*b*) added by FA 1968 s 60.
² Sub-s (1A) inserted by FA 1985 s 97 and repealed by FA 1993 s 205(3) and Sch 23 Pt VI in relation to resolutions passed after 27 July 1993.
³ Sub-s (1A) inserted by FA 1985 s 97 and repealed by FA 1993 s 205(3) and Sch 23 Pt VI in relation to resolutions passed after 27 July 1993.
⁴ Words in sub-s (1) inserted by FA 1993 s 205 in relation to resolutions passed after 27 July 1993.
⁵ Words in sub-s (3)(*a*) substituted by FA 1993 s 205 in relation to resolutions passed after 27 July 1993.
⁶ Words in sub-s (3)(*a*) substituted by FA 1993 s 205 in relation to resolutions passed after 27 July 1993.
⁷ Words in sub-s (4) substituted by FA 1993 s 205 in relation to resolutions passed after 27 July 1993.
⁸ Sub-s(3)(*aa*) inserted by F(No 2)A 1997 s 50(1), (3) in relation to resolutions passed after 31 July 1997.
⁹ Words in sub-s (1) repealed by FA 1998 Sch 3 para 1, Sch 27 Part III(2), with effect in relation to distributions made after 5 April 1999.

2 Payments and deductions made on account, and before renewal, of any temporary tax within s 1

(1) Any payment or deduction made on account of a temporary tax to which section 1 above applies and within one month after the date of its expiry shall, if the payment or deduction would have been a legal payment or deduction if the tax had not expired, be deemed to be a legal payment or deduction, subject to the condition that—

(*a*) if a resolution for the renewal or reimposition of the tax is not passed by the House of Commons within that month, or such a resolution is passed within that month but ceases to have statutory effect under the said section 1, any money so paid or deducted shall be repaid or made good, and

(*b*) if the tax is ultimately renewed or reimposed at a different rate, or with modifications, any amount paid or deducted which could not properly have been paid or deducted under the new conditions affecting the tax shall be repaid or made good.

(2) In this section "temporary tax" means a tax which has been imposed, or renewed or reimposed, for a limited period not exceeding eighteen months, and was in force or imposed during the previous financial year.

Commentary—*Simon's Direct Tax Service* **A1.104.**
Cross references—See TA 1988 s 822 (over-deductions from interest on loan capital etc made before passing of annual Act).

5 House of Commons resolution giving provisional effect to motions affecting taxation

(1) This section shall apply if the House of Commons resolves that provisional statutory effect shall be given to one or more motions to be moved by the Chancellor of the Exchequer, or some other Minister, and which, if agreed to by the House, would be resolutions—

(*a*) to which statutory effect could be given under section 1 of this Act, or
(*b*) to which section 3 of this Act could be applied ...¹
(*c*) ...¹

(2) Subject to subsection (3) below, on the passing of the resolution under subsection (1) above, sections 1 to 3 of this Act [[and section 822 of the Income and Corporation Taxes Act 1988]² (over-deductions from preference dividends before passing of annual Act)]¹ shall apply as if each motion to which the resolution applies had then been agreed to by a resolution of the House.

(3) Subsection (2) above shall cease to apply to a motion if that motion, or a motion containing the same proposals with modifications, is not agreed to by a resolution of the House (in this section referred to as "a confirmatory resolution") within the next ten days on which the House sits after the resolution under subsection (1) above is passed, and, if it ceases to apply, all such adjustments, whether by way of discharge or repayment of tax, or discharge of security, or otherwise, shall be made as may be necessary to restore the position to what it would have been if subsection (2) above had never applied to that motion, and to make good any deductions which have become unauthorised deductions.

(4) The enactments specified in subsection (2) above shall have effect as if—

(*a*) any confirmatory resolution passed within the said period of ten sitting days had been passed when the resolution under subsection (1) above was passed, and

(*b*) everything done in pursuance of the said subsection (2) by reference to the motion to which the confirmatory resolution relates had been done by reference to the confirmatory resolution,

but any necessary adjustments shall be made, whether by way of discharge or repayment of tax, or modification of the terms of any security, or further assessment, or otherwise, where the proposals in the confirmatory resolution are not the same as those in the original motion to which that resolution relates.

Commentary—*Simon's Direct Tax Service* **A1.104.**
Note—Sub-s (1)(*b*) is not relevant to this work.
Amendments—¹ Words in sub-s (2) substituted and sub-s (1)(*c*), and word immediately preceding it, repealed by FA 1993 s 205(1), (6), (7) Sch 23 Pt VI in relation to resolutions passed after 27 July 1993.
² Words in square brackets substituted by the Income and Corporation Taxes Act 1988 s 844 Sch 29 para 32 with effect from 5 April 1988.

6 Short title, repeals and saving as respects Northern Ireland

(1) This Act may be cited as the Provisional Collection of Taxes Act 1968.

(2), (3) ...¹

Note—Sub-s (2) repeals enactments specified in Sch. Effect has been given to these repeals where applicable in the relevant provisions of the earlier enactments.
Amendments—¹ Sub-s (3) repealed by Northern Ireland Constitution Act 1973 s 41(1)(*a*) and Sch 6 Pt 1, with effect from 18 July 1973.

FINANCE ACT 1969

(1969 Chapter 32)

An Act to grant certain duties, to alter other duties, and to amend the law relating to the National Debt and the Public Revenue, and to make further provision in connection with Finance.

[25th July 1969]

PART VI

MISCELLANEOUS

58 Disclosure of information for statistical purposes by Board of Inland Revenue

(1) For the purpose of any statistical survey conducted or to be conducted by the [Department of Employment]¹ [the Department of Trade and Industry or the [Office for National Statistics]¹²]⁶, the Board of Inland Revenue may disclose to an authorised officer of that Department or Office—

(*a*) the names and addresses of persons (in this section referred to as "employers") required under [section 203 of the Income and Corporation Taxes Act 1988]² (pay as you earn) to make deductions of tax from payments of, or on account of, emoluments to which that section applies; and

(*b*) information concerning the number of persons (in this section referred to as "employees") in receipt of emoluments paid by an employer.

(2) For the purpose of any statistical survey relating to earnings conducted or to be conducted by the [Office for National Statistics]¹², the Board of Inland Revenue may disclose to an authorised officer of [that office]¹¹ the name and address of the employer of any person who is one of a number of employees selected (as a statistical sample) for the purpose of that survey.

(3) Subsections (1) and (2) above shall have effect notwithstanding any obligation as to secrecy imposed on the Board or any officer of the Board under the Income Tax Management Act 1964 or otherwise.

(4) Subject to subsection (5) below, no information obtained by virtue of this section by an officer of the [Department of Employment]¹ [or of the Department of Trade and Industry or the [Office for National Statistics]¹²]⁶ may be disclosed except—

(*a*) to [an]³ officer of that Department or Office for the purpose of the statistical survey concerned, or

(*b*) to another department (including a department of the Government of Northern Ireland) for the purpose of a statistical survey conducted or to be conducted by that department, [or]⁴

[(*c*) to an authorised officer of any body specified in the first column of the following Table for the purposes of functions of that body under any enactment specified in relation to it in the second column of the Table.

TABLE

Body	Enactment
...	...[9]
The Northern Ireland Training Authority.	The Industrial Training (Northern Ireland) Order 1984.
A local planning authority within the meaning of [the Town and Country Planning Act 1990][8] and any board which exercises for any area the functions of such an authority.	[Part II of the Town and Country Planning Act 1990][8].
A planning authority as defined in [section 1 of the Town and Country Planning (Scotland) Act 1997][13].	Part II of the Town and Country Planning (Scotland) Act [1997].
The Welsh Development Agency.	The Welsh Development Agency Act 1975.
[Scottish Enterprise.][7]	[Part I of the Enterprise and New Towns (Scotland) Act 1990.][7]
...[14]	...[14]
[Highlands and Islands Enterprise.][7]	[Part I of the Enterprise and New Towns (Scotland) Act 1990.][7]
A development corporation within the meaning of the New Towns Act 1981.	Section 4 of the New Towns Act 1981.
A development corporation within the meaning of the New Towns (Scotland) Act 1968.	Section 3 of the New Towns (Scotland) Act 1968.
A new town commission within the meaning of the New Towns Act (Northern Ireland) 1965.	Section 7 of the New Towns Act (Northern Ireland) 1965.][4]

(5) Subsection (4) above does not apply to the disclosure of any such information as is mentioned in subsection (1) or subsection (2) above—

(a) in the form of a summary so framed as not to enable particulars relating to an employer or employee to be ascertained from it, or

(b) in the case of such information as is mentioned in subsection (1) above, with the consent of the employer concerned and, in the case of such information as is mentioned in subsection (2) above, with the consent of the employee concerned.

(6) If any person who has obtained any information by virtue of any provision of this section discloses that information otherwise than in accordance with paragraph (a) [paragraph (b) or paragraph (c) of subsection (4) above][5] or subsection (5) above, he shall be liable on summary conviction to a fine not exceeding [the prescribed sum],[10] or on conviction on indictment to imprisonment for a term not exceeding two years or to a fine or to both.

(7) References in this section to the [Department of Employment][1] [the Department of Trade and Industry or the [Office for National Statistics][12]][6] include references to any department of the Government of Northern Ireland carrying out similar functions.

Commentary—*Simon's Direct Tax Service* **A2.803.**
Cross references—See FA 1972 s 127 (disclosure of information between Revenue departments).
FA 1989 s 182 (unlawful disclosure of information).
Note—The reference to "the prescribed sum" in sub-s (6) is substituted by virtue of the Magistrates' Courts Act 1980 s 32(2). By the 1980 Act, s 32(9), as amended by the Criminal Justice Act 1991 s 17(2)(c), the prescribed sum is £5,000 but a different sum may be substituted by order under the 1980 Act, s 143.
Amendments—[1] Words "Department of Employment" in sub-ss (1), (4), (7) substituted by virtue of the Secretary of State for Trade and Industry Order, SI 1970/1537, art 3(2).
[2] Words in sub-s (1)(a) substituted by TA 1988 Sch 29 para 32 Table.
[3] Word in sub-s (4)(a) substituted by the Employment and Training Act 1973 s 4(6), with effect from 1 January 1974; see the Employment and Training Act 1973 (Commencement No 1) Order, SI 1973/2063.
[4] Sub-s (4)(c) and the word "or" preceding it added by F(No 2)A 1987, s 69(1), (2).
[5] Words in sub-s (6) substituted by F(No 2)A 1987, s 69(1), (3).
[6] Words in sub-ss (1), (4), (7) substituted by the Transfer of Functions (Economic Statistics) Order, SI 1989/992 Sch 2 para 1(1) with effect from 31 July 1989.
[7] Words in sub-s (4)(c) Table substituted by the Enterprise and New Towns (Scotland) Act 1990 Sch 4 para 2 with effect from 1 April 1991 by virtue of the Enterprise and New Towns (Scotland) Act 1990 Commencement Order, SI 1990/1840 art 4.
[8] Words in sub-s (4)(c) Table substituted by the Planning (Consequential Provisions) Act 1990 Sch 2 para 23.
[9] Entries in the Table in sub-s (4) repealed by the Trade Union Reform and Employment Rights Act 1993 Sch 10 with effect partly as from 1 April 1994 and partly as from 1 April 1995 (by virtue of the Trade Union Reform and Employment Rights Act 1993 (Commencement No 2 and Transitional Provisions) Order SI 1993/2503).
[10] See Note above.
[11] Words in sub-s (2) substituted by the Transfer of Functions (Education and Employment) Order, SI 1995/2986 art 11(1), Sch para 6 with effect from 1 January 1996.
[12] Words in sub-ss (1), (2), (4), (7) substituted by the Transfer of Functions (Registration and Statistics) Order 1996, SI 1996/273 art 5(1), Sch 2 para 17 with effect from 1 April 1996.
[13] Words in sub-s (4)(c) Table substituted by Planning (Consequential Provisions)(Scotland) Act 1997 Sch 2 para 18 with effect from 27 May 1997.
[14] Words in sub-s (4)(c) Table repealed by the Government of Wales Act 1998 Sch 18 Part IV with effect from 1 October 1998, by virtue of the Government of Wales Act 1998 (Commencement No 1) Order, SI 1998/2244.

TAXES MANAGEMENT ACT 1970

(1970 Chapter 9)

ARRANGEMENT OF SECTIONS

PART I

ADMINISTRATION

PART II

RETURNS OF INCOME AND GAINS

Income tax

Corporation tax

Capital gains

Partnerships

European Economic Interest Groupings

Records

PART III
OTHER RETURNS AND INFORMATION

PART IIIA
REFERRAL OF QUESTIONS DURING ENQUIRY

PART IV
ASSESSMENT AND CLAIMS

PART V

APPEALS AND OTHER PROCEEDINGS

Jurisdiction

Proceedings before Commissioners

Chargeable gains

Development land tax

An Act to consolidate certain of the enactments relating to income tax, capital gains tax and corporation tax, including certain enactments relating also to other taxes.

[12th March 1970]

Construction—FA 1988 s 127 to be construed as if it were contained in this Act; see FA 1988 s 127(6).

PART I

ADMINISTRATION

1 Taxes under care and management of the Board

(1) Income tax, corporation tax and capital gains tax shall be under the care and management of the Commissioners of Inland Revenue (in this Act referred to as "the Board"), and the definition of "inland revenue" in section 39 of the Inland Revenue Regulation Act 1890 shall have effect accordingly.

(2) The Board shall appoint inspectors and collectors of taxes who shall act under the direction of the Board.

[(2A) The Board may appoint a person to be an inspector or collector for general purposes or for such specific purposes as the Board think fit.][1]

[(2B) Where in accordance with the Board's administrative practices a person is authorised to act as an inspector or collector for specific purposes, he shall be deemed to have been appointed to be an inspector or collector for those purposes.][1]

(3) Any legal proceedings or administration act relating to any tax begun by one inspector or collector may be continued by another inspector or, as the case may be, another collector; and any inspector or collector may act for any division or other area.

Commentary—*Simon's Direct Tax Service* **A2.302, 401, 701.**
Cross references—See IRRA 1890 s 4 (appointment of collectors, inspectors and other persons).
SSC & BA 1992 Sch 2 para 6(2) (Revenue's powers of care and management under this section extended to the remission of interest payable under ss 86, 88 in respect of Class 4 National Insurance contributions).
Revenue & other press releases—IR 4-9-91 (special tax enquiry services for the deaf).
IR 13-8-91 (new Taxpayer's Charter).
IR 23-2-93 (new taxpayer service offices and taxpayer district offices to replace some existing assessment and collection offices, in restructuring programme to March 1994).
IR 2-6-93 (independent adjudicator appointed to deal with complaints from taxpayers. Complaints procedure).
IR 7-12-93 (new taxpayer service offices and taxpayer district offices: phase 2).
ICAEW TR 818 and TR 830 (applications to the Revenue for guidance or technical opinion).
Law Society 13-6-94 (letter from Deputy Chairman of Inland Revenue regarding disclosure in letters applying for clearance or confirmation of interpretation of the law).
IR Code of Practice 10: "Information and Advice" (provision of information and advice by Revenue; addresses for specific clearance applications).
Revenue Internal Guidance—Collection manual CM4.610 (the Board authorises the discharge of amounts which are irrecoverable or not worth pursuit under the general powers conferred on them by section 1).
Simon's Tax Cases—*IRC v National Federation of Self-Employed and Small Businesses Ltd* [1981] STC 260; *IRC v Nuttall* [1990] STC 194.
Amendments—¹ Sub-ss (2A), (2B) inserted by FA 1990 s 104(1), (3) and deemed always to have had effect.

2 General Commissioners

(1) For the purpose of exercising such powers relating to appeals and other matters as are conferred on them by the Taxes Acts [or by Part II of the Social Security Contributions (Transfer of Functions, etc) Act 1999][8] [or by Part III of the Social Security Contributions (Transfer of Functions, etc) (Northern Ireland) Order 1999][9] there shall be "Commissioners for the general purposes of the income tax" (in the Taxes Acts referred to as "General Commissioners") who shall act for the same separate areas in Great Britain as heretofore [or for the separate areas in Northern Ireland defined by an order made by the Lord Chancellor][4] (in the Taxes Acts referred to as "divisions").

(2) General Commissioners for divisions in England and Wales [or Northern Ireland][5] shall be appointed by, and shall hold office during the pleasure of, the Lord Chancellor.

(3) General Commissioners for divisions in Scotland shall be appointed by, and shall hold office during the pleasure of, [the Secretary of State][1-2] ...[3]

(4) In Scotland a sheriff shall be ex officio a General Commissioner for any division wholly or partly within his sheriffdom, and a salaried sheriff-substitute shall be ex officio a General Commissioner for any division wholly or partly within his district.

[(5) The Lord Chancellor or, in Scotland, the Secretary of State shall pay General Commissioners by way of travelling allowance or subsistence allowance sums of such amounts and in such circumstances as he may, with the approval of the Treasury, determine.][7]

(6) The Lord Chancellor or, in Scotland, the Secretary of State may by order create a new division or abolish an existing division or alter in any other respect the divisions or their boundaries; and any such order may contain such consequential and transitional provisions as the Lord Chancellor or the Secretary of State, as the case may be, thinks fit and may be revoked or varied by a subsequent order under this subsection.

...[6]

(7) A General Commissioner shall not continue in office after he attains the age of seventy-five years.

(8) The validity of any proceedings of General Commissioners shall not be affected by a defect in the appointment of any of them, or by a failure to observe the requirements of the last preceding subsection.

[(9) No action shall lie against a General Commissioner in respect of any act or omission of his—

(a) in the execution of his duty; and
(b) with respect to any matter within his jurisdiction.][10]

[(10) No action shall lie against a General Commissioner in respect of any act or omission of his—

(a) in the purported execution of his duty; but
(b) with respect to any matter not within his jurisdiction,

unless it is proved that he acted in bad faith.][10]

Commentary—*Simon's Direct Tax Service* **A2.502–504, 506, 508.**
Definition—"Local authority", TA 1988 s 519.
Cross references—See FA 1972 s 130 (compensation for loss of office, etc, by clerks to General Commissioners which is attributable to any order affecting a division made (whether before or after the passing of FA 1972) under sub-s (6) of this section);
FA 1973 s 41 (the alteration of local government areas due to take effect on 1 April 1974 (16 May 1975 in Scotland) is not to affect divisions, although orders may be made to take the changes into account).
F(No 2)A 1992 s 75 (General Commissioners may hold office by a different name).
Amendments—¹⁻² Words in sub-s (3) substituted by FA 1975 s 57(1)(a), with effect from 16 May 1975.
³ Words in sub-s (3) repealed by FA 1975 s 57(1)(b) and Sch 13 Pt II, with effect from 16 May 1975.
⁴ Words in sub-s (1) inserted by FA 1988 s 134(1), (4) with effect from 3 April 1989 by virtue of FA 1988 (Commencement) Order, SI 1989/473 subject to special provisions for proceedings instituted before 3 April 1989.
⁵ Words in sub-s (2) inserted by FA 1988 s 134(1), (4) with effect from 3 April 1989 by virtue of FA 1988 (Commencement) Order, SI 1989/473 subject to special provisions for proceedings instituted before 3 April 1989.
⁶ Words in sub-s (6) repealed by FA 1988 Sch 14 Pt IX with effect from 3 April 1989 by virtue of FA 1988 (Commencement) Order, SI 1989/473.

[7] Sub-s (5) substituted by F(No 2)A 1992 Sch 16 para 2(1), (5) with effect from 1 April 1994.

[8] Words in sub-s (1) inserted by the Social Security Contributions (Transfer of Functions, etc) Act 1999 Sch 7 para 1, with effect from 4 March 1999 by virtue of the Social Security Contributions (Transfer of Functions, etc) Act 1999 (Commencement No 1 and Transitional Provisions) Order, SI 1999/527 art 2(*a*), Sch 1.

[9] Words inserted in sub-s (1) by the Social Security Contributions (Transfer of Functions, etc) (Northern Ireland) Order, SI 1999/671 art 17 Sch 6 para 1, with effect from 1 April 1999 (by virtue of the Social Security Contributions (Transfer of Functions, etc) (1999 Order) (Commencement No 1 and Transitional Provisions) Order (Northern Ireland), SR 1999/149, art 2(*c*), Sch 2).

[10] Sub-ss (9), (10) inserted by the Access to Justice Act 1999, s 101 with effect from 1 April 2001 in relation to England, Wales, and Northern Ireland (by virtue of SI 2001/916).

Prospective amendment—Sub-ss (9), (10) to be inserted by the Access to Justice Act 1999, s 101 (in relation to Scotland) with effect from a day to be appointed.

[2A General Commissioners: costs and expenses in legal proceedings

(1) A court may not order a General Commissioner to pay costs or (in Scotland) expenses in any proceedings in respect of any act or omission of his in the execution (or purported execution) of his duty as a General Commissioner.

(2) Subsection (1) above does not apply in relation to—

(*a*) any proceedings in which a General Commissioner is being tried for an offence or is appealing against a conviction; or

(*b*) any proceedings in which it is proved that a General Commissioner acted in bad faith in respect of the matters giving rise to the proceedings.

(3) Where a court is prevented by subsection (1) above from ordering a General Commissioner to pay costs or expenses in any proceedings, the court may instead order the making by the relevant Minister of a payment in respect of the costs or expenses of a person in the proceedings.

(4) The relevant Minister may by regulations made by statutory instrument make provision specifying—

(*a*) circumstances when a court shall or shall not exercise the power conferred on it by subsection (3) above; and

(*b*) how the amount of any payment ordered under that subsection is to be determined.

(5) No regulations may be made under subsection (4) above unless a draft of the statutory instrument containing them has been laid before, and approved by a resolution of, each House of Parliament.

(6) In this section "relevant Minister" means the Lord Chancellor or, in Scotland, the Secretary of State.][1]

Regulations—See General Commissioners of Income Tax (Costs) Regulations, SI 2001/1304.

Amendments—[1]. This section inserted by the Access to Justice Act 1999, s 102 with effect from 1 April 2001 in relation to England, Northern Ireland, and Wales (by virtue of SI 2001/916).

Prospective amendment—This section to be inserted by the Access to Justice Act 1999, s 102 (in relation to Scotland) with effect from a day to be appointed.

3 Clerk to General Commissioners

(1) The General Commissioners for every division shall appoint a clerk and, if they think it necessary, an assistant clerk, and persons appointed under this subsection shall hold office during the pleasure of the Commissioners and act under their direction.

[(2) The Lord Chancellor or, in Scotland, the Secretary of State shall pay a clerk such remuneration in respect of his services as the Lord Chancellor or Secretary of State may, with the approval of the Treasury, determine.][2]

(3) [The Lord Chancellor or, in Scotland, the Secretary of State may, in such cases as he may in his discretion determine][3], pay to or in respect of any full-time clerk such pension [allowance][1] or gratuity, or make such provision for the payment of pension [allowance][1] or gratuity to or in respect of any full-time clerk, as [he may, with the approval of the Treasury, determine][3].

In this subsection "full-time clerk" means a clerk as regards whom [the Lord Chancellor or Secretary of State is satisfied][3] that he is required to devote substantially the whole of his time to the duties of his office.

(4) Without prejudice to the power of any General Commissioners to dismiss their clerk or assistant clerk, the Lord Chancellor or, in Scotland, the Secretary of State may, after consulting the General Commissioners for any division, dismiss their clerk or assistant clerk.

(5) A clerk or assistant clerk shall not continue in office after he has attained the age of seventy years unless the General Commissioners for whom he acts think it desirable in the public interest and extend his term of office; and the term shall not be extended beyond the age of seventy-five years.

Commentary—*Simon's Direct Tax Service* A2.509.

Amendments—[1] Word inserted in both places in sub-s (3) by the Superannuation Act 1972 s 29 and Sch 6 para 77, with effect from 25 March 1972: the Superannuation Act 1972 (Commencement No 1) Order, SI 1972/325 reg 2.

[2] Sub-s (2) substituted by F(No 2)A 1992 Sch 16 para 2(2)–(5), with effect from 1 April 1994.

[3] Words in sub-s (3) substituted by F(No 2)A 1992 Sch 16 para 2(2)–(5), with effect from 1 April 1994.

[3A General Commissioners and clerks: indemnity

(1) A General Commissioner or a clerk may be indemnified by the relevant Minister in respect of—

(a) any costs or (in Scotland) expenses which the General Commissioner or clerk reasonably incurs in or in connection with proceedings in respect of anything done or omitted in the exercise (or purported exercise) of his duty as a General Commissioner or clerk;

(b) any costs or expenses which he reasonably incurs in taking steps to dispute any claim which might be made in such proceedings;

(c) any damages awarded against him or costs or expenses ordered to be paid by him in any such proceedings; and

(d) any sums payable by him in connection with a reasonable settlement of any such proceedings or claim,

unless it is proved, in respect of matters giving rise to the proceedings or claim in question, that he acted in bad faith.

(2) A General Commissioner or a clerk shall be indemnified by the relevant Minister in respect of any such costs or expenses, damages or sums as are mentioned in subsection (1)(a) to (d) above if, in respect of the matters giving rise to the proceedings or claim in question, he acted reasonably and in good faith.

(3) Any question whether, or to what extent, a person is to be indemnified under this section shall be determined by the relevant Minister.

(4) A determination under subsection (3) above with respect to any such costs or expenses or sums as are mentioned in subsection (1)(a), (b) or (d) above may, if the person claiming to be indemnified so requests, be made in advance before they are incurred or the settlement made.

(5) Any such determination in advance for indemnity in respect of costs or expenses to be incurred—

(a) shall be subject to such limitations, if any, as the relevant Minister thinks proper and to the subsequent determination of the amount of the costs or expenses reasonably incurred; and

(b) shall not affect any other determination which may fall to be made in connection with the proceedings or claim in question.

(6) In this section "clerk" means—

(a) any person appointed to be a clerk or assistant clerk to the General Commissioners for any division; or

(b) a person who assists any such person;

and "relevant Minister" means the Lord Chancellor or, in Scotland, the Secretary of State.]¹

Amendment—¹ This section inserted by the Access to Justice Act 1999, s 103 with effect (in relation to England, Northern Ireland, and Wales) from 1 April 2001 (by virtue of SI 2001/916).

[4 Special Commissioners

(1) The Lord Chancellor shall, after consultation with the [Secretary of State]⁵, appoint such persons as he thinks fit as "Commissioners for the special purposes of the Income Tax Acts" (in the Taxes Acts referred to as "Special Commissioners") and shall designate one of the Special Commissioners as the Presiding Special Commissioner.

(2) No person shall be appointed under subsection (1) above [unless—

(a) he has a 10 year general qualification, within the meaning of section 71 of the Courts and Legal Services Act 1990;

(b) he is an advocate or solicitor in Scotland of at least 10 years' standing; or

(c) he is a member of the Bar of Northern Ireland or solicitor of the Supreme Court of Northern Ireland of at least 10 years' standing.]²

(3) If the Presiding Special Commissioner is temporarily absent or unable to act or there is a vacancy in his office, the Lord Chancellor may designate another Special Commissioner to act as deputy Presiding Special Commissioner and the Commissioner so designated shall, when so acting, have all the functions of the Presiding Special Commissioner.

[(3A) A Special Commissioner—

(a) may resign his office at any time; and

(b) shall vacate his office on the day on which he attains the age of seventy years;

but paragraph (b) above is subject to section 26(4) to (6) of the Judicial Pensions and Retirement Act 1993 (power to authorise continuance in office up to the age of 75).]³

(4) The Lord Chancellor may, if he thinks fit, and after consultation with the Lord Advocate, remove a Special Commissioner from office on the grounds of incapacity or misbehaviour.

(5) By virtue of their appointment the Special Commissioners shall have authority to execute such powers, and to perform such duties, as are assigned to them by any enactment.

(6) Such sums shall be allowed to Special Commissioners in respect of salary and incidental expenses and such pensions (including allowances and gratuities) shall be paid to, or in respect of, them as the Lord Chancellor may, with the approval of the Treasury, determine.

[(6A) Subsection (6) above, so far as relating to pensions (including allowances and gratuities), shall not have effect in relation to a person to whom Part I of the Judicial Pensions and Retirement Act 1993 applies, except to the extent provided by or under that Act.][4]

(7) Officers and staff may be appointed under section 27 of the Courts Act 1971 (court staff) for carrying out the administrative work of the Special Commissioners.][1]

Commentary—*Simon's Direct Tax Service* A2.513, 514.
Amendments—[1] This section substituted by FA 1984 Sch 22 para 1 and came into force on 1 January 1985 by virtue of FA 1984 (Commencement No 2) Order, SI 1984/1836.
[2] Words in sub-s (2) substituted by the Courts and Legal Services Act 1990 Sch 10 para 30 with effect from 1 January 1991 by virtue of the Courts and Legal Services Act 1990 (Commencement No 2) Order, SI 1990/2484.
[3] Sub-s (3A) inserted by the Judicial Pensions and Retirement Act 1993 s 26 and Sch 6 para 36(1) with effect from 31 March 1995 (by virtue of the Judicial Pensions and Retirement Act 1993 (Commencement) Order, SI 1995/631).
[4] Sub-s (6A) inserted by the Judicial Pensions and Retirement Act 1993 s 31 and Sch 8 para 8 with effect from 31 March 1995 (by virtue of the Judicial Pensions and Retirement Act 1993 (Commencement) Order, SI 1995/631).
[5] Words in sub-s (1) substituted by the Transfer of Functions (Lord Advocate and Secretary of State) Order, SI 1999/678 art 2(1), Sch with effect from 19 May 1999

[4A Deputy Special Commissioners

(1) If it appears to the Lord Chancellor expedient to do so in order to facilitate the performance of any functions of the Special Commissioners, he may, after consultation with the [Secretary of State][4], appoint a person to be a deputy Special Commissioner during such period or on such occasions as the Lord Chancellor thinks fit.

(2) A person shall not be qualified for appointment as a deputy Special Commissioner unless he is qualified for appointment as a Special Commissioner [(and, accordingly, no appointment of a person as a deputy Special Commissioner shall be such as to extend beyond the day on which he attains the age of seventy years, but subject to section 26(4) to (6) of the Judicial Pensions and Retirement Act 1993)][2].

(3) A deputy Special Commissioner while acting under this section shall have all the jurisdiction and functions of a Special Commissioner and any reference to a Special Commissioner in the following provisions of this Act or in any other enactment or any instrument made under any enactment (whenever passed or made) shall include a reference to a deputy Special Commissioner.

(4) The duty under section 6(1) below shall only apply to a deputy Special Commissioner on his first appointment to that office.

(5) ...[3]

(6) The Lord Chancellor may pay to any person appointed under this section such remuneration and allowances as he may, with the approval of the Treasury, determine.][1]

Commentary—*Simon's Direct Tax Service* A2.513, 514.
Amendments—[1] This section inserted by FA 1984 s 127 and Sch 22 para 1 and came into force on 1 January 1985 by virtue of FA 1984 (Commencement No 2) Order, SI 1984/1836.
[2] Words in sub-s (2) added by the Judicial Pensions and Retirement Act 1993 s 26 and Sch 6 para 36(2) with effect from 31 March 1995 (by virtue of the Judicial Pensions and Retirement Act 1993 (Commencement) Order, SI 1995/631).
[3] Sub-s (5) repealed by the Judicial Pensions and Retirement Act 1993 s 31 and Sch 9 with effect from 31 March 1995 (by virtue of the Judicial Pensions and Retirement Act 1993 (Commencement) Order, SI 1995/631).
[4] Words in sub-s (1) substituted by the Transfer of Functions (Lord Advocate and Secretary of State) Order, SI 1999/678 art 2(1), Sch with effect from 19 May 1999

5 General and Special Commissioners

(1) No General Commissioner or Special Commissioner shall act as such in relation to any matter in which he has a personal interest, or is interested on behalf of another person, except with the express consent of the parties to the proceedings.

(2) ...[1]

Commentary—*Simon's Direct Tax Service* A2.511, 514.
Simon's Tax Cases—*Silver v Inspector of Taxes* [1997] STC (SCD) 193.
Amendments—[1] Sub-s (2) repealed by the Criminal Justice Act 1972 Sch 6 Pt I, with effect from 30 March 1974; see the Criminal Justice Act 1972 (Commencement No 3) Order, SI 1973/1472.

6 Declarations on taking office

(1) Every person who is appointed to be—

(a) a General Commissioner or a Special Commissioner, or

(b) ...[1]

(c) a member of the tribunal established under section [706][2] of the principal Act (cancellation of tax advantages),

shall make a declaration in the form set out in Part I of Schedule 1 to this Act before another person holding the same office, or before a General Commissioner.

(2) Every person who is appointed to be a clerk or assistant clerk to the General Commissioners for any division, or who assists any such clerk, shall make a declaration in the form set out in Part I of Schedule 1 to this Act.

A clerk or assistant clerk shall make the declaration before a General Commissioner for the division, and a person who assists any such clerk shall make the declaration before such a General Commissioner or the clerk.

(3) Every person who is appointed to be a member of the Board shall make a declaration in the form set out in Part II of Schedule 1 to this Act before another member of the Board.

(4) Every person who is appointed an inspector or collector, or who is appointed by the Board to serve in any other capacity, shall make a declaration in the form set out in Part III of Schedule 1 to this Act before such person as the Board may direct.

(5) A declaration under this section shall be made as soon as may be after first appointment to the office in question.

Commentary—*Simon's Direct Tax Service* **A2.802.**
Simon's Tax Cases—*IRC v National Federation of Self-Employed and Small Businesses Ltd* [1981] STC 260.
Definition—''Principal Act'', s 118(1).
Cross references—s 4A(4) (duty under sub-s (1) above only applies to a deputy Special Commissioner on his first appointment).
Tax Credits Act 1999 s 5(6) (the reference to an offence relating to the inland revenue in any declaration for the purposes of this section includes a reference to an offence relating to the working families' tax credit and disabled person's tax credit).
Employment Act 2002 s 5 (the reference to an offence relating to inland revenue shall be taken to include a reference to an offence, relating to statutory paternity pay or statutory adoption pay.
Amendments—[1] Sub-s (1)(*b*) repealed by FA 1982 Sch 22 Pt X.
[2] Number substituted by TA 1988 Sch 29 para 32 Table.

PART II
RETURNS OF INCOME AND GAINS

Statement of Practice SP 5/83—Procedure for making a return with the aid of schedules attached to official return form.
Revenue & other press releases—Revenue Booklet SAT2 (1995) (detailed guidance on the self-assessment system).
Cross references—See TMA 1970 s 29 (powers of inspector to raise tax assessments where returns under this Part are incorrect or unsatisfactory).
TMA 1970 s 70(2) (a certificate of a collector that a penalty is payable under this Part and has not been paid is sufficient evidence).
TMA 1970 Sch 3A para 1 (any provision of this Part requiring a declaration as to correctness etc by a person making a return does not apply in the case of electronic lodgement of tax returns).
TA 1988 ss 253(2), 350(5) (power of Board to make regulations modifying the provisions of this Part in relation to advance corporation tax and income tax deducted under TA 1988 s 349 for which a company is liable to account).

Income tax

[7 Notice of liability to income tax and capital gains tax

(1) Every person who—

(*a*) is chargeable to income tax or capital gains tax for any year of assessment, and
(*b*) has not received a notice under section 8 of this Act requiring a return for that year of his total income and chargeable gains,

shall, subject to subsection (3) below, within six months from the end of that year, give notice to an officer of the Board that he is so chargeable.

(2) In the case of [persons who are][2] chargeable as mentioned in subsection (1) above as [the relevant trustees][2] of a settlement, that subsection shall have effect as if the reference to a notice under section 8 of this Act were a reference to a notice under section 8A of this Act.

(3) A person shall not be required to give notice under subsection (1) above in respect of a year of assessment if for that year his total income consists of income from sources falling within subsection (4) to (7) below and he has no chargeable gains.

(4) A source of income falls within this subsection in relation to a year of assessment if—

(*a*) all payments of, or on account of, income from it during that year, and
(*b*) all income from it for that year which does not consist of payments,

have or has been taken into account in the making of deductions or repayments of tax under section 203 of the principal Act.

(5) A source of income falls within this subsection in relation to any person and any year of assessment if all income from it for that year has been or will be taken into account—

(*a*) in determining that person's liability to tax, or
(*b*) in the making of deductions or repayments of tax under section 203 of the principal Act.

(6) A source of income falls within this subsection in relation to any person and any year of assessment if all income from it for that year is—

(*a*) income from which income tax has been deducted;
(*b*) income from or on which income tax is treated as having been deducted or paid; or
(*c*) income chargeable under Schedule F,

and that person is not for that year liable to tax at a rate other than the basic rate[, the Schedule F ordinary rate][6][, the lower rate or the starting rate][7].

(7) A source of income falls within this subsection in relation to any person and any year of assessment if all income from it for that year is [income on which][3] he could not become liable to tax under a self-assessment made under section 9 of this Act in respect of that year.

(8) If any person, for any year of assessment, fails to comply with subsection (1) above, he shall be liable to a penalty not exceeding the amount of the tax—

    (*a*) in which he is assessed under section 9 or 29 of this Act in respect of that year, and
    (*b*) which is not paid on or before the 31st January next following that year.][1]

[(9) For the purposes of this Act the relevant trustees of a settlement are—

    (*a*) in relation to income [(other than gains treated as arising under Chapter II of Part XIII of the principal Act)][5], the persons who are trustees when the income arises and any persons who subsequently become trustees; and
    [(*aa*) in relation to gains treated as arising under Chapter II of Part XIII of the principal Act, the persons who are trustees in the year of assessment in which the gains arise and any persons who subsequently become trustees; and][5]
    (*b*) in relation to chargeable gains, the persons who are trustees in the year of assessment in which the chargeable gains accrue and any persons who subsequently become trustees.][4]

Commentary—*Simon's Direct Tax Service* **A3.140, E1.805.**
Statement of Practice SP 1/96—For 1995–96 individuals who have not received a tax return within 12 months from the end of the tax year are required to notify the Revenue within that time of their chargeability to income tax and to specify each source of income separately.
For 1996–97 (self-assessment) individuals who have not received a tax return, are required within 6 months from the end of the tax year to notify the Revenue by 5 October of their chargeability to income tax and if necessary complete a return and send it back (with any payment due) by 31 January following.
Revenue Internal Guidance—Enquiry Handbook EH633 (common failure situations: taxpayer commencing to trade, creation of trust, realisation of chargeable gain by PAYE taxpayer, chargeable gain realised by interest in possession settlement where income declared by beneficiaries).
EH636 (no extra time under s 118(2)).
Definitions—"Board", s 118(1); "chargeable gain", s 118(1); "lower rate", TA 1988 s 832(1); "principal Act", s 118(1); "starting rate" TA 1988 s 832(1); "the relevant trustees", s 118(1).
Cross references—See TMA 1970 s 107A(2), (3) (recovery of penalties from the relevant trustees of a settlement).
Amendments—[1] This section substituted by FA 1994 s 196, Sch 19 Pt I para 1 with effect from the year 1995–96.
[2] Words in sub-s (2) substituted by FA 1995 ss 103(1), with effect from the year 1996–97.
[3] Words in sub-s (7) substituted by FA 1995, ss 103(7), 115(1) with effect from the year 1996–97.
[4] Sub-s (9) inserted by FA 1995, s 103(2), with effect from the year 1996–97.
[5] Inserted by FA 1998 Sch 14 para 5 with effect in relation to chargeable events happening on or after 6 April 1998.
[6] Words in sub-s (6) amended by F(No 2)A 1997 s 34, Sch 4 para 1 with effect from the year 1999–00.
[7] Words in sub-s (6) substituted by FA 1999 s 22(11), (12) with effect from the year 1999–00.

[8 Personal return

[(1) For the purpose of establishing the amounts in which a person is chargeable to income tax and capital gains tax for a year of assessment, [and the amount payable by him by way of income tax for that year,][6] he may be required by a notice given to him by an officer of the Board—

    (*a*) to make and deliver to the officer, on or before the day mentioned in subsection (1A) below, a return containing such information as may reasonably be required in pursuance of the notice, and
    (*b*) to deliver with the return such accounts, statements and documents, relating to information contained in the return, as may reasonably be so required.

(1A) The day referred to in subsection (1) above is—

    (*a*) the 31st January next following the year of assessment, or
    (*b*) where the notice under this section is given after the 31st October next following the year, the last day of the period of three months beginning with the day on which the notice is given ...][3]

[(1AA) For the purposes of subsection (1) above—

    (*a*) the amounts in which a person is chargeable to income tax and capital gains tax are net amounts, that is to say, amounts which take into account any relief or allowance a claim for which is included in the return; and
    (*b*) the amount payable by a person by way of income tax is the difference between the amount in which he is chargeable to income tax and the aggregate amount of any income tax deducted at source and any tax credits to which section 231 of the principal Act applies.][7]

(1B) In the case of a person who carries on a trade, profession, or business in partnership with one or more other persons, a return under this section shall include each amount which, in any relevant statement, is stated to be equal to his share of any income, [loss, tax, credit][4] or charge for the period in respect of which the statement is made.

(1C) In subsection (1B) above "relevant statement" means a statement which, as respects the partnership, falls to be made under section 12AB of this Act for a period which includes, or includes any part of, the year of assessment or its basis period.][2]

(2) Every return under this section shall include a declaration by the person making the return to the effect that the return is to the best of his knowledge correct and complete.

(3) A notice under this section may require different information, accounts and statements for different periods or in relation to different descriptions of source of income.

(4) Notices under this section may require different information, accounts and statements in relation to different descriptions of person.][1]

(5) In this section and sections 8A, 9 and 12AA of this Act, any reference to income tax deducted at source is a reference to income tax deducted or treated as deducted from any income or treated as paid on any income.][5]

Commentary—*Simon's Direct Tax Service* **A3.105, 106, 1631; E1.806.**
Statement of Practice SP A13—Tax returns and claims of old and infirm persons may be signed by their attorneys who have full knowledge of their tax affairs.
SP 5/83—Use of schedules in making personal tax return.
SP 5/87—Tax returns: the use of substitute forms and photocopies.
SP 4/91—Tax returns: their design and the information required in them.
Revenue Interpretation—RI 191—Incomplete returns and the use of provisional figures in returns.
Revenue & other press releases—Law Society 18-3-92 (tax returns, signature under enduring power of attorney: Return must be signed by taxpayer in person. Revenue will in principle accept signature of attorney where taxpayer is unable to sign because of physical inability or mental incapacity).
IR 18-5-93 (circumstances in which tax computations off large businesses or companies will be accepted rounded to the nearest £1,000).
IR Tax Bulletin June 1997 p 436 (completion of standard accounts information in self-assessment returns is essential).
IR 29-8-97 (new returns to be issued to trustees of approved pension schemes as from 1998–99; for 1997–98 a provisional return form is to be used).
PSO 5-9-97 (update 30: duties of trustees and administrators under self assessment).
IR Tax Bulletin June 2001 p 847 (the Revenue's position on signatures on the ITSA return (and other) forms; using provisional figures in returns, and rejecting unsatisfactory return forms).
Revenue Internal Guidance—Enquiry Handbook EH 37 (accounts and computations, P60s, dividend vouchers, copies of P11Ds etc not normally required with returns, but SC60s are required).
EH 260 (circumstances in which the Revenue will accept provisional figures entered on a return).
EH 723 (sub-s (1B) is mandatory: partner may not amend the amount of partnership profit etc allocated to him in the partnership statement).
Simon's Tax Cases—*Jones v O'Brien* [1988] STC 615; *Cox v Poole General Comrs and the IRC* [1990] STC 122; *Kingsley v Billingham* [1992] STC 132; *Alexander v Wallington General Comrs and IRC* [1993] STC 588.
s 8(1), *Moschi v General Comrs for Kensington* [1980] STC 1.
s 8(2), *R v HM Inspector of Taxes, ex p* [1974] STC 567.
Definitions—"Board", s 118(1); "notice", TA 1988 s 832(1); "return", s 118(1); "year of assessment", TA 1988 s 118(1).
Cross references—TMA 1970 s 7(1)(b) (taxpayer's obligation to notify inspector of taxes of his liability notwithstanding no notice for a return is issued).
TMA 1970 s 9(1) (a return under this section to include a self-assessment).
TMA 1970 s 12(1), (2) (application of this section in relation to CGT).
TMA 1970 s 12B (record keeping requirements).
TMA 1970 s 28C (determination of income tax and capital gains tax where a return is not delivered as required).
TMA 1970 s 29 (restrictions on assessments where loss of tax discovered following making of a return under this section).
TMA 1970 s 93 (penalty for failure to make a return in accordance with this section).
TMA 1970 s 95 (penalty for incorrect return made fraudulently or negligently).
TMA 1970 Sch 3A (returns issued under this section for 1996-97 onwards may be transmitted to the Revenue electronically).
FA 1974 s 24 (return of income of a person treated as employee to include emoluments, whether or not tax is chargeable on them);
TCGA 1992 s 3(6) (circumstances in which a statement by an individual will be sufficient compliance with any notice under this section).
Income Tax (Electronic Communications) Regulations, SI 2000/945 (delivery by electronic means of information in respect of income tax assessments).
Income Tax (Electronic Communications) (Incentive Payments) Regulations, SI 2001/56 reg 3 (incentive payments to be made to individuals and employers who submit returns to the Inland revenue using electronic communications).
Amendments—[1] This section and ss 8A, 9 substituted for ss 8, 9 by FA 1990 s 90(1), (5) with effect where a notice to deliver a return is or falls to be given after 5 April 1990.
[2] Sub-ss (1), (1A), (1B), (1C) substituted for sub-s (1) by FA 1994 ss 178(1), 199(1), (2)(a), with effect from the year 1996–97.
[3] Words omitted from sub-s (1A) (inserted by FA 1995 s104(1)) repealed by FA 1996 s 121(2), Sch 41 Pt V(6) with effect from the year 1996–97.
[4] Words in sub-s (1B) substituted by FA 1995 s 104(2) with effect from the year 1996–97.
[5] Sub-s (5) inserted by FA 1995 s 104(3) with effect from the year 1996–97.
[6] Words in sub-s (1) inserted by FA 1996 s 121(1) with effect from the year 1996–97.
[7] Sub-s (1AA) inserted by FA 1996 s 121(3) with effect from the year 1996–97.

[8A Trustee's return

[(1) For the purpose of establishing the amounts in which [the relevant trustees][3] of a settlement, and the settlors and beneficiaries, are chargeable to income tax and capital gains tax for a year of assessment, [and the amount payable by him by way of income tax for that year,][6] an officer of the Board may by a notice given to [any relevant trustee][3] require the trustee—

    (*a*) to make and deliver to the officer, on or before the day mentioned in subsection (1A) below, a return containing such information as may reasonably be required in pursuance of the notice, and
    (*b*) to deliver with the return such accounts, statements and documents, relating to information contained in the return, as may reasonably be so required;

and a notice may be given to any one trustee or separate notices may be given to each trustee or to such trustees as the officer thinks fit.

(1A) The day referred to in subsection (1) above is—

    (*a*) the 31st January next following the year of assessment, or
    (*b*) where the notice under this section is given after the 31st October next following the year, the last day of the period of three months beginning with the day on which the notice is given][2] ...[4]

[(1AA) For the purposes of subsection (1) above—

    (*a*) the amounts in which a person is chargeable to income tax and capital gains tax are net amounts, that is to say, amounts which take into account any relief or allowance a claim for which is included in the return; and (*b*) the amount payable by a person by way of income tax is the difference between the amount in which he is chargeable to income tax and the aggregate amount of any income tax deducted at source and any tax credits to which section 231 of the principal Act applies.][7]

(2) Every return under this section shall include a declaration by the person making the return to the effect that the return is to the best of his knowledge correct and complete.

(3) A notice under this section may require different information, accounts and statements for different periods or in relation to different descriptions of source of income.

(4) Notices under this section may require different information, accounts and statements in relation to different descriptions of settlement.][1]

[(5) The following references, namely—

(*a*) references in section 9 or 28C of this Act to a person to whom a notice has been given under this section being chargeable to tax; and

(*b*) references in section 29 of this Act to such a person being assessed to tax,

shall be construed as references to the relevant trustees of the settlement being so chargeable or, as the case may be, being so assessed.][5]

Commentary—*Simon's Direct Tax Service* A3.109.
Statement of Practice SP 4/91—Tax returns: their design and the information required in them.
Revenue & other press releases—IR 20-1-97 (tax obligations of trustees and certain beneficiaries of bare trusts).
Revenue Internal Guidance—Trust manual TM 3000–3-53 (Revenue practice regarding the issue of returns to trustees and the examination of those returns).
Definitions—"Board", s 118(1);"notice", TA 1988 s 832(1);"relevant trustees", s 118(1);"return", s 118(1);"year of assessment", TA 1988 s 832(1).
Cross references—See TMA 1970 s 8(5) (construction of references to income tax in this section).
TMA 1970 s 9(1) (returns under this section to include a self-assessment).
TMA 1970 s 12(1), (2) (application of this section in relation to CGT).
TMA 1970 s 12B (record-keeping requirements).
TMA 1970 s 28C (determination of income tax and capital gains tax where return not delivered as required).
TMA 1970 s 29 (restrictions on assessments where loss of tax discovered following making of a return under this section).
TMA 1970 s 93 (penalty for failure to make a return in accordance with this section).
TMA 1970 s 95 (penalty for incorrect return made fraudulently or negligently).
TMA 1970 Sch 3A (returns issued under this section for 1996-97 onwards may be transmitted to the Revenue electronically).
Amendments—[1] This section and s 8 above and s 9 substituted for ss 8, 9 by FA 1990 s 90(1), (5) with effect where a notice to deliver a return is or falls to be given after 5 April 1990.
[2] Sub-ss (1), (1A) substituted for sub-s (1) by FA 1994, ss 178(2), 199(1), (2)(*a*), with effect from the year 1996–97.
[3] Words in sub-s (1) substituted by FA 1995, s 103(3), with effect from the year 1996–97.
[4] Words in sub-s (1A) (inserted by FA 1995 s 104(1)(*b*)) repealed by FA 1996 s 121(2), Sch 41 Pt V(6) with effect from the year 1996–97.
[5] Sub-s (5) inserted by FA 1995 s 103(4) with effect from the year 1996–97.
[6] Words in sub-s (1) inserted by FA 1996 s 121(1) with effect from the year 1996–97.
[7] Sub-s (1AA) inserted by FA 1996 s 121(3) with effect from the year 1996–97.

[9 Returns to include self-assessment

[(1) Subject to [subsections (1A) and (2)][5], every return under section 8 or 8A of this Act shall include a self-assessment, that is to say—

(*a*) an assessment of the amounts in which, on the basis of the information contained in the return and taking into account any relief or allowance a claim for which is included in the return, the person making the return is chargeable to income tax and capital gains tax for the year of assessment; and

(*b*) an assessment of the amount payable by him by way of income tax, that is to say, the difference between the amount in which he is assessed to income tax under paragraph (*a*) above and the aggregate amount of any income tax deducted at source and any tax credits to which section 231 of the principal Act applies

[but nothing in this subsection shall enable a self-assessment to show as repayable any income tax treated as deducted or paid by virtue of section 233(1), 246D(1), 249(4), 421(1), 547(5) or 599A(5) of the principal Act.[4]][2]

[(1A) The tax to be assessed on a person by a self-assessment shall not include any tax which, under Chapter I or IV of Part XIV of the principal Act, is charged on the administrator of a scheme (within the meaning of section 658A of that Act) and is assessable by the Board in accordance with that section.][5]

(2) A person shall not be required to comply with subsection (1) above if he makes and delivers his return for a year of assessment—

(*a*) on or before the 30th September next following the year, or

(*b*) where the notice under section 8 or 8A of this Act is given after the 31st July next following the year, within the period of two months beginning with the day on which the notice is given.

(3) Where, in making and delivering a return, a person does not comply with subsection (1) above, an officer of the Board shall if subsection (2) above applies, and may in any other case—

(*a*) make the assessment on his behalf on the basis of the information contained in the return, and

(*b*) send him a copy of the assessment so made;

...[5]

[(3A) An assessment under subsection (3) above is treated for the purposes of this Act as a self-assessment and as included in the return.][5]

(4)–(6) ...][1]

Commentary—*Simon's Direct Tax Service* A3.108; E5.307.
Statement of Practice SP 5/87—Tax returns: the use of substitute forms and photocopies.
SP 4/91—Tax returns: their design and the information required in them.
Definitions—"Board", s 118(1); "filing date", ss 8(1A), 8A(1A); "notice", TA 1988 s 832(1); "return", TMA 1970 s 118(1); "year of assessment", TA 1988 s 832(1).
Cross references—TMA 1970 s 8(5) (construction of references to income tax in this section).
TMA 1970 s 8A(5) (construction of references to persons to whom a notice has been given under s 8A being chargeable to tax).
TMA 1970 s 12(4) (return under this section in relation to CGT to include certain particulars).
TMA 1970 s 12AB(4) (amendment of self-assessment under this section to give effect to amendments in a partnership statement).
TMA 1970 s 28A (amendment of self-assessment where enquiries are made under s 9A).
TMA 1970 s 28B (amendment of self-assessment where enquiries are made into a partnership return under s 12AC).
TMA 1970 28C (determination of tax under s 28C in absence of a return treated as a self-assessment under this section for the purposes of Parts VA, VI, IX and XI).
TMA 1970 s 30B (amendment of self-assessment under this section where, after a loss of tax is discovered, a related partnership statement is amended).
TMA 1970 s 33A (amendment of self-assessment where excess tax is charged by reason of an error or mistake made in a partnership statement).
TMA 1970 s 50(9) (amendment of self-assessment where amounts contained in an amended partnership statement are reduced or increased following an appeal).
TMA 1970 s 59A (requirement to make payments on account of income tax where, in the preceding year of assessment, a taxpayer was assessed to tax under this section).
TMA 1970 s 59B (payment of tax contained in a self-assessment under this section).
TMA 1970 s 93 (penalty for failure to make a return in accordance with this section).
TMA 1970 s 95 (penalty for incorrect return made fraudulently or negligently).
Income Tax (Electronic Communications) Regulations, SI 2000/945 (delivery by electronic means of information in respect of income tax assessments).
Education (Student Loans) (Repayment) Regulations, SI 2000/944 reg 17 (application of sub-ss (2)–(6) in connection with the repayment of student loans).
Income Tax (Electronic Communications) (Incentive Payments) Regulations, SI 2001/56 reg 3 (incentive payments to be made to individuals and employers who submit returns to the Inland Revenue using electronic communications).
Amendments—[1] This section (including the heading) substituted by FA 1994 ss 179, 199(1), (2)(a) with effect from the year 1996–97.
[2] Sub-s (1) substituted by FA 1996 s 121(4) with effect from the year 1996–97.
[3] Words in sub-s (1) inserted by FA 1996 s 122(1) with effect from the year 1996–97.
[4] Words in sub-s (1) substituted and sub-s (1A) inserted by FA 1998 s 98(2) with effect for the year 1998–99 and subsequent years of assessment and shall be deemed to have had effect for the years 1996–97 and 1997–98.
[5] Words in sub-s (3) repealed, sub-s (3A) inserted, and sub-ss (4)–(6) repealed by FA 2001 ss 88, 110, Sch 29 para 1, Sch 33 Pt II(13) with effect from the passing of FA 2001 in relation to returns whether made before or after the passing of FA 2001, and whether relating to periods before or after the passing of FA 2001. The words in sub-s (3) previously read—

"and references in this Act to a person's self-assessment include references to an assessment made on a person's behalf under this subsection."

Sub-ss (4)–(6) previously read—

"(4) Subject to subsection (5) below—

(a) at any time before the end of the period of nine months beginning with the day on which a person's return is delivered, an officer of the Board may by notice to that person so amend that person's self-assessment as to correct any obvious errors or mistakes in the return (whether errors of principle, arithmetical mistakes or otherwise); and
(b) at any time before the end of the period of twelve months beginning with the filing date, a person may by notice to an officer of the Board so amend his self-assessment as to give effect to any amendments to his return which he has notified to such an officer.

(5) No amendment of a self-assessment may be made under subsection (4) above at any time during the period—

(a) beginning with the day on which an officer of the Board gives notice of his intention to enquire into the return, and
(b) ending with the day on which the officer's enquiries into the return are completed.

(6) In this section and section 9A of this Act "the filing date" means the day mentioned in section 8(1A) or, as the case may be, section 8A(1A) of this Act."

[9ZA Amendment of personal or trustee return by taxpayer

(1) A person may amend his return under section 8 or 8A of this Act by notice to an officer of the Board.

(2) An amendment may not be made more than twelve months after the filing date.

(3) In this section "the filing date" means the day mentioned in section 8(1A) or, as the case may be, section 8A(1A) of this Act.][1]

Commentary—*Simon's Direct Tax Service* E1.807A.
Revenue Internal Guidance—Enquiry Handbook EH 148 (If an enquiry is opened into the return any amendment the taxpayer makes can only be given effect at the end of the enquiry).
Amendments—[1] This section inserted by FA 2001 s 88, Sch 29 para 2 with effect from the passing of FA 2001 in relation to returns whether made before or after the passing of FA 2001, and whether relating to periods before or after the passing of FA 2001.

[9ZB Correction of personal or trustee return by Revenue

(1) An officer of the Board may amend a return under section 8 or 8A of this Act so as to correct obvious errors or omissions in the return (whether errors of principle, arithmetical mistakes or otherwise).

(2) A correction under this section is made by notice to the person whose return it is.

(3) No such correction may be made more than nine months after—

(*a*) the day on which the return was delivered, or

(*b*) if the correction is required in consequence of an amendment of the return under section 9ZA of this Act, the day on which that amendment was made.

(4) A correction under this section is of no effect if the person whose return it is gives notice rejecting the correction.

(5) Notice of rejection under subsection (4) above must be given—

(*a*) to the officer of the Board by whom the notice of correction was given,

(*b*) before the end of the period of 30 days beginning with the date of issue of the notice of correction.]¹

Commentary—*Simon's Direct Tax Service* E1.807B.
Revenue Internal Guidance—Enquiry Handbook EH 144–147 (Revenue procedures concerning repairs/corrections to returns).
Amendments—¹ This section inserted by FA 2001 s 88, Sch 29 para 2 with effect from the passing of FA 2001 in relation to returns whether made before or after the passing of FA 2001, and whether relating to periods before or after the passing of FA 2001.

[9A Notice of enquiry

(1) An officer of the Board may enquire into a return under section 8 or 8A of this Act if he gives notice of his intention to do so ("notice of enquiry")—

(*a*) to the person whose return it is ("the taxpayer"),

(*b*) within the time allowed.

(2) The time allowed is—

(*a*) if the return was delivered on or before the filing date, up to the end of the period of twelve months after the filing date;

(*b*) if the return was delivered after the filing date, up to and including the quarter day next following the first anniversary of the day on which the return was delivered;

(*c*) if the return is amended under section 9ZA of this Act, up to and including the quarter day next following the first anniversary of the day on which the amendment was made.

For this purpose the quarter days are 31st January, 30th April, 31st July and 31st October.

(3) A return which has been the subject of one notice of enquiry may not be the subject of another, except one given in consequence of an amendment (or another amendment) of the return under section 9ZA of this Act.

(4) An enquiry extends to anything contained in the return, or required to be contained in the return, including any claim or election included in the return, subject to the following limitation.

(5) If the notice of enquiry is given as a result of an amendment of the return under section 9ZA of this Act—

(*a*) at a time when it is no longer possible to give notice of enquiry under subsection (2)(*a*) or (*b*) above, or

(*b*) after an enquiry into the return has been completed,

the enquiry into the return is limited to matters to which the amendment relates or which are affected by the amendment.

(6) In this section "the filing date" means the day mentioned in section 8(1A) or, as the case may be, section 8A(1A) of this Act.]¹

Commentary—*Simon's Direct Tax Service* E1.810.
Note—In sub-s (2)(*a*) above as it applies in relation to returns for years of assessment before the year 2001–02, "twelve months beginning with the date" is substituted for "up to the end of the period of twelve months after the filing date" (FA 2001 Sch 29 para 4(2)).
Revenue Internal Guidance—Enquiry Handbook EH 205–216 (Revenue procedures regarding co-ordination and liaison between network and specialist offices prior to opening and during the course of an enquiry).
EH 292 (Revenue procedures concerning the time limit for opening enquiries into returns or amendments).
EH 337 (enquiries into an amendment: Revenue procedures).
Amendments—¹ Sections 9A–9D substituted for s 9A by FA 2001 s 88, Sch 29 para 4(1) with effect from the passing of FA 2001 in relation to returns whether made before or after the passing of FA 2001, and whether relating to periods before or after the passing of FA 2001. Previously s 9A read—

"9A Power to enquire into returns

(1) An officer of the Board may enquire into—

(*a*) the return on the basis of which a person's self-assessment was made under section 9 of this Act, or

(*b*) any amendment of that return on the basis of which that assessment has been amended by that person, or

[(*c*) any claim or election included in the return (by amendment or otherwise).]²

if, before the end of the period mentioned in subsection (2) below, he gives notice in writing to that person of his intention to do so.

(2) The period referred to in subsection (1) above is—

(*a*) in the case of a return delivered or amendment made on or before the filing date, the period of twelve months beginning with that date;

(*b*) in the case of a return delivered or amendment made after that date, the period ending on the quarter day next following the first anniversary of the day on which the return or amendment was delivered or made;

and the quarter days for the purposes of this subsection are 31st January, 30th April, 31st July and 31st October.

(3) A return or amendment which has been enquired into under subsection (1) above shall not be the subject of a further notice under that subsection."

[9B Amendment of return by taxpayer during enquiry

(1) This section applies if a return is amended under section 9ZA of this Act (amendment of personal or trustee return by taxpayer) at a time when an enquiry is in progress into the return.

(2) The amendment does not restrict the scope of the enquiry but may be taken into account (together with any matters arising) in the enquiry.

(3) So far as the amendment affects the amount stated in the self-assessment included in the return as the amount of tax payable, it does not take effect while the enquiry is in progress and—

(*a*) if the officer states in the closure notice that he has taken the amendment into account and that—

(i) the amendment has been taken into account in formulating the amendments contained in the notice, or

(ii) his conclusion is that the amendment is incorrect,

the amendment shall not take effect;

(*b*) otherwise, the amendment takes effect when the closure notice is issued.

(4) For the purposes of this section the period during which an enquiry is in progress is the whole of the period—

(*a*) beginning with the day on which notice of enquiry is given, and

(*b*) ending with the day on which the enquiry is completed.][1]

Amendments—[1] Sections 9A–9D substituted for s 9A by FA 2001 s 88, Sch 29 para 4(1) with effect from 11 May 2001 in relation to returns whether made before or after the passing of FA 2001, and whether relating to periods before or after the passing of FA 2001.

[9C Amendment of self-assessment during enquiry to prevent loss of tax

(1) This section applies where an enquiry is in progress into a return as a result of notice of enquiry by an officer of the Board under section 9A(1) of this Act.

(2) If the officer forms the opinion—

(*a*) that the amount stated in the self-assessment contained in the return as the amount of tax payable is insufficient, and

(*b*) that unless the assessment is immediately amended there is likely to be a loss of tax to the Crown,

he may by notice to the taxpayer amend the assessment to make good the deficiency.

(3) In the case of an enquiry which under section 9A(5) of this Act is limited to matters arising from an amendment of the return, subsection (2) above only applies so far as the deficiency is attributable to the amendment.

(4) For the purposes of this section the period during which an enquiry is in progress is the whole of the period—

(*a*) beginning with the day on which notice of enquiry is given, and

(*b*) ending with the day on which the enquiry is completed.][1]

Amendments—[1] Sections 9A–9D substituted for s 9A by FA 2001 s 88, Sch 29 para 4(1) with effect from 11 May 2001 in relation to returns whether made before or after the passing of FA 2001, and whether relating to periods before or after the passing of FA 2001.

[9D Choice between different Cases of Schedule D

(1) Where in the case of a return under section 8 or 8A of this Act—

(*a*) alternative methods are allowed by the Tax Acts for bringing amounts into charge to tax,

(*b*) the return is made using one of those methods but could have been made using an alternative method, and

(*c*) an officer of the Board determines which of the alternative methods is to be used,

the officer's determination is final and conclusive, for the purposes of any enquiry into the return, as to the basis of charge to be used.

(2) For the purposes of this section the cases where the Tax Acts allow alternative methods for bringing amounts into charge to tax are where they may be brought into charge either—

(*a*) in computing profits chargeable to tax under Case I or II of Schedule D, or

(*b*) as amounts within Case III, IV or V of that Schedule.][1]

Amendments—[1] Sections 9A–9D substituted for s 9A by FA 2001 s 88, Sch 29 para 4(1) with effect from the passing of FA 2001 in relation to returns whether made before or after the passing of FA 2001, and whether relating to periods before or after the passing of FA 2001.

Corporation tax

10 Notice of liability to corporation tax

Commentary—*Simon's Direct Tax Service* A3.140, 803.

Amendments—This section repealed by FA 1998 ss 117, 165, Sch 19 para 1, Sch 27 Part III(28) with effect for accounting periods ending after 30 June 1999 (by virtue of Finance Act 1994, Section 199, (Appointed Day) Order, SI 1998/3173 art 2).

Sub-s (4) repealed by FA 1998 ss 31, 165, Sch 3 para 2 and Sch 27 Part III(2) with effect for accounting periods beginning after 5 April 1999.

11 Return of profits

Commentary—*Simon's Direct Tax Service* A3.110.
Simon's Tax Cases—s 11, *Slater Ltd v Comrs for the General Purposes of the Income Tax for the division of Beacontree* [2002] STC 246.
Amendments—This section repealed by FA 1998 ss 117, 165, Sch 19 para 1, Sch 27 Part III(28) with effect for accounting periods ending after 30 June 1999 (by virtue of Finance Act 1994, Section 199, (Appointed Day) Order, SI 1998/3173 art 2).

11AA Return of profits to include self-assessment

Amendments—This section repealed by FA 1998 ss 117, 165, Sch 19 para 1, Sch 27 Part III(28) with effect for accounting periods ending after 30 June 1999 (by virtue of Finance Act 1994, Section 199, (Appointed Day) Order, SI 1998/3173 art 2).

11AB Power to enquire into return of profits

Amendments—This section repealed by FA 1998 ss 117, 165, Sch 19 para 1, Sch 27 Part III(28) with effect for accounting periods ending after 30 June 1999 (by virtue of Finance Act 1994, Section 199, (Appointed Day) Order, SI 1998/3173 art 2).

11AC Modifications of sections 11AA and 11AB in relation to non-annual accounting of general insurance business

Amendments—This section repealed by FA 1998 ss 117, 165, Sch 19 para 1, Sch 27 Part III(28) with effect for accounting periods ending after 30 June 1999 (by virtue of Finance Act 1994, Section 199, (Appointed Day) Order, SI 1998/3173 art 2).

11AD Modifications of sections 11AA and 11AB for insurance companies with non-annual actuarial investigations

Amendments—This section repealed by FA 1998 ss 117, 165, Sch 19 para 1, Sch 27 Part III(28) with effect for accounting periods ending after 30 June 1999 (by virtue of Finance Act 1994, Section 199, (Appointed Day) Order, SI 1998/3173 art 2).

11AE Modifications of sections 11AA and 11AB for friendly societies with non-annual actuarial investigations

Amendments—This section repealed by FA 1998 ss 117, 165, Sch 19 para 1, Sch 27 Part III(28) with effect for accounting periods ending after 30 June 1999 (by virtue of Finance Act 1994, Section 199, (Appointed Day) Order, SI 1998/3173 art 2).

Capital gains

[11A Notice of liability to capital gains tax

Commentary—*Simon's Direct Tax Service* A3.140; E1.805.
Amendments—This section (as inserted by FA 1988 s 122(1)) repealed by FA 1995 s 115(3), (13), Sch 29 Pt VIII(14), with effect from the year 1995–96.

12 Information about chargeable gains

(1) ...[9]
(2) A notice under section 8 [or section 8A][6] ...[11] of this Act may require particulars of any assets acquired by the person on whom the notice was served (or if the notice relates to income or chargeable gains of some other person, of any assets acquired by that other person) in the period specified in the notice (being a period beginning not earlier than 6th April 1965) but excluding—
  [(*a*) any assets exempted by the following provisions of the [1992 Act][8], namely—
      (i) section [51(1)][8] (rights to winnings from pool betting, lotteries or games with prizes),
      (ii) section [121][8] (government non-marketable securities),
      (iii) section [263, 268 or 269][8] (passenger vehicles, decorations for valour or gallant conduct and foreign currency for personal expenditure)][1-2]
  (*b*) unless the amount or value of the consideration for its acquisition exceeded [£6,000][5], any asset which is tangible movable property and is not within the exceptions in [section [262(6)][8]][3] of the said Act (terminal markets and currency), or
  (*c*) any assets acquired as trading stock.
(3) The particulars required under this section may include particulars of the person from whom the asset was acquired, and of the consideration for the acquisition.
(4) ...[10]
(5) In this section "trading stock" has the meaning given by section [100(2)][4] of the principal Act.

Commentary—*Simon's Direct Tax Service* A3.106, 108.
Definitions—"the 1992 Act", s 118(1); "chargeable gain", TCGA 1992 s 15(2) by virtue of s 118(1); "principal Act", s 118(1); "return", s 118(1).
Amendments—[1-2]Sub-s (2)(*a*) substituted by CGTA 1979 s 157(2)–(4) and Sch 7 para 1(2), with effect from 22 March 1979.
[3] Word "section" in sub-s (2)(*b*) substituted by the Capital Gains Tax Act 1979 s 157(2), Sch 7 para 9 Table.
[4] Number in sub-s (5) substituted by TA 1988 Sch 29 para 32 Table.
[5] Amount in sub-s (2)(*b*) substituted by FA 1989 s 123(1)(*b*), (2) in relation to assets acquired after 5 April 1989.

TMA 1970

[6] Words in sub-s (2) inserted by FA 1990 s 90(2), (5).
[7] Words in sub-s (4) repealed by FA 1990 s 90(2), (5) and Sch 19 Pt V.
[8] Words in sub-s (2)(*a*), (*b*) substituted by TCGA 1992 Sch 10 para 2(1), (3).
[9] Sub-s (1), which was substituted by FA 1988 s 122(2), repealed by FA 1994 Sch 26 Pt V(23) with effect from the year 1996–97.
[10] Sub-s (4) repealed by FA 1994 Sch 26 Pt V(23) with effect from the year 1996–97.
[11] Words in sub-s (2) repealed by FA 1998 ss 117, 165, Sch 19 para 2, Sch 27 Part III(28) with effect in for accounting periods ending after 30 June 1999 (by virtue of Finance Act 1994, Section 199, (Appointed Day) Order, SI 1998/3173 art 2).

[Partnerships][1]

12AA Partnership return

[(1) Where a trade, profession or business is carried on by two or more persons in partnership, for the purpose of facilitating the establishment of the following amounts, namely—

(*a*) the amount in which each partner chargeable to income tax for any year of assessment is so chargeable [and the amount payable by way of income tax by each such partner][4], and

(*b*) the amount in which each partner chargeable to corporation tax for any period is so chargeable,

an officer of the Board may act under subsection (2) or (3) below (or both).

[(1A) For the purposes of subsection (1) above—

(*a*) the amount in which a partner is chargeable to income tax or corporation tax is a net amount, that is to say, an amount which takes into account any relief or allowance for which a claim is made; and

(*b*) the amount payable by a partner by way of income tax is the difference between the amount in which he is chargeable to income tax and the aggregate amount of any income tax deducted at source and any tax credits to which section 231 of the principal Act applies.][5]][2]

(2) An officer of the Board may by a notice given to the partners require such person as is identified in accordance with rules given with the notice [or a successor of his][6]—

(*a*) to make and deliver to the officer in respect of such period as may be specified in the notice, on or before such day as may be so specified, a return containing such information as may reasonably be required in pursuance of the notice, and

(*b*) to deliver with the return [such accounts, statements and documents, relating to information contained in the return,][3] as may reasonably be so required.

(3) An officer of the Board may by notice given to any partner require the partner [or a successor of his][6]—

(*a*) to make and deliver to the officer in respect of such period as may be specified in the notice, on or before such day as may be so specified, a return containing such information as may reasonably be required in pursuance of the notice, and

(*b*) to deliver with the return such accounts and statements as may reasonably be so required;

and a notice may be given to any one partner or separate notices may be given to each partner or to such partners as the officer thinks fit.

(4) In the case of a partnership which includes one or more individuals, the day specified in a notice under subsection (2) or (3) above shall not be earlier than—

(*a*) the 31st January next following the year of assessment concerned, or

(*b*) where the notice under this section is given after the 31st October next following the year, the last day of the period of three months beginning with the day on which the notice is given.

(5) In the case of a partnership which includes one or more companies, the day specified in a notice under subsection (2) or (3) above shall not be earlier than—

(*a*) the first anniversary of the end of the relevant period, or

(*b*) where the notice under this section is given more than nine months after the end of the relevant period, the last day of the period of three months beginning with the day on which the notice is given;

and the relevant period for the purposes of this subsection and subsection (6) below is the period in respect of which the return is required.

(6) Every return under this section shall include—

(*a*) a declaration of the name, residence and tax reference of each of the persons who have been partners—

(i) for the whole of the relevant period, or
(ii) for any part of that period,

and, in the case of a person falling within sub-paragraph (ii) above, of the part concerned; and

(*b*) a declaration by the person making the return to the effect that it is to the best of his knowledge correct and complete.

(7) Every return under this section shall also include, if the notice under subsection (2) or (3) above so requires—

(*a*) with respect to any disposal of partnership property during a period to which ...[7] the return relates, the like particulars as if the partnership were liable to tax on any chargeable gain accruing on the disposal, and (*b*) with respect to any acquisition of partnership property, the particulars required under section 12(2) of this Act [or paragraph 13 of Schedule 18 to the Finance Act 1998][9].

(8) A notice under this section may require different information, accounts and statements for different periods or in relation to different descriptions of source of income.

(9) Notices under this section may require different information, accounts and statements in relation to different descriptions of partnership.

(10) In this section "residence", in relation to a company, means its registered office.][1]

[(10A) In this Act a "partnership return" means a return in pursuance of a notice under subsection (2) or (3) above.][10]

[(11) In this Act "successor", in relation to a person who is required to make and deliver, or has made and delivered, [a partnership return][10], but is no longer available, means—

(*a*) where a partner is for the time being nominated for the purposes of this subsection by a majority of the relevant partners, that partner; and
(*b*) where no partner is for the time being so nominated, such partner as—

    (i) in the case of a notice under subsection (2) above, is identified in accordance with rules given with that notice; or
    (ii) in the case of a notice under subsection (3) above, is nominated for the purposes of this subsection by an officer of the Board;

and "predecessor" and "successor", in relation to a person so nominated or identified, shall be construed accordingly.][8]

[(12) For the purposes of subsection (11) above a nomination under paragraph (*a*) of that subsection, and a revocation of such a nomination, shall not have effect in relation to any time before notice of the nomination or revocation is given to an officer of the Board.][8]

[(13) In this section "relevant partner" means a person who was a partner at any time during the period for which the return was made or is required, or the personal representatives of such a person.][8]

Commentary—*Simon's Direct Tax Service* **E1.808, 808B; E5.307.**
Revenue Internal Guidance—Enquiry Handbook EH 865–871 (procedure for dealing with breakdown of partnership relationship).
Definitions—"Act", s 118(1); "the Board", s 118(1); "company", s 118(1); "notice", TA 1988 s 832(1); "principal Act", s 118(1); "return", s 118(1).
Cross references—See TMA 1970 s 8(5) (construction of references to income tax in this section).
TMA 1970 s 12AB(1) (a return under this section to include a partnership statement).
TMA 1970 s 12B (record-keeping requirements).
TMA 1970 s 93A (penalties for failure to deliver a partnership return).
TMA 1970 s 95 (penalties for incorrect return delivered fraudulently or negligently).
TMA 1970 Sch 3A (returns issued under this section may be transmitted to the Revenue electronically).
Amendments—[1] This section and heading preceding it inserted by FA 1994 ss 184, 199 and has effect from the year 1996–97 as it relates to income tax and capital gains tax and, as respects corporation tax, with effect in relation to accounting periods ending after 30 June 1999 (by virtue of Finance Act 1994, Section 199, (Appointed Day) Order, SI 1998/3173 art 2).
[2] Sub-ss (1), (1A) substituted for sub-s (1) by FA 1995, s 104(6), with effect from the year 1996–97 as it relates to income tax and capital gains tax and, as respects corporation tax, for accounting periods ending after 30 June 1999 (by virtue of SI 1998/3173 art 2). Note as to sub-s (1A), note 5 below.
[3] Words in sub-s (2)(*b*) substituted by FA 1995, s 115(4), with effect from the year 1996–97 as it relates to income tax and capital gains tax and, as respects corporation tax, for accounting periods ending after 30 June 1999 (by virtue of SI 1998/3173 art 2).
[4] Words in sub-s (1)(*a*) inserted by FA 1996 s 121(6) with effect from the year 1996–97 as it relates to income tax, and as respects corporation tax, for accounting periods ending after 30 June 1999 (by virtue of SI 1998/3173 art 2).
[5] Sub-s (1A) substituted by FA 1996 s 121(7) with effect from the year 1996–97 as it relates to income tax and, as respects corporation tax, for accounting periods ending on or after the appointed day (see note [1] above).
[6] Words in sub-ss (2), (3) inserted by FA 1996 s 123(1), (2) with effect from the year 1996–97 as it relates to income tax and capital gains tax and, as respects corporation tax, for accounting periods ending after 30 June 1999 (by virtue of SI 1998/3173 art 2).
[7] Words omitted from sub-s (7)(*a*) repealed by FA 1996 s 123(3), Sch 41 Pt V(6) with effect from the year 1996–97 as it relates to income tax and capital gains tax and, as respects corporation tax, for accounting periods ending after 30 June 1999 (by virtue of SI 1998/3173 art 2).
[8] Sub-ss (11)–(13) inserted by FA 1996 s 124(4) with effect from the year 1996–97 as it relates to income tax and capital gains tax and, as respects corporation tax, for accounting periods ending after 30 June 1999 (by virtue of SI 1998/3173 art 2).
[9] Words in sub-s (7) inserted by FA 1998 Sch 19 para 3 with effect for accounting periods ending after 30 June 1999 (by virtue of SI 1998/3173 art 2).
[10] Sub-s (10A) inserted, and words in sub-s (11) substituted for the words "a return in pursuance of a notice under subsection (2) or (3) above", by FA 2001 s 88, Sch 29 para 18 with effect from the passing of FA 2001 in relation to returns whether made before or after the passing of FA 2001, and whether relating to periods before or after the passing of FA 2001.

[12AB Partnership return to include partnership statement

[(1) Every [partnership return][9] shall include a statement (a partnership statement) of the following amounts, namely—

(*a*) in the case of [the period in respect of which the return is made and each period of account ending within that period,][4]—

    (i) the amount of income or loss from each source which, on the basis of the information contained in the return and taking into account any relief or allowance a section 42(7) claim for which is included in the return, has accrued to or has been sustained by the partnership for [the period in question][5], [(ia) the amount of the consideration which, on that basis, has accrued to the partnership in respect of each disposal of partnership property during that period,][6]

(ii) each amount of income tax which, on that basis, has been deducted or treated as deducted from any income of the partnership, or treated as paid on any such income, for that period,

(iii) the amount of each tax credit which, on that basis, has accrued to the partnership for that period, and

(iv) the amount of each charge which, on that basis, was a charge on the income of the partnership for that period; and

(*b*) in the case of each such period [as is mentioned in paragraph (*a*) above][7] and each of the partners, the amount which, on that basis and (where applicable) taking into account any such relief or allowance, is equal to his share of that income, loss, [consideration,][7] tax, credit or charge.][2]

(2)–(4) ...[8]

(5) In this section—

...[8]

...[10]

["section 42(7) claim" means a claim under any of the provisions mentioned in section 42(7) of this Act;

"tax credit" means a tax credit to which section 231 of the principal Act applies.][3][1]

Commentary—*Simon's Direct Tax Service* **E1.808.**
Definitions—"Act", s 118(1); "the Board", s 118(1); "filing date", s 12AB(5); "notice", TA 1988 s 832(1); "period of account", s 12AB(5); "predecessor", s 12AA(11); "return", s 118(1); "section 42(7) claim", s 12AB(5); "successor", s 12AA(11); "tax credit", s 12AB(5).
Cross references—See TMA 1970 s 28AB (amendment of partnership statement where notice of enquiry is given under s 12AC(1)).
TMA 1970 s 30B (Board may amend partnership statement where loss of tax discovered).
TMA 1970 s 33A(3) (amendment of partnership statement where excess tax is charged by reason of an error or mistake in it).
Amendments—[1] This section inserted by FA 1994 ss 185, 199 and has effect from the year 1996–97 as it relates to income tax and capital gains tax and, as respects corporation tax, with effect in relation to accounting periods ending after 30 June 1999 (by virtue of Finance Act 1994, Section 199, (Appointed Day) Order, SI 1998/3173 art 2).
[2] Sub-s (1) substituted by FA 1995, s 104(7), with effect from the year 1996–97 as it relates to income tax and capital gains tax and, as respects corporation tax, for accounting periods ending after 30 June 1999 (by virtue of SI 1998/3173 art 2).
[3] Sub-s (5) words "section 42(7) claim" and "tax credit" inserted by FA 1995, s 104(8), with effect from the year 1996–97 as it relates to income tax and capital gains tax and, as respects corporation tax, for accounting periods ending after 30 June 1999 (by virtue of SI 1998/3173 art 2).
[4] Words in sub-s (1)(*a*) substituted by FA 1996 s 123(5)(*a*) with effect from the year 1996–97 as it relates to income tax and capital gains tax and, as respects corporation tax, for accounting periods ending after 30 June 1999 (by virtue of SI 1998/3173 art 2).
[5] Words in sub-s (1)(*a*)(i) substituted by FA 1996 s 123(5)(*b*) with effect from the year 1996–97 as it relates to income tax and capital gains tax and, as respects corporation tax, for accounting periods ending after 30 June 1999 (by virtue of SI 1998/3173 art 2).
[6] Sub-s (1)(*ia*) inserted by FA 1996 s 123(5)(*c*) with effect from the year 1996–97 as it relates to income tax and capital gains tax and, as respects corporation tax, for accounting periods ending after 30 June 1999 (by virtue of SI 1998/3173 art 2).
[7] Words in sub-s (1)(*b*) inserted by FA 1996 s 123(5)(*d*) with effect from the year 1996–97 as it relates to income tax and capital gains tax and, as respects corporation tax, for accounting periods ending after 30 June 1999 (by virtue of SI 1998/3173 art 2).
[8] Sub-ss (2)–(4) repealed, in sub-s (5) definition of "filing date" repealed by FA 2001 ss 88, 110, Sch 29 para 3(1), Sch 33 Pt II(13) with effect from the passing of FA 2001 in relation to returns whether made before or after the passing of FA 2001, and whether relating to periods before or after the passing of FA 2001. Previously , the text read—

"(2) Subject to subsection (3) below—

(*a*) at any time before the end of the period of nine months beginning with the day on which a person's return is delivered, an officer of the Board may by notice to that person [or a successor][8] so amend that person's partnership statement as to correct any obvious errors or mistakes in the return (whether errors of principle, arithmetical mistakes or otherwise); and
(*b*) at any time before the end of the period of twelve months beginning with the filing date, a person may by notice to an officer of the Board so amend his [or a predecessor's partnership statement as to give effect to any amendments to the return in which it is included which he or a predecessor][9] has notified to such an officer.

(3) No amendment of a partnership statement may be made under subsection (2) above at any time during the period—

(*a*) beginning with the day on which an officer of the Board gives notice of his intention to enquire into the return, and
(*b*) ending with the day on which the officer's enquiries into the return are completed.

(4) Where a partnership statement is amended under subsection (2) above, the officer shall by notice to the partners amend—

(*a*) their self-assessment under section 9 of this Act, or
(*b*) their company tax return,

so as to give effect to the amendments of the partnership statement."
The definition of "filing date" in sub-s (5) previously read as follows—
"'filing date' means the day specified in the notice under subsection (2) or, as the case may be, subsection (3) of section 12AA of this Act;".
[9] Words in sub-s (1) substituted for the words "return under section 12AA of this Act" by FA 2001 s 88, Sch 29 para 19 with effect from the passing of FA 2001 in relation to returns whether made before or after the passing of FA 2001, and whether relating to periods before or after the passing of FA 2001.
[10] Definition of "period of account" repealed by FA 2002 s 141, Sch 40 Pt 3(16) with effect from 24 July 2002. The definition previously read thus—
" 'period of account', in relation to a partnership, means any period for which accounts are drawn up;".

[12ABA Amendment of partnership return by taxpayer

(1) A partnership return may be amended by the partner who made and delivered the return, or his successor, by notice to an officer of the Board.

(2) An amendment may not be made more than twelve months after the filing date.

(3) Where a partnership return is amended under this section, the officer shall by notice to each of the partners amend—

    (*a*) the partner's return under section 8 or 8A of this Act, or
    (*b*) the partner's company tax return,

so as to give effect to the amendment of the partnership return.

(4) In this section "the filing date" means the day specified in the notice under section 12AA(2) of this Act or, as the case may be, subsection (3) of that section.][1]

Amendments—[1] This section inserted by FA 2001 s 88, Sch 29 para 3(2) with effect from the passing of FA 2001 in relation to returns whether made before or after the passing of FA 2001, and whether relating to periods before or after the passing of FA 2001.

[12ABB Correction of partnership return by Revenue

(1) An officer of the Board may amend a partnership return so as to correct obvious errors or omissions in the return (whether errors of principle, arithmetical mistakes or otherwise).

(2) A correction under this section is made by notice to the partner who made and delivered the return, or his successor.

(3) No such correction may be made more than nine months after—

    (*a*) the day on which the return was delivered, or
    (*b*) if the correction is required in consequence of an amendment of the return under section 12ABA of this Act, the day on which that amendment was made.

(4) A correction under this section is of no effect if the person to whom the notice of correction was given, or his successor, gives notice rejecting the correction.

(5) Notice of rejection under subsection (4) above must be given—

    (*a*) to the officer of the Board by whom the notice of correction was given,
    (*b*) before the end of the period of 30 days beginning with the date of issue of the notice of correction.

(6) Where a partnership return is corrected under this section, the officer shall by notice to each of the partners amend—

    (*a*) the partner's return under section 8 or 8A of this Act, or
    (*b*) the partner's company tax return,

so as to give effect to the correction of the partnership return.

Any such amendment shall cease to have effect if the correction is rejected.][1]

Commentary—*Simon's Direct Tax Service* E1.808C.
Amendments—[1] This section inserted by FA 2001 s 88, Sch 29 para 3(2) with effect from the passing of FA 2001 in relation to returns whether made before or after the passing of FA 2001, and whether relating to periods before or after the passing of FA 2001.

[12AC Notice of enquiry

(1) An officer of the Board may enquire into a partnership return if he gives notice of his intention to do so ("notice of enquiry")—

    (*a*) to the partner who made and delivered the return, or his successor,
    (*b*) within the time allowed.

(2) The time allowed is—

    (*a*) if the return was delivered on or before the filing date, up to the end of the period of twelve months after the filing date;
    (*b*) if the return was delivered after the filing date, up to and including the quarter day next following the first anniversary of the day on which the return was delivered;
    (*c*) if the return is amended under section 12ABA of this Act, up to and including the quarter day next following the first anniversary of the day on which the amendment was made.

For this purpose the quarter days are 31st January, 30th April, 31st July and 31st October.

(3) A return which has been the subject of one notice of enquiry may not be the subject of another, except one given in consequence of an amendment (or another amendment) of the return under section 12ABA of this Act.

(4) An enquiry extends to anything contained in the return, or required to be contained in the return, including any claim or election included in the return, subject to the following limitation.

(5) If the notice of enquiry is given as a result of an amendment of the return under section 12ABA of this Act—

    (*a*) at a time when it is no longer possible to give notice of enquiry under subsection (2)(*a*) or (*b*) above, or
    (*b*) after an enquiry into the return has been completed,

the enquiry into the return is limited to matters to which the amendment relates or which are affected by the amendment.

(6) The giving of notice of enquiry under subsection (1) above at any time shall be deemed to include the giving of notice of enquiry—

    (a) under section 9A(1) of this Act to each partner who at that time has made a return under section 8 or 8A of this Act or at any subsequent time makes such a return, or

    (b) under paragraph 24 of Schedule 18 to the Finance Act 1998 to each partner who at that time has made a company tax return or at any subsequent time makes such a return.

(7) In this section "the filing date" means the day specified in the notice under section 12AA(2) of this Act or, as the case may be, subsection (3) of that section.]¹

Commentary—*Simon's Direct Tax Service* **E1.810.**
Note—In sub-s (2)(a) above as it applies in relation to returns for years of assessment before the year 2001–02, "twelve months beginning with that date" is substituted for "up to the end of the period of twelve months after the filing date" (FA 2001 Sch 29 para 5(2)).
Amendments—¹ Sections 12AC–12AE substitued for s 12AC by FA 2001 s 88, Sch 29 para 5(1) with effect from 11 May 2001 in relation to returns whether made before or after 11 May 2001, and whether relating to periods before or after 11 May 2001. Previously s 12AC read—

"12AC Power to enquire into partnership return
(1) An officer of the Board may enquire into—

    (a) the return on the basis of which a person's partnership statement was made under section 12AB of this Act, or
    (b) any amendment of that return on the basis of which that statement has been amended by that person [or a successor of that person]², [or]⁴,
    (c) any claim or election included in the return (by amendment or otherwise)]⁴

if, before the end of the period mentioned in subsection (2) below, he gives notice in writing of his intention to do so to that person or any successor of that person.

(2) The period referred to in subsection (1) above is—

    (a) in the case of a return delivered or amendment made on or before the filing date, the period of twelve months beginning with that date;
    (b) in the case of a return delivered or amendment made after that date, the period ending with the quarter day next following the first anniversary of the day on which the return or amendment was delivered or made;

and the quarter days for the purposes of this subsection are 31st January, 30th April, 31st July and 31st October.

(3) The giving of notice under subsection (1) above at any time shall be deemed to include—

    (a) the giving of notice under section 9A(1) of this Act to each partner who at that time has made a return under section 9 of this Act or at any subsequent time makes such a return;
    (b) the giving of notice of enquiry under Schedule 18 to the Finance Act 1998 to each partner who at that time has made a company tax return or at any subsequent time makes such a return.

(4) A return or amendment which has been enquired into under subsection (1) above shall not be the subject of a further notice under that subsection.
(5) In this section "the filing date" means the day specified in the notice under subsection (2) or, as the case may be, subsection (3) of section 12AA of this Act."

[12AD Amendment of partnership return by taxpayer during enquiry

(1) This section applies if a partnership return is amended under section 12ABA of this Act (amendment of partnership return by taxpayer) at a time when an enquiry is in progress into the return.

(2) The amendment does not restrict the scope of the enquiry but may be taken into account (together with any matters arising) in the enquiry.

(3) So far as the amendment affects any amount stated in the partnership statement included in the return, it does not take effect while the enquiry is in progress and—

    (a) if the officer states in the closure notice that he has taken the amendment into account and that—

        (i) the amendment has been taken into account in formulating the amendments contained in the notice, or
        (ii) his conclusion is that the amendment is incorrect,

    the amendment shall not take effect;
    (b) otherwise, the amendment takes effect when the closure notice is issued.

(4) Where the effect of an amendment is deferred under subsection (3) above—

    (a) no amendment to give effect to that amendment ("the deferred amendment") shall be made under section 12ABA(3) of this Act (consequential amendment of partners' returns) while the enquiry is in progress;
    (b) if the deferred amendment does not take effect but is taken into account as mentioned in subsection (3)(a)(i) above, section 28B(4) of this Act (amendment of partners' returns consequential on amendment of partnership return by closure notice) applies accordingly; and
    (c) if the deferred amendment takes effect under subsection (3)(b) above, any necessary amendment under section 12ABA(3) of this Act may then be made.

(5) For the purposes of this section the period during which an enquiry is in progress is the whole of the period—

    (a) beginning with the day on which notice of enquiry is given, and
    (b) ending with the day on which the enquiry is completed.]¹

Commentary—*Simon's Direct Tax Service* **E1.808B.**
Amendments—¹ Sections 12AC–12AE substitued for s 12AC by FA 2001 s 88, Sch 29 para 5(1) with effect from 11 May 2001 in relation to returns whether made before or after 11 May 2001, and whether relating to periods before or after 11 May 2001.

[12AE Choice between different Cases of Schedule D

(1) Where in the case of a partnership return—

    (*a*) alternative methods are allowed by the Tax Acts for bringing amounts into charge to tax,

    (*b*) the return is made using one of those methods but could have been made using an alternative method, and

    (*c*) an officer of the Board determines which of the alternative methods is to be used,

the officer's determination is final and conclusive, for the purposes of any enquiry into the return, as to the basis of charge to be used.

(2) For the purposes of this section the cases where the Tax Acts allow alternative methods for bringing amounts into charge to tax are those specified—

    (*a*) for income tax purposes, in section 9D(2) of this Act;

    (*b*) for corporation tax purposes, in paragraph 84(2) or (3) of Schedule 18 to the Finance Act 1998.][1]

Amendments—[1] Sections 12AC–12AE substituted for s 12AC by FA 2001 s 88, Sch 29 para 5(1) with effect from 11 May 2001 in relation to returns whether made before or after 11 May 2001, and whether relating to periods before or after 11 May 2001.

[European Economic Interest Groupings][1]

[12A European Economic Interest Groupings

(1) In this section "grouping" means a European Economic Interest Grouping formed in pursuance of Council Regulation (EEC) No 2137/85 of 25th July 1985 ("the Council Regulation"), whether registered in Great Britain, in Northern Ireland, or elsewhere.

(2) For the purposes of [securing that members of a grouping are assessed to income tax and capital gains tax or (as the case may be) corporation tax][2], an inspector may act under subsection (3) or (4) below.

(3) In the case of a grouping which is registered in Great Britain or Northern Ireland or has an establishment registered in Great Britain or Northern Ireland, an inspector may by a notice given to the grouping require the grouping—

    (*a*) to make and deliver to the inspector within the time limited by the notice a return containing such information as may be required in pursuance of the notice, and

    (*b*) to deliver with the return such accounts and statements as may be required in pursuance of the notice.

(4) In the case of any other grouping, an inspector may by a notice given to any member of the grouping resident in the United Kingdom, or if none is to any member of the grouping, require the member—

    (*a*) to make and deliver to the inspector within the time limited by the notice a return containing such information as may be required in pursuance of the notice, and

    (*b*) to deliver with the return such accounts and statements as may be required in pursuance of the notice,

and a notice may be given to any one of the members concerned or separate notices may be given to each of them or to such of them as the inspector thinks fit.

(5) Every return under this section shall include a declaration by the grouping or member making the return to the effect that the return is to the best of the maker's knowledge correct and complete.

(6) A notice under this section may require different information, accounts and statements for different periods, in relation to different descriptions of income or gains or in relation to different descriptions of member.

(7) Notices under this section may require different information, accounts and statements in relation to different descriptions of grouping.

(8) Subject to subsection (9) below, where a notice is given under subsection (3) above, everything required to be done shall be done by the grouping acting through its manager or, where there is more than one, any of them; but where the manager of a grouping (or each of them) is a person other than an individual, the grouping shall act through the individual, or any of the individuals, designated in accordance with the Council Regulation as the representative of the manager (or any of them).

(9) Where the contract for the formation of a grouping provides that the grouping shall be validly bound only by two or more managers acting jointly, any declaration required by subsection (5) above to be included in a return made by a grouping shall be given by the appropriate number of managers.][1]

Commentary—*Simon's Direct Tax Service* **D4.903.**
Statement of Practice SP 4/91—Tax returns: their design and the information required in them.
Definitions—"Inspector", s 118(1); "notice", TA 1988 s 832(1); "return", s 118(1).
Cross references—See TMA 1970 s 98B (penalty for failure to make a return by European Economic Interest Groupings).
Amendments—[1] This section inserted by FA 1990 Sch 11 paras 2, 5 with effect from 1 July 1989.
[2] Words in sub-s (2) substituted by FA 1994 ss 196, 199 and Sch 19 para 2 as respects income tax and capital gains tax with effect from the year 1996–97 and as respects corporation tax with effect in relation to accounting periods ending after 30 June 1999 (by virtue of Finance Act 1994, Section 199, (Appointed Day) Order, SI 1998/3173 art 2).

[Records]

12B Records to be kept for purposes of returns

(1) Any person who may be required by a notice under section 8, 8A ...[13] or 12AA of this Act (or under any of those sections as extended by section 12 of this Act) to make and deliver a return for a year of assessment or other period shall—

(a) keep all such records as may be requisite for the purpose of enabling him to make and deliver a correct and complete return for the year or period; and

[(b) preserve those records until the end of the relevant day, that is to say, the day mentioned in subsection (2) below or, where a return is required by a notice given on or before that day, whichever of that day and the following is the latest, namely—

(i) where enquiries into the return ...[14] are made by an officer of the Board, the day on which, by virtue of section [28A(1) or 28B(1)][14] of this Act, those enquiries are ...[14] completed; and

(ii) where no enquiries into the return ...[14] are so made, the day on which such an officer no longer has power to make such enquiries.][2]

(2) The day referred to in subsection (1) above is—

(a) in the case of a person carrying on a trade, profession or business alone or in partnership or a company, the fifth anniversary of the 31st January next following the year of assessment or (as the case may be) the sixth anniversary of the end of the period;

(b) in any other case, the first anniversary of the 31st January next following the year of assessment ...[3]

[(2A) Any person who—

(a) is required, by such a notice as is mentioned in subsection (1) above given at any time after the end of the day mentioned in subsection (2) above, to make and deliver a return for a year of assessment or other period; and

(b) has in his possession at that time any records which may be requisite for the purpose of enabling him to make and deliver a correct and complete return for the year or period,

shall preserve those records until the end of the relevant day, that is to say, the day which, if the notice had been given on or before the day mentioned in subsection (2) above, would have been the relevant day for the purposes of subsection (1) above.][4]

(3) In the case of a person carrying on a trade, profession or business alone or in partnership—

(a) the records required to be kept and preserved under subsection (1) [or (2A)][5] above shall include records of the following, namely—

(i) all amounts received and expended in the course of the trade, profession or business and the matters in respect of which the receipts and expenditure take place, and

(ii) in the case of a trade involving dealing in goods, all sales and purchases of goods made in the course of the trade; and

(b) the duty under that subsection shall include a duty to preserve until [the end of the relevant day][5] all supporting documents relating to such items as are mentioned in paragraph (a)(i) or (ii) above.

(4) [Except in the case of records falling within subsection (4A) below,][9] The duty under subsection (1) [or (2A)][6] above to preserve records may be discharged by the preservation of the information contained in them; and where information is so preserved a copy of any document forming part of the records shall be admissible in evidence in any proceedings before the Commissioners to the same extent as the records themselves.

[(4A) The records which fall within this subsection are—

(a) any statement in writing such as is mentioned in—

(i) subsection (1) of section 234 of the principal Act (amount of qualifying distribution and tax credit), or

(ii) subsection (1) of section 352 of that Act (gross amount, tax deducted, and actual amount paid, in certain cases where payments are made under deduction of tax),

which is furnished by the company or person there mentioned, whether after the making of a request or otherwise;

(b) any certificate or other record (however described) which is required by regulations under section 566(1) of the principal Act to be given to a sub-contractor (within the meaning of Chapter IV of Part XIII of that Act) on the making of a payment to which section 559 of that Act (deductions on account of tax) applies;

(c) any such record as may be requisite for making a correct and complete claim in respect of, or otherwise requisite for making a correct and complete return so far as relating to, an amount of tax—

(i) which has been paid under the laws of a territory outside the United Kingdom, or

(ii) which would have been payable under the law of such a territory but for a relief to which section 788(5) of the principal Act (relief for promoting development and relief contemplated by double taxation arrangements) applies.][10]

(5) [Subject to subsections (5A) and (5B)][11] below,][7] any person who fails to comply with subsection (1) [or (2A)][7] above in relation to a year of assessment or accounting period shall be liable to a penalty not exceeding £3,000.

[(5A) Subsection (5) above does not apply where the records which the person fails to keep or preserve are records which might have been requisite only for the purposes of claims, elections or notices which are not included in the return.][8]

[(5B) Subsection (5) above also does not apply where—

(a) the records which the person fails to keep or preserve are records falling within paragraph (a) of subsection (4A) above; and

(b) an officer of the Board is satisfied that any facts which he reasonably requires to be proved, and which would have been proved by the records, are proved by other documentary evidence furnished to him.][12]

(6) For the purposes of this section—

(a) a person engaged in the letting of property shall be treated as carrying on a trade; and

(b) "supporting documents" includes accounts, books, deeds, contracts, vouchers and receipts.][1]

Commentary—*Simon's Direct Tax Service* E1.809.
Revenue Interpretation RI 140—Revenue's view that use of optical imaging systems for keeping records is acceptable, if a complete and unaltered image is maintained. Employers and sub-contractors records and vouchers must be maintained in paper form.
Revenue Internal guidance—Investigations Handbook IH 1530 (background to this section and link with Companies Act 1985 s 221).
Enquiry Handbook EH 64 (penalties not imposed for failure to keep records except in the most serious cases, after consultation with Compliance Division).
EH 396 (where records are kept on a computer, the original documentation must be retained unless it has been filmed, microfiched or optically imaged; abstracts of original documents may not satisfy the requirements of s 12B).
EH 678 (records to be kept are those in taxpayer's possession at the time the return is received by him).
EH 681, 702 (penalties under sub-s (5) sought only in the more serious cases, eg where records have been destroyed deliberately or where there is a history of serious record-keeping failures).
Definitions—"Act", s 118(1);"the Board", s 118(1);"company", s 118(1);"notice", TA 1988 s 832(1);"the principal Act", s 118(1);"return", s 118(1);"trade", s 118(1).
Cross references—See TMA 1970 s 107A(2), (3) (recovery of penalties from the relevant trustees of a settlement).
Education (Student Loans) (Repayment) Regulations, SI 2000/944 reg 18 (application of this section in connection with the repayment of student loans).
Amendments—[1] This section and the heading preceding it inserted by FA 1994 ss 196, 199 and Sch 19 para 3 with effect from the year 1996–97 as respects income tax and capital gains tax and, as respects corporation tax, with effect in relation to accounting periods ending after 30 June 1999 (by virtue of Finance Act 1994, Section 199, (Appointed Day) Order, SI 1998/3173 art 2).
[2] Sub-s (1)(b) words substituted by FA 1995 ss 105(1), 103(7) with effect from 1996–97 as respects income tax and capital gains tax and, as respects corporation tax, for accounting periods ending after 30 June 1999 (by virtue of SI 1998/3173 art 2).
[3] Sub-s (2) words omitted repealed by FA 1995 ss 105(2), 103(7) Sch 29 Pt VIII(14) with effect from the same dates as are mentioned in note [2] above.
[4] Sub-s (2A) inserted by FA 1995 ss 105(3), 103(7) with effect from the same dates as are mentioned in note [2] above.
[5] Sub-s (3) words "or (2A)" inserted and the words "the end of the relevant day" substituted by FA 1995 ss 105(4), 103(7) with effect from the same dates as are mentioned in note [2] above.
[6] Sub-s (4) words "or (2A)" inserted by FA 1995 ss 105(6), 103(7) with effect from the same dates as are mentioned in note [2] above.
[7] Sub-s (5) words inserted by FA 1995 ss 105(6), 103(7) with effect from the same dates as are mentioned in note [2] above.
[8] Sub-s (5A) inserted by FA 1995 ss 105(7), 103(7) with effect from the same dates as are mentioned in note [2] above.
[9] Words in sub-s (4) inserted by FA 1996 s 124(2) with effect from the year 1996–97 as it relates to income tax and capital gains tax and, as respects corporation tax, for accounting periods ending after 30 June 1999 (by virtue of SI 1998/3173 art 2).
[10] Sub-s (4A) inserted by FA 1996 s 124(3) with effect from the year 1996–97 as it relates to income tax and capital gains tax and, as respects corporation tax, for accounting periods ending after 30 June 1999 (by virtue of SI 1998/3173 art 2) (and do not have effect in relation to any time before 29 April 1996 or to any records which a person fails to preserve before that date).
[11] Sub-s (5) words substituted for "subject to subsection (5A)" by FA 1996 s 126(4) with effect from the year 1996–97 as they relate to income tax and capital gains tax and, as respects corporation tax, for accounting periods ending after 30 June 1999 (by virtue of SI 1998/3173 art 2) (and do not have effect in relation to any time before 29 April 1996 or to any records which a person fails to preserve before that date).
[12] Sub-s (5B) inserted by FA 1996 s 124(5) with effect from the year 1996–97 as it relates to income tax and capital gains tax and, as respects corporation tax, for accounting periods ending after 30 June 1999 (by virtue of SI 1998/3173 art 2) (and does not have effect in relation to any time before 29 April 1996 or to any records which a person fails to preserve before that date).
[13] Words in sub-s (1) repealed by FA 1998 Sch 19 para 6, Sch 27 Part III(28) with effect in relation to accounting periods ending after 30 June 1999 (by virtue of SI 1998/3173 art 2).
[14] In sub-s (1)(b)(i) and (ii), the words "or any amendment of the return" repealed, "28A(1) or 28B(1)" substituted for "28A(5) or 28B(5)" and the words "treated as" repealed, by FA 2001 ss 88, 110, Sch 29 para 20, Sch 33 Pt II(13) with effect from the passing of FA 2001 in relation to returns whether made before or after the passing of FA 2001, and whether relating to periods before or after the passing of FA 2001.

PART III
OTHER RETURNS AND INFORMATION

Statement of Practice SP 5/83—Procedure for making a return with the aid of schedules attached to official return form.
Cross references—See TMA 1970 s 98 (penalty for failing to make a return or furnish information under this Part).
TA 1988 ss 253(2), 350(5) (power of Board to make regulations modifying the provisions of this Part in relation to advance corporation tax and income tax deducted under TA 1988 s 349 for which a company is liable to account).
Education (Student Loans) (Repayment) Regulations, SI 2000/944 reg 19 (application of this Part in connection with the repayment of student loans).

13 Persons in receipt of taxable income belonging to others

(1) Every person who, in whatever capacity, is in receipt of any money or value, or of any profits or gains from any of the sources mentioned in the Income Tax Acts, of or belonging to another person who is chargeable to income tax in respect thereof, or who would be so chargeable if he were resident in the United Kingdom and not an incapacitated person, shall, whenever required to do so by a notice given to him by an inspector, prepare and deliver, within the time mentioned in the notice, a return ...[1], signed by him, containing—

    (*a*) a statement of all such money, value, profits or gains, and
    (*b*) the name and address of every person to whom the same belong, and
    (*c*) a declaration whether every such person is of full age, ...[3], or is resident in the United Kingdom or is an incapacitated person.

(2) If any person described above is acting jointly with any other person, he shall, in like manner, deliver a return of the names and addresses of all persons joined with him at the time of delivery of the return mentioned in subsection (1) above.

[(3) A notice under this section shall not require information as to any money, value, profits or gains received in a year of assessment ending more than three years before the date of the giving of the notice.][2]

Commentary—*Simon's Direct Tax Service* **A3.115.**
Revenue & other press releases—Law Society 29–5–91 (Revenue instructions to inspectors on issue of returns to solicitors. Section 13 notices should not be issued indiscriminately, or where information is provided satisfactorily in another manner. If a nil return is received for two consecutive years, returns should only be issued every five years, until a receipt is returned).
Simon's Tax Cases—*Fawcett v Special Comrs and Lancaster Farmers' Auction Mart Co Ltd* [1997] STC 171.
Definitions—"Incapacitated person", s 118(1); "return", s 118(1).
Cross references—See TMA 1970 s 76 (making of a return under this section to be the only obligation of certain trustees, agents, etc).
Amendments—[1] Words in sub-s (1) repealed by FA 1970 Sch 8 Pt VII.
[2] Sub-s (3) added by FA 1988 s 123(1), (5) with respect to notices given after 29 July 1988.
[3] Words in sub-s (1)(*c*) repealed by FA 1988 Sch 14 Pt VIII with effect from the year 1990–91.

14 Return of lodgers and inmates

Every person, when required to do so by a notice served on him by an inspector, shall, within the time limited by the notice, prepare and deliver to the inspector a return, in writing, containing to the best of his belief—

    (*a*) the name of every lodger or inmate resident in his dwelling-house, and
    (*b*) the name and ordinary place of residence of any such lodger or inmate who has any ordinary place of residence elsewhere at which he can be assessed and who desires to be assessed at such ordinary place of residence.

Commentary—*Simon's Direct Tax Service* **A3.116.**
Definition—"Return", s 118(1).

[15 Return of employees' emoluments etc

(1) Every employer, when required to do so by notice from an officer of the Board, shall, within the time limited by the notice, prepare and deliver to the officer a return relating to persons who are or have been employees of his, containing the information required under the following provisions of this section.

(2) An employer shall not be required to include in his return information relating to any year of assessment if the notice is given more than five years after the 31st January next following that year.

(3) A notice under subsection (1) above—

    (*a*) shall specify the employees for whom a return is to be made and may, in particular, specify individuals (by name or otherwise) or all employees of an employer or all his employees who are or have been in employment to which Chapter II of Part V of the principal Act applies; and
    (*b*) shall specify the years of assessment or other periods with respect to which the information is to be provided.

(4) A notice under subsection (1) above may require the return to state the name and place of residence of an employee to whom it relates.

(5) A notice under subsection (1) above may require the return to contain, in respect of an employee to whom it relates, the following particulars—

    (*a*) in the case of relevant payments made by the employer, particulars of the payments;
    (*b*) in the case of relevant payments not falling within paragraph (*a*) above the making of which by another person has been arranged by the employer—
        (i) particulars of the payments; and
        (ii) the name and business address of the other person; and—
    (*c*) in the case of relevant payments not falling within either of the preceding paragraphs, the name and business address of any person who has, to the employer's knowledge, made the payments.

(6) Any payments made to an employee in respect of his employment are relevant payments for the purposes of this section, including—

(*a*) payments to him in respect of expenses (including sums put at his disposal and paid away by him);

(*b*) payments made on his behalf and not repaid; and

(*c*) payments to him for services rendered in connection with a trade or business, whether the services were rendered in the course of his employment or not.

(7) Where, for the purposes of his return, an employer apportions expenses incurred partly in or in connection with a particular matter and partly in or in connection with other matters—

(*a*) the return shall contain a statement that the sum included in the return is the result of such an apportionment; and

(*b*) if required to do so by notice from an officer of the Board, the employer shall prepare and deliver to the officer, within the time limited by the notice, a return containing full particulars as to the amount apportioned and the manner in which, and the grounds on which, the apportionment has been made.

(8) A notice under subsection (1) above may require the return—

(*a*) to state in respect of an employee to whom it relates whether any benefits are or have been provided for him (or for any other person) by reason of his employment, such as may give rise to charges to tax under the relevant sections, that is to say, sections 141, 142, 143, 144A, 145, 146 and 154 to 165 of the principal Act (miscellaneous benefits in cash or in kind); and

(*b*) if such benefits are or have been provided, to contain such particulars of those benefits as may be specified in the notice.

(9) Where such benefits are provided the notice may, without prejudice to subsection (8)(*b*) above, require the return to contain the following particulars—

(*a*) in the case of benefits which are or have been provided by the employer, particulars of the amounts which may be chargeable to tax by virtue of the relevant sections;

(*b*) in the case of benefits not falling within paragraph (*a*) above the provision of which by another person is or has been arranged by the employer—

(i) particulars of the amounts which may be so chargeable; and

(ii) the name and business address of the other person; and

(*c*) in the case of benefits not falling within either of the preceding paragraphs, the name and business address of any person who has, to the employer's knowledge, provided the benefits.

(10) Where it appears to an officer of the Board that a person has, in any year of assessment, been concerned in making relevant payments to, or providing benefits to or in respect of, employees of another, the officer may at any time up to five years after the 31st January next following that year by notice require that person—

(*a*) to deliver to the officer, within the time limited by the notice, such particulars of those payments or benefits, or of the amounts which may be chargeable to tax in respect of the benefits, as may be specified in the notice (so far as known to him); and

(*b*) to include with those particulars the names and addresses (so far as known to him) of the employees concerned.

(11) In determining, in pursuance of a notice under subsection (1) or (10) above, amounts which may be chargeable to tax by virtue of the relevant sections, a person—

(*a*) shall not make—

(i) any deduction or other adjustment which he is unable to show, by reference to information in his possession or otherwise available to him, is authorised or required by the relevant sections; or

(ii) any deduction authorised by section 141(3), 142(2), 145(3) or 156(8) of the principal Act; but

(*b*) subject to that, shall make all such deductions and other adjustments as may be authorised or required by the relevant sections.

(12) Where the employer is a body of persons, the secretary of the body or other officer (by whatever name called) performing the duties of secretary shall be treated as the employer for the purposes of this section.

Where the employer is a body corporate, that body corporate, as well as the secretary or other officer, shall be liable to a penalty for failure to comply with this section.

(13) In this section—

"arranged" includes guaranteed and in any way facilitated;

"employee" means an office holder or employee whose emoluments fall to be assessed under Schedule E, and related expressions are to be construed accordingly;

"relevant payments" has the meaning given by subsection (6) above; and

"the relevant sections" has the meaning given by subsection (8)(*a*) above.]'

Commentary—*Simon's Direct Tax Service* A3.117.
Definitions—"Act", s 118(1); "the Board", s 118(1); "Body of persons", s 118(1); "principal Act", s 118(1); "return", s 118(1)
Cross references—See TMA 1970 s 16A (agency workers).

FA 1974 s 24 (application of this section where employer not resident but duties performed for benefit of person resident or trading in UK).
Amendments—[1] This section substituted by FA 1995 s 106, with effect as respects payments made or benefits provided after 5 April 1996.

16 Fees, commissions, etc

(1) Every person carrying on a trade or business shall, if required to do so by notice from an inspector, make and deliver to the inspector a return of all payments of any kind specified in the notice made during a period so specified, being—

    (*a*) payments made in the course of the trade or business, or of such part of the trade or business as may be specified in the notice, for services rendered by persons not employed in the trade or business, or

    (*b*) payments for services rendered in connection with the formation, acquisition, development or disposal of the trade or business, or any part of it, by persons not employed in the trade or business, or

    (*c*) periodical or lump sum payments made in respect of any copyright[, public lending right, right in a registered design or design right][1].

(2) Every body of persons carrying on any activity which does not constitute a trade or business shall, if required to do so by notice from an inspector, make and deliver to the inspector a return of all payments of a kind specified in the notice made during a period so specified, being—

    (*a*) payments made in the course of carrying on the activity, or such part of the activity as may be specified in the notice, for services rendered by persons not employed by the said body of persons, or

    (*b*) periodical or lump sum payments made in respect of any copyright[, public lending right, right in a registered design or design right][1].

(3) A return required under either of the preceding subsections shall, if the trade or business or other activity is carried on by an unincorporated body of persons (other than a company), be made and delivered by the person who is or performs the duties of secretary of the body, and the notice shall be framed accordingly.

(4) A return under the preceding provisions of this section shall give the name of the person to whom each payment was made, the amount of the payment and such other particulars (including particulars as to the services or rights in respect of which the payment was made, the period over which any services were rendered and any business name and any business or home address of the person to whom payment was made) as may be specified in the notice.

(5) No person shall be required under the preceding provisions of this section to include in a return—

    (*a*) particulars of any payment from which income tax is deductible, or

    (*b*) particulars of payments made to any one person where the total of the payments to that person which would otherwise fall to be included in the return does not exceed £15, or

    (*c*) particulars of any payment made in a year of assessment ending more than three years before the service of the notice requiring him to make the return.

(6) ...[3]

(7) In this section—

    (*a*) references to payments for services include references to payments in the nature of commission of any kind and references to payments in respect of expenses incurred in connection with the rendering of services, and

    (*b*) references to the making of payments include references to the giving of any valuable consideration,

and the requirement imposed by subsection (4) above to state the amount of a payment shall, in relation to any consideration given otherwise than in the form of money, be construed as a requirement to give particulars of the consideration.

[(8) In subsection (2) above references to a body of persons include references to any department of the Crown, any public or local authority and any other public body.][2]

Commentary—*Simon's Direct Tax Service* A3.118.
Cross references—See TMA 1970 s 16A (agency workers).
Simon's Tax Cases—*Branch v Smith* [1985] STC 139.
Definitions—''Body of persons'', s 118(1); ''return'', s 118(1).
Amendments—[1] Words in sub-ss (1)(*c*), (2)(*b*) substituted by the Copyright, Designs and Patents Act 1988 Sch 7 para 13 with effect from 1 August 1989 by virtue of the Copyright, Designs and Patents Act 1988 (Commencement No 1) Order, SI 1989/816.
[2] Sub-s (8) added by FA 1988 s 124.
[3] Sub-s (6) repealed by FA 1989 s 164(6), (7)(*a*) and Sch 17 Pt VIII in relation to any failure to comply with a notice served after 26 July 1989.

[16A Agency workers

(1) Where—

    (*a*) any services which an individual renders or is under an obligation to render under a contract are treated under section 134(1) of the principal Act as the duties of an office or employment held by him; or (*b*) any remuneration receivable under or in consequence of arrangements to which subsection (6) of that section applies is treated under that subsection as emoluments of an office or employment held by an individual,

section 15 above shall apply as if that individual were employed—

(i) in a case within paragraph (*a*) above, by the persons or each of the persons from whom he receives any remuneration under or in consequence of the contract; and

(ii) in a case within paragraph (*b*) above, by the other party to the arrangements,

and section 16 above shall not apply to any payments made to that individual under or in consequence of that contract or those arrangements.

(2) In subsection (1) above ''remuneration'', in relation to an individual, does not include anything in respect of which he would not have been chargeable to tax under Schedule E if it had been receivable in connection with an office or employment held by him but, subject to that, includes every form of payment and all perquisites, benefits and profits whatsoever.][1]

Commentary—*Simon's Direct Tax Service* E4.204.
Definition—''The principal Act'', s 118(1).
Amendments—[1] This section inserted by TA 1988 Sch 29 para 6.

17 Interest paid or credited by banks etc without deduction of income tax

(1) Every person carrying on a trade or business who, in the ordinary course of the operations thereof, receives or retains money in such circumstances that interest becomes payable thereon which is paid or credited without deduction of income tax [or after deduction of income tax][2], and, in particular, every [such person who is a bank][7], shall, if required to do so by notice from an inspector, make and deliver to the inspector, within the time specified in the notice, a return of all interest paid or credited by him as aforesaid during a year [of assessment][1] specified in the notice in the course of his trade or business or any such part of his trade or business as may be so specified, giving the names and addresses of the persons to whom the interest was paid or credited and stating, in each case, the amount of the interest [actually paid or credited and (where the interest was paid or credited after deduction of income tax) the amount of the interest from which the tax was deducted and the amount of the tax deducted][2]:

Provided that—

(*a*) ...[4]

(*b*) the year specified in a notice under this subsection shall not be a year ending more than three years before the date of the service of the notice.

[(1A) In this section ''bank'' has the meaning given by section 840A of the principal Act.][8]

(2) Without prejudice to the generality of so much of subsection (1) above as enables different notices to be served thereunder in relation to different parts of a trade or business, separate notices may be served under that subsection as respects the transactions carried on at any branch or branches respectively specified in the notices, and any such separate notice shall, if served on the manager or other person in charge of the branch or branches in question, be deemed to have been duly served on the person carrying on the trade or business; and where such a separate notice is so served as respects the transactions carried on at any branch or branches, any notice subsequently served under the said subsection (1) on the person carrying on the trade or business shall not be deemed to extend to any transaction to which the said separate notice extends.

(3) This section shall, with any necessary adaptations, apply in relation to the National Savings Bank as if it were a trade or business carried on by the Director of Savings.

(4) This section shall apply only to money received or retained in the United Kingdom ...[5].

[(4A) If a person to whom any interest is paid or credited in respect of any money received or retained in the United Kingdom by notice in writing served on the person paying or crediting the interest—

(*a*) has declared that the person beneficially entitled to the interest is a company not resident in the United Kingdom, and

(*b*) has requested that the interest shall not be included in any return under this section,

the person paying or crediting the interest shall not be required to include the interest in any such return.][6]

(4B) ...[9]

(4C) ...[9]

[(5) The Board may by regulations provide as mentioned in all or any of the following paragraphs—

(*a*) that a return under subsection (1) above shall contain such further information as is prescribed if the notice requiring the return specifies the information and requires it to be contained in the return;

(*b*) that a person required to make and deliver a return under subsection (1) above shall furnish with the return such further information as is prescribed if the notice requiring the return specifies the information and requires it to be so furnished;

[(*c*) that if a person is required—

(i) to make and deliver a return under subsection (1) above;
(ii) to include information in such a return under any provision made under paragraph (*a*) above; or
(iii) to furnish information under any provision made under paragraph (*b*) above,

and the notice under subsection (1) above specifies the form in which the return is to be made and delivered, or the information is to be included or furnished, the person shall make and deliver the return, or include or furnish the information, in that form;][10]
(*d*) that a notice under subsection (1) above shall not require prescribed information;

and in this subsection "prescribed" means prescribed by the regulations.][3]

[The further information required as mentioned in paragraph (*a*) or (*b*) above may include, in prescribed cases, the name and address of the person beneficially entitled to the interest paid or credited.][10]

[(6) Regulations under subsection (5) above—

(*a*) shall be made by statutory instrument subject to annulment in pursuance of a resolution of the House of Commons,
[(*aa*) may make provision with respect to the furnishing of information by persons required—

(i) to make and deliver a return under subsection (1) above;
(ii) to include information in such a return under any provision made under subsection (5)(*a*) above; or
(iii) to furnish information under any provision made under subsection (5)(*b*) above,

including the inspection of books, documents and other records on behalf of the Board;][11]
(*b*) may make different provision in relation to different cases or descriptions of case, and
(*c*) may include such supplementary, incidental, consequential or transitional provisions as appear to the Board to be necessary or expedient.][3]

Commentary—*Simon's Direct Tax Service* **A3.120.**
Regulations—Income Tax (Interest Payments) (Information Powers) Regulations, SI 1992/15.
Simon's Tax Cases—*Eke v Knight* [1977] STC 198.
Definitions—"bank", TA 1988 s 840A; "the Board", s 118(1); "inspector", s 118(1); "interest", TA 1988 s 832(1); "notice", TA 1988 s 832(1); "the principal Act", s 118(1); "return", s 118(1); "trade", s 118(1).
Cross references—See IT (Building Societies) (Dividends and Interest) Regulations, SI 1990/2231 reg 12 (modified application of this section in relation to a building society).
Amendments—[1] Words in sub-s (1) inserted by FA 1988 s 123(2), (5) with respect to notices given after 29 July 1988.
[2] Words in sub-s (1) inserted by FA 1990 s 92(1), (2), (7) as regards a case where interest is paid or credited in the year 1991–92 or a subsequent year of assessment.
[3] Sub-ss (5), (6) inserted by FA 1990 s 92(1), (3), (7) as regards a case where interest is paid or credited in the year 1991–92 or a subsequent year of assessment.
[4] Sub-s (1) proviso (*a*) repealed by FA 1990 s 92(1), (2), (7) and Sch 19 Pt V as regards a case where interest is paid or credited in the year 1991–92 or a subsequent year of assessment.
[5] Words in sub-s (4) repealed by F(No 2)A 1992 s 29 and Sch 18, Pt VII(3) in respect of interest paid or credited after 16 July 1992.
[6] Sub-s (4A) inserted by F(No 2)A 1992 s 29 in respect of interest paid or credited after 16 July 1992.
[7] Words in sub-s (1) substituted by FA 1996 Sch 37 Pt III para 11(3) with effect in relation to interest paid on or after 29 April 1996.
[8] Sub-s (1A) inserted by FA 1996 Sch 24 Pt III para 11(1), (2)(*a*) with effect in relation to interest paid on or after 29 April 1996.
[9] Sub-ss (4B), (4C) repealed by FA 2000 s 145(1) with effect for amounts paid, credited or received after 5 April 2001.
[10] In sub-s (5), para (*c*) substituted, and words inserted by FA 2000 s 145(2) with effect for amounts paid, credited or received after 5 April 2001.
[11] Sub-s (6)(*aa*) inserted by FA 2000 s 145(3)) with effect for amounts paid, credited or received after 5 April 2001.

18 Interest paid without deduction of income tax

(1) Any person [by or through whom][8] any interest is paid in the year 1969–70 or any subsequent year of assessment without deduction of income tax [or after deduction of income tax][5] ...[1] shall, on being so required by a notice given to him by an inspector, furnish to the inspector, within the time limited by the notice—

(*a*) the name and address of the person to whom the interest has been paid or on whose behalf the interest has been received, and
(*b*) the amount of the interest [actually paid or received and (where the interest has been paid or received after deduction of income tax) the amount of the interest from which the tax has been deducted and the amount of the tax deducted][6],

and any person [by whom any such interest is received][8] on behalf of another person shall on being so required furnish to the inspector the name and address of the person on whose behalf the interest has been received, and [the amount actually received and (where the interest has been received after deduction of income tax) the amount of the interest from which the tax has been deducted and the amount of the tax deducted][6].

(2) The persons to whom [subsection (1) above][2] applies include any officer in any public office or in any department of the Crown.

(3) ...[9]

(3AA) ...[9]

[(3A) A notice under this section shall not require information with respect to interest paid [or received][8] in a year of assessment ending more than three years before the date of the giving of the notice.][4]

[(3B) The Board may by regulations provide as mentioned in all or any of the following paragraphs—

(a) that a person required to furnish information under subsection (1) above shall furnish at the same time such further information as is prescribed if the notice concerned specifies the information and requires it to be so furnished;

(b) that if a person is required to furnish information under subsection (1) above or under any provision made under paragraph (a) above, and the notice concerned specifies the form in which the information is to be furnished, the person shall furnish the information in that form;

(c) that a notice under subsection (1) above shall not require prescribed information;

and in this subsection "prescribed" means prescribed by the regulations.][7]

[The further information required as mentioned in paragraph (a) above may include, in prescribed cases, the name and address of the person beneficially entitled to the interest paid or received.][8]

[(3C) Regulations under subsection (3B) above—

(a) shall be made by statutory instruments subject to annulment in pursuance of a resolution of the House of Commons,

[(aa) may make provision with respect to the furnishing of information by persons required to furnish information under subsection (1) above, or under any provision made under subsection (3B)(a) above, including the inspection of books, documents and other records on behalf of the Board;][10]

(b) may make different provision in relation to different cases or descriptions of case, and

(c) may include such supplementary, incidental, consequential or transitional provisions as appear to the Board to be necessary or expedient.][7]

[(3D) For the purposes of this section interest shall be treated as received by any person if it is received by another person at his direction or with his consent.][11]

[(3E) For the purposes of this section the following shall be treated as interest—

(a) any dividend in respect of a share in a building society;

(b) any amount to which a person holding a relevant discounted security is entitled on the redemption of that security; and

(c) any foreign dividend.][11]

[(3F) In subsection (3E)(b) above "relevant discounted security" has the meaning given by paragraph 3 of Schedule 13 to the Finance Act 1996.][11]

[(3G) In subsection (3E)(c) above "foreign dividend" means any annual payment, interest or dividend payable out of, or in respect of the stocks, funds, shares or securities of—

(a) a body of persons that is not resident in the United Kingdom, or

(b) a government or public or local authority in a country outside the United Kingdom.".][11]

[(4) ...][3]

Commentary—*Simon's Direct Tax Service* A3.120.
Regulations—Income Tax (Interest Payments) (Information Powers) Regulations, SI 1992/15.
Definitions—"Bank", TA 1988 s 840A; "the Board", s 118(1); "inspector", s 118(1); "interest", TA 1988 s 832(1); "notice", TA 1988 s 832(1); "the principal Act", s 118(1).
Amendments—[1] Words in sub-s (1) which were inserted by TA 1988 Sch 29 para 7 repealed by FA 1988 Sch 14 Pt IV.
[2] Words in sub-s (2), substituted by TA 1988 Sch 29 para 7.
[3] Sub-s (4) which was inserted by TA 1988 Sch 29 para 7 repealed by FA 1988 Sch 14 Pt IV.
[4] Sub-s (3A) added by FA 1988 s 123(3), (5) with respect to notices given after 29 July 1988.
[5] Words in sub-s (1) inserted by FA 1990 s 92(4), (5), (8) as regards a case where interest is paid in the year 1991–92 or a subsequent year of assessment.
[6] Words in sub-s (1)(b) substituted by FA 1990 s 92(4), (5), (8) as regards a case where interest is paid in the year 1991–92 or a subsequent year of assessment.
[7] Sub-ss (3B), (3C) inserted by FA 1990 s 92(4), (6), (8) as regards a case where interest is paid in the year 1991–92 or a subsequent year of assessment.
[8] Sub-ss (1), (3A), (3B) amended by FA 2000 s 145(4), (6), (7) with effect for amounts paid, credited or received after 5 April 2001.
[9] Sub-ss (3), (3AA) repealed by FA 2000 s 145(5) with effect for amounts paid, credited or received after 5 April 2001.
[10] Sub-s (3C)(aa) inserted by FA 2000 s 145(8) with effect for amounts paid, credited or received after 5 April 2001.
[11] Sub-ss (3D)–(3G) substituted for sub-s (3D) by FA 2000 s 145(9) with effect for amounts paid, credited or received after 5 April 2001.

[18A Other payments and licences etc

(1) Any person by whom any payment out of public funds is made by way of grant or subsidy shall, on being so required by a notice given to him by an inspector, furnish to the inspector, within the time limited by the notice—

(a) the name and address of the person to whom the payment has been made or on whose behalf the payment has been received, and

(b) the amount of the payment so made or received,

and any person who receives any such payment on behalf of another person shall on being so required furnish to the inspector the name and address of the person on whose behalf the payment has been received, and its amount.

(2) Any person by whom licences or approvals are issued or a register is maintained shall, on being so required by a notice given to him by an inspector, furnish to the inspector, within the time limited by the notice—

(*a*) the name and address of any person who is or has been the holder of a licence or approval issued by the first-mentioned person, or to whom an entry in that register relates or related; and
(*b*) particulars of the licence or entry.

(3) the persons to whom this section applies include any department of the Crown, any public or local authority and any other public body.

(4) A notice is not to be given under this section unless (in the inspector's reasonable opinion) the information required is or may be relevant to any tax liability to which a person is or may be subject, or the amount of any such liability.

(5) A notice under this section shall not require information with respect to a payment which was made, or to a licence, approval or entry which ceased to subsist—

(*a*) before 6th April 1988; or
(*b*) in a year of assessment ending more than three years before the date of the giving of the notice.

(6) For the purposes of this section a payment is a payment out of public funds if it is provided directly or indirectly by the Crown, by any Government, public or local authority whether in the United Kingdom or elsewhere or by any Community institution.][1]

Commentary—*Simon's Direct Tax Service* **A3.118.**
Definition—''Inspector'', s 118(1).
Amendments—[1] This section inserted by FA 1988 s 125.

19 Information for purposes of Schedule A

(1) For the purpose of obtaining particulars of profits or gains chargeable to tax under Schedule A (or, for chargeable periods ending before 6th April 1970, under Case VIII of Schedule D), the inspector may by notice in writing require—

(*a*) any lessee, occupier or former lessee or occupier of land (including any person having, or having had, the use of land) to give such information as may be prescribed by the Board as to the terms applying to the lease, occupation or use of the land, and where any of those terms are established by any written instrument, to produce the instrument to the inspector,
(*b*) any lessee or former lessee of land to give such information as may be so prescribed as to any consideration given for the grant or assignment to him of the tenancy,
(*c*) any person who as agent manages land or is in receipt of rent or other payments arising from land to furnish the inspector with such particulars relating to payments arising therefrom as may be specified in the notice.

(2) Subsection (1) above shall apply in relation to sums chargeable to tax under Case VI of Schedule D by virtue of any provision of sections [34 to 36][1] of the principal Act as it applies to profits or gains chargeable to tax under Schedule A or Case VIII of Schedule D.

(3) In this section—

(*a*) ''lease'' includes an agreement for a lease, and any tenancy, but does not include a mortgage or heritable security, and ''lessee'' shall be construed accordingly but shall include the successor in title of a lessee,
(*b*) in relation to Scotland ''assignment'' means an assignation.

[(4) A notice under this section shall not require information with respect to—

(*a*) the terms applying to the lease, occupation or use of the land, or
(*b*) consideration given, or
(*c*) payments arising,

in a year of assessment ending more than three years before the date of the giving of the notice.][2]

Commentary—*Simon's Direct Tax Service* **A3.123.**
Definition—''Principal Act'', s 118(1).
Amendments—[1] Numbers in sub-s (2) substituted by TA 1988 Sch 29 para 32 Table.
[2] Sub-s (4) added by FA 1988 s 123(4), (5) with respect to notices given after 29 July 1988.

Production of accounts, books and other information

[19A Power to call for documents for purposes of certain enquiries

[(1) This section applies where an officer of the Board gives notice of enquiry under section 9A(1) or 12AC(1) of this Act to a person (''the taxpayer'').][6]

(2) For the purpose of [the enquiry][6], the officer may at the same or any subsequent time by notice in writing require the taxpayer, within such time (which shall not be less than 30 days) as may be specified in the notice—

(*a*) to produce to the officer such documents as are in the taxpayer's possession or power and as the officer may reasonably require for the purpose of determining whether and, if so, the extent to which [—

(i) the return is incorrect or incomplete, or

(ii) in the case of an enquiry which is limited under section 9A(5) or 12AC(5) of this Act, the amendment to which the enquiry relates is incorrect, and][6]

(*b*) to furnish the officer with such accounts or particulars as he may reasonably require for that purpose.

[(2A) The officer of the Board may also (whether or not he imposes a requirement under subsection (2) above), by a notice in writing, require the taxpayer, within such time (which shall be not less than 30 days) as may be specified in the notice—

(*a*) to produce to the officer such documents as are in the taxpayer's possession or power and as the officer may reasonably require for the purpose of making a determination for the purposes of section [9D(1)(*c*) or 12AE(1)(*c*)][6] of this Act, and

(*b*) to furnish the officer with such accounts or particulars as he may reasonably require for that purpose.][2]

(3) To comply with a notice under [subsection (2) or (2A)][3] above, copies of documents may be produced instead of originals; but—

(*a*) the copies must be photographic or otherwise by way of facsimile; and

(*b*) if so required by a notice in writing given by the officer, in the case of any document specified in the notice, the original must be produced for inspection by him within such time (which shall not be less than 30 days) as may be specified in the notice.

(4) The officer may take copies of, or make extracts from, any document produced to him under [subsection (2), (2A) or][4] (3) above.

(5) A notice under [subsection (2) or (2A)][3] above does not oblige the taxpayer to produce documents or furnish accounts or particulars relating to the conduct of [—

(*a*) any pending appeal by him, or

(*b*) any pending referral to the Special Commissioners under section 28ZA of this Act to which he is a party.][6]

(6) An appeal may be brought against any requirement imposed by a notice under subsection (2) above to produce any document or to furnish any accounts or particulars.

(7) An appeal under subsection (6) above must be brought within the period of 30 days beginning with the date on which the notice under [subsection (2) or (2A)][3] above is given.

(8) Subject to subsection (9) below, the provisions of this Act relating to appeals shall have effect in relation to an appeal under subsection (6) above as they have effect in relation to an appeal against an assessment to tax.

(9) On an appeal under subsection (6) above section 50(6) to (8) of this Act shall not apply but the Commissioners may—

(*a*) if it appears to them that the production of the document or the furnishing of the accounts or particulars was reasonably required by the officer of the Board for the purpose mentioned in [subsection (2) or (2A)][3] above, confirm the notice under that subsection so far as relating to the requirement; or

(*b*) if it does not so appear to them, set aside that notice so far as so relating.

(10) Where, on an appeal under subsection (6) above, the Commissioners confirm the notice under [subsection (2) or (2A)][3] above so far as relating to any requirement, the notice shall have effect in relation to that requirement as if it had specified 30 days beginning with the determination of the appeal.

[(11) The determination of the Commissioners of an appeal under subsection (6) above shall be final and conclusive (notwithstanding any provision having effect by virtue of section 56B of this Act).][5]

(12) Where this section applies by virtue of a notice given under section 12AC(1) of this Act, any reference in this section to the taxpayer includes a reference to any predecessor or successor of his.][1]

Commentary—*Simon's Direct Tax Service* D2.732; E1.811.
Revenue Internal Guidance—Enquiry Handbook EH 319, 398, 401 (Revenue consider that private bank accounts can be required, but will consider whether this is reasonable in each particular case).
EH 322–324 (other information which may be required).
EH 330, 377 (information is usually requested informally in the first instance; formal notice issued in cases of delay).
EH 345, 346 (initial meetings with taxpayer).
EH 347 (examination of records at taxpayer's premises).
EH 348, 403 (Revenue do not have the right to insist on a meeting with the taxpayer: if taxpayer refuses, then any questioning of taxpayer may have to be deferred to an appeal hearing).
EH 389 (interaction with s 20).
EH 397 (examples of s 19A information).
EH 403 (this section does not give Revenue right of access to taxpayer's premises, information relating to third parties or the right to general requests such as requests for "anything relevant to your return").
EH 753 (in the case of a partnership, the responsibility for complying with a notice lies with the nominated partner only and any failure to comply is his failure only, but any such failure may affect mitigation of penalties for other partners).
EH 967 (appeals under sub-s (6): Revenue will agree revised timescale in cases of genuine need: Commissioners do not have power to extend the time limit).
Simon's Tax Cases—*Mother v Inspector of Taxes* [1999] STC (SCD) 279; *Holly v Inspector of Taxes* [2000] STC (SCD) 50, *Guyer v Walton (Inspector of Taxes)* [2001] STC (SCD) 75.
s 19A(2), *Self-assessed v Inspector of Taxes* [1999] STC (SCD) 253.
s 19A(2)(*a*), (*b*), *Accountant v Inspector of Taxes* [2000] STC (SCD) 522.
Definitions—"Act", s 118(1); "the Board", s 118(1); "return", s 118(1).

Cross references—See TMA 1970 s 97AA (penalties for failure to produce documents in accordance with sub-ss (2), (2A), (3) above).

Education (Student Loans) (Repayment) Regulations, SI 2000/944 reg 19 (application of this section in connection with the repayment of student loans).

Amendments—[1] This section inserted by FA 1994 ss 187, 199 with effect from the year 1996–97 as respects income tax and capital gains tax and, as respects corporation tax, with effect in relation to accounting periods ending after 30 June 1999 (by virtue of Finance Act 1994, Section 199, (Appointed Day) Order, SI 1998/3173 art 2).

[2] Sub-s (2A) inserted by FA 1996 Sch 19 para 3(1) with effect from the year 1996–97 as respects income tax and capital gains tax and, as respects corporation tax, for accounting periods after 30 June 1999 (by virtue of SI 1998/3173 art 2).

[3] Words in sub-ss (3), (5), (7), (9)(a), (10) substituted by FA 1996 Sch 19 para 3(2) with effect from the year 1996–97 as respects income tax and capital gains tax and, as respects corporation tax, for accounting periods ending after 30 June 1999 (by virtue of SI 1998/3173 art 2).

[4] Words in sub-s (4) substituted by FA 1996 Sch 19 para 3(3) with effect from the year 1996–97 as respects income tax and capital gains tax and, as respects corporation tax, for accounting periods ending after 30 June 1999 (by virtue of SI 1998/3173 art 2).

[5] Sub-s (11) substituted by FA 1996 Sch 22 para 2 in relation to any proceedings relating to the year 1996–97 or any subsequent year of assessment and to any proceedings relating to an accounting period ending after 30 June 1999 (by virtue of SI 1998/3173 art 2).

[6] Sub-s (1) substituted, words in sub-s (2) substituted for the words "enquiring into the return or amendment", words in sub-s (2)(a) substituted for the words "the return is incorrect or incomplete or the amendment is incorrect, and"; in sub-s (2A), "9D(1)(c) or 12AE(1)(c)" substituted for "28A(7A)(d) or 28B(6A)(d)''; and words in sub-s (5) substituted for "any pending appeal by him", by FA 2001 s 88, Sch 29 para 21 with effect from the passing of FA 2001 in relation to returns whether made before or after the passing of FA 2001, and whether relating to periods before or after the passing of FA 2001. Sub-s (1) previously read as follows—

"(1) This section applies where an officer of the Board gives notice under section 9A(1) or 12AC(1) of this Act to any person (the taxpayer) of his intention to enquire into—

> (a) the return on the basis of which the taxpayer's self-assessment or partnership statement was made, or
> (b) any amendment of that return on the basis of which that assessment or statement has been amended by the taxpayer or
> (c) any claim or election included in the return (by amendment or otherwise) or
> (d) the period for which a return should have been made."

[20 Power to call for documents of taxpayer and others

(1) Subject to this section, an inspector may by notice in writing require [a person—

> (a) to deliver to him such documents as are in the person's possession or power and as (in the inspector's reasonable opinion) contain, or may contain, information relevant to—
>> (i) any tax liability to which the person is or may be subject, or
>> (ii) the amount of any such liability, or
> (b) to furnish to him such particulars as the inspector may reasonably require as being relevant to, or to the amount of, any such liability.][5]

(2) Subject to this section, the Board may by notice in writing require [a person—

> (a) to deliver to a named officer of the Board such documents as are in the person's possession or power and as (in the Board's reasonable opinion) contain, or may contain, information relevant to—
>> (i) any tax liability to which the person is or may be subject, or
>> (ii) the amount of any such liability, or
> (b) to furnish to a named officer of the Board such particulars as the Board may reasonably require as being relevant to, or to the amount of, any such liability.][6]

(3) Subject to this section, an inspector may, for the purpose of enquiring into the tax liability of any person ("the taxpayer"), by notice in writing require any [other person][7] to deliver to the inspector or, if the person to whom the notice is given so elects, to make available for inspection by a named officer of the Board, such documents as are in his possession or power and as (in the inspector's reasonable opinion) contain, or may contain, information relevant to any tax liability to which the taxpayer is or may be, or may have been, subject, or to the amount of any such liability [; and the persons who may be required to deliver or make available a document under this subsection include the Director of Savings.][8]

(4), (5) ...[9]

(6) The persons who may be treated as "the taxpayer" [for the purposes of this section][10] include a company which has ceased to exist and an individual who has died; ...[11]

(7) Notices under [subsection (1) or (3) above][3] are not to be given by an inspector unless he is authorised by the Board for its purposes; and—

> (a) a notice is not to be given by him except with the consent of a General or Special Commissioner; and
> (b) the Commissioner is to give his consent only on being satisfied that in all the circumstances the inspector is justified in proceeding under this section.

[(7A) A notice under subsection (2) above is not to be given unless the Board have reasonable grounds for believing—

> (a) that the person to whom it relates may have failed or may fail to comply with any provision of the Taxes Acts; and
> (b) that any such failure is likely to have led or to lead to serious prejudice to the proper assessment or collection of tax.][14]

[(7AB) A Commissioner who has given his consent under subsection (7) above shall neither take part in, nor be present at, any proceedings on, or related to, any appeal brought (*a*) in the case of a notice under subsection (1) above, by the person to whom the notice applies, or

(*b*) in the case of a notice under subsection (3) above, by the taxpayer concerned,

if the Commissioner has reason to believe that any of the required information is likely to be adduced in evidence in those proceedings.][15]

[(7AC) In subsection (7AB) above "required information" means any document or particulars which were the subject of the proposed notice with respect to which the Commissioner gave his consent.][15]

[(8) Subject to subsection (8A) below, a notice under subsection (3) above shall name the taxpayer with whose liability the inspector (or, where section 20B(3) below applies, the Board) is concerned.][12]

[(8A) If, on an application made by an inspector and authorised by order of the Board, a Special Commissioner gives his consent, the inspector may give such a notice as is mentioned in subsection (3) above but without naming the taxpayer to whom the notice relates; but such a consent shall not be given unless the Special Commissioner is satisfied—

(*a*) that the notice relates to a taxpayer whose identity is not known to the inspector or to a class of taxpayers whose individual identities are not so known;

(*b*) that there are reasonable grounds for believing that the taxpayer or any of the class of taxpayers to whom the notice relates may have failed or may fail to comply with any provision of the Taxes Acts;

(*c*) that any such failure is likely to have led or to lead to serious prejudice to the proper assessment or collection of tax; and

(*d*) that the information which is likely to be contained in the documents to which the notice relates is not readily available from another source.

(8B) A person to whom there is given a notice under subsection (8A) above may, by notice in writing given to the inspector within thirty days after the date of the notice under that subsection, object to that notice on the ground that it would be onerous for him to comply with it; and if the matter is not resolved by agreement, it shall be referred to the Special Commissioners, who may confirm, vary or cancel that notice.][4]

[(8C) In this section references to documents do not include—

(*a*) personal records (as defined in section 12 of the Police and Criminal Evidence Act 1984), or

(*b*) journalistic material (as defined in section 13 of that Act),

and references to particulars do not include particulars contained in such personal records or journalistic material.

(8D) Subject to subsection (8C) above, references in this section to documents and particulars are to those specified or described in the notice in question; and—

(*a*) the notice shall require documents to be delivered (or delivered or made available), or particulars to be furnished, within such time (which, except in the case of a notice under subsection (2) above, shall not be less than thirty days after the date of the notice) as may be specified in the notice; and

(*b*) the person to whom they are delivered, made available or furnished may take copies of them or of extracts from them.][13]

[(8E) An inspector who gives a notice under subsection (1) or (3) above shall also give to—

(*a*) the person to whom the notice applies (in the case of a notice under subsection (1) above), or

(*b*) the taxpayer concerned (in the case of a notice under subsection (3) above),

a written summary of his reasons for applying for consent to the giving of the notice.

(8F) Subsection (8E) above does not apply, in the case of a notice under subsection (3) above, if by virtue of section 20B(1B) a copy of that notice need not be given to the taxpayer.

(8G) Subsection (8E) above does not require the disclosure of any information—

(*a*) which would, or might, identify any person who has provided the inspector with any information which he took into account in deciding whether to apply for consent; or

(*b*) if the Commissioner giving the required consent has given a direction that that information is not to be subject to the obligation imposed by that subsection.

(8H) A General or Special Commissioner shall not give a direction under subsection (8G) above unless he is satisfied that the inspector has reasonable grounds for believing that disclosure of the information in question would prejudice the assessment or collection of tax.][15]

(9) To the extent specified in section 20B below, the above provisions are subject to the restrictions of that section.][1–2]

Commentary—*Simon's Direct Tax Service* **A3.151–154, 1633.**
Statement of Practice SP 5/90—The Revenue's interpretation of the scope of its powers under s 20, and the scope and limit of the exclusion of the three classes of documents by s 20B. It gives the same protection from disclosure to non-statutory audit papers as is given to statutory audit papers by s 20(3), (8A). It specifies the restrictions on the protection given to auditors' and tax advisers' communications relating to tax advice. It indicates the circumstances in which the Revenue will exercise its powers. It explains the scope of s 20BB.
Revenue & other press releases—Hansard 19–6–84 (Inspectors and taxpayers; transcript of meeting: the use of tape recorders by taxpayers to record meetings may be agreed provided the taxpayer provides a full transcript of the proceedings to the Revenue).

Hansard 5–11–92 (inspectors should not make tape recordings of interviews without taxpayer's knowledge or consent).
Revenue Internal Guidance—Enquiry Handbook EH 387 (powers under this section are not to be used in trivial or unsuitable cases, but equally, it is not necessary for the Revenue to demonstrate fraud or neglect; further s 20 notices are not linked to specific appeals or self–assessments, but can be issued regardless of whether or not there are open appeals).
EH 389 (interaction with s 19A).
Simon's Tax Cases—*Kempton v Special Comrs and IRC* [1992] STC 823; *R v Macdonald and IRC, ex p Hutchinson & Co Ltd* [1998] STC 680; *R v IRC, ex p Archon Shipping Corp* [1998] STC 1151; *Applicant v Inspector of Taxes* [1999] STC (SCD) 128.
s 20(1), *R v Macdonald and IRC, ex p Hutchinson & Co Ltd* [1998] STC 680; *R (on the application of Morgan Grenfell & Co Ltd) v Special Commissioner of Income Tax. CA* [2001] STC 497.
s 20(2), *R v IRC, ex p Taylor* [1990] STC 379.
s 20(3), *R v IRC, ex p T C Coombs & Co* [1991] STC 97; *R v O'Kane and Clarke, ex p Northern Bank Ltd* [1996] STC 1249; *R v IRC , ex p Mohammed* [1999] STC 129; *R v IRC, ex p Davis Frankel and Mead* [2000] STC 595; *R v IRC, ex p Banque Internationale à Luxembourg SA [2000] STC 708.*
s 20(3), (7) *R v IRC, ex p Lorimer* [2000] STC 751.
s 20(4), *Monarch Assurance Co Ltd v Special Comrs and IRC* [1986] STC 311; *R v IRC, ex p T C Coombs & Co* [1991] STC 97
s 20(7), *R v IRC, ex p T C Coombs & Co* [1991] STC 97; *R (on the application of Morgan Grenfell & Co Ltd) v Special Commissioner of Income Tax* [2000] STC 965.
s 20(7)(b), *R v IRC , ex p Mohammed* [1999] STC 129.
s 20(8A), *R v IRC, ex p Ulster Bank Ltd* [1997] STC 832; *R v Special Commissioner of Income Tax ex p IRC and R v IRC, ex p Ulster Bank Ltd* [2000] STC 537.
s 20(8D), *R v IRC, ex p Ulster Bank Ltd* [1997] STC 832; *R v Macdonald and IRC, ex p Hutchinson & Co Ltd* [1998] STC 680.
s 20(8E), (8G), *R v Macdonald and IRC, ex p Hutchinson & Co Ltd* [1998] STC 680.
s 20(8E)(b), (8G)(a), *R v IRC, ex p Continental Shipping Ltd SA and Atsiganos SA* [1996] STC 813.
Definitions—''The Board'', s 118(1);''document'', s 20D(3);''inspector'', s 118(1);''return'', s 118(1);''the Taxes Acts'', s 118(1).
Cross references—See TMA 1970 s 20B (restrictions on powers under this section).
TMA 1970 s 20BB (offence of falsifying etc documents required to be delivered by a notice under this section).
TMA 1970 s 20D (interpretation).
FA 1988 s 127(2)–(4), (6) (production of computer records etc).
FA 1990 s 125(1), (2)(a) (information for tax authorities in other Member States).
Tax Credits Act 1999 s 8 (this section applies to an employer's compliance with regulations made under Tax Credits Act 1999 s 6, concerning the employer's payment of the working families' tax credit and disabled person's tax credit, as it applies to a person's tax liability or its amount).
FA 2000 s 146(3), (4) (application of sub-ss (1)–(8), (8C)–(9) in relation to provisions on internation exchange of information).
Education (Student Loans) (Repayment) Regulations, SI 2000/944 reg 44 (application of this section in connection with the repayment of student loans).
Amendments—[1-2] This section and ss 20A to 20D, *post*, substituted for s 20 by FA 1976 Sch 6.
[3] Words in sub-s (7) substituted by FA 1988 s 126(2), (6) with respect to notices given after 29 July 1988.
[4] Sub-ss (8A), (8B) inserted by FA 1988 s 126(3), (6) with respect to notices given after 29 July 1988.
[5] Words in sub-s (1) substituted by FA 1989 s 142 with respect to notices given after 26 July 1989.
[6] Words in sub-s (2) substituted by FA 1989 s 142 with respect to notices given after 26 July 1989.
[7] Words in sub-s (3) substituted by FA 1989 s 142 with respect to notices given after 26 July 1989.
[8] Words in sub-s (3) added by FA 1989 s 142 with respect to notices given after 26 July 1989.
[9] Sub-ss (4), (5) repealed by FA 1989 s 142 and Sch 17 Pt VIII with respect to notices given after 26 July 1989.
[10] Words in sub-s (6) substituted by FA 1989 s 142.
[11] Words in sub-s (6) repealed by FA 1989 s 142 and Sch 17 Pt VIII with respect to notices given after 26 July 1989.
[12] Sub-s (8) substituted by FA 1989 s 142 and Sch 17 Pt VIII with respect to notices given after 26 July 1989.
[13] Sub-ss (8C), (8D) inserted by FA 1989 s 142 and Sch 17 Pt VIII with respect to notices given after 26 July 1989.
[14] Sub-s (7A) inserted by FA 1990 s 93 and applies to notices given after 25 July 1990.
[15] Sub-ss (7AB), (7AC), (8E)–(8H) inserted by FA 1994 s 255.

[20A Power to call for papers of tax accountant

(1) Where after the passing of the Finance Act 1976 a person—

    (*a*) is convicted of an offence in relation to tax (whenever committed) by or before any court in the United Kingdom; or

    (*b*) has [a penalty imposed on][3] him (whether before or after the passing of that Act) under section 99 of this Act,

and he has stood in relation to others as a tax accountant, an inspector authorised by the Board for the purpose of this section may by notice in writing require the person to deliver to him such documents as are in his possession or power and as (in the inspector's reasonable opinion) contain information relevant to any tax liability to which any client of his is or has been, or may be or have been, subject, or to the amount of any such liability.

[(1A) The reference to documents in subsection (1) above does not include—

    (*a*) personal records (as defined in section 12 of the Police and Criminal Evidence Act 1984), or

    (*b*) journalistic material (as defined in section 13 of that Act).][2]

[(1B) Subject to subsection (1A) above, the reference to documents in subsection (1) above is to those specified or described in the notice in question; and—

    (*a*) the notice shall require documents to be delivered within such time (which shall not be less than thirty days after the date of the notice) as may be specified in the notice; and

    (*b*) the inspector may take copies of them or of extracts from them.][2]

(2) Subsection (1) above does not have effect in relation to a person convicted or penalised as there mentioned for so long as an appeal is pending against the conviction or [penalty][3]; and—

    (*a*) for this purpose an appeal is to be treated as pending (where one is competent but has not been brought) until the expiration of the time for bringing it or, in the case of a conviction in Scotland, until the expiration of 28 days from the date of conviction; and

    (*b*) references here to appeal include further appeal but, in relation to the [imposition][3] of a penalty, do not include appeal against the amount of the penalty.

(3) A notice is not to be given to any person under this section unless with the consent of the appropriate judicial authority; and that authority is to give his consent only on being satisfied that in all the circumstances the inspector is justified in so proceeding.

(4) The power to give a notice under this section, by reference to a person's conviction or the [imposition on][3] him of a penalty, ceases at the expiration of the period of 12 months beginning with the date on which it was first exercisable in his case by virtue of that conviction or [penalty][3].

(5) To the extent specified in section 20B below, the above provisions are subject to the restrictions of that section.][1]

Commentary—*Simon's Direct Tax Service* A3.156.
Statement of Practice SP 5/90—The Revenue's interpretation of the scope of its powers under s 20, and the scope and limit of the exclusion of the three classes of documents by s 20B. It gives the same protection from disclosure to non-statutory audit papers as is given to statutory audit papers by s 20(3), (8A). It specifies the restrictions on the protection given to auditors' and tax advisers' communications relating to tax advice. It indicates the circumstances in which the Revenue will exercise its powers. It explains the scope of s 20BB.
Revenue & other press releases—ICAEW TR781 23–2–90 (guidance on ownership of books and records).
Note—FA 1976 was passed on 29 July 1976.
Definitions—''The Board'', s 118(1);''document'', s 20D(3);''inspector'', s 118(1);''tax'', s 118(1).
Cross references—See TMA 1970 s 20B (restrictions on powers under this section).
TMA 1970 s 20BB (offence of falsifying etc documents required to be delivered by a notice under this section).
TMA 1970 s 20D (interpretation).
FA 1988 s 127(2)–(4), (6) (production of computer records etc).
Amendments—[1] This section, s 20, *ante*, and ss 20B to 20D, *post*, substituted for s 20 by FA 1976 Sch 6.
[2] Sub-ss (1A), (1B) substituted for the last sentence of sub-s (1) by FA 1989 s 143 with respect to notices given after 26 July 1989.
[3] Words in sub-ss (1), (2), (4) substituted by FA 1989 s 168(1), (2).

[20B Restrictions on powers under ss 20 and 20A

(1) Before a notice is given to a person by an inspector under [section 20(1), (3) or (8A)][2], or under section 20A, the person must have been given a reasonable opportunity to deliver (or, in the case of section 20(3), to deliver or make available) the documents in question[, or to furnish the particulars in question][5]; and the inspector must not apply for consent under [section 20(7) or (8A)][3] or, as the case may be, section 20A(3), until the person has been given that opportunity.

[(1A) Subject to subsection (1B) below, where a notice is given to any person under section 20(3) the inspector shall give a copy of the notice to the taxpayer to whom it relates.][6]

[(1B) If, on an application by the inspector, a General or Special Commissioner so directs, a copy of a notice under section 20(3) need not be given to the taxpayer to whom it relates; but such a direction shall not be given unless the Commissioner is satisfied that the inspector has reasonable grounds for suspecting the taxpayer of fraud.][6]

(2) A notice under section 20(1) does not oblige a person to deliver documents [or furnish particulars][5] relating to the conduct of any pending appeal by him; a notice under section 20(3) [or (8A)][4] does not oblige a person to deliver or make available documents relating to the conduct of a pending appeal by the taxpayer; and a notice under section 20A does not oblige a person to deliver documents relating to the conduct of a pending appeal by the client.

''Appeal'' means appeal relating to tax.

(3) An inspector cannot under section 20(1) or (3) or under section 20A(1), give notice to a barrister, advocate or solicitor, but the notice must in any such case be given (if at all) by the Board; and accordingly in relation to a barrister, advocate or solicitor for references in section 20(3) and (4) and section 20A to the inspector there are substituted references to the Board.

(4) To comply with a notice under section 20(1) or section 20A(1), and as an alternative to delivering documents to comply with a notice under section 20(3) [or (8A)][4], copies of documents may be delivered instead of the originals; but—

(*a*) the copies must be photographic or otherwise by way of facsimile; and
(*b*) if so required by the inspector (or, as the case may be, the Board) in the case of any documents specified in the requirement, the original must be made available for inspection by a named officer of the Board (failure to comply with this requirement counting as failure to comply with the notice).

(5) A notice under section 20(3), [does not oblige a person][7] to deliver or make available any document the whole of which originates more than 6 years before the date of the notice.

(6) But subsection (5) does not apply where the notice is so expressed as to exclude the restrictions of that subsection; and it can only be so expressed where—

(*a*) the notice being given by an inspector with consent under section 20(7), the Commissioner giving consent has also given approval to the exclusion;
(*b*) the notice being given by the Board, they have applied to a General or Special Commissioner for, and obtained, that approval.

For this purpose the Commissioner gives approval only if satisfied, on the inspector's or the Board's application, that there is reasonable ground for believing that tax has, or may have been, lost to the Crown owing to the fraud of the taxpayer.

(7) A notice under section 20(3) in relation to a taxpayer who has died cannot be given ...[8] if more than 6 years have elapsed since the death.

(8) A notice under section 20(3) [or (8A)][4] or section 20A(1) does not oblige a barrister, advocate or a solicitor to deliver or make available, without his client's consent, any document with respect to which a claim to professional privilege could be maintained.

[(9) Subject to subsections (11) and (12) below, a notice under section 20(3) or (8A)—

   (*a*) does not oblige a person who has been appointed as an auditor for the purposes of any enactment to deliver or make available documents which are his property and were created by him or on his behalf for or in connection with the performance of his functions under that enactment, and

   (*b*) does not oblige a tax adviser to deliver or make available documents which are his property and consist of relevant communications.][9]

[(10) In subsection (9) above "relevant communications" means communications between the tax adviser and—

   (*a*) a person in relation to whose tax affairs he has been appointed, or
   (*b*) any other tax adviser of such a person,

the purpose of which is the giving or obtaining of advice about any of those tax affairs; and in subsection (9) above and this subsection "tax adviser" means a person appointed to give advice about the tax affairs of another person (whether appointed directly by that other person or by another tax adviser of his).][9]

[(11) Subject to subsection (13) below, subsection (9) above shall not have effect in relation to any document which contains information explaining any information, return, accounts or other document which the person to whom the notice is given has, as tax accountant, assisted any client of his in preparing for, or delivering to, the inspector or the Board.][9]

[(12) Subject to subsection (13) below, in the case of a notice under section 20(8A) subsection (9) above shall not have effect in relation to any document which contains information giving the identity or address of any taxpayer to whom the notice relates or of any person who has acted on behalf of any such person.][9]

[(13) Subsection (9) above is not disapplied by subsection (11) or (12) above in the case of any document if—

   (*a*) the information within subsection (11) or (12) is contained in some other document, and
   (*b*) either—

      (i) that other document, or a copy of it, has been delivered to the inspector or the Board, or
      (ii) that other document has been inspected by an officer of the Board.][9]

[(14) Where subsection (9) above is disapplied by subsection (11) or (12) above in the case of a document, the person to whom the notice is given either shall deliver the document to the inspector or make it available for inspection by an officer of the Board or shall—

   (*a*) deliver to the inspector (or, where subsection (3) above applies, the Board) a copy (which is photographic or otherwise by way of facsimile) of any parts of the document which contain the information within subsection (11) or (12), and

   (*b*) if so required by the inspector (or, as the case may be, the Board), make available for inspection by a named officer of the Board such parts of the document as contain that information;

and failure to comply with any requirement under paragraph (*b*) above shall constitute a failure to comply with the notice.][9][1]

Commentary—*Simon's Direct Tax Service* A3.151–153, 1680.
Statement of Practice SP 5/90—The Revenue's interpretation of the scope of its powers under s 20, and the scope and limit of the exclusion of the three classes of documents by s 20B. It gives the same protection from disclosure to non-statutory audit papers as is given to statutory audit papers by s 20(3), (8A). It specifies the restrictions on the protection given to auditors' and tax advisers' communications relating to tax advice. It indicates the circumstances in which the Revenue will exercise its powers. It explains the scope of s 20BB.
Simon's Tax Cases—*R v IRC, ex p Archon Shipping Corp* [1998] STC 1151.
s 20B(2), *R v IRC, ex p Banque Internationale à Luxembourg SA* [2000] STC 708
s 20B(3), *R v IRC, ex p Davis Frankel and Mead* [2000] STC 595.
s 20B(8), *R v IRC, ex p Goldberg* [1988] STC 524.
Definitions—"The Board", s 118(1); "document", s 20D(3); "General Commissioners", s 2; "inspector", s 118(1); "return", s 118(1); "Special Commissioners", s 4; "tax", s 118(1).
Cross references—See TMA 1970 s 20(9) (provisions of s 20 subject to restrictions of this section).
TMA 1970 s 20BB (offence of falsifying etc documents required to be delivered in accordance with sub-s (1) above).
TMA 1970 s 20D (interpretation).
FA 1990 s 125(1), (2)(*b*) (information for tax authorities in other Member States).
Tax Credits Act 1999 s 8 (this section, so far as it relates to TMA 1970 s 20, applies to an employer's compliance with regulations made under Tax Credits Act 1999 s 6, concerning the employer's payment of the working families' tax credit and disabled person's tax credit, as it applies to a person's tax liability or its amount).
Education (Student Loans) (Repayment) Regulations, SI 2000/944 reg 44 (application of this section in connection with the repayment of student loans).
Amendments—[1] This section, ss 20 and 20A, *ante*, and s 20C and 20D, *post*, substituted for s 20 by FA 1976 Sch 6.
[2] Words in sub-s (1) substituted by FA 1988 s 126(4), (6) with respect to notices given after 29 July 1988.
[3] Words in sub-s (1) substituted by FA 1988 s 126(4), (6) with respect to notices given after 29 July 1988.
[4] Words in sub-ss (2), (4), (8) inserted by FA 1988 s 126(4), (6) with respect to notices given after 29 July 1988.
[5] Words in sub-ss (1), (2) inserted by FA 1989 s 144 with respect to notices given after 26 July 1989.
[6] Sub-ss (1A), (1B) inserted by FA 1989 s 144 with respect to notices given after 26 July 1989.

[7] Words in sub-s (5) substituted by FA 1989 s 144 with respect to notices given after 26 July 1989.
[8] Words in sub-s (7) repealed by FA 1989 s 144 and Sch 17 Pt VIII with respect to notices given after 26 July 1989.
[9] Sub-ss (9)–(14) substituted for sub-s (9) by FA 1989 s 144 and Sch 17 Pt VIII with respect to notices given after 26 July 1989.

[20BA Orders for the delivery of documents

(1) The appropriate judicial authority may make an order under this section if satisfied on information on oath given by an authorised officer of the Board—

(*a*) that there is reasonable ground for suspecting that an offence involving serious fraud in connection with, or in relation to, tax is being, has been or is about to be committed, and

(*b*) that documents which may be required as evidence for the purposes of any proceedings in respect of such an offence are or may be in the power or possession of any person.

(2) An order under this section is an order requiring the person who appears to the authority to have in his possession or power the documents specified or described in the order to deliver them to an officer of the Board within—

(*a*) ten working days after the day on which notice of the order is served on him, or

(*b*) such shorter or longer period as may be specified in the order.

For this purpose a "working day" means any day other than a Saturday, Sunday or public holiday.

(3) Where in Scotland the information mentioned in subsection (1) above relates to persons residing or having places of business at addresses situated in different sheriffdoms—

(*a*) an application for an order may be made to the sheriff for the sheriffdom in which any of the addresses is situated, and

(*b*) where the sheriff makes an order in respect of a person residing or having a place of business in his own sheriffdom, he may also make orders in respect of all or any of the other persons to whom the information relates (whether or not they have an address within the sheriffdom).

(4) Schedule 1AA to this Act contains provisions supplementing this section.][1]

Cross references—See The Orders for the Delivery of Documents (Procedure) Regulations, SI 2000/2875 (procedural requirements in relation to orders specified within this section).
Criminal Justice and Police Act 2001 s 59(7) (application to appropriate judicial authority).
Amendments—[1] This section inserted by FA 2000 s 149(1) with effect from 28 July 2000.

[20BB Falsification etc of documents

(1) Subject to subsections (2) to (4) below, a person shall be guilty of an offence if he intentionally falsifies, conceals, destroys or otherwise disposes of, or causes or permits the falsification, concealment, destruction or disposal of, a document which—

(*a*) he has been required by a notice under section 20 or 20A above [or an order under section 20BA above][2], or

(*b*) he has been given an opportunity in accordance with section 20B(1) above,

to deliver, or to deliver or make available for inspection.

(2) A person does not commit an offence under subsection (1) above if he acts—

(*a*) with the written permission of a General or Special Commissioner, the inspector or an officer of the Board,

(*b*) after the document has been delivered or, in a case within section 20(3) or (8A) above, inspected, or

(*c*) after a copy has been delivered in accordance with section 20B(4) or (14) above and the original has been inspected.

(3) A person does not commit an offence under subsection (1)(*a*) above if he acts after the end of the period of two years beginning with the date on which the notice is given [or the order is made][2], unless before the end of that period the inspector or an officer of the Board has notified the person in writing that the notice [or order][2] has not been complied with to his satisfaction.

(4) A person does not commit an offence under subsection (1)(*b*) above if he acts—

(*a*) after the end of the period of six months beginning with the date on which an opportunity to deliver the document was given, or

(*b*) after an application for consent to a notice being given in relation to the document has been refused.

(5) A person guilty of an offence under subsection (1) above shall be liable—

(*a*) on summary conviction, to a fine not exceeding the statutory maximum;

(*b*) on conviction on indictment, to imprisonment for a term not exceeding two years or to a fine or to both.][1]

Commentary—*Simon's Direct Tax Service* A3.155.
Statement of Practice SP 5/90—This Statement sets out the Revenue's interpretation of the scope of its powers under s 20. It sets out the scope and limit of the exclusion of the three classes of documents by s 20B. It gives the same protection from disclosure to non-statutory audit papers as is given to statutory audit papers by s 20(3), (8A). It specifies the restrictions on the protection given to auditors' and tax advisers' communications relating to tax advice. It indicates the circumstances in which the Revenue will exercise its powers. It explains the scope of s 20BB.
Definitions—"The Board", s 118(1); "document", s 20D(3); "General Commissioners", s 2; "inspector", s 118(1); "Special Commissioners", s 4.
Cross references—See TMA 1970 s 20D (interpretation).

Education (Student Loans) (Repayment) Regulations, SI 2000/944 reg 44 (application of this section in connection with the repayment of student loans).

Amendments—[1] This section inserted by FA 1989 s 145 and applies to any falsification, concealment, destruction or disposal of a document occurring after 26 July 1989.
[2] Words in sub-ss (1), (3) inserted by FA 2000 s 149(3) with effect from 28 July 2000.

[20C Entry with warrant to obtain documents

(1) If the appropriate judicial authority is satisfied on information on oath given by an officer of the Board that—

(*a*) there is reasonable ground for suspecting that an offence involving [serious fraud][2] in connection with, or in relation to, tax [is being, has been or is about to be][3] committed and that evidence of it is to be found on premises specified in the information; and

(*b*) in applying under this section, the officer acts with the approval of the Board given in relation to the particular case,

the authority may issue a warrant in writing authorising an officer of the Board to enter the premises, if necessary by force, at any time within 14 days from the time of issue of the warrant, and search them.

[(1AA) The Board shall not approve an application for a warrant under this section unless they have reasonable grounds for believing that use of the procedure under section 20BA above and Schedule 1AA to this Act (order for production of documents) might seriously prejudice the investigation.][6]

[(1A) Without prejudice to the generality of the concept of serious fraud—

(*a*) any offence which involves fraud is for the purposes of this section an offence involving serious fraud if its commission had led, or is intended or likely to lead, either to substantial financial gain to any person or to serious prejudice to the proper assessment or collection of tax; and

(*b*) an offence which, if considered alone, would not be regarded as involving serious fraud may nevertheless be so regarded if there is reasonable ground for suspecting that it forms part of a course of conduct which is, or but for its detection would be, likely to result in serious prejudice to the proper assessment or collection of tax.][4]

[(1B) The powers conferred by a warrant under this section shall not be exercisable—

(*a*) by more than such number of officers of the Board as may be specified in the warrant;

(*b*) outside such times of day as may be so specified;

(*c*) if the warrant so provides, otherwise than in the presence of a constable in uniform.][4]

(2) Section 4A of the Inland Revenue Regulation Act 1890 (Board's functions to be exercisable by an officer acting under their authority) does not apply to the giving of Board approval under this section.

[(3) An officer who enters the premises under the authority of a warrant under this section may—

(*a*) take with him such other persons as appear to him to be necessary;

(*b*) seize and remove any things whatsoever found there which he has reasonable cause to believe may be required as evidence for the purposes of proceedings in respect of such an offence as is mentioned in subsection (1) above; and

(*c*) search or cause to be searched any person found on the premises whom he has reasonable cause to believe to be in possession of any such things;

but no person shall be searched except by a person of the same sex.][5]

[(3A) In the case of any information contained in a computer which is information that—

(*a*) an officer who enters the premises as mentioned in subsection (3) above has reasonable cause to believe may be required as evidence for the purposes mentioned in paragraph (*b*) of that subsection, and

(*b*) is accessible from the premises,

the power of seizure under that subsection includes a power to require the information to be produced in a form in which it can be taken away and in which it is visible and legible.][6]

[(4) Nothing in subsection (3) above authorises the seizure and removal of items subject to legal privilege.

(4A) In subsection (4) "items subject to legal privilege" means—

(*a*) communications between a professional legal adviser and his client or any person representing his client made in connection with the giving of legal advice to the client;

(*b*) communications between a professional legal adviser and his client or any person representing his client or between such an adviser or his client or any such representative and any other person made in connection with or in contemplation of legal proceedings and for the purposes of such proceedings; and

(*c*) items enclosed with or referred to in such communications and made—

    (i) in connection with the giving of legal advice; or

    (ii) in connection with or in contemplation of legal proceedings and for the purposes of such proceedings,

when they are in the possession of a person who is entitled to possession of them.

(4B) Items held with the intention of furthering a criminal purpose are not subject to legal privilege.][6]

[(5) An officer of the Board seeking to exercise the powers conferred by a warrant under this section or, if there is more than one such officer, that one of them who is in charge of the search—

(*a*) if the occupier of the premises concerned is present at the time the search is to begin, shall supply a copy of the warrant endorsed with his name to the occupier;

(*b*) if at that time the occupier is not present but a person who appears to the officer to be in charge of the premises is present, shall supply such a copy to that person; and

(*c*) if neither paragraph (*a*) nor paragraph (*b*) above applies, shall leave such a copy in a prominent place on the premises.][5]

[(6) Where entry to premises has been made with a warrant under this section, and the officer making the entry has seized any things under the authority of the warrant, he shall endorse on or attach to the warrant a list of the things seized.][5]

[(7) Subsections (10) to (12) of section 16 of the Police and Criminal Evidence Act 1984 (return, retention and inspection of warrants) apply to a warrant under this section (together with any list endorsed on or attached to it under subsection (6) above) as they apply to a warrant issued to a constable under any enactment.][5]

[(8) Subsection (7) above extends to England and Wales only.][5][1]

[(9) Where in Scotland the information mentioned in subsection (1) above relates to premises situated in different sheriffdoms—

(*a*) petitions for the issue of warrants in respect of all the premises to which the information relates may be made to the sheriff for a sheriffdom in which any of the premises is situated, and

(*b*) where the sheriff issues a warrant in respect of premises situated in his own sheriffdom, he shall also have jurisdiction to issue warrants in respect of all or any of the other premises to which the information relates.

This does not affect any power or jurisdiction of a sheriff to issue a warrant in respect of an offence committed within his own sheriffdom.][6]

Commentary—*Simon's Direct Tax Service* **A3.157.**
Simon's Tax Cases—s 20C(1), *R v Hunt* [1994] STC 819; *R v IRC, ex p Tamosius & Partners (a firm)* [1999] STC 1077.
s 20C(1), (3), *IRC v Rossminster Ltd* [1980] STC 42
s 20C(3), (4), *R v IRC, ex p Tamosius & Partners (a firm)* [1999] STC 1077.
Definitions—"The Board", s 118(1);"document", s 20D(3);"tax", s 118(1).
Cross references—See TMA 1970 s 20CC (Board's obligation to provide list of documents to be removed by virtue of this section).
TMA 1970 s 20D (interpretation).
Criminal Justice and Police Act 2001 s 50, Sch 1 Pt I (s 50 of that Act which provides additional powers of seizure from premises applies to the power of seizure conferred under the section above).
Criminal Justice and Police Act 2001 s 63 (powers to obtain hard copies of information stored in electronic form conferred by s 62(1)(*c*) of that Act include power under sub-s (3A) above).
Criminal Justice and Police Act 2001 s 65 (in relation to property seized in exercise of the power of seizure conferred by the section above, references to an item subject to legal privilege in Part 2 of that Act are construed in accordance with sub-s (4A) above).
Amendments—[1] This section, ss 20, 20A and 20B, *ante*, and s 20D, *post*, substituted by FA 1976 Sch 6.
[2] Words in sub-s (1)(*a*) substituted by FA 1989 s 146 with respect to warrants issued after 26 July 1989.
[3] Words in sub-s (1)(*a*) substituted by FA 1989 s 146 with respect to warrants issued after 26 July 1989.
[4] Sub-ss (1A), (1B) inserted by FA 1989 s 146 with respect to warrants issued after 26 July 1989.
[5] Sub-ss (3)–(8) substituted by for sub-ss (3)–(5) by FA 1989 s 146 with respect to warrants issued after 26 July 1989.
[6] Sub-ss (1AA), (3A), (9) inserted, and sub-ss (4), (4A), (4B) substituted for original sub-s (4), by FA 2000 s 150 with effect from 28 July 2000.
Prospective amendment—Amendments to be made to sub-s (3A) by Criminal Justice and Police Act 2001 ss 70, 138, Sch 2 Pt 2 para 13 with effect from such day as the Secretary of State may by order made by statutory instrument appoint.

[20CC Procedure where documents etc are removed

(1) An officer of the Board who removes anything in the exercise of the power conferred by section 20C above shall, if so requested by a person showing himself—

(*a*) to be the occupier of premises from which it was removed, or

(*b*) to have had custody or control of it immediately before the removal,

provide that person with a record of what he removed.

(2) The officer of the Board shall provide the record within a reasonable time from the making of the request for it.

(3) Where anything which has been removed by an officer of the Board as mentioned in subsection (1) above is of such a nature that a photograph or copy of it would be sufficient—

(*a*) for use as evidence at a trial for an offence, or

(*b*) for forensic examination or for investigation in connection with an offence,

it shall not be retained longer than is necessary to establish that fact and to obtain the photograph or copy.

(4) Subject to subsection (8) below, if a request for permission to be granted access to anything which—

(*a*) has been removed by an officer of the Board, and

(*b*) is retained by the Board for the purpose of investigating an offence, is made to the officer in overall charge of the investigation by a person who had custody or control of the thing immediately before it was so removed or by someone acting on behalf of any such person, the officer shall allow the person who made the request access to it under the supervision of an officer of the Board.

(5) Subject to subsection (8) below, if a request for a photograph or copy of any such thing is made to the officer in overall charge of the investigation by a person who had custody or control of the thing immediately before it was so removed, or by someone acting on behalf of any such person, the officer shall—

(a) allow the person who made the request access to it under the supervision of an officer of the Board for the purpose of photographing it or copying it, or

(b) photograph or copy it, or cause it to be photographed or copied.

(6) Where anything is photographed or copied under subsection (5)(b) above the photograph or copy shall be supplied to the person who made the request.

(7) The photograph or copy shall be supplied within a reasonable time from the making of the request.

(8) There is no duty under this section to grant access to, or to supply a photograph or copy of, anything if the officer in overall charge of the investigation for the purposes of which it was removed has reasonable grounds for believing that to do so would prejudice—

(a) that investigation;

(b) the investigation of an offence other than the offence for the purposes of the investigation of which the thing was removed; or

(c) any criminal proceedings which may be brought as a result of—

(i) the investigation of which he is in charge, or

(ii) any such investigation as is mentioned in paragraph (b) above.

(9) Any reference in this section to the officer in overall charge of the investigation is a reference to the person whose name and address are endorsed on the warrant concerned as being the officer so in charge.]¹

Commentary—*Simon's Direct Tax Service* A3.158.
Definitions—"The Board", s 118(1); "document", s 20D(3).
Cross references—See TMA 1970 s 20D (interpretation).
Criminal Justice and Police Act 2001 s 57 (retention of seized items).
Amendments—¹ This section inserted by FA 1989 s 147 with respect to warrants issued after 26 July 1989.

[20D Interpretation of ss 20 to [20CC]

(1) For the purposes of sections 20A[, 20BA]⁴ and 20C above, "the appropriate judicial authority" is—

(a) in England and Wales, a Circuit judge;

(b) in Scotland, a sheriff; and

(c) in Northern Ireland, a county court judge.

(2) For the purposes of sections 20 and 20A, a person stands in relation to another as tax accountant at any time when he assists the other in the preparation [or delivery of any information, return, accounts or other document which he knows will be, or is or are likely to be, used]² for any purpose of tax; and his clients are all those to whom he stands or has stood in that relationship.

[(3) Without prejudice to section 127 of the Finance Act 1988, in sections 20 to 20CC above "document" means, subject to sections 20(8C) and 20A(1A), anything in which information of any description is recorded.]³]¹

Commentary—*Simon's Direct Tax Service* A3.156, 157.
Definition—"return", s 118(1).
Amendments—¹ This section and ss 20 to 20C, *ante*, substituted for s 20 by FA 1976 Sch 6.
² Words in sub-s (2) substituted by FA 1989 s 148(2).
³ Sub-s (3) substituted by the Civil Evidence Act 1995 Sch 1 para 6 with effect from a day to be appointed. Sub-s (3) former wording as follows (as substituted by FA 1989 s 148(3), (4)): "(3) Without prejudice to section 127 of the Finance Act 1988 in sections 20 to 20CC above "document" has, subject to sections 20(8C) and 20A(1A), the same meaning as it has—

(a) in relation to England and Wales, in Part I of the Civil Evidence Act 1968

(b) in relation to Scotland, in Part III of the Law Reform (Miscellaneous Provisions) (Scotland) Act 1968 and

(c) in relation to Northern Ireland, in Part I of the Civil Evidence Act (Northern Ireland) 1971.".

⁴ Word in sub-s (1) inserted by FA 2000 s 149(4) with effect from 28 July 2000.

21 Stock jobbers' transactions

[(1) The Board may exercise the powers conferred by this section as respects, and in connection with, any business consisting in or involving dealings in securities; and for the purposes of this section it shall be immaterial whether those dealings are or, as the case may be, were—

(a) on behalf of persons other than the person carrying on the business;

(b) by that person on his own behalf; or

(c) a mixture of the two.]²

(2) With a view to obtaining information about [securities transactions]² in the course of a business within subsection (1) above, the Board may serve on the [person]² ...¹ by whom the business is or

has been carried on a notice requiring him to make available within a time specified in the notice, for inspection by an inspector or other officer of the Board, all such books, accounts and other documents in his possession or power as may be specified or described in the notice, being books, accounts or other documents which in the opinion of the Board contain or may contain information directly or indirectly relating to any such transactions.

(3) The Board may serve on any broker a notice requiring him to make available within a time specified in the notice, for inspection by an inspector or other officer of the Board, all such books, accounts or other documents in his possession or power as may be specified or described in the notice, being books, accounts or other documents which in the opinion of the Board contain or may contain information relating directly or indirectly to [securities transactions in the course of any business of a person other than the broker which is]² a business within subsection (1) above.

[(4) Where a person (''the recipient'') who is not a broker has directly or indirectly received from another person any payment which—

    (*a*) is made by that other person in the course of a business within subsection (1) above, and
    (*b*) is a payment treated by that other person as made in respect of interest on securities,

the Board may by notice in writing require the recipient to state, within a time specified in the notice, whether the amount received is in whole or in part received on behalf of, or for payment on to, a third person and (if it is) to furnish the name and address of that third person.

(4A) Where a person ('the payer') has directly or indirectly paid to another person any sum which—

    (*a*) constitutes a receipt by that other person in the course of a business within subsection (1) above, and
    (*b*) is a receipt treated by that other person as accruing in respect of interest on securities,

the Board may by notice in writing require the payer to state, within a time specified in the notice, whether the amount paid is in whole or in part received from, or paid on account of, a third person and (if it is) to furnish the name and address of that third person.]²

(5) If, for the purpose of obtaining (from any persons [at all]²) information directly or indirectly relating to any [securities transactions]² in the course of a business within subsection (1) above, any person in whose name any securities are registered is so required by notice in writing by the Board, he shall state whether or not he is the beneficial owner of those securities, and, if not the beneficial owner of those securities or any of them, shall furnish the name and address of the person or persons on whose behalf the securities are registered in his name.

[(5A) Where it appears to the Board that a person may have incurred a liability to pay or account for tax under Schedule 23A to the principal Act (manufactured payments), the Board may by notice served on that person require him, within such period (not being less than 28 days) as may be specified in the notice, to provide the Board with information which—

    (*a*) is available to that person; and
    (*b*) is or may be relevant to whether that person has incurred such a liability, or to the extent of such a liability.]²

(6) The Board may not exercise their powers under the preceding provisions of this section for the purpose of obtaining information relating to transactions in any year of assessment ending more than six years before the service of the notice.

[(7) In this section—

    ''broker'' means any person who is a member of a recognised investment exchange, within the meaning [given by section 285(1)(*a*) of the Financial Services and Markets Act 2000]³;
    ''interest'' includes dividends;
    ''securities'' includes shares and stock; and
    ''securities transaction'' means—

        (*a*) any transaction in securities;
        (*b*) any transaction under which a payment which is representative of any interest on a security has been, is to be or may be made; or
        (*c*) the making or receipt of such a payment.]²

Commentary—*Simon's Direct Tax Service* A3.126.
Revenue & other press releases—Code of Practice 5 (inspection of financial intermediaries' records).
Definition—''The Board'', s 832(1).
Cross references—See FA 1986 Sch 18 para 7(4), (5) (Board's powers to extend the scope of the definitions of ''broker'' and ''market maker'' in sub-s (7) with effect from an appointed day)—repealed by FA 1997 s 75, Sch 10 paras 15, 16(1), (3).
FA 1986 Sch 18 para 9(1)(*b*), (*c*), (3) (Board's powers to amend this section with effect from an appointed day)—repealed by FA 1997 s 76, Sch 10 paras 15, 16(1), (3).
Amendments—¹ Words in sub-s (2) repealed by FA 1973 Sch 21 para 5(*a*), and Sch 22 Pt IV.
² Sub-ss (1), (4), (4A), (7) and words in sub-s (2), (3), (5) substituted and sub-s (5A) inserted by FA 1997 s 76, Sch 10 paras 14(1)–(3), (5)–(9) 16(2), (3) for the purpose of conferring powers for obtaining information about (*a*) transactions entered into on or after 1 July 1997 (by virtue of the Finance Act 1997, Schedule 10, (Appointed Day) Order, SI 1997/991); and (*b*) payments made on or after 1 July 1997 (whether under such transactions or under transactions entered into before 1 July 1997), subject to the provision that nothing in FA 1997 Sch 10 Pt II shall affect the exercise, at any time on or after 1 July 1997, of the powers conferred apart from FA 1997 Sch 10 by TMA 1970 s 21, or by any regulations modifying that section, or TA 1988 s 737(8), for obtaining information about transactions entered into, or payments made, before that day.
³ Words in sub-s (7) substituted by the Financial Services and Markets Act 2000 (Consequential Amendments) (Taxes) Order, SI 2001/3629 art 3 with effect from 1 December 2001, immediately after the coming into force of the Financial Services and Markets Act 2000 ss 411, 432(1), Sch 20.

"Surtax"

22 Additional particulars for "surtax"

The Board may, ...[1], by notice in writing require any individual to furnish to them within such time as they may prescribe, not being less than twenty-eight days, such particulars as to the several sources of his income and the amount arising from each source, and as to the nature and the amount of any deductions claimed to be allowed therefrom, as they consider necessary.

Amendments—[1] Words repealed by FA 1971 ss 37, 38(1), Sch 6 paras 81, 83 and Sch 14 Pt II, with effect from the year 1973–74.

23 Power to obtain copies of registers of securities

(1) The Board may cause to be served upon any body corporate a notice requiring them to deliver to the Board within a specified time, being not less than twenty-one days, a copy, certified by a duly authorised officer of such body, of the whole of, or any specified class of entries in, any register containing the names of the holders of any securities issued by them.

(2) On delivery of the copy in accordance with the notice payment shall be made therefor at the rate of [25p][1] in respect of each one hundred entries.

(3) In this section, "security" includes shares, stock, debentures and debenture stock, and "entry" means, in relation to any register, so much thereof as relates to the securities held by any one person.

Commentary—*Simon's Direct Tax Service* **A3.124.**
Amendments—[1] Sum in sub-s (2) substituted by virtue of the Decimal Currency Act 1969 s 10(1).

24 Power to obtain information as to income from securities

(1) The Board may by notice in writing require—

(a) any person, being a registered or inscribed holder of any United Kingdom securities, who, in any year of assessment, has received on behalf of any other person any income arising from any such securities, or

(b) any person by or through whom, in any year of assessment, any income in respect of United Kingdom securities has been paid in any case where—

(i) the registered or inscribed holder of the securities is not the person to whom the income was paid or,

(ii) the securities are bearer securities,

to furnish them, within such time as may be specified in the notice (not being less than twenty-eight days) with particulars of the amounts so received or, as the case may be, paid in that year (other than amounts received or paid in that year on behalf of or to any one person which did not exceed in the aggregate the sum of £15), the securities to which those amounts respectively relate, and the names and addresses of the persons on whose behalf or to whom those amounts were respectively received or paid.

(2) The Board may similarly require any person who acts or has acted, directly or indirectly, as an intermediary or as one of a series of intermediaries between any such person as is specified in subsection (1)(a) or (b) above and the person or persons beneficially entitled to the income in question to furnish such information as the Board may require for the purpose of enabling them to ascertain the names and addresses of the person or persons beneficially entitled to the income and the respective amounts to which those persons were beneficially entitled.

(3) Nothing in this section shall impose on any bank the obligation to disclose any particulars relating to income from securities in cases where the person beneficially entitled to the income is not resident in the United Kingdom.

[(3A) In this section "bank" has the meaning given by section 840A of the principal Act.][1]

(4) In this section—

"securities" includes shares, stocks, bonds, debentures and debenture stock, and

"United Kingdom securities" means any securities issued by or on behalf of Her Majesty's Government in the United Kingdom or the Government of Northern Ireland and any securities of a body corporate incorporated in any part of the United Kingdom.

Commentary—*Simon's Direct Tax Service* **A3.125.**
Revenue & other press releases—Code of Practice 5 (inspection of financial intermediaries' records).
Amendments—[1] Sub-s (3A) inserted by FA 1996 Sch 37 Pt III para 11(1), (2)(c) with effect in relation to requirements imposed on or after 29 April 1996.

Chargeable gains

25 Issuing houses, stockbrokers, auctioneers, etc

(1) For the purpose of obtaining particulars of chargeable gains an inspector may by notice in writing require a return under any of the provisions of this section.

(2) An issuing house or other person carrying on a business of effecting public issues of shares or securities in any company, or placings of shares or securities in any company, either on behalf of the company, or on behalf of holders of blocks of shares or securities which have not previously been

the subject of a public issue or placing, may be required to make a return of all such public issues or placings effected by that person in the course of the business in the period specified in the notice requiring the return, giving particulars of the persons to or with whom the shares or securities are issued, allotted or placed, and the number or amount of the shares or securities so obtained by them respectively.

(3) A person not carrying on such a business may be required to make a return as regards any such public issue or placing effected by that person and specified in the notice, giving particulars of the persons to or with whom the shares or securities are issued, allotted, or placed and the number or amount of the shares or securities so obtained by them respectively.

(4) A member of a stock exchange in the United Kingdom, other than a [market maker][1], may be required to make a return giving particulars of any transactions effected by him in the course of his business in the period specified in the notice requiring the return and giving particulars of—

(a) the parties to the transactions,
(b) the number or amount of the shares or securities dealt with in the respective transactions, and
(c) the amount or value of the consideration.

(5) A person (other than a member of a stock exchange in the United Kingdom) who acts as an agent or broker in the United Kingdom in transactions in shares or securities may be required to make a return giving particulars of any such transactions effected by him after 5th April 1968 and in the period specified in the notice, and giving particulars of—

(a) the parties to the transactions,
(b) the number or amount of the shares or securities dealt with in the respective transactions, and
(c) the amount or value of the consideration.

(6) The committee or other person or body of persons responsible for managing a clearing house for any terminal market in commodities may be required to make a return giving particulars of any transactions effected through the clearing house in the period specified in the notice requiring the return and giving particulars of—

(a) the parties to the transactions,
(b) the amounts dealt with in those transactions respectively, and
(c) the amount or value of the consideration.

(7) An auctioneer, and any person carrying on a trade of dealing in any description of tangible movable property, or of acting as an agent or intermediary in dealings in any description of tangible movable property, may be required to make a return giving particulars of any transactions effected by or through him in which any asset which is tangible movable property is disposed of for a consideration the amount or value of which, in the hands of the recipient, exceeds [£6,000][3].

(8) No person shall be required under this section to include in a return particulars of any transaction effected more than three years before the service of the notice requiring him to make the return.

(9) In this section "company" and "shares" shall be construed in accordance with [sections 99 and 288(1) of the 1992 Act][4].

[(10) In this section "market maker", in relation to shares or securities, means a person who—

(a) holds himself out at all normal times in compliance with the rules of The Stock Exchange as willing to buy and sell shares or securities of the kind concerned at a price specified by him, and
(b) is recognised as doing so by the Council of The Stock Exchange.][2]

Commentary—*Simon's Direct Tax Service* A3.128.
Revenue & other press releases—Code of Practice 5 (inspection of financial intermediaries' records).
Revenue Internal Guidance—Capital gains manual CG 10350–10381 (returns are issued by the Taxes Information Distribution Office: details of Revenue procedures given).
Definitions—"the 1992 Act", s 118(1); "body of persons", s 118(1); "chargeable gain", TCGA 1992 s 15(2) by virtue of s 118(1); "return", s 118(1).
Cross references—See FA 1986 Sch 18 para 8(4), (5) (Board's powers to extend the scope of sub-ss (4), (5), (10) above with effect from an appointed day).
Amendments—[1] Words "market maker" in sub-s (4) substituted for the word "jobber" by FA 1986 Sch 18 para 8(1), (3) in relation to transactions on or after 27 October 1986.
[2] Sub-s (10) inserted by FA 1986 Sch 18 para 8(2), (3).
[3] Amount in sub-s (7) substituted by FA 1989 s 123(1)(c), (2) in relation to disposals after 5 April 1989.
[4] Words in sub-s (9) substituted by TCGA 1992 Sch 10 para 2(1), (4).

26 Nominee shareholders

(1) If, for the purpose of obtaining particulars of chargeable gains, any person in whose name any shares of a company are registered is so required by notice in writing by the Board or an inspector, he shall state whether or not he is the beneficial owner of those shares and, if not the beneficial owner of those shares or any of them, shall furnish the name and address of the person or persons on whose behalf the shares are registered in his name.

(2) In this section references to shares include references to securities and loan capital.

Commentary—*Simon's Direct Tax Service* A3.129.
Definition—"Chargeable gain", TCGA 1992 s 15(2) by virtue of s 118(1).

27 Settled property

(1) The Board may by notice in writing require any person, being a party to a settlement, to furnish them within such time as they may direct (not being less than twenty-eight days) with such particulars as they think necessary for the purposes of [the [1992 Act]²]¹.

(2) In this section ''settlement'' has the meaning given by [section 660G(1) and (2)]³ of the principal Act.

Commentary—*Simon's Direct Tax Service* A3.129.
Definitions—''the 1992 Act'', s 118(1); ''principal Act'', s 118(1).
Amendments—¹ Words in sub-s (1) substituted by CGTA 1979 s 157(2), Sch 7 para 8(b), Table, Pt II para 2.
² Words in sub-s (1) substituted by TCGA 1992 Sch 10 para 2(1), (2).
³ Words in sub-s (2) substituted by FA 1995 Sch 17 para 21, with effect from the year 1995–96 and applies to every settlement, wherever and whenever made or entered into.

28 Non-resident companies and trusts

[(1) A person holding shares or securities in a company which is not resident or ordinarily resident in the United Kingdom may be required by a notice by the Board to give such particulars as the Board may consider are required to determine whether the company falls within section 13 of the 1992 Act and whether any chargeable gains have accrued to that company in respect of which the person to whom the notice is given is liable to capital gains tax under that section.

(2) For the purposes of this section ''company'' and ''shares'' shall be construed in accordance with sections 99 and 288(1) of the 1992 Act.]¹

Definitions—''the 1992 Act'', s 118(1); ''chargeable gain'', TCGA 1992 s 15(2) by virtue of s 118(1).
Amendments—¹ This section substituted by TCGA 1992 Sch 10 para 2(1), (5) in relation to tax for the year 1992–93 and subsequent years and for chargeable periods beginning after 5 April 1992; see TCGA 1992 s 289.

[PART IIIA
REFERRAL OF QUESTIONS DURING ENQUIRY]¹

Amendments—¹ This Part inserted by FA 2001 s 88, Sch 29 para 6 with effect where the notice of enquiry is given after the passing of FA 2001, or where the enquiry is in progress immediately before the passing of FA 2001. An enquiry is in progress until the officer's enquiries fall to be treated as completed under TMA 1970 s 28A(5) or, as the case may be, TMA 1970 s 28B(5) (as those provisions had effect apart from FA 2001 Sch 29).

[28ZA Referral of questions during enquiry

(1) At any time when an enquiry is in progress under section 9A(1) or 12AC(1) of this Act, any question arising in connection with the subject-matter of the enquiry may be referred to the Special Commissioners for their determination.

(2) Notice of referral must be given—
    (a) jointly by the taxpayer and an officer of the Board,
    (b) in writing,
    (c) to the Special Commissioners.

(3) The notice of referral must specify the question or questions being referred.

(4) More than one notice of referral may be given under this section in relation to an enquiry.

(5) For the purposes of this section the period during which an enquiry is in progress is the whole of the period—
    (a) beginning with the day on which notice of enquiry is given, and
    (b) ending with the day on which the enquiry is completed.

(6) In this section ''the taxpayer'' means—
    (a) in relation to an enquiry under section 9A(1) of this Act, the person to whom the notice of enquiry was given;
    (b) in relation to an enquiry under section 12AC(1) of this Act, the person to whom the notice of enquiry was given or his successor.]¹

Commentary—*Simon's Direct Tax Service* E1.811A.
Amendments—¹ This section inserted by FA 2001 s 88, Sch 29 para 6 with effect where the notice of enquiry is given after the passing of FA 2001, or where the enquiry is in progress immediately before the passing of FA 2001. An enquiry is in progress until the officer's enquiries fall to be treated as completed under TMA 1970 s 28A(5) or, as the case may be, TMA 1970 s 28B(5) (as those provisions had effect apart from FA 2001 Sch 29).

[28ZB Withdrawal of notice of referral

(1) Either party may withdraw a notice of referral under section 28ZA of this Act by notice in accordance with this section.

(2) Notice of withdrawal must be given—
    (a) in writing,
    (b) to the other party to the referral and to the Special Commissioners,
    (c) before the first hearing by the Special Commissioners in relation to the referral.]¹

Commentary—*Simon's Direct Tax Service* **E1.811A.**
Amendments—[1] This section inserted by FA 2001 s 88, Sch 29 para 6 with effect where the notice of enquiry is given after the passing of FA 2001, or where the enquiry is in progress immediately before the passing of FA 2001. An enquiry is in progress until the officer's enquiries fall to be treated as completed under TMA 1970 s 28A(5) or, as the case may be, TMA 1970 s 28B(5) (as those provisions had effect apart from FA 2001 Sch 29).

[28ZC Regulations with respect to referrals

(1) The Lord Chancellor may make provision by regulations with respect to referrals to the Special Commissioners under—

(a) section 28ZA of this Act, or

(b) paragraph 31A of Schedule 18 to the Finance Act 1998.

(2) Regulations under subsection (1) above may, in particular—

(a) make provision with respect to any of the matters dealt with in the following provisions of this Act—

(i) section 50 (procedure before the Special Commissioners),

(ii) section 56 (statement of case for opinion of the High Court),

(iii) section 56A (appeals from the Special Commissioners), and

(iv) section 58 (proceedings in Northern Ireland), or

(b) provide for any of those provisions to apply, with such modifications as may be specified in the regulations, in relation to a referral to the Special Commissioners under the provisions mentioned in subsection (1) above.

(3) Regulations under subsection (1) above may—

(a) make different provision for different cases or different circumstances, and

(b) contain such supplementary, incidental, consequential and transitional provision as the Lord Chancellor thinks appropriate.

(4) Regulations under subsection (1) above shall—

(a) be made by statutory instrument, and

(b) be subject to annulment in pursuance of a resolution of either House of Parliament.

(5) In the following provisions any reference to an appeal includes a reference to a referral under section 28ZA of this Act or paragraph 31A of Schedule 18 to the Finance Act 1998—

(a) sections 56B, 56C and 56D of this Act (power of the Lord Chancellor to make regulations about the practice and procedure to be followed in connection with appeals to the Special Commissioners); and

(b) section 57 of this Act (power of the Board to make regulations about appeals relating to chargeable gains).

(6) Any regulations under section 56B or 57 of this Act which are in force immediately before the commencement of subsection (1) above shall apply in relation to referrals under section 28ZA of this Act or paragraph 31A of Schedule 18 to the Finance Act 1998, subject to any necessary modifications, as they apply in relation to appeals to the Special Commissioners.

(7) Regulations under this section relating to proceedings in Scotland shall not be made except with the consent of the Scottish Ministers.][1]

Commentary—*Simon's Direct Tax Service* **E1.811A.**
Amendments—[1] This section inserted by FA 2001 s 88, Sch 29 para 6 with effect where the notice of enquiry is given after the passing of FA 2001, or where the enquiry is in progress immediately before the passing of FA 2001. An enquiry is in progress until the officer's enquiries fall to be treated as completed under TMA 1970 s 28A(5) or, as the case may be, TMA 1970 s 28B(5) (as those provisions had effect apart from FA 2001 Sch 29).

[28ZD Effect of referral on enquiry

(1) While proceedings on a referral under section 28ZA of this Act are in progress in relation to an enquiry—

(a) no closure notice shall be given in relation to the enquiry, and

(b) no application may be made for a direction to give such a notice.

(2) For the purposes of this section proceedings on a referral are in progress where—

(a) notice of referral has been given,

(b) the notice has not been withdrawn, and

(c) the questions referred have not been finally determined.

(3) For the purposes of subsection (2)(c) above a question referred is finally determined when—

(a) it has been determined by the Special Commissioners, and

(b) there is no further possibility of that determination being varied or set aside (disregarding any power to give permission to appeal out of time).][1]

Commentary—*Simon's Direct Tax Service* **E1.811A.**
Amendments—[1] This section inserted by FA 2001 s 88, Sch 29 para 6 with effect where the notice of enquiry is given after the passing of FA 2001, or where the enquiry is in progress immediately before the passing of FA 2001. An enquiry is in progress until the officer's enquiries fall to be treated as completed under TMA 1970 s 28A(5) or, as the case may be, TMA 1970 s 28B(5) (as those provisions had effect apart from FA 2001 Sch 29).

[28ZE Effect of determination

(1) The determination of a question referred to the Special Commissioners under section 28ZA of this Act is binding on the parties to the referral in the same way, and to the same extent, as a decision on a preliminary issue in an appeal.

(2) The determination shall be taken into account by an officer of the Board—

    (*a*) in reaching his conclusions on the enquiry, and

    (*b*) in formulating any amendments of the return required to give effect to those conclusions.

(3) Any right of appeal under section 31(1)(*a*), (*b*) or (*c*) of this Act may not be exercised so as to reopen the question determined except to the extent (if any) that it could be reopened if it had been determined as a preliminary issue in that appeal.]¹

Commentary—*Simon's Direct Tax Service* **E1.811A.**
Amendments—¹ This section inserted by FA 2001 s 88, Sch 29 para 6 with effect where the notice of enquiry is given after the passing of FA 2001, or where the enquiry is in progress immediately before the passing of FA 2001. An enquiry is in progress until the officer's enquiries fall to be treated as completed under TMA 1970 s 28A(5) or, as the case may be, TMA 1970 s 28B(5) (as those provisions had effect apart from FA 2001 Sch 29).

PART IV
ASSESSMENT AND CLAIMS

Cross references—TA 1988 s 350(5) (power of Board to make regulations modifying the provisions of this Part in relation to advance corporation tax and income tax deducted under TA 1988 s 349 for which a company is liable to account).
IT (Sub-contractors in the Construction Industry) Regulations, SI 1993/743 reg 14 (this Part to apply to a formal determination of assessed amounts payable by contractor);
IT (Employment) Regulations, SI 1993/744 reg 49(7) (this Part to apply to a formal determination of assessed tax payable by employer).
Education (Student Loans) (Repayment) Regulations, SI 2000/944 reg 20 (application and modification of this Part in connection with the repayment of student loans).

[28A Completion of enquiry into personal or trustee return

(1) An enquiry under section 9A(1) of this Act is completed when an officer of the Board by notice (a "closure notice") informs the taxpayer that he has completed his enquiries and states his conclusions.

In this section "the taxpayer" means the person to whom notice of enquiry was given.

(2) A closure notice must either—

    (*a*) state that in the officer's opinion no amendment of the return is required, or

    (*b*) make the amendments of the return required to give effect to his conclusions.

(3) A closure notice takes effect when it is issued.

(4) The taxpayer may apply to the Commissioners for a direction requiring an officer of the Board to issue a closure notice within a specified period.

(5) Any such application shall be heard and determined in the same way as an appeal.

(6) The Commissioners hearing the application shall give the direction applied for unless they are satisfied that there are reasonable grounds for not issuing a closure notice within a specified period.]¹

Commentary—*Simon's Direct Tax Service* **D2.832; E1.810, 812.**
Revenue Internal Guidance—Enquiry Handbook EH 423 (circumstances under which Revenue will issue a closure notice where information has not been supplied or only partly supplied).
EH 428–435 (sub-s (2): conditions under which the Revenue may make a jeopardy amendment).
EH 436–442 (sub-s (4): taxpayer rights to apply to Commissioners for a closure notice to be issued).
EH 474 (examples of closure notices).
EH 491 (Revenue procedures where no amendment to self-assessment is necessary as a result of enquiries).
EH 492 (Revenue procedures where an amendment to self-assessment is necessary as a result of enquiries).
EH 498 (an outline of problems arising with 30-day periods).
EH 506 (where an enquiry has been closed before the taxpayer's 12 months for amending have expired a further amendment can be made by the taxpayer within that 12 months).
EH 520–524 (conclusion of enquiry: interaction with jeopardy amendments).
EH 525 (examples showing the effect of the section).
EH 535–545 (Revenue procedures regarding contract settlements).
Amendments—¹ This section substituted by FA 2001 s 88, Sch 29 para 8 with effect where the notice of enquiry is given after the passing of FA 2001, or where the enquiry is in progress immediately before the passing of FA 2001. An enquiry is in progress until the officer's enquiries fall to be treated as completed under TMA 1970 s 28A(5) (as that provision had effect apart from FA 2001 Sch 29). Previously, s 28A read—

"**28A Amendment of self-assessment where enquiries made**

(1) This section applies where an officer of the Board gives notice under section 9A(1) ...⁹ of this Act to any person (the taxpayer) of his intention to enquire into—

    (*a*) the return on the basis of which the taxpayer's self-assessment was made, or

    (*b*) any amendment of that return on the basis of which an amendment (the taxpayer's amendment) of that assessment has been made by the taxpayer [or]²

    (*c*) any claim or election included in the return (by amendment or otherwise).

(2) If, at any time before the officer's enquiries are completed, the officer is of opinion that—

    (*a*) the tax contained in the taxpayer's self-assessment is insufficient and, in a case falling within [subsection (1)(*b*) or (*c*) above]³, the deficiency is attributable (wholly or partly) to the taxpayer's amendment, and

    (*b*) unless the assessment is immediately so amended as to make good the deficiency or, as the case may be, so much of the deficiency as is so attributable, there is likely to be a loss of tax to the Crown, he may by notice to the taxpayer amend the assessment accordingly.

(3) At any time in the period of 30 days beginning with the day on which the officer's enquiries are completed, the taxpayer may so amend his self-assessment—

(a) as to make good any deficiency or eliminate any excess which, on the basis of the conclusions stated in the officer's notice under subsection (5) below, is a deficiency or excess which could be made good or eliminated under subsection (4) below; or

(b) in a case falling within subsection (1)(a) above where the return was made before the end of the period of twelve months beginning with the filing date, as to give effect to any amendments to the return which he has notified to the officer.

(4) If, at any time in the period of 30 days beginning immediately after the period mentioned in subsection (3) above, the officer is of opinion that—

(a) [any amount set out in the return]⁴ is insufficient or excessive, and

(b) in a case falling within [subsection (1)(b) or (c) above]³, the deficiency or excess is attributable (wholly or partly) to the taxpayer's amendment,

he may by notice to the taxpayer so amend the assessment as to make good or eliminate the deficiency or excess or, where paragraph (b) above applies, so much of the deficiency or excess as is so attributable.

(4A) If—

(a) any claim or election is included in the return,

(b) the officer is of opinion that the claim or election should be disallowed in whole or in part but that its disallowance to the extent he thinks appropriate would not require any amendment of the taxpayer's self-assessment, and

(c) the claim or election, so far as the officer thinks it should be disallowed, is not, before the end of the period mentioned in subsection (3) above, amended to the officer's satisfaction or withdrawn,

the officer shall, before the end of the period mentioned in subsection (4) above, give notice to the taxpayer of the extent to which he is disallowing the claim or election.

(4B) Subsection (4A)(c) above is without prejudice to any provision by virtue of which any claim or election is irrevocable or unamendable.

(5) Subject to subsection (6) below, the officer's enquiries shall be treated as completed at such time as he by notice—

(a) informs the taxpayer that he has completed his enquiries, and

(b) states his conclusions as to the amount of tax which should be contained in the taxpayer's self-assessment and as to any claims or elections into which he has enquired.

(6) At any time before a notice is given under subsection (5) above, the taxpayer may apply for a direction that the officer shall give such a notice within such period as may be specified in the direction.]⁷

(6A) Subject to subsection (7) below, an application under subsection (6) above shall be heard and determined in the same way as an appeal against an amendment of a self-assessment under subsection (2) or (4) above.

(7) The Commissioners hearing the application shall give the direction applied for unless they are satisfied that the officer has reasonable grounds for not giving the notice.

(7A) Where, in the case of any return made in respect of any chargeable period—

(a) alternative methods are allowed by the Tax Acts for bringing amounts into account in that return,

(b) the return is made or amended using one of those methods,

(c) a return could have been made in that case using an alternative method, and

(d) an officer of the Board determines which of the alternative methods is to be used by the Board in relation to the taxpayer for that period,

any enquiry into that return or into an amendment of it shall be conducted, and this section shall have effect, as if the only method allowed for the purposes of the Tax Acts were the method determined by the officer.

(7B) For the purposes of subsection (7A) above the cases where the Tax Acts allow alternative methods for bringing amounts into account in a return are—

(a) the case where those amounts may be brought into account either—

(i) in making a computation for the purposes of Case I or II of Schedule D; or

(ii) in making a computation for the purposes of any of Cases III to V of that Schedule;

(b) ..

(7C) ...

(8) In this section "filing date" means the day mentioned in section 8(1A) or section 8A(1A) of this Act, as the case may be."

28AA Amendment of return of profits made for wrong period

Amendments—This section repealed by FA 1998 Sch 19 para 9, Sch 27 Part III(28) with effect in relation to accounting periods ending after 30 June 1999 (by virtue of Finance Act 1994, Section 199, (Appointed Day) Order, SI 1998/3173 art 2).

28AB Provisions supplementary to section 28AA

Amendments—This section repealed by FA 1998 Sch 19 para 9, Sch 27 Part III(28) with effect in relation to accounting periods ending after 30 June 1999 (by virtue of Finance Act 1994, Section 199, (Appointed Day) Order, SI 1998/3173 art 2).

[28B Completion of enquiry into partnership return

(1) An enquiry under section 12AC(1) of this Act is completed when an officer of the Board by notice (a "closure notice") informs the taxpayer that he has completed his enquiries and states his conclusions.

In this section "the taxpayer" means the person to whom notice of enquiry was given or his successor.

(2) A closure notice must either—

(a) state that in the officer's opinion no amendment of the return is required, or

(b) make the amendments of the return required to give effect to his conclusions.

(3) A closure notice takes effect when it is issued.

(4) Where a partnership return is amended under subsection (2) above, the officer shall by notice to each of the partners amend—

(a) the partner's return under section 8 or 8A of this Act, or (*b*) the partner's company tax return,

so as to give effect to the amendments of the partnership return.

(5) The taxpayer may apply to the Commissioners for a direction requiring an officer of the Board to issue a closure notice within a specified period.

(6) Any such application shall be heard and determined in the same way as an appeal.

(7) The Commissioners hearing the application shall give the direction applied for unless they are satisfied that there are reasonable grounds for not issuing a closure notice within a specified period.][1]

Commentary—*Simon's Direct Tax Service* **E1.813.**
Revenue Internal Guidance—Enquiry Handbook EH 775 (summarises the relationship between this section and s 28A).
EH 789 (example showing the effect of this section).
Amendments—[1] This section substituted by FA 2001 s 88, Sch 29 para 9 with effect where the notice of enquiry is given after the passing of FA 2001, or where the enquiry is in progress immediately before the passing of FA 2001. An enquiry is in progress until the officer's enquiries fall to be treated as completed under TMA 1970 s 28B(5) (as that provision had effect apart from FA 2001 Sch 29). Previously, s 28B read—

"**28B Amendment of partnership statement where enquiries made**

(1) This section applies where an officer of the Board gives notice under section 12AC(1) of this Act to any person (the taxpayer) of his intention to enquire into—

    (*a*) the return on the basis of which the taxpayer's partnership statement was made, or
    (*b*) any amendment of that return on the basis of which an amendment (the taxpayer's amendment) of that statement has been made by the taxpayer [or]
    [(*c*) any claim or election included in the return (by amendment or otherwise)].

(2) At any time in the period of 30 days beginning with the day on which the officer's enquiries are completed, the taxpayer may so amend his partnership statement—

    (*a*) as to make good any deficiency or eliminate any excess which, on the basis of the conclusions stated in the officer's notice under subsection (5) below, is a deficiency or excess which could be made good or eliminated under subsection (3) below; or
    (*b*) in a case falling within subsection (1)(*a*) above where the return made before the end of the period of twelve months beginning with the filing date, as to give effect to any amendments to the return which he has notified to the officer.

(3) If, at any time in the period of 30 days beginning immediately after the period mentioned in subsection (2) above, the officer is of opinion that—

    (*a*) any amount contained in the taxpayer's partnership statement is insufficient or excessive, and
    (*b*) in a case falling within [subsection (1)(*b*) or (*c*) above], the deficiency or excess is attributable (wholly or partly) to the taxpayer's amendment,

he may by notice to the taxpayer so amend the statement as to make good or eliminate the deficiency or excess or, where paragraph (*b*) above applies, so much of the deficiency or excess as is so attributable.

(4) Where a partnership statement is amended under this section, the officer shall by notice to each of the partners amend—

    (*a*) the partner's self-assessment under section 9 of this Act, or
    (*b*) the partner's company tax return,

so as to give effect to the amendments of the partnership statement.

(5) Subject to subsection (6) below, the officer's enquiries shall be treated as completed at such time as he by notice—

    (*a*) informs the taxpayer that he has completed his enquiries, and
    (*b*) states his conclusions as to the amounts which should be contained in the taxpayer's partnership statement [and as to any claims or elections into which he has enquired.

(6) Subsections (6) and (7) of section 28A of this Act apply for the purposes of subsection (5) above as they apply for the purposes of subsection (5) of that section.
(6A) Where, in the case of any return made in relation to any period of account—

    (*a*) alternative methods are allowed by the Tax Acts for bringing amounts into account in that return,
    (*b*) the return is made or amended using one of those methods,
    (*c*) a return could have been made in that case using an alternative method, and
    (*d*) an officer of the Board determines which of the alternative methods is to be used by the Board in relation to the partnership for that period,

any enquiry into that return or into an amendment of it shall be conducted, and this section shall have effect, as if the only method allowed for the purposes of the Tax Acts were the method determined by the officer.

(6B) For the purposes of subsection (6A) above—

    (*a*) "period of account" has the same meaning as in section 12AB of this Act, and
    (*b*) the cases where alternative methods are allowed by the Tax Acts are those specified in section 28A(7B) of this Act or paragraph 84(2) or (3) of Schedule 18 to the Finance Act 1998.

(7) In this section "filing date" means the day specified in the notice under subsection (2) or, as the case may be, subsection (3) of section 12AA of this Act.
(8) Any reference in this section to the taxpayer includes a reference to any predecessor or successor of his."

[28C Determination of tax where no return delivered

[(1) This section applies where—

    (*a*) a notice has been given to any person under section 8 or 8A of this Act (the relevant section), and
    (*b*) the required return is not delivered on or before the filing date.][2]

[(1A) An officer of the Board may make a determination of the following amounts, to the best of his information and belief, namely—

    (*a*) the amounts in which the person who should have made the return is chargeable to income tax and capital gains tax for the year of assessment; and
    (*b*) the amount which is payable by him by way of income tax for that year;

and subsection (1AA) of section 8 or, as the case may be, section 8A of this Act applies for the purposes of this subsection as it applies for the purposes of subsection (1) of that section.][2]

(2) Notice of any determination under this section shall be served on the person in respect of whom it is made and shall state the date on which it is issued.

(3) Until such time (if any) as it is superseded by a self-assessment made under section 9 ...³ of this Act (whether by the taxpayer or an officer of the Board) on the basis of information contained in a return under the relevant section, a determination under this section shall have effect for the purposes of Parts VA, VI, IX and XI of this Act as if it were such a self-assessment.

(4) Where—

    (*a*) [proceedings have been commenced]⁵ for the recovery of any tax charged by a determination under this section; and

    (*b*) before those proceedings are concluded, the determination is superseded by such a self-assessment as is mentioned in subsection (3) above,

those proceedings may be continued as if they were proceedings for the recovery of so much of the tax charged by the self-assessment as is due and payable and has not been paid.

(5) No determination under this section, and no self-assessment superseding such a determination, shall be made otherwise than—

    (*a*) before the end of the period of five years beginning with the filing date; or

    (*b*) in the case of such a self-assessment, before the end of the period of twelve months beginning with the date of the determination.

(6) In this section "the filing date" means the day mentioned in section 8(1A) [or, as the case may be, section 8A(1A)]⁴ of this Act.]¹

Commentary—*Simon's Direct Tax Service* **E1.814.**
Revenue Internal Guidance—Enquiry Handbook EH 423 (completion notice may be issued in cases where there is delay in producing further information; this enables the Revenue to issue an amended self-assessment to the best of their judgement; matters can then proceed further on appeal).
Definitions—"Act", s 118(1); "the Board", s 118(1); "filing date", s 28C(6); "return", s 118(1); "year of assessment", TA 1988 s 832(1).
Cross references—See TMA 1970 s 8A(5) (construction of references in this section to a person to whom a notice has been given under s 8A being chargeable to tax).
FA 1994 s 197(1)(*b*) (references in the Tax Acts and Gains Tax Acts to a person being assessed or charged to tax by an assessment, to be construed as including a reference to a determination under this section).
Amendments—¹ This section inserted by FA 1994 ss 190, 199 with effect from the year 1996–97. (As originally enacted, this section was also to apply in relation to corporation tax with effect in relation to accounting periods after 30 June 1999 (by virtue of Finance Act 1994, Section 199, (Appointed Day) Order, SI 1998/3173 art 2).However, following amendments made by FA 1996 (see below), this section ceases to be relevant to corporation tax.
² Sub-ss (1), (1A) substituted for sub-s (1) by FA 1996 s 125(1) with effect from the year 1996–97.
³ Words omitted from sub-s (3) repealed by FA 1996 s 125(2), Sch 41 Pt V(6) with effect from the year 1996–97.
⁴ Words in sub-s (6) substituted by FA 1996 s 125(3) with effect from the year 1996–97.
⁵ Words in sub-s (4) substituted for the words "an officer of the Board has commenced any proceedings" by FA 2001 s 88, Sch 29 para 17 with effect for proceeedings begun after the passing of FA 2001.

28D Determination of corporation tax where no return delivered

Amendments—This section repealed by FA 1998 Sch 19 para 11, Sch 27 Part III(28) with effect in relation to accounting periods ending after 30 June 1999 (by virtue of Finance Act 1994, Section 199, (Appointed Day) Order, SI 1998/3173 art 2).

28E Determination of corporation tax where notice complied with in part

Amendments—This section repealed by FA 1998 Sch 19 para 11, Sch 27 Part III(28) with effect in relation to accounting periods ending after 30 June 1999 (by virtue of Finance Act 1994, Section 199, (Appointed Day) Order, SI 1998/3173 art 2).

28F Corporation tax determinations: supplementary

Amendments—This section repealed by FA 1998 Sch 19 para 11, Sch 27 Part III(28) with effect in relation to accounting periods ending after 30 June 1999 (by virtue of Finance Act 1994, Section 199, (Appointed Day) Order, SI 1998/3173 art 2).

[29 Assessment where loss of tax discovered

(1) If an officer of the Board or the Board discover, as regards any person (the taxpayer) and a [year of assessment]²—

    (*a*) that any [income which ought to have been assessed to income tax, or chargeable gains which ought to have been assessed to capital gains tax,]² have not been assessed, or

    (*b*) that an assessment to tax is or has become insufficient, or

    (*c*) that any relief which has been given is or has become excessive,

the officer or, as the case may be, the Board may, subject to subsections (2) and (3) below, make an assessment in the amount, or the further amount, which ought in his or their opinion to be charged in order to make good to the Crown the loss of tax.

(2) Where—

    (*a*) the taxpayer has made and delivered a return under [section 8 or 8A]² of this Act in respect of the relevant [year of assessment]², and

    (*b*) the situation mentioned in subsection (1) above is attributable to an error or mistake in the return as to the basis on which his liability ought to have been computed, the taxpayer shall not be assessed under that subsection in respect of the [year of assessment]² there mentioned if the return was in fact made on the basis or in accordance with the practice generally prevailing at the time when it was made.

(3) Where the taxpayer has made and delivered a return under [section 8 or 8A]² of this Act in respect of the relevant [year of assessment]², he shall not be assessed under subsection (1) above—

(a) in respect of the [year of assessment]² mentioned in that subsection; and

(b) ...² in the same capacity as that in which he made and delivered the return,

unless one of the two conditions mentioned below is fulfilled.

(4) The first condition is that the situation mentioned in subsection (1) above is attributable to fraudulent or negligent conduct on the part of the taxpayer or a person acting on his behalf.

(5) The second condition is that at the time when an officer of the Board—

(a) ceased to be entitled to give notice of his intention to enquire into the taxpayer's return under [section 8 or 8A]² of this Act in respect of the relevant [year of assessment]²; or

(b) informed the taxpayer that he had completed his enquiries into that return,

the officer could not have been reasonably expected, on the basis of the information made available to him before that time, to be aware of the situation mentioned in subsection (1) above.

(6) For the purposes of subsection (5) above, information is made available to an officer of the Board if—

(a) it is contained in the taxpayer's return under [section 8 or 8A]² of this Act in respect of the relevant [year of assessment]² (the return), or in any accounts, statements or documents accompanying the return;

(b) it is contained in any claim made as regards the relevant [year of assessment]² by the taxpayer acting in the same capacity as that in which he made the return, or in any accounts, statements or documents accompanying any such claim;

(c) it is contained in any documents, accounts or particulars which, for the purposes of any enquiries into the return or any such claim by an officer of the Board, are produced or furnished by the taxpayer to the officer, whether in pursuance of a notice under section 19A of this Act or otherwise; or

(d) it is information the existence of which, and the relevance of which as regards the situation mentioned in subsection (1) above—

(i) could reasonably be expected to be inferred by an officer of the Board from information falling within paragraphs (a) to (c) above; or

(ii) are notified in writing by the taxpayer to an officer of the Board.

(7) In subsection (6) above—

(a) any reference to the taxpayer's return under [section 8 or 8A]² of this Act in respect of the relevant [year of assessment]² includes—

(i) a reference to any return of his under that section for either of the two immediately preceding chargeable periods; and

(ii) where the return is under section 8 and the taxpayer carries on a trade, profession or business in partnership, a reference to [any partnership return with respect to the partnership]³ for the relevant [year of assessment]² or either of those periods; and

(b) any reference in paragraphs (b) to (d) to the taxpayer includes a reference to a person acting on his behalf.

(8) An objection to the making of an assessment under this section on the ground that neither of the two conditions mentioned above is fulfilled shall not be made otherwise than on an appeal against the assessment.

(9) Any reference in this section to the relevant [year of assessment]² is a reference to—

(a) in the case of the situation mentioned in paragraph (a) or (b) of subsection (1) above, the [year of assessment]² mentioned in that subsection; and

(b) in the case of the situation mentioned in paragraph (c) of that subsection, the [year of assessment]² in respect of which the claim was made.

(10) ...²]¹

Commentary—*Simon's Direct Tax Service* **A3.201, 202; E1.815**.
Statement of Practice SP 8/91, para 4—Discovery assessments; inspector's discovery powers.
SP 11/93—Pay and file—claims to capital allowances and group relief made outside normal time limit.
Revenue & other press releases—ICAEW TR760 6-9-89 (Revenue practice in case of new business; first return is issued thirteen months after the date of commencement and the first assessment one month later).
IR 31-5-96 (Revenue paper on operation of the discovery and disclosure rules under self-assessment).
Revenue Internal Guidance—Corporation tax manual CT 10503 (circumstances in which estimated assessments will be made under pay and file).
Investigation Handbook IH 200-550 (Revenue organisation of investigation work).
IH 640-644 (screening of accounts).
IH1000-1005 (background to accounts investigations).
IH 1200-1295 (selection of cases for investigation).
IH 1350-1380 (preparatory review of cases selected).
IH 1400-1425 (opening an investigation).
IH 1500-1586 (investigations: accounting systems and the role of accountants and auditors).
IH 1700-1867 (investigations: examination of records)

IH 1900-1940 (accounts investigations: business ratios).
IH 1975-2002 (investigations: use of business models).
IH 2050-2186 (use of capital statements, estimation of personal and private expenditure).
IH 2200-2297 (Revenue approach to cash hoards, betting winnings, legacies etc: evidence required to substantiate source of funds).
IH 2600-2658 (re-opening of earlier years tax liabilities: Revenue practice and procedures).
IH 3020-3031 (use of certificates of full disclosure).
IH 4000-4051, 6160-6190 (settlement of additional tax liabilities).
IH 4130-4141 (issue of protective assessments).
IH 5000-5111 (culpability of the taxpayer, meaning of "fraud", etc, reasonable excuses, taxpayer's defences).
Enquiry Handbook EH 420, 570 (under self-assessment, returns and enquiries procedures must be used where still in date: discovery assessment can be made only after the self-assessment has become final).
EH 565 (Information is not considered to be made available where the total amount of information supplied is so extensive that an officer could not have been reasonably expected to be aware of the significance of particular information and the officer's attention has not been drawn to it by the taxpayer or his agent).
EH 571 (conditions under which a discovery assessment can be made despite an enquiry window being available, or potentially available).
EH 595 (meaning of "disclosure" generally).
Simon's Tax Cases—*Honig v Sarsfield* [1986] STC 246; *IRC v Wilkinson* [1992] STC 454.
s 29(1)(*b*), *Jones v O'Brien* [1988] STC 615; *Phillimore v Heaton* [1989] STC 374; *Blackpool Marton Rotary Club v Martin* [1990] STC 1; *Hancock v IRC* [1999] STC (SCD) 287.
s 29(3), *Vickerman v Mason's Personal Representatives* [1984] STC 231; *Gray v Matheson* [1993] STC 178; [1996] STC (SCD) 381.
s 29(3)(*a*), *Duchy Maternity Ltd v Hodgson* [1985] STC 764.
s 29(3)(*b*), (4), *Hancock v IRC* [1999] STC (SCD) 287.
s 29(8), *Eke v Knight* [1977] STC 198.
Definitions—"Act", s 118(1);"the Board", s 118(1); "chargeable period", s 29(9); "return", s 118(1), "trade", s 118(1).
Cross references—See TMA 1970 s 8A(5) (construction of references in this section to a person to whom a notice has been given under s 8A being assessed to tax).
TMA 1970 s 30A (procedure for making assessments).
TMA 1970 s 43A(1) (extension of a time limit for claiming relief against assessments under sub-s (3) above).
TA 1988 s 369(7)(*a*) (application of sub-s (1)(*c*) of this section in relation to excessive or undue payments by the Board to lenders of MIRAS),
TA 1988 Sch 14 para 7(3)(*a*) (application of sub-s (1)(*c*) of this section in respect of excess repayment claims for tax deducted at source from life assurance premiums);
FA 1991 s 33(3)(*a*) (application of sub-s (1)(*c*) above to excessive relief on vocational training).
Lloyd's Underwriters (Tax) Regulations, SI 1995/351 regs 5, 6 (stop-loss insurance—late assessments).
FA 1995 s 73(4) (regulations may apply sub-s (1)(*c*) above to repayments of tax credits to venture capital trusts and investors).
Amendments—[1] This section (including the heading) substituted by FA 1994 ss 191, 199 with effect from the year 1996–97 as respects income tax and capital gains tax and, as respects corporation tax, with effect in relation to accounting periods ending after 30 June 1999 (by virtue of Finance Act 1994, (Appointed Day) Order, SI 1998/3173 art 2). In the case of partnerships commenced before 6 April 1994 it has effect from 1997–98.
[2] Words substituted in sub-s (1), (2), (3), (5)(*a*), (6)(*a*) and (7)(*a*), and words in sub-s (3)(*b*) repealed, by FA 1998 Sch 19 para 12 with effect in relation to accounting periods ending after 30 June 1999 (by virtue of SI 1998/3173 art 2).
[3] Words in sub-s (7)(*a*)(ii) substituted for the words "any return with respect to the partnership under section 12AA of this Act" by FA 2001 S 88, Sch 20 para 22 with effect from the passing of FA 2001 in relation to returns whether made before or after the passing of FA 2001, and whether relating to periods before or after the passing of FA 2001.

[30 Recovery of overpayment of tax, etc

(1) Where an amount of [income tax or capital gains tax][10] has been repaid to any person which ought not to have been repaid to him, that amount of tax may be assessed and recovered as if it were unpaid tax.

[(1A) Subsection (1) above shall not apply where the amount of tax which has been repaid is assessable under section 29 of this Act.][4]

[(1B) Subsections (2) to (8) of section 29 of this Act shall apply in relation to an assessment under subsection (1) above as they apply in relation to an assessment under subsection (1) of that section; and subsection (4) of that section as so applied shall have effect as if the reference to the loss of tax were a reference to the repayment of the amount of tax which ought not to have been repaid.][9]

(2) In any case where—

(*a*) a repayment of tax has been increased in accordance with section [824 ...][10] of the principal Act or section][2] [283 of the 1992 Act][5] (supplements added to repayments of tax, etc); and

(*b*) the whole or any part of that repayment has been paid to any person but ought not to have been paid to him; and

(*c*) that repayment ought not to have been increased either at all or to any extent;

then the amount of the repayment assessed under subsection (1) above may include an amount equal to the amount by which the repayment ought not to have been increased.

[(2A) ...][10][6]

(3) In any case where—

(*a*) a payment, other than a repayment of tax to which subsection (2) above applies, is increased in accordance with section [824 or 825 of the principal Act or section][2] [283 of the 1992 Act][5]; and

(*b*) that payment ought not to have been increased either at all or to any extent;

then an amount equal to the amount by which the payment ought not to have been increased may be assessed and recovered as if it were unpaid income tax ...[10].

[(3A) ...][10][6]

[(4) An assessment to income tax under this section shall be made under Case VI of Schedule D.][10][7]

[(4A) ...[10]][6]

[(5) An assessment under this section shall not be out of time under section 34 of this Act if it is made before the end of whichever of the following ends the later, namely—

(*a*) the [year of assessment][10] following that in which the amount assessed was repaid or paid as the case may be, or

(*b*) where a return delivered by the person concerned ...[11] is enquired into by an officer of the Board, the period ending with the day on which, by virtue of section [28A(1)][11] of this Act, [the enquiry is][11] completed.][9]

(6) Subsection (5) above is without prejudice to [section 36][3] of this Act.

(7) In this section any reference to an amount repaid or paid includes a reference to an amount allowed by way of set-off.][1]

Commentary—*Simon's Direct Tax Service* A3.243.
Concession B41—Claims to repayment of tax made outside statutory time limit.
Statement of Practice
SP 8/91, para 4—Discovery assessments; inspector's discovery powers.
Revenue Internal Guidance—Investigation handbook IH3240 (overpayment would include overpayment of tax credits, repayments effectively made by way of set-off and excessive payments of repayment supplement whether or not tax has also been over-repaid).
Definitions—''the 1992 Act'', s 118(1);''accounting period'', TA 1988 s 834(1);''the Board'', s 118(1);''company'', s 118(1).
Cross references—See TMA 1970 s 30A (procedure for making assessments).
Occupational Pension Schemes (Additional Voluntary Contributions) Regulations, SI 1987/1749 reg 11(1) (application of this section to excessive and undue payments by the Board to administrators in respect of tax deducted for employees' additional voluntary contributions).
Personal Pensions Schemes (Minimum Contributions under the Social Security Act 1986) Regulations, SI 1988/1012 reg 6(1) (application of this section to excessive or incorrect payments by the Secretary of State by way of minimum contributions).
TA 1988 s 369(7)(*b*) (application of this section in relation to MIRAS),
TA 1988 s 813(3), (6) (application of this section for the purpose of recovering from certain non-resident companies a fine for the violation of the provisions withdrawing the right of recovery of tax credits),
TA 1988 Sch 14 para 7(3)(*b*) (application of this section in respect of repayment claims for tax deducted at source from life assurance premiums),
TA 1988 Sch 19AB para 3(1), (1D) (excess provisional repayments of tax to insurance companies in respect of pensions business to be treated as corporation tax repaid which ought not to have been; modification of sub-s (5) above in relation to such excesses).
TA 1988 Sch 19AB para 4(3)(*c*) (interest on excessive provisional repayment of tax on account of an insurance company's pension business investment income to be treated for the purposes of this section as repayment of corporation tax which ought not to have been repaid);
TA 1988 Sch 19AB para 5(1), (7), (8) (pension business investment income: amendments of this section by F(No 2)A 1987 s 88 (see **Amendments** below) to have effect in relation to claims by an insurance company for repayment of tax paid on its pension business investment income);
Personal Pension Schemes (Relief at Source) Regulations, SI 1988/1013 reg 13 (application of this section for the purpose of the recovery from a scheme administrator of amounts refunded to him in excess of entitlement);
FA 1991 s 33(3)(*b*) (application of this section to excessive relief on vocational training);
Insurance Companies (Pension Business) (Transitional Provisions) Regulations, SI 1992/2326 reg 6(4) (provisional repayment of tax on account of an insurance company's pension business investment income; interest on the excess where the repayment exceeds maximum reduced entitlement to be treated for the purposes of this section as repayment of corporation tax which ought not to have been repaid).
Private Medical Insurance (Disentitlement to Tax Relief and Approved Benefits) Regulations, SI 1994/1518 reg 5 (adaptation of this section for the recovery of tax from payee of premium).
Lloyd's Underwriters (Tax) Regulations, SI 1995/351 regs 5, 6 (certain assessments relating to payments from stop-loss insurance on Lloyd's underwriters not to be out of time if made before the end of the following underwriting year, notwithstanding sub-s (5) above).
FA 2000 s 46(2) (exemption under FA 2000 s 46(1) for income of a charity is not granted in respect of income chargeable to tax under Schedule D Case VI by virtue of this section).
Amendments—[1] This section substituted by FA 1982 s 149(1).
[2] Words in sub-ss (2)(*a*), (3)(*a*) substituted by TA 1988 Sch 29 para 32 Table.
[3] Words in sub-s (6) substituted for the words ''sections 36, 37 and 39'' by FA 1989 s 149(3)(*a*).
[4] Sub-s (1A) inserted by FA 1990 s 105 and applies to tax repaid after 25 July 1990.
[5] Words in sub-ss (2)(*a*), (3)(*a*) substituted by TCGA 1992 Sch 10 para 2(1), (6).
[6] Sub-ss (2A), (3A), (4A) inserted by F(No 2)A 1987 s 88 and has effect with respect to recovery of repayments of corporation tax paid for accounting periods ending after 30 September 1993, recovery of repayments of income tax on payments received by a company in accounting periods ending after 30 September 1993 and recovery of interest on such repayments by virtue of Corporation Tax Acts (Provisions for Payment of Tax and Returns) (Appointed Days) Order, SI 1992/3066 art 2.
[7] Words in sub-s (4) added by F(No 2)A 1987 s 88 and has effect with respect to recovery of repayments of corporation tax paid for accounting periods ending after 30 September 1993, recovery of repayments of income tax on payments received by a company in accounting periods ending after 30 September 1993 and recovery of interest on such repayments by virtue of Corporation Tax Acts (Provisions for Payment of Tax and Returns) (Appointed Days) Order, SI 1992/3066 art 2.
[8] Words in sub-ss (2A), (3A) substituted by TA 1988 Sch 29 para 10(3).
[9] Words in sub-s (1B) inserted and sub-s (5) substituted by FA 1994 ss 196, 199 and Sch 19 para 4 with effect from the year 1996–97 as respects income tax and capital gains tax and, as respects corporation tax, with effect in relation to accounting periods ending after 30 June 1999 (by virtue of Finance Act 1994, Section 199, (Appointed Day) Order, SI 1998/3173 art 2).
[10] Words in sub-ss (2)(*a*), (3) and sub-ss (2A), (3A), (4A) repealed and words in sub-ss (1), (4) and (5)(*a*) substituted by FA 1998 Sch 19 para 13, Sch 27 Part III(28) with effect in relation to accounting periods ending after 30 June 1999 (by virtue of SI 1998/3173 art 2).
[11] In sub-s (5)(*b*), the words '', or an amendment of such a return,'' repealed, ''28A(1)'' substituted for ''28A(5)'', and words substituted for the words ''the officer's enquiries are treated as'', by FA 2001 ss 88, 110, Sch 29 para 23, Sch 33 Pt II(13) with effect from the passing of FA 2001 in relation to returns whether made before or after the passing of FA 2001, and whether relating to periods before or after the passing of FA 2001.

[30A Assessing procedure

(1) Except as otherwise provided, all assessments to tax which are not self-assessments shall be made by an officer of the Board.

(2) All income tax which falls to be charged by an assessment which is not a self-assessment may, notwithstanding that it was chargeable under more than one Schedule, be included in one assessment.

(3) Notice of any such assessment shall be served on the person assessed and shall state the date on which it is issued and the time within which any appeal against the assessment may be made.

(4) After the notice of any such assessment has been served on the person assessed, the assessment shall not be altered except in accordance with the express provisions of the Taxes Acts.

(5) Assessments to tax which under any provision in the Taxes Acts are to be made by the Board shall be made in accordance with this section.][1]

Commentary—*Simon's Direct Tax Service* E1.815.
Definitions—"the Board", s 118(1); "the Taxes Acts", s 118(1).
Amendments—[1] This section inserted by FA 1994 ss 196, 199 and Sch 19 para 5 with effect from the year 1996–97 as respects income tax and capital gains tax, and as respects corporation tax, with effect in relation to accounting periods ending after 30 June 1999 (by virtue of Finance Act 1994, Section 199, (Appointed Day) Order, SI 1998/3173 art 2), but so far as it relates to partnerships commenced before 6 April 1994, it has effect from the year 1997–98.

[30B Amendment of partnership statement where loss of tax discovered

(1) Where an officer of the Board or the Board discover, as regards a partnership statement made by any person (the representative partner) in respect of any period—

(a) that any profits which ought to have been included in the statement have not been so included, or

(b) that an amount of profits so included is or has become insufficient, or

(c) that any relief [or allowance][2] claimed by the representative partner is or has become excessive,

the officer or, as the case may be, the Board may, subject to subsections (3) and (4) below, by notice to that partner so [amend the partnership return][4] as to make good the omission or deficiency or eliminate the excess.

[(2) Where a partnership return is amended under subsection (1) above, the officer shall by notice to each of the relevant partners amend—

(a) the partner's return under section 8 or 8A of this Act, or

(b) the partner's company tax return,

so as to give effect to the amendments of the partnership return.][4]

(3) Where the situation mentioned in subsection (1) above is attributable to an error or mistake as to the basis on which the partnership statement ought to have been made, no amendment shall be made under that subsection if that statement was in fact made on the basis or in accordance with the practice generally prevailing at the time when it was made.

(4) No amendment shall be made under subsection (1) above unless one of the two conditions mentioned below is fulfilled.

(5) The first condition is that the situation mentioned in subsection (1) above is attributable to fraudulent or negligent conduct on the part of—

(a) the representative partner or a person acting on his behalf, or

(b) a relevant partner or a person acting on behalf of such a partner.

(6) The second condition is that at the time when an officer of the Board—

(a) ceased to be entitled to give notice of his intention to enquire into the representative partner's [partnership return][4]; or

(b) informed that partner that he had completed his enquiries into that return,

the officer could not have been reasonably expected, on the basis of the information made available to him before that time, to be aware of the situation mentioned in subsection (1) above.

(7) Subsections (6) and (7) of section 29 of this Act apply for the purposes of subsection (6) above as they apply for the purposes of subsection (5) of that section; and those subsections as so applied shall have effect as if—

(a) any reference to the taxpayer were a reference to the representative partner;

(b) any reference to the taxpayer's return under [section 8 or 8A][3] were a reference to the representative partner's [partnership return][4]; and

(c) sub-paragraph (ii) of paragraph (a) of subsection (7) were omitted.][3]

(8) An objection to the making of an amendment under subsection (1) above on the ground that neither of the two conditions mentioned above is fulfilled shall not be made otherwise than on an appeal against the amendment.

(9) In this section—

["profits"—

(a) in relation to income tax, means income,

(b) in relation to capital gains tax, means chargeable gains, and

(c) in relation to corporation tax, means profits as computed for the purposes of that tax;][3]

"relevant partner" means a person who was a partner at any time during the period in respect of which the partnership statement was made.

(10) Any reference in this section to the representative partner includes, unless the context otherwise requires, a reference to any successor of his.]¹

Commentary—*Simon's Direct Tax Service* E1.216, 813.
Revenue Internal Guidance—Enquiry Handbook EH 796 (reasons for discovery assessment to be given).
EH 804 (protective amendments to partners' self-assessments may be made whilst enquiries into partnership are in progress).
EH 809 (determination of appeal against discovery assessment on partner does not preclude the Revenue from making consequential amendments to self-assessments under sub-s (2)).
Definitions—"Act", s 118(1); "the Board", s 118(1); "profits", s 29 by virtue of s 30B(9); "relevant partner" s 30B(9).
Cross references—See TMA 1970 s 31(1), (1AA) (right of appeal against amendments to a partnership statement made under sub-s (1) above).
TMA 1970 ss 46B, 46C (certain questions in dispute on an appeal against an amendment under sub-s (1) above to be determined by the Special Commissioners).
TMA 1970 s 46D (questions as to the value of land in relation to the taxation of chargeable gains in dispute on an appeal against an amendment under sub-s (1) above to be determined by the Lands Tribunal).
Amendments—¹ This section inserted by FA 1994 ss 196, 199 and Sch 19 para 6 with effect from the year 1996–97 as respects income tax and capital gains tax and, as respects corporation tax, with effect in relation to accounting periods ending after 30 June 1999 (by virtue of Finance Act 1994, Section 199, (Appointed Day) Order, SI 1998/3173 art 2).
² Words in sub-s (1)(*c*) inserted by FA 1995 s 115(5), with effect from the year 1996–97 as respects income tax and capital gains tax and, as respects corporation tax, for accounting periods ending after 30 June 1999 (by virtue of SI 1998/3173 art 2).
³ Words in sub-ss (7)(*b*), (9) substituted by FA 1998 Sch 19 para 14 with effect in relation to accounting periods ending after 30 June 1999 (by virtue of SI 1998/3173 art 2).
⁴ Words in sub-s (1) substituted for the words "amend the statement", sub-s (2) substituted; and in sub-ss (6)(*a*), (7)(*b*), words substituted for the words "return under section 12AA of this Act", by FA 2001 s 88, Sch 29 para 24 with effect from the passing of FA 2001 in relation to returns whether made before or after the passing of FA 2001, and whether relating to periods before or after the passing of FA 2001. Sub-s (2) previously read as follows—

"(2) Where a partnership statement is amended under subsection (1) above, the officer shall by notice to each of the relevant partners amend—

    (*a*) the partner's self-assessment under section 9 of this Act, or
    (*b*) the partner's company tax return,

so as to give effect to the amendments of the partnership statement."

[31 Appeals: right of appeal

(1) An appeal may be brought against—

    (*a*) any amendment of a self-assessment under section 9C of this Act (amendment by Revenue during enquiry to prevent loss of tax),
    (*b*) any conclusion stated or amendment made by a closure notice under section 28A or 28B of this Act (amendment by Revenue on completion of enquiry into return),
    (*c*) any amendment of a partnership return under section 30B(1) of this Act (amendment by Revenue where loss of tax discovered), or
    (*d*) any assessment to tax which is not a self-assessment.

(2) An appeal under subsection (1)(*a*) above against an amendment of a self-assessment made while an enquiry is in progress shall not be heard and determined until the enquiry is completed.

(3) A determination under section 9D or 12AE of this Act (choice between different Cases of Schedule D) may not be questioned on an appeal under this section.

(4) This section has effect subject to any express provision in the Taxes Acts, including in particular any provision making one kind of assessment conclusive in an appeal against another kind of assessment.]¹

Commentary—*Simon's Direct Tax Service* A3.503, 1636; D2.735, 736; E1.838.
Amendments—¹ Sections 31–31D substituted for s 31 by FA 2001 s 88, Sch 29 para 11 with effect for—

    (*a*) amendments of a self-assessment under TMA 1970 s 9C as inserted by FA 2001 Sch 29 para 4,
    (*b*) closure notices issued under TMA 1970 s 28A(1) or 28B(1) as substituted by FA 2001 Sch 29 paras 8, 9,
    (*c*) amendments of partnership returns under TMA 1970 s 30B(1) where notice of the amendment is issued after the passing of FA 2001, and
    (*d*) assessments to tax which are not self-assessments where the notice of the assessment is issued after the passing of FA 2001.
Previously s 31 read as follows—

"31 Right of appeal

(1) Subject to subsection (1A) below, an appeal may be brought against—

    (*a*) an amendment under section 28A(2) or (4) of this Act of a self-assessment, or
    (*aa*) a decision contained in a notice under section 28A(4A) of this Act disallowing a claim or election in whole or in part, or
    (*b*) an amendment under section 28B(3) or 30B(1) of this Act of a partnership statement, or
    (*c*) an assessment to tax which is not a self-assessment,

by a notice of appeal in writing given within 30 days after the date on which the notice of amendment, the notice under section 28A(4A) of this Act or, as the case may be, the notice of assessment was issued.

(1AA) The matters that may be questioned on any appeal against—

    (*a*) an amendment under subsection (2) or (4) of section 28A of this Act,
    (*b*) a decision contained in a notice under subsection (4A) of that section disallowing a claim or election in whole or in part, or
    (*c*) an amendment under section 28B(3) or 30B(1) of this Act,

do not include any determination made for the purposes of section 28A(7A)(*d*) or 28B(6A)(*d*) of this Act.

(1A) An appeal against an amendment under subsection (2) of section 28A of this Act of a self-assessment shall not be heard and determined before the officer who made the amendment gives notice under subsection (5) of that section that he has completed his enquiries.
(2) The notice of appeal shall be given to the officer of the Board by whom the notice of amendment or assessment was given.
(3) An appeal against an assessment made—

    (*a*) by the Board, or

(*b*) under section 350 of the principal Act,

shall be to the Special Commissioners.

(4) Subject to subsection (3) above the appeal shall be to the General Commissioners, except that the appellant may elect (in accordance with section 46(1) of this Act) to bring the appeal before the Special Commissioners instead of the General Commissioners.

(5) The notice of appeal shall specify the grounds of appeal, but on the hearing of the appeal the Commissioners may allow the appellant to put forward any ground not specified in the notice, and take it into consideration if satisfied that the omission was not wilful or unreasonable.

(5A) An election under subsection (4) above shall be disregarded if—

(*a*) the appellant and the inspector or other officer of the Board agree in writing, at any time before the determination of the appeal, that it is to be disregarded; or

(*b*) the General Commissioners have given a direction under subsection (5C) below and have not revoked it.

(5B) At any time before the determination of an appeal in respect of which an election has been made under subsection (4) above, the inspector or other officer of the Board after giving notice to the appellant may refer the election to the General Commissioners.

(5C) On any such reference the Commissioners shall, unless they are satisfied that the appellant has arguments to present or evidence to adduce on the merits of the appeal, direct that the election be disregarded.

(5D) If, at any time after the giving of a direction under subsection (5C) above (but before the determination of the appeal) the General Commissioners are satisfied that the appellant has arguments to present or evidence to adduce on the merits of the appeal, they shall revoke the direction.

(5E) Any decision to give a direction under subsection (5C) above or revoke such a direction under subsection (5D) above shall be final.

(6) This section has effect subject to any express provision in the Taxes Acts, including in particular any provision under which an appeal lies to the Special Commissioners to the exclusion of the General Commissioners, any provision transferring jurisdiction to some other tribunal, and any provision making one kind of assessment conclusive in an appeal against another kind of assessment.''

[31A Appeals: notice of appeal

(1) Notice of an appeal under section 31 of this Act must be given—

(*a*) in writing,
(*b*) within 30 days after the specified date,
(*c*) to the relevant officer of the Board.

(2) In relation to an appeal under section 31(1)(*a*) or (*c*) of this Act—

(*a*) the specified date is the date on which the notice of amendment was issued, and
(*b*) the relevant officer of the Board is the officer by whom the notice of amendment was given.

(3) In relation to an appeal under section 31(1)(*b*) of this Act—

(*a*) the specified date is the date on which the closure notice was issued, and
(*b*) the relevant officer of the Board is the officer by whom the closure notice was given.

(4) In relation to an appeal under section 31(1)(*d*) of this Act—

(*a*) the specified date is the date on which the notice of assessment was issued, and
(*b*) the relevant officer of the Board is the officer by whom the notice of assessment was given.

(5) The notice of appeal must specify the grounds of appeal.

(6) On the hearing of the appeal the Commissioners may allow the appellant to put forward grounds not specified in the notice, and take them into consideration, if satisfied that the omission was not wilful or unreasonable.][1]

Commentary—*Simon's Direct Tax Service* **E1.838.**
Amendments—[1] Sections 31–31D substituted for s 31 by FA 2001 s 88, Sch 29 para 11 with effect for—

(*a*) amendments of a self-assessment under TMA 1970 s 9C as inserted by FA 2001 Sch 29 para 4,
(*b*) closure notices issued under TMA 1970 s 28A(1) or 28B(1) as substituted by FA 2001 Sch 29 paras 8, 9,
(*c*) amendments of partnership returns under TMA 1970 s 30B(1) where notice of the amendment is issued after the passing of FA 2001, and
(*d*) assessments to tax which are not self-assessments where the notice of the assessment is issued after the passing of FA 2001.

[31B Appeals: appeals to General Commissioners

(1) An appeal under section 31(1) of this Act shall be to the General Commissioners, subject to—

(*a*) section 31C of this Act (appeals to be brought to Special Commissioners),
(*b*) any provision made by or under Part V of this Act, and
(*c*) any other provision of the Taxes Acts providing for an appeal to be brought to the Special Commissioners to the exclusion of the General Commissioners.

(2) Subsection (1) above has effect subject to any election under section 31D of this Act (election to take appeal to Special Commissioners).][1]

Commentary—*Simon's Direct Tax Service* **E1.839.**
Amendments—[1] Sections 31–31D substituted for s 31 by FA 2001 s 88, Sch 29 para 11 with effect for—

(*a*) amendments of a self-assessment under TMA 1970 s 9C as inserted by FA 2001 Sch 29 para 4,
(*b*) closure notices issued under TMA 1970 s 28A(1) or 28B(1) as substituted by FA 2001 Sch 29 paras 8, 9,
(*c*) amendments of partnership returns under TMA 1970 s 30B(1) where notice of the amendment is issued after the passing of FA 2001, and
(*d*) assessments to tax which are not self-assessments where the notice of the assessment is issued after the passing of FA 2001.

[31C Appeals: appeals to Special Commissioners

(1) Unless the Special Commissioners otherwise direct, an appeal under section 31(1)(*a*), (*b*) or (*c*) of this Act shall be to the Special Commissioners if—

(*a*) the appeal relates to a return in relation to which notice of enquiry has been given under section 9A(1) or 12AC(1) of this Act, and
(*b*) notice has been given under section 28ZA of this Act referring a question relating to the subject-matter of that enquiry to the Special Commissioners.

This applies even if the notice of referral was subsequently withdrawn.

(2) An appeal under section 31(1)(*d*) of this Act (appeal against assessment other than self-assessment) shall be to the Special Commissioners if the assessment was made—

(*a*) by the Board, or
(*b*) under section 350 of the principal Act.][1]

Commentary—*Simon's Direct Tax Service* E1.839.
Amendments—[1] Sections 31–31D substituted for s 31 by FA 2001 s 88, Sch 29 para 11 with effect for—

(*a*) amendments of a self-assessment under TMA 1970 s 9C as inserted by FA 2001 Sch 29 para 4,
(*b*) closure notices issued under TMA 1970 s 28A(1) or 28B(1) as substituted by FA 2001 Sch 29 paras 8, 9,
(*c*) amendments of partnership returns under TMA 1970 s 30B(1) where notice of the amendment is issued after the passing of FA 2001, and
(*d*) assessments to tax which are not self-assessments where the notice of the assessment is issued after the passing of FA 2001.

[31D Appeals: election to bring appeal before Special Commissioners

(1) The appellant may elect (in accordance with section 46(1) of this Act) to bring before the Special Commissioners an appeal under section 31(1) of this Act that would otherwise be to the General Commissioners.

(2) Any such election above shall be disregarded if—

(*a*) the appellant and the inspector or other officer of the Board agree in writing, at any time before the determination of the appeal, that it is to be disregarded, or
(*b*) the General Commissioners have given a direction under subsection (5) below and have not revoked it.

(3) Where an election has been made under subsection (1) above, the inspector or other officer of the Board may refer the election to the General Commissioners.

(4) A reference under subsection (3) above must be made—

(*a*) after giving notice to the appellant, and
(*b*) before the determination of the appeal in respect of which the election has been made.

(5) On a reference under subsection (3) above the Commissioners shall, unless they are satisfied that the appellant has arguments to present or evidence to adduce on the merits of the appeal, direct that the election be disregarded.

(6) If at any time after giving a direction under subsection (5) above (but before the determination of the appeal) the General Commissioners are satisfied that the appellant has arguments to present or evidence to adduce on the merits of the appeal, they shall revoke the direction.

(7) A decision to give or revoke a direction under subsection (5) above shall be final.][1]

Amendments—[1] Sections 31–31D substituted for s 31 by FA 2001 s 88, Sch 29 para 11 with effect for—

(*a*) amendments of a self-assessment under TMA 1970 s 9C as inserted by FA 2001 Sch 29 para 4,
(*b*) closure notices issued under TMA 1970 s 28A(1) or 28B(1) as substituted by FA 2001 Sch 29 paras 8, 9,
(*c*) amendments of partnership returns under TMA 1970 s 30B(1) where notice of the amendment is issued after the passing of FA 2001, and
(*d*) assessments to tax which are not self-assessments where the notice of the assessment is issued after the passing of FA 2001.

Relief for excessive assessments

32 Double assessment

(1) If on a claim made to the Board it appears to their satisfaction that a person has been assessed to tax more than once for the same cause and for the same chargeable period, they shall direct the whole, or such part of any assessment as appears to be an overcharge, to be vacated, and thereupon the same shall be vacated accordingly.

(2) An appeal on a claim under this section shall lie to any of the bodies of Commissioners having jurisdiction to hear an appeal against the assessment, or the later of the assessments, to which the claim relates.

Commentary—*Simon's Direct Tax Service* A3.1007.
Simon's Tax Cases—s 32(1), *Martin v O'Sullivan* [1984] STC 258; *Bye v Coren* [1985] STC 113; *Salt v Fernandez* [1998] STC (SCD) 176.
Cross references—FA 1995 Sch 21 para 3(1), (2) (this section has effect, in the case of partnerships commenced before 6 April 1994, as respects each partner and the year 1996–97, as if the partnership had not been assessed to income tax for that year).

33 Error or mistake

[(1) If a person who has paid income tax or capital gains tax under an assessment (whether a self-assessment or otherwise) alleges that the assessment was excessive by reason of some error or mistake in a return, he may by notice in writing at any time not later than five years after the 31st January next following the year of assessment to which the return relates, make a claim to the Board for relief.][5]

(2) On receiving the claim the Board shall inquire into the matter and shall, subject to the provisions of this section, give by way of repayment such relief ...[1] in respect of the error or mistake as is reasonable and just:

...[4]

[(2A) No relief shall be given under this section in respect of—

 (a) an error or mistake as to the basis on which the liability of the claimant ought to have been computed where the return was in fact made on the basis or in accordance with the practice generally prevailing at the time when it was made; or

 (b) an error or mistake in a claim which is included in the return.][4]

(3) In determining the claim the Board shall have regard to all the relevant circumstances of the case, and in particular shall consider whether the granting of relief would result in the exclusion from charge to tax of any part of the profits of the claimant, and for this purpose the Board may take into consideration the liability of the claimant and assessments made on him in respect of chargeable periods other than that to which the claim relates.

(4) If any appeal is brought from the decision of the Board on the claim the Special Commissioners shall hear and determine the appeal in accordance with the principles to be followed by the Board in determining claims under this section; and neither the appellant nor the Board shall be entitled to [appeal under section 56A of this Act against the determination of the Special Commissioners except][3] on a point of law arising in connection with the computation of profits.

[(4A) ...][2]

(5) In this section ''profits''—

 (a) in relation to income tax, means income[, and][4]

 (b) in relation to capital gains tax, means chargeable gains,

 (c) ...[5]

Commentary—*Simon's Direct Tax Service* A3.1001–1006; E1.834.

Revenue Interpretation RI 65—Taxpayer cannot claim relief under this section where the substantive point was squarely in issue in the process of reaching agreement and determining the appeal under TMA 1970 s 54.

RI 154—Where error or mistake claim made by partnership in respect of locum and fixed costs insurance policies, premiums and benefits on such policies held by *all* partners must be given the same treatment.

Revenue Internal Guidance—Inspector's manual IM 3750-3756 (explanation of the section).

IM 3753b (failure to give notice of expenditure on machinery and plant under FA 1994 s 118 cannot be remedied by an error or mistake claim).

Simon's Tax Cases—*R v Special Comrs, ex p Tracy* [1996] STC 34; *Salt v Fernandez* [1998] STC (SCD) 278.

s 33(1), *Marsden v Gustar (Inspector of Taxes)* [2000] STC (SCD) 371; *Wall v IRC* [2002] STC(SCD) 122.

s 33(2), (4), *Arranmore Investment Co Ltd v IRC* [1973] STC 195.

s 33(4), *Eagerpath Ltd v Edwards* [2001] STC 26, CA.

Definitions—''Chargeable gain'', TCGA 1992 s 15(2) by virtue of s 118(1); ''return'', s 118(1).

Cross references—See FA 1994 s 118(7) (no relief under this section in respect of error or mistake consisting of a failure to satisfy the relevant condition for notification of expenditure on machinery and plant));

Lloyd's Underwriters (Tax) (1992–93 to 1996–97) Regulations, SI 1995/352 (extension of time limit for a claim under this section by Lloyd's underwriter and spouse).

Amendments—[1] Words in sub-s (2) repealed by FA 1971 ss 37(2), 38 and Sch 14 Pt II, with effect from the year 1973–74.

[2] Inserted by the Development Land Tax Act 1976 s 41 Sch 8 para 5; repealed, in respect of any disposal taking place on or after 19 March 1985, by virtue of FA 1985 s 98(6) Sch 27 Pt X.

[3] Words in sub-s (4) substituted by the General and Special Commissioners (Amendment of Enactments) Regulations, SI 1994/1813 reg 2(1), Sch 1 paras 1, 2, with effect from 1 September 1994.

[4] Proviso to sub-s (2) repealed and sub-s (2A) inserted by FA 1994 ss 196, 199 and Sch 19 para 8(2) and Sch 26 Pt V(23) as respects assessments to income tax and capital gains tax with effect from the year 1996–97 and as respects assessments to corporation tax with effect in relation to accounting periods ending after 30 June 1999 (by virtue of Finance Act 1994, Section 199, (Appointed Day) Order, SI 1998/3173 art 2).

[5] Sub-s (1) substituted and words in sub-s (5)(a)(c) repealed by FA 1998 Sch 19 para 15 with effect in relation to accounting periods ending after 30 June 1999 (by virtue of SI 1998/3173 art 2).

[33A Error or mistake in [partnership return][4]

(1) This section applies where, in the case of a trade, profession or business carried on by two or more persons in partnership, those persons allege that the tax charged by self-assessments of theirs ...[3] was excessive by reason of some error or mistake in a [partnership return][4].

(2) One of those persons (the representative partner) may, not later than five years after the filing date, by notice in writing make a claim to the Board for relief.

(3) On receiving the claim the Board shall inquire into the matter and shall, subject to subsection (5) below, so amend the [partnership return][4] so as to give such relief in respect of the error or mistake as is reasonable or just.

[(4) Where a partnership return is amended under subsection (3) above, the Board shall by notice to each of the relevant partners amend—

 (a) the partner's return under section 8 or 8A of this Act, or (*b*) the partner's company tax return,

so as to give effect to the amendments of the partnership return.]⁴

(5) No relief shall be given under this section in respect of an error or mistake as to the basis on which the liability of the partners ought to have been computed where the [partnership return]⁴ was in fact made on the basis or in accordance with the practice generally prevailing at the time when it was made.

(6) In determining the claim the Board—

   (*a*) shall have regard to all the relevant circumstances of the case, and
   (*b*) in particular shall consider whether the granting of relief would result in the exclusion from charge to tax of any part of the profits of any of the partners;

and for the purposes of this subsection the Board may take into consideration the liability of the partners and their self-assessments in respect of chargeable periods other than that to which the claim relates.

(7) If any appeal is brought from the decision of the Board on the claim, the Special Commissioners shall hear and determine the appeal in accordance with the principles to be followed by the Board in determining claims under this section.

[(8) Subject to subsection (8A) below, the determination of the Special Commissioners of an appeal under subsection (6) above shall be final and conclusive (notwithstanding any provision having effect by virtue of section 56B of this Act).]²

[(8A) Subsection (8) above does not apply in relation to a point of law arising in connection with the computation of profits.]²

(9) In this section—

   "filing date" has the same meaning as in section 12AC of this Act;
   "profits" has the same meaning as in section 33 of this Act;
   "relevant partner" means a person who was a partner at any time during the period in respect of which the [partnership return]⁴ was made.

(10) Any reference in this section to the representative partner includes, unless the context otherwise requires, a reference to any successor of his.]¹

Commentary—*Simon's Direct Tax Service* E1.833, 834.
Definitions—"Act", s 118(1); "the Board", s 118(1); "filing date", s 12AC by virtue of s 33A(9); "profits", s 33 by virtue of s 33A(9); "relevant partner", s 33A(9); "Special Commissioners", s 4; "trade", s 118(1);
Amendments—¹ This section inserted by FA 1994 ss 196, 199 and Sch 19 para 9 with effect from the year 1996–97 as respects income tax and capital gains tax and, as respects corporation tax, with effect in relation to accounting periods ending after 30 June 1999 (by virtue of Finance Act 1994, Section 199, (Appointed Day) Order, SI 1998/3173 art 2).
² Sub-ss (8), (8A) substituted by FA 1996 Sch 22 para 5 with effect in relation to any proceedings relating to the year 1996–97 or any subsequent year of assessment and in relation to any proceedings relating to an accounting period ending after 30 June 1999 (by virtue of SI 1998/3173 art 2).
³ Words in sub-s (1) repealed by and sub-s (4) substituted by FA 1998 Sch 19 para 16 with effect in relation to accounting periods ending after 30 June 1999 (by virtue of SI 1998/3173 art 2).
⁴ Words in heading, sub-ss (1), (3), (5), and (9) substituted for "partnership statement"; and sub-s (4) substituted, by FA 2001 s 88, Sch 29 para 25 with effect from the passing of FA 2001 in relation to returns whether made before or after the passing of FA 2001, and whether relating to periods before or after the passing of FA 2001. Sub s (4) previously read as follows—

   "(4) Where a partnership statement is amended under subsection (3) above, the Board shall by notice to each of the relevant partners amend—

   (*a*) the partner's self-assessment under section 9 of this Act, or
   (*b*) the partner's company tax return,
   so as to give effect to the amendments of the partnership statement."

Time limits

34 Ordinary time limit of six years

(1) Subject to the following provisions of this Act, and to any other provisions of the Taxes Acts allowing a longer period in any particular class of case, [an assessment to income tax or capital gains tax may be made at any time not later than five years after the 31st January next following the year of assessment to which it relates]¹

(2) An objection to the making of any assessment on the ground that the time limit for making it has expired shall only be made on an appeal against the assessment.

Commentary—*Simon's Direct Tax Service* A3.220.
Simon's Tax Cases—*Johnson v IRC* [1978] STC 196; *Amoco (UK) Exploration Co v IRC* [1983] STC 634.
s 34(1), *Larter v Skone James* [1976] STC 220.
Definitions—"the Taxes Act", s 118(1).
Cross references—See TMA 1970 s 30(5) (time limit for assessments under s 30).
TMA 1970 s 40 (time limit for assessing executors or administrators of a deceased person).
TCGA 1992 s 248(2) (exclusion of time limit for assessment to recover rollover relief given in respect of proceeds from compulsory acquisition of land).
FA 1993 s 178(3) (Lloyd's underwriters: payment to a member in respect of his loss under a stop-loss insurance policy or out of High Level Stop Loss Fund: extension of time limit where inspector is not notified of such payment within specified period).
Amendments—¹ Words in sub-s (1) substituted by FA 1998 Sch 19 para 17 with effect in relation to accounting periods ending after 30 June 1999 (by virtue of Finance Act 1994, Section 199, (Appointed Day) Order, SI 1998/3173 art 2).

35 Emoluments received after year for which they are assessable

Commentary—*Simon's Direct Tax Service* A3.229.
Amendments—This section repealed by FA 1998 s 165, Sch 27 Part III(9) in relation to payments or other benefits received after 5 April 1998, except where the payment or other benefit or the right to receive it has been brought into charge to tax before 6 April 1998.

[36 Fraudulent or negligent conduct

(1) An assessment on any person (in this section referred to as "the person in default") for the purpose of making good to the Crown a [loss of income tax or capital gains tax][5] attributable to his fraudulent or negligent conduct or the fraudulent or negligent conduct of a person acting on his behalf may be made at any time [not later than 20 years after the 31st January next following the year of assessment to which it relates][5]

[(2) Where the person in default carried on a trade, profession or business with one or more other persons at any time in the period for which the assessment is made, an assessment in respect of the profits or gains of the trade, profession or business for the purpose mentioned in subsection (1) above may be made not only on the person in default but also on his partner or any of his partners.][4]

(3) If the person on whom the assessment is made so requires, in determining the amount of the tax to be charged for any chargeable period in any assessment made for the purpose mentioned in subsection (1) above, effect shall be given to any relief or allowance to which he would have been entitled for that chargeable period on a claim or application made within the time allowed by the Taxes Acts.][1]

[(3A) In subsection (3) above, "claim or application" does not include an election under section 257BA of the principal Act (elections as to transfer of married couple's allowance)][3] [or under Schedule 13B to that Act (elections as to transfer of children's tax credit).][6]

[(4) Any act or omission such as is mentioned in section 98B below on the part of a grouping (as defined in that section) or member of a grouping shall be deemed for the purposes of subsection (1) above to be the act or omission of each member of the grouping.][2][1]

Commentary—*Simon's Direct Tax Service* A3.222–225.
Revenue Interpretation RI 155—Sub-s (2) does *not* preserve "joint liability" to tax on partnership profits, but simply allows Revenue to assess each partner on his revised profit share.
Revenue Internal Guidance—Capital gains CG 13720-13761 (time limit for elections is not extended by sub-s (3)).
Investigation handbook IH 4111 (a claim under sub-s (3) can be made before the assessment is finally determined).
IH4114 (effect of a late claim under sub-s (3) for deduction for family wages).
Simon's Tax Cases—*Kovak v Morris* [1985] STC 183; *Verdon v Honour* [1988] STC 809; *Rochester (UK) Ltd v Pickin,* [1998] STC (SCD) 138; *Re McGuckian* [2000] STC 65; *Billows v Hammond* [2000] STC (SCD) 430; *Last Viceroy Restaurant (a firm) v Jackson (Inspector of Taxes)* [2000] STC 1093.
Definitions—"the principal Act", s 118(1); "the Taxes Act", s 118(1).
Cross references—See TMA 1970 s 40 (time limit for assessing executors or administrators of a deceased person).
TMA 1970 s 118(3) (effect of assessment made in partnership name).
IT (Entertainers and Sportsmen) Regulations, SI 1987/530 reg 11(2)(*b*) (application of this section to assessments under reg 11).
TA 1988 Sch 3 paras 6, 6E(2) (tax deducted at source by banks, etc from foreign dividends, interest, etc and not paid over to the Revenue in time; assessments treated as relating to the year of assessment in which the relevant return quarter ends),
TA 1988 Sch 16 para 10(1) (this section to apply as modified to assessments to recover income tax on company payments which are not accounted for),
IT (Manufactured Overseas Dividends) Regulations, SI 1993/2004 reg 11(7) (this section to apply as modified to assessments under reg 11 in relation to manufactured overseas dividends),
FA 1993 s 178(3) (Lloyd's underwriters: payment to a member in respect of his loss under a stop-loss insurance or out of High Level Stop Loss Fund: extension of time limit under this section for assessment or further assessment),
FA 1993 Sch 19 para 8 (Lloyd's underwriters: assessment of individual members: individual member's liability under this section for acts of syndicate's managing agent).
Amendments—[1] This section substituted by FA 1989 s 149(1), (7), but does not affect the making of assessments for years of assessment before 1983–84 or for accounting periods ending before 1 April 1983.
[2] Sub-s (4) added by FA 1990 Sch 11 paras 4(1), (5) with effect from 1 July 1989.
[3] Sub-s (3A) inserted by F(No 2)A 1992 Sch 5 paras 9(1), (2), 10 in relation to tax for the year 1993–94 and subsequent years.
[4] Words in sub-s (1), and whole of sub-s (2), substituted by FA 1994 ss 196, 199 and Sch 19 para 11 with effect, as respects income tax and capital gains tax assessments, from the year 1996–97 and as respects corporation tax assessments, with effect in relation to accounting periods ending after 30 June 1999 (by virtue of Finance Act 1994, Section 199, (Appointed Day) Order, SI 1998/3173 art 2).
[5] Words in sub-s (1) substituted by FA 1998 Sch 19 para 18 with effect in relation to accounting periods ending after 30 June 1999 (by virtue of SI 1998/3173 art 2).
[6] Words in sub-s (3A) inserted by FA 1999 s 30(4), (5) with effect from the year 2001–02.

37 Neglect: income tax and capital gains tax

Commentary—*Simon's Direct Tax Service* A3.223.
Amendments—This section repealed by FA 1989 s 149(2), (7) and Sch 17 Pt VIII without affecting the making of assessments for years of assessment before 1983–84 or for accounting periods ending before 1 April 1983.

[37A Effect of assessment where allowances transferred

Where an assessment is made on any person for the purpose of making good a loss of tax wholly or partly attributable to [fraudulent or negligent conduct][2], the fact that the person's [liability to income tax or][4] total income for any year of assessment is assessed as greater than it was previously taken to be shall not affect the validity of [any income tax reduction or deduction from total income made in the case of that person's spouse][5] [or partner][7] by virtue of section [257BB][3] ...[6] or 265 of the principal Act [or paragraph 4 of Schedule 13B to that Act][7]; [and the entitlement in that case of the first-mentioned person for the year in question to any income tax reduction or deduction from total income shall be treated as correspondingly reduced][5].][1]

Commentary—*Simon's Direct Tax Service* A3.228.
Amendments—[1] This section inserted by FA 1988 Sch 3 para 30 with effect from the year 1990–91.
[2] Words substituted by FA 1989 s 149(4)(*a*)(i).
[3] "257BB" substituted by F(No 2)A 1992 Sch 5 paras 9(1), (3), 10 in relation to tax for the year 1993–94 and subsequent years.
[4] Words inserted by FA 1994 s 77(7) and Sch 8 para 13 with effect from the year 1994–95.
[5] Words substituted by FA 1994 s 77(7) and Sch 8 para 13 with effect from the year 1994–95.
[6] Word repealed by FA 1999 s 139, Sch 20 Pt III(3) with effect from the year 2000–01.
[7] Words inserted by FA 1999 s 30(4), (5) with effect from the year 2001–02.

38 Modification of s 37 in relation to partnerships

Commentary—*Simon's Direct Tax Service* A3.226.
Amendments—This section repealed by FA 1989 s 149(2), (7) and Sch 17 Pt VIII without affecting the making of assessments for years of assessment before 1983–84 or for accounting periods ending before 1 April 1983.

39 Neglect: corporation tax

Commentary—*Simon's Direct Tax Service* A3.226.
Amendments—This section repealed by FA 1989 s 149(2), (7) and Sch 17 Pt VIII without affecting the making of assessments for years of assessment before 1983–84 or for accounting periods ending before 1 April 1983.

40 Assessment on personal representatives

(1) For the purpose of the charge of tax on the executors or administrators of a deceased person in respect of the income, or chargeable gains, which arose or accrued to him before his death, the time allowed by section 34, 35 or 36 above shall in no case extend beyond the end of [the period of three years beginning with the 31st January next following the year of assessment][5] in which the deceased died.

(2) ...[2], for the purpose of making good to the Crown any loss of tax attributable to the [fraudulent or negligent conduct][3] of a person who has died, an assessment on his personal representatives to tax for any year of assessment ending not earlier than six years before his death may be made at any time before the end of [the period of three years beginning with the 31st January next following the year of assessment][5] in which he died.

(3) In [this section][1] "tax" means income tax or capital gains tax.

[(4) Any act or omission such as is mentioned in section 98B below on the part of a grouping (as defined in that section) or member of a grouping shall be deemed for the purposes of subsection (2) above to be the act or omission of each member of the grouping.][4]

Commentary—*Simon's Direct Tax Service* A3.227, 1682.
Revenue Internal Guidance—Enquiry Handbook EH 577 (in the case of a director, the Revenue will review the company's affairs; the time limit in sub-s (1) does not apply to the company).
EH 820–823 (the time limits under s 40 apply, in particular, to consequential amendments under s 30B(2) to the self-assessment of deceased partners in partnerships, but does not affect the time limit for amending the partnership statement).
Simon's Tax Cases—s 40(1), *Larter v Skone James* [1976] STC 220; *Honig v Sarsfield* [1986] STC 246.
Definitions—"Chargeable gain", TCGA 1992 s 15(2) by virtue of s 118(1); "year of assessment", TA 1988 s 832(1).
Cross references—See FA 1993 s 178(3) (Lloyd's underwriters: payment to a member in respect of his loss under a stop-loss insurance policy or out of High Level Stop Loss Fund: extension of time limit under this section for assessment or further assessment).
FA 1993 Sch 19 para 8 (acts or omissions of underwriting syndicate's managing agent treated as acts or omissions of each member for the purposes of this section).
Amendments—[1] Words in sub-s (3) substituted by FA 1985 s 93(7), Sch 25 Pt II para 5.
[2] Words in sub-s (2) repealed by FA 1989 Sch 17 Pt VIII.
[3] Words in sub-s (2) substituted by FA 1989 s 149(4)(*a*)(ii), (7).
[4] Sub-s (4) inserted by FA 1990 Sch 11 paras 4(2), 5 with effect from 1 July 1989.
[5] Words in sub-ss (1), (2) substituted by FA 1994 ss 196, 199(1), (2)(*a*) and Sch 19 para 12 with effect from the year 1996–97.

41 Leave of General or Special Commissioners required for certain assessments

Commentary—*Simon's Direct Tax Service* A3.222, 223.
Amendments—This section repealed by FA 1989 s 149(2), (7) and Sch 17 Pt VIII without affecting the making of assessments for years of assessment before 1983–84 or for accounting periods ending before 1 April 1983.

Corporation tax determinations

41A Determination procedure

Commentary—*Simon's Direct Tax Service* D2.720.
Amendments—This section repealed by FA 1998 Sch 19 para 19, Sch 27 Part III(28) with effect in relation to accounting periods ending after 30 June 1999 (by virtue of Finance Act 1994, Section 199, (Appointed Day) Order, SI 1998/3173 art 2).

41B Reduction of determination

Commentary—*Simon's Direct Tax Service* D2.720.
Amendments—This section repealed by FA 1998 Sch 19 para 19, Sch 27 Part III(28) with effect in relation to accounting periods ending after 30 June 1999 (by virtue of Finance Act 1994, Section 199, (Appointed Day) Order, SI 1998/3173 art 2).

41C Time limits

Commentary—*Simon's Direct Tax Service* **D2.720.**
Amendments—This section repealed by FA 1998 Sch 19 para 19, Sch 27 Part III(28) with effect in relation to accounting periods ending after 30 June 1999 (by virtue of Finance Act 1994, Section 199, (Appointed Day) Order, SI 1998/3173 art 2).

Claims

[42 Procedure for making claims etc

(1) Where any provision of the Taxes Acts provides for relief to be given, or any other thing to be done, on the making of a claim, this section shall, unless otherwise provided, have effect in relation to the claim.

[(1A) Subject to subsection (3) below, a claim for a relief, an allowance or a repayment of tax shall be for an amount which is quantified at the time when the claim is made.][3]

(2) Subject to [subsections (3) and (3A)][4] below, where notice has been given under section 8, 8A ...[5] or 12AA of this Act, a claim shall not at any time be made otherwise than by being included in a return under that section if it could, at that or any subsequent time, be made by being so included.

(3) [Subsections (1A) and (2)][4] above shall not apply in relation to any claim which falls to be taken into account in the making of deductions or repayments of tax under section 203 of the principal Act.

(3A), (3B) ...[10]

(4)–(4A) ...[5]

(5) The references in [this section][6] to a claim being included in a return include references to a claim being so included by virtue of an amendment of the return; ...[5]

(6) In the case of a trade, profession or business carried on by persons in partnership, a claim under any of the provisions mentioned in subsection (7) below shall be made—

(a) where subsection (2) above applies, by being included in a [partnership return][22], and
(b) in any other case, by such one of those persons as may be nominated by them for the purpose.

(7) The provisions are—

(a) [sections ...,[11] 84][7], 91B, 101(2), ...[18] , ...[11] 471, 472, ...[16], 504, 531, ...[17], 570, 571(4), ...[19], 723(3), 732(4), ...[20] of, and paragraphs 2, 6 and 11 of Schedule 5 to, the principal Act;
(b) section 43(5) of the Finance Act 1989;
[(c) sections 3, 83, 89, 129, 131, 135, 177, 183, 266, 268, 290, 355, 381 and 569 of the Capital Allowances Act; and][21]
[(d) sections 40B(5), 40D, 41 and 42 of the Finance (No 2) Act 1992.][21]

(8) A claim may be made on behalf of an incapacitated person by his trustee, guardian, tutor or curator; and a person who under Part VIII of this Act has been charged with tax on the profits of another person may make any such claim for relief by discharge or repayment of that tax.

(9) Where a claim has been made (whether by being included in a return under section 8, 8A, ...[5] or 12AA of this Act or otherwise) and the claimant subsequently discovers that an error or mistake has been made in the claim, the claimant may make a supplementary claim within the time allowed for making the original claim.

(10) This section [(except subsection (1A) above)][8] shall apply in relation to any elections ...[12] as it applies in relation to claims.

(11) Schedule 1A to this Act shall apply as respects any claim [or election][13] which—

(a) is made otherwise than by being included in a return under section 8, 8A, ...[5] or 12AA of this Act, ...[9]

[(11A) Schedule 1B to this Act shall have effect as respects certain claims for relief involving two or more years of assessment.][14]

(12) ...[15]

(13) In this section "profits"—

(a) in relation to income tax, means income, [and][5]
(b) in relation to capital gains tax, means chargeable gains, and
(c) ...[5]][1]

Commentary—*Simon's Direct Tax Service* **A3.606, 620.**
Concession C20—Claims to group relief in the form determined under sub-s (5) above may be signed by a person authorised by the claimant company as an alternative to the company secretary.
Statement of Practice SP A13—Declarations and returns under sub-s (5) of old and infirm persons may be signed by their attorneys who have full knowledge of their tax affairs.
SP 8/91, para 12—Discovery assessments; specific agreement: non-appeal cases.
Revenue Interpretation RI 48—Retrospective reduction(s) in CGT rate(s) applicable to individuals caused, for example, by terminal loss relief; claims for repayment of overpaid CGT by way of appeal under s 31 of this Act or alternatively under sub-s (7) above.
Revenue & other press releases—IR 30–3–88 (Revenue practice interim repayment claims: repayments are not made where the amount is £50 or less).
Code of Practice 1 (claims arising out of Inland Revenue error: delay in replying to letters or processing information: serious and persistent errors).

IR Tax Bulletin August 1995 p 246 (when making repayment claims, vouchers must be submitted to cover unused lower rate tax band income as well as income covered by personal allowances).

IR Tax Bulletin October 1996 p 350 (discusses claims given effect in PAYE codings under self-assessment).

Revenue Internal Guidance—Capital allowances manual CA 11120 (this section does not apply to capital allowances claimed in a return: it does apply to claims for plant and machinery allowances for special leasing; claims by mining concerns to carry back balancing allowances and in income tax cases, claims for patent allowances on non-trading expenditure).

Capital Gains manual CG 13720 (distinction between a claim and an election).

CG 13800–13812 (Revenue practice regarding late claims and elections).

CG 13850–13861 (withdrawal of claims and elections).

Claims manual RM 1000–1286 (Revenue procedure for dealing with repayment claims).

RM 1548–1600 (repayment claims: death of taxpayer: procedure for dealing with repayments after death).

RM 2584–2636 (repayment claims: repayment supplement; set off against other liabilities).

Enquiry Handbook EH 932, EH 933 (examples illustrating when claim can and cannot be made in a return).

Simon's Tax Cases—s 42(5), *Gallic Leasing Ltd v Coburn* [1991] STC 151.

Definitions—"Chargeable gain", TCGA 1992 s 15(2) by virtue of s 118(1);"company", s 118(1);"incapacitated person", s 118(1);"principal Act", s 118(1);"return", s 118(1);"the Taxes Acts", s 118(1);"trade", s 118(1).

Cross references—See TMA 1970 Sch 1B para 2(2) (sub-s (2) above not to apply to claims for losses incurred or payments made in one year to be given in an earlier year).

IT (Life Assurance Premium Relief) Regulations, SI 1978/1159 reg 10(1) (disapplication of this section to claims under these regulations by life office in respect of tax deducted at source from premiums);

IT (Interest Relief) Regulations, SI 1982/1236 reg 8A(2) (disapplication of this section to borrower's claim for payment of tax he has been unable to deduct from interest payments under MIRAS);

SI 1982/1236 reg 14(1) (disapplication of this section to lenders' claims in respect of tax deducted at source from interest payments under MIRAS);

IT (Entertainers and Sportsmen) Regulations, SI 1987/530 reg 13(2) (application of this section to claims under these regulations that tax payments have been excessive);

Occupational Pension Schemes (Additional Voluntary Contributions) Regulations, SI 1987/1749 reg 9(1) (disapplication of this section to claims under these regulations by administrators in respect of tax deducted at source from additional voluntary contributions);

Personal Pension Schemes (Relief at Source) Regulations, SI 1988/1013 reg 11(1) (disapplication of this section to claims under these regulations by administrators in respect of tax deducted at source from employees' personal pension contributions);

TA 1988 Sch 19AB para 1(6) (disapplication of this section to claims for provisional repayments of tax credits and deducted tax by an insurance company carrying on pension business).

TA 1988 Sch 19AB paras 1(7), 5(5) (insurance company carrying on pension business: provisional repayments of tax credits and tax deducted from payments received by the company to count as payments on account towards claims under sub-s (4) above);

Personal Equity Plan Regulations, SI 1989/469 reg 21(1) (disapplication of this section to claims under these regulations by plan managers for repayments of tax).

FA 1993 s 194(4) (modification of this section as regards claims for relief from double taxation in relation to petroleum revenue tax);

FA 1994 s 118(7) (no relief under this section in respect of error or mistake consisting of a failure to satisfy the relevant condition for notification of expenditure on machinery and plant).

FA 1998 Sch 18 (company tax returns, assessments and related matters in respect of accounting periods ending after 30 June 1999).

Amendments—[1] This section substituted by FA 1994 ss 196, 199 and Sch 19 para 13 with effect, as respects relief claims for income tax and capital gains tax, from the year 1996–97 and as respects relief claims for corporation tax, with effect in relation to accounting periods ending after 30 June 1999 (by virtue of Finance Act 1994, Section 199, (Appointed Day) Order, SI 1998/3173 art 2).

[2] Words in sub-s (7) inserted by FA 1995 s 97(2) with effect from the same dates as referred to in note [1].

[3] Sub-s (1A) inserted by FA 1995 s 107(1) with effect from the same dates as referred to in note [1].

[4] Words in sub-ss (2), (3) substituted by FA 1995 s 107(2), (3) with effect from the same dates as referred to in note [1].

[5] Words in sub-ss (2), (5), (9), and (11)(a), and sub-ss (4), (4A) and (13)(c) repealed, and words in sub-s (13)(a) inserted, by FA 1998 Sch 19 para 20 with effect in relation to accounting periods ending after 30 June 1999 (by virtue of SI 1998/3173 art 2). Sub-ss (4), (4A) also repealed, and sub-s (5) also amended, by F(No 2)A 1997 s 34, Sch 4 para 3, Sch 8 Pt II(9) with effect in relation to tax credits in respect of distributions made after 5 April 1999 for accounting periods ending after 30 June 1999.

[6] Sub-s (5) words substituted by FA 1995 s 107(7) with effect from the same dates as referred to in note [1].

[7] Sub-s (7)(a) words substituted by FA 1995 s 107(8) with effect from the same dates as referred to in note [1].

[8] Sub-s (10) words inserted by FA 1995 s 107(9) with effect from the same dates as referred to in note [1].

[9] Sub-s (11) words omitted repealed by FA 1995 s 107(10), Sch 29 Pt VIII(14) with effect from the same dates as referred to in note [1].

[10] Sub-ss (3A), (3B) (inserted by FA 1995 s 107(4)) repealed by FA 1996 s 128(1)(a), Sch 41 Pt V(6) with effect as respects claims made (or deemed to be made) from the year 1996–97.

[11] Words omitted from sub-s (7)(a) repealed by FA 1996 s 130(2), Sch 41 Pt V(7) with effect from the same dates as referred to in note [1].

[12] Words omitted from sub-s (10) repealed by FA 1996 s 130(3), Sch 41 Pt V(7) with effect from the same dates as referred to in note [1].

[13] Words "or election" in sub-s (11) substituted for the words "election or notice" by FA 1996 s 130(4) with effect from the same dates as referred to in note [1].

[14] Sub-s (11A) inserted by FA 1996 s 128(1)(c) with effect as respects claims made (or deemed to be made) from the year 1996–97.

[15] Sub-s (12) repealed by FA 1996 Sch 22 para 6, Sch 41 Pt V(12) with effect in relation to any proceedings relating to the year 1996–97 or any subsequent year of assessment and in relation to any proceedings relating to an accounting period ending on or after the appointed day (see note [1]).

[16] Number "484" omitted from sub-s (7)(a) repealed by FA 1996 Sch 41 Pt V(3) with effect from the year 1996–97 as respects income tax and, for the purposes of corporation tax, in relation to accounting periods ending after 31 March 1996, subject to transitional provisions in FA 1996 Sch 15.

[17] Words in sub-s (7)(a) repealed by FA 1996 s 128(1)(b), Sch 41 Pt V(6) with effect as respects claims made from the year 1997-1998.

[18] Words in sub-s (7)(a) repealed by FA 1997 s 113, Sch 17 Pt VI(2) with effect in relation to payments made after 5 April 1997.

[19] Words in sub-s (7)(a) repealed by FA 1998 s 165, Sch 27 Pt III(4) with effect for the year 1998-99 and subsequent years of assessment, and for corporation tax from 1 April 1998.

[20] Words in sub-s (7)(a) repealed by FA 2000 s 156, Sch 40 Pt II(13) with effect for claims made after 31 March 2000.

[21] Sub-ss (7)(c), (d) substituted by CAA 2001 s 578, Sch 2 para 1 with effect for income tax purposes, as respects allowances and charges falling to be made for chargeable periods ending after 5 April 2001, and for corporation tax purposes, as respects allowances and charges falling to be made for chargeable periods ending after 31 March 2001.

[22] Words in sub-s (6)(a) substituted for the words "return under section 12AA of this Act" by FA 2001 s 88, Sch 29 para a 26 with effect from the passing of FA 2001 in relation to returns whether made before or after the passing of FA 2001, and whether relating to periods before or after the passing of FA 2001.

43 Time limit for making claims

[(1) Subject to any provision of the Taxes Acts prescribing a longer or shorter period, no claim for relief in respect of income tax or capital gains tax may be made more than five years after the 31st January next following the year of assessment to which it relates.][1]

(2) A claim (including a supplementary claim) which could not have been allowed but for the making of an assessment to income tax or capital gains tax after the year of assessment to which the claim relates may be made at any time before the end of the year of assessment following that in which the assessment was made.

Commentary—*Simon's Direct Tax Service* **A3.620; E1.835.**
Concession B41—Claims to repayment of tax outside statutory time limits.
Statements of Practice SP 3/86—Relaxation of the time limit under this section in claims for relief from UK tax under double taxation agreements for payments to non-residents from UK discretionary trusts or UK estates.
Revenue & other press releases—ICAEW TR760 6–9–1989 (an election must be received by the Revenue. It will be accepted as having been received within the time limit if it is posted in reasonable expectation that it will be received in time).
Simon's Tax Cases—*Orakpo v Lane* [1996] STC (SCD) 43.
Cross references—See TA 1988 Sch 26 para 1(6) (application of this section to claims for group relief or relief for trading losses by UK controlled foreign companies);
FA 1993 s 194(4) (modification of this section as regards claims for relief from double taxation in relation to petroleum revenue tax).
Amendments—[1] Sub-s (1) substituted by FA 1998 Sch 19 para 21 with effect in relation to accounting periods ending after 30 June 1999 (by virtue of Finance Act 1994, Section 199, (Appointed Day) Order, SI 1998/3173 art 2).

[43A Further assessments: claims etc

(1) This section applies where—

    [(a) ...[4] by virtue of section 29 of this Act an assessment to income tax or capital gains tax is made on any person for a year of assessment, and][3]
    (b) the assessment is not made for the purpose of making good to the Crown any loss of tax attributable to his fraudulent or negligent conduct or the fraudulent or negligent conduct of a person acting on his behalf.

(2) Without prejudice to section 43(2) above but subject to section 43B below, where this section applies—

    (a) any relevant claim, election, application or notice which could have been made or given within the time allowed by the Taxes Acts may be made or given at any time within one year from the end of the [year of assessment][3] in which the assessment is made, and
    (b) any relevant claim, election, application or notice previously made or given may at any such time be revoked or varied—
        (i) in the same manner as it was made or given, and
        (ii) by or with the consent of the same person or persons who made, gave or consented to it (or, in the case of any such person who has died, by or with the consent of his personal representatives),

    except where by virtue of any enactment it is irrevocable.

[(2A) In subsection (2) above, ''claim, election, application or notice'' does not include an election under section 257BA of the principal Act (election as to transfer of married couple's allowance)][2] [or under Schedule 13B to that Act (elections as to transfer of children's tax credit).][5]

(3) For the purposes of this section and section 43B below, a claim, election, application or notice is relevant in relation to an assessment for a [year of assessment][3] if—

    (a) it relates to that [year of assessment][3] or is made or given by reference to an event occurring in that [year of assessment][3], and
    (b) it or, as the case may be, its revocation or variation has or could have the effect of reducing any of the liabilities mentioned in subsection (4) below.

(4) The liabilities referred to in subsection (3) above are—

    (a) the increased liability to tax resulting from the assessment,
    (b) any other liability to tax of the person concerned for—
        (i) the [year of assessment][3] to which the assessment relates, or
        (ii) any [year of assessment][3] which follows that [year of assessment][3] and ends not later than one year after the end of the [year of assessment][3] in which the assessment is made.

(5) Where a claim, election, application or notice is made, given, revoked or varied by virtue of subsection (2) above, all such adjustments shall be made, whether by way of discharge or repayment of tax or the making of assessments or otherwise, as are required to take account of the effect of the taking of that action on any person's liability to tax for any [year of assessment][3].

(6) The provisions of this Act relating to appeals against decisions on claims shall apply with any necessary modifications to a decision on the revocation or variation of a claim by virtue of subsection (2) above.][1]

Commentary—*Simon's Direct Tax Service* **A3.620.**
Concession B41—Claims to repayment of tax outside statutory time limit.
Statement of practice—Corporation tax pay and file—circumstances in which the Board will extend the time limit for making a claim.
Definitions—''the Taxes Acts'', s 118(1).

Amendments—[1] This section inserted by FA 1989 s 150 in relation to assessment notices issued after 26 July 1989.
[2] Sub-s (2A) inserted by F(No 2)A 1992 Sch 5 paras 9(1), (4), 10 in relation to tax for the year 1993–94 and subsequent years.
[3] Sub-s (1) and words in sub-ss (2)–(5) substituted by FA 1998 Sch 19 para 22 with effect in relation to accounting periods ending after 30 June 1999 (by virtue of Finance Act 1994, Section 199, (Appointed Day) Order, SI 1998/3173 art 2).
[4] Word "where" in sub-s (1)(*a*) repealed FA 1999 s 139, Sch 20 Pt III(21) with effect for accounting periods ending after 30 June 1999.
[5] Words in sub-s (2A) inserted by FA 1999 s 30(4), (5) with effect from the year 2001–02.

[43B Limits on application of section 43A

(1) If the effect of the exercise by any person of a power conferred by section 43A(2) above—

    (*a*) to make or give a claim, election, application or notice, or

    (*b*) to revoke or vary a claim, election, application or notice previously made or given,

would be to alter the liability to tax of another person, that power may not be exercised except with the consent in writing of that other person or, where he has died, his personal representatives.

(2) Where—

    (*a*) a power conferred by subsection (2) of section 43A above is exercised in consequence of an assessment made on a person, and

    (*b*) the exercise of the power increases the liability to tax of another person,

that section shall not apply by reason of any assessment made because of that increased liability.

(3) In any case where—

    (*a*) one or more relevant claims, elections, applications or notices are made, given, revoked or varied by virtue of the application of section 43A above in the case of an assessment, and

    (*b*) the total of the reductions in liability to tax which, apart from this subsection, would result from the action mentioned in paragraph (*a*) above would exceed the additional liability to tax resulting from the assessment,

the excess shall not be available to reduce any liability to tax.

(4) Where subsection (3) above has the effect of limiting either the reduction in a person's liability to tax for more than one period or the reduction in the liability to tax of more than one person, the limited amount shall be apportioned between the periods or persons concerned—

    (*a*) except where paragraph (*b*) below applies, in such manner as may be specified by the inspector by notice in writing to the person or persons concerned, or

    (*b*) where the person concerned gives (or the persons concerned jointly give) notice in writing to the inspector within the relevant period, in such manner as may be specified in the notice given by the person or persons concerned.

(5) For the purposes of paragraph (*b*) of subsection (4) above the relevant period is the period of 30 days beginning with the day on which notice under paragraph (*a*) of that subsection is given to the person concerned or, where more than one person is concerned, the latest date on which such notice is given to any of them.][1]

Commentary—*Simon's Direct Tax Service* **A3.620.**
Definitions—"Inspector", s 118(1); "notice", TA 1988 s 832(1).
Amendments—[1] This section inserted by FA 1989 s 150 in relation to assessment notices issued after 26 July 1989.

PART V
APPEALS AND OTHER PROCEEDINGS

Revenue Internal Guidance—Inspector's Manual IM5050–5108 (detailed guidance for inspectors on preparation of case for contentious hearing).
Cross references—See TMA 1970 s 19A(8), (9) (the provisions of this Part, except s 50(6)–(8), apply to an appeal against a requirement to produce certain documents for the purposes of enquiring into a return);
IT (Life Assurance Premium Relief) Regulations, SI 1978/1159 reg 10(5) (application of this Part to an appeal against Board's decision on annual claim by an insurer for recovery of tax deducted from life premium);
IT (Interest Relief) Regulations, SI 1982/1236 reg 14(5) (application of this Part to appeals against Board's decision on annual claims by lenders for recovery of tax deducted at source under MIRAS from interest);
Occupational Pension Schemes (Additional Voluntary Contributions) Regulations, SI 1987/1749 reg 9(5) (application of this Part to an appeal against Board's decision on annual claim by administrator for recovery of tax deducted from additional voluntary contributions);
TA 1988 s 62A(7) (application of provisions relating to appeals to apply to an appeal against a notice that the Revenue consider a change of accounting date as not having been made for *bona fide* commercial reasons);
TA 1988 ss 253(2), 350(5) (power of Board to make regulations applying or modifying this Part in relation to advance corporation tax and income tax deducted under TA 1988 s 349 for which a company is liable to account);
Profit-Related Pay (Shortfall Recovery) Regulations, SI 1988/640 reg 6(1) (determination of shortfall in deductions under a cancelled scheme to be treated as an assessment under this Part);
Personal Pension Schemes (Relief at Source) Regulations, SI 1988/1013 reg 11(5) (application of this Part to appeals against Board's decision on annual claim for recovery of tax by scheme administrator);
Personal Equity Plan Regulations, SI 1989/469 reg 13(3) (application of this Part to appeals against Board's withdrawal of approval of plan manager);
SI 1989/469 reg 21(5) (application of this Part to an appeal by a plan manager on Board's decision on annual claim for repayment of tax);
Private Medical Insurance (Tax Relief) Regulations, SI 1989/2387 reg 14(3) (application of this Part to an appeal against Board's failure to approve insurer or withdrawal of approval of qualifying insurer);
SI 1989/2387 regs 17(2), 18(5) (application of this Part to appeals against Board's refusal to certify contract or revocation of certification);

Tax-exempt Special Savings Account Regulations, SI 1990/2361 reg 9(3) (application of this Part to appeals against prohibition notices);

IT (Sub-contractors in the Construction Industry) Regulations, SI 1993/743 reg 14 (this Part to apply to a formal determination of assessed amounts payable by contractor);

IT (Employment) Regulations, SI 1993/744 reg 49(7) (this Part to apply to appeal against assessment of tax made on employer);

SI 1993/744 reg 100 (where place of employment and place where assessment was made are not in the same division, an appeal under this Part must be brought before the General Commissioners having jurisdiction for the place where assessment was made if the Inspector so elects);

IT (Manufactured Overseas Dividends) Regulations, SI 1993/2004 reg 11(10) (application of this Part to appeals against assessments to tax under reg 11 in relation to manufactured overseas dividend).

Tax Credits Act 1999 Sch 4 para 3(3) (provisions of this Act relating to appeals, except TMA 1970 s 50(6)–(8), apply to an appeal against a determination of a penalty under Tax Credits Act 1999 Sch 4 para 1 as they apply to an appeal against an assessment to tax.

Education (Student Loans) (Repayment) Regulations, SI 2000/944 reg 20 (application and modification of this Part in connection with the repayment of student loans).

Employment Act 2002 Sch 1 para 3 (the provisions of TMA 1970 relating to appeals, except TMA 1970 s 50(6)–(8), shall have effect for an appeal against a determination under EA 2002 Sch 1 para 1, as they have effect for an appeal against an assessment to tax).

Jurisdiction

44 General Commissioners

(1) Proceedings before the General Commissioners under the Taxes Acts shall, subject to the provisions of this section, be brought before the General Commissioners for the division in which the place given by the rules in Schedule 3 to this Act is situated.

(1A)–(1B) ...2

[(2) Where—

    (*a*) the parties to any proceedings under the Taxes Acts which are to be heard by any General Commissioners have agreed, whether before or after the institution of the proceedings, that the proceedings shall be brought before the General Commissioners for a division specified in the agreement; and

    (*b*) in the case of an agreement made before the time of the institution of the proceedings, neither party has determined that agreement by a notice served on the other party before that time,

the proceedings shall be brought before the General Commissioners for the division so specified, notwithstanding the said rules ...².]³

(3) In any case in which proceedings under the Taxes Acts may be brought at the election of any person before the Special Commissioners instead of before the General Commissioners, the Commissioners before whom the proceedings are to be brought or have been brought may, if they think fit, on an application made by the parties, arrange with the other Commissioners concerned for the transfer of the proceedings to those other Commissioners; and the proceedings may be so transferred notwithstanding that the election has been exercised, or that the time for exercising the election has expired without its being exercised.

[(3A) Where in any case (including one in which proceedings may be brought as mentioned in subsection (3) above)—

    (*a*) an appeal has been brought before the General Commissioners; and

    (*b*) those Commissioners consider that, because of the complexity of the appeal or the length of time likely to be required for hearing it, the appeal should be brought before the Special Commissioners;

the General Commissioners may, with the agreement of the Special Commissioners, and having considered any representations made to them by the parties, arrange for the transfer of the proceedings to the Special Commissioners.]¹

(4) No determination of any General Commissioners under the Taxes Acts shall be questioned, whether by a case stated under section 56 of this Act or otherwise, on the ground that this section did not authorise those General Commissioners to make the determination, except by a party by whom or on whose behalf an objection to the jurisdiction was made to those General Commissioners before or in the course of the proceedings leading to the determination.

(5) Anything to be done by the General Commissioners may, save as otherwise expressly provided by the Taxes Acts, [or by regulations under section 46A of this Act]⁴ be done by any two or more General Commissioners.

Commentary—*Simon's Direct Tax Service* A3.506.

Revenue & other press releases—IR 19–12–88 (tax appeals etc, place of hearing by General Commissioners: List of tax offices and linked divisions of General Commissioners responsible for substantive groups of companies and trusts).

Simon's Tax Cases—s 44(1), *Murphy v Elders* [1974] STC 34*; *R v O'Kane and Clarke, ex p Northern Bank Ltd* [1996] STC 1249.

s 44(4), *Re Sutherland & Partners' Appeal* [1993] STC 399.

s 44(5), *Toogood v Bristol General Comrs* [1977] STC 116.

Cross references—See FA 1988, s 134 (4), (7), (9) (application of this section, with effect from 3 April 1989 by virtue of FA 1988 (Commencement) Order, SI 1989/473, in relation to proceedings in Northern Ireland transferred from the Special Commissioners to the General Commissioners).

Modifications—Social Security Contributions (Decisions and Appeals) Regulations, SI 1999/1027 (as amended by SI 2001/4023) sub-ss (2), (3), (3A), (4) and (5) to apply (with modifications) to appeals to the tax appeal Commissioners under the Social Security Contributions (Transfer of Functions, etc) Act 1999 Pt II and the Social Security (Transfer of Functions, etc) (Northern Ireland) Order Pt III, as they apply to proceedings relating to income tax.

Amendments—¹ Sub-s (3A) inserted by FA 1984, Sch 22 para 5 and came into force on 1 January 1985 by virtue of FA 1984 (Commencement No 2) Order, SI 1984/1836.

is a question to be determined by the Special Commissioners.

(4) Any question as to the application of any of the following provisions of the principal Act is a question to be determined by the Special Commissioners—

    (*a*) Chapter IA or IB of Part XV (settlements);
    (*b*) Part XVI (administration of estates);
    (*c*) sections 740 and 743(1) (liability in respect of transfer of assets abroad);
    (*d*) section 747(4)(*a*) (liability in respect of controlled foreign company).

(5) Any question as to the application of—

    (*a*) section 830 of the principal Act, or
    (*b*) section 276 of the 1992 Act,

(liability in relation to territorial sea and designated areas) is a question to be determined by the Special Commissioners.][1]

Commentary—*Simon's Direct Tax Service* **E1.839.**
Definitions—"Chargeable gain", s 118(1);"company", s 118(1);"the principal Act", s 118(1);"return", s 118(1);"Special Commissioners" s 4;"the 1992 Act", s 118(1).
Cross references—See TMA 1970 s 57(3)(*c*) (regulations may provide for the giving of conditional decisions where questions on an appeal may go partly to one tribunal and partly to another).
Amendments—[1] Section substituted (with ss 46C, 46D) for former s 47 by FA 1996 Sch 22 para 7 with effect in relation to any proceedings relating to the year 1996–97 or any subsequent year of assessment and in relation to any proceedings relating to an accounting period ending after 30 June 1999 (by virtue of Finance Act 1994, Section 199, (Appointed Day) Order, SI 1998/3173 art 2).
[2] Sub-ss (2)(*a*)–(*c*) substituted; in sub-s (2)(*e*), words substituted for the words "an amendment under paragraph 7(3) of Schedule 1A to this Act of", and in sub-s (2)(*f*), words substituted for the words "notice under paragraph 7(3A)" by FA 2001 s 88, Sch 29 para 27 with effect from the passing of FA 2001 in relation to returns whether made before or after the passing of FA 2001, and whether relating to periods before or after the passing of FA 2001. Previously sub-s (2)(*a*)–(*c*) read as follows—

"(*a*) an appeal against an amendment of a self-assessment under—

    (i) section 28A(2) or (4) of this Act, or
    (ii) paragraph 30 or 34(2) of Schedule 18 to the Finance Act 1998;

(*b*) an appeal against a decision contained in a notice under section 28A(4A) of this Act disallowing a claim or election in whole or in part;
(*c*) an appeal against an amendment under section 28B(3) or 30B(1) of this Act of a partnership statement;".

[46C Jurisdiction of Special Commissioners over certain claims included in returns

(1) In so far as the question in dispute on an appeal to which this section applies concerns a claim made—

    (*a*) to the Board, or
    (*b*) under any of the provisions of the principal Act listed in subsection (3) below,

the question shall be determined by the Special Commissioners.

(2) This section applies to—

    [(*a*) an appeal against an amendment of a self-assessment under section 9C of this Act or paragraph 30 of Schedule 18 to the Finance Act 1998;][2]
    [(*b*) an appeal against an amendment of a return under paragraph 34(2) of Schedule 18 to the Finance Act 1998;][2]
    [(*c*) an appeal against a conclusion stated or amendment made by a closure notice under section 28A or 28B of this Act;][2]
    [(*d*) an appeal against an amendment of a partnership return under section 30B(1) of this Act.][2]

(3) The provisions of the principal act mentioned in subsection (1) above are—

    (*a*) section 121(1) and (2) (management expenses of owner of mineral rights);
    (*b*) sections 459 and 460 (exemption for certain friendly societies);
    (*c*) section 467 (exemption for certain trade unions and employers' associations);
    [(*d*) sections 527 and 536 (reliefs in respect of royalties);][3]
    (*e*) Chapter I of Part XVIII.][1]

Commentary—*Simon's Direct Tax Service* **E1.839.**
Definitions—"The Board", s 118(1);"the principal Act", s 118(1);"Special Commissioners", s 4.
Cross references—See TMA 1970 s 57(3)(*c*) (regulations may provide for the giving of conditional decisions where questions on an appeal may go partly to one tribunal and partly to another).
Amendments—[1] Section substituted (with ss 46B, 46D) for former s 47 by FA 1996 Sch 22 para 7 with effect in relation to any proceedings relating to the year 1996–97 or any subsequent year of assessment and in relation to any proceedings relating to an accounting period ending after 30 June 1999 (by virtue of Finance Act 1994, Section 199, (Appointed Day) Order, SI 1998/3173 art 2).
[2] Sub-s (2)(*a*)–(*d*) substituted for sub-s (2)(*a*), (*b*) by FA 2001 s 88,Sch 29 para 28 with effect from the passing of FA 2001 in relation to returns whether made before or after the passing of FA 2001, and whether relating to periods before or after the passing of FA 2001. Previously the text read as follows—

"(*a*) an appeal against an amendment of a self-assessment under—

    (i) section 28A(2) or (4) of this Act, or
    (ii) paragraph 30 or 34(2) of Schedule 18 to the Finance Act 1998;][2]

(*b*) an appeal against an amendment under section 28B(3) or 30B(1) of this Act of a partnership statement."
[3] Sub-s (3)(*d*) substituted by FA 2001 s 71(4), Sch 24 para 2 with effect for claims made in respect of payments actually receivable after 5 April 2001.

[46D Questions to be determined by Lands Tribunal

(1) In so far as the question in dispute on an appeal to which this section applies—

(*a*) is a question of the value of any land or of a lease of land, and

(*b*) arises in relation to the taxation of chargeable gains (whether under capital gains tax or corporation tax) or in relation to a claim under the 1992 Act,

the question shall be determined by the relevant Lands Tribunal.

(2) This section applies to—

[(*a*) an appeal against an amendment of a self-assessment under section 9C of this Act or paragraph 30 of Schedule 18 to the Finance Act 1998;]²

[(*aa*) an appeal against an amendment of a return under paragraph 34(2) of Schedule 18 to the Finance Act 1998;]²

[(*b*) an appeal against a conclusion stated or amendment made by a closure notice under section 28A or 28B of this Act;]²

[(*c*) an appeal against an amendment of a partnership return under section 30B(1) of this Act;]²

(*d*) an appeal against an assessment to tax which is not a self-assessment;

(*e*) an appeal against [a conclusion stated or amendment made by a closure notice under paragraph 7(2) of Schedule 1A to this Act relating to]² a claim or election made otherwise than by being included in a return;

(*f*) an appeal against a decision contained in a [closure notice under paragraph 7(3)]² of Schedule 1A to this Act disallowing in whole or in part a claim or election made otherwise than by being included in a return.

(3) In this section ''the relevant Lands Tribunal'' means—

(*a*) in relation to land in England and Wales, the Lands Tribunal;

(*b*) in relation to land in Scotland, the Lands Tribunal for Scotland;

(*c*) in relation to land in Northern Ireland, the Lands Tribunal for Northern Ireland.]¹

Commentary—*Simon's Direct Tax Service* **E1.839.**
Revenue Internal Guidance—Capital Gains manual CG 74501–74505 (referral of land valuations to Lands Tribunal).
CG 74000–75820 (procedure for obtaining valuations of land).
Definitions—''Chargeable gains'', s 118(1);''return'', s 118(1);''the 1992 Act'', s 118(1).
Cross references—See TMA 1970 s 57(3)(*c*) (regulations may provide for the giving of conditional decisions where questions on an appeal may go partly to one tribunal and partly to another).
Amendments—¹ Section substituted (with ss 46B, 46C) for former s 47 by FA 1996 Sch 22 para 7 with effect in relation to any proceedings relating to the year 1996–97 or any subsequent year of assessment and in relation to any proceedings relating to an accounting period ending after 30 June 1999 (by virtue of Finance Act 1994, Section 199, (Appointed Day) Order, SI 1998/3173 art 2).
² Sub-s (2)(*a*)–(*c*) substituted, in sub-s (2)(*e*), words substituted for the words ''an amendment under paragraph 7(3) of Schedule 1A to this Act of'', and in sub-s (2)(*f*), words substituted for the words ''notice under paragraph 7(3A)'', by FA 2001 s 88, Sch 29 para 29 with effect from the passing of FA 2001 in relation to returns whether made before or after the passing of FA 2001, and whether relating to periods before or after the passing of FA 2001. Previously sub-s (2)(*a*)–(*c*) read—

''(*a*) an appeal against an amendment of a self-assessment under—

(i) section 28A(2) or (4) of this Act, or

(ii) paragraph 30 or 34(2) of Schedule 18 to the Finance Act 1998;

(*b*) an appeal against a decision contained in a notice under section 28A(4A) of this Act disallowing a claim or election in whole or in part;

(*c*) an appeal against an amendment under section 28B(3) or 30B(1) of this Act of a partnership statement;''.

47 Special jurisdiction relating to tax on chargeable gains

Amendments—This section substituted by new ss 46B–46D above by FA 1996 Sch 22 para 7 with effect in relation to any proceedings relating to the year 1996–97 or any subsequent year of assessment and in relation to any proceedings relating to an accounting period ending after 30 June 1999 (by virtue of Finance Act 1994, Section 199, (Appointed Day) Order, SI 1998/3173 art 2).

47A Special jurisdiction relating to development land tax

Amendments—Inserted by the Development Land Tax Act 1976, s 41, Sch 8, Pt. I, para 13, but ceased to have effect in respect of any disposal taking place after 18 March 1985, by virtue of the repeal of the 1976 Act by FA 1985, s 98(6), Sch 27 Pt X.

[47B Special jurisdiction relating to Business Expansion Scheme

If and so far as the question in dispute on any appeal against the refusal of relief under [Chapter III of Part VII of the principal Act]² (relief for investment in corporate trades), or against an assessment withdrawing any such relief, is a question of the value of an interest in land (within the meaning of [section 294(5) of that Act]²), it shall be determined—

(*a*) if the land is in England and Wales, on a reference to the Lands Tribunal;

(*b*) if the land is in Scotland, on a reference to the Lands Tribunal for Scotland; and

(*c*) if the land is in Northern Ireland, on a reference to the Lands Tribunal for Northern Ireland.]¹

Commentary—*Simon's Direct Tax Service* **E1.818.**
Note—Business expansion scheme tax relief ceased to apply from 1 January 1994 and is replaced by Enterprise investment scheme; see TA 1988, ss 289–312.
Cross references—See Special Commissioners (Jurisdiction and Procedure) Regulations, SI 1994/1811 reg 22(2)(*c*) (final determination on appeal of market value of asset may be proved by certificate signed by clerk or registrar of tribunal under this section),

General Commissioners (Jurisdiction and Procedure) Regulations, SI 1994/1811 reg 23 (jurisdiction of tribunal to which question referred under this section by Special Commissioners),
General Commissioners (Jurisdiction and Procedure) Regulations, SI 1994/1812 reg 18(2)(c) (final determination on appeal of market value of asset may be proved by certificate signed by clerk or registrar of tribunal under this section),
General Commissioners (Jurisdiction and Procedure) Regulations, SI 1994/1812 reg 19 (jurisdiction of tribunal to which question referred under this section by General Commissioners).
Amendments—[1] This section inserted by FA 1986, Sch 9, para 1(2) and 22 in relation to shares issued after 18 March 1986.
[2] Words substituted by TA 1988, Sch 29, para 32 Table.

Proceedings before Commissioners

48 Application to appeals and other proceedings

(1) In the following provisions of this Part of this Act, unless the context otherwise requires—

"appeal" means any appeal to the General Commissioners or to the Special Commissioners under the Taxes Acts,

"the Commissioners" means the General Commissioners or the Special Commissioners as the case may be.

(2) The following provisions of this Part of this Act shall apply in relation to—

(a) appeals other than appeals against assessments, and

(b) proceedings which under the Taxes Acts are to be heard and determined in the same way as an appeal,

subject [to any necessary modifications, including (except in the case of applications under section 55 below) the omission of section 56 (9) below].[1]

Simon's Tax Cases—s 48(2), *R v HM Inspector of Taxes, ex p* [1974] STC 567.
Amendments—[1] Words in sub-s (2) substituted by F(No 2)A 1975, s 45(4) in relation to tax charged by assessment notice issued after 31 July 1975; see F(No 2)A 1975, s 44 (7).

49 Proceedings brought out of time

(1) An appeal may be brought out of time if on an application for the purpose an inspector or the Board is satisfied that there was a reasonable excuse for not bringing the appeal within the time limited, and that the application was made thereafter without unreasonable delay, and gives consent in writing; and the inspector or the Board, if not satisfied, shall refer the application for determination by the Commissioners.

(2) If there is a right to elect to bring the appeal before the Special Commissioners instead of before the General Commissioners, the Commissioners to whom an application under this section is to be referred shall be the General Commissioners unless the election has been exercised before the application is so referred.

Commentary—*Simon's Direct Tax Service* A3.510.
Revenue & other press releases—Association of British Chambers of Commerce 1–8–79 (inspectors by concession accept appeals which are late because of postal delays; due date for payment is similarly extended).
Revenue Internal Guidance—Inspector's Manual IM4901 (decision of Commissioners is final).
Simon's Tax Cases—*R v Hastings and Bexhill General Comrs and IRC, ex p Goodacre* [1994] STC 799.
s 49(1), *R v Special Comrs of the Income Tax Acts, ex p Magill* [1981] STC 479; *Bye v Coren* [1985] STC 113; *R v Special Comrs, ex p Fina Exploration Ltd* [1992] STC 1; *Consultants Ltd v Insp of Taxes* [2002] STC (SCD) 162.
Definitions—"Appeal", s 48(1); "Commissioners", s 48(1).

50 Procedure

(1)–(5) ...[2]

(6) If, on an appeal, it appears to the majority of the Commissioners present at the hearing, by examination of the appellant on oath or affirmation, or by other ...[2] evidence,—

(a) that, ...[6]the appellant is overcharged by a self-assessment;

(b) that, ...[6] any amounts contained in a partnership statement are excessive; or

(c) that the appellant is overcharged by an assessment other than a self-assessment,

the assessment or amounts shall be reduced accordingly, but otherwise the assessment or statement shall stand good.][3]

[(7) If, on an appeal, it appears to the Commissioners—

(a) that the appellant is undercharged to tax by a self-assessment ...[6]

(b) that any amounts contained in a partnership statement ...[6] are insufficient; or

(c) that the appellant is overcharged by an assessment other than a self-assessment,

the assessment or amounts shall be increased accordingly.][3]

[(7A) If, on appeal, it appears to the Commissioners that a claim or election [which was the subject of a decision contained in a closure notice under section 28A][6] of this Act should have been allowed or disallowed to an extent different from that specified in the notice, the claim or election shall be allowed or disallowed accordingly to the extent that appears to them appropriate, but otherwise the decision in the notice shall stand good.][4]

[(8) Where, on an appeal against an assessment [(other than a self-assessment)][3] which—

(a) assesses an amount which is chargeable to tax, and

(b) charges tax on the amount assessed,

it appears to the Commissioners as mentioned in subsection (6) or (7) above, they may, unless the circumstances of the case otherwise require, reduce or, as the case may be, increase only the amount assessed; and where any appeal is so determined the tax charged by the assessment shall be taken to have been reduced or increased accordingly.]¹

[(9) Where any amounts contained in a partnership statement are reduced under subsection (6) above or increased under subsection (7) above, an officer of the Board shall by notice to each of the relevant partners amend—

   [(*a*) the partner's return under section 8 or 8A of this Act, or]⁶
   (*b*) the partner's company tax return,

so as to give effect to the reductions or increases of those amounts.]⁵

Commentary—*Simon's Direct Tax Service* A3.530, 532, 533, 536.
Revenue & other press releases—Lord Chancellor's Department (guidance notes for appeals and other proceedings before the Special Commissioners).
Revenue Internal Guidance—Inspector's Manual IM4912a (onus of proof generally on taxpayer; where Revenue allege fraudulent or negligent conduct, onus on them to show such conduct, but onus remains with taxpayer regarding quantum of assessment).
As regards increase on appeal, onus is on the Revenue to show that the assessment is inadequate; standard of proof is the ordinary civil standard of balance of probabilities).
Simon's Tax Cases—*Wicker v Fraser* [1982] STC 505; *King v Walden* [2000] STC (SCD) 179.
s 50(5), *Banin v Mackinlay* [1985] STC 144; *Cassell v Crutchfield* [1995] STC 663.
s 50(6), *Owton Fens Properties Ltd v Redden* [1984] STC 618; *Barnes-Sherrocks v Mcintosh* [1989] STC 674; *Auckland v PAVH (International) Ltd* [1992] STC 712; *MacEachern v Carr* [1996] STC 282.
s 50(7), *Duchy Maternity Ltd v Hodgson* [1985] STC 764; *Cassell v Crutchfield* [1995] STC 663; *Horner v Madden* [1995] STC 802; *Glaxo Group Ltd v IRC* [1996] STC 191.
Definitions—''Appeal'', s 48(1); ''Commissioners'', s 48(1).
Cross references—See TMA 1970, s 100B(2) (sub–ss. (6)–(8) above not to apply on an appeal against a penalty determination by an officer of the Board).
TA 1988 s 62A(8) (disapplication of sub-ss (6)–(8) above in relation to appeals against a notice that the Revenue consider a change of accounting period as not having been made for *bona fide* commercial reasons).
Tax Credits Act 1999 Sch 4 para 3(3) (provisions of this Act relating to appeals, except sub-ss (6)–(8) above, apply to an appeal against a determination of a penalty under Tax Credits Act 1999 Sch 4 para 1 as they apply to an appeal against an assessment to tax.
Amendments—¹ Sub-s (8) added by F (No 2) A 1975, s 67 (2), and this section, as amended, to have effect and be deemed always to have had effect except that the addition of sub-s (8) does not affect the judgment of any court given in proceedings commenced before 29 April 1975; see F (No 2) A 1975, s 67(3).
² Sub-ss (1)–(5) and word in sub-s (6) repealed by the General and Special Commissioners (Amendment of Enactments) Regulations, SI 1994/1813, reg 2, Sch 1 paras 1, 6, 25(b), Sch 2 Pt I, with effect from 1 September 1994 in relation to proceedings before the General Commissioners in respect of which the General Commissioners (Jurisdiction and Procedure) Regulations, SI 1994/1812 apply, and in relation to proceedings before the Special Commissioners in respect of which the Special Commissioners (Jurisdiction and Procedure) Regulations, SI 1994/1811 apply.
³ Sub-ss (6), (7) substituted, and words in sub-s(8) and whole of sub-s(9) inserted by FA 1994 ss 196, 199 and Sch 19 para 17 with effect so far as they relate to income tax and capital gains tax from the year 1996–97 and, as respects corporation tax, with effect in relation to accounting periods ending after 30 June 1999 (by virtue of Finance Act 1994, Section 199, (Appointed Day) Order, SI 1998/3173 art 2).
⁴ Sub-s (7A) inserted by FA 1996 Sch 19 para 7 with effect from the year 1996–97 as respects income tax and capital gains tax and, as respects corporation tax, for accounting periods ending after 30 June 1999 (by virtue of SI 1998/3173 art 2).
⁵ Sub-s (9) substituted by FA 1998 Sch 19 para 27 with effect in relation to accounting periods ending after 30 June 1999 (by virtue of SI 1998/3173 art 2).
⁶ In sub-s (6)(*a*), the words ''by reason of an amendment under section 28A(2) or (4) of this Act or paragraph 30 or 34(2) of Schedule 18 to the Finance Act 1998'' repealed; in sub-s (6)(*b*), the words ''by reason of an amendment under section 28B(3) or 30B(1) of this Act,'' repealed; in sub-s (7)(*a*), the words ''which has been amended under section 28A(2) or (4) of this Act or paragraph 30 or 34(2) of Schedule 18 to the Finance Act 1998'' repealed; in sub-s (7)(b), the words ''which has been amended under section 28B(3) or 30B(1) of this Act'' repealed; in sub-s (7A), words substituted for the words ''specified in a notice under section 28A(4A)''; and sub-s (9)(*a*) substituted, by FA 2001 ss 88, 110, Sch 29 para 30, Sch 33 Pt II(13) with effect from the passing of FA 2001 in relation to returns whether made before or after the passing of FA 2001, and whether relating to periods before or after the passing of FA 2001. Sub-s (9)(*a*) previously read as follows—

''(*a*) the partner's self-assessment under section 9 of this Act, or''.

51 Power of Commissioners to obtain information from appellant

Commentary—*Simon's Direct Tax Service* A3.535.
Amendments—This section repealed by the General and Special Commissioners (Amendment of Enactments) Regulations, SI 1994/1813, reg 2, Sch 1, paras 1, 7, Sch 2, Pt. I, with effect from 1 September 1994 in relation to proceedings before the General Commissioners in respect of which the General Commissioners (Jurisdiction and Procedure) Regulations, SI 1994/1812 apply, and in relation to proceedings before the Special Commissioners in respect of which the Special Commissioners (Jurisdiction and Procedure) Regulations, SI 1994/1811 apply.

52 Evidence

Commentary—*Simon's Direct Tax Service* A3.518, 536, 539.
Amendments—This section repealed by the General and Special Commissioners (Amendment of Enactments) Regulations, SI 1994/1813, reg 2, Sch 1, paras 1, 7, Sch 2, Pt. I, with effect from 1 September 1994 in relation to proceedings before the General Commissioners in respect of which the General Commissioners (Jurisdiction and Procedure) Regulations, SI 1994/1812 apply, and in relation to proceedings before the Special Commissioners in respect of which the Special Commissioners (Jurisdiction and Procedure) Regulations, SI 1994/1811 apply.

[53 Appeals against summary determination of penalties

(1) An appeal shall lie to the High Court or, in Scotland, the Court of Session as the Court of Exchequer in Scotland, against the summary determination by the Commissioners of any penalty pursuant to regulations under section 56B of this Act.

(2) On any such appeal the court may either confirm or reverse the determination of the Commissioners or reduce or increase the sum determined.][1]

Commentary—*Simon's Direct Tax Service* **A3.535, 811.**
Simon's Tax Cases—*Boulton v Poole General Comrs and IRC* [1988] STC 709; *Delapage Ltd v Highbury General Comrs and IRC* [1992] STC 290; *Stoll v High Wycombe General Comrs and IRC* [1995] STC 91.
s 53(2), *Campbell v Rochdale General Comrs* [1975] STC 311; *QT Discount Foodstores Ltd v Warley General a Comrs and IRC* [1982] STC 40; *Beach v Willesden General Comrs* [1982] STC 157.
Definitions—''Appeal'', s 48(1); ''Commissioners'', s 48(1).
Amendments—[1] This section substituted by the General and Special Commissioners (Amendment of Enactments) Regulations, SI 1994/1813, reg 2(1), Sch 1, paras 1, 8, with effect from 1 September 1994 in relation to proceedings before the General Commissioners in respect of which the General Commissioners (Jurisdiction and Procedure) Regulations, SI 1994/1812 apply, and in relation to proceedings before the Special Commissioners in respect of which the Special Commissioners (Jurisdiction and Procedure) Regulations, SI 1994/1811 apply.

54 Settling of appeals by agreement

(1) Subject to the provisions of this section, where a person gives notice of appeal and, before the appeal is determined by the Commissioners, the inspector or other proper officer of the Crown and the appellant come to an agreement, whether in writing or otherwise, that the assessment or decision under appeal should be treated as upheld without variation, or as varied in a particular manner or as discharged or cancelled, the like consequences shall ensue for all purposes as would have ensued if, at the time when the agreement was come to, the Commissioners had determined the appeal and had upheld the assessment or decision without variation, had varied it in that manner or had discharged or cancelled it, as the case may be.

(2) Subsection (1) of this section shall not apply where, within thirty days from the date when the agreement was come to, the appellant gives notice in writing to the inspector or other proper officer of the Crown that he desires to repudiate or resile from the agreement.

(3) Where an agreement is not in writing—

(*a*) the preceding provisions of this section shall not apply unless the fact that an agreement was come to, and the terms agreed, are confirmed by notice in writing given by the inspector or other proper officer of the Crown to the appellant or by the appellant to the inspector or other proper officer; and

(*b*) the references in the said preceding provisions to the time when the agreement was come to shall be construed as references to the time of the giving of the said notice of confirmation.

(4) Where—

(*a*) a person who has given a notice of appeal notifies the inspector or other proper officer of the Crown, whether orally or in writing, that he desires not to proceed with the appeal; and

(*b*) thirty days have elapsed since the giving of the notification without the inspector or other proper officer giving to the appellant notice in writing indicating that he is unwilling that the appeal should be treated as withdrawn,

the preceding provisions of this section shall have effect as if, at the date of the appellant's notification, the appellant and the inspector or other proper officer had come to an agreement, orally or in writing, as the case may be, that the assessment or decision under appeal should be upheld without variation.

(5) The references in this section to an agreement being come to with an appellant and the giving of notice or notification to or by an appellant include references to an agreement being come to with, and the giving of notice or notification to or by, a person acting on behalf of the appellant in relation to the appeal.

Commentary—*Simon's Direct Tax Service* **A3.512–514.**
Revenue Interpretation RI 65—Where negotiations are in progress according to this section, taxpayer cannot claim relief for excessive assessment resulting from an error in his return, nor can the Revenue raise discovery assessment.
Revenue Internal Guidance—Inspector's Manual IM4902 (where there is a dispute as to whether an appeal has been settled by agreement, the matter is referred to the Commissioners to decide whether they have jurisdiction).
Statement of Practice SP 8/91, paras 7, 12—Discovery assessments; specific agreement: appeal and non-appeal cases.
Simon's Tax Cases—*Newidgets Manufacturing Ltd v Jones* [1999] STC (SCD) 193; *Schuldenfrei v Hilton* [1999] STC 821; *Rigby v Jayatilaka* [2000] STC 179; *Macniven (Inspector of Taxes) v Westmoreland Investments Ltd [2001] STC 237.*
s 54(1), *Delbourgo v Field* [1978] STC 234; *Gibson v General Comrs for Stroud and Morgan* [1989] STC 421; *IRC v West* [1991] STC 357.
s 54(4), *Beach v Willesden General Comrs* [1982] STC 157.
s 54(5), *IRC v West* [1991] STC 357.
Definitions—''Appeal'', s 48(1); ''Commissioners'', s 48(1).

[55 Recovery of tax not postponed

(1) This section applies to an appeal to the Commissioners against—

[(*a*) an amendment of a self-assessment—

    (i) under section 9C of this Act, or

    (ii) under paragraph 30 or 34(2) of Schedule 18 to the Finance Act 1998,

(*aa*) a conclusion stated or amendment made by a closure notice under section 28A or 28B of this Act,][14]

(*b*) an assessment to tax other than a self-assessment,][13] (*c*) an assessment to income tax made under Schedule 16 to the principal Act (income tax on company payments) other than an assessment charging tax the time for the payment of which is given by paragraph 4(1) or 9 of that Schedule, or

(*d*) a notice under subsection (1) or (3) of section 753 of that Act where, before the appeal is determined, the appellant is assessed to tax under section 747(4)(*a*) of that Act by reference to an amount of chargeable profits specified in that notice.]¹¹

(2) [Except as otherwise provided by the following provisions of this section]², the tax charged[—

(*a*) by the amendment or assessment, or

(*b*) where the appeal is against a conclusion stated by a closure notice, as a result of that conclusion,]¹⁴

shall be due and payable as if [there had been no appeal]⁶.

(3) If the appellant has grounds for believing that he is overcharged to tax by the [amendment or assessment[, or as a result of the conclusion stated in the closure notice,]¹⁴]¹², he may, by notice in writing given to the inspector within thirty days after [the specified date]¹⁴, apply to the Commissioners for a determination of the amount of tax the payment of which should be postponed pending the determination of the appeal.

A notice of application under this subsection shall state the amount in which the appellant believes that he is overcharged to tax and his grounds for that belief.

[(3A) An application under subsection (3) above may be made more than thirty days after [the specified date]¹⁴ if there is a change in the circumstances of the case as a result of which the appellant has grounds for believing that he is over-charged to tax by the [amendment or assessment]¹²[, or as a result of the conclusion stated in the closure notice]¹⁴.]³

(4) If, after any determination of the amount of tax the payment of which should be so postponed, there is a change in the circumstances of the case as a result of which either party has grounds for believing that the amount so determined has become excessive or, as the case may be, insufficient, he may, by notice in writing given to the other party at any time before the determination of the appeal, apply to the Commissioners for a further determination of that amount.

A notice of application under this subsection shall state the amount in which the applicant believes that the amount previously determined has become excessive or, as the case may be, insufficient and his grounds for that belief.

(5) An application under subsection (3) or (4) above shall be heard and determined in the same way as the appeal; and where any such application is heard and determined by any Commissioners, that shall not preclude them from hearing and determining the appeal or any application or further application under subsection (4) above.

(6) The amount of tax the payment of which shall be postponed pending the determination of the appeal shall be the amount (if any) in which it appears to the Commissioners, having regard to the representations made and any ...⁹ evidence adduced, that there are reasonable grounds for believing that the appellant is overcharged to tax; and—

[(*a*) in the case of a determination made on an application under subsection (3) above, other than an application made by virtue of subsection (3A) above, the date on which any tax the payment of which is not so postponed is due and payable shall be determined as if the tax were charged by an [amendment or assessment]¹² notice of which was issued on the date of that determination and against which there had been no appeal; and]⁷

[(*b*) in the case of a determination made on an application under subsection (4) above—

(i) the date on which any tax the payment of which ceases to be so postponed is due and payable shall be determined as if the tax were charged by an assessment notice of which was issued on the date of that determination and against which there had been no appeal; and

(ii) any tax overpaid shall be repaid.]⁷

[(6A) Where an appeal is brought against an [amendment or assessment]¹² to tax under section 4(4)(*a*) of the principal Act as well as against a notice under section 753(1) or (3) of that Act—

(*a*) an application under subsection (3) above may relate to matters arising on both appeals and, in determining the amount of tax the payment of which should be postponed, the Commissioners shall consider the matters so arising together; and

(*b*) if the Commissioners have determined the amount of tax the payment of which should be postponed solely in relation to one of the appeals, the bringing of the other appeal shall be taken to be a change of circumstances falling within subsection (4) above; and

(*c*) any reference in this section to the determination of the appeal shall be construed as a reference to the determination of the two appeals, but the determination of one before the other shall be taken to be a change of circumstances falling within subsection (4) above.]⁵

(7) If the appellant and [an inspector]⁸ come to an agreement, whether in writing or otherwise, as to the amount of tax the payment of which should be postponed pending the determination of the appeal, the like consequences shall ensue as would have ensued if the Commissioners had made a determination to that effect under subsection (6) above on the date when the agreement was come to, but without prejudice to the making of a further agreement or of a further determination under that subsection.

(8) Where an agreement is not in writing—

(*a*) subsection (7) above shall not apply unless the fact that an agreement was come to, and the terms agreed, are confirmed by notice in writing given by the inspector to the appellant or by the appellant to the inspector, and

(*b*) the reference in that subsection to the time when the agreement was come to shall be construed as a reference to the time of the giving of the notice of confirmation.

[(9) On the determination of the appeal—

(*a*) the date on which any tax payable in accordance with that determination is due and payable shall, so far as it is tax the payment of which had been postponed, or which would not have been charged by the [amendment or assessment]¹² [, or as a result of the conclusion stated in the closure notice,]¹⁴ if there had been no appeal, be determined as if the tax were charged by an [amendment or assessment]¹²—

(i) notice of which was issued on the date on which the inspector issues to the appellant a notice of the total amount payable in accordance with the determination, and

(ii) against which there had been no appeal; and

(*b*) any tax overpaid shall be repaid.]⁷

[(10) In subsection (3) above, ''inspector'' means the inspector or other officer of the Board—

(*a*) by whom the notice of amendment or assessment was issued, or

(*b*) in the case of an appeal against a conclusion stated or amendment made by a closure notice, by whom the closure notice was issued.]¹⁴

[(10A) In this section ''the specified date'' means the date of—

(*a*) the issue of the notice of amendment or assessment, or

(*b*) in the case of an appeal against a conclusion stated or amendment made by a closure notice, the issue of the closure notice.]¹⁴

[(10B) References in this section to an agreement being come to with an appellant, and to the giving of notice to or by an appellant, include references to an agreement being come to with, and the giving of notice to or by, a person acting on behalf of the appellant in relation to the appeal.]¹⁴

(11) ...⁴ the transfer of proceedings under this Act [or under regulations made pursuant to section 46A of this Act]¹⁰ from one body of Commissioners to another body of Commissioners shall not affect the validity of a determination under subsection (6) above.]¹

Commentary—*Simon's Direct Tax Service* **A3.1308.**
Revenue & other press releases—CCAB June 1982 (for purpose of subsection 3A, ''a change in circumstances'' includes case where further accounts work reveals additional relief is due).
ICAEW TR760 September 1989 (payment on account which exceeds amount charged by assessment should be accompanied by a brief clear explanation as to its allocation).
Revenue Internal Guidance—Assessed taxes manual AT4.303–4.304, AT6.609 (sub-s (3) to be construed strictly; action to be taken following communications with the Collector, Accounts Office from the taxpayer or his agent; list of circumstances in which collection of tax will not be suspended).
Company Taxation Manual COT (PF) 10422 (this procedure does not apply in relation to appeals against penalty determination. Nothing is payable until any appeal is determined).
Inspector's Manual IM5043 (sub-s (9) does not apply to income tax under Schedule E or to tax relating to an appeal against the refusal of a claim; however a refund may be made if taxpayer gives appropriate undertaking, notwithstanding any Revenue appeal to the courts).
Simon's Tax Cases—*Savacentre Ltd v IRC* [1995] STC 867.
s 55(2)(*b*), *Hallamshire Industrial Finance Trust Ltd v IRC* [1979] STC 237.
s 55(2), (3), *Parikh v Currie* [1978] STC 473.
s 55(4), *Savacentre Ltd v IRC* [1993] STC 344; *Sparrow Ltd v Insp of Taxes* [2001] STC(SCD) 206.
s 55(6), *Sparrow Ltd v Insp of Taxes* [2001] STC(SCD) 206.
s 55(7), *Sparrow Ltd v Insp of Taxes* [2001] STC(SCD) 206
s 55(9), *Re a debtor (No 1240/SD/91), ex p the debtor v IRC* [1992] STC 771.
Definitions—''Appeal'', s 48(1); ''Commissioners'', s 48(1); ''principal Act'', s 118(1).
Cross references—Pension Scheme Surpluses (Administration) Regulations, SI 1987/352 reg 6(6) (application of TMA 1970 to an assessment on an employer or administrator as if it were an assessment specified in sub-s (1) above).
TMA 1970 s 59C (surcharges on tax payable under this section but remaining unpaid).
TMA 1970 s 86 (interest on overdue tax).
IT (Entertainers and Sportsmen) Regulations, SI 1987/530 reg 14(2)(*a*) (this section to apply to assessment of tax under the Regulations);
TA 1988, s 306(8) (application for postponement of tax under sub-s (3) or (4) by an individual subscribing for EIS eligible shares in a qualifying company),
TA 1988, ss 374A(4), 375(4) (TMA 1970 applies to any assessment to recover tax relief incorrectly deducted from interest under MIRAS, as though such an assessment were one specified in s 55(1)),
TA 1988, Sch 27, para 19(3) (application of sub-ss (3A) onwards of this section to an application for postponement of tax on non-qualifying offshore fund pending its certification as a distributing fund);
FA 1993, Sch 19, para 5(1) (Lloyd's underwriters: determination by inspector of syndicate's profits: appeal by syndicate's managing agent against determination: modification of this section),
FA 1993, Sch 19, para 7(2) (Lloyd's underwriters: determination by inspector of syndicate member's profits: variation or modification of determination: this section to have effect.)
Special Commissioners (Jurisdiction and Procedure) Regulations, SI 1994/1811 (application under sub-s (11) with effect from 1 September 1994 in relation to proceedings before the Special Commissioners instituted after 31 August 1994).
General Commissioners (Jurisdiction and Procedure) Regulations, SI 1994/1812 (application under sub-s (11) with effect from 1 September 1994 in relation to proceedings before the General Commissioners instituted after 31 August 1994).
FA 2000 Sch 15 para 40(7) (no application shall be made under sub-ss (3), (4) above on the ground that the investing company is eligible for investment relief under the corporate venturing scheme unless a claim for the relief has been made by that company).
Amendments—¹ This section was substituted by F(No 2) A 1975, s 45(1) in relation to tax charged by assessment notices issued after 31 July 1975.

² Words in sub-s (2) substituted by FA 1982, s 8 (1), (4) in relation to assessment notices issued after 30 July 1982.
³ Sub-s (3A) inserted by FA 1982, s 68 (2)–(4) in relation to assessment notices issued after 30 July 1982.
⁴ Words in sub-s (11) repealed by FA 1984, Sch 23, Pt. XIII with effect from 1 January 1985 by virtue of FA 1984 (Commencement No 2) Order, SI 1984/1836.
⁵ Sub-s (6A) inserted by TA 1988 Sch 29, para 8.
⁶ Words in sub-s (2) substituted by FA 1989, s 56(2), (4) in respect of tax charged by assessment notices issued after 30 July 1982.
⁷ Sub-ss (6)(*a*), (6)(*b*), (9) substituted by FA 1989 s 56(2), (4) in respect of tax charged by assessment notices issued after 30 July 1982.
⁸ Words in sub-ss (7), (10) substituted by FA 1990, s 104(2), (4) where notice of appeal is given after 25 July 1990.
⁹ Word in sub-s (6) repealed by the General and Special Commissioners (Amendment of Enactments) Regulations, SI 1994/1813, reg 2, Sch 1, paras 1, 9, Sch 2, Pt I, with effect from 1 September 1994 in relation to proceedings before the General Commissioners in respect of which the General Commissioners (Jurisdiction and Procedure) Regulations, SI 1994/1812 apply, and in relation to proceedings before the Special Commissioners in respect of which the Special Commissioners (Jurisdiction and Procedure) Regulations, SI 1994/1811 apply.
¹⁰ Words in sub-s (11) inserted by the General and Special Commissioners (Amendment of Enactments) Regulations, SI 1994/1813, reg 2, Sch 1, paras 1, 9, Sch 2, Pt I, with effect from 1 September 1994 in relation to proceedings before the General Commissioners in respect of which the General Commissioners (Jurisdiction and Procedure) Regulations, SI 1994/1812 apply, and in relation to proceedings before the Special Commissioners in respect of which the Special Commissioners (Jurisdiction and Procedure) Regulations, SI 1994/1811 apply.
¹¹ Sub-s (1) substituted by FA 1994 ss 196, 199 and Sch 19 para 18(1) with effect so far as it relates to income tax and capital gains tax from the year 1996–97 and, in the case of corporation tax, with effect in relation to accounting periods ending after 30 June 1999 (by virtue of Finance Act 1994, Section 199, (Appointed Day) Order, SI 1998/3173 art 2).
¹² In sub-ss (3), (3A), (6), (6A), (9), (10) words substituted for the word ''assessment'' by FA 1994 ss 196, 199, Sch 19 para 18(2) with effect so far as they relate to income tax and capital gains tax from the year 1996–97 and, in the case of corporation tax, with effect in relation to accounting periods ending after 30 June 1999 (by virtue of SI 1998/3173 art 2).
¹³ Sub-ss (1)(*a*)(*b*) substituted by FA 1998 Sch 19 para 28 with effect in relation to accounting periods ending after 30 June 1999 (by virtue of SI 1998/3173 art 2).
¹⁴ Sub-s (1)(*a*), (*aa*) substituted for sub-s (1)(*a*), in sub-s (2) words substituted for the words ''by the amendment or assessment''; in sub-s (3) words inserted, and words substituted for the words ''the date of the issue of the notice of amendment or assessment''; in sub- (3A), words substituted for the words ''the date of the issue of the notice of amendment or assessment'', and words inserted; words in sub-s (9)(*a*) inserted, sub-ss (10)–(10B) substituted for sub-s (10), by FA 2001 s 88, Sch 29 para 31 with effect from the passing of FA 2001 in relation to returns whether made before or after the passing of FA 2001, and whether relating to periods before or after the passing of FA 2001.

Sub-s (1)(*a*) previously read as follows—

''(*a*) an amendment of a self-assessment under—

(i) section 28A(2) or (4) of this Act, or
(ii) paragraph 30 or 34(2) of Schedule 18 to the Finance Act 1998,''

Sub-s (10) previously read as follows—

''(10) In subsection (3) above ''inspector'' means the inspector or other officer of the Board by whom the notice of amendment or assessment was issued; and references in this section to an agreement being come to with an appellant and the giving of notice to or by an appellant include references to an agreement being come to with, and the giving of notice to or by, a person acting on behalf of the appellant in relation to the appeal.''

56 Statement of case for opinion of the High Court

(1), (2) ...⁴

(3) [Where a party to an appeal requires the Commissioners to state and sign a case under regulation 20(1) of the General Commissioners Regulations, he,]⁵ shall pay to the clerk to the Commissioners a fee of [£25]² for and in respect of the same, before he is entitled to have the case stated.

(4), (5) ...⁴

(6) The High Court shall hear and determine any question or questions of law [arising on a case stated and transmitted to the High Court under regulation 22 of the General Commissioners Regulations]⁶, and shall reverse, affirm or amend the determination in respect of which the case has been stated, or shall remit the matter to the Commissioners with the opinion of the Court thereon, or may make such other order in relation to the matter as to the Court may seem fit.

(7) The High Court may cause the case to be sent back for amendment, and thereupon the case shall be amended accordingly, and judgment shall be delivered after it has been amended.

(8) An appeal shall lie from the decision of the High Court to the Court of Appeal and thence to the House of Lords:

Provided that—

(*a*) no appeal shall lie to the House of Lords from the Court of Appeal unless leave has been given under and in accordance with section 1 of the Administration of Justice (Appeals) Act 1934, and
(*b*) this subsection has effect subject to Part II of the Administration of Justice Act 1969 (appeal from High Court to House of Lords).

(9) [Where a party to an appeal against an assessment has required a case to be stated under regulation 20(1) of the General Commissioners Regulations, then notwithstanding that the case]⁷ has been required to be stated or is pending before the High Court, tax shall be paid in accordance with the determination of the Commissioners who have been required to state the case:

Provided that, if the [amount charged by]³ the assessment is altered by the order or judgment of the High Court, then—

(*a*) if too much tax has been paid the amount overpaid shall be refunded with such interest, if any, as the High Court may allow; or
[(*b*) if too little tax has been charged, the amount undercharged shall be due and payable at the expiration of a period of thirty days beginning with the date on which the inspector issues to the

other party a notice of the total amount payable in accordance with the order or judgment of that Court.]¹

(10) All matters within the jurisdiction of the High Court under this section shall be assigned in Scotland to the Court of Session sitting as the Court of Exchequer, and an appeal shall lie from the decision under this section of the Court of Session, as the Court of Exchequer in Scotland, to the House of Lords.

(11) This section has effect in Northern Ireland subject to section 58 below.

Commentary—*Simon's Direct Tax Service* A3.543, 701–706, 708, 709.
Revenue & other press releases—Hansard 12–3–80 (costs of appeals: Revenue may not ask for costs where they are the appellants and taxpayer would suffer financial hardship or where important point of principle is at issue).
ICAEW TR760 September 1989 (when a case has been drafted, both parties can comment upon it before the Commissioners approve it).
Simon's Tax Cases—*R v HM Inspector of Taxes, ex p* [1974] STC 567; *R v Special Comrs of the Income Tax Acts, ex p Magill* [1981] STC 479; *Re Sutherland & Partners' Appeal* [1994] STC 387.
s 56(7), *Consolidated Goldfields plc v IRC* [1990] STC 357; *Fitzpatrick v IRC* [1991] STC 34; *Gordon v IRC* [1991] STC 174; *Kingsley v Billingham* [1992] STC 132.
s 56(9), *Re a debtor (No 960/SD/1992), ex p the debtor v IRC* [1993] STC 218.
Definitions—''Appeal'', s 48(1); ''Commissioners'', s 48(1); ''the General Commissioners Regulations'', s 118(1).
Cross references—See TMA 1970, s 44(4) (requirements for statement of case on question of General Commissioners' jurisdiction).
TMA 1970, s 58(2) (application of this section in relation to proceedings in Northern Ireland).
TMA 1970, s 100B(3) (appeals against penalty determinations to the High Court and the Court of Session, Scotland).
General Commissioners (Jurisdiction and Procedure) Regulations, SI 1994/1812, reg 20, (procedure where case stated for the opinion of the High Court).
Amendments—¹ In sub-s (9), para (*b*) of the proviso substituted by F (No 2) A 1975, s 45 (3) in relation to tax charged by assessment notice issued after 31 July 1975.
² Amount in sub-s (3) substituted by FA 1984, Sch 22, para 6 with effect from 1 January 1985 by virtue of FA 1984 (Commencement No 2) Order, SI 1984/1836.
³ Words in sub-s (9) proviso substituted by FA 1989, s 156 (3).
⁴ Sub-ss (1), (2), (4), (5) repealed by the General and Special Commissioners (Amendment of Enactments) Regulations, SI 1994/1813, reg 2, Sch 1, paras 1, 10(*a*), Sch 2, Pt I, with effect from 1 September 1994 in relation to proceedings before the General Commissioners in respect of which the General Commissioners (Jurisdiction and Procedure) Regulations, SI 1994/1812 apply, and in relation to proceedings before the Special Commissioners in respect of which the Special Commissioners (Jurisdiction and Procedure) Regulations, SI 1994/1811 apply.
⁵ Words in sub-s (3) substituted by the General and Special Commissioners (Amendment of Enactments) Regulations, SI 1994/1813, reg 2, Sch 1, paras 1, 10(*b*) with effect from 1 September 1994 in relation to proceedings before the General Commissioners in respect of which the General Commissioners (Jurisdiction and Procedure) Regulations, SI 1994/1812 apply, and in relation to proceedings before the Special Commissioners in respect of which the Special Commissioners (Jurisdiction and Procedure) Regulations, SI 1994/1811 apply.
⁶ Words in sub-s (6) substituted by the General and Special Commissioners (Amendment of Enactments) Regulations, SI 1994/1813, reg 2, Sch 1, paras 1, 10(*c*) with effect from 1 September 1994 in relation to proceedings before the General Commissioners in respect of which the General Commissioners (Jurisdiction and Procedure) Regulations, SI 1994/1812 apply, and in relation to proceedings before the Special Commissioners in respect of which the Special Commissioners (Jurisdiction and Procedure) Regulations, SI 1994/1811 apply.
⁷ Words in sub-s (9) substituted by the General and Special Commissioners (Amendment of Enactments) Regulations, SI 1994/1813, reg 2, Sch 1, paras 1, 10(*d*) with effect from 1 September 1994 in relation to proceedings before the General Commissioners in respect of which the General Commissioners (Jurisdiction and Procedure) Regulations, SI 1994/1812 apply, and in relation to proceedings before the Special Commissioners in respect of which the Special Commissioners (Jurisdiction and Procedure) Regulations, SI 1994/1811 apply.

[56A Appeals from the Special Commissioners

(1) If, in the case of any appeal to the Special Commissioners, the appellant or the inspector or other officer of the Board is dissatisfied in point of law—

    (*a*) with a decision in principle given under regulation 18 of the Special Commissioners Regulations;

    (*b*) with the decision finally determining the appeal[, other than a decision made in accordance with regulation 23(2)(*b*) of the Special Commissioners Regulations]²; or

    (*c*) with a decision under regulation 19 of those Regulations varying a decision such as is mentioned in paragraph (*a*) or (*b*) above or substituting for it a new decision,

he may appeal against that decision to the High Court.

(2) A party to any appeal in England and Wales who under subsection (1) above has the right to appeal against any decision to the High Court may instead appeal directly to the Court of Appeal if—

    (*a*) all the parties to the appeal consent;

    (*b*) the Special Commissioners certify that the decision involves a point of law relating wholly or mainly to the construction of an enactment which was fully argued before them and fully considered by them; and

    (*c*) the leave of the Court of Appeal has been obtained.

(3) Where a decision in principle or a decision finally determining an appeal is set aside or varied under regulation 19 of the Special Commissioners Regulations, an appeal against that decision under subsection (1) or (2) above that has not yet been determined shall be treated as withdrawn at the time the decision is set aside or varied.

(4) The High Court or, as the case may be, the Court of Appeal shall hear and determine any question of law arising on an appeal under subsection (1) or (2) above and may reverse, affirm or vary the decision appealed against, or remit the matter to the Special Commissioners with the Court's opinion on it, or make such other order in relation to the matter as the Court thinks fit.

(5) Subject to subsection (7) below and to Part II of the Administration of Justice Act 1969 (appeal from High Court to House of Lords), an appeal shall lie to the Court of Appeal and thence to the House of Lords from the decision of the High Court on an appeal in England and Wales under subsection (1) above.

(6) Subject to subsection (7) below, an appeal shall lie to the House of Lords from the decision of the Court of Appeal on an appeal under subsection (2) above.

(7) An appeal shall not lie to the House of Lords from the Court of Appeal unless leave has been given under and in accordance with section 1 of the Administration of Justice (Appeals) Act 1934.

(8) Where the decision appealed against under subsection (1) or (2) above is a decision on an appeal against an assessment, then notwithstanding that the appeal under that subsection is pending, tax shall be paid in accordance with the determination of the Special Commissioners who made that decision.

(9) If in such a case the amount charged by the assessment is altered by the order or judgment of the High Court or, as the case may be, the Court of Appeal, then—

(a) if too much tax has been paid the amount overpaid shall be refunded with such interest, if any, as the High Court or, as the case may be, the Court of Appeal may allow; or

(b) if too little tax has been charged, the amount undercharged shall be due and payable at the expiration of a period of thirty days beginning with the date on which the inspector issues to the other party a notice of the total amount payable in accordance with the order or judgment of the High Court or, as the case may be, the Court of Appeal.

(10) All matters within the jurisdiction of the High Court under this section shall be assigned in Scotland to the Court of Session sitting as the Court of Exchequer (references in this section to the High Court being construed accordingly); and an appeal shall lie from the decision under this section of the Court of Session, as the Court of Exchequer in Scotland, to the House of Lords.

(11) This section has effect in Northern Ireland subject to section 58 below.][1]

Commentary—*Simon's Direct Tax Service* A3.543, 701–704, 708.
Simon's Tax Cases—s 56A(4), *Denekamp v Pearce* [1998] STC 1120.
Definitions—"Appeal", s 48(1); "Board", s 118(1); "Commissioners", s 48(1).
Cross references—See TMA 1970 s 33(4) (restriction of appeals under this section in relation to an error or mistake claim to cases involving a point of law arising in connection with the computation of profits).
TMA 1970, s 58(2B), (2C) (application of this section in relation to proceedings in Northern Ireland).
Modifications—Referrals to the Special Commissioners Regulations, SI 2001/4024 reg 3 (modification of this section with effect from 31 January 2002 to apply to a referral to the Special Commissioners).
Amendments—[1] This section substituted by the General and Special Commissioners (Amendment of Enactments) Regulations, SI 1994/1813, reg 2(1), Sch 1, paras 1, 11, with effect from 1 September 1994 in relation to proceedings before the Special Commissioners in respect of which the Special Commissioners (Jurisdiction and Procedure) Regulations, SI 1994/1811 apply.
[2] Words added to sub-s (1)(b) with effect from 1 January 2000, in relation to proceedings before the Special Commissioners in relation to which the Special Commissioners Regulations apply.

[56B Regulations about practice and procedure

(1) The Lord Chancellor may, with the consent of the [Secretary of State][4], make regulations about the practice and procedure to be followed in connection with appeals.

(2) The regulations may in particular include provision—

(a) enabling the Commissioners to join as a party to an appeal a person who would not otherwise be a party;

(b) for requiring any party to an appeal to provide information and make documents available for inspection by [specified persons][2];

(c) for requiring persons to attend the hearing of an appeal to give evidence and produce documents;

(d) as to evidence generally in relation to appeals;

(e) enabling the Commissioners to review their decisions;

(f) for the imposition of penalties not exceeding an amount specified in the regulations;

(g) for the determination and recovery of penalties (imposed by virtue of paragraph (f) above or any other enactment) and for appeals against penalties.

[(2A) In subsection (2)(b) above "specified persons" means such of the following as may be specified in the regulations—

(a) the Commissioners;

(b) any party to the appeal;

(c) officers of the Board.][3]

(3) The regulations may also include provision—

(a) authorising or requiring the Commissioners, in circumstances prescribed in the regulations, to state a case for the opinion of a court;

(b) for an appeal to lie to a court on a question of law arising from a decision of the Commissioners;

(c) as to the practice and procedure to be followed in connection with cases so stated or such appeals.

(4) The regulations may—

(a) make different provision for different cases or different circumstances, and (*b*) contain such supplementary, incidental, consequential and transitional provision as the Lord Chancellor thinks appropriate.

(5) Provision made by virtue of any of subsections (1) to (4) above may include provision amending this or any other Act or any instrument made under an Act.

(6) Regulations under this section shall be made by statutory instrument subject to annulment in pursuance of a resolution of either House of Parliament.][1]

Regulations—Special Commissioners (Jurisdiction and Procedure) Regulations, SI 1994/1811.
General Commissioners (Jurisdiction and Procedure) Regulations, SI 1994/1812.
Definitions—"Board", s 118(1);"Commissioners", ss 2, 4, 4A.
Cross references—TMA 1970, s 56C (order for costs).
TMA 1970, s 56D (reports of decisions).
Special Commissioners (Jurisdiction and Procedure) Regulations, SI 1994/1811 (application with effect from 1 September 1994 in relation to proceedings before the Special Commissioners instituted after 31 August 1994).
General Commissioners (Jurisdiction and Procedure) Regulations, SI 1994/1812 (application with effect from 1 September 1994 in relation to proceedings before the General Commissioners instituted after 31 August 1994).
Amendments—[1] This section inserted by F(No 2)A 1992, Sch 16, paras 1, 4.
[2] Words substituted by FA 1994, s 254.
[3] Sub-s (2A) inserted by FA 1994 s 254.
[4] Words in sub-s (1) substituted by the Transfer of Functions (Lord Advocate and Secretary of State) Order, SI 1999/678 art 2(1), Sch with effect from 19 May 1999

[56C Power of Special Commissioners to order costs

(1) Regulations made under section 56B above may include provision for—

(*a*) the award by the Special Commissioners of the costs of, or incidental to, appeal hearings before them,
(*b*) the recovery of costs so awarded, and
(*c*) appeals against such awards.

(2) Any provision made by virtue of subsection (1)(*a*) above shall provide that the Special Commissioners shall not award costs against a party to an appeal unless they consider that he has acted wholly unreasonably in connection with the hearing in question.][1]

Definitions—"Special Commissioners", s 4.
Cross references—See Special Commissioners (Jurisdiction and Procedure) Regulations, SI 1994/1811, reg 21 (orders for costs procedure with effect from 1 September 1994 in respect of proceedings instituted after 31 August 1994).
Amendments—[1] This section inserted by F(No.2)A 1992, Sch 16, paras 1, 4.

[56D Power of Special Commissioners to publish reports of decisions

(1) Regulations made under section 56B above may include provision for the Special Commissioners to publish reports of such of their decisions as they consider appropriate.

(2) Any provision made by virtue of subsection (1) above shall provide that any report published, other than a report of an appeal that was heard in public, shall be in a form that so far as possible prevents the identification of any person whose affairs are dealt with in the report.

(3) No obligation of secrecy to which the Special Commissioners are subject (by virtue of this Act or otherwise) shall prevent their publishing reports of their decisions in accordance with any provision made by virtue of subsection (1) above.][1]

Revenue & other press releases—Special Commissioners 27-2-96 (no report will be published where the decision cannot be anonymised and to report it would defeat the ends of justice).
Definitions—"Special Commissioners", s 4.
Cross references—See Special Commissioners (Jurisdiction and Procedure) Regulations, SI 1994/1811 reg 20 (publication of decisions in principle or final determination with effect from 1 September 1994 in respect of proceedings instituted after 31 August 1994).
Amendments—[1] This section inserted by F(No 2)A 1992, Sch 16, paras 1, 4.

Chargeable gains

57 Regulations about appeals

(1) The Board may make regulations—

(*a*) as respects the conduct of appeals against assessments and decisions on claims under [the [1992 Act][4]][2],
(*b*) entitling persons, in addition to those who would be so entitled apart from the regulations, to appear on such appeals,
(*c*) regulating the time within which such appeals or claims may be brought or made,
(*d*) where the market value of an asset on a particular date, or an apportionment or any other matter, may affect the liability to capital gains tax of two or more persons, enabling any such person to have the matter determined by the tribunal having jurisdiction to determine that matter if arising on an appeal against an assessment, and prescribing a procedure by which the matter is not determined differently on different occasions,
(*e*) authorising an inspector or other officer of the Board, notwithstanding the obligation as to secrecy imposed by virtue of this or any other Act, to disclose to a person entitled to appear on such an appeal the market value of an asset as determined by an assessment or decision on a claim, or to disclose to a person whose liability to tax may be affected by the determination of the market

value of an asset on a particular date, or an apportionment or any other matter, any decision on the matter made by an inspector or other officer of the Board.

(2) ...[1]

(3) Regulations under this section may contain such supplemental and incidental provisions as appear to the Board to be expedient including in particular—

(a) provisions as to the choice of the Commissioners, whether a body of General Commissioners or the Special Commissioners, to hear the appeal where, in addition to the appellant against an assessment, or the claimant in the case of an appeal against the decision on a claim, and in addition to the inspector or other officer of the Board, some other person is entitled to be a party to the appeal, and

[(b) provisions corresponding to section 563 of the Capital Allowances Act (determination of apportionment affecting tax liability of two or more persons), and][6]

(c) provisions authorising the giving of conditional decisions where, under [section 46B, 46C or 46D][5] of this Act, ...[3], questions on an appeal against an assessment or a decision on a claim may go partly to one tribunal and partly to another.

(4) Regulations under this section—

(a) shall be made by statutory instrument subject to annulment in pursuance of a resolution of the House of Commons, and

(b) shall have effect notwithstanding anything in this Act.

Commentary—*Simon's Direct Tax Service* **A2.316.**
Regulations—Capital Gains Tax Regulations, SI 1967/149.
Definitions—"the 1992 Act", s 118(1); "appeal", s 48(1); "Commissioners", s 48(1).
Amendments—[1] Sub-s (2) repealed by FA 1971, Sch 14, Pt. III.
[2] Word "the" in sub-s (1)(a) substituted by CGTA 1979, s 157(2), Sch 7, para 8(a), Table, Pt I, para 1.
[3] Words in sub-s (3)(c) repealed by CGTA 1979, Sch 8.
[4] Words in sub-s (1)(a) substituted by TCGA 1992, Sch 10, para 2(1), (2).
[5] Words in sub-s (3)(c) substituted by FA 1996 Sch 22 para 8 with effect in relation to any proceedings relating to the year 1996–97 and subsequent years of assessment and any proceedings relating to an accounting period ending after 30 June 1999 (by virtue of Finance Act 1994, Section 199, (Appointed Day) Order, SI 1998/3173 art 2).
[6] Sub-s (3)(b) substituted by CAA 2001 s 578, Sch 2 para 2 with effect for income tax purposes, as respects allowances and charges falling to be made for chargeable periods ending after 5 April 2001, and for corporation tax purposes, as respects allowances and charges falling to be made for chargeable periods ending after 31 March 2001.

Development land tax

[57A Regulations about appeals]

Amendments—This section inserted by the Development Land Tax Act 1976, s 41, Sch 8, Pt. I, para 16, but ceased to have effect in respect of any disposal taking place after 18 March 1985, by virtue of the repeal of the 1976 Act by FA 1985, s 98(6), Sch 27, Pt X.

Procedural rules

[57B Commissioners: procedural rules]

Amendments—[1] This section inserted by FA 1984 Sch 22 para (4), repealed by F(No 2)A 1992, Sch 16, para 5 and Sch 18, Pt IX.

Northern Ireland

58 Proceedings in tax cases in Northern Ireland

(1) ...[1]

[(2) A case which is stated by the General Commissioners under regulation 22 of the General Commissioners Regulations in proceedings in Northern Ireland shall be a case for the opinion of the Court of Appeal in Northern Ireland, and the Taxes Acts shall have effect as if section 56 of this Act applied in relation to such proceedings—

(a) with the substitution for references to the High Court of references to the Court of Appeal in Northern Ireland, and

(b) with the omission of subsection (8) of that section,

and the procedure relating to the hearing and determination of the case by the Court of Appeal in Northern Ireland shall be that for the time being in force in Northern Ireland as respects cases stated by a county court in the exercise of its general jurisdiction.][3]

(2A) ...[4]

[(2B) The Taxes Acts shall have effect as if section 56A of this Act applied in relation to any appeal to the Special Commissioners constituting proceedings in Northern Ireland—

(a) with the substitution for references to the High Court of references to the Court of Appeal in Northern Ireland, and

(b) with the omission of subsections (2) and (5) to (7).][5]

[(2C) An appeal shall lie to the House of Lords in accordance with section 42 of the Judicature (Northern Ireland) Act 1978 from a decision of the Court of Appeal in Northern Ireland on a case stated under regulation 22 of the General Commissioners Regulations or on an appeal under section 56A of this Act.]⁵

[(3) For the purposes of this section—

(a) "proceedings in Northern Ireland" means proceedings as respects which the place given by the rules in Schedule 3 to this Act is in Northern Ireland;

(b) proceedings under section 102, 113(5), . . .⁶ 281(4), 343(10) or 783(9) of the principal Act (or the corresponding enactments repealed by that Act)[, paragraph 6 of Schedule 13B to that Act]⁷, section 11 of or paragraph 22 of Schedule 7 to the Income and Corporation Taxes Act 1970 or [section 563 of the Capital Allowances Act (determination of apportionment affecting tax liability of two or more persons)]⁸ shall be proceedings in Northern Ireland if the place given by the rules in Schedule 3 to this Act in relation to each of the parties concerned in the proceedings is in Northern Ireland,

and sections 21 and 22 of the Interpretation Act (Northern Ireland) 1954 shall apply as if references in those provisions to any enactment included a reference to this section.]²

(4) ...¹

Commentary—*Simon's Direct Tax Service* **A3.550, 551.**
Simon's Tax Cases—*IRC v McGuckian CA (NIC)* [1994] STC 888.
Definitions—"General Commissioners", s 2(1); "the General Commissioners Regulations", s 118(1); "Special Commissioners", s 4(1).
Cross references—See FA 1988, s 134 (4), (6), (9) (application of sub-s (3) of this section, with effect from 3 April 1989 by virtue of FA 1988 (Commencement) Order, SI 1989/473, where pending proceedings are transferred from Special Commissioners to General Commissioners, subject to any provision made under s 134(9)).
Modifications—Referrals to the Special Commissioners Regulations, SI 2001/4024 reg 4 (modification of this section to apply to a referral to the Special Commissioners).
Amendments—¹ Sub-ss (1), (4) repealed by FA 1988, s 134 (2), (4) and Sch 14, Pt. IX with effect from 3 April 1989 by virtue of FA 1988 (Commencement) Order, SI 1989/473, subject to any provision made under s 134(9).
² Sub-s (3) substituted by FA 1988, ss 134(4), (5), 135(2) with effect from 3 April 1989 by virtue of FA 1988 (Commencement) Order, SI 1989/473.
³ Sub-s (2) substituted by the General and Special Commissioners (Amendment of Enactments) Regulations, SI 1994/1813, reg 2(1), Sch 1, paras 1, 12(*a*), with effect from 1 September 1994 in relation to proceedings before the General Commissioners in respect of which the General Commissioners (Jurisdiction and Procedure) Regulations, SI 1994/1812 apply, and in relation to proceedings before the Special Commissioners in respect of which the Special Commissioners (Jurisdiction and Procedure) Regulations, SI 1994/1811 apply.
⁴ Sub-s (2A) repealed by the General and Special Commissioners (Amendment of Enactments) Regulations, SI 1994/1813, reg 2(1), Sch 1 paras 1, 12(*b*) with effect from 1 September 1994 in relation to proceedings before the General Commissioners in respect of which the General Commissioners (Jurisdiction and Procedure) Regulations, SI 1994/1812 apply, and in relation to proceedings before the Special Commissioners in respect of which the Special Commissioners (Jurisdiction and Procedure) Regulations, SI 1994/1811 apply.
⁵ Sub-ss (2B), (2C) inserted by the General and Special Commissioners (Amendment of Enactments) Regulations, SI 1994/1813, reg 2(1), Sch 1, paras 1, 12(*b*) with effect from 1 September 1994 in relation to proceedings before the General Commissioners in respect of which the General Commissioners (Jurisdiction and Procedure) Regulations, SI 1994/1812 apply, and in relation to proceedings before the Special Commissioners in respect of which the Special Commissioners (Jurisdiction and Procedure)
⁶ Word in sub-s (3)(*b*) repealed by FA 1999 s 139, Sch 20 Pt III(4) with effect from the year 2000–01.
⁷ Words in sub-s (3)(*b*) inserted by FA 1999 s 30(4), (5) with effect from the year 2001–02.
⁸ Words ib sub-s (3)(*b*) substituted by CAA 2001 s 578, Sch 2 para 3 with effect for income tax purposes, as respects allowances and charges falling to be made for chargeable periods ending after 5 April 2001, and for corporation tax purposes, as respects allowances and charges falling to be made for chargeable periods ending after 31 March 2001.

59 Election for county court in Northern Ireland

Amendments—This section repealed by FA 1988, s 134 (2), (4) and Sch 14, Pt. IX with effect from 3 April 1989 by virtue of FA 1988 (Commencement) Order, SI 1989/473.

[PART VA
PAYMENT OF TAX

Revenue & other press releases—Revenue Booklet SAT2 (1995) (detailed guidance on self-assessment).
IR 1–4–93 (Revenue accept payment by electronic funds transfer through BACS or CHAPS).
Revenue Internal Guidance—Assessed Taxes Manual AT14.104, AT14.715 (payments should be allocated in the first instance in accordance with taxpayer's original specific instructions and secondly to taxpayer's best advantage).
Cross references—See TMA 1970 s 70(2) (a certificate of a collector that a penalty or surcharge is payable under this Part and has not been paid is sufficient evidence).

*[Income tax and capital gains tax]*¹

Amendments—¹ Heading inserted by FA 1998 Sch 19 para 29 with effect in relation to accounting periods ending on or after the "self-assessment appointed day" (1 July 1999 by virtue of the Finance Act 1994, Section 199, (Appointed Day) Order, SI 1998/3173).

59A Payments on account of income tax

(1) [Subject to subsection (9) below,]² this section applies to any person (the taxpayer) as regards a year of assessment if as regards the immediately preceding year—

(a) he [is assessed]² to income tax under section 9 of this Act in any amount, and (*b*) that amount (the assessed amount) exceeds the amount of any income tax which has been deducted at source, and

(*c*) the amount of the excess (the relevant amount) is not less than such amount as may be prescribed by regulations made by the Board, and

(*d*) the proportion which the relevant amount bears to the assessed amount is not less than such proportion as may be so prescribed.

(2) Subject to subsection (3) below, the taxpayer shall make two payments on account of his liability to income tax for the year of assessment—

(*a*) the first on or before the 31st January in that year, and

(*b*) the second on or before the next following 31st July;

and, subject to [subsections [(4) to (4B)⁶]³ below, each of those payments on account shall be of an amount equal to 50 per cent of the relevant amount.

(3) If, at any time before the 31st January next following the year of assessment, the taxpayer makes a claim under this subsection stating—

(*a*) his belief that he will not be assessed to income tax for that year, or that the amount in which he will be so assessed will not exceed the amount of income tax deducted at source, and

(*b*) his grounds for that belief,

each of the payments on account shall not be, and shall be deemed never to have been, required to be made.

(4) If, at any time before the 31st January next following the year of assessment, the taxpayer makes a claim under this subsection stating—

(*a*) his belief that the amount in which he will be assessed to income tax for that year will exceed the amount of income tax deducted at source by a stated amount which is less than the relevant amount, and

(*b*) his grounds for that belief,

the amount of each of the payments on account required to be made shall be, and shall be deemed always to have been, equal to 50 per cent of the stated amount.

[(4A) If as regards the year immediately preceding the year of assessment—

(*a*) the taxpayer is assessed to income tax under section 9 of this Act after the date on or before which either payment on account is required to be made, or

(*b*) his assessment to income tax under that section is amended after that date,

then, subject to subsections (3) and (4) above [and subsection (4B) below]⁷ and to any subsequent application of this subsection, the amount of the payment on account shall be, and shall be deemed always to have been, equal to 50 per cent of the relevant amount as determined on the basis of the assessment or, as the case may be, the assessment as amended.]³

[(4B) If as regards the year immediately preceding the year of assessment the taxpayer is assessed to income tax under section 29 of this Act in any amount, then, subject to subsections (3) and (4) above and to any subsequent application of this subsection, the amount of each payment on account shall be, and shall be deemed always to have been, the total of—

(*a*) the amount which, immediately before the making of the assessment under section 29, is the amount of that payment, and

(*b*) an amount equal to 50 per cent of the amount in which he is assessed under that assessment;

and if that assessment is varied, the amount in which he is assessed under it shall be taken for the purposes of paragraph (*b*) above to be the amount of the assessment as varied.]⁸

(5) Where the taxpayer makes a claim under subsection (3) or (4) above [or subsection (4A) [or (4B)]⁹ above applies]⁴, there shall be made all such adjustments, whether by the repayment of amounts paid on account[, by the making of payments or further payments on account]⁴ or otherwise, as may be required to give effect to the provisions of that subsection.

(6) Where the taxpayer fraudulently or negligently makes any incorrect statement in connection with a claim under subsection (3) or (4) above, he shall be liable to a penalty not exceeding the difference between—

(*a*) the amount which would have been payable on account if he had made a correct statement, and

(*b*) the amount of the payment on account (if any) made by him.

(7) The provisions of the Income Tax Acts as to the recovery of income tax shall apply to an amount falling to be paid on account of tax in the same manner as they apply to an amount of tax.

[(8) In this section, in relation to a year of assessment, any reference to the amount of any income tax deducted at source is a reference to the amount by which the aggregate of the following, namely—

(*a*) any income tax deducted or treated as deducted from any income, or treated as paid on any income, in respect of the year, and

(*b*) any amounts which, in respect of the year, are to be deducted at source under section 203 of the principal Act in subsequent years, or are tax credits to which section 231 of that Act applies,

exceeds the aggregate of any amounts which, in the year, are deducted at source under the said section 203 in respect of previous years.]⁵

(9) If, at any time before the 31st January next following a year of assessment, an officer of the Board so directs—

(a) this section shall not apply, and shall be deemed never to have applied, as regards that year to any person specified in the direction; and

(b) there shall be made all such adjustments, whether by the repayment of amounts paid on account or otherwise, as may be required to give effect to the direction.][5]]1

[(10) Regulations under section 203 of the principal Act (PAYE) may provide that, for the purpose of determining the amount of any such excess as is mentioned in subsection (1) above, any necessary adjustments in respect of matters prescribed by the regulations shall be made to the amount of tax deducted at source under that section.][10]

Commentary—*Simon's Direct Tax Service* **E1.821.**
Regulations—IT (Payments on Account) Regulation, SI 1996/1654.
Revenue & other press releases—IR 29-7-96 (Revenue are to provide information from taxpayer statements of account to authorised agents).
IR Tax Bulletin October 1996 p 353 (discusses payments on account generally, and examines special features of 1996-97 payments on account).
IR Tax Bulletin December 1996 p 371 (calculation of 1996-97 payments on account: allocation of rental income and investment income received gross).
IR Tax Bulletin February 1997 p 387 (further guidance on 1996-97 payments on account, on claims under sub-s (4) to reduce payments and on statements of account; claims to reduce may be signed by an agent).
Revenue Internal Guidance—Assessed Taxes Manual AT 14.104, AT 14.715 (payments should be allocated in the first instance in accordance with taxpayer's specific instructions and secondly to taxpayer's best advantage).
Enquiry Handbook EH 678 (penalty under sub-s (6) is intended to prevent gross or persistent abuse: penalty will not be sought merely because the payments on account were less than they might have been).
Definitions—''The Board'', s 118(1); ''the Income Tax Acts'', IA 1978 Sch 1; ''the principal Act'', s 118(1); ''year of assessment'', TA 1988 s 832(1).
Cross references—See TMA 1970 s 86 (interest on overdue payments on account).
TMA 1970 s 107A(2) (recovery of amounts payable under this section from the relevant trustees of a settlement).
TA 1988 s 824(1)(a) (repayments of amounts paid under this section to be increased by a repayment supplement).
TA 1988 s 824(4) (order in which income tax repayments are to be attributed).
Taxation of Income from Land (Non-Residents) Regulations, SI 1995/2902 regs 20, 21 (application of this section to payments to the Board under TA 1988 s 42A in respect of Schedule A tax liabilities of non-resident landlords).
Note—The amount prescribed for the purposes of sub-s (1)(c) is £500 (from the year 1996/97) and the proportion prescribed for the purposes of sub-s (1)(d) is one to four (from the year 1997/98, no such proportion having been prescribed for 1996/97) (IT (Payments on Account) Regulations, SI 1996/1654.
Amendments—1 This section inserted, together with the preceding heading, by FA 1994 ss 192, 199(1), (2)(a) with effect from the year 1996–97.
2 Sub-s (1) words inserted and words in paragraph (a) substituted by FA 1995 s 108(1) with effect from the year 1996–97.
3 Words in sub-s (2) substituted and sub-s (4A) inserted by FA 1995 s 108(2), (3) with effect from the year 1996–97.
4 Sub-s (5) words inserted by FA 1995 s 108(4) with effect from the year 1996–97.
5 Sub-ss (8), (9) substituted for sub-s (8) by FA 1995 s 108(5) with effect from the year 1996–97.
6 Words in sub-s (2) substituted by FA 1996 Sch 18 para 2(2) with effect from the year 1996–97.
7 Words in sub-s (4A) inserted by FA 1996 Sch 18 para 2(3) with effect from the year 1996–97.
8 Sub-s (4B) inserted by FA 1996 Sch 18 para 2(4) with effect from the year 1996–97.
9 Words in sub-s (5) inserted by FA 1996 Sch 18 para 2(5) with effect from the year 1996–97.
10 Sub-s (10) inserted by FA 1996 s 126(1) with effect from the year 1996–97.

[59B Payment of income tax and capital gains tax

(1) Subject to subsection (2) below, the difference between—

(a) the amount of income tax and capital gains tax contained in a person's self-assessment under section 9 of this Act for any year of assessment, and

(b) the aggregate of any payments on account made by him in respect of that year (whether under section 59A of this Act or otherwise) and any income tax which in respect of that year has been deducted at source,

shall be payable by him or (as the case may be) repayable to him as mentioned in subsection (3) or (4) below [but nothing in this subsection shall require the repayment of any income tax treated as deducted or paid by virtue of section 233(1), 246D(1), 249(4), 421(1), 547(5) or 599A(5) of the principal Act.]3

(2) The following, namely—

(a) any amount which, in the year of assessment, is deducted at source under section 203 of the principal Act in respect of a previous year, and

(b) any amount which, in respect of the year of assessment, is to be deducted at source under that section in a subsequent year, or is a tax credit to which section 231 of that Act applies,

shall be respectively deducted from and added to the aggregate mentioned in subsection (1)(b) above.

(3) In a case where the person—

(a) gave the notice required by section 7 of this Act within six months from the end of the year of assessment, but

(b) was not given notice under section 8 or 8A of this Act until after the 31st October next following that year,

the difference shall be payable or repayable at the end of the period of three months beginning with the day on which the notice under section 8 or 8A was given.

(4) In any other case, the difference shall be payable or repayable on or before the 31st January next following the year of assessment.

[(4A) Where in the case of a repayment the return on the basis of which the person's self-assessment was made under section 9 of this Act is enquired into by an officer of the Board—

   (a) nothing in subsection (3) or (4) above shall require the repayment to be made before the day on which, by virtue of section [28A(1)][7] of this Act, [the enquiry is][7] completed; but

   (b) the officer may at any time before that day make the repayment, on a provisional basis, to such extent as he thinks fit.][4]

[(5) An amount of tax which is payable or repayable as a result of the amendment or correction of a self-assessment under—

   (a) section 9ZA, 9ZB, 9C or 28A of this Act (amendment or correction of return under section 8 or 8A of this Act), or

   (b) section 12ABA(3)(a), 12ABB(6)(a), 28B(4)(a), 30B(2)(a), 33A(4)(a) or 50(9)(a) of this Act (amendment of partner's return to give effect to amendment or correction of partnership return), is payable (or repayable) on or before the day specified by the relevant provision of Schedule 3ZA to this Act.][7]

[(5A) Where a determination under section 28C of this Act which has effect as a person's self-assessment is superseded by his self-assessment under section 9 of this Act, any amount of tax which is payable or repayable by virtue of the supersession shall be payable or (as the case may be) repayable on or before the day given by subsection (3) or (4) above.][5]

(6) Any amount of income tax or capital gains tax which is payable by virtue of an assessment made [otherwise than under section 9 of this Act shall, unless otherwise provided,][2] be payable on the day following the end of the period of 30 days beginning with the day on which the notice of assessment is given.

(7) In this section any reference to income tax deducted at source is a reference to income tax deducted or treated as deducted from any income or treated as paid on any income.][1]

[(8) Regulations under section 203 of the principal Act (PAYE) may provide that, for the purpose of determining the amount of the difference mentioned in subsection (1) above, any necessary adjustments in respect of matters prescribed by the regulations shall be made to the amount of tax deducted at source under that section.][6]

Commentary—*Simon's Direct Tax Service* **E1.822.**
Revenue Internal Guidance—Enquiry Handbook EH 74 (repayments are risk-assessed before processing).
EH 75 (making of a repayment does not preclude the issue of an enquiry notice at a later date).
EH 296 (repayment may be withheld pending completion of enquiry, but Revenue do not withhold more tax than is appropriate in the light of the perceived tax at risk).
Definitions—"The Board", s 118(1); "the principal Act", s 118(1); "year of assessment", TA 1988 s 832(1).
Cross references—See TMA 1970 s 59C (surcharges on tax payable under this section but remaining unpaid).
TMA 1970 s 86 (interest on tax payable under this section not paid by the date mentioned in sub-s (3) or (4) above as appropriate).
TMA 1970 s 107A(2) (recovery of amounts payable under this section from the relevant trustees of a settlement).
TA 1988 s 824(4) (repayment of income tax to be attributed first to income tax paid under this section).
Education (Student Loans) (Repayment) Regulations, SI 2000/944 reg 21 (application of sub-ss (4A), (5), (6) in connection with the repayment of student loans (sub-ss (5A), (7), (8) do not apply)).
Amendments—[1] This section inserted by FA 1994 ss 193, 199(1), (2)(a) with effect from the year 1996–97 but in the case of a partnership set up and commenced before 6 April 1994, with effect as respects each partner and the year 1996–97 subject to the modifications specified in FA 1995 Sch 21 para 3(1), (3).
[2] Words in sub-s (6) substituted by FA 1995, s 115(6), with effect from the year 1996–97.
[3] Words in sub-s (1) inserted by FA 1996 s 122(2) with effect from the year 1996–97.
[4] Sub-s (4A) inserted by FA 1996 s 127 with effect from the year 1996–97.
[5] Sub-s (5A) inserted by FA 1996 s 125(4) with effect from the year 1996–97.
[6] Sub-s (8) inserted by FA 1996 s 126(2) with effect from the year 1996–97.
[7] "28A(1)" substituted for "28A(5)", and words substituted for "the officer's enquiries are treated as" in sub-s (4A)(a); and sub-s (5) substituted, by FA 2001 s 88, Sch 29 para 14 with effect where the relevant day is after the passing of FA 2001. The "relevant day" means the first day of the period of 30 days specified in the relevant provision of TMA 1970 Sch 3ZA.
Sub-s (5) previously read as follows—

   "(5) Where a person's self-assessment under section 9 of this Act is amended under section 9(4), section 28A(2), (3) or (4) or section 30B(2) of this Act, any amount of tax which is payable or repayable by virtue of the amendment shall, subject to section 55(6) and (9) of this Act, be payable or (as the case may be) repayable—

     (a) in a case where notice of the amendment is given after, or less than 30 days before, the day given by subsection (3) or (4) above, on or before the day following the end of the period of 30 days beginning with the day on which notice is given; and

     (b) in any other case, on or before the day given by subsection (3) or (4) above."

[59C Surcharges on unpaid income tax and capital gains tax]

(1) This section applies in relation to any income tax or capital gains tax which has become payable by a person (the taxpayer) in accordance with section 55 or 59B of this Act.

(2) Where any of the tax remains unpaid on the day following the expiry of 28 days from the due date, the taxpayer shall be liable to a surcharge equal to 5 per cent of the unpaid tax.

(3) Where any of the tax remains unpaid on the day following the expiry of 6 months from the due date, the taxpayer shall be liable to a further surcharge equal to 5 per cent of the unpaid tax.

(4) Where the taxpayer has incurred a penalty under section 7, 93(5)[, 95 or 95A][2] of this Act, no part of the tax by reference to which that penalty was determined shall be regarded as unpaid for the purposes of subsection (2) or (3) above.

(5) An officer of the Board may impose a surcharge under subsection (2) or (3) above; and notice of the imposition of such a surcharge—

(*a*) shall be served on the taxpayer, and
(*b*) shall state the day on which it is issued and the time within which an appeal against the imposition of the surcharge may be brought.

(6) A surcharge imposed under subsection (2) or (3) above shall carry interest at the rate applicable under section 178 of the Finance Act 1989 from the end of the period of 30 days beginning with the day on which the surcharge is imposed until payment.

(7) An appeal may be brought against the imposition of a surcharge under subsection (2) or (3) above within the period of 30 days beginning with the date on which the surcharge is imposed.

(8) Subject to subsection (9) below, the provisions of this Act relating to appeals shall have effect in relation to an appeal under subsection (7) above as they have effect in relation to an appeal against an assessment to tax.

(9) On an appeal under subsection (7) above section 50(6) to (8) of this Act shall not apply but the Commissioners may—

(*a*) if it appears to them that, throughout the period of default, the taxpayer had a reasonable excuse for not paying the tax, set aside the imposition of the surcharge; or
(*b*) if it does not so appear to them, confirm the imposition of the surcharge.

(10) Inability to pay the tax shall not be regarded as a reasonable excuse for the purposes of subsection (9) above.

(11) The Board may in their discretion—

(*a*) mitigate any surcharge under subsection (2) or (3) above, or
(*b*) stay or compound any proceedings for the recovery of any such surcharge,

and may also, after judgment, further mitigate or entirely remit the surcharge.

(12) In this section—

"the due date", in relation to any tax, means the date on which the tax becomes due and payable;
"the period of default", in relation to any tax which remained unpaid after the due date, means the period beginning with that date and ending with the day before that on which the tax was paid.][1]

Commentary—*Simon's Direct Tax Service* **E1.823.**
Revenue Internal Guidance—Enquiry Handbook EH 30 (the imposition of a surcharge cannot be notified until a liability has been established on the basis of a self-assessment, amendment of a self-assessment or a determination).
EH 32 (surcharge notices are issued automatically by the revenue's computer).
EH 620 (inclusion of surcharge in enquiry contract settlement: adjustment where tax-geared penalty charged).
Definition—"The Board", s 118(1).
Note—In sub-s (6) the day appointed for which FA 1989 s 178(1) has effect is 9 March 1998 (Finance Act 1989, section 178(1), (Appointed Day) Order, SI 1998/311).
Cross references—See TMA 1970 s 107A(2)–(4) (recovery of surcharges from the relevant trustees of a settlement and modification of sub-s (9) above in relation thereto).
TA 1988 s 824(1)(*c*) (repayment of surcharge imposed under this section to be increased by a repayment supplement).
Education (Student Loans) (Repayment) Regulations, SI 2000/944 reg 22 (application of this section in connection with the repayment of student loans).
Amendments—[1] This section inserted by FA 1994 ss 194, 199(1), (2)(*a*) with effect from 1996–97.
[2] Words in sub-s (4) substituted by FA 1995 s 109(1), with effect from the year 1996–97. Note FA 1995 s 109(2) as to application of this section in relation to income tax or capital gains tax which is charged by an assessment made after 5 April 1998 and which is for the year 1995–96 or an earlier year of assessment.

[Corporation tax

59D General rule as to when corporation tax is due and payable

(1) Corporation tax for an accounting period is due and payable on the day following the expiry of nine months from the end of that period.

(2) If the tax payable is then exceeded by the total of any relevant amounts previously paid (as stated in the relevant company tax return), the excess shall be repaid.

(3) The tax payable means the amount computed in accordance with paragraph 8 of Schedule 18 to the Finance Act 1998.

(4) Relevant amounts previously paid means any of the following, so far as relating to the accounting period in question—

(*a*) any amount of corporation tax paid by the company and not repaid;
(*b*) any corporation tax refund surrendered to the company by another group company;
(*c*) any amount by which the sums available for set off under Step 4 of the calculation in paragraph 8 of Schedule 18 to the Finance Act 1998 (amounts set off against overall tax liability) exceeds the amount against which they may be set off under that provision;
(*d*) any amount treated as corporation tax paid in respect of profits of the company [by virtue of regulations under 559A][2] of the principal Act (deductions from payments to sub-contractors).

(5) This section has effect subject to section 59E.][1]

Commentary—*Simon's Direct Tax Service* **D2.841.**
Amendments—[1] Substituted by FA 1998 Sch 19 para 29 with effect in relation to accounting periods ending after 30 June 1999 (by virtue of Finance Act 1994, Section 199, (Appointed Day) Order, SI 1998/3173 art 2).
[2] Words in sub-s (4)(*d*) substituted by FA 2002 s 40(3), (4) with effect for deductions made under TA 1988 s 559 after 5 April 2002.

[59DA Claim for repayment in advance of liability being established

(1) This section applies where a company has paid an amount of corporation tax for an accounting period and the circumstances of the company change, so that the company has grounds for believing that the amount paid exceeds its probable tax liability although that liability has not been finally established.

(2) The company may, by notice given to an officer of the Board, claim repayment of the excess.

No such claim may be made before the date which under section 826 of the principal Act (interest on overpaid tax), subject to regulations under section 826A of that Act, is the material date in relation to that tax.

(3) The notice must state—

    (*a*) the amount which the company considers should be repaid, and
    (*b*) its grounds for believing that the amount paid exceeds its probable tax liability.

(4) If the company has appealed against an amendment of an assessment, or an assessment, relating to the tax liability in question, and the appeal has not been finally determined, it may apply to the Commissioners to whom the appeal stands referred for a determination of the amount which should be repaid to the company pending determination of the liability.

(5) Any claim under subsection (2) or application under subsection (4) shall be heard and determined in the same way as an appeal.

(6) If the company makes an application under section 55(3) or (4) (application to postpone payment pending determination of appeal), that application may be combined with an application under subsection (4) above.

(7) If a company makes a claim or application under this section before it has delivered a company tax return for the period in question, any deductions under section 559 of the principal Act (deductions from payments to certain subcontractors) shall be disregarded in considering whether the amount paid by the company exceeds its probable tax liability.

(8) This section has effect subject to section 59E.]¹

Commentary—*Simon's Direct Tax Service* **D2.833**.
Cross reference—Corporation Tax (Instalment Payments) Regulations, SI 1998/3175.
Amendments—¹ This section inserted by FA 1998 Sch 19 para 29 with effect for accounting periods ending after 30 June 1999 (by virtue of Finance Act 1994, Section 199, (Appointed Day) Order, SI 1998/3173 art 2).

[59E Further provision as to when corporation tax is due and payable

(1) The Treasury may by regulations make provision, in relation to companies of such descriptions as may be prescribed, for or in connection with treating amounts of corporation tax for an accounting period as becoming due and payable on dates which fall on or before the date on which corporation tax for that period would become due and payable apart from this section.

(2) Without prejudice to the generality of subsection (1) above, regulations under this section may make provision—

    (*a*) for or in connection with the determination of amounts of corporation tax which are treated as becoming due and payable under the regulations;
    (*b*) for or in connection with the determination of the dates on which amounts of corporation tax are treated as becoming due and payable under the regulations;
    (*c*) for or in connection with the making of payments to the Board in respect of amounts of corporation tax which are treated as becoming due and payable under the regulations;
    (*d*) for or in connection with the determination of the amount of any such payments as are mentioned in paragraph (*c*) above;
    (*e*) for or in connection with the determination of the dates on which any such payments as are mentioned in paragraph (*c*) above become due and payable;
    (*f*) for or in connection with any assumptions which are to be made for any purposes of the regulations;
    (*g*) for or in connection with the payment to the Board of interest on amounts of corporation tax which are treated as becoming due and payable under the regulations;
    (*h*) for or in connection with the repayment of amounts paid under the regulations;
    (*i*) for or in connection with the payment of interest by the Board on amounts paid or repaid under the regulations;
    (*j*) with respect to the furnishing of information to the Board;
    (*k*) with respect to the keeping, production or inspection of any books, documents or other records;
    (*l*) for or in connection with the imposition of such requirements as the Treasury think necessary or expedient for any purposes of the regulations;
    (*m*) for or in connection with appeals in relation to questions arising under the regulations.

(3) Regulations under this section may make provision—

    (*a*) for amounts of corporation tax for an accounting period to be treated as becoming due and payable on dates which fall within the accounting period;

(*b*) for payments in respect of any such amounts of corporation tax for an accounting period as are mentioned in paragraph (*a*) above to become due and payable on dates which fall within the accounting period.

(4) Where interest is charged by virtue of regulations under this section on any amounts of corporation tax for an accounting period which are treated as becoming due and payable under the regulations, the company shall, in such circumstances as may be prescribed, be liable to a penalty not exceeding twice the amount of that interest.

(5) Regulations under this section—

(*a*) may make such modifications of any provisions of the Taxes Acts, or
(*b*) may apply such provisions of the Taxes Acts,

as the Treasury think necessary or expedient for or in connection with giving effect to the provisions of this section.

(6) Regulations under this section which apply any provisions of the Taxes Acts may apply those provisions either without modifications or with such modifications as the Treasury think necessary or expedient for or in connection with giving effect to the provisions of this section.

(7) Regulations under this section—

(*a*) may make different provision for different purposes, cases or circumstances;
(*b*) may make different provision in relation to companies or accounting periods of different descriptions;
(*c*) may make such supplementary, incidental, consequential or transitional provision as appears to the Treasury to be necessary or expedient.

(8) Subject to subsection (9) below, regulations under this section may make provision in relation to accounting periods beginning before (as well as accounting periods beginning on or after) the date on which the regulations are made.

(9) Regulations under this section may not make provision in relation to accounting periods ending before the day appointed under section 199 of the Finance Act 1994 for the purposes of Chapter III of Part IV of that Act (corporation tax self-assessment).

(10) In this section—

"modifications" includes amendments, additions and omissions;
"prescribed" means prescribed by regulations made under this section.

(11) Any reference in this section to corporation tax includes a reference—

(*a*) to any amount due from a company under section 419 of the principal Act (loans to participators etc) as if it were an amount of corporation tax chargeable on the company;
(*b*) to any sum chargeable on a company under section 747(4)(*a*) of the principal Act (controlled foreign companies) as if it were an amount of corporation tax.][1]
[(*c*) to any sum chargeable on a company under section 501A(1) of the principal Act (supplementary charge in respect of ring fence trades) as if it were an amount of corporation tax chargeable on the company.][2]

Regulations—Corporation Tax (Instalment Payments) Regulations, SI 1998/3175; Corporation Tax (Instalment Payments) (Amendment) Regulations, SI 1999/1929.
Revenue & other press releases—IR Tax Bulletin April 1999 (quarterly instalment payments and group payment arrangements). IR 8-6-99 (guidance on Revenue's use of penalty powers in relation to corporation tax instalment payments).
Amendments—[1] This section inserted by FA 1998 s 30 with effect for accounting periods ending after 30 June 1999.
[2] Sub-s (11)(*c*) inserted by FA 2002 s 92(2) with effect from 24 July 2002.

PART VI

COLLECTION AND RECOVERY

Revenue & other press releases—Hansard 10–12–92 (bankruptcy proceedings taken only as a last resort).
Revenue Internal Guidance—Assessed taxes manual AT 1.101–1.303 (Revenue internal organisation and responsibilities).
AT 2.701–2.706 (Revenue procedures: issue of demands etc by computer).
AT 4.101–4.501 (Accounts Office procedures).
AT 6.101–6.612 (special cases).
AT 8.101–8.105 (accounting for payments received at Accounts Office).
AT 8.201–8.204 (procedure for dealing with dishonoured cheques).
AT 8.701–8.706 (overpayments and reallocations of payments).
Enforcement manual En 1.101–1.108 (division of responsibilities within the Inland Revenue).
En 4.801–4.821 (Revenue procedure where taxpayer applies for administration order).
Investigation Handbook IH 7156–7160 ("contrived" company liquidation: application of the Insolvency Act 1986 provisions).
Personal Contact Manual, PCM 3.1–3.28 (Revenue practice in personal calls to taxpayer's premises to collect outstanding tax).
PCM 4.1–4.16 (Revenue practice in relation to requests for additional time to pay).
Cross references—See the IT (Entertainers and Sportsmen) Regulations, SI 1987/530, reg 11(3)(*b*) (assessed tax on connected payments or transfers (as defined in TA 1988, s 556) to be treated for the purposes of this Part as income tax under Schedule D);
TA 1988 s 350(5) (power of Board to make regulations applying or modifying this Part in relation to advance corporation tax and income tax deducted under TA 1988, s 349 for which a company is liable to account).
Profit-Related Pay (Shortfall Recovery) Regulations, SI 1988/640, reg 6(1) (tax assessed on a scheme employer to be subject to the provisions of this Part);
IT (Sub-contractors in the Construction Industry) Regulations, SI 1993/743, reg 14 (this Part to apply to a formal determination of assessed amounts payable by contractor);

IT (Employment) Regulations, SI 1993/744, reg 49(7) (formal determination of tax payable by employer to be subject to the provisions of this Part).

Tax Credits Act 1999 Sch 4 paras 2(3), 4(3) (Part VI of this Act applies to penalties determined under Tax Credits Act 1999 Sch 4 paras 1, 4 as if it were tax charged in an assessment and due and payable).

Education (Student Loans) (Repayment) Regulations, SI 2000/944 reg 23 (application of this section in connection with the repayment of student loans).

Employment Act 2002 Sch 1 para 2 (TMA 1970 Pt 6 shall apply in relation to a penalty determined under EA 2002 Sch 1 para 1 as if it were tax charged in an assessment and due and payable).

60 Issue of demand notes and receipts

(1) Every collector shall, when the tax becomes due and payable, make demand of the respective sums given to him in charge to collect, from the persons charged therewith, or at the places of their last abode, or on the premises in respect of which the tax is charged, as the case may require.

(2) On payment of the tax, the collector shall if so requested give a receipt.

Commentary—*Simon's Direct Tax Service* **A3.1312.**
Revenue & other press releases—Hansard 8–2–93 (business facing temporary financial difficulties should contact Collector as soon as possible to agree payment method, including by instalments).
IR Code of Practice 6 (methods of paying tax and procedures adopted by Collector).
Revenue Internal Guidance—Corporation tax pay and file manual CT (PF) 11600–11613 (Revenue standard procedures).
Personal contact manual PCM 3.1–3.28 (personal calls to collect PAYE returns, outstanding tax etc).

Distraint and poinding

61 Distraint by collectors

(1) If a person neglects or refuses to pay the sum charged, upon demand made by the collector, [the collector may distrain upon the goods and chattels of the person charged (in this section referred to as "the person in default")][1].

(2) For the purpose of levying any such distress, [a justice of the peace, on being satisfied by information on oath that there is reasonable ground for believing that a person is neglecting or refusing to pay a sum charged, may issue a warrant in writing authorising a collector to][2] break open, in the daytime, any house or premises, calling to his assistance any constable.

Every such constable shall, when so required, aid and assist the collector in the execution of the warrant and in levying the distress in the house or premises.

(3) A levy or warrant to break open shall be executed by, or under the direction of, and in the presence of, the collector.

(4) A distress levied by the collector shall be kept for five days, at the costs and charges of the person [in default][3].

(5) If the person [in default][4] does not pay the sum due, together with the costs and charges ...[5], the distress shall be appraised by [one or more independent persons appointed by the collector][6], and shall be sold by public auction by the collector for payment of the sum due and all costs and charges.

... [7] any overplus coming by the distress, after the deduction of the costs and charges and of the sum due, shall be restored to the owner of the goods distrained.

[(6) The Treasury may by regulations make provision with respect to—

   (a) the fees chargeable on or in connection with the levying of distress, and
   (b) the costs and charges recoverable where distress has been levied;

and any such regulations shall be made by statutory instrument which shall be subject to annulment in pursuance of a resolution of the House of Commons.][8]

Commentary—*Simon's Direct Tax Service* **A3.1411.**
Regulations—Distraint by Collectors (Fees, Costs and Charges) Regulations, SI 1994/236.
Revenue Internal Guidance—Enforcement Manual En 2.101 (meaning of "distraint").
En 2.401–2.417 (procedure for carrying out a distraint; entry of premises; request for payment of tax; identification and seizure of goods; removal of goods).
En 2.500–2.517 (action following distraint: late claims and appeals; retention of goods; sale of goods; costs; recovery of any balance of tax due).
Cross references—See TMA 1970 s 69 (recovery of penalty, surchrge or interest).
Amendments—[1] Words in sub-s (1) substituted by FA 1989 s 152 with effect from 1 February 1994 by virtue of FA 1989, s 152, (Appointed Day) Order, SI 1994/87.
[2] Words in sub-s (2) substituted by FA 1989 s 152 with effect from 1 February 1994 by virtue of FA 1989, s 152, (Appointed Day) Order, SI 1994/87.
[3] Words in sub-s (4) substituted by FA 1989 s 152 with effect from 1 February 1994 by virtue of FA 1989, s 152, (Appointed Day) Order, SI 1994/87.
[4] Words in sub-s (5) substituted by FA 1989 s 152 with effect from 1 February 1994 by virtue of FA 1989 s 152, (Appointed Day) Order, SI 1994/87.
[5] Words in sub-s (5) repealed by FA 1989 s 152 with effect from 1 February 1994 by virtue of FA 1989 s 152, (Appointed Day) Order, SI 1994/87 and Sch 17 Pt. VIII.
[6] Words in sub-s (5) substituted by FA 1989 s 152 with effect from 1 February 1994 by virtue of FA 1989, s 152, (Appointed Day) Order, SI 1994/87.
[7] Words in sub-s (5) repealed by FA 1989 s 152 with effect from 1 February 1994 by virtue of FA 1989 s 152, (Appointed Day) Order, SI 1994/87 and Sch 17 Pt. VIII.
[8] Sub-s (6) added by FA 1989 s 152 with effect from 1 February 1994 by virtue of FA 1989 s 152, (Appointed Day) Order, SI 1994/87.

TMA 1970

62 Priority of claim for tax

(1) [If at any time at which any goods or chattels belonging to any person (in this section referred to as "the person in default") are][1] liable to be taken by virtue of any execution or other process, warrant, or authority whatever, or by virtue of any assignment, on any account or pretence whatever, except at the suit of the landlord for rent, [the person in default is in arrears in respect of any such sums as are referred to in subsection (1A) below, the goods or chattels may not be so taken unless on demand made by the collector"][1] the person at whose suit the execution or seizure is made, or to whom the assignment was made, pays or causes to be paid to the collector, before the sale or removal of the goods or chattels, all [such sums as have fallen due at or before the date of seizure][1]:

Provided that, where tax is claimed for more than one year, the person at whose instance the seizure has been made may, on paying to the collector the tax which is due for one whole year, proceed in his seizure in like manner as if no tax had been claimed.

[(1A) The sums referred to in subsection (1) above are—

    (*a*) sums due from the person in default on account of deductions of income tax from emoluments paid during the period of twelve months next before the date of seizure, being deductions which the person in default was liable to make under section 203 of the principal Act (pay as you earn) less the amount of the repayments of income tax which he was liable to make during that period; and

    (*b*) sums due from the person in default in respect of deductions required to be made by him for that period under section 559 of the principal Act (sub-contractors in the construction industry).][2]

(2) [If the sums referred to in subsection (1) above are not paid within ten days of the date of the demand referred to in that subsection, the collector may][3] distrain the goods and chattels notwithstanding the seizure or assignment, and [may proceed][3] to the sale thereof, as prescribed by this Act, for the purpose of obtaining payment of the whole of [those sums][3], and the reasonable costs and charges attending such distress and sale, and every collector so doing shall be indemnified by virtue of this Act.

Commentary—*Simon's Direct Tax Service* A3.1413.
Amendments—[1] Words in sub-s (1) substituted by FA 1989, s 153.
[2] Sub-s (1A) inserted by FA 1989 s 153.
[3] Words in sub-s (2) substituted by FA 1989 s 153.

[63 Recovery of tax in Scotland

(1) Subject to subsection (3) below, in Scotland, where any tax is due and has not been paid, the sheriff, on an application by the collector accompanied by a certificate by the collector—

    (*a*) stating that none of the persons specified in the application has paid the tax due by him;
    (*b*) stating that the collector has demanded payment under section 60 of this Act from each such person of the amount due by him
    (*c*) stating that 14 days have elapsed since the date of such demand without payment of the said amount; and
    (*d*) specifying the amount due and unpaid by each such person,

shall grant a summary warrant in a form prescribed by Act of Sederunt authorising the recovery, by any of the diligences mentioned in subsection (2) below, of the amount remaining due and unpaid.

(2) The diligences referred to in subsection (1) above are—

    (*a*) a poinding and sale in accordance with Schedule 5 to the Debtors (Scotland) Act 1987;
    (*b*) an earnings arrestment;
    (*c*) an arrestment and action of forthcoming or sale.

(3) Paragraph (*c*) of subsection (1) above shall not apply to an application under that subsection [insofar as it relates to sums due in respect of—][2]

    [(*a*) deductions of income tax which any person specified in the application was liable to make under section 203 of the principal Act (pay as you earn); or][2]
    [(*b*) deductions required to be made under section 559 of the principal Act (sub-contractors in the construction industry) by any person specified in the application.][2][1]

[(4) In this section references to amounts of tax due and references to sums due in respect of deductions include references to amounts which are deemed to be—

    (*a*) amounts of tax which the person is liable to pay by virtue of the Income Tax (Employments) Regulations 1973; or
    (*b*) amounts which the person is liable to pay by virtue of the Income Tax (Sub-Contractors in the Construction Industry) Regulations 1975.][3]

Commentary—*Simon's Direct Tax Service* A3.1414.
Definitions—"Collector", s 118(1); "principal Act", s 118(1); "tax", s 118(1).
Cross references—See TMA 1970 s 69 (recovery of penalty, surchrge or interest).
Modifications—Modification of this section in relation to the administration and collection of windfall tax by the Finance (No 2) Act 1997 Sch 2 para 15.
Amendments—[1] This section and s 63A below substituted for s 63 by the Debtors (Scotland) Act 1987, Sch 4, para 2 with effect from 30 November 1988 by virtue of the Debtors (Scotland) Act 1987 (Commencement No 2) Order, SI 1988/1818.
[2] Sub-s (3)(*a*), (*b*) and the preceding words substituted by FA 1989 s 154.
[3] Sub-s (4) added by FA 1989 s 154.

Prospective amendments—Sub-s (2)(*a*) repealed by the Abolition of Poindings and Warrant Sales Act 2001 s 3(1), Schedule, Pt 2 with effect from 31 December 2002 or such earlier date as the Scottish Ministers may by statutory instrument appoint.

[63A Sheriff officer's fees and outlays

(1) Subject to subsection (2) below and without prejudice to paragraphs 25 to 34 of Schedule 5 to the Debtors (Scotland) Act 1987 (expenses of poinding and sale), the sheriff officer's fees, together with the outlays necessarily incurred by him, in connection with the execution of a summary warrant shall be chargeable against the debtor.

(2) No fee shall be chargeable by the sheriff officer against the debtor for collecting, and accounting to the collector for, sums paid to him by the debtor in respect of the amount owing.][1]

Commentary—*Simon's Direct Tax Service* **A3.1414.**
Definition—"Collector", s 118(1).
Amendments—[1] This section and s 63 above substituted for s 63 by the Debtors (Scotland) Act 1987, Sch 4, para 2 with effect from 30 November 1988 by virtue of the Debtors (Scotland) Act 1987 (Commencement No 2) Order, SI 1988/1818.
Prospective amendments—In sub-s (1) words from "and without prejudice" to "poinding and sale)" repealed by the Abolition of Poindings and Warrant Sales Act 2001 s 3(1), Schedule, Pt 2 with effect from 31 December 2002 or such earlier date as the Scottish Ministers may by statutory instrument appoint.

64 Priority of claim for tax in Scotland

(1) [If at any time at which any moveable goods and effects belonging to any person (in this section referred to as "the person in default") are][1] liable to be taken by virtue of any poinding, sequestration for rent, or diligence whatever, or by any assignation, [the person in default is in arrears in respect of any such sums as are referred to in subsection (1A) below, the goods and effects may not be so taken unless on demand made by the collector][1], the person proceeding to take the said goods and effects pays [such sums as have fallen due at or before the date of poinding or, as the case may be, other diligence or assignation.][1]

[(1A) The sums referred to in subsection (1) above are—

(*a*) sums due from the person in default on account of deductions of income tax from emoluments paid during the period of twelve months next before the date of poinding, being deductions which the person in default was liable to make under section 203 of the principal Act (pay as you earn) less the amount of the repayments of income tax which he was liable to make during that period; and

(*b*) sums due from the person in default in respect of deductions required to be made by him for that period under section 559 of the principal Act (sub-contractors in the construction industry).][2]

(2) [If the sums referred to in subsection (1) above are not paid within ten days of the date of the demand referred to in that subsection, the sums shall][3], notwithstanding any [proceedings][3] for the purpose of taking the said moveable goods and effects, be recoverable by poinding and selling the said moveable goods and effects under warrant obtained in conformity with the provisions contained in section 63 above.

(3) ...

Commentary—*Simon's Direct Tax Service* **A3.1414.**
Amendments—[1] Words in sub-s (1) substituted by FA 1989 s 155.
[2] Sub-s (1A) inserted by FA 1989 s 155.
[3] Words in sub-s (2) substituted by FA 1989 s 155.
[4] Sub-s (3) repealed by FA 1989 s 187, Sch 17.
Prospective amendments—Sub-s (2) repealed by the Abolition of Poindings and Warrant Sales Act 2001 s 3(1), Schedule, Pt 2 with effect from 31 December 2002 or such earlier date as the Scottish Ministers may by statutory instrument appoint.

Court proceedings

65 Magistrates' courts

(1) [Any amount due and payable by way of income tax, capital gains tax or corporation tax which does not exceed £2,000][3] shall, without prejudice to any other remedy, be recoverable summarily as a civil debt by proceedings commenced in the name of a collector.

(2) All or any of the sums due in respect of tax from any one person and payable to any one collector (being sums which are by law recoverable summarily) may, whether or not they are due under one assessment, be included in the same complaint, summons, order, warrant or other document required by law to be laid before justices or to be issued by justices, and every such document as aforesaid shall, as respects each such sum, be construed as a separate document and its invalidity as respects any one such sum shall not affect its validity as respects any other such sum.

(3) Proceedings under this section ...[3] may be brought in England and Wales at any time within one year from the time when the matter complained of arose.

(4) It is hereby declared that in subsection (1) above the expression "recoverable summarily as a civil debt" in respect of proceedings in Northern Ireland means recoverable [in proceedings under Article 62 of the Magistrates' Courts (Northern Ireland) Order 1981][1].

[(5) The Treasury may by order made by statutory instrument increase the [sum][3] specified in subsection (1) above; and any such statutory instrument shall be subject to annulment in pursuance of a resolution of the Commons House of Parliament.][2]

Commentary—*Simon's Direct Tax Service* **A3.1410.**
Revenue Internal Guidance—Enforcement Manual En 3.101–3.108 (introduction to summary proceedings).
En 3.201–3.213 (preparation and issue of summons; service of summons; declaration of service etc).
En 3.301–3.309 (preparation and conduct of hearing).
En 3.401–3.422 (enforcement of distress warrants; judgment summons proceedings; committal hearings).
En 3.501–3.509 (dealing with late claims for relief, postponement applications, pleas in mitigation of penalties).
En 3.601–3.610 (court fees and court costs).
Cross references—See TMA 1970 s 67 (this section not applicable in Scotland).
TMA 1970 s 69 (recovery of penalty, surchrge or interest).
Amendments—[1] Words in sub-s (4) substituted by FA 1984, s 57 (1) (*a*), (*b*).
[2] Sub-s (5) added by FA 1984, s 57 (1) (*c*).
[3] Words in sub-ss (1) and (5) substituted and words in sub-s (3) repealed by FA 1998 Sch 19 para 30 with effect in relation to accounting periods ending after 30 June 1999 (by virtue of Finance Act 1994, Section 199, (Appointed Day) Order, SI 1998/3173 art 2).

66 County courts

(1) [Tax due and payable ...][6] may, in England and Wales, and in Northern Ireland where the amount does not exceed the limit specified in Article 10(1) of the County Courts (Northern Ireland) Order 1980,][3] without prejudice to any other remedy, be sued for and recovered from the person charged therewith as a debt due to the Crown by proceedings in a county court commenced in the name of a collector.

[(2) An officer of the Board who is authorised by the Board to do so may address the court in any proceedings under this section in a county court in England and Wales.][2]

(2A) ...[4]

[(3) In this section as it applies in Northern Ireland the expression "county court" shall mean a county court held for a division under the County Courts (Northern Ireland) Order 1980.][5]

(4) Sections 21 and 42 (2) of the Interpretation Act (Northern Ireland) 1954 shall apply as if any reference in those provisions to any enactment included a reference to this section, and Part III of the County Courts [(Northern Ireland) Order 1980][1] (general civil jurisdiction) shall apply for the purposes of this section in Northern Ireland.

Commentary—*Simon's Direct Tax Service* **A3.1402.**
Note—A county court has jurisdiction under this section with effect from 1 July 1991 whatever the amount involved in the proceedings: High Court and County Courts Jurisdiction Order, SI 1991/724, art 2.
The County Court Appeals Order, SI 1991/1877 prescribes the classes of county court proceedings in which an appeal to the Court of Appeal lies only with leave of a judge of the county court or of the Court of Appeal.
Where the appeal relates to the determination by the county court of proceedings for the recovery of tax under TMA 1970, s 66, leave of a judge of the county court or Court of Appeal must be obtained if the value of the appeal does not exceed £5,000. The value of the appeal for this purpose is the value of the claim (or counterclaim, if larger), but where the county court determination provides for the payment of a sum of money by way of debt, the value of the appeal cannot exceed that sum.
The Order comes into force on 1 October 1991 but does not affect appeals set down, or applications lodged with the Court of Appeal, before that date.
Revenue Internal Guidance—Enforcement Manual, En 4.207–4.224 (procedure for initiating proceedings: service of summons; particulars of claim; discovery of documents).
En 4.301–4.324 (action following service of summons).
En 4.501–4.511 (action following judgment).
En 4.701–4.710 (warrants of execution).
En 4.711–4.718 (garnishee proceedings: used mainly to obtain money from a debtor's bank or building society account).
En 4.719–4.726 (charging order: used where property has to be sold and there is a delay in the sale).
En 4.727–4.749 (attachment of earnings order, requiring employer to make deductions from payments of emoluments).
En 4.750–4.754 (bankruptcy and liquidation proceedings: not considered where only asset is matrimonial home and debt is less than £750).
En 4.755–4.781 (judgment summonses: only used as last resort or where instalment arrangement preferable to bankruptcy or liquidation).
En 4.801–4.821 (application by debtor for administration order).
Cross references—See TMA 1970 s 67 (this section not applicable in Scotland).
TMA 1970 s 69 (recovery of penalty, surchrge or interest).
Amendments—[1] Words in sub-s (4) substituted by the County Courts (Northern Ireland) Order, SI 1980,/397, Sch 1, Pt II.
[2] Sub-s (2) substituted by FA 1984, s 57 (2).
[3] Words in sub-s (1) substituted by the High Court and County Courts Jurisdiction Order, SI 1991/724, Schedule, with effect from 1 July 1991.
[4] Sub-s (2A) repealed by the High Court and County Courts Jurisdiction Order, SI 1991/724, Schedule, with effect from 1 July 1991.
[5] Sub-s (3) substituted by the High Court and County Courts Jurisdiction Order, SI 1991/724, Schedule, with effect from 1 July 1991.
[6] The words "under any assessment" in sub-s (1) repealed by FA 2001 ss 89(1), 110, Sch 33 Pt II(14) with effect for proceedings begun after the passing of FA 2001.

67 Inferior courts in Scotland

(1) In Scotland, [tax due and payable ...][4][1] may, without prejudice to any other remedy, be sued for and recovered from the person charged therewith as a debt due to the Crown by proceedings commenced in the name of a collector in the sheriff court ...[2].

[(1A) An officer of the Board who is authorised by the Board to do so may address the court in any proceedings under this section.][3]

(2) Section 65 and 66 above shall not apply in Scotland.

Commentary—*Simon's Direct Tax Service* **A3.1402.**
Cross references—TMA 1970 s 69 (recovery of penalty, surcharge or interest).

Amendments—¹ Words in sub-s (1) substituted by FA 1995 s 156(1), (2), (4), with effect for proceedings commenced on or after 1 May 1995.
² Words in sub-s (1) repealed by FA 1976, s 58 and Sch 15, Pt III, with effect from 1 September 1976.
³ Sub-s (1A) inserted by FA 1995 s 156(1), (3), (4), with effect for proceedings commenced on or after 1 May 1995.
⁴ The words "under any assessment" in sub-s (1) repealed by FA 2001 ss 89(1), 110, Sch 33 Pt II(14) with effect for proceedings begun after the passing of FA 2001.

68 High Court, etc

(1) Any tax may be sued for and recovered from the person charged therewith in the High Court as a debt due to the Crown, or by any other means whereby any debt of record or otherwise due to the Crown can, or may at any time, be sued for and recovered, as well as by the other means specially provided by this Act for levying the tax.

(2) All matters within the jurisdiction of the High Court under this section shall be assigned in Scotland to the Court of Session sitting as the Court of Exchequer.

Commentary—*Simon's Direct Tax Service* A3.1401.
Simon's Tax Cases—*Lord Advocate v Butt* [1992] STC 122.
Cross references—See TMA 1970 s 69 (recovery of penalty, surchrge or interest).

Supplemental

[69 Recovery of penalty, surcharge or interest

(1) This section applies to—

   (*a*) penalties imposed under Part II, VA or X of this Act or Schedule 18 to the Finance Act 1998;
   (*b*) surcharges imposed under Part VA of this Act; and
   (*c*) interest charged under any provision of this Act (or recoverable as if it were interest so charged).

(2) An amount by way of penalty, surcharge or interest to which this section applies shall be treated for the purposes of the following provisions as if it were an amount of tax.

(3) Those provisions are—

   (*a*) sections 61, 63 and 65 to 68 of this Act;
   (*b*) section 35(2)(*g*)(i) of the Crown Proceedings Act 1947 (rules of court: restriction of set-off or counterclaim where proceedings, or set-off or counterclaim, relate to tax) and any rules of court imposing any such restriction;
   (*c*) section 35(2)(*b*) of that Act as set out in section 50 of that Act (which imposes corresponding restrictions in Scotland).]¹

Commentary—*Simon's Direct Tax Service* A3.1320.
Amendments—¹ Section substituted by FA 2001 s 89(2) with effect for—

(*a*) to proceedings begun (or a counterclaim made) after the passing of FA 2001, and
(*b*) to a set-off first claimed after the passing of FA 2001.
Before substitution, this section read as follows—

"**69 Interest on tax**
A penalty imposed under Part II, VA or X of this Act [or under Schedule 18 to the Finance Act 1998, a surcharge imposed under Part VA of this Act and interest charged under Part IX of this Act or recoverable under section 826(8A) of the principal Act as if it were interest so charged shall be treated for the purposes—

(*a*) of sections 61, 63 and 65 to 68 above, and
(*b*) of section 35 (2)(*g*)(i) of the Crown Proceedings Act 1947 (rules of court to impose restrictions on set-off and counterclaim where the proceedings or set-off or counterclaim relate to tax) and of any rules of court (including county court rules) for England and Wales or Northern Ireland, which impose such a restriction, and
(*c*) of section 35(2)(*b*) of the said Act of 1947 as set out in section 50 of that Act (which imposes corresponding restrictions in Scotland).

as if it were tax charged and due and payable under the assessment to which it relates or, if it is a penalty or surcharge imposed in respect of, or if it is interest on, tax which is not in fact assessed or if it is interest recoverable under section 826(8A) of the principal Act, as if it were tax charged and due and payable under an assessment."

70 Evidence

(1) Where tax is in arrear, a certificate of the inspector or any other officer of the Board that tax has been charged and is due, together with a certificate of the collector that payment of the tax has not been made to him, or, to the best of his knowledge and belief, to any other collector, or to any person acting on his behalf or on behalf of another collector, shall be sufficient evidence that the sum mentioned in the certificate is unpaid and is due to the Crown; and any document purporting to be such a certificate as is mentioned in this subsection shall be deemed to be such a certificate until the contrary is proved.

(2) A certificate of a collector—

   [(*a*) that a penalty is payable under Part II, VA or X of this Act [or under Schedule 18 to the Finance Act 1998]³, that a surcharge is payable under Part VA of this Act or that interest is [payable under any provision of this Act or the principal Act]⁴, and
   (*b*) that payment of the penalty, surcharge or interest has not been made to him or, to the best of his knowledge and belief, to any other collector or to any person acting on his behalf or on behalf of another collector,]¹

shall be sufficient evidence that the sum mentioned in the certificate is unpaid and is due to the Crown, and any document purporting to be such a certificate as is mentioned in this subsection shall be deemed to be such a certificate unless the contrary is proved.

[*(3)* ...]²

(4) A written statement as to the wages, salaries, fees, and other emoluments paid for any period to the person against whom proceedings are brought under section 65, 66 or 67 of this Act, purporting to be signed by his employer for that period or by any responsible person in the employment of the employer, shall in such proceedings be prima facie evidence that the wages, salaries, fees and other emoluments therein stated to have been paid to the person charged have in fact been so paid.

Commentary—*Simon's Direct Tax Service* **A3.821, 1405, 1410.**
Definitions—''The Board'', s 118(1).
Amendments—¹ Words in sub-s (2) substituted by FA 1994 ss 196, 199 and Sch 19 para 21 with effect from the year 1996–97 as respects income tax and capital gains tax and, as respects corporation tax, with effect in relation to accounting periods ending after 30 June 1999 (by virtue of Finance Act 1994, Section 199, (Appointed Day) Order, SI 1998/3173 art 2).
² Sub-s (3), as substituted by FA 1989, s 160(3), repealed by FA 1994, ss 196, 199 and Sch 19, para 21 with effect from the year 1996–97 as respects income tax and capital gains tax and, as respects corporation tax, with effect in relation to accounting periods ending after 30 June 1999 (by virtue of SI 1998/3173 art 2).
³ Words in sub-s (2)(*a*) inserted by FA 1998 Sch 19 para 32 with effect in relation to accounting periods ending after 30 June 1999 (by virtue of SI 1998/3173 art 2).
⁴ Words in sub-s (2)(*a*) substituted for words ''payable under Part IX of this Act'' by FA 2001 s 89(3) with effect for certificates tendered in evidence after the passing of FA 2001.

[70A Payments by cheque

(1) For the purposes of this Act and the provisions mentioned in subsection (2) below, where—

    (*a*) any payment to an officer of the Board or the Board is made by cheque, and
    (*b*) the cheque is paid on its first presentation to the banker on whom it is drawn,

the payment shall be treated as made on the day on which the cheque was received by the officer or the Board.

(2) The provisions are—

    (*a*) sections 824 to 826 of the principal Act (repayment supplements and interest on tax overpaid); and
    (*b*) section 283 of the 1992 Act (repayment supplements).]¹

Commentary—*Simon's Direct Tax Service* **E1.824.**
Revenue & other press releases—IR 1–4–96 (details of when payments made to the Revenue are treated as received for the purpose of calculating interest).
Revenue Internal Guidance—Assessed Taxes Manual AT 8.301 (for sums over £500,000, the Revenue will obtain town clearing wherever possible).
Amendments—¹ This section inserted by FA 1994 Sch 19 para 22 with effect as respects payments by cheques which are received after 5 April 1996.

PART VII
PERSONS CHARGEABLE IN A REPRESENTATIVE CAPACITY, ETC.
Income tax

71 Bodies of persons

(1) Subject to [sections 6 to 12 and Parts VIII and XI]¹ of the principal Act (charge of corporation tax on companies), every body of persons shall be chargeable to income tax in like manner as any person is chargeable under the Income Tax Acts.

(2) Subject to section 108 of this Act, the chamberlain or other officer acting as treasurer, auditor or receiver for the time being of any body of persons chargeable to income tax shall be answerable for doing all such acts as are required to be done under the Income Tax Acts for the purpose of the assessment of the body and for payment of the tax.

(3) Every such officer as aforesaid may from time to time retain, out of any money coming into his hands on behalf of the body, so much thereof as is sufficient to pay the income tax charged upon the body, and shall be indemnified for all such payments made in pursuance of the Income Tax Acts.

Commentary—*Simon's Direct Tax Service* **A3.302.**
Definitions—''Body of persons'', s 118(1); ''principal Act'', s 118(1).
Amendments—¹ Words in sub-s (1) substituted by TA 1988, Sch 29, para 32 Table.

72 Trustees, guardians, etc of incapacitated persons

(1) The trustee, guardian, tutor, curator or committee of any incapacitated person having the direction, control or management of the property or concern of any such person, whether such person resides in the United Kingdom or not, shall be assessable and chargeable to income tax in like manner and to the like amount as that person would be assessed and charged if he were not an incapacitated person.

(2) The person who is chargeable in respect of an incapacitated person shall be answerable for all matters required to be done under the Income Tax Acts for the purpose of assessment and payment of income tax.

(3) Any person who has been charged under the Income Tax Acts in respect of any incapacitated person as aforesaid may retain, out of money coming into his hands on behalf of any such person, so much thereof from time to time as is sufficient to pay the tax charged, and shall be indemnified for all such payments made in pursuance of the Income Tax Acts.

Commentary—*Simon's Direct Tax Service* **A3.317.**
Definition—''Incapacitated person'', s 118(1).
Cross references—See Education (Student Loans) (Repayment) Regulations, SI 2000/944 reg 24 (application of this section in connection with the repayment of student loans).

73 Further provision as to infants

If a person chargeable to income tax is an infant, then his parent, guardian or tutor—

    (*a*) shall be liable for the tax in default of payment by the infant, and
    (*b*) on neglect or refusal of payment, may be proceeded against in like manner as any other defaulter, and
    (*c*) if he makes such payment, shall be allowed all sums so paid in his accounts.

Commentary—*Simon's Direct Tax Service* **A3.316, 317.**
Definition—''Infant'' (in relation to Scotland), s 118(1).
Cross references—See the Act of Legal Capacity (Scotland) Act 1991, s 11(2), (3) and Sch 1, para 33 (with effect from 25 September 1991 this section, in its application to Scotland, applies with the substitution of the words ''parent or guardian'' for the words ''parent, guardian or tutor'').

74 Personal representatives

(1) If a person chargeable to income tax dies, the executor or administrator of the person deceased shall be liable for the tax chargeable on such deceased person, and may deduct any payments made under this section out of the assets and effects of the person deceased.

(2) On neglect or refusal of payment, any person liable under this section may be proceeded against in like manner as any other defaulter.

Commentary—*Simon's Direct Tax Service* **A3.323.**
Cross references—See Education (Student Loans) (Repayment) Regulations, SI 2000/944 reg 24 (application of this section in connection with the repayment of student loans).

75 Receivers appointed by a court

(1) A receiver appointed by any court in the United Kingdom which has the direction and control of any property in respect of which income tax is charged in accordance with the provisions of the Income Tax Acts shall be assessable and chargeable with the tax in like manner and to the like amount as would be assessed and charged if the property were not under the direction and control of the court.

(2) Every such receiver shall be answerable for doing all matters and things required to be done under the Income Tax Acts for the purpose of assessment and payment of income tax.

Commentary—*Simon's Direct Tax Service* **A3.329.**
Cross references—See Education (Student Loans) (Repayment) Regulations, SI 2000/944 reg 24 (application of this section in connection with the repayment of student loans).

76 Protection for certain trustees, agents and receivers

(1) A trustee who has authorised the receipt of profits arising from trust property by, or by the agent of, the person entitled thereto shall not, if—

    (*a*) that person or agent actually received the profits under that authority, and
    (*b*) the trustee makes a return, as required by section 13 of this Act, of the name, address and profits of that person,

be required to do any other act for the purpose of the assessment of that person to income tax.

(2) An agent or receiver of any person resident in the United Kingdom, other than an incapacitated person, shall not, if he makes a return, as required by section 13 of this Act of the name, address and profits of that person, be required to do any other act for the purpose of the assessment of that person to income tax.

Commentary—*Simon's Direct Tax Service* **A3.329.**
Definitions—''Incapacitated person'', s 118(1); ''return'', s 118(1).
Cross references—See Education (Student Loans) (Repayment) Regulations, SI 2000/944 reg 24 (application of this section in connection with the repayment of student loans).

Capital gains tax

77 Application of Part VII to capital gains tax

(1) This Part of this Act (except section 76 above) shall apply in relation to capital gains tax as it applies in relation to income tax ... [1], and subject to any necessary modifications.

(2) This Part of this Act as applied by this section shall not affect the question of who is the person to whom chargeable gains accrue, or who is chargeable to capital gains tax, so far as that question is relevant for the purposes of any exemption, or of any provision determining the rate at which capital gains tax is chargeable.

Commentary—*Simon's Direct Tax Service* A3.317, 323.
Definitions—''Chargeable gain'', TCGA 1992, s 15(2) by virtue of s 118(1).
Amendments—¹ Words in sub-s (1) repealed by FA 1971, ss 37 (2), 38 (1) and Sch 14, Pt. II, with effect from the year 1973–74.

PART VIII
CHARGES ON NON-RESIDENTS
Income tax

78 Method of charging non-residents

Commentary—*Simon's Direct Tax Service* B3.118.
Amendments—This section repealed by FA 1995 s 162, Sch 29 Pt VIII(16), for the purposes of income tax and capital gains tax in relation to the year 1996–97 and subsequent years of assessment, and for the purposes of corporation tax, in relation to accounting periods beginning after 31 March 1996.

79 Profits from branch or agency

Commentary—*Simon's Direct Tax Service* B3.118.
Amendments—This section repealed by FA 1995 s 162, Sch 29 Pt VIII(16), for the purposes of income tax and capital gains tax in relation to the year 1996–97 and subsequent years of assessment, and for the purposes of corporation tax, in relation to accounting periods beginning after 31 March 1996.

80 Charge on percentage of turnover

Commentary—*Simon's Direct Tax Service* B3.121.
Amendments—This section repealed by FA 1995 s 162, Sch 29, Pt VIII(16), for the purposes of income tax and capital gains tax in relation to the year 1996–97 and subsequent years of assessment, and for the purposes of corporation tax, in relation to accounting periods beginning after 31 March 1996.

81 Taxation on basis of merchanting profit

Commentary—*Simon's Direct Tax Service* B3.122.
Amendments—This section repealed by FA 1995 s 162, Sch 29, Pt VIII(16), for the purposes of income tax and capital gains tax in relation to the year 1996–97 and subsequent years of assessment, and for the purposes of corporation tax, in relation to accounting periods beginning after 31 March 1996.

82 Savings

Commentary—*Simon's Direct Tax Service* B3.118, 123.
Amendments—This section repealed by FA 1995 s 162, Sch 29 Pt VIII(16), for the purposes of income tax and capital gains tax in relation to the year 1996–97 and subsequent years of assessment, and for the purposes of corporation tax, in relation to accounting periods beginning after 31 March 1996.

83 Responsibilities and indemnification of persons in whose name a non-resident person is chargeable

Commentary—*Simon's Direct Tax Service* A3.330.
Amendments—This section repealed by FA 1995 s 162, Sch 29 Pt VIII(16), for the purposes of income tax and capital gains tax in relation to the year 1996–97 and subsequent years of assessment, and for the purposes of corporation tax, in relation to accounting periods beginning after 31 March 1996.

Capital gains tax

84 Gains from branch or agency

Commentary—*Simon's Direct Tax Service* A3.330.
Amendments—This section repealed by FA 1995 s 162, Sch 29 Pt VIII(16), for the purposes of income tax and capital gains tax in relation to the year 1996–97 and subsequent years of assessment, and for the purposes of corporation tax, in relation to accounting periods beginning after 31 March 1996.

Corporation tax

85 Application of Part VIII to corporation tax

Amendments—This section repealed by FA 1995 s 162, Sch 29 Pt VIII(16), for the purposes of income tax and capital gains tax in relation to the year 1996–97 and subsequent years of assessment, and for the purposes of corporation tax, in relation to accounting periods beginning after 31 March 1996.

PART IX
INTEREST ON OVERDUE TAX

Cross references—See TMA 1970 s 70(2) (a certificate of a collector that interest is payable under this Part and has not been paid is sufficient evidence).
FA 1984 Sch 14 para 6(4) (this Part not to apply, subject to certain time limits, where capital gains tax due from beneficiaries on gains of non-resident trustees is postponed);
IT (Entertainers and Sportsmen) Regulations, SI 1987/530 reg 11(3)(b) (assessed tax on connected payments or transfers (as defined in TA 1988 s 556) to be treated for the purposes of this Part as income tax under Schedule D);
FA 1993 s 122(2) (application of this Part to public offices and departments of the Crown).

[86 Interest on overdue income tax and capital gains tax

(1) The following, namely—

(a) any amount on account of income tax which becomes due and payable in accordance with section 59A(2) of this Act, and

(b) any income tax or capital gains tax which becomes due and payable in accordance with section 55 or 59B of this Act,

shall carry interest at the rate applicable under section 178 of the Finance Act 1989 from the relevant date until payment.

(2) For the purposes of subsection (1)(a) above the relevant date is whichever of the dates mentioned in section 59A(2) of this Act is applicable; and for the purposes of subsection (1)(b) above the relevant date is—

(a) in any such case as is mentioned in subsection (3) of section 59B of this Act, the last day of the period of three months mentioned in that subsection; and

(b) in any other case, the date mentioned in subsection (4) of that section.

(3) Subsection (1) above applies even if the relevant date is a non-business day within the meaning of [section 92]² of the Bills of Exchange Act 1882.

(4) Subsection (5) below applies where as regards a year of assessment—

(a) any person makes a claim under subsection (3) or (4) of section 59A of this Act in respect of the amounts (the section 59A amounts) payable by him in accordance with subsection (2) of that section, and

(b) an amount (the section 59B amount) becomes payable by him

[(i)]³ in accordance with section 59B(3), (4) or (5) of this Act [or]³
[(ii) in accordance with section 59B(6) of this Act in respect of income tax assessed under section 29 of this Act.]³

(5) Interest shall be payable under this section as if each of the section 59A amounts had been equal to—

(a) the aggregate of that amount and 50 per cent of the section 59B amount, or

(b) the amount which would have been payable in accordance with subsection (2) of section 59A of this Act if the claim under subsection (3) or (4) of that section had not been made,

whichever is the less.

(6) In determining for the purposes of subsections (4) and (5) above what amount (if any) is payable by any person in accordance with section 59B(3), (4) or (5) of this Act [or, in respect of income tax assessed under section 29 of this Act, in accordance with section 59B(6) of this Act]⁴—

(a) it shall be assumed that both of the section 59A amounts have been paid, and

(b) no account shall be taken of any amount which has been paid on account otherwise than under section 59A(2) of this Act or is payable by way of capital gains tax.

(7) Subsection (8) below applies where as regards any person and a year of assessment—

(a) amounts (the section 59A amounts) become payable by him in accordance with section 59A(2) of this Act, and

(b) an amount (the section 59B amount) becomes repayable to him in accordance with section 59B(3), (4) or (5) of this Act.

(8) So much of any interest payable under this section on either of the section 59A amounts as is not attributable to the amount by which that amount exceeds 50 per cent of the section 59B amount shall be remitted.

(9) In determining for the purposes of subsections (7) and (8) above what amount (if any) is repayable to any person in accordance with section 59B(3), (4) or (5) of this Act, no account shall be taken of any amount which has been paid on account otherwise than under section 59A(2) of this Act or is payable by way of capital gains tax.]¹

Commentary—*Simon's Direct Tax Service* E1.825.
Note—This section is substituted by FA 1995 s 110(1), (2), (4) with effect from the year 1996–97 in so far as it relates to income tax and capital gains tax (other than in relation to partnerships whose trades, professions or businesses were set up and commenced before 6 April 1994). In the case of partnerships whose trades, professions or businesses were set up and commenced before 6 April 1994 it has effect from the year 1997–98 (see FA 1995 s 110(4) as inserted by FA 1996 s 131(1) and deemed always to have had effect), but for 1996–97 the old version of the section applied (see the *Yellow Tax Handbook*, 1998–99, 38th Edition, for the text of the old version).

This section also applies to liabilities for 1995–96 and earlier years which are assessed after 5 April 1998, by virtue of FA 1995 s 110(2).

For the interest rate applicable under sub-s (1) above, see SI 1989/1297 and the Note under s 89 (now repealed).

Revenue & other press releases—Certificates of tax deposit. Prospectus (Series 7), para 3 (use of to pay tax).

Hansard 17–11–86 (tax paid at a bank using the bank giro system is treated as paid on the date stamped on the payslip by the cashier).

ICAEW Tax 13/92 16 June 1992 (set-off of over payments against under payments is usually effected in the way which benefits taxpayer most: Guidance on procedure for set-off).

IR 1–4–93 (where tax is paid by electronic transfer, the date of payment is one working day immediately before the date value is received by the Revenue).

IR 27-1-97 (where statement of account under self-assessment issued late *in certain circumstances*, date from which interest accrues will be in practice be deferred).

Revenue Internal Guidance—Assessed Taxes Manual AT12.101-12.701 (individuals and partnerships: Revenue procedures for computing, collecting and mitigating interest).

AT13.801-13.803 (collection from non-resident entertainers and sportsmen).

AT13.901-13.903 (collection from Lloyd's agents).

AT14.200–14.218 (Revenue procedures for computing, collecting and instigating interest chargeable under this section).

AT14.501-14.511 (computation of interest).

AT14.507 (the ''effective date'' of payment may be earlier than the date of receipt: Table for calculation of effective date of payment in different circumstances and for different types of payment).

AT14.701-14.713 (procedure for dealing with objections to the charge to interest).

AT14.712 (the effective date of payment of an overpayment set-off is the date the inspector established that an overpayment existed, and therefore could have been repaid; the original date of payment of the amount set-off is immaterial).

Simon's Tax Cases—*R v IRC, ex p Barker* [1994] STC 731.

Definitions—''the 1992 Act'', s 118(1); ''accounting period'', TA 1988 s 834(1); ''interest'', TA 1988 s 832(1); ''principal Act'', s 118(1).

Cross references—See TMA 1970 s 70 (certificate from collector that interest is payable under this section is sufficient evidence of that fact).

TMA 1970 s 88 (exclusion of interest under this section where tax carries interest under s 88).

TMA 1970 s 91 (effect of reliefs on interest payable under this section).

TMA 1970 s 92 (interest relief where tax arrears arise by reason of exchange restrictions).

TMA 1970 s 107A(2) (recovery of interest from the relevant trustees of a settlement).

TA 1988 ss 306(9), 307(1) (application of this section to assessments relating to EIS relief).

TA 1988 s 369(7) (application of this section to MIRAS).

TA 1988 s 767B(1), (3) (avoidance of corporation tax by change in company ownership; measures to prevent avoidance and to charge interest).

TA 1988 Sch 14 para 7(3), (4) (application of this section to the recovery from a taxpayer of excess relief in respect of life assurance premiums).

FA 1991 s 33(3)(*c*), (3A) (application of this section in relation to tax relief claimed for vocational training).

FA 1995 s 71(4) (regulations may be made applying this section to repayments of tax credits to venture capital trusts and investors).

Amendments—[1] This section is substituted by FA 1995 s 110(1), (2), (4) with effect from the year 1996–97, other than in relation to partnerships whose trades, professions or businesses were set up and commenced before 6 April 1994, where it has effect from the year 1997–98. This section will also apply in relation to tax which is charged by an assessment made after 5 April 1998 which is for the year 1995–96 or earlier years in which case ''the relevant date'' means 31 January next following the relevant year: FA 1995 s 110(2), (3).

[2] Words in sub-s (3) substituted by FA 1996 s 131(2).

[3] Words in sub-s (4)(*b*) inserted by FA 1996 Sch 18 para 3(2) with effect from the year 1996–97 except in so far as it relates to partnerships whose trades, professions or businesses are set up and commenced before 6 April 1994 when it has effect from the year 1997–98.

[4] Words in sub-s (6) inserted by FA 1996 Sch 18 para 3(3) with effect from the year 1996–97 except in so far as it relates to partnerships whose trades, professions or businesses are set up and commenced before 6 April 1994 when it has effect from the year 1997–98.

[86A Interest on development land tax unpaid on reckonable date]

Amendments—This section inserted by Development Land Tax Act 1976 s 41, Sch 8 para 21, but ceased to have effect in respect of any disposal taking place after 18 March 1985, by virtue of the repeal of the 1976 Act by the Finance Act 1985 s 98(6), Sch 27 Pt X.

[87 Interest on overdue advance corporation tax and income tax on company payments

(1) Any tax assessable in accordance with Schedule ...[6] [16][3] to [the principal Act][3] shall carry interest at the [rate applicable under section 178 of the Finance Act 1989][5] from the date when the tax becomes due and payable until payment.

(2) Where—

(*a*) ...[6]

(*b*) income tax paid in respect of payments made in any return period is repaid or discharged under paragraph 5 of the said Schedule [16][3] in consequence of the receipt in a later return period of a payment on which income tax is borne by deduction,

the repayment or discharge shall not affect interest under this section on the tax so repaid or discharged for such time as is specified in subsection (3) below but, subject to that, this section shall apply as if any such tax which is repaid or discharged had never become payable.

(3) The time for which interest is not affected is—

(*a*) any time before the expiration of fourteen days from the end of the later return period, unless the return for that period is made earlier in those fourteen days; and

(*b*) if that return is made earlier in those fourteen days, any time ending before the date on which the return is made.

(4), (5) ...[4]

(6) In this section "return period" means a period for which a return is required to be made under the said Schedule ...[6] [16][3].

(7) It is hereby declared that this section applies to ...[6] income tax which, in accordance with [the said Schedule 16][6], is paid without the making of any assessment (but is paid after it is due), and that where the tax is charged by an assessment (whether or not any part of it has been paid when the assessment is made) this section applies as respects interest running before as well as after the making of the assessment].[1]

[(8) Tax assessable as mentioned in subsection (1) above shall carry interest from the date when it becomes due and payable even if that date is a non-business day within the meaning of section 92 of the Bills of Exchange Act 1882.][2]

Commentary—*Simon's Direct Tax Service* **A3.1324; D1.606, 617.**
Revenue & other press releases—Certificates of tax deposit Prospectus (Series 7), para 3 (use of to pay tax).
Hansard 17-11-86 (tax paid at a bank using the bank giro system is treated as paid on the date stamped on the payslip by the cashier).
ICAEW TR799 June 1990 (company in liquidation: interest under this section does not accrue beyond the date of commencement of liquidation, but interest under IA 1986 s 189 may arise from the later of the date of commencement of liquidation and the reckonable date).
IR 1-4-93 (where tax is paid by electronic transfer, the date of payment is one working day immediately before the date value is received by the Revenue).
Notes—For the interest rate applicable under sub-s (1) above, see SI 1989/1297 and the Note under s 89 (now repealed).
Cross references—See TMA 1970 s 70(2) (certificate from collector that interest is payable under this section is sufficient evidence of that fact).
IT (Entertainers and Sportsmen) Regulations, SI 1987/530 reg 14(2)(*b*) (modification of this section in its application to tax assessable under the Regulations);
IT (Building Societies) (Dividends and Interest) Regulations, SI 1990/2231 reg 10(4) (collection of income tax payable by building societies).
Amendments—[1] This section was substituted by FA 1972 s 111 and Sch 24 para 10, with effect from 6 April 1973.
[2] Sub-s (8) added by F(No 2)A 1975 s 46(3)(*b*) in relation to tax charged by assessment notice issued after 31 July 1975; see F(No 2)A 1975 s 44(7).
[3] Numbers and words in sub-ss (1) (2)(*b*), (6) substituted by TA 1988 Sch 29 para 32 Table.
[4] Sub-ss (4), (5) repealed by FA 1989 s 158(1)(*b*) and Sch 17 Pt VIII with effect, by virtue of FA 1989 s 158(1) and (2) (Appointed Days) Order, SI 1993/753 where tax is charged by an assessment relating to an accounting period beginning after 18 April 1993.
[5] Words in sub-s (1) substituted by FA 1989 s 179(1)(*b*)(i), (4) with effect from 18 August 1989 by virtue of FA 1989 s 178(1) (Appointed Day No 1) Order, SI 1989/1298.
[6] Words in sub-ss (1), (6), (7) and sub-s (2)(*a*) repealed, and words in sub-s (7) substituted, by FA 1998 Sch 3 para 3 with effect in relation to accounting periods beginning after 5 April 1999.

[87A Interest on overdue corporation tax etc

(1) Corporation tax shall carry interest at the [rate applicable under section 178 of the Finance Act 1989][3] from the date when the tax becomes due and payable (in accordance with [section 59D of this Act][9] until payment.

(2) Subsection (1) above applies even if the date when the tax becomes due and payable (as mentioned in that subsection) is a non-business day within the meaning of section 92 of the Bills of Exchange Act 1882.

(3) In relation to corporation tax assessed [or treated as assessed][15] by virtue of section [346(2) or 347(1) of the principal Act,][2] [section 137(4), 139(7) [or 190][17] ...[17] of the 1992 Act ...[16] [paragraph 75A(2) of Schedule 18 to the Finance Act 1998][14]][4] [or Schedule 28 of the Finance Act 2000][16] (which enable unpaid corporation tax assessed on a company to be assessed on other persons in certain circumstances), the reference in subsection (1) above to the date when the tax becomes due and payable is a reference to the date when it became due and payable by the company.

(4) ...[13]

[(4A) In a case where—
    (*a*) there is for an accounting period of a company ("the later period") [a non-trading deficit on the company's loan relationships,][10]
    (*b*) as a result of a claim under [section 83(2)(*c*) of the Finance Act 1996 or paragraph 4(3) of Schedule 11 to that Act the whole or part of the deficit for the later period is set off against profits][11] of an earlier accounting period ("the earlier period"), and
    [(*c*) if the claim had not been made, there would be an amount or, as the case may be, an additional amount of corporation tax for the earlier period which would carry interest in accordance with this section,][7]
[then, for the purposes of the determination at any time of whether any interest is payable under this section or of the amount of interest so payable, the amount mentioned in paragraph (*c*) above shall be taken to be an amount of unpaid corporation tax for the earlier period except so far as concerns interest for any time after the date on which any corporation tax for the later period became (or, as the case may be, would have become) due and payable [as mentioned in subsection (8) below][12].][8]][6]

[(4B) ...[13]

(5) A sum assessed on a company by such an assessment as is referred to in [section 252(5) of the principal Act][2] (recovery of payment of tax credit or interest on such a payment) shall carry interest at the [rate applicable under section 178 of the Finance Act 1989][3] from the date when the payment of tax credit or interest was made until the sum assessed is paid.][1]

[(6) In any case where—

(*a*) on a claim under section 393A(1) of the principal Act, the whole or any part of a loss incurred in an accounting period (the "later period") has been set off for the purposes of corporation tax against profits of a preceding accounting period (the "earlier period"),

(*b*) the earlier period does not fall wholly within the period of twelve months immediately preceding the later period, and

(*c*) if the claim had not been made, there would be an amount or, as the case may be, an additional amount of corporation tax for the earlier period which would carry interest in accordance with this section,

then, for the purposes of the determination at any time of whether any interest is payable under this section or of the amount of interest so payable, the amount mentioned in paragraph (*c*) above shall be taken to be an amount of unpaid corporation tax for the earlier period except so far as concerns interest for any time after the date on which any corporation tax for the later period became (or, as the case may be, would have become) due and payable [as mentioned in subsection (8) below][12].][5]

(7) ...[13]

[(8) In subsections (4), (4A) and (6) above, any reference to the date on which corporation tax for an accounting period became, or would have become, due and payable shall be construed on the basis that corporation tax for an accounting period becomes due and payable on the day following the expiry of nine months from the end of the accounting period.][12]

[(9) The power conferred by section 59E of this Act (alteration of date on which corporation tax becomes due and payable) does not include power to make provision in relation to subsection (4), (4A), (6) or (8) above the effect of which would be to change the meaning of references in subsection (4), (4A) or (6) above to the date on which corporation tax for an accounting period became, or would have become, due and payable (as mentioned in subsection (8) above).][12]

Commentary—*Simon's Direct Tax Service* **D2.708, 844.**
Regulations—Corporation Tax (Instalment Payments) Regulations, SI 1998/3175.
Revenue Internal Guidance—Corporation Tax Manual CT 10221–10223 (worked examples on sub-ss (4), (6)).
Corporation tax pay and file manual CT (PF) 11200-11247 (reallocation of overpayment: Revenue internal procedures).
Notes—TA 1988 ss 346, 347 referred to in sub-s (3) are re-enacted as TCGA 1992 ss 189, 190 respectively.
Definitions—"Accounting period", TA 1988 s 834(1); "advance corporation tax", TA 1988 s 14(1); "company", s 118(1); "loan relationship", TA 1988 s 834(1), FA 1996 s 81; "non-trading deficit", TA 1988 s 834(1), FA 1996 s 82; "surplus advance corporation tax", TA 1988 s 239(3); "tax credit", TA 1988 s 832(1).
Cross references—See TMA 1970 s 70(2) (a certificate of a collector that interest is payable and has not been paid is sufficient evidence).
TMA 1970 s 91(1A), (1B) (adjustment or repayment of interest charged under this section in the event of reduction or discharge of corporation tax).
TMA 1970 s 109(3) (interest on unpaid corporation tax chargeable in connection with loans by a close company to participators; date from which interest starts to be chargeable).
TMA 1970 s 109(3A) (interest on unpaid corporation tax chargeable in connection with loans by a close company to participators; period for which interest is chargeable where loan is repaid).
TA 1988 s 767B(1), (3) (avoidance of corporation tax by change in company ownership; measures to prevent avoidance and to charge interest);
TA 1988 Sch 19AB paras 3(3), 4(3)(*d*), 5(6) (provisional repayments of tax to an insurance company on its pension business income: application of this section with modification where repayments claimed are excessive);
Taxes (Interest Rate) Regulations, SI 1989/1297 regs 3A, 3ZA, 3ZB (applicable rates of interest on overdue corporation tax);
Insurance Companies (Pensions Business) (Transitional Provisions) Regulations, SI 1992/2326 reg 6(5), (6) (excessive claims by an insurance company for repayment of tax on its pension business investment income: modification of this section where repayment in excess of maximum reduced entitlement is recovered with interest under s 30 of this Act).
FA 1994 s 250(5) (disposal of assets by companies treated as non-resident; application of this section with modification where tax due under sub-s (4)).
Corporation Tax (Treatment of Unrelieved Surplus Advance Corporation Tax) Regulations, SI 1999/358 reg 21 (recovery of a sum equal to interest paid by a company under this section in relation to rules concerning the displacement of unrelieved surplus ACT).
FA 2000 Sch 15 para 63(2) (application of this section in relation to corporate venturing scheme).
Modifications—Modification of this section in relation to interest on unpaid amounts of a large company's total corporation tax liability for an accounting period: Corporation Tax (Instalment Payments) Regulations, SI 1998/3175 reg 7.
Amendments—[1] This section inserted by F(No 2)A 1987 s 85 with respect to accounting periods ending after 30 September 1993 by virtue of Corporation Tax Acts (Provisions for Payment of Tax and Returns) (Appointed Days) Order, SI 1992/3066 art 2(1), (2)(*a*).
[2] Words in sub-ss (3)–(5) substituted by TA 1988 Sch 29 para 10(4).
[3] Words in sub-ss (1), (5) substituted by FA 1989 s 179(1)(*b*)(i).
[4] Words in sub-s (3) substituted by TCGA 1992 Sch 10 para 2(9).
[5] Sub-ss (6), (7) substituted for sub-s (6) by FA 1993 Sch 14 para 4(2).
[6] Sub-s (4A) inserted by FA 1993 Sch 18 para 1.
[7] Sub-s (4A)(*c*) substituted by FA 1995 s 130, Sch 24 paras 7, 8(*a*) with effect from 23 March 1995, by virtue of the FA 1993 section 165, (Appointed Day) Order, SI 1994/3224.
[8] Words in sub-s (4A) substituted by FA 1995 s 130, Sch 24 paras 7, 8(*b*), with effect from 23 March 1995, by virtue of SI 1994/3224.
[9] Words in sub-s (1) substituted by FA 1994 ss 196, 199, Sch 19 para 24 with effect for accounting periods ending after 30 June 1999 (by virtue of Finance Act 1994, Section 199, (Appointed Day) Order, SI 1998/3173 art 2).
[10] Words in sub-s (4A)(*a*) substituted for "a relievable amount within the meaning of section 131 of the Finance Act 1993 (non-trading exchange gains and losses)" by FA 1996 Sch 14 para 1(1)(*a*) with effect for accounting periods ending after 31 March 1996, subject to transitional provisions in FA 1996 Sch 15.
[11] Words in sub-s (4A)(*b*) substituted by FA 1996 Sch 14 para 1(1)(*b*) with effect for account periods ending after 31 March 1996, subject to transitional provisions in FA 1996 Sch 15.
[12] Words in sub-ss (4A), (6) substituted, and sub-ss (8), (9) inserted, by FA 1998 Sch 4 para 4 with effect where the accounting period whose due and payable date falls to be determined is an accounting periods ending after 30 June 1999 (by virtue of SI 1998/3173 art 2).
[13] Sub-ss (4), (4B), (7) repealed by FA 1998 Sch 3 para 4 with effect in relation to the relevant periods beginning after 5 April 1999.

[14] Words in sub-s (3) substituted by FA 1999 s 92(5), (7) with effect for accounting periods ending after 30 June 1999.
[15] Words in sub-s (3) inserted by FA 2000 s 98, Sch 28 para 3(4)(*a*) with effect for corporation tax for accounting periods ending after 31 March 2000 and by FA 2000 s 102, Sch 29 para 9(2)(*a*) with effect in relation to gains accruing after 31 March 2000.
[16] Words in sub-s (3) inserted and repealed by FA 2000 ss 98, 156, Sch 28 para 3(4)(*b*), Sch 40 Pt II(11) with effect for corporation tax for accounting periods ending after 31 March 2000.
[17] Words in sub-s (3) inserted and repealed by FA 2000 ss 102, 156, Sch 29 para 9(2)(*b*), Sch 40 Pt II(12) with effect for gains accruing after 31 March 2000.

88 Interest on tax recovered to make good loss due to taxpayer's fault

Commentary—*Simon's Direct Tax Service* A3.820.
Amendments—This section repealed by FA 1996 Sch 18 para 4(1), Sch 41 Pt V(8) with effect from the year 1996–97 (except so far as relating to partnerships whose trades, professions or businesses were set up and commenced before 6 April 1994 when it applies with effect from the year 1997–98) and in relation to any income tax which is charged by an assessment made on or after 6 April 1998 and is for the year 1995–96 or any earlier year of assessment.

88A Determinations under section 88

Commentary—*Simon's Direct Tax Service* A3.821.
Amendments—This section (inserted by FA 1989 s 160(2)) is repealed by FA 1996 Sch 18 para 4(2)(*a*), Sch 41 Pt V(8) with effect from the year 1996–97 (except so far as relating to partnerships whose trades, professions or businesses were set up and commenced before 6 April 1994, where the repeal has effect from the year 1997–98) and in relation to any income tax which is charged by an assessment made on or after 6 April 1998 and is for the year 1995–96 or any earlier year of assessment.

89 The prescribed rate of interest

Commentary—*Simon's Direct Tax Service* A3.1322.
Amendments—This section repealed by FA 1989 Sch 17 Pt X with effect from 18 August 1989 by virtue of FA 1989 s 178(1) (Appointed Day No 1) Order, SI 1989/1298.

90 Disallowance of relief for interest on tax

[(1)][2] Interest payable under this Part of this Act—

[(*a*)][2] shall be paid without any deduction of income tax; and
[(*b*)][2] [subject to subsection (2) below,][1] shall not be allowed as a deduction in computing any income, profits or losses for any tax purposes.

[(2) Paragraph (*b*) of subsection (1) above does not apply in relation to interest under section 87 or 87A of this Act payable by a company within the charge to corporation tax.][1]

Commentary—*Simon's Direct Tax Service* A3.1320.
Cross references—See Education (Student Loans) (Repayment) Regulations, SI 2000/944 reg 25 (application of this section in connection with the repayment of student loans).
Amendments—[1] Words in sub-s (1) and sub-s (2) inserted by FA 1998 s 33 with effect in relation to interest on corporation tax for accounting periods ending after 30 June 1999 (by virtue of Finance Act 1994, Section 199, (Appointed Day) Order, SI 1998/3173 art 2)., and interest on tax assessable in accordance with TA 1988 Sch 13 or 16 for return periods in accounting periods ending on or after that day.
[2] Sub-s (1)(*a*) and (*b*) amended by FA 1998 s 33(2) with effect from 31 July 1998.

91 Effect on interest of reliefs

(1) Where any amount of interest is payable under section 86 ...[6] of this Act in relation to an assessment, and relief from tax charged by the assessment is given to any person by a discharge of any of that tax, such adjustment shall be made of the said amount, and such repayment shall be made of any amounts previously paid under [that section][6] in relation to the assessment, as are necessary to secure that the total sum, if any, paid or payable under [that section][10] in relation to the assessment, is the same as it would have been if the tax discharged had never been charged.

[(1A) Where interest is payable under section 87A of this Act in respect of an amount of corporation tax for an accounting period, and relief from tax is given by a discharge of any of that corporation tax—

(*a*) such adjustment shall be made of the amount of interest payable under that section in respect of corporation tax for that accounting period, and
(*b*) such repayment shall be made of any amounts of interest previously paid under that section in respect of that corporation tax,

as are necessary to secure that the total sum (if any) paid or payable under that section in respect of corporation tax for that accounting period is the same as it would have been if the tax discharged had never been charged.][3]

[(1B) Subsection (1A) above has effect subject to section 87A(4)[, (4A), (4B),][5] [(6) and (7)][4] of this Act.][3]

(2) [Subject to subsection (2A) below][3] where relief from tax paid for any chargeable period is given to any person by repayment, he shall be entitled to require that the amount repaid shall be treated for the purposes of this section, so far as it will go, as if it were a discharge of the tax charged on him (whether alone or together with other persons) by or by virtue of any assessment for or relating to the same chargeable period, so, however, that it shall not be applied to any assessment made after the relief was given and that it shall not be applied to more than one assessment so as to reduce, without extinguishing, the amount of tax charged thereby.

[(2A) In any case where—

(a) relief from corporation tax is given to any person by repayment, and

(b) that tax was paid for an accounting period ending after the day which is the appointed day for the purposes of section [10 of the principal Act][2],

that person shall be entitled to require that the amount repaid shall be treated for the purposes of this section, so far as it will go, as if it were a discharge of the corporation tax charged on him for that period.][3]

(3) Notwithstanding anything in the preceding provisions of this section, no relief, whether given by way of discharge or repayment, shall be treated for the purposes of this section as—

(a) ...[1]

(b) affecting tax charged by any assessment to income tax made under Schedule A or Schedule D if either—

(i) ...[1]

(ii) it arises in connection with income taxable otherwise than under Schedule A or Schedule D, or

(iii) it relates to a source income from which is taxable otherwise than under Schedule A or Schedule D, [or

(c) affecting tax charged at a rate other than the basic rate[, the lower rate or the starting rate][7] on income from which tax has been deducted (otherwise than under section [203][2] of the principal Act) or is treated as having been deducted, unless it is a relief from the tax so charged.][1]

(4) For the purposes of this section a relief from corporation tax or capital gains tax shall not be treated as affecting tax charged by any assessment unless the assessment is to the same tax.

Commentary—*Simon's Direct Tax Service* **A3.822.**
Definitions—"Lower rate", TA 1988 s 832(1); "starting rate", TA 1988 s 832(1).
Cross references—See TMA 1970 s 109(4), (5) (repayment of loans made by close company to participators before tax on such loans is paid; effect of the repayment on penalties and interest in respect of the tax).
Education (Student Loans) (Repayment) Regulations, SI 2000/944 reg 25 (application of this section in connection with the repayment of student loans).
Amendments—[1] Sub-s (3)(a), (b)(i) repealed and sub-s (3)(c) inserted by FA 1971 ss 37, 38(1), and Sch 6 para 88(a) and Sch 14 Pt II, with effect from 1973–74.
[2] Words in sub-s (2A)(b) and number in sub-s (3) substituted by TA 1988 Sch 29 paras 10(6), 32 Table.
[3] Sub-ss (1A), (1B), (2A) and words in sub-s (2) inserted by F(No 2)A 1987 s 86(5), (6), (7) with respect to accounting periods ending after 30 September 1993 by virtue of Corporation Tax Acts (Provisions for Payment of Tax and Returns) (Appointed Days) Order, SI 1992/3066 art 2(1), (2)(a).
[4] Words in sub-s (1B) inserted by FA 1993 Sch 14 para 5.
[5] Words in sub-s (1B) inserted by FA 1995 s 130, Sch 24 paras 7, 10, with effect from 23 March 1995, by virtue of the FA 1993 section 165, (Appointed Day) Order, SI 1994/3224.
[6] In sub-s (1) words repealed and words substituted by FA 1996 Sch 18 para 4(2)(b), Sch 41 Pt V(8) with effect from the year 1996–97 (except so far as relating to partnerships whose trades, professions or businesses were set up and commenced before 6 April 1994, where the amendments have effect from the year 1997–98) and in relation to any income tax which is charged by an assessment made on or after 6 April 1998 and is for the year 1995–96 or any earlier year of assessment.
[7] Words in sub-s (3)(c) substituted by FA 1999 s 22(11), (12) with effect from the year 1999–00.

92 Remission in certain cases of interest on tax in arrear by reason of exchange restrictions

(1) The provisions of this section shall have effect where the Board are satisfied as respects any tax carrying interest under section 86 of this Act—

(a) that the tax is in respect of income or chargeable gains arising in a country outside the United Kingdom, and

(b) that, as the result of action of the government of that country, it is impossible for the income or gains to be remitted to the United Kingdom, and

(c) that having regard to the matters aforesaid and to all the other circumstances of the case it is reasonable that the tax should for the time being remain uncollected,

and the Board allow the tax to remain uncollected accordingly.

(2) Interest on the said tax shall, subject to subsection (3) below, cease to run under the said section 86 as from the date on which the Board were first in possession of the information necessary to enable them to be satisfied as aforesaid and, if the said date is not later than three months from the time when the tax became due and payable, the interest thereon under the said section 86 in respect of the period before the said date shall be remitted.

(3) Where, under subsection (2) above, interest has ceased to run on any tax and thereafter demand is made by the collector or other proper officer for payment of all or any of that tax, interest under the said section 86 shall again begin to run from the date of the demand in respect of the amount demanded.

Provided that where all or any part of the amount demanded is paid not later than three months from the date of the demand, the interest under the said section 86 on the amount so paid running from the date of the demand shall be remitted.

Commentary—*Simon's Direct Tax Service* **A3.1323.**
Revenue Internal Guidance—Company Taxation Manual COT10219 (this section also applies to interest on corporation tax payable under s 87A).
Inspector's Manual IM 4151 (claims are dealt with by the collector).

Definition—"Chargeable gain", TCGA 1992 s 15(2) by virtue of s 118(1).
Cross references—See F(No 2)A 1987 s 86(3)(*a*) (references to s 86 in this section to include references to s 87A of this Act).

PART X
PENALTIES, ETC

Statement of Practice SP 2/88—Revenue's practice in relation to civil penalties and prosecutions for tax offences.
Revenue Press Releases & other material—IR Codes of Practice 8, 9 explain practice of Special Compliance Office in serious cases of tax evasion and avoidance.
Cross references—See TMA 1970 s 70(2) (a certificate of a collector that a penalty is payable under this Part and has not been paid is sufficient evidence).
TMA 1970 s 101 (for the purposes of ss 93–100 below, an assessment becomes conclusive if it cannot be varied on appeal).
TMA 1970 s 118(3) (effect of assessment made in partnership name).
FA 1993 s 122(2) (application of this Part to public offices and departments of the Crown).

[93 Failure to make return for income tax and capital gains tax

(1) This section applies where—

(*a*) any person (the taxpayer) has been required by a notice served under or for the purposes of section 8 or 8A of this Act (or either of those sections as extended by section 12 of this Act) to deliver any return, and

(*b*) he fails to comply with the notice.

(2) The taxpayer shall be liable to a penalty which shall be £100.

(3) If, on an application made to them by an officer of the Board, the General or Special Commissioners so direct, the taxpayer shall be liable to a further penalty or penalties not exceeding £60 for each day on which the failure continues after the day on which he is notified of the direction (but excluding any day for which a penalty under this subsection has already been imposed).

(4) If—

(*a*) the failure by the taxpayer to comply with the notice continues after the end of the period of six months beginning with the filing date, and

(*b*) no application is made under subsection (3) above before the end of that period,

the taxpayer shall be liable to a further penalty which shall be £100.

(5) Without prejudice to any penalties under subsections (2) to (4) above, if—

(*a*) the failure by the taxpayer to comply with the notice continues after the anniversary of the filing date, and

(*b*) there would have been a liability to tax shown in the return,

the taxpayer shall be liable to a penalty of an amount not exceeding the liability to tax which would have been so shown.

(6) No penalty shall be imposed under subsection (3) above in respect of a failure at any time after the failure has been remedied.

(7) If the taxpayer proves that the liability to tax shown in the return would not have exceeded a particular amount, the penalty under subsection (2) above, together with any penalty under subsection (4) above, shall not exceed that amount.

(8) On an appeal against the determination under section 100 of this Act of a penalty under subsection (2) or (4) above, neither section 50(6) to (8) nor section 100B(2) of this Act shall apply but the Commissioners may—

(*a*) if it appears to them that, throughout the period of default, the taxpayer had a reasonable excuse for not delivering the return, set the determination aside; or

(*b*) if it does not so appear to them, confirm the determination.

(9) References in this section to a liability to tax which would have been shown in the return are references to an amount which, if a proper return had been delivered on the filing date, would have been payable by the taxpayer under section 59B of this Act for the year of assessment.

(10) In this section—

"the filing date" means the day mentioned in section 8(1A) or, as the case may be, section 8A(1A) of this Act;

"the period of default", in relation to any failure to deliver a return, means the period beginning with the filing date and ending with the day before that on which the return was delivered.][1]

Commentary—*Simon's Direct Tax Service* **A3.804.**
Revenue Interpretation RI 191—Incomplete returns and the use of provisional figures in returns. Where an incomplete 1997–98 return is delivered to the Revenue by 31 January 1999 and is sent back for completion on or after 18 January 1999, the taxpayer is given 14 days in which to resubmit the return without penalty.
Revenue and other press releases—IR 3-2-98 (where return sent back for correction before 31 January 1998 was resubmitted by 11 February 1998, no penalty will be charged; examples of reasonable and non-reasonable excuses given).
IR Tax Bulletin October 1999 p 693 (Stamp duty reserve tax—changes to rates of interest; penalties for failure to notify liability; interaction with stamp duty).
Revenue Internal Guidance—Enquiry Handbook EH 21 (revised Revenue approach to the filing deadline for returns following the *Steeden* case: a late filing penalty is charged only when the return is not received by the end of 1 February).
EH 25 (fixed penalty notices are issued automatically by the Revenue's computer).

EH 626 (where fraud or negligence is not admitted, the onus is on the Revenue to establish that it has occurred: taxpayer may claim innocent error even where error is discovered by the Revenue; however, culpable error is not made innocent by taxpayer's voluntary disclosure).
EH 638, 639 (fixed penalties under sub-s (2), (4) are generated automatically by the Revenue's computer).
EH 640 (worked example of reduction under sub-s (7)).
EH 641 (daily penalty under sub-s (3) sought only in large cases or where there is some pressing reason for ensuring early submission of return).
EH 645 (amount of daily penalty determined by Revenue officer: the Commissioners merely decide in principle whether a daily penalty may be imposed; factors considered are general background, length of delays, likely amount of tax at stake, taxpayer's attitude and co-operation, whether taxpayer is habitual defaulter).
EH 650 (consideration of claim that return not received).
EH 651–656 (meaning of ''reasonable excuse'').
Simon's Tax Cases—*Jolley v Bolton General Comrs* [1986] STC 414; *Cox v Poole General Comrs* [1990] STC 122.
s 93(1), *Kenny v General Comrs for Wirral* [1975] STC 61; *Taylor v Bethnal Green General Comrs* [1977] STC 44; *Montague v Hampstead General Comrs and IRC* [1989] STC 818.
s 93(1)(a), *Alexander v Wallington General Comrs and IRC* [1993] STC 588.
s 93(2), *Caesar v Inspector of Taxes* [1998] STC (SCD) 1.
s 93(8)(a), *Steeden v Carver* [1999] STC (SCD) 283.
Definitions—''the Board'', s 118(1); ''filing date'', s 8(1A) by virtue of s 93(10); ''the period of default'', s 93(10); ''return'', s 118(1).
Cross references—See TMA 1970 s 100 (revision of penalties under sub-ss (2), (4) or (5) above if amount of tax taken into account discovered to be excessive).
TMA 1970 s 100C (proceedings before the Commissioners in relation to penalty under sub-s (1) above).
TMA 1970 s 107A(2)–(4) (recovery of penalties from the relevant trustees of a settlement and modification of sub-s (8) above in relation thereto).
Education (Student Loans) (Repayment) Regulations, SI 2000/944 reg 26 (application of this section in connection with the repayment of student loans).
Amendments—[1] This section (including the heading) substituted by FA 1994 ss 196, 199(1), (2)(a) and Sch 19 para 25 with effect from the year 1996–97.

[93A Failure to make partnership return

(1) This section applies where, in the case of a trade, profession or business carried on by two or more persons in partnership—

(a) a partner (the representative partner) has been required by a notice served under or for the purposes of section 12AA(2) or (3) of this Act to deliver any return, and
(b) he [or a successor of his][2] fails to comply with the notice.

(2) Each relevant partner shall be liable to a penalty which shall be £100.

(3) If, on an application made to them by an officer of the Board, the General or Special Commissioners so direct, each relevant partner shall be liable, for each day on which the failure continues after the day on which the representative partner [or a successor of his][2] is notified of the direction (but excluding any day for which a penalty under this subsection has already been imposed), to a further penalty or penalties not exceeding £60.

(4) If—

(a) the failure by the representative partner [or a successor of his][2] to comply with the notice continues after the end of the period of six months beginning with the filing date, and
(b) no application is made under subsection (3) above before the end of that period,

each relevant partner shall be liable to a further penalty which shall be £100.

(5) No penalty shall be imposed under subsection (3) above in respect of a failure at any time after the failure has been remedied.

(6) Where, in respect of the same failure to comply, penalties under subsection (2), (3) or (4) above are determined under section 100 of this Act as regards two or more relevant partners—

(a) no appeal against the determination of any of those penalties shall be brought otherwise than by the representative partner [or a successor of his][2];
(b) any appeal by that partner [or successor][2] shall be a composite appeal against the determination of each of those penalties; and
(c) section 100B(3) of this Act shall apply as if that partner [or successor][2] were the person liable to each of those penalties.

(7) On an appeal against a determination under section 100 of this Act of a penalty under subsection (2) or (4) above, neither section 50(6) to (8) nor section 100B(2) of this Act shall apply but the Commissioners may—

(a) if it appears to them that, throughout the period of default, [the person for the time being required to deliver the return (whether the representative partner or a successor of his) had a reasonable excuse for not delivering it][2], set the determination aside; or
(b) if it does not so appear to them, confirm the determination.

(8) In this section—

''the filing date'' means the day specified in the notice under section 12AA(2) or (3) of this Act;
''the period of default'', in relation to any failure to deliver a return, means the period beginning with the filing date and ending with the day before that on which the return was delivered;
''relevant partner'' means a person who was a partner at any time during the period in respect of which the return was required.][1]

Commentary—*Simon's Direct Tax Service* **E1.826.**
Revenue Internal Guidance—Enquiry Handbook EH 836, 837 (fixed penalties generated automatically by the Revenue's computer).
EH 651–656 (meaning of "reasonable excuse").
EH 838 (the amount of daily penalty is determined by the Revenue office: the Commissioner's function is to determine whether a daily penalty can be imposed: the penalty must be in the same amount for each partner).
Definitions—"the board", s 118(1); "the filing date", s 12AA(2), (3) by virtue of s 93A(8); "the period of default", s 93A(8); "relevant partner", s 93A, "successor", s 12AA(11); "trade", s 118(1).
Amendments—[1] This section inserted by FA 1994 ss 196, 199 and Sch 19 para 26 with effect from the year 1996–97 in relation to income tax and capital gains tax and, as respects corporation tax, with effect in relation to accounting periods ending after 30 June 1999 (by virtue of Finance Act 1994, Section 199, (Appointed Day) Order, SI 1998/3173 art 2).
[2] Words in sub-ss (1)(*b*), (3), (4), (6) inserted and words in sub-s (7)(*a*) substituted by FA 1996 s 123(8)–(11) with effect from the year 1996–97 as respects income tax and capital gains tax and, as respects corporation tax, for accounting periods ending after 30 June 1999 (by virtue of SI 1998/3173 art 2).

94 Failure to make return for corporation tax

Commentary—*Simon's Direct Tax Service* **A3.804A; D2.715.**
Concession B46—The Revenue will waive automatic penalty charges on late company end-of-year returns having a statutory filing date after 30 September 1995 where these are received on or before the last business day within 7 days following the statutory filing date.
Amendments—This section repealed by FA 1998 ss 117, 165, Sch 19 para 33, Sch 27 Part III(28) with effect in relation to accounting periods ending after 30 June 1999 (by virtue of Finance Act 1994, Section 199, (Appointed Day) Order, SI 1998/3173 art 2).

95 Incorrect return or accounts for income tax or capital gains tax

(1) Where a person fraudulently or negligently—

    (*a*) delivers any incorrect return of a kind mentioned in [section 8 or 8A of this Act (or either of those sections][3] as extended by section 12 of this Act ...[2]), or

    (*b*) makes any incorrect return, statement or declaration in connection with any claim for any allowance, deduction or relief in respect of income tax or capital gains tax, or

    (*c*) submits to an inspector or the Board or any Commissioners any incorrect accounts in connection with the ascertainment of his liability to income tax or capital gains tax,

he shall be liable to a penalty not exceeding [the amount of the difference specified in subsection (2) below.][1]

(2) The difference is that between—

    (*a*) the amount of income tax and capital gains tax payable for the relevant years of assessment by the said person (including any amount of income tax deducted at source and not repayable), and

    (*b*) the amount which would have been the amount so payable if the return, statement, declaration or accounts as made or submitted by him had been correct.

(3) The relevant years of assessment for the purposes of this section are, in relation to anything delivered, made or submitted in any year of assessment, that, the next following, and any preceding year of assessment; ...[3]

Commentary—*Simon's Direct Tax Service* **A3.805.**
Statement of Practice SP 2/88—Civil tax penalties and criminal prosecution cases.
Revenue Interpretation RI 195—Amending a self-assessment return under TMA 1970 s 9(4), or a partnership statement under TMA 1970 s 12AB(2), does not preclude penalty action by the Revenue in relation to incorrect figures included in the original return.
Revenue & other press releases—ICAEW TR788 8–1–90 (Revenue investigation procedure; independent taxation: Inspectors will respect confidentiality. In investigating one spouse they may require information from the other, such information will not be gratuitously given to the first spouse).
Code of Practice 2 (conduct of Inland Revenue investigations—superseded by Code of Practice 11 (Enquiries into tax returns by local tax offices)).
Revenue Internal Guidance—Enquiry handbook EH 665 (a penalty can still apply in respect of an original return even if an amendment has been made in the 12-month period following the filing date).
EH 676 (the offence is committed on the date when the incorrect return is submitted).
Investigation handbook IH 4725 (the taxpayer cannot delegate responsibility for his returns and is expected to sign them himself/herself).
Simon's Tax Cases—*Williams v Comrs for the Special Purposes of the Income Tax Acts* [1975] STC 167; *Jolley v Bolton General Comrs* [1986] STC 414; *Walsh v Croydon General Comrs and IRC* [1987] STC 456; *King v Walden* [2001] STC 822.
s 95(1), *Taylor v Bethnal Green General Comrs* [1977] STC 44; *Sparks v West Brixton General Comrs* [1977] STC 212.
s 95(1)(*a*), *Brodt v Wells General Comrs and IRC* [1987] STC 207.
Definitions—"Principal Act", s 118(1); "return", s 118(1).
Cross references—See TMA 1970 s 97 (supplementary provisions).
TMA 1970 s 107A(2), (3) (recovery of penalties from the relevant trustees of a settlement).
TA 1988 s 369(7)(*d*) (application of this section to excessive or undue payments by the Board to lenders in respect of MIRAS),
TA 1988 Sch 6A para 8(4) (claim for alternative calculation of shared van benefit deemed to be a claim for relief for the purposes of this section),
TA 1988 Sch 14 para 7(3)(*d*) (application of this section in respect of tax deducted at source from life insurance premiums);
Personal Equity Plan Regulations, SI 1989/469 reg 18(4) (deduction in respect of previous excessive relief or exemption treated as tax deducted at source and not repayable by virtue of sub-s 2(*a*)).
FA 1991 s 33(3)(*d*) (application of this section where incorrect return or accounts are submitted for tax relief claims on vocational training).
FA 1995 s 71(4) (regulations may be made applying this section to repayments of tax credits to venture capital trusts and investors).
Education (Student Loans) (Repayment) Regulations, SI 2000/944 reg 26 (application of this section in connection with the repayment of student loans).

Amendments—¹ Words in sub-s (1) substituted by FA 1989 s 163(1)(*a*), (2) in relation to returns, etc submitted after 26 July 1989.
² Words omitted repealed by FA 1988 s 148, Sch 14 Pt VIII with effect from the year 1990–91.
³ Words in sub-s (1)(*a*) substituted and words omitted from sub-s (3) repealed by FA 1994 ss 196, 199(1), (2)(*a*) and Sch 19 para 27 and Sch 26 Pt V(23) with effect from the year 1996–97.

[95A Incorrect partnership return or accounts

(1) This section applies where, in the case of a trade, profession or business carried on by two or more persons in partnership—

    (*a*) a partner (the representative partner)—

        (i) delivers an [incorrect partnership return]⁴, or

        (ii) makes any incorrect statement or declaration in connection with [a [partnership return]⁴]², or

        (iii) submits to an officer of the Board any incorrect accounts in connection with such a return, and

    (*b*) either he does so fraudulently or negligently, or his doing so is attributable to fraudulent or negligent conduct on the part of a relevant partner.

(2) Each relevant partner shall be liable to a penalty not exceeding the difference between—

    (*a*) the amount of income tax or corporation tax payable by him for the relevant period (including any amount of income tax deducted at source and not repayable), and

    (*b*) the amount which would have been the amount so payable if the return, statement, declaration or accounts made or submitted by the representative partner had been correct;

and in determining each such penalty, regard shall be had only to the fraud or negligence, or the fraudulent or negligent conduct, mentioned in subsection (1)(*b*) above.

(3) Where, in respect of the same return, statement, declaration or accounts, penalties under subsection (2) above are determined under section 100 of this Act as regards two or more relevant partners—

    (*a*) no appeal against the determination of any of those penalties shall be brought otherwise than by the representative partner [or a successor of his]³;

    (*b*) any appeal by that partner [or successor]³ shall be a composite appeal against the determination of each of those penalties; and

    (*c*) section 100B(3) of this Act shall apply as if that partner [or successor]³ were the person liable to each of those penalties.

(4) In this section—

    "relevant partner" means a person who was a partner at any time during the relevant period;

    "relevant period" means the period in respect of which the return was made.]¹

Commentary—*Simon's Direct Tax Service* E1.826.
Revenue Interpretation RI 195—Amending a self-assessment return under TMA 1970 s 9(4), or a partnership statement under TMA 1970 s 12AB(2), does not preclude penalty action by the Revenue in relation to incorrect figures included in the original return.
Definitions—"the Board", s 118(1); "relevant partner", s 95A(4); "relevant period", s 93A(4); "return", s 118(1); "successor", s 12AA(11); "trade", s 118(1).
Amendments—¹ This section inserted by FA 1994 ss 196, 199 and Sch 19 para 28 with effect from the year 1996–97 in relation to income tax and capital gains tax, and, as respects corporation tax, with effect in relation to accounting periods ending after 30 June 1999 (by virtue of Finance Act 1994, Section 199, (Appointed Day) Order, SI 1998/3173 art 2).
² Words in sub-s (1)(*a*)(ii) substituted by FA 1996 s 123(12) with effect from the year 1996–97 as respects income tax and capital gains tax and, as respects corporation tax, for accounting periods ending after 30 June 1999 (by virtue of SI 1998/3173 art 2).
³ Words in sub-s (3) inserted by FA 1996 s 123(13) with effect from the year 1996–97 as respects income tax and capital gains tax and, as respects corporation tax, for accounting periods ending after 30 June 1999 (by virtue of SI 1998/3173 art 2).
⁴ In sub-s (1), words in para (*a*)(i) substituted for the words "incorrect return of a kind mentioned in section 12AA of this Act"; and in para (*a*)(ii), words substituted for the words "return of such a kind", by FA 2001 s 88, Sch 29 para 32 with effect from the passing of FA 2001 in relation to returns whether made before or after the passing of FA 2001, and whether relating to periods before or after the passing of FA 2001.

96 Incorrect return or accounts for corporation tax

Commentary—*Simon's Direct Tax Service* A3.805.
Statement of Practice SP 2/88—Civil tax penalties and criminal prosecution cases.
Revenue & other press releases—Code of Practice 2 (conduct of Inland Revenue investigations).
Amendments—This section repealed by FA 1998 ss 117, 165, Sch 19 para 34, Sch 27 Part III(28) with effect in relation to accounting periods ending after 30 June 1999 (by virtue of Finance Act 1994, Section 199, (Appointed Day) Order, SI 1998/3173 art 2).

97 Incorrect return or accounts: supplemental

(1) Where any such return, statement, declaration or accounts as are mentioned in [section 95]¹ above were made or submitted by any person neither fraudulently nor negligently and it comes to his notice (or, if he has died, to the notice of his personal representatives) that they were incorrect, then, unless the error is remedied without unreasonable delay, the return, statement, declaration or accounts shall be treated for the purposes of those sections as having been negligently made or submitted by him.

(2) For the purpose of [section 95][1] above, any accounts submitted on behalf of any person shall be deemed to have been submitted by him unless he proves that they were submitted without his consent or connivance.

Commentary—*Simon's Direct Tax Service* A3.111.
Revenue & other press releases—ICAEW Tax 12/92 25–6–92 (guidance note Pay & File: Use of estimated figures on CT200 return acceptable if made to best of company's ability and the basis explained in covering letter; accurate figures submitted as soon as available bring company within s 97).
Definition—"Return", s 118(1).
Cross references—See the Personal Equity Plan Regulations, SI 1989/469 reg 28(4) (modification of this section in its application to PEPs).
Education (Student Loans) (Repayment) Regulations, SI 2000/944 reg 26 (application of this section in connection with the repayment of student loans).
Amendments—[1] Words in sub-ss (1) and (2) substituted by FA 1998 Sch 19 para 35 with effect in relation to accounting periods ending after 30 June 1999 (by virtue of Finance Act 1994, Section 199, (Appointed Day) Order, SI 1998/3173 art 2).

[97AA Failure to produce documents under section 19A

(1) Where a person fails to comply with a notice or requirement under [section 19A(2), (2A) or (3)][2] of this Act [or paragraph 6(2) or (3A)(b) of Schedule 1A to this Act][3], he shall be liable, subject to subsection (4) below—

(a) to a penalty which shall be £50, and

(b) if the failure continues after a penalty is imposed under paragraph (a) above, to a further penalty or penalties not exceeding the relevant amount for each day on which the failure continues after the day on which the penalty under that paragraph was imposed (but excluding any day for which a penalty under this paragraph has already been imposed).

(2) In subsection (1)(b) above 'the relevant amount' means—

(a) in the case of a determination of a penalty by an officer of the Board under section 100 of this Act, £30;

(b) in the case of a determination of a penalty by the Commissioners under section 100C of this Act, £150.

(3) An officer of the Board authorised by the Board for the purposes of section 100C of this Act may commence proceedings under that section for any penalty under subsection (1)(b) above, notwithstanding that it is not a penalty to which subsection (1) of section 100 of this Act does not apply by virtue of subsection (2) of that section.

(4) No penalty shall be imposed under subsection (1) above in respect of a failure within that subsection at any time after the failure has been remedied.][1]

Commentary—*Simon's Direct Tax Service* E1.826.
Revenue Internal Guidance—Enquiry Handbook EH 685–689 (Revenue procedure for imposing penalties).
Definitions—"the Board", s 118(1); "the relevant amount" s 97AA(2).
Cross references—See TMA 1970 s 107A(2), (3) (recovery of penalties from the relevant trustees of a settlement).
Amendments—[1] This section inserted by FA 1994 ss 196, 199 and Sch 19 para 29 with effect from the year 1996–97 in relation to income tax and capital gains tax or, as respects corporation tax, with effect in relation to accounting periods ending after 30 June 1999 (by virtue of Finance Act 1994, Section 199, (Appointed Day) Order, SI 1998/3173 art 2).
[2] Words in sub-s (1) substituted by FA 1996 Sch 19 para 3(4) with effect from the year 1996–97 in relation to income tax and capital gains tax and, as respects corporation tax, for accounting periods ending on after 30 June 1999 (by virtue of SI 1998/3173 art 2).
[3] Words in sub-s (1) inserted by FA 1998 Sch 19 para 36 with effect in relation to accounting periods ending after 30 June 1999 (by virtue of SI 1998/3173 art 2).

[97A Two or more tax-geared penalties in respect of same tax

Where two or more penalties—

(a) are incurred by any person and fall to be determined by reference to any income tax or capital gains tax with which he is chargeable for a year of assessment; ...[2]

(b) ...[2]

each penalty after the first shall be so reduced that the aggregate amount of the penalties, so far as determined by reference to any particular part of the tax, does not exceed whichever is or, but for this section, would be the greater or greatest of them, so far as so determined.][1]

Commentary—*Simon's Direct Tax Service* A3.802.
Revenue Internal Guidance—Investigation handbook IH4675 (worked example).
Amendments—[1] This section inserted by FA 1988 s 129; paragraph (a) came into effect from 1988–89 and paragraph (b) came into effect for accounting periods ending after 31 March 1989.
[2] Para (b) and word preceding it repealed by FA 1998 ss 117, 165, Sch 19 para 37, Sch 27 Part III(28) with effect in relation to accounting periods ending after 30 June 1999 (by virtue of Finance Act 1994, Section 199, (Appointed Day) Order, SI 1998/3173 art 2).

98 Special returns, etc

(1) [Subject to [the provisions of this section and][21–22] section 98A below, where][5] any person—

(a) has been required, by a notice served under or for the purposes of any of the provisions specified in the first column of the Table below, to deliver any return or other document, to furnish any particulars, to produce any document, or to make anything available for inspection, and he fails to comply with the notice, or (*b*) fails to furnish any information, give any certificate or produce any document or record in accordance with any of the provisions specified in the second column of the Table below,

he shall be liable, subject to [subsections (3) and (4) below—

    (i) to a penalty not exceeding £300, and
    (ii) if the failure continues after a penalty is imposed under paragraph (i) above, to a further penalty or penalties not exceeding £60 for each day on which the failure continues after the day on which the penalty under paragraph (i) above was imposed (but excluding any day for which a penalty under this paragraph has already been imposed).][6]

(2) [Subject to section 98A below, where][5] a person fraudulently or negligently furnishes, gives, produces or makes any incorrect information, certificate, document, record or declaration of a kind mentioned in any of the provisions specified in either column of the Table below, he shall be liable to a penalty not exceeding [£3,000][7].

[(3) No penalty shall be imposed under subsection (1) above in respect of a failure within paragraph (*a*) of that subsection at any time after the failure has been remedied.][8]

[(4) No penalty shall be imposed under paragraph (ii) of subsection (1) above in respect of a failure within paragraph (*b*) of that subsection at any time after the failure has been remedied.][8]

[(4A) If—

    (*a*) a failure to comply with section 350(1) of, or Schedule 16 to, the principal Act arises from a person's failure to deliver an account, or show the amount, of a payment, and
    (*b*) the payment is within subsection (4B) [or (4D)][88] below,

subsection (1) above shall have effect as if for "£300" there were substituted "£3,000" and as if for "£60" there were substituted "£600".

(4B) A payment is within this subsection if—

    (*a*) the payment is made by a company [or local authority][87] without an amount representing the income tax on the payment being deducted from the payment,
    (*b*) at the time the payment is made, the company [or authority][87]—

        (i) does not believe that [one][87] of the conditions specified in section 349B of the principal Act is satisfied, or
        (ii) where it believes that [one][87] of those conditions is satisfied, could not reasonably so believe,

    (*c*) the payment is one from which tax is deductible under section 349 of the principal Act unless the company [or authority][87] reasonably believes that one of those conditions is satisfied, and
    (*d*) [none][87] of those conditions is satisfied at the time the payment is made.

[(4C) In subsection (4B) above—

"company" includes a partnership of which any member is a company; and
"local authority" includes a partnership of which any member is a local authority.][87][83]

[(4D) A payment is within this subsection if—

    (*a*) it is a payment to which section 349(1) of the principal Act (requirement to deduct tax) applies,
    (*b*) it is made by a company which, purporting to rely on section 349E(1) of that Act (power for companies to take account of double taxation treaty relief when paying royalties), deducts less tax from the payment than required by section 349(1) of that Act, and
    (*c*) at the time the payment is made the payee (within the meaning of section 349E of that. Act) is not entitled to relief in respect of the payment under any arrangements under section 788 of that Act (double taxation relief) and the company—

        (i) does not believe that it is entitled to such relief, or
        (ii) if it does so believe, cannot reasonably do so.][88]

[(5) In the case of a failure to comply with section 765A(2)(*a*) or (*b*) of the principal Act, subsection (1) above shall have effect as if for "£300" there were substituted "£3,000" and as if for "£60" there were substituted "£600".][23]

[TABLE

1	2
Part III of this Act ...[9]	In the principal Act—
...[39]	...[10]
In the principal Act—	...[62]
[section 38(5);][10]	[regulations under section 42A;][40]
[section 42;][11]	...[11]
[regulations under section 42A;][40]	...[79]
[regulations under section 59E of this Act;][68]	[*regulations under section 51B*][48]
...[79]	...[80]
...[80]	section 136(6)
[*section 181(1);*][71]	...[2];

1

regulations under section 202;
section 217;
section 226(3) and (4);
section 234(7)(*b*), (8) and (9);
[section 246H;]³⁷
section 250(6) and (7);
section 272(7);
section 310(4) and (5);
[regulations under section 326C;]²⁰
regulations under section 333;
[regulations under section 333B;]⁵⁹
[regulations under section 431E(1) or 441A(3);]⁴⁶
regulations under section 476(1);
[regulations under section 477A(1);]²⁷
...¹²
section 482(3);
regulations under section 482(11);

section 483;
regulations under section 555(7);
section 561(8);
section 588(7);
regulations under section 602;
[regulations under section 605(1A)(*b*) to (*d*);]³⁵
[section 605(3)(*b*) and (4);]³⁶
regulations under section 612(3);
regulations under section 639;
[regulations under section 651A(1)(*b*) to (*d*);]⁶⁰
...⁷⁸
[section 660F;]⁴⁷
section 700(4);
section 708;
section 728;
section 729(11);⁵³
section 730(8);⁵⁷
...
section 745(1);
section 755;
[section 765A(2)(*b*);]²⁴⁻²⁵
[section 767C;]⁶¹
section 768(9);
...⁶⁴;
section 774(5);
section 778;
section 815;
...³¹;
Schedule 5, paragraph 10;
Schedule 9, [paragraph 6;]²⁶
Schedule 15, paragraph 14(5);
[Schedule 15B, paragraph 5(2);]⁴²
...¹⁶;
Schedule 22, paragraph 4.
[regulations under paragraph 11B(5) of Schedule 28B]⁷⁷

Section 32 of the Finance Act 1973.

2

[section 140G;]⁵⁸;
...⁶³
[*section 180(1);*]⁷¹
regulations under section 202;
regulations under section 203;
section 216;
section 226(1) and (2);
section 234(5), (6) and (7)(*a*);
section 250(1) to (5);
section 310(1), (2)[, 2A]⁸⁴ and (3);
section 313(5);
[regulations under section 326C;]²⁰
regulations under section 333;
[regulations under section 333B;]⁵⁹
section 350(1);
section 375(5);
[regulations under section 431E(1) or 441A(3);]⁴⁶
[regulations under section 444BB;]⁵⁰
[regulations under section 444BD;]⁵⁰
regulations under section 476(1);
[regulations under section 477A(1);]²⁷
[section 482(2);]¹³
regulations under section 482(11);
[section 552;]⁸⁵
[regulations under section 552ZA(6);]⁸⁵
regulations under section 555(7);
[regulations under section 566(1), (2) or (2A);]⁵¹
section 577(4);
section 588(6);
regulations under section 602;
[regulations under section 605(1A)(*a*);]³⁵
section 605(3)(*a*);
regulations under section 612(3);
regulations under section 639;
[regulations under section 651A(1)(*a*);]⁶⁰
[section 765A(2)(*a*);]²⁴⁻²⁵
...⁶⁴;
[...]³¹;
[*Schedule 13;*]⁶⁵
[*Schedule 13A, paragraphs 11, 12 and 13;*]⁵⁴ ⁶⁵
regulations under paragraph 7 of Schedule 14;
Schedule 15, paragraph 14(4);
[Schedule 15B, paragraph 5(1);]⁴²
Schedule 16;
Schedule 22, paragraph 2.
regulations under section [151 of the 1992 Act]²⁹.
[Sections 43(5) and (6), [45B(5), (6),]⁸² [45G(4) and (5),]⁸⁶ 118 to 120, 145(2) and (3) and 203 of the Capital Allowances Act]⁸¹
regulations 16 and 17 of the Income Tax (Interest Relief) Regulations 1982.
Paragraph 15(3) of Schedule 14 to the Finance Act 1984.
...¹⁹
[Section 85(1) and (2) of the Finance Act 1988.]³⁻⁴
[Regulations under section 57 of the Finance Act 1989.]¹⁷
...³²
...³⁸

1

Paragraph 2 of Schedule 15 to the Finance Act 1973.
Regulations under section [151 of the 1992 Act][29].
Paragraph [2(9) of Schedule 1 to the 1992 Act.][29].
...[81]
Section [98 of the 1992 Act][29].
Paragraph 15(1) of Schedule 14 to the Finance Act 1984.
Paragraph 6(1) of Schedule 22 to the Finance Act 1985.
[Section 79(6) of the 1992 Act][29].

[Section 73 of the Finance Act 1989.][14]

[Paragraphs 2 to 4 of Schedule 12 to the Finance Act 1989.][15]
[regulations under section 57 of the Finance Act 1989.][17]
[Section 235 of the 1992 Act][29].

[regulations under section 33 of the Finance Act 1991.][28]
[Paragraph 10 of Schedule 5 to the 1992 Act][29].

[section 86(12) of the Finance Act 1995.][44]

[paragraph 117 of Schedule 8 to the Finance Act 2000][73]
[paragraph 64 of Schedule 14 to the Finance Act 2000][74]
[paragraph 66 of Schedule 15 to the Finance Act 2000][75]
[Regulations under Schedule 33 to the Finance Act 2002.][89]

2

[regulations under section 33 of the Finance Act 1991.][28]
[section 28(2) of the Finance (No 2) Act 1992.][30]
[regulation 11(2) of the Income Tax (Manufactured Overseas Dividends) Regulations 1993.][33]
[Paragraphs 2 to 6 of Schedule 5A to the 1992 Act.][34]
[regulations under section 73 of the Finance Act 1995;][43]

[Section 110ZA of the Social Security Administration Act 1992][66]
[Section 104ZA of the Social Security Administration (Northern Ireland) Act 1992][69]
[Section 86(4) of the Finance Act 1999][70]
[paragraph 65 of Schedule 14 to the Finance Act 2000][74]
[paragraph 64 or 65 of Schedule 15 to the Finance Act 2000][75]
[Paragraph 93(2) of Schedule 22 to the Finance Act 2000][76]
[Paragraph 129 of Schedule 22 to the Finance Act 2000][76]
[Regulations under Schedule 33 to the Finance Act 2002.][89]

The references in this Table to regulations under section 602 have effect only for the purpose of giving effect to any provision mentioned in paragraphs (*a*) and (*b*) of subsection (2) of that section.][1]

Commentary—*Simon's Direct Tax Service* **A3.802.**
Simon's Tax Cases—*Shah v General Comrs for Hampstead* [1974] STC 438; *Comrs and related appeal* [1992] STC 290.
s 98(1), *Chapman v General Comrs of Income Tax for the District of Sheaf* [1975] STC 170; *Toogood v Bristol General Comrs* [1977] STC 116; *Boulton v Poole General Comrs* [1988] STC 709.
s 98(1)(ii), *Wilson v Leek General Comrs and IRC* [1994] STC 147.
Definitions—''The 1992 Act'', s 118(1); ''return'', s 118(1).
Cross references—See TMA 1970 s 100C (proceedings before the Commissioners in relation to penalty under sub-s (1) above). TA 1988 s 566(2E) (exclusion of penalty under this section in respect of matters giving rise to a penalty under s 566(2C) (inaccurate statements in connection with sub-contractors deductions)).
Manufactured Dividends (Tax) Regulations, SI 1997/993 reg 8(5), (6) (this Schedule to apply with modification to a return under that Regulation by a person, other than a UK resident company, who is liable to account for tax in respect of a manufactured dividend).
Education (Student Loans) (Repayment) Regulations, SI 2000/944 regs 7, 43 (application of this section in connection with the repayment of student loans).
Amendments —[1] The Table substituted by TA 1988 Sch 29 para 9.
[2] Words in column 2 repealed by FA 1988 Sch 14 Pt VI.
[3-4] Words in column 2 added by FA 1988 s 85(3).
[5] Words in sub-ss (1), (2) substituted by FA 1989 s 164.
[6] Words in sub-s (1) substituted by FA 1989 s 164 in relation to any failure to comply with a notice or to furnish information, give a certificate or produce a document or record beginning after 26 July 1989, and the furnishing, giving, producing or making of any incorrect information, certificate, document, record or declaration after 26 July 1989.
[7] Amount in sub-s (2) substituted by FA 1989 s 164.
[8] Sub-ss (3), (4) substituted for sub-s (3) by FA 1989 s 164.
[9] Words in column 1 repealed by FA 1989 s 164 and Sch 17 Pt VIII.
[10] Entry transferred from column 2 to column 1 by FA 1989 s 164.
[11] Entry transferred from column 2 to column 1 by FA 1989 s 164.
[12] Entry in column 1 repealed by FA 1989 s 164 and Sch 17 Pt VIII.
[13] Words in column 2 inserted by FA 1989 s 164.
[14] Words in column 1 added by FA 1989 s 73(9).
[15] Words in column 1 added by FA 1989 Sch 12 para 5.
[16] Words in column 1 repealed by FA 1989 Sch 17 Pt V with effect from 27 July 1989.
[17] Words in columns 1 and 2 added by FA 1989 s 57(2).
[18] ...
[19] Words in column 2 repealed by CAA 1990 Sch 2.
[20] Words in columns 1 and 2 inserted by FA 1990 s 28(2).
[21-22] Words in sub-s (1) inserted by FA 1990 s 68(3), (4) and apply to transactions carried out after 30 June 1990.
[23] Sub-s (5) inserted by FA 1990 s 68(3), (4) and apply to transactions carried out after 30 June 1990.

^{24–25} Words in columns 1 and 2 inserted by FA 1990 s 68(3), (4) and apply to transactions carried out after 30 June 1990.

²⁶ Words in column 1 substituted by FA 1990 Sch 14 paras 15, 19(1) with effect from 9 February 1988.

²⁷ Words in column 1 and 2 inserted by FA 1990 Sch 5 para 15.

²⁸ Words in columns 1 and 2 inserted by FA 1991 s 33(2).

²⁹ Words in columns 1 and 2 substituted by TCGA 1992 Sch 2 para 2(1), (10).

³⁰ Words in column 2 inserted by F(No 2)A 1992 s 28(4).

³¹ Words in columns 1 and 2 repealed by FA 1996 Sch 7 para 29, Sch 41 Pt V(2) with effect from the year 1996–97.

³² Words in column 2 repealed by F(No 2)A 1992 Sch 18 Pt VII(2) in relation to claims made after 16 July 1992.

³³ Words in column 2 inserted by IT (Manufactured Overseas Dividends) Regulations, SI 1993/2004 reg 11(13).

³⁴ Words in column 2 inserted by FA 1994 s 97(6).

³⁵ Words in columns 1 and 2 inserted by FA 1994 s 105(4)(*a*), (*c*).

³⁶ Words in column 1 substituted for the words "section 605(1), (2), (3) (*b*) and (4)" by FA 1994 s 105(4)(*b*), (5) with effect from 1 January 1996 by virtue of FA 1994, section 105 (Appointed Day) Order, SI 1995/3125.

³⁷ Words in column 1 inserted by FA 1994 Sch 16 para 10.

³⁸ Words in column 2 repealed by FA 1994 Sch 26, Pt V(10) where the relevant day falls on or after 3 May 1994.

³⁹ Words in column 1 repealed by the General and Special Commissioners (Amendment of Enactments) Regulations, SI 1994/1813 reg 2, Sch 1 paras 1, 13, Sch 2 Pt I.

⁴⁰ Words in columns 1 and 2 inserted by FA 1995 s 40(2).

⁴¹ Words in column 2 substituted by FA 1995 s 57(3), with effect on or after 1 May 1995.

⁴² Words in columns 1 and 2 inserted by FA 1995 s 71(3), (4) with effect for the year 1995–96 and subsequent years of assessment.

⁴³ Words in column 2 added by FA 1995 s 73(5).

⁴⁴ Words in column 1 added by virtue of FA 1995 s 86(12).

⁴⁵ ...

⁴⁶ Words in columns 1 and 2 inserted by FA 1995 s 51, Sch 8 para 50, in relation to accounting periods beginning after 31 October 1994.

⁴⁷ Words in column 1 substituted by FA 1995 s 74, Sch 17 para 23 with effect from the year 1995–96 and applies to every settlement wherever and whenever made or entered into.

⁴⁸ Words in column 2 (inserted by FA 1995 s 78(2)) repealed by FA 1998 s 165, Sch 27 Part (28) with effect in relation to payments of interest falling due after 31 March 1999 by virtue of SI 1999/619 art 2 (FA 1998 s 37(3).

⁴⁹ Words in columns 1 and 2 inserted by FA 1996 Sch 29 Pt II para 2(1).

⁵⁰ Words in column 2 inserted by FA 1996 Sch 32 para 2.

⁵¹ Words in column 2 substituted by FA 1996 s 178(2).

⁵² Words in column 2 substituted by FA 1996 Sch 29 Pt II para 2(2)(*b*).

⁵³ Words in column 1 repealed by FA 1996 Sch 41 Pt V(21) with effect as from a date to be appointed.

⁵⁴ Words in column 2 originally inserted by FA 1996 Sch 25 para 5 before repeal (see note ⁶⁵ below).

⁵⁵ Words in column 1 inserted by FA 1996 Sch 29 Pt II para 2(2)(*a*).

⁵⁶ ...

⁵⁷ Words "section 737(8)" repealed by FA 1997 Sch 18 Pt VI(10) with effect subject to FA 1997 Sch 10 para 16(3).

⁵⁸ Words in column 2 inserted by FA 1998 s 52(2) with effect from 31 July 1998.

⁵⁹ Words inserted by FA 1998 s 77 with effect from 31 July 1998.

⁶⁰ Words inserted by FA 1998 s 96 with effect from 31 July 1998.

⁶¹ Words inserted by FA 1998 s 115(2), (3) with effect in relation to changes in ownership occurring after 1 July 1997 other than any change occurring in pursuance of a contract entered into before 2 July 1997.

⁶² Words repealed by FA 1998 s 165, Sch 27 Part III(4) with effect for the year 1998–99 and subsequent years of assessment, and for corporation tax with effect from 1 April 1998.

⁶³ Words repealed by FA 1998 s 165, Sch 27 Part III(9) in relation to payments or other benefits received after 5 April 1998, except where the payment or other benefit or the right to receive it has been brought into charge to tax before 6 April 1998.

⁶⁴ Entry relating to section 772(1) and (3) of TA 1988 in the first column of the Table, and the entry relating to section 772(6) of that Act in the second column of the Table repealed by FA 1998 Sch 27 Part III(25) with effect in relation to accounting periods ending after 30 June 1999 (by virtue of Finance Act 1994, Section 199, (Appointed Day) Order, SI 1998/3173 art 2).

⁶⁵ Words in column 2 repealed by FA 1998 s 165, Sch 27 Part III(2) with effect in relation to accounting periods and return periods beginning after 5 April 1999.

⁶⁶ Words in column 2 inserted by the Social Security Contributions (Transfer of Functions, etc) Act 1999 Sch 5 para 1 with effect from 1 April 1999 by virtue of the Social Security Contributions (Transfer of Functions, etc) Act (Commencement No 1 and Transitional Provisions) Order, SI 1999/527 art 2, Sch 2.

⁶⁷ ...

⁶⁸ Words in column 1 inserted by FA 1999 s 89(1), (3) with effect for accounting periods ending after 30 June 1999.

⁶⁹ Words inserted in column 2 by the Social Security Contributions (Transfer of Functions, etc) (Northern Ireland) Order, SI 1999/671 art 5 Sch 4 para 1 with effect from 1 April 1999 (by virtue of the Social Security Contributions (Transfer of Functions, etc) (1999 Order) (Commencement No 1 and Transitional Provisions) Order (Northern Ireland), SR 1999/149, art 2(*c*), Sch 2).

⁷⁰ Words in column 2 inserted by FA 1999 s 86(9) with effect from 27 July 1999.

⁷¹ In column 1, the entry relating to TA 1988 s 181(1), and in column 2, the entry relating to TA 1988 s 180(1), repealed by FA 1997 Sch 18 Pt VI(3) with effect for any payment made by reference to a profit period beginning after 31 December 1999 in accordance with FA 1997 s 61(2), (3), but subject to FA 1997 Sch 18 Pt VI(3) note 2.

⁷² ...

⁷³ Words inserted in column 1 by FA 2000 s 47, Sch 8 para 117(4) with effect from 28 July 2000.

⁷⁴ Words in columns 1 and 2 inserted by FA 2000 s 62, Sch 14 paras 64(3), 65(3) with effect for any right to acquired shares granted after 28 July 2000.

⁷⁵ Words in columns 1 and 2 inserted by FA 2000 s 63(2), Sch 16 para 1 with effect for shares issued after 31 March 2000 but before 1 April 2010.

⁷⁶ Words in column 2 inserted by FA 2000 s 82, Sch 22 paras 93(4), 127(3) with effect from 28 July 2000.

⁷⁷ Words in column 1 inserted by FA 2000 s 65, Sch 18 para 8(2) with effect for exchanges of shares or securities (within the meaning of TA 1988 Sch 28B, para 11B(1)) taking effect after 20 March 2000.

⁷⁸ Words in column 1 repealed by FA 1998 ss 96(3)(*b*), 165, Sch 27 Part III(21) with effect from 1 October 2000.

⁷⁹ Words repealed by FA 2000 s 156, Sch 40 Pt II(17) with effect for relevant payments or receipts in relation to which the chargeable date for the purposes of this Chapter is after 31 March 2001.

⁸⁰ Words repealed by FA 2000 s 156, Sch 40 Pt II(17) with effect for payments of interest made after 31 March 2001.

⁸¹ Words in column 1 repealed, and words in column 2 substituted, by CAA 2001 ss 578, 580, Sch 2 para 4, Sch 4 with effect for income tax purposes, as respects allowances and charges falling to be made for chargeable periods ending after 5 April 2001, and for corporation tax purposes, as respects allowances and charges falling to be made for chargeable periods ending after 31 March 2001.

⁸² Words inserted by FA 2001 s 65, Sch 17 para 5 with effect for income tax purposes, as respects allowances and charges falling to be made for chargeable periods ending after 5 April 2001, and for corporation tax purposes, as respects allowances and charges falling to be made for chargeable periods ending after 31 March 2001.

⁸³ Sub-ss (4A)–(4C) inserted by FA 2001 s 85(2), (4) with effect for payments made after 31 March 2001.

⁸⁴ "2A" inserted by FA 2001 s 63, Sch 15 para 39 with effect for shares issued after 5 April 2001, for claims for relief under TA 1988 Pt VII Chapter III made for the year 2000–01 or any later year of assessment.

[85] Words in column 2 substituted by FA 2001 s 83, Sch 28 para 20 with effect for chargeable events happening after 5 April 2002.
[86] Words in column 2 inserted by FA 2002 s 63, Sch 21 paras 1, 7 with effect for expenditure incurred after 16 April 2002.
[87] In sub-s (4B), words inserted in paras (*a*)–(*c*), in para (*b*), word substituted for the word "either", in para (*d*), word substituted for the word "neither"; and sub-s (4C) substituted; by FA 2002 s 94(5)–(7) with effect for payments made after 30 September 2002. Sub-s (4C) previously read as follows—

"(4C) In subsection (4B) above "company" includes a partnership of which any member is a company.".
[88] Words in sub-s (4A)(*b*) inserted, and sub-s (4D) inserted, by FA 2002 s 96(3), (4) with effect for payments made after 30 September 2002.
[89] Words in both columns inserted by FA 2002 s 109, Sch 33 para 15 with effect from 24 July 2002.
Prospective amendments—Words "paragraph 42 of Schedule 16 to the Finance Act 2002" to be inserted in column 2 by FA 2002 s 57, Sch 17 para 1 with effect from such day as the Treasury may by order appoint.

[98A Special penalties in the case of certain returns

(1) Regulations under section 203(2) (PAYE) or 566(1) (sub-contractors) of the principal Act may provide that this section shall apply in relation to any specified provision of the regulations.

(2) Where this section applies in relation to a provision of regulations, any person who fails to make a return in accordance with the provision shall be liable—

[(*a*) to a penalty or penalties of the relevant monthly amount for each month (or part of a month) during which the failure continues, but excluding any month after the twelfth or for which a penalty under this paragraph has already been imposed,][2] and

(*b*) if the failure continues beyond twelve months, without prejudice to any penalty under paragraph (*a*) above, to a penalty not exceeding so much of the amount payable by him in accordance with the regulations for the year of assessment to which the return relates as remained unpaid at the end of 19th April after the end of that year.

(3) For the purposes of subsection (2)(*a*) above, the relevant monthly amount in the case of a failure to make a return—

(*a*) where the number of persons in respect of whom particulars should be included in the return is fifty or less, is £100, and

(*b*) where that number is greater than fifty, is £100 for each fifty such persons and an additional £100 where that number is not a multiple of fifty.

(4) Where this section applies in relation to a provision of regulations, any person who fraudulently or negligently makes an incorrect return of a kind mentioned in the provision shall be liable to a penalty not exceeding the difference between—

(*a*) the amount payable by him in accordance with the regulations for the year of assessment to which the return relates, and

(*b*) the amount which would have been so payable if the return had been correct.][1]

Commentary—*Simon's Direct Tax Service* **A3.806**.
Regulations—IT (Employments) Regulations, SI 1993/744.
Concession B46—The Revenue will waive penalty charges on late employers' and sub-contractors' end-of-year returns, for the year ended 5 April 1995 and subsequent years, where these are received on or before the last business day within 7 days following the statutory filing date (19 May).
Revenue & other press releases—IR 14-6-96 (Revenue restrict level of automatic penalties for late 1995-96 employers' and contractors' end-of-year returns).
IR Tax Bulletin April 1997 p 422 (Revenue restrict level of automatic penalties for late 1996/97 employers' and contractors' end-of-year returns).
Revenue Internal Guidance—*Audit Instructions, Aud 10.200–10.206 (Revenue practice in evaluating penalty position).*
Aud 10.300–10.301 (procedures for dealing with irregularities in the current year).
Aud 10.600–10.605 (computation of unpaid tax)
Aud 15.301 (imposition of penalties under sub-s (2)(b)).
Aud 15.401–15.402 (Revenue policy on mitigation: maximum percentages reduction are 20% for disclosure plus 10% for unprompted voluntary disclosure, 40% for co-operation and 40% for gravity).
Aud 16.205–16.217 (settlement of PAYE investigation by agreement, including instalment arrangements, with worked examples).
NOTE: the Audit Instructions manual has been superseded by the Employer Compliance Manual.
Employers section manual ES 2140–2150 (Revenue procedures relating to automatically issued penalty determinations).
Definitions—"The principal Act", s 118(1), "return", s 118(1); "year of assessment", TA 1988 s 832(1).
Cross references—See TMA 1970 s 100C (proceedings before the Commissioners in relation to penalty under sub-s (2)(a)(i) above).
IT (Employments) Regulations, SI 1993/744 reg 43(12) (this section to apply in relation to employer's end of year returns).
Amendments—[1] This section inserted by FA 1989 s 165.

[98B European Economic Interest Groupings

(1) In this section "grouping" means a European Economic Interest Grouping formed in pursuance of Council Regulation (EEC) No 2137/85 of 25th July 1985, whether registered in Great Britain, in Northern Ireland, or elsewhere.

[(2) Subsections (2A) to (4) below apply where a grouping or member of a grouping required by a notice given under section 12A of this Act to deliver a return or other document falls to comply with the notice.

(2A) The grouping or member shall be liable to a penalty not exceeding £300 multiplied by the number of members of the grouping at the time of the failure to comply.

(2B) If, on an application made to them by an officer of the Board, the General or Special Commissioners so direct, the grouping or member shall be liable, for each day on which the failure continues after the day on which the grouping or member is notified of the direction (but excluding any day for which a penalty under this subsection has already been imposed), to a further penalty or penalties not exceeding £60 multiplied by the number of members of the grouping at the end of that day.][2]

(3) No penalty shall be imposed under [subsection (2A) and (2B)][2] above in respect of a failure at any time after the failure has been remedied.

(4) If a grouping to which, or member to whom, a notice is given proves that there was no income or chargeable gain to be included in the return, the penalty under [subsection (2A) and (2B)][2] above shall not exceed £100.

(5) Where a grouping or member fraudulently or negligently delivers an incorrect return, accounts or statement, or makes an incorrect declaration in a return delivered, under section 12A above, the grouping or member shall be liable to a penalty not exceeding £3,000 multiplied by the number of members of the grouping at the time of delivery.][1]

Commentary—*Simon's Direct Tax Service* A3.802.
Definitions—"The Board", s 118(1); "chargeable gain", TCGA 1992 s 15(2) by virtue of s 118(1); "General Commissioners", s 2; "notice", TA 1988 s 832(1); "return", s 118(1); "Special Commissioners", s 4.
Cross references—See TMA 1970 s 40(4) (group's collective liability for a deceased member's tax evasion).
TMA 1970 s 100C (proceedings before the Commissioners in relation to penalty under sub-s (2)(*a*) above).
Amendments—[1] This section inserted by FA 1990 Sch 11 paras 3, 5 with effect from 1 July 1989.
[2] Sub-ss (2), (2A), (2B) substituted for sub-s (2) and words in sub-ss (3), (4), substituted for the words "subsection (2)" by FA 1994 ss 196, 199 and Sch 19 para 30 with effect from the year 1996–97 as respects income tax and capital gains tax and, as respects corporation tax, with effect in relation to accounting periods ending after 30 June 1999 (by virtue of Finance Act 1994, Section 199, (Appointed Day) Order, SI 1998/3173 art 2).

[99 Assisting in preparation of incorrect return etc

Any person who assists in or induces the preparation or delivery of any information, return, accounts or other document which—

(*a*) he knows will be, or is or are likely to be, used for any purpose of tax, and
(*b*) he knows to be incorrect,

shall be liable to a penalty not exceeding £3,000.][1]

Commentary—*Simon's Direct Tax Service* A3.805.
Revenue & other press releases—ICAEW 27-7-94 (guidelines on professional conduct in relation to taxation).
Revenue Internal Guidance—*Audit Instructions, Aud 15.102 (the onus is on the Revenue to show that the person concerned knew that the documents etc were incorrect).* NOTE: the Audit Instructions manual has been superseded by the Employer Compliance Manual.
Definition—"Return", s 118(1).
Cross references—See TMA 1970 s 103(3) (Board may determine penalty under this section and time limit for proceedings for such penalty).
Education (Student Loans) (Repayment) Regulations, SI 2000/944 reg 7 (application of this section to penalties in connection with the repayment of student loans by assessment to income tax or deduction of repayments by employers).
Amendments—[1] This section substituted by FA 1989 s 166 in relation to assistance and inducements occurring after 26 July 1989.

[99A Certificates of non-liability to income tax

If a person who gives a certificates of non-liability to income tax in pursuance of regulations under section 477A of the principal Act (building societies) or section 480B of that Act (deposit-takers)—

(*a*) gives the certificate fraudulently or negligently, or
(*b*) fails to comply with any undertaking contained in the certificate in pursuance of the regulations,

he shall be liable to a penalty not exceeding £3,000.][1]

Commentary—*Simon's Direct Tax Service* B5.224.
Amendments—[1] This section inserted by FA 1991 s 82. So far as relating to the giving of a certificate, it applies in relation to certificates given after 24 July 1991. So far as relating to failure to comply with an undertaking contained in a certificate, it applies in relation to certificates whenever given, but not so as to impose liability for a failure occurring before 25 July 1991.

[100 Determination of penalties by officer of Board

(1) Subject to subsection (2) below and except where proceedings for a penalty have been instituted under section 100D below ...[3], an officer of the Board authorised by the Board for the purposes of this section may make a determination imposing a penalty under any provision of the Taxes Acts and setting it at such amount as, in his opinion, is correct or appropriate.

(2) Subsection (1) above does not apply where the penalty is a penalty under—

(*a*) section 93(1) above as it has effect before the amendments made by section 162 of the Finance Act 1989 or section 93(1)(*a*) above as it has effect after those amendments,
(*b*) section 94(1) above as it has effect before the substitution made by section 83 of the Finance (No 2) Act 1987
(*c*) section 98(1) above as it has effect before the amendments made by section 164 of the Finance Act 1989 or section 98(1)(i) above as it has effect after those amendments, or
(*d*) paragraph (*a*)(i) of section 98A(2) above as it has effect by virtue of section 165(2) of the Finance Act 1989 [or][2]
[(*e*) section 98B(2)(*a*) above.][2]

(3) Notice of a determination of a penalty under this section shall be served on the person liable to the penalty and shall state the date on which it is issued and the time within which an appeal against the determination may be made.

(4) After the notice of a determination under this section has been served the determination shall not be altered except in accordance with this section or on appeal.

(5) If it is discovered by an officer of the Board authorised by the Board for the purposes of this section that the amount of a penalty determined under this section is or has become insufficient the officer may make a determination in a further amount so that the penalty is set at the amount which, in his opinion, is correct or appropriate.

(6) In any case where—

(a) a determination under this section is of a penalty under [section 93(2), (4) or (5) of this Act or][5] [paragraph 18(2) of Schedule 18 to the Finance Act 1998][4], and

(b) after the determination has been made it is discovered by an officer of the Board authorised by the Board for the purposes of this section that the amount which was taken into account as the relevant amount of tax is or has become excessive,

the determination shall be revised so that the penalty is set at the amount which is correct; and, where more than the correct amount has already been paid, the appropriate amount shall be repaid.][1]

Commentary—*Simon's Direct Tax Service* **A3.807, 1636.**
Revenue Internal Guidance—Corporation tax pay and file manual, CT (PF) 10420 (examples illustrating the determination of penalties).
Investigations Handbook IH 5500–5551 (Revenue practice on the imposition and mitigation of penalties in investigation cases, with examples).
IH 6000–6080 (investigation cases: offers of settlement: penalties included).
IH 6100–6142 (investigation cases: letter of offer).
IH 6260–6284 (Revenue acceptance of offer of settlement and subsequent procedures).
Simon's Tax Cases—*Cox v Poole General Comrs and the IRC* [1988] STC 66.
s 100(1), *Willey v IRC* [1985] STC 56.
s 100(6), *Brodt v Wells General Comrs and IRC* [1987] STC 207; *Walsh v Croydon General Comrs and IRC* [1987] STC 456; *Montague v Hampstead General Comrs and IRC* [1989] STC 818.
s 100(7), *Moschi v General Comrs for Kensington* [1980] STC 1; *Brodt v Wells General Comrs and IRC* [1987] STC 207, *Walsh v Croydon General Comrs and IRC* [1987] STC 456.
Cross references—See TMA 1970 s 100A (supplementary provisions).
TMA 1970 s 100B (appeals against penalty determinations under this section).
TMA 1970 s 100C(1) (proceedings for penalties to be before Commissioners where sub-s (2) above disapplies sub-s (1) above).
TMA 1970 s 113(1D) (procedure for serving notice of determination of interest under this section may be completed by other officer of Board once certain decisions have been taken);
FA 1988 s 134(8)(b) (proceedings begun in Northern Ireland under this section before 3 April 1989 not to be transferred to General Commissioners);
Special Commissioners (Jurisdiction and Procedures) Regulations, SI 1994/1811 reg 3 (parties to proceedings under this section not to have facility to serve notice on Clerk to fix date of hearing);
General Commissioners (Jurisdiction and Procedure) Regulations, SI 1994/1812 reg 1(2)(b) (General Commissioners Regulations do not apply to proceedings under this section in respect of which summons issued before 1 September 1994),
General Commissioners (Jurisdiction and Procedure) Regulations, SI 1994/1812 reg 3(1) (parties to proceedings under this section not to have facility to serve notice on Clerk to fix date of hearing).
Education (Student Loans) (Repayment) Regulations, SI 2000/944 reg 7 (application of this section to penalties in connection with the repayment of student loans by assessment to income tax or deduction of repayments by employers).
Amendments—[1] This section and ss 100A to 100D below substituted for s 100 by FA 1989 s 167.
[2] Sub-s (2)(e) and the preceding word "or" inserted by FA 1990 Sch 11 paras 3(2), 5 with effect from 1 July 1989.
[3] Words in sub-s (1) repealed by the General and Special Commissioners (Amendment of Enactments) Regulations, SI 1994/1813 reg 2, Sch 1 paras 1, 14, Sch 2 Pt I, as from 1 September 1994 in relation to proceedings before the General Commissioners in respect of which the General Commissioners Regulations, SI 1994/1812 apply or, as the case may be the Special Commissioners Regulations, SI 1994/1811 apply.
[4] Words in sub-s (6)(a) substituted by FA 1998 Sch 19 para 38 with effect in relation to accounting periods ending after 30 June 1999 (by virtue of Finance Act 1994, Section 199, (Appointed Day) Order, SI 1998/3173 art 2).
[5] Words in sub-s (6)(a) inserted by FA 2001 s 91 with effect for penalties determined at any time whether before or after the passing of FA 2001.

[100A Provisions supplementary to section 100

(1) Where a person who has incurred a penalty has died, a determination under section 100 above which could have been made in relation to him may be made in relation to his personal representatives, and any penalty imposed on personal representatives by virtue of this subsection shall be a debt due from and payable out of his estate.

(2) A penalty determined under section 100 above shall be due and payable at the end of the period of thirty days beginning with the date of the issue of the notice of determination.

(3) A penalty determined under section 100 above shall for all purposes be treated as if it were tax charged in an assessment and due and payable.][1]

Commentary—*Simon's Direct Tax Service* **A3.807, 1682.**
Simon's Tax Cases—*Sparks v West Brixton General Comrs* [1977] STC 212.
Cross references—See Education (Student Loans) (Repayment) Regulations, SI 2000/944 reg 7 (application of this section to penalties in connection with the repayment of student loans by assessment to income tax or deduction of repayments by employers).
Amendments—[1] This section and ss 100, 100B to 100D substituted for s 100 by FA 1989 s 167.

[100B Appeals against penalty determinations

(1) An appeal may be brought against the determination of a penalty under section 100 above and, subject to [sections 93, 93A and 95A of this Act][3] [and][4] the following provisions of this section, the

provisions of this Act relating to appeals shall have effect in relation to an appeal against such a determination as they have effect in relation to an appeal against an assessment to tax.

(2) [Subject to sections 93(8) and 93A(7) of this Act][3] on an appeal against the determination of a penalty under section 100 above section 50(6) to (8) of this Act shall not apply but—

  (*a*) in the case of a penalty which is required to be of a particular amount, the Commissioners may—

   (i) if it appears to them that no penalty has been incurred, set the determination aside,
   (ii) if the amount determined appears to them to be correct, confirm the determination, or
   (iii) if the amount determined appears to them to be incorrect, increase or reduce it to the correct amount,

  (*b*) in the case of any other penalty, the Commissioners may—

   (i) if it appears to them that no penalty has been incurred, set the determination aside,
   (ii) if the amount determined appears to them to be appropriate, confirm the determination,
   (iii) if the amount determined appears to them to be excessive, reduce it to such other amount (including nil) as they consider appropriate, or
   (iv) if the amount determined appears to them to be insufficient, increase it to such amount not exceeding the permitted maximum as they consider appropriate.

(3) Without prejudice to [any right to have a case stated under regulation 22 of the General Commissioners Regulations or any right of appeal under section 56A][2] of this Act, an appeal from a decision of the Commissioners against the amount of a penalty which has been determined under section 100 above or this section shall lie, at the instance of the person liable to the penalty, to the High Court or, in Scotland, to the Court of Session as the Court of Exchequer in Scotland; and on that appeal the court shall have the like jurisdiction as is conferred on the Commissioners by virtue of this section.][1]

Commentary—*Simon's Direct Tax Service* **A3.811.**
Regulations—General Commissioners (Jurisdiction and Procedure) Regulations, SI 1994/1812.
Revenue Internal Guidance—Enquiry Handbook EH 839 (an appeal against penalties imposed in a partnership case can be brought only by the representative partner and is a composite appeal against the determination of each relevant partner's liability).
Simon's Tax Cases—*King v Walden* [2000] STC (SCD) 179.
Cross references—See Education (Student Loans) (Repayment) Regulations, SI 2000/944 reg 7 (application of this section to penalties in connection with the repayment of student loans by assessment to income tax or deduction of repayments by employers).
Definitions—"the General Commissioners Regulations", s 118(1).
Amendments—[1] This section and ss 100, 100A, 100C, 100D substituted for s 100 by FA 1989 s 167.
[2] Words in sub-s (3) substituted by the General and Special Commissioners (Amendment of Enactments) Regulations, SI 1994/1813 reg 2(1), Sch 1 paras 1, 15, as from 1 September 1994 in relation to proceedings before the General Commissioners in respect of which the General Commissioners Regulations, SI 1994/1812 apply or, as the case may be the Special Commissioners Regulations, SI 1994/1811 apply.
[3] Words in sub-ss (1), (2) inserted by FA 1994 ss 196, 199 and Sch 19 para 31 with effect for income tax and capital gains tax from the year 1996–97 or, as respects corporation tax, with effect in relation to accounting periods ending after 30 June 1999 (by virtue of Finance Act 1994, Section 199, (Appointed Day) Order, SI 1998/3173 art 2).
[4] Word in sub-s (1) inserted by FA 1995, s 115(7), with effect for income tax and capital gains tax from the year 1996–97 or, as respects corporation tax, for accounting periods ending after 30 June 1999 (by virtue of SI 1998/3173 art 2).

[100C Penalty proceedings before Commissioners

(1) An officer of the Board authorised by the Board for the purposes of this section may commence proceedings before the General or Special Commissioners for any penalty to which subsection (1) of section 100 above does not apply by virtue of subsection (2) of that section.

(2) Proceedings under this section shall be by way of information in writing, made to the Commissioners, and upon summons issued by them to the defendant (or defender) to appear before them at a time and place stated in the summons; and they shall hear and decide each case in a summary way.

(3) Any penalty determined by the Commissioners in proceedings under this section shall for all purposes be treated as if it were tax charged in an assessment and due and payable.

(4) An appeal against the determination of a penalty in proceedings under this section shall lie to the High Court or, in Scotland, the Court of Session as the Court of Exchequer in Scotland—

  (*a*) by any party on a question of law, and
  (*b*) by the defendant (or, in Scotland, the defender) against the amount of the penalty.

(5) On any such appeal the court may—

  (*a*) if it appears that no penalty has been incurred, set the determination aside,
  (*b*) if the amount determined appears to be appropriate, confirm the determination,
  (*c*) if the amount determined appears to be excessive, reduce it to such other amount (including nil) as the court considers appropriate, or
  (*d*) if the amount determined appears to be insufficient, increase it to such amount not exceeding the permitted maximum as the court considers appropriate.][1]

Commentary—*Simon's Direct Tax Service* **A3.808.**
Cross references—See Education (Student Loans) (Repayment) Regulations, SI 2000/944 reg 7 (application of this section to penalties in connection with the repayment of student loans by assessment to income tax or deduction of repayments by employers).
Amendments—[1] This section and ss 100, 100A, 100B, 100D substituted for s 100 by FA 1989 s 167.

[100D Penalty proceedings before court

(1) Where in the opinion of the Board the liability of any person for a penalty arises by reason of the fraud of that or any other person, proceedings for the penalty may be instituted before the High Court or, in Scotland, the Court of Session as the Court of Exchequer in Scotland.

(2) Proceedings under this section which are not instituted (in England, Wales or Northern Ireland) under the Crown Proceedings Act 1947 by and in the name of the Board as an authorised department for the purposes of that Act shall be instituted—

    (a) in England and Wales, in the name of the Attorney General,
    (b) in Scotland, in the name of the [Advocate General for Scotland][2], and
    (c) in Northern Ireland, in the name of the Attorney General for Northern Ireland.

(3) Any proceedings under this section instituted in England and Wales shall be deemed to be civil proceedings by the Crown within the meaning of Part II of the Crown Proceedings Act 1947 and any such proceedings instituted in Northern Ireland shall be deemed to be civil proceedings within the meaning of that Part of that Act as for the time being in force in Northern Ireland.

(4) If in proceedings under this section the court does not find that fraud is proved but consider that the person concerned is nevertheless liable to a penalty, the court may determine a penalty notwithstanding that, but for the opinion of the Board as to fraud, the penalty would not have been a matter for the court.][1]

Commentary—*Simon's Direct Tax Service* **A3.809.**
Cross references—See Education (Student Loans) (Repayment) Regulations, SI 2000/944 reg 7 (application of this section to penalties in connection with the repayment of student loans by assessment to income tax or deduction of repayments by employers).
Amendments—[1] This section and ss 100, 100A–100C substituted for s 100 by FA 1989 s 167.
[2] Words in sub-s (2)(d) substituted by the Transfer of Functions (Lord Advocate and Advocate General for Scotland) Order, SI 1999/679 art 2, Sch with effect from 20 May 1999.

[101 Evidence for purposes of proceedings relating to penalties

An assessment which can no longer be varied by any Commissioners on appeal or by order of any court is sufficient evidence, for the purposes of—

    (a) the preceding provisions of this Part, and
    (b) the provisions of Schedule 18 to the Finance Act 1998 relating to penalties,

that the amounts in respect of which tax is charged in the assessment arose or were received as stated in the assessment.][1]

Commentary—*Simon's Direct Tax Service* **A3.802.**
Simon's Tax Cases—*King v Walden (Inspector of Taxes)* [2001] STC 822.
Definition—''Chargeable gain'', TCGA 1992 s 15(2) by virtue of s 118(1).
Amendments—[1] This section substituted by FA 1998 Sch 19 para 39 with effect in relation to accounting periods ending after 30 June 1999 (by virtue of Finance Act 1994, Section 199, (Appointed Day) Order, SI 1998/3173 art 2).

102 Mitigation of penalties

The Board may in their discretion mitigate any penalty, or stay or compound any proceedings for [a penalty][1], and may also, after judgment, further mitigate or entirely remit the penalty.

Commentary—*Simon's Direct Tax Service* **A3.813.**
Revenue Internal Guidance—Investigations Handbook IH 5500-5551 (Revenue practice on the impositions and mitigation of penalties in investigation cases, with examples).
Cross references—See Education (Student Loans) (Repayment) Regulations, SI 2000/944 reg 7 (application of this section to penalties in connection with the repayment of student loans by assessment to income tax or deduction of repayments by employers).
Amendments—[1] Words substituted by FA 1989 s 168(4).

[103 Time limits for penalties

(1) Subject to subsection (2) below, where the amount of a penalty is to be ascertained by reference to tax payable by a person for any period, the penalty may be determined by an officer of the Board, or proceedings for the penalty may be commenced before the Commissioners or a court—

    (a) at any time within six years after the date on which the penalty was incurred, or
    (b) at any later time within three years after the final determination of the amount of tax by reference to which the amount of the penalty is to be ascertained.

(2) Where the tax was payable by a person who has died, and the determination would be made in relation to his personal representatives, subsection (1)(b) above does not apply if the tax was charged in an assessment made later than six years after [the 31st January next following the chargeable period][2] for which it was charged.

(3) A penalty under section 99 of this Act may be determined by an officer of the Board, or proceedings for such a penalty may be commenced before a court, at any time within twenty years after the date on which the penalty was incurred.

(4) A penalty to which neither subsection (1) nor subsection (3) above applies may be so determined, or proceedings for such a penalty may be commenced before the Commissioners or a court, at any time within six years after the date on which the penalty was incurred or began to be incurred.][1]

Commentary—*Simon's Direct Tax Service* A3.810.
Revenue Internal Guidance—Corporation tax pay and file manual CT (PF) 10424 (examples illustrating the operation of the time limits).
Revenue Internal Guidance—Enquiry Handbook EH 700 (example illustrating sub-s (2)).
Simon's Tax Cases—s 103(2), *R v Inland Revenue Comrs , ex p Knight* [1973] STC 564.
s 103(3), *Willey v IRC* [1985] STC 56; *Carco Accessories Ltd v IRC* [1985] STC 518.
Cross references—See Education (Student Loans) (Repayment) Regulations, SI 2000/944 reg 7 (application of sub-ss (3), (4) to penalties in connection with the repayment of student loans by assessment to income tax or deduction of repayments by employers).
Amendments—[1] This section substituted by FA 1989 s 169, but it does not affect the application of TMA 1970 s 103(4) to proceedings under TMA 1970 s 100 as originally enacted.
[2] Words in sub-s (2) substituted by FA 1994 ss 196, 199 and Sch 19 para 32 with effect from the year 1996–97 in relation to income tax and capital gains tax and, as respects corporation tax, with effect in relation to accounting periods ending after 30 June 1999 (by virtue of Finance Act 1994, Section 199, (Appointed Day) Order, SI 1998/3173 art 2).

[103A Interest on penalties

A penalty under any of the provisions of [Part II, IV or VA][2] or this Part of this Act[, or Schedule 18 to the Finance Act 1998,][3] shall carry interest at the rate applicable under section 178 of the Finance Act 1989 from the date on which it becomes due and payable until payment.][1]

Commentary—*Simon's Direct Tax Service* E1.826.
Cross references—See TMA 1970 s 107A(2), (3) (recovery of interest from the relevant trustees of a settlement).
Notes—The day appointed for which FA 1989 s 178(1) has effect is 9 March 1998 (Finance Act 1989, section 178(1), (Appointed Day) Order, SI 1998/311).
Cross references—See Education (Student Loans) (Repayment) Regulations, SI 2000/944 reg 7 (application of this section to penalties in connection with the repayment of student loans by assessment to income tax or deduction of repayments by employers).
Amendments—[1] This section inserted by FA 1994 ss 196, 199 and Sch 19 para 33 in relation to income tax and capital gains tax with effect from the year 1996–97 or, as respects corporation tax, with effect in relation to accounting periods ending on or after the 'self-assessment appointed day' (1 July 1999).
[2] Words substituted by FA 1995, s 115(8), with effect from the year 1996–97 in relation to income tax and capital gains tax or, as respects corporation tax, with effect in relation to accounting periods ending on or after the 'self-assessment appointed day' (1 July 1999).
[3] Words inserted by FA 1998 Sch 19 para 40 with effect in relation to accounting periods ending after 30 June 1999 (by virtue of Finance Act 1994, Section 199, (Appointed Day) Order, SI 1998/3173 art 2).

104 Saving for criminal proceedings

The provisions of the Taxes Acts shall not, save so far as is otherwise provided, affect any criminal proceedings for any misdemeanour.

Commentary—*Simon's Direct Tax Service* A3.816.
Definitions—''The Taxes Acts'', s 118(1).
Cross references—See Education (Student Loans) (Repayment) Regulations, SI 2000/944 reg 7 (application of this section to penalties in connection with the repayment of student loans by assessment to income tax or deduction of repayments by employers).
Statement of Practice SP 2/88—Revenue's practice in relation to civil penalties and prosecutions for tax offences.

105 Evidence in cases of [fraudulent conduct]

(1) Statements made or documents produced by or on behalf of a person shall not be inadmissible in any such proceedings as are mentioned in subsection (2) below by reason only that it has been drawn to his attention that—

[(a) pecuniary settlements may be accepted instead of a penalty being determined, or proceedings being instituted, in relation to any tax,][1]

(b) though no undertaking can be given as to whether or not the Board will accept such a settlement in the case of any particular person, it is the practice of the Board to be influenced by the fact that a person has made a full confession of any [fraudulent conduct][1] to which he has been a party and has given full facilities for investigation,

and that he was or may have been induced thereby to make the statements or produce the documents.

(2) The proceedings mentioned in subsection (1) above are—

(a) any criminal proceedings against the person in question for any form of [fraudulent conduct][1] in connection with or in relation to tax, and

(b) any proceedings against him for the recovery of any [tax due from him, and][1]

[(c) any proceedings for a penalty or on appeal against the determination of a penalty.][1]

Commentary—*Simon's Direct Tax Service* A3.816, 1505.
Revenue & other press releases—IR 18–10–90 (Revenue practice in cases of fraud: In considering whether to institute criminal proceedings, Revenue are influenced by the fact that the taxpayer has made a full confession and has given full facilities for investigation into his affairs and for examination of such books, papers, documents or information as Board may consider necessary. Revenue may accept a monetary settlement from a taxpayer, but can give no assurance that they will do so).

Cross references—See Education (Student Loans) (Repayment) Regulations, SI 2000/944 reg 7 (application of this section to penalties in connection with the repayment of student loans by assessment to income tax or deduction of repayments by employers).
Amendments—¹ Sub-s (1)(*a*) and words in sub-s (1)(*b*), (2)(*a*), (*b*) substituted and sub-s (2)(*c*) inserted by FA 1989 ss 149(5), 168(5).

106 Refusal to allow a deduction of income tax, and avoidance of agreements for payment without deduction

(1) A person who refuses to allow a deduction of income tax authorised by the Taxes Acts to be made out of any payment shall incur a penalty of £50.

(2) Every agreement for payment of interest, rent or other annual payment in full without allowing any such deduction shall be void.

Commentary—*Simon's Direct Tax Service* **A3.429.**

Scotland

107 Criminal liability for false statements made to obtain allowances

(1) This section applies only in Scotland.

(2) If any person, for the purpose of obtaining any allowance, reduction, rebate or repayment in respect of tax, either for himself or for any other person, or, in any return made with reference to tax, knowingly makes any false statement or false representation, he shall be liable, on summary conviction, to imprisonment for a term not exceeding six months.

(3) Notwithstanding anything in the Summary Jurisdiction (Scotland) Act 1954 proceedings for an offence under this section may be commenced at any time within three years from the time when the offence was committed.

(4) The expression ''return'' in this section shall be construed without regard to the definition in section 118(1) of this Act.

Commentary—*Simon's Direct Tax Service* **A3.1503.**

PART XI
MISCELLANEOUS AND SUPPLEMENTAL
[Settlements

107A Relevant trustees

(1) Subject to the following provisions of this section, anything which for the purposes of this Act is done at any time by or in relation to any one or more of the relevant trustees of a settlement shall be treated for those purposes as done at that time by or in relation to the other or others of those trustees.

(2) Subject to subsection (3) below, where the relevant trustees of a settlement are liable—

(*a*) to a penalty under section 7, 12B, 93, 95 or 97AA of this Act or paragraph 2A of Schedule 1A to this Act, or to interest under section 103A of this Act on such a penalty;

(*b*) to make a payment in accordance with an assessment under section 30 of this Act, or to make a payment under section 59A or 59B of this Act;

(*c*) to a surcharge under section 59C of this Act, or to interest under that section on such a surcharge; or

(*d*) to interest under section 86 of this Act,

the penalty, interest, payment or surcharge may be recovered (but only once) from any one or more of those trustees.

(3) No amount may be recovered by virtue of subsection (2)(*a*) or (*c*) above from a person who did not become a relevant trustee until after the relevant time, that is to say—

(*a*) in relation to so much of a penalty under section 93(3) or 97AA(1)(*b*) of this Act as is payable in respect of any day, or to interest under section 103A of this Act on so much of such a penalty as is so payable, the beginning of that day;

(*b*) in relation to a penalty under any other provision of this Act mentioned in subsection (2)(*a*) above, or to interest under section 103A of this Act on such a penalty, the time when the relevant act or omission occurred; and

(*c*) in relation to a surcharge under subsection (2) or (3) of section 59C of this Act, or to interest under that section on such a surcharge, the beginning of the day mentioned in that subsection;

and in paragraph (*b*) above ''the relevant act or omission'' means the act or omission which caused the penalty to become payable.

(4) In a case where—

(*a*) subsection (2)(*a*) above applies in relation to a penalty under section 93 of this Act, or

(*b*) subsection (2)(*c*) above applies in relation to a surcharge under section 59C of this Act, subsection (8) of section 93 or, as the case may be, subsection (9) of section 59C of this Act shall have effect as if the reference to the taxpayer were a reference to each of the relevant trustees.][1]

Commentary—*Simon's Direct Tax Service* **E1.805.**
Definitions—''the relevant trustees'', s 118(1).
Amendments—[1] This section inserted, together with the preceding cross-heading, by FA 1995 s 103(5), (7), with effect in relation to income tax and capital gains tax for the year 1996–97 and subsequent years of assessment.

Companies

108 Responsibility of company officers

(1) Everything to be done by a company under the Taxes Acts shall be done by the company acting through the proper officer of the company [or, except where a liquidator has been appointed for the company, through such other person as may for the time being have the express, implied or apparent authority of the company to act on its behalf for the purpose][2], and service on a company of any document under or in pursuance of the Taxes Acts may be effected by serving it on the proper officer.

This subsection is without prejudice to Part VIII of this Act (charges on non-residents) as it applies to corporation tax.

(2) Corporation tax or other tax chargeable under the Corporation Tax Acts on a company which is not a body corporate, or which is a body corporate not incorporated under the [Companies Act 1985][1] or any other enactment forming part of the law of the United Kingdom, or by Charter, may, at any time after the tax becomes due, and without prejudice to any other method of recovery, be recovered from the proper officer of the company, and that officer may retain out of any money coming into his hands on behalf of the company sufficient sums to pay that tax, and, so far as he is not so reimbursed, shall be entitled to be indemnified by the company in respect of the liability so imposed on him.

(3) For the purposes of this section—

(*a*) the proper officer of a company which is a body corporate shall be the secretary or person acting as secretary of the company, except that if a liquidator has been appointed for the company the liquidator shall be the proper officer,
(*b*) the proper officer of a company which is not a body corporate or for which there is no proper officer within paragraph (*a*) above, shall be the treasurer or the person acting as treasurer, of the company.

Commentary—*Simon's Direct Tax Service* **A3.302.**
Concession C20—A company's claim to group relief may be signed by a person authorised by the company as an alternative to the company secretary.
Revenue & other press releases—ICAEW TR799 June 1990 (foreign company in liquidation: Revenue practice is to proceed against the company itself for a winding-up under IA 1986 Pt V).
Simon's Tax Cases—*R v Dimsey* [1999] STC 846.
Cross references—See TMA 1970 s 71(2) (accountability on tax matters of treasurer, auditor, etc of a body of persons).
Amendments—[1] Words in sub-s (2) substituted by the Companies Consolidation (Consequential Provisions) Act 1985 Sch 2 with effect from 1 July 1985.
[2] Words in sub-s (1) inserted by FA 1993 Sch 14 para 7.

[109 Corporation tax on close company in connection with loans to participators etc

(1) The provisions of [sections 419 and 420][3] of the principal Act (charge of tax in connection with loans by close companies to participators etc) directing that tax be assessed and recoverable as if it were an amount of corporation tax shall be taken as applying, subject to the provisions of the Taxes Act, and to any necessary modifications, all enactments applying generally to corporation tax, including those relating to the assessing, collecting and receiving of corporation tax, those conferring or regulating a right of appeal and those concerning administration, penalties, interest on unpaid tax and priority of tax in cases of insolvency under the law of any part of the United Kingdom.

(2) ...[2]

(3) For the purposes of section [87A][2] of this Act as applied by subsection (1) above, the date when tax [under the said section [419]][3] became due and payable shall be that determined in accordance with subsection [(3)][3] of that section][2].

[(3A) If—

[(*a*)][4] there is such a repayment of the whole or any part of a loan or advance as is referred to in subsection [(4) of section 419][3] of the principal Act, [or
(*b*) there is such a release or writing off of the whole or any part of the debt in respect of a loan or advance as is referred to in that subsection,][4]

interest under section 87A of this Act on so much of the tax under the said section [419][3] as is referable to the amount repaid[, released or written off][4] shall not be payable in respect of any period after the date on which the repayment was made [or the release or writing off occurred][4].][2]

(4) Section 91 of this Act shall not apply in consequence of any discharge or repayment of tax under section [419(4)][3] of the principal Act.

(5) For the purposes of the said section 91, a relief from tax under the said [sections 419 and 420][3] shall not be treated as affecting tax charged by any assessment unless the assessment is to tax under that section.][1]

Commentary—*Simon's Direct Tax Service* D2.724.
Definition—''Principal Act'', s 118(1).
Simon's Tax Cases—*Joint v Bracken Developments Ltd* [1994] STC 300; *Earlspring Properties Ltd v Guest* [1995] STC 479.
Amendments—[1] This section was substituted by FA 1972 s 111 and Sch 24 para 13, with effect from 6 April 1973.
[2] Sub-s (2) repealed, words in sub-s (3) substituted and sub-s (3A) inserted by F(No 2)A 1987 s 91 with respect to loans or advances made or treated as made in accounting periods ending after 30 September 1993 by virtue of Corporation Tax Acts (Provisions for Payment of Tax and Returns) (Appointed Days) Order, SI 1992/3066 art 2(1), (2)(a).
[3] Words in sub-ss (1), (3), (3A), (4), (5) substituted by TA 1988 Sch 29 paras 10(6), 32 Table.
[4] Words in sub-s (3A) inserted by FA 1998 Sch 3 para 6 with effect in relation to the release or writing off of the whole or part of a debt after 5 April 1999.

Valuation

110 Valuation of land: power of entry

Any person authorised in that behalf by the Board may, on producing if so required evidence of his authority, at any reasonable time enter on and inspect, with a view to establishing its annual value, any land the annual value of which falls to be determined for purposes of income tax or corporation tax.

Commentary—*Simon's Direct Tax Service* A3.538.

111 Valuation of assets; power to inspect

(1) If for the purposes of [the [1992 Act][2]][1] the Board authorise an inspector or other officer of the Board to inspect any property for the purpose of ascertaining its market value the person having the custody or possession of that property shall permit the inspector or other officer so authorised to inspect it at such reasonable times as the Board may consider necessary.

(2) If any person wilfully delays or obstructs an inspector or other officer of the Board acting in pursuance of this section he shall be liable on summary conviction to a fine not exceeding [level 1 on the standard scale][3].

Commentary—*Simon's Direct Tax Service* C2.126.
Definitions—''the 1992 Act'', s 118(1).
Amendments—[1] Word ''the'' in sub-s (1) substituted by CGTA 1979 s 157(2), Sch 7, para 8(a), Table, Pt I, para 1.
[2] Words in sub-s (1) substituted by TCGA 1992 Sch 10 para 2(1), (2).
[3] Words in sub-s (2) substituted by virtue of the Criminal Justice Act 1982 ss 38, 46.

Documents

112 Loss, destruction or damage to assessments, returns, etc

(1) Where any assessment to tax, or any duplicate of assessment to tax, or any return or other document relating to tax, has been lost or destroyed, or been so defaced or damaged as to be illegible or otherwise useless, the Commissioners, inspectors, collectors and other officers having powers in relation to tax may, notwithstanding anything in any enactment to the contrary, do all such acts and things as they might have done, and all acts and things done under or in pursuance of this section shall be as valid and effectual for all purposes as they would have been, if the assessment or duplicate of assessment had not been made, or the return or other document had not been made or furnished or required to be made or furnished:

Provided that, where any person who is charged with tax in consequence or by virtue of any act or thing done under or in pursuance of this section proves to the satisfaction of the Commissioners having jurisdiction in the case that he has already paid any tax for the same chargeable period in respect of the subject matter and on the account in respect of and on which he is so charged, relief shall be given to the extent to which the liability of that person has been discharged by the payment so made either by abatement from the charge or by repayment, as the case may require.

(2) In this section, ''the Commissioners'' means, as the case may require, either the Board or the General or Special Commissioners concerned.

[(3) The references in subsection (1) above to assessments to tax include references to determinations of penalties; and in its application to such determinations the proviso to that subsection shall have effect with the appropriate modifications.][1]

Commentary—*Simon's Direct Tax Service* A3.201.
Definition—''Return'', s 118(1).
Cross references—See Education (Student Loans) (Repayment) Regulations, SI 2000/944 reg 7 (application of this section in connection with the repayment of student loans by assessment to income tax or deduction of repayments by employers).
Amendments—[1] Sub-s (3) added by FA 1989 s 168(6).

113 Form of returns and other documents

(1) Any returns under the Taxes Acts shall be in such form as the Board prescribe, and in prescribing income tax forms under this subsection the Board shall have regard to the desirability of securing, so

far as may be possible, that no person shall be required to make more than one return annually of the sources of his income and the amounts derived therefrom.

[(1A) Any notice or direction requiring any return to be made under the Taxes Acts to an inspector or other officer of the Board may be issued or given in the name of that officer, or as the case may be in the name of the Board, by any officer of the Board, and so as to require the return to be made to the first-mentioned officer][1].

[(1B) Where the Board or an inspector or other officer of the Board have in accordance with section 29 of this Act [or paragraph 41 of Schedule 18 to the Finance Act 1998][4], or any other provision of the Taxes Acts, decided to make an assessment to tax, and have taken all other decisions needed for arriving at the amount of the assessment, they may entrust to some other officer of the Board responsibility for completing the assessing procedure, whether by means involving the use of a computer or otherwise, including responsibility for serving notice of the assessment on the person liable for tax][1].

(1C) ...[2]

[(1D) Where an officer of the Board has decided to impose a penalty under section 100 of this Act and has taken all other decisions needed for arriving at the amount of the penalty, he may entrust to any other officer of the Board responsibility for completing the determination procedure, whether by means involving the use of a computer or otherwise, including responsibility for serving notice of the determination on the person liable to the penalty.][3]

(2) Any return or assessment or other document relating to chargeable gains or tax on capital gains may be combined with one relating to income or income tax.

(3) Every assessment, [determination of a penalty][3] duplicate, warrant, notice of assessment[, of determination][3] or of demand, or other document required to be used in assessing, charging, collecting and levying tax [or determining a penalty][3] shall be in accordance with the forms prescribed from time to time in that behalf by the Board, and a document in the form prescribed and supplied or approved by them shall be valid and effectual.

Commentary—*Simon's Direct Tax Service* A3.105, 215.
Statements of Practice SP 5/87—Tax returns and other revenue forms may be submitted on facsimiles or photocopies provided Revenue's approval of their wording and design has been obtained in advance.
SP 4/91—Tax returns: their design and the information required in them.
SP 9/93—Form prescribed under sub-s (1) above for corporation tax return under pay and file.
Cross references—See Education (Student Loans) (Repayment) Regulations, SI 2000/944 reg 7 (application of this section in connection with the repayment of student loans by assessment to income tax or deduction of repayments by employers).
Definitions—"Chargeable gain", TCGA 1992 s 15(2) by virtue of s 118(1); "return", s 118(1).
Amendments—[1] Sub-ss (1A) and (1B) inserted by FA 1970 Sch 4 para 10.
[2] Sub-s (1C) (inserted by FA 1989 s 160(4)) repealed by FA 1996 Sch 18 para 4(2)(c), Sch 41 Pt V(8) with effect: from the year 1996–97 (except so far as relating to partnerships whose trades, professions or businesses were set up and commenced before 6 April 1994, where the repeal has effect from the year 1997–98) and in relation to any income tax which is charged by an assessment made after 5 April 1998 and is for the year 1995–96 or any earlier year of assessment.
[3] Sub-s (1D) and words in sub-s (3) inserted by FA 1989 s 168(7).
[4] Words in sub-s (1B) inserted by FA 1998 Sch 19 para 41 with effect in relation to accounting periods ending after 30 June 1999 (by virtue of Finance Act 1994, Section 199, (Appointed Day) Order, SI 1998/3173 art 2).

114 Want of form or errors not to invalidate assessments, etc

(1) An assessment [or determination][1], warrant or other proceeding which purports to be made in pursuance of any provision of the Taxes Acts shall not be quashed, or deemed to be void or voidable, for want of form, or be affected by reason of a mistake, defect or omission therein, if the same is in substance and effect in conformity with or according to the intent and meaning of the Taxes Acts, and if the person or property charged or intended to be charged or affected thereby is designated therein according to common intent and understanding.

(2) An assessment [or determination][1] shall not be impeached or affected—

(a) by reason of a mistake therein as to—

(i) the name or surname of a person liable, or
(ii) the description of any profits or property, or
(iii) the amount of the tax charged, or

(b) by reason of any variance between the notice and the assessment [or determination][1].

Commentary—*Simon's Direct Tax Service* A3.215.
Simon's Tax Cases—*Murphy v Elders* [1974] STC 34*; *Baylis v Gregory* [1988] STC 476; *Gallic Leasing Ltd v Coburn* [1989] STC 354.
s 114(1), *Bath and West Counties Property Trust Ltd v Thomas* [1978] STC 30*; *Baylis v Gregory* [1986] STC 22.
s 114(2), *Honig v Sarsfield* [1986] STC 246.
Cross references—See Education (Student Loans) (Repayment) Regulations, SI 2000/944 reg 7 (application of this section in connection with the repayment of student loans by assessment to income tax or deduction of repayments by employers).
Amendments—[1] Words in sub-ss (1), (2) inserted by FA 1989 s 160(5).

115 Delivery and service of documents

(1) A notice or form which is to be served under the Taxes Acts on a person may be either delivered to him or left at his usual or last known place of residence.

(2) Any notice or other document to be given, sent, served or delivered under the Taxes Acts may be served by post, and, if to be given, sent, served or delivered to or on any person by the Board, by

any officer of the Board, or by or on behalf of any body of Commissioners, may be so served addressed to that person—

(a) at his usual or last known place of residence, or his place of business or employment, or

(b) in the case of a company, at any other prescribed place and, in the case of a liquidator of a company, at his address for the purposes of the liquidation or any other prescribed place.

(3) In subsection (2) above "prescribed" means prescribed by regulations made by the Board, and the power of making regulations for the purposes of that subsection shall be exercisable by statutory instrument subject to annulment in pursuance of a resolution of the House of Commons.

(4) Notices to be given or delivered to, or served on, the General Commissioners shall be valid and effectual if given or delivered to or served on their clerk.

[(5) Nothing in this section applies to any notice or other document required or authorised by the General Commissioners Regulations or the Special Commissioners Regulations to be sent or delivered to, or served on, any person.][1]

Commentary—*Simon's Direct Tax Service* A3.102, 216, 516.
Simon's Tax Cases—s 115(2), *Re a debtor (No 1240/SD/91), ex p the debtor v IRC* [1992] STC 771.
Cross references—See Education (Student Loans) (Repayment) Regulations, SI 2000/944 reg 7 (application of this section in connection with the repayment of student loans by assessment to income tax or deduction of repayments by employers).
Amendments—[1] Sub-s (5) added by the General and Special Commissioners (Amendment of Enactments) Regulations SI 1994/1813, reg 2(1), Sch 1 paras 1, 16, as from 1 September 1994 in relation to proceedings before the General Commissioners in respect of which the General Commissioners Regulations SI 1994/1812 apply or, as the case may be to proceedings before the Special Commissioners where the Special Commissioners Regulations SI 1994/1811 apply.

[115A Electronic lodgement of tax returns, etc

Schedule 3A to this Act (which makes provision with respect to the electronic lodgement of tax returns and documents required in connection with tax returns) shall have effect.][1]

Commentary—*Simon's Direct Tax Service* A3.111; E1.806D.
Cross references—See Education (Student Loans) (Repayment) Regulations, SI 2000/944 reg 7 (application of this section in connection with the repayment of student loans by assessment to income tax or deduction of repayments by employers).
Amendments—[1] Section inserted by FA 1995 Sch 28 para 1.
Prospective amendment—This section will be repealed by FA 1999 s 139, Sch 20 Pt VII with effect on such day as the Treasury may by order appoint.

116 Receipts, etc exempt from stamp duty

Amendments—This section repealed by FA 1970 Sch 8 Pt V, with effect from 1 February 1971.

Northern Ireland

117 Action of ejectment in Northern Ireland

Unless other provision is made in that behalf by any enactment, an action of ejectment in Northern Ireland for non-payment of rent shall not be defeated on the ground that the person liable to pay the rent is entitled under the Income Tax Acts to a deduction which would reduce the amount due by him below a year's rent.

Interpretation

118 Interpretation

(1) In this Act, unless the context otherwise requires—

　"Act" includes an Act of the Parliament of Northern Ireland and "enactment" shall be construed accordingly,

　　"the Board" means the Commissioners of Inland Revenue,

　"body of persons" means any body politic, corporate or collegiate, and any company, fraternity, fellowship and society of persons, whether corporate or not corporate,

　"branch or agency" means any factorship, agency, receivership, branch or management, and "branch or agent" shall be construed accordingly,

　"chargeable gain" has the same meaning as in [the [1992 Act][10]][4],

　"chargeable period" means a year of assessment or a company's accounting period,

　"collector" means any collector of taxes,

　"company" has the meaning given by section [832(1)][6] of the principal Act (with section [468][6] of that Act),

　["the General Commissioners Regulations" means the General Commissioners (Jurisdiction and Procedure) Regulations 1994,][11]

　"incapacitated person" means any infant, person of unsound mind, lunatic, idiot or insane person,

　["infant", in relation to Scotland, except in section 73 of this Act, means a person under legal disability by reason of nonage, and, in the said section 73, means a person under the age of 18 years,][9]

　"inspector" means any inspector of taxes,
[8]
　["partnership return" has the meaning given by section 12AA(10A) of this Act,][15]

''the principal Act'' means the Income and Corporation Taxes Act [1988][6],
[''the relevant trustees'', in relation to a settlement, shall be construed in accordance with section 7(9) of this Act.][13]
''return'' includes any statement or declaration under the Taxes Acts,
[''the Special Commissioners Regulations'' means the Special Commissioners (Jurisdiction and Procedure) Regulations 1994,][11]
[''successor'', in relation to a person who is required to make and deliver, or has made and delivered, [a partnership return][15], and ''predecessor'' and ''successor'', in relation to the successor of such a person, shall be construed in accordance with section 12AA(11) of this Act;][14]
''tax'', where neither income tax nor capital gains tax nor corporation tax [nor development land tax][2] is specified, means any of those taxes [except that in sections 20, 20A, 20B, 20C and 20D it does not include development land tax][3],
''the Taxes Acts'' means this Act and—
  (*a*) the Tax Acts ...[7],
  (*b*) [the Taxation of Chargeable Gains Act 1992][10] and all other enactments relating to capital gains tax, [and
  (*c*) the Development Land Tax Act 1976 and any other enactment relating to development land tax][2],
[''the 1992 Act'' means the Taxation of Chargeable Gains Act 1992][10],
''trade'' includes every trade, manufacture, adventure or concern in the nature of trade.

(2) For the purposes of this Act, a person shall be deemed not to have failed to do anything required to be done within a limited time if he did it within such further time, if any, as the Board or the Commissioners or officer concerned may have allowed; and where a person had a reasonable excuse for not doing anything required to be done he shall be deemed [not to have failed to do it unless the excuse ceased and, after the excuse ceased, he shall be deemed][5] not to have failed to do it if he did it without unreasonable delay after the excuse had ceased ...[1]

(3) ...[12]

(4) For the purposes of this Act, the amount of tax covered by any assessment shall not be deemed to be finally determined until that assessment can no longer be varied, whether by any Commissioners on appeal or by the order of any court.

Commentary—*Simon's Direct Tax Service* **A1.151–155, 160.**
Concession C4—Where specified conditions are satisfied, tax is not charged on activities such as bazaars, jumble sales, carnivals, etc organised for charitable purposes although such activities may come within the definition of trade.
Statement of Practice SP 1/96—In considering whether it is reasonable that notification of chargeability for self-assessment was not made, Revenue will consider whether employee's explanation is a ''reasonable excuse'' for such a failure.
Revenue Internal Guidance—Corporation Tax Manual CT 10412 (''reasonable excuse'' under sub-s (2): detailed criteria given).
Simon's Tax Cases—*Nuttall v Barrett* [1992] STC 112; *Kingsley v Billingham* [1992] STC 132; *R v Special Comrs, ex p Tracy* [1996] STC 34; *King v Walden* [2000] STC (SCD) 179.
s 118(2), *R v Sevenoaks General Comrs and IRC, ex p Thorne* [1989] STC 560; *Orakpo v Lane* [1996] STC (SCD) 43.
Definitions—''The Tax Acts'', IA 1978 Sch 1.
Cross references—See Tax Credits Act 1999 s 10(3) (sub-s (2) above applies for the purposes of Tax Credits Act 1999 s 9(3), (6) concerning penalties for fraud etc relating to a claim for the working families' tax credit and disabled person's tax credit and failure to comply).
Education (Student Loans) (Repayment) Regulations, SI 2000/944 reg 7 (application of sub-s (2) in relation to the repayment of student loans by assessment to income tax or deduction of repayments by employers).
Employment Act 2002 s 11 (sub-s (2) above shall apply for the purposes of EA 2002 s 11(1), (3), (6) as it applies for the purposes of TMA 1970).
Amendments—[1] In sub-s (2), the proviso repealed by FA 1970 Sch 8 Pt VII.
[2] Words in the definition of ''tax'' and para (*c*) in the definition of ''the Taxes Acts'' in sub-s (1) added by the Development Land Tax Act 1976 Sch 8 para 32(*c*), (*d*).
[3] Words in the definition of ''tax'' in sub-s (1) inserted by FA 1976 s 57(2).
[4] Word ''the'' in definition of ''chargeable gain'' substituted by CGTA 1979 s 157(2), Sch 7, para 8(*a*), Table, Pt I, para 1.
[5] Words in sub-s (2) inserted by F(No 2)A 1987, s 94.
[6] Numbers in sub-s (1) substituted by TA 1988 Sch 29 para 32 Table.
[7] Words in sub-s (1) repealed by TA 1988 Sch 31.
[8] Definition of ''neglect'' repealed by FA 1989 Sch 17 Pt VIII.
[9] Definition of ''infant'' inserted by the Act of Legal Capacity (Scotland) Act 1991 s 11(2) and Sch 1 para 34 with effect from 25 September 1991.
[10] Words in the definitions of ''chargeable gain'' and ''the Taxes Acts'' para (*b*) substituted and definition of ''the 1992 Act'' inserted by TCGA 1992 Sch 10 para 2(1), (11).
[11] Definitions of ''the General Commissioners Regulations'' and ''the Special Commissioners Regulations'' inserted by the General and Special Commissioners (Amendment of Enactments) Regulations, SI 1994/1813 reg 2(1), Sch 1 paras 1, 17.
[12] Sub-s (3) repealed by FA 1994 ss 196, 199 and Sch 19 para 34(2) and Sch 26 Pt V(23) with effect from the year 1996–97 as respects income tax and capital gains tax (other than in relation to partnerships whose trades, professions or businesses were set up and commenced before 6 April 1994), and as respects corporation tax with effect in relation to accounting periods ending after 30 June 1999 (by virtue of SI 1998/3173 art 2). In the case of a partnership commenced before 6 April 1994 the repeal has effect from the year 1997–98.
[13] Definition of ''the relevant trustees'' inserted by FA 1995 s 103(6), with effect in relation to income tax and capital gains tax from the year 1996–97.
[14] Definition of ''successor'' substituted by FA 1996 s 114(14) with effect from the year 1996–97, as respects income tax and capital gains tax, and as respects corporation tax, for accounting periods ending after 30 June 1999 (by virtue of Finance Act 1994, Section 199, (Appointed Day) Order, SI 1998/3173 art 2).
[15] Definition of ''partnership return'' inserted; and in the definition of ''successor'', words substituted for the words ''a return under section 12AA of this Act'', by FA 2001 s 88, Sch 29 para 33 with effect from the passing of FA 2001 in relation to returns whether made before or after the passing of FA 2001, and whether relating to periods before or after the passing of FA 2001.

PART XII
GENERAL

119 Commencement and construction

(1) This Act shall come into force for all purposes on 6th April 1970 to the exclusion of the corresponding enactments repealed by the principal Act.

(2) This Act, and the repeals made by the principal Act, have effect subject to Schedule 4 to this Act.

(3) This Act, so far as it relates to income tax or corporation tax, shall be construed as one with the principal Act.

(4) This Act, so far as it relates to chargeable gains, shall be construed as one with [the [1992 Act]]²]¹.

Definition—"the 1992 Act", s 118(1); "principal Act", s 118(1).
Amendments—¹ Word "the" in sub-s (4) substituted by CGTA 1979 s 157(2), Sch 7, para 8(*a*), Table, Pt I, para 1.
² Words in sub-s (4) substituted by TCGA 1992 Sch 10 para 2(1), (2).

120 Short title

This Act may be cited as the Taxes Management Act 1970.

Commentary—*Simon's Direct Tax Service* **A2.402.**

SCHEDULES

SCHEDULE 1
FORMS OF DECLARATIONS
Section 6

PART I
GENERAL AND SPECIAL COMMISSIONERS AND OTHERS

"I, A.B., do solemnly declare that I will impartially and to the best of my ability execute [the duties of my office]1; and that I will not disclose any information received by me in the execution of [those duties]1 except for the purposes of [those duties]1 or for the purposes of any prosecution for an offence relating to [inland revenue]1, or in such other cases as may be required by law."

Commentary—*Simon's Direct Tax Service* **A2.402.**
Revenue & other press releases—IR 1-9-94 (disclosure in relation to Class 1A national insurance contributions).
Simon's Tax Cases—*IRC v National Federation of Self-Employed and Small Businesses Ltd* [1981] STC 260.
Cross references—See FA 1972 s 127 (disclosure to Customs & Excise).
FA 1978 s 77 (disclosure to tax authorities within EC).
SSAA 1992 s 122 (disclosure to DSS).
Amendments—¹ Words substituted by FA 1975 s 57(2), with effect from 13 March 1975.

PART II
COMMISSIONERS OF INLAND REVENUE

"I, A.B., do solemnly declare that I will not disclose any information received by me in the execution of my duties except for the purposes of those duties or for the purposes of any prosecution for an offence relating to inland revenue, or in such other cases as may be required by law."

PART III
INSPECTORS, COLLECTORS AND OTHER OFFICERS

"I, A.B., do solemnly declare that I will not disclose any information received by me in the execution of the duties which may from time to time be assigned to me by the Board of Inland Revenue except for the purposes of my duties, or to the Board of Inland Revenue or in accordance with their instructions, or for the purposes of any prosecution for an offence relating to inland revenue, or in such other cases as may be required by law."

[SCHEDULE 1AA

ORDERS FOR PRODUCTION OF DOCUMENTS][1]

Section 2BA

Cross references—See The Orders for the Delivery of Documents (Procedure) Regulations, SI 2000/2875 (procedural requirements in relation to orders specified within this Schedule).
Amendment—[1] This Schedule inserted by FA 2000 s 149(2), Sch 39 with effect from 28 July 2000.

[Introduction

1 The provisions of this Schedule supplement section 20BA.][1]

Amendment—[1] This Schedule inserted by FA 2000 s 149(2), Sch 39 with effect from 28 July 2000.

[Authorised officer of the Board

2—(1) In section 20BA(1) an ''authorised officer of the Board'' means an officer of the Board authorised by the Board for the purposes of that section.

(2) The Board may make provision by regulations as to—

(*a*) the procedures for approving in any particular case the decision to apply for an order under that section, and
(*b*) the descriptions of officer by whom such approval may be given.][1]

Regulations—The Orders for the Delivery of Documents (Procedure) Regulations, SI 2000/2875.
Amendment—[1] This Schedule inserted by FA 2000 s 149(2), Sch 39 with effect from 28 July 2000.

[Notice of application for order

3—(1) A person is entitled—

(*a*) to notice of the intention to apply for an order against him under section 20BA, and
(*b*) to appear and be heard at the hearing of the application,

unless the appropriate judicial authority is satisfied that this would seriously prejudice the investigation of the offence.

(2) The Board may make provision by regulations as to the notice to be given, the contents of the notice and the manner of giving it.][1]

Regulations—The Orders for the Delivery of Documents (Procedure) Regulations, SI 2000/2875.
Cross references—See The Orders for the Delivery of Documents (Procedure) Regulations, SI 2000/2875 reg 4 (notice of the intention to apply for order to which a person is entitled under para 3(1) above must be in writing).
Amendments—[1] This Schedule inserted by FA 2000 s 149(2), Sch 39 with effect from 28 July 2000.

[Obligations of person given notice of application

4—(1) A person who has been given notice of intention to apply for an order under section 20BA(4) shall not—

(*a*) conceal, destroy, alter or dispose of any document to which the application relates, or
(*b*) disclose to any other person information or any other matter likely to prejudice the investigation of the offence to which the application relates.

This is subject to the following qualifications.

(2) Sub-paragraph (1)(*a*) does not prevent anything being done—

(*a*) with the leave of the appropriate judicial authority,
(*b*) with the written permission of an officer of the Board,
(*c*) after the application has been dismissed or abandoned, or
(*d*) after any order made on the application has been complied with.

(3) Sub-paragraph (1)(*b*) does not prevent a professional legal adviser from disclosing any information or other matter—

(*a*) to, or to a representative of, a client of his in connection with the giving by the adviser of legal advice to the client; or
(*b*) to any person—

(i) in contemplation of, or in connection with, legal proceedings; and
(ii) for the purpose of those proceedings.

This sub-paragraph does not apply in relation to any information or other matter which is disclosed with a view to furthering a criminal purpose.

(4) A person who fails to comply with the obligation in sub-paragraph (1)(*a*) or (*b*) above may be dealt with as if he had failed to comply with an order under section 20BA.][1]

Amendment—[1] This Schedule inserted by FA 2000 s 149(2), Sch 39 with effect from 28 July 2000.

[Exception of items subject to legal privilege

5—(1) Section 20BA does not apply to items subject to legal privilege.

(2) For this purpose ''items subject to legal privilege'' means—

(*a*) communications between a professional legal adviser and his client or any person representing his client made in connection with the giving of legal advice to the client;

(*b*) communications between a professional legal adviser and his client or any person representing his client or between such an adviser or his client or any such representative and any other person made in connection with or in contemplation of legal proceedings and for the purposes of such proceedings; and

(*c*) items enclosed with or referred to in such communications and made—

(i) in connection with the giving of legal advice; or

(ii) in connection with or in contemplation of legal proceedings and for the purposes of such proceedings,

when they are in the possession of a person who is entitled to possession of them.

(3) Items held with the intention of furthering a criminal purpose are not subject to legal privilege.][1]

Amendment—[1] This Schedule inserted by FA 2000 s 149(2), Sch 39 with effect from 28 July 2000.

[Resolution of disputes as to legal privilege

6—(1) The Board may make provision by regulations for the resolution of disputes as to whether a document, or part of a document, is an item subject to legal privilege.

(2) The regulations may, in particular, make provision as to—

(*a*) the custody of the document whilst its status is being decided;

(*b*) the appointment of an independent, legally qualified person to decide the matter;

(*c*) the procedures to be followed; and

(*d*) who is to meet the costs of the proceedings.][1]

Regulations—The Orders for the Delivery of Documents (Procedure) Regulations, SI 2000/2875.
Amendments—[1] This Schedule inserted by FA 2000 s 149(2), Sch 39 with effect from 28 July 2000.

[Complying with an order

7—(1) The Board may make provision by regulations as to how a person is to comply with an order under section 20BA.

(2) The regulations may, in particular, make provision as to—

(*a*) the officer of the Board to whom the documents are to be produced,

(*b*) the address to which the documents are to be taken or sent, and

(*c*) the circumstances in which sending the documents by post complies with the order.

(3) Where an order under section 20BA applies to a document in electronic or magnetic form, the order shall be taken to require the person to deliver the information recorded in the document in a form in which it is visible and legible.][1]

Regulations—The Orders for the Delivery of Documents (Procedure) Regulations, SI 2000/2875.
Amendment—[1] This Schedule inserted by FA 2000 s 149(2), Sch 39 with effect from 28 July 2000.

[Procedure where documents are delivered

8—(1) The provisions of section 20CC(3) to (9) apply in relation to a document delivered to an officer of the Board in accordance with an order under section 20BA as they apply to a thing removed by an officer of the Board as mentioned in subsection (1) of section 20CC.

(2) In section 20CC(9) as applied by sub-paragraph (1) above the reference to the warrant concerned shall be read as a reference to the order concerned.][1]

Amendment—[1] This Schedule inserted by FA 2000 s 149(2), Sch 39 with effect from 28 July 2000.

[Sanction for failure to comply with order

9—(1) If a person fails to comply with an order made under section 20BA, he may be dealt with as if he had committed a contempt of the court.

(2) For this purpose ''the court'' means—

(*a*) in relation to an order made by a Circuit judge, the Crown Court;

(*b*) in relation to an order made by a sheriff, a sheriff court;

(*c*) in relation to an order made by a county court judge, a county court in Northern Ireland.][1]

Amendment—[1] This Schedule inserted by FA 2000 s 146(2), Sch 39 with effect from 28 July 2000.

[Notice of order etc

10 The Board may make provision by regulations as to the circumstances in which notice of an order under section 20BA, or of an application for such an order, is to be treated as having been given.][1]

Regulations—The Orders for the Delivery of Documents (Procedure) Regulations, SI 2000/2875.
Amendment—¹ This Schedule inserted by FA 2000 s 149(2), Sch 39 with effect from 28 July 2000.

[General provisions about regulations

11 Regulations under this Schedule—

(*a*) may contain such incidental, supplementary and transitional provision as appears to the Board to be appropriate, and

(*b*) shall be made by statutory instrument which shall be subject to annulment in pursuance of a resolution of either House of Parliament.]¹

Regulations—The Orders for the Delivery of Documents (Procedure) Regulations, SI 2000/2875.
Amendments—¹ This Schedule inserted by FA 2000 s 149(2), Sch 39 with effect from 28 July 2000.

[SCHEDULE 1A

CLAIMS ETC NOT INCLUDED IN RETURNS]¹

Section 42

Commentary—*Simon's Direct Tax Service* A3.608; E1.809, 832.
Revenue Internal Guidance—Claims Manual RM 1000–1286 (Revenue procedure for dealing with repayment claims).
RM 1548–1600 (repayment claims: death of taxpayer: procedure for dealing with repayments after death).
RM 2584–2636 (repayment claims: repayment supplement; set off against other liabilities).
Cross references—See TA 1988 Sch 13A para 5(2) (disapplication of this Schedule to claims to surrender ACT).
Amendments—This Schedule inserted by FA 1994 ss 196, 199 and Sch 19 para 35 with effect from the year 1996–97 as respects income tax and capital gains tax and, as respects corporation tax, with effect in relation to accounting periods ending after 30 June 1999 (by virtue of Finance Act 1994, Section 199, (Appointed Day) Order, SI 1998/3173 art 2).

Preliminary

[1 In this Schedule—

"claim" [means a claim or election]² as respects which this Schedule applies;

"partnership claim" means a claim made in accordance with section 42(6)(*b*) of this Act;

["profits"—

(*a*) in relation to income tax, means income,

(*b*) in relation to capital gains tax, means chargeable gains, and

(*c*) in relation to corporation tax, means profits as computed for the purposes of that tax;]³

"relevant partner", in relation to a partnership claim, means any person who was a partner at any time during the period in respect of which the claim is made;

"successor", in relation to a person who—

(*a*) has made a partnership claim, but

(*b*) is no longer a partner or is otherwise no longer available,

means such other partner who may at any time be nominated for the purposes of this paragraph by the majority of the partners at that time, and "predecessor" and "successor", in relation to a person so nominated, shall be construed accordingly.]¹

Amendments—¹ This Schedule inserted by FA 1994 ss 196, 199 and Sch 19 para 35 with effect from the year 1996–97 as respects income tax and capital gains tax and, as respects corporation tax, with effect in relation to accounting periods ending after 30 June 1999 (by virtue of Finance Act 1994, Section 199, (Appointed Day) Order, SI 1998/3173 art 2).
² Words in para 1 substituted by FA 1996 s 130(5) with effect from the year 1996–97 as respects income tax and capital gains tax and, as respects corporation tax, with effect in relation to accounting periods ending after 30 June 1999 (by virtue of SI 1998/3173 art 2).
³ Definition of "profits" substituted by FA 1998 Sch 19 para 42 with effect in relation to accounting periods ending after 30 June 1999 (by virtue of SI 1998/3173 art 2).

Making of claims

[2—(1) Subject to any provision in the Taxes Acts for a claim to be made to the Board, every claim shall be made to an officer of the Board.

(2) No claim requiring the repayment of tax shall be made unless the claimant has documentary proof that the tax has been paid by deduction or otherwise.

(3) A claim shall be made in such form as the Board may determine.

(4) The form of claim shall provide for a declaration to the effect that all the particulars given in the form are correctly stated to the best of the information and belief of the person making the claim.

(5) The form of claim may require—

(*a*) a statement of the amount of tax which will be required to be discharged or repaid in order to give effect to the claim;

[(*b*) such information as is reasonably required for the purpose of determining whether and, if so, the extent to which the claim is correct;

(*bb*) the delivery with the claim of such accounts, statements and documents, relating to information contained in the claim, as are reasonably required for the purpose mentioned in paragraph (*b*) above;]² and *(c)* any such particulars of assets acquired as may be required in a return by virtue of section 12 of this Act [or paragraph 13 of Schedule 18 to the Finance Act 1998][3].

(6) In the case of a claim made by or on behalf of a person who is not resident, or who claims to be not resident or not ordinarily resident or not domiciled, in the United Kingdom, an officer of the Board or the Board may require a statement or declaration in support of the claim to be made by affidavit.][1]

Commentary—*Simon's Direct Tax Service* E1.832.
Definitions—"The Board", s 118(1); "claim", Sch 1A para 1; "the Taxes Acts", s 118(1).
Cross references—See TA 1988 s 488(12) (co-operative housing associations: power to require delivery of an authority to use information in returns in connection with enquiries into claims under s 488).
Amendments—[1] This Schedule inserted by FA 1994 ss 196, 199 and Sch 19 para 35 with effect from the year 1996–97 as respects income tax and capital gains tax, and, as respects corporation tax, with effect in relation to accounting periods ending after 30 June 1999 (by virtue of Finance Act 1994, Section 199, (Appointed Day) Order, SI 1998/3173 art 2).
[2] Sub-para (5)(*b*), (*bb*) substituted for sub-para (*b*) by FA 1995 s 107(11), Sch 20 para 1 with effect from the year 1996–97 as respects income tax and capital gains tax, and, as respects corporation tax, with effect in relation to accounting periods ending after 30 June 1999 (by virtue of SI 1998/3173 art 2).
[3] Words in sub-para (5)(*c*) inserted by FA 1998 Sch 19 para 42 with effect in relation to accounting periods ending after 30 June 1999 (by virtue of SI 1998/3173 art 2).

[Keeping and preserving of records

2A—(1) Any person who may wish to make a claim in relation to a year of assessment or other period shall—

(*a*) keep all such records as may be requisite for the purpose of enabling him to make a correct and complete claim; and
(*b*) shall preserve those records until the end of the relevant day.

(2) In relation to a claim, the relevant day for the purposes of sub-paragraph (1) above is whichever of the following is the latest, namely—

(*a*) where enquiries into the claim or any amendment of the claim are made by an officer of the Board, the day on which, by virtue of paragraph [7(1)][4] below, those enquiries are ...[4] completed; and
(*b*) where no enquiries into the claim or any amendment of the claim are so made, the day on which such an officer no longer has power to make such enquiries.

(3) [Except in the case of records falling within section 12B(4A) of this Act [or paragraph 22(3) of Schedule 18 to the Finance Act 1998][3],][2] the duty under sub-paragraph (1) above to preserve records may be discharged by the preservation of the information contained in them; and where the information is so preserved a copy of any document forming part of the records shall be admissible in evidence in any proceedings before the Commissioners to the same extent as the records themselves.

(4) [Subject to sub-paragraph (5) below,][2] Any person who fails to comply with sub-paragraph (1) above in relation to any claim which is made for a year of assessment or accounting period shall be liable to a penalty not exceeding £3,000.][1]

[(5) Sub-paragraph (4) above does not apply where—

(*a*) the records which the person fails to keep or preserve are records falling within paragraph (*a*) of section 12B(4A) of this Act [or paragraph 22(3) of Schedule 18 to the Finance Act 1998][3]; and
(*b*) an officer of the Board is satisfied that any facts which he reasonably requires to be proved, and which would have been proved by the records, are proved by other documentary evidence furnished to him.][2]

Definitions—"The Board", s 118(1); "claim", Sch 1A para 1; "year of assessment", TA 1988 s 832(1).
Amendments—[1] This paragraph inserted by FA 1995 s 107(11), Sch 20 para 2 with effect from the year 1996–97 as respects income tax and capital gains tax and, as respects corporation tax, for accounting periods ending after 30 June 1999 (by virtue of Finance Act 1994, Section 199, (Appointed Day) Order, SI 1998/3173 art 2).
[2] Words in sub-paras (3), (4) and whole of sub-para (5) inserted by FA 1996 s 124(6)–(8) with effect from the year 1996–97 as respects income tax and capital gains tax and, as respects corporation tax, for accounting periods ending after 30 June 1999 (by virtue of SI 1998/3173 art 2).
[3] Words in sub-paras (3) and (5)(*a*) inserted by FA 1998 Sch 19 para 42 with effect in relation to accounting periods ending after 30 June 1999 (by virtue of SI 1998/3173 art 2).
[4] In sub-para (2)(*a*), "7(1)" substituted for "7(4)", and the words "treated as" repealed, by FA 2001 ss 88, 110, Sch 29 para 34(2), Sch 33 Pt II(13) with effect from the passing of FA 2001 in relation to returns whether made before or after the passing of FA 2001, and whether relating to periods before or after the passing of FA 2001.

Amendments of claims

[3—(1) Subject to sub-paragraph (2) below—

(*a*) at any time before the end of the period of nine months beginning with the day on which a claim is made, an officer of the Board may by notice to the claimant so amend the claim as to correct any obvious errors or mistakes in the [claim][3] (whether errors of principle, arithmetical mistakes or otherwise); and
(*b*) at any time before the end of the period of twelve months beginning with the day on which the claim is made, the claimant may amend his claim by notice to an officer of the Board.

(2) No amendment of a claim may be made under sub-paragraph (1) above at any time during the period—

(a) beginning with the day on which an officer of the Board gives notice of his intention to enquire into the claim, and

(b) ending with the day on which the officer's enquiries into the claim are completed.][1]

Commentary—*Simon's Direct Tax Service* **E1.832.**
Definitions—"The Board", s 118(1); "claim", Sch 1A para 1.
Amendments—[1] This Schedule inserted by FA 1994 ss 196, 199 and Sch 19 para 35 with effect from the year 1996–97 as respects income tax and capital gains tax and, as respects corporation tax, with effect in relation to accounting periods ending after 30 June 1999 (by virtue of Finance Act 1994, Section 199, (Appointed Day) Order, SI 1998/3173 art 2).
[2] Word in sub-para (1)(a) substituted by FA 1995 s 107(11), Sch 20 para 3 with effect from the year 1996–97 as respects income tax and capital gains tax and, as respects corporation tax, with effect in relation to accounting periods ending after 30 June 1999 (by virtue of SI 1998/3173 art 2).

Giving effect to claims and amendments

[4—(1) [Subject to sub-paragraphs [(1A), (3) and (4)][3] below and to any other provision in the Taxes Acts which otherwise provides,][2] An officer of the Board or the Board shall, as soon as practicable after a claim other than a partnership claim is made, or such a claim is amended under paragraph 3 above, give effect to the claim or amendment by discharge or repayment of tax.

[(1A) In relation to a claim which would otherwise fall to be taken into account in the making of deductions or repayments of tax under section 203 of the principal Act, sub-paragraph (1) above shall apply as if for the word "shall" there were substituted the word "may".][1]

(2) [Subject to [sub-paragraphs (3) and (4)][3] below,][2] An officer of the Board or the Board shall, as soon as practicable after a partnership claim is made, or such a claim is amended under paragraph 3 above, give effect to the claim or amendment, as respects each of the relevant partners, by discharge or repayment of tax.

[(3) Where any such claim or amendment as is mentioned in sub-paragraph (1) or (2) above is enquired into by an officer of the Board—

(a) that sub-paragraph shall not apply until the day on which, by virtue of paragraph [7(1)][4] below, [the enquiry is][4] completed; but

(b) the officer may at any time before that day give effect to the claim or amendment, on a provisional basis, to such extent as he thinks fit.][2]

[(4) Nothing in this paragraph applies in relation to a claim or an amendment of a claim if the claim is not one for discharge or repayment of tax.][3]][1]

Commentary—*Simon's Direct Tax Service* **E1.832.**
Definitions—"The Board", s 118(1); "claim", Sch 1A para 1; "partnership claim", Sch 1A para 1; "the principal Act", s 118(1); "the Taxes Acts", s 118(1).
Amendments—[1] This Schedule inserted by FA 1994 ss 196, 199 and Sch 19 para 35 with effect from the year 1996–97 as respects income tax and capital gains tax and, as respects corporation tax, with effect in relation to accounting periods ending after 30 June 1999 (by virtue of Finance Act 1994, Section 199, (Appointed Day) Order, SI 1998/3173 art 2).
[2] Words in sub-paras (1), (2) and sub-paras (1A), (3) inserted by FA 1995 s 107(11), Sch 20 para 4 with effect from the year 1996–97 as respects income tax and capital gains tax and, as respects corporation tax, with effect in relation to accounting periods ending after 30 June 1999 (by virtue of SI 1998/3173 art 2).
[3] Words in sub-paras (1), (2) substituted and sub-para (4) inserted by FA 1996 Sch 19 para 8 with effect from the year 1996–97 as respects income tax and capital gains tax and, as respects corporation tax, with effect in relation to accounting periods ending after 30 June 1999 (by virtue of SI 1998/3173 art 2).
[4] In sub-para (3)(a), "7(1)" substituted for "(7(4)", and words substituted for the words "the officer's enquiries are treated as" by FA 2001 s 88, Sch 29 para 34(3) with effect from the passing of FA 2001 in relation to returns whether made before or after the passing of FA 2001, and whether relating to periods before or after the passing of FA 2001.

Power to enquire into claims

[5—(1) An officer of the Board may enquire into—

(a) a claim made by any person, or

(b) any amendment made by any person of a claim made by him,

if, before the end of the period mentioned in sub-paragraph (2) below, he gives notice in writing of his intention to do so to that person or, in the case of a partnership claim, any successor of that person.

[(2) The period referred to in sub-paragraph (1) above is whichever of the following ends the latest, namely—

(a) the period ending with the quarter day next following the first anniversary of the day on which the claim or amendment was made;

(b) where the claim or amendment relates to a year of assessment, the period ending with the first anniversary of the 31st January next following that year; and

(c) where the claim or amendment relates to a period other than a year of assessment, the period ending with the first anniversary of the end of that period;

and the quarter days for the purposes of this sub-paragraph are 31st January, 30th April, 31st July and 31st October.

(3) A claim or amendment which has been enquired into under sub-paragraph (1) above shall not be the subject of—

(*a*) a further notice under that sub-paragraph; or

(*b*) if it is subsequently included in a return, a notice under [section 9A(1) or 12AC(1) of this Act or paragraph 24 of Schedule 18 to the Finance Act 1998][3].[2]][1]

Commentary—*Simon's Direct Tax Service* E1.832.

Revenue Internal Guidance—Enquiry Handbook EH 940 (where claim is made before submission of return, the Revenue have the option to enquire into the claim as part of an enquiry into the return).

Definitions—"The Board", s 118(1); "claim", Sch 1A para 1; "partnership claim", Sch 1A para 1; "return", s 118(1); "successor", Sch 1A para 1; "year of assessment", TA 1988 s 832(1).

Cross references—See TA 1988 s 488(11A) (co-operative housing associations: where an enquiry under this paragraph results in an amendment to the association's claim, the liability to tax of all concerned persons may be adjusted).

TA 1988 s 489(9A) (self-build societies: where an enquiry under this paragraph results in an amendment to a claim made by a self-build society, the liability to tax of the society for all relevant periods may be adjusted).

Amendments—[1] This Schedule inserted by FA 1994 ss 196, 199 and Sch 19 para 35 with effect from the year 1996–97 as respects income tax and capital gains tax and, as respects corporation tax, with effect in relation to accounting periods ending after 30 June 1999 (by virtue of Finance Act 1994, Section 199, (Appointed Day) Order, SI 1998/3173 art 2).

[2] Sub-paras (2), (3) substituted for sub-para (2) by FA 1995 s 107(11), Sch 20 para 5 with effect from the year 1996–97 as respects income tax and capital gains tax and, as respects corporation tax, for accounting periods ending after 30 June 1999 (by virtue of SI 1998/3173 art 2).

[3] Words in sub-para (3)(*b*) substituted by FA 1998 Sch 19 para 42 with effect in relation to accounting periods ending after 30 June 1999 (by virtue of SI 1998/3173 art 2).

Power to call for documents for purposes of enquiries

[**6**—(1) This paragraph applies where an officer of the Board gives notice under paragraph 5 above to any person (the claimant) of his intention to enquire into—

(*a*) a claim made by the claimant, or

(*b*) any amendment made by the claimant of such a claim.

(2) For the purpose of enquiring into the claim or amendment, the officer may at the same or any subsequent time by notice in writing require the claimant, within such time (which shall not be less than 30 days) as may be specified in the notice—

(*a*) to produce to the officer such documents as are in the claimant's possession or power and as the officer may reasonably require for the purpose of determining whether and, if so, the extent to which the claim or amendment is incorrect, and

(*b*) to furnish the officer with such accounts or particulars as he may reasonably require for that purpose.

[(3A) In complying with a notice under this paragraph copies of documents may be produced instead of originals, but—

(*a*) the copies must be photographic or other facsimiles, and

(*b*) the officer may by notice require the original to be produced for inspection.

A notice under paragraph (*b*) must specify the time (which must not be less than 30 days) within which the company is to comply with it.

(3B) The officer may take copies of, or make extracts from, any document produced to him under this paragraph.

(3C) A notice under this paragraph does not oblige the claimant to produce documents or provide accounts or information relating to the conduct of any pending appeal by the claimant.][2]

(4) Where this paragraph applies in relation to a partnership claim, any reference in this paragraph to the claimant includes a reference to any predecessor or successor of his.][1]

Commentary—*Simon's Direct Tax Service* E1.832.

Definitions—"The Board", s 118(1); "claim", Sch 1A para 1; "partnership claim", Sch 1A para 1; "predecessor", Sch 1A para 1; "successor", Sch 1A para 1.

Amendments—[1] This Schedule inserted by FA 1994 ss 196, 199 and Sch 19 para 35 with effect from the year 1996–97 as respects income tax and capital gains tax and, as respects corporation tax, with effect in relation to accounting periods ending after 30 June 1999 (by virtue of Finance Act 1994, Section 199, (Appointed Day) Order, SI 1998/3173 art 2).

[2] Sub-para (3) substituted and new sub-paras (3A), (3B) and (3C) inserted by FA 1998 Sch 19 para 42 with effect in relation to accounting periods ending after 30 June 1999 (by virtue of SI 1998/3173 art 2).

[Appeal against notice to produce documents, etc

6A—(1) An appeal may be brought against a requirement imposed by a notice under paragraph 6 to produce documents or provide accounts or information.

(2) Notice of appeal must be given—

(*a*) in writing,

(*b*) within 30 days after the notice was given to the claimant,

(*c*) to the officer of the Board by whom that notice was given.

(3) On an appeal under this paragraph the Commissioners—

(*a*) shall set aside the notice so far as it requires the production of documents, or the provision of accounts or information, which appears to them not reasonably required for the purposes of the enquiry, and

(*b*) shall confirm the notice so far as it requires the production of documents, or the provision of accounts or information, which appear to them are reasonably required for the purposes of the enquiry.

(4) A notice which is confirmed by the Commissioners (or so far as it is confirmed) has effect as if the period specified in it for complying was 30 days from the determination of the appeal.

(5) The decision of the Commissioners on an appeal under this paragraph is final and conclusive.]¹

Commentary—*Simon's Direct Tax Service* **E1.832.**
Amendments—¹ Paragraph inserted by FA 1998 Sch 19 para 42 with effect in relation to accounting periods ending after 30 June 1999 (by virtue of Finance Act 1994, Section 199, (Appointed Day) Order, SI 1998/3173 art 2).

[Completion of enquiry into claim

7—(1) An enquiry under paragraph 5 above is completed when an officer of the Board by notice (a "closure notice") informs the claimant that he has completed his enquiries and states his conclusions.

(2) In the case of a claim for discharge or repayment of tax, the closure notice must either—

(*a*) state that in the officer's opinion no amendment of the claim is required, or
(*b*) if in the officer's opinion the claim is insufficient or excessive, amend the claim so as to make good or eliminate the deficiency or excess.

In the case of an enquiry falling within paragraph 5(1)(*b*) above, paragraph (*b*) above only applies so far as the deficiency or excess is attributable to the claimant's amendment.

(3) In the case of a claim that is not a claim for discharge or repayment of tax, the closure notice must either—

(*a*) allow the claim, or
(*b*) disallow the claim, wholly or to such extent as appears to the officer appropriate.

(4) A closure notice takes effect when it is issued.

(5) The claimant may apply to the Commissioners for a direction requiring an officer of the Board to issue a closure notice within a specified period.

(6) Any such application shall be heard and determined in the same way as an appeal.

(7) The Commissioners hearing the application shall give the direction applied for unless they are satisfied that there are reasonable grounds for not issuing a closure notice within a specified period.

(8) In relation to a partnership claim, references in this paragraph to the claimant are to the person who made the claim or his successor.]¹

Commentary—*Simon's Direct Tax Service* **E1.832.**
Amendments—¹ Paragraph substituted by FA 2001 s 88, Sch 29 para 10 with effect where the notice of enquiry is given after the passing of FA 2001, or where the enquiry is in progress immediately before the passing of FA 2001. An enquiry is in progress until the officer's enquiries fall to be treated as completed under TMA 1970 Sch 1A para 7(4) (as that provision had effect apart from FA 2001 Sch 29). Para 7 previously read—

"*Amendments of claims where enquiries made*

7—(1) This paragraph applies where an officer of the Board gives notice under paragraph 5(1) above to any person (the claimant) of his intention to enquire into—

(*a*) a claim made by the claimant, or
(*b*) any amendment made by the claimant of such a claim.

(2) At any time in the period of 30 days beginning with the day on which the officer's enquiries are completed, the claimant may so amend his claim—

(*a*) as to eliminate or make good any excess or deficiency which, on the basis of the conclusions stated in the officer's notice under sub-paragraph (4) below, is an excess or deficiency which could be made good or eliminated under sub-paragraph (3) below; or
(*b*) as to give effect to any amendments to the claim which he has notified to the officer.

(3) If, at any time in the period of 30 days beginning immediately after the period mentioned in sub-paragraph (2) above, the officer is of opinion that—

(*a*) the claimant's claim is excessive or insufficient, and
(*b*) in a case falling within sub-paragraph (1)(*b*) above, the excess or deficiency is attributable (wholly or partly) to the claimant's amendment,

the officer may by notice to the claimant so amend the claim as to eliminate or make good the excess or deficiency or, where paragraph (*b*) above applies, so much of the excess or deficiency as is so attributable.

(3A) If, in the case of a claim which is not a claim for discharge or repayment of tax—

(*a*) the officer is of opinion that the claim should be disallowed in whole or in part, and
(*b*) the claim, so far as the officer thinks it should be disallowed, is not, before the end of the period mentioned in sub-paragraph (2) above, amended to the officer's satisfaction or withdrawn,

the officer shall, before the end of the period mentioned in sub-paragraph (3) above, give notice to the taxpayer of the extent to which he is disallowing the claim.

(3B) Sub-paragraph (3A)(*b*) above is without prejudice to any provision by virtue of which any claim is irrevocable or unamendable.

(4) Subject to sub-paragraph (5) below, the officer's enquiries shall be treated as completed at such time as he by notice—

(*a*) informs the claimant that he has completed his enquiries, and
(*b*) states his conclusions as to [whether the claim should be allowed in whole or in part and as to what amount (if any)]² should be the amount of the claimant's claim.

(5) Subsections (6) and (7) of section 28A of this Act apply for the purposes of sub-paragraph (4) above as they apply for the purposes of subsection (5) of that section.
(6) Where this paragraph applies in relation to a partnership claim, any reference in this paragraph to the claimant includes a reference to any predecessor or successor of his."

Giving effect to such amendments

[8—(1) An officer of the Board or the Board shall, within 30 days [after the date of issue of a closure notice amending a claim other than a partnership claim under paragraph 7(2)][2] above, give effect to the amendment by making such adjustment as may be necessary, whether—

(*a*) by way of assessment on the claimant, or

(*b*) by discharge of tax or, on proof to the satisfaction of the officer or the Board that any tax has been paid by the claimant by deduction or otherwise, by repayment of tax.

(2) An officer of the Board or the Board shall, within 30 days [after the date of issue of a closure notice amending a partnership claim under paragraph 7(2)][2] above, give effect to the amendment, as respects each of the relevant partners, by making such adjustment as may be necessary, whether—

(*a*) by way of assessment on the partner, or

(*b*) by discharge of tax or, on proof to the satisfaction of the officer or the Board that any tax has been paid by the partner by deduction or otherwise, by repayment of tax.

(3) An assessment made under sub-paragraph (1) or (2) above shall not be out of time if it is made within the time mentioned in that sub-paragraph.][1]

Definitions—"The Board", s 118(1); "claim", Sch 1A para 1; "partnership claim", Sch 1A para 1.
Amendments—[1] This Schedule inserted by FA 1994 ss 196, 199 and Sch 19 para 35 with effect from the year 1996–97 as respects income tax and capital gains tax and, as respects corporation tax, with effect in relation to accounting periods ending after 30 June 1999 (by virtue of Finance Act 1994, Section 199, (Appointed Day) Order, SI 1998/3173 art 2).
[2] In sub-para (1), words substituted for the words "of a claim other than a partnership claim being amended under paragraph 7(2) or (3)"; and in sub-para (2), words substituted for the words "of a partnership claim being amended under paragraph 7(2) or (3)", by FA 2001 s 88, Sch 29 para 34(4), (5) with effect from 11 May 2001 in relation to returns whether made before or after the passing of FA 2001, and whether relating to periods before or after the passing of FA 2001.

Appeals against such amendments

[9—(1) An appeal may be brought against—

(*a*) any conclusion stated or amendment made by a closure notice under paragraph 7(2) above, or

(*b*) any decision contained in a closure notice under paragraph 7(3) above.][3]

[(1A) Notice of the appeal must be given—

(*a*) in writing,

(*b*) within 30 days after the date on which the closure notice was issued,

(*c*) to the officer of the Board by whom the closure notice was given.][3]

(2) Where, in the case of such an appeal, the issues arising include—

(*a*) any question arising under section 278 of the principal Act (personal reliefs for non-residents);

(*b*) any question of residence, ordinary residence or domicile; or

(*c*) the question whether a fund is one to which section 615(3) of that Act applies (pension funds for service abroad),

the time for bringing the appeal shall be three months from the [date mentioned in sub-paragraph [(1A)(*b*)][3] above][2].

(3) On an appeal [against an [amendment made by a closure notice under paragraph 7(2) above][3]][2], the Commissioners may vary the amendment appealed against whether or not the variation is to the advantage of the appellant.

(4) Where [any such amendment][3] is varied, whether by the Commissioners or by the order of any court, paragraph 8 above shall (with the necessary modifications) apply in relation to the variation as it applied in relation to the amendment.][1]

[(5) If, on appeal, it appears to the Commissioners that a claim [which was the subject of a decision contained in a closure notice under paragraph 7(3)][3] above should have been allowed or disallowed to an extent different from that specified in the notice, the claim shall be allowed or disallowed accordingly to the extent that appears to them appropriate, but otherwise the decision in the notice shall stand good.][2]

Commentary—*Simon's Direct Tax Service* E1.832.
Definitions—"Claim", Sch 1A para 1; "notice", TA 1988 s 832(1); "the principal Act", s 118(1).
Amendments—[1] This Schedule inserted by FA 1994 ss 196, 199 and Sch 19 para 35 with effect from the year 1996–97 as respects income tax and capital gains tax and, as respects corporation tax, with effect in relation to accounting periods ending after 30 June 1999 (by virtue of Finance Act 1994, Section 199, (Appointed Day) Order, SI 1998/3173 art 2).
[2] Words in sub-paras (2), (3) substituted and sub-para (5) inserted by FA 1996 Sch 19 para 10 with effect from the year 1996–97 as respects income tax and capital gains tax and, as respects corporation tax, for accounting periods ending after 30 June 1999 (by virtue of SI 1998/3173 art 2).
[3] Sub-paras (1), (1A) substituted for sub-para (1); in sub-para (2), "(1A)(*b*)" substituted for (1), words in sub-para (3) substituted for the words "amendment under paragraph 7(3) above"; words in sub-para (4) substituted for the words "an amendment made under paragraph 7(3) above"; words in sub-para (5) substituted for the words "specified in a notice under paragraph 7(3A)", by FA 2001 s 88, Sch 29 para 12 with effect for closure notices issued under TMA 1970 Sch 1A para 7 as substituted by FA 2001 Sch 29 para 10. Previously sub-para (1) read—

"(1) An appeal may be brought against—

(*a*) an amendment under paragraph 7(3) above, or

(*b*) a decision contained in a notice under paragraph 7(3A) above,

by giving notice to the officer within 30 days after the date on which the notice of amendment or, as the case may be, the notice under paragraph 7(3A) above was issued."

[10 An appeal against [any conclusion stated or amendment made by a closure notice under paragraph 7(2) above relating to][2] a claim made—

   (*a*) to the Board,

   (*b*) under Part XVI of the principal Act (administration of estates), or

   (*c*) under any of the provisions of the principal Act listed in section 46C(3) of this Act,

shall be to the Special Commissioners.][1]

Commentary—*Simon's Direct Tax Service* **E1.832.**
Definitions—''The Board'', s 118(1); ''the principal Act'', s 118(1); ''Special Commissioners'', s 4.
Amendments—[1] This paragraph inserted by FA 1996 Sch 22 para 9 with effect in relation to any proceedings relating to the year 1996–97 and subsequent years of assessment and in relation to any proceedings relating to an accounting period ending after 30 June 1999 (by virtue of Finance Act 1994, Section 199, (Appointed Day) Order, SI 1998/3173 art 2).
[2] Words substituted for the words ''an amendment under paragraph 7(3) above of'' by FA 2001 s 88, Sch 29 para 12(7), (8) with effect for closure notices issued under TMA 1970 Sch 1A para 7 as substituted by FA 2001 Sch 29 para 10.

[11—(1) Subject to paragraph 10 above and the following provisions of this paragraph, an appeal under paragraph 9(1) above shall be to the General Commissioners.

(2) The appellant may elect (in accordance with section 46(1) of this Act) to bring the appeal before the Special Commissioners.

(3) Such an election shall be disregarded if—

   (*a*) the appellant and the officer of the Board agree in writing, at any time before the determination of the appeal, that it is to be disregarded; or

   (*b*) the General Commissioners have given a direction under sub-paragraph (5) below and have not revoked it.

(4) At any time before the determination of an appeal in respect of which an election has been made an officer of the Board after giving notice to the appellant may refer the election to the General Commissioners.

(5) On any such reference the Commissioners shall, unless they are satisfied that the appellant has arguments to present or evidence to adduce on the merits of the appeal, give a direction that the election be disregarded.

(6) If, at any time after the giving of such a direction (but before the determination of the appeal) the General Commissioners are satisfied that the appellant has arguments to present or evidence to adduce on the merits of the appeal, they shall revoke the direction.

(7) Any decision to give or revoke such a direction shall be final.

(8) If—

   (*a*) a person bringing an appeal under paragraph 9(1) above has another appeal pending to either body of Commissioners concerning an assessment on him, and

   (*b*) the appeals relate to the same source of income,

the appeal under paragraph 9(1) above shall be to the body of Commissioners before whom the appeal concerning the assessment is being brought.

(9) This paragraph is subject to provision made by or under Part V of this Act.][1]

Definitions—''The Board'', s 118(1); ''General Commissioners'', s 2; ''Special Commissioners'', s 4.
Amendments—[1] This paragraph inserted by FA 1996 Sch 22 para 9 with effect in relation to any proceedings relating to the year 1996–97 and subsequent years of assessment and in relation to any proceedings relating to an accounting period ending after 30 June 1999 (by virtue of Finance Act 1994, Section 199, (Appointed Day) Order, SI 1998/3173 art 2).

[SCHEDULE 1B

CLAIMS FOR RELIEF INVOLVING TWO OR MORE YEARS][1]

Section 42

Commentary—*Simon's Direct Tax Service* **A3.609; E1. 833.**
Revenue & other press releases—IR Tax Bulletin December 1996 p 361 (explains how Revenue will give effect to claims to carry back pension contributions—and see also IR Tax Bulletin June 1997 p 443).
Amendments—[1] This Schedule inserted by FA 1996 s 128(2), Sch 17 with effect as respects claims made (or deemed to be made) from the year 1996–97.

Preliminary

[1—(1) In this Schedule—

   (*a*) any reference to a claim includes a reference to an election or notice; and

   (*b*) any reference to the amount in which a person is chargeable to tax is a reference to the amount in which he is so chargeable after taking into account any relief or allowance for which a claim is made.][1]

[(2) For the purposes of this Schedule, two or more claims made by the same person are associated with each other if each of them are any of the following—

   (*a*) a claim to which this Schedule applies, or

(*b*) a claim to which Schedule 4A to the principal Act applies (creative artists: relief for fluctuating profits),

and the same year of assessment is the earlier year in relation to each of those claims.

(3) In sub-paragraph (2) above, any reference to claims includes—

(*a*) in the case of a claim to which this Schedule applies, a reference to amendments and revocations to which paragraph 4 below applies;

(*b*) in the case of a claim to which Schedule 4A to the principal Act applies, a reference to amendments and revocations to which paragraph 9 of that Schedule applies.]²

Commentary—*Simon's Direct Tax Service* **E1.833.**
Amendments—¹ This Schedule inserted by FA 1996 s 128(2), Sch 17 with effect as respects claims made (or deemed to be made) from the year 1996–97.
² Sub-paras (2), (3) substituted by FA 2001 s 71(4), Sch 24 para 3 with effect from the year 2001–02.

Loss relief

[**2**—(1) This paragraph applies where a person makes a claim requiring relief for a loss incurred or treated as incurred, or a payment made, in one year of assessment ("the later year") to be given in an earlier year of assessment ("the earlier year").

(2) Section 42(2) of this Act shall not apply in relation to the claim.

(3) The claim shall relate to the later year.

(4) Subject to sub-paragraph (5) below, the claim shall be for an amount equal to the difference between—

(*a*) the amount in which the person is chargeable to tax for the earlier year ("amount A"); and

(*b*) the amount in which he would be so chargeable on the assumption that effect could be, and were, given to the claim in relation to that year ("amount B").

(5) Where effect has been given to one or more associated claims, amounts A and B above shall each be determined on the assumption that effect could have been, and had been, given to the associated claim or claims in relation to the earlier year.

(6) Effect shall be given to the claim in relation to the later year, whether by repayment or set-off, or by an increase in the aggregate amount given by section 59B(1)(*b*) of this Act, or otherwise.

(7) For the purposes of this paragraph, any deduction made under section 62(2) of the 1992 Act (death: general provisions) in respect of an allowable loss shall be deemed to be made in pursuance of a claim requiring relief to be given in respect of that loss.]¹

Commentary—*Simon's Direct Tax Service* **E1.833.**
Revenue & other press releases—IR 21-3-96 (this para disapplied in practice as regards the carry-back of pension contributions from 1996-97 to 1995-96—but this para *will* apply to carry-backs from 1996-97 to 1994-95 (IR Tax Bulletin February 1997 p 396)).
IR Tax Bulletin December 1996 p 361 (explains how Revenue will give effect to claims to carry back pension contributions—and also see IR Tax Bulletin June 1997 p 443).
Definitions—"Claim", Sch 1B para 1; "the 1992 Act", s 118(1); "year of assessment", TA 1988 s 832(1).
Amendments—¹ This Schedule inserted by FA 1996 s 128(2), Sch 17 with effect as respects claims made (or deemed to be made) from the year 1996–97.

Relief for fluctuating profits of farming etc

[**3**—(1) This paragraph applies where a person who is or has been carrying on a trade of farming or market gardening claims that subsection (2) or (3) of section 96 of the principal Act shall have effect in relation to his profits from that trade for two consecutive years of assessment ("the earlier year" and "the later year").

(2) The claim shall relate to the later year.

(3) Subject to sub-paragraph (4) below, in so far as the claim relates to the profits of the earlier year, the claim shall be for an amount equal to the difference between—

(*a*) the amount in which the person is chargeable to tax for the earlier year ("amount A"); and

(*b*) the amount in which he would be so chargeable on the assumption that effect could be, and were, given to the claim in relation to that year ("amount B").

(4) Where effect has been given to one or more associated claims, amounts A and B above shall each be determined on the assumption that effect could have been, and had been, given to the associated claim or claims in relation to the earlier year.

(5) In so far as the claim relates to the profits of the earlier year, effect shall be given to the claim in relation to the later year by an increase in the amount of tax payable or, as the case may require, in the aggregate amount given by section 59B(1)(*b*) of this Act.

(6) Where this paragraph applies twice in relation to the same year of assessment, the increase or reduction in the amount of tax payable for that year which is required by sub-paragraph (5) above on the earlier application shall be disregarded in determining amounts A and B above for the purposes of the later application.]¹

Commentary—*Simon's Direct Tax Service* **E1.833.**
Revenue & other press releases—IR Tax Bulletin February 1997 p 393 (explains rules under this para for implementing farmers' averaging claims).

Definitions—"Claim", Sch 1B para 1; "the principal Act", s 118(1); "trade", s 118(1); "year of assessment", TA 1988 s 832(1).
Amendments—¹ This Schedule inserted by FA 1996 s 128(2), Sch 17 with effect as respects claims made (or deemed to be made) from the year 1996–97.

Relief claimed by virtue of section 96(9)

[4—(1) This paragraph applies where—

    (*a*) a person who claims that subsection (2) or (3) of section 96 of the principal Act shall have effect for two consecutive years of assessment ("the earlier year" and "the later year") makes or amends a claim for relief under any other provision of the Income Tax Acts for either of those years; and

    (*b*) the making or amendment of the claim would be out of time but for subsection (9) of that section.

(2) The claim or amendment shall relate to the later year.

(3) Subject to sub-paragraph (4) below, in so far as the claim or amendment relates to income of the earlier year, the amount claimed, or (as the case may be) the increase or reduction in the amount claimed, shall be equal to the difference between—

    (*a*) the amount in which the person is chargeable to tax for the earlier year ("amount A"); and

    (*b*) the amount in which he would be so chargeable on the assumption that effect could be, and were, given to the claim or amendment in relation to that year ("amount B").

(4) Where effect has been given to one or more associated claims, amounts A and B above shall each be determined on the assumption that effect could have been, and had been, given to the associated claim or claims in relation to the earlier year.

(5) In so far as the claim or amendment relates to income of the earlier year, effect shall be given to the claim or amendment in relation to the later year by an increase in the amount of tax payable or, as the case may require, in the aggregate amount given by section 59B(1)(*b*) of this Act.

(6) In this paragraph "amend" includes revoke and "amendment" shall be construed accordingly.]¹

Commentary—*Simon's Direct Tax Service* E1.833.
Definitions—"Claim", Sch 1B para 1; "Income Tax Acts", 1A 1978 Sch 1; "the principal Act", s 118(1); "year of assessment", TA 1988 s 832(1).
Amendments—¹ This Schedule inserted by FA 1996 s 128(2), Sch 17 with effect as respects claims made (or deemed to be made) from the year 1996–97.

Carry-back of post-cessation etc receipts

[5—(1) This paragraph applies where a person who has received a sum to which section 108 of the principal Act applies (election for carry-back) makes an election under that section requiring tax to be charged as if the sum were received on the date on which the discontinuance took place or, as the case may be, on the last day of the period at the end of which the change of basis took place; and in this paragraph—

    "the earlier year" means the year in which the sum is treated as received;

    "the later year" means the year in which the sum is received.

(2) The claim shall relate to the later year.

(3) Subject to sub-paragraph (4) below, the claim shall be for an amount equal to the difference between—

    (*a*) the amount in which the person is chargeable to tax for the earlier year ("amount A"); and

    (*b*) the amount in which he would be so chargeable on the assumption that effect could be, and were, given to the claim in relation to that year ("amount B").

(4) Where effect has been given to one or more associated claims, amounts A and B above shall each be determined on the assumption that effect could have been, and had been, given to the associated claim or claims in relation to the earlier year.

(5) In computing amount B for the purposes of this paragraph, no further deduction or relief shall be made or given in respect of any loss or allowance deducted in pursuance of section 105 of the principal Act.

(6) Effect shall be given to the claim in relation to the later year by an increase in the amount of tax payable.]¹

Commentary—*Simon's Direct Tax Service* E1.833.
Definitions—"Claim", Sch 1B para 1; "the principal Act", s 118(1).
Amendments—¹ This Schedule inserted by FA 1996 s 128(2), Sch 17 with effect as respects claims made (or deemed to be made) from the year 1996–97.

Backward spreading of certain payments

[6—*(1) This paragraph applies where a person who has received a payment to which any of the following sections applies, namely—*

    (a) section 534 of the principal Act (relief for copyright payments etc);

    (b) section 537A of that Act (relief for payments in respect of designs); and

(c) section 538 of that Act (relief for painters, sculptors and other artists),
makes a claim under subsection (1) of that section requiring that effect be given to the following
provisions of that section in connection with that payment.

(2) The claim shall relate to the year of assessment in which the payment in question is receivable
("the payment year"); and for the purposes of this sub-paragraph a payment shall be regarded as
receivable in the year of assessment in computing the amount of the profits or gains of which it
would, but for the relevant section, be included.

(3) Subject to sub-paragraph (4) below, in so far as the claim relates to the profits or gains of a
year of assessment earlier than the payment year ("the earlier year"), the claim shall be for an
amount equal to the difference between—

    (a) the amount in which the person is chargeable to tax for the earlier year ("amount A"); and
    (b) the amount in which he would be so chargeable on the assumption that effect could be, and
    were, given to the claim or amendment in relation to that year ("amount B").

(4) Where effect has been given to one or more associated claims, amounts A and B above shall
each be determined on the assumption that effect could have been, and had been, given to the
associated claim or claims in relation to the earlier year.

(5) In so far as the claim relates to the profits or gains of the earlier year, effect shall be given to
the claim in relation to the payment year by an increase in the amount of tax payable.]¹]²

Commentary—*Simon's Direct Tax Service* **E1.833.**
Definitions—"Claim", Sch 1B para 1; "the principal Act", s 118(1); "year of assessment", TA 1988 s 832(1).
Amendments—¹ Schedule inserted by FA 1996 s 128(2), Sch 17 with effect as respects claims made (or deemed to be made)
    from the year 1996–97.
² This paragraph repealed by FA 2001 s 110, Sch 33 Pt II(6) with effect for payments actually receivable after 5 April 2001.

SCHEDULE 2

JURISDICTION IN APPEALS ON CLAIMS

Section 42

Commentary—*Simon's Direct Tax Service* **A2.511; A3.503.**
Amendments—This Schedule (together with amendments prospectively made to it by FA 1994 ss 196, 199 and Sch 19 para 36)
    repealed by FA 1996 Sch 22 para 6, Sch 41 Pt V(12) with effect in relation to any proceedings relating to the year 1996–97 or
    any subsequent year of assessment, and in relation to any proceedings relating to an accounting period ending after 30 June
    1999 (by virtue of Finance Act 1994, Section 199, (Appointed Day) Order, SI 1998/3173 art 2).
Note—See the *Yellow Tax Handbook*, 1998–99, 38th Edition, for the text of this Schedule.

[SCHEDULE 3

RULES FOR ASSIGNING PROCEEDINGS TO GENERAL COMMISSIONERS]

Section 44(1)

Commentary—*Simon's Direct Tax Service* **E1.839.**
Amendments—This Schedule substituted by FA 1996 Sch 22 para 10 with effect in relation to any proceedings relating to the
    year 1996–97 and any subsequent year of assessment and in relation to any proceedings relating to an accounting period ending
    after 30 June 1999 (by virtue of Finance Act 1994, Section 199, (Appointed Day) Order, SI 1998/3173 art 2).

Introductory

[1 In this Schedule—
    "the relevant place" means the place referred to in section 44(1) of this Act, which is used to
      identify the General Commissioners before whom proceedings are to be brought; and
    "the taxpayer", in relation to any proceedings, means the party to the proceedings who is neither
      the Board nor an officer of the Board.]¹

Commentary—*Simon's Direct Tax Service* **E1.839.**
Amendments—¹ This Schedule substituted by FA 1996 Sch 22 para 10 with effect in relation to any proceedings relating to the
    year 1996–97 and any subsequent year of assessment and in relation to any proceedings relating to an accounting period ending
    after 30 June 1999 (by virtue of Finance Act 1994, Section 199, (Appointed Day) Order, SI 1998/3173 art 2).

General rule for income and capital gains tax proceedings

[2—(1) In the case of any proceedings relating to income tax or capital gains tax the relevant place
is whichever of the places specified in sub-paragraph (2) below is identified—
    (a) except where the proceedings are commenced by an officer of the Board, by an election made
    by the taxpayer; and
    (b) where the proceedings are so commenced, by an election made by the officer.

(2) Those places are—
    (a) the place (if any) in the United Kingdom which, at the time when the election is made, is the
    taxpayer's place of residence;
    (b) the place (if any) which at that time is the taxpayer's place of business in the United Kingdom;

(*c*) the place (if any) in the United Kingdom which at that time is the taxpayer's place of employment;

and, in the case of a place of employment, it shall be immaterial for the purposes of this paragraph whether the proceedings in question relate to matters connected with the employment of the taxpayer.

(3) Where the taxpayer fails to make an election for the purposes of this paragraph before the time limit given by paragraph 5 below, an officer of the Board may elect which of the places specified in sub-paragraph (2) above is to be the relevant place.

(4) In sub-paragraph (2)(*a*) above "place of residence" means—

(*a*) in relation to an election made by the taxpayer, his usual place of residence; and
(*b*) in relation to an election made by an officer of the Board, the taxpayer's usual place of residence or, if that is unknown, his last known place of residence.

(5) In sub-paragraph (2)(*b*) above "place of business" means—

(*a*) the place where the trade, profession, vocation or business with which the proceedings are concerned is carried on, or
(*b*) if the trade, profession, vocation or business is carried on at more than one place, the head office or place where it is mainly carried on.

(6) This paragraph does not apply in the case of any proceedings to which paragraph 3, 4 or 7 below applies.][1]

Commentary—*Simon's Direct Tax Service* **E1.839.**
Simon's Tax Cases—*R v Inland Revenue Comrs, ex p Knight* [1973] STC 564.
Definitions—"The Board", s 118(1); "the relevant place", Sch 3 para 1; "taxpayer", Sch 3 para 1; "trade", s 118(1).
Amendments—[1] This Schedule substituted by FA 1996 Sch 22 para 10 with effect in relation to any proceedings relating to the year 1996–97 and any subsequent year of assessment and in relation to any proceedings relating to an accounting period ending after 30 June 1999 (by virtue of Finance Act 1994, Section 199, (Appointed Day) Order, SI 1998/3173 art 2).

PAYE appeals

[**3**—(1) In the case of an appeal in exercise of a right of appeal conferred by regulations under section 203 of the principal Act, the relevant place is—

(*a*) except in a case falling in paragraph (*b*) below, the place determined by the regulations, and
(*b*) if the appellant elects for one of the places specified in paragraph 2(2) above to be the relevant place instead, the place identified by the election.

(2) This paragraph does not apply in the case of any proceedings to which paragraph 4 or 7 below applies.][1]

Commentary—*Simon's Direct Tax Service* **E1.839.**
Simon's Tax Cases—*Murphy v Elders* [1974] STC 34*.
Definitions—"the principal Act", s 118(1); "the relevant place", Sch 3 para 1.
Amendments—[1] This Schedule substituted by FA 1996 Sch 22 para 10 with effect in relation to any proceedings relating to the year 1996–97 and any subsequent year of assessment and in relation to any proceedings relating to an accounting period ending after 30 June 1999 (by virtue of Finance Act 1994, Section 199, (Appointed Day) Order, SI 1998/3173 art 2).

Corporation tax etc

[**4**—(1) In the case of the proceedings mentioned in sub-paragraph (2) below the relevant place is whichever of the places specified in sub-paragraph (3) below is identified—

(*a*) except where the proceedings are commenced by an officer of the Board, by an election made by the company or other body corporate which is a party to the proceedings ("the corporate taxpayer"); and
(*b*) where the proceedings are so commenced, by an election made by the officer.

(2) The proceedings are—

(*a*) proceedings relating to corporation tax;
(*b*) proceedings relating to income tax which are proceedings to which a company resident in the United Kingdom and within the charge to corporation tax is a party;
(*c*) proceedings relating to tax assessable under sections 419 and 420 of the principal Act (close company loans).

(3) The places are—

(*a*) the place where, at the time when the election is made, the corporate taxpayer carries on its trade or business;
(*b*) the place where, at that time, the head office or principal place of business of the corporate taxpayer is situated;
(*c*) the place where, at that time, the corporate taxpayer resides.

(4) Where the corporate taxpayer fails to make an election for the purposes of this paragraph before the time limit given by paragraph 5 below, an officer of the Board may elect which of the places specified in sub-paragraph (3) above is to be the relevant place.

(5) This paragraph does not apply in the case of any proceedings to which paragraph 7 below applies.][1]

Definitions—''The Board'', s 118(1); ''company'', s 118(1); ''the principal Act'', s 118(1); ''the relevant place'', Sch 3 para 1; ''taxpayer'', Sch 3 para 1; ''trade'', s 118(1).
Amendments—[1] This Schedule substituted by FA 1996 Sch 22 para 10 with effect in relation to any proceedings relating to the year 1996–97 and any subsequent year of assessment and in relation to any proceedings relating to an accounting period ending after 30 June 1999 (by virtue of Finance Act 1994, Section 199, (Appointed Day) Order, SI 1998/3173 art 2).

Procedure for making elections, etc

[5—(1) An election by a taxpayer for the purposes of this Schedule shall be made by notice in writing to an officer of the Board.

(2) The time limit for the making of such an election in relation to proceedings is—

(*a*) the time when the taxpayer gives notice of appeal or, if the proceedings are not an appeal, otherwise commences the proceedings; or
(*b*) such later date as the Board allows.

(3) Such an election shall be irrevocable.]](1)

Commentary—*Simon's Direct Tax Service* **E1.839.**
Definitions—''The Board'', s 118(1); ''taxpayer'', Sch 3 para 1.
Amendments—[1] This Schedule substituted by FA 1996 Sch 22 para 10 with effect in relation to any proceedings relating to the year 1996–97 and any subsequent year of assessment and in relation to any proceedings relating to an accounting period ending after 30 June 1999 (by virtue of Finance Act 1994, Section 199, (Appointed Day) Order, SI 1998/3173 art 2).

[6 An election by an officer of the Board for the purposes of this Schedule shall be made by notice in writing served on the taxpayer.]](1)

Simon's Tax Cases—*R v Inland Revenue Comrs , ex p Knight* [1973] STC 564.
Definitions—''The Board'', s 118(1); ''taxpayer'', Sch 3 para 1.
Amendments—[1] This Schedule substituted by FA 1996 Sch 22 para 10 with effect in relation to any proceedings relating to the year 1996–97 and any subsequent year of assessment and in relation to any proceedings relating to an accounting period ending after 30 June 1999 (by virtue of Finance Act 1994, Section 199, (Appointed Day) Order, SI 1998/3173 art 2).

Partnerships

[7 In the case of proceedings relating to a partnership to which a partner of that partnership is a party, the relevant place is—

(*a*) the place where the trade, profession or business of the partnership is carried on, or
(*b*) if the trade, profession or business is carried on at more than one place, the place where it is mainly carried on.]](1)

Commentary—*Simon's Direct Tax Service* **E1.839.**
Definitions—''The relevant place'', Sch 3 para 1; ''trade'', s 118(1).
Amendments—[1] This Schedule substituted by FA 1996 Sch 22 para 10 with effect in relation to any proceedings relating to the year 1996–97 and any subsequent year of assessment and in relation to any proceedings relating to an accounting period ending after 30 June 1999 (by virtue of Finance Act 1994, Section 199, (Appointed Day) Order, SI 1998/3173 art 2).

Directions by the Board

[8—(1) The Board may give a direction in relation to any class of proceedings specified in the direction that, notwithstanding the preceding provisions of this Schedule, the relevant place shall be taken to be a place in a division specified in the direction.

(2) A direction given under this paragraph shall not have effect in relation to any proceedings unless an officer of the Board has served on the taxpayer a notice in writing stating the effect of the direction in relation to those proceedings.

(3) A direction given under this paragraph shall not have effect if the taxpayer gives a notice in accordance with sub-paragraph (4) below objecting to the direction.

(4) The taxpayer gives a notice in accordance with this sub-paragraph if he gives it in writing to the Board within the period of 30 days beginning with the day on which the notice under sub-paragraph (2) above was served on him.]](1)

Commentary—*Simon's Direct Tax Service* **E1.839.**
Definitions—''The Board'', s 118(1); ''the relevant place'', Sch 3 para 1; ''taxpayer'', Sch 3 para 1.
Amendments—[1] This Schedule substituted by FA 1996 Sch 22 para 10 with effect in relation to any proceedings relating to the year 1996–97 and any subsequent year of assessment and in relation to any proceedings relating to an accounting period ending after 30 June 1999 (by virtue of Finance Act 1994, Section 199, (Appointed Day) Order, SI 1998/3173 art 2).

[9—(1) The Board may give directions for determining the relevant place in cases where—

(*a*) the proceedings fall within paragraph 2, 4 or 7 above, but there is no place falling within paragraph 2(2), 4(3) or, as the case may be, paragraph 7; or
(*b*) the relevant place would, apart from the direction, be a place outside the United Kingdom.

(2) A direction given under this paragraph by the Board shall not have effect in relation to any proceedings unless an officer of the Board has served on the taxpayer a notice in writing stating the effect of the direction in relation to those proceedings.

(3) A direction under sub-paragraph (1) above may be given in relation to—

(*a*) proceedings falling within that sub-paragraph;
(*b*) any class of such proceedings specified in the direction; or

(*c*) proceedings specified in the direction.]¹

Commentary—*Simon's Direct Tax Service* E1.839.
Definitions—"The Board", s 118(1); "the relevant place", Sch 3 para 1; "taxpayer", Sch 3 para 1.
Amendments—¹ This Schedule substituted by FA 1996 Sch 22 para 10 with effect in relation to any proceedings relating to the
year 1996–97 and any subsequent year of assessment and in relation to any proceedings relating to an accounting period ending
after 30 June 1999 (by virtue of Finance Act 1994, Section 199, (Appointed Day) Order, SI 1998/3173 art 2).

Other provisions

[10 The provisions of this Schedule have effect subject to sections 44(2), 46A and 57 of this Act,
sections 102(1), 113(5), 343(10) and 783(9) of the principal Act and [section 563 of the Capital
Allowances Act]²]¹

Definition—"The principal Act", s 118(1).
Amendments—¹ This Schedule substituted by FA 1996 Sch 22 para 10 with effect in relation to any proceedings relating to the
year 1996–97 and any subsequent year of assessment and in relation to any proceedings relating to an accounting period ending
after 30 June 1999 (by virtue of Finance Act 1994, Section 199, (Appointed Day) Order, SI 1998/3173 art 2).
² Words substituted by CAA 2001 s 578, Sch 2 para 5 with effect for income tax purposes, as respects allowances and charges
falling to be made for chargeable periods ending after 5 April 2001, and for corporation tax purposes, as respects allowances
and charges falling to be made for chargeable periods ending after 31 March 2001.

[SCHEDULE 3ZA

DATE BY WHICH PAYMENT TO BE MADE AFTER AMENDMENT OR CORRECTION OF SELF-ASSESSMENT]¹

Section 59B(5)

¹ This Schedule inserted by FA 2001 s 88, Sch 29 paras 15, 16 where the relevant day is after 10 May 2001. The "relevant day"
means the first day of the period of 30 days specified in the relevant provision of this Schedule.

[General

1—(1) This Schedule specifies the day by which tax has to be paid (or repaid) following the
amendment or correction of a self-assessment.

(2) If in any case the general rules in section 59B(3) and (4) of this Act give a later day, those rules
apply instead.

(3) The provisions of this Schedule have effect subject to section 55(6) and (9) of this Act (provisions
as to postponement of payment, etc in case of appeal).]¹

Amendments—¹ This paragraph inserted by FA 2001 s 88, Sch 29 paras 15, 16 where the relevant day is after 10 May 2001. The
"relevant day" means the first day of the period of 30 days specified in the relevant provision of this Schedule.

[Amendment of personal or trustee return by the taxpayer

2—(1) This paragraph applies where an amount of tax is payable or repayable as a result of the
amendment of a self-assessment under section 9ZA of this Act (amendment of personal or trustee
return by taxpayer).

(2) Subject to sub-paragraph (3) below, the amount is payable (or repayable) on or before the day
following the end of the period of 30 days beginning with the day on which the notice of amendment
was given.

(3) If section 9B(3) of this Act applies (amendment of self-assessment by taxpayer during enquiry:
deferral of effect), then—

(*a*) if the amendment is taken into account as mentioned in paragraph (*a*)(i) of that subsection,
paragraph 5 below (amendment of personal or trustee return by closure notice) applies accordingly;
and

(*b*) if the amendment takes effect under paragraph (*b*) of that subsection on the issue of the closure
notice, the amount is payable (or repayable) on or before the day following the end of the period
of 30 days beginning with the day on which the closure notice was given.]¹

¹ This paragraph inserted by FA 2001 s 88, Sch 29 paras 15, 16 where the relevant day is after 10 May 2001. The "relevant day"
means the first day of the period of 30 days specified in the relevant provision of this Schedule.

[Correction of personal or trustee return by Revenue

3—(1) This paragraph applies where an amount of tax is payable or repayable as a result of the
correction of a self-assessment under section 9ZB of this Act (correction of personal or trustee return
by the Revenue).

(2) The amount is payable (or repayable) on or before the day following the end of the period of 30
days beginning with the day on which the notice of correction was given.]¹

¹ This paragraph inserted by FA 2001 s 88, Sch 29 paras 15, 16 where the relevant day is after 10 May 2001. The "relevant day"
means the first day of the period of 30 days specified in the relevant provision of this Schedule.

[Amendment of personal or trustee return to prevent loss of tax

4—(1) This paragraph applies where an amount of tax is payable or repayable as a result of the amendment of a self-assessment under section 9C of this Act (amendment of personal or trustee return by Revenue to prevent loss of tax).

(2) The amount is payable (or repayable) on or before the day following the end of the period of 30 days beginning with the day on which the notice of amendment was given.]¹

¹ This paragraph inserted by FA 2001 s 88, Sch 29 paras 15, 16 where the relevant day is after 10 May 2001. The "relevant day" means the first day of the period of 30 days specified in the relevant provision of this Schedule.

[Amendment of personal or trustee return by closure notice

5—(1) This paragraph applies where an amount of tax is payable or repayable as a result of the amendment of a self-assessment under section 28A of this Act (amendment of personal or trustee return by closure notice following enquiry).

(2) The amount is payable (or repayable) on or before the day following the end of the period of 30 days beginning with the day on which the closure notice was given.]¹

¹ This paragraph inserted by FA 2001 s 88, Sch 29 paras 15, 16 where the relevant day is after 10 May 2001. The "relevant day" means the first day of the period of 30 days specified in the relevant provision of this Schedule.

[Amendment consequential on amendment of partnership return by taxpayer

6—(1) This paragraph applies where an amount of tax is payable or repayable as a result of the amendment of a self-assessment under section 12ABA(3)(*a*) of this Act (consequential amendment of partner's personal or trustee return where partnership return amended by taxpayer).

(2) The amount is payable (or repayable) on or before the day following the end of the period of 30 days beginning with the day on which the notice under section 12ABA(3)(*a*) of this Act was given.]¹

¹ This paragraph inserted by FA 2001 s 88, Sch 29 paras 15, 16 where the relevant day is after 10 May 2001. The "relevant day" means the first day of the period of 30 days specified in the relevant provision of this Schedule.

[Amendment consequential on correction of partnership return by Revenue

7—(1) This paragraph applies where an amount of tax is payable or repayable as a result of the amendment of a self-assessment under section 12ABB(6)(*a*) of this Act (consequential amendment of partner's personal or trustee return where partnership return corrected by Revenue).

(2) The amount is payable (or repayable) on or before the day following the end of the period of 30 days beginning with the day on which the notice under section 12ABB(6)(*a*) of this Act was given.]¹

¹ This paragraph inserted by FA 2001 s 88, Sch 29 paras 15, 16 where the relevant day is after 10 May 2001. The "relevant day" means the first day of the period of 30 days specified in the relevant provision of this Schedule.

[Amendment consequential on amendment of partnership return by closure notice

8—(1) This paragraph applies where an amount of tax is payable or repayable as a result of the amendment of a self-assessment under section 28B(4)(*a*) of this Act (consequential amendment of partner's personal or trustee return where partnership return amended by closure notice).

(2) The amount is payable (or repayable) on or before the day following the end of the period of 30 days beginning with the day on which the notice under section 28B(4)(*a*) of this Act was given.]¹

¹ This paragarph inserted by FA 2001 s 88, Sch 29 paras 15, 16 where the relevant day is after 10 May 2001. The "relevant day" means the first day of the period of 30 days specified in the relevant provision of this Schedule.

[Amendment consequential on amendment of partnership return to prevent loss of tax

9—(1) This paragraph applies where an amount of tax is payable or repayable as a result of the amendment of a self-assessment under section 30B(2)(*a*) of this Act (consequential amendment of partner's personal or trustee return where partnership return amended by Revenue to prevent loss of tax).

(2) The amount is payable (or repayable) on or before the day following the end of the period of 30 days beginning with the day on which the notice under section 30B(2)(*a*) of this Act was given.]¹

¹ This paragraph inserted by FA 2001 s 88, Sch 29 paras 15, 16 where the relevant day is after 10 May 2001. The "relevant day" means the first day of the period of 30 days specified in the relevant provision of this Schedule.

[Amendment consequential on amendment of partnership return by way of error or mistake relief

10—(1) This paragraph applies where an amount of tax is payable or repayable as a result of the amendment of a self-assessment under section 33A(4)(*a*) of this Act (consequential amendment of partner's personal or trustee return where partnership return amended by Revenue to afford relief in case of error or mistake).

(2) The amount is payable (or repayable) on or before the day following the end of the period of 30 days beginning with the day on which the notice under section 33A(4)(*a*) of this Act was given.]¹

[1] This paragraph inserted by FA 2001 s 88, Sch 29 paras 15, 16 where the relevant day is after 10 May 2001. The "relevant day" means the first day of the period of 30 days specified in the relevant provision of this Schedule.

[Amendment consequential on reduction or increase on appeal of amounts stated in partnership statement

11—(1) This paragraph applies where an amount of tax is payable or repayable as a result of the amendment of a self-assessment under section 50(9)(*a*) of this Act (consequential amendment of partner's personal or trustee return where partnership statement amended by Revenue following decision on appeal).

(2) The amount is payable (or repayable) on or before the day following the end of the period of 30 days beginning with the day on which the notice under section 50(9)(*a*) of this Act was given.]*[1]*

[1] This paragraph inserted by FA 2001 s 88, Sch 29 paras 15, 16 where the relevant day is after 10 May 2001. The "relevant day" means the first day of the period of 30 days specified in the relevant provision of this Schedule.

[SCHEDULE 3A

ELECTRONIC LODGEMENT OF TAX RETURNS, ETC][1]

Section 115A

Commentary—*Simon's Direct Tax Service* **A3.111A.**
Note—The provisions thus far specified (for 1996-97 and subsequent years) by virtue of para 2(1)(*b*) are TMA 1970 ss 8, 8A, 12AA, and this Schedule applies to notices under those provisions given after 1 March 1997 (Electronic Lodgement of Tax Returns Order, SI 1997/57.
Statement of Practice SP 1/97—Describes how the Revenue will operate the electronic lodgement service and the more detailed requirements of the service.
Cross references—See FA 1999 ss 132, 133 (power to provide for use of electronic communications).
Amendments—[1] This Schedule inserted by FA 1995 Sch 28 para 2.
Prospective amendment—This Schedule to be repealed by FA 1999 ss 133(3), (4), 139, Sch 20 Pt VII with effect from such day or days as the Treasury may by order appoint.

[PART I

TAX RETURNS: GENERAL

The basic rule

1—(1) Sub-paragraph (2) below applies where a person is—

(*a*) required by a notice to which this Schedule applies, or
(*b*) subject to any other requirement to which this Schedule applies,

to deliver or make a return to an officer of the Board or to the Board.

(2) The requirement to deliver or make the return shall be treated as fulfilled by the person subject to the requirement if—

(*a*) information is transmitted electronically in response to that requirement; and
(*b*) each of the conditions in Part III of this Schedule is met with respect to that transmission.

(3) Sub-paragraphs (4) and (5) below apply where the requirement to deliver or make the return is fulfilled by virtue of sub-paragraph (2) above.

(4) Any requirement—

(*a*) under any provision of Part II of this Act [or Schedule 18 to the Finance Act 1998][2] that the return include a declaration by the person making the return to the effect that the return is to the best of his knowledge correct and complete, or
(*b*) under or by virtue of any other provision of the Taxes Acts that the return be signed or include any description of declaration or certificate,

shall not apply.

(5) The time at which the requirement to deliver or make the return is fulfilled is the end of the day during which the last of the conditions in Part III of this Schedule to be met with respect to the transmission is met.

(6) In sub-paragraph (2)(*a*) above "information" includes any self-assessment, partnership statement, particulars or claim.][1]

Definitions—"The Board", s 118(1); "return", s 118(1); "the Taxes Acts", s 118(1).
Cross reference—See TMA 1970 Sch 3A paras 4–7 (conditions to be met in respect of transmission).
Amendments—[1] This Schedule inserted by FA 1995 Sch 28 para 2.
[2] Words in sub-para (4)(*a*) inserted by FA 1998 Sch 19 para 43 with effect in relation to accounting periods ending after 30 June 1999 (by virtue of Finance Act 1994, Section 199, (Appointed Day) Order, SI 1998/3173 art 2).
Prospective amendment—See note at the beginning of this Schedule.

[Returns to which Schedule applies

2—(1) This Schedule applies to a notice requiring a return to be delivered or made if—

(*a*) the notice is given under any provision of the Taxes Acts or of regulations made under the Taxes Acts;

(*b*) the provision is specified for the purposes of this Schedule by an order made by the Treasury; and

(*c*) the notice is given after the day appointed by the order in relation to notices under the provision so specified.

(2) This Schedule applies to any other requirement to deliver or make a return if—

(*a*) the requirement is imposed by any provision of the Taxes Acts or of regulations made under the Taxes Acts;

(*b*) the provision is specified for the purposes of this Schedule by an order made by the Treasury; and

(*c*) the requirement is required to be fulfilled within a period beginning after the day appointed by the order in relation to the specified provision.

(3) The power to make an order under this paragraph shall be exercisable by statutory instrument which shall be subject to annulment in pursuance of a resolution of the House of Commons.

(4) For the purposes of this Schedule, any reference to a requirement to deliver a return includes, in relation to regulations made under the principal Act, a reference to a requirement to render a return.]¹

Note—The provisions thus far specified (for 1996-97 and subsequent years) by virtue of sub-para (1)(*b*) are TMA 1970 ss 8, 8A 12AA, and, in relation to notices under those provisions, the day appointed pursuant to sub-para (1)(*c*) is 1 March 1997 (Electronic Lodgement of Tax Returns Order, SI 1997/57).
Definitions—''Return'', s 118(1); ''the Taxes Acts'', s 118(1).
Amendments—¹ This Schedule inserted by FA 1995 Sch 28 para 2.
Prospective amendment—See note at the beginning of this Schedule.

[PART II
DOCUMENTS SUPPORTING CERTAIN TAX RETURNS

3—(1) This paragraph applies where—

(*a*) a person is required by a notice to which this Schedule applies to deliver a return to an officer of the Board;

(*b*) the notice also requires any document other than the return (''a supporting document'') to be delivered;

(*c*) the provision under which the notice is given requires the supporting document to be delivered with the return;

(*d*) the notice states that the supporting document may be transmitted electronically; and

(*e*) the requirement to deliver the return is fulfilled by virtue of paragraph 1(2) of this Schedule.

(2) The requirement to deliver the supporting document shall be treated as fulfilled by the person subject to the requirement if—

(*a*) information is transmitted electronically in response to that requirement; and

(*b*) each of the conditions in Part III of this Schedule is met with respect to that transmission.

(3) If information is not transmitted electronically in response to the requirement to deliver the supporting document, that requirement shall have effect as a requirement to deliver the document on or before the day which is the last day for the delivery of the return.

(4) For the purposes of sub-paragraph (1)(*b*) above the reference to a document includes in particular a reference to any accounts, statements or reports.

(5) Where the requirement to deliver the supporting document is fulfilled by virtue of sub-paragraph (2) above, the time at which it is fulfilled is the end of the day during which the last of the conditions in Part III of this Schedule to be met with respect to the transmission is met.]¹

Definitions—''The Board'', s 118(1); ''return'', s 118(1).
Cross reference—See TMA 1970 Sch 3A para 4–7(conditions to be met in respect of transmission).
Amendments—¹ This Schedule inserted by FA 1995 Sch 28 para 2.
Prospective amendment—See note at the beginning of this Schedule.

[PART III
THE CONDITIONS

Approved persons

4—(1) The first condition is that the transmission must be made by a person approved by the Board.

(2) A person seeking approval under this paragraph shall be given notice of the grant or refusal of approval.

(3) A person may be approved for the purpose of transmitting the information—

(*a*) on behalf of another person or other persons; or

(*b*) on his own behalf.

(4) An approval under this paragraph may be withdrawn by notice with effect from such date as may be specified in the notice.

(5) A notice refusing or withdrawing an approval shall state the grounds for the refusal or withdrawal.

(6) A person who is refused approval or whose approval is withdrawn may appeal to the Special Commissioners against the refusal or withdrawal.

(7) The appeal shall be made by notice given to the Board before the end of the period of 30 days beginning with the day on which notice of the refusal or withdrawal was given to the appellant.

(8) The Special Commissioners shall not allow the appeal unless it appears to them that, having regard to all the circumstances, it is unreasonable for the approval to be refused or (as the case may be) withdrawn.

(9) If the Special Commissioners allow an appeal by a person who has been refused approval, they shall specify the date from which the approval is to have effect.]¹

Commentary—*Simon's Direct Tax Service* **E1.806D**.
Definition—"The Board", s 118(1).
Amendments—¹ This Schedule inserted by FA 1995 Sch 28 para 2.
Prospective amendment—See note at the beginning of this Schedule.

[Approved manner of transmission

5—(1) The second condition applies if the person who makes the transmission is notified by the Board of any requirements for the time being applicable to him as to the manner in which transmissions are to be made by him or as to the manner in which any description of transmission is to be made by him.

(2) The second condition is that the transmission must comply with the requirements so notified.

(3) The requirements referred to include in particular requirements as to—

    (*a*) the hardware or type of hardware, or
    (*b*) the software or type of software,

to be used to make transmissions or a description of transmissions.]¹

Commentary—*Simon's Direct Tax Service* **E1.806D**.
Definition—"The Board", s 118(1).
Amendments—¹ This Schedule inserted by FA 1995 Sch 28 para 2.
Prospective amendment—See note at the beginning of this Schedule.

[Content of transmission

6 The third condition is that the transmission must signify, in a manner approved by the Board, that before the transmission was made a hard copy of the information proposed to be transmitted was made and authenticated in accordance with Part IV of this Schedule.]¹

Commentary—*Simon's Direct Tax Service* **E1.806D**.
Definition—"The Board", s 118(1).
Cross reference—See TMA 1970 Sch 3A paras 8, 9 (authentification of hard copy of information transmitted).
Amendments—¹ This Schedule inserted by FA 1995 Sch 28 para 2.
Prospective amendment—See note at the beginning of this Schedule.

[Procedure for accepting electronic transmissions

7—(1) The fourth condition is that the information transmitted must be accepted for electronic lodgement.

(2) For the purposes of this Schedule, information is accepted for electronic lodgement if it is accepted under a procedure selected by the Board for the purposes of this Schedule.

(3) The selected procedure may in particular consist of or include the use of specially designed software.]¹

Commentary—*Simon's Direct Tax Service* **E1.806D**.
Definition—"The Board", s 118(1).
Amendments—¹ This Schedule inserted by FA 1995 Sch 28 para 2.
Prospective amendment—See note at the beginning of this Schedule.

[PART IV

HARD COPIES OF INFORMATION TRANSMITTED

Provisions about making of hard copies

8—(1) A hard copy is made in accordance with this Part of this Schedule if it is made under arrangements designed to ensure that the information contained in the hard copy is the information in fact transmitted.

(2) A hard copy is authenticated in accordance with this Part of this Schedule if—

(*a*) where the transmission is made in response to a requirement imposed by a notice under Part II of this Act [or Schedule 18 to the Finance Act 1998][2] to deliver a return, the hard copy is endorsed with a declaration by the relevant person that the hard copy is to the best of his knowledge correct and complete; and

(*b*) in any other case, if the hard copy is signed by the relevant person.

(3) In sub-paragraph (2) above "the relevant person" means—

(*a*) where the transmission is made as mentioned in sub-paragraph (2)(*a*) above, the person who, but for paragraph 1(4)(*a*) of this Schedule, would have been required to make the declaration there mentioned;

(*b*) in any other case, the person subject to the requirement to deliver or make the return or, in the case of a document other than a return, deliver the document.]¹

Commentary—*Simon's Direct Tax Service* **E1.806D.**
Definition—"Hard copy", Sch 3A, para 9.
Amendments—¹ This Schedule inserted by FA 1995 Sch 28 para 2.
² Words in sub-para (2)(*a*) inserted by FA 1998 Sch 19 para 43 with effect in relation to accounting periods ending after 30 June 1999 (by virtue of Finance Act 1994, Section 199, (Appointed Day) Order, SI 1998/3173 art 2).
Prospective amendment—See note at the beginning of this Schedule.

[Meaning of "hard copy"

9 In this Part of this Schedule "hard copy", in relation to information held electronically, means a printed out version of that information.]¹

Commentary—*Simon's Direct Tax Service* **E1.806D.**
Amendments—¹ This Schedule inserted by FA 1995 Sch 28 para 2.
Prospective amendment—See note at the beginning of this Schedule.

[PART V
STATUS OF INFORMATION
Exercise of powers

10—(1) Sub-paragraphs (2) to (5) below apply where information transmitted in response to a requirement to deliver or make a return is accepted for electronic lodgement.

(2) An officer of the Board shall have all the powers that he would have had if the information accepted had been contained in a return delivered by post.

(3) The Board shall have all the powers that they would have had if the information accepted had been contained in a return delivered by post.

(4) Where the information is transmitted in response to a notice given under any provision of Part II of this Act, any power which, if the information had been contained in a return delivered by post, a person would have had under this Act to amend the return—

(*a*) by delivering a document, or

(*b*) by notifying amendments,

to an officer of the Board, shall have effect as if the power enabled that person to deliver a statement of amended information to the officer.

(5) Any right that a person would have had, if the information transmitted had been contained in a return delivered by post, to claim that tax charged under an assessment was excessive by reason of some mistake or error in the return shall have effect as far as the claimant is concerned as if the information transmitted had been contained in a return delivered by post.

(6) Where information transmitted in response to a requirement to deliver a document other than a return is accepted for electronic lodgement, an officer of the Board shall have all the powers that he would have had if the information had been contained in a document delivered by post.

(7) This paragraph is subject to paragraph 11 of this Schedule.]¹

Commentary—*Simon's Direct Tax Service* **E1.806D.**
Definitions—"The Board", s 118(1); "return", s 118(1).
Amendments—¹ This Schedule inserted by FA 1995 Sch 28 para 2.
Prospective amendment—See note at the beginning of this Schedule.

[Proceedings

11—(1) Sub-paragraphs (2) to (4) below apply where—

(*a*) a person is required by a notice to which this Schedule applies, or subject to any other requirement to which this Schedule applies, to deliver or make a return; and

(*b*) that requirement is fulfilled by virtue of paragraph 1(2) of this Schedule.

(2) A hard copy shown to have been made and authenticated in accordance with Part IV of this Schedule for the purposes of the transmission in question shall be treated for the purposes of any proceedings as if it were a return delivered or made in response to the requirement.

(3) Sub-paragraph (4) below applies if no hard copy is shown to have been made and authenticated in accordance with Part IV of this Schedule for the purposes of the transmission in question.

(4) A hard copy certified by an officer of the Board to be a true copy of the information transmitted shall be treated for the purposes of any proceedings in relation to which the certificate is given as if it—

(a) were a return delivered or made in response to the requirement in question, and

(b) contained any declaration or signature which would have appeared on a hard copy made and authenticated in accordance with Part IV of this Schedule for the purposes of the transmission.

(5) Where—

(a) a person is required by a notice to which this Schedule applies to deliver any document other than a return, and

(b) that requirement is fulfilled by virtue of paragraph 3(2) of this Schedule,

sub-paragraphs (2) to (4) above shall apply as if any reference to a return delivered in response to the requirement were a reference to a document delivered in response to the requirement.

(6) In this paragraph—

"hard copy" has the same meaning as in Part IV of this Schedule; and

"proceedings" includes proceedings before the General or Special Commissioners or any tribunal having jurisdiction by virtue of any provision of the Taxes Acts.][1]

Commentary—*Simon's Direct Tax Service* **E1.806D.**
Definitions—"The Board", s 118(1); "hard copy", Sch 3A para 9; "return", s 118(1).
Amendments—[1] This Schedule inserted by FA 1995 Sch 28 para 2.
Prospective amendment—See note at the beginning of this Schedule.

SCHEDULE 4

SAVINGS AND TRANSITORY PROVISIONS

Section 119

(*Not reproduced*)

FINANCE ACT 1971

(1971 Chapter 68)

An Act to grant certain duties, to alter other duties, and to amend the law relating to the National Debt and the Public Revenue, and to make further provision in connection with Finance.

[5th August 1971]

PART II

INCOME TAX AND CORPORATION TAX

CHAPTER I

GENERAL

21 Occupational pension schemes

(1)–(5) ...[2]

[(6) Part II of Schedule 3 to this Act shall have effect.][1]

Amendments—[1] Sub-s (6) substituted by TA 1988 Sch 29 para 32 Table.
[2] Sub-ss (1)–(5) repealed by TA 1988 Sch 31.

PART V

MISCELLANEOUS

69 Citation, interpretation, construction, extent and repeals

(1) This Act may be cited as the Finance Act 1971.

(2) In this Act "the Taxes Act" means the Income and Corporation Taxes Act [1988][3].

(3) In this Act—

...[1]

Parts II and III, so far as they relate to income tax, shall be construed as one with the Income Tax Acts and, so far as they relate to corporation tax, shall be construed as one with the Corporation Tax Acts;

...[2]

(4) Except so far as the context otherwise requires, any reference in this Act to any enactment shall be construed as a reference to that enactment as amended, and as including a reference to that enactment as applied, by or under any other enactment, including this Act.

(5) Except as otherwise expressly provided, such of the provisions of this Act as relate to matters in respect of which the Parliament of Northern Ireland has power to make laws do not extend to Northern Ireland.

(6) If the Parliament of Northern Ireland passes provisions amending or replacing any enactment of that Parliament referred to in this Act the reference shall be construed as a reference to the enactment as so amended or, as the case may be, as a reference to those provisions.

(7) (*repeals enactments specified in Sch 14. Effect has been given to these repeals, where applicable, in the relevant provisions of the earlier enactments*).

Amendments—[1] Words in sub-s (3) repealed by the Customs and Excise Management Act 1979 s 177(3), Sch 6.
[2] Words in sub-s (3) repealed by CGTA 1979 s 158 and Sch 8.
[3] Year in sub-s (2) substituted by TA 1988 Sch 29 para 32 Table.

SCHEDULES

SCHEDULE 3

OCCUPATIONAL PENSION SCHEMES

Section 21

PART II

TAXATION OF REFUNDS OF CONTRIBUTIONS AND CERTAIN OTHER PAYMENTS

Schemes approved under old law
Taxation of refunds of contributions and commutation payments

8—(1) This paragraph has effect as respects any payment chargeable to tax for the year 1971–72 or any later year of assessment under Regulation 7, 8 or 13 of the Regulations dated November 10th

1921 made by the Board under section 32 of the Finance Act 1921 (which corresponds to section 208 of [the Income and Corporation Taxes Act 1970][1]).

(2) Where tax is chargeable under the said Regulation 7 (or Regulation 13 with that Regulation) then—

    (*a*) if the scheme relates to a trade, profession or vocation carried on by the employer, the payment shall be treated for the purposes of the Tax Acts as a receipt of that trade, profession or vocation receivable when the payment falls due or on the last day on which the trade, profession or vocation is carried on by the employer, whichever is the earlier;

    (*b*) if the scheme does not relate to such a trade, profession or vocation, the employer shall be charged to tax on the amount of the payment under Case VI of Schedule D.

(3) Where tax is chargeable under the said Regulation 8 (or Regulation 13 with that Regulation), [section 598 (2) to (4) of the Taxes Act][1] shall apply as they apply to tax chargeable under that paragraph.

(4) If at any time the scheme becomes an approved scheme (that is to say approved for the purposes of Chapter II of Part II of the Finance Act [1970 or Chapter I of Part XIV of the Taxes Act][1]) no tax shall be chargeable under the said Regulations on any payment made under the scheme after that time.

(5) The provisions of this paragraph shall have effect in substitution for the provisions of the said Regulations as to the rate of tax and the manner of charging tax, and the said Regulations 7, 8 and 13 shall not cease to be in force by reason of the provisions of this Act repealing the said section 208 of [the Income and Corporation Taxes Act 1970][1], or of the provisions of this Act under which in certain cases the said section 208 ceases to apply to a scheme before the date of that repeal.

Cross references—See TA 1988 s 599A(9) (tax charge on repayment of surplus funds to members of AVC schemes).
Amendments—[1] Words in sub-paras (1), (3), (4), (5) substituted by TA 1988 Sch 29 para 32 Table.

FINANCE ACT 1972

(1972 Chapter 41)

An Act to grant certain duties, to alter other duties, and to amend the law relating to the National Debt and the Public Revenue, and to make further provision in connection with Finance.

[27th July 1972]

PART V

TAXATION OF COMPANIES AND COMPANY DISTRIBUTIONS

111 Consequential amendments

(1) (*amends the enactments specified in Sch 24*).

(2) ...[1]

(3) This section has effect from 6th April 1973 and does not affect the operation of any enactment in relation to any previous time; and no amendment in the said Schedule 24 adapting an enactment so as to make it apply or refer to a provision of this Act instead of a provision repealed thereby shall be construed as affecting the operation of that enactment in relation to the repealed provision so far as concerns matters occurring before the repeal or otherwise unaffected by it.

Notes—FA 1972 Sch 24 not reproduced. Effect has been given to the amendments made by this Schedule where appropriate in earlier enactments.
Amendments—[1] Sub-s (2) repealed by TA 1988 Sch 31.

PART VII

MISCELLANEOUS

127 Disclosure of information between revenue departments

(1) No obligation as to secrecy or other restriction upon the disclosure of information imposed by statute or otherwise shall prevent either—

    (*a*) the Commissioners of Inland Revenue or an authorised officer of those Commissioners; or

    (*b*) the Commissioners of Customs and Excise or an authorised officer of those Commissioners;

from disclosing information to the other Commissioners or an authorised officer of the other Commissioners for the purpose of assisting them in the performance of their duties.

(2) Information obtained in pursuance of this section shall not be disclosed except—

(*a*) to the Commissioners or an authorised officer of the Commissioners on whose behalf it was obtained; or

(*b*) for the purpose of any proceedings connected with a matter in relation to which those Commissioners perform duties.

Commentary—*Simon's Direct Tax Service* **A2.802.**
Revenue & other press releases—IR 8-3-88 (information is exchanged between tax offices and C & E offices at local level).
Revenue Internal Guidance—Investigations Handbook IH 240 (Revenue practice on exchange of information).
IH 1280-1295 (Revenue use of information from Customs & Excise).
IH 6500–6512 (investigation cases: information supplied to Customs & Excise).
Cross references—FA 1989 s 182 (6) (disclosure of information made with lawful authority).

130 Compensation for loss of office etc by clerks to General Commissioners

(1) The Commissioners of Inland Revenue may, with the concurrence of the Minister for the Civil Service, by regulations provide for the payment out of money provided by Parliament of compensation to or in respect of any clerk to the General Commissioners for any division who suffers or has suffered loss of office or loss or diminution of emoluments which is attributable to any order affecting that division made (whether before or after the passing of this Act) under section 2(6) of the Taxes Management Act 1970 (alteration and abolition of divisions).

(2) Regulations under this section may—

(*a*) include provision as to the manner in which and the person to whom any claim for compensation under the regulations is to be made, and for the determination of all questions arising under the regulations;

(*b*) make different provision for different classes of persons and for different circumstances, and make, or authorise the Commissioners of Inland Revenue to make, exceptions and conditions;

(*c*) be framed so as to have effect from a date earlier than the making of the regulations,

but so that regulations having effect from a date earlier than their making shall not place any individual in a worse position than he would have been in if the regulations had been so framed as to have effect only from the date of their making.

(3) Regulations under this section shall be made by statutory instrument subject to annulment in pursuance of a resolution of either House of Parliament.

Commentary—*Simon's Direct Tax Service* **A2.509.**
Regulations—The Clerks to General Commissioners (Compensation) Regulations, SI 1973/900 (payments of compensation) have been made under this section.

131 Post-war credits

(1) On the repayment of any post-war credit, or payment to a building society of any amount outstanding under section 3 of the Income Tax (Repayment of Post-War Credits) Act 1959 the sum payable, inclusive of the interest, may be taken by the Commissioners of Inland Revenue as amounting to 138 per cent of the credit as notified under section 7 of the Finance Act 1941 or of the amount so outstanding, as the case may be.

(2) An application for such a repayment made before the applicant is qualified may, if he later becomes qualified, be treated as made on the date when he does so.

(3) No such repayment shall be made unless application therefor is made before such time (not earlier than the beginning of the year 1974) as the Treasury may by order direct.

Any order under this subsection shall be made by statutory instrument, which shall be laid before Parliament after being made, and may be varied by a subsequent order so as to extend the time for applications for repayment.

[(3A) An order under subsection (3) above may make different provision for different cases or classes of case and may provide that no amount shall be ascertained, recorded or notified under section 7 of the Finance Act 1941 after any such time as may be specified in the order.][1]

(4) In this section "post-war credit" has the same meaning as in the Income Tax (Repayment of Post-War Credits) Act 1959.

(5) This section shall be deemed to have had effect from the beginning of April 1972.

Commentary—*Simon's Direct Tax Service* **E2.1206.**
Regulations—Post-War Credit (Income Tax) Orders.
Amendments—[1]Sub-s (3A) inserted by FA 1976 s 59.

FINANCE ACT 1973

(1973 Chapter 51)

An Act to grant certain duties, to alter other duties, and to amend the law relating to the National Debt and the Public Revenue, and to make further provision in connection with Finance.

[25th July 1973]

PART III

INCOME TAX, CORPORATION TAX AND CAPITAL GAINS TAX

32 Information as to arrangements for transferring relief, etc

(1) If a company—

(a) makes a claim for group relief, or

(b) being a party to a leasing contract, as defined in section [395 of the Taxes Act 1988][2], claims relief as mentioned in subsection (1)(b) of that section, or

(c) being a member of a partnership, either claims any relief which, if subsection (2) of section [116 of that Act][2] applied in relation to it, it would not be entitled to claim, or makes a return which is treated as a claim by virtue of section [239(5) of that Act][2], or

(d) makes a claim under section [240 of that Act][2] (surrender of advance corporation tax),

and the inspector has reason to believe that any relevant arrangements may exist, or may have existed at any time material to the claim, then at any time after the claim (or return) is made he may serve notice in writing on the company requiring it to furnish him, within such time being not less than thirty days from the giving of the notice as he may direct, with—

(i) a declaration in writing stating whether or not any such arrangements exist or existed at any material time, or

(ii) such information as he may reasonably require for the purpose of satisfying himself whether or not any such arrangements exist or existed at any material time, or

(iii) both such a declaration and such information.

(2) In this section "relevant arrangements", in relation to a claim (including a return which is treated as a claim) falling within any of paragraphs (a) to (d) of subsection (1) above, means such arrangements as are referred to in that enactment which is specified in the corresponding paragraph below, that is to say,—

[(a) section 410(1) or (2) of or paragraph 5(3) of Schedule 18 to the Taxes Act 1988;

(b) section 395(1)(c) of that Act;

(c) section 116(1) of that Act;

(d) paragraph 5(3) of Schedule 18 to or section 240(11) of that Act.][3]

(3) In a case falling within paragraph (a) of subsection (1) above, a notice under that subsection may be served on the surrendering company, within the meaning of section [402 of the Taxes Act 1988][2], instead of or as well as on the company claiming relief.

(4) In a case falling within paragraph (c) of subsection (1) above, a notice under that subsection may be served on the partners instead of or as well as on the company alone, and accordingly may require them, instead of or as well as the company, to furnish the declaration, information or declaration and information concerned.

(5) ...[1]

(6) In this section, ...[1] "arrangements" means arrangements of any kind, whether in writing or not.

Commentary—*Simon's Direct Tax Service* A3.133.
Revenue Internal Guidance—Company Taxation Manual COT2684 (this provision is regarded as a long stop: inspectors are instructed to request information on the normal informal basis first).
Amendments—[1] Sub-s (5) and words in sub-s (6) repealed by TA 1988 Sch 31.
[2] Words in sub-ss (1)(b), (c), (d), (3) substituted by TA 1988 Sch 29 para 32 Table.
[3] Sub-s (2)(a)–(d) substituted by TA 1988 Sch 29 para 32 Table.

38 Territorial extension of charge to income tax, capital gains tax and corporation tax

(1) ...[3]

(2) [Schedule 15 to this Act shall have effect and in that Schedule][4]—

(a) "exploration or exploitation activities" means activities carried on in connection with the exploration or exploitation of so much of the seabed and subsoil and their natural resources as is situated in the United Kingdom or a designated area; and

(b) "exploration or exploitation rights" means rights to assets to be produced by exploration or exploitation activities or to interests in or to the benefit of such assets; and

(c) references to the disposal of exploration or exploitation rights include references to the disposal of shares deriving their value or the greater part of their value directly or indirectly from such rights, other than shares [listed][5] on a recognised stock exchange (within the meaning of the Corporation Tax Acts); and

(d) "shares" includes stock and any security as defined in section [254(1) of the Taxes Act 1988][2]; and

(e) "designated area" means an area designated by Order in Council under section 1(7) of the Continental Shelf Act 1964.

(3)–(5) ...[3]

(6) ...[1]

(7) This section shall have effect for the purposes of income tax and capital gains tax for the year 1973–74 and subsequent years of assessment and for the purposes of corporation tax for the financial year 1973 and subsequent years.

(8) ...[3]

Commentary—*Simon's Direct Tax Service* **D4.911.**
Simon's Tax Cases—s 38, s 38(6) *Clark v Oceanic Contractors Inc* [1983] STC 35.
Amendments—[1] Sub-s (6) repealed by TA 1988 Sch 31.
[2] Words in sub-ss (2)(*d*) substituted by TA 1988 Sch 29 para 32 Table.
[3] Sub-ss (1), (3)–(5), (8) repealed by TCGA 1992 Sch 12 with effect for 1992–93 and subsequent years of assessment.
[4] Words in sub-s (2) substituted by TCGA 1992 Sch 10 para 3(1).
[5] Word in sub-s (2)(*c*) substituted by FA 1996 Sch 38 para 1 with effect in relation to disposals of shares on or after 1 April 1996.

41 General Commissioners' divisions

The boundaries of any division specified by an order made or having effect as if made under section 2(6) of the Taxes Management Act 1970 and in operation immediately before—

    (*a*) 1st April 1974, if the division is in England or Wales; and
    (*b*) 16th May 1975, if the division is in Scotland;

shall remain the same on and after that day as if there were then no change of local government areas (but without prejudice to the making of new orders under that section).

Commentary—*Simon's Direct Tax Service* **A2.508.**

PART VI
MISCELLANEOUS AND GENERAL

59 Citation, interpretation, construction, extent and repeals

(1) This Act may be cited as the Finance Act 1973.

[(2) In this Act—

    (*a*) "the Taxes Act 1970" means the Income and Corporation Taxes Act 1970; and
    (*b*) "the Taxes Act 1988" means the Income and Corporation Taxes Act 1988.][2]

(3) In this Act—

    (*a*)–(*b*) ...
    (*c*) Part III, so far as it relates to income tax, shall be construed as one with the Income Tax Acts, so far as it relates to corporation tax, shall be construed as one with the Corporation Tax Acts and, so far as it relates to capital gains tax, shall be construed as one with [the Capital Gains Tax Act 1979][1];
    (*d*)–(*e*) ...

(4) Except so far as the context otherwise requires, any reference in this Act to any enactment shall be construed as a reference to that enactment as amended, and as including a reference to that enactment as applied, by or under any other enactment, including this Act.

(5) Except as otherwise expressly provided, such of the provisions of this Act to relate to matters in respect of which the Parliament of Northern Ireland has power to make laws do not extend to Northern Ireland.

(6) If the Parliament of Northern Ireland passes provisions amending or replacing any enactment of that Parliament referred to in this Act the reference shall be construed as a reference to the enactment as so amended or, as the case may be, as a reference to those provisions.

(7) The enactments mentioned in Schedule 22 to this Act (which include certain enactments which had ceased to have effect before the commencement of this Act) are hereby repealed to the extent specified in the third column of that Schedule, but subject to any provision at the end of any Part of that Schedule.

Note—Sub-s (3), paras (*a*), (*b*), and (*d*) were outside the scope of this work and have been repealed; sub-s (3)(*e*) is not relevant to this publication.
Amendments—[1] Words in sub-s (3)(*c*) substituted by CGTA 1979 s 157(2)–(4) and Sch 7 para 8 Table, Pt I. 5, with effect from 22 March 1979.
[2] Sub-s (2) substituted by TA 1988 Sch 29 para 32 Table.

SCHEDULES

SCHEDULE 15

TERRITORIAL EXTENSION OF CHARGE TO TAX—SUPPLEMENTARY PROVISIONS

Section 38

Information

2 The holder of any licence granted under the Petroleum (Production) Act 1934 shall, if required to do so by a notice served on him by an inspector, give to the inspector within the time limited by the notice (which shall not be less than thirty days) such particulars as may be required by the notice of—

    (*a*) transactions in connection with activities authorised by the licence as a result of which any person is or might be liable to tax by virtue of section [276 of the Taxation of Chargeable Gains Act 1992][3] or section 830 of the Taxes Act 1988][2]; and

    (*b*) [emoluments or other payments paid or payable in respect of duties or services][1] performed in an area in which those activities may be carried on under the licence and the persons to whom they were paid or are payable;

and shall take reasonable steps to obtain the information necessary to enable him to comply with the notice.

Commentary—*Simon's Direct Tax Service* **A3.134.**
Amendments—[1] Words in sub-para (*b*) substituted by FA 1978 s 29(3), (4).
[2] Words "or section 830 of the Taxes Act 1988" in para (*a*) substituted by TA 1988 Sch 29 para 32 Table (opening square bracket for this amendment superseded by later amendment to this provision).
[3] Words in para (*a*) substituted by TCGA 1992 Sch 10 para 3(2).

Collection

4—(1) Subject to the following provisions of this Schedule, where any tax is assessed by virtue of section [276 of the Taxation of Chargeable Gains Act 1992][3] or section 830 of the Taxes Act 1988][2] on a person not resident in the United Kingdom in respect of—

    (*a*) profits or gains from activities authorised, or carried on in connection with activities authorised, by a licence granted under the Petroleum (Production) Act 1934 or

    (*b*) profits or gains from, or chargeable gains accruing on the disposal of, exploration or exploitation rights connected with activities so authorised or carried on,

then, if the tax remains unpaid later than thirty days after it has become due and payable, the Board may serve a notice on the holder of the licence stating particulars of the assessment, the amount remaining unpaid and the date when it became payable, and requiring the holder of the licence to pay that amount, together with any interest due thereon under section 86 of the Taxes Management Act 1970 within thirty days of the service of the notice.

(2) Any amount which a person is required to pay by a notice under this paragraph may be recovered from him as if it were tax due and duly demanded from him; and he may recover any such amount paid by him from the person on whom the assessment was made.

[(3) A payment in pursuance of a notice under this paragraph shall not be allowed as a deduction in computing any income, profits or losses for any tax purposes.][1]

Commentary—*Simon's Direct Tax Service* **A3.1421.**
Cross references—See F(No 2)A 1987 s 86(3)(*b*) (licence holder's liability for interest on overdue corporation tax under TMA 1970 s 87A in addition to his liability for interest under TMA 1970 s 86);
FA 1988 s 130(7)(*e*) (securing payment from a migrating company of outstanding amount under this paragraph).
Amendments—[1] Sub-para (3) inserted by FA 1984 s 124(1).
[2] Words "or section 830 of the Taxes Act 1988" in sub-para (1) substituted by TA 1988 Sch 29 para 32 Table (opening square bracket for this amendment superseded by later amendment to this provision).
[3] Words in sub-para (1) substituted by TCGA 1992 Sch 10 para 3(2).

[**4A**—(1) Subject to the following provisions of this Schedule, the power of the Board under paragraph 4 above to serve a notice in respect of tax remaining unpaid as there mentioned shall also apply where—

    (*a*) tax is assessed on any person not resident in the United Kingdom as mentioned in paragraph 4 (1) (*a*) or (*b*) but more than one licence under the Petroleum (Production) Act 1934 is the basis for the assessment; or

    (*b*) tax assessed on any such person includes, but is not limited to, tax assessed on him as so mentioned (whether by reference to one or to more than one such licence);

but in any such case the amount the holder of any licence in question may be required to pay by a notice under that paragraph shall be the amount of the tax remaining unpaid under the assessment which is attributable to the profits or gains in respect of which that licence was the basis for the assessment, together with a corresponding proportion of any interest due as mentioned in paragraph 4 (1).

(2) For the purposes of sub-paragraph (1) above the amount of the tax remaining unpaid under the assessment which is attributable to the profits or gains in respect of which any licence in question was the basis for the assessment is such part of the total amount of that tax as bears to that total amount the same proportion as the proportion borne by the amount of the profits or gains in respect of which that licence was the basis for the assessment to the total amount of the profits or gains in respect of which the assessment was made.]¹

Commentary—*Simon's Direct Tax Service* **A3.1421.**
Amendments—¹ This paragraph inserted by FA 1984 s 124(2), (8) and applies in any case where a period of thirty days relevant for the purposes of the service of a notice under para 4 above in relation to any tax expires after 11 March 1984.

5 Paragraph 4 above does not apply to any assessment to tax under Schedule E.

6 Paragraph 4 above does not apply [in relation to the holder of any licence]¹ if the profits or gains arose or the chargeable gains accrued to the person on whom the assessment is made in consequence of a contract made by the holder of the licence before 23rd March 1973, unless he is a person connected with the holder within the meaning of section [839 of the Taxes Act 1988]² or the contract was substantially varied on or after that date.

Commentary—*Simon's Direct Tax Service* **A3.1421.**
Amendments—¹ Words inserted by FA 1984 s 124(3), (8) and apply in any case where a period of thirty days relevant for the purposes of the service of a notice under paragraph 4 above in relation to any tax expires after 11 March 1984.
² Words substituted by TA 1988 Sch 29 para 32 Table.

7 Where, on an application made by a person who will or might become liable to tax which, if remaining unpaid, could be recovered under paragraph 4 above from the holder of a licence, the Board are satisfied that the applicant will comply with any obligations imposed on him by the Taxes Acts, they may issue a certificate to the holder of the licence exempting him from the provisions of that paragraph with respect to any tax payable by the applicant; and where such a certificate is issued that paragraph shall not apply to any such tax which becomes due while the certificate is in force [or, if the certificate is cancelled under paragraph 8 below, to any such tax which becomes due after the cancellation of the certificate in respect of profits or gains arising while the certificate is in force (referred to below in this Schedule as pre-cancellation profits or gains)].¹

Commentary—*Simon's Direct Tax Service* **A3.1421.**
Amendments—¹ Words added by FA 1984 s 124(4).

[7A—(1) Paragraph 7 above is subject to the following provisions of this paragraph in any case where—

(a) after the cancellation of a certificate issued to the holder of a licence under that paragraph tax is assessed as mentioned in paragraph 4(1)(a) or (b) above on the person who applied for the certificate; and

(b) the relevant profits or gains include (but are not limited to) pre-cancellation profits or gains.

(2) In this paragraph ''the relevant profits or gains'' means—

(a) in a case where the amount of the tax remaining unpaid under the assessment which, but for paragraph 7 above, the holder of the licence could be required to pay by a notice under paragraph 4 above (referred to below in this paragraph as the amount otherwise applicable in his case) is the whole of the amount remaining unpaid, all the profits or gains in respect of which the assessment was made; or

(b) in a case where the amount otherwise applicable in his case falls under paragraph 4A above to be determined by reference to profits or gains in respect of which the licence was the basis for the assessment, the profits or gains in question.

(3) In any case to which this paragraph applies, the amount the holder of the licence may be required to pay by a notice under paragraph 4 shall be the amount otherwise applicable in his case reduced by the amount of the tax remaining unpaid under the assessment which is attributable to the pre-cancellation profits or gains, together with a corresponding proportion of any interest due as mentioned in paragraph 4 (1).

(4) For the purposes of sub-paragraph (3) above the amount of the tax remaining unpaid under the assessment which is attributable to the pre-cancellation profits or gains is such part of the amount otherwise applicable in the case of the holder of the licence as bears to the whole of the amount otherwise so applicable the same proportion as the proportion borne by the amount of the pre-cancellation profits or gains to the total amount of the relevant profits or gains.]¹

Commentary—*Simon's Direct Tax Service* **A3.1421.**
Amendments—¹ This paragraph inserted by FA 1984 s 124(5).

8 The Board may, by notice in writing to the holder of a certificate issued under paragraph 7 above, cancel the certificate from such date, not earlier than thirty days after the service of the notice, as may be specified in the notice.

[8A—(1) For the purposes of paragraphs 4A and 7A above and this paragraph, profits or gains in respect of which an assessment is made as mentioned in paragraph 4(1)(a) or (b) above are profits or gains in respect of which any licence in question was the basis for the assessment if those profits or gains fall within paragraph 4(1)(a) or (b) by reference to that licence.

(2) In determining—

(a) for the purposes of paragraph 4A (2) or 7A (4) above, the amount of the profits or gains in respect of which any licence was the basis for an assessment; or

(b) for the purposes of paragraph 7A (4) above, the amount of any pre-cancellation profits or gains;

the Board shall compute that amount as if for the purposes of making a separate assessment in respect of those profits or gains on the person on whom the assessment was made, making all such allocations and apportionments of receipts, expenses, allowances and deductions taken into account or made for the purposes of the actual assessment as appear to the Board to be just and reasonable in the circumstances.

(3) A notice under paragraph 4 above as it applies by virtue of paragraph 4A or 7A above shall give particulars of the manner in which the amount required to be paid was determined.

(4) References in paragraphs 4A, 7 and 7A above and in this paragraph to profits or gains include chargeable gains.]¹

Commentary—*Simon's Direct Tax Service* A3.1421.
Amendments—¹ This paragraph inserted by FA 1984 s 124(6).

9 In this Schedule ''The Taxes Acts'' has the same meaning as in the Taxes Management Act 1970.

FINANCE ACT 1974

(1974 Chapter 30)

An Act to grant certain duties, to alter other duties, and to amend the law relating to the National Debt and the Public Revenue, and to make further provision in connection with Finance.

[31st July 1974]

PART II

INCOME TAX, CORPORATION TAX AND CAPITAL GAINS TAX
(GENERAL)

24 Returns of persons treated as employees

Where a person performs in the United Kingdom for a continuous period of not less than thirty days duties of an office or employment and—

(a) the office or employment is under or with a person resident outside and not resident in the United Kingdom; but

(b) the duties are performed for the benefit of a person resident or carrying on a trade, profession or vocation in the United Kingdom;

section 15 of the Taxes Management Act 1970 (return of employees) [shall apply as if the person for whose benefit the duties were performed were the employer, but only so as to require him to make a return of the name and place of residence of the person performing the duties;]¹ and any notice given to him under section 8 of the Taxes Management Act 1970 may require a return of his income to include particulars of any emoluments paid to him, whether or not tax is chargeable on them.

Commentary—*Simon's Direct Tax Service* A3.117.
Amendments—¹ Words substituted by FA 1976 Sch 9 para 5 with effect from the year 1976–77.

INTERPRETATION ACT 1978

(1978 Chapter 30)

ARRANGEMENT OF SECTIONS

General provisions as to enactment and operation

An Act to consolidate the Interpretation Act 1889 and certain other enactments relating to the construction and operation of Acts of Parliament and other instruments, with amendments to give effect to recommendations of the Law Commission and the Scottish Law Commission.
[20th July 1978]

General provisions as to enactment and operation

1 Words of enactment

Every section of an Act takes effect as a substantive enactment without introductory words.

3 Judicial notice

Every Act is a public Act to be judicially noticed as such, unless the contrary is expressly provided by the Act.

4 Time of commencement

An Act or provision of an Act comes into force—

(*a*) where provision is made for it to come into force on a particular day, at the beginning of that day;
(*b*) where no provision is made for its coming into force, at the beginning of the day on which the Act receives the Royal Assent.

Interpretation and construction

5 Definitions

In any Act, unless the contrary intention appears, words and expressions listed in Schedule 1 to this Act are to be construed according to that Schedule.

Simon's Tax Cases—*IRC v Clydebridge Properties Ltd* [1980] STC 68*; *IRC v Frampton (Trustees of the Worthing Rugby Football Club)* [1985] STC 186*; *Starke (executors of Brown decd) v IRC* [1995] STC 689.

6 Gender and number

In any Act, unless the contrary intention appears,—

    (*a*) words importing the masculine gender include the feminine;

    (*b*) words importing the feminine gender include the masculine;

    (*c*) words in the singular include the plural and words in the plural include the singular.

Simon's Tax Cases—*Floor v Davis* [1976] STC 475*.

7 References to service by post

Where an Act authorises or requires any document to be served by post (whether the expression "serve" or the expression "give" or "send" or any other expression is used) then, unless the contrary intention appears, the service is deemed to be effected by properly addressing, pre-paying and posting a letter containing the document and, unless the contrary is proved, to have been effected at the time at which the letter would be delivered in the ordinary course of post.

Simon's Tax Cases—*Wing Hung Lai v Bale* [1999] STC (SCD) 238; *Holly v Inspector of Taxes [2000] STC (SCD) 50.*

10 References to the Sovereign

In any Act a reference to the Sovereign reigning at the time of the passing of the Act is to be construed, unless the contrary intention appears, as a reference to the Sovereign for the time being.

11 Construction of subordinate legislation

Where an Act confers power to make subordinate legislation, expressions used in that legislation have, unless the contrary intention appears, the meaning which they bear in the Act.

Statutory powers and duties

12 Continuity of powers and duties

(1) Where an Act confers a power or imposes a duty it is implied, unless the contrary intention appears, that the power may be exercised, or the duty is to be performed, from time to time as occasion requires.

(2) Where an Act confers a power or imposes a duty on the holder of an office as such, it is implied, unless the contrary intention appears, that the power may be exercised, or the duty is to be performed, by the holder for the time being of the office.

13 Anticipatory exercise of powers

Where an Act which (or any provision of which) does not come into force immediately on its passing confers power to make subordinate legislation, or to make appointments, give notices, prescribe forms or do any other thing for the purposes of the Act, then, unless the contrary intention appears, the power may be exercised, and any instrument made thereunder may be made so as to come into force, at any time after the passing of the Act so far as may be necessary or expedient for the purpose—

    (*a*) of bringing the Act or any provision of the Act into force; or

    (*b*) of giving full effect to the Act or any such provision at or after the time when it comes into force.

14 Implied power to amend

Where an Act confers power to make—

    (*a*) rules, regulations or byelaws; or

    (*b*) Orders in Council, orders or other subordinate legislation to be made by statutory instrument,

it implies, unless the contrary intention appears, a power, exercisable in the same manner and subject to the same conditions or limitations, to revoke, amend or re-enact any instrument made under the power.

Repealing enactments

15 Repeal of repeal

Where an Act repeals a repealing enactment, the repeal does not revive any enactment previously repealed unless words are added reviving it.

16 General savings

(1) Without prejudice to section 15, where an Act repeals an enactment, the repeal does not, unless the contrary intention appears,—

    (*a*) revive anything not in force or existing at the time at which the repeal takes effect;

    (*b*) affect the previous operation of the enactment repealed or anything duly done or suffered under that enactment;

(*c*) affect any right, privilege, obligation or liability acquired, accrued or incurred under that enactment;

(*d*) affect any penalty, forfeiture or punishment incurred in respect of any offence committed against that enactment;

(*e*) affect any investigation, legal proceeding or remedy in respect of any such right, privilege, obligation, liability, penalty, forfeiture or punishment;

and any such investigation, legal proceeding or remedy may be instituted, continued or enforced, and any such penalty, forfeiture or punishment may be imposed, as if the repealing Act had not been passed.

(2) This section applies to the expiry of a temporary enactment as if it were repealed by an Act.

17 Repeal and re-enactment

(1) Where an Act repeals a previous enactment and substitutes provisions for the enactment repealed, the repealed enactment remains in force until the substituted provisions come into force.

(2) Where an Act repeals and re-enacts, with or without modification, a previous enactment then, unless the contrary intention appears,—

(*a*) any reference in any other enactment to the enactment so repealed shall be construed as a reference to the provision re-enacted;

(*b*) in so far as any subordinate legislation made or other thing done under the enactment so repealed, or having effect as if so made or done, could have been made or done under the provision re-enacted, it shall have effect as if made or done under that provision.

Miscellaneous

18 Duplicated offences

Where an act or omission constitutes an offence under two or more Acts, or both under an Act and at common law, the offender shall, unless the contrary intention appears, be liable to be prosecuted and punished under either or any of those Acts or at common law, but shall not be liable to be punished more than once for the same offence.

19 Citation of other Acts

(1) Where an Act cites another Act by year, statute, session or chapter, or a section or other portion of another Act by number or letter, the reference shall, unless the contrary intention appears, be read as referring—

(*a*) in the case of Acts included in any revised edition of the statutes printed by authority, to that edition;

(*b*) in the case of Acts not so included but included in the edition prepared under the direction of the Record Commission, to that edition;

(*c*) in any other case, to the Acts printed by the Queen's Printer, or under the superintendence or authority of Her Majesty's Stationery Office.

(2) An Act may continue to be cited by the short title authorised by any enactment notwithstanding the repeal of that enactment.

20 References to other enactments

(1) Where an Act describes or cites a portion of an enactment by referring to words, sections or other parts from or to which (or from and to which) the portion extends, the portion described or cited includes the words, sections or other parts referred to unless the contrary intention appears.

(2) Where an Act refers to an enactment, the reference, unless the contrary intention appears, is a reference to that enactment as amended, and includes a reference thereto as extended or applied, by or under any other enactment, including any other provision of that Act.

Supplementary

21 Interpretation etc

(1) In this Act "Act" includes a local and personal or private Act; and "subordinate legislation" means Orders in Council, orders, rules, regulations, schemes, warrants, byelaws and other instruments made or to be made under any Act.

(2) This Act binds the Crown.

26 Commencement

This Act shall come into force on 1st January 1979.

27 Short title

This Act may be cited as the Interpretation Act 1978.

SCHEDULES

SCHEDULE 1

WORDS AND EXPRESSIONS DEFINED

Section 5

Simon's Tax Cases—*IRC v Clydebridge Properties Ltd* [1980] STC 68*; *IRC v Frampton (Trustees of the Worthing Rugby Football Club)* [1985] STC 186*; *Starke (executors of Brown decd) v IRC* [1995] STC 689.

Note: The years or dates which follow certain entries in the Schedule are relevant for the purposes of paragraph 4 of Schedule 2 (application to existing enactments).

Definitions

"Associated state" means a territory maintaining a status of association with the United Kingdom in accordance with the West Indies Act 1967. [16th February 1967]

"Bank of England" means, as the context requires, the Governor and Company of the Bank of England or the bank of the Governor and Company of the Bank of England.

"Bank of Ireland" means, as the context requires, the Governor and Company of the Bank of Ireland or the bank of the Governor and Company of the Bank of Ireland.

"British Islands" means the United Kingdom, the Channel Islands and the Isle of Man. [1889]

["British overseas territory" has the same meaning as in the British Nationality Act 1981.]

"British possession" means any part of Her Majesty's dominions outside the United Kingdom; and where parts of such dominions are under both a central and a local legislature, all parts under the central legislature are deemed, for the purposes of this definition, to be one British possession. [1889]

...

"Building regulations", in relation to England and Wales, [has the meaning given by section 122 of the Building Act 1984].

"Central funds", in an enactment providing in relation to England and Wales for the payment of costs out of central funds, means money provided by Parliament.

"Charity Commissioners" means the Charity Commissioners for England and Wales referred to in [section 1 of the Charities Act 1993].

"Church Commissioners" means the Commissioners constituted by the Church Commissioners Measure 1947.

"Colonial legislature", and "legislature" in relation to a British possession, mean the authority, other than the Parliament of the United Kingdom or Her Majesty in Council, competent to make laws for the possession. [1889]

"Colony" means any part of Her Majesty's dominions outside the British Islands except—

(*a*) countries having fully responsible status within the Commonwealth;

(*b*) territories for whose external relations a country other than the United Kingdom is responsible;

(*c*) associated states;

and where parts of such dominions are under both a central and a local legislature, all parts under the central legislature are deemed for the purposes of this definition to be one colony. [1889]

"Commencement", in relation to an Act or enactment, means the time when the Act or enactment comes into force.

"Committed for trial" means—

(*a*) *in relation to England and Wales, committed in custody or on bail by a magistrates' court pursuant to [section 6 of the Magistrates' Courts Act 1980], or by any judge or other authority having power to do so, with a view to trial before a judge and jury; [1889]*

(*b*) in relation to Northern Ireland, committed in custody or on bail by a magistrates' court pursuant to [Article 37 of the Magistrates' Courts (Northern Ireland) Order 1981], or by a court, judge, resident magistrate, justice of the peace or other authority having power to do so, with a view to trial on indictment. [1st January 1979]

"The Communities", "the Treaties" or "the Community Treaties" and other expressions defined by section 1 of and Schedule 1 to the European Communities Act 1972 have the meanings prescribed by that Act.

"Comptroller and Auditor General" means the Comptroller-General of the receipt and issue of Her Majesty's Exchequer and Auditor-General of Public Accounts appointed in pursuance of the Exchequer and Audit Departments Act 1866.

"Consular officer" has the meaning assigned by Article 1 of the Vienna Convention set out in Schedule 1 to the Consular Relations Act 1968.

["The Corporation Tax Acts" means the enactments relating to the taxation of the income and chargeable gains of companies and of company distributions (including provisions relating to income tax).]

"County court" means—

(*a*) in relation to England and Wales, a court held for a district under [the County Courts Act 1984]; [1846]

(*b*) in relation to Northern Ireland, a court held for a division under the County Courts [(Northern Ireland) Order 1980]. [1889]

"Court of Appeal" means—

(*a*) in relation to England and Wales, Her Majesty's Court of Appeal in England;

(*b*) in relation to Northern Ireland, Her Majesty's Court of Appeal in Northern Ireland.

"Court of summary jurisdiction", "summary conviction" and "Summary Jurisdiction Acts", in relation to Northern Ireland, have the same meanings as in Measures of the Northern Ireland Assembly and Acts of the Parliament of Northern Ireland.

"Crown Court" means—

(*a*) in relation to England and Wales, the Crown Court constituted by section 4 of the Courts Act 1971;

(*b*) in relation to Northern Ireland, the Crown Court constituted by section 4 of the Judicature (Northern Ireland) Act 1978.

"Crown Estate Commissioners" means the Commissioners referred to in section 1 of the Crown Estate Act 1961.

"England" means, subject to any alteration of boundaries under Part IV of the Local Government Act 1972 the area consisting of the countries established by section 1 of that Act, Greater London and the Isles of Scilly. [1st April 1974]

"Financial year" means, in relation to matters relating to the Consolidated Fund, the National Loans Fund, or moneys provided by Parliament, or to the Exchequer or to central taxes or finance, the twelve months ending with 31st March. [1889]

"Governor-General" includes any person who for the time being has the powers of the Governor-General, and "Governor", in relation to any British possession, includes the officer for the time being administering the government of that possession. [1889]

"High Court" means—

(*a*) in relation to England and Wales, Her Majesty's High Court of Justice in England;

(*b*) in relation to Northern Ireland, Her Majesty's High Court of Justice in Northern Ireland.

"The Income Tax Acts" means all enactments relating to income tax, including any provisions of the Corporation Tax Acts which relate to income tax.

"Land" includes buildings and other structures, land covered with water, and any estate, interest, easement, servitude or right in or over land. [1st January 1979]

"Land Clauses Acts" means—

(*a*) in relation to England and Wales, the Land Clauses Consolidation Act 1845 and the Lands Clauses Consolidation Acts Amendment Act 1860, and any Acts for the time being in force amending those Acts; [1889]

(*b*) in relation to Scotland, the Lands Clauses Consolidation (Scotland) Act 1845 and the Lands Clauses Consolidation Acts Amendment Act 1860, and any Acts for the time being in force amending those Acts; [1889]

(*c*) in relation to Northern Ireland, the enactments defined as such by section 46(1) of the Interpretation Act (Northern Ireland) 1954. [1889]

"Local land charges register", in relation to England and Wales, means a register kept pursuant to section 3 of the Local Land Charges Act 1975 and "the appropriate local land charges register" has the meaning assigned by section 4 of that Act.

"London borough" means a borough described in Schedule 1 to the London Government Act 1963 "inner London borough" means one of the boroughs so described and numbered from 1 to 12 and "outer London borough" means one of the boroughs so described and numbered from 13 to 32, subject (in each case) to any alterations made under Part IV of the Local Government Act 1972 [or Part II of the Local Government Act 1992].

"Lord Chancellor" means the Lord High Chancellor of Great Britain.

"Magistrates' court" has the meaning assigned to it—

(*a*) in relation to England and Wales, by [section 148 of the Magistrates' Courts Act 1980];

(*b*) in relation to Northern Ireland, by [Article 2(2) of the Magistrates' Courts (Northern Ireland) Order 1981].

"Month" means calendar month. [1850]

"National Debt Commissioners" means the Commissioners for the Reduction of the National Debt.

"Northern Ireland legislation" has the meaning assigned by section 24(5) of this Act. [1st January 1979]

"Oath" and "affidavit" include affirmation and declaration, and "swear" includes affirm and declare.

"Ordnance Map" means a map made under powers conferred by the Ordnance Survey Act 1841 or the Boundary Survey (Ireland) Act 1854.

"Parliamentary Election" means the election of a Member to serve in Parliament for a constituency. [1889]

"Person" includes a body of persons corporate or unincorporate. [1889]

"Police area", "police authority" and other expressions relating to the police have the meaning or effect described—

(a) in relation to England and Wales, by [section 101(1) of the Police Act 1996];

(b) in relation to Scotland, by sections 50 and 51(4) of the Police (Scotland) Act 1967.

["Police Service of Northern Ireland" and "Police Service of Northern Ireland Reserve" have the same meaning as in the Police (Northern Ireland) Act 2000.]

"The Privy Council" means the Lords and others of Her Majesty's Most Honourable Privy Council.

["Registered" in relation to nurses, midwives and health visitors, means registered in the register maintained by the United Kingdom Central Council for Nursing, Midwifery and Health Visiting by virtue of qualifications in nursing, midwifery or health visiting, as the case may be.]

"Registered medical practitioner" means a fully registered person within the meaning of [the Medical Act 1983]. [1st January 1979]

"Rules of Court" in relation to any court means rules made by the authority having power to make rules or orders regulating the practice and procedure of that court, and in Scotland includes Acts of Adjournal and Acts of Sederunt; and the power of the authority to make rules of court (as above defined) includes power to make such rules for the purpose of any Act which directs or authorises anything to be done by rules of court. [1889]

"Secretary of State" means one of Her Majesty's Principal Secretaries of State.

["Sewerage undertaker, in relation to England and Wales, shall be construed in accordance with [section 6 of the Water Industry Act 1991].]

"Sheriff", in relation to Scotland, includes sheriff principal. [1889]

["The standard scale", with reference to a fine or penalty for an offence triable only summarily,—

(a) in relation to England and Wales, has the meaning given by section 37 of the Criminal Justice Act 1982;

(b) in relation to Scotland, has the meaning given by section 289G of the Criminal Procedure (Scotland) Act 1975;

(c) in relation to Northern Ireland, has the meaning given by Article 5 of the Fines and Penalties (Northern Ireland) Order 1984.]

"Statutory declaration" means a declaration made by virtue of the Statutory Declarations Act 1835.

["Statutory maximum", with reference to a fine or penalty on summary conviction for an offence,—

(a) in relation to England and Wales, means the prescribed sum within the meaning of section 32 of the Magistrates' Courts Act 1980;

(b) in relation to Scotland, means the prescribed sum within the meaning of section 289B(6) of the Criminal Procedure (Scotland) Act 1975; and

(c) in relation to Northern Ireland, means the prescribed sum within the meaning of Article 4 of the Fines and Penalties (Northern Ireland) Order 1984.]

"Supreme Court" means—

(a) in relation to England and Wales, the Court of Appeal and the High Court together with the Crown Court;

(b) in relation to Northern Ireland, the Supreme Court of Judicature of Northern Ireland.

["The Tax Acts" means the Income Tax Acts and the Corporation Tax Acts.]

["Transfer for trial" means the transfer of proceedings against an accused to the Crown Court for trial under section 7 of the Magistrates' Courts Act 1980.]

"The Treasury" means the Commissioners of Her Majesty's Treasury.

["Trust of land" and "trustees of land", in relation to England and Wales, have the same meanings as in the Trusts of Land and Appointment of Trustees Act 1996.]

"United Kingdom" means Great Britain and Northern Ireland. [12th April 1927]

["Wales" means the combined area of counties which were created by section 20 of the Local Government Act 1972, as originally enacted, but subject to any alteration made under section 73 of that Act (consequential alteration of boundary following alteration of watercourse).]

["Water undertaker", in relation to England and Wales, shall be construed in accordance with [section 6 of the Water Industry Act 1991].]

"Writing" includes typing, printing, lithography, photography and other modes of representing or reproducing words in a visible form, and expressions referring to writing are construed accordingly.

...

Construction of certain expressions relating to offences

In relation to England and Wales—

(a) "indictable offence" means an offence which, if committed by an adult, is triable on indictment, whether it is exclusively so triable or triable either way;

(b) "summary offence" means an offence which, if committed by an adult, is triable only summarily;

(c) "offence triable either way" means an offence [, other than an offence triable on indictment only by virtue of Part V of the Criminal Justice Act 1988] which, if committed by an adult, is triable either on indictment or summarily;

and the terms "indictable", "summary" and "triable either way", in their application to offences, are to be construed accordingly.

In the above definitions references to the way or ways in which an offence is triable are to be construed without regard to the effect, if any, of [section 22 of the Magistrates' Courts Act 1980] on the mode of trial in a particular case.

[Construction of certain references to relationships

In relation to England and Wales—

(a) references (however expressed) to any relationship between two persons;

(b) references to a person whose father and mother were or were not married to each other at the time of his birth; and

(c) references cognate with references falling within paragraph (b) above,

shall be construed in accordance with section 1 of the Family Law Reform Act 1987. [4th April 1988]]

Cross references—See TA 1988 s 834(1) (meaning of "financial year" for the purposes of Corporation Tax Acts). Family Law Reform Act 1987: Section 1 of that Act reads as follows—

"1 General principle

(1) In this Act and enactments passed and instruments made after the coming into force of this section, references (however expressed) to any relationship between two persons shall, unless the contrary intention appears, be construed without regard to whether or not the father and mother of either of them, or the father and mother of any person through whom the relationship is deduced, have or had been married to each other at any time.

(2) In this Act and enactments passed after the coming into force of this section, unless the contrary intention appears—

(a) references to a person whose father and mother were married to each other at the time of his birth include; and

(b) references to a person whose father and mother were not married to each other at the time of his birth do not include,

references to any person to whom subsection (3) below applies, and cognate references shall be construed accordingly.

(3) This subsection applies to any person who—

(a) is treated as legitimate by virtue of section 1 of the Legitimacy Act 1976;

(b) is a legitimated person within the meaning of section 10 of that Act;

(c) is an adopted child within the meaning of Part IV of the Adoption Act 1976; or

(d) is otherwise treated in law as legitimate.

(4) For the purpose of construing references falling within subsection (2) above, the time of a person's birth shall be taken to include any time during the period beginning with—

(a) the insemination resulting in his birth; or

(b) where there was no such insemination, his conception,

and (in either case) ending with his birth."

Amendments—The definition of "British overseas territory" inserted by the British Overseas Territories Act 2002 s 1(3) with effect from 26 February 2002.

The definitions of "British subject" and "Commonwealth citizen" repealed by the British Nationality Act 1981 Sch 9.

Words in the definition of "Building regulations" substituted by the Building Act 1984 Sch 6 para 19.

Words in the definition of "Charity Commissioners" substituted by the Charities Act 1993 s 98(1) Sch 6 para 15.

Words in the definition of "Committed for trial" substituted by the Magistrates' Courts Act 1980 Sch 7 para 169 and the Magistrates' Courts (Northern Ireland) Order, SI 1981/1675 Sch 6 para 56. The whole of para(a) of this definition is repealed, as from a day to be appointed, by the Criminal Justice and Public Order Act 1994 Sch 4 para 28(a), Sch 11.

The definition of "The Corporation Tax Acts" substituted by FA 1987 s 71 Sch 15 para 12.

Words in the definition of "County court" substituted by the County Courts Act 1984 Sch 2 para 68 and the County Courts (Northern Ireland) Order, SI 1980/397 Sch 1 Pt II.

Words in the definition of "London borough" inserted by the Local Government Act 1992 s 27(1) Sch 3 para 21.

Words in para (a) of the definition of "Magistrates' court" substituted by the Magistrates' Courts Act 1980 s 154 Sch 7 para 169 and, in para (b), by the Magistrates' Court (Northern Ireland) Order, SI 1981/1675 art 170(2) Sch 6 Pt I para 56.

Words in the definition of "police area substituted by the Police Act 1996 Sch 7 para 32.

Definition of "Police Service of Northern Ireland" and "Police Service of Northern Ireland Reserve" inserted by the Police (Northern Ireland) Act 2000 s 78(1), Sch 6 para 5 with effect from 4 December 2001 (by virtue of SR 2001/396).

The definition of "Registered" inserted by the Nurses, Midwives and Health Visitors Act 1979 Sch 7 para 30.

Words in the definition of "Registered medical practitioner" substituted by the Medical Act 1983 Sch 5 para 18.

The definition of "Sewerage undertaker" inserted by the Water Act 1989 s 190(1), Sch 25 para 55(1), (2), as amended by the Water Consolidation (Consequential Provisions) Act 1991 s 2(1) Sch 1 para 32.

The definition of "The standard scale" inserted by the Criminal Justice Act 1988 s 170(1) Sch 15 para 58(a).

The definition of "Statutory maximum" inserted by the Criminal Justice Act 1988 s 170(1) Sch 15 para 58(b).

The definition of "The Tax Acts" substituted by FA 1987 s 71 Sch 15 para 12.

The definition "Transfer for trial" inserted by the Criminal Justice and Public Order Act 1994 Sch 4 para 28(b), as from a day to be appointed.

The definitions of "Trust of land" and trustees of land" inserted by the Trusts of Land and Appointment of Trustees Act 1996 s 25(1), Sch 3 para 16, as from a day to be appointed.

The definition of "Wales" substituted by the Local Government (Wales) Act 1994 Sch 2 para 9.

The definition of "Water undertaker" substituted for the definitions "Water authority" and "Water authority area" by the Water Act 1989 s 190(1) Sch 25 para 55(1), (3), as amended by the Water Consolidation (Consequential Provisions) Act 1991 s 2(1) Sch 1 para 32.

The entry relating to the construction of certain expressions relating to children is repealed by the Children Act 1989 s 108(7) Sch 15.

In the entry relating to the construction of certain expressions relating to offences (i) the words in the definition "offence triable either way" inserted by the Criminal Justice Act 1988 s 170(1) Sch 15 para 59; (ii) the words "section 22 of the Magistrates' Courts Act 1980" substituted by the Magistrates' Courts Act 1980 s 154 Sch 7 para 169.

The entry relating to the construction of references to relationships added at the end by the Family Law Reform Act 1987 s 33(1), Sch 2 para 73.
Prospective amendments—Definition of "Registered" to be substituted by the Nursing and Midwifery Order 2001, SI 2002/253, art 54, Sch 5 para 7 with effect from a date to be appointed. The substituted definition to read as follows—

"Registered" in relation to nurses and midwives, means registered in the register maintained under article 5 of the Nurses and Midwives Order 2001 by virtue of qualifications in nursing or midwifery, as the case may be."

SCHEDULE 2

APPLICATION OF ACT TO EXISTING ENACTMENTS

PART I

ACTS

1 The following provisions of this Act apply to Acts whenever passed—

Section 6(*a*) and (*c*) so far as applicable to enactments relating to offences punishable on indictment or on summary conviction

    Section 9
    Section 10
    Section 11 so far as it relates to subordinate legislation made after the year 1889
    Section 18
    Section 19(2).

2 The following apply to Acts passed after the year 1850—

    Section 1
    Section 3
    Section 6(*a*) and (*c*) so far as not applicable to such Acts by virtue of paragraph 1
    Section 15
    Section 17(1)

3 The following apply to Acts passed after the year 1889—

    Section 4
    Section 7
    Section 12
    Section 13
    Section 14 so far as it relates to rules, regulations or byelaws
    Section 16(1)
    Section 17(2)(*a*)
    Section 19(1)
    Section 20(1)

4—(1) Subject to the following provisions of this paragraph—

(*a*) paragraphs of Schedule 1 at the end of which a year or date ...¹ is specified [or described]² apply, so far as applicable, to Acts passed on or after the date, or after the year, so specified [or described]²; and
(*b*) paragraphs of the Schedule at the end of which no year or date is specified [or described]² apply, so far as applicable, to Acts passed at any time.

(4) The definition of "Lord Chancellor" does not apply to Acts passed before 1st October 1921 in which that expression was used in relation to Ireland only.

(5) The definition of "person", so far as it includes bodies corporate, applies to any provision of an Act whenever passed relating to an offence punishable on indictment or on summary conviction.

Note—Omitted provisions are outside the scope of this publication.
Amendments—¹ Words in sub-para (1)(*a*) repealed by the Family Law Reform Act 1987 s 33(1) Sch 2 para 74, Sch 4, with effect from 4 April 1988, by virtue of the Family Law Reform Act 1987 (Commencement No 1) Order, SI 1988/425.
² Words in sub-para (1)(*a*), (*b*) inserted by the Family Law Reform Act 1987 s 33(1) Sch 2 para 74, Sch 4, with effect from 4 April 1988, by virtue of the Family Law Reform Act 1987 (Commencement No 1) Order, SI 1988/425.

5 The following definitions shall be treated as included in Schedule 1 for the purposes specified in this paragraph—

(*a*) in any Act passed before 1st April 1974, a reference to England includes Berwick upon Tweed and Monmouthshire and, in the case of an Act passed before the Welsh Language Act 1967 Wales;
(*b*) in any Act passed before the commencement of this Act and after the year 1850, "land", includes messuages, tenements and hereditaments, houses and buildings of any tenure;
(*c*) in any Act passed before the commencement of the Criminal Procedure (Scotland) Act 1975 "the Summary Jurisdiction (Scotland) Acts" means Part II of that Act.

PART II
SUBORDINATE LEGISLATION

7 The definition in Schedule 1 of "county court", in relation to England and Wales, applies to Orders in Council made after the year 1846.

FINANCE ACT 1978

(1978 Chapter 42)

PART V
MISCELLANEOUS AND SUPPLEMENTARY

77 Disclosure of information to tax authorities in other member States

(1) No obligation as to secrecy imposed by statute or otherwise shall preclude the Commissioners of Inland Revenue or an authorised officer of those Commissioners from disclosing to the competent authorities of another member State any information required to be so disclosed by virtue of the Directive of the Council of the European Communities dated 19th December 1977 No 77/799/EEC.

(2) Neither the Commissioners nor an authorised officer shall disclose any information in pursuance of the said Directive unless satisfied that the competent authorities of the other State are bound by, or have undertaken to observe, rules of confidentiality with respect to the information which are not less strict than those applying to it in the United Kingdom.

(3) Nothing in this section shall permit the Commissioners of Inland Revenue or an authorised officer of those Commissioners to authorise the use of information disclosed by virtue of the said Directive other than for the purposes of taxation or to facilitate legal proceedings for failure to observe the tax laws of the receiving State.

Commentary—*Simon's Direct Tax Service* A2.803.
Revenue Internal Guidance—Investigations Handbook IH 421 (exchange of information is dealt with by London Special Compliance Office).
Note—Directive 77/799/EEC is reproduced in Part II of this publication.

FINANCE ACT 1982

(1982 Chapter 39)

An Act to grant certain duties, to alter other duties, and to amend the law relating to the National Debt and the Public Revenue, and to make further provision in connection with Finance.

[30th July 1982]

PART VI
OIL TAXATION

CHAPTER I
GENERAL

137 Expenditure met by regional development grants to be disregarded for certain purposes

(1) (*amends* Oil Taxation Act 1975 Sch 3 para 8(1)).

(2) ...[2]

(3) ...[2]

(4), (5) ...[1]

(6) ...[2]

(7) ...[2]

Commentary—*Simon's Direct Tax Service* B2.111.
Notes—The principal Act referred to in this section is the Oil Taxation Act 1975.
Regional development grants ceased to be made under Industrial Development Act 1982 after 31 August 1988 except on applications made before that date (Regional Development Grants (Termination) Act 1988 s 1).
Cross references—See TA 1988 s 495 (3) (certain expenditure met by regional development grants not to be disregarded notwithstanding the provisions of this section).

Amendments—[1] Sub-ss (4), (5) repealed by TA 1988 Sch 31.
[2] Sub-ss (2), (3), (6) and (7) repealed by CAA 2001 ss 578, 580, Sch 2 para 6, Sch 4 with effect for income tax purposes, as respects allowances and charges falling to be made for chargeable periods ending after 5 April 2001, and for corporation tax purposes, as respects allowances and charges falling to be made for chargeable periods ending after 31 March 2001.

FINANCE ACT 1984

(1984 Chapter 43)

An Act to grant certain duties, to alter other duties, and to amend the law relating to the National Debt and the Public Revenue, and to make further provision in connection with Finance.

[26th July 1984]

PART II

INCOME TAX, CORPORATION TAX AND CAPITAL GAINS TAX ETC

70 Postponement of tax due from beneficiaries on gains of non-resident trustees

(1) The provisions of Schedule 14 to this Act have effect in any case where,—

(a) before 6th April 1981, a chargeable gain accrued to the trustees of a settlement in such circumstances that section 17 of the Capital Gains Tax Act 1979 (non-resident trust) applies as respects that chargeable gain; and(a) before 6th April 1981, a chargeable gain accrued to the trustees of a settlement in such circumstances that section 17 of the Capital Gains Tax Act 1979 (non-resident trust) applies as respects that chargeable gain; and

(b) by virtue of that section a beneficiary under the settlement is treated for the purposes of that Act as if, in the year 1983–84 or any earlier year of assessment, an amount determined by reference to the chargeable gain which accrued to the trustees or, as the case may be, the whole or part of that gain had been a chargeable gain accruing to the beneficiary; and

(c) at 29th March 1983 some or all of the capital gains tax payable in respect of the chargeable gain accruing to the beneficiary had not been paid.

(2)   (amended CGTA 1979 s 17(3)(b)).

(3)   (amends FA 1981 s 80(8)).

(b) by virtue of that section a beneficiary under the settlement is treated for the purposes of that Act as if, in the year 1983–84 or any earlier year of assessment, an amount determined by reference to the chargeable gain which accrued to the trustees or, as the case may be, the whole or part of that gain had been a chargeable gain accruing to the beneficiary; and

(c) at 29th March 1983 some or all of the capital gains tax payable in respect of the chargeable gain accruing to the beneficiary had not been paid.

(2)   (amended CGTA 1979 s 17(3)(b)).

(3)   (amends FA 1981 s 80(8)).

(4) In this section and Schedule 14 to this Act "settlement", "settlor" and "settled property" have the same meaning as in section 17 of the Capital Gains Tax Act 1979.

In this section and Schedule 14 to this Act "settlement", "settlor" and "settled property" have the same meaning as in section 17 of the Capital Gains Tax Act 1979.

Cross references—See TCGA 1992 Sch 11 para 18(*b*) (notwithstanding repeal of this section by TCGA 1992 Sch 12, it continues to have effect in relation to tax postponed under Sch 14 of this Act).
Amendments—This section is repealed by TCGA 1992 s 290 Sch 12, subject to a saving in TCGA 1992 Sch 11 para 18(*b*) in relation to amounts of tax which are postponed under FA 1984 Sch 14.

CHAPTER IV

INSURANCE

73 Insurance business of registered friendly societies

(1)–(3) ...[1]

(4) In consequence of the preceding provisions of this section and subsection (5) below, in ...[2] section 7 of the Friendly Societies Act 1974 (societies which may be registered),—

(*aa*) paragraph (*aa*) of subsection (3), and
(*bb*) subsection (3A),

shall not have effect with respect to benefits secured by contracts made after 13th March 1984.

(5), (6) ...[1]

(7) If, after 13th March 1984, the committee of a registered society or branch whose rules make provision for it to carry on life or endowment business resolve to accept, in respect of any contract falling within subsection (8) below, premiums of amounts arrived at by deducting 15 percent from the premiums provided for by the rules of the society or branch (that is to say by deducting the same amount as, apart from section 72 above, would have been deductible by way of relief under section 19 of the Taxes Act),—

    (*aa*) the resolution shall be deemed to be permitted by the principal Act and the rules of the society or branch; and

    (*bb*) nothing in the principal Act shall require the registration of the resolution; and

    (c) together with the annual return of the society or branch for the year of account ending 31st December 1984, the society or branch shall send a copy of the resolution to the registrar.

(8) Subsection (7) above applies to any contract entered into by a registered society or branch—

    (*aa*) which is for the assurance under life or endowment business of any gross sum; and

    (*bb*) which is entered into pursuant to a proposal received by the society or branch on or before 13th March 1984; and

    (*cc*) which is one which the society might lawfully have entered into on that date; and

    (*dd*) which is entered into after 13th March 1984 and before 1st May 1984.

(9) In subsection (7) above "the principal Act" means, ...[2]

    (*bb*) the Friendly Societies Act 1974;

and subsections (7) and (8) above shall be construed as one with the principal Act.

Commentary—*Simon's Direct Tax Service* **A3.620; E2.1047.**
Amendments—[1] Sub-ss (1)–(3), (5), (6) repealed by TA 1988 Sch 31.
[2] Words in sub-ss (4), (9) repealed by Friendly Societies Act 1992 Sch 22 as from 1 January 1994 by virtue of the Friendly Societies Act 1992 (Commencement No 7 and Transitional Provisions and Savings) Order, SI 1993/3226.

SCHEDULES

SCHEDULE 14

BENEFICIARY'S LIABILITY FOR TAX ON GAINS OF NON-RESIDENT TRUSTEES

Section 70

Cross references—See TCGA 1992 Sch 11 para 18(*b*) (notwithstanding repeal of this Schedule by TCGA 1992 Sch 12, it continues to have effect in relation to tax postponed under this Schedule).
Amendments—This Schedule is repealed by TCGA 1992 s 290 Sch 12, subject to a saving in TCGA 1992 Sch 11 para 18(*b*) in relation to amounts of tax which are postponed under FA 1984 Sch 14.

Interpretation

1—*(1) In this Schedule—*

    "attributed gain", in relation to the beneficiary, means the chargeable gain which, as mentioned in paragraph (b) of subsection (1) of the principal section, is treated as accruing to him;

    "the beneficiary" means the beneficiary referred to in that paragraph and paragraph (c) of that subsection;

    "claim" means a claim under paragraph 2 (1) below;

    "close relative", in relation to any person, means his spouse or a child or remoter descendant of his;

    "ineligible gain" shall be construed in accordance with paragraph 2 (3) below;

    "offshore income gain" has the same meaning as in Chapter [V of Part XVII of the Taxes Act 1988];—[1](1) In this Schedule—

    "the principal Act" means the Capital Gains Tax Act 1979;

    "the principal section" means section 70 of this Act;

    "related settlement" shall be construed in accordance with paragraph 5 (6) below;

    "relevant benefit" shall be construed in accordance with paragraph 5 below; and

    "the relevant year of assessment", in relation to an attributed gain, means the year of assessment in which the gain is treated as accruing to the beneficiary.

(2) Subject to subsection (4) of the principal section, section 83 of the Finance Act 1981 (meaning of "capital payment" etc) applies for the purposes of this Schedule as it applies for the purposes of sections 80 to 82 of that Act.

(3) In any case where the beneficiary is a married woman, any reference in the following provisions of this Schedule to the payment of capital gains tax by the beneficiary shall be construed as including a reference to the payment by her husband of capital gains tax which, under subsection (1) of section 45 of the principal Act, is assessed and charged on him.

Amendments—[1] Words in sub-para (1) substituted by TA 1988 Sch 29 para 32 Table.

Claims for postponement of tax

2—*(1) Subject to sub-paragraph (3) below, in a case falling within the principal section, the provisions of this Schedule have effect to determine whether, on a claim made to the Board, payment of any of the capital gains tax referable to an attributed gain may be postponed and, if so, to what extent and for how long.*

(2) A claim must be made before 1st July 1985 or, if it is later, the expiry of the period of thirty days beginning with the date of the issue of a notice of assessment requiring the payment of an amount of capital gains tax assessed, in whole or in part, by reason of an attributed gain to which the claim relates.

(3) The provisions of this Schedule do not have effect to allow postponement of the payment of the capital gains tax referable to an attributed gain if the capital gains tax chargeable on the gain—

    (a) has previously been postponed under section 17(4) (b) of the principal Act (pre-6th April 1965 settlements); or

    (b) subject to sub-paragraph (4) below, carries interest, by virtue of section 88(1) of the Taxes Management Act 1970 (interest on tax recovered to make good tax lost due to fraud, wilful default or neglect), from the date on which the tax ought to have been paid until payment;

and an attributed gain falling within paragraph (a) or paragraph (b) above is in this Schedule referred to as an ineligible gain.

(4) Sub-paragraph (3) (b) above does not apply where the tax carries interest by reason only of the neglect of any person and that neglect is remedied before 1st July 1985.

(5) In relation to a claim, any reference in this Schedule to an attributed gain to which the claim relates is a reference to such a gain—

    (a) which is specified in the claim, and

    (b) which is not an ineligible gain, and

    (c) in respect of which the claim is not out of time by virtue of sub-paragraph (2) above,

and any reference to the settlement to which the claim relates is a reference to the settlement under which the beneficiary is a beneficiary and to the trustees of which accrued the chargeable gain which gives rise to the attributed gain or gains to which the claim relates.

(6) In a case where a claim relates to attributed gains accruing to the beneficiary by virtue of more than one settlement, the provisions of this Schedule shall have effect as if there were separate claims, each relating to the attributed gain or gains accruing by virtue of a single settlement.

(7) Without prejudice to the application of sub-paragraph (2) above in a case where the personal representatives of the beneficiary receive a notice of assessment requiring the payment by them of an amount of capital gains tax assessed, in whole or in part, by reason of an attributed gain, if—

    (a) before his death the beneficiary or, where paragraph 1(3) above applies, the beneficiary's husband received a notice of assessment requiring the payment by him of such an amount of capital gains tax, and

    (b) at the time of his death the period within which he might make a claim in respect of any of the tax assessed by that notice had not expired,

a claim by his personal representatives relating to that tax may be made at any time before the expiry of the period of six months beginning on the date of the death of the beneficiary or, as the case may be, her husband (or, if it is later, before 1st July 1985).

(8) In relation to any claim by the personal representatives of the beneficiary, references in this Schedule to the postponement of the payment of any tax shall be construed as references to the discharge of that tax and, accordingly, paragraphs 11 and 12 below do not apply where a claim is made by the personal representatives.

Commentary—*Simon's Direct Tax Service* **C4.462.**

Tax referable to attributed gains

3—*(1) Any reference in this Schedule to the tax referable to an attributed gain is a reference to the amount determined by multiplying the total capital gains tax on chargeable gains accruing to the beneficiary in the relevant year of assessment by a fraction—*

    (a) of which the numerator is the amount of the attributed gain; and

    (b) the denominator is the total of the chargeable gains accruing to the beneficiary in the relevant year of assessment.

Initial calculations relevant to tax which may be postponed

4—*(1) Where a claim is made, the determination referred to in paragraph 2(1) above shall, in the first instance, be made (in accordance with paragraph 6 below) by reference to—*

    (a) the amount defined in sub-paragraph (4) below as the unpaid tax;

    (b) the amount defined in sub-paragraph (5) below as the tax already paid; and

    (c) the aggregate value of any relevant benefits which, by virtue of paragraph 5 below, fall to be taken into account in relation to the claim.

(2) Subject to sub-paragraph (3) below, in this paragraph and paragraph 5 below "the base year" means the year of assessment which precedes the relevant year of assessment in relation to the attributed gain or, as the case may be, the earliest of the attributed gains to which the claim relates.

(3) Where the relevant year of assessment referred to in sub-paragraph (2) above is the year 1965–66, the base year is also that year of assessment.

(4) In relation to a claim "the unpaid tax" means the amount of tax—

    (a) which is referable to the attributed gain (or attributed gains) to which the claim relates; and
    (b) which remains unpaid at the date of the claim.

(5) In relation to a claim, "the tax already paid" means the amount of tax—

    (a) which has been paid at the date of the claim, excluding any tax which was so paid, or is or was otherwise borne, by the trustees of the settlement to which the claim relates; and
    (b) which is referable to any attributed gains—

        (i) which have accrued to the beneficiary by virtue of the settlement to which the claim relates; and
        (ii) for which the relevant year of assessment is, or is later than, the base year; and
        (iii) which are not ineligible gains.

Relevant benefits

5—*(1) The provisions of this paragraph have effect to determine what are the relevant benefits to be taken into account (as mentioned in paragraph 4(1)(c) above) in relation to a claim; and in the following provisions of this paragraph "the calculation period" means the period beginning at the beginning of the base year and ending on 9th March 1981.*

(2) Subject to sub-paragraph (3) below, if, under or by reference to the settlement to which the claim relates or a related settlement, the beneficiary received a capital payment from the trustees of the settlement—

    (a) at any time in the calculation period, or
    (b) after the end of that period but before 6th April 1984, in so far as that payment represented a chargeable gain which, before 6th April 1981, accrued to the trustees of the settlement to which the claim relates,

the amount of that capital payment is a relevant benefit.

(3) In any case where, apart from this sub-paragraph, sub-paragraph (2) above would bring into account, as a relevant benefit in relation to a claim, a capital payment received under or by reference to a related settlement, and either—

    (a) on a claim relating to the related settlement, the payment falls to be taken into account under this paragraph as a relevant benefit, or
    (b) it appears to the Board to be likely that the payment will fall to be so taken into account on a claim relating to the related settlement,

the payment shall not be taken into account as a relevant benefit in relation to the claim referred to in sub-paragraph (2) above except to the extent that it constitutes a surplus benefit by virtue of paragraph 6(5) below.

(4) If, at any time in the period beginning at the beginning of the base year and ending at the beginning of the year of assessment in which the claim is made, the beneficiary disposed of his interest in the settlement to which the claim relates in circumstances such that, by virtue of section 58(1) of the principal Act, no chargeable gain could accrue on the disposal, then the amount or value of the consideration for the disposal is a relevant benefit.

(5) Where the disposal referred to in sub-paragraph (4) above was made before 6th April 1984, the reference in that sub-paragraph to the consideration for the disposal shall be construed as a reference only to such consideration (if any) as was actually given for the disposal.

(6) For the purposes of this Schedule, a settlement is a related settlement in relation to the settlement to which a claim relates if, by the exercise in the base year or later (whether before or after the making of the claim) of a power conferred by one of the settlements, or by the combination of such an exercise and any other transactions, property of any description forming part of the settled property of one of the settlements is at any time appointed to the other settlement or otherwise dealt with so as to increase the value of the settled property of the other settlement.

The basic rules as to postponement

6—*(1) Unless on a claim the aggregate of—*

    (a) the unpaid tax (as defined in paragraph 4(4) above), and
    (b) the tax already paid (as defined in paragraph 4(5) above),

exceeds 30 per cent of the aggregate of the relevant benefits referred to in paragraph 4(1)(c) above, there is no postponement of the payment of any of the capital gains tax referable to the attributed gains to which the claim relates.

(2) Subject to the following provisions of this Schedule, the amount of capital gains tax payment of which is, on a claim, postponed by virtue of this Schedule is whichever is the smaller of—

(a) the unpaid tax; and

(b) the amount of the excess referred to in sub-paragraph (1) above;

and, where the amount in paragraph (b) above is the smaller, payment of tax assessed for a later year shall be postponed in priority to payment of tax assessed for an earlier year.

(3) Without prejudice to paragraph 2(8) above, if at any time after a claim is made the beneficiary dies, any tax the payment of which would, by virtue of this Schedule, still be postponed at the date of his death shall be discharged on that date.

(4) Notwithstanding anything in Part IX of the Taxes Management Act 1970 (interest on overdue tax), where payment of an amount of capital gains tax is postponed by virtue of this Schedule none of that tax shall carry interest (or be taken to have carried interest) for any period before the time when the tax becomes payable in accordance with paragraph 11 below.

(5) In any case where, by virtue of sub-paragraph (1) above, there is on a claim no postponement of the payment of capital gains tax, there shall be determined—

(a) whether there would still be no postponement if there were left out of account all relevant benefits (if any) referable to capital payments received under or by reference to a related settlement, and

(b) if so, what is the excess of all the other relevant benefits over 31/3 times the aggregate of the tax referred to in paragraphs (a) and (b) of sub-paragraph (1) above,

and so much of those other relevant benefits as are referable to capital payments falling within sub-paragraph (2) of paragraph 5 above and equal (or do not exceed) that excess shall be regarded as a surplus benefit for the purposes of sub-paragraph (3) of that paragraph.

Effect of subsequent capital payments received by the beneficiary

7—(1) The provisions of this paragraph apply if—

(a) on a claim there would, in accordance with paragraph 6(2) above, be an amount of capital gains tax payment of which is postponed by virtue of this Schedule; but

(b) before the beginning of the year of assessment in which the claim is made, the beneficiary has received from the trustees of the settlement to which the claim relates or a related settlement a capital payment which is not a relevant benefit and has not been brought into account under subsections (3) and (4) of section 80 of the Finance Act 1981 (new provisions as to gain of non-resident settlements) in determining whether chargeable gains or offshore income gains should be attributed to the beneficiary by reference to any trust gains for any previous year of assessment.

(2) If the amount of capital gains tax referred to in paragraph (a) of sub-paragraph (1) above exceeds 30 per cent of the aggregate of the amount of the capital payments which fall within paragraph (b) of that sub-paragraph, then, subject to paragraph 9 below, the amount of capital gains tax payment of which is postponed by virtue of this Schedule is an amount equal to that excess.

(3) If the amount of capital gains tax referred to in paragraph (a) of sub-paragraph (1) above is less than or equal to 30 per cent of the aggregate of the amount of the capital payments which fall within paragraph (b) of that sub-paragraph, then there is no postponement of the payment of any of that capital gains tax.

(4) In any case where—

(a) the amount of capital gains tax referred to in sub-paragraph (1)(a) above equals or exceeds 30 per cent of the aggregate of those capital payments falling within sub-paragraph (1)(b) above which the beneficiary has received from the trustees of the settlement to which the claim relates, and

(b) apart from this paragraph, those capital payments would fall to be brought into account under subsections (3) and (4) of section 80 of the Finance Act 1981 (new provisions as to gains of non-resident settlements) in determining whether chargeable gains or offshore income gains should be attributed to the beneficiary by reference to any trust gains for the year of assessment in which the claim is made,

then, as respects that year of assessment and any subsequent year, those capital payments shall be left out of account for the purposes of the said subsections (3) and (4).

(5) In any case where—

(a) the condition in sub-paragraph (4)(a) above is not fulfilled, but

(b) the condition in sub-paragraph (4)(b) above is fulfilled,

then, as respects the year of assessment in which the claim is made and any subsequent year, so much of the capital payments referred to in sub-paragraph (4) above as is equal to 31/3 times the amount of capital gains tax referred to in sub-paragraph (1)(a) above shall be left out of account for the purposes of subsections (3) and (4) of section 80 of the Finance Act 1981.

(6) Where, by virtue of sub-paragraph (4) or sub-paragraph (5) above, the whole or any part of a capital payment falls to be left out of account as mentioned in that sub-paragraph—

(a) the payment shall to the same extent be left out of account for the purposes of the application on any other occasion of any provision of paragraphs 7 to 12 of this Schedule; and

(b) section [740 of the Taxes Act 1988]1 (transfer of assets abroad: liability of non-transferors) shall have effect in relation to a benefit received by the beneficiary which, in whole or in part, consists of that payment as if, in the year of assessment in which the claim is made, chargeable gains equal to so much of that payment as falls to be so left out of account were, by reason of that payment, treated under section 80 of that act as accruing to the beneficiary.

(7) Where any capital payments falling within sub-paragraph (1)(b) above which the beneficiary has received from the trustees of the settlement to which the claim relates are not such as are referred to in sub-paragraph (4)(b) above, sub-paragraph (6)(a) above shall apply to each of those payments in like manner as if it had been such a payment as is referred to in sub-paragraph (4)(b) above and the amount of it to be left out of account had been determined accordingly under sub-paragraph (4) or sub-paragraph (5) above.

Amendments—¹ Words in sub-para (6)(*b*) substituted by TA 1988 Sch 29 para 32 Table.

8—*(1) The provisions of this paragraph apply if, in a case where paragraph 7 above applies, the amount of capital gains tax referred to in sub-paragraph (1)(a) of that paragraph exceeds 30 per cent of the aggregate of those capital payments falling within sub-paragraph (1)(b) of that paragraph which the beneficiary has received from the trustees of that settlement to which the claim relates.*

(2) In the following provisions of this paragraph—

(a) the capital payments falling within sub-paragraph (1)(b) of paragraph 7 above which the beneficiary has received otherwise than from the trustees of the settlement to which the claim relates are referred to as "related payments"; and

(b) any of those related payments which, apart from this paragraph, would fall to be brought into account as mentioned in sub-paragraph (4)(b) of paragraph 7 above is referred to as a "related section 80 payment".

(3) If sub-paragraph (2) of paragraph 7 above applies, then—

(a) as respects the year of assessment in which the claim is made and any subsequent year, any related section 80 payment shall be left out of account for the purposes of sub-paragraphs (3) and (4) of section 80 of the Finance Act 1981; and

(b) all the related payments shall be left out of account for the purposes of the application on any other occasion of any provision of paragraphs 7 to 12 of this Schedule.

(4) If sub-paragraph (3) of paragraph 7 above applies, then—

(a) as respects the year of assessment in which the claim is made and any subsequent year, so much of any related section 80 payment as is equal to 31/3 times the amount of capital gains tax released by that payment shall be left out of account for the purposes of subsections (3) and (4) of section 80 of the Finance Act 1981; and

(b) so much of each of the related payments as is equal to 31/3 times the amount of capital gains tax released by the payment shall be left out of account for the purposes mentioned in sub-paragraph (3)(b) above.

(5) For the purposes of sub-paragraph (4) above, the amount of capital gains tax released by a related payment shall be determined by the formula—

$$(A - B) \times \frac{C}{D}$$

where—

"A" is the capital gains tax referred to in sub-paragraph (1)(a) of paragraph 7 above;
"B" is an amount equal to 30 per cent of the aggregate of those capital payments falling within sub-paragraph (1)(b) of that paragraph which the beneficiary has received from the trustees of the settlement to which the claim relates;
"C" is the related payment in question; and
"D" is the aggregate of all the related payments.

(6) Where, by virtue of sub-paragraph (3)(a) or sub-paragraph (4)(a) above, the whole or any part of a related section 80 payment falls to be left out of account as mentioned in that sub-paragraph, section [740 of the Taxes Act 1988]1 shall have effect in relation to the benefit received by the beneficiary which, in whole or in part, consists of that payment as if, in the year of assessment in which the claim is made, chargeable gains equal to so much of that payment as falls to be so left out of account were, by reason of that payment, treated under section 80 of that Act as accruing to the beneficiary.

Amendments—¹ Words in sub-para (6) substituted by TA 1988 Sch 29 para 32 Table.

Effect of related benefits derived from payments received by close relatives of the beneficiary

9—*(1) The provisions of this paragraph apply if,—*

(a) on a claim, payment of an amount of capital gains tax determined in accordance with paragraph 6(2) or paragraph 7(2) above would, apart from this paragraph, be postponed by virtue of this Schedule; and

(b) as a result of a capital payment received by a close relative of the beneficiary, there is, in accordance with paragraph 10 below, a related benefit which falls to be taken into account in relation to the claim.

(2) If the amount of capital gains tax referred to in sub-paragraph (1)(a) above exceeds 30 per cent of the aggregate of the related benefits which fall to be taken into account in relation to the claim, then the amount of capital gains tax payment of which is postponed by virtue of this Schedule is an amount equal to that excess.

(3) If the amount of capital gains tax referred to in sub-paragraph (1)(a) above is less than or equal to 30 per cent of the aggregate of the related benefits which fall to be taken into account in relation to the claim, then there is no postponement of the payment of any of that capital gains tax.

Related benefits

10—(1) The provisions of this paragraph have effect to determine what are, in relation to a claim, the related benefits which are to be taken into account under paragraph 9 above.

(2) If, on or after 6th April 1984 and before the beginning of the year of assessment in which the claim is made, a close relative of the beneficiary has received from the trustees of the settlement to which the claim relates or a related settlement a capital payment which has not been brought into account under subsections (3) and (4) of section 80 of the Finance Act 1981 in determining whether chargeable gains or offshore income gains should be attributed to the close relative by reference to any trust gains for any previous year of assessment, then, subject to sub-paragraphs (3) and (4) below, that capital payment is a related benefit which falls to be taken into account in relation to the claim.

(3) A capital payment falling within sub-paragraph (2) above is not a related benefit which falls to be taken into account as mentioned in that sub-paragraph to the extent that it has already been taken into account on any previous operation of sub-paragraph (4) or sub-paragraph (5) of paragraph 7 above on the occasion of a claim in respect of which the close relative himself or a close relative of his or a person whose close relative he is was the beneficiary.

(4) A capital payment falling within sub-paragraph (2) above is not a related benefit which falls to be taken into account as mentioned in that sub-paragraph if the Board so direct on the grounds that it appears likely that the payment will fall to be taken into account, either as giving rise to a relevant benefit or under paragraph 7 above, in relation to such a claim as is referred to in sub-paragraph (3) above.

(5) Sub-paragraphs (3) to (6) of paragraph 8 above shall have effect for the purposes of this paragraph—

(a) as if any reference to a provision of paragraph 7 above were a reference to the corresponding provision of paragraph 9 above; and

(b) as if any reference to a related payment were a reference to a related benefit which falls to be taken into account as mentioned in sub-paragraph (2) above; and

(c) as if any reference to a related section 80 payment were a reference to a related benefit which falls to be taken into account as mentioned in sub-paragraph (2) above and which, apart from this paragraph, would fall to be taken into account under sub-paragraphs (3) and (4) of section 80 of the Finance Act 1981 in determining whether chargeable gains or offshore income gains should be attributed to the close relative concerned by reference to any trust gains for the year of assessment in which is made the claim referred to in sub-paragraph (2) above; and

(d) as if "B" in the formula in sub-paragraph (5) were nil; and

(e) as if any reference in sub-paragraph (6) to the beneficiary were a reference to the close relative concerned.

Commentary—*Simon's Direct Tax Service* **C4.462.**

Time when postponed tax becomes payable

11—(1) The provisions of this paragraph apply where, as a result of a claim, payment of an amount of capital gains tax, determined in accordance with paragraphs 6 to 9 above, is postponed by virtue of this Schedule; and, subject to sub-paragraph (6) below, any reference in the following provisions of this paragraph to postponed tax is a reference to tax the payment of which is so postponed.

(2) Postponed tax shall become payable in accordance with sub-paragraph (5) below if, at any time in the year of assessment in which the claim is made or any later year, the beneficiary disposes of his interest in the settlement to which the claim relates in circumstances such that, by virtue of section 58(1) of the principal Act, no chargeable gain could accrue on the disposal; and in sub-paragraph (5) below "the relevant consideration" means the amount or value of the consideration for such a disposal.

(3) Subject to paragraph 12 below, postponed tax shall become payable in accordance with sub-paragraph (5) below if in the year of assessment in which the claim is made or any later year, the beneficiary or a close relative of his receives a capital payment from the trustees of the settlement to which the claim relates or a related settlement.

(4) In the following provisions of this paragraph and paragraph 12 below, any reference to a material year of assessment is a reference to one in which the beneficiary disposes of his interest as mentioned in sub-paragraph (2) above or in which sub-paragraph (3) above applies.

(5) For any material year of assessment, so much of the postponed tax as does not exceed 30 per cent of the aggregate of—

    (a) the relevant consideration in respect of any disposal in that year, and
    (b) subject to paragraph 12 below, the capital payments received in that year as mentioned in sub-paragraph (3) above,

shall become payable as if it were capital gains tax assessed in respect of gains accruing in that year.

(6) If, for any material year of assessment, the amount of the postponed tax exceeds 30 per cent of the aggregate referred to in sub-paragraph (5) above, only the excess shall continue after the end of that year to be postponed tax for the purposes of this paragraph, but without prejudice to the subsequent operation of this paragraph in relation to a later year of assessment which is a material year.

(7) Where part, but not the whole, of any postponed tax becomes payable in accordance with sub-paragraph (5) above, tax assessed for an earlier year shall be regarded as becoming so payable before tax assessed for a later year.

Commentary—*Simon's Direct Tax Service* **C4.462.**

Balance of capital payments

12—*(1) If any capital payments received in any year of assessment as mentioned in paragraph 11(3) above fall to be brought into account for that year for the purposes of subsections (3) and (4) of section 80 of the Finance Act 1981, those capital payments shall be disregarded for the purposes of sub-paragraph (5) or, as the case may be, sub-paragraph (6) of paragraph 11 above except to the extent that the aggregate of those payments exceeds the chargeable gains and offshore income gains which in that year are treated under the said section 80 as accruing to the beneficiary or, as the case may be, the close relative; and any such excess is in the following provisions of this paragraph referred to as the balance of section 80 payments for that year.*

(2) Subject to the following provisions of this paragraph, as respects any year of assessment subsequent to a material year of assessment for which there is a balance of section 80 payments there shall be left out of account for the purposes of subsections (3) and (4) of section 80 of the Finance Act 1981 so much of the capital payments as made up that balance.

(3) If paragraph 11(6) above did not apply for any material year of assessment for which there is a balance of section 80 payments then, as respects years of assessment subsequent to that year, sub-paragraph (2) above shall apply only to so much of the capital payments mentioned therein as is equal to 31/3 times the amount of postponed tax released by that balance.

(4) For any material year of assessment, the amount of postponed tax released by a balance of section 80 payments for that year shall be determined by that formula—

$$(E - F) \times \frac{G}{H}$$

where

    "E" is the postponed tax, within the meaning of paragraph 11 above;
    "F" is an amount equal to 30 per cent of any consideration for that year which falls within sub-paragraph (5) (a) of that paragraph;
    "G" is the balance of the section 80 payments for that year; and
    "H" is the aggregate of the capital payments (including that balance) taken into account under sub-paragraph (5) (b) of that paragraph for that year.

(5) If, in a case where sub-paragraph (2) above applies in accordance with sub-paragraph (3) above, there were, for the material year of assessment concerned,—

    (a) a balance of section 80 payments derived from payments received by the beneficiary, and
    (b) another such balance derived from payments received by a close relative of his,

sub-paragraph (2) above shall apply (in accordance with sub-paragraph (3) above) to the capital payments which made up the balance derived from payments received by the beneficiary in priority to capital payments which made up the other balance.

(6) Subject to sub-paragraph (5) above, where there is more than one capital payment to which sub-paragraph (2) above applies, the proportion of each of them which is left out of account as mentioned in that sub-paragraph shall be the same.

(7) Where, by virtue of the preceding provisions of this paragraph, the whole or any part of a capital payment falls to be left out of account as mentioned in sub-paragraph (2) above, section [740 of the Taxes Act 1988]1 shall have effect in relation to a benefit which is received by the beneficiary or, as the case may be, a close relative of his and which, in whole or in part, consists of that payment as if, in the material year of assessment concerned, chargeable gains equal to so much of that payment as

falls to be so left out of account were, by reason of that payment, treated under section 80 of that Act as accruing to the beneficiary or, as the case may be, the close relative.

Commentary—*Simon's Direct Tax Service* **C4.462.**
Cross references—See TCGA 1992, Sch 11, para 18(*b*) (references to FA 1981, s 80 and s 80(3), (4) in this paragraph to include references to TCGA 1992, s 87 and s 87(4), (5)).
Amendments—¹ Words in sub-para (7) substituted by TA 1988, Sch 29, para 32 Table.

13—*(1) Where, by virtue of sub-paragraph (2) of paragraph 12 above, the whole or any part of a capital payment falls to be left out of account as mentioned in that sub-paragraph, it shall to the same extent be left out of account for the purposes of the application on any other occasion of any provision of paragraphs 7 to 12 of this Schedule.*

(2) Where sub-paragraph (6) of paragraph 11 above applies for any material year of assessment, any capital payments which—

   (a) fall to be taken into account under sub-paragraph (5)(b) of that paragraph for that year, and
   (b) are not such as to fall within paragraph 12(1) above,

shall be left out of account for the purposes referred to in sub-paragraph (1) above.

(3) Where sub-paragraph (6) of paragraph 11 above does not apply for any material year of assessment, so much of any capital payment falling within paragraphs (a) and (b) of sub-paragraph (2) above as is equal to 31/3 times the amount of postponed tax released by that payment shall be left out of account for the purposes referred to in sub-paragraph (1) above.

(4) The amount of postponed tax released by a capital payment shall be determined for the purposes of sub-paragraph (3) above by the formula in paragraph 12(4) above, except that, in applying that formula for those purposes, "G" shall be the amount of the capital payment in question.

(5) In this paragraph, "material year of assessment" shall be construed in accordance with paragraph 11(4) above.

Commentary—*Simon's Direct Tax Service* **C4.462.**

Second and later claims

14—*(1) This paragraph applies where—*

   (a) as a result of a claim (in this paragraph referred to as "the earlier claim"), payment of an amount of capital gains tax (in this paragraph referred to as "the original tax"), determined in accordance with paragraph 6 or paragraph 7 above, is or was postponed by virtue of this Schedule; and
   (b) after the making of the earlier claim, another claim (in this paragraph referred to as "the later claim") is made in relation to an attributed gain to which the earlier claim did not relate; and
   (c) the settlement to which the earlier and the later claims relate is the same.

(2) If the year of assessment which is the relevant year of assessment in relation to any attributed gain to which the later claim relates is earlier than the earliest year of assessment which is the relevant year of assessment in relation to any attributed gain to which the earlier claim related, then,—

   (a) the earlier claim and the postponement resulting from it shall be set aside; and
   (b) the provisions of this Schedule shall have effect as if (notwithstanding paragraph 2(2) above) the attributed gains to which the later claim relates included the attributed gains to which the earlier claim related.

(3) Where sub-paragraph (2) above does not apply and, at the time the later claim is made, payment of any of the original tax remains postponed by virtue of this Schedule, then, subject to sub-paragraph (4) below,—

   (a) paragraphs 4 to 10 above shall not apply in relation to the later claim; and
   (b) payment of the tax referable to the attributed gain or gains to which the later claim relates shall be postponed by virtue of this Schedule; and
   (c) paragraphs 11 and 12 above shall apply as if the payment of that tax had been postponed as a result of the earlier claim and, accordingly, that tax shall be added to the original tax.

(4) If, in a case where sub-paragraph (3) above applies, the relevant year of assessment in relation to an attributed gain (in this sub-paragraph referred to as "the later gain") to which the later claim relates is the same as the relevant year of assessment in relation to an attributed gain to which the earlier claim related,—

   (a) paragraph 3 above shall not apply in relation to the later gain; and
   (b) in relation to the later gain, the references in sub-paragraph (3) above to the tax referable to the gain shall be construed as references to the capital gains tax assessed by reason of the gain.

(5) Where sub-paragraph (2) above does not apply and, at the time the later claim is made, there is no longer any postponement of the payment of any of the original tax, then, in the application of the provisions of this Schedule in relation to the later claim, paragraph 4(2) above shall not apply and "the base year" for the purposes of paragraphs 4 and 5 above shall be that year of assessment which was the base year in relation to the earlier claim.

Information

15—(1) The Board may by notice in writing require any person to furnish them, within such time as they may direct, not being less than twenty-eight days, with such particulars as they think necessary for the purposes of section 70 of this Act and this Schedule.

(2) Subsections (2) to [(6) of section 745 of the Taxes Act 1988]1 shall have effect in relation to sub-paragraph (1) above as they have effect in relation to subsection (1) of that section; but, in the application of those subsections by virtue of this sub-paragraph, references to Chapter III of Part XVII of the Taxes Act shall be construed as references to section 70 of this Act and this Schedule.

(3) In any case where—

(a) a claim has been made, and

(b) as a result of the claim, payment of an amount of capital gains tax was postponed by virtue of this Schedule, and

(c) at a time when any of that tax remains unpaid, there is a disposal to which paragraph 11(2) above applies or the beneficiary or a close relative of his receives such a capital payment as is referred to in paragraph 11(3) above,

then, not later than three months after the end of the year of assessment in which the disposal occurs or the payment is received, the beneficiary shall inform the Board of the disposal or receipt, as the case may be.

Commentary—*Simon's Direct Tax Service* C4.463.
Amendments—¹ Words in sub-para (2) substituted by TA 1988, Sch 29, para 32 Table.

FILMS ACT 1985

(1985 Chapter 21)

6 Certification of master negatives, tapes and discs for purposes of section 72 of Finance Act 1982

(1) Schedule 1 to this Act shall have effect with respect to the certification by the Secretary of State of a master negative, tape or disc of a film as a qualifying film, tape or disc for the purposes of [section 40D of the Finance (No 2) Act 1992 (election relating to tax treatment of films expenditure)]².

(2) ... ¹

Commentary—*Simon's Direct Tax Service* B2.311; B3.1307.
Amendments—¹ Sub-s (2) repealed by CAA 1990, Sch 2.
² Words in sub-s (1) substituted by CAA 2001 s 578, Sch 2 para 8 with effect for income tax purposes, as respects allowances and charges falling to be made for chargeable periods ending after 5 April 2001, and for corporation tax purposes, as respects allowances and charges falling to be made for chargeable periods ending after 31 March 2001.

8 Short title, commencement and extent

(1) This Act may be cited as the Films Act 1985.

(2), (3) ...

Note—Sub-ss (2), (3) not relevant to this work.

SCHEDULE 1

CERTIFICATION FOR PURPOSES OF SECTION 72 OF FINANCE ACT 1982 IN CASE OF BRITISH FILMS

Sections 3, 5 and 6

Statement of Practice SP 1/93, paras 26–37—Effect on tax rules of certification under this Schedule depends on whether a film is completed before, on or after 10 March 1992.
Cross References—See F(No 2)A 1992 ss 41, 43 (relief for preliminary expenditure of a revenue nature incurred before a film is made).
F(No 2)A 1992 ss 42, 43 (relief for expenditure of a revenue nature incurred for production or acquisition of a film).

Preliminary

1—(1) In this Schedule—

"Commonwealth country" means the United Kingdom, any country for the time being specified in Schedule 3 to the British Nationality Act 1981 (countries whose citizens are Commonwealth citizens), and any territory for whose international relations Her Majesty's Government in the United Kingdom is responsible;

"film" includes any record, however made, of a sequence of visual images, which is a record capable of being used as a means of showing that sequence as a moving picture;

["film production activity", in relation to a film, means any activity undertaken for the purposes of the production of the film;][1]

"maker", in relation to a film, means the person by whom the arrangements necessary for the making of the film are undertaken;

"master disc", in relation to a film, means the original master film disc or the original master audio disc of the film;

"master negative", in relation to a film, means the original master negative of the film and its soundtrack (if any);

"master tape", in relation to a film, means the original master film tape or the original master audio tape of the film;

...[2]

[(2) For the purposes of this Schedule the production of a film is completed when the film is first in a form in which it can reasonably be regarded as ready for copies of it to be made and distributed for presentation to the general public.][3]

(3) Subject to sub-paragraph (4), each part of a series of films shall be treated as a separate film for the purposes of this Schedule.

[(4) The Secretary of State may direct that a number of films shall be treated as a single film for the purposes of this Schedule if—

(a) they form a series with not more than twenty-six parts;

(b) the combined playing time is not more than twenty-six hours; and

(c) in the opinion of the Secretary of State the series constitutes a self-contained work or is a series of documentaries with a common theme.][3]

(5) Any reference in this Schedule to a master negative, tape or disc certified under paragraph 3(1) or to a certificate issued under that provisions includes a reference to a master negative, tape or disc certified in pursuance of section 72 (7) (b) of the Finance Act 1982 as originally enacted or to a certificate issued in pursuance of that provision.

Amendments—[1] In sub-para (1) definition "film production activity" inserted by the Films (Modification of the Definition of "British Film") Order 1999, SI 1999/2386, arts 2(1), 3(1), (2), with effect from 27 August 1999, with a transitional provision allowing applicants to elect to proceed under this Schedule, as it stood before that date, until 27 August 2000.
[2] In sub-para (1) definitions "sound recording" and "studio" repealed by SI 1999/2386, arts 2(1), 3(3), with effect from 27 August 1999, with a transitional provision allowing applicants to elect to proceed under this Schedule, as it stood before that date, until 27 August 2000. Previous text read as follows—

"'sound recording' means a sound recording which is either an original recording or a re-recording;

'studio' (except in paragraph 5(1)(b) means a building or group of buildings constructed or adapted for the purpose of making films therein and includes any land occupied with such a building or group of buildings.".
[3] Sub-paras (2), (4) substituted by SI 1999/2386, arts 2(1), 4, 5, with effect from 27 August 1999, with a transitional provision allowing applicants to elect to proceed under this Schedule, as it stood before that date, until 27 August 2000.

Applications for certification of master negatives, tapes and discs

2—(1) An application for the certification by the Secretary of State of a master negative, master tape or master disc of a film as a qualifying film, qualifying tape or qualifying disc for the purposes of [section 40D of the Finance (No 2) Act 1992][1] may be made by any person who has incurred expenditure on the production or acquisition of that negative, tape, or disc.

(2) In sub-paragraph (1) the reference to the acquisition of a master negative, tape or disc includes a reference to the acquisition of any description of rights in it.

(3) On an application under this paragraph for the certification of a master negative, tape or disc the applicant shall—

(a) produce to the Secretary of State such books and other documents relating to it; and

(b) furnish to the Secretary of State such other information with respect to it,

as the Secretary of State may require for the purpose of determining the application.

(4) Any information furnished for the purposes of sub-paragraph (3) shall, if the Secretary of State so directs, be accompanied by a statutory declaration as to the truth of the information made by the person furnishing it.

Cross references—See the Films (Certification) Regulations, SI 1985/994 reg 3 (applications for certification under this paragraph).
Amendments—[1] Words in sub-para (1) substituted by CAA 2001 s 578, Sch 2 para 9(1) with effect for income tax purposes, as respects allowances and charges falling to be made for chargeable periods ending after 5 April 2001, and for corporation tax purposes, as respects allowances and charges falling to be made for chargeable periods ending after 31 March 2001.

Certification by Secretary of State of master negatives, tapes and discs

3—(1) If the Secretary of State is satisfied that a master negative, tape or disc with respect to which an application is made under paragraph 2 is a master negative, tape or disc of a film which, in his opinion, is a British film for the purposes of this Schedule, he shall certify that negative, tape or disc as a qualifying film, qualifying tape or qualifying disc for the purposes of [section 40D of the Finance (No 2) Act 1992][1].

(2) If the Secretary of State is for any reason not satisfied as mentioned in sub-paragraph (1) he shall refuse the application.

(3) If it appears to the Secretary of State that any negative, tape or disc certified by him under sub-paragraph (1) ought for any reason not to have been so certified he shall revoke its certification.

(4) Where an application is made under paragraph 2 in relation to a negative, tape or disc of a film which has already been certified by the Secretary of State under sub-paragraph (1) on a prior application, the Secretary of State may issue the applicant with a duplicate or copy of the certificate issued on that prior application.

Amendments—[1] Words in sub-para (1) substituted by CAA 2001 s 578, Sch 2 para 9(2) with effect for income tax purposes, as respects allowances and charges falling to be made for chargeable periods ending after 5 April 2001, and for corporation tax purposes, as respects allowances and charges falling to be made for chargeable periods ending after 31 March 2001.

British films for purposes of the Schedule

[**4**—(1) Subject to paragraph 5, a film is a British film for the purposes of this Schedule if all the requirements specified in sub-paragraphs (2) to (4) are satisfied with respect to it.

(2) The first requirement is that throughout the period during which the film is being made the maker of the film is—

(*a*) a person ordinarily resident in a member State; or
(*b*) a company which is registered in a member State and in the case of which the central management and control of business is exercised in a member State.

(3) The second requirement is that at least 70 per cent of the total expenditure incurred in the production of the film was incurred on film production activity carried out in the United Kingdom.

(4) The third requirement is that not less than the requisite amount of labour costs (as determined under paragraph 7) represents payments paid or payable in respect of the labour or services of—

(*a*) Commonwealth citizens,
(*b*) citizens of a member State, or
(*c*) persons ordinarily resident in a Commonwealth country or a member State.

(5) For the purpose of calculating the total expenditure incurred in the production of a film pursuant to sub-paragraph (3), the following shall be disregarded—

(*a*) any amount deducted under paragraph 7(2)(*a*) or, as the case may be, paragraph 7(2)(*b*) in calculating the amount which is the lesser amount for the purposes of paragraph 7(1);
(*b*) any expenditure incurred on the acquisition or licensing of copyright, trademarks or rights of a similar nature, other than copyright in works created for the purpose of their use in the film;
(*c*) any expenditure, including the payment of interest, incurred for the purposes of raising or servicing finance for making the film; and
(*d*) any business overheads attributable to the film.

(6) A state shall be treated for the purposes of this paragraph as if it were a member State if—

(*a*) it is party to an agreement under Article 310 of the Treaty establishing the European Community; and
(*b*) the agreement requires a maker of a film who is ordinarily resident or registered in that state to be treated for the purposes of this Schedule in the same way as a maker of a film who is ordinarily resident or registered in a member State.

(7) Her Majesty may by Order in Council provide for films to be treated as British films for the purposes of this Schedule if they are made in accordance with the terms of any agreement between Her Majesty's Government in the United Kingdom and any other government, international organisation or authority.][1]

Amendments—[1] This paragraph substituted by the Films (Modification of the Definition of "British Film") Order, SI 1999/2386, arts 2(1), 6, with effect from 27 August 1999, with a transitional provision allowing applicants to elect to proceed under this Schedule, as it stood before that date, until 27 August 2000.

Excluded films

[**5**—(1) Subject to sub-paragraph (2), a film is not a British film for the purposes of this Schedule by virtue of paragraph 4(1) if parts of the film are derived from—

(*a*) any film of which the master negative, tape or disc is certified under paragraph 3(1), or
(*b*) any film not made by the same maker as the first-mentioned film,

and the playing time of those parts exceeds 10 per cent of the total playing time of the film.

(2) The Secretary of State may direct that sub-paragraph (1) shall not apply in relation to a film if in his opinion—

(*a*) it is a documentary; and
(*b*) its subject matter makes it appropriate for sub-paragraph (1) not to be applied.][1]

Amendments—[1] This paragraph substituted by the Films (Modification of the Definition of "British Film") Order, SI 1999/2386, arts 2(1), 7, with effect from 27 August 1999, with a transitional provision allowing applicants to elect to proceed under this Schedule, as it stood before that date, until 27 August 2000.

Ascertainment of labour costs and playing time

6—(1) For the purposes of this Schedule the labour costs of a film shall be taken to be, subject to paragraph 8, the total amount of the payments paid or payable in respect of the labour or services of persons directly engaged in the making of the film, in so far as those payments are attributable to the making of that film, ...².

[(1A) The labour costs of a film shall not include payments in respect of copyright other than copyright in a work created for the purpose of use in the film.

(1B) The labour costs of a film shall not include payments which—

(*a*) are in respect of living expenses which a person incurs because it is not reasonably practicable for him to reside at his usual place of residence while directly engaged in the making of the film, and

(*b*) are reasonable in the opinion of the Secretary of State.]²

(2) For the purposes of sub-paragraph (1)—

(*a*) the author of the scenario of the film shall be deemed to be a person directly engaged in the making of the film;

(*b*) a person shall not be taken to be directly engaged in the making of a film by reason only—

(i) that he is financially interested in the making of the film or is engaged in a clerical capacity as a servant of an undertaking concerned with the making of the film; or

(ii) that he supplies goods used in the making of the film or is in the employment of a person who supplies such goods;

(*c*) payments paid or payable to a person who is engaged in an administrative capacity as an officer or servant of an undertaking concerned with the making of a film shall not be taken to be attributable to the making of the film except in so far as they are payments in respect of services directly concerned with the making of that film.

(3) ...¹

Amendments—¹ Sub-para (3) repealed by the Films (Modification of the Definition of "British Film") Order , SI 1999/2386, arts 2(1), 8, with effect from 27 August 1999, with a transitional provision allowing applicants to elect to proceed under this Schedule, as it stood before that date, until 27 August 2000.
² Words in sub-para (1) repealed and sub-ss (1A), (1B) inserted by the Films (Modification of the Definition of "British Film") Order , SI 2000/756, arts 2(1), (2), with effect from 10 March 2000 (note that an election to proceed (by SI 1999/2386 art 1(2)) under this Schedule, as it stood before 27 August 1999, until 27 August 2000, does not affect the application of SI 2000/756).

Determination of requisite amount of labour costs

7—(1) For the purposes of [paragraph 4(4)]¹ the requisite amount of the labour costs of a film shall be taken to be ...² whichever is the lesser of the two amounts specified in sub-paragraph (2) of this paragraph.

(2) The amounts referred to in sub-paragraph (1) are—

(*a*) the amount arrived at by applying the fraction [seven-tenths]¹ to the total labour costs of the film, after deducting from those costs, if the applicant on an application under paragraph 2 so desires, the amount of any payment which, as part of those costs, has been paid or is payable in respect of the labour or services of any one person who was not, while engaged in the making of the film—

(i) a Commonwealth citizen or a citizen of a member State, nor

(ii) a person ordinarily resident in a Commonwealth country or a member State; and

(*b*) the amount arrived at by applying the fraction [three-quarters]¹to the total labour costs of the film, after deducting from those costs the amount of any payments which, as part of those costs, have been paid or are payable in respect of the labour or services of any two persons neither of whom was, while engaged in the making of the film, such a citizen or person as is referred to in paragraph (*a*)(i) or (ii), and at least one of whom was so engaged in the capacity of an actor or actress and in no other capacity.

[(3) Paragraph 4(6) has effect for the purposes of this paragraph as it has effect for the purposes of paragraph 4.]³

Amendments—¹ In sub-paras (1), (2) words substituted by the Films (Modification of the Definition of "British Film") Order, SI 1999/2386, arts 2(1), 9(1), (2)(*a*), (3), (4) with effect from 27 August 1999, with a transitional provision allowing applicants to elect to proceed under this Schedule, as it stood before that date, until 27 August 2000.
² In sub-para (1) words repealed by SI 1999/2386, arts 2(1), 9(1), (2)(*b*), with effect from 27 August 1999, with a transitional provision allowing applicants to elect to proceed under this Schedule, as it stood before that date, until 27 August 2000.
³ Sub-para (3) substituted by SI 1999/2386, arts 2(1), 9(1), (5), with effect from 27 August 1999, with a transitional provision allowing applicants to elect to proceed under this Schedule, as it stood before that date, until 27 August 2000.

Power of Secretary of State to direct alteration of labour costs

8 Where it is material, in connection with an application under paragraph 2 in relation to a negative, tape or disc of a film, to ascertain the labour costs of the film or the proportion of those costs which represents payments in respect of the labour or services of persons of any particular class, then—

(*a*) if it appears to the Secretary of State that any sum which, as part of those costs, is paid or payable in respect of the labour or services of any particular person is so great as not to be a bona fide payment by way of remuneration for the said labour or services, the Secretary of State may direct that that sum, or part of that sum, shall be disregarded in ascertaining the said labour costs or the said proportion thereof, as the case may be; and

(b) if it appears to the Secretary of State that no sum or a sum so small as not bona fide to represent all the remuneration therefor is paid or payable as part of those costs in respect of the labour or services of any particular person, the Secretary of State may direct that such sum, or (as the case may be) such greater sum, as may be specified in the direction shall be treated as so paid or payable.

Determination of disputes

9—(1) Any person who is aggrieved by any decision of the Secretary of State to refuse an application under paragraph 2 or to revoke any certification under paragraph 3(1) may, subject to rules of court, apply to the High Court, and the decision of that Court shall be final.

(2) In relation to any person whose principal place of business is in Scotland, subparagraph (1) shall have effect as if for any reference to the High Court there were substituted a reference to the Court of Session.

Regulations and orders

10—(1) The Secretary of State may make regulations—

(a) prescribing the form of applications under paragraph 2;

(b) prescribing the particulars and evidence necessary for satisfying the Secretary of State that a film is a British film for the purposes of this Schedule;

(c) providing that any statutory declaration which is required by paragraph 2(4) to be made by any person shall be deemed to be properly made if it is made on his behalf by any such person as may be specified in the regulations.

(2) The Secretary of State with the approval of the Treasury may by order make such modifications of any of the provisions of paragraphs 1 and 4 to 8 as he considers appropriate; and any such order may contain such incidental, supplemental and transitional provisions as he considers appropriate in connection with the order.

(3) In sub-paragraph (2) "modifications" includes additions, omissions and alterations.

(4) Any regulations or order under this paragraph shall be made by statutory instrument.

(5) Any regulations under this paragraph shall be laid before Parliament after being made; but no order shall be made under this paragraph unless it has been laid before Parliament and approved by a resolution of each House.

Regulations—Films (Certification) Regulations, SI 1985/994.

BANKRUPTCY (SCOTLAND) ACT 1985

(1985 Chapter 66)

Note—This Act received Royal Assent on 30 October 1985.

Distribution of debtor's estate

51 Order of priority in distribution

(1) The funds of the debtor's estate shall be distributed by the permanent trustee to meet the following debts in the order in which they are mentioned—

(a) the outlays and remuneration of the interim trustee in the administration of the debtor's estate;

(b) the outlays and remuneration of the permanent trustee in the administration of the debtor's estate;

(c) where the debtor is a deceased debtor, deathbed and funeral expenses reasonably incurred and expenses reasonably incurred in administering the deceased's estate;

(d) the expenses reasonably incurred by a creditor who is a petitioner, or concurs in the petition, for sequestration;

(e) preferred debts (excluding any interest which has accrued thereon to the date of sequestration);

(f) ordinary debts, that is to say a debt which is neither a secured debt nor a debt mentioned in any other paragraph of this subsection;

(g) interest at the rate specified in subsection (7) below on—

    (i) the preferred debts;

    (ii) the ordinary debts,

between the date of sequestration and the date of payment of the debt;

(h) any postponed debt.

(2) In this Act "preferred debt" means a debt listed in Part I of Schedule 3 to this Act; and Part II of that Schedule shall have effect for the interpretation of the said Part I.

(3) In this Act "postponed debt" means—

(*a*) a loan made to the debtor, in consideration of a share of the profits in his business, which is postponed under section 3 of the Partnership Act 1890 to the claims of other creditors;

(*b*) a loan made to the debtor by the debtor's spouse;

(*c*) a creditor's right to anything vesting in the permanent trustee by virtue of a successful challenge under section 34 of this Act or to the proceeds of sale of such a thing.

(4) Any debt falling within any of paragraphs (*c*) to (*h*) of subsection (1) above shall have the same priority as any other debt falling within the same paragraph and, where the funds of the estate are inadequate to enable the debts mentioned in the paragraph to be paid in full, they shall abate in equal proportions.

(5) Any surplus remaining, after all the debts mentioned in this section have been paid in full, shall be made over to the debtor or to his successors or assignees; and in this subsection "surplus" includes any kind of estate but does not include any unclaimed dividend.

(6) Nothing in this section shall affect—

(*a*) the right of a secured creditor which is preferable to the rights of the permanent trustee; or

(*b*) any preference of the holder of a lien over a title deed or other document which has been delivered to the permanent trustee in accordance with a requirement under section 38(4) of this Act.

(7) The rate of interest referred to in paragraph (*g*) of subsection (1) above shall be whichever is the greater of—

(*a*) the prescribed rate at the date of sequestration; and

(*b*) the rate applicable to that debt apart from the sequestration.

Notes—Sub-ss (1), (3)–(7) have effect from 1 April 1986 and sub-s (2) has effect from 29 December 1986 by virtue of SI 1985/1924 and SI 1986/1913.

SCHEDULE 3

PREFERRED DEBTS

Section 51

Note—This Schedule was brought into effect on 29 December 1986 by virtue of s 78 and the Bankruptcy (Scotland) Act 1985 (Commencement No 2) Order, SI 1986/1913.

PART I

LIST OF PREFERRED DEBTS

Debts to Inland Revenue

1—(1) Sums due at the relevant date from the debtor on account of deductions of income tax from emoluments paid during the period of twelve months next before that date, being deductions which the debtor was liable to make under [section 203 of the Income and Corporation Taxes Act 1988][1] (pay as you earn), less the amount of the repayments of income tax which the debtor was liable to make during that period.

(2) Sums due at the relevant date from the debtor in respect of such deductions as are required to be made by the debtor for that period under [section 559 of the Income and Corporation Taxes Act 1988][1] (subcontractors in the construction industry).

Amendments—[1] Words in sub-paras (1), (2) substituted by virtue of TA 1988 Sch 29 para 32 Table.

PART II

INTERPRETATION OF PART I

Meaning of "the relevant date"

7 In Part I of this Schedule "the relevant date" means—

(*a*) in relation to a debtor (other than a deceased debtor), the date of sequestration; and

(*b*) in relation to a deceased debtor, the date of his death.

FINANCE ACT 1986

(1986 Chapter 41)

An Act to grant certain duties, to alter other duties, and to amend the law relating to the National Debt and the Public Revenue, and to make further provision in connection with Finance.

[25th July 1986]

PART II

INCOME TAX, CORPORATION TAX AND CAPITAL GAINS TAX

CHAPTER I
GENERAL
Employee shareholding

24 Approved profit sharing schemes: workers' co-operatives

(1)–(3) ...[1]

(4) Where, for the purpose of securing (and maintaining) approval of its profit sharing scheme in accordance with Part I of Schedule 9 to the [Taxes Act 1988][2], the rules of a society which is a workers' co-operative or which is seeking to be registered under the industrial and provident societies legislation as a workers' co-operative contain—

    (*a*) provision for membership of the society by the trustees of the scheme,

    (*b*) provision denying voting rights to those trustees, or

    (*c*) other provisions which appear to the registrar to be reasonably necessary for that purpose,

those provisions shall be disregarded in determining whether the society should be or continue to be registered under the industrial and provident societies legislation as a bona fide co-operative society.

(5) In subsection (4) above "the industrial and provident societies legislation" means—

    (*a*) the Industrial and Provident Societies Act 1965 or

    (*b*) the Industrial and Provident Societies Act (Northern Ireland) 1969,

and "registrar" has the same meaning as in each of those Acts and "co-operative society" has the same meaning as in section 1 of those Acts.

Commentary—*Simon's Direct Tax Service* **E4.533, 534.**
Amendments—[1] Sub-ss (1)–(3) repealed by TA 1988 s 844, Sch 31.
[2] Words in sub-s (4) substituted by TA 1988 Sch 29 para 32 Table.

CHAPTER IV
SECURITIES

63 Other provisions

Schedule 18 to this Act (which contains other provisions about securities) shall have effect.

Commentary—*Simon's Direct Tax Service* **A3.126.**

SCHEDULES

SCHEDULE 18

SECURITIES: OTHER PROVISIONS

Section 63

Information

7 ...

Note—Sub-paras (1)–(3) amend TMA 1970 s 21.
Amendments—[1] This paragraph repealed by FA 1997 Sch 10 paras 15, 16(2), (3), Sch 18 Pt VI(10) with effect for the purpose of conferring powers for obtaining information about (a) transactions entered into on or after 1 July 1997 by virtue of the Finance Act 1997, Schedule 10, (Appointed Day) Order, SI 1997/991; and (b) payments made on or after 1 July 1997 (whether under such transactions or under transactions entered into before 1 July 1997), subject to the provision that nothing in FA 1997 Sch 10 Pt II shall affect the exercise, at any time on or after 1 July 1997, of the powers conferred apart from FA 1997 Sch 10 by TMA 1970 s 21, or by any regulations modifying that section, or TA 1988 s 737(8), for obtaining information about transactions entered into, or payments made, before that day.

8—(1)–(3) (*amend* TMA 1970 s 25).

(4) The Board may by regulations provide that—

(*a*) subsections (4) and (5) of section 25 and paragraph (*a*) of subsection (10) (as inserted by sub-paragraph (2) above) shall have effect as if references to The Stock Exchange were to any recognised investment exchange or to any of those exchanges specified in the regulations, and

(*b*) paragraph (*b*) of subsection (10) shall have effect as if the reference to the Council of The Stock Exchange were to the investment exchange concerned.

(5) Regulations under sub-paragraph (4) above shall apply in relation to transactions effected on or after such day, after the day of The Stock Exchange reforms, as is specified in the regulations.

Miscellaneous

9 ...

Amendments—This paragraph repealed by FA 1997 Sch 10 paras 15, 16(2), (3) Sch 18 Pt VI (10) with effect for manufactured payments made after 30 June 1997, by virtue of SI 1997/991 art 2.

General

10—(1) In this Schedule "the day of The Stock Exchange reforms" means the day on which the rule of The Stock Exchange that prohibits a person from carrying on business as both a broker and a jobber is abolished.

(2) In this Schedule "recognised investment exchange" means a recognised investment exchange within the meaning [given by section 285(1)(*a*) of the Financial Services and Markets Act 2000][1].

(3) Any power to make regulations under this Schedule shall be exercisable by statutory instrument subject to annulment in pursuance of a resolution of the House of Commons.

Amendment—[1] Words in sub-s (2) substituted by the Financial Services and Markets Act 2000 (Consequential Amendments) (Taxes) Order, SI 2001/3629 arts 6, 12 with effect from 1 December 2001, immediately after the coming into force of the Financial Services and Markets Act 2000 ss 411, 432(1), Sch 20.

INSOLVENCY ACT 1986

(1986 Chapter 45)

Note—This Act received Royal Assent on 25 July 1986. By virtue of s 443 of this Act and SI 1986/1924, art 3 it has effect from 29 December 1986.

PART IV

WINDING UP OF COMPANIES REGISTERED UNDER THE COMPANIES ACTS

CHAPTER VIII

PROVISIONS OF GENERAL APPLICATION IN WINDING UP

Preferential debts

175 Preferential debts (general provision)

(1) In a winding up the company's preferential debts (within the meaning given by section 386 in Part XII) shall be paid in priority to all other debts.

(2) Preferential debts—

(*a*) rank equally among themselves after the expenses of the winding up and shall be paid in full, unless the assets are insufficient to meet them, in which case they abate in equal proportions; and

(*b*) so far as the assets of the company available for payment of general creditors are insufficient to meet them, have priority over the claims of holders of debentures secured by, or holders of, any floating charge created by the company, and shall be paid accordingly out of any property comprised in or subject to that charge.

PART XII

PREFERENTIAL DEBTS IN COMPANY AND INDIVIDUAL INSOLVENCY

Note—This Part to apply, from 1 December 1999 (by virtue of the Building Societies Act 1997 (Commencement No 3) Order, SI 1997/2668), to building societies as it does to companies, per Building Societies Act 1997 Sch 6 para 1.

PART XII

PREFERENTIAL DEBTS IN COMPANY AND INDIVIDUAL INSOLVENCY

386 Categories of preferential debts

(1) A reference in this Act to the preferential debts of a company or an individual is to the debts listed in Schedule 6 to this Act (money owed to the Inland Revenue for income tax deducted at source; ... [climate change levy,][2] social security and pension scheme contributions ...); and references to preferential creditors are to be read accordingly.

(2) In that Schedule ''the debtor'' means the company or the individual concerned.

(3) Schedule 6 is to be read with [Schedule 4 to the Pension Schemes Act 1993][1] (occupational pension scheme contributions).

Note—Words omitted from sub-s (1) are not relevant to this work.
Amendments—[1] Words in sub-s (3) substituted by the Pension Schemes Act 1993 s 190, Sch 8 para 18 with effect from 7 February 1994.
[2] Words in sub-s (1) inserted by FA 2000 s 30, Sch 7 para 3(a) with effect from 28 July 2000.

387 ''The relevant date''

(1) This section explains references in Schedule 6 to the relevant date (being the date which determines the existence and amount of a preferential debt).

(2) For the purposes of section 4 in Part I (meetings to consider company voluntary arrangement), the relevant date in relation to a company which is not being wound up is—

    (*a*) where an administration order is in force in relation to the company, the date of the making of that order, and
    (*b*) where no such order has been made, the date of the approval of the voluntary arrangement.

(3) In relation to a company which is being wound up, the following applies—

    (*a*) if the winding up is by the court, and the winding-up order was made immediately upon the discharge of an administration order, the relevant date is the date of the making of the administration order;
    [(*aa*) if the winding up is by the court and the winding-up order was made following conversion of administration into winding up by virtue of Article 37 of the EC Regulation, the relevant date is the date of the making of the administration order;
    (*ab*) if the company is deemed to have passed a resolution for voluntary winding up by virtue of an order following conversion of administration into winding up under Article 37 of the EC Regulation, the relevant date is the date of the making of the administration order;][1]
    (*b*) if the case does not fall within paragraph (*a*)[, (*aa*) or (*ab*)][1] and the company—

        (i) is being wound up by the court, and
        (ii) had not commenced to be wound up voluntarily before the date of the making of the winding-up order,

    the relevant date is the date of the appointment (or first appointment) of a provisional liquidator or, if no such appointment has been made, the date of the winding-up order;
    (*c*) if the case does not fall [paragraph (*a*), (*aa*), (*ab*) or (*b*)][1], the relevant date is the date of the passing of the resolution for the winding up of the company.

(4) In relation to a company in receivership (where section 40 or, as the case may be, section 59 applies), the relevant date is—

    (*a*) in England and Wales, the date of the appointment of the receiver by debenture-holders, and
    (*b*) in Scotland, the date of the appointment of the receiver under section 53(6) or (as the case may be) 54(5).

(5) For the purposes of section 258 in Part VIII (individual voluntary arrangements), the relevant date is, in relation to a debtor who is not an undischarged bankrupt, the date of the interim order made under section 252 with respect to his proposal.

(6) In relation to a bankrupt, the following applies—

    (*a*) where at the time the bankruptcy order was made there was an interim receiver appointed under section 286, the relevant date is the date on which the interim receiver was first appointed after the presentation of the bankruptcy petition;
    (*b*) otherwise, the relevant date is the date of the making of the bankruptcy order.

Amendments—[1] Sub-s (3), paras (*aa*), (*ab*) inserted, words in para (*b*) inserted, and words in para (*c*) substituted, by the Insolvency Act 1986 (Amendment) (No 2) Regulations, SI 2002/1240 regs 3, 16 with effect from 31 May 2002.
Prospective amendments—In sub-s (2)(*b*) for the words following ''date'' there is substituted ''on which the voluntary arrangement takes effect'' by the Insolvency Act 2000 s 2, Sch 2 para 11 with effect from a day to be appointed.

Sub-s (2A) inserted by the Insolvency Act 2000 s 1, Sch 1 para 9 with effect from a day to be appointed as follows—

"(2A) For the purposes of paragraph 31 of Schedule A1 (meetings to consider company voluntary arrangement where a moratorium under section 1A is in force), the relevant date in relation to a company is the date of filing.".

Words following "undischarged bankrupt" in sub-s (5) substituted by the Insolvency Act 2000 s 3, Sch 3 para 15 with effect from a day to be appointed as follows—

"(*a*) where an interim order has been made under section 252 with respect to his proposal, the date of that order, and
(*b*) in any other case, the date on which the voluntary arrangement takes effect.".

SCHEDULE 6

THE CATEGORIES OF PREFERENTIAL DEBTS

Section 386

Category 1: Debts due to Inland Revenue

1 Sums due at the relevant date from the debtor on account of deductions of income tax from emoluments paid during the period of 12 months next before that date.

The deductions here referred to are those which the debtor was liable to make under [section 203 of the Income and Corporation Taxes Act 1988][1] (pay as you earn), less the amount of the repayments of income tax which the debtor was liable to make during that period.

Amendments—[1] Words substituted by virtue of TA 1988 Sch 29 para 32 Table with effect for companies' accounting periods ending after 5 April 1988.

2 Sums due at the relevant date from the debtor in respect of such deductions as are required to be made by the debtor for that period under [section 559 of the Income and Corporation Taxes Act 1988][1] (sub-contractors in the construction industry).

Amendments—[1] Words substituted by virtue of TA 1988 Sch 29 para 32 Table with effect for companies' accounting periods ending after 5 April 1988.

Category 3: Social Security contributions

6 All sums which on the relevant date are due from the debtor on account of Class 1 or Class 2 contributions under the [Social Security Contributions and Benefits Act 1992][1] or the Social Security (Northern Ireland) Act 1975 and which became due from the debtor in the 12 months next before the relevant date.

Amendments—[1] Words substituted by SS(CP)A 1992 ss 4, 7(2), Sch 2 para 73 with effect from 1 July 1992.

7 All sums which on the relevant date have been assessed on and are due from the debtor on account of Class 4 contributions under either of those Acts of 1975, being sums which—

(*a*) are due to the Commissioners of Inland Revenue (rather than to the Secretary of State or a Northern Ireland department), and
(*b*) are assessed on the debtor up to 5th April next before the relevant date,

but not exceeding, in the whole, any one year's assessment.

BANKING ACT 1987

(1987 Chapter 22)

Note—The Banking Act 1987 has been repealed by the Financial Services and Markets Act 2000 (Consequential Amendments and Repeals) Order, SI 2001/3649 arts 1, 3(1)(*d*) with effect from 1 Decmber 2001.

66 Tax treatment of contributions and repayments

In computing for the purposes of the Tax Acts the profits or gains arising from the trade carried on by a contributory institution—

(*a*) *to the extent that it would not be deductible apart from this section, any sum expended by the institution in paying a contribution to the Fund may be deducted as an allowable expense;*
(*b*) *any payment which is made to the institution by the Board under section 55(2) above or pursuant to a scheme under section 63(2) above shall be treated as a trading receipt.*

FINANCE (NO 2) ACT 1987

(1987 Chapter 51)

An Act to grant certain duties, to alter other duties, and to amend the law relating to the National Debt and the Public Revenue, and to make further provision in connection with Finance.

[23rd July 1987]

CHAPTER V
TAXES MANAGEMENT PROVISIONS

Company returns

82 Return of profits

Amendments—This section repealed by FA 1998 s 165, Sch 27 Part III(28) for accounting periods ending after 30 June 1999 (by virtue of Finance Act 1994, Section 199, (Appointed Day) Order, SI 1998/3173 art 2).

83 Failure to make return for corporation tax

Amendments—This section repealed by FA 1998 s 165, Sch 27 Part III(28) for accounting periods ending after 30 June 1999 (by virtue of Finance Act 1994, Section 199, (Appointed Day) Order, SI 1998/3173 art 2).

Interest etc

85 Interest on overdue corporation tax etc

(*Inserts* TMA 1970 s 87A with respect to accounting periods ending after the appointed day).

Orders—Corporation Tax Acts (Provisions for Payment of Tax and Returns) (Appointed Days) Order, SI 1992/3066.

86 Supplementary provisions as to interest on overdue tax

(1) (*amends* TMA 1970 s 69; *repealed* by FA 2001 s 110, Sch 33 Pt II(14) with effect for proceedings begun, or a counterclaim made, and a set-off first claimed after the passing of FA 2001).

(2) (*repeals* TMA 1970 s 86(2)(*dd*) and para 5 of Table).

(3) References to section 86 of the Management Act in—

    (*aa*) sections 70 (2) and 92 of that Act (evidence, and remission of interest in certain cases), and
    (*bb*) paragraph 4 of Schedule 15 to the Finance Act 1973 (territorial extension of tax),

shall include a reference to section 87A of the Management Act.

(4)–(6) (*amend* TMA 1970 ss 88, 91(2) and *insert* ss 91(1A), (1B), (2A)).

(7) This section has effect with respect to accounting periods ending after the appointed day.

Orders—Corporation Tax Acts (Provisions for Payment of Tax and Returns) (Appointed Days) Order, SI 1992/3066.

88 Recovery of overpayment of tax etc

Amendments—This section repealed by FA 1998 s 165, Sch 27 Part III(28) for accounting periods ending after 30 June 1999 (by virtue of Finance Act 1994, Section 199, (Appointed Day) Order, SI 1998/3173 art 2).

91 Close companies: loans to participators

(1)–(3) (*Repeal* TMA 1970 s 109(2), *amend* TMA 1970 s 109(3) and *insert* TMA 1970 s 109(3A)).

(4) This section has effect with respect to loans or advances made (or treated as made) in any accounting period ending after the appointed day.

Orders—Corporation Tax Acts (Provisions for Payment of Tax and Returns) (Appointed Days) Order, SI 1992/3066.

95 Interpretation of Chapter V and consequential and supplementary provisions

(1) In this Chapter "the Management Act" means the Taxes Management Act 1970.

(2) Subject to subsection (3) below, any reference in this Chapter to the appointed day is a reference to such day as the Treasury may by order made by statutory instrument appoint, and different days may be so appointed for different provisions of this Chapter.

(3) No day may be appointed by virtue of subsection (2) above which falls earlier than 31st March 1992.

(4) The provisions of Schedule 6 to this Act shall have effect, being provisions consequential on and supplementary to the provisions of this Chapter.

Commentary—*Simon's Direct Tax Service* **D2.701.**
Orders—Corporation Tax Acts (Provisions for Payment of Tax and Returns) (Appointed Days) Order, SI 1992/3066.

SCHEDULE 6

MANAGEMENT PROVISIONS: SUPPLEMENTARY AND CONSEQUENTIAL PROVISIONS

Section 95

Companies' capital gains

1–8 (Paras 1, 3, 6, 8 *repealed by* TA 1988 Sch 31, paras 2, 4, 5, *repealed by* TCGA 1992 Sch 12, para 7 *repealed by* FA 1995 Sch 29 Pt VIII(16), *in relation to accounting periods beginning after 31 March 1996*).

INCOME AND CORPORATION TAXES ACT 1988

(1988 Chapter 1)

ARRANGEMENT OF PARTS

DESTINATION TABLE

For a table listing the provisions of the Income and Corporation Taxes Act 1970 and subsequent Finance Acts and other Acts which were re-enacted in the Income and Corporation Taxes Act 1988, see the Yellow Tax Handbook Part II.

ARRANGEMENT OF SECTIONS

PART I

THE CHARGE TO TAX

Income tax

Corporation tax

Small companies' rate

PART II
PROVISIONS RELATING TO THE SCHEDULE A CHARGE ...

CHAPTER IV

PROVISIONS SUPPLEMENTARY TO CHAPTERS II AND III

CHAPTER V

COMPUTATIONAL PROVISIONS

Deductions

Treatment of regional development and other grants and debts released etc

Special provisions

CHAPTER VI

DISCONTINUANCE ...

Valuation of trading stock etc

PART V

PROVISIONS RELATING TO THE SCHEDULE E CHARGE

CHAPTER I

SUPPLEMENTARY CHARGING PROVISIONS OF GENERAL APPLICATION

Miscellaneous provisions

Shareholdings, loans etc

Vouchers etc

Living accommodation

Payments on retirement, sick pay etc

CHAPTER II

EMPLOYEES EARNING £8,500 OR MORE AND DIRECTORS

Expenses

Benefits in kind

CHAPTER III
PROFIT-RELATED PAY
Preliminary

CHAPTER IV
OTHER EXEMPTIONS AND RELIEFS
Share option and profit sharing schemes

Contributions in respect of share option gains

Retirement benefits etc

Removal expenses and benefits

Foreign emoluments and earnings, pensions and certain travel facilities

Mileage allowances

Mileage allowances

Sporting and recreational facilities

Other expenses, subscriptions etc

CHAPTER V

ASSESSMENT, COLLECTION, RECOVERY AND APPEALS

PART VI

COMPANY DISTRIBUTIONS, TAX CREDITS ETC

CHAPTER I

TAXATION OF COMPANY DISTRIBUTIONS

CHAPTER II

MATTERS WHICH ARE DISTRIBUTIONS FOR THE PURPOSES OF THE

CORPORATION TAX ACTS

CHAPTER III

MATTERS WHICH ARE NOT DISTRIBUTIONS FOR THE PURPOSES OF THE
CORPORATION TAX ACTS

Payments of interest

Demergers

CHAPTER IV
TAX CREDITS

CHAPTER V
ADVANCE CORPORATION TAX AND FRANKED INVESTMENT INCOME

CHAPTER VA
FOREIGN INCOME DIVIDENDS

Election by company paying dividend

Recipient of foreign income dividend

Companies: payments and receipts

CHAPTER II
TAXATION OF INCOME OF SPOUSES
General rules

Separate assessments

Separate taxation

CHAPTER III
ENTERPRISE INVESTMENT SCHEME

PART VIII
TAXATION OF INCOME AND CHARGEABLE GAINS OF COMPANIES
Taxation of income

Chargeable gains

PART IX
ANNUAL PAYMENTS AND INTEREST
Annual payments

Relief for payments of interest (excluding MIRAS)

CHAPTER II
FRIENDLY SOCIETIES, TRADE UNIONS AND EMPLOYERS' ASSOCIATIONS
Unregistered friendly societies

Registered friendly societies

Trade unions and employers' associations

CHAPTER III
UNIT TRUST SCHEMES, DEALERS IN SECURITIES ETC
Unit trust schemes

Distributions of authorised unit trusts: general

Dividend and foreign income distributions

Interest distributions

PART XIII

MISCELLANEOUS SPECIAL PROVISIONS

CHAPTER I

INTELLECTUAL PROPERTY

Patents and know-how

Copyright and public lending right

Artists' receipts

CHAPTER II

LIFE POLICIES, LIFE ANNUITIES AND CAPITAL REDEMPTION POLICIES

CHAPTER III

ENTERTAINERS AND SPORTSMEN

CHAPTER IV

SUB-CONTRACTORS IN THE CONSTRUCTION INDUSTRY

CHAPTER V

SCHEMES FOR RATIONALISING INDUSTRY

CHAPTER VI

OTHER PROVISIONS

Relief for losses on unlisted shares in trading companies

Miscellaneous

PART XIV

PENSION SCHEMES, SOCIAL SECURITY BENEFITS, LIFE ANNUITIES ETC

CHAPTER I

RETIREMENT BENEFIT SCHEMES

Approval of schemes

Tax reliefs

Charge to tax in certain cases

Supplementary provisions

TA 1988

TA 1988

CHAPTER V
OFFSHORE FUNDS

Material interests in non-qualifying offshore funds

Charge to tax of offshore income gains

CHAPTER VI
MISCELLANEOUS

Migration etc of company

Change in ownership of company

Transactions between associated persons

PART XVIII

DOUBLE TAXATION RELIEF

CHAPTER I

THE PRINCIPAL RELIEFS

CHAPTER II

RULES GOVERNING RELIEF BY WAY OF CREDIT

General

Tax underlying dividends

Miscellaneous rules

*An Act to consolidate certain of the enactments relating to income tax and corporation tax, including
    certain enactments relating also to capital gains tax; and to repeal as obsolete section 339(1)
    of the Income and Corporation Taxes Act 1970 and paragraphs 3 and 4 of Schedule 11 to the
    Finance Act 1980.*   [9 February 1988]

PART I

THE CHARGE TO TAX

Income tax

1 The charge to income tax

(1) Income tax shall be charged in accordance with the provisions of the Income Tax Acts in respect
of all property, profits or gains respectively described or comprised in the [Schedules A, D, E and
F][9], set out in sections 15 to 20 or which in accordance with the Income Tax Acts are to be brought
into charge to tax under any of those Schedules or otherwise.

(2) Where any Act enacts that income tax shall be charged for any year, income tax shall be charged
for that year—

[(*aa*) in respect of so much of an individual's total income as does not exceed [£1,920][14], at such rate as Parliament may determine to be the starting rate for that year;][10]
(*a*) in respect of any income which does not fall within [paragraph (*aa*) above or][5] paragraph (*b*) below, at such rate as Parliament may determine to be the basic rate for that year;
[(*b*) in respect of so much of an individual's total income as exceeds [£29,900][13], at such higher rate as Parliament may determine][1];

but this subsection has effect subject to any provision of the Income Tax Acts providing for income tax to be charged at a different rate in certain cases.

[(2A) The amount up to which an individual's income is by virtue of subsection (2) above chargeable for any year at the starting rate shall be known as the starting rate limit.][10]

(3) The amount up to which an individual's income is by virtue of subsection (2) above chargeable for any year at the [starting rate][10] or the basic rate shall be known as the basic rate limit; ...[2]

(4) If the retail prices index for the month of [September][7] preceding a year of assessment is higher than it was for the previous [September][7], then, unless Parliament otherwise determines, subsection (2) above shall apply for that year as if for [each of the amounts specified][6] in that subsection as it applied for the previous year (whether by virtue of this subsection or otherwise) there were substituted an amount arrived at by increasing the amount for the previous year by the same percentage as the percentage increase in the retail prices index [and—

(*a*) if the result in the case of the amount specified in subsection (2)(*aa*) above is not a multiple of £10, rounding it up to the nearest amount which is such a multiple, and
(*b*) if the result in the case of the amount specified in subsection (2)(*b*) above is not a multiple of £100, rounding it up to the nearest amount which is such a multiple.][12]

[(5A) Subsection (4) above shall not require any change to be made in the amounts deductible or repayable under section 203 during the period beginning with 6th April and ending with 17th May in the year of assessment.][11]

(5) ...[8]

(6) The Treasury shall before each year of assessment make an order specifying the [amounts][6] which by virtue of subsection (4) above will be treated as specified for that year in subsection (2) above.

[(6A) Where income tax at the basic rate has been borne on income chargeable at the [starting rate][10] any necessary repayment of tax shall be made on the making of a claim.][4]

(7) Part VII contains general provisions relating to the taxation of income of individuals.

Commentary—*Simon's Direct Tax Service* **A1.104; E1.102, 104.**
Statement of Practice SP B1—This Statement sets out general principles applied in dealing with VAT in the computation of liability to income tax and corporation tax. It deals with the position of taxpayers who make exempt supplies, zero-rated supplies, taxable supplies and partly taxable supplies. It also deals with the position of taxpayers who have suffered bad debts.

Simon's Tax Cases—s 1(2), *Ang v Parrish* [1980] STC 3741*.
Definitions—"Act", s 832(1); "basic rate", s 832(1); "higher rates", s 831(1)(*b*); "profits or gains", s 833(1); "retail prices index", s 833(2); "Schedule A", s 15(1); "Schedule B", s 16(1); "Schedule C", s 17(1); "Schedule D", s 18(1); "Schedule E", s 19(1); "Schedule F", s 20(1); "starting rate", s 832(1); "total income", s 835(1); "year of assessment", s 832(1).
Note—The starting rate of income tax for 2002–03 is 10%, the basic rate is 22% and the higher rate is 40% (FA 2002 s 26).
Cross references—See TA 1988 s 1A (non-dividend savings income to be charged to tax at lower rate instead of starting rate and basic rate; dividend etc income to be charged at the Schedule F ordinary rate instead of the starting rate and basic rate, and at the Schedule F upper rate instead of the higher rate).
TA 1988 s 200 (exemption from income tax for payments to members of the House of Commons in respect of necessary overnight expenses or EU travel).
TA 1988 s 200ZA (exemption from income tax for payments to members of the Scottish Parliament, the National Assembly for Wales and the Northern Ireland Assembly in respect of necessary overnight expenses or EU travel).
TA 1988 s 203 (deduction of Sch E tax at source under PAYE).
TA 1988 s 686 (liability to additional rate of tax for certain income of discretionary trusts).
FA 2001 s 51(2) (sub-s (4) above does not apply for 2001–02 so far as it relates to the amount specified in sub-s (2)(*aa*) above).
FA 2002 s 27(*a*) (sub-s (5A) above has effect for 2002–03 as if "17th June" were substituted for "17th May").
Amendments—[1] Sub-s (2)(*b*) substituted by FA 1988 s 24(2).
[2] Words in sub-s (3) repealed by FA 1988 s 24(2)(*b*) and Sch 14 Pt IV with effect from the year 1988–89.
[3] The reference to Schedule B in sub-s (1) repealed by FA 1988 Sch 14 Pt V with effect from 6 April 1988.
[4] Sub-s (6A) inserted by FA 1992 s 9(1)–(8), (10) with effect from the year 1992–93.
[5] Words in sub-s (2)(*a*) inserted by FA 1992 s 9(1)–(8), (10) with effect from the year 1992–93.
[6] Words in sub-ss (4), (6) substituted by FA 1992 s 9(1)–(8), (10) with effect from the year 1992–93.
[7] "September" in sub-s (4) substituted by FA 1993 s 107(1), (2) with effect from the year 1994–95.
[8] Sub-s (5) repealed by FA 1993 Sch 23 Pt III(10) with effect from the year 1994–95.
[9] Words in sub-s (1) substituted by FA 1996 Sch 7 paras 2, 32 with from the year 1996–97.
[10] Sub-ss (2)(*aa*), (2A) and words in sub-ss (3), (6A) substituted by FA 1999 s 22(1)–(3), (6), (12), 25(2), (4) with effect from the year 1999–00.
[11] Sub-s (5A) inserted by FA 1999 s 25(2), (4) with effect from the year 1999–00.
[12] Words in sub-s (4) substituted by FA 1999 s 22(4), (12) with effect from the year 2000–01.
[13] Amount in sub-s (2)(*b*) specified by the Income Tax (Indexation) Order, SI 2002/707 art 2(2)(*b*) with effect for 2002–03.
[14] Amount in sub-s (2)(*aa*) specified by SI 2002/707 art 2(2)(*a*) with effect for 2002–03.

[1A Application of lower rate to income from savings and distributions

(1) Subject to sections 469(2)[, 686 and 720(5),][3], so much of any person's total income for any year of assessment as—

   (*a*) comprises income to which this section applies, and

   (*b*) in the case of an individual, is not[—

      (i) savings income falling within section 1(2)(*aa*), or

      (ii)][6] income falling within section 1(2)(*b*),

shall, by virtue of this section, be charged for that year at the [rate applicable in accordance with sub-section (1A) below][4], instead of at the rate otherwise applicable to it in accordance with section 1(2)(*aa*) and (*a*).

[(1AA) In subsection (1)(*b*)(i) above "savings income" means income to which this section applies other than—

   (*a*) income chargeable under Schedule F, or

   (*b*) equivalent foreign income falling within subsection (3)(*b*) below and chargeable under Case V of Schedule D.][6]

[(1A) The rate applicable in accordance with this subsection is—

   (*a*) in the case of income chargeable under Schedule F, the Schedule F ordinary rate;

   (*b*) in the case of equivalent foreign income falling within subsection (3)(*b*) below and chargeable under Case V of Schedule D, the Schedule F ordinary rate; and

   (*c*) in the case of any other income, the lower rate.][4]

[(1B) In relation to any year of assessment for which income tax is charged the lower rate is 20 per cent or such other rate as Parliament may determine.][5]

(2) Subject to subsection (4) below, this section applies to the following income—

   (*a*) any income chargeable under Case III of Schedule D other than—

      (i) relevant annuities and other annual payments that are not interest; and

      (ii) amounts so chargeable by virtue of section 119 ...[2];

   [(*aa*) any amount chargeable to tax under Case VI of Schedule D by virtue of section 714, 716 or 723;][3]

   (*b*) any income chargeable under Schedule F; and

   (*c*) subject to subsection (4) below, any equivalent foreign income.

(3) The income which is equivalent foreign income for the purposes of this section is any income chargeable under Case IV or V of Schedule D which—

   (*a*) is equivalent to a description of income falling within subsection (2)(*a*) above but arises from securities or other possessions out of the United Kingdom; or

   (*b*) consists in any such dividend or other distribution of a company not resident in the United Kingdom as would be chargeable under Schedule F if the company were resident in the United Kingdom.

(4) This section does not apply to—

   (*a*) any income chargeable to tax under Case IV or V of Schedule D which is such that section 65(5)(*a*) or (*b*) provides for the tax to be computed on the full amount of sums received in the United Kingdom; or

   (*b*) any amounts deemed by virtue of section 695(4)(*b*) or 696(6) to be income chargeable under Case IV of Schedule D.

[(5) For the purposes of subsection (1)(*b*) above and any other provisions of the Income Tax Acts—

   (*a*) so much of any person's income as comprises income to which this section applies shall be treated as the highest part of his income; and

   (*b*) so much of that part as consists of—

      (i) income chargeable under Schedule F (if any), and

      (ii) equivalent foreign income falling within subsection (3)(*b*) above and chargeable under Case V of Schedule D (if any),

shall be treated as the highest part of that part.][4]

(6) Subsection (5) above shall have effect subject to section 833(3) but shall otherwise have effect notwithstanding any provision requiring income of any description to be treated for the purposes of the Income Tax Acts (other than section 550) as the highest part of a person's income.

[(6A) Where income tax at the basic rate has been borne on income chargeable at the lower rate any necessary repayment of tax shall be made on the making of a claim.][5]

(7) In this section "relevant annuity" means any annuity other than a purchased life annuity to which section 656 applies or to which that section would apply but for section 657(2)(*a*).][1]

Commentary—*Simon's Direct Tax Service* E1.102.

Definitions—"Basic rate", s 832(1); "company", s 832(1); "Income Tax Acts", s 831(1)(*b*); "lower rate", s 832(1); "resident in the United Kingdom", FA 1988 s 66; "Schedule D", s 18; "Schedule F", s 20; "total income", s 835(1); "United Kingdom", s 830(1); "year of assessment", s 832(1).

Cross references—See TA 1988 s 1B (for 2000–01 the Schedule F ordinary rate is 10%, and the Schedule F upper rate is 32.5%). TA 1988 s 249(4) (stock dividends issued to an individual treated as income to which this section applies on which the individual has paid income tax at the lower rate).

TA 1988 s 421(1) (the amount of a loan to a participator in a close company which is released or written off is treated as income to which this section applies).
TA 1988 s 469(2) (income of unauthorised unit trust to which this section applies to be chargeable to tax at the basic rate instead of the lower rate).
TA 1988 s 686 (income of accumulation or discretionary trusts within this section to be charged to tax at the following rates: income within sub-ss (2)(*a*)(*aa*), (3)(*a*) above at the rate applicable to trusts; income within sub-ss (2)(*b*), (3)(*b*) above at the Schedule F trust rate).
TA 1988 s 689B(4) (trustees' expenses to be set against income falling within this section first, notwithstanding sub-ss (5), (6) above).
TA 1988 s 698A(1) (this section treated as applying to income which is treated under Part XVI (estates of deceased persons in course of administration) as having borne income tax at the lower rate).
TA 1988 s 698A(2) (income of residue of a deceased's estate paid indirectly through a trustee treated as income of the trustee to which this section applies).
TA 1988 Sch 23A para 3(2) (manufactured interest to constitute income of the recipient falling within this section).
Amendments—[1] This section inserted by FA 1996 s 73(1), (3) with effect from the year 1996–97 .
[2] Words omitted in sub-s (2)(*a*)(ii) repealed by FA 1997 Sch 18 Pt VI(2) with effect in relation to payments made after 5 April 1997.
[3] Words in sub-s (1) substituted, and sub-s (2)(aa) inserted, by FA 1998 s 100(1)(2) with effect from the year 1998–99.
[4] Sub-s (1A) inserted, words in sub-s (1) substituted for "lower rate", and sub-s (5) substituted, by F(No 2)A 1997 s 31(1)-(4), (6) in relation to distributions made after 5 April 1999.
[5] Sub-ss (1B), (6A) inserted by FA 1999 s 22(7), (12) with effect from the year 1999–00.
[6] Words in sub-s (1) and whole of sub-s (1AA) inserted by FA 2000 s 32 with effect from the year 2000–01 and deemed to have had effect for the year 1999–00.

[1B Rates of tax applicable to Schedule F income

(1) In the case of so much of an individual's income which consists of—

 (*a*) income chargeable under Schedule F (if any), and
 (*b*) equivalent foreign income falling within section 1A(3)(*b*) and chargeable under Case V of Schedule D (if any),

as is income falling within section 1(2)(*b*), income tax shall, by virtue of this subsection, be charged at the Schedule F upper rate, instead of at the rate otherwise applicable to it in accordance with section 1(2)(*b*).

(2) In relation to any year of assessment for which income tax is charged—

 (*a*) the Schedule F ordinary rate is 10 per cent, and
 (*b*) the Schedule F upper rate is 32.5 per cent,

or, in either case, such other rate as Parliament may determine.][1]

Amendments—[1] This section inserted by F(No 2)A 1997 s 31(5), (6) with effect in relation to distributions made after 5 April 1999.

2 Fractions of a pound, and yearly assessments

(1) The due proportion of income tax shall be charged for every fractional part of one pound.

(2) Every assessment and charge to income tax shall be made for a year commencing on the 6th April and ending on the following 5th April.

Commentary—*Simon's Direct Tax Service* **A1.144.**

3 Certain income charged at basic rate

Where a person is required to be assessed and charged with income tax in respect of any property, profits or gains out of which he makes any payment in respect of—

 (*a*) any annuity or other annual payment (not being interest); or
 (*b*) any royalty or other sum in respect of the user of a patent; ...[1]
 (*c*) ...[1]

he shall, in respect of so much of the property, profits or gains as is equal to the payment and may be deducted in computing his total income, be charged at the basic rate.

Commentary—*Simon's Direct Tax Service* **E1.501–503.**
Revenue Internal Guidance—Relief, RE 100–153 (meaning of "charges" (RE 100–RE 110); summary guide (RE 101); effect on tax liabilities with worked examples (RE 120–RE 131); failure to deduct tax at source (RE 140)).
Definitions—"Basic rate", s 832(1); "interest", s 832(1); "profits or gains", s 833(1); "total income", s 835(1).
Cross reference—See TA 1988 s 231(3) (tax credits may be set against income tax chargeable under this section).
Amendments—[1] Para (*c*), and preceding word "or", repealed by FA 1997 Sch 18 Pt VI(2) with effect in relation to payments made after 5 April 1997.

4 Construction of references in Income Tax Acts to deduction of tax

(1) Any provision of the Income Tax Acts requiring, permitting or assuming the deduction of income tax from any amount (otherwise than in pursuance of section 203) or treating income tax as having been deducted from or paid on any amount, shall, subject to any provision to the contrary, be construed as referring to deduction or payment of income tax at the basic rate in force for the relevant year of assessment.

[(1A) As respects deductions from, and tax treated as paid on, any such amounts as constitute or (but for the person whose income they are) would constitute income to which section 1A applies, subsection (1) above shall have effect with a reference to the lower rate in force for the relevant year of assessment substituted for the reference to the basic rate in force for that year.][1]

[(1B) To the extent that section 118E (paying and collecting agents: deduction of tax) applies in relation to foreign dividend income—

(*a*) subsections (1) and (1A) above shall not apply, and

(*b*) any provision of that section of the kind mentioned in subsection (1) above shall be construed as referring to deduction or payment of income tax at the Schedule F ordinary rate in force for the relevant year of assessment.

For this purpose ''foreign dividend income'' means any such dividend or other distribution of a company not resident in the United Kingdom as would be chargeable under Schedule F if the company were resident in the United Kingdom.]³

(2) For the purposes of [this section]², the relevant year of assessment shall be taken to be (except where otherwise provided)—

(*a*) if the amount is an amount payable wholly out of profits or gains brought into charge to tax, the year in which the amount becomes due;

(*b*) in any other case, the year in which the amount is paid.

Commentary—*Simon's Direct Tax Service* A3.401; E1.103.
Simon's Tax Cases—*IRC v Crawley* [1987] STC 147*.
Definitions—''Basic rate'', s 832(1); ''the Income Tax Acts'', s 831(1)(*b*); ''profits or gains'', s 833(1); ''year of assessment'', s 832(1).
Amendments—¹ Sub-s (1A) inserted by FA 1996 s 73(2), (3) in relation to payments after 5 April 1996.
² Words in sub-s (2) substituted by FA 1996 Sch 6 paras 2, 28 with effect from the year 1996–97.
³ Sub-s (1B) inserted by FA 2000 s 33 with effect for the year 2000–01 and deemed to have had effect for the year 1999–00.

5 Date for payment

Commentary—*Simon's Direct Tax Service* A3.1302, 1303.
Amendments—This section repealed by FA 1994 s 199(2), (3), Sch 26 Pt V(23) with effect for income tax and capital gains tax from the year 1996–97. For partnerships whose trades, professions or businesses were set up and commenced before 6 April 1994 the repeal has effect from 1997–98.

Corporation tax

6 The charge to corporation tax and exclusion of income tax and capital gains tax

(1) Corporation tax shall be charged on profits of companies, and the Corporation Tax Acts shall apply, for any financial year for which Parliament so determines, and where an Act charges corporation tax for any financial year the Corporation Tax Acts apply, without any express provision, for that year accordingly.

(2) The provisions of the Income Tax Acts relating to the charge of income tax shall not apply to income of a company (not arising to it in a fiduciary or representative capacity) if—

(*a*) the company is resident in the United Kingdom, or

(*b*) the income is, in the case of a company not so resident, within the chargeable profits of the company as defined for the purposes of corporation tax by section 11(2).

(3) A company shall not be chargeable to capital gains tax in respect of gains accruing to it so that it is chargeable in respect of them to corporation tax or would be so chargeable but for an exemption from corporation tax.

(4) In this section, sections 7 to 12, 114, 115 (but subject to subsection (7)), *242, 243²* ...³ and 248, Part VIII, Chapter IV of Part X and Part XI, except in so far as the context otherwise requires—

(*a*) ''profits'' means income and chargeable gains; and

(*b*) ''trade'' includes ''vocation'', and also includes an office or employment ...¹

(5) Part VIII contains general provisions relating to the taxation of profits of companies.

Commentary—*Simon's Direct Tax Service* D2.102.
Revenue Interpretation RI 143—Clarification of the due dates for payment of tax charged in composite partnership assessments for 1996–97.
Definitions—''Act'', s 832(1); ''capital gains tax'', s 831(5); ''chargeable gains'', s 832(1); ''company'', s 832(1), (2); ''the Corporation Tax Acts'', s 831(1)(*a*); ''the Income Tax Acts'', s 831(1)(*b*); ''trade'', s 832(1).
Cross references—See TA 1988 s 7(5) (sub-s (2) above to be given effect by means of a claim).
TA 1988 s 13 (corporation tax small companies' rate).
TA 1988 s 70(1) (in accordance with this section, corporation tax to be computed under Schedule D Cases I to VI on the full amount of profits or gains or income arising in an accounting period, subject only to authorised deduction).
TA 1988 s 468(1A) (from 1996, corporation tax in relation to authorised unit trusts to be charged at the lower rate of income tax).
FA 1989 ss 88, 88A (rate of corporation tax on the profits of a company carrying on life assurance business).
TCGA 1992 s 1(2) (companies to be chargeable to corporation tax in respect of chargeable gains in accordance with this section).
FA 1998 s 29 (subject to TA 1988 ss 13, 13AA, corporation tax to be charged for the financial year 2000 at 30%).
FA 1999 s 24 (corporation tax charged for the financial year 2000 at 30%).
FA 2000 s 35 (corporation tax charged for the financial year 2001 at 30%).
FA 2001 s 54 (corporation tax charged for the financial year 2002 at 30%).
FA 2002 s 30 (corporation tax charged for the financial year 2003 at 30%).
Modification—Sub-s (4) modified to apply for the purposes of TA 1988 Sch 19AC para 5B in relation to overseas life insurance companies with effect for accounting periods beginning after 31 December 1994.
Amendments—¹ Words in sub-s (4)(*b*) repealed by FA 1988 Sch 14 Pt V with effect from 6 April 1993.
² Figures in sub-s (4) repealed by F(No 2) A 1997 Sch 8 Pt II(4) with effect generally in relation to accounting periods beginning after 1 July 1997 but subject to the detailed provisions of F(No 2)A 1997 s 20(1)-(4).
³ In sub-s (4), '', 247'' repealed by FA 2001 s 110, Sch 33 Pt II(10) with effect for payments made after 11 May 2001.

7 Treatment of certain payments and repayment of income tax

(1) No payment made by a company resident in the United Kingdom shall be treated for any purpose of the Income Tax Acts as paid out of profits or gains brought into charge to income tax; nor shall any right or obligation under the Income Tax Acts to deduct income tax from any payment be affected by the fact that the recipient is a company not chargeable to income tax in respect of the payment.

(2) Subject to the provisions of the Corporation Tax Acts, where a company resident in the United Kingdom receives any payment on which it bears income tax by deduction, the income tax thereon shall be set off against any corporation tax assessable on the company ...[2] for the accounting period in which that payment falls to be taken into account for corporation tax (or would fall to be taken into account but for any exemption from corporation tax); ...[1]

(3) Subsection (2) above does not apply to a payment of relevant loan interest to which section 369 applies.

(4) References in this section to payments received by a company apply to any received by another person on behalf of or in trust for the company, but not to any received by the company on behalf of or in trust for another person.

(5)–(7) ...[2]

Commentary—*Simon's Direct Tax Service* **D1.616.**
Definitions—''Accounting period'', s 834(1); ''company'', s 832(1), (2); ''the Corporation Tax Acts'', s 831(1)(a); ''income tax'', s 832(4); ''the Income Tax Acts'', s 831(1)(b); ''profits'', s 6(4); ''profits or gains'', s 833(1); ''United Kingdom'', s 830(1).
Revenue Internal Guidance—Company Taxation Manual COT3355, 3356 (treatment of charges etc in the case of non-resident companies).
Cross references—See TA 1988 s 70(1) (in accordance with this section, corporation tax to be computed under Schedule D Cases I to VI on the full amount of profits or gains or income arising in an accounting period, subject only to authorised deduction).
TA 1988 s 687A(3)(a) (sub-s (2) above not to apply in the case of a payment by a discretionary trust to a company after 1 July 1997).
TA 1988 Sch 16 para 7 (avoidance of double relief under sub-s (2) above and Sch 16 (income tax on company payments which are not distributions)).
TA 1988 Sch 19AB para 1(7) (provisional repayment of tax and tax credit to an insurance company carrying on pension business).
TA 1988 Sch 19AB para 5(2), (3), (5) (provisional repayment of tax and tax credit to an insurance company carrying on pension business; transitional application of pay and file provisions).
Gilt-edged Securities (Tax on Interest) Regulations, SI 1995/3224 reg 15 (avoidance of double relief in respect of income tax on excess gilt interest received under both sub-s (2) above and SI 1995/3224).
Amendments—[1] Words in sub-s (2) repealed by FA 1990 s 98(1), (2), (5) and Sch 19 Pt V in relation to set off of income tax against corporation tax for accounting periods ending after 30 September 1993.
[2] Words ''by an assessment made'' in sub-s (2) and sub-ss (5)–(7) repealed by FA 1998 s 165, Sch 27 Part III(28) with effect in relation to accounting periods ending after 30 June 1999 (by virtue of Finance Act 1994, Section 199, (Appointed Day) Order, SI 1998/3173 art 2).

8 General scheme of corporation tax

(1) Subject to any exceptions provided for by the Corporation Tax Acts, a company shall be chargeable to corporation tax on all its profits wherever arising.

(2) A company shall be chargeable to corporation tax on profits accruing for its benefit under any trust, or arising under any partnership, in any case in which it would be so chargeable if the profits accrued to it directly; and a company shall be chargeable to corporation tax on profits arising in the winding up of the company, but shall not otherwise be chargeable to corporation tax on profits accruing to it in a fiduciary or representative capacity except as respects its own beneficial interest (if any) in those profits.

(3) Corporation tax for any financial year shall be charged on profits arising in that year; but [corporation tax shall be computed and chargeable (and any assessments shall accordingly be made)][2] by reference to accounting periods, and the amount chargeable (after making all proper deductions) of the profits arising in an accounting period shall, where necessary, be apportioned between the financial years in which the accounting period falls.

(4)–(6) ...[1]

Commentary—*Simon's Direct Tax Service* **D2.104, 105, 113.**
Revenue & other press releases—IR booklet IR 126 (1993) (corporation tax pay and file—a general guide).
Definitions—''Accounting period'', s 834(1); ''company'', s 832(1), (2); ''the Corporation Tax Acts'', s 831(1)(a); ''profits'', s 6(4).
Revenue Internal Guidance—Company Taxation Manual COT52 (Sub-s(3): apportionment by reference to transactions where that gives more accurate result than time basis).
Cross references—See TMA 1970 s 10 (notice of liability to corporation tax).
TA 1988 s 70(1) (in accordance with this section, corporation tax to be computed under Schedule D Cases I to VI on the full amount of profits or gains or income arising in an accounting period, subject only to authorised deduction).
See TA 1988 s 834(4): apportionment on a time basis.
Amendments—[1] Sub-ss (4)–(6) repealed by FA 1993 s 206(1) and Sch 23 Pt VI.
[2] Words in sub-s (3) substituted by virtue of a provision in the same subsection with effect with respect to any accounting period ending after 30 September 1993 by virtue of the Corporation Tax Acts (Provisions for Payment of Tax and Returns) (Appointed Days) Order, SI 1992/3066 art 2.

8A Resolutions to reduce corporation tax

Commentary—*Simon's Direct Tax Service* **A1.105; D2.113.**
Amendments—This section (inserted by FA 1993 s 206(2)) repealed by FA 1996 Sch 24 para 10, Sch 41 Pt V(13) with effect from 29 April 1996.

9 Computation of income: application of income tax principles

(1) Except as otherwise provided by the Tax Acts, the amount of any income shall for purposes of corporation tax be computed in accordance with income tax principles, all questions as to the amounts which are or are not to be taken into account as income, or in computing income, or charged to tax as a person's income, or as to the time when any such amount is to be treated as arising, being determined in accordance with income tax law and practice as if accounting periods were years of assessment.

(2) For the purposes of this section "income tax law" means, in relation to any accounting period, the law applying, for the year of assessment in which the period ends, to the charge on individuals of income tax, except that it does not include such of the enactments of the Income Tax Acts as make special provision for individuals in relation to matters referred to in subsection (1) above.

(3) Accordingly, for purposes of corporation tax, income shall be computed, and the assessment shall be made, under the like Schedules and Cases as apply for purposes of income tax, and in accordance with the provisions applicable to those Schedules and Cases, but (subject to the provisions of the Corporation Tax Acts) the amounts so computed for the several sources of income, if more than one, together with any amount to be included in respect of chargeable gains, shall be aggregated to arrive at the total profits.

(4) Without prejudice to the generality of subsection (1) above, any provision of the Income Tax Acts which confers an exemption from income tax, or which provides for a person to be charged to income tax on any amount (whether expressed to be income or not, and whether an actual amount or not), shall, except as otherwise provided, have the like effect for purposes of corporation tax.

(5) Where, by virtue of this section or otherwise, any enactment applies both to income tax and to corporation tax—

(a) it shall not be affected in its operation by the fact that they are distinct taxes but, so far as is consistent with the Corporation Tax Acts, shall apply in relation to income tax and corporation tax as if they were one tax, so that, in particular, a matter which in a case involving two individuals is relevant for both of them in relation to income tax shall in a like case involving an individual and a company be relevant for him in relation to that tax and for it in relation to corporation tax; and

(b) for that purpose references in any such enactment to a relief from or charge to income tax, or to a specified provision of the Income Tax Acts shall, in the absence of or subject to any express adaptation, be construed as being or including a reference to any corresponding relief from or charge to corporation tax, or to any corresponding provision of the Corporation Tax Acts.

(6) The provisions of the Income Tax Acts applied by this section do not include sections 1 to 5, 60 to 69, Part VII or sections 348 to 350 of this Act; and nothing in this section shall be taken to mean that income arising in any period is to be computed by reference to any other period (except in so far as this results from apportioning to different parts of a period income of the whole period).

Commentary—*Simon's Direct Tax Service* D2.202.
Definitions—"Accounting period", s 834(1); "company", s 832(1), (2); "the Corporation Tax Acts", s 831(1)(a); "income tax", s 832(4); "the Income Tax Acts", s 831(1)(b).
Revenue Internal Guidance—Company Taxation Manual COT132 (Sub-s(3): separate computation required for each source for any accounting period).
Simon's Tax Cases—*Re a debtor (No 1240/SD/91), ex p the debtor v IRC* [1992] STC 771.
Cross references—See TA 1988 s 30(4) (sub-s (1) does not apply to the computation of income of a company incurring expenditure on sea walls and deductions are apportioned between accounting periods).
TA 1988 s 70(1) (in accordance with this section, corporation tax to be computed under Schedule D Cases I to VI on the full amount of profits or gains or income arising in an accounting period, subject only to authorised deduction).
TA 1988 s 207 (determination of disputes as to domicile or ordinary residence under Schedule E paragraph 1).
FA 1995 s 39(1) (modification of s 15 not to apply for the purposes of corporation tax).

10 Time for payment of tax

Commentary—*Simon's Direct Tax Service* A3.1306; D2.705, 706.
Amendments—This section repealed by FA 1994 Sch 26 Pt V(23) with effect for accounting periods ending after 30 June 1999 (by virtue of Finance Act 1994, Section 199, (Appointed Day) Order, SI 1998/3173 art 2).

11 Companies not resident in United Kingdom

(1) A company not resident in the United Kingdom shall not be within the charge to corporation tax unless it carries on a trade in the United Kingdom through a branch or agency but, if it does so, it shall, subject to any exceptions provided for by the Corporation Tax Acts, be chargeable to corporation tax on all its chargeable profits wherever arising.

(2) For purposes of corporation tax the chargeable profits of a company not resident in the United Kingdom but carrying on a trade there through a branch or agency shall be—

(a) any trading income arising directly or indirectly through or from the branch or agency, and any income from property or rights used by, or held by or for, the branch or agency (but so that this paragraph shall not include distributions received from companies resident in the United Kingdom); and

[(b) such chargeable gains as are, by virtue of section 10(3) of the 1992 Act, to be, or be included in, the company's chargeable profits.][1]

(3) ...², where a company not resident in the United Kingdom receives any payment on which it bears income tax by deduction, and the payment forms part of, or is to be taken into account in computing, the company's income chargeable to corporation tax, the income tax thereon shall be set off against any corporation tax assessable on that income ...⁴ for the accounting period in which the payment falls to be taken into account for corporation tax; ...³

(4) Subsection (3) above does not apply to a payment of relevant loan interest to which section 369 applies.

Commentary—*Simon's Direct Tax Service* **D4.123, 537.**
Revenue Interpretation RI 49—Tax need not be deducted under s 349(2)(*c*) of this Act from interest paid to UK branch of non-resident company which is liable to corporation tax under this section.
Definitions—"The 1992 Act", s 831(3); "accounting period", s 834(1); "branch or agency", s 834(1); "capital gains tax", s 831(5); "chargeable gain", s 832(1); "company", s 832(1), (2); "the Corporation Tax Acts", s 831(1)(*a*); "distribution", ss 209(2), 832(1); "income tax", s 832(4); "interest", s 832(1); "profits", s 6(4); "resident in the United Kingdom", FA 1988 s 66; "trade", ss 6(4), 832(1); "United Kingdom", s 830(1).
Revenue Internal Guidance—Banking Manual BM 9.1.1–9.2.4.2 (taxation of foreign banks trading in the UK).
Company Taxation Manual COT3351 (a non-resident company not carrying on a trade through a branch or agency in the UK is chargeable to income tax on income arising in the UK, subject to ESC B13 (bank interest) and to double taxation agreements).
COT3352 (differences in taxation of resident and non-resident companies).
COT3361 (liability is not pursued in respect of FIDs received by a non-resident company; a non-qualifying distribution is neither income nor FII in the hands of a non-resident company).
Cross references—See TA 1988 s 70(1) (in accordance with this section, corporation tax to be computed under Schedule D Cases I to VI on the full amount of profits or gains or income arising in an accounting period, subject only to authorised deduction).
TA 1988 s 95(1A)(*e*) (modification of sub-s (2)(*a*) above in its application in relation to a relevant distribution received by a dealer).
TA 1988 s 687A(3)(*a*) (sub-s (3) above not to apply in the case of a payment by a discretionary trust to a company after 1 July 1997).
TA 1988 s 761(2), (4) (this section to have effect with certain modification in relation to tax on offshore income gains).
TA 1988 Sch 19AB para 5(3) (modification of sub-s (3) above in relation to provisional repayment of tax and tax credit claim by an insurance company carrying on pension business).
TA 1988 Sch 19AC, para 3 (modification of sub-s (2) and insertion of sub-s (2A) in relation to the application of this section to overseas life insurance companies).
FA 1993 Sch 9 para 2 (deemed disposal and reacquisition of assets at market value if the company referred to in sub-s (2) above is an overseas life insurance company).
FA 1994 s 219(4) (dividends forming part of the profits of a premiums trust fund of Lloyd's corporate member to be chargeable under Schedule D Case I notwithstanding anything in sub-s (2)(*a*) above).
Gilt-edged Securities (Tax on Interest) Regulations, SI 1995/3224 reg 15(3) (avoidance of double relief in respect of income tax on excess gilt interest received under both sub-s (3) above and SI 1995/3224).
Amendments—¹ Sub-s (2)(*b*) substituted by TCGA 1992 Sch 10 para 14(1), (2) in respect of accounting period beginning after 5 April 1992.
² Words in sub-s (3) repealed by FA 1993 Sch 23 Pt III(9) in relation to accounting periods beginning after 31 December 1992.
³ Words in sub-s (3) repealed by FA 1990 s 98(1), (4), (5), Sch 19 Pt V in relation to income tax falling to be set off against corporation tax for accounting periods ending after 30 September 1993.
⁴ Words "by an assessment made" in sub-s (3) repealed by FA 1998 s 165, Sch 27 Part III(28) for accounting periods ending after 30 June 1999 (by virtue of Finance Act 1994, Section 199, (Appointed Day) Order, SI 1998/3173 art 2).

11A Overseas life insurance companies: interpretation of sections 11B and 11C

Note—This section is treated as inserted as a modification of this Act in its application to overseas life insurance companies by s 444B of and Sch 19AC, paras 1, 4 to this Act in relation to accounting periods beginning after 31 December 1992.

11B Overseas life insurance companies: attribution of assets

Note—This section is treated as inserted as a modification of this Act in its application to overseas life insurance companies by s 444B of and Sch 19AC, paras 1, 4 to this Act in relation to accounting periods beginning after 31 December 1992.

11C Overseas life insurance companies: additional income and gains

Note—This section is treated as inserted as a modification of this Act in its application to overseas life insurance companies by s 444B of and Sch 19AC, paras 1, 4 to this Act in relation to accounting periods beginning after 31 December 1992.

12 Basis of, and periods for, assessment

(1) Except as otherwise provided by the Corporation Tax Acts, corporation tax shall be assessed and charged for any accounting period of a company on the full amount of the profits arising in the period (whether or not received in or transmitted to the United Kingdom) without any other deduction than is authorised by those Acts.

(2) An accounting period of a company shall begin for purposes of corporation tax whenever—

(*a*) the company, not then being within the charge to corporation tax, comes within it, whether by the company becoming resident in the United Kingdom or acquiring a source of income, or otherwise; or

(*b*) an accounting period of the company ends without the company then ceasing to be within the charge to corporation tax.

(3) An accounting period of a company shall end for purposes of corporation tax on the first occurrence of any of the following—

(*a*) the expiration of 12 months from the beginning of the accounting period;

(b) an accounting date of the company or, if there is a period for which the company does not make up accounts, the end of that period;

(c) the company beginning or ceasing to trade or to be, in respect of the trade or (if more than one) of all the trades carried on by it, within the charge to corporation tax;

(d) the company beginning or ceasing to be resident in the United Kingdom;

(e) the company ceasing to be within the charge to corporation tax.

(4) For the purposes of this section a company resident in the United Kingdom, if not otherwise within the charge to corporation tax, shall be treated as coming within the charge to corporation tax at the time when it commences to carry on business.

(5) [Subject to subsection (5A) below]² if a company carrying on more than one trade makes up accounts of any of them to different dates, and does not make up general accounts for the whole of the company's activities, subsection (3)(b) above shall apply with reference to the accounting date of such one of the trades [as the company may determine]².

[(5A) If the Board is of the opinion, on reasonable grounds, that a date determined by a company for the purposes of subsection (5) above is inappropriate, they may by notice direct that the accounting date of such other of the trades referred to in that subsection as appears to them to be appropriate shall be used instead.]³

(6) If a chargeable gain or allowable loss accrues to a company at a time not otherwise within an accounting period of the company, an accounting period of the company shall then begin for the purposes of corporation tax, and the gain or loss shall accrue in that accounting period.

(7) Notwithstanding anything in subsections (1) to (6) above, where a company is wound up, an accounting period shall end and a new one begin with the commencement of the winding up, and thereafter, subject to section 342(6), an accounting period shall not end otherwise than by the expiration of 12 months from its beginning or by the completion of the winding up.

For this purpose a winding up is to be taken to commence on the passing by the company of a resolution for the winding up of the company, or on the presentation of a winding up petition if no such resolution has previously been passed and a winding up order is made on the petition, or on the doing of any other act for a like purpose in the case of a winding up otherwise than under the Insolvency Act 1986.

[(7A) Notwithstanding anything in subsections (1) to (7) above, where [an insurance business transfer scheme has effect to transfer from a company to another person business which consists of the effecting or carrying out of contracts of long-term insurance]⁴, an accounting period of the company from which the business is transferred shall end with the day of the transfer.]¹

[(7B) In subsection (7A) above—

"contracts of long-term insurance" means contracts which fall within Part II of Schedule 1 to the Financial Services and Markets Act 2000 (Regulated Activities) Order 2001; and

"insurance business transfer scheme" means a scheme falling within section 105 of the Financial Services and Markets Act 2000 and—

(a) includes an excluded scheme falling within Case 2, 3 or 4 of subsection (3) of that section, but

(b) does not include a scheme for the transfer of business carried on by one or members or former underwriting members of Lloyd's.]⁴

(8) Where it appears to the inspector that the beginning or end of any accounting period of a company is uncertain, he may make an assessment on the company for such period, not exceeding 12 months, as appears to him appropriate, and that period shall be treated for all purposes as an accounting period of the company unless either—

(a) the inspector on further facts coming to his knowledge sees fit to revise it; or

(b) on an appeal against the assessment in respect of some other matter the company shows the true accounting periods;

and if on an appeal against an assessment made by virtue of this subsection the company shows the true accounting periods, the assessment appealed against shall, as regards the period to which it relates, have effect as an assessment or assessments for the true accounting periods, and there may be made such other assessments for any such periods or any of them as might have been made at the time when the assessment appealed against was made.

Commentary—*Simon's Direct Tax Service* D2.106, 107.
Concession C12—This Concession provides for the avoidance of payment of corporation tax more often than once a year by retail co-operative societies which prepare their accounts at half-yearly or quarterly intervals.
Statement of Practice SP 1/91—Procedure for a valid claim under this section.
Revenue Interpretation RI 21—Treatment of close investment-holding companies in liquidation.
Revenue Internal Guidance—Company Taxation Manual COT55 (Sub-s (8): whether accounting period uncertain is subjective; clearly uncertain when no accounts submitted).
COT56 (accounts made up to slightly varying date may be treated as for 12 months).
Revenue & other press releases—CCAB TR500 10-3-83 (successive accounts made up to slightly varying accounting dates can be treated as twelve month accounting periods subject to various conditions, but terminal date must not vary by more than four days either side of a mean date).
ICAEW TR799 June 1990 (neither filing of an administration order petition nor the making of an administration order brings about the end of an accounting period).
Simon's Tax Cases—s 12(1), *Pearce v Woodall-Duckham Ltd* [1978] STC 372*.
s 12(2), *Aproline Ltd v Littlejohn* [1995] STC (SCD) 201; *Walker v Centaur Clothes Group Ltd* [2000] STC 324.

s 12(3), *R v Special Comr, ex p Stipplechoice Ltd* [1985] STC 248*; *Aproline Ltd v Littlejohn* [1995] STC (SCD) 201.

s 12(3)(*c*), *N Ltd v Inspector of Taxes* [1996] STC (SCD) 346.

s 12(8), *R v Ward, R v Special Comr, ex p Stipplechoice Ltd (No 3)* [1989] STC 93*; *Kelsall v Stipplechoice Ltd* [1995] STC 681*.

Definitions—"Accounting date", s 834(1); "accounting period", s 834(1); "the Board", s 832(1); "company", s 832(1), (2); "the Corporation Tax Acts", s 831(1)(*a*); "inspector", s 832(1); "profits", s 6(4); "trade", ss 6(4), 832(1); "United Kingdom", s 830(1).

Cross references—See TA 1988 s 70(1) (in accordance with this section, corporation tax to be computed under Schedule D Cases I to VI on the full amount of profits or gains or income arising in an accounting period, subject only to authorised deduction).

TA 1988 s 342(5), (6) (application of sub-s (7) above where liquidation of a company is not completed in one accounting period).

TA 1988 s 751(3) (application of sub-ss (3), (5), (7) above to controlled foreign companies).

TA 1988 Sch 19AC para 4A(1) (reference to a transfer of the whole or part of a company's long term business in sub-s (7A) is treated as including a reference to a qualifying overseas transfer).

Modification—Sub-s (7A) modified so as to remove references to a scheme sanctioned by a court under Insurance Companies Act 1982 by the Friendly Societies (Modification of the Corporation Tax Acts), Regulations, SI 1997/473 reg 4.

Amendments—[1] Sub-s (7A) inserted by FA 1990 Sch 9 paras 3, 7 with effect for transfers of business after 31 December 1989.

[2] In sub-s (5) first words inserted and second words substituted (for words "as the Board may determine") by FA 1996 Sch 24 para 11(2) with effect where each of the different dates referred to in sub-s (5) of this section occurs after 30 June 1999 (by virtue of Finance Act 1994, Section 199, (Appointed Day) Order, SI 1998/3173 art 2).

[3] Sub-s (5A) inserted by FA 1996 Sch 24 para 11(3) with effect where each of the different dates referred to in sub-s (5) of this section occurs after 30 June 1999 (by virtue of SI 1998/3173 art 2).

[4] Words in sub-s (7A) substituted, and sub-s (7B) inserted, by the Financial Services and Markets Act 2000 (Consequential Amendments) (Taxes) Order, SI 2001/3629 arts 13, 14 with effect from 1 December 2001, immediately after the coming into force of the Financial Services and Markets Act 2000 ss 411, 432(1), Sch 20. SI 2001/3629 art 14 has effect in relation to any transfer under a scheme falling within the Financial Services and Markets Act 2000 s 105, including an excluded scheme falling within Case 2, 3 or 4 of the Financial Services and Markets Act 2000 s 105(3).

Small companies' rate

13 Small companies' relief

(1) Where in any accounting period the profits of [a company which—

    (*a*) is resident in the United Kingdom, and

    (*b*) is not a close investment-holding company (as defined in section 13A) at the end of that period,][1]

do not exceed the lower relevant maximum amount, the company may claim that the corporation tax charged on its basic profits for that period shall be calculated as if the rate of corporation tax (instead of being the rate fixed for companies generally) were such lower rate (to be known as the "small companies' rate") as Parliament may from time to time determine.

(2) Where in any accounting period the profits of any such company exceed the lower relevant maximum amount but do not exceed the upper relevant maximum amount, the company may claim that the corporation tax charged on its basic profits for that period shall be reduced by a sum equal to such fraction as Parliament may from time to time determine of the following amount—

$$(M-P) \times \frac{I}{P}$$

where—

    M is the upper relevant maximum amount;

    P is the amount of the profits; and

    I is the amount of the basic profits.

(3) The lower and upper relevant maximum amounts mentioned above shall be determined as follows—

    (*a*) where the company has no associated company in the accounting period, those amounts are [£300,000][2] and [£1,500,000][2] respectively;

    (*b*) where the company has one or more associated companies in the accounting period, the lower relevant maximum amount is [£300,000][2] divided by one plus the number of those associated companies, and the upper relevant maximum amount is [£1,500,000][2] divided by one plus the number of those associated companies.

(4) In applying subsection (3) above to any accounting period of a company, an associated company which has not carried on any trade or business at any time in that accounting period (or, if an associated company during part only of that accounting period, at any time in that part of that accounting period) shall be disregarded and for the purposes of this section a company is to be treated as an "associated company" of another at a given time if at that time one of the two has control of the other or both are under the control of the same person or persons.

In this subsection "control" shall be construed in accordance with section 416.

(5) In determining how many associated companies a company has got in an accounting period or whether a company has an associated company in an accounting period, an associated company shall be counted even if it was an associated company for part only of the accounting period, and two or more associated companies shall be counted even if they were associated companies for different parts of the accounting period.

(6) For an accounting period of less than 12 months the relevant maximum amounts determined in accordance with subsection (3) above shall be proportionately reduced.

[(7) For the purposes of this section the profits (but not the basic profits) of a company for an accounting period shall be taken to be the amount of its profits for that period on which corporation tax falls finally to be borne, with the addition of franked investment income other than franked investment income (if any) which the company (''the receiving company'') receives from a company resident in the United Kingdom which is—

(a) a 51 per cent subsidiary of the receiving company or of a company ...⁶ of which the receiving company is a 51 per cent subsidiary; or

(b) a trading or holding company which does not fall within [subsection (7A) below]⁶ and which is owned by a consortium the members of which include the receiving company.]⁴

[(7A) A company falls within this subsection if—

(a) it is a 75 per cent subsidiary of any other company, or

(b) arrangements of any kind (whether in writing or not) are in existence by virtue of which it could become such a subsidiary.]⁶

(8) For the purposes of this section the basic profits of a company for an accounting period shall be taken to be the amount of its profits for that period on which corporation tax falls finally to be borne.

[(8AA) Section 13ZA applies for the interpretation of subsection (7) above.]⁶

[(8AB) The reference in subsection (7) above to franked investment income received by a company applies to any such income received by another person on behalf of or in trust for the company, but not to any such income received by the company on behalf of or in trust for another person.]⁴

(8A) ...³

(9) ...⁵

Commentary—*Simon's Direct Tax Service* D2.109.
Concession C9—Circumstances in which, by Concession, companies not to be treated as associated, for purposes of small companies' relief.
Statements of Practice SP 1/91—Procedure for a valid claim under this section.
SP 5/94—Application of sub-s (4) to holding companies.
Revenue & other press releases—CCAB TR500 10-3-83 (UK branch or agency of a non-resident company may be entitled to have profits taxed at small companies rate if it can claim benefit of non-discrimination clause in the relevant double taxation agreement. Relief is governed by worldwide profits of company; associated companies wherever resident included in determining upper and lower maximum amounts).
Revenue Internal Guidance- Company Taxation Manual COT3059 (sub-s(4): whether trade or business carried on).
COT3073–3075 (sub-s(4): meaning of ''control'' and attribution of rights and powers of associates).
Simon's Tax Cases—*O'Neill and Brennan Construction Ltd v Jowett* [1997] STC (SCD) 170; *John M Harris (Design Partnership) Ltd v Lee* [1997] STC (SCD) 240; *Jowett v O'Neill and Brennan Construction Ltd* [1998] STC 482; *R v IRC, ex p Newfields Developments Ltd* [2001] STC 901; *Land Management Ltd V Fox (Insp of Taxes)* [2002] STC (SCD) 152.
Definitions—''Accounting period'', s 834(1); ''company'', s 832(1), (2); ''inspector'', s 832(1); ''small companies' rate'', s 13(1); ''United Kingdom'', s 830(1).
Cross references—See TA 1988 s 342(2)(b) (small companies' rate for final year of company in liquidation).
TA 1988 s 434(3A) (policyholders' share of franked investment income to be disregarded in calculating the franked investment income forming part of the profits of a resident life assurance company under sub-s (7) above).
TA 1988 s 434(3B) (policyholders' share of foreign income dividends to be disregarded in calculating the foreign income dividends forming part of the profits of a resident life assurance company under sub-s (7) above).
TA 1988 s 508A(1)(b) (the housing investment profits of an investment trust are excluded from its basic profits for the purposes of this section for any period for which it has eligible rental income).
FA 1989 s 88(4) (policy holder's fraction of profits to be disregarded in calculating for the purposes of this section a life assurance company's profits and basic profits);
FA 2000 s 36 (for the financial year 2000, the small companies' rate is 20 per cent and the fraction mentioned in sub-s (2) above is one fortieth).
FA 2001 s 55 (for the financial year 2001, the small companies' rate is 20 per cent and the fraction mentioned in sub-s (2) above is one fortieth).
FA 2002 s 31 (for the financial year 2002, the small companies' rate is 19 per cent and the fraction mentioned in sub-s (2) above is eleven four-hundredths).
Amendments—¹ Words in sub-s (1) substituted by FA 1989 s 105(1).
² Amounts in sub-s (3)(a), (b) substituted by FA 1994 s 86(2), (3) from the financial year 1994. Where this section has effect with different relevant maximum amounts in relation to different parts of a company's accounting period, those parts are to be treated as if they were separate accounting periods and the profits and basic profits of the company for that period are to be apportioned between those parts.
³ Sub-s (8A) (originally inserted by FA 1994 Sch 16 para 11) repealed, by F(No 2)A 1997 s 36(4), Sch 6 para 1, Sch 8 Pt II(11) with effect for accounting periods beginning after 5 April 1999.
⁴ Sub-s (7) substituted and sub-s (8AB) inserted by FA 1998 Sch 3 para 7 with effect in relation to distributions made after 5 April 1999.
⁵ Sub-s (9) repealed by FA 1999 s 139, Sch 20 Pt III(2) with effect from the financial year 2000.
⁶ Words in sub-s (7) repealed and substituted, sub-s (7A) inserted, and sub-s (8AA) substituted, by FA 2001 ss 86(1)–(4), (6), 110, Sch 33 Pt II(11) with effect for accounting periods ending after 31 March 2001.

[13ZA Interpretation of section 13(7)

(1) In determining for the purposes of section 13(7) whether one body corporate is a 51 per cent subsidiary of another, that other shall be treated as not being the owner of any share capital—

(a) which it owns indirectly, and

(b) which is owned directly by a body corporate for which a profit on the sale of the shares would be a trading receipt.

(2) Notwithstanding that at any time a company (''the subsidiary company'') is a 51 per cent subsidiary of another company (''the parent company'') it shall not be treated at that time as such a subsidiary for the purposes of section 13(7) unless, additionally, at that time—

(*a*) the parent company would be beneficially entitled to more than 50 per cent of any profits available for distribution to equity holders of the subsidiary company, and

(*b*) the parent company would be beneficially entitled to more than 50 per cent of any assets of the subsidiary company available for distribution to its equity holders on a winding-up.

(3) For the purposes of section 13(7) and this section—

(*a*) "trading or holding company" means a trading company or a company the business of which consists wholly or mainly in the holding of shares or securities of trading companies that are its 90 per cent subsidiaries;

(*b*) "trading company" means a company whose business consists wholly or mainly of the carrying on of a trade or trades;

(*c*) a company is owned by a consortium if 75 per cent or more of the ordinary share capital of the company is beneficially owned between them by companies of which none—

(i) beneficially owns less than 5 per cent of that capital,

(ii) would be beneficially entitled to less than 5 per cent of any profits available for distribution to equity holders of the company, or

(iii) would be beneficially entitled to less than 5 per cent of any assets of the company available for distribution to its equity holders on a winding up,

and those companies are called the members of the consortium.

(4) Schedule 18 (equity holders and assets etc available for distribution) applies for the purposes of subsections (2) and (3)(*c*) above as it applies for the purposes of section 413(7).][1]

Commentary—*Simon's Direct Tax Service* **D2.109.**
Amendments—[1] This section inserted by FA 2001 s 86(1), (5), (6) with effect for accounting periods ending after 31 March 2001.

[13AA Corporation tax starting rate

(1) Where in any accounting period the profits of a qualifying company do not exceed the first relevant amount, the company may, instead of making a claim under section 13(1), claim that the corporation tax charged on its basic profits for that period shall be calculated as if the rate of corporation tax were such rate (to be known as the 'corporation tax starting rate'), lower than the small companies' rate, as Parliament may from time to time determine.

(2) Where in any accounting period the profits of a qualifying company exceed the first relevant amount but do not exceed the second relevant amount, the company may, instead of making a claim under section 13(1), claim that the corporation tax charged on its basic profits for that period shall be—

(*a*) calculated as if the rate of corporation tax were the small companies' rate; and

(*b*) then reduced by the sum specified in subsection (3) below.

(3) That sum is the sum equal to such fraction as Parliament may from time to time determine of the following amount—

$$(R2 - P) \times \frac{I}{P}$$

where—

R2 is the second relevant amount;
P is the amount of the profits; and
I is the amount of the basic profits.

(4) The first and second relevant amounts mentioned above shall be determined as follows—

(*a*) where the company has no associated company in the accounting period, those amounts are £10,000 and £50,000 respectively;

(*b*) where the company has one or more associated companies in the accounting period—

(i) the first relevant amount is £10,000 divided by one plus the number of those associated companies, and

(ii) the second relevant amount is £50,000 divided by one plus the number of those associated companies.

(5) Subsections (4) and (5) of section 13 shall apply for the purposes of subsection (4) above as they apply for the purposes of subsection (3) of that section.

(6) For an accounting period of less than 12 months the relevant amounts determined in accordance with subsection (4) above shall be proportionately reduced.

(7) The profits and the basic profits of a company for an accounting period shall be determined for the purposes of this section as they are for the purposes of section 13.

(8) In this section "qualifying company", in relation to an accounting period, means a company which—

(*a*) is resident in the United Kingdom;

(*b*) is not a close investment-holding company (as defined in section 13A) at the end of that period; and (*c*) is not an investment trust which for that period has any eligible rental income (within the meaning of section 508A).][1]

Commentary—*Simon's Direct Tax Service* **D2.109A.**
Cross reference—See FA 2001 s 56 (for the financial year 2001, the starting rate is 10 per cent and the fraction mentioned in sub-s (3) above is one fortieth).
FA 2002 s 32 (for the financial year 2002, the starting rate is 0 per cent and the fraction mentioned in sub-s (3) above is nineteen four-hundredths).
Amendments—[1] This section inserted by FA 1999 s 28(1), (6) with effect for corporation tax from the financial year 2000, subject to FA 1999 s 28(7) (concerning accounting periods straddling 1 April 2000).

[13A Close investment-holding companies

(1) A close company is for the purposes of section 13(1) [or 13AA(8)][2] a "close investment-holding company" unless it complies with subsection (2) below.

(2) A company ("the relevant company") complies with this subsection in any accounting period if throughout that period it exists wholly or mainly for any one or more of the following purposes—

(*a*) the purpose of carrying on a trade or trades on a commercial basis,

(*b*) the purpose of making investments in land or estates or interests in land in cases where the land is, or is intended to be, let to persons other than—

(i) any person connected with the relevant company, or

(ii) any person who is the wife or husband of an individual connected with the relevant company, or is a relative, or the wife or husband of a relative, of such an individual or of the husband or wife of such an individual,

(*c*) the purpose of holding shares in and securities of, or making loans to, one or more companies each of which is a qualifying company or a company which—

(i) is under the control of the relevant company or of a company which has control of the relevant company, and

(ii) itself exists wholly or mainly for the purpose of holding shares in or securities of, or making loans to, one or more qualifying companies,

(*d*) the purpose of co-ordinating the administration of two or more qualifying companies,

(*e*) the purpose of a trade or trades carried on on a commercial basis by one or more qualifying companies or by a company which has control of the relevant company, and

(*f*) the purpose of the making, by one or more qualifying companies or by a company which has control of the relevant company, of investments as mentioned in paragraph (*b*) above.

(3) For the purposes of subsection (2) above, a company is a "qualifying company", in relation to the relevant company, if it—

(*a*) is under the control of the relevant company or of a company which has control of the relevant company, and

(*b*) exists wholly or mainly for either or both of the purposes mentioned in subsection (2)(*a*) or (*b*) above.

(4) Where a company is wound up, it shall not be treated as failing to comply with subsection (2) above in the accounting period that (by virtue of subsection (7) of section 12) begins with the time which is for the purposes of that subsection the commencement of the winding up, if it complied with subsection (2) above in the accounting period that ends with that time.

(5) In this section—

"control" shall be construed in accordance with section 416, and

"relative" has the meaning given by section 839(8).

(6) Section 839 shall apply for the purposes of this section.][1]

Commentary—*Simon's Direct Tax Service* **D3.202.**
Revenue Interpretation RI 21—Treatment of close investment-holding companies in liquidation.
Revenue Internal Guidance—Company Taxation Manual COT8162, 8163 (interpretation of "purpose" and "wholly or mainly").
COT8167 (group service companies).
Cross references—See TA 1988 s 231(3A) (restriction on payment of tax credits in relation to distributions by close investment-holding companies).
TA 1988 s 360(1) (interest relief in relation to loan to buy an interest in or lend money for the business of a close company complying with sub-s (2) above).
FA 1989 Sch 12, para. 1 (administrative provisions relating to close companies).
Amendments—[1] This section inserted by FA 1989 s 105(2), (3) in relation to accounting periods beginning after 31 March 1989.
[2] Words inserted in sub-s (1) by FA 1999 s 28(2), (6) with effect for corporation tax from the financial year 2000, subject to FA 1999 s 28(7) (concerning accounting periods straddling 1 April 2000).

Advance corporation tax

14 Advance corporation tax and qualifying distributions

(1) ...[1]

(2) In this Act "qualifying distribution" means any distribution other than—

(*a*) a distribution which, in relation to the company making it, is a distribution by virtue only of section 209(2)(*c*); or (*b*) a distribution consisting of any share capital or security which the company making the distribution has directly or indirectly received from the company by which the share capital or security was issued and which, in relation to the latter company, is a distribution by virtue only of section 209(2)(*c*).

(3)–(5) ...[1]

Commentary—*Simon's Direct Tax Service* D1.302, 303.
Definitions—"Company", s 832(1), (2); "the Corporation Tax Acts", s 831(1)(*a*); "distribution", s 209(2); "financial year 1988", s 834(1); "lower rate", s 832(1); "United Kingdom", s 830(1).
Cross references—See TA 1988 s 241 (calculation of ACT where the company receives franked investment income).
TA 1988 s 246F (calculation of ACT where company receives foreign income dividend).
Amendments—[1] Sub-ss (1), (3)–(5) repealed by FA 1998 Sch 3 para 8 with effect in relation to distributions made after 5 April 1999.

The six Schedules

15 Schedule A

(1) The Schedule referred to as Schedule A is as follows:—

[SCHEDULE A

1—(1) Tax is charged under this Schedule on the annual profits arising from a business carried on for the exploitation, as a source of rents or other receipts, of any estate, interest or rights in or over land in the United Kingdom.

(2) To the extent that any transaction is entered into for the exploitation, as a source of rents or other receipts, of any estate, interest or rights in or over land in the United Kingdom, it is taken to be entered into in the course of such a business.

(3) All businesses and transactions carried on or entered into by a particular person or partnership, so far as they are businesses or transactions the profits of which are chargeable to tax under this Schedule, are treated for the purposes of this Schedule as, or as entered into in the course of carrying on, a single business.

There are qualifications to this rule in the case of—

    (*a*) companies not resident in the United Kingdom (see subsection (1A) below); and
    (*b*) insurance companies (see sections 432AA and 441B(2A)).

(4) The receipts referred to in the expression "as a source of rents or other receipts" include—

    (*a*) payments in respect of a licence to occupy or otherwise to use land or the exercise of any other right over land, and
    (*b*) rentcharges, *ground annuals and feu duties* and other annual payments reserved in respect of, or charged on or issuing out of, the land.

2—(1) This Schedule does not apply to profits arising from the occupation of land.

(2) This Schedule does not apply to—

    (*a*) profits charged to tax under Case I of Schedule D under—
        –section 53(1) (farming and market gardening), or
        –section 55 (mines, quarries and other concerns);
    (*b*) receipts or expenses taken into account as trading receipts or expenses under section 98 (tied premises);
    (*c*) rent charged to tax under Schedule D under—
        –section 119 (rent, etc payable in connection with mines, quarries and other concerns), or
        –section 120(1) (certain rent, etc payable in respect of electric line wayleaves).

(3) The profits of a Schedule A business carried on by a company shall be computed without regard to items giving rise to—

–credits or debits within Chapter II of Part IV of the Finance Act 1996 (loan relationships), or
...[4]
[—credits or debits within Schedule 26 to the Finance Act 2002 (derivative contracts).][3]

This Schedule does not affect the operation of those provisions.

3—(1) For the purposes of this Schedule a right to use a caravan or houseboat, where the use to which the caravan or houseboat may be put in pursuance of the right is confined to use at a single location in the United Kingdom, is treated as a right deriving from an estate or interest in land in the United Kingdom.

(2) In sub-paragraph (1)—

    "caravan" has the meaning given by section 29(1) of the Caravan Sites and Control of Development Act 1960; and
    "houseboat" means a boat or similar structure designed or adapted for use as a place of human habitation.

4—(1) In the case of a furnished letting, any sum payable for the use of furniture shall be taken into account in computing the profits chargeable to tax under this Schedule in the same way as rent.

Expenses in connection with the provision of furniture shall similarly be taken into account in the same way as expenses in connection with the premises.

(2) A furnished letting means where—

    (*a*) a sum is payable in respect of the use of premises, and
    (*b*) the tenant or other person entitled to the use of the premises is also entitled, in connection with that use, to the use of furniture.

(3) This paragraph does not apply if the receipts and expenses are taken into account in computing the profits of a trade consisting in, or involving, making furniture available for use in premises.

(4) In this paragraph—

    (*a*) any reference to a sum includes the value of consideration other than money, and references to a sum being payable shall be construed accordingly; and
    (*b*) "premises" includes a caravan or houseboat within the meaning of paragraph 3.][2]

[(1A) In the case of a company which is not resident in the United Kingdom—

    (*a*) businesses carried on and transactions entered into by it the profits of which are within the charge to corporation tax under Schedule A, and
    (*b*) businesses carried on and transactions entered into by it the profits of which are within the charge to income tax under Schedule A,

are treated as separate Schedule A businesses.][2]

(2) ...[2]

(3) ...[1]

(4) Part II contains further provisions relating to the charge to tax under Schedule A.

Commentary—*Simon's Direct Tax Service* **A4.102, 105–108.**
Concession B4—A proportion of the expenditure on improvement of property to obviate maintenance and repairs is allowed as a deduction, subject to certain exceptions.
Concession B29—The owner of a caravan site who operates it as a trade may treat the income from letting caravan plots and caravans as trading income chargeable under Schedule D instead of under this Schedule.
Revenue Interpretation RI 135—Schedule A transitional rules.
RI 197—As from 1 April 1998, residential service charges received by occupier controlled flat management companies will ordinarily be outside the scope of Schedule A.
Revenue Decision RD 9—Rent income from letting surplus business accommodation; apportionment of outgoings on such accommodation between Schedule D and this Schedule.
Revenue & other press releases—IR 10-2-95 (Schedule A transitional arrangements: where it is clear that a source is likely to come to end shortly after 1995–96 then the existing Schedule A rules may be applied until the source ceases).
Revenue Internal Guidance—Company Taxation Manual COT201 (management expenses of investment companies must be dealt with under TA 1988 s 75 and not as Schedule A expenses).
Property Income Manual PIM4300 (where letting amounts to a trade it is within Schedule D Case I).
PIM4700 (letting of property situated outside the UK is within Schedule D Case V).
PIM2500 (criteria for determining dates of commencement and cessation of Schedule A business).
PIM5040 (accounts basis acceptable where annual accounts including a balance sheet are produced).
PIM5095 (treatment of flat management companies).
Simon's Tax Cases—*IRC v Church Comrs for England* [1975] STC 546*, *Gittos v Barclay* [1982] STC 390*.
s 15(1), *Jeffries v Stevens* [1982] STC 639*; *Griffiths v Jackson* [1983] STC 184*; *Beecham Group Ltd v Fair* [1984] STC 15*; *Mcclure v Petre* [1988] STC 749*.
Definitions—"Chargeable period", s 832(1); "inspector", s 832(1); "interest", s 832(1); "lease", s 24(6); "notice", s 832(1); "profits or gains", s 833(1); "rent", s 24(6); "Schedule B", s 16(1); "Schedule D", s 18(1); "tax", s 832(3); "United Kingdom", s 830(1).
Cross references—See IA 1978 Sch 1 ("land" includes buildings and other structures, land covered with water and any estate, interest, easement, servitude or right in or over land).
TA 1988 s 55 (profits or gains arising out of land from mines, quarries and other specified concerns to be chargeable under Schedule D Case I).
TA 1988 s 119 (rent payable in respect of land used in connection with a mine, quarry or other specified concern to be chargeable to tax under Schedule D).
TA 1988 s 120 (rent payable in respect of easements in connection with electric, telegraphic or telephonic wire or cable to be chargeable to tax under Schedule D).
TA 1988 s 375A (option to make deductions from relevant loan interest by borrower carrying on a Schedule A business).
TA 1988 s 379A (Schedule A losses (income tax)).
TA 1988 s 503 (profits from the commercial letting of furnished holiday accommodation in the United Kingdom to be chargeable to tax under Schedule D Case I).
F(No 2)A 1992 Sch 10 (calculation of Schedule A profits under Rent-a-Room scheme).
Amendments—[1] Sub-s (3) repealed by FA 1988 Sch 14 Pt V.
[2] Sub-s (1) (new Schedule A) substituted, sub-s (1A) inserted and sub-s (2) repealed by FA 1998 s 38, Sch 5 paras 1, 2 with effect for income tax purposes from 1998–99, and for corporation tax purposes from 1 April 1998, subject to the transitional provisions in FA 1998 Sch 5 Part IV.
[3] In sub-s (1), words substituted for the words "–qualifying payments within Chapter II of Part IV of the Finance Act 1994 (interest rate and currency contracts)." by FA 2002 s 83(1)(*b*), Sch 27 paras 1, 2 with effect for accounting periods beginning after 30 September 2002.
[4] In sub-s (1), the following words repealed by FA 2002 s 141, Sch 40 Pt 3(10) with effect for accounting periods beginning after 30 September 2002—

"–exchange gains or losses within Chapter II of Part II of the Finance Act 1993 (foreign exchange gains and losses), or".

Prospective amendments—Words in italics in para 1(4)(*b*) of sub-s (1) to be repealed by the Abolition of Feudal Tenure etc (Scotland) Act 2000 s 76(1), (2), Sch 12 Pt I para 50(1), Sch 13 Pt 1 with effect from a day to be appointed.

16 Schedule B

Amendments—This section repealed by FA 1988 Sch 14 Pt V with effect from 6 April 1988.

17 Schedule C

Commentary—*Simon's Direct Tax Service* **A6.102, 106.**
Amendments—This section repealed by FA 1996 Sch 7 paras 3, 32, Sch 41 Pt V(2) with effect, for the purposes of income tax from the year 1996–97, and for the purposes of corporation tax for accounting periods ending after 31 March 1996.

18 Schedule D

(1) The Schedule referred to as Schedule D is as follows—

SCHEDULE D

Tax under this Schedule shall be charged in respect of—

(*a*) the annual profits or gains arising or accruing—

    (i) to any person residing in the United Kingdom from any kind of property whatever, whether situated in the United Kingdom or elsewhere, and

    (ii) to any person residing in the United Kingdom from any trade, profession or vocation, whether carried on in the United Kingdom or elsewhere, and

    (iii) to any person, whether a Commonwealth citizen or not, although not resident in the United Kingdom from any property whatever in the United Kingdom or from any trade, profession or vocation exercised within the United Kingdom, and

(*b*) all interest of money, annuities and other annual profits or gains [not charged under Schedule A or E][1], and not specially exempted from tax.

(2) Tax under Schedule D shall be charged under the Cases set out in subsection (3) below, and subject to and in accordance with the provisions of the Tax Acts applicable to those Cases respectively.

(3) The Cases are—

Case I: tax in respect of any trade carried on in the United Kingdom or elsewhere [but not contained in Schedule A][2];

Case II: tax in respect of any profession or vocation not contained in any other Schedule;

Case III: tax in respect of—

    (*a*) any interest of money, whether yearly or otherwise, or any annuity or other annual payment, whether such payment is payable within or out of the United Kingdom, either as a charge on any property of the person paying the same by virtue of any deed or will or otherwise, or as a reservation out of it, or as a personal debt or obligation by virtue of any contract, or whether the same is received and payable half-yearly or at any shorter or more distant periods, but not including any payment chargeable under Schedule A, and

    (*b*) all discounts, and

    (*c*) income [from securities which is payable out of the public revenue of the United Kingdom or Northern Ireland][3];

Case IV: tax in respect of income arising from securities out of the United Kingdom ...[4]

Case V: tax in respect of income arising from possessions out of the United Kingdom not being income consisting of emoluments of any office or employment;

Case VI: tax in respect of any annual profits or gains not falling under any other Case of Schedule D and not charged by virtue of [Schedule A or E][5].

[(3A) For the purposes of corporation tax subsection (3) above shall have effect as if the following Case were substituted for Cases III and IV, that is to say—

"Case III: tax in respect of—

    (*a*) profits and gains which, as profits and gains arising from loan relationships, are to be treated as chargeable under this Case by virtue of Chapter II of Part IV of the Finance Act 1996;

    (*b*) any annuity or other annual payment which—

        (i) is payable (whether inside or outside the United Kingdom and whether annually or at shorter or longer intervals) in respect of anything other than a loan relationship; and

        (ii) is not a payment chargeable under Schedule A;

    (*c*) any discount arising otherwise than in respect of a loan relationship;"

and as if Case V did not include tax in respect of any income falling within paragraph (*a*) of the substituted Case III.][6]

[(3B) The references in Case IV of Schedule D to income arising from securities out of the United Kingdom, and in Case V of Schedule D to income arising from possessions out of the United Kingdom, shall be taken, in the case of relevant foreign holdings, to include references to the following—

(*a*) any proceeds of such a sale or other realisation of coupons for foreign dividends as is effected by a bank in the United Kingdom which pays the proceeds over or carries them into an account;
(*b*) any proceeds of a sale of such coupons to a dealer in coupons in the United Kingdom by a person who is not a bank or another dealer in coupons.][7]

[(3C) In this section "relevant foreign holdings" means—

(*a*) any securities issued by or on behalf of a government or a public or local authority in a country outside the United Kingdom; or
(*b*) any shares or securities issued by or on behalf of a body of persons not resident in the United Kingdom;

and "securities" here includes loan stock and similar securities.][7]

[(3D) In this section "foreign dividends" means—

(*a*) in relation to relevant foreign holdings falling within subsection (3C)(*a*) above, interest or annual payments payable out of the revenue of the government or authority in question; and
(*b*) in relation to relevant foreign holdings falling within subsection (3C)(*b*) above, any dividends, interest or annual payments payable in respect of the holdings in question.][7]

[(3E) In this section—

(*a*) "bank" has the meaning given by section 840A; and
(*b*) references to coupons include, in relation to any foreign dividends, warrants for and bills of exchange purporting to be drawn or made in payment of those dividends.][7]

(4) The provisions of Schedule D and of subsection (2) above are without prejudice to any other provision of the Tax Acts directing tax to be charged under Schedule D or under one or other of the Cases set out in subsection (3) above, and tax directed to be so charged shall be charged accordingly.

(5) [Parts III and IV contain][8] further provisions relating to the charge to tax under Schedule D.

Commentary—*Simon's Direct Tax Service* **B1.101, 102; B5.102.**
Concession A37—Fees received in respect of directorships are in strictness assessable on the recipient director under Schedule E. By Concession, however, they are assessed as partnership or company income if certain conditions are satisfied.
A40—This Concession exempts adoption allowances paid under approved adoption schemes which are in strictness liable to tax under Case III.
A57—Income tax is not charged under this Schedule in respect of an award made by an employer to an employee under a staff suggestion scheme where specified conditions are satisfied.
B13—Tax is not recovered from interest received gross by a person absent from the UK throughout tax year if certain conditions are satisfied.
B29—Treatment of income from caravan sites where there is both trading and associated letting income.
Statement of Practice SP 8/79—Reimbursed removal expenses and compensation for temporary loss of profits in relation to acquisition of property under compulsory powers.
SP 1/87—This statement sets out the Revenue's views on treatment of profits and losses arising from exchange rate fluctuations following the judgment of the House of Lords in *Pattison v Marine Midland Ltd*.
SP 16/91—Accountancy expenses arising out of accountancy investigations which are or which are not allowable under Schedule D Cases I and II.
Revenue Interpretation RI 18—Tax liability on compensation for loss of earnings while rendering services such as jury service.
RI 30—Insurance agents commission: treatment under Case I of commission repaid owing to early lapse of policy.
RI 52—Lump sum payment under exclusivity agreement: whether capital or revenue: if revenue, whether liable to tax under this section.
RI 192—Accountancy expenses arising out of self-assessment enquiries.
Revenue Decision RD 9—Rent income from letting surplus business accommodation; apportionment of outgoings on such accommodation between Schedule A and this Schedule.
Revenue & other press releases—CCAB October 1977 (examination of business accounts: selection and procedure). See also Practice Code 2.
CCAB September 1979 (examination of business accounts: use of gross profit margins).
CCAB TR500 10-3-83 (Concession B13 applies to discounts on bills of exchange received by non-residents and to disposals of certificates of deposit by non-residents).
ICAEW TR588 25-9-85 (year-end stock adjustments: valuation of trading stock sold intra-group where the purchaser company holds the stock at the year-end, vendor company may issue a credit note and show the stock at cost in its own accounts; Revenue will not normally seek to apply *Furniss v Dawson* principle in this case).
IR 7-11-89 (small businesses: detailed accounts not required where business turnover is less than a certain amount).
IR 18-5-93 (computations of business profits rounded to nearest £1,000 will be accepted by the Revenue where turnover is at least £5 million and basis adopted is satisfactory; but computations of chargeable gains, tax credit relief, accrued income under accrued income scheme, some capital allowances and CFC apportioned profits must be accurate).
IR 3-11-97 (new list of business economic notes).
Booklet IR150 paras 523–541 (computation of Case V profits from the letting of property outside the UK).
Revenue Internal Guidance—Banking manual BM 3.1.1–3.3.6.1 (banks: income derived from assets usually forms part of the Case I profit).
BM 4.1.1–4.3.3.2 (banks: treatment of profits and losses on realisation of assets under Case I).
BM 5.1.1–5.3.2 (banks: treatment of fees and other income under Case I).
BM 10.1.1–10.3.3.3 (banks: computation of profits and losses on transactions involving foreign exchange).
Inspector's manual IM 474–477 (insurance commissions: completion of profits).
IM 1508 (For purposes of a charge under Case III, meaning of "discount").
IM 1812a–1812h (adult carers and adult placement schemes: carers are liable under Case I or Case II: computation of profits considered at 1812e).
IM 1820a–1829 (athletes: employed or self employed; hobby status; sources and timing of income, expenses etc).
IM 1833 (bed and breakfast transactions by financial concerns: whether a Case I loss can be established).
IM 1838 (Financial concerns, consideration of the treatment of discounts on bills of exchange, whether the arising basis may be adopted in calculating Case I profits).
IM 1852–1854 (Financial concerns, securitisation of mortgage debts etc, consideration of status of the vehicle company, treatment of interest payments etc).

IM 1856–1859 (Before it is accepted that group finance companies are carrying on a trade cases should be critically examined and submitted to Financial Institutions Division (Financial Concerns)).
IM 1859 (group finance companies: international aspects).
IM 1880 (horse racing etc: treatment of sums received from the Horserace Betting Levy Board).
IM 1990 (Builders and developers: interest charged to work in progress or long term contracts, detailed guidance).
IM 2070–2072 (crematoria: receipts from the sale of niches are trading receipts).
IM 2060–2063 (cemeteries: treatment of capital expenditure).
IM 2090 (checktraders: computation of profits).
IM 2095 (childminders are usually taxed under Case I or Case II).
IM 2200–2213 (doctors and dentists: treatment under Case I or Case II).
IM 2250–2263 (farming: application of Case I principles).
IM 2266a–2283b (farming: various receipts and expenses).
IM 2286a–2287e (farming quotas).
IM 2291a–2297b (farming: stock valuations).
IM 2350b (stud farms: valuation; herd basis; losses; stallion syndicates).
IM 2363 (laying up grants and exploratory voyage grants for fishing vessels are trading receipts).
IM 2380 (whether foreign exchange transactions are part of a trade).
IM 2390–2393 (foster parents: treatment of allowances and expense reimbursements).
IM 2401a–2401c (franchising fees: when taxed as income).
IM 2402a–2402d (relief for franchising expenses).
IM 2410–2411 (grant-aided bodies: whether carrying on a trade).
IM 2420 (greyhound stadium proprietors: dogs owned for racing are dealt with on the renewals basis).
IM 2425–2428 (admission to historic houses: whether a trade is carried on).
IM 2601–2634 (Transactions in land, whether trading, time share schemes (IM 2628–2632)).
IM 2628–2632 (time share schemes: treatment under Case I).
IM 2670–2671d (leasing: commercial background).
IM 2672–2672i (accounting treatment of leasing transactions).
IM 2673–2678c (tax treatment of finance leases).
IM 2679 (operating leases: timing of rentals).
IM 2690–2701 (literary profits: computation under Cases I, II or VI).
IM 2920 (pawnbrokers: surplus on sale of pledges is part of the trading profit).
IM 2955 (profits from prostitution are within Case I or II if the activities are organised as a trade or profession).
IM 3030–3031 (research grants and fellowships: circumstances in which they fall within Schedule D).
IM 3100–3102 (solicitors: interest received gross by a solicitor on UK resident client's money is passed on to the client gross).
IM 3150–3152 (sub-postmasters may include remuneration under Schedule D Case I if a retail trade or business is carried on from the same premises).
IM 3155 (theatre backers: any excess of sums received over money advanced is normally assessed under Case III).
IM 3160 (timber merchants: purchases of standing timber are regarded as purchases of trading stock in certain circumstances).
IM 3161 (timber merchants: treatment of purchases of commercial woodlands).
IM 3220–3223 (underwriting of share issues: profits are within Case I or Case VI).
IM 3230a–3230h (video traders: treatment of tapes: capital allowances, renewals basis, valuation basis).
Schedule E manual SE 7050 (awards and bursaries by the Arts Council etc to writers, artists etc are trading or professional receipts).
Simon's Tax Cases—*Andrews v King* [1991] STC 481*; *Alongi v IRC* [1991] STC 517*; *Albon v anor v IRC* [1998] STC 1181; *Clarke v British Telecom Pension Scheme Trustees* [2000] STC 222.
s 18(1), *Alloway v Phillips* [1980] STC 490*; *Ditchfield v Sharp* [1983] STC 590*.
s 18(1)(a)(ii), *Tapenaze Ltd v Melluish* [2000] STC 189.
s 18(2), *Simpson v John Reynolds & Co (Insurances) Ltd* [1975] STC 271*; *Black Nominees Ltd v Nicol* [1975] STC 372*.
s 18(3), *Sugden v Kent (Inspector of Taxes)* [2001] STC (SCD) 158.
s 18(3) Sch D, Case I, *Taylor v Good* [1974] STC 148*; *Simpson v John Reynolds* [1974] STC 277*; *Dickenson v Downes* [1974] STC 539*.
s 18(3) Sch D, Case II, *Duff v Williamson* [1973] STC 434*.
s 18(3) Sch D, Case III, *Aplin v White* [1973] STC 322*; *re Euro Hotel (Belgravia) Ltd* [1975] STC 682*; *Ditchfield v Sharp* [1983] STC 590*.
s 18(3) Sch D, Case V, *Newstead v Frost* [1980] STC 123*.
Definitions—"Interest", s 832(1); "loan relationship", TA 1988 s 834(1), FA 1996 s 81; "person residing in the United Kingdom", s 336(1); "profits or gains", s 833(1); "tax", s 831(2); "the Tax Acts", s 831(2); "trade", s 832(1); "United Kingdom", s 830(1).
Cross references—See TA 1988 s 1A (certain income from savings and distributions chargeable to tax under Cases III, IV and V to be taxed at the lower rate).
TA 1988 s 314 (income from employment as a diver concerned with exploration or exploitation of the seabed to be chargeable to tax under Schedule D Case I).
TA 1988 s 331A (certain interest relating to student loans to be disregarded for income tax).
TA 1988 s 347A (exclusion from tax of annual payments which would otherwise fall within Schedule D Case III, subject to specified exceptions).
TA 1988 s 503 (profits from the commercial letting of furnished holiday accommodation in the United Kingdom to be chargeable to tax under Schedule D Case I).
TA 1988 s 580A (exclusion from income tax of annual payments under an insurance policy providing insurance against risk of illness, unemployment or that of trade).
F(No 2)A 1992 Sch 10 (calculation of Schedule D Case I profits under Rent-a-Room scheme).
Amendments—[1] Words in sub-s (1) substituted by FA 1996 Sch 7 paras 4(1), 32 with effect for the purposes of income tax from the year 1996–97 and as respects corporation tax for accounting periods ending after 31 March 1996.
[2] Words in sub-s (3), Case I, inserted by FA 1995 s 39(3)–(5), Sch 6 para 2, from the year 1995–96 (and so far as having effect for the purposes of corporation tax, in relation to accounting periods ending on or after 31 March 1995); however, this amendment does not apply in relation to certain sources of income which cease during the year 1995–96: FA 1995 s 39(5).
[3] Words in sub-s (3), Case III(c) substituted by FA 1996 Sch 7 paras 4(2)(a), 32 with effect from the year 1996–97.
[4] Words omitted from sub-s (3), Case IV repealed by FA 1996 Sch 7 paras 4(2)(b), 32, Sch 41 Pt V(2) with effect from the year 1996–97.
[5] Words in sub-s (3), Case VI substituted by FA 1996 Sch 7 paras 4(2)(c), 32 with effect for the purposes of income tax from the year 1996–97 and as respects corporation tax for accounting periods ending after 31 March 1996.
[6] Sub-s (3A) inserted by FA 1996 s 105, Sch 14 para 5 with effect in relation to accounting periods ending after 31 March 1996, subject to transitional provisions in FA 1996 Sch 15.
[7] Sub-ss (3B)–(3E) inserted by FA 1996 Sch 7 paras 4(3), 32 with effect for the purposes of income tax from the year 1996–97 and as respects corporation tax for accounting periods ending after 31 March 1996.
[8] Words in sub-s (5) substituted by FA 1996 Sch 7 paras 4(4), 32 with effect for the purposes of income tax from the year 1996–97 and as respects corporation tax for accounting periods ending after 31 March 1996.

19 Schedule E

(1) The Schedule referred to as Schedule E is as follows—

SCHEDULE E

1 Tax under this Schedule shall be charged in respect of any office or employment on emoluments therefrom which fall under one or more than one of the following Cases—

[Case I: any emoluments for any year of assessment in which the person holding the office or employment is resident and ordinarily resident in the United Kingdom, subject however to section 192 if the emoluments are foreign emoluments (within the meaning of that section) [...]⁴;]¹

[Case II: Any emoluments, in respect of duties performed in the United Kingdom, for any year of assessment in which the person holding the office or employment is not resident (or, if resident, not ordinarily resident) in the United Kingdom, subject however to section 192 if the emoluments are foreign emoluments (within the meaning of that section);]¹

[Case III: any emoluments for any year of assessment in which the person holding the office or employment is resident in the United Kingdom (whether or not ordinarily resident there) so far as the emoluments are received in the United Kingdom;]¹

and tax shall not be chargeable in respect of emoluments of an office or employment under any other paragraph of this Schedule.

2 Tax under this Schedule shall be charged in respect of every annuity, pension or stipend payable by the Crown or out of the public revenue of the United Kingdom or of Northern Ireland, other than annuities charged [under paragraph (*c*) of Case III of Schedule D]³.

3 Tax under this Schedule shall also be charged in respect of any pension which is paid otherwise than by or on behalf of a person outside the United Kingdom.

4 Where—

(*a*) any pension or annuity is payable in the United Kingdom by or through any public department, officer or agent of a government of a territory to which this paragraph applies (but otherwise than out of the public revenue of the United Kingdom or of Northern Ireland) to a person who has been employed in relevant service outside the United Kingdom in respect of that service, or

(*b*) any pension or annuity is so payable to the widow, child, relative or dependant of any such person as is mentioned above,

and the person in receipt of the pension or annuity is chargeable to tax as a person resident in the United Kingdom, the pension or annuity shall be chargeable to tax under this Schedule.

The territories to which this paragraph applies are—

(i) any country forming part of Her Majesty's dominions,

(ii) any other country for the time being mentioned in Schedule 3 to the British Nationality Act 1981 and

(iii) any territory under Her Majesty's protection;

and in this paragraph ''relevant service'' means the service of the Crown or service under the government of a territory to which this paragraph applies.

[**4A** Where (apart from this paragraph) emoluments from an office or employment would be for a year of assessment in which a person does not hold the office or employment, the following rules shall apply for the purposes of the Cases set out in paragraph 1 above—

(*a*) if in the year concerned the office or employment has never been held, the emoluments shall be treated as emoluments for the first year of assessment in which the office or employment is held;

(*b*) if in the year concerned the office or employment is no longer held, the emoluments shall be treated as emoluments for the last year of assessment in which the office or employment was held.]²

5 The preceding provisions of this Schedule are without prejudice to any other provision of the Tax Acts directing tax to be charged under this Schedule and tax so directed to be charged shall be charged accordingly.

(2) References in the Tax Acts to Cases I, II and III of Schedule E shall be taken as referring to the Cases under which tax is chargeable under paragraph 1 of that Schedule.

(3) Part V contains further provisions relating to the charge to tax under Schedule E.

Commentary—*Simon's Direct Tax Service* E4.102.
Concessions A11—Residence in the UK: year of commencement or cessation of residence.
A37—Director's fees received by partnerships and other companies.
A78—Residence in the UK: husband/wife accompanying or joining non-resident wife/husband abroad.
A90—Exemption for payments and training vouchers under the Employment Department's Jobmatch pilot scheme.
Statements of Practice SP 3/81—Individuals coming to the UK: ordinary residence.
SP 5/84—To simplify procedure, the emoluments of an employee (*a*) who is resident but not ordinarily resident in the UK, (*b*) who performs duties of a single employment in the UK and abroad and (*c*) who receives part of his emoluments in the UK and part abroad, are assessed under Schedule E Case II, subject to certain exception.
SP 13/91, para 9—Certain ex gratia award made on termination of an office or employment by retirement or death to be charged to tax under Schedule E.
SP 17/91—Residence in the UK: when ordinary residence is regarded as commencing where the period to be spent in the UK is less than 3 years.

Revenue Interpretation RI 45—Payment by employer of charges for employee's routine health checks or medical screening; circumstances of charge to tax under this section.

Revenue & other press releases—IR 30-3-83 (certain freelance workers in the film and allied industries to be taxed under Schedule E).

Hansard 10-2-86 (Police rent allowances: grants paid to policemen to compensate for tax on rent allowance paid in previous year is taxable).

ICAEW TR796 25-6-90 (performers/artists: standard Equity contracts earnings are assessable under Schedule E, except those with "reserved Schedule D" status; guidance on travel and subsistence expenses. Non-performers whether employed or self-employed, various contracts categorised).

IR 16-3-93 (Council Tax: where an employer pays an employee's liability, the amount is taxable on the employee, except in a case of "representative accommodation").

IR Tax Bulletin February 1997 p 387 (from 1997/98, tax equalisation payments made to take account of UK liability are considered to be referable to duties performed in the UK and are fully chargeable to tax under Case II).

IR Tax Bulletin June 2002 (tax equalisation emoluments are wholly referable to duties performed in the UK where the underlying tax liability is similarly wholly referable to duties performed in the UK).

Revenue Internal Guidance—Schedule E manual SE 00510 (introduction to this section)

SE 00520–595 (meaning of "emoluments")

SE 00600–610 (meaning of "from an office or employment")

The Employment Status Manual provides additional guidance on the meaning of "office" and "employment" and provides criteria for determining employed or self-employed status

SE 00620–750 (guidance on lump sum payments chargeable under s 19(1)1)

SE 01000 (list of particular items—alphabetical list showing where to find further guidance on whether a payment or benefit is chargeable as an emolument and any special rules that may apply)

SE 01704 (all subsistence payments and other payments in cash or in kind paid under the Employment Zone scheme to assist the participant in finding and keeping a job are exempt from tax)

SE 02100 (compensation for loss of office—whether payment chargeable s 19 or s 148)

SE 08001–08008 (emoluments: transfer of real property to employees and directors)

SE 10000 (travelling and subsistence payments—general and arrangement of guidance covering SE 10010–10300)

SE 11301–11311 (possible s 19 charge for accommodation)

SE 11521 (living accommodation: other liabilities in connection with living accommodation—meeting employee's liability)

SE 12810 (termination payments and benefits: introduction)

SE 12850 (common examples of termination payments and benefits taxable under s 19)

SE 12856 (termination payments and benefits: compromise agreements)

SE 12950 (termination payments and benefits: payments made under the Employment Rights Act 1996)

SE 12975 (termination payments and benefits: payments in lieu of notice (PILONs) and "gardening leave")

SE 12976 (termination payments and benefits: payments in lieu of notice (PILONs): contractual payments)

SE 12977 (termination payments and benefits: payments in lieu of notice (PILONs): customary payments)

SE 12979 (termination payments and benefits: payments in lieu of notice (PILONs): agreements)

SE 13270 (termination payments and benefits: valuation of non-cash benefits received on or after 6 April 1998)

SE 13735 (termination payments and benefits: contributions to an approved retirement benefits scheme etc—application of Statement of Practice 2/81 to s 19 charge)

SE 13750 (termination payments and benefits: redundancy)

SE 13765 (termination payments and benefits: redundancy payments made under contractual terms)

SE 13785 (termination payments and benefits: redundancy payments: Statement of Practice 1/1994)

SE 13825–13830 (termination payments and benefits: redundancy: site agreements for short-service employees)

SE 13834 (termination payments and benefits: severance payments under the Working Rule Agreement for the engineering construction industry)

SE 13900–14000 (examples of termination payments showing application of s 19 charge)

SE 15125 (non-approved "retirement benefits schemes": payments other than on retirement or death)

SE 21740 (charge under this section where loans released or written off)

SE 30525 (deductions for directors and officers liabilities in the years before 1995/96)

SE 40001–40021 (scope of Schedule E, the cases)

SE 40304 (Schedule E: interaction of Case II and III: Statement of Practice 5/84)

SE 41010 (meaning of "resident and ordinarily resident in the United Kingdom")

SE 42750 (introduction and arrangement of guidance on salary sacrifice, covering references SE 42755–42786)

SE 42810 (residence or employment in the UK: meaning of "resident" in the UK)

SE 50000 (tax treatment of particular occupations—alphabetical list of occupations where special tax treatments apply, references are in the range SE50010–71399). See also the Employment Status Manual which provides additional guidance on the status of workers in particular occupations.

SE 74001–74403 (pensions and annuities chargeable to income tax under Schedule E)

SE 76004 (taxable Social Security benefits are chargeable under Schedule E by virtue of s 19(1)1 (paragraph 5))

SE 76200 (Social Security benefits: industrial death benefit)

SE 76350 (Social Security benefits: statutory sick pay)

SE 76360 (Social Security benefits: Statutory Maternity Pay)

Inspector's Manual IM5343–5348 (examples involving international groups).

Simon's Tax Cases—*Nichols v Gibson* [1996] STC 1008*; *EMI Group Electronics Ltd v Coldicott* [1999] STC 803; *R v Dimsey* [1999] STC 846; *Sports Club plc and others v Insp of Taxes* [2000] STC (SCD) 443, *Mimtec Ltd v IRC* [2001] STC 101.

s 19(1), *Bootle v Bye* [1996] STC (SCD) 58*; *Richardson (Insp of Taxes) v Delaney* [2001] STC 1328; *Perro v Mansorth (Insp of Taxes)* [2001] STC (SCD) 179.

s 19(1) Sch E, *Shilton v Wilmshurst* [1991] STC 88*; *Mairs v Haughey* [1993] STC 569.

s 19(1) Sch E para 1, *Cooke v Blacklaws* [1985] STC 1*; *Shilton v Wilmshurst* [1988] STC 868*.

s 19(1) Sch E para 3, *Esslemont v Estill* [1980] STC 620*; *Johnson v Farquhar* [1992] STC 11*.

Definitions—"Annuity", s 133(2); "chargeable period", s 832(1); "emoluments", s 131(1); "pension", s 133(2); "resident in the United Kingdom", s 386(2); "United Kingdom", s 830(1).

Cross references—See TA 1988 s 190 (exemption for certain grants and payments made to members of the House of Commons, the European Parliament, the Scottish Parliament, the National Assembly for Wales and the Northern Ireland Assembly).

TA 1988 s 197 (exemption for travel facilities for members of the armed forces).

TA 1988 s 197A (exemption for provision of car, cycle and motorcycle parking facilities).

TA 1988 s 313 (certain sums received as contributions for restrictive undertakings chargeable under Schedule E).

TA 1988 s 314 (income from employment as a diver concerned in exploration or exploitation of the seabed to be chargeable to tax under Schedule D Case I and not Schedule E).

TA 1988 s 332 (special exemptions and reliefs in assessing tax under Schedule E chargeable on ministers of religion).

TA 1988 s 336(2) (temporary visitor treated as resident for Schedule E purposes only if present for at least six months).

TA 1988 s 588 (reimbursement by employer of certain expenses relating to qualifying training courses to be exempt from charge to tax under Schedule E).

TA 1988 s 595 (employer's contributions to an unapproved retirement benefits scheme to be chargeable to tax under Schedule E on the relevant employee).

TA 1988 s 596A(2), (8) (benefits received by an individual from an unapproved retirement benefits scheme to be chargeable to tax under Schedule E, subject to certain exceptions).

TA 1988 s 597 (pensions paid under approved retirement benefits schemes to be chargeable to tax under Schedule E).

TA 1988 s 600 (unauthorised payments out of approved retirement benefits schemes to be chargeable to tax under Schedule E).

TA 1988 s 608(4) (annuities paid out of superannuation funds approved before 6 April 1980 to be chargeable to tax under Schedule E).

TA 1988 s 613(3) (payments out of the House of Commons Members' Fund to be chargeable to tax under Schedule E).

TA 1988 s 617(1) (certain social security benefits to be chargeable to tax under Schedule E).

TA 1988 s 643(1) (contributions made by an employer to an approved personal pension scheme are not regarded as emoluments chargeable to tax under Schedule E).

TA 1988 s 643(5) (income withdrawals under approved personal pension arrangements to be chargeable to tax under Schedule E).

TA 1988 s 647(3) (unauthorised payments out of an approved personal pension scheme to or for the benefit of an individual to be chargeable to tax under Schedule E).

TA 1988 s 648 (contributions by an employer to an unapproved personal pension scheme to be emoluments chargeable to tax under Schedule E).

FA 1988 s 68 (priority share allocations to directors or employees in a public offer not to be treated as an emolument).

FA 1988 ss 77–80 (charge to tax under Schedule E in respect of unapproved employee share schemes).

See FA 1989 s 41(1)(a) (income tax in respect of pension, stipend or annuity chargeable under this section to be charged in the year it accrues irrespective of when it is paid).

Amendments—¹ Cases I, II, III substituted by FA 1989 s 36(2), (4) from the year 1989–90. Originally Case III read as follows and is reproduced for the benefit of FA 1989 s 39(1)(c)—

"Case III: where that person is resident in the United Kingdom (whether or not ordinarily resident there) any emoluments received in the United Kingdom in the chargeable period being emoluments either for that period or for an earlier period in which he has been resident there and any emoluments for that period received in the United Kingdom in an earlier period;".

² Paragraph 4A in sub-s (1) inserted by FA 1989 s 36(3), (5) where each of the years mentioned in sub-paras(a) or (b) (as the case may be) is 1989–90 or a subsequent year.

³ Words in para 2 in sub-s (1) substituted by FA 1996 Sch 7 paras 5, 32 with effect from the year 1996–97.

⁴ Words in sub-s (1) revoked by FA 1998 s 63(3) in connection with the repeal of TA 1988 s 193(1), with effect from 17 March 1998.

20 Schedule F

(1) The Schedule referred to as Schedule F is as follows—

SCHEDULE F

1 Subject to section [95(1A)(a)]⁴, income tax under this Schedule shall be chargeable for any year of assessment in respect of all dividends and other distributions in that year of a company resident in the United Kingdom which are not specially excluded from income tax, and for the purposes of income tax all such distributions shall be regarded as income however they fall to be dealt with in the hands of the recipient.

2 For the purposes of this Schedule and all other purposes of the Tax Acts [(other than section 95(1) [of this Act and section 219(4A) of the Finance Act 1994]⁶)]⁵ any such distribution in respect of which a person is entitled to a tax credit shall be treated as representing income equal to the aggregate of the amount or value of that distribution and the amount of that credit, and income tax under this Schedule shall accordingly be charged on that aggregate.

(2) [Except as provided by [section 171 of the Finance Act 1993]² [or section 219 of the Finance Act 1994]³ (underwriters)]¹ no distribution which is chargeable under Schedule F shall be chargeable under any other provision of the Income Tax Acts.

(3) Part VI contains further provisions relating to company distributions and tax credits.

Commentary—*Simon's Direct Tax Service* **D1.401.**
Revenue Interpretation RI 199—Taxation of Schedule F income received by trustees from 6 April 1999.
Definitions—"Company", s 832(1), (2); "the Income Tax Acts", s 831(1)(b); "the Tax Acts", s 831(2); "United Kingdom", s 830(1).
Cross references—See TA 1988 s 1A (income chargeable under Schedule F to be charged at the lower rate of tax).
Amendments—¹ Words in sub-s (2) inserted by FA 1988 s 61(1)(a), (5), with effect from the year 1988–89.
² Words in sub-s (2) substituted by FA 1993 s 183(1), 184(3) with effect from the year 1992–93.
³ Words in sub-s (2) inserted by FA 1994 s 219(5) with effect for accounting periods ending after 31 December 1993, or, as the case may require, for underwriting year 1994 and subsequent underwriting years.
⁴ Word in sub-s (1) para 1 substituted by FA 1997 Sch 7, para 8(2)(a), (3) with effect in relation to distributions made after 25 November 1996.
⁵ Words in sub-s (1) para 2 inserted by F(No 2)A 1997 s 24(10), (15) with effect in relation to any distribution made after 1 July 1997 and any payment which is representative of such a distribution.
⁶ Words in sub-s (1) para 2 inserted by F(No 2)A 1997 s 22 (5), (7) with effect in relation to distributions made after 1 July 1997.

PART II
PROVISIONS RELATING TO THE SCHEDULE A CHARGE ...¹

Cross references—See TA 1988 s 15 (the charge to Schedule A).
TA 1988 s 24 (construction of this Part).
Amendments—¹ Words omitted from heading to Part II by FA 1998 Sch 5 para 3 with effect from the year 1998–99 (income tax), and from 1 April 1998, subject to the transitional provisions in FA 1998 Sch 5 Part IV (corporation tax).

General

[21 Persons chargeable and basis of assessment (income tax only)

(1) Income tax under Schedule A shall be charged on and paid by the persons receiving or entitled to the income in respect of which the tax is directed by the Income Tax Acts to be charged.

(2) Income tax under Schedule A is charged on the full amount of the profits arising in the year of assessment.

(3) This section does not apply for the purposes of corporation tax.]¹

Commentary—*Simon's Direct Tax Service* **A4.107, 501.**
Concession B47—Allowance for wear and tear of furniture of 10 per cent of net rents in respect of income from furnished lettings of dwelling houses.
Concession A89—Relief for mortgage interest where property used for mixed purposes.
Revenue Interpretation RI 135—Schedule A transitional rules.
Revenue & other press releases—IR 10-2-95 (Inland Revenue guidance Notes on the transitional provisions which apply for 1995–96: old rules may be applied until a source ceases where it is clear that it is likely to end soon after 1995–96).
IR Tax Bulletin October 1996 p 349 (interest rate hedging instruments and deposits/bonds taken from tenants).
IR Tax Bulletin October 1996 p 349 (transitional: cessations after 5 April 1996 but before 6 April 1997—application of old rules).
IR Tax Bulletin December 1996 p 375 (considers admissibility as deduction under Schedule A of legal and professional costs of re-letting existing property).
Revenue Internal Guidance—Assessment Procedures Manual AP 1224–1228 (Schedule A assessments usually made by taxpayer's general claim district, but where agent involved, local district may assess 1995–96 and previous years).
AP 1244 (mortgagee in possession is assessable on rental profits receivable by him; basis of assessment explained).
AP 1320 (excess rents paid by close company to participator and treated as distribution are excluded from participator's Schedule A income).
AP 1368–1388 (accounts basis: Revenue practice).
Property Income Manual PIM 1100 (accruals basis applies, as does distinction between capital and revenue: cash basis not normally accepted).
PIM 2001 (deductions: application of the "wholly and exclusively" principle).
PIM 2020 (deduction for repairs and dilapidations).
PIM 2025 (deduction for rent paid).
PIM 2030 (deduction for rates and council tax).
PIM 2040 (deduction for insurance premiums).
PIM 2100, 2110 (deduction for interest given on accruals basis, but income tax may be deductible at source if paid to non-resident).
PIM 2120 (mortgage interest relief given under MIRAS unless taxpayer elects under TA 1988 s 375A).
PIM 2200 (deduction for legal and professional costs).
PIM 2210 (deduction for travelling expenses).
PIM 2220 (where property let uncommercially, there is a restriction on allowable expenses under TA 1988 s 74: expenses limited to rent arising from the property concerned).
Definitions— "the Income Tax Acts", s 831(1)(*b*); "Schedule A", s 15(1); "tax", s 831(2); "year of assessment", s 832(1).
Cross references— TA 1988 s 15(1) (items included in, and excluded from, the Schedule A computation).
TA 1988 s 96(11) (farmers averaging rules do not apply for Schedule A purposes).
TA 1988 s 375A (election for mortgage interest to be allowed as a Schedule A deduction).
TA 1988 s 65A(1), (2) (application of sub-ss (3) and (4) above to income from land overseas chargeable to income tax under Schedule D Case V).
TA 1988 s 82(6) (disapplication of the provisions of s 82 relating to interest paid to non-residents for computations under sub-s (3) above of income tax on the profits or gains of a Schedule A business).
TA 1988 s 87(10) (disapplication of the provisions of s 87 relating to taxable premiums for computations under sub-s (3) above).
TA 1988 s 98 (references to a trade in the provisions of s 98 relating to tied premises are not to be taken by virtue of sub-s (3) above as including a Schedule A business).
Amendments—¹ This section substituted by FA 1998 Sch 5 para 4 with effect from the year 1998–99.

[21A Computation of amount chargeable

(1) Except as otherwise expressly provided, the profits of a Schedule A business are computed in the same way as the profits of a trade are computed for the purposes of Case I of Schedule D.

(2) The following provisions apply in accordance with subsection (1)—

    section 72 (apportionment);
    the provisions of Chapter V of Part IV (computational provisions relating to the Schedule D charge), except as mentioned in subsection (4) below;
    section 577 (business entertainment expenses);
    section 577A (expenditure involving crime);
    sections 579 and 580 (redundancy payments);
    sections 588 and 589 (training courses for employees);
    sections 589A and 589B (counselling services for employees);
    section 73(2) of the Finance Act 1988 (consideration for restrictive undertakings);
    section 43 of the Finance Act 1989 (deductions in respect of certain emoluments);
    section 76 of that Act (expenses in connection with non-approved retirement benefit schemes);
    sections 112 and 113 of that Act (expenditure in connection with provision of security asset or service);
    sections 42 and 46(1) and (2) of the Finance Act 1998 (provisions as to computation of profits and losses).

(3) Section 74(1)(d) of this Act (disallowance of provisions for future repairs) applies in relation to a Schedule A business as if the reference to premises occupied for the purposes of the trade were to premises held for the purposes of the Schedule A business.

(4) The following provisions in Chapter V of Part IV of this Act do not apply, or are excepted from applying, in accordance with subsection (1)—

TA 1988

section 82 (interest paid to non-residents),
section 87 (treatment of premiums taxed as rent),
section 96 (farming and market gardening: relief for fluctuating profits), and
section 98 (tied premises: receipts and expenses treated as those of trade).][1]

[(5) Part I of Schedule 22 to the Finance Act 2001 (deduction for capital expenditure on remediation of contaminated land) applies in accordance with subsection (1), and the other Parts of that Schedule (further provision as to relief for remediation of contaminated land) have effect in relation to a Schedule A business in accordance with their provisions.][2]

Commentary—*Simon's Direct Tax Service* **A4.102.**
Definitions—''Schedule A'', s 15(1); ''Schedule D'', s 18(1).
Cross references—See TA 1988 s 65A(1), (2) (application of sub-ss (3) and (4) above to income from land overseas chargeable to income tax under Schedule D Case V).
TA 1988 s 82(6) (disapplication of the provisions of s 82 relating to interest paid to non-residents for computations under sub-s (3) above of income tax on the profits or gains of a Schedule A business).
TA 1988 s 87(10) (disapplication of the provisions of s 87 relating to taxable premiums for computations under sub-s (3) above).
TA 1988 s 98 (references to a trade in the provisions of s 98 relating to tied premises are not to be taken by virtue of sub-s (3) above as including a Schedule A business).
Amendments—[1] This section inserted by FA 1998 Sch 5 para 4 with effect from the year 1998–99 (income tax), and from 1 April 1998, subject to the transitional provisions in FA 1998 Sch 5 Part IV (corporation tax).
[2] Sub-s (5) inserted by FA 2001 s 70(3), Sch 23 para 1 with effect for accounting periods ending after 31 March 2001.

[21B Application of other rules applicable to Case I of Schedule D

The following provisions apply for the purposes of Schedule A in relation to a Schedule A business as they apply for the purposes of Case I of Schedule D in relation to a trade—

sections 103 to 106, 108, 109A and 110 (post-cessation receipts and expenses, etc);
section 113 (effect for income tax purposes of change in the persons engaged on trade);
section 337(1) (effect of company beginning or ceasing to carry on trade);
section 401(1) (pre-trading expenditure);
section 44 of and Schedule 6 to the Finance Act 1998 (change of accounting basis).][1]

Commentary—*Simon's Direct Tax Service* **A4.102.**
Definitions—''Schedule A'', s 15(1); ''Schedule D'', s 18(1).
Cross references—See TA 1988 s 65A(1), (2) (application of sub-ss (3) and (4) above to income from land overseas chargeable to income tax under Schedule D Case V).
TA 1988 s 82(6) (disapplication of the provisions of s 82 relating to interest paid to non-residents for computations under sub-s (3) above of income tax on the profits or gains of a Schedule A business).
TA 1988 s 87(10) (disapplication of the provisions of s 87 relating to taxable premiums for computations under sub-s (3) above).
TA 1988 s 98 (references to a trade in the provisions of s 98 relating to tied premises are not to be taken by virtue of sub-s (3) above as including a Schedule A business).
Amendments—[1] This section inserted by FA 1998 Sch 5 para 4 with effect from the year 1998–99 (income tax), and from 1 April 1998, subject to the transitional provisions in FA 1998 Sch 5 Part IV (corporation tax).

[21C The Schedule A charge and mutual business

(1) The following provisions have effect for the purpose of applying the charge to tax under Schedule A in relation to mutual business.

(2) The transactions or relationships involved in mutual business are treated as if they were transactions or relationships between persons between whom no relationship of mutuality existed.

(3) Any surplus arising from the business is regarded as a profit (and any deficit as a loss) if it would be so regarded if the business were not mutual.

(4) The person—

(*a*) to whom the profit arises for corporation tax purposes, or
(*b*) who is regarded as receiving or entitled to the profit for income tax purposes,

is the person who would satisfy that description if the business were not mutual business.

(5) Nothing in this section affects the operation of section 488 (co-operative housing associations).][1]

Commentary—*Simon's Direct Tax Service* **A4.102.**
Definition—''Schedule A'', s 15(1).
Cross references—See TA 1988 s 65A(1), (2) (application of sub-ss (3) and (4) above to income from land overseas chargeable to income tax under Schedule D Case V).
TA 1988 s 82(6) (disapplication of the provisions of s 82 relating to interest paid to non-residents for computations under sub-s (3) above of income tax on the profits or gains of a Schedule A business).
TA 1988 s 87(10) (disapplication of the provisions of s 87 relating to taxable premiums for computations under sub-s (3) above).
TA 1988 s 98 (references to a trade in the provisions of s 98 relating to tied premises are not to be taken by virtue of sub-s (3) above as including a Schedule A business).
Amendments—[1] Section inserted by FA 1998 Sch 5 para 5 with effect from the year 1998–99 (income tax), and from 1 April 1998, subject to the transitional provisions in FA 1998 Sch 5 Part IV (corporation tax).

22 Assessments

Commentary—*Simon's Direct Tax Service* **A4.501; D3.215.**
Amendments—[1] This section repealed by FA 1995 s 39, Sch 6 para 3, Sch 29 Pt VIII(1), with effect from the year 1995–96, except in relation to certain sources of income which ceased during the year 1995–96, and, so far as having effect for the purposes of corporation tax, in relation to accounting periods ending after 30 March 1995.

23 Collection from lessees and agents

Commentary—*Simon's Direct Tax Service* **A4.502.**
Amendments—[1] This section repealed by FA 1995 s 39, Sch 6 para 3, Sch 29 Pt VIII(1), with effect for income tax from the year 1995–96 and for corporation tax in relation to accounting periods ending after 30 March 1995, except in relation to certain sources of income which ceased during the year 1995–96.

24 Construction of Part II

(1) In this Part, except where the context otherwise requires—

"lease" includes an agreement for a lease, and any tenancy, but does not include a mortgage or heritable security, and "lessee", "lessor" and "letting" shall be construed accordingly;

"lessee" and "lessor" include respectively the successors in title of a lessee or a lessor;

"premises" includes any land; and

"premium" includes any like sum, whether payable to the immediate or a superior landlord or to a person connected (within the meaning of section 839) with the immediate or a superior landlord.

(2) For the purposes of this Part, any sum (other than rent) paid on or in connection with the granting of a tenancy shall be presumed to have been paid by way of premium except in so far as other sufficient consideration for the payment [can be][1] shown to have been given.

(3) Where paragraph (*c*) of section 38(1) applies, the premium, or an appropriate part of the premium, payable for or in connection with either lease mentioned in that paragraph may be treated as having been required under the other.

(4) References in this section to a sum shall be construed as including the value of any consideration, and references to a sum paid or payable or to the payment of a sum shall be construed accordingly.

(5) In the application of this Part to Scotland—

"assignment" means an assignation;

"intermediate landlord" means, where an occupying lessee is a sub-lessee, any person for the time being holding the interest of landlord under a sub-lease which comprises the property of which the occupying lessee is sub-lessee, but does not include the immediate landlord;

"premium" includes in particular a grassum payable to any landlord or intermediate landlord on the creation of a sub-lease; and

"reversion" means the interest of the landlord in the property subject to the lease.

(6) In Schedule A and in sections 25 to 31—

(*a*) references to a lease extend only to a lease conferring a right, as against the person whose interest is subject to the lease, to the possession of the premises;

(*b*) "rent" includes a payment by the tenant to defray the cost of work of maintenance of, or repairs to, the demised premises, not being work required by the lease to be carried out by the tenant; ...[2]

(7) ...[2]

Commentary—*Simon's Direct Tax Service* **A4.104, 308.**
Definition—"Schedule A", s 15(1).
Amendments—[1] Words in sub-s (2) substituted for the word "is" by FA 1996 s 134, Sch 20 para 1 with effect from the year 1996–97 as respects income tax and capital gains tax and, as respects corporation tax, for accounting periods ending after 30 June 1999 (by virtue of Finance Act 1994, Section 199, (Appointed Day) Order, SI 1998/3173 art 2).
[2] Para (*c*) and preceding word "and" in sub-s (6), and sub-s (7) repealed by FA 1998 s 165, Sch 27 Part III(4) with effect from the year 1998–99 (income tax), and from 1 April 1998, subject to the transitional provisions in FA 1998 Sch 5 Part IV (corporation tax).

Deductions and other allowances

25 Deductions from rent: general rules

Commentary—*Simon's Direct Tax Service* **A4.203, 301–310.**
Amendments—This section ceased to have effect by virtue of FA 1995 s 39(4), (5), Sch 6 para 4 with effect from the year 1995–96, except (*a*) in so far as this section applies to corporation tax by virtue of TA 1988 s 9; and (*b*) as regards income tax, for certain sources of income which ceased during the year 1995–96 (see FA 1995 s 39(5)). Section repealed by FA 1998 s 165, Sch 27 Part III(4) with effect from the year 1998–99 (income tax), and from 1 April 1998, subject to the transitional provisions in FA 1998 Sch 5 Part IV (corporation tax).

26 Deductions from rent: land managed as one estate

Commentary—*Simon's Direct Tax Service* **A4.311.**
Amendments—This section is repealed by FA 1998 s 39 with effect for income tax purposes after 5 April 2001, and for corporation tax purposes for accounting periods beginning on or after 1 April 2001.

27 Deductions from rent: maintenance funds for historic buildings

Commentary—*Simon's Direct Tax Service* **A4.312.**
Amendments—This section is repealed by FA 1998 s 39 with effect for income tax purposes after 5 April 2001, and for corporation tax purposes for accounting periods beginning on or after 1 April 2001.

28 Deductions from receipts other than rent

Amendments—This section ceased to have effect by virtue of FA 1995 s 39(4), (5), Sch 6 para 4 with effect from the year 1995–96, except (*a*) in so far as this section applies to corporation tax by virtue of TA 1988 s 9; and (*b*) as regards income tax, for certain sources of income which ceased during the year 1995–96 (see FA 1995 s 39(5)). Repealed by FA 1998 Sch 5 para 9 with effect from 1 April 1998, subject to the transitional provisions in FA 1998 Sch 5 Part IV (corporation tax) and from the year 1998–99 (income tax).

29 Sporting rights

Amendments—This section ceased to have effect by virtue of FA 1995 s 39(4), (5), Sch 6 para 4 with effect from the year 1995–96, except (*a*) in so far as this section applies to corporation tax by virtue of TA 1988 s 9; and (*b*) as regards income tax, for certain sources of income which ceased during the year 1995–96 (see FA 1995 s 39(5)). Repealed by FA 1998 Sch 5 para 10 with effect from 1 April 1998, subject to the transitional provisions in FA 1998 Sch 5 Part IV (corporation tax) and from the year 1998–99 (income tax).

30 Expenditure on making sea walls

(1) Where in any year of assessment the owner or tenant of any premises incurs any expenditure in the making of any sea wall or other embankment necessary for the preservation or protection of the premises against the encroachment or overflowing of the sea or any tidal river, he shall be treated [for the purpose of computing the profits of any Schedule A business carried on in relation to those premises][1] as making in that year of assessment and in each of the succeeding 20 years of assessment a payment in relation to the premises preserved or protected by the embankment of an amount equal to a twenty-first part of the expenditure and incurred [as an expense of the business for that year.][1]

(2) Where the whole of that person's interest in the premises or any part thereof is transferred (whether by operation of law or otherwise) to some other person—

(*a*) the amount of the payment which he would be so treated as making for the year of assessment in which the transfer takes place shall be treated as being made partly by the transferor and partly by the transferee, as may be just; and

(*b*) the transferee shall, to the exclusion of the transferor, be treated in any subsequent year—

(i) where the interest transferred is in the whole of the premises, as having made the whole of the payment for that year, and

(ii) where the interest transferred is in part only of the premises, as having made so much of the payment as is properly referable to that part of the premises.

(3) For the purposes of subsection (2) above, where an interest in any premises is a lease and that lease comes to an end, that interest shall be deemed to have been transferred—

(*a*) if an incoming lessee makes any payment to the outgoing lessee in respect of the embankment in question, to the incoming lessee, and

(*b*) in any other case, to the owner of the interest in immediate reversion on the lease and, in relation to Scotland, the expression "the owner of the interest in immediate reversion on the lease" shall be construed as a reference to the landlord.

(4) In relation to a company, section 9(1) shall not have effect so as to require references in this section to a year of assessment to be read as references to an accounting period, but any deduction authorised by this section shall be apportioned between the accounting periods (if more than one) comprising the year of assessment, other than any such period ended before the expenditure is incurred, or transfer takes place, by virtue of which the company is entitled to the deduction.

(5) This section shall not apply in relation to any expenditure in respect of which a capital allowance has been made.

Commentary—*Simon's Direct Tax Service* **A4.323.**
Revenue & other press releases—IR 10-2-95 (Schedule A transitional guidelines: old rules may be applied until a source ceases where it is clear that it will end soon after 1995–96).
Definitions—"Accounting period", s 834(1); "capital allowance", s 832(1); "company", s 832(1), (2); "lease", s 24(1), (6); "premises", s 24(1); "Schedule A business", s 832(1); "year of assessment", s 832(1).
Cross references—See TA 1988 s 31 (supplementary provisions).
Amendments—[1] Words in sub-s (1) substituted by FA 1998 s 38, Sch 5 para 11 with effect for income tax purposes from 1998–99, and for corporation tax purposes from 1 April 1998, subject to the transitional provisions in FA 1998 Sch 5 Part IV.

31 Provisions supplementary to sections 25 to 30

Amendments—This section ceased to have effect by virtue of FA 1995 s 39(4), (5), Sch 6 para 4 with effect from the year 1995–96, except (*a*) in so far as this section applies to corporation tax by virtue of TA 1988 s 9; and (*b*) as regards income tax, for certain sources of income which ceased during the year 1995–96 (see FA 1995 s 39(5)). Repealed by FA 1998 Sch 5 para 12 with effect from 1 April 1998, subject to the transitional provisions in FA 1998 Sch 5 Part IV (corporation tax) and from the year 1998–99 (income tax).

32 Capital allowances for machinery and plant used in estate management

Commentary—*Simon's Direct Tax Service* **A4.331.**
Modifications and amendments—This section was modified by FA 1995 s 39(4), (5), Sch 6 para 8 with effect from the year 1995–96; however, these modifications did not apply (*a*) in so far as this section applied to corporation tax by virtue of TA 1988 s 9; and (*b*) in relation to income tax, for certain sources of income which ceased during the year 1995–96 (see FA 1995 s 39(5)). It is repealed by FA 1997 Sch 15 paras 1, 9(1), Sch 18 Pt VI (11) with effect for the purposes of income tax from 1997–98, and for the purposes of corporation tax for accounting periods ending after 31 March 1997.

33 Agricultural land: allowance for excess expenditure on maintenance

Amendments—This section ceased to have effect by virtue of FA 1995 s 39(4), (5), Sch 6 para 4 with effect from the year 1995–96, except (a) in so far as this section applies to corporation tax by virtue of TA 1988 s 9; and (b) as regards income tax, for certain sources of income which ceased during the year 1995–96 (see FA 1995 s 39(5)). Repealed by FA 1998 Sch 5 para 13 with effect from 1 April 1998, subject to the transitional provisions in FA 1998 Sch 5 Part IV (corporation tax) and from 1998–99 (income tax).

Connected persons

33A Rents or receipts payable by a connected person

Amendments—This section ceased to have effect by virtue of FA 1995 s 39(4), (5), Sch 6 para 4 with effect from the year 1995–96, except (a) in so far as this section applies to corporation tax by virtue of TA 1988 s 9; and (b) as regards income tax, for certain sources of income which ceased during the year 1995–96 (see FA 1995 s 39(5)). Repealed by FA 1998 Sch 5 para 14 with effect from 1 April 1998, subject to the transitional provisions in FA 1998 Sch 5 Part IV (corporation tax) and from 1998–99 (income tax).

33B Rents or receipts relating to land in respect of which a connected person makes payments to a third party

Amendments—This section ceased to have effect by virtue of FA 1995 s 39(4), (5), Sch 6 para 4 with effect from the year 1995–96, except (a) in so far as this section applies to corporation tax by virtue of TA 1988 s 9; and (b) as regards income tax, for certain sources of income which ceased during the year 1995–96 (see FA 1995 s 39(5)). Section repealed by FA 1998 Sch 5 para 14 with effect from 1 April 1998, subject to the transitional provisions in FA 1998 Sch 5 Part IV (corporation tax) and from 1998–99 (income tax).

Premiums, leases at undervalue etc

34 [Treatment of premiums etc as rent][3]

(1) Where the payment of any premium is required under a lease, or otherwise under the terms subject to which a lease is granted, and the duration of the lease does not exceed 50 years, the landlord shall be treated for the purposes of the Tax Acts as [receiving when the lease is granted][2] an amount by way of rent (in addition to any actual rent) equal to—

$$P - \frac{(P \times Y)}{50}$$

where P is the premium and Y is the number of complete periods of 12 months (other than the first) comprised in the duration of the lease.

(2) Where the terms subject to which a lease is granted impose on the tenant an obligation to carry out any work on the premises, the lease shall be deemed for the purposes of this section to have required the payment of a premium to the landlord (in addition to any other premium) of an amount equal to the amount by which the value of the landlord's estate or interest immediately after the commencement of the lease exceeds what its then value would have been if those terms did not impose that obligation on the tenant.

(3) Subsection (2) above shall not apply in so far as the obligation requires the carrying out of work the payment for which would, if the landlord and not the tenant were obliged to carry it out, be deductible [as an expense of any Schedule A business carried on by the landlord][3].

(4) Where, under the terms subject to which a lease is granted, a sum becomes payable by the tenant in lieu of the whole or a part of the rent for any period, or as consideration for the surrender of the lease, the lease shall be deemed for the purposes of this section to have required the payment of a premium to the landlord (in addition to any other premium) of the amount of that sum; but—

(a) [in computing the profits of the Schedule A business of which the sum payable in lieu of rent is by virtue of this subsection to be treated as a receipt][2], the duration of the lease shall be treated as not including any period other than that in relation to which the sum is payable; and

(b) notwithstanding anything in subsection (1) above, rent treated as arising by virtue of this subsection shall be [deemed to be received][2] when the sum in question becomes payable by the tenant.

(5) Where, as a consideration for the variation or waiver of any of the terms of a lease, a sum becomes payable by the tenant otherwise than by way of rent, the lease shall be deemed for the purposes of this section to have required the payment of a premium to the landlord (in addition to any other premium) of the amount of that sum; but—

(a) in computing [the profits of the Schedule A business of which that sum is by virtue of this subsection to be treated as a receipt][2], the duration of the lease shall be treated as not including any period which precedes the time at which the variation or waiver takes effect, or falls after the time at which it ceases to have effect; and

(b) notwithstanding anything in subsection (1) above, rent treated as arising by virtue of this subsection shall be [deemed to be received][2] when the contract providing for the variation or waiver is entered into.

(6) Where a payment falling within subsection (1), (4) or (5) above is due to a person other than the landlord, [no amount shall fall under that subsection to be treated as a receipt of any Schedule A business carried on by the landlord; but that other person shall be taken to have received as income an amount equal to the amount which would otherwise fall to be treated as rent and to be chargeable

to tax as if he had received it in consequence of having, on his own account, entered into a transaction falling to be treated as mentioned in paragraph 1(2) of Schedule A][3].

(7) Subsection (6) above shall not apply in relation to any payment falling within subsection (5) above unless it is due to a person who is, within the meaning of section 839, connected with the landlord.

[(7A) An amount treated under this section as rent shall be taken into account in computing the profits of the Schedule A business in question for the chargeable period in which it is treated as received.][3]

(8) Where an amount by reference to which a person is chargeable to tax by virtue of this section is payable by instalments ("the tax instalments"), the tax chargeable by reference to that amount [may, at his option, be paid][3] by such instalments as the Board may allow over a period not exceeding eight years and ending not later than the time at which the last of the tax instalments is payable.

(9) ...[1]

Commentary—*Simon's Direct Tax Service* **A4.201, 202, 204–207.**
Revenue & other press releases—Hansard 22-6-72 ("undue hardship"—Revenue considers the resources made available by the particular transaction in permitting an instalment arrangement for payment in relation to a bona fide commercial transaction).
Revenue Internal Guidance—Assessed taxes manual, AT 6.611 (application to pay by instalments (made under sub-s (8)) should be sent to the inspector: communications with the collector or Accounts Office will be referred to the inspector).
Property Income Manual PIM1204 (no charge on assignment of lease: difference between grant and assignment of lease).
PIM1212–1218 ("hidden premiums": examples of items falling within sub-ss (2)–(6)).
PIM1220 (hardship applications under sub-s (8) are dealt with by the local office where the tax does not exceed £300,000).
Definitions—"Lease", s 24(1); "premium", s 24(1); "Schedule A", s 15(1); "the Tax Acts", s 831(2).
Cross references—See TA 1988 s 37(2), (3) (reduction of the chargeable amount under this section where the relevant lease is disposed of or a sub-lease granted).
TA 1988 s 38(1) (rules for ascertaining duration of leases for the purposes of this section).
TA 1988 s 39 (this section does not apply to pre-1963 leases).
TA 1988 s 42(1) (appeals against a determination under this section by persons other than the persons chargeable under this section).
TA 1988 s 87 (in computing profits under Schedule D Cases I or II a lessee may deduct a proportional part of a premium taxable under this section where the relevant land is used by the lessee for the purposes of that trade).
TA 1988 s 99(2) (trading receipts of dealers in land to be treated as reduced by the amount on which tax is chargeable by this section).
TA 1988 s 396(2) (Schedule D Case VI loss relief not available in respect of premiums taxed under this section).
TA 1988 s 550(7) (amounts chargeable to tax under this section are not included in total income when computing top-slicing relief in respect of gains from life and capital redemption policies and life annuity contracts).
TA 1988 s 746 (sums arising to persons resident in the Irish Republic).
TCGA 1992 Sch 8 para 5 (exclusion of premiums taxed under this section in computing gains),
TCGA 1992 Sch 8 para 7 (notional premiums taxed under this section treated as enhancement expenditure for the purposes of computing gains).
Amendments—[1] Sub-s (9) repealed by FA 1995 s 39(4), (5), Sch 29 Pt VIII(1) with effect for income tax purposes from 1995–96, except in relation to certain sources of income which ceased during 1995–96, and with effect for corporation tax purposes for accounting periods ending after 30 March 1995.
[2] Words in sub-ss (1), (4)(a), (b), (5)(a), (b) substituted by FA 1998 s 40 with effect in relation to amounts treated as received under this section after 16 March 1998.
[3] Rubric and words in sub-ss (3), (6), (8) substituted, and sub-s (7A) inserted by FA 1998 s 38, Sch 5 para 15 with effect for income tax purposes from 1998–99, and for corporation tax purposes from 1 April 1998, subject to the transitional provisions in FA 1998 Sch 5 Part IV.

35 Charge on assignment of lease granted at an undervalue

(1) This section applies to any lease of a duration not exceeding 50 years where the terms subject to which it was granted are such that the grantor, having regard to values prevailing at the time it was granted and on the assumption that the negotiations for the lease were at arm's length, could have required the payment of an additional sum by way of premium, or additional premium, for the grant of the lease; and in this section any such additional sum is referred to as the "amount foregone".

(2) On any assignment of a lease to which this section applies for a consideration—

(a) where the lease has not previously been assigned, exceeding the premium, if any, for which it was granted, or

(b) where the lease has been previously assigned, exceeding the consideration for which it was last assigned,

the amount of the excess, in so far as it is not greater than the amount foregone reduced by the amount of any such excess arising on a previous assignment of the lease, shall in the same proportion as the amount foregone would, under section 34(1), have fallen to be treated as rent if it had been a premium under the lease, be [deemed to have been received as income by the assignor and to have been received by him in consequence of his having entered into a transaction falling to be treated as mentioned in paragraph 1(2) of Schedule A][1].

[(2A) An amount deemed under this section to have been received as income by the assignor—

(a) is treated as received when the consideration mentioned in subsection (2) becomes payable, and

(b) shall be taken into account in computing the profits of the Schedule A business in question for the chargeable period in which it is treated as received.][1]

(3) If there is submitted to the inspector, by the grantor or any assignor or assignee of the lease, a statement showing whether or not a charge to tax arises or may arise under this section and, if so, the amount on which the charge arises or may arise, then, if the inspector is satisfied as to the accuracy of the statement, he shall certify the accuracy thereof.

Commentary—*Simon's Direct Tax Service* **A4.212.**
Revenue Internal Guidance—Property Income Manual PIM1222 (explanation of section with worked examples).
Definitions—"Assignment", s 24(5); "inspector", s 832(1); "lease", s 24(1); "premium", s 24(1); "Schedule D", s 18(1); "tax", s 832(3).
Cross references—See TA 1988 s 37(2), (3) (reduction of the amount chargeable to tax under this section where the relevant lease is disposed of or a sub-lease granted).
TA 1988 s 38(1) (rules for ascertaining duration of leases for the purposes of this section).
TA 1988 s 39 (this section does not apply to pre-1963 leases).
TA 1988 s 42(1) (appeals against a determination under this section by persons other than the persons chargeable under this section).
TA 1988 s 87 (in computing profits under Schedule D Cases I or II a lessee may deduct a proportional part of a premium taxable under this section where the relevant land is used by the lessee for the purposes of that trade).
TA 1988 s 99(2) (trading receipts of dealers in land to be treated as reduced by the amount on which tax is chargeable by this section).
TA 1988 s 396(2) (Schedule D Case VI loss relief not available in respect of leases taxed under this section).
TA 1988 s 746 (sums arising to persons resident in the Irish Republic).
TCGA 1992 Sch 8 para 6(2) (nothing in TCGA 1992 s 37 is to prevent sums brought into account under this section as receipts of a Schedule A business from being chargeable to capital gains tax).
F(No 2)A 1992 Sch 17 para 5(6) (privatisation of Northern Ireland Electricity: in ascertaining the duration of a lease granted as part of the transfer scheme for the purposes of this section, TA 1988 s 38(1)(*a*), (4) to be disregarded).
Amendments—[1] Words in sub-s (2) substituted, and sub-s (2A) inserted by FA 1998 s 38, Sch 5 para 16 with effect for income tax purposes from 1998–99, and for corporation tax purposes from 1 April 1998, subject to the transitional provisions in FA 1998 Sch 5 Part IV.

36 Charge on sale of land with right to reconveyance

(1) Where the terms subject to which an estate or interest in land is sold provide that it shall be, or may be required to be, reconveyed at a future date to the vendor or a person connected with him, [the following amount shall be deemed to have been received as income by the vendor and to have been received by him in consequence of his having entered into a transaction falling to be treated as mentioned in paragraph 1(2) of Schedule A, that is to say][1] any amount by which the price at which the estate or interest is sold exceeds the price at which it is to be reconveyed or, if the earliest date at which in accordance with those terms it would fall to be reconveyed is a date two years or more after the sale, [the amount of the excess][1] reduced by one-fiftieth thereof for each complete year (other than the first) in the period between the sale and that date.

(2) Where, under the terms of the sale, the date of the reconveyance is not fixed, then—

    (*a*) if the price on reconveyance varies with the date, the price shall be taken, for the purposes of this section, to be the lowest possible under the terms of the sale, and

    (*b*) there shall be repaid to the vendor, on a claim made before the expiry of six years after the reconveyance takes place, any amount by which tax assessed on him by virtue of this section exceeded the amount which would have been so assessed if that date had been treated for the purposes of this section as the date fixed by the terms of the sale.

(3) Where the terms of the sale provide for the grant of a lease directly or indirectly out of the estate or interest to the vendor or a person connected with him, this section shall, subject to subsection (4) below, apply as if the grant of the lease were a reconveyance of the estate or interest at a price equal to the sum of the amount of the premium (if any) for the lease and the value at the date of the sale of the right to receive a conveyance of the reversion immediately after the lease begins to run.

(4) Subsection (3) above shall not apply in any case where the lease is granted and begins to run within one month after the sale.

[(4A) An amount deemed under this section to have been received as income by the vendor—

    (*a*) is treated as received when the estate or interest is sold, and

    (*b*) shall be taken into account in computing the profits of the Schedule A business in question for the chargeable period in which it is treated as received.

(4B) For the purposes of subsection (4A)(*a*) an estate or interest in land is treated as sold when any of the following occurs—

    (*a*) an unconditional contract for its sale is entered into,

    (*b*) a conditional contract for its sale becomes unconditional, or

    (*c*) an option or right of pre-emption is exercised requiring the vendor to enter into an unconditional contract for its sale.][1]

(5) In this section references to a person connected with another shall be construed in accordance with section 839.

Commentary—*Simon's Direct Tax Service* **A4.213.**
Revenue Internal Guidance—Property Income Manual PIM1224, 1226 (explanation of section with worked examples).
PIM1228 ("Treasury arrangement" for avoiding charge in relation to mineral-bearing land).
Definitions—"Lease", s 24(5); "premium", s 24(1); "Schedule D", s 18(1); "tax", s 832(3).
Cross references—See TA 1988 s 38(1) (rules for ascertaining duration of leases for the purposes of this section).
TA 1988 s 39 (this section does not apply to pre-1963 leases).
TA 1988 s 42(1) (appeals against a determination under this section by persons other than the persons chargeable under this section).
TA 1988 s 99(2), (3) (trading receipts of dealers in land to be treated as reduced by the amount on which tax is chargeable by this section).
TA 1988 s 396(2) (Schedule D Case VI loss relief not available in respect of land taxed under this section).
TA 1988 s 746 (sums arising to persons resident in the Irish Republic).
TCGA 1992 Sch 8 para 5(3) (exclusion of capital gains tax on amount brought into account as a receipt of a Schedule A business under this section).
FA 1994 Sch 24 para 24 (railway privatisation: disapplication of this section to specified transactions).
Amendments—[1] Words in sub-s (1) substituted, and sub-ss (4A), (4B) inserted by FA 1998 s 38, Sch 5 para 17 with effect for income tax purposes from 1998–99, and for corporation tax purposes from 1 April 1998, subject to the transitional provisions in FA 1998 Sch 5 Part IV.

37 Premiums paid etc: deductions from premiums and rent received

(1) This section applies in any case where in respect of a lease of any premises—

[(a) any amount falls to be treated as a receipt of a Schedule A business by virtue of section 34 or 35, or

(b) any amount would fall to be so treated but for the operation of subsection (2) or (3) below,][2]

and [that amount][1] is in this section referred to as "the amount chargeable on the superior interest" and any such lease is referred to as "the head lease".

(2) Where—

(a) a lease is granted out of, or there is a disposition of, the head lease, and

(b) in respect of that grant or disposition a person would, apart from this subsection, [be treated by virtue of section 34 or 35 as receiving any amount as income in the course of carrying on a Schedule A business][2] ("the later chargeable amount"),

then the amount [which he shall be treated as having so received][2] shall, subject to subsection (3) below, be the excess (if any) of the later chargeable amount over the appropriate fraction of the amount chargeable on the superior interest.

(3) Where a person would, apart from subsection (2) above, be [treated by virtue of section 34 or 35 as having received any amount as income in the course of carrying on a Schedule A business and falls to be so treated][2] in respect of a lease or disposition which extends to a part only of the premises subject to the head lease, the amount [which he shall be treated as having so received][2] shall be the excess (if any) of the later chargeable amount over the appropriate fraction of the amount chargeable on the superior interest as, on a just apportionment, is attributable to that part of the premises.

(4) Subject to subsection (5) below, the person for the time being entitled to the head lease shall be treated for the [purpose, in computing the profits of a Schedule A business, of making deductions in respect of the disbursements and expenses of that business][2] as paying rent for those premises (in addition to any actual rent), becoming due from day to day, during any part of the period in respect of which the amount chargeable on the superior interest arose for which he was entitled to the head lease, and, in all, bearing to that amount the same proportion as that part of the period bears to the whole.

(5) Where subsection (2) above applies, subsection (4) above shall apply for the period in respect of which the later chargeable amount arose only if the appropriate fraction of the amount chargeable on the superior interest exceeds the later chargeable amount, and shall then apply as if the amount chargeable on the superior interest were reduced in the proportion which that excess bears to that appropriate fraction.

(6) Where subsection (3) above applies, subsections (4) and (5) above shall be applied separately to the part of the premises referred to in subsection (3) above and to the remainder of the premises, but as if for any reference to the amount chargeable on the superior interest there were substituted a reference to that amount proportionately adjusted.

(7) For the purposes of this section—

(a) the appropriate fraction of the amount chargeable on the superior interest is the fraction—

$$\frac{A}{B}$$

where—

A is the period in respect of which the later chargeable amount arose; and
B is the period in respect of which the amount chargeable on the superior interest arose;

and

(b) the period in respect of which an amount arose—

(i) where it arose under section 34, shall be the period treated in computing the amount as being the duration of the lease;

(ii) where it arose under section 35, shall be the period treated in computing the amount as being the duration of the lease remaining at the date of the assignment.

(8) Where the amount chargeable on the superior interest arose under section 34(2) by reason of an obligation which included the carrying out of work in respect of which any capital allowance has fallen or will fall to be made, subsections (1) to (6) above shall apply as if the obligation had not included the carrying out of that work and that amount had been calculated accordingly.

(9) An amount or part of an amount shall not be deducted under this section more than once from any sum, or from more than one sum, and shall not in any case be so deducted if it has been otherwise allowed as a deduction in computing the income of any person for tax purposes.

Commentary—*Simon's Direct Tax Service* **A4.221–223.**
Definitions—"Lease", s 24(1); "premises", s 24(1); "premium", s 24(1); "Schedule A", s 15(1); "tax", s 832(3).

Cross references—See TA 1988 s 87(5), (6) (interaction of this section and s 87 where premiums charged in respect of premises occupied by lessee for the purposes of a trade etc).

TCGA 1992 Sch 8 para 6(1) (reduction of loss accruing on grant of a sublease where under sub-s (4) above a person is treated as paying additional rent in consequence of granting the sublease).

Amendments—[1] Words in sub-s (1) substituted by FA 1990 Sch 14 paras 1, 2 and deemed always to have had effect.

[2] Sub-s (1)(a), (b) substituted, and words in sub-ss (2), (3), (4) substituted, by FA 1998 Sch 5 para 18 with effect for income tax purposes from 1998–99, and for corporation tax purposes from 1 April 1998, subject to the transitional provisions in FA 1998 Sch 5 Part IV.

38 Rules for ascertaining duration of leases

(1) In ascertaining the duration of a lease for the purposes of sections 34 to 36—

    (*a*) in any case where—

        (i) any of the terms of the lease (whether relating to forfeiture or any other matter) or any other circumstances render it unlikely that the lease will continue beyond a date falling before the expiry of the term of the lease, and

        (ii) the premium was not substantially greater than it would have been, on the assumptions required by subsections (3) and (4) below, had the term been one expiring on that date,

    the lease shall not be treated as having been granted for a term longer than one ending on that date;

    (*b*) where the terms of the lease include provision for the extension of the lease beyond a given date by notice given by the tenant, account may be taken of any circumstances making it likely that the lease will be so extended; and

    (*c*) where the tenant or a person connected with him (within the meaning of section 839) is or may become entitled to a further lease or the grant of a further lease (whenever commencing) of the same premises or of premises including the whole or part of the same premises, the term of the lease may be treated as not expiring before the term of the further lease.

(2) Subsection (1) above shall be applied by reference to the facts which were known or ascertainable at the time of the grant of the lease, or in relation to tax under section 34(5), at a time when the contract providing for the variation or waiver is entered into.

(3) It shall be assumed in applying subsection (1) above that all parties concerned, whatever their relationship, act as they would act if they were at arm's length.

(4) In any case where—

    (*a*) by the lease or in connection with the granting of it benefits were conferred other than—

        (i) vacant possession and beneficial occupation of the premises, or

        (ii) the right to receive rent at a reasonable commercial rate in respect of the premises, or

    (*b*) payments were made which would not be expected to be made by parties acting at arm's length if no other benefits had been so conferred,

it shall also be assumed, unless it [can be][1] shown that the benefits were not conferred or the payments made for the purpose of securing a tax advantage in the application of this Part, that the benefits would not have been conferred nor the payments made had the lease been for a term ending on the date mentioned in subsection (1)(*a*) above.

(5) Where an inspector has reason to believe that a person has information relevant to the ascertainment of the duration of a lease in accordance with subsections (1) to (4) above, the inspector may by notice require him to give, within a time specified in the notice, such information on the matters so specified as is in his possession; but a solicitor shall not be so required to do more, in relation to anything done by him on behalf of a client, than state that he is or was so acting and give the name and address of his client.

(6) In this section in relation to Scotland, the expression "term", where referring to the duration of a lease, means "period".

(7) This section has effect subject to paragraphs 2 and 3 of Schedule 30.

Commentary—*Simon's Direct Tax Service* A4.203.

Revenue Internal Guidance—Property Income Manual PIM1206 (interpretation of sub-ss (3), (4)).

PIM1207 (example on sub-s (1)).

Definitions—"Inspector", s 832(1); "lease", s 24(1); "notice", s 832(1); "premises", s 24(1); "premium", s 24(1); "tax", s 832(3).

Cross references—See TMA 1970 s 98 (failure to provide information required under sub-s (5) above may incur liability to a special-return penalty).

TA 1988 s 24(3) (premium for either lease mentioned in sub-s(1)(*c*) above may be treated as having been required under the other).

TA 1988 Sch 30 para 2 (scope of this section).

TA 1988 Sch 30 para 3 (modifications to sub-ss (1), (2) and (4) above in relation to leases granted between 13 June 1969 and 24 August 1971).

TA 1988 Sch 30 para 4 (rules for ascertaining the duration of leases where the provisions of this section do not apply).

F(No 2)A 1992 Sch 17 para 5(4), (6) (leases granted to successor companies under scheme for transfer of property, rights and liabilities of Northern Ireland Electricity: sub-ss (1)(*a*), (4) to be disregarded in determining duration of lease for purposes of CAA 1990 s 11 and TA 1988 s 35).

Amendments—[1] Words in sub-s (4) substituted for the word "is" by FA 1996 s 134, Sch 20 para 2 with effect for the purposes of income tax and capital gains tax from the year 1996–97 and, as respects corporation tax, for accounting periods ending after 30 June 1999 (by virtue of Finance Act 1994, Section 199, (Appointed Day) Order, SI 1998/3173 art 2).

39 Saving for pre-1963 leases, and special relief for individuals

(1) Subject to subsection (2) below, sections 34 to 36 shall not apply in relation to a lease granted, or an estate or interest in land sold, before the beginning of the year 1963–64 or in pursuance of a contract entered into before 4th April 1963.

(2) Section 34(5) shall apply to the variation or waiver of any terms of a lease (not being a variation or waiver made in pursuance of a contract entered into before 4th April 1963) notwithstanding that the lease was granted before the beginning of the year 1963–64.

(3) ...[1]

Commentary—*Simon's Direct Tax Service* A4.202.
Definitions—"Lease", s 24(1); "year of assessment", s 832(1).
Amendments—[1] Sub-s (3) repealed by FA 1988 s 75 and Sch 14 Pt IV with effect from the year 1988–89.

[Supplementary provisions][2]

40 Tax treatment of receipts and outgoings on sale of land

(1) Where—

(a) by virtue of a contract for the sale of an estate or interest in land there falls to be apportioned between the parties a receipt or outgoing in respect of the estate or interest which becomes due after the making of the contract but before the time to which the apportionment falls to be made, and

(b) a part of the receipt is therefore receivable by the vendor in trust for the purchaser or, as the case may be, a part of the outgoing is paid by the vendor as trustee for the purchaser,

the purchaser shall be treated for the purposes of tax under Schedule A as if that part had [been received or paid by him][2] immediately after the time to which the apportionment falls to be made.

(2) Where by virtue of such a contract there falls to be apportioned between the parties a receipt or outgoing in respect of the estate or interest which became due before the making of the contract, the parties shall be treated for the purposes of tax under Schedule A as if the contract had been entered into before the receipt or outgoing became due, and sub-section (1) above shall apply accordingly.

(3) Where on the sale of an estate or interest in land there is apportioned to the vendor a part of a receipt or outgoing in respect of the estate or interest which is to become receivable or be paid by the purchaser after the making of the apportionment, then for the purposes of tax under Schedule A—

(a) when the receipt becomes due or, as the case may be, the outgoing is paid, the amount of it shall be treated as reduced by so much thereof as was apportioned to the vendor, and

(b) the part apportioned to the vendor shall be treated as if it were of the same nature as the receipt or outgoing and [had been received or paid directly by him immediately before the time to which the apportionment is made][2].

(4) Any reference in subsection (1) or (2) above to a party to a contract shall include a person to whom the rights and obligations of that party under the contract have passed by assignment or otherwise.

[(4A) An amount deemed under this section to have been received or paid shall be taken into account in computing the profits of the Schedule A business in question for the period in which it is treated as received or paid.][2]

Commentary—*Simon's Direct Tax Service* A4.109.
Revenue Internal Guidance—Assessment procedures manual AP 1328 (worked examples).
Property Income Manual PIM 5157, 5158 (effect of s 40 with worked examples).
Definitions—"Assignment", s 24(5); "Schedule A", s 15(1); "Schedule D", s 18(1); "tax", s 832(3).
Amendments—[1] Sub-s (5) ceased to have effect by virtue of FA 1995 s 39(4), (5), Sch 6 para 4 with effect from the year 1995–96, except (a) in so far as this section applies to corporation tax by virtue of TA 1988 s 9; and (b) as regards income tax, for certain sources of income which ceased during the year 1995–96 (see FA 1995 s 39(5)).
[2] Words in sub-ss (1), (3)(b) and the heading before the section substituted, sub-s (4A) inserted, and sub-s (5) omitted by FA 1998 Sch 5 paras 19–20 with effect from 1 April 1998, subject to the transitional provisions in FA 1998 Sch 5 Part IV (corporation tax) and from the year 1998–99 (income tax).

41 Relief for rent etc not paid

Amendments—This section ceased to have effect by virtue of FA 1995 s 39(4), (5), Sch 6 para 4 with effect from the year 1995–96, except (a) in so far as this section applies to corporation tax by virtue of TA 1988 s 9; and (b) as regards income tax, for certain sources of income which ceased during the year 1995–96 (see FA 1995 s 39(5)). Repealed by FA 1998 Sch 5 para 21 with effect from 1 April 1998, subject to the transitional provisions in FA 1998 Sch 5 Part IV (corporation tax) and from the year 1998–99 (income tax).

42 Appeals against determinations under sections 34 to 36

(1) Where it appears to the inspector that the determination of any amount on which a person may be chargeable to tax by virtue of section 34, 35 or 36 may affect the liability to income tax, corporation tax or capital gains tax of other persons he may give notice to those persons as well as to the first-mentioned person of the determination he proposes to make and of the rights conferred on them by this section.

(2) Any person to whom such a notice is given may, within 30 days after the date on which it is given, object to the proposed determination by notice given to the inspector.

(3) Where notices have been given under subsection (1) above and no notice of objection is duly given under subsection (2) above the inspector shall make the determination as proposed in his notices and the determination shall not be called in question in any proceedings.

(4) Where a notice of objection is duly given the amount mentioned in subsection (1) above shall be determined in like manner as an appeal and shall be so determined by the Special Commissioners or such body of General Commissioners as may be agreed on by the person to be charged and all persons who have given notice of objection.

(5) All persons to whom notices have been given under subsection (1) above may take part in any proceedings under subsection (4) above and in any appeal arising out of those proceedings and shall be bound by the determination made in the proceedings or on appeal, whether or not they have taken part in the proceedings; and their successors in title shall also be so bound.

(6) A notice under subsection (1) above may, notwithstanding any obligation as to secrecy or other restriction on the disclosure of information, include a statement of the grounds on which the inspector proposes to make the determination.

(7) An inspector may by notice require any person to give within the time specified in the notice such information as appears to the inspector to be required for deciding whether to give a notice under subsection (1) above to any person.

Commentary—*Simon's Direct Tax Service* **A4.231.**
Revenue Internal Guidance—Property Income Manual PIM2340 (procedure where information from the two taxpayers involved does not agree).
Definitions—"Capital gains tax", s 831(5); "income tax", s 832(4); "inspector", s 832(1); "notice", s 832(1).
Cross reference—TMA 1970 s 98 (failure to provide information required by a notice served under this section may incur a liability to a special-return penalty).

[42A Non-residents and their representatives

(1) The Board may by regulations make provision for the charging, assessment, collection and recovery on or from prescribed persons falling within subsection (2) below of prescribed amounts in respect of the tax which is or may become chargeable under Schedule A on the income of any person who has his usual place of abode outside the United Kingdom (''the non-resident'').

(2) A person falls within this subsection if he is—
    (*a*) a person by whom any such sums are payable to the non-resident as fall, or would fall, to be treated as receipts of a Schedule A business carried on by the non-resident; or
    (*b*) a person who acts on behalf of the non-resident in connection with the management or administration of any such business.

(3) A person on whom any obligation to make payments to the Board is imposed by regulations under this section shall be entitled—
    (*a*) to be indemnified by the non-resident for all such payments; and
    (*b*) to retain, out of any sums otherwise due from him to the non-resident, or received by him on behalf of the non-resident, amounts sufficient for meeting any liabilities under the regulations to make payments to the Board which have been discharged by that person or to which he is subject.

(4) Without prejudice to the generality of the preceding provisions of this section, regulations under this section may include any or all of the following provisions, that is to say—
    (*a*) provision for the amount of any payment to be made to the Board in respect of the tax on any income to be calculated by reference to such factors as may be prescribed;
    (*b*) provision for the determination in accordance with any such regulations of the period for which, the circumstances in which and the times at which any payments are to be made to the Board;
    (*c*) provision for requiring the payment of interest on amounts which are not paid to the Board at the times required under any such regulations;
    (*d*) provision as to the certificates to be given in prescribed circumstances to the non-resident by a person falling within subsection (2) above, and as to the particulars to be included in any such certificate;
    (*e*) provision for the making of repayments of tax to the non-resident and for such repayments to be made in prescribed cases to persons falling within subsection (2) above;
    (*f*) provision for the payment of interest by the Board on sums repaid under any such regulations;
    (*g*) provision for the rights and obligations arising under any such regulations to depend on the giving of such notices and the making of such claims and determinations as may be prescribed;
    (*h*) provision for the making and determination of applications for requirements of any such regulations not to apply in certain cases, and for the variation or revocation, in prescribed cases, of the determinations made on such applications;
    (*i*) provision for appeals with respect to questions arising under any such regulations;
    (*j*) provision requiring prescribed persons falling within subsection (2)(*b*) above to register with the Board;
    (*k*) provision requiring persons registered with the Board and other prescribed persons falling within subsection (2) above to make returns and supply prescribed information to the Board and to make available prescribed books, documents and other records for inspection on behalf of the Board;

(*l*) provision for the partnership, as such, to be treated as the person falling within subsection (2) above in a case where a liability to make any payment under the regulations arises from amounts payable or things done in the course of a business carried on by any persons in partnership;

(*m*) provision which, in relation to payments to be made by virtue of this section in respect of any tax or to any sums retained in respect of such payments, applies (with or without modifications) any enactment or subordinate legislation having effect apart from this section with respect to cases in which tax is or is treated as deducted from any income.

(5) Interest required to be paid by any regulations under this section shall be paid without deduction of tax and shall not be taken into account in computing any income, profits or losses for any tax purposes.

(6) Regulations under this section may—

(*a*) make different provision for different cases; and

(*b*) contain such supplementary, incidental, consequential and transitional provision as appears to the Board to be appropriate;

and the provision that may be made by virtue of paragraph (*b*) above may include provision which, in connection with any other provision made by any such regulations, modifies the operation in any case of section 59A of the Management Act or Schedule 21 to the Finance Act 1995 (payments on account of income tax).

(7) In this section—

"prescribed" means prescribed by, or determined by an officer of the Board in accordance with, regulations made by the Board under this section; and

"subordinate legislation" has the same meaning as in the Interpretation Act 1978.

(8) ...²]¹

Commentary—*Simon's Direct Tax Service* **A4.503.**
Regulations—Taxation of Income from Land (Non-Residents) Regulations, SI 1995/2902.
Revenue and other press releases—Booklet "Non-resident landlords scheme: Guidance notes for letting agents and tenants" (full description of the non-resident landlords scheme; available from Financial Intermediaries and Claims Office, which administers the scheme).
Definitions—"The Board", s 832(1); "Management Act", s 831(3); "Schedule A", s 15(1), "tax", s 832(3), "United Kingdom", s 830(1).
Cross reference—TMA 1970 s 98 (failure to provide notices etc pursuant to Regulations made under this section may incur a liability to a special-return penalty).
Amendments—¹ This section inserted by FA 1995 s 40(1).
² Sub-s (8) repealed by FA 1998 Sch 5 para 22 with effect from 1 April 1998, subject to the transitional provisions in FA 1998 Sch 5 Part IV (corporation tax), and from the year 1998–99 (income tax).

43 Non-residents

Commentary—*Simon's Direct Tax Service* **A4.503.**
Amendments—This section repealed by FA 1995 s 40(3), Sch 29 Pt VIII(16), in relation to any payment made after 5 April 1996.

[Rent factoring
43A Finance agreement: interpretation

(1) A transaction is a finance agreement for the purposes of sections 43B to 43F if in accordance with [generally accepted accounting practice]² the accounts of a company which receives money under the transaction would record a financial obligation (whether in respect of a lease creditor or otherwise) in relation to that receipt.

(2) ...³

(3) The reference to a company's accounts in subsection (1) shall be taken to include a reference to the consolidated group accounts of a group of companies of which it is a member; and—

(*a*) "group of companies" means a set of companies which, if each were incorporated in Great Britain, would form a group within the meaning given by section 262(1) of the Companies Act 1985, and

(*b*) "consolidated group accounts" means accounts of a kind which would satisfy the requirements of section 227 of the Companies Act 1985.

(4) For the purposes of subsection (1) a company shall be treated as receiving any money which—

(*a*) falls to be taken into account as a receipt for the purpose of calculating the company's liability to corporation tax, or

(*b*) would fall to be taken into account as a receipt for that purpose if the company were resident in the United Kingdom.]¹

Commentary—*Simon's Direct Tax Service* **A4.106A.**
Amendments—¹ This section inserted, together with ss 43B–43G, by FA 2000 s 110 with effect for transactions entered into after 20 March 2000.
² In sub-s (1), words substituted for the words "normal accounting practice" by FA 2002 s 103(4)(*a*) with effect from 24 July 2002.
³ Sub-s (2) repealed by FA 2002 s 141, Sch 40 Pt 3(16) with effect from 24 July 2002 Sub-s (2) previously read as follows—

"(2) In subsection (1) "normal accounting practice" in relation to a company means normal accounting practice for a company incorporated in a part of the United Kingdom (irrespective of where the company is in fact incorporated)."

[43B Transfer of rent

(1) This section applies to a finance agreement if it transfers a right to receive rent in respect of land in the United Kingdom from one person to another, otherwise than by means of the grant of a lease of land in the United Kingdom.

(2) A person who receives a finance amount shall be treated for the purposes of the Tax Acts as receiving it—

(a) by way of rent,

(b) in the course of a business falling within paragraph 1(1) of Schedule A, and

(c) in the chargeable period in which the agreement is made;

and the finance amount shall be taken into account in computing the profits of the Schedule A business for the chargeable period in which the agreement is made.

(3) In subsection (2) "finance amount" means a receipt in respect of which section 43A(1) is satisfied.][1]

Commentary—*Simon's Direct Tax Service* **A4.106A.**
Amendments—[1] This section inserted, together with ss 43A, 43C–43G, by FA 2000 s 110 with effect for transactions entered into after 20 March 2000.

[43C Transfer of rent: exceptions, etc

(1) Section 43B shall not apply to a finance agreement if the term over which the financial obligation is to be reduced exceeds 15 years.

(2) Section 43B shall not apply to a finance agreement if—

(a) the arrangements for the reduction of the financial obligation substantially depend on a person's entitlement to an allowance under [the Capital Allowances Act (including enactments which under this Act are to be treated as contained in that Act)][2], and

(b) that person is not connected to the person from whom the right to receive rent is transferred.

(3) Section 43B shall not apply to a finance agreement if—

(a) section 36(1) applies (without reference to section 36(3)), or

(b) section 36(1) would apply (without reference to section 36(3)) if the price at which an estate or interest is sold were to exceed the price at which it is to be reconveyed.

(4) If—

(a) section 36(1) would apply in relation to a finance agreement by virtue only of section 36(3), and

(b) section 43B applies in relation to the agreement,

section 36(1) shall not apply.

(5) Section 43B shall not apply to a finance agreement if section 780 applies.

(6) Section 43B(2) shall not apply to a finance amount which is brought into account in computing the profits of a trade for the purposes of Case I of Schedule D (otherwise than by virtue of section 83 of the Finance Act 1989 (life assurance)).][1]

Commentary—*Simon's Direct Tax Service* **A4.106A.**
Amendments—[1] This section inserted, together with ss 43A, 43B, 43D–43G, by FA 2000 s 110 with effect for transactions entered into after 20 March 2000.
[2] Words substituted by CAA 2001 s 578, Sch 2 para 11 with effect for income tax purposes, as respects allowances and charges falling to be made for chargeable periods ending after 5 April 2001, and for corporation tax purposes, as respects allowances and charges falling to be made for chargeable periods ending after 31 March 2001.

[43D Interposed lease

(1) This section applies to a finance agreement under which—

(a) a lease is granted in respect of land in the United Kingdom,

(b) a premium is payable in respect of the lease, and

(c) section 43A(1) is satisfied by reference to the receipt of the premium.

(2) Where this section applies, the person to whom the premium is payable shall be treated for the purposes of the Tax Acts as receiving it—

(a) by way of rent,

(b) in the course of a business falling within paragraph 1(1) of Schedule A, and

(c) in the chargeable period in which the agreement is made;

and the premium shall be taken into account in computing the profits of the Schedule A business for the chargeable period in which the agreement is made.][1]

Commentary—*Simon's Direct Tax Service* **A4.106A.**
Amendments—[1] This section inserted, together with ss 43A–43C, 43E–43G, by FA 2000 s 110 with effect for transactions entered into after 20 March 2000.

[43E Interposed lease: exceptions, etc

(1) Section 43D shall not apply to a finance agreement if—

(a) the term over which the financial obligation is to be reduced exceeds 15 years, or (*b*) the length of the lease does not exceed 15 years, or

(*c*) the length of the lease is not significantly different from the term over which the financial obligation is to be reduced.

(2) For the purpose of subsection (1) the length of a lease shall be calculated in accordance with section 38.

(3) Section 43D shall not apply to a finance agreement if—

(*a*) the arrangements for the reduction of the financial obligation substantially depend on a person's entitlement to an allowance under [the Capital Allowances Act (including enactments which under this Act are to be treated as contained in that Act)][2], and

(*b*) that person is not connected to the person who grants the lease in respect of which the premium is payable.

(4) Section 43D(2) shall not apply where all or part of the premium is brought into account in computing the profits of a trade for the purposes of Case I of Schedule D (otherwise than by virtue of section 83 of the Finance Act 1989 (life assurance)).

(5) Section 34 shall not apply in relation to a premium to which section 43D(2) applies.][1]

Commentary—*Simon's Direct Tax Service* **A4.106A.**
Amendments—[1] This section inserted, together with ss 43A–43D, 43F, 43G, by FA 2000 s 110 with effect for transactions entered into after 20 March 2000.
[2] Words substituted by CAA 2001 s 578, Sch 2 para 12 with effect for income tax purposes, as respects allowances and charges falling to be made for chargeable periods ending after 5 April 2001, and for corporation tax purposes, as respects allowances and charges falling to be made for chargeable periods ending after 31 March 2001.

[43F Insurance business

(1) In the application of sections 43A to 43E to companies carrying on insurance business a reference to accounts does not include a reference to accounts required to be prepared under [Chapter 9 of the Prudential Sourcebook (Insurers)][2].

(2) Neither section 43B(2) nor section 43D(2) shall require any amount to be brought into account in a computation of profits of life assurance business, or any category of life assurance business, carried on by a company where the computation is made in accordance with the provisions of this Act applicable to Case I of Schedule D.

(3) Section 432A shall have effect in relation to any sum which is or would be treated as received by virtue of section 43B(2) or 43D(2) of this Act.

(4) Expressions used in this section and in Chapter I of Part XII have the same meaning in this section as in that Chapter.][1]

Commentary—*Simon's Direct Tax Service* **A4.106A.**
Amendments—[1] This section inserted, together with ss 43A–43E, 43G, by FA 2000 s 110 with effect for transactions entered into after 20 March 2000.
[2] Words in sub-s (1) substituted by the Financial Services and Markets Act 2000 (Consequential Amendments) (Taxes) Order, SI 2001/3629 arts 13, 15 with effect for periods of account ending after 30 November 2001.

[43G Interpretation

(1) This section applies for the purposes of sections 43A to 43F.

(2) In those sections—

"connected" in relation to persons has the meaning given by section 839,

"rent" includes any sum which is chargeable to tax under Schedule A,

"lease" includes an underlease, sublease, tenancy or licence and an agreement for any of those things, but does not include a mortgage or heritable security,

"premium" has the meaning given by section 24(1) (and, in relation to Scotland, section 24(5)), and subsections (4) and (5) of section 34 shall have effect in relation to sections 43A to 43F as they have effect in relation to section 34, and

"sum" has the meaning given by section 24(4).

(3) A reference to a transfer of a right to receive rent from one person to another includes a reference to any arrangement under which rent ceases to form part of the receipts taken into account for the purposes of calculating a company's liability to corporation tax or income tax.

(4) In calculating the term over which a financial obligation is to be reduced no account shall be taken of any period during which the arrangements for reduction differ from the arrangements which apply in a previous period if—

(*a*) the period begins after the financial obligation has been substantially reduced, and

(*b*) the different arrangements for reduction are not the result of a provision for periodic review, on commercial terms, of rent under a lease.][1]

Commentary—*Simon's Direct Tax Service* **A4.106A.**
Amendments—[1] This section inserted, together with ss 43A–43F, by FA 2000 s 110 with effect for transactions entered into after 20 March 2000.

PART III

[GOVERNMENT SECURITIES][1]

Cross references—See TA 1988 s 17 (the charge to Schedule C).
TA 1988 s 45 (interpretation of this Part).
Amendments—[1] Pt III heading substituted by FA 1996 Sch 7 paras 6, 32 with effect from the year 1996–97 for income tax purposes and for accounting periods ending after 31 March 1996 for corporation tax purposes.

General

44 Income tax: mode of charge

Commentary—*Simon's Direct Tax Service* A6.301.
Amendments—This section repealed by FA 1996 Sch 7 paras 7, 32, Sch 41 Pt V(2) with effect from the year 1996–97 for income tax purposes and for accounting periods ending after 31 March 1996 for corporation tax purposes.

45 Interpretation of Part III

Commentary—*Simon's Direct Tax Service* A6.102, 103, 106.
Amendments—This section repealed by FA 1996 Sch 7 paras 8, 32, Sch 41 Pt V(2) with effect from the year 1996–97 for income tax purposes and for accounting periods ending after 31 March 1996 for corporation tax purposes.

Government securities: exemptions from tax

46 Savings certificates and tax reserve certificates

(1) Subject to subsections (3) to (6) below, income arising from savings certificates shall not be liable to tax.

(2) Tax shall not be chargeable in respect of the interest on tax reserve certificates issued by the Treasury.

(3) Subsection (1) above does not apply to any savings certificates which are purchased by or on behalf of a person in excess of the amount which a person is for the time being authorised to purchase under regulations made by the Treasury or, as respects Ulster Savings Certificates, by the Department of Finance and Personnel.

(4) Subsection (1) above does not apply to Ulster Savings Certificates unless—

(a) the holder is resident and ordinarily resident in Northern Ireland when the certificates are repaid; or

(b) the certificates were purchased by him and he was so resident and ordinarily resident when they were purchased.

(5) A claim under this section in respect of Ulster Savings Certificates shall be made to the Board.

(6) In this section "savings certificates" means savings certificates issued under section 12 of the National Loans Act 1968 or section 7 of the National Debt Act 1958 or section 59 of the Finance Act 1920 and any war savings certificates as defined in section 9(3) of the National Debt Act 1972 together with any savings certificates issued under any corresponding enactment forming part of the law of Northern Ireland.

Commentary—*Simon's Direct Tax Service* A6.210.
Concession A34—Ulster savings certificates encashed after death of registered holder.
Definitions—"The Board", s 832(1); "interest", s 832(1); "tax", s 832(3); "Ulster Savings Certificates", s 832(1).
Cross reference—See TCGA 1992 s 121 (capital gains tax exemption for government non-marketable securities).

47 United Kingdom government securities held by non-residents

Commentary—*Simon's Direct Tax Service* A6.205; B5.215.
Amendments—This section repealed by FA 1996 s 154, Sch 28 para 1, Sch 41 Pt V(18) with effect from the year 1996–97 for income tax purposes and for accounting periods ending after 31 March 1996 for corporation tax purposes.

48 Securities of foreign states

Commentary—*Simon's Direct Tax Service* A6.104, 203; B5.216.
Amendments—This section repealed by FA 1996 Sch 7 paras 9, 32, Sch 41 Pt V(2) with effect for the purposes of income tax from the year 1996–97 and, as respects corporation tax, for accounting periods ending after 31 March 1996.

49 Stock and dividends in name of Treasury etc

(1) No tax shall be chargeable in respect of the stock or dividends transferred to accounts in the books of the Bank of England in the name of the Treasury or the National Debt Commissioners in pursuance of any Act of Parliament, but the Bank of England shall transmit to the Board an account of the total amount thereof.

(2) No tax shall be chargeable in respect of the stock or dividends belonging to the Crown, in whatever name they may stand in the books of the Bank of England.

[(3) In this section "dividends" means any interest, public annuities, dividends or shares of annuities.][1]

Commentary—*Simon's Direct Tax Service* A6.201.
Definitions—"Act", s 832(1); "the Board", s 832(1); "dividends", s 45; "tax", s 832(3).
Amendments—[1] Sub-s (3) inserted by FA 1996 Sch 7 paras 10, 32 with effect for the purposes of income tax from the year 1996–97 and, as respects corporation tax, for accounting periods ending after 31 March 1996.

Government securities: interest payable without deduction of tax

50 United Kingdom securities: Treasury directions for payment without deduction of tax

[(A1) The interest on [gilt-edged securities][4] (whenever issued and whatever the terms on which they were issued) shall be paid without deduction of income tax.][3]

(1) The Treasury may direct that any of the following securities, [in so far as they are not gilt-edged securities][3], that is to say—

(*a*) ...[4]

(*b*) any securities issued or deemed to be issued under the National Loans Act 1939 or issued under the National Loans Act 1968;

(*c*), (*d*) ...[4]

shall be issued, or shall be deemed to have been issued, subject to the condition that the interest thereon shall be paid without deduction of income tax; and subject to the provisions of this section the interest shall be so paid accordingly, ...[1]

(2) The holder of any registered securities the interest on which is by virtue of [subsection (A1) above or of][3] directions given under subsection (1) above payable without deduction of tax may make an application to the Bank under this subsection requesting that income tax shall be deducted from the interest on those securities before payment thereof.

(3) Where any such application is made, income tax in respect of the interest on those securities shall, so long as they remain registered in the name of the applicant and subject to the withdrawal of the application under subsection (5) below, be deducted and charged in the same manner as if they were not securities, [the interest on which is to be paid without deduction of income tax][3].

(4) An application under subsection (2) above shall be made in such form as the Bank with the approval of the Treasury may prescribe, and any application made less than [one month][2] before the date on which a payment of interest falls due shall only have effect as regards any payment of interest subsequent to that payment.

(5) An application made under subsection (2) above may at any time be withdrawn by notice to the Bank in such form as the Bank may with the approval of the Treasury prescribe, but an application so withdrawn shall, notwithstanding the withdrawal, continue to have effect as regards any interest payable less than [one month][2] after the date the notice is received at the Bank.

(6) Where any securities to which subsection (2) above applies are held on trust, the holders of the securities may make an application under that subsection in respect thereof without the consent of any other person, notwithstanding anything in the instrument creating the trust.

(7) In this section—

"the Bank" means the Bank of England or the Bank of Ireland as the case requires;

["gilt-edged securities" means any securities which—

(*a*) are gilt-edged securities for the purposes of the 1992 Act; or

(*b*) will be such securities on the making of any order under paragraph 1 of Schedule 9 to that Act the making of which is anticipated in the prospectus under which they were issued;][3] and

"registered" means entered in the register of the Bank.

Commentary—*Simon's Direct Tax Service* A6.206, A7.1101; B5.103.
Revenue & other press releases—HM Treasury 13-8-96 (interest on existing strippable gilts is to be paid gross from 7 June 1997).
Definitions—"Income tax", s 832(4); "interest", s 832(1); "notice", s 832(1); "tax", s 832(3); "United Kingdom", s 830(1).
Amendments—[1] Words omitted from sub-s (1) repealed by FA 1996 Sch 7 paras 11, 32 Sch 41 Pt V(2) with effect for the purposes of income tax from the year 1996–97 and, as respects corporation tax, for accounting periods ending after 31 March 1996.
[2] Words in sub-ss (4), (5) substituted, for the words "two months", by F(No 2)A 1997 s 37(1), (3)(*d*), (9) with effect in relation to applications made and notices given at any time on or after 31 July 1997.
[3] Sub-ss (1)–(3), (7) amended, and new sub-s (A1) inserted, by F(No 2)A 1997 s 37(1), (2), (3)(*a*)–(*c*), (4), (8) in relation to payments of interest falling due after 5 April 1998 (subject to F(No 2)A 1997 s 37(10)-(13)).
[3] Sub-s (1)(*a*), (*c*), (*d*) repealed by F(No 2)A 1997 s 52, Sch 8 Part II(13) with effect in relation to payments falling due after 5 April 1998.
[4] Words in sub-s (A1) substituted by FA 2000 s 112(1), (5) with effect for payments made after 31 March 2001

51 Treasury directions as respects Northern Ireland securities

(1) The Treasury may, on the application of the Department of Finance and Personnel, as respects any securities to which this section applies, direct that the securities specified in the direction shall be issued, or shall be deemed to have been issued, subject to the condition that the interest thereon shall be paid without deduction of income tax; and in relation to any securities so specified and the interest thereon, section 50 shall have effect as if—

(*a*) the securities were securities in respect of which a direction had been given by the Treasury under subsection (1) of that section;

(*b*) references in that section to "the Bank" were (notwithstanding subsection (7) of that section) references to the bank in the books of which the securities are registered or inscribed; and

(*c*) the references in subsections (4) and (5) of that section to the Treasury were references to the Department of Finance and Personnel.

(2) The securities to which this section applies are securities issued under section 11(1)(*c*) of the Exchequer and Financial Provisions Act (Northern Ireland) 1950 for money borrowed by the Department of Finance and Personnel for the purposes of making issues from the Consolidated Fund of Northern Ireland.

Commentary—*Simon's Direct Tax Service* **A6.206.**
Definitions—"Income tax", s 832(4); "interest", s 832(1).

[51AA Commencement of direction under section 50 or 51

A direction under section 50 or 51 that any security shall be deemed to have been issued subject to the condition that the interest thereon shall be paid without deduction of tax may provide that the direction is to have effect in relation only to payments of interest made on or after such date as may be specified in the direction.][1]

Commentary—*Simon's Direct Tax Service* **B5.103.**
Definition—"Interest", s 832(1).
Amendments—[1] This section inserted by FA 1996 s 155 with effect from 29 April 1996.

51A Gilt-edged securities held under authorised arrangements

Commentary—*Simon's Direct Tax Service* **B3.701.**
Amendments—This section repealed by F(No 2)A 1997 s 37(5), Sch 8 Part II(13) with effect in relation to payments of interest falling due after 5 April 1998 (subject to F(No 2)A 1997 s 37(10)–(13)).

51B Periodic accounting for tax on interest on gilt-edged securities

Commentary—*Simon's Direct Tax Service* **A7.1102, 1115.**
Amendments—This section (inserted by FA 1995 s 78(1)) repealed by FA 1998 s 37(1) with effect in relation to payments of interest falling due after 31 March 1999 by virtue of the Finance Act 1998, Section 37, (Appointed Day) Order, SI 1999/619.

52 Taxation of interest on converted government securities and interest which becomes subject to deduction

Commentary—*Simon's Direct Tax Service* **B5.103.**
Amendments—Section repealed by FA 1996 Sch 7 paras 12, 32, Sch 41 Pt V(2) with effect from the year 1996–97.

PART IV
PROVISIONS RELATING TO THE SCHEDULE D CHARGE
CHAPTER I
SUPPLEMENTARY CHARGING PROVISIONS

53 Farming and other commercial occupation of land (except woodlands)

(1) All farming and market gardening in the United Kingdom shall be treated as the carrying on of a trade or, as the case may be, of a part of a trade, and the [profits][2] thereof shall be charged to tax under Case I of Schedule D accordingly.

(2) All the farming carried on by any particular person or partnership or body of persons shall be treated as one trade.

(3) Subject to subsection (4) below, the occupation of land in the United Kingdom for any purpose other than farming or market gardening shall, if the land is managed on a commercial basis and with a view to the realisation of profits, be treated as the carrying on of a trade or, as the case may be, of a part of a trade, and the [profits][2] thereof shall be charged to tax under Case I of Schedule D accordingly.

[(4) Subsection (3) above shall not apply in relation to the occupation of land which comprises woodlands or is being prepared for use for forestry purposes.][1]

Commentary—*Simon's Direct Tax Service* **B3.501, 502, 601.**
Statement of Practice SP 5/81—Subject to certain conditions, expenses incurred in restoring drainage on waterlogged land are admitted as revenue expenditure in farm accounts.
Revenue Internal Guidance—Inspector's manual IM 2350B (stud farming is covered by this provision).
IM 2425-2428 (admission to historic houses: whether a trade is carried on).
Simon's Tax Cases—s 53(1), (2), *Sargent v Eayrs* [1973] STC 50*.
s 53(3), (4) *Webb v Conelee Properties Ltd* [1982] STC 913*.
s 53(4), *Jaggers (T/A Shide Trees) v Ellis* [1997] STC 1417.
Definitions—"Schedule D", s 18(1); "tax", s 832(3); "trade", s 832(1); "United Kingdom", s 830(1).
Cross references—See TA 1988 s 15 Sch A para 2(*c*) (Schedule A provisions do not apply to profits or gains charged to Schedule D by virtue of this section).
TA 1988 s 154(1) (cultivation of short rotation coppice to be regarded as farming).
Amendments—[1] Sub-s (4) substituted by FA 1988 Sch 6 para 6(7) with effect from 6 April 1988, but it did not apply where FA 1988 Sch 6 para 4(3) applied.
[2] Word in sub-ss (1), (3) substituted by FA 1998 Sch 7 para 1 with effect from 31 July 1998.

54 Woodlands managed on a commercial basis

Amendments—This section repealed by FA 1988 Sch 6 para 3(1), (7) and Sch 14, Pt V with effect from 15 March 1988.

55 Mines, quarries and other concerns

(1) [Profits][1] arising out of land in the case of any concern specified in subsection (2) below shall be charged to tax under Case I of Schedule D.

(2) The concerns are—

(a) mines and quarries (including gravel pits, sand pits and brickfields);

(b) ironworks, gasworks, salt springs or works, alum mines or works (not being mines falling within the preceding paragraph) and waterworks and streams of water;

(c) canals, inland navigation, docks and drains or levels;

(d) fishings;

(e) rights of markets and fairs, tolls, bridges and ferries;

(f) railways and other ways;

(g) other concerns of the like nature as any of the concerns specified in paragraphs (b) to (e) above.

Commentary—*Simon's Direct Tax Service* **B3.401–414.**
Definitions—"Schedule D", s 18(1).
Cross references—See TA 1988 s 15 Sch A para 2(c) (Schedule A provisions do not apply to profits or gains charged to Schedule D by virtue of this section).
TA 1988 s 59(2) (persons chargeable to tax in respect of concerns mentioned in this section).
TA 1988 s 119(1) (rent payable in respect of land connected with a concern specified in sub-s (2) above to be subject to deduction of tax at source under ss 348, 349).
Amendments—[1] Word substituted by FA 1998 Sch 7 para 1 with effect from 31 July 1998.

56 Transactions in deposits with and without certificates or in debts

(1) Subsection (2) below applies to the following rights—

(a) the right to receive the amount, with or without interest, stated in a certificate of deposit;

(b) the right to receive an amount payable with interest—

(i) in a transaction in which no certificate of deposit or security is issued, and

(ii) which is payable by a bank or similar institution or a person regularly engaging in similar transactions;

and the right to receive that interest.

(2) Profits or gains arising to a person from the disposal of a right to which this subsection applies or, except so far as it is a right to receive interest, from the exercise of any such right (whether by the person to whom the certificate was issued or by some other person, or, as the case may be, by the person who acquired the right in the transaction referred to in subsection (1) above or by some person acquiring it directly or indirectly from that person), shall, if not falling to be taken into account as a trading receipt, be treated as annual profits or gains chargeable to tax under Case VI of Schedule D.

(3) Subsection (2) above does not apply in the case of the disposal or exercise of a right to receive an amount stated in a certificate of deposit or interest on such an amount—

(a) if the person disposing of the right acquired it before 7th March 1973;

(b) to any profits or gains arising to a fund or scheme in the case of which provision is made by section 592(2), 613, 614(1) to (3) or 620(6) for exempting the whole or part of its income from income tax;

(c) in so far as they are applied to charitable purposes only, to any profits or gains arising to a charity within the meaning of section 506.

(3A)–(3D) ...[5]

(4) For the purposes of this section, profits or gains shall not be treated as falling to be taken into account as a trading receipt by reason only that they are included in the computation required [for the purposes of][3] section 76(2).

[(4A) This section and section 56A shall not apply for the purposes of corporation tax except in relation to rights in existence before 1st April 1996.][4]

[(4B) For the purposes of corporation tax, where any profits or gains arising from the disposal or exercise of a right in existence before 1st April 1996 are, or (if there were any) would be, chargeable under this section, nothing in Chapter II of Part IV of the Finance Act 1996 (loan relationships) shall require any amount relating to that disposal, or to the exercise of that right, to be brought into account for the purposes of that Chapter.][4]

(5) In this section—

"certificate of deposit" means a document relating to money, in any currency, which has been deposited with the issuer or some other person, being a document which recognises an obligation to pay a stated amount to bearer or to order, with or without interest, and being a document by the delivery of which, with or without endorsement, the right to receive that stated amount, with or without interest, is transferable; and

"security" has the same meaning as in section [132 of the 1992 Act][1].

Commentary—*Simon's Direct Tax Service* **A7.1204.**
Definitions—"the 1992 Act", s 831(3); "interest", s 832(1); "profits or gains", s 833(1); "Schedule D", s 18(1).
Revenue Internal Guidance—Company Taxation Manual COT13376 (worked example on sub-ss(3A)–(3D)).
Cross references—See TA 1988 s 56A (application of this section with modifications in respect of deposits of money without certificates).
TA 1988 s 398 (relief for losses in respect of transactions within this section).
TA 1988 s 608(2) (superannuation funds approved before 6 April 1980: tax exemption in respect of profits from disposal of right mentioned in sub-s (1)(a) above).
TA 1988 Sch 22 para 7(3) (pension fund surpluses: restriction on the exemption under sub-s (3)(b)).
Amendments—[1] Words in the definition of "security" in sub-s (5) substituted by TCGA 1992 Sch 10, para 14(1), (3) with effect from 6 April 1992.
[2] Sub-ss (3A)–(3D) inserted by FA 1993 Sch 18 para 2 with effect, broadly, for accounting periods commencing on or after 23 March 1995 (the date appointed for the commencement of FA 1993 Part II, Ch II): see FA 1993 s 165.
[3] Words in sub-s (4) substituted by FA 1996 s 164(4), (5) with effect for accounting periods beginning on or after 1 January 1996.
[4] Sub-ss (4A), (4B) inserted by FA 1996 ss 104, 105, Sch 14 para 6 with effect for accounting periods ending after 31 March 1996, subject to transitional provisions in FA 1996 Sch 15.
[5] Sub-ss (3A)–(3D) repealed by FA 2002 s 141, Sch 40 Pt 3(10) with effect for accounting periods beginning after 30 September 2002. Sub-ss (3A)–(3D) previously read as follows—

"(3A) Subsection (3B) below applies where—

(a) profits or gains arise from the disposal of a right to which subsection (2) above applies and fall to be charged to tax under Case VI of Schedule D by virtue of that subsection, and
(b) the profits or gains arise to a qualifying company.
(3B) For the purposes of the charge under Case VI the profits or gains—

(a) shall be increased by the amount of any non-trading exchange loss, or the aggregate of the amounts of any non-trading exchange losses, accruing to the company as regards the right for any accrual period or periods constituting or falling within the holding period;
(b) shall (after taking account of paragraph (a) above) be reduced by the amount of any non-trading exchange gain, or the aggregate of the amounts of any non-trading exchange gains, accruing to the company as regards the right for any accrual period or periods constituting or falling within the holding period.
(3C) For the purposes of subsections (3A) and (3B) above—

(a) "accrual period" and "qualifying company" have the same meanings as in Chapter II of Part II of the Finance Act 1993;
(b) the question whether a non-trading exchange gain or loss accrues to the company as regards the right for an accrual period shall be decided in accordance with that Chapter.][2]
[(3D) For the purposes of subsection (3B) above the holding period is the period which—

(a) begins when the company acquired (or last acquired) the right before the disposal, and

(b) ends when the disposal is made."

[56A Disposal or exercise of rights in pursuance of deposits

(1) This section applies where there is an arrangement under which—

(a) there is a right to receive an amount (with or without interest) in pursuance of a deposit of money,
(b) when the right comes into existence there is no certificate of deposit in respect of the right, and
(c) the person for the time being entitled to the right is entitled to call for the issue of a certificate of deposit in respect of the right.

(2) In such a case—

(a) the right shall be treated as not falling within section 56(1)(b), and
(b) if there is a disposal or exercise of the right before such time (if any) as a certificate of deposit is issued in respect of it, section 56(2) shall apply to it by virtue of this paragraph.

(3) In the application of section 56 by virtue of this section—

(a) subsection (2) shall have effect as if the words from "(whether" to "person)" read "(whether by the person originally entitled to the right or by some other person)", and
(b) subsection (3) shall have effect as if the words "stated in a certificate of deposit" read "under an arrangement".

(4) In this section "certificate of deposit" has the meaning given by section 56(5).][1]

Commentary—*Simon's Direct Tax Service* **A7.1204.**
Definitions—"Interest", s 832(1).
Cross reference—See TA 1988 s 56(4A) (this section does not apply for corporation tax purposes except in relation to rights in existence before 1 April 1996).
Amendments—[1] This section inserted by F(No 2)A 1992 Sch 8 paras 1, 6 in relation to arrangements made after 16 July 1992.

57 Deep discount securities

Commentary—*Simon's Direct Tax Service* **B5.414.**
Amendments—This section repealed by FA 1996 s 105, Sch 41 Pt V(3) with effect from the year 1996–97 as respects income tax, and, as respects corporation tax, for accounting periods ending after 31 March 1996, subject to transitional provisions in FA 1996 Sch 15.

58 Foreign pensions

(1) A pension which—

   (*a*) is paid by or on behalf of a person outside the United Kingdom, and

   (*b*) is not charged under paragraph 4 of Schedule E,

shall be charged to tax under Case V of Schedule D.

(2) Where—

   (*a*) a person has ceased to hold any office or employment, and

   (*b*) a pension or annual payment is paid to him, or to his widow or child or to any relative or dependant of his, by the person under whom he held the office or by whom he was employed, or by the successors of that person, and

   (*c*) that pension or annual payment is paid by or on behalf of a person outside the United Kingdom,

then, notwithstanding that the pension or payment is paid voluntarily, or is capable of being discontinued, it shall be deemed to be income for the purposes of assessment to tax and shall be assessed and charged to tax under Case V of Schedule D as income from a pension.

Commentary—*Simon's Direct Tax Service* B6.207; E4.126.
Definitions—"Schedule D", s 18(1); "Schedule E", s 19(1); "tax", s 832(3); "United Kingdom", s 830(1).
Cross reference—See TA 1988 s 833(5)(*b*) (pensions to which sub-s (2) above applies to be earned income).

59 Persons chargeable

(1) Subject to subsections (2) and (3) below, income tax under Schedule D shall be charged on and paid by the persons receiving or entitled to the income in respect of which the tax is directed by the Income Tax Acts to be charged.

(2) Income tax to be charged under Schedule D in respect of any of the concerns mentioned in section 55 shall be assessed and charged on the person carrying on the concern, or on the agents or other officers who have the direction or management of the concern or receive the profits thereof.

(3) Where, in accordance with that section, income tax is charged under Schedule D on the profits of markets or fairs, or on tolls, fisheries or any other annual or casual profits not distrainable, the owner or occupier or receiver of the profits thereof shall be answerable for the tax so charged, and may retain and deduct the same out of any such profits.

(4) Subsections (1) to (3) above shall not apply for the purposes of corporation tax.

Commentary—*Simon's Direct Tax Service* B3.403.
Concessions A37—Tax treatment of directors' fees received by partnerships and other companies.
B40—UK investment managers acting for non-resident clients.
Revenue Internal Guidance—Inspector's manual IM 3102 (interest received gross by a solicitor on UK resident client's money is passed on to the client gross).
Simon's Tax Cases—*Dawson v IRC* [1989] STC 473*.
s 59(1), *Dunmore v McGowan* [1978] STC 217*; *Macpherson v Bond* [1985] STC 678*; *Peracha v Miley* [1990] STC 512*.
Definitions—"The Income Tax Acts", s 831(1)(*b*); "Schedule D", s 18(1).

CHAPTER II

INCOME TAX: BASIS OF ASSESSMENT ETC

Statement of Practice SP 3/90—This Statement sets out the Revenue's practice with regard to certain bases of valuation of stocks and to changes in accounts in the basis of valuation of stocks and long-term contracts. It reflects the effects of relevant case law, including in particular the case of *Pearce v Woodall Duckham Ltd.*
Note—This Chapter is superseded with effect from the year 1994–95 in its application to trades etc commenced after 5 April 1994 and income from a source arising to a person on or after that date. Subject to exceptions noted in the annotations to particular sections and transitional provisions in FA 1994 Sch 20, it is superseded with effect from the year 1996–97 in its application to trades etc commenced before 6 April 1994 and income from a source arising to a person before that date. The new superseding provisions which have been enacted by FA 1994 ss 200–218 and Sch 20 are printed below; for the text of this Chapter as originally enacted (in connection with savings in FA 1994 Sch 20), reference should be made to the 1995–96 edition of the *Yellow Tax Handbook.*
For detailed commencement and transitional provisions, see FA 1994 s 218 and Sch 20.

Cases I and II

Revenue & other press releases—Revenue Booklet SAT 1(1995) (detailed guidance and worked examples on the basis of assessment for 1994–95 to 2001–02).

[60 Assessment on current year basis

(1) Subject to subsection (2) below and section 63A, income tax shall be charged under Cases I and II of Schedule D on the full amount of the [profits]² of the year of assessment.

(2) Where, in the case of a trade, profession or vocation, a basis period for the year of assessment is given by subsection (3) below or sections 61 to 63, the [profits]² of that period shall be taken to be the [profits]² of the year.

(3) Subject to sections 61 to 63, the basis period for a year of assessment is as follows—

(*a*) if the year is the first year of assessment in which there is an accounting date which falls not less than 12 months after the commencement date, the period of 12 months ending with that accounting date; and

(*b*) if there is a basis period for the immediately preceding year and that basis period is not given by section 61, the period of 12 months beginning immediately after the end of that basis period.

(4) In the case of a person who, if he had not died, would under the provisions of this section and sections 61 to 63A have become chargeable to income tax for any year, the tax which would have been so chargeable—

(*a*) shall be assessed and charged on his personal representatives, and

(*b*) shall be a debt due from and payable out of his estate.

(5) In this section and sections 61 to 63—

"accounting date", in relation to a year of assessment, means a date in the year to which accounts are made up or, where there are two or more such dates, the latest of those dates;

"the commencement date" and "the commencement year" mean respectively the date on which and the year of assessment in which the trade, profession or vocation is set up and commenced.][1]

Commentary—*Simon's Direct Tax Service* **E1.203.**
Definitions— "Schedule D", s 18(1); "trade", s 832(1); "year of assessment", s 832(1).
Revenue Interpretation RI 123—Changes of accounting date in advance of the transition to the current year basis.
RI 136—Changes of accounting date; transition to the current year basis.
RI 142—Acquisition of a business, successions and mergers under self-assessment.
Simon's Tax Cases—*A Firm v Honour* [1997] STC (SCD) 293; *Herbert Smith (a firm) v Honour* [1999] STC 173.
Cross references—See TA 1988 s 9(6) (this section not to apply in computing income for the purposes of corporation tax).
TA 1988 s 65(3) (this section to apply to profits of a trade etc assessable under Schedule D Cases IV and V but computed according to the rules applicable to Cases I and II).
TA 1988 s 72 (apportionment of profits, gains or losses to particular period).
TA 1988 s 111(4) (application of this section with modifications to determine partner's share in the profits or gains of a partnership).
FA 1994 Sch 20 para 2 (application of this section for the year 1996–97 to trades etc commencing before 6 April 1994 and continuing after 5 April 1997).
FA 1994 Sch 20 para 3(1), (2) (the provisions of s 60 as enacted before substitution by FA 1994 s 200 to apply where a trade etc commenced before 6 April 1994 ceases before 6 April 1997 or, if the Revenue so direct, before 6 April 1998; for the provisions of s 60 as previously enacted reference should be made to the 1995–96 edition).
FA 1994 Sch 20 para 3(3) (assessment for the year 1996–97 on a trade etc commenced before 6 April 1994 and ceasing in 1998–99 to be on an actual basis if the Revenue so direct).
Amendments—[1] This section substituted by FA 1994 ss 200, 218 with effect from the year 1994–95 for trades, professions or vocations set up and commenced after 5 April 1994 and with effect from the year 1996–97, subject to the transitional provisions in FA 1994 Sch 20, for trades, etc set up and commenced before 6 April 1994. For detailed commencement provisions, see FA 1994 s 218.
[2] Word in sub-ss (1), (2) substituted by FA 1998 Sch 7 para 1 with effect from 31 July 1998.

[61 Basis of assessment at commencement

(1) Notwithstanding anything in section 60, where the year of assessment is the commencement year, the computation of the [profits][2] chargeable to income tax under Case I or II of Schedule D shall be made on the [profits][2] arising in the year.

(2) Subject to section 63, where the year of assessment is the year next following the commencement year and—

(*a*) there is an accounting date in the year and the period beginning with the commencement date and ending with the accounting date is a period of less than 12 months; or

(*b*) the basis period for the year would, apart from this subsection, be given by section 62(2) and the period beginning with the commencement date and ending with the new date in the year is a period of less than 12 months,

the basis period for the year is the period of 12 months beginning with the commencement date.

(3) In this section "the new date" has the same meaning as in section 62.][1]

Commentary—*Simon's Direct Tax Service* **E1.206.**
Simon's Tax Cases—s 61(3), *Gascoine v Wharton* [1996] STC 1481.
Definitions—"Accounting date", s 60(5); "commencement date", s 60(5); "commencement year", s 60(5); "Schedule D", s 18(1); "year of assessment", s 832(1).
Revenue Interpretation RI 142—Acquisition of a business, successions and mergers under self-assessment.
Revenue Internal Guidance—Assessed taxes manual, AT 14.709 (first assessment not normally issued until 30 days after first twelve months trading, but assessment issued before then is not invalidated by being issued early).
Inspector's manual IM 2170 (dentists: change of practice is treated as the cessation of the old practice and the start of a new one).
Cross references—See TA 1988 s 9(6) (this section not to apply in computing income for the purposes of corporation tax).
TA 1988 s 60(4) (assessment on personal representatives in respect of a deceased person's tax liability).
TA 1988 s 65(3) (this section to apply to profits of a trade etc assessable under Schedule D Cases IV and V but computed according to the rules applicable to Cases I and II).
TA 1988 s 72 (apportionment of profits, gains or losses to particular period).
TA 1988 s 111(4) (application of this section with modifications to determine partner's share in the profits or gains of a partnership).
TA 1988 s 113(1), (2) (deemed cessation and recommencement where there is a change in the persons carrying on the trade etc subject to contrary election by partners).
FA 1994 Sch 20 para 2 (application of this section for the year 1996–97 to trades etc commencing before 6 April 1994 and continuing after 5 April 1997).
FA 1994 Sch 20 para 3(1), (2) (the provisions of s 61 as enacted before substitution by FA 1994 s 201 to apply where a trade etc commenced before 6 April 1994 ceases before 6 April 1997 or, if the Revenue so direct, before 6 April 1998; for the provisions of s 61 as previously enacted reference should be made to the 1995–96 edition).

FA 1994 Sch 20 para 3(3) (assessment for the year 1996–97 on a trade etc commenced before 6 April 1994 and ceasing in 1998–99 to be on an actual basis if the Revenue so direct).
Amendments—[1] This section substituted by FA 1994 s 201 with effect from the year 1994–95 for trades, professions or vocations set up and commenced after 5 April 1994 and with effect from the year 1996–97, subject to the transitional provisions in FA 1994 Sch 20, for trades, professions or vocations set up before 6 April 1994. For detailed commencement provisions, see FA 1994 s 218.
[2] Word in sub-ss (1), (2) substituted by FA 1998 Sch 7 para 1 with effect from 31 July 1998.

[62 Change of basis period

(1) Subsection (2) below applies where, in the case of a trade, profession or vocation—

(*a*) an accounting change, that is, a change from one accounting date ("the old date") to another ("the new date"), is made or treated as made in a year of assessment; and

(*b*) either section 62A applies or the year of assessment is the year next following or next but one following the commencement year.

(2) The basis period for the year of assessment is as follows—

(*a*) if the year is the year next following the commencement year or the relevant period is a period of less than 12 months, the period of 12 months ending with the new date in the year; and

(*b*) if the relevant period is a period of more than 12 months, that period;

and in this subsection "the relevant period" means the period beginning immediately after the end of the basis period for the preceding year and ending with the new date in the year.

(3) Where subsection (2) above does not apply as respects an accounting change made or treated as made in a year of assessment ("the first year"), this section and section 62A shall have effect in relation to the next following year ("the second year") as if the change had not been made or treated as made.

(4) As a consequence of subsection (3) above—

(*a*) an accounting change shall be treated as made in the second year if the date or, as the case may be, the latest date in that year to which accounts are made up is a date other than the date of the end of the basis period for the first year; and

(*b*) no such change shall be treated as made in the second year if that date is the date of the end of that period.

(5) For the purposes of this section an accounting change is made in the first year of assessment in which accounts are not made up to the old date, or accounts are made up to the new date, or both.][1]

Commentary—*Simon's Direct Tax Service* E1.201.
Definitions—"Accounting date", s 60(5); "commencement year", s 60(5); "trade", s 832(1); "year of assessment", s 832(1).
Revenue Interpretation RI 142—Acquisition of a business, successions and mergers under self-assessment.
Cross references—See TA 1988 s 9(6) (this section not to apply in computing income for the purposes of corporation tax).
TA 1988 s 60(4) (assessment on personal representatives in respect of a deceased person's tax liability).
TA 1988 s 63A (deduction for overlap profits where the basis period is given by sub-s (2)(*b*) above).
TA 1988 s 65(3) (this section to apply to profits of a trade etc assessable under Schedule D Cases IV and V but computed according to the rules applicable to Cases I and II).
TA 1988 s 72 (apportionment of profits, gains or losses to particular period).
TA 1988 s 111(4) (application of this section with modifications to determine partner's share in the profits or gains of a partnership).
TA 1988 s 113(1), (2) (deemed cessation and recommencement where there is a change in the persons carrying on the trade etc subject to contrary election by partners).
FA 1994 Sch 20 para 1(3) (application of this section as modified where trade etc commenced before 6 April 1994 continues after 5 April 1997 and its basis period is the 12 months ending with 5 April 1997).
FA 1994 Sch 20 para 2 (application of this section for the year 1996–97 to trades etc commencing before 6 April 1994 and continuing after 5 April 1997).
FA 1994 Sch 20 para 3(1), (2) (the provisions of s 62 as enacted before substitution by FA 1994 s 202 to apply where a trade etc commenced before 6 April 1994 ceases before 6 April 1997 or, if the Revenue so direct, before 6 April 1998; for the provisions of s 62 as previously enacted reference should be made to the 1995–96 edition).
FA 1994 Sch 20 para 3(3) (assessment for the year 1996–97 on a trade etc commenced before 6 April 1994 and ceasing in 1998–99 to be on an actual basis if the Revenue so direct).
Amendments—[1] This section substituted by FA 1994 s 202 with effect from the year 1994–95 for trades, professions or vocations set up and commenced after 5 April 1994 and with effect from the year 1996–97, subject to the transitional provisions in FA 1994 Sch 20, for trades, professions or vocations set up and commenced before 6 April 1994. For detailed commencement provisions, see FA 1994 s 218.

[62A Conditions for such a change

(1) This section applies in relation to an accounting change if the following are fulfilled, namely—

(*a*) the first and second conditions mentioned below, and

(*b*) either the third or the fourth condition so mentioned.

(2) The first condition is that the first accounting period ending with the new date does not exceed 18 months.

(3) The second condition is—

[(*a*) in the case of a trade, profession or vocation carried on by an individual, that notice of the accounting change is given to an officer of the Board in a return under section 8 of the Management Act on or before the day on which that return is required to be made and delivered under that section;

(*b*) in the case of a trade, profession or vocation carried on by persons in partnership, that notice of the accounting change is given to an officer of the Board in a return under section 12AA of that

Act on or before the day specified in relation to that return under subsection (2) or (3) of that section.]²

(4) The third condition is that no accounting change as respects which section 62(2) has applied has been made or treated as made in any of the five years immediately preceding the year of assessment.

(5) The fourth condition is that—

(a) the notice required by the second condition sets out the reasons for which the change is made; and

(b) either the officer is satisfied that the change is made for bona fide commercial reasons or he does not, within 60 days of receiving the notice, give notice to the person carrying on the trade, profession or vocation that he is not so satisfied.

(6) An appeal may be brought against the giving of a notice under subsection (5)(b) above within the period of 30 days beginning with the date on which the notice is given.

(7) Subject to subsection (8) below, the provisions of the Management Act relating to appeals shall have effect in relation to an appeal under subsection (6) above as they have effect in relation to an appeal against an assessment to tax.

(8) On an appeal under subsection (6) above section 50(6) to (8) of the Management Act shall not apply but the Commissioners may—

(a) if they are satisfied that the change is made for bona fide commercial reasons, set the notice under subsection (5)(b) above aside; or

(b) if they are not so satisfied, confirm that notice.

(9) Obtaining a tax advantage shall not be regarded as a bona fide commercial reason for the purposes of subsections (5) and (8) above.

(10) In this section—

(a) ''accounting period'' means a period for which accounts are made up, and

(b) expressions which are also used in section 62 have the same meanings as in that section.]¹

Commentary—*Simon's Direct Tax Service* **E1.218.**
Definitions—''Accounting change'', s 62(1)(a); ''the Board'', s 832(1); ''Commissioners'', s 2; ''Management Act'', s 831(3); ''notice'', s 832(1); ''trade'', s 832(1).
Cross references—See TA 1988 s 9(6) (this section not to apply in computing income for the purposes of corporation tax).
TA 1988 s 60(4) (assessment on personal representatives in respect of a deceased person's tax liability).
TA 1988 s 65(3) (this section to apply to profits of a trade etc assessable under Schedule D Cases IV and V but computed according to the rules applicable to Cases I and II).
TA 1988 s 111(4) (application of this section with modifications to determine partner's share in the profits or gains of a partnership).
FA 1994 Sch 20 para 2 (application of this section for the year 1996–97 to trades etc commencing before 6 April 1994 and continuing after 5 April 1997).
FA 1994 Sch 20 para 3(1), (2) (this section not to apply where a trade etc commenced before 6 April 1994 ceases before 6 April 1997 or, if the Revenue so direct, before 6 April 1998).
FA 1994 Sch 20 para 3(3) (assessment for the year 1996–97 on a trade etc commenced before 6 April 1994 and ceasing in 1998–99 to be on an actual basis if the Revenue so direct).
Amendments—¹ This section inserted by FA 1994 s 203 with effect from the year 1994–95 for trades, professions or vocations set up and commenced after 5 April 1994 and with effect from the year 1996–97, subject to the transitional provisions in FA 1994 Sch 20, for trades, professions or vocations set up and commenced before 6 April 1994. For detailed commencement provisions, see FA 1994 s 218.
² Sub-s (3)(a), (b) substituted by FA 1996 s 135, Sch 21 para 1 with effect from the year 1996–97.

[63 Basis of assessment on discontinuance

Where a trade, profession or vocation is permanently discontinued in a year of assessment other than the commencement year, the basis period for the year shall be the period beginning—

(a) where the year is the year next following the commencement year, immediately after the end of the commencement year, and

(b) in any other case, immediately after the end of the basis period for the preceding year of assessment,

and (in either case) ending with the date on which the trade, profession or vocation is permanently discontinued.]¹

Commentary—*Simon's Direct Tax Service* **E1.201.**
Revenue Internal Guidance—Inspector's manual IM 2170 (dentists: change of practice is treated as the cessation of the old practice and the start of a new one).
Simon's Tax Cases—*Watts (T/A A A Watts) v Hart* [1984] STC 548*; *Gilmore v Inspector of Taxes* [1999] STC (SCD) 269.
s 63(2), *R v IRC, ex p Barker* [1994] STC 731; *Gilmore v Inspector of Taxes* [1999] STC (SCD) 269.
Definitions—''Accounting date'', s 60(5); ''commencement year'', s 60(5); ''trade'', s 832(1); ''year of assessment'', s 832(1).
Cross references—See TA 1988 s 9(6) (this section not to apply in computing income for the purposes of corporation tax).
TA 1988 s 60(4) (assessment on personal representatives in respect of a deceased person's tax liability).
TA 1988 s 63A(3) (deduction for overlap profits where the basis period is given by this section).
TA 1988 s 65(3) (this section to apply to profits of a trade etc assessable under Schedule D Cases IV and V but computed according to the rules applicable to Cases I and II).
TA 1988 s 111(4) (application of this section with modifications to determine partner's share in the profits or gains of a partnership).
TA 1988 s 113(1), (2) (deemed cessation and recommencement where there is a change in the persons carrying on the trade etc subject to contrary election by partners).
TA 1988 s 804(5) (recapture of excess double taxation relief in respect of income of non-basis period on cessation under this section).

FA 1994 Sch 20 para 1(3) (application of this section as modified where trade etc commenced before 6 April 1994 continues after 5 April 1997 and its basis period is the 12 months ending with 5 April 1997).

FA 1994 Sch 20 para 2 (application of this section for the year 1996–97 to trades etc commencing before 6 April 1994 and continuing after 5 April 1997).

FA 1994 Sch 20 para 3(1), (2) (the provisions of s 63 as enacted before substitution by FA 1994 s 204 to apply where a trade etc commenced before 6 April 1994 ceases before 6 April 1997 or, if the Revenue so direct, before 6 April 1998; for the provisions of s 63 as previously enacted reference should be made to the 1995–96 edition).

FA 1994 Sch 20 para 3(3) (assessment for the year 1996–97 on a trade etc commenced before 6 April 1994 and ceasing in 1998–99 to be on an actual basis if the Revenue so direct).

Amendments—[1] This section substituted by FA 1994 s 204 with effect from the year 1994–95 for trades, professions or vocations set up and commenced after 5 April 1994 and with effect from the year 1996–97, subject to the transitional provisions in FA 1994 Sch 20, for trades, professions or vocations set up and commenced before 6 April 1994. For detailed commencement provisions, see FA 1994 s 218.

[63A Overlap profits and overlap losses

(1) Where, in the case of any trade, profession or vocation, the basis period for a year of assessment is given by section 62(2)(b), a deduction shall be made in computing the [profits][2] of that year of an amount equal to that given by the formula in subsection (2) below.

(2) The formula referred to in subsection (1) above is—

$$A \times \frac{B - C}{D}$$

where—

A = the aggregate of any overlap profits less the aggregate of any amounts previously deducted under subsection (1) above;

B = the number of days in the basis period;

C = the number of days in the year of assessment;

D = the aggregate of the overlap periods of any overlap profits less the aggregate number of days given by the variable "B–C" in any previous applications of this subsection.

(3) Where, in the case of any trade, profession or vocation, the basis period for a year of assessment is given by section 63, a deduction shall be made in computing the [profits][2] of that year of an amount equal to—

(a) the aggregate of any overlap profits, less

(b) the aggregate of any amounts deducted under subsection (1) above.

(4) Where, in the case of any trade, profession or vocation, an amount of a loss would, apart from this subsection, fall to be included in the computations for two successive years of assessment, that amount shall not be included in the computation for the second of those years.

(5) In this section—

"overlap profit" means an amount of [profits][2] which, by virtue of sections 60 to 62, is included in the computations for two successive years of assessment; and

"overlap period", in relation to an overlap profit, means the number of days in the period in which the overlap profit arose.][1]

Commentary—*Simon's Direct Tax Service* E1.201.
Revenue Interpretation RI 194—Recording overlap profit carried forward from 1997–98 on self-assessment returns.
Definitions—"trade", s 832(1); "year of assessment", s 832(1).
Cross references—See TA 1988 s 9(6) (this section not to apply when computing income for corporation tax purposes).
TA 1988 s 60(4) (assessment on personal representatives in respect of a deceased person's tax liability).
TA 1988 s 111(4) (application of this section with modifications to determine partner's share in the profits or gains of a partnership).
FA 1994 Sch 20 para 2 (application of this section with modifications for the year 1996–97 to trades etc commencing before 6 April 1994 and continuing after 5 April 1997).
FA 1994 Sch 20 para 3(3) (assessment for the year 1996–97 on a trade etc commenced before 6 April 1994 and ceasing in 1998–99 to be on an actual basis if the Revenue so direct).
FA 1994 Sch 20 para 6(4) (application of this section modified in relation to the basis period for 1996–97 as it applies to income assessable under Schedule D Cases IV and V and from a source arising before 6 April 1994 and continuing after 5 April 1998).
Amendments—[1] This section inserted by FA 1994 s 205 with effect from the year 1994–95 for trades, professions or vocations set up and commenced after 5 April 1994 and with effect from the year 1996–97, subject to the transitional provisions in FA 1994 Sch 20, for trades, professions or vocations set up and commenced before 6 April 1994. For detailed commencement provisions, see FA 1994 s 218.
[2] Word in sub-ss (1), (3), (5) substituted by FA 1998 Sch 7 para 1 with effect from 31 July 1998.

Cases III, IV and V

[64 Case III assessments

Income tax under Case III of Schedule D shall be computed on the full amount of the income arising within the year of assessment, and shall be paid on the actual amount of that income, without any deduction.][1]

Commentary—*Simon's Direct Tax Service* E1.311.
Simon's Tax Cases—*Beese v Mackinlay* [1980] STC 228*; *Moore v Austin* [1985] STC 673*; *Girvan v Orange Personal Communication Services Ltd* [1998] STC 567.
Definitions—"Schedule D", s 18(1); "year of assessment", s 832(1).
Cross references—See TA 1988 s 9(6) (disapplication of this section in computing income for purposes of corporation tax).
TA 1988 s 341 (payment of interest between related companies treated as received on the same day as paid).

FA 1988 s 38(8) (maintenance payments under obligations existing at 15 March 1988 assessable under Schedule D Case III on payments falling due in the year of assessment notwithstanding anything in this section).

FA 1994 Sch 20 para 4(2) (modification of this section as it applies to 1996–97).

FA 1994 Sch 20 para 5 (the provisions of s 64 as enacted before substitution by FA 1994 s 206 to apply for income from a source arising before 6 April 1994 and ceasing before 6 April 1998; for the provisions of s 64 as previously enacted reference should be made to the 1995–96 edition).

Amendments—[1] This section substituted by FA 1994 s 206 with effect from the year 1994–95 for income arising after 5 April 1994 and with effect from the year 1996–97, subject to the transitional provisions in FA 1994 Sch 20, for income arising before 6 April 1994. For detailed commencement provisions, see FA 1994 s 218.

65 Cases IV and V assessments: general

(1) Subject to the provisions of this section ...[1], income tax chargeable under Case IV or Case V of Schedule D shall be computed on the full amount of the income arising in ...[1] the year of assessment, whether the income has been or will be received in the United Kingdom or not, subject in the case of income not received in the United Kingdom—

(a) to the same deductions and allowances as if it had been so received, and

(b) to a deduction on account of any annuity or other annual payment (not being interest) payable out of the income to a person not resident in the United Kingdom.

(2) Subject to section 330, income tax chargeable under Case IV or V of Schedule D on income arising from any pension shall be computed on the amount of that income subject to a deduction of one-tenth of the amount of the income.

[(2A), (2B) ...][4]

(3) Income tax chargeable under Case IV or V of Schedule D on income which is immediately derived by a person from the carrying on by him of any trade, profession or vocation either solely or in partnership shall be computed in accordance with the rules applicable to Cases I and II of Schedule D [(including sections 60 to 63A and 113)][2]; and subsection (1)(a) above shall not apply. ...[2]

(4) [Subsections (1) to (3)][5] above [and section 65A below][7] shall not apply to any person who, [makes a claim to the Board stating][6] that he is not domiciled in the United Kingdom, or that, being a Commonwealth citizen or a citizen of the Republic of Ireland, he is not ordinarily resident in the United Kingdom.

(5) Where subsection (4) above applies the tax shall, ...[3], be computed—

(a) in the case of tax chargeable under Case IV, on the full amount, so far as the same can be computed, of the sums received in the United Kingdom in ...[3] the year of assessment, without any deduction or abatement; and

(b) in the case of tax chargeable under Case V, on the full amount of the actual sums received in the United Kingdom in ...[3] the year of assessment from remittances payable in the United Kingdom, or from property imported, or from money or value arising from property not imported, or from money or value so received on credit or on account in respect of any such remittances, property, money or value brought or to be brought into the United Kingdom, without any deduction or abatement other than is allowed under the provisions of the Income Tax Acts in respect of [profits][8] charged under Case I of Schedule D.

(6) For the purposes of subsection (5) above, any income arising from securities or possessions out of the United Kingdom which is applied outside the United Kingdom by a person ordinarily resident in the United Kingdom in or towards satisfaction of—

(a) any debt for money lent to him in the United Kingdom or for interest on money so lent, or

(b) any debt for money lent to him outside the United Kingdom and received in or brought to the United Kingdom, or

(c) any debt incurred for satisfying in whole or in part a debt falling within paragraph (a) or (b) above,

shall be treated as received by him in the United Kingdom (and, for the purposes of subsection (5)(b) above, as so received from remittances payable in the United Kingdom).

(7) Where a person ordinarily resident in the United Kingdom receives in or brings to the United Kingdom money lent to him outside the United Kingdom, but the debt for that money is wholly or partly satisfied before he does so, subsection (6) above shall apply as if the money had been received in or brought to the United Kingdom before the debt was so satisfied, except that any sums treated by virtue of that subsection as received in the United Kingdom shall be treated as so received at the time when the money so lent is actually received in or brought to the United Kingdom.

(8) Where—

(a) a person (''the borrower'') is indebted for money lent to him, and

(b) income is applied by him in such a way that the money or property representing it is held by the lender on behalf of or to the account of the borrower in such circumstances as to be available to the lender for the purpose of satisfying or reducing the debt by set-off or otherwise,

that income shall be treated as applied by the borrower in or towards satisfaction of the debt if, under any arrangement between the borrower and the lender, the amount for the time being of the borrower's indebtedness to the lender, or the time at which the debt is to be repaid in whole or in part, depends in any respect directly or indirectly on the amount or value so held by the lender.

(9) For the purposes of subsections (6) to (8) above—

(*a*) a debt for money lent shall, to the extent to which that money is applied in or towards satisfying another debt, be deemed to be a debt incurred for satisfying that other debt, and a debt incurred for satisfying in whole or in part a debt falling within paragraph (*c*) of subsection (6) above shall itself be treated as falling within that paragraph; and

(*b*) "lender" includes, in relation to any money lent, any person for the time being entitled to repayment.

Commentary—*Simon's Direct Tax Service* **E1.321, 323; E4.116**.
Concessions A55—Arrears of foreign pensions to be treated as having arisen in the years to which they relate if advantageous to taxpayer.
Statement of Practice SP 3/90—Stocks and long-term contracts.
Simon's Tax Cases—s 65(1), *Ockenden v Mackley* [1982] STC 513*,
s 65(4), (5), *Buswell v IRC* [1974] STC 266*; *Newstead v Frost* [1980] STC 123*.
Definitions—"The Board", s 832(1); "the Income Tax Acts", s 831(1)(*b*); "Schedule D", s 18(1); "trade", s 832(1); "United Kingdom", s 830(1); "year of assessment", s 832(1).
Cross references—See TA 1988 s 9(6) (this section not to apply when computing income for the purposes of corporation tax).
TA 1988 s 70(2) (a company's foreign trading income chargeable to corporation tax under Schedule D Case V to be computed according to the rules of Case I).
TA 1988 s 80(1) (provisions regarding an individual foreign trader who does not satisfy the Board as mentioned in sub-s (4) above).
TA 1988 s 347A(5) (certain foreign maintenance payments not allowed as a deduction under sub-s (1)(*b*) above).
TA 1988 s 391 (losses from trade etc carried on abroad; loss relief on income falling within sub-ss (2) and (3) above).
TA 1988 s 585 (relief for delayed remittances where income chargeable under Schedule D Case IV or V).
FA 1988 s 38(9) (no deduction to be made under sub-s (1)(*b*) on account of certain maintenance payments).
FA 1994 Sch 20 para 6 (application of this section with modifications for the year 1996–97 to income from a source arising before 6 April 1994 and continuing after 5 April 1998).
FA 1994 Sch 20 para 7 (this section to apply disregarding amendments made by FA 1994 s 207 in respect of income from a source arising before 6 April 1994 and ceasing before 6 April 1998).
Amendments—[1] In sub-s (1), words omitted repealed by FA 1994 ss 207(1), 218 and Sch 26 Pt V(24), with effect from the year 1994–95 for income from a source arising after 5 April 1994, and with effect from the year 1996–97 for income from a source arising before 6 April 1994, subject to the transitional provisions in FA 1994 Sch 20.
[2] In sub-s (3), words inserted and words omitted repealed by FA 1994 ss 207(2), (6), 218 and Sch 26 Pt V(24), with effect from the year 1994–95 for income from a source arising after 5 April 1994, and with effect from the year 1997–98 for income from a source arising before 6 April 1994, subject to the transitional provisions in FA 1994 Sch 20.
[3] In sub-s (5), words omitted repealed by FA 1994 ss 207(3), 218 and Sch 26 Pt V(24), with effect from the year 1994–95 for income from a source arising after 5 April 1994, and with effect from the year 1996–97 for income from a source arising before 6 April 1994, subject to the transitional provisions in FA 1994 Sch 20.
[4] Sub-ss (2A), (2B) were inserted by FA 1995 s 41(1), with effect from the year 1995–96 (note however for further commencement detail, FA 1995 s 41(5)–(10)). These sub-sections repealed by FA 1998 Sch 5 para 23 with effect from the year 1998–99 for income tax purposes, and from 1 April 1998 for corporation tax purposes, subject to the transitional provisions in FA 1998 Sch 5 Part IV.
[5] Words in sub-s (4) substituted for the words "Subsections (1), (2) and (3)" by FA 1995 s 41(1), with effect from the year 1995–96 (note however for further provisions as to commencement, FA 1995 s 41(5)–(10)).
[6] Words in sub-s (4) substituted by FA 1996 s 134, Sch 20 para 3 with effect from the year 1996–97.
[7] Words in sub-s (4) inserted by FA 1998 Sch 5 para 23 with effect from the year 1998–99 for income tax purposes, and from 1 April 1998 for corporation tax purposes, subject to the transitional provisions in FA 1998 Sch 5 Part IV.
[8] Word in sub-s (5)(*b*) substituted by FA 1998 Sch 7 para 1 with effect from 31 July 1998.

[65A Case V income from land outside UK: income tax

(1) This section applies where a person is chargeable to income tax under Case V of Schedule D in respect of income which—

(*a*) arises from a business carried on for the exploitation, as a source of rents or other receipts, of any estate, interest or rights in or over land outside the United Kingdom, and

(*b*) is not income to which section 65(3) applies (income immediately derived from carrying on a trade, profession or vocation).

(2) The provisions of Schedule A apply to determine whether income falls within subsection (1)(*a*) above as they would apply to determine whether the income fell within paragraph 1(1) of that Schedule if—

(*a*) the land in question were in the United Kingdom, or

(*b*) a caravan or houseboat which is to be used at a location outside the United Kingdom were to be used at a location in the United Kingdom.

(3) Any provision of the Taxes Acts which deems there to be a Schedule A business in the case of land in the United Kingdom applies where the corresponding circumstances arise with respect to land outside the United Kingdom so as to deem there to be a business within subsection (1)(*a*) above.

(4) All businesses and transactions carried on or entered into by a particular person or partnership, so far as they are businesses or transactions the income from which is chargeable to tax under Case V of Schedule D in accordance with this section, are treated for the purposes of the charge to tax under Case V as, or as entered into in the course of carrying on, a single business (an "overseas property business").

(5) The income from an overseas property business shall be computed for the purposes of Case V of Schedule D in accordance with the rules applicable to the computation of the profits of a Schedule A business.

Those rules apply separately in relation to—

(*a*) an overseas property business, and

(*b*) any actual Schedule A business of the person chargeable, as if each were the only Schedule A business carried on by that person.

(6) Sections 80 and 81 (expenses in connection with foreign trades and travel between trades etc) do not apply in relation to the computation of the profits of an overseas property business.

(7) Sections 503 and 504 of this Act ...[2] do not apply to the profits or losses of an overseas property business.

(8) Where under this section rules expressed by reference to domestic concepts of law apply in relation to land outside the United Kingdom, they shall be interpreted so as to produce the result that most closely corresponds with the result produced for Schedule A purposes in relation to land in the United Kingdom.][1]

Commentary—*Simon's Direct Tax Service* **A4.101.**
Definitions—"The 1990 Act", s 831(3); "Schedule A", s 15(1); "Schedule D", s 18(1); "tax", s 832(3).
Amendments—[1] Substituted by FA 1998 Sch 5 para 24 with effect from the year 1998–99 for income tax purposes, and from 1 April 1998, subject to the transitional provisions in FA 1998 Sch 5 Part IV, for corporation tax.
[2] Words in sub-s (7) repealed by CAA 2001 ss 578, 580, Sch 2 para 13, Sch 4 with effect for income tax purposes as respects allowances and charges falling to be made for chargeable periods ending after 5 April 2001.

66 Special rules for fresh income

Commentary—*Simon's Direct Tax Service* **E1.304.**
Amendments—This section repealed with effect from the year 1994–95 as respects income from a source arising after 5 April 1994 and with effect from the year 1996–97 as respects income from a source arising before 6 April 1994, subject to transitional provisions in FA 1994 Sch 20; see FA 1994 ss 207(4), 218 and Sch 26 Pt V(24).

67 Special rules where source of income disposed of or yield ceases

Commentary—*Simon's Direct Tax Service* **E1.305–307.**
Amendments—This section repealed with effect from the year 1994–95 as respects income from a source arising after 5 April 1994 and with effect from the year 1996–97 as respects income from a source arising before 6 April 1994, subject to transitional provisions in FA 1994 Sch 20; see FA 1994 ss 207(4), 218 and Sch 26 Pt V(24). It is retained here because of its continued application pursuant to FA 1995 s 86(11).

68 Special rules where property etc situated in Republic of Ireland

(1) Notwithstanding anything in [section 65][1], but subject to the provisions of this section, income tax chargeable under Case IV or V of Schedule D shall, in the case of property situated and [profits][2] arising in the Republic of Ireland, be computed on the full amount of the income arising in the year of assessment, whether the income has been or will be received in the United Kingdom or not, subject in the case of income not received in the United Kingdom—

    (a) to the same deductions and allowances as if it had been so received; and

    (b) to a deduction on account of any annuity or other annual payment (not being interest) payable out of the income to a person not resident in the United Kingdom.

(2) Subsection (1) above shall not apply—

    (a) to any income which is immediately derived by a person from the carrying on by him of any trade, profession or vocation, either solely or in partnership; or

    (b) to any income which arises from any pension.

(3) The tax in respect of any such income as is mentioned in subsection (2) above arising in the Republic of Ireland shall be computed either—

    (a) on the full amount thereof arising in the year of assessment; or

    (b) on the full amount thereof on an average of such period as the case may require and as may be directed by the inspector;

so that, according to the nature of the income, the tax may be computed on the same basis as that on which it would have been computed if the income had arisen in the United Kingdom, and subject in either case to a deduction on account of any annuity or other annual payment (not being interest) payable out of the income to a person not resident in the United Kingdom; and the person chargeable and assessable shall be entitled to the same allowances, deductions and reliefs as if the income had arisen in the United Kingdom.

The jurisdiction of the General or Special Commissioners on any appeal shall include jurisdiction to review the inspector's decision under this subsection.

(4) In charging any income which is excluded from subsection (1) above by subsection (2)(a) above there shall be the same limitation on reliefs as under section 391(2) in the case of income computed by virtue of section 65(3) in accordance with the rules applicable to Cases I and II of Schedule D.

(5) In charging income arising from a pension under subsection (3) above, a deduction of one-tenth shall be allowed unless it is the income of a person falling within section 65(4).

Commentary—*Simon's Direct Tax Service* **E1.328, F1.501.**
Statement of Practice SP 3/90—Stocks and long-term contracts.
Simon's Tax Cases—s 68(1), *Jones v O'Brien* [1988] STC 615*.
Definitions—"Inspector", s 832(1); "interest", s 832(1); "Schedule D", s 18(1); "tax", s 832(3); "trade", s 832(1); "United Kingdom", s 830(1); "year of assessment", s 832(1).
Cross references—See TA 1988 s 9(6) (this section not to apply when computing income for the purposes of corporation tax).
TA 1988 s 347A(5) (certain foreign maintenance payments not allowed as a deduction under sub-s (1)(b) above).
FA 1988 s 38(9) (no deduction to be made under sub-s (1)(b) above on account of certain maintenance payments).

FA 1994 Sch 20 para 7 (this section to apply disregarding amendments made by FA 1994 s 207 in respect of income from a source arising before 6 April 1994 and ceasing before 6 April 1988).
Amendments—[1] Words in sub-s (1) substituted with effect from the year 1994–95 as respects income from a source arising after 5 April 1994 and from the year 1996–97 as respects income from a source arising before 6 April 1994, subject to transitional provisions in FA 1994 Sch 20; see FA 1994 ss 207(5), 218.
[2] Word in sub-s (1) substituted by FA 1998 Sch 7 para 1 with effect from 31 July 1998.

Case VI

[69 Case VI assessments

Income tax under Case VI of Schedule D shall be computed on the full amount of the profits or gains arising in the year of assessment.][1]

Commentary—*Simon's Direct Tax Service* **B7.217.**
Revenue Interpretation RI 135—Schedule A transitional rules.
Definitions—"Profits or gains", s 833(1); "Schedule D", s 18(1); "year of assessment", s 832(1).
Cross references—See TA 1988 s 9(6) (this section not to apply when computing income for the purposes of corporation tax).
TA 1988 s 72 (apportionment of profits, gains or losses to particular periods).
TA 1988 ss 392, 396 (treatment of Schedule D Case VI losses).
TA 1988 s 577A (expenditure involving crime not deductible).
TA 1988 s 817 (deductions not allowed in computing profits or gains).
Amendments—[1] This section substituted by FA 1994 s 208 with effect from the year 1994–95 for profits or gains from a source arising after 6 April 1994 and with effect from the year 1996–97 for profits or gains from a source arising before 6 April 1994. For detailed commencement provisions, see FA 1994 s 218.

CHAPTER III
CORPORATION TAX: BASIS OF ASSESSMENT ETC

70 Basis of assessment etc

(1) In accordance with sections 6 to 12 and 337 to 344, for the purposes of corporation tax for any accounting period income shall be computed under Cases I to VI of Schedule D on the full amount of the profits or gains or income arising in the period (whether or not received in or transmitted to the United Kingdom), without any other deduction than is authorised by the Corporation Tax Acts.

(2) Where a company is chargeable to corporation tax in respect of a trade or vocation under Case V of Schedule D, the income from the trade or vocation shall be computed in accordance with the rules applicable to Case I of Schedule D.

(3) [Cases III and V][1] of Schedule D shall for the purposes of corporation tax extend to companies not resident in the United Kingdom, so far as those companies are chargeable to tax on income of descriptions which, in the case of companies resident in the United Kingdom, fall within those Cases (but without prejudice to any provision of the Tax Acts specially exempting non-residents from tax on any particular description of income).

Commentary—*Simon's Direct Tax Service* **D2.203; D4.123.**
Statement of Practice SP B1—This Statement sets out the general principles applied in dealing with VAT in the computation of liability to income tax and corporation tax. It deals with the position of taxpayers who make exempt supplies, zero-rated supplies and partly taxable supplies. It also deals with the position of taxpayers who have suffered bad debts.
SP C1—A percentage of the proceeds of certain football pools or small lotteries run by supporters' clubs or similar societies to be excluded in computing profits or gains.
Simon's Tax Cases—s 70(1), *Meat Traders Ltd v Cushing* [1997] STC (SCD) 245.
Definitions—"Accounting period", s 834(1); "company", s 832(1), (2); "Corporation Tax Acts", s 831(1)(*a*); "profits or gains", s 833(1); "Schedule D", s 18(1); "the Tax Acts", s 831(2); "trade", s 832(1); "United Kingdom", s 830(1).
Cross-references—See FA 2002 s 65(2) (postponement of charge to mark to market basis in certain cases).
Amendments—[1] Words in sub-s (3) substituted for "Cases IV and V" by FA 1996 ss 104, 105, Sch 14 para 7 with effect for accounting periods ending after 31 March 1996, subject to transitional provisions in FA 1996 Sch 15.

[70A Case V income from land outside UK: corporation tax

(1) This section applies where a company is chargeable to corporation tax under Case V of Schedule D in respect of income which—

(*a*) arises from a business carried on for the exploitation, as a source of rents or other receipts, of any estate, interest or rights in or over land outside the United Kingdom, and
(*b*) is not income to which section 70(2) applies (income from a trade or vocation).

(2) The provisions of Schedule A apply to determine whether income falls within subsection (1)(*a*) above as they would apply to determine whether the income fell within paragraph 1(1) of that Schedule if—

(*a*) the land in question were in the United Kingdom, or
(*b*) a caravan or houseboat which is to be used at a location outside the United Kingdom were to be used at a location in the United Kingdom.

(3) Any provision of the Taxes Acts which deems there to be a Schedule A business in the case of land in the United Kingdom applies where the corresponding circumstances arise with respect to land outside the United Kingdom so as to deem there to be a business within subsection (1)(*a*) above.

(4) All businesses and transactions carried on or entered into by a particular company or partnership, so far as they are businesses or transactions the income from which is chargeable to tax under Case V of Schedule D in accordance with this section, are treated for the purposes of the charge to tax

under Case V as, or as entered into in the course of carrying on, a single business (an "overseas property business").

(5) The income from an overseas property business shall be computed for the purposes of Case V of Schedule D in accordance with the rules applicable to the computation of the profits of a Schedule A business.

Those rules apply separately in relation to—

  (a) an overseas property business, and
  (b) any actual Schedule A business of the company chargeable,

as if each were the only Schedule A business carried on by that company.

(6) Sections 503 and 504 of this Act ...[2] do not apply to the profits or losses of an overseas property business.

(7) Where under this section rules expressed by reference to domestic concepts of law apply in relation to land outside the United Kingdom, they shall be interpreted so as to produce the result that most closely corresponds with the result produced for Schedule A purposes in relation to land in the United Kingdom.][1]

Commentary—*Simon's Direct Tax Service* E1.303, 304.
Amendments—[1] This section inserted by FA 1998 Sch 5 para 25 with effect from the year 1998–99 for income tax purposes, and from 1 April 1998 for corporation tax purposes, subject to the transitional provisions in FA 1998 Sch 5 Part IV.
[2] Words in sub-s (6) repealed by CAA 2001 s 578, 580, Sch 2 para 14, Sch 4 with effect for corporation tax purposes as respects allowances and charges falling to be made for chargeable periods ending after 31 March 2001.

CHAPTER IV

PROVISIONS SUPPLEMENTARY TO CHAPTERS II AND III

71 Computation of income tax where no profits in year of assessment

Where it is provided by the Income Tax Acts that income tax under Schedule D in respect of profits or gains or income from any source is to be computed by reference to the amount of the profits or gains or income of some period preceding the year of assessment, tax as so computed shall be charged for that year of assessment notwithstanding that no profits or gains or income arise from that source for or within that year.

Commentary—*Simon's Direct Tax Service* E1.303, 304.
Definitions—"Income tax", s 832(4); "Income Tax Acts", s 831(1)(b); "profits or gains", s 833(1); "Schedule D", s 18(1); "tax", s 832(3); "year of assessment", s 832(1).

72 Apportionments etc for purposes of Cases I, II and VI

(1) Where in the case of any profits or gains chargeable under Case I, II or VI of Schedule D it is necessary in order to arrive for the purposes of income tax or corporation tax at the profits or gains or losses of any year of assessment, accounting period or other period, to divide and apportion to specific periods the profits or gains or losses for any period for which the accounts have been made up, or to aggregate any such profits, gains or losses or any apportioned parts thereof, it shall be lawful to make such a division and apportionment or aggregation.

(2) Any apportionment under this section shall be made in proportion to the number of [days][1] in the respective periods.

Commentary—*Simon's Direct Tax Service* D2.208; E1.202.
Regulations—IT (Entertainers and Sportsmen) Regulations, SI 1987/530 reg 16 which supplements the provisions of this section.
Revenue Interpretation RI 193—Use of apportionments in calculation of transitional overlap profits under FA 1994 Sch 20 para 2(4).
Simon's Tax Cases—s 72(1), *Marshall Hus & Partners Ltd v Bolton* [1981] STC 18*.
Definitions—"Accounting period", s 834(1); "income tax", s 832(4); "profits or gains", s 833(1); "Schedule D", s 18(1); "year of assessment", s 832(1).
Amendments—[1] Word in sub-s (2) substituted by FA 1995 s 121.

73 Single assessments for purposes of Cases III, IV and V

Commentary—*Simon's Direct Tax Service* E1.302.
Amendments—This section repealed by FA 1995 ss 103(7), 115(9), Sch 29 Pt VIII(14), with effect, so far as relating to income tax and capital gains tax from the year 1996–97, and so far as relating to corporation tax as respects accounting periods ending after 30 June 1999 (by virtue of Finance Act 1994, Section 199, (Appointed Day) Order, SI 1998/3173 art 2).

CHAPTER V

COMPUTATIONAL PROVISIONS

Deductions

74 General rules as to deductions not allowable

[(1)][1] Subject to the provisions of the Tax Acts, in computing the amount of the [profits][7] to be charged under Case I or Case II of Schedule D, no sum shall be deducted in respect of—

(*a*) any disbursements or expenses, not being money wholly and exclusively laid out or expended for the purposes of the trade, profession or vocation;

(*b*) any disbursements or expenses of maintenance of the parties, their families or establishments, or any sums expended for any other domestic or private purposes distinct from the purposes of the trade, profession or vocation;

(*c*) the rent of the whole or any part of any dwelling-house or domestic offices, except any such part as is used for the purposes of the trade, profession or vocation, and where any such part is so used, the sum so deducted shall not, unless in any particular case it appears that having regard to all the circumstances some greater sum ought to be deducted, exceed two-thirds of the rent bona fide paid for that dwelling-house or those offices;

(*d*) any sum expended for repairs of premises occupied, or for the supply, repairs or alterations of any implements, utensils or articles employed, for the purposes of the trade, profession or vocation, beyond the sum actually expended for those purposes;

(*e*) any loss not connected with or arising out of the trade, profession or vocation;

(*f*) any capital withdrawn from, or any sum employed or intended to be employed as capital in, the trade, profession or vocation, but so that this paragraph shall not be treated as disallowing the deduction of any interest;

(*g*) any capital employed in improvements of premises occupied for the purposes of the trade, profession or vocation;

(*h*) any interest which might have been made if any such sums as aforesaid had been laid out at interest;

[(*j*) any debts except—

    (i) a bad debt ...[6];
    (ii) a debt or part of a debt released by the creditor wholly and exclusively for the purposes of his trade, profession or vocation as part of a relevant arrangement or compromise; and
    (iii) a doubtful debt to the extent estimated to be bad, meaning, in the case of the bankruptcy or insolvency of the debtor, the debt except to the extent that any amount may reasonably be expected to be received on the debt;][2]

(*k*) any average loss beyond the actual amount of loss after adjustment;

(*l*) any sum recoverable under an insurance or contract of indemnity;

(*m*) any annuity or other annual payment (other than interest) payable out of the [profits][7];

(*n*) any interest paid to a person not resident in the United Kingdom if and so far as it is interest at more than a reasonable commercial rate;

[(*o*) any interest in so far as the payment of that interest is or would be, otherwise than by virtue of section 375(2), either—

    (i) a payment of interest to which section 369 applies, or
    (ii) a payment of interest to which that section would apply but for section 373(5);][4]

(*p*) any royalty or other sum paid in respect of the user of a patent;

(*q*) ...[5]

[(2) In paragraph (*j*) of subsection (1) above "relevant arrangement or compromise" means—

    (*a*) a voluntary arrangement which has taken effect under or by virtue of the Insolvency Act 1986 or the Insolvency (Northern Ireland) Order 1989; or
    (*b*) a compromise or arrangement which has taken effect under section 425 of the Companies Act 1985 or Article 418 of the Companies (Northern Ireland) Order 1986.][3]

Commentary—*Simon's Direct Tax Service* B3.1202.

Regulations—European Single Currency (Taxes) Regulations, SI 1998/3177 (Deduction allowable for costs incurred by trading company in respect of euroconversion of its shares or other securities).

Concessions B7—The costs of benevolent gifts to a trader's local trade or charitable association is allowed as a deduction if specified conditions are satisfied.

Concession B38—Relief for trade receipts and trade debts, the proceeds of which cannot be remitted to the UK (under para (*j*) above unremittable debt proceeds are not relieved).

Statement of Practice SP A16—Living expenses for longer periods abroad for the purposes of UK trade or profession are allowable deductions.

SP A32—*Sharkey v Wernher* principle not to apply in cases where para (*b*) above applies.

SP C10—Valuation fees for providing in the directors' report particulars of significant changes in the fixed assets of a company are allowable deductions.

SP 5/81—Subject to certain conditions, expenses incurred in restoring drainage on waterlogged land are admitted as revenue expenditure in farm accounts.

SP 11/81—Relief for redundancy payments on partial discontinuance of trade if the payments satisfy the test in para (*b*) above.

SP 16/91—Accountancy expenses arising out of accounts investigations.

Revenue Interpretations RI 1—Expenditure on training courses for business proprietors.

RI 2—Revaluation of business assets in advance of disposal; disallowance of interest in computing profits.

RI 4—Disallowance in computing profits of legal expenses incurred by a company in respect of the purchase of its own shares.

RI 51—Long distance self-employed lorry drivers who use their lorries for overnight accommodation may claim relief under para (*a*) above for reasonable cost of evening meal and morning breakfast.

RI 57—Bank failures: relief for losses incurred by depositors.

RI 167—Where normal accounting practice requires employer contributions to a non-statutory Employee Share Ownership Trust to be treated as an asset in the accounts, such treatment should also be followed for tax purposes.

RI 168—Considers the circumstances in which expenditure on the training and development of employees may be disallowed either under sub-s (1)(*a*) above or because for tax purposes it counts as capital.

RI 192—Accountancy expenses arising out of self-assessment enquiries.

RI 200—Redundancy payments made to employees under pre-existing obligations which were a consequence of their employment for the purpose of the trade are not disallowed under sub-s (1)(*a*) merely because the cessation of trade crystallised the liability to pay.

Revenue Internal Guidance—Banking manual, BM 6.1.1–6.3.1.3 (banks: deduction for interest payable in computing Case I profits).

Banking manual BM 6.2.2.2.: (short interest payable for trade deductible under Case I, annual interest payable in the UK to bank deductible under Case I, other annual interest not deductible (loan relationships provisions apply for accounting periods ended after 31 March 1996 – see FA 1996 s 82); Chapter 7: relief for bad and doubtful debts).

BM 7.7.7–7.3.4.1 (banks: deduction for bad and doubtful debts).

Inspector's manual IM 1885 (bookmakers: deduction for permits to trade etc).

IM 1886 (bookmakers: contributions to the Horserace Betting Levy Board are allowable).

IM 1902 (breweries: no deduction for the cost of application for the removal of licences or payments to Guarantee Fund Trustees).

IM 1910 (breweries: trading results of managed houses are included in the general computation of brewery profits).

IM 1920–1925 (breweries: tied houses: admissible and inadmissible expenditure).

IM 1940a–1940j (builders: valuation procedures).

IM 1941–1978 (builders: other computational matters).

IM 1990 (builders: interest payable included in the cost of work in progress).

IM 260–2063 (cemeteries: treatment of capital expenditure).

IM 2681 (legal expenses of licensed houses: renewal of licence is allowable; first application, transfer or removal is not allowable).

IM 2960 (rents payable by public house tenants are apportioned between business and domestic elements on the basis of the facts).

IM 3122 (travelling and subsistence expenses of sub-contractors).

IM 3123–3124 (sub-contractors: business use of home).

Schedule E manual SE 42730 (consequential adjustment to Schedule E liability where director's remuneration disallowed).

Revenue & other press releases—Hansard 27-7-44 (key man insurance premiums are deductible if paid by an employer for an employee, including a director, to cover short term loss of profits arising from loss of the employee's services).

Hansard 27-7-44 and 1-8-44 (benefits arising under key man insurance policies are taxable as trading receipts under s 18, where premiums are allowable deductions).

Hansard 6-12-76 (a self-employed individual may deduct modest expenditure on meals consumed in the course of a travelling occupation or on infrequent business journeys).

Hansard 11-6-84 (expenditure entering architectural competitions or tendering for contracts is deductible, regardless of whether these are successful; expenditure on abortive planning applications, generally of capital nature is not).

ICAEW TR637 24-11-86 (expenditure for which no tax relief is available).

ICAEW TR799 June 1990 (a debt or part thereof "released" under a voluntary arrangement under IA 1986 Pt I does not automatically disapply s 74(*j*): the inspector will need to be satisfied the debt was bad or doubtful to the extent claimed. A "release" in excess of an amount arrived at on this basis is unlikely to be an allowable deduction).

IR 16-3-93 (Council Tax: where a property is let or used for business purposes, in whole or part, then an appropriate portion of the council tax is deductible in computing rental income or trading profits. An employer who pays an employee's liability as part of a remuneration package may deduct the amount in computing business profits).

ICAEW TAX 10/95 12-4-95 (relationship between accounting practice and tax computations on provisions for warranty claims, closure costs, disputed legal actions and losses on long-term contracts).

IR 30-4-96 (premiums on insurance policies to cover practice expenses, for example those of taking on a locum, in event of illness or incapacity is tax deductible).

IR Tax Bulletin April 1996 p 303 (criteria are listed under which the Revenue will accept a computation of car expenses using a fixed rate per business mile).

Simon's Tax Cases—s 74(1)(*a*), *McKnight v Sheppard* [1999] STC 669*; *Halifax plc v Davidson* [2000] STC (SCD) 251; *Woolwich plc v Davidson* [2000] STC (SCD) 302; *Northern Rock plc v Thorpe* [2000] STC (SCD) 317; *Alliance & Leicester plc v Hamer* [2000] STC (SCD) 332.

s 74(1)(*b*), *Watkis v Ashford Sparkes & Harward (a firm)* [1985] STC 451*; *Gazelle v Servini* [1995] STC (SCD) 324*; *Silk v Fletcher* [1999] STC (SCD) 220; *Salt v Buckley (Insp of Taxes)* [2001] STC(SCD) 262.

s 74(1)(*d*), (*g*) *Wynne-Jones v Bedale Auction Ltd* [1977] STC 50*; *Brown v Burnley Football and Athletic Co Ltd* [1980] STC 424*; *Gazelle v Servini* [1995] STC (SCD) 324*; *Jenners Princes Street Edinburgh Ltd v IRC* [1998] STC (SCD) 196.

s 74(1)(*e*), *Stockbroker v McKnight* [1996] STC (SCD) 103*; *Sycamore plc and Maple Ltd v Fir* [1997] STC (SCD) 1*; *McKnight v Sheppard* [1999] STC 669*.

s 74(1)(*f*), *RTZ Oil and Gas Ltd v Elliss* [1987] STC 512*; *Beauchamp* [1988] STC 714*; *Beauchamp v F W Woolworth plc* [1989] STC 510*; *Bullrun Inc v Insp of Taxes* [2000] STC (SCD) 384.

s 74(1)(*j*), *Taylor v Clatworthy*, [1996] STC (SCD) 506; *Sycamore plc and Maple Ltd v Fir*, [1997] STC (SCD) 1*.

s 74(1)(*l*), *Bolton v Halpern Woolf (a firm)* [1979] STC 761*.

Definitions—"Interest", s 832(1);.

Cross references—See TA 1988 s 79(1) (notwithstanding anything in this section, contributions to local enterprise agencies are deductible in computing profits or gains).

TA 1988 s 79A(1) (notwithstanding anything in this section, contributions to training and enterprise councils and local enterprise companies are deductible in computing profits or gains).

TA 1988 s 83 (notwithstanding anything in this section, patent fees and expenses are deductible in computing profits or gains).

TA 1988 s 86(1) (notwithstanding anything in this section, expenses in respect of an employee temporarily seconded to a charity or school are deductible in computing profits or gains).

TA 1988 s 89 (debts proving irrecoverable after deemed discontinuance to be deductible in computing subsequent profits or gains to the extent not allowed under sub-s (1)(*j*) above).

TA 1988 s 568(1) (notwithstanding anything in this section, contributions to schemes for rationalising industry are deductible expenses).

FA 1988 s 73(2) (notwithstanding anything in this section, any sum to which s 313 of this Act applies (consideration for certain restrictive undertakings) to be an allowable deduction from the profits or gains of a trade etc).

FA 1989 s 112(2) (the limitations of this section not to apply to expenditure incurred to acquire assets or services for personal physical security).

FA 1993 s 128(10) (notwithstanding anything in this section, certain foreign exchange losses to be deductible in computing profits or gains).

FA 1994 s 159(4) (notwithstanding anything in this section, loss on interest-rate and currency contracts held for trading purposes treated as a loss of the trade).

European Single Currency (Taxes) Regulations, SI 1998/3177 regs 4–6 (deductibility of costs of Euroconversion of shares and other securities).

Amendments—[1] "(1)" inserted by virtue of FA 1994 s 144(2).

[2] Para (*j*) substituted by FA 1994 s 144(1), (6) and has effect, for the purposes of determining (in computing the amount of profits or gains to be charged under Case I or Case II of Schedule D) whether any sum should be deducted in respect of any debt, in relation to debts—

(*a*) proved to be bad,

(*b*) released as part of—

   (i) a voluntary arrangement which has taken effect under or by virtue of the Insolvency Act 1986 or the Insolvency (Northern Ireland) Order 1989, or,

   (ii) a compromise or arrangement which has taken effect under section 425 of the Companies Act 1985 or Article 418 of the Companies (Northern Ireland) Order 1986, and

(*c*) estimated to be bad,

if the proof, release or estimation occurs after 29 November 1993. Note, however, as to proof, note 6 below.
[3] Sub-s (2) inserted by FA 1994 s 144(2).
[4] Sub-s (1)(*o*) substituted by FA 1994 s 81(5), (6), (7), Sch 9 para 1 and has effect—

    (*a*) in relation to payments of interest made after 5 April 1994 (whenever falling due); and
    (*b*) as respects relevant loan interest, in relation to any payments of interest becoming due after 5 April 1994 which have been made before that date but after 29 November 1993.

Any provision made before the passing of FA 1994 (3 May 1994) by reference to the basic rate of income tax and contained in any instrument or agreement under or in accordance with which payments of relevant loan interest have been or are to be made shall be taken, in relation to any such payment as is mentioned in (*a*) or (*b*) above, to have been made, instead, by reference to a rate which, in the case of that payment, is the applicable percentage for the purposes of TA 1988 s 369(1).
[5] Sub-s (1)(*q*) repealed by FA 1997 Sch 18 Pt VI(2) with effect in relation to payments made after 5 April 1997.
[6] Words in sub-s (1)(*j*)(i) repealed by FA 1996 s 134, Sch 20 para 4, Sch 41 Pt V(10) with effect for the purposes of income tax from the year 1996–97 and, as respects corporation tax, for accounting periods ending after 30 June 1999 (by virtue of Finance Act 1994, Section 199, (Appointed Day) Order, SI 1998/3173 art 2).
[7] Word substituted in sub-s (1) and (1)(m) by FA 1998 Sch 7 para 1 with effect from 31 July 1998.

75 Expenses of management: investment companies

(1) In computing for the purposes of corporation tax the total profits for any accounting period of an investment company resident in the United Kingdom there shall be deducted any sums disbursed as expenses of management (including commissions) for that period, except any such expenses as are deductible in computing profits apart from this section.

[(1A) The expenses of management of a company shall not include any expenses in relation to which a debit falls to be brought into account for the purposes of Chapter II of Part IV of the Finance Act 1996 (loan relationships) in computing the amount from which sums disbursed as expenses of management are deductible.][3]

(2) For the purposes of subsection (1) above there shall be deducted from the amount treated as expenses of management the amount of any income derived from sources not charged to tax, other than franked investment income, ...[1], ...[5] and any regional development grant. In this subsection "regional development grant" means a payment by way of grant under Part II of the Industrial Development Act 1982.

(3) Where in any accounting period of an investment company the expenses of management deductible under subsection (1) above, together with any charges on income paid in the accounting period wholly and exclusively for purposes of the company's business, exceed the amount of the profits from which they are deductible—

    (*a*) the excess shall be carried forward to the succeeding accounting period; and
    (*b*) the amount so carried forward to the succeeding accounting period shall be treated for the purposes of this section, including any further application of this subsection, as if it had been disbursed as expenses of management for that accounting period.

(4) For the purposes of this section there shall be added to a company's expenses of management in any accounting period the amount of any allowances falling to be made to the company for that period by virtue of [section 15(1)(*g*) of the Capital Allowances Act (plant and machinery allowances) so far as effect cannot be given to them under section 253(2) of that Act][6].

(5) Where an appeal against an assessment to corporation tax *or against a decision on a claim under section 242*[4] relates exclusively to the relief to be given under subsection (1) above, the appeal shall lie to the Special Commissioners, and if and so far as the question in dispute on any such appeal which does not lie to the Special Commissioners relates to that relief, that question shall, instead of being determined on the appeal, be referred to and determined by the Special Commissioners, and the Management Act shall apply as if that reference were an appeal.

(6) ...[2]

Commentary—*Simon's Direct Tax Service* **D4.403, 408, 409, 504.**
Regulations—European Single Currency (Taxes) Regulations, SI 1998/3177 (Costs incurred by investment company in respect of euroconversion of its shares or other securities to be treated as expenses of management).
Concessions B7—The costs of benevolent gifts to a trader's local trade or charitable association are allowed as a deduction if specified conditions are satisfied.
ESC B39—Contributions to overseas pension schemes.
Statement of Practice SP C10—Valuation fees for providing in the directors' report particulars of significant changes in the fixed assets of a company are expenses deductible under sub-s (1) above.
Revenue Interpretation RI 37—For the purpose of time limit in s 242(8)(*b*) of this Act, excess management expenses carried forward under sub-s (3) above to a later accounting period may be set off against surplus franked investment income within 6 years of the end of the later period.
RI 126—Revenue approach and factors to be considered in determining whether a company's business consists wholly or mainly in the making of investments.
Revenue Internal Guidance—Company Taxation Manual COT803 (deduction for management expenses automatic: no claim required; accruals basis acceptable).
COT805 (deduction for management expenses takes precedence over deduction of trading loss under TA 1988 s 393A).
COT830–850 (meaning of "management expenses" with examples).
Schedule E manual SE 42730 (consequential adjustment to Schedule E liability where director's remuneration disallowed).
Simon's Tax Cases—*Westmoreland Investments Ltd v Macniven* [1997] STC (SCD) 69; *Holdings Ltd v IRC* [1997] STC (SCD)144; *Johnson v The Prudential Assurance Co Ltd* [1998] STC 439.
s 75(1)(2), *Hoechst Finance Ltd v Gumbrell* [1983] STC 150*; *Cadbury Schweppes plc v Williams (Insp of Taxes)* [2002] STC(SCD) 115.
s 75(3), *Westmoreland Investments Ltd v Macniven* [1998] STC 1131.
Definitions—"Accounting period", s 834(1); "the 1990 Act", s 831(3); "capital allowance", s 832(1); "company", s 832(1), (2); "franked investment income", s 832(1); "investment company", s 130; "the Management Act", s 831(3); "profits", ss 6(4), 834(2); "tax", s 832(3); "United Kingdom", s 830(1).

Cross references—See TA 1988 s 76(1), (5) (expenses of management: insurance companies).

TA 1988 s 77(1) (incidental costs of obtaining loan finance treated as management expenses).

TA 1988 s 78(4) (incidental costs in securing a bank's acceptance of a discounted bill of exchange treated as management expenses).

TA 1988 s 79(2) (contributions by investment companies to local enterprise agencies treated as management expenses).

TA 1988 s 79A(2) (contributions by investment companies to training and enterprise councils and local enterprise companies are treated as management expenses).

TA 1988 s 84A(2)(*b*) (relief for costs of establishing share option or profit sharing schemes incurred by a company to which this section applies by virtue of s 76 below).

TA 1988 s 85(1) (payments by an investment company to trustees of an approved profit sharing scheme treated as management expenses).

TA 1988 s 85A(2)(*b*) (expenditure incurred in establishing an approved share option or profit sharing scheme by investment or insurance company treated as management expenses).

TA 1988 s 86(1) (expenses in respect of an employee temporarily seconded to a charity or educational establishment are deductible as expenses of management).

TA 1988 s 86A (tax relief for agents' expenses paid by employers for operating payroll deduction scheme for donations to charity by employees).

TA 1988 s 88 (payments by an investment company to Export Credit Guarantee Department are deductible as management expenses).

TA 1988 s 90(1) (certain additional payments to redundant employees allowable as expenses of management notwithstanding the permanent discontinuance of the business etc).

TA 1988 s 92(2) (regional development grants not to be deducted under sub-s (2) above).

TA 1988 s 242 (recovery of tax credits by set-off of management expenses against surplus of franked investment income).

TA 1988 s 400(2) (reduction of excess management expenses and charges on income allowed to be carried forward under sub-s (3) above where government investment in a company is written off).

TA 1988 s 403 (unrelieved management expenses of an investment company may be surrendered by way of group relief).

TA 1988 s 468(4) (this section to apply to an authorised unit trust whether or not it is an investment company and sums periodically appropriated for managers' remuneration treated as management expenses).

TA 1988 s 487(4) (a credit union is not an investment company for the purposes of this section).

TA 1988 s 577 (business entertaining expenses not to be treated as management expenses).

TA 1988 s 577A(2) (expenditure involving crime not to be treated as management expenses).

TA 1988 s 579(3) (extension of management expenses relief under this section to statutory redundancy payments).

TA 1988 s 586(2) (war risk premiums not to be treated as management expenses).

TA 1988 s 587(2)(*b*) (certain payments to employees in respect of war injuries not to be treated as expenses of management).

TA 1988 s 588(4) (extension of management expenses relief under this section to expenditure incurred in respect of training courses for employees).

TA 1988 s 589A(9) (certain expenditure on qualifying counselling services for employees to be treated as management expenses).

TA 1988 s 592(4)–(6) (extension of management expenses relief under this section to employer's contributions to an approved occupational pension scheme).

TA 1988 s 617(4) (secondary Class 1 contributions, Class 1A and Class 1B contributions *not* precluded from being allowable as management expenses under this section).

TA 1988 s 768B(6)–(9) (relief for management expenses, charges and capital allowances (under sub-s (4) above) following a change in ownership of an investment company within sub-s (1) resulting in the accounting period being divided).

TA 1988 s 768C (restriction of relief under this section in an accounting period beginning before a change in ownership of an investment company in which there is a disposal of an asset transferred intra group on which a chargeable gain arises).

TA 1988 Sch 19AC para 5(2) (application of sub-s (5) above as modified to overseas life insurance company).

TA 1988 Sch 27 para 4(3) (expenditure deductible under this section in computing an offshore fund's profits which include commodity income).

FA 1988 s 73(3) (any sum to which s 313 of this Act applies (consideration for restrictive undertakings) to be treated for the purposes of this section as management expenses).

FA 1989 s 44 (emoluments paid more than nine months after the end of the relevant period of account to be treated as expenses of management of period in which paid).

FA 1989 s 67(2)(*b*) (contributions to employee share ownership trusts to be treated as management expenses).

FA 1989 s 76(1), (4)(*b*) (the relief given by this section not to apply to certain management expenses of non-approved retirement benefits schemes).

FA 1989 ss 84(1), 86 (spreading of relief over a seven year period for certain management expenses incurred in accounting periods beginning after 31 December 1989 in relation to basic life assurance business).

FA 1989 ss 84(1), 87(5), (6) (limit on excess expenses of management that may be carried forward by insurance company under sub-s (3)(*a*) above).

European Single Currency (Taxes) Regulations, SI 1998/3177 regs 4–6 (deductibility of costs of Euroconversion of shares and other securities).

Amendments—[1] Words in sub-s (2) (originally inserted by FA 1994 Sch 16 para 12 with effect under the foreign income dividend provisions (ss 246A–246Y)) repealed by F(No 2)A 1997 s 36(4), Sch 6 para 2, Sch 8 Pt II(11) with effect in relation to distributions made after 5 April 1999.

[2] Sub-s (6) (originally inserted by FA 1994 Sch 16 para 12 with effect under the foreign income dividend provisions (ss 246A–246Y)) repealed by F(No 2)A 1997 s 36(4), Sch 6 para 2, Sch 8 Pt II(11) with effect in relation to distributions made after 5 April 1999.

[3] Sub-s (1A) inserted by FA 1996 ss 104, 105, Sch 14 para 8 with effect for accounting periods ending after 31 March 1996, subject to transitional provisions in FA 1996 Sch 15.

[4] Words in sub-s (5) repealed by F(No 2)A 1997 Sch 8 Pt II(4) with effect generally in relation to accounting periods beginning after 1 July 1997 but subject to the detailed provisions of F(No 2)A 1997 s 20(1)–(4).

[5] Words in sub-s (2) repealed by FA 1998 Sch 3 para 9 in relation to distributions made after 5 April 1999.

[6] Words in sub-s (4) substituted by CAA 2001 s 578, Sch 2 para 15 with effect for corporation tax purposes as respects allowances and charges falling to be made for chargeable periods ending after 31 March 2001.

76 Expenses of management: insurance companies

(1) Subject to the provisions of this section and of section 432, section 75 shall apply for computing the profits of a company carrying on life assurance business, whether mutual or proprietary, (and not charged to corporation tax in respect of it under Case I of Schedule D), whether or not the company is resident in the United Kingdom, as that section applies in relation to an investment company except that—

[(*aa*) where the whole or any part of a loss arising to the company in respect of its life assurance business in an accounting period is set off under section 393A or 403(1), there shall be deducted from the amount treated as the expenses of management for that period an amount equal to so much of the loss as, in the aggregate, is so set off, reduced by the amounts by which any losses for that period under section 436 [or 439B][19] fall to be reduced under section 434A(2)(b); and][15]

[(ab) section 75(1) shall have effect with the substitution for "in computing profits apart from this section" of—

> "(a) in computing income for the purposes of Schedule A, or
> (b) by virtue of section 121(3) in computing income from the letting of rights to work minerals in the United Kingdom"; and][15]

(a) there shall be deducted from the amount treated as the expenses of management for any accounting period the amount of any fines, fees or profits arising from reversions; and

(b) no deduction shall be made under section 75(2); [and][1]

[(c) there shall be deducted from the amount treated as the expenses of management for any accounting period any repayment or refund (in whole or in part) of a sum disbursed by the company (for that or any earlier period) as acquisition expenses; and][1]

[(ca) there shall also be deducted from the amount treated as the expenses of management for any accounting period any reinsurance commission earned in the period which is referable to [basic life assurance and general annuity business][7]; and][2]

[(d) the amount treated as expenses of management shall not include any amount in respect of expenses referable to ...[8][, pension business[, life reinsurance business][9] or overseas life assurance business][3]; and][1]

[(e) the amount of profits from which expenses of management may be deducted for any accounting period shall not exceed the net income and gains of that accounting period referable to [basic life assurance and general annuity business][7];][1]

[and for this purpose "net income and gains" means income and gains after deducting any reliefs or exemptions which fall to be applied before taking account of this section.][1]

[(2) Where, in the case of any such company, the amount mentioned in paragraph (a) of subsection (2A) below exceeds for any accounting period the amount mentioned in paragraph (b) of that subsection, the amount which by virtue of this section is to be deductible by way of management expenses for that period shall be equal to the basic deduction for that period reduced by the amount of the excess.][10]

[(2A) Those amounts are—

(a) the amount which would be the profits of the company's life assurance business for that period if computed in accordance with the provisions applicable to Case I of Schedule D and adjusted in respect of losses; and

(b) the amount (including any negative amount) produced by deducting the following aggregate amount from the company's relevant income for that period from its life assurance business, that is to say, the aggregate of—

> (i) the basic deduction,
> (ii) any non-trading deficit on the company's loan relationships which is produced for that period in relation to that business by a separate computation under paragraph 2 of Schedule 11 to the Finance Act 1996, [and][16]
> (iii) any amount which in pursuance of a claim under paragraph 4(3) of that Schedule is carried back to that period and (in accordance with paragraph 4(5) of that Schedule) applied in reducing profits of the company for that period, ...[16]
> (iv) ...[16]][10]

[(2B) For the purposes of subsection (2A) above a company's relevant income for any accounting period from its life assurance business is the sum of the following—

(a) the income and gains of the company's life assurance business for that accounting period; and

[(b) the franked investment income of, and foreign income dividends arising to, the company which are referable to its basic life assurance and general annuity business.][17]][10]

[(2C) The adjustment in respect of losses that is to be made for any accounting period under paragraph (a) of subsection (2A) above is a deduction of the amount equal to the unused part of the sum which—

(a) by reference to computations made in respect of the company's life assurance business in accordance with the provisions applicable to Case I of Schedule D, and

(b) disregarding section 434A(2),

would fall, in the case of the company, to be set off under section 393 against the company's income for that period.][10]

[(2D) For the purposes of subsection (2C) above, an amount is unused to the extent that it has not been taken into account for any previous accounting period in determining the amount by reference to which the following question was answered, namely, the question whether, and by how much, the amount deductible by virtue of this section by way of management expenses was less than the basic deduction.][10]

[(5) Subject to paragraph 4(11) to (13) of Schedule 11 to the Finance Act 1996, where the basic deduction for any period exceeds the amount which for that period is to be deductible by virtue of this section by way of management expenses, the amount to be carried forward by virtue of section

75(3) (including the amount to be so carried forward for the purpose of computing the amount of the basic deduction for any period) shall be increased by the amount of the excess.][10]

[(5A) In the preceding provisions of this section references to life assurance business and references to basic life assurance and general annuity business shall be deemed, in each case, to include references to capital redemption business.][11]

(6) The relief under this section available to an overseas life insurance company (within the meaning of section 431) in respect of its expenses of management shall be limited to expenses attributable to the life assurance business carried on by the company at or through its branch or agency in the United Kingdom [or to any capital redemption business carried on by the company at or through that branch or agency.][12]

(7) ...[22]

[(7A)][21] ...[22]

[(7B) The amounts which a company may treat as part of its expenses of management for the purposes of this section include amounts in respect of which relief is given under paragraph 22 of Schedule 22 to the Finance Act 2001 (relief in respect of expenditure on remediation of contaminated land which is management asset).][20]

[(8) In this section—

...[23]

"acquisition expenses" means expenses falling within paragraphs (*a*) to (*c*) of subsection (1) of section 86 of the Finance Act 1989;

...[23]

["basic deduction", in relation to an accounting period of an insurance company, means the amount which, by virtue of this section, would be deductible by way of management expenses for that period but for subsection (2) above;][13]

["capital redemption business" means any capital redemption business, within the meaning of section 458, which is business to which that section applies;][14]

...[23]

...[18]

and other expressions have the same meaning as in Chapter I of Part XII.][6]

Commentary—*Simon's Direct Tax Service* **D4.504.**
Regulations—IT (Insurance Companies) (Expenses of Management) Regulations, SI 1992/2744.
Revenue Interpretation RI 126—Revenue approach and factors to be considered in determining whether a company's business consists wholly or mainly in the making of investments.
Revenue Internal Guidance—Life assurance manual LAM 2.32 (management expenses in excess of life assurance business cannot be set off against non-life business income).
Life assurance manual (para 12.21: examples of items of expenditure which qualify and do not qualify: there must be a disbursement not merely a discount on premium and the disbursement must be for the accounting period so accruals basis applies; paras 12.31–12.62 relief for acquisition expenses; paras 12.71–12.91 set off and carry forward of management expenses).
Simon's Tax Cases—*Johnson v The Prudential Assurance Co Ltd* [1998] STC 439.
s 76(2), (3), *Utopia Assurance Co Ltd v Chaloner* [1996] STC (SCD) 204.
s 76(6), *Sun Life Assurance Co of Canada v Pearson* [1986] STC 335*.
Definitions—"Accounting period", s 834(1); "advance corporation tax", s 14(1); "basic life assurance and general annuity business", s 431F; "branch or agency", s 834(1); "company", s 832(1), (2); "distribution", ss 209(2), 832(1); "foreign income dividends", s 246A; "franked investment income", s 238(1); "investment company", s 130; "loan relationship", s 834(1), FA 1996 s 81; "non-trading deficit", s 834(1), FA 1996 s 82; "profits", ss 6(4), 834(2); "Schedule D", s 18(1); "tax", s 832(3); "United Kingdom", s 830(1).
Cross references—See TA 1988 s 85(1) (payments by an insurance company to trustees of an approved profit sharing Scheme treated as management expenses).
TA 1988 s 85A(2)(*b*) (expenditure incurred in establishing an approved share option or profit sharing scheme by an insurance company treated as management expenses).
TA 1988 s 86A (tax relief for agents' expenses paid by employers for operating payroll deduction scheme for donations to charity by employees).
TA 1988 s 88 (payments by an insurance company to Export Credit Guarantee Department are deductible as management expenses).
TA 1988 s 90(1) (certain additional payments to redundant employees allowable as expenses of management notwithstanding the permanent discontinuance of the business etc).
TA 1988 s 242 (recovery of tax credits by set-off of management expenses against surplus of franked investment income).
TA 1988 s 432(2) (industrial assurance business of insurance company to be treated separately from its ordinary life assurance business for the purposes of this section).
TA 1988 s 434 (nothing in s 208 to prevent taking into account franked investment income and foreign income dividends for the purposes of the calculation under sub-s (2) above).
TA 1988 s 434D(6) (capital allowances in respect of plant and machinery given for expenditure on management assets to be treated as additional management expenses).
TA 1988 s 458(1) (this section to be applied separately to capital redemption businesses to which it applies by virtue of sub-s (5A) above).
TA 1988 s 473 (application of s 473(3), (4) (conversion of securities held as circulating capital) in relation to computation under sub-s (2) above where old securities are equated with new securities).
TA 1988 s 579(3) (extension of management expenses relief under this section to statutory redundancy payments).
TA 1988 s 586(2) (war risk premiums not to be treated as expenses of management).
TA 1988 s 587(2) (certain payments to employees in respect of war injuries not to be treated as expenses of management).
TA 1988 s 592(4)–(6) (extension of management expenses relief under this section to employer's contributions to an approved occupational pension scheme).
TA 1988 s 617(4) (secondary Class 1 contributions and Class 1A contributions *not* precluded from being allowable as management expenses under this section).
TA 1988 Sch 19AC para 5 (modification of this section by insertion of sub-ss (6A), (6B) in relation to its application to overseas life insurance companies; references to franked investment income construed as being references to UK distribution income).

TA 1988 Sch 19AC para 5B (modification of this section to enable an overseas life insurance company to claim to set expenses of management against qualifying distributions).

TA 1988 Sch 19AC para 5C (reduction of relief under this section where the calculation of income of UK branch or agency of overseas life assurance business excludes profits or gains from a FOTRA security or any loan relationship represented by it).

FA 1989 s 67(2)(*b*) (contributions by insurance companies to trustees of qualifying employee share ownership trust to be treated as expenses of management).

FA 1989 ss 84(1), 86 (spreading of relief over a seven year period for certain management expenses incurred in accounting periods beginning after 31 December 1989 in relation to basic life assurance business).

FA 1989 ss 84(1), 87(5), (6) (limit on excess expenses of management that may be carried forward by insurance company under TA 1988 s 75(3)).

IT (Insurance Companies) (Expenses of Management) Regulations, SI 1992/2744 (relief under this section for levy imposed under LAUTRO Indemnity Scheme).

Modifications—Sub-ss (1), (7) modified so far as they apply to the life or endowment business carried on by friendly societies by the Friendly Societies (Modification of the Corporation Tax Acts) Regulations, SI 1997/473 reg 5.

This section shall have effect as if the reference in sub-s (1)(*d*) to expenses referable to different classes of life insurance business included a reference to apportionment of costs incurred by a company carrying on life assurance business in respect of a euroconversion of its shares or other securities between the different classes of life assurance business carried on by that company: see the European Single Currency (Taxes) Regulations, SI 1998/3177 reg 6(3).

Words inserted in sub-s (1)(*d*) in respect of individual savings account business carried out by insurance companies by the Individual Savings Account Regulations 1998, SI 1998/1871 reg 6, with effect from 6 April 1999.

Sub-s (5A), and words in sub-ss (6), (8), omitted in applying life assurance provisions of the Corporation Tax Acts to insurance companies carrying on capital redemption business with effect for accounting periods ending after 30 June 1999: see Insurance Companies (Capital Redemption Business) (Modification of the Corporation Tax Acts) Regulations, SI 1999/498 reg 4.

Amendments—[1] Sub-s (1)(*c*) and the preceding word "and", (*d*), (*e*) and the words following inserted by FA 1989 s 87(1)–(3), (5) with respect to accounting periods beginning after 31 December 1989.

[2] Sub-s (1)(*ca*) inserted by FA 1990 s 44(3), (4) with respect to accounting periods beginning after 31 December 1989.

[3] Words in sub-s (1)(*d*) substituted by FA 1990 Sch 7 paras 1, 10(1) with effect for accounting periods beginning after 31 December 1989.

[4] Words in sub-s (7) inserted by FA 1991 s 47(1), (4).

[5] Sub-s (7A) inserted by FA 1991 s 47(2).

[6] Sub-s (8) substituted by FA 1991 s 47(3).

[7] Words in sub-s (1)(*ca*), (*e*) substituted by FA 1991 Sch 7 paras 1, 18 with respect to accounting periods beginning after 31 December 1991.

[8] Words in sub-s (1)(*d*) repealed by FA 1991 Sch 7 paras 1, 18, and Sch 19 Pt V.

[9] Words in sub-s (1)(*d*) inserted by FA 1995 Sch 8 paras 7, 57, with effect in relation to accounting periods beginning after 31 December 1994.

[10] Sub-ss (2), (2A)–(2D), (5) substituted for sub-ss (2)–(5) by FA 1996 s 164(1), (5) with effect in relation to accounting periods beginning on or after 1 January 1996, subject to transitional provisions in FA 1996 s 164(6) to the effect that this section has effect in respect of such accounting periods: (*a*) as if the reference in sub-s (2D) to a previous accounting period included a reference to an accounting period beginning before 1 January 1996, and (*b*) in relation to such a previous accounting period, as if the references—(i) to the amount deductible by virtue of amendments made by FA 1996 s 164, and (ii) to the basic deduction, were to be construed by reference to whatever provisions had effect in relation to that previous period for purposes corresponding to those of that section as amended by FA 1996 s 164.

[11] Sub-s (5A) inserted by FA 1996 Sch 33 paras 1(1), 4 with effect in relation to accounting periods ending after 30 June 1999 (by virtue of Finance Act 1994, Section 199, (Appointed Day) Order, SI 1998/3173 art 2).

[12] Words in sub-s (6) inserted by FA 1996 Sch 33 paras 1(2), 4 with effect in relation to accounting periods ending after 30 June 1999 (by virtue of SI 1998/3173 art 2).

[13] In sub-s (8), definition "basic deduction" inserted by FA 1996 s 164(2), (5) with effect in relation to accounting periods beginning on or after 1 January 1996, subject to transitional provisions in FA 1996 s 164(6) noted at footnote 10 above.

[14] In sub-s (8), definition "capital redemption business" inserted by FA 1996 Sch 33 paras 1(3), 4 with effect in relation to accounting periods ending after 30 June 1999 (by virtue of SI 1998/3173 art 2).

[15] Sub-s (1)(*aa*), (*ab*) inserted by FA 1996 Sch 31 para 1 with effect for accounting periods beginning after 31 December 1995.

[16] Word "and" at the end of sub-s (2A)(*b*)(ii) inserted, and sub-s (2A)(*b*)(iv) and preceding word "and" repealed, by FA 1997 s 67(4)(*a*), (7), Sch 18 Pt VI(6) with effect in relation to accounting periods beginning after 5 March 1997.

[17] Sub-s (2B)(*b*) substituted by F(No 2)A 1997 s 23, Sch 3 para 1 with effect in relation to distributions made after 1 July 1997.

[18] In sub-s (8), definition "relevant franked investment income" repealed by F(No 2)A 1997 s 23, Sch 3 para 1, Sch 8 Pt II(6) with effect for distributions made after 1 July 1997. This definition was inserted by FA 1996 s 164(2), (5) with effect for accounting periods beginning after 31 December 1995 (subject to transitional provisions in FA 1996 s 164(6) noted at footnote 10 above).

[19] Words in sub-para (1)(*aa*) substituted FA 2000 s 97, Sch 27 para 7 with effect for accounting periods ending after 31 March 2000.

[20] Sub-s (7B) inserted by FA 2001 s 70(3), Sch 23 para 2 with effect for accounting periods ending after 31 March 2001.

[21] Sub-s (7A) substituted by the Financial Services and Markets Act 2000 ss 411, 432(1), (3), Sch 20 para 4, Sch 22 with effect 1 December 2001 (by virtue of SI 2001/3629).

[22] Sub-ss (7), (7A) repealed by the Financial Services and Markets Act 2000 (Consequential Amendments) (Taxes) Order, SI 2001/3629 arts 13, 16(1) with effect from 1 December 2001, immediately after the coming into force of the Financial Services and Markets Act 2000 ss 411, 432(1), Sch 20.

[23] In sub-s (8), definitions of "the 1986 Act", "authorised person", "investment business", "investor", "investor protection scheme", "prescribed", and "recognised self-regulating organisation" repealed by the Financial Services and Markets Act 2000 s 432(1), Sch 20 para 4 with effect from 1 December 2001 (by virtue of SI 2001/3538).

[76A Levies and repayments under the Financial Services and Markets Act 2000]

(1) In computing the amount of the profits to be charged under Case I of Schedule D arising from a trade carried on by an authorised person (other than an investment company)—

    (*a*) to the extent that it would not be deductible apart from this section, any sum expended by the authorised person in paying a levy may be deducted as an allowable expense;

    (*b*) any payment which is made to the authorised person as a result of a repayment provision is to be treated as a trading receipt.

[(2) "Levy" means—

    (*a*) a payment required under rules made under section 136(2) of the Financial Services and Markets Act 2000 ("the Act of 2000");

    (*b*) a levy imposed under the Financial Services Compensation Scheme;

    (*c*) a payment required under rules made under section 234 of the Act of 2000;

(*d*) a payment required under scheme rules in accordance with paragraph 15(1) of Schedule 17 to the Act of 2000;

(*e*) a payment required in accordance with the standard terms fixed under paragraph 18 of Schedule 17 to the Act of 2000 other than an award which is not an award of costs under costs rules.][2]

[(3) "Repayment provision" means—

(*a*) any provision made by virtue of section 136(7) or 214(1)(*e*) of the Act of 2000;

(*b*) any provision by scheme rules for fees to be refunded in specified circumstances.][2]

(4) "Authorised person" has the same meaning as in the Act of 2000.][1]

[(5) "Scheme rules" means the rules referred to in paragraph 14(1) of Schedule 17 to the Act of 2000.][2]

[(6) "Costs rules" means—

(*a*) rules made under section 230 of the Act of 2000;

(*b*) provision relating to costs contained in the standard terms fixed under paragraph 18 of Schedule 17 to the Act of 2000.][2]][1]

Amendments—[1] This section inserted by the Financial Services and Markets Act 2000 s 411 with effect from 1 December 2001 (by virtue of SI 2001/3538).
[2] Sub-ss (2), (3) substituted, and sub-ss (5), (6) added, by the Financial Services and Markets Act 2000 (Consequential Amendments) (Taxes) Order, SI 2001/3629 arts 13, 16(2)–(5) with effect from 1 December 2001 immediately after the coming into force of the Financial Services and Markets Act 2000 ss 411, 432(1), Sch 20.

[76B Levies and repayments under the Financial Services and Markets Act 2000: investment companies

(1) For the purposes of section 75 any sums paid by an investment company—

(*a*) by way of a levy, or

(*b*) as a result of an award of costs under costs rules,

shall be treated as part of its expenses of management.

(2) If a payment is made to an investment company as a result of a repayment provision, the company shall be charged to tax under Case VI of Schedule D on the amount of that payment.

(3) "Levy" has the meaning given in section [76A(2)].[2]

[(4) "Costs rules" has the meaning given in section 76A(6).][2]

(5) "Repayment provision" has the meaning given in section 76A(3).][1]

Amendments—[1] This section inserted by the Financial Services and Markets Act 2000 s 411 with effect from 1 December 2001 (by virtue of SI 2001/3538).
[2] Reference in sub-s (3) substituted, and sub-s (4) substituted by the Financial Services and Markets Act 2000 (Consequential Amendments) (Taxes) Order, SI 2001/3629 arts 13, 16(6)–(8) with effect from 1 December 2001, immediately after the coming into force of the Financial Services and Markets Act 2000 ss 411, 432(1), Sch 20.

77 Incidental costs of obtaining loan finance

(1) Subject to subsection (5) below, in computing the [profits][2] to be charged under Case I or II of Schedule D there may be deducted the incidental costs of obtaining finance by means of a qualifying loan or the issue of qualifying loan stock or a qualifying security; and the incidental costs of obtaining finance by those means shall be treated for the purposes of section 75 as expenses of management.

(2) Subject to subsections (3) and (4) below, in this section—

(*a*) "a qualifying loan" and "qualifying loan stock" mean a loan or loan stock the interest on which is deductible—

(i) in computing for tax purposes the [profits][2] of the person by whom the incidental costs in question are incurred; or[3]

(ii) *under section 338 against his total profits; and*[3]

(*b*) "qualifying security" means any deep discount security, as defined by paragraph 1 of Schedule 4, in respect of which the income elements, as defined by paragraph 4 of that Schedule, are deductible under paragraph 5(1) of that Schedule in computing the total profits of the company by which the incidental costs in question are incurred.

(3) Except as provided by subsection (4) below, a loan or loan stock which carries the right of conversion into or to the acquisition of—

(*a*) shares, or

(*b*) other securities not being a qualifying loan or qualifying loan stock,

is not a qualifying loan or qualifying loan stock if that right is exercisable before the expiry of the period of three years from the date when the loan was obtained or the stock issued.

(4) A loan or loan stock—

(*a*) which carries such a right as is referred to in subsection (3) above, and

(*b*) which by virtue of that subsection is not a qualifying loan or qualifying loan stock, shall nevertheless be regarded as a qualifying loan or qualifying loan stock, as the case may be, if the right is not, or is not wholly, exercised before the expiry of the period of three years from the date when the loan was obtained or the stock was issued.

(5) For the purposes of the application of subsection (1) above in relation to a loan or loan stock which is a qualifying loan or qualifying loan stock by virtue of subsection (4) above—

    (*a*) if the right referred to in subsection (4)(*a*) above is exercised as to part of the loan or stock within the period referred to in that subsection, only that proportion of the incidental costs of obtaining finance which corresponds to the proportion of the stock in respect of which the right is not exercised within that period shall be taken into account; and

    (*b*) in so far as any of the incidental costs of obtaining finance are incurred before the expiry of the period referred to in subsection (4) above they shall be treated as incurred immediately after that period expires.

(6) In this section "the incidental costs of obtaining finance" means expenditure on fees, commissions, advertising, printing and other incidental matters (but not including stamp duty), being expenditure wholly and exclusively incurred for the purpose of obtaining the finance (whether or not it is in fact obtained), or of providing security for it or of repaying it.

(7) This section shall not be construed as affording relief—

    (*a*) for any sums paid in consequence of, or for obtaining protection against, losses resulting from changes in the rate of exchange between different currencies; or

    (*b*) for the cost of repaying a loan or loan stock or a qualifying security so far as attributable to its being repayable at a premium or to its having been obtained or issued at a discount.

[(8) This section shall not apply for the purposes of corporation tax.][1]

Commentary—*Simon's Direct Tax Service* B3.1321; D2.215.
Revenue Interpretation RI 13—Premiums on life insurance policy taken out for obtaining loan are not "incidental costs" within this section.
RI 150—Considers *timing* of deductions under this section; deduction for incidental costs is due at same time as any other deduction in computing Schedule D Case I and II profits.
Simon's Tax Cases—s 77(6), *Focus Dynamics plc (formerly Eurovein plc) v Turner* [1999] STC (SCD) 71; *Cadbury Schweppes plc v Williams (Insp of Taxes)* [2002] STC(SCD) 115.
Definitions—"Company", s 832(1), (2); "interest", s 832(1); "Schedule D", s 18(1); "tax", s 832(3).
Amendments—[1] Sub-s (8) inserted by FA 1996 ss 104, 105, Sch 14 para 9 with effect for accounting periods ending after 31 March 1996, subject to transitional provisions in FA 1996 Sch 15.
[2] Word in sub-ss (1), (2)(*a*)(i) substituted by FA 1998 Sch 7 para 1 with effect from 31 July 1998.
[3] Sub-s (2)(*a*)(ii) and preceding word "or" repealed by FA 2002 ss 82, 141, Sch 25 paras 43, 44, Sch 40 Pt 3(12) with effect for accounting periods beginning after 30 September 2002.

78 Discounted bills of exchange

Amendments—[1] This section repealed by FA 1996 ss 104, 105, Sch 14 para 10, Sch 41 Pt V(3) with effect for accounting periods ending after 31 March 1996 except in relation to bills of exchange drawn before 1 April 1996 and subject to transitional provisions in FA 1996 Sch 15. Note that where any bill so drawn is paid on or after 1 April 1996: (*a*) the amount which subsection (2) above provides to be treated as a deduction against total profits and as a charge on income shall (instead of being so treated) be brought into account for the purposes of FA 1996 Part IV Chapter II as a non-trading debit; and (*b*) that amount shall be the only amount brought into account for the purposes of FA 1996 Part IV Chapter II in respect of the discount in question.

79 Contributions to local enterprise agencies

(1) Notwithstanding anything in section 74, but subject to the provisions of this section, where a person carrying on a trade, profession or vocation makes any contribution (whether in cash or in kind) to an approved local enterprise agency, any expenditure incurred by him in making the contribution may be deducted as an expense in computing the [profits][1] of the trade, profession or vocation for the purposes of tax if it would not otherwise be so deductible.

(2) Where any such contribution is made by an investment company any expenditure allowable as a deduction under subsection (1) above shall for the purposes of section 75 be treated as expenses of management.

(3) Subsection (1) above does not apply in relation to a contribution made by any person if either he or any person connected with him receives or is entitled to receive a benefit of any kind whatsoever for or in connection with the making of that contribution, whether from the agency concerned or from any other person.

(4) In this section "approved local enterprise agency" means a body approved by the Secretary of State for the purposes of this section; but he shall not so approve a body unless he is satisfied that—

    (*a*) its sole objective is the promotion or encouragement of industrial and commercial activity or enterprise in a particular area in the United Kingdom with particular reference to encouraging the formation and development of small businesses; or

    (*b*) one of its principal objectives is that set out in paragraph (*a*) above and it maintains or is about to maintain a fund separate from its other funds which is or is to be applied solely in pursuance of that objective;

and where the Secretary of State approves a body by virtue of paragraph (*b*) above, the approval shall specify the fund concerned and, in relation to a body so approved, any reference in this section to a contribution is a reference to a contribution which is made wholly to or for the purposes of that fund.

(5) A body may be approved under subsection (4) above whether or not it is a body corporate or a body of trustees or any other association or organisation and whether or not it is described as a local enterprise agency.

(6) A body may not be approved under subsection (4) above unless it is precluded, by virtue of any enactment, contractual obligation, memorandum or otherwise, from making any direct or indirect payment or transfer to any of its members, or to any person charged with the control and direction of its affairs, of any of its income or profit by way of dividend, gift, division, bonus or otherwise howsoever by way of profit.

(7) For the purposes of subsection (6) above, the payment—

(a) of reasonable remuneration for goods, labour or power supplied or for services rendered, or

(b) of reasonable interest for money lent, or

(c) of reasonable rent for any premises,

does not constitute a payment or transfer which is required to be so precluded.

(8) Any approval given by the Secretary of State may be made conditional upon compliance with such requirements as to accounts, provision of information and other matters as he considers appropriate; and if it appears to the Secretary of State that—

(a) an approved local enterprise agency is not complying with any such requirement, or

(b) one or other of the conditions for his approval contained in subsection (4) above or the precondition for his approval in subsection (6) above has ceased to be fulfilled with respect to an approved local enterprise agency,

he shall by notice withdraw his approval from the body concerned with effect from such date as he may specify in the notice (which may be a date earlier than the date on which the notice is given).

(9) In any case where—

(a) a contribution has been made to an approved local enterprise agency in respect of which relief has been given under subsection (1) above, and

(b) any benefit received in any chargeable period by the contributor or any person connected with him is in any way attributable to that contribution,

the contributor shall in respect of that chargeable period be charged to tax under Case I or Case II of Schedule D or, if he is not chargeable to tax under either of those Cases for that period, under Case VI of Schedule D on an amount equal to the value of that benefit.

(10) Section 839 applies for the purposes of subsections (3) and (9) above.

(11) This section applies to contributions made on or after 1st April 1982 *and before 1st April 2000*[2].

Commentary—*Simon's Direct Tax Service* **B3.1444.**
Definitions—''Chargeable period'', s 832(1); ''control'', s 840; ''interest'', s 832(1); ''Schedule D'', s 18(1); ''tax'', s 832(3); ''trade'', s 832(1); ''United Kingdom'', s 830(1).
Cross references—See the National Assembly for Wales (Transfer of Functions) Order, SI 1999/672 art 2, Sch 1 (functions exercisable under this section by a Minister of the Crown shall, so far as exercisable in relation to Wales, be exercisable by the National Assembly for Wales concurrently with the Minister with effect from 1 July 1999).
Amendments—[1] Word in sub-s (1) substituted by FA 1998 Sch 7 para 1 with effect from 31 July 1998.
[2] Words in sub-s (11) repealed by FA 2000 ss 88, 156, Sch 40 Pt II(9) with effect from 28 July 2000.

[79A Contributions to training and enterprise councils and local enterprise companies

(1) Notwithstanding anything in section 74, but subject to the provisions of this section, where a person carrying on a trade, profession or vocation makes any contribution (whether in cash or in kind) to a training and enterprise council [business link organisation][2] or a local enterprise company, any expenditure incurred by him in making the contribution may be deducted as an expense in computing the [profits][4] of the trade, profession or vocation for the purposes of tax if it would not otherwise be so deductible.

(2) Where any such contribution is made by an investment company any expenditure allowable as a deduction under subsection (1) above shall for the purposes of section 75 be treated as expenses of management.

(3) Subsection (1) above does not apply in relation to a contribution made by any person if either he or any person connected with him receives or is entitled to receive a benefit of any kind whatsoever for or in connection with the making of that contribution, whether from the council [organisation][2] or company concerned or from any other person.

(4) In any case where—

(a) relief has been given under subsection (1) above in respect of a contribution, and

(b) any benefit received in any chargeable period by the contributor or any person connected with him is in any way attributable to that contribution,

the contributor shall in respect of that chargeable period be charged to tax under Case I or Case II of Schedule D or, if he is not chargeable to tax under either of those Cases for that period, under Case VI of Schedule D on an amount equal to the value of that benefit.

(5) In this section—

TA 1988

[(*aa*) "business link organisation" means any person authorised by or on behalf of the Secretary of State to use a service mark (within the meaning of the Trade Marks (Amendment) Act 1984) designated by the Secretary of State for the purposes of this paragraph][3]

(*a*) "training and enterprise council" means a body with which the Secretary of State has made an agreement (not being one which has terminated) under which it is agreed that the body shall carry out the functions of a training and enterprise council, and

(*b*) "local enterprise company" means a company with which an agreement (not being one which has terminated) under which it is agreed that the company shall carry out the functions of a local enterprise company has been made by the *Scottish Development Agency, the Highlands and Islands Development Board,*[5] Scottish Enterprise or Highlands and Islands Enterprise.

(6) Section 839 applies for the purposes of subsections (3) and (4) above.

(7) This section applies to contributions made on or after 1st April 1990 [or, in the case of a contribution to a business link organisation, 30th November 1993][2] *and before 1st April 2000*[5].]¹

Commentary—*Simon's Direct Tax Service* B3.1444.
Definitions—"Chargeable period", s 832(1); "Schedule D", s 18(1); "tax", s 832(3); "trade", s 832(1).
Amendments—¹ This section inserted by FA 1990 s 76.
² Words in sub-ss (1), (3), (7) inserted by FA 1994 s 145(2), (3), (5).
³ Sub-s (5)(*aa*) inserted by FA 1994 s 145(2), (4).
⁴ Word in sub-s (1) substituted by FA 1998 Sch 7 para 1 with effect from 31 July 1998.
⁵ Words in sub-ss (5)(*b*), (7) repealed by FA 2000 ss 88, 156, Sch 40 Pt II(9) with effect from 28 July 2000.

80 Expenses connected with foreign trades etc

(1) This section applies in the case of a trade, profession or vocation carried on wholly outside the United Kingdom by an individual ("the taxpayer") who does not satisfy the Board as mentioned in section 65(4); and it is immaterial in the case of a trade or profession whether the taxpayer carries it on solely or in partnership.

(2) Expenses of the taxpayer—

(*a*) in travelling from any place in the United Kingdom to any place where the trade, profession or vocation is carried on;

(*b*) in travelling to any place in the United Kingdom from any place where the trade, profession or vocation is carried on; or

(*c*) on board and lodging for the taxpayer at any place where the trade, profession or vocation is carried on;

shall, subject to subsections (3) and (4) below, be treated for the purposes of section 74(*a*) as having been wholly and exclusively expended for the purposes of the trade, profession or vocation.

(3) Subsection (2) above does not apply unless the taxpayer's absence from the United Kingdom is occasioned wholly and exclusively for the purpose of performing the functions of the trade, profession or vocation or of performing those functions and the functions of any other trade, profession or vocation (whether or not one in the case of which this section applies).

(4) Where subsection (2) above applies and more than one trade, profession or vocation in the case of which this section applies is carried on at the place in question, the expenses shall be apportioned on such basis as is reasonable between those trades, professions or vocations; and the expenses so apportioned to a particular trade, profession or vocation shall be treated for the purposes of section 74(*a*) as having been wholly and exclusively expended for the purposes of that trade, profession or vocation.

(5) Where the taxpayer is absent from the United Kingdom for a continuous period of 60 days or more wholly and exclusively for the purpose of performing the functions of one or more trades, professions or vocations in the case of which this section applies, expenses to which subsection (6) below applies shall be treated in accordance with subsection (7) or (8) below (as the case may be).

(6) This subsection applies to the expenses of any journey by the taxpayer's spouse, or any child of his, between any place in the United Kingdom and the place of performance of any of those functions outside the United Kingdom, if the journey—

(*a*) is made in order to accompany him at the beginning of the period of absence or to visit him during that period; or

(*b*) is a return journey following a journey falling within paragraph (*a*) above;

but this subsection does not apply to more than two outward and two return journeys by the same person in any year of assessment.

(7) The expenses shall be treated for the purposes of section 74(*a*) as having been wholly and exclusively expended for the purposes of the trade, profession or vocation concerned (if there is only one).

(8) The expenses shall be apportioned on such basis as is reasonable between the trades, professions or vocations concerned (if there is more than one) and the expenses so apportioned to a particular trade, profession or vocation shall be treated for the purposes of section 74(*a*) as having been wholly and exclusively expended for the purposes of that trade, profession or vocation.

(9) In subsection (6) above "child" includes a stepchild and an illegitimate child but does not include a person who is aged 18 or over at the beginning of the outward journey.

(10) Nothing in this section shall permit the same sum to be deducted for more than one trade, profession or vocation in respect of expenses in computing [profits][1].

Commentary—*Simon's Direct Tax Service* **B3.103.**
Definitions—"The Board", s 832(1); "trade", s 832(1); "United Kingdom", s 830(1); "year of assessment", s 832(1).
Cross reference—See TA 1988 s 65A(2) (this section to be disregarded in computing the amount of profit or gains of a Schedule A business).
Amendments—[1] Word in sub-s (10) substituted by FA 1998 Sch 7 para 1 with effect from 31 July 1998.

81 Travel between trades etc

(1) Where a taxpayer (within the meaning of section 80) travels between a place where he carries on a trade, profession or vocation in the case of which section 80 applies and a place outside the United Kingdom where he carries on another trade, profession or vocation (whether or not one in the case of which that section applies) expenses of the taxpayer on such travel shall, subject to subsections (3) to (5) below, be treated for the purposes of section 74(a) as having been wholly and exclusively expended for the purposes of the trade, profession or vocation mentioned in subsection (2) below.

(2) The trade, profession or vocation is—

(a) the one carried on at the place of the taxpayer's destination; or
(b) if that trade, profession or vocation is not one in the case of which section 80 applies, the one carried on at the place of his departure.

(3) This section does not apply unless the journey was made—

(a) after performing functions of the trade, profession or vocation carried on at the place of departure; and
(b) for the purpose of performing functions of the trade, profession or vocation carried on at the place of destination.

(4) This section does not apply unless the taxpayer's absence from the United Kingdom is occasioned wholly and exclusively for the purpose of performing the functions of both the trades, professions or vocations concerned or of performing those functions and the functions of any other trade, profession or vocation.

(5) Where this section applies and more than one trade, profession or vocation in the case of which section 80 applies is carried on at the place of the taxpayer's destination or (in a case falling within subsection (2)(b) above) at the place of his departure, the expenses shall be apportioned on such basis as is reasonable between those trades, professions or vocations; and the expenses so apportioned to a particular trade, profession or vocation shall be treated for the purposes of section 74(a) as having been wholly and exclusively expended for the purposes of that trade, profession or vocation.

(6) Nothing in this section shall permit the same sum to be deducted for more than one trade, profession or vocation in respect of expenses in computing profits or gains.

Commentary—*Simon's Direct Tax Service* **B3.103.**
Definitions—"Profits or gains", s 833(1); "trade", s 832(1); "United Kingdom", s 830(1).
Cross reference—See TA 1988 s 65A(2) (this section to be disregarded in computing the amount of profit or gains of a Schedule A business).

82 Interest paid to non-residents

(1) In computing the [profits][2] arising from a trade, profession or vocation, no sum shall be deducted in respect of any annual interest paid to a person not resident in the United Kingdom unless—

(a) the person making the payment has deducted income tax from the payment in accordance with section 349(2) and accounts for the tax so deducted, or
(b) the conditions set out in subsection (2) below are satisfied.

(2) The conditions referred to in subsection (1)(b) above are as follows—

(a) that the trade, profession or vocation is carried on by a person residing in the United Kingdom, and
(b) that the liability to pay the interest was incurred exclusively for the purposes of the trade, profession or vocation, and
(c) that either—

(i) the liability to pay the interest was incurred wholly or mainly for the purposes of activities of the trade, profession or vocation carried on outside the United Kingdom, or
(ii) the interest is payable in a currency other than sterling, and

(d) that, under the terms of the contract under which the interest is payable, the interest is to be paid, or may be required to be paid, outside the United Kingdom, and
(e) that the interest is in fact paid outside the United Kingdom.

(3) Where the trade, profession or vocation is carried on by a partnership, subsection (1)(b) above shall not apply to any interest which is payable to any of the partners, or is payable in respect of the share of any partner in the partnership capital.

(4) Subsection (1)(b) above shall not apply where—

(a) the trade, profession or vocation is carried on by a body of persons over whom the person entitled to the interest has control; or (*b*) the person entitled to the interest is a body of persons over whom the person carrying on the trade, profession or vocation has control; or

(*c*) the person carrying on the trade, profession or vocation and the person entitled to the interest are both bodies of persons and some other person has control over both of them.

In this subsection, the references to a body of persons include references to a partnership, and ''control'' has the meaning given by section 840.

(5) If interest paid under deduction of tax in accordance with section 349(2) is deductible in computing the [profits][2] of a trade, profession or vocation the amount so deductible shall be the gross amount.

(6) This section does not apply for the purposes of corporation tax.[...][1]

Commentary—*Simon's Direct Tax Service* A4.332; B3.1324.
Definitions—''Body of persons'', s 832(1); ''income tax'', s 832(4); ''interest'', s 832(1); ''tax'', s 832(3); ''trade'', s 832(1); ''United Kingdom'', s 830(1).
Amendments—[1] Words in sub-s (6) added by FA 1995 s 39(4), (5), Sch 6 para 13, with effect from the year 1995–96 ; however, the amendment did not apply to certain sources of income which ceased during the year 1995–96 (see FA 1995 s 39(5)). These words repealed by FA 1998 s 165, Sch 27 Part III(4) with effect from the year 1998–99 for income tax purposes, and from 1 April 1998 for corporation tax purposes, subject to the transitional provisions in FA 1998 Sch 5 Part IV.
[2] Word in sub-ss (1), (5) substituted by FA 1998 Sch 7 para 1 with effect from 31 July 1998.

[82A Expenditure on research and development

(1) Notwithstanding anything in section 74, where a person carrying on a trade incurs expenditure not of a capital nature on research and development—

(*a*) related to that trade, and

(*b*) directly undertaken by him or on his behalf,

the expenditure incurred may be deducted as an expense in computing the profits of the trade for the purposes of tax.

(2) For this purpose expenditure on research and development does not include expenditure incurred in the acquisition of rights in, or arising out of, research and development.

Subject to that, it includes all expenditure incurred in carrying out, or providing facilities for carrying out, research and development.

(3) The reference in subsection (1) above to research and development related to a trade includes—

(*a*) research and development which may lead to or facilitate an extension of that trade;

(*b*) research and development of a medical nature which has a special relation to the welfare of workers employed in that trade.

(4) The same expenditure may not be taken into account under this section in relation to more than one trade.

(5) In this section ''research and development'' has the meaning given by section 837A and includes oil and gas exploration and appraisal.][1]

Commentary—*Simon's Direct Tax Service* B3.1421.
Amendments—[1] This section inserted by FA 2000 s 68, Sch 19 para 5(1) with effect for the purposes of income tax and capital gains tax from the year 2000–01 and for the purposes of corporation tax, for accounting periods ending after 31 March 2000.

[82B Payments to research associations, universities etc

(1) Notwithstanding anything in section 74, where a person carrying on a trade—

(*a*) pays any sum to a scientific research association that—

(i) has as its object the undertaking of scientific research related to the class of trade to which the trade he is carrying on belongs, and

(ii) is for the time being approved for the purposes of this section by the Secretary of State, or

(*b*) pays any sum to be used for such scientific research as is mentioned in paragraph (*a*) above to any such university, college research institute or other similar institution as is for the time being approved for the purposes of this section by the Secretary of State,

the sum paid may be deducted as an expense in computing the profits of the trade for the purposes of tax.

(2) In this section ''scientific research'' means any activities in the fields of natural or applied science for the extension of knowledge.

(3) The reference in this section to scientific research related to a class of trade includes—

(*a*) scientific research which may lead to or facilitate an extension of trades of that class;

(*b*) scientific research of a medical nature which has a special relation to the welfare of workers employed in trades of that class.

(4) If a question arises under this section whether, or to what extent, any activities constitute or constituted scientific research, the Board shall refer the question for decision to the Secretary of State.

The decision of the Secretary of State is final.

(5) The same expenditure may not be taken into account under this section in relation to more than one trade.][1]

Commentary—*Simon's Direct Tax Service* **B3.1422**.
Amendments—[1] This section inserted by FA 2000 s 68, Sch 19 para 5(1) with effect for the purposes of income tax and capital gains tax from the year 2000–01 and for the purposes of corporation tax, for accounting periods ending after 31 March 2000.

83 Patent fees etc and expenses

Notwithstanding anything in section 74, in computing the [profits][3] of a trade there may be deducted as expenses any fees paid or expenses incurred—

    (*a*) in obtaining for the purposes of the trade the grant of a patent, an extension of the term of a patent, the registration of a design or trade mark, [an extension of the period for which the right in a registered design subsists][1] or the renewal of registration of a trade mark, or
    (*b*) in connection with a rejected or abandoned application for a patent made for the purposes of the trade.

...[2]

Commentary—*Simon's Direct Tax Service* **B2.609**.
Definitions—"trade", s 832(1).
Cross reference—See TA 1988 s 526 (relief for patent expenses incurred otherwise than for purposes of trade).
Amendments—[1] Words in para (*a*) substituted by the Copyright, Designs and Patents Act 1988 Sch 7 para 36(1), (2) with effect from 1 August 1989 by virtue of the Copyright, Designs and Patents Act 1988 (Commencement No 1) Order 1989, SI 1989/816.
[2] Words repealed by the Trade Marks Act 1994 s 106(2), Sch 5, with effect from 31 October 1994, by virtue of the Trade Marks Act 1994 (Commencement) Order 1994, SI 1994/2550.
[3] Word substituted by FA 1998 Sch 7 para 1 with effect from 31 July 1998.

[83A Gifts in kind to charities etc

(1) This section applies where a person carrying on a trade, profession or vocation gives an article falling within subsection (2) below to—

    (*a*) a charity within the meaning of section 506, or
    (*b*) a body listed in section 507(1).

(2) An article falls within this subsection if—

    (*a*) it is an article manufactured, or of a class or description sold, by the donor in the course of his trade; ...[2]
    (*b*) ...[2]

(3) Subject to subsection (4) below, where this section applies in the case of the gift of an article—

    (*a*) no amount shall be required, in consequence of the donor's disposal of that article from trading stock, to be brought into account for the purposes of the Tax Acts as a trading receipt of the donor; ...[2]
    (*b*) ...[2]

(4) In any case where—

    (*a*) relief is given under subsection (3) above in respect of the gift of an article, and
    (*b*) any benefit received in any chargeable period by the donor or any person connected with him is in any way attributable to the making of that gift,

the donor shall in respect of that chargeable period be charged to tax under Case I or Case II of Schedule D or, if he is not chargeable to tax under either of those Cases for that period, under Case VI of Schedule D on an amount equal to the value of that benefit.

(5) Section 839 applies for the purposes of this section.][1]

Commentary—*Simon's Direct Tax Service* **B3.1445A**.
Cross-references—See FA 2002 Sch 18 para 9(3) (relief for donors in relation to community amateur sports clubs; this section has effect as if a registered club were a charity)
Amendments—[1] This section inserted by FA 1999 s 55(1), (3) with effect for gifts made on or after 27 July 1999.
[2] Word "or", and sub-ss (2)(*b*), (3)(*b*) repealed by CAA 2001 ss 578, 580, Sch 2 para 16, Sch 4 with effect for income tax purposes, as respects allowances and charges falling to be made for chargeable periods ending after 5 April 2001, and for corporation tax purposes, as respects allowances and charges falling to be made for chargeable periods ending after 31 March 2001.

[84 Gifts to educational establishments

(1) This section applies where a person carrying on a trade, profession or vocation ("the donor") makes a gift for the purposes of a designated educational establishment of—

    (*a*) an article manufactured, or of a class or description sold, by the donor in the course of his trade which qualifies as [plant or machinery][4] in the hands of the educational establishment; ...[5]
    (*b*) ...[5]

(2) For the purposes of this section, an article "[qualifies as plant or machinery][4] in the hands of an educational establishment" if, and only if, it is an article such that—

    (*a*) were the activities carried on by the educational establishment regarded as a trade carried on by a body of persons, and
    (*b*) had that body, at the time of the gift, incurred capital expenditure wholly and exclusively on the provision of an identical article for the purposes of those activities, and

(c) had the identical article belonged to that body in consequence of the incurring of that expenditure,

the identical article would be regarded for the purposes of [Part II of the Capital Allowances Act as plant or machinery]⁴ provided by the body for the purposes of that trade.

(3) Where this section applies—

(a) if the gift is of an article falling within paragraph (a) of subsection (1) above, then, for the purposes of the Tax Acts, no amount shall be required to be brought into account as a trading receipt of the donor in consequence of his disposal of that article from trading stock; ...⁵

(b) ...⁵

but this subsection shall not apply unless, within [the period specified in subsection (3A) below]², the donor makes a claim for relief under this subsection, specifying the article given and the name of the educational establishment in question.

[(3A) The period mentioned in subsection (3) above is—

(a) in the case of a claim with respect to income tax, the period ending with the first anniversary of the 31st January next following the year of assessment in whose basis period the gift is made;

(b) in the case of a claim with respect to corporation tax, the period of two years beginning at the end of the accounting period in which the gift is made.]³

[(3B) In paragraph (a) of subsection (3A) above "basis period" means—

(a) in relation to a year of assessment for which a basis period is given by sections 60 to 63, that basis period,

(b) in relation to a year of assessment for which no basis period is given by those sections, the year of assessment.]³

(4) In any case where—

(a) relief is given under subsection (3) above [or section 63(2) of the Capital Allowances Act]⁴ in respect of the gift of an article, and

(b) any benefit received in any chargeable period by the donor or any person connected with him is in any way attributable to the making of that gift,

the donor shall in respect of that chargeable period be charged to tax under Case I or Case II of Schedule D or, if he is not chargeable to tax under either of those Cases for that period, under Case VI of Schedule D on an amount equal to the value of that benefit.

(5) In this section "designated educational establishment" means any educational establishment designated, or of a category designated,—

(a) as respects Great Britain, in regulations made by the Secretary of State; or

(b) as respects Northern Ireland, in regulations made by the Department of Education for Northern Ireland;

and any such regulations may make different provision for different areas.

(6) If any question arises as to whether a particular establishment falls within a category designated in regulations under subsection (5) above, the Board shall refer the question for decision—

(a) in the case of an establishment in Great Britain, to the Secretary of State, or

(b) in the case of an establishment in Northern Ireland, to the Department of Education for Northern Ireland.

(7) The power of the Secretary of State to make regulations under subsection (5) above shall be exercisable by statutory instrument; and a statutory instrument containing any such regulations shall be subject to annulment in pursuance of a resolution of the House of Commons.

(8) Regulations made under subsection (5) above for Northern Ireland—

(a) shall be a statutory rule for the purposes of the Statutory Rules (Northern Ireland) Order 1979; and

(b) shall be subject to negative resolution within the meaning of section 41(6) of the Interpretation Act (Northern Ireland) 1954.

(9) Section 839 applies for the purposes of subsection (4) above.]¹

Commentary—*Simon's Direct Tax Service* **B3.1445.**
Regulations—Taxes (Relief for Gifts) (Designated Educational Establishments) Regulations, SI 1992/42.
Revenue Interpretation RI 151—considers donations of trading stock to charities.
Revenue Internal Guidance—Share Schemes Manual SSM 2.7 (costs of setting up a scheme are not allowable if options are granted or shares transferred before the date of scheme approval).
Definitions—"The 1990 Act", s 831(3); "accounting period", s 834(1);"connected", s 839; "Schedule D", s 18(1); "tax", s 832(3); "Tax Acts", s 831(2); "trade", s 832(1) "year of assessment", s 832(1).
Cross references—See the National Assembly for Wales (Transfer of Functions) Order, SI 1999/672 art 2, Sch 1 (functions exercisable under this section by a Minister of the Crown shall, so far as exercisable in relation to Wales, be exercisable by the National Assembly for Wales concurrently with the Minister with effect from 1 July 1999).
Amendments—¹ This section substituted by FA 1991 s 68 with respect to gifts made after 18 March 1991.
² Words in sub-s (3) substituted (for words "two years of making the gift") by FA 1996 s 135, Sch 21, para 2(2) with effect as respects income tax from the year 1996–97 and, as respects corporation tax, for accounting periods ending after 30 June 1999 (by virtue of Finance Act 1994, Section 199, (Appointed Day) Order, SI 1998/3173 art 2).
³ Sub-ss (3A), (3B) inserted by FA 1996 s 135, Sch 21 para 2(3) with effect as respects income tax from the year 1996–97 and, as respects corporation tax, for accounting periods ending on or after the appointed day under FA 1994 s 199 (1 July 1999).
⁴ Words in sub-ss (1), (2) substituted, and words in sub-s (4) inserted, by CAA 2001 s 578, Sch 2 para 17 with effect for income tax purposes, as respects allowances and charges falling to be made for chargeable periods ending after 5 April 2001, and for

corporation tax purposes, as respects allowances and charges falling to be made for chargeable periods ending after 31 March 2001.
[5] Sub-ss (1)(*b*), (3)(*b*), and words in sub-ss (1)(*a*), (3)(*a*) repealed by CAA 2001 ss 578, 580, Sch 2 para 17, Sch 4 with effect for income tax purposes, as respects allowances and charges falling to be made for chargeable periods ending after 5 April 2001, and for corporation tax purposes, as respects allowances and charges falling to be made for chargeable periods ending after 31 March 2001.

[84A Costs of establishing share option or profit sharing schemes: relief

(1) Subsection (2) below applies where—

(*a*) a company incurs expenditure on establishing a share option scheme which the Board approve and under which no employee or director obtains rights before such approval is given, or
(*b*) a company incurs expenditure on establishing a profit sharing scheme which the Board approve and under which the trustees acquire no shares before such approval is given.

(2) In such a case the expenditure—

(*a*) shall be deducted in computing for the purposes of Schedule D the [profits][2] of a trade carried on by the company, or
(*b*) if the company is an investment company or a company in the case of which section 75 applies by virtue of section 76, shall be treated as expenses of management.

(3) In a case where—

(*a*) subsection (2) above applies, and
(*b*) the approval is given after the end of the period of nine months beginning with the day following the end of the period of account in which the expenditure is incurred,

for the purpose of applying subsection (2) above the expenditure shall be treated as incurred in the period of account in which the approval is given (and not the period of account mentioned in paragraph (*b*) above).

(4) References in this section to approving are to approving under Schedule 9.

(5) This section applies where the expenditure is incurred on or after 1st April 1991.][1]

Commentary—*Simon's Direct Tax Service* **D2.269; E4.569, 580, 590.**
Definitions—"Board", s 832(1); "company", s 832(1), (2); "investment company", s 130; "profit sharing scheme", s 186; "Schedule D", s 18(1); "share option scheme", s 185; "trade", s 832(1).
Amendments—[1] This section inserted by FA 1991 s 42.
[2] Word in sub-s (2)(*a*) substituted by FA 1998 Sch 7 para 1 with effect from 31 July 1998.

85 Payments to trustees of approved profit sharing schemes

(1) Any sum expended in making a payment to the trustees of an approved profit sharing scheme by a company which is in relation to that scheme the grantor or a participating company—

(*a*) shall be deducted in computing for the purposes of Schedule D the [profits][1] of a trade carried on by that company; or
(*b*) if that company is an investment company or a company in the case of which section 75 applies by virtue of section 76, shall be treated as expenses of management,

if, and only if, one of the conditions in subsection (2) below is fulfilled.

(2) The conditions referred to in subsection (1) above are—

(*a*) that before the expiry of the relevant period the sum in question is applied by the trustees in the acquisition of shares for appropriation to individuals who are eligible to participate in the scheme by virtue of their being or having been employees or directors of the company making the payment; and
(*b*) that the sum is necessary to meet the reasonable expenses of the trustees in administering the scheme.

(3) For the purposes of subsection (2)(*a*) above "the relevant period" means the period of nine months beginning on the day following the end of the period of account in which the sum in question is charged as an expense of the company incurring the expenditure or such longer period as the Board may allow by notice given to that company.

(4) For the purposes of this section, the trustees of an approved profit sharing scheme shall be taken to apply sums paid to them in the order in which the sums are received by them.

(5) In this section—

"approved profit sharing scheme" means a profit sharing scheme approved under Schedule 9; and
"the grantor" and "participating company" have the meaning given by paragraph 1(3) and (4) of that Schedule.

Commentary—*Simon's Direct Tax Service* **D2.240, E4.569.**
Definitions—"Board", s 832(1); "company", s 832(1), (2); "investment company", s 130; "Schedule D", s 18(1); "trade", s 832(1).
Cross references—See FA 2000 s 50 (phasing out of relief for payments to trustees of profit sharing schemes).
Amendments—[1] Word in sub-s (1)(*a*) substituted by FA 1998 Sch 7 para 1 with effect from 31 July 1998.

[85A Costs of establishing employee share ownership trusts: relief

(1) Subsection (2) below applies where a company incurs expenditure on establishing a qualifying employee share ownership trust.

(2) In such a case the expenditure—

(*a*) shall be deducted in computing for the purposes of Schedule D the [profits][2] of a trade carried on by the company, or

(*b*) if the company is an investment company or a company in the case of which section 75 applies by virtue of section 76, shall be treated as expenses of management.

(3) In a case where—

(*a*) subsection (2) above applies, and

(*b*) the trust is established after the end of the period of nine months beginning with the day following the end of the period of account in which the expenditure is incurred,

for the purpose of applying subsection (2) above the expenditure shall be treated as incurred in the period of account in which the trust is established (and not the period of account mentioned in paragraph (*b*) above).

(4) In this section ''qualifying employee share ownership trust'' shall be construed in accordance with Schedule 5 to the Finance Act 1989.

(5) For the purposes of this section the trust is established when the deed under which it is established is executed.

(6) This section applies where the expenditure is incurred on or after 1st April 1991.][1]

Commentary—*Simon's Direct Tax Service* D2.241.
Definitions—''Company'', s 832(1), (2); ''investment company'', s 130; ''Schedule D'', s 18(1); ''trade'', s 832(1).
Cross reference—See FA 1989 s 67 (relief for company's contributions to qualifying employee share ownership trusts).
Amendments—[1] This section inserted by FA 1991 s 43 with effect for expenditure incurred after 31 March 1991.
[2] Word in sub-s (2)(*a*) substituted by FA 1998 Sch 7 para 1 with effect from 31 July 1998.

86 Employees seconded to charities and educational establishments

(1) If a person (''the employer'') carrying on a trade, profession, vocation or business for the purposes of which he employs a person (''the employee'') makes available to a charity, on a basis which is expressed and intended to be of a temporary nature, the services of the employee then, notwithstanding anything in section 74 or 75, any expenditure incurred (or disbursed) by the employer which is attributable to the employment of that employee shall continue to be deductible in the manner and to the like extent as if, during the time that his services are so made available to the charity, they continued to be available for the purposes of the employer's trade, business, profession or vocation.

(2) In subsection (1) above—

''charity'' has the same meaning as in section 506;

''deductible'' means deductible as an expense in computing the [profits][1] of the employer to be charged under Case I or II of Schedule D or, as the case may be, deductible as expenses of management for the purposes of section 75.

(3) With respect to expenditure attributable to the employment of a person on or after 26th November 1986 ...[2] this section shall have effect as if the references to a charity included references to any of the following bodies, that is to say—

[(*a*) in England and Wales, any body falling within subsection (4) below;

(*b*) in Scotland, any body falling within subsection (5) below;

(*c*) in Northern Ireland, any body falling within subsection (6) below; and][3]

(*d*) any other educational body which is for the time being approved for the purposes of this section by the Secretary of State or, in Northern Ireland, the Department of Education for Northern Ireland.

[(4) A body falls within this subsection if it is—

(*a*) a local education authority;

(*b*) an educational institution maintained by such an authority (including a grant-maintained school or a grant-maintained special school within the meaning of the Education Act 1996);

(*c*) an independent school, within the meaning of the Education Act 1996, whose registration under section 465 of that Act is final; or

(*d*) an institution within the further education sector, or the higher education sector, within the meaning of the Further and Higher Education Act 1992.

(5) A body falls within this subsection if it is—

(*a*) an education authority;

(*b*) an educational establishment managed by such an authority within the meaning of the Education (Scotland) Act 1980 (''the 1980 Act'');

(*c*) a public or grant-aided school within the meaning of the 1980 Act;

(*d*) a self-governing school within the meaning of the Self-Governing Schools etc (Scotland) Act 1989;

(*e*) an independent school within the meaning of the 1980 Act;

(*f*) a central institution within the meaning of the 1980 Act;

(*g*) an institution within the higher education sector within the meaning of section 56(2) of the Further and Higher Education (Scotland) Act 1992; or

(*h*) a college of further education within the meaning of section 36(1) of that Act.]

(6) A body falls within this subsection if it is—

(*a*) an education or library board within the meaning of the Education and Libraries (Northern Ireland) Order 1986;

(*b*) a college of education or a controlled, maintained, grant-maintained integrated, controlled integrated, voluntary or independent school within the meaning of that Order; or

(*c*) an institution of further education within the meaning of the Further Education (Northern Ireland) Order 1997.]³

Commentary—*Simon's Direct Tax Service* **B3.1203, 1424, 1441.**
Definitions— ''Schedule D'', s 18(1); ''trade'', s 832(1).
Amendments—¹ Word in sub-s (2) substituted by FA 1998 Sch 7 para 1 with effect from 31 July 1998.
² Words in sub-s (3) repealed by FA 1999 s 58(2), (5), Sch 20 Pt III(14) and deemed always to have had effect.
³ In sub-s (3) paras (*a*)–(*c*) substituted and sub-ss ss (4)–(6) inserted by FA 1999 s 58(3), (4), (6) with effect from the year 1999–00.

[86A Charitable donations: contributions to agent's expenses

(1) This section applies where—

(*a*) a person (the employer) is liable to make to any individual payments from which income tax falls to be deducted by virtue of section 203 and regulations under that section, and

(*b*) the employer withholds sums from those payments in accordance with a scheme falling within subsection (3) of section 202 and pays the sums to an agent (within the meaning of subsection (4)(*a*) of that section).

(2) Any relevant expenditure incurred by the employer on or after 16th March 1993—

(*a*) shall be deducted in computing for the purposes of Schedule D the [profits]² of a trade, profession or vocation carried on by the employer, or

(*b*) if the employer is an investment company or a company in the case of which section 75 applies by virtue of section 76, shall be treated as expenses of management.

(3) Relevant expenditure is expenditure incurred in making to the agent any payment in respect of expenses which have been or are to be incurred by the agent in connection with his functions under the scheme.]¹

Commentary—*Simon's Direct Tax Service* **E4.948.**
Definitions—''Investment company'', s 130; ''Schedule D'', s 18(1); ''trade'', s 832(1).
Amendments—¹ This section inserted by FA 1993 s 69 with effect for expenditure incurred after 15 March 1993.
² Word in sub-s (2)(*a*) substituted by FA 1998 Sch 7 para 1 with effect from 31 July 1998.

87 Taxable premiums etc

(1) This section applies where in relation to any land used in connection with a trade, profession or vocation—

[(*a*) any amount falls to be treated as a receipt of a Schedule A business by virtue of section 34 or 35, or

(*b*) any amount would fall to be so treated but for the operation of section 37(2) or (3);]³

and that amount is referred to below as ''the amount chargeable''.

(2) Subject to subsections (3) to (8) below, where—

(*a*) during any part of the relevant period the land in relation to which the amount chargeable arose is occupied by the person for the time being entitled to the lease as respects which it arose, and

(*b*) that occupation is for the purposes of a trade, profession or vocation carried on by him,

he shall be treated, in computing the [profits]⁵ of the trade, profession or vocation chargeable to tax under Case I or II of Schedule D, as paying in respect of that land rent for the period (in addition to any actual rent), becoming due from day to day, of an amount which bears to the amount chargeable the same proportion as that part of the relevant period bears to the whole.

(3) As respects any period during which a part only of the land in relation to which the amount chargeable arose is occupied as mentioned in subsection (2) above, that subsection shall apply as if the whole were so occupied, but the amount chargeable shall be treated as reduced by so much thereof as, on a just apportionment, is attributable to the remainder of the land.

(4) Where a person, although not in occupation of the land or any part of the land, deals with his interest in the land or that part as property employed for the purposes of a trade, profession or vocation carried on by him, subsections (2) and (3) above shall apply as if the land or part were occupied by him for those purposes.

(5) Where section 37(2) and (3) has effect in relation to a lease granted out of the interest referred to in subsection (4) above, subsections (5) and (6) of that section shall apply for modifying the operation of subsections (2) and (3) above as they apply for modifying the operation of subsection (4) of that section.

(6) In computing [profits][5] chargeable under Case I or II of Schedule D for any chargeable period, rent shall not by virtue of subsection (4) above be treated as paid by a person for any period in respect of land in so far as rent treated under section 37(4) as paid by him for that period in respect of the land has in any previous chargeable period been deducted, or falls in that chargeable period to be deducted under Part II.

(7) Where, in respect of expenditure on the acquisition of his interest in the land in relation to which the amount chargeable arose, a person has become entitled to an allowance under [Part 5 of the Capital Allowances Act in respect of expenditure falling within section 403 (mineral asset expenditure)][6] for any chargeable period, then—

    (a) if the allowance is in respect of the whole of the expenditure, no deduction shall be allowed him under this section for that or any subsequent chargeable period; or

    (b) if the allowance is in respect of part only of the expenditure ("the allowable part"), a deduction allowed him under this section for that or any subsequent chargeable period shall be the fraction—

$$\frac{A - B}{A}$$

of the amount which apart from this subsection would fall to be deducted, where—

    A is the whole of the expenditure, and

    B is the allowable part of the expenditure;

...[2].

(8) Where the amount chargeable arose under section 34(2) by reason of an obligation which included the carrying out of work in respect of which any capital allowance has fallen or will fall to be made, this section shall apply as if the obligation had not included the carrying out of that work and the amount chargeable had been calculated accordingly.

(9) In this section "the relevant period" means—

    (a) where the amount chargeable arose under section 34, the period treated in computing that amount as the duration of the lease;

    (b) where the amount chargeable arose under section 35, the period treated in computing that amount as the duration of the lease remaining at the date of the assignment.

(10) ...[4]

Commentary—*Simon's Direct Tax Service* A4.221–223; B3.1341, 1342.
Definitions—"The 1990 Act", s 831(3); "chargeable period", s 832(1); "interest", s 832(1); "Schedule A", s 15(1); "Schedule D", s 18(1); "tax", s 832(3); "trade", s 832(1).
Amendments—[1] Words in sub-s (7) substituted by CAA 1990 Sch 1 para 8(1), (5).
[2] Words in sub-s (7) repealed by CAA 1990 Sch 2.
[3] Sub-s (1)(a), (b) substituted by FA 1998 Sch 5 para 34 with effect from the year 1998–99 for income tax purposes, and from 1 April 1998 for corporation tax purposes, subject to the transitional provisions in FA 1998 Sch 5 Part IV.
[4] Sub-s (10) repealed by FA 1998 s 165, Sch 27 Part III with effect from the year 1998-99 for income tax purposes, and from 1 April 1998 for corporation tax purposes, subject to the transitional provisions in FA 1998 Sch 5 Part IV.
[5] Word in sub-ss (2), (6) substituted by FA 1998 Sch 7 para 1 with effect from 31 July 1998.
[6] Words in sub-s (7) substituted by CAA 2001 s 578, Sch 2 para 18 with effect for income tax purposes, as respects allowances and charges falling to be made for chargeable periods ending after 5 April 2001, and for corporation tax purposes, as respects allowances and charges falling to be made for chargeable periods ending after 31 March 2001.

88 Payments to Export Credits Guarantee Department

Any sums paid by a person to the Export Credits Guarantee Department under an agreement entered into under arrangements made by the Secretary of State in pursuance of section 11 of the Export Guarantees and Overseas Investment Act 1978 or with a view to entering into such an agreement, shall be included—

    (a) in the sums to be deducted in computing for the purposes of Case I or Case II of Schedule D the [profits][1] of any trade, profession or vocation carried on by that person; or

    (b) if that person is an investment company or a company in the case of which section 75 applies by virtue of section 76, in the sums to be deducted as expenses of management in computing the company's profits for the purposes of corporation tax;

whether or not they would fall to be so included apart from this section.

Commentary—*Simon's Direct Tax Service* D4.408, 504.
Simon's Tax Cases—*Nunn v Gray* [1997] STC (SCD) 175.
Definitions—"Company", s 832(1), (2); "Schedule D", s 18(1); "trade", s 832(1).
Amendments—[1] Word substituted by FA 1998 Sch 7 para 1 with effect from 31 July 1998.

88A Debts of overseas governments etc

Commentary—*Simon's Direct Tax Service* B3.1113.
Amendments—This section (inserted by FA 1990 s 74) repealed by FA 1996 ss 104, 105, Sch 41 Pt V(3) with effect for accounting periods ending after 31 March 1996, subject to transitional provisions in FA 1996 Sch 15.

88B Section 88A debts: restriction on deductions under section 74(j)

Commentary—*Simon's Direct Tax Service* B3.1113.
Amendments—This section (inserted by FA 1990 s 74) repealed by FA 1996 ss 104, 105, Sch 41 Pt V(3) with effect for accounting periods ending after 31 March 1996, subject to transitional provisions in FA 1996 Sch 15.

88C Section 88A debts: restriction on other deductions

Commentary—*Simon's Direct Tax Service* **B3.1113**.
Amendments—This section (inserted by FA 1990 s 74) repealed by FA 1996 ss 104, 105, Sch 41 Pt V(3) with effect for accounting periods ending after 31 March 1996, subject to transitional provisions in FA 1996 Sch 15.

89 Debts proving irrecoverable after event treated as discontinuance

Where section 113 or 337(1) applies to treat a trade, profession or vocation as discontinued by reason of any event, then, in computing for tax purposes the [profits][1] of the trade, profession or vocation in any period after the event, there may be deducted a sum equal to any amount proved during that period to be irrecoverable in respect of any debts credited in computing for tax purposes the [profits][1] for any period before the event (being debts the benefit of which was assigned to the persons carrying on the trade, profession or vocation after the event) in so far as the total amount proved to be irrecoverable in respect of those debts exceeds any deduction allowed in respect of them under section 74(*j*) in a computation for any period before the event.

Commentary—*Simon's Direct Tax Service* **E5.336**.
Definitions—"tax", s 832(3); "trade", s 832(1).
Amendments—[1] Word substituted by FA 1998 Sch 7 para 1 with effect from 31 July 1998.

90 Additional payments to redundant employees

(1) Where a payment is made by way of addition to a redundancy payment or to the corresponding amount of any other employer's payment and the additional payment would be—

    (*a*) allowable as a deduction in computing for the purposes of Schedule D the [profits][1] or losses of a trade, profession or vocation; or
    (*b*) eligible for relief under section 75 or 76 as expenses of management of a business,

but for the permanent discontinuance of the trade, profession, vocation or business, the additional payment shall, subject to subsection (2) below, be so allowable or so eligible notwithstanding that discontinuance and, if made after the discontinuance, shall be treated as made on the last day on which the trade, profession, vocation or business was carried on.

(2) Subsection (1) above applies to an additional payment only so far as it does not exceed three times the amount of the redundancy payment or of the corresponding amount of the other employer's payment.

(3) In this section references to the permanent discontinuance of a trade, profession, vocation or business include references to any occasion on which it is treated as permanently discontinued by virtue of section 113(1) or 337(1).

(4) In this section references to a redundancy payment or to the corresponding amount of an employer's payment shall be construed as in sections 579 and 580.

Commentary—*Simon's Direct Tax Service* **B3.1477**.
Revenue Interpretation RI 103—Timing of deductions for redundancy payments.
Revenue Interpretation RI 200—Deduction to be allowed for certain severance payments made on cessation of trade under pre-existing contractual or statutory obligations to employees taken on for the purposes of the trade.
Statement of Practice SP 11/81—Relief for additional redundancy payments on partial discontinuance of trade if the payments satisfy the test in s 74(*b*) of this Act.
Definitions—"Schedule D", s 18(1); "trade", s 832(1).
Amendments—[1] Word substituted by FA 1998 Sch 7 para 1 with effect from 31 July 1998.

91 Cemeteries

(1) In computing the [profits][1] or losses for any period of a trade which consists of or includes the carrying on of a cemetery, there shall be allowed as a deduction—

    (*a*) any capital expenditure incurred by the person engaged in carrying on the trade in providing any land in the cemetery sold during that period for the purpose of interments, and
    (*b*) the appropriate fraction of the residue at the end of that period of the relevant capital expenditure.

(2) Subject to subsection (3) below, the relevant capital expenditure is capital expenditure incurred for the purposes of the trade in question by the person engaged in carrying it on, being—

    (*a*) expenditure on any building or structure other than a dwelling-house, being a building or structure in the cemetery likely to have little or no value when the cemetery is full; and
    (*b*) expenditure incurred in providing land taken up by any such building or structure, and any other land in the cemetery not suitable or adaptable for use for interments and likely to have little or no value when the cemetery is full.

(3) Relevant capital expenditure—

    (*a*) does not include expenditure incurred on buildings or structures which have been destroyed before the beginning of the first period to which subsection (1) above applies in the case of the trade in question; and (*b*) of other expenditure incurred before that time, includes only the fraction—

$$\frac{A}{A + B}$$

where—

A is the number of grave-spaces which at that time were or could have been made available in the cemetery for sale, and
B is the number already sold.

(4) For the purposes of this section—

(*a*) the residue of any expenditure at the end of a period is the amount incurred before that time which remains after deducting—

(i) any amount allowed in respect of that expenditure under subsection (1)(*b*) above in computing the [profits][1] or losses of the trade for any previous period, and
(ii) if, after the beginning of the first period to which subsection (1) above applies in the case of a trade and before the end of the period mentioned at the beginning of this subsection, any asset representing that expenditure is sold or destroyed, the net proceeds of sale or, as the case may be, any insurance money or other compensation of any description received by the person carrying on the trade in respect of the destruction and any money received by him for the remains of the asset; and

(*b*) the appropriate fraction of the residue of any expenditure at the end of any period is—

$$\frac{A}{A + B}$$

where—

A is the number of grave-spaces in the cemetery sold in the period, and
B is the number of grave-spaces which at the end of the period are or could be made available in the cemetery for sale.

(5) Where in any chargeable period there is a change in the persons engaged in carrying on a trade which consists of or includes the carrying on of a cemetery, any allowance to be made under this section to the persons carrying on the trade after the change shall, whether or not it is to be assumed for other purposes that the trade was discontinued and a new trade set up and commenced, be computed—

(*a*) as if they had at all times been engaged in carrying on the trade;
(*b*) as if everything done to or by any of their predecessors in carrying on the trade had been done to or by them; and
(*c*) without regard to the price paid on any sale on the occasion of any such change.

(6) No expenditure shall be taken into account under both paragraph (*a*) and paragraph (*b*) of subsection (1) above, whether for the same or different periods.

(7) This section shall apply in relation to a trade which consists of or includes the carrying on of a crematorium and, in connection therewith, the maintenance of memorial garden plots, as it applies in relation to a trade which consists of or includes the carrying on of a cemetery, but subject to the modifications that—

(*a*) references to the cemetery or land in the cemetery shall be taken as references to the land which is devoted wholly to memorial garden plots, and
(*b*) references to grave-spaces shall be taken as references to memorial garden plots, and
(*c*) references to the sale or use of land for interments shall be taken as references to its sale or use for memorial garden plots.

(8) In this section—

(*a*) references to the sale of land include references to the sale of a right of interment in land, and to the appropriation of part of a memorial garden in return for a dedication fee or similar payment;
(*b*) references to capital expenditure incurred in providing land shall be taken as references to the cost of purchase and to any capital expenditure incurred in levelling or draining it or otherwise rendering it suitable for the purposes of a cemetery or a memorial garden; and
(*c*) the reference in subsection (4)(*a*)(ii) to subsection (1) above includes a reference to section 141 of the 1970 Act and section 22 of the Finance Act 1952 (which made similar provision to that made by this section).

[(9) Section 532 of the Capital Allowances Act (general rule excluding contributions) shall apply for the purposes of this section as it applies for the purposes of that Act.][2]

Commentary—*Simon's Direct Tax Service* B3.1131, 1132.
Definitions—''The 1990 Act'', s 831(3); ''trade'', s 832(1).
Cross reference—See TCGA 1992 s 41(4)(*c*) (allowance under this section included as capital allowance by reference to which capital losses are restricted).
FA 1997 Sch 12 para 11(11), (12) (clawback of allowances in any case where an occasion occurs after 25 November 1996 on which a ''major lump sum''—see FA 1997 Sch 12 para 3(2)—falls to be paid in the case of the lease of an asset.
Amendments—[1] Word in sub-ss (1), (4)(*a*)(i) substituted by FA 1998 Sch 7 para 1 with effect from 31 July 1998.
[2] Sub-s (9) substituted by CAA 2001 s 578, Sch 2 para 19 with effect for income tax purposes, as respects allowances and charges falling to be made for chargeable periods ending after 5 April 2001, and for corporation tax purposes, as respects allowances and charges falling to be made for chargeable periods ending after 31 March 2001.

[91A Waste disposal: restoration payments

(1) This section applies where on or after 6th April 1989 a person makes a site restoration payment in the course of carrying on a trade.

(2) Subject to subsection (3) below, for the purposes of income tax or corporation tax the payment shall be allowed as a deduction in computing the [profits][5] of the trade for the period of account in which the payment is made.

(3) Subsection (2) above shall not apply to so much of the payment as—

(*a*) represents expenditure which has been allowed as a deduction in computing the [profits][5] of the trade for any period of account preceding the period of account in which the payment is made, or

(*b*) represents capital expenditure in respect of which an allowance has been, or may be, made under the enactments relating to capital allowances.

(4) For the purposes of this section a site restoration payment is a payment made—

(*a*) in connection with the restoration of a site or part of a site, and

(*b*) in order to comply with any condition of a relevant licence, or any condition imposed on the grant of planning permission to use the site for the carrying out of waste disposal activities, or [any relevant obligation][2].

(5) For the purposes of this section waste disposal activities are the collection, treatment, conversion and final depositing of waste materials, or any of those activities.

(6) For the purposes of this section a relevant licence is—

(*a*) a disposal licence under Part I of the Control of Pollution Act 1974 or Part II of the Pollution Control and Local Government (Northern Ireland) Order 1978, or

(*b*) a waste management licence under Part II of the Environmental Protection Act 1990 or any corresponding provision for the time being in force in Northern Ireland, [or

[(*ba*) a permit under regulations under section 2 of the Pollution Prevention and Control Act 1999, or][6]

(*c*) any authorisation under the Radioactive Substances Act 1960 or the Radioactive Substances Act 1993 for the disposal of radioactive waste or any nuclear site licence under the Nuclear Installations Act 1965.][3]

[(7) For the purposes of this section a relevant obligation is—

(*a*) an obligation arising under an agreement made under—

(i) section 106 of the Town and Country Planning Act 1990 as originally enacted;

(ii) [section 75 of the Town and Country Planning (Scotland) Act 1997][4];

(*b*) a planning obligation entered into under section 106 of the Act of 1990, as substituted by section 12 of the Planning and Compensation Act 1991 or under section 299A of the Act of 1990;

(*c*) an obligation arising under or under an agreement made under any provision—

(i) corresponding to section 106 of the Town and Country Planning Act 1990 as originally enacted or as substituted by the Act of 1991 or to section 299A of the Act of 1990; and

(ii) for the time being in force in Northern Ireland.][2]

(8)...][7][1]

Commentary—*Simon's Direct Tax Service* **B3.1345.**
Revenue Internal Guidance—Inspector's manual IM 4330–4358 (examples of activities qualifying as restoration).
Definitions—"Income tax", s 832(4); "trade", s 832(1).
Cross reference—See FA 1997 Sch 12 para 11(11), (12) (clawback of allowances in any case where an occasion occurs after 25 November 1996 on which a "major lump sum"—see FA 1997 Sch 12 para 3(2)—falls to be paid in the case of the lease of an asset).
Amendments—[1] This section inserted by FA 1990 s 78.
[2] Words in sub-s (4)(*b*) and whole of sub-s (7) substituted by Planning and Compensation Act 1991 ss 83, 84(2) with effect from 25 October 1991 by virtue of the Planning and Compensation Act 1991 (Commencement No 3) Order 1991, SI 1991/2272.
[3] Sub-s (6)(*c*) and the preceding word "or" inserted by FA 1993 s 110(1), (3) with effect where the trade is begun after 31 March 1993.
[4] Words in sub-s (7) substituted by Planning (Consequential Provisions) (Scotland) Act 1997 Sch 2 para 41 with effect from 27 May 1997.
[5] Word in sub-ss (2), (3)(*a*) substituted by FA 1998 Sch 7 para 1 with effect from 31 July 1998.
[6] Sub-s (6)(*ba*) inserted with effect in England and Wales by the Pollution Prevention and Control (England and Wales) Regulations, SI 2000/1973 reg 39, Sch 10 para 1 with effect from 1 August 2000. With effect in Scotland, sub-s (6)(*ba*) is inserted as follows by the Pollution Prevention and Control (Scotland) Regulations, SI 2000/323 reg 36, Sch 10 para 2, with effect from 28 September 2000:
"(*ba*) a permit granted under regulations under section 2 of the Pollution Prevention and Control Act 1999, or".
[7] Sub-s (8) repealed by FA 2002 s 141, Sch 40 Pt 3(16) with effect from 24 July 2002. Sub-s (8) previously read as follows—
"(8) For the purposes of this section a period of account is a period for which an account is made up.".

[91B Waste disposal: preparation expenditure

(1) This section applies where a person—

(*a*) incurs, in the course of carrying on a trade, site preparation expenditure in relation to a waste disposal site (the site in question),

(*b*) holds, at the time the person first deposits waste materials on the site in question, a relevant licence which is then in force, (*c*) makes a claim for relief under this section in such form as the Board may direct, and

(*d*) submits such plans and other documents (if any) as the Board may require;

and it is immaterial whether the expenditure is incurred before or after the coming into force of this section.

(2) In computing the [profits][3] of the trade for a period of account ending after 5th April 1989, the allowable amount shall be allowed as a deduction for the purposes of income tax or corporation tax.

(3) In relation to a period of account (the period in question) the allowable amount shall be determined in accordance with the formula—

$$(A - B) \times \frac{C}{C + D}$$

(4) A is the site preparation expenditure incurred by the person at any time before the beginning of, or during, the period in question—

(*a*) in relation to the site in question, and

(*b*) in the course of carrying on the trade;

but this subsection is subject to subsections (5) and (9) below.

(5) A does not include any expenditure—

(*a*) which has been allowed as a deduction in computing the [profits][3] of the trade for any period of account preceding the period in question, or

(*b*) which constitutes capital expenditure in respect of which an allowance has been, or may be, made under the enactments relating to capital allowances.

(6) B is an amount equal to any amount allowed as a deduction under this section, if allowed—

(*a*) in computing the [profits][3] of the trade for any period of account preceding the period in question, and

(*b*) as regards expenditure incurred in relation to the site in question;

and if different amounts have been so allowed as regards different periods, B is the aggregate of them.

(7) C is the volume of waste materials deposited on the site in question during the period in question; but if the period is one beginning before 6th April 1989 C shall be reduced by the volume of any waste materials deposited on the site during the period but before that date.

(8) D is the capacity of the site in question not used up for the deposit of waste materials, looking at the state of affairs at the end of the period in question.

(9) Where any of the expenditure which would be included in A (apart from this subsection) was incurred before 6th April 1989, A shall be reduced by an amount determined in accordance with the formula—

$$E \times \frac{F}{F + G}$$

(10) For the purposes of subsection (9) above

(*a*) E is so much of the initial expenditure (that is, the expenditure which would be included in A apart from subsection (9) above) as was incurred before 6th April 1989,

(*b*) F is the volume of waste materials deposited on the site in question before 6th April 1989, and

(*c*) G is the capacity of the site in question not used up for the deposit of waste materials, looking at the state of affairs immediately before 6th April 1989.

[(10A) For the purposes of this section any expenditure incurred for the purposes of a trade by a person about to carry it on shall be treated as if it had been incurred by that person on the first day on which he does carry it on and in the course of doing so.][2]

(11) For the purposes of this section—

(*a*) a waste disposal site is a site used (or to be used) for the disposal of waste materials by their deposit on the site,

(*b*) in relation to such a site, site preparation expenditure is expenditure on preparing the site for the deposit of waste materials (and may include expenditure on earthworks),

(*c*) in relation to such a site, "capacity" means capacity expressed in volume,

(*d*) "relevant licence" has the same meaning as in section 91A, and

(*e*) ...[4]][1]

Commentary—*Simon's Direct Tax Service* **B3.1345.**
Revenue Interpretation RI 31—Meaning of "preparation expenditure" for the purposes of this section. **RI 225**—Distinction
between the capital costs of engineering a waste disposal site to receive waste and the revenue costs of creating internal cells.
Revenue Internal Guidance—Inspector's manual IM 3250 (examples of site preparation expenditure).
IM 3256 (worked example: calculation of relief).
Revenue & other press releases—IR Tax Bulletin October 2001 p 827 (Certain costs to count as capital expenditure).
Definitions—"The Board", s 832(1); "income tax", s 832(4); "trade", s 832(1).
Cross reference—See FA 1997 Sch 12 para 11(11), (12) (clawback of allowances in any case where an occasion occurs after 25
November 1996 on which a "major lump sum"—see FA 1997 Sch 12 para 3(2)—falls to be paid in the case of the lease of an
asset).
Amendments—[1] This section inserted by FA 1990 s 78.
[2] Sub-s (10A) inserted by FA 1993 s 110(2), (3) with effect where the trade is begun after 31 March 1993.

[3] Word in sub-ss (2), (5)(*a*), (6)(*a*) substituted by FA 1998 Sch 7 para 1 with effect from 31 July 1998.
[4] Sub-s (11)(*e*) repealed by FA 2002 s 141, Sch 40 Pt 3(16) with effect from 24 July 2002. Sub-s (11)(*e*) previously read as follows—

"(*e*) a period of account is a period for which an account is made up."

[91BA Waste disposal: entitlement of successor to allowances

(1) This section applies where—

    (*a*) site preparation expenditure has been incurred in relation to a waste disposal site,
    (*b*) that expenditure was incurred by a person in the course of carrying on a trade, and
    (*c*) on or after 21st March 2000—

        (i) that person ("the predecessor") ceases to carry on that trade, or ceases to carry it on so far as it relates to that site, and
        (ii) another person ("the successor") begins to carry on that trade, or to carry on in the course of a trade the activities formerly carried on by the predecessor in relation to that site.

(2) If the conditions specified in the following provisions of this section are met, then, for the purposes of section 91B above—

    (*a*) the trade carried on by the successor shall be treated as the same trade as that carried on by the predecessor, and
    (*b*) allowances shall be made to the successor (and not to the predecessor) as if everything done to or by the predecessor had been done to or by the successor.

(3) The first condition is that the whole of the site in question is transferred to the successor.

Provided the successor holds an estate or interest in the whole of the site, it need not be the same as that held by the predecessor.

(4) The second condition is that the successor, at the time he first deposits waste material at the site, holds a relevant licence in respect of the site which is then in force.

(5) Expressions used in this section have the same meaning as in section 91B.][1]

Commentary—*Simon's Direct Tax Service* **B3.1345**.
Amendments—[1] This section inserted by FA 2000 s 89 with effect from 28 July 2000.

[91C Mineral exploration and access

Where—

    (*a*) a person carrying on a trade incurs expenditure on mineral exploration and access as defined in [section 396(1) of the Capital Allowances Act][3] in an area or group of sands in which the presence of mineral deposits in commercial quantities has already been established, and
    (*b*) if the presence in that area or group of sands of mineral deposits in commercial quantities had not already been established, that expenditure would not have been allowed to be deducted in computing the [profits][2] of the trade for the purposes of tax,

that expenditure shall not be so deducted.][1]

Commentary—*Simon's Direct Tax Service* **B3.405**.
Definitions—"tax", s 832(3); "trade", s 832(1).
Amendments—[1] This section inserted by FA 1997 s 66(1), (3), (4) with effect in relation to expenditure which (*a*) is incurred on or after 26th November 1996; but (*b*) is not incurred before 26th November 1997 in pursuance of a contract entered into before 26th November 1996; the reference to expenditure incurred in pursuance of a contract entered into before 26th November 1996 does not, in the case of a contract varied on or after that date, include a reference to so much of any expenditure of the sort described in this section as exceeds the amount of expenditure of that sort that would have been incurred if that contract had not been so varied.
[2] Word substituted by FA 1998 Sch 7 para 1 with effect from 31 July 1998.
[3] Words substituted by CAA 2001 s 578, Sch 2 para 20 with effect for income tax purposes, as respects allowances and charges falling to be made for chargeable periods ending after 5 April 2001, and for corporation tax purposes, as respects allowances and charges falling to be made for chargeable periods ending after 31 March 2001.

Treatment of regional development and other grants and debts released etc

92 Regional development grants

(1) A regional development grant which, apart from this subsection, would be taken into account as a receipt in computing the profits of a trade, profession or vocation which are chargeable under Case I or II of Schedule D, shall not be taken into account as a receipt in computing those profits.

(2) A regional development grant which is made to an investment company—

    (*a*) shall not be taken into account as a receipt in computing its profits under Case VI of Schedule D; and
    (*b*) shall not be deducted, by virtue of section 75(2), from the amount treated as expenses of management.

(3) In this section "regional development grant" means a payment by way of grant under Part II of the Industrial Development Act 1982.

Commentary—*Simon's Direct Tax Service* **B3.912**.
Definitions—"Schedule D", s 18(1); "trade", s 832(1).
Cross reference—See Industrial Development Act 1982 Part II (Regional development grants ceased to be made after 31 March 1988 except on application made on or before that date: Regional Development Grants (Termination) Act 1988 s 1).

93 Other grants under Industrial Development Act 1982 etc

(1) A payment to which this section applies which is made to a person carrying on a trade the profits of which are chargeable under Case I of Schedule D shall be taken into account as a receipt in computing those profits; and any such payment which is made to an investment company shall be taken into account as a receipt in computing its profits under Case VI of Schedule D.

(2) This section applies to any payment which would not, apart from this section, be taken into account as mentioned in subsection (1) above, being a payment by way of a grant under—

(a) section 7 or 8 of the Industrial Development Act 1982 or section 7 or 8 of the Industry Act 1972; or

(b) section 1 of the Industries Development Act (Northern Ireland) 1966 or section 4 of the Industries Development Act (Northern Ireland) 1971; or

(c) any of Articles 7, 9 and 30 of the Industrial Development (Northern Ireland) Order 1982;

other than a grant designated as made towards the cost of specified capital expenditure or as made by way of compensation for the loss of capital assets and other than a grant falling within subsection (3) below.

(3) A payment by way of grant which is made—

(a) under Article 7 of the Order referred to in subsection (2)(c) above, and

(b) in respect of a liability for corporation tax (including a liability which has already been met),

shall not be taken into account as mentioned in subsection (1) above, whether by virtue of this section or otherwise.

Commentary—*Simon's Direct Tax Service* B3.929.
Definitions—"Investment company", s 130; "Schedule D", s 18(1); "trade", s 832(1).
Cross reference—See Industrial Development Act 1982 Part II (Regional development grants ceased to be made after 31 March 1988 except on application made on or before that date: Regional Development Grants (Termination) Act 1988 s 1).

94 Debts deducted and subsequently released

[(1)][1] Where, in computing for tax purposes the [profits][4] of a trade, profession or vocation, a deduction has been allowed for any debt incurred for the purposes of the trade, profession or vocation, then, if the whole or any part of the debt is thereafter released [otherwise than as part of a relevant arrangement or compromise][2], the amount released shall be treated as a receipt of the trade, profession or vocation arising in the period in which the release is effected.

[(2) In subsection (1) above "relevant arrangement or compromise" has the same meaning as in section 74.][3]

Commentary—*Simon's Direct Tax Service* B3.923.
Revenue Interpretation RI 50—Where all the assets and liabilities of a company are transferred to another company in the same group ("hive-across"), the transferor company is not liable to a charge under this section, subject to certain conditions.
RI 238—Revised interpretation as to the income tax treatment of trade debts written back to the profit and loss account.
Revenue & other press releases—ICAEW TR799 June 1990 (formal arrangement with creditors under IA 1986 Pt I brings about a "release" of a debt under s 94. A compromise in satisfaction of a debt under a voluntary arrangement gives rise to a "release". Failure to pay, bankruptcy or liquidation of the debtor does not give rise to a charge under s 94).
Definitions—"tax", s 832(3); "trade", s 832(1).
Amendments—[1] "(1)" inserted by virtue of FA 1994 s 144(4).
[2] Words in sub-s (1) inserted by FA 1994 s 144(3)(a), (7) in relation to a debt or part of it released after 29 November 1993.
[3] Sub-s (2) inserted by FA 1994 s 144(4).
[4] Word in sub-s (1) substituted by FA 1998 Sch 7 para 1 with effect from 31 July 1998.

95 [Taxation of dealers in respect of distributions etc][2]

[(1) Where a dealer—

(a) receives a relevant distribution, that is to say—

(i) any distribution which is made by a company resident in the United Kingdom ("a UK distribution"), or

(ii) any payment which is representative of a UK distribution, or

(b) makes any payment which is representative of a UK distribution,

the distribution or, as the case may be, the payment shall be taken into account in computing the profits of the dealer which are chargeable to tax in accordance with the provisions of this Act applicable to Case I or II of Schedule D.][2]

[(1A) Accordingly, where a dealer receives a [relevant distribution.][2]

(a) tax shall not be charged under Schedule F in respect of that distribution;

(b) ...[2]

(c) [section 208][2] shall not apply to that distribution; and

(d) ...[2]][1]

[(e) section 11(2)(a) shall have effect in relation to that distribution with the omission of the words "(but so that this paragraph shall not include distributions received from companies resident in the United Kingdom)".][2]

(1B) ...[2]

[(2) For the purposes of this section a person is a dealer in relation to any ...[2] distribution if—

(*a*) were there a sale by that person of the shares [or stock][2] in respect of which the distribution is made, and

(*b*) the circumstances of that sale were such that the price would not fall to be treated as a ...[2] distribution,

the price would be taken into account in computing the profits of that person which are chargeable to tax in accordance with the provisions of this Act applicable to Case I or II of Schedule D.][1]

[(2A) The reference in subsection (2) above to the profits of a person does not include the profits of that person in respect of insurance business or any category of insurance business.][2]

(3) ...[1]

(4), (5) ...[2]

Commentary—*Simon's Direct Tax Service* **D2.507.**
Simon's Tax Cases—s 95(1), (2), *Bibby v Prudential Assurance Co Ltd* and *Oakes v Equitable Life Assurance Society* [2000] STC 459.
Definitions—"Distribution", ss 209(2), 832(1); "Schedule D", s 18(1); "Schedule F", s 20(1); "tax", s 832(3).
Amendments—[1] Sub-ss (1), (1A), (1B), (2) substituted for sub-ss (1)–(3) by FA 1997 Sch 7 para 8 (1), (3) in relation to distributions made after 25 November 1996.
[2] Headnote, sub-s (1) and words in sub-s (1A) substituted, sub-ss (1A)(*b*), (*d*), (1B), (4), (5) and words in sub-s (2) repealed and sub-ss (1A)(*e*), (2A) and words in sub-s (2)(*a*) inserted by F(No 2)A 1997 s 24, Sch 8 Pt II(8) with effect in relation to any distribution made after 1 July 1997 and any payment which is representative of such a distribution.

Special provisions

[95A Creative artists: relief for fluctuating profits

Schedule 4A (which enables individuals to make an averaging claim in respect of profits derived wholly or mainly from creative works) shall have effect.

The provisions of that Schedule apply for the year 2000–01 and subsequent years of assessment (so that the first years which may be the subject of an averaging claim are 2000–01 and 2001–02).][1]

Commentary—*Simon's Direct Tax Service* **B3.835.**
Amendments—[1] Section inserted by FA 2001 s 71(1) with effect from 11 May 2001.

96 Farming and market gardening: relief for fluctuating profits

(1) Subject to the provisions of this section, a person who is or has been carrying on a trade of farming or market gardening in the United Kingdom may claim that subsection (2) or (3) below shall have effect in relation to his profits from that trade for any two consecutive years of assessment if his profits for either year do not exceed such part of his profits for the other year as is there specified.

(2) If the claimant's profits for either year do not exceed seven-tenths of his profits for the other year or are nil, his profits for each year shall be adjusted so as to be equal to one-half of his profits for the two years taken together or, as the case may be, for the year for which there are profits.

(3) If the claimant's profits for either year exceed seven-tenths but are less than three-quarters of his profits for the other year, his profits for each year shall be adjusted by adding to the profits that are lower and deducting from those that are higher an amount equal to three times the difference between them less three-quarters of those that are higher.

(4) No claim shall be made under this section—

(*a*) in respect of any year of assessment before a year in respect of which a claim has already been made under this section; or

(*b*) in respect of a year of assessment in which the trade is (or by virtue of section 113(1) is treated as) set up and commenced or permanently discontinued.

(5) Any adjustment under this section shall have effect for all the purposes of the Income Tax Acts (including any further application of this section where the second of any two years of assessment is the first of a subsequent pair) except that—

(*a*) subsection (2) above shall not prevent a person obtaining relief under those Acts for a loss sustained by him in any year of assessment;

(*b*) ...[1] and

(*c*) where, after a claim has been made under this section in respect of the profits for any two years of assessment, the profits for both or either of those years are adjusted for any other reason, this section shall have effect as if the claim had not been made but without prejudice to the making of a further claim in respect of those profits as so adjusted.

(6) This section applies to the profits of a trade carried on by a person in partnership as it applies to the profits of a sole trader ...[2]

(7) In this section references to profits from a trade for a year of assessment are references to the [profits][6] from that trade which are chargeable to income tax for that year before—

(*a*) any deduction for losses sustained in any year of assessment;

(*b*) ...[2]

(*c*) any deduction for relief under Schedule 9 to the Finance Act 1981 (stock relief).

(8) Any claim under this section shall be made by notice given to the inspector not later than [twelve months from the 31st January next following][3] the second of the years of assessment to which the

claim relates but any such further claim as is mentioned in subsection (5)(*c*) above shall not be out of time if made [before the 31st January next following][3] the year of assessment following that in which the adjustment is made.

[(9) Where a person makes a claim under this section, any claim by him for relief under any other provision of the Income Tax Acts for either of the two years of assessment—

(*a*) shall not be out of time if made before the end of the period during which the claim under this section is capable of being revoked; and

(*b*) if already made, may be amended or revoked before the end of that period;

and, in relation to a claim made by being included in a return, any reference in this subsection to amending or revoking the claim is a reference to amending the return by amending or, as the case may be, omitting the claim.][5]

(10) There shall be made all such alterations of assessments or repayments of tax (whether in respect of such profits as are mentioned in subsection (1) above or of other income of the person concerned) as may be required in consequence of any adjustment under this section.

(11) Nothing in this section shall be construed as applying to profits chargeable to corporation tax ...[4]

(12) This section applies where the first of the two years mentioned in subsection (1) above is the year 1987–88 or a subsequent year of assessment.

Commentary—*Simon's Direct Tax Service* **B3.541; E5.314.**
Concession A29—"Farming" includes intensive rearing of livestock or fish on a commercial basis for the production of food for human consumption.
Revenue Interpretation RI 139—Farmers' averaging and the transition to self-assessment.
Revenue Interpretation RI 190—Farmers' averaging and transitional overlap relief under FA 1994 Sch 20 para 2.
Revenue & other press releases—IR Tax Bulletin February 1997 p 392 (article explaining rules for making, calculating and implementing claims to farmers' averaging under self-assessment).
Simon's Tax Cases—s 96(7)(*c*), *Shaw v Samuel Montagu & Co Ltd* [1990] STC 538*.
Definitions—"The Income Tax Acts", s 831(1)(*b*); "inspector", s 832(1); "trade", s 832(1); "United Kingdom", s 830(1); "year of assessment", s 832(1).
Cross references—See TMA 1970 Sch 1B paras 3, 4 (provisions for dealing with claims under sub-ss (2), (3) above for two consecutive years of assessment).
Amendments—[1] Sub-s (5)(*b*) repealed by FA 1994 ss 216(3)(*a*), 258, Sch 26 Pt V(24) with effect from the year 1994–95 as respects trades set up and commenced after 5 April 1994 where the first of the two years of assessment to which the claim relates is 1995–96 or any subsequent year. For trades set up and commenced before 6 April 1994 the repeal has effect where the first of the two years of assessment to which the claim relates is 1996–97 or any subsequent year.
[2] Words omitted from sub-s (6) and sub-s (7)(*b*) repealed by FA 1994 ss 214(1)(*a*), (7), 216(3)(*a*), (5), 258, Sch 26 Pt V(24) with effect where the first of the two years of assessment to which the claim relates is 1995–96 or any subsequent year. For trades set up and commenced before 6 April 1994 the repeal has effect where the first of the two years of assessment to which the claim relates is 1996–97 or any subsequent year.
[3] Words in sub-s (8) substituted by FA 1994 ss 196, 199 and Sch 19 para 37 with effect where the first of the two years of assessment to which the claim relates is the year 1996–97 or any subsequent year.
[4] Words in sub-s (11) repealed by FA 1998 s 165, Sch 27 Part III(4) with effect from the year 1998–99 for income tax purposes, and from 1 April 1998 for corporation tax purposes, subject to the transitional provisions in FA 1998 Sch 5 Part IV.
[5] Sub-s (9) substituted by FA 1996 s 128(3), (11) with effect for claims made (or deemed to be made) in relation to the year 1996–97 and later years of assessment.
[6] Word in sub-s (7) substituted by FA 1998 Sch 7 para 1 with effect from 31 July 1998.

97 Treatment of farm animals etc

Schedule 5 shall have effect with respect to the treatment, in computing [profits][1] for the purposes of Case I of Schedule D, of animals and other living creatures kept for the purposes of farming or any other trade.

Commentary—*Simon's Direct Tax Service* **B3.515–522.**
Concession B37.—The herd basis: shares in animals.
Definitions—"Schedule D", s 18(1); "trade", s 832(1).
Amendments—[1] Word substituted by FA 1998 Sch 7 para 1 with effect from 31 July 1998.

[98 Tied premises: receipts and expenses treated as those of trade

(1) This section applies where a person ("the trader")—

(*a*) carries on a trade,

(*b*) in the course of the trade supplies, or is concerned in the supply of, goods sold or used on premises occupied by another person,

(*c*) has an estate or interest in those premises, and

(*d*) deals with that estate or interest as property employed for the purposes of the trade.

(2) Where this section applies the receipts and expenses in connection with the premises that would otherwise fall to be brought into account in computing the profits of a Schedule A business carried on by the trader shall instead be brought into account in computing the profits of the trade.

(3) Any necessary apportionment shall be made on a just and reasonable basis of receipts or expenses—

(*a*) which do not relate only to the premises concerned, or

(*b*) where the conditions in subsection (1) are met only in relation to part of the premises.

(4) This section applies to premises outside the United Kingdom as if the premises were in the United Kingdom.][1]

Commentary—*Simon's Direct Tax Service* **A4.104; B3.1121–1124.**
Definitions— ''interest'', s 832(1); s 833(1); ''Schedule A'', s 18(1); ''trade'', s 832(1); ''United Kingdom'', s 830(1).
Cross reference—See TCGA 1992 s 156(4) (lessor of tied premises (construed according to sub-s (2) of this section) to be treated as occupying premises only for purposes of relevant trade for purposes of rollover relief).
Amendments—[1] This section substituted by FA 1998 s 41 with effect from 17 March 1998 subject to the following transitional provisions in FA 1998, s 41(3)–(7)—

''(3) The above amendments have effect on and after 17th March 1998, subject to the following transitional provisions.
   In those provisions—
     'before commencement' and 'after commencement' mean, respectively, before 17th March 1998 and on or after that date; and
     'the new section 98' means the section as substituted by subsection (1) above.
(4) To the extent that receipts or expenses have been taken into account before commencement, they shall not be taken into account again under the new section 98 after commencement.
(5) To the extent that receipts or expenses would under the new section 98 have been brought into account before commencement, and were not so brought into account, they shall be brought into account immediately after commencement.
(6) If any estate, interest or rights in or over land is or are transferred from one person to another, the references in subsections (4) and (5) above to receipts or expenses being taken into account shall be construed as references to their being taken into account in relation to either of those persons.
(7) For the purposes of those subsections an amount is ''taken into account'' if—
   (*a*) it is brought into account for tax purposes, or
   (*b*) it would have been so brought into account if the person concerned were chargeable to tax.''

99 Dealers in land

(1) In computing for tax purposes the [profits][1] of a trade of dealing in land, there shall be disregarded—

   (*a*) so much of the cost of woodlands in the United Kingdom purchased in the course of the trade as is attributable to trees or saleable underwood growing on the land; and

   (*b*) where any amount has been disregarded under paragraph (*a*) above and, on a subsequent sale of the woodlands in the course of the trade, all or any of the trees or underwood to which the amount disregarded was attributable are still growing on the land, so much of the price for the land as is equal to the amount so disregarded in respect of those trees or underwood.

(2) In computing the [profits][1] of a trade of dealing in land, any trading receipt falling within subsection (1), (4) or (5) of section 34 or section 35 or 36 shall be treated as reduced by the amount on which tax is chargeable by virtue of that section.

(3) Where, on a claim being made under subsection (2)(*b*) of section 36, the amount on which tax was chargeable by virtue of that section is treated as reduced, subsection (2) above shall be deemed to have applied to the amount as reduced, and any such adjustment of liability to tax shall be made (for all relevant chargeable periods) whether by means of an assessment or otherwise, as may be necessary, and may be so made at any time at which it could be made if it related only to tax for the chargeable period in which that claim is made.

(4) Subsection (1) above shall not apply where the purchase mentioned in paragraph (*a*) of that subsection was made under a contract entered into before 1st May 1963.

Commentary—*Simon's Direct Tax Service* **A5.107.**
Definitions—''Chargeable period'', s 832(1); ''tax'', s 832(3); ''trade'', s 832(1); ''United Kingdom'', s 830(1).
Cross reference—See TA 1988 s 776(6) (transactions in land: taxation of capital gains: adjustments under sub-ss (2), (3) above to be taken into account in computing gains).
Amendments—[1] Word in sub-ss (1), (2) substituted by FA 1998 Sch 7 para 1 with effect from 31 July 1998.

CHAPTER VI
DISCONTINUANCE ...[1]

Statement of Practice
SP 3/90—Stocks and long-term contracts.
Amendments—[1] Words repealed by FA 1998 s 165, Sch 27 Pt III(6) in relation to a change of accounting basis taking effect after 5 April 1999.

Valuation of trading stock etc

100 Valuation of trading stock at discontinuance of trade

(1) In computing for any tax purpose the [profits][2] of a trade which has been discontinued, any trading stock belonging to the trade at the discontinuance shall be valued as follows—

   (*a*) if—

     (i) the stock is sold or transferred for valuable consideration to a person who carries on, or intends to carry on, a trade in the United Kingdom, and

     (ii) the cost of the stock may be deducted by the purchaser as an expense in computing for any tax purpose the [profits][2] of that trade,

   the value of the stock shall be taken to be the amount [determined in accordance with subsections (1A) to (1C) below; and][1]

   (*b*) if the stock does not fall to be valued under paragraph (*a*) above, its value shall be taken to be the amount which it would have realised if it had been sold in the open market at the discontinuance of the trade.

[(1A) Subject to subsections (1B) and (1C) below and to paragraph 2 of Schedule 12 to the Finance Act 1988 (gilt-edged securities and other financial trading stock), the value of any trading stock falling to be valued under paragraph (*a*) of subsection (1) above shall be taken—

(*a*) except where the person to whom it is sold or transferred is connected with the person who makes the sale or transfer, to be the amount (''the price actually received for it'') which is in fact realised on the sale or, as the case may be, which is in fact the value of the consideration given for the transfer; and

(*b*) if those persons are connected with each other, to be what would have been the price actually received for it had the sale or transfer been a transaction between independent persons dealing at arm's length.

(1B) In a case falling within subsection (1)(*a*) above—

(*a*) ...³

(*b*) stock sold in circumstances in which the amount realised on the sale would be taken to be an amount determined in accordance with paragraph 5 of Schedule 5 shall be taken to have the value so determined, instead of the value for which subsection (1A)(*a*) or (*b*) above provides.

(1C) If—

(*a*) trading stock is sold or transferred to a person in circumstances where paragraph (*b*) of subsection (1A) above would apply (apart from this subsection) for determining the value of the stock so sold or transferred,

(*b*) the amount which would be taken in accordance with that paragraph to be the value of all of the stock sold or transferred to that person is more than the acquisition value of that stock and also more than the price actually received for it, and

(*c*) both parties to the sale or transfer, by notice signed by them and sent to the inspector no later than two years after the end of the chargeable period in which the trade is discontinued, elect that this subsection shall apply,

then the stock sold or transferred to that person shall be taken to have a value equal to whichever is the greater (taking all the stock so sold or transferred together) of its acquisition value and the price actually received for it or, in a case where they are the same, to either of them.

(1D) In subsection (1C) above ''acquisition value'', in relation to any trading stock, means the amount which, in computing for any tax purposes the [profits]² of the discontinued trade, would have been deductible as representing the acquisition value of that stock if—

(*a*) the stock had, immediately before the discontinuance, been sold in the course of the trade for a price equal to whatever would be its value in accordance with subsection (1A)(*b*) above; and

(*b*) the period for which those [profits]² were to be computed began immediately before the sale.

(1E) Where any trading stock falls to be valued under subsection (1)(*a*) above, the amount determined in accordance with subsections (1A) to (1C) above to be the amount to be brought into account as the value of that stock in computing [profits]² of the discontinued trade shall also be taken, for the purpose of making any deduction in computing the [profits]² of any trade carried on by the purchaser, to be the cost of that stock to the purchaser.

(1F) For the purposes of this section two persons are connected with each other if—

(*a*) they are connected with each other within the meaning of section 839;

(*b*) one of them is a partnership and the other has a right to a share in the partnership;

(*c*) one of them is a body corporate and the other has control over that body;

(*d*) both of them are partnerships and some other person has a right to a share in each of them; or

(*e*) both of them are bodies corporate or one of them is a partnership and the other is a body corporate and, in either case, some other person has control over both of them;

and in this subsection the references to a right to a share in a partnership are references to a right to a share of the assets or income of the partnership and ''control'' has the meaning given by section 840.

(1G) In this section ''purchaser'', in relation to a transfer otherwise than by sale, means the person to whom the transfer is made.]¹

(2) For the purposes of this section ''trading stock'', in relation to any trade—

(*a*) means property of any description, whether real or personal, being either—

(i) property such as is sold in the ordinary course of the trade, or would be so sold if it were mature or if its manufacture, preparation or construction were complete; or

(ii) materials such as are used in the manufacture, preparation or construction of any such property as is referred to in sub-paragraph (i) above; and

(*b*) includes also any services, article or material which would, if the trade were a profession or vocation, be treated, for the purposes of section 101, as work in progress of the profession or vocation, and references to the sale or transfer of trading stock shall be construed accordingly.

[(3) Where trading stock falling to be valued under paragraph (*a*) of subsection (1) above is sold or transferred together with other assets, so much of the amount realised on the sale or, as the case may be, of the value of the consideration given for the transfer as on a just and reasonable apportionment is properly attributable to each asset shall be treated for the purposes of this section as the amount realised on the sale or, as the case may be, the value of the consideration given for the transfer, of that asset.]⁴

Commentary—*Simon's Direct Tax Service* **B3.1016.**
Concession D29—Relief under s 267(1) of TA 1970 for trading stock falling under sub-s (2) of this section transferred under the Insurance Companies Act 1982 s 49.
Statement of Practice SP 3/90—Stocks and long-term contracts.
Simon's Tax Cases—s 100(2), *Reed v Nova Securities Ltd* [1985] STC 124*.
Definitions— ''tax'', s 832(3); ''trade'', s 832(1); ''United Kingdom'', s 830(1).
Cross references—See TA 1988 s 102 (supplementary provisions).
TA 1988 s 113 (deemed discontinuance of trade etc upon change in persons carrying it on);
TA 1988 s 337(1) (cessation of trade by companies);
TA 1988 s 442(4) (exclusion of market valuation required under sub-s (1)(*b*) above where a resident subsidiary insurance company operating overseas ceases to be resident).
FA 1988 Sch 12 para 2 (building society's financial trading stock to be valued at cost for the purposes of sub-s (1) above at the time of its change into a company).
F(No 2)A 1992 s 42(8) (relief for film production or acquisition expenditure not to apply where film constitutes trading stock under sub-s (2) of this section).
Amendments—[1] Words in sub-s (1)(*a*) substituted and sub-ss (1A)–(1G) inserted, by FA 1995 s 140, in relation to any case in which a trade is discontinued at a time after 28 November 1994.
[2] Word in sub-ss (1), (1D), (1E) substituted by FA 1998 Sch 7 para 1 with effect from 31 July 1998.
[3] Sub-s (1B)(*a*) repealed by FA 2002 ss 105(1), 141, Sch 40 Pt 3(17) with effect from the date of 24 July 2002. Sub-s (1B)(*a*) previously read as follows—

    ''(*a*) stock consisting of debts to which section 88A(2) applies shall have the value for which paragraph (*a*) of subsection (1A) above provides even where the persons in question are connected with each other; and''.
[4] Sub-s (3) added by FA 2002 s 106 with effect where the sale or transfer in question takes place after 24 July 2002.

101 Valuation of work in progress at discontinuance of profession or vocation

(1) Where, in computing for any tax purpose the [profits][2] of a profession or vocation which has been discontinued, a valuation is taken of the work of the profession or vocation in progress at the discontinuance, that work shall be valued as follows—

    (*a*) if—

        (i) the work is transferred for money or any other valuable consideration to a person who carries on, or intends to carry on, a profession or vocation in the United Kingdom, and
        (ii) the cost of the work may be deducted by that person as an expense in computing for any tax purpose the [profits][2] of that profession or vocation,

    the value of the work shall be taken to be the amount paid or other consideration given for the transfer; and
    (*b*) if the work does not fall to be valued under paragraph (*a*) above, its value shall be taken to be the amount which would have been paid for a transfer of the work on the date of the discontinuance as between parties at arm's length.

(2) Where a profession or vocation is discontinued, and the person by whom it was carried on immediately before the discontinuance so elects by notice sent to the inspector at any time within [the period specified in subsection (2A) below][1]—

    (*a*) the amount (if any) by which the value of the work in progress at the discontinuance (as ascertained under subsection (1) above) exceeds the actual cost of the work shall not be brought into account in computing the [profits][2] of the period immediately before the discontinuance; but
    (*b*) the amount by which any sums received for the transfer of the work exceed the actual cost of the work shall be included in the sums chargeable to tax by virtue of section 103 as if it were a sum to which that section applies received after the discontinuance.

[(2A) The period mentioned in subsection (2) above is—

    (*a*) in the case of an election for the purposes of income tax, the period ending with the first anniversary of the 31st January next following the year of assessment in which the profession or vocation is discontinued;
    (*b*) in the case of an election for the purposes of corporation tax, the period of two years beginning at the end of the accounting period in which the profession or vocation is discontinued.][1]

(3) References in this section to work in progress at the discontinuance of a profession or vocation shall be construed as references to—

    (*a*) any services performed in the ordinary course of the profession or vocation, the performance of which was wholly or partly completed at the time of the discontinuance and for which it would be reasonable to expect that a charge would have been made on their completion if the profession or vocation had not been discontinued; and
    (*b*) any article produced, and any such material as is used, in the performance of any such services,

and references in this section to the transfer of work in progress shall include references to the transfer of any benefits and rights which accrue, or might reasonably be expected to accrue, from the carrying out of the work.

Commentary—*Simon's Direct Tax Service* **B4.206.**
Statement of Practice SP 3/90—Stocks and long-term contracts.
Revenue & other press releases—ICAEW Tax 7/95 20-2-95 Section A, paras (1)–(4): valuation of partnership work in progress on incorporation of a business.
Definitions—''accounting period'', s 834(1); ''inspector'', s 832(1); ''notice'', s 832(1); ''tax'', s 832(3); ''United Kingdom'', s 830(1); ''year of assessment'', s 832(1).
Cross references—See TA 1988 s 100(2)(*b*) (meaning of trading stock to include services etc that would be treated as work in progress of profession or vocation for purposes of this section).
TA 1988 s 102 (supplementary provisions).
TA 1988 s 113 (deemed discontinuance of trade etc upon change in persons carrying it on);

TA 1988 s 337(1) (cessation of trade by companies).
Amendments—[1] Words in sub-s (2) substituted for words "12 months after the discontinuance" and sub-s (2A) inserted by FA 1996 s 135, Sch 21 para 3 with effect as respects income tax from the year 1996–97 and, as respects corporation tax, for accounting periods ending after 30 June 1999 (by virtue of Finance Act 1994, Section 199, (Appointed Day) Order, SI 1998/3173 art 2).
[2] Word in sub-ss (1), (2) substituted by FA 1998 Sch 7 para 1 with effect from 31 July 1998.

102 Provisions supplementary to sections 100 and 101

(1) Any question arising under section 100(1)(*a*) or 101(1)(*a*) shall be determined as follows, for the purpose of computing for any tax purpose the [profits][2] of both the trades or, as the case may be, the professions or vocations concerned—

   (*a*) in a case where the same body of General Commissioners have jurisdiction with respect to [each of the persons whose trade, profession or vocation is one of those][1] concerned, the question shall be determined by those Commissioners unless all parties concerned agree that it shall be determined by the Special Commissioners;

   (*b*) in any other case, the question shall be determined by the Special Commissioners; and

   (*c*) the General or Special Commissioners shall determine the question in like manner as an appeal.

(2) Where, by virtue of section 113 or 337(1), a trade, profession or vocation is treated as having been permanently discontinued for the purpose of computing tax, it shall also be so treated for the purposes of sections 100 and 101; but those sections shall not apply in a case where a trade, profession or vocation carried on by a single individual is discontinued by reason of his death.

Commentary—*Simon's Direct Tax Service* **B3.1016; B4.206.**
Statement of Practice SP 3/90—Stocks and long-term contracts.
Definitions—"tax", s 832(3); "trade", s 832(1).
Cross references—See TMA 1970 s 58(3)(*b*) (proceedings under this section to be in Northern Ireland if the place given by certain rules in relation to the parties to the proceedings is in Northern Ireland).
TMA 1970 Sch 3 (rules for place of appeal proceedings to have effect subject to this section).
Amendments—[1] Words in sub-s (1)(*a*) substituted for words "both the trades, professions or vocations" by FA 1996 Sch 22 paras 11, 12 with effect in relation to any proceedings relating to the year 1996–97 or any subsequent year of assessment and in relation to any proceedings relating to an accounting period ending after 30 June 1999 (by virtue of Finance Act 1994, Section 199, (Appointed Day) Order, SI 1998/3173 art 2).
[2] Word in sub-s (1) substituted by FA 1998 Sch 7 para 1 with effect from 31 July 1998.

Case VI charges on receipts

Cross reference—See TA 1988 s 110 (supplemental provisions for the purposes of ss 103–109).

103 Receipts after discontinuance: earnings basis charge and related charge affecting conventional basis

(1) Where any trade, profession or vocation the [profits][4] of which are chargeable to tax under Case I or II of Schedule D has been permanently discontinued, tax shall be charged under Case VI of that Schedule in respect of any sums to which this section applies which are received after the discontinuance.

(2) Subject to subsection (3) below, this section applies to the following sums arising from the carrying on of the trade, profession or vocation during any period before the discontinuance (not being sums otherwise chargeable to tax)—

   (*a*) where the [profits][4] for that period were computed by reference to earnings, all such sums in so far as their value was not brought into account in computing the [profits][4] for any period before the discontinuance, and

   (*b*) where those [profits][4] were computed on a conventional basis (that is to say, were computed otherwise than by reference to earnings), any sums which, if those [profits][4] had been computed by reference to earnings, would not have been brought into the computation for any period before the discontinuance because the date on which they became due, or the date on which the amount due in respect thereof was ascertained, fell after the discontinuance.

(3) This section does not apply to any of the following sums—

   (*a*) sums received by a person beneficially entitled thereto who is not resident in the United Kingdom, or by a person acting on his behalf, which represent income arising directly or indirectly from a country or territory outside the United Kingdom, or

   (*b*) a lump sum paid to the personal representatives of the author of a literary, dramatic, musical or artistic work as consideration for the assignment by them, wholly or partially, of the copyright in the work, or

   [(*bb*) a lump sum paid to the personal representatives of the designer of a design in which design right subsists as consideration for the assignment by them, wholly or partially, of that right,][1]

   (*c*) sums realised by the transfer of trading stock belonging to a trade at the discontinuance of the trade, or by the transfer of the work of a profession or vocation in progress at its discontinuance.

Paragraph (*b*) above shall have effect in relation to public lending right as it has effect in relation to copyright.

(4) Where—

(*a*) in computing for tax purposes the [profits][4] of a trade, profession or vocation a deduction has been allowed for any debt incurred for the purposes of the trade, profession or vocation, and

(*b*) the whole or any part of that debt is thereafter released [otherwise than as part of a relevant arrangement or compromise][2], and

(*c*) the trade, profession or vocation has been permanently discontinued at or after the end of the period for which the deduction was allowed and before the release was effected,

subsections (1) to (3) above shall apply as if the amount released were a sum received after the discontinuance.

[(4A) In subsection (4)(*b*) above ''relevant arrangement or compromise'' has the same meaning as in section 74.][3]

(5) For the purposes of this section the value of any sum received in payment of a debt shall be treated as not brought into account in the computation of the [profits][4] of a trade, profession or vocation to the extent that a deduction has been allowed in respect of that sum under section 74(*j*).

Commentary—*Simon's Direct Tax Service* **B4.222, 223.**
Statement of Practice SP 3/90—Stocks and long-term contracts.
Revenue Interpretation RI 129—Timing of the recognition of VAT refunds paid to opticians.
Simon's Tax Cases—*Gilmore v Inspector of Taxes* [1999] STC (SCD) 269.
s 103(2), *Walker v O'Connor* [1996] STC (SCD) 218.
Definitions—''Permanent discontinuance'', s 110(2); ''Schedule D'', s 18(1); ''tax'', s 832(3); ''trade'', s 832(1); ''United Kingdom'', s 830(1).
Cross references—See TA 1988 s 21(5) (this section applies to a permanent discontinuance of a Schedule A business as it applies to a permanent discontinuance of a trade).
TA 1988 s 101(2) (application of this section where, on discontinuance of profession or vocation, consideration for sale of work in progress exceeds its costs).
TA 1988 s 104(3) (sums chargeable to tax under this section not to be subject to charge to tax under Schedule D, Case VI by virtue of TA 1988 s 104(1) on post-cessation receipts where profits of trade etc previously computed on conventional basis).
TA 1988 s 105(1) (allowable deductions in respect of sums chargeable under this section).
TA 1988 s 106 (amount on which tax is chargeable in the case of a transfer for value of the right to receive any sum to which this section applies).
TA 1988 s 107 (certain sums chargeable under this section to be treated as earned income).
TA 1988 s 108 (election for carry-back of any sum chargeable under this section and received not later than six years after discontinuance or change of basis).
TA 1988 s 109A(4A) (sums subsequently received in respect of a debt for which relief has been given under s 109A(4A) treated as ones to which this section applies).
TA 1988 s 110 (supplementary provisions).
TA 1988 s 491(7) (exclusion for double relief for losses, expenses etc under TA 1988 s 491(6) in respect of distribution of assets of body carrying on mutual business where relief already given under this section).
Amendments—[1] Sub-s (3)(*bb*) inserted by the Copyright, Designs and Patents Act 1988 Sch 7 para 36(3) with effect from 1 August 1989 by virtue of the Copyright, Designs and Patents Act 1988 (Commencement No 1) Order 1989, SI 1989/816.
[2] Words in sub-s (4)(*b*) inserted by FA 1994 s 144(3)(*b*), (7) in relation to a debt or part of it released after 29 November 1993.
[3] Sub-s (4A) inserted by FA 1994 s 144(5), (7) with effect in relation to the release of the whole or any part of a debt after 29 November 1993.
[4] Word in sub-ss (1), (2)(*a*), (2)(*b*), (4)(*a*), (5) substituted by FA 1998 Sch 7 para 1 with effect from 31 July 1998.

104 Conventional basis: general charge on receipts after discontinuance [or change of basis][2]

(1) Where any trade, profession or vocation the [profits][1] of which are chargeable to tax under Case I or II of Schedule D has been permanently discontinued, and the [profits][1] for any period before the discontinuance were computed on a conventional basis, tax shall be charged under Case VI of that Schedule in respect of any sums to which this subsection applies which are received on or after the discontinuance.

(2) Subject to subsection (3) below, subsection (1) above applies to all sums arising from the carrying on of the trade, profession or vocation during any period before the discontinuance, not being sums otherwise chargeable to tax, in so far as the amount or value of the sums was not brought into account in computing the [profits][1] for any period before the discontinuance.

(3) In subsection (2) above the reference to sums otherwise chargeable to tax includes any sums which (disregarding this section) are chargeable to tax under section 103 or to which that section would have applied but for subsection (3)(*a*) and (*b*) of that section.

(4), (5) ...[2]

(6) It is hereby declared that where work in progress at the discontinuance of a profession or vocation, or the responsibility for its completion, is transferred, the sums to which subsection (1) above applies include any sums received by way of consideration for the transfer, and any sums received by way of realisation by the transferee, on behalf of the transferor, of the work in progress transferred.

(7) ...[2]

Commentary—*Simon's Direct Tax Service* **B4.223.**
Statements of Practice SP A3—Tax liability under this section where a barrister elected to change from cash basis to earnings basis at the end of an accounting period and for work in progress at the time of the change. Statement (not reproduced) classified obsolete by IR 131 Supplement (November 1998).
SP A27—Tax liability under this section where accounts were prepared on a basis other than earnings or where a change is made to a basis other than earnings. Statement (not reproduced) classified obsolete by IR 131 Supplement (November 1998).
SP 3/90—Stocks and long-term contracts.
Revenue & other press releases—ICAEW Tax 7/95 20-2-95 Section A, paras 5–7: incorporation of partnership business, cash basis, if no consideration given for debtors and work in progress. The amount realised by the company will form part of the company's profits.

Definitions—"Conventional basis", s 110(4); "permanent discontinuance", s 110(2); "Schedule D", s 18(1); "tax", s 832(3); "trade", s 832(1); "work in progress", s 110(6).
Cross references—See TA 1988 s 105(1), (4) (allowable deductions in respect of sums chargeable under sub-ss (1), (4) above).
TA 1988 s 106 (amount on which tax is chargeable in the case of a transfer for value of the right to receive any sum to which this section applies).
TA 1988 s 107 (certain sums chargeable under this section to be treated as earned income).
TA 1988 s 108 (election for carry-back of any sum chargeable under this section and received not later than six years after discontinuance or change of basis).
TA 1988 s 109 (relief for individuals born before 6 April 1917).
TA 1988 s 110 (supplementary provisions).
Amendments—[1] Word in sub-ss (1), (2), (4), (5), (7) substituted by FA 1998 Sch 7 para 1 with effect from 31 July 1998.
[2] Words in section heading, and sub-ss (4), (5), (7) repealed by FA 1998 s 165, Sch 27 Pt III(6) in relation to a change of accounting basis taking effect after 5 April 1999.

105 Allowable deductions

(1) In computing the charge to tax in respect of sums received by any person which are chargeable to tax by virtue of section 103 or 104(1) (including amounts treated as sums received by him by virtue of section 103(4)), there shall be deducted from the amount which, apart from this subsection, would be chargeable to tax—

    (a) any loss, expense or debit (not being a loss, expense or debit arising directly or indirectly from the discontinuance itself) which, if the trade, profession or vocation had not been discontinued, would have been deducted in computing for tax purposes the [profits][2] of the person by whom it was carried on before the discontinuance, or would have been deducted from or set off against those [profits][2] as so computed, and

    (b) any capital allowance to which the person who carried on the trade, profession or vocation was entitled immediately before the discontinuance and to which effect has not been given by way of relief before the discontinuance.

(2) No amount shall be deducted under subsection (1) above if that amount has been allowed under any other provision of the Tax Acts [or by virtue of section 90(4) of the Finance Act 1995][1].

(3) No amount shall be deducted more than once under subsection (1) above; and—

    (a) any expense or debit shall be apportioned between a sum chargeable under section 103 and a sum chargeable under section 104(1) in such manner as may be just;

    (b) as between sums chargeable, whether under section 103 or 104(1), for one chargeable period and sums so charged for a subsequent chargeable period, any deduction in respect of a loss or capital allowance shall be made against sums chargeable for the earlier chargeable period;

    (c) subject to paragraph (b) above, as between sums chargeable for any chargeable period under section 103 and sums so chargeable under section 104(1), any deduction in respect of a loss or capital allowance shall be made against the last-mentioned sums rather than the first-mentioned;

but, in the case of a loss which is to be allowed after the discontinuance, not so as to authorise its deduction from any sum chargeable for a chargeable period preceding that in which the loss is incurred.

(4) ...[3]

Commentary—*Simon's Direct Tax Service* B4.225.
Statement of Practice SP 3/90—Stocks and long-term contracts.
Revenue Interpretation RI 25—Post-cessation professional indemnity insurance premiums: whether such premiums qualify as allowable deductions under this section.
Simon's Tax Cases—*Gilmore v Inspector of Taxes* [1999] STC (SCD) 269.
Definitions—"Capital allowance", s 832(1); "chargeable period", s 832(1); "tax", s 832(3); "the Tax Acts", s 831(2); "trade", s 832(1).
Cross references—See TA 1988 s 109A(3), (4), (4A) (no deduction to be made under this section in respect of which relief is claimed as post-cessation expenditure).
TA 1988 s 110 (supplementary provisions).
TA 1988 s 491(7) (avoidance of double relief in respect of loss etc of companies carrying on mutual business).
TA 1988 s 535(8) (amount of income treated as received in instalments in respect of copyright sold after 10 years or more, reduced by amounts deductible under sub-s (1) of this section).
Amendments—[1] Words in sub-s (2) added by FA 1995 s 90(6), (7), with effect in relation to payments made or treated as made after 28 November 1994.
[2] Word in sub-s (1)(a) substituted by FA 1998 Sch 7 para 1 with effect from 31 July 1998.
[3] Sub-s (4) repealed by FA 1998 s 165, Sch 27 Pt III(6) in relation to a change of accounting basis taking effect after 5 April 1999.

106 Application of charges where rights to payments transferred

(1) Subject to subsection (2) below, in the case of a transfer for value of the right to receive any sum to which section 103, 104(1) or 104(4) applies, any tax chargeable by virtue of either of those sections shall be charged in respect of the amount or value of the consideration (or, in the case of a transfer otherwise than at arm's length, in respect of the value of the right transferred as between parties at arm's length), and references in this Chapter, except section 101(2), to sums received shall be construed accordingly.

(2) Where a trade, profession or vocation is treated as permanently discontinued by reason of a change in the persons carrying it on, and the right to receive any sum to which section 103 or 104(1) applies is or was transferred at the time of the change to the persons carrying on the trade, profession or vocation after the change, tax shall not be charged by virtue of either of those sections, but any

sum received by those persons by virtue of the transfer shall be treated for all purposes as a receipt to be brought into the computation of the [profits][1] of the trade, profession or vocation in the period in which it is received.

Commentary—*Simon's Direct Tax Service* **B4.224.**
Statement of Practice SP 3/90—Stocks and long-term contracts.
Simon's Tax Cases—s 106(2), *Brewin v McVittie* [1999] STC (SCD) 5.
Definitions— "tax", s 832(3); "trade", s 832(1).
Cross reference—See TA 1988 s 110 (supplementary provisions).
Amendments—[1] Word in sub-s (2) substituted by FA 1998 Sch 7 para 1 with effect from 31 July 1998.

Reliefs

107 Treatment of receipts as earned income

Where an individual is chargeable to tax by virtue of section 103 or 104, and the [profits][1] of the trade, profession or vocation to which he was entitled before the discontinuance or, as the case may be, change of basis fell to be treated as earned income for the purposes of income tax, the sums in respect of which he is so chargeable shall also be treated as earned income for those purposes (but, in the case of sums chargeable by virtue of section 104, after any reduction in those sums under section 109).

Commentary—*Simon's Direct Tax Service* **B4.224.**
Statement of Practice SP 3/90—Stocks and long-term contracts.
Definitions—"Earned income", s 833(4); "income tax", s 832(4); "tax", s 832(3); "trade", s 832(1).
Cross reference—See TA 1988 s 110 (supplementary provisions).
Amendments—[1] Word substituted by FA 1998 Sch 7 para 1 with effect from 31 July 1998.

108 Election for carry-back

Where any sum is—

(a) chargeable to tax by virtue of section 103 or 104, and

(b) received in any year of assessment beginning not later than six years after the discontinuance or, as the case may be, change of basis by the person by whom the trade, profession or vocation was carried on before the discontinuance or change, or by his personal representatives,

that person or (in either case) his personal representatives may, by notice sent to [an officer of the Board within one year from the 31st January next following][1] that year of assessment, elect that the tax so chargeable shall be charged as if the sum in question were received on the date on which the discontinuance took place or, as the case may be, on the last day of the period at the end of which the change of basis took place; ...[1]

Commentary—*Simon's Direct Tax Service* **B4.226.**
Statement of Practice SP 3/90—Stocks and long-term contracts.
Simon's Tax Cases—*Gilmore v Inspector of Taxes* [1999] STC (SCD) 269.
Definitions—"The Board", s 832(1); "tax", s 832(3); "the Tax Acts", s 831(2); "year of assessment", s 832(1).
Cross reference—See TMA 1970 Sch 1B para 5 (provisions for dealing with elections for carry-back under this section).
TA 1988 s 110 (supplementary provisions).
Amendments—[1] Words substituted, and words omitted repealed, by FA 1996 s 128(4), (11), Sch 41 Pt V(6) with effect for claims made (or deemed to be made) in relation to the year 1996–97 and later years of assessment.

109 Charge under section 104: relief for individuals born before 6th April 1917

(1) If an individual born before 6th April 1917, or the personal representatives of such an individual, is chargeable to tax under section 104 and—

(a) the individual was engaged in carrying on a trade, profession or vocation on 18th March 1968, and

(b) the [profits][1] of the trade, profession or vocation were not computed by reference to earnings in the period in which that 18th March fell, or in any subsequent period ending before or with the relevant date,

the net amount with which he is so chargeable to tax shall be reduced by multiplying that net amount by the fraction given below.

(2) Where section 104(4) applies in relation to a change of basis taking place on a date before 19th March 1968, then, in relation to tax chargeable by reference to that change of basis, that earlier date shall be substituted for the date in subsection (1)(a) above and subsection (1)(b) above shall be omitted.

(3) The fraction referred to in subsection (1) above is—

(a) where on 5th April 1968 the individual had not attained the age of 52—

$$\frac{19}{20}$$

(b) where on that date he had attained the age of 52, but had not attained the age of 53—

$$\frac{18}{20}$$

and so on, reducing the fraction by—

$$\frac{1}{20}$$

for each year he had attained up to the age of 64;

(c) where on that date he had attained the age of 65, or any greater age—

$$\frac{5}{20}$$

(4) In this section—

"the net amount" with which a person is chargeable to tax under section 104 means the amount with which he is so chargeable after making any deduction authorised by section 105 but before giving any relief under this section; and

"relevant date"—

(a) in relation to tax under section 104(1), means the date of the permanent discontinuance, and

(b) in relation to tax under section 104(4), means the date of the change of basis.

(5) Subsections (1) to (4) above shall apply as follows as respects the net amount of any sum chargeable under section 104 which is assessed by reference to a sum accruing to a partnership—

(a) the part of that net amount which is apportioned to any partner (who is an individual), or the personal representative of such an individual, shall be a net amount with which that person is chargeable under that section, and

(b) if the part of that net amount which is so apportioned is a greater proportion of that amount than is the individual's share (that is to say, the part to be included in his total income) of the total amount of the partnership profits assessed to income tax for the three years of assessment ending with the year in which the discontinuance or change of basis took place, the amount of the reduction to be given by way of relief shall not exceed the amount of relief which would have been so given if the apportionment had been made by reference to his share of that total amount.

(6) For the purposes of this section the trade, profession or vocation carried on before a permanent discontinuance shall not be treated as the same as any carried after the discontinuance.

Commentary—*Simon's Direct Tax Service* **B4.227.**
Statement of Practice SP 3/90—Stocks and long-term contracts.
Definitions—"Permanent discontinuance", s 110(2); "tax", s 832(3); "total income", s 835(1); "trade", s 832(1).
Amendments—¹ Word in sub-s (1)(b) substituted by FA 1998 Sch 7 para 1 with effect from 31 July 1998.

[Relief for post-cessation expenditure

109A Relief for post-cessation expenditure

(1) Where in connection with a trade, profession or vocation formerly carried on by him which has been permanently discontinued a person makes, within seven years of the discontinuance, a payment to which this section applies, he may, by notice given within twelve months from the 31st January next following the year of assessment in which the payment is made, claim relief from income tax on an amount of his income for that year equal to the amount of the payment.

(2) This section applies to payments made wholly and exclusively—

(a) in remedying defective work done, goods supplied or services rendered in the course of the former trade, profession or vocation or by way of damages (whether awarded or agreed) in respect of any such defective work, goods or services; or

(b) in defraying the expenses of legal or other professional services in connection with any claim that work done, goods supplied or services rendered in the course of the former trade, profession or vocation was or were defective;

(c) in insuring against any liabilities arising out of any such claim or against the incurring of such expenses; or

(d) for the purpose of collecting a debt taken into account in computing the [profits]³ of the former trade, profession or vocation.

(3) Where a payment of any of the above descriptions is made in circumstances such that relief under this section is available, the following shall be treated as sums to which section 103 applies (whether or not they would be so treated apart from this subsection)—

(a) in the case of a payment within paragraph (a) or (b) of subsection (2) above, any sum received, by way of the proceeds of insurance or otherwise, for the purpose of enabling the payment to be made or by means of which it is reimbursed,

(b) in the case of a payment within paragraph (c) of that subsection, any sum (not falling within paragraph (a) above) received by way of refund of premium or otherwise in connection with the insurance, and

(c) in the case of a payment within paragraph (d) of that subsection, any sum received to meet the costs of collecting the debt;

and no deduction shall be made under section 105 respect of any such sums.

Where such a sum is received in a year of assessment earlier than that in which the related payment is made, it shall be treated as having been received in that later year and not in the earlier year; and any such adjustment shall be made, by way of modification of any assessment or discharge or repayment of tax, as is required to give effect to this subsection.

(4) Where a trade, profession or vocation carried on by a person has been permanently discontinued and subsequently an unpaid debt which was taken into account in computing the [profits][3] of that trade, profession or vocation and to the benefit of which he is entitled [is released in whole or in part as part of a relevant arrangement or compromise (within the meaning of section 74), he shall be treated as making a payment to which this section applies of—

> (*a*) an amount equal to the amount released, or
> (*b*) if he was entitled to only part of the benefit of the debt, an amount equal to an appropriate proportion of that amount.][2]

If any sum is subsequently received by him in payment of a debt for which relief has been given by virtue of this subsection, the sum shall be treated as one to which section 103 applies; and no deduction shall be made under section 105 in respect of any such sum.

[(4A) Where a trade, profession or vocation carried on by a person has been permanently discontinued and subsequently an unpaid debt which was taken into account in computing the [profits][3] of that trade, profession or vocation and to the benefit of which he is entitled, proves to be bad, then if—

> (*a*) in making a claim for a year of assessment under subsection (1) above he gives notice that the debt was bad in any part of that year, and
> (*b*) he has not given such a notice in respect of that debt in the making of any other such claim,

he shall be treated as making in that year a payment to which this section applies of an amount equal to the amount of the debt or, if he was entitled to only part of the benefit of the debt, to an appropriate proportion of that amount.

If any sum is subsequently received by him in payment of a debt for which relief has been given by virtue of this subsection, the sum shall be treated as one to which section 103 applies; and no deduction shall be made under section 105 in respect of any sum.][2]

(5) Where in the case of a trade, profession or vocation which has subsequently been permanently discontinued a deduction was made in computing the profits or losses of the trade, profession or vocation in respect of an expense not actually paid (an ''unpaid expense''), then—

> (*a*) if relief under this section in connection with that trade, profession or vocation is claimed in respect of any year of assessment, the amount of the relief shall be reduced by the amount of any unpaid expenses at the end of that year;
> (*b*) for the purposes of the application of paragraph (*a*) above in relation to a subsequent year of assessment, any amount by which relief under this section has been reduced by virtue of that paragraph shall be treated as having been paid in respect of the expense in question; and
> (*c*) if subsequently any amount is in fact paid in respect of an expense in respect of which a reduction has been made under paragraph (*a*), that amount (or, if less, the amount of the reduction) shall be treated as a payment to which this section applies.

(6) Relief shall not be given under this section in respect of an amount for which relief has been given or is available under any other provision of the Income Tax Acts.

In applying this subsection relief available under section 105 shall be treated as given in respect of other amounts before any amount in respect of which relief is available under this section.

(7) This section does not apply for the purposes of corporation tax.][1]

Commentary—*Simon's Direct Tax Service* B4.231–233.
Revenue Interpretation RI 130—Relief is given for payments made after 28 November 1994 and within seven years from the discontinuance. A claim must be made within two years of the end of the year of assessment in which the payment was made. Professional indemnity insurance premiums, in principle, will usually be allowable.
Definitions—''The Income Tax Acts'', s 831(1)(*b*); ''tax'', s 832(3); ''trade'', s 832(1); ''year of assessment'', s 832(1).
Cross reference—See FA 1995 s 90(4), (5) (claim to treat excess expenditure as an allowable capital loss of the same year).
Amendments—[1] Section and preceding heading inserted by FA 1995 s 90(1), (7), with effect in relation to payments made or treated as made after 28 November 1994. Note that, by virtue of FA 1995 s 90(2), sub-s (1) of this section had effect as respects the years 1994–95 and 1995–96 with the substitution for the words ''twelve months from the 31st January next following'' of the words ''two years after''.
[2] Words in sub-s (4) substituted and sub-s (4A) inserted by FA 1996 s 134, Sch 20 para 5(1), (2) with effect from the year 1996–97.
[3] Word in sub-ss (2)(*d*), (4), (4A) substituted by FA 1998 Sch 7 para 1 with effect from 31 July 1998.

Supplemental

110 Interpretation etc

(1) The following provisions have effect for the purposes of [sections 103 to 109A][2].

(2) For the purposes of those sections, any reference to the permanent discontinuance of a trade, profession or vocation includes a reference to the occurring of

> [(*a*) any event which, under section 113 or 337(1), is to be treated as equivalent to the permanent discontinuance of a trade, profession or vocation; or.

(b) in relation to a trade or profession carried on by a person in partnership with other persons, any event which, under subsection (4) of section 111, is to be treated as equivalent to the permanent discontinuance of his deemed trade or profession (within the meaning of that subsection)].[1]

(3) The [profits][3] of a trade, profession or vocation in any period shall be treated as computed by reference to earnings where all credits and liabilities accruing during that period as a consequence of its being carried on are brought into account in computing those [profits][3] for tax purposes, and not otherwise, and "earnings basis" shall be construed accordingly.

(4) "Conventional basis" has the meaning given by section 103(2), so that [profits][3] are computed on a conventional basis if computed otherwise than by reference to earnings.

(5) There is a change from a conventional basis to the earnings basis at the end of a period the [profits][3] of which were computed on a conventional basis if the [profits][3] of the next succeeding period are computed by reference to earnings; and, if the [profits][3] of two successive periods are computed on different conventional bases, a change of conventional basis occurs at the end of the earlier period.

(6) In sections 103 and 104—

   (a) "trading stock" has the meaning given by section 100(2);
   (b) references to work in progress at the discontinuance of a profession or vocation, and to the transfer of work in progress, are to be construed in accordance with section 101(3); and
   (c) the reference to work in progress at the time of a change of basis is also to be construed in accordance with section 101(3), substituting therein for this purpose references to the change of basis for references to the discontinuance.

Commentary—*Simon's Direct Tax Service* **B4.222–227, B4.231–233.**
Statement of Practice SP A27—Accounts on a cash basis. Statement (not reproduced) classified obsolete by IR 131 Supplement (November 1998).
SP 3/90—Stocks and long-term contracts.
Definitions—"trade", s 832(1).
Amendments—[1] Words in sub-s (2) substituted by FA 1994 s 215(1A) (as inserted by FA 1995 s 117(1)(b), (3)) with effect from the year 1994–95 in relation to partnerships whose trades, professions or businesses are set up and commenced after 5 April 1994 (but from 1995–96 for such partnerships which are controlled abroad), and with effect from the year 1997–98 in relation to partnerships etc set up and commenced before 6 April 1994: see FA 1994 s 215(4), (5), FA 1995 s 125(1).
[2] Words in sub-s (1) substituted by FA 1995 s 90(3), (7) with effect in relation to payments made or treated as made after 28 November 1994.
[3] Word in sub-ss (3)–(5) substituted by FA 1998 Sch 7 para 1 with effect from 31 July 1998.

[Change of residence][1]

[110A Change of residence

(1) Where there is a change of residence by an individual who is carrying on any trade, profession or vocation wholly or partly outside the United Kingdom and otherwise than in partnership with others, tax shall be chargeable, and loss relief may be claimed, as if the change —

   (a) constituted the permanent discontinuance of the trade, profession or vocation; and
   (b) was immediately followed, in so far as the trade, profession or vocation continues to be carried on by that individual, by the setting up and commencement of a new one;

but nothing in this subsection shall prevent any portion of a loss sustained before the change from being carried forward under section 385 and set against [profits][2] arising or accruing after the change.

(2) For the purposes of this section there is a change of residence by an individual if—

   (a) not being resident in the United Kingdom, he becomes so resident; or
   (b) being so resident, he ceases to be so resident.][1]

Commentary—*Simon's Direct Tax Service* **B3.101.**
Definitions—"Tax", s 832(3); "trade", s 832(1); "United Kingdom", s 830(1).
Amendments—[1] Section and preceding heading inserted by FA 1995 s 124(1), with effect from the year 1997–98 and also, in relation only to a trade, profession or vocation set up and commenced after 5 April 1994, as respects the years 1995–96 and 1996–97.
[2] Word in sub-s (1) substituted by FA 1998 Sch 7 para 1 with effect from 31 July 1998.

CHAPTER VII
PARTNERSHIPS AND SUCCESSIONS
General

[111 Treatment of partnerships

(1) Where a trade or profession is carried on by persons in partnership, the partnership shall not, unless the contrary intention appears, be treated for the purposes of the Tax Acts as an entity which is separate and distinct from those persons.

(2) So long as a trade or profession is carried on by persons in partnership, and any of those persons is chargeable to income tax, the [profits][2] or losses arising from the trade or profession ("the actual trade or profession") shall be computed for the purposes of income tax in like manner as if—

   (a) the partnership were an individual; and
   (b) that individual were an individual resident in the United Kingdom.

(3) A person's share in the [profits]² or losses arising from the actual trade or profession which for any period are computed in accordance with subsection (2) above shall be determined according to the interests of the partners during that period.

(4) Where a person's share in any [profits]² or losses is determined in accordance with subsection (3) above, sections 60 to 63A shall apply as if—

(*a*) that share of the [profits]² or losses derived from a trade or profession carried on by him alone;

(*b*) that trade or profession (''the deemed trade or profession'') had been set up and commenced by him at the time when he became a partner or, where the actual trade or profession was previously carried on by him alone, the time when the actual trade or profession was set up and commenced;

(*c*) as regards each year of assessment, any accounting date or accounting change of the actual trade or profession were also an accounting date or accounting change of the deemed trade or profession;

(*d*) subsection (2) of section 62 applied in relation to any accounting change of the deemed trade or profession if, and only if, on the assumption that the partnership were an individual, that subsection would apply in relation to the corresponding accounting change of the actual trade or profession; and

(*e*) the deemed trade or profession were permanently discontinued by him at the time when he ceases to be a partner or, where the actual trade or profession is subsequently carried on by him alone, the time when the actual trade or profession is permanently discontinued.

(5) Where section 62(2) does not apply in relation to any accounting change of the deemed trade or profession which is made or treated as made in the year of assessment next following or next but one following the commencement year, sections 60(3)(*a*) and 61(2)(*a*) shall apply as if the old date in that year were the accounting date.

(6) For the purpose of determining whether, on the assumption that the partnership were an individual, section 62(2) would apply in relation to an accounting change of the actual trade or profession—

(*a*) a notice may be given under subsection (3) of section 62A; and

(*b*) an appeal may be brought under subsection (6) of that section,

by such one of the partners as may be nominated by them for the purposes of this subsection.

(7) Where—

(*a*) subsections (2) and (3) above apply in relation to the [profits]² or losses of a trade or profession carried on by persons in partnership; and

(*b*) other income or other relievable losses accrue to those persons by virtue of their being partners,

those subsections shall apply as if references to the [profits]² or losses arising from the trade or profession included references to that other income or those other relievable losses.

(8) Where a person's share in any untaxed income from one or more sources, or in any relievable losses, is determined in accordance with subsection (3) as applied by subsection (7) above, sections 60 to 63A shall apply as if—

(*a*) that share of that income or of those losses were [profits]² or losses of a trade or profession carried on by that person alone;

(*b*) that trade or profession (''the second deemed trade or profession'') had been set up and commenced by him at the time when he became a partner;

(*c*) paragraphs (*c*) and (*d*) of subsection (4) and subsection (5) above applied in relation to the second deemed trade or profession as they apply in relation to the other deemed trade or profession;

(*d*) the second deemed trade or profession were permanently discontinued by him at the time when he ceases to be a partner; and

(*e*) each source of the income were treated as continuing until the second deemed trade or profession is treated as permanently discontinued.

(9) Where—

(*a*) the basis period for any year of assessment is given by section 62(2)(*b*) in the case of a person's second deemed trade or profession, or such a trade or profession is treated as permanently discontinued in any year of assessment; and

(*b*) the amount falling to be deducted under subsection (1) or (3) of section 63A exceeds that person's share, as determined in accordance with subsection (3) as applied by subsection (7) above, in any untaxed income,

the amount of the excess shall be deducted in computing that person's income for that year.

(10) Subsections (1) to (3) above apply in relation to persons in partnership by whom a business which is not a trade or profession is carried on as they apply in relation to persons in partnership by whom a trade or profession is carried on.

(11) In subsections (2) and (3) above as applied by subsection (10) above, references to the [profits]² or losses arising from the trade or profession shall have effect as references to any income or relievable losses arising from the business.

(12) In this section—

"accounting change" and "the old date" have the meanings given by section 62(1);

"accounting date" has the meaning given by section 60(5);

"the commencement year", in relation to the deemed trade or profession or the second deemed trade or profession, means the year of assessment in which that trade or profession is deemed to have been set up and commenced;

"income" means any income (whether or not chargeable under Schedule D);

"untaxed income" means income which is not—

    (*a*) income from which income tax has been deducted;

    (*b*) income from or on which income tax is treated as having been deducted or paid; or

    (*c*) income chargeable under Schedule F.

(13) In this section—

    (*a*) any reference to sections 60 to 63A includes a reference to those sections as applied in relation to losses by section 382(3) and (4) and section 385(1); and

    (*b*) any reference to a person becoming or ceasing to be a partner is a reference to his beginning or, as the case may be, ceasing to carry on the actual trade or profession in partnership with other persons.]¹

Commentary—*Simon's Direct Tax Service* E1.808; E5.301.

Revenue Interpretation RI 137—Clarification of the circumstances in which income from jointly owned property constitutes partnership income.

Definitions—"trade", s 832(1).

Cross references—See TA 1988 s 282A(4)(*b*) (disapplication for income from jointly held property of man and wife to unearned income to which this section applies).

TA 1988 s 510A(7) (disapplication of this section to members of an European Economic Interest Grouping).

Amendments—¹ This section was substituted by FA 1994 s 215(1), (4), (5) (as amended by FA 1995 s 117(2)), from the year 1994–1995 in relation to partnerships whose trades, professions or businesses are set up and commenced after 5 April 1994 (but from 1995–96 for such partnerships which are controlled abroad: see FA 1995 s 125(1)). The substitution has effect from the year 1997–98 in relation to partnerships etc set up and commenced before 6 April 1994. (As respects the year 1994–95 the section had effect as if sub-s (2)(*b*) and the word "and" preceding it were omitted; see FA 1995 s 117(4).)

² Word in sub-ss (2), (3), (4), (7), (8)(*a*), (11) substituted by FA 1998 Sch 7 para 1 with effect from 31 July 1998.

112 Partnerships controlled abroad

[(1) So long as a trade, profession or business is carried on by persons in partnership and any of those persons is not resident in the United Kingdom, section 111 shall have effect for the purposes of income tax in relation to the partner who is not so resident as if—

    (*a*) the reference in subsection (2)(*b*) to an individual resident in the United Kingdom were a reference to an individual who is not so resident; and

    (*b*) in subsection (4)(*a*), after "carried on" there were inserted "in the United Kingdom".

(1A) Where—

    (*a*) any persons are carrying on a trade, profession or business in partnership,

    (*b*) the trade, profession or business is carried on wholly or partly outside the United Kingdom,

    (*c*) the control and management of the trade, profession or business is situated outside the United Kingdom, and

    (*d*) any of the partners who is an individual resident in the United Kingdom satisfies the Board that he is not domiciled in the United Kingdom or that, being a Commonwealth citizen or a citizen of the Republic of Ireland, he is not ordinarily resident in the United Kingdom,

section 111 shall have effect in accordance with subsection (1) above as if that partner were not resident in the United Kingdom and, in addition (as respects that partner as an individual who is in fact resident in the United Kingdom), his interest as a partner, so far as it entitles him to a share of any [profits]³ arising from the carrying on of the trade, profession or business otherwise than within the United Kingdom, shall be treated for the purposes of Case V of Schedule D as if it were a possession outside the United Kingdom.

(1B) Where any persons are carrying on a trade or profession in partnership, the trade or profession is carried on wholly or partly outside the United Kingdom and an individual who is one of the partners changes his residence (within the meaning of section 110A), it shall be assumed for income tax purposes—

    (*a*) that that individual ceased to be a partner at the time of the change and became one again immediately afterwards; and

    (*b*) in relation to matters arising after the change, that the time when he became a partner is the time immediately after the change;

but nothing in this subsection shall, in relation to that individual, prevent any portion of a loss sustained before the change from being carried forward under section 385 and set against [profits]³ arising or accruing after the change.]¹

(4) In any case where—

    (*a*) a person resident in the United Kingdom (in this subsection and subsection (5) below referred to as "the resident partner") is a member of a partnership which resides [outside the United Kingdom or which carries on any trade, profession or business the control and management of which is situated outside the United Kingdom]²; and (*b*) by virtue of any arrangements falling within section 788 any of the income or capital gains of the partnership is relieved from tax in the United Kingdom,

the arrangements referred to in paragraph (*b*) above shall not affect any liability to tax in respect of the resident partner's share of any income or capital gains of the partnership.

(5) If, in a case where subsection (4) above applies, the resident partner's share of the income of the partnership consists of or includes a share in a qualifying distribution made by a company resident in the United Kingdom, then, notwithstanding anything in the arrangements, the resident partner (and not the partnership as a whole) shall be regarded as entitled to that share of the tax credit in respect of the distribution which corresponds to his share of the distribution.

(6) Section 115(5) has effect as respects the application of [subsections (4) and (5) above][2] where the partners in a partnership include a company.

Commentary—*Simon's Direct Tax Service* A3.303; B3.124; E5.338.
Revenue Internal Guidance—International tax handbook ITH 1600–1604 (background to the section).
ITH 1606 (sub-s (2) "business" includes a profession).
ITH 1612–1613 (determination of place of control and management).
ITH 1614 ("control" and "management" are separate concepts).
ITH 1619–1622 (discussion of *Newstead v Frost*, (1980) 53 TC 525).
ITH 1623–1625 (parallel overseas partnerships).
ITH 1626–1627, 1654–1660, 1667 (effect of double taxation agreements).
ITH 1635–1636 (importation of losses).
ITH 1639 (limited partnerships registered in the UK but claiming no business activities to be reviewed by International Division (Foreign Partnerships)).
ITH 1644–1645 (UK representative partners).
ITH 1664 (s 111 (old version) assessment is made up of shares of world-wide profits of UK partners and shares of UK profits of non-resident partners).
Simon's Tax Cases—*Padmore v IRC (No 2)* [2001] STC 280.
Definitions—"Company", s 832(1), (2); "control", s 840; "distribution", s 209(2); "qualifying distribution", s 832(1); "tax", s 832(3); "tax credit", s 832(1); "trade", s 832(1); "United Kingdom", s 830(1).
Cross references—See TA 1988 s 115(5) (application of this section where partners in a partnership include a company).
TA 1988 s 510A(7) (this section to have effect with modifications in relation to members of a European Economic Interest Grouping).
TCGA 1992 s 59 (determination of residence of partnerships in accordance with sub-ss (1), (2) above for purposes of capital gains tax).
Amendments—[1] Sub-ss (1)–(1B) substituted for sub-ss (1)–(3) and words in sub-s (4)(*a*), (6) substituted by FA 1995 s 125(1)–(3) with effect from the year 1997–98, and, so far as this Act has application with the amendments made by FA 1994 ss 215, 216 to partnerships whose trades, professions or businesses were set up and commenced after 5 April 1994, as respects the years 1995–96 and 1996–97.
[2] Words in sub-s (6) substituted by FA 1995 s 125(1), (3)(*b*) with effect from the year 1997–98, and so far as this Act has application with the amendments made by FA 1994 ss 215, 216, to partnerships whose trades, professions or businesses were set up and commenced after 5 April 1994, as respects the years 1995–96 and 1996–97.
[3] Word in sub-s (1A), (1B) substituted by FA 1998 Sch 7 para 1 with effect from 31 July 1998.

113 Effect, for income tax, of change in ownership of trade, profession or vocation

(1) Where there is a change in the persons engaged in carrying on any trade, profession or vocation chargeable under Case I or II of Schedule D, then, subject to the provisions of this section ...[1], the amount of the [profits][2] of the trade, profession or vocation on which income tax is chargeable for any year of assessment and the persons on whom it is chargeable, shall be determined as if the trade, profession or vocation had been permanently discontinued, and a new one set up and commenced, at the date of the change.

[(2) Where—

(*a*) there is such a change as is mentioned in subsection (1) above, and
(*b*) a person engaged in carrying on the trade, profession or vocation immediately before the change continues to be so engaged immediately after it,

subsection (1) above shall not apply to treat the trade, profession or vocation as discontinued or a new one as set up and commenced.][1]

(3)–(5) ...[1]

(6) In the case of the death of a person who, if he had not died, would under the provisions of this section have become chargeable to tax for any year, the tax which would have been so chargeable shall be assessed and charged upon his executors or administrators, and shall be a debt due from and payable out of his estate; ...[1]

(7) For the purposes of this section, a change in the personal representatives of any person, or in the trustees of any trust, shall not be treated as a change in the persons engaged in the carrying on any trade, profession or vocation carried on by those personal representatives or trustees as such.

Commentary—*Simon's Direct Tax Service* E5.332.
Statement of Practice SP 9/86—Basis on which the Revenue apply the provisions of this section in relation to partnership mergers and demergers.
Revenue Interpretation RI 173—Confirms that under the self-assessment rules for partnerships a fresh herd basis election is still required after a change in the membership of a farming partnership if herd basis is to continue, and gives details of the form of election required.
Revenue Decision RD 8—Late partnership continuation election.
Simon's Tax Cases—*Watts (T/A AA Watts) v Hart* [1984] STC 548*.
s 113(1), *Maidment v Kibby* [1993] STC 494*.
Definitions—"Apportionment", s 834(4); "the Board", s 832(1); "income tax", s 832(4); "inspector", s 832(1); "notice", s 832(1); "Schedule D", s 18(1); "tax", s 832(3); "trade", s 832(1); "year of assessment", s 832(1).

Cross references—TMA 1970 s 58(3)(*b*) (proceedings under sub-s (5) above to be in Northern Ireland if the place given by certain rules in relation to the parties to the proceedings is in Northern Ireland).
TA 1988 s 65(3) (disapplication of this section to income chargeable under Schedule D Case V but computed as under Schedule D Cases I and II).
TA 1988 s 89 (deduction of debts proving irrecoverable after event treated as discontinuance).
TA 1988 s 102(2) (valuation of stock and work in progress where trade etc is treated by this section as discontinued).
TA 1988 s 110(2) (charge under Schedule D Case VI on post-cessation receipts under TA 1988 ss 103–109 extended to events treated as a discontinuance under this section).
TA 1988 s 380(3) (deemed discontinuance disregarded for the purposes of set-off of losses against general income).
TA 1988 s 385(5) (deemed discontinuance disregarded for the purposes of carry-forward of loss relief).
TA 1988 s 782(9) (deemed discontinuance disregarded in the context of certain payments received in respect of leased assets).
TA 1988 s 804(5) (recapture of excess double-tax relief in respect of income of non-basis period on cessation under this section).
Amendments—[1] Words in sub-ss (1), (6) and whole of sub-ss (3)–(5) repealed, and sub-s (2) substituted (i) in relation to partnerships commenced before 6 April 1994 from the year 1997–98 and (ii) in relation to partnerships commenced after 5 April 1994 from the year 1994–95 (but from the year 1995–96 in relation to partnerships commenced after 5 April 1994 which are controlled abroad); see FA 1994 ss 215(4), (5), 216(1) and Sch 26 Pt V(24), as read with FA 1995 s 125(1).
[2] Word in sub-s (1) substituted by FA 1998 Sch 7 para 1 with effect from 31 July 1998.

Partnerships involving companies

114 Special rules for computing profits and losses

(1) So long as a trade[, profession or business][1] is carried on by persons in partnership, and any of those persons is a company, the profits and losses (including terminal losses) of the trade[, profession or business][1] shall be computed for the purposes of corporation tax in like manner, and by reference to the like accounting periods, as if the partnership were a company [and, subject to section 115(4), as if that company were resident in the United Kingdom][2], and without regard to any change in the persons carrying on the trade[, profession or business][1], except that—

   (*a*) references to distributions shall not apply; and
   (*b*) subject to section 116(5), no deduction or addition shall be made for charges on income, or for capital allowances and charges, nor in any accounting period for losses incurred in any other period nor for any expenditure to which section 401(1) applies; and
   (*c*) a change in the persons engaged in carrying on the trade[, profession or business][1] shall be treated as the transfer of the trade[, profession or business][1] to a different company if there continues to be a company so engaged after the change, but not a company that was so engaged before the change.

(2) A company's share in the profits or loss of any accounting period of the partnership, or in any matter excluded from the computation by subsection (1)(*b*) above, shall be determined according to the interests of the partners during that period, and corporation tax shall be chargeable as if that share derived from a trade[, profession or business][1] carried on by the company alone in its corresponding accounting period or periods; and the company shall be assessed and charged to tax for its corresponding accounting period or periods accordingly.

In this subsection "corresponding accounting period or periods" means the accounting period or periods of the company comprising or together comprising the accounting period of the partnership, and any necessary apportionment shall be made between corresponding accounting periods if more than one.

(3), (4) ...[3]

Commentary—*Simon's Direct Tax Service* D4.802, 810.
Statement of Practice SP 4/98—Application of loan relationships, foreign exchange and financial instruments legislation to partnerships which include companies.
Revenue Internal Guidance—International tax handbook ITH 1668 (non-resident partners in BVCA partnerships).
ITH 1672–1675 (status of overseas business organisations).
Company Taxation Manual COT3251–3260 (interpretation of s 114).
Definitions—"Accounting period", s 834(1); "apportionment", s 834(4); "capital allowances and charges", s 115(6); "charges on income", s 834(1); "company", s 832(1), (2); "distribution", s 209(2); "income tax", s 832(4); "profits", s 6(4); "trade", s 6(4); "year of assessment", s 832(1).
Cross references—See TA 1988 s 115 (supplementary provisions).
TA 1988 s 116(5) (application with modification of sub-s (2) above for the purposes of s 116).
TA 1988 s 510A(7) (sub-s (4) above not to apply to members of a European Economic Interest Grouping).
FA 1994 s 172(4) (interest rate and currency contracts: special rules for computing profits and losses in relation to such contracts accruing to partnerships involving qualifying companies).
Tonnage Tax Regulations, SI 2000/2303 (application of this section for the purposes of tonnage tax).
Amendments—[1] Words ", profession or business" inserted in each place (i) as respects partnerships commenced before 6 April 1994 from the year 1997–98 and (ii) as respects partnerships commenced after 5 April 1994 from the year 1994–95 (but from the year 1995–96 in relation to partnerships commenced after 5 April 1994 which are controlled abroad): see FA 1994 s 215(2)(*a*), (*b*), (4), (5), as read with FA 1995 s 125(1).
[2] Words in sub-s (1) inserted by FA 1995 s 125(4) with effect generally from the year 1997–98, but with effect also for the years 1995–96 and 1996–97 in respect of partnerships commenced after 5 April 1994.
[3] Sub-ss (3), (4) repealed by FA 1994 s 215 (3)(*a*), (4), (5), Sch 26 Pt V(24) (as amended in the case of s 215(3)(*a*) by FA 1995 s 117(1)(*d*), as read with FA 1995 s 125(1), with effect (I) as respects partnerships commenced before 6 April 1994 from the year 1997-98, and (ii) as respects partnerships commenced after 5 April 1994 from the year 1994-95 (but from the year 1995-96 as respects partnerships commenced after 5 April 1994 which are controlled abroad). Sub-s (3) was also repealed by FA 1995 Sch 29, Pt VIII(15).

115 Provisions supplementary to section 114

(1)–(3) ...[1]

[(4) So long as a trade, profession or business is carried on by persons in partnership and any of those persons is a company which is not resident in the United Kingdom, section 114 shall have effect in relation to that company as if—

    (a) the reference in subsection (1) to a company resident in the United Kingdom were a reference to a company that is not so resident; and

    (b) in subsection (2), after "carried on" there were inserted "in the United Kingdom through a branch or agency".][2]

[(5) Where the partners in a partnership include a company, subsections (4) and (5) of section 112 shall apply for the purposes of corporation tax as well as for the purposes of income tax, and section 114 shall have effect accordingly.][2]

(7) For the purposes of ...[3] section 114 "profits" shall not be taken as including chargeable gains.

Commentary—*Simon's Direct Tax Service* **D4.805–808.**
Definitions—"Accounting period", s 834(1); "apportionment", s 834(4); "capital allowance", s 832(1); "the Capital Allowances Acts", s 832(1); "charges on income", s 834(1); "company", s 832(1), (2); "control", s 840; "income tax", s 832(4); "profits", s 6(4); "profits or gains", s 833(1); "Schedule D", s 18(1); "trade", s 6(4); "United Kingdom", s 830(1); "year of assessment", s 832(1).
Amendments—[1] Sub-ss (1), (2), (3), (6) repealed (i) in relation to partnerships commenced before 6 April 1994 from the year 1997–98 and (ii) in relation to partnerships commenced after 5 April 1994 from the year 1994–95 (but from the year 1995–96 in relation to partnerships commenced after 5 April 1994 which are controlled abroad): see FA 1994 s 215(3)(b), (4), (5) and Sch 26 Pt V(24), as read with FA 1995 s 125(1).
[2] Sub-ss (4), (5) substituted by FA 1995 s 125(5) from the year 1997–98, and so far as this Act has application with the amendments made by FA 1994 ss 215, 216 (cf note [1] above) to partnerships whose trades, professions or businesses were set up and commenced after 5 April 1994, as respects the years 1995–96 and 1996–97.
[3] Words omitted in sub-s (7) repealed by FA 1995 Sch 29 Pt VIII(16), with effect in relation to any cases in relation to which s 112 *ante* has effect as amended by FA 1995 s 125.

116 Arrangements for transferring relief

(1) The provisions of subsection (2) below shall apply in relation to a company ("the partner company") which is a member of a partnership carrying on a trade if arrangements are in existence (whether as part of the terms of the partnership or otherwise) whereby—

    (a) in respect of the whole or any part of the value of, or of any portion of, the partner company's share in the profits or loss of any accounting period of the partnership, another member of the partnership or any person connected with another member of the partnership receives any payment or acquires or enjoys, directly or indirectly, any other benefit in money's worth; or

    (b) in respect of the whole or any part of the cost of, or of any portion of, the partner company's share in the loss of any accounting period of the partnership, the partner company or any person connected with that company receives any payment or acquires or enjoys, directly or indirectly, any other benefit in money's worth, other than a payment in respect of group relief to the partner company by a company which is a member of the same group as the partner company for the purposes of group relief.

(2) In any case where the provisions of this subsection apply in relation to the partner company—

    (a) the company's share in the loss of the relevant accounting period of the partnership and its share in any charges on income, within the meaning of section 338, paid by the partnership in that accounting period shall not be available for set-off for the purposes of corporation tax except against its share in the profits of the trade carried on by the partnership; and

    (b) except in accordance with paragraph (a) above, no trading losses shall be available for set-off for the purposes of corporation tax against the company's share in the profits of the relevant accounting period of the partnership; and

    (c) except in accordance with paragraphs (a) and (b) above, no amount which, apart from this subsection, would be available for relief against profits shall be available for set-off for the purposes of corporation tax against so much of the company's total profits as consists of its share in the profits of the relevant accounting period of the partnership; and

    (d) ...[1]

(3) In subsection (2) above "relevant accounting period of the partnership" means any accounting period of the partnership in which any such arrangements as are specified in subsection (1) above are in existence or to which any such arrangements apply.

(4) If a company is a member of a partnership and tax in respect of any profits of the partnership is chargeable under Case VI of Schedule D, this section shall apply in relation to the company's share in the profits or loss of the partnership as if—

    (a) the profits or loss to which the company's share is attributable were the profits of, or the loss incurred in, a trade carried on by the partnership; and

    [(b) any allowance to be given effect under Part 2 of the Capital Allowances Act in respect of a special leasing of plant or machinery were an allowance to be given effect in calculating the profits of that trade.][2]

(5) For the purposes of this section, subsection (2) of section 114 shall have effect for determining a company's share in the profits or loss of any accounting period of a partnership as if, in subsection (1)(*b*) of that section, the words ''or for capital allowances and charges'' were omitted.

(6) In this section ''arrangements'' means arrangements of any kind whether in writing or not.

(7) Section 839 shall apply for the purposes of this section.

Commentary—*Simon's Direct Tax Service* D4.810.
Definitions—''Accounting period'', s 834(1); ''the 1990 Act'', s 831(3); ''advance corporation tax'', s 14(1); ''charges on income'', s 834(1); ''company'', s 832(1), (2); ''group relief'', s 834(1); ''Schedule D'', s 18(1); ''tax'', s 832(3); ''trade'', s 832(1).
Cross references—FA 1973 s 32(3) (Revenue information power in respect of claims to which this section may apply).
Corporation Tax (Treatment of Unrelieved Surplus Advance Corporation Tax) Regulations, SI 1999/358 reg 14(3), (5) (where sub-s (2) above applies in relation to a company which is a member of a partnership, no unrelieved surplus ACT may be set against its liability to corporation tax on its share of the profits of the relevant accounting period of the partnership; ''relevant accounting period'' shall be construed in accordance with sub-s (3) above).
Amendments—[1] Sub-s (2)(*d*) repealed by FA 1998 Sch 3 para 10 with effect in relation to accounting periods beginning after 5 April 1999.
[2] Sub-s (4)(*b*) substituted by CAA 2001 s 578, Sch 2 para 21 with effect for income tax purposes, as respects allowances and charges falling to be made for chargeable periods ending after 5 April 2001, and for corporation tax purposes, as respects allowances and charges falling to be made for chargeable periods ending after 31 March 2001.

Limited partners

117 Restriction on relief: individuals

(1) An amount which may be given ...[2] to an individual under section 353, 380 or 381 below ...[2]—

(*a*) in respect of a loss sustained by him in a trade, or of interest paid by him in connection with the carrying on of a trade, in a relevant year of assessment; ...[2]

(*b*) ...[2]

may be given ... otherwise than against income consisting of [profits][1] arising from the trade only to the extent that the amount given ... or (as the case may be) the aggregate amount does not exceed the relevant sum.

(2) In this section—

''limited partner'' means—

(i) a person who is carrying on a trade as a limited partner in a limited partnership registered under the Limited Partnership Act 1907;

(ii) a person who is carrying on a trade as a general partner in a partnership, who is not entitled to take part in the management of the trade and who is entitled to have his liabilities, or his liabilities beyond a certain limit, for debts or obligations incurred for the purposes of the trade discharged or reimbursed by some other person; or

(iii) a person who carries on a trade jointly with others and who, under the law of any territory outside the United Kingdom, is not entitled to take part in the management of the trade and is not liable beyond a certain limit for debts or obligations incurred for the purposes of the trade;

''relevant year of assessment'' means a year of assessment at any time during which the individual carried on the trade as a limited partner;

''the aggregate amount'' means the aggregate of any amounts given *or allowed*[3] to him at any time under section 353, 380 or 381 below *or section [141 of the 1990 Act]*[3]—

(*a*) in respect of a loss sustained by him in the trade, or of interest paid by him in connection with carrying it on, in a relevant year of assessment; *or*[3]

(*b*) *as an allowance falling to be made to him for a relevant year of assessment either in taxing the trade or by way of discharge or repayment of tax to which he is entitled by reason of his participation in the trade*[3]

''the relevant sum'' means the amount of his contribution to the trade as at the appropriate time; and

''the appropriate time'' is the end of the relevant year of assessment in which the loss is sustained or the interest paid or for which the allowance falls to be made (except that where he ceased to carry on the trade during that year of assessment it is the time when he so ceased).

(3) A person's contribution to a trade at any time is the aggregate of—

(*a*) the amount which he has contributed to it as capital and has not, directly or indirectly, drawn out or received back (other than anything which he is or may be entitled so to draw out or receive back at any time when he carries on the trade as a limited partner or which he is or may be entitled to require another person to reimburse to him), and

(*b*) the amount of any [profits][1] of the trade to which he is entitled but which he has not received in money or money's worth.

(4) To the extent that an allowance is taken into account in computing [profits][1] or losses in the year of the loss by virtue of section 383(1) it shall, for the purposes of this section, be treated as falling to be made in the year of the loss (and not the year of assessment for which the year of loss is the basis year).

Commentary—*Simon's Direct Tax Service* E5.332, 335.
Definitions—''The 1990 Act'', s 831(3); ''interest'', s 832(1); ''tax'', s 832(3); ''trade'', s 832(1); ''United Kingdom'', s 830(1); ''year of assessment'', s 832(1).

Cross reference—See TA 1988 s 118 (restriction of loss relief for companies trading as limited partners).
Modification—CAA 2001 Sch 2 para 22(3) (repeals made by CAA 2001 Sch 2 para 22(2) not to exclude from an individual's aggregate amount for the purposes of this section any amounts included in the individual's aggregate amount at any time before the chargeable period to which CAA 2001 applies).
Amendments—[1] Word in sub-ss (1), (3)(b), (4) substituted by FA 1998 Sch 7 para 1 with effect from 31 July 1998.
[2] Words in sub-s (1), and sub-s (1)(b) repealed by CAA 2001 ss 578, 580, Sch 2 para 22(1), Sch 4 with effect for income tax purposes as respects allowances and charges falling to be made for chargeable periods ending after 5 April 2001.
[3] Words in sub-s (2), and sub-s (2)(b) repealed by CAA 2001 ss 578, 580, Sch 2 para 22(2), Sch 4 subject to CAA 2001 Sch 2 para 22(3) with effect for income tax purposes as respects allowances and charges falling to be made for chargeable periods ending after 5 April 2001.

118 Restriction on relief: companies

(1) An amount which may be given ...[4] under section 338, [393A(1)][2] or [403][3] below ...[4]—

    (a) in respect of a loss incurred by a company in a trade, or of charges paid by a company in connection with the carrying on of a trade, in a relevant accounting period; ...[4]

    (b) ...[4]

may be given ...[4] to that company (''the partner company'') otherwise than against [profits][3] arising from the trade, or to another company, only to the extent that the amount given ...[4] or (as the case may be) the aggregate amount does not exceed the relevant sum.

(2) In this section—

    ''relevant accounting period'' means an accounting period of the partner company at any time during which it carried on the trade as a limited partner (within the meaning of section 117(2));

    ''the aggregate amount'' means the aggregate of any amounts given *or allowed*[5] to the partner company or another company at any time under section 338, [393A(1)][1] or [403][2] below *or section [145 of the 1990 Act]*[5]—

        (a) in respect of a loss incurred by the partner company in the trade, or of charges paid by it in connection with carrying it on, in any relevant accounting period; *or*[5]

        (b) *as an allowance falling to be made to the partner company for any relevant accounting period either in taxing the trade or by way of discharge or repayment of tax to which it is entitled by reason of its participation in the trade;*[5]

    ''the relevant sum'' means the amount of the partner company's contribution (within the meaning of section 117(3)) to the trade as at the appropriate time; and

    ''the appropriate time'' is the end of the relevant accounting period in which the loss is incurred or the charges paid or for which the allowance falls to be made (except that where the partner company ceased to carry on the trade during that accounting period it is the time when it so ceased).

Commentary—*Simon's Direct Tax Service* **Division D4.8.**
Simon's Tax Cases—*Nunn v Gray* [1997] STC (SCD) 175.
Definitions—''Accounting period'', s 834(1); ''the 1990 Act'', s 831(3); ''company'', s 832(1), (2); ''tax'', s 832(3); ''trade'', s 832(1).
Modification—CAA 2001 Sch 2 para 22(3) (repeals made by CAA 2001 Sch 2 para 22(2) not to exclude from a company's aggregate amount for the purposes of this section any amounts included in the company's aggregate amount at any time before the chargeable period to which CAA 2001 applies).
Amendments—[1] ''393A(1)'' substituted in sub-ss (1), (2) by FA 1991 Sch 15 para 4 with effect for losses incurred in accounting periods ending after 31 March 1991.
[2] ''403'' substituted in sub-ss (1), (2) for ''403(1) to (3) and (7)'' by FA 1998 Sch 5 para 35 with effect from 1998–99 for income tax purposes, and from 1 April 1998 for corporation tax purposes, subject to the transitional provisions in FA 1998 Sch 5 Part IV.
[3] Word in sub-s (1) substituted by FA 1998 Sch 7 para 1 with effect from 31 July 1998.
[4] Words in sub-s (1), and sub-s (1)(b) repealed by CAA 2001 ss 578, 580, Sch 2 para 23(1), Sch 4 with effect for corporation tax purposes as respects allowances and charges falling to be made for chargeable periods ending after 31 March 2001.
[5] Words in sub-s (2), and sub-s (2)(b) repealed by CAA 2001 ss 578, 580, Sch 2 para 2, Sch 4 subject to CAA 2001 para 23 (3), with effect for corporation tax purposes as respects allowances and charges falling to be made for chargeable periods ending after 31 March 2001.

[Limited liability partnerships

118ZA Treatment of limited liability partnerships

(1) For the purposes of the Tax Acts, where a limited liability partnership carries on a trade, profession or other business with a view to profit—

    (a) all the activities of the partnership are treated as carried on in partnership by its members (and not by the partnership as such),

    (b) anything done by, to or in relation to the partnership for the purposes of, or in connection with, any of its activities is treated as done by, to or in relation to the members as partners, and

    (c) the property of the partnership is treated as held by the members as partnership property.

References in this subsection to the activities of the limited liability partnership are to anything that it does, whether or not in the course of carrying on a trade, profession or other business with a view to profit.

(2) For all purposes, except as otherwise provided, in the Tax Acts—

    (a) references to a partnership include a limited liability partnership in relation to which subsection (1) above applies,

    (b) references to members of a partnership include members of such a limited liability partnership, (*c*) references to a company do not include such a limited liability partnership, and

(*d*) references to members of a company do not include members of such a limited liability partnership.

(3) Subsection (1) above continues to apply in relation to a limited liability partnership which no longer carries on any trade, profession or other business with a view to profit—

(*a*) if the cessation is only temporary, or

(*b*) during a period of winding up following a permanent cessation, provided—

(i) the winding up is not for reasons connected in whole or in part with the avoidance of tax, and

(ii) the period of winding up is not unreasonably prolonged,

but subject to subsection (4) below.

(4) Subsection (1) above ceases to apply in relation to a limited liability partnership—

(*a*) on the appointment of a liquidator or (if earlier) the making of a winding-up order by the court, or

(*b*) on the occurrence of any event under the law of a country or territory outside the United Kingdom corresponding to an event specified in paragraph (*a*) above.]¹

Commentary—*Simon's Direct Tax Service* **E5.306**.
Amendments—¹ This section (which was originally inserted by the Limited Liability Partnerships Act 2000 s 10(1)) substituted by FA 2001 s 75(1), (6) with effect from 6 April 2001.

[118ZB Restriction on relief

Sections 117 and 118 have effect in relation to a member of a limited liability partnership as in relation to a limited partner, but subject to sections 118ZC and 118ZD.]¹

Commentary—*Simon's Direct Tax Service* **E5.348**.
Amendments—¹ This section inserted by the Limited Liability Partnerships Act 2000 s 10(1) with effect from 6 April 2001 (by virtue of SI 2000/3316 art 2). For the full text of that Act, see *Halsbury's Statutes* (4th edn) PARTNERSHIP.

[118ZC Member's contribution to trade

(1) Subsection (3) of section 117 does not have effect in relation to a member of a limited liability partnership.

(2) But, for the purposes of that section and section 118, such a member's contribution to a trade at any time (''the relevant time'') is the greater of—

(*a*) the amount subscribed by him, and

(*b*) the amount of his liability on a winding up.

(3) The amount subscribed by a member of a limited liability partnership is the amount which he has contributed to the limited liability partnership as capital, less so much of that amount (if any) as—

(*a*) he has previously, directly or indirectly, drawn out or received back,

(*b*) he so draws out or receives back during the period of five years beginning with the relevant time,

(*c*) he is or may be entitled so to draw out or receive back at any time when he is a member of the limited liability partnership, or

(*d*) he is or may be entitled to require another person to reimburse to him.

(4) The amount of the liability of a member of a limited liability partnership on a winding up is the amount which—

(*a*) he is liable to contribute to the assets of the limited liability partnership in the event of its being wound up, and

(*b*) he remains liable so to contribute for the period of at least five years beginning with the relevant time (or until it is wound up, if that happens before the end of that period).]¹

Commentary—*Simon's Direct Tax Service* **E5.348**.
Amendments—¹ This section inserted by the Limited Liability Partnerships Act 2000 s 10(1) with effect from 6 April 2001 (by virtue of SI 2000/3316 art 2). For the full text of that Act, see *Halsbury's Statutes* (4th edn) PARTNERSHIP.

[118ZD Carry forward of unrelieved losses

(1) Where amounts relating to a trade carried on by a member of a limited liability partnership are, in any one or more chargeable periods, prevented from being given or allowed by section 117 or 118 as it applies otherwise than by virtue of this section (his ''total unrelieved loss''), subsection (2) applies in each subsequent chargeable period in which—

(*a*) he carries on the trade as a member of the limited liability partnership, and

(*b*) any of his total unrelieved loss remains outstanding.

(2) Sections 380, 381, 393A(1) and 403 (and sections 117 and 118 as they apply in relation to those sections) shall have effect in the subsequent chargeable period as if—

(*a*) any loss sustained or incurred by the member in the trade in that chargeable period were increased by an amount equal to so much of his total unrelieved loss as remains outstanding in that period, or (*b*) (if no loss is so sustained or incurred) a loss of that amount were so sustained or incurred.

(3) To ascertain whether any (and, if so, how much) of a member's total unrelieved loss remains outstanding in the subsequent chargeable period, deduct from the amount of his total unrelieved loss the aggregate of—

(*a*) any relief given under any provision of the Tax Acts (otherwise than as a result of subsection (2)) in respect of his total unrelieved loss in that or any previous chargeable period, and

(*b*) any amount given or allowed in respect of his total unrelieved loss as a result of subsection (2) in any previous chargeable period (or which would have been so given or allowed had a claim been made).][1]

Commentary—*Simon's Direct Tax Service* **E5.348**.
Amendments—[1] This section inserted by the Limited Liability Partnerships Act 2000 s 10(1) with effect from 6 April 2001 (by virtue of SI 2000/3316 art 2). For the full text of that Act, see *Halsbury's Statutes* (4th edn) PARTNERSHIP.

[CHAPTER VIIA
PAYING AND COLLECTING AGENTS][1]

Commentary—*Simon's Direct Tax Service* **Division A7.9**.
Revenue and other press releases—
IR Tax Bulletin August 2001 p 867 (outlines changes made by FA 2000 and FA 2001 to the rules requiring deduction of tax at source from certain payments of interest).
Cross references—See TA 1988 ss 348(3), 349(1), (3) (provisions for deduction of tax from certain annual and other payments not to apply to any payment which is a relevant payment for the purposes of this Chapter).
Amendments—This Chapter (ss 118A–118K) repealed by FA 2000 ss 111(1), (6)(*a*), 156, Sch 40 Pt II(17) with effect for relevant payments or receipts in relation to which the chargeable date for the purposes of this Chapter is after 31 March 2001.

CHAPTER VIII
MISCELLANEOUS AND SUPPLEMENTAL

119 Rent etc payable in connection with mines, quarries and similar concerns

(1) Where rent is payable in respect of any land or easement, and either—

(*a*) the land or easement is used, occupied or enjoyed in connection with any of the concerns specified in section 55(2); or

(*b*) the lease or other agreement under which the rent is payable provides for the recoupment of the rent by way of reduction of royalties or payments of a similar nature in the event of the land or easement being so used, occupied or enjoyed,

the rent shall, subject to section 122 [and section 201 of the 1992 Act][1], be charged to tax under Schedule D, ...[2]

(2) Where the rent is rendered in produce of the concern, it shall, ...[3], be charged under Case III of Schedule D, and the value of the produce so rendered shall be taken to be the amount of the profits or income arising therefrom.

(3) For the purposes of this section—

"easement" includes any right, privilege or benefit in, over or derived from land; and

"rent" includes a rent service, rentcharge, fee farm rent, *feuduty* or other rent, toll, duty, royalty or annual or periodical payment in the nature of rent, whether payable in money or money's worth or otherwise.

Commentary—*Simon's Direct Tax Service* **B3.415**.
Definitions—"the 1992 Act", s 831(3); "Deduction of income tax", s 4(1); "Schedule D", s 18(1); "tax", s 832(3).
Cross references—See TA 1988 s 120 (treatment of rents in respect of electric-line wayleaves not falling within sub-s (1) of this section).
TA 1988 s 821(3) (recovery of tax underdeducted from rent etc falling within this section before passing of annual Finance Act).
Amendments—[1] Words in sub-s (1) inserted by TCGA 1992 Sch 10 para 14(1), (4).
[2] Words omitted from sub-s (1) repealed by FA 1995 s 145(1), (3), Sch 29 Pt VIII(22), with effect in relation to payments made after 1 May 1995.
[3] Words omitted from sub-s (2) repealed by FA 1995 Sch 29 Pt VIII(22), with effect in relation to payments made after 1 May 1995.
Prospective amendments—Words in italics in sub-s (3) to be repealed by the Abolition of Feudal Tenure etc (Scotland) Act 2000 s 76(1), (2), Sch 12 Pt I para 50(2), Sch 13 Pt 1 with effect from a day to be appointed.

120 Rent etc payable in respect of electric line wayleaves

(1) [Subject to subsection (1A) below][1] where rent is payable in respect of any easement enjoyed in the United Kingdom in connection with any electric, telegraphic or telephonic wire or cable (not being such an easement as is mentioned in section 119(1)), the rent shall be charged to tax under Schedule D, ...[1]

[(1A) If—

(*a*) the profits and gains arising to any person for any chargeable period include both rent in respect of any such easement as is mentioned in subsection (1) above and amounts which are charged to tax under Schedule A, and (*b*) some or all of the land to which the easement relates is included in the land by reference to which the amounts charged under Schedule A arise,

then, for that period, that rent shall be charged to tax under Schedule A, instead of being charged under Schedule D.][2]

(2)–(4) ...[3]

(5) In this section—

(*a*) "easement" and "rent" have the same meanings as in section 119;

(*b*) the reference to easements enjoyed in connection with any electric, telegraphic or telephonic wire or cable includes (without prejudice to the generality of that expression) references to easements enjoyed in connection with any pole or pylon supporting any such wire or cable, or with any apparatus (including any transformer) used in connection with any such wire or cable;
...[3]

(*c*) ...[3]

Commentary—*Simon's Direct Tax Service* **B3.1181.**
Definitions—"Chargeable period", s 832(1); "profits or gains", s 833(1); "Schedule A", s 15(1); "Schedule D", s 18(1); "tax", s 832(3); "United Kingdom", s 830(1).
Cross references—See TA 1988 s 3 (rent etc subject to deduction of tax under ss 348, 349 to be charged at the basic rate).
TA 1988 s 74(1)(*q*) (any rent etc falling under sub-s (1) above not allowable as a deduction (subject to sub-s (4) above) in computing profits or gains of a trade, profession or vocation).
TA 1988 s 387(3)(*c*) (payments under sub-s (4) of this section may not be carried forward as losses against future profits).
TA 1988 s 821(3) (recovery of under–deducted tax from payments to which this section applies made before passing of annual Finance Act).
Amendments—[1] Words in sub-s (1) inserted and words omitted repealed by FA 1997 s 60(1), (2), (5) Sch 17 Pt VI (2) with effect in relation to payments made after 5 April 1997.
[2] Sub-s (1A) inserted by FA 1997 s 60(1), (3), (5) with effect in relation to payments made after 6 April 1997.
[3] Sub-ss (2)–(4) and words omitted in sub-s (5) repealed by FA 1997 s 60(1), (4), (5), Sch 17 Pt VI(2) with effect in relation to payments made after 5 April 1997.

121 Management expenses of owner of mineral rights

[(1) Where for any year of assessment rights to work minerals in the United Kingdom are let, the lessor shall be entitled to deduct in determining the amount chargeable to income tax in respect of the rent or royalties for that year, any sums wholly, exclusively and necessarily disbursed by him as expenses of management or supervision of those minerals in that year.][1]

(3) In computing for the purposes of corporation tax the income of a company for any accounting period from the letting of rights to work minerals in the United Kingdom, there may be deducted any sums disbursed by the company wholly, exclusively and necessarily as expenses of management or supervision of those minerals in that period.

Commentary—*Simon's Direct Tax Service* **A3.504.**
Definitions—"Accounting period", s 834(1); "company", s 832(1), (2); "income tax", s 832(4); "tax", s 832(3); "United Kingdom", s 830(1); "year of assessment", s 832(1).
Cross references—See TMA 1970 s 46C (Special Commissioners to have jurisdiction on an appeal against an amendment to a self-assessment or partnership statement where the question in dispute concerns a claim made under sub-s (1) above).
TA 1988 s 587(2)(*b*) (certain payments to employees in respect of war injuries to be disallowed in computing expenses of management under this section).
TA 1988 s 617(4) (secondary Class 1 contributions or Class 1A contributions may be deducted in computing expenses of management under this section).
Amendments—[1] Sub-s (1) substituted for sub-ss (1), (2) as originally enacted by FA 1995 s 145(2), (3), with effect in relation to payments made after 1 May 1995.

122 Relief in respect of mineral royalties

(1) Subject to the following provisions of this section, a person resident or ordinarily resident in the United Kingdom who in any year of assessment or accounting period is entitled to receive any mineral royalties under a mineral lease or agreement shall be treated—

(*a*) for the purposes of income tax, or as the case may be for the purposes of corporation tax on profits exclusive of chargeable gains, as if the total of the mineral royalties receivable by him under that lease or agreement in that year or period and any management expenses available for set-off against those royalties in that year or period were each reduced by one-half; ...[2]

(*b*) ...[2];

and this section shall have effect notwithstanding any provision of section 119(1) making the whole of certain kinds of mineral royalties chargeable to tax under Schedule D, ...[3]

(2) For the purposes of subsection (1)(*a*) above, "management expenses available for set-off" against royalties means—

(*a*) where section 121 applies in respect of the royalties, any sum brought into account under subsection (1) of that section in determining the amount of the repayment of income tax in respect of those royalties or, as the case may be, deductible from those royalties under subsection (2) of that section in computing the income of a company for the purposes of corporation tax; and

(*b*) if the royalties are chargeable to tax under Schedule A, any sums deductible under Part II as payments made in respect of management of the property concerned;

and if neither paragraph (*a*) nor paragraph (*b*) above applies, the reference in subsection (1)(*a*) above to management expenses available for set-off shall be disregarded.

(3) ...[2]

(4) Where subsection (1) above applies in relation to mineral royalties receivable under a mineral lease or agreement by a person not chargeable to corporation tax in respect of those royalties, then, in so far as the amount of income tax paid, by deduction or otherwise, by him in respect of those mineral royalties in any year of assessment exceeds the amount of income tax for which he is liable in respect of those royalties by virtue of subsection (1)(*a*) above—

(*a*) the amount of the excess shall in the first instance be set against the tax for which he is chargeable by virtue of [section 201(1) of the 1992 Act][1]; and

(*b*) on the making of a claim in that behalf, he shall be entitled to repayment of tax in respect of the balance of that excess.

(5) In this section references to mineral royalties refer only to royalties receivable on or after 6th April 1970, and the expression ''mineral royalties'' means so much of any rents, tolls, royalties and other periodical payments in the nature of rent payable under a mineral lease or agreement as relates to the winning and working of minerals; and the Board may by regulations—

(*a*) provide whether, and to what extent, payments made under a mineral lease or agreement and relating both to the winning and working of minerals and to other matters are to be treated as mineral royalties; and

(*b*) provide for treating the whole of such payments as mineral royalties in cases where the extent to which they relate to matters other than the winning and working of minerals is small.

(6) In this section—

''minerals'' means all minerals and substances in or under land which are ordinarily worked for removal by underground or surface working but excluding water, peat, top-soil and vegetation; and

''mineral lease or agreement'' means—

(*a*) a lease, profit à prendre, licence or other agreement conferring a right to win and work minerals in the United Kingdom;

(*b*) a contract for the sale, or a conveyance, of minerals in or under land in the United Kingdom; and

(*c*) a grant of a right under section 1 of the Mines (Working Facilities and Support) Act 1966 other than an ancillary right within the meaning of that Act.

(7) In the application of this section to Northern Ireland—

(*a*) references to mineral royalties include references to periodical payments—

(i) of compensation under section 29 or 35 of the Mineral Development Act (Northern Ireland) 1969 (''the 1969 Act'') or under section 4 of the Petroleum (Production) Act (Northern Ireland) 1964 (''the 1964 Act''); and

(ii) made as mentioned in section 37 of the 1969 Act or under section 55(4)(*b*) of that Act or under section 11 of the 1964 Act (payments in respect of minerals to persons entitled to a share of royalties under section 13(3) of the Irish Land Act 1903); and

(*b*) in its application to any such payments as are mentioned in paragraph (*a*) above, references to the mineral lease or agreement under which mineral royalties are payable shall be construed as references to the enactment under which the payments are made.

(8) ...[2]

Commentary—*Simon's Direct Tax Service* **B3.416.**
Regulations—Mineral Royalties (Tax) Regulations, SI 1971/1035.
Definitions—''The 1992 Act'', s 831(3); ''accounting period'', s 834(1); ''chargeable gain'', s 832(1); ''deduction of income tax'', s 4(1); ''income tax'', s 832(4); ''Schedule A'', s 15(1); ''Schedule D'', s 18(1); ''tax'', s 832(3); ''United Kingdom'', s 830(1); ''year of assessment'', s 832(1).
Simon's Tax Cases—*Padmore v IRC* [2000] STC (SCD) 356.
Cross references—See TA 1988 s 28 (deductions from receipts other than rent to have effect subject to this section). TA 1988 s 119 (deduction of tax from rent etc payable in connection with mines, quarries etc; to have effect subject to this section).
Amendments—[1] Words in sub-s (4)(*a*) substituted by TCGA 1992 Sch 10 para 14(1), (5) with effect from 6 April 1992.
[2] Sub-ss (1)(*b*) (and the word ''and'' preceding it), (3), (8) repealed by TCGA 1992 Sch 12 with effect from 6 April 1992.
[3] Words omitted from sub-s (1) repealed by FA 1995 Sch 29 Pt VIII(22), with effect in relation to payments made after 1 May 1995.

123 Foreign dividends

Commentary—*Simon's Direct Tax Service* **A6.107.**
Amendments—This section repealed by FA 1996 Sch 7 paras 13, 32, Sch 41 Pt V(2) with effect as respects income tax from the year 1996–97 and, as respects corporation tax, for accounting periods ending after 31 March 1996.

124 Interest on quoted Eurobonds

Commentary—*Simon's Direct Tax Service* **A6.108.**
Revenue and other press releases—IR Tax Bulletin August 2001 p 867 (Gross payments of interest).
Amendments—This section repealed by FA 2000 ss 111(2)(*b*), (6)(*b*), 156, Sch 40 Pt II(17) with effect for payments of interest made after 31 March 2001.

125 Annual payments for non-taxable consideration

(1) Any payment to which this subsection applies shall be made without deduction of income tax, shall not be allowed as a deduction in computing the income or total income of the person by whom it is made and shall not be a charge on income for the purposes of corporation tax.

(2) Subject to the following provisions of this section, subsection (1) above applies to any payment which—

(*a*) is an annuity or other annual payment charged with tax under Case III of Schedule D, not being interest; and

(*b*) is made under a liability incurred for consideration in money or money's worth all or any of which is not required to be brought into account in computing for the purposes of income tax or corporation tax the income of the person making the payment.

(3) Subsection (1) above does not apply to—

(*a*) any payment which in the hands of the recipient is income falling within [section 660A(8) or 9(*a*)][1];

(*b*) any payment made to an individual under a liability incurred in consideration of his surrendering, assigning or releasing an interest in settled property to or in favour of a person having a subsequent interest;

(*c*) any annuity granted in the ordinary course of a business of granting annuities; or

(*d*) any annuity charged on an interest in settled property and granted at any time before 30th March 1977 by an individual to a company whose business at that time consisted wholly or mainly in the acquisition of interests in settled property or which was at that time carrying on life assurance business in the United Kingdom.

(4) In the application of this section to Scotland the references in subsection (3) above to settled property shall be construed as references to property held in trust.

(5) Subsection (1) above applies to a payment made after 5th April 1988 irrespective of when the liability to make it was incurred.

Commentary—*Simon's Direct Tax Service* **D2.210; E1.503.**
Revenue Internal Guidance—Inspector's manual IM 4865–4866 (application of sub-s (3): circumstances in which cases are to be referred to head office).
Definitions—"Deduction of income tax", s 4(1); "income tax", s 832(4); "interest", s 832(1); "Schedule D", s 18(1); "total income", s 835(1); "United Kingdom", s 830(1).
Cross references—See TA 1988 s 338(7) (payment to which sub-s (1) above applies is not a charge on income for corporation tax purposes).
FA 1989 s 59 (this section to apply to covenanted subscriptions to certain charities notwithstanding enjoyment of certain benefits by the covenantor in return for the subscription).
Amendments—[1] Words in sub-s (3)(*a*) substituted by FA 1995 s 74, Sch 17 para 2, with effect from the year 1995–96 (and apply to every settlement, wherever and whenever made or entered into).

[126 Treasury securities issued at a discount]

Commentary—*Simon's Direct Tax Service* **B5.219.**
Amendments—This section repealed by FA 1996 s 105, Sch 41 Pt V(3) with effect for the purposes of income tax from the year 1996–97 and for the purposes of corporation tax for accounting periods ending after 31 March 1996, subject to transitional provisions in FA 1996 Sch 15.

[126A Charge to tax on appropriation of securities and bonds]

Commentary—*Simon's Direct Tax Service* **C2.803.**
Amendments—This section (inserted by TCGA 1992 Sch 10 para 14(6)) repealed by FA 1996 s 105, Sch 41 Pt V(3) with effect for accounting periods ending after 31 March 1996, subject to transitional provisions in FA 1996 Sch 15.

127 Enterprise allowance

(1) This section applies to—

(*a*) payments known as enterprise allowance and made—

[(i)][3] [(whether before or after the coming into force of section 25 of the Employment Act 1988)][1] in pursuance of arrangements under section 2(2)(*d*) of the Employment and Training Act 1973 [or

(ii) under subsection (4)(*c*) of section 2 of the Enterprise and New Towns (Scotland) Act 1990 in relation to arrangements under subsection (3) of that section;][3] and

(*b*) corresponding payments made in Northern Ireland by the Department of Economic Development.

(2) Any such payment which would (apart from this section) be charged to tax under Case I or II of Schedule D shall be charged to tax under Case VI of that Schedule.

(3) Nothing in subsection (2) above shall prevent such a payment—

(*a*) being treated for the purposes of section 623(2)(*c*) or 833(4)(*c*) as immediately derived from the carrying on or exercise of a trade, profession or vocation; ...[2]

(*b*) ...[2]

Commentary—*Simon's Direct Tax Service* **B7.217.**
Definitions—"Schedule D", s 18(1); "tax", s 832(3); "trade", s 832(1).
Amendments—¹ Words in sub-s (1)(*a*) substituted by the Employment Act 1988 Sch 3 para 15.
² Sub-s (3)(*b*) and the preceding word "or" repealed by FA 1989 Sch 17 Pt V.
³ Sub-s (1) amended by the Enterprise and New Towns (Scotland) Act 1990 Sch 4 para 15 with effect from 1 April 1991 by virtue of the Enterprise and New Towns (Scotland) Act 1990 Commencement Order, SI 1990/1840.

[127A Futures and options: transactions with guaranteed returns

Schedule 5AA (which makes provision for the taxation of the profits and gains arising from transactions in futures and options that are designed to produce guaranteed returns) shall have effect.]¹

Commentary—*Simon's Direct Tax Service* **B7.204.**
Amendments—¹ This section inserted by FA 1997, 80(1), (6), with effect for chargeable periods ending on or after 5 March 1997 in relation to profits and gains realised, and losses sustained, on or after that date.

128 Commodity and financial futures etc: losses and gains

[(1)]³ [For the purposes of income tax,]³ any gain arising to any person in the course of dealing in commodity or financial futures or in qualifying options, which [is not chargeable to tax in accordance with Schedule 5AA and]² [apart from this subsection]³ would constitute profits or gains chargeable to tax under Schedule D otherwise than as the profits of a trade, shall not be chargeable to tax under [Schedule D]².

[(2) For the purposes of corporation tax, any gain arising to any company in the course of dealing in financial futures or in qualifying options, which apart from this subsection would constitute profits or gains chargeable to tax under Schedule D otherwise than as the profits of a trade, shall not be chargeable to tax under Case V or VI of Schedule D.]³

[3]³ In this section "commodity or financial futures" and "qualifying options" have the same meaning as in section [143 of the 1992 Act]¹, and the reference to a gain arising in the course of dealing in commodity or financial futures includes any gain which is regarded as arising in the course of such dealing by virtue of subsection [(3)]¹ of that section.

Commentary—*Simon's Direct Tax Service* **B7.204.**
Statement of Practice SP 14/91—Tax treatment of transactions in financial futures and options.
Simon's Tax Cases—*Griffin (Inspector of Taxes) v Citibank Investments* [2000] STC 1010; *HSBC Life (UK) Ltd v Stubbs (Insp of Taxes), Nationwide Life Ltd v Crisp (Insp of Taxes), Abbey Life Assurance Co Ltd v Colclough (Insp of Taxes), TSB Life Ltd v Colclough (Insp of Taxes), Lloyds TSB Life Assurance Co Ltd v Colclough (Insp of Taxes)* [2002] STC(SCD) 9.
Definitions—"the 1992 Act", s 831(3); "profits or gains", s 833(1); "Schedule D", s 18(1); "tax", s 832(3); "trade", s 832(1).
Cross references—See TA 1988 s 399(1) (restriction on relief in respect of losses from commodity etc dealings).
TA 1988 s 436(5) (nothing in this section to affect operation of TA 1988 s 436 in charging profits of insurance company from pension business as separate trade under Schedule D Case VI).
TA 1988 s 439B(5) (nothing in this section to affect computation of profits arising to resident insurance company from life reinsurance business).
TA 1988 s 441(6) (nothing in this section to affect operation of TA 1988 s 441 in charging overseas life-assurance business of resident insurance company).
TCGA 1992 s 143(1) (gains or losses from non-trading transactions in commodity and financial futures treated as capital gains or losses).
Amendments—¹ Words substituted by TCGA 1992 Sch 10 para 14(1), (7).
² Words inserted or substituted by FA 1997 s 80(3), (6), with effect for chargeable periods ending on or after 5 March 1997 in relation to profits and gains realised, and losses sustained, on or after that date.
³ Sub-ss (1), (3) numbered as such, in sub-s (1), words inserted, and words substituted for the words "apart from this section", and sub-s (2) inserted, by FA 2002 s 83(1)(*b*), (3) Sch 27 paras 1, 3 with effect for accounting periods beginning after 30 September 2002.

129 Stock lending

Commentary—*Simon's Direct Tax Service* **A7.702.**
Amendments—This section repealed by FA 1997 s 76, Sch 10 paras 1(1), 7(1), Sch 18 Pt VI(10) with effect in relation to, and to transfer under, any arrangement made on or after 1 July 1997 by virtue of the Finance Act 1997, Schedule 10, (Appointed Day) Order, SI 1997/991.

129A Stock lending: interest on cash collateral

Amendments—This section inserted by FA 1995 s 85(1), in relation to approved stock lending arrangements entered into after 1 May 1995, and repealed by FA 1997 s 76, Sch 10 paras 1(2), 7(1), Sch 18 Pt VI(10) with effect in relation to and to transfers under, any arrangement made on or after 1 July 1997 by virtue of the Finance Act 1997, Schedule 10, (Appointed Day) Order, SI 1997/991.

[129B Stock lending fees

(1) The income which, as income deriving from investments of a description specified in any of the relevant provisions, is eligible for relief from tax by virtue of that provision shall be taken to include any relevant stock lending fee.

(2) For the purposes of this section the relevant provisions are sections 592(2), 608(2)(*a*), 613(4), 614(3), 620(6) and 643(2).

(3) In this section "relevant stock lending fee", in relation to investments of any description, means any amount, in the nature of a fee, which is payable in connection with [any]² stock lending

arrangement relating to investments which, but for any transfer under the arrangement, would be investments of that description.

[(4) In this section "stock lending arrangement" has the same meaning as in section 263B of the 1992 Act.]²]¹

Commentary—*Simon's Direct Tax Service* B3.1007.
Revenue Internal Guidance—Inspector's manual IM 4305 (case under which stock lending fees should be taxed).
Definition— "tax", s 832(3).
Amendments—¹ Section inserted by FA 1996 s 157 with effect in relation to any arrangements entered into after 1 January 1996.
² Word in sub-s (3) substituted and whole of sub-s (4) substituted by FA 1997 Sch 10 paras 2, 7(1) with effect in relation to, and to transfers under, any arrangement made on or after 1 July 1997 by virtue of the Finance Act 1997, Schedule 10, (Appointed Day) Order, SI 1997/991.

130 Meaning of "investment company" for purposes of Part IV

In this Part of this Act "investment company", means any company whose business consists wholly or mainly in the making of investments and the principal part of whose income is derived therefrom, but includes any savings bank or other bank for savings except any which, for the purposes of the Trustee Savings Bank Act 1985 is a successor or a further successor to a trustee savings bank.

Commentary—*Simon's Direct Tax Service* D4.403.
Revenue Interpretation RI 126—Revenue approach and factors to be considered in determining whether a company's business consists wholly or mainly in the making of investments.
Revenue Internal Guidance—Company Taxation Manual COT810–816 (meaning of "investment company").
Simon's Tax Cases—*White House Drive Residents' Association Ltd v Worsley* [1997] STC (SCD) 63; *Cook v Medway Housing Society Ltd* [1997] STC 90; *Macniven v Westmoreland Investments Ltd* [1997] STC 1103.

PART V
PROVISIONS RELATING TO THE SCHEDULE E CHARGE

Revenue Internal Guidance—Schedule E manual, SE 12815 (termination payments and benefits; interaction with benefits received during employment).

CHAPTER I
SUPPLEMENTARY CHARGING PROVISIONS OF GENERAL APPLICATION
Miscellaneous provisions

Cross reference—See TA 1988 s 19 (charge to tax under Schedule E).

131 Chargeable emoluments

(1) Tax under Case I, II or III of Schedule E shall, except as provided to the contrary by any provision of the Tax Acts, be chargeable on the full amount of the emoluments falling under that Case, subject to such deductions only as may be authorised by the Tax Acts, and the expression "emoluments" shall include all salaries, fees, wages, perquisites and profits whatsoever.

(2) Tax under Case III of Schedule E shall be chargeable whether or not tax is chargeable in respect of the same office or employment under Case I or II of that Schedule, but shall not be chargeable on any emoluments falling under Case I or II ...¹.

Commentary—*Simon's Direct Tax Service* E4.401.
Concessions A6—Exemption on supply of free coal or on cash payments in lieu of free coal to miners.
A22—Tax is not charged on long service award made at ten-year intervals to directors and employees who have been in the employment for twenty years or more. The award should not be in cash and its cost should be as specified in the Concession.
A37—Fees received in respect of directorships are in strictness assessable on the recipient director under Schedule E. By Concession, however, they are assessed as partnership or company income if certain conditions are satisfied.
A61—Exemption for heating, lighting, etc expenses paid to clergymen.
A70—Small gifts to employees and their family by third parties and staff Christmas parties, annual dinner dance, etc are tax free up to specified costs.
A74—Free or subsidised meals to staff (or vouchers to obtain them) on employer's business premises or in a staff canteen are tax free, subject to conditions and exceptions.
A75—Theatrical entertainers transition to Schedule E with effect from 6 April 1990 where earnings are from engagements under "standard contracts" or contracts of employment.
Statements of practice SP 4/97—Taxation of commissions, cashbacks and discounts.
Simon's Tax Cases—*Tyrer v Smart* [1979] STC 34*.
s 131(1), *McGregor v Randall* [1984] STC 223*; *Wilson v Alexander* [1986] STC 365*; *Hamblett v Godfrey* [1987] STC 60*; *Singh v Williams* [2000] STC (SCD) 404.
Revenue Internal Guidance—Schedule E manual SE 00520–00590 (meaning of "emoluments").
SE 11310 (charge can arise where employee allowed to sub-let employer's accommodation—"money's worth" principle).
SE 31610 et seq. (introduces the principal rules that allow deductions from the emoluments of an office or employment).
SE 33001 (Foreign Earnings Deduction (FED) prior to 17 March 1998—FED is a deduction against Case I charge not an exemption, no question of chargeability under Case III).
SE 40301 (Schedule E Case III: general, explanation of sub-s (2)).
Definitions—"Chargeable period", s 832(1); "Schedule E", s 19(1); "tax", s 832(3); "the Tax Acts", s 831(2).
Cross references—See TA 1988 s 145(4) (exceptions to taxation of living accommodation provided to employees).
TA 1988 s 146A (emoluments in respect of the provision of living accommodation to be calculated first under s 145 or 146 and only to the extent of any excess under general Schedule E charge).
TA 1988 s 197(2) (exemption in respect of leave travel facilities for the armed forces).
Amendments—¹ Words in sub-s (2) repealed by FA 1989 s 42(1), (2) and Sch 17 Pt IV.

132 Place of performance, and meaning of emoluments received in the UK

(1) Where a person ordinarily performs the whole or part of the duties of his office or employment in the United Kingdom, then, for the purposes of Cases I and II of Schedule E, his emoluments for any period of absence from the office or employment shall be treated as emoluments for duties performed in the United Kingdom, except in so far as [they would, but for that absence][1] have been emoluments for duties performed outside the United Kingdom.

(2) Where an office or employment is in substance one the duties of which fall in the chargeable period to be performed outside the United Kingdom, then, for the purposes of Cases I and II of Schedule E, there shall be treated as so performed any duties performed in the United Kingdom the performance of which is merely incidental to the performance of the other duties outside the United Kingdom.

(3) Subsection (2) above shall not be construed as affecting any question under section [192A][2] or paragraph 3 of Schedule 12 as to where any duties are performed or whether a person is absent from the United Kingdom.

(4) For the purposes of Cases I and II of Schedule E, but subject to section 194(7) and paragraph 5 of Schedule 12, the following duties shall be treated as performed in the United Kingdom, namely—

    (a) the duties of any office or employment under the Crown which is of a public nature and the emoluments of which are payable out of the public revenue of the United Kingdom or of Northern Ireland; and

    (b) any duties which a person performs on a vessel engaged on a voyage not extending to a port outside the United Kingdom, or which a person resident in the United Kingdom performs on a vessel or aircraft engaged on a voyage or journey beginning or ending in the United Kingdom or on a part beginning or ending in the United Kingdom of any other voyage or journey.

(5) For the purposes of Case III of Schedule E, emoluments shall be treated as received in the United Kingdom if they are paid, used or enjoyed in, or in any manner or form transmitted or brought to, the United Kingdom, and subsections (6) to (9) of section 65 shall apply for the purposes of this subsection as they apply for the purposes of subsection (5) of that section.

Commentary—*Simon's Direct Tax Service* **E4.120.**
Concessions A25—Sub-s (4)(a) not to apply to duties performed by locally engaged non-resident staff with earnings not exceeding a specified limit.
Concession A27—Mortgage interest relief for persons falling within sub-s (4)(a) performing their duties overseas.
Concession A84—Income tax not chargeable on daily subsistence allowances paid by the EC to detached national experts who are treated by virtue of sub-s (4) as Crown Servants performing their duties in the UK.
Simon's Tax Cases—s 132(1), *Leonard v Blanchard* [1993] STC 259*.
s 132(4)(a), *Caldicott v Varty* [1976] STC 418*.
Revenue Internal Guidance—Schedule E manual SE 33035 (Foreign Earnings Deduction (FED): location of duties for crown servants).
SE 40202–40208 (further information on location of duties).
SE 40302–40303 (meaning of "received in the United Kingdom").
Definitions—"Chargeable period", s 832(1); "emoluments", s 131(1); "Schedule E", s 19(1); "United Kingdom", s 830(1).
Cross references—See TA 1988 s 194(7) (modification of sub-s (4)(b) above in calculating deduction for travel in respect of overseas employment on a vessel).
TA 1988 Sch 12 para 5 (certain duties performed on board vessel or aircraft to be treated as performed outside the UK, not withstanding sub-s 4(b) of this section).
FA 1989 s 54(9)(b) (Crown servants performing duties abroad specified in sub-s (4)(a) to be treated as UK resident for purpose of medical insurance relief).
Personal Equity Plan Regulations, SI 1989/469 regs 7(2)(c)(ii), 9(3)(c) (Crown servants performing duties abroad specified in sub-s (4)(a) to be eligible to invest in PEP).
FA 1991 s 32(8) (relief for expenses in connection with vocational training incurred by an individual performing duties treated by virtue of sub-s (4)(a) as performed in the UK).
Amendments—[1] Words in sub-s (1) substituted by FA 1996 Sch 20 para 6 with effect from the year 1996–97.
[2] Word in sub-s (3) substituted by FA 1998 s 63(3) with effect in relation to emoluments attributable to qualifying periods beginning on or after 17 March 1998, and emoluments attributable to qualifying periods beginning before 17 March 1998 which are received on or after that date.

133 Voluntary pensions

(1) Where—

    (a) a person has ceased to hold any office or employment, and

    (b) a pension or annual payment is paid to him, or to his widow or child, or to any relative or dependant of his, by the person under whom he held the office or by whom he was employed, or by the successors of that person, and

    (c) that pension or annual payment is paid otherwise than by or on behalf of a person outside the United Kingdom,

then, notwithstanding that the pension or payment is paid voluntarily or is capable of being discontinued, it shall be deemed to be income for the purposes of assessment to tax, and shall be assessed and charged under Schedule E.

(2) For the avoidance of doubt, it is hereby declared that the expressions "annuity" and "pension" in Schedule E include respectively an annuity and a pension which is paid voluntarily or is capable of being discontinued.

Commentary—*Simon's Direct Tax Service* **E4.127, 466.**
Concession A62—Pensions or increased pensions awarded to employees who suffer work-related injury or illness are not taxed.
Revenue Internal Guidance—Schedule E manual SE 74011 (circumstances in which s 133 applies).
SE 74101 (pensions strictly assessable on the amounts which the pensioner is entitled to in the year of assessment rather than receipts basis; examples given of how to deal with pensions paid in advance).
SE 74151 (pensions provided in a form other than cash may give rise to s 133 liability).
Definitions—"Child", ss 831(4), 832(5); "Schedule E", s 19(1); "tax", s 832(3); "United Kingdom", s 830(1).
Cross references—See TA 1988 s 58 (foreign pensions paid by or on behalf of a person outside the UK).
TA 1988 s 833(5)(b) ("earned income" to include pensions charged to tax under this section).
FA 1989 s 41(1)(b) (a pension or annual payment chargeable to income tax under this section to be charged in the year in which it accrued irrespective of when it is paid).

134 Workers supplied by agencies

(1) Subject to the provisions of this section, where—

(a) an individual ("the worker") renders or is under an obligation to render personal services to another person ("the client") and is subject to, or to the right of, supervision, direction or control as to the manner in which he renders those services; and

(b) the worker is supplied to the client by or through a third person ("the agency") and renders or is under an obligation to render those services under the terms of a contract between the worker and the agency ("the relevant contract"); and

(c) remuneration receivable under or in consequence of that contract would not, apart from this section, be chargeable to income tax under Schedule E,

then, for all the purposes of the Income Tax Acts, the services which the worker renders or is under an obligation to render to the client under that contract shall be treated as if they were the duties of an office or employment held by the worker, and all remuneration receivable under or in consequence of that contract shall be treated as emoluments of that office or employment and shall be assessable to income tax under Schedule E accordingly.

(2) Subsection (1)(b) above includes cases in which the third person is an unincorporated body of which the worker is a member.

(3) Subsection (1) above shall apply whether or not the worker renders or is under an obligation to render the services in question as a partner in a firm or a member of an unincorporated body; and where, in any case in which that subsection applies, the worker is a partner in a firm or a member of such a body, remuneration receivable under or in consequence of the relevant contract shall be treated for all the purposes of the Income Tax Acts as income of the worker and not as income of the firm or body.

(4) For the purposes of this section, any remuneration which the client pays or provides by reason of the worker being a person who renders or is under an obligation to render the services in question shall be treated as receivable in consequence of the relevant contract.

(5) Subsection (1) above shall not apply—

(a) if the services in question are services as an actor, singer, musician or other entertainer or as a fashion, photographic or artist's model; or

(b) if the services in question are rendered wholly in the worker's own home or at other premises which are neither under the control or management of the client nor premises at which the worker is required, by reason of the nature of the services, to render them.

(c) [...][1]

(6) Where an individual enters into arrangements with another person with a view to the rendering of personal services by the individual, being arrangements such that, if and when he renders any such services as a result of the arrangements, those services will be treated under subsection (1) above as if they were the duties of an office or employment held by him, then for all purposes of the Income Tax Acts any remuneration receivable under or in consequence of the arrangements shall be treated as emoluments of an office or employment held by the individual and shall be assessable to income tax under Schedule E accordingly.

(7) In this section "remuneration", in relation to an individual, does not include anything in respect of which he would not have been chargeable to tax under Schedule E if it had been receivable in connection with an office or employment held by him but, subject to that, includes every form of payment and all perquisites, benefits and profits whatsoever.

Commentary—*Simon's Direct Tax Service* **E4.225.**
Revenue Decision RD4—Operation of PAYE by a company supplying a worker to an agency.
Revenue Internal Guidance—Schedule E manual SE 11930 (PAYE avoidance: agencies and offshore employers—application of s 134).
See also the Employment Status Manual which provides additional guidance on the operation of s 134.
Simon's Tax Cases—*Bhadra v Ellam* [1988] STC 239*.
Definitions—"Emoluments", s 131(1); "income tax", s 832(4); "the Income Tax Acts", s 831(1)(b); "Schedule E", s 19(1); "tax", s 832(3).
Cross reference—See TMA 1970 s 16A(1) (returns in respect of agency workers).
Amendments—[1] Sub-s (5)(c) repealed by FA 1998 ss 55(1), 165, Sch 27 Part III(7) with effect from 6 April 1998 in relation to any payments made on or after that date, other than any made in respect of services before that date, and any payments made before 6 April 1998 in respect of services to be rendered on or after that date.

Shareholdings, loans etc

Cross reference—See TA 1988 s 140 (further interpretation of ss 135–139).

135 Gains by directors and employees from share options

(1) Subject to section 185, where a person realises a gain by the exercise, or by the assignment or release, of a right to acquire shares in a body corporate obtained by that person as a director or employee of that or any other body corporate, he shall be chargeable to tax under Schedule E on an amount equal to the amount of his gain, as computed in accordance with this section.

(2) Without prejudice to section 185, where tax may by virtue of this section become chargeable in respect of any gain which may be realised by the exercise of a right which is not capable of being exercised more than [ten][1] years after it is obtained, tax shall not be chargeable under any other provision of the Tax Acts in respect of the receipt of the right.

(3) Subject to section 136(4)—

    (*a*) the gain realised by the exercise of any such right at any time shall be taken to be the difference between the amount that a person might reasonably expect to obtain from a sale in the open market at that time of the shares acquired and the amount or value of the consideration given whether for them or for the grant of the right; and

    (*b*) the gain realised by the assignment or release of any such right shall be taken to be the difference between the amount or value of the consideration for the assignment or release and the amount or value of the consideration given for the grant of the right;

(a just apportionment being made of any entire consideration given for the grant of the right to acquire those shares and other shares or otherwise for the grant of the right to acquire those shares and for something besides).

(4) For the purposes of subsection (3) above, neither the consideration given for the grant of the right nor any such entire consideration as is mentioned in that subsection shall be taken to include the performance of any duties in or in connection with the office or employment by reason of which the right was granted, and no part of the amount or value of the consideration given for the grant shall be deducted more than once under that subsection.

(5) Where such a right as is mentioned in subsection (1) above is obtained as mentioned therein and is capable of being exercised later than [ten][1] years after it is obtained, and the receipt of the right is chargeable to tax under any other provision of the Tax Acts, then—

    [(*a*) the amount so charged shall be deducted from any amount which is chargeable under subsection (1) above by reference to the gain realised by the exercise, assignment or release of that right; and][2]

    (*b*) for the purpose of any such charge to tax in relation to the receipt of the right, the value of the right shall be taken to be not less than the market value at the time the right is obtained—

        (i) of the shares which may be acquired by the exercise of the right, or

        (ii) of shares for which shares so acquired may be exchanged,

    reduced by the amount or value (or, if variable, the least amount or value) of the consideration for which the shares may be so acquired.

(6) Subject to subsection (7) below, a person shall, in the case of a right granted by reason of his office or employment, be chargeable to tax under this section in respect of a gain realised by another person—

    (*a*) if the right was granted to that other person, or

    (*b*) if the other person acquired the right otherwise than by or under an assignment made by way of a bargain at arm's length, or if the two are connected persons at the time when the gain is realised,

but in a case within paragraph (*b*) above the gain realised shall be treated as reduced by the amount of any gain realised by a previous holder on an assignment of the right.

(7) A person shall not be chargeable to tax by virtue of subsection (6)(*b*) above in respect of any gain realised by another person if the first-mentioned person was divested of the right by operation of law on his bankruptcy or otherwise, but the other person shall be chargeable to tax in respect of the gain under Case VI of Schedule D.

(8) In any case where—

    (*a*) a person has obtained any such right to acquire shares as is mentioned in sub-section (1) above ("the first right"); and

    (*b*) as to any of the shares to which the first right relates, he omits or undertakes to omit to exercise the right or grants or undertakes to grant to another a right to acquire the shares or any interest in them; and

    (*c*) in consideration for or otherwise in connection with that omission, grant or undertaking, he receives any benefit in money or money's worth;

he shall be treated for the purposes of this section and section 136 as realising a gain by the assignment or release of the first right, so far as it relates to the shares in question, for a consideration equal to the amount or value of the benefit referred to in paragraph (*c*) above.

TA 1988

(9) Where subsection (8) above has had effect on any occasion, nothing in that subsection affects the application of this section in relation to a gain realised on a subsequent occasion, except that on that subsequent occasion so much of the consideration given for the grant of the first right as was deducted on the first occasion shall not be deducted again.

Commentary—*Simon's Direct Tax Service* **E4.512–514.**
Revenue & other press releases—IR 5-10-89 (an employee or director who ceases to be resident in the UK: no liability arises under this section on the exercise of options falling within s 140(1)(*a*)); but see IR 7-3-94: this exemption withdrawn from 6-4-94 for employees not resident or ordinarily resident; also withdrawn from 6-4-94 the 100 per cent foreign earnings deduction). See also new edition of IR 16.
Share Scheme Lawyers Group 17-7-95 (Revenue agree that a payment to an employee for cancellation or surrender of share options is not subject to PAYE, even though all or part of it may be within Sch E).
IR Booklet IR 16 (Share acquisitions by directors and employees — explanatory notes).
Construction—TCGA 1992 s 120(4) to be construed as one with this section; see TCGA 1992 s 120(7).
Simon's Tax Cases—*Ball v Phillips* [1990] STC 675*; *Hunt v Murphy* [1992] STC 41*.
s 135(1), (2), (5) *Williamson v Dalton* [1981] STC 753*; *AZ v BY* [1998] STC (SCD) 10.
Revenue Internal Guidance—Schedule E manual SE 11853 (potential charge arises under s 135 where an employee is granted an option over shares in a scheme not approved by the Inland Revenue when the option is exercised, assigned or released—see Share Schemes Manual 3.1).
SE 11862 (under sub-s (8) when an employee assigns or releases an option an income tax charge arises on the difference between the amount paid to the employee and the amount (if any) paid for the option).
Share Schemes Manual SSM 3.17 (when an option is sold or given up in return, or partly in return for another option, an income tax charge arises when the second option is exercised, not when the first option is sold or given up).
SSM 7.4 (sub-s (5): worked example illustrating application of this section).
Definitions—"Connected persons", s 839; "director", s 136(5); "employee", s 136(5); "market value", s 140(3); "release", s 136(5); "Schedule D", s 18(1); "Schedule E", s 19(1); "shares", s 136(5); "tax", s 832(3); "the Tax Acts", s 831(2).
Cross references—See TA 1988 s 136 (supplementary provisions).
TA 1988 s 137 (payment of tax under s 135 by instalments).
TA 1988 s 140 (further interpretation).
TA 1988 s 185(8) (reduction of gain under this section on rights acquired at a discount under approved share option schemes which are charged to tax under s 185(6A)).
TA 1988 s 187A (relief for contributions in respect of share option gains).
TCGA 1992 s 120(4) (relief for gains chargeable under sub-s (1) or (6) above where gains are realised by exercise of right to acquire shares).
FA 2000 Sch 14 Pt VI (taxation of share options in respect of the grant of a qualifying enterprise management incentive option).
Amendments—[1] Amount in sub-ss (2) and (5) inserted by FA 1998 s 49(1) with effect in relation to rights obtained after 5 April 1998.
[2] Sub-s (5)(*a*) substituted by FA 2002 s 37, Sch 6 para 1 with effect from the year 2002–03.

136 Provisions supplementary to section 135

(1) If a right to acquire shares in a body corporate is assigned or released in whole or in part for a consideration which consists of or comprises another right to acquire shares in that or any other body corporate, that other right shall not be treated as consideration for the assignment or release, but section 135 and this section shall apply in relation to it as they apply in relation to the right assigned or released and as if the consideration for its acquisition—

(*a*) did not include the value of the right assigned or released, but
(*b*) did include the amount or value of the consideration given for the grant of the right assigned or released so far as that has not been offset by any valuable consideration for the assignment or release other than the consideration consisting of the other right.

(2) If—

(*a*) as a result of two or more transactions a person ceases to hold a right to acquire shares in a body corporate and he or a connected person comes to hold another right to acquire shares in that or any other body corporate (whether or not acquired from the person to whom the other right was assigned), and
(*b*) any of those transactions was effected under arrangements to which two or more persons holding rights in respect of which tax may be chargeable under this section were parties,

those transactions shall be treated for the purposes of subsection (1) above as a single transaction whereby the one right is assigned for a consideration which consists of or comprises the other right.

(3) Subsection (2) above applies in relation to two or more transactions whether they involve an assignment preceding, coinciding with or subsequent to an acquisition.

(4) In the case of a right to acquire shares granted before 3rd May 1966—

(*a*) the amount of the gain realised at any time by the exercise, or by the assignment or release, of the right shall not exceed the difference between the market value of those shares at that time and their market value on 3rd May 1966 (and no gain shall be treated as so realised unless the later value exceeds the earlier value); and
(*b*) subsection (2) of section 135 shall not affect tax chargeable under Case I of Schedule E in respect of the receipt of the right, but the amount, if any, on which tax is so chargeable shall be taken into account under subsection (3)(*a*) and (*b*) of that section in relation to the gain realised by the exercise or by the assignment or release, of the right as if that amount formed part (in addition to any other amount) of the consideration for the grant of the right.

(5) For the purposes of this section and section 135—

(*a*) references to the release of a right include references to agreeing to the restriction of the exercise of the right;
(*b*) "director" means—

(i) in relation to a body corporate the affairs of which are managed by a board of directors or similar body, a member of that board or similar body;

(ii) in relation to a body corporate the affairs of which are managed by a single director or similar person, that director or person;

(iii) in relation to a body corporate the affairs of which are managed by the members themselves, a member of the body corporate;

and includes any person who is to be or has been a director;

(*c*) ''employee'', in relation to a body corporate, includes any person taking part in the management of the affairs of the body corporate who is not a director, and includes a person who is to be or has been an employee; and

(*d*) in so far as the context permits, ''shares'' includes stock;

and this section and section 135 shall apply in relation to any securities issued by a body corporate as they apply to shares in that body corporate.

(6) Where in any year of assessment a body corporate grants a right in respect of which tax may become chargeable under section 135, or allots or transfers any shares in pursuance of such a right, or receives notice of the assignment of such a right or provides any benefit in money or money's worth—

(*a*) for the assignment or for the release in whole or in part of such a right; or

(*b*) for or in connection with an omission or undertaking to omit to exercise such a right; or

(*c*) for or in connection with the grant or undertaking to grant a right to acquire shares or an interest in shares to which such a right relates;

it shall deliver particulars thereof in writing to the inspector not later than [92 days][1] after the end of that year.

[(7) A body corporate is not obliged to deliver particulars under subsection (6) above which it has already given in a notice under paragraph 2 of Schedule 14 to the Finance Act 2000 (enterprise management incentives: notice required for option to be qualifying option).

In other respects the obligations imposed by that subsection and that paragraph are independent of each other.

(8) The duty of a body corporate under subsection (6) above to deliver particulars of any matter includes a duty to deliver particulars of any secondary Class 1 contributions payable in connection with that matter that—

(*a*) are recovered as mentioned in section 187A(2)(*a*), or

(*b*) are met as mentioned in section 187A(3).

In this subsection ''secondary Class 1 contributions'' has the same meaning as in section 187A.][2]

Commentary—*Simon's Direct Tax Service* **E4.513.**
Definitions—''Connected person'', s 839; ''market value'', s 140(3); ''Schedule E'', s 19(1); ''tax'', s 832(3).
Cross references—See TMA 1970 s 98 Table 2 (penalty for failure to provide information required under sub-s (6)).
TA 1988 s 140 (further interpretation).
Amendments—[1] Words in sub-s (6) substituted by FA 2000 s 56(3) with effect where the event giving rise to the duty to deliver particulars occurs after 5 April 2000.
[2] Sub-ss (7), (8) inserted by FA 2000 s 56(4) with effect from 28 July 2000. Sub-s (8) has effect for any amounts recovered or met as mentioned in TA 1988 s 187A(2)(*a*) or (3) whether before or after this date.

137 Payment of tax under section 135 by instalments

(1) In any case where—

(*a*) for any year of assessment a person is chargeable to tax under Schedule E, by virtue of section 135, on an amount equal to a gain realised by the exercise of a right to acquire shares which was obtained before 6th April 1984; and

(*b*) the shares acquired in the exercise of that right were acquired for a consideration which, subject to subsection (2) below, was not less than the market value (determined as for the purposes of the [1992][1] Act) of shares of the same class at the time the right was granted or, if the right was granted before 6th April 1982, 90 per cent of that market value; and

(*c*) following an assessment for the year in which that right was exercised (''the relevant year'') an amount of tax chargeable by virtue of section 135 in respect of the amount referred to in paragraph (*a*) above and exceeding £250 is payable to the collector pursuant to regulations under section 203; and

(*d*) the person concerned makes an election in accordance with subsection (3) below,

he shall be entitled to pay tax by instalments in accordance with subsection (4) below.

(2) Shares which are acquired for a consideration less than that required by paragraph (*b*) of subsection (1) above by reason only of a diminution in the market value of shares of that class (determined as for the purposes of the [1992][1] Act) which is attributable solely to the share capital of the company issuing the shares being varied after the right to acquire the shares was granted, shall for the purposes of that paragraph be regarded as having been acquired for a consideration not less than that required by that paragraph.

(3) An election under this section shall be made by notice to the inspector before the expiry of the period of 60 days beginning immediately after the end of the relevant year.

TA 1988

(4) Where an election has been made under this section the tax referred to in subsection (1)(c) above shall, subject to subsection (5) and (6) below, be paid in five equal instalments as follows—

(a) the first shall be due and payable at the expiry of the period of 14 days beginning on the date on which application for the tax is made pursuant to regulations under section 203;

(b) the fifth shall be due and payable on the last day of the fifth year following the end of the relevant year; and

(c) the second, third and fourth instalments shall be due on such dates as will secure, so far as may be, that the interval between any two consecutive dates is the same.

(5) In any case where the date which, apart from this subsection, would be the due date for the fifth instalment of tax under subsection (4) above is earlier than the due date referred to in paragraph (a) of that subsection, all five instalments shall be due on the later date.

(6) Tax which, by virtue of an election under this section, is not yet due and payable in accordance with subsection (4) above may nevertheless be paid at any time and shall become due and payable forthwith if the person who made the election becomes bankrupt under the law of any part of the United Kingdom.

(7) Subject to any other provision of the Income Tax Acts requiring income of any description to be treated as the highest part of a person's income, for the purposes of paragraph (c) of subsection (1) above in determining what tax is chargeable on a person by virtue of section 135 in respect of the amount referred to in paragraph (a) of that subsection, that amount shall be treated as the highest part of his income for the relevant year.

Commentary—*Simon's Direct Tax Service* E4.512.
Simon's Tax Cases—*Hunt v Murphy* [1992] STC 41*.
Definitions—''the 1992 Act'', s 831(3); ''company'', s 832(1), (2); ''highest part of a person's income'', s 833(3); ''the Income Tax Acts'', s 831(1)(b); ''inspector'', s 832(1); ''notice'', s 832(1); ''Schedule E'', s 19(1); ''tax'', s 832(3); ''United Kingdom'', s 830(1); ''year of assessment'', s 832(1).
Cross references—TA 1988 s 550 (provisions for top-slicing relief for gains in respect of life policies, life-annuity contracts and capital redemption policies to have precedence over similar provision in sub-s (7) of this section).
TA 1988 s 833(3) (certain income to be disregarded for purposes of determination under sub-s (7) of this section).
TCGA 1992 ss 272, 273 (valuation provisions for purposes of tax on chargeable gains).
Amendments—[1] Year in sub-ss (1)(b), (2) substituted by TCGA 1992 Sch 10 para 14(1), (9).

138 Share acquisitions by directors and employees

Commentary—*Simon's Direct Tax Service* E4.525.
Amendments—This section repealed by FA 1988 s 88(1) and Sch 14 Pt VI with effect for acquisitions after 25 October 1987.

139 Provisions supplementary to section 138

Commentary—*Simon's Direct Tax Service*—E4.523.
Amendments—This section repealed by FA 1988 Sch 14 Pt VI for acquisitions after 25 October 1987.

140 Further interpretation of sections 135 to 139

(1) For the purposes of section 135, 136, 138 or 139, a right to acquire shares is obtained by a person as a director or employee (within the meaning of the section in question) of a body corporate—

(a) if it is granted to him by reason of his office or employment as such a director or employee who is chargeable to tax in respect of that office or employment under Case I of Schedule E; or

(b) if the right is assigned to him and was granted by reason of any such office or employment of his to some other person;

and paragraph (a) above shall apply to a right granted by reason of a person's office or employment after he has ceased to hold it if it would apply to a right so granted in the last chargeable period in which he did hold it.

(2) For those purposes any question whether a person is connected with another shall be determined in accordance with section 839.

(3) For those purposes—

''market value'' has the same meaning as, for the purposes of the [1992][1] Act, it has by virtue of section [272][1] of that Act; and

''securities'' has the meaning given by section 254(1).

Commentary—*Simon's Direct Tax Service* E4.513.
Definitions—''The 1992 Act'', s 831(3); ''chargeable period'', s 832(1); ''connected persons'', s 839; ''Schedule E'', s 19(1).
Amendments—[1] Year and number in sub-s (3) substituted by TCGA 1992 Sch 10 para 14(1), (11).

[140A Conditional acquisition of shares

(1) This section applies where—

(a) a beneficial interest in any shares in a company (''the employee's interest'') is acquired by any person (''the employee'') as a director or employee of that or another company; and

(b) the employee acquires that interest on terms that make his interest in the shares only conditional.

(2) ...[2]

(3) [If the terms on which the employee acquires the employee's interest are such that his interest in the shares in question will cease to be only conditional within five years after his acquisition of the interest][2], there shall (subject to the following provisions of this section) be no tax chargeable on the employee under Schedule E in respect of his acquisition of the interest except any tax which is so chargeable by virtue only of section 135 or 162.

(4) If [(whether or not subsection (3) above applies)][2]—

(a) the shares cease, without the employee ceasing to have a beneficial interest in them, to be shares in which the employee's interest is only conditional, or

(b) the employee, not having become chargeable by virtue of this subsection in relation to the shares, sells or otherwise disposes of the employee's interest or any other beneficial interest in them,

he shall, for the year of assessment in which they so cease, or in which the sale or other disposal takes place, be chargeable to tax under Schedule E on the amount specified in subsection (5) below.

(5) That amount is the amount (if any) by which the sum of the deductible amounts is exceeded by the market value of the employee's interest immediately after that interest ceases to be only conditional or, as the case may be, at the time of the sale or other disposal.

(6) For the purposes of subsection (5) above the market value of the employee's interest at any time is the amount that might reasonably be expected to be obtained from a sale of that interest in the open market at that time.

(7) For those purposes the deductible amounts are—

(a) the amount or value of the consideration given for the employee's interest;

(b) any amounts on which the employee has become chargeable to tax under Schedule E in respect of his acquisition of the employee's interest;

(c) any amounts on which the employee has, by reference to an event occurring not later than the time of the event by virtue of which a charge arises under this section, become chargeable to tax in respect of the shares under section 78 or 79 of the Finance Act 1988 (unapproved employee share schemes).

(8) Where the employee dies holding the employee's interest this section shall have effect—

(a) as if he had disposed of that interest immediately before his death; and

(b) as if the market value of the interest at the time of that disposal were to be determined for the purposes of subsection (5) above on the basis-

(i) that it is known that the disposal is being made immediately before the employee's death; and

(ii) that any restriction on disposal subject to which the employee holds the shares is to be disregarded in so far as it is a restriction terminating on his death.

(9) Any reference in this section or section 140B or 140C to shares in a company includes a reference to securities issued by a company; and the references in subsection (7)(c) above to an event include references to the expiry of a period.][1]

Commentary—*Simon's Direct Tax Service* E4.526.
Revenue & other press releases—IR Tax Bulletin June 1998 p 545 (Remuneration for employees in shares subject to forfeiture—article concerning awards of shares where, if certain conditions are not met, those shares may be forfeit before the employee is free to dispose of the shares).
IR Tax Bulletin April 2000 p 731 (Employee Share Plans—conditional shares and related topics).
Revenue Internal Guidance—Schedule E manual SE 11855, Share Schemes Manual 4.11 (PAYE avoidance: shares subject to forfeiture, application of this section).
SE 11863 (PAYE on share transactions: example involving this section).
Cross references—TA 1988 s 136(5) (applies for the purposes of this section but see exceptions in FA 1998 s 53(8)).
TA 1988 s 140H (supplementary definitions and explanations for terms used in this section).
TA 1988 s 839 (connected persons).
FA 2000 Sch 8 para 80(1) (no charge to tax by virtue of this section on a participant of an employee share ownership plan when any provision for forfeiture to which shares are subject, in accordance with FA 2000 Sch 8 para 65, is varied or removed).
FA 2000 Sch 14 para 55 (amount of relief under that Schedule is treated as deductible for the purpose of any charge under this section in respect of shares acquired under an enterprise management incentive option).
Amendments—[1] Section inserted by FA 1998 s 50(1) with effect in relation to interests acquired after 16 March 1998.
[2] Sub-s (2) repealed and words in sub-ss (3), (4) substituted by FA 1999 ss 42, 139, Sch 20 Pt III(8) with effect for shares acquired after 26 July 1999.

[140B Consideration for shares conditionally acquired

(1) This section applies in relation to any shares for determining the amount or value of the consideration referred to in section 140A(7)(a).

(2) Subject to the following provisions of this section, that consideration is any given by—

(a) the employee; or

(b) in a case where section 140H(1)(b) applies and the shares were acquired by another person, that other person,

in respect of the acquisition of an interest in the shares.

(3) The amount or value of the consideration given by any person for an interest in the shares shall include—

(a) the amount or value of any consideration given for a right to acquire those shares; and (*b*) the amount or value of any consideration given for anything by virtue of which the employee's interest in the shares ceases to be only conditional.

(4) Where any consideration is given partly in respect of one thing and partly in respect of another, the amount given in respect of the different things shall be determined on a just and reasonable apportionment.

(5) The consideration which for the purposes of this section is taken to be given wholly or partly for anything shall not include the performance of any duties of or in connection with the office or employment by reference to which the interest in the shares in question has been acquired by a person as a director or employee of a company.

(6) No amount shall be counted more than once in the computation of the amount or value of any consideration.

(7) Subsections (1) to (3) of section 136 shall apply for determining for the purposes of subsection (3)(*a*) above the amount or value of the consideration given for a right to acquire any shares as they apply for determining such an amount for the purposes of section 135.]¹

Commentary—*Simon's Direct Tax Service* **E4.526.**
Cross references—TA 1988 s 136(5) (applies for the purposes of this section but see exceptions in FA 1998 s 53(8)).
TA 1988 s 140H (supplementary definitions and explanations for terms used in this section).
TA 1988 s 839 (Connected persons).
Amendments—¹ Section inserted by FA 1998 s 50(1) with effect in relation to interests acquired on or after 17 March 1998.

[140C Cases where interest to be treated as only conditional

(1) For the purposes of sections 140A and 140B (but subject to the following provisions of this section) a beneficial interest in shares is only conditional for so long as the terms on which the person with that interest is entitled to it—

(*a*) provide that, if certain circumstances arise, or do not arise, there will be a transfer, reversion or forfeiture as a result of which that person will cease to be entitled to any beneficial interest in the shares; and
(*b*) are not such that, on the transfer, reversion or forfeiture, that person will be entitled in respect of his interest to receive an amount equal to or more than the amount that might reasonably be expected (if there were no provision for transfer, reversion or forfeiture) to be obtained from a sale of that interest in the open market at that time.

[(1A) A person shall not for the purposes of sections 140A and 140B be taken, in relation to any shares in a company or any security, to have an interest which is only conditional by reason only that one or more of subsections (2) to (4) below applies in relation to him.]²

(2) [This subsection applies in relation to a person if]³, in a case where there is no restriction on the meeting of calls by that person, the shares—

(*a*) are unpaid or partly paid; and
(*b*) may be forfeited for non-payment of calls.

(3) [This subsection applies in relation to a person if]³ the articles of association of the company require him to offer the shares for sale [or transfer them if he ceases to be an officer or employee of the company or of one or more group companies or of any group company.]³

[(3A) This subsection applies in relation to a person if he may be required to offer the shares for sale or transfer them, if, as a result of misconduct, he ceases to be an officer or employee of the company or of one or more group companies or of any group company.]²

(4) [This subsection applies in relation to a person if]³ the security may be redeemed on payment of any amount.

(5) In subsection (1) above the references, in relation to the terms of a person's entitlement, to circumstances arising include references—

(*a*) to the expiration of a period specified in or determined under those terms or the death of that person or any other person; and
(*b*) to the exercise by any person of any power conferred on him by or under those terms.]¹

[(6) For the purposes of this section—

(*a*) a company is a "group company" in relation to another company if they are members of the same group, and
(*b*) companies are taken to be members of the same group if, and only if, one is a 51 per cent subsidiary of the other or both are 51 per cent subsidiaries of a third company.]²

Commentary—*Simon's Direct Tax Service* **E4.526.**
Cross references—TA 1988 s 136(5) (applies for the purposes of this section but see exceptions in FA 1998 s 53(8)).
TA 1988 s 140H (supplementary definitions and explanations for terms used in this section).
TA 1988 s 839 (Connected persons).
Amendments—¹ Section inserted by FA 1998 s 50(1) with effect for interests acquired after 16 March 1998.
² Sub-ss (1A), (3A), (6) inserted by FA 1999 s 43(2), (5)–(7) and deemed always to have had effect.
³ Sub-ss (2), (3), (4) amended by FA 1999 s 43(3), (4), (7) and deemed always to have had effect.

[140D Convertible shares

(1) This section applies where a person ("the employee") has acquired convertible shares in a company as a director or employee of that or another company.

(2) For the purposes of this section shares are convertible wherever they—

(a) confer on the holder an immediate or conditional entitlement to convert them into shares of a different class; or

(b) are held on terms that authorise or require the grant of such an entitlement to the holder if certain circumstances arise, or do not arise.

(3) The employee shall be chargeable to tax under Schedule E if, at a time when he has a beneficial interest in them, the shares are converted into shares of a different class in pursuance of any entitlement to convert them that has been conferred on the holder.

(4) A charge by virtue of this section shall be a charge for the year of assessment in which the conversion occurs on the amount of the gain from the conversion.

(5) The amount of the gain from the conversion is the amount (if any) by which the market value at the time of the conversion of the shares into which the convertible shares are converted exceeds the sum of the deductible amounts.

(6) The deductible amounts are—

(a) the amount or value of any consideration given for the convertible shares;

(b) the amount or value of any consideration given for the conversion in question;

(c) any amounts on which the employee has become chargeable to tax under Schedule E in respect of his acquisition of those shares;

(d) any amounts on which the employee has, by reference to an event occurring not later than the time of the conversion, become chargeable to tax in respect of the shares under section 78 or 79 of the Finance Act 1988 (unapproved employee share schemes);

(e) if the convertible shares were acquired through a series of conversions each of which was a taxable conversion, the amount of the gain from each conversion, so far as not falling within paragraph (c) above.

(7) In subsection (6) above the reference to a taxable conversion is a reference to any conversion which—

(a) gave rise to a gain on which the employee was chargeable to tax by virtue of this section, or

(b) would have given rise to such a gain but for the fact that the market value of the shares at the time of the conversion did not exceed the sum of the deductible amounts.

(8) Tax shall not be chargeable by virtue of this section if—

(a) the conversion is a conversion of shares of one class only ("the original class") into shares of one other class only ("the new class");

(b) all shares of the original class are converted into shares of the new class; and

(c) one of the conditions in subsection (9) below is fulfilled.

(9) The conditions referred to in subsection (8) above are—

(a) that immediately before the conversion the majority of the company's shares of the original class are held otherwise than by or for the benefit of—

(i) directors or employees of the company;

(ii) an associated company of the company; or

(iii) directors or employees of such an associated company; and

(b) that immediately before the conversion the company is employee-controlled by virtue of holdings of shares of the original class.

(10) Tax shall not be chargeable by virtue of this section where the interest which the employee acquires in the shares into which the convertible shares are converted is an interest which (within the meaning given for the purposes of section 140A by section 140C) is only conditional.]¹

Commentary—*Simon's Direct Tax Service* **E4.527.**
Revenue Internal Guidance—Share Schemes Manual 4.13–4.15 (application of this section).
Cross references—TA 1988 s 136(5) (applies for the purposes of this section but see exceptions in FA 1998 s 53(8)).
TA 1988 s 140H (supplementary definitions and explanations for terms used in this section).
TA 1988 s 839 (Connected persons).
FA 2000 Sch 14 para 55 (amount of relief under that Schedule is treated as deductible for the purpose of any charge under this section in respect of shares acquired under an enterprise management incentive option).
Amendments—¹ Inserted by FA 1998 s 51(1) with effect in relation to shares acquired on or after 17 March 1998.

[140E Consideration for convertible shares

(1) This section applies in relation to any shares for determining the amount or value of the consideration referred to in section 140D(6)(a) or (b).

(2) Subject to the following provisions of this section, the consideration referred to in section 140D(6)(a) is any consideration given by—

(a) the employee; or

(b) in a case where section 140H(1)(b) applies and the shares were acquired by another person, that other person, in respect of the acquisition of the shares.

(3) The amount or value of the consideration given by any person for any shares shall include the amount or value of any consideration given for a right to acquire those shares.

(4) Where any consideration is given partly in respect of one thing and partly in respect of another, the amount given in respect of the different things shall be determined on a just and reasonable apportionment.

(5) The consideration which for the purposes of this section is taken to be given wholly or partly for anything shall not include the performance of any duties of or in connection with the office or employment by reference to which the shares in question have been acquired by a person as a director or employee of a company.

(6) No amount shall be counted more than once in the computation of the amount or value of any consideration.

(7) Subsections (1) to (3) of section 136 shall apply for determining for the purposes of subsection (3) above the amount or value of the consideration given for a right to acquire any shares as they apply for determining such an amount for the purposes of section 135.]¹

Commentary—*Simon's Direct Tax Service* E4.527.
Cross references—TA 1988 s 136(5) (applies for the purposes of this section but see exceptions in FA 1998 s 53(8)).
TA 1988 s 140H (supplementary definitions and explanations for terms used in this section).
TA 1988 s 839 (Connected persons).
Amendments—¹ Section inserted by FA 1998 s 51(1) with effect in relation to shares acquired on or after 17 March 1998.

[140F Supplemental provision with respect to convertible shares.

(1) Where—

(a) a person has an interest in any convertible shares at the time of his death,
(b) those shares are converted into shares of a different class either on his death or within the following twelve months, and
(c) the conversion takes place wholly or partly as a consequence of his death,

section 140D shall have effect as if the conversion had taken place immediately before his death and had been in pursuance of an entitlement to convert conferred on the deceased.

(2) In section 140D(2) the references, in relation to the terms of a person's entitlement, to circumstances arising include references—

(a) to the expiration of a period specified in or determined under those terms or the death of that person or any other person; and
(b) to the exercise by any person of any power conferred on him by or under those terms.

(3) For the purposes of section 140D, the market value of any shares at any time is the amount that might reasonably be expected to be obtained from a sale of the shares in the open market at that time.

(4) In this section and section 140D "associated company" has the same meaning as it has for the purposes of Part XI by virtue of section 416.

(5) For the purposes of section 140D a company is employee-controlled by virtue of holdings of shares of a class if—

(a) the majority of the company's shares of that class (other than any held by or for the benefit of an associated company) are held by or for the benefit of employees or directors of the company or a company controlled by the company; and
(b) those directors and employees are together able as holders of the shares to control the company.

(6) The provisions of sections 140D and 140E and this section apply in relation to an interest in shares as they apply in relation to shares.

(7) Section 840 (control) applies for the purposes of this section.]¹

Commentary—*Simon's Direct Tax Service* E4.526.
Cross references—TA 1988 s 136(5) (applies for the purposes of this section but see exceptions in FA 1998 s 53(8)).
TA 1988 s 140H (supplementary definitions and explanations for terms used in this section).
TA 1988 s 839 (Connected persons).
Amendments—¹ Section inserted by FA 1998 s 51(1) with effect in relation to shares acquired on or after 17 March 1998.

[140G Information for the purposes of sections 140A to 140F

(1) Where—

(a) any person provides any individual with an interest in shares which is only conditional, and
(b) the circumstances are such that—
    (i) the acquisition of that interest by that individual, or
    (ii) its subsequently ceasing to be only conditional,
    (iii) its subsequent disposal, or
    (iv) the death of the individual,

gives rise or may give rise to a charge under section 140A on that individual,

each of the relevant persons shall deliver to an officer of the Board particulars in writing of the interest and its provision.

(2) Where—

    (*a*) a person has an interest in any shares which is only conditional,

    (*b*) those shares cease to be shares in which that person's interest is only conditional or are disposed of or that person dies, and

    (*c*) that event gives rise to a charge under section 140A(4),

each of the relevant persons shall deliver to an officer of the Board particulars in writing of the shares and the event.

(3) Where—

    (*a*) any person has provided any individual with any convertible shares in a company,

    (*b*) those shares are subsequently converted into shares of a different class, and

    (*c*) the circumstance are such that the conversion gives rise or may give rise to a charge under section 140D on that individual,

each of the relevant persons shall deliver to an officer of the Board particulars in writing of the shares and their conversion.

(4) For the purposes of this section the relevant persons are—

    (*a*) the person who is providing, or who provided, the shares in question; and

    (*b*) the person under or with whom the office or employment is or was held by reference to which the charge may arise or has arisen.

(5) Particulars required to be delivered under this section must be delivered no later than thirty days after the end of the year of assessment in which the interest is provided, the event occurs or the conversion takes place.

(6) Expressions used in this section and in section 140A or 140D above have the same meanings in this section as in section 140A or, as the case may be, section 140D.][1]

Commentary—*Simon's Direct Tax Service* **E4.527.**
Cross references—TA 1988 s 136(5) (applies for the purposes of this section but see exceptions in FA 1998 s 53(8)).
TA 1988 s 140H (supplementary definitions and explanations for terms used in this section).
TA 1988 s 839 (Connected persons).
Amendments—[1] Section inserted by FA 1998 s 52(1) with effect from 31 July 1998.

[140H Construction of sections 140A to 140G

(1) For the purposes of sections 140A to 140G and this section, a person acquires any shares or securities as a director or employee of a company if—

    (*a*) he acquires them in pursuance of a right conferred on him, or an opportunity offered to him, by reason of his office or employment as a director or employee of the company; or

    (*b*) the shares or securities are, or a right or opportunity in pursuance of which he acquires them is, assigned to him after being acquired by, conferred on or, as the case may be, offered to some other person by reason of the assignee's office or employment as a director or employee of the company.

(2) Subject to subsection (3) below, the references in subsection (1) above to a right or opportunity conferred or offered by reason of a person's office or employment shall be taken to include—

    (*a*) a reference to one so conferred or offered after he has ceased to hold it; and

    (*b*) a reference to one that arises from the fact that any shares which a person acquires as a director or employee (or is treated as so acquiring by virtue of this paragraph) are convertible for the purposes of section 140D.

(3) For the purposes of this section—

    (*a*) the references in subsections (1) and (2) above to a person's office or employment are references only to an office or employment in respect of which he is chargeable to tax under Case I of Schedule E; but

    (*b*) subsection (2)(*a*) above shall not apply where a right or opportunity conferred or offered in the last chargeable period in which the office or employment was held by the person in question would not have fallen to be taken into account for the purposes of subsection (1)(*a*) above.

(4) Without prejudice to subsection (2)(*b*) above where—

    (*a*) a person has acquired an interest in any shares or securities which is only conditional or has acquired any convertible shares,

    (*b*) he acquired that interest or those shares as a director or employee of a company, or is treated by virtue of this subsection as having done so, and

    (*c*) as a result of any two or more transactions—

        (i) he ceases to be entitled to that interest or those shares, and

        (ii) he or a connected person becomes entitled to any interest in any shares or securities which is only conditional or to any convertible shares,

he shall be treated for the purposes of sections 140A to 140G as if the interest or shares to which he becomes entitled were also acquired by him as a director or employee of the company in question.

(5) Sections 140C and 140D(2) have effect for the purposes of subsection (4) above as they have effect for the purposes of sections 140A and 140B and section 140D respectively.

(6) References in sections 140A to 140G or this section to the terms on which a person is entitled to an interest in shares or securities include references to any terms imposed by any contract or arrangement or in any other way.

(7) References in this section to shares or to securities include references to an interest in shares or, as the case may be, securities.

(8) Subsection (5) of section 136 applies for the purposes of sections 140A to 140G and this section as it applies for the purposes of that section but as if—

(*a*) references to a body corporate were references to a company;

(*b*) at the end of paragraph (*d*) there were inserted "or any other interest of a member of a company"; and

(*c*) the words after paragraph (d) were omitted.

(9) Section 839 applies for the purposes of this section.]¹

Commentary—*Simon's Direct Tax Service* **E4.527.**
Cross references—TA 1988 s 839 (Connected persons).
Amendments—¹ Section inserted by FA 1998 s 53 with effect from 31 July 1998.

Vouchers etc

141 Non-cash vouchers

(1) Subject to the following provisions of this section and section 157(3), where a non-cash voucher provided for an employee by reason of his employment is received by the employee, then, for the purposes of the Income Tax Acts—

(*a*) he shall be treated as having received in the relevant year of assessment an emolument from his employment of an amount equal to [the expense incurred ("the chargeable expense")—

(i) by the person at whose cost the voucher and the money, goods or services for which it is capable of being exchanged are provided,

(ii) in or in connection with that provision;]⁵ and

(*b*) any money, goods or services obtained by the employee or any other person in exchange for the voucher shall be disregarded;

...⁷.

(2) In subsection (1)(*a*) above "the relevant year of assessment" means—

(*a*) in relation to a cheque voucher, the year of assessment in which the voucher is handed over in exchange for money, goods or services (a voucher which is posted being treated as handed over at the time of posting); and

(*b*) in relation to any other non-cash voucher, the year of assessment in which the chargeable expense is incurred or, if later, the year of assessment in which the voucher is received by the employee.

(3) There shall be deductible under section 198, 201 [201AA]⁸ or 332(3) from the amount taxable under subsection (1) above such amounts, if any, as would have been so deductible if the cost of the goods or services in question had been incurred by the employee out of his emoluments.

(4) The chargeable expense shall be treated as reduced by any part of that expense made good to the person incurring it by the employee.

(5) Where a non-cash voucher provided for an employee by reason of his employment is appropriated to him (whether by attaching it to a card held for him or in any other way), subsections (1) and (2) above shall have effect as if the employee had received the voucher at the time when it was so appropriated.

(6) [Subsection (1)]¹ above shall not apply in relation to a transport voucher provided for an employee of a passenger transport undertaking under arrangements in operation on 25th March 1982 and intended to enable that employee or a relation of his to obtain passenger transport services provided by—

(*a*) his employer;

(*b*) a subsidiary of his employer;

(*c*) a body corporate of which his employer is a subsidiary; or

(*d*) another passenger transport undertaking.

[(6A) Subsection (1) above shall not apply in relation to a non-cash voucher to the extent that it is used by the employee to obtain the use of a car parking space at or near his place of work.]²

[(6B) Subsection (1) above shall not apply in relation to any non-cash voucher to the extent that it is used to obtain entertainment (including hospitality of any kind) for the employee or a relation of his, if—

(*a*) [the person at whose cost the voucher and the entertainment are provided]⁶ is neither his employer nor a person connected with his employer;

(*b*) neither his employer nor a person connected with his employer has directly or indirectly procured the provision of the entertainment; and (*c*) the entertainment is not provided either in recognition of particular services which have been performed by him in the course of his employment or in anticipation of particular services which are to be so performed by him;

and section 839 shall apply for determining whether persons are connected for the purposes of this subsection.][3]

[(6C) Subsection (1) above shall not apply in relation to a non-cash voucher to the extent that it is used by the employee to obtain goods, services or money where—

(*a*) obtaining the goods or services is incidental to his being away from his usual place of abode during a qualifying absence from home or, as the case may be, the money is obtained for the purpose of being used to obtain goods or services which would be so incidental;

(*b*) the authorised maximum is not exceeded in relation to that qualifying absence; and

(*c*) the cost of obtaining the goods or services would not be deductible as mentioned in subsection (3) above if incurred by the employee out of his emoluments.][9]

[(6D) Subsections (3) to (5) of section 200A shall apply as they apply for the purposes of that section for construing the references in subsection (6C) above to a qualifying absence from home and for determining, for the purposes of that subsection, whether the authorised maximum is exceeded.][9]

(7) In this section—

"cheque voucher" means a cheque provided for an employee and intended for use by him wholly or mainly for payment for particular goods or services or for goods or services of one or more particular classes; and, in relation to a cheque voucher, references to a voucher being exchanged for goods or services shall be construed accordingly;

"passenger transport undertaking" means an undertaking whose business consists wholly or mainly in the carriage of passengers and includes a subsidiary of such an undertaking;

"subsidiary" means a wholly owned subsidiary within the meaning of section [736][4] of the Companies Act 1985;

"transport voucher" means any ticket, pass or other document or token intended to enable a person to obtain passenger transport services (whether or not in exchange for it) and, in relation to a transport voucher, references to a voucher being exchanged for services shall be construed as references to it being exchanged for, or otherwise being used to procure, services; and

"non-cash voucher" does not include a cash voucher within the meaning of section 143 but, subject to that, means any voucher, stamp or similar document or token capable of being exchanged (whether singly or together with other such vouchers, stamps, documents or tokens and whether immediately or only after a time) for money, goods or services (or for any combination of two or more of those things) and includes a transport voucher and a cheque voucher.

Commentary—*Simon's Direct Tax Service* E4.432.
Concessions A2—Exemption for luncheon vouchers not exceeding 15p per day.
A70—Small gifts to employees and their family by third parties and staff Christmas parties, annual dinner dance, etc are tax free up to specified costs.
A74—Free or subsidised meals to staff (or vouchers to obtain them) on employer's business premises or in a staff canteen are tax free, subject to conditions and exceptions.
Statement of Practice SP 6/85—Expenses which are to be included in the calculation of the amount assessable under this section in relation to incentive awards.
Revenue & other press releases—IR 16-5-95 (Revenue guidance notes for employees on the exemption for incidental overnight expenses).
Revenue Internal Guidance—Schedule E manual, SE 01550 (applies this section where an employer meets the cost of employees' medical expenses or arranges for them to be met under an insurance policy and the medical treatment is obtained or the bills are paid by means of vouchers).
SE 06300 (all employees provided with season tickets for ordinary commuting journeys receive an emolument chargeable under this section).
SE 11260 (deduction under sub-s (3) from incentive awards unlikely to be permitted).
SE 16000 (vouchers and credit-tokens: table of contents, covering references SE 16010–16220).
SE 16030 (table summarizing Revenue procedures where vouchers and credit-tokens supplied or used).
SE 16040 (meaning of non-cash voucher).
SE 16045 (non-cash voucher: when does Schedule E charge arise?).
SE 16050 (meaning of cheque voucher).
SE 16060 (meaning of transport voucher).
SE 16070 (transport vouchers: exemption for employees of passenger transport undertakings earning at a rate less than £8,500 a year)
SE 16075 (transport vouchers: exemption for former British Rail employees earning at a rate less than £8,500 a year).
SE 16100 (exclusions from the scope of the non-cash voucher and credit token legislation).
SE 16120 (meaning of "received by or appropriated to" an employee).
SE 16140 (amount and year of charge: table for the various types of voucher).
SE 16150 (expenses incurred in providing a voucher or credit token—Statement of Practice SP 6/85).
SE 16170 (deductions which may be given).
SE 16180 (conditions where dispensations can be granted).
SE 20101 (amounts chargeable under this section to be included when calculating whether employment has emoluments at a rate of £8,500 a year or more, unless covered by a dispensation).
SE 21835–21840 (conditions to be satisfied for exemption under sub-s (6B)).
SE 50100 (exemption from charge where travel facilities provided for members of the naval, military or air forces of the Crown going on, or returning from, leave).
Definitions—"Emoluments", s 131(1); "employees", s 144(5); "the Income Tax Acts", s 831(1)(*b*); "non-cash voucher", s 141(7) by virtue of s 144(5); "relation", s 144(5); "year of assessment", s 832(1).
Cross references—See TMA 1970 s 15(8) (requirement on employer to give notice to Revenue of benefits falling within this section).

TA 1988 s 144 (supplementary provisions).
TA 1988 s 144A (where employee fails to make good to employer tax accounted for in respect of the receipt of a non-cash voucher, he is charged to tax under Schedule E on the amount of that tax).
TA 1988 s 157(3) (no charge arises under this section on non–cash vouchers used in connection with car benefit).
TA 1988 s 159AA(3)(b) (no charge arises under this section on non-cash vouchers used in connection with van benefit).
TA 1988 s 159AC(3)(b) (no charge arises under this section on non-cash vouchers used in connection with heavier commercial vehicle benefit).
TA 1988 s 167(2) (application of this section for taxation of benefits provided for directors and higher–paid employees).
TA 1988 s 197(2) (exemption in respect of leave travel facilities for the armed forces).
TA 1988 s 197AA(6) (no charge to tax under this section for vouchers evidencing an employee's right to use a works bus service for qualifying journeys.)
TA 1988 s 197AC (no charge to tax under this section for vouchers evidencing an employee's right to use a cycle or cyclist's safety equipment provided for qualifying journeys).
TA 1988 s 197G (no charge arises under this section on non-cash vouchers used in connection with sporting and recreational facilities).
TA 1988 s 202B(8) (deemed emoluments under sub-s (1)(a) above to be treated for purposes of assessment as received at the time specified in that subsection).
TA 1988 ss 203G, 203J (taxation at source of non-cash vouchers under PAYE).
IT (Employments) Regulations, SI 1993/744 reg 46(1)(d), (2), (5), (6) (returns to be rendered by an employer in respect of any deemed emolument under this section).
FA 1994 Sch 24 para 27 (railway privatisation: sub-s (6) above to have effect in certain circumstances to exempt travel vouchers paid after privatisation to employees of British Rail).
IT (Employments) (Notional Payments) Regulations, SI 1944/1212 reg 6 (time when notional payment is treated as made by employer in respect of non-cash vouchers).
FA 1999 s 49 (sub-s (6A) above applies in relation to motor cycle parking spaces and facilities for parking cycles as it applies to car parking spaces with effect from the year 1999–00).
Amendments—[1] Words in sub-s (6) substituted by FA 1988 s 46(1), (5).
[2] Sub-s (6A) inserted by FA 1988 s 46(1), (5).
[3] Sub-s (6B) inserted by FA 1988 s 47(1), (4).
[4] Number in definition of "subsidiary" in sub-s (7) substituted by the Companies Act 1989 s 144(4), Sch 18 para 46.
[5] Words in sub-s (1)(a) substituted by FA 1994 s 89(1), (2)(a).
[6] Words in sub-s (6B)(a) substituted by FA 1994 s 89(1), (3).
[7] Words in sub-s (1) repealed by FA 1994 s 89(1), (2)(b) and Sch 26 Pt V(6).
[8] Words in sub-s (3) inserted by FA 1995 s 91(2), (3) with effect from the year 1995–96.
[9] Sub-ss (6C), (6D) inserted by FA 1995 s 93(1), (5) with effect for determining emoluments received by any person after 5 April 1995.

142 Credit-tokens

(1) Subject to the provisions of this section and section 157(3), where a credit-token is provided for an employee by reason of his employment, then, for the purposes of the Income Tax Acts—

(a) on each occasion on which the employee uses the credit-token to obtain money, goods or services he shall be treated as having received an emolument from his employment of an amount equal to [the expense incurred—

(i) by the person at whose cost the money, goods or services are provided,
(ii) in or in connection with that provision;][3] and

(b) any money, goods or services obtained by the employee by use of the credit-token shall be disregarded.

(2) There shall be deductible under section 198, 201 [201AA][4] or 332(3) from the amount taxable under subsection (1) above such amounts, if any, as would have been so deductible if the cost of the goods or services in question had been incurred by the employee out of his emoluments.

(3) The expense incurred by the person [mentioned in subsection (1)(a)(i) above][3] shall be treated as reduced by any part of that expense made good to that person by the employee.

[(3A) Subsection (1) above shall not apply in relation to a credit-token to the extent that it is used by the employee to obtain the use of a car parking space at or near his place of work.][1]

[(3B) Subsection (1) above shall not apply in relation to any credit-token to the extent that it is used to obtain entertainment (including hospitality of any kind) for the employee or a relation of his, if—

(a) the person [mentioned in subsection (1)(a)(i) above][3] is neither his employer nor a person connected with his employer;
(b) neither his employer nor a person connected with his employer has directly or indirectly procured the provision of the entertainment; and
(c) the entertainment is not provided either in recognition of particular services which have been performed by him in the course of his employment or in anticipation of particular services which are to be so performed by him;
and section 839 shall apply for determining whether persons are connected for the purposes of this subsection.][2]

[(3C) Subsection (1) above shall not apply in relation to a credit-token to the extent that it is used by the employee to obtain goods, services or money where—

(a) obtaining the goods or services is incidental to his being away from his usual place of abode during a qualifying absence from home or, as the case may be, the money is obtained for the purpose of being used to obtain goods or services which would be so incidental;
(b) the authorised maximum is not exceeded in relation to that qualifying absence; and
(c) the cost of obtaining the goods or services would not be deductible as mentioned in subsection (2) above if incurred by the employee out of his emoluments.][5]

[(3D) Subsections (3) to (5) of section 200A shall apply as they apply for the purposes of that section for construing the references in subsection (3C) above to a qualifying absence from home and for determining, for the purposes of that subsection, whether the authorised maximum is exceeded.][5]

(4) In this section "credit-token" means a card, token, document or other thing given to a person by another person who undertakes—

(*a*) that on the production of it (whether or not some other action is also required) he will supply money, goods and services (or any of them) on credit; or
(*b*) that where, on the production of it to a third party (whether or not some other action is also required) the third party supplies money, goods and services (or any of them), he will pay the third party for them (whether or not taking any discount or commission);

but does not include a non-cash voucher or a cash voucher.

(5) For the purposes of subsection (4) above, the use of an object to operate a machine provided by the person giving the object, or by a third party, shall be treated as production of the object to that person or, as the case may be, third party.

Commentary—*Simon's Direct Tax Service* **E4.433.**
Statement of Practice SP 6/85—Expenses which are to be included in the calculation of the amount assessable under this section in relation to incentive awards.
Revenue Internal Guidance—Schedule E manual, SE 11260 (deduction under sub-s (2) from incentive awards unlikely to be permitted).
SE 16000 (vouchers and credit-tokens: table of contents, covering references SE 16010–16220).
SE 16090 (meaning of credit- token).
SE 16100 (exclusions from the scope of the non-cash voucher and credit token legislation).
SE 16140 (amount and year of charge: table for the various types of voucher).
SE 16150 (expenses incurred in providing a voucher or credit token—Statement of Practice SP 6/85).
SE 16170 (deductions which may be given).
SE 16180 (conditions where dispensations can be granted).
SE 21835–21840 (conditions to be satisfied for exemption under sub-s (3B)).
Definitions—"Cash voucher", s 143(3) by virtue of s 144(5); "emoluments", s 131(1); "employee", s 144(5); "non-cash voucher", s 141(7) by virtue of s 144(5).
Cross references—See TMA 1970 s 15(8) (requirement to employer to give notice to Revenue of benefits falling within this section).
TA 1988 s 144 (supplementary provisions).
TA 1988 s 144A (where employee fails to make good to employer tax accounted for in respect of the receipt of a non-cash voucher, he is charged to tax under Schedule E on the amount of that tax).
TA 1988 s 157(3) (no charge arises under this section on credit-token used in connection with car benefit).
TA 1988 s 159AA(3)(*b*) (no charge arises under this section on credit-tokens used in connection with van benefit).
TA 1988 s 159AC(3)(*b*) (no charge arises under this section on credit-tokens used in connection with heavier commercial vehicle benefit).
TA 1988 s 167(2) (application of this section for taxation of benefit. provided for directors and higher-paid employees).
TA 1988 s 202B(8) (deemed emoluments under sub-s (1)(*a*) above to be treated for the purposes of assessment as received at the time specified in that subsection).
TA 1988 ss 203H, 203J (taxation at source of credit-tokens under PAYE).
IT (Employments) Regulations, SI 1993/744 reg 46(1)(*d*), (2), (5), (6) (returns to be rendered by an employer in respect of any deemed emolument under this section).
IT (Employments) (Notional Payments) Regulations, SI 1994/1212 reg 4 (exclusion of certain credit-tokens from taxation at source under PAYE).
FA 1999 s 49 (sub-s (3A) above applies in relation to motor cycle parking spaces and facilities for parking cycles as it applies to car parking spaces with effect from the year 1999–00).
Amendments—[1] Sub-s (3A) inserted by FA 1988 s 46(2), (5).
[2] Sub-s (3B) inserted by FA 1988 s 48(1), (3).
[3] Words in sub-ss (1)(*a*), (3), (3B)(*a*) substituted by FA 1994 s 89(4)–(7).
[4] Words in sub-s (2) inserted by FA 1995 s 91(2), (3) with effect from the year 1995–96.
[5] Sub-ss (3C), (3D) inserted by FA 1995 s 93(2), (5) with effect for determining emoluments received by any person after 5 April 1995.

143 Cash vouchers taxable under PAYE

(1) Where a cash voucher provided for an employee by reason of his employment is received by the employee, then, subject to subsection (5) below, for the purposes of the Income Tax Acts—

(*a*) [he shall be treated as having received][1], at the time when he receives the voucher, an emolument of his employment equal to the sum of money for which the voucher is capable of being exchanged as mentioned in subsection (3) below; and
(*b*) any money obtained by the employee or any other person in exchange for the voucher shall be disregarded.

(2) Where a cash voucher provided for an employee by reason of his employment is appropriated to him (whether by attaching it to a card held for him or in any other way), subsections (1) and (5) of this section shall have effect as if the employee had received the voucher at the time when it was so appropriated.

(3) In this section "cash voucher" (subject to subsection (4) below) means any voucher, stamp or similar document capable of being exchanged (whether singly or together with such other vouchers, stamps or documents, and whether immediately or only after a time) for a sum of money greater than, equal to or not substantially less than the expense incurred [by the person at whose cost the voucher is provided][1] (whether or not it is also capable of being exchanged for goods or services), except that it does not include—

(*a*) any document intended to enable a person to obtain payment of the sum mentioned in the document, being a sum which if paid to him directly would not have been chargeable to income tax under Schedule E; or

(*b*) a savings certificate the accumulated interest payable in respect of which is exempt from tax (or would be so exempt if certain conditions were satisfied).

(4) Where—

(*a*) a voucher, stamp or similar document is capable of being exchanged (as mentioned above) for a sum of money substantially less than the expense incurred [by the person at whose cost the voucher, stamp or similar document is provided]¹, and

(*b*) the difference or part of the difference represents the cost to that person of providing benefits in connection with sickness, personal injury or death,

then, in determining whether the voucher, stamp or document is a cash voucher within the meaning of this section, [the expense incurred by the person mentioned in paragraph (*a*) above shall be treated as reduced by the difference or part of the difference mentioned in paragraph (*b*) above.]¹

(5) Subsection (1) above shall not apply to a cash voucher received by an employee if, at the time when the voucher is received, the scheme under which it was issued is a scheme approved by the Board for the purposes of this subsection; and the Board shall not approve a scheme for those purposes unless satisfied that it is practicable for income tax in respect of all payments made in exchange for vouchers issued under the scheme to be deducted in accordance with regulations under section 203.

Commentary—*Simon's Direct Tax Service* E4.431.
Revenue Internal Guidance—Schedule E manual SE 16000 (vouchers and credit-tokens: table of contents, covering references SE 16010–16220).
SE 16110 (meaning of cash voucher).
SE 16120 (meaning of "received by or appropriated to" an employee).
SE 16140 (amount and year of charge: table for the various types of voucher).
SE 16150 (expenses incurred in providing a voucher or credit token—Statement of Practice SP 6/85).
SE 20101 (amounts chargeable under this section to be included when calculating whether employment has emoluments at a rate of £8,500 a year or more, unless covered by a dispensation).
Definitions—"The Board", s 832(1); "emoluments", s 131(1); "employee", s 144(5); "the Income Tax Acts", s 831(1)(*b*); "interest", s 832(1); "Schedule E", s 19(1); "tax", s 832(3).
Cross references—See TMA 1970 s 15(8) (requirement on employer to give notice to Revenue of benefits falling within this section).
TA 1988 s 144 (supplementary provisions).
TA 1988 s 144A (where employee fails to make good to employer tax accounted for in respect of the receipt of a non-cash voucher, he is charged to tax under Schedule E on the amount of that tax).
TA 1988 s 167(2) (application of this section for taxation of benefits provided for directors and higher-paid employees).
TA 1988 s 202B(8) (deemed emoluments under sub-s (1)(*a*) above to be treated for the purposes of assessment as received at the time specified in that subsection).
TA 1988 ss 203I–203L (cash vouchers under this section to be treated as assessable income of employee for PAYE regulations).
IT (Employments) Regulations, SI 1993/744 reg 46(1)(*d*), (5), (6) (returns to be rendered by an employer in respect of benefits giving rise to a charge to tax under this section).
IT (Employments) (Notional Payments) Regulations, SI 1994/1212 reg 5 (exclusion of certain cash vouchers from taxation at source under PAYE).
Amendments—¹ Words in sub-ss (1), (3), (4) substituted by FA 1994 s 89(8)–(11).

144 Supplementary provisions

(1) If a person furnishes to the inspector a statement of the cases and circumstances in which non-cash vouchers[, credit-tokens or cash vouchers]¹ are provided for any employees (whether his own or those of anyone else) and the inspector is satisfied that no additional tax is payable under section [141, 142 or 143]¹ by reference to the vouchers or tokens mentioned in the statement, the inspector shall notify the person accordingly and nothing in those sections shall apply to the provision of those vouchers or tokens or their use.

(2) The inspector may, if in his opinion there is reason to do so, by notice served on the person to whom the notification under subsection (1) above was given, revoke the notification, either as from the date of its making or as from such later date as may be specified in the notice under this subsection; and all such income tax becomes chargeable, and all such returns are to be made by that person and by the employees in question, as would have been chargeable or would have had to be made in the first instance if the notification under subsection (1) above had never been given or, as the case may be, it had ceased to have effect on the specified date.

(3) For the purposes of sections [141, 142 and 143]¹ where a person incurs expense in or in connection with the provision [of]¹ vouchers or credit-tokens for two or more employees as members of a group or class, the expense incurred in respect of any one of them shall be taken to be such part of that expense as is just and reasonable.

(4) For the purposes of sections 141, 142 and 143 and this section—

(*a*) a non-cash voucher, cash voucher or credit-token provided for an employee by his employer shall be deemed to be provided for him by reason of his employment; and

(*b*) any reference to a non-cash voucher, cash voucher or credit-token being provided for or received by an employee includes a reference to it being provided for or received by a relation of his.

[(4A) Section 142(1) has effect as if—

(4) Subject to subsection (5) below, subsection (1) above does not apply to accommodation provided for the employee in any of the following cases—

(*a*) where it is necessary for the proper performance of the employee's duties that he should reside in the accommodation;

(*b*) where the accommodation is provided for the better performance of the duties of his employment, and his is one of the kinds of employment in the case of which it is customary for employers to provide living accommodation for employees;

(*c*) where there is a special threat to his security, special security arrangements are in force and he resides in the accommodation as part of those arrangements;

and in any such case there is no charge to tax under Schedule E (either by virtue of this section or under section 131 or otherwise) in respect of a liability for rates on the premises being discharged for or on behalf of the employee or the employee being reimbursed for the discharge of that liability.

(5) If the accommodation is provided by a company and the employee is a director of the company or of an associated company, then, except in a case where paragraph (*c*) of subsection (4) above applies, no exemption is given by virtue of that subsection unless, for each employment of his which is employment as director of the company or an associated company, the following conditions are fulfilled, that is—

(*a*) he has no material interest in the company, and

(*b*) either his employment is as a full-time working director or the company is non-profit-making (meaning that neither does it carry on a trade nor do its functions consist wholly or mainly in the holding of investments or other property) or is established for charitable purposes only.

(6) If by reason of a person's employment accommodation is provided for others being members of his family or household, he is to be treated under subsections (1) to (3) above as if it were accommodation provided for him.

(7) For the purposes of this section, living accommodation provided for an employee, or for members of his family or household, by his employer is deemed to be provided by reason of his employment unless—

(*a*) the employer is an individual, and ...² he makes the provision in the normal course of his domestic, family or personal relationships; or

(*b*) the accommodation is provided by a local authority for an employee of theirs, and ...² the terms on which it is provided are no more favourable than those on which similar accommodation is provided by the authority for persons who are not their employees but are otherwise similarly circumstanced.

(8) For the purposes of this section—

(*a*) a company is associated with another if one has control of the other or both are under the control of the same person; and

(*b*) the expressions "employment", "family or household", "director", "full-time working director", "material interest" and (in relation to a body corporate) "control" shall be construed in accordance with subsections (2), (4) and (8) to (12) of section 168 as if this section were included in Chapter II of this Part.

Commentary—*Simon's Direct Tax Service* **E4.412, 620.**
Concessions A56—Determination of the "annual value" for the purposes of this section of accommodation provided to employees in Scotland.
A60—Where specified conditions are satisfied, free board and lodging provided to agricultural employees is not assessed to tax. However, any such employee who opts for higher gross wage by forgoing free board and lodging is assessed to tax on the gross wage even if he pays his employer for board and lodging.
A91—Where accommodation is provided to more than one employee in the same period, the total charge under this section will not exceed the amount chargeable if it had been provided to one employee.
Revenue Internal Guidance—Schedule E manual, SE 01020 (s 145 does not apply to board and lodging).
SE 11300 (table of contents on application of s 145 provisions, references in the range SE 11301–11442).
SE 11501–11506 (part of premises used for business purposes. See SE 11300 for list of contents).
SE 20101 (amounts chargeable under this section to be included when calculating whether employment has emoluments at a rate of £8,500 a year or more).
SE 31618 (example of deduction from living accommodation charge).
SE 60020 (ministers of religion may be chargeable under this section if the minister is engaged purely on administrative duties).
SE 65805 (application of this section and effect of gross pay for local authority officials and employees).
SE 66625 (provision of housing for certain mineworkers may be regarded as exempt under sub-s (4)).
SE 68150 (police officer provided with living accommodation by the police authority not chargeable under this section).
SE 68310 (prison governors, officers and chaplains, who, by reason of their employment, occupy living accommodation provided by the prison authority are within the exemption from charge provided by sub-s (4)).
Revenue & other press releases—IR 7-7-83 (living accommodation provided for employee: accommodation outside UK: definition in s 837 implies tax is charged on full commercial rent. Revenue will consider cases where injustice arises).
IR 19-4-90 (valuation of benefit following end of domestic rating).
Simon's Tax Cases—*Stones v Hall* [1989] STC 138*; *R v Dimsey; R v Allen* [1999] STC 846.
s 145(1), (4), *Vertigan v Brady* [1988] STC 91*.
Definitions—"Annual value", s 837; "emoluments", s 131(1); "local authority", s 519(4) by virtue of s 832(1); "Schedule E", s 19(1).
Cross references—See TMA 1970 s 15(8) (requirement on employer to give notice to Revenue of benefits falling within this section).
TA 1988 s 146 (additional charge in respect of certain living accommodation).
TA 1988 s 163(1) (s 163 to apply where a charge to tax would arise under this section but for sub-s (4)).
TA 1988 s 167(2) (application of this section for taxation of benefits provided for directors and higher-paid employees).
TA 1988 s 202B(9) (deemed emoluments under sub-s (1) above to be treated for purposes of assessment as received at the time specified in that subsection).

TA 1988 Sch 11A para 24 (exemption for removal expenses and benefits provided to an employee by reason of relocation of his employment or commencement of a new employment);

IT (Employments) Regulations, SI 1993/744 reg 46(1)(*d*), (2), (5), (6) (returns to be rendered by an employer of any deemed emolument under this section).

Amendments—[1] Words omitted from sub-s (1) repealed by FA 1996 s 106(1), Sch 41 Pt V(4) with effect from the year 1996–97.

[2] Words omitted from sub-s (7) repealed by FA 1996 Sch 20 para 7, Sch 41 Pt V(10) with effect from the year 1996–97.

146 Additional charge in respect of certain living accommodation

(1) This section applies where—

(*a*) living accommodation is provided for a person in any period, by reason of his employment;

(*b*) by virtue of section 145 he is treated for the purposes of Schedule E as being in receipt of emoluments of an amount calculated by reference to the value to him of that accommodation, or would be so treated if there were disregarded any sum made good by him to those at whose cost the accommodation is provided; and

(*c*) the cost of providing the accommodation exceeds £75,000.

(2) Where this section applies, the employee shall be treated for the purposes of Schedule E as being in receipt of emoluments (in addition to those which he is treated as receiving by virtue of section 145) of an amount equal to the additional value to him of the accommodation for the period, less so much of any rent paid by the employee, in respect of the accommodation, to the person providing it as exceeds the value to the employee of the accommodation for the period (as determined under section 145).

(3) The additional value of the accommodation to the employee in any period is the rent which would have been payable for that period if the premises had been let to him at an annual rent equal to the appropriate percentage of the amount by which the cost of providing the accommodation exceeds £75,000.

(4) For the purposes of this section, the cost of providing any living accommodation shall be taken to be the aggregate of—

(*a*) the amount of any expenditure incurred in acquiring the estate or interest in the property held by a relevant person; and

(*b*) the amount of any expenditure incurred by a relevant person before the year of assessment in question on improvements to the property.

(5) The aggregate amount mentioned in subsection (4) above shall be reduced by the amount of any payment made by the employee to a relevant person, so far as that amount represents a reimbursement of any such expenditure as is mentioned in paragraph (*a*) or (*b*) of that subsection or represents consideration for the grant to the employee of a tenancy of the property.

(6) Subject to subsection (8) below, where throughout the period of six years ending with the date when the employee first occupied the property, any estate or interest in the property was held by a relevant person (whether or not it was the same estate, interest or person throughout), the additional value shall be calculated as if in subsection (4) above—

(*a*) the amount referred to in paragraph (*a*) were the market value of that property as at that date; and

(*b*) the amount referred to in paragraph (*b*) did not include expenditure on improvements made before that date.

(7) In this section, "relevant person" means any of the following—

(*a*) the person providing the accommodation;

(*b*) where the person providing the accommodation is not the employee's employer, that employer;

(*c*) any person, other than the employee, who is connected with a person falling within paragraph (*a*) or (*b*) above.

(8) Subsection (6) above does not apply where the employee first occupied the property before 31st March 1983.

(9) Any amount which is deductible, by virtue of section 145(3), from an amount to be treated as emoluments under that section may, to the extent to which it exceeds the amount of those emoluments, be deductible from the amount to be treated as emoluments under this section.

(10) For the purposes of this section, living accommodation shall be treated as provided for a person by reason of his employment if it is so treated for the purposes of section 145; and "employment" has the same meaning in this section as in that.

(11) In this section—

"the appropriate percentage" means the rate [applicable for the purposes of section 160][1] as at the beginning of the year of assessment in question;

"property", in relation to any living accommodation, means the property consisting of that accommodation;

"market value", in relation to any property, means the price which that property might reasonably be expected to fetch on a sale in the open market with vacant possession, no reduction being made, in estimating the market value, on account of any option in respect of the property held by the employee, or a person connected with him, or by any of the persons mentioned in subsection (7) above; and

"tenancy" includes a sub-tenancy;

and section 839 shall apply for the purposes of this section.

Commentary—*Simon's Direct Tax Service* E4.413.
Concessions A91—Amount chargeable under this section where accommodation is provided to more than one employee in the same period will not exceed the amount which would have been chargeable if it had been provided to one employee; where the charge to tax under s 145 is calculated by reference to open market rent, there is no additional charge under this section.
Revenue Internal Guidance—Schedule E manual, SE 11402 (when a charge can arise under s 145 and 146).
SE 11408 (no charge under s 145 or 146 where accommodation provided by someone other than employer to a pensioner or ex-employee. But if continued use of living accommodation is provided after termination of employment see SE12805 onwards).
SE 11410 (living accommodation provided to more than one employee in the same period—ESC A91(*a*)).
SE 11471–11484 (properties costing more than £75000: measure of the extra charge. See SE 11300 for list of contents).
SE 11501–11506 (part of premises used for business purposes. See SE 11300 for list of contents).
SE 65805 (application of this section and effect of gross pay for local authority officials and employees).
Revenue & other press releases—IR 18-8-88 (notwithstanding s 146(6), a charge arises only when the cost of a property (plus expenditure on improvements before the year of assessment) exceeds £75,000).
IR 22-11-90 (from 6 April 1989, where two or more properties are made available to the same employee, the £75,000 limit applies separately to each one).
Definitions—"Connected persons", s 839; "emoluments", s 131(1); "Schedule E", s 19(1); "year of assessment", s 832(1).
Cross reference—See TMA 1970 s 15(8) (requirement on employer to give notice to Revenue of benefits falling within this section).
IT (Employments) Regulations, SI 1993/744 reg 46(1)(*d*), (2), (5), (6) (returns to be rendered by an employer of any deemed emoluments under this section).
Amendments—[1] Words in the definition of "the appropriate percentage" substituted by FA 1989 s 179(5) with effect from the year 1990–91 by virtue of FA 1989 s 178(1) (Appointed Day No 1) Order 1989, SI 1989/1298 and FA 1989 s 179(5).

[146A Priority of rules applying to living accommodation

(1) This section applies where, within the meaning of section 145, living accommodation is provided in any period for any person by reason of his employment.

(2) The question whether the employee is to be treated under section 145 or 146 as in receipt of emoluments in respect of the provision of the accommodation shall be determined before any other question whether there is an amount falling to be treated in respect of the provision of that accommodation as emoluments.

(3) Tax under Schedule E in respect of the provision of the accommodation shall be chargeable on the employee otherwise than in pursuance of sections 145 and 146 to the extent only that the amount on which it is chargeable by virtue of those sections is exceeded by the amount on which it would be chargeable apart from those sections.][1]

Commentary—*Simon's Direct Tax Service* E4.412.
Definitions—"Emoluments", s 131(1); "Schedule E", s 19(1).
Amendments—[1] Section inserted by FA 1996 s 106(2) with effect from the year 1996–97.

147 Occupation of Chevening House

Section 145 shall not apply in relation to the occupation of Chevening House or any other premises held on the trusts of the trust instrument set out in the Schedule to the Chevening Estate Act 1959 by a person nominated in accordance with those trusts.

Payments on retirement, sick pay etc

[148 Payments and other benefits in connection with termination of employment, etc

(1) Payments and other benefits not otherwise chargeable to tax which are received in connection with—

(*a*) the termination of a person's employment, or

(*b*) any change in the duties of or emoluments from a person's employment,

are chargeable to tax under this section if and to the extent that their amount exceeds £30,000.

[(2) For the purposes of this section "benefit" includes anything which, disregarding any exemption—

(*a*) would be an emolument of the employment, or

(*b*) would be chargeable to tax as an emolument of the employment,

if received for the performance of the duties of the employment.][2]

[(2A) But subsection (1) does not apply—

(*a*) to any payment or other benefit received in connection with any change in the duties of, or emoluments from, a person's employment to the extent that it is a benefit which, if received for the performance of the duties of the employment, would fall within paragraph 1(1) of Schedule 11A, or

(*b*) to any payment or other benefit received in connection with the termination of a person's employment—

(i) that is a benefit which, if received for the performance of the duties of the employment, would fall within section 155(1) or (5), 155AA, 156A, 157(3), 159AA(3), 159AC(3), 200B(2)(*b*), 200E(2)(*b*), 588(1), 589A or 643(1), or

     (ii) to the extent that it is a benefit which, if so received, would not be included in the emoluments of that person by virtue of section 200D(1) or 200J(2).][2]

(3) An amount chargeable to tax under this section is income chargeable under Schedule E for the year of assessment in which the payment or other benefit is received.

The right to receive the payments or other benefits is not itself regarded as a benefit for this purpose.

(4) For the purposes of this section—

   (*a*) a cash benefit is treated as received—

     (i) when payment is made of or on account of the benefit, or
     (ii) the recipient becomes entitled to require payment of or on account of the benefit; and

   (*b*) a non-cash benefit is treated as received when it is used or enjoyed.

(5) This section applies—

   (*a*) whether the payment or other benefit is provided by the employer or former employer or by another person, and
   (*b*) whether or not the payment or other benefit is provided in pursuance of a legal obligation.

(6) This section has effect subject to Schedule 11, which contains provisions extending, restricting and otherwise supplementing the provisions of this section.

(7) In this section and that Schedule "employment" includes an office and related expressions have a corresponding meaning.][1]

Commentary—*Simon's Direct Tax Service* E4.805–807.
Concessions A10—Exemption for payments from overseas provident funds for termination of employment overseas.
A81—Exemption for legal costs recovered by an employee incurred for a legal action against his employer for compensation for loss of employment. See also RI 61.
Statements of Practice SP 2/81—Exemption for employer's contributions to retirement benefits schemes on termination of employment and purchases of annuities from former employees.
SP 13/91, para 10—Payment for redundancy caused by accident.
SP 1/94—Exemption for genuine non-statutory redundancy payments.
SP 3/96—Revenue will not attribute part of a termination payment made in settlement of employment claims to restrictive covenants under s 313, where they formed part of the terms of employment and are reaffirmed in the settlement.
Revenue Interpretation RI 61—Exemption for legal costs recovered by an employee incurred for a legal action against his employer for compensation for loss of employment. See also Concession A81.
Revenue & other press releases—ICAEW TR851 6-11-91 (See SP13/91 transfer of a company car as part of an ex-gratia severance package falls within a 148(3) if not otherwise chargeable to income tax).
IR 17-3-97 (Revenue to apply special arrangements for employment termination agreements entered into from 6 April 1996, which will offer taxpayers a simpler approach to taxing benefits in kind that continue to be paid or made available after the year of termination).
IR Tax Bulletin June 1997 p 427 (gives information on the operation of the arrangements announced in IR press release 17-3-97 for taxing continuing non-cash benefits provided as part of an employment termination settlement).
IR Tax Bulletin October 1998 p 582 (changes to employment termination legislation under FA 1998).
Revenue Internal Guidance—Schedule E manual, SE 02100 (compensation for loss of office—whether payment chargeable s 19 or s 148).
SE 12800 (termination payments and benefits—table of contents, covering references SE 12805–14000).
SE 12810 (order of applying the legislation; redundancy payments (as defined in SE 13800) will always be within s 148).
SE 12815 (interaction with benefits received during employment).
SE 12830 (common questions with cross-references to instructions).
SE 12852 (examples of other reasons for payments to be considered if payment looks too large to be "compensation for loss of office or employment").
SE 13050 (foreign aspects; application of *Nichols v Gibson* (68 TC 611)).
SE 12975 (distinguishing between payments in lieu of notice (PILONs) and "gardening leave" and establishing the date of termination).
SE 13735 (contributions to an approved retirement benefits scheme etc—application of Statement of Practice 2/1981).
SE 13740 (payments to meet legal costs—application of Concession ESC A81).
SE 13750 (redundancy payments—application of *Mairs v Haughey* (66 TC 273)).
SE 13830 (redundancy: site agreements for short-service employees—table showing the types of payment most frequently made under "site agreements" and the appropriate tax treatment).
SE 13844–13855 (reports by employers of payments and benefits within s 148: settlements made on or after 6 April 1998, application of paragraph 15 Schedule 11 ICTA 1988 and Statutory Instrument 1999/70).
SE 15022 (non-approved "retirement benefits schemes": meaning of "retirement", payments in cases of early retirement can be chargeable under this section as compensation for loss of employment).
SE 15024 (non-approved "retirement benefits schemes": ill-health and "retirement"—payments will often be chargeable under this section subject to any claim to the disability exemption (see SE 13610)).
SE 21007 (interaction of the benefits legislation with the taxing of termination payments—payments not to be treated as benefits even though wholly or partly exempt from tax).
SE 21746 (loans written off on termination of employment—charge under s 160(2) takes precedence denying the benefit of the £30,000 exemption).
SE 23555 (treatment of cars available after employment ceases).
SE 42250 (link between the basis of assessment and the operation of PAYE—deduction of PAYE tax from termination etc payments).
SE 50640 (Death Benefit Schemes in the construction industry not within s 148).
SE 64615 (possibility of charge under this section on commission "received" by insurance agents not covered by Statement of Practice 4/97).
SE 65870 (terminal gratuities for non-pensionable service made since 6 July 1995 under the Local Government Superannuation (Gratuities) Regulations 1995—redundancy lump sums chargeable under this section).
SE 65875 (re-settlement compensation, lump sum compensation for premature retirement and redundancy and reorganisation compensation paid to an employee of a Local Authority, River Board, Harbour Board or other similar body is chargeable under s 148. The re-settlement compensation must not be paid for more than 52 weeks).
SE 66690 (payments in lieu of free coal: lump sum payments received by mineworkers on redundancy for surrendering their rights to free coal or cash in lieu fall to be treated as payments made on the termination of employment within s 148).
SE 68228 (sub-postmasters: payments on termination of office, redundancy payments and closure payments chargeable under this section).

SE 70400 (steel industry employees: payments during retraining under schemes set up by the European Community (Iron and Steel Employees Re-adaptation Benefits Scheme) chargeable under this section).

SE 74011 (voluntary pensions: isolated gifts in respect of the termination of the employment could be charged under this section).

Simon's Tax Cases—*Allan v IRC* [1994] STC 943*; *Horner v Hasted* [1995] STC 766; *Nichols v Gibson* [1996] STC 1008*; *Richardson (Insp of Taxes) v Delaney* [2001] STC 1328.

s 148(1), (2), (4), *Warnett v Jones* [1980] STC 131*.

s 148(2), *Williams v Simmonds* [1981] STC 715*.

s 148(6), *Larter v Skone James* [1976] STC 22*.

Definitions—"Earned income", s 833(4), (5); "emoluments", s 131(1); "inspector", s 832(1); "Schedule E", s 19(1); "tax", s 832(3); "year of assessment", s 832(1).

Cross references—See TMA 1970 s 98 (failure to provide information required under sub-s (7) above may incur liability to a special-return penalty).

TA 1988 s 161(5) (amount charged under this section not thereby excluded from charge on release on termination of employment of a beneficial loan made to a director or higher-paid employees).

TA 1988 s 190 (certain payments to members of Parliament and others to be taken into account under this section).

TA 1988 s 191 (lump sum benefits from approved retirement benefits schemes exempt from charge under Schedule E).

TA 1988 s 191 (certain job release scheme allowances for payments made within one year of pensionable age not to be treated as income).

TA 1988 s 202B(8) (deemed emoluments under sub-s (4) above to be treated for the purposes of assessment as received at the time specified in that subsection).

TA 1988 s 550(7) (amounts chargeable to tax under this section to be ignored in computing top-slicing relief in respect of gains from life and capital redemption policies and life annuity contracts).

TA 1988 s 580(3) (statutory redundancy payments to be taken into account for the purposes of this section).

TA 1988 s 589A (exemption from charge to tax under Schedule E of qualifying counselling services in connection with termination of employment).

TA 1988 s 596A(8) (lump sum paid to an employee on retirement not to be taxed under this section if employer contributed towards it and if taxed under s 595).

TA 1988 Sch 11 para 1 (relief in respect of tax chargeable by virtue of this section).

TA 1988 Sch 11 para 3 (relief where payment chargeable under this section includes payment for foreign service).

FA 1995 s 92(10) (exemption from tax under this section in respect of payments connected with certain employment related expenses after cessation of employment).

IT (Employments) Regulations, SI 1993/744 reg 46ZA (information provided to the Revenue by employers in respect of termination payments and other benefits exceeding £30,000).

Amendments—[1] This section substituted by FA 1998 s 58(1) with effect in relation to payments or other benefits received on or after 6 April 1998, except where the payment or other benefit or the right to receive it has been brought into charge to tax before that date.

[2] Sub-ss (2), (2A) substituted for sub-s (2) by FA 2002 s 37, Sch 6 para 5 with effect from the year 2002–03.

149 Sick pay

(1) Where a person holding an employment is absent from work for any period by reason of sickness or disability, any sums which—

(*a*) are paid to, or to the order or for the benefit of, that person (or a member of his family or household) in respect of any such absence from work; and

(*b*) are, by reason of his employment, paid as a result of any arrangements entered into by his employer,

shall be chargeable to income tax under Schedule E as emoluments of the employment ...[1] if, apart from this section, they would not be so chargeable ...[1].

(2) Where the funds for making payments under any arrangements are attributable partly to contributions made by the employer and partly to contributions made by the persons employed by him, subsection (1) above shall apply only to such part of the sums paid as a result of the arrangements as it is just and reasonable to regard as attributable to the employer's contributions.

(3) In this section "employment" means an office or employment the emoluments of which fall to be assessed under Schedule E and related expressions shall be construed accordingly; and the reference to a person's family or household is to his spouse, his sons and daughters and their spouses, his parents and his dependants.

Commentary—*Simon's Direct Tax Service* **E4.424.**

Revenue Internal Guidance—Schedule E manual SE 06400 (sick pay and injury payments (other than Statutory Sick Pay)—list of guidance).

SE 06410 (sick pay and injury payments—sick pay funded by the employer, application of s 149).

SE 06430 (sick pay and injury payments—sick pay funded partly by the employer and partly by employees, part funded by employer liable to tax under Schedule E).

SE 06460 (sick pay and injury payments—sick pay funded partly by the employer and partly by employees—examples).

Definitions—"Emoluments", s 131(1); "Schedule E", s 19(1).

Cross reference—See TA 1988 s 154(2) (any benefits which would be chargeable to tax under this section are not taxable benefits for employees earning £8,500 or more and directors).

Amendments—[1] Words in sub-s (1) repealed by FA 1989 ss 42(1), (3), (6), 187(1) and Sch 17 Pt IV.

150 Job release scheme allowances, maternity pay and statutory sick pay

The following payments shall be charged to income tax under Schedule E by virtue of this section if they would not otherwise be, that is to say—

(*a*) allowances paid under a scheme of the kind described in the Job Release Act 1977 being a scheme which provides for the payment of allowances for periods beginning earlier than one year before the date on which the recipient attains pensionable age, as defined in that Act;

(*b*) ...[1]

(*c*) payments of statutory sick pay within the meaning of section 1 of the Social Security and Housing Benefits Act 1982 or, in Northern Ireland, Article 3 of the Social Security (Northern Ireland) Order 1982; and (*d*) payments of statutory maternity pay under Part V of the Social Security Act 1986 or, in Northern Ireland, under Part VI of the Social Security (Northern Ireland) Order 1986.

[(*e*) payments of statutory paternity pay or statutory adoption pay under Part 12ZA or 12ZB of the Social Security Contributions and Benefits Act 1992 or, in Northern Ireland, under any corresponding legislation in force there.][2]

Commentary—*Simon's Direct Tax Service* **E4.128.**
Notes—Provisions mentioned in paras (*c*) and (*d*) are re-enacted by the Social Security Contributions and Benefits Act 1992 s 151; Social Security Contributions and Benefits (Northern Ireland) Act 1992 s 147; Social Security Contributions and Benefits Act 1992 Pt XII and Social Security Contributions and Benefits (Northern Ireland) Act 1992 Pt XII respectively.
Revenue Internal Guidance—Schedule E manual, SE 76350 (social security benefits: statutory sick pay—where payments of SSP do not arise from an employment, s 150(*c*) ensures that the payments are still chargeable under Schedule E).
SE 76360 (social security benefits: Statutory Maternity Pay (where payments of SMP do not arise from an employment, s 150(*d*) ensures that the payments are still chargeable under Schedule E).
Definition—''Schedule E'', s 19(1).
Cross references—TA 1988 s 191 (certain job release scheme allowances made within one year of pensionable age not to be treated as income).
FA 1995 s 128(3) (income chargeable under this section is excluded income for the purposes of limiting income chargeable on non-residents).
Amendments—[1] Para (*b*) repealed by the Employment Rights Act 1996 Sch 3 Pt I with effect from 22 August 1996.
[2] Para (*e*) inserted by FA 2002 s 35 with effect from 24 July 2002.

151 Income support etc

(1) Subject to the following provisions of this section, payments to any person of income support under the Social Security Act 1986 in respect of any period shall be charged to income tax under Schedule E if during that period—

(*a*) his right to income support is subject to the condition specified in section 20(3)(*d*)(i) of that Act (availability for employment); or
(*b*) he is one of a married or unmarried couple and section 23 of that Act (trade disputes) applies to him but not to the other person;

(2) In this section ''married couple'' and ''unmarried couple'' have the same meaning as in Part II of the Social Security Act 1986.

(3) Where the amount of income support paid to any person in respect of any week or part of a week exceeds the taxable maximum for that period as defined below, the excess shall not be taxable.

(4) Where payments of unemployment benefit and payments of income support are made to any person in respect of the same week or part of a week, the amount taxable in respect of that period in respect of those payments shall not exceed the taxable maximum for that period within the meaning of subsection (3) above.

(5) For the purposes of subsections (3) and (4) above, the taxable maximum in respect of a week shall be determined in accordance with subsections (6) to (8) below and the taxable maximum in respect of part of a week shall be equal to one-sixth of the taxable maximum in respect of a week multiplied by the number of days in the part.

(6) Where the income support is paid to one of a married or unmarried couple in a case not falling within subsection (1)(*b*) above, the taxable maximum in respect of a week shall be equal to the aggregate of—

(*a*) the weekly rate specified for the week in question in relation to unemployment benefit in paragraph 1 of Part I of Schedule 4 to the Social Security Act 1975; and
(*b*) the increase for an adult dependant specified for that week in paragraph 1(*a*) of Part IV of that Schedule.

(7) Where the income support is paid to one of a married or unmarried couple in a case falling within subsection (1)(*b*) above, the taxable maximum in respect of a week shall—

(*a*) if the applicable amount (within the meaning of Part II of the Social Security Act 1986) consists only of an amount in respect of them, be equal to one half of that amount; and
(*b*) if the applicable amount includes other amounts, be equal to one half of the portion of it which is included in respect of them.

(8) Where the income support is paid to a person who is not one of a married or unmarried couple, the taxable maximum in respect of a week shall be equal to the weekly rate referred to in subsection (6)(*a*) above.

(9) In its application to Northern Ireland this section shall have effect as if—

(*a*) for the references to the Social Security Act 1986 to Part II of that Act and to sections 20(3)(*d*)(i) and 23 of that Act there were substituted respectively references to the Social Security (Northern Ireland) Order 1986, Part III of that Order and Articles 21(3)(*d*)(i) and 24 of that Order; and
(*b*) for the references to paragraph 1 of Part I of Schedule 4 to the Social Security Act 1975 and paragraph 1(*a*) of Part IV of that Schedule there were substituted respectively references to paragraph 1 of Part I of Schedule 4 to the Social Security (Northern Ireland) Act 1975 and paragraph 1(*a*) of Part IV of that Schedule.

TA 1988

Commentary—*Simon's Direct Tax Service* **E4.129.**
Notes—SSA 1986 ss 20, 23 and corresponding Northern Ireland provisions referred to in sub-ss (1), (9) above are re-enacted in
  Social Security Contributions and Benefits Act 1992 ss 124(1)(*d*)(i), 126 and Social Security Contributions and Benefits
  (Northern Ireland) Act 1992 ss 123(1)(*d*)(i), 125.
SSA 1986 Pt II referred to in sub-ss (2), (7) above is re-enacted in Social Security Contributions and Benefits Act 1992 Pt VII.
SSA 1975 Sch 4, Pts I, IV and corresponding Northern Ireland provisions referred to in sub-ss (6), (9) above are re-enacted in
  Social Security Contributions and Benefits Act 1992 Sch 4 Pt I, para 1 and Pt IV, para 1(*a*) and Social Security Contributions
  and Benefits (Northern Ireland) Act 1992 Sch 4 Pt I, para 1 and Pt IV para 1(*a*).
Revenue Internal Guidance—Schedule E manual SE 65980 (Local Government Councillors and Civic Dignitaries: DETR
  guidance—Part Three. Members' allowances and the social security system: income support affected by receipt of allowances).
SE 76190 (Social Security benefits: income support, explanation of amounts taxable).
Cross reference—See FA 1989 s 41(1)(*c*) (income support chargeable to income tax under this section to be charged in the year
  in which it accrues irrespective of when it is paid).

[151A Jobseeker's allowance

(1) Subject to the following provisions of this section, payments to any person of a jobseeker's
allowance in respect of any period shall be charged to income tax under Schedule E.

(2) Where the amount of a jobseeker's allowance paid to any person in respect of any week or part
of a week exceeds the taxable maximum for that period as defined below, the excess shall not be
taxable.

(3) For the purposes of subsection (2) above, the taxable maximum in respect of a week shall be
determined in accordance with subsections (4) to (8) below and the taxable maximum in respect of
part of a week shall be equal to one-seventh of the taxable maximum in respect of a week multiplied
by the number of days in the part.

(4) Where an income-based jobseeker's allowance is paid to one of a married or unmarried couple,
in a case which does not fall within subsection (8) below, the taxable maximum in respect of a week
shall be equal to the portion of the applicable amount which is included in respect of them for that
week.

(5) Where a contribution-based jobseeker's allowance is paid to a person ("the claimant") who is a
member of a married or unmarried couple, the taxable maximum in respect of a week shall be equal
to the portion of the applicable amount which would be included in respect of them if an income-
based jobseeker's allowance was payable to the claimant for that week.

(6) Where an income-based jobseeker's allowance is paid to a person who is not a member of a
married or unmarried couple, the taxable maximum in respect of a week shall be equal to the age-
related amount which would be applicable to him if a contribution-based jobseeker's allowance was
payable to him for that week.

(7) Where a contribution-based jobseeker's allowance is paid to a person who is not a member of a
married or unmarried couple, the taxable maximum in respect of a week shall be equal to the age-
related amount which is applicable to him for that week.

(8) Where an income-based jobseeker's allowance is paid to a person ("the claimant") who is a
member of a married or unmarried couple, the other member of which is prevented by section 14 of
the Jobseekers Act 1995 (trade disputes) or any corresponding enactment in Northern Ireland from
being entitled to a jobseeker's allowance, the taxable maximum in respect of a week shall be equal
to half the portion of the applicable amount which is included in respect of them for that week.

(9) In this section—

  "age-related amount" and "applicable amount" mean the amounts determined as such in
    accordance with regulations made under section 4 of the Jobseekers Act 1995 or, for Northern
    Ireland, regulations made under any corresponding enactment in Northern Ireland;
  and "contribution-based jobseeker's allowance", "income-based jobseeker's allowance",
    "married couple" and "unmarried couple" have the same meanings as in the Jobseekers Act
    1995 or, for Northern Ireland, the same meanings as in any corresponding enactment in Northern
    Ireland.][1]

Commentary—*Simon's Direct Tax Service* **E4.128.**
Revenue Internal Guidance—Schedule E manual, SE 01700–01706 (Employment Zone scheme—interaction with jobseeker's
  allowance).
SE 65980 (Local Government Councillors and Civic Dignitaries: DETR guidance—Part Three. Members' allowances and the
  social security system: interaction of jobseeker's allowance with allowances paid by local authorities).
SE 76220–76222 (Social Security benefits: details of jobseeker's allowance and how much is taxable).
SE 76223 (Social Security benefits: tax treatment of jobseeker's allowance during strikes and back to work bonus).
SE 76224 (Social Security benefits: benefit paid during layoffs—procedures for recipients of jobseeker's allowance also known
  as 'temporary stop' claimants).
SE 76225 (Social Security benefits: relationship between jobseeker's allowance and other benefits).
SE 76226 (Social Security benefits: payments under the Employment Protection Acts—amount paid initially as jobseeker's
  allowance is regarded instead as an advance payment of the award).
SE 76300–76302 (Social security benefits: operational issues relevant to jobseeker's allowance).
Definition—"Schedule E", s 19.
Cross reference—See TA 1988 s 617(2)(*ab*) (payments of jobseeker's allowance not to be treated as income except for payments
  taxable under this section).
Amendments—[1] This section inserted by the Jobseekers Act 1995 Sch 2 para 12, as from 2 September 1996 (see Jobseekers Act
  1995 (Commencement No 4) Order 1996, SI 1996/2208).

152 Notification of amount taxable under section 151

(1) A benefit officer may by notice notify a person who is taxable in respect of any unemployment benefit[, jobseeker's allowance][1] or income support of the amount on which he is taxable and any such notification shall state the date on which it is issued and shall inform the person to whom it is given that he may object to the notification by notice given within 60 days after the date of issue of the notification.

(2) Where—

    (*a*) no objection is made to a notification of an amount under subsection (1) above within the period specified in that subsection (or such further period as may be allowed by virtue of subsection (5) below); or

    (*b*) an objection is made but is withdrawn by the objector by notice,

that amount shall not be questioned in any appeal against any assessment in respect of income including that amount.

(3) Where—

    (*a*) an objection is made to a notification of an amount under subsection (1) above within the period specified in that subsection (or such further period as may be allowed by virtue of subsection (5) below), and

    (*b*) the benefit officer and the objector come to an agreement that the amount notified should be varied in a particular manner, and

    (*c*) the officer confirms the agreement to vary in writing,

then, subject to subsection (4) below, that amount as so varied shall not be questioned in any appeal against any assessment in respect of income including that amount.

(4) Subsection (3) above shall not apply if, within 60 days from the date when the agreement was come to, the objector gives notice to the benefit officer that he wishes to repudiate or resile from the agreement.

(5) An objection to a notification may be made later than 60 days after the date of the issue of the notification if, on an application for the purpose—

    (*a*) a benefit officer is satisfied that there was a reasonable excuse for not objecting within that time, and

    (*b*) the objection was made thereafter without unreasonable delay, and

    (*c*) the officer gives consent in writing;

and if the officer is not so satisfied he shall refer the application for determination—

    (i) by the General Commissioners for the division in which the objector ordinarily resides or,

    (ii) in a case where an appeal has been made against an assessment in respect of income including the amount in question, the General Commissioners or the Special Commissioners having jurisdiction in that appeal.

(6) Where a benefit officer has notified an amount to a person under subsection (1) above, he may by another notice notify the person of an alteration in the amount previously notified and, if he does so, the original notification shall be cancelled and this section shall apply to such a subsequent notification as it applies to the original notification.

(7) In this section "benefit officer" means the appropriate officer, [in Great Britain, of the Department for Work and Pensions][2], or, in Northern Ireland, of the Department of Health and Social Services.

Commentary—*Simon's Direct Tax Service* **E4.129.**
Revenue Internal Guidance—Schedule E manual, SE 71435 (appeals involving taxable jobseeker's allowance—overview).
SE 76303–76305 and SE 76308 (social security benefits: operational issues—the procedure for written objections under this section).
SE 76306 (Social security benefits: operational issues—procedures for dealing with appeals against Schedule E assessments on jobseeker's allowance).
SE 76309 (Social security benefits: operational issues—procedures when objection or appeal settled).
Definition—"Notice", s 832(1).
Amendments—[1] Words in sub-s (1) inserted by the Jobseekers Act 1995 Sch 2 para 13, as from 7 October 1996 (see Jobseekers Act 1995 (Commencement No 4) Order 1996, SI 1996/2208).
[2] Words in sub-s (7) substituted by the Secretaries of State for Education and Skills and for Work and Pensions Order, SI 2002/1397 art 12, Schedule para 6 with effect from 27 June 2002.

CHAPTER II
[EMPLOYEES EARNING £8,500 OR MORE AND DIRECTORS][1]

Concession A4—Certain modifications to the general rule under this Chapter of treating travelling and hotel expenses as taxable emoluments.
A5—Circumstances in which a "cheap or interest-free loan" is exempt from a charge under this Chapter.
A5—Where a director or employee needs the company of his wife because of his precarious health when travelling abroad on business, wife's travelling expenses paid by employer are exempt from a charge under this Chapter.
Revenue Interpretation RI 45—Routine medical check-ups or screening provided by employer for employees; whether benefit in kind.
Cross references—See TMA 1970 s 15(3)(*a*) (employer may be required to give notice to all employees who are in employment to which this Chapter applies).
TA 1988 s 168 (interpretation).

IT (Employments) Regulations, SI 1993/744 reg 46(1)(*b*), (3) (contents of returns to be rendered by employer in respect of an employee within this Chapter).
FA 2000 Sch 12 para 11 (deemed Schedule E payment treated as part of worker's emoluments from an intermediary for the purposes of determining whether it is employment to which this Chapter applies).
Amendments—[1] Heading substituted by FA 1989 s 53(2)(*a*).

Expenses

153 Payments in respect of expenses

(1) Subject to the provisions of this Chapter [and sections 197AD and 197AE][3], where in any year a person is employed in [employment to which this Chapter applies][1] and by reason of his employment there are paid to him in respect of expenses any sums which, apart from this section, are not chargeable to tax as his income, those sums are to be treated as emoluments of the employment and accordingly chargeable to income tax under Schedule E.

(2) Subsection (1) above is without prejudice to any claim for deductions under section [197AG,][3]198, 201 [201AA][2] or 332(3).

(3) The reference in subsection (1) above to sums paid in respect of expenses includes any sums put at the employee's disposal by reason of his employment and paid away by him.

Commentary—*Simon's Direct Tax Service* E4.604.
Concession A5—Removal expenses: concessionary treatment up to 5 April 1993; transitional provisions.
A67—Employees moved to higher cost housing area: concessionary treatment up to 5 April 1993; transitional provisions.
Statement of Practice SP A6—This statement sets out the procedure to be followed by the employers in respect of expenses, benefits and fees affected by VAT and accountable under Schedule E.
Revenue Internal Guidance—Schedule E Manual, SE 01110 (expenses payments and reimbursements—general scope of s 153).
SE 10000 (travelling and subsistence payments—general, application of s 153).
SE 10150 (motor mileage allowances paid for business travel in employee's own car—basis of charge, application of s 153).
SE 20101 (amounts chargeable under this section to be included when calculating whether employment has emoluments at a rate of £8,500 a year or more, unless covered by a dispensation).
SE 20501 (meaning of 'by reason of the employment').
SE 20601 (expenses payments of directors and employees within Pt V Ch II: scope).
SE 20602 (expenses payments are not chargeable by virtue of this section if they are already chargeable by virtue of some other provision).
SE 20603 (examples of expenses payments chargeable by virtue of this section).
SE 20604 (a payment made by an employer direct to a third party in respect of expenses is not within this section).
SE 20605 (employees chargeable under Case III of Sch E—include expenses payments in the UK as chargeable emoluments as well as those remitted to the UK).
SE 21835 (third party entertainment—need for internal report where Revenue believes liability on third party entertaining could arise under s 19(1)1 or s 153).
SE 31616 (example of deduction from expenses charge under sub-s (2)).
SE 31980–31985 (spouses on business trips—expenses will be assessable on the employee under this section, conditions for obtaining a deduction, application of Concession A4).
SE 32805 (working from home—one-man service companies—example of charge under this section).
Simon's Tax Cases—*Smith v Fox* [1989] STC 378*
Definitions—"Emoluments", s 131(1): "employment", s 168(2); "employment to which this Chapter applies", s 167; "Schedule E", s 19(1).
Cross references—See TA 1988 s 157(3) (charging provisions in respect of car benefits).
TA 1988 s 159AA(3)(*c*) (charging provisions in respect of van benefit).
TA 1988 s 159AC(3)(*c*) (exemption provisions in respect of heavier commercial vehicle supplied to an employee and not used by him wholly or mainly for private purposes).
TA 1988 s 193 (deduction in respect of certain travel expenses relating to overseas employment).
TA 1988 s 194 (deduction in respect of certain reimbursed travel expenses between the United Kingdom and place of work abroad).
TA 1988 s 195 (deduction in respect of certain reimbursed travel expenses of employee not domiciled in the United Kingdom).
TA 1988 s 197A (exemption for reimbursed expenses in connection with certain car parking facilities).
TA 1988 ss 197B–197F (restriction on charge to tax in respect of reimbursed expenses in connection with mileage allowances for use of own car).
TA 1988 s 198 (relief for expenses incurred wholly, exclusively and necessarily in the performance of the duties of an office or employment).
TA 1988 s 200 (exemption for certain travel and subsistence allowances of MPs).
TA 1988 s 200A (relief for incidental overnight expenses).
TA 1988 s 200AA (relief for certain transport and subsistence reimbursements made by the Crown to holders of certain Government offices).
TA 1988 s 332 (relief for certain expenses of ministers of religion).
TA 1988 s 588 (exemption for certain reimbursed expenses relating to retraining courses).
TA 1988 s 589A (exemption for certain reimbursed expenses relating to counselling services in connection with termination of employment).
TA 1988 Sch 11A (certain reimbursed removal expenses to be exempt).
Amendments—[1] Words in sub-s (1) substituted by FA 1989 s 53(2)(*b*).
[2] Words in sub-s (2) inserted by FA 1995 s 91(2), (3) with effect from the year 1995–96.
[3] Words in sub-s (1), (2) inserted by FA 2001 s 57(3), (4), Sch 12 Pt II para 1 with effect from the year 2002–03.

Benefits in kind

154 General charging provision

(1) Subject to section 163, where in any year a person is employed in [employment to which this Chapter applies][1] and—

(*a*) by reason of his employment there is provided for him, or for others being members of his family or household, any benefit to which this section applies; and

(*b*) the cost of providing the benefit is not (apart from this section) chargeable to tax as his income, there is to be treated as emoluments of the employment, and accordingly chargeable to income tax under Schedule E, an amount equal to whatever is the cash equivalent of the benefit.

(2) The benefits to which this section applies are accommodation (other than living accommodation), entertainment, domestic or other services, and other benefits and facilities of whatsoever nature (whether or not similar to any of those mentioned above in this subsection), excluding however—

　　(a) any benefit consisting of the right to receive, or the prospect of receiving, any sums which would be chargeable to tax under section 149; and

　　(b) any benefit chargeable under section 157, 158, [159AA,]³ ...⁴ 160 or 162;

and subject to the exceptions provided for by [sections 155[, 155ZA]⁶[, 155ZB,]⁶ [, 155AA]⁴[, 155A and 156A]⁵]².

(3) For the purposes of this section and sections 155[, 155ZA]⁶ and 156, the persons providing a benefit are those at whose cost the provision is made.

Commentary—*Simon's Direct Tax Service* **E4.611, 612.**
Concessions A65—Exemption for expenses paid by employees of oil and gas staff for transfers of staff between mainland and oil rigs.
A70—Small gifts to employees and their family by third parties and staff Christmas parties, annual dinner dance, etc are tax free up to specified costs.
A72—Exemption for the provision by an employer of pension, annuity, etc for the benefit of an employee's family on death or retirement of the employee.
A85—Exemption for costs incurred by the provider of an asset where the asset is transferred by an employee or director to their employer or other; normal vendor's costs borne by someone other than the director or employee remain chargeable.
Statements of Practice SP 6/85—Expenses which are to be included in the calculation of the amount assessable under this section in relation to incentive awards.
SP 5/88—Circumstances in which a car telephone provided by an employer may or may not be taxable under this section.
SP A6—The statement sets out the procedure to be followed by the employers in respect of expenses, benefits and fees affected by VAT and accountable under Schedule E.
SP A7—Where an employer incurs expense in providing a benefit (including a benefit of the use of employer's property) affected by VAT, the Schedule E liability extends to expenditure inclusive of VAT, whether or not any part of VAT is recoverable.
Revenue Interpretation RI 45—Routine medical check-ups or screening provided by employer for employees; whether benefit in kind.
RI 112—Relocation packages and guaranteed selling price schemes.
Revenue Internal Guidance—Inspector's manual IM 5325–5337 (information from company accounts is passed to district dealing with directors etc).
Schedule E manual, SE 01020 (board and lodging—chargeable under this section on the cost to the employer of providing the benefit, less any amount made good by the employee).
SE 01100 (examination grants to employees—chargeable under this section where employee has emoluments at the rate of £8,500 a year or more).
SE 11322 (board and lodging and other accommodation which is not living accommodation, possible charge under this section).
SE 11522 (living accommodation: other liabilities in connection with living accommodation—employer's liability providing benefit to employee, application of this section).
SE 13905 (termination payments and benefits: interaction with benefits received during employment—example showing how to calculate the taxable amounts for the year of assessment in which the termination occurs).
SE 20101 (benefits chargeable under this section to be included when calculating whether employment has emoluments at a rate of £8,500 a year or more, unless covered by a dispensation).
SE 20501 (meaning of ''by reason of the employment'').
SE 20504 (meaning of provided for an employee's family or household).
SE 20505 (provision to a family member employed by the same employer as the employee).
SE 20510 (the person providing a benefit is deemed to be the person at whose cost the provision is made, not necessarily the person who physically ''hands over'' the benefit to the employee).
SE 21000 (general index of benefits chargeable under Pt V Ch II covering references SE 21001–21241).
SE 21241 (sick pay schemes: employers' contributions exempt under sub-s (2)).
SE 21600 (alphabetical index of rules relating to particular benefits and expenses payments, covering references SE 21601–21855).
SE 21900 (exemption for workplace nurseries—purpose of the legislation is that exemption should only apply when charge to tax would otherwise be under this section).
SE 22900–22920 (treatment of benefits which are trivial in amount).
SE 23005 (examples of exclusion from charge where benefit is of a car chargeable under s 157).
SE 23043 (application of this section where a car 'unsuitable for use as a private vehicle' is so used).
SE 31980 (spouses on business trips—expenses will be assessable on the employee under this section).
SE 31991 (overseas conferences, seminars and study tours—example of charge under this section).
SE 50100 (exemption from charge where travel facilities provided for members of the naval, military or air forces of the Crown going on, or returning from, leave).
SE 64630 (insurance agents: possibility of charge under this section where an employee, in connection with his or her own policy or purchase, pays a discounted premium or price to an employer).
SE 67191 (workers on offshore oil and gas rigs or platforms: free transfers from and to mainland, application of Concession A65).
Revenue & other press releases—IR 2-11-84 and 18-1-90 (incentive awards and prizes for employees (Taxed Award Schemes) voluntary arrangements for collecting tax where employer wishes to pay employee's tax liability on awards provided).
IR 480 (1993) (guide to expenses payments and benefits for directors and certain employees).
ICAEW TR786 15-3-90 (exam prizes are within the scope of this section).
IR Tax Bulletin October 2000 p 779 (calculating the cash equivalent of a benefit when there is part business and part private use).
Simon's Tax Cases—*Templeton v Jacobs* [1996] STC 991; *R v Dimsey; R v Allen* [1999] STC 846; *Sports Club plc and others v Insp of Taxes* [2000] STC (SCD) 443.
s 154(1), *Wicks v Firth* [1983] STC 25*; *Pepper v Hart* [1990] STC 6*
Definitions—''Emoluments'', s 131(1); ''employment'', s 168(2); ''family or household'', s 168(4); ''Schedule E'', s 19(1).
Cross references—See TMA 1970 s 15(8) (employer may be required to give notice of benefits that may give rise to a charge under this section).
TA 1988 s 155 (exceptions from the general charge).
TA 1988 s 155AA (exception for mobile telephone made available to employees).
TA 1988 s 155A(1) (exception for care for children).
TA 1988 s 156 (cash equivalents of benefits charged under s 154).
TA 1988 s 156A (limited exemption in respect of computer equipment provided to employees).
TA 1988 s 159(3) (this section not to apply to pooled cars).

TA 1988 s 159AC(2) (this section not to apply to benefit of heavier commercial vehicle made available to employees).
TA 1988 ss 165, 331 (exclusion of certain scholarships from tax charge under this section).
TA 1988 s 197(2) (exemption in respect of leave travel facilities for the armed forces).
TA 1988 s 197AA (exemption for provision for employees of a works bus service.)
TA 1988 s 197AB (exemption for financial or other support for a public transport bus service used by employees for qualifying journeys).
TA 1988 s 197AC (exemption for cycles and cyclist's safety equipment provided to employees for qualifying journeys).
TA 1988 s 197G (exemption for the provision of certain sporting and recreational facilities).
TA 1988 s 200AA (relief for certain transport and subsistence benefits provided to certain Government office holders by the Crown).
TA 1988 s 588 (exemption for the provision of certain retraining services).
TA 1988 s 589A (exemption for the provision of certain counselling services in connection with termination of employment).
IT (Employments) Regulations, SI 1993/744 reg 46(1)(d), (3), (5), (6) (contents of returns to be made by employers in respect of benefits giving rise to a charge to tax under this section).
IT (Benefits in Kind) (Exemption for Welfare Counselling) Regulations, SI 2000/2080 (exemption for welfare counselling).
Amendments—[1] Words in sub-s (1) substituted by FA 1989 s 53(2)(b).
[2] Words in sub-s (2) substituted by FA 1990 s 21(2), (3).
[3] "159AA," in sub-s (2)(b) inserted by FA 1993 Sch 4 paras 1, 2.
[4] Sub-s (2) amended by FA 1999 ss 44(3), (6), 139, Sch 20 Pt III(9) with effect from the year 1999–00.
[5] Words in sub-s (2) substituted by FA 1999 s 45(2), (3) with effect from the year 1999–00.
[6] Words in sub-ss (2), (3) inserted by FA 2000 s 57, Sch 10 paras 1, 2(2), 3(2) with effect from the year 2000–01.

155 Exceptions from the general charge

(1) Where the benefit of a car [or van][3] is taxable under section 157 [or 159AA][3], section 154 does not apply to any benefit in connection with the car [or van][3] other than a benefit in connection with the provision of a driver for the car [or van][3].

[(1A) Section 154 does not apply to a benefit consisting in the provision for the employee of a car parking space at or near his place of work.][1]

[(1B) Section 154 does not apply in the case of a benefit provided for the employee himself where—

(a) the provision of the benefit is incidental to the employee's being away from his usual place of abode during a qualifying absence from home;

(b) the authorised maximum is not exceeded in relation to that qualifying absence; and

(c) the cost of the benefit would not be deductible as mentioned in section 156(8) if incurred by the employee out of his emoluments.][4]

[(1C) Subsections (3) to (5) of section 200A shall apply as they apply for the purposes of that section for construing the references in subsection (1B) above to a qualifying absence from home and for determining, for the purposes of that subsection, whether the authorised maximum is exceeded.][4]

(2) ...[5]

(3) Where living accommodation is provided by reason of a person's employment—

(a) alterations and additions to the premises concerned which are of a structural nature, and

(b) repairs to the premises of a kind which, if the premises were let under a lease to which section 11 of the Landlord and Tenant Act 1985 (repairing obligations) applies, would be the obligation of the lessor under the covenants implied by subsection (1) of that section,

are not benefits to which section 154 applies.

(4) Section 154 does not apply to a benefit consisting in the provision by the employee's employer for the employee himself, or for the spouse, children or dependants of the employee, of any pension, annuity, lump sum, gratuity or other like benefit to be given on the employee's death or retirement.

(5) Section 154 does not apply to a benefit consisting in the provision by the employee's employer of meals in any canteen in which meals are provided for the staff generally.

(6) Section 154 does not apply where the benefit consists—

(a) in providing the employee with medical treatment outside the United Kingdom (including providing for him to be an in-patient) in a case where the need for the treatment arises while the employee is outside the United Kingdom for the purpose of performing the duties of his employment; or

(b) in providing insurance for the employee against the cost of such treatment in such a case;

and for the purpose of this subsection, medical treatment includes all forms of treatment for, and all procedures for diagnosing, any physical or mental ailment, infirmity or defect.

[(7) Section 154 does not apply to a benefit consisting in the provision of entertainment (including hospitality of any kind) for the employee, or for members of his family or household, if—

(a) the person providing the benefit is neither his employer nor a person connected with his employer;

(b) neither his employer nor a person connected with his employer has directly or indirectly procured its provision; and

(c) it is not provided either in recognition of particular services which have been performed by the employee in the course of his employment or in anticipation of particular services which are to be so performed by him;

and section 839 shall apply for determining whether persons are connected for the purposes of this subsection.][2]

Commentary—*Simon's Direct Tax Service* **E4.612.**
Concessions A70—Small gifts to employees by third parties and staff Christmas parties.
A74—Meals provided for employees.
Statement of Practice SP 5/88—Circumstances in which a car telephone provided by an employer is not excepted from the general charge.
Notes—Landlord and Tenant Act 1985 s 11(1) mentioned in sub-s (3)(b) above reads—

"**11** Repairing obligations in short leases

(1) In a lease to which this section applies (as to which, see sections 13 and 14) there is implied a covenant by the lessor—

(a) to keep in repair the structure and exterior of the dwelling-house (including drains, gutters and external pipes),
(b) to keep in repair and proper working order the installations in the dwelling-house for the supply of water, gas and electricity and for sanitation (including basins, sinks, baths and sanitary conveniences, but not other fixtures, fittings and appliances for making use of the supply of water, gas or electricity), and
(c) to keep in repair and proper working order the installations in the dwelling-house for space heating and heating water.".

Revenue Internal Guidance—Schedule E manual SE 13300 (termination payments and benefits—sub-s (5) does not apply for s 148 purposes).
SE 21241 (table of benefits and reimbursed expenses exempt from tax, giving references for guidance on this section).
SE 21601 (particular accommodation, supplies and services on the employer's premises).
SE 21611 (particular benefits: alterations, additions and repairs to living accommodation).
SE 21670–21677 (subsidised meals including canteen meals and working lunches, Concession A74).
SE 21685 (sub-s (1A)—the application of "at or near" should not be rigidly applied: an exemption should not be denied simply because there is a car park nearer to the place of work).
SE 21766 (sub-s (6)—the exemption does not extend to the cost of treatment for family or household members).
SE 21835–21840 (conditions to be satisfied for exemption under sub-s (7)).
SE 23005 (provision of a season ticket for a toll bridge not covered by sub-s (1)).
SE 23007 (cash equivalent of the benefit of the chauffeur is calculated in the same way as other benefits in kind).
SE 23550 (transfer of ownership of the car to the employee: sub-s 1 will cease to apply after car has been transferred).
SE 42780 (salary sacrifice: contributions to an approved retirement benefits scheme—income tax effects, application of sub-s (4) with example at SE 42785).
Simon's Tax Cases—*Stones v Hall* [1989] STC 138*.
s 155(2), *Templeton v Jacobs* [1996] STC 991.
Definitions—"Car", s 168(5); "children", ss 831(4), 832(5); "emoluments", s 131(1); "employment", s 168(2); "United Kingdom", s 830(1).
Cross references—See FA 1999 s 49 (sub-s (1A) above applies in relation to motor cycle parking spaces and facilities for parking cycles as it applies to car parking spaces with effect from the year 1999–00).
Amendments—[1] Sub-s (1A) inserted by FA 1988 s 46(3), (5).
[2] Sub-s (7) added by FA 1988 s 49(1), (3).
[3] Words in sub-s (1) inserted by FA 1993 Sch 4 paras 1, 3 with effect from the year 1993–94.
[4] Sub-ss (1B), (1C) inserted by FA 1995 s 93(3), (5) with effect for determining what emoluments are received by any person after 5 April 1995.
[5] Sub-s (2) repealed by FA 2000 s 156, Sch 40 Pt II(2) with effect from the year 2000–01.

[155ZA Accommodation, supplies or services used in performing duties of employment]

(1) Section 154 does not apply to a benefit consisting in the provision of accommodation, supplies or services used by the employee in performing the duties of his employment if the following conditions are met.

(2) Where the benefit is provided on premises occupied by the employer or other person providing it, the only condition is that any use of it for private purposes by the employee or members of his family or household is not significant.

(3) Where the benefit is provided otherwise than on premises occupied by the employer or other person providing it, the conditions are—

(a) that the sole purpose of providing the benefit is to enable the employee to perform the duties of his employment,
(b) that any use of it for private purposes is not significant, and
(c) that it is not an excluded benefit.

(4) The Treasury may make provision by regulations as to what is an excluded benefit for the purposes of subsection (3)(c) above.

The regulations may provide that a benefit is an excluded benefit only if such conditions as may be prescribed are met as to the terms on which, and persons to whom, it is provided.

(5) Subject to any such regulations, the provision of any of the following is an excluded benefit (whatever the terms and whoever it is provided to)—

(a) a motor vehicle, boat or aircraft;
(b) a benefit that involves—

(i) the extension, conversion or alteration of any living accommodation, or
(ii) the construction, extension, conversion or alteration of a building or other structure on land adjacent to and enjoyed with such accommodation.

(6) For the purposes of this section—

(a) use "for private purposes" means any use that is not use in performing the duties of the employee's employment; and
(b) use that is at the same time use in performing the duties of an employee's employment and use for private purposes counts as use for private purposes.][1]

Revenue & other press releases—IR Tax Bulletin October 2000 p 779 (Revenue explanation of how this section operates in practice).
Amendments—[1] This section inserted by FA 2000 s 57, Sch 10 paras 1, 2(1) with effect from the year 2000–01.

[155ZB Power to provide for exemption of minor benefits

(1) The Treasury may make provision by regulations for exempting from section 154 such minor benefits as may be specified in the regulations.

(2) Any exemption conferred by regulations under this section is conditional on the benefit being made available to the employer's employees generally on similar terms.]¹

[(3) If by virtue of regulations under this section there is no charge to tax under section 154 in respect of a benefit (or there would be no charge if the employee were in employment to which Chapter 2 of Part 5 applied), there is no charge to tax under section 141 (non-cash vouchers) in respect of a voucher evidencing the employee's entitlement to the benefit.]²

Regulations—See the Income Tax (Exemption of Minor Benefits) Regulations, SI 2002/205 (exemption for the provision of qualifying meals for employees who cycle to work; and for the provision to employees of works buses for the purpose of making certain journeys).
The Income Tax (Benefits in Kind) (Exemption for Employment Costs resulting from Disability) Regulations, SI 2002/1596 (exemption, with effect from 9 July 2002, for hearing aids and other equipment, services or facilities made available to disabled employees to enable them to fulfil the duties of their employment).
Amendments—¹ This section inserted by FA 2000 s 57, Sch 10 paras 1, 3(1) with effect from the year 2000–01.
² Sub-s (3) added by FA 2002 s 36 with effect from the year 2002–03.

[155AA Mobile telephones

(1) Section 154 does not apply where the benefit consists in a mobile telephone being made available (without any transfer of the property in it) to the employee or to a member of his family or household.

(2) In this section "mobile telephone" means wireless telegraphy apparatus designed or adapted for the purpose of transmitting and receiving spoken messages so as to provide a telephone which—

(*a*) is connected to a public telecommunication system (within the meaning of the Telecommunications Act 1984); and

(*b*) is not physically connected to a land-line;

but does not include any cordless telephone or any telepoint telephone.

(3) The mobile telephones to which the exemption provided by this section applies include any mobile telephone provided in connection with a car, van or heavier commercial vehicle, notwithstanding that the vehicle is made available as mentioned in section 157, section 159AA or, as the case may be, section 159AC.

(4) In this section "cordless telephone" means wireless telegraphy apparatus which (whether or not provided in connection with a car, van or heavier commercial vehicle)—

(*a*) is designed or adapted for the purpose of transmitting and receiving spoken messages so as to provide a wireless extension to a telephone, and

(*b*) is used only as such an extension to a telephone that is physically connected to a land-line.

(5) In this section "telepoint telephone" means wireless telegraphy apparatus which (whether or not provided in connection with a car, van or heavier commercial vehicle) is used for the purpose of a short-range radio communications service utilising frequencies between 864 and 868 megahertz (inclusive).

(6) In this section "heavier commercial vehicle" has the same meaning as in section 159AC.]¹

Commentary—*Simon's Direct Tax Service* **E4.617.**
Revenue Internal Guidance—Schedule E manual, SE 21780 (mobile telephones—1999/2000 onwards, guidance on application of this section, examples where Schedule E charge may still arise). For periods prior to 1999/2000 see SE 21781–21786.
SE 23123 (mobile telephones do not count as accessories for car benefit purposes).
SE 32945 (tax treatment of mobile phones generally)
Cross references—See TA 1988 s 168A(11) (mobile telephones are not "accessories" for the purpose of computing the cash equivalent of the benefit of a car made available to an employee).
Amendments—¹ This section inserted by FA 1999 s 44(1), (6) with effect from the year 1999–00.

[155A Care for children

(1) Where a benefit consists in the provision for the employee of care for a child, section 154 does not apply to the benefit to the extent that it is provided in qualifying circumstances.

(2) For the purposes of subsection (1) above the benefit is provided in qualifying circumstances if—

(*a*) the child falls within subsection (3) below,

(*b*) the care is provided on premises which are not domestic premises,

(*c*) the condition set out in subsection (4) below or the condition set out in subsection (5) below (or each of them) is fulfilled, and

(*d*) in a case where the registration requirement applies, it is met.

(3) The child falls within this subsection if—

(*a*) he is a child for whom the employee has parental responsibility,

(*b*) he is resident with the employee, or

(*c*) he is a child of the employee and maintained at his expense.

(4) The condition is that the care is provided on premises which are made available by the employer alone.

(5) The condition is that—

(*a*) the care is provided under arrangements made by persons who include the employer,

(*b*) the care is provided on premises which are made available by one or more of those persons, and

(*c*) under the arrangements the employer is wholly or partly responsible for financing and managing the provision of the care.

(6) The registration requirement applies where—

(*a*) the premises on which the care is provided are required to be registered under ...[3] or section 11 of the Children and Young Persons Act (Northern Ireland) 1968, ...[3]

(*b*) any person providing the care is required to be registered under ...[3] [or Part XA][2] of the Children Act 1989 with respect to the premises on which it is provided[, or

(*c*) the provision of such care constitutes the provision of a care service (within the meaning of the Registration of Care (Scotland) Act 2001 (asp 8)),][3]

and the requirement is met if the premises are so registered or (as the case may be) the person is so registered [or the care service is registered under that Act of 2001.][3]

(7) In subsection (3)(*c*) above the reference to a child of the employee includes a reference to a stepchild of his.

(8) In this section—

"care" means any form of care or supervised activity, whether or not provided on a regular basis, but excluding supervised activity provided primarily for educational purposes;

"child" means a person under the age of eighteen;

"domestic premises" means any premises wholly or mainly used as a private dwelling;

"parental responsibility" has the meaning given in section 3(1) of the Children Act 1989.][1]

Commentary—*Simon's Direct Tax Service* E4.623.
Revenue Internal Guidance—Schedule E manual SE 21900 (exemption for workplace nurseries: purpose of the legislation and table showing arrangement of guidance, covering references SE 21905–21960).
Amendments—[1] This section inserted by FA 1990 s 21 with effect from the year 1990–91.
[2] Words in sub-s (6) inserted by the Care Standards Act 2000 s 116, Sch 4 para 13 with effect from 2 July 2001 (by virtue of SI 2001/2041).
[3] In sub-s (6), words repealed, para (*c*) inserted, and words inserted, by the Regulation of Care (Scotland) Act 2001 ss 79, 81(2), Sch 3 para 14 with effect from 1 April 2002 (by virtue of SSI 2002/162).

156 Cash equivalents of benefits charged under section 154

(1) The cash equivalent of any benefit chargeable to tax under section 154 is an amount equal to the cost of the benefit, less so much (if any) of it as is made good by the employee to those providing the benefit.

(2) Subject to the following subsections, the cost of a benefit is the amount of any expense incurred in or in connection with its provision, and (here and in those subsections) includes a proper proportion of any expense relating partly to the benefit and partly to other matters.

(3) Where the benefit consists in the transfer of an asset by any person, and since that person acquired or produced the asset it has been used or has depreciated, the cost of the benefit is deemed to be the market value of the asset at the time of transfer.

(4) Where the asset referred to in subsection (3) above is not a car and before the transfer a person (whether or not the transferee) has been chargeable to tax in respect of the asset in accordance with subsection (5) below, the amount which under subsection (3) above is deemed to be the cost of the benefit shall (if apart from this subsection it would be less) be deemed to be—

(*a*) the market value of the asset at the time when it was first applied (by those providing the benefit in question) for the provision of any benefit for a person, or for members of his family or household, by reason of his employment, less

(*b*) the aggregate of the amounts taken into account as the cost of the benefit in charging tax in accordance with subsection (5) below in the year or years up to and including that in which the transfer takes place.

(5) Where the benefit consists in an asset being placed at the employee's disposal, or at the disposal of others being members of his family or household, for his or their use (without any transfer of the property in the asset), or of its being used wholly or partly for his or their purposes, then the cost of the benefit in any year is deemed to be—

(*a*) the annual value of the use of the asset ascertained under subsection (6) below; plus

(*b*) the total of any expense incurred in or in connection with the provision of the benefit excluding—

(i) the expense of acquiring or producing it incurred by the person to whom the asset belongs; and

(ii) any rent or hire charge payable for the asset by those providing the benefit.

(6) Subject to subsection (7) below, the annual value of the use of the asset, for the purposes of subsection (5) above—

(*a*) in the case of land, is its annual value determined in accordance with section 837; and (*b*) in any other case is 20 per cent of its market value at the time when it was first applied (by those providing the benefit in question) in the provision of any benefit for a person, or for members of his family or household, by reason of his employment.

(7) Where there is payable, by those providing the benefit, any sum by way of rent or hire-charge for the asset, the annual amount of which is equal to, or greater than, the annual value of the use of the asset as ascertained under subsection (6) above, that amount shall be substituted for the annual value in subsection (5)(*a*) above.

(8) From the cash equivalent there are deductible in each case under section 198, 201 [201AA][1] or 332(3) such amounts (if any) as would have been so deductible if the cost of the benefit had been incurred by the employee out of his emoluments.

(9) In the case of assets first applied before 6th April 1980 by those providing the benefit in question in the provision of any benefit for a person, or for members of his family or household, by reason of his employment—

(*a*) subsection (4) above shall not have effect; and

(*b*) in subsection (6)(*b*) above for the words "20 per cent" there shall be substituted the words "10 per cent".

Commentary—*Simon's Direct Tax Service* E4.613.
Concessions A65—Exemption for travelling expenses paid by employers of oil and gas staff for travelling by the staff between oil rigs and home.
A85—Where an asset is transferred by an employee or director to his employer, cost for the purpose of sub-s (1) includes (*a*) the price or other consideration given, plus any costs normally met by the vendor but borne by someone other than the employee, (*b*) other costs incurred by the provider are ignored. Normal vendor's costs in connection with the transfer are chargeable under s 154.
Statements of Practice SP A6—Effect of VAT on Schedule E tax.
SP A7—Effect of VAT on Schedule E tax in respect of perquisites.
Revenue Interpretation RI 112—Relocation packages and guaranteed selling price schemes.
Revenue Internal Guidance—Schedule E manual SE 20506 (joint benefits of husband and wife—application of sub-s (2)).
SE 21102 (cash equivalent—general rule).
SE 21110 (cash equivalent of 'in house benefits'—marginal additional expense, application of sub-s (2) including consideration of *Pepper v Hart* (65TC 421)).
SE 21111 (cash equivalent of 'in house benefits'—marginal additional expense—examples).
SE 21120 (what is meant by 'making good').
SE 21121 (when must making good take place?).
SE 21200–21201 (apportionment of the cash equivalent of the benefit—general application of sub-s (2)).
SE 21210 (examples of deductions for necessary expenses under sub-s (8)).
SE 21615–21620 (assets placed at the disposal of a director or employee—guidance on application of sub-s (5) and (6) including worked example).
SE 21621 (asset unavailable for part of a year—annual value has to be apportioned).
SE 21625 (asset also used in the business or by other employees—apportionment of the full amount of a benefit is required).
SE 21626 (asset used by the employee partly for private purposes and partly for work purposes—chargeable benefit may be reduced).
SE 21640–21660 (assets transferred to a director or employee—general outline, interaction with Section 19(1)1, application of sub-s (2)–(4) and worked examples).
SE 21704 (discounts—if the discounted amount the employee pays exceeds the expense incurred by the employer in providing the goods or services the cash equivalent of the benefit will be nil; guidance on the "expense incurred by the employer").
SE 21732 (assets hired or rented by employer—application of sub-s (7)).
SE 21763 (medical insurance—apportionment of group premiums, application of sub-s (2) in these circumstances).
Revenue & other press releases—IR 21-1-93 (in-house benefits in kind: application of marginal cost rule to goods and services sold in normal course of employer's business, services and facilities provided in-house and assets used in the business and made available for employee's private use).
IR Tax Bulletin October 2000 p 779 (calculating the cash equivalent of a benefit when there is part business and part private use).
Simon's Tax Cases—s 156(1), (2), *Stones v Hall* [1989] STC 138*; *Pepper v Hart* [1992] STC 898*.
Definitions—"Annual value" (of land), s 837; "car", s 168(5); "emoluments", s 131(1); "employment", s 168(2); "family or household", s 168(4); "market value", s 168(7).
Amendments—[1] Words in sub-s (8) inserted by FA 1995 s 91(2), (3) with effect from the year 1995–96.

[156A Limited exemption for computer equipment

(1) This section applies to a benefit consisting in the provision of computer equipment if, in the case of a person ("the employee") who is in employment to which this Chapter applies—

(*a*) that equipment is provided by being made available to the employee or to a member of his family or household;

(*b*) it is so made available without any transfer of property in the equipment to the employee or to a member of his family or household; and

(*c*) it is so made available in a case in which the arrangements for providing employees of the employer with the benefit of computer equipment comply with subsection (2) below.

(2) The arrangements for providing the employees of the employer with the benefit of computer equipment comply with this subsection unless—

(*a*) the only arrangements for making computer equipment available to such employees, or to members of their families or households, are arrangements that are confined to cases where the employee in question is a director of a company; or

(*b*) the arrangements (taking them all together) for making computer equipment available to employees of the employer, or to members of their families or households, are such that it is made available on terms that are more favourable in some or all of the cases where the employee in question is a director of a company than in one or more cases where he is not.

(3) Section 154 applies for any year of assessment to—

(*a*) the benefits to which this section applies that are provided in that year and consist in the making available to the employee of any equipment, and

(*b*) the benefits to which this section applies that are provided in that year and consist in the making available to members of his family or household of any equipment,

to the extent only that the amount which (disregarding this section) would be taken to be the aggregate cash equivalent of the benefits falling within paragraphs (*a*) and (*b*) above exceeds £500.

(4) For the purposes of this section ''computer equipment'' includes printers, scanners, modems, discs and other peripheral devices designed to be used by being connected to or inserted in a computer.

(5) In this section references to making computer equipment available—

(*a*) include references to the provision, together with any computer equipment made available, of a right to use computer software; but

(*b*) do not include references to the provision of a benefit consisting in access to, or the use of, any public telecommunication system (within the meaning of the Telecommunications Act 1984).][1]

Commentary—*Simon's Direct Tax Service* **E4.612**.
Revenue Internal Guidance—Schedule E manual, SE 21697–21701 (computers—partial exemption 1999/2000 onwards: explanation of the rules with examples).
Amendments—[1] This section inserted by FA 1999 s 45(1), (3) with effect from the year 1999–00.

157 Cars available for private use

(1) Where in any year in the case of a person employed in [employment to which this Chapter applies][1], a car is made available (without any transfer of the property in it) either to himself or to others being members of his family or household, and—

(*a*) it is so made available by reason of his employment and it is in that year available for his or their private use; and

(*b*) the benefit of the car is not (apart from this section) chargeable to tax as the employee's income,

there is to be treated as emoluments of the employment, and accordingly chargeable to income tax under Schedule E, an amount equal to whatever is the cash equivalent of that benefit in that year.

[(2) The cash equivalent of the benefit in the year concerned shall be ascertained in accordance with Schedule 6.][2]

(3) Where in any year the benefit of a car is chargeable to tax under this section as the employee's income he shall not be taxable—

(*a*) under Schedule E in respect of the discharge of any liability of his in connection with the car;

(*b*) under section 141 or 142 in respect of any non-cash voucher or credit-token to the extent that it is used by him [or a relation of his (within the meaning of section 144)][4]—

    (i) for obtaining money which is spent on goods or services in connection with the car; or

    (ii) for obtaining such goods or services;

(*c*) under section 153 in respect of any payment made to him in respect of expenses incurred by him in connection with the car.

(4)–(5) ...[3]

Commentary—*Simon's Direct Tax Service* **E4.625, 626**.
Concession A71—Circumstances in which company cars for family members are exempt from tax.
Statements of Practice SP A6—Effect of VAT on Schedule E tax.
SP A7—Effect of VAT on Schedule E tax in respect of perquisites.
Revenue Internal Guidance—Schedule E manual SE 00570 (car benefit charge under this section takes precedence over any potential ''*Heaton v Bell*'' charge under s 19(1)1, because of the anti-avoidance provision in s 157A).
SE 13906 (termination payments and benefits: example of interaction with benefits received during employment where this section is involved).
SE 20101 (expenditure provided in connection with a car still included when calculating whether employment has emoluments at a rate of £8,500 a year or more).
SE 23000 (cars available for private use—table of contents covering references 23001–23007).
SE 23050 (meaning of 'made available').
SE 23053 (meaning of 'without any transfer of the property in it').
SE 23055 (employee car purchase schemes—tax consequences).
SE 23060—23062 (meaning of 'made available by reason of the employment').
SE 23070–23075 (cars provided by the employer for members of the employee's family or household—removal of tax charge in certain circumstances—ESC A71).
SE 23320 (calculating the car benefit charge 1999/2000 onwards—general).
SE 23550 (transfer of ownership of the car to the employee: sub-s (3) will cease to apply after car has been transferred).
SE 23555 (treatment of cars available after employment ceases).
SE 23600 (cars provided for home to work travel of severely disabled employees, ESC A59 applies to exempt benefit if certain conditions satisfied).
SE 23601 (cars provided for home to work travel of severely disabled employees; calculation of car benefit charge where a taxable benefit still arises).
SE 23640–23643 (cars provided for employees in the motor industry; detail as to when there is a car benefit charge, calculations and record keeping).
SE 23680 (cars provided for severely disabled employees; cases where a taxable benefit still arises—example).
SE 23771 (interaction of sub-s 3 and fuel scale charge—car fuel ''scale charge'' replaces any tax liability that would otherwise arise in respect of fuel supplied for a car available for private use).
SE 23790 (car and fuel benefits: Class 1A NICs payable by employers).

Simon's Tax Cases—*Wilson v Alexander* [1986] STC 365*; *Brown v Ware* [1995] STC (SCD) 155; *Clark v Bye* [1997] STC 311; *Henwood v Clarke* [1997] STC 789.
s 157(1), *Gilbert v Hemsley* [1981] STC 703*; *R v Walton General Comrs, ex p Wilson* [1983] STC 464*; *Gurney v Richards* [1989] STC 682*; *IRC v Quigley* [1995] STC 931.
Definitions—"Car", s 168(5); "emoluments", s 131(1); "employment", s 168(2); "family or household", s 168(4); "made available", s 168(6); "private use", s 168(5); "Schedule E", s 19(1); "year", ss 168(13), 832(1).
Cross references—See TMA 1970 s 15(8) (return to include benefit which may give rise to a charge under this section).
TA 1988 s 155AA(3) (no benefit to arise by virtue of a mobile telephone provided in connection with a benefit under this section).
TA 1988 s 158(1) (taxation of fuel provided for cars to which this section applies).
TA 1988 s 159(3) (this section not to apply to pooled cars).
IT (Employments) Regulations, SI 1993/744 reg 46(1)(*d*), (3), (5), (6) (contents of returns to be made by employers in respect of benefits giving rise to a charge to tax under this section).
Amendments—[1] Words in sub-s (1) substituted by FA 1989 s 53(2)(*b*).
[2] Sub-s (2) substituted by FA 1993 Sch 3 paras 1, 2, 7 with effect from the year 1994–95.
[3] Sub-ss (4), (5) repealed by FA 1993 Sch 3 paras 1, 2, 7 and Sch 23 Pt III(3) with effect from the year 1994–95.
[4] Words in sub-s (3)(*b*) inserted by FA 2002 s 37, Sch 6 para 3(*a*) with effect from the year 2002–03.

[157A Cars available for private use: cash alternative, etc

Where, in any year in the case of a person employed in employment to which this Chapter applies—

(*a*) a car is made available as mentioned in section 157, and
(*b*) an alternative to the benefit of the car is offered,

the mere fact that the alternative is offered shall not make the benefit chargeable to tax under section 19(1).][1]

Commentary—*Simon's Direct Tax Service* E4.625.
Revenue Internal Guidance—Schedule E manual, SE 00570 (car benefit charge takes precedence over any potential "*Heaton v Bell*" charge under s 19(1)1).
SE 23300 (mere fact that a cash alternative is offered does not change the method of calculation of the cash equivalent of the car benefit).
Definitions—"Car", s 168(5); "employment", s 168(2); "tax", s 832(3).
Amendments—[1] Section inserted by FA 1995 s 43(1), (4) with effect from the year 1995–96.

158 Car fuel

(1) Where in any year in the case of a person employed in [employment to which this Chapter applies][1] fuel is provided by reason of his employment for a car [the benefit of which is chargeable to tax under section 157 as his income,][5] an amount equal to whatever is the cash equivalent of that benefit in that year shall be treated as emoluments of the employment and, accordingly, shall be chargeable to income tax under Schedule E.

[(2) Subject to the provisions of this section, the cash equivalent of that benefit shall be ascertained from—

(*a*) Table A below where the car has an internal combustion engine with one or more reciprocating pistons and is not a diesel car;
(*b*) Table AB below where the car has an internal combustion engine with one or more reciprocating pistons and is a diesel car;
(*c*) Table B below where the car does not have an internal combustion engine with one or more reciprocating pistons.

[TABLE A

Cylinder capacity of car in cubic centimetres	Cash equivalent
1,400 or less	£2,240
More than 1,400 but not more than 2,000	£2,850
More than 2,000	£4,200

TABLE AB

Cylinder capacity of car in cubic centimetres	Cash equivalent
2,000 or less	£2,850
More than 2,000	£4,200

TABLE B

Description of car	Cash equivalent
Any car	£4,200][8]

[(2A) For the purposes of subsection (2) above a diesel car is a car which uses heavy oil as fuel; and "heavy oil" here means heavy oil as defined by section 1(4) of the Hydrocarbon Oil Duties Act 1979.][2]

[(2B) For the purposes of Tables A and AB in subsection (2) above a car's cylinder capacity is the capacity of its engine calculated as for the purposes of [the Vehicle Excise and Registration Act 1994][6].][2]

(3) Without prejudice to the generality of subsection (1) above, fuel is provided for a car if—

    (*a*) any liability in respect of the provision of fuel for the car is discharged;

    (*b*) a non-cash voucher or a credit-token is used to obtain fuel for the car or money which is spent on such fuel;

    (*c*) any sum is paid in respect of expenses incurred in providing fuel for the car.

In this subsection "non-cash voucher" and "credit-token" have the meanings given by section 141(7) and 142(4) respectively.

(4) The Treasury may by order taking effect from the beginning of any year beginning after it is made substitute a different Table for [any][3] of the Tables in subsection (2) above.

(5) Where [paragraph 6][4] of Schedule 6 applies to reduce the cash equivalent of the benefit of the car for which the fuel is provided, the same reduction shall be made to the cash equivalent of the benefit of the fuel ascertained under subsection (2) above.

(6) [...][7] if in the relevant year—

    (*a*) the employee is required to make good to the person providing the fuel the whole of the expense incurred by him in or in connection with the provision of fuel for his private use and he does so; or

    (*b*) the fuel is made available only for business travel;

the cash equivalent is nil.

[(7) ...][7]

Commentary—*Simon's Direct Tax Service* **E4.629.**
Statements of Practice SP A6—Effect of VAT on Schedule E tax.
SP A7—Effect of VAT on Schedule E tax in respect of perquisites.
Revenue Internal Guidance—Schedule E manual SE 23750–23786 (explanation of charge, rates, guidance in specific situations, examples).
SE 23790 (car and fuel benefits: Class 1A NICs payable by employers).
Definitions—"Business travel", s 168(5); "car", s 168(5); "emoluments", s 131(1); "employment", s 168(2); "made available", s 168(6); "Schedule E", s 19(1); "year", ss 168(13), 832(1).
Cross references—See TMA 1970 s 15(8) (return to include benefits which may give rise to a charge under this section).
IT (Employments) Regulations, SI 1993/744 reg 46(1)(*d*), (3), (5), (6) (contents of returns to be made by employers in respect of benefits giving rise to a charge to tax under this section).
Amendments—[1] Words in sub-s (1) substituted by FA 1989 s 53(2)(*b*).
[2] Sub-ss (2), (2A), (2B) substituted for sub-s (2) by F(No 2)A 1992 s 53 with effect from the year 1992–93.
[3] Word in sub-s (4) substituted by F(No 2)A 1992 s 53 with effect from the year 1992–93.
[4] Words in sub-s (5) substituted by FA 1993 Sch 3 paras 1, 6(2), 7 with effect from the year 1994–95.
[5] Words in sub-s (1) substituted by FA 1995 s 43(2), (4) with effect from the year 1995–96.
[6] Words in sub-s (2B) substituted by the Vehicle Excise and Registration Act 1994 s 63, Sch 3 para 22.
[7] Sub-s (7), and words in sub-s (6), inserted by FA 1997 s 62(3), (5) with effect from the year 1998–99, but repealed with effect from 1998–99 by FA 1998 s 165, Sch 27 Pt III(10).
[8] Tables A, AB and B in sub-s (2) substituted by the Income Tax (Cash Equivalents of Car Fuel Benefits) Order, SI 2002/706 with effect from 6 April 2002.
Prospective amendments—This section to be amended by FA 2002 s 34 with effect from 2003–04.

159 Pooled cars

(1) This section applies to any car [which][1] has for any year been included in a car pool for the use of the employees of one or more employers.

(2) A car is to be treated as having been so included for a year if—

    (*a*) in that year it was made available to, and actually used by, more than one of those employees and, in the case of each of them, it was made available to him by reason of his employment but it was not in that year ordinarily used by one of them to the exclusion of the others; and

    (*b*) in the case of each of them any private use of the car made by him in that year was merely incidental to his other use of it in the year; and

    (*c*) it was in that year not normally kept overnight on or in the vicinity of any residential premises where any of the employees was residing, except while being kept overnight on premises occupied by the person making the car available to them.

(3) Where this section applies to a car, then for the year in question the car is to be treated under sections 154 and 157 as not having been available for the private use of any of the employees.

(4)–(6) ...[2]

Commentary—*Simon's Direct Tax Service* **E4.630A.**
Statement of Practice SP 2/96—Interpretation of the meaning of private use which is "merely incidental" to business use; provision of car with driver for employee to work on confidential papers in the car on the way home is private use.
Revenue Internal Guidance—Schedule E manual SE 23800 (pooled cars and vans: general).
SE 23801 (meaning of private use "merely incidental" to its business use—sub-s (2)(*b*)).
SE 23802 ("de minimis" private use, application of Statement of Practice SP 2/96, conditions under which private use, which is not merely incidental to business use, can be ignored).
SE 23803 (meaning of "not normally kept overnight"—sub-s (2)(*c*)—60% test).

SE 23806 (Revenue procedures for establishing pooled car status from 1996/97 onwards).
SE 23810 (intervals of three or four years will usually be appropriate for checking pooled car status).
SE 23811 (use of "pooled cars" by chauffeurs: use of the car privately at weekends or for holidays will mean car ceases to qualify as a pooled car).
SE 23813 (inadequate parking facilities or security risk at employer's premises does not eliminate requirement to satisfy sub-s (2)(c)).
SE 23815 (carrying confidential papers and working in a chauffeur-driven vehicle on a private journey does not ensure that pool vehicle status is not lost; internal report necessary before claim is refused).
Definitions—"Car", s 168(5); "employment", s 168(2); "made available", s 168(6); "private use", s 168(5); "year", ss 168(13), 832(1).
Cross reference—See TA 1988 s 159AB (application with modifications of this section in relation to vans made available to employees for private use).
Amendments—¹ Words in sub-s (1) substituted by FA 1996 Sch 20 para 8(a) with effect from the year 1996–97.
² Sub-ss (4)–(6) repealed by FA 1996 Sch 20 para 8(b), Sch 41 Pt V(10) with effect from the year 1996–97.

[159AA Vans available for private use

(1) Where in any year, in the case of a person employed in employment to which this Chapter applies, a van is made available (without any transfer of the property in it) either to himself or to others being members of his family or household, and—

   (a) it is so made available by reason of his employment and it is in that year available for his or their private use, and

   (b) the benefit of the van is not (apart from this section) chargeable to tax as the employee's income,

there is to be treated as emoluments of the employment, and accordingly chargeable to income tax under Schedule E, an amount equal to whatever is the cash equivalent of that benefit in that year.

(2) The cash equivalent of the benefit in the year concerned shall be ascertained in accordance with Schedule 6A.

(3) Where in any year the benefit of a van is chargeable to tax under this section as the employee's income, he shall not be taxable—

   (a) under Schedule E in respect of the discharge of any liability of his in connection with the van;

   (b) under section 141 or 142 in respect of any non-cash voucher or credit-token to the extent that it is used by him [or a relation of his (within the meaning of section 144)]²—

      (i) for obtaining money which is spent on goods or services in connection with the van, or

      (ii) for obtaining such goods or services;

   (c) under section 153 in respect of any payment made to him in respect of expenses incurred by him in connection with the van.]¹

Commentary—*Simon's Direct Tax Service* E4.630.
Revenue & other press releases—IR 136 (guide for employers and employees).
Revenue Internal Guidance—Schedule E manual SE 22051–22068 (description of legislation).
SE 22069 (amount of van scale charges—step-by-step calculation).
SE 22078 (worked example).
References on rules relating to shared vans can be found under TA 1988 Sch 6A ICTA.
Definitions—"Emoluments", s 131(1); "employment", s 168(2); "family or household", s 168(4); "made available", s 168(6); "private use", s 168(5); "Schedule E", s 19(1); "year", ss 168(13), 832(1).
Cross references—See TMA 1970 s 15(8) (return to include benefits which may give rise to a charge to tax under this section).
TA 1988 155AA(3) (no benefit to arise by virtue of a mobile telephone provided in connection with a benefit in this section).
TA 1988 Sch 6A para 1 (shared vans).
IT (Employments) Regulations, SI 1993/744 reg 46(1)(d), (3), (5), (6) (contents of returns to be made by employers in respect of benefits giving rise to a charge to tax under this section).
Amendments—¹ This section inserted by FA 1993 Sch 4 paras 4, 8 with effect from the year 1993–94.
² Words in sub-s (3)(b) inserted by FA 2002 s 37, Sch 6 para 3(b) with effect from the year 2002–03.

[159AB Pooled vans

Section 159 shall apply in relation to vans as it applies in relation to cars, and for the purposes of the application of that section to vans—

   (a) any reference in that section to a car shall be construed as a reference to a van,

   (b) the reference in subsection (1) of that section to a car pool shall be construed as a reference to a van pool, and

   (c) the reference in subsection (3) of that section to section 157 shall be construed as a reference to section 159AA.]¹

Commentary—*Simon's Direct Tax Service* E4.630A.
Statement of Practice SP 2/96—Interpretation of the meaning of private use which is "merely incidental" to business use.
Revenue Internal Guidance—Schedule E manual, SE 22061 (general rules on exceptions to the charge for vans).
SE 23800–23813 (meaning of provisions applicable to pooled vans: *for detail see references under s 159*).
Amendments—¹ This section inserted by FA 1993 Sch 4 paras 4, 8 with effect from the year 1993–94.

[159AC Heavier commercial vehicles available for private use

(1) This section applies where in any year—

   (a) a heavier commercial vehicle is made available to an employee in circumstances such that, had that vehicle been a van, the benefit so provided would have been chargeable to tax under section 159AA, and

   (b) the employee's use of the vehicle is not wholly or mainly private use.

(2) Section 154 shall not apply to—

  (a) the benefit so provided, or

  (b) any benefit in connection with the vehicle other than a benefit in connection with the provision of a driver for the vehicle.

(3) The employee shall not be taxable—

  (a) under Schedule E in respect of the discharge of any liability of his in connection with the vehicle;

  (b) under section 141 or 142 in respect of any non-cash voucher or credit-token to the extent that it is used by him [or a relation of his (within the meaning of section 144)]²—

    (i) for obtaining money which is spent on goods or services in connection with the vehicle, or

    (ii) for obtaining such goods or services;

  (c) under section 153 in respect of any payment made to him in respect of expenses incurred by him in connection with the vehicle.

(4) In this section "heavier commercial vehicle" means a mechanically propelled road vehicle which is—

  (a) of a construction primarily suited for the conveyance of goods or burden of any description, and

  (b) of a design weight exceeding 3,500 kilograms;

and "design weight" here means the weight which the vehicle is designed or adapted not to exceed when in normal use and travelling on a road laden.

(5) In this section—

  (a) "private use", in relation to a vehicle made available to an employee, means any use other than for his business travel, and

  (b) "business travel" means travelling which the employee is necessarily obliged to do in the performance of the duties of his employment.]¹

Commentary—*Simon's Direct Tax Service* E4.630.
Revenue Internal Guidance—Schedule E manual, SE 22300 (explanation of exemption).
SE 22301 (explanation of sub-s (4) "heavier commercial vehicle").
SE 22302 (scope of exemption—explanation of sub-ss (2) and (3)).
SE 22303 (availability of vehicle which is not exempt charged in the same way as availability of any other asset which is not a car).
Definitions—"Made available", s 168(6); "Schedule E", s 19(1); "year", ss 168(13), 832(1).
Cross references—TA 1988 155AA(3) (no benefit to arise by virtue of a mobile telephone provided in connection with a benefit in this section).
Amendments—¹ This section inserted by FA 1993 s 74(1), (3) with effect from the year 1993–94.
² Words in sub-s (3)(b) inserted by FA 2002 s 37, Sch 6 para 3(c) with effect from the year 2002–03.

159A Mobile telephones

Commentary—*Simon's Direct Tax Service* E4.617.
Amendments—This section repealed by FA 1999 ss 44(2), (6), 139, Sch 20 Pt III(9) with effect from the year 1999–00.

160 Beneficial loan arrangements

(1) Where in the case of a person employed in [employment to which this Chapter applies]¹ there is outstanding for the whole or part of a year a loan (whether to the employee himself or a relative of his) of which the benefit is obtained by reason of his employment and—

  (a) no interest is paid on the loan for that year; or

  (b) the amount of interest paid on it for the year is less than interest at the official rate,

[an amount equal to whatever is the cash equivalent of the benefit of the loan for that year shall, subject to the provisions of this Chapter, be treated as emoluments of the employment, and accordingly chargeable to tax under Schedule E; and where that amount is so treated, the employee is to be treated as having paid interest on the loan in that year of the same amount.]⁶

[(1A) Interest treated as paid by virtue of subsection (1) above—

  (a) shall be treated as paid for all the purposes of the Tax Acts (other than this Chapter, including Schedule 7), but shall not be treated for any purpose as income of the person making the loan or be treated as relevant loan interest to which section 369 applies, and

  (b) shall be treated as accruing during, and paid by the employee at the end of, the year or, if different, the period in the year during which he is employed in employment to which this Chapter applies and the loan is outstanding.]⁶

[(1B) Where, in relation to any year—

  (a) there are loans between the same lender and borrower which are aggregable with each other,

  (b) the lender elects, by notice given to the inspector, for aggregation to apply in the case of that borrower, and

  (c) that notice is given before the end of the period of 92 days after the end of that year,

TA 1988

all the loans between that lender and that borrower which are aggregable with each other shall be treated for the purposes of subsections (1) and (1A) above and Part II of Schedule 7 as a single loan.][11]

[(1BA) For the purposes of subsection (1B) above loans are aggregable with each other for any year where—

(a) in the case of each of the loans, there is a time in that year, while the loan is outstanding as to any amount, when the lender is a close company and the borrower a director of that company;

(b) the benefit of each of the loans is obtained by reason of the borrower's employment;

(c) in the case of each of the loans, there is no time in that year when a rate of interest is applied to the loan which is equal to or more than whatever is the official rate at that time;

(d) the loans are loans made in the same currency; and

(e) none of the loans is a qualifying loan.][11]

[(1C) ...[14]][6]

(2) Where in the case of a person employed in [employment to which this Chapter applies][1]—

(a) there is in any year released or written off the whole or part of a loan (whether to the employee himself or a relative of his, and whether or not such a loan as is mentioned in subsection (1) above), and

(b) the benefit of that loan was obtained by reason of his employment,

then there is to be treated as emoluments of the employment, and accordingly chargeable to income tax under Schedule E, an amount equal to that which is released or written off.

[(3) Where—

(a) there was outstanding, at any time when a person was in employment to which this Chapter applies, the whole or part of a loan to him (or a relative of his) the benefit of which was obtained by reason of his employment, and

(b) that employment has terminated or ceased to be employment to which this Chapter applies,

subsection (2) above applies as if the employment had not terminated or, as the case may be, had not ceased to be employment to which this Chapter applies.][2]

[(3A) Where subsection (3) above applies, a loan which—

(a) is applied directly or indirectly to the replacement of any such loan as is mentioned in paragraph (a) of that subsection, and

(b) would, if the employment referred to in that subsection had not terminated or, as the case may be, ceased to be employment to which this Chapter applies, have been a loan the benefit of which was obtained by reason of that employment,

shall, unless it is a loan the benefit of which was obtained by reason of other employment, be treated as a loan the benefit of which was obtained by reason of that employment.][9]

(4) Part I of Schedule 7 has effect as to what is meant by the benefit of a loan obtained by reason of a person's employment; the cash equivalent of the benefit is to be ascertained in accordance with Part II of that Schedule; ...[8]

[(4A) Where an assessment for any year in respect of a loan has been made or determined on the footing that the whole or part of the interest payable on the loan for that year was not in fact paid, but it is subsequently paid, then, on a claim in that behalf, the cash equivalent for that year shall be recalculated so as to take that payment into account and the assessment shall be adjusted accordingly.][5]

(5) In this section, sections 161[, 161A][14][, 161B][14] and 162 and [Schedules 7 and 7A][15]—

(a) "loan" includes any form of credit;

(b) ...[10]

(c) references to making a loan include arranging, guaranteeing or in any way facilitating a loan (related expressions being construed accordingly); and

(d) references to the official rate of interest are to the [rate applicable under section 178 of the Finance Act 1989][3-4];

[and, without prejudice to the generality of section 178 of the Finance Act 1989 regulations under that section may make different provision in relation to a loan outstanding for the whole or part of a year if—

(i) it was made in the currency of a country or territory outside the United Kingdom,

(ii) the benefit of the loan is obtained by reason of the employment of a person who normally lives in that country or territory, and

(iii) that person has lived in that country or territory at some time in the period of six years ending with that year][7].

(6) For the purposes of this section and section 161, a person is a relative of another person if he or she is—

(a) the spouse of that other; or

(b) a parent or remoter forebear, child or remoter issue, or brother or sister of that other or of the spouse of that other; or

(c) the spouse of a person falling within paragraph (b) above.

(7) Subject to section 161, this section applies to loans whether made before or after this Act is passed.

Commentary—*Simon's Direct Tax Service* **E4.631, 632.**

Concession A5—Exemption from a charge under this section where the beneficial loan exceeds Sch 7 Pt III relief limit only because it co-exists with a qualifying bridging loan to pay for removal expenses.

Statement of Practice SP 7/79—This section not to apply in respect of money advanced by an employer in respect of expenses necessarily incurred by an employee in performing his duties, subject to certain conditions.

Revenue Internal Guidance—Schedule E manual SE 03123–03125 (removal or transfer costs: bridging loans provided by the employer—the normal charge under this section may be eligible for exemption or reduction if the other relocation expenses and benefits qualifying for exemption do not exceed the £8,000 limit; procedure and example).

SE 03126 (removal or transfer costs: non-eligible expenses and benefits—compensation payments for "loss on sale", charge to tax under this section where employer lends money, or waives a loan, to cover shortfall).

SE 03136 (removal or transfer costs: relocation companies—guaranteed sale price schemes—property not sold to employer nor to relocation company—example showing that receipt of guaranteed sale price is not the receipt of sale proceeds, but a loan chargeable under this section).

SE 21741 (loans written off—special rules, explanation of sub-ss (2) and (3)).

SE 21745 (loans written off after retirement or ceasing to be within a UK charge to tax in respect of the loan- explanation of sub-s 3).

SE 21748 (loans written off—loans made by close companies, instruction not to treat any amount released or written off, which has been treated as the borrower's income under s 421, as also chargeable under this section).

SE 26100 (index of guidance on beneficial loans, covering references 26101–26520).

SE 26102 (not necessary for the loan to be advantageous to the recipient for a chargeable benefit to arise).

SE 66780 (tax treatment of NHS employees—advances of salary for house purchase are not emoluments within s 19 but give rise to charge to tax under this section).

Revenue & other press releases—ICAEW TAX 11/93 9-7-93 (where a loan or overdrawn balance is cleared by voting remuneration or a dividend, it is not regarded as cleared until the date on which the remuneration or dividend is voted—see para 41. As regards sub-s (4A), the benefit can be re-calculated only if the obligation to pay the interest existed during the fiscal year concerned—see para 36).

IR Tax Bulletin October 1994 p 161 (details of whether a loan made to an employee prior to his coming to the UK is within the provisions).

IR Booklet IR 145 (Low interest loans provided by employers—a guide for employees).

IR 25-1-00 Deregulatory change setting official rate of interest on beneficial loans in advance.

IR 19-2-01 Benefits in kind: loans provided by employers—official rate of interest to remain unchanged at 6.25% for the 2001–02 tax year.

Simon's Tax Cases—*Williams v Todd* [1988] STC 676*; *Harvey v Williams* [1998] STC (SCD) 215; *Gold v Inspector of Taxes*; *HCB Ltd v Inspector of Taxes* [1998] STC (SCD) 222; *Grant v Watton* [1999] STC 330.

s 160(1), (5), (5)(*a*) *West v Crossland* [1999] STC 147.

Definitions—"Child", ss 831(4), 832(5); "close company", s 832(1); "director", s 168(8); "emoluments", s 131(1); "employment", s 832(1); "inspector", s 168(2); "interest", s 832(1); "Schedule E", s 19(1); "year", ss 168(13), 832(1).

Cross references—See TMA 1970 s 15(8) (return to include benefits which may give rise to a charge under this section).

TA 1988 s 161(1), (1A), (1B) (certain beneficial loans not to be treated as emoluments).

TA 1988 s 162 (application of this section where shares are sold to directors or higher-paid employees at an under-value).

TA 1988 s 191B (beneficial loan arrangements in respect of removal expenses on change of residence of an employee).

TA 1988 Sch 7 para 3(1) (cash equivalent for the purposes of this section of two or more loans).

IT (Employments) Regulations, SI 1993/744 reg 46(1)(*d*), (3), (5), (6) (contents of returns to be made by employers in respect of benefits giving rise to a charge to tax under this section).

Amendments—[1] Words in sub-ss (1), (2) substituted by FA 1989 s 53(2)(*b*).

[2] Sub-s (3) substituted by FA 1989 s 53(2)(*c*).

[3-4] Words in sub-s (5)(*d*) substituted by FA 1989 s 179(1)(*g*).

[5] Sub-s (4A) inserted by FA 1991 s 27(6), Sch 6 para 1.

[6] Sub-ss (1A)–(1C) and words following sub-s (1)(*b*) substituted for the words following sub-s (1)(*b*) by FA 1994 s 88(1), (6) with effect from the year 1994–95. See however note [11] below.

[7] Words following para (*d*) in sub-s (5) added by FA 1994 s 88(2), (6) with effect from the year 1994–95.

[8] Words in sub-s (4) repealed by FA 1994 Sch 26 Pt V(5) with effect from the year 1994–95.

[9] Sub-s (3A) inserted by FA 1995 s 45(3), (5) with effect from the year 1995–96 (and applies to loans made before or after 1 May 1995).

[10] Sub-s (5)(*b*) repealed by FA 1995 s 45(2), (5), Sch 29 Pt VIII(3), with effect from the year 1995–96.

[11] Sub-ss (1B), (1BA) substituted for sub-s (1B) by FA 1996 s 107(1) with effect from the year 1996–97 and apply to loans whenever made.

[12] Word in sub-s (1C)(*b*) substituted by FA 1998 Sch 7 para 1 with effect from 31 July 1998.

[13] Words in sub-s (1C)(*a*) repealed by FA 1999 s 139, Sch 20 Pt III(7) with effect for payments of interest made—

–after 5 April 2000;

–after 8 March 1999 and before 6 April 2000 in respect of interest falling due after 5 April 2000; or

–after 8 March 1999 and before 6 April 2000 under a scheme made for a tax avoidance purpose after 8 March 1999.

[14] Sub-s (1C) repealed, and words in sub-s (5) inserted, by FA 2000 ss 57, 156, Sch 10 paras 1, 4(2), 5(3)(*a*), Sch 40 Pt II(2) with effect from the year 2000–01.

[15] Words in sub-s (5) substituted by FA 2000 s 57, Sch 10 paras 1, 5(3)(*b*) with effect from the year 2000–01.

161 Exceptions from section 160

[(1) The cash equivalent of the benefit of any such loan as is referred to in section 160(1) is not to be treated as emoluments of the employment if—

    (*a*) at no time in the year does the amount outstanding on the loan (or, if two or more such loans as are referred to in section 160(1) are outstanding in the year, the aggregate of the amounts outstanding on them) exceed £5000, or

    (*b*) where paragraph (*a*) above does not apply, the loan is not a qualifying loan and at no time in the year does the amount outstanding on the loan (or, if two or more such loans as are referred to in section 160(1) and are not qualifying loans are outstanding in the year, the aggregate of the amounts outstanding on them) exceed £5000.][1]

[(1A), (1B) ...[3]][1]

(2) Where the amount of interest paid on a loan for the year in which it is made is not less than interest at the official rate applying for that year for the purposes of section 160 and the loan is made—

(*a*) for a fixed and invariable period; and

(*b*) at a fixed and invariable rate of interest,

subsection (1) of that section shall not apply to the loan in any subsequent year by reason only of an increase in the official rate since the year in which the loan was made.

(3) Where a loan was made at any time before 6th April 1978—

(*a*) for a fixed and invariable period; and

(*b*) at a fixed and invariable rate of interest,

section 160(1) shall not apply to the loan if ...[2] the rate of interest is not less than such rate as could have been expected to apply to a loan on the same terms (other than as to the rate of interest) made at that time between persons not connected with each other (within the meaning of section 839) dealing at arm's length.

(4) If the employee ...[2] derived no benefit from a loan made to a relative of his, section 160(1) and (2) above shall not apply to that loan.

(5) Section 160(2) does not apply where the amount released or written off is chargeable to income tax as income of the employee apart from that section, except—

(*a*) where it is chargeable only by virtue of section 148; or

(*b*) to the extent that the amount exceeds the sums previously falling to be treated as the employee's income under section 677.

(6) On the employee's death—

(*a*) a loan within subsection (1) of section 160 ceases to be outstanding for the purposes of the operation of that subsection; and .

(*b*) no charge arises under subsection (2) of that section by reference to any release or writing-off which takes effect on or after the death.

(7) Section 160(2) does not apply to benefits received in pursuance of arrangements made at any time with a view to protecting the holder of shares acquired before 6th April 1976 from a fall in their market value.

Commentary—*Simon's Direct Tax Service* **E4.631.**
Statement of Practice SP 7/79—Extends this section to money advanced by an employer in respect of expenses necessarily incurred by an employee in performing his duties, subject to certain conditions.
Revenue Internal Guidance—Schedule E manual SE 21744 (death of a relative to whom a loan has been made does not prevent a tax charge).
SE 21746 (loans written off on termination of employment—explanation of sub-s (5)(*a*), charge under s 160(2) takes precedence denying the benefit of the £30,000 exemption).
SE 21747 (loans written off: loans made by trustees of settlement of which borrower or their spouse is a settlor –explanation of sub-s (5)(*b*), where tax liability has arisen under s 677 only the excess of the amount released or written off over the amount already taxed is chargeable under s 160(2)).
SE 26135 (exemptions from charge- table giving references for particular circumstances, including worked examples, 26140–26153).
Simon's Tax Cases—*Williams v Todd* [1988] STC 676*.
s 161(1A), *West v O'Neill* [1999] STC 147.
Definitions—''Interest'', s 832(1); ''loan'', s 160(5), (7); ''official rate'', s 160(5), (7); ''qualifying loan'', s 160(1C); ''relative'', s 160(6); ''year'', ss 168(13), 832(1).
Cross reference—See FA 1994 s 88(5) (loans made before 1 June 1994: sub-ss (1A), (1B) determination as respects fees, commission and incidental expenses).
Amendments—[1] Sub-ss (1), (1A), (1B) substituted for sub-s (1) by FA 1994 s 88(3), (6) with effect from the year 1994–95.
[2] Words omitted from sub-ss (3), (4) repealed by FA 1996 Sch 20 para 9, Sch 41 Pt V(10) with effect from the year 1996–97.
[3] Sub-ss (1A), (1B) repealed by FA 2000 ss 57, 156, Sch 10 paras 1, 5(4), Sch 40 Pt II(2) with effect from the year 2000–01.

[161A Treatment of qualifying loans

(1) In this Chapter a ''qualifying loan'' means a loan made to a person where, assuming interest is paid on the loan (whether or not it is in fact paid), the whole or part of the interest paid on it for the year—

(*a*) is eligible for relief under section 353 or would be so eligible but for subsection (2) of that section, or

(*b*) is deductible in computing the amount of the profits to be charged—

(i) under Case I or II of Schedule D in respect of a trade, profession or vocation carried on by him, or

(ii) under Schedule A in respect of a Schedule A business carried on by him.

(2) Section 160(1) does not apply to a loan in any year in which, on the assumption mentioned in subsection (1) above, the whole of the interest paid on it is eligible for relief or deductible as mentioned in that subsection.][1]

Amendments—[1] This section inserted by FA 2000 s 57, Sch 10 paras 1, 4(1) with effect from the year 2000–01.

[161B Beneficial loans: loans on ordinary commercial terms

(1) Section 160(1) does not apply to a loan on ordinary commercial terms.

(2) Schedule 7A to this Act has effect as to what is meant by a loan on ordinary commercial terms.][1]

Revenue Internal Guidance—Schedule E manual, SE 26158–26165 (these paras provide explanations of the rules that relating to the former s 161(1A) and (1B)—exemption for 'commercial' loans, which may be of relevance).
Amendments—[1] This section inserted by FA 2000 s 57, Sch 10 paras 1, 5(1) with effect from the year 2000–01.

162 Employee shareholdings

(1) Where [after 6th April 1976][1]—

(a) a person employed or about to be employed in [employment to which this Chapter applies][2] (''the employee''), or a person connected with him, acquires shares in a company (whether the employing company or not); and

(b) the shares are acquired at an under-value in pursuance of a right or opportunity available by reason of his employment,

section 160(1) and Schedule 7 apply as if the employee had the benefit of an interest-free loan obtained by reason of his employment (''the notional loan'').

(2) The provisions of this section have effect subject to sections 185 and 186; and in this section—

(a) references to shares being acquired at an under-value are references to shares being acquired either without payment for them at the time or being acquired for an amount then paid which is less than the market value of fully paid up shares of that class (in either case with or without obligation to make payment or further payment at some later time); and

(b) any reference, in relation to any shares, to the under-value on acquisition is a reference to the market value of fully paid up shares of that class less any payment then made for the shares.

(3) The amount initially outstanding of the notional loan is so much of the under-value on acquisition as is not chargeable to tax as an emolument of the employee; and—

(a) the loan remains outstanding until terminated under subsection (4) below; and

(b) payments or further payments made for the shares after the initial acquisition go to reduce the amount outstanding of the notional loan.

(4) The notional loan terminates on the occurrence of any of the following events—

(a) the whole amount of it outstanding is made good by means of payments or further payments made for the shares; or

(b) the case being one in which the shares were not at the time of acquisition fully paid up, any outstanding or contingent obligation to pay for them is released, transferred or adjusted so as no longer to bind the employee or any person connected with him; or

(c) the shares are so disposed of by surrender or otherwise that neither he nor any such person any longer has a beneficial interest in the shares; or

(d) the employee dies.

(5) If the notional loan terminates as mentioned in subsection (4)(b) or (c) above, there is then for the year in which the event in question occurs the same charge to income tax on the employee, under section 160(2) [(and where appropriate section 160(3))][2], as if an amount equal to the then outstanding amount of the notional loan had been released or written off from a loan within that section.

(6) Where after 6th April 1976 shares are acquired, whether or not at an under-value but otherwise as mentioned in subsection (1) above, and—

(a) the shares are subsequently disposed of by surrender or otherwise so that neither the employee nor any person connected with him any longer has a beneficial interest in them; and

(b) the disposal is for a consideration which exceeds the then market value of the shares,

then for the year in which the disposal is effected the amount of the excess is treated as emoluments of the employee's employment and accordingly chargeable to income tax under Schedule E.

[(7) If at the time of the event giving rise to a charge by virtue of subsection (6) above the employment in question has terminated, that subsection shall apply as if it had not.][2]

(8) No charge arises under subsection (6) above by reference to any disposal effected after the death of the employee, whether by his personal representatives or otherwise.

(9) This section applies in relation to acquisition and disposal of an interest in shares less than full beneficial ownership (including an interest in the proceeds of sale of part of the shares but not including a share option) as it applies in relation to the acquisition and disposal of shares, subject to the following modifications—

(a) for references to the shares acquired there shall be substituted references to the interest in shares acquired;

(b) for the reference to the market value of the shares acquired there shall be substituted a reference to the proportion corresponding to the size of the interest of the market value of the shares in which the interest subsists;

(c) for the reference to shares of the same class as those acquired there shall be substituted a reference to shares of the same class as those in which the interest subsists; and

(d) for the reference to the market value of fully paid up shares of that class there shall be substituted a reference to the proportion of that value corresponding to the size of the interest.

(10) In this section—

(a) ''shares'' includes stock and also includes securities as defined in section 254(1);

(b) ''acquisition'' in relation to shares includes receipt by way of allotment or assignment or otherwise howsoever;

(c) any reference to payment for shares includes giving any consideration in money or money's worth or making any subscription, whether in pursuance of a legal liability or not;

(*d*) "market value" has the same meaning as, for the purposes of the [1992][3] Act, it has by virtue of section [272][3] of that Act;

and section 839 applies for the purposes of this section.

(11) This section, in respect of any shares or any interest in shares, operates only to include an amount in emoluments so far as any amount corresponding to it, and representing the same benefit, does not otherwise fall to be so included under the Tax Acts.

Commentary—*Simon's Direct Tax Service* **E4.621.**
Revenue Internal Guidance—Schedule E manual SE 21230 (special valuation rules for certain benefits—explanations for this section are in the share scheme manual).
Share Schemes Manual SSM 6.20–6.56 (Revenue interpretation of this section including worked examples).
SSM 11.5 (treatment of an exercised share option where the option was granted by reason of an employment within Case II or Case III of Schedule E).
Simon's Tax Cases—*IRC v Herd* [1993] STC 436*.
Definitions—"Company", s 832(1), (2); "connected person", s 839, by virtue of sub-s (10); "emoluments", s 131(1); "employment", s 168(2); "loan", s 160(5), (7); "Schedule E", s 19(1); "the Tax Acts", s 831(2).
Cross references—See TCGA 1992 s 120(3) (relief from tax on chargeable gains in respect of shares chargeable under sub-s (5) above).
IT (Employments) Regulations, SI 1993/744 reg 46(1)(*d*), (3), (5), (6) (contents of returns to be made by employers in respect of benefits giving rise to a charge to tax under this section).
FA 2000 Sch 8 para 78(2) (an employee is not chargeable to tax under Schedule E by virtue of sub-s (1) in respect of an award to him of shares under an employee share ownership plan).
FA 2000 Sch 14 para 54 (no charge under sub-s (1) where shares acquired on the exercise of an enterprise management incentive option; any charge under sub-s (6) is not affected).
Amendments—[1] Words in sub-s (1) inserted by FA 1988 Sch 13 para 3.
[2] Words in sub-s (1) and whole of sub-s (7) substituted and words in sub-s (5) inserted by FA 1989 s 53(2).
[3] Year and number in sub-s (10)(*d*) substituted by TCGA 1992 Sch 10 para 14(1), (11).

163 Expenses connected with living accommodation

(1) This section applies where, in the case of a person employed in [employment to which this Chapter applies][1], living accommodation is provided by reason of the employment and, accordingly, a charge to tax would arise in his case under section 145 but for the case being one of those specified in subsection (4) of that section.

(2) Where, by reason of expenditure incurred in one or more of the following, that is to say,—

(*a*) heating, lighting or cleaning the premises concerned;
(*b*) repairs to the premises, their maintenance or decoration;
(*c*) the provision in the premises of furniture or other appurtenances or effects which are normal for domestic occupation;

or by reason of such expenditure being reimbursed to the employee, an amount falls to be included in the emoluments of his employment, that amount shall not exceed the limit specified in subsection (3) below.

(3) That limit is—

(*a*) 10 per cent of the net amount of the emoluments of the employment or, if the accommodation is provided for a period of less than a year, so much of that percentage of the net amount as is attributable to the period; less
(*b*) where the expenditure is incurred by a person other than the employee, so much as is properly attributable to the expenditure of any sum made good by the employee to that other.

(4) The net amount of the emoluments of a person's employment for the purposes of subsection (3) above is the amount of those emoluments (leaving out of account the expenditure in question) after—

(*a*) any capital allowance; and
(*b*) any deductions allowable under section [197AG,][2] 198, 199, 201, 332(3), 592(7), 594 or 619(1)(*a*);

and, for the purposes of this subsection, in the case of employment by a company there shall be taken into account, as emoluments of the employment, the emoluments of any employment by an associated company.

(5) For the purposes of subsection (4) above, a company is an associated company of another if one of them has control of the other or both are under the control of the same person.

Commentary—*Simon's Direct Tax Service* **E4.620.**
Statements of Practice SP A6—Effect of VAT on Schedule E tax.
SP A7—Effect of VAT on Schedule E tax in respect of perquisites.
Revenue Internal Guidance—Schedule E manual SE 11522 (living accommodation: other liabilities in connection with living accommodation—employer's liability providing benefit to employee, application of this section).
SE 21720–21728 (explanation of rules including worked examples).
SE 66625 (provision of housing to mineworkers: charge on ancillary services may be subject to the limitation provided by this section).
Definitions—"Capital allowance", s 832(1); "company", s 832(1), (2); "control", ss 168(12), 840; "emoluments", s 131(1); "employment", s 168(2); "year", ss 168(13), 832(1).
Cross references—See TA 1988 s 154(1) (this section to apply for the purposes of s 154 (taxation of benefits in kind)).
IT (Employments) Regulations, SI 1993/744 reg 46(1)(*d*), (3), (5), (6) (contents of returns to be made by employers in respect of benefits giving rise to a charge to tax under this section).
Amendments—[1] Words in sub-s (1) substituted by FA 1989 s 53(2)(*b*).
[2] Word in sub-s (4)(*b*) inserted by FA 2001 s 57(3), (4), Sch 12 Pt II para 2 with effect from the year 2002–03.

164 Director's tax paid by employer

(1) Subject to the provisions of this Chapter, where in any year a person (''the recipient'') is employed as a director of a company and—

(a) a payment of, or on account of, income assessable to income tax under Schedule E as emoluments of that employment is made to him in circumstances in which the person making the payment is required, by regulations made under section 203, to deduct an amount of income tax on making the payment; and

(b) the whole of that amount is not so deducted but is, or any part of it is, accounted for to the Board by someone other than the recipient;

the amount so accounted for to the Board, less so much (if any) as is made good by the recipient to that other person or so deducted, shall be treated as emoluments of the employment and accordingly chargeable to income tax under Schedule E.

(2) A person shall not be treated, for the purposes of subsection (1) above, as employed as a director of a company if he has no material interest in the company and either paragraph (a) or paragraph (b) of section 167(5) is satisfied.

(3) Where an amount treated as emoluments of a person's employment, by subsection (1) above, is accounted for to the Board at a time when the employment has come to an end, those emoluments shall be treated, for the purposes of the Income Tax Acts, as having arisen in the year in which the employment ended; but that subsection shall not apply in relation to any amount accounted for to the Board after the death of the director in question.

Commentary—*Simon's Direct Tax Service* **E4.619.**
Revenue Internal Guidance—Schedule E manual, SE 21790–21795 (explanation of rules including worked example).
Definitions—''The Board'', s 832(1); ''company'', s 832(1), (2); ''director'', s 168(8), (9); ''emoluments'', s 131(1); ''employment'', s 168(2); ''the Income Tax Acts'', s 831(1)(b); ''material interest'', s 168(11); ''Schedule E'', s 19(1); ''year'', ss 168(13), 832(1).
Cross references—See TMA 1970 s 15(8) (return to include benefits which may give rise to charge under this section).
IT (Employments) Regulations, SI 1993/744 reg 46(1)(d), (3), (5), (6) (contents of returns to be made by employers in respect of benefits giving rise to a charge to tax under this section).

165 Scholarships

(1) Nothing in section 331 shall be construed as conferring on any person other than the person holding the scholarship in question any exemption from the charge to tax under section 154.

(2) For the purposes of this Chapter, any scholarship provided for a member of a person's family or household shall, without prejudice to any other provision of this Chapter, be taken to have been provided by reason of that person's employment if it is provided under arrangements entered into by, or by any person connected with, his employer (whether or not those arrangements require the employer or connected person to contribute directly or indirectly to the cost of providing the scholarship).

(3) Section 154 does not apply to a benefit consisting in a payment in respect of a scholarship—

(a) provided from a trust fund or under a scheme; and

(b) held by a person receiving full-time instruction at a university, college, school or other educational establishment; and

(c) which would not be regarded, for the purposes of this Chapter, as provided by reason of a person's employment were subsection (2) above and section 168(3) to be disregarded;

if, in the year in which the payment is made, not more than 25 per cent of the total amount of the payments made from that fund, or under that scheme, in respect of scholarships held as mentioned in paragraph (b) above is attributable to relevant scholarships.

(4) This section does not have effect in relation to any payment if—

(a) it is made in respect of a scholarship awarded before 15th March 1983, and

(b) the first payment in respect of the scholarship was made before 6th April 1984; and

(c) in relation to payments made after 5th April 1989, the person holding the scholarship is receiving full-time instruction at the university, college, school or other educational establishment at which he was receiving such instruction on—

    (i) 15th March 1983, in a case where the first payment in respect of the scholarship was made before that date; or

    (ii) the date on which the first such payment was made, in any other case.

(5) For the purposes of subsection (4)(c) above, a payment made before 6th April 1989 in respect of any period beginning on or after that date shall be treated as made at the beginning of that period.

(6) In this section—

(a) ''scholarship'' includes an exhibition, bursary or other similar educational endowment;

(b) ''relevant scholarship'' means a scholarship which is provided by reason of a person's employment (whether or not that employment is [employment to which this Chapter applies]¹); and for the purposes of this definition ''employment'' includes an office or employment whose emoluments do not fall to be assessed under Schedule E but would fall to be so assessed if the employee were resident, and ordinarily resident, and all the duties of the employment were performed wholly, in the United Kingdom;

and section 839 applies for the purposes of this section.

Commentary—*Simon's Direct Tax Service* **E4.618.**
Revenue Internal Guidance—Schedule E manual SE 21006 (in *Wicks v Firth* 56TC318 payments made as scholarships to the children of an employee within TA 1988 Pt V Ch II were held to be benefits within s 154 but exempt from charge by s 331. The exemption was subsequently removed in most cases by this section).
SE 30000 (table of contents giving explanation of charge and procedures followed, covering references 30001–30008).
Definitions—"Connected persons", s 839 by virtue of sub-s (6); "employment", ss 165(6)(*b*), 168(2); "family or household", s 168(4); "United Kingdom", s 830(1); "year", ss 168(13), 832(1).
Amendments—¹ Words in sub-s (6)(*b*) substituted by FA 1989 s 53(2)(*b*).

General supplementary provisions

166 Notice of nil liability under this Chapter

(1) If a person furnishes to the inspector a statement of the cases and circumstances in which payments of a particular character are made, or benefits or facilities of a particular kind are provided, for any employees (whether his own or those of anyone else), and the inspector is satisfied that no additional tax is payable under this Chapter by reference to the payments, benefits or facilities mentioned in the statement, the inspector shall notify the person accordingly; and then nothing in this Chapter applies to those payments, or to the provision of those benefits or facilities, or otherwise for imposing any additional charge to income tax.

(2) The inspector may, if in his opinion there is reason to do so, by notice served on the person to whom notification under subsection (1) above was given, revoke the notification, either as from the date of its making or from such later date as may be specified in the notice under this subsection; and then all such income tax becomes chargeable, and all such returns are to be made by that person and by the employees in question as would have been chargeable or would have had to be made in the first instance if the notification under subsection (1) had never been given or, as the case may be, it had ceased to have effect on the specified date.

(3) In relation to a notification given before 6th April 1988, the reference in subsection (2) above to income tax includes a reference to income tax chargeable under the corresponding enactment's in force before that date, and accordingly, where the notification is revoked for any period before that date, that subsection has effect in relation to years of assessment before the year 1988–89.

(4) The validity of any notification given under section 199 of the 1970 Act which was continued in force by paragraph 14 of Schedule 9 to the Finance Act 1976 shall not be affected by the repeal of that paragraph by this Act but shall continue in force as if made under subsection (1) above in relation to tax liability under sections 153 to 156; and subsection (2) above shall apply accordingly.

Commentary—*Simon's Direct Tax Service* **E4.651.**
Revenue Internal Guidance—Schedule E manual SE 30050 (index of instructions relating to dispensations covering references SE 30051–30098).
SE 32645 (no general prohibition on the inclusion of entertaining expenses in a dispensation).
SE 36770 (motor vehicles: contributions from employers to wear and tear covered by a dispensation, capital allowances to be restricted "to such an extent as would be just and reasonable having regard to all the relevant circumstances of the case".
SE 70717 (Association of University and College Lecturers: expenses payments received from an employer, general rules as to when reimbursement of expenses will not be taxed).
Revenue & other press releases—IR 69 (guidance on how to apply for dispensation).
Definitions—"Inspector", s 832(1); "notice", s 832(1); "the 1970 Act", s 831(3); "year of assessment", s 832(1); "the year 1988–89", s 832(1).
Cross reference—See FA 2001 s 58(2) (a notice under sub-s (1) above is a nil-liability notice for the purposes of FA 2001 s 58 concerning mileage allowances).

[167 Employment to which this Chapter applies

(1) This Chapter applies—

　(*a*) to employment as a director of a company (but subject to subsection (5) below), and
　(*b*) to employment with emoluments at the rate of £8,500 a year or more.

(2) [Subject to subsection (2B) below]³ for this purpose emoluments are to be calculated—

　(*a*) on the basis that they include all such amounts as come, or would but for section 157(3) come, into charge under this Chapter or section 141, 142, 143 or 145, and
　(*b*) without any deduction under section [197AG,]⁴ 198, 201 or 332(3).

[(2A) ...²]

[(2B) Where, in any relevant year—

　(*a*) a car is made available as mentioned in section 157, and
　(*b*) an alternative to the benefit of the car is offered,

subsection (2)(*a*) above shall have effect as if, in connection with the benefit of the car, the amount produced under subsection (2C) below together with any amounts falling within (2D) below were the amounts to be included in the emoluments.]³

[(2C) The amount produced under this subsection is the higher of—

　(*a*) the amount equal to the aggregate of—

　　(i) whatever is the cash equivalent (ascertained in accordance with Schedule 6) of the benefit of the car; and

(ii) whatever is the cash equivalent (ascertained in accordance with section 158) of the benefit of any fuel provided, by reason of the employee's employment, for the car; and

(b) the amount which would be chargeable to tax under section 19(1), if the benefit of the car were chargeable under that section by reference to the alternative offered to that benefit.][3]

[(2D) The amounts which fall within this subsection are those which would come into charge under section 141, 142 or 153 if the section in question applied in connection with the car.][3]

(3) Where a person is employed in two or more employments by the same employer and either—

(a) the total of the emoluments of those employments (applying this section) is at the rate of £8,500 a year or more; or

(b) this Chapter applies (apart from this subsection) to one or more of those employments,

this Chapter shall apply to all the employments.

(4) All employees of a partnership or body over which an individual or another partnership or body has control are to be treated for the purposes of this section (but not for any other purpose) as if the employment were an employment by the individual or by that other partnership or body as the case may be.

(5) This Chapter shall not apply to a person's employment by reason only of its being employment as a director of a company (without prejudice to its application by virtue of subsection (1)(b) or (3) above) if he has no material interest in the company and either—

(a) his employment is as a full-time working director; or

(b) the company is non-profit making (meaning that neither does it carry on a trade nor do its functions consist wholly or mainly in the holding of investments or other property) or is established for charitable purposes only.][1]

Commentary—*Simon's Direct Tax Service* E4.602.
Simon's Tax Cases—*R v Dimsey* [1999] STC 846.
Revenue Internal Guidance—Schedule E manual, SE 20101–20105 (working out if an employment has emoluments at a rate of £8,500 a year or more, application of s167(2) including worked example).
SE 20106 (employee with more than one employment—deciding whether each employment has emoluments of £8,500 a year or more).
SE 20110 (the effect of changes in rates of pay during the year).
SE 20111 (employee with employment for only part of a year).
SE 20115 (employee with emoluments falling in Case III of Schedule E, take the full emoluments arising whether in the UK or abroad, not restricted to those received in the UK).
SE 20200 (meaning of 'director').
SE 20201–20212 (exclusions provided by sub-s (5), including meaning of "material interest", "full-time working director", "non-profit-making" and "established for charitable purposes only").
SE 23006 (effect of expenses etc. paid in connection with a provided car included even though the expenses etc themselves are not separately chargeable to tax).
SE 30081 (expenses payments and benefits covered by a dispensation do not count as emoluments in deciding if an employee is earning £8,500 or more).
Definitions—"Basic rate", s 832(1); "car", s 168(5); "company", s 832(1), (2); "control", ss 168(12), 840; "director", s 168(8), (9); "emoluments", ss 131(1), 167(2); "employment", s 168(2); "full-time working director", s 168(10); "lower rate", s 832(1); "material interest", s 168(11); "tax", s 832(3); "trade", s 832(1).
Cross reference—See TMA 1970 s 15(3)(a) (employer may be required to give notice of all employees who are in employment to which this Chapter applies).
Amendments—[1] This section substituted by FA 1989 s 53(1).
[2] Sub-s (2A) repealed by FA 1994 Sch 26 Pt V(5) with effect from the year 1994–95 (previously inserted by FA 1991 s 27(6), Sch 6 para 2).
[3] Words in sub-s (2) and sub-ss (2B)–(2D) inserted by FA 1995 s 43(3), (4) with effect from the year 1995–96.
[4] Word in sub-s (2)(b) to be inserted by FA 2001 s 57(3), (4), Sch 12 Pt II para 3 with effect from the year 2002–03.

168 Other interpretative provisions

(1) The following provisions of this section apply for the interpretation of expressions used in this Chapter.

(2) Subject to section 165(6)(b), "employment" means an office or employment the emoluments of which fall to be assessed under Schedule E; and related expressions shall be construed accordingly.

(3) For the purposes of this Chapter—

(a) all sums paid to an employee by his employer in respect of expenses, and

(b) all such provision as is mentioned in this Chapter which is made for an employee, or for members of his family or household, by his employer,

are deemed to be paid to or made for him or them by reason of his employment, except any such payment or provision [which is made by the employer, being an individual, in the normal course of his domestic, family or personal relationships][6].

(4) References to members of a person's family or household are to his spouse, his sons and daughters and their spouses, his parents and his servants, dependants and guests.

(5) As respects cars, the following definitions apply—

(a) "car" means any mechanically propelled road vehicle except—

(i) a vehicle of a construction primarily suited for the conveyance of goods or burden of any description,

(ii) a vehicle of a type not commonly used as a private vehicle and unsuitable to be so used,

(iii) a motor cycle as defined in section 190(4) of the Road Traffic Act 1972 and

(iv) an invalid carriage as defined in section 190(5) of that Act;

(*b*) the age of a car at any time is the interval between the date of its first registration and that time;

[(*c*) "business travel", in relation to any employee, means any travelling the expenses of which, if incurred out of the emoluments of his employment, would [(in the absence of sections 197AD to 197AF)]⁸ be deductible under section 198;]⁷

[(*d*) the date of a car's first registration is the date on which it was first registered under [the Vehicle Excise and Registration Act 1994]⁵ or under corresponding legislation of any country or territory;]⁴

[(*e*) the price of a car as regards a year shall be determined in accordance with the provisions contained in or made under sections 168A to 168G; and]⁴

(*f*) "private use", in relation to a car made available to any person, or to others being members of his family or household, means any use otherwise than for his business travel.

[(5A) As respects vans, the following definitions apply—

(*a*) "van" means a mechanically propelled road vehicle which is—

(i) of a construction primarily suited for the conveyance of goods or burden of any description, and

(ii) of a design weight not exceeding 3,500 kilograms,

and which is not a motor cycle as defined in section 185(1) of the Road Traffic Act 1988;

(*b*) the age of a van at any time is the interval between the date of its first registration and that time;

[(*c*) "business travel", in relation to any employee, means any travelling the expenses of which, if incurred out of the emoluments of his employment, would [(in the absence of sections 197AD to 197AF)]⁸ be deductible under section 198;]⁷

(*d*) the date of a van's first registration is the date on which it was first registered under [the Vehicle Excise and Registration Act 1994]⁵ or under corresponding legislation of any country or territory;

(*e*) "design weight" means the weight which a vehicle is designed or adapted not to exceed when in normal use and travelling on a road laden; and

(*f*) "private use", in relation to a van made available to any person, or to others being members of his family or household, means any use otherwise than for his business travel.]³

(6) For the purposes of this Chapter—

(*a*) a car made available in any year to an employee, or to others being members of his family or household, by reason of his employment is deemed to be available in that year for his or their private use unless the terms on which the car is made available prohibit such use and no such use is made of the car in that year;

(*b*) a car made available to an employee, or to others being members of his family or household, by his employer is deemed to be made available to him or them by reason of his employment (unless the employer is an individual and [the car is]⁶ made so available in the normal course of his domestic, family or personal relationships);

[(*c*) a van made available in any year to an employee, or to others being members of his family or household, by reason of his employment is deemed to be available in that year for his or their private use unless the terms on which the van is made available prohibit such use and no such use is made of the van in that year;

(*d*) a van made available to an employee, or to others being members of his family or household, by his employer is deemed to be made available to him or them by reason of his employment (unless the employer is an individual and [the van is]⁶ made so available in the normal course of his domestic, family or personal relationships).]³

(7) For the purposes of section 156, the market value of an asset at any time is the price which it might reasonably have been expected to fetch on a sale in the open market at that time.

(8) Subject to subsection (9) below, "director" means—

(*a*) in relation to a company whose affairs are managed by a board of directors or similar body, a member of that board or similar body;

(*b*) in relation to a company whose affairs are managed by a single director or similar person, that director or person; and

(*c*) in relation to a company whose affairs are managed by the members themselves, a member of the company,

and includes any person in accordance with whose directions or instructions the directors of the company (as defined above) are accustomed to act.

(9) A person is not under subsection (8) above to be deemed to be a person in accordance with whose directions or instructions the directors of the company are accustomed to act by reason only that the directors act on advice given by him in a professional capacity.

(10) "Full-time working director" means a director who is required to devote substantially the whole of his time to the service of the company in a managerial or technical capacity.

(11) A person shall be treated as having a material interest [in a company if he, either on his own or with one or more associates, or if any associate of his with or without such other associates,—

(*a*) is the beneficial owner of, or able, directly or through the medium of other companies, or by any other indirect means to control, more than 5 per cent of the ordinary share capital of the company, or

(*b*) in the case of a close company, possesses, or is entitled to acquire, such rights as would, in the event of the winding-up of the company or in any other circumstances, give an entitlement to receive more than 5 per cent of the assets which would then be available for distribution among the participators.]¹

In this subsection "associate" has the same meaning as in section 417(3), except that for this purpose "relative" in that subsection has the meaning given by section 160(6)[, and "participator" has the meaning given by section 417(1)]².

(12) "Control", in relation to a body corporate or partnership, has the meaning given to it by section 840; and the definition of "control" in that section applies (with the necessary modifications) in relation to an unincorporated association as it applies in relation to a body corporate.

(13) "Year" means year of assessment (except where the expression is used with reference to the age of a car).

Commentary—*Simon's Direct Tax Service* E4.603.
Revenue Internal Guidance—Schedule E manual, SE 01040 (Christmas presents or bonuses—all directors and employees who earn at a rate of £8,500 per year or more are taxable on any cash gifts which they may receive from their employer).
SE 11210 (incentive awards to an employee's family or dependants: different definitions of the family circle depending upon whether vouchers are used, or awards are obtained in some other way and taxable under this part of ICTA).
SE 11412 (living accommodation: avoidance areas, application of sub-s (8)).
SE 11413 (living accommodation: avoidance area—shadow directors, application of sub-s (8), provisions are brought into the living accommodation legislation by s 145(8)(*b*)).
SE 20202 (meaning of "full-time working director").
SE 20213 (meaning of "control")
SE 20502 (the one exception to sub-s (3) is when the employer is an individual and he can show that the payment was made or the benefit was provided in the normal course of his domestic family or personal relationships, eg a father who employs his son will normally be able to show that a Christmas present he gives to his son is not "by reason of the employment").
SE 20504 (meaning of provided for an employee's family or household)
SE 20505 (provision to a family member employed by the same employer as the employee).
SE 21619 (meaning of market value).
SE 22065 (meaning of van).
SE 22066 (meaning of "design weight").
SE 23020 and 23020a (meaning of car, including flow-chart)
SE23030 (meaning of "construction").
SE 23031 (meaning of "primarily suited").
SE 23040 (meaning of "type"—as in 'of a type not commonly used').
SE 23041 (meaning of "not commonly used as a private vehicle").
SE 23042 (meaning of "unsuitable for use as a private vehicle").
SE 23043 (treatment of emergency vehicles).
SE 23044 (treatment of 'off road' vehicles).
SE 23081 (meaning of "available for private use").
Simon's Tax Cases—*R v Dimsey* [1999] STC 846.
s 168(3), *Wicks v Firth* [1983] STC 25*.
s 168(5)(*a*)(ii), *Gurney v Richards* [1989] STC 682*.
s 168(6)(*a*), *Gilbert v Hemsley* [1981] STC 703*.
Definitions—"Close company", ss 414(1), 832(1); "company", s 832(1), (2); "emoluments", s 131(1); "ordinary share capital", s 832(1); "Schedule E", s 19(1); "total income", s 835(1); "United Kingdom", s 830(1).
Amendments—¹ Sub-s (11)(*a*) (and the preceding words), (*b*) substituted by FA 1989 Sch 12 para 8 in relation to accounting periods beginning after 31 March 1989.
² Words in sub-s (11) added by FA 1989 Sch 12 para 8 in relation to accounting periods beginning after 31 March 1989.
³ Sub-ss (5A), (6)(*c*), (*d*) inserted by FA 1993 Sch 4 paras 1, 6, 8 with effect from the year 1993–94.
⁴ Sub-ss (5)(*d*), (*e*) substituted by FA 1993 Sch 3 paras 1, 3, 7 with effect from the year 1994–95.
⁵ Words in sub-ss (5)(*d*), (5A)(*d*) substituted by the Vehicle Excise and Registration Act 1994 Sch 3 para 22.
⁶ Words in sub-ss (3), (6)(*b*), (*d*) substituted by FA 1996 Sch 20 para 10 with effect from the year 1996–97.
⁷ Sub-ss (5)(*c*) and (5A)(*c*) substituted by FA 1997 s 62(4), (5) with effect from the year 1998–99.
⁸ Words inserted in sub-ss (5)(*c*), (5A)(*c*) by FA 2001 s 57(3), (4), Sch 12 Pt II para 4 with effect from the year 2002–03.

[168A Price of a car as regards a year

(1) Subject to the provisions contained in or made under [sections 168AB to 168G]³ for the purposes of this Chapter the price of a car as regards a year is—

(*a*) its list price, if it has one, or
(*b*) its notional price, if it has no list price;

and in this section any reference to the relevant car is to the particular car whose price as regards a year is being determined.

(2) The relevant car has a list price if a price was published by the car's manufacturer, importer or distributor (as the case may be) as the inclusive price appropriate for a car of that kind if sold in the United Kingdom singly in a retail sale in the open market on the relevant day.

(3) In a case where—

(*a*) subsection (2) above applies, and
(*b*) at the time when the relevant car was first made available to the employee the only qualifying accessories available with it were standard accessories,

the list price of the car is the price published as mentioned in subsection (2) above.

(4) In a case where—

(*a*) subsection (2) above applies,

(b) at the time when the relevant car was first made available to the employee a qualifying accessory which was an optional accessory was available with it, and

(c) in relation to each such accessory then available with the car a price was published by the car's manufacturer, importer or distributor (as the case may be) as the inclusive price appropriate for an equivalent accessory if sold with a car of the same kind as the relevant car in the United Kingdom singly in a retail sale in the open market on the relevant day,

the list price of the car is the price found under subsection (5) below.

(5) The price referred to in subsection (4) above is the total of—

(a) the price published as mentioned in subsection (2) above, and

(b) the price, or the sum of the prices, published as mentioned in subsection (4) above in relation to the optional accessory or (as the case may be) the optional accessories.

(6) In a case where—

(a) subsection (2) above applies, and

(b) at the time when the relevant car was first made available to the employee a qualifying accessory falling within subsection (7) below was available with the car,

the list price of the car is the price which would have been its list price under subsection (3) or (4) above (as the case may be) if no such accessory had been available with it at that time.

(7) An accessory falls within this subsection if—

(a) it is an optional accessory, and

(b) no price was published by the relevant car's manufacturer, importer or distributor (as the case may be) as the inclusive price appropriate for an equivalent accessory if sold with a car of the same kind as the relevant car in the United Kingdom singly in a retail sale in the open market on the relevant day.

(8) The notional price of a car is the price which might reasonably have been expected to be its list price if its manufacturer, importer or distributor (as the case may be) had published a price as the inclusive price appropriate for an equivalent car if sold in the United Kingdom singly in a retail sale in the open market on the relevant day; and "equivalent car" here means a car—

(a) of the same kind as the relevant car, and

(b) with accessories equivalent to the qualifying accessories available with the relevant car at the time when it was first made available to the employee.

(9) For the purposes of this section—

(a) the inclusive price is the price inclusive of any charge for delivery by the manufacturer, importer or distributor to the seller's place of business and of any relevant tax and, in the case of an accessory, of any charge for fitting it,

(b) the relevant day is the day immediately before the date of the relevant car's first registration,

(c) a standard accessory is an accessory equivalent to an accessory which, in arriving at the price published as mentioned in subsection (2) above, is assumed to be available with cars of the same kind as the relevant car, and

(d) an optional accessory is an accessory other than a standard accessory;

and "relevant tax" here means any customs or excise duty, any tax chargeable as if it were a duty of customs, any value added tax and any car tax.

(10) For the purposes of this section a qualifying accessory is an accessory which—

(a) is made available for use with the car without any transfer of the property in it,

(b) is made available by reason of the employee's employment,

(c) is attached to the car (whether or not permanently), and

(d) is not an accessory necessarily provided for use in the performance of the duties of the employee's employment.

(11) For the purposes of this section "accessory" includes any kind of equipment, but does not include a mobile telephone within the meaning given by [section 155AA(2)][4] [or equipment which falls within section 168AA [or 168AB(1).][3]][2]

(12) For the purposes of this section the time when a car is first made available to an employee is the earliest time when the car is made available, by reason of his employment and without any transfer of the property in it, either to him or to others being members of his family or household.][1]

Commentary—*Simon's Direct Tax Service* E4.627.

Revenue Internal Guidance—Schedule E SE 23100 and 23100a (price of the car as regards the year—general, including flow-chart)

SE 23101 (list price of a car—general).

SE 23102 (meaning of "relevant day").

SE 23103 (meaning of "inclusive price").

SE 23104 (treatment of imported cars).

SE 23120 (accessories—general).

SE 23125 (meaning of "standard accessory").

SE 23126 (meaning of "optional accessory").

SE 23127 (meaning of "qualifying accessory").

SE 23130 (car accessories made available at the time the car is first made available; optional accessories included in the list price of the car).

SE 23140 (notional price—general).

SE 23156 (car accessories—treatment of personalised car number plates).

SE 23185 (worked example involving accessories).
SE 23187 (calculation of price as regards a year; notional price—example).
Revenue & other press releases—IR 27-9-93 (list price of car may be obtained from (i) manufacturers' list price (ii) specialist organisations publishing details of list prices (iii) manufacturers offering support services (iv) some leasing companies (v) original invoice. Minor accessories fitted after delivery of car are ignored).
Cross references—See TA 1988 s 168AA(4) (sub-s (12) above applies for the purposes of equipment being made available to enable a disabled person to use a car).
IT (Car Benefits) (Replacement Accessories) Regulations, SI 1994/777 regs 3–5 (replacement accessories; ascertainment of price of car where replacement accessories are inferior or superior to the replaced accessories).
Definitions—"Car", s 168(5); "employment", s 168(2); "family or household", s 168(4); "first registration", s 168(5); "made available", s 168(6); "United Kingdom", s 830(1); "year", ss 168(13), 832(1).
Amendments—[1] This section inserted by FA 1993 Sch 3 paras 1, 4, 7 with effect from the year 1994–95.
[2] Words in sub-s (11) inserted by FA 1995 s 44(1), (3) with effect from the year 1995–96.
[3] Words "sections 168AB to 168G" substituted for "sections 168B to 168G" in sub-s (1), and words "or 168AB(1)" inserted in sub-s (11), by FA 1998 s 60(1)(2) from the year 1998–99.
[4] Words in sub-s (11) substituted by FA 1999 s 44(4), (6) with effect from the year 1999–00.

[168AA Equipment to enable disabled person to use car

(1) Equipment falls within this section if it is designed solely for use by a chronically sick or disabled person.

(2) Equipment also falls within this section if—

(*a*) at the time when the car is first made available to the employee, the employee holds a disabled person's badge, and

(*b*) the equipment is made available for use with the car because the equipment enables him to use the car in spite of the disability entitling him to hold the badge.

(3) In subsection (2) above "disabled person's badge" means a badge—

(*a*) which is issued to a disabled person under section 21 of the Chronically Sick and Disabled Persons Act 1970 or section 14 of the Chronically Sick and Disabled Persons (Northern Ireland) Act 1978 (or which has effect as if so issued), and

(*b*) which is not required to be returned to the issuing authority under or by virtue of the section in question.

(4) Subsection (12) of section 168A applies for the purposes of this section as it applies for the purposes of that.][1]

Commentary—*Simon's Direct Tax Service* **E4.627A.**
Revenue Internal Guidance—Schedule E manual, SE 23121 (car accessories; exceptions—equipment for disabled persons).
Definitions—"Car", s 168(5); "made available", s 168(6).
Amendments—[1] This section inserted by FA 1995 s 44(2), (3) with effect from the year 1995–96.

[168AB Equipment etc to enable car to run on road fuel gas

(1) Equipment by means of which the car is capable of running on road fuel gas shall not be regarded as an accessory for the purposes of section 168A.

(2) Where the car is manufactured in such way as to be capable of running on road fuel gas, the price of the car as regards each relevant year shall be treated as the price given by section 168A, reduced by so much of that price as it is reasonable to attribute to the car's being manufactured in that way rather than in such a way as to be capable of running only on petrol.

(3) In this section "road fuel gas" means any substance which is gaseous at a temperature of 15°C and under a pressure of 1013·25 millibars, and which is for use as fuel in road vehicles.][1]

[(4) This section does not apply in relation to cars to which paragraph 5 of Schedule 6 to this Act applies (bi-fuel cars taxed by reference to CO_2 emissions figure).][2]

Commentary—*Simon's Direct Tax Service* **E4.627.**
Revenue Internal Guidance—Schedule E manual, SE 23107 (cars manufactured to run on road fuel gases).
SE 23122 (car accessories; exceptions—cost of converting car to run on road fuel gases).
Definitions—"Car", s 168(5).
Amendments—[1] This section inserted by FA 1998 s 60(3) with effect from the year 1998–99.
[2] Sub-s (4) inserted by FA 2000 s 59, Sch 11 para 2 with effect from the year 2002–03.

[168B Price of a car: accessories not included in list price

(1) This section applies where a car has a list price and in any year there are available with the car qualifying accessories which—

(*a*) fall within section 168A(7), and

(*b*) were available with the car at the time when it was first made available to the employee.

(2) As regards that year the price of the car shall be treated as the price found under [sections 168A and 168AB][2], increased by the price of the accessories.

(3) For the purposes of this section the price of an accessory is—

(*a*) its list price, if it has one, or

(*b*) its notional price, if it has no list price.

(4) The list price of an accessory is the price published by or on behalf of its manufacturer, importer or distributor (as the case may be) as the inclusive price appropriate for such an accessory if sold in the United Kingdom singly in a retail sale in the open market at the relevant time; and the relevant

time is the time immediately before the accessory concerned is first made available for use with the car (which may be before the car is first made available to the employee).

(5) The notional price of an accessory is the inclusive price which it might reasonably have been expected to fetch if sold in the United Kingdom singly in a retail sale in the open market immediately before it is first made available for use with the car (which may be before the car is first made available to the employee).

(6) Where the accessory is permanently attached to the car the sale assumed by subsection (4) or (5) above is one under which the seller is to attach it.

(7) For the purposes of this section the inclusive price is the price inclusive of—

(*a*) any charge for delivery by the manufacturer, importer or distributor to the seller's place of business, and

(*b*) any customs or excise duty, any tax chargeable as if it were a duty of customs and any value added tax.

(8) Subsections (10) to (12) of section 168A apply for the purposes of this section as they apply for the purposes of that.][1]

Commentary—*Simon's Direct Tax Service* **E4.627A.**
Revenue Internal Guidance—Schedule E manual, SE 23131 (car accessories made available at the time the car is first made available; optional accessories not included in list price—to be added to price of the car).
SE 23132 (list price of an accessory).
SE 23133 (notional price of an accessory).
SE 23135 (inclusive price of an optional accessory).
SE 23185 (worked example involving accessories).
Definitions—"Car", s 168(5); "made available", s 168(6); "United Kingdom", s 830(1); "year", ss 168(13), 832(1).
Cross reference—See IT (Car Benefits) (Replacement Accessories) Regulations, SI 1994/777 regs 3–5 (replacement accessories; ascertainment of price of car where replacement accessories are inferior or superior to the replaced accessories).
Amendments—[1] This section inserted by FA 1993 Sch 3 paras 1, 4, 7 with effect from the year 1994–95.
[2] Words in sub-s (2) substituted by FA 1998 s 60(4) with effect from the year 1998–99.

[168C Price of a car: accessories available after car first made available

(1) This section applies where in any year there are available with a car qualifying accessories which—

(*a*) were not available with the car at the time when it was first made available to the employee, and

(*b*) were not made available with the car before 1st August 1993,

but any accessory whose price is less than £100 shall be ignored for the purposes of this section.

(2) As regards that year the price of the car shall be treated as the price found under [sections 168A to 168B][2], increased by the price of the accessories.

(3) Subsections (10) to (12) of section 168A apply for the purposes of this section as they apply for the purposes of that.

(4) Subsections (3) to (6) of section 168B apply for the purposes of this section as they apply for the purposes of that, but ignoring for the purposes of this section the words "(which may be before the car is first made available to the employee)".

(5) The Treasury may by order substitute for the sum for the time being specified in subsection (1) above a sum of a greater amount; and any such substitution shall have effect as regards such years as are specified in the order.][1]

Commentary—*Simon's Direct Tax Service* **E4.627A.**
Revenue Internal Guidance—Schedule E manual SE 23150 (accessories provided after the car is first made available).
SE 23185 (worked example involving accessories).
Definitions—"Car", s 168(5); "made available", s 168(6); "year", ss 168(13), 832(1).
Cross reference—See IT (Car Benefits) (Replacement Accessories) Regulations, SI 1994/777 regs 3–5 (replacement accessories; ascertainment of price of car where replacement accessories are inferior or superior to the replaced accessories).
Amendments—[1] This section inserted by FA 1993 Sch 3 paras 1, 4, 7 with effect from the year 1994–95.
[2] Words in sub-s (2) substituted by FA 1998 s 60(5) with effect from the year 1998–99.

[168D Price of a car: capital contributions

(1) This section applies where the employee contributes a capital sum to expenditure on the provision of—

(*a*) the car, or

(*b*) any qualifying accessories which are taken into account under sections 168A to 168C in determining the price of the car as regards a year.

(2) As regards each relevant year the price of the car shall be treated as the price found under sections 168A to 168C, reduced by the appropriate amount; and relevant years are the year in which the capital sum is contributed and all subsequent years in which section 157 applies in the case of the car and the employee.

(3) As regards a relevant year the appropriate amount is whichever is the smaller of—

(*a*) the amount found under subsection (4) below as regards the year, and

(*b*) £5,000.

(4) As regards a relevant year the amount referred to in subsection (3) above is the amount of the capital sum, or the total amount of all the capital sums, which the employee has contributed (whether in the year in question or earlier) to expenditure on the provision of—

   (*a*) the car, or

   (*b*) any qualifying accessories which are taken into account under sections 168A to 168C in determining the price of the car as regards the year in question.

(5) Subsections (10) and (11) of section 168A apply for the purposes of this section as they apply for the purposes of that.

(6) The Treasury may by order substitute for the sum for the time being specified in subsection (3)(*b*) above a sum of a greater amount; and any such substitution shall have effect as regards such years as are specified in the order.][1]

Commentary—*Simon's Direct Tax Service* **E4.627.**
Revenue Internal Guidance—Schedule E manual SE 23160 (reduction of the price of the car as regards a year because of capital contributions, Revenue expects to see the payment made at or about the time when the car or accessory in question is provided).
SE 23161 (limit on the amount allowable).
SE 23162 (years when amount is allowed; relates only to the car to which the contribution was made and only for that employee).
SE 23163 (treatment of repayments of capital contributions).
SE 23185 (worked example involving capital contributions).
Definitions—''Car'', s 168(5); ''year'', ss 168(13), 832(1).
Cross reference—See IT (Car Benefits) (Replacement Accessories) Regulations, SI 1994/777 regs 3–5 (replacement accessories; ascertainment of price of car where replacement accessories are inferior or superior to the replaced accessories).
Amendments—[1]This section inserted by FA 1993 Sch 3 paras 1, 4, 7 with effect from the year 1994–95.

[168E Price of a car: replacement accessories

(1) The Treasury may make regulations under this section as regards any case where—

   (*a*) a qualifying accessory is available with a car in any year, and

   (*b*) the accessory (the replacing accessory) replaces another accessory (the replaced accessory).

(2) Regulations under this section may provide that as regards the year—

   (*a*) the price of the car shall be found as if the replacement had not been made and the replacing accessory were a continuation of the replaced accessory, or

   (*b*) sections 168A to 168D shall apply to the car with such modifications to take account of the fact that the replacement has been made as are prescribed by the regulations.

(3) The regulations may—

   (*a*) provide as mentioned in subsection (2)(*a*) above as regards some cases and as mentioned in subsection (2)(*b*) above as regards others;

   (*b*) provide under subsection (2)(*b*) above that sections 168A to 168D shall apply with different modifications in different cases.][1]

Commentary—*Simon's Direct Tax Service* **E4.627A.**
Regulation—IT (Car Benefits) (Replacement Accessories) Regulations, SI 1994/777.
Revenue Internal Guidance—Schedule E manual, SE 23155 (replacement accessories).
Definitions—''Car'', s 168(5); ''year'', ss 168(13), 832(1).
Amendments—[1]This section inserted by FA 1993 Sch 3 paras 1, 4, 7 with effect from the year 1994–95.

[168F Price of a car: classic cars

(1) This section applies where—

   (*a*) the price of a car as regards a year, found under the provisions contained in or made under sections 168A to 168E, is less than the market value of the car for the year,

   (*b*) the age of the car at the end of the year is 15 years or more, and

   (*c*) the market value of the car for the year is £15,000 or more.

(2) In such a case—

   (*a*) the price of the car as regards the year is not the amount found under the provisions contained in or made under sections 168A to 168E;

   (*b*) the price of the car as regards the year is the market value of the car for the year;

but paragraph (*b*) above is subject to subsection (5) below.

(3) The market value of a car for a year is the price which the car might reasonably have been expected to fetch on a sale in the open market on the material day, on the assumption that any qualifying accessories available with the car on the material day are included in the sale.

(4) For the purposes of subsection (3) above the material day is—

   (*a*) the last day of the year concerned, or

   (*b*) if earlier, the last day in the year on which the car is available to the employee.

(5) Where the employee contributes a capital sum to expenditure on the provision of—

   (*a*) the car, or

   (*b*) any qualifying accessories which are taken into account under subsection (3) above in determining the price of the car as regards a year,

TA 1988

as regards each relevant year the price of the car shall be treated as the market value of the car for the year, reduced by the appropriate amount.

(6) For the purposes of subsection (5) above relevant years are the year in which the capital sum is contributed and all subsequent years in which section 157 applies in the case of the car and the employee.

(7) For the purposes of subsection (5) above the appropriate amount, in relation to a relevant year, is whichever is the smaller of—

(*a*) the amount found under subsection (8) below as regards the year, and

(*b*) £5,000.

(8) As regards a particular year the amount referred to in subsection (7) above is the amount of the capital sum, or the total amounts of all the capital sums, which the employee has contributed (whether in the year or earlier) to expenditure—

(*a*) on the provision of the car, or

(*b*) on the provision of any qualifying accessories which are taken into account in determining the price of the car as regards the year.

(9) Subsections (10) and (11) of section 168A apply for the purposes of this section as they apply for the purposes of that.

(10) For the purposes of this section the last day in a year on which a car is available to an employee is the last day in the year on which the car is made available, by reason of his employment and without any transfer of the property in it, either to him or to others being members of his family or household.

(11) The Treasury may by order—

(*a*) substitute for the sum for the time being specified in subsection (1)(*c*) above a sum of a greater amount;

(*b*) substitute for the sum for the time being specified in subsection (7)(*b*) above a sum of a greater amount;

and any such substitution shall have effect as regards such years as are specified in the order.][1]

Commentary—*Simon's Direct Tax Service* **E4.627.**
Revenue Internal Guidance—Schedule E manual, SE 23170 (classic cars—general).
SE 23171 (price of a classic car as regards a year).
SE 23172 (market value—if bought in a poor state of repair and restored during the year, then it is the market value of the restored vehicle on the material day which is needed to calculate the car benefit charge and not the cost of the earlier purchase).
SE 23173 (capital contributions for classic cars).
SE 23174 (meaning of "material day").
SE 23186 (calculation of price as regards a year; classic car—example).
Definitions—"Age of car", s 168(5); "car", s 168(5); "employment", s 168(2); "family or household", s 168(4); "made available", s 168(6); "year", ss 168(13), 832(1).
Amendments—[1] This section inserted by FA 1993 Sch 3 paras 1, 4, 7 with effect from the year 1994–95.

[168G Price of a car: cap for expensive car

(1) Where the price of a car as regards a year (as found under the provisions contained in or made under sections 168A to 168F) exceeds £80,000, the price of the car as regards the year is £80,000 and not the price as so found.

(2) The Treasury may by order substitute for the sum for the time being specified in subsection (1) above a sum of a greater amount; and any such substitution shall have effect as regards such years as are specified in the order.][1]

Commentary—*Simon's Direct Tax Service* **E4.627.**
Revenue Internal Guidance—Schedule E manual, SE 23179 (price cap for expensive cars—same for all cars, classic or otherwise).
SE 23336 (worked example involving expensive car).
Definitions—"Car", s 168(5); "year", ss 168(13), 832(1).
Amendments—[1] This section inserted by FA 1993 Sch 3 paras 1, 4, 7 with effect from the year 1994–95.

[CHAPTER III
PROFIT-RELATED PAY][1]

Regulations—Profit-Related Pay (Shortfall Recovery) Regulations, SI 1988/640 reg 3 which requires, when a scheme is cancelled, a return to be made showing shortfall in deductions.
Revenue & other press releases—IR 28-7-98 (national minimum wage legislation and tax-relieved profit-related pay).
Revenue Internal Guidance—Profit-related pay unit manual gives a detailed exposition of the law relating to profit-related pay schemes.
Schedule E manual, SE 03050 (tax relief for employees who receive profit-related pay (PRP)).
Amendments—[1] By FA 1997 s 62(2), this Chapter shall not have effect for any payment made by reference to a profit period beginning after 31 December 1999; and accordingly a scheme shall not be registered under this Chapter if the only payments for which it provides are payments by reference to profit periods beginning after 31 December 1999, and registration under this Chapter shall end on that date. Sections 169–184 are accordingly repealed by FA 1997 Sch 18 Pt VI(3) in accordance with FA 1997 s 61(2), (3), but subject to FA 1997 Sch Pt VI(3) note 2.
See FA 1998 Sch 11 for transitional provisions to prevent the manipulation of profit periods during the phasing out of the relief.

Preliminary

[169 Interpretation

(1) In this Chapter—

"*employment*" *means an office or employment whose emoluments fall to be assessed under Schedule E, and related expressions have corresponding meanings;*

"*employment unit*" *means an undertaking, or that part of an undertaking, to which a profit-related pay scheme*

"*pay*" *(except in the expression "profit-related pay") means emoluments paid under deduction of tax pursuant to section 203, reduced by any amounts included in them by virtue of Chapter II of Part V;*

"*profit period*" *means an accounting period by reference to which any profit-related pay is calculated;*

"*profit-related pay*" *means emoluments from an employment which are paid in accordance with a profit-related pay scheme;*

"*profit-related pay scheme*" *means a scheme providing for the payment of emoluments calculated by reference to profits;*

"*profits*", *or* "*losses*", *in relation to a profit period, means the amount shown in the account prepared for that period in accordance with the relevant profit-related pay scheme as the profit, or as the case may be the loss, on ordinary activities after taxation;*

"*registered scheme*" *means a profit-related pay scheme registered under this Chapter;*

"*scheme employer*" *means the person on whose application a profit-related pay scheme is or may be registered under this Chapter.*

(2) References in this Chapter to the employees to whom a profit-related pay scheme relates are references to the employees who will receive any payments of profit-related pay under the scheme.][1]

Commentary—*Simon's Direct Tax Service* **E4.301–305.**
Revenue & other press releases—IR Notes for Guidance (PRP2) (information and explanation of statutory requirements of a PRP scheme).
PRP Unit December 1993 (guidance notes for employers regarding changes effective from 1-12-93).
Revenue Internal Guidance—Profit-related pay unit manual PRP 3.200-3.222 (meaning and determination of "employment unit").
Definitions—"Accounting period", s 834(1); "emoluments", s 131(1); "Schedule E", s 19(1).
Amendments—This section repealed by FA 1997 Sch 18 Pt VI(3); see the corresponding note at the beginning of this Chapter.

170 Taxation of profit-related pay

Commentary—*Simon's Direct Tax Service* **E4.302.**
Amendments—This section repealed by FA 1989 s 42(4), Sch 17 Pt IV, and by FA 1997 Sch 18 Pt VI(3) (see the corresponding note at the beginning of the Chapter).

The relief

[171 Relief from tax

(1) [The whole][2] *of any profit-related pay to which this section applies shall be exempt from income tax.*

(2) This section applies to any profit-related pay paid to an employee by reference to a profit period and in accordance with a registered scheme, but only so far as it does not exceed the lower of the two limits specified in the following provisions of this section.

(3) The first of the limits referred to in subsection (2) above is one fifth of the aggregate of—

(a) the pay (but not any profit-related pay) paid to the employee in the profit period in respect of his employment in the employment unit concerned (or, if the employee is eligible to receive profit-related pay by reference to part only of the period, so much of his pay, but not any profit-related pay, as is paid in that part); and

(b) the profit-related pay paid to him by reference to that period in respect of that employment.

(4) The second of the limits referred to in subsection (2) above is [£1,000][1] *(or, if the profit period is less than 12 months, or the employee is eligible to receive profit-related payprofit period, a proportionately reduced amount).]*[3]

Commentary—*Simon's Direct Tax Service* **E4.302.**
Definitions—"Employment", s 169(1); "employment unit", s 169(1); "pay", s 169(1); "profit period", s 169(1); "profit-related pay", s 169(1); "registered scheme", s 169(1).
Cross reference—See TA 1988 s 172(1) (exclusion of relief under this section).
Amendments—[1] Amount in sub-s (4) substituted by FA 1997 s 61(1)(b) with effect for profit-related pay paid by reference to a profit period beginning after 31 December 1998 and before 1 January 2000. The amount was "£2,000" with effect for profit-related pay paid by reference to profit periods beginning after 31 December 1997 and before 1 January 1999 (by virtue of FA 1997 s 61(1)(a)).
[2] Words in sub-s (1) substituted for the words "one half" by FA 1991 s 37 in relation to profit-related pay paid by reference to profit periods beginning after 31 March 1991.
[3] This section repealed by FA 1997 Sch 18 Pt VI(3); see the corresponding note at the beginning of this Chapter.

[172 Exceptions from tax

(1) Profit-related pay shall not be exempt from income tax by virtue of section 171 if—

    (a) it is paid to an employee in respect of his employment in an employment unit during a time when he also has another employment; and

    (b) he receives in respect of that other employment during that time profit-related pay which is exempt from income tax by virtue of that section.

(2) Subject to subsection (3) below, profit-related pay in respect of which no secondary Class I contributions under Part I of the Social Security Act 1975 or Part I of the Social Security (Northern Ireland) Act 1975 are payable shall not be exempt from income tax by virtue of section 171.

(3) Subsection (2) above shall not apply to profit-related pay in respect of which no [secondary Class 1 contributions]¹ are payable only because the employee's earnings are below the [secondary threshold]³ for such contributions.]²

Commentary—*Simon's Direct Tax Service* **E4.302.**
Notes—SSA 1975 Pt I and SS (Northern Ireland) A 1975 Pt I referred to in sub-s (2) are re-enacted in Social Security Contributions and Benefits Act 1992 Pt I.
Definitions—''Employment'', s 169(1); ''employment unit'', s 169(1); ''profit-related pay'', s 169(1).
Amendments—¹ Words in sub-s (3) substituted by the Social Security Act 1998 Sch 7 para 16 with effect from 6 April 1999, by virtue of the Social Security Act 1998 (Commencement No 3) Order, SI 1999/418 art 2(3).
² This section repealed by FA 1997 Sch 18 Pt VI(3); see the corresponding note at the beginning of this Chapter.
³ Words in sub-s (3) substituted by the Welfare Reform and Pensions Act 1999 s 84 Sch 12 paras 73, 74, with effect from 6 April 2000.

Registration

[173 Persons who may apply for registration

(1) Where the emoluments of all the employees to whom a profit-related pay scheme relates are paid by the same person, an application to register the scheme under this Chapter may be made to the Board by that person.

(2) Where subsection (1) above does not apply to a profit-related pay scheme, no application to register it may be made unless all the persons who pay emoluments to employees to whom the scheme relates are bodies corporate which are members of the same group; and in that case an application may be made by the parent company of the group.

(3) In subsection (2) above—

    ''group'' means a body corporate and its 51 per cent subsidiaries, and

    ''parent company'' means that body corporate; and

in applying for the purposes of this section the definition of ''51 per cent subsidiary'' in section 838, any share capital of a registered industrial and provident society (within the meaning of section 486) shall be treated as ordinary share capital.]¹

Commentary—*Simon's Direct Tax Service* **E4.303.**
Definitions—''The Board'', s 832(1); ''emoluments'', s 131(1); ''employees to whom a profit-related pay scheme relates'', s 169(2); ''51 per cent subsidiary'', s 838; ''ordinary share capital'', s 832(1); ''profit-related pay scheme'', s 169(1).
Revenue Internal Guidance—Profit-related pay unit manual PRP 2.100–2.118 (requirements and duties of scheme employers). PRP 2.500–2.521 (special cases, including non-resident employers, doctors, mutual concerns and exempt concerns).
Cross reference—See TA 1988 s 177 (change of Scheme employer).
Amendments—¹ This section repealed by FA 1997 Sch 18 Pt VI(3); see the corresponding note at the beginning of this Chapter.

[174 Excluded employments

(1) No application may be made to register a scheme under this Chapter if any employment to which the scheme relates is—

    (a) employment in an office under the Crown or otherwise in the service of the Crown; or

    (b) employment by an excluded employer.

(2) For the purposes of this section ''excluded employer'' means—

    (a) a person in an employment within subsection (1) above;

    (b) a body under the control of the Crown, or of one or more persons acting on behalf of the Crown;

    (c) a local authority;

    (d) a body under the control of one or more local authorities, or of the Crown (or one or more persons acting on behalf of the Crown) and one or more local authorities.

(3) For the purposes of this section a person has control of a body only if one or more of the following conditions is satisfied—

    (a) in the case of a body whose affairs are managed by its members, he has the power to appoint more than half of the members;

    (b) in the case of a body having a share capital, he holds more than half of its issued share capital;

    (c) in the case of a body whose members vote in general meeting, he has the power to exercise more than half of the votes exercisable in general meeting;

    (d) the articles of association or other rules regulating the body give him the power to secure that the affairs of the body are conducted in accordance with his wishes.

(4) For the purposes of this section a person shall be taken to possess rights and powers possessed by—

(a) a person appointed by him to an office by virtue of which the rights or powers are exercisable; or

(b) a body which he controls;

including rights and powers which such an officer or body is taken to possess by virtue of this subsection.

(5) Subsections (3) and (4) above apply with the necessary modifications for the purpose of determining whether persons together have control of a body.][1]

Commentary—*Simon's Direct Tax Service* **E4.303.**
Revenue Internal Guidance—Profit-related pay unit manual PRP 2.200–2.207 (Revenue interpretation of this section).
Definitions—"Body of persons", s 832(1); "employment", s 169(1); "local authority", s 519(4) by virtue of s 832(1).
Cross reference—See TA 1988 s 178(1) (cancellation of a scheme where circumstances after registration are such that this section would apply).
Amendments—[1] This section repealed by FA 1997 Sch 18 Pt VI(3); see the corresponding note at the beginning of this Chapter.

[175 Applications for registration

(1) An application for the registration of a profit-related pay scheme under this Chapter—

(a) shall be in such form as the Board may prescribe;

(b) shall contain a declaration by the applicant that the scheme complies with the requirements of Schedule 8;

[(c) shall contain an undertaking by the applicant that the emoluments paid to any employee to whom the scheme relates and to whom minimum wage legislation applies will satisfy that legislation without taking account of profit-related pay;][3]

(d) shall specify the profit period or periods to which the scheme relates;

(e) shall be supported by such information as the Board may require.

(2) An application for the registration of a profit-related pay scheme under this Chapter shall be accompanied by a report by an independent accountant, in a form prescribed by the Board, to the effect that in his opinion—

(a) the scheme complies with the requirements of Schedule 8;

(b) the books and records maintained and proposed to be maintained by the applicant are adequate for the purpose of enabling the documents required by section 180(1) to be produced.

(3) ...[1]

[(4) In subsection (1) above "minimum wage legislation" means the provisions relating to remuneration in ...[2]*, the Wages Councils (Northern Ireland) Order 1982, the Agricultural Wages Act 1948 the Agricultural Wages (Scotland) Act 1949 and the Agricultural Wages (Regulation) (Northern Ireland) Order 1977.]*[3]*]*[4]

Commentary—*Simon's Direct Tax Service* **E4.308.**
Revenue & other press releases—IR 28-7-98 (national minimum wage legislation and tax-relieved profit-related pay).
Definitions—"The Board", s 832(1); "emoluments", s 131(1); "employee to whom the scheme relates", s 169(2); "independent accountant", s 184; "profit-period", s 169(1); "profit-related pay", s 169(1); "profit-related pay scheme", s 169(1).
Cross reference—See TA 1988 s 178(1) (cancellation of a scheme failing compliance with sub-s (1)(c) above).
Amendments—[1] Sub-s (3) repealed by FA 1989 Sch 4 para 10(2)(a) and Sch 17 Pt IV.
[2] Words in sub-s (4) repealed by the Trade Union Reform and Employment Rights Act 1993 Sch 10 with effect from 30 August 1993 by virtue of the Trade Union Reform and Employment Rights Act 1993 (Commencement No 1 and Transitional Provisions) Order 1993, SI 1993/1908.
[3] Sub-ss (1)(c), (4) repealed by FA 1999 ss 46(1), 139, Sch 20 Pt III(10) with effect for applications for the registration of a PRP scheme made after 27 July 1998.
[4] This section repealed by FA 1997 Sch 18 Pt VI(3); see the corresponding note at the beginning of this Chapter.

[176 Registration

(1) If an application for registration of a profit-related pay scheme under this Chapter is made more than three months ...[1] *before the beginning of the profit period, or the first of the profit periods, to which the scheme relates, then subject to subsection (2) below, the Board shall register the scheme before the beginning of that period.*

(2) If the Board are not satisfied that an application made as mentioned in subsection (1) above complies with the requirements of this Chapter, they may within 30 days after the day on which they receive the application—

(a) refuse the application; or

(b) by notice to the applicant either require him to amend the application or require him to give them such further information as may be specified in the notice, and in either case to do so within such time, not exceeding 30 days after the day on which the notice is given, as may be so specified.

(3) If a notice under subsection (2) above is complied with and the Board are satisfied that the application complies with the requirements of this Chapter, the Board shall register the scheme before the beginning of the profit period.

(4) If a notice under subsection (2) above is complied with but remain not satisfied that the application complies with the requirements of this Chapter, the Board shall refuse the application.

(5) If a notice under subsection (2) above is not complied with but the Board are before the beginning of the profit period satisfied that the application complies with the requirements of this Chapter, the Board may register the scheme before the beginning of the period; but if they do not do so, the application shall be regarded as having been refused.

(6) If an application for registration of a profit-related pay scheme under this Chapter is made within the period of three months before the beginning of the profit period, or the first of the profit periods, to which the scheme relates, then—

(a) if before the beginning of the profit period the Board are satisfied that the application complies with the requirements of this Chapter, they shall register the scheme before the beginning of the period; but

(b) in any other case, the application shall be regarded as having been refused.

(7) After registering a scheme under this Chapter, the Board shall by notice inform the applicant that they have done so.

(8) The Board shall give notice to the applicant if they refuse his application under subsection (2) or (4) above.

(9) For the purposes of this section an application does not comply with the requirements of this Chapter if the scheme to which it relates does not comply with the requirements of Schedule 8.]²

Commentary—*Simon's Direct Tax Service* **E4.308.**
Former enactment—F(No 2)A 1987 s 8.
Definitions—''The Board'', s 832(1); ''notice'', s 832(1); ''profit period'', s 169(1); ''profit-related pay scheme'', s 169(1).
Cross reference—See TA 1988 s 182 (appeal against Board's refusal to register a scheme under sub-s (2) or (4) above).
Amendments—¹ Words in sub-s (1) repealed by FA 1989 Sch 4 para 10(2)(a) and Sch 17 Pt IV.
² This section repealed by FA 1997 Sch 18 Pt VI(3); see the corresponding note at the beginning of this Chapter.

[177 Change of scheme employer

(1) Where—

(a) a scheme employer ceases to fulfil the conditions which section 173 requires to be fulfilled by an applicant for registration of the scheme; and

(b) he is succeeded by a person who would be eligible to apply for registration to the scheme; and

(c) there is otherwise no other material change in the employment unit or in the circumstances relating to the scheme;

the scheme employer and his successor may make a joint written application to the Board under this section for the amendment of the registration of the scheme.

(2) If on receiving an application under this section the Board are satisfied—

(a) that the conditions in subsection (1)(a), (b) and (c) above are fulfilled; and

(b) that, apart from the change of scheme employer, there would be no grounds for cancelling the registration of the scheme,

the Board shall amend the registration of the scheme by substituting the successor for the previous scheme employer.

(3) An application under this section shall be made before the end of the period of one month beginning with the date of the succession.

(4) Where the Board amend the registration of a scheme under this section, this Chapter shall (subject to any necessary modifications) have effect as if the successor had been the scheme employer throughout.

(5) The Board shall give notice to the applicants if they refuse an application under this section.]¹

Commentary—*Simon's Direct Tax Service* **E4.311.**
Revenue Internal Guidance—Profit-related pay unit manual PRP 2.300–2.318 (detailed explanation of this section with examples).
Definitions—''The Board'', s 832(1); ''employment unit'', s 169(1); ''scheme employer'', s 169(1).
Cross reference—See TA 1988 s 182 (appeal against Board's refusal to register amendment).
Amendments—¹ This section repealed by FA 1997 Sch 18 Pt VI(3); see the corresponding note at the beginning of this Chapter.

[177A Death of scheme employer

(1) Where a scheme employer has died, his personal representatives may make a written application to the Board under this section for the amendment of the registration of the scheme.

(2) If on receiving an application under this section the Board are satisfied that, apart from the death of the scheme employer, there would be no grounds for cancelling the registration of the scheme, the Board shall amend the registration of the scheme by substituting the personal representatives for the deceased scheme employer.

(3) An application under this section shall be made before the end of the period of one month beginning with the date of the grant of probate or letters of administration or, in Scotland, confirmation of executors.

(4) Where the Board amend the registration of a scheme under this section, this Chapter shall (subject to any necessary modifications) have effect as if the personal representatives had been the scheme employer throughout.

(5) The Board shall give notice to the personal representatives if they refuse an application under this section.][1]

Commentary—*Simon's Direct Tax Service* **E4.311.**
Revenue Internal Guidance—Profit-related pay unit manual PRP 2.400–2.407 (responsibilities of personal representatives).
Cross reference—See TA 1988 s 182 (appeal against Board's refusal of an application under this section).
Amendments—[1] This section inserted by FA 1989 Sch 4 paras 1, 3 and repealed by FA 1997 Sch 18 Pt VI(3); see the corresponding note at the beginning of this Chapter.

[177B Alteration of scheme's terms

(1) The alteration of the terms of a registered scheme shall not of itself invalidate the registration of the scheme.

(2) Subsection (1) above is without prejudice to the power of cancellation conferred on the Board by section 178(3A); but the power conferred by section 178(3A) shall not be exercisable by virtue of an alteration registered in accordance with this section.

(3) Where the terms of a registered scheme have been altered, the scheme employer may apply to the Board for the registration of the alteration.

(4) An application under subsection (3) above—

> *(a) shall be in such form as the Board may prescribe;*
> *(b) shall be made within the period of one month beginning with the day on which the alteration is made;*
> *(c) shall contain a declaration by the applicant that the alteration is within subsection (8) below and that the scheme as altered complies with the requirements of Schedule 8 (either as that Schedule had effect when the scheme was registered, or as it then had effect but subject to one or more subsequent amendments specified in the declaration);*
> *(d) shall be accompanied by a report by an independent accountant, in a form prescribed by the Board, to the effect that in his opinion the alteration is within subsection (8) below and the scheme as altered complies with the requirements of Schedule 8 (either as that Schedule had effect when the scheme was registered, or as it then had effect but subject to one or more subsequent amendments specified in the report).*

(5) The Board shall not more than three months after the day on which they receive an application under subsection (3) above either register the alteration or refuse the application; and in either case they shall give notice of their decision to the applicant.

(6) Subject to subsection (7) below, the Board shall register an alteration on an application under subsection (3) above.

(7) The Board may refuse an application under subsection (3) above if they are not satisfied—

> *(a) that the application complies with the requirements of subsection (4) above, or*
> *(b) that the declaration referred to in subsection (4)(c) above is true.*

(8) An alteration is within this subsection if—

> *(a) it relates to a term which is not relevant to the question whether the scheme complies with the requirements of Schedule 8; or*
> *(b) it relates to a term identifying any person (other than the scheme employer) who pays the emoluments of employees to whom the scheme relates; or*
> *(c) it consists of the addition of a term making provision for an abbreviated profit period of the kind referred to in paragraph 10(3) of Schedule 8; or*
> *(d) it amends the provisions by reference to which the employees to whom the scheme relates may be identified, and does so only for the purposes of profit periods which begin after the date on which the alteration is made; or*
> *(e) it relates to a provision of a kind referred to in paragraph 13(4) or (5) or 14(3), (4) or (5) of Schedule 8 (as those provisions have effect at the time of the application for registration of the alteration), and has effect only for the purposes of profit periods beginning after the date on which the alteration is made; or*
> *(f) it amends the provisions as to when payments will be made to employees, and does so only for the purposes of profit periods beginning after the date on which the alteration is made; or*
> *(g) the scheme did not comply with the requirements of Schedule 8 when it was registered, and the alteration—*
>> *(i) is made in order to bring the scheme into compliance with the requirements of that Schedule (either as it had effect when the scheme was registered or as it has effect at the time of the application for registration of the alteration), and*
>> *(ii) is made for the purposes of the first and any subsequent profit period to which the scheme relates, and*
>> *(iii) is made within two years of the beginning of the first profit period, and*
>> *(iv) does not invalidate (in whole or in part) any payment of profit-related pay already made under the scheme.]*[1]

Commentary—*Simon's Direct Tax Service* **E4.308A.**
Cross references—See TA 1988 s 182 (appeal against Board's refusal to register alteration).
FA 1995 s 136(10) (alteration of existing profit-related pay scheme to take account of amendments made by s 136 to be treated as being within sub-s (8) above).
Amendments—[1] This section inserted by FA 1989 Sch 4 paras 1, 3 and repealed by FA 1997 Sch 18 Pt VI(3); see the corresponding note at the beginning of this Chapter.

[178 Cancellation of registration

(1) If after a scheme has been registered under this Chapter it appears to the Board—

(a) that the scheme has not been or will not be administered in accordance with [its terms or in accordance with]¹ this Chapter in relation to a profit period; or
(b) that the circumstances relating to the scheme have during a profit period become such that (if it were not registered) an application to register it under this Chapter would be excluded by section 174; or
(c) in the case of a scheme which employs (as the method of determining the distributable pool for a profit period) the method described as method B in paragraph 14 of Schedule 8, that losses were incurred in a profit period or in the preceding period of 12 months; ...⁵
(d) ...⁵

the Board may cancel the registration and, subject to [subsections (5) and (5A)]² below, the cancellation shall have effect from the beginning of that profit period.

(2) If after a scheme has been registered under this Chapter it appears to the Board—

(a) that at the time of registration the scheme did not comply with the requirements of Schedule 8 or that the application did not comply with the requirements of this Chapter; ...⁴
(b) ...⁴

the Board may cancel the registration with effect from the beginning of the profit period (or first profit period) to which the scheme related.

(3) If after a scheme has been registered under this Chapter the scheme employer fails to comply with the requirements of section 180 in relation to a profit period, the Board may cancel the registration with effect from the beginning of that profit period.

[(3A) Where the terms of a registered scheme have been altered, then, subject to section 177B(2), the Board may cancel the registration of the scheme with effect from the beginning of the profit period during which the alteration took effect or with effect from the beginning of any later profit period.]³

[(3B) If after an alteration of the terms of a scheme has been registered under section 177B it appears to the Board—

(a) that the application for registration of the alteration did not comply with the requirements of subsection (4) of that section, or
(b) that the declaration referred to in subsection (4)(c) of that section was false,

the Board may cancel the registration of the scheme with effect from the beginning of the profit period during which the alteration took effect or with effect from the beginning of any later profit period.]³

(4) If the scheme employer by notice requests the Board to cancel the registration of the scheme with effect from the beginning of a profit period specified in the notice, the Board shall comply with the request.

(5) Where—

(a) the scheme employer has given to the Board in accordance with section 181(3) notice of a change in the employment unit, or in the circumstances relating to the scheme, which is a ground for cancellation of the registration of the scheme by virtue of subsection (1)(a) or (b) above, and
(b) the Board are satisfied that the change is not brought about with a view to the registration of a new scheme, and
(c) in the notice the scheme employer requests the Board to cancel the registration of the scheme with effect from the date of the change,

then, if the notice is given before the end of the period of one month beginning with that day, the Board shall comply with the request.

[(5A) Where—

(a) the scheme employer has died, and
(b) his personal representatives by notice request the Board to cancel the registration of the scheme with effect from the date of death,

then, if the notice is given before the end of the period of one month beginning with the date of the grant of probate or letters of administration or, in Scotland, confirmation of executors, the Board shall comply with the request.]³

(6) The Board shall give notice to the scheme employer of the cancellation of a scheme's registration.]⁶

Commentary—*Simon's Direct Tax Service* E4.310.
Concession B33—Subject to certain conditions, a scheme registered before 3 February 1989 will not be cancelled on the grounds that all employees cannot participate in it on similar terms.
Simon's Tax Cases—s 178(5), *Colours Ltd (formerly Spectrum Ltd) v IRC*, [1998] STC (SCD) 93.
Definitions—"The Board", s 832(1); "employment", s 169(1); "employment unit", s 169(1); "losses", s 169(1); "notice", s 832(1); "profit period", s 169(1); "scheme employer", s 169(1).
Amendments—¹ Words in sub-s (1)(a) inserted by FA 1988 Sch 13 para 4.

² Words in sub-s (1) substituted by FA 1989 Sch 4 para 4(1), (2).
³ Sub-ss (3A), (3B), (5A) inserted by FA 1989 Sch 4 para 4(1), (3), (4).
⁴ Sub-s (2)(*b*) and the word "or" preceding it repealed by FA 1989 Sch 4 para 10(2)(*a*) and Sch 17 Pt IV.
⁵ Sub-s (1)(*d*) and preceding word "or" repealed by FA 1999 ss 46(2), (3), 139, Sch 20 Pt III(10) with effect only for failures to comply taking place after 27 July 1998; but deemed so to have had effect at all times after that date.
⁶ This section repealed by FA 1997 Sch 18 Pt VI(3); see the corresponding note at the beginning of this Chapter.

Administration

[179 Recovery of tax from scheme employer

(1) This section applies where—

(a) payments of profit-related pay are made to an employee in accordance with a registered scheme; and

(b) in consequence of the relief given by this Chapter in respect of registered schemes, less income tax is deducted from the payments in accordance with section 203 than would have been deducted if the scheme had not been registered; and

(c) the registration of the scheme is subsequently cancelled with effect from a time before that relevant for the purposes of the relief.

(2) Where this section applies, an amount equal to the shortfall in the deductions made in accordance with section 203 shall be payable by the scheme employer to the Board; and regulations under that section may include provision as to the collection and recovery of any such amount.

[(3) Where—

(a) the scheme employer has died, but

(b) his personal representatives have not been substituted for him as the scheme employer by virtue of section 177A,

the reference in subsection (2) above to the scheme employer shall be construed as a reference to the personal representatives.]¹

[(4) Where—

(a) a payment to which this section applies was made by a person other than the scheme employer, and

(b) the scheme employer is not resident in the United Kingdom,

then in relation to that payment the reference in subsection (2) above to the scheme employer shall include a reference to the person by whom the payment was made.]¹]²

Commentary—*Simon's Direct Tax Service* **E4.313.**
Definitions—"The Board", s 832(1); "profit-related pay", s 169(1); "registered scheme", s 169(1); "scheme employer", s 169(1).
Amendments—¹ Sub-ss (3), (4) inserted by FA 1989 Sch 4 para 5.
² This section repealed by FA 1997 Sch 18 Pt VI(3); see the corresponding note at the beginning of this Chapter.

[180 Annual returns etc

(1) After every profit period of a registered scheme, the scheme employer shall, within the period allowed by subsection (2) below, send to the Board—

(a) a return in such form and containing such information as the Board may prescribe; and

(b) a report by an independent accountant in such form and containing such information as the Board may prescribe and stating that in his opinion the terms of the scheme have been complied with in respect of the profit period.

(2) Subject to subsection (3) below, the period allowed for complying with subsection (1) above is—

(a) seven months from the end of the profit period if the employment unit to which the scheme relates is an undertaking or part of an undertaking of a public company; and

(b) ten months from the end of the profit period in any other case.

(3) If before the end of the period allowed by subsection (2) above the scheme employer gives the Board notice that an extension of three months has been allowed under [section 244(3)]² of the Companies Act 1985 or under [Article 252(3)]³ of the Companies (Northern Ireland) Order 1986, in relation to a financial year of the employer which corresponds with the profit period in question, then the period allowed by subsection (2) above shall be correspondingly extended.

(4) In subsection (2)(a) above, "public company" has the meaning given by section 1(3) of the Companies Act 1985 or Article 12(3) of the Companies (Northern Ireland) Order 1986.

[(5) Where—

(a) the scheme employer has died, but

(b) his personal representatives have not been substituted for him as the scheme employer by virtue of section 177A,

the reference in subsection (1) above to the scheme employer shall be construed as a reference to the personal representatives.]¹]⁴

Commentary—*Simon's Direct Tax Service* **A3.117; E4.309.**
Definitions—"The Board", s 832(1); "employment unit", s 169(1); "independent accountant", s 184; "notice", s 832(1); "profit period", s 169(1); "registered scheme", s 169(1); "scheme employer", s 169(1).
Amendments—¹ Sub-s (5) inserted by FA 1989 Sch 4 para 6.
² Words in sub-s (3) substituted by the Companies Act 1989 Sch 10 para 38 with effect from 1 April 1990 by virtue of the Companies Act 1989 (Commencement No 4, Transitional and Savings Provisions) Order, SI 1990/355.
³ Words in sub-s (3) substituted by the Companies (Northern Ireland) Order 1990, SI 1990/593 Sch 10 para 30(1).
⁴ This section repealed by FA 1997 Sch 18 Pt VI(3); see the corresponding note at the beginning of this Chapter.

[181 Other information

(1) The Board may by notice require any person to give them, within a period of 30 days or such longer period as may be specified in the notice, any information which is so specified and which—

(a) that person has or can reasonably be required to obtain; and
(b) the Board consider they need to have in order to perform their functions under this Chapter.

(2) Without prejudice to the generality of subsection (1)(b) above, the Board may in particular require a person under subsection (1) to give them—

(a) information to enable them to determine whether the registration of a scheme should be cancelled;
(b) information to enable them to determine the liability to tax of any person who is or has been an employee to whom a registered scheme relates or who pays or has paid emoluments to such an employee;
(c) information about the administration of a profit-related pay scheme which is or has been a registered scheme;
(d) information about any change of person paying emoluments to employees to whom a registered scheme relates.

(3) The scheme employer of a registered scheme shall by notice inform the Board without delay if he becomes aware of anything that is or may be a ground for cancellation of the registration of the scheme.

[(4) Where the scheme employer has died, his personal representatives shall inform the Board of his death by notice given before the end of the period of one month beginning with the date of the grant of probate or letters of administration or, in Scotland, confirmation of executors.]¹]²

Commentary—*Simon's Direct Tax Service* **A3.117; E4.309.**
Definitions—"The Board", s 832(1); "emoluments", s 131(1); "employees to whom a registered scheme relates", s 169(2); "notice", s 832(1); "profit-related pay scheme", s 169(1); "registered scheme", s 169(1); "scheme employer", s 169(1); "tax", s 832(3).
Amendments—¹ Sub-s (4) inserted by FA 1989 Sch 4 para 7.
² This section repealed by FA 1997 Sch 18 Pt VI(3); see the corresponding note at the beginning of this Chapter.

[182 Appeals

(1) An appeal to the Special Commissioners may be made by a scheme employer—

(a) against a refusal by the Board under section 176(2) or (4) of an application for registration of the scheme;
(b) against a refusal by the Board of an application under section 177;
[(bb) against a refusal by the Board of an application under section 177B(3);]¹
(c) against the cancellation by the Board of the registration of the scheme.

[(1A) An appeal to the Special Commissioners may be made by the personal representatives of a scheme employer against a refusal by the Board of an application under section 177A.]¹

(2) An appeal under this section shall be made by notice given to the Board within 30 days of the day on which the [appellant]² was notified of the refusal or, as the case may be, the cancellation.]³

Commentary—*Simon's Direct Tax Service* **E4.308, 310, 311.**
Definitions—"The Board", s 832(1); "notice", s 832(1); "scheme employer", s 169(1).
Amendments—¹ Sub-ss (1)(bb), (1A) inserted by FA 1989 Sch 4 para 8(1), (2), (3).
² Word in sub-s (2) substituted by FA 1989 Sch 4 para 8(1), (4).
³ This section repealed by FA 1997 Sch 18 Pt VI(3); see the corresponding note at the beginning of this Chapter.

Supplementary

[183 Partnerships

For the purposes of this Chapter the members of a partnership which is a scheme employer shall be treated as a single continuing body of persons notwithstanding any change in their identity.]¹

Commentary—*Simon's Direct Tax Service* **E4.303.**
Revenue Internal Guidance—Profit-related pay unit manual PRP 2.111 (status of salaried partners).
Definition—"Scheme employer", s 169(1).
Amendments—¹ This section repealed by FA 1997 Sch 18 Pt VI(3); see the corresponding note at the beginning of this Chapter.

[184 Independent accountants

(1) For the purposes of this Chapter, "independent accountant", in relation to a profit-related pay scheme, means a person who—

(a) [is eligible for appointment as a company auditor under section 25 of the Companies Act 1989]¹ [or Article 28 of the Companies (Northern Ireland) Order 1990]⁴; and
(b) is not excluded by subsections (2) to [(4)]¹ below.

(2) A person is not an independent accountant in relation to a profit-related pay scheme if—

    (a) he is the employer of employees to whom the scheme relates; or

    (b) he is a partner[, or an officer][2] or an employee of, or partner of an employee of, a person within subsection (3) below; or

    (c) he is [a partner or][2] an employee of a person within paragraph *(b)* above.

(3) The persons within this subsection are—

    (a) any person having employees to whom the scheme relates;

    (b) any body corporate which is the subsidiary or holding company of a body corporate within paragraph *(a)* above or a subsidiary of such a body's holding company.

(4) For the purposes of this section—

    (a) an auditor of a company is not to be regarded as an [officer or][2] employee of it; and

    (b) "holding company" and "subsidiary" are to be construed in accordance with section 736 of the Companies Act 1985 or Article 4 of the Companies (Northern Ireland) Order 1986.

(5) ...[3]

(6) ...[5]][6]

Commentary—*Simon's Direct Tax Service* **E4.308.**
Definitions—"Employees to whom the scheme relates", s 169(2); "profit-related pay scheme", s 169(1).
Amendments—[1] Words in sub-s (1)(a), (b) substituted by the Companies Act 1989 (Eligibility for Appointment as Company Auditor) (Consequential Amendments) Regulations, SI 1991/1997 Schedule para 68, subject to following transitional provision in reg 4—

"**4** None of the amendments specified in the Schedule to these Regulations shall have the effect that a person is required to resign from or otherwise surrender an appointment, or that the appointment of a person must be terminated, before the date on which the person's appointment would, apart from these Regulations, have expired."
[2] Words in sub-ss (2)(b), (c), (4)(a) inserted by the Companies Act 1989 (Eligibility for Appointment as Company Auditor) (Consequential Amendments) Regulations, SI 1991/1997 Schedule para 68, subject to the transitional provision in reg 4.
[3] Sub-s (5) repealed by the Companies Act 1989 (Eligibility for Appointment as Company Auditor) (Consequential Amendments) Regulations, SI 1991/1997 Schedule para 68, subject to the transitional provision in reg 4.
[4] Words in sub-s (1)(a) substituted by the Companies (1990 Order) (Eligibility for Appointment as Company Auditor) (Consequential Amendments) Regulations (Northern Ireland) 1993, S.R. 1993/No 67, reg 2, Schedule para 18, subject to savings and transitional provisions contained in regs 3, 4 thereof making provision as to the effect when a partnership which is not a legal person is appointed as a company auditor and provision concerning the position of persons holding an appointment as company auditor on 29 March 1993.
[5] Sub-s (6) repealed by the Companies Act 1989 Part II (Consequential Amendments) Regulations, SI 1995/1163 reg 3 with effect from 23 May 1995.
[6] This section repealed by FA 1997 Sch 18 Pt VI(3); see the corresponding note at the beginning of this Chapter.

CHAPTER IV

OTHER EXEMPTIONS AND RELIEFS

Share option and profit sharing schemes

185 Approved share option schemes

(1) The provisions of this section shall apply where, in accordance with the provisions of an approved share option scheme, an individual obtains a right to acquire shares in a body corporate by reason of his office or employment as a director or employee of that or any other body corporate and he obtains that right—

    (a) in the case of a savings-related share option scheme, on or after 15th November 1980; or

    (b) in the case of any other share option scheme, on or after 6th April 1984.

(2) [Subject to subsection (6) below][4], tax shall not be chargeable under any provision of the Tax Acts in respect of the receipt of the right.

(3) Subject to subsections (4) and, except where paragraph 27(3) of Schedule 9 applies, (5) below, if he exercises the right in accordance with the provisions of the scheme at a time when it is approved—

    (a) tax shall not be chargeable under any provision of the Tax Acts in respect of the exercise nor under [section 78 or 79 of the Finance Act 1988 in respect of the shares][1];

    (b) section [17(1) of the 1992 Act][3] (assets deemed to be acquired at market value) shall not apply in calculating the consideration for the acquisition of the shares by him or for any corresponding disposal of them to him.

(4) [Subsection (3) above][2] shall not apply in respect of a right, obtained by a person under a scheme which is a savings-related share option scheme, which is exercised within three years of its being obtained by virtue of a provision included in a scheme pursuant to paragraph 21 of Schedule 9.

(5) Subsection (3) above shall not apply in relation to the exercise by any person of a right in accordance with the provisions of a scheme which is not a savings-related share option scheme if—

    (a) the period beginning with his obtaining the right and ending with his exercising it is less than three, or greater than ten, years; or

    (b) the right is exercised within three years of the date on which he last exercised (in circumstances in which subsection (3) above applied) any right obtained under the scheme or under any other approved share option scheme which is not a savings-related share option scheme (any such right exercised on the same day being disregarded).

[(6) Where, in the case of a right obtained by a person under a scheme which is not a savings-related share option scheme, the aggregate of—

   (*a*) the amount or value of any consideration given by him for obtaining the right, and
   (*b*) the price at which he may acquire the shares by exercising the right,

is less than the market value, at the time he obtains the right, of the same quantity of issued shares of the same class, he shall be chargeable to tax under Schedule E for the year of assessment in which he obtains the right on the amount of the difference; and the amount so chargeable shall be treated as earned income, whether or not it would otherwise fall to be so treated.]⁴

(7) For the purposes of section [38(1)(*a*) of the 1992 Act]³ (computation of chargeable gains: allowable expenditure) the consideration given for shares acquired in the exercise of the right shall be taken to have included that part of any amount on which income tax is payable in accordance with subsection [(6)]⁴ above which is attributable to the shares disposed of.

This subsection applies whether or not the exercise is in accordance with the provisions of the scheme and whether or not the scheme is approved at the time of the exercise.

(8) Where a person is chargeable to tax under subsection [(6)]⁴ above on any amount (the ''amount of the discount'') and subsequently, in circumstances in which subsection (3) above does not apply—

   (*a*) he is chargeable to tax under section 135, the amount of the gain on which he is chargeable to tax under that section shall be reduced by that part of the amount of the discount which is attributable to the shares in question; or
   (*b*) he is treated by virtue of section 162 as having had the benefit of a notional interest-free loan, the amount of the notional loan initially outstanding shall be reduced by that part of the amount of the discount which is attributable to the shares in question.

(9) Where the provisions of a scheme which is not a savings-related share option scheme are approved in pursuance of an application made under paragraph 1 of Schedule 10 to the Finance Act 1984 before 1st January 1985 (and the approval has not been withdrawn), this section shall apply in relation to any right obtained before 1st July 1985 as if the scheme containing those provisions had been approved under that Schedule during the period beginning with the date on which that right was obtained and ending with the date on which those provisions were actually so approved.

(10) In this section ''savings-related share option scheme'' has the meaning given by Schedule 9.

Commentary—*Simon's Direct Tax Service* E4.578, 588.
Revenue Decision RD5—Linkage between approved discretionary employee share option scheme and ''phantom'' share scheme.
Revenue & other press releases—IR Booklet IR 97 (Approved SAYE share option schemes).
IR Booklet IR 98 (Approved SAYE share option schemes—explanatory note).
IR Booklet IR 101 (Approved company share option plans).
IR Booklet IR 102 (Approved company share option plans—explanatory notes).
Revenue Internal Guidance—Share Schemes Manual SSM 2.34 (sub-s (4): Revenue interpretation of this sub-section).
SSM 2.96–2.97 (worked examples covering the effects of the exercise of a share option (with or without tax relief) and late sale of shares).
Simon's Tax Cases—*IRC v Reed International plc* [1995] STC 889.
s 185(1), *IRC v Burton Group plc* [1990] STC 242; *IRC v Eurocopy plc* [1991] STC 707; *Cricket plc v Inspector of Taxes* [1998] STC (SCD) 10.
Definitions—''the 1992 Act'', s 831(3); ''approved'', s 187(2); ''earned income'', s 833(4), (5); ''market value'', s 187(2); ''savings-related share option scheme'', s 187(2); ''Schedule E'', s 19(1); ''scheme'', s 187(2); ''shares'', s 187(2); ''tax'', s 832(3); ''the Tax Acts'', s 831(2); ''year of assessment'', s 832(1).
Cross references—See TA 1988 s 162(2) (extension of this section where shares are sold to directors or higher-paid employees at an under-value).
TA 1988 s 187 (interpretation of this section).
TCGA 1992 s 120(6) (relief for chargeable gains accruing on disposal of shares acquired in exercise of a right under sub-s (1) above and chargeable to tax under sub-s (6) above).
Amendments—¹ Words in sub-s (3)(*a*) substituted by FA 1988 s 89 in relation to acquisitions after 25 October 1987.
² Words in sub-s (4) substituted by FA 1991 s 39(2), (4), (8) in relation to rights obtained after 31 December 1991.
³ Words in sub-ss (3)(*b*), (7) substituted by TCGA 1992 Sch 10 para 14(1), (12).
⁴ Words in sub-ss (2), (7), (8) and whole of sub-s (6) substituted by FA 1996 s 114 with effect in relation to rights obtained after 28 April 1996.

186 Approved profit sharing schemes

(1) The provisions of this section apply where, after 5th April 1979 [and before 1st January 2003]⁴, the trustees of an approved profit sharing scheme appropriate shares—

   (*a*) which have previously been acquired by the trustees, and
   (*b*) as to which the conditions in Part II of Schedule 9 are fulfilled,

to an individual who participates in the scheme (''the participant'').

(2) Notwithstanding that, by virtue of such an appropriation of shares as is mentioned in subsection (1) above, the beneficial interest in the shares passes to the participant to whom they are appropriated—

   (*a*) the value of the shares at the time of the appropriation shall be treated as not being income of his chargeable to tax under Schedule E; and
   (*b*) he shall not be chargeable to income tax under that Schedule by virtue of [section 78 or 79 of the Finance Act 1988 in respect of the shares]¹ or by virtue of section 162 in any case where the shares are appropriated to him at an under-value within the meaning of that section.

(3) Subject to the provisions of this section and paragraph 4 of Schedule 10, if, in respect of or by reference to any of a participant's shares, the trustees become or the participant becomes entitled, before the release date, to receive any money or money's worth ("a capital receipt"), the participant shall be chargeable to income tax under Schedule E for the year of assessment in which the entitlement arises on the appropriate percentage (determined as at the time the trustees become or the participant becomes so entitled) of so much of the amount or value of the receipt as exceeds the appropriate allowance for that year, as determined under subsection (12) below.

(4) If the trustees dispose of any of a participant's shares at any time before the release date or, if it is earlier, the date of the participant's death, then, subject to subsections (6) and (7) below, the participant shall be chargeable to income tax under Schedule E for the year of assessment in which the disposal takes place on the appropriate percentage of the locked-in value of the shares at the time of the disposal.

(5) Subject to paragraphs 5 and 6(6) of Schedule 10, the locked-in value of a participant's shares at any time is—

    (*a*) if prior to that time he has become chargeable to income tax by virtue of subsection (3) above on a percentage of the amount or value of any capital receipt which is referable to those shares, the amount by which their initial market value exceeds the amount or value of that capital receipt or, if there has been more than one such receipt, the aggregate of them; and

    (*b*) in any other case, their initial market value.

(6) Subject to subsection (7) below, if, on a disposal of shares falling within subsection (4) above, the proceeds of the disposal are less than the locked-in value of the shares at the time of the disposal, subsection (4) above shall have effect as if that locked-in value were reduced to an amount equal to the proceeds of the disposal.

(7) If, at any time prior to the disposal of any of a participant's shares, a payment was made to the trustees to enable them to exercise rights arising under a rights issue, then, subject to subsection (8) below, subsections (4) and (6) above shall have effect as if the proceeds of the disposal were reduced by an amount equal to that proportion of that payment or, if there was more than one, of the aggregate of those payments which, immediately before the disposal, the market value of the shares disposed of bore to the market value of all the participant's shares held by the trustees at that time.

(8) For the purposes of subsection (7) above—

    (*a*) no account shall be taken of any payment to the trustees if or to the extent that it consists of the proceeds of a disposal of rights arising under a rights issue; and

    (*b*) in relation to a particular disposal the amount of the payment or, as the case may be, of the aggregate of the payments referred to in that subsection shall be taken to be reduced by an amount equal to the total of the reduction (if any) previously made under that subsection in relation to earlier disposals;

and any reference in subsection (7) or paragraph (*a*) above to the rights arising under a rights issue is a reference to rights conferred in respect of a participant's shares, being rights to be allotted, on payment, other shares or securities or rights of any description in the same company.

(9) If at any time the participant's beneficial interest in any of his shares is disposed of, the shares in question shall be treated for the purposes of the relevant provisions as having been disposed of at that time by the trustees for (subject to subsection (10) below) the like consideration as was obtained for the disposal of the beneficial interest; and for the purposes of this subsection there is no disposal of the participant's beneficial interest if and at the time when—

    (*a*) in England and Wales or Northern Ireland, that interest becomes vested in any person on the insolvency of the participant or otherwise by operation of law, or

    (*b*) in Scotland, that interest becomes vested in a judicial factor, in a trustee on the participant's sequestrated estate or in a trustee for the benefit of the participant's creditors.

(10) If—

    (*a*) a disposal of shares falling with subsection (4) above is a transfer to which paragraph 2(2)(*c*) of Schedule 9 applies, or

    [(*b*) any other disposal falling within that subsection is not at arm's length,]²

    (*c*) a disposal of shares falling within [that subsection]² is one which is treated as taking place by virtue of subsection (9) above and takes place within the period of retention,

then for the purposes of the relevant provisions the proceeds of the disposal shall be taken to be equal to the market value of the shares at the time of the disposal.

(11) Where the trustees of an approved scheme acquire any shares as to which the requirements of Part II of Schedule 9 are fulfilled and, within the period of 18 months beginning with the date of their acquisition, those shares are appropriated in accordance with the scheme, section 686 shall not apply to income consisting of dividends on those shares received by the trustees; and, for the purpose of determining whether any shares are appropriated within that period, shares which were acquired at an earlier time shall be taken to be appropriated before shares of the same class which were acquired at a later time.

(12) For the purposes of subsection (3) above, "the appropriate allowance", in relation to any year of assessment, means a sum which, subject to a maximum of [£60]³, is the product of multiplying

£20 by 1 plus the number of years which fall within the period of [three years][3] immediately preceding the year in question and in which shares were appropriated to the participant under the scheme; and if in any year (and before the release date) the trustees become or the participant becomes entitled, in respect of or by reference to any of his shares, to more than one capital receipt, the receipts shall be set against the appropriate allowance for that year in the order in which they are received.

(13) Schedule 10 shall have effect with respect to profit sharing schemes.

Commentary—*Simon's Direct Tax Service* E4.561–563.
Revenue & other press releases—IR Booklet IR 95 (Approved profit sharing schemes).
IR Booklet IR 96 (Approved profit sharing schemes—explanatory notes).
Definitions—''Appropriate percentage'', s 187(2); ''approved'', s 187(2); ''capital receipt'', s 187(2); ''initial market value'', s 187(2); ''locked-in value'', s 187(2); ''market value'', s 187(2); ''participant'', s 187(2); ''participant's shares'', s 187(2); ''period of retention'', s 187(2); ''release date'', s 187(2); ''the relevant provisions'', s 187(2); ''Schedule E'', s 19(1); ''scheme'', s 187(2); ''shares'', s 187(2); ''the trustees'', s 187(2); ''year of assessment'', s 832(1).
Cross references—See TA 1988 s 162(2) (extension of this section where shares are sold to directors or higher-paid employees at an under-value).
TA 1988 s 187 (interpretation).
TCGA 1992 s 238(2)(*a*) (for capital gains tax, no deduction to be made from the consideration for disposal of shares by reason only that an amount determined under this section is chargeable to income tax under sub-s (3) or (4) above).
TCGA 1992 s 238(2)(*b*) (any charge to income tax by virtue of sub-s (3) above to be disregarded in determining whether a distribution is a capital distribution).
TCGA 1992 s 238(2)(*c*) (part disposal of a holding of shares or other securities acquired at different times).
TCGA 1992 s 238(2)(*d*) (a gain accruing on an appropriation of shares to which sub-s (11) above applies not to be a chargeable gain).
Amendments—[1] Words in sub-s (2)(*b*) substituted by FA 1988 s 89 in relation to acquisitions after 25 October 1987.
[2] Sub-s (10)(*b*) and words in sub-s (10)(*c*) substituted by FA 1996 Sch 20 para 11 with effect from the year 1996–97.
[3] Words in sub-s (12) substituted by FA 1996 s 118 with effect from the year 1997–98.
[4] Words in sub-s (1) inserted by FA 2000 s 49(3) with effect from 28 July 2000.

187 Interpretation of sections 185 and 186 and Schedules 9 and 10

(1) In sections 185 and 186, this section and Schedules 9 and 10 ''the relevant provisions'' means those sections (including this section) and Schedules.

(2) For the purposes of the relevant provisions, except where the context otherwise requires—

''appropriate percentage'' shall be construed in accordance with paragraph 3 of Schedule 10;
''approved'', in relation to a scheme, means approved under Schedule 9;
''associated company'' has the same meaning as in section 416, except that, for the purposes of paragraph 23 of Schedule 9, subsection (1) of that section shall have effect with the omission of the words ''or at any time within one year previously'';
''bonus date'' has the meaning given by paragraph 17 of Schedule 9;
''capital receipt'' means money or money's worth to which the trustees of or a participant in a profit sharing scheme become or becomes entitled as mentioned in section 186(3), but subject to paragraph 4 of Schedule 10;
''certified contractual savings scheme'' has the meaning given by section 326;
''control'' has the same meaning as in section 840;
''grantor'', in relation to any scheme, means the company which has established the scheme;
''group scheme'' and, in relation to such a scheme, ''participating company'' have the meanings given by paragraph 1(3) and (4) of Schedule 9;
''initial market value'', in relation to shares in a profit sharing scheme, has the meaning given by paragraph 30(4) of Schedule 9;
''locked-in value'', in relation to any shares, shall be construed in accordance with section 186(5);
''market value'' has the same meaning as in Part VIII of the [1992][5] Act;
''new holding'' has the meaning given by section [126(1)(*b*) of the 1992 Act][5];
''participant'', in relation to a profit sharing scheme, means an individual to whom the trustees of the scheme have appropriated shares;
''participant's shares'', in relation to a participant in a profit sharing scheme, means, subject to paragraph 5(4) of Schedule 10, shares which have been appropriated to the participant by the trustees;
...[6];
''period of retention'' has the meaning given by paragraph 2 of Schedule 10;
''release date'', in relation to any of the shares of a participant in a profit sharing scheme, means the [third][7] anniversary of the date on which they were appropriated to him;
''relevant amount'', in relation to a participant in a profit sharing scheme, means an amount which is [not less than £3,000 and not more than £8,000][3] but which, subject to that, is 10 per cent of his salary (determined under subsection (5) below) for the year of assessment in question or the preceding year of assessment, whichever is the greater;
''relevant requirements'' has the meaning given by paragraph 1 of Schedule 9;
''savings-related share option scheme'' has the meaning given by paragraph 1 of Schedule 9;
''scheme'' means a savings-related share option scheme, a share option scheme which is not a savings-related share option scheme or a profit sharing scheme, as the context may require;
''shares'' includes stock;
[''specified age'', in relation to a scheme, means the age specified in pursuance of paragraph 8A of Schedule 9 as the specified age for the purposes of the scheme;][4]

"the trustees", in relation to an approved profit sharing scheme or the shares of a participant in such a scheme, means the body of persons for the establishment of which the scheme must provide as mentioned in paragraph 30 of Schedule 9; and

"the trust instrument", in relation to an approved profit sharing scheme, means the instrument referred to in paragraph 30(1)(c) of Schedule 9.

(3) For the purposes of the application of the relevant provisions in relation to any share option scheme or profit sharing scheme, a person has a material interest [in a company if he, either on his own or with one or more associates, or if any associate of his with or without such other associates,—

[(a) is the beneficial owner of, or able, directly or through the medium of other companies, or by any other indirect means to control, more than 25 per cent or, in the case of a share option scheme which is not a savings-related share option scheme, more than 10 per cent, of the ordinary share capital of the company, or

(b) where the company is a close company, possesses, or is entitled to acquire, such rights as would, in the event of the winding-up of the company or in any other circumstances, give an entitlement to receive more than 25 per cent, or in the case of a share option scheme which is not a savings-related share option scheme more than 10 per cent, of the assets which would then be available for distribution among the participators.]]¹

In this subsection "associate" has the meaning given by section 417(3) and (4) [and "participator" has the meaning given by section 417(1)]².

(4) Subsection (3) above shall have effect subject to the provisions of Part VI of Schedule 9.

(5) For the purposes of subsection (2) above, a participant's salary for a year of assessment means such of the emoluments of the office or employment by virtue of which he is entitled to participate in a profit sharing scheme as are liable to be paid in that year under deduction of tax pursuant to section 203 after deducting therefrom amounts included by virtue of Chapter II of this Part.

(6) Section 839 shall apply for the purposes of the relevant provisions.

(7) For the purposes of the relevant provisions a company is a member of a consortium owning another company if it is one of a number of companies which between them beneficially own not less than three-quarters of the other company's ordinary share capital and each of which beneficially owns not less than one-twentieth of that capital.

(8) Where the disposal referred to in section 186(4) is made from a holding of shares which were appropriated to the participant at different times, then, in determining for the purposes of the relevant provisions—

(a) the initial market value and the locked-in value of each of those shares, ...⁸

(b) ...⁸

the disposal shall be treated as being of shares which were appropriated earlier before those which were appropriated later.

(9) Any of the relevant provisions with respect to—

(a) the order in which any of a participant's shares are to be treated as disposed of for the purposes of those provisions, or

(b) the shares in relation to which an event is to be treated as occurring for any such purpose,

shall have effect in relation to a profit sharing scheme notwithstanding any direction given to the trustees with respect to shares of a particular description or to shares appropriated to the participant at a particular time.

(10) In the relevant provisions "workers' co-operative" means a registered industrial and provident society, within the meaning of section 486, which is a co-operative society and the rules of which include provisions which secure—

(a) that the only persons who may be members of it are those who are employed by, or by a subsidiary of, the society and those who are the trustees of its profit sharing scheme; and

(b) that, subject to any provision about qualifications for membership which is from time to time made by the members of the society by reference to age, length of service or other factors of any description, all such persons may be members of the society;

and in this subsection "co-operative society" has the same meaning as in section 1 of the Industrial and Provident Societies Act 1965 or, as the case may be, the Industrial and Provident Societies (Northern Ireland) Act 1969.

Commentary—*Simon's Direct Tax Service* **E4.563.**
Revenue & other press releases—ICAEW TR511 August 1983 ("salary" in sub-s (5) means salary net of pension contributions).
Note—SSA 1975 Sch 20 referred to in the definition of "pensionable age" in sub-s (2) is re-enacted in Social Security Contributions and Benefits Act 1992 s 122(1).
Definitions—"the 1992 Act", s 831(3); "Body of persons", s 832(1); "company", s 832(1), (2); "emoluments", s 131(1); "ordinary share capital", s 832(1); "year of assessment", s 832(1).
Cross references—See TA 1988 Sch 10 para 6(4) (charge to tax under Schedule E in respect of profit-sharing scheme shares to be applied first to shares that are not excess or unauthorised but without prejudice to sub-s (8) above).
TCGA 1992 s 238(2)(a) (for capital gains tax, no deduction to be made from the consideration for disposal of shares by reason only that an amount determined under this section is chargeable to income tax under s 186(3) or (4) of this Act).
TCGA 1992 s 238(2)(c) (part disposal of a holding of shares or other securities acquired at different times).
Amendments—¹ Sub-s (3)(a) (and the preceding words), (b) substituted by FA 1989 Sch 12 para 9 in relation to accounting periods beginning after 31 March 1989.
² Words in sub-s (3) added by FA 1989 Sch 12 para 9 in relation to accounting periods beginning after 31 March 1989.

³ In sub-s (2) in the definition of "relevant amount" words substituted by FA 1991 s 41 with effect from the year 1991–92.
⁴ Definition of "specified age" in sub-s (2) inserted by FA 1991 s 38(4).
⁵ Year in the definition of "market value" and words in the definition of "new holding" in sub-s (2) substituted by TCGA 1992 Sch 10 para 14(1), (13).
⁶ Definition of "pensionable age" in sub-s (2) repealed by the Pensions Act 1995 Sch 4 Pt III para 12(a), Sch 7 Pt II with effect from 19 July 1995.
⁷ Word "third" in sub-s (2) the definition of "release date" substituted for word "fifth" by FA 1996 s 116(1) with effect in relation to shares of a participant in a profit sharing scheme if the third anniversary of the appropriation of the shares to the participant occurs on or after 29 April 1996. By virtue of FA 1996 s 116(3), if the third anniversary of the appropriation of any shares to a participant in a profit sharing scheme has occurred, but the fifth anniversary of their appropriation to him has not occurred, before that date, then, in the application of ss 186 and 187 of, and Schs 9 and 10 to, this Act in relation to those shares, the release date shall be 29 April 1996.
⁸ Words omitted in sub-s (8)(a) and sub-s (8)(b) repealed by FA 1996 s 117(2), Sch 41 Pt V(5) with effect in relation to the occurrence, on or after 29 April 1996, of events by reason of whose occurrence any provision of s 186 or 187 of, or Sch 9 or 10 to, this Act charges an individual to income tax under Schedule E.

[Contributions in respect of share option gains

187A Relief for contributions in respect of share option gains

(1) Where a person ("the earner") is chargeable of tax under section 135 on a gain, relief is available under this section if—

(a) an agreement has been entered into allowing the secondary contributor to recover from the earner the whole or part of any secondary Class 1 contributions in respect of the gain, or

(b) an election is in force which has the effect of transferring to the earner the whole or part of the liability to pay secondary Class 1 contributions in respect of the gain.

(2) The amount of the relief is the total of—

(a) any amount that, in pursuance of any such agreement as is mentioned in subsection (1)(a), is recovered in respect of the gain by the secondary contributor not later than 60 days after the end of the year of assessment in which occurred the event giving rise to the charge to tax under section 135; and

(b) the amount of any liability in respect of that gain that, by virtue of any such election as is mentioned in subsection (1)(b), has become the earner's liability.

(3) Where notice of withdrawal of approval of any such election is given, relief under subsection (2)(b) is limited to so much of the earner's liability in respect of the gain as is met before the end of the 60th day after the end of the year of assessment in which occurred the event giving rise to the charge under section 135.

(4) Relief under this section shall be given by way of deduction from the amount of the gain on which the earner is chargeable to tax under section 135.

(5) Any such deduction does not affect the amount of the gain for the purpose of—

(a) section 120(4) of the Taxation of Chargeable Gains Act 1992 (amount treated as consideration for acquisition of shares), or

(b) section 4(4)(a) of the Contributions and Benefits Act (amount treated as remuneration for contributions purposes).

(6) The agreements and elections referred to in this section are those having effect under paragraph 3A or 3B of Schedule 1 to the Contributions and Benefits Act.

References to approval in relation to an election are to approval by the Inland Revenue under paragraph 3B of that Schedule.

(7) In this section—

"the Contributions and Benefits Act" means the Social Security Contributions and Benefits Act 1992 or the Social Security Contributions and Benefits (Northern Ireland) Act 1992; and

"secondary Class 1 contributions" and "secondary contributor" have the same meaning as in that Act.]¹

Commentary—*Simon's Direct Tax Service* **E4.513.**
Modification—Application of this section in relation to the Social Security Contributions (Share Options) Act 2001: Social Security Contributions (Share Options) Act 2001 s 4.
Amendments—¹ This section inserted by FA 2000 s 56(1) with effect for any agreement or election having effect as mentioned in sub-s (6), whether made before or after 28 July 2000.

Retirement benefits etc

188 Exemptions from section 148

Amendments—This section repealed by FA 1998 s 165, Sch 27 Part III(9) with effect in relation to payments or benefits received after 5 April 1998, except where the payment or other benefit, or the right to receive it, has been brought into charge to tax before 6 April 1998 (FA 1998 s 58(4)).

189 Lump sum benefits on retirement

[(1)]³ A lump sum paid to a person [(whether on his retirement from an office or employment or otherwise)]¹ shall not be chargeable to income tax under Schedule E if—

(*a*) it is paid in pursuance of any such scheme or fund as was described in section 221(1) and (2) of the 1970 Act or as is described in section 596(1) [and is not expected from this paragraph by subsection (2) or (3) below][3]; or

(*b*) ...[2]

(*c*) it is paid under approved personal pension arrangements (within the meaning of Chapter IV of Part XIV).

[(2) Subsection (1)(*a*) above does not apply to a payment of compensation for loss of office or employment, or for loss or diminution of emoluments, unless

(*a*) the loss or diminution is due to ill-health, or

(*b*) the payment is properly regarded as earned by past service.

(3) Subsection (1)(*a*) above does not apply to a payment chargeable to tax under section 600 (payments not authorised by rules of scheme).][3]

Commentary—*Simon's Direct Tax Service* **E4.802, 805D.**
Revenue Internal Guidance—Schedule E manual, SE 04800 (retirement lump sums—general).
SE 13660 (termination payments and benefits—more examples of exemptions).
Definitions—''The 1970 Act'', s 831(3); ''Schedule E'', s 19(1).
Amendments—[1] Words substituted by FA 1988 s 57 and this section as so amended is deemed always to have had effect.
[2] Para (*b*) repealed by FA 1994 s 108(7)(*b*) and Sch 26 Pt V(12) in relation to any benefit provided after 30 November 1993 except under a scheme or arrangement entered into before 1 December 1993 with no variation on or after that date to counter the effect of the repeal; see FA 1994 s 108(8).
[3] Words in sub-s (1) substituted and sub-ss (2) and (3) inserted by FA 1998 Sch 9 Part II with effect from 6 April 1998, except where the payment or other benefit, or the right to receive it, has been brought into charge to tax before that date.

[190 Payments to MPs and others

(1) Grants and payments to which this section applies shall be exempt from income tax under Schedule E as emoluments, but without prejudice to any charge to tax under section 148 (payments in connection with termination of employment, etc).

(2) This section applies to grants and payments if they are made—

(*a*) in pursuance of a resolution of the House of Commons to a person ceasing to be a member of that House on a dissolution of Parliament;

(*b*) under section 13 of the Parliamentary Pensions etc. Act 1984 or section 4 of the Ministerial and other Pensions and Salaries Act 1991 (grants to persons ceasing to hold certain Ministerial and other offices); or

(*c*) under section 3 of the European Parliament (Pay and Pensions) Act 1979 (resettlement grants for persons ceasing to be Representatives).

(3) This section also applies to grants and payments if they are not pension payments and they are made—

(*a*) under section 81(3) of the Scotland Act 1998—

(i) to a person ceasing to be a member of the Scottish Parliament on the dissolution of the Scottish Parliament, or

(ii) to a person ceasing to hold an office corresponding to a relevant office;

(*b*) under section 18(1) of the Government of Wales Act 1998 to a person ceasing to be a member of the National Assembly for Wales on the expiry of his term of office; or

(*c*) under section 48(1) of the Northern Ireland Act 1998—

(i) to a person ceasing to be a member of the Northern Ireland Assembly on the dissolution of the Assembly, or

(ii) to a person ceasing to hold an office corresponding to a relevant office.

(4) In subsection (3) above ''a relevant office'' has the same meaning as in section 4 of the Ministerial and other Pensions and Salaries Act 1991.][1]

Commentary—*Simon's Direct Tax Service* **E4.334, 805F.**
Amendments—[1] This section substituted by FA 1999 s 52, Sch 5 para 1 with effect from the year 1999–00.

191 Job release scheme allowances not to be treated as income

(1) A payment on account of an allowance to which this section applies shall not be treated as income for any purposes of the Income Tax Acts.

(2) This section applies to any allowance paid since the beginning of 1977 by the Secretary of State or the Department of Economic Development under any scheme of the kind described in the Job Release Act 1977 being a scheme which provides for the payment of allowances for periods beginning not earlier than one year before the date on which the recipient attains pensionable age as defined in that Act.

Commentary—*Simon's Direct Tax Service* **E4.332.**
Definition—''The Income Tax Acts'', s 831(1)(*b*).

[Removal expenses and benefits

191A Removal expenses and benefits

Schedule 11A to this Act (which relates to the payment of expenses, and the provision of benefits, in respect of removals) shall have effect.]¹

Commentary—*Simon's Direct Tax Service* **E4.491.**
Concessions A5—Removal expenses and cheap or interest-free loans: concessionary treatment until 5 April 1993.
A67—Payments to employees moved to higher cost housing areas: concessionary treatment until 5 April 1993.
Revenue Internal Guidance—Schedule E manual, SE 03100–03140 (Removal or transfer costs—qualifying expenses and benefits).
Amendments—¹ This section inserted by FA 1993 Sch 5 para 1.

[191B Removal benefits: beneficial loan arrangements

(1) This section applies where—

(*a*) there is a change in the residence of an employee,
(*b*) the conditions mentioned in paragraph 5(1) to (3) of Schedule 11A are fulfilled in relation to the change (construing the reference in paragraph 5(1) to paragraphs 3(2) and 4(2) of that Schedule as a reference to this subsection),
(*c*) a qualifying loan is raised by the employee in connection with the change and is made before the relevant day, and
(*d*) section 160(1) applies (or would apply apart from this section) in respect of the employee and the loan.

(2) For the purposes of this section a loan is a qualifying loan if (and only if)—

(*a*) the employee has an interest in his former residence,
(*b*) he disposes of that interest in consequence of the change of residence,
(*c*) he acquires an interest in his new residence, and
(*d*) the reason, or one of the reasons, for the loan being raised is that a period elapses between the date when expenditure is incurred in connection with the acquisition of the employee's interest in his new residence and the date when the proceeds of the disposal of the employee's interest in his former residence are available.

(3) The reference in subsection (1) above to a loan raised by the employee includes a reference to a loan raised by one or more members of the employee's family or household or by the employee and one or more members of his family or household.

(4) References in subsection (2) above to the employee having, disposing of or acquiring an interest in a residence include references to—

(*a*) one or more members of the employee's family or household having, disposing of or acquiring such an interest;
(*b*) the employee and one or more members of his family or household having, disposing of or acquiring such an interest;

and references to the employee's interest shall be construed accordingly.

(5) This section does not apply unless the total of the amounts mentioned in subsection (6) below is less than the qualifying limit for the time being specified in paragraph 24(9) of Schedule 11A.

(6) The amounts referred to in subsection (5) above are—

(*a*) the aggregate of the amounts of any sums which, by reason of the employee's employment and in connection with the change of residence, are paid to him, or to another person on his behalf, in respect of qualifying removal expenses, and
(*b*) the aggregate of any amounts represented by qualifying removal benefits which, by reason of the employee's employment and in connection with the change of residence, are provided for him or for others being members of his family or household.

(7) For the purposes of subsection (6) above—

(*a*) references to qualifying removal expenses and qualifying removal benefits shall be construed in accordance with Schedule 11A, and
(*b*) the reference to any amounts represented by qualifying removal benefits shall be construed in accordance with paragraph 24 of that Schedule.

(8) Where this section applies, for the purposes of section 160 and Schedule 7 the loan mentioned in subsection (1)(*c*) above shall be treated as if it had been made on the day after the day on which the relevant period expires; and the relevant period is a period, of the appropriate number of days, beginning with the day on which the loan is actually made.

(9) Where the loan is discharged on or before the day on which the relevant period expires subsection (8) above shall not apply; and in such a case the loan shall be ignored for the purposes of section 160 and Schedule 7.

(10) For the purposes of subsection (8) above the appropriate number is the number given by the following formula—

$$\frac{A \times B}{C \times D}$$

(11) For the purposes of subsection (10) above—

A is the amount by which the qualifying limit for the time being specified in paragraph 24(9) of Schedule 11A exceeds the total mentioned in subsection (5) above;
B is 365;
C is the maximum amount of the loan outstanding in the period beginning with the time when the loan is actually made and ending with the end of the relevant day;
D is the official rate of interest, within the meaning given by section 160(5), in force at the time when the loan is actually made.

(12) Where the number given by the formula set out in subsection (10) above is not a whole number, it shall be rounded up to the nearest whole number.

(13) An assessment in respect of the loan for a year of assessment ending before the relevant day may be made or determined on the assumption that the condition mentioned in subsection (5) above will not be fulfilled in relation to the change of residence; but where an assessment has been made or determined on that assumption and that condition is fulfilled in relation to the change, on a claim in that behalf the assessment shall be adjusted accordingly.

(14) ...²

(15) Any reference in this section to the relevant day is to the day which, by virtue of paragraph 6 of Schedule 11A, is the relevant day in relation to the change of residence concerned.

(16) Paragraphs 25 to 27 of Schedule 11A apply for the purposes of this section as they apply for the purposes of that Schedule.]¹

Commentary—*Simon's Direct Tax Service* **E4.637.**
Concessions A5—Removal expenses and cheap or interest-free loans: concessionary treatment until 5 April 1993.
A67—Payments to employees moved to higher cost housing areas: concessionary treatment until 5 April 1993.
Revenue Internal Guidance—Schedule E manual SE 03123 (bridging loans—loans provided by the employer—background).
SE 03124 (loans provided by the employer—procedure).
SE 03125 (loans provided by the employer—example).
Amendments—¹ This section inserted by FA 1993 Sch 5 para 1.
² Sub-s (14) repealed by FA 1994 Sch 26 Pt V(5) with effect from the year 1994–95.

Foreign emoluments and earnings, pensions and certain travel facilities

192 Relief from tax for foreign emoluments

(1) In this Part "foreign emoluments" means the emoluments of a person not domiciled in the United Kingdom from an office or employment under or with any person, body of persons or partnership resident outside, and not resident in, the United Kingdom, but shall be taken not to include the emoluments of a person resident in the United Kingdom from an office or employment under or with a person, body of persons or partnership resident in the Republic of Ireland.

(2) Where the duties of an office or employment are performed wholly outside the United Kingdom and the emoluments from the office or employment are foreign emoluments, the emoluments shall be excepted from Case I of Schedule E.

(3) If it appears to the Board on a claim made by the holder of an office or employment that out of any foreign emoluments from the office or employment he has made payments in circumstances corresponding to those in which the payments would have reduced his liability to income tax, the Board may allow those payments as a deduction in computing the amount of the emoluments.

(4) ...

(5) Paragraph 2(2) and (3) of Schedule 12 shall have effect with the necessary modifications in relation to the amount of emoluments to be excepted under subsection (2) above as they have effect in relation to the amount of emoluments in respect of which a deduction is allowed under section 193(1), and, subject to that, for the purposes of subsections (2) and (4) above the amount of any emoluments shall be taken to be the amount remaining after any capital allowance and after any deductions under subsection (3) above or section 193(4), 194(1), 195(7), [197AG,]¹ 198, 199, 201, 332, 592 or 594.

Commentary—*Simon's Direct Tax Service* **E4.115.**
Note—Sub-s (4) is spent.
Revenue Internal Guidance—Schedule E manual SE 32661 (examples of corresponding payments deductible under sub-s (3)).
SE 32665 (corresponding payments: procedure to obtain relief).
SE 32671 (contributions to a foreign superannuation scheme—claims will be referred to PSO).
SE 32675 (alimony and maintenance paid under the order of a foreign court—relief only available in respect of payments made on or before 5 April 1994).
SE 32681 (interest paid that is not eligible for relief under s 353 because it is paid to a foreign lender may qualify under sub-s 3)
SE 40031 (meaning of "foreign emoluments").
SE 40102 (exception from Case I in respect of foreign emoluments arising from duties performed wholly outside the UK—explanation of sub-s (2) and Revenue procedures in case of claim).
SE 40103–40104 (dual contract arrangements, procedures and example).
SE 40205 (Crown servants may not claim exception from Case I of Schedule E provided by sub-s (2)).

SE 40301 (emoluments excepted from Case I by sub-s 2 may be charged under Case III).

Definitions—"The Board", s 832(1); "body of persons", s 832(1); "capital allowance", s 832(1); "Case I of Schedule E", s 19(2); "Case II of Schedule E", s 19(2); "emoluments", s 131(1); "United Kingdom", s 830(1); "year of assessment", s 832(1); "the year 1984–85", s 832(1).

Cross references—See TA 1988 s 207 (determination of disputes as to domicile or ordinary residence under this section).

TA 1988 s 347A(5) (certain foreign maintenance payments not allowed as a deduction under sub-s (3) above).

TA 1988 s 391 (losses from trade etc carried on abroad; loss relief on income falling within sub-ss (2), (3) and (4) above).

FA 1988 s 38(9) (no deduction to be made under sub-s (3) above on account of certain maintenance payments).

Amendments—[1] Word in sub-s (5) inserted by FA 2001 s 57(3), (4), Sch 12 Pt II para 5 with effect from the year 2002–03.

[192A Foreign earnings deduction for seafarers

(1) Where in any year of assessment—

(*a*) the duties of an employment as a seafarer are performed wholly or partly outside the United Kingdom, and

(*b*) any of those duties are performed in the course of a qualifying period (within the meaning of Schedule 12) which falls wholly or partly in that year and consists of at least 365 days,

then, in charging tax under Case I of Schedule E on the amount of the emoluments from that employment attributable to that period, or to so much of it as falls in that year of assessment, there shall be allowed a deduction equal to the whole of that amount.

(2) In subsection (1) employment "as a seafarer" means an employment consisting of the performance of duties on a ship (or of such duties and others incidental to them).

(3) For the purposes of this section a "ship" does not include—

(*a*) any offshore installation within the meaning of the Mineral Workings (Offshore Installations) Act 1971, or

(*b*) what would be such an installation if the references in that Act to controlled waters were to any waters.

(4) Schedule 12 has effect for the purpose of supplementing this section.][1]

Commentary—*Simon's Direct Tax Service* E4.709.

Note—The question whether emoluments are attributable to a qualifying period beginning before 17 March 1998 shall be determined without reference to any arrangements entered into on or after that date (FA 1998 s 63(7)).

Revenue Internal Guidance—Schedule E manual, SE 33221 (Foreign Earnings Deduction (FED) for "seafarers": meaning of "seafarer" and "ship" on and after 17 March 1998).

SE 33222 (meaning of "offshore installation" on and after 17 March 1998).

SE 33223 (examples of "offshore installation" and ships on and after 17 March 1998).

SE 33301 (example of seafarer's calculation of qualifying period after 17 March 1998).

SE 70245(the Foreign Earnings Deduction was withdrawn from all employees with the exception of "seafarers" on 17 March 1998).

Amendments—[1] This section inserted by FA 1998 s 63(2) with effect in relation to emoluments attributable to qualifying periods beginning on or after 17 March 1998 and emoluments attributable to qualifying periods beginning before 17 March 1998 which are received on or after that date.

193 Foreign earnings and travel expenses

(1) ...[1]

(2) Subsections (3) and (4) below apply where a person ("the employee") who is resident and ordinarily resident in the United Kingdom holds an office or employment ("the overseas employment") the duties of which are performed wholly outside the United Kingdom and the emoluments from which are not foreign emoluments.

(3) For the purposes of section 198(1) there shall be treated as having been necessarily incurred in the performance of the duties of the overseas employment expenses of the employee in travelling from any place in the United Kingdom to take up the overseas employment and in travelling to any place in the United Kingdom on its termination; and if travel is partly for a purpose mentioned in this subsection and partly for another purpose this subsection applies only to such part of the expenses as is properly attributable to the former purpose.

(4) Where, for the purpose of enabling the employee to perform the duties of the overseas employment—

(*a*) board and lodging outside the United Kingdom is provided for him and the cost of it is borne by or on behalf of his employer; or

(*b*) he incurs expenses out of the emoluments of the employment on such board and lodging for himself and those expenses are reimbursed by or on behalf of his employer,

there shall be allowed, in charging tax under Case I of Schedule E on the emoluments from that employment, a deduction of an amount equal to so much of that cost, or, as the case may be, those expenses as falls to be included in those emoluments.

Where board and lodging is partly for the purpose mentioned in this subsection and partly for another purpose, this subsection applies only to such part of the cost or expenses as is properly attributable to the former purpose.

(5) Subsection (6) below applies where a person resident and ordinarily resident in the United Kingdom—

(*a*) holds two or more offices or employments the duties of one or more of which are performed wholly or partly outside the United Kingdom; and

(b) travels from one place having performed there duties of one office or employment to another place for the purpose of performing duties of another office or employment (the emoluments from which are not foreign emoluments);

and either or both of those places is outside the United Kingdom.

(6) For the purposes of section 198(1) expenses incurred by such a person on such travel shall be treated as having been necessarily incurred in the performance of the duties which he is to perform at his destination; and if travel is partly for the purpose of performing those duties and partly for another purpose this subsection applies only to such part of the expenses as is properly attributable to the former purpose.

(7) References in the Income Tax Acts (including any provision of this Act, but without prejudice to any express reference to subsection (3) above) to section 198 and to deductions allowable under sections 198, 199, 201 or 332 shall be construed as including a reference to subsection (3) above and to deductions allowable under that subsection.

Commentary—*Simon's Direct Tax Service* **E4.709.**
Statement of Practice SP 18/91—Foreign earnings deductions. Statement (not reproduced) classified obsolete by IR 131 Supplement (November 1998).
Revenue & other press releases—IR 12-2-1980 (earnings from foreign employments, 100 per cent deduction applies to all emoluments of the qualifying period, whether or not any return visits to UK are in performance of the duties).
Revenue Internal Guidance—Schedule E manual SE 02720 (personal incidental expenses: where travelling expense qualifies under this section, except sub-s 4, relief will be available for personal incidental expenses under s 200A).
SE 03116 (where travel expenses of employee and spouse and family are eligible for relief under this section; will not also count as 'removal expenses' so full £8,000 exemption still available).
SE 30079 (dispensations may be given for travelling and subsistence expenses incurred on international journeys provided that the expenses would be fully allowable under this section).
SE 34002 (distinction between expenses deductible under this section and s 198).
SE 34010 (special rules for employees travelling to work outside the UK: introduction).
SE 34020 (employee's initial and terminal journeys, application of sub-ss (2) and (3)).
SE 34030 (employee's board and lodging at the overseas workplace, application of sub-ss (2) and (4)).
SE 34080 (employee with two or more employments: journeys between them where the duties of one or more of the employments are performed wholly or partly abroad, application of sub-ss (5) and (6)).
SE 34100 (overseas conferences and study tours: allowable expenses).
SE 34110 (treatment of journeys to and from oil or gas rigs in the United Kingdom Designated Area).
SE 34120 (meaning of "expenses borne or reimbursed by or on behalf of the employer").
SE 34130 (meaning of "travelling expenses").
Simon's Tax Cases—s 193 *Lavery v Macleod* [2000] STC (SCD) 118; *Clark v Perks* [2001] STC 1254.
s 193(1), *Robins v Durkin* [1988] STC 588*; *Carstairs (Inspector of Taxes) v Sykes* [2000] STC 1103.
Definitions—"Case I of Schedule E", s 19(2); "emoluments", s 131(1); "foreign emoluments", s 192(1); "the Income Tax Acts", s 831(1)(b); "United Kingdom", s 830(1); "year of assessment", s 832(1).
Cross references—See TA 1988 s 132(3) (place of performance of duties of office or employment).
TA 1988 ss 194(9), 195(12) (avoidance of double relief).
TA 1988 Sch 12 para 1A (emoluments for the purposes of sub-s (1) above to be the amount after any capital allowance and certain deductions).
FA 1991 s 46 (workers in Kuwait and Iraq in period of 62 days ending with 2 August 1990 may have shorter absence treated as qualifying period of absence).
Amendments—¹ Sub-s (1) repealed by FA 1998 s 63(1) with effect in relation to emoluments attributable to qualifying periods beginning on or after 17 March 1998, and emoluments attributable to qualifying periods beginning before 17 March 1998 which are received on or after that date.

194 Other foreign travel expenses

(1) Where—

(a) travel facilities are provided for any journey to which this subsection applies and the cost of them is borne by or on behalf of the employer; or
(b) expenses are incurred out of the emoluments of any office or employment mentioned in subsection (2), (3) or (5) below on any such journey and those expenses are reimbursed by or on behalf of the employer,

there shall be allowed, in charging tax under Case I of Schedule E on the emoluments from that office or employment, a deduction of an amount equal to so much of that cost or, as the case may be, those expenses as falls to be included in those emoluments.

(2) Subsection (1) above applies where a person is absent from the United Kingdom for a continuous period of 60 days or more for the purpose of performing the duties of one or more offices or employments and applies to travel of the following descriptions between any place in the United Kingdom and the place of performance of any of those duties outside the United Kingdom, that is to say—

(a) any journey by his spouse or any child of his—

(i) accompanying him at the beginning of the period of absence; or
(ii) to visit him during that period;

(b) any return journey following a journey of a kind described in paragraph (a) above;

but that subsection does not extend to more than two outward and two return journeys by the same person in any year of assessment.

For the purposes of this subsection "child" includes a stepchild and an illegitimate child but does not include a person who is aged 18 or over at the beginning of the outward journey.

(3) Where a person holds an office or employment the duties of which are performed partly outside the United Kingdom, subsection (1) above applies, subject to subsection (4) below, to any journey by him—

(a) from any place in the United Kingdom to the place of performance of any of those duties outside the United Kingdom;

(b) from the place of performance of any of those duties outside the United Kingdom to any place in the United Kingdom.

(4) Subsection (1) does not apply by virtue of subsection (3) unless the duties concerned can only be performed outside the United Kingdom and the journey is made wholly and exclusively for the purpose—

(a) where the journey falls within subsection (3)(a), of performing the duties concerned; or

(b) where the journey falls within subsection (3)(b), of returning after performing the duties concerned.

(5) Where a person is absent from the United Kingdom for the purposes of performing the duties of one or more offices or employments, subsection (1) above applies, subject to subsection (6) below, to—

(a) any journey by him from the place of performance of any of those duties outside the United Kingdom to any place in the United Kingdom;

(b) any return journey following a journey of a kind described in paragraph (a) above.

(6) Subsection (1) does not apply by virtue of subsection (5) unless the duties concerned can only be performed outside the United Kingdom and the absence mentioned in subsection (5) was occasioned wholly and exclusively for the purpose of performing the duties concerned.

(7) For the purpose of applying this section in a case where the duties of the office or employment or (as the case may be) any of the offices or employments are performed on a vessel, in section 132(4)(b) the words from "or which" to the end shall be ignored.

(8) In such a case as is mentioned in subsection (7) above, subsection (4) above shall have effect as if "the duties concerned" in paragraphs (a) and (b) read "the duties concerned, or those duties and other duties of the office or employment".

(9) Where apart from this subsection a deduction in respect of any cost or expenses is allowable under a provision of this section or section 193 and a deduction in respect of the same cost or expenses is also allowable under another provision of this section or section 193 or of any other enactment, a deduction in respect of the cost or expenses may be made under either, but not both, of those provisions.

(10) References in the Income Tax Acts (including any provision of this Act, but without prejudice to any express reference to subsection (1) above) to section 198 and to deductions allowable under sections 198, 199, 201 or 332 shall be construed as including a reference to subsection (1) above and to deductions allowable under that subsection.

Commentary—*Simon's Direct Tax Service* E4.709.
Revenue Internal Guidance—Schedule E manual SE 02720 (personal incidental expenses: where travelling expense qualifies under this section relief will be available for personal incidental expenses under s 200A).
SE 03116 (where travel expenses of employee and spouse and family are eligible for relief under this section; will not also count as 'removal expenses' so full £8,000 exemption still available).
SE 34002 (distinction between expenses deductible under this section and s 198).
SE 34003 (example of expenses that may be deducted under this and other sections).
SE 34010 (special rules for employees travelling to work outside the United Kingdom: introduction).
SE 34025 (employee's interim journeys to and from the United Kingdom, application of sub-ss (1), (5) and (6)).
SE 34040 (employee's journeys from and to the United Kingdom, application of sub-ss (1), (3) and (4)).
SE 34050 (travelling expenses of the employee's family, application of sub-ss (1) and (2)).
SE 34060 (travelling expenses of the employee's family: the "60 day test" and examples).
SE 34070 (travelling expenses of the employee's family: meaning of "place where the duties are performed").
SE 34090 (duties performed partly overseas: seafarers, application of sub-ss (7) and (8)).
SE 34100 (overseas conferences and study tours: allowable expenses).
SE 34110 (treatment of journeys to and from oil or gas rigs in the United Kingdom Designated Area).
SE 34120 (meaning of "expenses borne or reimbursed by or on behalf of the employer").
SE 34130 (meaning of "travelling expenses").
SE 34140 (foreign travel: inter-relationship of the statutory rules, ss 194 and 195).
SE 34150 (prohibition of double deductions).
SE 70240 (tax treatment of seafarers—location of duties for tax purposes, special rules to be found at SE 34090).
Definitions—"Case I of Schedule E", s 19(2); "child", sub-s (2), ss 831(4), 832(5); "the Income Tax Acts", s 831(1)(b); "United Kingdom", s 830(1); "year of assessment", s 832(1).
Cross references—See TA 1988 s 132(2) (place of performance of duties).
TA 1988 s 195(12) (avoidance of double relief).

195 Travel expenses of employees not domiciled in the United Kingdom

(1) Subject to subsection (2) below, this section applies in the case of an office or employment in respect of which a person ("the employee") who is not domiciled in the United Kingdom is in receipt of emoluments for duties performed in the United Kingdom.

(2) This section does not apply unless subsection (3) below is satisfied in respect of a date on which the employee arrives in the United Kingdom to perform duties of the office or employment; and where subsection (3) is so satisfied, this section applies only for a period of five years beginning with that date.

(3) This subsection is satisfied in respect of a date if the employee—

   (*a*) was not resident in the United Kingdom in either of the two years of assessment immediately preceding the year of assessment in which the date falls; or

   (*b*) was not in the United Kingdom for any purpose at any time during the period of two years ending with the day immediately preceding the date.

(4) Where subsection (3) above is satisfied (by virtue of paragraph (*a*) of that subsection) in respect of more than one date in any year of assessment, only the first of those dates is relevant for the purposes of this section.

(5) Subsection (7) below applies to any journey by the employee—

   (*a*) from his usual place of abode to any place in the United Kingdom in order to perform any duties of the office or employment there; or

   (*b*) to his usual place of abode from any place in the United Kingdom after performing such duties there.

(6) Where the employee is in the United Kingdom for a continuous period of 60 days or more for the purpose of performing the duties of one or more offices or employments in the case of which this section applies, subsection (7) below applies to any journey by his spouse, or any child of his, between his usual place of abode and the place of performance of any of those duties in the United Kingdom, if the journey—

   (*a*) is made to accompany him at the beginning of that period or to visit him during it; or

   (*b*) is a return journey following a journey falling within paragraph (*a*) above;

but subsection (7) as it applies by virtue of this subsection does not extend to more than two journeys to the United Kingdom and two return journeys by the same person in any year of assessment.

(7) Subject to subsection (8) below, where—

   (*a*) travel facilities are provided for any journey to which this subsection applies and the cost of them is borne by or on behalf of a person who is an employer in respect of any office or employment in the case of which this section applies; or

   (*b*) expenses are incurred out of the emoluments of any office or employment in the case of which this section applies on such a journey and those expenses are reimbursed by or on behalf of the employer;

there shall be allowed, in charging tax under Case I or II of Schedule E on the emoluments from the office or employment concerned, a deduction of an amount equal to so much of that cost or, as the case may be, those expenses as falls to be included in those emoluments.

(8) If a journey is partly for a purpose mentioned in subsection (5) or (6) above and partly for another purpose, only so much of the cost or expenses referred to in subsection (7) as is properly attributable to the former purpose shall be taken into account in calculating any deduction made under subsection (7) as it applies by virtue of subsection (5) or, as the case may be, (6).

(9) For the purposes of this section a person's usual place of abode is the country (outside the United Kingdom) in which he normally lives.

(10) In subsection (6) above "child" includes a step-child and an illegitimate child but does not include a person who is aged 18 or over at the beginning of the journey to the United Kingdom.

(11) References in the Income Tax Acts (including any provision of this Act, but without prejudice to any express reference to subsection (7) above) to section 198 and to deductions allowable under section 198, 199, 201 or 332 shall be construed as including a reference to subsection (7) above and to deductions allowable under it.

(12) Where apart from this subsection a deduction in respect of any cost or expenses is allowable under a provision of this section and a deduction in respect of the same cost or expenses is also allowable under another provision of this section or of any other enactment, a deduction in respect of the cost or expenses may be made under either, but not both, of those provisions.

(13) Where by virtue of subsection (3) of section 38 of the Finance Act 1986 any provision of section 37 of that Act applied in the case of any employee at any time during the year 1984–85 or 1985–86 (and that section applied to him immediately before 6th April 1988), this section shall apply in his case for the years 1988–89 to 1990–91 as if the following were substituted for subsections (2) to (4)—

   "(2) This section does not apply after 5th April 1991.".

Commentary—*Simon's Direct Tax Service* **E4.709.**
Revenue Interpretation—**RI 237**—sets out the Revenue's view as to what constitutes a continuous period of 60 days or more.
Revenue Internal Guidance—Schedule E manual SE 02720 (personal incidental expenses: where travelling expense qualifies under this section, except sub-s 6, relief will be available for personal incidental expenses under s 200A).
SE 03116 (where a foreign national comes to the UK for employment travel expenses of the spouse and family may be eligible for relief under this section; will not also count as 'removal expenses' so full £8,000 exemption still available).
SE 30079 (dispensations may be given for travelling and subsistence expenses incurred on international journeys provided that the expenses would be fully allowable under this section and certain procedures are followed).
SE 34140 (foreign travel: inter-relationship of the statutory rules, ss 194 and 195).
SE 34150 (prohibition of double deductions).
SE 35000 (travelling expenses: employees working but not domiciled in the UK—explanation of this section and list of instructions covering references SE 35001–35140).
Definitions—"Case I or II of Schedule E", s 19(2); "child", sub-s (10), ss 831(4), 832(5); "emoluments", s 131(1); "the Income Tax Acts", s 831(1)(*b*); "United Kingdom", s 830(1); "year of assessment", s 832(1); "the year 1984–85" etc, s 831(3).

196 Foreign pensions

A deduction of one-tenth of its amount shall be allowed in charging any pension or annuity to tax under paragraph 4 of Schedule E.

Commentary—*Simon's Direct Tax Service* **E1.329; E4.126, 314.**
Revenue Internal Guidance—Schedule E manual, SE 74006 (annuities and pensions from overseas governments chargeable under paragraph 4).
SE 74201 (pensions: deductions, application of this section).
Definition—"Schedule E", s 19(1).
Cross reference—See TA 1988 s 391 (losses from trade etc carried on abroad; loss relief on income falling within this section).

197 Leave travel facilities for the armed forces

(1) No charge to tax under Schedule E shall arise in respect of travel facilities provided for members of the naval, military or air forces of the Crown going on, or returning from, leave.

(2) Subsection (1) above applies whether the charge would otherwise have arisen under section 131, 141 or 154 and applies not only to travel vouchers and warrants for particular journeys but also to allowances and other payments for and in respect of leave travel, whether or not a warrant was available.

Commentary—*Simon's Direct Tax Service* **E4.431, 432.**
Revenue Internal Guidance—Schedule E manual, SE 21733 (leave travel facilities for the Armed Forces, application of this section).
SE 50100 (tax treatment of armed forces—situations in which exemption applies).
Definition—"Schedule E", s 19(1).

[197A Car parking facilities

Any expenditure incurred in paying or reimbursing expenses in connection with the provision for, or use by, a person holding an office or employment of a car parking space at or near his place of work shall not be regarded as an emolument of the office or employment for any purpose of Schedule E.][1]

Commentary—*Simon's Direct Tax Service* **E4.604.**
Cross references—See FA 1999 s 49 (this section applies in relation to motor cycle parking spaces and facilities for parking cycles as it applies to car parking spaces with effect from the year 1999–00).
Revenue Internal Guidance—Schedule E manual, SE 01030 (car parking facilities at or near the place of work—application of this section including cross-references to other relevant instructions).
Amendments—[1]This section inserted by FA 1988 s 46(4), (5).

[197AA Works bus services

(1) There is no charge to tax under section 154 (taxable benefits: general charging provision)[, or under section 157 (charge on provision of car for private use),][2] in respect of the provision for employees of a works bus service.

(2) A "works bus service" means a service provided by means of a bus[, or a minibus,][2] for conveying employees of one or more employers on qualifying journeys.

(3) For the purposes of this section—

"bus" means a road passenger vehicle with a seating capacity of 12 or more; and
["minibus" means a vehicle constructed or adapted for the carriage of passengers which has a seating capacity of 9 or more, but less than 12;][2]
"qualifying journey", in relation to an employee, means a journey—

(a) between his home and workplace, or
(b) between one workplace and another,

in connection with the performance of the duties of the employment.

(4) The exemption conferred by this section is subject to the following conditions—

(a) the service must be available generally to employees of the employer (or each employer) concerned;
(b) the main use of the service must be for qualifying journeys by those employees.

(5) The exemption is also subject to substantial compliance with the condition that the service must be used only by the employees for whom it is provided or their children.

For this purpose "children" includes stepchildren and illegitimate children but does not include children aged 18 or over.

(6) If under this section there is no charge to tax under section 154 [or 157][2] (or would be no charge if the employee were in employment to which Chapter II of Part V applies), there is no charge to tax under section 141 (non-cash vouchers) in respect of a voucher evidencing the employee's entitlement to use the service.

(7) In this section—

"employment" includes an office and related expressions have a corresponding meaning; and "workplace" means a place at which the employee's attendance is necessary in the performance of the duties of the employment.

(8) For the purposes of this section the seating capacity of a vehicle is determined in the same way as for the purposes of Part III of Schedule 1 to the Vehicle Excise and Registration Act 1994 (vehicle excise duty on buses), whether or not the vehicle is a bus within the meaning of that Part.][1]

[(9) In determining whether a vehicle is a minibus for the purposes of this section, no account shall be taken of seats in relation to which relevant construction and use requirements are not met.

In this subsection "construction and use requirements" has the same meaning as in Part II of the Road Traffic Act 1988 or, in Northern Ireland, Part III of the Road Traffic (Northern Ireland) Order 1995.][2]

Commentary—*Simon's Direct Tax Service* **E4.612**.
Revenue Internal Guidance—Schedule E manual, SE 21850 (exemption for works buses).
Amendments—[1] This section inserted by FA 1999 s 48 with effect from the year 1999–00.
[2] Words in sub-ss (1), (2), (6) inserted; in sub-s (3), definition of "minibus" inserted; and sub-s (9) added, by FA 2001 s 60 with effect from the year 2002–03.

[197AB Support for public transport bus services

(1) There is no charge to tax under section 154 (taxable benefits: general charging provision) in respect of financial or other support for a public transport road service used by employees of one or more employers for qualifying journeys.

(2) For this purpose—

"public transport road service" means a public passenger transport service provided by means of a road vehicle; and
"qualifying journey", in relation to an employee, means [the whole or part of][2] a journey—

(*a*) between his home and workplace, or
(*b*) between one workplace and another,

in connection with the performance of the duties of the employment.

[(3) Except in the case of a local bus service, the exemption conferred by this section is subject to the condition that the terms on which the service is available to the employees mentioned in subsection (1) must not be more favourable than those available to other passengers.][2]

[(3A) The exemption conferred by this section is in every case subject to the condition that the service must be available generally to employees of the employer (or each employer) concerned.][2]

(4) In this section—

"employment" includes an office and related expressions have a corresponding meaning; and
["local bus service" means a local service as defined by section 2 of the Transport Act 1985;][2]
"workplace" means a place at which the employee's attendance is necessary in the performance of the duties of the employment.][1]

[(5) If under this section there is no charge to tax under section 154 (or there would be no charge if the employee were in employment to which Chapter 2 of Part 5 applied), there is no charge to tax under section 141 (non-cash vouchers) in respect of a voucher evidencing the employee's entitlement to use the service.][2]

Commentary—*Simon's Direct Tax Service* **E4.612**.
Revenue Internal Guidance—Schedule E manual, SE 21855 (exemption for subsidies to public bus services).
Amendments—[1] This section inserted by FA 1999 s 48 with effect from the year 1999–00.
[2] In sub-s (2), words inserted, sub-ss (3), (3A) substituted for sub-s (3); in sub-s (4), definition of "local bus service" inserted; and sub-s (5) added; by FA 2002 s 33 with effect from 2002–03.

[197AC Provision of cycle or cyclist's safety equipment

(1) There is no charge to tax under section 154 (taxable benefits: general charging provision) in respect of the provision for an employee of—

(*a*) a cycle, or
(*b*) cyclist's safety equipment,

without any transfer of the property in the cycle or equipment.

(2) In this section "cycle" has the meaning given by section 192(1) of the Road Traffic Act 1988, and "cyclist" has a corresponding meaning.

(3) The exemption conferred by subsection (1) above is subject to the condition that the benefit or facility in question must be available generally to employees of the employer concerned.

(4) The exemption is also subject to the condition that the employee must use the cycle or safety equipment mainly for qualifying journeys.

For this purpose "qualifying journey", in relation to an employee, means a journey—

(*a*) between his home and workplace, or
(*b*) between one workplace and another,

in connection with the performance of the duties of the employment.

(5) If under this section there is no charge to tax under section 154 (or would be no charge if the employee were in employment to which Chapter II of Part V applies), there is no charge to tax under section 141 (non-cash vouchers) in respect of a voucher evidencing the employee's entitlement to use the cycle or safety equipment in question.

(6) In this section—

"employment" includes an office and related expressions shall be construed accordingly; and

"workplace" means a place at which the employee's attendance is necessary in the performance of the duties of the employment.]¹

Commentary—*Simon's Direct Tax Service* **E4.612**.
Revenue Internal Guidance—Schedule E manual, SE 21664 (conditions to be satisfied for exemption under this section).
Amendments—¹ This section inserted by FA 1999 s 50(1), (3) with effect from the year 1999–00.

[Mileage allowances

197AD Mileage allowance payments

(1) There is no charge to tax under Schedule E in respect of approved mileage allowance payments for a qualifying vehicle.

(2) Mileage allowance payments are amounts (other than passenger payments within the meaning of section 197AE(2)) paid to an employee in respect of expenses in connection with the use by him for business travel of a qualifying vehicle.

(3) Mileage allowance payments are approved only if, or to the extent that, for a tax year, the total amount of all the mileage allowance payments made to the employee for the kind of vehicle in question does not exceed the approved amount for mileage allowance payments applicable to that kind of vehicle.

(4) Subsection (1) above does not apply if—

(a) the employee is a passenger in the vehicle, or
(b) the vehicle is a company vehicle.]¹

Commentary—*Simon's Direct Tax Service* **E4.705**.
Amendments—¹ This section inserted by FA 2001 s 57(1), (4) with effect from the year 2002–03.

[197AE Passenger payments

(1) There is no charge to tax under Schedule E in respect of approved passenger payments made to an employee for a car or van (whether or not it is a company vehicle) if—

(a) mileage allowance payments (within the meaning of section 197AD(2)) are made to the employee for the car or van, and
(b) if the car or van is made available to the employee by reason of his employment, he is chargeable to tax in respect of it under section 157 or 159AA (cars and vans made available for private use).

(2) Passenger payments are amounts paid to an employee because, while using a car or van for business travel, he carries one or more qualifying passengers in it.

"Qualifying passenger" means a passenger who is also an employee for whom the travel is business travel.

(3) Passenger payments are approved only if, or to the extent that, for a tax year, the total amount of all the passenger payments made to the employee does not exceed the approved amount for passenger payments.

(4) Section 168(6) (when cars and vans are made available by reason of employment) applies for the purposes of subsection (1)(b) above.]¹

Commentary—*Simon's Direct Tax Service* **E4.705**.
Amendments—¹ This section inserted by FA 2001 s 57(1), (4) with effect from the year 2002–03.

[197AF Mileage allowance relief

(1) An employee is entitled to mileage allowance relief for a tax year if the employee uses a qualifying vehicle for business travel and—

(a) no mileage allowance payments are made to him for the kind of vehicle in question for the tax year, or
(b) the total amount of all the mileage allowance payments made to him for the kind of vehicle in question for the tax year is less than the approved amount for mileage allowance payments applicable to that kind of vehicle.

(2) Subsection (1) above does not apply if—

(a) the employee is a passenger in the vehicle, or
(b) the vehicle is a company vehicle.

(3) The amount of mileage allowance relief to which an employee is entitled for a tax year is—

(a) if subsection (1)(a) above applies, the approved amount for mileage allowance payments applicable to the kind of vehicle in question;

(b) if subsection (1)(b) above applies, the difference between the total amount of all the mileage allowance payments made to the employee for the kind of vehicle in question and the approved amount for mileage allowance payments applicable to that kind of vehicle.

(4) In this section "mileage allowance payments" has the meaning given by section 197AD(2).][1]

Commentary—*Simon's Direct Tax Service* **E4.705.**
Amendments—[1] This section inserted by FA 2001 s 57(1), (4) with effect from the year 2002–03.

[197AG Giving effect to mileage allowance relief

(1) Mileage allowance relief to which an employee is entitled for a tax year is given effect as follows.

(2) Where any emoluments of the employment fall within Case I or II of Schedule E, the relief is allowed as a deduction from those emoluments in calculating the amount chargeable to tax for that tax year.

(3) In the case of emoluments chargeable under Case III of Schedule E for a tax year there may be deducted from those emoluments the amount of any mileage allowance relief—

(a) for that tax year, and
(b) for any earlier tax year in which the employee was resident in the United Kingdom,

which might have been deducted from the emoluments of the employment for the tax year for which the employee is entitled to the relief if those emoluments had been chargeable under Case I of Schedule E.

(4) Subsection (3) above applies only to the extent that the mileage allowance relief cannot be deducted under subsection (2) above.

(5) A deduction shall not be made twice, whether under subsection (2) or (3) above, in respect of the same mileage allowance relief.][1]

Commentary—*Simon's Direct Tax Service* **E4.705.**
Amendments—[1] This section inserted by FA 2001 s 57(1), (4) with effect from the year 2002–03.

[197AH Interpretation of sections 197AD to 197AG

Schedule 12AA to this Act defines terms used in sections 197AD to 197AG.][1]

Commentary—*Simon's Direct Tax Service* **E4.705.**
Amendments—This section inserted by FA 2001 s 57(1), (4) with effect from the year 2002–03.

Mileage allowances

197B Limit on chargeable mileage profit

...

Commentary—*Simon's Direct Tax Service* **E4.705.**
Revenue & other press releases—IR 8-12-97 (fixed profit car scheme rates for 1998–99).
Amendment—This section repealed by FA 2001 s 110, Sch 33 Pt II(1) with effect from the year 2002–03.

197C Definition of mileage profit

...

Commentary—*Simon's Direct Tax Service* **E4.705.**
Amendment—This section repealed by FA 2001 s 110, Sch 33 Pt II(1) with effect from the year 2002–03.

197D Definition of taxed mileage profit

...

Commentary—*Simon's Direct Tax Service* **E4.705.**
Amendment—This section repealed by FA 2001 s 110, Sch 33 Pt II(1) with effect from the year 2002–03.

197E Exception from section 197B

...

Commentary—*Simon's Direct Tax Service* **E4.705.**
Amendment—This section repealed by FA 2001 s 110, Sch 33 Pt II(1) with effect from the year 2002–03.

197F Other interpretative provisions

...

Commentary—*Simon's Direct Tax Service* **E4.705.**
Amendment—This section repealed by FA 2001 s 110, Sch 33 Pt II(1) with effect from the year 2002–03.

TA 1988

[Sporting and recreational facilities][1]

[197G Sporting and recreational facilities

(1) No charge to tax under Schedule E shall arise in respect of the provision to any person in employment with any employer, or to any member of the family or household of such a person, of—

(*a*) any benefit to which this section applies; or

(*b*) any non-cash voucher which is capable of being exchanged only for a benefit to which this section applies.

(2) This section applies, subject to subsections (3) to (5) below, to any benefit consisting in, or in a right or opportunity to make use of, any sporting or other recreational facilities provided so as to be available generally to, or for use by, the employees of the employer in question.

(3) Except in such cases as may be prescribed, this section does not apply to any benefit consisting in—

(*a*) an interest in, or the use of, any mechanically propelled vehicle;

(*b*) an interest in, or the use of, any holiday or other overnight accommodation or any facilities which include, or are provided in association with, a right or opportunity to make use of any such accommodation;

(*c*) a facility provided on domestic premises;

(*d*) a facility provided so as to be available to, or for use by, members of the public generally;

(*e*) a facility which is used neither wholly nor mainly by persons whose right or opportunity to use it derives from employment (whether with the same employer or with different employers); or

(*f*) a right or opportunity to make use of any facility falling within any of the preceding paragraphs.

(4) For the purposes of subsection (3)(*e*) above a person's right or opportunity to use any facility shall be taken to derive from employment if, and only if—

(*a*) it derives from his being or having been an employee of a particular employer or a member of the family or household of a person who is or has been such an employee; and

(*b*) the facility is one which is provided so as to be available generally to the employees of that employer.

(5) The Treasury may by regulations provide—

(*a*) that such benefits as may be prescribed shall not be benefits to which this section applies; and

(*b*) that such other benefits as may be prescribed shall be benefits to which this section applies only where such conditions as may be prescribed are satisfied in relation to the terms on which, and the persons to whom, they are provided.

(6) In this section—

"domestic premises" means any premises used wholly or mainly as a private dwelling or any land or other premises belonging to, or enjoyed with, any premises so used;

"non-cash voucher" has the same meaning as in section 141;

"prescribed" means prescribed by regulations made by the Treasury;

"vehicle" includes any ship, boat or other vessel, any aircraft and any hovercraft;

and section 168(2) and (4) shall apply for the purposes of this section as it applies for the purposes of Chapter II of this Part.]*[1]*

Commentary—*Simon's Direct Tax Service* **E4.612.**
Revenue Internal Guidance—Schedule E manual, SE 22850 (exemption for sports and recreation facilities—table of contents covering references SE 22850–22865).
Definitions—"Employment", s 197F; "family or household", s 168(4); "Schedule E", s 19(1).
Amendments—[1] This section inserted by FA 1993 s 75 with effect from the year 1993–94.

Other expenses, subscriptions etc

198 Relief for necessary expenses

[(1) If the holder of an office or employment is obliged to incur and defray out of the emoluments of the office or employment—

(*a*) qualifying travelling expenses, or

(*b*) any amount (other than qualifying travelling expenses) expended wholly, exclusively and necessarily in the performance of the duties of the office or employment,

there may be deducted from the emoluments to be assessed the amount so incurred and defrayed.

(1A) "Qualifying travelling expenses" means—

(*a*) amounts necessarily expended on travelling in the performance of the duties of the office or employment, or

(*b*) other expenses of travelling which—

(i) are attributable to the necessary attendance at any place of the holder of the office or employment in the performance of the duties of the office or employment, and

(ii) are not expenses of ordinary commuting or private travel.

What is ordinary commuting or private travel for this purpose is defined in Schedule 12A.

(1B) Expenses of travel by the holder of an office or employment between two places at which he performs duties of different offices or employments under or with companies in the same group are treated as necessarily expended in the performance of the duties which he is to perform at his destination.

For this purpose companies are taken to be members of the same group if, and only if, one is a 51% subsidiary of the other or both are 51% subsidiaries of a third company.][1]

(2) Subject to subsection (3) below, where the emoluments for any duties do not fall within Case I or II of Schedule E, then in relation to those or any other emoluments of the office or employment, subsection (1) above ...[3] shall apply as if the performance of those duties did not belong to that office or employment.

(3) There may be deducted from any emoluments chargeable under Case III of Schedule E the amount of—

(a) any expenses defrayed out of those emoluments, and
(b) any other expenses defrayed in the United Kingdom in the chargeable period or in an earlier chargeable period in which the holder of the office or employment has been resident in the United Kingdom,

being in either case expenses for which a deduction might have been made under subsection (1) above from emoluments of the office or employment if they had been chargeable under Case I of Schedule E for the chargeable period in which the expenses were incurred; but a deduction shall not be made twice, whether under this subsection or otherwise, in respect of the same expenses from emoluments of the office or employment.

[(4) No deduction shall be made under this section in respect of expenditure incurred by—

(a) a member of the House of Commons, or
(b) a member of the Scottish Parliament, or
(c) a member of the National Assembly for Wales, or
(d) a member of the Northern Ireland Assembly,

in, or in connection with, the provision or use of residential or overnight accommodation to enable him to perform his duties as such a member in or about the place where the body of which he is a member sits or the constituency or region for which he has been returned.][2].

[(5) No deduction may be made under this section in respect of qualifying travelling expenses incurred in connection with the use by an employee or office-holder of a vehicle that is not a company vehicle if—

(a) mileage allowance payments (within the meaning of section 197AD(2)) are made to that person in respect of the use of the vehicle; or
(b) mileage allowance relief is available in respect of the use of the vehicle by that person.
"Company vehicle" has the meaning given by paragraph 6 of Schedule 12AA.][4]

Commentary—*Simon's Direct Tax Service* E4.701.
Concessions—**A1**—Flat rate allowances for costs of tools and special clothing agreed with Trade Unions.
A5—Exemption for removal expenses and interest on bridging loan borne by employer where employee changes job.
A58—Reasonable travelling, subsistence, overnight accommodation, etc allowances made by employers during public transport disruption are not taxed.
A59—Provision of alternative means of transport or financial assistance made to severely disabled employees incapable of using public transport to enable them to travel to work is not taxed.
A64—External training courses: circumstances in which expenditure incurred by an employee is deductible.
A66—Where an employer pays for an employee's journey between work and home on occasions when the employee is required to work late, the employee is not liable to tax if specified conditions are satisfied.
Concession—(unnumbered)—New arrangements to ensure consistent treatment of travelling and subsistence allowances paid to operatives and site-based staff in the construction and allied industries, with retrospective effect from 6 April 1981.
Statements of Practice—**SP 16/80**—Payments by employers to reimburse extra travelling and subsistence expenses incurred by full-time long-distance drivers are tax free. Where such expenses are not reimbursed by employers, they are deducted in calculating total income of the drivers. The expenses must have been incurred wholly, exclusively and necessarily in the performance of duties.
SP A6—This statement sets out the procedure to be followed by the employers in respect of expenses, benefits and fees affected by VAT and accountable under Schedule E.
Revenue Internal Guidance—Schedule E manual, SE 02710 (personal incidental expenses not allowable under this section).
SE 02720 (personal incidental expenses: where travelling expense qualifies under this section relief will be available for personal incidental expenses under s 200A).
SE 11260 (unlikely that an employee who has received an incentive award will be able to justify a deduction from that award under this section).
SE 11501 (living accommodation: example of an ordinary house in which one room was used exclusively as an office—possibility of a deduction under this section).
SE 15530 (amount to be deducted under this section should normally include the full amount of VAT, whether or not the employer may subsequently recover all or part of it from Customs & Excise).
SE 16025 and SE 16030 (relief under this section where vouchers and credit-tokens have been supplied).
SE 20102 (working out if an employment has emoluments at a rate of £8,500 a year or more—no deduction for expenses under this section).
SE 21210 (benefits which are used for business entertaining will not usually qualify for a deduction under this section).
SE 21626 (asset used by the employee partly for private purposes and partly for work purposes—by treating the value of the benefit as if it were expenditure business proportion can qualify for deduction under this section).
SE 21670 (subsidised meals including canteen meals and working lunches—may be non-taxable where the employee or director's meal is part of business entertaining for which there is a matching deduction under this section).
SE 22062 and 23080 (van and car scale charge respectively—private use and business travel: travel has to pass the test imposed by this section).
SE 23776 (car fuel benefit: does not apply to employee's own car where, if fuel is provided, deduction is available under this section).

SE 23778 (car fuel benefit: fares allowances paid under Working Rule Agreements in the building, civil engineering and electrical contracting industries; use the tests imposed by this section to quantify business travel).
SE 30077 (entertaining expenses: dispensation will be refused where there is any doubt whether particular items of entertaining would be fully allowable to the employee as an expenses deduction under this section).
SE 31615–31618 (explanation, and examples, of deductions from 'expenses and benefits' available under this section).
SE 31620–31622 (introduction to the Schedule E expenses rule).
SE 31623 (list of instructions where Revenue have agreed that particular deductions can be made from the emoluments of particular groups of employees e.g. doctors, examiners, actors etc).
SE 31624 (list of instructions where guidance can be found on specific expenses eg books, clothing, medical expenses etc).
SE 31630–31665 (key words and phrases used in this section explained in detail with case law references and practical examples).
SE 31700–31720 (internal procedures for dealing with expense claims).
SE 31750–31751 (expenses that are deductible from income charged under Case III of Schedule E).
SE 31800 (travel expenses: general table of contents covering references SE 31805–31992).
SE 32000 (travel expenses 1998/1999 and later years: table of contents covering references SE 32005–32325).
SE 32400 (other expenses: alphabetical table of contents covering references SE 32405–32560 and the letters A–E).
SE 32565 (entertaining expenses: table of contents covering references SE 32565–32650a).
SE 32700 (other expenses: alphabetical table of contents covering references SE 32700–32951 and the letters F–T).
SE 34001–34003 (travelling expenses: employees working abroad—consider s 198 first).
SE 35001–35003 (travelling expenses: employees working but not domiciled in the UK—consider s 198 first).
SE 36800 (pocket calculators normally dealt with as minor items for which a deduction may be due under this section).
SE 36880 (no deduction for capital allowances can be given from emoluments chargeable under Case III of Schedule E—sub-s 2).
SE 36890 (if deductions allowable under this section exceed the emoluments from the employment, no deduction for the excess can be given against other income).
SE 42390 (emoluments received after the death of an employee or office holder: the personal representatives can only claim deductions for expenses incurred by the employee or office holder).
Revenue & other press releases—Hansard 1-11-76 (UK resident director or employee of foreign subsidiary of UK parent may deduct board and lodging expenses incurred in visiting the foreign subsidiary in the course of his duties).
Hansard 6-11-86 (recurrent registration fees payable by nurses to UK Central Council for Nursing, Midwifery and Health Visiting are deductible under s 201; initial registration fees are not deductible either under s 198 or s 201).
IR Tax Bulletin December 1997 (The new tax rules on employee travel and subsistence—general scope).
IR Tax Bulletin February 1998 (The new tax rules on employee travel and subsistence—taxation of employees' travel expenses).
IR Tax Bulletin April 1998 (The new tax rules on employee travel and subsistence—explanation of the provision which denies relief for journeys that are substantially 'ordinary commuting', and practical examples).
IR 5-3-99 (deductions for fire fighters and healthcare workers in respect of uniform cleaning and maintenance costs).
Simon's Tax Cases—*Miners v Atkinson* [1997] STC 58; *Clark v Bye* [1997] STC 311; *Baird v Williams* [1999] STC 635, *Ansell (Inspector of Taxes) v Brown* [2001] STC 1166.
Sub-s (1), *Ben Nevis v IRC* [2001] STC (SCD) 144; *Snowdon v Charnock (Inspector of Taxes)* [2001] STC (SCD) 152; *Kirkwood (Inspector of Taxes) v Evans* [2001] STC (SCD) 231.
Sub-s (1A); *Kirkwood (Inspector of Taxes) v Evans* [2001] STC (SCD) 231.
Definitions—''The 1990 Act'', s 831(3); ''Case I or II of Schedule E'', s 19(2); ''Case III of Schedule E'', s 19(2); ''chargeable period'', s 832(1); ''emoluments'', s 131(1); ''United Kingdom'', s 830(1).
Cross references—See TA 1988 s 141(3) (relief under this section for non-cash vouchers provided to employees).
TA 1988 s 142(2) (relief under this section for credit–token provided to employees).
TA 1988 s 145(3) (relief under this section for living accommodation provided to employees).
TA 1988 s 156(8) (taxation of benefits in kind; allowable deductions under this section).
TA 1988 s 167(2) (exclusion of deductions. under this section in calculating value of benefits provided for directors and employees earning £8,500 or more).
TA 1988 s 193(3) (travelling expenses connected with overseas employment to be treated as satisfying sub-s (1) above).
TA 1988 ss 193(7), 194(10), 195(11) (construction of references to this section in the Income Tax Acts).
TA 1988 s 198A (interpretation of this section).
TA 1988 s 200 (exemption from income tax for payments to members of the House of Commons in respect of necessary overnight expenses or EU travel).
TA 1988 s 200ZA (exemption from income tax for payments to members of the Scottish Parliament, the National Assembly for Wales and the Northern Ireland Assembly in respect of necessary overnight expenses or EU travel).
TA 1988 s 617(4) (secondary Class 1 contributions and Class 1A contributions *not* precluded from being deductible under this section).
FA 2000 Sch 12 para 11 (deemed Schedule E payment treated as part of worker's emoluments from an intermediary for the purposes of this section).
Amendments—¹ Sub-ss (1)–(1B) substituted for sub-s (1) by FA 1998 s 61(1) with effect from the year 1998–99, replacing the FA 1997 s 62(1), (5) amendments which were due to become effective on the same date.
² Sub-s (4) substituted by FA 1999 s 52, Sch 5 para 2(2) with effect from the year 1999–00.
³ Words in sub-s (2) repealed by CAA 2001 ss 578, 580, Sch 2 para 25, Sch 4 with effect for income tax purposes as respects allowances and charges falling to be made for chargeable periods ending after 5 April 2001.
⁴ Sub-s (5) added by FA 2001 s 57(3), (4), Sch 12 Pt II para 6 with effect from the year 2002–03.

198A Interpretation of section 198

Commentary—*Simon's Direct Tax Service* E4.708.
Amendments—This section repealed by FA 1998 s 165, Sch 27 Part III(10) with effect from the year 1998–99.

199 Expenses necessarily incurred and defrayed from official emoluments

(1) Subject to the provisions of subsection (2) below, where the Treasury are satisfied with respect to any class of persons in receipt of any salary, fees or emoluments payable out of the public revenue that such persons are obliged to lay out and expend money wholly, exclusively and necessarily in the performance of the duties in respect of which such salary, fees or emoluments are payable, the Treasury may fix such sum as in the opinion of the Treasury represents a fair equivalent of the average annual amount laid out and so expended by persons of that class, and in charging income tax on that salary or those fees or emoluments there shall be deducted from the amount thereof the sums so fixed by the Treasury.

(2) If any such person would, but for the provisions of subsection (1) above, be entitled to deduct a larger amount than the sum so fixed, that amount may be deducted instead of the sum so fixed.

Commentary—*Simon's Direct Tax Service* **E4.703**.
Simon's Tax Cases—*Shaw v Tonkin* [1988] STC 186*.
Revenue Internal Guidance—Schedule E manual, SE 60720 (enquiries re deductions under this section to be referred to the appropriate PD office).
Definition—"Emoluments", s 131(1).
Cross reference—See TA 1988 ss 193(7), 194(10), 195(11) (construction of references to this section in the Income Tax Acts).

200 Expenses of Members of Parliament

[(1)][1] An allowance—

    (*a*) which is paid to a Member of the House of Commons; and

    (*b*) for which provision is made by resolution of that House, and

    (*c*) which is expressed to be in respect of additional expenses necessarily incurred by the Member in staying overnight away from his only or main residence for the purpose of performing his parliamentary duties, either in the London area, as defined in such a resolution, or in his constituency,

shall not be regarded as income for any purpose of the Income Tax Acts.

[(2) A sum which is paid to a Member of the House of Commons in accordance with any resolution of that House providing for Members of that House to be reimbursed in respect of [EU travel expenses][2] shall not be regarded as income for any purpose of the Income Tax Acts.][1]

[(3) For the purposes of subsection (2) above "EU travel expenses" are the cost of, and any additional expenses incurred in, travelling between the United Kingdom and—

    (*a*) any European Union institution in Brussels, Luxembourg or Strasbourg, or

    (*b*) the national parliament of another member State [or of a candidate country][3].][2]

[(4) In subsection (3) above "candidate country" means Bulgaria, Cyprus, the Czech Republic, Estonia, Hungary, Latvia, Lithuania, Malta, Poland, Romania, the Slovak Republic, Slovenia or Turkey.][3]

[(5) The Treasury shall by order made by statutory instrument make such amendments to the definition in subsection (4) above as are necessary to secure that the countries listed are those that are from time to time candidates for membership of the European Union.][3]

Commentary—*Simon's Direct Tax Service* **E4.334**.
Definition—"The Income Tax Acts", s 831(1)(*b*).
Cross reference—See FA 1993 s 124(3) (tax adjustments in view of sub-s (2) above).
Amendments—[1] Sub-s (2) inserted and section as originally enacted numbered sub-s (1) by FA 1993 s 124(1), (2) in relation to sums paid after 31 December 1991.
[2] Words in sub-s (2) substituted, and sub-s (3) inserted, by FA 1999 s 51 with effect for sums paid after 31 March 1999.
[3] Words in sub-s (3)(*b*) inserted, and sub-ss (4), (5) inserted, by FA 2002 s 41 with effect for sums paid after 31 March 2002.

[200ZA Expenses of members of Scottish Parliament, National Assembly for Wales or Northern Ireland Assembly

(1) This section applies to payments made—

    (*a*) to members of the Scottish Parliament under section 81(2) of the Scotland Act 1998,

    (*b*) to members of the National Assembly for Wales under section 16(2) of the Government of Wales Act 1998, or

    (*c*) to members of the Northern Ireland Assembly under section 47(2) of the Northern Ireland Act 1998.

(2) If a payment to which this section applies is expressed to be made in respect of necessary overnight expenses or EU travel expenses, the payment shall not be regarded as income for any purpose of the Income Tax Acts.

(3) For the purposes of subsection (2) above—

"necessary overnight expenses" are additional expenses necessarily incurred by the member for the purpose of performing duties as a member in staying overnight away from the member's only or main residence, either in the area in which the body of which he is a member sits or in the constituency or region for which he has been returned, and

"EU travel expenses" are the cost of, and any additional expenses incurred in, travelling between the United Kingdom and—

    (*a*) any European institution in Brussels, Luxembourg or Strasbourg, or

    (*b*) the national parliament of another member State [or of a candidate country][2].

[(4) In subsection (3) above "candidate country" means Bulgaria, Cyprus, the Czech Republic, Estonia, Hungary, Latvia, Lithuania, Malta, Poland, Romania, the Slovak Republic, Slovenia or Turkey.][2]

[(5) The Treasury shall by order made by statutory instrument make such amendments to the definition in subsection (4) above as are necessary to secure that the countries listed are those that are from time to time candidates for membership of the European Union.][2]

Commentary—*Simon's Direct Tax Service* **E4.612**.
Amendments—[1] This section inserted by FA 1999 s 52, Sch 5 para 2(1) with effect from the year 1999–00.
[2] Words in sub-s (3)(*b*) inserted, and sub-ss (4), (5) inserted, by FA 2002 s 41 with effect for sums paid after 31 March 2002.

[200AA Incidental benefits for holders of certain offices etc

(1) A person holding any of the offices mentioned in subsection (2) below shall not be charged to tax under Schedule E in respect of—

(*a*) any transport or subsistence provided or made available by or on behalf of the Crown to the office-holder or any member of his family or household; or

(*b*) the payment of re-imbursement by or on behalf of the Crown of any expenses incurred in connection with the provision of transport or subsistence to the office-holder or any member of his family or household.

(2) Those offices are—

(*a*) any office in Her Majesty's Government in the United Kingdom, and

(*b*) any other office which is one of the offices and positions in respect of which salaries are payable under section 1 of the Ministerial and other Salaries Act 1975 (whether or not the person holding it is a person to whom a salary is paid or payable under the Act)[, and

(*c*) any office under the Scotland Act 1998, the Government of Wales Act 1998 or the Northern Ireland Act 1998 that corresponds to any of the offices mentioned in paragraph (*a*) or (*b*) above][3].

(3) ...[2]

(4) References in this section to a member of the family or household of an office-holder shall be construed in accordance with section 168(4).

(5) References in this section to the provision of transport to any person include references to the following—

(*a*) the provision or making available to that person of any car (whether with or without a driver);

(*b*) the provision of any fuel for a car provided or made available to that person;

(*c*) the provision of any other benefit in connection with a car provided or made available to that person.

(6) In this section—

"car" means any mechanically propelled road vehicle; and

"subsistence" includes food and drink and temporary living accommodation.][1]

Commentary—*Simon's Direct Tax Service* **E4.612.**
Definitions—''Family or household'', s 168(4); ''Schedule E'', s 19(1); ''tax'', s 832(1); ''United Kingdom'', s 830(1).
Amendments—[1] Section inserted by FA 1996 s 108 with effect from the year 1996–97.
[2] Sub-s (3) repealed by FA 1999 ss 44(5), (6), 139, Sch 20 Pt III(9) with effect from the year 1999–00.
[3] Sub-s (2)(*c*), and preceding word ''and'', inserted by FA 1999 s 52, Sch 5 para 3 with effect from the year 1999–00.

[200A Incidental overnight expenses

(1) Subject to subsection (2) below, sums paid to or on behalf of any person holding an office or employment, to the extent that they are paid wholly and exclusively for the purpose of defraying, or of being used for defraying, any expenses which—

(*a*) are incidental to that person's being away from his usual place of abode during a qualifying absence from home, but

(*b*) would not be deductible under sections 193, 194, [195 or 332 or (in the absence of sections 197AD to 197AF) 198][4] if incurred out of that person's emoluments,

shall not be regarded as emoluments of the office or employment for any purpose of Schedule E.

(2) Subsection (1) above shall not apply in the case of any qualifying absence in relation to which the authorised maximum is exceeded.

(3) For the purposes of this section a qualifying absence from home, in relation to a person holding an office or employment, is any continuous period throughout which that person is obliged to stay away from his usual place of abode and during which he—

(*a*) has at least one overnight stay away from that place; but

(*b*) does not on any occasion stay overnight at a place other than a place the expenses of travelling to which are...[2]—

(i) expenses incurred out of his emoluments and deductible, otherwise than by virtue of section 193(4), 194(2) or 195(6), under any of the provisions mentioned in subsection (1)(*b*) above, or

(ii) expenses which would be so deductible if so incurred [or][2]

[(iii) expenses the amount of which, having been paid or reimbursed by the person under whom he holds that office or employment, is excluded from his emoluments in pursuance of section 200B, or

(iv) expenses the amount of which would be so excluded if it were so paid or reimbursed][2][,
or

(v) expenses the amount of which, having been paid or reimbursed by the person under whom he holds that office or employment, is excluded from his emoluments in pursuance of section 200E, or

(vi) expenses the amount of which would be so excluded if it were so paid or reimbursed.][3]

(4) In this section ''the authorised maximum'', in relation to each qualifying absence from home by any person, means the aggregate amount equal to the sum of the following amounts—

(*a*) £5 for every night (if any) during that absence which is a night the whole of which is spent by that person in the United Kingdom; and

(*b*) £10 for every night (if any) during that absence which is a night the whole or any part of which is spent by that person outside the United Kingdom.

(5) For the purposes of this section the authorised maximum is exceeded in relation to a qualifying absence from home by any person if that maximum is exceeded by the amount which, in the absence of subsection (2) above and of the other requirements of this Act that that maximum is not exceeded, would fall by virtue of this section and sections 141(6C), 142(3C) and 155(1B) to be disregarded, in relation to that qualifying absence, in determining the amount of that person's emoluments.

(6) The Treasury may by order increase either or both of the sums for the time being specified in subsection (4)(*a*) and (*b*) above; and such an order shall have effect for determining what emoluments are received by any person on or after the date when the order comes into force.][1]

Commentary—*Simon's Direct Tax Service* **E4.708.**
Revenue & other press releases—IR 16-5-95 (Revenue guidance notes for employers on exemption for incidental overnight expenses).
Revenue Internal Guidance—Schedule E manual, SE 02700 (personal incidental expenses—table of contents).
SE 02710 (personal incidental expenses—general explanation of exemption from charge and no deduction given for incidental expenses incurred by the employee that are not reimbursed by the employer unless the expenses are deductible under Section 198(1)).
SE 02720 (meaning of qualifying absence).
SE 02730 (how the tax free limits operate).
SE 02740 (other areas to be checked when policing personal incidental expenses).
SE 02750–02770 (personal incidental expenses—examples).
Definitions—"Emoluments", s 131(1); "Schedule E", s 19(1); "United Kingdom", s 830(1).
Amendments—[1] Section inserted by FA 1995 s 93(4), (5) with effect for determining what emoluments are received by any person after 5 April 1995.
[2] Word omitted from sub-s (3)(*b*) repealed and sub-paras (*b*)(ii), (iv) and word "or" preceding them inserted, by FA 1997 s 63(2), (3), Sch 18 Pt VI(4) with effect from the year 1997–98.
[3] Sub-s (3)(*b*)(v), (vi) and word in sub-s (3)(*b*)(iv) inserted by FA 2000 s 58(2), (3) with effect from the year 2000–01.
[4] Words in sub-s (1)(*b*) substituted by FA 2001 s 57(3), (4), Sch 12 Pt II para 7 with effect from the year 2002–03.

[200B Work-related training provided by employers

(1) This section applies for the purposes of Schedule E where any person ('the employer') incurs expenditure on providing work-related training for a person ('the employee') who holds an office or employment under him.

(2) Subject to section 200C, the emoluments of the employee from the office or employment shall not be taken to include—

(*a*) any amount in respect of that expenditure; or

(*b*) any amount in respect of the benefit of the work-related training provided by means of that expenditure.

(3) For the purposes of this section the employer shall be taken to incur expenditure on the provision of work-related, training in so far only as he incurs expenditure in paying or reimbursing—

(*a*) the cost of providing any such training to the employee; or

(*b*) any related costs.

(4) In subsection (3) above 'related costs', in relation to any work-related training provided to the employee, means—

(*a*) any costs which are incidental to the employee's undertaking the training and are incurred wholly and exclusively as a result of his doing so;

(*b*) any expenses incurred in connection with an assessment (whether by examination or otherwise) of what the employee has gained from the training; and

(*c*) the cost of obtaining for the employee any qualification, registration or award to which he has or may become entitled as a result of undertaking the training or of undergoing such an assessment.

(5) In this section 'work-related training' means any training course or other activity which is designed to impart, instil, improve or reinforce any knowledge, skills or personal qualities which—

(*a*) is or, as the case may be, are likely to prove useful to the employee when performing the duties of any relevant employment; or

(*b*) will qualify him, or better qualify him—

(i) to undertake any relevant employment; or

(ii) to participate in any charitable or voluntary activities that are available to be undertaken in association with any relevant employment.

(6) In this section 'relevant employment', in relation to the employee, means—

(*a*) any office or employment which he holds under the employer or which he is to hold under the employer or a person connected with the employer;

(*b*) any office or employment under the employer or such a person to which he has a serious opportunity of being appointed; or

(*c*) any office or employment under the employer or such a person as respects which he can realistically expect to have such an opportunity in due course.

(7) Section 839 (meaning of 'connected person') applies for the purposes of this section.][1]

Commentary—*Simon's Direct Tax Service* **E2.1301.**
Revenue Internal Guidance—Schedule E manual SE 01200 (introduction to reliefs for further education and training costs including table of contents covering references SE 01210–01300).
SE 01210 (general explanation of rules including fact that employees with self-financed training not reimbursed by the employer are within the vocational training relief rules, guidance at SE 32525).
SE 01220 (meaning of "work-related training").
SE 01230 (meaning of "relevant employment").
SE 01240 (meaning of "related costs").
SE 02720 (personal incidental expenses: where travelling expense qualifies under this section relief will be available for personal incidental expenses under s 200A).
SE 21707 (exemption provided by this section can apply to benefits provided to directors and employees within Pt V Ch II).
Definitions—"Emoluments", s 131(1); "Schedule E", s 19(1).
Cross reference—See TA 1988 s 200C (expenditure excluded from this section).
Amendments—[1] This section inserted by FA 1997 s 63(1), (3) with effect from the year 1997-98.

[200C Expenditure excluded from section 200B

(1) Section 200B shall not apply in the case of any expenditure to the extent that it is incurred in paying or reimbursing the cost of any facilities or other benefits provided or made available to the employee for one or more of the following purposes, that is to say—

(*a*) enabling the employee to enjoy the facilities or benefits for entertainment or recreational purposes unconnected with the imparting, instilling, improvement or reinforcement of knowledge, skills or personal qualities falling within section 200B(5)(*a*) or (*b*);

(*b*) rewarding the employee for the performance of the duties of his office or employment under the employer, or for the manner in which he has performed them;

(*c*) providing the employee with an employment inducement which is unconnected with the imparting, instilling, improvement or reinforcement of knowledge, skills or personal qualities falling within section 200B(5)(*a*) or (*b*).

[(2) Section 200B shall not apply in the case of any expenditure incurred in paying or reimbursing any expenses of travelling or subsistence, except to the extent that, on the assumptions in subsection (2A) below—

(*a*) mileage allowance relief would be available in respect of those expenses if no mileage allowance payments (within the meaning of section 197AD(2)) had been made; or

(*b*) those expenses would be deductible under section 198.][2]

[(2A) The assumptions are—

(*a*) that the employee undertook the training in question in the performance of the duties of his office or employment under the employer; and

(*b*) that the employee incurred the expenses in question out of the emoluments of that office or employment.][2]

(3) Section 200B shall not apply in the case of any expenditure incurred in paying or reimbursing the cost of providing the employee with, or with the use of, any asset except where—

(*a*) the asset is provided or made available for use only in the course of the training;

(*b*) the asset is provided or made available for use in the course of the training and in the performance of the duties of the employee's office or employment but not for any other use;

(*c*) the asset consists in training materials provided in the course of the training; or

(*d*) the asset consists in something made by the employee in the course of the training or incorporated into something so made.

(4) Section 200B shall apply in the case of expenditure in connection with anything that is a qualifying course of training for the purposes of section 588 to the extent only that section 588(1) does not have effect.

(5) Section 200B shall not apply in the case of any expenditure incurred in enabling the employee to meet, or in reimbursing him for, any payment in respect of which there is an entitlement to relief under section 32 of the Finance Act 1991 (vocational training).

(6) In subsection (1) above the reference to enjoying facilities or benefits for entertainment or recreational purposes includes a reference to enjoying them in the course of any leisure activity.

(7) In this section—

"employment inducement", in relation to the employee, means an inducement to remain in, or to accept, any office or employment with the employer or a person connected with the employer;

"subsistence" includes food and drink and temporary living accommodation; and

"training materials" means stationery, books or other written material, audio or video tapes, compact disks or floppy disks.

(8) Section 839 (meaning of "connected person") applies for the purposes of this section.][1]

Commentary—*Simon's Direct Tax Service* **E2.1301.**
Revenue Internal Guidance—Schedule E manual SE 01250 (excluded expenditure and apportionment of costs: the marginal cost of the reward element should be taxed; examples given).
SE 01260 (travel and subsistence costs, application of sub-s (2)).
SE 01280 (provision of assets, application of sub-s (3)).
SE 01290 (inter-action with other training provisions, application of sub-s (4) and (5)).
Amendments—[1] This section inserted by FA 1997 s 63(1), (3) with effect from the year 1997–98.
[2] Sub-ss (2), (2A) substituted for sub-s (2) by FA 2001 s 57(3), (4), Sch 12 Pt II para 8 with effect from the year 2002–03.

[200D Other work-related training

(1) For the purposes of Schedule E, where—

(*a*) any person ('the employee') who holds an office or employment under another ('the employer') is provided by reason of that office or employment with any benefit,

(*b*) that benefit consists in any work-related training or is provided in connection with any such training, and

(*c*) the amount which (apart from this section and sections 200B and 200C) would be included in respect of that benefit in the emoluments of the employee ('the chargeable amount') is or includes an amount that does not represent expenditure incurred by the employer,

the questions whether and to what extent those emoluments shall in fact be taken to include an amount in respect of that benefit shall be determined in accordance with those sections as if the benefit had been provided by means of a payment by the employer of an amount equal to the whole of the chargeable amount.

(2) In this section 'work-related training' has the same meaning as in section 200B.][1]

Commentary—*Simon's Direct Tax Service* E2.1301.
Revenue Internal Guidance—Schedule E manual SE 01270 (incidental overnight expenses, within the limits set by s 200AA, can be paid tax free to employees on training courses as they are when paid to an employee who is away on business).
SE 01300 (exemption extended to provision of work-related training by third parties).
Definitions—''Emoluments'', s 131(1); ''Schedule E'', s 19(1).
Amendments—[1] This section inserted by FA 1997 s 63(1), (3) with effect from the year 1997–98.

[200E Education and training funded by employers

(1) This section applies for the purposes of Schedule E where any person (in this section, and sections 200F and 200G, called ''the employer'') incurs expenditure—

(*a*) by making a payment to a person (''the provider'') in respect of the costs of any qualifying education or training provided by the provider to a fundable employee of the employer (in this section, and sections 200F and 200G, called ''the employee''), or

(*b*) in paying or reimbursing any related costs.

(2) Subject to sections 200F to 200H, the emoluments of the employee from the office or employment shall not be taken to include—

(*a*) any amount in respect of that expenditure, or

(*b*) any amount in respect of the benefit of the education or training provided by means of that expenditure.

(3) In subsection (1) above ''related costs'', in relation to any qualifying education or training provided to the employee, means—

(*a*) any costs that are incidental to the employee's undertaking the education or training and are incurred wholly and exclusively as a result of his doing so;

(*b*) any expenses incurred in connection with an assessment (whether by examination or otherwise) of what the employee has gained from the education or training; and

(*c*) the cost of obtaining for the employee any qualification, registration or award to which he has or may become entitled as a result of undertaking the education or training or of undergoing such an assessment.

(4) In this section ''qualifying education or training'' means education or training of a kind that qualifies for grants whose payment is authorised by—

(*a*) regulations under section 108 or 109 of the Learning and Skills Act 2000, or

(*b*) regulations under section 1 of the Education and Training (Scotland) Act 2000.

(5) For the purposes of this section, a person is a fundable employee of the employer if—

(*a*) he holds, or has at any time held, an office or employment under the employer, and

(*b*) he holds an account that qualifies under section 104 of the Learning and Skills Act 2000 or he is a party to qualifying arrangements.

(6) In subsection (5) above ''qualifying arrangements'' means arrangements which qualify under—

(*a*) section 105 or 106 of the Learning and Skills Act 2000, or

(*b*) section 2 of the Education and Training (Scotland) Act 2000.][1]

Commentary—*Simon's Direct Tax Service* E2.130.
Cross references—See TA 1988 s 200F (exclusion of expenditure not directly related to training).
TA 1988 s 200G (exclusion of expenditure if contributions not generally available to staff).
TA 1988 s 200H (exclusion of expenditure otherwise relieved).
Amendment—[1] This section inserted by FA 2000 s 58(1), (3) with effect from the year 2000–01.

[200F Section 200E: exclusion of expenditure not directly related to training

(1) Section 200E shall not apply in the case of any expenditure to the extent that it is incurred in paying or reimbursing the cost of any facilities or other benefits provided or made available to the employee for either or both of the following purposes, that is to say—

(*a*) enabling the employee to enjoy the facilities or benefits for entertainment or recreational purposes;

TA 1988

(*b*) rewarding the employee for the performance of the duties of his office or employment under the employer, or for the manner in which he has performed them.

[(2) Section 200E shall not apply in the case of any expenditure incurred in paying or reimbursing any expenses of travelling or subsistence, except to the extent that, on the assumptions in subsection (2A) below—

(*a*) mileage allowance relief would be available in respect of those expenses if no mileage allowance payments (within the meaning of section 197AD(2)) had been made; or

(*b*) those expenses would be deductible under section 198.][2]

[(2A) The assumptions are—

(*a*) that the employee undertook the education or training in question in the performance of the duties of—

(i) his office or employment under the employer, or

(ii) where the employee no longer holds an office or employment under the employer, the last office or employment that he did hold under the employer; and

(*b*) that the employee incurred the expenses in question out of the emoluments of that office or employment.][2]

(3) Section 200E shall not apply in the case of any expenditure incurred in paying or reimbursing the cost of providing the employee with, or with the use of, any asset except where—

(*a*) the asset is provided or made available for use only in the course of the education or training;

(*b*) the asset is provided or made available for use in the course of the education or training and in the performance of the duties of the employee's office or employment but not to any significant extent for any other use;

(*c*) the asset consists in training materials provided in the course of the education or training; or

(*d*) the asset consists in something made by the employee in the course of the education or training or incorporated into something so made.

(4) In subsection (1) above the reference to enjoying facilities or benefits for entertainment or recreational purposes includes a reference to enjoying them in the course of any leisure activity.

(5) In this section—

"subsistence" includes food and drink and temporary living accommodation; and

"training materials" means stationery, books or other written material, audio or video tapes, compact disks or floppy disks.][1]

Commentary—*Simon's Direct Tax Service* **E2.130.**
Amendment—[1] This section inserted by FA 2000 s 58(1), (3) with effect from the year 2000–01.
[2] Sub-ss (2), (2A) substituted for sub-s (2) by FA 2001 s 57(3), (4), Sch 12 Pt II para 9 with effect from the year 2002–03.

[200G Section 200E: exclusion of expenditure if contributions not generally available to staff

(1) Section 200E shall not apply to any expenditure incurred in respect of—

(*a*) the costs of any education or training provided to the employee, or

(*b*) any related costs,

unless the expenditure is incurred in giving effect to fair-opportunity arrangements that were in place at the time when the employer agreed to incur the expenditure.

In this subsection "related costs", in relation to any education or training provided to the employee, has the meaning given by section 200E(3).

(2) For the purposes of subsection (1) above "fair-opportunity arrangements" are in place at any time if at that time arrangements are in place that provide—

(*a*) for the making of contributions by the employer to costs arising from qualifying education or training being undertaken by persons who hold, or have held, an office or employment under the employer, and

(*b*) for such contributions to be generally available, on similar terms, to the persons who at that time hold an office or employment under the employer.

In this subsection "qualifying education or training" has the same meaning as in section 200E.

(3) The Treasury may by regulations make provision specifying the persons or other entities under whom Crown servants are to be treated for the purposes of this section as holding office or employment; and such regulations may—

(*a*) deem a description of Crown servants (or two or more such descriptions taken together) to be an entity for the purposes of the regulations;

(*b*) make different provision for different descriptions of Crown servants.

In this subsection "Crown servant" means a person holding an office or employment under the Crown.][1]

Commentary—*Simon's Direct Tax Service* **E2.130.**
Cross references—See Individual Learning Accounts (Separate Employers Under the Crown) Regulations, SI 2000/2076 (Crown servants treated as holding office or employment for the purposes of this section).
Amendment—[1] This section inserted by FA 2000 s 58(1), (3) with effect from the year 2000–01.

[200H Section 200E: exclusion of expenditure otherwise relieved

Section 200E does not apply to expenditure to the extent that—

    (*a*) section 200B (expenditure on work-related training) applies to it, or

    (*b*) section 588(1) (expenditure on retraining courses) has effect in respect of it.]¹

Commentary—*Simon's Direct Tax Service* **E2.130.**
Amendment—¹ This section inserted by FA 2000 s 58(1), (3) with effect from the year 2000–01.

[200J Education or training funded by third parties

(1) This section applies where—

    (*a*) any person (''the employee'') who holds, or has at any time held, an office or employment under another (''the employer'') is provided by reason of that office or employment with any benefit,

    (*b*) that benefit consists in any qualifying education or training or is provided in connection with any such education or training, and

    (*c*) the amount which (apart from this section and sections 200E to 200H) would be included in respect of that benefit in the emoluments of the employee (''the chargeable amount'') is or includes an amount that does not represent expenditure incurred by the employer.

(2) For the purposes of Schedule E, the questions whether and to what extent those emoluments shall be taken to include an amount in respect of that benefit shall be determined in accordance with sections 200E to 200H as if the benefit had been provided by means of a payment by the employer of an amount equal to the whole of the chargeable amount.

(3) In this section ''qualifying education or training'' has the same meaning as in section 200E.]¹

Commentary—*Simon's Direct Tax Service* **E2.130.**
Amendment—¹ This section inserted by FA 2000 s 58(1), (3) with effect from the year 2000–01.

201 Fees and subscriptions to professional bodies, learned societies etc

(1) Subject to the provisions of this section, the following may be deducted from the emoluments of any office or employment to be assessed to tax, if defrayed out of those emoluments, that is to say—

    (*a*) any fee or contribution mentioned in subsection (2) below, and

    (*b*) any annual subscription paid to a body of persons approved for the purposes of this section by the Board.

(2) The fees and contributions referred to in subsection (1)(*a*) above are—

    (*a*) the fee payable in respect of the retention of a name in the Register of Architects;

    (*b*) the fee payable in respect of the retention of a name in the dentists register or in a roll or record kept for a class of ancillary dental workers;

    (*c*) the fee payable in respect of the retention of a name in either of the registers of ophthalmic opticians or in the register of dispensing opticians;

    (*d*) the annual fee payable by a registered patent agent;

    (*e*) the fee payable in respect of the retention of a name in the register of pharmaceutical chemists;

    (*f*) the fee and contribution to the Compensation Fund or Guarantee Fund payable on the issue of a solicitor's practising certificate; and

    (*g*) the annual fee payable by a registered veterinary surgeon or by a person registered in the Supplementary Veterinary Register.

(3) The Board may, on the application of the body, approve for the purposes of this section any body of persons not of a mainly local character whose activities are carried on otherwise than for profit and are solely or mainly directed to all or any of the following objects—

    (*a*) the advancement or spreading of knowledge (whether generally or among persons belonging to the same or similar professions or occupying the same or similar positions);

    (*b*) the maintenance or improvement of standards of conduct and competence among the members of any profession;

    (*c*) the indemnification or protection of members of any profession against claims in respect of liabilities incurred by them in the exercise of their profession.

(4) If the activities of a body approved for the purposes of this section are to a significant extent directed to objects other than those mentioned in subsection (3) above, the Board may determine that such specified part only of any annual subscription paid to the body may be deducted under this section as corresponds to the extent to which its activities are directed to objects mentioned in that subsection; and in doing so the Board shall have regard to all relevant circumstances and, in particular, to the proportions of the body's expenditure attributable to the furtherance of objects so mentioned and other objects respectively.

(5) A fee, contribution or subscription shall not be deducted under this section from the emoluments of any office or employment unless—

    (*a*) the fee is payable in respect of a registration (or retention of a name in a roll or record) or certificate which is a condition, or one of alternative conditions, of the performance of the duties of the office or employment or, as the case may be, the contribution is payable on the issue of such a certificate; or (*b*) the subscription is paid to a body the activities of which, so far as they are directed to the objects mentioned in subsection (3) above, are relevant to the office or employment, that is to say, the performance of the duties of the office or employment is directly affected by the knowledge concerned or involves the exercise of the profession concerned.

(6) Any approval given and any determination made under this section may be withdrawn, and any such determination varied, so as to take account of any change of circumstances; and where a body is approved for the purposes of this section in pursuance of an application made before the end of any year of assessment, a deduction may be made under this section in respect of a subscription paid to the body in that year, whether the approval is given before or after the end of the year.

(7) Any body aggrieved by the failure of the Board to approve the body for the purposes of this section, or by their withdrawal of the approval, or by any determination made by them under this section or the variation of or refusal to withdraw or vary such a determination may, by notice given to the Board within 30 days from the date on which the body is notified of their decision, require the matter to be determined by the Special Commissioners, and the Special Commissioners shall thereupon hear and determine the matter in like manner as an appeal.

Commentary—*Simon's Direct Tax Service* **E4.717.**
Revenue & other press releases—Hansard 6-11-86 (recurrent registration fees payable by nurses to UK Central Council for Nursing, Midwifery and Health Visiting are deductible under s 201; initial registration fees are not deductible either under s 198 or s 201).
Hansard 30-3-90 (professional subscription paid during a period of unemployment is usually allowable against relevant employment income of the same tax year).
Law Society 24-2-93 (s 201(2)(*f*) applies to solicitors employed in private practice or where an employee's duties include activities for which a current solicitors practising certificate is required as a condition of employment: no benefit arises if the employer pays or reimburses the fee).
IR 18-12-96 (new list of approved professional bodies).
Simon's Tax Cases—*Shaw v Tonkin* [1988] STC 186*; *Singh v Williams* [2000] STC (SCD) 404.
Revenue Internal Guidance—Schedule E manual, SE 20102 (working out if an employment has emoluments at a rate of £8,500 a year or more—no deduction for expenses under this section).
SE 30075 (professional subscriptions to be included in a dispensation if relief would have been available to the employee under this section).
SE 32880 (professional fees and subscriptions—introduction).
SE 32885 (treatment of trade union subscriptions).
SE 32890 (fees and contributions to named bodies, application of subs (2)).
SE 32895 (annual subscriptions to approved bodies, application of sub-s (3)).
SE 32900 (subscriptions paid under a deed of covenant: treated as a charge rather than a deduction under this section unless taxpayer requests otherwise, example given).
SE 32905 (list of statutory fees and approved bodies).
SE 32910 (claims to become an approved body; dealt with only at Head Office).
SE 32915 (examination of individual claims to relief; no relief for an entrance fee or a life membership subscription).
SE 42390 (emoluments received after the death of an employee or office holder: the personal representatives can only claim deductions for expenses incurred by the employee or office holder).
SE 66190 (tax treatment of lorry drivers: employed lorry driver meeting the renewal cost of an LGV licence (formerly HGV licence) and any related medical expense costs can treat these costs as deductible under this section).
Definitions—"The Board", s 832(1); "body of persons", s 832(1); "emoluments", s 131(1); "notice", s 832(1); "year of assessment", s 832(1).
Cross references—See TA 1988 s 141(3) (relief under this section for non–cash vouchers provided to employees).
TA 1988 s 142(2) (relief under this section for credit-tokens provided to employees).
TA 1988 s 156(8) (allowable deductions under this section in computing the cash equivalent of fees and subscriptions to professional bodies etc provided as a benefit in kind).
TA 1988 s 167(2) (exclusion of deductions under this section in calculating value of benefits provided for directors and higher-paid employee).
TA 1988 ss 193(7), 194(10), 195(11) (construction of references to this section in the Income Tax Acts).

[201AA Employee liabilities and indemnity insurance

(1) Subject to the provisions of this section, the following may be deducted from the emoluments of any office or employment to be assessed to tax, if defrayed out of those emoluments, that is to say—

(*a*) any amount paid in or towards the discharge of a qualifying liability of the person who is the holder of the office or employment;

(*b*) costs or expenses incurred in connection with any claim that that person is subject to such a liability or with any proceedings relating to or arising out of such a claim; and

(*c*) so much (if any) of any premium paid under a qualifying contract of insurance as relates to the indemnification of that person against a qualifying liability or to the payment of any such costs or expenses.

(2) For the purposes of this section a liability is a qualifying liability, in relation to any office or employment, if it is imposed either—

(*a*) in respect of any acts or omissions of a person in his capacity as the holder of that office or employment or in any other capacity in which he acts in the performance of the duties of that office or employment; or

(*b*) in connection with any proceedings relating to or arising out of a claim that a person is subject to a liability imposed in respect of any such acts or omissions.

(3) For the purposes of this section a qualifying contract of insurance is a contract of insurance which—

(*a*) so far as the risks insured against are concerned, relates exclusively to one or more of the matters mentioned in subsection (4) below;

(*b*) is not connected with any other contract;

(*c*) does not contain provision entitling the insured, in addition to cover for the risks insured against and any right to renew the policy, to receive any payment or other benefit the entitlement to which is something to which a significant part of the premium under the contract is reasonably attributable; and

(*d*) is a contract the period of insurance under which does not exceed two years (except by virtue of one or more renewals each for a period of two years or less) and is not a contract which the insured is required to renew for any period.

(4) The matters referred to in subsection (3)(*a*) above in relation to any contract of insurance are the following, that is to say—

(*a*) the indemnification of any person holding any office or employment against any qualifying liability;

(*b*) the indemnification of any person against any vicarious liability in respect of acts or omissions giving rise, in the case of another, to such a qualifying liability;

(*c*) the payment of some or all of the costs or expenses incurred by or on behalf of that or any other person in connection with any claim that a person is subject to a liability to which the insurance relates or with any proceedings relating to or arising out of such a claim; and

(*d*) the indemnification of any person against any loss from the payment by him (whether or not in discharge of any liability) to a person holding an office or employment under him of any amount in respect of a qualifying liability or of any such costs or expenses.

(5) For the purposes of this section a contract of insurance is connected with another contract at any time at or after the time when they have both been entered into if—

(*a*) either of them was entered into by reference to the other or with a view to enabling the other to be entered into on particular terms or to facilitating the other being entered into on particular terms; and

(*b*) the terms on which either of them was entered into would have been significantly different if it had not been entered into in anticipation of the other being entered into or if the other had not also been entered into.

(6) Two or more contracts of insurance shall not be prevented by virtue of paragraph (*b*) of subsection (3) above from being qualifying contracts if—

(*a*) they each satisfy the requirements of paragraphs (*a*), (*c*) and (*d*) of that subsection; and

(*b*) the only respects in which there is a significant difference between the terms on which any of those contracts is entered into and what would have been those terms if the other contract or contracts had not been entered into consist in such reductions of premium as are reasonably attributable to—

(i) the fact that, where different contracts have been entered into as part of a single transaction, the premium under each of the contracts has been fixed by reference to the appropriate proportion of what would have been the premium under a single contract relating to all the risks covered by the different contracts; or

(ii) the fact that the contract in question contains a right to renew or is entered into by way of renewal or in pursuance of such a right.

(7) For the purpose of determining the different parts of any premium under any contract of insurance which are to be treated for the purposes of this section as paid in respect of the different risks, different persons and different offices and employments to which the contract relates, such apportionment of that premium shall be made as may be reasonable.

(8) Where it would be unlawful for a person under whom any other person holds any office or employment to enter into a contract of insurance in respect of liabilities of any description or in respect of costs or expenses of any description, no deduction may be made under this section in respect of—

(*a*) the discharge of any liability of that other person which is a liability of that description; or

(*b*) any costs or expenses incurred by or on behalf that other person which are costs or expenses of that description.

(9) References in this section to a premium, in relation to a contract of insurance, are references to any amount payable under the contract to the insurer.][1]

Commentary—*Simon's Direct Tax Service* E4.718A.
Revenue Interpretation RI 131—Clarification of certain points on how employees' liability and indemnity relief operates.
Revenue Internal Guidance—Schedule E manual, SE 30500 (index of guidance on directors and officers liabilities covering references SE 30501—30534).
Definitions—"Emoluments", s 131(3); "tax", s 832(3).
Cross references—See TA 1988 s 141(3) (relief under this section for non-cash vouchers provided to employees.)
TA 1988 s 142 (relief under this section for credit tokens provided to employees).
TA 1988 s 156(8) (allowable deduction under this section in computing the cash equivalent of employee liability and indemnity insurance provided as benefit in kind).
FA 1995 s 84 (deductions available for post employment employee liability and indemnity insurance payments made by former employee).
Amendments—[1] This section inserted by FA 1995 s 91(1), (3) with effect from the year 1995–96.

[201A Expenses of entertainers

(1) Where emoluments of an employment to which this section applies fall to be charged to tax for a year of assessment for which this section applies, there may be deducted from the emoluments of the employment to be charged to tax for the year—

(a) fees falling within subsection (2) [or (2A)]² below, and

(b) any additional amount paid by the employee in respect of value added tax charged by reference to those fees.

(2) Fees fall within this subsection if—

(a) they are paid by the employee to another person,

(b) they are paid under a contract made between the employee and the other person, who agrees under the contract to act as an agent of the employee in connection with the employment,

(c) at each time any of the fees are paid the other person carries on an employment agency with a view to profit ...³,

(d) they are calculated as a percentage of the emoluments of the employment or as a percentage of part of those emoluments, and

(e) they are defrayed out of the emoluments of the employment falling to be charged to tax for the year concerned.

[(2A) Fees fall within this subsection if—

(a) they are paid by the employee in pursuance of an arrangement under which a bona fide co-operative society agrees, or the members of such a society agree, to act as agent of the employee in connection with the employment,

(b) they are calculated as a percentage of the emoluments of the employment or as a percentage of part of those emoluments, and

(c) they are defrayed out of the emoluments of the employment falling to be charged to tax for the year concerned.]²

(3) For the purposes of subsection (2) above—

(a) "employment agency" means an employment agency within the meaning given by section 13(2) of the Employment Agencies Act 1973, ...³

(b) ...³

[(3A) Subsection (3) of section 1 of the Industrial and Provident Societies Act 1965 (co-operative society does not include profit-making society) shall apply for the purposes of subsection (2A)(a) above as it applies for the purposes of that section.]²

(4) The amount which may be deducted by virtue of this section shall not exceed 17·5 per cent of the emoluments of the employment falling to be charged to tax for the year concerned.

[(4A) Subject to subsection (4) above, a deduction by virtue of this section as regards a particular employment and a particular year of assessment may be based on fees falling within subsection (2) above or fees falling within subsection (2A) above, or both.]²

(5) This section applies to employment as an actor, singer, musician, dancer or theatrical artist.

(6) This section applies for the year 1990–91 and subsequent years of assessment.]¹

Commentary—*Simon's Direct Tax Service* E4.715.
Note—The Industrial and Provident Societies Act 1965 s 1(3) reads—

"(3) In this section, the expression "co-operative society" does not include a society which carries on, or intends to carry on, business with the object of making profits mainly for the payment of interest, dividends or bonuses on money invested or deposited with, or lent to, the society or any other persons."

Revenue Internal Guidance—Schedule E manual, SE 62800 and 62810 (fees paid to agents, application of this section).
Definitions—"Emoluments", s 131(1); "year of assessment", s 832(1); "the year 1990–91", etc, s 832(1).
Cross reference—See FA 1991 s 69(7) (necessary adjustment by way of discharge or repayment of tax etc in consequence of retrospective amendments to this section by FA 1991 s 69).
Amendments—¹This section inserted by FA 1990 s 77.
² Words in sub-s (1)(a) and whole of sub-ss (2A), (3A), (4A) inserted by FA 1991 s 69 with effect from the year 1990–91.
³ Words in sub-ss (2), (3) repealed by the Deregulation and Contracting Out Act 1994 s 81(1), Sch 17 with effect from 3 January 1995.

202 Donations to charity: payroll deduction scheme

(1) This section applies where an individual ("the employee") is entitled to receive payments from which income tax falls to be deducted by virtue of section 203 and regulations under that section, and the person liable to make the payments ("the employer") withholds sums from them.

(2) If the conditions mentioned in subsections (3) to (7) below are fulfilled the sums shall, in assessing tax under Schedule E, be allowed to be deducted as expenses incurred in the year of assessment in which they are withheld.

(3) The sums must be withheld in accordance with a scheme which is (or is of a kind) approved by the Board at the time they are withheld and which either contains provisions falling within subsection (4)(a) below, or contains provisions falling within subsection (4)(a) below and provisions falling within subsection (4)(b) below.

(4) The provisions are that—

(*a*) the employer is to pay sums withheld to a person ("the agent") who is approved by the Board at the time they are withheld, and the agent is to pay them to a charity or charities;

(*b*) the employer is to pay sums withheld directly to a charity which (or charities each of which) is at the time the sums are withheld approved by the Board as an agent for the purpose of paying sums to other charities.

(5) The sums must be withheld in accordance with a request by the employee that they be paid to a charity or charities in accordance with a scheme approved (or of a kind approved) by the Board.

(6) The sums must constitute gifts by the employee to the charity or charities concerned, ...² and must fulfil any conditions set out in the terms of the scheme concerned.

(7) ...²

(8) The circumstances in which the Board may grant or withdraw approval of schemes (or kinds of schemes) or of agents shall be such as are prescribed by the Treasury by regulations; and the circumstances so prescribed (whether relating to the terms of schemes or the qualifications of agents or otherwise) shall be such as the Treasury think fit.

(9) The Treasury may by regulations make provision—

(*a*) that a participating employer or agent shall comply with any notice which is served on him by the Board and which requires him within a prescribed period to make available for the Board's inspection documents of a prescribed kind or records of a prescribed kind;

(*b*) that a participating employer or agent shall in prescribed circumstances furnish to the Board information of a prescribed kind;

(*c*) for, and with respect to, appeals to the Special Commissioners against the Board's refusal to grant, or their withdrawal of, approval of any scheme (or any kind of scheme) or agent;

(*d*) generally for giving effect to subsections (1) to (7) above.

In this subsection "prescribed" means prescribed by the regulations.

(10) For the purposes of subsection (9) above a person is a participating employer or agent if he is an employer or agent who participates, or has at any time participated, in a scheme under this section.

(11) In this section "charity" has the same meaning as in section 506 [and includes each of the bodies mentioned in section 507]².

Commentary—*Simon's Direct Tax Service* **E4.948.**
Regulations—Charitable Deductions (Approved Schemes) Regulations, SI 1986/2211.
Revenue & other press releases—ICAEW TR631 22-8-86 (confirmation in Parliament pensioners can qualify under the scheme; a charity can be both an agent and a recipient; a condition of being an agent is a willingness to serve all employees and all charities).
IR 5-10-87 (payroll giving scheme for charities: list of approved agency charities).
Revenue Internal Guidance—Schedule E manual, SE 20104 (notes on calculating whether an employment has emoluments of £8,500 a year or more, deductions under this section are made).
SE 74201 (pensions: any sum withheld by a pension provider as a donation to charity under a payroll deduction scheme is allowable as a deduction in any assessment made on the pension).
Definitions—"The Board", s 832(1); "notice", s 832(1); "Schedule E", s 19(1); "year of assessment", s 832(1).
Cross references—See TA 1988 s 86A (tax relief for agents' expenses paid by employers for operating schemes under this section).
FA 1990 s 25(2)(*d*) (donations to charity by individuals).
FA 2000 s 38 (where an agent pays sum from an employer to charity he must pay a supplement equal to 10% of that sum to the charity with effectfor sums withheld after 5 April 2000 and before 6 April 2003).
Amendments—¹ Amount in sub-s (7) substituted by FA 1996 s 109 with effect from the year 1996–97.
² Words in sub-ss (6), (7) repealed, and words in sub-s (11) inserted, by FA 2000 ss 38(5), (7), 156, Sch 40 Pt II(1) with effect for sums withheld after 5 April 2000.

CHAPTER V
ASSESSMENT, COLLECTION, RECOVERY AND APPEALS

[202A Assessment on receipts basis

(1) As regards any particular year of assessment—

(*a*) income tax shall be charged under Cases I and II of Schedule E on the full amount of the emoluments received in the year in respect of the office or employment concerned;

(*b*) income tax shall be charged under Case III of Schedule E on the full amount of the emoluments received in the United Kingdom in the year in respect of the office or employment concerned.

(2) Subsection (1) above applies—

(*a*) whether the emoluments are for that year or for some other year of assessment;

(*b*) whether or not the office or employment concerned is held at the time the emoluments are received or (as the case may be) received in the United Kingdom.

(3) Where subsection (1) above applies in the case of emoluments received, or (as the case may be) received in the United Kingdom, after the death of the person who held the office or employment concerned, the charge shall be a charge on his executors or administrators; and accordingly income tax—

(*a*) shall be assessed and charged on the executors or administrators, and

(*b*) shall be a debt due from and payable out of the deceased's estate.

(4) Section 202B shall have effect for the purposes of subsection (1)(*a*) above.]¹

TA 1988

Commentary—*Simon's Direct Tax Service* **E4.103.**
Revenue Internal Guidance—Schedule E manual, SE 33021 (where an employee is entitled to a Foreign Earnings Deduction
(FED) the deduction is given in the year the emolument is received although this may be different to the year the emoluments
attracted the FED; example given).
SE 42200 (introduction and arrangement of guidance on the basis of assessment covering references SE 42205–42700).
SE 42700 (table of contents giving the guidance on waivers of remuneration covering references SE 42705–42725).
Cross references—See FA 1989 s 39(3) (income tax to be charged in accordance with this section where foreign emoluments
for earlier years are received in the year 1989–90 or subsequently),
FA 1989 s 40(2) (income tax to be charged in accordance with this section where emoluments for later years have been paid
before the year 1989–90).
FA 1989 s 40(4) (income tax to be charged in accordance with this section where foreign emoluments for later years are received
before the year 1989–90).
Amendments—[1] This section inserted by FA 1989 s 37 and applies where the year of assessment mentioned in sub-s (1) above
is 1989–90 or a subsequent year even if the emoluments concerned are for a year before 1989–90. However, this section does
not apply in the case of an employee who died before 6 April 1989.

[202B Receipts basis: meaning of receipt

(1) For the purposes of section 202A(1)(a) emoluments shall be treated as received at the time found in accordance with the following rules (taking the earlier or earliest time in a case where more than one rule applies)—

(a) the time when payment is made of or on account of the emoluments;

(b) the time when a person becomes entitled to payment of or on account of the emoluments;

(c) in a case where the emoluments are from an office or employment with a company, the holder of the office or employment is a director of the company and sums on account of the emoluments are credited in the company's accounts or records, the time when sums on account of the emoluments are so credited;

(d) in a case where the emoluments are from an office or employment with a company, the holder of the office or employment is a director of the company and the amount of the emoluments for a period is determined before the period ends, the time when the period ends;

(e) in a case where the emoluments are from an office or employment with a company, the holder of the office or employment is a director of the company and the amount of the emoluments for a period is not known until the amount is determined after the period has ended, the time when the amount is determined.

(2) Subsection (1)(c), (d) or (e) above applies whether or not the office or employment concerned is that of director.

(3) Paragraph (c), (d) or (e) of subsection (1) above applies if the holder of the office or employment is a director of the company at any time in the year of assessment in which the time mentioned in the paragraph concerned falls.

(4) For the purposes of the rule in subsection (1)(c) above, any fetter on the right to draw the sums is to be disregarded.

(5) In subsection (1) above "director" means—

(a) in relation to a company whose affairs are managed by a board of directors or similar body, a member of that board or similar body,

(b) in relation to a company whose affairs are managed by a single director or similar person, that director or person, and

(c) in relation to a company whose affairs are managed by the members themselves, a member of the company.

(6) In subsection (1) above "director", in relation to a company, also includes any person in accordance with whose directions or instructions the company's directors (as defined in subsection (5) above) are accustomed to act; and for this purpose a person is not to be deemed to be a person in accordance with whose directions or instructions the company's directors are accustomed to act by reason only that the directors act on advice given by him in a professional capacity.

(7) Subsections (1) to (6) above shall have effect subject to subsections (8) to (11) below.

(8) In a case where section 141(1)(a), 142(1)(a), [or 143(1)(a)][2] treats a person as receiving or being paid an emolument or emoluments at a particular time, for the purposes of section 202A(1)(a) the emolument or emoluments shall be treated as received at that time; and in such a case subsections (1) to (6) above shall not apply.

(9) In a case where section 145(1) treats a person as receiving emoluments, for the purposes of section 202A(1)(a) the emoluments shall be treated as received in the period referred to in section 145(1); and in such a case subsections (1) to (6) above shall not apply.

(10) In a case where section 154(1), 157(1), 158(1), 160(1), 160(2), 162(6) or 164(1) treats an amount as emoluments, for the purposes of section 202A(1)(a) the emoluments shall be treated as received in the year referred to in section 154(1) or the other provision concerned; and in such a case subsections (1) to (6) above shall not apply.

(11) In a case where—

(a) emoluments take the form of a benefit not consisting of money, and

(b) subsection (8), (9) or (10) above does not apply,

for the purposes of section 202A(1)(*a*) the emoluments shall be treated as received at the time when the benefit is provided; and in such a case subsections (1) to (6) above shall not apply.]¹

Commentary—*Simon's Direct Tax Service* **E4.108.**
Revenue Internal Guidance—Schedule E manual SE 42210 (table setting out the basis of assessment to be used for particular types of payment, and benefits in kind).
SE 42260 (meaning of "received").
SE 42270 (actual payment happens when the income comes into the control of the employee so that they are able to deal with it for their own use and benefit, examples given).
SE 42290 (entitlement to payment of emoluments: for non-director employees, the terms of service agreed by the employer and employee determine the date—not necessarily the same as the date on which an employee acquires a right to be paid, examples given).
SE 42300 (entitlement to director's emoluments: two main ways in which directors become entitled to be paid emoluments).
SE 42310 (crediting of emoluments in the accounts or records of the company: for directors only, any fetter on the director's right to draw the emolument is disregarded for Schedule E and PAYE purposes).
SE 42320 (limited scope of the "crediting" rule: only applies when an *emolument* is credited, entry in the accounts or records for "remuneration" which is not yet an emolument is not caught. Three examples given).
SE 42330 (director's emoluments fixed before the end of the period for which they are due: treated as being received, and paid, at the end of that period, example given).
SE 42340 (director's emoluments fixed after the end of the period for which they are due: treated as being received, and paid, at the time the amount is determined, example given).
SE 42350 (directors' emoluments conditional on results: emoluments are not determined for the purposes of SE 42340 until the underlying information is available to calculate the amount due).
SE 42700 (table of contents giving the guidance on waivers of remuneration covering references SE 42705–42725).
Cross references—See TA 1988 s 203A(5) (application of sub-ss (5) and (6) above for the purposes of s 203A(1) (meaning of payment for PAYE)).
FA 1989 s 38(1) (application of this section for the purposes of FA 1989 s 38(1)(*d*) (Schedule E: unpaid emoluments)).
FA 1989 s 43(12) (application of this section for the purposes of FA 1989 s 43 (Schedule D: computation)).
FA 1989 s 44(11) (application of this section for the purposes of FA 1989 s 44 (investment and insurance companies: computation)).
Amendments—¹ This section inserted by FA 1989 s 37 and applies where the year of assessment mentioned in s 202A(1) above is 1989–90 or a subsequent year even if the emoluments concerned are for a year before 1989–90. However, this section does not apply in the case of an employee who died before 6 April 1989.
² Words substituted by FA 1998 Sch 9 Part II with effect from 6 April 1998.

203 Pay as you earn

(1) On the making of any payment of, or on account of, any income assessable to income tax under Schedule E, income tax shall, subject to and in accordance with regulations made by the Board under this section, be deducted or repaid by the person making the payment, notwithstanding that when the payment is made no assessment has been made in respect of the income and notwithstanding that the income is in whole or in part income for some year of assessment other than the year during which the payment is made.

(2) The Board shall make regulations with respect to the assessment, charge, collection and recovery of income tax in respect of all income assessable thereto under Schedule E, and those regulations may, in particular, include provision—

(*a*) for requiring any person making any payment of, or on account of, any such income, when he makes the payment, to make a deduction or repayment of income tax calculated by reference to tax tables prepared by the Board, and for rendering persons who are required to make any such deduction or repayment accountable to, or, as the case may be, entitled to repayment from, the Board;

(*b*) for the production to and inspection by persons authorised by the Board of wages sheets and other documents and records for the purpose of satisfying themselves that income tax has been and is being deducted, repaid and accounted for in accordance with the regulations;

(*c*) for the collection and recovery, whether by deduction from any such income paid in any later year or otherwise, of income tax in respect of any such income which has not been deducted or otherwise recovered during the year;

[(*d*) for requiring the payment of interest on sums due to the Board which are not paid by the due date, for determining the date (being not less than 14 days after the end of the year of assessment in respect of which the sums are due) from which such interest is to be calculated and for enabling the repayment of remission of such interest;

(*dd*) for requiring the payment of interest on sums due from the Board and for determining the date ...⁵ from which such interest is to be calculated;]¹

(*e*) for the assessment and charge of income tax by the inspector in respect of income to which this section applies; and

(*f*) for appeals with respect to matters arising under the regulations which would otherwise not be the subject of an appeal;

and any such regulations shall have effect notwithstanding anything in the Income Tax Acts.

(3) The deductions of income tax required to be made by regulations under subsection (2)(*a*) above may be required to be made at the basic rate or other rates in such cases or classes of cases as may be provided for by the regulations.

[(3A) Regulations under this section may include provision for income tax in respect of any of a person's income for the year 1989–90 or any earlier year of assessment to be collected and recovered (whether by deduction from income assessable under Schedule E or otherwise) from the person's spouse if—

(*a*) the income was income to which section 279 applied, and

(*b*) the tax has not been deducted or otherwise recovered before 6th April 1990.][3]

(4) ...[4]

(5) Regulations under this section shall not affect any right of appeal to the General or Special Commissioners which a person would have apart from the regulations.

(6) The tax tables referred to in subsection (2)(*a*) above shall be constructed with a view to securing that so far as possible—

(*a*) the total income tax payable in respect of any income assessable under Schedule E for any year of assessment is deducted from such income paid during that year; and

(*b*) the income tax deductible or repayable on the occasion of any payment of, or on account of, any such income is such that the total net income tax deducted since the beginning of the year of assessment bears to the total income tax payable for the year the same proportion that the part of the year which ends with the date of the payment bears to the whole year.

(7) In subsection (6) above references to the total income tax payable for the year shall be construed as references to the total income tax estimated to be payable for the year in respect of the income in question, subject to a provisional deduction for allowances and reliefs, and subject also, if necessary, to an adjustment for amounts overpaid or remaining unpaid on account of income tax in respect of income assessable under Schedule E for any previous year.

(8) For the purpose of estimating the total income tax payable as mentioned in subsection (6)(*a*) above, it may be assumed in relation to any payment of, or on account of, income assessable under Schedule E that the income paid in the part of the year of assessment which ends with the making of the payment will bear to the income for the whole of that year the same proportion as that part of the year bears to the whole year.

[(9) Interest required to be paid by regulations under subsection (2) above shall be paid without any deduction of income tax and shall not be taken into account in computing any income, profits or losses for any tax purposes.][2]

[(10) Without prejudice to the generality of the powers conferred by the preceding provisions of this section, regulations under this section may include provision as to the manner of proving any of the matters for which the regulations provide and, in particular, of proving the contents or transmission of anything that, by virtue of the regulations, takes an electronic form or is transmitted to any person by electronic means.][6]

Commentary—*Simon's Direct Tax Service* **E4.902, 905.**
Regulations—IT (Employments) Regulations, SI 1993/744.
Profit-Related Pay (Shortfall Recovery) Regulations, SI 1988/640.
IT (Employments) (Notional Payments) Regulations, SI 1994/1212.
Statement of Practice SP A11—Informal end of year adjustments.
Revenue & other press releases—IR 13-2-81 (travelling and subsistence payments, site based staff, employees in the construction and allied industries: Revenue have agreed similar procedures may be applied in respect of payments made as apply to operatives covered by Working Rule Agreements).
IR 15-4-86 ("call-out" fees payable to volunteer lifeboatmen are taxable, but tax need not be deducted at source under PAYE where this is the only payment made).
IR 2-9-88 (agricultural gangmasters: Agricultural Compliance Unit enforces operation of PAYE).
MAFF 16-1-91 (overseas students working in Home Office approved Seasonal Agricultural Workers Scheme, P38(s) procedure).
IRCWG1 and CWG2 (1997) (Employer's quick guide and Employer's further guide to PAYE and NICS).
ICAEW TAX 11/93 9-7-93 paras 18–20 (detailed guidance on whether a payment is "of or on account of" emoluments, paras 22–23 (a payment on account of director's remuneration may also be a loan within ss 160, 419 if PAYE not operated).
Code of Practice 3 (inspection of employers' records).
Revenue Internal Guidance—Inspector's manual IM 5343–5352 (international assignment of labour; head office personnel working in UK (IM 5346); dual contracts (IM 6348); share schemes (IM 5350)).
Simon's Tax Cases—*Clark v Oceanic Contractors Inc* [1983] STC 35*; *Booth v Mirror Group Newspapers plc* [1992] STC 615; *IRC v Herd* [1993] STC 436*; *Sports Club plc and others v Insp of Taxes* [2000] STC (SCD) 443.
s 203(1), *DTE Financial Services Ltd v Wilson* [2001] STC 777; *Paul Dunstall Organisation Ltd v Hedges* [1999] STC (SCD) 26.
s 203(2), (3), (5), *Edwards v Clinch* [1981] STC 617*; *R v Walton General Comrs, ex p Wilson* [1983] STC 464*.
Definitions—"Basic rate", s 832(1); "the Board", s 832(1); "the Income Tax Acts", s 831(1)(*b*); "inspector", s 832(1); "interest", s 832(1); "Schedule E", s 19(1); "year of assessment", s 832(1).
Cross references—See TMA 1970 s 59A(10) (regulations under this section may provide for adjustments to PAYE for the purposes of determining the excess of income tax assessed over income tax deducted at source in the preceding year).
TMA 1970 s 59B(8) (regulations under this section may provide for adjustments to PAYE deductions for the purpose of determining the difference between income tax and CGT contained in a self-assessment and amounts paid on account thereof or tax deducted at source).
TMA 1970 Sch 3 para 3 (place of assignment of PAYE appeals).
Insolvency Act 1986 Sch 6 (PAYE outstanding in respect of previous 12 months to be preferential debt on insolvency or bankruptcy).
TA 1988 s 1(5A) (from 1999–00, any changes in the income tax bands resulting from statutory indexation need not be applied for the purposes of PAYE until after 17 May in that year).
TA 1988 s 4(1) (requirement that income tax deducted at source be at basic rate not to apply to PAYE deductions).
TA 1988 s 5(1) (general provisions for date of payment of income tax not to apply to tax deductible under this section).
TA 1988 s 179(2) (where registration of profit-related pay scheme lapses, any shortfall in deductions under this section to be made good by scheme employer).
TA 1988 s 257C(2A) (from 1999–00, any changes in the allowances resulting from statutory indexation need not be applied for the purposes of PAYE until after 17 May in that year).
TA 1988 s 597 (PAYE deductions to be made from pensions and annuities paid under approved retirement-benefit schemes).
TA 1988 s 608(4) (PAYE deductions to be made from annuities paid out of pre-6 April 1980 approved superannuation funds).
TA 1988 s 643(5) (income withdrawals under approved personal pension arrangements to be subject to PAYE).
TA 1988 s 659B(9)(*a*) (authorised person acting on behalf of an EC insurance company providing pensions to discharge duty to account for PAYE on annuities).

TA 1988 Sch 10 para 7 (PAYE deductions to be made from proceeds of disposal of participant's shares in and capital receipts from approved profit-sharing scheme).
FA 1988 s 130(7)(a) (company migration: provisions to secure payment of tax due under this section by a migrating company).
FA 1994 s 139 (regulations may apply PAYE to payments of incapacity benefit).
Amendments—¹ Sub-s (2)(d), (dd) substituted for sub-s (2)(d) by FA 1988 s 128(1).
² Sub-s (9) added by FA 1988 s 128(2).³ Sub-s (3A) inserted by FA 1988 Sch 3 para 4.
⁴ Sub-s (4) repealed by FA 1989 s 45(3) and Sch 17 Pt IV.
⁵ Words omitted from sub-s (2)(dd) repealed by FA 1994 ss 196, 199(1), (2)(a), 258, Sch 19 Pt II para 38 and Sch 26 Pt V(23) with effect from the year 1996–97.
⁶ Sub-s (10) inserted by FA 1998 s 119 with effect from 31 July 1998.
Prospective amendment—Words "and, in particular" onwards in sub-s (10) will be repealed by FA 1999 s 139, Sch 20 Pt VII with effect on such day as the Treasury may by order appoint.

[203A PAYE: meaning of payment

(1) For the purposes of section 203 and regulations under it a payment of, or on account of, any income assessable to income tax under Schedule E shall be treated as made at the time found in accordance with the following rules (taking the earlier or earliest time in a case where more than one rule applies)—

(a) the time when the payment is actually made;

(b) the time when a person becomes entitled to the payment;

(c) in a case where the income is income from an office or employment with a company, the holder of the office or employment is a director of the company and sums on account of the income are credited in the company's accounts or records, the time when sums on account of the income are so credited;

(d) in a case where the income is income from an office or employment with a company, the holder of the office or employment is a director of the company and the amount of the income for a period is determined before the period ends, the time when the period ends;

(e) in a case where the income is income from an office or employment with a company, the holder of the office or employment is a director of the company and the amount of the income for a period is not known until the amount is determined after the period has ended, the time when the amount is determined.

(2) Subsection (1)(c), (d) or (e) above applies whether or not the office or employment concerned is that of director.

(3) Paragraph (c), (d) or (e) of subsection (1) above applies if the holder of the office or employment is a director of the company at any time in the year of assessment in which the time mentioned in the paragraph concerned falls.

(4) For the purposes of the rule in subsection (1)(c) above, any fetter on the right to draw the sums is to be disregarded.

(5) Subsections (5) and (6) of section 202B shall apply for the purposes of subsection (1) above as they apply for the purposes of section 202B(1).]¹

Commentary—*Simon's Direct Tax Service* E4.920.
Revenue & other press releases—IR 28-7-89 paras 15–17 (as regards sub-s (1)(c), a general provision for directors' remuneration is not caught, and a provision for remuneration to which a director will become entitled on fulfilment of conditions does not become a credit of earnings until the conditions are satisfied, eg approval of accounts at AGM. As regards sub-s (4), a "fetter", which merely delays payment, does not include a condition).
IR 28-7-89 para 22 (as regards sub-s (1)(e), where directors' remuneration is based on profits, the amount is determined not when the formula is decided upon, but when all information required to calculate the amount of remuneration becomes available).
ICAEW TAX 11/93 9-7-93 paras 27–28 (as regards sub-s (1)(b), where a director has a prior unconditional right to draw remuneration which is provided at the year-end, PAYE must be applied when the entitlement arises. Subsequent withdrawals from his account have no tax consequences as long as it is not overdrawn),
ICAEW TAX 11/93 9-7-93 para 29 (where remuneration is paid and subjected to PAYE, but is not approved, it must be repaid and Inland Revenue should be informed for necessary adjustments).
Revenue Internal Guidance—Schedule E manual SE 42240 (definition of the meaning of "payment" for PAYE purposes is the same as the definition of "receipt" for the purpose of assessing money emoluments, subject to the exception of payments chargeable under s 148. Guidance on the meaning of payment and receipt at SE 42260 onwards therefore applies both for assessment and self-assessment purposes, and for the collection of tax under PAYE).
SE 42270 (actual payment happens when the income comes into the control of the employee so that they are able to deal with it for their own use and benefit, examples given).
SE 42310 (application of sub-s (1)(c)).
SE 42320 (limited scope of the "crediting" rule: only applies when an *emolument* is credited, entry in the accounts or records for "remuneration" which is not yet an emolument is not caught. Three examples given.).
SE 42330 (director's emoluments fixed before the end of the period for which they are due: treated as being received, and paid, at the end of that period, example given).
SE 42340 (director's emoluments fixed after the end of the period for which they are due: treated as being received, and paid, at the time the amount is determined, example given).
SE 42350 (directors' emoluments conditional on results: emoluments are not determined for the purposes of SE 42340 until the underlying information is available to calculate the amount due).
Definitions—"Schedule E", s 19(1); "year of assessment", s 832(1).
Amendments—¹ This section inserted by FA 1989 s 45(1), (2), (4), (5) and has effect to determine whether anything occurring after 27 July 1989 constitutes a payment for the purposes of this section, but subject to FA 1989 s 45(5).

[203B PAYE: payment by intermediary

(1) Subject to subsection (2) below, where any payment of, or on account of, assessable income of an employee is made by an intermediary of the employer, the employer shall be treated, for the

purposes of PAYE regulations, as making a payment of that income of an amount equal to the amount determined in accordance with subsection (3) below.

(2) Subsection (1) above does not apply if the intermediary (whether or not he is a person to whom section 203 and PAYE regulations apply) deducts income tax from the payment he makes and accounts for it in accordance with PAYE regulations.

(3) The amount referred to is—

> (a) if the amount of the payment made by the intermediary is an amount to which the recipient is entitled after deduction of any income tax, the aggregate of the amount of that payment and the amount of any income tax due; and
> (b) in any other case, the amount of the payment made by the intermediary.

(4) For the purposes of this section, a payment of, or on account of, assessable income of an employee is made by an intermediary of the employer if it is made—

> (a) by a person acting on behalf of the employer and at the expense of the employer or a person connected with him; or
> (b) by trustees holding property for any persons who include or class of persons which includes the employee.

(5) Section 839 applies for the purposes of subsection (4) above.][1]

Commentary—*Simon's Direct Tax Service* **E4.909A.**
Revenue Internal Guidance—Schedule E manual, SE 11931 and 11932 (PAYE avoidance: agencies and offshore employers, table showing who has to operate PAYE for agency workers, cases of difficulty to be referred to Personal Tax Division).
SE 11941 (example of payment by an overseas intermediary in cash).
Simon's Tax Cases—*DTE Financial Services Ltd v Wilson* [2001] STC 777.
Definitions—"Assessable", s 203L; "employee", s 203L; "PAYE regulations", s 203L.
Cross reference—See TA 1988 s 144A (payments free of tax).
TA 1988 s 203J (accounting for tax for payments treated as made by virtue of this section).
Amendments—[1] This section inserted by FA 1994 s 125.

[203C PAYE: employee of non-UK employer

(1) This subsection applies where—

> (a) an employee during any period works for a person ("the relevant person") who is not his employer;
> (b) any payment of, or on account of, assessable income of the employee in respect of work done in that period is made by a person who is the employer or an intermediary of the employer [or of the relevant person][2];
> (c) PAYE regulations do not apply to the person making the payment or, if he makes the payment as an intermediary of the employer, [or of the relevant person][2] the employer; and
> (d) income tax is not deducted or accounted for in accordance with the regulations by the person making the payment or, if he makes the payment as an intermediary of the employer, [or of the relevant person][2] the employer.

(2) Where subsection (1) above applies, the relevant person shall be treated, for the purposes of PAYE regulations, as making a payment of the assessable income of the employee of an amount equal to the amount determined in accordance with subsection (3) below.

(3) The amount referred to is—

> (a) if the amount of the payment actually made is an amount to which the recipient is entitled after deduction of any income tax, the aggregate of the amount of that payment and the amount of any income tax due; and
> (b) in any other case, the amount of the payment actually made.

[(3A) Where, by virtue of any of sections 203F to 203I, an employer would be treated for the purposes of PAYE regulations (if they applied to him) as making a payment of any amount to an employee, this section shall have effect—

> (a) as if the employer were also to be treated for the purposes of this section as making an actual payment of that amount; and
> (b) as if paragraph (a) of subsection (3) above were omitted.

(3B) References in this section to the making of any payment by an intermediary of the relevant person shall be construed in accordance with subsection (4) of section 203B as if references in that subsection to the employer were references to the relevant person.][2]

(4) In this section and sections 203D and 203E "work", in relation to an employee, means the performance of any duties of the office or employment of the employee and any reference to his working shall be construed accordingly.

(5) Subsections (4) and (5) of section 203B apply for the purposes of this section as they apply for the purposes of that section.][1]

Commentary—*Simon's Direct Tax Service* **E4.909B.**
Revenue Internal Guidance—Schedule E manual, SE 11931 and 11932 (PAYE avoidance: agencies and offshore employers, table showing who has to operate PAYE for agency workers, cases of difficulty to be referred to Personal Tax Division).
SE 11942 (example of payment by an overseas intermediary in readily convertible assets).
Definitions—"Assessable", s 203L; "employee", s 203L; "PAYE regulations", s 203L.
Cross reference—See TA 1988 s 144A (payments free of tax).

TA 1988 s 203J (accounting for tax for payments treated as made by virtue of this section).
FA 2000 Sch 8 paras 95(8), 96(4) (this section does not apply in certain cases in relation to shares ceasing to be subject to the employee share ownership plan and related capital receipts).
Amendments—This section inserted by FA 1994 s 126.
² Words in sub-s (1)(*b*), (*c*), (*d*) and whole of sub-ss (3A), (3B) inserted by FA 1998 s 69 with effect in relation to payments made, assets provided and vouchers received at any time after 5 April 1998 and in relation to any use of a credit-token on or after that date.

[203D PAYE: employee non-resident, etc

(1) This section applies in relation to an employee in a year of assessment only if—

(*a*) he is not resident or, if resident, not ordinarily resident in the United Kingdom; and
(*b*) he works or will work in the United Kingdom and also works or is likely to work outside the United Kingdom.

(2) Where in relation to any year of assessment it appears to an officer of the Board that—

(*a*) some of the income of an employee to whom this section applies is assessable to income tax under Case II of Schedule E, but
(*b*) an as yet unascertainable proportion of the income may prove not to be assessable,

the officer may, on an application made by the appropriate person, give a direction for determining a proportion of any payment made in that year of, or on account of, income of the employee which shall be treated for the purposes of PAYE regulations as a payment of assessable income of the employee.

(3) In this section "the appropriate person" means—

(*a*) the person designated by the employer for the purposes of this section; or
(*b*) if no person is so designated, the employer.

(4) An application for a direction under subsection (2) above shall provide such information as is available and is relevant to the giving of the direction.

(5) A direction under subsection (2) above—

(*a*) shall specify the employee to whom and the year of assessment to which it relates;
(*b*) shall be given by notice to the appropriate person; and
(*c*) may be withdrawn by notice to the appropriate person from a date specified in the notice.

(6) The date so specified may not be earlier than thirty days from the date on which the notice of the withdrawal is given.

(7) Where—

(*a*) a direction under subsection (2) above has effect in relation to an employee to whom this section applies, and
(*b*) a payment of, or on account of, the income of the employee is made in the year of assessment to which the direction relates,

the proportion of the payment determined in accordance with the direction shall be treated for the purposes of PAYE regulations as a payment of assessable income of the employee.

(8) Where in any year of assessment—

(*a*) no direction under subsection (2) above has effect in relation to an employee to whom this section applies, and
(*b*) any payment is made of, or on account of, the income of the employee,

the entire payment shall be treated for the purposes of PAYE regulations as a payment of assessable income of the employee.

(9) Subsections (7) and (8) above are without prejudice to—

(*a*) any assessment in respect of the income of the employee in question; and
(*b*) any right to repayment of income tax overpaid and any obligation to pay income tax underpaid.]¹

Commentary—*Simon's Direct Tax Service* **E4.988.**
Revenue Internal Guidance—Schedule E manual, SE 11931 and 11932 (PAYE avoidance: agencies and offshore employers, table showing who has to operate PAYE for agency workers, cases of difficulty to be referred to Personal Tax Division).
Definitions—"Assessable", s 203L; "the Board", s 832(1); "Case II of Schedule E", s 19(2); "employee", s 203L; "notice", s 832(1); "PAYE regulations", s 203L; "United Kingdom", s 830(1); "work", s 203C; "year of assessment", s 832(1).
Cross reference—See TA 1988 s 144A (payments free of tax).
TA 1988 s 203J (accounting for tax for payments treated as made by virtue of this section).
Amendments—¹ This section inserted by FA 1994 s 126.

[203E PAYE: mobile UK workforce

(1) This subsection applies where it appears to the Board that—

(*a*) a person ("the relevant person") has entered into or is likely to enter into an agreement that employees of another person ("the contractor") shall in any period work for, but not as employees of, the relevant person;
(*b*) payments of, or on account of, assessable income of the employees in respect of work done in that period are likely to be made by or on behalf of the contractor; and

(*c*) PAYE regulations would apply on the making of such payments but it is likely that income tax will not be deducted or accounted for in accordance with the regulations.

(2) Where subsection (1) above applies, the Board may give a direction that, if—

(*a*) any employees of the contractor work in any period for, but not as employees of, the relevant person, and

(*b*) any payment is made by the relevant person in respect of work done by the employees in that period,

income tax shall be deducted in accordance with the provisions of this section by the relevant person on making that payment.

(3) A direction under subsection (2) above—

(*a*) shall specify the relevant person and the contractor to whom it relates;

(*b*) shall be given by notice to the relevant person; and

(*c*) may at any time be withdrawn by notice to the relevant person.

(4) The Board shall take such steps as are reasonably practicable to ensure that the contractor is supplied with a copy of any notice given under subsection (3) above which relates to him.

(5) Where—

(*a*) a direction under subsection (2) above has effect, and

(*b*) any employees of the contractor specified in the direction work for, but not as employees of, the relevant person so specified,

income tax shall, subject to and in accordance with PAYE regulations, be deducted by the relevant person on making any payment in respect of that work as if so much of the payment as is attributable to work done by each employee were a payment of assessable income of that employee.]¹

Commentary—*Simon's Direct Tax Service* **E4.909C.**
Revenue Internal Guidance—Schedule E manual, SE 11931 and 11932 (PAYE avoidance: agencies and offshore employers, table showing who has to operate PAYE for agency workers, cases of difficulty to be referred to Personal Tax Division).
Definitions—"Assessable", s 203L; "the Board", s 832(1); "employee", s 203L; "PAYE regulations", s 203L; "work", s 203C.
Cross reference—See TA 1988 s 144A (payments free of tax).
TA 1988 s 203J (accounting for tax for payments treated as made by virtue of this section).
Amendments—¹ This section inserted by FA 1994 s 126.

[203F PAYE: tradeable assets

(1) Where any assessable income of an employee is provided in the form of [a readily convertible asset]², the employer shall be treated, for the purposes of PAYE regulations, as making a payment of that income of an amount equal to the amount specified in subsection (3) below.

[(2) In this section "readily convertible asset" means—

(*a*) an asset capable of being sold or otherwise realised on a recognised investment exchange (within the meaning [given by section 285(1)(*a*) of the Financial Services and Markets Act 2000]⁶) or on the London Bullion Market;

(*b*) an asset capable of being sold or otherwise realised on a market for the time being specified in PAYE regulations;

(*c*) an asset consisting in the rights of an assignee, or any other rights, in respect of a money debt that is or may become due to the employer or any other person;

(*d*) an asset consisting in, or in any right in respect of, any property that is subject to a fiscal warehousing regime;

(*e*) an asset consisting in anything that is likely (without anything being done by the employee) to give rise to, or to become, a right enabling a person to obtain an amount or total amount of money which is likely to be similar to the expense incurred in the provision of the asset;

(*f*) an asset for which trading arrangements are in existence; or

(*g*) an asset for which trading arrangements are likely to come into existence in accordance with any arrangements of another description existing when the asset is provided or with any understanding existing at that time.

(3) The amount referred to is the amount which, on the basis of the best estimate that can reasonably be made, is the amount of income likely to be chargeable to tax under Schedule E in respect of the provision of the asset.

(3A) For the purposes of this section trading arrangements for any asset provided to any person exist whenever there exist any arrangements the effect of which in relation to that asset is to enable that person, or a member of his family or household, to obtain an amount or total amount of money that is, or is likely to be, similar to the expense incurred in the provision of that asset.

(3B) References in this section to enabling a person to obtain an amount of money shall be construed—

(*a*) as references to enabling an amount to be obtained by that person by any means at all, including, in particular-

(i) by using any asset or other property as security for a loan or advance, or

(ii) by using any rights comprised in or attached to any asset or other property to obtain any asset for which trading arrangements exist; and (*b*) as including references to cases where a person is enabled to obtain an amount as a member of a class or description of persons, as well as where he is so enabled in his own right.

(3C) For the purposes of this section an amount is similar to the expense incurred in the provision of any asset if it is, or is an amount of money equivalent to—

(*a*) the amount of the expense so incurred; or
(*b*) a greater amount; or
(*c*) an amount that is less than that amount but not substantially so.][3]

(4) For the purposes of [this section][4], "asset" does not include—

(*a*) any payment actually made of, or on account of, assessable income;
(*b*) any non-cash voucher, credit-token or cash voucher (as defined in sections 141 to 143); or
(*c*) any description of property for the time being excluded from the scope of this section by PAYE regulations.

(5) Subject to subsection (4) above, for the purposes of [this section][4] "asset" includes any property and in particular any [investment of a kind specified in Part III of the Financial Services and Markets Act 2000 (Regulated Activities) Order 2001.][6]][1]

[(6) In this section—

"EEA State" means a State which is a Contracting Party to the Agreement on the European Economic Area signed at Oporto on 2nd May 1992 as adjusted by the Protocol signed at Brussels on 17th March 1993;
"family or household" has the same meaning as it has, by virtue of section 168(4), in Chapter II of this Part;
"fiscal warehousing regime" means–

(*a*) a warehousing regime or fiscal warehousing regime (within the meaning of sections 18 to 18F of the Value Added Tax Act 1994); or
(*b*) any corresponding arrangements in an EEA State other than the United Kingdom;

"money" includes money expressed in a currency other than sterling or in the European currency unit (as for the time being defined in Council Regulation No. 3180/78/EEC or any Community instrument replacing it); and
"money debt" means any obligation which falls to be, or may be, settled–

(*a*) by the payment of money, or
(*b*) by the transfer of a right to settlement under an obligation which is itself a money debt.][5]

Commentary—*Simon's Direct Tax Service* **E4.909D**.
Regulations—IT (Employments) (Notional Payments) Regulations, SI 1994/1212.
Revenue & other press releases—IR Tax Bulletin February 1997 p 385 (updated article addressing some of the practical considerations of operating PAYE on payments in the form of tradeable assets).
IR Tax Bulletin August 1998 p 563 (Applying PAYE to remuneration in the form of readily convertible assets).
Revenue Internal Guidance—Schedule E manual, SE 03604 (non-cash consideration given to an employee for entering into a restrictive covenant caught by this section).
SE 11800 (PAYE avoidance: non-cash remuneration—table of contents for this section covering references SE 11801–11827, includes examples).
SE 11840 (enhancing the value of an existing asset: before 6 April 1998 this section applied if assets were "tradeable assets").
SE 11850 (employer required to operate PAYE if shares awarded to an employee, or acquired on exercise of an option, give rise to a Schedule E charge and are readily convertible assets).
SE 11852 (shares as readily convertible assets: share awards after 26 November 1996).
SE 11860–11861 and SE 11863 (examples of PAYE on share transactions).
SE 11900–11902 (the amount on which to operate PAYE).
SE 11931 and 11932 (PAYE avoidance: agencies and offshore employers, table showing who has to operate PAYE for agency workers, cases of difficulty to be referred to Personal Tax Division).
SE 11940 (example of payments by an agency in readily convertible assets).
SE 12000–12005 (non-cash remuneration before 6 April 1998 including examples).
SE 12010–12020 (the "tradeable asset" rules).
SE 64605 (tax treatment of insurance agents: Statement of Practice SP 4/97—where commission or other taxable income is provided in the form of tradable assets rather than cash, PAYE applies under this section).
Simon's Tax Cases—*DTE Financial Services Ltd v Wilson* [2001] STC 777.
Definitions—"Assessable", s 203L; "employee", s 203L; "PAYE regulations", s 203L; "trading arrangements", s 203K.
Cross reference—See TA 1988 s 144A (payments free of tax).
TA 1988 s 203J (accounting for tax for payments treated as made by virtue of this section).
FA 2000 Sch 8 para 94 (application of sub-s (3) in relation to shares ceasing to be subject to an employee share ownership plan).
Amendments—[1] This section inserted by FA 1994 s 127.
[2] Words in sub-s (1) substituted by FA 1998 s 65(2) with effect in relation to any asset provided after 5 April 1998 and deemed, in accordance with FA 1998 s 65(7), to have come into force on that date.
[3] Sub-ss (2), (3), (3A), (3B), (3C) substituted by FA 1998 s 65(3) with effect in relation to any asset provided after 5 April 1998 and deemed, in accordance with FA 1998 s 65(7), to have come into force on that date.
[4] Words in sub-ss (4), (5) substituted by FA 1998 s 65(4) with effect in relation to any asset provided after 5 April 1998 and deemed, in accordance with FA 1998 s 65(7), to have come into force on that date.
[5] Sub-s (6) inserted by FA 1998 s 65(5) with effect in relation to any asset provided after 5 April 1998 and deemed, in accordance with FA 1998 s 65(7), to have come into force on that date.
[6] Words in sub-ss (2)(*a*), (5) substituted by the Financial Services and Markets Act 2000 (Consequential Amendments) (Taxes) Order, SI 2001/3629 arts 13, 17 with effect from 1 December 2001, immediately after the coming into force of the Financial Services and Markets Act 2000 ss 411, 432(1), Sch 20.

[203FA PAYE: enhancing the value of an asset

(1) Where—

(*a*) any assessable income of an employee is provided in the form of anything enhancing the value of an asset in which the employee or a member of his family or household already has an interest, and

(*b*) that asset, with its value enhanced, would be treated as a readily convertible asset for the purposes of section 203F if assessable income were provided to the employee in the form of that asset at the time of the enhancement,

that section shall have effect (subject to subsection (2) below) as if the employee had been provided, at that time, with assessable income in the form of the asset (with its value enhanced), instead of with whatever enhanced its value.

(2) Where section 203F has effect in accordance with subsection (1) above, subsection (3) of that section shall apply as if the reference in subsection (3) of that section to the provision of the asset were a reference to the enhancement of its value.

(3) Subject to subsection (4) below, any reference in this section to enhancing the value of an asset is a reference to—

(*a*) the provision of any services by which that asset or any right or interest in it is improved or otherwise made more valuable,

(*b*) the provision of any property the addition of which to the asset in question improves it or otherwise increases its value, or

(*c*) the provision of any other enhancement by the application of money or property to the improvement of the asset in question or to securing an increase in its value or in the value of any right or interest in it.

(4) PAYE regulations may make provision excluding such matters as may be described in the regulations from the scope of what constitutes enhancing the value of an asset for the purposes of this section.

(5) Expressions used in this section and in section 203F have the same meanings in this section as in that section.][1]

Commentary—*Simon's Direct Tax Service* **E4.909D.**
Revenue Internal Guidance—Schedule E manual, SE 03604 (non-cash consideration given to an employee for entering into a restrictive covenant caught by this section).
SE 11840 (PAYE avoidance: enhancing the value of an existing asset).
SE 11841 (enhancing an asset: example—premium paid to an existing life assurance policy).
SE 11862 (PAYE on share transactions: example 3—option cancelled in return for payment).
SE 11931 and 11932 (PAYE avoidance: agencies and offshore employers, table showing who has to operate PAYE for agency workers, cases of difficulty to be referred to Personal Tax Division).
SE 12000–12005 (non-cash remuneration before 6 April 1998 including examples).
SE 12010–12020 (the "tradeable asset" rules).
SE 12030–12102 (non-cash remuneration: handling of cases; Revenue has responsibility for NIC; procedures for dealing with cases; guidance on NIC charge).
Amendments—[1] Section inserted by FA 1998 s 66(1) with effect in relation to any assessable income provided after 5 April 1998 and deemed, in accordance with FA 1998 s 66(3), to have come into force on that date.

[203FB PAYE: gains from share options etc

(1) This section applies where an event occurs by virtue of which an amount is assessable on any person ("the relevant person") by virtue of section 135, 140A(4) or 140D.

(2) If that event is the exercise of a right to acquire shares, section 203F shall have effect, subject to [subsection (6A)][2] below, as if the relevant person were being provided—

(*a*) at the time he acquires the shares in exercise of that right, and

(*b*) in respect of the office or employment by reason of which he was granted the right,

with assessable income in the form of those shares.

(3) If that event is the assignment or release of a right to acquire shares, sections 203 to 203F shall have effect, subject to [subsection (6A)][2] below—

(*a*) in so far as the consideration for the assignment or release takes the form of a payment, as if so much of that payment as does not exceed the amount assessable by virtue of section 135 were a payment of assessable income of the relevant person; and

(*b*) in so far as that consideration consists in the provision of an asset, as if the provision of that asset were the provision—

(i) to the relevant person, and

(ii) in respect of the office or employment by reason of which he was granted the right,

of assessable income in the form of that asset.

(4) If that event is an event falling within subsection (4)(*a*) or (*b*) of section 140A, sections 203 to 203F shall have effect, subject to subsection (7) below, as if—

(*a*) the provision to the relevant person of the employee's interest in the shares included the provision to him at the time of the event of a further interest in those shares; and

(*b*) the further interest were not subject to any terms by virtue of which it would fall for the purposes of section 140A to be treated as only conditional.

(5) If that event is an event falling within subsection (3) of section 140D, sections 203 to 203F shall have effect, subject to subsection (7) below, as if the original provision to the relevant person of the convertible shares or securities included the provision to him at the time of the event of the shares or securities into which they are converted.

(6) Subsection (5) above shall apply in a case where the convertible shares or securities were themselves acquired by means of a taxable conversion (as defined in section 140D(7)), or by a series of such conversions, as if the reference to the original provision of the convertible shares or securities were a reference to the provision of the shares or securities which were converted by the earlier or earliest conversion.

[(6A) Where section 203F has effect in accordance with subsection (2) or (3) above, subsection (3) of section 203F shall apply as if the reference in that subsection to the amount of income likely to be chargeable to tax under Schedule E in respect of the provision of the asset were a reference to the amount on which tax is likely to be chargeable by virtue of section 135 in respect of the event in question, reduced by the amount of any relief likely to be available under section 187A.][2]

(7) Where section 203F has effect in accordance with [subsection (4) or (5) above][2], subsection (3) of section 203F shall apply as if the reference in that subsection to the amount of income likely to be chargeable to tax under Schedule E in respect of the provision of the asset were a reference to the amount on which tax is likely to be chargeable by virtue of [section 140A or 140D][2] in respect of the event in question.

(8) PAYE regulations may make provision for excluding payments from the scope of subsection (3)(*a*) above in such circumstances as may be specified in the regulations.

(9) In this section "asset" means—

    (*a*) any asset within the meaning of section 203F; or

    (*b*) any non-cash voucher, credit-token or cash voucher (as defined for the purposes of section 141, 142 or, as the case may be, 143).

(10) Expressions used in this section and in any of sections 135 and 140A to 140H have the same meanings in this section as in that section, and any reference in this section to—

    (*a*) an event falling within subsection (4)(*a*) or (*b*) of section 140A, or

    (*b*) an event falling within subsection (3) of section 140D,

includes a reference to an event which is treated for the purposes of that section as such an event by virtue of section 140A(8) or 140F(1).][1]

Commentary—*Simon's Direct Tax Service* **E4.909D.**
Revenue Internal Guidance—Schedule E manual, SE 03604 (non-cash consideration given to an employee for entering into a restrictive covenant caught by this section).
SE 11800 (PAYE avoidance: non-cash remuneration—table of contents for this section covering references SE 11850–11863, includes examples).
SE 11931 and 11932 (PAYE avoidance: agencies and offshore employers, table showing who has to operate PAYE for agency workers, cases of difficulty to be referred to Personal Tax Division).
SE 12000–12005 (non-cash remuneration before 6 April 1998 including examples).
SE 12010–12020 (the "tradeable asset" rules).
SE 12030–12102 (non-cash remuneration: handling of cases; Revenue has responsibility for NIC; procedures for dealing with cases; guidance on NIC charge).
Modification—The reference in sub-s (6A) above to relief likely to be available under TA 1988 s 187A is treated as not including a reference to any relief available by virtue of Social Security Contributions (Share Options) Act 2001 s 4 in respect of any liability which is prevented from arising, or is treated as not having arisen, by virtue of s 2(1)(*a*) or (*b*) or (4) of that Act: Social Security Contributions (Share Options) Act 2001 s 4.
Amendments—[1] This section inserted by FA 1998 s 67(1) with effect in relation to events occurring after 5 April 1998 and deemed, in accordance with FA 1998 s 67(3), to have come into force at that date.
[2] Words in sub-ss (2), (3) substituted for words "subsection (7)"; words in sub-s (7) substituted for words "any of the preceding provisions of this section" and "section 135, 140A or 140D" respectively; and sub-s (6A) inserted by FA 2000 s 56(2) with effect where the event giving rise to the charge to tax occurs after 28 July 2000.

[203G PAYE: non-cash vouchers

(1) Where a non-cash voucher to which this section applies is received by an employee, the employer shall be treated, for the purposes of PAYE regulations, as making a payment of assessable income of the employee of an amount equal to the amount ascertained in accordance with section 141(1)(*a*).

(2) This section applies to a non-cash voucher to which section 141(1) applies if—

    (*a*) either of the two conditions set out below is fulfilled with respect to the voucher; and

    (*b*) the voucher is not of a description for the time being excluded from the scope of this section by PAYE regulations.][1]

[(3) The first condition is fulfilled with respect to a non-cash voucher if it is capable of being exchanged for anything which, if provided to the employee at the time when the voucher is received, would fall to be regarded as a readily convertible asset for the purposes of section 203F.

(4) The second condition is fulfilled with respect to a non-cash voucher if (but for section 203F(4)(*b*)) it would itself fall to be regarded as a readily convertible asset for the purposes of section 203F.

(5) Subsection (5) of section 141 (time of receipt of voucher appropriated to employee) shall apply for the purposes of this section as it applies for the purposes of subsections (1) and (2) of that section.][2]

Commentary—*Simon's Direct Tax Service* **E4.909D.**
Revenue Internal Guidance—Schedule E manual, SE 03604 (non-cash consideration given to an employee for entering into a restrictive covenant caught by this section).
SE 11910 (PAYE avoidance: PAYE on vouchers and credit tokens).
SE 11931 and 11932 (PAYE avoidance: agencies and offshore employers, table showing who has to operate PAYE for agency workers, cases of difficulty to be referred to Personal Tax Division).
SE 12000–12005 (non-cash remuneration before 6 April 1998 including examples).
SE 12010–12020 (the "tradeable asset" rules).
SE 12030–12102 (non-cash remuneration: handling of cases; Revenue has responsibility for NIC; procedures for dealing with cases; guidance on NIC charge).
Definitions—"Assessable", s 203L; "employee", s 203L; "PAYE regulations", s 203L; "trading arrangements", s 203K.
Cross reference—See TA 1988 s 144A (payments free of tax).
TA 1988 s 203J (accounting for tax for payments treated as made by virtue of this section).
IT (Employments) (Notional Payments) Regulations, SI 1994/1212 reg 6 (non-cash vouchers, time of payment).
Amendments—[1] This section inserted by FA 1994 s 128.
[2] Sub-ss (3)–(5) substituted by FA 1998 s 68(1) with effect in relation to non-cash vouchers or cash vouchers received after 5 April 1998, and in relation to any use of a credit-token on or after that date, and deemed, in accordance with FA 1998 s 68(5), to have come into force on that date.

[203H PAYE: credit-tokens

(1) Subject to subsection (3) below, on each occasion on which an employee uses a credit-token provided to him by reason of his employment to obtain—

(*a*) money, or

[(*b*) anything which, if provided to the employee at the time when the credit-token is used, would fall to be regarded as a readily convertible asset for the purposes of section 203F,][2]

the employer shall be treated, for the purposes of PAYE regulations, as making a payment of assessable income of the employee of an amount equal to the amount ascertained in accordance with section 142(1)(*a*).

(2) [...][2]

(3) PAYE regulations may make provision for excluding from the scope of this section any description of use of a credit-token.

(4) In this section "credit-token" has the same meaning as in section 142.][1]

Commentary—*Simon's Direct Tax Service* **E4.909D.**
Revenue Internal Guidance—Schedule E manual, SE 03604 (non-cash consideration given to an employee for entering into a restrictive covenant caught by this section).
SE 11910 (PAYE avoidance: PAYE on vouchers and credit tokens).
SE 11931 and 11932 (PAYE avoidance: agencies and offshore employers, table showing who has to operate PAYE for agency workers, cases of difficulty to be referred to Personal Tax Division).
SE 12000–12005 (non-cash remuneration before 6 April 1998 including examples)
SE 12010–12020 (the "tradeable asset" rules).
SE 12030–12102 (non-cash remuneration: handling of cases; Revenue has responsibility for NIC; procedures for dealing with cases; guidance on NIC charge).
Definitions—"Assessable", s 203L; "employee", s 203L; "PAYE regulations", s 203L; "trading arrangements", s 203K.
Cross reference—See TA 1988 s 144A (payments free of tax).
See TA 1988 s 203J (accounting for tax for payments treated as made by virtue of this section).
IT (Employments) (Notional Payments) Regulations, SI 1994/1212 reg 3 (exclusion of property from s 203F).
Amendments—[1] This section inserted by FA 1994 s 129.
[2] Sub-s (1)(*b*) substituted, and sub-s (2) repealed by FA 1998 s 68(2) with effect in relation to non-cash vouchers or cash vouchers received after 5 April 1998, and in relation to any use of a credit-token on or after that date, and deemed, in accordance with FA 1998 s 68(5), to have come into force on that date.

[203I PAYE: cash vouchers

(1) Subject to subsection (2) below, where a cash voucher to which section 143(1) applies is received by an employee, the employer shall be treated, for the purposes of PAYE regulations, as making a payment of assessable income of the employee of an amount equal to the amount ascertained in accordance with section 143(1)(*a*).

(2) PAYE regulations may make provision for excluding from the scope of this section the provision of cash vouchers in such description of circumstances as may be specified in the regulations.][1]

[(3) Subsection (2) of section 143 (time of receipt of voucher appropriated to employee) shall apply for the purposes of this section as it applies for the purposes of subsections (1) and (5) of that section.][2]

Commentary—*Simon's Direct Tax Service* **E4.909D.**
Revenue Internal Guidance—Schedule E manual, SE 03604 (non-cash consideration given to an employee for entering into a restrictive covenant caught by this section).
SE 11910 (PAYE avoidance: PAYE on vouchers and credit tokens).
SE 11931 and 11932 (PAYE avoidance: agencies and offshore employers, table showing who has to operate PAYE for agency workers, cases of difficulty to be referred to Personal Tax Division).
SE 12000–12005 (non-cash remuneration before 6 April 1998 including examples).
SE 12010–12020 (the "tradeable asset" rules).
SE 12030–12102 (non-cash remuneration: handling of cases; Revenue has responsibility for NIC; procedures for dealing with cases; guidance on NIC charge).
Definitions—"Assessable", s 203L; "employee", s 203L; "PAYE regulations", s 203L.
Cross reference—See TA 1988 s 144A (payments free of tax).
See TA 1988 s 203J (accounting for tax for payments treated as made by virtue of this section).
IT (Employments) (Notional Payments) Regulations, SI 1994/1212 reg 5 (exclusion of cash vouchers from s 203I).
Amendments—[1] This section inserted by FA 1994 s 130.
[2] Sub-s (3) inserted by FA 1998 s 68(3) with effect in relation to non-cash vouchers or cash vouchers received after 5 April 1998, and in relation to any use of a credit-token on or after that date, and deemed, in accordance with FA 1998 s 68(5), to have come into force on that date.

[203J s 203B to s 203I: accounting for tax

(1) Where an employer makes a notional payment of assessable income of an employee, the obligation to deduct income tax shall have effect as an obligation on the employer to deduct income tax at such time as may be prescribed by PAYE regulations from any payment or payments he actually makes of, or on account of, such income of that employee.

(2) For the purposes of this section—

(*a*) a notional payment is a payment treated as made by virtue of any of sections 203B, 203C and 203F to 203I, other than a payment whose amount is determined in accordance with section 203B(3)(*a*) or 203C(3)(*a*); and

(*b*) any reference to an employer includes a reference to a person who is treated as making a payment by virtue of section 203C(2).

(3) Where, by reason of an insufficiency of payments actually made, the employer is unable to deduct the amount (or the full amount) of the income tax as required by virtue of subsection (1) above, the obligation to deduct income tax shall have effect as an obligation on the employer to account to the Board at such time as may be prescribed by PAYE regulations for an amount of income tax equal to the amount of income tax he is required, but is unable, to deduct.

(4) PAYE regulations may make provision—

(*a*) with respect to the time when any notional payment (or description of notional payment) is made;

(*b*) applying (with or without modifications) any specified provisions of the regulations for the time being in force in relation to deductions from actual payments to amounts accounted for in respect of any notional payments;

(*c*) with respect to the collection and recovery of amounts accounted for in respect of notional payments.

(5) Any amount which an employer deducts or for which he accounts as mentioned in subsections (1) and (3) above shall be treated as an amount paid by the employee in question in respect of his liability to income tax for such year of assessment as may be specified in PAYE regulations.][1]

Commentary—*Simon's Direct Tax Service* **E4.949.**
Revenue Internal Guidance—Schedule E manual, SE 03604 (non-cash consideration given to an employee for entering into a restrictive covenant caught by this section).
SE 11931 and 11932 (PAYE avoidance: agencies and offshore employers, table showing who has to operate PAYE for agency workers, cases of difficulty to be referred to Personal Tax Division).
SE 11950 (application of sub-s 2)
SE 12000–12005 (non-cash remuneration before 6 April 1998 including examples).
SE 12010–12020 (the "tradeable asset" rules)
SE 12030–12102 (non-cash remuneration: handling of cases; Revenue has responsibility for NIC; procedures for dealing with cases; guidance on NIC charge).
Definitions—"Assessable", s 203L; "the Board", s 832(1); "employee", s 203L; "PAYE regulations", s 203L.
Cross reference—See TA 1988 s 144A (payments free of tax).
IT (Employments) (Notional Payments) Regulations, SI 1994/1212 regs 7, 8 (deduction of income tax and accounting for income tax where inability to deduct).
FA 2000 Sch 8 para 95(4) (application of sub-s (1) in relation to shares ceasing to be subject to the employee share ownership plan).
Amendments—[1] This section inserted by FA 1994 s 131.

[203K Trading arrangements

(1)–(3) ...[2]

(4) PAYE regulations may exclude any description of arrangements from being trading arrangements for the purposes of sections 203F to 203H.][1]

Commentary—*Simon's Direct Tax Service* **E4.909D.**
Revenue Internal Guidance—Schedule E manual, SE 03604 (non-cash consideration given to an employee for entering into a restrictive covenant caught by this section).
SE 11824 (readily convertible assets: example—property held in a "bonded" warehouse).
SE 11931 and 11932 (PAYE avoidance: agencies and offshore employers, table showing who has to operate PAYE for agency workers, cases of difficulty to be referred to Personal Tax Division).
SE 12000–12005 (non-cash remuneration before 6 April 1998 including examples).
SE 12010–12020 (the "tradeable asset" rules).
SE 12030–12102 (non-cash remuneration: handling of cases; Revenue has responsibility for NIC; procedures for dealing with cases; guidance on NIC charge).
Simon's Tax Cases—*DTE Financial Services Ltd v Wilson* [2001] STC 777.
Definitions—"PAYE regulations", s 203L.
Amendments—[1] This section inserted by FA 1994 s 131.
[2] Sub-ss (1)–(3) repealed by FA 1998 s 165, Sch 27 Part III(12) with effect in relation to assets provided and non-cash vouchers received at any time after 5 April 1998, and in relation to any use of a credit-token on or after that date.

[203L S 203B to s 203K: interpretation, etc

[(1) Subject to subsections (1A) and (1B) below and section 203J(2)(*b*), in sections 203B to 203J—

"employee" means a person who holds or has held any office or employment under or with another person; and "employer"—

(*a*) in relation to an employee, means a person under or with whom that employee holds or has held an office or employment; and

(*b*) in relation to any assessable income of an employee, means the person who is the employer of that employee in relation to the office or employment in respect of which that income is or was provided or, as the case may be, by reference to which it falls to be regarded as assessable.

(1A) Subject to subsection (1B) below, where the remuneration receivable by an individual under or in consequence of any contract falls to be treated under section 134 (agency workers) as the emoluments of an office or employment, sections 203B to 203K (except section 203E) shall have effect as if that person held that office or employment under or with the agency.

(1B) Where—

(*a*) the remuneration receivable by an individual under or in consequence of any contract falls to be so treated under section 134, and

(*b*) a payment of, or on account of, assessable income of that individual is made by a person acting on behalf of the client and at the expense of the client or a person connected with the client,

section 203B and, in relation to any payment treated as made by the client under section 203B, section 203J shall have effect in relation to that payment as if the client and not the agency were the employer for the purposes of sections 203B to 203K.

(1C) In subsections (1A) and (1B) above "the agency" and "the client" have the same meanings as in section 134; and section 839 applies for the purposes of those subsections.

(2) In sections 203B to 203K and in this section "assessable" means assessable to income tax under Schedule E.][2]

(3) In sections 203B to 203K and this section "PAYE regulations" means regulations under section 203.

(4) PAYE regulations made by virtue of any of sections 203B to 203K may—

(*a*) make different provision for different classes of case;

(*b*) contain such incidental, consequential and supplementary provision as appears to the Board to be expedient.][1]

Commentary—*Simon's Direct Tax Service* **E4.909A–909D.**
Revenue Internal Guidance—Schedule E manual, SE 03604 (non-cash consideration given to an employee for entering into a restrictive covenant caught by this section).
SE 11920 (PAYE avoidance: award of non-cash remuneration to a former employee).
SE 11930 (PAYE avoidance: agencies and offshore employers—general).
SE 11931 and 11932 (PAYE avoidance: agencies and offshore employers, table showing who has to operate PAYE for agency workers, cases of difficulty to be referred to Personal Tax Division).
SE 11940 (example of payments by an agency in readily convertible assets).
SE 11941 (example of payment by an overseas intermediary in cash).
SE 11942 (example of payment by an overseas intermediary in readily convertible assets).
SE 12030–12102 (non-cash remuneration: handling of cases; Revenue has responsibility for NIC; procedures for dealing with cases; guidance on NIC charge).
Definition—"Schedule E", s 19.
Amendments—[1] This section inserted by FA 1994 s 131.
[2] Sub-ss (1), (1A), (1B), (1C), (2) substituted by FA 1998 s 69(3) with effect in relation to payments made, assets provided and vouchers received at any time after 5 April 1998 and in relation to any use of a credit-token on or after that date.

204 PAYE repayments

Without prejudice to the generality of section 203, regulations under that section may provide that no repayment of income tax shall be made under that section to any person if at any time—

(*a*) he has claimed unemployment benefit in respect of a period including that time; or

[(*aa*) he has claimed a jobseeker's allowance in respect of a period including that time; or][1]

(*b*) he has claimed a payment of income support under the Social Security Act 1986 or the Social Security (Northern Ireland) Order 1986 in respect of a period including that time and his right to that income support is subject to the condition specified in section 20(3)(*d*)(i) of that Act or, in Northern Ireland, Article 21(3)(*d*)(i) of that Order (availability for employment); or

(*c*) he is disqualified at the time from receiving unemployment benefit by virtue of section 19 of the Social Security Act 1975 or of section 19 of the Social Security (Northern Ireland) Act 1975 (loss of employment due to stoppage of work) or would be so disqualified if he otherwise satisfied the conditions for entitlement; [or][1]

[(*d*) he is prevented at the time from being entitled to a jobseeker's allowance by section 14 of the Jobseekers Act 1995 (trade disputes) or any corresponding enactment in Northern Ireland or would be so prevented if he otherwise satisfied the conditions for entitlement;][1]

and such regulations may make different provision with respect to persons falling within paragraph (*c*) [or (*d*)][1] above from that made with respect to other persons.

Commentary—*Simon's Direct Tax Service* **E4.952, 953.**
Regulations—IT (Employments) Regulations, SI 1993/744.
Notes—SSA 1986 s 20 and SS (Northern Ireland) Order 1986, art 21 referred to in para (*b*) above are re-enacted in Social Security Contributions and Benefits Act 1992 s 124(1)(*d*)(i) and Social Security Contributions and Benefits (Northern Ireland) Act 1992 s 123(1)(*d*)(i).
SSA 1975 s 19 and SS (Northern Ireland) A 1975, s 19 referred to in para (*c*) above are re-enacted in Social Security Contributions and Benefits Act 1992 s 27 and Social Security Contributions and Benefits (Northern Ireland) Act 1992 s 27.

Simon's Tax Cases—*IRC v Herd* [1992] STC 264*.
Amendments—[1] Para (*aa*), para (*d*) and the word "or" immediately preceding it, and the words "or (*d*)" inserted by the Jobseekers Act 1995 Sch 2 para 14, as from 2 September 1996 (see the Jobseekers Act 1995 (Commencement No 4) Order 1996, SI 1996/2208).

[205 Assessments unnecessary in certain circumstances

(1) Subject to the provisions of this section, no assessment need be made in respect of income assessable to income tax for any year of assessment if the income has been taken into account in the making of deductions or repayments of income tax by virtue of regulations made under section 203.

(2) Subsection (1) above does not apply if the total net tax deducted in the year in question from the income is not the same as it would have been if—

    (*a*) all the relevant circumstances had been known to all parties throughout the year;

    (*b*) deductions and repayments had throughout the year been made accordingly; and

    (*c*) the deductions and repayments had been so made by reference to cumulative tax tables.

(3) Nothing in this section shall be construed as preventing an assessment (whether under section 9 of the Management Act or otherwise) being made in respect of income assessable to income tax for any year of assessment.

(4) A person as regards whose income for a year of assessment deductions or repayments have been made may by notice, given not later than five years after the 31st October next following that year, require an officer of the Board to give him notice under section 8 of that Act in respect of that year.

(5) In this section—

    (*a*) "cumulative tax tables" means tax tables prepared under section 203 which are so framed as to require the tax which is to be deducted or repaid on the occasion of each payment made in the year to be ascertained by reference to a total of emoluments paid in the year up to the time of making that payment; and

    (*b*) any reference to the total net tax deducted shall be construed as a reference to the total income tax deducted during the year by virtue of regulations made under section 203, less any income tax repaid by virtue of any such regulations.][1]

Commentary—*Simon's Direct Tax Service* **E4.971.**
Revenue Internal Guidance—Schedule E manual, SE 71405 (assessments, appeals and other procedures: this section provides that assessments are not needed when PAYE gets things right in the tax year but the section also gives taxpayers the right to self assess for any year).
Definitions—"The Board", s 832(1); "emoluments", s 131(1); "Management Act", s 831(3); "notice", s 832(1); "year of assessment", s 832(1).
Amendments—[1] This section substituted by FA 1995 ss 103(7), 111(1), with effect from the year 1996–97.

206 Additional provision for certain assessments

Where an assessment to income tax ...[1] is made as respects income which—

    (*a*) has been taken into account in the making of deductions or repayments of tax under section 203, and

    (*b*) was received not less than 12 months before the beginning of the year of assessment in which the assessment is made,

then, if the assessment is made after the expiration of the period of 12 months immediately following the year of assessment for which it is made, it shall be made in accordance with the practice generally prevailing at the expiration of that period.

Commentary—*Simon's Direct Tax Service* **E4.971.**
Revenue Internal Guidance—Schedule E manual SE 42440 (assessments made after a change of practice: general introduction; application of this section rare; cases to be submitted to Personal Tax Division).
SE 42450 (income to which the change of practice rule applies).
SE 42460 (cases involving exemption from tax and application of *Walters v Tickner* (66TC174)).
SE 42470 (emoluments from offices and employments and the basis of assessment: assessments made after a change of practice—how the change of practice rule applies).
SE 74251 (rules apply to pensions and annuities).
Simon's Tax Cases—*Walters v Tickner* [1993] STC 624*.
Definition—"Year of assessment", s 832(1).
Amendments—[1] Words repealed by FA 1995 ss 103(7), 111(2), Sch 29 Pt VIII(14), with effect from the year 1996–97.

[206A PAYE settlement agreements

(1) PAYE regulations may make provision falling within subsection (2) below about the sums which, as sums in respect of income tax under Schedule E on emoluments of a person's employees, are to be the sums for which the employer is to be accountable to the Board from time to time.

(2) That provision is provision under which the accountability of the employer, and the sums for which he is to be accountable, are to be determined, to such extent as may be prescribed, in accordance with an agreement between the Board and the employer ("a PAYE settlement agreement"), instead of under PAYE regulations made otherwise than by virtue of this section.

(3) PAYE regulations may provide for a PAYE settlement agreement to allow sums for which an employer is to be accountable to the Board in accordance with the agreement—

    (*a*) to be computed, in cases where there are two or more persons holding employments to which the agreement relates, by reference to a number of those persons all taken together;

(*b*) to include sums representing income tax on an estimated amount taken, in accordance with the agreement, to be the aggregate of the cash equivalents and other amounts chargeable to tax in respect of—

(i) taxable benefits provided or made available by reason of the employments to which the agreement relates; and

(ii) expenses paid to the persons holding those employments;

and

(*c*) to be computed in a manner under which the sums for which the employer is accountable do not necessarily represent an amount of income tax payable in respect of income which (apart from the regulations) is assessable under Schedule E on persons holding employments to which the agreement relates.

(4) PAYE regulations may provide—

(*a*) for an employer who is accountable to the Board under a PAYE settlement agreement for any sum to be so accountable without that sum, or any other sum, being treated for any prescribed purpose as tax deducted from emoluments;

(*b*) for an employee to have no right to be treated as having paid tax in respect of sums for which his employer is accountable under such an agreement;

(*c*) for an employee to be treated, except—

(i) for the purposes of the obligations imposed on his employer by such an agreement, and

(ii) to such further extent as may be prescribed,

as relieved from any prescribed obligations of his under the Income Tax Acts in respect of emoluments from an employment to which the agreement relates; and

(*d*) for such emoluments to be treated as excluded from the employee's income for such further purposes of the Income Tax Acts, and to such extent, as may be prescribed.

(5) For the purposes of any PAYE regulations made by virtue of this section it shall be immaterial that any agreement to which they relate was entered into before the coming into force of the regulations.

(6) PAYE regulations made by virtue of this section may—

(*a*) make different provision for different cases; and

(*b*) contain such incidental, supplemental, consequential and transitional provision as the Board may think fit.

(7) Without prejudice to the generality of subsection (6) above, the transitional provision that may be made by virtue of that subsection includes transitional provision for any year of assessment which—

(*a*) for the purposes of the regulations, treats sums accounted for in that year before the coming into force of the regulations as accounted for in accordance with an agreement as respects which the regulations have effect after they come into force; and

(*b*) provides, by reference to any provision made by virtue of paragraph (*a*) above, for income arising in that year before the coming into force of the regulations to be treated as income in relation to which modifications of the Income Tax Acts contained in the regulations apply.

(8) Without prejudice to the generality of subsection (6) above, any power of the Board to make PAYE regulations with respect to sums falling to be accounted for under such regulations shall include power to make the corresponding provision with respect to sums falling, by virtue of this section, to be accounted for in accordance with a PAYE settlement agreement.

(9) In this section—

"employment" means any office or employment the emoluments from which are (or, apart from any regulations made by virtue of this section, would be) assessable to tax under Schedule E, and cognate expressions shall be construed accordingly;

"PAYE regulations" means regulations under section 203;

"prescribed" means prescribed by PAYE regulations;

"taxable benefit", in relation to an employee, means any benefit provided or made available, otherwise than in the form of a payment of money, to the employee or to a person who is, for the purposes of Chapter II of this Part, a member of his family or household;

and references in this section to a time before the coming into force of any regulations include references to a time before the commencement of section 110 of the Finance Act 1996 (by virtue of which this section was inserted in this Act).][1]

Commentary—*Simon's Direct Tax Service* E4.968.
Regulations—IT (Employments) Regulations, SI 1993/744, regs 80A–80N.
Statement of Practice SP 5/96—PAYE settlement agreements.
Definitions—"The Board", s 832(1); "emoluments", s 131(1); "Income Tax Acts", s 831(1)(*b*); "member of a person's family or household", s 168(4); "Schedule E", s 19(1); "tax", s 832(3); "year of assessment", s 832(1).
Amendments—[1] Section inserted by FA 1996 s 110.

207 Disputes as to domicile or ordinary residence

Where a dispute arises under paragraph 1 of Schedule E or under section 192 whether a person is or has been ordinarily resident or domiciled in the United Kingdom, the question shall be referred to and determined by the Board; but any person who is aggrieved by their decision on the question may, by notice to that effect given to them within three months from the date on which notice is given to him, make an application to have the question heard and determined by the Special Commissioners, and where such an application is so made, the Special Commissioners shall hear and determine the question in like manner as an appeal.

Commentary—*Simon's Direct Tax Service* **E6.106.**
Statement of Practice SP 3/81—Individuals coming to the UK: ordinary residence.
Definitions—"The Board", s 832(1); "notice", s 832(1); "Schedule E", s 19(1); "United Kingdom", s 832(1).
Cross reference—See TCGA 1992 s 9(2) (this section also applies in relation to capital gains tax).

PART VI
COMPANY DISTRIBUTIONS, TAX CREDITS ETC

Cross references—See TA 1988 s 254 (interpretation).

CHAPTER I
TAXATION OF COMPANY DISTRIBUTIONS

207A Application of lower rate to company distributions

Commentary—*Simon's Direct Tax Service* **D1.401.**
Amendments—This section repealed by FA 1996 Sch 41 Pt V(1) with effect from the year 1996–97 (previously inserted by FA 1993, s 77(1), (2), (5)).

208 UK company distributions not generally chargeable to corporation tax

Except as otherwise provided by the Corporation Tax Acts, corporation tax shall not be chargeable on dividends and other distributions of a company resident in the United Kingdom, nor shall any such dividends or distributions be taken into account in computing income for corporation tax.

Commentary—*Simon's Direct Tax Service* **D1.101; D2.105.**
Statement of Practice SP 4/89—Where an incorporated shareholder receives a distribution arising from a company's purchase of its own shares, the distribution is treated as capital gains and charged to corporation tax. This practice applies where the purchase of own shares takes place after 19 April 1989.
Definitions—"The Corporation Tax Acts", s 831(1)(*a*); "distributions", s 209(2).
Cross references—See TA 1988 s 95(1A) (treatment of qualifying distribution to which FA 1997 Sch 7 applies (special treatment for certain distributions) received by a dealer).
TA 1988 s 434(1) (in relation to distributions made before 2 July 1997, this section does not prevent franked investment income and foreign income dividends being taken into account in the computation of policy holder's share of profits of a life assurance company for the purposes of FA 1989 s 89(7) and in limiting relief for expenses of management under TA 1988 s 76(2)).
TA 1988 s 434(1) (in relation to distributions made after 1 July 1997, this section does not apply to the charge to corporation tax on the life assurance profits of an insurance company computed under Schedule D Case I or to the computation of such profits).
TA 1988 s 440B(1A) (nothing in this section is to prevent foreign income dividends from being taken into account in the computation of a company's life assurance business profits under Schedule D Case I).
TA 1988 s 438(3) (franked investment income to be taken into account in computing income of a life assurance company's pension business).
TA 1988 s 441A(1) (this section not to apply to a distribution in respect of any asset of an insurance company's overseas life assurance fund).
FA 1994 s 219(4) (distributions of a UK company to be included in the profits of a Lloyd's corporate member notwithstanding this section).

CHAPTER II
MATTERS WHICH ARE DISTRIBUTIONS FOR THE PURPOSES OF THE CORPORATION TAX ACTS

Cross references—See FA 1995 s 152(3)(*b*) (Treasury may make regulations modifying this Chapter in its application to open-ended investment companies).

209 Meaning of "distribution"

(1) The following provisions of this Chapter, together with section 418, shall, subject to [any express exceptions][6], have effect with respect to the meaning of "distribution" and for determining the persons to whom certain distributions are to be treated as made, but references in the Corporation Tax Acts to distributions of a company shall not apply to distributions made in respect of share capital in a winding up.

(2) In the Corporation Tax Acts "distribution", in relation to any company, means—

(*a*) any dividend paid by the company, including a capital dividend;
(*b*) subject to subsections (5) and (6) below, any other distribution out of assets of the company (whether in cash or otherwise) in respect of shares in the company, except so much of the distribution, if any, as represents repayment of capital on the shares or is, when it is made, equal in amount or value to any new consideration received by the company for the distribution;
(*c*) subject to section 230, any redeemable share capital or any security issued by the company in respect of shares in or securities of the company otherwise than wholly for new consideration, or

such part of any redeemable share capital or any security so issued as is not properly referable to new consideration;

(*d*) any interest or other distribution out of assets of the company in respect of securities of the company, where they are securities under which the consideration given by the company for the use of the principal thereby secured represents more than a reasonable commercial return for the use of that principal, except so much, if any, of any such distribution as represents that principal and so much as represents a reasonable commercial return for the use of that principal;

[(*da*) any interest or other distribution out of assets of the company ("the issuing company") in respect of securities issued by that company which are held by another company where—

    (i) the issuing company is a 75 per cent subsidiary of the other company or both are 75 per cent subsidiaries of a third company, and

    (ii) the whole or any part of the distribution represents an amount which would not have fallen to be paid to the other company if the companies had been companies between whom there was (apart from in respect of the securities in question) no relationship, arrangements or other connection (whether formal or informal),

except so much, if any, of any such distribution as does not represent such an amount or as is a distribution by virtue of paragraph (*d*) above or an amount representing the principal secured by the securities;]³

(*e*) any interest or other distribution out of assets of the company in respect of securities of the company (except so much, if any, of any such distribution as represents the principal thereby secured and except so much of any distribution as falls within [paragraph (*d*) or (*da*)]³ above), where the securities are—

    (i) securities issued as mentioned in paragraph (*c*) above, but excluding securities issued before 6th April 1965 in respect of shares and securities issued before 6th April 1972 in respect of securities; or

    (ii) securities convertible directly or indirectly into shares in the company or securities issued after 5th April 1972 and carrying any right to receive shares in or securities of the company, not being (in either case) securities [listed]⁴ on a recognised stock exchange nor issued on terms which are reasonably comparable with the terms of issue of securities so [listed]⁴; or

    (iii) securities under which the consideration given by the company for the use of the principal secured is to any extent dependent on the results of the company's business or any part of it; or

    (iv)–(v) ...³

    (vi) securities which are connected with shares in the company, and for this purpose securities are so connected if, in consequence of the nature of the rights attaching to the securities or shares and in particular of any terms or conditions attaching to the right to transfer the shares or securities, it is necessary or advantageous for a person who has, or disposes of or acquires, any of the securities also to have, or to dispose of or to acquire, a proportionate holding of the shares; [or]¹

    [(vii) equity notes issued by the company ("the issuing company") and held by a company which is associated with the issuing company or is a funded company;]¹

(*f*) any such amount as is required to be treated as a distribution by subsection (4) below or section 210.

(3) Without prejudice to section 254(11), no amount shall be regarded for the purposes of [subsection (2)(*d*), (*da*)]³ and (*e*) above as representing the principal secured by a security issued after 5th April 1972 in so far as it exceeds any new consideration which has been received by the company for the issue of the security.

[(3A) Where any security of a company is issued at a premium representing new consideration—

(*a*) the references in subsection (2)(*d*), (*da*) and (*e*) above to so much of any distribution as represents, or is an amount representing, the principal secured by a security shall be construed, in relation to a distribution in respect of the security issued at a premium, as references to the aggregate of—

    (i) so much of the distribution as represents, or is an amount representing, that principal, and

    (ii) so much of it as represents, or is an amount representing, the premium; and

(*b*) the reference in subsection (2)(*d*) above to so much of any distribution as represents a reasonable commercial return for the use of the principal secured by a security shall be construed, in relation to a distribution in respect of the security issued at a premium, as a reference to the aggregate of—

    (i) so much of the distribution as represents a reasonable commercial return for the use of that principal, and

    (ii) so much of it as (when regard is had to the extent to which distributions represent the premium) represents a reasonable commercial return for the use of the premium.]⁵

[(3AA) If, in the case of any security issued by a company, the amount of new consideration received by the company for the issue of the security exceeds the amount of the principal secured by the security—

(*a*) the amount of the principal so secured shall be treated for the purposes of paragraph (*d*) of subsection (2) above as increased to the amount of the new consideration so received; and

(*b*) subsection (3A) above, so far as relating to that paragraph, shall not have effect in relation to the security;

but this subsection is subject to sections 209A and 209B.][8]

[(3B) For the purposes of subsection (2)(*e*)(iii) above the consideration given by the company for the use of the principal secured shall not be treated as being to any extent dependent on the results of the company's business or any part of it by reason only of the fact that the terms of the security provide—

(*a*) for the consideration to be reduced in the event of the results improving, or

(*b*) for the consideration to be increased in the event of the results deteriorating.][7]

(4) Where on a transfer of assets or liabilities by a company to its members or to a company by its members, the amount or value of the benefit received by a member (taken according to its market value) exceeds the amount or value (so taken) of any new consideration given by him, the company shall, subject to subsections (5) and (6) below, be treated as making a distribution to him of an amount equal to the difference.

(5) Subsection (4) above shall not apply where the company and the member receiving the benefit are both resident in the United Kingdom and either the former is a subsidiary of the latter or both are subsidiaries of a third company also so resident; and any amount which would apart from this subsection be a distribution shall not constitute a distribution by virtue of subsection (2)(*b*) above.

(6) No transfer of assets (other than cash) or of liabilities between one company and another shall constitute, or be treated as giving rise to, a distribution by virtue of subsection (2)(*b*) or (4) above if they are companies—

(*a*) both of which are resident in the United Kingdom and neither of which is a 51 per cent subsidiary of a company not so resident; and

(*b*) which, neither at the time of the transfer nor as a result of it, are under common control.

For the purposes of this subsection two companies are under common control if they are under the control of the same person or persons, and for this purpose "control" shall be construed in accordance with section 416.

(7) The question whether one body corporate is a subsidiary of another for the purpose of subsection (5) above shall be determined as a question whether it is a 51 per cent subsidiary of that other, except that that other shall be treated as not being the owner—

(*a*) of any share capital which it owns directly in a body corporate, if a profit on a sale of the shares would be treated as a trading receipt of its trade; or

(*b*) of any share capital which it owns indirectly, and which is owned directly by a body corporate for which a profit on the sale of the shares would be a trading receipt; or

(*c*) of any share capital which it owns directly or indirectly in a body corporate not resident in the United Kingdom.

(8) For the purposes of subsection (2)(*c*) above—

(*a*) the value of any redeemable share capital shall be taken to be the amount of the share capital together with any premium payable on redemption, or in a winding up, or in any other circumstances; and

(*b*) the value of any security shall be taken to be the amount of the principal thereby secured (including any premium payable at maturity or in a winding up, or in any other circumstances);

and in determining the amount of the distribution constituted by the issue of any redeemable share capital or any security, the capital or security shall be taken at that value.

[(8A) For the purposes of paragraph (*da*) of subsection (2) above subsections (2) to (4) of section 808A shall apply as they apply for the purposes of a special relationship provision such as is mentioned in that section but as if—

(*a*) the references in those subsections to the relationship in question were references to any relationship, arrangements or other connection between the issuing company and the other company mentioned in sub-paragraph (ii) of that paragraph; and

(*b*) the provision in question required no account to be taken, in the determination of any of the matters mentioned in subsection (8B) below, of (or of any inference capable of being drawn from) any other relationship, arrangements or connection (whether formal or informal) between the issuing company and any person, except where that person—

(i) has no relevant connection with the issuing company, or

(ii) is a company that is a member of the same UK grouping as the issuing company.][3]

[(8B) The matters mentioned in subsection (8A)(*b*) above are the following—

(*a*) the appropriate level or extent of the issuing company's overall indebtedness;

(*b*) whether it might be expected that the issuing company and a particular person would have become parties to a transaction involving the issue of a security by the issuing company or the making of a loan, or a loan of a particular amount, to that company; and

(*c*) the rate of interest and other terms that might be expected to be applicable in any particular case to such a transaction.][3]

[(8C) For the purposes of subsection (8A) above a person has a relevant connection with the issuing company if he is connected with it within the terms of section 839 or that person (without being so connected to the issuing company) is—

(*a*) an effective 51 per cent subsidiary of the issuing company; or

(*b*) a company of which the issuing company is an effective 51 per cent subsidiary.][3]

[(8D) For the purposes of subsection (8A) above any question as to what constitutes the UK grouping of which the issuing company is a member or as to the other members of that grouping shall be determined as follows—

(*a*) where the issuing company has no effective 51 per cent subsidiaries and is not an effective 51 per cent subsidiary of a company resident in the United Kingdom, the issuing company shall be taken to be a member of a UK grouping of which it is itself the only member;

(*b*) where the issuing company has one or more effective 51 cent subsidiaries and is not an effective 51 per cent subsidiary of a company resident in the United Kingdom, the issuing company shall be taken to be a member of a UK grouping of which the only members are the issuing company and its effective 51 per cent subsidiaries; and

(*c*) where the issuing company is an effective 51 per cent subsidiary of a company resident in the United Kingdom ('the UK holding company'), the issuing company shall be taken to be a member of a UK grouping of which the only members are—

(i) the UK holding company or, if there is more than one company resident in the United Kingdom of which the issuing company is an effective 51 per cent subsidiary, such one of them as is not itself an effective 51 per cent subsidiary of any of the others, and

(ii) the effective 51 per cent subsidiaries of the company which is a member of that grouping by virtue of sub-paragraph (i) above.][3]

[(8E) For the purposes of subsections (8C) and (8D) above section 170(7) of the 1992 Act shall apply for determining whether a company is an effective 51 per cent subsidiary of another company but shall so apply as if the question whether the effective 51 per cent subsidiaries of a company resident in the United Kingdom ('the putative holding company') include either—

(*a*) the issuing company, or

(*b*) a company of which the issuing company is an effective 51 per cent subsidiary,

were to be determined without regard to any beneficial entitlement of the putative holding company to any profits or assets of any company resident outside the United Kingdom.][3]

[(8F) References in subsections (8D) and (8E) above to a company that is resident in the United Kingdom shall not include references to a company which is a dual resident company for the purposes of section 404.][3]

[(9) For the purposes of subsection (2)(*e*)(vii) above a security is an equity note if as regards the whole of the principal or as regards any part of it—

(*a*) the security's terms contain no particular date by which it is to be redeemed,

(*b*) under the security's terms the date for redemption, or the latest date for redemption, falls after the expiry of the permitted period,

(*c*) under the security's terms redemption is to occur after the expiry of the permitted period if a particular event occurs and the event is one which (judged at the time of the security's issue) is certain or likely to occur, or

(*d*) the issuing company can secure that there is no particular date by which the security is to be redeemed or that the date for redemption falls after the expiry of the permitted period;

and the permitted period is the period of 50 years beginning with the date of the security's issue.][2]

[(10) For the purposes of subsection (2)(*e*)(vii) above and subsection (11) below a company is associated with the issuing company if—

(*a*) the issuing company is a 75 per cent subsidiary of the other company,

(*b*) the other company is a 75 per cent subsidiary of the issuing company, or

(*c*) both are 75 per cent subsidiaries of a third company.][2]

[(11) For the purposes of subsection (2)(*e*)(vii) above a company is a funded company if there are arrangements involving the company being put in funds (directly or indirectly) by the issuing company or a company associated with the issuing company.][2]

Commentary—*Simon's Direct Tax Service* **D2.511.**
Concessions C2—Distributions by a loan or money society to its members by way of dividend or interest are not regarded as distributions within this section; hence no ACT liability, but income tax liability.
Concession C15—Exemption from ACT liability on the dissolution of an unincorporated social or recreational association.
Concession C16—Dissolution of company under Companies Act 1985 s 652: circumstances in which distribution to shareholders may be treated as a capital receipt, certain assurance which must be given.
Concession C18—Payments of interest to non-resident companies treated as deductions and not as distributions under sub-s (2)(*e*)(iv) above.
Revenue & other press releases—CCAB June 1970 (an amount not treated as a distribution under s 209(5) will not be treated as a distribution under any other provision of s 209).
CCAB 26-6-73 (s 209 is not applied to the distribution of assets to the members of an unincorporated association in a winding-up; See also Concession C15). s 839 (connected persons).
Law Society 15-2-93 (s 209(2)(*e*)(vii) does not relate only to interest paid to a non-resident; it is not affected by provisions of double tax agreements which override s 209(2)(*e*)(iv), (v). The definition of equity note s 209(9) is not extended by s 254(1) to include money advanced without the issue of a security. A demand loan is not an equity note even if not repaid within the permitted period. The ownership of shares in a company is not, of itself, treated as "power to secure" within s 209(9)(*d*). The taking of a deposit by a bank from an unconnected customer who may himself hold an equity note issued by the bank is not an "arrangement" s 209(11)).

ICAEW 19-3-93 (1. "equity note" does not include: a loan repayable on demand, a bank overdraft, normal inter-company balances, or a loan which is not a "security"; 2. "arrangements" means more than a mere happening: the legislation is aimed at payments between associated companies which may insert another company in a drain between them in order to frustrate the legislation).

IR Tax Bulletin May 1993 p 68 (points arising on the scope of this section in relation to equity notes).

Revenue Internal Guidance—International tax handbook ITH 1249–1251 (subs (2)(*e*)(vii); background to the "equity notes" legislation).

Company Taxation Manual COT1550 (sub-s (2): "principal secured" means the amount that the borrower must pay on redemption of the security; meaning of "reasonable commercial return").

COT1751 (sub-s (2)(*b*): purchase of own shares: identification of shares acquired and calculation of amount of capital repaid).

COT1552 (equity mortgage may be within sub-s (2)(*e*)(iii); there is no territorial limitation on sub-s (2)(*e*)(vii)).

COT2007a (treatment of ultra vires dividends, date of payment of dividends, dividend waivers and uncashed dividends).

COT2611 (an amount which is not within sub-s (4) because it is excluded by sub-s (5) is not within sub-s (2)(*b*)).

Simon's Tax Cases—s 209(1), (2), *Addy v IRC* [1975] STC 601*.

Definitions—"The Corporation Tax Acts", s 831(1)(*a*); "new consideration", s 254(1); "security", s 254(1); "share", s 254(1); "51 per cent subsidiary", s 838; "75 per cent subsidiary", s 838.

Cross references—See TA 1988 s 211(1) (what constitutes repayment of share capital for the purposes of this section).

TA 1988 s 212(1) (matters which are not distributions for the purposes of this section).

TA 1988 s 230 (issue of certain share capital not to constitute a distribution within sub-s (2) above).

TA 1988 s 209A (sub-s (3AA) above does not apply where there is link to shares of company or associated company)

TA 1988 s 209B (sub-s (3AA) above does not apply where there are or have been certain hedging arrangements)

FA 1988 Sch 12 para 6(1) (on the transfer of a building society's business to a company, qualifying benefits conferred on members are not treated as distribution within the meaning of the Corporation Tax Acts).

Amendments—[1] Sub-s (2)(*e*)(vii) and the preceding word "or" inserted by F(No 2)A 1992 s 31 with effect where the interest or other distribution is paid after 14 May 1992.

[2] Sub-ss (9)–(11) inserted by F(No 2)A 1992 s 31 with effect where the interest or other distribution is paid after 14 May 1992.

[3] Sub-ss (2)(*da*), (8A)–(8F) inserted; words in sub-s (2)(*e*), (3) substituted; and sub-s (2)(*e*)(iv), (v) repealed, by FA 1995 s 87(1)–(3), Sch 29 Pt VIII(12), with effect generally in relation to any interest or other distribution paid after 28 November 1994 (for detailed transitional commencement provision, see FA 1995 s 87(8)).

[4] Word in sub-s (2)(*e*)(ii) substituted by FA 1996 Sch 34 para 6(1), (2)(*b*), (4) with effect in relation to any interest paid or other distribution made on or after 1 April 1996.

[5] Sub-s (3A) inserted by FA 1996 Sch 14 para 11 with effect in relation to distributions made after 31 March 1996.

[6] Words in sub-s (1) substituted by FA 2000 s 40(9), (11) with effect for payments made after 31 March 2000. Accounting periods straddling 1 April 2000 are treated as separate accounting periods for the purpose of this amendment.

[7] Sub-s (3B) inserted by FA 2000 s 86(1) with effect for payments made after 20 March 2000.

[8] Sub-s (3AA) inserted by FA 2002 s 102(1), (3) with effect for interest and other distributions out of assets of a company in respect of securities of the company where the interest is paid, or the distribution is made, after 16 April 2002.

[209A Section 209(3AA): link to shares of company or associated company

(1) Subsection (3AA) of section 209 does not apply in relation to a security issued by a company (the "issuing company") if the security is one which to a significant extent reflects dividends or other distributions in respect of, or fluctuations in the value of, shares in one or more companies each of which is—

  (*a*) the issuing company; or

  (*b*) an associated company of the issuing company;

but this subsection is subject to the following provisions of this section.

(2) Subsection (1) above does not prevent subsection (3AA) of section 209 above from applying in relation to a security if—

  (*a*) the issuing company is a bank or securities house;

  (*b*) the security is issued by the issuing company in the ordinary course of its business; and

  (*c*) the security reflects dividends or other distributions in respect of, or fluctuations in the value of, shares in companies falling within paragraph (*a*) or (*b*) of subsection (1) above by reason only that the security reflects fluctuations in a qualifying index.

(3) In subsection (2)(*c*) above "qualifying index" means an index whose underlying subject matter includes both—

  (*a*) shares in one or more companies falling within paragraph (*a*) or (*b*) of subsection (1) above, and

  (*b*) shares in one or more companies falling within neither of those paragraphs,

and which is an index such that the shares falling within paragraph (*b*) above represent a significant proportion of the market value of the underlying subject matter of the index.

(4) In this section—

"bank" has the meaning given by section 840A;

"securities house" means any person—

  (*a*) who is authorised for the purposes of the Financial Services and Markets Act 2000; and

  (*b*) whose business consists wholly or mainly of dealing in financial instruments as principal;

and in paragraph (*b*) above "financial instrument" has the meaning given by section 349(5) and (6).

(5) For the purposes of this section a company is an "associated company" of another at any time if at that time one has control of the other or both are under the control of the same person or persons.

(6) For the purposes of subsection (5) above, "control", in relation to a company, means the power of a person to secure—

(*a*) by means of the holding of shares or the possession of voting power in or in relation to the company or any other company, oror

(*b*) by virtue of any powers conferred by the articles of association or other document regulating the company or any other company,

that the affairs of the company are conducted in accordance with his wishes.

(7) There shall be left out of account for the purposes of subsection (6) above—

(*a*) any shares held by a company, and

(*b*) any voting power or other powers arising from shares held by a company,

if a profit on a sale of the shares would be treated as a trading receipt of a trade carried on by the company and the shares are not, within the meaning of Chapter 1 of Part 12, assets of an insurance company's long-term insurance fund (see section 431(2)).]¹

Amendments—¹ This section inserted by FA 2002 s 102(2), (3) with effect for interest and other distributions out of assets of a company in respect of securities of the company where the interest is paid, or the distribution is made, after 16 April 2002.

[209B Section 209(3AA): hedging arrangements

(1) Subsection (3AA) of section 209 does not at any time apply in relation to a security issued by a company (the ''issuing company'') if at that time, or any earlier time on or after 17th April 2002, there are or have been any hedging arrangements that relate to some or all of the company's liabilities under the security.

(2) Subsection (1) above does not prevent subsection (3AA) of section 209 from applying in relation to a security at any time if—

(*a*) conditions 1 to 4 below are satisfied in relation to any such hedging arrangements at that time; and

(*b*) at all earlier times on or after 17th April 2002 when there have been hedging arrangements that relate to some or all of the company's liabilities under the security, conditions 1 to 4 below were satisfied in relation to those hedging arrangements.

(3) Where subsection (3AA) of section 209 at any time ceases to apply in relation to a security by virtue of this section, subsection (2)(*d*) of that section shall have effect in relation to the security as from that time as it would have had effect if subsection (3AA) had never applied in relation to the security.

(4) Condition 1 is that the hedging arrangements do not constitute, include, or form part of, any scheme or arrangement the purpose or one of the main purposes of which is the avoidance of tax or stamp duty.

(5) Condition 2 is that the hedging arrangements are such that, where for the purposes of corporation tax a deduction in respect of the security falls to be made at any time by the issuing company, then at that time, or within a reasonable time before or after it, any amounts intended under the hedging arrangements to offset some or all of that deduction arise—

(*a*) to the issuing company; or

(*b*) to a company which is a member of the same group of companies as the issuing company.

(6) Condition 3 is that the whole of every amount arising as mentioned in subsection (5) above is brought into charge to corporation tax—

(*a*) by a company falling within paragraph (*a*) or (*b*) of that subsection, or

(*b*) by two or more companies, taken together, each of which falls within paragraph (*a*) or (*b*) of that subsection.

(7) Condition 4 is that for the purposes of corporation tax any deductions in respect of expenses of establishing or administering the hedging arrangements are reasonable, in proportion to the amounts required to be brought into charge to corporation tax by subsection (6) above.

(8) For the purposes of this section ''hedging arrangements'', in relation to a security, means any scheme or arrangement for the purpose, or for purposes which include the purpose, of securing that an amount of income or gain accrues, or is received or receivable, whether directly or indirectly, which is intended to offset some or all of the amounts which fall to be brought into account, in accordance with generally accepted accounting practice, in respect of amounts accruing or falling to be paid in accordance with the terms of the security.

(9) Any reference in this section to two companies being members of the same group of companies is a reference to their being members of the same group of companies for the purposes of Chapter 4 of Part 10 of this Act (group relief).]¹

Amendments—¹ This section inserted by FA 2002 s 102(2), (3) with effect for interest and other distributions out of assets of a company in respect of securities of the company where the interest is paid, or the distribution is made, after 16 April 2002.

210 Bonus issue following repayment of share capital

(1) Where a company—

(*a*) repays any share capital or has done so at any time after 6th April 1965, and

(*b*) at or after the time of that repayment issues any share capital as paid up otherwise than by the receipt of new consideration, the amount so paid up shall, except as provided by any provision of the Corporation Tax Acts, be treated as a distribution made in respect of the shares on which it is paid up, except in so far as that amount exceeds the amount or aggregate amount of share capital so repaid less any amounts previously so paid up and treated by virtue of this subsection as distributions.

(2) Subsection (1) above shall not apply where the repaid share capital consists of fully paid preference shares—

(a) if those shares existed as issued and fully paid preference shares on 6th April 1965 and throughout the period from that date until the repayment those shares continued to be fully paid preference shares, or

(b) if those shares were issued after 6th April 1965 as fully paid preference shares wholly for new consideration not derived from ordinary shares and throughout the period from their issue until the repayment those shares continued to be fully paid preference shares.

(3) Except in relation to a company within paragraph D of section 704, subsection (1) above shall not apply if the issue of share capital mentioned in paragraph (b) of that subsection—

(a) is of share capital other than redeemable share capital; and

(b) takes place after 5th April 1973 and more than ten years after the repayment of share capital mentioned in paragraph (a) of that subsection.

(4) In this section—

"ordinary shares" means shares other than preference shares;
"preference shares" means shares—

(a) which do not carry any right to dividends other than dividends at a rate per cent of the nominal value of the shares which is fixed, and

(b) which carry rights in respect of dividends and capital which are comparable with those general for fixed-dividend shares [listed in the Official List of][1] the Stock Exchange; and

"new consideration not derived from ordinary shares" means new consideration other than consideration—

(a) consisting of the surrender, transfer or cancellation of ordinary shares of the company or any other company or consisting of the variation of rights in ordinary shares of the company or any other company, or

(b) derived from a repayment of share capital paid in respect of ordinary shares of the company or of any other company.

Commentary—*Simon's Direct Tax Service* **D1.108.**
Revenue & other press releases—CCAB June 1968 (where a bonus issue of shares is treated as a distribution, the net amount of the distribution is treated as an addition to the acquisition cost of the holding for CGT purposes).
Definitions—"The Corporation Tax Acts", s 831(1)(a); "distribution", s 209(2); "new consideration", s 254(1); "share", s 254(1).
Cross references—See TA 1988 s 211(1) (what constitutes repayment of share capital for the purposes of this section).
TA 1988 s 214(1) (in the event of a demerger of companies, certain chargeable payments not to be treated as repayment of capital for the purposes of this section).
TA 1988 s 230 (issue of certain share capital not to be treated "as paid up otherwise than by the receipt of new consideration" for the purpose of this section).
Amendments—[1] Words in sub-s (4) substituted by FA 1996 Sch 38 para 7(1), (2)(a), (3) with effect in relation to share capital repaid after 31 March 1996.

211 Matters to be treated or not to be treated as repayments of share capital

(1) Where—

(a) a company issues any share capital as paid up otherwise than by the receipt of new consideration, or has done so after 6th April 1965; and

(b) any amount so paid up does not fall to be treated as a qualifying distribution or, where the issue took place before 6th April 1973, did not fall to be treated as a distribution;

then, except as otherwise provided by any provision of the Corporation Tax Acts, for the purposes of sections 209 and 210, distributions afterwards made by the company in respect of shares representing that share capital shall not be treated as repayments of share capital, except to the extent to which those distributions, together with any relevant distributions previously so made, exceed the amounts so paid up (then or previously) on such shares after 6th April 1965 and not falling to be treated as qualifying distributions or, where the share capital was issued before 6th April 1973, as distributions.

(2) Except in relation to a company within paragraph D of section 704, subsection (1) above shall not prevent a distribution being treated as a repayment of share capital if it is made—

(a) more than ten years after the issue of share capital mentioned in paragraph (a) of that subsection; and

(b) in respect of share capital other than redeemable share capital.

(3) In subsection (1) above "relevant distribution" means so much of any distribution made in respect of shares representing the relevant share capital as apart from that subsection would be treated as a repayment of share capital, but by virtue of that subsection cannot be so treated.

(4) For the purposes of subsection (1) above all shares of the same class shall be treated as representing the same share capital, and where shares are issued in respect of other shares, or are

directly or indirectly converted into or exchanged for other shares, all such shares shall be treated as representing the same share capital.

(5) Where share capital is issued at a premium representing new consideration, the amount of the premium is to be treated as forming part of that share capital for the purpose of determining under this Chapter whether any distribution made in respect of shares representing the share capital is to be treated as a repayment of share capital.

(6) Subsection (5) above shall not have effect in relation to any part of the premium after that part has been applied in paying up share capital.

(7) Subject to subsection (5) above, premiums paid on redemption of share capital are not to be treated as repayments of capital.

Commentary—*Simon's Direct Tax Service* **D1.104.**
Definitions—"The Corporation Tax Acts", s 831(1)(*a*); "distribution", s 209(2); "new consideration", s 254(1); "qualifying distribution", s 14(2), by virtue of s 832(1); "share", s 254(1).
Cross references—See TA 1988 s 214(1) (in the event of a demerger of companies, certain chargeable payments not to be treated as repayment of capital for the purposes of this section).
TA 1988 s 230 (issue of certain share capital not to be treated "as paid up otherwise than by the receipt of new consideration" for the purpose of this section).

CHAPTER III

MATTERS WHICH ARE NOT DISTRIBUTIONS FOR THE PURPOSES OF THE CORPORATION TAX ACTS

Cross references—See FA 1988 Sch 12 para 6(1) (on the transfer of a building society's business to a company, qualifying benefits conferred on members are not distributions).
FA 1995 s 152 (Treasury may make regulations modifying this Chapter in its application to open-ended investment companies).

Payments of interest

212 Interest etc paid in respect of certain securities

(1) Any interest or other distribution—

(*a*) which is paid out of the assets of a company ("the borrower") to another company which is within the charge to corporation tax; and

(*b*) which is so paid in respect of securities of the borrower which fall within [paragraph (*da*) of section 209(2) or][2] any of sub-paragraphs (i) to (iii) and (vi) [and (vii)][1] of paragraph (*e*) of section 209(2); and

(*c*) which does not fall within paragraph (*d*) of section 209(2),

shall not be a distribution for the purposes of the Corporation Tax Acts unless the application of this subsection is excluded by subsection (2) or (3) below.

(2) Subsection (1) above does not apply in the case of any interest or other distribution which is paid in respect of a security of the borrower falling within section 209(2)(*e*)(iii) if—

(*a*) the principal secured does not exceed £100,000; and

(*b*) the borrower is under an obligation to repay the principal and interest before the expiry of the period of five years beginning on the date on which the principal was paid to the borrower; and

(*c*) that obligation either was entered into before 9th March 1982 or was entered into before 1st July 1982 pursuant to negotiations which were in progress on 9th March 1982; and

(*d*) where the period for repayment of either principal or interest is extended after 8th March 1982 (but paragraph (*b*) above still applies), the interest or other distribution is paid within the period which was applicable immediately before that date;

and for the purposes of paragraph (*c*) above negotiations shall not be regarded as having been in progress on 9th March 1982 unless, before that date, the borrower had applied to the lender for a loan and had supplied the lender with any documents required by him to support the application.

(3) [Without prejudice to subsection (4) below,][2] subsection (1) above does not apply in a case where the company to which the interest or other distribution is paid is entitled under any enactment, other than section 208, to an exemption from tax in respect of that interest or distribution [and does not apply in relation to any interest or distribution falling within section 209(2)(*da*) if that interest or distribution is otherwise outside the matters in respect of which that company is within the charge to corporation tax.][2]

[(4) Where any interest or other distribution is paid to a charity (within the meaning of section 506) or to any of the bodies mentioned in section 507, the interest or distribution so paid shall not be a distribution for the purposes of the Corporation Tax Acts if it would otherwise fall to be treated as such a distribution by virtue only of paragraph (*da*) of section 209(2).][2]

Commentary—*Simon's Direct Tax Service* **D1.106.**
Definitions—"The Corporation Tax Acts", s 831(1)(*a*); "distribution", s 209(2); "interest", s 832(1); "security", s 254(1).
Amendments—[1] Words in sub-s (1)(*b*) inserted by F(No 2)A 1992 s 31(3), (4) where interest etc is paid after 14 May 1992.
[2] Words in sub-ss (1)(*b*), (3) inserted, and sub-s (4) inserted, by FA 1995 s 87(4), with effect in relation to any interest or other distribution paid after 28 November 1994 (for detailed transitional commencement provision, see FA 1995 s 87(8)).

Demergers

Statements of Practice SP 13/80—Revenue's practice for applying certain provisions contained in ss 213–218 below.
SP 5/85, para 4—The division of a company involving the transfer of shares in a subsidiary to a newly formed company by way of a demerger is regarded as a scheme of reconstruction even though the distributing and the transferee companies have no common shareholder.
Revenue & other press releases—IR Tax Bulletin October 1994 p 162 (tax treatment of exempt demergers where the shares in the distributing company are held by trustees).
Revenue Internal Guidance—Company Taxation Manual COT1732 (whether legal costs of demerger allowable).
Cross references—See TA 1988 s 218 (interpretation of ss 213–217).

213 Exempt distributions

(1) The provisions of this section and sections 214 to 218 have effect for facilitating certain transactions whereby trading activities carried on by a single company or group are divided so as to be carried on by two or more companies not belonging to the same group or by two or more independent groups.

(2) References in the Corporation Tax Acts to distributions of a company shall not apply to any distribution—

    (*a*) which falls within subsection (3) below, and
    (*b*) in respect of which the conditions specified in subsections (4) to (12) below are satisfied;

and any such distribution is referred to in this section as an "exempt distribution".

(3) The following distributions fall within this subsection—

    (*a*) a distribution consisting of the transfer to all or any of its members by a company ("the distributing company") of shares in one or more companies which are its 75 per cent subsidiaries;
    (*b*) a distribution consisting of the transfer by a company ("the distributing company") to one or more other companies ("the transferee company or companies") of—

        (i) a trade or trades; or
        (ii) shares in one or more companies which are 75 per cent subsidiaries of the distributing company,

    and the issue of shares by the transferee company or companies to all or any of the members of the distributing company;

and in this section and sections 214 to 217 references to a relevant company are to the distributing company, to each subsidiary whose shares are transferred as mentioned in paragraph (*a*) or (*b*)(ii) above and to each transferee company mentioned in paragraph (*b*) above.

(4) Each relevant company must be resident in the United Kingdom at the time of the distribution.

(5) The distributing company must at the time of the distribution be either a trading company or a member of a trading group and each subsidiary whose shares are transferred as mentioned in subsection (3)(*a*) or (*b*)(ii) above must at that time be either a trading company or the holding company of a trading group.

(6) In a case within subsection [(3)(*a*)][1] above—

    (*a*) the shares must not be redeemable, must constitute the whole or substantially the whole of the distributing company's holding of the ordinary share capital of the subsidiary and must confer the whole or substantially the whole of the distributing company's voting rights in the subsidiary; and
    (*b*) subject to subsections (7) and (12)(*b*) below, the distributing company must after the distribution be either a trading company or the holding company of a trading group.

(7) Subsection (6)(*b*) above does not apply if the transfer relates to two or more 75 per cent subsidiaries of the distributing company and that company is dissolved without there having been after the distribution any net assets of the company available for distribution in a winding up or otherwise.

(8) In a case within subsection (3)(*b*) above—

    (*a*) if a trade is transferred the distributing company must either not retain any interest or retain only a minor interest in that trade;
    (*b*) if shares in a subsidiary are transferred those shares must constitute the whole or substantially the whole of the distributing company's holding of the ordinary share capital of the subsidiary and must confer the whole or substantially the whole of the distributing company's voting rights in the subsidiary;
    (*c*) the only or main activity of the transferee company or each transferee company after the distribution must be the carrying on of the trade or the holding of the shares transferred to it;
    (*d*) the shares issued by the transferee company or each transferee company must not be redeemable, must constitute the whole or substantially the whole of its issued ordinary share capital and must confer the whole or substantially the whole of the voting rights in that company; and
    (*e*) subject to subsections (9) and (12)(*b*) below, the distributing company must after the distribution be either a trading company or the holding company of a trading group.

(9) Subsection (8)(*e*) above does not apply if there are two or more transferee companies each of which has a trade or shares in a separate 75 per cent subsidiary of the distributing company transferred

to it and the distributing company is dissolved without there having been after the distribution any net assets of the company available for distribution in a winding up or otherwise.

(10) The distribution must be made wholly or mainly for the purpose of benefiting some or all of the trading activities which before the distribution are carried on by a single company or group and after the distribution will be carried on by two or more companies or groups.

(11) The distribution must not form part of a scheme or arrangements the main purpose or one of the main purposes of which is—

(a) the avoidance of tax (including stamp duty); or
(b) without prejudice to paragraph (a) above, the making of a chargeable payment, as defined by section 214, or what would be such a payment if any of the companies mentioned in that section were an unquoted company; or
(c) the acquisition by any person or persons other than members of the distributing company of control of that company, of any other relevant company or of any company which belongs to the same group as any such company; or
(d) the cessation of a trade or its sale after the distribution.

In paragraph (c) above "group" means a company which has one or more 51 per cent subsidiaries together with that or those subsidiaries.

(12) Where the distributing company is a 75 per cent subsidiary of another company—

(a) the group (or, if more than one, the largest group) to which the distributing company belongs at the time of the distribution must be a trading group;
(b) subsections (6)(b) and (8)(e) above shall not apply; and
(c) the distribution must be followed by one or more other distributions falling within subsection (3)(a) or (b)(ii) above which satisfy the conditions of this section and result in members of the holding company of the group (or, if more than one, the largest group) to which the distributing company belonged at the time of the distribution becoming members of—

(i) the transferee company or each transferee company to which a trade was transferred by the distributing company; or
(ii) the subsidiary or each subsidiary whose shares were transferred by the distributing company; or
(iii) a company (other than that holding company) of which the company or companies mentioned in sub-paragraph (i) or (ii) above are 75 per cent subsidiaries.

Commentary—*Simon's Direct Tax Service* **D1.502.**
Concession C11—A company does not fail to comply with this section if after distribution it retains sufficient funds to meet cost of liquidation and negligible amount of share capital. Share capital will be regarded as negligible if it amounts to £5,000 or less.
Statements of Practice SP 13/80—Meanings of "exempt distribution", "ordinary share capital" and "substantially the whole" in the context of sub-ss (6)(a), (8)(b), (d), "any interest or retain only a minor interest in that trade" in the context of sub-s (8)(a), "after" in the context of sub-ss (6)(b), (8)(c), (l), (11)(d).
The concurrent sale of another company in the same group as a subsidiary being demerged does not *necessarily* fall under sub-s (11)(c).
Definitions—"Chargeable payment", s 214(2) by virtue of s 218(1); "company", s 832(1), (2); "control", s 416(2)–(6), by virtue of s 218(1); "the Corporation Tax Acts", s 831(1)(a); "distributing company", s 218(1); "distribution", s 209(2); "group", s 218(1); "holding company, s 218(1); "member", s 218(1); "relevant company", s 218(1); "shares", s 218(1); "trade", s 218(1); "trading company", s 218(1); "trade group", s 218(1); "unquoted company", s 218(1); "75 per cent subsidiary", s 218(2), (3).
Cross references—See TA 1988 s 217(1) (inspector's powers to ask for information on certain matters within this section).
TCGA 1992 s 192(2) (relief from tax on chargeable gains accruing on demergers).
Amendments—¹ "(3)(a)" in sub-s (6) substituted by FA 1990 Sch 14 paras 1, 3 and deemed always to have had effect.

214 Chargeable payments connected with exempt distributions

(1) If within five years after the making of an exempt distribution there is a chargeable payment—

(a) the amount or value of the payment shall be treated as income chargeable to tax under Case VI of Schedule D;
(b) unless the payment is a transfer of money's worth, sections 349(1) and 350 shall apply to the payment as if it were an annual sum payable otherwise than out of profits or gains charged to income tax;
(c) the payment shall be regarded as a distribution for the purposes of [section 337A(1)]¹; and
(d) the payment shall not (if it otherwise would) be treated as a repayment of capital for the purposes of section 210 or 211.

(2) In this section "a chargeable payment" means any payment made otherwise than for bona fide commercial reasons or forming part of a scheme or arrangement the main purpose or one of the main purposes of which is the avoidance of tax (including stamp duty), being a payment which—

(a) a company concerned in an exempt distribution makes directly or indirectly to a member of that company or of any other company concerned in that distribution; and
(b) is made in connection with, or with any transaction affecting, the shares in that or any such company; and
(c) is not a distribution or exempt distribution or made to another company which belongs to the same group as the company making the payment.

(3) Where a company concerned in an exempt distribution is an unquoted company subsection (2)(*a*) above shall have effect as if any reference to the making of a payment by, or to a member of, a company concerned in the exempt distribution included a reference to the making of a payment by or to any other person in pursuance of a scheme or arrangements made with the unquoted company or, if the unquoted company is—

(*a*) under the control of five or fewer persons; and

(*b*) not under the control of (and only of) a company which is not itself under the control of five or fewer persons,

with any of the persons mentioned in paragraph (*a*) above.

(4) References in this section to a company concerned in an exempt distribution are to any relevant company and to any other company which was connected with any such company for the whole or any part of the period beginning with the exempt distribution and ending with the making of the payment which is in question under this section.

(5) For the purposes of subsection (4) above and this subsection a company shall be deemed to have been connected in the period referred to in that subsection with each company to which a company connected with it was connected in that period.

(6) References in this section to a payment include references to a transfer of money's worth including the assumption of a liability.

Commentary—*Simon's Direct Tax Service* **D1.503.**
Revenue & other press releases—IR 27–7–90 (clearance applications: details).
Definitions—"Control", s 416(2)–(6) by virtue of s 218(1); "distribution", s 209(2); "exempt distribution", s 213(2) by virtue of s 218(1); "group", s 218(1); "member", s 218(1); "profits or gains", s 833(1); "relevant company", s 218(1); "Schedule D", s 18(1); "unquoted company", s 218(1).
Cross references—See TA 1988 s 217(2), (3) (inspector's powers to ask for information on certain matters within this section).
FA 2000 s 46(2) (exemption under FA 2000 s 46(1) for income of a charity is not granted in respect of income chargeable to tax under Schedule D Case VI by virtue of this section).
Amendments—[1] Words in sub-s (1)(*c*) substituted for "337(2), and 338(2)(*a*)" by FA 2002 s 84(2), Sch 30 para 1(3) with effect from the date of Royal Assent of FA 2002.

215 Advance clearance by Board of distributions and payments

(1) A distribution shall be treated as an exempt distribution in any case in which, before the distribution is made, the Board have, on the application of the distributing company, notified that company that the Board are satisfied that it will be such a distribution.

(2) A payment shall not be treated as a chargeable payment in any case in which, before the payment is made, the Board have, on the application of the person intending to make it, notified him that they are satisfied that it will be made for bona fide commercial reasons and will not form part of any scheme or arrangements the main purpose, or one of the main purposes, of which is the avoidance of tax (including stamp duty).

(3) A company which becomes or ceases to be connected with another company may make an application under subsection (2) above as respects any payments that may be made by it at any time after becoming or ceasing to be so connected (whether or not there is any present intention to make any payments); and where a notification is given by the Board on such an application no payment to which the notification relates shall be treated as a chargeable payment by reason only of the company being or having been connected with the other company.

(4) References in subsections (2) and (3) above to a payment shall be construed as in section 214.

(5) Any application under this section shall be in writing and shall contain particulars of the relevant transactions and the Board may, within 30 days of the receipt of the application or of any further particulars previously required under this subsection, by notice require the applicant to furnish further particulars for the purposes of enabling the Board to make their decision; and if any such notice is not complied with within 30 days or such longer period as the Board may allow, the Board need not proceed further on the application.

(6) The Board shall notify their decision to the applicant within 30 days of receiving the application or, if they give a notice under subsection (5) above, within 30 days of the notice being complied with.

(7) If the Board notify the applicant that they are not satisfied as mentioned in sub-section (1) or (2) above or do not notify their decision to the applicant within the time required by subsection (6) above, the applicant may within 30 days of the notification or of that time require the Board to transmit the application, together with any notice given and further particulars furnished under subsection (5) above, to the Special Commissioners; and in that event any notification by the Special Commissioners shall have effect for the purposes of this section as if it were a notification by the Board.

(8) If any particulars furnished under this section do not fully and accurately disclose all facts and circumstances material for the decision of the Board or the Special Commissioners, any resulting notification that the Board or Commissioners are satisfied as mentioned in subsection (1) or (2) above shall be void.

Commentary—*Simon's Direct Tax Service* **D1.504.**
Statement of Practice SP 13/80—Procedure for the purposes of sub-s (1) above.
Revenue Internal Guidance—Company Taxation Manual COT1727–1730 (district procedures).
Definitions—"The Board", s 832(1); "chargeable payment", ss 214(2) by virtue of a 218(1); "company", s 832(1), (2); "distributing company", s 218(1); "distribution", s 209(2); "exempt distribution", s 218(1).

216 Returns

(1) Where a company makes an exempt distribution it shall within 30 days after the distribution make a return to the inspector giving particulars of the distribution and of the circumstances by reason of which it is exempt.

(2) Where within five years after the making of an exempt distribution a person makes a chargeable payment which consists of a transfer of money's worth, he shall within 30 days after the transfer make a return to the inspector giving particulars—

    (*a*) of the transaction effecting the transfer;
    (*b*) of the name and address of the recipient or each recipient and the value of what is transferred to him or each of them; and
    (*c*) if the transfer is accompanied by a chargeable payment consisting of a payment of money, of that payment.

(3) Subject to subsection (4) below, where within five years after the making of an exempt distribution a person makes a payment or a transfer of money's worth which would be a chargeable payment but for the fact that it is made for bona fide commercial reasons and does not form part of any such scheme or arrangements as are mentioned in section 214(2), that person shall within 30 days after making the payment or transfer make a return to the inspector giving particulars—

    (*a*) in the case of a transfer, of the transaction by which it is effected;
    (*b*) of the name and address of the recipient or each recipient and the amount of the payment made, or the value of what is transferred, to him or each of them; and
    (*c*) of the circumstances by reason of which the payment or transfer is not a chargeable payment.

(4) Subsection (3) above does not apply where the payment or transfer is one in relation to which a notification under section 215(3) has effect.

Commentary—*Simon's Direct Tax Service* **D1.505.**
Statement of Practice SP 13/80—Sufficiency of a clearance notification made under s 215(1) above for the purposes of sub-s (1) of this section.
Definitions—''Chargeable payment'', s 214(2) by virtue of s 218(1); ''distribution'', s 209(2); ''exempt distribution'', s 218(1).
Cross references—See TA 1988 s 217(2) (inspector's powers to ask for information on certain matters within this section).

217 Information

(1) Where a distribution falling within section 213(3) has been made and the inspector has reason to believe that it may form part of any such scheme or arrangements as are mentioned in section 213(11), he may by notice require any relevant company or any person controlling any such company to furnish him within such time, not being less than 30 days, as may be specified in the notice with—

    (*a*) a declaration in writing stating whether or not, according to information which the company or that person has or can reasonably obtain, any such scheme or arrangements exist or have existed;
    (*b*) such other information as the inspector may reasonably require for the purposes of section 213(11) and the company or that person has or can reasonably obtain.

(2) If the inspector has reason to believe that a person has not delivered an account or made a return which he is required to deliver or make by virtue of section 214(1)(*b*) or 216(2) or (3) in respect of any payment or transfer, he may by notice require that person to furnish him within such time, not being less than 30 days, as may be specified in the notice with such information relating to the payment or transfer as he may reasonably require for the purposes of section 214.

(3) If the inspector has reason to believe that a payment or transfer has been made within five years after the making of an exempt distribution and that the payment or transfer is a chargeable payment by reason of the existence of any such scheme or arrangements as are mentioned in section 214(3), he may by notice require the person making the payment or transfer or, if that person is a company, any person controlling it to furnish him within such time, not being less than 30 days, as may be specified in the notice with—

    (*a*) a declaration in writing stating whether or not, according to information which that person has, or can reasonably obtain, any such scheme or arrangements exist or have existed;
    (*b*) such other information as the inspector may reasonably require for the purposes of section 214 and that person has or can reasonably obtain.

(4) Any recipient of a chargeable payment and any person on whose behalf such a payment is received shall, if so required by the inspector, state whether the payment received by him or on his behalf is received on behalf of any person other than himself and, if so, the name and address of that person.

Commentary—*Simon's Direct Tax Service* **D1.501, 505.**
Definitions—''Chargeable payment'', s 214(2) by virtue of s 218(1); ''distribution'', s 832(1); ''exempt distribution'', s 218(1); ''relevant company'', s 218(1).

218 Interpretation of sections 213 to 217

(1) In sections 213 to 217—

"chargeable payment" has the meaning given by section 214(2);

"control" shall be construed in accordance with section 416(2) to (6);

"distributing company" has the meaning given by section 213(3);

"exempt distribution" has the meaning given by section 213(2);

"group", except in section 213(11)(*c*), means a company which has one or more 75 per cent subsidiaries together with that or those subsidiaries;

"holding company" means a company whose business (disregarding any trade carried on by it) consists wholly or mainly of the holding of shares or securities of one or more companies which are its 75 per cent subsidiaries;

"member", where the reference is to a member of a company, does not, except in section 214(2)(*a*), include a person who is a member otherwise than by virtue of holding shares forming part of the company's ordinary share capital;

"relevant company" has the meaning given by section 213(3);

"shares" includes stock;

"trade", except in subsection (3) below, does not include dealing in shares, securities, land, trades or commodity futures and "trading activities" shall be construed accordingly;

"trading company" means a company whose business consists wholly or mainly of the carrying on of a trade or trades;

"trading group" means a group the business of whose members, taken together, consists wholly or mainly in the carrying on of a trade or trades; and

"unquoted company" means a company which does not satisfy the condition that its shares or some class thereof (disregarding debenture or loan stock, preferred shares or preferred stock) are listed in the Official List of the Stock Exchange and are dealt in on the Stock Exchange regularly or from time to time, so however that this definition does not apply to a company under the control of (and only of) one or more companies to which this definition does not apply.

(2) In determining for the purposes of section 213(3) to (9) whether a company whose shares are transferred by the distributing company is a 75 per cent subsidiary of the distributing company there shall be disregarded any share capital of the first-mentioned company which is owned indirectly by the distributing company.

(3) In determining for the purposes of sections 213 to 217 whether one company is a 75 per cent subsidiary of another, the other company shall be treated as not being the owner of—

(*a*) any share capital which it owns directly in a body corporate if a profit on a sale of the shares would be treated as a trading receipt of its trade; or

(*b*) any share capital which it owns indirectly and which is owned directly by a body corporate for which a profit on the sale of the shares would be a trading receipt.

(4) Section 839 applies for the purposes of sections 213 to 217.

Commentary—*Simon's Direct Tax Service* **D1.501–505.**
Definitions—"Company", s 832(1), (2); "trade", s 832(1).

Purchase of own shares

Cross references—See TA 1988 s 229 (interpretative provisions for ss 219–228).

219 Purchase by unquoted trading company of own shares

(1) References in the Corporation Tax Acts to distributions of a company shall not include references to a payment made by a company on the redemption, repayment or purchase of its own shares if the company is an unquoted trading company or the unquoted holding company of a trading group and either—

(*a*) the redemption, repayment or purchase is made wholly or mainly for the purpose of benefiting a trade carried on by the company or by any of its 75 per cent subsidiaries, and does not form part of a scheme or arrangement the main purpose or one of the main purposes of which is—

(i) to enable the owner of the shares to participate in the profits of the company without receiving a dividend, or

(ii) the avoidance of tax; and

the conditions specified in sections 220 to 224, so far as applicable, are satisfied in relation to the owner of the shares; or

(*b*) the whole or substantially the whole of the payment (apart from any sum applied in paying capital gains tax charged on the redemption, repayment or purchase) is applied by the person to whom it is made in discharging a liability of his for inheritance tax charged on a death and is so applied within the period of two years after the death;

and in sections 220 to 224—

"the purchase" means the redemption, repayment or purchase referred to in subsection (1)(*a*) above; and "the vendor" means the owner of the shares at the time it is made.

(2) Where, apart from this subsection, a payment falls within subsection (1)(*b*) above, subsection (1) above shall not apply to the extent that the liability in question could without undue hardship have been discharged otherwise than through the redemption, repayment or purchase of shares in the company or another unquoted company which is a trading company or the holding company of a trading group.

Commentary—*Simon's Direct Tax Service* **D2.508, 509.**
Statement of Practice SP 2/82—Company's purchase of own shares, "trade benefit test".
Revenue Interpretation RI 4—Disallowance in computing profits of legal expenses incurred by a company in respect of the purchase of its own shares.
Revenue & other press releases—Hansard 17-3-88 (as regards sub-s (2), where the company has surplus funds sufficient to discharge IHT liability on the death of a controlling shareholder, the Revenue's view is that there is no hardship since the liability can be met by dividend payments).
ICAEW TR745 April 1989 (a holding company is not disqualified merely because it owns properties which are rented to qualifying subsidiaries for trading purposes, or merely because it lends money to such subsidiaries for trading purposes).
Simon's Tax Cases—s 219(1)(*a*), *Moody v Tyler* [2000] STC 296.
Definitions—"Company", s 832(1), (2); "the Corporation Tax Acts", s 831(1)(*a*); "distribution", s 209(2); "holding company", s 229(1); "shares", s 229(1); "trade", s 229(1); "trading company", s 229(1); "trading group", s 229(1); "unquoted company", s 229(1); "75 per cent subsidiary", s 838.
Cross references—See TA 1988 s 225(1) (advance clearance by the Board of payments to which this section applies).
TA 1988 s 226 (returns and information in respect of payments to which this section applies).

220 Conditions as to residence and period of ownership

(1) The vendor must be resident and ordinarily resident in the United Kingdom in the year of assessment in which the purchase is made and if the shares are held through a nominee the nominee must also be so resident and ordinarily resident.

(2) The residence and ordinary residence of trustees shall be determined for the purposes of this section as they are determined under section [69 of the 1992 Act][1] for the purposes of that Act.

(3) The residence and ordinary residence of personal representatives shall be taken for the purposes of this section to be the same as the residence and ordinary residence of the deceased immediately before his death.

(4) The references in this section to a person's ordinary residence shall be disregarded in the case of a company.

(5) The shares must have been owned by the vendor throughout the period of five years ending with the date of the purchase.

(6) If at any time during that period the shares were transferred to the vendor by a person who was then his spouse living with him then, unless that person is alive at the date of the purchase but is no longer the vendor's spouse living with him, any period during which the shares were owned by that person shall be treated for the purposes of subsection (5) above as a period of ownership by the vendor.

(7) Where the vendor became entitled to the shares under the will or on the intestacy of a previous owner or is the personal representative of a previous owner—

(*a*) any period during which the shares were owned by the previous owner or his personal representatives shall be treated for the purposes of subsection (5) above as a period of ownership by the vendor, and

(*b*) that subsection shall have effect as if it referred to three years instead of five.

(8) In determining whether the condition in subsection (5) above is satisfied in a case where the vendor acquired shares of the same class at different times—

(*a*) shares acquired earlier shall be taken into account before shares acquired later, and

(*b*) any previous disposal by him of shares of that class shall be assumed to be a disposal of shares acquired later rather than of shares acquired earlier.

(9) If for the purposes of capital gains tax the time when shares were acquired would be determined under any provision of Chapter II of Part IV of the [1992][1] Act (reorganisation of share capital, conversion of securities, etc) then, unless the shares were allotted for payment or were comprised in share capital to which section 249 applies, it shall be determined in the same way for the purposes of this section.

Commentary—*Simon's Direct Tax Service* **D2.507.**
Definitions—"The 1992 Act", s 831(3); "company", s 832(1), (2); "personal representatives", s 229(1); "the purchase", s 219(1); "shares", s 229(1); "the vendor", s 219(1); "year of assessment", s 832(1).
Amendments—[1] Words in sub-ss (2), (9) substituted by TCGA 1992 Sch 10 para 14(1), (14).

221 Reduction of vendor's interest as shareholder

(1) If immediately after the purchase the vendor owns shares in the company, then, subject to section 224, the vendor's interest as a shareholder must be substantially reduced.

(2) If immediately after the purchase any associate of the vendor owns shares in the company then, subject to section 224, the combined interests as shareholders of the vendor and his associates must be substantially reduced.

(3) The question whether the combined interests as shareholders of the vendor and his associates are substantially reduced shall be determined in the same way as is (under the following subsections) the question whether a vendor's interest as a shareholder is substantially reduced, except that the vendor shall be assumed to have the interests of his associates as well as his own.

(4) Subject to subsection (5) below, the vendor's interest as a shareholder shall be taken to be substantially reduced if and only if the total nominal value of the shares owned by him immediately after the purchase, expressed as a fraction of the issued share capital of the company at that time, does not exceed 75 per cent of the corresponding fraction immediately before the purchase.

(5) The vendor's interest as a shareholder shall not be taken to be substantially reduced where—

(*a*) he would, if the company distributed all its profits available for distribution immediately after the purchase, be entitled to a share of those profits, and

(*b*) that share, expressed as a fraction of the total of those profits, exceeds 75 per cent of the corresponding fraction immediately before the purchase.

(6) In determining for the purposes of subsection (5) above the division of profits among the persons entitled to them, a person entitled to periodic distributions calculated by reference to fixed rates or amounts shall be regarded as entitled to a distribution of the amount or maximum amount to which he would be entitled for a year.

(7) In subsection (5) above "profits available for distribution" has the same meaning as it has for the purposes of Part VIII of the Companies Act 1985 except that for the purposes of that subsection the amount of the profits available for distribution (whether immediately before or immediately after the purchase) shall be treated as increased—

(*a*) in the case of every company, by £100, and

(*b*) in the case of a company from which any person is entitled to periodic distributions of the kind mentioned in subsection (6) above, by a further amount equal to that required to make the distribution to which he is entitled in accordance with that subsection;

and where the aggregate of the sums payable by the company on the purchase and on any contemporaneous redemption, repayment or purchase of other shares of the company exceeds the amount of the profits available for distribution immediately before the purchase, that amount shall be treated as further increased by an amount equal to the excess.

(8) References in this section to entitlement are, except in the case of trustees and personal representatives, references to beneficial entitlement.

Commentary—*Simon's Direct Tax Service* D2.507.
Revenue & other press releases—ICAEW TR745 April 1989 (purchase in instalments: the "substantial reduction" test must be satisfied after each instalment, but an unconditional sale with payment by instalments applies the test to all the shares sold).
Definitions—"The purchase", s 219(1); "shares", s 229(1); "the vendor", s 219(1).
Cross references—See TA 1988 s 222(8) (extension of the application of sub-ss (6) and (7) above).

222 Conditions applicable where purchasing company is member of group

(1) Subject to section 224, where the company making the purchase is immediately before the purchase a member of a group and—

(*a*) immediately after the purchase the vendor owns shares in one or more other members of the group (whether or not he then owns shares in the company making the purchase), or

(*b*) immediately after the purchase the vendor owns shares in the company making the purchase and immediately before the purchase he owned shares in one or more other members of the group,

the vendor's interest as a shareholder in the group must be substantially reduced.

(2) In subsections (5) to (7) below "relevant company" means the company making the purchase and any other member of the group in which the vendor owns shares immediately before or immediately after the purchase, but subject to subsection (4) below.

(3) Subject to section 224, where the company making the purchase is immediately before the purchase a member of a group and at that time an associate of the vendor owns shares in any member of the group, the combined interests as shareholders in the group of the vendor and his associates must be substantially reduced.

(4) The question whether the combined interests as shareholders in the group of the vendor and his associates are substantially reduced shall be determined in the same way as is (under the following subsections) the question whether a vendor's interest as a shareholder in a group is substantially reduced, except that the vendor shall be assumed to have the interests of his associates as well as his own (and references in subsections (5) to (7) below to a relevant company shall be construed accordingly).

(5) The vendor's interest as a shareholder in the group shall be ascertained by—

(*a*) expressing the total nominal value of the shares owned by him in each relevant company as a fraction of the issued share capital of the company,

(*b*) adding together the fractions so obtained, and

(*c*) dividing the result by the number of relevant companies (including any in which he owns no shares).

(6) Subject to subsection (7) below, the vendor's interest as a shareholder in the group shall be taken to be substantially reduced if and only if it does not exceed 75 per cent of the corresponding interest immediately before the purchase.

(7) The vendor's interest as a shareholder in the group shall not be taken to be substantially reduced if—

    (*a*) he would, if every member of the group distributed all its profits available for distribution immediately after the purchase (including any profits received by it on a distribution by another member), be entitled to a share of the profits of one or more of them, and

    (*b*) that share, or the aggregate of those shares, expressed as a fraction of the aggregate of the profits available for distribution of every member of the group which is—

        (i) a relevant company, or
        (ii) a 51 per cent subsidiary of a relevant company,

    exceeds 75 per cent of the corresponding fraction immediately before the purchase.

(8) Subsections (6) and (7) of section 221 shall apply for the purposes of subsection (7) above as they apply for the purposes of subsection (5) of that section.

(9) Subject to the following subsections, in this section "group" means a company which has one or more 51 per cent subsidiaries, but is not itself a 51 per cent subsidiary of any other company, together with those subsidiaries.

(10) Where the whole or a significant part of the business carried on by an unquoted company ("the successor company") was previously carried on by—

    (*a*) the company making the purchase, or

    (*b*) a company which is (apart from this subsection) a member of a group to which the company making the purchase belongs,

the successor company and any company of which it is a 51 per cent subsidiary shall be treated as being a member of the same group as the company making the purchase (whether or not, apart from this subsection, the company making the purchase is a member of a group).

(11) Subsection (10) above shall not apply if the successor company first carried on the business there referred to more than three years before the time of the purchase.

(12) For the purposes of this section a company which has ceased to be a 51 per cent subsidiary of another company before the time of the purchase shall be treated as continuing to be such a subsidiary if at that time there exist arrangements under which it could again become such a subsidiary.

Commentary—*Simon's Direct Tax Service* **D2.507.**
Statement of Practice SP 2/82—Company's purchase of own shares, claims for relief.
Definitions—"Company", s 832(1), (2); "the purchase", s 219(1); "shares", s 229(1); "unquoted company", s 229(1); "the vendor", s 219(1); "51 per cent subsidiary", s 838.

223 Other conditions

(1) Subject to section 224, the vendor must not immediately after the purchase be connected with the company making the purchase or with any company which is a member of the same group as that company.

In this subsection "group" has the same meaning as it has for the purposes of section 222.

(2) Subject to section 224, the purchase must not be part of a scheme or arrangement which is designed or likely to result in the vendor or any associate of his having interests in any company such that, if he had those interests immediately after the purchase, any of the conditions in sections 221 and 222 and subsection (1) above could not be satisfied.

(3) A transaction occurring within one year after the purchase shall be deemed for the purposes of subsection (2) above to be part of a scheme or arrangement of which the purchase is also part.

Commentary—*Simon's Direct Tax Service* **D2.507.**
Statement of Practice SP 2/82, para 8—Sub-s (2) does not apply where personal representatives or beneficiaries sell shares which came into their ownership on a death if the deceased had purchased them before his death.
Definitions—"The purchase", s 219(1); "the vendor", s 219(1).
Cross references—See TA 1988 s 226 (information to be furnished to the inspector about any scheme or arrangement mentioned in sub-s. (2) above).

224 Relaxation of conditions in certain cases

Where—

    (*a*) any of the conditions in sections 221 to 223 which are applicable are not satisfied in relation to the vendor, but

    (*b*) he proposed or agreed to the purchase in order that the condition in section 221(2) or 222(3) could be satisfied in respect of the redemption, repayment or purchase of shares owned by a person of whom he is an associate,

then, to the extent that that result is produced by virtue of the purchase, section 219(1)(*a*) shall have effect as if the conditions in sections 221 to 223 were satisfied in relation to the vendor.

Commentary—*Simon's Direct Tax Service* **D2.507.**
Definitions—"The purchase", s 219(1); "shares", s 229(1); "the vendor", s 229(1).

225 Advance clearance of payments by Board

(1) A payment made by a company on the redemption, repayment or purchase of its own shares shall be deemed—

(*a*) to be one to which section 219 applies if, before it is made, the Board have on the application of the company notified the company that they are satisfied that the section will apply; and

(*b*) to be one to which section 219 does not apply if, before it is made, the Board have on the application of the company notified the company that they are satisfied that the section will not apply.

(2) An application under this section shall be in writing and shall contain particulars of the relevant transactions; and the Board may, within 30 days of the receipt of the application or of any further particulars previously required under this subsection, by notice require the applicant to furnish further particulars for the purpose of enabling the Board to make their decision.

(3) If a notice under subsection (2) above is not complied with within 30 days or such longer period as the Board may allow, the Board need not proceed further on the application.

(4) The Board shall notify their decision to the applicant within 30 days of receiving the application or, if they give a notice under subsection (2) above, within 30 days of the notice being complied with.

(5) If particulars furnished under this section do not fully and accurately disclose all facts and circumstances material for the decision of the Board, any resulting notification by the Board shall be void.

Commentary—*Simon's Direct Tax Service* **D2.509.**
Statement of Practice SP 2/82—Procedure for obtaining clearance under this section.
Revenue & other press releases—ICAEW TR745 April 1989 (clearance under this section does not automatically imply clearance under s 707; separate clearance should be obtained).
Definitions—''The Board'', s 832(1); ''company'', s 832(1), (2); ''payment made by a company'', s 229(1); ''shares'', s 229(1).

226 Returns and information

(1) A company which treats a payment made by it as one to which section 219 applies shall within 60 days after making the payment make a return to the inspector giving particulars of the payment and of the circumstances by reason of which that section is regarded as applying to it.

(2) Where a company treats a payment made by it as one to which section 219(1)(*a*) applies, any person connected with the company who knows of any such scheme or arrangement affecting the payment as is mentioned in section 223(2) shall, within 60 days after he first knows of both the payment and the scheme or arrangement, give a notice to the inspector containing particulars of the scheme or arrangement.

(3) Where the inspector has reason to believe that a payment treated by the company making it as one to which section 219(1)(*a*) applies may form part of a scheme or arrangement of the kind referred to therein or in section 223(2), he may by notice require the company or any person who is connected with the company to furnish him within such time, not being less than 60 days, as may be specified in the notice with—

(*a*) a declaration in writing stating whether or not, according to information which the company or that person has or can reasonably obtain, any such scheme or arrangement exists or has existed, and

(*b*) such other information as the inspector may reasonably require for the purposes of the provision in question and the company or that person has or can reasonably obtain.

(4) The recipient of a payment treated by the company making it as one to which section 219 applies, and any person on whose behalf such a payment is received, shall if so required by the inspector state whether the payment received by him or on his behalf is received on behalf of any person other than himself and, if so, the name and address of that person.

Commentary—*Simon's Direct Tax Service* **D2.507.**
Definitions—''Company'', s 832(1), (2); ''inspector'', s 832(1); ''person connected with a company'', s 228(1).

227 Associated persons

(1) Any question whether a person is an associate of another in relation to a company shall be determined for the purposes of sections 219 to 226 and 228 in accordance with the following provisions of this section.

(2) A husband and wife living together are associates of one another, a person under the age of 18 is an associate of his parents, and his parents are his associates.

(3) A person connected with a company is an associate of the company and of any company controlled by it, and the company and any company controlled by it are his associates.

(4) Where a person connected with one company has control of another company, the second company is an associate of the first.

(5) Where shares in a company are held by trustees (other than bare trustees) then in relation to that company, but subject to subsection (8) below, the trustees are associates of—

(*a*) any person who directly or indirectly provided property to the trustees or has made a reciprocal arrangement for another to do so,

(*b*) any person who is, by virtue of subsection (2) above, an associate of a person within paragraph (*a*) above, and

(*c*) any person who is or may become beneficially entitled to a significant interest in the shares;

and any such person is an associate of the trustees.

(6) Where shares in a company are comprised in the estate of a deceased person, then in relation to that company the deceased's personal representatives are associates of any person who is or may become beneficially entitled to a significant interest in the shares, and any such person is an associate of the personal representatives.

(7) Where one person is accustomed to act on the directions of another in relation to the affairs of a company, then in relation to that company the two persons are associates of one another.

(8) Subsection (5) above shall not apply to shares held on trusts which—

(*a*) relate exclusively to an exempt approved scheme as defined in Chapter I of Part XIV, or

(*b*) are exclusively for the benefit of the employees, or the employees and directors, of the company referred to in that subsection or of companies in a group to which that company belongs, or their dependants (and are not wholly or mainly for the benefit of directors or their relatives);

and for the purposes of this subsection "group" means a company which has one or more 51 per cent subsidiaries, together with those subsidiaries.

(9) For the purposes of subsections (5) and (6) above a person's interest is significant if its value exceeds 5 per cent of the value of all the property held on the trusts or, as the case may be, comprised in the estate concerned, excluding any property in which he is not and cannot become beneficially entitled to an interest.

Commentary—*Simon's Direct Tax Service* **D2.507.**
Definitions—"Company", s 832(1), (2); "control", s 840 by virtue of s 229(1); "person connected with a company", s 228(1); "personal representatives", s 229(1); "shares", s 229(1); "51 per cent subsidiary", s 838.

228 Connected persons

(1) Any question whether a person is connected with a company shall be determined for the purposes of sections 219 to 227 in accordance with the following provisions of this section.

(2) A person is connected with a company if he directly or indirectly possesses or is entitled to acquire more than 30 per cent of—

(*a*) the issued ordinary share capital of the company, or

(*b*) the loan capital and issued share capital of the company, or

(*c*) the voting power in the company.

(3) Where a person—

(*a*) acquired or became entitled to acquire loan capital of a company in the ordinary course of a business carried on by him, being a business which includes the lending of money, and

(*b*) takes no part in the management or conduct of the company,

his interest in that loan capital shall be disregarded for the purposes of subsection (2) above.

(4) A person is connected with a company if he directly or indirectly possesses or is entitled to acquire such rights as would, in the event of the winding up of the company or in any other circumstances, entitle him to receive more than 30 per cent of the assets of the company which would then be available for distribution to equity holders of the company; and for the purposes of this subsection—

(*a*) the persons who are equity holders of the company, and

(*b*) the percentage of the assets of the company to which a person would be entitled,

shall be determined in accordance with paragraphs 1 and 3 of Schedule 18, taking references in paragraph 3 to the first company as references to an equity holder and references to a winding up as including references to any other circumstances in which assets of the company are available for distribution to its equity holders.

(5) A person is connected with a company if he has control of it.

(6) References in this section to the loan capital of a company are references to any debt incurred by the company—

(*a*) for any money borrowed or capital assets acquired by the company, or

(*b*) for any right to receive income created in favour of the company, or

(*c*) for consideration the value of which to the company was (at the time when the debt was incurred) substantially less than the amount of the debt (including any premium thereon).

(7) For the purposes of this section a person shall be treated as entitled to acquire anything which he is entitled to acquire at a future date or will at a future date be entitled to acquire.

(8) For the purposes of this section a person shall be assumed to have the rights or powers of his associates as well as his own.

Commentary—*Simon's Direct Tax Service* **D2.507.**
Definitions—"Company", s 832(1), (2); "control", s 840 by virtue of s 229(1); "ordinary share capital", s 832(1).

229 Other interpretative provisions

(1) In sections 219 to 228—

''control'' has the meaning given by section 840;

''holding company'' means a company whose business (disregarding any trade carried on by it) consists wholly or mainly of the holding of shares or securities of one or more companies which are its 75 per cent subsidiaries;

''personal representatives'' means persons responsible for administering the estate of a deceased person;

''quoted company'' means a company whose shares (or any class of whose shares) are listed in the official list of a stock exchange;

''shares'' includes stock;

''trade'' does not include dealing in shares, securities, land or futures and ''trading activities'' shall be construed accordingly;

''trading company'' means a company whose business consists wholly or mainly of the carrying on of a trade or trades;

''trading group'' means a group the business of whose members, taken together, consists wholly or mainly of the carrying on of a trade or trades, and for this purpose ''group'' means a company which has one or more 75 per cent subsidiaries together with those subsidiaries; and

''unquoted company'' means a company which is neither a quoted company nor a 51 per cent subsidiary of a quoted company.

(2) References in sections 219 to 228 to the owner of shares are references to the beneficial owner except where the shares are held on trusts (other than bare trusts) or are comprised in the estate of a deceased person, and in such a case are references to the trustees or, as the case may be, to the deceased's personal representatives.

(3) References in sections 219 to 228 to a payment made by a company include references to anything else that is, or would but for section 219 be, a distribution.

Commentary—*Simon's Direct Tax Service* **D2.504.**
Statement of Practice SP 18/80—Securities dealt in on the Stock Exchange Unlisted Securities Market: status and valuation for tax purposes.
Definitions—''Company'', s 832(1), (2); ''51 per cent subsidiary, s 838; ''75 per cent subsidiary'', s 838.

Stock dividends

230 Stock dividends: distributions

Any share capital to which section 249 applies and which is issued by a company ...[1] as mentioned in subsection (4), (5) or (6) of that section ...[1] (read ...[1] with subsection (3) of that section)—

(*a*) shall, notwithstanding section 209(2)(*c*), not constitute a distribution within the meaning of section 209(2); and

(*b*) for purposes of sections 210 and 211 shall not be treated as issued ''as paid up otherwise than by the receipt of new consideration''.

Commentary—*Simon's Direct Tax Service* **D1.202.**
Definitions—''Company'', s 832(1), (2); ''close company'', s 414(1) by virtue of s 832(1); ''new consideration'', s 254(1).
Cross references—See TA 1988 s 250(7) (tax returns for the purposes of this section).
Amendments—[1] Words repealed by FA 1989 Sch 17 Pt V in relation to accounting periods beginning after 31 March 1989.

CHAPTER IV
TAX CREDITS

231 Tax credits for certain recipients of qualifying distributions

(1) Subject to sections [231AA,][8] [231AB,][12]...[5][...[13] and [469(2A)][9][4], [section 171(2B) of the Finance Act 1993 and section 219(4B) of the Finance Act 1994,][7] where[, in any year of assessment for which income tax is charged][9] a company resident in the United Kingdom makes a qualifying distribution and the person receiving the distribution is another such company or a person resident in the United Kingdom, not being a company, the recipient of the distribution shall be entitled to a tax credit equal to such proportion of the amount or value of the distribution as corresponds to [the tax credit fraction in force when][9] the distribution is made.

[(1A) The tax credit fraction is one-ninth.][9]

[(2) [Subject to sections 231A and 241(5)][6], a company resident in the United Kingdom which is entitled to a tax credit in respect of a distribution may claim to have the amount of the credit paid to it if—

(*a*) the company is wholly exempt from corporation tax or is only not exempt in respect of trading income; or

(*b*) the distribution is one in relation to which express exemption is given (otherwise than by section 208), whether specifically or by virtue of a more general exemption from tax, under any provision of the Tax Acts.][10]

(3) [Subject to section (3AA) below,][11] a person, not being a company resident in the United Kingdom, who is entitled to a tax credit in respect of a distribution may claim to have the credit set against the income tax chargeable on his income under section 3 or on his total income for the year of assessment in which the distribution is made *[and [subject to subsections (3A) to (3D) below]*[1] *where the credit exceeds that income tax, to have the excess paid to him]*[11].

[(3AA) For any year of assessment, the aggregate amount of the tax credits in respect of which claims are made under subsection (3) above by any person must not exceed the aggregate amount of the tax credits in respect of such qualifying distributions (if any) as are brought into charge to tax in the case of that person.][3]

(3A)–(3D) ...[3]

(4) Where a distribution mentioned in subsection (1) above is, or falls to be treated as, or under any provision of the Tax Acts is deemed to be, the income of a person other than the recipient, that person shall be treated for the purposes of this section as receiving the distribution (and accordingly the question whether he is entitled to a tax credit in respect of it shall be determined by reference to where he, and not the actual recipient, is resident); ...[2]

(5) ...[2]

Commentary—*Simon's Direct Tax Service* **D1.402.**
Definitions—"Advance corporation tax", s 834(1); "company", s 832(1), (2); "qualifying distribution", s 14(2) by virtue of s 832(1); "the Tax Acts", s 831(2); "tax credit", s 832(1); "total income", s 835(1); "year of assessment", s 832(1).
Revenue Internal Guidance—Company Taxation Manual COT8169 (examples of the operation of sub-s (3A)–(3D)).
Simon's Tax Cases—*Union Texas Petroleum Corporation v Critchley* [1990] STC 305*; *Getty Oil Co v Steele* [1990] STC 434*.
s 231(3), *R v IRC, ex p Camacq Corporation* [1989] STC 785; *Guild (as Trustees of the William Muir (Bond 9) Ltd Employees' Share Scheme) v IRC* [1993] STC 444.
Cross references—See TA 1988 s 231B(4) (no claim possible under sub-s (2) or (3) above where certain arrangements entered into to pass on the value of a tax credit).
TA 1988 s 246(6) (modification of the application of sub-s (1) above as it applies on a change of rate of ACT).
TA 1988 s 246C (no tax credit under sub-s (1) above for foreign income dividend).
TA 1988 s 247(2) (dividends paid under a group income election are excluded from this section).
TA 1988 s 438(4) (that section — pension business of an insurance company—to be disregarded in determining whether the condition in sub-s (2)(*a*) or (*b*) above is satisfied).
TA 1988 s 441A(2) (except as provided by regulations made under s 441A(3), an insurance company is not entitled to a tax credit relating to a distribution in respect of any asset of its overseas life assurance fund).
TA 1988 s 788(3) (double taxation arrangements: right to tax credit under this section in respect of qualifying distributions made to non–resident companies by resident companies).
TA 1988 s 812(1), (4) (restriction on a claim for set–off of tax credit under sub-s (3) above where the credit accrues under double taxation arrangements to a company connected with a unitary state).
TA 1988 Sch 19AC para 5A (overseas life-insurance company to be entitled to such a tax credit in respect of certain qualifying distributions as it would if it were resident in the UK).
FA 1989 Sch 12 para 1 (administrative provisions relating to close companies);
FA 1993 s 78(3) (rate of ACT for calculating tax credit under sub-s (1) above for financial year 1993).
FA 1993 s 171(2B) (sub-s (1) above not to apply to a post - 1 July 1997 distribution in respect of any asset of a non-corporate Lloyd's underwriting member's premiums trust fund).
FA 1994 s 219(4B) (sub-s (1) above not to apply to a post - 1 July 1997 distribution in respect of any asset of a corporate Lloyd's underwriting member's premiums trust fund).
FA 1994 s 221(2) (repayments of tax credits on pre - 2 July 1997 investment income to be made to corporate members of Lloyd's notwithstanding sub-s (2) above).
Amendments—[1] Words in sub-s (3) inserted by FA 1989 s 106(1).
[2] Words in sub-s (4) and whole of sub-s (5) repealed by FA 1989 Sch 17 Pt IV with effect in accordance with FA 1989 ss 110, 111.
[3] Sub-s (3AA) inserted, and sub-ss (3A)–(3D) repealed, by F(No 2)A 1997 ss 30(4), (5), Sch 8 Pt II(9), with effect for distributions after 5 April 1999. The insertion of sub-s (3AA) is subject to F(No 2)A 1997 s 30(9), (10), and is also subject to the amendments to F(No 2)A 1997 concerning tax-credit payments to ISAs and PEPs set out in FA 1998 s 76.
[4] Words in sub-s (1) substituted by FA 1990 Sch 7 para 2.
[5] Number in sub-s (1) repealed by FA 1997 Sch 18 Pt VI(7) with effect in relation to distributions made after 25 November 1996
[6] Words in sub-s (2) inserted, by F(No 2)A 1997 s 19(1), (3) in relation to qualifying distributions made after 1 July 1997.
[7] Words in sub-s (1) inserted by F(No 2)A 1997 s 22(6), (7) with effect in relation to distributions made after 1 July 1997.
[8] Word in sub-s (1) inserted by FA 1998 s 102(1), (9) in relation to qualifying distributions made after 7 April 1998, if the manufactured dividend representative of the distribution is paid (or treated for the purposes of TA 1988 Sch 23 as paid) after 5 April 1999.
[9] Words in sub-s (1) inserted and substituted, sub-s (1A) inserted by F(No 2)A 1997 ss 30(1)–(7), (9), (11), 34, Sch 4 para 4 (subject to the amendments to F(No 2)A 1997 concerning tax-credit payments to ISAs and PEPs set out in FA 1998 s 76) with effect in relation to distributions made after 5 April 1999, and by FA 1998 ss 76, 102 in relation to distributions made and manufactured dividends paid (or treated for the purposes of TA 1988 Sch 23 as paid) after 5 April 1999. Sub-s (1) previously read as follows—
"(1) Subject to sections 231AA, 247 and 441A, section 171(2B) of the Finance Act 1993 and section 219(4B) of the Finance Act 1994, where a company resident in the United Kingdom makes a qualifying distribution and the person receiving the distribution is another such company or a person resident in the United Kingdom, not being a company, the recipient of the distribution shall be entitled to a tax credit equal to such proportion of the amount or value of the distribution as corresponds to the rate of advance corporation tax in force for the financial year in which the distribution is made."
[10] Sub-s (2), repealed by F(No 2)A 1997 Sch 8 Pt II(9) with effect in relation to distributions made after 5 April 1999. This repeal does not have effect in relation to distributions to insurance companies in respect of investments of so much of the insurance companies' long term business fund as is referable to its individual savings account business (see Individual Savings Account (Insurance Companies) Regulations, SI 1998/1871 reg 4), or in relation to certain distributions to friendly societies made before 6 April 2004 (see FA 1998 s 90(1)).
[11] First set of words in sub-s (3) substituted for "Subject to section 231A", and final words in sub-s (3) repealed, by F(No 2)A 1997 s 30(5), Sch 8 Pt II(9) with effect in relation to distributions made after 5 April 1999. These amendments are subject to F(No 2)A 1997 s 30(9), (10) and are also subject to the amendments to F(No 2)A 1997 concerning tax-credit payments to ISAs and PEPs set out in FA 1998 s 76.
[12] Word in sub-s (1) inserted by FA 1998 s 102(2) with effect in relation to manufactured distributions paid (or treated for the purposes of TA 1988 Sch 23A as paid) after 5 April 1999.
[13] In sub-s (1), ", 247" repealed by FA 2001 s 110, Sch 33 Pt II(10) with effect for payments made after 11 May 2001.

[231AA No tax credit for borrower under stock lending arrangement or interim holder under repurchase agreement

(1) A person shall not be entitled to a tax credit under section 231 in respect of a qualifying distribution if—

   (*a*) he is the borrower under a stock lending arrangement or the interim holder under a repurchase agreement;
   (*b*) the qualifying distribution is, or is a payment representative of, a distribution in respect of securities to which the arrangement or agreement relates; and
   (*c*) a manufactured dividend representative of that distribution is paid by that person in respect of securities to which the arrangement or agreement relates.

(2) In this section "stock lending arrangement" has the same meaning as in section 263B of the 1992 Act and, in relation to any such arrangement, any reference to the borrower, or the securities to which the arrangement relates, shall be construed accordingly.

(3) For the purposes of this section the cases where there is a repurchase agreement are the following—

   (*a*) any case falling within subsection (1) of section 730A; and
   (*b*) any case which would fall within that subsection if the sale price and the repurchase price were different;

and, in any such case, any reference to the interim holder, or the securities to which the agreement relates, shall be construed accordingly.

(4) For the purposes of this section "manufactured dividend" has the same meaning as in paragraph 2 of Schedule 23A (and any reference to a manufactured dividend being paid accordingly includes a reference to a payment falling by virtue of section 736B(2) or 737A(5) to be treated for the purposes of Schedule 23A as if it were made).][1]

Commentary—*Simon's Direct Tax Service* **D1.402.**
Amendments—[1] This section inserted by FA 1998 s 102(1), (9) with effect in relation to qualifying distributions made after 7 April 1998 if the manufactured dividend representative of the distribution is paid (or treated for the purposes of TA 1988 Sch 23A as paid) after 5 April 1998.

[231AB No tax credit for original owner under repurchase agreement in respect of certain manufactured dividends

(1) A person shall not be entitled to a tax credit under section 231 in respect of a qualifying distribution if—

   (*a*) he is the original owner under a repurchase agreement;
   (*b*) the qualifying distribution is a manufactured dividend paid to that person by the interim holder under the repurchase agreement in respect of securities to which the agreement relates; and
   (*c*) the repurchase agreement is not such that the actual dividend which the manufactured dividend represents is receivable otherwise than by the original owner.

(2) For the purposes of this section the cases where there is a repurchase agreement are the following—

   (*a*) any case falling within subsection (1) of section 730A; and
   (*b*) any case which would fall within that subsection if the sale price and the repurchase price were different;

and, in any such case, any reference to the original owner, the interim holder, or the securities to which the agreement relates, shall be construed accordingly.

(3) Subsection (4) of section 231AA applies for the purposes of this section as it applies for the purposes of that section.][1]

Amendments—[1] This section inserted by FA 1998 s 102(2), (10) with effect in relation to manufactured distributions paid (or treated for the purposes of TA 1988 Sch 23A as paid) after 5 April 1999.

[231A Restrictions on the use of tax credits by pension funds

Definitions—"Qualifying distribution", s 14(2) by virtue of s 832(1); "tax credit", s 832(1); "year of assessment", s 832(1).
Amendments—This section (inserted by F(No 2)A 1997 s 19(2), (3)) repealed by F(No 2)A 1997 s 30(8), (11), Sch 8 Pt II(9) with effect in relation to distributions made after 5 April 1999.

[231B Consequences of certain arrangements to pass on the value of a tax credit

(1) This section applies in any case where—

   (*a*) a person ("A") is entitled to a tax credit in respect of a qualifying distribution;
   (*b*) arrangements subsist such that another person ("B") obtains, whether directly or indirectly, a payment representing any of the value of the tax credit;
   (*c*) the arrangements (whether or not made directly between A and B) were entered into for an unallowable purpose; and
   (*d*) the condition in subsection (2) below is satisfied.

(2) The condition is that if B had been the person entitled to the tax credit and the qualifying distribution to which it relates, and had received the distribution when it was made, then—

(a) B would not have been entitled to obtain any payment under section 231(2) or (3) in respect of the tax credit; and

(b) if B is a company, B could not have used the income consisting of the distribution to frank a distribution actually made in the accounting period in which it would have received the distribution to which the tax credit relates.

(3) This section does not apply if and to the extent that any other provision of the Tax Acts has the effect of cancelling or reducing the tax advantage which would otherwise be obtained by virtue of the arrangements.

(4) Where this section applies—

(a) no claim shall be made under section 231(2) for payment of the amount of the tax credit;

(b) no claim shall be made under section 231(3) ...[2] in respect of the tax credit;

(c) the income consisting of the distribution in respect of which A is entitled to the tax credit shall not be regarded for the purposes of section 241 as franked investment income; and

(d) no claim shall be made under section 35 of the Finance (No. 2) Act 1997 (transitional relief) for payment of an amount determined by reference to that distribution.

(5) For the purposes of this section, the question whether any arrangements were entered into for an "unallowable purpose" shall be determined in accordance with subsections (6) and (7) below.

(6) Arrangements are entered into for an unallowable purpose if the purposes for which at least one person is a party to the arrangements include a purpose which is not amongst the business or other commercial purposes of that person.

(7) Where one of the purposes for which a person enters into any arrangements is the purpose of securing that that person or another obtains a tax advantage, that purpose shall be regarded as a business or other commercial purpose of the person only if it is neither the main purpose, nor one of the main purposes, for which the person enters into the arrangements.

(8) Any reference in this section to a person obtaining a tax advantage includes a reference to a person obtaining a payment representing any of the value of a tax credit in circumstances where, had the person obtaining the payment been entitled to the tax credit and the qualifying distribution to which it relates, that person—

(a) would not have been entitled to obtain any payment under section 231(2) or (3) in respect of the tax credit; and

(b) if that person is a company, could not have used the income consisting of the distribution to frank a distribution actually made in the accounting period in which it would have received the distribution to which the tax credit relates.

(9) If an amount representing any of the value of a tax credit to which a person is entitled is applied at the direction of, or otherwise in favour of, some other person (whether by way of set off or otherwise), that case shall be treated for the purposes of this section as one where that other person obtains a payment representing any of the value of the tax credit.

(10) In determining for the purposes of subsections (2)(b) and (8)(b) above whether a company could have used the income consisting of the distribution in question to frank a distribution of the company, the company shall be taken to use its actual franked investment income to frank distributions before using the income consisting of the distribution in question.

(11) References in this section to using franked investment income to frank a distribution of a company have the same meaning as in Chapter V of Part VI.

(12) In this section—

"arrangements" means arrangements of any kind, whether in writing or not (and includes a series of arrangements, whether or not between the same parties);

"business or other commercial purposes" includes the efficient management of investments;

"franked investment income" has the same meaning as in Chapter V of Part VI and references to income consisting of a distribution shall be construed accordingly;

"tax advantage" has the same meaning as in Chapter I of Part XVII.][1]

Definitions—"Company", s 832(1), (2); "distribution", s 209; "franked investment income", s 238(1); "qualifying distribution", s 14(2) by virtue of s 832(1); "tax advantage", s 709(1); "tax credit", s 832(1).
Cross references—See TA 1988 s 231A (restrictions on use of tax credits by pension funds).
Amendments—[1] This section inserted by F(No 2)A 1997 s 28 with effect in relation to qualifying distributions made after 1 July 1997.
[2] Words in sub-s (4)(b) repealed by F(No 2)A 1997 s 34, Sch 4 para 26, Sch 8 Pt II(10) with effect in relation to distributions made after 5 April 1999.

232 Tax credits for non-UK residents

(1) An individual who, having made a claim in that behalf, is entitled to relief under Chapter I of Part VII by virtue of section 278(2) in respect of any year of assessment shall be entitled to a tax credit in respect of any qualifying distribution received by him in that year to the same extent as if he were resident in the United Kingdom.

(2), (3) ...[1]

Commentary—*Simon's Direct Tax Service* **D1.404.**
Simon's Tax Cases—s 232(3), *R v IRC, ex p Camacq Corporation* [1989] STC 785.
Definitions—''Qualifying distribution'', s 14(2) by virtue of s 832(1); ''tax credit'', s 832(1); ''year of assessment'', s 832(1).
Amendments—¹ Sub-ss (2), (3) repealed by F(No 2)A 1997 s 34, Sch 4 para 5, Sch 8 Pt II(9) with effect in relation to distributions made after 5 April 1999.

233 Taxation of certain recipients of distributions and in respect of non-qualifying distributions

(1) Where in any year of assessment the income of any person, not being a company resident in the United Kingdom, includes a distribution in respect of which that person is not entitled to a tax credit—

     [(*a*) that person shall be treated as having paid income tax at the [Schedule F ordinary rate]⁴ on the amount or value of the distribution;

     (*b*) no repayment shall be made of any income tax treated by virtue of paragraph (*a*) above as having been paid;]²

     (*c*) the amount or value of the distribution shall be treated ...¹ for the purposes of sections 348 and 349(1) as not brought into charge to income tax.

[(1A) Where in any year of assessment the income of any person who is not a company includes a qualifying distribution in respect of which that person, not being resident in the United Kingdom, is not entitled to a tax credit—

     (*a*) the amount or value of the distribution so far as it is comprised in—

         [(i) income on which that person falls to be treated as having paid income tax at the [Schedule F ordinary rate]⁴ by virtue of paragraph (*a*) of subsection (1) above, or]²

         [(ii) income to which section 686 applies,]³

     shall be deemed for the purposes of [that subsection]² or, as the case may be, that section to be the sum which if reduced by an amount equal to income tax on that sum at the [Schedule F ordinary rate]⁴ would be equal to the amount or value of the distribution actually made; and

     (*b*) that person shall be treated for the purposes of section 686 as having paid tax at the [Schedule F ordinary rate]⁴ on any amount which under paragraph (*a*) above is deemed to be the amount or value of the distribution for the purpose of that section;

but no repayment shall be made of any income tax treated by virtue of this subsection as having been paid.

(1B) Where in any year of assessment the income of any trustees which is chargeable to income tax in accordance with section 686 includes any non-qualifying distribution (within the meaning of subsection (2) below), the trustees' liability under any assessment made in respect of income tax at the rate applicable to trusts on the amount or value of the distribution, or on any part of the distribution, shall be reduced by a sum equal to income tax at the [Schedule F ordinary rate]⁴ on so much of the distribution as is assessed at the [Schedule F trust rate]⁴.]¹

(2) Where a person has paid tax (''the tax paid'') in respect of excess liability on, or on any part of, a non-qualifying distribution, then if, apart from this subsection, he would be liable to pay an amount of tax in respect of excess liability on, or on any part of, a repayment of the share capital or of the principal of the security which constituted that non-qualifying distribution, he shall be so liable only to the extent (if any) to which that amount exceeds the amount of the tax paid.

In this subsection—

     ''excess liability'' means the excess of liability to income tax over what it would be if all income tax [were charged—

         (*a*) in the case of income chargeable under Schedule F, at the Schedule F ordinary rate, and

         (*b*) in the case of any other income, at the lower rate;

     to the exclusion of the higher rate, the Schedule F upper rate or, as the case may be, the Schedule F trust rate.]⁴

     ''non-qualifying distribution'' means a distribution which is not a qualifying distribution.

Commentary—*Simon's Direct Tax Service* **D1.403.**
Definitions—''Basic rate'' s 832(1); ''company'', s 832(1), (2); ''distribution'', s 832(1); ''higher rate'', s 832(1); ''lower rate'', s 832(1); ''qualifying distribution'', s 14(2) by virtue of s 832(1); ''Schedule F ordinary rate'', s 832(1); ''Schedule F trust rate'', s 832(1); ''security'', s 254(1); ''tax credit'', s 832(1); ''year of assessment'', s 832(1).
Cross references—See TA 1988 s 246D(5) (sub-ss (1), (1A) above not to apply to foreign income dividend).
Amendments—¹ Words omitted from sub-s (1)(*c*) repealed and sub-ss (1A), (1B) inserted by FA 1993 Sch 6 paras 2, 25(1), Sch 23 Pt III(6) with effect from the year 1993–94.
² Sub-s (1)(*a*), (*b*) and words in sub-s (1A)(*a*) substituted by FA 1996 s 122(3), (4) for the purposes of income tax and capital gains tax, from the year 1996–97, and as respects corporation tax for accounting periods ending on or after the appointed day being a day not earlier than 1 April 1996.
³ Sub-s (1A)(*a*)(ii) substituted by FA 1997 Sch 7 para 12(3), (4) with effect from the year 1996–97.
⁴ Words in sub-ss (1)–(1B), (2) substituted by F(No 2)A 1997 s 34, Sch 4 para 6 with effect for distributions made after 5 April 1999.

234 Information relating to distributions

(1) Without prejudice to [section 234A]² *but subject to section 95(1A)(c)*⁴, a company which makes a qualifying distribution shall, if the recipient so requests in writing, furnish to him a statement in writing showing the amount or value of the distribution and (whether or not the recipient is a person

entitled to a tax credit in respect of the distribution) the amount of the tax credit to which a recipient who is such a person is entitled in respect of that distribution.

(2) The duty imposed by subsection (1) above shall be enforceable at the suit or instance of the person requesting the information.

(3), (4) ...[3]

(5) Where a company makes a distribution which is not a qualifying distribution it shall make a return to the inspector—

(a) within 14 days from the end of the accounting period in which the distribution is made; or
(b) if the distribution is made on a date not falling in an accounting period, within 14 days from that date.

(6) A return under subsection (5) above shall contain—

(a) particulars of the transaction giving rise to the distribution; and
(b) the name and address of the person, or each of the persons, receiving the distribution, and the amount or value of the distribution received by him or by each of them.

(7) Where it is not in the circumstances apparent whether a transaction gives rise to a distribution in respect of which a return is required to be made under subsection (5) above, the company shall—

(a) within the time within which such a return would be required to be made if the transaction did give rise to such a distribution, make a return to the inspector containing particulars of the transaction in question; and
(b) if required by a notice served on the company by the inspector, furnish him with the time specified in the notice with such further information in relation to the transaction as he may reasonably require.

(8) If it appears to the inspector that particulars of any transaction ought to have been and have not been included in a return under subsection (5) or (7) above, he may by a notice served on the company require the company to furnish him within the time specified in the notice with such information relating thereto as he may reasonably require.

(9) Any power which the inspector may exercise under [paragraphs 2 to 4 of Schedule 12 to the Finance Act 1989 for the purposes of the relevant provisions (as defined in paragraph 1 of that Schedule)][2] may be exercised by him for the purposes of subsections (5) to (8) above.

Commentary—*Simon's Direct Tax Service* **D1.608.**
Definitions—"Accounting period", s 834(1); "company", s 832(1), (2); "deduction of income tax", s 4(1); "distribution", s 832(1); "inspector", s 832(1); "notice", s 832(1); "qualifying distribution", s 14(2) by virtue of s 832(1); "tax credit", s 832(1).
Cross references—See TMA 1970 s 98 (special return penalties in respect of failures to provide information or make returns under this section).
TA 1988 s 253 (power to modify or replace sub-ss (5)–(9) above).
IT (Dividend Manufacturing) Regulations, SI 1992/569 reg 16 (approved manufactured payment; sub-s (3) above not to apply unless the payee requires a written statement as mentioned in sub-s(3)).
Venture Capital Trusts Regulations, SI 1995/1979 reg 21 (application of this section to certain distributions of venture capital trusts).
Amendments—[1] Words in sub-s (9) substituted by FA 1989 Sch 12 para 11.
[2] Words in sub-s (1) substituted by F(No 2)A 1992 s 32(2).
[3] Sub-ss (3), (4) repealed by F(No 2)A 1992 s 32(2), (4) and Sch 18 Pt VII(4) in relation to distributions begun after 16 July - 1992.
[4] Words in sub-s (1) (as amended by FA 1997 Sch 7 para 8(2)(b), (3) with effect in relation to distributions made after 25 November 1996) repealed by F(No 2)A 1997 s 24(11), (15), Sch 8 Pt II(8) with effect in relation to any distribution made after 1 July 1997 and any payment which is representative of such a distribution.

[234A Information relating to distributions: further provisions]

(1) This section applies where dividend or interest is distributed by a company which is—

(a) a company within the meaning of the Companies Act 1985 or the Companies (Northern Ireland) Order 1986, or
(b) a company created by letters patent or by or in pursuance of an Act.

(2) If the company makes a payment of dividend or interest to any person, and subsection (3) below does not apply, within a reasonable period the company shall send an appropriate statement to that person.

(3) If the company makes a payment of dividend or interest into a bank or building society account held by any person, within a reasonable period the company shall send an appropriate statement to either—

(a) the bank or building society concerned, or
(b) the person holding the account.

(4) In a case where—

(a) a statement is received by a person under subsection (2) or (3)(b) above,
(b) the whole or part of the sum concerned is paid to or on behalf of the person as nominee for another person, and
(c) the nominee makes a payment of the sum or part to the other person and sub- section (5) below does not apply,

within a reasonable period the nominee shall send an appropriate statement to that person.

(5) In a case where—

(*a*) a statement is received by a person under subsection (2) or (3)(*b*) above,

(*b*) the whole or part of the sum concerned is paid to or on behalf of the person as nominee for another person, and

(*c*) the nominee makes a payment of the sum or part into a bank or building society account held by the other person,

within a reasonable period the nominee shall send an appropriate statement to either the bank or building society concerned or the other person.

(6) In the case of a payment of interest which is not a qualifying distribution or part of a qualifying distribution, references in this section to an appropriate statement are to a written statement showing—

(*a*) the gross amount which, after deduction of the income tax appropriate to the interest, corresponds to the net amount actually paid,

(*b*) the rate and the amount of income tax appropriate to such gross amount,

(*c*) the net amount actually paid, and

(*d*) the date of the payment.

(7) In the case of a payment of dividend or interest which is a qualifying distribution or part of a qualifying distribution, references in this section to an appropriate statement are to a written statement showing—

(*a*) the amount of the dividend or interest paid,

(*b*) the date of the payment, and

(*c*) the amount of the tax credit to which a person is entitled in respect of the dividend or interest, or to which a person would be so entitled if he had a right to a tax credit in respect of the dividend or interest.

(8) In this section "send" means send by post.

[(8A) In this section "bank" has the meaning given by section 840A.][2]

(9) If a person fails to comply with subsection (2), (3), (4) or (5) above, the person shall incur a penalty of £60 in respect of each offence, except that the aggregate amount of any penalties imposed under this subsection on a person in respect of offences connected with any one distribution of dividends or interest shall not exceed £600.

(10) The Board may by regulations provide that where a person is under a duty to comply with subsection (2), (3), (4) or (5) above, the person shall be taken to comply with the subsection if the person either—

(*a*) acts in accordance with the subsection concerned, or

(*b*) acts in accordance with rules contained in the regulations;

and subsection (9) above shall be construed accordingly.

(11) Regulations under subsection (10) above may make different provision for different circumstances.][1]

Commentary—*Simon's Direct Tax Service* **D1.204.**
Concession C30—Requirement for an authorised unit trust or open-ended investment company to issue tax vouchers in respect of a waived distribution is relaxed in certain circumstances.
Definitions—"Building society", s 832(1); "the Board", s 832(1); "interest", s 832(1); "qualifying distribution", s 832(1); "tax credit", s 832(1).
Cross references—See TA 1988 s 246G (information relating to foreign income dividend).
TA 1988 s 468(3) (extension of this section to authorised unit trusts).
FA 2000 Sch 8 para 89(4) (sub-s (4) above does not apply in relation to any amount applied by the trustees in acquiring dividend shares on behalf of a participant in an employee share ownership plan).
FA 2000 Sch 8 paras 90, 92(3), 93(4) (application of sub-ss (4)–(11) in relation to repayments of excess cash dividends, the treatment of cash dividends retained and later paid out, and the charge on dividend shares ceasing to be subject to an employee share ownership plan).
Amendments—[1] This section inserted by F(No 2)A 1992 s 32(1), (4) in relation to distributions begun after 16 July 1992.
[2] Sub-s (8A) inserted by FA 1996 Sch 37 paras 2(1), (2)(*a*), 7 with effect in relation to payments made on or after 29 April 1996.

[235 Distributions of exempt funds etc

Commentary—*Simon's Direct Tax Service* **A7.1202.**
Amendments—This section repealed by F(No 2)A 1997 s 34, Sch 4 para 7, Sch 8 Pt II(9) with effect in relation to distributions made after 5 April 1999.

[236 Provisions supplementary to section 235

Commentary—*Simon's Direct Tax Service* **A7.1202.**
Amendments—This section repealed by F(No 2)A 1997 s 34, Sch 4 para 7, Sch 8 Pt II(9) with effect in relation to distributions made after 5 April 1999.

[237 Disallowance of reliefs in respect of bonus issues

Commentary—*Simon's Direct Tax Service* **A7.1203.**
Amendments—This section repealed by F(No 2)A 1997 s 34, Sch 4 para 7, Sch 8 Pt II(9) with effect in relation to distributions made after 5 April 1999.

CHAPTER V

ADVANCE CORPORATION TAX AND FRANKED INVESTMENT INCOME

Revenue and other press releases—
IR 16-2-99 (operation of ''shadow'' ACT rules, with worked example).
Cross references—See TA 1988 s 434(3) (policy holders' share of granted investment income on investments held for life assurance business not to be used to frank distributions for the purposes of this Chapter).
TA 1988 s 441A(8) (franked investment income of insurance company not to be used under this Chapter to frank distributions in respect of assets of its overseas life assurance fund where any part of the tax credit is payable to the company).
Corporation Tax (Treatment of Unrelieved Surplus Advance Corporation Tax) Regulations, SI 1999/358 (''shadow'' ACT rules for the relief of past surplus ACT from 6 April 1999).

238 Interpretation of terms and collection of ACT

Commentary—*Simon's Direct Tax Service* D1.301.
Amendments—This section repealed by FA 1998 Sch 3 para 11 with effect for accounting periods beginning after 5 April 1999.

239 Set-off of ACT against liability to corporation tax

Commentary—*Simon's Direct Tax Service* D1.311–313.
Cross references—See FA 1998 Sch 3 para 12(3)–(6) (no ACT shall, by virtue of sub-s (4), shall be treated as paid in respect of distributions made in accounting periods beginning after 5 April 1999; determination of the limit under sub-s (2) on the set-off of ACT for an accounting period straddling 6 April 1999).
Amendments—This section repealed by FA 1998 Sch 3 para 12 with effect in relation to accounting periods beginning after 5 April 1999.

240 Set-off of company's surplus ACT against subsidiary's liability to corporation tax

Commentary—*Simon's Direct Tax Service* D2.644.
Amendments—This section repealed by FA 1998 Sch 3 para 13 with effect in relation to accounting periods of the surrendering company (as defined in sub-s (1)) beginning after 5 April 1999.

241 Calculation of ACT where company receives franked investment income

Commentary—*Simon's Direct Tax Service* D1.304.
Amendments—This section repealed by FA 1998 Sch 3 para 14 with effect in relation to accounting periods beginning after 5 April 1999.

242 Set-off of losses etc against surplus of franked investment income

Commentary—*Simon's Direct Tax Service* D2.413, 414.
Amendments—This section repealed by F(No 2)A 1997 s 20(1), (2), (5), Sch 8 Pt II(4). As regards claims under this section, the repeal has effect for accounting periods beginning after 1 July 1997. As regards restoration of losses under sub-ss (5), (6), the repeal has effect where the later accounting period mentioned in sub-s (5)(*b*) begins after that date. In both cases, see also F(No 2)A 1997 s 20(4) for provisions affecting accounting periods straddling 2 July 1997.

243 Set-off of loss brought forward

Commentary—*Simon's Direct Tax Service* D2.414.
Amendments—This section repealed by F(No 2)A 1997 s 20(1), (2), (5), Sch 8 Pt II(4). As regards claims under this section, the repeal has effect for accounting periods beginning after 1 July 1997. As regards sub-s (4), the repeal has effect where the later accounting period mentioned in section 242(5)(*b*) begins after that date. In both cases, see also F(No 2)A 1997 s 20(4) for provisions affecting accounting periods straddling 2 July 1997.

244 Further provisions relating to claims under section 242 or 243

Commentary—*Simon's Direct Tax Service* D2.413, 414.
Amendments—This section repealed by F(No 2)A 1997 s 20(1), (3), (5), Sch 8 Pt II(4). As regards sub-s (1), the repeal has effect for accounting periods beginning after 1 July 1997. As regards sub-s (2), no amount may be deducted under para (*a*), or carried forward and deducted under para (*b*), for any accounting period beginning after that date. See also F(No 2)A 1997 s 20(4) for provisions affecting accounting periods straddling 2 July 1997.

245 Calculation etc of ACT on change of ownership of company

Commentary—*Simon's Direct Tax Service* D1.313.
Amendments—This section repealed by FA 1998 Sch 3 para 15 with effect in relation to changes in ownership (within the meaning of this section) occurring after 5 April 1999.

[245A Restriction on application of section 240 in certain circumstances]

Commentary—*Simon's Direct Tax Service* D1.313.
Amendments—This section repealed by FA 1998 Sch 3 para 16 with effect in relation to changes in ownership (within the meaning of this section) occurring after 5 April 1999 (previously inserted by FA 1989 s 98).

[245B Restriction on set-off where asset transferred after change in ownership of company]

Commentary—*Simon's Direct Tax Service* D1.313.
Amendments—This section (inserted by FA 1989 s 98) repealed by FA 1998 Sch 3 para 17 with effect in relation to disposals after 5 April 1999 (previously inserted by FA 1989 s 98). In relation to an accounting period beginning before and ending on

or after 6 April 1999, the reference in TA 1988 s 245B(4)(*a*) to the end of the relevant period shall be taken to be a reference to the end of a period which ends on 5 April 1999.

246 Charge of ACT at previous rate until new rate fixed, and changes of rate

Amendments—This section repealed by FA 1998 Sch 3 para 18 with effect in relation to distributions made after 5 April 1999.

[CHAPTER VA
FOREIGN INCOME DIVIDENDS][1]

Commentary—*Simon's Direct Tax Service* **Division D1.7.**
Amendments—[1] This Chapter (inserted by FA 1994 Sch 16 para 1) repealed by F(No 2)A 1997 s 36(4), Sch 6 para 3, Sch 8 Pt II(11) (previously inserted by FA 1994 Sch 16 para 1). The repeal has effect (*a*) as regards ss 246A-246E, 246G, in relation to distributions made after 5 April 1999, (*b*) as regards ss 246F, 246H-246J, 246N-246Y, for accounting periods beginning after 5 April 1999 and (*c*) as regards ss 246K-246M, for accounting periods of the parent (within the meaning of those sections) beginning after 5 April 1999. See F(No 2)A 1997 Sch 6 paras 22, 23 for transitional provisions.

[Election by company paying dividend

246A Election by company paying dividend]

Commentary—*Simon's Direct Tax Service* **D1.702.**
Amendments—This section repealed by F(No 2)A 1997 s 36(4), Sch 6 para 3, Sch 8 Pt II(11) with effect in relation to distributions made after 5 April 1999.

[246B Procedure for making election]

Commentary—*Simon's Direct Tax Service* **D1.702.**
Amendments—This section repealed by F(No 2)A 1997 s 36(4), Sch 6 para 3, Sch 8 Pt II(11) with effect in relation to distributions made after 5 April 1999.

[Recipient of foreign income dividend]

[246C No tax credit for recipient]

Commentary—*Simon's Direct Tax Service* **D1.701.**
Definitions—"Distribution", s 832(1); "tax credit", s 832(1).
Amendments—This section repealed by F(No 2)A 1997 s 36(4), Sch 6 para 3, Sch 8 Pt II(11) with effect in relation to distributions made after 5 April 1999.

[246D Individuals etc]

Commentary—*Simon's Direct Tax Service* **D1.707.**
Amendments—This section repealed by F(No 2)A 1997 s 36(4), Sch 6 para 3, Sch 8 Pt II(11) with effect in relation to distributions made after 5 April 1999.

[Companies: payments and receipts]

[246E Foreign income dividend not franked payment]

Commentary—*Simon's Direct Tax Service* **D1.706.**
Amendments—This section repealed by F(No 2)A 1997 s 36(4), Sch 6 para 3, Sch 8 Pt II(11) with effect in relation to distributions made after 5 April 1999.

[246F Calculation of ACT where company receives foreign income dividend]

Commentary—*Simon's Direct Tax Service* **D1.706.**
Amendments—This section repealed by F(No 2)A 1997 s 36(4), Sch 6 para 3, Sch 8 Pt II(11) with effect for accounting periods beginning after 5 April 1999.

[246G Information relating to foreign income dividends]

Commentary—*Simon's Direct Tax Service* **D1.704.**
Amendments—This section repealed by F(No 2)A 1997 s 36(4), Sch 6 para 3, Sch 8 Pt II(11) with effect in relation to distributions made after 5 April 1999.

[246H Power of inspector to require information]

Commentary—*Simon's Direct Tax Service* **D1.731.**
Amendments—This section repealed by F(No 2)A 1997 s 36(4), Sch 6 para 3, Sch 8 Pt II(11) with effect for accounting periods beginning after 5 April 1999.

[Foreign source profit and distributable foreign profit

246I Foreign source profit and distributable foreign profit]

Commentary—*Simon's Direct Tax Service* **D1.703.**
Amendments—This section repealed by F(No 2)A 1997 s 36(4), Sch 6 para 3, Sch 8 Pt II(11) with effect for accounting periods beginning after 5 April 1999.

[Matching of dividend with distributable foreign profit

246J Matching of dividend with distributable foreign profit]

Commentary—*Simon's Direct Tax Service* **D1.704.**
Amendments—This section repealed by F(No 2)A 1997 s 36(4), Sch 6 para 3, Sch 8 Pt II(11) with effect for accounting periods beginning after 5 April 1999.

[246K Matching: subsidiaries]

Commentary—*Simon's Direct Tax Service* **D1.705.**
Amendments—This section repealed by F(No 2)A 1997 s 36(4), Sch 6 para 3, Sch 8 Pt II(11) with effect for accounting periods of the parent beginning after 5 April 1999.

[246L Requirement as to subsidiaries]

Commentary—*Simon's Direct Tax Service* **D1.705.**
Amendments—This section repealed by F(No 2)A 1997 s 36(4), Sch 6 para 3, Sch 8 Pt II(11) with effect for accounting periods of the parent beginning after 5 April 1999.

[246M Matching: further provisions]

Commentary—*Simon's Direct Tax Service* **D1.705.**
Amendments—This section repealed by F(No 2)A 1997 s 36(4), Sch 6 para 3, Sch 8 Pt II(11) with effect for accounting periods of the parent beginning after 5 April 1999.

[Repayment or set-off of advance corporation tax

246N ACT to be repaid or set off against corporation tax liability]

Commentary—*Simon's Direct Tax Service* **D1.711.**
Amendments—This section repealed by F(No 2)A 1997 s 36(4), Sch 6 para 3, Sch 8 Pt II(11) with effect for accounting periods beginning after 5 April 1999.

[246P Notional foreign source advance corporation tax]

Commentary—*Simon's Direct Tax Service* **D1.712.**
Amendments—This section repealed by F(No 2)A 1997 s 36(4), Sch 6 para 3, Sch 8 Pt II(11) with effect for accounting periods beginning after 5 April 1999.

[246Q Repayment or set-off: supplementary]

Commentary—*Simon's Direct Tax Service* **D1.713.**
Amendments—This section repealed by F(No 2)A 1997 s 36(4), Sch 6 para 3, Sch 8 Pt II(11) with effect for accounting periods beginning after 5 April 1999.

[246R Supplementary claims]

Commentary—*Simon's Direct Tax Service* **D1.713.**
Amendments—This section repealed by F(No 2)A 1997 s 36(4), Sch 6 para 3, Sch 8 Pt II(11) with effect for accounting periods beginning after 5 April 1999.

[International headquarters companies

246S International headquarters companies]

Commentary—*Simon's Direct Tax Service* **D1.721.**
Amendments—This section repealed by F(No 2)A 1997 s 36(4), Sch 6 para 3, Sch 8 Pt II(11) with effect for accounting periods beginning after 5 April 1999.

[246T Liability to pay ACT displaced]

Commentary—*Simon's Direct Tax Service* **D1.722.**
Amendments—This section repealed by F(No 2)A 1997 s 36(4), Sch 6 para 3, Sch 8 Pt II(11) with effect for accounting periods beginning after 5 April 1999.

[246U Settlement of liability by IHC as to ACT]

Commentary—*Simon's Direct Tax Service* **D1.722.**
Amendments—This section repealed by F(No 2)A 1997 s 36(4), Sch 6 para 3, Sch 8 Pt II(11) with effect for accounting periods beginning after 5 April 1999.

[246V Settlement of liability by non-IHC as to ACT]

Commentary—*Simon's Direct Tax Service* **D1.722.**
Amendments—This section repealed by F(No 2)A 1997 s 36(4), Sch 6 para 3, Sch 8 Pt II(11) with effect for accounting periods beginning after 5 April 1999.

[246W Payments and repayments where further matching takes place]

Commentary—*Simon's Direct Tax Service* **D1.723.**
Amendments—This section repealed by F(No 2)A 1997 s 36(4), Sch 6 para 3, Sch 8 Pt II(11) with effect for accounting periods
   beginning after 5 April 1999.

[Adjustments

246X Adjustments where profits or foreign tax altered]

Commentary—*Simon's Direct Tax Service* **D1.714.**
Amendments—This section repealed by F(No 2)A 1997 s 36(4), Sch 6 para 3, Sch 8 Pt II(11) with effect for accounting periods
   beginning after 5 April 1999.

[Application of this Chapter

246Y Application of this Chapter]

Commentary—*Simon's Direct Tax Service* **D1.701.**
Amendments—This section repealed by F(No 2)A 1997 s 36(4), Sch 6 para 3, Sch 8 Pt II(11) with effect for accounting periods
   beginning after 5 April 1999.

TA 1988

CHAPTER VI
MISCELLANEOUS AND SUPPLEMENTAL
Group income

[247 Dividends etc paid by one member of a group to another

(1) ...[4]

[(1A) A company falls within this subsection if—

   (a) it is a 75 per cent subsidiary of any other company, or
   *(b) arrangements of any kind (whether in writing or not) are in existence by virtue of which it
   could become such a subsidiary.][1]*

(2), (3) ...[4]

*(4) Where a company ("the recipient company") receives from another company ("the payer
company"), both being bodies corporate resident in the United Kingdom, any payments which are
[deductible payments in relation to the payer company for the purposes of corporation tax][2] and
either—*

   [(a) the payer company is—

      *(i) a 51 per cent subsidiary of the other or of a company so resident of which the other is a
      51 per cent subsidiary, or*
      *(ii) a trading or holding company which does not fall within subsection (1A) above and which
      is owned by a consortium the members of which include the recipient company, or][4]*

   (b) the recipient company is a 51 per cent subsidiary of the payer company,

*then, subject to the following provisions of this section, the recipient company and the payer company
may jointly elect that this subsection shall apply to any such payments received from the payer
company by the recipient company, and so long as the election is in force those payments may be
made without deduction of income tax and neither section 349 nor section 350 shall apply thereto.*

*[(4A) The reference in subsection (4) above to a payment which is a deductible payment in relation
to a company for the purposes of corporation tax is a reference to any payment which is—*

   (a) a charge on income of that company for those purposes; or
   *(b) a payment of interest in relation to which a debit falls to be brought into account in the case
   of that company for the purposes of Chapter II of Part IV of the Finance Act 1996 (loan
   relationships).][2]*

*(5) [Subsection (4) above shall not apply to payments received by a company on any investments, if
a profit on the sale of those investments would be treated as a trading receipt of that company][4]*

(5A)–(5D) ...[3]

(6) Where—

   ...[4]

   *(b) the payer company purports by virtue of an election under subsection (4) above to make any
   payment without deduction of income tax,*

and ...[4] *income tax ought to have been deducted,* ...[4] *the inspector may make such assessments,
adjustments or set-offs as may be required for securing that the resulting liabilities to tax (including
interest on unpaid tax) of the* ...[4] *payer company and the* ...[4] *recipient company are, so far as possible,
the same as they would have been if* ...[4] *the income tax had been duly deducted.*

(7) Where tax assessed under subsection (6) above on the ...[4] *payer company is not paid by that
company before the expiry of the period of three months from the date on which that tax is payable,*

that tax shall, without prejudice to the right to recover it from that company, be recoverable from the ...[4] recipient company.

(8) In determining for the purposes of this section whether one body corporate is a 51 per cent subsidiary of another, that other shall be treated as not being the owner—

(a) of any share capital which it owns directly or indirectly in a body corporate not resident in the United Kingdom, or

(b) of any share capital which it owns indirectly, and which is owned directly by a body corporate for which a profit on the sale of the shares would be a trading receipt.

[(8A) Notwithstanding that at any time a company ("the subsidiary company") is a 51 per cent subsidiary of another company ("the parent company") it shall not be treated at that time as such a subsidiary for the purposes of this section unless, additionally, at that time—

(a) the parent company would be beneficially entitled to more than 50 per cent of any profits available for distribution to equity holders of the subsidiary company; and

(b) the parent company would be beneficially entitled to more than 50 per cent of any assets of the subsidiary company available for distribution to its equity holders on a winding-up.][1]

(9) For the purposes of this section—

(a) "trading or holding company" means a trading company or a company the business of which consists wholly or mainly in the holding of shares or securities of trading companies which are its 90 per cent subsidiaries;

(b) "trading company" means a company whose business consists wholly or mainly of the carrying on of a trade or trades; and

[(c) a company is owned by a consortium if 75 per cent or more of the ordinary share capital of the company is beneficially owned between them by companies resident in the United Kingdom of which none—

(i) beneficially owns less than 5 per cent of that capital,

(ii) would be beneficially entitled to less than 5 per cent of any profits available for distribution to equity holders of the company, or

(iii) would be beneficially entitled to less than 5 per cent of any assets of the company available for distribution to its equity holders on a winding-up,

and those companies are called the members of the consortium.][1]

[(9A) Schedule 18 shall apply for the purposes of subsections (8A) and (9)(c) above as it applies for the purposes of section 413(7).][1]

(10) References in this section to ...[4] payments received by a company apply to any received by another person on behalf of or in trust for the company, but not to any received by the company on behalf of or in trust for another person ...[4].][5]

Commentary—*Simon's Direct Tax Service* D2.605–610.
Concession C10—Groups of companies: arrangements.
Statement of Practice SP 3/93—Interpretation of "arrangements" in sub-s (1A)(b) above.
Revenue & other press releases—CCAB June 1965 (intra-group dividends can be paid partly subject to ACT, notwithstanding a group income election).
IR 24-2-78 (Revenue view, where an election under s 247(4) is in force, intra-group payments must be paid gross).
CCAB TR340 16-5-79 (Revenue procedure for making elections and model form of words).
Revenue Internal Guidance—Banking manual BM 6.2.4.4 (interest which is a distribution under s 209 cannot be paid under group dividend election).
International tax handbook ITH 437-438 (use of group dividend to repatriate overseas profits of earlier years may be challenged).
Life assurance manual LAM 2.68-2.71 (application of sub-s (5) to life assurance companies).
Company Taxation Manual COT2621 (notice under sub-s (3) must be given within 14 days after the end of the quarter in which the dividend was paid: retrospective notices will not be accepted).
COT2631–2633, 2916, 2917 (no specified form of election, but notice should set out the facts necessary to show the group relationship: multiple elections are acceptable).
COT2635, 2920 (election may be retrospective only if there would be no disturbance to assessments which have become final and conclusive, or claims to which effect has already been given).
COT3110 (election becomes ineffective when parent company or consortium member goes into liquidation).
Definitions—"Advance corporation tax", s 14(1); "distribution", s 832(1); "company", s 832(1), (2); "the Corporation Tax Acts", s 831(1)(a); "deduction of income tax", s 4(1); "franked investment income", s 832(1); "inspector", s 832(1); "interest", s 832(1); "ordinary share capital", s 832(1); "profit", s 6(4); "security", s 254(1); "share", s 254(1); "51 per cent subsidiary", s 838; "90 per cent subsidiary", s 838; "tax credit", s 832(1); "trade", s 6(4); "United Kingdom", s 830(1).
Cross references—See TA 1988 s 246A(10) (revocation of election made under sub-s (1) above where a company elects to treat dividend paid by it as foreign income dividend).
TA 1988 s 248 (supplementary provisions).
TA 1988 Sch 13, para 2(2) (return of franked payments in consequence of a notice under sub-s (3) above).
TA 1988 Sch 24, para 6 (certain resident companies controlling foreign companies barred from making the election under sub-ss (1), (4) above).
Amendments—[1] Sub-ss (1A), (8A), (9A) inserted and sub-s (9)(c) substituted by FA 1989 s 99 in relation to dividends and other sums paid after 26 July 1989.
[2] Words in sub-s (4) substituted and sub-s (4A) inserted by FA 1996 Sch 14 para 13(1), (2) with effect for accounting periods ending after 31 March 1996, subject to transitional provisions in FA 1996 Sch 15.
[3] Sub-ss (5A)–(5D) repealed by F(No 2)A 1997 s 36(4), Sch 6 para 4, Sch 8 Pt II(11) with effect in relation to distributions made after 5 April 1999 (sub-ss (5B)–(5D) and words in sub-s (5A) originally inserted by FA 1997 Sch 7 para 10 and sub-s (5A) originally inserted by FA 1994 Sch 16 para 13).
[4] Sub-ss (1), (2), (3) and words in sub-s (6), (7), (10) repealed, sub-s (4)(a) substituted and sub-s (5) amended by FA 1998 Sch 3 para 19 with effect in relation to distributions made after 5 April 1999.
[5] This section repealed by FA 2001 ss 85(5), (6), 110, Sch 33 Pt II(10) with effect for payments made after 11 May 2001.

[248 Provisions supplementary to section 247

(1) The Board may make regulations with respect to the procedure to be adopted for giving effect to section 247 and as to the information and evidence to be furnished by a company in connection with that section and, subject to the provisions of such regulations, an election under that section ("the election") shall be made by notice to the inspector which shall set out the facts necessary to show that the companies are entitled to make the election.

(2) The election shall not have effect in relation to ...[1] payments paid less than three months after the giving of the notice and before the inspector is satisfied that the election is validly made, and has so notified the companies concerned; but shall be of no effect if within those three months the inspector notifies the companies concerned that the validity of the election is not established to his satisfaction.

(3) The companies concerned shall have the like right of appeal against any decision that the validity of the election is not established as the company paying the ...[1] payments would have if it were an assessment made on that company, and Part V of the Management Act shall apply accordingly.

(4) The election shall cease to be in force if at any time the companies cease to be entitled to make the election, and on that happening each company shall forthwith notify the inspector.

(5) Either of the companies making the election may at any time give the inspector notice revoking the election; and any such notice shall have effect from the time it is given.

(6) The Board shall not make any regulations under subsection (1) above unless a draft of them has been laid before and approved by a resolution of the House of Commons.][2]

Commentary—*Simon's Direct Tax Service* **D2.608.**
Definitions—"The Board", s 832(1); "company", s 832(1), (2); "inspector", s 832(1); "the Management Act", s 831(3).
Cross references—See IT (Building Societies) Regulations, SI 1986/482 reg 6(3) (application of this section with modifications in relation to gross payments by a building society to its 51 per cent subsidiary company).
Amendments—[1] Words in sub-ss (2), (3) repealed by FA 1998 Sch 3 para 20 with effect in relation to distributions made after 5 April 1999.
[2] This section repealed by FA 2001 ss 85(5), (6), 110, Sch 33 Pt II(10) with effect for payments made after 11 May 2001.

Stock dividends

249 Stock dividends treated as income

(1) Subject to subsections (7) to (9) below, this section applies to any of the following share capital, that is to say—

(a) any share capital issued by a company resident in the United Kingdom in consequence of the exercise by any person of an option conferred on him to receive in respect of shares in the company (whether the last-mentioned shares were issued before or after the coming into force of this section) either a dividend in cash or additional share capital; and
(b) any bonus share capital issued by a company so resident in respect of any shares in the company of a relevant class (whether the last-mentioned shares were issued before or after the coming into force of this section).

(2) For the purposes of subsection (1)(b) above a class of shares is a relevant class if—

(a) shares of that class carry the right to receive bonus share capital in the company of the same or a different class; and
(b) that right is conferred by the terms on which shares of that class were originally issued or by those terms as subsequently extended or otherwise varied.

(3) Where a company issues any share capital in a case in which two or more persons are entitled thereto, the following provisions of this section ...[1] shall have effect as if the company had issued to each of those persons separately a part of that share capital proportionate to his interest therein on the due date of issue.

(4) Subject to the following provisions of this section, where a company issues any share capital in a case in which an individual is beneficially entitled to that share capital, that individual shall be treated as having received on the due date of issue income of an amount which, if reduced by an amount equal to income tax on that income at the [Schedule F ordinary rate][5] for the year of assessment in which that date fell, would be equal to the appropriate amount in cash, and—

(a) the individual shall be treated as having paid income tax at the [Schedule F ordinary rate][5] on that income or, if his total income is reduced by any deductions, on so much of it as is part of his total income as so reduced;
(b) no repayment shall be made of income tax treated by virtue of paragraph (a) above as having been paid; and
(c) that income shall be treated [[(without prejudice to paragraph (a) above) as if it were income to which section 1A applies [as it applies to income chargeable under Schedule F][6], but][4] [shall be treated][3]][2] for the purposes of sections 348 and 349(1) as not brought into charge to income tax.

(5) Where a company issues any share capital to the personal representatives of a deceased person as such during the administration period, the amount of income which, if the case had been one in which an individual was beneficially entitled to that share capital, that individual would have been

treated under subsection (4) above as having received shall be deemed for the purposes of Part XVI to be part of the aggregate income of the estate of the deceased.

This subsection shall be construed as if it were contained in Part XVI.

(6) Where a company issues any share capital to trustees in respect of any shares in the company held by them (or by them and one or more other persons) in a case in which a dividend in cash paid to the trustees in respect of those shares would have been to any extent income to which section 686 applies, then—

(a) there shall be ascertained the amount of income which, if the case had been one in which an individual was beneficially entitled to that share capital, that individual would have been treated under subsection (4) above as having received; and

(b) income of that amount shall be treated as having arisen to the trustees on the due date of issue and as if it had been chargeable to income tax at the [Schedule F ordinary rate][6]; and

(c) paragraphs (a) to (c) of subsection (4) above shall, with the substitution of "income" for "total income" and with all other necessary modifications, apply to that income as they apply to income which an individual is treated as having received under that subsection.

(7) This section does not apply to—

(a) any share capital of which the due date of issue is earlier than 6th April 1975; or

(b) any share capital issued by a company in respect of shares in the company which confer on the holder a right to convert or exchange them into or for shares in the company of a class which is not a relevant class for the purposes of subsection (1)(b) above where the due date of issue of the share capital so issued precedes the earlier of the following dates, namely—

(i) the day next after the earliest date after 5th August 1975 on which conversion or exchange of the shares could be effected by an exercise of that right; and

(ii) 6th April 1976 or, in the case of share capital issued by an investment trust, 6th April 1977.

(8) Where, in a case within subsection (4) above, the share capital in question is issued in respect of shares in the company issued before 6th April 1975 which confer on the holder a right to convert or exchange them into or for shares of a different class, this section shall not apply to so much (if any) of any bonus share capital issued by the company after 5th April 1976 in connection with an exercise of that right as would have been issued if that right had been exercised so as to effect the conversion or exchange of the shares on the earliest possible date after 5th April 1975; and subsections (5) and (6) above shall, where applicable, have effect accordingly.

(9) Where any bonus share capital falling within subsection (1)(b) above is after 5th April 1975 converted into or exchanged for shares in the company in question of a different class, then—

(a) this section shall not apply to any shares in the company issued, in connection with the conversion or exchange, in consideration of the cancellation, extinguishment or acquisition by the company of that bonus share capital; but

(b) section 230(a) and (b) shall apply to any shares in the company issued, in connection with the conversion or exchange, in consideration of the cancellation, extinguishment or acquisition by the company of so much of that bonus share capital as caused an individual to be treated under subsection (4) above as having received an amount of income on the due date of issue (or would have done so if the case had been one in which an individual was beneficially entitled to that share capital).

Commentary—*Simon's Direct Tax Service* **D1.202.**
Revenue Internal Guidance—Capital gains manual CG 33800-33817 (background to the legislation; application to trusts; effect on capital gains tax computation).
CG 58763 (worked example).
Definitions—"Appropriate amount in cash", s 251(2); "bonus share capital", s 251(1); "company", s 832(1), (2); "due date of issue", s 251(1); "lower rate", s 832(1); "option conferred", s 251(1); "Schedule F ordinary rate", s 832(1); "shares", s 254(1); "total income", s 835(1); "year of assessment", s 832(1).
Cross references—See TA 1988 s 250 (Tax Returns for the purposes of this section).
TA 1988 s 251 (interpretation of this section).
TA 1988 s 699A(1)(a), (4)(a) (sums included in the aggregate income of the deceased by virtue of sub-s (5) above, to be treated as having income tax at the lower rate).
TCGA 1992 s 141(1) (issue of stock dividends as new holding on reorganisation of companies: appropriate amount in cash treated as income under this section treated as additional expenditure for chargeable gains tax purposes),
TCGA 1992 s 142(1) (issue of stock dividends to bare trustees: appropriate amount in cash treated as income under this section treated as additional expenditure for capital gains tax purposes).
FA 1997 Sch 7 para 4 (exercise of option within sub-s (1)(a) above does not in itself render a qualifying distribution one to which FA 1997 Sch 7 applies (special treatment for certain distributions)).
Amendments—[1] Words in sub-s (3) repealed by FA 1989 Sch 17 Pt V.
[2] Words (outer) in sub-s (4)(c) inserted by F(No 2)A 1992 s 19(4).
[3] Words substituted by FA 1993 ss 77(3)(a), (5), with effect from the year 1993–94.
[4] Words from "without prejudice to" to "but" in sub-s (4)(c) substituted by FA 1996 s 73 Sch 6 para 6, 28, with effect from the year 1996–97.
[5] Words in sub-ss (4), (6)(b) substituted for "lower rate" by F(No 2)A 1997 s 34, Sch 4 para 10 with effect in relation to share capital, within the meaning of this section, issued after 5 April 1999.
[6] Words in sub-s (4)(c) inserted by F(No 2)A 1997 s 34, Sch 4 para 10 with effect in relation to share capital, within the meaning of this section, issued after 5 April 1999.

250 Returns

(1) A company shall for each of its accounting periods make, in accordance with this section, returns to the inspector of all share capital to which section 249 applies (''relevant share capital'') and which was issued by it in that period.

(2) A return shall be made for—

(a) each complete quarter falling within the accounting period, that is to say, each of the periods of three months ending with 31st March, 30th June, 30th September or 31st December which falls within that period;

(b) each part of the accounting period which is not a complete quarter and ends on the first (or only), or begins immediately after the last (or only), of those dates which falls within the accounting period;

(c) if none of those dates falls within the accounting period, the whole accounting period.

(3) A return for any period for which a return is required to be made under this section (a ''return period'') shall be made within 30 days from the end of that period.

(4) No return need be made under this section by a company for any period in which it has issued no relevant share capital.

(5) The return made by a company for any return period shall state—

(a) the date on which any relevant share capital issued by it in the period was issued and, if different, the date on which the company was first required to issue it;

(b) particulars of the terms on which any such share capital so issued by it was issued; and

(c) what is, in relation to any such share capital so issued, the appropriate amount in cash.

(6) If it appears to the inspector that a company ought to have, but has not, made a return for any return period, he may (notwithstanding subsection (4) above) by notice require the company to make a return for that period within such time (not being less than 30 days) as may be specified in the notice; and a return required to be made under this subsection shall, if such be the case, state that no relevant share capital was issued in the period in question.

(7) As regards any share capital included in a return made under this section by a company, the inspector may by notice require the company to furnish him within such time (not being less than 30 days) as may be specified in the notice with such further information relating thereto as he may reasonably require for the purposes of sections 230 and 249, this section and section 251 ...[1].

Commentary—*Simon's Direct Tax Service* **D1.610.**
Definitions—''Accounting period'', s 834(1); ''appropriate amount in cash'', s 251(2); ''company'', s 832(1), (2); ''inspector'', s 832(1); ''notice'', s 832(1).
Cross references—See TA 1988 s 251 (interpretation of this section).
Amendments—[1] Words in sub-s (7) repealed by FA 1989 Sch 17 Pt V.

251 Interpretation of sections 249 and 250

(1) For the purposes of sections 249 and 250—

(a) ''bonus share capital'', in relation to a company, means share capital issued by the company otherwise than wholly for new consideration or such part of any share capital so issued as is not properly referable to new consideration;

(b) ''due date of issue'', in relation to any share capital issued by a company, means the earliest date on which the company was required to issue that share capital;

(c) an option to receive either a dividend in cash or additional share capital is conferred on a person not only where he is required to choose one or the other, but also where he is offered the one subject to a right, however expressed, to choose the other instead, and a person's abandonment of, or failure to exercise, such a right is to be treated as an exercise of the option;

and in section 254 the definition of ''security'' (in subsection (1)) and subsections (5) and (11) shall not apply.

(2) In sections 249 and 250 ''the appropriate amount in cash'', in relation to any share capital to which section 249 applies—

(a) in a case where that share capital was issued—

(i) in consequence of the exercise of an option such as is mentioned in section 249(1)(a); or

(ii) in a quantity which is determined by or determines the amount of a dividend in cash payable in respect of share capital in the company of a different class,

and where the relevant cash dividend is not substantially greater nor substantially less than the market value of that share capital on the relevant date, means the amount of the relevant cash dividend or, in a case in which section 249(3) applies, a due proportion of that amount;

(b) in a case where paragraph (a) above does not apply, means the market value of that share capital on the relevant date or, in a case in which section 249(3) applies, a due proportion of that market value.

(3) In subsection (2) above—

''the relevant cash dividend'', in a case falling within subsection (2)(a)(i) above, means the cash dividend mentioned in section 249(1)(a) or, in a case falling within subsection (2)(a)(ii) above, means the cash dividend there mentioned (subject to subsection (4) below);

"the relevant date", in the case of share capital listed in the Stock Exchange Daily Official List, means the date of first dealing and, in the case of share capital not so listed, means the due date of issue;

"market value", in relation to any share capital in a company, means, subject to the provisions applied by subsections (5) and (6) below, the price which that share capital might reasonably be expected to fetch on a sale in the open market.

(4) Where, in a case falling within subsection (2)(*a*)(ii) above, the company on the occasion on which it issues the share capital in question also issues a dividend in cash ("the accompanying cash dividend") in respect of the shares in the company in respect of which that share capital is issued, "the relevant cash dividend" means the cash dividend mentioned in subsection (2)(*a*)(ii) above reduced by the amount of the accompanying cash dividend.

(5) Section [272(3) of the 1992 Act][1] (market value of shares or securities [quoted][2] in the Stock Exchange Daily Official List) shall apply for the purposes of subsection (3) above as it applies for the purposes of that Act.

(6) In the case of shares or securities which are not quoted on a recognised stock exchange at the time when their market value for the purposes of subsection (2) above falls to be determined, subsection (3) of section [273 of the 1992 Act][1] shall apply with respect to the determination of their market value for those purposes as it applies with respect to a determination falling within subsection (1) of that section.

Commentary—*Simon's Direct Tax Service* **D1.202; D3.312.**
Statement of Practice SP A8—"substantially greater" or "substantially less" in the context of sub-s (2)(*a*) above means a difference of 15 per cent or more.
Definitions—"Company", s 832(1), (2); "new consideration", s 254(1); "recognised stock exchange", s 841; "shares", s 254(1); "the 1992 Act", s 831(3).
Amendments—[1] Words in sub-ss (5), (6) substituted by TCGA 1992 Sch 10 para 14(1), (16).
[2] Words in sub-s (5) substituted by FA 1996 Sch 38 para 8 with effect where the relevant date falls after 31 March 1996.

Supplemental

252 Rectification of excessive set-off etc of ACT or tax credit

(1) If an inspector discovers that—
... [1]
(*b*) any set-off or payment of tax credit,

ought not to have been made, or is or has become excessive, the inspector may make any such assessments as may in his judgment be required for recovering any tax that ought to have been paid or any payment of tax credit that ought not to have been made and generally for securing that the resulting liabilities to tax (including interest on unpaid tax) of the persons concerned are what they would have been if only such set-offs or payments had been made as ought to have been made.

(2) In any case where—
(*a*) interest has been paid under section 826 on a payment of tax credit; and
(*b*) interest ought not to have been paid on that payment, either at all or to any extent,

an assessment under this section may be made for recovering any interest that ought not to have been paid.

(3) Where—
(*a*) an assessment is made under this section to recover tax credit paid to a company in respect of franked investment income received by the company in an accounting period; and
(*b*) more than one payment of tax credit has been made in respect of that period,

any sum recovered shall as far as possible be treated as relating to a payment of tax credit made later rather than to a payment made earlier.

(4) Subsections (2) and (3) above shall have effect in relation to payments of tax credit claimed in respect of accounting periods ending after such day as may be appointed for the purpose of those subsections by order made by the Treasury, not being earlier than 31st March 1992.

(5) The Management Act shall apply to any assessment under this section for recovering a payment of tax credit or interest on such a payment as if it were an assessment to income tax for the year of assessment, or in the case of a company, corporation tax for the accounting period, in respect of which the payment was claimed, and as if that payment represented a loss of tax to the Crown; and any sum charged by any such assessment shall, subject to any appeal against the assessment, be due within 14 days after the issue of the notice of assessment.

Commentary—*Simon's Direct Tax Service* **D1.314, 405.**
Statement of Practice SP 8/91, para 4—Discovery of excessive set-offs etc and assessments or further assessments to make good tax losses.
Revenue Internal Guidance—Corporation tax pay and file manual CT (PF) 10218 (interest on tax charged by assessment under sub-s (1)(*b*) runs from the date of payment or set off of tax credit to the date the sum assessed is paid).
Notes—The appointed day for the purposes of sub-ss (2)–(4) above is 30 September 1993 by virtue of the Corporation Tax Acts (Provisions for Payment of Tax and Returns) (Appointed Days) Order, SI 1992/3066 art 2.
Definitions—"Accounting period", s 834(1); "advance corporation tax", s 14(1); "company", s 832(1), (2); "franked investment income", s 832(1); "inspector", s 832(1); "interest", s 832(1); "the Management Act", s 831(3); "tax credit", s 832(1); "year of assessment", s 832(1).
Cross references—See TMA 1970 s 87A(5) (interest on tax credit or interest recovered under sub-s (5) above);

FA 1989 s 157 (transitional provisions in respect of a charge of interest on corporation tax assessed under sub-s (1) above for the period from 14 March 1989 to 30 September 1993);
FA 1993 s 80(8) (excessive set-off of special payments to charities made to compensate them for reduced repayments of tax resulting from reduction in tax credits occasioned by reduction in ACT rate).
Venture Capital Trust Regulations, SI 1995/1979 reg 20 (assessments to recover tax credits paid in respect of distributions by venture capital trusts following withdrawal of provisional approval).
Amendments—[1] Sub-s (1)(a) repealed by FA 1998 Sch 3 para 21 with effect in relation to accounting periods beginning after 5 April 1999.

253 Power to modify or replace section 234(5) to (9) and Schedule 13

(1) The Board may by regulations—

(a) modify, supplement or replace any of the provisions of subsections (5) to (9) of section 234 for the purpose of requiring companies resident in the United Kingdom to make returns and give information to the inspector in respect of distributions made by them, whether before or after the passing of this Act, which are not qualifying distributions;
...[1]

and references in this Act and in any other enactment to section 234(5) to (9) ...[1] shall be construed as including references to any such regulations.

...[1]

(3) Regulations under this section may—

(a) make different provision for different descriptions of companies and for different circumstances and may authorise the Board, where in their opinion there are special circumstances justifying it, to make special arrangements as respects ...[1] the repayment of income tax borne by a company or the payment to a company of amounts in respect of any tax credit to which it is entitled;
(b) include such transitional and other supplemental provisions as appear to the Board to be expedient or necessary.

(4) The Board shall not make any regulations under this section unless a draft of them has been laid before and approved by a resolution of the House of Commons.

Commentary—*Simon's Direct Tax Service* **D1.601.**
Definitions—"Advance corporation tax", s 14(1); "the Board", s 832(1); "company", s 832(1), (2); "distribution", s 832(1); "inspector", s 832(1); "the Management Act", s 832(1); "qualifying distribution", s 14(2), by virtue of s 832(1); "tax credit", s 832(1).
Amendments—[1] Sub-ss (1)(b), (2), and words in sub-ss (1) and (3)(a), repealed by FA 1998 Sch 3 para 22 with effect in relation to accounting periods beginning after 5 April 1999.

254 Interpretation of Part VI

(1) In this Part, except where the context otherwise requires—

"new consideration" means, subject to subsections (5) and (6) below, consideration not provided directly or indirectly out of the assets of the company, and in particular does not include amounts retained by the company by way of capitalising a distribution;
"security" includes securities not creating or evidencing a charge on assets, and interest paid by a company on money advanced without the issue of a security for the advance, or other consideration given by a company for the use of money so advanced, shall be treated as if paid or given in respect of a security issued for the advance by the company;
"share" includes stock, and any other interest of a member in a company;

and in this section "a 90 per cent group" means a company and all of its 90 per cent subsidiaries.

(2) In this Part, the expression "in respect of shares in the company" and "in respect of securities of the company", in relation to a company which is a member of a 90 per cent group, mean respectively in respect of shares in that company or any other company in the group and in respect of securities of that company or any other company in the group.

(3) Without prejudice to section 209(2)(b) as extended by subsection (2) above, in relation to a company which is a member of a 90 per cent group, "distribution" includes anything distributed out of assets of the company (whether in cash or otherwise) in respect of shares in or securities of another company in the group.

(4) Nothing in subsections (2) and (3) above shall require a company to be treated as making a distribution to any other company which is in the same group and is resident in the United Kingdom.

(5) Where share capital has been issued at a premium representing new consideration, any part of that premium afterwards applied in paying up share capital shall be treated as new consideration also for that share capital, except in so far as the premium has been taken into account under section 211(5) so as to enable a distribution to be treated as a repayment of share capital.

(6) Subject to subsection (7) below, no consideration derived from the value of any share capital or security of a company, or from voting or other rights in a company, shall be regarded for the purposes of this Part as new consideration received by the company unless the consideration consists of—

(a) money or value received from the company as a qualifying distribution;
(b) money received from the company as a payment which for those purposes constitutes a repayment of that share capital or of the principal secured by the security; or

(*c*) the giving up of the right to the share capital or security on its cancellation, extinguishment or acquisition by the company.

(7) No amount shall be regarded as new consideration by virtue of subsection (6)(*b*) or (*c*) above in so far as it exceeds any new consideration received by the company for the issue of the share capital or security in question or, in the case of share capital which constituted a qualifying distribution on issue, the nominal value of that share capital.

(8) Where two or more companies enter into arrangements to make distributions to each other's members, all parties concerned (however many) may for the purposes of this Part be treated as if anything done by any one of those companies had been done by any of the others.

(9) A distribution shall be treated under this Part as made, or consideration as provided, out of assets of a company if the cost falls on the company.

(10) References in this Part to issuing share capital as paid up apply also to the paying up of any issued share capital.

(11) Where securities are issued at a price less than the amount repayable on them, and are not [listed][1] on a recognised stock exchange, the principal secured shall not be taken for the purposes of this Part to exceed the issue price, unless the securities are issued on terms reasonably comparable with the terms of issue of securities so quoted.

(12) For the purposes of this Part a thing is to be regarded as done in respect of a share if it is done to a person as being the holder of the share, or as having at a particular time been the holder, or is done in pursuance of a right granted or offer made in respect of a share; and anything done in respect of shares by reference to share holdings at a particular time is to be regarded as done to the then holders of the shares or the personal representatives of any share holder then dead.

This subsection shall apply in relation to securities as it applies in relation to shares.

Commentary—*Simon's Direct Tax Service* D1.102, 104.
Definitions—"Company", s 832(1), (2); "distribution", s 832(1); "qualifying distribution", s 14(2) by virtue of s 832(1); "recognised stock exchange", s 841.
Revenue Internal Guidance—Company Taxation Manual COT1535 (sub-s(12): transfer of asset to associate of shareholder may be in respect of shares).
Amendments—[1] Word in sub-s (11) substituted by FA 1996 Sch 38 para 6(1), (2)(*d*), (6) with effect in relation to securities issued after 31 March 1996.

255 "Gross rate" and "gross amount" of distributions to include ACT

Commentary—*Simon's Direct Tax Service* D1.203.
Amendments—[1] This section repealed by FA 1998 Sch 3 para 23 with effect in relation to distributions made after 5 April 1999.

PART VII
GENERAL PROVISIONS RELATING TO TAXATION OF INCOME OF INDIVIDUALS

Cross references—See TA 1988 s 9(6) (the provisions of this Part do not apply in computing income for the purposes of corporation tax).

CHAPTER I
PERSONAL RELIEFS

Revenue Internal Guidance—Trust manual TM 3300-3301 (trustees of settlements are not entitled to personal reliefs).
Cross references—See TMA 1970 Sch 2 para 2 (appeal from an inspector's decision on a claim under this Chapter to be to the General Commissioners).
TA 1988 s 232(1) (entitlement to a tax credit in respect of qualifying distribution received by an individual entitled to relief under this Chapter by virtue of s 278(2)).
TA 1988 s 289A(5)(*a*) EIS relief is offset in priority to relief under this Chapter).
TA 1988 s 347B(5B)(*a*) (relief for analysing maintenance payments is given in priority to relief under this Chapter).
TA 1988 s 353(1H) (relief for certain interest payments is given in priority to relief under this Chapter).
TA 1988 s 835(5) (relief given under this Chapter by way of deductions from total income to be deducted after any other deduction).
TA 1988 Sch 15B para 1 (tax relief on qualifying investments in venture capital trusts is offset against tax liability, for any year of assessment, in priority to relief under this Chapter).
FA 1989 s 54(3C) (relief for medical insurance premiums is given in priority to relief under this Chapter).
FA 1995 Sch 15 para 1(6) (relief for investments in venture capital trusts is given in priority to relief under this Chapter).

The reliefs

256 General

[(1)][2] An individual who makes a claim in that behalf or, in the case of relief under section 266, who satisfies the conditions of that section, shall be entitled to such relief as is specified in sections 257 to 274, subject however to the provisions of sections 275 to 278 ...[1]

[(2) Where under any provision of this Chapter the relief to which a person is entitled for any year of assessment consists in an income tax reduction calculated by reference to a specified amount, the effect of that relief shall be that the amount of that person's liability for that year to income tax on his total income shall be the amount to which he would have been liable apart from that provision less whichever is the smaller of—

(*a*) the amount equal to [10 per cent][3] of the specified amount; and

(*b*) the amount which reduces his liability to nil.][2]

[(3) In determining for the purposes of subsection (2) above the amount of income tax to which a person would be liable apart from any provision providing for an income tax reduction, no account shall be taken—

(*a*) . . .[5]

(*b*) where that provision is section 262(1), of any income tax reduction under any of the other provisions of this Chapter . . .[5]; or

(*c*) whatever that provision—

    (i) of any relief by way of a reduction of liability to tax which is given in accordance with any arrangements having effect by virtue of section 788 or by way of a credit under section 790(1); or

    (ii) of any tax at the basic rate on so much of that person's income as is income the income tax on which he is entitled to charge against any other person or to deduct, retain or satisfy out of any payment;

. . .[4]][2]

Commentary—*Simon's Direct Tax Service* E1.102A; E2.103.
Cross references—See TA 1988 s 257BB(1)(*b*), (3)(*b*) (amount of relief which a spouse may claim to be transferred to him/her in respect of married couple's allowance where the other spouse's entitlement is determined under sub-s(2)(*b*) above).
TA 1988 s 262(3) (widow's bereavement allowance).
Amendments—[1] Words repealed by FA 1988 Sch 14 Pt VIII with effect from the year 1990–91.
[2] "(1)" added and sub-ss (2), (3) inserted by FA 1994 s 77(1), (7) with effect from the year 1994–95.
[3] Words in sub-s (2)(*a*) substituted by FA 1998 s 27(1)(*a*) with effect from the year 1999–00 and subsequent years of assessment.
[4] Words after sub-s (3)(*c*) repealed by FA 1999 ss 35(1), (3), 139, Sch 20 Pt III(4) with effect from the year 2000–01.
[5] Sub-s (3)(*a*) and words in sub-s (3)(*b*) repealed by virtue of FA 1999 s 35(4) with effect for the year 2000–01.

[257 Personal allowance

(1) The claimant shall be entitled to a deduction from his total income of [£4,615][4].

(2) If the claimant ...[3] is at any time within the year of assessment of the age of 65 or upwards, he shall be entitled to a deduction from his total income of [£6,100][4] (instead of the deduction provided for by subsection (1) above).

(3) If the claimant ...[3] is at any time within the year of assessment of the age of [75][2] or upwards, he shall be entitled to a deduction from his total income of [£6,370][4] (instead of the deduction provided for by subsection (1) or (2) above).

(4) For the purposes of subsections (2) and (3) above a person who would have been of or over a specified age within the year of assessment if he had not died in the course of it shall be treated as having been of that age within that year.

(5) In relation to a claimant whose total income for the year of assessment exceeds [£17,900][4], subsections (2) and (3) above shall apply as if the amounts specified in them were reduced by [one half][2] of the excess (but not so as to reduce those amounts below that specified in subsection (1) above).][1]

Commentary—*Simon's Direct Tax Service* E2.201, 302, 304.
Concession A102—With effect from 6 April 2001, contributions to an approved personal pension scheme can reduce an individual's total income for the purposes only of determining the level of age-related allowances available under TA 1988 ss 257(5), 257A(5).
Revenue Internal Guidance—Relief RE 70–73 (calculation of "total income", no deduction for reliefs given in terms of tax).
Simon's Tax Cases—s 257(1), *Nabi v Heaton* [1983] STC 344*; *Rignell v Andrews* [1990] STC 410*.
s 257(1)(*a*), *Holmes v Mitchell* [1991] STC 25*.
Definitions—"Total income", s 835(1); "year of assessment", s 832(1).
Cross references—FA 1990 s 25(9A) (for the purposes of sub-s (5) above, with regards to an individual who makes a gift to charity, his total income is to be treated as reduced by the aggregate amount of gifts from which tax is treated as deducted by virtue of FA 1990 s 25(6)).
See TA 1988 s 257C (indexation of amounts in this section).
TA 1988 s 835(5) (deductions under sub-ss (1), (2), (3) and s 265 to be ignored in computing "total income" for the purposes of sub-s (5));
FA 1988 s 38 (maintenance payments under existing obligations: 1989–90 onwards);
IT (Employments) Regulations, SI 1993/744 regs 10–13 (coding).
FA 2002 s 28(1) (for 2003–04, the amount specified in sub-s (1) above shall be taken to be £4,615).
FA 2002 s 29(1)(*a*) (for 2003–04, the amount specified in sub-s (2) above shall be taken to be £6,610).
FA 2002 s 29(1)(*b*) (for 2003–04, the amount specified in sub-s (3) above shall be taken to be the indexed amount (the amount that would apply by virtue of TA 1988 s 257C(1)) plus £240).
Amendments—[1] This section and ss 257A–257F substituted for s 257 by FA 1988 s 33 with effect from the year 1990–91. S 257B further substituted by ss 257BA, 257BB by F(No 2)A 1992 Sch 5 paras 1, 2, 10 with effect from 1993–94.
[2] Words in sub-ss (3), (5) substituted by FA 1989 s 33(4)(*a*), (5)(*b*) with effect from the year 1990–91.
[3] Words omitted from sub-ss (2), (3) repealed by FA 1996 Sch 20 para 13, Sch 41 Pt V(10) with effect from the year 1996–97.
[4] Amounts in sub-ss (1), (2), (3), (5) substituted for the year 2002–03 by the Income Tax (Indexation) (No 2) Order, SI 2001/3773 art 2(1), (2).

[257AA Children's tax credit

(1) If a qualifying child (or more than one) is resident with the claimant during the whole or part of the year of assessment, the claimant shall be entitled to an income tax reduction, to be known as a children's tax credit.

(2) The reduction shall be calculated by reference to [£5,290]².

[(2A) For a year of assessment during the whole or part of which a qualifying baby (or more than one) is resident with the claimant, subsection (2) above has effect as if the amount specified there were increased by £5,200.]³

(3) Where any part of the claimant's income for the year of assessment falls within section 1(2)(b), his children's tax credit for the year shall be calculated as if the amount specified in subsection (2) above were reduced by £2 for every £3 of that part of his income.

[(3A) Where subsection (2A) above applies, the reference in subsection (3) above to the amount specified in subsection (2) above is to the higher amount applicable by virtue of subsection (2A) above.]³

(4) In this section "qualifying child" means, in relation to a person—

　(a) a child of his who has not attained the age of 16, or
　(b) a child who has not attained the age of 16 and who is maintained by, and at the expense of, the person for any part of the year of assessment;

and "child" includes illegitimate child and stepchild.

[(4A) In this section "qualifying baby", in relation to a year of assessment, means a qualifying child born in that year.]³

(5) Schedule 13B (which modifies this section where a child lives with more than one adult during a year of assessment) shall have effect.]¹

Amendments—¹ This section inserted by FA 1999 s 30(1), (5) with effect from the year 2001–02.
² Amount in sub-s (2) substituted by the Income Tax (Indexation) Order, SI 2002/707 art 2(3) with effect for 2002–03.
³ Sub-ss (2A), (3A), (4A) inserted by FA 2001 s 53(1)–(3), (5) with effect from the year 2002–03.

[257A Married couple's allowance

(1) . . .⁸

(2) [If the claimant is, for the whole or any part of the year of assessment, a married man whose wife is living with him, and]³ either of them [was born before 6th April 1935]⁸, he shall be entitled [for that year to an income tax reduction calculated by reference to [£5,465]⁹ . . .⁸]⁴ . . .⁸,

(3) [If the claimant is, for the whole or any part of the year of assessment, a married man whose wife is living with him, and]³ either of them—

　[(a)]⁸ is at any time within that year of the age of [75]² or upwards, [and
　(b) was born before 6th April 1935,]⁸

he shall be entitled [for that year to an income tax reduction calculated by reference to [£5,535]⁹ (instead of to the reduction]⁴ provided for by subsection . . .⁸ (2) above).

(4) For the purposes of [subsection (3)]⁸ above a person who would have been of or over [the age of 75]⁸ within the year of assessment if he had not died in the course of it shall be treated as having been of that age within that year.

(5) In relation to a claimant whose total income for the year of assessment exceeds [£17,900]⁹, subsections (2) and (3) above shall apply as if the amounts specified in them were reduced by—

　(a) [one half]² of the excess, less
　(b) any reduction made in his allowance under section 257 by virtue of subsection (5) of that section ...⁶

[(5A) The amounts specified in subsections (2) and (3) above shall not by virtue of subsection (5) above be treated as reduced below [£2,110]⁹.]⁷

(6) A man shall not be entitled by virtue of this section to more than one [income tax reduction]⁵ for any year of assessment; and in relation to a claim by a man who becomes married in the year of assessment and has not previously in the year been entitled to relief under this section, this section shall have effect as if the amounts specified in [subsections (2) and (3)]⁸ above were reduced by one twelfth for each month of the year ending before the date of the marriage.

In this subsection "month" means a month beginning with the 6th day of a month of the calendar year.]¹

[(7) A man who is entitled for any year of assessment to an income tax reduction under this section, or to make a claim for such a reduction, shall not be entitled for that year to any income tax reduction under section 257AA.]¹⁰

[(8) Where—

　(a) a woman is married to and living with a man for the whole or any part of a year of assessment, and
　(b) that man is entitled for that year to an income tax reduction under this section, or to make a claim for such a reduction,

no child shall be regarded for any of the purposes of section 257AA or Schedule 13B as resident with that woman at any time in that year when she is married to and living with that man.]¹⁰

[(9) A person may, by notice to an officer of the Board, elect to give up his entitlement for any year of assessment to an income tax reduction under this section; and where he does so and the election is not subsequently revoked, that person shall be taken for the purposes of this section to have no entitlement for that year to a reduction under this section, or to make a claim for such a reduction.]¹⁰

Commentary—*Simon's Direct Tax Service* **E1.102A; E2.202, 303, 304.**
Concession A102—With effect from 6 April 2001, contributions to an approved personal pension scheme can reduce an individual's total income for the purposes only of determining the level of age-related allowances available under TA 1988 ss 257(5), 257A(5).
Revenue & other press releases—Hansard 16-2-78 (a married man can claim only one married couple's allowance even if he has more than one wife).
Revenue Internal Guidance—Independent taxation handbook, In 340-347 (meaning of "married"). Relief RE 70–73 (calculation of "total income", no deduction for reliefs given in terms of tax).
Definitions—"Total income", s 835(1); "year of assessment", s 832(1).
Cross references—See FA 1990 s 25(9A) (for the purposes of sub-s (5) above, with regards to an individual who makes a gift to charity, his total income is to be treated as reduced by the aggregate amount of gifts from which tax is treated as deducted by virtue of FA 1990 s 25(6)).
TA 1988 s 257BA (elections by spouses as to transfer of relief under this section).
TA 1988 s 257BB (transfer to wife of relief under this section which husband cannot utilise).
TA 1988 s 257C (indexation of amounts in this section).
TA 1988 s 257F (transitional provisions applying this section to separated couples).
TA 1988 s 259 (extension of the relief under sub-s (1) above in respect of children).
TA 1988 s 261 (where a husband elects to have marriage disregarded so as to claim additional relief for children, marriage is also disregarded for the purposes of this section).
TA 1988 s 261A (reduction of relief in respect of children of separated parents by the amount of relief under this section).
TA 1988 s 282 (construction of references to husband and wife living together).
TA 1988 s 835(5) (deductions under s 257(1), (2), (3) and s 265 to be ignored in computing "total income" for the purposes of sub-s (5));
FA 1988 s 38(5) (recipient of maintenance payments under existing obligations may deduct from total income the amount specified under sub-s (1) above).
IT (Employments) Regulations, SI 1993/744 regs 10–13 (coding);
Amendments—¹ This section and ss 257, 257B–257F substituted for s 257 by FA 1988 s 33 with effect from the year 1990–91. S 257B further substituted by ss 257BA, 257BB by F(No 2)A 1992 Sch 5 paras 1, 2, 10 with effect from 1993–94.
² Words in sub-ss (3), (5)(a) substituted by FA 1989 s 33(8)(a), (9)(b) with effect from the year 1990–91.
³ Words in sub-ss (2), (3) substituted by FA 1996 Sch 20 para 14 with effect from the year 1996–97.
⁴ Words in sub-ss (2), (3) substituted by FA 1994 s 77(2), (7) with effect from the year 1994–95.
⁵ Words in sub-s (6) substituted by FA 1994 s 77(7) and Sch 8 para 1 with effect from the year 1994–95.
⁶ Words in sub-s (5) repealed by FA 1999 s 31(6), (11), Sch 20 Pt III(3) with effect from the year 1999–00.
⁷ Sub-s (5A) inserted by FA 1999 s 30(7), (11) with effect from the year 1999–00. TA 1988 s 257C (indexation) applies in relation to this subsection, but only from the year 2000–01 (FA 1999 s 32(5)).
⁸ Sub-s (1) and words in sub-ss (2), (3) repealed, inserted, words in sub-s (3) inserted, and words in sub-ss (2), (4), (6) substituted by FA 1999 s 31(1)–(5), (8), (10), Sch 20 Pt III(3) with effect from the year 2000–01.
⁹ Amounts in sub-ss (2), (3), (5), (5A) specified for the year 2002–03 by virtue of the Income Tax (Indexation) (No 2) Order, SI 2001/3773 art 2(1), (3).
¹⁰ Sub-s (7), (8), (9) inserted by FA 1999 s 31(9), (12) with effect from the year 2001–02.

[257BA Elections as to transfer of relief under section 257A

(1) A woman may elect that for any year of assessment for which her husband is entitled to relief under section 257A—

    (a) she shall be entitled (on making a claim) [to an income tax reduction calculated by reference to]² one half of the amount specified in [section 257A(5A)]³ for that year, and
    (b) the amount [by reference to which the calculation of the income tax reduction to which he is entitled under section 257A is to be made]² shall be reduced accordingly.

(2) A husband and wife may jointly elect that for any year of assessment for which the husband is entitled to relief under section 257A—

    (a) she shall be entitled (on making a claim) [to an income tax reduction calculated by reference to]² the amount specified in [section 257A(5A)]³ for that year, and
    (b) the amount [by reference to which the calculation of the income tax reduction to which he is entitled under section 257A is to be made]² shall be reduced accordingly . . .⁴

(3) A man may elect that for any year of assessment for which his wife is entitled to relief by virtue of an election under subsection (2) above—

    (a) he shall be entitled (on making a claim) [to an income tax reduction calculated by reference to]² one half of the amount specified in [section 257A(5A)]³ for that year (in addition to [any income tax reduction to which he is already entitled]² under section 257A), and
    (b) the amount [by reference to which the calculation of the income tax reduction to which she is entitled by virtue of that election is to be made]² shall be reduced accordingly.

(4) An election under this section shall be made by giving notice to the inspector in such form as the Board may determine and—

    (a) subject to subsections (5) and (7) below, shall be made before the first year of assessment for which it is to have effect, and
    (b) shall have effect for that and each succeeding year of assessment for which the husband is entitled to relief under section 257A, subject to its withdrawal under subsection (8) below or a subsequent election under this section.

(5) An election may be made during the first year of assessment for which it is to have effect if that is the year of assessment in which the marriage takes place.

(6) Where subsection (5) above applies, the references in subsections (1)(*a*), (2)(*a*) and (3)(*a*) above to the amount specified for the year of assessment in [section 257A(5A)][3] shall be read as references to that amount reduced in accordance with section 257A(6).

(7) An election may be made within the first thirty days of the first year of assessment for which it is to have effect if before that year the inspector has been given written notification that it is intended to make the election.

(8) The person or persons by whom an election was made may withdraw it by giving notice to the inspector in such form as the Board may determine; but the withdrawal shall not have effect until the year of assessment after the one in which the notice is given.

(9) A woman shall not be entitled by virtue of an election under this section to more than one [income tax reduction][3] for any year of assessment.][1]

Commentary—*Simon's Direct Tax Service* **E2.202, 303.**
Revenue Internal Guidance—Independent taxation handbook, In 470-472 (general explanation of the section).
In 473 (year of marriage: effect of an election under this section).
Definitions—''The Board'', s 832(1); ''inspector'', s 832(1); ''notice'', s 832(1); ''total income'', s 835(1); ''year of assessment'', s 832(1).
Cross references—See TA 1988 s 257BB(1) (transfer to wife of unused married couple's allowance under s 257A in addition to any transfer elected under this section).
TA 1988 s 257BB(3) (husband's entitlement to relief elected under this section which wife cannot utilise).
TA 1988 s 261A (reduction of relief in respect of children of separated parents by the amount of relief under this section).
TA 1988 s 262(2), (3) (treatment of married couple's allowance transferred to a widow by virtue of an election under this section in a case where she is also entitled to bereavement allowance).
FA 1994 Sch 8 para 2(3) (an election made under this section for the year 1994–95 to have effect in accordance with this section as amended by FA 1994 Sch 8 para 2 even if made before the passing of FA 1994).
Amendments—[1] This section and s 257BB substituted for s 257B by F(No 2)A 1992 Sch 5 paras 1, 2, 10 in relation to tax from the year 1993–94.
[2] Words in sub-ss (1)–(3) substituted by FA 1994 s 77(7) and Sch 8 para 2 with effect from the year 1994–95.
[3] Words in sub-ss (1)(*a*), (2)(*a*), (3)(*a*), (6), (9) substituted by FA 1999 s 32(1), (3) with effect from the year 1999–00.
[4] Words in sub-s (2) repealed by FA 1999 ss 32(1), (4), 129, Sch 20 Pt III(3) with effect from the year 2000–01.

[257BB Transfer of relief under section 257A where relief exceeds income

(1) Where—

    (*a*) a man is entitled to relief under section 257A, but

    [(*b*) the amount of the reduction to which he is entitled is determined in accordance with section 256(2)(*b*) [(read with section 25(6)(*c*) of the Finance Act 1990 where applicable)][6] or, by virtue of his having no income tax liability to which that reduction is applicable, is nil,

his wife shall be entitled (in addition to any reduction to which she is entitled by virtue of an election under section 257BA) to an income tax reduction calculated by reference to an amount equal to the unused part of the amount by reference to which her husband's income tax reduction fell to be calculated in pursuance of section 257A and any election under section 257BA.][2]

(2) Subsection (1) above shall not apply for a year of assessment unless the claimant's husband gives notice to the inspector that it is to apply.

(3) Where—

    (*a*) a woman is entitled to relief by virtue of an election under section 257BA, but

    [(*b*) the amount of the reduction to which she is entitled is determined in accordance with section 256(2)(*b*) [(read with section 25(6)(*c*) of the Finance Act 1990 where applicable)][6] or, by virtue of her having no income tax liability to which that reduction is applicable, is nil,

her husband shall be entitled (in addition to any other reduction to which he is entitled by virtue of section 257A) to an income tax reduction calculated by reference to an amount equal to the unused part of the amount by reference to which his wife's income tax reduction fell to be calculated in pursuance of that election.][2]

[(3A) In this section references, in relation to such an amount as is mentioned in subsection (1)(*b*) or (3)(*b*), to the unused part of an amount by reference to which any income tax reduction fell to be calculated are references to so much of it (including, where the amount so mentioned is nil, all of it) as has no practical effect on the determination of the amount so mentioned.][3]

(4) Subsection (3) above shall not apply for a year of assessment unless the claimant's wife gives notice to the inspector that it is to apply.

(5) Any notice under subsection (2) or (4) above—

    (*a*) shall be given [on or before the fifth anniversary of the 31st January next following][5] the end of the year of assessment to which it relates,

    (*b*) shall be in such form as the Board may determine, and

    (*c*) shall be irrevocable.

(6) ...[4]][1]

Commentary—*Simon's Direct Tax Service* **E2.202, 303.**
Concession A86—From 1994–95 allowance also given by concession for the previous year provided evidence of blindness already obtained at the end of that year, subject to normal time limits for claims.

Definitions—''The Board'', s 832(1); ''inspector'', s 832(1); ''notice'', s 832(1); ''total income'', s 835(1); ''year of assessment'', s 832(1).
Cross references—See TA 1988 s 257D(10) (claim by husband for transitional relief under s 257D to serve also as a notice under sub-s (2) above).
TA 1988 s 265(6) (notice under s 265(5) (notice to transfer to spouse blind person's unused allowance) to have effect for sub-s (2) above as well).
Amendments—[1] This section and s 257BA substituted for s 257B by F(No 2)A 1992 Sch 5 paras 1, 2, 10 in relation to tax from the year 1993–94. The old s 257B was substituted by FA 1988 s 33 with effect from the year 1990–91.
[2] Sub-s (1)(*b*) and the words following it and sub-s (3)(*b*) and the words following it substituted by FA 1994 s 77(7) and Sch 8 para 3 with effect from the year 1994–95.
[3] Sub-s (3A) inserted by FA 1994 s 77(7) and Sch 8 para 3 with effect from the year 1994–95.
[4] Sub-s (6) repealed by FA 1994 s 77(7), Sch 8 para 3 and Sch 26, Pt V(1) with effect from the year 1994–95.
[5] Words in sub-s (5)(*a*) substituted by FA 1996 Sch 21 para 4 with effect from the year 1996–97.
[6] Words in sub-ss (1)(*b*), (3)(*b*) inserted by FA 2000 s 39(8), (10) with effect for gifts made after 5 April 2000 which are not covenanted payments and covenanted payments falling to be made after that date.

[257C Indexation of amounts in sections 257 and 257A

(1) If the retail prices index for the month of [September][3] preceding a year of assessment is higher than it was for the previous [September][3], then, unless Parliament otherwise determines, [sections 257, 257AA(2) and 257A][6] shall apply for that year as if for each amount specified in them as they applied for the previous year (whether by virtue of this section or otherwise) there were substituted an amount arrived at by increasing the amount for the previous year by the same percentage as the percentage increase in the retail prices index, and—

(*a*) if in the case of an amount specified in sections 257(5) and 257A(5) the result is not a multiple of £100, rounding it up to the nearest amount which is such a multiple;
(*b*) if in the case of any other amount the increase is not a multiple of £10, rounding the increase up to the nearest amount which is such a multiple.

[(2A) Subsection (1) above shall not require any change to be made in the amounts deductible or repayable under section 203 during the period beginning with 6th April and ending with 17th May in the year of assessment.][5]

(2) ...[4]

(3) The Treasury shall in each year of assessment make an order specifying the amounts which by virtue of subsection (1) above will be treated as specified for the following year of assessment in [sections 257, [257AA(2)] and 257A][6].

(4) ...[2].][1]

Commentary—*Simon's Direct Tax Service* E1.104.
Definitions—''Retail prices index'', s 833(2); ''year of assessment'', s 832(1); ''the year 1990–91'', etc, s 832(1).
Cross-reference—
See TA 1988 s 265 (this section also to have effect for the application of that section—blind person's allowance).
FA 1999 s 32(5) (this section shall apply in relation to TA 1988 s 257A(5A), but only from the year 2000–01).
FA 2002 s 27(*b*) (sub-s (2A) above as it has effect for the application of TA 1988 ss 257AA(2), 265 shall have effect for 2002–03 as if ''17th June'' were substituted for ''17th May'').
FA 2002 s 28(2) (sub-s (1) above, so far as it relates to the amount specified in TA 1988 s 257(1) shall not apply for 2003–04).
FA 2002 s 29(2) (sub-s (1) above, so far as it relates to the amounts specified in TA 1988 s 257(2), (3), shall not apply for 2003–04 (except as it applies for the purposes of FA 2002 s 29(1)(*b*)).
Regulations—Income Tax (Indexation) (No 2) Order, SI 2000/2996 art 2(1), (3) (specifies amounts in ss 257, 257A for the year 2001–02).
Amendments—[1] This section and ss 257, 257A, 257B, 257D–257F substituted for s 257 by FA 1988 s 33 with effect from the year 1990–91. S 257B further substituted by ss 257BA, 257BB by F(No 2)A 1992 Sch 5 paras 1, 2, 10 with effect from 1993–94.
[2] Sub-s (4) repealed by FA 1990 Sch 19 Pt IV.
[3] ''September'' in sub-s (1) substituted by FA 1993 s 107(1), (3)(*a*), (8) with effect from the year 1994–95.
[4] Sub-s (2) repealed by FA 1993 s 107(1), (3)(*b*), (8) and Sch 23 Pt III(10) with effect from the year 1994–95.
[5] Sub-s (2A) inserted by FA 1999 s 25(3), (4) with effect from the year 1999–00.
[6] Words substituted in sub-ss (1), (3) by FA 1999 s 30(3), (6) with effect for the purposes of the application of s 257AA concerning the married couple's allowance from the year 2002–03.
Prospective amendments—Words ''257AA(2) and (2A)'' in sub-ss (1), (3) to be substituted by FA 2001 s 53(4), (7) with effect for the purposes of the application of TA 1988 s 257AA from the year 2003–04.

257D Transitional relief: husband with excess allowances

Commentary—*Simon's Direct Tax Service* E2.203.
Amendments—This section repealed by FA 1999 ss 32(2), (4), 139, Sch 20 Pt III(3) with effect from the year 2000–01.

257E Transitional relief: the elderly

Commentary—*Simon's Direct Tax Service* E2.302.
Amendments—This section repealed by FA 1999 s 32(2), (4), 139, Sch 20 Pt III(3) with effect from the year 2000–01.

257F Transitional relief: separated couples

Commentary—*Simon's Direct Tax Service* E2.204.
Amendments—This section repealed by FA 1999 ss 32(2), (4), 139, Sch 20 Pt III(3) with effect from the year 2000–01.

258 Widower's or widow's housekeeper

Amendments—This section repealed by FA 1988 s 25(3), Sch 14 Pt IV.

TA 1988

259 Additional relief in respect of children

Commentary—*Simon's Direct Tax Service* E1.102A; E2.502.
Amendments——This section repealed by FA 1999 ss 32, 139, Sch 20 Pt III(4) with effect from the year 2000–01.

260 Apportionment of relief under section 259

Commentary—*Simon's Direct Tax Service* E2.502.
Amendments—This section repealed by FA 1999 ss 32, 139, Sch 20 Pt III(4) with effect from the year 2000–01.

261 Claims under section 259 for year of marriage

Commentary—*Simon's Direct Tax Service* E2.202.
Amendments—This section repealed by FA 1999 ss 32, 139, Sch 20 Pt III(4) with effect from the year 2000–01.

261A Additional relief in respect of children for year of separation

Commentary—*Simon's Direct Tax Service* E1.102A; E2.502.
Amendments—This section repealed by FA 1999 ss 32, 139, Sch 20 Pt III(4) with effect from the year 2000–01.

262 Widow's bereavement allowance

Simon's Tax Cases—*R (oao Wilkinson) v IRC* [2002] STC 347.
Amendments—This section repealed by FA 1999 ss 34, 139, Sch 20 Pt III(5) with effect for deaths occurring after 5 April 2000.

263 Dependent relatives

Amendments—This section repealed by FA 1988 s 25(3), Sch 14 Pt IV.

264 Claimant depending on services of a son or daughter

Amendments—This section repealed by FA 1988 s 25(3), Sch 14 Pt IV.

[265 Blind person's allowance

(1) If the claimant ...[7] is a registered blind person for the whole or any part of the year of assessment, he shall be entitled to a deduction of [£1,480][9] from his total income.

[(1A) Section 257C (indexation) shall have effect (using the rounding up rule in subsection (1)(*b*) of that section) for the application of this section for the year 1998–99 and any subsequent year of assessment as it has effect for the application of sections 257 and 257A.][8]

(2) Where—

(*a*) a person entitled to relief under subsection (1) above is a married man whose wife is living with him for the whole or any part of the year of assessment, but

(*b*) the amount which he is entitled to deduct from his total income by virtue of that subsection exceeds what is left of his total income after all other deductions have been made from it,

his wife shall be entitled to a deduction from her total income of an amount equal to the excess.

(3) In determining for the purposes of subsection (2)(*b*) above the amount that is left of a person's total income for a year of assessment after other deductions have been made from it, there shall be disregarded any deduction made—

(*a*) ...[6]

(*b*) ...[5]

[(*c*) on account of any payments to which section 593(2) or 639(3) applies,][2]

[(*d*) ...][4]
...[10]

(4) Subsections (2) and (3) above shall have effect where a wife is entitled to relief under subsection (1) above as they have effect where the husband is entitled to that relief, but with the appropriate modifications ...[3]

(5) Subsections (2) to (4) above shall not apply for a year of assessment unless the person entitled to relief under subsection (1) has given to the inspector written notice that they are to apply; and any such notice—

(*a*) shall be given [on or before the fifth anniversary of the 31st January next following][7] the end of the year of assessment to which it relates,

(*b*) shall be in such form as the Board may determine, and

(*c*) shall be irrevocable.

(6) A notice given under subsection (5) above in relation to a year of assessment by a husband shall have effect also as a notice under [section 257BB(2)][3].

(7) In this section "registered blind person" means a person registered as a blind person in a register compiled under section 29 of the National Assistance Act 1948 or, in the case of a person ordinarily resident in Scotland or Northern Ireland, a person who is a blind person within the meaning of section 64(1) of that Act.][1]

Commentary—*Simon's Direct Tax Service* **E2.801, 802.**
Concession A86—From 1994-95 allowance also given by concession for the previous year provided evidence of blindness already obtained at the end of that year, subject to normal time limit, for claims.
Revenue Internal Guidance—Independent taxation handbook IN 690–725 (transfer of allowance including worked examples).
Definitions—''The Board'', s 832(1); ''inspector'', s 832(1); ''total income'', s 835(1); ''year of assessment'', s 832(1).
Cross references—See TMA 1970 s 37A (assessment to make good a loss of tax through fraudulent or negligent conduct not to affect the validity of spouse's relief under this section).
TA 1988 s 257(10) (notice by husband giving effect to transitional allowances under s 257D for wife to have effect as a notice under sub-s (5) above also, where relevant).
TA 1988 s 282 (construction of references to husband and wife living together).
Amendments—[1] This section substituted by FA 1988 Sch 3 paras 1, 8 with effect from the year 1990–91.
[2] Sub-s (3)(c) and word therein inserted by FA 1989 ss 33(1), (10), 57(4).
[3] Words in sub-s (4) repealed and words in sub-s (6) substituted by F(No 2)A 1992 Sch 5 paras 1, 8, 10, Sch 18 Pt VII with effect in relation to tax from the year 1993–94.
[4] Sub-s (3)(d) repealed by FA 1994 Sch 10 para 3 and Sch 26 Pt V(3) in relation to private medical insurance premiums paid after 5 April 1994 (previously inserted by FA 1989 s 57(4)).
[5] Sub-s (3)(b) repealed by FA 1994 s 77(7), Sch 8 para 10 and Sch 26, Pt V(1),(17)—
(a) with effect from the year 1994–95 where it referred to TA 1988 ss 257A, 257BA and
(b) in relation to shares issued after 31 December 1993 with effect from the year 1993–94 where it referred to TA 1988 s 289.
[6] Sub-s (3)(a) repealed by FA 1994 Sch 26 Pt V(2) in relation to mortgage interest paid after 5 April 1994 (whenever due) and payments due after that date but made between 30 November 1993 and 5 April 1994.
[7] Words omitted from sub-s (1) repealed and words in sub-s (5)(a) substituted by FA 1996 Sch 20 para 19, Sch 21 para 6, Sch 41 Pt V(10) with effect from the year 1996–97.
[8] Sub-s (1A) inserted by FA 1997 s 56(2).
[9] Amount in sub-s (1) specified for the year 2002–03 by virtue of the Income Tax (Indexation) Order, SI 2002/707 art 2(4).
[10] Sub-s (3)(e) and preceding word ''or'' repealed by FA 1999 s 139, Sch 20 Pt III(15) with effect for payments made after 31 August 2000.

266 Life assurance premiums

(1) Subject to the provisions of this section, sections 274 and 619(6) and Schedules 14 and 15, an individual who pays any such premium as is specified in subsection (2) below or makes a payment falling within subsection (7) below shall (without making any claim) be entitled to relief under this section.

(2) The premiums referred to in subsection (1) above are any premiums paid by an individual under a policy of insurance or contract for a deferred annuity, where—

   (a) the payments are made to—

      [(i) a person who has permission under Part 4 of the Financial Services and Markets Act 2000 or under paragraph 15 of Schedule 3 to that Act (as a result of qualifying for authorisation under paragraph 12(1) of that Schedule) to effect or carry out contracts of long-term insurance; or

      (ii) a member of the Society who effects or carries out contracts of long-term insurance in accordance with Part 19 of the Financial Services and Markets Act 2000;][7] or

      (iv) in the case of a deferred annuity, the National Debt Commissioners; and

   (b) the insurance or, as the case may be, the deferred annuity is on the life of the individual or on the life of his spouse; and

   (c) the insurance or contract was made by him or his spouse.

(3) Subject to subsections (7), (10) and (11) below, no relief under this section shall be given—

   (a) except in respect of premiums payable under policies for securing a capital sum on death, whether in conjunction with any other benefit or not;

   (b) in respect of premiums payable under any policy issued in respect of an insurance made after 19th March 1968 unless the policy is a qualifying policy;

   (c) in respect of premiums payable under any policy issued in respect of an insurance made after 13th March 1984, except where the relief relates to part only of any such payment as falls within subsection (6) below;

   (d) in respect of premiums payable during the period of deferment in respect of a policy of deferred assurance.

(4) Subject to subsections (6) to (8) below, relief under this section in respect of any premiums paid by an individual in a year of assessment shall be given by making good to the person to whom they are paid any deficiency arising from the deductions authorised under subsection (5) below; and this section and Schedule 14 shall have effect in relation to any premium or part of a premium which is paid otherwise than in the year of assessment in which it becomes due and payable as if it were paid in that year.

(5) Subject to the provisions of Schedule 14—

   (a) an individual resident in the United Kingdom who is entitled to relief under this section in respect of any premium may deduct from any payment in respect of the premium and retain an amount equal to [12·5 per cent][1] of the payment; and

   (b) the person to whom the payment is made shall accept the amount paid after the deduction in discharge of the individual's liability to the same extent as if the deduction had not been made and may recover the deficiency from the Board.

(6) Where—

   (a) a person is entitled to relief under this section in respect of part only of a payment made to a [friendly society][3]; and (*b*) the insurance or contract was made by the society in the course of tax exempt life or endowment business (as defined in section 466(2)), [and]⁵

[(*c*) the insurance or contract is not excluded by subsection (6A) below,]⁵

subsection (4) above shall not apply with respect to that relief but there shall be deducted from his total income an amount equal to one-half of that part of the payment.

[(6A) For the purposes of subsection (6)(*c*) above, an insurance or contract is excluded by this subsection if it is made on or after 1st September 1996 and affords provision for sickness or other infirmity (whether bodily or mental), unless—

(*a*) it also affords assurance for a gross sum independent of sickness or other infirmity;

(*b*) not less than 60 per cent of the amount of the premiums is attributable to the provision afforded during sickness or other infirmity; and

(*c*) there is no bonus or addition which may be declared or accrue upon the assurance of the gross sum.]⁶

(7) Where a person makes a payment to a trade union as defined in section 28(1) of the Trade Union and Labour Relations Act 1974 and part of that payment is attributable to the provision of superannuation, life insurance or funeral benefits, he shall be entitled to relief under this section in respect of that part of the payment, but—

(*a*) subsection (4) above shall not apply; and

(*b*) there shall be deducted from his total income an amount equal to one-half of that part of the payment.

This subsection shall also apply in relation to any payment made to an organisation of persons in police service but only where the annual amount of the part of the payment attributable to the provision of the benefits in question is £20 or more.

(8) Where the individual is not resident in the United Kingdom but is entitled to relief by virtue of section 278(2), subsection (4) above shall not apply but (subject to section 278(3)) the like relief shall be given to him under paragraph 6 of Schedule 14.

(9) Subsections (5) and (8) above shall apply in relation to an individual who is not resident in the United Kingdom but is a member of the armed forces of the Crown or the [spouse]² of such a member as if the individual were so resident.

(10) Subsection (3)(*b*) above shall not apply—

(*a*) to any policy of life insurance having as its sole object the provision on an individual's death or disability of a sum substantially the same as any amount then outstanding under a mortgage of his residence, or of any premises occupied by him for the purposes of a business, being a mortgage the principal amount secured by which is repayable by instalments payable annually or at shorter regular intervals; or

(*b*) to any policy of life insurance issued in connection with an approved scheme as defined in Chapter I of Part XIV.

In the application of this subsection to Scotland, for any reference to a mortgage there shall be substituted a reference to a heritable security within the meaning of the Conveyancing (Scotland) Act 1924 (but including a security constituted by ex facie absolute disposition or assignation).

(11) Subsection (3)(*a*) and (*d*) above shall not affect premiums payable—

(*a*) under policies or contracts made in connection with any superannuation or bona fide pension scheme for the benefit of the employees of any employer, or of persons engaged in any particular trade, profession, vocation or business, or for the benefit of the [spouse, widow, widower or children or other dependants of any such employee or person,]²

(*b*) under policies taken out by teachers in the schools known in the year 1918 as secondary schools, pending the establishment of a superannuation or pension scheme for those teachers.

(12) Schedule 14 shall have effect for the purpose of modifying, for certain cases, and supplementing the provisions of this section.

[(13) In this section and Schedule 14, "friendly society" means the same as in the Friendly Societies Act 1992 (and includes any society that by virtue of section 96(2) of that Act is to be treated as a registered friendly society within the meaning of that Act).]⁴

[(14) In subsection (2)(*a*)—

"contracts of long-term insurance" means contracts which fall within Part II of Schedule 1 to the Financial Services and Markets Act 2000 (Regulated Activities) Order 2001; and

"member of the Society" has the same meaning as in Lloyd's Act 1982.]⁷

Commentary—*Simon's Direct Tax Service* **E2.1001, 1031, 1032, 1034, 1038, 1047.**
Concession A32—Revenue will continue to give relief after 5 April 1980 for life assurance premiums on certain non-qualifying policies which would have qualified under TA 1970 s 19(4)(*b*).
Statements of Practice SP 4/79—Premium relief not allowed on life policies for children under 12 if taken out on or after 1 March 1979 and until the age of 12 for policies taken out after 1 March 1979 but before 1 September 1979. But see **SP 11/79** below.
SP 11/79—This Statement contains exceptions to the terms of SP 4/79 above. Relief is allowed on premiums on industrial branch juvenile policies and similar policies issued by registered Friendly Societies as part of their tax exempt business, subject to the limit in TA 1988 Sch 14 para 2. Relief is allowed also on premiums on ordinary branch juvenile policies other than Friendly Societies policies, subject to certain conditions.

SP 4/97—Taxation of persons receiving or becoming entitled to commission, cashbacks or discounts, including under life insurance and personal pensions.
Simon's Tax Cases—*Legal & General Assurance Society Ltd v, IRC* [1996] STC (SCD) 419*.
Definitions—"Total income", s 835(1); "year of assessment", s 832(1).
Cross references—See TA 1988 s 268 (claw-back of tax relief on life assurance premiums in the event of conversion or surrender of policy within four years).
TA 1988 s 269 (claw-back of tax relief on life assurance premiums in the event of surrender of policy after four years).
TA 1988 s 270 (reduction of relief under this section where claw-back under ss 268 or 269 made).
TA 1988 s 274 (limit on relief under this section).
TA 1988 s 592(9) (exclusion of relief under this section in respect of employee's contributions to an approved occupational pension scheme).
TA 1988 s 594(1) (exclusion of relief under this section in respect of employee's contributions to statutory superannuation scheme).
TA 1988 s 595(1) (extension of relief under this section to an employee whose employer makes payments for the employee's benefit to a retirement benefit scheme).
TA 1988 s 657(2) (purchased life annuities).
Friendly Societies (Life Assurance Premium Relief) Regulations, SI 1977/1143 Sch 1 para 2 (contributions made by members of registered friendly societies deemed to have been made net);
Industrial Assurance (Life Assurance Premium Relief) Regulations, SI 1977/1144 Sch 1 para 2 (contributions by members to policy under prescribed industrial assurance scheme deemed to be made net).
IT (Life Assurance Premium Relief) Regulations, SI 1978/1159 reg 11 (Board may require information from policyholders for the purposes of this section).
Amendments—[1] "12·5 per cent" in sub-s (5)(*a*) substituted by FA 1988 s 29 with effect from 6 April 1989.
[2] Words in sub-ss (9), (11)(*a*) substituted by FA 1988 Sch 3 paras 1, 9 with effect from the year 1990–91.
[3] Words in sub-ss (2)(*a*)(iii), (6)(*a*) substituted by F(No 2)A 1992 Sch 9 paras 1, 2, 22 with effect from 19 February 1993 by virtue of F(No 2)A 1992 Sch 9 (Appointed Day) Order, SI 1993/236.
[4] Sub-s (13) added by F(No 2)A 1992 Sch 9 paras 1, 2, 22 with effect from 19 February 1993 by virtue of F(No 2)A 1992 Sch 9 (Appointed Day) Order, SI 1993/236.
[5] Words in sub-s (6) inserted by FA 1996 s 171(3).
[6] Sub-s (6A) inserted by FA 1996 s 171(4).
[7] Words in sub-s (2)(*a*) substituted, and sub-s (14) added, by the Financial Services and Markets Act 2000 (Consequential Amendments) (Taxes) Order, SI 2001/3629 arts 13, 18 with effect from 1 December 2001, immediately after the coming into force of the Financial Services and Markets Act 2000 ss 411, 432(1), Sch 20.

267 Qualifying policies

Schedule 15, Part I of which contains the basic rules for determining whether or not a policy is a qualifying policy, Part II of which makes provision for the certification etc of policies as qualifying policies and Part III of which modifies Parts I and II in their application to certain policies issued by non-resident companies, shall have effect for the purpose of determining whether or not a policy is a qualifying policy; and, accordingly, any reference in this Act to a qualifying policy shall be construed in accordance with that Schedule.

Commentary—*Simon's Direct Tax Service* **E2.1032, 1042, 1048.**

268 Early conversion or surrender of life policies

(1) Where a policy of life insurance to which this section applies has been issued and, within four years from the making of the insurance in respect of which it was issued, any of the following events happens, that is to say—

    (*a*) the surrender of the whole or part of the rights conferred by the policy;
    (*b*) the falling due (otherwise than on death) of a sum payable in pursuance of a right conferred by the policy to participate in profits; and
    (*c*) the conversion of the policy into a paid-up or partly paid-up policy;

the body by whom the policy was issued shall pay to the Board, out of the sums payable by reason of the surrender or, as the case may be, out of the sum falling due or out of the fund available to pay the sums which will be due on death or on the maturity of the policy, a sum determined in accordance with the following provisions of this section, unless the body is wound up and the event is a surrender or conversion effected in connection with the winding-up.

(2) The sum payable under subsection (1) above shall, subject to the following provisions of this section, be equal to the lower of the following, that is to say—

    (*a*) the appropriate percentage of the premiums payable under the policy up to the happening of the event; and
    (*b*) the surrender value of the policy at the time of the happening of the event less the complementary percentage of the premiums mentioned in paragraph (*a*) above.

(3) If the event is one of those mentioned below, the sum payable to the Board shall not exceed the following limit, that is to say—

    (*a*) if it is the surrender of part of the rights conferred by the policy, the value of the rights surrendered at the time of the surrender;
    (*b*) if it is the conversion of the policy into a partly paid-up policy, the surrender value at the time of the conversion, of so much of the policy as is paid up; and
    (*c*) if it is the falling due of a sum, that sum.

(4) If the event was preceded by the happening of such an event as is mentioned in subsection (1) above, subsection (2) above shall apply—

    (*a*) as if the lower of the amounts mentioned therein were reduced by the sum paid under this section in respect of the earlier event; and (*b*) if the earlier event was such an event as is mentioned in paragraph (*a*) or (*c*) of subsection (3) above, as if the surrender value of the policy were increased by the amount which, under that paragraph, limited or might have limited the sum payable under this section in respect of the earlier event.

(5) For the purposes of this section the appropriate percentage, in relation to any event, is the percentage equal to the following fraction of the percentage found by doubling that mentioned in section 266(5)(*a*) as in force for the year of assessment in which the event happened, that is to say—

(*a*) if the event happens in the first two of the four years mentioned in subsection (1) above, three-sixths;

(*b*) if it happens in the third of those years, two-sixths; and

(*c*) if it happens in the last of those years, one-sixth;

and the complementary percentage, in relation to any event, is 100 per cent less the appropriate percentage.

(6) Where the annual amount of the premiums payable under a policy of life insurance is at any time increased (whether under the policy or by any contract made after its issue) so as to exceed by more than 25 per cent—

(*a*) if the insurance was made on or before 26th March 1974, the annual amount as at that date, or

(*b*) in the case of any other insurance, the first annual amount so payable,

the additional rights attributable to the excess shall be treated for the purposes of this section as conferred by a new policy issued in respect of an insurance made at that time, and the excess shall be treated as premiums payable under the new policy.

(7) This section applies to any policy of life insurance which is a qualifying policy unless—

(*a*) it is a policy in respect of the premiums on which relief under section 266 is not available by virtue of subsection (3)(*c*) of that section; or

(*b*) it is a policy of life insurance issued in connection with an approved scheme, as defined in Chapter I of Part XIV;

and in relation to a policy of life insurance issued in respect of an insurance made before 27th March 1974 applies only in accordance with subsection (6) above.

Commentary—*Simon's Direct Tax Service* E2.1051.
Concession A41—Where under Sch 15, para 1(8) of this Act the commencement date of a policy is back-dated by not more than three months, the earlier date is taken as the date of the policy for the purposes of this section.
Definitions—"The Board", s 832(1); "year of assessment", s 832(1).
Cross references—See TA 1988 s 270 (supplementary provisions).
TA 1988 s 271(1) (deemed surrender of a life policy issued after 26 March 1974 in consequence of a loan on the policy).
TA 1988 s 272 (collection of sums payable under this section).
TA 1988 Sch 14, para 3(4) (increases in capital sums treated as made by virtue of Sch 14, para 3(3) to be disregarded for the purposes of sub-s (6) above).
TA 1988 Sch 15, para 20 (rules applicable for the purposes of this section where a new qualifying policy replaces an old qualifying policy after 24 March 1982 as a result of a variation in the life or lives being assured).

269 Surrender etc of policies after four years

(1) Where a policy of life insurance to which this section applies has been issued and, in the fifth or any later year from the making of the insurance in respect of which it was issued, either of the following events happens, that is to say—

(*a*) the surrender of the whole or part of the rights conferred by the policy; and

(*b*) the falling due (otherwise than on death or maturity) of a sum payable in pursuance of a right conferred by the policy to participate in profits;

then, if either of those events has happened before, the body by whom the policy was issued shall pay to the Board, out of the sums payable by reason of the surrender, or, as the case may be, out of the sum falling due, a sum determined in accordance with the following provisions of this section.

(2) The sum payable under subsection (1) above shall, subject to the following provisions of this section, be equal to the applicable percentage of the lower of the following—

(*a*) the total of the premiums which are payable in that year under the policy; and

(*b*) the sums payable by reason of the surrender or, as the case may be, the sum falling due;

and the percentage to be applied for this purpose shall be a percentage equal to that mentioned in section 266(5)(*a*) as in force for the year of assessment in which the event happens.

(3) Where, after a sum has become payable under subsection (1) above, and within the same year from the making of the insurance, another such event happens as is mentioned therein, the sums payable under that subsection in respect of both or all of the events shall not exceed the applicable percentage of the total mentioned in subsection (2)(*a*) above.

(4) Where, on the happening of an event in the fifth or any later year from the making of the insurance, any sum is payable under subsection (1) of section 268 as applied by subsection (6) of that section as well as under subsection (1) above, subsection (2) above shall apply as if the sums or sum mentioned in paragraph (*b*) thereof were reduced by the sum payable under that section.

(5) This section applies to any policy of life insurance which is a qualifying policy unless—

(*a*) it is a policy in respect of the premiums on which relief under section 266 is not available by virtue of subsection (3)(*c*) of that section; or

(*b*) it is a policy issued in the course of an industrial insurance business; or

(*c*) it was issued in respect of an insurance made before 27th March 1974.

Commentary—*Simon's Direct Tax Service* **E2.1052.**
Concession A41—Where under Sch 15, para 1(8) of this Act the commencement date of a policy is back-dated by not more than three months, the earlier date is taken as the date of the policy for the purposes of this section.
Definitions—"The Board", s 832(1); "qualifying policy", s 832(1); "year of assessment", s 832(1).
Cross references—See TA 1988 s 270 (supplementary provisions).
TA 1988 s 271(1) (deemed surrender of a life policy issued after 26 March 1974 in consequence of a loan on the policy).
TA 1988 s 272 (collection of sums payable under this section).
TA 1988 Sch 15, para 20 (rules applicable for the purposes of this section where a new qualifying policy replaces an old qualifying policy after 24 March 1982 as a result of a variation in the life or lives being assured).

270 Provisions supplementary to sections 268 and 269

(1) Where on the happening of an event in relation to a policy of life insurance a sum is payable under section 268 or 269, relief under section 266 in respect of the relevant premiums paid under the policy shall be reduced by the sum so payable or, as the case may be, by so much of the sum as does not exceed the amount of that relief (or as does not exceed so much of that amount as remains after any previous reduction under this section).

(2) For the purposes of this section the relevant premiums are—

(*a*) in relation to a sum payable under section 268, the premiums payable under the policy up to the happening of the event by reason of which the sum is payable; and

(*b*) in relation to a sum payable under section 269, the premiums payable in the year (from the making of the insurance) in which the event happens by reason of which the sum is payable.

(3) Where the relevant premiums are payable in more than one year of assessment the reduction in relief under this section shall, so far as possible, reduce relief for an earlier year of assessment before reducing relief for a later one.

(4) Any sum paid under section 268 or 269 by reason of any event shall be treated—

(*a*) as between the parties, as received by the person by whom the premiums under the policy were paid; and

(*b*) for the purposes of section 266, as a sum paid by that person in satisfaction of his liability resulting from the reduction of relief under this section;

and where that sum exceeds that liability he shall be entitled, on a claim made by him not later than six years after the end of the year of assessment in which the event happens, to repayment of the excess.

Commentary—*Simon's Direct Tax Service* **E2.1053.**
Concession A41—Where under Sch 15, para 1(8) of this Act the commencement date of a policy is back-dated by not more than three months, the earlier date is taken as the date of the policy for the purposes of this section.
Definitions—"Year of assessment", s 832(1).
Cross references—See TA 1988 s 271(1) (deemed surrender of a life policy issued after 26 March 1974 in consequence of a loan on the policy).
TA 1988 Sch 15, para 20 (rules applicable for the purposes of this section where a new qualifying policy replaces an old qualifying policy after 24 March 1982 as a result of a variation in the life or lives being assured).

271 Deemed surrender in cases of certain loans

(1) Where—

(*a*) under section 547 a gain arising in connection with a policy ...[1] would be treated as forming part of an individual's total income; and

(*b*) the policy was issued in respect of an insurance made after 26th March 1974 or ...[1]; and

(*c*) any sum is at any time after the making of the insurance ...[1] lent to or at the direction of that individual by or by arrangement with the body issuing the policy ...[1];

then, subject to subsection (2) below, the same results shall follow under section 268 to 270 as if at the time the sum was lent there had been a surrender of part of the rights conferred by the policy ...[1] and the sum had been paid as consideration for the surrender (and if the policy is a qualifying policy, whether or not the premiums under it are eligible for relief under section 266, those results shall follow under section 269, whether or not a gain would be treated as arising on the surrender).

(2) Subsection (1) above does not apply—

(*a*) in relation to a policy if—

(i) it is a qualifying policy; and

(ii) either interest at a commercial rate is payable on the sum lent or the sum is lent to a full-time employee of the body issuing the policy for the purpose of assisting him in the purchase or improvement of a dwelling used or to be used as his only or main residence; ...[1]

(*b*) ...[1]

Commentary—*Simon's Direct Tax Service* **E3.510.**
Definitions—"Qualifying policy", s 832(1); "total income", s 835(1).
Amendments—[1] Words in sub-s (1) and sub-s (2)(*b*) and the preceding word "or" repealed by FA 1994 Sch 17 para 2, Sch 26, Pt V(22) and are deemed always to have had effect.

272 Collection of sums payable under sections 268 and 269

(1) Any body by whom a policy to which section 268 or 269 applies has been issued shall, within 30 days of the end of each period of 12 months ending with 31st March in every year, make a return to the collector of the sums which, in that period, have become payable by it under either of those sections.

(2) Any sum which is to be included in a return made under subsection (1) above shall be due at the time by which the return is to be made and shall be paid without being demanded.

(3) Where any sum which was or ought to have been included in such a return is not paid by the end of the period for which the return was to be made, it may be recovered by an assessment as if it were income tax for the year of assessment in which that period ends; and where it appears to the inspector that a sum which ought to have been so included had not been included or that a return is not correct he may make such an assessment to the best of his judgment.

(4) All the provisions of the Income Tax Acts relating to the assessment and collection of tax, interest on unpaid tax, appeals and penalties shall, with the necessary modifications, apply in relation to sums due under this section; and for the purposes of those provisions so far as they relate to interest on unpaid tax, a sum assessed in pursuance of this section shall be treated as having been payable when it would have been payable had it been included in a return under subsection (1) above.

(5) Where, on an appeal against an assessment made in pursuance of this section, it is determined that a greater sum has been assessed than was payable, the excess, if paid, shall be repaid.

(6) Where a body has paid a sum which is payable under section 268 or 269 it shall give within 30 days to the person by whom the sum is, under section 270(4), treated as received a statement specifying that sum and showing how it has been arrived at.

(7) The Board or an inspector may, by notice served on the body by whom a policy to which section 268 or 269 applies has been issued, require the body, within such time, not being less than 30 days, as may be specified in the notice—

(*a*) to furnish such particulars; or
(*b*) to make available for inspection by an officer authorised by the Board such books and other documents in the possession or under the control of the body;

as the Board or officer may reasonably require for the purposes of those sections or this section.

Commentary—*Simon's Direct Tax Service* E2.1054.
Definitions—"The Board", s 832(1); "collector", s 832(1); "the Income Tax Acts", s 831(1)(*b*); "inspector", s 832(1); "interest", s 832(1); "year of assessment", s 832(1).
Cross references—See TMA 1970 s 98 (liability to a special return penalty in respect of a failure to provide information required under sub-s (7) above).

[273 Payments securing annuities

Subject to sections 274, 617(3) and 619(6), if the claimant is, under any Act of Parliament or under any terms and conditions of employment, liable to the payment of any sum, or to the deduction from any salary or stipend of any sum, for the purpose of securing a deferred annuity to a widow or widower of the claimant or provision for the claimant's children after the claimant dies, the claimant shall be entitled to a deduction from the amount of income tax on which he or she is chargeable equal to income tax at the basic rate on the amount of the sum which he or she has paid or which has been deducted from his or her salary or stipend.][1]

Commentary—*Simon's Direct Tax Service* E2.1003.
Definitions—"Act", s 832(1); "basic rate", s 832(1).
Cross references—See TA 1988 s 274 (limit on relief under this section).
TA 1988 s 276 (effect on relief under this section of charges on income).
TA 1988 s 592(9) (exclusion of relief under this section in respect of employee's contributions to an approved occupational pension scheme).
TA 1988 s 594(1) (exclusion of relief under this section in respect of employee's contributions to statutory superannuation scheme).
TA 1988 s 657(2) (purchased life annuities).
Amendments—[1] This section substituted by FA 1988 Sch 3 paras 1, 10 with effect from the year 1990–91.

274 Limits on relief under sections 266 and 273

(1) The aggregate of the premiums or other sums in respect of which relief is given to any person under section 266 shall not exceed £1,500 in any year of assessment or one-sixth of that person's total income, whichever is the greater.

(2) The aggregate of the relief given under sections 266 and 273 in respect of premiums or sums payable for securing any benefits other than capital sums on death shall not exceed the amount of the income tax calculated at the appropriate rate on £100.

(3) In subsection (2) above "the appropriate rate"—

(*a*) in relation to premiums to which section 266 applies, means [12·5 per cent.][1];
(*b*) in relation to other payments, means the basic rate of income tax.

(4) War insurance premiums shall not be taken into account in calculating the limits of one-sixth of total income or of £100 mentioned in this section.

In this subsection "war insurance premiums" means any additional premium or other sum paid in order to extend an existing life insurance policy to risks arising from war or war service abroad, and any part of any premium or other sum paid in respect of a life insurance policy covering those risks, or either of them, which [is][2] attributable to those risks, or either of them.

Commentary—*Simon's Direct Tax Service* **E2.1035.**
Definitions—"Basic rate", s 832(1); "total income", s 835(1); "year of assessment", s 832(1).
Cross-references—See TA 1988 s 835(5) (deductions under s 257(1), (2), (3) and s 265 to be ignored in computing "total income" for the purposes of this section.
Amendments—[1] "12·5 per cent" in sub-s (3)(*a*) substituted by FA 1988 s 29 with effect from 6 April 1989.
[2] Word in sub-s (4) substituted by FA 1996 Sch 20 para 20 with effect from the year 1996–97.

Supplemental

275 Meaning of "relative"

Amendments—This section repealed by FA 1988 Sch 14 Pt IV with effect from the year 1988–89.

276 Effect on relief of charges on income

(1) Where any of the claimant's income is income the income tax on which (at the basic rate) he is entitled to charge against any other person, or to deduct, retain or satisfy out of any payment, he shall not be entitled to relief under this Chapter in respect of that income, except to the extent, if any, that the relief would exceed tax at the basic rate on that income.

[(1A) In subsection (1) above the references to relief under this Chapter do not include references to relief consisting in such an income tax reduction as is mentioned in section 256(2).][1]

(2) Notwithstanding subsection (1) above, relief under section 273 may be given to the extent that the deduction from tax provided for by that section can be made from so much of the income tax with which the claimant is chargeable as exceeds what would be the amount of that tax if all income tax were chargeable at the basic rate to the exclusion of any other rate.

Commentary—*Simon's Direct Tax Service* **E1.501.**
Revenue Internal Guidance—Relief RE 100–153 (meaning of "charges" (RE 100, RE 110); summary guide (RE 101); effect on tax liabilities with worked examples (RE 120–131); failure to deduct tax at source (RE 140)).
Definition—"Basic rate", s 832(1).
Amendments—[1] Sub-s (1A) inserted by FA 1994 s 77(7) and Sch 8 para 11 with effect from the year 1994–95.

277 Partners

(1) ...[1] the following persons having joint interests, that is to say—

(*a*) coparceners, joint tenants, or tenants in common of the profits of any property, and
(*b*) joint tenants, or tenants of land or tenements in partnership, being in the actual and joint occupation thereof in partnership, who are entitled to the profits thereof in shares, ...[1]
(*c*) ...[1]

may claim any relief under this Chapter according to their respective shares and interests, and any such claims which are proved may be dealt with in the same manner as in the case of several interests.

(2) ...[1]

Commentary—*Simon's Direct Tax Service* **E5.317.**
Definitions—"The Income Tax Acts", s 831(1)(*b*); "trade", s 832(1).
Amendments—[1] Words repealed by FA 1994 ss 215(3)(*c*), (4), (5), 258, Sch 26, Pt V(24) with effect (i) as respects partnerships whose trades, professions or businesses are set up and commenced on or after 6 April 1994 from the year 1994–95, and (ii) as respects such partnerships commenced before 6 April 1994 from the year 1997–98 (but see FA 1995 s 125(1) as regards partnerships controlled abroad).

278 Non-residents

(1) Subject to the provisions of this section, no relief under this Chapter shall be given in the case of any individual who is not resident in the United Kingdom.

(2) ...[1] subsection (1) above shall not apply in the case of any individual who ...[2]

(*a*) is a Commonwealth citizen or [an EEA national][2]; or
(*b*) is a person who is or who has been employed in the service of the Crown, or who is employed in the service of any missionary society or in the service of any territory under Her Majesty's protection; or
(*c*) is resident in the Isle of Man or the Channel Islands; or
(*d*) has previously resided within the United Kingdom, and is resident abroad for the sake of his or her health, or the health of a member of his or her family resident with him or her; or
(*e*) is a widow whose late husband[, or a widower whose late wife,][1] was in the service of the Crown.

[(2A) ...][3]

(3)–(7) ...[1]

(8) Any claim which an individual is entitled to make by virtue of subsection (2) above shall be made to the Board.

[(9) In this section "EEA national" means a national of any State, other than the United Kingdom, which is a Contracting Party to the Agreement on the European Economic Area signed at Oporto on 2nd May 1992, as adjusted by the Protocol signed at Brussels on 17th March 1993.][2]

Commentary—*Simon's Direct Tax Service* E6.201–202.
Concessions A14—Relief in respect of residuary income received during the administration period of deceased's person's estate by a non-resident legatee.
B13—No action is taken to recover tax on gross interest payments to a non-resident except so far as it can be set-off in a claim under this section.
B18—Relief for payments to a non-resident made by trustees out of a discretionary trust otherwise taxable under s 687(2) of this Act.
Statement of Practice SP 3/86—Procedure for giving tax relief under double taxation agreements in respect of payments to a non-resident from a UK discretionary trust or a UK estate.
Revenue Interpretation RI 158—Explains application of this section to residents of Hong Kong following transfer of sovereignty on 30 June 1997.
Simon's Tax Cases—s 278(2), (3), *IRC v Addison* [1984] STC 540*.
Definitions—"The Board", s 832(1); "total income", s 835(1); "year of assessment", s 832(1).
Cross references—See TA 1988 s 232(1) (entitlement to a tax credit in respect of qualifying distribution received by an individual entitled to relief by virtue of sub-s (2) above).
TA 1988 s 266(8) (relief for life assurance premiums paid by a non-resident to whom sub-s (2) above applies to be given on claim and not by deduction at source).
FA 1995 s 128(1) (restriction of income tax chargeable on non-residents to be calculated disregarding personal allowances to which non-resident entitled by virtue of sub-s (2) above).
Amendments—[1] Words in sub-s (2)(*e*) inserted and words in sub-s (2) and whole of sub-ss (3)–(7) repealed by FA 1988 s 31, Sch 14 Pt IV with effect from the year 1990–91.
[2] Words omitted from sub-s (2) repealed and words in sub-s (2)(*a*) and whole of sub-s (9) inserted by FA 1996 s 145, Sch 20 para 21, Sch 41 Pt V(10) with effect from the year 1996–97.
[3] Sub-s (2A) repealed by FA 1999 s 139, Sch 20 Pt III(3) with effect from the year 2000–01 (previously inserted by FA 1988 s 31).

CHAPTER II
TAXATION OF INCOME OF SPOUSES
General rules

279 Aggregation of wife's income with husband's

Amendments—This section repealed by FA 1988 s 32 and Sch 14 Pt VIII with effect from the year 1990–91.

280 Transfer of reliefs

Amendments—This section repealed by FA 1988 Sch 14 Pt VIII with effect from the year 1990–91.

281 Tax repayments to wives

Amendments—This section repealed by FA 1988 Sch 14 Pt VIII with effect from the year 1990–91.

[282 Construction of references to husband and wife living together

A husband and wife shall be treated for income tax purposes as living together unless—

(*a*) they are separated under an order of a court of competent jurisdiction, or by deed of separation, or

(*b*) they are in fact separated in such circumstances that the separation is likely to be permanent.][1]

Commentary—*Simon's Direct Tax Service* E5.102.
Revenue Internal Guidance—Relief RE 1040–1045 (Revenue practice in dealing with differences of opinion).
RE 1050–1065 (treatment where couples separate).
RE 1080 (reconciliation after period of separation).
RE 1090–1091 (divorce).
Simon's Tax Cases—*Gubay v Kington* [1984] STC 99*; *Ward-Stemp v Griffin* [1988] STC 47*.
s 282(2), *Gubay v Kington* [1981] STC 721*.
Amendments—[1] This section substituted by FA 1988 Sch 3 paras 1, 11 with effect from the year 1990–91.

[282A Jointly held property

(1) Subject to the following provisions of this section, income arising from property held in the names of a husband and his wife shall for the purposes of income tax be regarded as income to which they are beneficially entitled in equal shares.

(2) Subsection (1) above shall not apply to income to which neither the husband nor the wife is beneficially entitled.

(3) Subsection (1) above shall not apply to income—

(*a*) to which either the husband or the wife is beneficially entitled to the exclusion of the other, or
(*b*) to which they are beneficially entitled in unequal shares,

if a declaration relating to it has effect under section 282B.

(4) Subsection (1) above shall not apply to—

(*a*) earned income, or
(*b*) income which is not earned income but to which section 111 applies.

(5) Subsection (1) above shall not apply to income to which the husband or the wife is beneficially entitled if or to the extent that it is treated by virtue of any other provision of the Income Tax Acts as the income of the other of them or of a third party.

(6) References in this section to a husband and his wife are references to a husband and wife living together.]¹

Commentary—*Simon's Direct Tax Service* **E5.103A.**
Revenue Internal Guidance—Independent taxation handbook, In 115-139 (operation of this section).
In 126 (meaning of "beneficially entitled").
In 129-139 (scope of sub-s (1): computation for new sources, years of marriage and separation).
Definitions—"Earned income", s 835(1); "Income Tax Acts", s 831(1).
Amendments—¹ This section inserted by FA 1988 s 34 with effect from the year 1990–91.

[282B Jointly held property: declarations

(1) The declaration referred to in section 282A(3) is a declaration by both the husband and the wife of their beneficial interests in—

   (a) the income to which the declaration relates, and
   (b) the property from which that income arises.

(2) Subject to the following subsections, a declaration shall have effect under this section in relation to income arising on or after the date of the declaration; but a declaration made before 6th June 1990 shall also have effect in relation to income arising before that date.

(3) A declaration shall not have effect under this section unless notice of it is given to the inspector, in such form and manner as the Board may prescribe, within the period of 60 days beginning with the date of the declaration.

(4) A declaration shall not have effect under this section in relation to income from property if the beneficial interests of the husband and the wife in the property itself do not correspond to their beneficial interests in the income.

(5) A declaration having effect under this section shall continue to have effect unless and until the beneficial interests of husband and wife in either the income to which it relates, or the property from which the income arises, cease to accord with the declaration.]¹

Commentary—*Simon's Direct Tax Service* **E5.103A.**
Revenue Internal Guidance—Independent taxation handbook, In 140-158 (scope of this section; declarations procedure; date from which declaration effective; date from which declaration ceases).
In 162 (worked example).
Definitions—"The Board", s 832(1); "inspector", s 832(1); "notice", s 832(1).
Amendments—¹ This section inserted by FA 1988 s 34 with effect from the year 1990–91.

Separate assessments

283 Option for separate assessment

Amendments—This section repealed by FA 1988 Sch 14 Pt VIII with effect from the year 1990–91.

284 Effect of separate assessment on personal reliefs

Amendments—This section repealed by FA 1988 Sch 14 Pt VIII with effect from the year 1990–91.

285 Collection from wife of tax assessed on husband but attributable to her income

Amendments—This section repealed by FA 1988 Sch 14 Pt VIII with effect from the year 1990–91.

286 Right of husband to disclaim liability for tax on deceased wife's income

Amendments—This section repealed by FA 1988 Sch 14 Pt VIII with effect from the year 1990–91.

Separate taxation

287 Separate taxation of wife's earnings

Amendments—This section repealed by FA 1988 Sch 14 Pt VIII with effect from the year 1990–91.

288 Elections under section 287

Amendments—This section repealed by FA 1988 Sch 14 Pt VIII with effect from the year 1990–91.

CHAPTER III
[ENTERPRISE INVESTMENT SCHEME]¹

Note—For the provisions of this Chapter as applicable to the Business Expansion Scheme which was abolished in relation to shares issued after 31 December 1993, see *Yellow Tax Handbook*, 1993–94, 32nd edition. Note that as so applicable this chapter is amended by FA 1995 s 68 and FA 1998 Schedule 13 Part IV.
Revenue & other press releases—IR Booklet IR37 (guide for investors).

Revenue Internal Guidance—Assessment procedures manual AP 4970–4986 (procedures regarding withdrawal of relief). Inspector's Manual IM 6925–7044 (Revenue procedures in relation to the EIS).

Inspector's Manual IM 6972 (sub-s (1)(*b*) not satisfied if the money has already been advanced to the company).

Definitions—''Appraisal licence'', s 312(1); ''associate'', s 312(1); ''arrangements'' s 312(1); ''basic rate'', s 832(1); ''the Board'', s 832(1); ''close company'', s 832(1); ''company'', s 832(1); ''connected'', s 291(2); ''connected persons'', ss 291A, 291B; ''control'', s 312(1); ''debenture'', s 312(1); ''designated period'', s 291(6); ''development licence'', s 312(1); ''director'', s 312(1); ''disposal of shares'', s 312(3); ''distribution'', s 832(1); ''eligible for relief'', s 289(1); ''eligible shares'', s 289(7); ''exploration licence'', s 312(1); ''51 per cent subsidiary'', s 312(1); ''film'', s 298(5); ''General Commissioners'', TMA 1970 s 2; ''inspector'', s 832(1); ''issue of shares'', s 289B(4); ''lower rate'', s 832(1); ''modified appraisal licence'', s 312(1); ''new consideration'', s 312(1); ''the 1984 regulations'', s 312(1); ''Northern Ireland licence'', s 312(1); ''notice'', s 832(1); ''oil'', s 312(1); ''oil exploration'', s 312(1); ''oil extraction activity'', s 312(1); ''oil rig'', s 298(5); ''ordinary share capital'', ss 312(1), 832(1); ''pleasure craft'', s 298(5); ''profits or gains'', s 833(1); ''qualifying business activity'', s 289(2); ''qualifying company'', s 293; ''qualifying trade'', s 297; ''recognised stock exchange'', s 841; ''related person'', s 291A(2); ''relevant period'', s 312(1A); ''relevant shares'', s 289A(3); ''relief'', s 312(1); ''relief attributable to shares'', s 289B(1); ''research and development'', s 837A; ''Schedule D'', s 18; ''sound recording'', s 298(5); ''Special Commissioners'', TMA 1970 s 4; ''subsidiary'', ss 308, 312(1); ''total income'', s 835; ''trade'', ss 298(3), 832(1); ''United Kingdom'', s 830; ''unquoted company'', s 312(1), (1B)–(1E); ''value received'', ss 300, 303; ''year of assessment'', s 832(1).

Cross references—See TMA 1970 s 47B (question of land valuation in appeals over refusal of relief under this Chapter to be determined by Lands Tribunal).

TA 1988 s 360(3A) (interest relief not available for loan to acquire shares where claim made under this Chapter in respect of those shares).

TCGA 1992 ss 150A, 150B (CGT provisions in respect of EIS eligible shares).

TCGA 1992 s 164MA (exclusion of CGT roll-over relief in respect of EIS eligible shares).

TCGA 1992 s 231 (exclusion of CGT roll-over relief in respect of EIS eligible shares disposed of to an employee share ownership trust).

Amendments—[1] The heading substituted by FA 1994 Sch 15 paras 1, 2 with effect for shares issued after 31 December 1993, for 1993–94 and subsequent years of assessment.

[289 Eligibility for relief]

(1) For the purposes of this Chapter, an individual is eligible for relief, subject to the following provisions of this Chapter, if—

(*a*) eligible shares in a qualifying company for which he has subscribed [wholly in cash][3] are issued to him and, under section 291, he qualifies for relief in respect of those shares,

[(*aa*) at the time when they are issued the shares are fully paid up (disregarding for this purpose any undertaking to pay cash to the company at a future date),][3]

(*b*) the shares [and all other shares comprised in the same issue][3] are issued in order to raise money for the purpose of a qualifying business activity,

[(*ba*) the requirements of subsection (1A) below are satisfied in relation to the company,][2] ...[9]

[(*c*) at least 80% of the money raised by the issue mentioned in paragraph (*b*) above is employed wholly for the purpose of the activity mentioned in that paragraph not later than the time mentioned in subsection (3) below, and][8]

[(*d*) all of the money so raised is employed wholly for that purpose not later than 12 months after that time.][8][3].

[(1A) The requirements of this subsection are satisfied in relation to a qualifying company if throughout the relevant period the active company—

[(*a*) is a company which—

(i) is such a company as is mentioned in section 293(2)(*a*), and

(ii) if it is a subsidiary of the qualifying company, is a 90 per cent subsidiary of that company, or][4]

(*b*) would be [a company falling within paragraph (*a*) above][4] if its purposes were disregarded to the extent that they consist in the carrying on of activities such as are mentioned in section 293(3D)(*a*) and (*b*) and (3E)(*a*), or

(*c*) is a [90 per cent subsidiary][3] of the qualifying company and falls within subsection (1B) below.][2]

[(1B) A subsidiary of the qualifying company falls within this subsection if—

(*a*) apart from purposes capable of having no significant effect (other than in relation to incidental matters) on the extent of its activities, it exists wholly for the purpose of carrying on activities such as are mentioned in section 293(3D)(*b*); or

(*b*) it has no profits for the purposes of corporation tax and no part of its business consists in the making of investments.][2]

[(1C) In subsection (1A) above 'the active company' means the qualifying company or, where the qualifying business activity mentioned in subsection (1) above consists in a subsidiary of that company carrying on or preparing to carry on a qualifying trade [or research and development][7], that subsidiary.][2]

[(1D) [Subsections (4A) and (6)][6] of section 293 shall apply in relation to the requirements of subsection (1A) above as [they apply][6] in relation to subsection (2) of that section.][2]

(2) In this Chapter ''qualifying business activity'', in relation to a company, means—

(*a*) the company or any subsidiary—

(i) carrying on a qualifying trade which, on the date the shares are issued, it is carrying on, or

(ii) preparing to carry on a qualifying trade which, on that date, it intends to carry on wholly or mainly in the United Kingdom and which it begins to carry on within two years after that date,

but only if, at any time in the relevant period when the qualifying trade is carried on, it is carried on wholly or mainly in the United Kingdom, [or][7]

(b) the company or any subsidiary carrying on research and development—

(i) which, on the date the shares are issued, it is carrying on or which it begins to carry on immediately afterwards, and

(ii) from which it is intended that a qualifying trade which the company or any subsidiary will carry on wholly or mainly in the United Kingdom will be derived,

but only if, at any time in the relevant period when the research and development or the qualifying trade derived from it is carried on, it is carried on wholly or mainly in the United Kingdom, ...[7]

(c) ...[7]

(3) The time referred to in subsection (1)(c) above is—

(a) the end of the period of twelve months beginning with the issue of the eligible shares, ...

(b) in the case of money raised only for the purpose referred to in subsection (2)(a) above, the end of that period or, if later, the end of the period of twelve months beginning when the company or subsidiary concerned begins to carry on the qualifying trade,

and for the purposes of this Chapter, [conditions in subsection (1)(c) and (d) above do][8] not fail to be satisfied by reason only of the fact that an amount of money which is not significant is employed for another purpose.

(4)–(5) ...[7]

(6) An individual is not eligible for relief in respect of any shares unless the shares are subscribed [for][3], and issued, for bona fide commercial purposes and not as part of a scheme or arrangement the main purpose or one of the main purposes of which is the avoidance of tax.

(7) In this Chapter ''eligible shares'' means new ordinary shares which, throughout [the period—

(a) beginning with the issue of the shares, and

(b) ending immediately before the termination date relating to those shares,][5]

carry no present or future preferential right to dividends or to a company's assets on its winding up and no present or future ...[3] right to be redeemed.

(8) Section 312(1A)(b) applies to determine the relevant period for the purposes of this section.][1]

[(9) In this section ''90 per cent subsidiary'', in relation to the qualifying company, means a subsidiary of a kind which the company might hold by virtue of section 308 if—

(a) the references in subsection (2) of that section to 75 per cent were references to 90 per cent; and

(b) subsection (4) of that section were omitted.][3]

Commentary—*Simon's Direct Tax Service* E3.135.

Note—For the text of this section as applicable to the Business Expansion Scheme which was abolished in relation to shares issued after 31 December 1993, see *Yellow Tax Handbook*, 1993–94, 32nd edition.

Statements of Practice SP 2/94—Interpretation of sub-s (2), ''qualifying trade'' for holdings of shares issued before 6 April 1998. Revenue will look at totality of activities, locations of capital assets at which business processes are performed and where employees customarily carry out their duties. No one factor is decisive, but over half of the aggregate activities must take place in the UK.

SP 3/00—Enterprise Investment Schemes—location of activity.

Revenue Interpretation RI 148—Explains practical consequences of issuing shares to raise money for more than one ''qualifying business activity'' (see sub-s (2)) and expands on definition of that term.

Simon's Tax Cases—*Barclays Bank plc v IRC* [1993] STC 639; *National Westminster Bank plc v IRC* [1994] STC 580.

s 289(1)(a), *Thompson v Hart* [2000] STC 381.

Definitions—See at the beginning of this Chapter.

Cross references—See TA 1988 s 297(9) (trade consisting substantially of oil extraction activities is a qualifying trade for the purposes of sub-s (2)(c) above).

TA 1988 s 307 (withdrawal or reduction of relief with consequent tax assessment).

TA 1988 s 310(2) (inspector to be informed if relief given is not due).

TA 1988 s 310(5) (inspector's powers to obtain information where he suspects relief is not due).

Amendments—[1] This section and ss 289A, 289B substituted for s 289 (which was in respect of Business Expansion Scheme) by FA 1994 s 137(1), (2) and Sch 15 paras 1, 2 in relation to EIS shares issued after 31 December 1993, with effect from the year 1993–94.

[2] Sub-ss (1)(ba), (1A)-(1D) inserted by FA 1997 Sch 8 para 2 with effect in accordance with Sch 8 para 1.

[3] Words in sub-s (1)(a), (b), (1)(aa), (6), (9) inserted, words in sub-s (1)(c), (1A)(c) substituted and word in sub-s (7) repealed by FA 1998 Sch 13 para 1 with effect in relation to shares issued after 5 April 1998.

[4] Sub-s (1A)(a) and words in sub-s (1A)(b) substituted by FA 1999 s 71 with effect for shares issued after 5 April 1999.

[5] Words in sub-s (7) substituted for words ''the period of five years begiiniing with the date on which they are issued'' by FA 2000 s 64, Sch 17 para 1 with effect for shares issued after 5 April 2000.

[6] Words in sub-s (6) substituted by FA 2000 s 64, Sch 17 para 9(2) with effect—

(a) for shares issued after 20 March 2000, and

(b) in respect of the application of TA 1988 s 293 after that date for shares—

(i) that were issued after 31 December 1993 but before 21 March 2000, and

(ii) to which income tax relief or deferral relief was attributable immediately before 21 March 2000.

Before substitution, the words read ''Subsection (6)'' and ''it applies'' respectively.

[7] Words in sub-s (1C) substituted for the words '', research and development or oil exploration''; in sub-s (2), word ''or'' inserted in para (a), and para (c) repealed; sub-ss (4), (5) repealed by FA 2001 ss 63, 110, Sch 15 paras 2, 10, 40, Sch 33 Pt II(3) with effect—

(a) in relation to shares issued after 6 March 2001, and

(*b*) in respect of the application of TA 1988 Pt VII Chapter III and TCGA 1992 Sch 5B after 6 March 2001 in relation to shares—

    (i) that were issued after 31 December 1993 but before 7 March 2001, and

    (ii) to which income tax relief or deferral relief was attributable immediately before 7 March 2001.

Sub-s (2)(*c*) previously read as follows—

  "(*c*) the company or any subsidiary carrying on oil exploration—

    (i) which, on the date the shares are issued, it is carrying on or begins to carry on immediately afterwards, and

    (ii) from which it is intended that a qualifying trade which the company or any subsidiary will carry on wholly or mainly in the United Kingdom will be derived,

but only if, at any time in the relevant period when the oil exploration or the qualifying trade derived from it is carried on, it is carried on wholly or mainly in the United Kingdom.''

Sub-ss (4), (5) previously read as follows—

  "(4) Subsection (2)(*c*) above shall not apply unless—

    (*a*) throughout the period of three years beginning with the date on which the shares were issued, the company or any subsidiary holds an exploration licence which was granted to it, or to another subsidiary,

    (*b*) the exploration is carried out solely within the area to which the licence applies, and

    (*c*) on the date on which the shares were issued, neither the company nor any subsidiary held an appraisal licence or a development licence relating to that area or any part of that area.

    (5) Where, at any time after the issue of the shares but before the end of the period mentioned in subsection (4)(*a*) above, the company or any subsidiary comes to hold an appraisal licence or development licence which relates to the area, or any part of the area, to which the exploration licence relates, the exploration licence and that other licence shall be treated for the purposes of subsection (4)(*a*) above as a single exploration licence.''

[8] Sub-s (1)(*c*), (*d*) substituted for sub-s (1)(*c*), and words in sub-s (3) substituted for the words "condition in subsection (1)(*c*) above does" by FA 2001 s 63, Sch 15 paras 6, 40 with effect—

    (*a*) in relation to shares issued after 6 March 2001, and

    (*b*) in respect of the application of TA 1988 Pt VII Chapter III and TCGA 1992 Sch 5B after 6 March 2001 in relation to shares—

    (i) that were issued after 31 December 1993 but before 7 March 2001, and

    (ii) to which income tax relief or deferral relief was attributable immediately before 7 March 2001.

Sub-s (1)(*c*) previously read—

  "(*c*) the money raised by the issue is employed not later than the time mentioned in subsection (3) below wholly for the purpose of [the activity mentioned in paragraph (*b*) above.''

[9] Word "and" in sub-s (1) repealed by FA 2001 s 110, Sch 33 Pt II(3) with effect—

    (*a*) in relation to shares issued after 6 March 2001, and

    (*b*) in respect of the application of TA 1988 Pt VII Chapter III and TCGA 1992 Sch 5B after 6 March 2001 in relation to shares—

    (i) that were issued after 31 December 1993 but before 7 March 2001, and

    (ii) to which income tax relief or deferral relief was attributable immediately before 7 March 2001.

[289A Form of relief

(1) Where an individual eligible for relief in respect of any amount subscribed for eligible shares makes a claim, then, subject to the following provisions of this Chapter, the amount of his liability for the year of assessment in which the shares were issued (''the current year'') to income tax on his total income shall be the following amount.

(2) That amount is the amount to which he would be so liable apart from this section less whichever is the smaller of—

    (*a*) an amount equal to tax at the lower rate for the current year on the amount or, as the case may be, the aggregate of the amounts subscribed for eligible shares issued in that year in respect of which he is eligible for relief, and

    (*b*) the amount which reduces his liability to nil.

(3) Subject to subsection (4) below, if in the case of any issue of relevant shares, that is, shares—

    (*a*) which are issued before 6th October in the current year, and

    (*b*) in respect of the amount subscribed for which the individual is eligible for relief,

the individual so requests in his claim, subsection (1) above shall apply as if, in respect of such part of that issue as may be specified in his claim, the shares had been issued in the preceding year of assessment; and his liability to income tax for both years of assessment shall be determined accordingly.

(4) Not more than half of the relevant shares comprised in any issue may be treated by virtue of subsection (3) above as issued in the previous year; and the number of relevant shares (comprised in any issues) so treated as issued in a particular year shall not be such that the total amount subscribed for them exceeds [£25,000][2].

(5) In determining for the purposes of subsection (2) above the amount of income tax to which a person would be liable apart from this section, no account shall be taken of—

    (*a*) any income tax reduction under Chapter I of Part VII of this Act or under section 347B,

    (*b*) any income tax reduction under section 353(1A),

    (*c*) any income tax reduction under section 54(3A) of the Finance Act 1989

    (*d*) any relief by way of a reduction of liability to tax which is given in accordance with any arrangements having effect by virtue of section 788 or by way of a credit under section 790(1), or

    (*e*) any tax at the basic rate on so much of that person's income as is income the income tax on which he is entitled to charge against any other person or to deduct, retain or satisfy out of any payment.

(6) A claim for relief shall not be allowed unless subsection (7) below is complied with but, where it is complied with, the relief may be given at any time when it appears that the conditions for the relief may be satisfied.

(7) This subsection is complied with if—

(a) in the case of shares issued for the purpose of a qualifying business activity falling within paragraph (a) of section 289(2), the company or subsidiary concerned has carried on the trade for four months, [and]⁴

(b) in the case of shares issued for the purpose of a qualifying business activity falling within paragraph (b) of that subsection or within both paragraph (a) and paragraph (b) of that subsection, the company or subsidiary concerned has carried on the research and development for four months, ...⁴

(c) ...⁴

(8) Where—

(a) the company or subsidiary concerned, by reason of its being wound up, or dissolved without winding up, carries on a trade for a period shorter than four months, and

(b) it is shown that the winding up or dissolution was for bona fide commercial reasons and not as part of a scheme or arrangement the main purpose or one of the main purposes of which was the avoidance of tax,

subsection (7)(a) above shall have effect as if it referred to that shorter period.

[(8A) Where the company or subsidiary concerned, by reason of anything done as a consequence of its being in administration or receivership, carries on a trade for a period shorter than four months, subsection (7)(a) above shall have effect as if it referred to that shorter period.

This applies only if—

(a) the making of the order in question, and

(b) everything done as a consequence of the company being in administration or receivership,

is for bona fide commercial reasons and is not part of a scheme or arrangement the main purpose or one of the main purposes of which is the avoidance of tax.]³

(9) ...⁵]¹

Commentary—*Simon's Direct Tax Service* E3.143 .
Definitions—See at the beginning of this Chapter.
Cross references—TA 1988 s 289B (attribution of relief to shares).
TA 1988 s 299(4) (withdrawal of relief where disposal of eligible shares before end of relevant period).
TA 1988 s 304(2) (inter vivos transfer between husband and wife: transferee to be treated as having received relief under this section).
TA 1988 s 306(1) (time limits for claims).
TA 1988 s 311(2B) (modification of this section where shares held by nominees, bare trustees and approved investment funds for individuals).
TA 1988 Sch 15B para 1 (tax relief on qualifying investments in venture capital trusts is offset against tax liability for any year of assessment in priority to relief under this section).
See FA 1990, s 25(6), (7) (where any gift made by an individual (a "donor") in a year of assessment is a qualifying donation, then for that year sub-s (3) above shall have effect in its application to him as if any reference to income tax which he is entitled to charge against any person included a reference to the tax treated as deducted from the gift).
TCGA 1992 s 150A(3) (where an individual's tax liability is reduced under this section, there is corresponding restriction on EIS exemption).
TCGA 1992 s 150A(3) (where relief restricted to less than 20 per cent, capital gains tax exemption also restricted).
TCGA 1992 Sch 58 (interaction with capital gains tax relief for reinvestment into EIS shares).
FA 1995 Sch 15 para 1 (in computing the amount of relief available for investment in venture capital trusts, relief under this section is disregarded).
Amendments—¹ This section, s 289 and s 289B substituted for s 289 (which was in respect of Business Expansion Scheme) by FA 1994 s 137(1), (2) and Sch 15 paras 1, 2 in relation to EIS shares issued after 31 December 1993 with effect from the year 1993–94.
² Amount in sub-s (4) substituted by FA 1998 Sch 13 para 2 with effect in relation to shares issued on or after 6 April 1998.
³ Sub-s (8A) inserted by FA 2000 s 64, Sch 17 para 9(3) with effect—

(a) in relation to shares issued after 20 March 2000, and
(b) in respect of the application of TA 1988 s 293 after that date in relation to shares—
    (i) that were issued after 31 December 1993 but before 21 March 2000, and
    (ii) to which income tax relief or deferral relief was attributable immediately before 21 March 2000.
⁴ The word "and" inserted in sub-para 7(a), and sub-para 7(c) and preceding word "and" repealed, by FA 2001 ss 63, 110, Sch 15 paras 3, 40, Sch 33 Pt II(3) with effect—

(a) in relation to shares issued after 6 March 2001, and
(b) in respect of the application of TA 1988 Pt VII Chapter III and TCGA 1992 Sch 5B after 6 March 2001 in relation to shares—
    (i) that were issued after 31 December 1993 but before 7 March 2001, and
    (ii) to which income tax relief or deferral relief was attributable immediately before 7 March 2001,
Sub-para 7(c) previously read as follows—

"(c) in the case of shares issued for the purpose of a qualifying business activity falling within paragraph (c) of that subsection, the company or subsidiary concerned has carried on the exploration for four months."
⁵ Sub-s (9) repealed by FA 2001 s 63, Sch 15 para 9 with effect for repayments of tax after 6 March 2001.
Prospective amendments—Sub-s (5)(ca) to be inserted by FA 2002 s 57, Sch 17 para 2 with effect from such day as the Treasury may by order appoint. This amendment shall have effect for years of assessment ending on or after the appointed day.
Sub-s (5)(ca) as inserted to read as follows—

"(ca) any income tax reduction under paragraph 19(2) of Schedule 16 to the Finance Act 2002 (community investment tax relief),".

[289B Attribution of relief to shares

(1) References in this Chapter, in relation to any individual, to the relief attributable to any shares or issue of shares shall be read, subject to the provisions of this Chapter providing for the reduction or withdrawal of relief, as references to any reduction made in the individual's liability to income tax which is attributed to those shares or that issue in accordance with this section.

(2) Where an individual's liability to income tax is reduced in any year of assessment ("the current year") under section 289A, then—

(*a*) where the reduction is given by reason of an issue of shares made (or treated as made) in the current year, the amount of the reduction shall be attributed to that issue, and
(*b*) where the reduction is given by reason of two or more issues of shares made (or treated as made) in the current year, the reduction—

(i) shall be apportioned between those issues in the same proportions as the amounts subscribed by the individual for each issue, and
(ii) shall be attributed to those issues accordingly.

(3) Where under this section an amount of any reduction of income tax is attributed to an issue of shares ("the original issue") in a company to an individual—

(*a*) a proportionate part of that amount shall be attributed to each share comprised in the original issue, and
(*b*) if any [corresponding bonus shares in that company][2] are issued to him at any subsequent time—

(i) a proportionate part of the total amount attributed immediately before that time to shares comprised in the original issue shall be attributed to each of the shares in the holding comprising those shares and the bonus shares, and
(ii) this Chapter shall apply as if the original holding had comprised all those shares.

[(3A) In subsection (3) above "corresponding bonus shares" means bonus shares which—

(*a*) are issued in respect of the shares comprised in the original issue; and
(*b*) are of the same class, and carry the same rights, as those shares.][2]

[(4) Subject to subsection (5) below, in this Chapter references (however expressed) to an issue of eligible shares in any company to an individual are references to any eligible shares in the company that are of the same class and are issued to him on the same day.][3]

(5) Where section 289A(1) applies in the case of any issue of shares as if part of the issue had been issued in a previous year, this section and [sections 299(4) and 306(1)][3] shall have effect as if that part and the remainder were separate issues of shares (and that part had been issued on a day in the previous year).

(6) Where, at a time when any relief is attributable to, or to any part of, any issue of shares, the relief falls to be withdrawn or reduced under this Chapter—

(*a*) where it falls to be withdrawn, the relief attributable to each of the shares in question shall be reduced to nil, and
(*b*) where it falls to be reduced by any amount, the relief attributable to each of the shares in question shall be reduced by a proportionate part of that amount.][1]

Commentary—*Simon's Direct Tax Service* E3.144.
Definitions—See at the beginning of this Chapter.
Cross references—See TA 1988 s 311(2B) (modification of this section in its application to shares held by nominees, bare trustees and approved investment funds for individuals).
Amendments—[1] This section, s 289 and s 289A substituted for s 289 (which was in respect of Business Expansion Scheme) by FA 1994 s 137(1), (2) and Sch 15 paras 1, 2 in relation to EIS shares issued after 31 December 1993 with effect from the year 1993–94.
[2] Words in sub-s (3)(*b*) substituted and sub-s (3A) inserted by FA 1998 Sch 13 para 3 with effect in relation to bonus shares issued on or after 6 April 1998.
[3] Sub-s (4) substituted and words in sub-s (5) substituted by FA 1998 Sch 13 para 3 with effect in relation to shares issued on or after 6 April 1998.

290 Minimum and maximum subscriptions

(1) Subject to section 311(3), the relief shall not be given in respect of any amount subscribed by an individual for eligible shares issued to him by any company in any year of assessment unless the amount or total amount subscribed by him for the eligible shares issued to him by the company in that year is £500 or more.

[(2) An individual shall not be eligible for relief in any year of assessment in respect of any amount subscribed for eligible shares exceeding [£150,000][2] (whether the shares are issued in that or a subsequent year).][1]

Commentary—*Simon's Direct Tax Service* E3.141.
Note—For the text of this section as applicable to the Business Expansion Scheme which was abolished in relation to shares issued after 31 December 1993, see *Yellow Tax Handbook*, 1993–94, 32nd edition.
Definitions—See at the beginning of this Chapter.
Cross references—See TA 1988 s 311(3) (minimum instrument prescribed by sub-s (1) above not to apply to investment via approved fund).
FA 1994 Sch 15 para 3(3), (4) (eligibility for relief in respect of the year 1993-94).

Amendments—[1] Sub-s (2) substituted by FA 1994 Sch 15 paras 1, 3(1), (2) with effect from the year 1994–95.
[2] Amount in sub-s (2) substituted by FA 1998 Sch 13 para 4 with effect for shares issued after 5 April 1998.

[290A Restriction of relief where amounts raised exceed permitted maximum]

[(1) Where—

(a) a company raises any amount through the issue of eligible shares, and
(b) the aggregate of that amount and of all other amounts (if any) so raised within the period mentioned in subsection (2) below exceeds £1 million,

the relief shall not be given in respect of the excess.]2

(2) The period referred to in subsection (1) above is—

(a) the period of 6 months ending with the date of the issue of the shares; or
(b) the period beginning with the preceding 6th April and ending with the date of that issue,

whichever is the longer.

(3) In determining the aggregate mentioned in subsection (1) above, no account shall be taken of any amount—

(a) which is subscribed by a person other than an individual who qualifies for relief; or
(b) as respects which relief is precluded by section 290 or this section.

(4) Where—

(a) at any time within the relevant period, the company in question or any of its subsidiaries carries on any trade or part of a trade in partnership, or as a party to a joint venture, with one or more other persons; and
(b) that other person, or at least one of those other persons, is a company,

the reference to [£1 million]3 in subsection (1) above shall have effect as if it were a reference to—

$$\frac{[£1 \text{ million}]^3}{1+A,}$$

where A is the total number of companies (apart from the company in question or any of its subsidiaries) which, during the relevant period, are members of any such partnership or parties to any such joint venture.

(5) Where this section precludes the giving of relief on claims in respect of shares issued to two or more individuals, the available relief shall be divided between them in proportion to the amounts which have been respectively subscribed by them for the shares to which their claims relate and which would, apart from this section, be eligible for relief.

(6) Where—

(a) in the case of a company falling within subsection (2)(a) of section 293, the qualifying trade or each of the qualifying trades is a trade to which subsection (7) below applies; [or]6
[(aa) in the case of a company falling within subsection 2(aa) of that section—

(i) it satisfies the requirements of subsection (6A) below, and
(ii) each of its subsidiaries is a shipping company,]6

subsections (1) and (4) above shall have effect as if for the amount there specified there were substituted £5 million.

[(6A) A company satisfies the requirements of this subsection if, apart from purposes capable of having no significant effect (other than in relation to incidental matters) on the extent of its activities, the company exists wholly—

(a) for the purpose of carrying on activities such as are mentioned in section 293(3D)(a) and (b); or
(b) for the purpose of carrying on one or more qualifying trades which or each of which is a trade to which subsection (7) below applies; or
(c) for any combination of the purposes mentioned in paragraphs (a) and (b) above]6

[(6B) For the purposes of subsection (6) above a subsidiary of a company falling within section 293(2)(aa) is a shipping company if—

(a) that subsidiary satisfies the requirements of subsection (6A) above, or
(b) it would satisfy those requirements if the reference in subsection (6A)(a) above to section 293(3D)(a) and (b) included a reference to section 293(3E)(a), or
(c) it has no profits for the purposes of corporation tax and no part of its business consists in the making of investments.]6

(7) This subsection applies to a trade if it consists, wholly or substantially wholly, of operating or letting ships, other than oil rigs or pleasure craft, and—

(a) every ship operated or let by the company carrying on the trade is beneficially owned by the company;
(b) every ship beneficially owned by the company is registered in the United Kingdom;
(c) throughout the relevant period the company is solely responsible for arranging the marketing of the services of its ships; and

(*d*) the conditions mentioned in section 297(7) are satisfied in relation to every letting by the company.

(8) Where—

(*a*) any of the requirements mentioned in paragraphs (*a*) to (*c*) of subsection (7) above are not satisfied in relation to any ships; or

(*b*) any of the conditions referred to in paragraph (*d*) of that subsection are not satisfied in relation to any lettings,

the trade shall not thereby be precluded from being a trade to which that subsection applies if the operation or letting of those ships, or, as the case may be, those lettings do not amount to a substantial part of the trade.

(9) The Treasury may by order amend any of the foregoing provisions of this section by substituting a different amount for the amount for the time being specified there.

(10) ...5

(11) In this section—

"let" means let on charter and "letting" shall be construed accordingly;

"oil rig" and "pleasure craft" have the same meanings as in section 297;

...5.]1

[(12) Section 312(1A)(*b*) applies to determine the relevant period for the purposes of this section.]4]
7

Commentary—*Simon's Direct Tax Service* **E3.136.**
For the text of this section as applicable to the Business Expansion Scheme which was abolished in relation to shares issued after 31 December 1993, see *Butterworths Yellow Tax Handbook*, 1993–94, 32nd edition.
Revenue Internal Guidance—Inspector's manual IM 6503b (sub-s (4) examples illustrating rules for "relevant periods").
Definitions—See at the beginning of this Chapter.
Cross references—See TA 1988 s 289B(5) (application of this section where relief in respect of part of an issue of shares carried back).
FA 1994 Sch 15 para 4(2) ("amounts raised through the issue of eligible shares" include amounts raised before 1 January 1994 under the old scheme(BES)).
Amendments—1 This section (ie sub-ss (1)–(11)) inserted by FA 1988 s 51(1)(*b*) and deemed always to have had effect.
2 Sub-s (1) substituted by FA 1994 s 137(1), (2) and Sch 15 paras 1, 4 in relation to shares issued after 31 December 1993, with effect from the year 1993–94 and subsequent years of assessment.
3 Amount in sub-s (4) substituted by FA 1994 s 137(1), (2) and Sch 15 paras 1, 4 in relation to shares issued after 31 December 1993, with effect from the year 1993–94 and subsequent years of assessment.
4 Sub-s (12) added by FA 1994 s 137(1), (2) and Sch 15 paras 1, 4 in relation to shares issued after 31 December 1993, with effect from the year 1993–94 and subsequent years of assessment.
5 Sub-s (10) and the definition of "prospectus" in sub-s (11) repealed by FA 1994 s 137(1), (2), Sch 15 paras 1, 4 and Sch 26, Pt V(17) in relation to shares issued after 31 December 1993, with effect from the year 1993–94 and subsequent years of assessment and Sch 26, Pt V(17).
6 Sub-s (6)(*aa*) and preceding word "or" substituted for sub-s(6)(*b*), (*c*), and sub-ss (6A), (6B) inserted, by FA 1997 Sch 8 para 3 with effect in accordance with Sch 8 para 1.
7 Section repealed by FA 1998 Sch 13 para 5 with effect for shares issued after 5 April 1998.

[291 Individuals qualifying for relief

(1) An individual qualifies for relief in respect of eligible shares in a company (referred to in this section and sections 291A and 291B as the "issuing company") if—

(*a*) he subscribes for the shares on his own behalf; and

[(*b*) subject to section 291A(4), he is not at any time in the period—

(i) beginning two years before the issue of the shares, and

(ii) ending immediately before the termination date relating to those shares,

connected with the company (whether before or after its incorporation).]4.

(2) For the purposes of this section ...2, an individual is connected with the issuing company if he, or an associate of his, is—

(*a*) an employee of, or of a partner of, the issuing company or any subsidiary,

(*b*) a partner of the issuing company or any subsidiary, or

(*c*) subject to section 291A, a director of, or of a company which is a partner of, the issuing company or any subsidiary,

or if he, or an associate of his, is so connected by virtue of section 291B.

[(3) In subsection (2) above "subsidiary", in relation to the issuing company, means a company which at any time in the relevant period is a 51 per cent subsidiary of the issuing company, whether or not it is such a subsidiary while the individual concerned or his associate is such an employee, partner or director as is mentioned in that subsection.]2

(4) For the purposes of subsections (2) and (3) above and section 291A, in the case of a person who is both a director and an employee of a company—

(*a*) references (however expressed) to him in his capacity as a director of the company include him in his capacity as an employee of the company, but

(*b*) (apart from that) he is not to be treated as an employee of the company.

(5) Section 312(1A)(*a*) applies to determine the relevant period for the purposes of this section and sections 291A and 291B.]1

(6) ...[5]

Commentary—*Simon's Direct Tax Service* **E3.106.**
Note—For the text of this section as applicable to the Business Expansion Scheme which was abolished in relation to shares issued after 31 December 1993, see *Yellow Tax Handbook*, 1993–94, 32nd edition.
Concession
A76—Concession for holdings of shares issued before 6 April 1998 as regards connection with issuing company condition in sub-s (1)(*b*).
Simon's Tax Cases—s 291(1)(*c*), *Wild v Cannavan* [1997] STC 966.
s 291(4), (8), *Cook v Billings* [1999] STC 661; *Cook (Inspector of Taxes) v Billings and related appeals* [2001] STC 16, CA.
Definitions—See at the beginning of this Chapter.
Cross references—See TA 1988 s 289B(5) (application of this section where relief in respect of part of an issue of shares carried back).
TA 1988 s 307(6)–(8A) (withdrawal or reduction of relief with consequent tax assessment; interest on tax).
TA 1988 s 310(1) (requirement to inform inspector of events leading to withdrawal of relief).
TA 1988 s 310(1) (inspector to be informed if relief given is not due).
TA 1988 s 310(5) (inspector's powers to obtain information where he suspects relief is not due).
Amendments—[1] This section substituted, together with ss 291A, 291B, for s 291 by FA 1994 s 137(1), (2), Sch 15 paras 1, 5 in relation to EIS shares issued after 31 December 1993 with effect from the year 1993–94.
[2] Words substituted in sub-s (3), repealed in sub-s (2) by FA 1998 Sch 13 para 6 with effect in relation to shares issued after 5 April 1998.
[3] Sub-s (6) substituted by FA 2000 s 64, Sch 17 para 2 with effect for shares issued after 5 April 2000. Previously sub-s (6) read—

"(6) In this Chapter 'the seven year period', in relation to relief in respect of any eligible shares issued by a company, means the period beginning two years before, and ending five years after, the issue of the shares."
[4] Sub-s (1)(*b*) substituted by FA 2001 s 63, Sch 15 paras 10, 40 with effect—

(*a*) in relation to shares issued after 6 March 2001, and
(*b*) in respect of the application of TA 1988 Pt VII Chapter III and TCGA 1992 Sch 5B after 6 March 2001 in relation to shares—

(i) that were issued after 31 December 1993 but before 7 March 2001, and
(ii) to which income tax relief or deferral relief was attributable immediately before 7 March 2001.
Sub-s (1)(*b*) previously read—

"(*b*) subject to section 291A(4), he is not at any time in [the [designated] period connected with the company (whether before or after its incorporation)".
[5] Sub-s (6) repealed by FA 2001 S 110, Sch 33 Pt II(3) with effect—

(*a*) in relation to shares issued after 6 March 2001, and
(*b*) in respect of the application of TA 1988 Pt VII Chapter III and TCGA 1992 Sch 5B after 6 March 2001 in relation to shares—

(i) that were issued after 31 December 1993 but before 7 March 2001, and
(ii) to which income tax relief or deferral relief was attributable immediately before 7 March 2001.
Sub-s (6) previously read—

"(6) In this Chapter "the designated period", in relation to any eligible shares issued by a company, means the period—

(*a*) beginning two years before the issue of the shares, and
(*b*) ending immediately before the termination date relating to those shares."

[291A Connected persons: directors

(1) An individual is not connected with the issuing company by reason only that he, or an associate of his, is a director of that or another company unless he or his associate (or a partnership of which he or his associate is a member)—

(*a*) receives a payment from the issuing company or a related person during [the period mentioned in section 291(1)(*b*)][5], or
(*b*) is entitled to receive such a payment in respect of that period or any part of it.

(2) In this section—

(*a*) "related person", in relation to the issuing company, means—

(i) any company of which the individual or his associate is a director and which is a subsidiary or a partner of the issuing company or of a subsidiary, and
(ii) any person connected with the issuing company or with a company falling within sub-paragraph (i) above, and

(*b*) any reference to a payment to an individual includes a payment made to him indirectly or to his order or for his benefit.

(3) For the purposes of subsection (1) above there shall be disregarded—

(*a*) any payment or reimbursement of travelling or other expenses wholly, exclusively and necessarily incurred by him or his associate in the performance of his duties as a director,
(*b*) any interest which represents no more than a reasonable commercial return on money lent to the issuing company or a related person,
(*c*) any dividend or other distribution which does not exceed a normal return on the investment,
(*d*) any payment for the supply of goods which does not exceed their market value,
(*e*) any payment of rent for any property occupied by the issuing company or a related person which does not exceed a reasonable and commercial rent for the property, and
(*f*) any reasonable and necessary remuneration which—

(i) is paid for services rendered to the issuing company or related person in the course of a trade or profession (not being secretarial or managerial services or services of a kind provided by the person to whom they are rendered), and

(ii) is taken into account in computing the [profits]³ of the trade or profession under Case I or II of Schedule D or would be so taken into account if it fell in a period on the basis of which those [profits]³ are assessed under that Schedule.

(4) An individual ("the subscriber") who subscribes for eligible shares ("the relevant shares") may qualify for the relief notwithstanding his connection with the company at any time in the relevant period if—

(*a*) he is so connected by reason only of his, or his associate's, being a director of, or of a company which is a partner of, the issuing company or a subsidiary in receipt of, or entitled to receive, remuneration as such, and

(*b*) the following conditions are satisfied;

and in this subsection and subsection (5) below "remuneration" includes any benefit or facility.

(5) The conditions are that—

(*a*) in relation to the director (whether he is the subscriber or his associate), his remuneration, or the remuneration to which he is entitled, (leaving out of account any reasonable and necessary remuneration falling within subsection (3)(*f*) above) consists only of remuneration which is reasonable remuneration for services rendered to the company of which he is a director in his capacity as such,

(*b*) the subscriber was issued with eligible shares (whether the relevant shares or a previous issue of eligible shares) at a time when he had never been—

(i) connected with the issuing company, or

[(ii) involved in carrying on (whether on his own account or as a partner, director or employee) the whole or any part of the trade carried on by the issuing company or a subsidiary, and]²

(*c*) where the issue of the relevant shares did not satisfy paragraph (*b*) above, they were not issued after the end of the period—

[(i)]⁴ beginning with the date of the latest issue of eligible shares which satisfied that paragraph, [and

(ii) ending immediately before the termination date relating to those eligible shares,]⁴

and in paragraph (*b*) above "trade" includes any business, profession or vocation ...².

(6) In this section "subsidiary", in relation to the issuing company, means a 51 per cent subsidiary of the issuing company.]¹

Commentary—*Simon's Direct Tax Service* E3.110, 111.
Concession A76—Concession for holdings of shares issued before 6 April 1998 as regards connection with the issuing company within s 291(11)(*b*) for the purpose of EIS relief, subject to sub-s (4).
Revenue Internal Guidance—Inspector's Manual IM6937 (examples illustrating s 291A).
Definitions—See at the beginning of this Chapter.
Cross references—See TA 1988 s 289B(5) (application of this section where relief carried back in respect of part of a share issue).
TA 1988 s 291(2) (meaning of "individual connected with issuing company").
TA 1988 s 291(4) (application of this section to a person who is both a director and employee).
TA 1988 s 291(5) ("the relevant period" is determined by s 312(1A)(*a*)).
Amendments—¹ This section substituted, together with ss 291, 291B, for s 291 by FA 1994 s 137(1), (2), Sch 15 paras 1, 5 in relation to EIS shares issued after 31 December 1993 with effect from the year 1993–94.
² Sub-s (5)(*b*)(ii) substituted, and certain words in sub-s (5) repealed by FA 1998 Sch 13 para 7 with effect in relation to shares issued after 5 April 1998.
³ Word in sub-s (3)(*f*)(ii) substituted by FA 1998 Sch 7 para 1 with effect from 31 July 1998.
⁴ Word "(i)" in sub-s (5)(*c*) substituted for words "of five years", and sub-s (5)(*c*)(ii), and word "and" preceding it inserted by FA 2000 s 64, Sch 17 para 3 with effect for shares issued after 5 April 2000.
⁵ Words in sub-s (1)(*a*) substituted for the words "the designated period" by FA 2001 s 63, Sch 15 paras 11, 40 with effect—

(*a*) in relation to shares issued after 6 March 2001, and
(*b*) in respect of the application of TA 1988 Pt VII Chapter III and TCGA 1992 Sch 5B after 6 March 2001 in relation to shares—
(i) that were issued after 31 December 1993 but before 7 March 2001, and
(ii) to which income tax relief or deferral relief was attributable immediately before 7 March 2001.

[291B Connected persons: persons interested in capital etc of company

(1) An individual is connected with the issuing company if he directly or indirectly possesses or is entitled to acquire more than 30 per cent of—

(*a*) the issued ordinary share capital of the company or any subsidiary,

(*b*) the loan capital and issued share capital of the company or any subsidiary, or

(*c*) the voting power in the company or any subsidiary.

(2) An individual is connected with the issuing company if he directly or indirectly possesses or is entitled to acquire such rights as would, in the event of the winding up of the company or any subsidiary or in any other circumstances, entitle him to receive more than 30 per cent of the assets of the company or subsidiary (the "company in question") which would then be available for distribution to equity holders of the company in question.

(3) For the purposes of subsection (2) above—

(*a*) the persons who are equity holders of the company in question, and

(*b*) the percentage of the assets of the company in question to which the individual would be entitled, shall be determined in accordance with paragraphs 1 and 3 of Schedule 18, taking references in paragraph 3 to the first company as references to an equity holder and references to a winding up as including references to any other circumstances in which assets of the company in question are available for distribution to its equity holders.

(4) An individual is connected with a company if he has control of it or of any subsidiary.

(5) Where an individual subscribes for shares in a company with which (apart from this subsection) he is not connected, he shall nevertheless be treated as connected with it if he subscribes for the shares as part of any arrangement which provides for another person to subscribe for shares in another company with which (assuming it to be an issuing company) that or any other individual who is a party to the arrangement is connected.

[(5A) An individual is not connected with a company by reason only of the fact that one or more shares in the company are held by him, or by an associate of his, at a time when the company—

    (*a*) has not issued any shares other than subscriber shares; and
    (*b*) has not begun to carry on, or to make preparations for carrying on, any trade or business.]²

[(6) In this section "subsidiary", in relation to the issuing company, means a company which at any time in the relevant period is a 51 per cent subsidiary of the issuing company, whether or not it is such a subsidiary while the individual concerned has, or is entitled to acquire, such capital, voting power, rights or control as are mentioned in this section.]²

(7) For the purposes of this section the loan capital of a company shall be treated as including any debt incurred by the company—

    (*a*) for any money borrowed or capital assets acquired by the company,
    (*b*) for any right to receive income created in favour of the company, or
    (*c*) for consideration the value of which to the company was (at the time when the debt was incurred) substantially less than the amount of the debt (including any premium on it).

(8) For the purposes of this section an individual shall be treated as entitled to acquire anything which he is entitled to acquire at a future date or will at a future date be entitled to acquire, and there shall be attributed to any person any rights or powers of any other person who is an associate of his.

(9) In determining for the purposes of this section whether an individual is connected with a company, no debt incurred by the company or any subsidiary by overdrawing an account with a person carrying on a business of banking shall be treated as loan capital of the company or subsidiary if the debt arose in the ordinary course of that business.

(10) Section 840 applies for the purposes of this section.]¹

Commentary—*Simon's Direct Tax Service* **E3.107.**
Revenue Internal Guidance—Inspector's manual IM 6527 (sub-s (8) includes ability to obtain possession of shares, votes etc through a contractual right or other arrangement).
Revenue Internal Guidance—Inspector's Manual IM6941 (example illustrating s 291B).
Definitions—See at the beginning of this Chapter.
Cross references—See TA 1988 s 291(2) (meaning of "individual connected with issuing company").
TA 1988 s 291(5) ("the relevant period" is determined by s 312(1A)(*a*)).
TA 1988 s 303 (effect on sub-s (1) above where a member of a company receives or is entitled to receive value from the company).
TA 1988 s 310(5), (6) (information powers where inspector has reason to believe relief is not due by reason of sub-s (5) above).
Amendments—¹ This section substituted, together with ss 291, 291A, for s 291 by FA 1994 s 137(1), (2), Sch 15 paras 1, 5 in relation to EIS shares issued after 31 December 1993 with effect from the year 1993–94.
² Sub-s (5A) inserted and sub-s (6) substituted by FA 1998 Sch 13 para 8 with effect in relation to shares issued on or after 6 April 1998.

292 Parallel trades

[(1) An individual is not eligible for relief in respect of any shares in a company if, at the date mentioned in subsection (2) below—]¹

    (*a*) he is one of a group of persons—
        (i) who control the company; or
        (ii) to whom belongs an interest amounting in the aggregate to more than a half share in the trade carried on by the company;
    (*b*) he is also an individual, or one of a group of persons—
        (i) controlling another company; or
        (ii) to whom belongs an interest amounting in the aggregate to more than a half share in another trade; and
    (*c*) the trade carried on by the company, or a substantial part of it—
        (i) is concerned with the same or similar types of property or parts thereof or provides the same or similar services or facilities; and
        (ii) serves substantially the same or similar outlets or markets;

as the other trade or (as the case may be) the trade carried on by the other company.

(2) The date mentioned in subsection (1) above is—

    (*a*) the date on which the shares are issued; or
    (*b*) if later, the date on which the company begins to carry on the trade.

(3) For the purposes of subsection (1) above—

(a) the persons to whom a trade belongs, and (where a trade belongs to two or more persons) their respective shares in that trade, shall be determined in accordance with section 344(1)(a) and (b), (2) and (3); and

(b) any interest, rights or powers of a person who is an associate of another person shall be treated as those of that other person.

(4) For the purposes of this section—

(a) references to a company's trade include references to the trade of [any company which is a 51 per cent subsidiary of that company on the date referred to in subsection (2) above][1]; and

(b) "trade" in the expressions "another trade", "other trade" and "trade carried on by the other company" includes any business, profession or vocation.

[(5) This section shall not apply where the shares mentioned in subsection (1) above are issued on or after 29th November 1994.][2]

Commentary—*Simon's Direct Tax Service* E3.113.
Note—For the text of this section as applicable to the Business Expansion Scheme which was abolished in relation to shares issued after 31 December 1993, see *Yellow Tax Handbook*, 1993–94, 32nd edition.
Definitions—See at the beginning of this Chapter.
Amendments—[1] Words in sub-ss (1), (4)(a) substituted by FA 1994 s 137(1), (2), Sch 15 para 6 in relation to EIS shares issued after 31 December 1993 with effect from the year 1993–94.
[2] Sub-s (5) inserted by FA 1995 s 66(2), with effect as this Chapter has effect in relation to shares issued after 31 December 1993.

293 Qualifying companies

[(1) Subject to section 294, a company is a qualifying company (whether it is resident in the United Kingdom or elsewhere) if it complies with the requirements of this section.][2]

[(1A) At the beginning of the relevant period, the company must be—

(a) an unquoted company, and
(b) a company to which subsection (1B) below does not apply.][12]

[(1B) This subsection applies to a company—

(a) if arrangements are in existence for it to cease to be an unquoted company; or
(b) if—
(i) arrangements are in existence for it to become a subsidiary of another company ("the new company") by virtue of an exchange of shares, or shares and securities, in relation to which section 304A (certain exchanges resulting in acquisition of share capital by new company) applies, and
(ii) arrangements have been made with a view to the new company ceasing to be an unquoted company.][12]

[(2) The company must, throughout the relevant period, ...[12] be—

(a) a company which exists wholly for the purpose of carrying on one or more qualifying trades or which so exists apart from purposes capable of having no significant effect (other than in relation to incidental matters) on the extent of the company's activities, or
[(aa) the parent company of a trading group.][7]][2]

[(3) In this section "qualifying subsidiary", in relation to a company, means a subsidiary of a kind which that company may hold by virtue of section 308.][2]

[(3A) For the purposes of this section a company is the parent company of a trading group if—

(a) it has one or more subsidiaries;
(b) each of its subsidiaries is a qualifying subsidiary of the company; and
(c) the requirements of subsection (3B) below are fulfilled by what would be the business of the company and its subsidiaries if all the activities, taken together, of the company and its subsidiaries were regarded as one business.][7]

[(3B) A business fulfils the requirements of this subsection if neither the business nor a substantial part of it consists in, or in either of, the following, that is to say—

(a) activities falling within section 297(2)(a) to (g) but not within subsection (3C) below; and
(b) activities [(other than research and development ...[11])][8] carried on otherwise than in the course of a trade.][7]

[(3C) The activities falling within this subsection are—

(a) the receiving of royalties or licence fees in circumstances where [the requirement mentioned in section 297(4) is][13] satisfied in relation to the company receiving them;
(b) the letting of ships, other than oil rigs or pleasure craft, on charter in circumstances where the requirements mentioned in paragraphs (a) to (d) of section 297(6) are satisfied in relation to the company so letting them.][7]

[(3D) Activities of a company or of any of its subsidiaries shall be disregarded for the purposes of subsections (3A) to (3C) above to the extent that they consist in—

(a) the holding of shares in or securities of, or the making of loans to, one or more of the company's subsidiaries; or

(b) the holding and managing of property used by the company or any of its subsidiaries for the purposes of—

    (i) research and development from which it is intended that a qualifying trade to be carried on by the company or any of its subsidiaries will be derived; or

    (ii) one or more qualifying trades so carried on.][7]

[(3E) Activities of a subsidiary of a company shall also be disregarded for the purposes of subsections (3A) to (3C) above to the extent that they consist in—

    (a) the making of loans to the company; or

    (b) in the case of a mainly trading subsidiary, activities carried on otherwise than in pursuance of its main purpose.][7]

[(3F) For the purposes of subsection (3E) above—

    (a) 'mainly trading subsidiary' means a subsidiary which, apart from purposes capable of having no significant effect (other than in relation to incidental matters) on the extent of its activities, exists wholly for the purpose of carrying on one or more qualifying trades; and

    (b) that purpose shall be taken to be its main purpose.][7]

(4) ...[5]

[(4A) A company which is in administration or receivership shall not be regarded as ceasing to comply with subsection (2) above by reason of anything done as a consequence of its being in administration or receivership.

This subsection has effect subject to subsection (4B) and subsection (5) below.

(4B) Subsection (4A) applies only if—

    (a) the making of the order in question, and

    (b) everything done as a consequence of the company being in administration or receivership,

is for bona fide commercial reasons and is not part of a scheme or arrangement the main purpose or one of the main purposes of which is the avoidance of tax.][10]

(5) Without prejudice to the generality of subsection (2) above, but subject to subsection (6) below, a company ceases to comply with that subsection if before the end of the relevant period a resolution is passed, or an order is made, for the winding up of the company (or, in the case of a winding up otherwise than under the Insolvency Act 1986 or the [Insolvency (Northern Ireland) Order 1989][1], any other act is done for the like purpose) or the company is dissolved without winding up.

(6) A company shall not be regarded as ceasing to comply with subsection (2) above if it does so by reason of being wound up or dissolved without winding up and—

    (a) [...][9] the winding up or dissolution is for bona fide commercial reasons and not part of a scheme or arrangement the main purpose or one of the main purposes of which is the avoidance of tax; *and*[10]

    (b) *the company's net assets, if any, are distributed to its members or dealt with as bona vacantia before the end of the relevant period or, in the case of a winding up, the end (if later) of three years from the commencement of the winding up*[10]

[(6A) The value of the relevant assets—

    (a) must not exceed £15 million immediately before the issue of the eligible shares; and

    (b) must not exceed £16 million immediately afterwards.

(6B) Subject to subsection (6C) below, the reference in subsection (6A) above to the value of the relevant assets is a reference—

    (a) in relation to a time when the company did not have any qualifying subsidiaries, to the value of the gross assets of the company at that time; and

    (b) in relation to any other time, to the aggregate value at that time of the gross assets of all the companies in the company's group.

(6C) For the purposes of subsection (6B) above assets of any member of the company's group that consist in rights against, or in shares in or securities of, another member of the group shall be disregarded.

(6D) In subsections (6B) and (6C) above references, in relation to any time, to the company's group are references to the company and its qualifying subsidiaries at that time.][8]

(7) ...[8]

[(8) Subject to section 304A, the company must not at any time in the relevant period—

    (a) control (whether on its own or together with any person connected with it) any company which is not a qualifying subsidiary, or

    (b) be—

        (i) a 51% subsidiary of another company, or

        (ii) under the control of another company (or of another company and any other person connected with that other company), without being a 51% subsidiary of that other company,

and no arrangements must be in existence at any time in that period by virtue of which the company could fall within paragraph (a) or (b) above (whether during that period or otherwise).

(8AA) In subsection (8)(b) above ''control'' has the meaning given by section 840.][10]

[(8A) Section 312(1A)(*b*) applies to determine the relevant period for the purposes of this section and sections 294, 295 and 296.][4]

[(8B) In arriving at the relevant period for the purposes of sections 294 to 296 any time falling on or after 29th November 1994 shall be ignored; and subsection (8A) above shall have effect subject to the preceding provisions of this subsection.][6]

(9)–(11) ...[5]

Commentary—*Simon's Direct Tax Service* E3.115.
Statement of Practice SP 2/00—Enterprise Investment Schemes—value of "gross assets".
Revenue Interpretation RI 14—Qualifying company ceasing to trade; effect on "qualifying" status.
Revenue & other press releases—IR 20–2–95 (shares listed on the AIM are not "quoted").
Hansard 18-2-97 (Standing Committee B (twelfth sitting): Finance Bill debate) (for the purposes of sub-s (3B), "a substantial part" means "80%").
Revenue Internal Guidance—Inspector's manual IM 6553 (sub-s (2)(*b*) temporary investment of surplus funds in bank deposit does not disqualify company).
Note—For the text of this section as applicable to the Business Expansion Scheme which was abolished in relation to shares issued after 31 December 1993, see *Yellow Tax Handbook*, 1993–94, 32nd edition.
Definitions—See at the beginning of this Chapter.
Cross references—See TA 1988 s 290A(6) (£5 million EIS finance limit for ship chartering company).
TA 1988 s 298 (meaning of "controlling interest" for the purposes of sub-s (9) above).
TA 1988 s 307(6)–(8A) (withdrawal or reduction of relief with consequent tax assessment; interest on tax).
TA 1988 s 310(2) (inspector to be informed if relief given is not due).
TA 1988 s 310(5) (inspector's powers to obtain information where he suspects relief is not due).
Amendments—[1] Words in sub-s (5) substituted by the Insolvency (Northern Ireland) Order 1989, SI 1989/2405 Sch 9 para 59.
[2] Sub-ss (1)–(3) substituted by FA 1994 s 137(1), (2) and Sch 15 paras 1, 7 in relation to EIS shares issued after 31 December 1993 with effect from the year 1993–94.
[3] Words in sub-s (7) inserted by FA 1994 s 137(1), (2) and Sch 15 paras 1,7.
[4] Sub-ss (8), (8A) substituted for sub-s (8) by FA 1994 s 137(1), (2) and Sch 15 paras 1,7.
[5] Sub-ss (4), (9)–(11) repealed by FA 1994 s 137(1), (2) and Sch 15 paras 1,7 and Sch 26, Pt V(17).
[6] Sub-s (8B) inserted by FA 1995 s 66(3), with effect as this Chapter has effect for shares issued after 31 December 1993.
[7] Sub-s (2)(*aa*) substituted for sub-s (2)(*b*), and sub-ss (3A)-(3F) inserted, by FA 1997 Sch 8 para 4 with effect in accordance with Sch 8 para 1.
[8] Words in sub-s (3B)(*b*) inserted, sub-ss (6A)–(6D) inserted, sub-s (7) repealed and words in sub-s (8) substituted by FA 1998 Sch 13 para 9 with effect in relation to shares issued after 5 April 1998.
[9] Words in sub-s (6)(*a*) repealed by FA 1998 Sch 13 para 9 in relation to events occurring after 5 April 1998.
[10] Sub-ss (4A), (4B) inserted, sub-s (6)(*b*) and the word "and" preceding it repealed and sub-ss (8), (8AA) substituted for original sub-s (8), by FA 2000 ss 64, 156, Sch 17 paras 9(1), 10, 11, 12, Sch 40 Pt II(5) with effect—

(*a*) for shares issued after 20 March 2000, and
(*b*) in respect of the application of TA 1988 s 293 after that date for shares—
(i) that were issued after 31 December 1993 but before 21 March 2000, and
(ii) to which income tax relief or deferral relief was attributable immediately before 21 March 2000.

Sub-s (8) previously read—

"(8) Subject to sections 304A and 308, the company must not—

(*a*) at any time in the relevant period control (or together with any person connected with it control) another company or be under the control of another company (or another company and any other person connected with that other company), or
(*b*) at any such time be a 51 per cent subsidiary of another company or itself have a 51 per cent subsidiary,

and no arrangements must be in existence at any time in that period by virtue of which the company could fall within paragraph (*a*) or (*b*) above."

[11] The words "and oil exploration" in sub-s (3B)(*b*) repealed by FA 2001 ss 63,110, Sch 15 paras 4, 40, Sch 33 Pt II(3) with effect—

(*a*) in relation to shares issued after 6 March 2001, and
(*b*) in respect of the application of TA 1988 Pt VII Chapter III and TCGA 1992 Sch 5B after 6 March 2001 in relation to shares—
(i) that were issued after 31 December 1993 but before 7 March 2001, and
(ii) to which income tax relief or deferral relief was attributable immediately before 7 March 2001.

[12] Sub-ss (1A), (1B) inserted, and in sub-s (2), the words "be an unquoted company and" repealed, by FA 2001 ss 63, 110, Sch 15 paras 12, 40, Sch 33 Pt II(3) with effect—

(*a*) in relation to shares issued after 6 March 2001, and
(*b*) in respect of the application of TA 1988 Pt VII Chapter III and TCGA 1992 Sch 5B after 6 March 2001 in relation to shares—
(i) that were issued after 31 December 1993 but before 7 March 2001, and
(ii) to which income tax relief or deferral relief was attributable immediately before 7 March 2001.

[13] Words in sub-s (3C) substituted for the words "the requirements mentioned in paragraphs (*a*) and (*b*) of section 297(4) or (5) are" by FA 2001 s 63, Sch 15 para 14 with effect for shares issued after 6 April 2000, and deemed always to have had effect.

294 Companies with interests in land

...

Commentary—*Simon's Direct Tax Service* E3.120.
Notes—For the text of this section as applicable to the Business Expansion Scheme which was abolished in relation to shares issued after 31 December 1993, see *Yellow Tax Handbook*, 1993–94, 32nd edition.
This section *effectively* repealed for EIS purposes with effect after 28 November 1994 by TA 1988 s 293(8B) as inserted by FA 1995 s 66(3). For text see *Yellow Tax Handbook*, 2000–01, 40th edition.

295 Valuation of interests in land for purposes of section 294(1)(*b*)

...

Commentary—*Simon's Direct Tax Service* E3.120.
Notes—For the text of this section as applicable to the Business Expansion Scheme which was abolished in relation to shares issued after 31 December 1993, see *Yellow Tax Handbook*, 1993–94, 32nd edition.
This section *effectively* repealed for EIS purposes with effect after 28 November 1994 by TA 1988 s 293(8B) as inserted by FA 1995 s 66(3). For text see *Yellow Tax Handbook*, 2000–01, 40th edition.

296 Section 294 disapplied where amounts raised total £50,000 or less

...

Commentary—*Simon's Direct Tax Service* **E3.120.**
Notes—For the text of this section as applicable to the Business Expansion Scheme which was abolished in relation to shares
  issued after 31 December 1993, see *Yellow Tax Handbook*, 1993–94, 32nd edition.
This section *effectively* repealed for EIS purposes with effect after 28 November 1994 by TA 1988 s 293(8B) as inserted by
  FA 1995 s 66(3). For text see *Yellow Tax Handbook*, 2000–01, 40th edition.

297 Qualifying trades

(1) ...[7] A trade is a qualifying trade if it complies with the requirements of this section.

(2) Subject to subsection (9) below, the trade must not at any time in the relevant period consist of
one or more of the following activities if that activity amounts, or those activities when taken
together amount, to a substantial part of the trade—

(*a*) dealing in [land, in commodities or futures or in shares, securities or other financial
instruments][2];
(*b*) dealing in goods otherwise than in the course of an ordinary trade of wholesale or retail
distribution;
(*c*) banking, insurance, money-lending, debt-factoring, hire-purchase financing or other financial
activities;
(*d*) ...[9]
(*e*) leasing (including letting ships on charter or other assets on hire) or receiving royalties or
licence fees;
(*f*) providing legal or accountancy services;
[(*fa*) property development;
(*fb*) farming or market gardening;
(*fc*) holding, managing or occupying woodlands, any other forestry activities or timber production;
(*fd*) operating or managing hotels or comparable establishments or managing property used as an
hotel or comparable establishment;
(*fe*) operating or managing nursing homes or residential care homes, or managing property used
as a nursing home or residential care home;][6]
(*g*) providing services or facilities for any trade carried on by another person [(other than a
company of which the company providing the services or facilities is the subsidiary)][3] which
consists to any substantial extent of activities within any of paragraphs (*a*) to [(*fe*)][6] above and in
which a controlling interest is held by a person who also has a controlling interest in the trade
carried on by the company;
(*h*), (*j*) ...[4]

(3) For the purposes of subsection (2)(*b*) above—

(*a*) a trade of wholesale distribution is one in which the goods are offered for sale and sold to
persons for resale by them, or for processing and resale by them, to members of the general public
for their use or consumption;
(*b*) a trade of retail distribution is one in which the goods are offered for sale and sold to members
of the general public for their use or consumption;
(*c*) a trade is not an ordinary trade of wholesale or retail distribution if—

(i) it consists to a substantial extent of dealing in goods of a kind which are collected or held
as an investment or of that activity and any other activity of a kind falling within subsection
[(2)(*a*) to (*g*)][5] above, taken together; and
(ii) a substantial proportion of those goods are held by the company for a period which is
significantly longer than the period for which a vendor would reasonably be expected to hold
them while endeavouring to dispose of them at their market value; and

(*d*) in determining whether a trade is an ordinary trade of wholesale or retail distribution regard
shall be had to the extent to which it has the following features, that is to say—

(i) the goods are bought by the trader in quantities larger than those in which he sells them;
(ii) the goods are bought and sold by the trader in different markets;
(iii) the trader employs staff and incurs expenses in the trade in addition to the cost of the
goods and, in the case of a trade carried on by a company, in addition to any remuneration
paid to any person connected with it;
(iv) there are purchases or sales from or to persons who are connected with the trader;
(v) purchases are matched with forward sales or vice versa;
(vi) the goods are held by the trader for longer than is normal for goods of the kind in
question;
(vii) the trade is carried on otherwise than at a place or places commonly used for wholesale
or retail trade;
(viii) the trader does not take physical possession of the goods;

those features in sub-paragraphs (i) to (iii) being regarded as indications that the trade is such an
ordinary trade and those in sub-paragraphs (iv) to (viii) being regarded as indications of the
contrary.

TA 1988

[(3A) For the purposes of this Chapter the activities of a person shall not be taken to fall within paragraph (fd) or (fe) of subsection (2) above except where that person has an estate or interest in, or is in occupation of, the hotels or comparable establishments or, as the case may be, the nursing homes or residential care homes.][6]

[(4) A trade shall not be treated as failing to comply with this section by reason only that at some time in the relevant period it consists to a substantial extent in the receiving of royalties or licence fees if the royalties and licence fees (or all but for a part that is not a substantial part in terms of value) are attributable to the exploitation of relevant intangible assets.

(5) For this purpose an intangible asset is a "relevant intangible asset" if the whole or greater part (in terms of value) of it has been created—

    (a) by the company carrying on the trade, or
    (b) by a company which at all times during which it created the intangible asset was—

        (i) the parent company of the company carrying on the trade, or
        (ii) a qualifying subsidiary of that parent company.

(5A) For the purposes of subsection (5) above—

    (a) in the case of an intangible asset that is intellectual property, references to the creation of the asset by a company are to its creation in circumstances in which the right to exploit it vests in the company (whether alone or jointly with others);
    (b) "parent company" means a company that—

        (i) has one or more 51% subsidiaries, but
        (ii) is not itself a 51% subsidiary of another company; and

    (c) a subsidiary of the parent company referred to in subsection (5)(b) above is a "qualifying subsidiary" of that company if it is a subsidiary of a kind which the parent company may hold by virtue of section 308.

For the purposes of paragraph (c) above, section 308 shall have effect as if the references in that section to the qualifying company were to that parent company.

(5B) For the purposes of subsections (4) to (5A) above "intangible asset" means any asset which falls to be treated as an intangible asset in accordance with [generally accepted accounting practice][10].
...[11]

(5C) In subsection (5A)(a) above "intellectual property" means—

    (a) any patent, trade mark, registered design, copyright, design right, performer's right or plant breeder's right; and
    (b) any rights under the law of a country or territory outside the United Kingdom which correspond or are similar to those falling within paragraph (a) above.][8]

(6) A trade shall not be treated as failing to comply with this section by reason only of its consisting of letting ships, other than oil rigs or pleasure craft, on charter if—

    (a) every ship let on charter by the company carrying on the trade is beneficially owned by the company;
    (b) every ship beneficially owned by the company is registered in the United Kingdom; and
    (c) throughout the relevant period the company is solely responsible for arranging the marketing of the services of its ships; and
    (d) the conditions mentioned in subsection (7) below are satisfied in relation to every letting on charter by the company;

but where any of the requirements mentioned in paragraphs (a) to (d) above are not satisfied in relation to any lettings of such ships, the trade shall not thereby be treated as failing to comply with this section if those lettings and any other activity of a kind falling within subsection [(2)(a) to (g)][5] above do not, when taken together, amount to a substantial part of the trade.

(7) The conditions are that—

    (a) the letting is for a period not exceeding 12 months and no provision is made at any time (whether in the lease or otherwise) for extending it beyond that period otherwise than at the option of the lessee;
    (b) during the period of the letting there is no provision in force (whether made in the lease or otherwise) for the grant of a new letting to end, otherwise than at the option of the lessee, more than 12 months after that provision is made;
    (c) the letting is by way of a bargain made at arm's length between the company and a person who is not connected with it;
    (d) under the terms of the charter the company is responsible as principal—

        (i) for taking, throughout the period of the charter, management decisions in relation to the ship, other than those of a kind generally regarded by persons engaged in trade of the kind in question as matters of husbandry; and
        (ii) for defraying all expenses in connection with the ship throughout that period, or substantially all such expenses, other than those directly incidental to a particular voyage or to the employment of the ship during that period; and

(*e*) no arrangements exist by virtue of which a person other than the company may be appointed to be responsible for the matters mentioned in paragraph (*d*) above on behalf of the company;

but this subsection shall have effect, in relation to any letting between the company in question and its subsidiary, or between it and another company of which it is a subsidiary or between it and a company which is a subsidiary of the same company of which it is a subsidiary, as if paragraph (*c*) were omitted.

(8) The trade must, during the relevant period, be conducted on a commercial basis and with a view to the realisation of profits.

(9)...⁹.

Commentary—*Simon's Direct Tax Service* **E3.126.**

Note—For the text of this section as applicable to the Business Expansion Scheme which was abolished in relation to shares issued after 31 December 1993, see *Yellow Tax Handbook*, 1993–94, 32nd edition.

Revenue Internal Guidance—Inspector's manual IM 6582 (sub-s (2)(*a*) "commodities" is restricted to things dealt in on a commodities market; purchase of commodity in market for use in manufacturing trade is not disqualified).

IM 6584 (sub-s (2) "substantial" is judged by any reasonable measure eg turnover or capital employed; if excluded activities account for less than 20 per cent of total, that is not substantial).

IM 6585 (sub-s (3) no objection taken where type of goods is such that only a small and specialised group of people likely to buy or use them).

IM 6587 (sub-s (4) production includes development stages, eg preparation of screenplay, budgets, engagement of actors etc and arrangements for distribution).

Definitions—See at the beginning of this Chapter.

Simon's Tax Cases—s 297(2)(*f*), *Castleton Management Services Ltd v Kirkwood (Inspector of Taxes)* [2001] STC 95.

Cross references—See TA 1988 s 290A(6), (7) (£5 million EIS finance limit for ship chartering company).

TA 1988 s 298 (meaning of "controlling interest" and "trade" for the purposes of this section).

TA 1988 s 307(6)–(8A) (withdrawal or reduction of relief with consequent tax assessment; interest on tax).

TA 1988 s 310 (inspector to be informed if relief given is not due).

Revenue Interpretation RI 120—Consideration of kinds of "non-qualifying activities" under sub-s (2)(*e*)—leasing, receiving royalties and receiving licence fees.

Amendments—¹ Words omitted from sub-s (1) repealed by FA 1994 Sch 15 para 10, Sch 26, Pt V(17) in relation to EIS shares issued after 31 December 1993 with effect from the year 1993–94.

² Words in sub-ss (2)(*a*), (5) substituted by FA 1994 s 137(1), (2) and Sch 15 para 10 in relation to shares issued after 31 December 1993 with effect from the year 1993–94.

³ Words in sub-s (2)(*g*) inserted by FA 1994 s 137(1), (2) and Sch 15 para 10 in relation to shares issued after 31 December 1993 with effect from the year 1993–94.

⁴ Sub-s (2)(*h*), (*j*) repealed by FA 1994 s 137(1), (2) and Sch 15 para 10 and Sch 26 Pt V(17) in relation to EIS shares issued after 31 December 1993.

⁵ Words in sub-ss (3)(*c*)(i), (6) substituted by FA 1997 Sch 8 para 5 with effect in accordance with Sch 8 para 1.

⁶ Sub-ss (2)(*fa*)–(*fe*), (3A) inserted, and word substituted in sub-s (2)(*g*) by FA 1998 Sch 12 para 1 with effect in relation to shares issued after 16 March 1998.

⁷ Words in sub-s (1) repealed by FA 1998 Sch 13 para 10 with effect in relation to shares issued after 5 April 1998.

⁸ Sub-ss (4)–(5C) substituted for original sub-ss (4), (5) by FA 2000 s 64, Sch 17 para 13 with effect for shares issued after 5 April 2000. Sub-ss (4), (5) previously read—

"(4) A trade shall not be treated as failing to comply with this section by reason only of its consisting to a substantial extent of receiving royalties or licence fees if—

(*a*) the company carrying on the trade is engaged throughout the relevant period in—

(i) the production of films; or

(ii) the production of films and the distribution of films produced by it in the relevant period; and

(*b*) all royalties and licence fees received by it in that period are in respect of films produced by it in that period or sound recordings in relation to such films or other products arising from such films.

(5) A trade shall not be treated as failing to comply with this section by reason only that it consists to a substantial extent of receiving royalties or licence fees if—

(*a*) the company carrying on the trade is engaged in research and development throughout the relevant period; and

(*b*) all royalties and licence fees received by it in that period are attributable to research and development which it has carried out."

⁹ Sub-ss (2)(*d*), (9) repealed by FA 2001 ss 63, 110, Sch 15 paras 5, 40, Sch 33 Pt II(3) with effect—

(*a*) in relation to shares issued after 6 March 2001, and

(*b*) in respect of the application of TA 1988 Pt VII Chapter III and TCGA 1992 Sch 5B after 6 March 2001 in relation to shares—

(i) that were issued after 31 December 1993 but before 7 March 2001, and

(ii) to which income tax relief or deferral relief was attributable immediately before 7 March 2001.

Sub-s (2)(*d*) previously read—

"(*d*) oil extraction activities;"

Sub-s (9) previously read—

"(9) A trade which consists to any substantial extent of oil extraction activities shall, if it would be a qualifying trade were it not for subsection (2)(*d*) above, be treated as a qualifying trade for the purposes of section 289(2)(*c*)."

¹⁰ In sub-s (5B), words substituted for the words "normal accounting practice" by FA 2002 s 103(4)(*a*) with effect from 24 July 2002.

¹¹ Words in sub-s (5B) repealed by FA 2002 s 141, Sch 40 Pt 3(16) with effect from 24 July 2002. Words previously read thus—

"For this purpose "normal accounting practice" means normal accounting practice in relation to the accounts of companies incorporated in any part of the United Kingdom.".

298 Provisions supplementary to sections 293 and 297

(1) For the purposes of [section 297]⁶ a person has a controlling interest in a trade—

(*a*) in the case of a trade carried on by a company, if—

(i) he controls the company;

(ii) the company is a close company and he or an associate of his is a director of the company and the beneficial owner of, or able directly or through the medium of other companies or by any other indirect means to control, more than 30 per cent of the ordinary share capital of the company; or

(iii) not less than half of the trade could in accordance with section 344(2) be regarded as belonging to him;

(b) in any other case, if he is entitled to not less than half of the assets used for, or the income arising from, the trade.

(2) For the purposes of subsection (1) above, there shall be attributed to any person any rights or powers of any other person who is an associate of his.

(3) References in this section and section 297 to a trade shall be construed without regard to so much of the definition of "trade" in section 832(1) as relates to adventures or concerns in the nature of trade; but the foregoing provisions do not affect the construction of references in section 297(2)(g) or subsection (1) above to a trade carried on by a person other than the company and those references shall be construed as including a reference to any business, profession or vocation.

[(4) The Treasury may by order amend [sections 293 and 297][4] and this section in such manner as they consider expedient.][1]

(5) In section 297—

"film" means an original master negative of a film, an original master film disc or an original master film tape;

["nursing home" means any establishment which exists wholly or mainly for the provision of nursing care for persons suffering from sickness, injury or infirmity or for women who are pregnant or have given birth to children;][5]

"oil rig" means any ship which is an offshore installation for the purposes of the Mineral Workings (Offshore Installations) Act 1971;

"pleasure craft" means any ship of a kind primarily used for sport or recreation;

["property development" means the development of land—

(a) by a company which has, or at any time has had, an interest in the land, and

(b) with the sole or main object of realising a gain from the disposal of an interest in the land when it is developed;

"residential care home" means any establishment which exists wholly or mainly for the provision of residential accommodation, together with board and personal care, for persons in need of personal care by reason of old age, mental or physical disabilities, past or present dependence on alcohol or drugs or any past illnesses or past or present mental disorders;][5]

...[3]; and

"sound recording" means, in relation to a film, its sound track, original master audio disc or, as the case may be, original master audio tape;

[and section 312(1A)(b) shall apply to determine the relevant period for the purposes of that section][2].

[(5A) References in this section, in relation to an hotel, to a comparable establishment are references to a guest house, hostel or other establishment the main purpose of maintaining which is the provision of facilities for overnight accommodation (whether with or without catering services).

(5B) Subject to subsection (5C) below, the reference in subsection (5) above to an interest in land is a reference to—

(a) any estate, interest or right in or over land, including any right affecting the use or disposition of land; or

(b) any right to obtain such an estate, interest or right from another which is conditional on the other's ability to grant the estate, interest or right.

(5C) References in this section to an interest in land do not include references to—

(a) the interest of a creditor (other than a creditor in respect of a rentcharge) whose debt is secured by way of mortgage, an agreement for a mortgage or a charge of any kind over land; or

(b) in the case of land in Scotland, the interest of a creditor in a charge or security of any kind over land.][5]

(6)–(8) ...[3]

Commentary—*Simon's Direct Tax Service* **E3.126.**
Note—For the text of this section as applicable to the Business Expansion Scheme which was abolished in relation to shares issued after 31 December 1993, see *Yellow Tax Handbook*, 1993–94, 32nd edition.
Revenue Internal Guidance—Inspector's manual IM 6580 (sub-s (3) trade includes farming and market gardening, quarries and gravel pits, commercial letting of furnished holiday accommodation).
Definitions—See at the beginning of this Chapter.
Amendments—[1] Sub-s (4) substituted by FA 1994 Sch 15 para 11.
[2] Words in sub-s (5) inserted by FA 1994 Sch 15 para 11.
[3] Sub-ss (6)–(8) and the definition of "property development" in sub-s (5) repealed by FA 1994 Sch 15 para 11 and Sch 26, Pt V(17) in relation to EIS shares issued after 31 December 1993 with effect from the year 1993–94.
[4] Words substituted in sub-s (4) by FA 1998 s 70(2) with effect in relation to shares issued on or after 17 March 1998.
[5] Definitions in sub-s (5), and sub-ss (5A)–(5C) inserted by FA 1998 Sch 12 para 2 with effect in relation to shares issued on or after 17 March 1998.
[6] Words substituted in sub-s (1) by FA 1998 Sch 13 para 11 with effect in relation to shares issued on or after 6 April 1998.

[299 Disposal of shares

(1) [Subject to section 304(1), where an individual makes, before the end of the relevant period, any disposal of eligible shares to which relief is attributable][2], then—

    (*a*) if the disposal is made otherwise than by way of a bargain made at arm's length, [the relief][2] attributable to those shares shall be withdrawn, and

    (*b*) in the case of any disposal made by way of a bargain made at arm's length—

        (i) if, apart from this subsection, the relief attributable to those shares is greater than the amount mentioned in subsection (2) below, it shall be reduced by that amount, and

        (ii) if sub-paragraph (i) above does not apply, [the relief][2] attributable to those shares shall be withdrawn.

(2) The amount referred to in subsection (1) above is an amount equal to tax at the lower rate for the year of assessment for which the relief was given on the amount or value of the consideration which the individual receives for the shares.

(3) Where, in relation to [any issue of eligible shares held by any individual][3], the disposal referred to in subsection (1) above is a disposal of part of [the issue][3], that subsection shall apply to the relief that was attributable to that part.

(4) Where an individual's liability to income tax has been reduced in any year of assessment under section 289A in respect of any issue of [eligible][2] shares [issued in that year (or treated by section 289B(5) as so issued][3] and the amount of the reduction (''A'') is less than the amount (''B'') which is equal to tax at the lower rate for that year on the amount subscribed for the issue, subsection (2) above shall have effect as if the amount or value referred to in that subsection were reduced by multiplying it by the fraction—

$$\frac{A}{B}$$

(5) Where an option, the exercise of which would bind the grantor to purchase any shares, is granted to an individual during the relevant period, any relief attributable to the shares to which the option relates shall be withdrawn.

[(5A) The shares to which such an option relates shall be taken to be those which, if—

    (*a*) the option were exercised immediately after the grant; and

    (*b*) any shares in the company acquired by the individual after the grant were disposed of immediately after being acquired,

would be treated for the purposes of this section as disposed of in pursuance of the option.][3]

[(6) Where shares of any class in a company have been acquired by an individual on different days, any disposal by him of shares of that class shall be treated for the purposes of this section as relating to those acquired on an earlier day rather than to those acquired on a later day.

(6A) Where shares of any class in a company have been acquired by an individual on the same day, any of those shares disposed of by him shall be treated for the purposes of this section as disposed of in the following order, namely—

    (*a*) first any to which neither relief under this Chapter nor deferral relief is attributable;

    (*b*) next any to which deferral relief, but not relief under this Chapter, is attributable;

    (*c*) next any to which relief under this Chapter, but not deferral relief, is attributable; and

    (*d*) finally any to which both relief under this Chapter and deferral relief are attributable;

and in this subsection and subsection (6C) below ''deferral relief'' has the same meaning as in Schedule 5B to the 1992 Act.

(6B) Any shares falling within paragraph (*c*) or (*d*) of subsection (6A) above which are treated by section 289B(5) as issued on an earlier day shall be treated as disposed of before any other shares falling within that paragraph.

(6C) The following, namely—

    (*a*) any shares to which relief under this Chapter is attributable and which were transferred to an individual as mentioned in section 304; and

    (*b*) any shares to which deferral relief, but not relief under this Chapter, is attributable and which were acquired by an individual on a disposal to which section 58 of the 1992 Act applies,

shall be treated for the purposes of subsections (6) and (6A) above as acquired by him on the day on which they were issued.

(6D) In a case to which section 127 of the 1992 Act applies [(including a case where that section applies by virtue of any enactment relating to chargeable gains)][5], shares comprised in the new holding shall be treated for the purposes of subsections (6) and (6A) above as acquired when the original shares were acquired.

In this subsection ''new holding'' and ''original shares'' [have the same meaning as in section 127 of the 1992 Act (or, as the case may be, that section as applied by virtue of the enactment concerned)][5]][2]

(7) ...[2]

(8) For the purposes of this section—

(*a*) ...[3]

(*b*) references to a disposal of shares include references to the grant of an option the exercise of which would bind the grantor to sell the shares, and

(*c*) section 312(1A)(*a*) applies to determine the relevant period.][1]

Commentary—*Simon's Direct Tax Service* **E3.146.**
Note—For the text of this section as applicable to the Business Expansion Scheme which was abolished in relation to shares issued after 31 December 1993, see *Yellow Tax Handbook*, 1993–94, 32nd edition.
Definitions—See at the beginning of this Chapter.
Cross references—See TA 1988 s 304 (disposal of shares between spouses not subject to sub-s (1) above).
TA 1988 s 307(4) (withdrawal or reduction of relief in respect of disposals falling under sub-s (1)(*b*) above; no assessment to tax to be made for subsequent event unless it occurs when the individual is connected with the company).
TA 1988 s 307(6)–(8A) (withdrawal or reduction of relief with consequent tax assessment; interest on tax).
TA 1988 s 310 (inspector to be informed if relief given is not due).
Amendments—[1] This section substituted by FA 1994 s 137(1), (2) and Sch 15 para 12 in relation to shares issued after 31 December 1993 with effect from the year 1993–94.
[2] Words in sub-s (1), substituted, words in sub-s (4) inserted, sub-ss (6), (6A)–(6D) substituted, and sub-s (7) repealed by FA 1998 Sch 13 para 12 with effect in relation to disposals made after 5 April 1998.
[3] Words in sub-s (3) substituted and in sub-s (4) inserted, sub-s (8)(*a*) repealed by FA 1998 Sch 13 para 12 with effect in relation to shares issued after 5 April 1998.
[4] Sub-s (5A) inserted by FA 1998 Sch 13 para 12 with effect in relation to options granted on or after 6 April 1998.
[5] Words substituted in sub-s (6D), as that section applies to shares issued after 31 December 1993, by FA 2002 s 45, Sch 9 paras 4(1), (2), 7, 8 with effect for disposals after 16 April 2002. Sub-s (6D) previously read as follows—

"(6D) In a case to which section 127 of the 1992 Act applies (whether or not by virtue of section 135(3) of that Act), shares comprised in the new holding shall be treated for the purposes of subsections (6) and (6A) above as acquired when the original shares were acquired.

In this subsection "new holding" and "original shares" shall be construed in accordance with sections 126, 127, 135 and 136 of the 1992 Act.".

[299A Loan linked investments

(1) [An individual is not eligible for relief in respect of any shares in a company if][2]—

(*a*) there is a loan made by any person, at any time in the relevant period, to that individual or any associate of his; and

(*b*) the loan is one which would not have been made, or would not have been made on the same terms, if that individual had not subscribed for those shares or had not been proposing to do so.

(2) References in this section to the making by any person of a loan to any individual or an associate of his include references—

(*a*) to the giving by that person of any credit to that individual or any associate of his; and

(*b*) to the assignment or assignation to that person of any debt due from that individual or any associate of his;

and the references in section 307(6)(*ca*) to the making of a loan shall be construed accordingly.][1]

[(3) Section 312(1A)(*a*) applies to determine the relevant period for the purposes of this section.][2]

Commentary—*Simon's Direct Tax Service* **E3.149.**
Note—For the text of this section as applicable to the Business Expansion Scheme which was abolished in relation to shares issued after 31 December 1993, see *Yellow Tax Handbook*, 1993–94, 32nd edition.
Statements of practice P 3/94—For holdings of shares issued before 6 April 1998, loans made to acquire shares and available to other borrowers on the same terms do not necessarily preclude relief, but "eligible shares" or, associated rights specified as security for the loan would.
SP 6/98—For holdings of shares issued after 5 April 1998, loans made to acquire shares do not necessarily preclude relief; the test is whether the lender makes the loan on terms which are influenced by the fact that the borrower, or an associate of the borrower, has acquired, or is proposing to acquire, the shares.
Revenue Internal Guidance—Inspector's manual IM 6542 (this section applies where loan is given on security of shares or where repayment date is to date of disposal of shares).
Simon's Tax Cases—*National Westminster Bank plc v IRC* [1994] STC 580.
Definitions—See at the beginning of this Chapter.
Cross references—See TA 1988 s 307(*ca*) (reckonable date for interest on overdue tax where relief is withdrawn by virtue of this section).
TA 1988 s 310 (inspector to be informed if relief given is not due).
Amendments—[1] This section (ie sub-ss (1), (2)) inserted by FA 1993 s 111(1), (4) with effect where claim for relief is made after 15 March 1993.
[2] Words in sub-s (1) substituted and sub-s (3) inserted by FA 1994 s 137(1), (2), Sch 15 para 13 in relation to EIS shares issued after 31 December 1993 with effect from the year 1993–94.

[299B Pre-arranged exits

(1) An individual is not eligible for relief in respect of any shares in a company if the relevant arrangements include—

(*a*) arrangements with a view to the subsequent repurchase, exchange or other disposal of those shares or of other shares in or securities of the same company;

(*b*) arrangements for or with a view to the cessation of any trade which is being or is to be or may be carried on by the company or a person connected with the company;

(*c*) arrangements for the disposal of, or of a substantial amount of, the assets of the company or of a person connected with the company;

(*d*) arrangements the main purpose of which, or one of the main purposes of which, is (by means of any insurance, indemnity or guarantee or otherwise) to provide partial or complete protection for persons investing in shares in that company against what would otherwise be the risks attached to making the investment.

(2) The arrangements referred to in subsection (1)(*a*) above do not include any arrangements with a view to such an exchange of shares, or shares and securities, as is mentioned in section 304A(1).

(3) The arrangements referred to in subsection (1)(*b*) and (*c*) above do not include any arrangements applicable only on the winding up of a company except in a case where—

(*a*) the relevant arrangements include arrangements for the company to be wound up; or
(*b*) the company is wound up otherwise than for bona fide commercial reasons.

(4) The arrangements referred to in subsection (1)(*d*) above do not include any arrangements which are confined to the provision—

(*a*) for the company itself, or
(*b*) in the case of a company which is a parent company of a trading group, for the company itself, for the company itself and one or more of its subsidiaries or for one or more of its subsidiaries,

of any such protection against the risks arising in the course of carrying on its business as it might reasonably be expected so to provide in normal commercial circumstances.

(5) The reference in subsection (4) above to the parent company of a trading group shall be construed in accordance with the provision contained for the purposes of section 293 in that section.

(6) In this section "the relevant arrangements" means—

(*a*) the arrangements under which the shares are issued to the individual; and
(*b*) any arrangements made before the issue of the shares to him in relation to or in connection with that issue.

(7) *In this section "arrangements" includes any scheme, agreement or understanding, whether or not legally enforceable.*[2]]

Commentary—*Simon's Direct Tax Service* **E3.141.**
Definitions—See at the beginning of this Chapter.
Amendments—[1] This section inserted by FA 1998 s 71(1) with effect in relation to shares issued after 1 July 1997.
[2] Sub-s (7) repealed by FA 2000 s 156, Sch 40 Pt II(5) with effect—

(*a*) in relation to shares issued after 20 March 2000, and
(*b*) in respect of the application of TA 1988 s 312 after that date in relation to shares—
　(i) that were issued after 31 December 1993 but before 21 March 2000, and
　(ii) to which income tax relief or deferral relief was attributable immediately before 21 March 2000.

300 Value received from company

[(1) Subsection (1A) below applies where an individual who subscribes for eligible shares in a company receives any value [(other than insignificant value)][5] from the company at any time in the [period of restriction][5].][2]

[(1A) Where any relief is attributable to those shares, then (unless the amount of the relief has already been reduced on account of the value received)—

(*a*) if it is greater than the amount mentioned in subsection (1B) below, it shall be reduced by that amount, and
(*b*) if paragraph (*a*) above does not apply, the relief shall be withdrawn.][1]

[(1AA) This section is subject to section 300A.][5]

[(1B) The amount referred to in subsection (1A) above is an amount equal to tax at the lower rate for the year of assessment for which the relief was given on the amount of the value received; and section 299(4) above applies for the purposes of this subsection as it applies for the purposes of subsection (2) of that section.][1]

[(1BA) Where—

(*a*) an individual subscribes for two or more issues of eligible shares in a company, being issues comprising shares in respect of which the individual obtains relief, and
(*b*) the individual receives any value from the company at any time in the periods of restriction relating to the shares comprised in two or more of those issues,

this section has effect in relation to the shares comprised in each of the issues referred to in paragraph (*b*) above as if the amount of the value received were reduced by multiplying it by the fraction specified in subsection (1BB) below.][5]

[(1BB) The fraction is—

$$\frac{A}{B}$$

where—

A is the amount subscribed by the individual for the eligible shares comprised in the issue in question, and
B is the aggregate of that amount and the corresponding amount or amounts for eligible shares comprised in the other issue or issues.][5]

[(1BC) Where—

(*a*) an individual who subscribes for eligible shares in a company receives value (''the relevant receipt'') from the company during the period of restriction,

(*b*) the individual has received from the company one or more receipts of insignificant value at a time or times—

(i) during that period, but

(ii) not later than the time of the relevant receipt, and

(*c*) the aggregate amount of the value of the receipts within paragraphs (*a*) and (*b*) above is not an amount of insignificant value,

the individual shall be treated for the purposes of this Chapter as if the relevant receipt had been a receipt of an amount of value equal to the aggregate amount.

For this purpose a receipt does not fall within paragraph (*b*) above if it has previously been aggregated under this subsection.]⁵

[(1C) [Any reference in subsection (1), (1BA) or (1BC) above to the receipt of value (however expressed) from a company includes a reference]⁵ to the receipt of value from a person who at any time in the relevant period is connected with the company, whether or not he is so connected at the time when the individual concerned receives the value from him; and other references to the company in this section and section 301 shall be read accordingly.]²

[(1D) Notwithstanding anything in subsection (2) below, for the purposes of this section an individual is not to be treated as receiving value from a company by reason only of the payment to him, or any associate of his, of any remuneration for services rendered to the company as a director if the remuneration is reasonable remuneration.]¹

[(1E) Section 291(4) applies for the purposes of subsection (1D) above as it applies for the purposes of section 291A, and the reference in subsection (1D) above to the payment of remuneration includes the provision of any benefit or facility.]¹

(2) For the purposes of this section an individual receives value from the company if the company—

(*a*) repays, redeems or repurchases any of its share capital or securities which belong to the individual or makes any payment to him for giving up his right to any of the company's share capital or any security on its cancellation or extinguishment;

(*b*) repays any debt owed to the individual other than a debt which was incurred by the company—

(i) on or after the date on which he subscribed for the shares in respect of which the relief is claimed; and

(ii) otherwise than in consideration of the extinguishment of a debt incurred before that date;

(*c*) makes to the individual any payment for giving up his right to any debt (other than a debt in respect of a payment of the kind mentioned in section [291A(3)(*a*) or (*f*)]¹ or an ordinary trade debt) on its extinguishment;

(*d*) releases or waives any liability of the individual to the company or discharges, or undertakes to discharge, any liability of his to a third person;

(*e*) makes a loan or advance to the individual which has not been repaid in full before the issue of the shares in respect of which relief is claimed;

(*f*) provides a benefit or facility for the individual;

(*g*) transfers an asset to the individual for no consideration or for consideration less than its market value or acquires an asset from him for consideration exceeding its market value; or

(*h*) makes to him any other payment except a payment of the kind mentioned in [any of the paragraphs of section 291A(3)]¹ or a payment in discharge of an ordinary trade debt.

(3) For the purposes of this section an individual also receives value from the company if he receives in respect of ordinary shares held by him any payment or asset in a winding up or in connection with a dissolution of the company, being a winding up or dissolution falling within section 293(6).

(4) The value received by an individual is—

(*a*) in a case within paragraph (*a*), (*b*) or (*c*) of subsection (2) above, the amount [received]⁵ by the individual or, if greater, the market value of the shares, securities or debt in question;

(*b*) in a case within paragraph (*d*) of that subsection, the amount of the liability;

(*c*) in a case within paragraph (*e*) of that subsection, the amount of the loan or advance reduced by the amount of any repayment made before the issue of the shares in respect of which relief is claimed;

(*d*) in a case within paragraph (*f*) of that subsection, the cost to the company of providing the benefit or facility less any consideration given for it by the individual;

(*e*) in a case within paragraph (*g*) of that subsection, the difference between the market value of the asset and the consideration (if any) given for it;

(*f*) in a case within paragraph (*h*) of that subsection, the amount of the payment; and

(*g*) in a case within subsection (3) above, the amount of the payment or, as the case may be, the market value of the asset.

(5) For the purposes of this section an individual also receives value from the company if any person who would, for the purposes of section 291, be treated as connected with the company—

(*a*) purchases any of its share capital or securities which belong to the individual; or (*b*) makes any payment to him for giving up any right in relation to any of the company's share capital or securities;

and the value received by the individual is the amount [received][5] by the individual or, if greater, the market value of the shares or securities in question.

[(6) Where by reason of an individual's disposal of shares in a company any relief attributable to those shares is withdrawn or reduced under section 299, the individual shall not be treated for the purposes of this section as receiving value from the company in respect of the disposal.][3]

Commentary—*Simon's Direct Tax Service* **E3.147.**
Note—For the text of this section as applicable to the Business Expansion Scheme which was abolished in relation to shares issued after 31 December 1993, see *Yellow Tax Handbook*, 1993–94, 32nd edition.
Revenue Internal Guidance—Inspector's manual IM 6611 (sub-s (5) operates whether the sale of shares precedes or follows the subscription of the shares).
Revenue Internal Guidance—Inspector's Manual IM7029 (example illustrating operation of sub-s (5)).
Definitions—See at the beginning of this Chapter.
Cross references—See TA 1988 s 301 (supplementary provisions).
TA 1988 s 307(6)–(8A) (withdrawal or reduction of relief with consequent tax assessment; interest on tax).
TA 1988 s 310(1), (2), (7) (inspector to be informed if relief given is not due).
TCGA 1992 s 150B(1) (enterprise investment scheme: reduction of relief by amount of value received under sub-s (1A)(*a*) above).
Amendments—[1] Sub-ss (1), (1A)–(1E) substituted for sub-s (1) and words in sub-s (2)(*c*), (*h*) substituted by FA 1994 s 137(1), (2), Sch 15 para 14 in relation to EIS shares issued after 31 December 1993 with effect from the year 1993–94.
[2] Sub-ss (1), (1C) substituted by FA 1998 Sch 13 para 13 with effect in relation to shares issued on or after 6 April 1998.
[3] Sub-s (6) inserted by FA 1998 Sch 13 para 13 with effect in relation to disposals made on or after 6 April 1998.
[4] Words in sub-s (1) substituted for words "seven year" by FA 2000 s 64, Sch 17 para 4 with effect for shares issued after 5 April 2000.
[5] Words in sub-s (1) inserted, words substituted for the words "designated period", sub-s (1AA), (1BA)–(1BC) inserted, words in sub-s (1C) substituted for the words "References in subsection (1) above to the receipt of value from a company include references", and in sub-ss (4), (5), the word "received" substituted for "receivable", by FA 2001 s 63, Sch 15 paras 15, 40 with effect—

(*a*) in relation to shares issued after 6 March 2001, and
(*b*) in relation to shares issued before that date, in respect of the application of TA 1988 Pt VII Chapter III and TCGA 1992 Sch 5B in relation to—
(i) value received (within the meaning of TA 1988 s 300 or TCGA 1992 Sch 5B para 13 of Schedule 5B), and
(ii) repayments made,
on or after that date.

[300A Receipt of replacement value

(1) Where—

(*a*) any relief attributable to any eligible shares comprised in an issue of shares subscribed for by an individual ("the individual") would, in the absence of this section, be reduced or withdrawn under section 300 by reason of a receipt of value within subsection (2) or (5) of that section ("the original value"),
(*b*) the original supplier receives value ("the replacement value") from the original recipient by virtue of a qualifying receipt, and
(*c*) the amount of the replacement value is not less than the amount of the original value,

the receipt of the original value shall be disregarded for the purposes of section 300.

This is subject to subsections (7) and (8) below.

(2) For the purposes of this section—

"the original recipient" means the person who receives the original value, and
"the original supplier" means the person from whom that value was received.

(3) Where the amount of the original value is, by virtue of subsection (1BA) of section 300, treated as reduced for the purposes of that section as it applies in relation to the eligible shares in question, the reference in subsection (1)(*c*) above to the amount of the original value shall be read as a reference to the amount of that value disregarding the reduction.

(4) A receipt of the replacement value is a qualifying receipt for the purposes of subsection (1) above if it arises—

(*a*) by reason of the original recipient doing one or more of the following—

(i) making a payment to the original supplier, other than a payment which falls within paragraph (*c*) below or to which subsection (5) below applies;
(ii) acquiring any asset from the original supplier for a consideration the amount or value of which is more than the market value of the asset;
(iii) disposing of any asset to the original supplier for no consideration or for a consideration the amount or value of which is less than the market value of the asset;

(*b*) where the receipt of the original value was within section 300(2)(*d*), by reason of an event the effect of which is to reverse the event which constituted the receipt of the original value; or
(*c*) where the receipt of the original value was within section 300(5), by reason of the original recipient repurchasing the share capital or securities in question, or (as the case may be) reacquiring the right in question, for a consideration the amount or value of which is not less than the amount of the original value.

(5) This subsection applies to—

(*a*) any payment for any goods, services or facilities, provided (whether in the course of a trade or otherwise) by—

    (i) the original supplier, or

    (ii) any other person who, at any time in the period of restriction, is an associate of, or connected with, that supplier (whether or not he is such an associate, or so connected, at the material time),

which is reasonable in relation to the market value of those goods, services or facilities;

(*b*) any payment of any interest which represents no more than a reasonable commercial return on money lent to—

    (i) the original recipient, or

    (ii) any person who, at any time in the period of restriction, is an associate of his (whether or not he is such an associate at the material time);

(*c*) any payment for the acquisition of an asset which does not exceed its market value;

(*d*) any payment, as rent for any property occupied by—

    (i) the original recipient, or

    (ii) any person who, at any time in the period of restriction, is an associate of his (whether or not he is such an associate at the material time),

of an amount not exceeding a reasonable and commercial rent for the property;

(*e*) any payment in discharge of an ordinary trade debt; and

(*f*) any payment for shares in or securities of any company in circumstances that do not fall within subsection (4)(*a*)(ii) above.

(6) For the purposes of this section, the amount of the replacement value is—

(*a*) in a case within paragraph (*a*) of subsection (4) above, the aggregate of—

    (i) the amount of any payment within sub-paragraph (i) of that paragraph, and

    (ii) the difference between the market value of any asset to which sub-paragraph (ii) or (iii) of that paragraph applies and the amount or value of the consideration (if any) received for it,

(*b*) in a case within subsection (4)(*b*) above, the same as the amount of the original value, and

(*c*) in a case within subsection (4)(*c*) above, the amount or value of the consideration received by the original supplier,

and section 300(4) and (5) shall apply for the purposes of determining the amount of the original value.

(7) The receipt of the replacement value by the original supplier shall be disregarded for the purposes of this section, as it applies in relation to the eligible shares, to the extent to which that receipt has previously been set (under this section) against any receipts of value which are, in consequence, disregarded for the purposes of section 300 as that section applies in relation to those shares or any other shares subscribed for by the individual.

(8) The receipt of the replacement value by the original supplier ("the event") shall be disregarded for the purposes of this section if—

(*a*) the event occurs before the start of the period of restriction, or

(*b*) in a case where the event occurs after the time the original recipient receives the original value, it does not occur as soon after that time as is reasonably practicable in the circumstances, or

(*c*) where an appeal has been brought by the individual against an assessment to withdraw or reduce any relief attributable to the eligible shares by reason of the receipt of the original value, the event occurs more than 60 days after the amount of relief which falls to be withdrawn has been finally determined.

But nothing in this section requires the replacement value to be received after the original value.

(9) Subsection (10) below applies where—

(*a*) the receipt of the replacement value by the original supplier is a qualifying receipt (for the purposes of subsection (1) above) in consequence of which any receipts of value are disregarded for the purposes of section 300 as that section applies in relation to the shares in question or any other shares subscribed for by the individual in question, and

(*b*) the event which gives rise to the receipt is (or includes) a subscription for shares by—

    (i) the individual, or

    (ii) any person who, at any time in the period of restriction, is an associate of his, whether or not he is such an associate at the material time.

(10) Where this subsection applies, the person who subscribes for the shares as mentioned in subsection (9)(*b*) above shall not—

(*a*) be eligible for any relief under this Chapter in relation to those shares or any other shares in the same issue, or

(*b*) by virtue of his subscription for those shares or any other shares in the same issue, be treated as making a qualifying investment for the purposes of Schedule 5B to the 1992 Act (enterprise investment scheme: reinvestment).

(11) In this section—

(*a*) any reference to a payment to a person (however expressed) includes a reference to a payment made to him indirectly or to his order or for his benefit, and

(*b*) references to "the period of restriction" are to the period of restriction relating to the shares mentioned in subsection (1)(*a*) above.]¹

Commentary—*Simon's Direct Tax Service* **E3.147A**.
Amendments—¹ This section inserted by FA 2001 s 63, Sch 15 paras 16, 40 with effect—
(*a*) in relation to shares issued after 6 March 2001, and
(*b*) in relation to shares issued before that date, in respect of the application of TA 1988 Pt VII Chapter III and TCGA 1992 Sch 5B in relation to—
    (i) value received (within the meaning of TA 1988 s 300 or TCGA 1992 Sch 5B para 13 of Schedule 5B), and
    (ii) repayments made,
on or after that date.

301 Provisions supplementary to section 300

(1), (2) ...¹

(3) For the purposes of section 300(2)(*d*) a company shall be treated as having released or waived a liability if the liability is not discharged within 12 months of the time when it ought to have been discharged.

(4) For the purposes of section 300(2)(*e*) there shall be treated as if it were a loan made by the company to the individual—

(*a*) the amount of any debt (other than an ordinary trade debt) incurred by the individual to the company; and

(*b*) the amount of any debt due from the individual to a third person which has been assigned to the company.

[(4A) For the purposes of this section and [sections 300 and 300A]⁴, an individual who acquires any eligible shares on such a transfer as is mentioned in section 304 shall be treated as if he subscribed for those shares.]²

(5) In this section and [sections 300 and 300A]⁴, "an ordinary trade debt" means any debt for goods or services supplied in the ordinary course of a trade or business where [any credit]³ given does not exceed six months and is not longer than that normally given to the customers of the person carrying on the trade or business.

(6) In this section and section 300—

(*a*) any reference to a payment or transfer to an individual includes a reference to a payment or transfer made to him indirectly or to his order or for his benefit; and

(*b*) any reference to an individual includes a reference to an associate of his and any reference to the company includes a reference to any person connected with the company.

[(6A) Section 312(1A)(*a*) applies to determine the relevant period for the purposes of section 300.]¹

(7) ...¹

Commentary—*Simon's Direct Tax Service* **E3.132**.
Note—For the text of this section as applicable to the Business Expansion Scheme which was abolished in relation to shares issued after 31 December 1993, see *Yellow Tax Handbook*, 1993–94, 32nd edition.
Revenue Internal Guidance—Inspector's Manual IM7026 (example illustrating operation of sub-s (6)).
Definitions—See at the beginning of this Chapter.
Cross references—See TA 1988 s 300(1C) (references to receipt of value from a company to include receipt of value from a 51 per cent subsidiary).
TA 1988 s 310(7) (inspector to be informed when value for eligible shares is received from the issuing company by the shareholder).
Amendments—¹ Sub-s (6A) inserted and sub-ss (1), (2), (7) repealed by FA 1994 s 137(1), (2), Sch 15 para 15, Sch 26, Pt V(17) in relation to EIS shares issued after 31 December 1993 with effect from the year 1993–94.
² Sub-s (4A) inserted by FA 1998 Sch 13 para 14 with effect in relation to value received (within the meaning of TA 1988 s 300) on or after 6 April 1998.
³ Words in sub-s (5) substituted by FA 1998 Sch 13 para 14 with effect in relation to shares issued on or after 6 April 1998.
⁴ Words in sub-ss (4A), (5) substituted for the words "section 300" by FA 2001 s 63, Sch 15 paras 17, 40 with effect—
(*a*) in relation to shares issued after 6 March 2001, and
(*b*) in relation to shares issued before that date, in respect of the application of TA 1988 Pt VII Chapter III and TCGA 1992 Sch 5B in relation to—
    (i) value received (within the meaning of TA 1988 s 300 or TCGA 1992 Sch 5B para 13 of Schedule 5B), and
    (ii) repayments made,
on or after that date.

[301A Receipts of insignificant value: supplementary provision

(1) In this section and section 300 references to a receipt of insignificant value (however expressed) are references to a receipt of an amount of insignificant value.

This is subject to subsection (3) below.

(2) For the purposes of this section and section 300 "an amount of insignificant value" means an amount of value which—

(*a*) does not exceed £1,000, or

(*b*) if it exceeds that amount, is insignificant in relation to the amount subscribed by the individual in question for the eligible shares in question.

(3) For the purposes of section 300, if, at any time in the period—

(*a*) beginning one year before the eligible shares in question are issued, and

(*b*) expiring at the end of the issue date,

arrangements are in existence which provide for the individual in question to receive or to be entitled to receive, at any time in the period of restriction relating to those shares, any value from the company that issued those shares, no amount of value received by the individual shall be treated as a receipt of insignificant value.

(4) For the purposes of this section—

(*a*) references to the individual include references to any person who, at any time in the period of restriction relating to the shares in question, is an associate of his (whether or not he is such an associate at the material time), and

(*b*) the reference in subsection (3) above to the company includes a reference to any person who, at any time in the period of restriction relating to the shares in question, is connected with the company (whether or not that person is so connected at the material time).

(5) For the purposes of this section, an individual who acquires any eligible shares on such a transfer as is mentioned in section 304 shall be treated as if he subscribed for those shares.][1]

Commentary—*Simon's Direct Tax Service* **E3.147**.
Amendments—[1] This section inserted by FA 2001 s 63, Sch 15 paras 18, 49 with effect—

(*a*) in relation to shares issued after 6 March 2001, and
(*b*) in relation to shares issued before that date, in respect of the application of TA 1988 Pt VII Chapter III and TCGA 1992 Sch 5B in relation to—
  (i) value received (within the meaning of TA 1988 s 300 or TCGA 1992 Sch 5B para 13 of Schedule 5B), and
  (ii) repayments made,
on or after that date.

302 Replacement capital

[(1) Any relief attributable to any shares in a company held by an individual shall be withdrawn if—

(*a*) at any time in the relevant period, the company or any subsidiary—

  (i) begins to carry on as its trade or as part of its trade a trade which was previously carried on at any time in that period otherwise than by the company or any subsidiary, or
  (ii) acquires the whole, or a greater part, of the assets used for the purposes of a trade previously so carried on, and

(*b*) subsection (2) below applies in relation to that individual.][1]

(2) This subsection applies in relation to an individual where—

(*a*) any person or group of persons to whom an interest amounting in the aggregate to more than a half share in the trade (as previously carried on) belonged, at any time in the relevant period, is or are a person or group of persons to whom such an interest in the trade carried on by the company belongs or has, at any such time, belonged; or

(*b*) any person or group of persons who control or, at any such time, have controlled the company is or are a person or group of persons who, at any such time, controlled another company which previously carried on the trade;

and the individual is that person or one of those persons.

(3) [Any relief attributable to any shares in a company held by an individual shall be withdrawn if][1]—

(*a*) the company comes to acquire all of the issued share capital of another company, at any time in the relevant period; and

(*b*) any person or group of persons who control or have, at any such time, controlled the company is or are a person or group of persons who, at any such time, controlled that other company;

and that individual is that person or one of those persons.

(4) For the purposes of subsection (2) above—

(*a*) the persons to whom a trade belongs and, where a trade belongs to two or more persons, their respective shares in that trade shall be determined in accordance with section 344(1)(*a*) and (*b*), (2) and (3); and

(*b*) any interest, rights or powers of a person who is an associate of another person shall be treated as those of that other person.

[(4A) In determining whether any relief attributable to any shares in a company (the "issuing company") held by a person who—

(*a*) is a director of, or of a company which is a partner of, the issuing company or any subsidiary, and

(*b*) is in receipt of, or entitled to receive, remuneration as such a director falling within section 291A(5)(*a*),

is to be withdrawn, the second reference in paragraph (*b*) of each of subsections (2) and (3) above and, so far as relating to those paragraphs, in subsection (1)(*a*)(i) above to any time in the relevant period shall be read as a reference to any time before the end of the relevant period.

(4B) Section 291(4) applies for the purposes of subsection (4A) above as it applies for the purposes of section 291A, and in subsection (4A) above "remuneration" includes any benefit or facility.][1]

(5) In this section—

["subsidiary" means a company which would be a subsidiary if the relevant period for the purposes of section 308 were the period referred to in section 312(1A)(*a*)]¹; and

"trade" includes any business, profession or vocation, and references to a trade previously carried on include references to part of such a trade;

[and section 312(1A)(*a*) applies to determine the relevant period for the purposes of this section.]¹

Commentary—*Simon's Direct Tax Service* **E3.151.**
Note—For the text of this section as applicable to the Business Expansion Scheme which was abolished in relation to shares issued after 31 December 1993, see *Yellow Tax Handbook*, 1993–94, 32nd edition.
Definitions—See at the beginning of this Chapter.
Cross references—See TA 1988 s 307(6)–(8A) (withdrawal or reduction of relief with consequent tax assessment; interest on tax).
TA 1988 s 310 (inspector to be informed if relief given is not due).
Amendments—¹ Sub-s (1), words in sub-s (3) and definition of "subsidiary" in sub-s (5) substituted, and sub-ss (4A), (4B) and words in sub-s (5) inserted, by FA 1994 s 137(1), (2), Sch 15 para 16 in relation to EIS shares issued after 31 December 1993 with effect from the year 1993–94.

303 Value received by persons other than claimants

[(1) Where, in the case of an issue of eligible shares in a company, any relief is attributable to any shares comprised in the issue which are held by an individual, subsection (1A) below shall apply if at any time in the [period of restriction]⁸ the company or any subsidiary—

(*a*) repays, redeems or repurchases any of its share capital which belongs to any member other than that individual or a person who falls within subsection (1B) below, or
(*b*) makes any payment to any such member for giving up his right to any of the share capital of the company or subsidiary on its cancellation or extinguishment.

(1A) The relief—

(*a*) if it is greater than the amount mentioned in subsection (1C) below, shall be reduced by that amount, and
(*b*) if paragraph (*a*) above does not apply, shall be withdrawn.

[(1AA) This section is subject to [sections 303AA and 303A]⁸.]⁶

(1B) A person falls within this sub-paragraph if the repayment, redemption, repurchase or payment in question—

(*a*) causes any relief attributable to his shares in the company to be withdrawn or reduced by virtue of section 299 or 300(2)(*a*), or
(*b*) gives rise to a qualifying chargeable event (within the meaning of paragraph 14(4) of Schedule 5B to the 1992 Act) in respect of him[, or
(*c*) causes any investment relief [attributable to shares held by that person]⁸ (within the meaning of Schedule 15 to the Finance Act 2000) to be withdrawn or reduced by virtue of paragraph 46 (disposal of shares) or 49(1)(*a*) (repayment etc of share capital or securities) of that Schedule]⁶[,

or it would have the effect mentioned in paragraph (*a*), (*b*) or (*c*) above were it not a receipt of insignificant value for the purposes of section 300 above, paragraph 13 of Schedule 5B to the 1992 Act or paragraph 47 of the Finance Act 2000, as the case may be.]⁸

(1C) The amount referred to in subsection (1A) above is an amount equal to tax at the lower rate for the year of assessment for which the relief was given—

(*a*) where subsection (1) above does not apply in the case of any other individual, on the amount [received]⁸ by the member;
(*b*) where that subsection also applies in the case of one or more other individuals, on the appropriate fraction of that amount;

and subsection (4) of section 299 applies for the purposes of this subsection as it applies for the purposes of subsection (2) of that section.

(1D) In subsection (1C) above "the appropriate fraction" is—

$$\frac{A}{B}$$

where—

A = the amount subscribed by the individual for eligible shares which are comprised in the issue and to which relief is or, but for subsection (1A)(*b*) above, would be attributable;
B = the aggregate of that amount and the amount or amounts subscribed by the other individual or individuals for such shares.

(2) Where the repayment, redemption, repurchase or payment mentioned in subsection (1) above falls within [the applicable periods]⁷ for two or more issues of eligible shares in the company, subsection (1A) above shall have effect in relation to each of those issues as if the amount receivable by the member were reduced by multiplying it by the fraction—

$$\frac{C}{D}$$

where—

    C = the amount subscribed by individuals for eligible shares which are comprised in the issue and to which relief is or, but for subsection (1A)(b) above, would be attributable;

    D = the aggregate of that amount and the corresponding amount or amounts for the other issue or issues.][5]

[(2A) For the purposes of subsection (2) above "the applicable period" for an issue of eligible shares is—

    (a) if the shares were issued before 6th April 2000, the period beginning two years before the issue of the shares and ending immediately before the fifth anniversary of the issue date,

    [(b) if the shares were issued on or after 6th April 2000 but before 7th March 2001, the period beginning two years before the issue of the shares and ending immediately before the termination date relating to those shares,][8]

    [(c) in any other case, the period of restriction for the issue.][8]][7]

(3)–(7) ...[8]

(8) ...[4]

(9) Where—

    (a) a company issues share capital ("the original shares") of nominal value equal to the authorised minimum (within the meaning of the Companies Act 1985) for the purposes of complying with the requirements of section 117 of that Act (public company not to do business unless requirements as to share capital complied with); and

    (b) after the registrar of companies has issued the company with a certificate under section 117, it issues eligible shares;

subsection (1) above shall not apply in relation to any redemption of any of the original shares within 12 months of the date on which those shares were issued.

In relation to companies incorporated under the law of Northern Ireland references in this subsection to the Companies Act 1985 and to section 117 of that Act shall have effect as references to the Companies (Northern Ireland) Order 1986 and to Article 127 of that Order.

[(9A) References in this section [and section 303AA][8] to a subsidiary of a company are references to a company which at any time in the relevant period is a 51 per cent subsidiary of the first mentioned company, whether or not it is such a subsidiary at the time of the repayment, redemption, repurchase or payment in question ...[9].][5]

[(9B) Section 312(1A)(a) applies to determine the relevant period for the purposes of this section.][3]

(10)–(11) ...[4]

Commentary—*Simon's Direct Tax Service* E3.148.
Note—For the text of this section as applicable to the Business Expansion Scheme which was abolished in relation to shares issued after 31 December 1993, see *Yellow Tax Handbook*, 1993–94, 32nd edition.
Revenue Internal Guidance—Inspector's manual IM 6614 (sub-ss (3)–(7) explanation with worked examples).
Definitions—See at the beginning of this Chapter.
Cross references—See TA 1988 s 307(6)–(8A) (withdrawal or reduction of relief with consequent tax assessment; interest on tax).
TA 1988 s 310(2) (inspector to be informed if relief given is not due).
TA 1988 s 310(7) (inspector to be informed where value for eligible shares is received from the issuing company by the shareholder).
Amendments—[1] Sub-ss (1), (1A), (1B) substituted for sub-s (1) by FA 1994 s 137(1), (2) and Sch 15 para 17 in relation to EIS shares issued after 31 December 1993 with effect from the year 1993–94.
[2] Section numbers in sub-s (3) substituted by FA 1994 s 137(1), (2) and Sch 15 para 17 in relation to EIS shares issued after 31 December 1993 with effect from the year 1993–94.
[3] Sub-ss (9A), (9B) inserted by FA 1994 s 137(1), (2) and Sch 15 para 17 in relation to EIS shares issued after 31 December 1993 with effect from the year 1993–94.
[4] Sub-ss (8), (10), (11) repealed by FA 1994 s 137(1), (2), Sch 15 para 17 and Sch 26, Pt V(17) in relation to EIS shares issued after 31 December 1993 with effect from the year 1993–94.
[5] Sub-ss (1)–(2), (9A) and words in sub-s (3) substituted by FA 1998 Sch 13 para 15 with effect in relation to shares issued on or after 6 April 1998.
[6] Sub-ss (1AA) and (1B)(c) and word "or" preceding it, inserted by FA 2000 s 63(2), Sch 16 para 2(1), (2) with effect for shares issued after 31 March 2000 but before 1 April 2010.
[7] Words in sub-ss (1), (3) substituted for "seven year", words in sub-s (2) substituted for "the seven year period" and sub-s (2A) inserted by FA 2000 s 64, Sch 17 para 5 with effect for shares issued after 5 April 2000.
[8] Words in sub-s (1) substituted for the words "designated period", words in sub-s (1AA) substituted for the words "section 303A", words in sub-s (1B), and para (c) inserted, word in sub-s (1C)(a) substituted for "receivable", sub-s (2A)(b), (c) substituted for sub-s (2A)(b); sub-ss (3)–(7) repealed, and words inserted in sub-s (9A) by FA 2001 ss 63, 110, Sch 15 paras 19, 40, Sch 33 Pt II(3) with effect—

    (a) in relation to shares issued after 6 March 2001, and

    (b) in relation to shares issued before that date, in respect of the application of TA 1988 Pt VII Chapter III and TCGA 1992 Sch 5B in relation to—

        (i) value received (within the meaning of TA 1988 s 300 or TCGA 1992 Sch 5B para 13 of Schedule 5B), and

        (ii) repayments made,

on or after that date.
Previously, sub-s (2A)(b) read—

    "(b) in any other case, the designated period for the issue."
Previously, sub-ss (3)–(7) read—

    "(3) Where at any time in the designated period a member of a company receives or is entitled to receive any value from the company within the meaning of this subsection, then, for the purposes of section 291B(1) in its application to any subsequent time—

        (a) the amount of the company's issued ordinary share capital; and

(b) the amount of the part of that capital which consists of the shares which (within the meaning of section 291B) the individual directly or indirectly possesses or is entitled to acquire, and the amount of the part consisting of the remainder,

shall each be treated as reduced in accordance with subsection (4) below.

(4) The amount of each of the parts mentioned in subsection (3)(b) above shall be treated as equal to such proportion of that amount as the amount subscribed for that part less the relevant value bears to the amount subscribed; and the amount of the issued share capital shall be treated as equal to the sum of the amounts treated under this subsection as the amount of those parts respectively.

(5) In subsection (4) above "the relevant value", in relation to each of the parts there mentioned, means the value received by the member or members entitled to the shares of which that part consists.

(6) For the purposes of subsection (3) above a member of a company receives or is entitled to receive value from the company in any case in which an individual would receive value from the company by virtue of section 300(2)(d), (e), (f), (g) or (h) (but treating as excepted from paragraph (h) all payments made for full consideration) and the value received shall be determined as for the purposes of that section.

(6A) The reference in subsection (3) above to the receipt of value from a company includes the receipt of value from a subsidiary, and the reference to the company in subsection (6) above shall be read accordingly.

(7) For the purposes of subsection (3) above a person shall be treated as entitled to receive anything which he is entitled to receive at a future date or will at a future date be entitled to receive."

[9] The words "or, as the case may be, the receipt of value in question" in sub-s (9A) repealed by FA 2001 s 110, Sch 33 Pt II(3) with effect—

(a) in relation to shares issued on or after 7 March 2001, and
(b) in relation to shares issued before that date, in respect of the application of TA 1988 Pt VII Chapter III and TCGA 1992 Sch 5B in relation to—
   (i) value received (within the meaning of TA 1988 s 300 or TCGA 1992 Sch 5B para 13) and
   (ii) repayments made,
on or after that date.

[303AA Insignificant repayments disregarded for purposes of section 303(1)

(1) Any repayment shall be disregarded for the purposes of section 303(1) (repayments etc which cause withdrawal or reduction of relief) if whichever is the greater of—

   (a) the market value of the shares to which it relates ("the target shares") immediately before the event occurs, and

   (b) the amount received by the member in question,

is insignificant in relation to the market value of the remaining issued share capital of the company in question (or, as the case may be, subsidiary in question) immediately after the event occurs.

This is subject to subsection (4) below.

(2) For the purposes of this section "repayment" means a repayment, redemption, repurchase or payment mentioned in section 303(1) (repayments etc which cause withdrawal or reduction of relief).

(3) For the purposes of subsection (1) above it shall be assumed that the target shares are cancelled at the time the repayment is made.

(4) Where an individual subscribes for eligible shares in a company, subsection (1) above does not apply to prevent section 303(1) having effect in relation to those shares if, at a relevant time, arrangements are in existence that provide—

   (a) for a repayment by the company or any subsidiary of the company (whether or not it is such a subsidiary at the time the arrangements are made), or
   (b) for anyone to be entitled to such a repayment,

at any time in the period of restriction relating to those shares.

(5) For the purposes of subsection (4) above "a relevant time" means any time in the period—

   (a) beginning one year before the eligible shares were issued, and
   (b) expiring at the end of the issue date.][1]

Commentary—*Simon's Direct Tax Service* E3.148.
Amendments—[1] This section inserted by FA 2001 s 63, Sch 15 paras 20, 40 with effect—
(a) in relation to shares issued after 6 March 2001, and
(b) in relation to shares issued before that date, in respect of the application of TA 1988 Pt VII Chapter III and TCGA 1992 Sch 5B in relation to—
   (i) value received (within the meaning of TA 1988 s 300 or TCGA 1992 Sch 5B para 13 of Schedule 5B), and
   (ii) repayments made,
on or after that date.

[303A Restriction on withdrawal of relief under section 303

(1) Subsections (4) and (7) below apply where, by reason of a repayment, any investment relief which is attributable under Schedule 15 to the Finance Act 2000 to any shares is withdrawn under paragraph 56(2) of that Schedule.

[(2) For the purposes of this section "repayment" has the meaning given in section 303AA(2) above.][2]

(3) For the purposes of this section "the relevant amount" is the amount determined by the formula—

$$X - 5Y$$

Where—
   X is the amount of the repayment, and
   Y is the aggregate amount of investment relief withdrawn by reason of the repayment.

(4) Where the relevant amount does not exceed £1,000 the repayment shall be disregarded for the purposes of section 303(1), unless repayment arrangements are in existence at any time in the period—

   (a) beginning one year before the shares mentioned in subsection (1) above are issued, and
   (b) expiring at the end of the issue date of those shares.

(5) For this purpose ''repayment arrangements'' means arrangements which provide—

   (a) for a repayment by the company that issued the shares (''the issuing company'') or any subsidiary of that company, or
   (b) for anyone to be entitled to such a repayment,

at any time.

(6) Subsection (5)(a) above applies in relation to a subsidiary of the issuing company whether or not it is such a subsidiary—

   (a) at the time of the repayment mentioned in subsection (1) above, or
   (b) when the arrangements were made.

(7) Where the repayment is not disregarded by virtue of subsection (4) above, the amount receivable by reason of the repayment shall be treated for the purposes of section 303(1C)(a) as an amount equal to the relevant amount.

(8) ...[2]

(9) In this section—

   (a) ''investment relief'' has the same meaning as in [Schedule 15 to the Finance Act 2000 (corporate venturing scheme)][2]; and
   (b) references to the withdrawal of investment relief include its reduction.][1]

Commentary—*Simon's Direct Tax Service* **E3.148**.
Amendments—[1] This section inserted by FA 2000 s 63(2), Sch 16 para 2(1), (3) with effect for shares issued after 31 March 2000 but before 1 April 2010.
[2] Sub-s (2) substituted, sub-s (8) repealed, and words in sub-s (9)(a) substituted for the words ''that Schedule'' by FA 2001 ss 63, 110 Sch 15 paras 21, 40, Sch 33 Pt II(3) with effect—

   (a) in relation to shares issued on or after 7 March 2001, and
   (b) in relation to shares issued before that date, in respect of the application of TA 1988 Pt VII Chapter III and TCGA 1992 Sch 5B in relation to—
      (i) value received (within the meaning of TA 1988 s 300 or TCGA 1992 Sch 5B para 13 of Schedule 5B), and
      (ii) repayments made,

on or after that date.
Previously, sub-s (2) read—

''(2) For the purposes of this section ''repayment'' means a repayment, redemption, repurchase or payment mentioned in paragraph 56(1) of that Schedule (repayments etc which cause withdrawal of investment relief).''
Previously, sub-s (8) read—

''(8) Where, but for the existence of paragraph 57(1) of Schedule 15 to the Finance Act 2000 (repayments causing insignificant changes to share capital to be disregarded), any investment relief would be withdrawn by reason of a repayment, the repayment shall be disregarded for the purposes of section 303(1).''.

[304 Husband and wife

(1) Section 299(1) shall not apply to a disposal of shares to which an amount of relief is attributable made by a married man to his wife or a married woman to her husband at a time when they are living together.

(2) Where such shares issued to one of them (''the transferor'') are transferred to the other (''the transferee'') by a transaction inter vivos to which that section does not apply, this Chapter shall have effect, in relation to any subsequent disposal or other event, as if—

   (a) the transferee were the person who had subscribed for the shares,
   (b) the transferee's liability to income tax had been reduced under section 289A in respect of those shares for the same year of assessment as that for which the transferor's liability was so reduced and, accordingly, that amount of relief had continued to be attributable to the shares notwithstanding the transfer.

(3) Any assessment for reducing or withdrawing the relief by reason of any such disposal or other event shall be made on the transferee.][1]

[(4) Subsections (6) to (6D) of section 299 shall apply for the purposes of this section as they apply for the purposes of that section.][2]

Commentary—*Simon's Direct Tax Service* **E3.146**.
For the text of this section as applicable to the Business Expansion Scheme which was abolished in relation to shares issued after 31 December 1993, see *Yellow Tax Handbook*, 1993–94, 32nd edition.
Definitions—See at the beginning of this Chapter.
Cross references—See TA 1988 s 310 (inspector to be informed if relief given is not due).
Amendments—[1] This section substituted by FA 1994 s 137(1), (2) and Sch 15 para 18 in relation to EIS shares issued after 31 December 1993 with effect from the year 1993–94.
[2] Sub-s (4) inserted by FA 1998 Sch 13 para 16 with effect in relation to disposals made on or after 6 April 1998.

[304A Acquisition of share capital by new company

(1) This section applies where—

(*a*) a company (''the new company'') in which the only issued shares are subscriber shares acquires all the shares (''old shares'') in another company (''the old company'');

(*b*) the consideration for the old shares consists wholly of the issue of shares (''new shares'') in the new company;

(*c*) the consideration for new shares of each description consists wholly of old shares of the corresponding description;

(*d*) new shares of each description are issued to the holders of old shares of the corresponding description in respect of and in proportion to their holdings;

(*e*) at some time before the issue of the new shares—

(i) the old company issued eligible shares; and

(ii) a certificate in relation to those eligible shares was issued by that company for the purposes of subsection (2) of section 306 and in accordance with that section; and

(*f*) before the issue of the new shares, the Board have, on the application of the new company or the old company, notified that company that the Board are satisfied that the exchange of shares—

(i) will be effected for bona fide commercial reasons; and

(ii) will not form part of any such scheme or arrangements as are mentioned in section 137(1) of the 1992 Act.

(2) For the purposes of this Chapter—

(*a*) the exchange of shares shall not be regarded as involving any disposal of the old shares or any acquisition of the new shares; and

(*b*) any relief under this Chapter which is attributable to any old shares shall be attributable instead to the new shares for which they are exchanged.

(3) Where, in the case of any new shares held by an individual to which relief becomes so attributable, the old shares for which they were exchanged were subscribed for by and issued to the individual, this Chapter shall have effect as if—

(*a*) the new shares had been subscribed for by him at the time when, and for the amount for which, the old shares were subscribed for by him;

(*b*) the new shares had been issued to him by the new company at the time when the old shares were issued to him by the old company;

(*c*) the claim for relief made in respect of the old shares had been made in respect of the new shares; and

(*d*) his liability to income tax had been reduced under section 289A in respect of the new shares for the same year of assessment as that for which his liability was so reduced in respect of the old shares.

(4) Where, in the case of any new shares held by an individual to which relief becomes so attributable, the old shares for which they are exchanged were transferred to the individual as mentioned in section 304, this Chapter shall have effect in relation to any subsequent disposal or other event as if—

(*a*) the new shares had been subscribed for by him at the time when, and for the amount for which, the old shares were subscribed for;

(*b*) the new shares had been issued by the new company at the time when the old shares were issued by the old company;

(*c*) the claim for relief made in respect of the old shares had been made in respect of the new shares; and

(*d*) his liability to income tax had been reduced under section 289A in respect of the new shares for the same year of assessment as that for which the liability of the individual who subscribed for the old shares was so reduced in respect of those shares.

(5) Where relief becomes so attributable to any new shares—

(*a*) this Chapter shall have effect as if anything which, under section 306(2), 307(1A) or 310, has been done, or is required to be done, by or in relation to the old company had been done, or were required to be done, by or in relation to the new company; and

(*b*) any appeal brought by the old company against a notice under section 307(1A)(*b*) may be prosecuted by the new company as if it had been brought by that company.

(6) For the purposes of this section old shares and new shares are of a corresponding description if, on the assumption that they were shares in the same company, they would be of the same class and carry the same rights; and in subsection (1) above references to shares, except in the expressions ''eligible shares'' and ''subscriber shares'', include references to securities.

(7) Nothing in section 293(8) shall apply in relation to such an exchange of shares, or shares and securities, as is mentioned in subsection (1) above or arrangements with a view to such an exchange.

(8) Subsection (2) of section 138 of the 1992 Act shall apply for the purposes of subsection (1)(*f*) above as it applies for the purposes of subsection (1) of that section.]¹

Commentary—*Simon's Direct Tax Service* **E3.121.**
Definitions—See at the beginning of this Chapter.

Amendments—[1] This section inserted by FA 1998 Sch 13 para 17 with effect in relation to new shares (within the meaning of TA 1988 s 304A) issued on or after 6 April 1998.

[305 Reorganisation of share capital

(1) Subsection (2) below applies where—

(a) there is by virtue of any allotment in the relevant period, being such an allotment for payment as is mentioned in section 126(2)(a) of the 1992 Act, a reorganisation affecting ordinary shares,

(b) immediately before the reorganisation an amount of relief ("X") is attributable to the shares, and

(c) both—

(i) the amount subscribed for the shares ("Z"), and

(ii) the market value of the shares immediately before the reorganisation,

exceed the market value of the shares immediately after the reorganisation.

(2) Where this subsection applies, the relief attributable to the shares shall be reduced by the following amount—

$$\frac{X \times Y}{Z}$$

where "Y" is whichever is the smaller of the amounts by which Z, and the market value of the shares immediately before the reorganisation, exceed the market value of the shares immediately after the reorganisation.

(3) Subsection (2) above also applies where—

(a) an individual, who at any time in the relevant period has received, or become entitled to receive, in respect of any ordinary shares in a company, a provisional allotment of shares in or debentures of the company, disposes of his rights, and

(b) that subsection would have applied if he had not disposed of the rights but the allotment had been made to him by virtue of those rights.

(4) Section 312(1A)(a) applies to determine the relevant period for the purposes of this section.][1]

[(5) Subsection (2) above shall not apply where the reorganisation occurs on or after 29th November 1994.][2]

[(6) Subsection (2) above shall not apply by virtue of subsection (3) above where the rights are disposed of on or after 29th November 1994.][2]

Note—For the text of this section as applicable to the Business Expansion Scheme which was abolished in relation to shares issued after 31 December 1993, see *Yellow Tax Handbook*, 1993–94, 32nd edition.
Definitions—See at the beginning of this Chapter.
Cross references—See TA 1988 s 307(6)–(8A) (withdrawal or reduction of relief with consequent tax assessment; interest on tax).
Amendments—[1] This section substituted by FA 1994 s 137(1), (2) and Sch 15 para 19 in relation to EIS shares issued after 31 December 1993 with effect from the year 1993–94.
[2] Sub-ss (5), (6) inserted by FA 1995 s 66(4), with effect as this Chapter has effect in relation to EIS shares issued on or after 1 January 1994.

[305A Relief for loss on disposal of shares

(1) Section 574 shall apply on the disposal by an individual of shares to which relief is attributable as it applies to a disposal by him of shares in a qualifying trading company for which he has subscribed ("qualifying trading company" and "subscribed" having for this purpose the same meaning as in that section).

(2) For the purposes of that section (as applied by this) sections 575(1) and (3) and [576(1) to (3)][2] shall apply.][1]

Commentary—*Simon's Direct Tax Service* E3.146.
Definitions—See at the beginning of this Chapter.
Amendments—[1] This section inserted by FA 1994 s 137(1), (2) and Sch 15 para 20 in relation to EIS shares issued after 31 December 1993 with effect from the year 1993–94.
[2] Words in sub-s (2) substituted by FA 1998 Sch 13 para 18 with effect in relation to disposals made on or after 6 April 1998.

306 Claims

(1) A claim for relief in respect of eligible shares issued by a company in any year of assessment [(or treated by section 289B(5) as so issued)][7] shall be made—

[(a) not earlier than the time the requirement in section 289A(6) is first satisfied; and][8]

[(b) not later than the fifth anniversary of the 31st January next following that year of assessment].[5]

(2) [No claim for relief in respect of eligible shares in a company may be made unless the person making the claim has received from the company][6] a certificate issued by the company in such form as the Board may direct and certifying that[,except so far as they fall to be satisfied by that person, the conditions for the relief][7], are satisfied in relation to those shares.

[(3) Before issuing a certificate for the purposes of subsection (2) above a company shall furnish the inspector with a statement to the effect that, except so far as they fall to be satisfied by the persons to whom eligible shares comprised in the share issue have been issued, the conditions for the relief—

(*a*) are satisfied in relation to that issue; and

(*b*) have been so satisfied at all times since the beginning of the relevant period.][7]

[(3A) A company may not furnish an inspector with a statement in respect of any shares issued in any year of assessment—

(*a*) later than two years after the end of that year of assessment, or

(*b*) if the period of four months referred to in subsection (1)(*a*) above ended after the end of that year, later than two years after the end of that period. ...][7][2]

[(4) No certificate shall be issued for the purposes of subsection (2) above without the authority of the inspector; but where the company, or a person connected with the company, has given notice to the inspector under section 310(2) or paragraph 16(2) or (4) of Schedule 5B to the 1992 Act, the authority must be given or renewed after the receipt of the notice.

(5) Any statement under subsection (3) above shall be in such form as the Board may direct and shall contain—

(*a*) such additional information as the Board may reasonably require, including in particular information relating to the persons who have requested the issue of certificates under subsection (2) above;

(*b*) a declaration that the statement is correct to the best of the company's knowledge and belief; and

(*c*) such other declarations as the Board may reasonably require.][7]

(6) Where a company has issued a certificate for the purposes of subsection (2) above, or furnished a statement under subsection (3) above and—

(*a*) the certificate or statement is made fraudulently or negligently; or

(*b*) the certificate was issued in contravention of subsection (4) above;

the company shall be liable to a penalty not exceeding [£3,000][1].

(7) For the purposes of regulations made under section 203 no regard shall be had to the relief unless a claim for it has been duly made and admitted.

(8) No application shall be made under section 55(3) or (4) of the Management Act (application for postponement of payment of tax pending appeal) on the ground that the applicant is [eligible for][3] the relief unless a claim for the relief has been duly made by him.

(9) For the purposes of section 86 of the Management Act (interest on overdue tax), tax charged by an assessment—

(*a*) shall be regarded as due and payable notwithstanding that relief from the tax (whether by discharge or repayment) is subsequently given on a claim for the relief; but

(*b*) shall, unless paid earlier or due and payable later, be regarded as paid on the date of the making of the claim on which the relief is given;

and section 91 of that Act (effect on interest of reliefs) shall not apply in consequence of any discharge or repayment for giving effect to the relief.

(10) For the purposes of the provisions of the Management Act relating to appeals against decisions on claims, the refusal of the inspector to authorise the issue of a certificate under subsection (2) above shall be taken to be a decision refusing a claim made by the company.

...[4]

[(11) Section 312(1A)(*b*) applies to determine the relevant period for the purposes of this section.][2]

Commentary—*Simon's Direct Tax Service* E3.142.

Note—For the text of this section as applicable to the Business Expansion Scheme which was abolished in relation to shares issued after 31 December 1993, see *Yellow Tax Handbook*, 1993–94, 32nd edition.

Revenue Internal Guidance—Inspector's Manual IM7011–7014 (procedure on request for advance assurance).

IM7015–7020 (procedure for examination of form EIS1 and issue of form EIS2).

Definitions—See at the beginning of this Chapter.

Cross references—See TA 1988 s 310(3) (inspector to be informed where a certificate is issued under sub-s (2) above and by virtue of s 294 relief may not be due).

TA 1988 s 311(4) (modification of sub-s (2) above where relief is claimed for shares held by an approved investment fund as nominee for an individual).

TA 1988 s 311(6) (disapplication of sub-s (6) above to a certificate issued by managers of an approved investment fund confirming investment).

Amendments—[1] Amount in sub-s (6) substituted by FA 1989 s 170(3), (6) in relation to things done or omitted after 26 July 1989.

[2] Sub-ss (3A), (11) inserted by FA 1994 s 137(1), (2) and Sch 15 para 21 in relation to EIS shares issued after 31 December 1993 with effect from the year 1993–94.

[3] Words in sub-s (8) substituted by FA 1994 s 137(1), (2) and Sch 15 para 21 in relation to EIS shares issued after 31 December 1993 with effect from the year 1993–94.

[4] Words in sub-s (10) repealed by FA 1994 s 137(1), (2), Sch 15 para 21and Sch 26, Pt V(17) in relation to EIS shares issued after 31 December 1993 with effect from the year 1993–94.

[5] Sub-s (1)(*b*) substituted by FA 1996 Sch 21 para 7 with effect from the year 1996–97.

[6] Words in sub-s (2) substituted by FA 1996 Sch 20 para 22 with effect in relation to shares issued after 5 April 1996.

[7] Words in sub-s (1) inserted, words in sub-s (2), sub-ss (3)–(5) substituted, and words in sub-s (3A) repealed by FA 1998 Sch 13 para 19 with effect in relation to shares issued after 5 April 1998.

[8] Sub-s (1)(*a*) substituted by FA 2001 s 63, Sch 15 para 22 with effect for shares issued after 5 April 2001. Previously sub-s (1)(*a*) read as follows—

"(*a*) not earlier than the end of the period of four months mentioned in section 289A(7)(*a*), (*b*) or (*c*), as the case may be; and"

TA 1988

307 Withdrawal of relief

(1) Where any relief has been given which is subsequently found not to have been due, it shall be withdrawn by the making of an assessment to tax under Case VI of Schedule D for the year of assessment for which the relief was given; ...[6].

[(1A) Relief may not be withdrawn, in relation to shares issued by a company on any date, on the ground that the company is not a qualifying company or that the requirements of [section 289(1)(b), (ba), (c) or (d)][10] are not met unless—

(a) the company has given notice under section 310 [or paragraph 16(2) or (4) of Schedule 5B to the 1992 Act][8], or

(b) an inspector has given notice to the company stating that, by reason of that ground, the whole or any part of the relief given to individuals to whom the shares were issued on that date was not, in his opinion, due.][3]

[(1B) The giving of notice by an inspector under subsection (1A) above shall be taken, for the purposes of the provisions of the Management Act relating to appeals against decisions on claims, to be a decision refusing a claim made by the company.][3]

[(1C) Where any issue has been determined on an appeal brought by virtue of paragraph 1A(6) of Schedule 5B to the 1992 Act (appeal against notice that shares never have been, or have ceased to be, eligible shares), the determination shall be conclusive for the purposes of any appeal brought by virtue of subsection (1B) above on which that issue arises.][8]

[(2) Subject to subsections (3) to (7) below, no assessment for withdrawing relief may be made, and no notice may be given under subsection (1A) above, more than six years after the end of the year of assessment—

(a) in which the time mentioned in section 289(3) falls, or

(b) in which the event by reason of which the claimant ceases to be eligible for relief occurs,

whichever is the later.][3]

(3) No assessment for withdrawing relief in respect of shares issued to any person shall be made by reason of any event occurring after his death.

(4) Where a person has, by a disposal or disposals to which section 299(1)(b) applies, disposed of all the [eligible shares][8] issued to him by a company, no assessment for withdrawing relief in respect of any of those shares shall be made by reason of any subsequent event unless it occurs at a time when he is connected with the company within the meaning of section 291.

(5) Subsection (2) above is without prejudice to section 36 of the Management Act ([fraudulent or negligent conduct][1]).

(6) In its application to an assessment made by virtue of this section, section 86 of the Management Act (interest on overdue tax) shall have effect as if [the relevant date][7] were—

(a) in the case of relief withdrawn by virtue of section [289(6) [or 299B(1)][9]][5]—

(i) so far as effect has been given to the relief in accordance with regulations under section 203, 5th April in the year of assessment in which effect was so given;

(ii) so far as effect has not been so given, the date on which the relief was granted;

[(aa) in the case of relief withdrawn by virtue of [section 289(1)(c) or (d)][10], the date on which the relief was granted;][4]

(b) in the case of relief withdrawn by virtue of [section 289(1)(ba), 291][8], 293, 297, 302, 303(1) or 305 in consequence of any event after the grant of the relief, the date of that event;

(c) in the case of relief withdrawn by virtue of section 299(1) in consequence of a disposal after the grant of the relief, the date of the disposal;

[(cca) in the case of relief withdrawn by virtue of section 299(5), the date on which the option was granted;][4]

[(ca) in the case of relief withdrawn by virtue of section 299A in consequence of the making of any loan after the grant of the relief, the date of the making of the loan;][2]

(d) in the case of relief withdrawn by virtue of section 300 in consequence of a receipt of value after the grant of the relief, the date of the receipt.

(7) For the purposes of subsection (6) above the date on which the relief is granted is the date on which a repayment of tax for giving effect to the relief was made or, if there was no such repayment, the date on which the inspector issued a notice to the claimant showing the amount of tax payable after giving effect to the relief.

(8) Where a company has ceased to be a qualifying company in consequence of the operation of section 294, subsection (6) above shall apply as if the relief was withdrawn in consequence of an event which occurred at the time when the company so ceased to be a qualifying company.

[(8A) References in this section to the withdrawal of relief include its reduction.][4]

(9) ...[6].

Commentary—*Simon's Direct Tax Service* E3.152, 153.
Note—For the text of this section as applicable to the Business Expansion Scheme which was abolished in relation to shares issued after 31 December 1993, see *Yellow Tax Handbook*, 1993–94, 32nd edition.
Definitions—See at the beginning of this Chapter.
Cross references—See TA 1988 s 299A(2) (construction of reference to "the making of a loan" in sub-s (6)(ca) above).

Amendments—¹ Words in sub-s (5) substituted for the words "fraud and wilful default) and section 37 of that Act (neglect)" by FA 1989 s 149(4)(*b*), (7) but without affecting the making of assessment for years before 1983–84 or for accounting periods ending before 1 April 1983. (As amended the subsection now applies for the purposes of EIS.)
² Sub-s (6)(*ca*) inserted by FA 1993 s 111(3), (4) with effect where claim for relief is made after 15 March 1993.
³ Sub-ss (1A), (1B), (2) substituted for sub-s (2) by FA 1994 s 137(1), (2) and Sch 15 para 22 in relation to EIS shares issued after 31 December 1993 with effect from the year 1993–94.
⁴ Sub-ss (6)(*aa*), (*cca*), (8A) inserted by FA 1994 s 137(1), (2) and Sch 15 para 22 in relation to EIS shares issued after 31 December 1993 with effect from the year 1993–94.
⁵ Section number in sub-s (6)(*a*) substituted by FA 1994 s 137(1), (2) and Sch 15 para 22 in relation to EIS shares issued after 31 December 1993 with effect from the year 1993–94.
⁶ Sub-s (9) and words in sub-s (1) repealed by FA 1994 s 137(1), (2), Sch 15 para 22 and Sch 26, Pt V(17) in relation to EIS shares issued after 31 December 1993 with effect from the year 1993–94.
⁷ Words in sub-s (6) substituted by FA 1996 Sch 18 para 5 with effect from the year 1996–97 and in relation to any income tax charged by an assessment made after 5 April 1998 which is for the year 1995–96 or any earlier year of assessment.
⁸ Words in sub-ss (4), (6)(*b*) substituted, words in sub-s (1A), and sub-s (1C) inserted by FA 1998 Sch 13 para 20 with effect in relation to shares issued on or after 6 April 1998.
⁹ Words in sub-s (6)(*a*) inserted by FA 1998 s 71(2) with effect in relation to shares issued after 1 July 1997.
¹⁰ Words in sub-s (1A) substituted for the words "section 289(1)(*b*), (*ba*) or (c)", and words in sub-s (6)(*aa*) substituted for the words "section 289(1)(c)", by FA 2001 s 63, Sch 15 paras 7, 40 with effect—
  (*a*) in relation to shares issued after 6 March 2001, and
  (*b*) in respect of the application of TA 1988 Pt VII Chapter III and TCGA 1992 Sch 5B after 6 March 2001 in relation to shares—
    (i) that were issued after 31 December 1993 but before 7 March 2001, and
    (ii) to which income tax relief or deferral relief was attributable immediately before 7 March 2001.

308 Application to subsidiaries

(1) A qualifying company may, in the relevant period, have one or more subsidiaries if—

(*a*) the conditions mentioned in subsection (2) below are satisfied in respect of the subsidiary or, as the case may be, each subsidiary and, except as provided by subsection (3) below, continue to be so satisfied until the end of the relevant period; ...²

(*b*) ...²

(2) The conditions referred to are—

(*a*) that the qualifying company, or another of its subsidiaries, possesses not less than [75 per cent]³ of the issued share capital of, and not less than [75 per cent]³ of the voting power in, the subsidiary;

(*b*) that the qualifying company, or another of its subsidiaries, would in the event of a winding up of the subsidiary or in any other circumstances be beneficially entitled to receive not less than [75 per cent]³ of the assets of the subsidiary which would then be available for distribution to the equity holders of the subsidiary;

(*c*) that the qualifying company or another of its subsidiaries is beneficially entitled to not less than [75 per cent]³ of any profits of the subsidiary which are available for distribution to the equity holders of the subsidiary;

(*d*) that no person other than the qualifying company or another of its subsidiaries has control of the subsidiary within the meaning of section 840; and

(*e*) that no arrangements are in existence by virtue of which the conditions in paragraphs (*a*) to (*d*) above could cease to be satisfied.

(3) The conditions shall not be regarded as ceasing to be satisfied by reason only of the subsidiary or the qualifying company being wound up, or dissolved without winding up, if—

(*a*) it is shown that the winding up or dissolution is for bona fide commercial reasons and not part of a scheme or arrangement the main purpose or one of the main purposes of which is the avoidance of tax; and

(*b*) the net assets, if any, of the subsidiary or, as the case may be, the qualifying company are distributed to its members or dealt with as bona vacantia before the end of the relevant period, or in the case of a winding up, the end (if later) of three years from the commencement of the winding up.

(4) The conditions shall not be regarded as ceasing to be satisfied by reason only of the disposal by the qualifying company or (as the case may be) by another subsidiary, within the relevant period, of all its interest in the subsidiary if it is shown that the disposal is for bona fide commercial reasons and not part of a scheme or arrangement the main purpose or one of the main purposes of which is the avoidance of tax.

(5) For the purposes of this section—

(*a*), (*b*) ...²

(*c*) the persons who are equity holders of a subsidiary and the percentage of the assets of a subsidiary to which an equity holder would be entitled shall be determined in accordance with paragraphs 1 and 3 of Schedule 18, taking references in paragraph 3 to the first company as references to an equity holder and references to a winding up as including references to any other circumstances in which assets of the subsidiary are available for distribution to its equity holders.

[(5A) Section 312(1A)(*b*) applies to determine the relevant period for the purposes of this section.]¹

(6) ...¹

Commentary—*Simon's Direct Tax Service* E3.117.
Note—For the text of this section as applicable to the Business Expansion Scheme which was abolished in relation to shares issued after 31 December 1993, see *Yellow Tax Handbook*, 1993–94, 32nd edition.
Definitions—See at the beginning of this Chapter.

Cross references—See TA 1988 s 310(5) (inspector's powers to obtain information where he suspects relief is not due).
Amendments—¹ Sub-s (5A) inserted and sub-s (6) repealed by FA 1994 s 137(1), (2), Sch 15 para 23, Sch 26, Pt V(17) in relation to EIS shares issued after 31 December 1993 with effect from the year 1993–94.
² Sub-s (1)(*b*) and preceding word "and", and sub-s (5)(*a*), (*b*) repealed by FA 1997 Sch 8 para 6, Sch 18 Pt VI(8) with effect in accordance with Sch 8 para 1.
³ Percentage amounts in sub-s (2) substituted by FA 1998 Sch 13 para 21 with effect in relation to shares issued on or after 6 April 1998 (formerly 75 per cent).

309 Further provisions as to subsidiaries

Amendments—This section repealed by FA 1994 s 137(1), (2), Sch 15 para 24 and Sch 26, Pt V(17) in relation to EIS shares issued after 31 December 1993 with effect from the year 1993–94.

310 Information

(1) Where an event occurs by reason of which any relief given to an individual falls to be withdrawn by virtue of sections 291, 299, [299A or 300]⁴ [or would fall to be withdrawn under section 300 were it not for the application of section 300A]⁷, the individual shall within 60 days of his coming to know of the event give a notice to the inspector containing particulars of the event.

(2) Where an event occurs by reason of which any relief in respect of any shares in a company falls to be withdrawn by virtue of section [[289(1)(*ba*), (*c*) or (*d*)]⁶, 293]⁴, 300, 302 or 303[, or would fall to be withdrawn under section 300 were it not for the application of section 300A,]⁷—

  (*a*) the company; and
  (*b*) any person connected with the company who has knowledge of that matter;

shall within 60 days of the event or, in the case of a person within paragraph (*b*) above, of his coming to know of it, give a notice to the inspector containing particulars of the event ...⁴.

[(2A) Where—

  (*a*) a person is required to give notice under subsection (1) or (2) above of an event by reason of which any relief in respect of any shares in a company—

    (i) falls to be withdrawn under section 300, or
    (ii) would fall to be so withdrawn were it not for the application of section 300A, and

  (*b*) that person has knowledge of the replacement value received (or expected to be received) from the original recipient by the original supplier by reason of a qualifying receipt,

the notice shall include particulars of that receipt of the replacement value (or expected receipt).
In this subsection "the replacement value", "the original recipient", "the original supplier" and "qualifying receipt" shall be construed in accordance with section 300A.]⁷

(3) Where—

  (*a*) a company has issued a certificate under section 306(2) in respect of any eligible shares in the company; and
  (*b*) it appears to the company, or to any person connected with the company who has knowledge of the matter, that section 294 may have effect to deny relief in respect of those shares;

the company or (as the case may be) that person or (where it so appears to each of them) both the company and that person shall give notice to the inspector setting out the particulars of the case.

(4) If the inspector has reason to believe—

  [(*a*)]⁷ that a person has not given a notice which he is required to give under subsection (1) or (2) above in respect of any event, or under subsection (3) above in respect of any particular case, [or
  (*b*) that a person has given or received value (within the meaning of section 300(2) or (5)) which, but for the fact that the amount given or received was an amount of insignificant value (within the meaning of section 301A(2)), would have triggered a requirement to give a notice under subsection (1) or (2) above, or
  (*c*) that a person has made or received any repayment (within the meaning of section 303AA(2)) which, but for the fact that it falls to be disregarded for the purposes of section 303(1) by virtue of section 303AA(1), would have triggered a requirement to give a notice under subsection (2) above,

the inspector may]⁷ by notice require that person to furnish him within such time (not being less than 60 days) as may be specified in the notice with such information relating to the event or case as the inspector may reasonably require for the purposes of this Chapter.

(5) Where relief is claimed in respect of shares in a company and the inspector has reason to believe that it may not be due by reason of any such arrangement or scheme as is mentioned in section [289(6), 291B(5)]², 293(8)[, 299B(1)]⁵ or 308(2)(*e*), he may by notice require any person concerned to furnish him within such time (not being less than 60 days) as may be specified in the notice with—

  (*a*) a declaration in writing stating whether or not, according to the information which that person has or can reasonably obtain, any such arrangement or scheme exists or has existed;
  (*b*) such other information as the inspector may reasonably require for the purposes of the provision in question and as that person has or can reasonably obtain.

[(6) For the purposes of subsection (5) above the persons who are persons concerned are—

  (*a*) in relation to section 289(6), the claimant, the company and any person controlling the company;

(b) in relation to section 291B(5), the claimant;

(c) in relation to section 293(8) or 308(2)(e), the company and any person controlling the company; and

(d) in relation to section 299B(1), the claimant, the company and any person connected with the company;

and for those purposes references in this subsection to the claimant include references to any person to whom the claimant appears to have made a transfer such as is mentioned in section 304(1) of any of the shares in question.][5]

(7) Where relief has been given in respect of shares in a company—

(a) any person who receives from the company any payment or asset which may constitute value received (by him or another) for the purposes of sections [300 and 303(3)][4]; and

(b) any person on whose behalf such a payment or asset is received,

shall, if so required by the inspector, state whether the payment or asset received by him or on his behalf is received on behalf of any person other than himself and, if so, the name and address of that person.

(8) Where relief has been claimed in respect of shares in a company, any person who holds or has held shares in the company and any person on whose behalf any such shares are or were held shall, if so required by the inspector, state whether the shares which are or were held by him or on his behalf are or were held on behalf of any person other than himself and, if so, the name and address of that person.

(9) No obligation as to secrecy imposed by statute or otherwise shall preclude the inspector from disclosing to a company that relief has been given or claimed in respect of a particular number or proportion of its shares.

[(9A) References in this section to withdrawal of relief include its reduction.][4]

(10)–(11) ...[3].

Commentary—*Simon's Direct Tax Service* E3.155.
Note—For the text of this section as applicable to the Business Expansion Scheme which was abolished in relation to shares issued after 31 December 1993, see *Yellow Tax Handbook*, 1993–94, 32nd edition.
Revenue & other press releases—IR 1-8-94 (guidelines for approval of funds published).
Definitions—See at the beginning of this Chapter.
Cross references—See TMA 1970 s 98 (liability to special return penalties in respect of failures to give notifications or provide information and declarations required under this section).
Amendments—[1] "299A," in sub-s (1) inserted by FA 1993 s 111(2).
[2] Section numbers in sub-ss (1), (2), (5), (6) substituted by FA 1994 Sch 15 para 25.
[3] Sub-ss (10), (11) repealed by FA 1994 s 137(1), (2), Sch 15 para 25 and Sch 26, Pt V(17) in relation to EIS shares issued after 31 December 1993 with effect from the year 1993–94.
[4] Words in sub-ss (1), (2), (7) substituted, words in sub-s (2) repealed, and sub-s (9A) inserted by FA 1998 Sch 13 para 22 with effect in relation to events occurring after 5 April 1998.
[5] Words in sub-s (5) inserted, and sub-s (6) substituted by FA 1998 s 71(3)–(4) with effect in relation to shares issued after 1 July 1997.
[6] Words in sub-s (2) substituted for the words "289(1)(ba) or (c)" by FA 2001 s 63, Sch 15 paras 8, 40 with effect—

(a) in relation to shares issued after 6 March 2001, and
(b) in respect of the application of TA 1988 Pt VII Chapter III and TCGA 1992 Sch 5B after 6 March 2001 in relation to shares—
(i) that were issued after 31 December 1993 but before 7 March 2001, and
(ii) to which income tax relief or deferral relief was attributable immediately before 7 March 2001.
[7] Words in sub-ss (1), (2), and the whole of sub-s (2A) inserted, in sub-s (4), "(a)" added, and words substituted by FA 2001 s 63, Sch 15 paras 23, 40 with effect for events occurring after 6 March 2001.

311 Nominees, bare trustees and approved investment funds

(1) Shares subscribed for, issued to, held by or disposed of for an individual by a nominee shall be treated for the purposes of this Chapter as subscribed for, issued to, held by or disposed of by that individual.

(2) [Where eligible shares are held on a bare trust for two or more beneficiaries][2], this Chapter shall have effect (with the necessary modifications) as if—

(a) each beneficiary had subscribed as an individual for all of those shares; and

(b) the amount subscribed by each beneficiary was equal to the total amount subscribed on the issue of those shares divided by the number of beneficiaries.

[(2A) Subsection (2B) below applies where an individual claims relief in respect of eligible shares in a company and—

(a) the shares have been issued to the managers of an approved fund as nominee for the individual;

(b) the fund has closed, that is to say, no further investments in the fund are to be accepted; and

(c) the amounts which the managers have, as nominee for the individual, subscribed for eligible shares issued within six months after the closing of the fund represent not less than 90 per cent of his investment in the fund;

and in this section "the managers of an approved fund" means the person or persons having the management of an investment fund approved for the purposes of this section by the Board.][1]

[(2B) [In any case where this subsection applies, sections 289A and 289B shall have effect as if][2]—

(*a*) any reference to the year of assessment or other period in which the shares are issued were a reference to the year of assessment or other period in which the fund closes; and

(*b*) any reference to the time of the issue of the shares, or the time of the subscription for the shares, were a reference to the time of the closing of the fund.]¹

[(3) Section 290(1) shall not apply where the amount is subscribed as nominee for an individual by the managers of an approved fund.]¹

(4) Where an individual claims relief in respect of eligible shares in a company which have been issued to the managers of an approved fund as nominee for that individual, section 306(2) shall apply—

[(*a*) as if it required the certificate referred to in that section to be issued by the company to the managers; and

(*b*) as if it provided that no claim for relief may be made unless the person making the claim has received from the managers]³ a certificate issued by the managers, in such form as the Board may authorise, certifying that the managers hold certificates issued to them by the companies concerned, for the purposes of sections 306(2), in respect of the holdings of eligible shares shown on the managers' certificate.

(5) The managers of an approved fund may be required by a notice given to them by an inspector or other officer of the Board to deliver to the officer, within the time limited by the notice, a return of the holdings of eligible shares shown on certificates issued by them in accordance with subsection (4) above in the year of assessment to which the return relates.

(6) Section 306(6) shall not apply in relation to any certificate issued by the managers of an approved fund for the purposes of subsection (4) above.

Commentary—*Simon's Direct Tax Service* E3.156.
Note—For the text of this section as applicable to the Business Expansion Scheme which was abolished in relation to shares issued after 31 December 1993, see *Yellow Tax Handbook*, 1993–94, 32nd edition.
Definitions—See at the beginning of this Chapter.
Amendments—¹ Sub-ss (2A), (2B), (3) substituted for sub-s (3) by FA 1988 s 53, originally in relation to approved funds closing after 15 March 1988.
² Words in sub-ss (2), (2B) substituted by FA 1994 s 137(1), (2) and Sch 15 para 26 in relation to EIS shares issued after 31 December 1993 with effect from the year 1993–94.
³ Words in sub-s (4) substituted by FA 1996 s 134(3) Sch 20 para 23 with effect in relation to shares issued after 5 April 1996.

312 Interpretation of Chapter III

(1) In this Chapter—

["arrangements" includes any scheme, agreement or understanding, whether or not legally enforceable;]¹³

"associate" has the meaning given in subsections (3) and (4) of section 417 except that in those subsections "relative" shall not include a brother or sister;

...¹⁸

"control", except in sections [291B(4)[, 293(8)(*b*)]¹³ and 308(2)]⁵, shall be construed in accordance with section 416(2) to (6);

"debenture" has the meaning given by section 744 of the Companies Act 1985;

...¹⁸

"director" shall be construed in accordance with section 417(5);

["eligible for relief" has the meaning given by section 289(1);]²

["eligible shares" has the meaning given by section 289(7);]²

...¹⁸

...⁹;

...¹⁸

... .¹⁰

...¹⁸

"ordinary shares" means shares forming part of a company's ordinary share capital;

["the period of restriction", in relation to any eligible shares issued by a company, means the period—

(*a*) beginning one year before the shares are issued, and

(*b*) ending immediately before the termination date relating to the shares;]¹⁷

...⁹;

["relief" means relief under this Chapter;]¹⁰

["research and development" has the meaning given by section 837A;]¹⁴

*"the seven year period" has the meaning given by section 291(6);*¹⁵

["subsidiary", in relation to any company (except in the expression "51 per cent subsidiary" or where otherwise defined), means a subsidiary of that company of a kind which that company may hold under section 308;]³

["51 per cent subsidiary", in relation to any company, means (except in the case of references to a company which is a 51 per cent subsidiary on a particular date or at a particular time) a company which is a 51 per cent subsidiary of that company at any time in the relevant period (applying subsection (1A)(*a*) below);]³ [

"termination date" in relation to any eligible shares issued by a company, means the third anniversary of the issue date or if—

(a) the shares were issued wholly or mainly in order to raise money for the purpose of a qualifying business activity falling within section 289(2)(a) (company meeting trading activities requirement by reason of the company or a subsidiary carrying on or preparing to carry on a qualifying trade), and

(b) the company or subsidiary concerned had not begun to carry on the trade in question on the issue date,

the third anniversary of the date on which it begins to carry on that trade; and][11]

["unquoted company" means a company none of whose shares, stocks, debentures or other securities are marketed to the general public;][4]

...[18]

[(1A) In any provision of this Chapter "relevant period", in relation to any eligible shares issued by a company, means whichever of the following periods is applied for the purposes of that provision—

(a) the period beginning either—

(i) with the incorporation of the company, or

(ii) if the company was incorporated more than two years before the date on which the shares were issued, two years before that date,

and ending immediately before the termination date relating to the shares, and

(b) the period beginning with the issue of the shares and ending immediately before the termination date relating to them.][11]

[(1B) For the purposes of the definition of "unquoted company" in subsection (1) above, shares, stocks, debentures or other securities are marketed to the general public if they are—

(a) listed on a recognised stock exchange,

(b) listed on a designated exchange in a country outside the United Kingdom, or

(c) ...[10] dealt in outside the United Kingdom by such means as may be designated.][7]

[(1C) In subsection (1B) above "designated" means designated by an order made by the Board for the purposes of that subsection; and an order made for the purposes of paragraph (b) of that subsection may designate an exchange by name, or by reference to any class or description of exchanges, including a class or description framed by reference to any authority or approval given in a country outside the United Kingdom.][7]

[(1D) Section 828(1) does not apply to an order made for the purposes of subsection (1B) above.][7]

[(1E) Where a company is an unquoted company at the time when any shares are issued [("the relevant time")][16], it shall not be treated for the purposes of this Chapter as ceasing to be an unquoted company in relation to those shares at any subsequent time by reason only that any shares, stocks, debentures or other securities of the company are at that time—

[(a) listed on a stock exchange that is a recognised stock exchange by virtue of an order made under section 841, or

(b) listed on an exchange, or dealt in by any means, designated by an order made for the purposes of subsection (1B) above,

if the order was made after the relevant time][16].][7]

(2) Section 839 applies for the purposes of this Chapter other than [section 291, section 291A(1), (4) and (5) and section 291B][10].

[(2A) References in this Chapter to a company being in administration or receivership shall be construed as follows—

(a) references to a company being "in administration" are to there being in force in relation to it—

(i) an administration order under Part II of the Insolvency Act 1986 or Part III of the Insolvency (Northern Ireland) Order 1989, or

(ii) any corresponding order under the law of a country or territory outside the United Kingdom;

(b) references to a company being "in receivership" are to there being in force in relation to it—

(i) an order for the appointment of an administrative receiver, a receiver and manager or a receiver under Chapter I or II of Part III of the Insolvency Act 1986 or Part IV of the Insolvency (Northern Ireland) Order 1989, or

(ii) any corresponding order under the law of a country or territory outside the United Kingdom.][12]

(3) References in this Chapter to a disposal of shares include references to a disposal of an interest or right in or over the shares and an individual shall be treated for the purposes of this Chapter as disposing of any shares which he is treated by virtue of section [[136][19] of the 1992 Act][1] as exchanging for other shares.

[(4) In this Chapter—

(a) references in any provision to the reduction of any relief attributable to any shares include a reference—

(i) to the reduction of the relief to nil, and

(ii) where no relief has yet been given, to the reduction of the amount which apart from that provision would be the relief, and

(b) references to the withdrawal of any relief, in respect of any shares, are to the withdrawal of the relief attributable to those shares or, in a case where no relief has yet been given, to ceasing to be eligible for relief in respect of those shares.][8]

[(4A) In this Chapter references (however expressed) to an issue of eligible shares in any company are to any eligible shares in the company that are of the same class and are issued on the same day.

(4B) For the purposes of this Chapter shares in a company shall not be treated as being of the same class unless they would be so treated if dealt with on the Stock Exchange.][10]

[(5) For the purposes of this Chapter, the market value at any time of any asset shall be taken to be the price which it might reasonably be expected to fetch on a sale at that time in the open market free from any interest or right which exists by way of security in or over it.][8]

(6) References in this Chapter to relief given to an individual in respect of eligible shares, and to the withdrawal of such relief, include respectively references to relief given to him in respect of those shares at any time after he has disposed of them and references to the withdrawal of such relief at any such time.

(7)–(8) ...[18]

Commentary—*Simon's Direct Tax Service* **Division E3.1.**
Note—For the text of this section as applicable to the Business Expansion Scheme which was abolished in relation to shares issued after 31 December 1993, see *Yellow Tax Handbook*, 1993–94, 32nd edition.
Revenue Interpretation RI 148—Where there is more than one "qualifying business activity" (see TA 1988 s 289(2)), "relevant period" under sub-s (1A)(b) above lasts until latest date has been reached.
Revenue Internal Guidance—Inspector's manual IM 6720 ("associate": separated spouse remains associated but not divorced spouse; other relatives are associated only if there is a blood relationship; illegitimate child is associate but not step-child).
Definitions—See at the beginning of this Chapter.
Amendments—[1] Words in sub-s (3) substituted by TCGA 1992 Sch 10 para 14(1),(18).
[2] Definitions of "eligible for relief", "eligible shares" in sub-s (1) inserted by FA 1994 Sch 15 para 27.
[3] Definitions of "relief", "subsidiary", "51 per cent subsidiary" in sub-s (1) substituted for the definitions of "the relief" and "relief" by FA 1994 Sch 15 para 27.
[4] Definition of "unquoted company" in sub-s (1) substituted by FA 1994 Sch 15 para 27.
[5] Section numbers in the definition of "control" in sub-s (1) substituted by FA 1994 Sch 15 para 27.
[6] Section numbers in sub-ss (2), (7) substituted by FA 1994 Sch 15 para 27.
[7] Sub-ss (1A)–(1E) inserted by FA 1994 s 137(1), (2) and Sch 15 para 27 in relation to EIS shares issued after 31 December 1993 with effect from the year 1993–94.
[8] Sub-ss (4), (5) substituted by FA 1994 s 137(1), (2) and Sch 15 para 27 in relation to EIS shares issued after 31 December 1993 with effect from the year 1993–94.
[9] Definitions of "fixed-rate preference share capital" and "the relevant period" in sub-s (1) repealed by FA 1994 s 137(1), (2), Sch 15 para 27 and Sch 26, Pt V(17) in relation to EIS shares issued after 31 December 1993 with effect from the year 1993–94.
[10] Definition of "new consideration" and words in sub-s (1A), (1B)(c) repealed, new definitions of "relief" and "research and development" substituted, words in sub-ss (2), (7) substituted, and sub-ss (4A)–(4B) inserted by FA 1998 Sch 13 para 23 with effect in relation to shares issued after 5 April 1998.
[11] Word "and" in definition of "51 per cent subsidiary" substituted by new definition of "termination date", and sub-s (1A) substituted by FA 2000 s 64, Sch 17 para 6 with effect for shares issued after 5 April 2000. Sub-s (1A) previously read—

"(1A) In any provision of this Chapter 'relevant period', in relation to relief in respect of any eligible shares issued by a company, means whichever of the following periods is applied for the purposes of that provision ...—

(a) the period beginning with the incorporation of the company (or, if the company was incorporated more than two years before the date on which the shares were issued, beginning two years before that date) and ending five years after the issue of the shares, and

(b) the period beginning with the date on which the shares were issued and ending either—

(i) three years after that date, or

(ii) in a case falling within section 289(2)(a) where the company or subsidiary concerned had not begun to carry on the trade in question on that date, three years after the date on which it begins to carry on that trade."

[12] Sub-s (2A) inserted by FA 2000 s 64, Sch 17 para 9(4) with effect—

(a) for shares issued after 20 March 2000, and

(b) in respect of the application of TA 1988 s 293 after that date for shares—

(i) that were issued after 31 December 1993 but before 21 March 2000, and

(ii) to which income tax relief or deferral relief was attributable immediately before 21 March 2000.

[13] Definition of "arrangements" and words in definition of "control" inserted by FA 2000 s 64, Sch 17 para 14 with effect—

(a) for shares issued after 20 March 2000, and

(b) in respect of the application of TA 1988 s 312 after that date for shares—

(i) that were issued after 31 December 1993 but before 21 March 2000, and

(ii) to which income tax relief or deferral relief was attributable immediately before 21 March 2000.

[14] Definition of "research and development" substituted by FA 2000 s 64, Sch 17 para 15(1), (2) with effect for shares issued after 5 April 2000, in accordance with FA 2000 Sch 17 para 15(3). Definition previously read "'research and development' means any activity which is intended to result in a patentable invention (within the meaning of the Patents Act 1977) or in a computer program;"

[15] Definition of "the seven year period" repealed by FA 2000 s 156, Sch 40 Pt II(5) with effect for shares issued after 5 April 2000.

[16] In sub-s (1E), words inserted, and words substituted for the words "listed on an exchange, or dealt in by any means, designated by such an order if the order was made after the shares were issued" by FA 2001 s 63, Sch 15 paras 13, 40 with effect—

(a) in relation to shares issued after 6 March 2001, and

(b) in respect of the application of TA 1988 Pt VII Chapter III and TCGA 1992 Sch 5B after 6 March 2001 in relation to shares—

(i) that were issued after 31 December 1993 but before 7 March 2001, and

(ii) to which income tax relief or deferral relief was attributable immediately before 7 March 2001.

[17] In sub-s (1), definition of "the period of restriction" inserted by FA 2001 s 63, Sch 15 paras 24, 40 with effect—

(a) in relation to shares issued after 6 March 2001, and

(*b*) in respect of the application of TA 1988 Pt VII Chapter III and TCGA 1992 Sch 5B after 6 March 2001 in relation to shares—

    (i) that were issued after 31 December 1993 but before 7 March 2001, and

    (ii) to which income tax relief or deferral relief was attributable immediately before 7 March 2001.

[18] In sub-s (1), the word "and", and definitions repealed, and sub-ss (7), (8) repealed by FA 2001 s 110, Sch 33 Pt II(3) with effect—

    (*a*) in relation to shares issued after 6 March 2001, and

    (*b*) in respect of the application of TA 1988 Pt VII Chapter III and TCGA 1992 Sch 5B after 6 March 2001 in relation to shares—

    (i) that were issued after 31 December 1993 but before 7 March 2001, and

    (ii) to which income tax relief or deferral relief was attributable immediately before 7 March 2001.

The relevant definitions read as follows—

"'appraisal licence' means an appraisal licence incorporating the model clauses set out in Schedule 4 to the 1984 Regulations or a Northern Ireland licence granted for the five year renewal term and includes in either case any modified appraisal licence;
'the designated period' has the meaning given by section 291(6);
'development licence' means a development licence incorporating the model clauses set out in Schedule 5 to the 1984 Regulations or a Northern Ireland licence granted for the 30 year renewal term and includes in either case any modified development licence;
'exploration licence' means an exploration licence incorporating the model clauses set out in Schedule 3 to the 1984 Regulations or a Northern Ireland licence granted for the initial term and includes in either case any modified exploration licence;
'modified appraisal licence', 'modified development licence' and 'modified exploration licence' mean, respectively, any appraisal licence, development licence or exploration licence in which any of the relevant model clauses have been modified or excluded by the Secretary of State or in Northern Ireland the Department of Economic Development;
'Northern Ireland licence' means a licence granted under the Petroleum (Production) Act (Northern Ireland) 1964 and incorporating the model clauses set out in Schedule 2 to the Petroleum Production (Licences) Regulations (Northern Ireland) 1965, and in relation to such a licence the references above to "the initial term", "the 30 year renewal term" and "the five year renewal term" shall be construed in accordance with Clause 2 of Schedule 2 to those Regulations;
'oil' and 'oil extraction activities' have the same meanings as they have in Chapter V of Part XII;
'oil exploration' means searching for oil;
'the 1984 Regulations' means the Petroleum (Production) (Landward Areas) Regulations 1984."

[19] In sub-s (3) figure "136" substituted for "136(1)" by FA 2002 s 45, Sch 9 paras 4(1), (3), 7(1), 8 with effect for disposals after 16 April 2002.

CHAPTER IV
SPECIAL PROVISIONS

313 Taxation of consideration for certain restrictive undertakings

[(1) Where an individual who holds, has held, or is about to hold, an office or employment gives in connection with his holding that office or employment an undertaking (whether absolute or qualified, and whether legally valid or not) the tenor or effect of which is to restrict him as to his conduct or activities, any sum to which this section applies shall be treated as an emolument of the office or employment, and accordingly shall be chargeable to tax under Schedule E, for the year of assessment in which it is paid.

(2) This section applies to any sum which—

    (*a*) is paid, in respect of the giving of the undertaking or its total or partial fulfilment, either to the individual or to any other person; and

    (*b*) would not, apart from this section, fall to be treated as an emolument of the office or employment.

(3) Where the individual has died before the payment of any sum to which this section applies, subsections (1) and (2) above shall have effect as if that sum had been paid immediately before his death.

(4) Where valuable consideration otherwise than in the form of money is given in respect of the giving of the undertaking or its total or partial fulfilment, subsections (1) to (3) above shall have effect as if a sum had instead been paid equal to the value of that consideration.][1]

(6) In this section—

    (*a*) "office or employment" means any office or employment whatsoever such that the emoluments thereof, if any, are or would be chargeable to income tax under Case I or II of Schedule E; and

    (*b*) references to the giving of valuable consideration do not include references to the mere assumption of an obligation to make over or provide valuable property, rights or advantages, but do include references to the doing of anything in or towards the discharge of such an obligation.

Commentary—*Simon's Direct Tax Service* **E4.481, 482.**
Statements of Practice SP 3/96—Revenue will not attribute part of a termination payment made in settlement of employment claims to restrictive covenants which formed part of the terms of employment and are reaffirmed in the settlement.
Revenue Internal Guidance—Schedule E manual, SE 03600 (general introduction and list of instructions covering references SE 03610–03626, including examples).
SE 12810 (termination payments and benefits: applying the legislation, check for chargeability under this section).
SE 13900 (termination payments and benefits: example involving charge under this section).
Simon's Tax Cases—*Vaughan-Neil v IRC* [1979] STC 644*.
Definitions—"Basic rate", s 832(1); "Case I or II of Schedule E", s 19(2); "deduction of income tax", s 4(1); "the Income Tax Acts", s 831(1)(*b*); "total income", s 835(1); "year of assessment", s 832(1).
Cross references—See TA 1988 s 188(1)(*b*) (sums paid under this section are exempt from the charge to tax on termination payments under s 148).
FA 1988 s 73(2) (notwithstanding anything in s 74 of this Act (deductions not allowable), any sum to which this section applies to be an allowable deduction from the profits or gains of a trade etc),
FA 1988 s 73(3) (any sum to which this section applies to be treated as management expenses in the case of investment companies).

Amendments—¹ Sub-ss (1)–(4) substituted for sub-ss (1)–(5) by FA 1988 s 73 for sums paid or treated as paid in respect of the giving of, or the total or partial fulfilment of, undertakings given after 8 June 1988.

314 Divers and diving supervisors

(1) Where the duties of any employment which are performed by a person in the United Kingdom or a designated area consist wholly or mainly—

(a) of taking part, as a diver, in diving operations concerned with the exploration or exploitation of the seabed, its subsoil and their natural resources; or

(b) of acting, in relation to any such diving operations, as a diving supervisor,

the Income Tax Acts shall have effect as if the performance by that person of those duties constituted the carrying on by him of a trade within Case I of Schedule D; and accordingly Schedule E shall not apply to the emoluments from the employment so far as attributable to his performance of those duties.

(2) In this section "designated area" means any area designated under section 1(7) of the Continental Shelf Act 1964.

Commentary—*Simon's Direct Tax Service* E5.701, 703.
Revenue Internal Guidance—Schedule E manual, SE 67115 (as regards divers and diving supervisors see the *Employment Status Manual*).
Definitions—"Emoluments", s 131(1); "the Income Tax Acts", s 831(1)(b); "Schedule D", s 18(1); "Schedule E", s 19(1).

315 Wounds and disability pensions

(1) Income from wounds and disability pensions to which this subsection applies shall be exempt from income tax and shall not be reckoned in computing income for any purposes of the Income Tax Acts.

(2) Subsection (1) above applies to—

(a) wounds pensions granted to members of the naval, military or air forces of the Crown;

(b) retired pay of disabled officers granted on account of medical unfitness attributable to or aggravated by naval, military or air-force service;

(c) disablement or disability pensions granted to members, other than commissioned officers, of the naval, military or air forces of the Crown on account of medical unfitness attributable to or aggravated by naval, military or air-force service;

(d) disablement pensions granted to persons who have been employed in the nursing services of any of the naval, military or air forces of the Crown on account of medical unfitness attributable to or aggravated by naval, military or air-force service; and

(e) injury and disablement pensions payable under any scheme made under the Injuries in War (Compensation) Act 1914 the Injuries in War Compensation Act 1914 (Session 2) and the Injuries in War (Compensation) Act 1915 or under any War Risks Compensation Scheme for the Mercantile marine.

(3) Where the amount of any retired pay or pensions to which subsection (1) above applies is not solely attributable to disablement or disability, the relief conferred by that subsection shall extend only to such part as is certified by the [Secretary of State]¹, after consultation with the appropriate government department, to be attributable to disablement or disability.

Commentary—*Simon's Direct Tax Service* E4.317, 319.
Revenue Internal Guidance—Schedule E manual, SE 74008 (payments exempted from or not charged to tax as pensions includes wounds and disability pensions paid in respect of service with HM Forces).
SE 74301 (pensions: particular occupations: armed forces pensions and allowances).
Definition—"The Income Tax Acts", s 831(1)(b).
Amendments—¹ Words in sub-s (3) substituted by the Transfer of Functions (War Pensions etc) Order, SI 2001/3506 art 5, Schedule para 2 with effect from 31 December 2001.

316 Allowances, bounties and gratuities

(1) Where, under the scheme relating to men in the Armed Forces of the Crown announced on behalf of His Majesty's Government in the United Kingdom on 15th April 1946 or under any other scheme certified by the Treasury to make analogous provision for classes of persons to whom the first-mentioned scheme does not apply, a person who has served in the armed forces of the Crown at any time during the continuance in force of the Emergency Powers (Defence) Act 1939 voluntarily undertakes to serve therein for a further period, any sum payable to him in pursuance of the scheme out of moneys provided by Parliament by way of gratuity at the end of his further period of service shall not be regarded as income for any income tax purposes.

(2) Where, under the scheme relating to members of the Women's Royal Naval Service, the Auxiliary Territorial Service and the Women's Auxiliary Air Force announced on behalf of His Majesty's Government in the United Kingdom on 20th November 1946, or under any other scheme certified by the Treasury to make analogous provision for classes of persons to whom the first-mentioned scheme does not apply, a woman who has served in or with the armed forces of the Crown at any time during the continuance in force of the Emergency Powers (Defence) Act 1939 voluntarily undertakes to serve in or with those forces for a further period, any sum payable to her in

pursuance of the scheme out of moneys provided by Parliament by way of gratuity at the end of her further period of service shall not be regarded as income for any income tax purposes.

(3) Any allowance payable out of the public revenue to or in respect of any class of persons, being members of the armed forces of the Crown, as respects which the Treasury certifies either—

(*a*) that it is payable to the persons in question in lieu of food or drink normally supplied in kind to members of the armed forces, or

(*b*) that it is payable in respect of the persons in question as a contribution to the expenses of a mess,

shall not be regarded as income for any income tax purposes.

(4) The sums known as training expenses allowances payable out of the public revenue to members of the reserve and auxiliary forces of the Crown, and the sums payable by way of bounty out of the public revenue to such members in consideration of their undertaking prescribed training and attaining a prescribed standard of efficiency, shall not be treated as income for any income tax purpose.

(5) Any sum which, in pursuance of the scheme as to service emoluments contained in the Command Paper laid before Parliament in August 1950, becomes payable out of moneys provided by Parliament by way of bounty to a person who, having served in the armed forces of the Crown, voluntarily undertakes to serve for a further period shall not be regarded as income for any income tax purpose.

Commentary—*Simon's Direct Tax Service* E4.320–322.
Revenue Internal Guidance—Schedule E manual, SE 50110 (reserve and auxiliary forces: taxable payments; exempt payments, application of sub-ss (4) and (5)).
SE 74301 (pensions: particular occupations: armed forces pensions and allowances).
Definition—''Emoluments'', s 131(1).

317 Victoria Cross and other awards

The following shall be disregarded for all the purposes of the Income Tax Acts—

(*a*) annuities and additional pensions paid to holders of the Victoria Cross;
(*b*) annuities and additional pensions paid to holders of the George Cross;
(*c*) annuities paid to holders of the Albert Medal or of the Edward Medal;
(*d*) additional pensions paid to holders of the Military Cross;
(*e*) additional pensions paid to holders of the Distinguished Flying Cross;
(*f*) additional pensions paid to holders of the Distinguished Conduct Medal;
(*g*) additional pensions paid to holders of the Conspicuous Gallantry Medal;
(*h*) additional pensions paid to holders of the Distinguished Service Medal;
(*i*) additional pensions paid to holders of the Military Medal;
(*j*) additional pensions paid to holders of the Distinguished Flying Medal;

where paid by virtue of holding the award.

Commentary—*Simon's Direct Tax Service* E4.318.
Revenue Internal Guidance—Schedule E manual, SE 74008 (payments exempted from or not charged to tax as pensions includes pensions paid to holders of certain awards for gallantry).
SE 74301 (pensions: particular occupations: armed forces pensions and allowances).

318 Other pensions in respect of death due to war service etc

(1) Payments of pensions or allowances to which this section applies shall not be treated as income for any purposes of the Income Tax Acts.

(2) This section applies to—

(*a*) any pension or allowance payable by or on behalf of the [Department of Social Security][1] under so much of any Order in Council, Royal Warrant, order or scheme as relates to death due to—

(i) service in the armed forces of the Crown or war-time service in the merchant navy, or
(ii) war injuries;

(*b*) any pension or allowance at similar rates and subject to similar conditions which is payable by the Ministry of Defence in respect of death due to peacetime service in the armed forces of the Crown before 3rd September 1939; and

(*c*) any pension or allowance which is payable under the law of a country other than the United Kingdom and is of a character substantially similar to a pension or allowance falling within paragraph (*a*) or (*b*) above.

(3) Where a pension or allowance falling within subsection (2) above is withheld or abated by reason of the receipt of another pension or allowance not falling within that subsection, there shall be treated as falling within that subsection so much of the other pension or allowance as is equal to the pension or allowance that is withheld or, as the case may be, to the amount of the abatement.

Commentary—*Simon's Direct Tax Service* E4.319.
Revenue Internal Guidance—Schedule E manual, SE 74008 (payments exempted from or not charged to tax as pensions includes certain pensions paid to war widows and other dependants of deceased servicemen).
SE 74301 (pensions: particular occupations: armed forces pensions and allowances).
SE 76103 (war widow's pensions are exempt and pensions to other dependants of a deceased member of HM Forces etc can also qualify).
SE 76104 (cases of difficulty to be reported to Head Office).

Definition—"The Income Tax Acts", s 831(1)(*b*).
Amendments—¹ Words in sub-s (2)(*a*) substituted by the Transfer of Functions (Health and Social Security) Order 1988, SI 1988/1843.

319 Crown servants: foreign service allowance

[(1)]¹ Where any allowance to any person in the service of the Crown is certified ...¹ to represent compensation for the extra cost of having to live outside the United Kingdom in order to perform his duties, that allowance shall not be regarded as income for any income tax purpose.

[(2) A certificate under subsection (1) shall be given by the Treasury, the Secretary of State, the Lord Chancellor, the Chancellor of the Exchequer, the Minister of Agriculture, Fisheries and Food, the Minister for the Civil Service, the Lord President of the Council, the Lord Privy Seal, the Attorney General or the [Secretary of State for Scotland]².]¹

Commentary—*Simon's Direct Tax Service* E4.324.
Concession A44—Education allowances under Overseas Service Aid Scheme are exempt from income tax if the UK Government has agreed not to tax them.
Amendments—¹ Section numbered as sub-s (1), words omitted repealed and sub-s (2) added by the Transfer of Functions (Foreign Service Allowance) Order 1996, SI 1996/313.
² Words in sub-s (2) substituted by virtue of the Transfer of Functions (Lord Advocate and Secretary of State) Order, SI 1999/678 art 2(1), Schedule with effect from 19 May 1999.

320 Commonwealth Agents-General and official agents etc

(1) An Agent-General who is resident in the United Kingdom shall be entitled to the same immunity from income tax as that to which the head of a mission so resident is entitled under the Diplomatic Privileges Act 1964.

(2) Any person having or exercising any employment to which this subsection applies (not being a person employed in any trade, business or other undertaking carried on for the purposes of profit) shall be entitled to the same immunity from income tax as that to which a member of the staff of a mission is entitled under the Diplomatic Privileges Act 1964.

(3) The employments to which subsection (2) above applies are the employment in the United Kingdom as—

  (*a*) a member of the personal staff of any Agent-General; or
  (*b*) an official agent for, or for any state or province of, any of the countries for the time being mentioned in Schedule 3 to the British Nationality Act 1981 or the Republic of Ireland; or
  (*c*) an official agent for any self-governing colony,

of a person certified by the High Commissioner of the country in question or, as the case may be, by the Agent-General for the state, province or self-governing colony in question to be ordinarily resident outside the United Kingdom and to be resident in the United Kingdom solely for the purpose of the performance of his duties as such member or official agent.

(4) In this section—

  "Agent-General" means the Agent-General for any state or province of a country within subsection (3)(*b*) above or for any self-governing colony;
  "High Commissioner" includes the head of the mission of a country within subsection (3)(*b*) above by whatever name called;
  "mission" has the same meaning as in the Diplomatic Privileges Act 1964 and references to the head of a mission and a member of the staff of a mission shall be construed in accordance with that Act;
  "self-governing colony" means any colony certified by a Secretary of State to be a self-governing colony.

Commentary—*Simon's Direct Tax Service* E5.401.
Concession A39—Extension of relief under this section to certain Hong Kong officials.
Cross references—See TCGA 1992 s 11 (relief for Agents-General, official agents etc from capital gains tax).
Definition—"Trade", s 832(1).

321 Consuls and other official agents

(1) Income arising from any office or employment to which this section applies shall be exempt from income tax, and no account shall be taken of any such income in estimating the amount of income for any income tax purposes.

(2) The offices and employments to which this section applies are the following, that is to say—

  (*a*) the office of a consul in the United Kingdom in the service of any foreign state; and
  (*b*) the employment of an official agent in the United Kingdom for any foreign state, not being an employment exercised by a Commonwealth citizen or a citizen of the Republic of Ireland or exercised in connection with any trade, business or other undertaking carried on for the purposes of profit.

(3) In this section—

  "consul" means a person recognised by Her Majesty as being a consul-general, consul, vice-consul or consular agent; and "official agent" means a person, not being a consul, who is employed on the staff of any consulate, official department or agency of a foreign state, not being a department or agency which carries on any trade, business or other undertaking for the purposes of profit.

Commentary—*Simon's Direct Tax Service* **E5.401.**
Simon's Tax Cases—s 321(2)(*b*), *Caglar v Billingham* [1996] STC (SCD) 150.
Definition—"Trade", s 832(1).

322 Consular officers and employees

(1) Where a consular officer or employee in the United Kingdom of any foreign state to which this section applies—

(*a*) is not a British citizen, a British Dependent Territories citizen[, a British National (Overseas)][1] or a British Overseas citizen, and

(*b*) is not engaged in any trade, profession, vocation or employment in the United Kingdom, otherwise than as such a consular officer or employee, and

(*c*) either is a permanent employee of that state or was not ordinarily resident in the United Kingdom immediately before he became a consular officer or employee in the United Kingdom of that state;

then any income of his falling within Case IV or V of Schedule D shall be exempt from income tax, ...[2]

(2) Without prejudice to section 321, the income arising from a person's employment in the United Kingdom as a consular employee of any foreign state to which this section applies shall be exempt from income tax, except in the case of a person who is not a national of that state but is a British citizen, a British Dependent Territories citizen[, a British National (Overseas)][1] or a British Overseas citizen.

(3) For the purposes of this section "consular employee" includes any person employed, for the purposes of the official business of a consular officer, at any consulate or consular establishment or at any other premises used for those purposes.

(4) This section shall apply to any foreign state to which Her Majesty by Order in Council directs that it shall apply for the purpose of giving effect to any consular convention or other arrangement with that state making similar provision in the case of Her Majesty's consular officers or employees in that state.

(5) An Order in Council under subsection (4) above—

(*a*) may limit the operation of this section in relation to any state in such manner as appears to Her Majesty to be necessary or expedient having regard to the arrangement with that state;

(*b*) may be made so as to have effect from a date earlier than the making of the Order or the passing of this Act (but not earlier than the coming into force of the arrangement with regard to which it is made); and

(*c*) may contain such transitional provisions as appear to Her Majesty to be necessary or expedient;

and any statutory instrument under this section shall be subject to annulment in pursuance of a resolution of the House of Commons.

Commentary—*Simon's Direct Tax Service* **E5.401.**
Definitions—"Schedule D", s 19(1); "trade", s 832(1).
Cross references—See TCGA 1992 s 271(1)(*f*) (any gain accruing to a consular officer or employee, within the meaning of this section, on the disposal of assets which were situated outside the UK at the time of disposal, shall not be chargeable).
Amendments—[1] Words in sub-ss (1)(*a*), (2) inserted by FA 1990 Sch 14 paras 1, 4(1) and are deemed always to have had effect. [2] Words omitted from sub-s (1) repealed by FA 1996 Sch 7 paras 15, 32, Sch 41 Pt V(2) with effect from the year 1996–97.

323 Visiting forces

(1) The emoluments paid by the government of any designated country to any member of a visiting force of that country who is not a British citizen, a British Dependent Territories citizen[, a British National (Overseas)][1] or a British Overseas citizen shall be exempt from income tax.

(2) A period during which a member of a visiting force to whom subsection (1) above applies is in the United Kingdom by reason solely of his being a member of that force shall not be treated for the purposes of income tax either as a period of residence in the United Kingdom or as creating a change of his residence or domicile.

(3) Subsection (2) above shall not affect the operation of section 278 in relation to any person for any year of assessment.

(4) In subsections (1) and (2) above references to a visiting force shall apply to a civilian component of such a force as they apply to the force itself; and those subsections shall be construed as one with the Visiting Forces Act 1952 but so that, for the purposes of this section, references to a designated country shall be substituted in that Act for references to a country to which a provision of that Act applies.

(5) For the purpose of conferring on persons attached to any designated allied headquarters the like benefits as are conferred by subsections (1) and (2) above on members of a visiting force or civilian component, any members of the armed forces of a designated country shall, while attached to any such headquarters, be deemed to constitute a visiting force of that country, and there shall be a

corresponding extension of the class of persons who may be treated as members of a civilian component of such a visiting force.

(6) In the case of persons of any category for the time being agreed between Her Majesty's government in the United Kingdom and the other members of the North Atlantic Council—

(*a*) employment by a designated allied headquarters shall be treated for the purposes of subsection (2) above as if it were service as a member of a visiting force of a designated country; and

(*b*) the emoluments paid by a designated allied headquarters to persons employed by such a headquarters shall be exempt from income tax.

(7) The exemption conferred by subsection (6)(*b*) above shall cease to apply to British citizens, British Dependent Territories citizens[, British Nationals (Overseas)][1] and British Overseas citizens if it becomes unnecessary that it should so apply for the purpose of giving effect to any agreement between parties to the North Atlantic Treaty.

(8) For the purposes of this section—

"allied headquarters" means any international military headquarters established under the North Atlantic Treaty, and

"designated" means designated for the purpose in question by or under any Order in Council made for giving effect to any international agreement.

Commentary—*Simon's Direct Tax Service* E5.403.
Notes—The following countries and allied Headquarters are designated for the purposes of this section by the Visiting Forces and Allied Headquarters (Income Tax and Capital Gains Tax) (Designation) Orders, SI 1961/580, SI 1964/924, SI 1998/1513 and SI 1998/1514. For the continuity of these Orders, see Sch 30, para 21 of this Act.

Countries
Albania, Armenia, Austria, Azerbaijan, Belarus, Belgium, Bulgaria, Canada, Czech Republic, Denmark, Estonia, Germany, Finland, France, Georgia, Greece, Hungary, Italy, Kazakhstan, Kyrgyzstan, Latvia, Lithuania, Luxembourg, Macedonia, Moldova, the Netherlands, Norway, Poland, Portugal, Romania, Russia, Slovak Republic, Slovenia, Spain, Sweden, Switzerland, Turkey, Trukmenistan, Ukraine, United States of America and Uzbekistan.

Allied Headquarters
Channel Committee, Channel Command, Eastern Atlantic Area Command, Supreme Headquarters Allied Powers Europe, Allied Command Atlantic Headquarters, Headquarters of the Supreme Allied Commander Atlantic (SACLANT), Headquarters Eastern Atlantic (EASTLANT), Headquarters Maritime Air Eastern Atlantic (MARAIREASTLANT), Headquarters Submarine Forces Eastern Atlantic (SUBEASTLANT), Headquarters Allied Forces North Western Europe (AFNORTHWEST), Headquarters Allied Naval Forces North Western Europe (NAVNORTHWEST), Headquarters Allied Air Forces North Western Europe (AIRNORTHWEST), NATO Airborne Early Warning Force Headquarters and NATO E-3A Component.

Definitions—"Emoluments", s 131(1); "year of assessment", s 832(1).
Cross references—See TCGA 1992 s 11(1) (visits to the UK by members of forces not to have any effect on their non-resident, non-domiciled status for the purposes of capital gains tax).
Amendments—[1] Words in sub-ss (1), (7) inserted by FA 1990 Sch 14 paras 1, 4(2) and deemed always to have had effect.

324 Designated international organisations

(1) The Treasury may by order designate for the purposes of this section—

(*a*) any international organisation—

(i) if one of its members is the United Kingdom or any of the Communities; and

(ii) if the agreement under which that member became a member provides for exemption from tax, in relation to the organisation, of the kind for which provision is made by this section; or

(*b*) any of the Communities or the European Investment Bank.

(2) Where an organisation has been so designated, a person not resident in the United Kingdom shall not be liable to income tax in respect of income from any security issued by the organisation if he would not be liable but for the fact that—

(*a*) the security or income is issued, made payable or paid in the United Kingdom or in sterling; or

(*b*) the organisation maintains an office or other place of business in the United Kingdom.

Commentary—*Simon's Direct Tax Service* D4.338.

325 Interest on deposits with National Savings Bank

Where the total income of an individual for the year of assessment includes, or would but for this section include, any sums paid or credited in respect of interest on deposits with the National Savings Bank, other than investment deposits, those sums shall be disregarded for all purposes of the Income Tax Acts, other than the furnishing of information, if or in so far as they do not exceed £70; ...[1].

Commentary—*Simon's Direct Tax Service* B5.103.
Definitions—"The Income Tax Acts", s 831(1)(*b*); "interest", s 832(1); "total income", s 835(1).
Amendments—[1] Words repealed by FA 1988 Sch 14 Pt VIII with effect from the year 1990–91.

326 Interest etc under contractual savings schemes

(1) Any terminal bonus, or interest or other sum, payable under a certified contractual savings scheme—

    (*a*) in respect of money raised under section 12 of the National Loans Act 1968 or

    (*b*) in respect of shares in a building society, [or]¹

    [(*c*) in respect of money paid to [a person falling within section 840A(1)(*b*)]¹²]¹ [or]⁶

    [(*d*) in respect of money paid to a relevant European institution,]⁶

shall [not be regarded as income for any income tax purposes]⁴.

(2) In this section ''certified contractual savings scheme'' means, except in relation to a building society [or [a person falling within section 840A(1)(*b*)]¹² [or a relevant European institution]⁷]², [a share option linked scheme]⁵—

    (*a*) governed by regulations made under section [11 of the National Debt Act 1972]³; and

    (*b*) providing for periodical contributions by individuals for a specified period, and the repayment in accordance with the regulations of contributions together with any additional sum by way of bonus or interest, and

    (*c*) certified by the Treasury as qualifying for exemption under this section.

(3) In this section ''certified contractual savings scheme'' means, in relation to a building society, [a share option linked scheme]⁵—

    (*a*) providing for periodical contributions by individuals for a specified period, being contributions by way of investment in shares in the building society, and

    (*b*) certified by the Treasury as [fulfilling such requirements as the Treasury may specify for the purposes of this section]⁹, and as qualifying for exemption under this section.

[(4) In this section ''certified contractual savings scheme'' means, in relation to [a person falling within section 840A(1)(*b*)]¹² [a share option linked scheme]⁵—

    (*a*) providing for periodical contributions by individuals for a specified period, and

    (*b*) certified by the Treasury as [fulfilling such requirements as the Treasury may specify for the purposes of this section]⁹, and as qualifying for exemption under this section.]¹

[(5) In this section ''certified contractual savings scheme'' means, in relation to a relevant European institution, a share option linked scheme—

    (*a*) providing for periodical contributions by individuals for a specified period, and

    (*b*) certified by the Treasury as [fulfilling such requirements as the Treasury may specify for the purposes of this section]⁹, and as qualifying for exemption under this section.]⁸

[(6) Any terminal bonus, interest or other sum payable under a scheme shall not be treated as payable under a certified contractual savings scheme for the purposes of this section if—

    (*a*) the contract under which the sum is payable provides for contributions to be made by way of investment in a building society or to be made to [a person falling within section 840A(1)(*b*)]¹² or to a relevant European institution, and

    (*b*) neither the requirement under subsection (7) below nor that under subsection (8) below is fulfilled.]¹⁰

[(7) The requirement under this subsection is that—

    (*a*) when the contract is entered into there is Treasury authorisation for the society[, person]¹² or institution concerned to enter into contracts under the scheme, and

    (*b*) the authorisation was given without any conditions being imposed.]¹⁰

[(8) The requirement under this subsection is that—

    (*a*) when the contract is entered into there is Treasury authorisation for the society[, person]¹² or institution concerned to enter into contracts under the scheme,

    (*b*) the authorisation was given subject to conditions being met, and

    (*c*) the conditions are met when the contract is entered into.]¹⁰

[(9) Schedule 15A to this Act (which contains provisions supplementing this section) shall have effect.]¹¹

Commentary—*Simon's Direct Tax Service* **B5.210.**
Definition— ''Interest'', s 832(1).
Cross references—See FA 1988 Sch 12, para 7(*a*) (building societies change of status: continuation of tax exemption under this section where contractual savings schemes are in operation before change of status);
TCGA 1992 s 271(4) (any bonus to which this section applies to be disregarded for purposes of capital gains tax).
FA 1995 Sch 12, para 7 (occasions where a terminal bonus, interest or other sum payable under a scheme shall not be treated as payable under a certified contractual savings scheme for the purposes of this section).
FA 1995 Sch 12, para 8 (Treasury may make Regulations under this section).
Amendments—¹ Sub-ss (1)(*c*) (and the preceding word ''or''), (4) inserted by FA 1990 s 29 with effect from 26 July 1990.
² Words in sub-s (2) inserted by FA 1990 s 29 with effect from 26 July 1990.
³ Words in sub-s (2)(*a*) substituted by FA 1990 Sch 14 paras 1, 5 and deemed always to have had effect.
⁴ Words in sub-s (1) substituted by FA 1990 s 29 with effect from 26 July 1990.
⁵ Words in sub-ss (2)–(4) substituted by FA 1995 Sch 12 para 2, with effect for schemes not certified as mentioned in sub-ss (2)(*c*), (3)(*b*), (4)(*b*) above before 1 December 1994.
⁶ Sub-s (1)(*d*) inserted by FA 1995 Sch 12 para 3(2) for schemes established after 1 May 1995.
⁷ Words in sub-s (2) inserted by FA 1995 Sch 12 para 3(3).
⁸ Sub-s (5) inserted by FA 1995 Sch 12, para 3(4).

[9] Words in sub-ss (3)(*b*), (4)(*b*), (5)(*b*) (as noted at 8 above) substituted for the words ''corresponding to a scheme certified under subsection (2) above'' by FA 1995 Sch 12 para 4, for schemes not certified as mentioned in sub-ss (3)(*b*), (4)(*b*), (5)(*b*) above, before such day as the Treasury may by order appoint.

[10] Sub-ss (6)–(8) added by FA 1995 Sch 12 para 5, for schemes not certified as mentioned in sub-ss (3)(*b*), (4)(*b*), (5)(*b*) above, before a day to be appointed under FA 1995 Sch 12 para 4(3).

[11] Sub-s (9) added by FA 1995 Sch 12 para 6(1).

[12] Words in sub-ss (1)(*c*), (2), (4) and (6)(*a*) substituted, and the word ''person'' in sub-ss (7)(*a*), (8)(*a*) inserted, by the Financial Services and Markets Act 2000 (Consequential Amendments) (Taxes) Order, SI 2001/3629 arts 13, 19 with effect from 1 December 2001, immediately after the coming into force of the Financial Services and Markets Act 2000 ss 411, 432(1), Sch 20.

[326A Tax-exempt special savings accounts

(1) Subject to the provisions of section 326B, any interest or bonus payable on a deposit account in respect of a period when it is a tax-exempt special savings account shall not be regarded as income for any income tax purposes.

(2) An account is a ''tax-exempt special savings account'' for the purposes of this section if the conditions set out in subsections (3) to (9) below and any further conditions prescribed by regulations made by the Board are satisfied when the account is opened; and subject to section 326B it shall continue to be such an account until the end of the period of five years beginning with the day on which it is opened, or until the death of the account-holder if that happens earlier.

(3) The account must be opened on or after 1st January 1991 [and before 6th April 1999][3] by an individual aged 18 or more.

(4) The account must be with a building society or [a person falling within section 840A(1)(*b*)][4] [or a relevant European institution][2].

(5) The account must be identified as a tax-exempt special savings account and the account-holder must not simultaneously hold any other such account (with the same or any other society[, person][4] or institution).

(6) The account must not be a joint account.

(7) The account must not be held on behalf of a person other than the account-holder.

(8) The account must not be connected with any other account held by the account-holder or any other person; and for this purpose an account is connected with another if—

(*a*) either was opened with reference to the other, or with a view to enabling the other to be opened on particular terms, or with a view to facilitating the opening of the other on particular terms, and

(*b*) the terms on which either was opened would have been significantly less favourable to the holder if the other had not been opened.

(9) There must not be in force a notice given by the Board to the society[, person][4] or institution prohibiting it from operating new tax-exempt special savings accounts.][1]

[(10) In this section ''relevant European institution'' means an EEA firm of the kind mentioned in paragraph 5(*b*) of Schedule 3 to the Financial Services and Markets Act 2000 which has permission under paragraph 15 of that Schedule (as a result of qualifying for authorisation under paragraph 12 of that Schedule) to accept deposits.][4]

Commentary—*Simon's Direct Tax Service* **E3.401, 402.**

Concession A79—A curator bonis in Scotland may operate a TESSA on behalf of an incapacitated person aged 18 or over, subject to certain conditions.

A92—From 1 January 1996 institutions authorised to operate TESSAs to include European authorised institutions by virtue of SI 1995/3236.

Definitions—''The Board'', s 832(1); ''interest'', s 832(1); ''notice'', s 832(1); ''United Kingdom'', s 830(1).

Cross references—See TA 1988 s 326BB(4) (accounts not to be connected accounts for the purposes of sub-s (8) merely because one of them is a follow-up account).

TA 1988 s 326C (supplementary provisions).

Tax-exempt Special Savings Account Regulations, SI 1990/2361 reg 3(*a*) (additional condition to be satisfied for exemption under this section),

Tax-exempt Special Savings Account Regulations, SI 1990/2361 reg 15(*b*) (information relating to a non-TESSA account with which an account is connected within the meaning of sub-s (8) above),

Tax-exempt Special Savings Account Regulations, SI 1990/2361 reg 16(*b*) (inspection of records relating to a non-TESSA account with which an account is connected within the meaning of sub-s (8) above);

IT (Interest Payments) (Information Powers) Regulations, SI 1992/15 reg 4(4) (a return under TMA 1970 s 17 or s 18 to contain further information in respect of payments on TESSA accounts);

TCGA 1992 s 271(4) (any bonus to which this section applies to be disregarded for purposes of capital gains tax).

Amendments—[1] This section inserted by FA 1990 s 28(1).

[2] Words in sub-s (4) inserted by FA 1995 s 63(2), for accounts opened after 1 January 1996 (by virtue of the Finance Act 1995, section 63(2) (Appointed Day) Order SI 1995/3236.

[3] Words in sub-s (3) inserted by FA 1998 s 78 with effect from 31 July 1998.

[4] Words in sub-s (4) substituted, words in sub-ss (5) and (9) inserted, and sub-s (10) substituted, by the Financial Services and Markets Act 2000 (Consequential Amendments) (Taxes) Order, SI 2001/3629 arts 13, 20(1)–(5) with effect from 1 December 2001, immediately after the coming into force of the Financial Services and Markets Act 2000 ss 411, 432(1), Sch 20.

[326B Loss of exemption for special savings accounts

(1) A tax-exempt special savings account shall cease to be such an account if at any time after it is opened any of the conditions set out in subsections (4) to (8) of section 326A, or any further condition prescribed by regulations made by the Board, is not satisfied, or if any of the events mentioned in subsection (2) below occurs.

(2) The events referred to in subsection (1) above are—

(*a*) the deposit of more than £3,000 in the account during the period of 12 months beginning with the day on which it is opened, more than £1,800 in any of the succeeding periods of 12 months, or more than £9,000 in total;

(*b*) a withdrawal from the account which causes the balance to fall below an amount equal to the aggregate of—

(i) all the sums deposited in the account before the time of the withdrawal, and

(ii) an amount equal to income tax at the [applicable rate on any interest or bonus paid on the account before that time;][2]

(*c*) the assignment of any rights of the account-holder in respect of the account, or the use of such rights as security for a loan.

[(2A) In subsection (2)(*b*)(ii) above "the applicable rate" means—

(*a*) in the case of interest or bonus paid before 6th April 1996, the basic rate for the year of assessment in which the payment was made; and

(*b*) in any other case, the lower rate for the year of assessment in which it was made.][3]

(3) If at any time an account ceases to be a tax-exempt special savings account by virtue of subsection (1) above, the Income Tax Acts shall have effect as if immediately after that time the society[, person][4] or institution had credited to the account an amount of interest equal to the aggregate of any interest and bonus payable in respect of the period during which the account was a tax-exempt special savings account.][1]

Commentary—*Simon's Direct Tax Service* **E3.401.**
Definitions—''Basic rate'', s 832(1); ''the Income Tax Acts'', s 831(1)(*b*); ''interest'', s 832(1); ''lower rate'', s 832(1).
Cross references—See TA 1988 s 326BB(2) (application of sub-s(2)(*a*) to follow up accounts as if £3,000 was reference to the total amount deposited).
TA 1988 s 326C (supplementary provisions).
Tax-exempt Special Savings Account Regulations, SI 1990/2361 reg 12(3)(*c*), (*h*) (return of accounts ceasing to be tax-exempt and return of tax deductions from income of accounts ceasing to be tax-exempt for reasons mentioned in sub-s (1) above).
Tax-exempt Special Savings Account Regulations, SI 1990/2361 reg 13(3)(*b*)(vi) (return of individual account ceasing to be tax-exempt for reasons mentioned in sub-s (1) above).
Tax-exempt Special Savings Account (Relevant European Institutions) Regulations, SI 1995/3239 reg 7 (sub-s (3) above has effect also for accounts held with European institutions which cease to qualify by virtue of Part II of the regulations).
Amendments—[1] This section inserted by FA 1990 s 28(1).
[2] Words in sub-s (2)(*b*)(ii) substituted by FA 1996 Sch 6 para 7(1) with effect as respects withdrawals after 5 April 1995.
[3] Sub-s (2A) inserted by FA 1996 Sch 6 para 7(2) with effect as respects withdrawals after 5 April 1996.
[4] Words ''person'' in sub-s (3) inserted by the Financial Services and Markets Act 2000 (Consequential Amendments) (Taxes) Order, SI 2001/3629 arts 13, 20(6) with effect from 1 December 2001, immediately after the coming into force of the Financial Services and Markets Act 2000 ss 411, 432(1), Sch 20.

[326BB Follow-up TESSAs

(1) Subsection (2) below applies where—

(*a*) an individual, within the period of six months from the day on which a tax-exempt special savings account held by him matured, opens another account (''a follow-up account'') which is a tax-exempt special savings account at the time it is opened; and

(*b*) the total amount deposited in the matured account, before it matured, exceeded £3,000.

(2) In relation to the follow-up account section 326B(2)(*a*) shall apply as if the reference to £3,000 were a reference to the total amount so deposited.

(3) For the purposes of subsection (1) above a tax-exempt special savings account held by an individual matures when a period of five years throughout which the account was a tax-exempt special savings account comes to an end.

(4) An account is not connected with another account for the purposes of section 326A(8) merely because one of them is a follow-up account.][1]

Commentary—*Simon's Direct Tax Service* **E3.401.**
Cross references—See TA 1988 ss 326C(1B), 326D(11) (sub-s (3) above applies for the purposes of the Revenue making regulations for follow-up TESSAs).
Tax-exempt Special Savings Account Regulations, SI 1990/2361 regs 3(*cc*), 7A, 7B (sub-s (2) above does not apply unless the institution holds a maturity certificate or, where the matured account and follow up are with the same institution, the equivalent records).
Amendments—[1] Section inserted by FA 1995 s 62(2).

[326C Tax-exempt special savings accounts: supplementary

(1) The Board may make regulations—

(*a*) prescribing conditions additional to those set out in section 326A which must be satisfied if an account is to be or remain a tax-exempt special savings account;

(*b*) making provision for the giving by the Board to building societies and other [persons and][4] institutions of notices prohibiting them from operating new tax-exempt special savings accounts, including provision about appeals against the giving of notices;

(*c*) requiring building societies and other [persons and][4] institutions operating or proposing to operate tax-exempt special savings accounts to give information or send documents to the Board or to make documents available for inspection;

[(*cc*) providing that subsection (2) of section 326BB does not apply in relation to a follow-up account unless at such time as may be prescribed by the regulations the building society[, person][4] or institution with which the account is held has a document of a prescribed description containing such information as the regulations may prescribe;][2]

[(*cd*) requiring building societies and other [persons and][4] institutions operating tax-exempt special savings accounts which mature to give to the individuals who have held them certificates containing such information as the regulations may prescribe;][2]

(*d*) making provision as to the transfer of tax-exempt special savings accounts from one building society[, person][4] or institution to another;

(*e*) generally for supplementing the provisions of sections 326A and [326B and 326BB][3].][1]

[(1A) In paragraph (*cc*) of subsection (1) above "document" includes a record kept by means of a computer; and regulations made by virtue of that paragraph may prescribe different documents for different cases.][2]

[(1B) Subsection (3) of section 326BB applies for the purposes of subsection (1) above as it applies for the purposes of subsection (1) of that section.][2]

(2) The reference in section 326A to a deposit account shall be taken to include a reference to a share account with a building society, and accordingly that section, [sections 326B and 326BB][3] and subsection (1) above shall apply to such an account with the necessary modifications.

Commentary—*Simon's Direct Tax Service* **E3.401.**
Regulations—Tax-exempt Special Savings Account Regulations, SI 1990/2361.
Tax-exempt Special Savings Account (Relevant European Institutions) Regulations, SI 1995/3239.
Definitions—"The Board", s 832(1); "follow-up account", s 326BB(1)(*a*); "notice", s 832(1).
Amendments—[1] This section inserted by FA 1990 s 28(1).
[2] Sub-ss (1)(*cc*), (*cd*), (1A), (1B) inserted by FA 1995 s 62(3), (5).
[3] Words in sub-ss (1)(*e*), (2) substituted by FA 1995 s 62(4), (6).
[4] Words in sub-s (1) inserted by the Financial Services and Markets Act 2000 (Consequential Amendments) (Taxes) Order, SI 2001/3629 arts 13, 20(7) with effect from 1 December 2001, immediately after the coming into force of the Financial Services and Markets Act 2000 ss 411, 432(1), Sch 20.

[326D Tax-exempt special savings accounts: tax representatives

(1) Without prejudice to the generality of section 326C(1), the Board may make regulations providing that an account held with a relevant European institution shall not be a tax-exempt special savings account at the time it is opened, or shall cease to be a tax-exempt special savings account at a given time, unless at the time concerned one of the following three requirements is fulfilled.

(2) The first requirement is that—

(*a*) a person who falls within subsection (5) below is appointed by the institution to be responsible for securing the discharge of prescribed duties which fall to be discharged by the institution, and

(*b*) his identity and the fact of his appointment have been notified to the Board by the institution.

(3) The second requirement is that there are other arrangements with the Board for a person other than the institution to secure the discharge of such duties.

(4) The third requirement is that there are other arrangements with the Board designed to secure the discharge of such duties.

(5) A person falls within this subsection if—

(*a*) he is not an individual and has a business establishment in the United Kingdom, or

(*b*) he is an individual and is resident in the United Kingdom.

(6) Different duties may be prescribed as regards different institutions or different descriptions of institution.

(7) The regulations may provide that—

(*a*) the first requirement shall not be treated as fulfilled unless the person concerned is of a prescribed description;

(*b*) the appointment of a person in pursuance of that requirement shall be treated as terminated in prescribed circumstances.

(8) The regulations may provide that—

(*a*) the second requirement shall not be treated as fulfilled unless the person concerned is of a prescribed description;

(*b*) arrangements made in pursuance of that requirement shall be treated as terminated in prescribed circumstances.

(9) The regulations may provide as mentioned in subsection (10) below as regards a case where—

(*a*) in accordance with the first requirement a person is at any time appointed to be responsible for securing the discharge of duties, or

(*b*) in accordance with the second requirement there are at any time arrangements for a person to secure the discharge of duties.

(10) In such a case the regulations may provide that the person concerned—

(*a*) shall be entitled to act on the institution's behalf for any of the purposes of the provisions relating to the duties;

(*b*) shall secure (where appropriate by acting on the institution's behalf) the institution's compliance with and discharge of the duties;

(*c*) shall be personally liable in respect of any failure of the institution to comply with or discharge any such duty as if the duties imposed on the institution were imposed jointly and severally on the institution and the person concerned.

(11) Regulations under this section may include provision that section 326B(3) shall have effect as if the reference to subsection (1) included a reference to the regulations.

(12) In this section ''prescribed'' means prescribed by the regulations.]¹

Commentary—*Simon's Direct Tax Service* **E3.401.**
Regulations—Tax-exempt Special Savings Account (Relevant European Institutions) Regulations, SI 1995/3239.
Definitions—''The Board'', s 832(1); ''United Kingdom'', s 830(1).
Amendments—¹ Section inserted by FA 1995 s 63(4).

327 Disabled person's vehicle maintenance grant

A grant made under paragraph 2 of Schedule 2 to the National Health Service Act 1977 or section 46(3) of the National Health Service (Scotland) Act 1978 (cost of maintenance etc of vehicles belonging to disabled persons) or under Article 30 of the Health and Personal Social Services (Northern Ireland) Order 1972 to any person owning a vehicle shall not be treated as income for any purpose of the Income Tax Acts.

Commentary—*Simon's Direct Tax Service* **E4.328.**
Definition—''The Income Tax Acts'', s 831(1)(*b*).

328 Funds in court

Amendments—This section repealed by FA 1999 ss 68(2), (3), 139, Sch 20 Pt III(17) with effect for any income arising to a common investment fund after 5 April 1999, and any distribution made by such a fund for a distribution period beginning after that date. See FA 1999 s 68(4) for transitional rules for a common investment fund in existence on 5 April 1999.

329 Interest on damages for personal injuries

(1) The following interest shall not be regarded as income for any income tax purpose—

(*a*) any interest on damages in respect of personal injuries to a plaintiff or any other person, or in respect of a person's death, which is included in any sum for which judgment is given by virtue of a provision to which this paragraph applies; and

(*b*) any interest on damages or solatium in respect of personal injuries sustained by a pursuer or by any other person, decree for payment of which is included in any interlocutor by virtue of section 1 of the Interest on Damages (Scotland) Act 1958.

(2) The provisions to which subsection (1)(*a*) above applies are—

(*a*) section 3 of the Law Reform (Miscellaneous Provisions) Act 1934;
(*b*) section 17 of the Law Reform (Miscellaneous Provisions) Act (Northern Ireland) 1937;
(*c*) section 35A of the Supreme Court Act 1981;
(*d*) section 69 of the County Courts Act 1984;
(*e*) section 33A of the Judicature (Northern Ireland) Act 1978; and
(*f*) Article 45A of the County Courts (Northern Ireland) Order 1980.

(3) A payment in satisfaction of a cause of action, including a payment into court, shall not be regarded as income for any income tax purpose to the extent to which it is in respect of interest which would fall within subsection (1) above if included in a sum for which a judgment is given or if decree for payment of it were included in an interlocutor.

(4) In this section ''personal injuries'' includes any disease and any impairment of a person's physical or mental condition.

Commentary—*Simon's Direct Tax Service* **B5.210.**
Concession A30—The exemption under this section is extended to interest on damages awarded for personal injuries or death by a foreign court provided the interest is exempt in the country in which the award is made.
Definition—''Interest'', s 832(1).

[329AA Personal injury damages in the form of periodical payments

(1) Where—

(*a*) an agreement is made settling a claim or action for damages for personal injury on terms whereby the damages are to consist wholly or partly of periodical payments; or

(*b*) a court awarding damages for personal injury makes an order incorporating such terms,

the payments shall not for the purposes of income tax be regarded as the income of any of the persons mentioned in subsection (2) below and accordingly shall be paid without any deduction under section 348(1)(*b*) or 349(1).

(2) The persons referred to in subsection (1) above are—

(*a*) the person (''A'') entitled to the damages under the agreement or order;

(*b*) any person who, whether in pursuance of the agreement or order or otherwise, receives the payments or any of them on behalf of A;

(*c*) any trustee who, whether in pursuance of the agreement or order or otherwise, receives the payments or any of them on trust for the benefit of A under a trust under which A is during his lifetime the sole beneficiary.

(3) The periodical payments referred to in subsection (1) above, or any of them, may, if the agreement or order mentioned in that subsection or a subsequent agreement so provides, consist of payments under one or more annuities purchased or provided for, or for the benefit of, A by the person by whom the payments would otherwise fall to be made.

(4) Sums paid to, or for the benefit of, A by a trustee or trustees shall not be regarded as his income for the purposes of income tax if made out of payments which by virtue of this section are not to be regarded for those purposes as income of the trustee or trustees.

(5) In this section "personal injury" includes any disease and any impairment of a person's physical or mental condition.

(6) For the purposes of this section a claim or action for personal injury includes—

(*a*) such a claim or action brought by virtue of the Law Reform (Miscellaneous Provisions) Act 1934;
(*b*) such a claim or action brought by virtue of the Law Reform (Miscellaneous Provisions) Act (Northern Ireland) 1937;
(*c*) such a claim or action brought by virtue of the Damages (Scotland) Act 1976;
(*d*) a claim or action brought by virtue of the Fatal Accidents Act 1976;
(*e*) a claim or action brought by virtue of the Fatal Accidents (Northern Ireland) Order 1977.

(7) In relation to such an order as is mentioned in paragraph (*b*) of subsection (1) above "damages" includes an interim payment which the court, by virtue of rules of court in that behalf, orders the defendant to make to the plaintiff; and where, without such an order, the defendant agrees to make a payment on account of the damages that may be awarded against him in such an action as is mentioned in paragraph (*a*) of that subsection, that paragraph shall apply to the payment and the agreement as it applies to damages and to such an agreement as is there mentioned.

(8) In the application of subsection (7) above to Scotland for references to the plaintiff and the defendant there shall be substituted references to the pursuer and the defender.]¹

Commentary—*Simon's Direct Tax Service* **B5.310.**
Cross references—TA 1988 s 329AB (application of this section to compensation for personal injury annuities under the criminal injuries compensation scheme and other appointed schemes).
Amendments—¹ This section inserted by FA 1996 s 150 Sch 26 (superseding former ss 329A, 329B) with effect for payments received after 29 April 1996 irrespective of when the agreement or order was made or took effect.

[329AB Compensation for personal injury under statutory or other schemes

(1) Section 329AA applies to annuity payments under an award of compensation made under the Criminal Injuries Compensation Scheme as it applies to payments of damages in that form under such an agreement or order as is mentioned in subsection (1) of that section.

(2) In subsection (1) above "the Criminal Injuries Compensation Scheme" means—

(*a*) the scheme established by arrangements made under the Criminal Injuries Compensation Act 1995; or
(*b*) arrangements made by the Secretary of State for compensation for criminal injuries and in operation before the commencement of that scheme.

(3) If it appears to the Treasury that any other scheme or arrangement, whether established by statute or otherwise, makes provision for the making of periodical payments by way of compensation for personal injury within the meaning of section 329AA, the Treasury may by order apply that section to those payments with such modifications as the Treasury consider necessary.]¹

Commentary—*Simon's Direct Tax Service* **B5.310.**
Amendments—¹ Section inserted by FA 1996 s 150 Sch 26 (sub-ss (1), (2) superseding former s 329C) with effect for payments received after 8 November 1995 (the date the Criminal Injuries Compensation Act 1995 received Royal Assent).

329A Annuities purchased for certain persons

Cross references—See TA 1988 s 329B(4) (sub-ss (6)–(10) above apply for the purposes of annuities assigned in favour of certain persons).
Amendments—This section inserted by FA 1995 s 142 and repealed by FA 1996 s 150(2), (4) Sch 41 Pt V(16) (being replaced by s 329AA *ante*) but not so as to affect the operation of this section for payments received before 29 April 1996.

329B Annuities assigned in favour of certain persons

Amendments—This section inserted by FA 1995 s 142 and repealed by FA 1996 s 150(2), (4) Sch 41 Pt V(16) (being replaced by s 329AA *ante*) but not so as to affect the operation of this section for payments received before 29 April 1996.

329C Annuities: criminal injuries

Amendments—This section (inserted by the Criminal Injuries Compensation Act 1995 s 8) repealed by FA 1996 s 150(3), (4) Sch 41 Pt V(16) (being replaced by s 329AB(1), (2) *above* for payments received after 8 November 1995.

330 Compensation for National-Socialist persecution

Annuities and pensions payable under any special provision for victims of National-Socialist persecution which is made by the law of the Federal Republic of Germany or any part of it or of Austria shall not be regarded as income for any income tax purpose.

Commentary—*Simon's Direct Tax Service* **E1.329.**

331 Scholarship income

(1) Income arising from a scholarship held by a person receiving full-time instruction at a university, college, school or other educational establishment shall be exempt from income tax, and no account shall be taken of any such income in computing the amount of income for income tax purposes.

(2) In this section ''scholarship'' includes an exhibition, bursary or any other similar educational endowment.

Commentary—*Simon's Direct Tax Service* **E4.325.**
Statement of Practice SP 4/86—Circumstances in which scholarships awarded by employers to employees are exempt from tax.

Revenue Internal Guidance—Schedule E manual SE 06200 (scholarship income: table of contents explaining application of this section and covering references SE 06200–06214).
Simon's Tax Cases—*Walters v Tickner* [1993] STC 624*.
s 331(1), *Wicks v Firth* [1983] STC 25*.
Cross references—See TA 1988 s 165(1) (taxation of scholarships by virtue of a person's employment as director or higher-paid employee).

[331A Student loans: certain interest to be disregarded

(1) If—

　　(a) a loan is made to a person under any of the relevant student loan provisions,
　　(b) an amount is recovered from him in respect of the loan,
　　(c) an amount is repaid to him in respect of the amount recovered, and
　　(d) interest is paid to him in respect of the amount repaid, the interest shall be disregarded for all purposes of income tax.

(2) For the purposes of subsection (1) above the relevant student loan provisions are—

　　(a) section 22 of the Teaching and Higher Education Act 1998;
　　(b) section 73(f) of the Education (Scotland) Act 1980;
　　(c) Article 3 of the Education (Student Support) (Northern Ireland) Order 1998.][1]

Commentary—*Simon's Direct Tax Service* **B5.210.**
Amendments—[1] This section inserted by FA 1999 s 60 with effect from 27 July 1999.

332 Expenditure and houses of ministers of religion

(1) Subsection (2) below applies where an interest in any premises belongs to a charity or any ecclesiastical corporation and (in right of that interest)—

　　(a) the persons from time to time holding any full-time office as clergyman or minister of any religious denomination, or
　　(b) any particular person holding such an office,

have or has a residence in those premises from which to perform the duties of the office.

(2) In the case of such a clergyman or minister, for the purposes of income tax with which he may be chargeable under Schedule E, there shall be disregarded—

　　(a) the making good to him, in consequence of his being the holder of his office, of statutory amounts payable in connection with the premises or statutory deductions falling to be made in connection therewith, except in so far as an amount or deduction is properly attributable to a part of the premises in respect of which he receives rent;
　　(b) the payment on his behalf, except as aforesaid, of such a statutory amount; and
　　(c) unless he is in [employment to which Chapter II of Part V applies][1], the value to him of any expenses incurred in connection with the provision in the premises of living accommodation for him, being expenses incurred in consequence of his being the holder of his office.

(3) In assessing the income tax chargeable (whether under Schedule E or any other Schedule) upon a clergyman or minister of any religious denomination, the following deductions may be made from any profits, fees or emoluments of his profession or vocation—

　　(a) any sums of money paid or expenses incurred by him wholly, exclusively and necessarily in the performance of his duty as a clergyman or minister;
　　(b) such part of the rent (not exceeding one-quarter) as the inspector by whom the assessment is made may allow, paid by him in respect of a dwelling-house any part of which is used mainly and substantially for the purposes of his duty as such clergyman or minister; and
　　(c) in respect of expenses borne by him in the maintenance, repairs, insurance or management of any premises in which, in right of such an interest as is mentioned in subsection (1) above, he has such a residence as is mentioned in that subsection, such part of the expenses as, together with any

deduction allowable in respect of such expenses under paragraph (*a*) above, is equal to one-quarter of the amount of the expenses.

On an appeal to the General Commissioners or Special Commissioners, the Commissioners shall have jurisdiction to review the inspector's decision under paragraph (*b*) above.

[(3A) No deduction may be made under subsection (3) above in respect of qualifying travelling expenses incurred in connection with the use by a clergyman or minister of a vehicle that is not a company vehicle if—

(*a*) mileage allowance payments are made to that person in respect of the use of the vehicle; or
(*b*) mileage allowance relief is available in respect of the use of the vehicle by that person.][2]

[(3B) In subsection (3A)—

"company vehicle" has the meaning given by paragraph 6 of Schedule 12AA;
"mileage allowance payments" has the meaning given by section 197AD(2); and
"qualifying travelling expenses" has the meaning given by section 198(1A).][2]

(4) In this section "statutory amount" and "statutory deduction" mean an amount paid and a deduction made in pursuance of any provision contained in or having the force of an Act.

Commentary—*Simon's Direct Tax Service* **E4.712.**
Revenue Internal Guidance—Schedule E manual, SE 02720 (personal incidental expenses: where travelling expense qualifies under this section relief will be available for personal incidental expenses under s 200A).
SE 20102 (working out if an employment has emoluments at a rate of £8,500 a year or more—no deduction for expenses under this section).
SE 60001 (Ministers of religion: overview).
SE 60007–60011 (application of sub-s 2 and Extra Statutory Concession A61).
SE 60013–60014 (statutory amounts and statutory deductions under sub-s (2) and (4)).
SE 60015 (heating, lighting, cleaning, gardening; lower paid employees, application of ESC A61).
SE 60040 (allowable expenses: overview).
SE 60044 (property expenses, application of sub-s (3)).
SE 60046–60048 (list of allowable items).
Definitions—"Emoluments", s 131(1); "inspector", s 832(1); "Schedule E", s 19(1).
Cross references—See TA 1988 s 141(3) (relief under sub-s (3) above for non-cash vouchers).
TA 1988 s 142(2) (relief under sub-s (3) above for credit-tokens).
TA 1988 s 145(3) (relief under sub-s (3) above for living accommodation).
TA 1988 s 156(8) (taxation of benefits in kind; allowable deductions under this section).
TA 1988 s 167(2) (exclusion of deductions under sub-s (3) above in calculating value of benefits provided for directors and higher-paid employees).
TA 1988 ss 193(7), 194(10), 195(11) (construction of references to this section in the Income Tax Acts).
TA 1988 s 167(4) (secondary Class 1 contributions and Class 1A contributions *not* precluded from being deductible under sub-s (3)(*a*) above).
Amendments—[1] Words in sub-s (2)(*c*) substituted by FA 1989 s 53(2)(*f*).
[2] Sub-ss (3A), (3B) inserted by FA 2001 s 57(3), (4), Sch 12 Pt II para 10 with effect from the year 2002–03.

[332A Venture capital trusts: relief

Schedule 15B shall have effect for conferring relief from income tax in respect of investments in venture capital trusts and distributions by such trusts.][1]

Commentary—*Simon's Direct Tax Service* **Division E3.6.**
Definition—"Venture capital trust", s 842AA.
Amendments—[1] Section inserted by FA 1995 s 71(1), with effect from the year 1995–96.

333 Personal equity plans

(1) The Treasury may make regulations providing that an individual who invests under a plan shall be entitled to relief from income tax in respect of the investments.

[(1A) The plans for which provision may be made by the regulations include, in particular, a plan in the form of an account the subscriptions to which are to be invested in one or more of the ways authorised by the regulations; and, accordingly, references in this section, or in any other enactment, to a plan manager include references to the manager of such an account.][2]

(2) The regulations shall set out the conditions subject to which plans are to operate and the extent to which investors are to be entitled to relief from tax.

(3) In particular, the regulations may—

(*a*) specify the description of individuals who may invest and the kind of investments they may make;
(*b*) specify maximum investment limits ...[2]
(*c*) provide that investments are to be held by persons ("plan managers") on behalf of investors;
(*d*) specify how relief from tax is to be claimed by, and granted to, investors or plan managers on their behalf;
(*e*) provide that plans and plan managers must be such as are approved by the Board;
(*f*) specify the circumstances in which approval may be granted and withdrawn.
[(*g*) provide for plans to be treated as being of different kinds, according to criteria set out in the regulations;][1]
[(*h*) provide that the Board may register a plan as being of a particular kind;][1]
[(*i*) make different provision as to different kinds of plan;][1]

[(*j*) provide for investment by an individual under more than one plan in the same year of assessment.]¹

(4) The regulations may include provision—

  (*a*) that in prescribed circumstances—

    (i) an investor under a plan shall cease to be, and be treated as not having been, entitled to relief from tax in respect of the investments; and

    (ii) he or the plan manager concerned (depending on the terms of the regulations) shall account to the Board for tax from which relief has already been given on the basis that the investor was so entitled;

  (*b*) that an investor under a plan or the plan manager concerned (depending on the terms of the regulations) shall account to the Board either—

    (i) for tax from which relief has been given in circumstances such that the investor was not entitled to it; [or

    (ii) for an amount determined in accordance with the regulations to be the amount which is to be taken to represent such tax]²

  (*c*) adapting, or modifying the effect of, any enactment relating to income tax in order to—

    (i) secure that investors under plans are entitled to relief from tax in respect of investments;

    (ii) secure that investors under plans cease to be, and are treated as not having been, so entitled;

    (iii) secure that investors under plans or plan managers account for tax [and other amounts]² as mentioned in paragraph (*a*) or (*b*) above;

  [(*ca*) adapting or modifying the provisions of Chapter II of Part XIII in relation to cases where—

    (i) an investor ceases to be, and is treated as not having been, entitled to relief from tax in respect of investments; or

    (ii) an investor who was not entitled to relief has been given relief on the basis that he was;

  (*cb*) securing that plan managers (as well as investors) are liable to account for amounts becoming due from investors as a consequence of any regulations made by virtue of paragraph (ca) above;

  (*cc*) that an investor under a plan or a plan manager is, in prescribed cases where relief has been given to which there was no entitlement, to be liable to a penalty of a prescribed amount, instead of to any obligation to account as mentioned in paragraph (*b*) or (cb) above;

  (*cd*) that liabilities equivalent to any of those which, by virtue of any of the preceding paragraphs of this subsection, may be imposed in cases where relief has been given to which there was no entitlement are to arise (in place of the liabilities to tax otherwise arising) in other cases where, in relation to any plan—

    (i) a prescribed contravention of, or failure to comply with, the regulations, or

    (ii) the existence of such other circumstances as may be prescribed, would have the effect (subject to the provision made by virtue of this paragraph) of excluding or limiting an entitlement to relief;]²

  (*d*) that a person who is, or has at any time been, either an investor under a plan or a plan manager—

    (i) shall comply with any notice which is served on him by the Board and which requires him within a prescribed period to make available for the Board's inspection documents (of a prescribed kind) relating to a plan or to investments which are or have been held under it;

    (ii) shall, within a prescribed period of being required to do so by the Board, furnish to the Board information (of a prescribed kind) about a plan or about investments which are or have been held under it;

  (*e*) generally for the purpose of bringing plans into existence, and generally for the purpose of the administration of plans and the administration of income tax and corporation tax in relation to them.

(5) In this section ''prescribed'' means prescribed by the regulations.

Commentary—*Simon's Direct Tax Service* E3.301–311.
Regulations—Personal Equity Plan Regulations, SI 1989/469.
Individual Savings Account Regulations, SI 1998/1870.
Revenue & other press releases—IR 17-12-86 (list of registered PEP managers, updated quarterly, is available from Public Enquiry Room, Somerset House).
IR 6-10-89 (new share issues may be subscribed to outside a PEP and transferred into it).
IR Tax Bulletin April 1997 p 418 (explains the rules whereby certain shares when a building society or insurance company transfers its business to a company may be transferred into a PEP).
Definition—''The Board'', s 832(1).
Cross references—See TCGA 1992 s 151(2) (extension of the application of sub-ss (2) to (5) of this section for capital gains tax).
Amendments—¹ Sub-s (3)(*g*)–(*j*) inserted by FA 1991 s 70.
² Sub-ss (1A), (4)(*b*)(ii), (*ca*)–(*cd*) inserted, words in sub-s (4)(*c*) inserted, and words in sub-s (3)(*b*) repealed by FA 1998 ss 75, 165, Sch 27 Pt III(15) with effect from 31 July 1998.

[333A Personal equity plans: tax representatives

(1) Regulations under section 333 may include provision that a European institution cannot be a plan manager unless one of the following three requirements is fulfilled.

(2) The first requirement is that—

(*a*) a person who falls within subsection (5) below is for the time being appointed by the institution to be responsible for securing the discharge of prescribed duties which fall to be discharged by the institution, and

(*b*) his identity and the fact of his appointment have been notified to the Board by the institution.

(3) The second requirement is that there are for the time being other arrangements with the Board for a person other than the institution to secure the discharge of such duties.

(4) The third requirement is that there are for the time being other arrangements with the Board designed to secure the discharge of such duties.

(5) A person falls within this subsection if—

(*a*) he is not an individual and has a business establishment in the United Kingdom, or

(*b*) he is an individual and is resident in the United Kingdom.

(6) Different duties may be prescribed as regards different institutions or different descriptions of institution.

(7) The regulations may provide that—

(*a*) the first requirement shall not be treated as fulfilled unless the person concerned is of a prescribed description;

(*b*) the appointment of a person in pursuance of that requirement shall be treated as terminated in prescribed circumstances.

(8) The regulations may provide that—

(*a*) the second requirement shall not be treated as fulfilled unless the person concerned is of a prescribed description;

(*b*) arrangements made in pursuance of that requirement shall be treated as terminated in prescribed circumstances.

(9) The regulations may provide as mentioned in subsection (10) below as regards a case where—

(*a*) in accordance with the first requirement a person is for the time being appointed to be responsible for securing the discharge of duties, or

(*b*) in accordance with the second requirement there are for the time being arrangements for a person to secure the discharge of duties.

(10) In such a case the regulations may provide that the person concerned—

(*a*) shall be entitled to act on the institution's behalf for any of the purposes of the provisions relating to the duties;

(*b*) shall secure (where appropriate by acting on the institution's behalf) the institution's compliance with and discharge of the duties;

(*c*) shall be personally liable in respect of any failure of the institution to comply with or discharge any such duty as if the duties imposed on the institution were imposed jointly and severally on the institution and the person concerned.

(11) In this section—

[(*a*) "European institution" means an EEA firm of the kind mentioned in paragraph 5(*a*), (*b*) or (*c*) of Schedule 3 to the Financial Services and Markets Act 2000 which is an authorised person for the purposes of that Act as a result of qualifying for authorisation under paragraph 12 of that Schedule;]²

(*b*) "prescribed" means prescribed by the regulations.

(12) The preceding provisions of this section shall apply in the case of a relevant authorised person as they apply in the case of a European institution; and "relevant authorised person" here means [a firm which is an authorised person for the purposes of the Financial Services and Markets Act 2000 as a result of qualifying for authorisation under paragraph 2 of Schedule 4 to that Act.]²]¹

Commentary—*Simon's Direct Tax Service* E3.303.
Regulations—Personal Equity Plan Regulations, SI 1989/469 regs 11, 11A.
Individual Savings Account Regulations, SI 1998/1870.
Definitions—"The Board", s 832(1); "United Kingdom", s 830(1).
Amendments—¹ Section inserted by FA 1995 s 64(1).
² Sub-s (11) and words in sub-s (12) substituted by the Financial Services and Markets Act 2000 (Consequential Amendments) (Taxes) Order, SI 2001/3629 arts 13, 21 with effect from 1 December 2001, immediately after the coming into force of the Financial Services and Markets Act 2000 ss 411, 432(1), Sch 20.

[333B Involvement of insurance companies with plans and accounts

(1) The Treasury may make regulations providing exemption from tax for income from, and chargeable gains in respect of, investments and deposits of so much of an insurance company's [long-term insurance fund]³ as is referable to section 333 business.

(2) The Treasury may by regulations modify the effect of section 30(4) of the Finance (No 2) Act 1997 (which repeals section 231(2) of the Taxes Act 1988 with effect from 6th April 1999) in relation to distributions which—

(*a*) are made before 6th April 2004; and

(*b*) are received by an insurance company in respect of investments of so much of its [long-term insurance fund][3] as is referable to section 333 business.

(3) Regulations under this section may make provision for insurance companies that are not resident in the United Kingdom to be treated, in relation to investments of so much of their [long-term insurance fund][3] as are referable to section 333 business—

(*a*) as if they were so resident for the purposes of any enactment conferring an entitlement to, or to the payment of, tax credits in respect of investments; and

(*b*) as if such other conditions of any entitlement to, or to the payment of, tax credits were also satisfied.

(4) Regulations under section 333 or this section may include provision which, in relation to insurance companies that are not resident in the United Kingdom—

(*a*) requires a person to be appointed to be responsible for securing the discharge of any duties to which such an insurance company is subject under the regulations; and

(*b*) confers rights and powers, and imposes liabilities, on a person so appointed;

and, without prejudice to the generality of paragraphs (*a*) and (*b*) above, regulations made by virtue of this subsection may include any provision corresponding to any that, in relation to a European institution, may be made under section 333A.

(5) Regulations under this section may provide that an insurance company—

(*a*) shall comply with any notice served on it by the Board which requires it, within a prescribed period, to make available for the Board's inspection documents (of a prescribed kind) relating to, or to matters connected with, its past or present section 333 business; and

(*b*) shall, within a prescribed period of being required to do so by the Board, furnish to the Board information (of a prescribed kind) about its past or present section 333 business or any matters connected with it.

(6) Any power of the Treasury under this section to make provision by regulations in relation to insurance companies shall include power by regulations to make such corresponding provision in relation to friendly societies as the Treasury think fit.

(7) Regulations under this section may—

(*a*) for purposes connected with any exemption from tax conferred by virtue of subsection (1) above, apply or modify any provision made by or under the Tax Acts;

(*b*) make different provision for different cases;

(*c*) include such incidental, supplemental, consequential and transitional provision as the Treasury may consider appropriate.

(8) Without prejudice to the generality of the powers conferred by subsection (7) above, the provision that may be made in connection with an exemption from tax conferred by virtue of subsection (1) above shall include provision for section 436 to apply (with any such modifications as may be prescribed) in relation to section 333 business as it applies in relation to pension business.

(9) In this section—

"friendly society" has the same meaning as in Chapter II of Part XII;

["insurance company" means an undertaking carrying on the business of effecting or carrying out contracts of insurance and, for the purposes of this definition, "contract of insurance" has the meaning given by Article 3(1) of the Financial Services and Markets Act 2000 (Regulated Activities) Order 2001;][2]

"[long-term insurance fund][3]" has the same meaning as in Chapter I of Part XII;

"prescribed" means prescribed by regulations under this section;

"section 333 business", in relation to an insurance company, means the business of the company that is attributable to the making of investments with that company under plans for which provision is made by regulations under section 333.][1]

Commentary—*Simon's Direct Tax Service* E3.303.
Regulations—Individual Savings Account Regulations, SI 1998/1870.
Individual Savings Account (Insurance Companies) Regulations, SI 1998/1871.
Individual Savings Account (Amendment) Regulations, SI 1998/3174.
Definitions—"The Board", s 832(1); "United Kingdom", s 830(1).
Amendments—[1] This section inserted by FA 1998 s 77 with effect from 31 July 1998.
[2] Definition of "insurance company" substituted by the Financial Services and Markets Act 2000 (Consequential Amendments) (Taxes) Order, SI 2001/3629 arts 13, 22 with effect from 1 December 2001, immediately after the coming into force of the Financial Services and Markets Act 2000 ss 411, 432(1), Sch 20.
[3] Words in sub-ss (1), (2)(*b*), (3) and (9) substituted by SI 2001/3629 arts 13, 52(1)(*a*) with effect from 1 December 2001, immediately after the coming into force of the Financial Services and Markets Act 2000 ss 411, 432(1), Sch 20.

CHAPTER V
RESIDENCE OF INDIVIDUALS

Concession A11—Residence in the UK: year of commencement or cessation of residence.
Revenue and other press releases—
Revenue booklet IR 20 (residents and non-residents—liability to tax in the UK).

334 Commonwealth citizens and others temporarily abroad

Every Commonwealth citizen or citizen of the Republic of Ireland—

(*a*) shall, if his ordinary residence has been in the United Kingdom, be assessed and charged to income tax notwithstanding that at the time the assessment or charge is made he may have left the United Kingdom, if he has so left the United Kingdom for the purpose only of occasional residence abroad, and

(*b*) shall be charged as a person actually residing in the United Kingdom upon the whole amount of his profits or gains, whether they arise from property in the United Kingdom or elsewhere, or from any allowance, annuity or stipend, or from any trade, profession, employment or vocation in the United Kingdom or elsewhere.

Commentary—*Simon's Direct Tax Service* **E6.102.**
Simon's Tax Cases—*Reed v Clark* [1985] STC 323*.
Revenue Internal Guidance—Schedule E manual, SE 42820 (residence or employment in the United Kingdom: resident in more than one country).
Definitions—''Profits or gains'', s 831(1); ''trade'', s 832(1).

335 Residence of persons working abroad

(1) Where—

(*a*) a person works full-time in one or more of the following, that is to say, a trade, profession, vocation, office or employment; and

(*b*) no part of the trade, profession or vocation is carried on in the United Kingdom and all the duties of the office or employment are performed outside the United Kingdom;

the question whether he is resident in the United Kingdom shall be decided without regard to any place of abode maintained in the United Kingdom for his use.

(2) Where an office or employment is in substance one of which the duties fall in the year of assessment to be performed outside the United Kingdom there shall be treated for the purposes of this section as so performed any duties performed in the United Kingdom the performance of which is merely incidental to the performance of the other duties outside the United Kingdom.

Commentary—*Simon's Direct Tax Service* **E6.102.**
Revenue Interpretation RI 40—Interpretation of ''full-time'' used in sub-s (1)(*a*) above.
Definitions—''Trade'', s 832(1); ''year of assessment'', s 832(1).

336 Temporary residents in the United Kingdom

(1) A person shall not be charged to income tax under Schedule D as a person residing in the United Kingdom, in respect of profits or gains received in respect of possessions or securities out of the United Kingdom, if—

(*a*) he is in the United Kingdom for some temporary purpose only and not with any view or intent of establishing his residence there, and

(*b*) he has not actually resided in the United Kingdom at one time or several times for a period equal in the whole to six months in any year of assessment,

but if any such person resides in the United Kingdom for such a period he shall be so chargeable for that year.

(2) For the purposes of Cases I, II and III of Schedule E, a person who is in the United Kingdom for some temporary purpose only and not with the intention of establishing his residence there shall not be treated as resident in the United Kingdom if he has not in the aggregate spent at least six months in the United Kingdom in the year of assessment, but shall be treated as resident there if he has.

[(3) The question whether—

(*a*) a person falls within subsection (1)(*a*) above, or

(*b*) for the purposes of subsection (2) above a person is in the United Kingdom for some temporary purpose only and not with the intention of establishing his residence there,

shall be decided without regard to any living accommodation available in the United Kingdom for his use.][1]

Commentary—*Simon's Direct Tax Service* **E6.102.**
Statement of Practice SP 2/91—Relaxation of the rule in sub-s (1)(*a*) above where a stay in the UK is extended because of exceptional circumstances.
Revenue Internal Guidance—Schedule E manual, SE 42820 (residence or employment in the UK: resident in more than one country).
Definitions—''Case I, II and III of Schedule E'', s 19(2); ''profits or gains'', s 832(1); ''Schedule D'', s 18(1); ''year of assessment'', s 832(1).
Amendments—[1] Sub-s (3) inserted by FA 1993 s 208(1), (4) with effect from the year 1993–94.

PART VIII

TAXATION OF INCOME AND CHARGEABLE GAINS OF COMPANIES

Taxation of income

[337 Company beginning or ceasing to carry on trade

(1) Where a company begins or ceases—

(*a*) to carry on a trade, or

(*b*) to be within the charge to corporation tax in respect of a trade, the company's income shall be computed as if that were the commencement or, as the case may be, the discontinuance of the trade, whether or not the trade is in fact commenced or discontinued.

(2) Subsection (1) applies to a Schedule A business or overseas property business as it applies to a trade.]¹

Commentary—*Simon's Direct Tax Service* **D2.203, 204.**
Concession C23—Relief for annual interest payable by a bank or a similar concern for the purpose of its trade of borrowing and lending, notwithstanding sub-s (2)(*b*) above.
Statement of Practice SP 2/90—This Statement explains the procedure to be followed by migrating companies in respect of their obligations under FA 1988 s 130. Any liability to tax under this section must be included in the information supplied by the migrating companies.
Revenue Interpretation RI 3—Effect on Case I computation of interest charged to work in progress of property development companies.
Revenue Internal Guidance—Banking manual BM 6.223 (meaning of "yearly" interest; para 1.2.5: meaning of bank carrying on bona fide banking business in the UK).
Company Taxation Manual COT160 (sub-s (1): any special rules relating to commencement or cessation apply, eg. TA 1988 s 100 (trading stock), s 89 (bad debts) and ss 103–110 (post cessation receipts)).
COT3413, 3431 (s 337 can apply when a UK resident company becomes non-resident, or vice versa).
Simon's Tax Cases—s 337(2), *IRC v Cookson* [1977] STC 140*; *Rank Xerox Ltd v Lane* [1978] STC 449*.
Definitions—"Company", s 832(1), (2); "the Corporation Tax Acts", s 831(1)(*a*); "interest", s 832(1); "Schedule A", s 15(1); "Schedule D"; "trade", s 6(4).
Cross references—See TA 1988 s 70(1) (in accordance with this section, corporation tax to be computed under Schedule D Cases I to VI on the full amount of profits or gains or income arising in an accounting period, subject only to authorised deduction).
TA 1988 s 89 (deduction for debts proving irrecoverable after event treated as discontinuance).
TA 1988 s 102(2) (valuation of stock and work in progress where trade etc is treated by sub-s (1) above as discontinued).
TA 1988 s 110(2) (extension of sub-s (1) above for the purposes of ss 103–109A).
TA 1988 s120(4)–example of provision expressly authorising a deduction (easements paid by a radio relay concern).
TA 1988 s 214(1) (certain payments connected with demergers to be regarded as distributions for the purposes of sub-s (2) above).
TA 1988 s 388(2) (any annuity or other annual payment within sub-s (2A) above excluded from being a charge on income).
TA 1988 s 434B(2) (nothing in sub-s (2A) above to prevent an annuity or other annual payment paid wholly or partly as mentioned therein from being treated as a charge on income in computing the profits of a basic life assurance and general annuity business otherwise than under Schedule D Case I).
Amendments—¹ This section substituted by FA 2002 s 84(2), Sch 30 para 1(1) with effect from 24 July 2002. This section previously read as follows—

"**337 Companies beginning or ceasing to carry on a trade**

(1) Where a company begins or ceases to carry on a trade, or to be within the charge to corporation tax in respect of a trade, the company's income shall be computed as if that were the commencement or, as the case may be, discontinuance of the trade, whether or not the trade is in fact commenced or discontinued.

(2) Subject *to subsection (3) below and* to any other provision of the Corporation Tax Acts which expressly authorises such a deduction, no deduction shall be made in computing income from any source—

(*a*) in respect of dividends or other distributions; nor

(*b*) in respect of any [annuity or other annual payment which is not interest] or in respect of any such other payments as are mentioned in section 348(2), but not including sums which are, or but for any exemption would be, chargeable under Schedule A.

[(2A) In computing any profits or losses of a company in accordance with the provisions of this Act applicable to Case I of Schedule D, subsection (2)(*b*) above shall not prevent the deduction of any annuity or other annual payment which is payable by a company wholly or partly in satisfaction of any claim under an insurance policy in relation to which the company is the insurer.]

[(2B) The reference in subsection (2A) above to an annuity payable wholly or partly in satisfaction of a claim under an insurance policy shall be taken, in relation to an insurance company (within the meaning of Chapter I of Part XII), to include a reference to every annuity payable by that company; and [the reference in section 338(2)] to an annuity paid wholly or partly as mentioned in subsection (2A) above shall be construed accordingly.]

(3) In computing income from a trade, subsection (2)(b) above shall not prevent the deduction of yearly interest payable in the United Kingdom on an advance from a bank carrying on a bona fide banking business in the United Kingdom."

[337A Computation of company's profits or income: exclusion of general deductions

(1) For the purposes of corporation tax, subject to any provision of the Corporation Tax Acts expressly authorising a deduction—

(*a*) a company's profits shall be computed without any deduction in respect of dividends or other distributions, and

(*b*) a company's income from any source shall be computed without any deduction in respect of charges on income.

(2) In computing a company's income from any source for the purposes of corporation tax—

(*a*) no deduction shall be made in respect of interest except in accordance with Chapter 2 of Part 4 of the Finance Act 1996 (loan relationships); and (*b*) no deduction shall be made in respect of losses from intangible fixed assets within Schedule 29 to the Finance Act 2002 except in accordance with that Schedule.][1]

Commentary—*Simon's Direct Tax Service* B5.101.
Revenue Interpretation RI 157—This section can only apply for corporation tax purposes and does not preclude deduction for interest for companies within income tax provisions, for example non-UK resident companies with only UK property income.
Revenue Internal Guidance—International tax handbook ITH 1100-1143 (interest payable abroad: application of the pre-FA 1996 legislation).
Definitions—"Company", s 832(1); "interest", s 832(1).
Amendments—[1] Section substituted by FA 2002 s 84(2), Sch 30 para 1(1) with effect from 24 July 2002.
This section previously read as follows—

> **"337A Interest payable by companies**
>
> No deduction shall be made in respect of interest in computing a company's income from any source except in accordance with Chapter II of Part IV of the Finance Act 1996 (loan relationships)."

[338 Charges on income deducted from total profits

(1) Charges on income are allowed as deductions from a company's total profits in computing the corporation tax chargeable for an accounting period.

(2) They are deducted from the company's total profits for the period as reduced by any other relief from tax other than group relief.

(3) The amount of the deduction is limited to the amount that reduces the company's total profits for the period to nil.

(4) Except as otherwise provided, a deduction is allowed only in respect of payments made by the company in the accounting period concerned.

(5) The above provisions are subject to any express exceptions in the Corporation Tax Acts.][1]

Commentary—*Simon's Direct Tax Service* D2.209–213.
Revenue Interpretation RI 3—Effect on Case I computation of interest charged to work in progress of property development companies.
Revenue Internal Guidance—Banking manual BM 6.223 (meaning of "yearly" interest; para 1.2.5: meaning of bank carrying on bona fide banking business in the UK.
Company Taxation Manual COT902 (sub-s (5)(*b*): meaning of "valuable and sufficient consideration").
International tax handbook ITH 1101–1109, 1120–1121 (sub-s (4) nature of interest; source of interest; application of sub-s (4)).
ITH 1126–1131 (sub-s (4)(*b*) Eurobond interest).
Revenue & other press releases—ICAEW TR799 June 1990 (interest payable under IA 1986 s 189 is not normally regarded as annual interest).
Simon's Tax Cases—*Macarthur v Greycoat Estates Mayfair Ltd* [1996] STC 1*.
s 338(1), *Commercial Union Assurance Co plc v Shaw* [1999] STC 109; *Prudential Assurance Co Ltd v Bibby* [1999] STC 952.
s 338(2)(*a*), *Wilcock v Frigate Investments Ltd* [1982] STC 198*; *Westmoreland Investments Ltd v Macniven*, [1997] STC (SCD) 69.
s 338(3), *Rank Xerox Ltd v Lane* [1978] STC 449*; *Westmoreland Investments Ltd v Macniven* [1998] STC 1131; *MacNivan (Inspector of Taxes) v Westmoreland Investments Ltd* [2001] STC 237.
s 338(3)(*a*), (*b*), *Mink v Inspector of Taxes* [1999] STC (SCD) 17.
s 338(5)(*a*), *Westmoreland Investments Ltd v Macniven* [1998] STC 1131.
Definitions—"Accounting period", s 834(1); "branch or agency", s 834(1); "company", s 832(1), (2); "group relief", s 834(1); "loan relationship", FA 1996 s 81; "profits", s 6(4); "Schedule A", s 15(1); "Schedule D", s 18(1); "trade", s 6(4).
Cross references—TA 1988 s 70(1) (in accordance with this section, corporation tax to be computed under Schedule D Cases I to VI on the full amount of profits or gains or income arising in an accounting period, subject only to authorised deduction).
TA 1988 s 78(2) (discount on a discounted bill of exchange not treated as a charge on income under sub-s (1) above).
TA 1988 s 118(1) (restriction on loss relief where an individual carries on a trade as a limited partner).
TA 1988 s 214(1) (certain chargeable payments connected with demergers to be regarded as distributions for the purposes of sub-s (2)(*a*) above).
TA 1988 s 242 (set-off of annual charges against surplus of franked investment income).
TA 1988 s 393A(8) (loss relief against profits of earlier accounting periods not to be given to avoid interference with relief under this section).
TA 1988 s 407(1) (group relief to be allowed as a deduction against a company's total profits as reduced by the relief under sub-s. (1) above).
TA 1988 s 434B (notwithstanding sub-s (2) above, annuities and other annual payments by an insurer in satisfaction of a claim to be deducted in computing income from insurance company's basic life assurance and general annuity business).
TA 1988 s 494 (modification of this section in its application to a company carrying out oil extraction activities etc).
TA 1988 Sch 19AC para 5B (modification of this section to enable an overseas life insurance company to claim to set charges against qualifying distributions).
TA 1988 Sch 23A, para 4(2)(*b*) (modified application of sub-s (4)(*a*) above for manufactured overseas dividends).
Double Taxation Relief (Taxes on Income)(General) Regulations 1970, SI 1970/488, reg 6 (payments complying with a Revenue notice shall be treated for the purposes of s 338 as if tax had been deducted and accounted for).
Amendments—
[1] Sections 338–338B substituted for this section by FA 2002 s 84(2), Sch 30 para 1 with effect from 24 July 2002. This section previously read as follows—

> **"338 Allowance of charges on income and capital**
>
> (1) Subject to sections 339, 494 and 787, in computing the corporation tax chargeable for any accounting period of a company any charges on income paid by the company in the accounting period, so far as paid out of the company's profits brought into charge to corporation tax, shall be allowed as deductions against the total profits for the period as reduced by any other relief from tax, other than group relief.
>
> (2) Subject to the following subsections, [to sections 339] and to any other express exceptions, "charges on income" means for the purposes of corporation tax—
>
> [(*za*) amounts allowed as charges on income under section 587B(2)(*a*)(ii);]
> (*a*) payments of any description mentioned in subsection (3) below, not being dividends or other distributions of the company [or payments falling within paragraph (*b*) below]; and
> (*b*) payments which are qualifying donations (within the meaning of section 339);

but no payment which is deductible in computing profits or any description of profits for purposes of corporation tax [nor any annuity or other annual payment which (without being so deductible) is paid wholly or partly as mentioned in section 337(2A)] shall be treated as a charge on income.

(3) Subject to subsections (4) to (6) below, the payments referred to in subsection (2)(*a*) above are—

(*a*) [any annuity or annual payment payable otherwise than in respect of any of the company's loan relationships] and any such other payments as are mentioned in section 348(2) but not including sums which are or, but for any exemption would be, chargeable under Schedule A; ...

(*b*) ...

(4) No such payment as is mentioned in subsection (3)(*a*) above made by a company to a person not resident in the United Kingdom shall be treated as a charge on income unless the company is so resident and either—

(*a*) the company deducts income tax from the payment in accordance with section 349, and accounts under Schedule 16 for the tax so deducted, or

[(*aa*) the person beneficially entitled to the income in respect of which the payment is made is a company not resident in the United Kingdom (''the non-resident company''), the non-resident company carries on a trade in the United Kingdom through a branch or agency and the payment falls to be brought into account in computing the chargeable profits (within the meaning given by section 11(2)) of the non-resident company, or]

(*b*), (*c*) ...

(*d*) the payment is one payable out of income brought into charge to tax under Case IV or V of Schedule D.

(5) No such payment made by a company as is mentioned in subsection (3) above shall be treated as a charge on income if—

(*a*) the payment ... is charged to capital or the payment is not ultimately borne by the company; or

(*b*) the payment is not made under a liability incurred for a valuable and sufficient consideration (and, in the case of a company not resident in the United Kingdom, incurred wholly and exclusively for the purposes of a trade [which is or is to be] carried on by it in the United Kingdom through a branch or agency), and is not [a qualifying donation] (within the meaning of section 339).

(6) ...

(7) Any payment to which section 125(1) applies shall not be a charge on income for the purposes of corporation tax.''

[338A Meaning of ''charges on income'']

(1) This section defines what payments or other amounts are ''charges on income'' for the purposes of corporation tax.

This section has effect subject to any express exceptions in the Corporation Tax Acts.

(2) Subject to the following provisions of this section, the following (and only the following) are charges on income—

(*a*) annuities or other annual payments that meet the conditions specified in section 338B;

(*b*) qualifying donations within the meaning of section 339 (qualifying donations to charity);

(*c*) amounts allowed as charges on income under section 587B(2)(*a*)(ii) (gifts of shares etc to charity).

(3) No payment that is deductible in computing profits or any description of profits for the purposes of corporation tax shall be treated as a charge on income.

(4) No payment shall be treated as a charge on income if (without being so deductible) it is—

(*a*) an annuity payable by an insurance company, or

(*b*) an annuity or other annual payment payable by a company wholly or partly in satisfaction of any claim under an insurance policy in relation to which the company is the insurer.

In paragraph (*a*) ''insurance company'' has the same meaning as in Chapter 1 of Part 12.]¹

Amendments—¹ This section (and TA 1988 ss 338, 338B) substituted for TA 1988 s 338 by FA 2002 s 84(2), Sch 30 para 1(2) with effect from 24 July 2002.

[338B Charges on income: annuities or other annual payments]

(1) An annuity or other annual payment is a charge on income if—

(*a*) the requirements specified in subsection (2) are met, and

(*b*) it is not excluded from being a charge on income for the purposes of corporation tax—

(i) by any of the following provisions of this section, or

(ii) by any other provision of the Corporation Tax Acts.

(2) The requirements are that the payment—

(*a*) is made under a liability incurred for a valuable and sufficient consideration,

(*b*) is not charged to capital,

(*c*) is ultimately borne by the company, and

(*d*) in the case of a company not resident in the United Kingdom, is incurred wholly and exclusively for the purposes of a trade which is or is to be carried on by it in the United Kingdom through a branch or agency.

(3) An annuity or other annual payment made to a person not resident in the United Kingdom shall be treated as a charge on income only if the following conditions are met.

(4) The conditions are that the company making the payment is resident in the United Kingdom and that either—

(*a*) the company deducts tax from the payment in accordance with section 349, and accounts under Schedule 16 for the tax so deducted, or

(*b*) the person beneficially entitled to the income in respect of which the payment is made is a company that is not resident in the United Kingdom but which carries on a trade in the United

Kingdom through a branch or agency and the payment falls to be brought into account in computing the chargeable profits (within the meaning given by section 11(2) of that company, or

(c) the payment is one payable out of income brought into charge to tax under Case V of Schedule D.

(5) An annuity or other annual payment is not a charge on income if—

(a) it is payable in respect of the company's loan relationships, or

(b) it is a royalty to which Schedule 29 to the Finance Act 2002 applies (intangible fixed assets).

(6) Nothing in this section prevents an annuity or other annual payment from being a charge on income if it is a qualifying donation (within the meaning of section 339).][1]

Amendments—[1] This section (and TA 1988 ss 338, 338A) substituted for TA 1988 s 338 by FA 2002 s 84(2), Sch 30 para 1(2) with effect from 24 July 2002.

339 Charges on income: donations to charity

(1) A qualifying donation is a payment [of a sum of money][4] made by a company to a charity, other than—

[(a) a payment which, by reason of any provision of the Taxes Acts (within the meaning of the Management Act) except section 209(4), is to be regarded as a distribution; and][6]

(b) a payment which is deductible in computing profits or any description of profits for purposes of corporation tax.

(2), (3), (3A) ...[6]

[(3B) A payment made by a close company is not a qualifying donation if—

(a) it is made subject to a condition as to repayment, or

(b) the company or a connected person receives a benefit in consequence of making it and either the relevant value in relation to the payment exceeds [the limit imposed by subsection (3DA) below][6] or the amount to be taken into account for the purposes of this paragraph in relation to the payments exceeds £250.

(3C) For the purposes of subsections (3B) above and (3D) below, the relevant value in relation to a payment to a charity is—

(a) where there is one benefit received in consequence of making it which is received by the company or a connected person, the value of that benefit;

(b) where there is more than one benefit received in consequence of making it which is received by the company or a connected person, the aggregate value of all the benefits received in consequence of making it which are received by the company or a connected person.

(3D) The amount to be taken into account for the purposes of subsection (3B)(b) above in relation to a payment to a charity is an amount equal to the aggregate of—

(a) the relevant value in relation to the payment, and

(b) the relevant value in relation to each payment already made to the charity by the company in the accounting period in which the payment is made which is a qualifying donation within the meaning of this section.][2]

[(3DA) The limit imposed by this subsection is—

(a) where the amount of the payment does not exceed £100, 25 per cent of the amount of the payment;

(b) where the amount of the payment exceeds £100 but does not exceed £1,000, £25;

(c) where the amount of the payment exceeds £1,000, 2.5 per cent of the amount of the payment.

(3DB) Where a benefit received in consequence of making a payment—

(a) consists of the right to receive benefits at intervals over a period of less than twelve months;

(b) relates to a period of less than twelve months; or

(c) is one of a series of benefits received at intervals in consequence of making a series of payments at intervals of less than twelve months,

the value of the benefit shall be adjusted for the purposes of subsection (3C) above and the amount of the payment shall be adjusted for the purposes of subsection (3DA) above.

(3DC) Where a benefit, other than a benefit which is one of a series of benefits received at intervals, is received in consequence of making a payment which is one of a series of payments made at intervals of less than twelve months, the amount of the payment shall be adjusted for the purposes of subsection (3DA) above.

(3DD) Where the value of a benefit, or the amount of a payment, falls to be adjusted under subsection (3DB) or (3DC) above, the value or amount shall be multiplied by 365 and the result shall be divided by—

(a) in a case falling within subsection (3DB)(a) or (b) above, the number of days in the period of less than twelve months;

(b) in a case falling within subsection (3DB)(c) or (3DC) above, the average number of days in the intervals of less than twelve months;

and the reference in subsection (3DB) to subsection (3C) above is a reference to that subsection as it applies for the purposes of subsection (3B) above.][7]

[(3E) A payment made by a close company is not a qualifying donation if it is conditional on, or associated with, or part of an arrangement involving, the acquisition of property by the charity, otherwise than by way of gift, from the company or a connected person.][2]

[(3F) ...[6]][2]

[(3G) A payment made by a company is not a qualifying donation if the company is itself a charity.][2]

[(4) Where a company gives a sum of money to a charity, the gift shall in the hands of the charity be treated for the purposes of this Act as if it were an annual payment.][6]

(5) ...[3]

(6), (7) ...[6]

[(7AA) Where—

(a) a qualifying donation to a charity is made by a company which is wholly owned by a charity, and

(b) the company makes a claim for the donation, or any part of it, to be deemed for the purposes of section 338 to be a charge on income paid in an accounting period falling wholly or partly within the period of nine months ending with the date of the making of the donation,

the donation or part shall be deemed for those purposes to be a charge on income paid in that accounting period, and not in any later period.

A claim under this subsection must be made within the period of two years immediately following the accounting period in which the donation is made, or such longer period as the Board may allow.][6]

[(7AB) For the purposes of this section a company is wholly owned by a charity if it is either—

(a) a company with an ordinary share capital every part of which is owned by a charity (whether or not the same charity); or

(b) a company limited by guarantee in whose case every person who—

(i) is beneficially entitled to participate in the divisible profits of the company, or

(ii) will be beneficially entitled to share in any net assets of the company available for distribution on its winding up,

is or must be a charity or a company wholly owned by a charity.][5]

[(7AC) For the purposes of subsection (7AB) above ordinary share capital of a company shall be taken to be owned by a charity if there is a charity which—

(a) within the meaning of section 838 directly or indirectly owns that share capital; or

(b) would be taken so to own that share capital if references in that section to a body corporate included references to a charity which is not a body corporate.][5]

[(7A) In subsections (3B) to (3E) above references to a connected person are to a person connected with—

(a) the company, or

(b) a person connected with the company;

and section 839 applies for the purposes of this subsection.][3]

(8) ...[6]

(9) For the purposes of this section "charity" includes [each of the bodies mentioned in section 507, and ...[6]][1] any Association of a description specified in section 508, but, subject to that, in this section "charity" has the same meaning as in section 506.

Commentary—*Simon's Direct Tax Service* **D2.212, 212A.**
Revenue Interpretation RI 196—Interpretation of the word "like" in the phrase "like annual payments" in sub-s (8), and explanation of how a tax effective deed can be written to include formula-based payments.
Revenue & other press releases—ICAEW TR588 25-9-85 (Revenue do not normally challenge the covenanting to charity of the profits of a trading subsidiary, provided there is no circularity eg. an interest free loan-back).
IR Tax Bulletin June 1997 p 438 (outlines, with illustrative examples, the operation of sub-ss (7AA)-(7AC) re charity owned companies).
IR 8-12-97 (fixed profit car scheme rates for 1998–99).
Revenue Internal Guidance—Company Taxation Manual COT1525 (covenanted donation to a charity is a charge, not a distribution, even if recipient is a shareholder).
Definitions—"Accounting period", s 834(1); "charge on income", s 338(2); "close company", s 414(1) by virtue of s 832(1); "company", s 832(1), (2); "the Corporation Tax Acts", s 831(1)(a); "distribution", s 209(2) by virtue of s 832(1); "ordinary share capital", s 832(1); "profits", s 6(4); "the Tax Acts", s 831(2).
Cross references—See TA 1988 s 70(1) (in accordance with this section, corporation tax to be computed under Schedule D Cases I to VI on the full amount of profits or gains or income arising in an accounting period, subject only to authorised deduction).
TA 1988 s 338(1) (s 338 allowances of charges on income and capital) to have effect subject to this section).
TA 1988 s 352 (payees' right to obtain certificate of deduction where tax under this section is deducted).
Amendments—[1] Words in sub-s (9) substituted by FA 1989 s 60(2), (4) in respect of payments due after 13 March 1989.
[2] Sub-ss (3A)–(3G), (7A) inserted by FA 1990 s 26(4), (5), (6) in relation to payments made after 30 September 1990.
[3] Sub-s (5) repealed by FA 1990 s 27(2), (4) and Sch 19 Pt IV in relation to accounting periods ending after 30 September 1990.
[4] Words in sub-s (1) inserted by FA 1990 s 26(2).
[5] Sub-ss (7AA)–(7AC) inserted by FA 1997 s 64 with effect in relation to donations made in accounting periods beginning after 31 March 1997.
[6] Words in sub-ss (1), (3B)(b), and whole of sub-ss (4), (7AA) substituted, sub-ss (2), (3), (3A), (3F), (6), (7), (8) and words in sub-s (9) repealed by FA 2000 ss 40(1)–(4), (6)–(8), (11), 156, Sch 40 Pt II(1) with effect for payments made after 31 March 2000. For the purposes of these amendments, so much of an accounting period as falls before 1 April 2000 and so much of it as falls after 31 March 2000 are treated as separate accounting periods.

⁷ Sub-ss (3DA)–(3DD) inserted by FA 2000 s 40(1), (5), (11) with effect for payments made after 31 March 2000. For the purposes of these amendments, so much of an accounting period as falls before 1 April 2000 and so much of it as falls after 31 March 2000 are treated as separate accounting periods.

339A Maximum qualifying donations

Amendments—This section repealed by FA 1991 s 71(1), (3) and Sch 19 Pt V for accounting periods beginning after 18 March 1991.

340 Charges on income: interest payable to non-residents

Commentary—*Simon's Direct Tax Service* **D2.214.**
Amendments—This section repealed by FA 1996 Sch 14 para 17, Sch 41 Pt V(3) with effect for accounting periods ending after 31 March 1996, subject to transitional provisions in FA 1996 Sch 15.

341 Payments of interest etc between related companies

Commentary—*Simon's Direct Tax Service* **D1.616; D2.209.**
Amendments—This section repealed by FA 1996 Sch 14 para 17, Sch 41 Pt V(3) with effect for accounting periods ending after 31 March 1996, subject to transitional provisions in FA 1996 Sch 15.

342 Tax on company in liquidation

(1) In this section references to a company's final year are references to the financial year in which the affairs of the company are completely wound up, and references to a company's penultimate year are references to the last financial year preceding its final year.

(2) Subject to subsection (3) [or (3A)]³ below—

(*a*) corporation tax shall be charged on the profits of the company arising in the winding-up in its final year at the rate of corporation tax fixed or proposed for the penultimate year; but

(*b*) where the corporation tax charged on the company's income included in those profits falls to be calculated or reduced in accordance with section 13, it shall be so calculated or reduced in accordance with such rate or fraction fixed or proposed for the penultimate year as is applicable under that section.

(3) If, before the affairs of the company are completely wound up, any of the rates or fractions mentioned in subsection (2) above has been fixed or proposed for the final year, that subsection shall have effect in relation to that rate or fraction as if for the references to the penultimate year there were substituted references to the final year.

[(3A) If, in the case of the company's final accounting period, the income (if any) which consists of interest received or receivable by the company under section 826 does not exceed £2,000, that income shall not be subject to corporation tax.

In this subsection ''the company's final accounting period'' means the accounting period of the company which, in accordance with section 12(7), ends by reason of the completion of the winding up.]³

(4) An assessment on the company's profits for an accounting period which falls after the commencement of the winding-up shall not be invalid because made before the end of the accounting period.

(5) In making an assessment after the commencement of the winding-up of the company but before the date when its affairs are completely wound up, [the liquidator may]¹, act on an assumption as to when that date will fall, so far as it governs section 12(7).

(6) The assumption of the wrong date shall not alter the company's final and penultimate year, and, if the right date is later, an accounting period shall end on the date assumed, and a new accounting period shall begin and section 12(7) shall thereafter apply [as if the winding-up had commenced with the beginning of that new accounting period]².

(7) References in this section to a rate or fraction fixed or proposed are references to a rate or fraction fixed by an Act passed before the completion of the winding-up or, if not so fixed, proposed by a Budget resolution (and without regard to any subsequent Act); except that if a rate or fraction so fixed is proposed to be altered by a Budget resolution any such reference to it is a reference to it as proposed to be so altered.

In this subsection ''Budget resolution'' means a resolution of the House of Commons for fixing any such rate or fraction as is mentioned in this section.

(8) Where the winding-up commenced before the company's final year, paragraphs (*a*) and (*b*) of subsection (2) (but not subsection (3)) above shall apply in relation to the company's profits arising at any time in its penultimate year.

(9) Any assessment made by virtue of section 8(4) shall be subject to any such adjustment by discharge or repayment of tax or by a further assessment as may be required to give effect to this section.

Definitions—''Accounting period'', s 834(1); ''Act'', s 832(1); ''company'', s 832(1), (2); ''inspector'', s 832(1); ''profits'', s 6(4).

Revenue Internal Guidance—Company Taxation Manual COT3122 (Revenue review of file when company goes into liquidation).

Cross references—See TA 1988 s 70(1) (in accordance with this section, corporation tax to be computed under Schedule D Cases I to VI on the full amount of profits or gains or income arising in an accounting period, subject to authorised deductions).

Amendments—[1] Words in sub-s (5) substituted for words "the inspector may, with the concurrence of the liquidation" by FA 1996 Sch 24 para 12(1), (2), (4) with effect in relation to the winding up of a company if the date on which the affairs of the company are completely wound up does not occur before the appointed day (1 July 1999 by virtue of Finance Act 1994, Section 199, (Appointed Day) Order, SI 1998/3173 art 2).

[2] Words in sub-s (6) substituted for the words "as if that new accounting period began with the commencement of the winding up" by FA 1996 Sch 24 para 12(1), (3), (4) with effect in relation to the winding up of a company if the date on which the affairs of the company are completely wound up does not occur before the appointed day, (1 July 1999 by virtue of SI 1998/3173 art 2).

[3] Words in sub-s (2) and new sub-s (3A) inserted by FA 1998 Sch 4 para 6 with effect for final accounting periods ending after 30 June 1999 (by virtue of SI 1998/3173 art 2).

343 Company reconstructions without a change of ownership

(1) Where, on a company ("the predecessor") ceasing to carry on a trade, another company ("the successor") begins to carry it on, and—

    (a) on or at any time within two years after that event the trade or an interest amounting to not less than a three-fourths share in it belongs to the same persons as the trade or such an interest belonged to at some time within a year before that event; and

    (b) the trade is not, within the period taken for the comparison under paragraph (a) above, carried on otherwise than by a company which is within the charge to tax in respect of it;

then the Corporation Tax Acts shall have effect subject to subsections (2) to (6) below.

In paragraphs (a) and (b) above references to the trade shall apply also to any other trade of which the activities comprise the activities of the first mentioned trade.

(2) The trade shall not be treated as permanently discontinued nor a new trade as set up and commenced for the purpose of the allowances and charges provided for by [the Capital Allowances Act (including enactments which under this Act are to be treated as contained in that Act)][4]; but—

    (a) there shall be made to or on the successor in accordance with those Acts all such allowances and charges as would, if the predecessor had continued to carry on the trade, have fallen to be made to or on it; and

    (b) the amount of any such allowance or charge shall be computed as if—

       (i) the successor had been carrying on the trade since the predecessor began to do so, and

       (ii) everything done to or by the predecessor had been done to or by the successor (but so that no sale or transfer which on the transfer of the trade is made to the successor by the predecessor of any assets in use for the purpose of the trade shall be treated as giving rise to any such allowance or charge).

The preceding provisions of this subsection shall not apply if the successor is a dual resident investing company (within the meaning of section 404) which begins to carry on the trade after 31st March 1987.

(3) ...[1] subject to subsection (4) below and to any claim made by the predecessor under section [393A(1)][1], the successor shall be entitled to relief under section 393(1), as for a loss sustained by the successor in carrying on the trade, for any amount for which the predecessor would have been entitled to ...[2] relief if it had continued to carry on the trade.

(4) Where the amount of relevant liabilities exceeds the value of relevant assets, the successor shall be entitled to relief by virtue of subsection (3) above only if, and only to the extent that, the amount of that excess is less than the amount mentioned in that subsection.

This subsection does not apply where the predecessor ceased to carry on the trade or part of a trade before 19th March 1986 nor, in a case where subsection (7) below applies, in relation to any earlier event, within the meaning of that subsection, which occurred before that date (but without prejudice to its application in relation to any later event which occurred on or after that date).

[(4A) Subsection (2A) of section 393A shall not apply to any loss which (but for this subsection) would fall within subsection (2B) of that section by virtue of the predecessor's ceasing to carry on the trade, and subsection (7) of that section shall not apply for the computation of any such loss.][3]

(5) Any securities, within the meaning of section 731, which at the time when the predecessor ceases to carry on the trade form part of the trading stock belonging to the trade shall be treated for the purposes of that section as having been sold at that time in the open market by the predecessor and as having been purchased at that time in the open market by the successor.

(6) ...[1]

(7) Where the successor ceases to carry on the trade within the period taken for the comparison under subsection (1)(a) above and on its doing so a third company begins to carry on the trade, ...[1], subsections (2) to [(5)][1] above shall apply both in relation to that event (together with the new predecessor and successor) and to the earlier event (together with the original predecessor and successor), but so that—

    (a) in relation to the earlier event "successor" shall include the successor at either event; and

    (b) in relation to the later event "predecessor" shall include the predecessor at either event;

and if the conditions of this subsection are thereafter again satisfied, it shall apply again in like manner.

(8) Where, on a company ceasing to carry on a trade, another company begins to carry on the activities of the trade as part of its trade, then that part of the trade carried on by the successor shall be treated for the purposes of this section as a separate trade, if the effect of so treating it is that subsection (1) or (7) above has effect on that event in relation to that separate trade; and where, on a company ceasing to carry on part of a trade, another company begins to carry on the activities of that part as its trade or part of its trade, the predecessor shall for purposes of this section be treated as having carried on that part of its trade as a separate trade if the effect of so treating it is that subsection (1) or (7) above has effect on that event in relation to that separate trade.

(9) Where under subsection (8) above any activities of a company's trade fall, on the company ceasing or beginning to carry them on, to be treated as a separate trade, such apportionments of receipts, expenses, assets or liabilities shall be made as may be just.

(10) Where, by virtue of subsection (9) above, any item falls to be apportioned and, at the time of the apportionment, it appears that it is material as respects the liability to tax (for whatever period) of two or more companies, any question which arises as to the manner in which the item is to be apportioned shall be determined, for the purposes of the tax of all those companies—

(a) in a case where the same body of General Commissioners have jurisdiction with respect to all those companies, by those Commissioners, unless all the companies agree that it shall be determined by the Special Commissioners;
(b) in a case where different bodies of Commissioners have jurisdiction with respect to those companies, by such of those bodies as the Board may direct, unless all the companies agree that it shall be determined by the Special Commissioners; and
(c) in any other case, by the Special Commissioners,

and any such Commissioners shall determine the question in like manner as if it were an appeal except that all those companies shall be entitled to appear and be heard by the Commissioners who are to make the determination or to make representations to them in writing.

(11) Any relief obtainable under this section by way of discharge or repayment of tax shall be given on the making of a claim.

(12) In the application of this section to any case in relation to which subsection (4) above does not apply—

(a) subsection (9) above shall have effect with the substitution for the words following "separate trade" of the words "any necessary apportionment shall be made of receipts or expenses"; and
(b) subsection (10) above shall have effect with the substitution for "item" of "sum".

Commentary—*Simon's Direct Tax Service* D2.515.
Statement of Practice SP 10/91, para 9—Where a trade is split into separate trades, and this section applies to any such separate trade, the split may not by itself be regarded for corporation tax purposes as "a major change in the nature or conduct of a trade or business".
Revenue & other press releases—CCAB TR500 10-3-83 (writing down allowance apportioned on a time basis where transfer of a trade occurs part way through an accounting period; FYA to company incurring expenditure; balancing adjustments are not apportioned; where part of a trade is transferred CA pool is apportioned on a just and reasonable basis).
Revenue Internal Guidance—Capital allowances manual CA 15400 (application of this section to capital allowances).
Simon's Tax Cases—s 343(1), (8), (9), *Falmer Jeans Ltd v Rodin* [1990] STC 270*.
s 343(3), *Rolls-Royce Motors Ltd v Bamford* [1976] STC 162*.
Definitions—"Apportionment", s 834(4); "the Board", s 832(1); "the Capital Allowances Acts", s 832(1); "company", s 832(1), (2); "the Corporation Tax Acts", s 831(1)(*a*); "trade", s 6(4).
Cross references—TMA 1970 s 58(3)(*b*) proceedings under sub-s (10) of this section to be in Northern Ireland if the place given by certain rules in relation to the parties to the proceedings is in Northern Ireland);
TA 1988 s 70(1) (in accordance with this section, corporation tax to be computed under Schedule D Cases I to VI on the full amount of profits or gains or income arising in an accounting period, subject only to authorised deduction).
TA 1988 s 344 (supplemental provisions).
TA 1988 s 768(5) (change in ownership of company: disallowance of trading losses).
TA 1988 Sch 24, para 8 (transfer of trade between resident companies and controlled foreign companies).
FA 1994 Sch 24 para 15 (modification of this section in respect of trading losses as it applies to railway privatisations).
FA 1994 Sch 24 para 20 (disapplication of this section in respect of continuity of capital allowances as it applies to railway privatisations).
Amendments—[1] Words in sub-ss (3), (7) substituted and sub-s (6) and words in sub-ss (3), (7) repealed by FA 1991 s 73(4), (5) and Sch 15 para 7 and Sch 19, Pt V for losses incurred in accounting periods ending after 31 March 1991 and for losses so incurred the repeal is deemed to have had effect at all times.
[2] Word "claim" in sub-s (3) repealed by FA 1993 Sch 14 para 8(1),(2) and Sch 23 Pt III(11) for set off of losses in accounting periods ending after 30 September 1993 by virtue of amendment to s 393(1) of this Act by FA 1990 s 99(1), (2), (4) and Corporation Tax Acts (Provisions for Payment of Tax and Returns) (Appointed Days) Order, SI 1992/3066 art 2(1),(2)(*b*).
[3] Sub-s (4A) inserted by F(No 2)A 1997 s 39(7), (8) in respect of any loss incurred in an accounting period ending after 1 July 1997, subject to transitional provisions in F(No 2)A 1997 s 39(9)–(12) for accounting periods straddling that date.
[4] Words in sub-s (2) substituted by CAA 2001 s 578, Sch 2 para 26 with effect for corporation tax purposes, as respects allowances and charges falling to be made for chargeable periods ending after 31 March 2001.

344 Company reconstructions: supplemental

(1) For the purposes of section 343—

(a) a trade carried on by two or more persons shall be treated as belonging to them in the shares in which they are entitled to the profits of the trade;

(*b*) a trade or interest in a trade belonging to any person as trustee (otherwise than for charitable or public purposes) shall be treated as belonging to the persons for the time being entitled to the income under the trust; and

(*c*) a trade or interest in a trade belonging to a company shall, where the result of so doing is that subsection (1) or (7) of section 343 has effect in relation to an event, be treated in any of the ways permitted by subsection (2) below.

(2) For the purposes of section 343, a trade or interest in a trade which belongs to a company engaged in carrying it on may be regarded—

(*a*) as belonging to the persons owning the ordinary share capital of the company and as belonging to them in proportion to the amount of their holdings of that capital, or

(*b*) in the case of a company which is a subsidiary company, as belonging to a company which is its parent company, or as belonging to the persons owning the ordinary share capital of that parent company, and as belonging to them in proportion to the amount of their holdings of that capital,

and any ordinary share capital owned by a company may, if any person or body of persons has the power to secure by means of the holding of shares or the possession of voting power in or in relation to any company, or by virtue of any power conferred by the articles of association or other document regulating any company, that the affairs of the company owning the share capital are conducted in accordance with his or their wishes, be regarded as owned by the person or body of persons having that power.

(3) For the purposes of subsection (2) above—

(*a*) references to ownership shall be construed as references to beneficial ownership;

(*b*) a company shall be deemed to be a subsidiary of another company if and so long as not less than three-quarters of its ordinary share capital is owned by that other company, whether directly or through another company or other companies, or partly directly and partly through another company or other companies;

(*c*) the amount of ordinary share capital of one company owned by a second company through another company or other companies, or partly directly and partly through another company or other companies, shall be determined in accordance with section 838(5) to (10); and

(*d*) where any company is a subsidiary of another company, that other company shall be considered as its parent company unless both are subsidiaries of a third company.

(4) In determining, for the purposes of section 343, whether or to what extent a trade belongs at different times to the same persons, persons who are relatives of one another and the persons from time to time entitled to the income under any trust shall respectively be treated as a single person, and for this purpose ''relative'' means husband, wife, ancestor, lineal descendant, brother or sister.

(5) For the purposes of section 343(4), relevant assets are—

(*a*) assets which were vested in the predecessor immediately before it ceased to carry on the trade, which were not transferred to the successor and which, in a case where the predecessor was the predecessor on a previous application of section 343, were not by virtue of subsection (9) of that section apportioned to a trade carried on by the company which was the successor on that application; and

(*b*) consideration given to the predecessor by the successor in respect of the change of company carrying on the trade;

and for the purposes of paragraph (*b*) above the assumption by the successor of any liabilities of the predecessor shall not be treated as the giving of consideration to the predecessor by the successor.

(6) For the purposes of section 343(4), relevant liabilities are liabilities which were outstanding and vested in the predecessor immediately before it ceased to carry on the trade, which were not transferred to the successor and which, in a case where the predecessor was the predecessor on a previous application of section 343, were not by virtue of subsection (9) of that section apportioned to a trade carried on by the company which was the successor on that application; but a liability representing the predecessor's share capital, share premium account, reserves or relevant loan stock is not a relevant liability.

(7) For the purposes of section 343(4)—

(*a*) the value of assets (other than money) shall be taken to be the price which they might reasonably be expected to have fetched on a sale in the open market immediately before the predecessor ceased to carry on the trade; and

(*b*) the amount of liabilities shall be taken to be their amount at that time.

(8) Where the predecessor transferred a liability to the successor but the creditor concerned agreed to accept settlement of part of the liability as settlement of the whole, the liability shall be treated for the purposes of subsection (6) above as not having been transferred to the successor except as to that part.

(9) A liability representing the predecessor's share capital, share premium account, reserves or relevant loan stock shall, for the purposes of subsection (6) above, be treated as not doing so if, in the period of one year ending with the day on which the predecessor ceased to carry on the trade, the liability arose on a conversion of a liability not representing its share capital, share premium account, reserves or relevant loan stock.

(10) Where a liability of the predecessor representing its relevant loan stock is not a relevant liability for the purposes of section 343(4) but is secured on an asset of the predecessor not transferred to the successor, the value of the asset shall, for the purposes of section 343(4), be reduced by an amount equal to the amount of the liability.

(11) In this section ''relevant loan stock'' means any loan stock or similar security (whether secured or unsecured) except any in the case of which subsection (12) below applies.

(12) This subsection applies where, at the time the liability giving rise to the loan stock or other security was incurred, the person who was the creditor was carrying on a trade of lending money.

Commentary—*Simon's Direct Tax Service* **D2.515, 516.**
Simon's Tax Cases—*J H & S (Timber) Ltd v Quirk* [1973] STC 111*.
s 344(1), (2), (3)(*a*), *Ayerst v C & K* [1975] STC 345*.
Definitions—''Body of persons'', s 832(1); ''company'', s 832(1), (2); ''ordinary share capital'', s 832(1); ''profits'', s 6(4); ''trade'', s 6(4).
Cross references—See TA 1988 s 70(1) (in accordance with this section, corporation tax to be computed under Schedule D Cases I to VI on the full amount of profits or gains or income arising in an accounting period, subject only to authorised deduction).

Chargeable gains

345 Computation of chargeable gains

Amendments—This section repealed by TCGA 1992 Sch 12 and re-enacted in TCGA 1992 s 8 from the year 1992–93.

346 Capital distribution of chargeable gains: recovery of tax from shareholder

Amendments—This section repealed by TCGA 1992 Sch 12 and re-enacted in TCGA 1992 s 189 from the year 1992–93.

347 Tax on one member of group recoverable from another member

Amendments—This section repealed by TCGA 1992 Sch 12 and re-enacted in TCGA 1992 s 190 from the year 1992–93.

PART IX
ANNUAL PAYMENTS AND INTEREST

Cross references—See FA 1988 s 43(3) (interest paid by a housing association or a self-build society on a home improvement loan made after 5 April 1988 not to be relevant loan interest for the purposes of this Part),
FA 1988 s 44(6) (interest paid by a housing association or a self-build society on a loan for residence of dependent relative or former spouse made after 5 April 1988 not to be relevant loan interest for the purposes of this Part).

Annual payments

[347A General rule

(1) A payment to which this section applies shall not be a charge on the income of the person liable to make it, and accordingly—

(*a*) his income shall be computed without any deduction being made on account of the payment, and

(*b*) the payment shall not form part of the income of the person to whom it is made or of any other person.

(2) This section applies to any annual payment made by an individual which would otherwise be within the charge to tax under Case III of Schedule D except—

(*a*) a payment of interest;
(*b*) ...[4]
(*c*) a payment made for bona fide commercial reasons in connection with the individual's trade, profession or vocation; and
(*d*) a payment to which section 125(1) applies.

(3) This section applies to a payment made by personal representatives (within the meaning given in section 701(4)) where—

(*a*) the deceased would have been liable to make the payment if he had not died, and
(*b*) this section would have applied to the payment if he had made it.

(4) A maintenance payment arising outside the United Kingdom shall not be within the charge to tax under Case V of Schedule D if, because of this section, it would not have been within the charge to tax under Case III had it arisen in the United Kingdom; and for this purpose ''maintenance payment'' means a periodical payment (not being an instalment of a lump sum) which satisfies the conditions set out in paragraphs (*a*) and (*b*) of section 347B(5).

(5) No deduction shall be made under section 65(1)(*b*)[, 68(1)(*b*) or 192(3)][2] on account of an annuity or other annual payment which would not have been within the charge to tax under Case III of Schedule D if it had arisen in the United Kingdom.][1]

(6) References in subsection (2) above to an individual include references to a Scottish partnership in which at least one partner is an individual.

(7), (8) ...[4]

Commentary—*Simon's Direct Tax Service* **B5.301–303; E1.501–503.**
Concession A12—Although maintenance payments paid by a non-resident under a UK court order or agreement is income from a UK source, relief by way of credit under TA 1988 s 793 is allowed if the conditions specified in the Concession are met.
Revenue Interpretation RI 196—Interpretation of the word ''like'' in the phrase ''like annual payments'' in sub-s (7), and explanation of how a tax effective deed can be written to include formula-based payments.
Revenue Internal Guidance—Relief RE 100–153 (meaning of ''charges'' (RE 110); summary guide (RE 101); effect on tax liability with worked examples (RE 120–131); failure to deduct tax at source (RE 140)).
Definitions—''Interest'', s 832(1); ''Schedule D'', s 18(1); ''trade'', s 832(1); ''United Kingdom'', s 830(1).
Cross references—See FA 1988 s 38(3A) (rate of relief for maintenance payments under an obligation which arose before 15 March 1988);
FA 1988 Sch 3 para 32 (this section to apply to annual payments between spouses living together even where made under an obligation arising before 15 March 1988).
FA 1994 s 79(1), (2) (modifications of this section for maintenance payments becoming due after 5 April 1994; payment under an existing obligation for the benefit of a person attaining 21 after 5 April 1994 but on or before the day the payment became due).
FA 1995 Sch 17 para 4 (application of this section to payments which are treated as income of the payer (by virtue of TA 1988 Part XV, Ch IA) notwithstanding that it is made under an existing obligation within FA 1988 s 36(3)).
FA 1999 s 36(7) (with effect for any payment falling due after 5 April 2000, this section and TA 1988 s 347B shall have effect, notwithstanding anything in FA 1988 s 36(3), for a payment made in pursuance of an existing obligation (within the meaning of s 36(3)) as they have effect for a payment made otherwise than in pursuance of such an obligation).
Amendments—[1] This section inserted by FA 1988 s 36(1), (3)–(5) for any payment falling due after 14 March 1988 unless made in pursuance of an existing obligation as defined.
[2] Words in sub-s (5) inserted by F(No 2)A 1992 s 60 with effect from the year 1992–93.
[3] Sub-ss (7), (8) inserted by FA 1995 s 74, Sch 17 Pt II, para 4(2), with effect from the year 1995–96 (and apply to every settlement wherever and whenever made or entered into).
[4] Words in sub-s (2)(b), and whole of sub-ss (7), (8) repealed by FA 2000 ss 41(2), (9), 156, Sch 40 Pt II(1) with effect for covenanted payments falling to be made by individuals after 5 April 2000 or made by companies after 31 March 2000.

[347B Qualifying maintenance payments

(1) [Subject to subsection (1A) below][12] in this section ''qualifying maintenance payment'' means a periodical payment which—

    (a) is made under an order made by a court [in a member State][6], or under a written agreement the [law applicable to][4] which is the law of [a member State or of a part of a member State][6],

    (b) is made by one of the parties to a marriage (including a marriage which has been dissolved or annulled) either—

        (i) to or for the benefit of the other party and for the maintenance of the other party, or

        (ii) to the other party for the maintenance by the other party of any child of the family,

    (c) is due at a time when—

        (i) the two parties are not a married couple living together, and

        (ii) the party to whom or for whose benefit the payment is made has not remarried, and

    (d) is not a payment in respect of which relief from tax is available to the person making the payment under any provision of the Income Tax Acts other than this section.

[(1A) A periodical payment is not a qualifying maintenance payment unless either of the parties to the marriage mentioned in subsection (1)(b) above was born before 6th April 1935.][12]

(2) ...[9] subject to [subsection (3)][12] below, a person making a claim for the purpose shall be entitled, [for a year of assessment to an income tax reduction calculated by reference to][7] an amount equal to the aggregate amount of any qualifying maintenance payments made by him which fall due in that year.

(3) [The amount by reference to which any income tax reduction is to be calculated under this section shall be limited to][7] the amount [specified in [section 257A(5A)][12] for the year][2].

(4), (5) ...[12]

[(5A) Where any person is entitled under this section for any year of assessment to an income tax reduction calculated by reference to the amount determined in accordance with [subsections (2) and (3)][12] above (''the relevant amount''), the amount of that person's liability for that year to income tax on his total income shall be the amount to which he would have been liable apart from this section less whichever is the smaller of—

    (a) the amount equal to [10 per cent][11] of the relevant amount; and

    (b) the amount which reduces his liability to nil;

...[11]

[(5B) In determining for the purposes of subsection (5A) above the amount of income tax to which a person would be liable apart from any income tax reduction under this section, no account shall be taken of—

    (a) any income tax reduction under Chapter I of Part VII;

    (b) any relief by way of a reduction of liability to tax which is given in accordance with any arrangements having effect by virtue of section 788 or by way of a credit under section 790(1); or (*c*) any tax at the basic rate on so much of that person's income as is income the income tax on which he is entitled to charge against any other person or to deduct, retain or satisfy out of any payment.][8]

(6) ...[3]

(7) In this section—

"child of the family", in relation to the parties to a marriage, means a person under 21 years of age—

(*a*) who is a child of both those parties, or

(*b*) who (not being a person who has been boarded out with them by a public authority or voluntary organisation) has been treated by both of them as a child of their family;

"periodical payment" does not include an instalment of a lump sum."

[(8) In [subsection (1)(*a*)][12] above, the reference to an order made by a court in the United Kingdom includes a reference to a maintenance assessment.][5]

[(9) Where—

(*a*) any periodical payment is made under a maintenance assessment by one of the parties to a marriage (including a marriage which has been dissolved or annulled),

(*b*) the other party to the marriage is, for the purposes of the Child Support Act 1991 or (as the case may be) the Child Support (Northern Ireland) Order 1991, a parent of the child or children with respect to whom the assessment has effect,

(*c*) the assessment was not made under section 7 of the Child Support Act 1991 (right of child in Scotland to apply for maintenance assessment), and

(*d*) any of the conditions mentioned in subsection (10) below is satisfied,

this section shall have effect as if the payment had been made to the other party for the maintenance by that other party of that child or (as the case may be) those children.][5]

[(10) The conditions are that—

(*a*) the payment is made to the Secretary of State in accordance with regulations made under section 29 of the Child Support Act 1991 by virtue of subsection(3)(*a*)(ii) of that section;

(*b*) the payment is made to the Department of Health and Social Services for Northern Ireland in accordance with regulations made under Article 29 of the Child Support (Northern Ireland) Order 1991, by virtue of paragraph (3)(*a*)(ii) of that Article;

(*c*) the payment is retained by the Secretary of State in accordance with regulations made under section 41 of that Act;

(*d*) the payment is retained by the Department of Health and Social Services for Northern Ireland in accordance with regulations made under Article 38 of that Order.][5]

[(11) In this section "maintenance assessment" means a maintenance assessment made under the Child Support Act 1991 or the Child Support (Northern Ireland) Order 1991.][5]

[(12) Where any periodical payment is made to the Secretary of State or to the Department of Health and Social Services for Northern Ireland—

(*a*) by one of the parties to a marriage (including a marriage which has been dissolved or annulled), and

[(*b*) under an order—

(i) made under section 106 of the Social Security Administration Act 1992 or section 101 of the Social Security Administration (Northern Ireland) Act 1992 (recovery of expenditure on benefit from person liable for maintenance) in respect of income support claimed by the other party to the marriage; or

(ii) made by virtue of section 23 of the Jobseekers Act 1995 (recovery of sums in respect of maintenance), or any corresponding enactment in Northern Ireland, in respect of an income-based jobseeker's allowance claimed by the other party to the marriage,][10]

this section shall have effect as if the payment had been made to the other party to the marriage to or for the benefit, and for the maintenance, of that other party or (as the case may be) to that other party for the maintenance of the child or children concerned.][5]][11]

[(13) In subsection (12) above "income-based jobseeker's allowance" has the same meaning as in the Jobseekers Act 1995, or, for Northern Ireland, the same meaning as in any corresponding enactment in Northern Ireland.][10]

Commentary—*Simon's Direct Tax Service* **E5.104, 105.**

Concession A12—Although maintenance payments paid by a non-resident under a UK court order or agreement is income from a UK source, relief by way of credit under TA 1988 s 793 is allowed if the conditions specified in the Concession are met.

A52—Relief for maintenance payments made under a court order or other legally binding agreement before the charges introduced by FA 1988.

Statement of Practice SP 15/80—Relief for maintenance payments including payment of school fees paid direct to the child or school under court order etc made before the charges introduced by FA 1988.

Revenue Internal Guidance—Inspector's manual IM 3900 (where VAT is chargeable on the payment, income tax need not be deducted from the VAT).

Simon's Tax Cases—*Billingham v John* [1998] STC 120; *Otter v Andrews* [1999] STC (SCD) 67; *Norris v Edgson* [2000] STC 494.

Definitions—"The Income Tax Acts", s 831(1)(*b*); "total income", s 835(1); "United Kingdom", s 830(1); "year of assessment", s 832(1).

Cross references—See TA 1988 s 289A(5)(*a*) (relief in respect of EIS to be given in priority to relief under this section).

TA 1988 TA 1988 s 347A(4) (exemption for foreign maintenance payments satisfying conditions in sub-s (5) above).

TA 1988 Sch 15B para 1 (tax relief on qualifying investments in venture capital trusts is offset against tax liability, for any year of assessment, in priority to relief under this section).

FA 1988 s 38(3A) (modification of this section as it applies to give relief for maintenance payments under obligations arising before 15 March 1988).

FA 1988 Sch 3 para 32 (this section to apply to annual payments between spouses living together even where made under obligations arising before 15 March 1988).

FA 1989 s 54(3C) (medical insurance relief given in priority to relief under this section).

FA 1991 s 32(2B) (vocational training relief given in priority to relief under this section).

FA 1995 Sch 15 para 1(6) (relief for investment in venture capital trusts given in priority to relief under this section).

FA 1999 s 36(7) (with effect for any payment falling due after 5 April 2000, this section and TA 1988 s 347A shall have effect, notwithstanding anything in FA 1988 s 36(3), for a payment made in pursuance of an existing obligation (within the meaning of s 36(3)) as they have effect for a payment made otherwise than in pursuance of such an obligation).

Amendments—[1] This section inserted by FA 1988 s 36(1), (3)–(5) for any payment falling due after 14 March 1988 unless made in pursuance of an existing obligation as defined.

[2] Words in sub-s (3) substituted by FA 1988 Sch 3 para 13 with effect from the year 1990–91.

[3] Sub-s (6) repealed by FA 1988 Sch 14 Pt VIII with effect from the year 1990–91.

[4] Words in sub-s (1)(a) substituted by the Contracts (Applicable Law) Act 1990 s 5 and Sch 4 para 6.

[5] Sub-ss (8)–(12) added by F(No 2)A 1992 s 62(1), (4), (6) with effect from 6 April 1993 by virtue of F(No 2)A 1992 s 62 (Commencement) Order, SI 1992/2642 and so far as concerns orders under sub-s(12)(b) above, only for payments falling due after 6 April 1993.

[6] Words in sub-s (1)(a) substituted by F(No 2)A 1992 s 61 with effect from the year 1992–93.

[7] Words in sub-ss (2), (3), (5) substituted by FA 1994 s 79(1), (3)–(5) for maintenance payments becoming due after 5 April 1994.

[8] Sub-ss (5A), (5B) inserted by FA 1994 s 79(1), (6) for maintenance payments becoming due after 5 April 1994.

[9] Words in sub-s (2) repealed by FA 1994 s 79(1), (3)(a) and Sch 26 Pt V(1) for maintenance payments becoming due after 5 April 1994.

[10] Sub-s (12)(b) substituted, and sub-s (13) added, by the Jobseekers Act 1995 Sch 2 paras 11, 15, as from 7 October 1996 (see the Jobseekers Act 1995 (Commencement No 4) Order 1996, SI 1996/2208).

[11] Words in sub-s (5A)(a) substituted and words after sub-s (5A)(b) repealed by FA 1998 s 27 and Sch 27 Part III(1) with effect for the year 1999–00 and subsequent years of assessment.

[12] Sub-s (1A) and words in sub-s (1) inserted, words in sub-ss (2), (3), (5A), (8) substituted, and sub-ss (4), (5) repealed by FA 1999 ss 36, 139, Sch 20 Pt III(6) with effect for any payment falling due after 5 April 2000.

Prospective amendments—In sub-ss (8), (9) for the words "maintenance assessment" there shall be substituted "maintenance calculation", in subsection (9)(b) and (c), for the words "the assessment" there shall be substituted "the calculation", and whole of sub-s (11) to be substituted by the Child Support, Pensions and Social Security Act 2000 ss 26, 86, Sch 3 para 8(1), (2) with effect from a day to be appointed. Sub-s (11) as substituted will read as follows—

"(11) In this section "maintenance calculation" means a maintenance calculation made under the Child Support Act 1991 or a maintenance assessment made under the Child Support (Northern Ireland) Order 1991.".

348 Payments out of profits or gains brought into charge to income tax: deduction of tax

(1) Subject to any provision to the contrary in the Income Tax Acts, where any annuity or other annual payment charged with tax under Case III of Schedule D, not being interest, is payable wholly out of profits or gains brought into charge to income tax—

(a) the whole of the profits or gains shall be assessed and charged with income tax on the person liable to the annuity or other annual payment, without distinguishing the annuity or other annual payment; and

(b) the person liable to make the payment, whether out of the profits or gains charged with income tax or out of any annual payment liable to deduction, or from which a deduction has been made, shall be entitled on making the payment to deduct and retain out of it a sum representing the amount of income tax thereon; and

(c) the person to whom the payment is made shall allow the deduction on receipt of the residue of the payment, and the person making the deduction shall be acquitted and discharged of so much money as is represented by the deduction, as if that sum had been actually paid; and

(d) the deduction shall be treated as income tax paid by the person to whom the payment is made.

(2) Subject to any provision to the contrary in the Income Tax Acts, where—

(a) any royalty or other sum paid in respect of the user of a patent; ...[2]

(b) ...[2]

is paid wholly out of profits or gains brought into charge to income tax, the person making the payment shall be entitled on making the payment to deduct and retain out of it a sum representing the amount of the income tax thereon.

(3) This section does not apply to ...[1] any payment to which section 687 applies ...[4] [or to any payment which is a qualifying donation for the purposes of section 25 of the Finance Act 1990][3].

Commentary—*Simon's Direct Tax Service* A3.235, 403.

Concession A16—Where an annuity etc is paid in a later year out of untaxed income, but could have been paid in the due year out of taxed income, the payer is not required to account for tax notwithstanding ss 349(1), 350(1) below. Similar relief is allowed to trusts and non-trading institutions.

A52—Relief for maintenance payments made under a court order or other legally binding agreement before the charges introduced by FA 1988.

Revenue & other press releases—IR 6-12-95 (effect of change in basic rate of tax with effect from 6 April 1996).

Revenue Internal Guidance—Relief manual RE 100, 110 (meaning of "charges").

RE 101 (flow charts illustrating the treatment of charges).

RE 114 (treatment of partnership charges).

RE 124 (taxed income which cannot be used to cover charges).

Simon's Tax Cases—*Essex County Council v Ellam* [1989] STC 317*; *Tenbry Investments Ltd v Peugeot Talbot Motor Co Ltd* [1992] STC 791*; *Moodie v IRC* [1993] STC 188*.

s 348(1), *IRC v Plummer* [1979] STC 793*; *Moodie v IRC* [1990] STC 475*.

s 348(2), *Rank Xerox Ltd v Lane* [1978] STC 449*.

Definitions—"The Income Tax Acts", s 831(1)(b); "profits or gains", s 833(1); "Schedule D", s 18(1).

Cross references—See TA 1988 s 4 (deduction of income tax to be at the basic or lower rate).

TA 1988 s 120 (rent payable in respect of electric line wayleaves to be subject to deduction of tax under this section).

TA 1988 s 233(1) (distributions received by persons not entitled to a tax credit to be treated as not brought into the charge to income tax for the purposes of this section).

TA 1988 s 235(3) (distributions received by exempt funds etc to be treated as not brought into the charge to income tax for the purposes of this section).

TA 1988 s 237(5) (tax creditor relating to bonus issues not to be set off against income tax chargeable under this section).

TA 1988 s 246D(2) (foreign income dividend received by an individual treated as income not brought into charge to income tax).

TA 1988 s 249(4)(c) (stock dividends treated as income not brought into the charge to income tax for the purposes of this section).

TA 1988 s 329AA, 329AB (personal injury damages and compensation under the Criminal Injuries Compensation Scheme in the form of periodical payments to be made without deduction of tax).

TA 1988 s 337(2) (where a company begins or ceases to trade, no deduction in respect of payments mentioned in sub-s (2) above to be made in computing income).

TA 1988 s 352 (payee's right to obtain certificate of deduction where tax under this section is deducted).

TA 1988 s 477A(7) (notwithstanding this section, interest payments to a building society to be made gross).

TA 1988 s 486(2) (notwithstanding this section, payment of interest by a registered industrial and provident society to be made gross).

TA 1988 s 547(5) (where in certain circumstances an individual's total income is deemed to include a gain treated as arising in connection with life and capital redemption policies and life annuity contracts, the gain to be treated for the purposes of this section as not brought into charge to income tax).

TA 1988 s 597(2) (Board may direct temporary deduction of tax under this section in respect of certain pensions).

TA 1988 s 648A(2) (Board may direct temporary deduction of tax in respect of annuities acquired with approved pension funds).

TA 1988 s 687(1) (disapplication of this section to payments out of discretionary trusts).

TA 1988 s 699A(6) (untaxed estate income within this section treated as income not brought into charge to income tax).

TA 1988 s 704(A)(f) (cancellation of tax advantage from dividend stripping).

FA 1994 Sch 20 para 11(7) (deemed income on recovery of excess double taxation relief obtained in respect of opening years of trade not to be treated as income brought into charge to income tax).

Amendments—[1] Words in sub-s (3) repealed by FA 1988 Sch 14 Pt IV for payments made after 5 April 1989.

[2] Sub-s (2)(b) and the word "or" preceding it repealed by FA 1997 Sch 18 Pt VI(2) with effect for payments made after 5 April 1997.

[3] Words in sub-s (3) inserted by FA 2000 s 41(3), (9) with effect for covenanted payments falling to be made by individuals after 5 April 2000 or made by companies after 31 March 2000.

[4] Words in sub-s (3) repealed by FA 2000 s 156, Sch 40 Pt II(17) with effect for relevant payments or receipts for which the chargeable date for the purposes of Pt IV, Ch VIIA is after 31 March 2001.

349 Payments not out of profits or gains brought into charge to income tax, and annual interest

(1) Where—

(a) any annuity or other annual payment charged with tax under Case III of Schedule D, not being interest; or

(b) any royalty or other sum paid in respect of the user of a patent;...[16]

(c) ...[16]

is not payable or not wholly payable out of profits or gains brought into charge to income tax, the person by or through whom any payment thereof is made shall, on making the payment, deduct out of it a sum representing the amount of income tax thereon.

This subsection does not apply to any payment to which section 687 applies ...[18] [or to any payment which is a qualifying donation (within the meaning of section 339) or a qualifying donation for the purposes of section 25 of the Finance Act 1990][17].

(2) Subject to subsection (3) below and to any other provision to the contrary in the Income Tax Acts, where any yearly interest of money chargeable to tax under Case III of Schedule D [(as that Schedule has effect apart from the modification made for the purposes of corporation tax by section 18(3A))][9] is paid—

(a) otherwise than in a fiduciary or representative capacity, by a company [(other than a building society)][3] or local authority; or

(b) by or on behalf of a partnership of which a company is a member; or

(c) by any person to another person whose usual place of abode is outside the United Kingdom;

the person by or through whom the payment is made shall, on making the payment, deduct out of it a sum representing the amount of income tax thereon for the year in which the payment is made.

(3) Subsection (2) above does not apply—

(a) to interest payable [on an advance from a bank, if at the time when the interest is paid the person beneficially entitled to the interest is within the charge to corporation tax as respects the interest][10]; or

(b) to interest paid by [a bank in the ordinary course of its][13] business; or

[(ba) to interest paid on deposits with the National Savings Bank; or][15]

(c) to any [payment of interest on a quoted Eurobond][19]; or

(d) to any payment to which section 369 ...[2a] applies; [or][2]

...[18]

[(f) to any payment in respect of which a liability to deduct income tax is imposed by section 480A(1); or][2]

[(g) to any payment in respect of which a liability to deduct income tax would be imposed by section 480A(1) if conditions prescribed by regulations under section 480B were not fulfilled;][2] [or][7]

[(h) to any payment in respect of which a liability to deduct income tax would, but for section 481(5)(k), be imposed by section 480A(1).][7] [or

(i) in the case of a person who is authorised for the purposes of the Financial Services and Markets Act 2000 and whose business consists wholly or mainly of dealing in financial instruments as principal, to interest paid by that person in the ordinary course of his business.][22]

...[1]

[(3AA) In this section "bank" has the meaning given by section 840A.][11]

[(3AB) An order under section 840A(1)(d) designating an organisation as a bank for the purposes of paragraph (a) of subsection (3) above may provide that that paragraph shall apply to the organisation as if the words from "if" to the end were omitted.][12]

[(3A) Subject to subsection (3B) below and to any other provision to the contrary in the Income Tax Acts, where—

(a) any dividend or interest is paid in respect of a security issued by a building society other than a qualifying certificate of deposit [and other than a qualifying deposit right][6],
(b) the security was [listed][14], or capable of being [listed][14], on a recognised stock exchange at the time the dividend or interest became payable,

the person by or through whom the payment is made shall, on making the payment, deduct out of it a sum representing the amount of income tax thereon for the year in which the payment is made.][4]

[(3B) Subsection (3A) above does not apply to any [payment of interest on a quoted Eurobond][19].][4]

[(3C) Subject to any provision to the contrary in the Income Tax Acts, where any UK public revenue dividend is paid, the person by or through whom the payment is made shall, on making the payment, deduct out of it a sum representing the amount of income tax on it for the year in which the payment is made.][21]

[(4) In [this section][5]—

"dividend" has the same meaning as in section 477A;
["qualifying certificate of deposit" means a certificate of deposit, as defined in section 56(5), under which—

(a) the amount payable by the issuing society, exclusive of interest, is not less than £50,000 (or, for a deposit denominated in foreign currency, not less than the equivalent of £50,000 at the time when the deposit is made), and
(b) the obligation of the society to pay that amount arises after a period of not more than five years beginning with the date on which the deposit is made; and][5]

["qualifying deposit right" means a right to receive an amount (with or without interest) in pursuance of a deposit of money, where—

(a) the right subsists under an arrangement falling within section 56A,
(b) no certificate of deposit, as defined in section 56(5), has been issued in respect of the right at the time the dividend or interest concerned is paid, and
(c) the conditions set out in paragraphs (a) and (b) in the definition of "qualifying certificate of deposit" apply; and][6]

["quoted Eurobond" means any security that—

(i)   is issued by a company,
(ii) is listed on a recognised stock exchange, and
(iii) carries a right to interest;"][20]

["security" includes share.][5]

["UK public revenue dividend" means any income from securities which is paid out of the public revenue of the United Kingdom or Northern Ireland, but does not include interest on local authority stock.][21]][2]

[(5) For the purposes of subsection (3)(i) above, a financial instrument includes—

(a) any money,
(b) any shares or securities,
(c) an option, future or contract for differences if, but only if, its underlying subject-matter is (or is primarily) a financial instrument, or financial instruments, and
(d) an instrument the underlying subject-matter of which is (or is primarily) creditworthiness.][22]

[(6) For the purposes of subsection (5) above, the "underlying" subject-matter of an instrument the effect of which depends on an index or factor is the matter by reference to which the index or factor is determined.][22]

Commentary—*Simon's Direct Tax Service* A3.236, 404, 405; D4.728, 730.
Concessions A16—Where an annuity etc is paid in a later year out of untaxed income, but could have been paid in the due year out of taxed income, the payer is not required to account for tax notwithstanding sub-s (1) above. Similar relief is allowed to trusts and non-trading institutions.
A89—Interest on a loan to buy a property used for both residential and business purposes may be allowed in part under this section and in part as a deduction in computing profits or losses.
C17—Annual swap fees which are not deductible from trading income are treated as annual payments for corporation tax purposes. Where such fees are paid to or by recognised UK banks or swap dealers, deduction of fees as a charge will not be conditional on tax having been deducted and accounted for to the Revenue. The concession does not apply to annual swap fees for currency swaps after the company's commencement day (the first day of the company's first accounting period beginning after 22 March 1995). As regards interest swaps held at commencement day see FA 1994 s 148.
A94—Profits and losses of theatre backers (angels), payers may deduct tax under sub-s (1) but are not obligated to do so.

Statements of Practice SP C5—Interest payable to a bank in the UK on a foreign currency loan is treated for the purposes of this section as payable in the UK and consequently is payable gross.

SP 12/91—Interpretation of the words "in the ordinary course" in sub-s (3)(*b*) above for interest paid before 29 April 1996.

SP 4/96—Interpretation of sub-s (3)(*b*) above for interest paid after 28 April 1996.

Revenue Interpretation RI 49—Tax need not be deducted under sub-s (2)(*c*) above from interest paid to UK branch of non-resident company which is liable to corporation tax under s 11 of this Act.

RI 207—The obligation to deduct tax under sub-s (2) is not affected by the taxation of interest received from a loan relationship as part of a company's Case I profit under FA 1996 s 80.

RI 209—Tax need not be deducted under sub-s (2) from interest payable under the Late Payment of Commercial Debts (Interest) Act 1998 as it is not yearly interest.

Revenue Internal Guidance—Inspector's manual IM 3103 (a solicitor may be charged under this section if he is a person through whom payment is made).

IM 3922 (deduction of tax is required only from payments of an income nature; whether a lump sum is income or capital).

IM 3900 (where VAT is chargeable on the payment, income tax need not be deducted from the VAT).

IM 3940 (sub-s (2) criteria for deciding whether interest within Schedule D Case III).

IM 3942 (capitalised interest: tax is deductible only when payment is made).

IM 3961 (a non-resident payer has the same right to deduct tax as a resident payer).

Relief manual RE 100, 110 (meaning of "charges").

RE 101 (flow charts illustrating the treatment of charges).

RE 114 (treatment of partnership charges).

RE 124 (taxed income which cannot be used to cover charges).

Revenue & other press releases—IR 10-11-78 (interest paid under s 349(3)(*b*) by a bank refers to interest paid directly; if paid through an agent, who is within TMA 1970 s 78, the agent must deduct tax from any annual interest.

IR 6-12-95 (effect of change in basic rate of tax with effect from 6 April 1996).

IR Tax Bulletin August 2001 p 867 (outlines changes made by FA 2000 and FA 2001 to the rules requiring deduction of tax at source from certain payments of interest).).

Simon's Tax Cases—s 349(1), *Fitzleet Estates Ltd v Cherry* [1977] STC 397*; *Mcburnie v Tacey* [1984] STC 347*; *IRC v Crawley* [1987] STC 147*; *Tenbry Investments Ltd v Peugeot Talbot Motor Co Ltd* [1992] STC 791.

s 349(2), *re Euro Hotel (Belgravia) Ltd* [1975] STC 682*; *Chevron Petroleum (UK) Ltd v BP Petroleum Development Ltd* [1981] STC 689*; *Hafton Properties Ltd v mchugh* [1987] STC 16*.

s 349(3)(*a*), (*b*), *Hafton Properties Ltd v mchugh* [1987] STC 16*.

Definitions—"Deduction of income tax", s 4(1); "the Income Tax Acts", s 831(1)(*b*); "local authority", s 832(1); "Schedule D", s 18(1).

Cross references—See Double Taxation Relief (Taxes on Income) (General) Regulations, SI 1970/488 regs 6, 7, 9 (tax treated as deducted under this section where relief from the requirement to deduct is conferred by a double tax treaty).

TA 1988 s 4 (deduction of income tax to be at the basic or lower rate).

TA 1988 s 43(1), (2) (application of sub-s (1) above to profits or gains of non-residents chargeable under Schedule A or Schedule D Case VI).

TA 1988 s 120 (rent payable in respect of electric line wayleaves to be subject to deduction of tax under this section).

TA 1988 s 124 (sub-s (2) above does not apply to interest on quoted Eurobonds where certain conditions met).

TA 1988 s 214(1) (application of sub-s (1) above in relation to certain chargeable payments connected with demergers).

TA 1988 s 233(1) (distributions received by persons not entitled to a tax credit to be treated as not brought into the charge to income tax for the purposes of this section).

TA 1988 s 235(3) (distributions received by exempt funds etc to be treated as not brought into the charge to income tax for the purposes of this section).

TA 1988 s 237(5) (tax creditor relating to bonus issues not to be set off against income tax chargeable under this section).

TA 1988 s 246D(2) (foreign income dividend received by an individual treated as income not brought into charge to income tax).

TA 1988 s 247(4) (this section not to apply to certain annual payments between members of a group of companies).

TA 1988 s 249(4)(*c*) (stock dividends treated as income not brought into the charge to income tax).

TA 1988 ss 329AA, 329AB (personal injury damages and compensation under the Criminal Injuries Compensation Scheme in the form of periodical payments to be made without deduction of tax).

TA 1988 s 349E (payment of royalties overseas to which sub-s (1) above applies).

TA 1988 s 350 (tax returns and accountability for payments made under this section).

TA 1988 s 352 (payee's right to obtain certificate of deduction where tax under this section is deducted).

TA 1988 s 387 (carry-forward as losses of annual payments taxed under this section, subject to certain exceptions).

TA 1988 s 421(1)(*c*) (deemed income on release of a loan by a close company to be treated as not brought into the charge to income tax for the purposes of this section).

TA 1988 ss 468M, 468N (interest distributions of authorised unit trusts).

TA 1988 s 477A(7) (notwithstanding this section, interest payments to a building society to be made gross).

TA 1988 s 480A(3) (deduction of tax from interest payment by deposit takers).

TA 1988 s 486(2) (notwithstanding this section, payment of interest by a registered industrial and provident society to be made gross).

TA 1988 s 486(3) (application of sub-s (2) above to interest payment made to a non-resident by a registered industrial and provident society).

TA 1988 s 524(3),(4)(*a*) (taxation of receipts from sale by a non-resident of patent rights).

TA 1988 s 536(1),(3) (application of sub-s (1) above to the taxation of royalties etc for a copyright owned by a non-resident).

TA 1988 s 537 (application of sub-s (1) above to the taxation of royalties etc for a public lending right owned by a non-resident).

TA 1988 s 537B(1) (application of sub-s (1) above to the taxation of royalties etc for a design right owned by a non-resident).

TA 1988 s 547(5) (where in certain circumstances an individual's total income is deemed to include a gain treated as arising in connection with life and capital redemption policies and life annuity contracts, the gain to be treated for the purposes of sub-s (1) of this section as not brought into charge to income tax).

TA 1988 s 582A(4), (5) (sub-ss (1), (2) above not to apply to payments by designated international organisations).

TA 1988 s 597(2) (Board may direct the temporary deduction of tax under this section in respect of pensions).

TA 1988 s 648A(2) (Board may direct the temporary deduction of tax under this section in respect of annuities acquired with an approved pension).

TA 1988 s 687(1) (disapplication of sub-s (1) above to payments out of discretionary trusts).

TA 1988 s 699A(6) (untaxed estate income within this section treated as income not brought into charge to income tax for purpose of sub-s (1) above).

TA 1988 s 704(A)(*f*) (cancellation of tax advantage from dividend stripping).

TA 1988 s 777(9) (Board may direct that certain payments made to non-residents in connection with the sale of income or transactions in land be made under deduction of tax under sub-s (1) above).

TA 1988 Sch 23A, para 4(2) (gross amount of manufactured overseas dividend to be treated as an annual payment within this section).

IT (Building Societies) (Annual Payments) Regulations, SI 1991/512 regs 2, 3(1)(*a*) (time and manner of collection of income tax from building societies);

IT (Manufactured Interest) Regulations, SI 1992/2074 reg 5 (tax treatment for the purposes of sub-s (2) above of interest on UK securities paid gross by a resident company under stock exchange rules);

FA 1994 s 174 (interest rate and currency contracts: qualifying payments made by qualifying companies as defined in FA 1994 ss 153, 154: no withholding tax to be levied on such payments).

European Investment Bank (Designated International Organisation) Order, SI 1996/1179 (applies sub-s (3AB) above to the European Investment Bank).

Amendments—[1] Words in sub-s (3) repealed by FA 1988 Sch 14 Pt IV for payments made after 5 April 1989.

[2] Sub-ss (3)(*f*), (g), preceding word ''or'' and sub-s (4) inserted by FA 1990 Sch 5 para 10 as regards a payment made after 5 April 1991.

[3] Words in sub-s (2)(*a*) inserted by FA 1991 Sch 11 para 1(1),(2).

[4] Sub-ss (3A), (3B) inserted by FA 1991 Sch 11 para 1(1),(4).

[5] Words in sub-s (4) substituted by FA 1991 Sch 11 para 1(1),(5).

[6] Words in sub-s (3A)(*a*) and definition of ''qualifying deposit right'' in sub-s (4) inserted by F(No 2)A 1992 Sch 8 paras 2, 6 for arrangements made after 16 July 1992.

[7] Sub-s (3)(*h*) and the preceding word ''or'' inserted by FA 1993 s 59.

[8] Words omitted from sub-s (1)(*c*) repealed by FA 1995 Sch 29 Pt VIII(22), with effect for payments made after 1 May 1995.

[9] Words in sub-s (2) inserted by FA 1996 Sch 14 para 18 with effect from the year 1996–97.

[10] Words in sub-s (3)(*a*) substituted for ''in the United Kingdom on an advance from a bank carrying on a bone fide banking business in the United Kingdom'' by FA 1996 Sch 37 para 3(*a*) with effect for interest payable on and after 29 April 1996 but subject to the transitional provisions in FA 1996 Sch 37 para 8(1)–(6).

[11] Sub-s (3AA) inserted by FA 1996 Sch 37 para 2(1), (2)(*b*) with effect, so far as relating to sub-s (3)(*a*), in relation to interest payable on and after 29 April 1996 but subject to the transitional provisions in FA 1996 Sch 37 para 8(1)–(6), and so far as relating to sub-s (3)(*b*), in relation to interest paid on or after that date on an advance made on or after that date see (FA 1996 Sch 37 para 8(7)).

[12] Sub-s (3AB) inserted by FA 1996 Sch 37 para 4.

[13] Words in sub-s (3)(*b*) substituted for ''such a bank in the ordinary course of that'' by FA 1996 Sch 37 para 3(*b*), 8(7) applying in relation to interest paid on or after 29 April 1996 on an advance made on or after that day. However, by virtue of FA 1996 Sch 37 para 8(8), in relation to interest paid on an advance made before that date, sub-s (3)(*b*) has effect as if for the words ''such a bank'' there were substituted ''a bank carrying on a bona fide banking business in the United Kingdom'' (and sub-s (3AA) is to be disregarded).

[14] Word in sub-s (3A)(*b*) substituted by FA 1996 Sch 38 para 6(1), (2)(*e*), (7) with effect for dividends or interest which became payable after 31 March 1996.

[15] Sub-s (3)(*ba*) inserted by FA 1997 s 78 with effect for interest whenever paid (including interest paid before the passing of FA 1997).

[16] Sub-s (1)(*c*) and the word ''or'' preceding it repealed by FA 1997 Sch 18 Pt VI(2) with effect for payments made after 5 April 1997.

[17] Words in sub-s (1) inserted by FA 2000 s 41(4), (9) with effect for covenanted payments falling to be made by individuals after 5 April 2000 or made by companies after 31 March 2000.

[18] Words in sub-s (1) and whole of sub-s (3)(*e*) repealed by FA 2000 s 156, Sch 40 Pt II(17) with effect for relevant payments or receipts in relation to which the chargeable date for the purposes of Pt IV, Ch VIIA is after 31 March 2001.

[19] Words in sub-ss (3)(*c*) and (3B) substituted by FA 2000 s 111(2)(*a*) with effect for payments of interest made after 31 March 2001.

[20] In sub-s (4), definition of ''quoted Eurobond'' inserted by FA 2000 s 111(2)(*b*) with effect for payments of interest made after 31 March 2001.

[21] Sub-s (3C) and definition of ''UK public revenue dividend'' in sub-s (4) inserted by FA 2000 s 112(2), (3), (5) with effect for payments made after 31 March 2001.

[22] Sub-s (3)(*i*), (5) and (6) added by FA 2002 s 95 with effect for the payment of interest after 30 September 2002.

[349A Exceptions to section 349 for payments between companies etc

(1) The provisions specified in subsection (3) below (which require tax to be deducted on making certain payments) do not apply to a payment made by a company [or a local authority][2] if, at the time the payment is made, the company [or authority][2] reasonably believes that one of the conditions specified in section 349B is satisfied.

(2) Subsection (1) above has effect subject to any directions under section 349C.

(3) The provisions are—

section 349(1) (certain annuities and other annual payments, and royalties and other sums paid for use of UK patents),

section 349(2)(*a*) and (*b*) (UK interest),

section 349(3A) (dividend or interest on securities issued by building societies), and

section 524(3)(*b*) (which provides for section 349(1) to apply to proceeds of sale of UK patent rights).

(4) References in subsection (3) above to any provision of section 349 do not include that provision as applied—

(*a*) under section 777(9) (directions applying section 349(1) to certain payments to non-residents), or

(*b*) by paragraph 4(2) of Schedule 23A (manufactured overseas dividends to be treated as annual payments within section 349).

(5) References in this section to the company by which a payment is made do not include a company acting as trustee or agent for another person.

(6) For the purposes of this section—

[(*a*)][2] a payment by a partnership is treated as made by a company if any member of the partnership is a company][1] [and

(*b*) a payment by a partnership is treated as made by a local authority if any member of the partnership is a local authority.][2]

Commentary—*Simon's Direct Tax Service* A3.426.

Revenue and other press releases—IR Tax Bulletin August 2001 p 867 (outlines changes made by FA 2000 and FA 2001 to the rules requiring deduction of tax at source from certain payments of interest).

Amendments—[1] This section inserted by FA 2001 s 85(1), (4) with effect for payments made after 31 March 2001.

[2] Words in sub-s (1) inserted, in sub-s (6), "(a)" inserted, and para (b) added, by FA 2002 s 94(1), (7) with effect for payments made after 30 September 2002.

[349B The conditions mentioned in section 349A(1)

(1) The first of the conditions mentioned in section 349A(1) is that the person beneficially entitled to the income in respect of which the payment is made is—

   (a) a company resident in the United Kingdom, ...[3]

   (b) ...[3].

(2) The second of those conditions is that—

   (a) the person beneficially entitled to the income in respect of which the payment is made is a company not resident in the United Kingdom ("the non-resident company"),

   (b) the non-resident company carries on a trade in the United Kingdom through a branch or agency, and

   (c) the payment falls to be brought into account in computing the chargeable profits (within the meaning given by section 11(2)) of the non-resident company.][1]

[(3) The third of those conditions is that the payment is made to—

   (a) a local authority;

   (b) a health service body within the meaning of section 519A(2);

   (c) a public office or department of the Crown to which section 829(1) applies;

   (d) a charity (within the meaning of section 506(1));

   (e) a body for the time being mentioned in section 507(1) (bodies that are allowed the same exemption from tax as charities the whole income of which is applied to charitable purposes);

   (f) an Association of a description specified in section 508 (scientific research organisations);

   (g) the United Kingdom Atomic Energy Authority;

   (h) the National Radiological Protection Board;

   (i) the administrator (within the meaning of section 611AA) of a scheme entitled to exemption under section 592(2) or 608(2)(a) (exempt approved schemes and former approved superannuation funds);

   (j) the trustees of a scheme entitled to exemption under section 613(4) (Parliamentary pension funds);

   (k) the persons entitled to receive the income of a fund entitled to exemption under section 614(3) (certain colonial, etc pension funds);

   (l) the trustees or other persons having the management of a fund entitled to exemption under section 620(6) (retirement annuity trust schemes); or

   (m) a person holding investments or deposits for the purposes of a scheme entitled to exemption under section 643(2) (approved personal pension schemes).][2]

[(4) The fourth of those conditions is that—

   (a) the person to whom the payment is made is, or is the nominee of, the plan manager of a plan,

   (b) an individual investing under the plan is entitled to exemption by virtue of regulations under section 333 (personal equity plans and individual savings accounts), and

   (c) the plan manager receives the payment in respect of investments under the plan.][2]

[(5) The fifth of those conditions is that—

   (a) the person to whom the payment is made is a society or institution with whom tax-exempt special savings accounts (within the meaning of section 326A) may be held, and

   (b) the society or institution receives the payment in respect of investments held for the purposes of such accounts.][2]

[(6) The sixth of those conditions is that the person beneficially entitled to the income in respect of which the payment is made is a partnership each member of which is—

   (a) a person or body mentioned in subsection (3) above, or

   (b) a person or body mentioned in subsection (7) below.][2]

[(7) The persons and bodies referred to in subsection (6)(b) above are—

   (a) a company resident in the United Kingdom;

   (b) a company that—

     (i) is not resident in the United Kingdom,

     (ii) carries on a trade there through a branch or agency, and

     (iii) is required to bring into account, in computing its chargeable profits (within the meaning of section 11(2)), the whole of any share of that payment that falls to it by reason of sections 114 and 115;

   (c) the European Investment Fund.][2]

[(8) The Treasury may by order amend—

   (a) subsection (3) above;

   (b) subsection (7) above;

so as to add to, restrict or otherwise alter the persons and bodies falling within that subsection.][2]

Commentary—*Simon's Direct Tax Service* A3.426.
Revenue and other press releases—IR Tax Bulletin August 2001 p 867 (outlines changes made by FA 2000 and FA 2001 to the rules requiring deduction of tax at source from certain payments of interest).
Amendments—[1] This section inserted by FA 2001 s 85(1), (4) with effect for payments made after 31 March 2001.
[2] Sub-ss (3)–(8) added by FA 2002 s 94(2), (7) with effect for payments made after 30 September 2002.

³ Sub-s (1)(*b*) and word "or" preceding it repealed by FA 2002 s 141, Sch 40 Pt 3(14) with effect for payments made after 30 September 2002. Sub-s (1)(*b*) previously read thus—

"(*b*) a partnership each member of which is a company resident in the United Kingdom."

[349C Directions disapplying section 349A(1)

(1) The Board may give a direction to a company [or a local authority] directing that section 349A(1) is not to apply in relation to any payment that—

    (*a*) is made by the company [or authority] after the giving of the direction, and
    (*b*) is specified in the direction or is of a description so specified.

(2) Such a direction shall not be given unless the Board have reasonable grounds for believing as respects each payment to which the direction relates that it is likely that [none] of the conditions specified in section 349B will be satisfied in relation to the payment at the time the payment is made.

(3) A direction under this section may be varied or revoked by a subsequent such direction.

[(4) In this section—

    "company" includes a partnership of which any member is a company; and
    "local authority" includes a partnership of which any member is a local authority.]²]¹

Commentary—*Simon's Direct Tax Service* A3.426.
Revenue and other press releases—IR Tax Bulletin August 2001 p 867 (outlines changes made by FA 2000 and FA 2001 to the rules requiring deduction of tax at source from certain payments of interest).
Amendments—¹ This section inserted by FA 2001 s 85(1), (4) with effect for payments made after 31 March 2001.
² Words in sub-s (1) inserted, and in sub-s (2), words substituted for the words "neither", and sub-s (4) substituted, by FA 2002 s 94(3) by FA 2002 s 94(3), (7) with effect for payments made after 30 September 2002. Sub-s (4) previously read as follows—

    "(4) In this section "company" includes a partnership of which any member is a company."

[349D Section 349A(1): consequences of reasonable but incorrect belief

(1) Where—

    (*a*) a payment is made by a company [or local authority]² without an amount representing the income tax on the payment being deducted from the payment,
    (*b*) at the time the payment is made, the company [or authority]² reasonably believes that one of the conditions specified in section 349B is satisfied,
    (*c*) if the company [or authority]² did not so believe, tax would be deductible from the payment under section 349, and
    (*d*) [none]² of the conditions specified in section 349B is satisfied at the time the payment is made,

section 350 applies as if the payment were within section 349 (and Schedule 16 applies as if tax were deductible from the payment under section 349).

[(2) In this section—

    "company" includes a partnership of which any member is a company; and
    "local authority" includes a partnership of which any member is a local authority.]²]¹

Commentary—*Simon's Direct Tax Service* A3.426.
Revenue and other press releases—IR Tax Bulletin August 2001 p (outlines changes made by FA 2000 and FA 2001 to the rules requiring deduction of tax at source from certain payments of interest).
Amendments—¹ This section inserted by FA 2001 s 85(1), (4) with effect for payments made after 31 March 2001.
² Words inserted in sub-s (1), in sub-s (1)(*d*), word substituted for the word "neither", and sub-s (2) substituted, by FA 2002 s 94(4), (7) with effect for payments made after 30 September 2002. Sub-s (2) previously read as follows—

    "(2) In this section "company" includes a partnership of which any member is a company."

[349E Deductions under section 349(1): payment of royalties overseas

(1) Where—

    (*a*) a company makes a payment of a royalty to which section 349(1) applies, and
    (*b*) the company reasonably believes that, at the time the payment is made, the payee is entitled to relief in respect of the payment under any arrangements under section 788 (double taxation relief),

the company may, if it thinks fit, calculate the sum to be deducted from the payment under section 349(1) by reference to the rate of income tax appropriate to the payee pursuant to the arrangements.

(2) But, where the payee is not at that time entitled to such relief, section 350 and Schedule 16 shall have effect as if subsection (1) above never applied in relation to the payment.

(3) Where the Board are not satisfied that the payee will be entitled to such relief in respect of one or more payments to be made by a company, they may direct the company that subsection (1) above is not to apply to the payment or payments.

(4) A direction under subsection (3) above may be varied or revoked by a subsequent such direction.

(5) In this section—

    "payee", in relation to a payment, means the person beneficially entitled to the income in respect of which the payment is made; and
    "royalty" includes—

    (*a*) any payment received as a consideration for the use of, or the right to use, any copyright, patent, trade mark, design, process or information, or

    (*b*) any proceeds of sale of all or any part of any patent rights.

(6) Paragraph 3(1) of Schedule 18 to the Finance Act 1998 (c 36) (requirement to make return in respect of information relevant to application of Corporation Tax Acts) has effect as if the reference to the Corporation Tax Acts included a reference to this section.

(7) Paragraph 20 of that Schedule (penalties for incorrect returns), in its application to an error relating to information required in a return by virtue of subsection (6) above, has effect as if—

    (*a*) the reference in sub-paragraph (1) to a tax-related penalty were a reference to an amount not exceeding £3000, and

    (*b*) sub-paragraphs (2) and (3) were omitted.]¹

Amendments—¹This section inserted by FA 2002 s 96(1), (4) with effect for payments made after 30 September 2002.

350 Charge to tax where payments made under section 349

(1) Where any payment within section 349 is made by or through any person, that person shall forthwith deliver to the inspector an account of the payment, and shall be assessable and chargeable with income tax at the [applicable rate]¹ on the payment, or on so much thereof as is not made out of profits or gains brought into charge to income tax.

[(1A) In subsection (1) above "the applicable rate" means the rate which is applicable to the payment under section 4 [(or, where the payment is one to which subsection (1) of section 349E applies, the rate referred to in that subsection)]².]¹

(2) In section 349(1) any reference to a payment or sum as being not payable, or not wholly payable, out of profits or gains brought into charge to income tax shall be construed as a reference to it as being payable wholly or in part out of a source other than profits or gains brought into charge; and any such reference elsewhere in the Tax Acts shall be construed accordingly.

(3) All the provisions of the Income Tax Acts relating to persons who are to be chargeable with income tax, to income tax assessments, and to the collection and recovery of income tax, shall, so far as they are applicable, apply to the charge, assessment, collection and recovery of income tax under this section.

(4) Section 349 and this section have effect subject to the provisions of Schedule 16 which has effect for the purpose of regulating the time and manner in which companies resident in the United Kingdom—

    (*a*) are to account for and pay income tax in respect of payments from which tax is deductible under section 349, and

    (*b*) are to be repaid income tax in respect of payments received by them;

and for that purpose the Board may by regulations modify, supplement or replace any of the provisions of Schedule 16; and references in this Act and in any other enactment to any of those provisions shall be construed as including references to any such regulations.

(5) Without prejudice to the generality of subsection (4) above, regulations under that subsection may, in relation to income tax for which a company is liable to account, modify any provision of Parts II to VI of the Management Act or apply any such provision with or without modifications.

(6) Regulations under this section may—

    (*a*) make different provision for different descriptions of companies and for different circumstances and may authorise the Board, where in their opinion there are special circumstances justifying it, to make special arrangements as respects income tax for which a company is liable to account or the repayment of income tax borne by a company;

    (*b*) include such transitional and other supplemental provisions as appear to the Board to be expedient or necessary.

(7) The Board shall not make any regulations under this section unless a draft of them has been laid before and approved by a resolution of the House of Commons.

Commentary—*Simon's Direct Tax Service* **A3.238, 406, 407.**
Regulations—IT (Building Societies) (Annual Payments) Regulations, SI 1991/512.
Concessions A16—Where an annuity etc is paid in a later year out of untaxed income, but could have been paid in the due year out of taxed income, the payer is not required to account for tax notwithstanding sub-s (1) above. Similar relief is allowed to trusts and non-trading institutions.
Revenue Internal Guidance—Assessed taxes manual AT 6.606 (Revenue collection procedures).
Independent taxation handbook, In 1160 (married couple's charges are dealt with independently).
Inspector's manual IM 3103 (a solicitor may be charged under this section if he is a person through whom payment is made).
IM 3942 (the liability does not arise until the interest etc is paid: capitalisation of interest does not constitute payment).
Revenue & other press releases—IR Tax Bulletin October 2001 p 827 (Interest on s 350 assessments).
Simon's Tax Cases—*Fitzleet Estates Ltd v Cherry* [1977] STC 397*; *Mcburnie v Tacey* [1984] STC 347*; *IRC v Crawley* [1987] STC 147*.
Definitions—"Basic rate", s 832(1); "the Board", s 832(1); "the Income Tax Acts", s 831(1)(*b*); "inspector", s 832(1); "the Management Act", s 831(3); "profits or gains", s 833(1); "the Tax Acts", s 832(1).
Cross references—See TMA 1970 s 31(3)(*b*) (an appeal against an assessment under this section to be made to the Special Commissioners);
TMA 1970 s 98 (liability to a special return penalty in respect of failure to information under sub-s (1) above).
TA 1988 s 9(6) (this section does not apply for the computation of income for corporation tax purposes).

TA 1988 s 43(1), (2) (application of this section to profits or gains of non-residents chargeable under Schedule A or Schedule D Case VI).

TA 1988 s 214(1) (application of this section in relation to certain chargeable payments connected with demergers).

TA 1988 s 247(4) (disapplication of this section to charges on income paid under a group income election).

TA 1988 s 477A(7) (notwithstanding this section, tax not to be deductible from interest payable on advances from a building society).

TA 1988 s 486(2) (notwithstanding this section, payment of interest by a registered industrial and provident society to be made gross).

TA 1988 s 524(4) (taxation of receipts from sale by a non-resident of patent rights).

TA 1988 s 704(A)(f) (cancellation of tax advantage from dividend stripping).

TA 1988 s 737(1), (1A), (2) (manufactured dividends: treatment of tax deducted at the lower rate and construction of sub-s (1) above accordingly).

TA 1988 Sch 23A, para 4(2)(b) (modified application of sub-s (4) above in relation to manufactured overseas dividends).

FA 1988 s 130(7)(b) (company migration: provisions to secure payment by a migrating company of income tax in respect of payments under sub-s (4)(a) above),

FA 1991 Sch 11 para 3(2) (sub-s (4) above to be treated as if the second reference to regulations included a reference to FA 1991 Sch 11 para 3(1)),

FA 1991 Sch 11, para 3(3) (regulations under sub-s (4) above may repeal FA 1991 Sch 11 para 3(1),(2)).

IT (Dividend Manufacturing) Regulations, SI 1992/569 reg 13(2) (disapplication of sub-s (1) above to the payment of certain manufactured dividends).

Amendments—[1] Words in sub-s (1) substituted, and sub-s (1A) inserted, by FA 1996 Sch 6 para 8 with effect from the year 1996–97.
[2] Words in sub-s (1A) inserted by FA 2002 s 96(2), (4) with effect for payments made after 30 September 2002.

[350A UK public revenue dividends: deduction of tax

(1) The Board may by regulations—

    (a) make provision as to the time and manner in which persons who under section 349(3C) deduct sums representing income tax out of payments of UK public revenue dividends are to account for and pay those sums; and

    (b) otherwise modify the provisions of sections 349 and 350 in their application to such dividends;

and in this section "UK public revenue dividend" has the same meaning as in section 349.

(2) Regulations under this section may—

    (a) make different provision for different descriptions of UK public revenue dividend and for different circumstances;

    (b) make special provision for UK public revenue dividends which—

      (i) are payable to the Bank of Ireland out of the public revenue of the United Kingdom, or

      (ii) are entrusted to the Bank of Ireland for payment and distribution and are not payable by that Bank out of its principal office in Belfast;

    (c) include such transitional and other supplementary provisions as appear to the Board to be necessary or expedient.

(3) No regulations under this section shall be made unless a draft of them has been laid before and approved by a resolution of the House of Commons.][1]

Amendments—[1] This section inserted by FA 2000 s 112(4), (5) with effect for payments made after 31 March 2001.

351 Small maintenance payments

Commentary—*Simon's Direct Tax Service* **E5.107.**
Amendments—This section repealed by FA 1988 Sch 14 Pt IV in relation to payments made after 5 April 1989 and in relation to orders and variations made after 5 April 1989.

352 Certificates of deduction of tax

(1) A person making any payment which is subject to deduction of income tax by virtue of section 339, 348, 349[, 480A or 687 or by virtue of regulations under s 477A(1)][1] shall, if the recipient so requests in writing, furnish him with a statement in writing showing the gross amount of the payment, the amount of tax deducted, and the actual amount paid.

(2) The duty imposed by subsection (1) above shall be enforceable at the suit or instance of the person requesting the statement.

Commentary—*Simon's Direct Tax Service* **A3.402.**
Definition—"Deduction of income tax", s 4(1).
Cross references—See IT (Dividend Manufacturing) Regulations, SI 1992/569 reg 23 reg 21 (provision of certificates relating to payments of approved manufactured dividends),
IT (Dividend Manufacturing) Regulations, SI 1992/569 reg 23 (provision of certificates relating to tax deducted under s 737(1) of this Act).
Amendments—[1] Words in sub-s (1) substituted by FA 1990 Sch 5 para 11 as regards a payment made after 5 April 1991.

Relief for payments of interest (excluding MIRAS)

Note—Relief for interest on mortgage loans is withdrawn by FA 1999 s 38, Sch 4 with effect for interest paid—

  – after 5 April 2000;
  – after 8 March 1999 and before 6 April 2000 in respect of interest falling due after 5 April 2000; or
  – after 8 March 1999 and before 6 April 2000 under a scheme made for a tax avoidance purpose after 8 March 1999.

Statement of Practice SP A34—Where mortgaged property passes on death, there is continuity of interest relief if the deceased was entitled to the relief. Also, the relief is transferred to a new loan used in paying off the inherited mortgage.

Cross references—See TA 1988 ss 357A–357C (continuity of mortgage interest relief where the borrower buys a new home and the original loan for the previous home is secured by the new home).

353 General provision

[(1) Where a person pays interest in any year of assessment, that person, if he makes a claim to the relief, shall for that year of assessment be entitled (subject to [sections 359][6] to 368) to relief in accordance with this section in respect of so much (if any) of the amount of that interest as is eligible for relief under this section by virtue of [sections 359][6] to 365.][1]

[(1A) Where a person is entitled for any year of assessment to relief under this section in respect of any amount of interest which—

(a) is eligible for that relief by virtue of section ...[6] 365, ...[5]

(b) ...[5]

that relief shall consist in an income tax reduction for that year calculated by reference to that amount.][2]

[(1B) Where a person is entitled for any year of assessment to relief under this section in respect of any amount of interest which—

(a) is eligible for that relief otherwise than by virtue of section ...[6] 365, ...[5]

(b) ...[5]

that relief shall consist (subject to [section 237(5)(b)][4]) in a deduction or set-off of that amount from or against that person's income for that year.][2]

(1C), (1D) ...[2,5]

[(1E) Where any person is entitled for any year of assessment to relief under this section in respect of any amount of interest which is eligible for that relief partly as mentioned in subsection (1A) above and partly as mentioned in subsection (1B) above, that amount of interest shall be apportioned between the cases to which each of those subsections applies without regard to what parts of the total amount borrowed remain outstanding but according to ...[5]—

(a) the proportions of the total amount borrowed which were applied for different purposes; ...[5]

(b) ...[5]

and subsection (1A) or (1B) above shall apply accordingly in relation to the interest apportioned to the case to which that subsection applies.][2]

[(1F) Where any person is entitled under this section for any year of assessment to an income tax reduction calculated by reference to an amount of interest, the amount of that person's liability for that year to income tax on his total income shall be the amount to which he would have been liable apart from this section less whichever is the smaller of—

(a) the amount equal to the applicable percentage of that amount of interest; and

(b) the amount which reduces his liability to nil.][2]

[(1G) In subsection (1F) above, the "applicable percentage" means [23 per cent][7].][6]

[(1H) In determining for the purposes of subsection (1F) above the amount of income tax to which a person would be liable apart from any income tax reduction under this section, no account shall be taken of—

(a) any income tax reduction under Chapter I of Part VII or section 347B;

(b) any relief by way of a reduction of liability to tax which is given in accordance with any arrangements having effect by virtue of section 788 or by way of a credit under section 790(1); or

(c) any tax at the basic rate on so much of that person's income as is income the income tax on which he is entitled to charge against any other person or to deduct, retain or satisfy out of any payment.][2]

(2) This section does not apply to a payment of relevant loan interest to which section 369 applies.

(3) Relief under this section shall not be given in respect of—

(a) interest on a debt incurred by overdrawing an account or by debiting the account of any person as the holder of a credit card or under similar arrangements; or

(b) where interest is paid at a rate in excess of a reasonable commercial rate, so much of the interest as represents the excess.

(4), (5) ...[3]

Commentary—*Simon's Direct Tax Service* E1.531.
Concession A89—Relief for interest on a loan to buy a property used for both residential and business purposes may in certain circumstances be allowed partly under this section and as a deduction in the computation of profits or losses.
Revenue Interpretation RI 58—Location of source of interest.
RI 111–Provision of certificates of interest paid to borrowers.
Revenue Decision RD 3—Beneficial loan; interest on an overdraft on a director's loan account falls within sub-s (3)(a) above.
Revenue & other press releases—IR 22-1-80 and 17-2-82 (relief for interest payments: whether interest is within Sch D Case III depends on location of the source and residence of debtor. Interest payable to a non-resident in a foreign country under a foreign specialty contract not secured on UK real property is outside the scope of Sch D Case III. The existence of a foreign specialty contract is not vital).
Revenue Internal Guidance—Independent taxation handbook, In 1150-1151 (non-MIRAS loans).
In 1108-1110 (procedure for dealing with claims for main residence relief).
Simon's Tax Cases—*Hughes v Viner* [1985] STC 235*; *Orakpo v Lane* [1996] STC (SCD) 43; *Lancaster v IRC* [2000] STC (SCD) 138.

s 353(1), *Cairns v macdiarmid* [1983] STC 178*; *Hughes v Viner* [1985] STC 235*.
s 353(3)(*a*), *Walcot-Bather v Golding* [1979] STC 707*; *Hughes v Viner* [1985] STC 235*; *Lawson v Brooks* [1992] STC 76*.
Definitions—"Basic rate", s 832(1); "the Board", s 832(1); "interest", s 832(1); "Schedule D", s 18(1); "total income", s 835(1); "year of assessment", s 832(1).
Cross references—See TA 1988 s 117(1) (restriction on interest relief where an individual carries on a trade as a limited partner).
TA 1988 s 235(3) (interest relief under this section not available for set-off against distributions from an exempt fund).
TA 1988 s 237(5) (interest relief under this section not available for set-off against income from bonus issues).
TA 1988 s 356B(1) (husband and wife living together may elect that interest paid by one be treated as paid by the other).
TA 1988 s 357A–357C (continuity of mortgage interest relief where the borrower buys a new home and the original loan for the previous home is secured by the new home).
TA 1988 s 366 (supply of information by person claiming relief under this section).
TA 1988 s 370(2) (definition by reference to this section of "relevant loan interest" for interest relief under MIRAS).
TA 1988 s 390 (carry forward of interest paid in connection with a trade and not fully relieved under this section).
TA 1988 s 704(A)(*g*) (cancellation of tax advantage from dividend stripping).
TA 1988 s 787 (restriction of relief where interest paid as part of a scheme with the sole or main purpose of tax reduction).
TA 1988 Sch 15B para 1 (tax relief on qualifying investments in venture capital trusts is offset against tax liability, for any year of assessment, in priority to relief under sub-s (1A)).
FA 1988 Sch 6 para 3(3)(*b*), (4)(*b*), (5) , (7) (interest paid after 14 March 1988 in relation to commercial woodlands not eligible for relief under this section),
FA 1989 s 54(3C) (medical insurance relief to be given in priority to relief under sub-s (1A) above).
FA 1991 s 32(2B) (vocational training relief given in priority to relief under this section).
FA 1995 Sch 15 (relief for investments in venture capital trusts to be given in priority to relief under sub-s (1A) above).
FA 1999 s 38(1) (withdrawal of relief for interest on mortgage loans where the interest is paid—

– after 5 April 2000;
– after 8 March 1999 and before 6 April 2000 in respect of interest falling due after 5 April 2000; or
– after 8 March 1999 and before 6 April 2000 under a scheme made for a tax avoidance purpose after 8 March 1999.)

Amendments—[1] Sub-s (1) substituted by FA 1994 s 81(1) with effect generally from 6 April 1994; for detailed commencement provisions, see FA 1994 s 81(6), (7).
[2] Sub-ss (1A)–(1H) inserted by FA 1994 s 81(2) with effect generally from 6 April 1994; for detailed commencement provisions, see FA 1994 s 81(6), (7) (sub-ss (1C), (1D) since repealed: see note below).
[3] Sub-ss (4), (5) repealed by FA 1994 Sch 9 para 3 and Sch 26, Pt V(2) with effect generally from 6 April 1994; see FA 1994 s 81(6).
[4] Words in sub-s (1B) substituted by FA 1995 s 42(2)(*a*), with effect for any payment of interest made after 5 April 1995, except for certain interest payments on loans in respect of which the source of Schedule A income ceased during 1995–96: see FA 1995 s 42(3)–(5).
[5] Words omitted from sub-ss (1A), (1B) and (1E), and whole of sub-ss (1C), (1D), repealed by FA 1995 s 42(2), Sch 29 Pt VIII(2), with effect for any payment of interest made after 5 April 1995, except for certain interest payments on loans in respect of which the source of Schedule A income ceased during 1995–96: see FA 1995 s 42(3)–(5).
[6] Words in sub-s (1) and whole of sub-s (1G) substituted, and words in sub-ss (1A), (1B) repealed, by FA 1999 s 38(8), Sch 4 paras 1(2)–(4), 18(5), Sch 20 Pt III(7) with effect for payments of interest made—

– after 5 April 2000;
– after 8 March 1999 and before 6 April 2000 in respect of interest falling due after 5 April 2000; or
– after 8 March 1999 and before 6 April 2000 under a scheme made for a tax avoidance purpose after 8 March 1999.
[7] Words in sub-s (1G) substituted by FA 2000 s 83(2), (4) with effect for payments of interest made after 5 April 2000.

354 Loans to buy land etc

Commentary—*Simon's Direct Tax Service* **E1.535.**
Amendments—This section repealed by FA 1999 s 38(8), Sch 4 paras 2, 18(5), Sch 20 Pt III(7) with effect for payments of interest made—

– after 5 April 2000;
– after 8 March 1999 and before 6 April 2000 in respect of interest falling due after 5 April 2000; or
– after 8 March 1999 and before 6 April 2000 under a scheme made for a tax avoidance purpose after 8 March 1999.

355 Matters excluded from section 354

Commentary—*Simon's Direct Tax Service* **E1.535.**
Amendments— This section repealed by FA 1999 s 38(8), Sch 4 paras 2, 18(5), Sch 20 Pt III(7) with effect for payments of interest made—

– after 5 April 2000;
– after 8 March 1999 and before 6 April 2000 in respect of interest falling due after 5 April 2000; or
– after 8 March 1999 and before 6 April 2000 under a scheme made for a tax avoidance purpose after 8 March 1999.

356 Job-related accommodation

Commentary—*Simon's Direct Tax Service* **E1.546.**
Amendments—This section repealed by FA 1999 s 38(8), Sch 4 paras 2, 18(5), Sch 20 Pt III(7) with effect for payments of interest made—

– after 5 April 2000;
– after 8 March 1999 and before 6 April 2000 in respect of interest falling due after 5 April 2000; or
– after 8 March 1999 and before 6 April 2000 under a scheme made for a tax avoidance purpose after 8 March 1999.

[356A Limit on relief for home loans: residence basis]

Commentary—*Simon's Direct Tax Service* **E1.539.**
Amendments—This section (inserted by FA 1988 s 42(1), (4) with effect from 1 August 1988) repealed by FA 1999 s 38(8), Sch 4 paras 2, 18(5), Sch 20 Pt III(7) with effect for payments of interest made—

– after 5 April 2000;
– after 8 March 1999 and before 6 April 2000 in respect of interest falling due after 5 April 2000; or
– after 8 March 1999 and before 6 April 2000 under a scheme made for a tax avoidance purpose after 8 March 1999.

TA 1988

[356B Residence basis: married couples]

Commentary—*Simon's Direct Tax Service* E1.539.
Amendments—This section (inserted by FA 1988 s 42(1), (4) and substituted by Sch 3 para 14 to that Act) repealed by FA 1999 s 38(8), Sch 4 paras 2, 18(5), Sch 20 Pt III(7) with effect for payments of interest made—
– after 5 April 2000;
– after 8 March 1999 and before 6 April 2000 in respect of interest falling due after 5 April 2000; or
– after 8 March 1999 and before 6 April 2000 under a scheme made for a tax avoidance purpose after 8 March 1999.

[356C Payments to which sections 356A and 356B apply]

Commentary—*Simon's Direct Tax Service* E1.539.
Amendments—This section (inserted by FA 1988 s 42(1), (4) with effect from 1 August 1988) repealed by FA 1999 s 38(8), Sch 4 paras 2, 18(5), Sch 20 Pt III(7) with effect for payments of interest made—
– after 5 April 2000;
– after 8 March 1999 and before 6 April 2000 in respect of interest falling due after 5 April 2000; or
– after 8 March 1999 and before 6 April 2000 under a scheme made for a tax avoidance purpose after 8 March 1999.

[356D Provisions supplementary to sections 356A to 356C]

Commentary—*Simon's Direct Tax Service* E1.539.
Amendments—This section (inserted by FA 1988 s 42(1), (4) with effect from 1 August 1988) repealed by FA 1999 s 38(8), Sch 4 paras 2, 18(5), Sch 20 Pt III(7) with effect for payments of interest made—
– after 5 April 2000;
– after 8 March 1999 and before 6 April 2000 in respect of interest falling due after 5 April 2000; or
– after 8 March 1999 and before 6 April 2000 under a scheme made for a tax avoidance purpose after 8 March 1999.

357 Limit on amount of loan eligible for relief by virtue of section 354

Commentary—*Simon's Direct Tax Service* E1.538, 539.
Amendments—This section repealed by FA 1999 s 38(8), Sch 4 paras 2, 18(5), Sch 20 Pt III(7) with effect for payments of interest made—
– after 5 April 2000;
– after 8 March 1999 and before 6 April 2000 in respect of interest falling due after 5 April 2000; or
– after 8 March 1999 and before 6 April 2000 under a scheme made for a tax avoidance purpose after 8 March 1999.

[357A Substitution of security]

Commentary—*Simon's Direct Tax Service* A3.431; E1.535.
Amendments—This section (inserted by FA 1993 s 56) repealed by FA 1999 s 38(8), Sch 4 paras 2, 18(5), Sch 20 Pt III(7) with effect for payments of interest made—
– after 5 April 2000;
– after 8 March 1999 and before 6 April 2000 in respect of interest falling due after 5 April 2000; or
– after 8 March 1999 and before 6 April 2000 under a scheme made for a tax avoidance purpose after 8 March 1999.

[357B Treatment of loans following security substitution]

Commentary—*Simon's Direct Tax Service* A3.431; E1.535.
Amendments—[1] This section (inserted by FA 1993 s 56) repealed by FA 1999 s 38(8), Sch 4 paras 2, 18(5), Sch 20 Pt III(7) with effect for payments of interest made—
– after 5 April 2000;
– after 8 March 1999 and before 6 April 2000 in respect of interest falling due after 5 April 2000; or
– after 8 March 1999 and before 6 April 2000 under a scheme made for a tax avoidance purpose after 8 March 1999.

[357C Substitution of security: supplemental]

Commentary—*Simon's Direct Tax Service* A3.431; E1.535.
Amendments—[1] This section (inserted by FA 1993 s 56) repealed by FA 1999 s 38(8), Sch 4 paras 2, 18(5), Sch 20 Pt III(7) with effect for payments of interest made—
– after 5 April 2000;
– after 8 March 1999 and before 6 April 2000 in respect of interest falling due after 5 April 2000; or
– after 8 March 1999 and before 6 April 2000 under a scheme made for a tax avoidance purpose after 8 March 1999.

[358 Relief where borrower deceased]

Commentary—*Simon's Direct Tax Service* E1.540.
Amendments—This section repealed by FA 1999 s 38(8), Sch 4 paras 2, 18(5), Sch 20 Pt III(7) with effect for payments of interest made—
– after 5 April 2000;
– after 8 March 1999 and before 6 April 2000 in respect of interest falling due after 5 April 2000; or
– after 8 March 1999 and before 6 April 2000 under a scheme made for a tax avoidance purpose after 8 March 1999.

359 Loan to buy machinery or plant

(1) Where an individual is a member of a partnership which, under [section 264 of the Capital Allowances Act][1], is entitled to a capital allowance or liable to a balancing charge for [any period of account in respect of plant or machinery][1] belonging to the individual, any interest paid by him in [that period of account][1] on a loan to defray money applied as capital expenditure on the provision

of [that plant or machinery][1] is eligible for relief under section 353, except interest falling due and payable more than three years after the end of [the period of account][1] in which the debt was incurred.

(2) Where the machinery or plant is in use partly for the purposes of the trade, profession or vocation carried on by the partnership and partly for other purposes, such part only of the interest is eligible for relief under section 353 as is just and reasonable to attribute to the purposes of the trade, profession or vocation, having regard to all the relevant circumstances and, in particular, to the extent of the use for those other purposes.

(3) Where the holder of an office or employment—

(a) is under [Part 2 of the Capital Allowances Act][1] entitled to a capital allowance or liable to a balancing charge, (or would be so entitled or liable but for some contribution made by the employer), for any year of assessment in respect of [plant or machinery][1] belonging to him and in use for the purposes of the office or employment; and
(b) pays interest in that year on a loan to defray money applied as capital expenditure on the provision of that [plant or machinery][1];

the interest so paid is eligible for relief under section 353 unless it is interest falling due and payable more than three years after the end of the year of assessment in which the debt was incurred.

(4) Where the machinery or plant is in use partly for the purposes of the office or employment and partly for other purposes, such part only of the interest is eligible for relief under section 353 as it is just and reasonable to attribute to the purposes of the office or employment, having regard to all the relevant circumstances and, in particular, to the extent of the use for those other purposes.

Commentary—*Simon's Direct Tax Service* **E1.533.**
Revenue Internal Guidance—Schedule E manual SE 31890 (interest on car loans).
SE 32860 (application of sub-ss (3) and (4)).
SE 36900 (relief depends on the employee's entitlement to capital allowances, not on whether such allowances are actually claimed).
Definitions—"The 1990 Act", s 831(3); "capital allowance", s 832(1); "interest", s 832(1); "trade", s 832(1); "year of assessment", s 832(1).
Cross references—See TA 1988 s 367 (supplementary provisions).
Amendments—[1] Words in sub-ss (1), (3) substituted by CAA 2001 s 578, Sch 2 para 27 with effect for income tax purposes as respects allowances and charges falling to be made for chargeable periods ending after 5 April 2001.

360 Loan to buy interest in close company

(1) Subject to the following provisions of this section and sections 361 to 364, interest is eligible for relief under section 353 if it is interest on a loan to an individual to defray money applied—

(a) in acquiring any part of the ordinary share capital of a close company [complying with section 13A(2)][2]; or
(b) in lending money to such a close company which is used wholly and exclusively for the purposes of the business of the company or of any associated company of it which is a close company satisfying any of those conditions; or
(c) in paying off another loan interest on which would have been eligible for relief under section 353 had the loan not been paid off (on the assumption, if the loan was free of interest, that it carried interest);

and either the conditions stated in subsection (2) below or those stated in subsection (3) below are satisfied.

(2) The conditions first referred to in subsection (1) above are—

(a) that, when the interest is paid, the company continues to [comply with section 13A(2)][2] and the individual has a material interest in the company; and
(b) that he shows that in the period from the application of the proceeds of the loan to the payment of the interest he has not recovered any capital from the company, apart from any amount taken into account under section 363(1); and
(c) that, if the company exists wholly or mainly for the purpose of holding investments or other property, no property held by the company is used as a residence by the individual;

but the condition in paragraph (c) above shall not apply in a case where the individual has worked for the greater part of his time in the actual management or conduct of the business of the company, or of an associated company of the company.

(3) The conditions secondly referred to in subsection (1) above are—

(a) that, when the interest is paid, the company continues to [comply with section 13A(2)][2] and the individual holds any part of the ordinary share capital of the company; and
(b) that in the period from the application of the proceeds of the loan to the payment of the interest the individual has worked for the greater part of his time in the actual management or conduct of the company or of an associated company of the company; and
(c) that he shows in the period from the application of the proceeds of the loan to the payment of the interest he has not recovered any capital from the company, apart from any amount taken into account under section 363(1).

[(3A) Interest shall not be eligible for relief under section 353 by virtue of paragraph (a) of subsection (1) above in respect of shares acquired on or after 14th March 1989 if at any time the person by whom they are acquired, or that person's husband or wife, makes a claim for relief in respect of them under Chapter III of Part VII][1] [or makes a claim in respect of them under Schedule 5B to the 1992 Act.][3]

[(4) Subject to section 360A, in this section expressions to which a meaning is assigned by Part XI have that meaning.][2]

Commentary—*Simon's Direct Tax Service* E1.547.
Concession A43—This concession extends relief available under ss 360–363 where (*a*) a partnership is incorporated into a co-operative, a close company or an employee controlled company, or (*b*) shares in any of these are changed for, or replaced by shares in any one of these types of company, or (*c*) a partnership reconstruction involving a merger or demerger.
Statement of Practice SP 3/78—For the purposes of sub-s (1) above, it is not necessary for a company to be a close company throughout the period between the use of the loan and the payment of interest.
Revenue Interpretations RI 12—Interest on loan for acquiring loan stock not qualifying for relief under this section after the loan stock is converted to share capital.
RI 15—Independent taxation of husband and wife: interest relief on certain joint loans.
RI 62—Interpretation of the words "actual management or conduct" in sub-ss (2), (3) above.
Revenue & other press releases—ICAEW Tax 15/92 16-11-92 (investment in convertible stock: RI 12 re-affirmed).
ICAEW Tax 15/92 16-11-92 (Revenue practice: relief allowed as long as trading commences within a reasonable time after the investment is made and the company remains close and trading).
Revenue Internal Guidance—Inspector's manual IM 3804 ("greater part of his time" in sub-s (3)(*b*) means more than half of the normal working day; the period can be taken as a whole, so that the work need not be continuous).
Simon's Tax Cases—*Lord v Tustain* [1993] STC 755; *Cohen v Petch* [1999] STC (SCD) 207.
s 360(1), *Hendy v Hadley* [1980] STC 292*.
s 362(1)(*b*), *Badger v Major* [1997] STC (SCD) 218; *Gold v Inspector of Taxes* [1998] STC (SCD) 222; *Major v Brodie* [1998] STC 491; *Grant v Watton* [1999] STC 330.
Definitions—"Close company", s 832(1); "interest", s 832(1); "ordinary share capital", s 832(1).
Cross references—See TA 1988 ss 363, 367 (supplementary provisions).
FA 1988 Sch 6 para 3(3)(*b*)(i), (4)(*b*), (5), (7) (interest paid after 14 March 1988 in relation to commercial woodlands not eligible for relief under this section).
Amendments—[1] Sub-s (3A) inserted and sub-s (4) substituted by FA 1989 ss 47, 48(1).
[2] Words in sub-ss (1)(*a*), (2)(*a*), (3)(*a*) substituted by FA 1989 Sch 12 para 12 in relation to interest paid after 26 July 1989.
[3] Words in sub-s (3A) inserted by FA 1998 s 79(1) with effect in relation to shares acquired on or after 6 April 1998.

[360A Meaning of "material interest" in section 360

(1) For the purposes of section 360(2)(*a*) an individual shall be treated as having a material interest [in a company if he, either on his own or with one or more associates, or if any associate of his with or without such other associates,—

(*a*) is the beneficial owner of, or able, directly or through the medium of other companies, or by any other indirect means to control, more than 5 per cent of the ordinary share capital of the company, or

(*b*) possesses, or is entitled to acquire, such rights as would, in the event of the winding-up of the company or in any other circumstances, give an entitlement to receive more than 5 per cent of the assets which would then be available for distribution among the participators.][2]

(2) Subject to the following provisions of this section, in subsection (1) above "associate", in relation to an individual, means—

(*a*) any relative or partner of the individual;

(*b*) the trustee or trustees of a settlement in relation to which the individual is, or any relative of his (living or dead) is or was, a settlor ("settlement" and "settlor" having the same meaning as in [Chapter IA of Part XV (see section 660G(1) and (2))][3]; and

(*c*) where the individual is interested in any shares or obligations of the company which are subject to any trust, or are part of the estate of a deceased person, the trustee or trustees of the settlement concerned or, as the case may be, the personal representative of the deceased.

(3) In relation to any loan made after 5th April 1987, there shall be disregarded for the purposes of subsection (2)(*c*) above—

(*a*) the interest of the trustees of an approved profit sharing scheme (within the meaning of section 187) in any shares which are held by them in accordance with the scheme and have not yet been appropriated to an individual; and

(*b*) any rights exercisable by those trustees by virtue of that interest.

(4) In relation to any loan made on or after the day on which the Finance Act 1989 was passed, where the individual has an interest in shares or obligations of the company as a beneficiary of an employee benefit trust, the trustees shall not be regarded as associates of his by reason only of that interest unless subsection (6) below applies in relation to him.

(5) In subsection (4) above "employee benefit trust" has the same meaning as in paragraph 7 of Schedule 8, except that in its application for this purpose paragraph 7(5)(*b*) shall have effect as if it referred to the day on which the Finance Act 1989 was passed instead of to 14th March 1989.

(6) This subsection applies in relation to an individual if at any time on or after the day on which the Finance Act 1989 was passed—

(*a*) the individual, either on his own or with any one or more of his associates, or

(*b*) any associate of his, with or without other such associates,

has been the beneficial owner of, or able (directly or through the medium of other companies or by any other indirect means) to control, more than 5 per cent of the ordinary share capital of the company.

(7) Sub-paragraphs (9) to (12) of paragraph 7 of Schedule 8 shall apply for the purposes of subsection (6) above in relation to an individual as they apply for the purposes of that paragraph in relation to an employee.

(8) In relation to any loan made before 14th November 1986, where the individual is interested in any shares or obligations of the company which are subject to any trust, or are part of the estate of a deceased person, subsection (2)(c) above shall have effect as if for the reference to the trustee or trustees of the settlement concerned or, as the case may be, the personal representative of the deceased there were substituted a reference to any person (other than the individual) interested in the settlement or estate, but subject to subsection (9) below.

(9) Subsection (8) above shall not apply so as to make an individual an associate as being entitled or eligible to benefit under a trust—

(a) if the trust relates exclusively to an exempt approved scheme as defined in section 592; or
(b) if the trust is exclusively for the benefit of the employees, or the employees and directors, of the company or their dependants (and not wholly or mainly for the benefit of directors or their relatives), and the individual in question is not (and could not as a result of the operation of the trust become), either on his own or with his relatives, the beneficial owner of more than 5 per cent of the ordinary share capital of the company;

and in applying paragraph (b) above any charitable trusts which may arise on the failure or determination of other trusts shall be disregarded.

(10) In this section [''participator'' has the meaning given by section 417(1)][2] and ''relative'' means husband or wife, parent or remoter forebear, child or remoter issue or brother or sister.][1]

Commentary—*Simon's Direct Tax Service* **E1.547.**
Definitions—''Company'', s 832(1), (2); ''distribution'', s 832(1); ''ordinary share capital'', s 832(1).
Note—FA 1989 was passed on 27 July 1989.
Cross references—TA 1988 ss 363, 367 (supplementary provisions).
Amendments—[1] This section inserted by FA 1989 s 48(2) in relation to accounting periods beginning after 31 March 1989.
[2] Words in sub-ss (1), (10) substituted by FA 1989 s 107, Sch 12 para 13, in relation to accounting periods beginning after 31 March 1989.
[3] Words in sub-s (2)(b) substituted by FA 1995 s 74, Sch 17 para 5, with effect from the year 1995–96 (and apply to every settlement wherever and whenever made or entered into).

361 Loan to buy interest in co-operative or employee-controlled company

(1) Subject to the following provisions of this section and sections 363 and 364, interest is eligible for relief under section 353 if it is interest on a loan to an individual to defray money applied—

(a) in acquiring a share or shares in a body which is a co-operative as defined by section 363(5); or
(b) in lending money to any such body which is used wholly and exclusively for the purposes of the business of that body or of a subsidiary of that body; or
(c) in paying off another loan interest on which would have been eligible for relief under section 353 had the loan not been paid off (on the assumption, if it was free of interest, that it carried interest);

and the conditions in subsection (2) below are satisfied.

(2) The conditions referred to in subsection (1) above are—

(a) that the loan was made after 10th March 1981;
(b) that, when the interest is paid, the body continues to be a co-operative; and
(c) that in the period from the application of the proceeds of the loan to the payment of the interest the individual has worked for the greater part of his time as an employee of the body or of a subsidiary of the body; and
(d) that he shows that in that period he has not recovered any capital from the body apart from any taken into account under section 363(1).

(3) Subject to sections 362 to 365, interest is eligible for relief under section 353 if it is interest on a loan to an individual to defray money applied—

(a) in acquiring any part of the ordinary share capital of an employee-controlled company; or
(b) in paying off another loan, interest on which would have been eligible for relief under section 353 had the loan not been paid off (on the assumption, if it was free of interest, that it carried interest);

and the conditions stated in subsection (4) below are satisfied.

(4) The conditions referred to in subsection (3) above are that—

(a) the company is, throughout the period beginning with the date on which the shares are acquired and ending with the date on which the interest is paid—
 (i) an unquoted company resident in the United Kingdom and not resident elsewhere; and
 (ii) a trading company or the holding company of a trading group;
(b) the shares are acquired before, or not later than 12 months after, the date on which the company first becomes an employee-controlled company;
(c) during the year of assessment in which the interest is paid the company either—
 (i) first becomes an employee-controlled company; or

(ii) is such a company throughout a period of at least nine months;

(*d*) the individual ...¹ is a full-time employee of the company throughout the period beginning with the date on which the proceeds of the loan are applied and ending with the date on which the interest is paid or, if at that date he has ceased to be such an employee, ending with whichever is the later of—

(i) the date on which he ceased to be such an employee;

(ii) the date 12 months before the payment of the interest; and

(*e*) the individual shows that in the period from the application of the proceeds of the loan to the payment of the interest he has not recovered any capital from the company, apart from any amount taken into account under section 363(1).

(5) For the purposes of this section a company is employee-controlled at any time when more than 50 per cent—

(*a*) of the issued ordinary share capital of the company, and

(*b*) of the voting power in the company,

is beneficially owned by persons who ...¹ are full-time employees of the company.

[(6) Where an individual owns beneficially more than 10 per cent of the issued ordinary share capital of, or voting power in, a company, the excess shall be treated for the purposes of subsection (5) above as being owned by an individual who is not a full-time employee of the company.]¹

(8) In this section—

"full-time employee", in relation to a company, means a person who works for the greater part of his time as an employee or director of the company or of a 51 per cent subsidiary of the company;

"holding company" means a company whose business (disregarding any trade carried on by it) consists wholly or mainly of the holding of shares or securities of one or more companies which are its 75 per cent subsidiaries;

"trading company" means a company whose business consists wholly or mainly of the carrying on of a trade or trades;

"trading group" means a group the business of whose members taken together consists wholly or mainly of the carrying on of a trade or trades, and for this purpose "group" means a company which has one or more 75 per cent subsidiaries together with those subsidiaries; and

"unquoted company" means a company none of whose shares are listed in the Official List of the Stock Exchange.

Commentary—*Simon's Direct Tax Service* **E1.548, 549.**
Concession A43—This concession extends relief available under ss 360–363 where (*a*) a partnership is incorporated into a cooperative, a close company or an employee controlled company, or (*b*) shares in any one of these are exchanged for, or replaced by shares in one of these types of company, or (*c*) a partnership reconstruction involving a merger or demerger.
Revenue & other press releases—ICAEW Tax 7/95 20-2-95 (Section B: uncorporation of partnership business, company non-close, extension of concession A43 to allow relief for interest on former partners' loan).
Definitions—"Co-operative", s 363(5); "company", s 832(1), (2); "interest", s 832(1); "ordinary share capital", s 832(1); "subsidiary", s 363(5); "51 per cent subsidiary", s 838; "75 per cent subsidiary", s 838; "year of assessment", s 832(1).
Cross references—See TA 1988 ss 363, 367 (supplementary provisions).
FA 1988 Sch 3 para 15(3) (interest paid on a loan made after 5 April 1990 to defray money applied in paying off another loan not eligible for relief under sub-s (3)(*b*) of this section unless certain conditions apply),
FA 1988 Sch 6 para 3(3)(*b*)(i), (4)(*b*), (5), (7) (interest paid after 14 March 1988 in relation to commercial woodlands not eligible for relief under this section),
Amendments—¹ Words in sub-ss (4)(*d*), (5) repealed and sub-s (6) substituted for sub-ss (6), (7) by FA 1988 Sch 3 para 15(1), (2), Sch 14, Pt VIII in relation to payments of interest made after 5 April 1990 unless the proceeds of the loan were used before that date to defray money applied as mentioned in sub-s (3) above.

362 Loan to buy into partnership

(1) Subject to sections 363 to 365, interest is eligible for relief under section 353 if it is interest on a loan to an individual to defray money applied—

(*a*) in purchasing a share in a partnership; or

(*b*) in contributing money to a partnership by way of capital or premium, or in advancing money to a partnership, where the money contributed or advanced is used wholly for the purposes of the trade, profession or vocation carried on by the partnership; or

(*c*) in paying off another loan interest on which would have been eligible for relief under that section had the loan not been paid off (on the assumption, if the loan was free of interest, that it carried interest);

and the conditions stated in subsection (2) below are satisfied.

(2) The conditions referred to in subsection (1) above are—

(*a*) that, throughout the period from the application of the proceeds of the loan until the interest was paid, the individual has been a member of the partnership [otherwise than—

(i) as a limited partner in a limited partnership registered under the Limited Partnerships Act 1907, or

(ii) as a member of an investment LLP;]¹; and

(*b*) that he shows that in that period he has not recovered any capital from the partnership, apart from any amount taken into account under section 363(1).

Commentary—*Simon's Direct Tax Service* **E1.550.**
Concession A43—This concession extends relief available under ss 360–363 where (*a*) a partnership is incorporated into a cooperative, a close company or an employee controlled company, or (*b*) shares in any one of these are exchanged for, or replaced by shares in one of these types of company, or (*c*) a partnership reconstruction involving a merger or demerger.
Statement of Practice SP A33—This Statement extends the application of this section to salaried partners who are allowed independence of action in handling the affairs of clients.
Revenue Interpretations RI 15—Independent taxation of husband and wife: interest relief on certain joint loans.
RI 41—Interest relief under this section ceases if the borrower leaves the partnership and this is so even if he is unable to withdraw his capital at the time of leaving.
Simon's Tax Cases—*Lancaster v IRCs* [2000] STC (SCD) 138.
Definition—"Interest", s 832(1).
Cross references—See TA 1988 ss 363, 367 (supplementary provisions).
FA 1988 Sch 6 para 3(3)(*b*)(i), (4)(*b*), (5), (7) (interest paid after 14 March 1988 in relation to commercial woodlands not eligible for relief under this section).
Amendments—¹ Words in sub-s (2)(*a*) substituted by FA 2001 s 76, Sch 25 para 9 with effect from 6 April 2001 (by virtue of SI 2000/3316 art 2).

363 Provisions supplementary to sections 360 to 362

(1) If at any time after the application of the proceeds of the loan the individual has recovered any amount of capital from the close company, co-operative, employee-controlled company or partnership without using that amount in repayment of the loan, he shall be treated for the purposes of sections 353, 360, 361 and 362 as if he had at that time repaid that amount out of the loan, so that out of the interest otherwise eligible for relief (or, where section 367(4) applies, out of the proportion so eligible) and payable for any period after that time there shall be deducted an amount equal to interest on the amount of capital so recovered.

(2) The individual shall be treated as having recovered an amount of capital from the close company, co-operative, employee-controlled company or partnership if—

(*a*) he receives consideration of that amount or value for the sale, exchange or assignment of any part of the ordinary share capital of the company or of his share or shares in the co-operative or of his interest in the partnership, or of any consideration of that amount or value by way of repayment of any part of that ordinary share capital or of his share or shares in the co-operative; or
(*b*) the close company, co-operative, employee-controlled company or partnership repays that amount of a loan or advance from him or the partnership returns that amount of capital to him; or
(*c*) he receives consideration of that amount or value for assigning any debt due to him from the close company, co-operative, employee-controlled company or partnership;

and where a sale or assignment is not a bargain made at arm's length, the sale or assignment shall be deemed to be for a consideration of an amount equal to the market value of what is disposed of.

(3) In the application of this section to Scotland for the word "assignment" wherever it occurs there shall be substituted the word "assignation".

(4) Section 360, or, as the case may be, 361(2) or (4) or 362(2) and subsections (1) to (3) above, shall apply to a loan within section 360(1)(*c*), 361(1)(*c*) or (3)(*b*) or 362(1)(*c*) as if it, and any loan it replaces, were one loan, and so that—

(*a*) references to the application of the proceeds of the loan were references to the application of the proceeds of the original loan; and
(*b*) any restriction under subsection (1) above which applies to any loan which has been replaced shall apply to the loan which replaces it.

(5) In this section and sections 361 and 362—

"co-operative" means a common ownership enterprise or a co-operative enterprise as defined in section 2 of the Industrial Common Ownership Act 1976; and
"subsidiary" has the same meaning as for the purposes of section 2 of that Act.

Commentary—*Simon's Direct Tax Service* **E1.551.**
Revenue Interpretation RI 12—Interest relief: loans to invest in close companies.
Revenue Internal Guidance—Inspector's manual IM 3834 (partnerships: unless there are separate capital accounts and drawings accounts, drawings are matched with profits as far as possible).
Definitions—"Close company", s 832(1); "ordinary share capital", s 832(1).

364 Loan to pay inheritance tax

(1) Interest is eligible for relief under section 353 if it is interest on a loan to the personal representatives of a deceased person, the proceeds of which are applied—

(*a*) in paying, before the grant of representation or confirmation, capital transfer tax or inheritance tax payable on the delivery of the personal representatives' account and attributable to the value of personal property to which the deceased was beneficially entitled immediately before his death and which vests in the personal representatives or would vest in them if the property were situated in the United Kingdom; or
(*b*) in paying off another loan interest on which would have been eligible for that relief by virtue of this section if the loan had not been paid off (on the assumption, if the loan was free of interest, that it carried interest);

and the interest is paid in respect of a period ending within one year from the making of the loan within paragraph (*a*) above.

(2) If or to the extent that any relief in respect of interest eligible for it under subsection (1) above cannot be given against income of the year in which the interest is paid because of an insufficiency of income in that year, it may instead be given against income of the preceding year of assessment, and so on; and if or to the extent that it cannot be so given it may instead be given against income of the year following that in which the interest is paid, and so on.

(3) Sufficient evidence of the amount of capital transfer tax or inheritance tax paid as mentioned in subsection (1)(a) above and of any statements relevant to its computation may be given by the production of a document purporting to be a certificate from the Board.

(4) For the purposes of subsections (1) to (3) above—

(a) references to capital transfer tax or inheritance tax include any interest payable on that tax; and

(b) references to interest in respect of a period ending within a given time apply whether or not interest continues to run after that time.

Commentary—*Simon's Direct Tax Service* **C4.106; E1.552.**
Definitions—''The Board'', s 832(1); ''interest'', s 832(1); ''year of assessment'', s 832(1).
Cross references—See TA 1988 s 366 (information to be provided by person claiming interest relief by virtue of sub-s (2) above to include interest for the year for which claim would have been made but for an insufficiency of income).
TA 1988 s 367 (supplementary provisions).

365 Loan to buy life annuity

(1) Subject to the following provisions of this section, interest is eligible for relief under section 353 if it is interest on a loan in respect of which the following conditions are satisfied—

[(aa) that the loan was made before 9th March 1999;][2]

(a) that the loan was made as part of a scheme under which not less than nine-tenths of the proceeds of the loan were applied to the purchase by the person to whom it was made of an annuity ending with his life or with the life of the survivor of two or more persons (''the annuitants'') who include the person to whom the loan was made;

(b) that at the time the loan was made the person to whom it was made or each of the annuitants had attained the age of 65 years;

(c) that the loan was secured on land in the United Kingdom or the Republic of Ireland and the person to whom it was made or one of the annuitants owns an estate or interest in that land; and

(d) that, if the loan was made after 26th March 1974, the person to whom it was made or each of the annuitants [used the land on which it was secured as his only or main residence immediately before 9th March 1999,][3].

[(1AA) Where—

(a) a loan made on or after 9th March 1999 was made in pursuance of an offer made by the lender before that date, and

(b) the offer was either in writing or evidenced by a note or memorandum made by the lender before that date,

the loan shall be deemed for the purposes of subsection (1)(aa) above to have been made before that date.][2]

[(1AB) Subject to subsection (1AC) below, the conditions in paragraphs (aa) and (a) of subsection (1) above shall be treated as satisfied in relation to a loan (''the new loan'') if—

(a) the new loan was made on or after the day on which the Finance Act 1999 was passed;

(b) the new loan was made as part of a scheme (''the scheme'') under which the whole or any part of the proceeds of the loan was used to defray money applied in paying off another loan (''the old loan''); and

(c) the conditions in subsection (1) above were, or were treated by virtue of this subsection as, satisfied with respect to the old loan.

(1AC) If only part of the proceeds of the new loan was used to defray money applied in paying off the old loan, subsection (1AB) above applies only if, under the scheme, not less than nine-tenths of the remaining part of the proceeds of the new loan was applied to the purchase by the person to whom it was made of an annuity ending with his life or with the life of the survivor of two or more persons who include him.

(1AD) In subsection (1AC) above ''the remaining part'' means the part of the proceeds of the new loan that was not used to defray money applied in paying off the old loan.][3]

[(1A) The condition in subsection (1)(d) above shall be treated as satisfied in relation to a loan if—

(a) the person to whom the loan was made, or any of the annuitants, ceased to use the land as his only or main residence at a time falling within the period of twelve months ending with 8th March 1999, and

(b) the intention at that time of the person to whom the loan was made, or each of the annuitants owning an estate or interest in the land, was to take steps, before the end of the period of twelve months after the day on which the land ceased to be so used, with a view to the disposal of his estate or interest.][3]

[(1B) If it appears to the Board reasonable to do so, having regard to all the circumstances of a particular case, they may direct that in relation to that case subsection (1A) above shall have effect as if for the reference to 12 months there were substituted a reference to such longer period as meets the circumstances of that case.]¹

(2) Interest is not eligible for relief by virtue of this section unless it is payable by the person to whom the loan was made or by one of the annuitants.

(3) If the loan was made after 26th March 1974 interest on it is eligible for relief by virtue of this section only to the extent that the amount on which it is payable does not exceed [the sum of £30,000]⁴; and if the interest is payable by two or more persons the interest payable by each of them is so eligible only to the extent that the amount on which it is payable does not exceed such amount as bears to [that sum]⁴ the same proportion as the interest payable by him bears to the interest payable by both or all of them.

Commentary—*Simon's Direct Tax Service* **E1.553.**
Definitions—''the Board'', s 832(1); ''estate or interest'', s 354(4); ''interest'', s 832(1); ''year of assessment'', s 832(1).
Cross references—See IT (Interest Relief) Regulations, SI 1982/1236 reg 4 (a loan qualifying for relief under this section is specified for the purposes of s 374(1)(*d*) of this Act);
TA 1988 s 367 (supplementary provisions).
TA 1988 s 370(2) (definition by reference to this section of ''relevant loan interest'' for interest relief under MIRAS).
TA 1988 s 373(1) (''limited loan'' provisions under MIRAS).
FA 1993 s 57(6) (Board's power to extend the power specified in sub-s (1A) above where the condition specified in sub-s (1)(*d*) above ceases to be fulfilled before 16 March 1993).
Amendments—¹ Sub-s (1B) inserted by FA 1993 s 57,(3), (5) with effect for payments of interest made after 15 March 1993, whenever falling due; see also Cross references to FA 1993 s 57(6) above.
²Sub-s (1)(*aa*), and sub-s (1AA), inserted by FA 1999 s 39 with effect from the year 1998–99.
³Words in sub-s (1)(*d*) and whole of sub-s (1A) substituted and sub-ss (1AB)–(1AD) inserted by FA 1999 s 40 with effect for any payment of interest made after 26 July 1999.
⁴ Words in sub-s (3) substituted by FA 2000 s 83(1), (4) with effect for payments of interest made after 5 April 2000.

366 Information

(1) A person who claims relief under section 353 in respect of any payment of interest shall furnish to the inspector a statement in writing by the person to whom the payment is made, showing—

    (*a*) the date when the debt was incurred;
    (*b*) the amount of the debt when incurred;
    (*c*) the interest paid in the year of assessment for which the claim is made (or, in the case of relief by virtue of section ...¹ 364(2), the year of assessment for which the claim would be made but for an insufficiency of income); and
    (*d*) the name and address of the debtor.

(2) Where any such interest as is mentioned in section 353 is paid, the person to whom it is paid shall, if the person who pays it so requests in writing, furnish him with such statement as regards that interest as is mentioned in subsection (1) above; and the duty imposed by this subsection shall be enforceable at the suit or instance of the person making the request.

(3) Subsections (1) and (2) above do not apply to interest paid to a building society, or to a local authority.

Commentary—*Simon's Direct Tax Service* **E1.527.**
Revenue Interpretation RI 111—Provision of certificates of interest paid to borrowers.
Definitions—''Building society'', s 832(1); ''inspector'', s 832(1); ''interest'', s 832(1); ''local authority'', s 519 by virtue of s 832(1); ''year of assessment'', s 832(1).
Cross references—See TA 1988 s 367 (supplementary provisions).
Amendments—¹ Words omitted from sub-s (1)(*c*) repealed by FA 1995 Sch 29 Pt VIII(2), with effect for any payment of interest made after 5 April 1995, except for certain interest payments on loans in respect of which the source of Schedule A income ceased during 1995–96: see FA 1995 s 42(3)–(5).

367 Provisions supplementary to sections 354 to 366

(1) ...¹

(2) Sections ...¹ 360 to 364 do not apply to a loan unless it is made—

    (*a*) in connection with the application of money, and
    (*b*) on the occasion of, or within what is in the circumstances a reasonable time from, the application of the money;

and those sections do not apply to a loan the proceeds of which are applied for some other purpose before being applied as mentioned in those sections.

(3) For the purposes of [sections 359]¹ to 364, the giving of credit for any money due from the purchaser under any sale shall be treated as the making of a loan to defray money applied by him in making the purchase.

(4) Where part only of a debt fulfils the conditions required under [sections 359]¹ to 364 for interest on the debt to be eligible for relief under section 353, such proportion of the interest shall be treated as eligible for relief under that section as is equal to the portion of the debt fulfilling those conditions at the time of the application of the money in question.

(5) In [section]¹ 365(3) references to the qualifying maximum for the year of assessment are references to such sum as Parliament may determine for the purpose for that year.

Commentary—*Simon's Direct Tax Service* **E1.535–540.**
Note—The qualifying maximum in sub-s (5) for the year 1999–00 is £30,000 by virtue of FA 1999 s 37.
Simon's Tax Cases—s 367(1)(2), *Hughes v Viner* [1985] STC 235*.

s 367(2), *Badger v Major* [1997] STC (SCD) 218; *Cohen v Petch* [1999] STC (SCD) 207.
s 367(3), *Gold v Inspector of Taxes* [1998] STC (SCD) 222; *Grant v Watton* [1999] STC 330.
Definitions—"Interest", s 832(1); "year of assessment", s 832(1).
Amendments—[1] Sub-s (1) and words in sub-s (2) repealed and words in sub-ss (3)–(5) substituted by FA 1999 s 38(8), Sch 4 paras 3, 18(5), Sch 20 Pt III(7) with effect for payments of interest made—

after 5 April 2000;

after 8 March 1999 and before 6 April 2000 in respect of interest falling due after 5 April 2000; or

after 8 March 1999 and before 6 April 2000 under a scheme made for a tax avoidance purpose after 8 March 1999).

368 Exclusion of double relief etc

(1) Interest in respect of which relief is given under section 353 shall not be allowable as a deduction [for any purpose of the Income Tax Acts except so far as it is so allowable in accordance with subsection (1B) of that section][1].

(2) Relief shall not be given under section 353 against income chargeable to corporation tax, and shall not be given against any other income of a company, except where both of the following conditions are satisfied, that is to say—

(*a*) that the company is not resident in the United Kingdom; and

(*b*) that the interest cannot be taken into account in computing corporation tax chargeable on the company.

(3) Where interest on any debt or liability is taken into account in the computation of [profits][3] or losses for the purposes of [Schedule A or][2] Case I or II of Schedule D no relief shall be given under section 353—

(*a*) in respect of the payment of that interest; or

(*b*) in respect of interest on the same debt or liability which is paid in any year of assessment for which that computation is relevant.

(4) Where relief is given under section 353 in respect of the interest paid in any year of assessment on any debt or liability—

(*a*) that interest shall not be taken into account in the computation of [profits][3] or losses for the purposes of [Schedule A or][2] Case I or II of Schedule D for any year of assessment; and

(*b*) interest on that debt or liability shall not be taken into account in that computation for any year of assessment for which the interest so paid could have been taken into account but for the relief.

(5) For the purposes of subsections (3) and (4) above, all interest capable of being taken into account in such a computation as is mentioned in those subsections which is payable by any person on money advanced to him on current account, whether advanced on one or more accounts or by the same or separate banks or other persons, shall be treated as interest payable on the same debt.

(6) References in subsections (3) and (4) above to relief given or an amount taken into account are references to relief given or an amount taken into account on a claim or in an assessment which has been finally determined.

Commentary—*Simon's Direct Tax Service* E1.530.
Concession A89—Relief for interest on a loan to buy a property used for both residential and business purposes may in certain circumstances be allowed partly under this section and under TA 1988 s 353.
Definitions—"Company", s 832(1), (2); "the Income Tax Acts", s 831(1)(*b*); "interest", s 832(1); "Schedule D", s 18(1); "year of assessment", s 832(1).
Amendments—[1] Words in sub-s (1) substituted by FA 1994 Sch 9 para 9 with effect generally from 6 April 1994; for detailed commencement provisions, see FA 1994 s 81(5), (6), (7).
[2] Words in sub-ss (3), (4) inserted by FA 1995 Sch 6 para 17, with effect for the year 1995–96 and subsequent years of assessment, except for the purposes of corporation tax where the insertion has effect for accounting periods ending after 30 March 1995, or where the source of income ceased in the year 1995–96: see FA 1995 s 39(4), (5).
[3] Word in sub-ss (3), (4)(*a*) substituted by FA 1998 Sch 7 para 1 with effect from 31 July 1998.

Mortgage interest relief at source

Statement of Practice SP A34—Where mortgaged property passes on death, there is continuity of interest relief if the deceased was entitled to the relief. Also, the relief is transferred to a new loan used in paying off the inherited mortgage.
Cross references—See TA 1988 s 356B(1) (for the purposes of ss 369–379 below, husband and wife may jointly elect that interest paid by one be treated as paid by the other).
TA 1988 ss 357A–357C (continuity of mortgage interest relief where the borrower buys a new home and the original loan for the previous home is secured by the new home).
TA 1988 s 378 (regulations to bring housing associations, self-build societies, etc within MIRAS provisions).
FA 1988 s 43(3) (interest paid by a housing association or a self-build society on a home improvement loan made after 5 April 1988 not to be relevant loan interest for the purposes of tax relief under the following provisions),
FA 1988 s 44(6) (interest paid by a housing association or a self-build society on a loan for residence of dependent relative or former spouse made after 5 April 1988 not to be relevant loan interest for the purposes of tax relief under the following provisions);
IT (Interest Relief) (Housing Associations) Regulations, SI 1988/1347 reg 3 (application of ss 369–377 (with modifications) to housing associations).

369 Mortgage interest payable under deduction of tax

(1) If a person who is a qualifying borrower makes a payment of relevant loan interest to which this section applies, he shall be entitled, on making the payment, to deduct and retain out of it a sum equal to [the applicable percentage thereof.][3]

[(1A) In subsection (1) above "the applicable percentage" means [23 per cent][8].][7]

(2) Where a sum is deducted under subsection (1) above from a payment of relevant loan interest—

    (*a*) the person to whom the payment is made shall allow the deduction on receipt of the residue;

    (*b*) the borrower shall be acquitted and discharged of so much money as is represented by the deduction as if the sum had been actually paid; and

    (*c*) the sum deducted shall be treated as income tax paid by the person to whom the payment is made.

[(3) The following payments, that is to say—

    (*a*) payments of relevant loan interest to which this section applies, and

    (*b*) payments which would be such payments but for section 373(5),

shall not be allowable as deductions for any purpose of the Income Tax Acts except in so far as they fall to be treated as such payments by virtue only of section 375(2) and would be allowable apart from this subsection.]²

(3A)–(5B) ...²

(6) Any person by whom a payment of relevant loan interest to which this section applies is received shall be entitled to recover from the Board, in accordance with regulations, an amount which by virtue of subsection (2)(*c*) above is treated as income tax paid by him; and any amount so recovered shall be treated for the purposes of the Tax Acts in like manner as the payment of relevant loan interest to which it relates.

[(7) The following provisions of the Management Act, namely—

    [(*a*) section 29(1)(*c*) (excessive relief) as it has effect apart from section 29(2) to (10) of that Act;]⁴

    (*b*) section 30 (tax repaid in error etc) [apart from subsection (1B)]⁴,

    (*c*) [section 86]⁵ (interest), and

    (*d*) section 95 (incorrect return or accounts),

shall apply in relation to an amount which is paid to any person by the Board as an amount recoverable in accordance with regulations made by virtue of subsection (6) above but to which that person is not entitled as if it were income tax which ought not to have been repaid and, where that amount was claimed by that person, as if it had been repaid [as respects a chargeable period]⁶ as a relief which was not due.]¹

[(8) In the application of section 86 of the Management Act by virtue of subsection (7) above in relation to sums due and payable by virtue of an assessment made for the whole or part of a year of assessment ("the relevant year of assessment") under section 29(1)(*c*) or 30 of that Act, as applied by that subsection, the relevant date—

    (*a*) is 1st January in the relevant year of assessment in a case where the person falling within subsection (6) above has made a relevant interim claim; and

    (*b*) in any other case, is the later of the following dates, that is to say—

        (i) 1st January in the relevant year of assessment; or

        (ii) the date of the making of the payment by the Board which gives rise to the assessment.]⁵

[(9) In this section—

    "financial year", in relation to any person, means a financial year of that person for the purposes of the relevant regulations;

    "interim claim" means an interim claim within the meaning of the relevant regulations;

    "relevant interim claim" means, in relation to an assessment made for a period coterminous with, or falling wholly within, a person's financial year, an interim claim made for a period falling wholly or partly within that financial year; and

    "the relevant regulations" means regulations made under section 378(3) for the purposes of subsection (6) above.]⁵

Commentary—*Simon's Direct Tax Service* A3.430.

Concessions A89—Relief for interest on a loan to buy a property used for both business and residential purposes may be allowed in part under MIRAS and in part as a deduction in computing profits or losses.

Revenue & other press releases—IRCU 7–12–89 (MIRAS under independent taxation).

IR February 1994 (guidance note to lenders: changes in rate of tax relief under MIRAS).

IR 17-3-94 (MIRAS payments due between 1 and 5 April 1994).

Simon's Tax Cases—*Tither v IRC* [1990] STC 416*.

Definitions—"Basic rate", s 832(1); "the Board", s 832(1); "Income Tax Acts", s 831(1)(*b*); "qualifying borrower", s 379; "relevant loan interest", s 379; "the Tax Acts", s 831(2); "year of assessment", s 832(1).

Cross references—See TA 1988 ss 7(3), 11(4) (income tax borne by deduction at source under this section not to be available for set off against corporation tax).

TA 1988 s 74(1)(*o*) (deduction of relevant loan interest in computing profits and gains—general rules as to deductions not allowable).

TA 1988 s 160(1A) (interest treated as paid on a beneficial loan by an employee borrower is not to be treated as relevant loan interest under this section).

TA 1988 ss 357A–357C (continuity of mortgage interest relief where the borrower buys a new home and the original loan for the previous home is secured by the new home).

TA 1988 s 374 (conditions for application of this section).

TA 1988 s 375 (interest ceasing to be relevant loan interest).

TA 1988 s 375A (disapplication of this section to certain payments of interest to be deducted in computing the profits or gains of a Schedule A business).

TA 1988 s 477 (provisions prohibiting deduction of tax from payments of interest to building societies do not apply to interest to which this section applies).

IT (Interest Relief) Regulations, SI 1982/1236 reg 8A (repayment claim by a borrower who has not been able to deduct the full amount allowed to be deducted by sub-s (1) above,

IT (Interest Relief) Regulations, SI 1982/1236 regs 9, 13 (repayment claims by lenders under sub-s (6) above),

IT (Interest Relief) Regulations, SI 1982/1236 reg 16 (information to be provided to the Board by a borrower or a lender);

IT (Interest Relief) (Housing Associations) Regulations, SI 1988/1347 reg 4 (modification of sub-s (1) above in its application to a housing association);

FA 1994 s 81(7) (references in loan agreements made before 3 May 1994 to the basic rate to be construed as references to the applicable percentage under sub-s (1) above).

FA 1999 s 38(2) (sub-s (1) above does not apply in respect of interest on mortgage loans dealt with under MIRAS where the interest is paid—

–after 5 April 2000;

–after 8 March 1999 and before 6 April 2000 in respect of interest falling due after 5 April 2000; or

–after 8 March 1999 and before 6 April 2000 under a scheme made for a tax avoidance purpose after 8 March 1999).

Amendments—[1] Sub-s (7) inserted by FA 1993 s 58, but does not apply in relation to any payment if it, or the claim on which it is made, is made before 27 July 1993.

[2] Sub-s (3) substituted for sub-ss (3), (3A), (3B), (4), (5), (5A), (5B) by FA 1994 s 81(4) with effect generally from 6 April 1994; for detailed commencement provisions, see FA 1994 s 81(5), (6), (7).

[3] Words in sub-s (1) substituted by FA 1994 s 81(3).

[4] Sub-s (7)(a) substituted and words in sub-s (7)(b) inserted by FA 1996 Sch 18 paras 6(2)(a), (b), 17(1), (2), with effect for the purposes of income tax from the year 1996–97 and, so far as relating to partnerships whose trades, professions or businesses were set up and commenced before 6 April 1994, with effect from the year 1997–98.

[5] Words in sub-s (7)(c) substituted and sub-ss (8), (9) inserted, by FA 1996 Sch 18 paras 6(2)(c), (3), 17(3), (4), with effect from the year 1996–97 and in relation to income tax which is charged by an assessment made on or after 6 April 1998 which is for the year 1995–96 or any earlier year of assessment; and so far as relating to partnerships whose trades, professions or businesses were set up and commenced before 6 April 1994 with effect from the year 1997–98 and in relation to income tax which is charged by an assessment made after 5 April 1998 which is for the year 1995–96 or any earlier year of assessment.

[6] Words in sub-s (7) inserted by FA 1996 Sch 18 paras 6(2)(d), 17(8) but do not apply in relation to any payment if the payment, or the claim on which it is made, was made before 29 April 1996.

[7] Sub-s (1A) substituted by FA 1999 s 38(8), Sch 4 paras 4, 18(5) with effect for payments of interest made—

–after 5 April 2000;

–after 8 March 1999 and before 6 April 2000 in respect of interest falling due after 5 April 2000; or

–after 8 March 1999 and before 6 April 2000 under a scheme made for a tax avoidance purpose after 8 March 1999).

[8] Words in sub-s (1A) substituted by FA 2000 s 83(3), (4) with effect for payments of interest made after 5 April 2000.

370 Relevant loan interest

(1) Subject to this section and [sections 373][3] to 376, in this Part ''relevant loan interest'' means interest which is paid and payable in the United Kingdom to a qualifying lender and to which subsection (2) ...[3] below applies.

(2) Subject to subsection (4) below, this subsection applies to interest if, disregarding section 353(2) [and any other provision applying to interest falling to be treated as relevant loan interest][1]—

(a) it is interest falling within section ...[3] 365; and

(b) apart [(where applicable) from][1] section ...[3] 365(3), the whole of the interest either would be eligible for relief under section 353 or would be taken into account in a computation of profits or gains or losses for the purposes of Case I, II or VI of Schedule D for any year of assessment; ...[3]

(c) ...[3]

(3), (4) ...[3]

(5) In determining whether subsection (2) above applies to any interest, [section 365 shall][3] have effect as if the words ''or the Republic of Ireland'' were omitted.

(6) ...[3]

(6A) ...[2]

(7) ...[3]

Commentary—*Simon's Direct Tax Service* A3.431.

Simon's Tax Cases—s 370(2)(b), *R v Inspector of Taxes, ex p Kelly* [1991] STC 566.

Definitions—''Caravan'', s 367(1); ''house-boat'', s 367(1); ''interest'', s 832(1); ''qualifying lender'', s 379; ''relevant loan interest'', s 379; ''Schedule D'', s 18(1); ''year of assessment'', s 832(1).

Cross references—See TA 1988 s 375(6) (notice to be given by Board if any provision of this section may not be fulfilled).

TA 1988 s 375(9) (disclosure of information relating to a loan in respect of which an option notice has been given as required by sub-s (3)(a) above).

IT (Interest Relief) Regulations, SI 1982/1236 reg 7B (modification of sub-s (3) above in determining whether interest payable by certain trustees is relevant loan interest);

IT (Interest Relief) (Housing Associations) Regulations, SI 1988/1347 regs 5–5D (modification of this section in its application to housing associations).

Amendments—[1] Words in sub-s (2) substituted by FA 1994 Sch 9 para 10 with effect generally from 6 April 1994; for detailed commencement provisions, see FA 1994 s 81(5), (6), (7).

[2] Sub-s (6A) repealed by FA 1995 Sch 29 Pt VIII(2), with effect for any payment of interest made after 5 April 1995, except for certain interest payments on loans in respect of which the source of Schedule A income ceased during 1995–96: see FA 1995 s 42(3)–(5) (previously inserted by FA 1994 Sch 9 para 10 with effect generally from 6 April 1994).

[3] Words in sub-ss (1), (5) and words in sub-ss (1), (2) and sub-ss (3), (4), (6), (7) repealed by FA 1999 s 38(8), Sch 4 paras 5, 18(5), Sch 20 Pt III(7) with effect for payments of interest made—

–after 5 April 2000;

–after 8 March 1999 and before 6 April 2000 in respect of interest falling due after 5 April 2000; or

–after 8 March 1999 and before 6 April 2000 under a scheme made for a tax avoidance purpose after 8 March 1999.

371 Second loans

Commentary—*Simon's Direct Tax Service* A3.431.

Amendments—This section repealed by FA 1993 s 57(4)(b) and Sch 23, Pt III(1) in relation to payments of interest made after 15 March 1993, but subject to FA 1993 s 57(6), (7) (now, in part, repealed).

372 Home improvement loans

Commentary—*Simon's Direct Tax Service* **A3.431.**
Amendments—This section repealed by FA 1999 s 38(8), Sch 4 paras 6, 18(5), Sch 20 Pt III(7) with effect for payments of
interest made—
 –after 5 April 2000;
 –after 8 March 1999 and before 6 April 2000 in respect of interest falling due after 5 April 2000; or
 –after 8 March 1999 and before 6 April 2000 under a scheme made for a tax avoidance purpose after 8 March 1999.

373 Loans in excess of the qualifying maximum, and joint borrowers

(1) The provisions of this section have effect in relation to a loan where, by virtue of . . .[1] section
365(3), only part of the interest on the loan would (apart from section 353(2)) be eligible for relief
under section 353; and in this section any such loan is referred to as a "limited loan".

(2) None of the interest on a limited loan is relevant loan interest unless—

    (a) the loan is made on or after 6th April 1987; or
    (b) the qualifying lender to whom the interest is payable has given notice to the Board in
    accordance with regulations that he is prepared to have limited loans of a description which
    includes that limited loan brought within the tax deduction scheme.

(3), (4) . . .[1]

(5) Where the condition in paragraph (a) or (b) of subsection (2) above is fulfilled . . .[1] only so much
of the interest as (apart from section 353(2)) would be eligible for relief under section 353 is relevant
loan interest.

(6) Where a loan on which interest is payable by the borrower was made jointly to the borrower and
another person who is not the borrower's husband or wife, the interest on the loan is not relevant
loan interest unless—

    (a) each of the persons to whom the loan was made is a qualifying borrower; and
    (b) in relation to each of them considered separately, the whole of that interest is relevant loan
    interest, in accordance with [section 370][1] and this section.

(7) In subsection (6) above references to the borrower's husband or wife do not include references
to a separated husband or wife, . . .[1]

Commentary—*Simon's Direct Tax Service* **A3.431.**
Definitions—"The Board", s 832(1); "interest", s 832(1); "qualifying borrower", s 379; "qualifying lender", s 379;
"regulations", s 379; "relevant loan interest", s 379; "separated" s 379.
Cross references—See TA 1988 s 375(6) (notice to be given by Board where it appears that any provision of this section may
not be fulfilled).
IT (Interest Relief) (Housing Associations) Regulations, SI 1988/1347 reg 6 (modification of sub-ss (1)–(5) above in their
application to housing associations).
Amendments—[1] Words in sub-ss (1), (5), (7), and sub-ss (3), (4), repealed and words in sub-s (6)(b) substituted by FA 1999
s 38(8), Sch 4 paras 7, 18(5), Sch 20 Pt III(7) with effect for payments of interest made—
 –after 5 April 2000;
 –after 8 March 1999 and before 6 April 2000 in respect of interest falling due after 5 April 2000; or
 –after 8 March 1999 and before 6 April 2000 under a scheme made for a tax avoidance purpose after 8 March 1999.

374 Conditions for application of section 369

(1) Section 369 does not apply to any relevant loan interest unless—

    (a) in the case of a loan of a description specified by regulations for the purposes of this paragraph,
    the borrower or, in the case of joint borrowers, each of them has given notice to the lender in the
    prescribed form certifying—

        (i) that he is a qualifying borrower; and
        (ii) that the interest is relevant loan interest; and
        (iii) such other matters as may be prescribed; or

    (b) the Board have given notice to the lender and the borrower that the interest may be paid under
    deduction of tax; or
    (c) . . .[1]
    (d) the loan to which the interest relates is of a description specified by regulations for the
    purposes of this paragraph and was made—

        (i) if sub-paragraph (2) of paragraph 2 of Schedule 7 to the Finance Act 1982 applied to
        interest on the loan which became due on or after a date earlier than 6th April 1983, being a
        date specified by the Board in pursuance of sub-paragraph (5) of that paragraph, before that
        earlier date; or
        (ii) if the qualifying lender is a building society or a local authority, before 1st April 1983; or
        (iii) if sub-paragraphs (i) and (ii) above do not apply and the interest falls within section
        370(2), before 6th April 1983.

(2) Where notice has been given as mentioned in paragraph (a) or (b) of subsection (1) above,
section 369 applies to any relevant loan interest to which the notice relates and which becomes due
on or after the relevant date, as defined by subsection (3) below; and in a case falling within paragraph
. . .[1] (d) of subsection (1) above, section 369 applies to the relevant loan interest referred to in that
paragraph.

(3) In subsection (2) above "the relevant date" means—

(a) in the case of a notice under subsection (1)(a) above, the date the notice is given, and

(b) in the case of a notice under subsection (1)(b) above, a date specified in the notice as being the relevant date (which may be earlier than the date so specified as the date from which the interest may be paid under deduction of tax).

Commentary—*Simon's Direct Tax Service* A3.431, 432.
Regulations—IT (Interest Relief) Regulations, SI 1982/1236 regs 3, 4 (specification of loans for the purposes of sub-s(1)(a), (d)).

Definitions—"The Board", s 832(1); "building society", s 832(1); "interest", s 832(1); "local authority", s 519(4) by virtue of s 832(1); "notice", s 832(1); "prescribed", s 379; "qualifying borrower", s 379; "qualifying lender", s 379; "regulations", s 379; "relevant loan interest", s 379.
Cross references—See IT (Interest Relief) (Housing Associations) Regulations, SI 1988/1347, reg 7 (modification of sub-s (1)(c) above in its application to housing associations).
Amendments—[1] Sub-ss (1)(c) and words in sub-s (2) repealed by FA 1999 s 38(8), Sch 4 paras 8, 18(5), Sch 20 Pt III(7) with effect for payments of interest made—
–after 5 April 2000;
–after 8 March 1999 and before 6 April 2000 in respect of interest falling due after 5 April 2000; or
–after 8 March 1999 and before 6 April 2000 under a scheme made for a tax avoidance purpose after 8 March 1999.

[374A Interest which never has been relevant loan interest etc

(1) This section applies where, in the case of any loan, interest on the loan never has been relevant loan interest or the borrower never has been a qualifying borrower.

(2) Without prejudice to subsection (3) below, in relation to a payment of interest—

(a) as respects which either of the conditions mentioned in paragraphs (a) and (b) of section 374(1) is fulfilled, and

(b) from which a deduction was made as mentioned in section 369(1),

section 369 shall have effect as if the payment of interest were a payment of relevant loan interest made by a qualifying borrower.

(3) Nothing in subsection (2) above shall be taken as regards the borrower as entitling him to make any deduction or to retain any amount deducted and, accordingly, where any amount has been deducted, he shall be liable to make good that amount and an officer of the Board may make such assessments as may in his judgment be required for recovering that amount.

(4) The Management Act shall apply to an assessment under subsection (3) above as if it were an assessment to income tax for the year of assessment in which the deduction was made . . .[2]

(5) If the borrower fraudulently or negligently makes any false statement or representation in connection with the making of any deduction, he shall be liable to a penalty not exceeding the amount deducted.][1]

Commentary—*Simon's Direct Tax Service* A3.431; E1.828.
Definitions—"The Board", s 832(1); "interest", s 832(1); "the Management Act", s 831(3); "qualifying borrower", s 379; "year of assessment", s 832(1).
Amendments—[1] This section inserted by FA 1995 s 112(1), (5), in relation to deductions made by borrowers, and payments made to the Board, after 1 May 1995.
[2] Words in sub-s (4) repealed by FA 1996 Sch 18 paras 7, 17(5), (6), Sch 41 Pt V(8) with effect (i) generally from the year 1996–97 and (ii) (except for the repeal of sub-s (4)(a) and the words "and as if" preceding that paragraph) in relation to any income tax which is charged by an assessment made after 5 April 1998 which is for the year 1995–96 or any earlier year of assessment.

375 Interest ceasing to be relevant loan interest etc

(1) If at any time—

(a) the interest on a loan ceases to be relevant loan interest; or

(b) a person making payments of relevant loan interest ceases to be a qualifying borrower;

the borrower shall give notice of the fact to the lender.

(2) Without prejudice to subsection (3) below, in relation to a payment of interest—

(a) which is due after the time referred to in subsection (1) above and before the date on which notice is given under that subsection, and

[(aa) as respects which any of the conditions mentioned in section 374(1) is fulfilled, and][2]

(b) from which a deduction was made as mentioned in section 369(1),

section 369 shall have effect as if the payment were a payment of relevant loan interest made by a qualifying borrower.

(3) Nothing in subsection (2) above [shall be taken as regards the borrower as entitling him to any deduction or to retain any amount deducted and, accordingly, where any amount that has been deducted exceeds the amount which ought to have been deducted][1], he shall be liable to make good the excess and an inspector may make such assessments as may in his judgment be required for recovering the excess.

[(4) The Management Act shall apply to an assessment under subsection (3) above [as if it were an assessment to income tax for the year of assessment in which the deduction was made][3].][2]

[(4A) If there is any unreasonable delay in the giving of a notice under subsection (1) above, the borrower shall be liable to a penalty not exceeding so much of the aggregate amount that he is liable to make good under subsection (3) above as is attributable to that delay.][2]

(5) If, as a result of receiving a notice under subsection (1) above or otherwise, a qualifying lender has reason to believe that any interest is not longer relevant loan interest or that a borrower is no longer a qualifying borrower, the lender shall furnish the Board with such information as is in his possession with respect to those matters.

(6) Where it appears to the Board that any of the provisions of sections 370 to 373 is not or may not be fulfilled with respect to any interest, or that a qualifying borrower has or may have ceased to be a qualifying borrower, they shall give notice of that fact to the lender and the borrower specifying the description of relevant loan interest concerned or, as the case may be, that the borrower has or may have ceased to be a qualifying borrower.

(7) Section 369 shall not apply to any payment of relevant loan interest of a description to which a notice under subsection (6) above relates and which becomes due or is made after such date as may be specified in the notice and before such date as may be specified in a further notice given by the Board to the lender and the borrower.

(8) In any case where—

(a) section 369 applies to any relevant loan interest by virtue of a notice under section 374(1)(b), and

(b) the relevant date specified in the notice is earlier than the date from which the interest begins to be paid under deduction of tax, and

(c) a payment of that interest was made on or after the relevant date but not under deduction of tax,

regulations may provide for a sum to be paid by the Board of an amount equal to that which the borrower would have been able to deduct from that payment by virtue of section 369 if it had been made after the relevant date.

[(8A) In any case where an amount to which a person is not entitled is paid to him by the Board in pursuance of regulations made by virtue of subsection (8) above, regulations may—

(a) provide for an officer of the Board to make such assessments as may in his judgment be required for recovering that amount from that person; and

(b) make provision corresponding to that made by subsection (4A) above and subsections (4) and (5) of section 374A.][2]

[(8B) Subsections (1), (5) and (6) above shall not apply where interest ceases to be relevant loan interest by virtue of section 35 of the Finance Act 1999.][4]

(9), (10) . . .[4]

Commentary—*Simon's Direct Tax Service* **A3.431, 432.**
Definitions—"The Board", s 832(1); "inspector", s 832(1); "interest", s 832(1); "the Management Act", s 831(3); "notice", s 832(1); "qualifying borrower", s 379; "qualifying lender", s 379; "regulations", s 379; "relevant loan interest", s 379.
Cross references—See TMA 1970 s 98 (liability to special return penalty for failure to provide information under sub-s (5) above).
TA 1988 s 74(1)(o) (deduction of interest to which sub-s (2) above applies in computing profits or gains of a trade, profession or vocation).
TA 1988 s 824(2B) (repayment by the Board under sub-s (8) above to be increased by repayment supplement).
Amendments—[1] Words in sub-s (3) substituted by FA 1994 Sch 9 para 11 with effect generally from 6 April 1994; for detailed commencement provisions, see FA 1994 s 81(5), (6), (7).
[2] Sub-ss (2)(aa), (8A) inserted and sub-ss (4), (4A) substituted for sub-s (4), by FA 1995 s 112(2)–(4), (5), in relation to deductions made by borrowers, and payments made by the Board, after 1 May 1995.
[3] Words in sub-s (4) substituted by FA 1996 Sch 18 paras 8, 17(1) with effect from the year 1996–97.
[4] Sub-s (8B) inserted by FA 1999 s 38(8), Sch 4 paras 9(1), 18(5) with effect for payments of interest made—
–after 5 April 2000;
–after 8 March 1999 and before 6 April 2000 in respect of interest falling due after 5 April 2000; or
–after 8 March 1999 and before 6 April 2000 under a scheme made for a tax avoidance purpose after 8 March 1999.
[5] Sub-ss (9), (10) repealed by FA 1999 s 38(8), Sch 4 paras 9(2), 18(1), Sch 20 Pt III(7) with effect for any loan the only payments under which are payments of interest made under FA 1999 s 38(3), (4) (as described in note [4] above).

[375A Option to deduct interest for the purposes of Schedule A]

Definitions—"The Board", s 832(1); "interest", s 832(1); "profits or gains", s 833(1); "qualifying borrower", "relevant loan interest", s 379; "Schedule A", s 15(1); "year of assessment", s 832(1).
Amendments—This section repealed by FA 1999 s 38(8), Sch 4 paras 10, 18(5), Sch 20 Pt III(7) with effect for payments of interest made—
–after 5 April 2000;
–after 8 March 1999 and before 6 April 2000 in respect of interest falling due after 5 April 2000; or
–after 8 March 1999 and before 6 April 2000 under a scheme made for a tax avoidance purpose after 8 March 1999.

376 Qualifying borrowers and qualifying lenders

(1) Subject to subsection (2) below, an individual is a qualifying borrower with respect to the interest on any loan.

(2) In relation to interest paid at a time when the borrower or the borrower's husband or wife holds an office or employment in respect of the emoluments of which he or she would but for some special exemption or immunity from tax be chargeable to tax under Case I, II or III of Schedule E, the borrower is not a qualifying borrower.

(3) In subsection (2) above references to the borrower's husband or wife do not include references to a separated husband or wife, ...[7]

(4) The following bodies are qualifying lenders:—

(*a*) a building society;

(*b*) a local authority;

(*c*) the Bank of England;

(*d*) ...[8]

[(*e*) a person who has permission under Part 4 of the Financial Services and Markets Act 2000 to effect or carry out contracts of long-term insurance;][9]

(*f*) any company to which property and rights belonging to a trustee savings bank were transferred by section 3 of the Trustee Savings Bank Act 1985;

(*g*) ...[9]

(*h*) a development corporation within the meaning of the New Towns Act 1981 or the New Towns (Scotland) Act 1968;

(*j*) the Commission for the New Towns;

(*k*) the Housing Corporation;

[(*ka*) the Secretary of State if the loan is made by him under section 79 of the Housing Associations Act 1985;][1]

(*l*) the Northern Ireland Housing Executive;

(*m*) [Scottish Homes][6];

(*n*) the Development Board for Rural Wales;

(*o*) the Church of England Pensions Board;

[(*p*) any body which is for the time being registered under section 376A.][9]

(4A) ...[9]

(5) ...[5]

(6) ...[7]

Commentary—*Simon's Direct Tax Service* **A3.433.**
Revenue & other press releases—IR 16-7-98 (updated register of approved qualifying lenders published).
Simon's Tax Cases—s 376(1)–(3), *Tither v IRC* [1990] STC 416*.
Definitions—"The Board", s 832(1); "building society", s 832(1); "Case I, II or III of Schedule E", s 19(2); "company", s 832(1), (2); "emoluments", s 131(1); "interest", s 832(1); "local authority", s 519(4) by virtue of s 832(1); "prescribed", s 379; "qualifying borrower", s 379; "qualifying lender", s 379; "separated" s 379; "90 per cent subsidiary", s 838.
Cross references—See TA 1988 s 376A (register of qualifying lenders for the purposes of sub-s (4) above).
IT (Interest Relief) (Housing Associations) Regulations, SI 1988/1347 reg 3 (a housing association borrowing from a qualifying lender on the security of a freehold or leasehold estate is treated as a qualifying borrower within sub-s (1) above).
Amendments—[1] Sub-s (4)(*ka*) substituted by the Government of Wales Act 1998 Sch 16 para 55 with effect from 1 November 1998, by virtue of the Government of Wales Act 1998 (Commencement No 1) Order 1998, SI 1998/2244.
[2] ...
[3] ...
[4] Words in sub-s (4)(*p*) substituted by FA 1994 s 142(1).
[5] Sub-s (5) repealed by FA 1994 s 142(1), Sch 26, Pt V (19).
[6] Words in sub-s (4)(*m*) substituted by the Housing (Scotland) Act 1988 s 3(3), Sch 2 para 1.
[7] Words in sub-s (3), and whole of sub-s (6), repealed by FA 1999 s 38(8), Sch 4 paras 11 , 18(5), Sch 20 Pt III(7) with effect for payments of interest made—
  –after 5 April 2000;
  –after 8 March 1999 and before 6 April 2000 in respect of interest falling due after 5 April 2000; or
  –after 8 March 1999 and before 6 April 2000 under a scheme made for a tax avoidance purpose after 8 March 1999.
[8] Sub-s (4)(*d*) repealed by the Postal Services Act 2000 (Consequential Modifications No 1) Order, SI 2001/1149 art 3, Sch 2 with effect from 26 March 2001.
[9] In sub-s (4), paras (*e*) and (*p*) substituted, and para (*g*) repealed, and sub-s (4A) repealed, by the Financial Services and Markets Act 2000 (Consequential Amendments) (Taxes) Order, SI 2001/3629 arts 13, 23 with effect from 1 December 2001, immediately after the coming into force of the Financial Services and Markets Act 2000 ss 411, 432(1), Sch 20.

[376A The register of qualifying lenders

(1) The Board shall maintain, and publish in such manner as they consider appropriate, a register for the purposes of section 376(4).

[(1A) The following are entitled to be registered—

(*a*) a person who has permission under Part 4 of the Financial Services and Markets Act 2000—

(i) to accept deposits; or

(ii) to effect or carry out contracts of general insurance;

(*b*) a 90 per cent subsidiary of a person mentioned in—

(i) section 376(4)(*e*); or

(ii) paragraph (*a*) above;

(*c*) any other body whose activities and objects appear to the Board to qualify it for registration.][2]

(2) If the Board are satisfied that an applicant for registration is entitled to be registered, they may register the applicant generally or in relation to any description of loan specified in the register, with effect from such date as may be so specified; and a body which is so registered shall become a qualifying lender in accordance with the terms of its registration.

(3) The registration of any body may be varied by the Board—

(*a*) where it is general, by providing for it to be in relation to a specified description of loan, or

(*b*) where it is in relation to a specified description of loan, by removing or varying the reference to that description of loan, and where they do so, they shall give the body written notice of the variation and of the date from which it is to have effect.

(4) If it appears to the Board at any time that a body which is registered under this section would not be entitled to be registered if it applied for registration at that time, the Board may by written notice given to the body cancel its registration with effect from such date as may be specified in the notice.

(5) The date specified in a notice under subsection (3) or (4) above shall not be earlier than the end of the period of 30 days beginning with the date on which the notice is served.

(6) Any body which is aggrieved by the failure of the Board to register it under this section, or by the variation or cancellation of its registration, may, by notice given to the Board before the end of the period of 30 days beginning with the date on which the body is notified of the Board's decision, require the matter to be determined by the Special Commissioners; and the Special Commissioners shall thereupon hear and determine the matter in like manner as an appeal.][1]

Commentary—*Simon's Direct Tax Service* A3.433.
Revenue & other press releases—IR 16-7-98 (updated register of approved qualifying lenders published).
Definitions—"The Board", s 832(1); "notice", s 832(1); "qualifying lender", s 379; "Special Commissioners", TMA 1970 s 4.
Cross references—See FA 1994 s 142(3), (4) (qualifying lenders prescribed under s 376 before the date on which FA 1994 is passed are entitled to be registered under this section).
Amendments—[1] This section inserted by FA 1994 s 142(2).
[2] Sub-s (1A) inserted by the Financial Services and Markets Act 2000 (Consequential Amendments) (Taxes) Order, SI 2001/3629 arts 13, 24 with effect from 1 December 2001, immediately after the coming into force of the Financial Services and Markets Act 2000 ss 411, 432(1), Sch 20.

377 Variation of terms of repayment of certain loans

Amendments—This section repealed by FA 1999 s 38(8), Sch 4 paras 12, 18(5), Sch 20 Pt III(7) with effect for payments of interest made—
–after 5 April 2000;
–after 8 March 1999 and before 6 April 2000 in respect of interest falling due after 5 April 2000; or
–after 8 March 1999 and before 6 April 2000 under a scheme made for a tax avoidance purpose after 8 March 1999.

378 Supplementary regulations

(1), (2) . . .[1]

(3) The Board may by regulations make provision—

    (*a*) for the purposes of any provision of sections 369 to [376A][2] which relates to any matter or thing to be specified by or done in accordance with regulations;
    (*b*) for the application of those sections in relation to loan interest paid by personal representatives and trustees;
    (*c*) with respect to the furnishing of information by borrowers or lenders, including, in the case of lenders, the inspection of books, documents and other records on behalf of the Board;
    (*d*) for, and with respect to, appeals to the General Commissioners or the Special Commissioners against the refusal of the Board to issue a notice under section 374(1)(*b*) or the issue of a notice under section 375(6) or (7); and
    (*e*) generally for giving effect to sections 369 to [376A].[1]

(4) . . .[1]

Regulations—IT (Interest Relief) Regulations, SI 1982/1236. See also Sch 30, para 21 of this Act.
IT (Interest Relief) (Housing Associations) Regulations, SI 1988/1347. See also Sch 30, para 21 of this Act.
Definitions—"The Board", s 832(1); "qualifying lender", s 379; "regulations", s 379.
Amendments—[1] Sub-ss (1), (2), (4) repealed and word in sub-s (3) substituted by FA 1999 s 38(8), Sch 4 paras 13, 18(5), Sch 20 Pt III(7) with effect for payments of interest made—
–after 5 April 2000;
–after 8 March 1999 and before 6 April 2000 in respect of interest falling due after 5 April 2000; or
–after 8 March 1999 and before 6 April 2000 under a scheme made for a tax avoidance purpose after 8 March 1999.

379 Interpretation of sections 369 to 378

In sections 369 to 378—

    ["contracts of general insurance" means contracts which fall within Part I of Schedule 1 to the Financial Services and Markets Act 2000 (Regulated Activities) Order 2001 and "contracts of long-term insurance" means contracts which fall within Part II of that Schedule;][3]
    "prescribed", . . .[1], means prescribed by the Board;
    "qualifying borrower" has the meaning given by section 376(1) to (3);
    "qualifying lender" has the meaning given by section 376(4) . . .[2] ;
    "regulations", . . .[2] means regulations made by the Board under section 378;
    "relevant loan interest" has the meaning given by section 370(1);
    ["separated" means separated under an order of a court of competent jurisdiction or by deed of separation or in such circumstances that the separation is likely to be permanent.][2]

Commentary—*Simon's Direct Tax Service* A3.431–433.
Definition—"The Board", s 832(1).
Amendments—[1] Words in definition of "prescribed" repealed by FA 1994 Sch 26 Pt V(19).

[2] Words in definitions of "regulations and qualifying lender" repealed and definition of "separated" inserted by FA 1999 s 38(8), Sch 4 paras 14, 18(5), Sch 20 Pt III(7) with effect for payments of interest made—

–after 5 April 2000;

–after 8 March 1999 and before 6 April 2000 in respect of interest falling due after 5 April 2000; or

–after 8 March 1999 and before 6 April 2000 under a scheme made for a tax avoidance purpose after 8 March 1999.

[3] Definition of "contracts of general insurance" inserted by the Financial Services and Markets Act 2000 (Consequential Amendments) (Taxes) Order, SI 2001/3629 arts 13, 25 with effect from 1 December 2001, immediately after the coming into force of the Financial Services and Markets Act 2000 ss 411, 432(1), Sch 20.

PART X

LOSS RELIEF AND GROUP RELIEF

CHAPTER I
LOSS RELIEF: INCOME TAX

Statement of Practice C11—Revenue practice to accept informal claims to loss relief carried forward in relation to income tax under Schedule D Cases I, II, VI, subject to certain conditions as regards formulation of claims.

Revenue Interpretation RI 57—Bank failures: relief for losses incurred by depositors.

Revenue Internal Guidance—Inspector's manual IM 3360 (a claim may be withdrawn up to the time at which a decision on the claim is given; an attempted withdrawal within 30 days thereafter is treated as an appeal).

IM 3361 (a claim may be increased by way of a supplementary claim).

Cross references—See TA 1988 s 401 (relief under this Chapter for pre-trading expenditure).

[*Losses from Schedule A business or overseas property business*][1]

Amendments—[1] Substituted by FA 1998 Sch 5 para 26 with effect for 1998–99 and subsequent years of assessment for income tax purposes.

[379A Schedule A losses

(1) Subject to the following provisions of this section, where for any year of assessment any person sustains any loss in a Schedule A business carried on by him either solely or in partnership—

(a) the loss shall be carried forward to the following year of assessment and, to the extent that it does not exceed them, set against any [profits][3] of that business for the year to which it is carried forward; and

(b) where there are no [profits][3] for the following year or the [profits][3] for that year are exceeded by the amount of the loss, the loss or, as the case may be, the remainder of it shall be so carried forward to the next following year, and so on.

(2) Subsection (3) below shall apply where a loss is sustained in a Schedule A business for any year of assessment ("the year of the loss") and one or both of the following conditions is satisfied, that is to say—

(a) the amount of the ...[2] capital allowances treated as expenses of that business in computing that loss exceeds, by any amount ("the net capital allowances"), the amount of any charges under [the Capital Allowances Act][4] which are treated as receipts of that business in computing that loss;

(b) the Schedule A business has been carried on in relation to land that consists of or includes an agricultural estate to which allowable agricultural expenses deducted in computing that loss are attributable;

...[2]

(3) Where the person carrying on the Schedule A business in a case to which this subsection applies makes a claim, in relation to the year of the loss or the year following that year, for relief under this subsection in respect of the loss—

(a) relief from income tax may be given, for the year to which the claim relates, on an amount of that person's income for that year which is equal to the amount of relief available for that year in respect of the loss; and

(b) the loss which is to be or has been carried forward under subsection (1) above shall be treated as reduced (if necessary to nil) by an amount equal to the amount on which relief is given;

but a claim for relief under this subsection shall not be made after the end of twelve months from the 31st January next following the end of the year to which it relates and shall be accompanied by all such amendments as may be required by virtue of paragraph (b) above of any [return made by the claimant under section 8 or 8A][5] of the Management Act.

(4) Subject to subsection (5) below, the reference in subsection (3) above to the amount of the relief available for any year in respect of a loss is a reference to whichever is the smallest of the following amounts, that is to say—

(a) the amount of the relievable income for the year to which the claim relates;

(b) the loss sustained in the Schedule A business in the year of the loss; and

(c) the amount which, according to whether one or both of the conditions mentioned in subsection (2) above is satisfied in relation to the year of the loss, is equal—

(i) to the net capital allowances,
(ii) to the amount of the allowable agricultural expenses for the year of the loss, or
(iii) to the sum of the net capital allowances and the amount of those expenses.

(5) Where relief under subsection (3) above is given in respect of a loss in relation to either of the years in relation to which relief may be claimed in respect of that loss, relief shall not be available in respect of the same loss for the other year except, in a case where the relief already given is of an amount determined in accordance with subsection (4)(*a*) above, to the extent that the smaller of the amounts applicable by virtue of subsection (4)(*b*) and (*c*) above exceeds the amount of relief already given.

(6) For the purposes of subsection (4)(*a*) above the amount of relievable income for any year, in relation to any person, shall be equal to the amount of his income for that year—

(*a*) after effect has been given to subsection (1) above in relation to any amount carried forward to that year in respect of a loss sustained in any year before the year of the loss, and
(*b*) in the case of a claim under subsection (3) above in relation to the year of the loss, after effect has been given to any claim under that subsection in respect of a loss sustained in the preceding year.

(7) For the purposes of this section the loss sustained in any Schedule A business shall be computed in like manner as the [profits]³ arising or accruing from such a business are computed under the provisions of the Income Tax Acts applicable to Schedule A.

(8) In this section 'allowable agricultural expenses', in relation to an agricultural estate, means any disbursements or expenses attributable to the estate which are deductible in respect of maintenance, repairs, insurance or management of the estate and otherwise than in respect of the interest payable on any loan.

(9) For the purposes of this section the amount of any disbursements or expenses attributable to an agricultural estate shall be determined as if—

(*a*) disbursements and expenses were to be disregarded to the extent that they would not have been attributable to the estate if it did not include the parts of it used wholly for purposes other than purposes of husbandry, and
(*b*) disbursements and expenses in respect of parts of the estate used partly for purposes of husbandry and partly for other purposes were to be reduced to an extent corresponding to the extent to which those parts were used for other purposes.

(10) In this section—

"agricultural estate" means any land (including any houses or other buildings) which is managed as one estate and which consists of or includes any agricultural land; and
"agricultural land" means land, houses or other buildings in the United Kingdom occupied wholly or mainly for the purposes of husbandry.]¹

Commentary—*Simon's Direct Tax Service* **A4.410.**
Revenue Internal Guidance—Property Income Manual PIM4210 (no claim required for loss carry forward under sub-s (1)).
Revenue and other press releases—
Booklet IR150 paras 423–478 (explanation of the loss relief provisions).
Definitions—"Schedule A", s 15(1), "United Kingdom", s 832(1), "year of assessment", s 832(1).
Cross references—See TA 1988 s 26(2A) (excess expenses related to land managed as one estate to be disregarded in computing Schedule A losses).
TA 1988 s 27(3)(*b*) (relief available to trustees of a maintenance fund under sub-s (2)(*b*) above to be available to the owner of other part of estate instead where election made under s 27(2)).
FA 1995 s 41(8) (this section does not apply before the year 1998–99 the computation of income from overseas property and chargeable under Schedule D Case V).
FA 1995 Sch 6 para 19(2), (3) (interest which would have been available for carry-forward to 1995–96 under Part II or former s 355(4) may be treated as a loss brought forward under sub-s (1)).
Amendments—¹ Section, and preceding heading, inserted by FA 1995 s 39(4), Sch 6 para 19(1), with effect generally from the year 1995–96; note FA 1995 Sch 6 para 19(2)–(4). However, the section printed above does not apply in relation to certain sources of income which ceased during the year 1995–96: see FA 1995 s 39(5).
² Words omitted in sub-s (2) repealed by FA 1997 Sch 15 paras 2(1), 9(1), Sch 18 Pt VI(II) with effect for 1997–98 and subsequent years of assessment.
³ Word substituted in sub-ss (1)(*a*), (1)(*b*), (7) by FA 1998 Sch 7 para 1 with effect from 31 July 1998.
⁴ Words in sub-s (2)(*a*) substituted by CAA 2001 s 578, Sch 2 para 28 with effect for income tax purposes as respects allowances and charges falling to be made for chargeable periods ending after 5 April 2001.
⁵ In sub-s (3), words substituted for the words "self-assessment previously made by the claimant under section 9" by FA 2001 s 88, Sch 29 para 35(2) with effect from the passing of FA 2001 in relation to returns whether made before or after the passing of FA 2001, and whether relating to periods before or after the passing of FA 2001.

[379B Losses from overseas property business

The provisions of section 379A apply in relation to an overseas property business as they apply in relation to a Schedule A business.]¹

Commentary—*Simon's Direct Tax Service* **A4.410.**
Amendments—¹ This section inserted by FA 1998 Sch 5 para 27 with effect for 1998–99 and subsequent years of assessment.

TA 1988

Trade etc losses

380 Set-off against general income

[(1) Where in any year of assessment any person sustains a loss in any trade, profession, vocation or employment carried on by him either solely or in partnership, he may, by notice given within [twelve months from the 31st January next following][4] that year, make a claim for relief from income tax on—

(a) so much of his income for that year as is equal to the amount of the loss or, where it is less than that amount, the whole of that income; or

(b) so much of his income for the last preceding year as is equal to that amount or, where it is less than that amount, the whole of that income;

but relief shall not be given for the loss or the same part of the loss both under paragraph (a) and under paragraph (b) above.][2]

[(2) Any relief claimed under paragraph (a) of subsection (1) above in respect of any income shall be given in priority to any relief claimed in respect of that income under paragraph (b) of that subsection.][2]

(3) ...[3]

(4) ...[1]

Commentary—*Simon's Direct Tax Service* **E1.602, 603; E4.722.**
Concession A8—Loss relief for capital allowances unused on the cessation of a business.
A87—Revenue will by concession allow relief for the loss of the year to the normal accounting date in the tax year rather than calculating the loss on a strict basis, except broadly where relief has been claimed under s 381, or in the opening or closing years of a business, or where an election for the continuation basis of assessment has been made by a partnership under s 113(2).
A88—Revenue's calculation of cessation adjustment in the case of businesses commenced before 6 April 1994 which cease before 5 April 1997 where relief has been allowed under this section.
Revenue Interpretation RI 17—Order of priority for loss relief claims under sub-ss (1), (2) above.
RI 47—Claims for relief under this section and under FA 1991 s 72 (trading losses set against capital gains) may be made separately subject to certain conditions.
RI 57—Bank failures: relief for losses incurred by depositors.
RI 114—Clarification of the time limits for making claims under Concession A87.
R1 234—Guidance on making anticipated loss claims.
Revenue Internal Guidance—Inspector's manual IM 3351, 3420 (current year basis period *must* be used as from 1997/98 and, may be used concessionally for earlier years).
IM 3354–3355 (relief not given unless claim made: procedure set out).
IM 3357–3361 (late claims circumstances in which Board will accept claim).
IM 3365-3371 (explanation of the section with historical comments).
IM 3427, IM 3490–3494 (worked examples).
IM 4885 ("contrived" losses: circumstances in which cases will be referred to Special Investigations Section).
Simon's Tax Cases—s 380(1), *Butt v Haxby* [1983] STC 239*; *IRC v Matthew's Executors* [1984] STC 38*; *Reed v Young* [1985] STC 25*; *Wannell v Rothwell* [1996] STC 450*; *Privet v IRC* [2001] STC (SCD) 119.
Definitions—"Notice", s 832(1); "profits or gains", s 833(1); "Schedule D", s 18(1); "trade", s 832(1); "year of assessment", s 832(1).
Cross references—See TMA 1970 Sch 1B para 2 (method of giving effect to claim where loss carried back to an earlier year of assessment).
TA 1988 s 117(1) (restriction on loss relief where an individual carries on a trade as a limited partner).
TA 1988 s 382 (supplementary provisions).
TA 1988 s 384 (conditions to be satisfied for a claim for loss relief under this section).
TA 1988 s 385(1) (a loss not fully relieved under this section may be carried forward against subsequent profits).
TA 1988 s 391 (application of this section to losses incurred in a trade assessable under Schedule D Cases IV or V).
TA 1988 s 397(1) (restriction on loss relief in case of farming or market gardening).
TA 1988 s 399(2) (restriction on relief under this section in respect of losses from commodity etc dealings).
TA 1988 s 458(2) (how loss on capital redemption business is ascertained for the purposes of this section).
TA 1988 s 503 (for the purposes of this section, all lettings of furnished holiday accommodation treated as a single trade chargeable to tax under Schedule D Case I).
TA 1988 s 574(2) (relief for losses on disposal of shares in a qualifying trading company to have priority over relief under this section).
TA 1988 s 693 (severance for purposes of this section of a settlement which is partly for benefit of maintenance of historic and qualifying properties and partly for benefit of other purposes).
FA 1991 s 72 (relief for trading loss as cannot be set off against income and has not been taken into account for relief under this section);
Lloyd's Underwriters (Tax) (1992–93 to 1996–97) Regulations, SI 1995/352 Sch (extension of time limit in sub-s (1) above where a claim falls to be made by a Lloyd's member, spouse, or both);
Amendments—[1] Sub-s (4) repealed by FA 1988 Sch 14 Pt V with effect from 6 April 1993.
[2] Sub-ss (1), (2) substituted by FA 1994 s 209(1), (7) (as amended, and deemed always to have had such effect, by FA 1995 s 118 Sch 20 para 8), with effect in relation to trades etc set up and commenced after 5 April 1994, as respects losses sustained in the year 1994–95 and subsequent years of assessment; and in relation to trades etc set up and commenced before 6 April 1994, as respects losses sustained in the year 1996–97 and subsequent years of assessment.
[3] Sub-s (3) ceased to apply—

–in relation to a sole trader who commenced his trade on or after 6 April 1994, with effect from the year 1994–95
–in relation to a sole trader who commenced his trade before 6 April 1994, with effect from the year 1996–97
–in relation to a partnership commenced after 5 April 1994, with effect from the year 1994–95
–in other cases, with effect from the year 1997–98.
See FA 1994 ss 215(4), (5), 216(3)(b), 218 and Sch 26 Pt V(24) but see FA 1995 s 125(1) as regards partnerships controlled abroad.
[4] Words in sub-s (1) substituted by FA 1994 ss 209(1), 218(5) and Sch 20 para 8 with effect from the year 1996–97.

381 Further relief for individuals for losses in early years of trade

(1) Where an individual carrying on a trade sustains a loss in the trade in—

(a) the year of assessment in which it is first carried on by him; or

(b) any of the next three years of assessment;

he may, by notice given [on or before the first anniversary of the 31st January next following][3] the year of assessment in which the loss is sustained, make a claim for relief under this section.

(2) Subject to section 492 and this section, relief shall be given under subsection (1) above from income tax on [so much of the claimant's income as is equal to the amount of the loss or, where it is less than that amount, the whole of that income],[1] being income for the three years of assessment last preceding that in which the loss is sustained, taking income for an earlier year before income for a later year.

(3) Relief shall not be given for the same loss or the same portion of a loss both under subsection (1) above and under any other provision of thå Income Tax Acts.

(4) Relief shall not be given under subsection (1) above in respect of a loss sustained in any period unless ...[4] the trade was carried on throughout that period on a commercial basis and in such a way that profits in the trade (or, where the carrying on of the trade forms part of a larger undertaking, in the undertaking as a whole) could reasonably be expected to be realised in that period or within a reasonable time thereafter.

(5) Relief shall not be given under subsection (1) above in respect of a loss sustained by an individual in a trade if—

(a) at the time when it is first carried on by him he is married to and living with another individual who has previously carried on the trade; and
(b) the loss is sustained in a year of assessment later than the third year of assessment after that in which the trade was first carried on by the other individual.

(6) ...[2]

(7) This section applies, with the necessary modifications, in relation to a profession or vocation as it applies in relation to a trade.

Commentary—*Simon's Direct Tax Service* E1.621.
Revenue Interpretation R1 234—Guidance on making anticipated loss claims.
Revenue Internal Guidance—Inspector's manual IM 3500-3510 (explanation of the relief).
IM 3501 (relief not available where individual recommences a trade after a break).
IM 3507 (if trade commercial for part of year, then part of loss may be allowed).
Simon's Tax Cases—*Butt v Haxby* [1983] STC 239*; *Gascoine v Wharton* [1996] STC 1481; [1998] STC (SCD) 116*; *Gamble v Rowe* [1998] STC 1247*.
s 381(1), (4), *Walls v Livesey* [1995] STC (SCD) 12; *Brown v Richardson* [1997] STC (SCD) 233; *Wannell v Rothwell* [1996] STC 450*.
Definitions—''The Income Tax Acts'', s 831(1)(b); ''notice'', s 832(1); ''profits or gains'', s 833(1); ''trade'', s 832(1); ''year of assessment'', s 832(1).
Cross references—See IT (Entertainers and Sportsmen) Regulations, SI 1987/530 reg 15(4) (for the purposes of this section an entertainer's ''world-wide'' trade (as defined) and TA 1988 s 556 trade to be treated as the same trade, but subject to relief under this section available for a limited period);
TMA 1970 Sch 1B para 2 (method of giving effect to claim where loss carried back to an earlier year of assessment).
TA 1988 s 117(1) (restriction on loss relief where an individual carries on a trade as a limited partner).
TA 1988 s 382 (supplementary provisions).
TA 1988 s 383 (capital allowances to be treated as a loss to increase the amount of claim under this section, subject to restrictions under ss 117 and 384).
TA 1988 s 384 (conditions to be satisfied for a claim for loss relief under this section).
TA 1988 s 385 (carry forward of losses).
TA 1988 s 391 (application of this section to losses incurred in a trade assessable under Schedule D Cases IV or V).
TA 1988 s 399(2) (restriction on relief under this section in respect of losses from commodity etc dealings).
TA 1988 s 503 (for the purposes of this section, all lettings of furnished holiday accommodation treated as a single trade chargeable to tax under Schedule D Case I).
TA 1988 s 574(2) (relief for losses on disposal of shares in a qualifying trading company to have priority over relief under this section).
TA 1988 s 693 (severance for purposes of this section of a settlement which is partly for benefit of maintenance of historic and qualifying properties and partly for benefit of other purposes).
Lloyd's Underwriters (Tax) (1992–93 to 1996–97) Regulations, SI 1995/352 Sch (extension of time limit in sub-s (1) above where a claim falls to be made by a Lloyd's member, spouse, or both).
Amendments—[1] Words in sub-s (2) substituted by FA 1994 s 209(2), (7) (as amended, and deemed always to have had such effect, by FA 1995 s 118), with effect in relation to trades etc set up and commenced after 5 April 1994, as respects losses sustained in the year 1994–95 and subsequent years of assessment; and in relation to trades etc set up and commenced before 6 April 1994, as respects losses sustained in the year 1996–97 and subsequent years of assessment.
[2] Sub-s (6) ceased to apply—
–in relation to a sole trader who commenced his trade on or after 6 April 1994, with effect from the year 1994–95
–in relation to a sole trader who commenced his trade before 6 April 1994, with effect from the year 1996–97
–in relation to a partnership commenced after 5 April 1994, with effect from the year 1994–95
–in other cases, with effect from the year 1997–98.
See FA 1994 ss 215(4), (5), 216(3)(c), 218 and Sch 26 Pt V(24), but see FA 1995 s 125(1) as regards partnerships controlled abroad.
[3] Words in sub-s (1) substituted by FA 1996 Sch 21 para 10 with effect from the year 1996–97.
[4] Words omitted from sub-s (4) repealed by FA 1996 Sch 20 para 24 Sch 41 Pt V(10) with effect from the year 1996–97.

382 Provisions supplementary to sections 380 and 381

(1), (2) ...[1]

[(3) Subject to subsection (4) below, for the purposes of sections 380 and 381, the amount of a loss sustained in a trade, profession or vocation shall be computed in like manner and in respect of the same period as the [profits][3] arising or accruing from the trade, profession or vocation are computed under the provisions of the Income Tax Acts applicable to Case I or II of Schedule D.][2]

[(4) An amount of a loss which, apart from this subsection, would fall to be included in the computations for two successive years of assessment shall not be included in the computation for the second of those years.][2]

Commentary—*Simon's Direct Tax Service* E1.602.
Simon's Tax Cases—*Butt v Haxby* [1983] STC 239*.
s 382(4), *Gascoine v Wharton* [1996] STC 1481.
Definitions—"The Income Tax Acts", s 831(1)(b); "occupation of woodlands", s 6(4); "Schedule D", s 18(1); "trade", s 832(1); "year of assessment", s 832(1).
Cross references—See TA 1988 s 391 (application of this section to losses incurred in a trade assessable under Schedule D Cases IV or V).
TA 1988 s 503 (for the purposes of this section, all lettings of furnished holiday accommodation treated as a single trade chargeable to tax under Schedule D Case I).
TA 1988 s 693 (severance for purposes of this section of a settlement which is partly for benefit of maintenance of historic and qualifying properties and partly for benefit of other purposes).
FA 1991 s 72(8) (further relief for trading loss).
Amendments—[1] Sub-ss (1), (2) repealed by FA 1988 Sch 14 Pt VIII in relation to loss relief given for the year 1990–91 and for subsequent years.
[2] Sub-ss (3), (4) substituted by FA 1994 s 209(3), (7) (as amended and deemed always to have had effect by FA 1995 s 118) in relation to trades etc set up and commenced after 5 April 1994, as respects losses sustained in the year 1994–95 and subsequent years of assessment; and in relation to trades etc set up and commenced before 6 April 1994, as respects losses sustained in the year 1997–98 and subsequent years of assessment.
[3] Word in sub-s (3) substituted by FA 1998 Sch 7 para 1 with effect from 31 July 1998.

383 Extension of right of set-off to capital allowances

Commentary—*Simon's Direct Tax Service* E1.605.
Amendments—This section ceased to apply with effect from the year 1994–95 as respects trades, etc set up commenced after 5 April 1994 and from the year 1997–98 as respects trades, etc set up commenced before 6 April 1994; see FA 1994 ss 211(2), 214(1)(b), 218 and Sch 26 Pt V(24).

384 Restrictions on right of set-off

(1) Subject to subsection (2) below, a loss ...[1] shall not be available for relief under section 380 unless ...[4], for the year of assessment in which the loss is claimed to have been sustained, the trade was being carried on on a commercial basis and with a view to the realisation of profits in the trade or, where the carrying on of the trade formed part of a larger undertaking, in the undertaking as a whole.

(2) Subsection (1) above shall not apply—

(a) to a loss made ...[1] by any person in the exercise of functions conferred by or under any enactment (including an enactment contained in a local or private Act); ...[1]

(b) ...[1]

(3) Where during a year of assessment there is a change in the manner in which a trade is being carried on, it shall be treated for the purposes of this section as having been carried on throughout the year in the way in which it was being carried on by the end of the year.

(4) Subject to subsection (5) below, where a trade is (or falls to be treated as being) carried on for a part only of a year of assessment by reason of its being (or falling to be treated as being) set up and commenced, or discontinued, or both, in that year, subsections (1) to (3) above shall have effect in relation to the trade as regards that part of that year as if any reference to the manner of carrying on the trade for or by the end of that year were a reference to the manner of carrying it on for or by the end of that part of that year.

(5) ...[3]

(6) [There shall be disregarded for the purposes of sections 380 and 381 so much of any loss as derives from any allowances][2] made to an individual [under Part 2 of the Capital Allowances Act in respect of expenditure incurred on the provision of plant or machinery][6] for leasing in the course of a trade unless—

(a) the trade is carried on by him (alone or in partnership) for a continuous period of at least six months in, or beginning or ending in, [the year of assessment in which the loss was sustained][3]; and

(b) he devotes substantially the whole of his time to carrying it on (alone or in partnership) throughout that year or if it is set up or permanently discontinued (or both) in that year, for a continuous period of at least six months beginning or ending in that year.

(7) Subsection (6) above shall apply also to expenditure incurred by an individual on the provision for the purposes of a trade carried on by him (alone or in partnership) of an asset which is not to be leased if payments in the nature of royalties or licence fees are to accrue from rights granted by him in connection with that asset.

(8) Where relief has been given in a case to which subsection (6) above applies it shall be withdrawn by the making of an assessment under Case VI of Schedule D.

[(9) Where at any time a trade is carried on so as to afford a reasonable expectation of profit, it shall be treated for the purposes of subsection (1) above as being carried on at that time with a view to the realisation of profits.][5]

(10) Subsections (1) to (5) and (9) above—

(*a*) apply to professions and vocations as they apply to trades, with references to a commercial basis construed accordingly; and

(*b*) have effect without prejudice to section 397;

...[6]

[(11) Expressions used in subsections (6) to (8) and in Part 2 of the Capital Allowances Act have same meaning in those subsections as in that Part; and those subsections are without prejudice to section 384A.][6]

Commentary—*Simon's Direct Tax Service* **E1.606.**
Concession B5—A non-commercial farm owner precluded by this section from claiming loss relief may claim the relief as allowed by s 33 of this Act for maintenance, repairs and insurance of his agricultural land.
Revenue Internal Guidance—Inspector's manual IM 2238 (farming losses: test of commerciality).
IM 3375-3379 (the Revenue are looking for extreme cases, but the onus is on the claimant to show commerciality).
Simon's Tax Cases—s 384(1), (2), (9), *Walls v Livesey* [1995] STC (SCD) 12; *Wannell v Rothwell* [1996] STC 450*; *Delian Enterprises (a partnership) v Ellis* [1999] STC (SCD) 103.
Definitions—"The 1990 Act", s 831(3); "Act", s 832(1); "capital allowance", s 832(1); "Schedule D", s 18(1); "trade", s 832(1); "year of assessment", s 832(1).
Cross references—See TA 1988 s 391 (application of this section to losses incurred in a trade chargeable to tax under Schedule D Cases IV or V).
TA 1988 s 503 (for the purposes of this section, all lettings of furnished holiday accommodation treated as a single trade chargeable to tax under Schedule D Case I).
TA 1988 s 503(1A) (this section modified in its application to furnished holiday accommodation).
TA 1988 s 693 (severance for purposes of this section of a settlement which is partly for benefit of maintenance of historic and qualifying properties and partly for benefit of other purposes).
Amendments—[1] Sub-ss (1), (2)(*a*)(*b*) words omitted repealed by FA 1994 ss 211(2), 214(1)(*c*), 258 and Sch 26 Pt V(24) with effect from the year 1994–95 as respects trades etc commenced after 5 April 1994 and from the year 1997–98 as respects trades commenced before 5 April 1994.
[2] Words in sub-s (6) substituted by FA 1994 s 214(2) with effect from the year 1994–95 as respects trades etc commenced after 5 April 1994 and with effect from the year 1997–98 as respects trades etc commenced before 6 April 1994.
[3] Sub-s (5) ceased to apply in relation to partnerships commenced after 5 April 1994 with effect from the year 1994–95 and in relation to partnerships commenced before 6 April 1994 with effect from the year 1997–98; see FA 1994 ss 215(4), (5), 216(3)(*d*), 218 and Sch 26 Pt V(24), but see FA 1995 s 125(1) as regards partnerships controlled abroad.
[4] Words omitted from sub-s (1) repealed by FA 1996 Sch 20 para 25(1), Sch 41 Pt V(10) with effect from the year 1996–97.
[5] Sub-s (9) substituted by FA 1996 Sch 20 para 25(2) with effect from the year 1996–97.
[6] Words in sub-s (6) substituted, words in sub-s (10) repealed, and sub-s (11) added by CAA 2001 ss 578, 580, Sch 2 para 29, Sch 4 with effect for income tax purposes as respects allowances and charges falling to be made for chargeable periods ending after 5 April 2001.

[384A Restriction of set-off of allowances against general income

(1) Relief shall not be given to an individual under sections 380 and 381 by reference to a first-year allowance under Part 2 of the Capital Allowances Act (plant and machinery allowances) in the circumstances specified in subsection (2) or (4) below.

(2) The circumstances are that the allowance is in respect of expenditure incurred on the provision of plant or machinery for leasing in the course of a qualifying activity and—

(*a*) at the time when the expenditure was incurred, the qualifying activity was carried on by the individual in question in partnership with a company (with or without other partners), or

(*b*) a scheme has been effected or arrangements have been made (whether before or after that time) with a view to the qualifying activity being so carried on by that individual.

(3) For the purposes of subsection (2) above letting a ship on charter shall be regarded as leasing it if, apart from this subsection, it would not be so regarded.

(4) The circumstances are that the allowance is made in connection with—

(*a*) a qualifying activity which at the time when the expenditure was incurred was carried on by the individual in partnership or which has subsequently been carried on by him in partnership or transferred to a person who was connected with him, or

(*b*) an asset which after that time has been transferred by the individual to a person who was connected with him or, at a price lower than its market value, to any other person,

and the condition in subsection (5) below is met.

(5) The condition is that a scheme has been effected or arrangements have been made (whether before or after the time referred to in subsection (4) above) such that the sole or main benefit that might be expected to accrue to the individual from the transaction under which the expenditure was incurred was the obtaining of a reduction in tax liability by means of relief under sections 380 and 381.

(6) Where relief has been given in circumstances in which subsection (1) applies it shall be withdrawn by the making of an assessment under Case VI of Schedule D.

(7) Section 839 (how to tell whether persons are connected) applies for the purposes of subsection (4) above.

(8) Expressions used in this section and in Part 2 of the Capital Allowances Act have the same meaning as in that Part.][1]

Amendments—[1] Inserted by CAA 2001 s 578, Sch 2 para 30 with effect for income tax purposes as respects allowances and charges falling to be made for chargeable periods ending after 5 April 2001.

385 Carry-forward against subsequent profits

[(1) Where a person has, in any trade, profession or vocation carried on by him either alone or in partnership, sustained a loss (to be computed as mentioned in subsections (3) and (4) of section 382) in respect of which relief has not been wholly given either under section 380 or any provision of the Income Tax Acts—

    (*a*) he may make a claim requiring that any part of the loss for which relief has not been so given shall be set off for the purposes of income tax against the income of the trade, profession or vocation for subsequent years of assessment; and

    (*b*) where he makes such a claim, the income from the trade, profession or vocation in any subsequent year of assessment shall be treated as reduced by that part of the loss, or by so much of that part as cannot, on that claim, be relieved against such income of an earlier year of assessment.][2]

(2) ...[3]

(3) ...[4]

(4) Where in any year of assessment relief cannot be given, or cannot be wholly given, in respect of a loss carried forward under this section because the amount of the [profits][5] of the trade assessed under Case I of Schedule D for that year is insufficient, any interest or dividends being interest or dividends—

    (*a*) on investments arising in that year, and

    (*b*) which would fall to be taken into account as trading receipts in computing the [profits][5] of the trade for the purposes of assessment under that Case but for the fact that they have been subjected to tax under other provisions of the Income Tax Acts,

shall be treated for the purposes of the application of this section as if they were [profits][5] on which the person carrying on the trade was assessed under that Case in respect of that trade for that year of assessment, and relief shall be given accordingly by repayment or otherwise.

(5) ...[3]

(6) ...[1]

(7) In so far as relief in respect of any loss has been given to any person under this section, that person shall not be entitled to claim relief in respect of that loss under any other provision of the Income Tax Acts.

(8) ...[4]

Commentary—*Simon's Direct Tax Service* E1.610; E5.333.
Concession B19—Unused trading losses which cannot be carried forward under this section may be set off against a balancing charge arising when a trader sells an industrial building after the trade has ceased.
Revenue Internal Guidance—Inspector's manual IM 3354–5 (relief not given unless claim made, procedure set out).
IM 3357–3361 (late claims circumstances in which Board will accept claim).
IM 3528 (no carry forward where business passes to surviving spouse).
IM 3532–3536 (carry forward restricted where other reliefs given: worked examples).
IM 3541 (where estimated assessment has become final and conclusive, a claim may still be made to set-off losses of basis period).
IM 3545 (under existing system, two claims required; one to establish the loss, and the other to set if off in the required year).
Simon's Tax Cases—*Richardson v Jenkins* [1995] STC 95.
s 385(1)(2), *Reed v Young* [1985] STC 25*.
Definitions—"Capital allowance", s 832(1); "the Income Tax Acts", s 831(1)(*b*); "interest", s 832(1); "Schedule D", s 18(1); "total income", s 835(1); "trade", s 832(1); "year of assessment", s 832(1).
Cross references—See TA 1988 s 110A(1) (deemed discontinuance on change of residence by an individual carrying on a trade partly in and partly outside the UK does not prevent the carry-forward of losses under this section).
TA 1988 s 386 (where an individual or partnership trade is transferred to a company, unrelieved losses of the trade may be set-off against the company's income by a claim under this section).
TA 1988 s 390 (interest not fully relieved under s 353 to be treated as a loss carried forward under this section).
TA 1988 s 391 (application of this section to losses incurred in a trade chargeable to tax under Schedule D Cases IV or V).
TA 1988 s 458(2) (how loss to be carried forward under sub-s (1) above is ascertained for determining relief under sub-s (4) above in the case of capital redemption business).
TA 1988 s 492(4) (relief in accordance with this section for ring fence losses).
TA 1988 s 503 (for the purposes of this section, all lettings of furnished holiday accommodation treated as a single trade chargeable to tax under Schedule D Case I).
TA 1988 s 693 (severance for purposes of this section of a settlement which is partly for benefit of maintenance of historic and qualifying properties and partly for benefit of other purposes).
IT (Entertainers and Sportsmen) Regulations, SI 1987/530 reg 15(2) (for the purposes of this section an entertainer's "worldwide" trade (as defined) and TA 1988 s 556 trade to be treated as the same trade).
FA 1991 s 72(8) (references in sub-s (1) above to s 380 to include references to relief for losses against capital gains under FA 1991 s 72).
FA 1998 s 56(4) (deemed discontinuance of trade at the end of 1997–98 for construction workers supplied by agencies but old and new trade treated as the same for the purposes of this section).
Amendments—[1] Sub-s (6) repealed by FA 1988 Sch 14 Pt V with effect from 6 April 1993.
[2] Sub-s (1) substituted by FA 1994 s 209(4), (7) (as amended, and deemed always to have had effect by FA 1995 s 118): in relation to trades etc set up and commenced after 5 April 1994, as respects losses sustained in the year 1994–95 and subsequent years of assessment; and in relation to trades etc set up and commenced before 6 April 1994, as respects losses sustained in the year 1997–98 and subsequent years of assessment.
[3] Sub-ss (2), (5) ceased to have effect in relation to partnerships whose trades, professions or businesses are set up and commenced after 5 April 1994 with effect from the year 1994–95 and in relation to such partnerships commenced before 6 April 1994 with effect from the year 1997–98; see FA 1994 ss 215(4), (5), 216(3)(*e*), 218 and Sch 26 Pt V(24), but see FA 1995 s 125(1) as regards partnerships controlled abroad.
[4] Sub-ss (3), (8) ceased to have effect: in relation to trades etc set up and commenced after 5 April 1994, as respects losses sustained in the year 1994–95 and subsequent years of assessment; and in relation to trades etc set up and commenced before

6 April 1994, as respects losses sustained in the year 1997–98 and subsequent years of assessment: see FA 1994 s 209(5), (7), Sch 26 Pt V(24) (as amended, and deemed always to have had such effect, by FA 1995 s 118).
[5] Word in sub-s (4) substituted by FA 1998 Sch 7 para 1 with effect from 31 July 1998.

386 Carry-forward where business transferred to a company

(1) Where—

(a) a business carried on by any individual, or any individuals in partnership, has been transferred to a company in consideration solely or mainly of the allotment of shares in the company to that individual or those individuals; and

(b) in the case of any individual to whom, or to whose nominee or nominees, shares have been so allotted, his total income for any year of assessment throughout which he is the beneficial owner of the shares, and throughout which the company carries on the business, includes any income derived by him from the company, whether by way of dividends on those shares or otherwise;

then, subject to subsection (2) below, section 385 (except subsection (5)) shall apply as if the income so derived were [profits][2] on which that individual was assessed under Schedule D in respect of that business for that year.

(2) Where under section 385 as applied by subsection (1) above a loss falls to be deducted from or set off against any income for any year of assessment, the deduction or set-off shall be made in the first place against that part, if any, of the income in respect of which the individual has been, or is liable to be, assessed to tax for that year.

(3) This section, in its application to the year of assessment in which a business is transferred, shall have effect as if, for the reference in subsection (1)(b) to the year of assessment throughout which the individual is the beneficial owner of the shares and the business is carried on by the company, there were substituted a reference to the period from the date of the transfer to the following 5th April.

(4) ...[1]

Commentary—*Simon's Direct Tax Service* E1.613.
Revenue Internal Guidance—Inspector's manual IM 3354–5 (relief not given unless claim made, procedure set out).
IM 3357–3361 (late claims circumstances in which Board will accept claim).
IM 3551 (relief available where consideration expressed in cash, but whole amount subscribed for shares).
Definitions—"Company", s 832(1), (2); "Schedule D", s 18(1); "total income", s 835(1); "year of assessment", s 832(1).
Cross references—See TA 1988 s 387 (treatment of certain amounts taxed under s 350 as losses for the purposes of this section).
TA 1988 s 391 (application of this section to losses incurred in a trade chargeable to tax under Schedule D Cases IV or V).
TA 1988 s 503 (for the purposes of this section, all lettings of furnished holiday accommodation treated as a single trade chargeable to tax under Schedule D Case I).
TA 1988 s 693 (severance for purposes of this section of a settlement which is partly for benefit of maintenance of historic and qualifying properties and partly for benefit of other purposes).
Amendments—[1] Sub-s (4) ceased to have effect in relation to partnerships whose trades, professions or businesses are set up and commenced after 5 April 1994 with effect from the year 1994–95 and in relation to such partnerships commenced before 6 April 1994 with effect from the year 1997–98; see FA 1994 ss 215(4), (5), 216(3)(f), 218 and Sch 26 Pt V(24), but see FA 1995 s 125(1) as regards partnerships controlled abroad.
[2] Word in sub-s (1) substituted by FA 1998 Sch 7 para 1 with effect from 31 July 1998.

387 Carry-forward as losses of amounts taxed under section 350

(1) Subject to the provisions of this section, where under section 350 a person has been assessed to income tax in respect of a payment made wholly and exclusively for the purposes of a trade, profession or vocation, the amount on which tax has been paid under that assessment shall be treated for the purposes of sections 385 and 386 as though it were a loss sustained in that trade, profession or vocation, and relief in respect of the loss shall be allowed accordingly.

(2) Relief shall not be allowed by virtue of this section in respect of any payment, or part of a payment, which is not ultimately borne by the person assessed, or which is charged to capital.

(3) This section shall not apply—

(a) to any payment falling within section 349(2);
(b) to any payment falling within section 349 by virtue of section 43(1);
(c) ...[2]
(d) to any capital sum paid in respect of any patent rights assessed under section 349(1) by virtue of section 524;
(e) to any payment of, or on account of, copyright royalties to which section 536 applies [or royalties in respect of a right in a design to which section 537B applies][1]; ...[3]
(f) ...[3]

Commentary—*Simon's Direct Tax Service* A3.407; E1.615.
Revenue Internal Guidance—Inspector's manual IM 3554 (where tax is assessed at a reduced rate under a double taxation agreement, relief is due as though tax had been charged at the basic rate).
Simon's Tax Cases—*Scorer v Olin Energy Systems Ltd* [1982] STC 800*.
Definition—"Trade", s 832(1).
Cross references—See TA 1988 s 503 (for the purposes of this section, all lettings of furnished holiday accommodation treated as a single trade).
TA 1988 s 693 (severance for purposes of this section of a settlement which is partly for benefit of maintenance of historic and qualifying properties and partly for benefit of other purposes).
Amendments—[1] Words in sub-s (3)(e) inserted by the Copyright, Designs and Patents Act 1988 Sch 7 para 36(4).
[2] Sub-s (3)(c) repealed by FA 1997 Sch 18 Pt VI(2) with effect in relation to payments made after 5 April 1997.

[3] Sub-s (3)(*f*) and word "or" preceding it repealed by FA 1997 Sch 18 Pt VI(10) with effect in relation to payments made on or after 1 July 1997 by virtue of the Finance Act 1997, Schedule 10, (Appointed Day) Order, SI 1997/991.

388 Carry-back of terminal losses

(1) Where a trade, profession or vocation is permanently discontinued in the year 1988–89 or any later year, and any person then carrying it on, either alone or in partnership, has sustained therein a loss to which this section applies ("a terminal loss"), that person may, subject to the provisions of this section and of section 389, make a claim requiring that the amount of the terminal loss shall, as far as may be, be deducted from or set off against the amount of [profits][3] on which he has been charged to income tax under Schedule D in respect of the trade, profession or vocation for [the year of assessment in which the discontinuance occurs and the three years last preceding it][1]; and there shall be made all such reductions of assessments or repayments of tax as may be necessary to give effect to the claim.

(2) Relief shall not be given in respect of the same matter both under this section and under some other provision of the Income Tax Acts.

(3) Any relief under this section shall be given as far as possible from the assessment for a later rather than an earlier year.

(4) Where—

  (*a*) a claim under this section is made in respect of a terminal loss sustained in a trade, and
  (*b*) relief cannot be given, or cannot be wholly given, against the [profits][3] of the trade charged to income tax under Schedule D for any year because the amount of those [profits][3] is insufficient,

any relevant interest or dividends arising in that year shall be treated for the purposes of the application of this section as if they were [profits][3] on which the person carrying on the trade was assessed under Case I of Schedule D in respect of that trade for that year of assessment, and relief shall be given accordingly by repayment or otherwise.

For the purposes of this subsection "any relevant interest or dividends" means interest or dividends which would fall to be taken into account as trading receipts in computing the [profits][3] of the trade for the purpose of assessment under Case I of Schedule D but for the fact that they have been subjected to tax under other provisions of the Income Tax Acts.

(5) The [profits][3] on which a person or partnership has been charged to income tax for any year of assessment shall be treated for the purposes of any relief under this section from the assessment for that year as reduced by the amount of those [profits][3] applied in making any payment from which income tax was deducted, but was not accounted for because the payment was made out of profits or gains brought into charge to income tax; and the like reduction shall be made in the amount of the terminal loss for which relief may be given under this section from the assessments for earlier years unless the payment was one which, if not made out of profits or gains brought into charge to income tax—

  (*a*) could have been assessed to income tax under section 350, and
  (*b*) if so assessed, could have been treated as a loss by virtue of section 387.

(6) The question whether a person has sustained any and, if so, what terminal loss in a trade, profession or vocation shall be determined for the purposes of this section by taking the amounts (if any) of the following, in so far as they have not otherwise been taken into account so as to reduce or relieve any charge to tax—

  (*a*) the loss sustained by him in the trade, profession or vocation in the year of assessment in which it is permanently discontinued;
  (*b*) ...[2]
  (*c*) the loss sustained by him in the trade, profession or vocation in the part of the preceding year of assessment beginning 12 months before the discontinuance; ...[2]
  (*d*) ...[2]

(7) ...[2] for the purposes of paragraphs (*a*) and (*c*) of that subsection the amount of a loss shall, subject to the provisions of this section, be computed in the same way as [profits][3] under the provisions of the Income Tax Acts applicable to Cases I and II of Schedule D.

Commentary—*Simon's Direct Tax Service* E1.622.
Note—The words "that subsection" in sub-s (7) refer to sub-s (6).
Concession A8—Capital allowances unused on the termination of a business: concessionary relief where relief under this section is not available.
Revenue Internal Guidance—Inspector's manual IM 3354–5 (relief not given unless claim made procedure set out).
IM 3357–3361 (late claims: circumstances in which Board will accept claim).
IM 3580-3593 (explanation of the relief).
Definitions—"The year 1988–89", s 832(1); "capital allowance", s 832(1); "the Income Tax Acts", s 831(1)(*b*); "interest", s 832(1); "Schedule D", s 18(1); "total income", s 835(1); "trade", s 832(1); "year of assessment", s 832(1).
Cross references—See TMA 1970 Sch 1B para 2 (method of giving effect to claim where loss carried back to an earlier year of assessment).
TA 1988 s 383 (treatment of capital allowances of partnership in year of permanent discontinuance for the purposes of claims under this section).
TA 1988 s 389(1) (application of ss 387,458 and 474 for the purposes of this section).
TA 1988 s 389(3), (4) (adaptation of this section in relation to a claim under it where a trade etc has been carried on in partnership for three years prior to its discontinuance or deemed discontinuance).
TA 1988 s 390 (interest not fully relieved under s 353 to be treated for the purposes of this section as a loss sustained at the date of payment).

TA 1988 s 391 (application of this section to losses incurred in a trade assessable to tax under Schedule D Cases IV or V).

TA 1988 s 503 (for the purposes of this section, all lettings of furnished holiday accommodation treated as a single trade chargeable to tax under Schedule D Case I).

IT (Entertainers and Sportsmen) Regulations, SI 1987/530 reg 15(3) (circumstances in which an entertainer may obtain relief for losses for which relief under this section is not available);

Lloyd's Underwriters (Tax) Regulations, SI 1995/351 reg 14 (cessation of underwriting business).

Amendments—[1] Words in sub-s (1) substituted by FA 1994 s 209(6), (7) (as amended, and deemed always to have had such effect, by FA 1995 s 118), with effect: in relation to trades etc set up and commenced after 5 April 1994, as respects losses sustained in the year 1994–95 and subsequent years of assessment; and in relation to trades etc set up and commenced before 6 April 1994, as respects losses sustained in the year 1996–97 and subsequent years of assessment.

[2] Sub-ss (6), (7) words repealed by FA 1994 ss 211(2), 214(1)(*d*) and Sch 26 Pt V(24) with effect from the year 1994–95 as respects trades etc commenced after 5 April 1994 and from 1997–98 as respects trades commenced before 6 April 1994.

[3] Word in sub-ss (1), (4), (5), (7) substituted by FA 1998 Sch 7 para 1 with effect from 31 July 1998.

389 Supplementary provisions relating to carry-back of terminal losses

(1) Sections 387, 458 and 474 shall apply to the computation of losses, or of profit or loss, for any purpose of this section or section 388 as they apply to any such computation for the corresponding purposes of section 385.

(2) Where on the permanent discontinuance of a trade which consists of or includes the working of a mine, oil well or other source of mineral deposits within the meaning of [Part 5 of the Capital Allowances Act][3], a claim for relief is made both under section 388 above and [section 355 of that Act][3] (carry-back of balancing allowances), the balancing allowance in respect of which the claim is made under [section 355][3] shall be left out of account for the purposes of section 388(6), but relief under section 388 shall be given in priority to relief under [section 355][3].

(3) ...[2]

[(4) For the purposes of this section and section 388 a trade, profession or vocation shall be treated as discontinued, and a new one as set up and commenced, when it is so treated for the purposes of section 111 or 113.][2]

(5)–(7) ...[2]

(8) ...[1]

Commentary—*Simon's Direct Tax Service* **E1.622.**
Revenue Internal Guidance—Inspector's manual IM 3582 (sub-s (1): as regards application of s 387, any assessment under s 350 for penultimate year is apportioned on a time basis).
Definitions—"The 1990 Act", s 831(3); "occupation of woodlands", s 6(4); "profits or gains", s 833(1); "Schedule D", s 18(1); "total income", s 835(1); "trade", s 832(1); "year of assessment", s 832(1).
Cross references—See TA 1988 s 390 (interest not fully relieved under s 353 to be treated for the purposes of this section as a loss sustained at the date of payment).
TA 1988 s 391 (application of this section to losses incurred in a trade assessable to tax under Schedule D Cases IV or V).
TA 1988 s 503 (for the purposes of this section, all lettings of furnished holiday accommodation treated as a single trade chargeable to tax under Schedule D Case I).
FA 1995 s 125(1) (partnerships controlled abroad).
Amendments—[1] Sub-s (8) repealed by FA 1988 Sch 14 Pt V with effect from 6 April 1993.
[2] Sub-ss (3), (5)–(7) repealed and sub-s (4) substituted by FA 1994 ss 211(2), 214(1)(*e*), 215(4), (5), 216(3)(*g*), (4), 218, Sch 26 Pt V(24) for partnerships whose trades, professions or businesses are set up and commenced after 5 April 1994 with effect from the year 1994–95 and for such partnerships commenced before 6 April 1994 with effect from the year 1997–98.
[3] Words in sub-s (2) substituted by CAA 2001 s 578, Sch 2 para 31 with effect for income tax purposes as respects allowances and charges falling to be made for chargeable periods ending after 5 April 2001.

390 Treatment of interest as a loss for purposes of carry-forward and carry-back

Where—

(*a*) a payment of interest eligible for relief under section 353 is money wholly and exclusively laid out or expended for the purposes of a trade, profession or vocation the profits of which are chargeable to tax under Case I or II of Schedule D, and

(*b*) full effect cannot be given to such relief in respect of the payment by reason of a want or deficiency of income of the year of assessment in which the payment is made,

the amount unallowed may be carried forward to succeeding years of assessment as if it were a loss carried forward under section 385, or may be treated for the purposes of sections 388 and 389 as a loss sustained at the date of payment.

Commentary—*Simon's Direct Tax Service* **E1.622.**
Definitions—"Interest", s 832(1); "Schedule D", s 18(1); "trade", s 832(1); "year of assessment", s 832(1).
Cross references—See TA 1988 s 503 (for the purposes of this section, all lettings of furnished holiday accommodation treated as a single trade chargeable to tax under Schedule D Case I).

391 Losses from trade etc carried on abroad

(1) Subject to the following provisions of this section, sections 380 to 386 and 388 and 389, so far as applicable, shall apply in relation to a loss incurred by any person in the carrying on of a trade, profession or vocation chargeable in accordance with section 65(3) as they apply to a loss incurred in a trade, profession or vocation chargeable to tax under Case I or II of Schedule D.

(2) Relief shall not be given by virtue of subsection (1) above except on income falling within section 65(2) or (3), 192(2), (3) or (4) or 196.

Commentary—*Simon's Direct Tax Service* **E1.330, 625.**
Definitions—"Schedule D", s 18(1); "trade", s 832(1).
Cross references—See TA 1988 s 68(4) (limitation on relief on loss from trade carried on in the Republic of Ireland).

Case VI losses

Statement of Practice SP C11—Revenue practice to accept informal claims to loss relief under Schedule D Case VI, subject to certain conditions as regards formulation of claims.

392 Case VI losses

(1) Where in any year of assessment a person sustains a loss in any transaction, whether he was engaged therein solely or in partnership, being a transaction of such a nature that, if any profits had arisen therefrom, he would have been liable to be assessed to income tax in respect thereof under Case VI of Schedule D, he may make a claim requiring—

(a) that the amount of the loss sustained by him shall, as far as may be, be deducted from or set off against the amount of any profits or gains arising from any transaction in respect of which he is assessed for that year under that Case, and

(b) that any portion of the loss for which relief is not so given shall, as far as may be, be carried forward and deducted from or set off against the amount of any profits or gains arising from any transaction in respect of which he is assessed to income tax under that Case for any subsequent year of assessment.

(2) In the application of this section to a loss sustained by a partner in a partnership, "the amount of any profits or gains arising from any transaction in respect of which he is assessed" shall be taken to mean in respect of any year such portion of the amount on which the partnership is assessed under Case VI of Schedule D in respect of any transaction as falls to be taken into account in computing his total income for that year.

(3) Any relief under this section by way of the carrying forward of the loss shall be given as far as possible from the first subsequent assessment in respect of any profits or gains arising from any transaction in respect of which he is assessed under Case VI of Schedule D for any year, and, so far as it cannot be so given, then from the next such assessment, and so on.

(4) This section does not apply to any loss sustained in a transaction falling within section 34, 35 or 36.

(5) So far as a claim under this section concerns the amount of the loss for any year of assessment, it must be made [on or before the fifth anniversary of the 31st January next following][1] the year of assessment in question; but the question whether any and if so how much relief on that amount should be given under this section against tax for any year of assessment may be the subject of a separate claim made [on or before the fifth anniversary of the 31st January next following][1] that year of assessment.

Commentary—*Simon's Direct Tax Service* E1.626.
Definitions—"Profits or gains", s 833(1); "Schedule D", s 18(1); "total income", s 835(1); "year of assessment", s 832(1).
Cross references—See TA 1988 s 398 (circumstances in which relief under this section is available against interest on deposits).
Amendments—[1] Words in sub-s (5) substituted by FA 1996 Sch 21 para 11 with effect from the year 1996–97.

CHAPTER II
LOSS RELIEF: CORPORATION TAX

Revenue Interpretation RI 57—Bank failures: relief for losses incurred by depositors.
Revenue Internal Guidance—International tax handbook ITH 419-430 ("importation" of losses of foreign branches and subsidiaries).
Cross references—See TA 1988 s 434A (limitation on loss relief under this Chapter in the case of a life assurance company).

[Losses from Schedule A business or overseas property business

392A Schedule A losses

(1) Where a company incurs a Schedule A loss in an accounting period, the loss shall be set off for the purposes of corporation tax against the company's total profits for that period.

(2) To the extent that a company's Schedule A loss cannot be set off under subsection (1), it shall, if the company continues to carry on the Schedule A business in the succeeding accounting period, be carried forward to that period and be treated for the purposes of this section as a Schedule A loss of that period.

(3) Where an investment company ceases to carry on a Schedule A business but continues to be an investment company, any Schedule A loss that cannot be used under the preceding provisions shall be carried forward to the succeeding accounting period and be treated for the purposes of section 75 as if it had been disbursed as expenses of management for that period.

(4) In this section—

(a) a "Schedule A loss" means a loss incurred by a company in a Schedule A business carried on by it; and

(b) "investment company" has the same meaning as in Part IV.

(5) The preceding provisions of this section apply to a Schedule A business only to the extent that it is carried on—

    (*a*) on a commercial basis, or

    (*b*) in the exercise of statutory functions.

(6) For the purposes of subsection (5)(*a*)—

    (*a*) a business or part is not carried on on a commercial basis unless it is carried on with a view to making a profit, but if it is carried on so as to afford a reasonable expectation of profit it is treated as carried on with a view to making a profit; and

    (*b*) if there is a change in the manner in which a business or part is carried on, it is treated as having been carried on throughout an accounting period in the way in which it was being carried on by the end of the period.

(7) In subsection (5)(*b*) "statutory functions" means functions conferred by or under any enactment (including an enactment contained in a local or private Act)[1].

Commentary—*Simon's Direct Tax Service* **D2.411.**
Amendments—[1] This section inserted by FA 1998 Sch 5 para 28 with effect from 1 April 1998, subject to the transitional provisions in FA 1998 Sch 5 Part IV.

[*Losses from overseas property business*

392B Losses from overseas property business

(1) Where in any accounting period a company incurs a loss in an overseas property business (whether carried on by it solely or in partnership)—

    (*a*) the loss shall be carried forward to the succeeding accounting period and set against any profits of the business for that period,

    (*b*) if there are no profits of the business for that period, or if the profits for that period are exceeded by the amount of the loss, the loss or the remainder of it shall be carried forward again and set against any profits of the business for the next succeeding accounting period,

and so on.

(2) Subsections (5) to (7) of section 392A apply in relation to relief under subsection (1) above and an overseas property business as they apply in relation to relief under section 392A(1) to (3) and a Schedule A business.][1]

Commentary—*Simon's Direct Tax Service* **D2.411.**
Amendments—[1] This section inserted by FA 1998 Sch 5 para 28 with effect from 1 April 1998, subject to the transitional provisions in FA 1998 Sch 5 Part IV.

Trade etc losses

393 Losses other than terminal losses

(1) Where in any accounting period a company carrying on a trade incurs a loss in the trade, [the loss shall][1] be set off for the purposes of corporation tax against any trading income from the trade in succeeding accounting periods; and (so long as the company continues to carry on the trade) its trading income from the trade in any succeeding accounting period shall then be treated as reduced by the amount of the loss, or by so much of that amount as cannot, [under this subsection][1] or on a claim (if made) under [section 393A(1)][2] be relieved against income or profits of an earlier accounting period.

(2)–(6) ...[2]

(7) The amount of a loss incurred in a trade in an accounting period shall be computed for the purposes of this section in the same way as trading income from the trade in that period would have been computed.

(8) For the purposes of this section "trading income" means, in relation to any trade, the income which falls or would fall to be included in respect of the trade in the total profits of the company; but where—

    (*a*) in an accounting period a company incurs a loss in a trade in respect of which it is within the charge to corporation tax under Case I or V of Schedule D, and

    (*b*) in any later accounting period to which the loss or any part of it is carried forward under subsection (1) above relief in respect thereof cannot be given, or cannot wholly be given, because the amount of the trading income of the trade is insufficient,

any interest or dividends on investments which would fall to be taken into account as trading receipts in computing that trading income but for the fact that they have been subjected to tax under other provisions shall be treated for the purposes of subsection (1) above as if they were trading income of the trade.

(9) Where in an accounting period the charges on income paid by a company—

    (*a*) exceed the amount of the profits against which they are deductible, and

    (*b*) include payments made wholly and exclusively for the purposes of a trade carried on by the company, then, up to the amount of that excess or of those payments, whichever is the less, the charges on income so paid shall in computing a loss for the purposes of subsection (1) above be deductible as if they were trading expenses of the trade.

(10) In this section references to a company carrying on a trade refer to the company carrying it on so as to be within the charge to corporation tax in respect of it.

(11) ...[1,2]

Commentary—*Simon's Direct Tax Service* B2.366; D2.402–406, 408.
Concession B19—Unused trading losses which cannot be carried forward under this section may be set off against a balancing charge arising when a trader sells an industrial building after the trade has ceased.
C5—Items of income regarded as trading income for the purposes of sub-s (8) above in the case of a registered industrial and provident society.
Statement of Practice SP C11—Revenue practice to accept informal claims to loss relief under sub-s (1) above, subject to certain conditions as regards formulation of claims.
Revenue Interpretation RI 57—Bank failures: relief for losses incurred by depositors.
Revenue & other press releases—CCAB TR500 10-3-83 (interest paid on current account and trade interest will normally qualify for relief under s 393(8); also interest received from temporary lodgement of current working capital in a bank deposit account is within Case I).
Simon's Tax Cases—s 393(1), *Rolls-Royce Motors Ltd v Bamford* [1976] STC 162*; *Robroyston Brickworks Ltd v IRC* [1976] STC 329*; *Willis v Peeters Picture Frames Ltd* [1983] STC 453*; *Nuclear Electric plc v Bradley* [1996] STC 405.
s 393(8), *Bank Line Ltd v Inland Revenue* [1974] STC 342*; *Nuclear Electric plc v Bradley* [1996] STC 405.
s 393(9), *Commercial Union Assurance Co plc v Shaw* [1999] STC 109.
Definitions—"Accounting period", s 834(1); "charges on income", s 338(2) by virtue of s 834(1); "company", s 832(1), (2); "profits", s 6(4) by virtue of s 834(2); "Schedule D", s 18(1); "trade", s 6(4) by virtue of s 834(2).
Cross references—See TMA 1970 s 41A(9) (determination of amount of losses computed in accordance with sub-s (7) above).
TA 1988 s 242(5) (treatment of loss, for which relief was previously given by set off against franked investment income, in subsequent accounting periods).
TA 1988 s 243 (set–off of brought forward losses against surplus of franked investment income).
TA 1988 s 343(3) (terminal loss relief provisions in relation to company reconstructions without change of ownership).
TA 1988 s 393A (set off of losses against profits of the same or an earlier accounting period).
TA 1988 s 395(1) (restriction on relief under sub-s (1) above in respect of losses incurred on leasing contracts).
TA 1988 s 400(2) (reduction of relief under sub-s (1) above where government investment in a company is written off).
TA 1988 s 411A (group relief by way of substitution for loss relief under this section).
TA 1988 s 458(2) (how loss on capital redemption business is ascertained for the purposes of this section).
TA 1988 s 492(4) (relief in accordance with sub-s (1) above for ring fence losses from oil extraction activities).
TA 1988 s 503 (for the purposes of this section, all lettings of furnished holiday accommodation treated as a single trade chargeable to tax under Schedule D Case I).
TA 1988 s 518(3) (harbour reorganisation schemes: transferee to be entitled to transferor's losses carried forward).
TA 1988 s 768(1) (relief under this section not available where within three years there is a change in ownership of a company coupled with a change in the nature of trade or a change in ownership at a time when trade is negligible).
TA 1988 s 808 (restriction on deduction of interest or dividends from trading income by non-resident giving rise to losses under this section).
TA 1988 Sch 17A, para 10(6), (7) (group relief claims under Sch 17A; consent to surrender loss relieved under sub-s (1) above).
F(No 2)A 1992 s 65(1)(*a*) (life assurance business: I minus E basis: effect on the I minus E basis of a claim under sub-s (1) above in respect of a trading loss).
FA 1993 s 78(10) (calculation of surplus franked investment income to be taken into account under sub-s (1) above by virtue of s 243(1) to be by reference to the lower rate).
FA 1993 Sch 14 para 8 (amendments to various provisions of TA 1988 where a loss under sub-s (1) above may be set off without making a claim).
FA 1994 Sch 24 para 15 (modification of the application of this section to successor companies under a railway privatisation).
FA 2000 Sch 20 paras 19, 23 (for the purposes of this section, a company's trading loss for a period for which it claims an R&D tax credit is reduced by the amount surrendered; certain deemed trading losses treated as brought forward under this section).
Amendments—[1] Words in sub-s (1) substituted and words in sub-s (11) repealed by FA 1990 s 99(1), (2) for accounting periods ending after 30 September 1993 by virtue of FA 1990 s 99(4) and Corporation Tax Acts (Provisions for Payment of Tax and Returns) (Appointed Days) Order, SI 1992/3066 art 2(1), (2)(*b*).
[2] Words in sub-s (1) substituted and sub-ss (2)–(6) and words in sub-s (11) repealed by FA 1991 s 73(2), (4), (5), Sch 15 para 8, Sch 19 Pt V for losses incurred in accounting periods ending after 31 March 1991 and in relation to losses so incurred this section is deemed to have had effect at all times as amended (sub-ss (2)–(6) superseded by s 393A below).

[393A Losses: set off against profits of the same, or an earlier, accounting period

(1) Subject to section 492(3), where in any accounting period ending on or after 1st April 1991 a company carrying on a trade incurs a loss in the trade, then, subject to subsection (3) below, the company may make a claim requiring that the loss be set off for the purposes of corporation tax against profits (of whatever description)—

    (*a*) of that accounting period, and
    (*b*) if the company was then carrying on the trade and the claim so requires, of preceding accounting periods falling wholly or partly within the period specified in subsection (2) below;

and, subject to that subsection and to any relief for an earlier loss, the profits of any of those accounting periods shall then be treated as reduced by the amount of the loss, or by so much of that amount as cannot be relieved under this subsection against profits of a later accounting period.

(2) The period referred to in paragraph (*b*) of subsection (1) above [is (subject to subsection (2A) below) the period of twelve months][3] immediately preceding the accounting period in which the loss is incurred; but the amount of the reduction that may be made under that subsection in the profits of an accounting period falling partly before the beginning of that period shall not exceed a part of those profits proportionate to the part of the accounting period falling within that period.

[(2A) This section shall have effect in relation to any loss to which this subsection applies as if, in subsection (2) above, the words 'three years' were substituted for the words 'twelve months'.

(2B) Where a company ceases to carry on a trade at any time, subsection (2A) above applies to the following—

(a) the whole of any loss incurred in that trade by that company in an accounting period beginning twelve months or less before that time; and

(b) the part of any loss incurred in that trade by that company in an accounting period ending, but not beginning, in that twelve months which is proportionate to the part of that accounting period falling within that twelve months.

(2C) Where—

(a) a loss is incurred by a company in a ring fence trade carried on by that company, and

(b) the accounting period in which the loss is incurred is an accounting period for which an allowance under [section 164 of the Capital Allowances Act (abandonment expenditure incurred before cessation of ring fence trade)][4] is made to that company,

subsection (2A) above applies to so much of the amount of that loss not falling within subsection (2B) above as does not exceed the amount of that allowance.][3]

(3) Subsection (1) above shall not apply to trades falling within Case V of Schedule D; and a loss incurred in a trade in any accounting period shall not be relieved under that subsection unless—

(a) the trade is one carried on in the exercise of functions conferred by or under any enactment (including an enactment contained in a local or private Act), or

(b) [for][2] that accounting period the trade was being carried on on a commercial basis and with a view to the realisation of gain in the trade or in any larger undertaking of which the trade formed part;

but this subsection is without prejudice to section 397.

(4) For the purposes of subsection (3) above—

[(a) where at any time a trade is carried on so as to afford a reasonable expectation of gain, it shall be treated as being carried on at that time with a view to the realisation of gain; and][2]

(b) where in an accounting period there is a change in the manner in which a trade is being carried on, it shall be treated as having throughout the accounting period been carried on in the way in which it was being carried on by the end of that period.

(5) ...[4]

(6) ...[4]

(7) [Subject to subsection (7A) below,][3] where a company ceases to carry on a trade, subsection (9) of section 393 shall apply in computing for the purposes of this section a loss in the trade in [an accounting period ending with the cessation, or ending at any time in the twelve months immediately preceding the cessation,][3] as it applies in computing a loss in an accounting period for the purposes of subsection (1) of that section.

[(7A) For the purposes of this section where—

(a) subsection (7) above has effect for computing the loss for any accounting period, and

(b) that accounting period is one beginning before the beginning of the twelve months mentioned in that subsection,

the part of that loss that is not the part falling within subsection (2B)(b) above shall be treated as reduced (without any corresponding increase in the part of the loss that does fall within subsection (2B)(b) above) by an amount equal to so much of the aggregate of the charges on income treated as expenses by virtue of subsection (7) above as is proportionate to the part of the accounting period that does not fall within those twelve months.][3]

(8) Relief shall not be given by virtue of subsection (1)(b) above in respect of a loss incurred in a trade so as to interfere with any relief under section 338 in respect of payments made wholly and exclusively for the purposes of that trade.

(9) For the purposes of this section—

(a) the amount of a loss incurred in a trade in an accounting period shall be computed in the same way as trading income from the trade in that period would have been computed;

(b) "trading income" means, in relation to any trade, the income which falls or would fall to be included in respect of the trade in the total profits of the company; and

(c) references to a company carrying on a trade refer to the company carrying it on so as to be within the charge to corporation tax in respect of it.

(10) A claim under subsection (1) above may only be made within the period of two years immediately following the accounting period in which the loss is incurred or within such further period as the Board may allow.

(11) In any case where—

(a) by virtue of [section 165 of the Capital Allowances Act (abandonment expenditure within 3 years of ceasing ring fence trade)][4] the qualifying expenditure of the company for the chargeable period related to the cessation of its ring fence trade is treated as increased by any amount, or

(b) by virtue of [section 416 of that Act (expenditure on restoration within 3 years of ceasing to trade)][4] any expenditure is treated as qualifying expenditure incurred by the company on [the last day of trading][4], then, in relation to any claim under subsection (1) above to the extent that it relates to an increase falling within paragraph (*a*) above or to expenditure falling within paragraph (*b*) above, subsection (10) above shall have effect with the substitution of ''five years'' for ''two years''.][1]

[(12) In this section ''ring fence'' has the same meaning as in [section 162 of the Capital Allowances Act][4].][3]

Commentary—*Simon's Direct Tax Service* D2.405.
Concession B5—A non-commercial farming company precluded by sub-s (3) above from claiming loss relief may claim relief under s 33 of this Act for maintenance, repairs and insurance.
Revenue Internal Guidance—Inspector's manual IM 4885 (''contrived'' losses: circumstances in which cases will be referred to Special Investigations Section).
Company Taxation Manual COT452 (circumstances in which late claim will be accepted).
COT453 (sub-s (4)(*a*): ''gain'' means commercial profit rather than profit as computed for tax purposes).
Simon's Tax Cases—*Camcrown Ltd v McDonald* [1999] STC (SCD) 255.
Definitions—''Accounting period'', s 834(1); ''Board'', s 832(1); ''capital allowance'', s 832(1); ''chargeable period'', s 832(1); ''company'', s 832(1), (2); ''profits'', s 6(4); ''ring fence trade'', s 502(1); ''tax'', s 832(3); ''trade'', s 832(1).
Cross references—See TMA 1970 s 87A(6) (interest on overdue corporation tax: in calculating the interest, no account to be taken in certain circumstances of any losses carried back, and surplus ACT thereby carried back, under sub-s (1) above);
TA 1988 s 118 (restriction of relief under this section where a company carries on a trade as limited partner).
TA 1988 s 242 (set-off of losses etc against surplus of franked investment income).
TA 1988 s 343(4A) (where trade is treated by that section as continuing, following a company reconstruction without change of ownership, sub-ss (2A), (7) above do not apply to any loss which would otherwise fall within sub-s (2B) above by virtue of the predecessor company's ceasing to carry on the trade).
TA 1988 s 393(1) (interaction with relief for losses carried forward).
TA 1988 s 395(1) (limitation of relief under sub-s (1) above in respect of losses on leasing contracts of machinery or plant).
TA 1988 s 397(2) (exclusion of relief for certain losses in farming or market gardening).
TA 1988 s 399(2) (exclusion of relief for certain losses from dealings in commodity futures).
TA 1988 s 400(4) (write-off of government investment).
TA 1988 s 403 (losses which may be surrendered by way of group relief).
TA 1988 s 407 (relationship between group relief and other relief).
TA 1988 s 434(2) (insurance companies: franked investment income).
TA 1988 s 458(2) (determination of amount of relief in respect of losses of a capital redemption business).
TA 1988 s 492(3) (restriction on relief against ring fence profits from oil extraction activities).
TA 1988 s 503(1) (commercial letting of furnished holiday accommodation to be treated as trade for the purposes of sub-s (1) above chargeable to tax under Schedule D Case I).
TA 1988 s 518(3) (harbour reorganisation schemes: entitlement of transferee to carried forward losses of transferor subject to claims under this section).
TA 1988 s 768A(1) (change in ownership of a company coupled with change in the nature of the trade or change in ownership occurring while trade negligible: disallowance of carry back of trading losses).
TA 1988 s 808 (restriction on deduction of interest or dividends from trading income by non-resident so as to give rise to losses).
TA 1988 s 825(4) (restriction on repayment supplement relating to claim for repayment resulting from carry-back of loans).
TA 1988 s 826(7A)–(7B) (interest on overpaid tax).
TA 1988 Sch 19AC para 5B (modification of this section to enable an overseas life insurance company to claim to set losses against qualifying distributions).
TA 1988 Sch 26, para 1(3) (set off of losses under sub-s (1) against profits of a controlled foreign company apportioned to the claimant).
F(No 2)A 1992 s 65(1)(*a*) (life assurance business: I minus E basis: effect on the I minus E basis of a claim under sub-s (1) above in respect of a trading loss);
FA 1993 s 133 (priorities of relief under sub-s (1) above and FA 1993 provisions in respect of relief for non-trading exchange losses).
FA 2000 Sch 20 para 23(2) (tax relief for expenditure on R&D: certain trading losses may not be set against profits of preceding accounting period under sub-s (1)(*b*) above)
Amendments—[1] This section inserted by FA 1991 s 73(1), (4) in relation to losses incurred in accounting periods ending after 31 March 1991.
[2] Word in sub-s (3)(*b*) and sub-s (4)(*a*) substituted by FA 1996 Sch 20 para 26 with respect to accounting periods ending after 30 June 1999 (by virtue of Finance Act 1994, Section 199, (Appointed Day) Order, SI 1998/3173 art 2).
[3] Sub-ss (2A)–(2C), (7A), (12) and words in sub-s (7) inserted, and words in sub-ss (2), (7) substituted by F(No 2)A 1997 s 39 in respect of any loss incurred in an accounting period ending after 1 July 1997, but see F(No 2)A 1997 s 39(9)-(12) for transitional provisions for accounting periods straddling that date.
[4] Words in sub-ss (2C)(*b*), (11) and (12) substituted, and sub-ss (5), (6) repealed, by CAA 2001 ss 578, 580 Sch 2 para 32, Sch 4 with effect for corporation tax purposes with respect to allowances and charges falling to be made for chargeable periods ending after 31 March 2001.

394 Terminal losses

Amendments—This section repealed by FA 1991 Sch 19 Pt V in relation to losses incurred in accounting periods ending after 31 March 1991 and in relation to losses so incurred the repeal of this section is deemed to have had effect at all times.

395 Leasing contracts and company reconstructions

(1) Subject to the provisions of this section, if—

   (*a*) under a contract entered into on or after 6th March 1973 a company (''the first company'') incurs capital expenditure on the provision of [plant or machinery][2] which the first company lets to another person by another contract (a ''leasing contract''); and

   (*b*) apart from this subsection, the first company would be entitled [under section 393(1) or in pursuance of a claim under section 393A(1) to relief][1] in respect of losses incurred on the leasing contract; and

   (*c*) in the accounting period for which a first-year allowance, [within the meaning of Part 2 of the Capital Allowances Act][2], in respect of the expenditure referred to in paragraph (*a*) above is made to the first company, arrangements are in existence by virtue of which, at some time during or after the expiry of that accounting period, a successor company will be able to carry on any part of the first company's trade which consists of or includes the performance of all or any of the obligations which, apart from the arrangements, would be the first company's obligations under the leasing contract;

then, in the accounting period specified in paragraph (c) above and in any subsequent accounting period, the first company shall not be entitled ...[1] as mentioned in paragraph (b) above except in computing its profits (if any) arising under the leasing contract.

(2) For the purposes of this section a company is a successor of the first company if the circumstances are such that—

     (a) section 343 applies in relation to the first company and the other company as the predecessor and the successor within the meaning of that section; or

     (b) the two companies are connected with each other within the terms of section 839.

(3) For the purposes of this section losses incurred on a leasing contract and profits arising under such a contract shall be computed as if the performance of the leasing contract were a trade begun to be carried on by the first company, separately from any other trade which it may carry on, at the commencement of the letting under the leasing contract.

(4) In determining whether the first company would be entitled ...[1] as mentioned in subsection (1)(b) above, any losses incurred on the leasing contract shall be treated as incurred in a trade carried on by that company separately from any other trade which it may carry on.

(5) In this section "arrangements" means arrangements of any kind whether in writing or not.

Commentary—*Simon's Direct Tax Service* **D2.409.**
Definitions—''The 1990 Act'', s 831(3); ''accounting period'', s 834(1); ''company'', s 832(1), (2); ''profits'', ss 6(4), 834(2); ''trade'', ss 6(4), 834(2).
Cross references—See FA 1973 s 32(1) (power of inspector to enquire into the existence of certain arrangements in connection with claims under sub-s (1)(b) or (c) above).
Amendments—[1] Words in sub-s (1)(b) substituted and words in sub-ss (1), (4) repealed by FA 1993 Sch 14 para 8(3), Sch 23 Pt III(11) in relation to accounting periods ending after 30 September 1993 by virtue of FA 1990 s 99(4), FA 1993 Sch 14 para 8(1) and Corporation Tax Acts (Provisions for Payment of Tax and Returns) (Appointed Days) Order, SI 1992/3066 art 2(1), (2)(b).
[2] Words in sub-ss (1)(a), (c) substituted by CAA 2001 s 578, Sch 2 para 33 with effect for corporation tax purposes with respect to allowances and charges falling to be made for chargeable periods ending after 31 March 2001.

Case VI losses

Statement of Practice SP C11—Revenue practice to accept informal claims to loss relief under Schedule D Case VI, subject to certain conditions as regards formulation of claims.

396 Case VI losses

(1) Subject to subsection (2) below, where in any accounting period a company incurs a loss in a transaction in respect of which the company is within the charge to corporation tax under Case VI of Schedule D, [the loss shall][1] be set off against the amount of any income arising from transactions in respect of which the company is assessed to corporation tax under that Case for the same or any subsequent accounting period; and the company's income in any accounting period from such transactions shall then be treated as reduced by the amount of the loss, or by so much of that amount as cannot be relieved under this section against income of an earlier accounting period.

(2) This section shall not apply to a loss incurred in a transaction falling within section 34, 35 or 36.

(3) ...[1]

Commentary—*Simon's Direct Tax Service* **D2.412.**
Definitions—''Accounting period'', s 834(1); ''company'', s 832(1), (2); ''Schedule D'', s 18(1).
Cross references—See TA 1988 s 396 (set off of losses against interest from certain deposits).
TA 1988 s 436(4) (this section not to apply to a loss incurred by an insurance company on its annuity or pension business).
TA 1988 s 439B(4) (this section not to apply to loss incurred by resident insurance company from life reinsurance business).
TA 1988 s 441(5) (this section not to apply to a loss incurred by a resident insurance company on its overseas business).
FA 1993 s 129(9) (this section not to apply to a non-trading exchange loss and a non-trading exchange gain not to be regarded for the purposes of sub-s (1) above as income).
FA 1993 Sch 14 para 8 (amendment of various provisions of TA 1988 where losses may be set off under this section without making a loan).
Amendments—[1] Words in sub-s (1) substituted and sub-s (3) repealed by FA 1990 s 99(1), (3), Sch 19 Pt V in relation to accounting periods ending after 30 September 1993 by virtue of FA 1990 s 99(4) and Corporation Tax Acts (Provisions for Payment of Tax and Returns) (Appointed Days) Order, SI 1992/3066 art 2(1), (2)(b).

CHAPTER III

LOSS RELIEF: MISCELLANEOUS PROVISIONS

397 Restriction of relief in case of farming and market gardening

(1) Any loss incurred in a trade of farming or market gardening shall be excluded from section 380 if in each of the prior five years a loss[, computed without regard to capital allowances,][2] was incurred in carrying on that trade; ...[2]

(2) Any loss incurred in any accounting period by a company in carrying on a trade of farming or market gardening shall be excluded from section [393A(1)][1] if a loss, computed without regard to capital allowances, was incurred in carrying on that trade in that accounting period, and in each of the chargeable periods wholly or partly comprised in the prior five years.

(3) Subsections (1) and (2) above shall not restrict relief for any loss or for any capital allowance, [in any case]³—

(a) [where]³ the whole of the farming or market gardening activities in the year next following the prior five years are of such a nature, and carried on in such a way, as would have justified a reasonable expectation of the realisation of profits in the future if they had been undertaken by a competent farmer or market gardener, but

(b) [where]³, if that farmer or market gardener had undertaken those activities at the beginning of the prior period of loss, he could not reasonably have expected the activities to become profitable until after the end of the year next following the prior period of loss.

(4) Subsections (1) and (2) above shall not restrict relief where the carrying on of the trade forms part of, and is ancillary to, a larger trading undertaking.

(5) In this section—

...⁴

"chargeable period", in relation to a company, means any accounting period, ...⁴

"prior five years"—

(a) in relation to a loss incurred in a year of assessment, means the last five years of assessment before that year, and

(b) in relation to a loss incurred in a company's accounting period, means the last five years before the beginning of the accounting period;

"prior period of loss" means the prior five years, except that, if losses were incurred in the trade in successive years of assessment or chargeable periods amounting in all to a period longer than five years (and ending when the prior five years end), it means that longer period, and in applying this definition to a chargeable period of a company "losses" means losses computed without regard to capital allowances; and

"farming" and "market gardening" shall be construed in accordance with the definitions of those terms in section 832, but as if those definitions were not restricted to activities in the United Kingdom.

(6) ...⁴

(7) In ascertaining for the purposes of this section whether a loss was incurred in any part of the prior five years or earlier, the rules applicable to Case I of Schedule D shall be applied; and in this section "loss computed without regard to capital allowances" means, in relation to a chargeable period of a company, a loss so ascertained, [but disregarding—

(a) any allowance or charge under the Capital Allowances Act (including enactments which under this Act are to be treated as contained in that Act); and

(b) any provision of that Act requiring allowances and charges to be treated as expenses and receipts of the trade]⁴

(8) Subsections (1) and (2) above shall not restrict relief for any loss or capital allowance if the trade was set up and commenced within the prior five years, and, for the purposes of this subsection, a trade shall be treated as discontinued, and a new trade set up, in any event which under any of the provisions of the Tax Acts is to be treated as equivalent to the permanent discontinuance or setting up of a trade.

(9) For the purposes of subsection (8) above a trade shall not be treated as discontinued if, under section 343(2), it is not to be treated as discontinued for the purpose of capital allowances and charges.

(10) Where at any time there has been a change in the persons engaged in carrying on a trade, this section shall, notwithstanding subsection (8) above, apply to any person who was engaged in carrying on the trade immediately before and immediately after the change as if the trade were the same before and after without any discontinuance, and as if—

(a) a husband and his wife were the same person, and

(b) a husband or his wife were the same person as any company of which either the husband or the wife has control, or of which the two of them have control;

and accordingly relief from income tax or from corporation tax may be restricted under this section by reference to losses some of which are incurred in years of assessment and some, computed without regard to capital allowances, are incurred in a company's chargeable periods.

In this subsection "control" has the same meaning as in Part XI.

Commentary—*Simon's Direct Tax Service* **B3.531.**
Concession B5—A non-commercial farm owner precluded by this section from claiming loss relief may claim the relief allowed by s 33 of this Act for maintenance, repairs and insurance of his agricultural land.
Concession B55—Temporary concession relaxing the rules which restrict loss relief in cases where there has been a run of losses of more than five years.
Revenue Internal Guidance—Inspector's manual IM 2340a–2340d (operation of the five-year rule, with examples).
IM 2341a (in determining whether sub-s (3) applies, the whole of the farming activities must be considered).
IM 2341b (in sub-s (4), the word "ancillary" means "subservient and annexed to").
IM 2342 (attempts to create a profit every six years will be investigated).
IM 2350g (stud farming is accepted as a long-term activity).
Definitions—"The 1990 Act", s 831(3); "accounting period", s 834(1); "capital allowance", s 832(1); "the Capital Allowances Acts", s 832(1); "company", s 832(1), (2); "control", s 416(1) by virtue of sub-s (10); "Schedule D", s 18(1); "the Tax Acts", s 831(2); "trade", s 832(1); "year of assessment", s 832(1).

Cross references—See TA 1988 s 393A(3) (restrictions on relief for losses against the same or earlier periods under s 393A(3) are without prejudice to this section).
Amendments—¹ '"393A(1)"' in sub-s (2) substituted by FA 1991 Sch 15 para 10.
² Sub-s (1) words inserted and repealed by FA 1994 ss 214(3), 258, Sch 26 Pt V(24) with effect from the year 1994–95 with respect to trades etc commenced after 5 April 1994 and from the year 1997–98 with respect to trades etc commenced before 6 April 1994.
³ Words in sub-s (3) substituted for "if it is shown that" and "that" by FA 1996 Sch 20 para 27 with effect from the year 1996–97 with respect to income tax, and, with respect to corporation tax, for accounting periods ending after 30 June 1999 (by virtue of Finance Act 1994, Section 199, (Appointed Day) Order, SI 1998/3173 art 2).
⁴ Definition of "basis year", words in definition of "chargeable period", sub-s (6) repealed, and words in sub-s (7) substituted, by CAA 2001 ss 578, 580, Sch 2 para 34, Sch 4 with effect for income tax purposes, with respect to allowances and charges falling to be made for chargeable periods ending after 5 April 2001, and for corporation tax purposes, with respect to allowances and charges falling to be made for chargeable periods ending after 31 March 2001.

398 Transactions in deposits with and without certificates or in debts

Where a person sustains a loss on the exercise or disposal of a right to receive any amount, being a right to which section 56(2) applies, in a case where—

(*a*) if a profit had arisen from that exercise or disposal, that profit would have been chargeable to tax by virtue of section 56(2), and

(*b*) he is chargeable to tax under Schedule ... D² in respect of interest payable on that amount,

then the amount of that interest shall be included in the amounts against which [the amount of his loss may be set off in pursuance of a claim under section 392 or, as the case may be, against which the amount of his loss may be set off under section 396]¹.

Commentary—*Simon's Direct Tax Service* **A7.1204.**
Definitions—"Interest", s 832(1); "Schedule D", s 18(1).
Amendments—¹ Words substituted by FA 1993 Sch 14 para 8(4) in relation to accounting periods ending after 30 September 1993 by virtue of FA 1990 s 99(4), FA 1993 Sch 14 para 8(1) and Corporation Tax Acts (Provisions for Payment of Tax and Returns) (Appointed Days) Order, SI 1992/3066 art 2(1), (2)(*b*).
² Words omitted from para (*b*) repealed by FA 1996 Sch 7 para 16, Sch 41 Pt V(2) with effect from the year 1996–97 with respect to income tax, and, with respect to corporation tax, for accounting periods ending after 31 March 1996.

399 Dealings in commodity futures etc: withdrawal of loss relief

(1) If, apart from section [143(1) of the 1992 Act]² or [section 128(1) above]⁴, gains arising to any person in the course of dealing in commodity or financial futures or in qualifying options would constitute, [for the purposes of the Income Tax Acts]⁴, profits or gains chargeable to tax under Schedule D otherwise than as the profits of a trade, then any loss arising in the course of that dealing shall not be allowable against profits or gains which are chargeable to tax under Schedule D.

[(1A) Subsection (1) above does not apply to a loss arising from a transaction to which Schedule 5AA applies.]³

[(1B) If, apart from section 143(1) of the 1992 Act or section 128(2) above, gains arising in the course of dealing in financial futures or in qualifying options would constitute, for the purposes of the Corporation Tax Acts, profits and gains chargeable to tax under Case V or VI of Schedule D, then any loss arising in the course of that dealing shall not be allowable against profits and gains which are chargeable to tax under Case V or VI of Schedule D.]⁴

(2) Relief shall not be given to any person under section 380, 381 or [393A(1)]¹ in respect of a loss sustained in a trade of dealing in commodity futures if—

(*a*) the loss was sustained in a trade carried on in partnership and that person or one or more of the other partners was a company; and

(*b*) a scheme has been effected or arrangements have been made (whether by the partnership agreement or otherwise) such that the sole or main benefit that might be expected to accrue to that person from his interest in the partnership was the obtaining of a reduction in tax liability by means of any such relief.

(3) Where relief has been given in a case to which subsection (2) above applies it shall be withdrawn by the making of an assessment under Case VI of Schedule D.

(4) Subsection (2) above does not apply where the scheme was effected or the arrangements were made wholly before 6th April 1976.

(5) In this section "commodity futures", "financial futures" and "qualifying options" have the same meanings as in section [143 of the 1992 Act]², and the reference in sub-section (1) to a loss arising in the course of dealing in commodity or financial futures includes any loss which is regarded as arising in the course of such dealing by virtue of sub-section [143(3)]² of that section.

Commentary—*Simon's Direct Tax Service* **D2.408.**
Definitions—"the 1992 Act", s 831(3); "company", s 831(1), (2); "profits or gains", s 833(1); "Schedule D", s 18(1); "the Tax Acts", s 832(1); "trade", s 832(1).
Cross references—See TA 1988 s 436(5) (nothing in sub-s (1) above to offset the operation of provisions for the separate charge to tax on the profits of the pension business of an insurance company).
TA 1988 s 439B(5) (sub-s (1) above not to affect computation of profits arising to a resident insurance company from life reinsurance business).
TA 1988 s 441(6) (sub-s (1) above not to apply in computing profits arising to a resident insurance company from its overseas business).
Amendments—¹ '"393A(1)"' in sub-s (2) substituted by FA 1991 Sch 15 para 11.
² Words in sub-ss (1), (5) substituted by TCGA 1992 Sch 10 para 14(1), (19).

[3] Sub-s (1A) inserted by FA 1997 s 80(4), (6), with effect for chargeable periods ending on or after 5 March 1997 in relation to profits and gains realised, and losses sustained, on or after that date.

[4] In sub-s (1), words substituted for the words "section 128 above" and for the words "for the purposes of the Tax Acts", and sub-s (1B) inserted, by FA 2002 s 83(1)(b), (3) Sch 27 paras 1, 4 with effect for accounting periods beginning after 30 September 2002.

400 Write-off of government investment

(1) Where any amount of government investment in a body corporate is written-off on or after 6th April 1988, an amount equal to the amount written-off shall be set off against the body's tax losses as at the end of the accounting period ending last before the write-off date and, to the extent to which that amount exceeds those losses, against the body's tax losses as at the end of the next accounting period and so on.

(2) For the purposes of subsection (1) above a body's tax losses as at the end of an accounting period are—

(a) any losses which under section 393(1) are ...[3] available for relief against its trading income for the next accounting period;

(b) in the case of an investment company, any expenses of management or charges on income which under section 75(3) are available for carry forward to the next accounting period;

[(bb) any losses which—

  (i) under section 392A(2) or 392B are carried forward to the next accounting period, or

  (ii) under section 392A(3) are treated as management expenses disbursed in the next accounting period;][5]

(c) any allowances which under [section 260(2) of the Capital Allowances Act][8] are available for carry forward to the next accounting period;

(d) any amount paid by way of charges on income so far as it exceeds the company's profit for the period and is not taken into account under 75(3) or 393(9); and

(e) any allowable losses available under section [8 of the 1992 Act][2] so far as not allowed in that or a previous accounting period.

(3) The set off to be made under subsection (1) above for any accounting period shall be made first against the amounts in paragraphs (a) to (d) of subsection (2) above and, so far as it cannot be so made, against the amount in paragraph (e) of that subsection.

(4) For the purposes of subsection (1) above there shall be excluded from a body's tax losses as at the end of the accounting period ending last before the write-off date any amounts in respect of which a claim has been made before the write-off date under section [393A(1)][1] or 402 of this Act or [section 260(3) of the Capital Allowances Act][8] but the body's tax losses as at the end of any subsequent accounting period shall be determined as if no such claim had been made on or after that date.

(5) Any amount that could be set off under subsection (1) above against a body's tax losses as at the end of an accounting period (or could be so set off if that body then had any such losses) may be set off against the tax losses of any other body corporate which at the end of that period is a member of the same group as the first-mentioned body, or partly against the tax losses of one member of that group and partly against those of the other or any of the others, as may be just and reasonable.

(6) Expenditure shall not be treated for the purposes of [section 532 or 536 of the Capital Allowances Act][8] or section [50 of the 1992 Act][2] as met by the Crown by reason only of the writing-off of any government investment in the body in question and a sum shall not by reason only of any such writing-off be treated as not having been deductible in computing the [profits][6] of that body for the purposes of Case I or II of Schedule D.

(7) For the purposes of this section an amount of government investment in a body corporate is written-off—

(a) if its liability to repay any money lent to it out of public funds by a Minister of the Crown [or the Scottish Ministers][7] is extinguished;

(b) if any of its shares for which a Minister of the Crown has[, or the Scottish Ministers have,][7] subscribed out of public funds are cancelled; or

(c) if its commencing capital debt is reduced otherwise than by being paid off or its public dividend capital is reduced otherwise than by being repaid (including, in either case, a reduction to nil);

and the amount written-off and the write-off date are the amount in respect of which the liability is extinguished and the date on which it is extinguished, the amount subscribed for the shares that are cancelled and the date of cancellation or the amount of reduction in the commencing capital debt or public dividend capital and the date of the reduction, as the case may be.

(8) In subsection (7) above "commencing capital debt" means any debt to a Minister of the Crown [or the Scottish Ministers][7] assumed as such under an enactment and "public dividend capital" means any amount paid by a Minister of the Crown [or the Scottish Ministers][7] under an enactment in which that amount is so described or under an enactment corresponding to an enactment in which a payment made on similar terms to another body is so described.

(9) This section shall not have effect in relation to any amount written-off if and to the extent to which it is replaced by money lent, or a payment made, out of public funds or by shares subscribed for, whether for money or money's worth, by a Minister of the Crown [or the Scottish Ministers][7].

[(9A) Nothing in section 80(5) of the Finance Act 1996 (matters to be brought into account in the case of loan relationships only under Chapter II of Part IV of that Act) shall be construed as preventing this section from applying where a government investment in a body corporate is written off by the extinguishment, in whole or in part, of any liability under a loan relationship.][4]

(10) In this section—

"body corporate" means any body corporate which is a company for the purposes of corporation tax;

"group" means a company having one or more 51 per cent subsidiaries and that or those subsidiaries; and

"Minister of the Crown" includes a Northern Ireland department.

Commentary—*Simon's Direct Tax Service* D2.411.
Revenue Internal Guidance—Life assurance manual (Chapter 18: Inland Revenue interpretation of taxation of friendly societies).
Definitions—"The 1990 Act", s 831(3); "the 1992 Act", s 831(3); "accounting period", s 834(1); "loan relationship", s 834(1), FA 1996 s 81; "Schedule D", s 18(1).
Cross references—See TCGA 1992 s 8(1) (in computing company's chargeable gains the allowable losses are losses as reduced by virtue of this section).
FA 1994 Sch 24 para 16 (this section not to have effect on the extinguishment of certain liabilities in connection with a rail privatisation).
Amendments—[1] "393A(1)" in sub-s (4) substituted by FA 1991 Sch 15 para 12.
[2] Words in sub-ss (2)(e), (6) substituted by TCGA 1992 Sch 10 para 14(1), (20).
[3] Words omitted from sub-s (2)(a) repealed by FA 1993 Sch 14 para 8(5) and Sch 23 Pt III(11) in relation to accounting periods ending after 30 September 1993 by virtue of FA 1990 s 99(4), FA 1993 Sch 14 para 8(1) and Corporation Tax Acts (Provisions for Payment of Tax and Returns) (Appointed Days) Order, SI 1992/3066 art 2(1), (2)(b).
[4] Sub-s (9A) inserted by FA 1996 Sch 14 para 19 with effect for accounting periods ending after 31 March 1996.
[5] Sub-s (2)(bb) inserted by FA 1998 Sch 5 para 36 with effect for 1998–99 and subsequent years of assessment for income tax purposes and from 1 April 1998 for corporation tax, subject to the transitional provisions in FA 1998 Sch 5 Part IV.
[6] Word in sub-s (6) substituted by FA 1998 Sch 7 para 1 with effect from 31 July 1998.
[7] Words in sub-ss (7)–(9) inserted by the Scotland Act 1998 (Consequential Modifications) (No 2) Order, SI 1999/1820 Sch 2 Pt I para 87(1), (2) with effect from 1 July 1999.
[8] Words in sub-ss (2)(c), (4), (6) substituted by CAA 2001 s 578, Sch 2 para 35 with effect for income tax purposes, with respect to allowances and charges falling to be made for chargeable periods ending after 5 April 2001, and for corporation tax purposes, with respect to allowances and charges falling to be made for chargeable periods ending after 31 March 2001.

401 Relief for pre-trading expenditure

(1) Where a person incurs expenditure for the purposes of a trade, profession or vocation before the time when he begins to carry it on and the expenditure—

(a) is incurred not more than [seven][1] years before that time; and
(b) is not allowable as a deduction in computing his [profits][6] from the trade, profession or vocation for the purposes of Case I or II of Schedule D but would have been so allowable if incurred after that time,

the expenditure shall be [treated as incurred on the day on which the trade, profession or vocation is first carried on by him].[2]

[(1AA) Subsection (1) above shall not apply to any expenditure in relation to which any debit falls, or (but for subsection (1AB) below) would fall, to be brought into account for the purposes of Chapter II of Part IV of the Finance Act 1996 (loan relationships).

(1AB) Where, in the case of any company—

(a) a non-trading debit is given for any accounting period for the purposes of Chapter II of Part IV of the Finance Act 1996 (loan relationships), and
(b) an election for the purposes of this section is made by that company with respect to that debit within the period of 2 years beginning with the end of that accounting period,

that debit shall not be brought into account for the purposes of that Chapter as a non-trading debit for that period, but subsection (1AC) below shall apply instead.

(1AC) If a company—

(a) begins to carry on a trade within the period of seven years after the end of the accounting period for which a non-trading debit is given for the purposes of Chapter II of Part IV of the Finance Act 1996 (loan relationships),
(b) that debit is such that, if it had been given for the accounting period in which the company begins to carry on that trade, it would have been brought into account by reference to that trade in accordance with section 82(2) of that Act (trading debits and credits), and
(c) an election is or has been made with respect to that debit under subsection (1AB) above,

that debit shall be treated for the purposes of that Chapter as if it were a debit for the accounting period in which the company begins to carry on the trade and shall be brought into account for that period in accordance with section 82(2) of that Act.][4]

[(1A) ...][3]

[(1B) ...][5]

(2) ... [2]

Commentary—*Simon's Direct Tax Service* **B3.1204.**
Revenue Interpretation RI 32—Relief under this section is not available for pre-trading expenditure incurred by another person.
RI 117—For income tax, where a business commences after 5 April 1995, relief for pre-trading expenditure is given by deduction in computing taxable profits. A separate income tax loss relief claim is not necessary.
Definitions—"Accounting Period", s 834(1); "charge on income", s 834(1); "company", s 832(1); "non-trading debit", FA 1996 s 74(3); "profits or gains", s 833(1); "Schedule A", s 15(1); "Schedule A business", s 832(1); "Schedule D", s 18(1); "trade", s 832(1); "year of assessment", s 832(1).
Revenue Internal Guidance—Company Taxation Manual COT12372 (relief for pre-trading loan relationship debits will not be refused where the company has no pre-trading accounting period).
Cross references—See TA 1988 s 114(1) (restriction on relief under sub-s (1) above where partners in a partnership include a company).
TA 1988 s 503 (for the purposes of this section, all lettings of furnished holiday accommodation treated as a single trade chargeable to tax under Schedule D Case I).
FA 2000 Sch 20 para 26(2) (no account is taken of this section under the transitional provisions for tax relief for expenditure on R&D).
FA 2001 Sch 22 para 32(2) (no account taken of this section under the transiitional provisions concerning remediation of contaminated land).
Amendments—[1] Word in sub-s (1)(*a*) substituted by FA 1993 s 109 where the time when the person begins to carry on the trade etc falls after 31 March 1993.
[2] Words in sub-s (1) substituted, and sub-s (2) repealed, by FA 1995 s 120, Sch 29 Pt VIII(15), with effect with respect to trades, professions and vocations which are set up and commenced after 5 April 1995.
[3] Sub-s (1A) repealed by FA 1996 Sch 14 para 20(2), Sch 41 Pt V(3) with effect in relation to accounting periods ending after 31 March 1996, subject to transitional provisions in FA 1996 Sch 15.
[4] Sub-ss (1AA)–(1AC) inserted by FA 1996 Sch 14 para 20(1) with effect in relation to accounting periods ending after 31 March 1996, subject to transitional provisions in FA 1996 Sch 15.
[5] Sub-s (1B) repealed by FA 1998 s 165, Sch 27 Part III(4) with effect from 1998–99 and subsequent years of assessment for income tax purposes, and from 1 April 1998 for corporation tax, subject to the transitional provisions in FA 1998 Sch 5 Part IV.
[6] Word in sub-s (1) substituted by FA 1998 Sch 7 para 1 with effect from 31 July 1998.

CHAPTER IV
GROUP RELIEF

Cross references—See FA 1973 s 32(1) (power of inspector to enquire into certain arrangements in connection with claims for group relief).
TA 1988 s 413 (interpretation of this Chapter).
TA 1988 s 434A (limitation on group relief under this Chapter in the case of a life assurance company).
TA 1988 s 492(8) (restriction of group relief with respect to ring-fenced profits of the claimant company from oil extraction activities).
TA 1988 Sch 26 para 1 (circumstances in which a company to which profits of a controlled foreign company are apportioned may set-off group relief).
FA 1998 Sch 18 Part VIII (claims for group relief for accounting periods ending after 30 June 1999).

402 Surrender of relief between members of groups and consortia

(1) Subject to and in accordance with this Chapter and section 492(8), relief for trading losses and other amounts eligible for relief from corporation tax may, in the cases set out in subsections (2) and (3) below, be surrendered by a company ("the surrendering company") and, on the making of a claim by another company ("the claimant company") may be allowed to the claimant company by way of a relief from corporation tax called "group relief".

(2) Group relief shall be available in a case where the surrendering company and the claimant company are both members of the same group.

A claim made by virtue of this subsection is referred to as a "group claim".

(3) Group relief shall also be available in the case of a surrendering company and a claimant company either where one of them is a member of a consortium and the other is—

(*a*) a trading company which is owned by the consortium and which is not a 75 per cent subsidiary of any company; or

(*b*) a trading company—

(i) which is a 90 per cent subsidiary of a holding company which is owned by the consortium; and

(ii) which is not a 75 per cent subsidiary of a company other than the holding company; or

(*c*) a holding company which is owned by the consortium and which is not a 75 per cent subsidiary of any company;

or, in accordance with section 406, where one of them is a member of a group of companies and the other is owned by a consortium and another company is a member of both the group and the consortium.

A claim made by virtue of this subsection is referred to as "a consortium claim".

[(3A) Group relief is not available unless the following condition is satisfied in the case of both the surrendering company and the claimant company.

(3B) The condition is that the company is resident in the United Kingdom or is a non-resident company carrying on a trade in the United Kingdom through a branch or agency.][1]

(4) A consortium claim shall not be made ...[2] if a profit on a sale of the share capital of the other company or its holding company which the member owns would be treated as a trading receipt of that member.

(5) Subject to the provisions of this Chapter, two or more claimant companies may make claims relating to the same surrendering company, and to the same accounting period of that surrendering company.

(6) A payment for group relief—

(*a*) shall not be taken into account in computing profits or losses of either company for corporation tax purposes, and

(*b*) shall not for any of the purposes of the Corporation Tax Acts be regarded as a distribution or a charge on income;

and in this subsection "a payment for group relief" means a payment made by the claimant company to the surrendering company in pursuance of an agreement between them as respects an amount surrendered by way of group relief, being a payment not exceeding that amount.

Commentary—*Simon's Direct Tax Service* **D2.622, 623, 625.**
Revenue Interpretation RI 224—Circumstances in which Delaware Limited Liability Companies (DLLCs) can be regarded as issuing "ordinary share capital" for the purposes of TA 1988 ss 402–413.
Simon's Tax Cases—*J Sainsbury plc v O'Connor* [1991] STC 318*; *Gallic Leasing Ltd v Coburn* [1991] STC 699*.
s 402(1), (2), *A W Chapman Ltd v Hennessey* [1982] STC 214*; *Gallic Leasing Ltd v Coburn* [1989] STC 354*; *Farmer v Bankers Trust International Ltd* [1990] STC 564*.
s 402(3), *Imperial Chemical Industries plc v Colmer* [1999] STC 1089*.
s 402(3)(*b*)–(*d*), *Irving v Tesco Stores (Holdings) Ltd* [1982] STC 881*.
s 402(5), (6), *Gallic Leasing Ltd v Coburn* [1989] STC 354*.
Definitions—"Accounting period", s 834(1); "charges on income", s 834(1); "claimant company", s 413(2); "company", s 413(2); "company owned by a consortium", s 413(6); "consortium claim", s 413(2); "the Corporation Tax Acts", s 831(1)(*a*); "group claim", s 413(2); "group relief", s 413(2); "holding company", s 413(3); "members of the same group", s 413(3); "member's share in a consortium", s 413(8), (9); "non-resident company" s 413(2); "profits", s 6(4); "relevant accounting period", s 413(2); "surrendering company", s 413(2); "trade", s 6(4); "trading company", s 413(2); "75 per cent subsidiary", ss 413(4), 838; "90 per cent subsidiary", ss 413(7), 838.
Cross references—See TA 1988 s 400(4) (reduction of tax losses in consequence of write–off of government investment; effect of a claim for relief under this section made before write-off).
TA 1988 s 403(9) (consortium claim for losses etc to be surrendered by way of group relief).
TA 1988 s 410(2) (restriction of group relief where arrangements exist for transfer of company to another group or consortium).
F(No 2)A 1992 s 65(1)(*c*), (*d*) (life assurance business: I minus E basis: effect on the I minus E basis of a claim under sub-ss(2), (3) above in respect of a trading loss).
FA 1993 s 141(3) (deferral of tax on unrealised exchange gains accruing to a company on capital borrowed on long-term basis to be measured by profits without regard to claims under this section).
FA 2000 Sch 20 para 22 (tax relief for expenditure on R&D: restriction on consortium relief under sub-s (3) above).
Amendments—[1] Sub-ss (3A), (3B) inserted by FA 2000 s 97, Sch 27 paras 1, 6(1), (4) with effect for accounting periods ending after 31 March 2000. This amendment does not have effect for any determination as to whether the qualifying conditions for the purposes of TA 1988 s 403A(9) were met at any time before 1 April 2000.
[2] Words in sub-s (4) repealed by FA 2000 ss 100(3)(*a*), (5), 156, Sch 40 Pt II(11) and deemed always to have had effect.

[403 Amounts which may be surrendered by way of group relief

(1) If in an accounting period (the "surrender period") the surrendering company has—

(*a*) trading losses, excess capital allowances or a non-trading deficit on its loan relationships, or

(*b*) charges on income, Schedule A losses[, management expenses or a non-trading loss on intangible fixed assets][2] available for group relief,

the amount may, subject to the provisions of this Chapter, be set off for the purposes of corporation tax against the total profits of the claimant company for its corresponding accounting period.

(2) Trading losses, excess capital allowances and a non-trading deficit on the company's loan relationships are eligible for surrender as group relief even if the surrendering company has other profits of the surrender period against which they could be set.

Further provision about relief in respect of amounts eligible for surrender under this subsection is contained in sections 403ZA to 403ZC.

(3) Charges on income, Schedule A losses[management expenses and a non-trading loss on intangible fixed assets][2] are available for surrender as group relief only to the extent that in aggregate they exceed the surrendering company's gross profits for the surrender period.

Any excess surrendered shall be taken to consist first of charges on income, then Schedule A losses, [management expenses and finally a non-trading loss on intangible fixed assets][2].

Further provision about relief in respect of amounts available for surrender under this subsection is contained in section 403ZD.

(4) This section has effect subject to—

section 404 (limitation of group relief in relation to certain dual resident companies), and
sections 492(8) and 494A (oil extraction activities: availability of group relief against ring fence profits).][1]

Commentary—*Simon's Direct Tax Service* **D2.624.**
Revenue Interpretation RI 224—Circumstances in which Delaware Limited Liability Companies (DLLCs) can be regarded as issuing "ordinary share capital" for the purposes of TA 1988 ss 402–413.
Simon's Tax Cases—s 403(7), (8), *MEPC Holdings Ltd v Taylor (Inspector of Taxes)* [2000] STC (SCD) 504.
Revenue Internal Guidance—Life Assurance Manual, paras 13.111–13.113 (life company may not surrender excess management expenses: losses may be surrendered but there is then a restriction of relief for management expenses; charges may be surrendered but not those pensions and overseas life annuities which are deductible in computing Case VI profits; capital allowances given by discharge or repayment may also be surrendered).
Cross references—See TMA 1970 s 41A (determination of amounts available for surrender under sub-ss (3), (4) or (7) above by inspector).

TA 1988 s 118(1) (restriction on loss relief where an individual carries on a trade as a limited partner).
TA 1988 ss 403A–403C (restrictions on relief where accounting periods of claimant and surrendering company do not wholly coincide).
TA 1988 s 404(1) (limitation of group relief under this section in relation to certain dual resident companies).
TA 1988 s 405(4) (consortium claims: profits referred to in sub-s (9)(*b*) above to be treated as reduced by potential group relief).
TA 1988 s 406(2) (consortium claims: fraction of profits referred to in sub-s (9)(*b*) on claims made by companies grouped with a link company).
TA 1988 s 409(3) (meanings of certain references in this section for group relief purposes where two companies become or cease to be group members).
TA 1988 s 494(4) (modification of sub-s (7) above to the surrender of excess charges not allowable against ring-fenced profits from oil extraction activities).
TA 1988 s 787(3) (restriction of relief where interest paid as part of a scheme or arrangement to reduce tax).
FA 1993 s 131(3) (group relief for non-trading exchange losses).
Amendments—¹ This section substituted by FA 1998 Sch 5 para 29 with effect from 1 April 1998 for corporation tax, subject to the transitional provisions in FA 1998 Sch 5 Part IV.
² In sub-s (1)(*b*), words substituted for the words "or management expenses which are", in sub-s (3), words substituted for the words "and management expenses" and "and finally management expenses" by FA 2002 s 84(2), Sch 30 para 2(1) with effect from 24 July 2002.

[403ZA Amounts eligible for group relief: trading losses

(1) For the purposes of section 403 a trading loss means a loss incurred by the surrendering company in the surrender period in carrying on a trade, computed as for the purposes of section 393A(1).

(2) That section does not apply to a trading loss which would be excluded from section 393A(1) by—

   (*a*) section 393A(3) (foreign trades and certain trades not carried on with a view to gain), or
   (*b*) section 397 (farming and market gardening: restriction on loss relief).

(3) Where a company owned by a consortium—

   (*a*) has in any relevant accounting period incurred a trading loss, and
   (*b*) has profits (of whatever description) of that accounting period against which that loss could be set off under section 393A(1),

the amount of the loss available to a member of the consortium on a consortium claim shall be determined on the assumption that the company has made a claim under section 393A(1) requiring the loss to be so set off.

(4) Where the company mentioned in subsection (3) is a group/consortium company, the amount of the loss available under that subsection shall be determined before any reduction is made under section 405(1) to (3).]¹

Commentary—*Simon's Direct Tax Service* D2.625.
Revenue Interpretation RI 224—Circumstances in which Delaware Limited Liability Companies (DLLCs) can be regarded as issuing "ordinary share capital" for the purposes of TA 1988 ss 402–413.
Definitions—"Accounting period", s 834(1); "company", s 413(2); "company owned by a consortium", s 413(6); "consortium claim", s 413(2); "relevant accounting period", s 413(2); "surrendering company", s 413(2); "trade", s 6(4).
Amendments—¹ This section inserted by FA 1998 Sch 5 para 29 with effect from 1 April 1998 for corporation tax, subject to the transitional provisions in FA 1998 Sch 5 Part IV.

[403ZB Amounts eligible for group relief: excess capital allowances.

(1) For the purposes of section 403 excess capital allowances means capital allowances falling to be made to the surrendering company for [the surrender period to the extent that they are to be given effect under section 260 of the Capital Allowances Act (special leasing: excess allowance).]²

(2) In determining the amount of the allowances falling to be made for the surrender period, no account shall be taken of any allowances carried forward from an earlier period.

(3) The amount of the company's income of the relevant class means its amount before deduction of—

   (*a*) losses of any other period, or
   (*b*) capital allowances.]¹

Commentary—*Simon's Direct Tax Service* D2.626.
Revenue Interpretation RI 224—Circumstances in which Delaware Limited Liability Companies (DLLCs) can be regarded as issuing "ordinary share capital" for the purposes of TA 1988 ss 402–413.
Definitions—"company" s 413(2); "surrendering company" s 413(2).
Amendments—¹ This section inserted by FA 1998 Sch 5 para 29 with effect from 1 April 1998 for corporation tax, subject to the transitional provisions in FA 1998 Sch 5 Part IV.
² Words substituted by CAA 2001 s 578, Sch 2 para 36 with effect for corporation tax purposes as respects allowances and charges falling to be made for chargeable periods ending after 31 March 2001.

[403ZC Amounts eligible for group relief: non-trading deficit on loan relationships.

(1) For the purposes of section 403 a non-trading deficit on its loan relationships means a deficit of the surrendering company to which section 83 of the Finance Act 1996 applies.

(2) *Section 403 applies to such a deficit only to the extent that a claim is duly made under section 83(2) of the Finance Act 1996 for it to be treated as eligible for group relief.²]¹*

Commentary—*Simon's Direct Tax Service* D2.628.
Revenue Interpretation RI 224—Circumstances in which Delaware Limited Liability Companies (DLLCs) can be regarded as issuing "ordinary share capital" for the purposes of TA 1988 ss 402–413.
Definitions—"Group relief" ss 413(2), 402(1); "surrendering company" s 413(2).

Amendments—[1] This section inserted by FA 1998 Sch 5 para 29 with effect from 1 April 1998 for corporation tax, subject to the transitional provisions in FA 1998 Sch 5 Part IV.

[2] Sub-s (2) repealed by FA 2002 ss 82, 141, Sch 25 paras 43, 45, Sch 40 Pt 3(12) with effect for accounting periods beginning after 30 September 2002.

[403ZD Other amounts available by way of group relief

(1) References in section 403 to charges on income, Schedule A losses and management expenses shall be construed as follows.

(2) Charges on income means the aggregate of the amounts paid by the surrendering company in the surrender period by way of charges on income.

(3) A Schedule A loss means a loss incurred by the surrendering company in the surrender period in a Schedule A business carried on by the company.

It does not include—

(a) an amount treated as such a loss by section 392A(2) (losses carried forward from earlier period), or

(b) a loss which would be excluded from section 392A by subsection (5) of that section (certain businesses not carried on with a view to gain).

(4) Management expenses means the aggregate of the amounts disbursed by the surrendering company for the surrender period which are deductible under section 75(1) (expenses of management of investment company).

It does not include an amount deductible only by virtue of section 75(3) or 392A(3) (amounts carried forward from earlier periods).

(5) References in this section to section 75 do not include that section as applied by section 76 to companies carrying on life assurance business.][1]

[(6) A non-trading loss on intangible fixed assets means a non-trading loss on intangible fixed assets, within the meaning of Schedule 29 to the Finance Act 2002, for the surrender period.

It does not include so much of any such loss as is attributable to an amount being carried forward under paragraph 35(3) of that Schedule (amounts carried forward from earlier periods).][2]

Commentary—*Simon's Direct Tax Service* **D2.628A.**
Revenue Interpretation RI 224—Circumstances in which Delaware Limited Liability Companies (DLLCs) can be regarded as issuing "ordinary share capital" for the purposes of TA 1988 ss 402–413.
Definitions—"Company" s 413(2); "surrendering company" s 413(2).
Amendments—[1] This section inserted by FA 1998 Sch 5 para 29 with effect from 1 April 1998 for corporation tax, subject to the transitional provisions in FA 1998 Sch 5 Part IV.
[2] Sub-s (6) added by FA 2002 s 84(2), Sch 30 para 2(2) with effect from 24 July 2002.

[403ZE Computation of gross profits

(1) For the purposes of section 403 the surrendering company's gross profits of the surrender period means its profits for that period—

(a) without any deduction in respect of such losses, allowances and other amounts as are mentioned in paragraph (a) or (b) of subsection (1) of that section, and

(b) without any deduction falling to be made—

(i) in respect of losses, allowances or other amounts of any other period (whether or not of a description within subsection (1) of that section), or

(ii) by virtue of section 75(3) or 392A(3) (other amounts carried forward).

(2) References in this section to section 75 do not include that section as applied by section 76 to companies carrying on life assurance business.][1]

Commentary—*Simon's Direct Tax Service* **D2.624.**
Revenue Interpretation RI 224—Circumstances in which Delaware Limited Liability Companies (DLLCs) can be regarded as issuing "ordinary share capital" for the purposes of TA 1988 ss 402–413.
Definitions—"Surrendering company" s 413(2).
Amendments—[1] This section inserted by FA 1998 Sch 5 para 29 with effect from 1 April 1998 for corporation tax, subject to the transitional provisions in FA 1998 Sch 5 Part IV.

[403A Limits on group relief

(1) The amount which, on a claim for group relief, may be set off against the total profits of the claimant company for an accounting period ('the claim period'), and accordingly the amount to which any consent required in respect of that claim may relate, shall not exceed whichever is the smaller of the following amounts—

(a) the unused part of the surrenderable amount for the overlapping period; and

(b) the unrelieved part of the claimant company's total profits for the overlapping period.

(2) For the purposes of any claim for group relief—

(a) the unused part of the surrenderable amount for the overlapping period is the surrenderable amount for that period reduced by the amount of any prior surrenders attributable to the overlapping period; and (*b*) the unrelieved part of the claimant company's total profits for the overlapping period is the amount of its total profits for that period reduced by the amount of any previously claimed group relief attributable to the overlapping period.

(3) For the purposes of any claim for group relief—

(*a*) the surrenderable amount for the overlapping period is so much of the surrenderable amount for the accounting period of the surrendering company to which the claim relates as is attributable, on an apportionment in accordance with section 403B, to the overlapping period;

(*b*) the surrenderable amount for an accounting period of the surrendering company is the total amount for that accounting period of the losses and other amounts which (disregarding this section and section 403C) are available in that company's case for set off by way of group relief; and

(*c*) the amount of the claimant company's total profits for the overlapping period is so much of its total profits for the claim period as is attributable, on an apportionment in accordance with section 403B, to the overlapping period.

(4) In relation to any claim for group relief ('the relevant claim') the amount of the prior surrenders attributable to the period which is the overlapping period in the case of the relevant claim is equal to the aggregate amount (if any) produced by—

(*a*) taking the amount of every claim for group relief (whether a group claim or a consortium claim) which—

(i) has been made before the relevant claim,

(ii) was made in respect of the whole or any part of the amount which, in relation to the relevant claim, is the surrenderable amount for the accounting period of the surrendering company to which the claim relates, and

(iii) has not been withdrawn;

(*b*) treating the amount of group relief which (having regard to the provisions of this section) is allowable under each such claim as an amount of relief for the period which is the overlapping period in the case of that claim;

(*c*) determining how much of each amount treated in accordance with paragraph (*b*) above as an amount of relief for a particular period is attributable, on an apportionment in accordance with section 403B, to the period (if any) which is common to both—

(i) that period; and

(ii) the period which is the overlapping period in the case of the relevant claim; and

(*d*) aggregating all the amounts determined under paragraph (*c*) above in respect of the previously made claims.

(5) In relation to any claim for group relief ('the relevant claim'), the amount of previously claimed group relief attributable to the period which is the overlapping period in the case of that claim is the aggregate amount produced by—

(*a*) taking the amount of every claim for group relief (whether a group claim or a consortium claim) which—

(i) has been made before the relevant claim,

(ii) was a claim to set off an amount by way of group relief against the claimant company's total profits for the period which, in relation to the relevant claim, is the claim period, and

(iii) has not been withdrawn;

(*b*) treating the amount of group relief which (having regard to the provisions of this section) is allowable under each such claim as an amount of relief for the period which is the overlapping period in the case of that claim;

(*c*) determining how much of each amount treated in accordance with paragraph (*b*) above as an amount of relief for a particular period is attributable, on an apportionment in accordance with section 403B, to the period (if any) which is common to both—

(i) that period; and

(ii) the period which is the overlapping period in the case of the relevant claim; and

(*d*) aggregating all the amounts determined under paragraph (*c*) above in respect of the previously made claims.

(6) For the purposes of this section the amount of group relief allowable on any claim ('the finalised claim') shall fall to be determined as at the time when that claim ceases to be capable of being withdrawn as if—

(*a*) every claim that became incapable of being withdrawn before that time were a claim made before the finalised claim, and

(*b*) every claim that remains capable of being withdrawn at that time were a claim made after the finalised claim.

(7) Subject to subsection (6) above and without prejudice to any power to withdraw and resubmit claims, where (but for this subsection) more than one claim for group relief would be taken for the purposes of subsections (4) and (5) above to have been made at the same time, those claims shall be deemed, instead, to have been made—

(*a*) in such order as the company or companies making them may, by notice to any officer of the Board, elect or, as the case may be, jointly elect; and

(*b*) if there is not such election, in such order as an officer of the Board may direct.

(8) In this section 'the overlapping period', in relation to a claim for group relief, means (subject to subsection (9) below an section 406(3) and (7)) the period which is common to both—

(*a*) the claim period; and

(*b*) the accounting period of the surrendering company to which the claim relates.

(9) For the purposes of this section any time in the period which, in relation to any claim for group relief, is common to both the accounting periods mentioned in subsection (8) above but which is a time when the qualifying conditions were not satisfied—

(*a*) shall be treated as not comprised in the period which is the overlapping period in the case of that claim; and

(*b*) shall be treated instead, in relation to each of those accounting periods, as if it constituted a part of that accounting period which was not common to both periods.

(10) For the purposes of subsection (9) above the qualifying conditions are satisfied in relation to any claim for group relief at the following times, that is to say—

(*a*) if the claim is a group claim, whenever the claimant company and the surrendering company are both members of the same group [and the condition specified in section 402(3B) is satisfied in the case of both companies][2]; and

(*b*) if the claim is a consortium claim, whenever the conditions specified in section 402(3) for the making of that claim [and the condition specified in section 402(3B)][2] are satisfied in the case of the claimant company and the surrendering company.][1]

[403B Apportionments under section 403A

(1) Subject to subsection (2) below, where an apportionment falls to be made under section 403A for the purpose of determining how much of an amount for any period (''the first period'') is attributable to any other period (''the second period'') which comprises the whole or a part of the first period—

(*a*) the whole of that amount shall be attributed to the second period if the first and second periods begin and end at the same times; and

(*b*) in any other case, the apportionment shall be made on a time basis according to how much of the first period coincides with the second period.

(2) Where the circumstances of a particular case are such that the making on the time basis mentioned in subsection (1)(*b*) above of some or all of the apportionments to be made in that case would work in a manner that would be unjust or unreasonable in relation to any person, those apportionments shall be made instead (to the extent only that is necessary in order to avoid injustice and unreasonableness) in such other manner as may be just and reasonable.][1]

[403C Amount of relief in consortium cases

(1) In the case of a consortium claim the amount that may be set off against the total profits of the claimant company is limited by this section.

(2) Where the claimant company is a member of the consortium, the amount that may be set off against the total profits of that company for the overlapping period is limited to the relevant fraction of the surrenderable amount.

That fraction is whichever is the lowest in that period of the following percentages—

(a) the percentage of the ordinary share capital of the surrendering company that is beneficially owned by the claimant company;

(b) the percentage to which the claimant company is beneficially entitled of any profits available for distribution to equity holders of the surrendering company; and

(c) the percentage to which the claimant company would be beneficially entitled of any assets of the surrendering company available for distribution to its equity holders on a winding-up.

If any of those percentages have fluctuated in that period, the average percentage over the period shall be taken.

(3) Where the surrendering company is a member of the consortium, the amount that may be set off against the total profits of the claimant company for the overlapping period is limited to the relevant fraction of the claimant company's total profits for the overlapping period.

That fraction is whichever is the lowest in that period of the following percentages—

(a) the percentage of the ordinary share capital of the claimant company that is beneficially owned by the surrendering company;

(b) the percentage to which the surrendering company is beneficially entitled of any profits available for distribution to equity holders of the claimant company; and

(c) the percentage to which the surrendering company would be beneficially entitled of any assets of the claimant company available for distribution to its equity holders on a winding-up.

If any of those percentages have fluctuated in that period, the average percentage over the period shall be taken.

(4) In any case where the claimant or surrendering company is a subsidiary of a holding company which is owned by a consortium, for the references in subsection (2) or (3) above to the claimant or surrendering company there shall be substituted references to the holding company.

(5) Expressions used in this section and in section 403A have the same meanings in this section as in that section.

(6) Schedule 18 has effect for supplementing this section.]¹

Commentary—*Simon's Direct Tax Service* **D2.633.**
Revenue Interpretation RI 224—Circumstances in which Delaware Limited Liability Companies (DLLCs) can be regarded as issuing "ordinary share capital" for the purposes of TA 1988 ss 402–413.
Definitions—"claimant company", ss 402(1), 413(2); "consortium claim", s 413(2); "overlapping period", s 403A(8); "profits", s 6(4); "surrendering company", ss 402(1), 413(2).
Cross references—See TA 1988 s 406(3), (7) (application of TA 1988 ss 403A–403C in relation to a consortium claim made by a group member or consortium company in circumstances where a company is a member of both a group and a consortium).
Amendments—¹ This section substituted by FA 2000 s 100(1), (5) and deemed always to have had effect.

[403D Relief for or in respect of non-resident companies

(1) In determining for the purposes of this Chapter the amounts for any accounting period of the losses and other amounts available for surrender by way of group relief by a non-resident company, no loss or other amount shall be treated as so available except in so far as—

(a) it is attributable to activities of that company the income and gains from which for that period are, or (were there any) would be, brought into account in computing the company's chargeable profits for that period for corporation tax purposes;

(b) it is not attributable to activities of the company which are made exempt from corporation tax for that period by any double taxation arrangements; and

(c) no part of—

(i) the loss or other amount, or

(ii) any amount brought into account in computing it,

corresponds to, or is represented in, any amount which, for the purposes of any foreign tax, is (in any period) deductible from or otherwise allowable against non-UK profits of the company or any other person.

(2) In determining for the purposes of sections 403A and 403C the total profits for an accounting period of a non-resident company, there shall be disregarded—

(a) amounts not falling to be comprised for corporation tax purposes in the chargeable profits of the company for that accounting period, and

(b) so far as not falling within paragraph (a) above, any amounts arising from activities which are made exempt from corporation tax for that period by any double taxation arrangements.

(3) In this section "non-UK profits", in relation to any person, means amounts which—

(a) are taken for the purposes of any foreign tax to be the amount of the profits, income or gains on which (after allowing for deductions) that person is charged with that tax, and

(b) are not amounts corresponding to, and are not represented in, the total profits (of that or any other person) for any accounting period, or amounts taken into account in computing such amounts.

(4) Subsection (2) above applies for the purposes of subsection (3)(*b*) above as it applies for the purposes of sections 403A and 403C.

(5) For the purposes of this section an amount shall not be taken to be an amount which for the purposes of any foreign tax is deductible from or otherwise allowable against any non-UK profits of any person by reason only that it is—

    (*a*) an amount of profits brought into account for the purpose of being excluded from the profits that are non-UK profits of that person by reference to that foreign tax; or

    (*b*) an amount brought into account in computing the amount of any profits falling to be so excluded.

(6) So much of the law of any territory outside the United Kingdom as for the purposes of any foreign tax makes the deductibility of any amount dependent on whether or not it is deductible for tax purposes in the United Kingdom shall be disregarded for the purposes of this section.

(7) For the purposes of this section activities of a company are made exempt from corporation tax for any period by double taxation arrangements if the effect of any such arrangements is that the income and gains (if any) arising for that period from those activities is to be disregarded in computing the company's chargeable profits.

(8) In this section "double taxation arrangements" means any arrangements having effect by virtue of section 788.

(9) In this section "foreign tax" means any tax chargeable under the law of any territory outside the United Kingdom which—

    (*a*) is charged on income and corresponds to United Kingdom income tax; or

    (*b*) is charged on income or chargeable gains or both and corresponds to United Kingdom corporation tax;

but for the purposes of this section a tax shall not be treated as failing to correspond to income tax or corporation tax by reason only that it is chargeable under the law of a province, state or other part of a country, or is levied by or on behalf of a municipality or other local body.

(10) In determining for the purposes of this section whether any activities are made exempt from corporation tax for any period by any double taxation arrangements any requirement that a claim is made before effect is given to any provision of the arrangements shall be disregarded.

Commentary—*Simon's Direct Tax Service* **D2.633A.**
Definitions—"Company" s 413(2); "non-resident company" s 413(2).
Revenue Interpretation RI 224—Circumstances in which Delaware Limited Liability Companies (DLLCs) can be regarded as issuing "ordinary share capital" for the purposes of TA 1988 ss 402–413.
Revenue & other press releases—IR Tax Bulletin October 2000 p 783 (Revenue explanation and examples of how this section applies in practice).
Amendments—¹ This section inserted by FA 2000 s 97, Sch 27 Pt I paras 4, 6(1), (4) with effect for accounting periods ending after 31 March 2000. This section does not have effect for any determination as to whether the qualifying conditions for the purposes of TA 1988 s 403A(9) were met at any time before 1 April 2000.

403E Relief for overseas losses of UK resident companies

(1) In determining, for the purposes of this Chapter, the amounts for any accounting period of the losses and other amounts available for surrender by way of group relief by any company resident in the United Kingdom ("the resident company"), a loss or other amount shall be treated as not so available in so far as it—

    (*a*) is attributable to an overseas branch or agency of that company, and

    (*b*) is a loss or other amount falling within subsection (2) below.

(2) Subject to subsection (3) below, a loss or other amount attributable to an overseas branch or agency falls within this subsection if the whole or any part of it is, or represents, an amount which, for the purposes of foreign tax under the law of the territory where that branch or agency is situated, is (in any period) deductible from or otherwise allowable against non-UK profits of a person other than the resident company.

(3) A loss or other amount does not fall within subsection (2) above if it is referable to life assurance business (within the meaning of Chapter I of Part XII) carried on by the resident company.

(4) The reference in subsections (1) and (2) above to a loss or other amount attributable to an overseas branch or agency of a company is a reference to the loss or other amount (if any) that would be surrenderable by that company by way of group relief if the amount surrenderable by that company were computed—

    (*a*) by reference only to that branch or agency, and

    (*b*) by the application in relation to that branch or agency of principles corresponding in all material respects to those applicable for the purposes of corporation tax to the computation of the equivalent losses or other amounts in the case of the UK branch or agency of a non-resident company.

(5) In subsection (4)(*b*) above the reference to the UK branch or agency of a non-resident company is a reference to any branch or agency through which a company which is not resident in the United Kingdom carries on a trade in the United Kingdom.

TA 1988

(6) References in this section to an overseas branch or agency of a company are references to any branch or agency through which that company carries on a trade in a territory outside the United Kingdom.

(7) In this section "foreign tax" and "non-UK profits" have the same meaning as in section 403D.

(8) Where the deductibility of any amount for the purposes of any foreign tax is dependent on whether or not that amount, or a corresponding amount, is deductible for tax purposes in the United Kingdom, this section shall have effect as if that amount were deductible for the purposes of that foreign tax if, and only if, the resident company is treated for the purposes of that tax as resident in the territory where that tax is charged.]¹

Commentary—*Simon's Direct Tax Service* **D2.633B.**
Definitions—"Group relief" s 413(2); "non-resident company" s 413(2).
Revenue Interpretation RI 224—Circumstances in which Delaware Limited Liability Companies (DLLCs) can be regarded as issuing "ordinary share capital" for the purposes of TA 1988 ss 402–413.
Revenue & other press releases—IR Tax Bulletin October 2000 p 783 (Revenue explanation and examples of how this section applies in practice).
Amendments—¹ This section inserted by FA 2000 s 97, Sch 27 Pt I paras 4, 6(2), (4) with effect for accounting periods ending after 31 March 2000. By virtue of FA 2000 Sch 27 para 6(2), nothing in this section has effect for the determination of the amount available for surrender—

 (*a*) for an accounting period ending before 1 April 2000, or
 (*b*) for an accounting period beginning before 1 April 2000 and ending on or after that date if or to the extent that the loss or other amount is attributable to the part of the period falling before that date.
Any apportionment necessary for the purposes of paragraph (*b*) shall be made on a time basis except where that would work in an unjust or unreasonable manner in relation to any person, in which case it shall be made in such manner as may be just and reasonable.

404 Limitation of group relief in relation to certain dual resident companies

(1) Notwithstanding any other provision of this Chapter, no loss or other amount shall be available for set off by way of group relief in accordance with section 403 if, in the material accounting period of the company which would otherwise be the surrendering company, that company is for the purposes of this section a dual resident investing company.

(2) In this section "the material accounting period" means, according to the kind of group relief which would be appropriate, the accounting period—

 [(*a*) in which the trading loss or Schedule A loss is incurred; or
 (*aa*) in which the non-trading deficit on the company's loan relationships arises; or]²
 (*b*) for which the capital allowances fall to be made; or
 (*c*) for which the expenses of management are disbursed; or
 (*d*) for which the amount is paid by way of charges on income;

but subsection (1) above does not have effect unless the material accounting period begins on or after 1st April 1987.

(3) In Schedule 17—

 (*a*) Part I has effect where an accounting period of a company in which it is a dual resident investing company begins before and ends on or after 1st April 1987 and references in subsections (1) and (2) above to the material accounting period shall be construed accordingly; and
 (*b*) Part II has effect with respect to the time at which certain interest and other payments are to be treated as paid.

(4) A company is for the purposes of this section a dual resident company in any accounting period in which—

 (*a*) it is resident in the United Kingdom; and
 (*b*) it is also within a charge to tax under the laws of a territory outside the United Kingdom—

  (i) because it derives its status as a company from those laws; or
  (ii) because its place of management is in that territory; or
  (iii) because under those laws it is for any other reason regarded as a resident in that territory for the purposes of that charge.

(5) In any accounting period throughout which it is not a trading company, a dual resident company is for the purposes of this section an investing company.

(6) In any accounting period of a dual resident company in which it is a trading company, the company is nevertheless for the purposes of this section an investing company if—

 (*a*) in that period it carries on a trade of such a description that its main function or one of its main functions consists of all or any of the following, namely—

  (i) acquiring and holding, directly or indirectly, shares, securities or investments of any other description, including interests in companies (resident outside, as well as in, the United Kingdom) with which the dual resident company is connected, within the terms of section 839;
  [(*ia*) making payments in relation to which, being payments under loan relationships, any debits fall to be brought into account for the purposes of Chapter II of Part IV of the Finance Act 1996;]¹
  (ii) making payments which, by virtue of any enactment, are charges on income for the purposes of corporation tax;

(iii) making payments (of interest or other sums) which are similar to those referred to in sub-paragraph (ii) above but which are deductible in computing the profits of the company for the purposes of corporation tax;

(iv) obtaining funds (by borrowing or in any other manner whatsoever) for the purpose of, or otherwise in connection with, any of the activities referred to in sub-paragraphs (i) to (iii) above; or

(*b*) it does not fall within paragraph (*a*) above, but in that accounting period it carries on all or any of the activities referred to in sub-paragraphs (i) to (iv) of that paragraph and does so—

(i) to an extent which does not appear to be justified by any trade which it does carry on; or

(ii) for a purpose which does not appear to be appropriate to any such trade

(*c*) ...[2]

[(7) In this section "debtor relationship" has the same meaning as in Chapter II of Part IV of the Finance Act 1996][1]

Commentary—*Simon's Direct Tax Service* **D2.621.**
Revenue Interpretation RI 224—Circumstances in which Delaware Limited Liability Companies (DLLCs) can be regarded as issuing "ordinary share capital" for the purposes of TA 1988 ss 402–413.
Revenue Internal Guidance—International Tax Handbook ITH 1241–1242 (background to the section).
Company Taxation Manual COT3453, 3456 (meaning of dual resident company and dual resident investing company).
Definitions—"Accounting period", s 834(1); "capital allowance", s 832(1); "charges on income", s 338(2) by virtue of s 834(1); "company", s 413(2); "group relief", s 402(1) by virtue of s 413(2); "loan relationship", FA 1996 s 81; "profits", s 6(4); "trade", s 6(4); "trading company", s 413(3); "United Kingdom", s 830(1).
Amendments—[1] Sub-ss (6)(*ia*), (7) inserted by FA 1996 Sch 14 para 21 with effect for accounting periods ending after 31 March 1996, subject to transitional provisions in FA 1996 Sch 15.
[2] Sub-s (2)(*a*), (2)(*aa*) substituted, and sub-s (6)(*c*) repealed by FA 1998 Sch 5 para 37 with effect from 1 April 1998 for corporation tax, subject to the transitional provisions in FA 1998 Sch 5 Part IV.

405 Claims relating to losses etc of members of both group and consortium

(1) For the purposes of a consortium claim in respect of the loss or other amount of any relevant accounting period of a group/consortium company, that loss or other amount shall be treated as reduced (or, as the case may be, extinguished) by first deducting therefrom the potential relief attributable to group claims.

(2) Subject to subsection (3) below, in relation to the loss or other amount of a relevant accounting period of a group/consortium company, the potential relief attributable to group claims is the aggregate amount of group relief that would be claimed if every company which, as a member of the same group of companies as the group/consortium company, could make a group claim in respect of that loss or other amount made such a claim for an amount which, when set against the claimant company's total profits for its corresponding accounting period, would equal those profits.

(3) Where for any accounting period another member of the group of companies of which the group/consortium company is a member has a loss or other amount available for relief and one or more group claims is or are in fact made in respect of that loss or other amount, account shall be taken of the relief so claimed before determining (in relation to the loss or other amount of the group/consortium company) the potential relief attributable to group claims under subsection (2) above.

(4) In any case where—

(*a*) a consortium claim is made by a group/consortium company in respect of a loss or other amount of an accounting period of a member of the consortium, and

(*b*) the corresponding accounting period of the group/consortium company is a relevant accounting period,

the total profits of the corresponding accounting period of the group/consortium company against [which an amount may by virtue of that claim be set off by way of group relief][1] shall be treated as reduced (or as the case may be extinguished) by deducting therefrom the potential relief available to the group/consortium company by way of group claims.

(5) Subject to subsection (6) below, in relation to a relevant accounting period of a group/consortium company, the potential relief available to the company by way of group claims is the maximum amount of group relief that could be claimed by the company for that accounting period on group claims relating to the losses or other amounts available for relief of other members of the group of companies of which the group/consortium company is a member.

(6) Where another member of the group of companies of which the group/consortium company is a member in fact makes one or more group claims in respect of losses or other amounts of other members of the group, account shall be taken of the relief already claimed by that company in determining the potential relief available to the group/consortium company by way of group claims under subsection (5) above.

Commentary—*Simon's Direct Tax Service* **D2.634.**
Revenue Interpretation RI 224—Circumstances in which Delaware Limited Liability Companies (DLLCs) can be regarded as issuing "ordinary share capital" for the purposes of TA 1988 ss 402–413.
Definitions—"Accounting period", s 834(1); "company", s 413(2); "consortium claim", s 413(2); "group claim", s 413(2); "group/consortium company", s 413(2); "group relief", s 402(1) by virtue of s 413(2); "relevant accounting period", s 413(2).

TA 1988

Amendments—¹ Words in sub-s (4) substituted by F(No 2)A 1997 s 41, Sch 7 paras 4, 9 with effect in relation to any claim for
group relief if the accounting period of either the claimant company or the surrendering company ends after 1 July 1997 and
the overlapping period (see TA 1988 s 403A(8)) would not fall entirely before that date. See also F(No 2)A 1997 Sch 7
para 9(3)-(5) for transitional provisions where the overlapping period straddles 2 July 1997.

406 Claims relating to losses etc of consortium company or group member

(1) In this section—

(a) "link company" means a company which is a member of a consortium and is also a member
of a group of companies; and

(b) "consortium company", in relation to a link company, means a company owned by the
consortium of which the link company is a member; and

(c) "group member", in relation to a link company, means a company which is a member of the
group of which the link company is also a member but is not itself a member of the consortium
of which the link company is a member.

(2) Subject to subsections (3) and (4) below, where the link company could (disregarding any
deficiency of profits) make a consortium claim in respect of the loss or other amount eligible for
relief of a relevant accounting period of a consortium company, a group member may make any
consortium claim which could be made by the link company; and the fraction which is [the relevant
fraction for the purposes of section 403C]¹ where a group member is the claimant company shall be
the same as [it would be]¹ if the link company were the claimant company.

[(3) Sections 403A to 403C shall have effect in relation to a consortium claim made by a group
member by virtue of subsection (2) above as if any time when the claimant company was not a
member of the group—

(a) were not comprised in the period which is the overlapping period in the case of that claim;
and

(b) were to be treated instead as if it constituted a part of the claim period which did not coincide
with any part of the accounting period of the surrendering company to which the claim relates.]¹

(4) The maximum amount of relief which, in the aggregate, may be claimed by group members and
the link company by consortium claims relating to the loss or other amount of a relevant accounting
period of a consortium company shall not exceed the relief which could have been claimed by the
link company (disregarding any deficiency of profits) if subsections (2) and (3) above had not been
enacted.

(5) Subject to subsections (6) to (8) below, where a group member has for a relevant accounting
period a loss or other amount available for relief, a consortium company may make any claim in
respect of that loss or other amount which it could make if the group member were a member of the
consortium at all times when the link company was such a member, but not at any other time.

(6) The fraction which is [the relevant fraction for the purposes of section 403C]¹ in relation to a
consortium claim made by virtue of subsection (5) above shall be the same as [it would be]¹ if the link
company were the surrendering company, except that the [overlapping period in respect of which the
relevant fraction]² is to be ascertained shall be that of the group member which is in fact the
surrendering company.

[(7) Sections 403A to 403C shall have effect in relation to a consortium claim made by a consortium
company by virtue of subsection (5) above as if any time when the surrendering company was not a
member of the group—

(a) were not comprised in the period which is the overlapping period in the case of that claim;
and

(b) were to be treated instead as if it constituted a part of the claim period that did not coincide
with any part of the accounting period of the surrendering company to which the claim relates.]¹

(8) For any accounting period of a consortium company ("the claimant company's accounting
period") the maximum amount of relief which, in the aggregate, may be claimed by that company
by consortium claims relating to the losses or other amounts of accounting periods of the link
company and group members shall not exceed [the maximum amount of relief available to the
claimant company]¹ on a consortium claim in respect of which—

(a) the link company was the surrendering company; and

(b) the link company's accounting period was the same as the claimant company's accounting
period.

Commentary—*Simon's Direct Tax Service* D2.622.
Revenue Interpretation RI 224—Circumstances in which Delaware Limited Liability Companies (DLLCs) can be regarded as
issuing "ordinary share capital" for the purposes of TA 1988 ss 402–413.
Definitions—"Accounting period", s 834(1); "claim period", s 403A(1) "claimant company", s 402(1) by virtue of s 413(2);
"consortium claim", s 413(2); "overlapping period", s 403A(8); "relevant accounting period", s 413(2); "surrendering
company" ss 402(1), 413(2).
Cross references—See TA 1988 s 402(3) (group relief to be available between companies in accordance with the section where
one is a consortium company, one a member of a group and another is a member of both the group and consortium).
TA 1988 s 409(6), (7) (restriction of group relief where the surrendering company or the claimant company is not a member of a
consortium for the whole of an accounting period).
Amendments—¹ Words in sub-ss (2), (6), (8) and whole of sub-ss (3), (7), substituted by F(No 2)A 1997 s 41, Sch 7 paras 5, 9
with effect in relation to any claim for group relief if the accounting period of either the claimant company or the surrendering

company ends after 1 July 1997 and the overlapping period (see TA 1988 s 403A(8)) would not fall entirely before that date (but see F(No 2)A 1997 Sch 7 para 9(3)–(5) for transitional provisions where the overlapping period straddles 2 July 1997).
² Words in sub-s (6) substituted by FA 2000 s 100(2), (5) and deemed always to have had effect.

407 Relationship between group relief and other relief

(1) Group relief for an accounting period shall be allowed as a deduction against the claimant company's total profits for the period—

(*a*) before reduction by any relief derived from a subsequent accounting period, but
(*b*) as reduced by any other relief from tax (including relief in respect of charges on income under section 338(1) [of this Act or by virtue of section 83 of, or paragraph 4 of Schedule 11 to, the Finance Act 1996 (non-trading deficits)]³ determined on the assumption that the company makes all relevant claims under section [393A(1)]¹ of this Act and [section 260(3) of the Capital Allowances Act]⁴ (set-off of capital allowances against total profits).

(2) For the purposes of this section "relief derived from a subsequent accounting period" means—

(*a*) relief under section [393A(1)(*b*)]¹ in respect of a loss incurred in an accounting period after the accounting period the profits of which are being computed; and
(*b*) relief under [section 260(3) of the Capital Allowances Act]⁴ in respect of capital allowances falling to be made for an accounting period after the accounting period the profits of which are being computed; [and]²
[(*c*) relief in pursuance of a claim under section 83(2) of, or paragraph 4 of Schedule 11 to, the Finance Act 1996 (non-trading deficits) in respect of any deficit for a deficit period after the accounting period the profits of which are being computed.]³

(3) The reductions to be made in total profits of an accounting period against which any relief derived from a subsequent accounting period is to be set off shall include any group relief for that first-mentioned accounting period.

Commentary—*Simon's Direct Tax Service* **D2.634.**
Revenue Interpretation RI 224—Circumstances in which Delaware Limited Liability Companies (DLLCs) can be regarded as issuing "ordinary share capital" for the purposes of TA 1988 ss 402–413.
Definitions—"Accounting period", s 834(1); "capital allowance", s 832(1); "company", s 413(2); "group relief", s 402(1) by virtue of s 413(2); "profits", s 6(4).
Revenue Internal Guidance—Company Taxation Manual COT2950–2985 (explanation of consortium relief with many worked examples).
COT2701 (worked example).
Cross references—See TA 1988 s 409(2) (apportionment of group relief under sub-s (1) above where two companies become or cease to be group members).
Amendments—¹ Words in sub-ss (1)(*b*), (2)(*a*) substituted by FA 1991 Sch 15 para 14.
² Word "and" in sub-s (2)(*b*) inserted by FA 1993 Sch 18 para 4.
³ Words in sub-s (1)(*b*) inserted and sub-s (2)(*c*) substituted by FA 1996 Sch 14 para 22(1), (2) with effect in relation to accounting periods ending after 31 March 1996, subject to transitional provisions in FA 1996 Sch 15.
⁴ Words in sub-s (1)(*b*), (2)(*b*) substituted by CAA 2001 s 578, Sch 2 para 37 with effect for corporation tax purposes as respects allowances and charges falling to be made for chargeable periods ending after 31 March 2001.

[408 Corresponding accounting periods

Commentary—*Simon's Direct Tax Service* **D2.632.**
Amendments—This section repealed by F(No 2)A 1997 s 41, Sch 7 paras 6, 9, Sch 8 Pt II(14) with effect for any claim for group relief if the accounting period of either the claimant company or the surrendering company ends after 1 July 1997 and the overlapping period (see TA 1988 s 403A(8)) would not fall entirely before that date (but see F(No 2)A 1997 Sch 7 para 9(3)–(5) for transitional provisions where the overlapping period straddles 2 July 1997).

[409 Companies joining or leaving group or consortium

Commentary—*Simon's Direct Tax Service* **D2.632.**
Amendments—This section repealed by F(No 2)A 1997 s 41, Sch 7 paras 6, 9, Sch 8 Pt II(14) with effect for any claim for group relief if the accounting period of either the claimant company or the surrendering company ends after 1 July 1997 and the overlapping period (see TA 1988 s 403A(8)) would not fall entirely before that date (but see F(No 2)A 1997 Sch 7 para 9(3)–(5) for transitional provisions where the overlapping period straddles 2 July 1997).

410 Arrangements for transfer of company to another group or consortium

(1) If, apart from this section, two companies ("the first company" and "the second company") would be treated as members of the same group of companies and—

(*a*) in an accounting period one of the two companies has trading losses or other amounts eligible for relief from corporation tax which it would, apart from this section, be entitled to surrender by way of group relief; and
(*b*) arrangements are in existence by virtue of which, at some time during or after the expiry of that accounting period—

  (i) the first company or any successor of it could cease to be a member of the same group of companies as the second company and could become a member of the same group of companies as a third company; or
  (ii) any person has or could obtain, or any persons together have or could obtain, control of the first company but not of the second; or

(iii) a third company could begin to carry on the whole or any part of a trade which, at any time in that accounting period, is carried on by the first company and could do so either as a successor of the first company or as a successor of another company which is not a third company but which, at some time during or after the expiry of that accounting period, has begun to carry on the whole or any part of that trade;

then, for the purposes of this Chapter, the first company shall be treated as not being a member of the same group of companies as the second company.

(2) If a trading company is owned by a consortium or is a 90 per cent subsidiary of a holding company which is owned by a consortium and—

(*a*) in any accounting period the trading company or a member of the consortium has trading losses or other amounts eligible for relief from corporation tax which it would, apart from this section, be entitled to surrender by way of group relief; and

(*b*) arrangements are in existence by virtue of which—

(i) the trading company or any successor of it could, at some time during or after the expiry of that accounting period, become a 75 per cent subsidiary of a third company; or

(ii) any person who owns, or any persons who together own, less than 50 per cent of the ordinary share capital of the trading company has or together have, or could at some time during or after the expiry of that accounting period obtain, control of the trading company; or

(iii) any person, other than a holding company of which the trading company is a 90 per cent subsidiary, either alone or together with connected persons, holds or could obtain, or controls or could control the exercise of not less than 75 per cent of the votes which may be cast on a poll taken at a general meeting of that trading company in that accounting period or in any subsequent accounting period; or

(iv) a third company could begin to carry on, at some time during or after the expiry of that accounting period, the whole or any part of a trade which, at any time in that accounting period, is carried on by the trading company and could do so either as a successor of the trading company or as a successor of another company which is not a third company but which, at some time during or after the expiry of that accounting period, has begun to carry on the whole or any part of that trade;

then, for the purposes of this Chapter, the trading company shall be treated as though it did not (as the surrendering company or the claimant company) fall within section 402(3).

(3) In any case where a trading company is a 90 per cent subsidiary of a holding company which is owned by a consortium, any reference in subsection (2) above to the trading company, other than a reference in paragraph (*b*)(iv), shall be construed as including a reference to the holding company.

(4) In this section "third company" means a company which, apart from any provision made by or under any such arrangements as are specified in paragraph (*b*) of either subsection (1) or subsection (2) above, is not a member of the same group of companies as the first company or, as the case may be, the trading company or the holding company to which subsection (2) above applies.

(5) In subsections (1) and (2) above—

"arrangements" means arrangements of any kind whether in writing or not;

"connected persons" shall be construed in accordance with section 839 [but as if subsection (7) of that section (persons acting together to control a company are connected) were omitted][1]; and

"control" has the meaning assigned by section 840.

(6) For the purposes of subsections (1) and (2) above a company is the successor of another if it carries on a trade which, in whole or in part, the other company has ceased to carry on and the circumstances are such that—

(*a*) section 343 applies in relation to the two companies as the predecessor and the successor within the meaning of that section; or

(*b*) the two companies are connected with each other within the meaning of section 839.

(7) Where by virtue of any enactment a Minister of the Crown or Northern Ireland department has power to give directions to a statutory body as to the disposal of assets belonging to, or to a subsidiary of, that body, the existence of that power shall not be regarded as constituting or as having at any time constituted an arrangement within the meaning of this section.

Commentary—*Simon's Direct Tax Service* **D2.637, 638.**
Concession C10—"First refusal agreements" are not regarded as arrangements for the purposes of this section.
Statement of Practice SP 3/93—Interpretation of "arrangements" in sub-ss (1), (2) above.
Revenue Interpretation RI 160—Sub-s (2)(*b*)(iii) will only apply where there is a *continuing* commitment by two or more members, holding at least 75% of the votes, to ensure that consortium company operates in accordance with their collective will.
RI 224—Circumstances in which Delaware Limited Liability Companies (DLLCs) can be regarded as issuing "ordinary share capital" for the purposes of TA 1988 ss 402–413.
Revenue & other press releases—IR 31-1-80 (group relief: effect of arrangements for transfer of a group company does not affect group relief entitlement for earlier accounting periods TA 1988 s 12. Revenue view of when arrangements come into existence).
IR 16-1-84 (where preference shares carry voting rights in the event of non-payment of preference dividends and common control over claimant and surrendering company could be broken, Revenue regard such rights as "arrangements" under s 410(1)(*b*) for all periods in which they exist, not just accounting periods when there was entitlement to vote).

ICAEW TR799 June 1990 (arrangements by an administrator for the sale of shares in subsidiaries, even if the company subject to the order does not lose beneficial ownership of the shares in the subsidiaries, would by virtue of ss 240(11), 410(1)(b) cut off entitlement to group relief and set off by the subsidiaries of surrendered ACT).
Revenue Internal Guidance—Company Taxation Manual COT2678 (example of arrangements caught under this section). COT2683 (arrangements may exist at any time material to the group relief claim).
Simon's Tax Cases—s 410(1)(b), *Pilkington Brothers Ltd v IRC* [1982] STC 103*; *Irving v Tesco Stores (Holdings) Ltd* [1982] STC 881*; *Scottish and Universal Newspapers Ltd v Fisher* [1996] STC (SCD) 311.
Definitions—"Accounting period", s 834(1); "company", s 413(2); "group relief", s 402(1) by virtue of s 413(2); "holding company", s 413(3); "members of the same group", s 413(8), (9); "ordinary share capital", s 832(1); "trade", s 6(4); "trading company", s 413(3); "75 per cent subsidiary", ss 413(4), 838; "90 per cent subsidiary", ss 413(4), 838.
Cross references—See FA 1973 s 32 (power of inspector to enquire into the existence of arrangements referred to in sub-ss (1) or (2) above).
FA 1994 Sch 24 para 17 (certain arrangements and powers under Railways Act 1993 relating to railway privatisations not to constitute arrangements under this section).
Amendments—[1] Words in sub-s (5) inserted by FA 1997 s 68 with effect from 19 March 1997.

411 Exclusion of double allowances

(1) Relief shall not be given more than once in respect of the same amount, whether by giving group relief and by giving some other relief (in any accounting period) to the surrendering company, or by giving group relief more than once.

(2)–(9) ...[1]

(10) ...[2], any reference in [the Capital Allowances Act, except Parts 6 and 10][2] to an allowance made includes a reference to an allowance which would be made but for the granting of group relief, or but for that and but for an insufficiency of profits or other income against which to make it.

Commentary—*Simon's Direct Tax Service* **D2.632.**
Revenue Interpretation RI 224—Circumstances in which Delaware Limited Liability Companies (DLLCs) can be regarded as issuing "ordinary share capital" for the purposes of TA 1988 ss 402–413.
Definitions—"Accounting period", s 834(1); "company", s 413(2); "consortium claim", s 413(2); "group relief", s 402(1) by virtue of s 413(2); "profits", s 6(4); "surrendering company", s 402(1) by virtue of s 413(2).
Amendments—[1] Sub-ss (2)–(9) repealed by F(No 2)A 1997 s 41, Sch 7 paras 6, 9, Sch 8 Pt II(14) with effect for any claim for group relief if the accounting period of either the claimant company or the surrendering company ends after 1 July 1997 and the overlapping period (see TA 1988 s 403A(8)) would not fall entirely before that date (but see F(No 2)A 1997 Sch 7 para 9(3)–(5) for transitional provisions where the overlapping period straddles 2 July 1997).
[2] Words in sub-s (10) repealed, and substituted, by CAA 2001 ss 578, 580, Sch 2 para 38, Sch 4 with effect for corporation tax purposes as respects allowances and charges falling to be made for chargeable periods ending after 31 March 2001.

411A Group relief by way of substitution for loss relief

Commentary—*Simon's Direct Tax Service* **D2.625.**
Amendments—This section repealed by FA 1999 s 93, Sch 11 para 1 and Sch 20 Pt III(21) with effect for accounting periods ending after 30 June 1999.

[412 Claims and adjustments

(1) Claims for group relief are dealt with in Part VIII of Schedule 18 to the Finance Act 1998.

(2) Paragraph 73 of that Schedule provides for assessments or other adjustments where group relief has been given which is or has become excessive.][1]

Commentary—*Simon's Direct Tax Service* **D2.640.**
Revenue Interpretation RI 224—Circumstances in which Delaware Limited Liability Companies (DLLCs) can be regarded as issuing "ordinary share capital" for the purposes of TA 1988 ss 402–413.
Simon's Tax Cases—*Gallic Leasing Ltd v Coburn* [1991] STC 699*.
s 412(1), *A W Chapman Ltd v Hennessey* [1982] STC 214*.
s 412(1)(c), *Gallic Leasing Ltd v Coburn* [1989] STC 354*; *Farmer v Bankers Trust International Ltd* [1990] STC 564*.
Cross references—See FA 2000 s 46(1) (exemption under FA 2000 s 46(1) for income of a charity is not granted in respect of income chargeable to tax under Schedule D Case VI by virtue of this section).
Amendments—[1] This section substituted by FA 1998 Sch 19 para 46 with effect in relation to accounting periods ending after 30 June 1999 (by virtue of Finance Act 1994, Section 199, (Appointed Day) Order, SI 1998/3173 art 2).

413 Interpretation of Chapter IV

(1) The following provisions of this section have effect for the interpretation of this Chapter.

(2) In this Chapter—

"claimant company" has the meaning given by section 402(1);
["company" means any body corporate;][4]
"consortium claim" means a claim for group relief made by virtue of section 402(3);
"group claim" means a claim for group relief made by virtue of section 402(2);
"group/consortium company" means a company which is both a member of a group of companies and a company owned by a consortium;
"group relief" has the meaning given by section 402(1);
["non-resident company" means a company that is not resident in the United Kingdom;][4]
"relevant accounting period" means an accounting period beginning after 31st July 1985; and
"surrendering company" has the meaning given by section 402(1).

[(2A) For the purposes of group relief an accounting period of the claimant company which falls wholly or partly within an accounting period of the surrendering company shall be taken to correspond to that accounting period of the surrendering company.][1]

(3) For the purposes of this Chapter—

    (*a*) two companies shall be deemed to be members of a group of companies if one is the 75 per cent subsidiary of the other or both are 75 per cent subsidiaries of a third company;

    (*b*) "holding company" means a company the business of which consists wholly or mainly in the holding of shares or securities of companies which are its 90 per cent subsidiaries and which are trading companies; and

    (*c*) "trading company" means a company the business of which consists wholly or mainly in the carrying on of a trade or trades.

(4) In applying for the purposes of this Chapter the definition of "75 per cent subsidiary" in section 838, any share capital of a registered industrial and provident society shall be treated as ordinary share capital.

(5) ...[4] In determining for the purposes of this Chapter whether one company is a 75 per cent subsidiary of another, the other company shall be treated as not being the owner—

    (*a*) of any share capital which it owns directly in a body corporate if a profit on a sale of the shares would be treated as a trading receipt of its trade; or

    (*b*) of any share capital which it owns indirectly, and which is owned directly by a body corporate for which a profit on a sale of the shares would be a trading receipt; ...[4]

    (*c*) ...[4]

(6) References to a company being owned by a consortium shall be construed in accordance with paragraph (*a*) below except for the purposes of the definition of "group/consortium company" in subsection (2) above and of sections [403ZA(3)][2], 406(1)(*b*) and 409(5), (6) and (7), and for those purposes shall be construed in accordance with paragraph (*b*) below—

    (*a*) a company is owned by a consortium if three-quarters or more of the ordinary share capital of the company is beneficially owned between them by companies of which none beneficially owns less than one-twentieth of that capital;

    (*b*) a company is owned by a consortium if—

      (i) it is either such a trading company as is referred to in paragraph (*a*) or (*b*) of subsection (3) of section 402 or such a holding company as is referred to in paragraph (*c*) of that subsection, and

      (ii) three-quarters or more of the ordinary share capital of the company or, in the case of a company within section 402(3)(*b*), of its holding company is beneficially owned between them by companies of which none beneficially owns less than one-twentieth of that capital;

and the companies which so own three-quarters or more of that ordinary share capital are in this Chapter called the members of the consortium.

(7) Notwithstanding that at any time a company ("the subsidiary company") is a 75 per cent subsidiary or a 90 per cent subsidiary of another company ("the parent company") it shall not be treated at that time as such a subsidiary for the purposes of this Chapter unless, additionally at that time—

    (*a*) the parent company is beneficially entitled to not less than 75 per cent or, as the case may be, 90 per cent of any profits available for distribution to equity holders of the subsidiary company; and

    (*b*) the parent company would be beneficially entitled to not less than 75 per cent or, as the case may be, 90 per cent of any assets of the subsidiary company available for distribution to its equity holders on a winding-up.

(8), (9) ...[3]

(10) Schedule 18 shall have effect for supplementing this section.

Commentary—*Simon's Direct Tax Service* D2.621–623.
Statement of Practice SP C6—Revenue applies a weighted average taking into account the length of time instead of the average under sub-s (8) above.
Revenue Interpretation RI 224—Circumstances in which Delaware Limited Liability Companies (DLLCs) can be regarded as issuing "ordinary share capital" for the purposes of TA 1988 ss 402–413.
Revenue & other press releases—ICAEW TR588 25-9-85 (creation of a UK holding company to facilitate claims and surrenders of group relief, Revenue do not normally seek to apply *Furniss v Dawson* principle where all the companies are UK resident).
ICAEW TR799 June 1990 (the making of an administration order does not, by itself, break the group relationship, but the approval of the administrators' proposals under Insolvency Act 1986 s 24 might do so).
ICAEW TAX 15/92 16-11-92 (holding company s 413(3)(*b*), Sch 25, para 12 includes a company with a single 90% trading subsidiary).
Revenue Internal Guidance—Life assurance manual LAM 2.68-2.72 (application of sub-s (5) to life assurance companies).
Simon's Tax Cases—*J Sainsbury plc v O'Connor* [1990] STC 516*.
s 413(3), (5), (6), *Imperial Chemical Industries plc v Colmer* [1999] STC 1089*.
s 413(7), *J Sainsbury plc v O'Connor* [1991] STC 318*.
s 413(7)–(10), *Tilcon Ltd v Holland* [1981] STC 365*.
Definitions—"Accounting period", s 834(1); "ordinary share capital", s 832(1); "profits", s 6(4); "trade", s 6(4).
Cross references—See TA 1988 ss 403A–403C (as regards sub-s (2A) above, the said sections impose restrictions on group relief where the two accounting periods do not wholly coincide).
Amendments—[1] Sub-s (2A) inserted by F(No 2)A 1997 s 41, Sch 7 paras 7, 9, with effect in relation to any claim for group relief if the accounting period of either the claimant company or the surrendering company end after 1 July 1997 and the overlapping period (see TA 1988 s 403A(8)) would not fall entirely before that date (but see F(No 2)A 1997 Sch 7 para 9(3)–(5) for transitional provisions where the overlapping period straddles 2 July 1997).
[2] Words in sub-s (6) substituted by FA 1998 Sch 5 para 38 with effect from 1 April 1998 for corporation tax, subject to the transitional provisions in FA 1998 Sch 5 Part IV.
[3] Sub-ss (8), (9) repealed by FA 2000 ss 100(3)(*b*), (5), 156, Sch 40 Pt II(11) and deemed always to have had effect.

⁴ Definitions "company" and "non-resident company" inserted, and words in sub-s (5) repealed, by FA 2000 ss 97, 156, Sch 27 paras 2, 6(1), (4), Sch 40 Pt II(11) with effect for accounting periods ending after 31 March 2000. These amendments do not have effect for any determination as to whether the qualifying conditions for the purposes of TA 1988 s 403A(9) were met at any time before 1 April 2000.

PART XI
CLOSE COMPANIES

CHAPTER I
INTERPRETATIVE PROVISIONS

414 Close companies

(1) For the purposes of the Tax Acts, a "close company" is one which is under the control of five or fewer participators, or of participators who are directors, except that the expression does not apply—

(a) to a company not resident in the United Kingdom;
(b) to a registered industrial and provident society within the meaning of section 486(12) or to a building society;
(c) to a company controlled by or on behalf of the Crown, and not otherwise a close company; or
(d) to a company falling within section 415 or subsection (5) below.

[(2) Subject to section 415 and subsection (5) below, a company resident in the United Kingdom (but not falling within subsection (1)(b) above) is also a close company if five or fewer participators, or participators who are directors, together possess or are entitled to acquire—

(a) such rights as would, in the event of the winding-up of the company ("the relevant company") on the basis set out in subsection (2A) below, entitle them to receive the greater part of the assets of the relevant company which would then be available for distribution among the participators, or
(b) such rights as would in that event so entitle them if any rights which any of them or any other person has as a loan creditor (in relation to the relevant company or any other company) were disregarded.]¹

[(2A) In the notional winding-up of the relevant company, the part of the assets available for distribution among the participators which any person is entitled to receive is the aggregate of—

(a) any part of those assets which he would be entitled to receive in the event of the winding-up of the company, and
(b) any part of those assets which he would be entitled to receive if—

(i) any other company which is a participator in the relevant company and is entitled to receive any assets in the notional winding-up were also wound up on the basis set out in this subsection, and
(ii) the part of the assets of the relevant company to which the other company is entitled were distributed among the participators in the other company in proportion to their respective entitlement to the assets of the other company available for distribution among the participators.]¹

[(2B) In the application of subsection (2A) above to the notional winding-up of the other company and to any further notional winding-up required by paragraph (b) of that subsection (or by any further application of that paragraph), references to "the relevant company" shall have effect as references to the company concerned.]¹

[(2C) In ascertaining under subsection (2) above whether five or fewer participators, or participators who are directors, together possess or are entitled to acquire rights such as are mentioned in paragraph (a) or (b) of that subsection—

(a) a person shall be treated as a participator in or director of the relevant company if he is a participator in or director of any other company which would be entitled to receive assets in the notional winding-up of the relevant company on the basis set out in subsection (2A) above, and
(b) except in the application of subsection (2A) above, no account shall be taken of a participator which is a company unless the company possesses or is entitled to acquire the rights in a fiduciary or representative capacity.]¹

[(2D) Subsections (4) to (6) of section 416 apply for the purposes of subsections (2) and (2A) above as they apply for the purposes of subsection (2) of that section.]¹

(3) ...¹

(4) For the purposes of this section—

(a) a company is to be treated as controlled by or on behalf of the Crown if, but only if, it is under the control of the Crown or of persons acting on behalf of the Crown, independently of any other person, and (*b*) where a company is so controlled, it shall not be treated as being otherwise a close company unless it can be treated as a close company as being under the control of persons acting independently of the Crown.

(5) A company is not to be treated as a close company—

(*a*) if—

(i) it is controlled by a company which is not a close company, or by two or more companies none of which is a close company; and

(ii) it cannot be treated as a close company except by taking as one of the five or fewer participators requisite for its being so treated a company which is not a close company;

(*b*) if it cannot be treated as a close company except by virtue of [paragraph (*a*) of subsection (2) above or paragraph (*c*) of section 416(2) and it would not be a close company if the references in those paragraphs][1] to participators did not include loan creditors who are companies other than close companies.

(6) References in subsection (5) above to a close company shall be treated as applying to any company which, if resident in the United Kingdom, would be a close company.

(7) If shares in any company ("the first company") are held on trust for an exempt approved scheme as defined in section 592, then, unless the scheme is established wholly or mainly for the benefit of persons who are, or are dependants of, directors or employees or past directors or employees of—

(*a*) the first company; or

(*b*) an associated company of the first company; or

(*c*) a company which is under the control of any director or associate of a director of the first company or of two or more persons each of whom is such a director or associate; or

(*d*) a close company;

the persons holding the shares shall, for the purposes of subsection (5) above, be deemed to be the beneficial owners of the shares and, in that capacity, to be a company which is not a close company.

Commentary—*Simon's Direct Tax Service* D3.102, 110.
Definitions—"Apportionment", s 834(4); "associate", s 417(3); "associated company", s 416(1); "building society", s 832(1); "company", s 832(1), (2); "control", s 416(2); "director", s 417(5); "loan creditor", s 417(7)–(9); "participator", s 417(1); "the Tax Acts", s 832(1).
Amendments—[1] Sub-ss (2)–(2D) substituted for sub-s (2), words in sub-s (5)(*b*) substituted and sub-s (3) repealed by FA 1989 s 104, Sch 17 Pt V with effect from 1 April 1989.

415 Certain quoted companies not to be close companies

(1) Subject to the following provisions of this section, a company is not to be treated as being at any time a close company if—

(*a*) shares in the company carrying not less than 35 per cent of the voting power in the company (and not being shares entitled to a fixed rate of dividend, whether with or without a further right to participate in profits) have been allotted unconditionally to, or acquired unconditionally by, and are at that time beneficially held by, the public, and

(*b*) any such shares have within the preceding 12 months been the subject of dealings on a recognised stock exchange, and the shares have within those 12 months been [listed][1] in the official list of a recognised stock exchange.

(2) Subsection (1) above shall not apply to a company at any time when the total percentage of the voting power in the company possessed by all of the company's principal members exceeds 85 per cent.

(3) For the purposes of subsection (1) above shares in a company shall be deemed to be beneficially held by the public if, and only if, they—

(*a*) fall within subsection (4) below, and

(*b*) are not within the exceptions in subsection (5) below,

and a corresponding construction shall be given to the reference to shares which have been allotted unconditionally to, or acquired unconditionally by, the public.

(4) Shares shall fall within this subsection (as being beneficially held by the public)—

(*a*) if beneficially held by a company resident in the United Kingdom which is not a close company, or by a company not so resident which would not be a close company if it were so resident, or

(*b*) if held on trust for an exempt approved scheme as defined in section 592, or

(*c*) if they are not comprised in a principal member's holding.

(5) Shares shall not be deemed to be held by the public if they are held—

(*a*) by any director or associate of a director of the company, or

(*b*) by any company which is under the control of any such director or associate, or of two or more persons each of whom is such a director or associate, or

(*c*) by any associated company of the company, or

(*d*) as part of any fund the capital or income of which is applicable or applied wholly or mainly for the benefit of, or of the dependants of, the employees or directors, or past employees or directors, of the company, or of any company within paragraph (*b*) or (*c*) above.

References in this subsection to shares held by any person include references to any shares the rights or powers attached to which could, for the purposes of section 416, be attributed to that person under subsection (5) of that section.

(6) For the purposes of this section—

(a) a person is a principal member of a company if he possesses a percentage of the voting power in the company of more than 5 per cent and, where there are more than five such persons, if he is one of the five persons who possess the greatest percentages or if, because two or more persons possess equal percentages of the voting power in the company, there are no such five persons, he is one of the six or more persons (so as to include those two or more who possess equal percentages) who possess the greatest percentages, and

(b) a principal member's holding consists of the shares which carry the voting power possessed by him.

(7) In arriving at the voting power which a person possesses, there shall be attributed to him any voting power which, for the purposes of section 416, would be attributed to him under subsection (5) or (6) of that section.

(8) In this section "shares" include stock.

Commentary—*Simon's Direct Tax Service* **D3.114.**
Revenue Internal Guidance—Company taxation manual CT 6211 (Revenue interpretation of this section).
Definitions—"Associate", s 417(3); "associated company", s 416(1); "company", s 832(1), (2); "control", s 416(2); "director", s 417(5); "profits", s 6(4); "recognised stock exchange", s 841.
Amendments—[1] Word in sub-s (1) substituted by FA 1996 Sch 38 para 6(1), (2)(f), (8) with effect in relation to periods of 12 months ending after 31 March 1996.

416 Meaning of "associated company" and "control"

(1) For the purposes of this Part, ...[1], a company is to be treated as another's "associated company" at a given time if, at that time or at any other time within one year previously, one of the two has control of the other, or both are under the control of the same person or persons.

(2) For the purposes of this Part, a person shall be taken to have control of a company if he exercises, or is able to exercise or is entitled to acquire, direct or indirect control over the company's affairs, and in particular, but without prejudice to the generality of the preceding words, if he possesses or is entitled to acquire—

(a) the greater part of the share capital or issued share capital of the company or of the voting power in the company; or

(b) such part of the issued share capital of the company as would, if the whole of the income of the company were in fact distributed among the participators (without regard to any rights which he or any other person has as a loan creditor), entitle him to receive the greater part of the amount so distributed; or

(c) such rights as would, in the event of the winding-up of the company or in any other circumstances, entitle him to receive the greater part of the assets of the company which would then be available for distribution among the participators.

(3) Where two or more persons together satisfy any of the conditions of subsection (2) above, they shall be taken to have control of the company.

(4) For the purposes of subsection (2) above a person shall be treated as entitled to acquire anything which he is entitled to acquire at a future date, or will at a future date be entitled to acquire.

(5) For the purposes of subsections (2) and (3) above, there shall be attributed to any person any rights or powers of a nominee for him, that is to say, any rights or powers which another person possesses on his behalf or may be required to exercise on his direction or behalf.

(6) For the purposes of subsections (2) and (3) above, there may also be attributed to any person all the rights and powers of any company of which he has, or he and associates of his have, control or any two or more such companies, or of any associate of his or of any two or more associates of his, including those attributed to a company or associate under subsection (5) above, but not those attributed to an associate under this subsection; and such attributions shall be made under this subsection as will result in the company being treated as under the control of five or fewer participators if it can be so treated.

Commentary—*Simon's Direct Tax Service* **D3.107, 112.**
Concession C8—For the purposes of sub-s (2)(c) above, a money broker is not a participator of a company carrying on business as stock jobber by reason of short term loans or advances.
C9—Companies are not associated merely because they are treated under sub-ss (2)–(4) above as controlled by the same loan creditor if apart from the common creditor there is no other connection between the companies. Also companies are not associated by reason of taking into account fixed rate preference shares (defined in s 95(5) of this Act) if certain conditions exist. Also it depends on the facts as to whether companies are associated because a person can exercise the rights and powers of his associates described in sub-s (2)(b), (c) above. Trustee companies which hold rights and powers and thereby exercise control not to be treated as associates where the rights are held in trust and there is no other connection between the companies.
Revenue & other press releases—IR 21-10-83 (associated companies: two companies are under the control of the same person or persons only if an irreducible group of persons having control of one company is identical with an irreducible group of persons having control of the second company. An irreducible group of persons is one which has control but which would not have control if any one of them were excluded).
Revenue Internal Guidance—Company taxation manual CT 6201–6206 (meaning of "control").
Simon's Tax Cases—*R v IRC, ex p Newfields Developments Ltd* [2001] STC 901.
Definitions—"Associate", s 417(3); "loan creditor", s 417(7)–(9); "participator", s 417(1).

Amendments—¹ Words in sub-s (1) repealed by FA 1989 Sch 17 Pt V in relation to accounting periods beginning after 31 March 1989.

417 Meaning of "participator", "associate", "director" and "loan creditor"

(1) For the purposes of this Part, a "participator" is, in relation to any company, a person having a share or interest in the capital or income of the company, and, without prejudice to the generality of the preceding words, includes—

(a) any person who possesses, or is entitled to acquire, share capital or voting rights in the company;

(b) any loan creditor of the company;

(c) any person who possesses, or is entitled to acquire, a right to receive or participate in distributions of the company (construing "distributions" without regard to section 418) or any amounts payable by the company (in cash or in kind) to loan creditors by way of premium on redemption; and

(d) any person who is entitled to secure that income or assets (whether present or future) of the company will be applied directly or indirectly for his benefit.

In this subsection references to being entitled to do anything apply where a person is presently entitled to do it at a future date, or will at a future date be entitled to do it.

(2) The provisions of subsection (1) above are without prejudice to any particular provision of this Part requiring a participator in one company to be treated as being also a participator in another company.

(3) For the purposes of this Part "associate" means, in relation to a participator—

(a) any relative or partner of the participator;

(b) the trustee or trustees of any settlement in relation to which the participator is, or any relative of his (living or dead) is or was, a settlor ("settlement" and "settlor" having here the same meaning as in [Chapter IA of Part XV (see section 660G(1) and (2))]¹; and

(c) where the participator is interested in any shares or obligations of the company which are subject to any trust, or are part of the estate of a deceased person—

(i) the trustee or trustees of the settlement concerned or, as the case may be, the personal representatives of the deceased; and

(ii) if the participator is a company, any other company interested in those shares or obligations;

and has a corresponding meaning in relation to a person other than a participator.

(4) In subsection (3) above "relative" means husband or wife, parent or remoter forebear, child or remoter issue, or brother or sister.

(5) For the purposes of this Part "director" includes any person occupying the position of director by whatever name called, any person in accordance with whose directions or instructions the directors are accustomed to act, and any person who—

(a) is a manager of the company or otherwise concerned in the management of the company's trade or business, and

(b) is, either on his own or with one or more associates, the beneficial owner of, or able, directly or through the medium of other companies or by any other indirect means, to control 20 per cent or over of the ordinary share capital of the company.

(6) In subsection (5)(b) above the expression "either on his own or with one or more associates" requires a person to be treated as owning or, as the case may be, controlling what any associate owns or controls, even if he does not own or control share capital on his own.

(7) Subject to subsection (9) below, for the purposes of this Part "loan creditor", in relation to a company, means a creditor in respect of any debt incurred by the company—

(a) for any money borrowed or capital assets acquired by the company; or

(b) for any right to receive income created in favour of the company; or

(c) for consideration the value of which to the company was (at the time when the debt was incurred) substantially less than the amount of the debt (including any premium thereon);

or in respect of any redeemable loan capital issued by the company.

(8) Subject to subsection (9) below, a person who is not the creditor in respect of any debt or loan capital to which subsection (7) above applies but nevertheless has a beneficial interest therein shall, to the extent of that interest, be treated for the purposes of this Part as a loan creditor in respect of that debt or loan capital.

(9) A person carrying on a business of banking shall not be deemed to be a loan creditor in respect of any loan capital or debt issued or incurred by the company for money lent by him to the company in the ordinary course of that business.

Commentary—*Simon's Direct Tax Service* **D3.103–106.**

Concession C9—For the purpose of small companies marginal relief, TA 1988 s 13, where there is no substantial trading interdependence between the companies, "relative" defined in sub-s (4) above does not include a relative other than spouse and minor children.

Revenue & other press releases—CCAB June 1968 (holders of units in a unit trust are not "associates" merely by reason of their common membership of the trust).

Revenue Internal Guidance—Company Taxation Manual COT6112, 6204 (meaning of "entitled to acquire" and "entitled to secure" in sub-s (1)).
COT6113 (where interest is treated as a distribution under s 209, the creditor is a loan creditor).
COT6115 (separated spouses are associates, but not divorced spouses; half-brothers are associates but not step-brothers).
COT6116 (meaning of "interested in" in sub-s (3)(*a*)).
COT6211 (sub-s (4)(*a*): where the company holding the shares goes into liquidation, this does not of itself render the company in which it holds shares close).
Cross references—See FA 1989 Sch 12, paras 2–4 (Revenue information powers).
Definitions—"Control", s 416(2); "ordinary share capital", s 832(1); "trade", s 6(4).
Amendments—¹ Words in sub-s (3)(*b*) substituted by FA 1995 s 74, Sch 17 para 6, with effect from the year 1995–96 (and apply to every settlement, wherever and whenever made or entered into).

Additional matters to be treated as distributions

418 "Distribution" to include certain expenses of close companies

(1) Subject to such exceptions as are mentioned in section 209(1), in the Corporation Tax Acts "distribution", in relation to a close company, includes, unless otherwise stated, any such amount as is required to be treated as a distribution by subsection (2) below.

(2) Subject to subsection (3) below, where a close company incurs expense in or in connection with the provision for any participator of living or other accommodation, of entertainment, of domestic or other services, or of other benefits or facilities of whatever nature, the company shall be treated as making a distribution to him of an amount equal to so much of that expense as is not made good to the company by the participator.

(3) Subsection (2) above shall not apply to expense incurred in or in connection with the provision—

(*a*) for a person employed in [employment to which Chapter II of Part V applies]¹ of such benefits as are mentioned in any of sections 154 to 165; or
(*b*) of living accommodation for any person if the accommodation is (within the meaning of section 145) provided by reason of his employment; or
(*c*) for the spouse, children or dependants of a person employed by the company of any pension, annuity, lump sum, gratuity or other like benefit to be given on that person's death or retirement.

(4) The amount of the expense to be taken into account under subsection (2) above as a distribution shall be the same as would under Chapter II of Part V be the cash equivalent of the resultant benefit to the participator.

(5) Subsection (2) above shall not apply if the company and the participator are both resident in the United Kingdom and—

(*a*) one is a subsidiary of the other or both are subsidiaries of a third company also so resident, and
(*b*) the benefit to the participator arises on or in connection with a transfer of assets or liabilities by the company to him, or to the company by him.

(6) The question whether one body corporate is a subsidiary of another for the purposes of subsection (5) above shall be determined as a question whether it is a 51 per cent subsidiary of that other, except that that other shall be treated as not being the owner—

(*a*) of any share capital which it owns directly in a body corporate if a profit on a sale of the shares would be treated as a trading receipt of its trade; or
(*b*) of any share capital which it owns indirectly, and which is owned directly by a body corporate for which a profit on a sale of the shares would be a trading receipt; or
(*c*) of any share capital which it owns directly or indirectly in a body corporate not resident in the United Kingdom.

(7) Where each of two or more close companies makes a payment to a person who is not a participator in that company, but is a participator in another of those companies, and the companies are acting in concert or under arrangements made by any person, then each of those companies and any participator in it shall be treated as if the payment made to him had been made by that company.

This subsection shall apply, with any necessary adaptations, in relation to the giving of any consideration, and to the provision of any facilities, as it applies in relation to the making of a payment.

(8) For the purposes of this section any reference to a participator includes an associate of a participator, and any participator in a company which controls another company shall be treated as being also a participator in that other company.

Commentary—*Simon's Direct Tax Service* D3.117.
Revenue & other press releases—CCAB June 1978 (a close company providing money for purchase of shares by trustees of a profit sharing scheme approved under s 186 is not treated as making a distribution).
Revenue Internal Guidance—Company Taxation Manual COT6609 (Schedule E rule applies only for determining the amount of any benefit: it does not extend the scope of s 418).
COT6610 (s 418 is not applied to benefits which are chargeable under Schedule E on a director or employee).
COT6616 (s 418 applies to money benefits as well as to benefits in kind).
COT6617 (s 418 also catches excessive amounts of pensions, annual payments, rents, royalties etc to the extent that they are disallowed in the company's corporation tax computation).
COT6619 (treatment of benefits provided for exempt or lower rate participators).

Definitions—"Close company", s 832(1); "the Corporation Tax Acts", s 831(1)(*a*); "director", s 417(5); "distribution", s 209(2) by virtue of s 832(1); "employment", s 6(4); "participator", s 417(1); "profit", s 6(4); "trade", s 6(4); "51 per cent subsidiary", s 838.
Amendments—[1] Words in sub-s (3)(*a*) substituted by FA 1989 s 53(2)(*f*).

CHAPTER II
CHARGES TO TAX IN CONNECTION WITH LOANS

419 Loans to participators etc

(1) Subject to the following provisions of this section and section 420, where a close company, otherwise than in the ordinary course of a business carried on by it which includes the lending of money, makes any loan or advances any money to an individual who is a participator in the company or an associate of a participator, there shall be [due][1] from the company, as if it were an amount of corporation tax chargeable on the company for the accounting period in which the loan or advance is made, an amount equal to [25 per cent of the amount of the loan or advance][4].

In relation to a loan or advance made in an accounting period ending after the day, not being earlier than 31st March 1992, appointed by order by the Treasury for the purpose of this provision, this subsection shall have effect with the substitution for "assessed on and recoverable" of "due".

(2) For the purposes of this section the cases in which a close company is to be regarded as making a loan to any person include a case where—

(*a*) that person incurs a debt to the close company; or
(*b*) a debt due from that person to a third party is assigned to the close company;

and then the close company shall be regarded as making a loan of an amount equal to the debt.

[(3) Tax due by virtue of this section in relation to any loan or advance shall be due and payable [in accordance with section 59D of the Management Act][3] on the day following the expiry of nine months from the end of the accounting period in which the loan or advance was made.][2]

(4) Where a close company has made a loan or advance which gave rise to a charge to tax on the company under subsection (1) above and

[(*a*)][5] the loan or advance or any part of it is repaid to the company, [or
(*b*) the whole or part of the debt in respect of the loan or advance is released or written off,][5]

relief shall be given from that tax, or a proportionate part of it ...[3].

Relief under this subsection shall be given on a claim, which must be made within six years from the end of the financial year in which the repayment is made [or the release or writing off occurs.][5]

[(4A) Where

[(*a*)][5] the repayment of the whole or any part of a loan or advance occurs on or after the day on which tax by virtue of this section becomes due in relation to that loan or advance [or,
(*b*) the release or writing off of the whole or any part of the debt in respect of a loan or advance occurs on or after the day on which tax by virtue of this section becomes due in relation to that loan or advance,][5]

relief in respect of the repayment[, release or writing off][5] shall not be given under subsection (4) above at any time before the expiry of nine months from the end of the accounting period in which the repayment[, release or writing off][5] occurred.][2]

[(4B) Schedule 1A to the Taxes Management Act 1970 (claims and elections not included in return) applies to a claim for relief under subsection (4) above unless—

(*a*) the claim is included (by amendment or otherwise) in the return for the period in which the loan or advance was made, and
(*b*) the relief may be given at the time the claim is made.][3]

(5) Where, under arrangements made by any person otherwise than in the ordinary course of a business carried on by him—

(*a*) a close company makes a loan or advance which, apart from this subsection, does not give rise to any charge on the company under subsection (1) above, and
(*b*) some person other than the close company makes a payment or transfers property to, or releases or satisfies (in whole or in part) a liability of, an individual who is a participator in the company or an associate of a participator,

then, unless in respect of the matter referred to in paragraph (*b*) above there falls to be included in the total income of the participator or associate an amount not less than the loan or advance, this section shall apply as if the loan or advance had been made to him.

(6) In subsections (1) and (5)(*b*) above the references to an individual shall apply also to a company receiving the loan or advance in a fiduciary or representative capacity, ...[2]

(7) For the purposes of this section any participator in a company which controls another company shall be treated as being also a participator in that other company.

Commentary—*Simon's Direct Tax Service* **D3.401–406.**
Revenue Interpretation RI 16—A single loan to a participator may not constitute a loan in the ordinary course of business for the purposes of sub-s (1) above.

Revenue & other press releases—ICAEW TR806 August 1990 (Revenue view, an assessment under s 419 is not restricted to an accounting period but can be raised for a quarter in which a loan is advanced, although such assessments are rare).

Revenue Internal Guidance—Company Taxation Manual COT 6650 (the lending of money, to be part of the ordinary business of a company, must be the lending of money in general, in the sense, for example, that money lending is part of the ordinary business of a registered money lender or bank).

COT 6650 (loan to the trustees of a settlement or to a partnership can be caught: see s 417(3)).

COT 6650a (treatment of irrecoverable loans in the case of insolvent company).

COT 6652 (Revenue approach to the aggregating of separate accounts).

COT 6662 (procedure where loan repaid).

COT 6664 (procedure where borrower dies).

COT 6665 (loan to trustees: procedure where trust comes to an end).

COT 10700 (interest is charged under TMA 1970 s 87A on tax paid late).

Enquiry Handbook EH 1082 (Revenue procedures concerning enquiry work in relation to this section).

Investigations handbook IH 7150 ("bed and breakfasting" of loans to participators will be challenged).

Schedule E manual, SE 21748 (loans written off—loans made by close companies).

SE 26500–26510 (beneficial loans: interaction between Schedule E and other tax charges, loans from close companies).

Simon's Tax Cases—*Joint v Bracken Developments Ltd* [1994] STC 300; *Earlspring Properties Ltd v Guest* [1995] STC 479*; [1998] STC (SCD) 222; *Grant v Watton* [1999] STC 330; *Brennan (Inspector of Taxes) v Deanby Investment Co Ltd* [2001] STC 536.

s 419(1), *Stephens v T Pittas Ltd* [1983] STC 576*.

Definitions—"Accounting period", s 834(1); "advance corporation tax", s 14(1); "associate", s 417(3); "close company", s 414(1) by virtue of s 832(1); "participator", s 417(1); "tax", s 832(3).

Cross references—See TMA 1970 s 109 (interpretation of references in this section to assessment and recovery of tax as if it were corporation tax).

TMA 1970 Sch 3 para 4 (rules for assigning proceedings to particular Commissioners).

TA 1988 s 421 (taxation of borrower when loan under this section is rebased or written off).

TA 1988 s 421(4) (s 421 to be construed as one with this section).

TA 1988 s 422 (extension of this section to loans by companies controlled by close companies; and s 422 to be construed as one with this section).

TA 1988 s 825(4) (repayment supplement on tax repaid on a claim under sub-s (4) above).

TA 1988 s 826(4) (interest on repayment of tax made on a claim under sub-s (4) above).

FA 1989 Sch 12, para 1(*a*) (administrative provisions relating to close companies).

Amendments—[1] Words in sub-s (1) substituted by virtue of provisions in the same subsection which read—

"In relation to a loan or advance made in an accounting period ending after the day, not being earlier than 31st March 1992, appointed by order by the Treasury for the purpose of this provision, this subsection shall have effect with the substitution for 'assessed on and recoverable' of 'due'."

The appointed day is 30 September 1993 (by virtue of Corporation Tax Acts (Provisions for Payment of Tax and Returns) (Appointed Days) Order, SI 1992/3066 art 2(1), 2(*b*)).

[2] Sub-s (3) substituted, sub-s (4A) inserted and words in sub-s (6) repealed by FA 1996 s 173, Sch 41 Pt V(25) with effect in relation to any loan or advance made in an accounting period ending after 30 March 1996.

[3] Words inserted in sub-s (3), repealed in sub-s (4) and sub-s (4B) inserted by FA 1998 Sch 19 para 47 with effect in relation to accounting periods ending after 30 June 1999 (by virtue of Finance Act 1994, Section 199, (Appointed Day) Order, SI 1998/3173 art 2).

[4] Words in sub-s (1) substituted by FA 1998 Sch 3 para 24 with effect in relation to loans or advances made after 5 April 1999.

[5] Words in sub-ss (4), (4A) inserted by FA 1998 Sch 3 para 24 with effect in relation to the release or writing off of the whole or part of a debt after 5 April 1999.

420 Exceptions from section 419

(1) Section 419(2)(*a*) shall not apply to a debt incurred for the supply by the close company of goods or services in the ordinary course of its trade or business unless the credit given exceeds six months or is longer than that normally given to the company's customers.

(2) Section 419(1) shall not apply to a loan made to a director or employee of a close company, or of an associated company of the close company, if—

    (*a*) neither the amount of the loan, nor that amount when taken together with any other outstanding loans which—

        (i) were made by the close company or any of its associated companies to the borrower ...[1]; and

        (ii) if made before 31st March 1971, were made for the purpose of purchasing a dwelling which was or was to be the borrower's only or main residence;

    exceeds £15,000 and the outstanding loans falling within sub-paragraph (ii) above do not together exceed £10,000; and

    (*b*) the borrower works full-time for the close company or any of its associated companies; and

    (*c*) the borrower does not have a material interest in the close company or in any associated company of the close company;

but if the borrower acquires such a material interest at a time when the whole or part of any such loan made after 30th March 1971 remains outstanding the close company shall be regarded as making to him at that time a loan of an amount equal to the sum outstanding.

Section 168(11) shall apply for the purpose of determining whether a person has, for the purpose of this subsection, a material interest in a company, but with the omission of the words following "417(3)".

Commentary—*Simon's Direct Tax Service* D3.404.

Simon's Tax Cases—*Earlspring Properties Ltd v Guest* [1993] STC 473*.

Definitions—"Associated company", s 416(1); "close company", s 832(1); "director", s 417(5); "trade", s 6(4).

Cross references—See TMA 1970 s 109 (interpretation of references in this section to assessment and recovery of tax as if it were corporation tax).

TMA 1970 Sch 3 para 4 (rules for assigning proceedings to particular Commissioners).

TA 1988 s 422 (extension of this section to loans by companies controlled by close companies; and s 422 to be construed as one with this section).

FA 1989 Sch 12, para 1(*a*) (administrative provisions relating to close companies).

Amendments—¹ Words in sub-s (2)(*a*)(i) repealed by FA 1988 Sch 3 para 16 and Sch 14, Pt VIII where the loan first mentioned in sub-s (2) of this section is made after 5 April 1990.

421 Taxation of borrower when loan under section 419 released etc

(1) Subject to the following provisions of this section, where a company is assessed or liable to be assessed under section 419 in respect of a loan or advance and releases or writes off the whole or part of the debt in respect of it, then—

(*a*) for the purpose of computing the total income of the person to whom the loan or advance was made, a sum equal to the amount so released or written off shall be treated as income received by him after deduction of income tax [at the [Schedule F ordinary rate]⁵]² from a corresponding gross amount;

(*b*) no repayment of income tax shall be made in respect of that income and [he shall not be liable to pay]³ income tax at the [Schedule F ordinary rate]⁵ on that income;

(*c*) the income included by virtue of paragraph (*a*) above in his total income [shall be treated [(without prejudice to paragraph (*b*) above) as if it were income to which section 1A applies [by virtue of subsection (2)(*b*) of that section]⁵, but]⁴, notwithstanding the preceding provisions of this subsection, shall be treated]¹ for the purposes of sections 348 and 349(1) as not brought into charge to income tax;

(*d*) for the purpose of determining whether any or what amount of tax is, by virtue of paragraph (*a*) above, to be taken into account as having been deducted from a gross amount in the case of an individual whose total income is reduced by any deductions so much only of that gross amount shall be taken into account as is part of his total income as so reduced.

(2) If the loan or advance referred to in subsection (1) above was made to a person who has since died, or to trustees of a trust which has come to an end, this section, instead of applying to the person to whom it was made, shall apply to the person from whom the debt is due at the time of release or writing off (and if it is due from him as personal representative, within the meaning of Part XVI, the amount treated as received by him shall accordingly be included for the purposes of that Part in the aggregate income of the estate) and subsection (1) above shall apply accordingly with the necessary modifications.

(3) This section shall not have effect in relation to a loan or advance made to a person if any sum falls in respect of the loan or advance to be included in his income by virtue of section 677, except so far as the amount released or written off exceeds the sums previously falling to be so included (without the addition for income tax provided for by subsection (6) of that section).

(4) This section shall be construed as one with section 419.

Commentary—*Simon's Direct Tax Service* **D3.407.**
Revenue Internal Guidance—Company Taxation Manual COT6663 (amount charged under s 421 in respect of a loan to a director or employee is not charged under Schedule E).
Schedule E manual, SE 21748 (loans written off—loans made by close companies).
Simon's Tax Cases—*Collins v Addies; Greenfield v Bains* [1992] STC 746*.
Definitions—"Basic rate", s 832(1); "company", s 832(1), (2); "deduction of income tax", s 4(1); "lower rate", s 832(1); "Schedule F ordinary rate", s 832(1); "total income", s 835(1).
Cross references—See TA 1988 s 422(5) (extension of s 419 to loans by companies controlled by close companies).
TA 1988 s 677(3) (avoidance of double tax charge in respect of a loan to a settlor taxed under this section).
TA 1988 s 701(8) (extension of sub-s (2) above to s 701(8)).
FA 1989 Sch 12, para 1(*a*) (administrative provisions relating to close companies).
Amendments—¹ Words in sub-s (1)(*c*) substituted by F(No 2)A 1992 s 19(6), (7) with effect from the year 1992–93.
² Words in sub-s (1)(*a*) inserted by the Finance Act 1993 s 77(4)(a), (5) with effect from the year 1993–94.
³ Words in sub-s (1)(*b*) substituted by FA 1996 s 122(6) with effect from the year 1996–97.
⁴ Words in sub-s (1)(*c*) substituted by FA 1996 Sch 6 para 9 with effect from the year 1996–97.
⁵ Words in sub-s (1)(*a*), (*b*) substituted for "lower rate", and words in sub-s (1)(*c*) inserted, by F(No 2)A 1997 s 34, Sch 4 para 11 with effect in relation to the release or writing off of the whole or part of a debt after 5 April 1999.

422 Extension of section 419 to loans by companies controlled by close companies

(1) Subject to subsection (4) below, where a company which is controlled by a close company makes a loan which, apart from this section, does not give rise to a charge under subsection (1) of section 419, that section and section 420 shall apply as if the loan had been made by the close company.

(2) Subject to subsection (4) below, where a company which is not controlled by a close company makes a loan which, apart from this section, does not give rise to a charge under subsection (1) of section 419 and a close company subsequently acquires control of it, that section and section 420 shall apply as if the loan had been made by the close company immediately after the time when it acquired control.

(3) Where two or more close companies together control the company that makes or has made the loan, subsections (1) and (2) above shall have effect—

(*a*) as if each of them controlled that company; and

(*b*) as if the loan had been made by each of those close companies,

but the loan shall be apportioned between those close companies in such proportion as may be appropriate having regard to the nature and amount of their respective interests in the company that makes or has made the loan.

(4) Subsections (1) and (2) above do not apply if it is shown that no person has made any arrangements (otherwise than in the ordinary course of a business carried on by him) as a result of which there is a connection—

    (*a*) between the making of the loan and the acquisition of control; or

    (*b*) between the making of the loan and the provision by the close company of funds for the company making the loan;

and the close company shall be regarded as providing funds for the company making the loan if it directly or indirectly makes any payment or transfers any property to, or releases or satisfies (in whole or in part) a liability of, the company making the loan.

(5) Where, by virtue of this section, sections 419 and 420 have effect as if a loan made by one company had been made by another, any question under those sections or section 421 whether—

    (*a*) the company making the loan did so otherwise than in the ordinary course of a business carried on by it which includes the lending of money;

    (*b*) the loan or any part of it has been repaid to the company;

    (*c*) the company has released or written off the whole or part of the debt in respect of the loan,

shall be determined by reference to the company that makes the loan.

(6) This section shall be construed as one with section 419 and section 420 and in this section—

    (*a*) ''loan'' includes advance; and

    (*b*) references to a company making a loan include references to cases in which the company is, or if it were a close company would be, regarded as making a loan by virtue of section 419(2).

Commentary—*Simon's Direct Tax Service* D3.403.
Revenue Internal Guidance—Company Taxation Manual COT6669–6675 (examples illustrating the application of s 422 and procedure).
Definitions—''Close company'', s 832(1); ''company'', s 832(1), (2); ''control'', s 416(2).
Cross references—See FA 1989 Sch 12, para 1(*a*) (administrative provisions relating to close companies).

CHAPTER III

APPORTIONMENT OF UNDISTRIBUTED INCOME ETC

Amendments—This Chapter (ss 423-430) repealed by FA 1989 s 103(1) and Sch 17 Pt V in relation to accounting periods beginning after 31 March 1989, subject to FA 1989 s 103(2).

PART XII

SPECIAL CLASSES OF COMPANIES AND BUSINESSES

CHAPTER I

INSURANCE COMPANIES, UNDERWRITERS AND CAPITAL REDEMPTION BUSINESS

Revenue Interpretation RI 30—Insurance agents commission: treatment under Case I of commission repaid by an agent owing to early lapse of policy.
Revenue Internal Guidance—Life assurance manual gives a detailed exposition of all aspects of the taxation of life assurance companies.
Cross references—See FA 1999 s 81 (charge to tax on disposal of investment assets of general insurance group of companies previously transferred intra-group under terms of a Concession).

Insurance companies: general

431 Interpretative provisions relating to insurance companies

(1) This section has effect for the interpretation of this Chapter.

(2) Unless the context otherwise requires—

    ''annuity business'' means the business of granting annuities on human life;
    ...[5]

    [''basic life assurance and general annuity business'' has the meaning given by section 431F;][8]

    [''closing'' and ''opening'', in relation to a period of account, refer respectively to the position at the end and at the beginning of the period and, in relation to an accounting period, refer respectively to the position at the end and at the beginning of the period of account in which the accounting period falls;][1]

    [''closing liabilities'' includes liabilities assumed at the end of the period of account concerned in consequence of the declaration of reversionary bonuses or a reduction in premiums;][1]

    [''contract of insurance'' has the meaning given by Article 3(1) of the Financial Services and Markets Act 2000 (Regulated Activities) Order 2001 and ''contract of long-term insurance'' means any contract which falls within Part II of Schedule 1 to that Order;][14]

    [...[4]]
    ...[5]

[...¹¹]¹

["insurance business transfer scheme" means a scheme falling within section 105 of the Financial Services and Markets Act 2000, including an excluded scheme falling within Case 2, 3 or 4 of subsection (3) of that section;

"insurance company" means—

    (*a*) a person (other than a friendly society) who has permission under Part 4 of the Financial Services and Markets Act 2000 to effect or carry out contracts of insurance, or

    (*b*) an EEA firm of the kind mentioned in paragraph 5(*d*) of Schedule 3 to that Act or a firm qualifying for authorisation under Schedule 4 to that Act which—

        (i) carries on business which consists of the effecting or carrying out of contracts of insurance, and

        (ii) carries on that business through a branch or agency in the United Kingdom;]¹⁵

[...¹³]¹

["liabilities", in relation to an insurance company, means the [long-term liabilities of the company determined for the purposes of the company's periodical return on actuarial principles in accordance with section 5.6 of the Prudential Sourcebook (Insurers) (excluding any that have been reinsured);]¹⁴]¹

"life assurance business" includes annuity business;

["life reinsurance business" has the meaning given by section 431C;"]⁸

["linked assets", and related expressions, shall be construed in accordance with section 432ZA;]⁹

["long-term business" means business which consists of the effecting or carrying out of contracts of long-term insurance;]¹⁴

["[long-term insurance]¹⁶" means the fund maintained by an insurance company in respect of its [long-term]¹⁷ business...¹¹;]¹

["long-term liabilities" means liabilities of an insurance company arising under or in connection with contracts for long-term business (including liabilities arising from deposit back arrangements within the meaning given by section 11.1 of the Prudential Sourcebook (Insurers));]¹⁵

...⁶

[...¹¹]¹

...⁶

["overseas life assurance business" has the meaning given by section 431D;]⁹

["overseas life assurance fund" shall be construed in accordance with Schedule 19AA;]¹

"overseas life insurance company" means an insurance company [not resident in]³ the United Kingdom but carrying on life assurance business through a branch or agency in the United Kingdom; ...⁵

["pension business" has the meaning given by section 431B;]⁸

"periodical return", in relation to an insurance company, means a return deposited with [Financial Services Authority under section 9.6 of the Prudential Sourcebook (Insurers)]¹⁵;

["the Prudential Sourcebook (Insurers)" means the Interim Prudential Sourcebook for Insurers made by the Financial Services Authority under the Financial Services and Markets Act 2000;]¹⁴

...⁵

["reinsurance business" includes retrocession business;]⁸

...²

["value", in relation to assets of an insurance company, means the value of the assets as taken into account for the purposes of the company's periodical return;]¹

["with-profits liabilities" means liabilities in respect of policies or contracts under which the policy holders or annuitants are eligible to participate in surplus;]¹.

[(2A), (3)–(6) ...]¹⁰

Commentary—*Simon's Direct Tax Service* **D4.501, 515.**
Regulations—Insurance Companies (Capital Redemption Business) (Modification of the Corporation Tax Acts) Regulations SI 1999/498.
Revenue Internal Guidance—Life assurance manual LAM 2.4-2.8 (meaning of "insurance company").
Definitions—"Accounting period", s 834(1).
Cross references—See TA 1988 s 444B and Sch 19AC para 6 (modification of sub-s (2) above in relation to overseas life insurance companies).
TA 1988 Sch 28 para 3(6) (calculation of offshore unindexed gain of a life assurance company; s 431 to have effect as if Sch 28, para 3(4) were included in this Chapter).
Modifications—Sub-s (2) is modified, so as to add and substitute definitions, and insert sub-ss (7)–(14), so far as applies to the life or endowment business carried on by this section, by the Friendly Societies (Modification of the Corporation Tax Acts) Regulations, SI 1997/473 regs 6, 7.
In sub-s (2), a definition of "individual savings account business" is inserted in respect of individual savings account business of insurance companies by the Individual Savings Account Regulations 1998, SI 1998/1871 reg 7, with effect from 6 April 1999.
In sub-s (2), a definition of "capital redemption business" inserted, and definition of "life assurance business" amended, in applying life assurance provisions of the Corporation Tax Acts to insurance companies carrying on capital redemption business with effect for accounting periods ending after 30 June 1999: see Insurance Companies (Capital Redemption Business) (Modification of the Corporation Tax Acts) Regulations, SI 1999/498 reg 5.
Amendments—¹ Definitions in sub-s (2) inserted by FA 1990 Sch 6 para 1(1), (2)(*b*), but subject to the provisions in paras 11, 12 of that Schedule.
² Definitions of "policyholders' fraction" and "shareholders' fraction" inserted by FA 1989 Sch 8 para 1 in sub-s (2) repealed by FA 1990 Sch 19 Pt IV and the definitions are deemed never to have had effect; see FA 1990 s 45(11).
³ Words in the definition of "overseas life insurance company" in sub-s (2) substituted by FA 1993 s 103(1), (3) for accounting periods beginning after 31 December 1992.

[4] Definition of "foreign income dividends" in sub-s (2) (originally inserted by FA 1994 Sch 16 para 4) repealed by F(No 2)A 1997 s 36(4), Sch 6 para 5, Sch 8 Pt II(11) with effect for accounting periods beginning after 5 April 1999.

[5] Definitions in sub-s (2) of "'general annuity business' and 'pension business'", "annuity fund", "basic life assurance business", "basic life assurance and general annuity business", "UK distribution income" and the word "and", omitted from the end of the definition "overseas life insurance company" repealed by FA 1995 Sch 29 Pt VIII(5) with effect for accounting periods beginning after 31 December 1994.

[6] Definitions in sub-s (2) of "offshore income gain" and "overseas life assurance business" repealed and definition of "overseas life assurance business" inserted, by FA 1995 Sch 8 paras 1, 55(1), Sch 29 Pt VIII(5) with effect for accounting periods beginning after 31 October 1994 (subject to FA 1995 Sch 8 para 55(2)).

[7] ...

[8] Definitions of "basic life assurance and general annuity business", "life reinsurance business", "pension business" and "reinsurance business" in sub-s (2) inserted by FA 1995 Sch 8 paras 1, 57 for accounting periods beginning after 31 December 1994.

[9] Definition "linked assets" in sub-s (2) substituted by FA 1995 Sch 8 paras 11(1), 57 with effect for accounting periods beginning after 31 December 1994.

[10] Sub-ss (2A), (3)–(6) repealed by FA 1995 Sch 29 Pt VIII(5), with effect for accounting periods beginning after 31 December 1994.

[11] In sub-s (2) definitions "industrial assurance business", "ordinary long term business" and "ordinary life assurance business" and words in italics in definition "long term business fund" repealed by FA 1996 Sch 41 Pt V(26) with effect for accounting periods beginning after 31 December 1995.

[12] ...

[13] Definition of "investment reserve" repealed by FA 2000 ss 109(9)(a), (10), 156, Sch 40 Pt II(16) with effect for accounting periods beginning after 31 December 1999 and ending after 20 March 2000.

[14] Definition of "closing liabilities" and "the Prudential Sourcebook" (Insurers) inserted, words in the definition of "liabilities" substituted, and definition of "long-term business" substituted, by the Financial Services and Markets Act 2000 (Consequential Amendments) (Taxes) Order, SI 2001/3629 arts 13, 26(1), (2), (4), (5), (8) with effect from 1 December 2001, immediately after the coming into force of the Financial Services and Markets Act 2000 ss 411, 432(1), Sch 20.

[15] Definition of "insurance business transfer scheme" and "insurance company" substituted for definition of "insurance company", definition of "long-term liabilities" inserted, and words in the definition of "periodical return" substituted by SI 2001/3629 arts 13, 26(1), (3), (6), (7), (9) with effect for periods of account ending after 30 November 2001.

[16] Words in sub-s (2) substituted by SI 2001/3629 arts 13, 52(1)(b) with effect from 1 December 2001 (immediately after the coming into force of the Financial Services and Markets Act 2000 ss 411, 432(1), Sch 20).

[17] Words in sub-s (2) substituted by SI 2001/3629 arts 13, 52(2)(a) with effect from 1 December 2001 (immediately after the coming into force of the Financial Services and Markets Act 2000 ss 411, 432(1), Sch 20).

431AA Relevant benefits for purposes of section 431(4)(d) and (e)

Amendments—This section repealed by FA 1995 Sch 29 Pt VIII(5)), with effect for accounting periods beginning after 31 December 1994 (originally inserted by FA 1994 s 143(1), (4), (5)).

[431A Amendment of Chapter etc

Where it is expedient to do so in consequence of the exercise of any power under the [Financial Services and Markets Act 2000, in so far as that Act relates to insurance companies,][2] the Treasury may by order amend the provisions of this Chapter and any other provision of the Tax Acts so far as relating to insurance companies.][1]

Commentary—*Simon's Direct Tax Service* **D4.526.**
Definitions—"Tax Acts"; s 831(2).
Amendments—[1] This section inserted by FA 1990 Sch 6 para 2.
[2] Words substituted by the Financial Services and Markets Act 2000 (Consequential Amendments) (Taxes) Order, SI 2001/3629 arts 13, 27 with effect from 1 December 2001, immediately after the coming into force of the Financial Services and Markets Act 2000 ss 411, 432(1), Sch 20.

[Classes of life assurance business]1

[431B Meaning of "pension business"

(1) In this Chapter "pension business" means so much of a company's life assurance business as is referable to contracts of the following descriptions or to the reinsurance of liabilities under such contracts.

(2) The descriptions of contracts are—

(a) any contract with an individual who is, or would but for an insufficiency of profits or gains be, chargeable to income tax in respect of relevant earnings (as defined in section 623(1) and (2)) from a trade, profession, vocation, office or employment carried on or held by him, being a contract approved by the Board under section 620 or a substituted contract within the meaning of section 622(3);

(b) any contract (including a contract of insurance) entered into for the purposes of, and made with the persons having the management of, an exempt approved scheme as defined in Chapter I of Part XIV, being a contract so framed that the liabilities undertaken by the insurance company under the contract correspond with liabilities against which the contract is intended to secure the scheme;

(c) any contract made under approved personal pension arrangements within the meaning of Chapter IV of Part XIV;

(d) any annuity contract entered into for the purposes of—

(i) a scheme which is approved or is being considered for approval under Chapter I of Part XIV;

(ii) a scheme which is a relevant statutory scheme for the purposes of Chapter I of Part XIV; or

(iii) a fund to which section 608 applies,

being a contract which is made with the persons having the management of the scheme or fund, or those persons and a member of or contributor to the scheme or fund, and by means of which relevant benefits (see subsections (3) and (4) below), and no other benefits, are secured;

(*e*) any annuity contract which is entered into in substitution for a contract within paragraph (*d*) above [or this paragraph][2] and by means of which relevant benefits (see subsections (3) and (4) below), and no other benefits, are secured;

[(*ea*) any contract which is entered into, for purposes connected with giving effect to any pension sharing order or provision made in relation to a contract falling within paragraph (*d*) or (*e*) above or this paragraph and by means of which relevant benefits (see subsections (3) and (4) below), and no other benefits, are secured;][2]

(*f*) any contract with the trustees or other persons having the management of a scheme approved under section 620 or, subject to subsection (5) below, of a superannuation fund which was approved under section 208 of the 1970 Act, being a contract which—

(i) was entered into for the purposes only of that scheme or fund or, in the case of a fund part only of which was approved under section 208, for the purposes only of that part of that fund, and

(ii) (in the case of a contract entered into or varied after 1st August 1956) is so framed that the liabilities undertaken by the insurance company under the contract correspond with liabilities against which the contract is intended to secure the scheme or fund (or the relevant part of the fund).

[(2A) For the purposes of subsection (2)(*d*) above the members of and contributors to a scheme or fund shall be deemed to include any person who by virtue of any pension sharing order or provision (within the meaning of Part XIV) has become entitled to any credit as against the persons having the management of the scheme or fund.][2]

(3) For the purposes of [subsection (2)(*d*) to (*ea*)] above "relevant benefits" means relevant benefits as defined by section 612(1) which correspond—

(*a*) where subsection (2)(*d*)(i) above applies, or subsection (2)(*e*) [or (*ea*)][2] above applies and the contract within subsection (2)(*d*) was entered into for the purposes of a scheme falling within subsection (2)(*d*)(i), with benefits that could be provided by a scheme approved under Chapter I of Part XIV;

(*b*) where subsection (2)(*d*)(ii) above applies, or subsection (2)(*e*) [or (*ea*)][2] above applies and the contract within subsection (2)(*d*) was entered into for the purposes of a scheme falling within subsection (2)(*d*)(ii), with benefits that could be provided by a scheme which is a relevant statutory scheme for the purposes of Chapter I of Part XIV;

(*c*) where subsection (2)(*d*)(iii) above applies, or subsection (2)(*e*) [or (*ea*)][2] above applies and the contract within subsection (2)(*d*) was entered into for the purposes of a fund falling within subsection (2)(*d*)(iii), with benefits that could be provided by a fund to which section 608 applies.

(4) For the purposes of subsection (3)(*a*), (*b*) or (*c*) above a hypothetical scheme or fund (rather than any particular scheme or fund), and benefits provided by a scheme or fund directly (rather than by means of an annuity contract), shall be taken.

(5) Subsection (2)(*f*) above shall not apply to a contract where the fund in question was approved under section 208 of the 1970 Act unless—

(*a*) immediately before 6th April 1980 premiums paid under the contract with the trustees or other persons having the management of the fund fell within section 323(4) of that Act (premiums referable to pension business); and

(*b*) the terms on which benefits are payable from the fund have not been altered since that time; and

(*c*) section 608 applies to the fund.

(6) In subsection (5) above "premium" includes any consideration for an annuity.][1]

Commentary—*Simon's Direct Tax Service* **D4.501.**
Regulations—Insurance Companies (Capital Redemption Business) (Modification of the Corporation Tax Acts) Regulations SI 1999/498.
Definitions—'Life assurance business'', s 431(2); "profits or gains", s 833(1).
Cross references—See TA 1988 s 438(8) (avoidance of double relief for insurance company's pension business under sub-s (2)(*c*) above and under s 438).
Modifications—Words in sub-s (1) inserted in applying life assurance provisions of the Corporation Tax Acts to insurance companies carrying on capital redemption business with effect for accounting periods ending after 30 June 1999: see Insurance Companies (Capital Redemption Business) (Modification of the Corporation Tax Acts) Regulations, SI 1999/498 reg 6.
Amendments—[1] This section, and preceding heading, inserted by FA 1995 Sch 8 paras 2, 57 with effect for accounting periods beginning after 31 December 1994.
[2] Words in sub-s (2)(*e*), and whole of sub-ss (2)(*ae*), (2A) inserted, and in sub-s (3) first words substituted, and other words inserted, by FA 1999 s 79 Sch 10 para 1, with effect in accordance with the commencement provisions contained in FA 1999 Sch 10 para 18. Words substituted in sub-s (3) previously read "subsection (2)(*d*) and (*e*)".

[431C Meaning of "life reinsurance business"

(1) In this Chapter "life reinsurance business" means reinsurance of life assurance business other than pension business or business of any description excluded from this section by regulations made by the Board.

(2) Regulations under subsection (1) above may describe the excluded business by reference to any circumstances appearing to the Board to be relevant.]¹

Commentary—*Simon's Direct Tax Service* **D4.501.**
Regulations—Insurance Companies (Taxation of Reinsurance Business) Regulations, SI 1995/1730 reg 11. Simon's Tax Cases—*Royal London Mutual Assurance Society Ltd v Barrett (Insp of Taxes)* [2002] STC(SCD) 61.
Definitions—''The Board'', s 832(1); ''life assurance business'', s 431(2); ''pension business'', s 431(2).
Modifications—Words inserted in sub-s (1) in respect of individual savings account business of Insurance Companies by the Individual Savings Account Regulations, SI 1998/1871 reg 8, with effect from 6 April 1999.
Amendments—¹ This section inserted by FA 1995 Sch 8 paras 2, 57 with effect for accounting periods beginning after 31 December 1994.

[431D Meaning of ''overseas life assurance business''

(1) In this Chapter ''overseas life assurance business'' means life assurance business, other than pension business[, life reinsurance business or business of any description excluded from this section by regulations made by the Board'']², which—

    (*a*) in the case of life assurance business other than reinsurance business, is business with a policy holder or annuitant not residing in the United Kingdom, and
    (*b*) in the case of reinsurance business, is—

        (i) reinsurance of life assurance business with a policy holder or annuitant not residing in the United Kingdom, or
        (ii) reinsurance of business within sub-paragraph (i) above or this sub-paragraph.

[(2) Regulations under subsection (1) above may describe the excluded business by reference to any circumstances appearing to the Board to be relevant.
(3) The Board may by regulations—

    (*a*) make provision as to the circumstances in which a trustee who is a policy holder or annuitant residing in the United Kingdom is to be treated for the purposes of this section as not so residing; and
    (*b*) provide that nothing in Chapter II of Part XIII shall apply to a policy or contract which constitutes overseas life assurance business by virtue of any such provision as is mentioned in paragraph (*a*) above.

(4) Regulations under subsection (1) or (3) above may contain such supplementary, incidental, consequential or transitional provision as appears to the Board to be appropriate.]²]¹

Commentary—*Simon's Direct Tax Service* **D4.524.**
Definitions—''Branch or agency'', s 834(1); ''company'', s 832(1); ''insurance company'', s 431(2); ''life assurance business'', s 431(2); ''life reinsurance business'', s 431(2); ''pension business'', s 431(2); ''reinsurance business'', s 431(2); ''United Kingdom'', s 832(1).
Cross references—See TA 1988 Sch 19AC para 6A (modification of sub-s (1) above in relation to overseas life insurance companies).
Insurance Companies (Overseas Life Assurance Business) (Excluded Business) Regulations, SI 2000/2089 (life assurance business is excluded from this section if it is of a description which does not fall within circumstances set out in the regulations).
Simon's Tax Cases—*Royal London Mutual Assurance Society Ltd v Barrett (Insp of Taxes)* [2002] STC(SCD) 61.
Modifications—Words inserted in sub-s (1) in respect of individual savings account business of Insurance Companies by the Individual Savings Account Regulations, SI 1998/1871 reg 8, with effect from 6 April 1999.
Amendments—¹˙¹This section inserted by FA 1995 Sch 8 paras 2, 55 with effect for accounting periods beginning after 31 October 1994 (subject to FA 1995 Sch 8 para 55(2), (3)).
² Words in sub-s (1) substituted for words ''or life reinsurance business'' and sub-ss (2)–(8) substituted by sub-ss (2)–(4) by FA 2000 s 108 with effect from 28 July 2000. By virtue of FA 2000 s 108(3), where any policy or contract for any life assurance business was made before 22 August 2000 (appointed by virtue of the Finance Act 2000, Section 108(3), (Appointed Day) Order, SI 2000/2082), these amendments shall not have effect for determining whether the business is overseas life assurance business. Sub-ss (2)–(8) previously read—

    ''(2) Subject to subsections (5) and (7) below, in subsection (1) above the references to life assurance business with a policy holder or annuitant do not include life assurance business with a person who is an individual if—

      (*a*) the policy holder or annuitant is not beneficially entitled to the rights conferred by the policy or contract for the business, or
      (*b*) any benefits under the policy or contract for the business are or will be payable to a person other than the policy holder or annuitant (or his personal representatives) or to a number of persons not including him (or them).

    (3) For the purposes of subsection (2) above any nomination by a policy holder or annuitant of an individual or individuals as the recipient or recipients of benefits payable on death shall be disregarded.
    (4) Subject to subsections (5) and (7) below, in subsection (1) above the references to life assurance business with a policy holder or annuitant do not include life assurance business with a person who is not an individual.
    (5) Subsections (2) and (4) above do not apply if—

      (*a*) the rights conferred by the policy or contract for the business are held subject to a trust,
      (*b*) the settlor does not reside in the United Kingdom, and
      (*c*) each beneficiary is either an individual not residing in the United Kingdom or a charity.

    (6) In subsection (5) above—

      (*a*) ''settlor'' means the person, or (where more than one) each of the persons, by whom the trust was directly or indirectly created (and for this purpose a person shall, in particular, be regarded as having created the trust if he provided or undertook to provide funds directly or indirectly for the purposes of the trust or made with any other person a reciprocal arrangement for that other person to create the trust),
      (*b*) ''beneficiary'' means any person who is, or will or may become, entitled to any benefit under the trust (including any person who may become so entitled on the exercise of a discretion by the trustees of the trust), and
      (*c*) ''charity'' means a person or body of persons established for charitable purposes only;

and for the purpose of that subsection an individual who is a trustee (of any trust) shall not be regarded as an individual.
    (7) Subsections (2) and (4) above do not apply if the policy or contract for the business was effected solely to provide benefits for or in respect of—

      (*a*) persons all, or all but an insignificant number, of whom are relevant overseas employees, or (*b*) spouses, widows, widowers, children or dependants of such persons.

(8) In subsection (7) above "relevant overseas employees" means persons who are not residing in the United Kingdom and are—

(*a*) employees of the policy holder or annuitant,

(*b*) employees of a person connected with the policy holder or annuitant, or

(*c*) employees in respect of whose employment there is established a superannuation fund to which section 615(3) applies;

and section 839 applies for the purposes of this subsection.".

[431E Overseas life assurance business: regulations

(1) The Board may by regulations make provision for giving effect to section 431D.

(2) Such regulations may, in particular—

(*a*) provide that, in such circumstances as may be prescribed, any prescribed issue as to whether business is or is not overseas life assurance business (or overseas life assurance business of a particular kind) shall be determined by reference to such matters (including the giving of certificates or undertakings, the giving or possession of information or the making of declarations) as may be prescribed,

(*b*) require companies to obtain certificates, undertakings, information or declarations from policy holders or annuitants, or from trustees or other companies, for the purposes of the regulations,

(*c*) make provision for dealing with cases where any issue such as is mentioned in paragraph (*a*) above is (for any reason) wrongly determined, including provision allowing for the imposition of charges to tax (with or without limits on time) on the insurance company concerned or on the policy holders or annuitants concerned,

(*d*) require companies to supply information and make available books, documents and other records for inspection on behalf of the Board, and

(*e*) make provision (including provision imposing penalties) for contravention of, or non-compliance with, the regulations.

(3) The regulations may—

(*a*) make different provision for different cases, and

(*b*) contain such supplementary, incidental, consequential or transitional provision as appears to the Board to be appropriate.][1]

Commentary—*Simon's Direct Tax Service* **D4.524.**
Regulations—Insurance Companies (Overseas Life Assurance Business) (Compliance) Regulations 1995, SI 1995/3237.
Insurance Companies (Overseas Life Assurance Business) (Tax Credit) Regulations 1995, SI 1995/3238.
Definitions—"Insurance company", s 431(2); "overseas life assurance business", s 431(2).
Amendments—[1] Section inserted by FA 1995 Sch 8 paras 2, 55 with effect for accounting periods beginning after 31 October 1994 (subject to FA 1995 Sch 8 para 55(2)).

[431F Meaning of "basic life assurance and general annuity business"

In this Chapter "basic life assurance and general annuity business" means life assurance business (including reinsurance business) other than pension business, life reinsurance business or overseas life assurance business.][1]

Commentary—*Simon's Direct Tax Service* **D4.524.**
Definitions—"Life assurance business", s 431(2); "life reinsurance business", s 431(2); "overseas life assurance business", s 431(2); "pension business", s 431(2); "reinsurance business", s 431(2).
Modifications—Words inserted in respect of individual savings account business of Insurance Companies by the Individual Savings Account Regulations, SI 1998/1871 reg 9, with effect from 6 April 1999.
Amendments—[1] Section inserted by FA 1995 Sch 8 paras 2, 57 with effect for accounting periods beginning after 31 December 1994.

[Separation of different categories of business][1]

Amendments—[1] Cross-heading inserted by FA 1995 Sch 8 paras 51(2), 57 with effect for accounting periods beginning after 31 December 1994.

432 Separation of different [categories][1] of business

(1) Where an insurance company carries on life assurance business in conjunction with insurance business of any other [category][1] the life assurance business shall, for the purposes of the Corporation Tax Acts, be treated as a separate business from any other [category][1] of business carried on by the company.

(2) ...[2]

Commentary—*Simon's Direct Tax Service* **D4.503.**
Revenue Internal Guidance—Life Assurance manual, Chpts 2–5 (detailed explanation of the I–E basis of assessment, Chpts 6, 7 the Schedule D Case I basis).
Life Assurance manual, para 11.6 (premiums and claims relating to PHI business normally established by reference to forms 41 and 42 of DTI return).
Definitions—"The Corporation Tax Acts", s 831(1)(*a*); "insurance company", s 431(2); "life assurance business", s 431(2).
Modification—Sub-s (3) inserted in so far as this the section applies to the life or endowment business carried on by friendly societies by the Friendly Societies (Modification of the Corporation Tax Acts) Regulations, SI 1997/473 reg 8.
Amendments—[1] In the heading and in sub-s (1) word "category" substituted for "class" by FA 1995 Sch 8 paras 12(3), 51(3), 57 with effect for accounting periods beginning after 31 December 1994.
[2] Sub-s (2) repealed by FA 1996 s 167(1), Sch 41 Pt V(26) with effect for accounting periods beginning after 31 December 1995.

[432ZA Linked assets

(1) In this Chapter "linked assets" means assets of an insurance company which are identified in its records as assets by reference to the value of which benefits provided for under a policy or contract are to be determined.

(2) Linked assets shall be taken—

(a) to be linked to [long-term][4] business of a particular category if the policies or contracts providing for the benefits concerned are policies or contracts the effecting of which constitutes the carrying on of business of that category; and

(b) to be linked solely to [long-term][4] business of a particular category if all (or all but an insignificant proportion) of the policies or contracts providing for the benefits concerned are policies or contracts the effecting of which constitutes the carrying on of business of that category.

(3) Where an asset is linked to more than one category of [long-term][4], a part of the asset shall be taken to be linked to each category; and references in this Chapter to assets linked (but not solely linked) to any category of business shall be construed accordingly.

(4) Where subsection (3) above applies, the part of the asset linked to any category of business shall be a proportion determined as follows—

(a) where in the records of the company values are shown for the asset in funds referable to particular categories of business, the proportion shall be determined by reference to those values;

(b) in any other case [the proportion A/B where—

A is the total of the linked liabilities of the company which are liabilities of the internal linked fund in which the asset is held and are referable to that category of business;
B is the total of the linked liabilities of the company which are liabilities of that fund.][2]

(5) For the purposes of sections 432A to 432F—

(a) income arising in any period from assets linked but not solely linked to a category of business,
(b) gains arising in any period from the disposal of such assets, and
(c) increases and decreases in the value of such assets,

shall be treated as arising to that category of business in the proportion which is the mean of the proportions determined under subsection (4) above at the beginning and end of the period.

[(6) In this section—

"internal linked fund", in relation to an insurance company, means an account—

(a) to which linked assets are appropriated by the company; and
(b) which may be divided into units the value of which is determined by the company by reference to the value of those assets;

"linked liabilities" means liabilities in respect of benefits to be determined by reference to the value of linked assets.][3]

(7) In the case of a policy or contract the effecting of which constitutes a class of life assurance business the fact that it also constitutes [long-term][4] business other than life assurance business shall be disregarded for the purposes of this section unless the benefits to be provided which constitute [long-term][4] business other than life assurance business are to be determined by reference to the value of assets.][1]

Commentary—*Simon's Direct Tax Service* **D4.526.**
Definitions—"Insurance company", s 431(2); "life assurance company", s 431(2); "life assurance business", s 431(2); "long term business", s 431(2).
Cross references—See FA 1996 Sch 11 para 3A(3) (referable debits or credits in relation to special loan relatioships provisions for insurers).
Amendments—[1] This section inserted by FA 1995 Sch 8 paras 11(2), 57 with effect for accounting periods beginning after 31 December 1994.
[2] Words in sub-s (4)(b) substituted by FA 2000 s 109(1), (10) with effect for accounting periods beginning after 31 December 1999 and ending after 20 March 2000.
[3] Sub-s (6) substituted by FA 2000 s 109(2), (10) with effect for accounting periods beginning after 31 December 1999 and ending after 20 March 2000.
[4] Words in sub-ss (2)(a), (b), (3), (7) substituted by the Financial Services and Markets Act 2000 (Consequential Amendments) (Taxes) Order, SI 2001/3629 arts 13, 52(2)(b) with effect from 1 December 2001 (immediately after the coming into force of the Financial Services and Markets Act 2000 ss 411, 432(1), Sch 20).

[432A Apportionment of income and gains

[(1) This section has effect where in any period an insurance company carries on more than one category of business and it is necessary for the purposes of the Corporation Tax Acts to determine in relation to the period what parts of—

(a) income arising from the assets of the company's [long-term insurance fund][9], or
(b) gains or losses accruing on the disposal of such assets,

are referable to any category of business.][2]

[(2) The categories of business referred to in subsection (1) above are—

(a) pension business;
(b) life reinsurance business;
(c) overseas life assurance business;

[(*d*) basic life assurance and general annuity business; and][5]

(*f*) [long-term][10] business other than life assurance business.][2]

[(3) Income arising from, and gains or losses accruing on the disposal of, assets linked to any category of business (apart from overseas life assurance business) shall be referable to that category of business.][2]

(4) Income arising from, and gains or losses accruing on the disposal of, assets of the overseas life assurance fund (and no other assets) shall be referable to overseas life assurance business.

(5) There shall be referable to any category of business (apart from overseas life assurance business) the relevant fraction of any income, gains or losses not directly referable to [any category][2] of business.

(6) For the purposes of subsection (5) above "the relevant fraction", in relation to a category of business, is the fraction of which—

(*a*) the numerator is the aggregate of—

(i) the mean of the opening and closing liabilities of the category, reduced [(but not below nil)][6] by the mean of the opening and closing [net values][7] of any assets directly referable to the category, and

(ii) the mean of the appropriate parts of the opening and closing amounts of the investment reserve; and

[(*b*) the denominator is the aggregate of—

(i) the numerator given by paragraph (*a*) above; and

(ii) the numerators given by that paragraph in relation to the other categories of business.][7]

[(7) For the purposes of subsections (5) and (6) above—

(*a*) income, gains or losses are directly referable to a category of business if referable to that category by virtue of subsection (3) or (4) above, and

(*b*) assets are directly referable to a category of business if income arising from the assets is, and gains or losses accruing on the disposal of the assets are, so referable by virtue of subsection (3) above.][4]

[(8) In subsection (6) above "appropriate part", in relation to the investment reserve, means—

(*a*) where none (or none but an insignificant proportion) of the liabilities of the [long-term][10] business are with-profits liabilities, the part of that reserve which bears to the whole the proportion A/B where—

A is the amount of the liabilities of the category of business in question;
B is the whole amount of the liabilities of the [long-term][10] business; and

(*b*) in any other case, the part of that reserve which bears to the whole the proportion C/D where—

C is the amount of the with-profits liabilities of the category of business in question;
D is the whole amount of the with-profits liabilities of the [long-term] business.][8]

[(9) Where a company carries on overseas life assurance business—

(*a*) references in this section to liabilities do not include liabilities of that business, and

(*b*) the appropriate part of the investment reserve as defined by paragraph 4(2)(*a*) of Schedule 19AA shall be left out of account in determining that reserve for the purposes of this section.][4]

[(9A) In this section and sections 432C and 432D "net value", in relation to any assets, means the excess of the value of the assets over any liabilities which—

(*a*) represent a [loan relationship][11]; and

(*b*) are liabilities of an internal linked fund in which the assets are held;

and in this subsection "internal linked fund" has the same meaning as in section 432ZA.

(9B) In this section—

"investment reserve", in relation to an insurance company, means the excess of the value of the assets of the company's [long-term][10] business over the aggregate of—

(*a*) the liabilities of that business; and

(*b*) any liabilities of the [long-term insurance fund][9] which represent a [loan relationship][11];

...][11][6]

(10) ...][3][1]

Commentary—*Simon's Direct Tax Service* **D4.526.**

Definitions—"Basic life assurance and general annuity business", s 431(2); "Corporation Tax Acts", s 831(1)(*a*); s 431(2); "insurance company", s 431(2); "life assurance business", s 431(2); "life reinsurance business", s 431(2); "linked assets", s 431(2); "long term business", s 431(2); "long term business fund", s 431(2); "overseas life assurance fund", s 431(2); "pension business", s 431(2); "with-profits liabilities", s 431(2).

Cross references—See TA 1988 s 432ZA(5) (treatment of income and gains from assets linked but not solely linked to a category of business).

TA 1988 Sch 5AA para 9 (treatment for purposes of this section of income and losses from disposals of futures and options producing a guaranteed return).

TA 1988 Sch 19AB, para 1(3) (insurance company carrying on pension business; provisional repayments on account of tax credits and deducted tax: determination of "the relevant fraction" under sub-s (5) above for the purposes of the provisional repayments).

FA 1996 Sch 11 para 3A(5) (application of sub-ss (6), (8) above in relation to special loan relationships provisions for insurers).

FA 1997 Sch 12 para 19(4) (application of this section in relation to notional rents in respect of certain leased assets).

Modifications—TA 1988 Sch 19AC, para 7 (modification of this section in relation to overseas life insurance companies).
This section is modified so far as it applies to the life or endowment business carried on by friendly societies, non-directive societies and certain directive and non-directive societies by the Friendly Societies (Modification of the Corporation Tax Acts) Regulations, SI 1997/473 regs 9–13.
New sub-s (2)(*aa*) inserted in respect of individual savings account business carried on by insurance companies by the Individual Savings Account Regulations, SI 1998/1871 reg 10, with effect from 6 April 1999.
Amendments—[1] This section inserted by FA 1990 Sch 6 para 4, but subject to the provisions in paras 10, 11 of that Schedule.
[2] Sub-ss (1)–(3) and words in sub-ss (5), (6) substituted by FA 1995 Sch 8 paras 13(2), (3), 57 with effect for accounting periods beginning after 31 December 1994.
[3] Sub-s (10) repealed by FA 1993 s 91(2)(*a*) and Sch 23 Pt III(8) for accounting periods beginning after 31 December 1992.
[4] Sub-ss (7), (9) substituted by FA 1995 Sch 8 paras 13(4), (5), 57 with effect for accounting periods beginning after 31 December 1994.
[5] Sub-s (2)(*d*) substituted for sub-s (2)(*d*), (*e*) by FA 1996 s 167(2) with effect for accounting periods beginning after 31 December 1995.
[6] Words in sub-s (6)(*a*) and whole of sub-ss (9A), (9B) inserted by FA 2000 s 109(3)(*a*), (4), (6), (10) with effect for accounting periods beginning after 31 December 1999 and ending after 20 March 2000.
[7] Words in sub-s (6)(*a*)(i) substituted for word "value" and whole of sub-s (6)(*b*), substituted by FA 2000 s 109(3)(*b*), (4), (5), (10) with effect for accounting periods beginning after 31 December 1999 and ending after 20 March 2000.
[8] Sub-s (8) substituted by FA 2000 s 109(5), (10) with effect for accounting periods beginning after 31 December 1999 and ending after 20 March 2000.
[9] Words in sub-s (1)(*a*), (9B) substituted by the Financial Services and Markets Act 2000 (Consequential Amendments) (Taxes) Order, SI 2001/3629 arts 13, 52(1)(*c*) with effect from 1 December 2001 (immediately after the coming into force of the Financial Services and Markets Act 2000 ss 411, 432(1), Sch 20).
[10] Words in sub-ss (2)(*f*), (8)(*a*), (*b*), (9B) substituted by SI 2001/3629 arts 13, 52(2)(*c*) with effect from 1 December 2001 (immediately after the coming into force of the Financial Services and Markets Act 2000 ss 411, 432(1), Sch 20).
[11] In sub-s (9A)(*a*), and in the definition of "investment reserve" in sub-s (9B)(*b*), words substituted for the words "money debt"; and in sub-s (9B), definition of "money debt" repealed; by FA 2002 ss 82, 141, Sch 25 paras 43, 46, Sch 40 Pt 3(12) with effect for accounting periods beginning after 30 September 2002. Definition of "money debt" previously read as follows—
"money debt" has the same meaning as in Chapter II of Part IV of the Finance Act 1996.".

[432AA Schedule A business or overseas property business

(1) An insurance company is treated as carrying on separate Schedule A businesses, or overseas property businesses, in accordance with the following rules.

(2) The exploitation of land held as an asset of the company's [long-term insurance fund][2] is treated as a separate business from the exploitation of land not so held. (3) The exploitation of land held as an asset of the company's overseas life assurance fund is treated as a separate business from the exploitation of other land held as an asset of its [long-term insurance fund][2].

(4) The exploitation of land held as an asset linked to any of the following categories of business is regarded as a separate business—

    (*a*) pension business;
    (*b*) life reinsurance business;
    (*c*) basic life assurance and general annuity business;
    (*d*) [long-term][3] business other than life assurance business.

(5) Accordingly, the exploitation of land held as an asset of the company's business fund otherwise than as mentioned in subsection (3) or (4) is treated as a separate business from any other.

(6) In this section "land" means any estate, interest or rights in or over land.][1]

Commentary—*Simon's Direct Tax Service* **D4.526.**
Modifications—Sub-s (4) modified so far as it applies to the life or endowment business carried on by friendly societies after 31 March 1998 by the Friendly Societies (Modification of the Corporation Tax Acts) Regulations, SI 1997/473 reg 13A (as inserted by SI 1999/2636).
New sub-s (4)(*aa*) inserted in sub-s (1) in respect of individual savings account business of Insurance Companies by the Individual Savings Account Regulations, SI 1998/1871 reg 11, with effect from 6 April 1999.
Amendments—[1] This section inserted by FA 1998 Sch 5 para 39 with effect from 1998–99 and subsequent years of assessment for income tax purposes and from 1 April 1998 for corporation tax, subject to the transitional provisions in FA 1998 Sch 5 Part IV.
[2] Words in sub-ss (2), (3) substituted by the Financial Services and Markets Act 2000 (Consequential Amendments) (Taxes) Order, SI 2001/3629 arts 13, 52(1)(*d*), with effect from 1 December 2001 (immediately after the coming into force of the Financial Services and Markets Act 2000 ss 411, 432(1), Sch 20).
[3] Words in sub-s (4)(*d*) substituted by SI 2001/3629 arts 13, 52(2)(*d*), with effect from 1 December 2001 (immediately after the coming into force of the Financial Services and Markets Act 2000 ss 411, 432(1), Sch 20).

[432AB Losses from Schedule A business or overseas property business

(1) This section applies to any loss arising in a Schedule A business or overseas property business.

(2) A loss arising from any category of business mentioned in section 432A(2) shall be apportioned under that section in the same way as income.

(3) So far as a loss is referable to basic life assurance and general annuity business, it shall be treated as if it were an amount of expenses of management under section 76 disbursed for the accounting period in which the loss arose.

(4) Where a company is treated under section 432AA as carrying on—

    (*a*) more than one Schedule A business, or
    (*b*) more than one overseas property business,

then, in relation to either kind of business, the reference in subsection (3) above to a loss referable to basic life assurance and general annuity business shall be construed as a reference to any aggregate net loss after setting the losses from those businesses which are so referable against any profits from those businesses that are so referable.

(5) The provisions of section 392A or 392B (loss relief) do not apply to a loss referable to life assurance business or any category of life assurance business.

(6) Where a company is treated under section 432AA as carrying on—

    (*a*) more than one Schedule A business, or

    (*b*) more than one overseas property business,

and, in relation to either kind of business, there are losses and profits referable to business which is not life assurance business, those losses shall be set against those profits before being used under section 392A or 392B.][1]

Commentary—*Simon's Direct Tax Service* **D4.526.**
Modification—This section modified so far as it applies to the life or endowment business carried on by friendly societies after 31 March 1998 by the Friendly Societies (Modification of the Corporation Tax Acts) Regulations, SI 1997/473 reg 13B (as inserted by SI 1999/2636).
Amendments—[1] This section inserted by FA 1998 Sch 5 para 39 with effect from 1998–99 and subsequent years of assessment for income tax purposes and from 1 April 1998 for corporation tax, subject to the transitional provisions in FA 1998 Sch 5 Part IV.

[432B Apportionment of receipts brought into account

(1) This section and [sections 432C to 432F][2] have effect where it is necessary in accordance with section 83 of the Finance Act 1989 to determine what parts of any items [brought into account, within the meaning of that section,][3] are referable to life assurance business or any class of life assurance business.

[(2) Where for that purpose reference falls to be made to more than one account recognised for the purposes of that section, the provisions of sections 432C to 432F apply separately in relation to each account.][3]

(3) Sections 432C and 432D apply where the business with which an account is concerned ("the relevant business") relates exclusively to policies or contracts under which the policy holders or annuitants are not eligible to participate in surplus; and [sections 432E and 432F apply][2] where the relevant business relates wholly or partly to other policies or contracts.][1]

Commentary—*Simon's Direct Tax Service* **D4.526.**
Revenue Internal Guidance—Life assurance manual, Chpt 8 (detailed explanation of apportionment of income between classes of business).
Life assurance manual LAM 8.22-8.25 (link with DTI form 40).
LAM 8.101–8.102 (consolidation of Case VI computations of separate funds to give overall Case VI profit).
Cross references—See TA 1988 s 432ZA(5) (treatment of income and gains arising from assets linked but not solely linked to a category of business).
TA 1988 Sch 19AC para 8 (modification of this section in its application to an overseas life insurance company).
FA 1990 Sch 6, para 12(5) and Sch 7, para 10 (omission in this section of references to "overseas life assurance business" as respects accounting periods ending on 31 December 1989).
Amendments—[1] This section inserted by FA 1990 Sch 6 para 4, but subject to the provisions in paras 10, 11 of that Schedule.
[2] Words in sub-ss (1), (3) substituted by FA 1995 Sch 8 paras 17(1), 53 with effect for accounting periods ending after 31 December 1993 (note, however, FA 1995 Sch 8 para 53(2)).
[3] Words in sub-s (1) and whole of sub-s (2) substituted by FA 1995 Sch 8 paras 16(2), 57 with effect for accounting periods beginning after 31 December 1994.

[432C Section 432B apportionment: income of non-participating funds

(1) To the extent that the amount brought into account as income is attributable to assets [linked][2] to [pension business, life reinsurance business, basic life assurance and general annuity business or [long-term][6] business other than life assurance business][2], it shall be referable to the category of business concerned.

(2) To the extent that that amount is attributable to assets of the overseas life assurance fund [or land in the United Kingdom linked to overseas life assurance business][3], it shall be referable to overseas life assurance business.

(3) There shall be referable to any category of business (apart from overseas life assurance business) the relevant fraction of so much of the amount brought into account as income as is not directly referable to [any category of business][2].

(4) For the purposes of subsection (3) above "the relevant fraction", in relation to a category of business, is the fraction of which—

    (*a*) the numerator is the mean of the opening and closing liabilities of the relevant business so far as referable to the category, reduced [(but not below nil)][4] by the mean of the opening and closing [net values][5] of any assets of the relevant business directly referable to the category; and

    [(*b*) the denominator is the aggregate of—

        (i) the numerator given by paragraph (*a*) above; and

        (ii) the numerators given by that paragraph in relation to the other categories of business.][5]

(5) For the purposes of subsections (3) and (4) above—

    (*a*) ...[5]

    (*b*) the part of the amount brought into account as income which is directly referable to a category of business is the part referable to the category by virtue of subsection (1) [or (2)][4] above and assets are directly referable to a category of business if such part of the amount brought into account as income as is attributable to them is so referable.

[(6) For the purposes of this section, where a company carries on overseas life assurance business 'liabilities' does not include liabilities of that business.][2]][1]

Commentary—*Simon's Direct Tax Service* **D4.526.**
Revenue Internal Guidance—Life assurance manual LAM 8.31-8.42 (explanation of this section).
Definitions—"Basic life assurance and general annuity business", s 431(2); "life assurance business", s 431(2); "life reinsurance business", s 431(2); "linked assets", s 431(2); "long term business", s 431(2); "overseas life assurance business", s 431(2); "overseas life assurance fund", s 431(2); "value", s 431(2).
Cross references—See TA 1988 s 432ZA(5) (treatment of income and gains arising from assets linked but not solely linked to a category of business).
TA 1988 s 432B(3) (this section applies where the business relates exclusively to policies or contracts under which policy holders of annuitants are not eligible to participate in surpluses).
TA 1988 Sch 19AC para 8(3) (modification of this section as it applies to overseas life companies).
Modifications—Words inserted in sub-s (1) in respect of individual savings account business of Insurance Companies by the Individual Savings Account Regulations, SI 1998/1871 reg 12, with effect from 6 April 1999.
Amendments—[1] This section inserted by FA 1990 Sch 6 para 4, but subject to the provisions in paras 11, 12 of that Schedule.
[2] Words in sub-ss (1), (3) and whole of sub-s (6) substituted, and sub-s (5)(a) repealed, by FA 1995 Sch 8 paras 12(1)(a), 14(2), (3), (5), 57, Sch 29 Pt VIII(5), with effect for accounting periods beginning after 31 December 1994.
[3] Words in sub-s (2) inserted by FA 1995 Sch 8 paras 3, 55 with effect for accounting periods beginning after 31 October 1994 (subject to FA 1995 Sch 8 para 55(2)).
[4] Words in sub-ss (4)(a), (5)(b) inserted by FA 2000 s 109(3), (4), (7), (10) with effect for accounting periods beginning after 31 December 1999 and ending after 20 March 2000.
[5] Words "net values" in sub-s (4)(a) substituted for word "value", and the whole of sub-s (4)(b) substituted, by FA 2000 s 109(3), (4), (10) with effect for accounting periods beginning after 31 December 1999 and ending after 20 March 2000.
[6] Words in sub-s (1) substituted by the Financial Services and Markets Act 2000 (Consequential Amendments) (Taxes) Order, SI 2001/3629 arts 13, 52(2)(e) with effect from 1 December 2001 (immediately after the coming into force of the Financial Services and Markets Act 2000 ss 411, 432(1), Sch 20).

[432D Section 432B apportionment: value of non-participating funds

(1) To the extent that the amount brought into account as the increase or decrease in the value of assets is attributable to assets [linked][2] to [pension business, life reinsurance business, basic life assurance and general annuity business or [long-term][5] business other than life assurance business][2], or to assets of the overseas life assurance fund which are [linked][5] to overseas life assurance business, it shall be referable to the category of business concerned.

(2) There shall be referable to any category of business the relevant fraction of the amount brought into account as the increase or decrease in the value of assets except so far as the amount is attributable to assets which are directly referable to [any category of business][2].

[(3) For the purposes of subsection (2) above "the relevant fraction", in relation to a category of business, is the fraction of which—

(a) the numerator is the mean of the opening and closing liabilities of the relevant business so far as referable to the category, reduced [(but not below nil)][3] by the mean of the opening and closing [net values][4] of any assets of the relevant business directly referable to the category; and

[(b) the denominator is the aggregate of—

(i) the numerator given by paragraph (a) above; and

(ii) the numerators given by that paragraph in relation to the other categories of business.][4]][2]

[(4) For the purposes of subsections (2) and (3) above, the part of the amount brought into account as the increase or decrease in the value of assets which is directly referable to a category of business is the part referable to the category by virtue of subsection (1) above and assets are directly referable to a category of business if such part of the amount brought into account as the increase or decrease in the value of assets as is attributable to them is so referable.][2]][1]

Commentary—*Simon's Direct Tax Service* **D4.526.**
Definitions—"Basic life assurance and general annuity business", s 431(2); "life assurance business", s 431(2); "life reinsurance business", s 431(2); "long term business", s 431(2); "overseas life assurance business", s 431(2); "overseas life assurance fund", s 431(2); "pension business", s 431(2); "value", s 431(2).
Cross references—See TA 1988 s 432ZA(5) (treatment of income and gains arising from assets linked but not solely linked to a category of business).
TA 1988 s 432B(3) (this section applies where the business relates exclusively to policies or contracts under which policy holders of annuitants are not eligible to participate in surpluses).
TA 1988 Sch 19AC para 8(3) (modification of this section as it applies to overseas life companies).
Modifications—Words inserted in sub-s (1) in respect of individual savings account business of Insurance Companies by the Individual Savings Account Regulations, SI 1998/1871 reg 12, with effect from 6 April 1999.
Amendments—[1] This section inserted by FA 1990 Sch 6 para 4, but subject to the provisions in paras 11, 12 of that Schedule.
[2] Words in sub-ss (1), (2) substituted and whole of sub-ss (3), (4) substituted for original sub-s (3) by FA 1995 Sch 8 paras 12(1)(a), 15(2)–(4), 57 with effect for accounting periods beginning after 31 December 1994.
[3] Words in sub-s (3)(a) inserted by FA 2000 s 109(3), (4), (10) with effect for accounting periods beginning after 31 December 1999 and ending after 20 March 2000.
[4] Words "net values" in sub-s (3)(a) substituted for word "value", and the whole of sub-s (3)(b) substituted, by FA 2000 s 109(3), (4), (10) with effect for accounting periods beginning after 31 December 1999 and ending after 20 March 2000.
[5] Words substituted by the Financial Services and Markets Act 2000 (Consequential Amendments) (Taxes) Order, SI 2001/3629 arts 13, 52(2)(f) with effect from 1 December 2001 (immediately after the coming into force of the Financial Services and Markets Act 2000 ss 411, 432(1), Sch 20).

[432E Section 432B apportionment: participating funds

(1) The part of the net amount [to be taken into account in accordance with section 83(2) of the Finance Act 1989 (that is to say, the aggregate amount to be taken into account as receipts reduced

by the aggregate amount to be taken into account as expenses)][3] which is referable to a particular category of business [shall be the amount determined in accordance with subsection (2) below or, if greater, the amount determined in accordance with subsection (3) below.][2]

(2) For the purposes of subsection (1) above there shall be determined the amount which is such as to secure—

(a) in a case where the relevant business is mutual business, that

$$CS - CAS = (S - AS) \times \frac{CAS}{AS}$$

where—

S is the surplus of the relevant business;

AS is so much of that surplus as is allocated to persons entitled to the benefits provided for by the policies or contracts to which the relevant business relates;

CAS is so much of the surplus so allocated as is attributable to policies or contracts of the category of business concerned; and

CS is so much of the surplus of the relevant business as would remain if the relevant business were confined to business of the category concerned.

(3) For the purposes of subsection (1) above there shall also be determined the aggregate of—

(a) the applicable percentage of what is left of the mean of the opening and closing liabilities of the relevant business so far as referable to the category of business concerned after deducting from it the mean of the opening and closing values of any assets of the relevant business [linked][3] to that category of business, and

(b) the part of the net amount mentioned in subsection (1) above that is attributable to assets [linked][3] to that category of business.

(4) For the purposes of subsection (3) above ''the applicable percentage'', in any case, is such percentage as may be determined for that case by or in accordance with an order made by the Treasury.

(5) Where the part of the net amount referable to a particular category or categories of business (''the subsection (3) category or categories'') is the amount determined in accordance with subsection (3) above, the amount determined in accordance with subsection (2) above in relation to any other category (''the relevant category'') shall be reduced by—

$$\frac{XY}{Z}$$

where—

X is the excess of the amount determined in accordance with subsection (3) above in the case of the subsection (3) category (or each of them) over the amount determined in its case (or the case of each of them) in accordance with subsection (2) above;

Y is so much of the surplus of the relevant business as is allocated to persons entitled to the benefits provided for by policies or contracts of the relevant category; and

Z is so much of the surplus of the relevant business as is allocated to persons entitled to the benefits provided for by policies or contracts of the category (or each of the categories) which is not a subsection (3) category.

[References in this subsection to the amount determined in accordance with subsection (3) above are to that amount after making any deduction required by section 432F.][2]

(6) Where the category of business concerned is overseas life assurance business—

(a) if the part of the income brought into account that is attributable to assets of the overseas life assurance fund not [linked][3] to overseas life assurance business is greater than the amount arrived at under subsection (3)(a) above, this section shall have effect as if that part of that income were the amount so arrived at; ...[4]

(b) ...[4]][1]

Commentary—*Simon's Direct Tax Service* **D4.526.**
Orders—Life Assurance (Apportionment of Receipts of Participating Funds) (Applicable Percentage) Order, SI 1990/1541.
Revenue Internal Guidance—Life Assurance Manual, LAM 8.51–8.89 (detailed explanation of this section).
LAM 8.61-8.67 (''needs basis'' computation).
Definitions—''Overseas life assurance business'', s 431(2); ''overseas life assurance fund'', s 431(2); ''relevant business'', s 432B(3).
Cross references—See TA 1988 s 432ZA(5) (treatment of income and gains arising from assets linked but not solely linked to a category of business).
TA 1988 s 432B(3) (this section applies where the business does not relate exclusively to policies or contracts under which policy holders of annuitants are not eligible to participate in surpluses).
TA 1986 s 432F (apportionment: supplementary provisions).
TA 1988 Sch 19AC para 8(3) (modification of this section as it applies to overseas life companies).
Modification—This section is modified so far as it applies to the life or endowment business carried on by friendly societies by the Friendly Societies (Modification of the Corporation Tax Acts) Regulations, SI 1997/473 reg 14.
Amendments—[1] This section inserted by FA 1990 Sch 6 para 4, but subject to the provisions in paras 11, 12 of that Schedule.
[2] Words in sub-s (1) substituted and words in sub-s (5) added by FA 1995 Sch 8 paras 17(2), 53 with effect for accounting periods ending after 31 December 1993 (note, however, FA 1995 Sch 8 para 55(1), (2)).
[3] Words in sub-ss (1), (3)(a), (b), (6)(a) substituted by FA 1995 Sch 8 paras 12(a), 16(3), 57 with effect for accounting periods beginning after 31 December 1994.

⁴ Sub-s (6)(*b*) and word preceding it repealed by F(No 2)A 1997 s 23, Sch 3 para 2, Sch 8 Pt II(6) with effect in relation to distributions made after 1 July 1997.

[432F Section 432B apportionment: supplementary provisions

(1) The provisions of this section provide for the reduction of the amount determined in accordance with section 432E(3) ("the subsection (3) figure") for an accounting period in which that amount exceeds, or would otherwise exceed, the amount determined in accordance with section 432E(2) ("the subsection (2) figure").

(2) For each category of business in relation to which section 432E falls to be applied there shall be determined for each accounting period the amount (if any) by which the subsection (2) figure, after making any reduction required by section 432E(5), exceeds the subsection (3) figure ("the subsection (2) excess").

(3) Where there is a subsection (2) excess, the amount shall be carried forward and if in any subsequent accounting period the subsection (3) figure exceeds, or would otherwise exceed, the subsection (2) figure, it shall be reduced by the amount or cumulative amount of subsection (2) excesses so far as not previously used under this subsection.

(4) Where in an accounting period that amount is greater than is required to bring the subsection (3) figure down to the subsection (2) figure, the balance shall be carried forward and aggregated with any subsequent subsection (2) excess for use in subsequent accounting periods.]¹

Commentary—*Simon's Direct Tax Service* **D4.526.**
Concession C27—Where a company has set a subsection (2) excess arising in accounting periods beginning after 31 December 1990 and ending before 1 January 1994 against a subsection (3) excess arising in an accounting period ending after 31 December 1993 but without exhausting those subsection (2) excesses, the unexhausted amount may be carried forward to the next accounting period in which a subsection (3) excess arises in respect of the same category of business, but no further.
Revenue Internal Guidance—Life assurance manual LAM 8.91-8.100 (operation of this section with examples).
Definition—"Accounting period", s 834(1).
Cross references—See TA 1988 s 432ZA(5) (treatment of income and gains arising from assets linked but not solely linked to a category of business).
TA 1988 s 432B(3) (this section applies where the business does not relate exclusively to policies or contracts under which policy holders of annuitants are not eligible to participate in surpluses).
TA 1988 s 444A(3A) treatment of the subsection (2) excess on a transfer of the whole or part of the long term business of an insurance company).
TA 1988 Sch 19AC para 8(3) (modification of this section as it applies to overseas life companies).
FA 1995 Sch 8 para 53(2) (sub-s (2) figure treated as increased by an amount not exceeding the sub-s (2) excess for accounting periods beginning after 31 December 1989 and ending before 1 January 1994 in the first period ending after 31 December 1993 in which the sub-s (3) figure exceeds the sub-s (2) figure).
Modification—Sub-s (1) is modified so far as it applies to the life or endowment business carried on by friendly societies by the Friendly Societies (Modification of the Corporation Tax Acts) Regulations, SI 1997/473 reg 15.
Amendments—¹ This section inserted by FA 1995 Sch 8 paras 17(3), 53 with effect for accounting periods ending after 31 December 1993 (note, however, FA 1995 Sch 8 para 55(1), (2)).

433 Profits reserved for policy holders and annuitants

Definitions—"Accounting period", s 834(1); "insurance company", s 431(2); "life assurance business", s 431(2); "Schedule D", s 18(1).
Amendments—This section repealed by FA 1989 s 84(5)(*a*), Sch 8 para 2 and Sch 17, Pt IV with effect from 14 March 1989, but subject to FA 1989 s 84(6).

[Miscellaneous provisions relating to life assurance business]1

Amendments—¹ Cross heading inserted by FA 1995 Sch 8 paras 51(4), 57 with effect for accounting periods beginning after 31 December 1994.

434 Franked investment income etc

[(1) Section 208 shall not apply in relation to—
  (*a*) the charge to corporation tax on the life assurance profits of an insurance company computed in accordance with the provisions of this Act applicable to Case I of Schedule D; or
  (*b*) any computation of such profits in accordance with those provisions.

(1A) Paragraph 2 of Schedule F shall not have effect for the purposes of subsection (1)(*a*) or (*b*) above ...⁷.

(1B) The reference in subsection (1) above to the life assurance profits of an insurance company is a reference to the profits of the company—
  (*a*) in respect of its life assurance business; or
  (*b*) in respect of any category of life assurance business which it carries on.]⁶

(2) ...⁵

(3) ...⁸

[(3A) The policy holders' [share]⁵ of the franked investment income from investments held in connection with a company's life assurance business shall be left out of account in determining, under subsection (7) of section 13, the franked investment income forming part of the company's profits for the purposes of that section.]¹

(3B)–(3D) ...³

(4), (5) ...¹

(6) ...⁹

[(6A) For the purposes of this section—

    (a) "the policy holders' share" of any franked investment income is so much of that income as is not the shareholders' share within the meaning of section 89 of the Finance Act 1989 ...⁴

    (aa)–(ac) ...³

    (b) "the policy holders' share of the relevant profits" has the same meaning as in section 88 of that Act.]²

(7) ...⁵

(8) ...⁹

Commentary—*Simon's Direct Tax Service* **D4.512, 514.**
Revenue Internal Guidance—Life Assurance Manual, paras 14.41–14.50 (explanation of sub-s (6) above) para 14.48 (worked example).
Definitions—"Company", s 832(1), (2); "foreign income dividend", s 431(2); "franked investment income", s 832(1); "life assurance business", s 431(2); "Schedule D", s 18(1); "Schedule F", s 20(1); "tax credit", s 832(1).
Cross references—See TA 1988 s 444B and Sch 19AC para 9 (modification of this section in relation to overseas life insurance companies).
FA 1990 s 45(10) (the amendments made to this section by FA 1990 s 45(4)–(7) to have the same effect as, by virtue of FA 1989 s 84(5)(b), they would have had if they had been made by FA 1989 Sch 8);
F(No 2)A 1992 s 65(2), (5) (the application of sub-ss (1), (1A) above does not prevent the application of the I minus E basis to a company's life assurance business).
FA 1993 s 78(6), (11) (rate of tax credit for calculating franked investment income for the purposes of this section from the financial year 1993).
Amendments—¹ Sub-ss (3), (3A) substituted for sub-s (3) as originally enacted and sub-ss (4), (5) repealed by FA 1989 s 84(5)(b), Sch 8 para 3, Sch 17, Pt IV with effect (subject to FA 1989 s 84(6)) in respect to accounting periods beginning after 31 December 1989 including the 1990 component period as defined in FA 1989 s 84(3).
² Sub-s (6A) inserted by FA 1990 s 45(7), (10) with effect for accounting periods beginning after 31 December 1989 including the 1990 component period as defined in FA 1989 s 84(3).
³ Sub-ss (3B)–(3D), (6A)(aa)–(ac) (originally inserted by FA 1994 Sch 16 para 5(1), (4), (5)) repealed by F(No 2)A 1997 s 36(4), Sch 6 para 6, Sch 8 Pt II(11) with effect for accounting periods beginning after 5 April 1999.
⁴ Word "and" in sub-s (6A)(a) repealed by FA 1994 Sch 16 para 5(1), (5), Sch 26, Pt V(16).
⁵ Sub-ss (2), (7) repealed by FA 1995 Sch 29 Pt VIII(5), with effect for accounting periods beginning after 31 December 1994.
⁶ Sub-ss (1), (1A), (1B) substituted for sub-s (1) by F(No 2)A 1997 s 23, Sch 3 para 3(1), (2), (5) with effect for distributions made after 1 July 1997.
⁷ Words in sub-s (1A) repealed by F(No 2)A 1997 s 34, Sch 4 para 27, Sch 8 Pt II(10) with effect for distributions made after 5 April 1999.
⁸ Sub-s (3) (substituted by FA 1995 Sch 8 paras 19(3), 57) repealed by FA 1998 Sch 3 para 25 with effect for franked investment income which is attributable to distributions made after 5 April 1999.
⁹ Sub-ss (6), (8) repealed by FA 1998 Sch 3 para 25 for accounting periods beginning after 5 April 1999.

[434A Computation of losses and limitation on relief

(1) ...⁵

[(2) Where for any accounting period the loss arising to an insurance company from its life assurance business falls to be computed in accordance with the provisions of this Act applicable to Case I of Schedule D—

    (a) the loss resulting from the computation shall be reduced (but not below nil) by the aggregate of—

        (i) the aggregate amount treated as a charge on income in computing for the period, otherwise than in accordance with those provisions, the profits or losses of the company's life assurance business; and

        (ii) any relevant non-trading deficit for that period on the company's debtor relationships; and

        [(iii) any loss for that period under section 441; and]⁶

    (b) if the whole or any part of that loss as so reduced is set off—

        (i) under section 393A, or

        (ii) under section 403(1),

any losses for that period under section 436 [or 439B]⁶ shall be reduced to nil, unless the aggregate of those losses exceeds the total of the amounts set off as mentioned in sub-paragraphs (i) and (ii) above, in which case each of those losses shall be reduced by an amount which bears to that total the proportion which the loss in question bears to that aggregate.]³

[(2A) The reference in subsection [(2)(a)(ii)]⁴ above to a relevant non-trading deficit for any period on a company's debtor relationships is a reference to the non-trading deficit on the company's loan relationships which would be produced by any separate computation made under paragraph 2 of Schedule 11 to the Finance Act 1996 for the company's basic life assurance and general annuity business if credits and debits given in respect of the company's creditor relationships (within the meaning of Chapter II of Part IV of that Act) were disregarded.]²

(3) In the case of a company carrying on life assurance business, no relief shall be allowable—

    [(a) under Chapter II (loss relief) or Chapter IV (group relief) of Part X, or

    (b) in respect of any amount representing a non-trading deficit on the company's loan relationships that has been computed otherwise than by reference to debits and credits referable to that business,]²

against the policy holders' share of the relevant profits for any accounting period.

For the purposes of this subsection "the policy holders' share of the relevant profits" has the same meaning as in section 88 of the Finance Act 1989.][1]

Commentary—*Simon's Direct Tax Service* **D4.513.**
Definitions—"Accounting period", s 834(1); "foreign income dividends", s 431(2); "franked investment income", s 832(1); "insurance company", s 431(2); "life assurance business", s 431(2); "loan relationship", s 834(1), FA 1996 s 81; "non-trading deficit", s 834(1), FA 1996 s 82.
Cross references—See TA 1988 Sch 19AC para 9A (modification of this section in its application to an overseas life insurance company).
F(No 2)A 1992 s 65(2), (5) (the application of this section does not prevent the application of the I minus E basis to a company's life assurance business).
Amendments—[1] This section substituted by FA 1995 Sch 8 paras 20, 57 with effect for accounting periods beginning after 31 December 1994.
[2] Sub-s (2A) inserted and words in sub-s (3) substituted by FA 1996 Sch 14 para 23(2), (3) with effect for accounting periods ending after 31 March 1996, subject to transitional provisions in FA 1996 Sch 15.
[3] Sub-s (2) substituted by FA 1996 Sch 31 para 2(1)(a), (2) with effect for accounting periods beginning after 31 December 1995 and ending after 31 March 1996. For the transitional modifications applying to sub-s (2) with effect for accounting periods beginning after 31 December 1995 and ending before 31 March 1996, see FA 1996 Sch 31 para 2(3).
[4] Words in sub-s (2A) substituted by FA 1996 Sch 31 para 2(1)(b) with effect for accounting periods beginning after 31 December 1995 and ending after 31 March 1996.
[5] Sub-s (1) repealed by F(No 2)A 1997 s 23, Sch 3 para 4, Sch 8 Pt II(6) with effect for accounting periods beginning after 1 July 1997.
[6] Sub-s (2)(a)(iii) inserted and words in sub-s (2)(b) substituted by FA 2000 s 97, Sch 27 Pt II paras 8, 12(1) with effect for accounting periods ending after 31 March 2000.

[434AA Treatment of annuities]

Cross references—This section is treated as inserted as a modification of this Act as it relates to overseas life insurance companies—see TA 1988 Sch 19AC para 9B.

[434B Treatment of interest and annuities

(1) ...[2]

(2) ...[3]][1]

Amendments—[1] Section inserted by FA 1995 Sch 8 paras 21(1), 57 with effect for accounting periods beginning after 31 December 1994.
[2] Sub-s (1) repealed by FA 1996 s 165(3), Sch 41 Pt V(25) with effect for accounting periods beginning after 31 December 1995.
[3] Sub-s (2) repealed by FA 1997 s 67(4), (7), Sch 18 Pt VI(6) with effect for accounting periods beginning after 5 March 1997.

[434C Interest on repayment of advance corporation tax]

Definitions—"Advance corporation tax", s 14(1); "distributions", s 832(1); "life assurance business", s 431(2).
Amendments—[1] This section repealed by FA 1998 Sch 3 para 26 with effect for distributions made after 5 April 1999 (originally inserted by FA 1995 Sch 8 paras 22, 54).

434D Capital allowances: management assets

Amendments—This section repealed by CAA 2001 ss 578, 580, Sch 2 para 39, Sch 4 with effect for corporation tax purposes in relation to allowances and charges falling to be made for chargeable periods ending after 31 March 2001.

434E Capital allowances: investment assets

Amendments—This section repealed by CAA 2001 ss 578, 580, Sch 2 para 39, Sch 4 with effect for corporation tax purposes with respect to allowances and charges falling to be made for chargeable periods ending after 31 March 2001.

435 Taxation of gains reserved for policy holders and annuitants

Amendments—This section repealed by FA 1989 s 84(5)(b), Sch 8 para 5 and Sch 17, Pt IV with effect, subject to FA 1989 s 84(6), with respect to accounting periods beginning after 31 December 1989 including the 1990 component period as defined in FA 1989 s 84(3).

436 [Pension business][10]: separate charge on profits

(1) Subject to the provisions of this section, profits arising to an insurance company from ...[5] pension business shall be treated as income within Schedule D, and be chargeable under Case VI of that Schedule, and for that purpose—

(*a*) [that business][6] shall be treated separately, and

(*b*) subject to paragraph (*a*) above, and to subsection (3) below, the profits therefrom shall be computed in accordance with the provisions of this Act applicable to Case I of Schedule D.

(2) Subsection (1) above shall not apply to an insurance company charged to corporation tax in accordance with the provisions applicable to Case I of Schedule D in respect of the profits of its ordinary life assurance business.

(3) In making the computation referred to in subsection (1) above—

(*a*) [sections 82 and 83 of the Finance Act 1989][1] shall apply with the necessary modifications and in particular with the omission of all references to policy holders (other than holders of policies referable to pension business) [and of the words [and any amounts of tax which are expended on behalf of][14] in section 82(1)(*a*)][3];

[(*aa*) ...][12]

(*b*) ...[2]

(*c*) there may be set off against the profits any loss, to be computed on the same basis as the profits, which has arisen from pension business ...[7] in any previous accounting period or year of assessment;

(*d*) [*where the computation in question is of profits arising to an insurance company from pension business—*

[(*i*) *group income so far as referable to pension business shall be deducted from the receipts to be taken into account,*][4]

[...][11]][13]

(*e*) *distributions which are not qualifying distributions shall not be taken into account where the computation in question is of the profits arising to an insurance company or overseas life insurance company from* ...[8] *pension business.*[13]

(4) Section 396 shall not be taken to apply to a loss incurred by a company on its ...[9] pension business.

(5) Nothing in section 128 or 399(1) shall affect the operation of this section.

Commentary—*Simon's Direct Tax Service* D4.520, 521.
Revenue Internal Guidance—Life Assurance Manual, Ch 9 (explanation of the computation of Case VI profits on general annuity and pension business).
Life assurance manual LAM 2.84, 2.85 (the charge under Case VI applies in particular to mutual companies).
LAM 9.31-9.44 (computation of Case VI profits).
Simon's Tax Cases—*Sun Life Assurance Co of Canada v Pearson* [1984] STC 461*.
s 436(1), *Bibby v Prudential Assurance Co Ltd and Oakes v Equitable Life Assurance Society* [2000] STC 459.
Definitions—"Accounting period", s 834(1); "annuity business", s 431(2); "general annuity business", s 431(2); "insurance company", s 431(2); "overseas life insurance company", s 431(2); "pension business", s 431(2); "profits or gains", s 833(1); "qualifying distribution", s 14(2) by virtue of s 832(1); "Schedule D", s 18(1); "year of assessment", s 832(1).
Cross references—See TA 1988 s 434A(2)(*a*) (insurance company's Schedule D Case I loss from life assurance business to be reduced by losses under this section).
TA 1988 s 434E (capital allowances and charges in respect of investment assets to be ignored in computing profits under this section).
TA 1988 s 438(3), (3AA) exclusion from the charge to corporation tax of franked investment income and foreign income dividends of an insurance company does not prevent their being taken into account in computing income under this section).
TA 1988 s 444A(3) (treatment of losses which would have been available under sub-s (3)(*c*) above upon a transfer of whole or part of the long term business of an insurance company).
TA 1988 s 808 (receipts of a non-resident carrying on a business in the UK of interest, dividends or royalties treated as tax-exempt under a double tax treaty are not to be excluded in computing losses for the purposes of this section).
TA 1988 Sch 19AC para 10 (UK distribution income or foreign income dividends of an overseas life company are to be taken into account in computing to income from a pension business under this section notwithstanding s 11(2)).
FA 1989 s 43(13) (the reference "this Act" in sub-s(1)(*b*) above to include a reference to FA 1989 s 43);
FA 1991 Sch 7 para 17(3)(*b*) (transitional provisions for an insurance company's unrelieved general annuity losses suffered before 1 January 1992).
Modifications—This section is modified so far as it applies to the life or endowment business carried on by certain non-directive societies by the Friendly Societies (Modification of the Corporation Tax Acts) Regulations 1997, SI 1997/473 regs 19, 20, 20A.
Words inserted throughout this section in respect of individual savings account business of Insurance Companies by the Individual Savings Account Regulations, SI 1998/1871 reg 13, with effect from 6 April 1999.
Amendments—[1] Words in sub-s (3)(*a*) substituted for the words "section 433" by FA 1989 s 84(4), (5)(*a*) and Sch 8 para 6 with effect from 14 March 1989, but subject to FA 1989 s 84(6).
[2] Sub-s (3)(*b*) repealed by FA 1989 s 87(4) and Sch 17 Pt IV with respect to accounting periods beginning after 31 December 1989, but subject to FA 1989 ss 84(1)–(3), 87(5) in relation to a straddling period as defined in those provisions and subject also to FA 1989 s 84(6). Sub-s(3)(*b*) read—

"(*b*) no deduction shall be allowed in respect of any expenses of management deductible under section 76;".
[3] Words in sub-s (3)(*a*) added by FA 1990 s 43(2) with effect from 14 March 1989, but subject to FA 1990 s 43(3).
[4] Sub-s (3)(*d*)(i) substituted by FA 1990 Sch 6 para 5, with effect from 1 January 1990, but subject to the provisions in FA 1990 Sch 6 paras 11, 12. Sub-s(3)(*d*)(i) originally read—
"(i) group income shall not be taken into account as part of those profits, and".
[5] Words omitted from sub-s (1) repealed by FA 1991 Sch 7 para 4 and Sch 19, Pt V with respect to accounting periods beginning after 31 December 1991.
[6] Words in sub-s (1)(*a*) substituted by FA 1991 Sch 7 para 4.
[7] Words omitted from sub-s (3)(*c*) repealed by FA 1991 Sch 7 para 4 and Sch 19, Pt V with respect to accounting periods beginning after 31 December 1991.
[8] Words omitted from sub-s (3)(*e*) repealed by FA 1991 Sch 7 para 4 and Sch 19, Pt V with respect to accounting periods beginning after 31 December 1991.
[9] Words omitted from sub-s (4) repealed by FA 1991 Sch 7 para 4 and Sch 19, Pt V with respect to accounting periods beginning after 31 December 1991.
[10] Words in heading substituted for the words "Annuity business and pension business", by FA 1995 Sch 8 paras 51(5), 57 with effect for accounting periods beginning after 31 December 1994.
[11] Words omitted from sub-s (3)(*d*) repealed by FA 1995 Sch 29 Pt VIII(5), with effect for accounting periods beginning after 31 December 1994.
[12] Sub-s (3)(*aa*) (inserted by FA 1995 Sch 8 paras 16(4), 57) repealed by FA 1996 Sch 31 para 7(1)(*a*), Sch 41 Pt V(23) with effect for periods of account beginning after 31 December 1995.
[13] Sub-s (3)(*d*), (*e*) repealed by F(No 2)A 1997 s 23, Sch 3 para 5, Sch 8 Pt II(6) with effect for distributions made after 1 July 1997.
[14] Words in sub-s (3)(*a*) substituted for words "tax or" by FA 2000 s 103, Sch 30 para 18(3) with effect for periods of account beginning after 31 March 2000.

[437 General annuity business

[(1A) In the computation, otherwise than in accordance with the provisions applicable to Case I of Schedule D, of the profits for any accounting period of a company's life assurance business, new annuities paid by the company in that period shall be brought into account by treating an amount equal to the income limit for that period as a sum disbursed as expenses of management of the company for that period.]³

[(1C) For the purposes of this section [(but subject to subsections (1CA) to (1CD) below)]⁴—

    (a) "new annuity" means any annuity, so far as paid under a contract made by an insurance company in an accounting period beginning on or after 1st January 1992 and so far as referable to the company's basic life assurance and general annuity business;

    (b) "the income limit" for an accounting period of an insurance company is the difference between—

        (i) the total amount of the new annuities paid by the company in that accounting period; and

        (ii) the total of the capital elements contained in the new annuities so paid; and

    (c) the capital element contained in an annuity shall be determined in accordance with Chapter V of Part XIV, but for this purpose—

        (i) it is immaterial whether or not an annuitant claims any relief to which he is entitled under that Chapter; and

        (ii) where, by virtue of subsection (2) of section 657, section 656 does not apply to an annuity, the annuity shall be treated as containing the capital element that it would have contained apart from that subsection.]¹

[(1CA) Where a new annuity ("the actual annuity") is a steep-reduction annuity, the income limit for an accounting period of the company paying the annuity shall be computed for the purposes of this section as if—

    (a) the contract providing for the actual annuity provided instead for the annuities identified by subsections (1CB) and (1CC) below; and

    (b) the consideration for each of those annuities were to be determined by the making of a just and reasonable apportionment of the consideration for the actual annuity.

(1CB) The annuities mentioned in subsection (1CA)(a) above are—

    (a) an annuity the payments in respect of which are confined to the payments in respect of the actual annuity that fall to be made before the earliest time for the making in respect of the actual annuity of a reduced payment such as is mentioned in section 437A(1)(c); and

    (b) subject to subsection (1CC) below, an annuity the payments in respect of which are all the payments in respect of the actual annuity other than those mentioned in paragraph (a) above.

(1CC) Where an annuity identified by paragraph (b) of subsection (1CB) above ("the later annuity") would itself be a steep-reduction annuity, the annuities mentioned in subsection (1CA)(a) above—

    (a) shall not include the later annuity; but

    (b) shall include, instead, the annuities which would be identified by subsection (1CB) above (with as many further applications of this subsection as may be necessary for securing that none of the annuities mentioned in subsection (1CA)(a) above is a steep-reduction annuity) if references in that subsection to the actual annuity were references to the later annuity.

(1CD) Subsections (1CA) to (1CC) above shall be construed in accordance with section 437A.]⁴

[(1D) In any case where—

    (a) a payment in respect of an annuity is made by an insurance company under a group annuity contract made in an accounting period beginning before 1st January 1992,

    (b) the company's liabilities first include an amount in respect of that annuity in an accounting period beginning on or after that date, and

    (c) the company's liability in respect of that annuity is referable to its basic life assurance and general annuity business,

the payment shall be treated for the purposes of this section, other than this subsection, as if the group annuity contract had been made in an accounting period beginning on or after 1st January 1992 (and, accordingly, as payment of a new annuity).]¹

[(1E) In any case where—

    (a) a payment in respect of an annuity is made by a reinsurer under a reinsurance treaty made in an accounting period beginning before 1st January 1992,

    (b) the reinsurer's liabilities first include an amount in respect of that annuity in an accounting period beginning on or after that date, and

    (c) the reinsurer's liability in respect of that annuity is referable to its basic life assurance and general annuity business,

the payment shall, as respects the reinsurer, be treated for the purposes of this section, other than this subsection, as if the reinsurance treaty had been made in an accounting period beginning on or after 1st January 1992 (and, accordingly, as payment of a new annuity).]¹

[(1F) In this section—

    "group annuity contract" means a contract between an insurance company and some other person under which the company undertakes to become liable to pay annuities to or in respect of such persons as may subsequently be specified or otherwise ascertained under or in accordance with the contract (whether or not annuities under the contract are also payable to or in respect of persons who are specified or ascertained at the time the contract is made);

"reinsurance treaty" means a contract under which one insurance company is obliged to cede, and another (in this section referred to as a "reinsurer") to accept, the whole or part of a risk of a class or description to which the contract relates.]¹

(2)–(5) ...¹

(6) ...²

Commentary—*Simon's Direct Tax Service* D4.516, 520.
Revenue Internal Guidance—Life Assurance Manual LAM 9.51-9.54 (computation of Case VI profits). LAM 13.11–13.54 (relief for general annuities as charges).
Definitions—"Accounting period", s 834(1); "annuity fund", s 431(2); "branch or agency", s 834(1); "charges on income", s 338(2) by virtue of s 834(1); "company", s 832(1), (2); "distribution", s 832(1); "franked investment income", s 832(1); "general annuity business", s 431(2); "insurance company", s 431(2); "profits or gains", s 833(1).
Modification— This section is modified in its application to the life or endowment business carried on by friendly societies by the Friendly Societies (Modification of the Corporation Tax Acts) Regulations, SI 1997/473 reg 21.
Amendments—¹ Sub-ss (1A)–(1F) substituted for original sub-s (1) and sub-ss (2)–(5) repealed by FA 1991 ss 48, 123, Sch 7 paras 4(4), (5), 18, Sch 19 Pt V. This version of this section has effect with respect to accounting periods beginning after 31 December 1991; see FA 1991 Sch 7 para 18. For the version having effect with respect to accounting periods beginning before 1 January 1992, see *Yellow Tax Handbook*, 1993–94, 32nd edition.
² Sub-s (6) repealed by FA 1995 Sch 29 Pt VIII(5), with effect for accounting periods beginning after 31 December 1994.
³ Sub-s (1A) substituted for sub-ss (1A), (1B) by FA 1997 s 67(1), (7), with effect for accounting periods beginning after 5 March 1997.
⁴ Words in sub-s (1C), and sub-ss (1CA)-(1CD), inserted by FA 1997 s 67(2), (8), with effect for accounting periods ending on or after 5 March 1997 but not so as to affect the computation of the capital elements contained in any annuity payments made before that date.

[437A Meaning of "steep-reduction annuity" etc

(1) For the purposes of section 437 an annuity is a steep-reduction annuity if—

(*a*) the amount of any payment in respect of the annuity (but not the term of the annuity) depends on any contingency other than the duration of a human life or lives;

(*b*) the annuitant is entitled in respect of the annuity to payments of different amounts at different times; and

(*c*) those payments include a payment ("a reduced payment") of an amount which is substantially smaller than the amount of at least one of the earlier payments in respect of that annuity to which the annuitant is entitled.

(2) Where there are different intervals between payments to which an annuitant is entitled in respect of any annuity, the question whether or not the conditions in subsection (1)(*b*) and (*c*) above are satisfied in the case of that annuity shall be determined by assuming—

(*a*) that the annuitant's entitlement, after the first payment, to payments in respect of that annuity is an entitlement to payments at yearly intervals on the anniversary of the first payment; and

(*b*) that the amount to which the annuitant is assumed to be entitled on each such anniversary is equal to the annuitant's assumed entitlement for the year ending with that anniversary.

(3) For the purposes of subsection (2) above an annuitant's assumed entitlement for any year shall be determined as follows—

(*a*) the annuitant's entitlement to each payment in respect of the annuity shall be taken to accrue at a constant rate during the interval between the previous payment and that payment; and

(*b*) his assumed entitlement for any year shall be taken to be equal to the aggregate of the amounts which, in accordance with paragraph (*a*) above, are treated as accruing in that year.

(4) In the case of an annuity to which subsection (2) above applies, the reference in section 437(1CB)(*a*) to the making of a reduced payment shall be construed as if it were a reference to the making of a payment in respect of that annuity which (applying subsection (3)(*a*) above) is taken to accrue at a rate that is substantially less than the rate at which at least one of the earlier payments in respect of that annuity is taken to accrue.

(5) Where—

(*a*) any question arises for the purposes of this section whether the amount of any payment in respect of any annuity—

(i) is substantially smaller than the amount of, or

(ii) accrues at a rate substantially less than,

an earlier payment in respect of that annuity, and

(*b*) the annuitant or, as the case may be, every annuitant is an individual who is beneficially entitled to all the rights conferred on him as such an annuitant,

that question shall be determined without regard to so much of the difference between the amounts or rates as is referable to a reduction falling to be made as a result of the occurrence of a death.

(6) Where the amount of any one or more of the payments to which an annuitant is entitled in respect of an annuity depends on any contingency, his entitlement to payments in respect of that annuity shall be determined for the purposes of section 437(1CA) to (1CC) and this section according to whatever (applying any relevant actuarial principles) is the most likely outcome in relation to that contingency.

(7) Where any agreement or arrangement has effect for varying the rights of an annuitant in relation to a payment in respect of any annuity, that payment shall be taken, for the purposes of section

437(1CA) to (1CC) and this section, to be a payment of the amount to which the annuitant is entitled in accordance with that agreement or arrangement.

(8) References in this section to a contingency include references to a contingency that consists wholly or partly in the exercise by any person of any option.][1]

Commentary—*Simon's Direct Tax Service* **D4.520A.**
Amendments—[1]Section inserted by FA 1997 s 67(3), (8) with effect for accounting periods ending on or after 5 March 1997 but not so as to affect the computation of the capital elements contained in any annuity payments made before that date.

438 Pension business: exemption from tax

(1) Exemption from corporation tax shall be allowed in respect of income from, and chargeable gains in respect of, investments and deposits of so much of an insurance company's [long-term insurance fund][6], as is referable to pension business.

(2) The exemption from tax conferred by subsection (1) above shall not exclude any sums from being taken into account as receipts in computing profits or losses for any purpose of the Corporation Tax Acts.

(3), (3AA) ...[3]

[(4) This section shall be disregarded in determining, in relation to an insurance company which is entitled to a tax credit in respect of a distribution, whether the condition in paragraph (*a*) or (*b*) of section 231(2) is satisfied.][3]

(5) ...[7]

(6), (6A)–(6E), (7) ...[4]

(8) Nothing in sections [431B(2)(*c*)][2] or 643(2) of this Act or section [271(1)(*h*) of the 1992 Act][1] shall be construed as affording relief in respect of any sums to be brought into account under this section.

(9) ...[5]

Commentary—*Simon's Direct Tax Service* **D4.517, 521.**
Simon's Tax Cases—s 438(4), *Utopia Assurance Co Ltd v Chaloner* [1996] STC (SCD) 204.
Definitions—"The 1992 Act", s 831(3); "accounting period", s 834(1); "annuity fund", s 431(2); "the Board", s 832(1); "chargeable gain", s 832(1); "the Corporation Tax Acts", s 831(1)(*a*); "distribution", s 832(1); "foreign income dividend", s 431(2); "franked investment income", s 832(1); "insurance company", s 431(2); "long term business fund", s 431(2); "notice", s 832(1); "pension business", s 431(2); "tax credit", s 832(1).
Cross references—See TA 1988 s 440B(2) (modification of this section where the profits of a company's life assurance business are charged to tax under Schedule D Case I).
TA 1988 s 592(11) (sums brought into account under this section not to be eligible for relief as income of an exempt approved retirement benefit scheme).
TA 1988 Sch 19AC para 10 (modification of this section by the insertion of sub-s (3A) in its application to an overseas life company).
TCGA 1992 s 117A(7) (to the extent that this section requires a disposal to be treated as made on a no gain/no loss basis, it does not apply to certain assets representing foreign currency loan relationships).
FA 1993 s 78(6), (7) (rate of tax credit for calculating franked investment income for the purposes of this section from the financial year 1993);
Manufactured Payments and Transfer of Securities (Tax Relief) Regulations, SI 1995/3036 reg 3(2) (manufactured payments made to an insurance company are eligible for relief under this section to the extent they are referable to the company's pension business).
Manufactured Payments and Transfer of Securities (Tax Relief) Regulations, SI 1995/3036 reg 4(2) (price differentials on sales and repurchases of securities which are deemed to be interest payments to an insurance company to be eligible for relief under this section).
Modifications—Words inserted in sub-s (1) in respect of individual savings account business of Insurance Companies by the Individual Savings Account Regulations, SI 1998/1871 reg 14, with effect from 6 April 1999.
Amendments—[1]Words in sub-s (8) substituted by TCGA 1992 Sch 10 para 14(1), (21).
[2]Words in sub-s (8) substituted by FA 1995 Sch 8 paras 4, 29, 57 with effect for accounting periods beginning after 31 December 1994.
[3]Sub-ss (3), (3AA), (5) repealed and sub-s (4) substituted by F(No 2)A 1997 s 23, Sch 3 para 6(1), (2), (3), (7) with effect for distributions made after 1 July 1997.
[4]Sub-ss (6), (6A)–(6E), (7) repealed by F(No 2)A 1997 s 23, Sch 3 para 6(1), (5), (8), (9) with effect for accounting periods beginning after 1 July 1997. Any distributions made after that date are left out of account in determining the franked investment income or foreign income dividends arising to an insurance company for that accounting period.
[5]Sub-s (9) repealed by F(No 2)A 1997 s 23, Sch 3 para 6(1), (6), (8) with effect for accounting periods beginning after 1 July 1997.
[6]Words in sub-s (1) substituted by the Financial Services and Markets Act 2000 (Consequential Amendments) (Taxes) Order, SI 2001/3629 arts 13, 52(1)(*e*) with effect from 1 December 2001 (immediately after the coming into force of the Financial Services and Markets Act 2000 ss 411, 432(1), Sch 20).

[438A Pension business: payments on account of tax credits and deducted tax
Schedule 19AB shall have effect.][1]

Amendments—[1]This section (inserted by FA 1991 s 49(1), (3) for accounting periods beginning after 1 October 1992 by virtue of FA 1991 s 49 (Appointed Day) Order, SI 1992/1746) repealed by FA 2001 ss 87, 110, Sch 33 Pt II(12) with effect in accordance with FA 2001 s 87.

[438B Income or gains arising from property investment LLP

(1) Where an asset held by an insurance company as an asset of its [long-term insurance fund][2] is held by the company as a member of a property investment LLP, the policy holders' share of any income arising from, or chargeable gains accruing on the disposal of, the asset which—

(*a*) is attributable to the company, and

(*b*) would otherwise be referable by virtue of section 432A to pension business,

shall be treated for the purposes of the Corporation Tax Acts as referable to basic life assurance and general annuity business.

(2) For the purposes of this section the property business of the insurance company for the purposes of which the asset is held shall be treated as a separate business.

''Property business'' means a Schedule A business or overseas property business.

(3) Where (apart from this subsection) an insurance company would not be carrying on basic life assurance and general annuity business, it shall be treated as carrying on such business if any income or chargeable gains of the company are treated as referable to the business by virtue of subsection (1) above.

(4) A company may be charged to tax by virtue of this section—

(*a*) notwithstanding section 439A, and

(*b*) whether or not the income or chargeable gains to which subsection (1) above applies is taken into account in computing the profits of the company for the purposes of any charge to tax in accordance with Case I of Schedule D.

(5) The policy holders' share of income or chargeable gains to which subsection (1) above applies—

(*a*) shall not be treated as relevant profits for the purposes of section 88 of the Finance Act 1989 (corporation tax on policy holders' fraction of profits), and

(*b*) shall not be treated as part of the BLAGAB profits for the purposes of section 88A of that Act (lower corporation tax rate on certain profits);

but the whole of the income or gains to which that subsection applies shall be chargeable to tax at the rate provided by section 88 of that Act.

(6) So far as income is brought into account as mentioned in section 83(2) of the Finance Act 1989, sections 432B to 432F (apportionment of receipts brought into account) have effect as if subsection (1) above did not apply.][1]

Modifications—Friendly Societies (Modification of the Corporation Tax Acts) Regulations, SI 1997/473 reg 21A (income and chargeable gains of a friendly society are treated as referable to the society's taxable basic life assurance or general annuity business).
SI 1997/473 reg 21B (method for computing the proportion of the assets of a friendly society held for the purposes of long-term business where the society does not have a long-term insurance fund).
Amendments—[1] Section inserted by FA 2001 s 76, Sch 25 with effect from 6 April 2001.
[2] Words in sub-s (1) substituted by the Financial Services and Markets Act 2000 (Consequential Amendments) (Taxes) Order, SI 2001/3629 arts 13, 52(1)(*f*) with effect from 1 December 2001 (immediately after the coming into force of the Financial Services and Markets Act 2000 ss 411, 432(1), Sch 20).

[438C Determination of policy holders' share for purposes of s 438B

(1) For the purposes of section 438B the policy holders' share of any income or chargeable gains to which subsection (1) of that section applies is what remains after deducting the shareholders' share.

(2) The shareholders' share is found by applying to the whole the fraction—

$$\frac{A}{B}$$

where—

A is the amount of the profits of the company for the period which are chargeable to tax under section 436; and

B is an amount equal to the excess of—

(*a*) the amount taken into account as receipts of the company in computing those profits (apart from premiums and sums received by virtue of a claim under a reinsurance contract), over

(*b*) the amounts taken into account as expenses in computing those profits.

(3) Where there is no such excess as is mentioned in subsection (2) above, or where the profits are greater than any excess, the whole of the income or gains is treated as the shareholders' share.

(4) Subject to that, where there are no profits none of the income or gains is treated as the shareholders' share.][1]

Amendments—[1] Section inserted by FA 2001 s 76, Sch 25 para 5 with effect from 6 April 2001.

439 Restricted government securities

[(1) For the purposes of this Chapter restricted government securities shall be treated as linked solely to pension business.][1]

[(2) In this section—][1]

...[2]

''restricted government securities'' means, subject to the following provisions of this section, government securities issued on the condition that, except in such circumstances as may be specified in the conditions of issue, they are to be held by insurance companies against and applied solely towards meeting pension business liabilities.

(6) Subject to subsection (7) below, the following Treasury Stock, namely—

   (*a*) 2 per cent Index-linked Treasury Stock 1996;
   (*b*) 2 per cent Index-linked Treasury Stock 2006;
   (*c*) 21/2 per cent Index-linked Treasury Stock 2011;

are not restricted government securities for the purposes of this section.

(7) If any of the index-linked stock referred to in subsection (6) above was on 27th March 1982 held by an insurance company against and applied solely towards meeting the liabilities of the company's pension business, then—

   (*a*) if and so long as the stock continues to be so held by that company, it shall continue to be treated as restricted government securities for the purposes of this section; and
   (*b*) if the stock ceases to be restricted government securities otherwise than by virtue of being actually disposed of or redeemed, on the day on which it so ceases the stock shall be deemed for the purposes of corporation tax, including ...[3] corporation tax on chargeable gains, to have been disposed of and immediately re-acquired at its market value on that date.

(8) ...[1]

Commentary—*Simon's Direct Tax Service* **D4.509.**
Definitions—"The 1979 Act", s 831(3); "accounting period", s 834(1); "chargeable gain", s 832(1); "insurance company", s 431(2); "pension business", s 431(2).
Amendments—[1] Sub-s (1) substituted for sub-ss (1)–(4), words in sub-s (2) substituted and sub-s (8) repealed by FA 1990 Sch 6 para 7, Sch 19 Pt IV with effect from 1 January 1990, but subject to the provisions in FA 1990 Sch 6 paras 11, 12.
[2] Words in sub-s (2) repealed by FA 1990 Sch 6 para 7.
[3] Words in sub-s (7) repealed by FA 1990 Sch 19 Pt IV.

[439A Taxation of pure reinsurance business

If a company does not carry on life assurance business other than reinsurance business, and none of that business is of a type excluded from this section by regulations made by the Board, the profits of that business shall be charged to tax in accordance with Case I of Schedule D and not otherwise.][1]

Commentary—*Simon's Direct Tax Service* **D4.509.**
Regulations—Insurance Companies (Taxation of Reinsurance Business) Regulations, SI 1995/1730 reg 12.
Revenue Internal Guidance—Life assurance manual LAM 2.101-2.105 (background information on types of reinsurance business).
Definitions—"The Board", s 832(1); "life assurance business", s 431(2); "Schedule D", s 18(1).
Cross references—See TA 1988 s 441B(4)(*a*) (notwithstanding this section, income arising from UK land held by an insurance company as an asset linked to its overseas life assurance business may be charged to tax).
Amendments—[1] Section inserted by FA 1995 Sch 8 paras 26, 57 with effect for accounting periods beginning after 31 December 1994.

[439B Life reinsurance business: separate charge on profits

(1) Where a company carries on life reinsurance business and the profits arising from that business are not charged to tax in accordance with the provisions applicable to Case I of Schedule D, then, subject as follows, those profits shall be treated as income within Schedule D and be chargeable to tax under Case VI of that Schedule, and for that purpose—

   (*a*) that business shall be treated separately, and
   (*b*) subject to paragraph (*a*) above, the profits from it shall be computed in accordance with the provisions of this Act applicable to Case I of Schedule D.

(2) Subsection (1) above does not apply to so much of reinsurance business of any description excluded from that subsection by regulations made by the Board.

Regulations under this subsection may describe the excluded business by reference to any circumstances appearing to the Board to be relevant.

(3) In making the computation referred to in subsection (1) above—

   (*a*) sections 82(1), (2) and (4) and 83 of the Finance Act 1989 shall apply with the necessary modifications and in particular with the omission of the words [and any amounts of tax which are expended on behalf of][4] in section 82(1)(*a*), [and][2]
   (*b*) ...[2]
   (*c*) there may be set off against the profits any loss, to be computed on the same basis as the profits, which has arisen from life reinsurance business in any previous accounting period beginning on or after 1st January 1995.

(4) Section 396 shall not be taken to apply to a loss incurred by a company on life reinsurance business.

(5) Nothing in section 128 or 399(1) shall affect the operation of this section.

(6) Gains accruing to a company which are referable to its life reinsurance business shall not be chargeable gains.

(7) ...[3]][1]

Commentary—*Simon's Direct Tax Service* **D4.509.**
Revenue Internal Guidance—Life assurance manual LAM 9.81-9.86 (computation of Case VI profits).

Definitions—"Accounting period", s 834(1); "Act", s 832(1); "chargeable gains", s 832(1); "foreign income dividends", s 431(2); "franked investment income", s 832(1); "life reinsurance business", s 431(2); "Schedule D", s 18(1).

Cross references—See TA 1988 s 434A(2)(a) (an insurance company's Schedule D Case I losses from its life assurance business are reduced by losses under this section).

TA 1988 s 434E (capital allowances and charges on investment assets to be ignored in computing profits under this section).

TA 1988 s 444A(3) (treatment of losses which would have been available under sub-s (3)(c) above upon the transfer of the whole or part of the long term business of an insurance company).

TA 1988 Sch 19AC, para 10A (modification of this section in relation to an overseas life insurance company).

Amendments—[1] Section inserted by FA 1995 Sch 8 paras 27, 57 with effect in relation to accounting periods beginning after 31 December 1994.

[2] Sub-s (3)(b) repealed, and word at end of sub-s (3)(a) added, by FA 1996 Sch 31 para 7(1), (2), Sch 41 Pt V(23) with effect for periods of account beginning after 31 December 1995.

[3] Sub-s (7) repealed by F(No 2)A 1997, s 23, Sch 3 para 7, Sch 8 Pt II(6) with effect for distributions made after 1 July 1997.

[4] Words in sub-s (3)(a) substituted for words "tax or" by FA 2000 s 103, Sch 30 para 18(3) with effect for periods of account beginning after 31 March 2000.

[440 Transfers of assets etc

(1) If at any time an asset (or a part of an asset) held by an insurance company ceases to be within one of the categories set out in subsection (4) below and comes within another of those categories, the company shall for the purposes of corporation tax be deemed to have disposed of and immediately re-acquired the asset (or part) for a consideration equal to its market value at that time.

(2) Where—

    [(a) an asset is acquired by a company as a result of an insurance business transfer scheme which has effect to transfer long-term business from any person ("the transferor") to the company, and][7]
    (b) the asset (or part of it) is within one of the categories set out in subsection (4) below immediately before the acquisition and is within another of those categories immediately afterwards,

the transferor shall for the purposes of corporation tax be deemed to have disposed of and immediately re-acquired the asset (or part) immediately before the acquisition for a consideration equal to its market value at that time.

[(2A) Where under subsection (1) or (2) above there is a deemed disposal and re-acquisition of any asset representing a loan relationship of a company, any authorised accounting method used as respects that asset for the purposes of Chapter II of Part IV of the Finance Act 1996 shall be applied as respects that asset as if the asset that is deemed to be disposed of and the asset that is deemed to be re-acquired were different assets.][6]

[(2B) Where under subsection (1) or (2) above there is a deemed disposal and re-acquisition of any derivative contract of a company, any authorised accounting method used as respects that contract for the purposes of Schedule 26 to the Finance Act 2002 shall be applied as respects that contract as if the contract that is deemed to be disposed of and the contract that is deemed to be re-acquired were different assets.][9]

(3) Where, apart from this subsection, section [171 or 173 of the 1992 Act][3] (transfers within a group) would apply to a disposal or acquisition by an insurance company of an asset (or part of an asset) which, immediately before the disposal or (as the case may be) immediately after the acquisition, is within one of the categories set out in [paragraphs (a) to (e)][2] of subsection (4) below, that section shall not apply to the disposal or acquisition.

[(4) The categories referred to in subsections (1) to (3) above are—

    (a) assets linked solely to pension business;
    (b) assets linked solely to life reinsurance business;
    (c) assets of the overseas life assurance fund;
    (d) assets linked solely to basic life assurance and general annuity business;
    (e) assets of the [long-term insurance fund][8] not within any of the preceding paragraphs;
    (f) other assets.][4]

(5) In this section "market value" has the same meaning as in the [1992][3] Act.

[(6) In a case where the profits of a company's life assurance business are charged to tax in accordance with Case I of Schedule D this section has effect with the modification specified in section 440B(3).][5]][1]

Commentary—*Simon's Direct Tax Service* D4.532.

Revenue Internal Guidance—Life assurance manual LAM 2.42-2.48 (transfers of assets between businesses).

Definitions—"the 1970 Act", s 831(3); "the 1992 Act", s 831(3); "basic life assurance business", s 431(2); "insurance company", s 431(2); "loan relationship", s 834(1), FA 1996 s 81; "long term business", s 431(2); "overseas life assurance fund", s 431(2); "pension business", s 431(2); "Schedule D", s 18(1).

Cross references—See TA 1988 s 440B(3) (modification of this section in its application where profits of a company's life assurance business are charged to tax under Schedule D, Case I; sub-ss (1), (2) apply as if the only categories of assets referred to in sub-s (4) were assets of the long term business fund and other assets).

TA 1988 Sch 19AC, para 10AA, 10B (modification of this section in its application to overseas life insurance companies).

FA 1990 Sch 6 para 12(8) (no disposal or re-acquisition to be deemed to occur by virtue of this section by reason only of the coming into force of any provision of s 440A below),

Modifications—This section is modified so far as it applies to the life or endowment business carried on by friendly societies, and, in some cases, in relation to specified transactions, by the Friendly Societies (Modification of the Corporation Tax Acts) Regulations, SI 1997/473 regs 22-25.

Words inserted in sub-s (4)(a) in respect of individual savings account business of Insurance Companies by the Individual Savings Account Regulations, SI 1998/1871 reg 15, with effect from 6 April 1999.

Amendments—[1] This section and s 440A below substituted for s 440 by FA 1990 Sch 6 para 8 with respect to accounting periods beginning after 31 December 1989, but subject to the provisions in FA 1990 Sch 6 paras 11, 12.
[2] Words in sub-s (3) substituted for words "paragraphs (*a*) to (*d*)" by FA 1995 Sch 8 paras 5(2), 57 with effect for accounting periods beginning after 31 December 1994.
[3] Words in sub-ss (3), (5) substituted by TCGA 1992 Sch 10 para 14(1), (22).
[4] Sub-s (4) substituted by FA 1995 Sch 8 paras 5(3), 57 with effect for accounting periods beginning after 31 December 1994.
[5] Sub-s (6) added by FA 1995 Sch 8 paras 28(3), 57 with effect for accounting periods beginning after 31 December 1994.
[6] Sub-s (2A) inserted by FA 1996 Sch 14 para 25 with effect for accounting periods ending after 31 March 1996, subject to transitional provisions in FA 1996 Sch 15.
[7] Sub-s (2)(*a*) substituted by the Financial Services and Markets Act 2000 (Consequential Amendments) (Taxes) Order, SI 2001/3629 arts 13, 28 with effect from 1 December 2001, immediately after the coming into force of the Financial Services and Markets Act 2000 ss 411, 432(1), Sch 20. SI 2001/3629 art 28 has effect in relation to any transfer under a scheme falling within the Financial Services and Markets Act 2000 s 105, including an excluded scheme falling within Case 2, 3 or 4 of the Financial Services and Markets Act 2000 s 105(3).
[8] Words in sub-s (4)(*e*) substituted by SI 2001/3629 arts 13, 52(1)(*g*) with effect from 1 December 2001 (immediately after the coming into force of the Financial Services and Markets Act 2000 ss 411, 432(1), Sch 20).
[9] Sub-s (2B) inserted by FA 2002 s 83(1)(*b*), (3) Sch 27 paras 1, 5 with effect for accounting periods beginning after 30 September 2002.

[440A Securities

(1) Subsection (2) below applies where the assets of an insurance company include securities of a class all of which would apart from this section be regarded for the purposes of corporation tax on chargeable gains as one holding.

(2) Where this subsection applies—

[(*a*) so many of the securities as are identified in the company's records as securities by reference to the value of which there are to be determined benefits provided for under policies or contracts the effecting of all (or all but an insignificant proportion) of which constitutes the carrying on of—

    (i) pension business, or

    (ii) life reinsurance business, or

    (iii) basic life assurance and general annuity business,

shall be treated for the purposes of corporation tax as a separate holding linked solely to that business,][3]

(*c*) so many of the securities as are included in the overseas life assurance fund shall be treated for those purposes as a separate holding which is an asset of that fund,

(*d*) so many of the securities as are included in the company's [long-term insurance fund][5] but do not fall within any of the preceding paragraphs shall be treated for those purposes as a separate holding which is an asset of that fund (but not of any of the descriptions mentioned in those paragraphs), and

(*e*) any remaining securities shall be treated for those purposes as a separate holding which is not of any of the descriptions mentioned in the preceding paragraphs.

(3) Subsection (2) above also applies where the assets of an insurance company include securities of a class and apart from this section some of them would be regarded as a 1982 holding, and the rest as a [section 104 holding][4], for the purposes of corporation tax on chargeable gains.

(4) In a case within subsection (3) above—

(*a*) the reference in any paragraph of subsection (2) above to a separate holding shall be construed, where necessary, as a reference to a separate 1982 holding and a separate [section 104 holding][4], and

(*b*) the questions whether such a construction is necessary in the case of any paragraph and, if it is, how many securities falling within the paragraph constitute each of the two holdings shall be determined in accordance with paragraph 12 of Schedule 6 to the Finance Act 1990 and the identification rules applying on any subsequent acquisitions and disposals.

(5) Section [105 of the 1992 Act][2] shall have effect where subsection (2) above applies as if securities regarded as included in different holdings by virtue of that subsection were securities of different kinds.

[(6) In this section—

"1982 holding" has the same meaning as in section 109 of the 1992 Act;

["section 104 holding][4]" has the same meaning as in section 104(3) of that Act; and

"securities" means shares, or securities of a company, and any other assets where they are of a nature to be dealt in without identifying the particular assets disposed of or acquired.][2]

[(7) In a case where the profits of a company's life assurance business are charged to tax in accordance with Case I of Schedule D this section has effect with the modification specified in section 440B(4).][3]][1]

Commentary—*Simon's Direct Tax Service* **D4.532.**
Definitions—"The 1992 Act", s 831(3); "chargeable gains", s 832(1); "insurance company", s 431(2); "overseas life assurance fund", s 431(2); "pension business", s 431(2).
Cross references—See TA 1988 s 440B(4) (modification of this section in its application where profits of a company's life assurance business are charged to tax in accordance with Schedule D, Case I: so far as sub-s (2) is concerned as regards securities in the company's records identified as securities by reference to the value of which are to be determined benefits provided under policies or contracts the effecting of which constitutes the carrying on of long term business shall be treated as a separate holding linked to that business for corporation tax purposes. Holdings outside this description will be treated as a separate holding for corporation tax purposes).

TA 1988 Sch 19AC, para 11 (modification of this section in relation to overseas life insurance companies).
FA 1990 Sch 6 para 12(8) (no disposal or re-acquisition to be deemed to occur by virtue of s 440 above by reason only of the coming into force of any provision of this section);
Modifications— Sub-s (2) modified so far as it applies to the life or endowment business carried on by friendly societies and certain non-directive societies by the Friendly Societies (Modification of the Corporation Tax Acts) Regulations, SI 1997/473 reg 26.
Words inserted in sub-s (2)(*a*)(i) in respect of individual savings account business of Insurance Companies by the Individual Savings Account Regulations, SI 1998/1871 reg 16, with effect from 6 April 1999.
Amendments—[1] This section and s 440 above substituted for s 440 by FA 1990 Sch 6 para 8 with respect to accounting periods beginning after 31 December 1989, but subject to the provisions in FA 1990 Sch 6 paras 11, 12.
[2] Sub-s (6) and words in sub-s (5) substituted by TCGA 1992 Sch 10 para 14(1), (23).
[3] Sub-s (2)(*a*) substituted for former paras (*a*), (*b*) and sub-s (7) added by FA 1995 Sch 8 paras 6, 57 with effect for accounting periods beginning after 31 December 1994.
[4] Words in sub-ss (3), (4), (6) substituted by FA 1998 s 123(5) with effect for any disposal after 5 April 1998 of any securities (whenever acquired).
[5] Words in sub-s (2)(*d*) substituted by the Financial Services and Markets Act 2000 (Consequential Amendments) (Taxes) Order, SI 2001/3629 arts 13, 52(1)(*h*) with effect from 1 December 2001 (immediately after the coming into force of the Financial Services and Markets Act 2000 ss 411, 432(1), Sch 20).

[440B Modifications where tax charged under Case I of Schedule D

(1) The following provisions apply where the profits of a company's life assurance business are charged to tax in accordance with Case I of Schedule D.

[(1A) ...[2]]

(2) ...[3]

(3) Section 440(1) and (2) apply as if the only categories set out in subsection (4) of that section were—

   (*a*) assets of the [long-term insurance fund][4], and
   (*b*) other assets.

(4) Section 440A applies as if for paragraphs (*a*) to (*e*) of subsection (2) there were substituted—

   ''(*a*) so many of the securities as are identified in the company's records as securities by reference to the value of which there are to be determined benefits provided for under policies or contracts the effecting of all (or all but an insignificant proportion) of which constitutes the carrying on of [long-term][5] business , shall be treated for the purposes of corporation tax as a separate holding linked solely to that business, and
   (*b*) any remaining securities shall be treated for those purposes as a separate holding which is not of the description mentioned in the preceding paragraph.''.

(5) Section 212(1) of the 1992 Act does not apply, but without prejudice to the bringing into account of any amounts deferred under section 213(1) or 214A(2) of that Act from any accounting period beginning before 1st January 1995.][1]

Commentary—*Simon's Direct Tax Service* **D4.503.**
Revenue Internal Guidance—Life assurance manual LAM 2.21-2.27 (application of this section).
Definitions—''The 1992 Act'', s 831(3); ''life assurance business'', s 431(2); ''long term business'', s 431(2); ''long term business fund'', s 431(2); ''Schedule D'', s 18(1); ''tax'', s 832(3).
Modifications—Sub-ss (3) and (4) are treated as substituted in the application of this section to an overseas life assurance company, see TA 1988 Sch 19AC para 10C.
Amendments—[1] Section inserted by FA 1995 Sch 8 paras 28(1), 57 with effect for accounting periods beginning after 31 December 1994.
[2] Sub-s (1A) (inserted by FA 1996 Sch 27 para 5 with effect for accounting periods beginning after 31 December 1995) repealed by F(No 2)A 1997 s 23, Sch 3 para 8(1), (2), (4), Sch 8 Pt II(6) with effect for distributions made 1 July 1997.
[3] Sub-s (2) repealed by F(No 2)A 1997 s 23, Sch 3 para 8(1), (3), (5), Sch 8 Pt II(6) with effect for accounting periods beginning after 1 July 1997.
[4] Words in sub-s (3)(*a*) substituted by the Financial Services and Markets Act 2000 (Consequential Amendments) (Taxes) Order, SI 2001/3629 arts 13, 52(1)(*i*) with effect from 1 December 2001 (immediately after the coming into force of the Financial Services and Markets Act 2000 ss 411, 432(1), Sch 20).
[5] Words in sub-s (4)(*a*) substituted by SI 2001/3629 arts 13, 52(2)(*g*) with effect from 1 December 2001 (immediately after the coming into force of the Financial Services and Markets Act 2000 ss 411, 432(1), Sch 20).

[441 Overseas life assurance business

(1) This section and section 441A shall apply for an accounting period of an insurance company ...[2] if during the period the company carries on overseas life assurance business.

(2) Subject to the provisions of this section and section 441A, profits arising to the company from the overseas life assurance business shall be treated as income within Schedule D, and be chargeable under Case VI of that Schedule, and for that purpose—

   (*a*) that business shall be treated separately, and
   (*b*) subject to paragraph (*a*) above, the profits from it shall be computed in accordance with the provisions of this Act applicable to Case I of Schedule D.

(3) Subsection (2) above shall not apply if the company is charged to corporation tax in accordance with the provisions applicable to Case I of Schedule D in respect of the profits of its life assurance business.

(4) In making the computation referred to in subsection (2) above—

(*a*) sections 82(1), (2) and (4) and 83 of the Finance Act 1989 shall apply with the necessary modifications and in particular with the omission of the words [and any amounts of tax which are expended on behalf of]⁵ in section 82(1)(*a*), [and]³

[(*aa*) ...]³

(*b*) there may be set off against the profits any loss, to be computed on the same basis as the profits, which has arisen from overseas life assurance business in any previous accounting period beginning on or after 1st January 1990.

(5) Section 396 shall not be taken to apply to a loss incurred by a company on overseas life assurance business.

(6) Nothing in section 128 or 399(1) shall affect the operation of this section.

(7) ...⁴

(8) Gains accruing on the disposal by a company of assets of its overseas life assurance fund shall not be chargeable gains.]¹

Commentary—*Simon's Direct Tax Service* **D4.524.**
Revenue Internal Guidance—Life assurance manual LAM 10.61-10.67 (computation of Case VI profits).
Definitions—"Accounting period", s 834(1); "chargeable gains", s 832(1); "insurance company", s 431(2); "overseas life assurance business", s 431(2); "overseas life assurance fund", s 431(2); "profits", s 833(1); "Schedule D", s 18(1).
Cross references—See TMA 1970 Sch 2 para 2 (appeals from decisions by inspectors under this section to be exclusively to the Special Commissioners).
TA 1970 s 434A(2)(*a*) (an insurance company's Schedule D Case I losses from its life assurance business are reduced by losses under this section).
TA 1988 s 434E (capital allowances and charges on investment assets to be ignored in computing profits under this section).
TA 1988 s 444A(3) (treatment of losses which would have been available under sub-s (4)(*b*) above upon the transfer of the whole or part of the long term overseas life assurance business of an insurance company).
TA 1988 s 804A(1) (restriction of credit for foreign tax against tax charged under this section).
Modification—Sub-s (4) modified so far as it applies to the life or endowment business carried on by non-directive societies, and this section modified so far as it applies to the life or endowment business carried on by friendly societies, by the Friendly Societies (Modification of the Corporation Tax Acts) Regulations, SI 1997/473 reg 28.
Amendments—¹ This section and s 441A below substituted for s 441 by FA 1990 Sch 7 paras 3, 10(1) with effect for accounting periods beginning after 31 December 1989.
² Words in sub-s (1) repealed by FA 1995 Sch 8 para 30, Sch 29, Pt VIII(5), for accounting periods beginning after 31 October 1994 (note however FA 1995 Sch 8 para 55(2)).
³ Words in sub-s (4)(*aa*) (inserted by FA 1995 Sch 8 paras 16(5), 57) repealed, and word "and" at end of sub-s (4)(*a*) added, by FA 1996 Sch 31 para 7(1)(*c*), (2), Sch 41 Pt V(23) with effect for periods of account beginning after 31 December 1995.
⁴ Sub-s (7) repealed by FA 1995 Sch 29 Pt VIII(5) for accounting periods beginning after 31 December 1994.
⁵ Words in sub-s (4)(*a*) substituted for words "tax or" by FA 2000 s 103, Sch 30 para 18(3) with effect for periods of account beginning after 31 March 2000.

441A Section 441: distributions

(1) ...²

(2)–(8) ...¹

Amendments—¹ Sub-ss (2)–(8) repealed by F(No 2)A 1997 s 34, Sch 4 para 28, Sch 8 Pt II(10) with effect for distributions made after 5 April 1999.
² Sub-s (1) repealed by F(No 2)A 1997 s 23, Sch 23 para 9(1), (2), (4), Sch 8 Pt II(6) with effect for distributions made after 1 July 1997.

[441B Treatment of UK land

(1) This section applies to land in the United Kingdom which—

(*a*) is held by a company as an asset linked to the company's overseas life assurance business, or
(*b*) is held by a company which is charged to tax under Case I of Schedule D in respect of its life assurance business as an asset by reference to the value of which benefits under any policy or contract are to be determined, where the policy or contract (or, in the case of a reinsurance contract, the underlying policy or contract) is held by a person not residing in the United Kingdom.

(2) Income arising from land to which this section applies shall be treated for the purposes of this Chapter as referable to basic life assurance and general annuity business.

[(2A) For the purposes of subsection (2) above a Schedule A business for the exploitation of any land to which this section applies shall be treated as a separate business from any other such business.]²

(3) Where (apart from this subsection) an insurance company would not be carrying on basic life assurance and general annuity business it shall be treated as carrying on such business if any income of the company is treated as referable to such business by subsection (2) above.

(4) A company may be charged to tax by virtue of this section—

(*a*) notwithstanding section 439A, and
(*b*) whether or not the income to which subsection (2) above relates is taken into account in computing the profits of the company for the purposes of any charge to tax in accordance with Case I of Schedule D.

(5) In this section "land" has the same meaning as in Schedule 19AA.]¹

Commentary—*Simon's Direct Tax Service* **D4.524.**
Definitions—"Basic life assurance and general annuity business", s 431(2); "insurance company", s 431(2); "land", Sch 19AA para 4(3); "overseas life assurance business", s 431(2); "Schedule D", s 18(1); "tax", s 832(3); "United Kingdom", s 830(1).

Amendments—[1] Section inserted by FA 1995 Sch 8 paras 32, 55 with effect for accounting periods beginning after 31 October 1994 (but note FA 1995 Sch 8 para 55(2)).
[2] Sub-s (2A) inserted by FA 1998 Sch 5 para 41 with effect from 1998–99 and subsequent years of assessment for income tax purposes, and from 1 April 1998 for corporation tax, subject to the transitional provisions in FA 1998 Sch 5 Part IV.

442 Overseas business of UK companies

(1) Subsections (2) and (3) below apply where a company resident in the United Kingdom carries on insurance business outside the United Kingdom through a branch or agency and—

(a) that business, or part of it, together with the whole assets of the company used for the purposes of that business or part (or together with the whole of those assets other than cash), is transferred to a company not resident in the United Kingdom;

(b) the business or part is so transferred wholly or partly in exchange for shares, or for shares and loan stock, issued by the transferee company to the transferor company; and

(c) the shares so issued, either alone or taken together with any other shares in the transferee company already held by the transferor company, amount in all to not less than one quarter of the ordinary share capital of the transferee company.

(2) In making any computation in accordance with the provisions of this Act applicable to Case I of Schedule D of the profits or losses of the transferor company for the accounting period in which the transfer occurs, there shall be disregarded any profit or loss in respect of any asset transferred which, apart from this subsection, would fall to be taken into account in making that computation.

(3) Where by virtue of subsection (2) above any profit or loss is disregarded in making any computation ...[2] the profit or loss shall be treated for the purposes of the [1992 Act][1] as a chargeable gain or allowable loss accruing to the transferor company on the transfer.

(4) Where at any time a company resident in the United Kingdom—

(a) which carries on insurance business wholly outside the United Kingdom, and

(b) the whole or part of whose ordinary share capital is beneficially owned by one or more companies resident in the United Kingdom,

ceases to be resident in the United Kingdom, the profits or losses of the company in respect of that business for the accounting period ending at that time shall be computed for tax purposes without regard to the whole, or, as the case may be, a corresponding part of any profit or loss in respect of any asset which, apart from this subsection, would fall to be calculated in accordance with section 100(1)(b) and taken into account in making that computation.

Commentary—*Simon's Direct Tax Service* **D4.529.**
Revenue Internal Guidance—Life Assurance Manual, paras 10.61–10.67 (computation of Case VI profits).
Definitions—"The 1992 Act", s 831(3); "accounting period", s 834(1); "allowable loss", s 834(1); "branch or agency", s 834(1); "chargeable gain", s 832(1); "company", s 832(1), (2); "ordinary share capital", s 832(1); "Schedule D", s 18(1).
Cross references—See TCGA 1992 s 140C(8) (sub-s (3) above to be ignored in computing the chargeable gain in relation to transfer by a UK resident company to a member state company of a trade which the transferor company carried on in a member state through a branch or agency).
Amendments—[1] Words in sub-s (3) substituted by TCGA 1992 Sch 10 para 14(1), (24).
[2] Words omitted in sub-s (3) repealed by FA 1996 Sch 41 Pt V(24) with effect for accounting periods beginning after 31 December 1995.

[442A Taxation of investment return where risk reinsured

(1) Where an insurance company reinsures any risk in respect of a policy or contract attributable to its basic life assurance and general annuity business, the investment return on the policy or contract shall be treated as accruing to the company over the period of the reinsurance arrangement and shall be charged to tax under Case VI of Schedule D.

(2) The Board may make provision by regulations as to the amount of investment return to be treated as accruing in each accounting period during which the reinsurance arrangement is in force.

(3) The regulations may, in particular, provide that the investment return to be treated as accruing to the company in respect of a policy or contract in any accounting period shall be calculated by reference to—

(a) the aggregate of the sums paid by the company to the reinsurer during that accounting period and any earlier accounting periods by way of premium or otherwise;

(b) the aggregate of the sums paid by the reinsurer to the company during that accounting period and any earlier accounting periods by way of commission or otherwise;

(c) the aggregate amount of the net investment return treated as accruing to the company in any earlier accounting periods, that is to say, net of tax at such rate as may be prescribed; and

(d) such percentage rate of return as may be prescribed.

(4) The regulations shall provide that the amount of investment return to be treated as accruing to the company in respect of a policy or contract in the final accounting period during which the policy or contract is in force is the amount, ascertained in accordance with regulations, by which the profit over the whole period during which the policy or contract, and the reinsurance arrangement, were in force exceeds the aggregate of the amounts treated as accruing in earlier accounting periods.

If that profit is less than the aggregate of the amounts treated as accruing in earlier accounting periods, the difference shall go to reduce the amounts treated by virtue of this section as arising in that accounting period from other policies or contracts, and if not fully so relieved may be carried forward and set against any such amounts in subsequent accounting periods.

(5) Regulations under this section—

(*a*) may exclude from the operation of this section such descriptions of insurance company, such descriptions of policies or contracts and such descriptions of reinsurance arrangements as may be prescribed;

(*b*) may make such supplementary provision as to the ascertainment of the investment return to be treated as accruing to the company as appears to the Board to be appropriate, including provision requiring payments made during an accounting period to be treated as made on such date or dates as may be prescribed; and

(*c*) may make different provision for different cases or descriptions of case.

(6) In this section "prescribed" means prescribed by regulations under this section.][1]

Commentary—*Simon's Direct Tax Service* **D4.509.**
Regulations—Insurance Companies (Taxation of Reinsurance Business) Regulations, SI 1995/1730.
Definitions—"Accounting period", s 834(1); "basic life assurance and general annuity business", s 431(2); "the Board", s 832(1); "insurance company", s 431(2); "Schedule D", s 18(1); "tax", s 832(3).
Cross references—See Insurance Companies (Taxation of Reinsurance Business) Regulations, SI 1995/1730 regs 3–8 (calculation of investment return on reinsurance arrangements).
Insurance Companies (Taxation of Reinsurance Business) Regulations, SI 1995/1730 regs 9, 10 (exclusion of certain reinsurance arrangements and policies and contracts from this section).
Modifications—Sub-s (7) treated as inserted in the applications of this section to an overseas life assurance company, see TA 1988 Sch 19AC para 11B.
Sub-s (1) modified so far as it applies to the life or endowment business carried on by friendly societies by the Friendly Societies (Modification of the Corporation Tax Acts) Regulations, SI 1997/473 reg 29.
Amendments—[1] This section inserted by FA 1995 Sch 8 paras 34, 57 with effect for accounting periods beginning after 31 December 1994 (subject to FA 1995 Sch 8 para 57(2)).

443 Life policies carrying rights not in money

Where any investments or other assets are or have been, in accordance with a policy issued in the course of life assurance business carried on by an insurance company, transferred to the policy holder on or after 6th April 1967, the policy holder's acquisition of the assets, and the disposal of them to him, shall be deemed to be for a consideration equal to the market value of the assets for the purposes of computing income in accordance with Case I or VI of Schedule D.

Commentary—*Simon's Direct Tax Service* **D4.518.**
Definitions—"Insurance company", s 431(2); "life assurance business", s 431(2); "Schedule D", s 18(1).
Cross references—See TCGA 1992 s 204(3) (policyholder's acquisition of assets deemed to be at market value for capital gains tax purposes).

444 Life policies issued before 5th August 1965

(1) This section applies in relation to policies of life assurance issued before 5th August 1965 by a company carrying on life assurance business, being policies which—

(*a*) provide for benefits consisting to any extent of investments of a specified description or of a sum of money to be determined by reference to the value of such investments, but

(*b*) do not provide for the deduction from those benefits of any amount by reference to tax chargeable in respect of chargeable gains.

(2) Where—

(*a*) the investments of the company's life assurance fund, so far as referable to those policies, consist wholly or mainly of investments of the description so specified, and

(*b*) on the company becoming liable under any of those policies for any such benefits (including benefits to be provided on the surrender of a policy), a chargeable gain accrues to the company from the disposal, in meeting or for the purpose of meeting that liability, of investments of that description forming part of its life assurance fund, or would so accrue if the liability were met by or from the proceeds of such a disposal,

then the company shall be entitled as against the person receiving the benefits to retain out of those benefits a part not exceeding in amount or value corporation tax, at the rate specified in subsection (3) below, in respect of the chargeable gain referred to in paragraph (*b*) above, computed without regard to any amount retained under this subsection.

(3) The amount to be retained under subsection (2) above shall, subject to subsection (4) below, be computed by reference to the rate of corporation tax for the time being in force or, if no rate of corporation tax has yet been fixed for the financial year, the rate last in force.

(4) In so far as the chargeable gain represents or would represent a gain belonging or allocated to, or reserved for, policy holders, the amount to be retained shall be computed by reference to a rate of tax not exceeding 37.5 per cent.

Commentary—*Simon's Direct Tax Service* **D4.518.**
Definitions—"Chargeable gain", s 832(1); "company", s 832(1), (2); "life assurance business", s 431(2).

[444A Transfers of business

[(1) Subject to subsection (7) below, this section applies where an insurance business transfer scheme has effect to transfer long-term business from one person ("the transferor") to another ("the transferee").][6]

(2) Any expenses of management which (assuming the transferor had continued to carry on the business transferred after the transfer) would have been deductible by the transferor under sections 75 and 76 in computing profits for an accounting period following the period which ends with the day on which the transfer takes place shall, instead, be treated as expenses of management of the transferee (and deductible in accordance with those sections, as modified in the case of acquisition expenses by section 86(6) to (9) of the Finance Act 1989 and in the case of expenses to which subsection (6) or (7) of section 87 of that Act applies by that subsection).

(3) Any loss which (assuming the transferor had continued to carry on the business transferred after the transfer)—

(a) would have been available under section 436(3)(c) [or 439B(3)(c)][3] to be set off against profits of the transferor for the accounting period following that which ends with the day on which transfer takes place, or

(b) where [the transfer relates to any overseas life assurance business or][4] in connection with the transfer the transferor also transfers the whole or part of any [such][4] business, would have been so available under section 441(4)(b),

shall, instead, be treated as a loss of the transferee (and available to be set off against profits of the same class of business as that in which it arose).

[(3A) Any subsection (2) excess (within the meaning of section 432F(2)) which (assuming the transferor had continued to carry on the business transferred after the transfer) would have been available under section 432F(3) or (4) to reduce a subsection (3) figure (within the meaning of section 432F(1)) of the transferor in an accounting period following that which ends with the day on which transfer takes place—

(a) shall, instead, be treated as a subsection (2) excess of the transferee, and

(b) shall be taken into account in the first accounting period of the transferee ending after the date of the transfer (to reduce the subsection (3) figure or, as the case may be, to produce or increase a subsection (2) excess for that period),

in relation to the revenue account of the transferee dealing with or including the business transferred.][5]

(4) Where acquisition expenses are treated as expenses of management of the transferee by virtue of subsection (2) above, the amount deductible for the first accounting period of the transferee ending after the transfer takes place shall be calculated as if that accounting period began with the day after the transfer.

(5) Where the transfer is of part only of the transferor's [long-term][7] business , [subsection (2), (3) or (3A)][5] above shall apply only to such part of any amount to which it would otherwise apply as is appropriate.

(6) Any question arising as to the operation of subsection (5) above shall be determined by the Special Commissioners who shall determine the question in the same manner as they determine appeals; but both the transferor and transferee shall be entitled to appear and be heard or to make representations in writing.

(7) Subject to subsection (8) below, this section shall not apply unless the transfer is effected for bona fide commercial reasons and does not form part of a scheme or arrangements of which the main purpose, or one of the main purposes, is avoidance of liability to corporation tax.

(8) Subsection (7) above shall not affect the operation of this section in any case where, before the transfer, the Board have, on the application of the transferee, notified the transferee that the Board are satisfied that the transfer will be effected for bona fide commercial reasons and will not form part of any scheme or arrangements such as are mentioned in that subsection; and subsections (2) to (5) of section [138 of the 1992 Act][2] shall have effect in relation to this subsection as they have effect in relation to subsection (1) of that section.]][1]

Commentary—*Simon's Direct Tax Service* **D4.528.**
Concession C29—Additional relief given for pre-1 January 1992 general annuity losses where long-term business is transferred.
Revenue Internal Guidance—Life assurance manual LAM 16.31-16.35 (explanation of this section).
LAM 16.62 (clearance applications are dealt with by FID1 (Insurance Group)).
LAM 16.91-16.101 (domestication of business).
Definitions—"Accounting period", s 834(1); "the Board", s 832(1); "the 1992 Act", s 831(3); "insurance company", s 431(2); "long term business", s 431(2); "overseas life assurance business", s 431(2).
Cross references—See TA 1988 Sch 19AC para 11C (references to a qualifying overseas transfer treated as being included in sub-s (1) above in its application to an overseas life assurance company).
Modifications— Friendly Societies (Modification of the Corporation Tax Acts) Regulations 1997, SI 1997/473 reg 3 (the provisions of the Corporation Tax Acts which apply on the transfer of the whole or part of the long term business of an insurance company to another company are to have effect where the transferee is a friendly society).
Sub-s (1) above to have effect as if the words "in accordance with a scheme sanctioned by a court under Part I of Schedule 2C to the Insurance Companies Act 1982" were omitted in relation to specified transactions, see Friendly Societies (Modification of the Corporation Tax Acts) Regulations SI 1997/473 reg 30.
For the modification of sub-s (3A) above in relation to a transfer taking place at the end of an accounting period of the transferor beginning after 31 December 1989 and ending before 1 January 1994, see **Amendments** note 5 below.

Amendments—[1] This section inserted by FA 1990 Sch 9 paras 4, 7 with effect where transfers of business take place after 31 December 1989.
[2] Words in sub-s (8) substituted by TCGA 1992 Sch 10 para 14(1), (25).
[3] Words in sub-s (3)(*a*) inserted by FA 1995 Sch 8 paras 27(2), 57 with effect for accounting periods beginning after 31 December 1994.
[4] Words in sub-s (3)(*b*) inserted and substituted by FA 1995 s 53, Sch 9 para 1(2)(*b*), (3), with effect for any transfers sanctioned or authorised after 30 June 1994.
[5] Sub-s (3A) inserted and words in sub-s (5) substituted by FA 1995 Sch 8 paras 17(4), (5), 53 with effect for accounting periods ending after 31 December 1993.
[6] Sub-s (1) substituted by the Financial Services and Markets Act 2000 (Consequential Amendments) (Taxes) Order, SI 2001/3629 arts 13, 29 with effect from 1 December 2001, immediately after the coming into force of the Financial Services and Markets Act 2000 ss 411, 432(1), Sch 20. SI 2001/3629 art 29 has effect in relation to any transfer under a scheme falling within the Financial Services and Markets Act 2000 s 105, including an excluded scheme falling within Case 2, 3 or 4 of the Financial Services and Markets Act 2000 s 105(3).
[7] Words in sub-s (5) substituted by the Financial Services and Markets Act 2000 (Consequential Amendments) (Taxes) Order, SI 2001/3629 arts 13, 52(2)(*h*) with effect from 1 December 2001 (immediately after the coming into force of the Financial Services and Markets Act 2000 ss 411, 432(1), Sch 20).

[Provisions applying in relation to overseas life insurance companies]1

[444B Modification of Act in relation to overseas life insurance companies

Schedule 19AC (which makes modifications of this Act in relation to overseas life insurance companies) shall have effect.][1]

Amendments—[1] This section inserted by FA 1993 s 97(1).

[Equalisation reserves]1

[444BA Equalisation reserves for general business

(1) Subject to the following provisions of this section and to sections 444BB to 444BD, the rules in subsection (2) below shall apply in making any computation, for the purposes of Case I or V of Schedule D, of the profits or losses for any accounting period of an insurance company whose business has at any time been or included business in respect of which it was required, by virtue of [equalisation reserves rules][2], to maintain an equalisation reserve.

(2) Those rules are—

(*a*) that amounts which, in accordance with [equalisation reserves rules][2], are transferred into the equalisation reserve in respect of the company's business for the accounting period in question are to be deductible;

(*b*) that amounts which, in accordance with any such regulations, are transferred out of the reserve in respect of the company's business for that period are to be treated as receipts of that business; and

(*c*) that it must be assumed that all such transfers as are required by [equalisation reserves rules][2] to be made into or out of the reserve in respect of the company's business for any period are made as required.

(3) Where an insurance company having any business in respect of which it is required, by virtue [equalisation reserves rules][2], to maintain an equalisation reserve ceases to trade—

(*a*) any balance which exists in the reserve at that time for the purposes of the Tax Acts shall be deemed to have been transferred out of the reserve immediately before the company ceases to trade; and

(*b*) that transfer out shall be deemed to be a transfer in respect of the company's business for the accounting period in which the company so ceases and to have been required by [equalisation reserves rules][2].

(4) Where—

(*a*) an amount is transferred into an equalisation reserve in respect of the business of an insurance company for any accounting period,

(*b*) the rule in subsection (2)(*a*) above would apply to the transfer of that amount but for this subsection,

(*c*) that company by notice in writing to an officer of the Board makes an election in relation to that amount for the purposes of this subsection, and

(*d*) the notice of the election is given not more than two years after the end of that period,

the rule mentioned in subsection (2)(*a*) above shall not apply to that transfer of that amount and, instead, the amount transferred (the "unrelieved transfer") shall be carried forward for the purposes of subsection (5) below to the next accounting period and (subject to subsection (6) below) from accounting period to accounting period.

(5) Where—

(*a*) in accordance with [equalisation reserves rules][2], a transfer is made out of an equalisation reserve in respect of an insurance company's business for any accounting period,

(*b*) the rule in subsection (2)(*b*) above would apply to the transfer but for this subsection, and

(*c*) the accounting period is one to which any amount representing one or more unrelieved transfers has been carried forward under subsection (4) above, that rule mentioned in subsection (2)(*b*) above shall not apply to that transfer except to the extent (if any) that the amount of the transfer exceeds the aggregate of the amounts representing unrelieved transfers carried forward to that period.

(6) Where in the case of any company—

(*a*) any amount representing one or more unrelieved transfers is carried forward to an accounting period in accordance with subsection (4) above, and

(*b*) by virtue of subsection (5) above the rule in subsection (2)(*b*) above does not apply to an amount representing the whole or any part of any transfer out of an equalisation reserve in respect of the company's business for that period,

the amount mentioned in paragraph (*a*) above shall not be carried forward under subsection (4) above to the next accounting period except to the extent (if any) that it exceeds the amount mentioned in paragraph (*b*) above.

(7) To the extent that any actual or assumed transfer in accordance with [equalisation reserves rules][2] of any amount into an equalisation reserve is attributable to arrangements entered into wholly or mainly for tax purposes—

(*a*) the rule in subsection (2)(*a*) above shall not apply to that transfer; and

(*b*) the making of that transfer shall be disregarded in determining, for the purposes of the Tax Acts, whether and to what extent there is subsequently any requirement to make a transfer into or out of the reserve in accordance with [equalisation reserves rules][2];

and this subsection applies irrespective of whether the insurance company in question is a party to the arrangements.

(8) For the purposes of this section the transfer of an amount into an equalisation reserve is attributable to arrangements entered into wholly or mainly for tax purposes to the extent that the arrangements to which it is attributable are arrangements—

(*a*) the sole or main purpose of which is, or

(*b*) the sole or main benefit accruing from which might (but for subsection (7) above) be expected to be,

the reduction by virtue of this section of any liability to tax.

(9) Where—

(*a*) any transfer made into or out of an equalisation reserve maintained by an insurance company is made in accordance with [equalisation reserves rules][2] in respect of business carried on by that company over a period ("the equalisation period"), and

(*b*) parts of the equalisation period are in different accounting periods,

the amount transferred shall be apportioned for the purposes of this section between the different accounting periods in the proportions that correspond to the number of days in the equalisation period that are included in each of those accounting periods.

(10) The Treasury may by regulations provide in relation to any accounting periods ending on or after 1st April 1996 for specified transitional provisions contained in [equalisation reserves rules][2] to be disregarded for the purposes of the Tax Acts in determining how much is required, on any occasion, to be transferred into or out of any equalisation reserve in accordance with [the rules][2].

[(11) In this section, and in sections 444BB to 444BD, "equalisation reserves rules" means the rules in Chapter 6 of the Prudential Sourcebook (Insurers).][2][1]

Commentary—*Simon's Direct Tax Service* **D4.503.**
Regulations—Insurance Companies (Reserves) (Tax) Regulations, SI 1996/2991.
Definitions—"Accounting period", s 834(1); "the Board", s 832(1); "insurance company", s 431(2); "Schedule D", s 18(1); "the Tax Acts", s 831(2).
Cross references—See TA 1988 ss 444BB–444BD (Treasury may make provisions modifying this section in particular cases).
Amendments—[1] This section (and preceding heading) inserted by FA 1996 Sch 32 para 1.
[2] Words substituted by the Financial Services and Markets Act 2000 (Consequential Amendments) (Taxes) Order, SI 2001/3629 arts 13, 30(1)–(4), (9) with effect for periods of account ending after 30 November 2001.

[444BB Modification of s 444BA for mutual or overseas business and for non-resident companies

(1) The Treasury may by regulations make provision modifying section 444BA so as, in cases mentioned in subsection (2) below—

(*a*) to require—

(i) sums by reference to which the amount of any transfer into or out of an equalisation reserve falls to be computed, or

(ii) the amount of any such transfer,

to be apportioned between different parts of the business carried on for any period by an insurance company; and

(*b*) to provide for the purposes of corporation tax for the amounts taken to be transferred into or out of an equalisation reserve to be computed disregarding any such sum or, as the case may be, any such part of a transfer as is attributed, in accordance with the regulations, to a part of the business described for the purpose in the regulations.

(2) Those cases are cases where an insurance company which, in accordance with [equalisation reserves rules][2], is required to make transfers into or out of an equalisation reserve in respect of any business carried on by that company for any period is carrying on, for the whole or any part of that period—

(a) any business the income and gains of which fall to be disregarded in making a computation of the company's profits in accordance with the rules applicable to Case I of Schedule D, or

(b) any business by reference to which double taxation relief is afforded in respect of any income or gains.

(3) Section 444BA shall have effect (subject to any regulations under subsection (1) above) in the case of an equalisation reserve maintained by an insurance company which—

(a) is not resident in the United Kingdom, and

(b) carries on business in the United Kingdom through a branch or agency,

only if such conditions as may be prescribed by regulations made by the Treasury are satisfied in relation to that company and in relation to transfers into or out of that reserve.

(4) Regulations under this section prescribing conditions subject to which section 444BA is to apply in the case of any equalisation reserve maintained by an insurance company may—

(a) contain conditions imposing requirements on the company to furnish the Board with information with respect to any matters to which the regulations relate, or to produce to the Board documents or records relating to any such matters; and

(b) provide that, where any prescribed condition is not, or ceases to be, satisfied in relation to the company or in relation to transfers into or out of that reserve, there is to be deemed for the purposes of the Tax Acts to have been a transfer out of that reserve of an amount determined under the regulations.

(5) Regulations under this section may—

(a) provide for apportionments under the regulations to be made in such manner, and by reference to such factors, as may be specified or described in the regulations;

(b) make different provision for different cases;

(c) contain such supplementary, incidental, consequential and transitional provision as the Treasury may think fit;

(d) make provision having retrospective effect in relation to accounting periods beginning not more than one year before the time when the regulations are made;

and the powers conferred by this section in relation to transfers into or out of any reserve shall be exercisable in relation to both actual and assumed transfers.

(6) In this section "double taxation relief" means—

(a) relief under double taxation arrangements which takes the form of a credit allowed against corporation tax, or

(b) unilateral relief under section 790(1) which takes that form;

and "double taxation arrangements" here means arrangements having effect by virtue of section 788.][1]

Commentary—*Simon's Direct Tax Service* **D4.538.**
Regulations—Insurance Companies (Reserves) (Tax) Regulations, SI 1996/2991.
Non-resident Companies (General Insurance Business) Regulations, SI 1999/1408.
Definitions—"Accounting period", s 834(1); "the Board", s 832(1); "insurance company", s 431(2); "Schedule D", s 18(1).
Cross references—See TMA 1970 s 98 (penalties for failure to provide information etc required by regulations made under this section).
Amendments—[1] This section inserted by FA 1996 Sch 32 para 1.
[2] Words substituted by the Financial Services and Markets Act 2000 (Consequential Amendments) (Taxes) Order, SI 2001/3629 arts 13, 30(1), (9) with effect for periods of account ending after 30 November 2001.

[444BC Modification of s 444BA for non-annual accounting etc

(1) The Treasury may by regulations make provision modifying the operation of section 444BA in relation to cases where an insurance company has, for the purpose of preparing the documents it is required to prepare for the purposes of section [9.3 of the Prudential Sourcebook (Insurers)][2], applied for any period an accounting method described in paragraph 52 or 53 of Schedule 9A to the Companies Act 1985 (accounting on a non-annual basis).

(2) Subsection (5) of section 444BB applies for the purposes of this section as it applies for the purposes of that section.][1]

Commentary—*Simon's Direct Tax Service* **D4.538.**
Regulations—Insurance Companies (Reserves) (Tax) Regulations, SI 1996/2991.
Definition—"Insurance company", s 431(2).
Amendments—[1] This section inserted by FA 1996 Sch 32 para 1.
[2] Words substituted by the Financial Services and Markets Act 2000 (Consequential Amendments) (Taxes) Order, SI 2001/3629 arts 13, 30(5), (9) with effect for periods of account ending after 30 November 2001.

[444BD Applications of 444BA rules to other equalisation reserves

(1) The Treasury may by regulations provide for section 444BA to have effect, in such cases and subject to such modifications as may be specified in the regulations, in relation to any equivalent

reserves as it has effect in relation to equalisation reserves maintained by virtue of [equalisation reserves rules][2].

(2) For the purposes of this section a reserve is an equivalent reserve if—

    (*a*) it is maintained, otherwise than by virtue of [equalisation reserves rules][2], either—

        [(i) by an EEA firm of the kind mentioned in paragraph 5(*d*) of Schedule 3 to the Financial Services and Markets Act 2000 which has permission under paragraph 15 of that Schedule (as a result of qualifying for authorisation under paragraph 12(1) of that Schedule) to effect or carry out contracts of insurance in the United Kingdom, or][2]

        [(ii) by a firm which has permission under paragraph 4 of Schedule 4 to that Act (as a result of qualifying for authorisation under paragraph 2 of that Schedule) to effect or carry out contracts of insurance in the United Kingdom, or][2]

        [(iii) in respect of any business which consists of the effecting or carrying out of contracts of insurance and which is carried on outside the United Kingdom by a company resident in the United Kingdom;][2]

    (*b*) the purpose for which, or the manner in which, it is maintained is such as to make it equivalent to an equalisation reserve maintained by virtue of [equalisation reserves rules][2].

(3) For the purposes of this section a reserve is also an equivalent reserve if it is maintained in respect of any credit insurance business in accordance with requirements imposed either—

    (*a*) by or under any enactment, or

    (*b*) under so much of the law of any territory as secures compliance with the requirements of Article 1 of the credit insurance directive (equalisation reserves for credit insurance).

(4) Without prejudice to the generality of subsection (1) above, the modifications made by virtue of that subsection may—

    (*a*) provide for section 444BA to apply in the case of an equivalent reserve only where such conditions as may be specified in the regulations are satisfied in relation to the company maintaining the reserve or in relation to transfers made into or out of it; and

    (*b*) contain any other provision corresponding to any provision which, in the case of a reserve maintained by virtue of [equalisation reserves rules][2], may be made under sections 444BA to 444BC.

(5) Subsections (4) and (5) of section 444BB shall apply for the purposes of this section as they apply for the purposes of that section.

(6) Without prejudice to the generality of section 444BB(5), the transitional provision which by virtue of subsection (5) above may be contained in regulations under this section shall include—

    (*a*) provision for treating the amount of any transfers made into or out of an equivalent reserve in respect of business carried on for any specified period as increased by the amount by which they would have been increased if no transfers into the reserve had been made in respect of business carried on for an earlier period; and

    (*b*) provision for excluding from the rule in section 444BA(2)(*b*) so much of any amount transferred out of an equivalent reserve as represents, in pursuance of an apportionment made under the regulations, the transfer out of that reserve of amounts in respect of which there has been no entitlement to relief by virtue of section 444BA(2)(*a*).

(7) In this section—

    ["credit insurance business" means business which consists of the effecting or carrying out of contracts of insurance against risks of loss to the persons insured arising from—

        (*a*) the insolvency of debtors of theirs, or

        (*b*) from the failure (otherwise than through insolvency) of debtors of theirs to pay their debts when due;][2]

    "the credit insurance directive" means Council Directive 87/343/EEC of 22nd June 1987 amending, as regards credit insurance and suretyship insurance, First Directive 73/239 on the co-ordination of laws, regulations and administrative provisions relating to the taking-up and pursuit of the business of direct insurance other than life assurance; ...[2]

    ...][1]

Commentary—*Simon's Direct Tax Service* D4.538.
Regulations—Insurance Companies (Reserves) (Tax) Regulations, SI 1996/2991.
Non-resident Companies (General Insurance Business) Regulations, SI 1999/1408.
Definitions—"Company", s 832(1); "resident in the United Kingdom", FA 1988 s 66.
Cross references—See TMA 1970 s 98 (penalties for failure to provide information etc required by regulations made under this section).
Amendments—[1] This section inserted by FA 1996 Sch 32 para 1.
[2] Words in sub-ss (1), (2), (4) substituted, sub-s (2)(*a*)(i)–(iii), and definition of "credit insurance business" substituted, definition of "EC Company" and the word "and" immediately before it repealed, by the Financial Services and Markets Act 2000 (Consequential Amendments) (Taxes) Order, SI 2001/3629 arts 13, 30(1), (6)–(9) with effect for periods of account ending after 30 November 2001.

[444C Modification of section 440]

Amendments—This section repealed by FA 1995 Sch 29 Pt VIII(5), with effect generally for accounting periods beginning after 31 December 1994 (and so far as relating to sub-s (2)(*a*) above in relation to accounting periods beginning after 31 October 1994 (subject to FA 1995 Sch 8 para 55(2)). The section was originally inserted by FA 1993 s 98.

[444D Qualifying distributions, tax credits, etc]

Amendments—[1] This section repealed by FA 1995 Sch 29 Pt VIII(5), with effect for accounting periods beginning after 31 December 1994 (originally inserted by FA 1993 s 99(1), (3)).

[444E Income from investments attributable to BLAGAB, etc]

Commentary—*Simon's Direct Tax Service* **D4.537.**
Amendments—[1] This section repealed by FA 1995 Sch 29 Pt VIII(5), with effect for accounting periods beginning after 31 December 1994 (originally inserted by FA 1993 s 100(1), (3)).

Provisions applying only to overseas life insurance companies

445 Charge to tax on investment income

Amendments—[1] This section repealed by FA 1993 s 103(2)(*a*), (3) and Sch 23 Pt III(9) for accounting periods beginning after 31 December 1992.

446 Annuity business

Amendments—Sub-s (4) repealed by FA 1990 Sch 19 Pt IV with respect to accounting periods beginning after 31 December 1989, but subject to the provisions in FA 1990 Sch 6 paras 11, 12.
Sub-ss (2), (3) and the words "and general annuity business" in sub-s (1) repealed by FA 1991 Sch 7 paras 7(1), 18 and Sch 19, Pt V with respect to accounting periods beginning after 31 December 1991.
Sub-s (1) repealed by FA 1993 s 103(2)(*b*), (3) and Sch 23 Pt III(9) for accounting periods beginning after 31 December 1992.

447 Set-off of income tax and tax credits against corporation tax

Amendments—Sub-s (3) repealed by FA 1991 Sch 7 paras 7, 18 and Sch 19, Pt V with respect to accounting periods beginning after 31 December 1991.
Sub-ss (1), (2), (4) repealed by FA 1993 s 103(2)(*c*) and Sch 23 Pt III(9) for accounting periods beginning after 31 December 1992.

448 Qualifying distributions and tax credits

Amendments—This section repealed by FA 1993 s 103(2)(*d*) and Sch 23 Pt III(9) for accounting periods beginning after 31 December 1992.

449 Double taxation agreements

Amendments—This section repealed by FA 1993 s 103(2)(*e*) and Sch 23 Pt III(9) for accounting periods beginning after 31 December 1992.

Underwriters

450 Assessment, set-off of losses and reinsurance

Amendments—Sub-ss (1)–(5A) repealed by FA 1993 Sch 23 Pt III(12) with effect from the year of assessment 1992–93.
Sub-s (6) repealed by FA 1993 Sch 23 Pt III(12) for acquisitions or disposals made, or treated as made, after 31 December 1993.

451 Regulations

Amendments—This section repealed by FA 1993 Sch 23 Pt III(12) with effect from the year of assessment 1992–93.

452 Special reserve funds

Amendments—This section repealed by FA 1993 Sch 23 Pt III(12) with effect from the year of assessment 1992–93.

453 Payments into premiums trust fund on account of losses

Amendments—This section repealed by FA 1993 Sch 23 Pt III(12) with effect from the year of assessment 1992–93.

454 Income tax consequences on payments into and out of special reserve fund

Amendments—This section repealed by FA 1993 Sch 23 Pt III(12) with effect from the year of assessment 1992–93.

455 Income tax consequences on death of underwriter

Amendments—This section repealed by FA 1993 Sch 23 Pt III(12) with effect from the year of assessment 1992–93.

456 Unearned income, variation of arrangements and cancellation of approval etc

Amendments—This section repealed by FA 1993 Sch 23 Pt III(12) with effect from the year of assessment 1992–93.

457 Interpretation of sections 450 to 456

Amendments—This section repealed by FA 1993 Sch 23 Pt III(12) with effect from the year of assessment 1992–93.

Capital redemption business

458 Capital redemption business

(1) Where any person carries on capital redemption business in conjunction with business of any other class, the capital redemption business shall, for the purposes of the Corporation Tax Acts (including the provisions about corporation tax on chargeable gains) and the Income Tax Acts, be treated as a separate business from any other class of business carried on by that person [and where section 76 applies by virtue of subsection (5A) of that section, it shall apply separately to capital redemption business][3].

(2) In ascertaining whether and to what extent any person has incurred a loss on his capital redemption business for the purposes of section 380 or sections 393 and [393A(1)][1]—

(*a*) any profits derived from investments held in connection with the capital redemption business (including franked investment income of [...][2] a company resident in the United Kingdom) shall be treated as part of the profits of that business, and

(*b*) in determining whether any, and if so what, relief can be given under section 385(4) in the case of capital redemption business, the loss which may be carried forward under subsection (1) of that section shall be similarly computed.

[(3) In this section "capital redemption business" means any business in so far as it—

[(*a*) consists of the effecting on the basis of actuarial calculations, and the carrying out, of contracts of insurance under which, in return for one or more fixed payments, a sum or series of sums of a specified amount become payable at a future time or over a period; and

(*b*) is not life assurance business.][4]][3]

(4) This section shall not apply to any capital redemption business in so far as it consists of carrying out contracts of insurance effected before 1st January 1938.

Commentary—*Simon's Direct Tax Service* D4.530.
Regulations—Insurance Companies (Capital Redemption Business) (Modification of the Corporation Tax Acts) Regulations SI 1999/498.
Definitions—"Chargeable gain", s 832(1); "company", s 832(1), (2); "the Corporation Tax Acts", s 831(1)(*a*); "foreign income dividend", s 431(2); "franked investment income", s 832(1); "the Income Tax Acts", s 831(1)(*b*); "life assurance business", s 431(2).
Cross references—See TA 1988 s 389(1) (this section to apply for the purposes of s 389 (carry-back of terminal losses).
TCGA 1992 s 213(1A) (spreading over seven accounting periods of gains and losses treated as accruing from deemed disposals of capital redemption business assets);
FA 1993 s 78(6) (rate of tax credit for calculating franked investment income for the purposes of this section from the financial year 1993).
Modifications—Sub-ss (1), (2) omitted in applying life assurance provisions of the Corporation Tax Acts to insurance companies carrying on capital redemption business with effect for accounting periods ending after 30 June 1999: see Insurance Companies (Capital Redemption Business) (Modification of the Corporation Tax Acts) Regulations, SI 1999/498 reg 7.
Amendments—[1] "393A(1)" in sub-s (2) substituted by FA 1991 Sch 15 para 16.
[2] Words in sub-s (2)(*a*) (originally inserted by FA 1994 Sch 16 para 7) repealed by F(No 2)A 1997 s 36(4), Sch 6 para 7, Sch 8 Pt II(11) with effect for distributions made after 5 April 1999.
[3] Words in sub-s (1) inserted and sub-s (3) substituted by FA 1996 s 168(1), Sch 33 para 2 with effect for accounting periods ending after 30 June 1999 (by virtue of Finance Act 1994, Section 199, (Appointed Day) Order, SI 1998/3173 art 2).
[4] Sub-s (3)(*a*), (*b*) substituted by the Financial Services and Markets Act 2000 (Consequential Amendments) (Taxes) Order, SI 2001/3629 arts 13, 31 with effect from 1 December 2001, immediately after the coming into force of the Financial Services and Markets Act 2000 ss 411, 432(1), Sch 20.

[458A Capital redemption business: power to apply life assurance provisions

(1) The Treasury may by regulations provide for the life assurance provisions of the Corporation Tax Acts to have effect in relation to companies carrying on capital redemption business as if capital redemption business were, or were a category of, life assurance business.

(2) Regulations under this section may provide that the provisions applied by the regulations are to have effect as respects capital redemption business with such modifications and exceptions as may be provided for in the regulations.

(3) Regulations under this section may—

(*a*) make different provision for different cases;

(*b*) include such incidental, supplemental, consequential and transitional provision (including provision modifying provisions of the Corporation Tax Acts other than the life assurance provisions) as the Treasury consider appropriate; and

(*c*) include retrospective provision.

(4) In this section references to the life assurance provisions of the Corporation Tax Acts are references to the following—

(*a*) the provisions of this Chapter so far as they relate to life assurance business or companies carrying on such business; and

(*b*) any other provisions of the Corporation Tax Acts making separate provision by reference to whether or not the business of a company is or includes life assurance business or any category of insurance business that includes life assurance business.

(5) In this section "capital redemption business" has the same meaning as in section 458.]¹

Commentary—*Simon's Direct Tax Service* **D4.530.**
Regulations—Insurance Companies (Capital Redemption Business) (Modification of the Corporation Tax Acts) Regulations, SI 1999/498.
Definitions—"Company", s 832(1); "the Corporation Tax Acts", s 831(1)(*a*); "life assurance business", s 431(2).
Amendments—¹ This section inserted by FA 1996 s 168(3).

CHAPTER II
FRIENDLY SOCIETIES, TRADE UNIONS AND EMPLOYERS' ASSOCIATIONS

Cross references—See TA 1988 s 466 (interpretation).

Unregistered friendly societies

459 Exemption from tax

An unregistered friendly society [(that is, a friendly society which is neither an incorporated friendly society nor a registered friendly society)]¹ whose income does not exceed £160 a year shall, on making a claim, be entitled to exemption from income tax and corporation tax (whether on income or chargeable gains).

Commentary—*Simon's Direct Tax Service* **D4.618.**
Definition—"incorporated friendly society", s 466(2); "registered friendly society", s 466(2).
Cross references—See TMA 1970 s 46C (Special Commissioners have jurisdiction on an appeal against an amendment to a self-assessment or partnership statement where the question in dispute concerns a claim under this section).
TMA 1970 Sch 2 para 2 (appeal from a decision of the inspector under this section to be exclusively to the Special Commissioners).
Amendments—¹ Words inserted by F(No 2)A 1992 Sch 9 paras 1, 4, 22 with effect from 19 February 1993 by virtue of F(No 2)A 1992 Sch 9 (Appointed Day) Order, SI 1993/236.

Registered friendly societies

460 Exemption from tax in respect of life or endowment business

(1) Subject to subsection (2) below, a [friendly society]¹¹ shall, on making a claim, be entitled to exemption from income tax and corporation tax (whether on income or chargeable gains) on its profits arising from life or endowment business.

(2) Subsection (1) above—

(*a*) shall not, subject to section 462, exempt a [registered friendly society]¹² registered after 31st December 1957 which at any time in the period of three months ending 3rd May 1966 entered into any transaction in return for a single premium, being a transaction forming part of its life or endowment business;

[(*aa*) shall not, subject to section 462, exempt an incorporated friendly society which, before its incorporation, was a registered friendly society such as is mentioned in paragraph (*a*) above,]¹³

(*b*) shall not apply to profits arising from pension business;

(*c*) shall not apply to profits arising from life or endowment business consisting—

[(zai) where the profits relate to contracts made on or after the day on which the Finance Act 1995 was passed, of the assurance of gross sums under contracts under which the total premiums payable in any period of 12 months exceed £270 or of the granting of annuities of annual amounts exceeding £156;]¹⁷

[(ai) where the profits relate to contracts made on or after the day on which the Finance Act 1991 was passed [but before the day on which the Finance Act 1995 was passed]¹⁷, of the assurance of gross sums under contracts under which the total premiums payable in any period of 12 months exceed £200 or of the granting of annuities of annual amounts exceeding £156;]⁴

(i) where the profits relate to contracts made after [31st August 1990 but before the day on which the Finance Act 1991 was passed]⁵, of the assurance of gross sums under contracts under which the total premiums payable in any period of 12 months exceed [£150]¹ or of the granting of annuities of annual amounts exceeding £156;

[(ia) where the profits relate to contracts made after 31st August 1987 but before 1st September 1990, of the assurance of gross sums under contracts under which the total premiums payable in any period of 12 months exceed £100 [or of the granting of annuities of annual amounts exceeding £156⁶;]²

(ii) where the profits relate to contracts made after 13th March 1984 but before 1st September 1987, of the assurance of gross sums exceeding £750 or of the granting of annuities of annual amounts exceeding £156;

(iii) where the profits relate to contracts made before 14th March 1984, of the assurance of gross sums exceeding £500 or of the granting of annuities of annual amounts exceeding £104; ...⁷

[(*ca*) shall not apply to so much of the profits arising from life or endowment business as is attributable to contracts for the assurance of gross sums made on or after 20th March 1991 and expressed at the outset not to be made in the course of tax exempt life or endowment business;]⁷

[(*cb*) shall not apply to profits arising from investments, deposits or other property held as a member of a property investment LLP;]²¹[and]⁷

(*d*) as respects other life or endowment business ("tax exempt life or endowment business"), has effect subject to the following provisions of this Chapter.

(3) In determining for the purposes [of [subsection (2)(*c*)(zai), (ai),]¹⁸, (i) or (ia)]⁸ above the total premiums payable in any period of 12 months—

(*a*) where those premiums are payable more frequently than annually, there shall be disregarded an amount equal to 10 per cent of those premiums; and

(*b*) so much of any premium as is charged on the ground that an exceptional risk of death is involved shall be disregarded;

and in applying the limit of £156 in [[subsection (2)(*c*)(zai), (ai),]¹⁸, (i) or (ia)]⁹ above, any bonus or addition declared upon an annuity shall be disregarded.

(4) In applying the limits referred to in subsection (2)(*c*)(ii) and (iii) above, any bonus or addition which either is declared upon an assurance of a gross sum or annuity or accrues upon such an assurance by reference to an increase in the value of any investments shall be disregarded.

[(4A) Subsection (4B) below applies to contracts for the assurance of gross sums under tax exempt life or endowment business made after 31st August 1987 and before the day on which [the Finance Act 1995]¹⁹ was passed.]¹⁰

[(4B) Where the amount payable by way of premium under a contract to which this subsection applies is increased by virtue of a [variation made—

(*a*) in the period beginning with 25th July 1991 and ending with 31st July 1992, or

(*b*) in which the period beginning with the day on which the Finance Act 1995 was passed and ending with 31st March 1996,

the contract shall, for the purposes of subsection (2)(*c*) above, be treated, in relation to any profits relating to it as varied, as made at the time of the variation.]²⁰]¹⁰

(5) A [friendly society]¹¹ is within this subsection if its rules make no provision for it to carry on life or endowment business consisting of the assurance of gross sums exceeding £2,000 or of the granting of annuities of annual amounts exceeding £416.

(6) In the case of a [friendly society]¹¹ within subsection (5) above—

(*a*) subsection (2)(*c*)(iii) above shall have effect with the substitution of references to £2,000 and £416 respectively for the references to £500 and £104; and

(*b*) references in this Chapter to tax exempt life or endowment business shall be construed accordingly.

(7) Where at any time a [friendly society]¹¹ within subsection (5) above amends its rules so as to cease to be within that subsection, any part of its life or endowment business consisting of business which—

(*a*) relates to contracts made before that time; and

(*b*) immediately before that time was tax exempt life or endowment business,

shall thereafter continue to be tax exempt life or endowment business for the purposes of this Chapter.

(8) Where at any time a [friendly society]¹¹ not within subsection (5) above amends its rules so as to bring itself within that subsection, any part of its life or endowment business consisting of business which—

(*a*) related to contracts made before that time; and

(*b*) immediately before that time was not tax exempt life or endowment business,

shall thereafter continue not to be tax exempt life or endowment business for the purposes of this Chapter.

(9) Where at any time a [friendly society]¹¹ not within subsection (5) above acquires by way of transfer of engagements or amalgamation from another [friendly society]¹¹ any life or endowment business consisting of business which—

(*a*) relates to contracts made before that time; and

(*b*) immediately before that time was tax exempt life or endowment business,

that business shall thereafter continue to be tax exempt life or endowment business for the purposes of this Chapter.

(10) Where at any time a [friendly society]¹¹ within subsection (5) above acquires by way of transfer of engagements or amalgamation from another [friendly society]¹¹ any life or endowment business consisting of business which—

(*a*) relates to contracts made before that time; and

(*b*) immediately before that time was not tax exempt life or endowment business,

that business shall thereafter continue not to be tax exempt life or endowment business for the purposes of this Chapter.

[(10A) [Where at any time an insurance business transfer scheme has effect to transfer to a friendly society long-term business,]²², any life or endowment business which relates to contracts included in the transfer shall not thereafter be tax exempt life or endowment business for the purposes of this Chapter.][3]

[(10B) In subsection (10A) "insurance business transfer scheme" means a scheme falling within section 105 of the Financial Services and Markets Act 2000, including an excluded scheme falling within Case 2, 3 or 4 of subsection (3) of that section.][22]

(11) Where at any time a [friendly society][11] ceases ...[23] by virtue of [section 91 of the Friendly Societies Act 1992][14] (conversion into company) to be registered under [that Act][23], any part of its life or endowment business consisting of business which—

    (a) relates to contracts made before that time; and

    (b) immediately before that time was tax exempt life or endowment business,

shall thereafter continue to be tax exempt life or endowment business for the purposes of this Chapter.

(12) For the purposes of the Corporation Tax Acts any part of a company's business which continues to be tax exempt life or endowment business by virtue of subsection (11) above shall be treated as a separate business from any other business carried on by the company.

Commentary—*Simon's Direct Tax Service* **D4.604–607.**
Note—FA 1995 was passed on 1 May 1995.
Simon's Tax Cases—*Homeowners Friendly Society Ltd v Barrett* [1995] STC (SCD) 90.
Definitions—"Chargeable gain", s 832(1); "the Corporation Tax Acts", s 831(1)(a); "friendly society", s 466(2); "incorporated friendly society", s 466(2); "insurance company", s 466(2); "life or endowment business", s 466(1); "long term business", "pension business", s 466(2); "registered friendly society", s 466(2); "tax exempt life or endowment business", s 466(2).
Cross references—See TMA 1970 s 46C (Special Commissioners to have jurisdiction on an appeal against an amendment of a self-assessment or partnership statement where the question in dispute concerns a claim made under this section).
TMA 1970 Sch 2 para 2 (appeal from a decision by an inspector under this section to be exclusively to the Special Commissioners).
TA 1988 s 462A (election by a registered friendly society for this section not to apply to tax exempt business).
TA 1988 Sch 14, para 3(4) (increases in capital sums treated as made by virtue of Sch 14, para 3(3) to be disregarded for the purposes of this section).
TA 1988 Sch 19AC para 11C (overseas life companies: sub-s (10A) above to be treated as including a qualifying overseas transfer).
FA 1993 s 121 (repayment of tax on investment income accruing in accounting periods beginning after 31 December 1993 from tax exempt activities of a friendly society carrying on exempt and non-exempt activities);
Insurance Companies (Overseas Life Assurance Business) (Compliance) Regulations 1995, SI 1995/3237 reg 3A (those regulations not to apply to any business of a friendly society the profits of which are exempt under sub-s (1) above).
Modification—Sub-s (2) modified so far as it applies to the life or endowment business carried on by friendly societies by the Friendly Societies (Modification of the Corporation Tax Acts) Regulations, SI 1997/473 reg 30A, as amended by SI 1998/1871 and SI 1998/3174.
Amendments—[1] Amount in sub-s (2)(c)(i) substituted by FA 1990 s 49(1)(a).
[2] Sub-s (2)(c)(ia) inserted by FA 1990 s 49(1)(b).
[3] Sub-s (10A) inserted by FA 1990 Sch 9 paras 6, 7 in relation to transfers of business taking place after 31 December 1989.
[4] Sub-s (2)(c)(ai) inserted by FA 1991 Sch 9 para 1(1)–(3).
[5] Words in sub-s (2)(c)(i) substituted by FA 1991 Sch 9, para 1(1), (2), (4).
[6] Words in sub-s (2)(c)(ia) inserted by FA 1991 Sch 9, para 1(1), (2), (5).
[7] Sub-s (2)(ca) inserted and the preceding word "and" deleted by FA 1991 Sch 9, para 1(1), (2), (6).
[8] Words in sub-s (3) substituted by FA 1991 Sch 9, para 1(1), (7)(a).
[9] Words in sub-s (3) substituted by FA 1991 Sch 9 para 1(1), (7)(b).
[10] Sub-ss (4A), (4B) inserted by FA 1991 Sch 9, para 1(1), (8).
[11] Words in sub-ss (1), (5)–(11) substituted by F(No 2)A 1992 Sch 9 paras 1, 5, 22 with effect from 19 February 1993 by virtue of F(No 2)A 1992 Sch 9 (Appointed Day) Order, SI 1993/236.
[12] Words in sub-s (2)(a) substituted by F(No 2)A 1992 Sch 9 paras 1, 5, 22 with effect from 19 February 1993 by virtue of F(No 2)A 1992 Sch 9 (Appointed Day) Order, SI 1993/236.
[13] Sub-s (2)(aa) inserted by F(No 2)A 1992 Sch 9 paras 1, 5, 22 with effect from 19 February 1993 by virtue of F(No 2)A 1992 Sch 9 (Appointed Day) Order, SI 1993/236.
[14] Words in sub-s (11) substituted by F(No 2)A 1992 Sch 9 paras 1, 5, 22 with effect from 19 February 1993 by virtue of F(No 2)A 1992 Sch 9 (Appointed Day) Order, SI 1993/236.
[15–16] ...
[17] Words in sub-s (2) inserted by FA 1995 Sch 10 para 1(2), (3).
[18] Words in sub-s (3) substituted by FA 1995 Sch 10, para 1(4).
[19] Words in sub-s (4A) substituted by FA 1995 Sch 10, para 1(5).
[20] Words in sub-s (4B) substituted by FA 1995 Sch 10, para 1(6).
[21] Sub-s (2)(cb) inserted by FA 2001 s 76, Sch 25 para 8(1) with effect from 6 April 2001.
[22] Words in sub-s (10A) substituted, and sub-s (10B) inserted, by the Financial Services and Markets Act 2000 (Consequential Amendments) (Taxes) Order, SI 2001/3629 arts 13, 32(2), (3) with effect from 1 December 2001, immediately after the coming into force of the Financial Services and Markets Act 2000 ss 411, 432(1), Sch 20. The amendments made by SI 2001/3629 arts 13, 32(2), (3) have effect in relation to any scheme falling within the Financial Services and Markets Act 2000 s 105, including an excluded scheme falling within Case 2, 3 or 4 of the Financial Services and Markets Act 2000 s 105(3).
[23] In sub-s (11), words substituted, and words repealed, by SI 2001/3629 arts 13, 32(4) with effect from 1 December 2001, immediately after the coming into force of the Financial Services and Markets Act 2000 ss 411, 432(1), Sch 20.

461 Taxation in respect of other business

(1) Subject to the following provisions of this section, a registered friendly society other than a society to which subsection (2) below applies shall, on making a claim, be entitled to exemption from income tax and corporation tax (whether on income or chargeable gains) on its profits other than those arising from life or endowment business.

(2) This subsection applies to any society registered after 31st May 1973 unless—

    (a) its business is limited to the provision, in accordance with the rules of the society, of benefits for or in respect of employees of a particular employer or such other group of persons as is for the time being approved for the purposes of this section by the [Board][2]; or (*b*) it was registered before 27th March 1974 and its rules limit the aggregate amount which may be paid by a member by way of contributions and deposits to not more than £1 per month or such greater amount as the [Board][2] may authorise for the purposes of this section;

and also applies to any society registered before 1st June 1973 with respect to which a direction under subsection [(7)][2] below is in force.

(3) If a society to which subsection (2) above applies, after 26th March 1974 or such later date as may be specified in a direction under this section, makes a payment to a member in respect of his interest in the society and the payment is made otherwise than in the course of life or endowment business and exceeds the aggregate of any sums paid by him to the society by way of contributions or deposits, after deducting from that aggregate the amount of—

(*a*) any previous payment so made to him by the society after that date, and

(*b*) any earlier repayment of such sums paid by him,

the excess shall be treated for the purposes of corporation tax and income tax as a qualifying distribution.

[(3A) The exemption conferred by subsection (1) above does not apply to profits arising from investments, deposits or other property held as a member of a property investment LLP.][1]

(4) Where a registered friendly society—

(*a*) at any time ceases ...[2] by virtue of [section 91 of the Friendly Societies Act 1992][4] (conversion into company) to be registered under [that Act][2]; and

(*b*) immediately before that time was exempt from income tax or corporation tax on profits arising from any business carried on by it other than life or endowment business,

the company into which the society is converted shall be so exempt on its profits arising from any part of that business which relates to contracts made before that time so long as there is no increase in the scale of benefits which it undertakes to provide in the course of carrying on that part of its business.

(5) For the purposes of the Corporation Tax Acts any part of a company's business in respect of the profits from which the company is exempt by virtue of subsection (4) above shall be treated as a separate business from any other business carried on by the company.

(6) If—

(*a*) a friendly society registered before 1st June 1973 begins after 26th March 1974 to carry on business other than life or endowment business or, in the opinion of [the Board][2], begins to carry on business other than life or endowment business on an enlarged scale or of a new character; and

(*b*) it appears to [the Board][2], having regard to the restrictions imposed by this section on friendly societies registered later, that for the protection of the revenue it is expedient to do so;

[the Board may give a direction to the society under subsection (7) below.][2]

[(7) A direction under this subsection is that (and has the effect that) the society to which it is given is to be treated for the purposes of this Act as a society registered after 31st May 1973 with respect to business carried on after the date of the direction.][2]

[(8) A society to which a direction is given may, within 30 days of the date on which it is given, appeal against the direction to the Special Commissioners on the ground that—

(*a*) it has not begun to carry on business as mentioned in subsection (6)(*a*) above; or

(*b*) the direction is not necessary for the protection of the revenue.][2]

[(9) If a registered friendly society in respect of which a direction is in force under subsection (7) above becomes an incorporated friendly society, the direction shall continue to have effect, so that the incorporated friendly society shall be treated for the purposes of this Act as a society registered after 31st May 1973.][2]

(10) For the purposes of this section a registered friendly society formed on the amalgamation of two or more friendly societies shall be treated as registered before 1st June 1973 if at the time of the amalgamation subsection (2) above did not apply to any of the societies amalgamated, but otherwise shall be treated as registered at that time.

[(11) For the purposes of this section and section 461C—

(*a*) any group of persons which was approved for the purposes of this section (as mentioned in subsection (2)(*a*) above) immediately before 1st December 2001 shall be treated as having been approved for the purposes of this section by the Board on that date;

(*b*) any greater amount which was authorised for the purposes of this section (as mentioned in subsection (2)(*b*) above) immediately before 1st December 2001 shall be treated as having been authorised for the purposes of this section by the Board on that date; and

(*c*) where a direction that subsection (2) above applies to a society was in force immediately before 1st December 2001, a direction in relation to that society shall be treated as having been made under subsection (7) above by the Board on that date.][2]

Commentary—*Simon's Direct Tax Service* **D4.610.**
Definitions—"Chargeable gain", s 832(1); "company", s 832(1), (2); "the Corporation Tax Acts", s 831(1)(*a*); "friendly society", s 466(2); "life or endowment business", s 466(1); "qualifying distribution", ss 14(2), 832(1).
Cross references—See TA 1988 ss 461A–461C (taxation in respect of other business of friendly societies).

TA 1988 Sch 14, para 3(4) (increases in capital sums treated as made by virtue of Sch 14, para 3(3) to be disregarded for the purposes of sub-s (1) above).
FA 1993 s 121 (repayment of tax on investment income accruing in accounting periods beginning after 31 December 1993 from tax exempt activities of a friendly society carrying on exempt and non-exempt activities);
Amendments—[1] Sub-s (3A) inserted by FA 2001 s 76, Sch 25 para 8(2) with effect from 6 April 2001.
[2] Words in sub-ss (2), (4)(a), (6) substituted, figure in sub-s (2) substituted, words in sub-s (4)(a) repealed, sub-ss (7)–(9) substituted, and sub-s (11) added, by the Financial Services and Markets Act 2000 (Consequential Amendments) (Taxes) Order, SI 2001/3629 arts 13, 33 with effect from 1 December 2001, immediately after the coming into force of the Financial Services and Markets Act 2000 ss 411, 432(1), Sch 20.

[461A Taxation in respect of other business: incorporated friendly societies qualifying for exemption

(1) For the purposes of sections 461B and 461C, a "qualifying society" is an incorporated friendly society which—

(*a*) immediately before its incorporation, was a registered friendly society to which section 461(2) did not apply,

(*b*) was formed otherwise than by the incorporation of a registered friendly society or the amalgamation of two or more friendly societies and satisfies subsection (2) below, or

(*c*) was formed by the amalgamation of two or more friendly societies and satisfies subsection (3) below,

and in respect of which no direction under section 461C(5) is in force.

(2) A society satisfies this subsection if its business is limited to the provision, in accordance with the rules of the society, of benefits for or in respect of employees of a particular employer or such other group of persons as is for the time being approved for the purposes of this section by the [Board][2].

(3) If at the time of the amalgamation referred to in subsection (1)(c) above—

(*a*) section 461(2) applied to none of the registered friendly societies being amalgamated (if any), and

(*b*) all of the incorporated friendly societies being amalgamated (if any) were qualifying societies,

the society formed by the amalgamation satisfies this subsection.][1]

[(4) For the purposes of this section and section 461C, any group of persons which was approved for the purposes of this section (as mentioned in subsection (2) above) by the Friendly Societies Commission immediately before 1st December 2001 shall be treated as having been approved for the purposes of this section by the Board on that date.][2]

Commentary—*Simon's Direct Tax Service* **D4.611, 616.**
Definitions—"Friendly society", s 466(2); "incorporated friendly society", s 466(2); "registered friendly society", s 466(2).
Cross references—See TA 1988 s 461C (withdrawal of "qualifying" status from incorporated friendly society).
Amendments—[1] This section inserted by F(No 2)A 1992 Sch 9 paras 1, 7, 22 with effect from 19 February 1993 by virtue of F(No 2)A 1992 Sch 9 (Appointed Day) Order, SI 1993/236.
[2] Words in sub-s (2) substituted, and sub-s (4) added, by the Financial Services and Markets Act 2000 (Consequential Amendments) (Taxes) Order, SI 2001/3629 arts 13, 34 with effect from 1 December 2001, immediately after the coming into force of the Financial Services and Markets Act 2000 ss 411, 432(1), Sch 20.

[461B Taxation in respect of other business: incorporated friendly societies etc

(1) Subject to the following provisions of this section, a qualifying society shall, on making a claim, be entitled to exemption from income tax and corporation tax (whether on income or chargeable gains) on its profits other than those arising from life or endowment business.

(2) Subsection (1) above shall not apply to any profits arising or accruing to the society from, or by reason of its interest in, a body corporate which is a subsidiary (within the meaning of the Friendly Societies Act 1992) of the society or of which the society has joint control (within the meaning of that Act).

[(2A) Subsection (1) above shall not apply to any profits arising or accruing to the society from or by reason of its membership of a property investment LLP.][2]

(3) If an incorporated friendly society which is not a qualifying society makes a payment to a member in respect of his interest in the society and the payment is made otherwise than in the course of life or endowment business and exceeds the aggregate of any sums paid by him to the society by way of contributions or deposits, after deducting from that aggregate the amount of—

(*a*) any previous payment so made to him by the society, and

(*b*) any earlier repayment of such sums paid by him,

the excess shall be treated for the purposes of corporation tax and income tax as a qualifying distribution.

(4) In relation to an incorporated friendly society which, immediately before its incorporation, was a registered friendly society to which section 461(2) applied—

(*a*) the references in subsection (3) above to sums paid to the society shall include sums paid to the registered friendly society,

(*b*) the reference in subsection (3)(a) above to any payment made by the society shall include any payment made by the registered friendly society after 26 March 1974 or such later date as was specified in any direction under section 461[(7)][3] relating to it, and (*c*) the reference in subsection (3)(*b*) above to any repayment shall include any repayment made by the registered friendly society.

(5) Where a qualifying society at any time ceases by virtue of section 91 of the Friendly Societies Act 1992 (conversion into company) to be registered under that Act, the company into which the society is converted shall be exempt from income tax or corporation tax on its profits arising from any part of its business, other than life or endowment business, which relates to contracts made before that time.

(6) Subsection (5) above shall apply so long as there is no increase in the scale of benefits which the company undertakes to provide in the course of carrying on the relevant part of its business.

(7) Any part of a company's business to which an exemption under subsection (5) above relates shall be treated for the purposes of the Corporation Tax Acts as a separate business from any other business carried on by the company.]¹

Commentary—*Simon's Direct Tax Service* D4.611, 612, 616.
Definitions—"Chargeable gains", s 832(1); "Corporation Tax Acts", s 831(1); "friendly society", s 466(2); "incorporated friendly society", s 466(2); "life or endowment business", s 466(1); "profits", s 833(1); "qualifying distribution", s 832(1); "qualifying society", s 461A; "registered friendly society", s 466(2).
Cross references—See FA 1993 s 121 (repayment of tax on investment income accruing in accounting periods beginning after 31 December 1993 from tax exempt activities of a friendly society carrying on exempt and non-exempt activities);
Amendments—¹ This section inserted by F(No 2)A 1992 Sch 9 paras 1, 7, 22 with effect from 19 February 1993 by virtue of F(No 2)A 1992 Sch 9 (Appointed Day) Order, SI 1993/236.
² Sub-s (2A) inserted by FA 2001 s 76, Sch 25 para 8(3) with effect from 6 April 2001.
³ Figure in sub-s (4)(*b*) substituted by the Financial Services and Markets Act 2000 (Consequential Amendments) (Taxes) Order, SI 2001/3629 arts 13, 35 with effect from 1 December 2001, immediately after the coming into force of the Financial Services and Markets Act 2000 ss 411, 432(1), Sch 20.

[461C Taxation in respect of other business: withdrawal of "qualifying" status from incorporated friendly society
(1) Subject to subsection (2) below, subsections (3) [and (4)]² below apply where a qualifying society—
(*a*) begins to carry on business other than life or endowment business, or
(*b*) in the opinion of the [Board]², begins to carry on business other than life or endowment business on an enlarged scale or of a new character.
(2) Subsections (3) [and (4)]² below do not apply if—
(*a*) the society's business is limited to the provision, in accordance with the rules of the society, of benefits for or in respect of employees of a particular employer or such other group of persons as is for the time being approved for the purposes of section 461 or 461A by the [Board]², or
(*b*) the society's rules limit the aggregate amount which may be paid by a member by way of contributions and deposits to not more than £1 per month or such greater amount as is authorised for the purposes of section 461.
(3) If it appears to the [Board]², having regard to the restrictions imposed by section 461 on registered friendly societies registered after 31st May 1973, that for the protection of the revenue it is expedient to do so, the [Board² may [give a direction to the society under subsection (4) below.]²
[(4) A direction under this subsection is that (and has the effect that) the society to which it is given shall cease to be a qualifying society as from the date of the direction.]²
[(5) A society to which a direction is given may, within 30 days of the date on which it is given, appeal against the direction to the Special Commissioners on the ground that—
(*a*) it has not begun to carry on business as mentioned in subsection (1) above;
(*b*) subsections (3) and (4) above do not apply to it by reason of subsection (2) above; or
(*c*) the direction is not necessary for the protection of the revenue.]²]¹

Commentary—*Simon's Direct Tax Service* D4.611.
Definitions—"Friendly society", s 466(2); "life or endowment business", s 466(1); "qualifying society", s 461A; "registered friendly society", s 466(2).
Amendments—¹ This section inserted by F(No 2)A 1992 Sch 9 paras 1, 7, 22 with effect from 19 February 1993 by virtue of F(No 2)A 1992 Sch 9 (Appointed Day) Order, SI 1993/236.
² Words in sub-ss (1)–(3) substituted, and sub-ss (4), (5) substituted for sub-ss (4)–(7), by the Financial Services and Markets Act 2000 (Consequential Amendments) (Taxes) Order, SI 2001/3629 arts 13, 36 with effect from 1 December 2001, immediately after the coming into force of the Financial Services and Markets Act 2000 ss 411, 432(1), Sch 20.

462 Conditions for tax exempt business
(1) Subject to subsections (2) to (4) below, section 460(1) shall not apply to so much of the profits arising from tax exempt life or endowment business as is attributable to a policy which, by virtue of paragraph 6(2) of Schedule 15—
(*a*) is not a qualifying policy; and
(*b*) would not be a qualifying policy if all policies with other friendly societies were left out of account.
(2) [Section 460(2)(*a*) or (*aa*)]¹ and subsection (1) above shall not withdraw exemption under section 460(1) for profits arising from any part of a life or endowment business relating to contracts made not later than 3rd May 1966.

(3) If, with respect to a policy issued in respect of an insurance made on or after 1st June 1984 and before 19th March 1985 for the assurance of a gross sum, there is or has been an infringement of any of the conditions in paragraph 3(2) to (11) of Schedule 15, section 460(1) shall not apply to so much as is attributable to that policy of the profits of the [friendly society or registered branch][1] concerned which arise from tax exempt life or endowment business.

(4) Nothing in subsection (3) above shall be taken to affect the status of a policy as a qualifying policy.

Commentary—*Simon's Direct Tax Service* **D4.605.**
Definitions—''Friendly society'', s 466(2); ''life or endowment business'', s 466(1); ''policy'', s 466(2); ''qualifying policy'', s 832(1); ''registered branch'', s 466(2); ''tax exempt life or endowment business'', s 466(2).
Cross references—See TA 1988 s 462A(8)(*b*) (election by a registered friendly society to waive exemption for profits from certain contracts: modification of sub-s (1) above in its application to the society).
Amendments—[1] Words in sub-ss (2), (3) substituted by F(No 2)A 1992 Sch 9 paras 1, 8, 22 with effect from 19 February 1993 by virtue of F(No 2)A 1992 Sch 9 (Appointed Day) Order, SI 1993/236.

[462A Election as to tax exempt business

(1) Where a registered friendly society has tax exempt life or endowment business which includes contracts—

    (*a*) made before 20th March 1991, and
    (*b*) expressed at the outset not to be made in the course of such business,

the society may by notice to the inspector elect that section 460(1) shall not apply to so much of the profits arising from such business as is attributable to such contracts.

(2) Where a registered friendly society has tax exempt life or endowment business which includes contracts falling within subsection (3) below, the society may by notice to the inspector elect that section 460(1) shall not apply to so much of the profits arising from such business as is attributable to such contracts.

(3) A contract falls within this subsection if—

    (*a*) at the outset, it is neither expressed to be made in the course of tax exempt life or endowment business nor expressed not to be so made but is assumed by the society not to be so made, and
    (*b*) the policy issued in pursuance of it falls within paragraph 21(1)(*b*) of Schedule 15.

(4) An election under subsection (2) above shall only be valid if the society satisfies the inspector (or the Commissioners on appeal) that it is possible to identify all the contracts to which the election relates.

(5) If the inspector decides that he is not satisfied as mentioned in subsection (4) above, he shall give notice of his decision to the society; and section 42(3), (4) and (9) of, and paragraph 1(1) to (1E) of Schedule 2 to, the Management Act shall apply in relation to such a decision of an inspector on a claim.

(6) An election under subsection (1) or (2) above shall have effect for accounting periods ending on or after the day on which the Finance Act 1991 was passed.

(7) No election under subsection (1) or (2) above may be made after 31st July 1992.

(8) Where a friendly society has made an election under subsection (1) or (2) above, then, for any accounting period for which the election has effect—

    (*a*) section 460(1) shall apply to profits arising from life or endowment business which would have been included in the society's tax exempt life or endowment business had no account been taken of the contracts to which the election relates, and
    (*b*) section 462(1), in its application to the society, shall have effect with the insertion after ''societies'' of ''and all policies issued in pursuance of contracts to which an election under section 462A(1) or (2) relates''.][1]

[(9) If a friendly society which (or a branch of which) has made an election under subsection (1) or (2) above becomes an incorporated friendly society, the election shall have effect in relation to the incorporated friendly society as it had effect in relation to the society (or branch) which made the election (and accordingly, in relation to accounting periods of the incorporated friendly society, ''the society'' in subsection (8)(*a*) and (*b*) above shall be read as referring to the incorporated friendly society).][2]

Commentary—*Simon's Direct Tax Service* **D4.607, 616.**
Note—FA 1991 was passed on 25 July 1991.
Definitions—''Accounting period'', s 834(1); ''Commissioners'', TMA 1970 s 48(1); ''friendly society'', s 466(2); ''incorporated friendly society'', s 466(2); ''inspector'', s 832(1); ''life or endowment business'', s 466(1); ''Management Act'', s 831(3); ''notice'', s 832(1); ''registered friendly society'', s 466(3), (4); ''tax exempt life or endowment business'', s 466(2).
Amendments—[1] This section inserted by FA 1991 Sch 9 para 2.
[2] Sub-s (9) added by F(No 2)A 1992 Sch 9 paras 1, 9, 22 with effect from 19 February 1993 by virtue of F(No 2)A 1992 Sch 9 (Appointed Day) Order, SI 1993/236.

463 Life or endowment business: application of the Corporation Tax Acts

[(1)][1] Subject to section 460(1), the Corporation Tax Acts shall apply to the life or endowment business carried on by [friendly societies][2] in the same way as they apply to mutual life assurance business [(or other [long-term][4] business)][3] carried on by insurance companies, so however that the

Treasury may by regulations provide that those Acts as so applied shall have effect subject to such modifications and exceptions as may be prescribed by the regulations, and those regulations may in particular require any part of any business to be treated as a separate business.

[(2) The provisions of the Corporation Tax Acts which apply on the transfer of the whole or part of the [long-term][4] business of an insurance company to another company shall apply in the same way—

(*a*) on the transfer of the whole or part of the business of a friendly society to another friendly society (and on the amalgamation of friendly societies), and

(*b*) on the transfer of the whole or part of the business of a friendly society to a company which is not a friendly society (and on the conversion of a friendly society into such a company),

so however that the Treasury may by regulations provide that those provisions as so applied shall have effect subject to such modifications and exceptions as may be prescribed by the regulations.][2]

[(3) The Treasury may by regulations provide that the provisions of the Corporation Tax Acts which apply on the transfer of the whole or part of the [long-term][4] business of an insurance company to another company shall have effect where the transferee is a friendly society subject to such modifications and exceptions as may be prescribed by the regulations.][2]

[(4) Regulations under this section may make different provision for different cases and may include provision having retrospective effect.][2]

Commentary—*Simon's Direct Tax Service* **D4.608.**
Regulations—Friendly Societies (Modification of the Corporation Tax Acts) Regulations, SI 1997/463.
Definitions—"The Corporation Tax Acts", s 831(1)(*a*); "friendly society", s 466(2); "insurance company", ss 431, 466(2); "life assurance business", s 466(2); "life or endowment business", s 466(1); "long term business", ss 431, 466; "registered friendly society", s 466(2).
Cross references—See FA 1993 s 121(4) (s 121 (repayments and payments to friendly societies) is without prejudice to sub-s (1) above).
Amendments—[1] Sub-s (1) numbered as such and sub-ss (2), (3), (4) added by FA 1990 s 50.
[2] Words in sub-s (1) substituted by F(No 2)A 1992 Sch 9 paras 1, 10, 22 with effect from 19 February 1993 by virtue of F(No 2)A 1992 Sch 9 (Appointed Day) Order, SI 1993/236.
[3] Words in sub-s (1) inserted by FA 1996 s 171(5), (6) with effect for accounting periods ending after 31 August 1996.
[4] Words in sub-ss (1), (2), (3) substituted by the Financial Services and Markets Act 2000 (Consequential Amendments) (Taxes) Order, SI 2001/3629 arts 13, 52(2)(*i*) with effect from 1 December 2001 (immediately after the coming into force of the Financial Services and Markets Act 2000 ss 411, 432(1), Sch 20).

464 Maximum benefits payable to members

(1) Subject to subsections (2) and (3) below, a member of a [friendly society or registered branch][5] shall not be entitled to have at any time outstanding contracts with any one or more such societies or branches (taking together all such societies or branches throughout the United Kingdom) for the assurance of—

(*a*) more than £750 by way of gross sum under tax exempt life or endowment business;

(*b*) more than £156 by way of annuity under tax exempt life or endowment business.

In any case where the member's outstanding contracts were all made before 14th March 1984 this subsection shall have effect with the substitution for "£750" and "£156" of "£2,000" and "£416" respectively.

(2) Subsection (1)(*a*) above shall not apply as respects sums assured under contracts made after 31st August 1987.

(3) With respect to contracts for the assurance of gross sums under tax exempt life or endowment business, a member of a [friendly society or registered branch][5] shall not be entitled to have outstanding with any one or more such societies or branches (taking together all such societies or branches throughout the United [Kingdom)—][1]

[(*zza*) contracts under which the total premiums payable in any period of 12 months exceed £270; or][9]

[(*za*) contracts [made before the day on which the Finance Act 1995 was passed and][9] under which the total premiums payable in any period of 12 months exceed £200; or][2]

[(*a*) contracts [made before the day on which the Finance Act 1991 was passed and][3] under which the total premiums payable in any period of 12 months exceed £150; or

(*b*) contracts made before 1st September 1990 under which the total premiums payable in any period of 12 months exceed £100,

unless all those contracts were made before 1st September 1987.][1]

(4) In applying the [limits][1] in subsection (3) above, the premiums under any contract for an annuity which was made before 1st June 1984 by a new society shall be brought into account as if the contract were for the assurance of a gross sum.

[(4A) Subsection (4B) below applies to contracts for the assurance of gross sums under tax exempt life or endowment business made after 31st August 1987 and before the day on which [the Finance Act 1995][10] was passed.][4]

[(4B) Where the amount payable by way of premium under a contract to which this subsection applies is increased by virtue of a [variation made—

(*a*) in the period beginning with 25th July 1991 and ending with 31st July 1992, or (*b*) in the period beginning with the day on which the Finance Act 1995 was passed and ending with 31st March 1996,

the contract shall, for the purposes of subsection (3) above, be treated, in relation to times when the contract has effect as varied, as made at the time of the variation.]¹¹]⁴

(5) In applying the limits in this section there shall be disregarded—

(*a*) any bonus or addition which either is declared upon assurance of a gross sum or annuity or accrues upon such an assurance by reference to an increase in the value of any investments;

(*b*) any approved annuities as defined in section 620(9) or any policy of insurance or annuity contract by means of which the benefits to be provided under an occupational pension scheme as defined in [section 1 of the Pension Schemes Act 1993]⁸ are secured;

(*c*) any increase in a benefit under a friendly society contract, as defined in section 6 of the Decimal Currency Act 1969 resulting from the adoption of a scheme prescribed or approved in pursuance of subsection (3) of that section; and

(*d*) so far as concerns the total premiums payable in any period of 12 months—

(i) 10 per cent of the premiums payable under any contract under which the premiums are payable more frequently than annually; and

(ii) £10 of the premiums payable under any contract made before 1st September 1987 by a [friendly society other than]⁶ a new society; and

(iii) so much of any premium as is charged on the ground that an exceptional risk of death is involved.

(6) In applying the limits in this section in any case where a member has outstanding with one or more society or branch one or more contracts made after 13th March 1984 and one or more contracts made on or before that date, any contract for an annuity which was made before 1st June 1984 by a new society shall be regarded not only as a contract for the annual amount concerned but also as a contract for the assurance of a gross sum equal to 75 per cent of the total premiums which would be payable under the contract if it were to run for its full term or, as the case may be, if the member concerned were to die at the age of 75 years.

(7) A [friendly society or registered branch]⁵ may require a member to make and sign a statutory declaration that the total amount assured under outstanding contracts entered into by that member with any one or more [friendly societies or registered branches]⁷ (taking together all such societies or branches throughout the United Kingdom) does not exceed the limits applicable by virtue of this section and that the total premiums under those contracts do not exceed those limits.

Commentary—*Simon's Direct Tax Service* **D4.614.**
Notes—FA 1995 was passed on 1 May 1995.
Definitions—"Friendly society", s 466(2); "new society", s 466(2); "policy", s 466(2); "registered branch", s 466(2); "registered friendly society", s 466(2); "tax exempt life or endowment business", s 466(2).
Cross references—See TA 1988 Sch 14 para 3(4) (increases in capital sums treated as made by virtue of Sch 14, para 3(3) to be disregarded for the purposes of this section).
TA 1988 Sch 15, para 6(2) (contract is not a "qualifying policy" where it involves breach by a member of the limits in this section).
Amendments—¹ Words in sub-ss (3), (4) substituted by FA 1990 s 49(3), (4).
² Sub-s (3)(*za*) inserted by FA 1991 Sch 9 para 3(1), (2).
³ Words in sub-s (3)(*a*) inserted by FA 1991 Sch 9, para 3(1), (3).
⁴ Sub-ss (4A), (4B) inserted by FA 1991 Sch 9, para 3(1), (4).
⁵ Words in sub-ss (1), (3), (7) substituted by F(No 2)A 1992 Sch 9 paras 1, 11, 22 with effect from 19 February 1993 by virtue of F(No 2)A 1992 Sch 9 (Appointed Day) Order, SI 1993/236.
⁶ Words in sub-s (5)(*d*)(ii) substituted by F(No 2)A 1992 Sch 9 paras 1, 11, 22 with effect from 19 February 1993 by virtue of F(No 2)A 1992 Sch 9 (Appointed Day) Order, SI 1993/236.
⁷ Words in sub-s (7) substituted by F(No 2)A 1992 Sch 9 paras 1, 11, 22 with effect from 19 February 1993 by virtue of F(No 2)A 1992 Sch 9 (Appointed Day) Order, SI 1993/236.
⁸ Words in sub-s (5)(*b*) substituted by the Pensions Schemes Act 1993 s 190, Sch 8 para 20(1).
⁹ Sub-s (3)(*zza*) inserted by FA 1995 Sch 10 para 2(2), (3).
¹⁰ Words in sub-s (4A) substituted by FA 1995 Sch 10, para 2(4).
¹¹ Words in sub-s (4B) substituted by FA 1995 Sch 10, para 2(5).

465 Old societies

(1) In this section "old society" means a friendly society which is not a new society.

(2) This section applies if, on or after 19th March 1985, an old society—

(*a*) begins to carry on tax exempt life or endowment business; or

(*b*) in the opinion of the Board begins to carry on such business on an enlarged scale or of a new character.

(3) If it appears to the Board, having regard to the restrictions placed on qualifying policies issued by new societies by paragraphs 3(1)(*b*) ...¹ and 4(3)(*b*) of Schedule 15, that for the protection of the revenue it is expedient to do so, the Board may give a direction to the old society under subsection (4) below.

(4) A direction under this subsection is that (and has the effect that) the old society to which it is given is to be treated for the purposes of this Act as a new society with respect to business carried on after the date of the direction.

(5) An old society to which a direction is given may, within 30 days of the date on which it is given, appeal against the direction to the Special Commissioners on the ground that—

(*a*) it has not begun to carry on business as mentioned in subsection (2) above; or

(*b*) that the direction is not necessary for the protection of the revenue.

[(6) If a registered friendly society in respect of which a direction is in force under subsection (4) above becomes an incorporated friendly society, the direction shall continue to have effect, so that the incorporated friendly society shall be treated for the purposes of this Act as a new society.]²

Commentary—*Simon's Direct Tax Service* **D4.615.**
Simon's Tax Cases—*R v HM Treasury, ex p Daily Mail and General Trust plc* [1987] STC 157*.
s 465(1), *R v HM Treasury and IRC, ex p Daily Mail and General Trust plc* [1988] STC 787*.
Definitions—"The Board", s 832(1); "friendly society", s 466(2); "incorporated friendly society", s 466(2); "new society", s 466(2); "qualifying policy", s 832(1); "registered friendly society", s 466(2); "tax exempt life or endowment business", s 466(2).
Amendments—¹ Words "and (*c*)" in sub-s (3) repealed by FA 1991 Sch 19 Pt V in relation to policies issued in pursuance of contracts made after 24 July 1991.
² Sub-s (6) added by F(No 2)A 1992 Sch 9 paras 1, 12, 22 with effect from 19 February 1993 by virtue of F(No 2)A 1992 Sch 9 (Appointed Day) Order, SI 1993/236.

[465A Assets of branch of registered friendly society to be treated as assets of society after incorporation

(1) This section applies where any assets of a branch of a registered friendly society have been identified in a scheme under section 6(5) of the Friendly Societies Act 1992 (property, rights etc excluded from transfer to the society on its incorporation).

(2) In relation to any time after the incorporation of the society, the assets shall be treated for the purposes of the Tax Acts as assets of the society (and, accordingly, any tax liability arising in respect of them shall be a liability of the society rather than of the branch).

(3) Where, by virtue of this section, tax in respect of any of the assets becomes chargeable on and is paid by the society, the society may recover from the trustees in whom those assets are vested the amount of the tax paid.]¹

Commentary—*Simon's Direct Tax Service* **D4.616.**
Definitions—"Registered friendly society", s 466(2); "Tax Acts", s 831(2).
Amendments—¹ This section inserted by F(No 2)A 1992 Sch 9 paras 1, 13, 22 with effect from 19 February 1993 by virtue of F(No 2)A 1992 Sch 9 (Appointed Day) Order, SI 1993/236.

466 Interpretation of Chapter II

[(1) In this Chapter "life or endowment business" means, subject to subsections (1A) and (1B) below,—

(*a*) any business [of effecting or carrying out contracts of insurance which fall within paragraphs I, II or III of Part II of Schedule 1 to the Financial Services and Markets Act 2000 (Regulated Activities) Order 2001;]⁵

(*b*) pension business;

(*c*) any other life assurance business;

(*d*) any business within [paragraph IV of Part II]⁵ of that Schedule, if—

(i) the contract is one made before 1st September 1996; or

(ii) the contract is one made on or after 1st September 1996 and the effecting and carrying out of the contract also constitutes business within [paragraphs I, II or III of Part II]⁵ of that Schedule.]²

[(1A) Life or endowment business does not include the issue, in respect of a contract made before 1st September 1996, of a policy affording provision for sickness or other infirmity (whether bodily or mental), unless—

(*a*) the policy also affords assurance for a gross sum independent of sickness or other infirmity;

(*b*) not less than 60 per cent of the amount of the premiums is attributable to the provision afforded during sickness or other infirmity; and

(*c*) there is no bonus or addition which may be declared or accrue upon the assurance of the gross sum.]²

[(1B) Life or endowment business does not include the assurance of any annuity the consideration for which consists of sums obtainable on the maturity, or on the surrender, of any other policy of assurance issued by the friendly society, being a policy of assurance forming part of the tax exempt life or endowment business of the friendly society.]²

(2) In this Chapter—

["friendly society", without qualification, means (except in section 459) an incorporated friendly society or a registered friendly society;]³

["incorporated friendly society" means a society incorporated under the Friendly Societies Act 1992;]³

["insurance company" shall be construed in accordance with section 431;]⁴

"life assurance business" means the issue of, or the undertaking of liability under, policies of assurance upon human life, or the granting of annuities upon human life, not being industrial assurance business;

["[long-term]⁶ business" shall be construed in accordance with section 431;]⁴

["new society" means—

(*a*) a registered friendly society which was registered after 3rd May 1966 or which was registered in the period of three months ending on that date but which at no time earlier than that date carried on any life or endowment business, or

(*b*) an incorporated friendly society other than one which, before its incorporation, was a registered friendly society not within paragraph (*a*) above;][3]

"pension business" shall be construed in accordance with section 431;

"policy", in relation to life or endowment business, includes an instrument evidencing a contract to pay an annuity upon human life;

["registered branch" means the same as in the Friendly Societies Act 1992 (and includes any branch that by virtue of section 96(3) of that Act is to be treated as a registered branch);][3]

["registered friendly society" means the same as in the Friendly Societies Act 1992 (and includes any society that by virtue of section 96(2) of that Act is to be treated as a registered friendly society);][3]

...[1]

"tax exempt life or endowment business" has, subject to subsections (7) to (11) of section 460, the meaning given by subsection (2)(*d*) of that section, that is to say, it means (subject to those subsections) life or endowment business other than business profits arising from which are excluded from subsection (1) of that section by subsection (2)(*b*) or (*c*) of that section (read, where appropriate, with subsection (6) of that section);

and references in sections 460 to 465 and this subsection to a friendly society [include, in the case of a registered friendly society, references to any branch of that society][3].

(3) It is hereby declared that for the purposes of this Chapter (except where provision to the contrary is made) a [friendly society][3] formed on the amalgamation of two or more friendly societies is to be treated as different from the amalgamated societies.

(4) A registered friendly society formed on the amalgamation of two or more friendly societies shall, for the purposes of this Chapter, be treated as registered not later than 3rd May 1966 if at the time of the amalgamation—

(*a*) all the friendly societies amalgamated were registered friendly societies eligible for the exemption conferred by section 460(1); and

(*b*) at least one of them was not a new society;

or, if the amalgamation took place before 19th March 1985, the society was treated as registered not later than 3rd May 1966 by virtue of the proviso to section 337(4) of the 1970 Act.

[(5) An incorporated friendly society formed on the amalgamation of two or more friendly societies shall, for the purposes of this Chapter, be treated as a society which, before its incorporation, was a registered friendly society registered not later than 3rd May 1966 if at the time of the amalgamation—

(*a*) all the friendly societies amalgamated were registered friendly societies eligible for the exemption conferred by section 460(1); and

(*b*) at least one of them was not a new society.][3]

Commentary—*Simon's Direct Tax Service* **D4.603, 615.**
Cross references—Sch 15, para 5 (interpretation of Sch 15, paras 3, 5).
Modifications—Words inserted in sub-s (2) in respect of individual savings account business of Insurance Companies by the Individual Savings Account Regulations, SI 1998/1871 reg 17, with effect from 6 April 1999.
Amendments—[1] Definition of "registrar" in sub-s (2) repealed by the Friendly Societies Act 1992 Sch 22 Pt I with effect from 1 January 1994 by virtue of the Friendly Societies Act 1992 (Commencement No 6 and Transitional Provisions) Order 1993, SI 1993/2213.
[2] Sub-ss (1), (1A), (1B) substituted for sub-s (1) by FA 1996 s 171(1).
[3] Definitions of "friendly society", "incorporated friendly society", "registered branch", "registered friendly society" inserted, definition of "new society" and words in sub-ss (2), (3) substituted and sub-s (5) added by F(No 2)A 1992 Sch 9 paras 1, 14, 22 with effect from 19 February 1993 by virtue of SI 1993/236.
[4] Definitions "insurance company" and "long term business" in sub-s (2) inserted by FA 1996 s 171(2).
[5] Words in sub-s (1)(*a*), (*d*) substituted by the Financial Services and Markets Act 2000 (Consequential Amendments) (Taxes) Order, SI 2001/3629 arts 13, 37 with effect from 1 December 2001, immediately after the coming into force of the Financial Services and Markets Act 2000 ss 411, 432(1), Sch 20.
[6] Words in sub-s (2) substituted by SI 2001/3629 arts 13, 52(2)(*j*) with effect from 1 December 2001, immediately after the coming into force of the Financial Services and Markets Act 2000 ss 411, 432(1), Sch 20.

Trade unions and employers' associations

467 Exemption for trade unions and employers' associations

(1) A trade union which is precluded by Act of Parliament or by its rules from assuring to any person a sum exceeding [£4,000][2] by way of gross sum or [£825][2] by way of annuity shall on making a claim be entitled—

(*a*) to exemption from income tax and corporation tax in respect of its income which is not trading income and which is applicable and applied for the purpose of provident benefits;

(*b*) to exemption from tax in respect of chargeable gains which are applicable and applied for the purpose of provident benefits.

(2) In this section "provident benefits" includes any payment, expressly authorised by the rules of the trade union, which is made to a member during sickness or incapacity from personal injury or while out of work, or to an aged member by way of superannuation, or to a member who has met with an accident, or has lost his tools by fire or theft, and includes a payment in discharge or aid of

funeral expenses on the death of a member or the [spouse][1] of a member or as provision for the children of a deceased member.

(3) In determining for the purposes of this section whether a trade union is by Act of Parliament or its rules precluded from assuring to any person a sum exceeding [£825][2] by way of annuity, there shall be disregarded any approved annuities (as defined in section 620(9)).

[(3A) The Treasury may by order substitute for any figure for the time being specified in this section such greater figure as may be specified in the order; and any amendment made in exercise of the power conferred by this subsection shall have effect in relation to such income or gains as may be specified in the order.][3]

(4) In this section "trade union" means—

(a) any trade union the name of which is entered in the list of trade unions maintained by the [Certification Officer][4] under [section 2 of the Trade Union and Labour Relations (Consolidation) Act 1992][7];

(b) any employers' association the name of which is entered in the list of employers' associations maintained by the [Certification Officer][4] under [section 123 of the Trade Union and Labour Relations (Consolidation) Act 1992][7] and which on 30th September 1971 was a registered trade union for the purposes of section 338 of the 1970 Act; ...[5]

[(ba) any trade union the name of which is entered in the list of trade unions maintained by the Certification Officer for Northern Ireland under Article 5 of the Industrial Relations (Northern Ireland) Order 1992;][6]

[(bb) any employers' association the name of which is entered in the list of employers' associations maintained by the Certification Officer for Northern Ireland under Article 5 of the Industrial Relations (Northern Ireland) Order 1992 and which immediately before the coming into operation of that Article was a trade union for the purposes of this section; and][6]

(c) the Police Federation for England and Wales, the Police Federation for Scotland, the Police Federation for Northern Ireland and any other organisation of persons in police service which has similar functions.

Commentary—*Simon's Direct Tax Service* **D4.636.**
Statement of Practice SP 1/84—Legal expenses for unfair dismissal cases before a tribunal, legal expenses in connection with accident or injury claims and administration expenses of providing provident benefits are regarded as payments for the purpose of provident benefits.
Revenue Internal Guidance—Capital Gains Tax Manual CG 67600–67603 (sub-s (1)(b): rollover relief under TCGA 1992 s 158 may be available where gains not wholly exempt).
Definition—"Chargeable gain", s 832(1).
Cross references—See TMA 1970 s 46C (Special Commissioners have jurisdiction on an appeal against an amendment of a self-assessment or partnership statement where the question in dispute concerns a claim under this section).
TMA 1970 Sch 2 para 2 (appeal against a decision by an inspector under this section to be exclusively to the Special Commissioners).
Amendments—[1] Word in sub-s (2) substituted by FA 1988 Sch 3 para 17 in relation to chargeable periods beginning after 5 April 1990.
[2] Sums in sub-ss (1), (3) substituted by FA 1991 s 74(1)–(3), (6) in relation to income or gains which are applicable and applied as mentioned in this section after 31 March 1991.
[3] Sub-s (3A) inserted by FA 1991 s 74(1), (4).
[4] Words in sub-s (4)(a), (b) substituted by FA 1991 s 74(1), (5)(a), (7) and deemed always to have had effect.
[5] Word "and" at end of sub-s (4)(b) deleted by virtue of FA 1991 s 74(5)(b).
[6] Sub-s (4)(ba), (bb) substituted for sub-s (4)(ba) by the Industrial Relations (Northern Ireland Consequential Amendment) Order, SI 1992/808 with effect from 1 July 1992 .
[7] Words in sub-s (4)(a), (b) substituted by the Trade Union and Labour Relations (Consolidation) Act 1992 Sch 2, para 37.

CHAPTER III
UNIT TRUST SCHEMES, DEALERS IN SECURITIES ETC
Unit trust schemes

Modifications—With specified modifications and exceptions, the Tax Acts and TCGA 1992 are to have effect for open-ended investment companies as they have effect for authorised unit trusts (per the Open-ended Investment Companies (Tax) Regulations, SI 1997/1154 regs 3-5).

468 Authorised unit trusts

(1) In respect of income arising to the trustees of an authorised unit trust, and for the purposes of the provisions relating to relief for capital expenditure, the Tax Acts shall have effect as if—

(a) the trustees were a company resident in the United Kingdom; and
(b) the rights of the unit holders were shares in the company;

[but paragraph (b) above is without prejudice to the making of distributions which are interest distributions (within the meaning of section 468L) to unit holders.][3]

[(1A) In relation to any authorised unit trust the rate of corporation tax for the financial year 1996 and subsequent financial years shall be deemed to be the rate at which income tax at the lower rate is charged for the year of assessment which begins on 6th April in the financial year concerned [and sections 13 and 13AA shall not apply][10].][9]

(2) ...[7]

(3) References in the Corporation Tax Acts to a body corporate shall be construed in accordance with [subsection (1) above][4], and section [234A][2] shall apply with any necessary modifications.

(4) Section 75 shall apply in relation to an authorised unit trust whether or not it is an investment company within the meaning of section 130; and sums periodically appropriated for managers' remuneration shall be treated for the purposes of section 75 as sums disbursed as expenses of management.

(5) ...[1]

(6) [Subject to subsections (7) to (9) below][5] in this section—

     "authorised unit trust" means, as respects an accounting period, a unit trust scheme in the case of which an order under section [243 of the Financial Services and Markets Act 2000][11] is in force during the whole or part of that accounting period;

     ...[8]

     "unit holder" means a person entitled to a share of the investments subject to the trusts of a unit trust scheme; and

     "unit trust scheme" has the same meaning as in section 469.

[(7) Each of the parts of an umbrella scheme shall be regarded for the purposes of this Chapter as an authorised unit trust and the scheme as a whole shall not be so regarded.][6]

[(8) In this section, "umbrella scheme" means a unit trust scheme—

     (*a*) which provides arrangements for separate pooling of the contributions of the participants and the profits or income out of which payments are to be made to them;

     (*b*) under which the participants are entitled to exchange rights in one pool for rights in another; and

     (*c*) in the case of which an order under section [243 of the Financial Services and Markets Act 2000][11] is in force;

and any reference to a part of an umbrella scheme is a reference to such of the arrangements as relate to a separate pool.][6]

[(9) In relation to a part of an umbrella scheme, any reference—

     (*a*) to investments subject to the trusts of an authorised unit trust, shall have effect as a reference to such of the investments as under the arrangements form part of the separate pool to which the part of the umbrella scheme relates; and

     (*b*) to a unit holder, shall have effect as a reference to a person for the time being having rights in that separate pool.][6]

Statement of Practice SP 3/97—Investment trusts investing in authorised unit trusts or open-ended investment companies: tax implications.

Revenue & other press releases—IR 12-7-96 (Government announces that it intends to block the emerging use of derivative instruments by unit trusts to deliver artificially tax-advantaged returns).

Definitions—"Accounting period", s 834(1); "company", s 832(1), (2); "the Corporation Tax Acts", s 831(1)(*a*); "financial year", s 834(1); "lower rate", s 832(1); "Schedule C", s 17(1); "Schedule D", s 18(1); "the Tax Acts", s 831(2).

Cross references—See TA 1988 s 592(10) (sub-s (2) above not to apply to authorised unit trusts which are also exempt approved retirement benefit schemes).

TA 1988 Sch 5AA para 1(2)(*c*) (para 1(1) of that Schedule (certain disposals of futures or options to be charged as income under Schedule D Case VI) *not* to apply to profits arising to an authorised unit trust).

FA 1989 s 80(1), (2) (disapplication of sub-s (5) of this section in its application to gilt unit trusts);

FA 1990 s 52(3), (4) (assessment of the trustees' liability to income tax in respect of income chargeable under Schedule D Case III in the last distribution period to which sub-s (5) above applies).

Modification—This section is modified, in relation to open-ended investment companies, by the Open-ended Investment Companies (Tax) Regulations, SI 1997/1154, regs 5–7, 9, 10.

Amendments—[1] Sub-s (5) repealed by FA 1990 s 52(2) and Sch 19 Pt IV with effect as regards distribution periods beginning after 31 December 1990.

[2] "234A" in sub-s (3) substituted for "234(3) and (4)" by F(No 2)A 1992 s 32(3), (4) in relation to distributions begun after 16 July 1992.

[3] Words in sub-s (1) inserted by FA 1994 Sch 14 paras 3, 7 in relation to distribution periods beginning after 31 March 1994, but subject to FA 1994 Sch 14 para 7(2).

[4] Words in sub-s (3) substituted by FA 1994 Sch 14 paras 3, 7 in relation to distribution periods beginning after 31 March 1994, but subject to FA 1994 Sch 14 para 7(2).

[5] Words in sub-s (6) inserted by FA 1994 s 113(1), (4) and have effect after 31 March 1994 in relation to unit trust schemes and their participants, but subject to FA 1994 s 113(5)–(11).

[6] Sub-ss (7)–(9) added by FA 1994 s 113(2), (4) and have effect after 31 March 1994 in relation to unit trust schemes and their participants, but subject to FA 1994 s 113(5)–(11).

[7] Sub-s (2) repealed by FA 1994 Sch 14 paras 3, 7, Sch 26 Pt V(13) in relation to distribution periods beginning after 31 March 1994, but subject to FA 1994 Sch 14 para 7(2).

[8] Definition of "distribution period" in sub-s (6) repealed by FA 1994 Sch 14 paras 3, 7, Sch 26 Pt V(13) in relation to distribution periods beginning after 31 March 1994, but subject to FA 1994 Sch 14 para 7(2).

[9] Sub-s (1A) inserted by FA 1996 Sch 6 para 10(1), (2) with effect for any accounting period ending after 31 March 1996.

[10] Words in sub-s (1A) inserted by FA 1999 s 28(3), (6) with effect for corporation tax from the financial year 2000, subject to FA 1999 s 28(7) (concerning accounting periods straddling 1 April 2000).

[11] Words in sub-ss (6), (8) substituted by the Financial Services and Markets Act 2000 s 432(1), Sch 20 para 4 with effect from 1 December 2001 (by virtue of SI 2001/3538).

[468AA Authorised unit trusts: futures and options

(1) Trustees shall be exempt from tax under Case I of Schedule D in respect of income if—

     (a) the income is derived from transactions relating to futures contracts or options contracts, and

(b) the trustees are trustees of a unit trust scheme *which is an* authorised unit trust *as respects the accounting period in which the income is derived.*

(2) *For the purposes of subsection (1) above a contract is not prevented from being a futures contract or an options contract by the fact that any party is or may be entitled to receive or liable to make, or entitled to receive and liable to make, only a payment of a sum (as opposed to a transfer of assets other than money) in full settlement of all obligations.*

(3) ...²]¹

Note—This section repealed by FA 2002 ss 83(1)(b), (3) 141, Sch 27 para s 1, 6, Sch 40 Pt 3(13) with effect for accounting periods beginning after 30 September 2002.
Commentary—*Simon's Direct Tax Service* **D4.1311.**
Definitions—''Accounting period'', s 834(1); ''Schedule D'', s 18(1).
Cross references—See the Open-ended Investment Companies (Tax) Regulations, SI 1997/1154 regs 9, 11 (specific modifications of this section as it has effect in its application to open-ended investment companies).
Modification—This section is modified, in relation to open-ended investment companies, by the Open-ended Investment Companies (Tax) Regulations, SI 1997/1154, regs 9, 11.
Amendments—¹ This section inserted by FA 1990 s 81(1), (5) with effect for income derived after 25 July 1990.
² Sub-s (3) repealed by FA 1999 s 139, Sch 20 Pt III(17), with effect from 27 July 1999.

[468A Certified unit trusts]

Amendments—This section (inserted by FA 1989 s 78) repealed by FA 1990 Sch 19 Pt IV with effect as regards accounting periods ending after 31 December 1990.

[468B Certified unit trusts: corporation tax]

Amendments—This section (inserted by FA 1989 s 78) repealed by FA 1990 s 52(5) and Sch 19 Pt IV with effect as regards accounting periods ending after 31 December 1990.

[468C Certified unit trusts: distributions]

Amendments—This section (inserted by FA 1989 s 78) repealed by FA 1990 s 52(6) and Sch 19 Pt IV with effect as regards distribution periods ending after 31 December 1990.

[468D Funds of funds: distributions]

Amendments—This section (inserted by FA 1989 s 79) repealed by FA 1990 s 52(7) and Sch 19 Pt IV with effect as regards distribution periods ending after 31 December 1990.

[468E Authorised unit trusts: corporation tax]

Amendments—This section (inserted by FA 1990 s 51) is repealed by FA 1996 Sch 6 para 10(3), Sch 41 Pt V(1) with effect for any accounting period ending after 31 March 1996 (except so far as relating to the financial year 1995).

[468EE Corporation tax: cases where lower rate applies]

Amendments—This section (inserted by FA 1994 s 111(2)) is repealed by FA 1996 Sch 6 para 10(3), Sch 41 Pt V(1) with effect for any accounting period ending after 31 March 1996 (except so far as relating to the financial year 1995).

[468F Authorised unit trusts: distributions]

Amendments—This section (inserted by FA 1990 s 51) repealed by FA 1994 Sch 14 paras 4, 7 and Sch 26, Pt V(13) for distribution periods beginning after 31 March 1994, but subject to FA 1994 Sch 14 para 7(2).

[468G Dividends paid to investment trusts]

Amendments—This section (inserted by FA 1990 s 51) repealed by FA 1994 Sch 14 paras 4, 7 and Sch 26, Pt V(13) for distribution periods beginning after 31 March 1994, but subject to FA 1994 Sch 14 para 7(2).

[Distributions of authorised unit trusts: general]1

[468H Interpretation

(1) This section has effect for the interpretation of sections 468I to 468R.

(2) The making of a distribution by an authorised unit trust to a unit holder includes investing an amount on behalf of the unit holder in respect of his accumulation units.

(3) In relation to an authorised unit trust—

(a) ''distribution period'' means a period by reference to which the total amount available for distribution to unit holders is ascertained; and

(b) ''distribution accounts'' means accounts showing how that total amount is computed.

(4) The distribution date for a distribution period of an authorised unit trust is—

(a) the date specified by or in accordance with the terms of the trust for any distribution for that distribution period; or

(b) if no date is so specified, the last day of that distribution period.

(5) ...²

(6) Sections 468I [to 468Q]³ do not apply to an authorised unit trust which is also an approved personal pension scheme (within the meaning of Chapter IV of Part XIV).]¹

Commentary—*Simon's Direct Tax Service* **D4.1315.**
Concession C30—Subject to conditions, an authorised unit trust or open-ended investment company will not be treated for tax purposes as making distributions of the total amount shown in its "distribution accounts" as available for distribution to investors in respect of a distribution period for which it waives a distribution (or accumulation) in accordance with *de minimis* provisions in Financial Services Regulations.
Definitions—"Authorised unit trust", s 832(1); "distribution", s 832(1); "unit holder", s 832(1).
Modification—This section is modified, in relation to open-ended investment companies, by the Open-ended Investment Companies (Tax) Regulations, SI 1997/1154, reg 9.
Amendments—¹ This section inserted by FA 1994 Sch 14 paras 1, 2, 7 in relation to distribution periods beginning after 31 March 1994, but subject to FA 1994 Sch 14 para 7(2).
² Sub-s (5) repealed by F(No 2)A 1997 s 36(4), Sch 6 para 8(1)(a), (8), Sch 8 Pt II(11) with effect for distribution periods beginning after 5 April 1999.
³ Words in sub-s (6) substituted by F(No 2)A 1997 s 36(4), Sch 6 para 8(1)(b), (9) with effect for distribution periods the distribution date for which falls after 5 April 1999.

[468I Distribution accounts

(1) The total amount shown in the distribution accounts as available for distribution to unit holders shall be shown as available for distribution in one of the ways set out below.

(2) It may be shown as available for distribution as dividends ...².

(3) ...²

(4) It may be shown as available for distribution as yearly interest.

(5), *(5A)* ...²

(6) Amounts deriving from income under Schedule A may not be included in any amount shown in the distribution accounts as available for distribution as yearly interest.

(7) ...²]¹

Commentary—*Simon's Direct Tax Service* **D4.1315, 1317, 1318, 1336.**
Concession C 30—Subject to conditions, an authorised unit trust or open-ended investment company will not be treated for tax purposes as making distributions of the total amount shown in its "distribution accounts" as available for distribution to investors in respect of a distribution period for which it waives a distribution (or accumulation) in accordance with *de minimis* provisions in Financial Services Regulations.
Definitions—"Distribution", s 832(1); "distribution accounts", s 468H(3); "foreign income dividend", s 468H(5); "Schedule A", s 15; "unit holder", s 832(1).
Cross references—See TA 1988 s 468H (interpretation).
TA 1988 s 468H(6) (this section does not apply to an authorised unit trust which is also an approved personal pension scheme).
Open-ended Investment Companies (Tax) Regulations, SI 1997/1154 regs 9, 12 (specific modifications of this section as it has effect in its application to open-ended investment companies).
Modification—This section is modified, in relation to open-ended investment companies, by the Open-ended Investment Companies (Tax) Regulations 1997, SI 1997/1154, regs 9, 12.
Amendments—¹ This section inserted by FA 1994 Sch 14 paras 1, 2, 7 in relation to distribution periods beginning after 31 March 1994, but subject to FA 1994 Sch 14 para 7(2).
² Words in sub-s (2), and sub-ss (3), (5), (5A), (7), repealed by F(No 2)A 1997 s 36(4), Sch 6 para 8(2), (9), Sch 8 Pt II(11) with effect for distribution periods the distribution date for which falls after 5 April 1999.

[Dividend and foreign income distributions]1

[468J Dividend distributions

(1) Subsection (2) below applies where the total amount ...² shown in the distribution accounts as available for distribution to unit holders is shown as available for distribution as dividends ...².

(2) The Tax Acts shall have effect as if the total amount ...² were dividends on shares paid on the distribution date by the company referred to in section 468(1) to the unit holders in proportion to their rights.

(3) ...²

(4) In the following provisions of this Chapter "a dividend distribution" means a dividend treated as paid by virtue of subsection (2) above.]¹

Commentary—*Simon's Direct Tax Service* **D4.1316.**
Definitions—"Authorised unit trust", s 832(1); "distribution", s 832(1); "distribution account", s 468H(3); "distribution date", s 468H(3); "foreign income dividend", s 468H(5); "the Tax Acts", s 831(2); "unit holder", s 832(1).
Cross references—See TA 1988 s 468H (interpretation).
TA 1988 s 468H(6) (this section does not apply to an authorised unit trust which is also an approved personal pension scheme).
TA 1988 s 468Q (dividend distribution to corporate unit holder).
Modification—This section is modified, in relation to open-ended investment companies, by the Open-ended Investment Companies (Tax) Regulations 1997, SI 1997/1154, reg 9.
Amendments—¹ This section inserted by FA 1994 Sch 14 paras 1, 2, 7 in relation to distribution periods beginning after 31 March 1994, but subject to FA 1994 Sch 14 para 7(2).
² Words in sub-ss (1), (2) and whole of sub-s (3) repealed by F(No 2)A 1997 s 36(4), Sch 6 para 8(3), (9), Sch 8 Pt II(11) with effect for distribution periods the distribution date for which falls after 5 April 1999.

[468K Foreign income distributions

Definitions—"Authorised unit trust", s 832(1); "distribution", s 832(1); "distribution account", s 468H(3); "distribution date", s 468H(3); "foreign income dividend", s 468H(5); "the Tax Acts", s 831(2); "unit holder", s 832(1).
Cross references—See TA 1988 s 468H (interpretation).

TA 1988 s 468H(6) (this section does not apply to an authorised unit trust which is also an approved personal pension scheme).
Amendments—¹ This section (originally inserted by FA 1994 Sch 14, paras, 1, 2, 7 for distribution periods beginning after 31 March 1994, but subject to FA 1994 Sch 14 para 7(2)) is repealed by F(No 2)A 1997 s 36(4), Sch 6 para 8(4), (9), Sch 8 Pt II(11) with effect for distribution periods the distribution date for which falls after 5 April 1999.

*[Interest distributions]*¹

[468L Interest distributions

(1) Subsection (2) below applies where the total amount shown in the distribution accounts as available for distribution to unit holders is shown as available for distribution as yearly interest.

[(1A) For the purposes of this Chapter no amount shall be shown as so available unless the authorised unit trust in question satisfies the qualifying investments test throughout the distribution period.]²

(2) The Tax Acts shall have effect (subject to what follows) as if the total amount were payments of yearly interest made on the distribution date by the company referred to in section 468(1) to the unit holders in proportion to their rights.

(3) In the following provisions of this Chapter ''an interest distribution'' means a payment of yearly interest treated as made by virtue of subsection (2) above.

(4) The obligation under section 349(2) to deduct a sum in its application to an interest distribution is subject to sections 468M and 468N (and, in its application to an interest distribution to a unit holder in respect of his accumulation units, is an obligation to deduct a sum out of the amount being invested on the unit holder's behalf).

(5) [Nothing in subsection (2) above or Chapter II of Part IV of the Finance Act 1996 (loan relationships) shall require any amount relating to an interest distribution to be brought into account for the purposes of that Chapter otherwise than by virtue of paragraph 4(4) of Schedule 10 to that Act; but the interest distributions of an authorised unit trust for a distribution period]³ shall be allowed as a deduction against the profits of the authorised unit trust for the accounting period in which the last day of that distribution period falls.

(6) The deduction mentioned in subsection (5) above may be made—

(*a*) in computing the total profits for the accounting period, after the deduction of any expenses deductible in computing profits apart from section 75 and either before or after the deduction under that section of sums disbursed as expenses of management; or

(*b*) against total profits as reduced by any other relief from tax or against total profits not so reduced.

(7) Where in any accounting period the amount deductible by virtue of subsection (5) above exceeds the amount from which the deduction is made—

(*a*) the excess may be carried forward to the succeeding accounting period; and

(*b*) the amount so carried forward shall be treated as if it were deductible in that succeeding accounting period by virtue of subsection (5) above.

[(8) For the purposes of this section an authorised unit trust satisfies the qualifying investments test throughout a distribution period (''the relevant period'') if at all times in that period, the market value of the qualifying investments exceeds 60 per cent of the market value of all the investments of that trust.]²

[(9) Subject to subsection (13) below, in this section ''qualifying investments'', in relation to an authorised unit trust, means the investments of that trust which are of any of the following descriptions—

(*a*) money placed at interest;

(*b*) securities;

(*c*) shares in a building society;

(*d*) qualifying entitlements to a share in the investments of another authorised unit trust.

[(*e*) qualifying shares in an open-ended investment company.]⁴]²

[(*f*) derivative contracts whose underlying subject matter consists wholly of any one or more of the matters referred to in paragraphs (*a*) to (*e*) above;]⁶

[(*g*) contracts for differences whose underlying subject matter consists wholly of interest rates or creditworthiness or both of those matters.]⁶

[(10) For the purposes of subsection (9) above an entitlement to a share in the investments of another authorised unit trust is a qualifying entitlement at any time in the relevant period if, and only if, the other authorised unit trust would itself (on the relevant assumption) satisfy the qualifying investments test throughout that period.]²

[(11) For the purposes of subsection (10) above the relevant assumption is that the only investments of the other authorised unit trust which are to be regarded as qualifying investments are those falling within paragraphs (*a*) to (*c*)[, (*f*) and (*g*)]⁶ of subsection (9) above.]²

[(12) In this section ''security'' does not include shares in a company; and references in this section to investments of an authorised unit trust are references to investments subject to the trusts of that authorised unit trust but do not include references to cash awaiting investment.]²

[(12A) For the purposes of subsection (9) above shares in an open-ended investment company are qualifying shares at any time in the relevant period if, and only if, throughout that period the aggregate market value of those investments of the company falling within paragraphs (*a*) to (*c*) of that subsection exceeds 60 per cent of the market value of all its investments.

(12B) In subsection (12A) above references to investments of an open-ended investment company are references to investments comprised in the scheme property of that company, but do not include references to cash awaiting investment.

(12C) In this section—

    "collective investment scheme" has the meaning given by section [235 of the Financial Services and Markets Act 2000][5];

    "open-ended investment company" means, subject to subsection (12D) below, an open-ended investment company within the meaning given by section [236 of the Financial Services and Markets Act 2000][5] which is incorporated in the United Kingdom;

    "scheme property" of an open-ended investment company means, subject to subsection (12E)(*b*) below, the property subject to the collective investment scheme constituted by the company.

(12D) Each of the parts of an umbrella company shall be regarded for the purposes of subsections (9) and (12A) above as an open-ended investment company and the umbrella company as a whole shall not be so regarded and shall not be regarded as a company.

(12E) In relation to a part of an umbrella company—

    (*a*) references in subsections (12A) and (12B) above to investments of an open-ended investment company shall have effect as references to such of the investments as under the arrangements referred to in subsection (12F) below form part of the separate pool to which that part of the umbrella company relates;

    (*b*) the reference in subsection (12B) above to the scheme property of an open-ended investment company shall have effect as if it were a reference to such property subject to the collective investment scheme constituted by the umbrella company as is comprised in the separate pool to which that part of the umbrella company relates;

    (*c*) a person for the time being having rights in that part shall be regarded as the owner of shares in the open-ended investment company which that part is deemed to be by virtue of subsection (12D) above, and not as the owner of shares in the umbrella company itself.

(12F) In subsections (12D) and (12E) above "umbrella company" means a company—

    (*a*) which falls within the definition of "open-ended investment company" in section [236 of the Financial Services and Markets Act 2000][5],

    (*b*) which is incorporated in the United Kingdom,

    (*c*) whose instrument of incorporation provides for arrangements for such pooling as is mentioned in section [235(3)(*a*)][5] of that Act in relation to separate parts of the scheme property of the company, and

    (*d*) the owners of shares in which are entitled to exchange rights in one part for rights in another;

and any reference to a part of an umbrella company is a reference to such of the arrangements as relate to a separate pool.

(12G) For the purposes of subsections (12E) and (12F) above, "owner of shares" in relation to an open-ended investment company means—

    (*a*) the beneficial owner of the shares, or

    (*b*) where the shares are held on trust (other than a bare trust), the trustees of the trust, or

    (*c*) where the shares are comprised in the estate of a deceased person, the deceased's personal representatives.]

[(12H) For the purposes of this section—

    "contract for differences" has the same meaning as in paragraph 12 of Schedule 26 to the Finance Act 2002;

    "derivative contract" means—

        (*a*) a contract which is a derivative contract within the meaning of that Schedule, or

        (*b*) a contract which is, in the accounting period in question, treated as if it were a derivative contract by virtue of paragraph 36 of that Schedule (contracts relating to holdings in unit trust schemes, open-ended investment companies and offshore funds);

    "underlying subject matter" has the same meaning as in paragraph 11 of that Schedule.][6]

[(13) The Treasury may by order amend subsection (9) above so as to extend or restrict the descriptions of investments of an authorised unit trust that are qualifying investments.][2]

[(14) An order made by the Treasury under subsection (13) above may—

    (*a*) make different provision for different cases; and

    (*b*) contain such incidental, supplemental, consequential and transitional provision as the Treasury may think fit;

and, without prejudice to the generality of paragraph (*b*) above, such an order may make such incidental modifications of subsection (11) above as the Treasury may think fit.][2][1]

Commentary—*Simon's Direct Tax Service* **D4.1318, 1319.**
Definitions—"Accounting period", s 834(1); "authorised unit trust", s 832(1); "company", s 832(1) "distribution", s 832(1); "distribution account", s 468H(3); "distribution date", s 468H(3); "distribution period", s 468H(3); "the Tax Acts", s 831(2); "unit holder", s 832(1).
Cross references—See TA 1988 s 468H (interpretation).
TA 1988 s 468H(6) (this section does not apply to an authorised unit trust which is also an approved personal pension scheme).
Modification—This section is modified, in relation to open-ended investment companies, by the Open-ended Investment Companies (Tax) Regulations, SI 1997/1154, regs 5, 7, 9, 13.
Amendments—[1] This section inserted by FA 1994 Sch 14 paras 1, 2, 7 in relation to distribution periods beginning after 31 March 1994, but subject to FA 1994 Sch 14 para 7(2).
[2] Sub-ss (1A), (8)–(14) inserted by FA 1996 Sch 6 para 11 with effect for distribution periods ending after 31 March 1996.
[3] Words in sub-s (5) substituted by FA 1996 Sch 14 para 26 with effect for accounting periods ending after 31 March 1996, subject to transitional provisions in FA 1996 Sch 15.
[4] Sub-s (9)(*e*) added, and sub-ss (12A)-(12G) inserted, by the Authorised Unit Trusts (Interest Distributions) (Qualifying Investments) Order, SI 1997/212, with effect from 25 February 1997.
[5] In sub-s (12C), words in the definition of "collective investment scheme" and "open-ended investment company" substituted, and in sub-s (12F), words in para (*a*) and figure in para (*c*) substituted, by the Financial Services and Markets Act 2000 (Consequential Amendments) (Taxes) Order, SI 2001/3629 arts 13, 38 with effect from 1 December 2001, immediately after the coming into force of the Financial Services and Markets Act 2000 ss 411, 432(1), Sch 20.
[6] In sub-s (9), paras (*f*), (*g*) inserted, words in sub-s (11) inserted, and sub-s (12H) inserted, by FA 2002 s 83(1)(*b*), (3) Sch 27 para s 1, 7 with effect for accounting periods beginning after 30 September 2002.

[468M Deduction of tax (simple case)]

(1) Subsection (2) below applies where—

(*a*) an interest distribution is made for a distribution period to a unit holder; and
(*b*) the gross income entered in the distribution accounts for the purpose of computing the total amount available for distribution to unit holders derives from eligible income entirely.

(2) Where this subsection applies, the obligation to deduct under section 349(2) shall not apply to the interest distribution to the unit holder if the residence condition is on the distribution date fulfilled with respect to him.

(3) Section 468O makes provision with respect to the circumstances in which the residence condition is fulfilled with respect to a unit holder.

(4) Subject to subsection (5) below, in this Chapter "eligible income" means—

(*a*) any interest on a security which falls within paragraph 5(5)(*d*) of Schedule 19AA;
(*b*) ...[4]
[(*cc*) any foreign dividends (as defined by section 18(3D)) and any proceeds falling within section 18(3B)(*a*) or (*b*);][2]
(*f*) any other amount, if it is not subject to income tax by deduction.

(5) "Eligible income" does not include—

(*a*) franked investment income;
(*b*) income under Schedule A;
(*c*) ...[3]
(*d*) any amount afforded relief from taxation imposed under the laws of a territory outside the United Kingdom under arrangements having effect by virtue of section 788 in relation to that territory.][1]

Commentary—*Simon's Direct Tax Service* **D4.1319.**
Definitions—"Distribution", s 832(1); "distribution account", s 468H(3); "distribution date", s 468H(3); "distribution period", s 468H(3); "franked investment income", s 832(1); "interest", s 832(1); "interest distribution", s 468L(3); "Schedule A", s 15; "unit holder", s 832(1); "United Kingdom", s 830.
Cross references—See TA 1988 s 468H (interpretation).
TA 1988 s 468H(6) (this section does not apply to an authorised unit trust which is also an approved personal pension scheme).
Modification—This section is modified, in relation to open-ended investment companies, by the Open-ended Investment Companies (Tax) Regulations, SI 1997/1154, reg 9.
Amendments—[1] This section inserted by FA 1994 Sch 14 paras 1, 2, 7 in relation to distribution periods beginning after 31 March 1994, but subject to FA 1994 Sch 14 para 7(2).
[2] Sub-s (4)(*cc*) substituted for sub-s (4)(*c*)–(*e*) by FA 1996 Sch 7 para 17 with effect for purposes of income tax from the year 1996–97 and so far as relating to corporation tax for accounting periods ending after 31 March 1996.
[3] Sub-s (5)(*c*) repealed by F(No 2)A 1997 s 36(4), Sch 6 para 8(5), (8), Sch 8 Pt II(11) with effect for distribution periods beginning after 5 April 1999.
[4] Sub-s (4)(*b*) repealed by FA 2000 s 156, Sch 40 Pt II(17) with effect for payments of interest made after 31 March 2001.

[468N Deduction of tax (mixed funds)]

(1) Subsection (2) below applies where—

(*a*) an interest distribution is made for a distribution period to a unit holder; and
(*b*) the gross income entered in the distribution accounts for the purposes of computing the total amount available for distribution to unit holders does not derive from eligible income entirely.

(2) Where this subsection applies, the obligation to deduct under section 349(2) shall not apply to the relevant amount of the interest distribution to the unit holder if the residence condition is on the distribution date fulfilled with respect to him.

(3) Section 468O makes provision with respect to the circumstances in which the residence condition is fulfilled with respect to a unit holder.

(4) This is how to calculate the relevant amount of the interest distribution—

$$R = A \times \frac{B}{C}$$

Where—

R = the relevant amount;

A = the amount of the interest distribution before deduction of tax to the unit holder in question;

B = such amount of the gross income as derives from eligible income;

C = the amount of the gross income.

(5) In subsection (4) above the references to the gross income are references to the gross income entered as mentioned in subsection (1)(b) above.]¹

Commentary—*Simon's Direct Tax Service* **D4.1319.**
Definitions—''Distribution'', s 832(1); ''distribution account'', s 468H(3); ''distribution date'', s 468H(3); ''distribution period'', s 468H(3); ''eligible income'', s 468M(4), (5); ''franked investment income'', s 832(1); ''interest distribution'', s 468L(3); ''unit holder'', s 832(1).
Modification—This section is modified, in relation to open-ended investment companies, by the Open-ended Investment Companies (Tax) Regulations, SI 1997/1154, reg 9.
Cross references—See TA 1988 s 468H (interpretation).
TA 1988 s 468H(6) (this section does not apply to an authorised unit trust which is also an approved personal pension scheme).
Amendments—¹ This section inserted by FA 1994 Sch 14 paras 1, 2, 7 in relation to distribution periods beginning after 31 March 1994, but subject to FA 1994 Sch 14 para 7(2).

[468O Residence condition

(1) For the purposes of sections 468M and 468N, the residence condition is fulfilled with respect to a unit holder if—

(a) there is a valid declaration made by him that he is not ordinarily resident in the United Kingdom; or

(b) he holds the rights as a personal representative of a unit holder and—

(i) before his death the deceased made a declaration valid at the time of his death that he was not ordinarily resident in the United Kingdom; or

(ii) the personal representative has made a declaration that the deceased, immediately before his death, was not ordinarily resident in the United Kingdom.

(2) For the purposes of sections 468M and 468N, the residence condition is also fulfilled with respect to a unit holder if the unit holder is a company and there is a valid declaration made by the company that it is not resident in the United Kingdom.

(3) The Board may by regulations make such provision as appears to them to be necessary or expedient modifying the application of this section and section 468P in relation to interest distributions made to or received under a trust.

(4) Regulations under subsection (3) above may—

(a) make different provision for different cases; and

(b) contain such supplementary, incidental, consequential or transitional provision as appears to the Board to be appropriate.]¹

Commentary—*Simon's Direct Tax Service* **D4.1319.**
Regulations—IT (Authorised Unit Trusts) (Interest Distributions) Regulations, SI 1994/2318.
Definitions—''The Board'', s 832(1); ''company'', s 832(1); ''interest distribution'', s 468L(3); ''unit holder'', s 832(1); ''United Kingdom'', s 830.
Cross references—See TA 1988 s 468H (interpretation).
TA 1988 s 468H(6) (this section does not apply to an authorised unit trust which is also an approved personal pension scheme).
TA 1988 s 468P (residence declaration).
Modifications—This section has effect with the substitution of sub-ss (1) and (2) above in relation to an interest distribution made to or received under a trust, see IT (Authorised Unit Trusts) (Interest Distributions) Regulations, SI 1994/2318 regs 3, 4 and 6.
This section is modified, in relation to open-ended investment companies, by the Open-ended Investment Companies (Tax) Regulations, SI 1997/1154, reg 9.
Amendments—¹ This section inserted by FA 1994 Sch 14 paras 1, 2, 7 in relation to distribution periods beginning after 31 March 1994, but subject to FA 1994 Sch 14 para 7(2).

[468P Residence declarations

(1) A declaration made for the purposes of section 468O must—

(a) be in such form as may be required or authorised by the Board;

(b) be made in writing to the trustees of the authorised unit trust in question; and

(c) contain any details or undertakings required by subsections (2) to (4) below.

(2) A declaration made as mentioned in section 468O(1)(a) or (b)(i) must contain—

(a) the name and principal residential address of the person making it; and

(b) an undertaking that he will notify the trustees if he becomes ordinarily resident in the United Kingdom.

(3) A declaration made as mentioned in section 468O(1)(b)(ii) must contain the name of the deceased and his principal residential address immediately before his death.

(4) A declaration made as mentioned in section 468O(2) must contain—

(*a*) the name of the company making it and the address of its registered or principal office; and
(*b*) an undertaking that the company will notify the trustees if it becomes resident in the United Kingdom.

(5) For the purposes of determining whether an interest distribution should be made with or without any deduction, the trustees may not treat a declaration as valid if—

(*a*) they receive a notification in compliance with an undertaking under subsection (2) or (4) above that the person in question has become ordinarily resident or, as the case may be, resident in the United Kingdom; or
(*b*) they come into possession of information by some other means which indicates that the person in question is or may be ordinarily resident or, as the case may be, resident in the United Kingdom;

but, subject to that, they are entitled to treat the declaration as valid.

(6) The trustees shall, on being required to do so by a notice given by an officer of the Board, make available for inspection by such an officer any declarations made to them under this section or any specified declaration or description of declarations.

(7) Where a notice has been given to the trustees under subsection (6) above, the declarations shall be made available within such time as may be specified in the notice and the person carrying out the inspection may take copies of or extracts from them.

(8) The Board may by regulations make provision for giving effect to this section, including in particular provision requiring trustees and managers of authorised unit trusts to supply information and make available books, documents and other records for inspection on behalf of the Board.

(9) Regulations under subsection (8) above may—

(*a*) make different provision for different cases; and
(*b*) contain such supplementary, incidental, consequential or transitional provision as appears to the Board to be appropriate.]¹

Commentary—*Simon's Direct Tax Service* **D4.1319.**
Regulations—IT (Authorised Unit Trusts) (Interest Distributions) Regulations, SI 1994/2318.
Definitions—"Authorised unit trust", s 832(1); "the Board", s 832(1); "company", s 832(1); "interest distribution", s 468L(3); "notice", s 832(1); "United Kingdom", s 830.
Cross references—See TA 1988 s 468H (interpretation).
TA 1988 s 468H(6) (this section does not apply to an authorised unit trust which is also an approved personal pension scheme).
Modifications—This section has effect with the substitution of sub-s (2) and of words in sub-ss (1)(*c*), (5)(*a*), (*b*) above and the omission of sub-ss (3) and (4) above in relation to an interest distribution made to or received under a trust, see IT (Authorised Unit Trusts) (Interest Distributions) Regulations, SI 1994/2318 regs 3, 5, 6.
This section is modified, in relation to open-ended investment companies, by the Open-ended Investment Companies (Tax) Regulations, SI 1997/1154, reg 9.
Amendments—¹ This section inserted by FA 1994 Sch 14 paras 1, 2, 7 in relation to distribution periods beginning after 31 March 1994, but subject to FA 1994 Sch 14 para 7(2).

*[Distributions to corporate unit holder]*¹

[468Q Dividend distribution to corporate unit holder

(1) Subsection (2) below applies where—

(*a*) a dividend distribution for a distribution period is made to a unit holder by the trustees of an authorised unit trust; and
(*b*) on the distribution date for that distribution period the unit holder is within the charge to corporation tax.

(2) For the purpose of computing corporation tax chargeable in the case of the unit holder the unfranked part of the dividend distribution shall be deemed—

(*a*) to be an annual payment and not a dividend distribution, ...² or an interest distribution; and
(*b*) to have been received by the unit holder after deduction of income tax at the lower rate for the year of assessment in which the distribution date falls, from a corresponding gross amount.

(3) This is how to calculate the unfranked part of the dividend distribution—

$$\left[U = \frac{A \times C}{D} \right]^2$$

Where—

U = the unfranked part of the dividend distribution to the unit holder;
A = the amount of the dividend distribution;
...²
[C = such amount of the gross income as does not derive from franked investment income, as reduced by an amount equal to the trustees' net liability to corporation tax in respect of the gross income]³
[D = the amount of the gross income, as reduced by an amount equal to the trustees' net liability to corporation tax in respect of the gross income]³

[(3A) Any reference in this section to the trustees' net liability to corporation tax in respect of the gross income is a reference to the amount of the liability of the trustees of the authorised unit trust to corporation tax in respect of that gross income less the amount (if any) of any reduction of that liability which is given or falls to be given in accordance with any arrangements having effect by virtue of section 788 or by way of a credit under section 790(1).][3]

(4) ...[2]

(5) Where the unit holder is on the distribution date the manager of the scheme, subsection (2) above shall not apply in so far as the rights in respect of which the dividend distribution is made are held by him in the ordinary course of his business as manager of the scheme.

[(5A) Where, in relation to a dividend distribution, any tax is deemed to have been deducted by virtue of the application of subsection (2)(b) above, the amount to which the unit holder is entitled by way of repayment of that tax shall not exceed the amount of the unit holder's portion of the trustees' net liability to corporation tax in respect of the gross income.

(5B) For the purposes of subsection (5A) above the unit holder's portion shall be determined by reference to the proportions in which unit holders have rights in the authorised unit trust in the distribution period in question.

(5C) The trustees of the authorised unit trust shall in the appropriate statement sent to the unit holder under section 234A include a statement showing their net liability to corporation tax in respect of the gross income.][3]

(6) For the purposes of this section the references to the gross income are references to the gross income entered in the distribution accounts for the purpose of computing the total amount available for distribution to unit holders for the distribution period in question.][1]

Commentary—*Simon's Direct Tax Service* D4.1316.
Definitions—"Authorised unit trust", s 832(1); "basic rate", s 832(1); "distribution account", s 468H(3); "distribution date", s 468H(3); "distribution period", s 468H(3); "foreign income distribution", s 468K; "franked investment income", s 832(1); "franked investment income", s 832(1); "interest distribution", s 468L(3); "lower rate", s 832(1); "unit holder", s 832(1); "year of assessment", s 832(1).
Cross references—See TA 1988 s 468H (interpretation).
TA 1988 s 468H(6) (this section does not apply to an authorised unit trust which is also an approved personal pension scheme).
TA 1988 s 468R(2) (modification of this section in its application to foreign income distributions to corporate unit holders).
Modification—This section is modified, in relation to open-ended investment companies, by the Open-ended Investment Companies (Tax) Regulations, SI 1997/1154, reg 9.
Amendments—[1] This section inserted by FA 1994 Sch 14 paras 1, 2, 7 in relation to distribution periods beginning after 31 March 1994, but subject to FA 1994 Sch 14 para 7(2).
[2] Words in sub-s (2)(a), and whole of sub-s (4), repealed and in sub-s (3) formula substituted, and definition of "B" repealed by F(No 2)A 1997 s 36(4), Sch 6 para 8(6), (8), Sch 8 Pt II(11) with effect for distribution periods beginning after 5 April 1999.
[3] In sub-s (3) definitions of "C" and "D" substituted and sub-ss (3A), (5A), (5B), (5C) inserted by FA 1998 Sch 3 para 27, with effect for distribution periods beginning after 5 April 1999.

[468R Foreign income distribution to corporate unit holder]

Amendments—[1] This section repealed by F(No 2)A 1997 s 36(4), Sch 6 para 8(7), (9), Sch 8 Pt II(11) with effect for distribution periods the distribution date for which falls after 5 April 1999 (originally inserted by FA 1994 Sch 14 paras 1, 2, 7).

469 Other unit trusts

(1) This section applies to—

    (a) any unit trust scheme [that is neither an authorised unit trust nor an umbrella scheme][2]; ...[6]
    (b) ...[6]

except where the trustees of the scheme are not resident in the United Kingdom.

(2) Income arising to the trustees of the scheme shall be regarded for the purposes of the Tax Acts as income of the trustees (and not as income of the unit holders) [and, in the case of income to which section 1A applies, chargeable to income tax at the basic rate, instead of at the [rate applicable in accordance with subsection (1A) of that section][8]][5]; and the trustees (and not the unit holders) shall be regarded as the persons to or on whom allowances or charges are to be made under the provisions of those Acts relating to relief for capital expenditure.

[(2A) Section 231(1) shall not apply where the recipent of the distribution there mentioned is the trustees of the scheme.][8]

[(2B) Section 233(1) shall not apply where the person there mentioned is the trustees of the scheme.][8]

(3) For the purposes of the Tax Acts the unit holders shall be treated as receiving annual payments (made by the trustees under deduction of tax) in proportion to their rights.
...[6]

(4) The total amount of those annual payments in respect of any distribution period shall be the amount which, after deducting income tax at the basic rate in force for the year of assessment in which the payments are treated as made, is equal to the aggregate amount shown in the accounts of the scheme as income available for payment to unit holders or for investment.

(5) The date on which the annual payments are treated as made shall be the date or latest date provided by the terms of the scheme for any distribution in respect of the distribution period in question, except that, if—

    (a) the date so provided is more than 12 months after the end of the period; or
    (b) no date is so provided,

the date on which the payments are treated as made shall be the last day of the period.

[(5A) Subsection (5B) below applies where for any year of assessment—

    (*a*) the trustees are (or, apart from this subsection, would be) chargeable under section 350 with tax on payments treated as made by them under subsection (3) above, and

    (*b*) there is an uncredited surplus in the case of the scheme.]¹

[(5B) Where this subsection applies, the amount on which the trustees would otherwise be so chargeable shall be reduced—

    (*a*) if the surplus is greater than that amount, to nil, or

    (*b*) if it is not, by an amount equal to the surplus.]¹

[(5C) For the purposes of subsections (5A) and (5B) above whether there is an uncredited surplus for a year of assessment in the case of a scheme (and, if so, its amount) shall be ascertained by—

    (*a*) determining, for each earlier year of assessment in which the income on which the trustees were chargeable to tax by virtue of subsection (2) above exceeded the amount treated by subsection (3) above as annual payments received by the unit holders, the amount of the excess,

    (*b*) aggregating the amounts determined in the case of the scheme under paragraph (*a*) above, and

    (*c*) deducting from that aggregate the total of any reductions made in the case of the scheme under subsection (5B) above for earlier years of assessment.]¹

[(5D) The references in subsection (5C)(*a*) above to subsections (2) and (3) above include references to subsections (2) and (3) of section 354A of the 1970 Act.]¹

(6) In this section "distribution period" [means a period beginning on or after 1st April 1987 over which income from the investments subject to the trusts is aggregated for the purposes of ascertaining the amount available for distribution to unit holders, but]⁴—

    (*a*) if the scheme does not make provision for distribution periods, then for the purposes of this section its distribution periods shall be taken to be successive periods of 12 months the first of which began with the day on which the scheme took effect; and

    (*b*) if the scheme makes provision for distribution periods of more than 12 months, then for the purposes of this section each of those periods shall be taken to be divided into two (or more) distribution periods, the second succeeding the first after 12 months (and so on for any further periods).

[(6A) In this section "umbrella scheme" has the same meaning as in section 468.]³

(7) In this section "unit trust scheme" has the same meaning as in the [Financial Services and Markets Act 2000]⁹ except that the Treasury may by regulations provide that any scheme of a description specified in the regulations shall be treated as not being a unit trust scheme for the purposes of this section.

(8) Regulations under this section may contain such supplementary and transitional provisions as appear to the Treasury to be necessary or expedient.

(9) Sections 686[, 686A]⁸ and 687 shall not apply to a scheme to which this section applies [except as respects income to which section 686 is treated as applying by virtue of paragraph 7 of Schedule 5AA]⁷.

(10) Section 720(5) shall not apply in relation to profits or gains treated as received by the trustees of a scheme to which this section applies if or to the extent that those profits or gains represent accruals of interest (within the meaning of Chapter II of Part XVII) which are treated as income in the accounts of the scheme.

(11) This section shall have effect in relation to distribution periods beginning on or after 6th April 1987.

Commentary—*Simon's Direct Tax Service* D4.1325–1327.

Regulations—IT (Definition of Unit Trust Scheme) Regulations, SI 1988/267.

IT (Pension Funds Pooling Schemes) Regulations, SI 1996/1585.

Concession B34—In calculating relief under sub-s (5A) above, an amount, calculated as specified in the Concession, in respect of all distribution periods beginning before 6 April 1987 may be included. That amount is treated as an "excess amount" under sub-s (5C)(*a*).

Revenue Internal Guidance—Inspector's manual IM 4181 (foreign income: double tax relief: worked example).

IM 4186 (sub-ss (5), (6) apply to interim distributions).

IM 4188 (returned equalisation is not a distribution and is a capital receipt of the unit holder).

IM 4189 (unrecovered income distributed to the manager is part of income available for distribution and is an annual payment received by the manager).

IM 4190 (sub-s (4) for interim distributions only, the annual payment is the amount actually distributed).

IM 4192–4205 (liability under s 350: worked examples).

Definitions—"Authorised unit trust", s 832(1); "basic rate", s 832(1); "deduction of income tax", s 4(1); "profits or gains", s 833(1); "the Tax Acts", s 831(2); "unit holders", s 832(1); "year of assessment", s 832(1).

Cross references—See TA 1988 s 246D(4) (treatment of foreign income dividend received by trustees of unit trust scheme).

TA 1988 s 592(10) (sub-s (3) above not to apply to authorised unit trusts which are also exempt approved retirement benefit schemes in certain circumstances).

FA 1990 Sch 10 para 19 (transfer or redemption of qualifying convertible securities by trustees not to be chargeable to tax at the rate applicable to trusts to the extent that the income is income of a scheme under this section).

F(No 2)A 1997 s 29 (qualifying distribution made between 2 July 1997 and 5 April 1999 inclusive and falling to be treated as income of a unit trust within this section is to be treated as if it were a foreign income dividend).

IT (Pension Funds Pooling Schemes) Regulations, SI 1996/1585 reg 3 (unit trust scheme which is a pension funds pooling scheme is treated as *not* being a unit trust scheme for purposes of this section).

Modification—This section is modified, in relation to open-ended investment companies, by the Open-ended Investment Companies (Tax) Regulations, SI 1997/1154, regs 5, 7, 9, 13.

Amendments—¹ Sub-ss (5A)–(5D) inserted by FA 1988 s 71.

[469A Court common investment funds

(1) The Tax Acts shall have effect in relation to any common investment fund established under section 42 of the Administration of Justice Act 1982 (common investment funds for money paid into court) as if—

   (*a*) the fund were an authorised unit trust;
   (*b*) the person who is for the time being the investment manager of the fund were the trustee of that authorised unit trust; and
   (*c*) the persons whose interests entitle them, as against the Accountant General, to share in the fund's investments were the unit holders in that authorised unit trust.

(2) In this section "the Accountant General" means (subject to subsection (3) below) the Accountant General of the Supreme Court of Judicature in England and Wales or the Accountant General of the Supreme Court of Judicature of Northern Ireland.

(3) Where in the case of any common investment fund a person other than the Accountant General is authorised by the Lord Chancellor to hold shares in the fund, the reference in subsection (1)(*c*) above to the Accountant General shall include a reference to that other person.][1]

Commentary— *Simon's Direct Tax Service* **D4.1340.**
Definitions—"common investment fund", FA 1999 s 68(5).
Cross references—See FA 1999 s 68(4) (transitional rules concerning common investment funds in existence on 5 April 1999).
Amendments—[1] This section inserted by FA 1999 s 68(1), (3) with effect for any income arising to a common investment fund after 5 April 1999, and any distribution made by such a fund for a distribution period beginning after that date.

470 Transitional provisions relating to unit trusts

Amendments—Sub-s (2) ceased to have effect on 29 April 1988 by virtue of sub-s (3) and TA 1988 (Appointed Day) Order, SI 1988/745. Sub-ss (1), (3) spent.

Dealers in securities, banks and insurance businesses

471 Exchange of securities in connection with conversion operations, nationalisation etc

Commentary—*Simon's Direct Tax Service* **D4.412.**
Amendments—This section repealed by FA 1998 s 101(1) with effect for exchanges made after 31 July 1998.

472 Distribution of securities issued in connection with nationalisation etc

Commentary—*Simon's Direct Tax Service* **D4.412.**
Amendments—This section repealed by FA 1998 s 101(2) with effect for issues of securities occurring after 31 July 1998.

473 Conversion etc of securities held as circulating capital

(1) Subsections (3) and (4) below shall have effect where a transaction to which this section applies occurs in relation to any securities ("the original holding")—

   (*a*) to which a person carrying on a banking business, an insurance business or a business consisting wholly or partly in dealing in securities is beneficially entitled; and
   (*b*) which are such that a profit on their sale would form part of the trading profits of that business.

(2) This section applies to any transaction which ...[5]—

   (*a*) [results][5] in the original holding being equated with a new holding by virtue of sections [126 to 136 of the 1992 Act][1] (capital gains tax roll-over relief in cases of conversion etc); or
   (*b*) [is][5] treated by virtue of section [134][1] of that Act (compensation stock) as an exchange for a new holding which does not involve a disposal of the original holding.
...[3]

[(2A) This section does not apply to securities in respect of which unrealised profits or losses, calculated by reference to the fair value of the securities at the end of a period of account, are taken into account in the period of account in which the transaction mentioned in subsection (2) above occurs.][5]

[(2B) Subsection (2A) above shall be disregarded in determining for the purposes of section 65 of the Finance Act 2002 (election to continue postponement of mark to market) whether an asset was held by a person on 1st January 2002.][5]

(3) Subject to subsection (4) below, in making any computation in accordance with the provisions of this Act applicable to Case I of Schedule D of the profits or losses of the business—

(*a*) the transaction shall be treated as not involving any disposal of the original holding, and

(*b*) the new holding shall be treated as the same asset as the original holding.

(4) Where under the transaction the person concerned receives or becomes entitled to receive any consideration in addition to the new holding, subsection (3) above shall have effect as if references to the original holding were references to the proportion of it which the market value of the new holding at the time of the transaction bears to the aggregate of that value and the market value at that time (or, if it is cash, the amount) of the consideration.

(5) ...[2]

(6) In this section "securities" includes shares, any security within the meaning of section [132 of the 1992 Act][1] and any rights, interests or options which by virtue of section [[135(5), 136(5)][4], 147 or 99][1] of that Act are treated as shares for the purposes of sections [126 to 136][1] of that Act.

(7) In determining for the purposes of subsection (2)(*a*) above whether a transaction [results][5] in the original holding being equated with a new holding by virtue of section [135 or 136 of the 1992 Act][1] the reference in section [137(1)][1] of that Act to capital gains tax shall be construed as a reference to income tax.

Commentary—*Simon's Direct Tax Service* **D4.412.**
Concession D27—Where consideration for disposal of shares by an investment dealing company includes a right to an unascertained number of new shares at a later date (earn out element), this concession allows any CGT to be deferred if certain conditions are satisfied.
Definitions—"The 1992 Act", s 831(3); "Schedule D", s 18(1).
Cross references—See TA 1988 s 730C(5) (disapplication of sub-ss (3), (4) in relation to exchanges of gilt-edged securities for strips of that security and consolidation of strips into a gilt-edged security).
FA 1999 s 81(9) (application of this section in relation to acquisitions disregarded under insurance companies concession).
Amendments—[1] Words in sub-ss (2), (5), (6), (7) substituted by TCGA 1992 Sch 10 para 14(1), (27).
[2] Sub-s (5) repealed by FA 1996 Sch 41 Pt V(24) with effect for accounting periods beginning after 31 December 1995.
[3] Words after sub-s (2)(*b*) repealed by FA 1998 Sch 27 Part III(23) with effect for exchanges made after 31 July 1998.
[4] Figures "135(5), 136(5)" substituted for "135(5)" by FA 2002 s 45, Sch 9 paras 4(1), (4), 7(1), 8(2) with effect for transactions to which this section applies occurring after 16 April 2002.
[5] In sub-s (2), words ", if the securities were not such as are mentioned in subsection (1)(*b*) above" repealed; in sub-ss (2)(*a*), (7), word substituted for the words "would result"; in sub-s (2)(*b*), word substituted for the words "would be"; and sub-ss (2A), (2B) inserted by FA 2002 ss 67(1), (2), (4)(*a*), 141, Sch 40 Pt 3(8) with effect for periods of account ending after 31 July 2001.

474 Treatment of tax-free income

Commentary—*Simon's Direct Tax Service* **B3.1112.**
Amendments—This section repealed by FA 1996 Sch 7 para 18 (sub-ss (1), (3)), Sch 28 para 2 (sub-s (2)), Sch 41 Pt V(2), (18) with effect from the year 1996–97 for the purposes of income tax, and as respects corporation tax for accounting periods ending after 31 March 1996.

475 Tax-free Treasury securities: exclusion of interest on borrowed money

[(1) This section has effect where a banking business, an insurance business or a business consisting wholly or partly in dealing in securities—

(*a*) is carried on in the United Kingdom by a person not ordinarily resident there; and

(*b*) in computing for any of the purposes of the Tax Acts the profits arising from, or loss sustained, in the business, any amount which would otherwise be brought into account is disregarded by virtue of a condition subject to which any 3½ % War Loan 1952 or after was issued;

and for this purpose insurance business includes insurance business of any category.][2]

(2) Up to the amount determined under this section ("the amount ineligible for relief"), interest on money borrowed for the purposes of the business—

(*a*) shall be excluded in any computation under the Tax Acts of the profits (or losses) arising from the business ...[1], and

[(*b*) shall not be brought into account by way of any debit given for the purposes of Chapter II of Part IV of the Finance Act 1996 (loan relationships).][3]

(3) Subject to subsection (4) below, in determining the amount ineligible for relief, account shall be taken of all money borrowed for the purposes of the business which is outstanding in the accounting or basis period, up to the total cost of the [3½ % War Loan 1952 or after][2] held for the purpose of the business in that period.

(4) Where the person carrying on the business is a company, account shall not be taken of any borrowed money carrying interest which, apart from subsection (2) above, does not fall to be included in the computations under paragraph (*a*) of that subsection, [or to be brought into account by way of a debit given for the purposes of Chapter II of Part IV of the Finance Act 1996 (loan relationships).][3]

(5) ...[2] the amount ineligible for relief shall be equal to a year's interest on the amount of money borrowed which is to be taken into account under subsection (3) above at a rate equal to the average rate of interest in the accounting or basis period on money borrowed for the purposes of the business, except that in the case of a period of less than 12 months interest shall be taken for that shorter period instead of for a year.

(6), (7) ...[2]

(8) For the purposes of this section the cost of a holding of [3½ % War Loan 1952 or after][2] which has fluctuated in the accounting or basis period shall be the average cost of acquisition of the initial holding, and of any subsequent acquisitions in the accounting or basis period, applied to the average amount of the holding in the accounting or basis period, ...[2]

(9) In this section "accounting or basis period" means the company's accounting period or the period by reference to which the profits or gains arising in the year of assessment are to be computed.

Commentary—*Simon's Direct Tax Service* **B3.1112.**
Definitions—"Accounting period", s 834(1); "company", s 832(1), (2); "interest", s 832(1); "profits or gains", s 833(1); "the Tax Acts", s 831(2); "year of assessment", s 832(1).
Amendments—[1] Words omitted from sub-s (2)(a) repealed by FA 1995 Sch 8 paras 25(1)(b), 55, Sch 29 Pt VIII(5), with effect for accounting periods beginning after 31 October 1994 (subject to FA 1995 Sch 8 para 55(2)).
[2] Sub-s (1) and words in sub-ss (3), (8) substituted and words in sub-ss (5), (8) and whole of sub-ss (6), (7) repealed by FA 1996 Sch 28 para 3, Sch 41 Pt V(18) with effect for accounting periods ending after 31 March 1996.
[3] Sub-s (2)(b) and words in sub-s (4) substituted by FA 1996 Sch 14 para 27 with effect for accounting periods ending after 31 March 1996, subject to transitional provisions in FA 1996 Sch 15.

CHAPTER IV
BUILDING SOCIETIES, BANKS, SAVINGS BANKS, INDUSTRIAL AND PROVIDENT SOCIETIES AND OTHERS

476 Building societies: regulations for payment of tax

Amendments—This section repealed by FA 1990 Sch 5 para 2 and Sch 19, Pt IV with effect from the year 1991–92.

477 Investments becoming or ceasing to be relevant building society investments

Amendments—This section repealed by FA 1990 Sch 5 para 3 and Sch 19, Pt IV with effect after 5 April 1991.

[477A Building societies: regulations for deduction of tax

(1) The Board may by regulations make provision with respect to any year of assessment requiring any building society—

(a) in such cases as may be prescribed by the regulations to deduct out of any dividend or interest paid or credited in the year in respect of shares in, or deposits with or loans to, the society a sum representing the amount of income tax on it, and
(b) to account for and pay any amount required to be deducted by the society by virtue of this subsection.

[(1A) Regulations under subsection (1) above may not make provision with respect to any dividend or interest paid or credited, on or after the day on which the Finance Act 1991 was passed, in respect of a security (other than a qualifying certificate of deposit [and other than a qualifying deposit right][3]) which was [listed][5], or capable of being [listed][5], on a recognised stock exchange at the time the dividend or interest became payable.][2]

(2) Regulations under subsection (1) above may—

(a) make provision with respect to the furnishing of information by building societies or their investors, including, in the case of societies, the inspection of books, documents and other records on behalf of the Board;
(b) contain such incidental and consequential provisions as appear to the Board to be appropriate, including provisions requiring the making of returns.

[(2A) Without prejudice to the generality of subsection (2)(a) above, regulations under subsection (1) above may make provision with respect to the furnishing of information to or by building societies corresponding to any provision that is made by, or may be made under, section 482 with respect to the furnishing of information to or by deposit-takers.][8]

(3) For any year of assessment to which regulations under subsection (1) above apply, dividends or interest payable in respect of shares in, or deposits with or loans to, a building society shall be dealt with for the purposes of corporation tax as follows—

[(a) [to the extent that it would not otherwise fall to be so regarded,][9] liability to pay the dividends or interest shall be treated for the purposes of Chapter II of Part IV of the Finance Act 1996 as a liability arising under a loan relationship of the building society;
(aa) if the dividends or interest are payable to a company, [then, to the extent that they would not otherwise fall to be so regarded,][9] they shall be treated for those purposes as payable to that company in pursuance of a right arising under a loan relationship of that company;][6]

TA 1988

(*b*) no part of any such dividends or interest paid or credited in the year of assessment shall be treated as a distribution of the society or as franked investment income of any company resident in the United Kingdom.

[(3A), (3B), (3C) ...][4]

(4) Subsection (3)(*a*) above shall apply to any terminal bonus paid by the society under a certified contractual savings scheme as if it were a dividend on a share in the society.

(5) Notwithstanding anything in sections 64, 66 and 67, for any year of assessment to which regulations under subsection (1) above apply income tax chargeable under Case III of Schedule D shall, in the case of any relevant sum, be computed on the full amount of the income arising in the year of assessment.

(6) For the purposes of subsection (5) above a sum is relevant if it is a sum in respect of which a liability to deduct income tax—

(*a*) is imposed by regulations under subsection (1) above, or

(*b*) would be so imposed if a certificate were not supplied, in accordance with the regulations, to the effect that the person beneficially entitled to the sum is unlikely to be liable to pay any amount by way of income tax for the year of assessment in which the sum is paid.

(7) Notwithstanding anything in sections 348 to 350, for any year of assessment to which regulations under subsection (1) above apply income tax shall not be deducted upon payment to the society of any interest on advances, being interest payable in that year.

(8) ...[7]

(9) In this section "dividend" has the meaning given by regulations under subsection (1) above, but any sum which is paid by a building society by way of dividend and which is not paid under deduction of income tax shall be treated for the purposes of Schedule D as paid by way of interest.][1]

[(10) In this section—

"qualifying certificate of deposit" has the same meaning as in section 349, and

["qualifying deposit right" has the meaning given by section 349(4), reading "paid" as "paid or credited", and][3]

"security" includes share.][2]

Commentary—*Simon's Direct Tax Service* **B5.221; D4.703, 705, 727.**
Regulations—IT (Building Societies) (Dividends and Interest) Regulations, SI 1990/2231.
IT (Building Societies) (Audit Powers) Regulations, SI 1992/10.
Concession C22—This concession extends relief under sub-s (3)(*a*) above on dividends and interest shown as *payable* in a building society's accounts.
Definitions—"The Board", s 832(1); "company", s 832(1), (2); "franked investment income", s 832(1); "interest", s 832(1); "loan relationship", s 834(1), FA 1996 s 81; "recognised stock exchange", s 841(1); "Schedule D", s 18; "year of assessment", s 832(1).
Cross references—See TMA 1970 s 99A (penalty for fraud or negligence in relation to a certificate of non-liability to tax issued by virtue of regulations under this section).
TA 1988 s 352(1) (certificate of deduction of tax at source made by virtue of regulations under this section).
TA 1988 s 482A (investments of persons not ordinarily resident in the UK; exclusion of audit powers conferred by sub-s (2)(*a*) above).
FA 1988 Sch 12 para 6(1) (conferral of qualifying benefits on members of a building society which is undergoing a change of status is not to be regarded as the payment or crediting of a dividend for the purposes of this section).
Amendments—[1] This section inserted by FA 1990 Sch 5 para 4 with effect from the year 1991–92.
[2] Sub-ss (1A), (10) inserted by FA 1991 Sch 11 para 2.
[3] Words in sub-ss (1A), (10) inserted by F(No 2)A 1992 Sch 8 paras 3, 6 in relation to arrangements made after 16 July 1992.
[4] Sub-ss (3A), (3B), (3C) (as inserted by FA 1991 s 52(2), (3)) repealed by FA 1996 Sch 14 para 28(2), Sch 41 Pt V(3) with effect for accounting periods ending after 31 March 1996, subject to transitional provisions in FA 1996 Sch 15.
[5] Words in sub-s (1A) substituted by FA 1996 Sch 38 para 6(1), (2)(*g*), (7) with effect for dividends or interest which became payable after 31 March 1996.
[6] Sub-s (3)(*a*), (*aa*) substituted for sub-s (3)(*a*) by FA 1996 Sch 14 para 28(1) with effect for accounting periods ending after 31 March 1996, subject to transitional provisions in FA 1996 Sch 15.
[7] Sub-s (8) repealed by FA 1999 s 139, Sch 20 Pt III(7) with effect for payments of interest made—
–after 5 April 2000;
–after 8 March 1999 and before 6 April 2000 in respect of interest falling due after 5 April 2000; or
–after 8 March 1999 and before 6 April 2000 under a scheme made for a tax avoidance purpose after 8 March 1999.
[8] Sub-s (2A) inserted by FA 2000 s 111(4) with effect from 28 July 2000.
[9] Words inserted in sub-s (3)(*a*), (*aa*) by FA 2002 s 82, Sch 25 paras 43, 47 with effect for accounting periods beginning after 30 September 2002.

[477B Building societies: incidental costs of issuing qualifying shares

(1) In computing for the purposes of corporation tax the income of a building society from the trade carried on by it, there shall be allowed as a deduction, if subsection (2) below applies, the incidental costs of obtaining finance by means of issuing shares in the society which are qualifying shares.

[(1A) A deduction shall not be allowed by virtue of subsection (1) above to the extent that the costs in question fall to be brought into account as debits for the purposes of Chapter 2 of Part 4 of the Finance Act 1996 (loan relationships).][3]

(2) This subsection applies if any amount payable in respect of the shares by way of dividend or interest is deductible in computing for the purposes of corporation tax the income of the society from the trade carried on by it.

(3) In subsection (1) above, "the incidental costs of obtaining finance" means expenditure on fees, commissions, advertising, printing and other incidental matters (but not including stamp duty), being

expenditure wholly and exclusively incurred for the purpose of obtaining the finance (whether or not it is in fact obtained), or of providing security for it or of repaying it.

(4) This section shall not be construed as affording relief—

(*a*) for any sums paid in consequence of, or for obtaining protection against, losses resulting from changes in the rate of exchange between different currencies, or

(*b*) for the cost of repaying qualifying shares so far as attributable to their being repayable at a premium or to their having been issued at a discount.

(5) In this section—

"dividend" has the same meaning as in section 477A, and

"qualifying share" has the same meaning as in section [117(4) of the 1992 Act.][2]

Commentary—*Simon's Direct Tax Service* **D4.705.**
Definitions—"the 1992 Act", s 831(3); "trade", s 832 (1).
Amendments—[1] This section inserted by FA 1991 Sch 10 para 3 for costs incurred after 24 July 1991.
[2] Words in sub-s (5) substituted by TCGA 1992 Sch 10 para 14(1), (28).
[3] Sub-s (1A) inserted by FA 2002 s 82, Sch 25 paras 43, 48 with effect for accounting periods beginning after 30 September 2002.

478 Building societies: time for payment of tax

Amendments—This section repealed by FA 1994 s 199(2), Sch 26 Pt V(23) for accounting periods ending after 30 June 1999 (by virtue of Finance Act 1994, Section 199, (Appointed Day) Order, SI 1998/3173 art 2).

479 Interest paid on deposits with banks etc

Commentary—*Simon's Direct Tax Service* **D4.1116, 1117.**
Amendments—This section repealed by FA 1990 Sch 5 para 5 and Sch 19, Pt IV as regards interest paid or credited after 5 April 1991.

480 Deposits becoming or ceasing to be composite rate deposits

Commentary—*Simon's Direct Tax Service* **D4.1118.**
Amendments—This section repealed by FA 1990 Sch 5 para 6 and Sch 19, Pt IV with effect as regards any time falling after 5 April 1991.

[480A Relevant deposits: deduction of tax from interest payments

(1) Any deposit-taker making a payment of interest in respect of a relevant deposit shall, on making the payment, deduct out of it a sum representing the amount of income tax on it for the year of assessment in which the payment is made.

(2) Any payment of interest out of which an amount is deductible under subsection (1) above shall be a relevant payment for the purposes of Schedule 16 whether or not the deposit-taker making the payment is resident in the United Kingdom.

(3) Schedule 16 shall apply in relation to any payment which is a relevant payment by virtue of subsection (2) above—

(*a*) with the substitution for any reference to a company of a reference to a deposit-taker,

(*b*) as if paragraph 5 applied only in relation to payments received by the deposit-taker and falling to be taken into account in computing his income chargeable to corporation tax, and

(*c*) as if in paragraph 7 the reference to section 7(2) included a reference to sections 11(3) and 349(1).

(4) In relation to any deposit-taker who is not a company, Schedule 16 shall have effect as if—

(*a*) paragraph 5 were omitted, and

(*b*) references to accounting periods were references to periods for which the deposit-taker makes up his accounts.

(5) For the purposes of this section, crediting interest shall be treated as paying it.][1]

Commentary—*Simon's Direct Tax Service* **B5.222; D4.1102.**
Revenue & other press releases—Law Society 4-3-92 (client monies held by solicitors under various headings: detailed application of rules s 480A).
Law Society 9-9-92 (further guidance re monies held by solicitors).
IR 9-2-94 (per EEA Agreement, these provisions apply to any European Union or European Economic Area deposit taker operating a branch in the UK).
IR 30-4-01 (compensation paid by banks on unclaimed accounts held by Holocaust victims are exempt from income tax).
Cross references—See TMA 1970 s 17(4B), (4C) (returns of interest not to include interest where there is no obligation to deduct tax under sub-s (1) above).
TA 1988 s 349(3)(*f*)–(*h*) (no deduction made under s 349(2) from payments which are subject to deduction under sub-s (1) above).
TA 1988 s 352(1) (certificate of deduction of tax at source made under this section).
TA 1988 s 480B(1) (regulations disapplying sub-s (1) above).
TA 1988 s 481 (meaning of "deposit taker", "deposit" and "relevant deposits" for the purposes of this section).
IT (Deposit-takers) (Interest Payments) Regulations, SI 1990/2232 reg 4(1) (sub-s (1) above not to apply in certain circumstances),
IT (Deposit-takers) (Interest Payments) Regulations, SI 1990/2232 reg 6(3)(*d*) (Board may issue notice requiring deduction of tax under sub-s (1) above in certain circumstances in which a certificate of non-liability to tax ceases to be valid),
IT (Deposit-takers) (Interest Payments) Regulations, SI 1990/2232 reg 8(1) (Board may require deposit-taker to deduct tax under sub-s (1) with respect to certain obsolescent accounts),
IT (Deposit-takers) (Interest Payments) Regulations, SI 1990/2232 reg 9(4), (6) (circumstances in which deduction of tax is to be made under sub-s (1) in respect of joint accounts),

IT (Deposit-takers) (Interest Payments) Regulations, SI 1990/2232 reg 11(2) (information to be provided by deposit-taker in respect of interest payments and tax deductions).
Amendments—[1] This section inserted by FA 1990 Sch 5 para 7 as regards interest paid or credited after 5 April 1991.

[480B Relevant deposits: exception from section 480A

(1) The Board may by regulations provide that section 480A(1) shall not apply as regards a payment of interest if such conditions as may be prescribed by the regulations are fulfilled.

(2) In particular, the regulations may include—

(a) provision for a certificate to be supplied to the effect that the person beneficially entitled to a payment is unlikely to be liable to pay any amount by way of income tax for the year of assessment in which the payment is made;

(b) provision for the certificate to be supplied by that person or such other person as may be prescribed by the regulations;

(c) provision about the time when, and the manner in which, a certificate is to be supplied;

(d) provision about the form and contents of a certificate.

(3) Any provision included under subsection (2)(d) above may allow the Board to make requirements, in such manner as they see fit, as to the matters there mentioned.

(4) For the purposes of this section, crediting interest shall be treated as paying it.][1]

Commentary—*Simon's Direct Tax Service* B5.223.
Regulations—IT (Deposit-takers) (Interest Payments) Regulations, SI 1990/2232.
Cross references—See TMA 1970 s 99A (penalty for fraud or negligence in relation to a certificate of non-liability to tax issued by virtue of regulations under this section).
Amendments—[1] This section inserted by FA 1990 Sch 5 para 7 as regards interest paid or credited after 5 April 1991.

[480C Relevant deposits: computation of tax on interest

Notwithstanding anything in sections 64, 66 and 67, income tax chargeable under Case III of Schedule D on interest in respect of a relevant deposit shall be computed on the full amount of the income arising in the year of assessment.][1]

Commentary—*Simon's Direct Tax Service* B5.228.
Cross references—See TA 1988 s 481 (meaning of "relevant deposit" for the purposes of this section).
Amendments—[1] This section inserted by FA 1990 Sch 5 para 7 as regards interest paid or credited after 5 April 1991.

481 "Deposit-taker", "deposit" and "relevant deposit"

(1) In this section "the relevant provisions" means ...[4] this section and section 482.

[(1A) In this section "the relevant provisions" also means sections 480A and 480C.][1]

(2) In the relevant provisions "deposit-taker" means any of the following—

(a) the Bank of England;

[(b) any person falling within section 840A(1)(b) whose permission under Part 4 of the Financial Services and Markets Act 2000 includes permission to accept deposits which are relevant deposits;][10]

[(ba) any company within the meaning of the Companies Act 1985—

(i) in respect of which a resolution has been passed by a local authority under section 48(3) of the Banking Act 1979 or section 103(3) of the Banking Act 1987; and

(ii) which is exempt from the prohibition imposed by section 19 of the Financial Services and Markets Act 2000 in relation to the acceptance of deposits which are relevant deposits;][10]

(c) ...[9]

[(ca) any local authority;][1]

(d) ...[2]

(e) ...[2]; and

(f) any person or class of person who receives deposits in the course of his business or activities and which is for the time being prescribed by order made by the Treasury for the purposes of this paragraph.

(3) In the relevant provisions "deposit" means a sum of money paid on terms under which it will be repaid with or without interest and either on demand or at a time or in circumstances agreed by or on behalf of the person making the payment and the person to whom it is made.

(4) For the purposes of the relevant provisions a deposit is a relevant deposit if, but only if—

(a) the person who is beneficially entitled to any interest in respect of the deposit is an individual or, where two or more persons are so entitled, all of them are individuals; or

(b) in Scotland, the person who is so entitled is a partnership all the partners of which are individuals; or

(c) the person entitled to any such interest receives it as a personal representative in his capacity as such; [or][7]

[(d) any interest in respect of the deposit is income arising to the trustees of a discretionary or accumulation trust in their capacity as such;][7]

and the deposit is not prevented from being a relevant deposit by [any of subsections (5) to (5B)][7] below.

[(4A) For the purposes of the relevant provisions a trust is a discretionary or accumulation trust if it is such that some or all of any income arising to the trustees would fall (unless treated as income of the settlor ...[8]) to be comprised for the year of assessment in which it arises in income to which section 686 applies.][7]

(5) A deposit is not a relevant deposit if—

    (*a*) a qualifying certificate of deposit has been issued in respect of it or it is a qualifying time deposit;

    (*b*) it is a debt on a debenture ("debenture" having the meaning given in section 744 of the Companies Act 1985) issued by the deposit-taker;

    (*c*) it is a loan made by a deposit-taker in the ordinary course of his business or activities;

    (*d*) it is a debt on a security which is listed on a recognised stock exchange;

    (*e*) it is a general client account deposit;

    (*f*) it forms part of a premiums trust fund (within the meaning of [section 184 of the Finance Act 1993) of an underwriting or former underwriting member][6] of Lloyd's;

    (*g*) ...[10]

    (*h*) in the case of a deposit-taker resident in the United Kingdom for the purposes of income tax or corporation tax, it is held at a branch of his situated outside the United Kingdom;

    (*j*) in the case of a deposit-taker who is not so resident, it is held otherwise than at a branch of his situated in the United Kingdom; or

    (*k*) the appropriate person has declared in writing to the deposit-taker liable to pay interest in respect of the deposit ...[7]—

        (i) [in a case falling within subsection (4)(*a*) or (*b*) above, that][7] at the time when the declaration is made, the person who is beneficially entitled to the interest is not, or, as the case may be, all the persons who are so entitled are not, ordinarily resident in the United Kingdom;

        (ii) in a case falling within subsection (4)(*c*) above[, that][7] the deceased was, immediately before his death, not ordinarily resident in the United Kingdom.

        [(iii) in a case falling within subsection (4)(*d*) above, that, at the time when the declaration is made, the trustees are not resident in the United Kingdom and do not have any reasonable grounds for believing that any of the beneficiaries of the trust is an individual who is ordinarily resident in the United Kingdom or a company which is resident in the United Kingdom.][7]

[(5A) In a case where—

    (*a*) there is an arrangement falling within section 56A,

    (*b*) the deposit is with a deposit-taker,

    (*c*) no certificate of deposit, as defined in section 56(5), has been issued in respect of the right at the time the interest mentioned in section 480A or 480C is paid, and

    (*d*) the conditions set out in paragraphs (*a*) and (*b*) in the definition of "qualifying certificate of deposit" in section 482(6) apply,

the deposit is not a relevant deposit.][5]

[(5B) In a case falling within subsection (4)(*d*) above, a deposit shall not be taken to be a relevant deposit in relation to a payment of interest in respect of that deposit if—

    (*a*) the deposit was made before 6th April 1995; and

    (*b*) the deposit-taker has not, at any time since that date but before the making of the payment, been given a notification by the Board or any of the trustees in question that interest in respect of that deposit is income arising to the trustees of a discretionary or accumulation trust.][7]

(6) The Treasury may by order make amendments in this section and sections [480A, 480C][3] ...[4] and 482 providing for deposits of a kind specified in the order to be or, as the case may be, not to be relevant deposits in relation to all deposit-takers or such deposit-takers or classes of deposit-takers as may be so specified.

Commentary—*Simon's Direct Tax Service* B5.221; D4.1104, 1105.

Orders—Various bodies have been prescribed under sub-s (2)(*f*) above as deposit-takers by the Income Tax (Prescribed Deposit-takers) (No 1) Order, SI 1984/1801, the Income Tax (Composite Rate) (Prescribed Deposit-takers) Order, SI 1985/1696 and the Income Tax (Prescribed Deposit-takers) Order, SI 1992/3234.

Definitions—"Appropriate person", s 482(6); "the Board", s 832(1); "company", s 832(1), (2); "general client account deposit", s 482(6); "interest", s 832(1); "qualifying certificate of deposit", s 482(6); "qualifying time deposit", s 482(6); "recognised stock exchange", s 841.

Cross-references—See TMA 1970 s 17(4B), (4C) (returns of interest not to include interest which as a result of a declaration under sub-s(5)(*k*) above is not subject to deduction of tax at source);

Personal Equity Plan Regulations, SI 1989/469 reg 17(2)(*a*) (interest on a cash deposit in a PEP is not treated as a relevant deposit under sub-s (4) above).

IT (Deposit-takers) (Audit Powers) Regulations, SI 1992/12 reg 3(2) (Revenue's powers to require information for determining whether, having regard to this section, a gross payment of interest on non-relevant or excluded deposits is in order),

FA 1995 s 86(12) (Board's power to require information from trustees relating to notifications under sub-s (5B) above).

IT (Prescribed Deposit-Takers) Order, SI 2001/1968 (a person authorised for the purposes of FSMA 2000 and whose business consists wholly or mainly of dealing in financial instruments as principal to a class of person prescribed in relation to all relevant deposits).

Amendments—[1] Sub-ss (1A), (2)(*ca*) inserted by FA 1990 Sch 5 para 8(1)–(3).

[2] Sub-s (2)(*d*), (*e*) repealed by FA 1990 Sch 5 para 8(1), (3), (5) and Sch 19, Pt IV as regards interest paid or credited after 5 April 1991.

[3] Numbers in sub-s (6) inserted by FA 1990 Sch 5 para 8(1), (4).

[4] References in sub-ss (1), (6) above to ss 479, 480 repealed by FA 1990 Sch 19 Pt IV.

[5] Sub-s (5A) inserted by F(No 2)A 1992 Sch 8 paras 4, 6 in relation to arrangements made after 16 July 1992.

[6] Words in sub-s (5)(*f*) substituted by FA 1993 s 183(2) with effect from the year 1992–93 by virtue of FA 1993 s 184(3).

[7] Words in sub-s (4) inserted and substituted respectively, sub-ss (4A), (5B) and words in sub-s (5) inserted, and words omitted from sub-s (5) repealed, in relation to any payments made after 5 April 1996, by FA 1995 s 86(1)–(4), (10), Sch 29 Pt VIII(11).

[8] Words in sub-s (4A) repealed by FA 1997 Sch 18 Pt VI(7) with effect from the year 1996-97.
[9] Sub-s (2)(c) repealed by the Postal Services Act 2000 (Consequential Modifications No 1) Order, SI 2001/1149 art 3, Sch 2 with effect from 26 March 2001.
[10] Sub-s (2)(b), (ba) substituted for sub-s (2)(b), and sub-s (5)(g) repealed, by the Financial Services and Markets Act 2000 (Consequential Amendments) (Taxes) Order, SI 2001/3629 arts 13, 39 with effect from 1 December 2001, immediately after the coming into force of the Financial Services and Markets Act 2000 ss 411, 432(1), Sch 20.

482 Supplementary provisions

(1) For the purposes of sections ...[4] 481 and this section, any amount which is credited as interest in respect of a relevant deposit shall be treated as a payment of interest.

(2) A declaration under section 481(5)(k) shall—

[(a) if made under sub-paragraph (i) or (iii), contain an undertaking by the person making it that where—

(i) the individual or any of the individuals in respect of whom it is made becomes ordinarily resident in the United Kingdom,

(ii) the trustees or any company in respect of whom it is made become or becomes resident in the United Kingdom, or

(iii) an individual who is ordinarily resident in the United Kingdom or a company which is resident in the United Kingdom becomes or is found to be a beneficiary of a trust to which the declaration relates,

the person giving the undertaking will notify the deposit-taker accordingly; and][5]

(b) in any case, be in such form as may be prescribed or authorised, and contain such information as may reasonably be required, by the Board.

[(2A) A declaration under section 481(5)(k)(i) must contain—

(a) in a case falling within section 481(4)(a), the name and principal residential address of the individual who is beneficially entitled to the interest or, where two or more individuals are so entitled, of each of them;

(b) in a case falling within section 481(4)(b), the name and principal residential address of each of the partners.][6]

(3) A deposit-taker shall, on being so required by notice given to him by an inspector, make all declarations which have been made to him under section 481(5) available for inspection by the inspector or by a named officer of the Board.

(4) Where a notice has been given to a deposit-taker under subsection (3) above, the declarations shall be made available within such time as may be specified in the notice, and the person to whom they are to be made available may take copies of or extracts from them.

(5) A deposit-taker shall treat every deposit made with him as a relevant deposit unless satisfied that it is not a relevant deposit, but where he has satisfied himself that a deposit is not a relevant deposit he shall be entitled to continue to so treat it until such time as he is in possession of information which can reasonably be taken to indicate that the deposit is or may be a relevant deposit.

[(5A) The persons who are to be taken for the purposes of section 481(5)(k)(iii) and subsection (2) above to be the beneficiaries of a discretionary or accumulation trust shall be every person who, as a person falling wholly or partly within any description of actual or potential beneficiaries, is either—

(a) a person who is, or will or may become, entitled under the trust to receive the whole or any part of any income under the trust; or

(b) a person to or for the benefit of whom the whole or any part of any such income may be paid or applied in exercise of any discretion conferred by the trust;

and for the purposes of this subsection references, in relation to a trust, to income under the trust shall include references to so much (if any) of any property falling to be treated as capital under the trust as represents amounts originally received by the trustees as income.][5]

(6) In section 481(5)—

"appropriate person", in relation to a deposit, means any person who is beneficially entitled to any interest in respect of the deposit or entitled to receive any such interest [in his capacity as a personal representative or as a trustee of a discretionary or accumulation trust][5] or to whom any such interest is payable;

"general client account deposit" means a deposit, held by the deposit-taker in a client account (other than one which is identified by the deposit-taker as one in which sums are held only for one or more particular clients of the person whose account it is) in respect of which that person is required by provision made under any enactment to make payments representing interest to some or all of the clients for whom, or on whose account, he received the sums deposited in the account;

"qualifying certificate of deposit" means a certificate of deposit, as defined in section 56(5), which is issued by a deposit-taker and under which—

(a) the amount payable by the deposit-taker, exclusive of interest, is not less than £50,000 (or, for a deposit denominated in foreign currency, not less than the equivalent of £50,000 at the time when the deposit is made); and

(b) the obligation of the deposit-taker to pay that amount arises after a period of not [more than five years][2] beginning with the date on which the deposit is made; and "qualifying time deposit" means a deposit which is made by way of loan for an amount which is not less than £50,000 (or, for a deposit denominated in foreign currency, not less than the equivalent of £50,000 at the time when the deposit is made) and on terms which—

   [(*a*) require repayment of the deposit at a specified time falling before the end of the period of five years beginning with the date on which the deposit is made;][3]

   (*b*) do not make provision for the transfer of the right to repayment; and

   (*c*) prevent partial withdrawals of, or additions to, the deposit.

...[4]

(7) For the purposes of section 481(5)(*h*) and (*j*) a deposit is held at a branch of a deposit-taker if it is recorded in his books as a liability of that branch.

(8) A certificate of deposit, as defined in section 56(5), which was issued before 13th March 1984 on terms which provide for interest to be payable on the deposit at any time after 5th April 1985 (whether or not interest is payable on it before that date) shall, if it is not a qualifying certificate of deposit, be treated for the purposes of section 481(5) as if it were a qualifying certificate of deposit.

(9) Any deposit which was made before 6th July 1984 but which is not a qualifying time deposit shall, where it is made on terms which—

   (*a*) do not make provision for the transfer of the right to repayment;

   (*b*) prevent partial withdrawals of, or additions to, the deposit; and

   (*c*) require—

      (i) the deposit-taker to repay the sum at the end of a specified period which ends after 5th April 1985; or

      (ii) in a case where interest is payable only at the time of repayment of the deposit, the deposit-taker to repay the sum on demand or on notice;

be treated for the purposes of section 481(5) as if it were a qualifying time deposit.

(10) An order under section 481(2)(*f*) may prescribe a person or class of person in relation to all relevant deposits or only in relation to relevant deposits of a kind specified in the order.

(11) The Board may by regulations make provision—

   (*a*) ...[6]

   [(*aa*) with respect to the furnishing of information by depositors or deposit-takers, including, in the case of deposit-takers, the inspection of books, documents and other records on behalf of the Board; and][1]

   [(*ab*) with respect to—

      (i) the manner and form in which a notification for the purposes of section 481(5B) is to be given or may be withdrawn, and

      (ii) the circumstances in which the deposit-taker is to be entitled to delay acting on such a notification,

   and][5]

   (*b*) generally for giving effect to sections 479 to 481 and this section.

[(11A) In subsection (11)(*aa*) above the reference to depositors is to persons who are appropriate persons (within the meaning given by subsection (6) above) in relation to deposits.][1]

(12) Regulations under subsection (11) above or an order under section 481(6) may contain such incidental and consequential provision as appears to the Board or the Treasury, as the case may be, to be appropriate.

Commentary—*Simon's Direct Tax Service* **D4.1115.**
Regulations—IT (Composite Rate) (Non-residents) Regulations, SI 1985/1702. For the continuity of the Regulations, see Sch 30, para 21 of this Act.
IT (Deposit-takers) (Interest Payments) Regulations, SI 1990/2232.
IT (Deposit-takers) (Audit Powers) Regulations, SI 1992/12.
IT (Deposit-takers) (Non-residents) Regulations, SI 1992/14.
Deposit Takers (Interest Payments) (Discretionary or Accumulation Trusts) Regulations, SI 1995/1370.
Concession B13—A non-resident's tax liability on untaxed interest payment from general client account or on untaxed profit from disposal of certificates of deposit as defined in sub-s (6) above is not pursued except so far as can be recovered against repayment claim.
Definitions—"The Board", s 832(1); "deposit", s 481(3); "deposit-taker", s 481(2); "inspector", s 832(1); "interest", s 832(1); "notice", s 832(1); "relevant deposit", s 481(4).
Cross-references—See TMA 1970 s 17(4B), (4C) (returns of interest not to include interest on deposits which are not relevant deposits by virtue of sub-s (5) above).
TMA 1970 s 98 (special return penalties in relation to a failure to provide information required under sub-s (2) or make available declarations in accordance with sub-s (3) above).
TA 1988 s 481 (meaning of "deposit taker", "deposit" and "relevant deposit" for the purposes of this section).
TA 1988 s 482A (investments of persons not ordinarily resident in the UK; exclusion of audit powers conferred by sub-s (11)(*aa*) above).
IT (Deposit-takers) (Audit Powers) Regulations, SI 1992/12 reg 3(2) (Revenue's powers to require information for determining whether having regard to this section a gross payment of interest on non-relevant or excluded deposits is in order).
Amendments—[1] Sub-ss (11)(*aa*), (11A) inserted by FA 1990 Sch 5 para 9(4), (5).
[2] Words in para (*b*) of the definition of "qualifying certificate of deposit" in sub-s (6) substituted by FA 1990 Sch 5 para 9(1), (2), (6) with effect as regards interest paid or credited after 5 April 1991.
[3] Para (*a*) of the definition of "qualifying time deposit" substituted by FA 1990 Sch 5 para 9(1), (3), (6) with effect as regards interest paid or credited after 5 April 1991.
[4] References in sub-s (1) to ss 479, 480 and words in sub-s (6) repealed by FA 1990 Sch 19, Pt IV.

[5] Words in sub-ss (2), (6) substituted and sub-s (5A) and words in sub-s (11) inserted in relation to any payments made after 5 April 1996 by FA 1995 s 86(5)–(8), (10).
[6] Sub-s (2A) inserted, and sub-s (11)(a) repealed by FA 2000 ss 111(3), (6)(c), 156, Sch 40 Pt II(17) with effect for declarations made under TA 1988 s 481(5)(k)(i) after 5 April 2001.

[482A Audit powers in relation to non-residents

...

Regulations—IT (Building Societies) (Audit Powers) Regulations, SI 1992/10.
IT (Deposit-takers) (Audit Powers) Regulations, SI 1992/12.
Definitions—"Board", s 832 (1); "United Kingdom", s 830 (1).
Amendments—This section repealed by FA 2000 ss 145(10), (11) with effect for amounts paid, credited or received after 5 April 2001.

483 Determination of reduced rate for building societies and composite rate for banks etc

Amendments—Sub-ss (1)–(3), (5) repealed by FA 1990 Sch 5 para 12 and Sch 19 Pt IV. Sub-s (4) is spent.

484 Savings banks: exemption from tax

Amendments—This section repealed by FA 1996 Sch 14 para 29 Sch 41 Pt V(3) with effect for the purposes of corporation tax for accounting periods ending after 31 March 1996 and so far as relating to income tax from the year 1996–97, subject to transitional provisions in FA 1996 Sch 15.

485 Savings banks: supplemental

Commentary—*Simon's Direct Tax Service* B5.103.
Amendments—This section repealed by FA 1996 Sch 13 para 27, Sch 37 Pt V(3) with effect for the purposes of corporation tax for accounting periods ending after 31 March 1996 and so far as relating to income tax from the year 1996–97, subject to transitional provisions in FA 1996 Sch 15.

486 Industrial and provident societies and co-operative associations

(1) Notwithstanding anything in the Tax Acts, share interest or loan interest paid by a registered industrial and provident society shall not be treated as a distribution; [but interest payable by such a society (whether as share interest or loan interest) shall be treated for the purposes of corporation tax as interest under a loan relationship of the society.][1]

(2) Notwithstanding anything in sections 348 to 350, any share interest or loan interest paid by a registered industrial and provident society, except any to which subsection (3) below applies, shall be paid without deduction of income tax.

(3) This subsection applies to any share interest or loan interest payable to a person whose usual place of abode is not within the United Kingdom, and in any such case section 349(2) shall apply to the payment as it applies to a payment of yearly interest, and income tax shall be deducted accordingly.

(4) Any share interest or loan interest paid by a registered industrial and provident society shall be chargeable under Case III of Schedule D.

(5) Where at any time, by virtue of this section, the income of a person from any source, not having previously been chargeable by direct assessment on that person, becomes so chargeable, section 66(3) shall apply as if the source of that income were a new source of income acquired by that person at that time.

(6) Every registered industrial and provident society shall, within three months after the end of any accounting period of the society, deliver to the inspector a return showing—

(a) the name and place of residence of every person to whom the society has by virtue of this section paid without deduction of income tax sums amounting to more than £15 in that period; and

(b) the amount so paid in that period to each of those persons.

(7) If for any accounting period a return under subsection (6) above is not duly made by a registered industrial and provident society, share and loan interest paid by the society in that period shall [not be brought into account in that period for the purposes of Chapter II of Part IV of the Finance Act 1996 (loan relationships).][2]

(8) If in the course of, or as part of, a union or amalgamation of two or more registered industrial and provident societies, or a transfer of engagements from one registered industrial and provident society to another, there is a disposal of an asset by one society to another, both shall be treated for the purposes of corporation tax in respect of chargeable gains as if the asset were acquired from the society making the disposal for a consideration of such amount as would secure that neither a gain nor a loss would accrue to that society on the disposal.

(9) Subsections (1) and (8) above shall have effect as if references to a registered industrial and provident society included any co-operative association established and resident in the United Kingdom, and having as its object or primary object to assist its members in the carrying on of agricultural or horticultural businesses on land occupied by them in the United Kingdom or in the carrying on of businesses consisting in the catching or taking of fish or shellfish.

(10) It is hereby declared that, in computing, for the purposes of any provision of the Tax Acts relating to [profits][10] chargeable under Case I of Schedule D (''the tax computation''), any [profits][2] of—

(*a*) any registered industrial and provident society which does not sell to persons not members thereof: or

(*b*) any registered industrial and provident society the number of the shares in which is not limited by its rules or practice;

there are to be deducted as expenses any sums which—

    (i) represent a discount, rebate, dividend or bonus granted by the company to members or other persons in respect of amounts paid or payable by or to them on account of their transactions with the company, being transactions which are taken into account in the tax computation; and

    (ii) are calculated by reference to those amounts or to the magnitude of those transactions and not by reference to the amount of any share or interest in the capital of the company.

(11) No dividends or bonus deductible in computing income as mentioned in subsection (10) above shall be regarded as a distribution.

(12) In this section—

''co-operative association'' means a body of persons having a written constitution from which the Minister is satisfied, having regard to the provision made as to the manner in which the income of the body is to be applied for the benefit of its members and all other relevant provisions, that the body is in substance a co-operative association;

''the Minister'' means—

    the [Secretary of State][3], as regards England and Wales;
    the Secretary of State, as regards Scotland; and
    the Department of Agriculture for Northern Ireland, as regards Northern Ireland;

''registered industrial and provident society'' means a society registered or deemed to be registered under the Industrial and Provident Societies Act 1965 or under the Industrial and Provident Societies Act (Northern Ireland) 1969;

''share interest'' means any interest, dividend, bonus or other sum payable to a shareholder of the society by reference to the amount of his holding in the share capital of the society;

''loan interest'' means any interest payable by the society in respect of any mortgage, loan, loan stock or deposit;

and references to the payment of share interest or loan interest include references to the crediting of such interest.

Commentary—*Simon's Direct Tax Service* D4.321, 625–628, 635.
Concession C13—For the purposes of this section, members of the basic level agricultural co-operative associations are treated as members of second and third tier.
Definitions—''Accounting period'', s 834(1); ''body of persons'', s 832(1); ''chargeable gain'', s 832(1); ''charges on income'', ss 338(2), 834(1); ''deduction of income tax'', s 4(1); ''distribution'', ss 209(2), 832(1); ''inspector'', s 832(1); ''loan relationship'', s 834(1), FA 1996 s 81; ''Schedule D'', s 18(1); ''the tax Acts'', s 831(2); ''trade'', s 832(1).
Cross references—See TA 1988 s 487(2) (failure to make timely return under sub-s (6) above by credit union results in loss of exclusion from credits on certain loans).
TCGA 1992 s 35 (rebasing for assets held at 31 March 1982 not to apply for disposal under sub-s (8) above unless election for rebasing of all assets so held is made).
TCGA 1992 s 117A(7), (8) (to the extent that sub-s (8) above treats disposals as made on a no gain/no loss basis, it does not apply to disposals of certain foreign currency debts involving companies).
TCGA 1992 s 117B(5), (6) (to the extent that sub-s (8) above treats disposals as made on a no gain/no loss basis, it does not apply to disposals of certain foreign currency denominated holdings in unit trusts and offshore funds treated as a right under a creditor relationship of a company).
FA 1995 s 131 (disapplication of sub-s (8) above in relation to disposals of certain qualifying assets under transitional provisions for exchange gains or losses).
Amendments—[1] Words in sub-ss (1), (7) substituted by FA 1996 Sch 14 para 30 with effect for accounting periods ending after 31 March 1996, subject to transitional provisions in FA 1996 Sch 15.
[2] Word in sub-s (10) substituted by FA 1998 Sch 7 para 1 with effect from 31 July 1998.
[3] In sub-s (12), words substituted for the words ''Minister of Agriculture, Fisheries and Food'' by the Ministry of Agriculture, Fisheries and Food (Dissolution) Order, SI 2002/794 art 5(a), Sch 1 para 31 with effect from 27 March 2002.

487 Credit unions

(1) Subject to subsection (2) below, in computing for the purposes of corporation tax the income of a credit union for any accounting period—

(*a*) neither the activity of the credit union in making loans to its members nor in placing on deposit or otherwise investing from time to time its surplus funds shall be regarded as the carrying on of a trade or part of a trade; and

[(*b*) no credits shall be brought into account for the purposes of Chapter II of Part IV of the Finance Act 1996 in respect of any loan relationship of a credit union as respects which a member of the union stands in the position of a debtor as respects the debt in question.][1]

(2) Paragraph (*b*) of subsection (1) above shall not apply to an accounting period of a credit union for which the credit union is obliged to make a return under section 486(6) and has not done so within three months after the end of that accounting period or such longer period as the inspector shall allow.

(3) [An annuity or other annual payment (not being a payment of share interest or loan interest) which is]¹ paid or payable by a credit union in any accounting period shall [not]¹ be deductible in computing for the purposes of corporation tax the income of the credit union for that period from any trade carried on by it or be treated for those purposes as a charge on income.

[(3A) No debits shall be brought into account for the purposes of Chapter II of Part IV of the Finance Act 1996 in respect of any loan relationship of a credit union as respects which a member of the union stands in the position of a creditor as respects the debt in question.]¹

(4) A credit union shall not be regarded as an investment company for the purposes of section 75 above or [Part 2 of the Capital Allowances Act (plant and machinery allowances)]².

(5) In this section—

"credit union" means a society registered as a credit union under the Industrial and Provident Societies Act 1965 or the Credit Unions (Northern Ireland) Order 1985;

"share interest" and "loan interest" have the same meaning as in section 486;

"surplus funds", in relation to a credit union, means funds not immediately required for its purposes;

and references to the payment of share interest or loan interest include references to the crediting of such interest.

Commentary—*Simon's Direct Tax Service* **D4.644.**
Definitions—"The 1970 Act", s 831(3); "accounting period", s 834(1); "charges on income", s 338(2) by virtue of s 834(1); "inspector", s 832(1); "loan relationship", s 834(1), FA 1996 s 81; "Schedule D", s 18(1); "trade", s 832(1).
Amendments—¹ Sub-s (1)(b) and words in sub-s (3) substituted or inserted, and sub-s (3A) inserted by FA 1996 Sch 14 para 31 with effect for accounting periods ending after 31 March 1996, subject to transitional provisions in FA 1994 Sch 15.
² Words in sub-s (4) substituted by CAA 2001 s 578, Sch 2 para 40 with effect for corporation tax purposes with respect to allowances and charges falling to be made for chargeable periods ending after 31 March 2001.

488 Co-operative housing associations

(1) Where a housing association makes a claim in that behalf for any year or part of a year of assessment during which the association was approved for the purposes of this section—

(a) rent to which the association was entitled from its members for the year or part shall be disregarded for tax purposes; and

(b) any yearly interest payable by the association for the year or part shall be treated for tax purposes [in relation to the association as if there were no interest so payable]⁸

(c) . . .⁸

(2) Where the property, or any of the properties, to which any such interest as is mentioned in paragraph (b) of subsection (1) above relates is for any period not subject to a tenancy—

(a) that paragraph shall not apply in relation to so much of the interest as is attributable to the property not subject to a tenancy; . . .⁸

(b) . . .⁸

(3) . . .⁵

(4) Where a claim under subsection (1) above has effect, any adjustment of the liability to tax of . . .⁸ the association which is required in consequence of the claim may be made by an assessment or by repayment or otherwise, as the case may require.

(5) Where a housing association makes a claim in that behalf for an accounting period or part of an accounting period during which it was approved for the purposes of this section, the housing association shall be exempt from corporation tax on chargeable gains accruing to it in the accounting period or part on the disposal by way of sale of any property which has been or is being occupied by a tenant of the housing association.

(6) References in this section to the approval of an association shall be construed as references to approval—

(a) by the Secretary of State in the case of a housing association in Great Britain;

(b) by the Head of the Department of the Environment for Northern Ireland in the case of a housing association in Northern Ireland;

and an association shall not be approved unless the approving authority is satisfied—

(i) that the association is, or is deemed to be, duly registered under the Industrial and Provident Societies Act 1965 or the Industrial and Provident Societies Act (Northern Ireland) 1969, and is a housing association within the meaning of the Housing Associations Act 1985 or [Article 3 of the Housing (Northern Ireland) Order 1992]¹

(ii) that the rules of the association restrict membership to persons who are tenants or prospective tenants of the association, and preclude the granting or assignment (or, in Scotland, the granting or assignation) of tenancies to persons other than members; and

(iii) that the association satisfies such other requirements as may be prescribed by the approving authority, and will comply with such conditions as may for the time being be so prescribed.

(7) An approval given for the purposes of this section shall have effect as from such date (whether before or after the giving of the approval) as may be specified by the approving authority and shall cease to have effect if revoked.

[(7A) The Secretary of State may delegate any of his functions under subsections (6) and (7)—

   (*a*) to the Housing Corporation, in the case of a body registered as a social landlord in the register maintained by the Housing Corporation under Part 1 of the Housing Act 1996,

   (*b*) ...[7]

to such extent and subject to such conditions as he may specify.][4]

(8) The Secretary of State as respects Great Britain, or the Head of the Department of the Environment for Northern Ireland as respects Northern Ireland, may make regulations for the purpose of carrying out the provisions of this section; and, from the coming into operation of regulations under this subsection prescribing requirements or conditions for the purposes of subsection (6)(iii) above, "prescribed" in subsection (6)(iii) above shall mean prescribed by or under such regulations.

The power to make regulations under this subsection shall be exercisable by the Secretary of State by statutory instrument and by the Head of the Department of the Environment for Northern Ireland by statutory rule for the purposes of the Statutory Rules (Northern Ireland) Order 1979.

[(9) A claim under this section may be made at any time not later than two years after the end of the year of assessment or accounting period to which, or to a part of which, it relates.][2]

(10) Subject to subsection (11) below, [no claim shall be made under this section unless][3] during the year or accounting period, or part thereof, to which the claim relates—

   (*a*) no property belonging to the association making the claim was let otherwise than to a member of the association;

   (*b*) no property let by the association, and no part of such property, was occupied, whether solely or as joint occupier, by a person not being a member of the association;

   (*c*) the association making the claim satisfies the conditions specified in subsection (6)(i) and (ii) above and has complied with the conditions prescribed under subsection (6)(iii) for the time being in force; and

   (*d*) any covenants required to be included in grants of tenancies by those conditions have been observed.

For the purposes of paragraph (*b*) above occupation by any other person in accordance with the will, or the provisions applicable on the intestacy, of a deceased member, shall be treated during the first six months after the death as if it were occupation by a member.

[(11) A housing association may make a claim under this section notwithstanding anything in subsection (10) above, if the association reasonably considers that the requirements of that subsection are substantially complied with.][2]

[(11A) If as a result of an enquiry—

   (*a*) [into a company tax return][6] in which a claim under this section by a housing association is included, or

   (*b*) under paragraph 5 of Schedule 1A to that Act into a claim under this section by a housing association, or an amendment of such a claim,

an amendment is made to the association's [return][6] or, as the case may be, to the claim, the liability of [the association][8] to tax for all relevant years or accounting periods may also be adjusted by the making of assessments or otherwise.][2]

[(12) ...][8]

489 Self-build societies

(1) Where a self-build society makes a claim in that behalf for any year or part of a year of assessment during which the society was approved for the purposes of this section, rent to which the society was entitled from its members for the year or part shall be disregarded for tax purposes.

(2) Where a claim under subsection (1) above has effect, any adjustment of the society's liability to tax which is required in consequence of the claim may be made by an assessment or by repayment or otherwise, as the case may require.

(3) Where a self-build society makes a claim in that behalf for an accounting period or part during which it was approved for the purposes of this section, the society shall be exempt from corporation tax on chargeable gains accruing to it in the accounting period or part thereof on the disposal of any land to a member of the society.

(4) References in this section to the approval of a self-build society are references to its approval by the Secretary of State, and the Secretary of State shall not approve a self-build society for the purposes of this section unless he is satisfied—

  (a) that the society is, or is deemed to be, duly registered under the Industrial and Provident Societies Act 1965; and
  (b) that the society satisfies such other requirements as may be prescribed by or under regulations under subsection (6) below and will comply with such conditions as may for the time being be so prescribed.

(5) An approval given for the purposes of this section shall have effect as from such date (whether before or after the giving of the approval) as may be specified by the Secretary of State and shall cease to have effect if revoked by him.

[(5A) The Secretary of State may delegate any of his functions under subsections (4) and (5) to—

  (a) the Housing Corporation, where the society has its registered office in England for the purposes of the Industrial and Provident Societies Act 1965,
  (b) ...⁴

to such extent and subject to such conditions as he may specify.]²

(6) The Secretary of State may by statutory instrument make regulations for the purpose of carrying out the provisions of this section; and a statutory instrument containing any such regulations shall be subject to annulment in pursuance of a resolution of the House of Commons.

[(7) A claim under this section may be made at any time not later than two years after the end of the year of assessment or accounting period to which, or to a part of which, it relates.]¹

(8) Subject to subsection (9) below, [no claim shall be made under this section unless]¹ during the year or accounting period, or part thereof, to which the claim relates—

  (a) no land owned by the society was occupied, in whole or in part and whether solely or as joint occupier, by a person who was not, at the time of his occupation, a member of the society; and
  (b) the society making the claim satisfies the condition specified in paragraph (a) of subsection (4) above and has complied with the conditions prescribed under paragraph (b) of that subsection and for the time being in force;

and for the purposes of paragraph (a) above, occupation by any other person in accordance with the will, or the provisions applicable on the intestacy, of a deceased member, shall be treated during the first six months after the death as if it were occupation by a member.

[(9) A self-build society may make a claim under this section notwithstanding anything in subsection (8) above, if the society reasonably considers that the requirements of that subsection are substantially complied with.]¹

[(9A) If as a result of an enquiry—

  (a) [into a company tax return]³ in which a claim under this section by a self-build society is included, or
  (b) under paragraph 5 of Schedule 1A to that Act into a claim under this section by a self-build society or an amendment of such a claim,

an amendment is made to the society's [return]³ or, as the case may be, to the claim, the society's liability to tax for all relevant years or accounting periods may also be adjusted by the making of assessments or otherwise.]¹

(10) A claim under this section shall be in such form and contain such particulars as may be prescribed by the Board.

(11) In this section—

  "self-build society" has the same meaning as in the Housing Associations Act 1985 or, in Northern Ireland, Part VII of the Housing (Northern Ireland) Order 1981; and
  "rent" includes any sums to which a self-build society is entitled in respect of the occupation of any of its land under a licence or otherwise.

(12) In the application of this section to Northern Ireland—

  (a) any reference in subsections (4) and (5) above to the Secretary of State shall be construed as a reference to the Department of the Environment for Northern Ireland;
  (b) the reference in subsection (4)(a) to the Industrial and Provident Societies Act 1965 shall be construed as a reference to the Industrial and Provident Societies Act (Northern Ireland) 1969; and
  (c) for subsection (6) there shall be substituted the following subsection—

  "(6) The Department of the Environment for Northern Ireland may by statutory rule for the purpose of the Statutory Rules (Northern Ireland) Order 1979 make regulations for the purpose of carrying out the provisions of this section; and a statutory rule containing any such regulations shall be subject to negative resolution within the meaning of section 41(6) of the Interpretation Act (Northern Ireland) 1954''.

Commentary—*Simon's Direct Tax Service* **D4.639.**
Regulations—IT (Interest Relief) (Housing Associations) Regulations, SI 1988/1347.
Definitions—''Accounting period'', s 834(1); ''the Board'', s 832(1); ''chargeable gains'', s 832(1); ''inspector'', s 832(1); ''the Management Act'', s 831(3); ''year of assessment'', s 832(1).
Cross references—See TA 1988 s 378 (application of MIRAS provisions to self-build societies).
The National Assembly for Wales (Transfer of Functions) Order, SI 1999/672 art 2, Sch 1 (functions exercisable under this section by a Minister of the Crown shall, so far as exercisable in relation to Wales, be exercisable by the National Assembly for Wales concurrently with the Minister with effect from 1 July 1999).
Amendments—[1] Sub-ss (7) and (9) and (9A) (for sub-s (9)) and words in sub-s (8) substituted by FA 1996 Sch 20 para 29(2)–(4) with effect for the purposes of income tax from the year 1996–97 and for the purposes of corporation tax for accounting periods ending after 30 June 1999 (by virtue of Finance Act 1994, Section 199, (Appointed Day) Order, SI 1998/3173 art 2).
[2] Sub-s (5A) inserted by Housing Act 1996 Sch 3 para 8 with effect from 1 October 1996 by virtue of the Housing Act 1996 (Commencement No 3 and Transitional Provisions) Order, SI 1996/2402 art 3.
[3] Words in sub-s (9A) substituted by FA 1998 Sch 19 para 49 with effect in relation to accounting periods ending after 30 June 1999 (by virtue of SI 1998/3173 art 2).
[4] Sub-s (5A)(b) repealed by the Government of Wales Act 1998 Sch 16 para 57 with effect from 1 November 1998, by virtue of the Government of Wales Act 1998 (Commencement No 1) Order 1998, SI 1998/2244.

490 Companies carrying on a mutual business or not carrying on a business

(1) Subject to subsection (2) below, where a company carries on any business of mutual trading or mutual insurance or other mutual business the provisions of the Tax Acts relating to distributions shall apply to distributions made by the company notwithstanding that they are made to persons participating in the mutual activities of that business and derive from those activities, but shall so apply only to the extent to which the distributions are made out of profits of the company which are brought into charge to corporation tax or out of franked investment income ...[3] ...[1].

(2) In the case of a company carrying on any mutual life assurance business, the provisions of the Tax Acts relating to distributions shall not apply to distributions made to persons participating in the mutual activities of that business and derived from those activities; ...[2]

(3) Subject to subsections (1) and (2) above, the fact that a distribution made by a company carrying on any such business is derived from the mutual activities of that business and the recipient is a person participating in those activities shall not affect the character which the payment or other receipt has for purposes of corporation tax or income tax in the hands of the recipient.

(4) Where a company does not carry on, and never has carried on, a trade or a business of holding investments, and is not established for purposes which include the carrying on of a trade or of such a business, the provisions of the Tax Acts relating to distributions shall apply to distributions made by the company only to the extent to which the distributions are made out of profits of the company which are brought into charge to corporation tax or out of franked investment income ...[1].

(5) ...[1]

Commentary—*Simon's Direct Tax Service* **D4.322–324.**
Concession C15—Distribution of assets to members on dissolution of unincorporated social or recreational association; option to treat the distribution as capital receipts instead of s 209 of this Act applying to it.
Definitions—''Company'', s 832(1), (2); ''distributions'', s 832(1); ''charges on income'', s 338(2) by virtue of s 834(1); ''franked investment income'', s 832(1); ''profits'', s 6(4) by virtue of s 834(2); ''the Tax Acts'', s 831(2); ''trade'', ss 6(4), 834(2).
Cross references—See FA 1993 s 78(6) (rate of tax credit for calculating franked investment income for the purposes of this section from the financial year 1993).
Amendments—[1] Words in sub-ss (1), (4) and whole of sub-s (5) (originally inserted by FA 1994 Sch 16 para 14) repealed by F(No 2)A 1997 s 36(4), Sch 6 para 9, Sch 8 Pt II(11) with effect for distributions made after 5 April 1999.
[2] Words in sub-s (2) repealed by FA 1997 Sch 18 Pt VI(6) with effect for accounting periods beginning after 5 March 1997.
[3] Words in sub-s (1) repealed by FA 1998 Sch 3 para 28 with effect for distributions made after 5 April 1999.

491 Distribution of assets of body corporate carrying on mutual business

(1) Where any person receives any money or money's worth—

(a) forming part of the assets of a body corporate, other than assets representing capital; or
(b) forming part of the consideration for the transfer of the assets of a body corporate, other than assets representing capital, as part of a scheme of amalgamation or reconstruction which involves the winding up of the body corporate; or
(c) consisting of the consideration for a transfer or surrender of a right to receive anything falling under paragraph (a) of (b) above, being a receipt not giving rise to any charge to tax on the recipient apart from this section,

and the body corporate has at any time carried on a trade which consists of or includes the conducting of any mutual business (whether confined to members of the body corporate or not), and is being or has been wound up or dissolved, the provisions of this section shall apply to the receipt.

(2) If a transfer or surrender of a right under subsection (1)(c) above is not at arm's length, the person making the transfer or surrender shall, for the purposes of this section, be deemed then to have received consideration equal to the value of the right.

(3) If in respect of a payment of any amount made to the body corporate for the purposes of its mutual business any deduction has been allowed for the purposes of tax in computing the [profits][2] or losses of a trade, then—

(*a*) if at the time of the receipt the recipient is the person, or one of the persons, carrying on that trade, the amount or value of the receipt shall be treated for the purposes of tax as a trading receipt of that trade; and

(*b*) if at the time of the receipt the recipient is not the person, or one of the persons, carrying on that trade, but was the person, or one of the persons, carrying on that trade when any payment was made to the body corporate for the purposes of its mutual business in respect of which a deduction was allowed for the purposes of tax in computing the [profits][2] or losses of the trade, the recipient shall, subject to subsection (6) below, be charged under Case VI of Schedule D for the chargeable period in which the receipt falls on an amount equal to the amount or value of the receipt.

(4) Subsection (3)(*a*) above applies notwithstanding that, as a result of a change in the persons carrying on the trade, the [profits][2] are under section 113 or 337(1) determined as if it had been permanently discontinued and a new trade set up and commenced.

(5) Where an individual is chargeable to tax by virtue of subsection (3)(*b*) above and the [profits][2] of the trade there mentioned fell to be treated as earned income for the purposes of the Income Tax Acts, the sums in respect of which he is so chargeable shall also be treated for those purposes as earned income.

(6) If the trade mentioned in subsection (3)(*b*) above was permanently discontinued before the time of the receipt, then in computing the charge to tax under subsection (3)(*b*) above there shall be deducted from the amount or value of the receipt—

(*a*) any loss, expense or debit (not being a loss, expense or debit arising directly or indirectly from the discontinuance itself) which, if the trade had not been discontinued, would have been deducted in computing for tax purposes the [profits][2] or losses of the person by whom it was carried on before the discontinuance, or would have been deducted from or set off against those profits as so computed, and

(*b*) any capital allowance to which the person who carried on the trade was entitled immediately before the discontinuance and to which effect has not been given by way of relief before discontinuance.

(7) Relief shall not be given under subsection (6) above or under section 105(1) in respect of any loss, expense, debit or allowance if and so far as it has been so given by reference to another charge to tax under this section or under section 103.

(8) For the purposes of subsection (1) above assets representing capital consist of—

(*a*) assets representing any loan or other capital subscribed, including income derived from any investment of any part of that capital, but not including profits from the employment of that capital for the purposes of the mutual business of the body corporate;

(*b*) assets representing any [profits][2] charged to tax as being [profits][2] of any part of the trade carried on by the body corporate which does not consist of the conducting of any mutual business;

(*c*) (so far as not comprised in paragraphs (*a*) and (*b*) above) assets representing taxed income from any investments.

(9) In this section "mutual business" includes any business of mutual insurance or mutual trading.

(10) Subsections (3) to (7) above shall apply with any necessary modifications—

(*a*) to a profession or vocation; and

(*b*) ...[1];

as they apply to a trade.

(11) It is hereby declared that the description of trades in subsection (1) above does not include any trade all the [profits][2] of which are chargeable to tax and, in particular, does not include such a trade carried on by any registered industrial and provident society.

Commentary—*Simon's Direct Tax Service* **B3.239.**
Definitions—"Capital allowance", s 832(1); "chargeable period", s 832(1); "earned income", s 833(4), (5); "the Income Tax Acts", s 831(1)(*b*); "Schedule D", s 18(1); "trade", s 832(1).
Amendments—[1] Sub-s (10)(*b*) repealed by FA 1988 Sch 14 Pt V with effect from 6 April 1993.
[2] Word in sub-ss (3)–(6), (8), (11) substituted by FA 1998 Sch 7 para 1 with effect from 31 July 1998.

CHAPTER V
PETROLEUM EXTRACTION ACTIVITIES

Revenue Internal Guidance—Oil taxation office ring fence corporation tax manual gives a detailed exposition of the provisions of this chapter.
Cross references—See TA 1988 s 502 (interpretation of this Chapter).

492 Treatment of oil extraction activities etc for tax purposes

(1) Where a person carries on as part of a trade—

(*a*) any oil extraction activities; or

(b) any of the following activities, namely, the acquisition, enjoyment or exploitation of oil rights; or

(c) activities of both those descriptions,

those activities shall be treated for all purposes of income tax, and for the purposes of the charge of corporation tax on income, as a separate trade, distinct from all other activities carried on by him as part of the trade.

(2) Relief in respect of a loss incurred by a person shall not be given under section 380 or 381 against income arising from oil extraction activities or from oil rights ("ring fence income") except to the extent that the loss arises from such activities or rights.

(3) Relief in respect of a loss incurred by a person shall not be given under section [393A(1)][2] against his ring fence profits except to the extent that the loss arises from oil extraction activities or from oil rights.

(4) In any case where—

(a) in any chargeable period a person incurs a loss in activities ("separate activities") which, for that or any subsequent chargeable period, are treated by virtue of subsection (1) above as a separate trade for the purposes specified in that subsection; and

(b) in any subsequent chargeable period any of his trading income is derived from activities ("related activities") which are not part of the separate activities but which, apart from subsection (1) above, would together with those activities constitute a single trade,

then, notwithstanding anything in that subsection, the amount of the loss may be set off, in accordance with section 385 or 393(1), against so much of his trading income in any subsequent chargeable period as is derived from the related activities.

(5) Subject to subsection (7) below, a capital allowance which is to be given to any person by discharge or repayment of tax shall not to any extent be given effect under [section 258 of the Capital Allowances Act] by deduction from or set off against his ring fence income.

(6) Subject to subsection (7) below, a capital allowance which is to be given to any person by discharge or repayment of tax shall not to any extent be given effect under [section 259 or 260 of the Capital Allowances Act] by deduction from or set off against his ring fence profits.

(7) Subsection (5) or (6) above shall not apply to a capital allowance which falls to be made to a company for any accounting period in respect of an asset used in the relevant accounting period by a company associated with it and so used in carrying on oil extraction activities.

For the purposes of this subsection, the relevant accounting period is that in which the allowance in question first falls to be made to the company (whether or not it can to any extent be given effect in that period under [section 259 of the Capital Allowances Act][2]).

(8) On a claim for group relief made by a claimant company in relation to a surrendering company, group relief shall not be allowed against the claimant company's ring fence profits except to the extent that the claim relates to losses incurred by the surrendering company that arose from oil extraction activities or from oil rights.

Commentary—*Simon's Direct Tax Service* **D4.1002.**
Statement of Practice SP 14/93—Companies which habitually dispose of all their UK produced oil at non arm's length but price it on a consistent and reasonable arm's length value may apply for that value rather than market value to be used for the purposes of this section.
Revenue Internal Guidance—Oil taxation office ring fence corporation tax manual OTRF 6.1-6.80 (treatment of intangible drilling costs).
OTRF 8.1.1-8.10.5 (computation of profits from oil extraction activities).
Definitions—"The 1990 Act", s 831(3); "accounting period", s 834(1); "capital allowance", s 832(1); "chargeable period", s 832(1); "group relief", s 834(1); "oil extraction activities", s 502(1); "oil rights", s 502(1); "ring fence income", s 502(1); "ring fence profits", s 502(1); "trade", s 832(1).
Cross references—See TA 1988 s 402(1) (s 402 (surrender of loss relief between group members) is subject to sub-s (8) above).
TCGA 1922 s 198 (relief for replacement of business assets used in connection with a ring-fence trade).
Amendments—[1] "393A(1)" in sub-s (3) substituted by FA 1991 Sch 15 para 17.
[2] Words in sub-ss (5), (6) and (7) substituted by CAA 2001 s 578, Sch 2 para 41 with effect for income tax purposes, as respects allowances and charges falling to be made for chargeable periods ending after 5 April 2001, and for corporation tax purposes, as respects allowances and charges falling to be made for chargeable periods ending after 31 March 2001.

493 Valuation of oil disposed of or appropriated in certain circumstances

(1) Where a person disposes of any oil in circumstances such that the market value of that oil in a particular month falls to be taken into account under section 2 of the Oil Taxation Act 1975 ("the 1975 Act"), otherwise than by virtue of paragraph 6 of Schedule 3 to that Act, in computing for the purposes of petroleum revenue tax the assessable profit or allowable loss accruing to him in any chargeable period from an oil field (or as would so fall but for section 10 of that Act), then—

(a) for all purposes of income tax, and

(b) for the purposes of the charge of corporation tax on income,

the disposal of the oil and its acquisition by the person to whom it was disposed of shall be treated as having been for a consideration equal to the market value of the oil as so taken into account under section 2 of that Act (or as would have been so taken into account under that section but for section 10 of that Act).

(2) Where a person makes a relevant appropriation of any oil without disposing of it and does so in circumstances such that the market value of that oil in a particular month falls to be taken into account under section 2 of the 1975 Act in computing for the purposes of petroleum revenue tax the assessable profit or allowable loss accruing to him in any chargeable period from an oil field (or would so fall but for section 10 of that Act), then for all the purposes of income tax and for the purposes of the charge of corporation tax on income, he shall be treated—

(*a*) as having, at the time of the appropriation—

(i) sold the oil in the course of the separate trade consisting of activities falling within section 492(1)(*a*) or (*b*); and

(ii) bought it in the course of the separate trade consisting of activities not so falling; and

(*b*) as having so sold and bought it at a price equal to its market value as so taken into account under section 2 of the 1975 Act (or as would have been so taken into account under that section but for section 10 of that Act).

In this subsection "relevant appropriation" has the meaning given by section 12(1) of the 1975 Act.

(3) Where—

(*a*) a person disposes otherwise than in a sale at arm's length (as defined in paragraph 1 of Schedule 3 to the 1975 Act) of oil acquired by him in the course of oil extraction activities carried on by him or by virtue of oil rights held by him, and

(*b*) subsection (1) above does not apply in relation to the disposal,

then, for all purposes of income tax and for the purposes of the charge of corporation tax on income, the disposal of the oil and its acquisition by the person to whom it was disposed of shall be treated as having been for a consideration equal to the market value of the oil in the calendar month in which the disposal was made.

(4) If a person appropriates oil acquired by him in the course of oil extraction activities carried on by him or by virtue of oil rights held by him and the appropriation is to refining or to any use except for production purposes of an oil field, within the meaning of Part I of the 1975 Act, then, unless subsection (2) above applies, for all purposes of income tax and for the purposes of the charge of corporation tax on income—

(*a*) he shall be treated as having, at the time of the appropriation, sold and bought the oil as mentioned in subsection (2)(*a*)(i) and (ii) above; and

(*b*) that sale and purchase shall be deemed to have been at a price equal to the market value of the oil in the calendar month in which it was appropriated.

(5) For the purposes of subsections (3) and (4) above—

(*a*) "calendar month" means a month of the calendar year; and

(*b*) paragraph 2 of Schedule 3 to the 1975 Act shall apply as it applies for the purposes of Part I of that Act, but with the following modifications, that is to say—

(i) for sub-paragraph (2)(*f*) there shall be substituted—

"(*f*) the contract is for the sale of the whole quantity of oil of which the market value falls to be ascertained for the purposes of section 493(3) or (4) of the Income and Corporation Taxes Act 1988 and of no other oil; and for the avoidance of doubt it is hereby declared that the terms as to payment which are to be implied in the contract shall be those which are customarily contained in contracts for sale at arm's length of oil of the kind in question."; and

(ii) sub-paragraphs (3) and (4) shall be omitted.

Commentary—*Simon's Direct Tax Service* **D4.1003.**
Statement of Practice SP 14/93—Companies which habitually dispose of all their UK produced oil at non arm's length but price it on a consistent and reasonable arm's length value may apply for that value rather than market value to be used for the purposes of this section.
Definitions—"Allowable loss", s 834(1); "chargeable period", s 832(1); "oil", s 502(1); "oil field", s 502(1).

494 Charges on income

(1) Section 338 [of this Act and Chapter II of Part IV of the Finance Act 1996 (loan relationships)][1] shall have effect subject to the following provisions of this section.

[(2) Debits shall not be brought into account for the purposes of Chapter II of Part IV of the Finance Act 1996 in respect of any loan relationship of a company in any manner that results in a reduction of what would otherwise be the company's ring fence profits except—

(*a*) to the extent that the loan relationship is in respect of money borrowed by the company which has been—

(i) used to meet expenditure incurred by the company in carrying on oil extraction activities or in acquiring oil rights otherwise than from a connected person; or

(ii) appropriated to meeting expenditure to be so incurred by the company;

(*b*) in the case of debits falling to be brought into account by virtue of subsection (4) of section 84 of that Act in respect of a loan relationship that has not been entered into, to the extent that the relationship would have been one entered into for the purpose of borrowing money to be used or appropriated as mentioned in paragraph (*a*) above;

(*c*) in the case of debits in respect of [a relationship to which section 100 of that Act applies,][3], to the extent that—

[(i)][3] the payment of interest under that relationship is expenditure incurred as mentioned in sub-paragraph (i) of paragraph (*a*) above; [or
(ii) the exchange loss arising from that relationship is in respect of a money debt on which the interest payable (if any) is, or would be, such expenditure;

as the case may be;][3] and
(*d*) [in the case of a net debit for an accounting period][3] in respect of a debtor relationship of the company which is a creditor relationship of a company associated with the company, to the extent that (subject always to paragraph (a) above) [the net debit][3] does not exceed what, having regard to—

(i) all the terms on which the money was borrowed, and
(ii) the standing of the borrower,

would be [the net debit][3] representing a reasonable commercial rate of return on the money borrowed.

In this subsection "debtor relationship" and "creditor relationship" have the same meanings as in Chapter II of Part IV of the Finance Act 1996, and references to a loan relationship, in relation to the borrowing of money, do not include references to [any relationship to which section 100 of that Act applies][3].][1]

[For the purposes of paragraph (d) above, the net debit for an accounting period in respect of a debtor relationship of a company is the amount if any by which—

(i) the aggregate of the debits for the period in respect of the relationship, exceeds

(ii) the credits in respect of exchange gains arising from the relationship for the period.][3]

Section 839 shall apply for the purposes of this subsection.

[(2ZA) Credits in respect of exchange gains from a company's loan relationships shall not be brought into account for the purposes of Chapter 2 of Part 4 of the Finance Act 1996 in respect of any loan relationship of a company in any manner that results in an increase of what would otherwise be the company's ring fence profits, except to the extent that, if the credit had been a debit in respect of an exchange loss from the relationship, it would have been brought into account by virtue of any of paragraphs (*a*) to (*c*) of subsection (2) above.][3]

[(2A) Where any debit [or credit][3]—

(*a*) falls to be brought into account for the purposes of Chapter II of Part IV of the Finance Act 1996 in respect of any loan relationship of a company, but
(*b*) in accordance with subsection (2) [or (2ZA)][3] above cannot be brought into account in a manner that results in any reduction [or, as the case may be, increase][3] of what would otherwise be the company's ring fence profits,

then (notwithstanding anything in section 82(2) of that Act) that debit [or credit][3] shall be brought into account for those purposes as a non-trading debit [or, as the case may be, non-trading credit][3].][1]

[(2B) Where, in accordance with subsection (2) above, any proportion (including the whole) of a net debit, within the meaning of paragraph (*d*) of that subsection, cannot be brought into account in a manner that results in any reduction of what would otherwise be the company's ring fence profits, subsection (2A) above shall apply—

(*a*) separately in relation to that proportion of each of the debits and each of the credits brought into account in determining the amount of the net debit, and
(*b*) on the assumption that that proportion of each of those debits and credits falls within paragraph (*b*) of that subsection.][3]

(3) Where a company pays to a company associated with it a charge on income ...[1], the charge shall not be allowable to any extent under section 338 against the first-mentioned company's ring fence profits.

(4), (5) ...[2]

Commentary—*Simon's Direct Tax Service* **D4.1004.**
Revenue Internal Guidance—Ring fence corporation tax manual 9.2 (OTO policy on acceptable levels of debt).
Definitions—"Accounting period", s 834(1); "associated", s 502(3), (4); "charges on income", s 338 by virtue of s 834(1); "company", s 832(1), (2); "loan relationship", s 834(1), FA 1996 s 81; "oil extraction activities", s 502(1); "oil rights", s 502(1); "ring fence profits", s 502(1).
Amendments—[1] Words in sub-s (1) inserted, words in sub-s (2) substituted and words in sub-s (3) repealed by FA 1996 Sch 14 para 32, Sch 41 Pt V(3) with effect for accounting periods ending after 31 March 1996, subject to transitional provisions in FA 1996 Sch 15.
[2] Sub-ss (4), (5) repealed by FA 1998 s 165, Sch 27 Part III(4) with effect for 1998–99 and subsequent years of assessment for income tax purposes, and from 1 April 1998 for corporation tax, subject to the transitional provisions in FA 1998 Sch 5 Part IV.
[3] Words inserted in sub-ss (2), (2A); in sub-s (2)(c), words substituted for the words "a loan relationship deemed to exist for the purposes of section 100 of that Act", "(i)" inserted, and para (ii) inserted; in sub-s (2)(d), words substituted for the words "in the case of debits", and also for the words "the debit", and "any loan relationship deemed to exist for the purposes of section 100 of that Act"; and sub-ss (2ZA), (2B) inserted, by FA 2002 s 79, Sch 23 para 17 with effect for accounting periods beginning after 30 September 2002.

TA 1988

[494AA Sale and lease-back

(1) This section applies where—

(a) a company (''the seller'') carrying on a trade has disposed of an asset which was used for the purposes of that trade, or an interest in such an asset;
(b) the asset is used, under a lease, by the seller or a company associated with the seller (''the lessee'') for the purposes of a ring fence trade carried on by the lessee; and
(c) the lessee uses the asset before the end of the period of two years beginning with the disposal.

(2) Subject to subsection (4) below, subsection (3) below applies to so much (if any) of the expenditure incurred by the lessee under the lease as—

(a) falls, in accordance with [generally accepted accounting practice]², to be treated in the accounts of the lessee as a finance charge; ...³
(b) ...³

(3) The expenditure shall not be allowable in computing for the purposes of Schedule D the profits of the ring fence trade.

(4) Expenditure shall not be disallowed by virtue of subsection (3) above to the extent that the disposal referred to in subsection (1) above is made for a consideration which—

(a) is used to meet expenditure incurred by the seller in carrying on oil extraction activities or in acquiring oil rights otherwise than from a company associated with the seller; or
(b) is appropriated to meeting expenditure to be so incurred by the seller.

(5) Where any expenditure—

(a) would apart from subsection (3) above be allowable in computing for the purposes of Schedule D the profits of the ring fence trade for an accounting period, but
(b) by virtue of that subsection is not so allowable,

that expenditure shall be brought into account for the purposes of Chapter II of Part IV of the Finance Act 1996 as if it were a non-trading debit in respect of a loan relationship of the lessee for that accounting period.

(6) In this section, ''lease'', in relation to an asset, has the same meaning as in sections 781 to 784.]¹

Commentary—*Simon's Direct Tax Service* **D4.1004.**
Definitions—''Ring fence trade'', s 502(1).
Amendments—¹ This section inserted by FA 1999 s 99 with effect for assets, or interests in assets, disposed of after 8 March 1999, subject to FA 1999 s 99(3).
² In sub-s (2), words substituted for the words ''normal accountancy practice'' by FA 2002 s 103(4)(a) with effect from 24 July 2002.
³ Sub-s (2)(b) and word ''or'' repealed by FA 2002 s 141, Sch 40 Pt 3(16) with effect from 24 July 2002. Sub-s (2)(b) previously read as follows—

''(b) would so fall if the lessee were a company incorporated in the United Kingdom.''.

[494A Computation of amount available for surrender by way of group relief

(1) In section 403(3) (availability of charges, Schedule A losses and management expenses for surrender as group relief) the reference to the gross profits of the surrendering company for an accounting period does not include the company's relevant ring fence profits for that period.

(2) If for that period—

(a) there are no charges on income paid by the company that are allowable under section 338, or
(b) the only charges on income so allowable are charges to which section 494(3) above applies,

all the company's ring fence profits are relevant ring fence profits.

(3) In any other case the company's relevant ring fence profits are so much of its ring fence profits as exceeds the amount of the charges on income paid by the company as—

(a) are allowable under section 338 for that period, and
(b) are not charges to which section 494(3) above applies.]¹

Commentary—*Simon's Direct Tax Service* **D4.1004.**
Amendments—¹ This section inserted by FA 1998 Sch 5 para 30 for 1998–99 and subsequent years of assessment for income tax purposes, and from 1 April 1998 for corporation tax, subject to the transitional provisions in FA 1998 Sch 5 Part IV.

495 Regional development grants

(1) Subsection (2) below applies in any case where—

(a) a person has incurred expenditure (by way of purchase, rent or otherwise) on the acquisition of an asset in a transaction to which paragraph 2 of Schedule 4 to the 1975 Act applies (transactions between connected persons and otherwise than at arm's length), and
(b) the expenditure incurred by the other person referred to in that paragraph in acquiring, bringing into existence or enhancing the value of the asset as mentioned in that paragraph has been or is to be met by a regional development grant and, in whole or in part, falls to be taken into account under [Part 2, 3 or 6 of the Capital Allowances Act (capital allowances relating to plant and machinery, industrial buildings or research and development)]¹

(2) Where this subsection applies, for the purposes of the charge of income tax or corporation tax on the income arising from those activities of the person referred to in paragraph (a) of subsection

(1) above which are treated by virtue of section 492(1) as a separate trade for those purposes, the expenditure referred to in that paragraph shall be treated as reduced by the amount of the regional development grant referred to in paragraph (*b*) of that subsection.

(3) Subsections (4) to (6) below apply where—

(*a*) expenditure incurred by any person in relation to an asset in any relevant period ("the initial period") has been or is to be met by a regional development grant; and

(*b*) notwithstanding the provisions of section 137 of the Finance Act 1982 and subsections (1) and (2) above, in determining that person's liability to income tax or corporation tax for the initial period the whole or some part of that expenditure falls to be taken into account under [Part 2, 3 or 6 of the Capital Allowances Act][1]; and

(*c*) in a relevant period subsequent to the initial period either expenditure on the asset becomes allowable under section 3 or 4 of the 1975 Act or the proportion of any such expenditure which is allowable is different as compared with the initial period;

and in subsections (4) to (6) below the subsequent relevant period referred to in paragraph (*c*) above is referred to as "the adjustment period".

(4) Where this subsection applies—

(*a*) there shall be redetermined for the purposes of subsections (5) and (6) below the amount of the expenditure referred to in subsection (3)(*a*) above which would have been taken into account as mentioned in subsection (3)(*b*) if the circumstances referred to in subsection (3)(*c*) had existed in the initial period; and

(*b*) according to whether the amount as so redetermined is greater or less than the amount actually taken into account as mentioned in subsection (3)(*b*), the difference is in subsections (5) and (6) below referred to as the increase or the reduction in the allowance.

(5) If there is an increase in the allowance, then, for the purposes of the provisions referred to in subsection (3)(*b*) above, an amount of capital expenditure equal to the increase shall be deemed to have been incurred by the person concerned in the adjustment period on an extension of or addition to the asset referred to in subsection (3)(*a*) above.

(6) If there is a reduction in the allowance, then, for the purpose of determining the liability to income tax or corporation tax of the person concerned, he shall be treated as having received in the adjustment period, as income of the trade in connection with which the expenditure referred to in subsection (3)(*a*) above was incurred, a sum equal to the amount of the reduction in the allowance.

(7) In this section—

"regional development grant" [means a grant falling within section 534(1) of the Capital Allowances Act][1]; and

"relevant period" means an accounting period of a company or a year of assessment.

Commentary—*Simon's Direct Tax Service* **D4.1011.**
Definitions—"The 1975 Act", s 502(1); "the 1990 Act", s 831(3); "accounting period", s 834(1); "year of assessment", s 832(1).
Amendments—[1] Words in sub-ss (1), (3) and (7) substituted by CAA 2001 s 578, Sch 2 para 42 with effect for income tax purposes, as respects allowances and charges falling to be made for chargeable periods ending after 5 April 2001, and for corporation tax purposes, as respects allowances and charges falling to be made for chargeable periods ending after 31 March 2001.

496 Tariff receipts

(1) Any sum which—

(*a*) constitutes a tariff receipt of a person who is a participator in an oil field, and

(*b*) constitutes consideration in the nature of income rather than capital, and

(*c*) would not, apart from this subsection, be treated for the purposes of this Chapter as a receipt of the separate trade referred to in section 492(1),

shall be so treated for those purposes.

(2) To the extent that they would not otherwise be so treated, the activities of a participator in an oil field or a person connected with him in making available an asset in a way which gives rise to tariff receipts of the participator shall be treated for the purposes of this Chapter as oil extraction activities.

(3) In determining for the purposes of subsection (1) above whether any sum constitutes a tariff receipt of a person who is a participator, no account shall be taken of any sum which—

(*a*) is in fact received or receivable by a person connected with the participator, and

(*b*) constitutes a tariff receipt of the participator,

but in relation to the person by whom such a sum is actually received, subsection (1) above shall have effect as if he were a participator and as if the condition in paragraph (*a*) of that subsection were fulfilled.

(4) References in this section to a person connected with a participator include references to a person with whom the person is associated within the meaning of paragraph 11 of Schedule 2 to the Oil Taxation Act 1983.

Commentary—*Simon's Direct Tax Service* **D4.1002.**
Definitions—"Oil extraction activities", s 502(1); "oil field", s 502(1); "participator", s 502(1).

[497 Restriction on setting ACT against income from oil extraction activities etc

Commentary—*Simon's Direct Tax Service* **D4.1005.**
Amendments—This section repealed by FA 1998 Sch 3 para 29 with effect for accounting periods beginning after 5 April 1999.

[498 Limited right to carry back surrendered ACT

Commentary—*Simon's Direct Tax Service* **D4.1006.**
Amendments—This section repealed by FA 1998 Sch 3 para 30 with effect for accounting periods of the surrendering company (as defined in TA 1988 s 240(1)) beginning after 5 April 1999.

[499 Surrender of ACT where oil extraction company etc owned by a consortium

Commentary—*Simon's Direct Tax Service* **D4.1006A.**
Amendments—This section repealed by FA 1998 Sch 3 para 31 with effect for distributions made after 5 April 1999.

500 Deduction of PRT in computing income for corporation tax purposes

(1) Where a participator in an oil field has paid any petroleum revenue tax with which he was chargeable for a chargeable period, then, in computing for corporation tax the amount of his income arising in the relevant accounting period from oil extraction activities or oil rights, there shall be deducted an amount equal to that petroleum revenue tax.

(2) There shall be made all such adjustments of assessments to corporation tax as are required in order to give effect to subsection (1) above.

(3) For the purposes of subsection (1) above, the relevant accounting period, in relation to any petroleum revenue tax paid by a company, is—

(*a*) the accounting period of the company in or at the end of which the chargeable period for which that tax was charged ends; or
(*b*) if that chargeable period ends after the accounting period of the company in or at the end of which the trade giving rise to the income referred to above is permanently discontinued, that accounting period.

(4) [Subject to the following provisions of this section][1] if some or all of the petroleum revenue tax in respect of which a deduction has been made under subsection (1) above is subsequently repaid, that deduction shall be reduced or extinguished accordingly; and any additional assessment to corporation tax required in order to give effect to this subsection may be made at any time not later than six years after the end of the [calendar year][1] in which the first-mentioned tax was repaid.

[(5) If, in a case where paragraph 17 of Schedule 2 to the 1975 Act applies, an amount of petroleum revenue tax in respect of which a deduction has been made under subsection (1) above is repaid by virtue of an assessment under that Schedule or an amendment of such an assessment, then, so far as concerns so much of that repayment as constitutes the appropriate repayment,—

(*a*) subsection (4) above shall not apply; and
(*b*) the following provisions of this section shall apply in relation to the company which is entitled to the repayment.

(6) In subsection (5) above and the following provisions of this section—

(*a*) "the appropriate repayment" has the meaning assigned by sub-paragraph (2) of paragraph 17 of Schedule 2 to the 1975 Act;
(*b*) in relation to the appropriate repayment, a "carried back loss" means an allowable loss which falls within sub-paragraph (1)(*a*) of that paragraph and which (alone or together with one or more other carried back losses) gives rise to the appropriate repayment;
(*c*) in relation to a carried back loss, "the operative chargeable period" means the chargeable period in which the loss accrued; and
(*d*) in relation to the company which is entitled to the appropriate repayment, "the relevant accounting period" means the accounting period in or at the end of which ends the operative chargeable period or, if the company's ring fence trade is permanently discontinued before the end of the operative chargeable period, the last accounting period of that trade.

(7) In computing for corporation tax the amount of the company's income arising in the relevant accounting period from oil extraction activities or oil rights there shall be added an amount equal to the appropriate repayment; but this subsection has effect subject to subsection (8) below in any case where—

(*a*) two or more carried back losses give rise to the appropriate repayment; and
(*b*) the operative chargeable period in relation to each of the carried back losses is not the same; and
(*c*) if subsection (6)(*d*) above were applied separately in relation to each of the carried back losses there would be more than one relevant accounting period.

(8) Where paragraphs (*a*) to (*c*) of subsection (7) above apply, the appropriate repayment shall be treated as apportioned between each of the relevant accounting periods referred to in paragraph (*c*) of that subsection in such manner as to secure that the amount added by virtue of that subsection in relation to each of those relevant accounting periods is what it would have been if—

(*a*) relief for each of the carried back losses for which there is a different operative chargeable period had been given by a separate assessment or amendment of an assessment under Schedule 2 to the 1975 Act; and

(*b*) relief for a carried back loss accruing in an earlier chargeable period had been so given before relief for a carried back loss accruing in a later chargeable period.

(9) Any additional assessment to corporation tax required in order to give effect to the addition of an amount by virtue of subsection (7) above may be made at any time not later than six years after the end of the calendar year in which is made the repayment of petroleum revenue tax comprising the appropriate repayment.

(10) In this section "allowable loss" and "chargeable period" have the same meaning as in Part I of the 1975 Act and "calendar year" means a period of twelve months beginning on 1st January.]¹

Commentary—*Simon's Direct Tax Service* **D4.1007.**
Definitions—"The 1975 Act", s 502(1); "accounting period", s 834(1); "chargeable period", s 832(1); "oil extraction activities", s 502(1); "oil field", s 502(1); "oil rights", s 502(1); "participator", s 502(1); "ring fence trade", s 502(1).
Cross references—See OTA 1983 Sch 2 para 11(2) (treatment of connected or associated user of an asset used in connection with an oil field).
OTA 1983 Sch 2 para 12(1) (treatment of a participator in an oil field in relation to purchases by him in certain circumstances of oil at the place of extraction).
Amendments—¹ First words in sub-s (4) inserted and second words in sub-s (4) and sub-ss (5)–(10) (for sub-s (5)) substituted by FA 1990 s 62.

501 Interest on repayment of PRT

Where any amount of petroleum revenue tax paid by a participator in an oil field is, under any provision of Part I of the 1975 Act, repaid to him with interest, the amount of the interest paid to him shall be disregarded in computing the amount of his income for the purposes of corporation tax.

Commentary—*Simon's Direct Tax Service* **D4.1007.**
Definitions—"The 1975 Act", s 502(1); "interest", s 832(1); "oil field", s 502(1); "participator", s 502(1).

[501A Supplementary charge in respect of ring fence trades

(1) Where in any accounting period beginning on or after 17th April 2002 a company carries on a ring fence trade, a sum equal to 10 per cent of its adjusted ring fence profits for that period shall be charged on the company as if it were an amount of corporation tax chargeable on the company.

(2) A company's adjusted ring fence profits for an accounting period are the amount which, on the assumption mentioned in subsection (3) below, would be determined for that period (in accordance with this Chapter) as the profits of the company's ring fence trade chargeable to corporation tax.

(3) The assumption is that financing costs are left out of account in computing—

(*a*) the amount of the profits or loss of any ring fence trade of the company's for each accounting period beginning on or after 17th April 2002; and

(*b*) where for any such period the whole or part of any loss relief is surrendered to the company in accordance with section 492(8), the amount of that relief or, as the case may be, that part.

(4) For the purposes of this section, "financing costs" means the costs of debt finance.

(5) In calculating the costs of debt finance for an accounting period the matters to be taken into account include—

(*a*) any costs giving rise to debits in respect of debtor relationships of the company under Chapter 2 of Part 4 of the Finance Act 1996 (loan relationships)[, other than debits in respect of exchange losses from such relationships (see section 103(1A) and (1B) of that Act);]²

[(*b*) any exchange gain or loss from a debtor relationship, within the meaning of that Chapter (see section 103(1A) and (1B) of that Act), in relation to debt finance;]²

[(*c*) any credit or debit falling to be brought into account under Schedule 26 to the Finance Act 2002 (derivative contracts) in relation to debt finance;]³

(*d*) the financing cost implicit in a payment under a finance lease; and

(*e*) any other costs arising from what would be considered in accordance with generally accepted accounting practice to be a financing transaction.

(6) Where an amount representing the whole or part of a payment falling to be made by a company—

(*a*) falls (or would fall) to be treated as a finance charge under a finance lease for the purposes of accounts relating to that company and one or more other companies and prepared in accordance with generally accepted accounting practice, but

(*b*) is not so treated in the accounts of the company,

the amount shall be treated for the purposes of this section as financing costs falling within subsection (5)(*d*) above.

(7) If—

(*a*) in computing the adjusted ring fence profits of a company for an accounting period, an amount falls to be left out of account by virtue of subsection (5)(*d*) above, but

(*b*) the whole or any part of that amount is repaid,

the repayment shall also be left out of account in computing the adjusted ring fence profits of the company for any accounting period.

(8) In this section "finance lease" means any arrangements—

(*a*) which provide for an asset to be leased or otherwise made available by a person to another person ("the lessee"), and

(*b*) which, under generally accepted accounting practice,—

(i) fall (or would fall) to be treated, in the accounts of the lessee or a person connected with the lessee, as a finance lease or a loan, or

(ii) are comprised in arrangements which fall (or would fall) to be so treated.

(9) For the purposes of applying subsection (8)(*b*) above, the lessee and any person connected with the lessee are to be treated as being companies which are incorporated in a part of the United Kingdom.

(10) In this section "accounts", in relation to a company, includes any accounts which—

(*a*) relate to two or more companies of which that company is one, and

(*b*) are drawn up in accordance with—

(i) section 227 of the Companies Act 1985, or

(ii) Article 235 of the Companies (Northern Ireland) Order 1986.][1]

Cross-references—See FA 2002 s 93 (supplementary charge: transitional provisions).
Amendments—[1] This section inserted by FA 2002 s 91.
[2] In sub-s (5), words in para (*a*) inserted, and para (*b*) substituted, by FA 2002 s 79, Sch 23 para 18 with effect for accounting periods beginning after 30 September 2002. Para (*b*) previously read as follows—

"(*b*) any exchange gain or loss, within the meaning of Chapter 2 of Part 2 of the Finance Act 1993, in relation to debt finance;".
[3] Sub-s (5)(*c*) substituted by FA 2002 s 83(1)(*b*), (3) Sch 27 paras 1, 8 with effect for accounting periods beginning after 30 September 2002. Sub-s (5)(*c*) previously read as follows—

"(*c*) any trading profit or loss, under Chapter 2 of Part 4 of the Finance Act 1994 (interest rate and currency contracts), in relation to debt finance;".

[501B Assessment, recovery and postponement of supplementary charge

(1) Subject to subsection (3) below, the provisions of section 501A(1) relating to the charging of a sum as if it were an amount of corporation tax shall be taken as applying, subject to the provisions of the Taxes Acts, and to any necessary modifications, all enactments applying generally to corporation tax, including—

(*a*) those relating to returns of information and the supply of accounts, statements and reports;

(*b*) those relating to the assessing, collecting and receiving of corporation tax;

(*c*) those conferring or regulating a right of appeal; and

(*d*) those concerning administration, penalties, interest on unpaid tax and priority of tax in cases of insolvency under the law of any part of the United Kingdom.

(2) Accordingly (but without prejudice to subsection (1) above) the Management Act shall have effect as if any reference to corporation tax included a reference to a sum chargeable under section 501A(1) as if it were an amount of corporation tax.

(3) In any regulations made under section 32 of the Finance Act 1998 (as at 17th April 2002, the Corporation Tax (Treatment of Unrelieved Surplus Advance Corporation Tax) Regulations 1999)—

(*a*) references to corporation tax do not include a reference to a sum chargeable on a company under section 501A(1) as if it were corporation tax; and

(*b*) references to profits charged to corporation tax do not include a reference to adjusted ring fence profits, within the meaning of section 501A(1).

(4) In this section "the Taxes Acts" has the same meaning as in the Management Act.][1]

Cross-references—See FA 2002 s 93 (supplementary charge: transitional provisions).
Amendments—[1] This section inserted by FA 2002 s 92(1).

502 Interpretation of Chapter V

(1) In this Chapter—

"the 1975 Act" means the Oil Taxation Act 1975;

"oil" means any substance won or capable of being won under the authority of a licence granted under either [Part I of the Petroleum Act 1998][4] or the Petroleum (Production) Act (Northern Ireland) 1964, other than methane gas won in the course of operations for making and keeping mines safe;

"oil extraction activities" means any activities of a person—

(*a*) in searching for oil in the United Kingdom or a designated area or causing such searching to be carried out for him; or

(*b*) in extracting or causing to be extracted for him oil at any place in the United Kingdom or a designated area under rights authorising the extraction and held by him or, if the person in question is a company, by the company or a company associated with it; or

(*c*) in transporting or causing to be transported for him ...[3] oil extracted at any such place not on dry land under rights authorising the extraction and so held [where the transportation is—

(i) to the place where the oil is first landed in the United Kingdom, or

(ii) to the place in the United Kingdom or, in the case of oil first landed in another country, the place in that or any other country (other than the United Kingdom) at which the seller in a sale at arm's length could reasonably be expected to deliver it or, if there is more than one such place, the one nearest to the place of extraction][3]; or

(*d*) in effecting or causing to be effected for him the initial treatment or initial storage of oil won from any oil field under rights authorising its extraction and so held;

"oil field" has the same meaning as in Part I of the 1975 Act;
"oil rights" means rights to oil to be extracted at any place in the United Kingdom or a designated area, or to interests in or to the benefit of such oil;
"participator" has the same meaning as in Part I of the 1975 Act; and
"ring fence income" means income arising from oil extraction activities or oil rights; and
"ring fence profits" has the [meaning given by sub-s (1A) below][2] or, in any case where that subsection does not apply, means ring fence income; [and][1]
["ring fence trade" means activities which—

     (*a*) fall within any of paragraphs (*a*) to (*c*) of subsection (1) of section 492; and
     (*b*) constitute a separate trade (whether by virtue of that subsection or otherwise).][1]

[(1A) Where in accordance with section 197(3) of the 1992 Act a person has an aggregate gain for any chargeable period, that gain and his ring fence income (if any) for that period together constitute his ring fence profits for the purposes of this Chapter.][2]

(2) For the purposes of subsection (1) above—

(*a*) "designated area" means an area designated by Order in Council under section 1(7) of the Continental Shelf Act 1964;
(*b*) "initial treatment" has the same meaning as in Part I of the 1975 Act; and
(*c*) the definition of "initial storage" in section 12(1) of the 1975 Act shall apply but, in its application for those purposes in relation to the person mentioned in subsection (1)(*d*) above and to oil won from any one oil field shall have effect as if the reference to the maximum daily production rate of oil for the field as there mentioned were a reference to that person's share of that maximum daily production rate, that is to say, a share thereof proportionate to his share of the oil won from that field.

(3) For the purposes of this Chapter two companies are associated with one another if—

(*a*) one is a 51 per cent subsidiary of the other;
(*b*) each is a 51 per cent subsidiary of a third company; or
(*c*) one is owned by a consortium of which the other is a member.

[(3A) Section 413(6) applies for the purposes of subsection (3)(*c*) above but as if section 413 were modified as follows—

(*a*) as if the definition of "company" in subsection (2) were omitted;
(*b*) as if at the beginning of subsection (5) there were inserted "References in this Chapter to a company apply only to bodies corporate resident in the United Kingdom; and"; and
(*c*) as if in that subsection, after the word "receipt", in the second place where it occurs, there were inserted "; or

     (*c*) of any share capital which it owns directly or indirectly in a body corporate not resident in the United Kingdom".][5]

(4) Without prejudice to subsection (3) above, for the purposes of this Chapter, two companies are also associated with one another if one has control of the other or both are under the control of the same person or persons; and in this subsection "control" shall be construed in accordance with section 416.

Commentary—*Simon's Direct Tax Service* **D4.1008.**
Definitions—"the 1992 Act", s 831(3); "51 per cent subsidiary", s 838.
Cross references—See F(No 2)A 1992 s 55(3) (definitions of "initial treatment" and "initial storage" as they have effect by virtue of sub-s (2) above for the purposes of this Chapter; amendments to the definitions by F(No 2)A 1992 Sch 15 para 3 to have effect with respect to chargeable periods ending after 27 November 1991).
Amendments—[1] Definition of "ring fence trade" and the preceding word "and" in sub-s (1) added by FA 1990 s 62(3).
[2] Words in the definition of "ring fence profits" substituted and sub-s (1A) inserted by TCGA 1992 Sch 10 para 14(1), (30).
[3] In the definition of "oil extraction activities" words in para (*c*) inserted and repealed by F(No 2)A 1992 s 55(1), (2), Sch 18 Pt VII(7) with respect to chargeable periods ending after 27 November 1991.
[4] Words in sub-s (1) substituted by the Petroleum Act 1998 s 50, Sch 4 para 25 with effect from 15 February 1999 (by virtue of the Petroleum Act 1998 (Commencement No 1) Order, SI 1999/161).
[5] Words at end of sub-s (3) substituted for words "Section 413(6) shall apply for the purposes of paragraph (*c*) above." by new sub-s (3A) by FA 2000 s 97, Sch 27 paras 9, 12(2) with effect wherever this section falls to be construed, so far as it applies TA 1988 Pt X Ch IV, as applying the provisions amended by FA 2000 Sch 27 Pt I.

CHAPTER VI
MISCELLANEOUS BUSINESSES AND BODIES

Concession C3—This Concession gives a measure of tax relief to holiday clubs and thrift funds which are formed annually to organise savings for holidays.

[503 Letting of furnished holiday accommodation treated as a trade for certain purposes

(1) For the purposes specified in subsection (2)—

(*a*) a Schedule A business which consists in, or so far as it consists in, the commercial letting of furnished holiday accommodation in the United Kingdom shall be treated as if it were a trade the profits of which are chargeable to tax under Case I of Schedule D, and

(*b*) all such lettings made by a particular person or partnership or body of persons shall be treated as one trade.

The "commercial letting of furnished holiday accommodation" is defined below in section 504.

(2) Subsection (1) above applies for the purposes of—

(*a*) Chapters I and II of Part X (loss relief for income tax and corporation tax), and

(*b*) sections 623(2)(*c*), 644(2)(*c*) and 833(4)(*c*) (income regarded as relevant earnings for pension purposes or as earned income).

(3) Chapter I of Part X (loss relief for income tax) as applied by this section has effect with the following adaptations—

(*a*) no relief shall be given to an individual under section 381 (relief for losses in early years of trade) in respect of a year of assessment if any of the accommodation in respect of which the trade is carried on in that year was first let by that person as furnished accommodation more than three years before the beginning of that year of assessment;

(*b*) section 384 (restrictions on right of set-off) has effect with the omission of subsections (6) to (8) and the words after paragraph (*b*) in subsection (10) (which relate to certain losses attributable to capital allowances);

(*c*) section 390 (treatment of interest as loss) has effect as if the reference to a trade the profits of which are chargeable to tax under Case I of Schedule D were a reference to the Schedule A business so far as it is treated as a trade.

(4) Where there is a letting of accommodation only part of which is holiday accommodation, such apportionments shall be made for the purposes of this section as are just and reasonable.

(5) Relief shall not be given for the same loss, or the same portion of a loss, both under a provision of Part X as applied by this section and under any other provision of the Tax Acts.][1]

Commentary—*Simon's Direct Tax Service* B7.206.
Revenue Interpretation RI 28—Rollover relief: commercial letting of furnished holiday accommodation in excess of 30 days.
Revenue & other press releases—IR 17-5-84 (furnished holiday lettings and caravans these provisions are relieving provisions and do not change basis of assessment of furnished holiday letting assessed to tax under Sch D Case I but provide additional reliefs where lettings do not amount to a trade).
Booklet IR150 paras 410–422 (outline of s 503).
Booklet IR150 paras 423–500 (explanation of the loss relief provisions).
Revenue Internal Guidance—Property Income Manual PIM4120 (profits not chargeable to Class IV NICs; where property closed for part of year all insurance, interest etc is allowed provided there is no private use).
Definitions—"The Tax Acts", s 831(2); "commercial letting", s 504(2); "furnished accommodation", s 504(2); "holiday accommodation", s 504(2); "Schedule D", s 18(1); "trade", s 832(1); "year of assessment", s 832(1).
Cross references—See TA 1988 s 65A(3) (this section to be disregarded in computing income from land overseas etc chargeable to income tax under Schedule D Case V).
TA 1988 s 504 (supplementary provisions).
Amendments—[1] This section substituted by FA 1998 s 38, Sch 5 para 42 with effect for income tax purposes from 1998–99, and for corporation tax purposes from 1 April 1998, subject to the transitional provisions in FA 1998 Sch 5 Part IV.

504 Supplementary provisions

(1) This section has effect for the purposes of section 503.

(2) A letting—

(*a*) is a commercial letting if it is let on a commercial basis and with a view to the realisation of profits; and

(*b*) is of furnished accommodation if the tenant is entitled to the use of furniture.

(3) Accommodation shall not be treated as holiday accommodation for the purposes of this section unless—

(*a*) it is available for commercial letting to the public generally as holiday accommodation for periods which amount, in the aggregate, to not less than 140 days;

(*b*) the periods for which it is so let amount in the aggregate to at least 70 days; and

(*c*) for a period comprising at least seven months (which need not be continuous but includes any months in which it is let as mentioned in paragraph (*b*) above) it is not normally in the same occupation for a continuous period exceeding 31 days.

(4) Any question whether accommodation let by any person other than a company is, at any time in a year of assessment, holiday accommodation shall be determined—

(*a*) if the accommodation was not let by him as furnished accommodation in the preceding year of assessment but is so let in the following year of assessment, by reference to the 12 months beginning with the date on which he first so let it in the year of assessment;

(*b*) if the accommodation was let by him as furnished accommodation in the preceding year of assessment but is not so let in the following year of assessment, by reference to the 12 months ending with the date on which he ceased so to let it in the year of assessment; and

(*c*) in any other case, by reference to the year of assessment.

(5) Any question whether accommodation let by a company is at any time in an accounting period holiday accommodation shall be determined—

   (a) if the accommodation was not let by it as furnished accommodation in the period of 12 months immediately preceding the accounting period but is so let in the period of 12 months immediately following the accounting period, by reference to the 12 months beginning with the date in the accounting period on which it first so let it;

   (b) if the accommodation was let by it as furnished accommodation in the period of 12 months immediately preceding the accounting period but is not so let by it in the period of 12 months immediately following the accounting period, by reference to the 12 months ending with the date in the accounting period on which it ceased so to let it;

   (c) in any other case, by reference to the period of 12 months ending with the last day of the accounting period.

(6) Where, in any year of assessment or accounting period, a person lets furnished accommodation which is treated as holiday accommodation for the purposes of this section in that year or period ("the qualifying accommodation"), he may make a claim under this subsection, within [the time specified in subsection (6A) below][1], for averaging treatment to apply for that year or period to that and any other accommodation specified in the claim which was let by him as furnished accommodation during that year or period and would fall to be treated as holiday accommodation in that year or period if subsection (3)(b) above were satisfied in relation to it.

[(6A) The time mentioned in subsection (6) above is—

   (a) in the case of a claim for the purposes of income tax, the period ending with the first anniversary of the 31st January next following the year of assessment in which the accommodation was let;

   (b) in the case of a claim for the purposes of corporation tax, the period of two years beginning at the end of the accounting period in which the accommodation was let.][1]

(7) Where a claim is made under subsection (6) above in respect of any year of assessment or accounting period, any such other accommodation shall be treated as being holiday accommodation in that year or period if the number of days for which the qualifying accommodation and any other such accommodation was let by the claimant as mentioned in subsection (3)(a) above during the year or period amounts on average to at least 70.

(8) Qualifying accommodation may not be specified in more than one claim in respect of any one year of assessment or accounting period.

(9) For the purposes of this section a person lets accommodation if he permits another person to occupy it, whether or not in pursuance of a lease; and "letting" and "tenant" shall be construed accordingly.

Commentary—*Simon's Direct Tax Service* **B7.206.**
Revenue Interpretation RI 28—Rollover relief: commercial letting of furnished holiday accommodation in excess of 30 days.
Revenue Internal Guidance—Property Income Manual PIM4100 (Revenue take a broad view of "commercial"; close season lettings may contribute to cost even if they do not contribute a profit; "furnished" implies sufficient furniture for normal occupation).
PIM4110 (examples illustrating sub-s (3); "normally" is construed as meaning regular or usual: genuine cases not denied relief due to exceptional or unforeseen circumstances).
Simon's Tax Cases—s 504(2)(a), *Walls v Livesey* [1995] STC (SCD) 12; *Brown v Richardson* [1997] STC (SCD) 233.
Definitions—"Accounting period", s 834(1); "company", s 832(1), (2); "year of assessment", s 832(1).
Cross references—See TMA 1970 s 42(6), (7) (procedure for claims by partnership under this section).
TA 1988 s 65A(3) (this section to be disregarded in computing income from land overseas etc chargeable to income tax under Schedule D Case V).
Amendments—[1] Words in sub-s (6) and sub-s (6A) inserted by FA 1996 Sch 21 para 14 with effect in relation to income tax from the year 1996–97 and for the purposes of corporation tax as respects accounting periods ending after 30 June 1999 (by virtue of Finance Act 1994, Section 199, (Appointed Day) Order, SI 1998/3173 art 2).

505 Charities: general

(1) Subject to subsections (2) and (3) below, the following exemptions shall be granted on a claim in that behalf to the Board—

   [(a) exemption from tax under Schedules A and D in respect of any profits or gains arising in respect of rents or other receipts from an estate, interest or right in or over any land (whether situated in the United Kingdom or elsewhere) to the extent that the profits or gains—

      (i) arise in respect of rents or receipts from an estate, interest or right vested in any person for charitable purposes; and

      (ii) are applied to charitable purposes only;][5]

   (b) ...[1]

   (c) exemption—

      (i) ...[6]

      [(ii) from tax under Case III of Schedule D,][5]

      [(iia) from tax under Case IV or V of Schedule D in respect of income equivalent to income chargeable under Case III of that Schedule but arising from securities or other possessions outside the United Kingdom, (iib) from tax under Case V of Schedule D in respect of income consisting in any such dividend or other distribution of a company not resident in the United Kingdom as would be chargeable to tax under Schedule F if the company were so resident, and][5]

[(iic) from tax under Case VI of Schedule D in respect of non-trading gains on intangible fixed assets under Schedule 29 to the Finance Act 2002, and][8]

(iii) from tax under Schedule F in respect of any distribution,

where the income in question forms part of the income of a charity, or is, according to rules or regulations established by Act of Parliament, charter, decree, deed of trust or will, applicable to charitable purposes only, and so far as it is applied to charitable purposes only;

[(*d*) exemption from tax under Schedule D in respect of public revenue dividends on securities which are in the name of trustees, to the extent that the dividends are applicable and applied only for the repair of—

(i) any cathedral, college, church or chapel, or
(ii) any building used only for the purposes of divine worship;][6]

(*e*) exemption from tax under Schedule D in respect of the profits of any trade carried on by a charity [(whether in the United Kingdom or elsewhere)][5], if the profits are applied solely to the purposes of the charity and either—

(i) the trade is exercised in the course of the actual carrying out of a primary purpose of the charity; or
(ii) the work in connection with the trade is mainly carried out by beneficiaries of the charity.

[(*f*) exemption from tax under Schedule D in respect of profits accruing to a charity from a lottery if—

(i) the lottery is promoted and conducted in accordance with section 3 or 5 of the Lotteries and Amusements Act 1976 or Article 133 or 135 of the Betting, Gaming, Lotteries and Amusements (Northern Ireland) Order 1985; and
(ii) the profits are applied solely to the charity's purposes.][3]

[(1A) In subsection (1)(*d*) above "public revenue dividends" means—

(*a*) income from securities which is payable out of the public revenue of the United Kingdom or Northern Ireland;
(*b*) income from securities issued by or on behalf of a government or a public or local authority in a country outside the United Kingdom.][6]

(2) Any payment which—

(*a*) is received by a charity from another charity; and
(*b*) is not made for full consideration in money or money's worth; and
(*c*) is not chargeable to tax apart from this subsection; and
(*d*) is not, apart from this subsection, of a description which (on a claim) would be eligible for relief from tax by virtue of any provision of subsection (1) above;

shall be chargeable to tax under Case III of Schedule D but shall be eligible for relief from tax under subsection (1)(*c*) above as if it were an annual payment.

(3) If in any chargeable period of a charity—

(*a*) its relevant income and gains are not less than £10,000; and
(*b*) its relevant income and gains exceed the amount of its qualifying expenditure; and
(*c*) the charity incurs, or is treated as incurring, non-qualifying expenditure;

relief shall not be available under either subsection (1) above or section [256 of the 1992 Act][2] for so much of the excess as does not exceed the non-qualifying expenditure incurred in that period.

(4) In relation to a chargeable period of less than 12 months, subsection (3) above shall have effect as if the amount specified in paragraph (*a*) of that subsection were proportionately reduced.

(5) In subsection (3) above "relevant income and gains" means—

(*a*) income which apart from subsection (1) above would not be exempt from tax together with any income which is taxable notwithstanding that subsection; and
(*b*) gains which apart from section [256 of the 1992 Act][2] would be chargeable gains together with any gains which are chargeable gains notwithstanding that section.

(6) Where by virtue of subsection (3) above there is an amount of a charity's relevant income and gains for which relief under subsection (1) above and section [256 of the 1992 Act][2] is not available, the charity may, by notice to the Board, specify which items of its relevant income and gains are, in whole or in part, to be attributed to that amount, ...[7]; and if within 30 days of being required to do so by the Board, a charity does not give notice under this subsection, the items of its relevant income and gains which are to be attributed to the amount in question shall be such as the Board may determine.

(7) Where it appears to the Board that two or more charities acting in concert are engaged in transactions of which the main purpose or one of the main purposes is the avoidance of tax (whether by the charities or by any other person), the Board may by notice given to the charities provide that, for such chargeable periods as may be specified in the notice, subsection (3) above shall have effect in relation to them with the omission of paragraph (*a*).

(8) An appeal may be brought against a notice under subsection (7) above as if it were notice of the decision of the Board on a claim made by the charities concerned.

Commentary—*Simon's Direct Tax Service* **C4.518–523, 527; D2.1145.**
Concession C4—Where specified conditions are satisfied, tax is not charged on activities such as bazaars, jumble sales, carnivals etc organised by charities or voluntary organisations for charitable purposes.
D47—Temporary loss of charitable status due to reversion of school and other sites: no adverse effect on CGT or income tax exemption.
Statement of Practice SP 3/87—Procedure adopted by the Revenue to minimise delay in making repayment to charities on covenanted and other income.
Revenue & other press releases—IR & HM Customs & Excise 23-11-89 (tax treatment of disaster funds; guidelines for organisers).
IR Leaflet CB(1) (''Setting up a charity in Scotland'' available from Inland Revenue, Claims (Scotland)).
IR 13-8-93 (new form R68(TR) to be used to claim payment of tax credit on UK company dividends up to 5 April 1997).
Code of Practice 4 (inspection of charities' records).
IR booklet charities series 2 (''Trading by charities'' available from Inland Revenue, FICO (Charities Technical)).
Simon's Tax Cases—s 505(1), *IRC v Helen Slater Charitable Trust Ltd* [1981] STC 471*; *IRC v Sheppard (Trustees of the Woodland Trust) (No 2)* [1993] STC 240*.
s 505(1)(*a*), *IRC v Church Comrs for England* [1975] STC 546*.
s 505(1)(*c*)(iii), *Guild (as Trustees of the William Muir (Bond 9) Ltd Employees' Share Scheme) v IRC* [1993] STC 444.
Definitions—''The 1992 Act'', s 831(3); ''the Board'', s 832(1); ''chargeable period'', s 832(1); ''charity'', s 506(1); ''distribution'', s 832(1); ''interest'', s 832(1); ''non-qualifying expenditure'', s 506(1); ''notice'', s 832(1); ''qualifying expenditure'', s 506(1); ''Schedule A'', s 15(1); ''Schedule D'', s 18(1); ''Schedule F'', s 20(1); ''trade'', s 832(1).
Cross references—See TA 1988 s 506(2) (for the purposes of this section, expenditure not actually incurred in a year to be treated as incurred in that year if the charity was committed to incur it).
TCGA 1992 s 256(1) (tax exemption on chargeable gains accruing to charities);
F(No 2)A 1992 s 28 (powers to inspect charities' records where a claim for exemption is made under sub-s (1) above);
FA 2000 s 46 (tax exemption for small trades etc if a charity's gross income is within the requisite limit as specified in s 46(4)).
Amendments—[1] Sub-s (1)(*b*) repealed by FA 1988 Sch 14 Pt V.
[2] Words in sub-ss (3), (5)(*b*), (6) substituted by TCGA 1992 Sch 10 paras 14(1), (31).
[3] Sub-s (1)(*f*) inserted by FA 1995 s 138(1), (2) with effect for chargeable periods beginning, in the case of a company, after 31 March 1995, and in any other case, after 5 April 1995.
[4] Words in sub-s (6) substituted by FA 1995 s 74(2), Sch 17 Pt II, para 7, with effect from the year 1995–96 (and apply to every settlement, wherever and whenever made or entered into).
[5] Sub-s (1)(*a*) and sub-s (1)(*c*)(ii), (iia), (iib) substituted (latter for sub-s (1)(*c*)(ii)) and words in sub-s (1)(*e*) inserted by FA 1996 s 146 with effect for the purposes of income tax from the year 1996–97 and for the purposes of corporation tax for accounting periods ending after 31 March 1996.
[6] Sub-s (1)(*c*)(i) repealed, sub-s (1)(*d*) is substituted and sub-s (1A) inserted by FA 1996 Sch 7 para 19, Sch 41 Pt V(2) with effect as respects income tax from the year 1996–97, and for the purposes of corporation tax, for accounting periods ending after 31 March 1996.
[7] Words in sub-s (6) repealed by FA 2000 ss 41(5), (9), 156, Sch 40 Pt II(1) with effect for covenanted payments falling to be made by individuals after 5 April 2000 or made by companies after 31 March 2000.
[8] Sub-s (1)(*c*)(iic) inserted by FA 2002 s 84(2), Sch 30 para 3 with effect from 24 July 2002.

506 Qualifying expenditure and non-qualifying expenditure

(1) In this section, section 505 and Schedule 20—

''charity'' means any body of persons or trust established for charitable purposes only;
''qualifying expenditure'', in relation to a chargeable period of a charity, means, subject to subsection (3) below, expenditure incurred in that period for charitable purposes only; and
''non-qualifying expenditure'' means expenditure which is not qualifying expenditure.

(2) For the purposes of section 505 and subsection (1) above, where expenditure which is not actually incurred in a particular chargeable period properly falls to be charged against the income of that chargeable period as being referable to commitments (whether or not of a contractual nature) which the charity has entered into before or during that period, it shall be treated as incurred in that period.

(3) A payment made (or to be made) to a body situated outside the United Kingdom shall not be qualifying expenditure by virtue of this section unless the charity concerned has taken such steps as may be reasonable in the circumstances to ensure that the payment will be applied for charitable purposes.

(4) If in any chargeable period a charity—

(*a*) invests any of its funds in an investment which is not a qualifying investment, as defined in Part I of Schedule 20; or
(*b*) makes a loan (not being an investment) which is not a qualifying loan, as defined in Part II of that Schedule;

then, subject to subsection (5) below, the amount so invested or lent in that period shall be treated for the purposes of this section as being an amount of expenditure incurred by the charity, and, accordingly, as being non-qualifying expenditure.

(5) If, in any chargeable period, a charity which has in that period made an investment or loan falling within subsection (4) above—

(*a*) realises the whole or part of that investment; or
(*b*) is repaid the whole or part of that loan;

any further investment or lending in that period of the sum realised or repaid shall, to the extent that it does not exceed the sum originally invested or lent, be left out of account in determining the amount which, by virtue of subsection (4) above, is treated as non-qualifying expenditure incurred in that period.

(6) If the aggregate of the qualifying and non-qualifying expenditure incurred by a charity in any chargeable period exceeds the relevant income and gains of that period, Part III of Schedule 20 shall have effect to treat, in certain cases, some or all of that excess as non-qualifying expenditure incurred in earlier periods.

Commentary—*Simon's Direct Tax Service* **C4.528.**
Statement of Practice SP 3/87—Procedure adopted by the Revenue to minimise delay in making repayment to charities on covenanted and other income.
Definition—"Chargeable period", s 832(1).

507 The National Heritage Memorial Fund, the Historic Buildings and Monuments Commission for England and the British Museum

(1) There shall on a claim in that behalf to the Board be allowed in the case of—

   (a) the Trustees of the National Heritage Memorial Fund;
   (b) the Historic Buildings and Monuments Commission for England;
   [(c) the Trustees of the British Museum;][1]
   [(d) the Trustees of the [Natural History Museum][3];][1]
   [(e) ...][4]

such exemption from tax as falls to be allowed under section 505 in the case of a charity the whole income of which is applied to charitable purposes.

(2) ...[2]

Commentary—*Simon's Direct Tax Service* **C4.551; D4.331.**
Simon's Tax Cases—s 506(1), *IRC v Oldham TEC* [1996] STC 1218.
Cross references—See F(No 2)A 1992 s 28 (powers to inspect records where a claim for exemption is made under this section);
Amendments—[1] Sub-s (1)(c), (d) inserted by FA 1989 s 60(1), (4) in relation to accounting periods ending after 13 March 1989.
[2] Sub-s (2) repealed by FA 1989 Sch 17 Pt IV.
[3] Words in sub-s (1)(d) substituted by the Museums and Galleries Act 1992 Sch 8 para 1(8) with effect from 1 September 1992 by virtue of Museums and Galleries Act 1992 (Commencement) Order, SI 1992/1874.
[4] Sub-s (1)(e) repealed by the United Kingdom Ecolabelling Board (Abolition) Regulations, SI 1999/931 reg 9 with effect from 19 April 1999.

508 Scientific research organisations

(1) Where—

   (a) an Association which has as its object the undertaking of scientific research which may lead to or facilitate an extension of any class or classes of trade is approved for the purposes of this section by the Secretary of State; and
   (b) the memorandum of association or other similar instrument regulating the functions of the Association precludes the direct or indirect payment or transfer to any of its members of any of its income or property by way of dividend, gift, division, bonus or otherwise howsoever by way of profit;

there shall, on a claim in that behalf to the Board, be allowed in the case of the Association such exemption from tax as falls to be allowed under section 505 in the case of a charity the whole income of which is applied to charitable purposes.

(2) The condition specified in paragraph (b) of subsection (1) above shall not be deemed not to be complied with in the case of any Association by reason only that the memorandum or other similar instrument regulating its functions does not prevent the payment to its members of reasonable remuneration for goods, labour or power supplied, or for services rendered, of reasonable interest for money lent, or of reasonable rent for any premises.

(3) In this section "scientific research" means any activities in the fields of natural or applied science for the extension of knowledge.

Commentary—*Simon's Direct Tax Service* **C4.535, 540.**
Concession C31—The criteria applied in determining whether a body is a scientific research association.
Revenue & other press releases—DTI 4-9-98 (Changes to tax exemption scheme for scientific research).
Definitions—"The Board", s 832(1); "trade", s 832(1).
Cross references—See TCGA 1992 s 271(6)(b) (an Association within this section exempt from tax in respect of all chargeable gains);
F(No 2)A 1992 s 28 (powers to inspect records where a claim for exemption is made under this section).

[508A Investment trusts investing in housing

(1) Where any company that is an investment trust has eligible rental income for any accounting period—

   (a) the rate of corporation tax chargeable for any financial year on the trust's housing investment profits for that period shall be deemed to be the small companies' rate for that year; and
   (b) its housing investment profits for that period shall be treated for the purposes of section 13 as excluded from its basic profits for that period.

(2) For the purposes of this section—

   (a) a company's eligible rental income for any period is so much of its income for that period as consists in rents or other receipts deriving from lettings by the company of eligible properties; and (*b*) its housing investment profits for any period are so much of its profits for that period as represents the amount chargeable to tax under Schedule A in respect of its eligible rental income for that period.

(3) In computing the amount mentioned in subsection (2)(*b*) above for any period, deductions shall be made which (except in so far as they exceed the amount from which they are deducted) are, in aggregate, not less than the sum of the following amounts—

(*a*) every amount which is both—

(i) deductible (otherwise than as a debit brought into account under Chapter II of Part IV of the Finance Act 1996) in the computation of any income of the company, or of its total profits, for that period, and

(ii) referable to, or to activities connected with, the letting by the company on assured tenancies of dwelling-houses that are eligible properties when so let,

and

(*b*) any amount that is so referable that would represent a non-trading deficit on the company's loan relationships for that period.

(4) For the purposes of subsection (3) above any question—

(*a*) whether for any period there is an amount referable to any matter that would represent a non-trading deficit on a company's loan relationships, or

(*b*) as to what that amount is for that period,

shall be determined by computing whether and to what extent there would for that period have been a non-trading deficit on the company's loan relationships if debits and credits fell to be brought into account under Chapter II of Part IV of the Finance Act 1996 to the extent only that they are referable to that matter.]¹

Commentary—*Simon's Direct Tax Service* **D4.428.**
Definitions—"Accounting period", s 834(1); "financial year", s 834(1); "investment trust", s 842; "loan relationship", s 834(1), FA 1996 s 81; "non-trading deficit", s 834(1), FA 1996 s 82; "Schedule A", s 15; "small companies' rate", s 13.
Cross references—See TA 1988 s 508B (interpretation).
Amendments—¹ This section inserted by FA 1996 Sch 30 para 1 with effect for accounting periods beginning after 28 April 1996.

[508B Interpretation of section 508A

(1) In section 508A "eligible property", in relation to a company, means (subject to the following provisions of this section) any dwelling-house as respects which the following conditions are satisfied—

(*a*) the company first acquired an interest in the dwelling-house on or after 1st April 1996;

(*b*) that interest was not, at the time when it was acquired, subject to any letting or to any statutory tenancy;

(*c*) at that time no arrangements had been made by the company or any person connected with it for the letting of the dwelling-house;

(*d*) the interest of the company in the dwelling-house is a freehold interest or an interest under a long lease at a low rent;

(*e*) the consideration given by the company for the acquisition of its interest in the dwelling-house did not exceed—

(i) £125,000, in the case of a dwelling-house in Greater London, or

(ii) £85,000, in any other case;

(*f*) the dwelling-house is let by the company under an assured tenancy and is neither—

(i) let by the company in consideration of a premium within the meaning of Schedule 8 to the 1992 Act, nor

(ii) a dwelling-house in respect of which the person to whom it is let or any associate of his has been granted any option to purchase.

(2) For the purposes of paragraph (*b*) of subsection (1) above, no account shall be taken of any shorthold tenancy or statutory shorthold tenancy to which the interest became subject before the time when it was acquired.

(3) For the purposes of paragraph (*c*) of subsection (1) above, no account shall be taken of any arrangements made by a person connected with the company in question before the time when the interest was acquired by the company if—

(*a*) that person had an interest in the dwelling-house when he made those arrangements;

(*b*) that person did not dispose of his interest at any time after the arrangements were entered into and before the company acquired its interest; and

(*c*) the arrangements were such as to confer a relevant entitlement on a person who, at the time when the company acquired its interest, was a tenant under any shorthold tenancy of the dwelling-house (or any part of it).

(4) For the purposes of subsection (3)(*c*) above a relevant entitlement is an entitlement of a tenant under a shorthold tenancy of any premises, on the coming to an end of that tenancy, to such a further tenancy of the same or substantially the same premises as will itself be a shorthold tenancy.

(5) For the purposes of this section the consideration given by a company for the acquisition of an interest in a dwelling-house shall be taken (subject to subsection (6) below) to include—

(a) any amount expended by the company on the construction or renovation of the dwelling-house or on any conversion by virtue of which that dwelling-house came to be usable as such;

(b) any amount so expended by a person connected with the company; and

(c) any consideration given by a person connected with the company for the acquisition of any such interest in the dwelling-house as—

(i) is subsequently acquired by the company, or

(ii) is held by such a person at the same time as the company holds its interest in the premises.

(6) Where a company has acquired any interest in a dwelling-house from a person connected with that company—

(a) amounts expended by that person as mentioned in paragraph (a) of subsection (5) above, and

(b) the amount of any consideration given by that person for an interest in the dwelling-house,

shall be treated by virtue of that subsection as included in the consideration given by the company to the extent only that the aggregate of those amounts exceeds the consideration given by that company to that person for the interest acquired from that person by the company.

(7) In section 508A and this section—

"associate" has the meaning given by subsections (3) and (4) of section 417;

"assured tenancy" means—

(a) any letting which is an assured tenancy for the purposes of the Housing Act 1988 or the Housing (Scotland) Act 1988, or

(b) any tenancy in Northern Ireland which complies with such requirements or conditions as may be prescribed by regulations made by the Department of the Environment for Northern Ireland;

"letting" includes a letting by virtue of an agreement for a lease or under a licence, and "let" shall be construed accordingly;

"long lease", in relation to the interest of a company in any dwelling-house, means a lease for a term of years certain of which at least 21 years remains unexpired at the time when that interest was acquired by the company;

"low rent" means a rent at an annual rate not exceeding—

(a) £1,000, in the case of a dwelling-house in Greater London; and

(b) £250, in any other case;

"rent" has the same meaning as it has for the purposes of Schedule A in its application to companies within the charge to corporation tax;

"shorthold tenancy" means any letting which is an assured shorthold tenancy for the purposes of the Housing Act 1988 or a short assured tenancy for the purposes of the Housing (Scotland) Act 1988;

"statutory shorthold tenancy" means—

(a) a statutory periodic tenancy within the meaning of the Housing Act 1988 which arose on the coming to an end of an assured shorthold tenancy which was a fixed term tenancy, or

(b) a statutory assured tenancy within the meaning of the Housing (Scotland) Act 1988 which arose on the coming to an end of a short assured tenancy;

"statutory tenancy"—

(a) in relation to England and Wales, has the same meaning as in the Rent Act 1977;

(b) in relation to Scotland, has the same meaning as in the Rent (Scotland) Act 1984; and

(c) in relation to Northern Ireland, has the same meaning as in the Rent (Northern Ireland) Order 1978.

(8) Section 839 shall apply for the purposes of this section.

(9) Section 508A shall have effect where—

(a) a company acquires an interest in any dwelling-house, and

(b) a person connected with the company has previously acquired an interest in the dwelling-house, being an interest subsequently acquired by the company or one held by that person at the same time as the company holds its interest,

as if references in this section (except in subsection (3) above) to the time when the company first acquired an interest in the premises included references to the time when the person connected with the company first acquired his interest.

(10) The Treasury may, if they think fit, by order vary the figures for the time being specified in paragraph (e) of subsection (1) above; and an order under this subsection may make different provision for different localities in Greater London or elsewhere.

(11) In the application of this section to Scotland—

(a) references to acquiring an interest shall be construed, if there is a contract to acquire the interest, as references to entering into that contract;

(b) references to the freehold interest shall be construed as references to the estate or interest of the proprietor of the *dominium utile* or, in the case of property other than feudal property, of the owner;

(c) in the definition of "long lease" in subsection (7) above, the word "certain" shall be omitted.

(12) Regulations made for the purposes of paragraph (b) of the definition of "assured tenancy" in subsection (7) above shall be made by statutory rule for the purposes of the Statutory Rules (Northern Ireland) Order 1979, and shall be subject to negative resolution within the meaning of section 41(6) of the Interpretation Act (Northern Ireland) 1954.][1]

Commentary—*Simon's Direct Tax Service* **D4.423.**
Definitions—"Company", s 832(1), (2); "connected", s 839; "Schedule A", s 15.
Amendments—[1] This section inserted by FA 1996 Sch 30 para 1 with effect for accounting periods beginning after 28 April 1996.

509 Reserves of marketing boards and certain other statutory bodies

(1) Where a body established by or under any enactment and having as its object, or one of its objects, the marketing of an agricultural product or the stabilising of the price of an agricultural product is required, by or under any scheme or arrangements approved by or made with a Minister of the Crown or government department, to pay the whole or part of any surplus derived from its trading operations or other trade receipts into a reserve fund satisfying the conditions specified in subsection (2) below, then, in computing for the purposes of tax the [profits][1] or losses of the body's trade—

(a) there shall be allowed as deductions any sums so required to be paid by the body into the reserve fund out of the [profits][1] of the trade, and

(b) there shall be taken into account as trading receipts any sums withdrawn by the body from the fund, except so far as they are so required to be paid to a Minister or government department, or are distributed to producers of the product in question or refunded to persons paying any levy or duty.

(2) The conditions to be satisfied by the reserve fund are as follows—

(a) that no sum may be withdrawn from the fund without the authority or consent of a Minister of the Crown or government department; and

(b) that where money has been paid to the body by a Minister of the Crown or government department in connection with arrangements for maintaining guaranteed prices, or in connection with the body's trading operations, and is repayable to that Minister or department, sums afterwards standing to the credit of the fund are required as mentioned in subsection (1) above to be applied in whole or in part in repaying the money; and

(c) that the fund is reviewed by a Minister of the Crown at intervals fixed by or under the scheme or arrangements in question, and any amount by which it appears to the Minister to exceed the reasonable requirements of the body is withdrawn therefrom.

(3) In this section references to a Minister of the Crown or government department include references to a Head of a Department or a Department in Northern Ireland, and references to producers of a product include references to producers of one type or quality of a product from another.

Commentary—*Simon's Direct Tax Service* **B3.1171.**
Definitions—"trade", s 832(1).
Amendments—[1] Word in sub-s (1) substituted by FA 1998 Sch 7 para 1 with effect from 31 July 1998.

510 Agricultural societies

(1) Profits or gains arising to an agricultural society from any exhibition or show held for the purposes of the society shall be exempt from tax if applied solely to the purposes of the society.

(2) In this section "agricultural society" means any society or institution established for the purpose of promoting the interests of agriculture, horticulture, livestock breeding or forestry.

Commentary—*Simon's Direct Tax Service* **D4.312.**
Revenue Internal Guidance—Inspector's manual IM 1813 (other income is taxable in the normal way; claims for charitable status are referred to Financial Intermediaries and Claims Office).
Definition—"Profits or gains", s 833(1).

[510A European Economic Interest Groupings

(1) In this section "grouping" means a European Economic Interest Grouping formed in pursuance of Council Regulation (EEC) No 2137/85 of 25th July 1985, whether registered in Great Britain, in Northern Ireland, or elsewhere.

(2) Subject to the following provisions of this section, for the purposes of charging tax in respect of income and gains a grouping shall be regarded as acting as the agent of its members.

(3) In accordance with subsection (2) above—

(a) for the purposes mentioned in that subsection the activities of the grouping shall be regarded as those of its members acting jointly and each member shall be regarded as having a share of its property, rights and liabilities; and (*b*) for the purposes of charging tax in respect of [chargeable gains][3] a person shall be regarded as acquiring or disposing of a share of the assets of the grouping not only where there is an acquisition or disposal of assets by the grouping while he is a member of it, but also where he becomes or ceases to be a member of a grouping or there is a change in his share of the property of the grouping;

[but paragraph (*a*) above is subject to subsection (6A) below.][3]

(4) Subject to subsection (5) below, for the purposes of this section a member's share of any property, rights or liabilities of a grouping shall be determined in accordance with the contract under which the grouping is established.

(5) Where the contract does not make provision as to the shares of members in the property, rights or liabilities in question a member's share shall be determined by reference to the share of the profits of the grouping to which he is entitled under the contract (and if the contract makes no provision as to that, the members shall be regarded as having equal shares).

(6) ...[2] where any trade or profession is carried on by a grouping it shall be regarded for the purposes of charging tax in respect of income and gains as carried on in partnership by the members of the grouping.

[(6A) Chapter 2 of Part 4 of the Finance Act 1996 (loan relationships) shall have effect in relation to a grouping as it has effect in relation to a partnership (see in particular section 87A of, and paragraphs 19 and 20 of Schedule 9 to, that Act).][3]

(7), (8) ...[2]][1]

Commentary—*Simon's Direct Tax Service* **D4.902.**
Revenue Internal Guidance—International tax handbook ITH 1679 (nature of an EEIG).
European Economic Interest Groupings Handbook EEIG 7–22 (Revenue internal procedures).
EEIG 31–41 (general tax treatment; whether trade carried on).
EEIG 49–72 (taxation of trading profits: partnership treatment).
EEIG 81–86 (capital allowances).
EEIG 91–96 (taxation of chargeable gains).
EEIG 101–144 (non-trading EEIGs).
EEIG 151–159 (payments under deduction of tax: company rules apply).
EEIG 161–164 (operation of PAYE: EEIG can be a person paying emoluments).
EEIG 171–173 (payments to sub-contractors: EEIG may be a contractor or a subcontractor).
EEIG 181 (foreign entertainers and sportsmen).
EEIG 191–198 (annual returns).
EEIG 201–205 (penalties).
Definition—"Trade", s 832(1).
Amendments—[1] This section inserted by FA 1990 Sch 11 paras 1, 5 with effect from 1 July 1989.
[2] Words omitted in sub-s (6), and whole of sub-ss (7), (8), repealed with effect for groupings whose trades or professions were set up and commenced after 5 April 1994, for the years 1995–96 and 1996–97 and in other cases with effect from the year 1997–98, by FA 1995 Sch 29 Pt VIII(16).
[3] In sub-s (3)(*b*), words substituted for the word "gains", words inserted after that sub-section; and sub-s (6A) inserted; by FA 2002 s 82, Sch 25 paras 43, 49 with effect for accounting periods beginning after 30 September 2002.

511 The Electricity Council and Boards, the Northern Ireland Electricity Service and the Gas Council

(1)–(3) ...[2]

(4), (5) ...[1]

(6) ...[2]

(7) The Corporation Tax Acts shall apply in relation to the trade of the Gas Council as if before the beginning of April 1962 it had consisted of the trades of the Area Boards (within the meaning of the Gas Act 1948), and (without prejudice to the generality of the foregoing) allowances and balancing charges shall be made to or on the Gas Council accordingly by reference to the capital expenditure of Area Boards and to the allowances made to Area Boards in respect of that expenditure.

Revenue Internal Guidance—International Tax Handbook ITH 300–371 (residence: central management and control test: background to FA 1988 s 66 and FA 1994 s 249).
Definitions—"The Corporation Tax Acts", s 831(1)(*a*); "trade", s 832(1).
Amendments—[1] Sub-ss (4), (5) repealed by Electricity (Northern Ireland) Order, SI 1992/231 Sch 14.
[2] Sub-ss (1)–(3), (6) repealed by the Electricity Act 1989 Sch 18 with effect from 9 November 2001 (by virtue of SI 2001/3419).

512 Atomic Energy Authority and National Radiological Protection Board

(1) The United Kingdom Atomic Energy Authority and the National Radiological Protection Board shall be entitled to exemption from income tax and corporation tax—

(*a*) under [Schedule A][1];
(*b*) under Schedule D in respect of any yearly interest or other annual payment [or in respect of public revenue dividends][1] received by the Authority or Board;
(*c*) under Schedule F in respect of distributions received by the Authority or Board.

(2) Income arising from investments or deposits held for the purposes of any pension scheme provided and maintained by the Authority shall be treated for the purposes of this section as if that income and the source thereof belonged to the Authority.

[(3) In subsection (1) above "public revenue dividends" means—

(*a*) income from securities which is payable out of the public revenue of the United Kingdom or Northern Ireland;

(*b*) income from securities issued by or on behalf of a government or a public or local authority in a country outside the United Kingdom.]¹

Commentary—*Simon's Direct Tax Service* **D4.333.**
Definitions—"Schedule A", s 15(1); "Schedule B", s 16(1); "Schedule D", s 18(1); "Schedule F", s 20(1).
Cross references—See TA 1988 s 231A (tax credits not repayable in respect of qualifying distributions made after 1 July 1997 to pension funds—see sub-s (2) above).
Amendments—¹ Words in sub-s (1)(*a*) substituted, words in sub-s (1)(*b*) inserted and sub-s (3) inserted by FA 1996 Sch 7 para 20 with effect for the purposes of income tax from the year 1996–97 and for the purposes of corporation tax for accounting periods ending after 31 March 1996.

513 British Airways Board and National Freight Corporation

(1) Subject to subsection (2) below, the successor company in which the property, rights, liabilities and obligations of the British Airways Board are vested by the Civil Aviation Act 1980 shall be treated for all purposes of corporation tax as if it were the same person as the British Airways Board; and the successor company to which the undertaking of the National Freight Corporation is transferred by the Transport Act 1980 shall be treated for those purposes as if it were the same person as the National Freight Corporation.

(2) The transfer by the Civil Aviation Act 1980 from the British Airways Board to the successor company of liability for any loan made to the Board shall not affect any direction in respect of the loan which has been given by the Treasury under section 581.

(3) A successor company shall not by virtue of subsection (1) above be regarded as a body falling within section [170(12) of the 1992 Act]¹.

Commentary—*Simon's Direct Tax Service* **B3.246.**
Definition—"The 1992 Act", s 831(3).
Amendments—¹ Words in sub-s (3) substituted by TCGA 1992 Sch 10 para 14(1), (32).

514 Funds for reducing the National Debt

Where any property is held upon trust in accordance with directions which are valid and effective under section 9 of the Superannuation and other Trust Funds (Validation) Act 1927 (which provides for the validation of trust funds for the reduction of the national debt), any income arising from that property or from any accumulation of any such income, and any profits of any description otherwise accruing to the property and liable to be accumulated under the trust, shall be exempt from income tax.

Commentary—*Simon's Direct Tax Service* **C4.536.**

515 Signatories to Operating Agreement for INMARSAT

(1) An overseas signatory to the Operating Agreement made pursuant to the Convention on the International Maritime Satellite Organisation which came into force on 16th July 1979 shall be exempt from income tax and corporation tax in respect of any payment received by that signatory from the Organisation in accordance with that Agreement.

(2) In this section "an overseas signatory" means a signatory other than one designated for the purposes of the Agreement by the United Kingdom in accordance with the Convention.

Commentary—*Simon's Direct Tax Service* **D4.336.**

516 Government securities held by non-resident central banks

(1) Tax shall not be chargeable on [income from securities which is payable out of the public revenue of the United Kingdom and which is]¹ income of any bank or issue department of a bank to which this subsection for the time being applies.

(2) Subsection (1) above shall not prevent any [such income]¹ being taken into account in computing profits or gains or losses of a business carried on in the United Kingdom.

(3) A bank or issue department of a bank to which this subsection for the time being applies shall be exempt from tax in respect of chargeable gains accruing to it.

(4) Her Majesty may by Order in Council direct that subsection (1) or (3), or both, shall apply to any bank, or to its issue department, if it appears to Her Majesty that the bank is not resident in the United Kingdom and is entrusted by the government of a territory outside the United Kingdom with the custody of the principal foreign exchange reserves of that territory.

(5) No recommendation shall be made to Her Majesty in Council to make an order under this section unless a draft of the order has been laid before the House of Commons and has been approved by resolution of that House.

Commentary—*Simon's Direct Tax Service* **A7.914.**
Amendments—¹ Words in sub-ss (1), (2) substituted by FA 1996 Sch 7 para 21 with effect for the purposes of income tax from the year 1996–97 and for the purpose of corporation tax for accounting periods ending after 31 March 1996.

517 Issue departments of the Reserve Bank of India and the State Bank of Pakistan

There shall be exempt from tax any profits or income arising or accruing to the issue department of the Reserve Bank of India constituted under an Act of the Indian legislature called the Reserve Bank of India Act 1934 or to the issue department of the State Bank of Pakistan constituted under certain orders made under section 9 of the Indian Independence Act 1947.

Commentary—*Simon's Direct Tax Service* **D4.332.**

518 Harbour reorganisation schemes

(1) This section has effect where the trade of any body corporate other than a limited liability company is transferred to a harbour authority by or under a certified harbour reorganisation scheme which provides also for the dissolution of the transferor.

(2) For the purposes of the Corporation Tax Acts, the trade shall not be treated as permanently discontinued, nor shall a new trade be treated as set up and commenced.

(3) The transferee shall be entitled to relief from corporation tax under section 393(1), as for a loss sustained by it in carrying on the transferred trade or any trade of which it comes to form part, for any amount which, if the transferor had continued to carry it on, would have been available to the transferor for carry-forward against chargeable profits of succeeding accounting periods, but subject to any claim made by the transferor under section [393A(1)][1].

(4) There shall be made to or on the transferee in accordance with [the Capital Allowances Act (including enactments which under this Act are to be treated as contained in that Act)][3] all such allowances and charges as would, if the transferor had continued to carry on the trade, have fallen to be made to or on it under those Acts and the amount of any such allowance or charge shall be computed as if the transferee had been carrying on the trade since the transferor had begun to do so and as if everything done to or by the transferor had been done to or by the transferee.

(5) No sale or transfer which on the transfer of the trade is made by the transferor to the transferee of any assets in use for the purposes of the trade shall be treated as giving rise to any such allowance or charge as is mentioned in subsection (4) above.

(6) ...[2]

(7) The transferee shall be entitled to relief from corporation tax in respect of chargeable gains for any amount for which the transferor would have been entitled to claim relief in respect of allowable losses if it had continued to carry on the trade.

(8) Where part only of such trade is transferred to a harbour authority by or under a certified harbour organisation scheme, and the transferor continues to carry on the remainder of the trade, or any such trade is, by or under a certified harbour reorganisation scheme which provides also for the dissolution of the transferor, transferred in parts to two or more harbour authorities, this section shall apply as if the transferred part, or each of the transferred parts, had at all times been a separate trade.

(9) Where a part of any trade is to be treated by virtue of subsection (8) above as having been a separate trade over any period there shall be made any necessary adjustments of accounting periods, and such apportionments as may be just of receipts, expenses, allowances or charges.

Subsection (10) of section 343 shall apply to any apportionment under this subsection as it applies to an apportionment under subsection (9) of that section.

(10) In this section—

"harbour authority" has the same meaning as in the Harbours Act 1964;

"harbour reorganisation scheme" means any statutory provision providing for the management by a harbour authority of any harbour or group of harbours in the United Kingdom, and "certified", in relation to any harbour reorganisation scheme, means certified by a Minister of the Crown or government department as so providing with a view to securing, in the public interest, the efficient and economical development of the harbour or harbours in question;

"limited liability company" means a company having a limit on the liability of its members;

"statutory provision" means any enactment, or any scheme, order or other instrument having effect under an enactment, and includes an enactment confirming a provisional order; and

"transferor", in relation to a trade, means the body from whom the trade is transferred, whether or not the transfer is effected by that body.

Commentary—*Simon's Direct Tax Service* **D2.539.**
Definitions—"Accounting period", s 834(1); "allowable loss", s 834(1); "Capital Allowance Acts", s 832(1); "chargeable gains", s 832(1); "the Corporation Tax Acts", s 831(1)(a); "trade", s 832(1).
Amendments—[1] "393A(1)" in sub-s (3) substituted by FA 1991 Sch 15 para 19.
[2] Sub-s (6) repealed by FA 1991 Sch 15 para 19 and Sch 19 Pt V.
[3] Words in sub-s (4) substituted by CAA 2001 s 578, Sch 2 para 43 with effect for corporation tax purposes as respects allowances and charges falling to be made for chargeable periods ending after 31 March 2001.

519 Local authorities

(1) A local authority in the United Kingdom—

(a) shall be exempt from all charge to income tax in respect of its income;

(b) shall be exempt from corporation tax;

and so far as the exemption from income tax conferred by this subsection calls for repayment of tax, effect shall be given thereto by means of a claim.

(2) Subsection (1) above shall apply to a local authority association as it applies to a local authority.

(3) In this Act "local authority association" means any incorporated or unincorporated association—

(a) of which all the constituent members are local authorities, groups of local authorities or local authority associations, and

(b) which has for its object or primary object the protection and furtherance of the interests in general of local authorities or any description of local authorities;

and for this purpose, if a member of an association is a representative of or appointed by any authority, group of authorities or association, that authority, group or association (and not he) shall be treated as a constituent member of the association.

(4) ...[1]

Commentary—*Simon's Direct Tax Service* **D4.301.**
Cross references—See TCGA 1992 s 271(3) (exemption from capital gains tax for local authorities).
Amendments—[1] Sub-s (4) repealed by FA 1990 Sch 18 para 5(1), (2) and Sch 19, Pt IV with effect from 1 April 1990.

[519A Health Service bodies

(1) A health service body—

(a) shall be exempt from income tax in respect of its income, and
(b) shall be exempt from corporation tax,

and, so far as the exemption from income tax conferred by this subsection calls for repayment of tax, effect shall be given thereto by means of a claim.

(2) In this section "health service body" means—

[(a) a Health Authority established under section 8 of the National Health Service Act 1977;
(aa) a Special Health Authority established under section 11 of that Act;][3]
[(ab) a Primary Care Trust][4]
(b) a National Health Service trust established under Part I of the National Health Service and Community Care Act 1990;
(c) ...[4];
(d) a Health Board or Special Health Board, the Common Services Agency for the Scottish Health Service and a National Health Service trust respectively constituted under sections 2, 10 and 12A of the National Health Service (Scotland) Act 1978;
(e) a State Hospital Management Committee constituted under section 91 of the Mental Health (Scotland) Act 1984;
(f) the Dental Practice Board;
(g) the Scottish Dental Practice Board; ...[2]
(h) the Public Health Laboratory Service Board.][1]
[(i) a Health and Social Services Board and the Northern Ireland Central Services Agency for the Health and Social Services established under Articles 16 and 26 respectively of the Health and Personal Social Services (Northern Ireland) Order 1972;][2]
[(j) a special health and social services agency established under the Health and Personal Social Services (Special Agencies) (Northern Ireland) Order 1990; and][2]
[(k) a Health and Social Services trust established under the Health and Personal Social Services (Northern Ireland) Order 1991.][2]

Commentary—*Simon's Direct Tax Service* **D4.303.**
Cross references—See TCGA 1992 s 271(3) (exemption from capital gains tax for health service bodies).
Amendments—[1] This section inserted by the National Health Service and Community Care Act 1990 s 61(1).
[2] Sub-s (2)(i), (j), (k) added the word "and" in sub-s (2)(g) repealed by the Health and Personal Social Services (Northern Ireland Consequential Amendments) Order, SI 1991/195.
[3] Sub-s (2)(a), (aa) substituted for sub-s (2)(a), and sub-s (2)(c) repealed, by the Health Authorities Act 1995 Sch 1 para 114, Sch 3 with effect from 1 April 1996.
[4] Sub-s (2)(ab) inserted by the Health Act 1999 s 65 Sch 4 para 73 with effect from 1 April 2000.

PART XIII
MISCELLANEOUS SPECIAL PROVISIONS

CHAPTER I
INTELLECTUAL PROPERTY
Patents and know-how

Cross references—TA 1988 s 533 (interpretation of ss 520–532).

520 Allowances for expenditure on purchase of patent rights: post-31st March 1986 expenditure

Commentary—*Simon's Direct Tax Service* B2.603, 604.
Amendments—This section repealed by CAA 2001 ss 578, 580, Sch 2 para 44, Sch 4 with effect for income tax purposes, as respects allowances and charges falling to be made for chargeable periods ending after 5 April 2001, and for corporation tax purposes, as respects allowances and charges falling to be made for chargeable periods ending after 31 March 2001.

521 Provisions supplementary to section 520

Commentary—*Simon's Direct Tax Service* B2.603, 607.
Amendments—This section repealed by CAA 2001 ss 578, 580, Sch 2 para 44, Sch 4 with effect for income tax purposes, as respects allowances and charges falling to be made for chargeable periods ending after 5 April 2001, and for corporation tax purposes, as respects allowances and charges falling to be made for chargeable periods ending after 31 March 2001.

522 Allowances for expenditure on purchase of patent rights: pre-1st April 1986 expenditure

Commentary—*Simon's Direct Tax Service* B2.605.
Amendments—This section repealed by CAA 2001 ss 578, 580, Sch 2 para 44, Sch 4 with effect for income tax purposes, as respects allowances and charges falling to be made for chargeable periods ending after 5 April 2001, and for corporation tax purposes, as respects allowances and charges falling to be made for chargeable periods ending after 31 March 2001.

523 Lapses of patent rights, sales etc

Commentary—*Simon's Direct Tax Service* B2.606.
Amendments—This section repealed by CAA 2001 ss 578, 580, Sch 2 para 44, Sch 4 with effect for income tax purposes, as respects allowances and charges falling to be made for chargeable periods ending after 5 April 2001, and for corporation tax purposes, as respects allowances and charges falling to be made for chargeable periods ending after 31 March 2001.

524 Taxation of receipts from sale of patent rights

(1) Subject to subsection (2) below, where a person resident in the United Kingdom sells all or any part of any patent rights and the net proceeds of the sale consist wholly or partly of a capital sum, he shall, subject to the provisions of this Chapter, be charged to tax under Case VI of Schedule D, for the chargeable period in which the sum is received by him and successive chargeable periods, being charged in each period on the same fraction of the sum as the period is of six years (or such less fraction as has not already been charged).

(2) If the person by notice served on [an officer of the Board within the period specified in subsection (2A) below][1], elects that the whole of the sum shall be charged to tax for [the chargeable period in which it was received][1], it shall be charged to tax accordingly.

[(2A) The period mentioned in subsection (2) above is—

    (*a*) in the case of an election for the purposes of income tax, the period ending with the first anniversary of the 31st January next following the year of assessment in which the sum was received;

    (*b*) in the case of an election for the purposes of corporation tax, the period of two years beginning at the end of the accounting period in which the sum was received.][1]

(3) Subject to subsection (4) below, where a person not resident in the United Kingdom sells all or any part of any patent rights and the net proceeds of the sale consist wholly or partly of a capital sum, and the patent is a United Kingdom patent, then, subject to the provisions of this Chapter—

    (*a*) he shall be chargeable to tax in respect of that sum under Case VI of Schedule D; and

    (*b*) section 349(1) shall apply to that sum as if it was an annual sum payable otherwise than out of profits or gains charged to income tax; and

    (*c*) all other provisions of the Tax Acts shall, save as therein otherwise provided, have effect accordingly.

(4) If, [on or before the first anniversary of the 31st January next following][1] the year of assessment in which the sum is paid, the person to whom it is paid, by notice to the Board, elects that the sum shall be treated for the purpose of income tax for that year and each of the five succeeding years as if one-sixth thereof, and no more, were included in his income chargeable to tax for all those years respectively, it shall be so treated, and all such repayments and assessments of tax for each of those years shall be made as are necessary to give effect to the election, but—

    (*a*) the election shall not affect the amount of tax which is to be deducted and assessed under section 349(1) and 350; and

    (*b*) where any sum is deducted under section 349(1), any adjustments necessary to give effect to the election shall be made by way of repayment of tax; and

    (*c*) those adjustments shall be made year by year and as if one-sixth of the sum deducted had been deducted in respect of tax for each year, and no repayment of, or of any part of, that portion of the tax deducted which is to be treated as deducted in respect of tax for any year shall be made unless and until it is ascertained that the tax ultimately falling to be paid for that year is less than the amount of tax paid for that year.

(5) In subsections (3) and (4) above, "tax" shall mean income tax or, in subsection (3) in a case where the seller of the patent rights, being a company, would be within the charge to corporation tax in respect of any proceeds of the sale not consisting of a capital sum, corporation tax.

(6) Where subsection (3) applies to charge a company to corporation tax in respect of a sum paid to it, subsection (4) shall not apply, but the company may, by notice given to the Board not later than two years after the end of the accounting period in which the sum is paid, elect that the sum shall be treated as arising rateably in the accounting periods ending not later than six years from the beginning of that in which the sum is paid (being accounting periods during which the company remains within the charge to corporation tax in respect of any proceeds of the sale not consisting of a capital sum), and there shall be made all such repayments of tax and assessments to tax as are necessary to give effect to any such election.

(7) Subject to subsections (8) and (9) below, where the person selling all or any part of any patent rights ("the seller") acquired the rights sold, or the rights out of which they were granted, by purchase and the price paid by him consisted wholly or partly of a capital sum, the preceding provisions of this section shall apply as if any capital sum received by him when he sells the rights were reduced by the amount of that sum.

(8) Where between the purchase and the sale the seller has sold part of the rights acquired by him and the net proceeds of that sale consist wholly or partly of a capital sum, the amount of the reduction falling to be made under subsection (7) above in respect of the subsequent sale shall be itself reduced by the amount of that sum.

(9) Nothing in subsections (7) and (8) above shall affect the amount of income tax which is to be deducted and assessed under section 349(1) and (3) by virtue of subsection (3) above, and, where any sum is deducted under section 349(1), any adjustment necessary to give effect to the provisions of this subsection shall be made by way of repayment of tax.

(10) A claim for relief under this section shall be made to the Board.

Commentary—*Simon's Direct Tax Service* B3.844, 846, 847.
Revenue Internal Guidance—Capital allowances manual CA 75200, 75210 (explanation of this section with examples).
Definitions—"Accounting period", s 834(1); "the Board", s 832(1); "chargeable period", s 832(1); "company", s 832(1), (2); "inspector", s 832(1); "notice", s 832(1); "profits or gains", s 833(1); "Schedule D", s 18(1); "sells all or any part of any patent rights", see s 533(2); "the Taxes Acts", s 831(2); "United Kingdom", s 830(1); "United Kingdom patent", s 533(1); "year of assessment", s 832(1).
Cross references—See TA 1988 s 525 (withdrawal of payment of tax by instalments under this section in the event of death, winding up or partnership change).
Amendments—¹ Words in sub-s (2) substituted, sub-s (2A) inserted, and words in sub-s (4) substituted by FA 1996 s 135, Sch 21 para 15 with effect for the purposes of income tax from the year 1996–97 and for the purposes of corporation tax as respects accounting periods ending after 30 June 1999 (by virtue of Finance Act 1994, Section 199, (Appointed Day) Order, SI 1998/3173 art 2).

525 Capital sums: death, winding up or partnership change

(1) Where a person on whom, by reason of the receipt of a capital sum, a charge falls or would otherwise fall to be made under section 524 dies or, being a body corporate, commences to be wound up—

    (*a*) no sums shall be charged under that section on that person for any chargeable period subsequent to that in which the death takes place or the winding up commences; and

    (*b*) the amount falling to be charged for the chargeable period in which the death occurs or the winding up commences shall, subject to subsection (2) below, be increased by the total amounts which, but for the death or winding up, would have fallen to be charged for subsequent chargeable periods.

(2) In the case of a death the personal representatives may, by notice served on the inspector not later than 30 days after notice has been served on them of the charge falling to be made by virtue of subsection (1) above, require that the income tax payable out of the estate of the deceased by reason of the increase provided for by that subsection shall be reduced so as not to exceed the total amount of income tax which would have been payable by him or out of his estate by reason of the operation of section 524 in relation to that sum, if, instead of the amount falling to be charged for the year in which the death occurs being increased by the whole amount of the sums charged for subsequent years, the several amounts falling to be charged for the years beginning with that in which the capital sum was received and ending with that in which the death occurred had each been increased by that whole amount divided by the number of those years.

(3) Where, under [section 559 of the Capital Allowances Act (effect of successions)]² as applied by section 532, a charge under section 524 falls to be made on two or more persons jointly as being the persons for the time being carrying on a trade, and that trade is discontinued, subsection (1) above shall have effect in relation to the discontinuance as it has effect where a body corporate commences to be wound up.

(4) Where subsection (3) above applies—

    (*a*) the additional sum which, under subsection (1) above, falls to be charged for the chargeable period in which the discontinuance occurs shall be apportioned among the members of the partnership immediately before the discontinuance, according to their respective interests in the partnership profits before the discontinuance, and each partner (or, if he is dead, his personal representatives) shall be charged separately for his proportion; and

(*b*) each partner (or, if he is dead, his personal representatives) shall have the same right to require a reduction of the total income tax payable by him or out of his estate by reason of the increase as would have been exercisable by the personal representatives under subsection (2) above in the case of a death, and that subsection shall have effect accordingly, but as if references to the amount of income tax which would have been payable by the deceased or out of his estate in the event therein mentioned were a reference to the amount of income tax which would in that event have fallen to be paid or borne by the partner in question or out of his estate.

(5) ...[1]

Commentary—*Simon's Direct Tax Service* **B3.849.**
Definitions—''The 1990 Act'', s 831(3); ''chargeable period'', s 832(1); ''income tax'', s 832(4); ''inspector'', s 832(1); ''notice'', s 832(1); ''trade'', s 832(1).
Amendments—[1] Sub-s (5) repealed by FA 1988 Sch 14 Pt VIII in relation to tax paid or borne etc for the year 1990–91 or a subsequent year.
[2] Words in sub-s (3) substituted by CAA 2001 s 578, Sch 2 para 45 with effect for income tax purposes, as respects allowances and charges falling to be made for chargeable periods ending after 5 April 2001, and for corporation tax purposes, as respects allowances and charges falling to be made for chargeable periods ending after 31 March 2001.

526 Relief for expenses

(1) Where—

(*a*) a person, otherwise than for the purposes of a trade carried on by him, pays any fees or incurs any expenses in connection with the grant or maintenance of a patent, or the obtaining of an extension of a term of a patent, or a rejected or abandoned application for a patent, and

(*b*) those fees or expenses would, if they had been paid or incurred for the purposes of a trade, have been allowable as a deduction in estimating the [profits][1] of that trade,

there shall be made to him, for the chargeable period in which those expenses were paid or incurred, an allowance equal to the amount thereof.

(2) Where a patent is granted in respect of any invention, an allowance equal to so much of the net amount of any expenses incurred by an individual who, whether alone or in conjunction with any other person, actually devised the invention as is properly ascribable to the devising thereof (not being expenses in respect of which, or of assets representing which, an allowance falls to be made under any other provision of the Income Tax Acts) shall be made to that individual for the year of assessment in which the expenses were incurred.

Commentary—*Simon's Direct Tax Service* **B2.609.**
Definitions—''Chargeable period'', s 832(1); ''the Income Tax Acts'', s 831(1) (*b*); ''trade'', s 832(1); ''year of assessment'', s 832(1).
Cross references—See TA 1988 s 528 (manner of making allowances under this section).
Amendments—[1] Word in sub-s (1) substituted by FA 1998 Sch 7 para 1 with effect from 31 July 1998.

527 Spreading of royalties over several years

(1) Where a royalty or other sum to which section 348 or 349(1) applies is paid in respect of the user of a patent, and that user extended over a period of six complete years or more, the person receiving the payment may on the making of a claim require that the income tax or corporation tax payable by him by reason of the receipt of that sum shall be reduced so as not to exceed the total amount of income tax or corporation tax which would have been payable by him if that royalty or sum had been paid in six equal instalments at yearly intervals, the last of which was paid on the date on which the payment was in fact made.

(2) Subsection (1) above shall apply in relation to a royalty or other sum where the period of the user is two complete years or more but less than six complete years as it applies to the royalties and sums mentioned in that subsection, but with the substitution for the reference to six equal instalments of a reference to so many equal instalments as there are complete years comprised in that period.

(3) ...[1]

(4) Nothing in this section shall apply to any sum to which section 349(1) applies by virtue of section 524(3)(*b*).

Commentary—*Simon's Direct Tax Service* **B3.845.**
Cross references—See TMA 1970 s 46C (Special Commissioners to have jurisdiction over questions in dispute for an appeal against an amendment to a self-assessment or partnership statement) concerning a claim under this section.
Amendments—[1] Sub-s (3) repealed by FA 1988 Sch 14 Pt VIII with effect from the year 1990–91.

528 Manner of making allowances and charges

(1) ...[1]

(2) Where an allowance falls to be made to a person for any year of assessment [section 526 as that provision applies][1] for the purposes of income tax, and the allowance is not to be made in taxing a trade—

(*a*) the amount of the allowance shall be deducted from or set off against his income from patents for that year of assessment, and

(b) if the amount to be allowed is greater than the amount of his income from patents for that year of assessment, the balance shall be deducted from or set off against his income from patents for the next year of assessment, and so on for subsequent years of assessment, and tax shall be discharged or repaid accordingly.

Relief shall be given under this subsection on the making of a claim.

(3) Where an allowance falls to be made to a company for any accounting period [section 526 as that provision applies][1] for the purposes of corporation tax, and is not to be made in taxing a trade—

(a) the allowance shall, as far as may be, be given effect by deducting the amount of the allowance from the company's income from patents of the accounting period;

(b) where the allowance cannot be given full effect under paragraph (a) above in that period by reason of a want or deficiency of income from patents, then (so long as the company remains within the charge to corporation tax) the amount unallowed shall be carried forward to the succeeding accounting period, and shall be treated for the purposes of that paragraph, and of any further application of this paragraph, as the amount of a corresponding allowance for that period.

[(3A) In this section references to a person's or a company's income from patents are references to that income after any allowance has been deducted from or set off against it under section 479 or 480 of the Capital Allowances Act.][1]

(4) ...[1]

Commentary—*Simon's Direct Tax Service* B2.608.
Definitions—"Accounting period", s 834(1); "chargeable period", s 832(1); "company", s 832(1), (2); "income from patents", s 533(1); "patent rights", s 533(1); "Schedule D", s 18(1); "tax", s 832(3); "trade", s 832(1); "year of assessment", s 832(1).
Amendments—[1] Sub-ss (1), (4) repealed, words in sub-ss (2), (3) substituted, and sub-s (3A) inserted, by CAA 2001 ss 578, 580, Sch 2 para 46, Sch 4 with effect for income tax purposes, with respect to allowances and charges falling to be made for chargeable periods ending after 5 April 2001, and for corporation tax purposes, with respect to allowances and charges falling to be made for chargeable periods ending after 31 March 2001.

529 Patent income to be earned income in certain cases

(1) Subject to subsection (2) below, any income from patent rights arising to an individual where the patent was granted for an invention actually devised by him, whether alone or jointly with any other person, shall be treated for all purposes as earned income.

(2) Where any part of the rights in question or of any rights out of which they were granted has at any time belonged to any other person, so much only of that income shall be treated as earned income as is not properly attributable to the rights which have belonged to that other person.

Commentary—*Simon's Direct Tax Service* B3.850.
Definitions—"Earned income", s 833(4), (5); "patent rights", s 533(1).

530 Disposal of know-how

Commentary—*Simon's Direct Tax Service* B2.616, 617.
Amendments—This section repealed by CAA 2001 ss 578, 580, Sch 2 para 47, Sch 4 with effect for income tax purposes, as respects allowances and charges falling to be made for chargeable periods ending after 5 April 2001, and for corporation tax purposes, as respects allowances and charges falling to be made for chargeable periods ending after 31 March 2001.

531 Provisions supplementary to section 530

(1) Subject to subsection (7) below, where, after 19th March 1968, a person disposes of know-how which has been used in a trade carried on by him, and continues to carry on the trade after the disposal, the amount or value of any consideration received by him for the disposal shall—

(a) if it is received in respect of the disposal of know-how after 31st March 1986, so far as it is not brought into account [as a disposal value under section 462 of the Capital Allowances Act][1], nor is chargeable to tax as a revenue or income receipt;

(b) in any other case, so far as it is not chargeable to tax as a revenue or income receipt,

be treated for all purposes as a trading receipt.

(2) Subject to subsection (3) below, where, after 19th March 1968, a person disposes of a trade or part of a trade and, together with that trade or part, of know-how used in it, any consideration received by him for the know-how shall be dealt with in relation both to him and to the person acquiring the know-how, if that person provided the consideration, and for the purposes of corporation tax, income tax and capital gains tax, as a payment for goodwill.

(3) Subsection (2) above shall not apply—

(a) to either of the persons concerned if they so elect by notice given jointly to the inspector within two years of the disposal, or

(b) to the person acquiring the know-how if the trade in question was, before the acquisition, carried on wholly outside the United Kingdom;

...[1]

(4) Subject to subsections (5) and (7) below, any consideration received by a person for the disposal of know-how shall—

    (*a*) if it is received in respect of the disposal of know-how after 31st March 1986 and is not
brought into account [as a disposal value under section 462 of the Capital Allowances Act][1], or

    (*b*) if it is neither chargeable to tax under subsection (1) above or otherwise as a revenue or
income receipt, nor dealt with in relation to him as a payment for goodwill as mentioned in
subsection (2) above, (whether the disposal took place before or after 31st March 1986),

be treated as a profit or gain chargeable to tax under Case VI of Schedule D.

(5) Where the person concerned has incurred expenditure wholly and exclusively in the acquisition
or disposal of the know-how, the amount which would apart from this subsection be treated as a
profit or gain chargeable to tax under Case VI of Schedule D shall be reduced by the amount of that
expenditure; but a deduction shall not be twice made in respect of the same expenditure, whether
under this subsection or otherwise.

(6) Where subsection (4) above has effect in the case of an individual who devised the know-how in
question, whether alone or jointly with any other person, the amount in respect of which he is
chargeable to tax by virtue of that subsection shall be treated for all purposes as earned income.

(7) Subsections (1) and (3) to (6) above ...[1] shall not apply on any sale of know-how where the buyer
is a body of persons over whom the seller has control, or the seller is a body of persons over whom
the buyer has control, or both the seller and the buyer are bodies of persons and some other person
has control over both of them; and subsection (2) above shall apply in any such case with the
omission of the words "Subject to subsection (3) below".

In this subsection references to a body of persons include references to a partnership.

(8) Where in connection with any disposal of know-how a person gives an undertaking (whether
absolute or qualified, and whether legally valid or not) the tenor or effect of which is to restrict his
or another's activities in any way, any consideration received in respect of the giving of the
undertaking or its total or partial fulfilment shall be treated for the purposes of this section as
consideration received for the disposal of the know-how.

Commentary—*Simon's Direct Tax Service* **B2.616, 617; B3.863–866.**
Definitions—"Body of persons", s 832(1); "capital gains tax", s 831(5); "control", s 840; "earned income", s 833(4), (5);
    "inspector", s 832(1); "know-how", s 533(7); "notice", s 832(1); "profit or gain", s 833(1); "Schedule D", s 18(1); "tax",
    s 832(3); "trade", s 832(1); "United Kingdom", s 830(1).
Amendments—[1] Words in sub-ss (1), (3) and (4) substituted, and words in sub-ss (3) and (7) repealed, by CAA 2001 ss 578,
    580, Sch 2 para 48, Sch 4 with effect for income tax purposes, as respects allowances and charges falling to be made for
    chargeable periods ending after 5 April 2001, and for corporation tax purposes, as respects allowances and charges falling to
    be made for chargeable periods ending after 31 March 2001.

[532 Application of Capital Allowances Act

The Tax Acts have effect as if sections 524 to 529 and 531, this section and section 533 were
contained in the Capital Allowances Act.][1]

Commentary—*Simon's Direct Tax Service* **B2.607.**
Definitions—"The Tax Acts", s 831(2).
Amendments—[1] This section substituted by CAA 2001 s 578, Sch 2 para 49 with effect for income tax purposes, as respects
    allowances and charges falling to be made for chargeable periods ending after 5 April 2001, and for corporation tax purposes,
    as respects allowances and charges falling to be made for chargeable periods ending after 31 March 2001.

533 Interpretation of sections 520 to 532

(1) In [sections 524 to 529][2]—

    "income from patents" means—

        (*a*) any royalty or other sum paid in respect of the user of a patent; and

        (*b*) any amount on which tax is payable for any chargeable period by virtue of section ...[2] 524
    or 525 [or section 472(5) of, or paragraph 100 of Schedule 3 to, the Capital Allowances Act][2];

    ...[2]

    "patent rights" means the right to do or authorise the doing of anything which would, but for that
    right, be an infringement of a patent;

    "United Kingdom patent" means a patent granted under the laws of the United Kingdom.

(2) Subject to subsection (3) below, in [sections 524 to 529][2] any reference to the sale of part of
patent rights includes a reference to the grant of a licence in respect of the patent in question, and
any reference to the purchase of patent rights includes a reference to the acquisition of a licence in
respect of a patent.

(3) If a licence granted by a person entitled to any patent rights is a licence to exercise those rights
to the exclusion of the grantor and all other persons for the whole of the remainder of the term for
which the right subsists, the grantor shall be treated for the purposes of [sections 524 to 529][2] as
thereby selling the whole of the rights.

(4) Where, under sections 46 to 49 of the Patents Act 1949[, sections 55 to 59 of the Patents Act
1977][1] or any corresponding provisions of the law of any country outside the United Kingdom, an
invention which is the subject of a patent is made, used, or exercised or vended by or for the service
of the Crown or the government of the country concerned, [sections 524 to 529][2] shall have effect as
if the making, user, exercise or vending of the invention had taken place in pursuance of a licence,
and any sums paid in respect thereof shall be treated accordingly.

(5) Expenditure incurred in obtaining a right to acquire in the future patent rights as respects any invention in respect of which the patent has not yet been granted shall be deemed for all the purposes of [sections 524 to 529][2] to be expenditure on the purchase of patent rights, and if the patent rights are subsequently acquired the expenditure shall be deemed for those purposes to have been expenditure on the purchase of those rights.

(6) Any sum received from a person which by virtue of subsection (5) above is deemed to be expenditure incurred by him on the purchase of patent rights shall be deemed to be proceeds of a sale of patent rights.

(7) In sections [section 531][2] "know-how" means any industrial information and techniques likely to assist in the manufacture or processing of goods or materials, or in the working of a mine, oil-well or other source of mineral deposits (including the searching for, discovery or testing of deposits or the winning of access thereto), or in the carrying out of any agricultural, forestry or fishing operations.

Commentary—*Simon's Direct Tax Service* **B2.602, 615; B3.861**.
Definitions—"Chargeable period", s 832(1); "tax", s 832(3); "United Kingdom", s 830(1).
Amendments—[1] Words in sub-s (4) inserted by FA 1988 Sch 13 para 5.
[2] Words in sub-ss (1)–(5), (7) substituted; in the definition of "income from patents", "520(6), 523(3)," repealed, and words inserted; definition of "the commencement of the patent" repealed by CAA 2001 ss 578, 580, Sch 2 para 50, Sch 4 with effect for income tax purposes, as respects allowances and charges falling to be made for chargeable periods ending after 5 April 2001, and for corporation tax purposes, as respects allowances and charges falling to be made for chargeable periods ending after 31 March 2001.

Copyright and public lending right

[534 Relief for copyright payments etc

(1) Where—

(a) an author of a literary, dramatic, musical or artistic work assigns the copyright in the work wholly or partially, or grants any interest in the copyright by licence; and
(b) the consideration for the assignment or grant consists wholly or partially of a payment to which this section applies, being a payment the whole amount of which would, but for this section, be included in computing the amount of his profits or gains for a single year of assessment; and
(c) the author was engaged on the making of the work for a period of more than 12 months;

he may, on making a claim, require that effect shall be given to the following provisions of this section in connection with that payment.

(2) If the period for which he was engaged on the making of the work does not exceed 24 months, then, for all income tax purposes, one-half only of the amount of the payment shall be treated as having become receivable on the date on which it actually became receivable, and the remaining half shall be treated as having become receivable 12 months before that date.

(3) If the period for which he was engaged on the making of the work exceeds 24 months, then, for all income tax purposes, one-third only of the amount of the payment shall be treated as having become receivable on the date on which it actually became receivable, and one-third shall be treated as having become receivable 12 months, and one-third 24 months, before that date.

(4) This section applies to—

(a) a lump sum payment, including an advance on account of royalties which is not returnable, and
(b) any payment of or on account of royalties or sums payable periodically,

except that it shall not by virtue of paragraph (b) above apply to payments in respect of the copyright in any work which only become receivable more than two years after its first publication.

[(5) A claim under this section with respect to any payment to which it applies by virtue only of subsection (4)(b) above—

(a) shall have effect as a claim with respect to all qualifying payments, that is to say, all such payments in respect of the copyright in the same work which are receivable by the claimant, whether before or after the claim; and
(b) where qualifying payments are so receivable in two or more years of assessment, shall be treated for the purposes of the Management Act as if it were two or more separate claims, each in respect of the qualifying payments receivable in one of those years.][1]

[(5A) A claim under this section may be made at any time within one year from the 31st January next following—

(a) in the case of such a claim as is mentioned in subsection (5) above, the latest year of assessment in which a qualifying payment is receivable; and
(b) in the case of any other claim, the year of assessment in which the payment in question is receivable.][1]

[(5B) For the purposes of subsections (5) and (5A) above, a payment shall be regarded as receivable in the year of assessment in computing the amount of the profits or gains of which it would, but for this section, be included.][1]

(6) A claim cannot be made under this section in respect of a payment if a prior claim has been made under section 535 as respects that payment.

[(6A) In the case of persons carrying on a trade, profession or business in partnership, no claim may be made under any of the following provisions, namely—

    (a) this section and section 535;
    (b) section 537 as it has effect in relation to this section and section 535; and
    (c) section 537A and section 538,

in respect of any payment or sum receivable on or after 6th April 1996; and nothing in any of those provisions shall be construed as applying to profits chargeable to corporation tax.]²

(7) In this section—

    (a) "author" includes a joint author; and
    (b) any reference to the first publication of a work is a reference to the first occasion on which the work or a reproduction of it is published, performed or exhibited.]³

Commentary—*Simon's Direct Tax Service* **B3.816.**
Definitions—"The Management Act", s 831(3); "profits or gains", s 833(1); "trade", s 832(1); "year of assessment", s 832(1).
Cross references—See TMA 1970 s 46C (Special Commissioners to have jurisdiction on an appeal against amendments to a self-assessment or partnership statement where the question in dispute concerns a claim made under this section).
TMA 1970 Sch 1B para 6 (effect of claims under sub-s (1) above in relation to earlier years of assessment).
TA 1988 s 537 (this section to have effect also in relation to public lending right).
Amendments—¹ Sub-ss (5)–(5B) substituted for sub-s (5) by FA 1996 s 128(5), (11) with effect as respects claims made (or deemed to be made) in relation to the year 1996–97 and subsequent years of assessment.
² Sub-s (6A) inserted by FA 1996 s 128(6).
³ Section repealed by FA 2001 ss 71(3), 110, Sch 33 Pt II(6) with effect for payments actually receivable after 5 April 2001.

[535 Relief where copyright sold after ten years or more

(1) Where not less than ten years after the first publication of the work the author of a literary, dramatic, musical or artistic work assigns the copyright in the work wholly or partially, or grants any interest in the copyright by licence, and—

    (a) the consideration for the assignment or grant consists wholly or partially of a lump sum payment the whole amount of which would, but for this section, be included in computing the amount of his profits or gains for a single year of assessment, and
    (b) the copyright or interest is not assigned or granted for a period of less than two years,

he may by making a claim require that effect shall be given to the following provisions of this section in connection with that payment.

(2) Except where the copyright or interest is assigned or granted for a period of less than six years, the amount of the payment shall for income tax purposes be treated as becoming receivable in six equal instalments at yearly intervals the first of which becomes receivable on the date when the payment actually became receivable.

(3) Where the copyright or interest is assigned or granted for a period of less than six years, the amount of the payment shall for income tax purposes be treated as becoming receivable in a number of equal instalments at yearly intervals the first of which becomes receivable on the date when the payment actually became receivable, the number being the number of whole years in that period.

(4) ...¹, if the author dies, any instalment which under this section would, but for the death, be treated as becoming receivable after the death shall for income tax purposes be treated as becoming receivable on the date when the last instalment before the death is to be treated as becoming receivable.

(5) ...¹

(6) If—

    (a) the payment would, apart from this section, have been taken into account in assessing the profits or gains of a profession or vocation, and
    (b) the profession or vocation is permanently discontinued (otherwise than on death) after the date on which the payment actually became receivable,

any instalment which under this section would, but for the discontinuance, be treated as receivable on a date after the discontinuance shall for income tax purposes be treated as becoming receivable when the last instalment before the discontinuance is to be treated as becoming receivable, ...¹

(7) ...¹

(8) In any case where—

    (a) but for this section, the payment would be included in computing any profits or gains chargeable to tax under Case VI of Schedule D, and
    (b) any amount would be deductible from that payment in computing those profits or gains (whether under the general provisions relating to Case VI or under section 105(1)),

the amount which, under this section, is to be treated as receivable in instalments shall be the amount of the payment after that deduction, and effect shall not be given to that deduction in any other way.

[(8A) No claim for relief made under subsection (1) above shall be allowed unless it is made within one year from the 31st January next following the year of assessment in which the payment is receivable; and for the purposes of this subsection a payment shall be regarded as receivable in the

year of assessment in computing the amount of the profits or gains of which it would, but for this section, be included.][1]

(9) A claim cannot be made under this section in respect of a payment if a prior claim has been made under section 534 as respects that payment.

(10) Where it is necessary, in order to give effect to a claim or election under this section, or as a result of the claim or election, to make any adjustment by way of an assessment on any person, the assessment shall not be out of time if it is made within one year of the final determination of the claim or, as the case may be, within one year from the giving of notice of the election.

(11) In this section—

"author" includes a joint author;

"lump sum payment" includes an advance on account of royalties which is not returnable;

and any reference to the first publication of a work is a reference to the first occasion on which the work or a reproduction of it is published, performed or exhibited.]*[2]

Commentary—*Simon's Direct Tax Service* **B3.816.**
Definitions—"Notice", s 832(1); "profits or gains", s 833(1); "Schedule D", s 18(1); "year of assessment", s 832(1).
Cross references—See TA 1988 s 534(6A) (no claim may be made under this section by a person carrying on a trade, profession or business in partnership; and this section does not apply to profits chargeable to corporation tax).
TA 1988 s 537 (this section to have effect also in relation to public lending right).
Amendments—[1] Words in sub-ss (4), (6), and whole of sub-ss (5), (7), repealed and sub-s (8A) inserted by FA 1996 s 128(7), (8), (11), Sch 41 Pt V(6) with effect for claims made (or deemed to be made) from the year 1996–97.
[2] Section repealed by FA 2001 ss 71(3), 110, Sch 33 Pt II (6) with effect for payments actually receivable after 5 April 2001.

536 Taxation of royalties where owner abroad

(1) Subject to the provisions of this section, where the usual place of abode of the owner of a copyright is not within the United Kingdom, section 349(1) shall apply to any payment of or on account of any royalties or sums paid periodically for or in respect of that copyright as it applies to annual payments not payable out of profits or gains brought into charge to income tax.

(2) In subsection (1) above—

["copyright" does not include copyright in—

    (i) a cinematograph film or video recording, or

    (ii) the sound-track of such a film or recording, so far as it is not separately exploited; and][1]

"owner of a copyright" includes a person who, notwithstanding that he has assigned a copyright to some other person, is entitled to receive periodical payments in respect of that copyright;

and the reference to royalties or sums paid periodically for or in respect of a copyright does not include royalties or sums paid in respect of copies of works which ...[2] have been exported from the United Kingdom for distribution outside the United Kingdom.

(3) Subject to subsection (4) below, where any payment to which subsection (1) above applies is made through an agent resident in the United Kingdom and that agent is entitled as against the owner of the copyright to deduct any sum by way of commission in respect of services rendered, the amount of the payment shall for the purposes of section 349(1) be taken to be diminished by the sum which the agent is so entitled to deduct.

(4) Where the person by or through whom the payment is made does not know that any such commission is payable or does not know the amount of any such commission, any income tax deducted by or assessed and charged on him shall be computed in the first instance on, and the account to be delivered of the payment shall be an account of, the total amount of the payment without regard being had to any diminution thereof....[2]

(5) The time of the making of a payment to which subsection (1) above applies shall, for all tax purposes, be taken to be the time when it is made by the person by whom it is first made and not the time when it is made by or through any other person.

(6) Any agreement for the making of any payment to which subsection (1) above applies in full and without deduction of income tax shall be void.

Commentary—*Simon's Direct Tax Service* **A3.423; B3.819.**
Revenue & other press releases—Hansard 10-11-69 (provisions do not apply to payments made to professional authors, or in circumstances where a double taxation agreement provides exemption).
Revenue Internal Guidance—Inspector's manual IM 4000–4030 (meaning of "copyright", "usual place of abode"; effect of double taxation agreements; form of certificate of deduction of tax).
Definitions—"Income tax", s 832(4); "United Kingdom", s 830(1).
Cross references— Hansard Vol 791, col 31 (provisions do not apply to payments made to professional authors, or in circumstances where a double taxation agreement provides exemption).
TMA 1970 s 46C (Special Commissioners have jurisdiction on an appeal against an amendment of a self assessment or partnership statement where the question in dispute concerns a claim under this section).
TA 1988 s 537 (this section to have effect also in relation to public lending right).
TA 1988 s 821(3) (recovery of under–deducted tax from payments to which this section applies made before passing of annual Act).
Amendments—[1] Definition of "copyright" in sub-s (2) substituted by the Copyright, Designs and Patents Act 1988 Sch 7 para 36(5) with effect from 1 August 1989 by virtue of the Copyright, Designs and Patents Act 1988 (Commencement No 1) Order 1989, SI 1989/816.
[2] Words in italics in sub-ss (2), (4) repealed by FA 1995 s 115(10), Sch 29 Pt VIII(14), with effect for income tax and capital gains tax from the year 1996–97, and for corporation tax for accounting periods ending after 30 June 1999 (by virtue of Finance Act 1994, Section 199, (Appointed Day) Order, SI 1998/3173 art 2).

537 Public lending right

[Section 536][1] shall have effect in relation to public lending right as [it has][1] effect in relation to copyright.

Commentary—*Simon's Direct Tax Service* **B3.814, 834.**
Cross references—See TA 1988 s 534(6A) (to the extent this section has effect in relation to ss 534 and 535, no claim may be made under it by persons carrying on a trade, profession or business in partnership, and it does not apply to profits chargeable to corporation tax).
TA 1988 s 821(3) (recovery of under-deducted tax from payments to which this section applies made before passing of annual Act).
Amendments—[1] Words substituted by FA 2001 s 71(4), Sch 24 para 4 with effect for payments actually receivable after 5 April 2001.

[Designs]

537A Relief for payments in respect of designs

(1) Where the designer of a design in which design right subsists assigns that right, or the author of a registered design assigns the right in the design, wholly or partially, or grants an interest in it by licence, and—

(a) the consideration for the assignment or grant consists, in whole or in part, of a payment to which this section applies, the whole amount of which would otherwise be included in computing the amount of his profits or gains for a single year of assessment, and

(b) he was engaged in the creation of the design for a period of more than 12 months,

he may, on making a claim, require that effect shall be given to the following provisions in connection with that payment.

(2) If the period for which he was engaged in the creation of the design does not exceed 24 months, then, for all income tax purposes, one-half only of the amount of the payment shall be treated as having become receivable on the date on which it actually became receivable and the remaining half shall be treated as having become receivable 12 months before that date.

(3) If the period for which he was engaged in the creation of the design exceeds 24 months, then, for all income tax purposes, one-third only of the amount of the payment shall be treated as having become receivable on the date on which it actually became receivable, and one-third shall be treated as having become receivable 12 months, and one-third 24 months, before that date.

(4) This section applies to—

(a) a lump sum payment, including an advance on account of royalties which is not returnable, and

(b) any other payment of or on account of royalties or sums payable periodically which does not only become receivable more than two years after articles made to the design or, as the case may be, articles to which the design is applied are first made available for sale or hire.

[(5) A claim under this section with respect to any payment to which it applies by virtue only of subsection (4)(b) above—

(a) shall have effect as a claim with respect to all qualifying payments, that is to say, all such payments in respect of rights in the design in question which are receivable by the claimant, whether before or after the claim; and

(b) where qualifying payments are so receivable in two or more years of assessment, shall be treated for the purposes of the Management Act as if it were two or more separate claims, each in respect of the qualifying payments receivable in one of those years.][1]

[(5A) A claim under this section may be made at any time within one year from the 31st January next following—

(a) in the case of such a claim as is mentioned in subsection (5) above, the latest year of assessment in which a qualifying payment is receivable; and

(b) in the case of any other claim, the year of assessment in which the payment in question is receivable.][1]

[(5B) For the purposes of subsections (5) and (5A) above, a payment shall be regarded as receivable in the year of assessment in computing the amount of the profits or gains of which it would, but for this section, be included.][1]

(6) In this section—

(a) "designer" includes a joint designer, and

(b) any reference to articles being made available for sale or hire is to their being so made available anywhere in the world by or with the licence of the design right owner or, as the case may be, the proprietor of the registered design.][2]

Commentary—*Simon's Direct Tax Service* **B3.833.**
Definitions—"The Management Act", s 831(3); "profits or gains", s 833(1); "year of assessment" s 832(1).
Cross references—See TMA 1970 Sch 1B para 6 (effect of claims under sub-s (1) above in relation to earlier years of assessment).
TA 1988 s 534(6A) (no claim may be made under this section by persons carrying on a trade, profession or business in partnership; and this section does not apply to profits chargeable to corporation tax).
Amendments—[1] Sub-ss (5)–(5B) substituted for sub-s (5) by FA 1996 s 128(9), (11) with effect as respects claims made (or deemed to be made) in relation to the year 1996–97 or later years of assessment.

[2] This section (which was inserted by the Copyright, Designs and Patents Act 1988 Sch 7 para 36(6) with effect from 1 August 1989 by virtue of the Copyright, Designs and Patents Act 1988 (Commencement No 1) Order 1989, SI 1989/816) repealed by FA 2001 ss 71(3), 110, Sch 33 Pt II(6) with effect for payments actually receivable after 5 April 2001.

[537B Taxation of design royalties where owner abroad

(1) Where the usual place of abode of the owner of a right in a design is not within the United Kingdom, section 349(1) shall apply to any payment of or on account of any royalties or sums paid periodically for or in respect of that right as it applies to annual payments not payable out of profits or gains brought into charge to income tax.

(2) In subsection (1) above—

(*a*) "right in a design" means design right or the right in a registered design,

(*b*) the reference to the owner of a right includes a person who, notwithstanding that he has assigned the right to some other person, is entitled to receive periodical payments in respect of the right, and

(*c*) the reference to royalties or other sums paid periodically for or in respect of a right does not include royalties or sums paid in respect of articles which ...[2] have been exported from the United Kingdom for distribution outside the United Kingdom.

(3) Where a payment to which subsection (1) above applies is made through an agent resident in the United Kingdom and that agent is entitled as against the owner of the right to deduct any sum by way of commission in respect of services rendered, the amount of the payment shall for the purposes of section 349(1) be taken to be diminished by the sum which the agent is entitled to deduct.

(4) Where the person by or through whom the payment is made does not know that any such commission is payable or does not know the amount of any such commission, any income tax deducted by or assessed and charged on him shall be computed in the first instance on, and the account to be delivered of the payment shall be an account of, the total amount of the payment without regard being had to any diminution thereof ...[2]

(5) The time of the making of a payment to which subsection (1) above applies shall, for all tax purposes, be taken to be the time when it is made by the person by whom it is first made and not the time when it is made by or through any other person.

(6) Any agreement for the making of any payment to which subsection (1) above applies in full and without deduction of income tax shall be void.][1]

Commentary—*Simon's Direct Tax Service* **B3.834.**
Definitions—"Income tax", s 832(4); "profits or gains", s 833(1); United Kingdom", s 830(1).
Cross references—See TA 1988 s 821(3) (recovery of under–deducted tax from payments to which this section applies made before passing of annual Act).
Amendments—[1] This section inserted by the Copyright, Designs and Patents Act 1988 Sch 7 para 36(6) with effect from 1 August 1989 by virtue of the Copyright, Designs and Patents Act 1988 (Commencement No 1) Order 1989, SI 1989/816.
[2] Words in sub-ss (2), (4) printed in italics repealed by FA 1995 s 115(10), Sch 29 Pt VIII(14), with effect for income tax and capital gains tax from the year 1996–97, and for corporation tax in respect of accounting periods ending after 30 June 1999 (by virtue of Finance Act 1994, Section 199, (Appointed Day) Order, SI 1998/3173 art 2).

Artists' receipts

[538 Relief for painters, sculptors and other artists

(1) Where the artist obtains any sum for the sale of a painting, sculpture or other work of art, or by way of commission or fee for the creation of the work of art, and—

(a) he was engaged on the making of the work of art for a period of more than 12 months, or

(b) he was engaged for a period of more than 12 months in making a number of works of art for an exhibition, and the work is one of them,

he may, by making a claim, require that effect shall be given to the following provisions of this section as respects that sum.

(2) If the period for which he was engaged on the making of the work does not exceed 24 months, then, for all income tax purposes, one-half only of the amount of the payment shall be treated as having become receivable on the date on which it actually became receivable, and the remaining half shall be treated as having become receivable 12 months before that date.

(3) If the period for which he was engaged on the making of the work exceeds 24 months, then, for all income tax purposes, one-third only of the amount of the payment shall be treated as having become receivable on the date on which it actually became receivable, and one-third shall be treated as having become receivable 12 months, and one-third 24 months, before that date.

[(4) No claim for relief made under subsection (1) above shall be allowed unless it is made within one year from the 31st January next following the year of assessment in which the payment is receivable; and for the purposes of this subsection a payment shall be regarded as receivable in the year of assessment in computing the amount of the profits or gains of which it would, but for this section, be included.][1]*]*[2]

Commentary—*Simon's Direct Tax Service* **B3.814, 817.**
Definition—"Income tax", s 832(4).
Cross references—See TMA 1970 s 46C (Special Commissioners have jurisdiction on an appeal against amendment of a self assessment or partnership statement where the question in dispute concerns a claim under this section).

TMA 1970 Sch 1B para 6 (effect of claims made under sub-s (1) above in relation to earlier years of assessment).
TA 1988 s 534(6A) (no claim may be made under this section by persons carrying on a trade, profession or business in partnership; and this section does not apply to profits chargeable to corporation tax).
Amendments—¹ Sub-s (4) inserted by FA 1996 s 128(10), (11) with effect as respects claims made (or deemed to be made) in relation to the year 1996–97 and subsequent years of assessment.
² Section repealed by FA 2001 ss 71(3), 110, Sch 33 Pt II (6) with effect for payments actually receivable after 5 April 2001.

CHAPTER II
LIFE POLICIES, LIFE ANNUITIES AND CAPITAL REDEMPTION POLICIES

Concession B42—Free gifts not exceeding specified amount in value made by insurance companies in connection with insurance policies are disregarded for the purposes of this Chapter.
A96 (IR 4-2-97)—For the purposes of this Chapter, no account will be taken of an alteration to the terms of a policy if a number of specified conditions are satisfied.
Statement of Practice SP 6/92—Accident insurance policies which provide protection only without investment element: for the purposes of this Chapter, no gains accrue from such policies.
Simon's Tax Cases—*Sugden v Kent (Inspector of Taxes)* [2001] STC (SCD) 158.
Modifications—Application of this Chapter, with modifications, in computing gains of personal portfolio bonds on which there is a yearly tax charge for years ending after 5 April 2000: see the Personal Portfolio Bonds (Tax) Regulations, SI 1999/1029.

539 Introductory

(1) This Chapter shall have effect for the purposes of imposing, in the manner and to the extent therein provided, charges to tax, ...², in respect of gains to be treated in accordance with this Chapter as arising in connection with policies of life insurance, contracts for life annuities and capital redemption policies.

(2) Nothing in this Chapter shall apply—

(a) to any policy of life insurance having as its sole object the provision on an individual's death or disability of a sum substantially the same as any amount then outstanding under a mortgage of his residence, or of any premises occupied by him for the purposes of a business, being a mortgage the principal amount secured by which is repayable by instalments payable annually or at shorter regular intervals; or

(b) to any policy of life insurance issued in connection with an approved scheme, as defined in Chapter I of Part XIV; or

(c) to a policy of insurance which constitutes, or is evidence of, a contract for the time being approved under section 621[; or

(d) to any policy of life insurance held in connection with a personal pension scheme, within the meaning of Chapter IV of Part XIV, for the time being approved under that Chapter.]⁵

In the application of this subsection to Scotland, for the reference to a mortgage there shall be substituted a reference to a heritable security within the meaning of the Conveyancing (Scotland) Act 1924 (but including a security constituted by ex facie absolute disposition or assignation).

(3) In this Chapter—

"assignment", in relation to Scotland, means an assignation;

"capital redemption policy" means any [contract]⁴ effected in the course of a capital redemption business as defined in section 458(3); and

["friendly society" means the same as in the Friendly Societies Act 1992 (and includes any society that by virtue of section 96(2) of that Act is to be treated as a registered friendly society within the meaning of that Act);]³

"life annuity" means any annuity to which sections 656 and 657 apply and any annuity the contract for which is made on or after 1st June 1984 by a friendly society or branch thereof in the course of life or endowment business as defined in section 466.

[(3A) References in this Chapter to assignment of the whole of, or assignment of part of or a share in, the rights conferred by a policy or contract shall, in any case where section 546A applies, be construed in accordance with that section.]⁶

(4) For the purposes of this Chapter the falling due of a sum payable in pursuance of a right conferred by a policy or contract to participate in profits shall be treated as the surrender of rights conferred by the policy or contract.

(5) This Chapter shall have effect only as respects policies of life insurance issued in respect of insurances made after 19th March 1968, contracts for life annuities entered into after that date, and capital redemption policies effected after that date.

(6) A policy of life insurance issued in respect of an insurance made on or before 19th March 1968 shall be treated for the purposes of subsection (5) above and the following provisions of this Chapter as issued in respect of one made after that date if it is varied after that date so as to increase the benefits secured or to extend the term of the insurance.

(7) A variation effected before the end of the year 1968 shall be disregarded for the purposes of subsection (6) above if its only effect was to bring into conformity with paragraph 2 of Schedule 9 to the Finance Act 1968 (which is re-enacted, as amended, by paragraph 2 of Schedule 15 to this

Act) a policy previously conforming therewith except as respects the amount guaranteed on death, and no increase was made in the premiums payable under the policy.

(8) Subsections (1) to (7) above do not apply in relation to section 554.

[(9) A policy of life insurance issued in respect of an insurance made before 14th March 1989 shall be treated for the purposes of sections 540(5A), 547(8) and 548(3A) as issued in respect of one made on or after that date if it is varied on or after that date so as to increase the benefits secured or to extend the term of the insurance; and any exercise of rights conferred by the policy shall be regarded for this purpose as a variation.][1]

Commentary—*Simon's Direct Tax Service* **D4.612; E3.502.**
Definition—"Tax", s 832(3).
Amendments—[1] Sub-s (9) added by FA 1989 Sch 9 paras 1, 2, 8 with effect from 14 March 1989.
[2] Words in sub-s (1) repealed by FA 1989 Sch 17 Pt V in relation to accounting periods beginning after 31 March 1989.
[3] Definition of "friendly society" in sub-s (3) inserted by F(No 2)A 1992 Sch 9 paras 1, 15, 22 with effect from 19 February 1993 by virtue of F(No 2)A 1992 Sch 9 (Appointed Day) Order, SI 1993/236.
[4] Word "contract" in sub-s (3) substituted for word "insurance" by FA 1996 s 168(4), (6) with effect as respects contracts effected on or after the appointed day under FA 1994 s 199 (1 July 1999 by virtue of Finance Act 1994, Section 199, (Appointed Day) Order, SI 1998/3173 art 2).
[5] Sub-(2)(d) and preceding word "or" inserted by FA 2000 s 61, Sch 13 paras 1, 2 with effect from the year 2000–01.
[6] Sub-s (3A) inserted by FA 2001 s 83, Sch 28 para 2 with effect, in the case of any policy or contract, in relation to any year (within the meaning given by TA 1988 s 546(4)) beginning after 5 April 2001.

540 Life policies: chargeable events

(1) Subject to the provisions of this section, in this Chapter "chargeable event" means, in relation to a policy of life insurance—

(a) if it is not a qualifying policy, any of the following—

(i) any death giving rise to benefits under the policy;
(ii) the maturity of the policy;
(iii) the surrender in whole of the rights conferred by the policy;
(iv) the assignment for money or money's worth of those rights; and
(v) [subject to section 546B(3)(a),][3] an excess of the reckonable aggregate value mentioned in subsection (2) of section 546 over the allowable aggregate amount mentioned in subsection (3) of that section, being an excess occurring at the end of any year (as defined in subsection (4) of that section) except, if it ends with another chargeable event, the final year; and

(b) if it is a qualifying policy (whether or not the premiums thereunder are eligible for relief under section 266), any of the above events, but—

(i) in the case of death or maturity, only if the policy is converted into a paid-up policy before the expiry of ten years from the making of the insurance, or, if sooner, of three-quarters of the term for which the policy is to run if not ended by death or disability;
(ii) in the case of a surrender or assignment or [(subject to section 546B(3)(a))][3] such an excess as is mentioned in paragraph (a)(v) above, only if it is effected or occurs within that time, or the policy has been converted into a paid-up policy within that time.

(2) The maturity of a policy is not a chargeable event in relation thereto if—

(a) a new policy is issued in consequence of the exercise of an option conferred by the maturing policy, and
(b) the whole of the sums becoming payable under the maturing policy are retained by the company with whom the insurance was made and applied in the payment of one or more premiums under the new policy,

unless the circumstances are such that the person making the insurance in respect of which the new policy is issued was an infant when the former policy was issued, and the former policy was one securing a capital sum payable either on a specified date falling not later than one month after his attaining 25 or on the anniversary of the policy immediately following his attainment of that age.

(3) Except as provided by section 544, no event is a chargeable event in relation to a policy issued in respect of an insurance made before 26th June 1982 if the rights conferred by the policy have at any time before that date and before the event been assigned for money or money's worth and are not at the time of the event held by the original beneficial owner.

(4) No account shall be taken for the purposes of [subsections (1) and (3) above][1] of any assignment effected by way of security for a debt, or on the discharge of a debt secured by the rights or share concerned, or of any assignment between spouses living together.

(5) Where subsection (1)(b) applies to a policy which has been varied so as to increase the premiums payable thereunder, it shall so apply as if the references in subsection (1)(b)(i) to the making of the insurance and the term of the policy were references respectively to the taking effect of the variation and the term of the policy as from the variation.

[(5A) Sub-paragraphs (i) and (ii) of subsection (1)(b) above shall not apply in relation to a policy issued in respect of an insurance made on or after 14th March 1989 if, immediately before the happening of the event, the rights conferred by the policy were in the beneficial ownership of a company, or were held on trusts created, or as security for a debt owed, by a company.][2]

(6) This section has effect subject to paragraph 20 of Schedule 15.

Commentary—*Simon's Direct Tax Service* **E3.506.**
Concession A41—For the purpose of calculating the chargeable event period under sub-s (1) above, the commencement date of a policy is regarded to be the earlier date where it is back-dated by not more than three months for the purpose of Sch 15, para 1(8) of this Act.
B42—Free gifts not exceeding specified amount in value made by insurance companies in connection with insurance policies are disregarded for the purposes of this Chapter.
Definition—"Qualifying policy", s 832(1).
Cross references—See TA 1988 s 539(9) (a policy in respect of an insurance made before 14 March 1989 to fall under sub-s (5A) above if certain variations to the policy are made on or after that date).
TA 1988 s 546 (calculation of certain amounts for the purposes of this section).
TA 1988 s 550 (top–slicing relief).
TA 1988 s 552 (insurer's duty to inform the Revenue of the happening of any chargeable event).
TA 1988 s 553 (this section to have effect with modifications where a new qualifying policy is substituted for an old non-qualifying policy).
TA 1988 Sch 15, para 20 (rules applicable for the purposes of this section where a new qualifying policy replaces an old qualifying policy after 24 March 1982 as a result of a variation in the life or lives being assured).
Amendments—[1] Words in sub-s (4) substituted by FA 1989 Sch 9 paras 1, 3, 8.
[2] Sub-s (5A) inserted by FA 1989 Sch 9 paras 1, 3, 8 with effect from 14 March 1989.
[3] Words in sub-s (1) inserted by FA 2001 s 83, Sch 28 para 3 with effect, in the case of any policy or contract, in relation to any year (within the meaning given by TA 1988 s 546(4)) beginning after 5 April 2001.

541 Life policies: computation of gain

(1) On the happening of a chargeable event in relation to any policy of life insurance, there shall be treated as a gain arising in connection with the policy—

(*a*) if the event is a death, the excess (if any) of the surrender value of the policy immediately before the death, plus the amount or value of any relevant capital payments, over the sum of the following—

  (i) the total amount previously paid under the policy by way of premiums; and
  (ii) the total amount treated as a gain by virtue of paragraph (*d*) below [or section 546C(7)(*b*)][2] on the previous happening of chargeable events;

(*b*) if the event is the maturity of the policy, or the surrender in whole of the rights thereby conferred, the excess (if any) of the amount or value of the sum payable or other benefits arising by reason of the event, plus the amount or value of any relevant capital payments, over the sum of the following—

  (i) the total amount previously paid under the policy by way of premiums; and
  (ii) the total amount treated as a gain by virtue of paragraph (*d*) below [or section 546C(7)(*b*)][2] on the previous happening of chargeable events;

(*c*) if the event is an assignment, the excess (if any) of the amount or value of the consideration, plus the amount or value of any relevant capital payments or[, subject to subsection (3A) below,][3] of any previously assigned share in the rights conferred by the policy, over the sum of the following—

  (i) the total amount previously paid under the policy by way of premiums; and
  (ii) the total amount treated as a gain by virtue of paragraph (*d*) below [or section 546C(7)(*b*)][2] on the previous happening of chargeable events;

(*d*) if the event is the occurrence of such an excess as is mentioned in section 540(1)(*a*)(v), the amount of the excess [(subject to section 546B(3)(*a*))][2].

(2) Where, in a case falling within subsection (1)(*b*) above, a right to periodical payments arises by reason of the event, there shall be treated as payable by reason thereof an amount equal to the capital value of those payments at the time the right arises.

(3) Where, in a case falling within subsection (1)(*c*) above, the assignment is between persons who are connected with each other within the meaning of section 839, the assignment shall be deemed to have been made for a consideration equal to the market value of the rights or share assigned.

[(3A) The amount or value of such a previously assigned share as is mentioned in paragraph (*c*) of subsection (1) above falls to be brought into account for the purposes of that paragraph only where that share was so assigned—

(*a*) in a year (as defined in section 546(4)) beginning on or before 5th April 2001; or
(*b*) for money or money's worth in a year (as so defined) beginning on or after 6th April 2001.][3]

(4) ...[2]

[(4A) Where, immediately before the happening of the chargeable event, the rights conferred by a qualifying endowment policy are held as security for a debt owed by a company, then, if—

(*a*) the conditions in subsection (4B) below are satisfied,
(*b*) the amount of the debt exceeds the total amount previously paid under the policy by way of premiums, and
(*c*) the company makes a claim for the purpose within two years after the end of the accounting period in which the chargeable event happens,

this section shall have effect as if the references in subsection (1)(*a*) and (*b*) to that total amount were references to the amount of the debt.][1]

[(4B) The conditions referred to in subsection (4A) above are—

(*a*) that, throughout the period beginning with the making of the insurance and ending immediately before the happening of the chargeable event, the rights conferred by the policy have been held as security for a debt owed by the company;

(*b*) that the capital sum payable under the policy in the event of death during the term of the policy is not less than the amount of the debt when the insurance was made;

(*c*) that any sum payable under the policy by reason of the chargeable event is applied in repayment of the debt (except to the extent that its amount exceeds the amount of the debt);

(*d*) that the debt was incurred to defray money applied—

    (i) in purchasing an estate or interest in land to be occupied by the company for the purposes of a trade carried on by it, or

    (ii) for the purpose of the construction, extension or improvement (but not the repair or maintenance) of buildings which are or are to be so occupied.][1]

[(4C) If the amount of the debt is higher immediately before the happening of the chargeable event than it was at some earlier time during the period mentioned in subsection (4B)(*a*) above, the amount to be taken into account for the purposes of subsection (1) above shall be the lowest amount at which it stood during that period.][1]

[(4D) If during the period mentioned in subsection (4B)(*a*) above the company incurs a debt by borrowing in order to repay another debt, subsections (4B) and (4C) above shall have effect as if, where appropriate, references to either debt included references to the other.][1]

(5) In this section—

(*a*) "relevant capital payments" means, in relation to any policy, any sum or other benefit of a capital nature, other than one attributable to a person's disability, paid or conferred under the policy before the happening of the chargeable event; and

(*b*) references in this subsection and (in relation to premiums) in subsection (1) above to "the policy" include references to any related policy, that is to say, to any policy in relation to which the policy is a new policy within the meaning of paragraph 17 of Schedule 15, and any policy in relation to which that policy is such a policy, and so on; [and[1]

(*c*) "qualifying endowment policy" means a policy which is a qualifying policy by virtue of paragraph 2 of Schedule 15;][1]

and the provisions of this section are subject to paragraph 20 of Schedule 15.

(6) There shall be disregarded for the purposes of this section any amount which was treated under section 72(9) of the Finance Act 1984 as an additional premium.

Commentary—*Simon's Direct Tax Service* **E3.506, 517.**
Definition—"Chargeable event", ss 540, 542, 545.
Cross references—See TA 1988 s 547 (method of charging tax on a gain treated as arising under this section).
TA 1988 s 549 (relief for deficiency where excess mentioned in sub-s (1)(*a*), (*b*) above is treated as a gain and part of an individual's total income).
TA 1988 Sch 15, para 20 (rules applicable for the purposes of this section where a new qualifying policy replaces an old qualifying policy after 24 March 1982 as a result of a variation in the life or lives being assured).
FA 1997 s 79 ("relevant capital payments" to include payment of a "relevant excepted benefit", as defined in that section).
Modifications—Sub-s (1)(*a*), (*b*), (*c*) modified in computing gains of personal portfolio bonds on which there is a yearly tax charge for years ending after 5 April 2000: see Personal Portfolio Bonds (Tax) Regulations, SI 1999/1029 reg 6(4).
Amendments—[1] Sub-ss (4A)–(4D) and sub-s (5)(*c*) inserted by FA 1989 Sch 9 paras 4, 8 with effect from 14 March 1989.
[2] Words in sub-s (1) inserted, and sub-s (4) repealed, by FA 2001 ss 83, 110, Sch 28 para 4, Sch 33 Pt II(9) with effect, in the case of any policy or contract, in relation to any year (within the meaning given by TA 1988 s 546(4)) beginning after 5 April 2001.
[3] Words in sub-s (1)(*c*) inserted, and sub-s (3A) inserted, by FA 2002 s 87(1)–(4), (11) with effect for any assignment after 5 April 2002 of the rights conferred by a policy or contract.

542 Life annuity contracts: chargeable events

(1) Subject to subsections (2) and (3) below, in this Chapter "chargeable event" means, in relation to any contract for a life annuity—

(*a*) the surrender in whole of the rights conferred by the contract, or

(*b*) the assignment for money or money's worth of those rights, or

(*c*) [subject to section 546B(3)(*a*),][1] an excess of the reckonable aggregate value mentioned in subsection (2) of section 546 over the allowable aggregate amount mentioned in subsection (3) of that section, being an excess occurring at the end of any year (as defined in subsection (4) of that section) except, if it ends with another chargeable event, the final year.

(2) Where the terms of a contract provide for the payment of a capital sum as an alternative, in whole or in part, to payments by way of annuity, the taking of the capital sum shall be treated for the purposes of this section and section 543 as a surrender in whole or in part of the rights conferred by the contract, and where the terms of the contract provide for the payment of a capital sum on death and the contract was made on or after 10th December 1974, the death shall be treated for those purposes as a surrender in whole of the rights conferred by the contract.

(3) Except as provided by section 544, an event referred to in subsection (1) above [or section 546C(7)(*a*)][2] is not a chargeable event in relation to any contract made before 26th June 1982 if the rights conferred by the contract have at any time before that date and before the event been assigned for money or money's worth and are not at the time of the event held by the original beneficial owner.

(4) Subsection (4) of section 540 shall, with any necessary modifications, apply for the purposes of this section as it applies for the purposes of that section.

Commentary—*Simon's Direct Tax Service* **E3.507.**
Cross references—See TA 1988 s 546 (calculation of certain amounts for the purposes of this section).
TA 1988 s 550 (top–slicing relief).
TA 1988 s 552 (insurer's duty to inform the Revenue of the happening of any chargeable event).
Amendments—¹ Words in sub-s (1)(*c*), (3) inserted by FA 2001 s 83, Sch 28 para 5 with effect, in the case of any policy or contract, in relation to any year (within the meaning given by TA 1988 s 546(4)) beginning after 5 April 2001.

543 Life annuity contracts: computation of gain

(1) On the happening of a chargeable event in relation to any contract for a life annuity, there shall be treated as a gain arising in connection with the contract—

(*a*) if the event is the surrender in whole of the rights conferred by the contract, the excess (if any) of the amount payable by reason of the event plus the amount or value of any relevant capital payments over the sum of the following—

(i) the total amount previously paid under the contract, whether by way of premiums or as lump sum consideration, reduced, if before the happening of the event one or more payments have been made on account of the annuity, by the capital element in that payment or payments, as determined in accordance with section 656; and

(ii) the total amount treated as a gain by virtue of paragraph (*c*) below [or section 546C(7)(*b*)]¹ on the previous happening of chargeable events;

(*b*) if the event is an assignment, the excess (if any) of the amount or value of the consideration, plus the amount or value of any relevant capital payments or[, subject to subsection (2A) below,]² of any previously assigned share in the rights conferred by the contract, over the sum of the following—

(i) the amount specified in paragraph (*a*)(i) above; and

(ii) any amount treated as a gain by virtue of paragraph (*c*) below [or section 546C(7)(*b*)]¹ on the previous happenings of chargeable events;

(*c*) if the event is the occurrence of such an excess as is mentioned in section 542(1), the amount of the excess [(subject to section 546B(3)(*a*))]¹.

(2) Subsection (3) of section 541 shall apply for the purposes of subsection (1) above as it applies for the purposes of subsection (1)(*c*) of that section, and subsection (4) of that section shall apply for the purposes of this section with the substitution of references to the contract for references to the policy.

[(2A) The amount or value of such a previously assigned share as is mentioned in paragraph (*b*) of subsection (1) above falls to be brought into account for the purposes of that paragraph only where that share was so assigned—

(*a*) in a year (as defined in section 546(4)) beginning on or before 5th April 2001; or

(*b*) for money or money's worth in a year (as so defined) beginning on or after 6th April 2001.]²

(3) In this section "relevant capital payments" means, in relation to any contract, any sum or other benefit of a capital nature paid or conferred under the contract before the happening of the chargeable event.

Commentary—*Simon's Direct Tax Service* **E3.507, 517.**
Concession B42—Free gifts not exceeding specified amount in value made by insurance companies in connection with insurance policies are disregarded for the purposes of this Chapter.
Definitions—"Chargeable event", ss 540, 542, 545; "life annuity", s 539(3).
Modifications—Sub-s (1)(*a*), (*b*) modified in computing gains of personal portfolio bonds on which there is a yearly tax charge for years ending after 5 April 2000: see Personal Portfolio Bonds (Tax) Regulations, SI 1999/1029 reg 6(5).
Cross references—See TA 1988 s 542(2) (treatment for the purposes of this section of a capital sum taken as an alternative to annuity payments).
TA 1988 s 547 (method of charging tax on a gain treated as arising under this section).
TA 1988 s 549 (relief for deficiency where excess mentioned in sub-s (1)(*a*) above is treated as a gain and part of an individual's total income).
Amendments—¹ Words in sub-s (1) inserted by FA 2001 s 83, Sch 28 para 6 with effect, in the case of any policy or contract, in relation to any year (within the meaning given by TA 1988 s 546(4)) beginning after 5 April 2001.
² Words in sub-s (1)(*b*) inserted, and sub-s (2A) inserted, by FA 2002 s 87(1), (5)–(7), (11) with effect for any assignment after 5 April 2002 of the rights conferred by a policy or contract.

544 Second and subsequent assignment of life policies and contracts

(1) In this section "assigned policy" means a policy of life assurance—

(*a*) which was issued in respect of an insurance made before 26th June 1982; and

(*b*) the rights conferred by which have been assigned for money or money's worth before that date; and

(*c*) in relation to which an event occurring on or after that date would not, apart from this section, be a chargeable event.

(2) In this section "assigned contract" means a contract for a life annuity—

(*a*) which was made before 26th June 1982; and

(*b*) the rights conferred by which have been assigned for money or money's worth before that date; and

(c) in relation to which an event occurring on or after that date would not, apart from this section, be a chargeable event.

(3) In any case where after 23rd August 1982—

(a) the rights conferred by an assigned policy or, as the case may be, an assigned contract are again assigned for money or money's worth; or
(b) a payment is made by way of premium or as lump sum consideration under the policy or contract; or
(c) subject to subsections (5) and (7) below, a sum is lent by or by arrangement with the body issuing the policy or, as the case may be, the body with which the contract was made;

section 540(3) shall cease to apply to the policy or section 542(3) shall cease to apply to the contract, as the case may be.

(4) No account shall be taken for the purposes of subsection (3)(a) above of any assignment effected by way of security for a debt, or on the discharge of a debt secured by the rights concerned, or of an assignment between spouses living together.

(5) Subsection (3)(c) above does not apply unless—

(a) the policy was issued in respect of an insurance made after 26th March 1974 or, as the case may be, the contract was entered into after that date; and
(b) the sum concerned is lent to or at the direction of the individual who, in accordance with subsection (6) below, is at the time of the loan the chargeable individual.

(6) The individual who is at any time the chargeable individual for the purposes of subsection (5)(b) above shall be determined as follows—

(a) if at the time the rights conferred by the policy or contract are vested in an individual as beneficial owner or are held on trusts created by an individual (including such trusts as are referred to in section 547(1)(a)), that individual is the chargeable individual; and
(b) if at that time those rights are held as security for a debt owned by an individual, that individual is the chargeable individual.

(7) Subsection (3)(c) above does not apply in relation to a policy if—

(a) it is a qualifying policy; and
(b) either interest at a commercial rate is payable on the sum lent or the sum is lent to a full-time employee of the body issuing the policy for the purpose of assisting him in the purchase or improvement of a dwelling-house to be used as his only or main residence.

(8) Where section 540(3) or 542(3) ceases to apply to an assigned policy or assigned contract by virtue of paragraph (c) of subsection (3) above, the lending of the sum concerned shall be regarded for the purposes of the Income Tax Acts (other than that paragraph) as taking place immediately after the time at which section 540(3) or, as the case may be, 542(3) ceases so to apply.

Commentary—*Simon's Direct Tax Service* E3.508.
Definitions—"Chargeable event", ss 540, 542, 545; "life annuity", s 539(3); "qualifying policy", s 832(1).

545 Capital redemption policies

(1) Subject to subsection (2) below, in this Chapter "chargeable event" means, in relation to a capital redemption policy, any of the following—

(a) the maturity of the policy, except where the sums payable on maturity are annual payments chargeable to tax under Schedule D;
(b) the surrender in whole of the rights conferred by the policy;
(c) the assignment for money or money's worth of those rights; and
(d) [subject to section 546B(3)(a),][1] an excess of the reckonable aggregate value mentioned in subsection (2) of section 546 over the allowable aggregate amount mentioned in subsection (3) of that section, being an excess occurring at the end of any year (as defined in subsection (4) of that section), except, if it ends with another chargeable event, the final year.

(2) Subsection (4) of section 540 shall apply for the purposes of this section as it applies for purposes of that section.

(3) The provisions of section 541, except subsection (3), shall, so far as appropriate and subject to subsection (4) below, apply to capital redemption policies as they apply to policies of life assurance.

(4) Where a chargeable event happens in relation to a capital redemption policy which has previously been assigned for money or money's worth, section 541 shall have effect in relation thereto as if, for the references to the total amount previously paid under the policy by way of premiums, there were substituted references to the amount or value of the consideration given for the last such assignment, plus the total amount of the premiums paid under the policy since that assignment.

Commentary—*Simon's Direct Tax Service* E3.509, 517.
Concession B42—Free gifts not exceeding specified amount in value made by insurance companies in connection with insurance policies are disregarded for the purposes of this Chapter.
Definitions—"Capital redemption policy", s 539(3); "Schedule D", s 18(1).
Cross references—See TA 1988 s 546 (calculation of certain amounts for the purposes of this section).
TA 1988 s 547 (method of charging tax on a gain treated as arising under this section).
TA 1988 s 550 (top-slicing relief).
TA 1988 s 552 (insurer's duty to inform the Revenue of the happening of any chargeable event).

Amendments—¹ Words in sub-s (1)(*d*) inserted by FA 2001 s 83, Sch 28 para 7 with effect, in the case of any policy or contract, in relation to any year (within the meaning given by TA 1988 s 546(4)) beginning after 5 April 2001.

546 Calculation of certain amounts for purposes of sections 540, 542 and 545

(1) For the purposes of sections 540, 542 and 545, there shall be calculated as at the end of each year—

  (*a*) the value, as at the time of surrender or assignment, of any part of or share in the rights conferred by the policy or contract which—

    [(i)]¹ has been [assigned for money or money's worth, or surrendered]¹ during the period ending with the end of that year and beginning with the commencement of the first year which falls wholly after 13th March 1975 [or
    (ii) has been assigned otherwise than for money or money's worth during that period but in a year beginning on or before 5th April 2001;]¹ and

  (*b*) the appropriate portion of any payment made up to the end of that period by way of premium or as a lump sum consideration;

and the appropriate portion of any payment shall be one-twentieth for the year in which it is made, increased by a further one-twentieth for each of the subsequent years, up to a maximum of nineteen, but excluding therefrom any such one-twentieth for any year before that first year.

(2) The reckonable aggregate value referred to in those sections shall be—

  (*a*) the sum of the values calculated under subsection (1) above; less
  (*b*) the sum of the values so calculated for a previous year and brought into account on the previous happening of a chargeable event.

(3) The allowable aggregate amount referred to in those sections shall be—

  (*a*) the aggregate of the appropriate portions calculated under subsection (1) above; less
  (*b*) the aggregate of the appropriate portions so calculated for a previous year and brought into account on the previous happening of a chargeable event.

(4) In this section "year" means the 12 months beginning with the making of the insurance or contract and any subsequent period of 12 months; except that—

  (*a*) death, the maturity of the policy or the surrender of the rights conferred by the policy or contract shall be treated as ending the final year; and
  (*b*) if the final year would by virtue of paragraph (*a*) above begin and end in the same year of assessment, the final year and the year preceding it shall together be one year.

(5) There shall be disregarded for the purposes of this section any amount which was treated under section 72(9) of the Finance Act 1984 as an additional premium.

[(6) Where any part of or share in the rights conferred by a policy or contract is assigned, the value of the part or share, as at the time of the assignment, shall be taken for the purposes of this section to be its surrender value at that time.]¹

Commentary—*Simon's Direct Tax Service* E3.505.
Definitions—"Chargeable event", ss 540, 542, 545; "year of assessment", s 832(1).
Cross references—See TA 1988 s 541(4) (how calculation under this section is to be made if a policy is assigned).
See the Personal Portfolio Bonds (Tax) Regulations, SI 1999/1029 reg 5 (this section is relevant for the purpose of computing gains arising on personal portfolio bonds)
Amendments—¹ Words in sub-s (1) inserted, and sub-s (6) inserted by FA 2001 s 83, Sch 28 para 8 with effect, in the case of any policy or contract, in relation to any year (within the meaning given by TA 1988 s 546(4)) beginning after 5 April 2001.

[546A Treatment of certain assignments etc involving co-ownership

(1) This section applies in any case where—

  (*a*) as a result of any transaction (the "material transaction") the whole or part of or a share in the rights conferred by a policy or contract ("the material interest") becomes beneficially owned by one person or by two or more persons jointly or in common ("the new ownership");
  (*b*) immediately before the material transaction, the material interest was in the beneficial ownership of one person or of two or more persons jointly ("the old ownership"); and
  (*c*) at least one person who is a member of the old ownership is also a member of the new ownership.

(2) In any such case, the material transaction shall, in accordance with the following provisions of this section, be taken for the purposes of this Chapter (other than this section) to be one or more assignments, of part only of the rights conferred by the policy or contract.

(3) For the purposes of this Chapter (other than this section), the members of the old ownership shall be treated—

  (*a*) where the old ownership consists of two or more persons beneficially entitled jointly, as if the material interest had been in their beneficial ownership in equal shares instead of jointly;
  (*b*) where the new ownership consists of two or more persons beneficially entitled jointly, as if the result of the material transaction had been that the material interest was in the beneficial ownership of those persons in equal shares instead of jointly; and

(c) as if the material transaction had been the assignment by each member of the old ownership of so much (if any) of his old share as exceeds his new share (or, if he does not have a new share, the whole of his old share).

(4) In this section—

"new share", in relation to the material interest and a person who is a member of the new ownership, means—

(a) if there is only one member of the new ownership, the material interest;
(b) if there are two or more members of the new ownership beneficially entitled to the material interest in common, the member's share in the material interest; or
(c) if there are two or more members of the new ownership beneficially entitled to the material interest jointly, the share attributed to the member by subsection (3)(b) above;

"old share", in relation to the material interest and a person who is a member of the old ownership, means—

(a) if there is only one member of the old ownership, the material interest; or
(b) if there are two or more members of the old ownership, the share attributed to the member by subsection (3)(a) above.]¹

Amendments—¹ This section inserted by FA 2001 s 83, Sch 28 para 9 with effect, in the case of any policy or contract, in relation to any year (within the meaning given by TA 1988 s 546(4)) beginning after 5 April 2001.

[546B Special provision in respect of certain section 546 excesses

(1) This section applies in relation to a policy or contract in any case where—

(a) a section 546 excess occurs at the end of any year (including the final year, whether or not ending with a terminal chargeable event); and
(b) the condition in subsection (2) below is satisfied in relation to that year.

[This subsection is subject to subsection (1A) below.]²

[(1A) In the case of a policy which is a qualifying policy (whether or not the premiums under the policy are eligible for relief under section 266) this section applies only if—

(a) the section 546 excess occurs within the time described in section 540(1)(b)(i); or
(b) the policy has been converted into a paid-up policy within that time.]²

(2) The condition is that—

(a) during the year there has been an assignment for money or money's worth of part of or a share in the rights conferred by the policy or contract; or
(b) during the year there has been both—

(i) an assignment, otherwise than for money or money's worth, of the whole or part of or a share in the rights conferred by the policy or contract; and
(ii) an earlier surrender of part of or a share in the rights conferred by the policy or contract.

(3) Where this section applies—

(a) the occurrence of the section 546 excess shall be treated for the purposes of this Chapter as not being a chargeable event; but
(b) the amount of the section 546 excess shall be charged to tax in accordance with the provisions of section 546C.

(4) In this section—

"final year" has the meaning given by section 546(4);
"section 546 excess", in relation to any year, means an excess, occurring at the end of the year, of—

(a) the reckonable aggregate value mentioned in subsection (2) of section 546,

over

(b) the allowable aggregate amount mentioned in subsection (3) of that section;

"terminal chargeable event" means any chargeable event other than—

(a) an assignment for money or money's worth of the whole of the rights conferred by the policy or contract;
(b) the occurrence of a section 546 excess; or
(c) a chargeable event by virtue of section 546C(7)(a);

"year" has the meaning given by section 546(4).]¹

Cross references—Personal Portfolio Bonds (Tax) Regulations, SI 1999/1029 reg 5 (modification of this section, with effect from 17 August 2001, for the purpose of computing gains arising from personal portfolio bonds).
Amendments—¹ Sections 546B–546D inserted by FA 2001 s 83, Sch 28 para 10 with effect, in the case of any policy or contract, in relation to any year (within the meaning given by TA 1988 s 546(4)) beginning after 5 April 2001.
² Words inserted in sub-s (1), and sub-s (1A) inserted, by FA 2002 s 87(8)–(10), (12). These amendments have effect, and shall be taken always to have had effect, for any policy, in relation to any year (as defined in TA 1988 s 546(4)) beginning after 5 April 2001.

[546C Charging the section 546 excess to tax where section 546B applies

(1) This section applies where, in relation to any policy or contract, the amount of a section 546 excess occurring at the end of any year falls to be charged to tax in accordance with this section by virtue of section 546B(3)(*b*).

(2) The following amounts shall be calculated as at the end of that year—

(*a*) the aggregate of the values calculated under section 546(1)(*a*) in respect of any part of or share in the rights conferred by the policy or contract which has been assigned for money or money's worth, or surrendered, during the year;

(*b*) the amount by which—

(i) the reckonable aggregate value mentioned in section 546(2), as at the end of the year,

exceeds

(ii) the aggregate calculated under paragraph (*a*) above; and

(*c*) the amount by which—

(i) the allowable aggregate amount mentioned in section 546(3), as at the end of the year,

exceeds

(ii) the amount calculated under paragraph (*b*) above.

(3) In this section—

(*a*) "relevant transaction" means any assignment for money or money's worth, or any surrender, of a part of or share in the rights conferred by the policy or contract which has happened during the year;

(*b*) "transaction value", in relation to any relevant transaction, means the value calculated in accordance with section 546(1)(*a*) in the case of that transaction;

(*c*) "the amount of available premium" means—

(i) in relation to the earliest relevant transaction, the amount calculated under subsection (2)(*c*) above (that amount being taken to be nil if there is no such excess as is there mentioned); and

(ii) in relation to each successive relevant transaction, that amount as successively reduced under subsections (5) to (7) below.

(4) Subsection (5) below shall apply successively to each of the relevant transactions that happened in the year, in the order in which they happened.

If the year is the final year and ends with a terminal chargeable event, this subsection is subject to section 546D.

(5) Where this subsection applies in relation to a relevant transaction—

(*a*) the transaction value shall be compared to the amount of available premium; and

(*b*) if the amount of available premium exceeds or is equal to the transaction value, subsection (6) below shall apply in relation to the transaction; but

(*c*) if the transaction value exceeds the amount of available premium, subsection (7) below shall apply in relation to the transaction.

(6) Where this subsection applies in relation to a relevant transaction—

(*a*) the amount of available premium shall be reduced (or further reduced) by the transaction value; and

(*b*) that reduction shall have effect in relation to the next subsequent relevant transaction.

(7) Where this subsection applies in relation to a relevant transaction—

(*a*) the relevant transaction shall for the purposes of this Chapter be a chargeable event in relation to the policy or contract, except as provided by sections 540(3) and 542(3);

(*b*) a gain of an amount equal to that by which the transaction value exceeds the amount of available premium shall be treated for the purposes of this Chapter as arising in connection with the policy or contract on the happening of that chargeable event; and

(*c*) in relation to any subsequent relevant transaction, the amount of available premium shall be reduced to nil.

(8) Where the whole or any part of the amount of any gain treated as arising by subsection (7)(*b*) above falls to be treated under any provision of section 547 as forming part of the income of any body or person for—

(*a*) the year of assessment in which the chargeable event in question happened, or

(*b*) the accounting period in which it happened,

that year of assessment or accounting period shall be taken to be the one which includes the end of the year as at which the section 546 excess in question occurs, instead of the one (if different) in which the relevant transaction happened.

(9) Where this section applies in relation to the final year and that year ends with a terminal chargeable event—

(*a*) effect shall be given to this section before applying the provisions of this Chapter in relation to the terminal chargeable event; and (*b*) in applying this Chapter in relation to the terminal chargeable event, any chargeable event by virtue of subsection (7)(*a*) above accordingly falls to be regarded as having occurred before the terminal chargeable event.

(10) This section shall be construed as one with section 546B.][1]

Cross references—See the Overseas Insurers (Tax Representatives) Regulations, SI 1999/881 Schedule para 1 (extension of the definition of "gain", with effect from 17 August 2001, to include gains treated as arising under this section).
Personal Portfolio Bonds (Tax) Regulations, SI 1999/1029 reg 5 (modification of this section, with effect from 17 August 2001, for the purpose of computing gains arising from personal portfolio bonds).
Amendments—[1] Sections 546B–546D inserted by FA 2001 s 83, Sch 28 para 10 with effect, in the case of any policy or contract, in relation to any year (within the meaning given by TA 1988 s 546(4)) beginning after 5 April 2001.

[546D Modifications of s 546C for final year ending with terminal chargeable event

(1) This section applies in any case where the year mentioned in section 546C(4) is the final year and that year ends with a terminal chargeable event.

(2) In any such case there shall be calculated, as at the end of the year, the amount of the gain ("the gains limit") that would have been treated as arising on the happening of the terminal chargeable event, apart from the application of sections 546B and 546C in relation to that year.

(3) Subsection (5) of section 546C shall apply successively to each of the relevant transactions that happened in the year, in the order in which they happened, unless and until the transaction in question (the "final transaction") is such that the aggregate of—

(*a*) its transaction value apart from subsection (4) below, and
(*b*) the sum of the transaction values of any relevant transactions to which subsection (5) of that section has previously applied,

exceeds the gains limit.

(4) If, in the case of the final transaction,—

(*a*) the aggregate mentioned in subsection (3) above exceeds the gains limit, but
(*b*) the sum mentioned in paragraph (*b*) of that subsection is less than that limit,

subsection (5) of section 546C shall apply in relation to that transaction, but for the purposes of subsections (5) to (7) of that section its transaction value shall be reduced to an amount equal to the difference between the gains limit and the sum mentioned in paragraph (*b*) above.

(5) Except as provided by subsection (4) above, subsection (5) of section 546C shall not apply in relation to the final transaction or any subsequent relevant transaction.

(6) This section shall be construed as one with sections 546B and 546C.][1]

Cross references—See the Personal Portfolio Bonds (Tax) Regulations, SI 1999/1029 reg 5 (modification of this section, with effect from 17 August 2001, for the purpose of computing gains arising from personal portfolio bonds).
Amendments—[1] Sections 546B–546D inserted by FA 2001 s 83, Sch 28 para 10 with effect, in the case of any policy or contract, in relation to any year (within the meaning given by TA 1988 s 546(4)) beginning after 5 April 2001.

547 Method of charging gain to tax

(1) Where under section 541, 543[, 545 or 546C][13] a gain is to be treated as arising in connection with any policy or contract—

(*a*) if, immediately before the happening of the chargeable event in question, the rights conferred by the policy or contract were vested in an individual as beneficial owner, or were held on trusts created by an individual ...[9] or as security for a debt owed by an individual, the amount of the gain shall be deemed to form part of that individual's total income for the year in which the event happened;
[(*b*) if, immediately before the happening of that event, those rights were in the beneficial ownership of a company, or were held on trusts created, or as security for a debt owed, by a company, the amount of the gain shall be deemed to form part of the company's income (chargeable under Case VI of Schedule D) for the accounting period in which the event happened;][1]
(*c*) if, immediately before the happening of that event, those rights were vested in personal representatives, within the meaning of Part XVI, the amount of the gain [(so far as it is not otherwise comprised in that income)][7] shall be deemed for the purposes of that Part to be part of the aggregate income of the estate of the deceased.
[(*d*) if, immediately before the happening of that event,—

    (i) those rights were held on trusts, and the person who created the trusts was not resident in the United Kingdom or had died or (in the case of a company or foreign institution) had been dissolved or wound up or had otherwise come to an end, or
    (ii) those rights were held as security for a debt owed by trustees,

subsection (9) or (10) below (as the case may be) shall apply in relation to the amount of the gain;

(*e*) if, immediately before the happening of that event, those rights—

    (i) were in the beneficial ownership of a foreign institution, or
    (ii) were held as security for a debt owed by a foreign institution,

subsection (11) below shall apply in relation to the amount of the gain.][10]

[(1A) In their application in relation to a gain which is treated as arising by virtue of section 546C(7)(*b*), subsection (1) above and subsections (9) to (11) below are subject to section 546C(8).]¹³

(2) Nothing in subsection (1) above shall apply to any amount which is chargeable to tax apart from that subsection.

(3) ...⁹

[(4) References in subsection (1) above to the rights conferred by a policy or contract are, in the case of an assignment or surrender of only a part of or share in any rights, references to that part or share.]¹³

(5) Subject to subsections (6) and (7) below and section 550, where by virtue of [subsection (1)(*a*)]¹¹ above, a sum is included in an individual's total income—

   (*a*) ...⁸ he shall be treated as having paid income tax at the basic rate on that sum or, if his total income is reduced by any deductions, on so much of that sum as is part of his total income as so reduced;

   (*b*) no repayment shall be made of the income tax treated by virtue of paragraph (*a*) above as having been paid; and

   (*c*) the sum so included shall be treated [as income which is not chargeable at the [starting rate]¹²and]⁵ for the purposes of sections 348 and 349(1) as not brought into charge to income tax.

[(5AA) If, in a case falling within subsection (1)(*d*) above, a sum forms part of the income of trustees by virtue of subsection (9)(*a*) below, subsection (5) above shall (subject to subsections (6) and (7) below and section 553(6)) apply in relation to the trustees and that sum—

   (*a*) as it applies in relation to an individual and a sum included in his total income by virtue of subsection (1)(*a*) above, but

   (*b*) with the omission from paragraph (*a*) of the words from ''or'' to the end of that paragraph.]¹⁰

[(5A) Where a gain is to be treated under section 543 [or 546C(7)(*b*)]¹³ as arising in connection with a contract for a life annuity made—

   (*a*) after 26th March 1974, and

   (*b*) unless the contract falls, or has at any time fallen, to be regarded as not forming part of any insurance company or friendly society's basic life assurance and general annuity business the income and gains of which are subject to corporation tax, in an accounting period of the insurance company or friendly society beginning before 1st January 1992,

subsection (6) below shall apply in relation to the gain unless [subsection (6A) or (7)]⁶ below applies in relation to it.]³

(6) [Where this subsection applies in relation to such a gain as is mentioned in subsection (5A) above]⁴—

   (*a*) this section shall have effect, in relation to the gain, as if subsection (5) were omitted; and

   (*b*) the gain shall be chargeable to tax under Case VI of Schedule D; but

   (*c*) any relief under section 550 shall be computed as if this subsection had not been enacted.

[(6A) Subsection (6) above shall not apply in relation to a gain treated as arising in connection with a contract for a life annuity in any case where the Board are satisfied, on a claim made for the purpose—

   (*a*) that the company liable to make payments under the contract (''the grantor'') has not, at any time (''a relevant time'') between the date on which it entered into the contract and the date on which the gain is treated as arising, been resident in the United Kingdom;

   (*b*) that at all relevant times the grantor has—

      (i) as a body deriving its status as a company from the laws of a territory outside the United Kingdom,

      (ii) as a company with its place of management in such a territory, or

      (iii) as a company falling, under the laws of such a territory, to be regarded, for any other reason, as resident or domiciled in that territory,

   been within a charge to tax under the laws of that territory;

   (*c*) that that territory is a territory within the European Economic Area when the gain is treated as arising;

   (*d*) that the charge to tax mentioned in paragraph (*b*) above has at all relevant times been such a charge made otherwise than by reference to profits as (by disallowing their deduction in computing the amount chargeable) to require sums payable and other liabilities arising under contracts of the same class as the contract in question to be treated as sums or liabilities falling to be met out of amounts subject to tax in the hands of the grantor;

   (*e*) that the rate of tax fixed for the purposes of that charge in relation to the amounts subject to tax in the hands of the grantor (not being amounts arising or accruing in respect of investments that are of a particular description for which a special relief or exemption is generally available) has at all relevant times been at least 20 per cent; and

   (*f*) that none of the grantor's obligations under the contract in question to pay any sum or to meet any other liability arising under that contract is or has been the subject, in whole or in part, of any reinsurance contract relating to anything other than the risk that the annuitant will die or will suffer any sickness or accident;

and subsection (6) above shall also not apply where the case would fall within paragraphs (*a*) to (*f*) above if references to a relevant time did not include references to any time when the contract fell to be regarded as forming part of so much of any basic life assurance and general annuity business the income and gains of which were subject to corporation tax as was being carried on through a branch or agency in the United Kingdom.][6]

(7) Where under section 541[, 543 or 546C(7)(*b*)][13] a gain is to be treated as arising in connection with a policy issued by a friendly society in the course of tax exempt life or endowment business, this section shall have effect in relation to the gain as if subsection (5) were omitted, but any relief under section 550 shall be computed as if this subsection had not been enacted.

[(7A) Where, in the case of any gain—

    (*a*) this section has effect by virtue of subsection (5A) or (7) above with the omission of subsection (5) above, and

    (*b*) the rights conferred by the contract or policy were vested immediately before the happening of the chargeable event in question in personal representatives within the meaning of Part XVI,

the gain shall be deemed for the purposes of income tax to be income of the personal representatives as such.][7]

[(8) Subsection (1)(*b*) above shall not have effect as respects—

    (*a*) a policy of life insurance issued in respect of an insurance made before 14th March 1989,

    (*b*) a contract for a life annuity made before that date, or

    (*c*) a capital redemption policy issued in respect of an insurance made before that date, or issued by a company resident in the United Kingdom in respect of an insurance made on or after that date.][1]

[(9) If, in a case falling within subsection (1)(*d*) above, the trustees were resident in the United Kingdom immediately before the happening of the chargeable event in question, the amount of the gain—

    (*a*) shall be deemed to form part of the income of the trustees for the year of assessment in which the chargeable event happened; and

    (*b*) shall be chargeable to income tax at the rate applicable to trusts for that year.

(10) If, in a case falling within subsection (1)(*d*) above, the trustees were not resident in the United Kingdom immediately before the happening of the chargeable event in question, then, for the purpose of determining whether an individual ordinarily resident in the United Kingdom has a liability for income tax in respect of the amount of the gain, section 740 shall apply as if—

    (*a*) the amount of the gain constituted income becoming payable to the trustees; and

    (*b*) that income were income arising to the trustees in the year of assessment in which the chargeable event happened.

(11) In a case falling within subsection (1)(*e*) above, for the purpose of determining whether an individual ordinarily resident in the United Kingdom has a liability for income tax in respect of the amount of the gain, section 740 shall apply as if—

    (*a*) the amount of the gain constituted income becoming payable to the foreign institution; and

    (*b*) that income were income arising to the foreign institution in the year of assessment in which the chargeable event happened.

(12) For the purposes of this section, property held for the purposes of a foreign institution shall be regarded as in the beneficial ownership of the foreign institution.][10]

[(13) In this section—

"basic life assurance and general annuity business" has the same meaning as in Chapter I of Part XII.][3]

["foreign institution" means a person which is a company or other institution resident or domiciled outside the United Kingdom.][10]

[(14) Any reference in this section to trusts created by an individual includes a reference to trusts arising under—

    (*a*) section 11 of the Married Women's Property Act 1882;

    (*b*) section 2 of the Married Women's Policies of Assurance (Scotland) Act 1880; or

    (*c*) section 4 of the Law Reform (Husband and Wife) Act (Northern Ireland) 1964;

and references to the settlor or to the person creating the trusts shall be construed accordingly.][10]

Commentary—*Simon's Direct Tax Service* **D4.612; E3.510, 513.**

Definitions—"Accounting period", s 834(1); "basic rate", "the Board", s 832(1); "branch or agency", s 834(1); "chargeable event", ss 540, 542, 545; "close company", ss 414, 415, by virtue of s 832(1); "distributable income", Sch 19 para 4; "friendly society", s 539; "income tax", s 832(4); "life annuity", s 539(3); "Schedule D", s 18(1); "starting rate" s 832(1); "tax", s 834(1); "total income", s 835(1); "United Kingdom", s 830(1).

Cross references—See TA 1988 s 271(1) (deemed surrender of a life policy issued after 26 March 1974 in consequence of a loan on the policy).

TA 1988 s 539(9) (a policy in respect of an insurance made before 14 March 1989 to fall under sub-s (8) above if certain variations are made to the policy on or after that date).

TA 1988 s 548 (where sub-s (1)(*a*), (*b*) above apply, the policy or contract is treated as surrendered (subject to certain exceptions) if a loan is made on the security of a post–26 March 1974 policy or contract).

TA 1988 s 548(1) (where sub-s (1)(*a*), (*b*) above apply, a loan secured by an insurance or contract made after 26 March 1974).

TA 1988 s 550 (top–slicing relief).

TA 1988 s 551 (right of a beneficiary under a trust to recover tax from trustees where sub-s (1)(*a*) above applies to the beneficiary).

TA 1988 s 553(6) (this section to have effect with modification in relation to non-resident policies and off-shore capital redemption policies).

TA 1988 s 701(8) (extension of sub-s (1)(*c*) above to s 701(8)).

TCGA 1992 s 6(3) (taxation of capital gains at income tax rates: the higher rate not to apply to the whole of the amount which is deemed to be included in the total income by virtue of sub-s (1)(*a*) above).

FA 1995 s 56(3) (power of Board to make regulations to extend the scope of sub-s (6A) above to include cases which fulfil the conditions specified in the regulations at any time (including before the regulations were made)).

FA 2000 s 46(2) (exemption under FA 2000 s 46(1) for income of a charity is not granted in respect of income chargeable to tax under Schedule D Case VI by virtue of sub-s (1)(*b*), (6) above).

Modifications—Sub-ss (1), (5A), (7) modified in computing gains of personal portfolio bonds on which there is a yearly tax charge for years ending after 5 April 2000: see Personal Portfolio Bonds (Tax) Regulations, SI 1999/1029 reg 6(3).

Amendments—[1] Sub-s (1)(*b*) substituted by FA 1989 Sch 9 paras 1, 5, 8 in relation to chargeable events in accounting periods beginning after 31 March 1989.

[2] Sub-s (8) inserted by FA 1989 Sch 9 paras 1, 5, 8 in relation to chargeable events in accounting periods beginning after 31 March 1989.

[3] Sub-s (5A) and sub-s (9) (which has since been renumbered sub-s (13) by FA 1998 Sch 14 para 1(8)) inserted by FA 1991 Sch 7 para 9(1), (3).

[4] Words in sub-s (6) substituted by FA 1991 Sch 7, para 9(2).

[5] Words in sub-s (5)(*c*) inserted by F(No 2)A 1992 s 19(4), (7) with effect from the year 1992–93.

[6] Words in sub-s (5A) substituted, and sub-s (6A) inserted, by FA 1995 s 56(1), (4), in relation to any gain arising after 28 November 1994 and in relation to any gain arising before that date the income tax on which has not been the subject of an assessment that became final and conclusive on or before that date.

[7] Words in sub-s (1)(*c*), and whole of sub-s (7A), inserted by FA 1995 s 76(2), (6), with effect from the year 1995–96.

[8] Words omitted from sub-s (5)(*a*) repealed by FA 1996 ss 121(8), 122(7)(*a*), Sch 41 Pt V(6) with effect from the year 1996–97.

[9] Words in sub-s (1), and sub-s (3) repealed by FA 1998 Sch 14 para 1 with effect in relation to chargeable events happening after 5 April 1998.

[10] Sub-s (1)(*d*), (*e*), sub-ss (5AA), (9)–(12), words in sub-s (13) and sub-s (14) inserted by FA 1998 Sch 14 para 1 with effect in relation to chargeable events happening after 5 April 1998. However, note that TA 1988 s 547(1)(*d*) shall not have effect in relation to the amount of a gain if—

(*a*) the gain is treated as arising on the happening of a chargeable event after 5 April 1998 in relation to a pre-commencement policy or contract; and

(*b*) the trusts in question were created before 17 March 1998 and the person, or (disregarding s 547A(6) of that Act) at least one of the persons, who created them was an individual who died before that date.

"Pre-commencement policy or contract" means—

(*a*) a policy of life insurance issued in respect of an insurance made before 17 March 1998,

(*b*) a contract for a life annuity made before that date, or

(*c*) a capital redemption policy where the contract was effected before that date,

but does not include a policy or contract varied on or after that date so as to increase the benefits secured or to extend the term of the insurance, annuity or capital redemption policy (any exercise of rights conferred by the policy or contract being regarded for this purpose as a variation).

[11] Words in sub-ss (4), (5) substituted by FA 1998 Sch 14 para 1 with effect in relation to chargeable events happening after 5 April 1998.

[12] Words in sub-s (5)(*c*) substituted by FA 1999 s 22(8), (12) with effect from the year 1999–00.

[13] Words in sub-ss (1), (7) substituted, sub-s (1A) inserted, sub-s (4) substituted, and words in sub-s (5A) inserted by FA 2001 s 83, Sch 28 para 11 with effect, in the case of any policy or contract, in relation to any year (within the meaning given by TA 1988 s 546(4)) beginning after 5 April 2001.

[547A Method of charging gain to tax: multiple interests

(1) Where, immediately before the happening of a chargeable event, two or more persons have relevant interests in the rights conferred by the policy or contract in question, section 547 shall have effect in relation to each of those persons as if that person had been the only person with a relevant interest in those rights, but with references to the amount of the gain construed as references to his proportionate share of the amount of the gain.

[(2) References in this section to the rights conferred by a policy or contract are, in the case of an assignment or surrender of only a part of or share in any rights, references to that part or share.][2]

(3) For the purposes of this section, a person has a "relevant interest" in the rights conferred by a policy or contract—

(*a*) in the case of an individual, if a share in the rights is vested in him as beneficial owner, or is held on trusts created, or as security for a debt owed, by him;

(*b*) in the case of a company, if a share in the rights is in the beneficial ownership of the company, or is held on trusts created, or as security for a debt owed, by the company;

(*c*) in the case of personal representatives, if a share in the rights is vested in them;

(*d*) in the case of trustees—

    (i) if a share in the rights is held by them, and the person who created the trusts is not resident in the United Kingdom or has died or (in the case of a company or foreign institution) has been dissolved or wound up or has otherwise come to an end; or

    (ii) if a share in the rights is held as security for a debt owed by them;

(*e*) in the case of a foreign institution, if a share in the rights is in the beneficial ownership of the foreign institution, or is held as security for a debt owed by the foreign institution.

(4) For the purposes of subsection (1) above, a person's "proportionate share" of the amount of a gain is that share of it which is proportionate to the share of the rights by reference to which he has the relevant interest in question.

(5) Where, immediately before the happening of a chargeable event, the rights conferred by the policy or contract in question are, or a share in those rights is, held as security for one or more debts owed by two or more persons, this section shall have effect in relation to the chargeable event as if—

(a) each of those persons were instead the sole debtor in respect of a separate debt; and
(b) the security for that separate debt were the appropriate share of the security for the actual debt or debts (so far as consisting of the rights, or a share in the rights, conferred by the policy or contract);

and for the purposes of paragraph (b) above the appropriate share, in the case of any person, is a share which is proportionate to that share of the actual debt or, as the case may be, the aggregate of the two or more actual debts, for which he is liable as between the debtors.

(6) Where, immediately before the happening of a chargeable event, the rights conferred by the policy or contract in question are, or a share in those rights is, held on trusts created by two or more persons, this section shall have effect in relation to that chargeable event as if—

(a) each of those persons had instead been the sole settlor in relation to a separate share of the rights or share so held; and
(b) that separate share were proportionate to the share which originates from him of the whole of the property subject to the trusts immediately before the happening of the chargeable event.

(7) The reference in subsection (6)(b) above to the share of the property which originates from a person is a reference to the share of the property which consists of—

(a) property which that person has provided directly or indirectly for the purposes of the trusts;
(b) property representing property which that person has so provided; and
(c) so much of any property which represents both property so provided and other property as, on a just apportionment, represents the property so provided.

(8) References in subsection (7) above to property which a person has provided directly or indirectly—

(a) include references to property which has been provided directly or indirectly by another in pursuance of reciprocal arrangements with the person, but
(b) do not include references to property which the person has provided directly or indirectly in pursuance of reciprocal arrangements with another.

(9) References in subsection (7) above to property which represents other property include references to property which represents accumulated income from that other property.

(10) Where immediately before the happening of a chargeable event—

(a) the rights conferred by the policy or contract in question are, or a share in those rights is, held subject to any trusts, and
(b) different shares of the whole of the property subject to those trusts originate (within the meaning of subsection (6)(b) above) from different persons,

the rights or share shall, in relation to that chargeable event, be taken for the purposes of this section to be held on trusts created by those persons.

(11) Where the rights conferred by a policy or contract are, or an interest in any such rights is, in the beneficial ownership of two or more persons jointly, the rights or interest shall be treated for the purposes of this section as if they were in the beneficial ownership of those persons in equal shares.

(12) A non-fractional interest in the rights conferred by a policy or contract shall be treated for the purposes of this section as if it were instead such a share in those rights as may justly and reasonably be regarded for those purposes as representing the non-fractional interest.

(13) For the purposes of subsection (12) above, a "non-fractional interest" in the rights conferred by a policy or contract is an interest in some or all of those rights which is not a share in all of those rights (otherwise than by virtue only of subsection (2) above).

(14) This section applies in a case where the same person has two or more relevant interests in the rights conferred by a policy or contract as it applies in a case where two or more persons have separate relevant interests, unless—

(a) that person is the only person with a relevant interest in those rights, and
(b) he has all the relevant interests in the same capacity,

in which case section 547 applies.

(15) In this section—

　"foreign institution" has the same meaning as in section 547;
　"personal representatives" has the same meaning as in Part XVI.

(16) Subsections (12) and (14) of section 547 apply for the purposes of this section as they apply for the purposes of that section.]¹

Commentary—*Simon's Direct Tax Service* E3.510, 513.
Amendments—¹ This section inserted by FA 1998 Sch 14 para 2 with effect in relation to chargeable events happening after 5 April 1998.
² Sub-s (2) substituted by FA 2001 s 83, Sch 28 para 12 with effect, in the case of any policy or contract, in relation to any year (within the meaning given by TA 1988 s 546(4)) beginning after 5 April 2001.

548 Deemed surrender of certain loans

(1) Where—

(a) under section 547 a gain arising in connection with a policy or contract would be treated as forming part of an individual's total income [or the income of a company]¹; and

(b) the policy was issued in respect of an insurance made after 26th March 1974 or the contract was made after that date; and

(c) any sum is at any time after the making of the insurance or contract lent to or at the direction of that individual [or company][1] by or by arrangement with the body issuing the policy or, as the case may be, the body with which the contract was made;

then, subject to [subsections (3) and (3A)][1] below, the same results shall follow under this Chapter as if at the time the sum was lent there had been a surrender of part of the rights conferred by the policy or contract and the sum had been paid as consideration for the surrender.

(2) If the whole or any part of the sum is repaid the repayment shall be treated, for the purpose of computing any gain arising on the happening, at the end of the final year, of a chargeable event, as a payment of a premium or lump sum consideration.

(3) Subsections (1) and (2) above do not apply in relation—

[(a) to a policy if it is a qualifying policy and interest at a commercial rate is payable on the sum lent;][2]

(b) to a contract if and to the extent that interest on the sum lent is eligible for relief under section 353 by virtue of section 365.

[(3A) Subsections (1) and (2) do not apply where the rights conferred by the policy or contract are in the beneficial ownership of a company, or are held on trusts created, or as security for a debt owed, by a company, if the policy was issued in respect of an insurance made before 14th March 1989 or the contract was made before that date.][1]

(4) In this section "final year" has the same meaning as in section 546.

Commentary—*Simon's Direct Tax Service* E3.510.
Concession A42—This section may not be applied where a policyholder exercises a loan-back option connected with a concurrent retirement annuity contract with the same insurer.
Definitions—"Chargeable event", ss 540, 542, 545; "qualifying policy", s 832(1); "total income", s 835(1).
Cross references—See TA 1988 s 539(9) (a policy in respect of an insurance made before 14 March 1989 to fall under sub-s (3A) above if certain variations are made to the policy on or after that date).
Amendments—[1] Words in sub-s (1)(a), (c) inserted and other words in sub-s (1) substituted, and sub-s (3A) inserted by FA 1989 Sch 9 paras 1, 6, 8 with effect from 14 March 1989.
[2] Sub-s (3)(a) substituted by FA 1999 s 38(8), Sch 4 paras 16, 18(3) with effect for loans made after 5 April 2000.

549 Certain deficiencies allowable as deductions

(1) Subject to subsections (2) below, where such an excess as is mentioned in section 541(1)(a) or (b) or 543(1)(a)—

(a) would be treated as a gain arising in connection with a policy or contract, and

(b) would form part of an individual's total income for the year of assessment in which the final year ends,

a corresponding deficiency occurring at the end of the final year shall be allowable as a deduction from his total income for that year of assessment, so far as it does not exceed the total amount treated as a gain by virtue of section 541(1)(d), [543(1)(c) or 546C(7)(b)][6] on the previous happenings of chargeable events.

(2) Except where the deficiency mentioned in subsection (1) above occurs in connection with a contract for a life annuity made after 26th March 1974, [but in an accounting period of the insurance company or friendly society beginning before 1st January 1992,][1] the deduction allowable under that subsection shall be made only for the purposes of ascertaining the individual's excess liability, that is to say, the excess (if any) of his liability to income tax over what it would be if all income tax not chargeable [[at the starting rate][5] were chargeable at the basic rate, or (so far as applicable in accordance with [section 1A][3]) the lower rate,][2] [or the Schedule F ordinary rate][4] to the exclusion of [the higher rate and the Schedule F upper rate.][4].

(3) In this section "final year" has the same meaning as in section 546.

Commentary—*Simon's Direct Tax Service* E3.511.
Definitions—"Basic rate", s 832(1); "chargeable events", ss 540, 542, 545; "friendly society", s 539; "higher rate", s 832(1); "income tax", s 832(4); "life annuity", s 539(3); "lower rate", s 832(1); "Schedule F ordinary rate", s 832(1); "Schedule F upper rate", s 832(1); "starting rate", s 832(1); "total income", s 835(1); "year of assessment", s 832(1).
Cross references—See TCGA 1992 s 6(2)(a) (taxation of capital gains at income tax rates: higher rate exemption in respect of the amount deducted under sub-s (2) above).
Amendments—[1] Words in sub-s (2) inserted by FA 1991 Sch 7 para 9(4).
[2] Words in sub-s (2) substituted by FA 1993 Sch 6 paras 6, 25(1) with effect from the year of assessment 1993–94.
[3] Words in sub-s (2) substituted by FA 1996 Sch 6 paras 13, 28 with effect from the year 1996–97.
[4] Words "or the Schedule F ordinary rate" inserted, and words "the higher rate and the Schedule F upper rate" substituted, in sub-s (2) by F(No 2)A 1997 s 34, Sch 4 para 13 with effect from the year 1999–00.
[5] Words in sub-s (2) substituted by FA 1999 s 22(9), (12) with effect from the year 1999–00.
[6] Words in sub-s (1) substituted by FA 2001 s 82, Sch 28 para 13 with effect, in the case of any policy or contract, in relation to any year (within the meaning given by TA 1988 s 546(4)) beginning after 5 April 2001.

550 Relief where gain charged at a higher rate

(1) The following provisions of this section shall have effect for the purposes of giving relief, on a claim in that behalf being made by him to the Board, in respect of any increase in an individual's liability to tax which is attributable to one or more amounts being included in his total income for a year of assessment by virtue of section 547(1)(a).

(2) Where one amount only is so included, there shall be computed—

　(*a*) the tax which would be chargeable in respect of the amount if relief under this section were not available and it constituted the highest part of the claimant's total income for the year, and

　(*b*) the tax (if any) which would be chargeable in respect of the amount if calculated, in accordance with subsection (3) below, by reference to its appropriate fraction;

and the relief shall consist of a reduction or repayment of tax equal to the difference between the two amounts of tax so computed, or, if tax would not be chargeable on a calculation by reference to the appropriate fraction, of a reduction or repayment of the tax equal to the tax computed under paragraph (*a*) above.

(3) In subsection (2) above "appropriate fraction" means, in relation to any amount, such a sum as bears thereto the same proportion as that borne by one to the number of complete years for which the policy or contract has run before the happening of the chargeable event; and the computation required by paragraph (*b*) of that subsection shall be made by applying to the amount in question such rate or rates of income tax, other than the basic rate [or the[starting rate][2]][1], as would apply if it were reduced to that fraction and, as so reduced, still constituted the highest part of the claimant's total income for the year.

(4) For the purposes of subsection (3) above the number of years for which a policy of life insurance has run before the happening of a chargeable event shall be calculated, where appropriate, from the issue of the earliest related policy, meaning, any policy in relation to which the policy is a new policy within the meaning of paragraph 17 of Schedule 15, any policy in relation to which that policy is such a policy, and so on.

(5) Where a chargeable event on the happening of which an amount is included in an individual's total income by virtue of section 547(1)(*a*) follows the happening of another chargeable event in relation to the same policy or contract, and each of those events is such an excess as is mentioned in section 540(1)(*a*)(v), 542(1) or 545(1)(*d*), subsection (3) and (4) above shall have effect in relation to that amount as if the number of complete years referred to in subsection (3) were the number of complete years elapsing between that other event (or, if more that one, the last of them) and the first-mentioned event.

[(5A) For the purposes of this section, a chargeable event by virtue of section 546C(7)(*a*)—

　(*a*) shall be treated as being such a chargeable event as is mentioned in subsection (5) above; and

　(*b*) accordingly, in computing any number of complete years, shall be treated as happening at the end of the year (within the meaning given by section 546(4)) as at which occurs the excess that gives rise to it.][3]

(6) Where by virtue of section 547(1)(*a*) two or more amounts are included in an individual's total income for any year of assessment, subsections (2) and (3) above shall apply as if they together constituted a single amount, but with the appropriate fraction of the whole determined by adding together the appropriate fractions of the individual amounts.

(7) A provision of this section requiring tax to be calculated as if an amount constituted the highest part of a claimant's total income shall apply notwithstanding any other provision of the Income Tax Acts directing any other amount to be treated as the highest part thereof, but, for the purposes of this section, a claimant's total income shall be deemed not to include any amount in respect of which he is chargeable to tax under section 34, 35, 36 or 148.

Commentary—*Simon's Direct Tax Service* E3.514, 517.
Definitions—"Basic rate", s 832(1); "the Board", s 832(1); "chargeable event", ss 540, 542, 545; "highest part of the claimant's total income", see s 833(3); "income tax", s 832(4); "the Income Tax Acts", s 831(1)(*b*); "starting rate" s 832(1); "total income", s 835(1).
Cross references—See TCGA 1992 s 6(3) (taxation of capital gains at income tax rates: top slicing relief in respect of capital gains tax).
Modifications—This section omitted in computing gains of personal portfolio bonds on which there is a yearly tax charge for years ending after 5 April 2000: see Personal Portfolio Bonds (Tax) Regulations, SI 1999/1029 reg 6(3).
Amendments—[1] Words in sub-s (3) inserted by F(No 2)A 1992 s 19(2), (7) with effect from the year 1992–93.
[2] Words in sub-s (3) substituted by FA 1999 s 22(8), (12) with effect from the year 1999–00.
[3] Sub-s (5A) inserted by FA 2001 s 83, Sch 28 para 14 with effect, in the case of any policy or contract, in relation to any year (within the meaning given by TA 1988 s 546(4)) beginning after 5 April 2001.

551 Right of individual to recover tax from trustees

(1) Where—

　(*a*) an amount is included in an individual's income by virtue of section 547(1)(*a*), and

　(*b*) the [rights, or the part or share,][1] in question were held immediately before the happening of the chargeable event on trust,

the individual shall be entitled to recover from the trustees, to the extent of any sums, or to the value of any benefits, received by them by reason of the event, an amount equal to that (if any) by which the tax with which he is chargeable for the year of assessment in question, reduced by the amount of any relief available under section 550 in respect of the amount so included, exceeds the tax with which he would have been chargeable for the year if that amount had not been so included.

(2) Where, for the purposes of relief under section 550, two or more amounts are to be treated as one, the reduction required by subsection (1) above on account of the relief available in respect of any of them shall consist of a proportionate part of the relief available in respect of their aggregate.

(3) An individual may require the Board to certify any amount recoverable by him by virtue of this section, and the certificate shall be conclusive evidence of the amount.

Commentary—*Simon's Direct Tax Service* E3.516.
Definitions—"The Board", s 832(1); "chargeable event", ss 540, 542, 545; "tax", s 832(3); "year of assessment", s 832(1).
Amendments—¹ Words in sub-s (1)(*b*) substituted by FA 2001 s 83, Sch 28 para 15 with effect, in the case of any policy or contract, in relation to any year (within the meaning given by TA 1988 s 546(4)) beginning after 5 April 2001.

[551A Right of company to recover tax from trustees

(1) Where—

> (*a*) an amount is included in a company's income by virtue of section 547(1)(*b*), and
> (*b*) the [rights, or the part or share,]² in question were held immediately before the happening of the chargeable event on trust,

the company shall be entitled to recover from the trustees, to the extent of any sums, or to the value of any benefits, received by them by reason of the event, the amount (if any) by which T1 exceeds T2.

(2) For the purposes of subsection (1) above—

> T1 is the tax with which the company is chargeable for the accounting period in question; and
> T2 is the tax with which the company would have been chargeable for the accounting period if the amount mentioned in subsection (1)(*a*) above had not been included as there mentioned.

(3) A company may require the Board to certify any amount recoverable by the company by virtue of this section, and the certificate shall be conclusive evidence of the amount.]¹

Commentary—*Simon's Direct Tax Service* E3.516.
Amendments—¹ This section inserted by FA 1998 Sch 14 para 3 with effect in relation to chargeable events happening after 5 April 1998.
² Words in sub-s (1)(*b*) substituted by FA 2001 s 82, Sch 28 para 16 with effect, in the case of any policy or contract, in relation to any year (within the meaning given by TA 1988 s 546(4)) beginning after 5 April 2001.

[552 Information: duty of insurers

(1) Where a chargeable event within the meaning of this Chapter has happened in relation to any policy or contract, the body by or with whom the policy or contract was issued, entered into or effected shall—

> (*a*) unless satisfied that no gain is to be treated as arising by reason of the event, deliver to the appropriate policy holder before the end of the relevant three month period a certificate specifying the information described in subsection (5) below; and
> (*b*) if the condition in paragraph (*a*) or (*b*) of subsection (2) below is satisfied, deliver to the inspector before the end of the relevant three month period a certificate specifying the information described in subsection (5) below together with the name and address of the appropriate policy holder.

(2) For the purposes of this section—

> (*a*) the condition in this paragraph is that the event is an assignment for money or money's worth of the whole of the rights conferred by the policy or contract; or
> (*b*) the condition in this paragraph is that the amount of the gain, or the aggregate amount of the gain and any gains connected with it, exceeds one half of the basic rate limit for the relevant year of assessment.

(3) If, in the case of every certificate which a body delivers under subsection (1)(*a*) above which relates to a gain attributable to a year of assessment (or, where the appropriate policy holder is a company, the corresponding financial year), the body also delivers to the inspector—

> (*a*) before the end of the relevant three month period for the purposes of subsection (1)(*b*) above,
> (*b*) by a means prescribed by the Board for the purposes of this subsection under section 552ZA(5), and
> (*c*) in a form so prescribed in the case of that means,

a certificate specifying the same information as the certificate under subsection (1)(*a*) together with the name and address of the appropriate policy holder, the body shall be taken to have complied with the requirements of subsection (1)(*b*) above in relation to that year of assessment, and the corresponding financial year, so far as relating to the chargeable events to which the certificates relate.

(4) Where a certificate is not required to be delivered under subsection (1)(*b*) above in the case of any chargeable event—

> (*a*) the inspector may by notice require the body to deliver to him a copy of any certificate that the body was required to deliver under subsection (1)(*a*) above which relates to the chargeable event; and
> (*b*) it shall be the duty of the body to deliver such a copy within 30 days of receipt of the notice.

(5) The information to be given to the appropriate policy holder pursuant to subsection (1)(*a*) above or the inspector pursuant to subsection (1)(*b*) above is—

> (*a*) any unique identifying designation given to the policy or contract;

(b) the nature of the chargeable event and—

   (i) the date on which it happened; and

   (ii) if it is a chargeable event by virtue of section 546C(7)(a), the date on which the year ends;

(c) if the event is the assignment of all the rights conferred by the policy or contract, such of the following as may be required for computing the amount of the gain to be treated as arising by virtue of this Chapter—

   (i) the amount or value of any relevant capital payments;

   (ii) the amounts previously paid under the policy or contract by way of premiums or otherwise by way of consideration for an annuity;

   (iii) the capital element in any payment previously made on account of an annuity;

   (iv) the value of any previously assigned parts of or shares in the rights conferred by the policy or contract;

   (v) the total of the amounts of gains treated as arising on previous chargeable events by reason, or in consequence, of the occurrence of a section 546 excess at the end of a year;

(d) except where paragraph (c) above applies, the amount of the gain treated as arising by reason of the event;

(e) the number of years relevant for computing the appropriate fraction of the gain for the purposes of section 550(3), apart from section 553(8);

(f) on the assumption that section 547(1)(a) has effect in relation to the gain—

   (i) whether an individual would fall to be treated as having paid income tax at the basic rate on the amount of the gain in accordance with section 547(5)(a); and

   (ii) if so, except in a case where paragraph (c) above applies, the amount of such tax that would fall to be so treated as paid.

(6) For the purposes of subsection (1)(a) above, the relevant three month period is whichever of the following periods ends the latest—

(a) the period of three months following the happening of the chargeable event;

(b) if the event is a surrender or assignment which is a chargeable event by virtue of section 546C(7)(a), the period of three months following the end of the year in which the event happens;

(c) if the event is a death or an assignment of the whole of the rights or a surrender or assignment which is a chargeable event by virtue of section 546C(7)(a), the period of three months beginning with receipt of written notification of the event.

(7) For the purposes of subsection (1)(b) above, the relevant three month period is whichever of the following periods ends the latest—

(a) the period of three months following the end of the year of assessment, or, where the policy holder is a company, the financial year, in which the event happened;

(b) if the event is a surrender or assignment which is a chargeable event by virtue of section 546C(7)(a), the period of three months following the end of the year in which the event happens;

(c) if the event is a death or an assignment, the period of three months beginning with receipt of written notification of the event;

(d) if a certificate under subsection (1)(b) above would not be required in respect of the event apart from the happening of another event, and that other event is one of those mentioned in paragraph (c) above, the period of three months beginning with receipt of written notification of that other event.

(8) For the purposes of this section the cases where a gain is connected with another gain are those cases where—

(a) both gains arise in connection with policies or contracts containing obligations which, immediately before the chargeable event, were obligations of the same body;

(b) the policy holder of those policies or contracts is the same;

(c) both gains are attributable to the same year of assessment or, where the policy holder is a company, to the same financial year;

(d) the terms of the policies or contracts are the same, apart from any difference in their maturity dates; and

(e) the policies or contracts were issued in respect of insurances made, or were entered into or effected, on the same date.

(9) For the purposes of this section, the year of assessment or financial year to which a gain is attributable is—

(a) in the case of a gain treated as arising by virtue of section 546C(7)(b), the year of assessment or financial year which includes the end of the year as at which the section 546 excess in question occurs; or

(b) in any other case, the year of assessment or financial year in which happens the chargeable event by reason of which the gain is treated as arising.

(10) In this section—

"amount", in relation to any gain, means the amount of the gain apart from section 553(3);

"appropriate policy holder" means—

(*a*) in relation to an assignment of part of or a share in the rights conferred by a policy or contract, any person who is both—

(i) the policy holder, or one of the policy holders, immediately before the assignment; and

(ii) the assignor or one of the assignors; and

(*b*) in relation to any other chargeable event, the person who is the policy holder immediately before the happening of the event;

"financial year" means a period of 12 months beginning with 1st April;

"the relevant year of assessment", in the case of any gain, means—

(*a*) the year of assessment to which the gain is attributable, or

(*b*) if the gain arises to a company, the year of assessment which corresponds to the financial year to which the gain is attributable;

"section 546 excess" has the meaning given in section 546B(4);

"year", in relation to any policy or contract, has the meaning given by section 546(4).

(11) For the purposes of this section a year of assessment and a financial year correspond to each other if the financial year ends with 31st March in the year of assessment.

(12) This section is supplemented by section 552ZA.]¹

Commentary—*Simon's Direct Tax Service* E3.503.
Regulations—Life Assurance and Other Policies (Keeping of Information and Duties of Insurers) Regulations, SI 1997/265.
Definitions—"The Board", s 832(1); "chargeable event", ss 540, 542, 545; "inspector", s 832(1); "notice", s 832(1).
Cross references—See the Overseas Insurers (Tax Representatives) Regulations, SI 1999/881 (duties of overseas insurer's tax representative).
Modifications—Sub-s (1)(*c*) modified in computing gains of personal portfolio bonds on which there is a yearly tax charge for years ending after 5 April 2000: see Personal Portfolio Bonds (Tax) Regulations, SI 1999/1029 reg 6(7).
Amendments—¹ This section substituted by FA 2001 s 83, Sch 28 para 18 with effect for chargeable events happening after 5 April 2002.

[552ZA Information: supplementary provisions

(1) This section supplements section 552 and shall be construed as one with it.

(2) Where the obligations under any policy or contract of the body that issued, entered into or effected it ("the original insurer") are at any time the obligations of another body ("the transferee") to whom there has been a transfer of the whole or any part of a business previously carried on by the original insurer, section 552 shall have effect in relation to that time, except where the chargeable event—

(*a*) happened before the transfer, and

(*b*) in the case of a death or an assignment, is an event of which the notification mentioned in subsection (6) or (7) of that section was given before the transfer,

as if the policy or contract had been issued, entered into or effected by the transferee.

(3) Where, in consequence of section 546C(7)(*a*), paragraph (*a*) or (*b*) of section 552(1) requires certificates to be delivered in respect of two or more surrenders, happening in the same year, of part of or a share in the rights conferred by the policy or contract, a single certificate may be delivered under the paragraph in question in respect of all those surrenders (and may treat them as if they together constituted a single surrender) unless between the happening of the first and the happening of the last of them there has been—

(*a*) an assignment of part of or a share in the rights conferred by the policy or contract; or

(*b*) an assignment, otherwise than for money or money's worth, of the whole of the rights conferred by the policy or contract.

(4) Where the appropriate policy holder is two or more persons—

(*a*) section 552(1)(*a*) requires a certificate to be delivered to each of them; but

(*b*) nothing in section 552 or this section requires a body to deliver a certificate under subsection (1)(*a*) of that section to any person whose address has not been provided to the body (or to another body, at a time when the obligations under the policy or contract were obligations of that other body).

(5) A certificate under section 552(1)(*b*) or (3)—

(*a*) shall be in a form prescribed for the purpose by the Board; and

(*b*) shall be delivered by any means prescribed for the purpose by the Board;

and different forms, or different means of delivery, may be prescribed for different cases or different purposes.

(6) The Board may by regulations make such provision as they think fit for securing that they are able—

(*a*) to ascertain whether there has been or is likely to be any contravention of the requirements of section 552 or this section; and

(*b*) to verify any certificate under that section.

(7) Regulations under subsection (6) above may include, in particular, provisions requiring persons to whom premiums under any policy are or have at any time been payable—

(*a*) to supply information to the Board; and

(*b*) to make available books, documents and other records for inspection on behalf of the Board.

(8) Regulations under subsection (6) above may—

(*a*) make different provision for different cases; and

(*b*) contain such supplementary, incidental, consequential or transitional provision as appears to the Board to be appropriate.]¹

Amendments—This section substituted for TA 1988 s 552 by FA 2001 s 83, Sch 28 para 18 with effect for chargeable events happening after 5 April 2002.

[552A Tax representatives

(1) This section has effect for the purpose of securing that, where it applies to an overseas insurer, another person is the overseas insurer's tax representative.

(2) In this section "overseas insurer" means a person who is not resident in the United Kingdom who carries on a business which consists of or includes the effecting and carrying out of

(*a*) policies of life insurance;

(*b*) contracts for life annuities; or

(*c*) capital redemption policies

(3) This section applies to an overseas insurer—

(*a*) if the condition in subsection (4) below is satisfied on the designated day; or

(*b*) where that condition is not satisfied on that day, if it has subsequently become satisfied.

(4) The condition mentioned in subsection (3) above is that—

(*a*) there are in force relevant insurances the obligations under which are obligations of the overseas insurer in question or of an overseas insurer connected with him; and

(*b*) the total amount or value of the gross premiums paid under those relevant insurances is £1 million or more.

(5) In this section "relevant insurance" means any policy of life insurance, contract for a life annuity or capital redemption policy in relation to which this Chapter has effect and in the case of which—

(*a*) the holder is resident in the United Kingdom;

(*b*) the obligations of the insurer are obligations of a person not resident in the United Kingdom; and

(*c*) those obligations are not attributable to a branch or agency of that person's in the United Kingdom.

(6) Before the expiration of the period of three months following the day on which this section first applies to an overseas insurer, the overseas insurer must nominate to the Board a person to be his tax representative.

(7) A person shall not be a tax representative unless—

(*a*) if he is an individual, he is resident in the United Kingdom and has a fixed place of residence there, or

(*b*) if he is not an individual, he has a business establishment in the United Kingdom,

and, in either case, he satisfies such other requirements (if any) as are prescribed in regulations made for the purpose by the Board.

(8) A person shall not be an overseas insurer's tax representative unless—

(*a*) his nomination by the overseas insurer has been approved by the Board; or

(*b*) he has been appointed by the Board.

(9) The Board may by regulations make provision supplementing this section; and the provision that may be made by any such regulations includes provision with respect to—

(*a*) the making of a nomination by an overseas insurer of a person to be his tax representative;

(*b*) the information which is to be provided in connection with such a nomination;

(*c*) the form in which such a nomination is to be made;

(*d*) the powers and duties of the Board in relation to such a nomination;

(*e*) the procedure for approving, or refusing to approve, such a nomination, and any time limits applicable to doing so;

(*f*) the termination, by the overseas insurer or the Board, of a person's appointment as a tax representative;

(*g*) the appointment by the Board of a person as the tax representative of an overseas insurer (including the circumstances in which such an appointment may be made);

(*h*) the nomination by the overseas insurer, or the appointment by the Board, of a person to be the tax representative of an overseas insurer in place of a person ceasing to be his tax representative;

(*j*) circumstances in which an overseas insurer to whom this section applies may, with the Board's agreement, be released (subject to any conditions imposed by the Board) from the requirement that there must be a tax representative;

(*k*) appeals to the Special Commissioners against decisions of the Board under this section or regulations under it.

(10) The provision that may be made by regulations under subsection (9) above also includes provision for or in connection with the making of other arrangements between the Board and an overseas insurer for the purpose of securing the discharge by or on behalf of the overseas insurer of the relevant duties, within the meaning of section 552B.

(11) Section 839 (connected persons) applies for the purposes of this section.

(12) In this section—

"the designated day" means such day as the Board may specify for the purpose in regulations;
"tax representative" means a tax representative under this section.][1]

Commentary—*Simon's Direct Tax Service* E3.503.
Regulations—Overseas Insurers (Tax Representatives) Regulations, SI 1999/881.
Amendments—[1] This section inserted by FA 1998 s 87 with effect from 31 July 1998.

[552B Duties of overseas insurers' tax representatives

(1) It shall be the duty of an overseas insurer's tax representative to secure (where appropriate by acting on the overseas insurer's behalf) that the relevant duties are discharged by or on behalf of the overseas insurer.

[(2) For the purposes of this section "the relevant duties" are—

(a) the duties imposed by section 552,
(b) the duties imposed by section 552ZA(2), (4) or (5), and
(c) any duties imposed by regulations made under subsection (6) of section 552ZA by virtue of subsection (7) of that section,

so far as relating to relevant insurances under which the overseas insurer in question has any obligations.][2]

(3) An overseas insurer's tax representative shall be personally liable—

(a) in respect of any failure to secure the discharge of the relevant duties, and
(b) in respect of anything done for purposes connected with acting on the overseas insurer's behalf,

as if the relevant duties were imposed jointly and severally on the tax representative and the overseas insurer.

(4) In the application of this section in relation to any particular tax representative, it is immaterial whether any particular relevant duty arose before or after his appointment.

(5) This section has effect in relation to relevant duties relating to chargeable events happening on or after the day by which section 552A(6) requires the nomination of the overseas insurer's first tax representative to be made.

(6) Expressions used in this section and in section 552A have the same meaning in this section as they have in that section.][1]

Commentary—*Simon's Direct Tax Service* E3.503.
Cross references—See the Overseas Insurers (Tax Representatives) Regulations, SI 1999/881 (duties of overseas insurer's tax representative).
Amendments—[1] This section inserted by FA 1998 s 87 with effect from 31 July 1998.
[2] Sub-s (2) substituted by FA 2001 s 83, Sch 28 para 19 with effect for chargeable events happening after 5 April 2002.

553 Non-resident policies and off-shore capital redemption policies

(1) If, in the case of a substitution of policies falling within paragraph 25(1) or (3) of Schedule 15, the new policy is a qualifying policy, section 540 shall have effect with the following modifications—

(a) the surrender of the rights conferred by the old policy shall not be a chargeable event (within the meaning of that section); and
(b) the new policy shall be treated as having been issued in respect of an insurance made on the day referred to in paragraph 26 of that Schedule.

(2) If at any time [the conditions in paragraph 24(3) of Schedule 15 to this Act are not fulfilled][1] with respect to a new non-resident policy which has previously become a qualifying policy, then, from that time onwards, this Chapter shall apply in relation to the policy as if it were not a qualifying policy.

(3) Subject to subsection[s (5) and (5A)][5] below, on the happening of a chargeable event in relation to a new non-resident policy or a new offshore capital redemption policy, the amount which, apart from this subsection, would by virtue of section 541 [or 546C(7)(b)][6] be treated as a gain arising in connection with the policy shall be reduced by multiplying it by the fraction—

$$\frac{A}{B}$$

where—

A is the number of days on which the policy holder was resident in the United Kingdom in the period for which the policy has run before the happening of the chargeable event; and
B is the number of days in that period.

(4) The calculation of the number of days in the period referred to in subsection (3) above shall be made in like manner as is provided in section 550(4), substituting a reference to the number of days for the reference to the number of years.

(5) If, on the happening of the chargeable event referred to in subsection (3) above or at any time during the period referred to in that subsection, the policy is or was held by a trustee resident outside the United Kingdom or by two or more trustees any of whom is or was so resident, no reduction shall be made under that subsection unless—

    (*a*) the policy was issued in respect of an insurance made on or before 19th March 1985; and
    (*b*) on that date the policy was held by a trustee who was so resident or, as the case may be, by two or more trustees any of whom was so resident.

[(5A) If, on the happening of the chargeable event referred to in subsection (3) above or at any time during the period referred to in that subsection, the policy is or was held by a foreign institution, no reduction shall be made under that subsection unless—

    (*a*) the policy was issued in respect of an insurance made on or before 16th March 1998; and
    (*b*) on that date the policy was held by a foreign institution.]⁵

(6) Subject to [subsections (6A) and (7)]² below, where, under section 541 [or 546C(7)(*b*)]⁶, a gain (reduced in accordance with subsection (3) above) is to be treated as arising in connection with a new non-resident policy or a new offshore capital redemption policy—

    (*a*) section 547 shall have effect, in relation to the gain, as if subsection (5) were omitted; and
    (*b*) the gain shall be chargeable to tax under Case VI of Schedule D;

but any relief under section 550 shall be computed as if this subsection had not been enacted.

[(6A) Paragraphs (*a*) and (*b*) of subsection (6) above do not apply to a gain in a case where the Board are satisfied, on a claim made for the purpose—

    (*a*) that the insurer has not, at any time ("a relevant time") between the making of the insurance and the date on which the gain is treated as arising, been resident in the United Kingdom;
    (*b*) that at all relevant times the insurer has—

        (i) as a body deriving its status as a company from the laws of a territory outside the United Kingdom,
        (ii) as a company with its place of management in such a territory, or
        (iii) as a company falling, under the laws of such a territory, to be regarded, for any other reason, as resident or domiciled in that territory,

    been within a charge to tax under the laws of that territory;
    (*c*) that that territory is a territory within the European Economic Area when the gain is treated as arising;
    (*d*) that the charge to tax mentioned in paragraph (*b*) above has at all relevant times been such a charge made otherwise than by reference to profits as (by disallowing their deduction in computing the amount chargeable) to require sums payable and other liabilities arising under policies of the same class as the policy in question to be treated as sums or liabilities falling to be met out of amounts subject to tax in the hands of the insurer;
    (*e*) that the rate of tax fixed for the purposes of that charge in relation to the amounts subject to tax in the hands of the insurer (not being amounts arising or accruing in respect of investments that are of a particular description for which a special relief or exemption is generally available) has at all relevant times been at least 20 per cent; and
    (*f*) that none of the insurer's obligations under the policy in question to pay any sum or to meet any other liability arising under that policy is or has been the subject, in whole or in part, of any reinsurance contract relating to anything other than the risk that the person whose life is insured by the policy will die or will suffer any sickness or accident;

and paragraphs (*a*) and (*b*) of subsection (6) above shall also not apply where the case would fall within paragraphs (*a*) to (*f*) above if references to a relevant time did not include references to any time when the conditions required to be fulfilled in relation to that time for the purposes of subsection (7) below were fulfilled.]²

(7) Paragraphs (*a*) and (*b*) of subsections (6) above do not apply to a gain arising in connection with a new non-resident policy if the conditions in [sub-paragraph (3)]¹ of paragraph 24 of Schedule 15 are fulfilled at all times between the date on which the policy was issued and the date on which the gain is treated as arising.

[(7A) Where, in the case of a gain to which subsection (6)(*a*) and (*b*) above applies, the rights conferred by the policy were vested immediately before the happening of the chargeable event in question in personal representatives within the meaning of Part XVI, the gain shall be deemed for the purposes of income tax to be income of the personal representatives as such.]³

(8) Where a claim is made under section 550 in respect of the amount of a gain treated as arising in connection with a new non-resident policy or a new offshore capital redemption policy (with or without other amounts), the "appropriate fraction" which, in accordance with subsection (2) of that section, is to be applied to that amount shall be modified by deducting from the number of complete years referred to in subsection (3) of that section any complete years during which the policy holder was not resident in the United Kingdom.

(9) Subsection (5) of section 550 shall not apply in relation to a new non-resident policy or a new offshore capital redemption policy.

(10) In this section—

> "chargeable event" has, subject to subsection (1) above, the meaning given by section 540 or, as the case may be, 545 [or 546C(7)(a)][6];
> ["foreign institution" has the same meaning as in section 547;][5]
> "new non-resident policy" has the meaning given by paragraph 24 of Schedule 15; and
> "new offshore capital redemption policy" means a capital redemption policy, as defined in section 539(3), which—
>> (a) is issued in respect of [a contract][4] made after 22nd February 1984; and
>> (b) is so issued by a company resident outside the United Kingdom.

Commentary—*Simon's Direct Tax Service* E3.512.
Definitions— "The Board", s 832(1); "capital redemption policy", s 539(3); "qualifying policy", s 832(1); "Schedule D", s 18(1); "tax", s 832(3); "United Kingdom", s 830(1).
Cross references—See FA 2000 s 46(2) (exemption under FA 2000 s 46(1) for income of a charity is not granted in respect of income chargeable to tax under Schedule D Case VI by virtue of sub-s (6) above).
Modifications—Sub-ss (3), (6), (10) modified in computing gains of personal portfolio bonds on which there is a yearly tax charge for years ending after 5 April 2000: see Personal Portfolio Bonds (Tax) Regulations, SI 1999/1029 reg 6(8).
Amendments—[1] Words in sub-s (2) substituted for the words "neither the conditions in sub-paragraph (3) nor those in sub-paragraph (4) of paragraph 24 of Schedule 15 are fulfilled" and words in sub-s (7) substituted for the words "either sub-paragraph (3) or sub-paragraph (4)" by FA 1995 s 55(8), but not so as to affect the operation of Pt XIII, Ch II of this Act in relation to any policy in relation to which the conditions in Sch 15 para 24(4), as it then had effect, were fulfilled at times in accounting periods before those in relation to which FA 1993 s 103 had effect.
[2] Words in sub-s (6) substituted, and sub-s (6A) inserted, by FA 1995 s 5(2), (4), in relation to any gain arising after 28 November 1994 and in relation to any gain arising before that date the income tax on which has not been the subject of an assessment that became final and conclusive on or before that date.
[3] Sub-s (7A) inserted by FA 1995 s 76(3), (6), with effect from the year 1995–96.
[4] In sub-s (10) words in definition of "new offshore capital redemption policy" substituted by FA 1996 s 168(5), (6) with effect as respects contracts effected after 30 June 1999 (by virtue of Finance Act 1994, Section 199, (Appointed Day) Order, SI 1998/3173 art 2).
[5] Words in sub-s (3) substituted, sub-s (5A) inserted and definition in sub-s (10) inserted by FA 1998 Sch 14 para 4 with effect in relation to chargeable events happening after 5 April 1998.
[6] Words inserted in sub-ss (3), (6) and (10) by FA 2001 s 83, Sch 28 para 17 with effect, in the case of any policy or contract, in relation to any year (within the meaning given by TA 1988 s 546(4)) beginning after 5 April 2001.

[553A Overseas life assurance business

(1) A policy of life insurance which, immediately before the happening of a chargeable event or a relevant event—

> (a) is an overseas policy, but
> (b) is not a new non-resident policy,

shall, in relation to that event, be treated for the purposes of this Chapter as if it were a new non-resident policy.

(2) A policy of life insurance which, immediately before the happening of a relevant event—

> (a) is an overseas policy, and
> (b) is a new non-resident policy,

shall, in relation to that event, be taken for the purposes of this Chapter not to be a qualifying policy.

(3) Where a chargeable event happens in relation to a new non-resident policy, section 553(7) shall not have effect in relation to the gain treated as arising in connection with the policy on the happening of the chargeable event.

(4) In this section—

> "new non-resident policy" means a new non-resident policy as defined in paragraph 24 of Schedule 15 (and in subsections (2) and (3) above includes a policy treated as such by virtue of subsection (1) above);
> "overseas policy" means a policy of life insurance which, by virtue of section 431D(1)(a), forms part of the overseas life assurance business of an insurance company or friendly society;
> "relevant event", in relation to a policy of life insurance, means an event which would be a chargeable event in relation to that policy if the policy were assumed not to be a qualifying policy.

(5) This section applies in relation to chargeable events and relevant events happening on or after 17th March 1998 in relation to policies of life insurance issued in respect of insurances made on or after that date.

(6) A policy of life insurance issued in respect of an insurance made before 17th March 1998 shall be treated for the purposes of this section as issued in respect of one made on or after that date if it is varied on or after that date so as to increase the benefits secured or to extend the term of the insurance; and any exercise of rights conferred by the policy shall be regarded for this purpose as a variation.][1]

Commentary—*Simon's Direct Tax Service* E3.512.
Amendments—[1] This section inserted by FA 1998 s 88 with effect from 31 July 1998.

[553B Overseas life assurance business: capital redemption policies

(1) A capital redemption policy which immediately before the happening of a chargeable event

(*a*) is an overseas policy, but

(*b*) is not a new offshore capital redemption policy,

shall, in relation to that event, be treated for the purposes of this Chapter as if it were a new offshore capital redemption policy.

(2) In this section

"new offshore capital redemption policy" has the same meaning as in section 553;

"overseas policy" means a capital redemption policy which, by virtue of section 431D(1)(*a*), forms part of the overseas life assurance business of an insurance company.

(3) This section applies in relation to capital redemption policies where the contract is made after the coming into force of the first regulations under section 458A in consequence of which capital redemption business forms part of the overseas life assurance business of an insurance company.]¹

Commentary—*Simon's Direct Tax Service* **E3.512.**
Amendments—¹ This section inserted by FA 1998 s 88 with effect from 31 July 1998.

[553C Personal portfolio bonds

(1) The Treasury may by regulations make provision imposing a yearly charge to tax in relation to personal portfolio bonds ("yearly" being construed for this purpose by reference to years as defined in section 546(4)).

(2) Subject to any provision to the contrary made by the regulations, any charge to tax under this section is in addition to any other charge to tax under this Chapter.

(3) The regulations may make provision with respect to or in connection with all or any of the following—

(*a*) the method by which the charge to tax, or any relief, allowance or deduction against or in respect of the tax, is to be imposed or given effect;

(*b*) the person who is to be liable for the tax;

(*c*) the periods for or in respect of which the tax is to be charged;

(*d*) the amounts in respect of which, or by reference to which, the tax is to be charged;

(*e*) the period or periods by reference to which those amounts are to be determined;

(*f*) the rate or rates at which the tax is to be charged;

(*g*) any reliefs, allowances or deductions which are to be given or made against or in respect of the tax;

(*h*) the administration of the tax.

(4) The provision that may be made by the regulations includes provision for imposing the charge to tax by a method which involves—

(*a*) treating an event described in the regulations as if it were a chargeable event;

(*b*) treating an amount determined in accordance with the regulations as if it were a gain treated as arising on the happening of a chargeable event;

(*c*) deeming an amount determined in accordance with the regulations to be income of a person or body of persons (or to be part of the aggregate income of the estate of a deceased person); or

(*d*) applying section 740, with or without modification, in relation to an amount determined in accordance with the regulations.

(5) The provision that may be made in the regulations includes provision for the amount or amounts in respect of which, or by reference to which, the tax is to be charged for periods beginning after the coming into force of the regulations to be determined in whole or in part by reference to periods beginning or ending, premiums paid, or events happening, before, on or after the day on which the Finance Act 1998 is passed.

(6) The regulations may make provision excluding, or applying (with or without modification), other provisions of this Chapter in relation to policies or contracts which are also personal portfolio bonds.

(7) In this section, "personal portfolio bond" means a policy of life insurance, contract for a life annuity or capital redemption policy under whose terms—

(*a*) some or all of the benefits are determined by reference to the value of, or the income from, property of any description (whether or not specified in the policy or contract) or fluctuations in, or in an index of, the value of property of any description (whether or not so specified); and

(*b*) some or all of the property, or such an index, may be selected by, or by a person acting on behalf of, the holder of the policy or contract or a person connected with him (or the holder of the policy or contract and a person connected with him);

but a policy or contract is not a personal portfolio bond if the only property or index which may be so selected is of a description prescribed for this purpose in the regulations.

(8) The regulations may prescribe additional conditions which must be satisfied if a policy or contract is to be a personal portfolio bond.

(9) The regulations—

(a) may make different provision for different cases, different circumstances or different periods; and

(b) may make incidental, consequential, supplemental or transitional provision.

(10) In this section, "holder", in the case of a policy or contract held by two or more persons, includes a reference to any of those persons.

(11) Section 839 (connected persons) applies for the purposes of this section.]¹

Commentary—*Simon's Direct Tax Service* **E3.512.**
Regulations—Personal Portfolio Bonds (Tax) Regulations, SI 1999/1029.
Amendments—¹ This section inserted by FA 1998 s 89 with effect from 31 July 1998.

554 Borrowings on life policies to be treated as income in certain cases

(1) Where—

(a) under any contract or arrangements made on or after 7th April 1949, provision is made for the making to any person, at intervals until the happening of an event or contingency dependent on human life, of payments by way of loan; and

(b) under the contract or arrangements, the loans are secured upon a policy of life assurance which assures moneys payable on the happening of such an event or contingency and need not be repaid until the policy moneys become payable; and

(c) the amount of the moneys payable on the happening of the event or contingency is made by the policy to increase by reference to the length of a period ending on the happening of that event or contingency;

the payments made by way of loan shall be treated for tax purposes as annual payments falling within Case III of Schedule D, or, if they are made to a person residing in the United Kingdom and the contract or arrangements were made outside the United Kingdom, as income from a possession out of the United Kingdom and, for income tax, as falling within section 65(1).

(2) The amount of the moneys payable under a policy of life assurance shall not be deemed for the purposes of this section to be made to increase by reference to the length of a period ending on the happening of an event or contingency dependent on human life by reason only that those moneys are to increase from time to time if profits are made by the person liable under the policy.

(3) This section shall not apply to any payments by way of loan if the Board are satisfied as respects those payments that it is not one of the objects of the contract or arrangements under which the payments are made that the recipient of them should enjoy the advantages which would, apart from any question of liability to tax, be enjoyed by a person in receipt of payments of the same amounts paid at the same times by way of annuity.

Commentary—*Simon's Direct Tax Service* **B5.103.**
Definitions—"The Board", s 832(1); "income tax", s 832(4); "Schedule D", s 18(1); "tax", s 832(3); "United Kingdom", s 830(1).
Cross references—See TA 1988 s 539(8) (s 539(1)–(7) not to apply in relation to this section).

CHAPTER III
ENTERTAINERS AND SPORTSMEN

555 Payment of tax

(1) Where a person who is an entertainer or sportsman of a prescribed description performs an activity of a prescribed description in the United Kingdom ("a relevant activity"), this Chapter shall apply if he is not resident in the United Kingdom in the year of assessment in which the relevant activity is performed.

(2) Where a payment is made (to whatever person) and it has a connection of a prescribed kind with the relevant activity, the person by whom it is made shall on making it deduct out of it a sum representing income tax and shall account to the Board for the sum.

(3) Where a transfer is made (to whatever person) and it has a connection of a prescribed kind with the relevant activity, the person by whom it is made shall account to the Board for a sum representing income tax.

(4) The sums mentioned in subsections (2) and (3) above shall be such as are calculated in accordance with prescribed rules but shall in no case exceed the relevant proportion of the payment concerned or of the value of what is transferred, as the case may be; and "relevant proportion" here means a proportion equal to the basic rate of income tax for the year of assessment in which the payment or, as the case may be, the transfer is made.

(5) In this Chapter—

(a) references to a payment include references to a payment by way of loan of money; and

(b) references to a transfer do not include references to a transfer of money but, subject to that, include references to a temporary transfer (as by way of loan) and to a transfer of a right (whether or not a right to receive money).

(6) This section shall not apply to payments or transfers of such a kind as may be prescribed.

(7) Regulations may—

(*a*) make provision enabling the Board to serve notices requiring persons who make payments or transfers to which subsection (2) or (3) above applies to furnish to the Board particulars of a prescribed kind in respect of payments or transfers;

(*b*) make provision requiring persons who make payments or transfers to which subsection (2) or (3) above applies to make, at prescribed times and for prescribed periods, returns to the Board containing prescribed information about payments or transfers and the income tax for which those persons are accountable in respect of them;

(*c*) make provision for the collection and recovery of such income tax, provision for assessments and claims to be made in respect of it, and provision for the payment of interest on it;

(*d*) adapt, or modify the effect of, any enactment relating to income tax for the purpose of making any such provision as is mentioned in paragraphs (*a*) to (*c*) above.

(8) Where in accordance with subsections (2) to (7) above a person pays a sum to the Board, they shall treat it as having been paid on account of a liability of another person to income tax or corporation tax; and the liability and the other person shall be such as are found in accordance with prescribed rules.

(9) Where the sum exceeds the liability concerned, the Board shall pay such of the sum as is appropriate to the other person mentioned in subsection (8) above.

(10) Where no liability is found as mentioned in subsection (8) above, the Board shall pay the sum to the person to whom the payment or transfer to which subsection (2) or (3) above applies, and which gave rise to the payment of the sum concerned to the Board, was made.

(11) In construing references to a sum in subsections (8) to (10) above, anything representing interest shall be ignored.

Commentary—*Simon's Direct Tax Service* E5.802, 803, 808.
Revenue Internal Guidance—Assessed taxes manual AT 6.603 (Revenue collection procedures).
Definitions—"The Board", s 832(1); "income tax", s 832(4); "notices", s 832(1); "Regulations", s 558(6); "United Kingdom", s 830(1); "year of assessment", s 832(1).
Cross references—See TA 1988 s 558 (supplementary provisions).
IT (Entertainers and Sportsmen) Regulations, SI 1987/530 reg 2(1) (definitions of "connected payments or transfers" and "entertainers"),
IT (Entertainers and Sportsmen) Regulations, SI 1987/530 reg 3 (payments or transfers having connection and payments not having connection of a prescribed kind with a relevant activity),
IT (Entertainers and Sportsmen) Regulations, SI 1987/530 regs 4, 5 (prescribed rules for calculating the sums mentioned in sub-ss (2)–(4) above),
IT (Entertainers and Sportsmen) Regulations, SI 1987/530 reg 6 (definition of "relevant activity"),
IT (Entertainers and Sportsmen) Regulations, SI 1987/530 regs 9–14 (regulations for the purposes of sub-ss (7)–(10) above),
IT (Entertainers and Sportsmen) Regulations, SI 1987/530 reg 17 (prescribed rules for the purposes of sub-s (4) above);
FA 1988 s 130(7)(*c*)(iii), (9) (company migration: provisions for securing payment by migrating company of tax under this section and FA 1986 Sch 11 paras 1–4).
FA 2000 Sch 12 para 6 (FA 2000 Sch 12 (concerning the provision of services through an intermediary) does not apply to payments subject to deduction of tax under this section).

556 Activity treated as trade etc and attribution of income

(1) Where a payment is made (to whatever person) and it has a connection of the prescribed kind with the relevant activity, the activity shall be treated for the purposes of the Tax Acts as performed in the course of a trade, profession or vocation exercised by the entertainer or sportsman within the United Kingdom, to the extent that (apart from this subsection) it would not be so treated.

This subsection shall not apply where the relevant activity is performed in the course of an office or employment.

(2) Where a payment is made to a person who fulfils a prescribed description but is not the entertainer or sportsman and the payment has a connection of the prescribed kind with the relevant activity—

(*a*) the entertainer or sportsman shall be treated for the purposes of the Tax Acts as the person to whom the payment is made; and

(*b*) the payment shall be treated for those purposes as made to him in the course of a trade, profession or vocation exercised by him within the United Kingdom (whether or not he would be treated as exercising such a trade, profession or vocation apart from this paragraph).

(3) Regulations may provide—

(*a*) for the deduction, in computing any [profits][1] of the entertainer or sportsman arising from the payment, of expenses incurred by other persons in relation to the payment;

(*b*) that any liability to tax (whether of the entertainer or sportsman or of another person) which would, apart from subsection (2) above, arise in relation to the payment shall not arise or shall arise only to a prescribed extent.

(4) References in this section to a payment include references to a transfer.

(5) This section shall not apply unless the payment or transfer is one to which section 555(2) or (3) applies, and subsections (2) and (3) above shall not apply in such circumstances as may be prescribed.

Commentary—*Simon's Direct Tax Service* **E5.804, 805.**
Definitions— "relevant activity", s 555(1); "Regulations", s 558(6); "tax", s 832(3); "the Tax Acts", s 831(2); "trade", s 832(1); "United Kingdom", s 830(1).
Cross references—See IT (Entertainers and Sportsmen) Regulations, SI 1987/530 reg 7 (descriptions of persons other than entertainers mentioned in sub-s (2) above),

IT (Entertainers and Sportsmen) Regulations, SI 1987/530 reg 8 (regulation for computing profits or gains under sub-s (3) above).
Amendments—¹ Word in sub-s (3)(*a*) substituted by FA 1998 Sch 7 para 1 with effect from 31 July 1998.

557 Charge on [profits]¹

(1) Where income tax is chargeable under Case I or II of Schedule D on the [profits]¹ arising from payment (made to whatever person) and the payments have a connection of the prescribed kind with relevant activities of the entertainer or sportsman, such tax shall be charged—

(*a*) as if those payments were received in the course of one trade, profession or vocation exercised by the entertainer or sportsman within the United Kingdom separately from any other trade, profession or vocation exercised by him; and

(*b*) for each of assessment, on the full amount of the [profits]¹ arising in the year from those payments.

(2) Regulations may—

(*a*) provide for the apportionment of [profits]¹ between different trades, professions or vocations of the entertainer or sportsman;

(*b*) provide for the apportionment between different years of assessment of the [profits]¹ arising from relevant activities of the entertainer or sportsman;

(*c*) provide for losses sustained in any trade, profession or vocation of the entertainer or sportsman to be deducted from or set off against the [profits]¹ of another trade, profession or vocation of the entertainer or sportsman;

(*d*) provide that prescribed provisions of the Tax Acts about losses, or about expenditure, shall not apply (or shall apply with prescribed modifications) in prescribed circumstances relating to the entertainer or sportsman.

(3) References in subsection (2)(*a*) and (*c*) above to a trade, profession or vocation of the entertainer or sportsman include references to that first mentioned in subsection (1)(*a*) above as well as to any other exercised by him.

(4) References in this section to a payment include references to a transfer.

(5) This section shall not apply in the case of a payment or transfer unless it is one to which section 555(2) or (3) applies.

Commentary—*Simon's Direct Tax Service* **E5.804.**
Definitions—''Apportionment'', s 834(4); ''Regulations'', s 558(6); ''relevant activity'', s 555(1); ''Schedule D'', s 18(1); ''the Tax Acts'', s 831(2); ''trade'', s 832(1); ''United Kingdom'', s 830(1); ''year of assessment'', s 832(1).
Cross references—See IT (Entertainers and Sportsmen) Regulations, SI 1987/530 reg 16 (regulations for the purposes of sub-s (2) above).
Amendments—¹ Word in section heading, and sub-ss (1), (2)(*a*)–(*c*) substituted by FA 1998 Sch 7 para 1 with effect from 31 July 1998.

558 Supplementary provisions

(1) A payment to which subsection (2) of section 555 applies shall be treated for the purposes of the Tax Acts as not diminished by the sum mentioned in that subsection.

(2) Regulations may provide that for the purposes of the Tax Acts the value of what is transferred by a transfer to which section 555(3) applies shall be calculated in accordance with prescribed rules.

(3) In particular, rules may include provision for the calculation of an amount representing the actual worth of what is transferred, for that amount to be treated as a net amount corresponding to a gross amount from which income tax at the basic rate has been deducted, and for the gross amount to be taken to be the value of what is transferred.

(4) No obligation as to secrecy imposed by statute or otherwise shall preclude the Board or an authorised officer of the Board from disclosing to any person who appears to the Board to have an interest in the matter information which may be relevant to determining whether section 555(2) or (3) applies to a payment or transfer.

(5) Regulations may make provision generally for giving effect to this Chapter, and may make different provision for different cases or descriptions of case.

(6) In this Chapter—

''regulations'' means regulations made by the Treasury; and
''prescribed'' means prescribed by regulations.

Commentary—*Simon's Direct Tax Service* **E5.803, 809.**
Regulations—IT (Entertainers and Sportsmen) Regulations, SI 1987/530. For continuity, see Sch 30, para 21 of this Act.
Definitions—''Basic rate'', s 832(1); ''the Board'', s 832(1); ''the Tax Acts'', s 831(2).

CHAPTER IV
SUB-CONTRACTORS IN THE CONSTRUCTION INDUSTRY

Regulations—IT (Sub-contractors in the Construction Industry) Regulations, SI 1993/743.
Concession (unnumbered)—New arrangements to ensure consistent treatment of travelling and subsistence allowances paid to operations and site-based staff in the construction and allied industries, with retrospective effect from 6 April 1981.
Revenue & other press releases—IR 28-7-97 (new scheme to be implemented on 1 August 1999).

IR Booklet IR 148/CA 69 (Are your workers employed or self-employed? A guide for tax and national insurance for contractors in the construction industry).
IR Booklet IR 157 (Workers in building and construction—help with tax for employees and the self-employed).
IR Tax Bulletin April 1997 p 405 (explains what contractors were expected to have done by 5 April 1997 in relation to the employment status of their workers and includes worked examples illustrating decisions on employment status for tax and NIC purposes).
IR Tax Bulletin December 1998 p 615 (guidance on turnover tests).
IR Tax Bulletin April 1999 p 635 (qualification for CIS5 exemption certificate).
IR Tax Bulletin June 1999 p 667 (turnover tests and change in concern).
Revenue Internal Guidance—The Construction Industry Scheme manual gives a detailed explanation of the provisions of this chapter.
Cross references—See TA 1988 s 560 (persons who are sub-contractors or contractors for purposes of this Chapter).
TA 1988 s 566 (general powers to make regulations under this Chapter).
Finance Act 1995, Section 139(3), (Appointed Day) Order, SI 1998/2620 art 4 (certificates under TA 1988 s 561 for periods ending after 31 July 1999 cease to have effect at the end of 31 July 1999).

559 Deductions on account of tax etc from payments to certain sub-contractors

(1) Subject to [the following provisions of this section][2], where a contract relating to construction operations is not a contract of employment but—

    (*a*) one party to the contract is a sub-contractor; and
    (*b*) another party to the contract (''the contractor'') either is a sub-contractor under another such contract relating to all or any of the construction operations or is a person to whom section 560(2) applies,

this section shall apply to any payments which are made under the contract and are so made by the contractor to—

    (i) the sub-contractor;
    (ii) a person nominated by the sub-contractor or the contractor; or
    (iii) a person nominated by a person who is a sub-contractor under another such contract relating to all or any of the construction operations.

[(1A) Subsection (1) above shall not apply to any payment made under the contract in question that is chargeable to income tax under Schedule E by virtue of section 134(1).][2]

(2) Subsection (1) above shall not apply to any payment made under the contract in question if the person to whom it is made or, if it is made to a nominee, each of the following persons, that is to say, the nominee, the person who nominated him and the person for whose labour (or, where that person is a company, for whose employees' or officers' labour) the payment is made, is excepted from this section in relation to those payments by virtue of section 561.

(3) ...[4]

[(3A) Subsection (1) above shall not apply to a payment made under any contract if such conditions as may be prescribed in regulations made by the Board are satisfied in relation to the payment and the person making it.][5]

(4) On making a payment to which this section applies the contractor shall deduct from it a sum equal to [the relevant percentage][7] of so much of the payment as is not shown to represent the direct cost to any other person of materials used or to be used in carrying out the construction operations to which the contract under which the payment is to be made relates; ...[8]

[(4A) In subsection (4) above 'the relevant percentage', in relation to a payment, means such percentage (not exceeding the percentage which is the basic rate for the year of assessment in which the payment is made) as the Treasury may by order determine.][7]

(5), (5A) ...[8]

(6) ...[1]

(7) For the purposes of this Chapter a payment (including a payment by way of loan) that has the effect of discharging an obligation under a contract relating to construction operations shall be taken to be made under the contract; and if—

    (*a*) the obligation is to make a payment to a person within subsection (1)(i) to (iii) above, but
    (*b*) the payment discharging that obligation is made to a person not within those paragraphs,

the payment shall for those purposes be taken to be made to the first-mentioned person.

(8) ...[8]

Commentary—*Simon's Direct Tax Service* **E5.501–505, 506, 525.**
Note—The relevant percentage determined for the purposes of sub-ss (4), (4A) is 18 per cent by the Income and Corporation Taxes Act 1988, Section 559(4A), Order, SI 2000/921 art 2, with effect from 6 April 2000.
SSA 1975 and SS (Northern Ireland) A 1975 referred to in sub-s (8) are re-enacted as Social Security Contributions and Benefits Act 1992 and Social Security Contributions and Benefits (Northern Ireland) Act 1992 respectively.
Regulations—IT (Sub-contractors in the Construction Industry) Regulations, SI 1993/743.
Concession B23—Payments not exceeding specified amount made by the local managers of the bodies mentioned in s 560(2)(*b*)–(*f*) below for minor repairs or maintenance work are excluded from the tax deduction scheme within this section.
Revenue & other press releases—IR booklet IR 14/15 (1982) (comprehensive guide for sub-contractors; IR 116 (1992) sub-contractors with tax certificates; IR 117 (1992) sub-contractors without tax certificates).
IR 31-7-96 (new guidelines issued on the making of provisional tax repayments before end of tax year).
Revenue Internal Guidance—Construction Industry Scheme manual CIS 1017 (sub-s (3A): a small payment is a payment where the contract value, net of materials, is less than £1000).
CIS 1027 (definition of CIS terms).
CIS 1311 (disputes concerning the scope of construction payments).

CIS 1405–1450 (definition of "payment" and Revenue procedures relating to payments).

CIS 7013 (sub-s (4): where a payment by a contractor is made without a deduction to an uncertified subcontractor but the contractor subsequently pays a sum to the Revenue, no credit can be given to the subcontractor as the sum was not "deducted" at the time of payment).

CIS 7023 (disputes between contractor and subcontractor).

Inspector's manual IM 3121 (this legislation does not affect the question whether a sub-contractor is within Schedule D or Schedule E).

Simon's Tax Cases—s 559(1), (2)(*a*), (4)–(6), (8), *Slater v Richardson Bottoms Ltd* [1979] STC 630*.

Definitions—"The Board", s 832(1); "company", s 832(1), (2); "construction operations", s 567; "income tax", s 832(4); "trade", s 832(1).

Cross references—See TMA 1970 s 7(4)(*b*) (duty to notify inspector of taxes of liability to tax in respect of income consisting of a payment under this section);

TA 1988 s 566(2A) (regulations may require a person making payments under this section to check the validity of registration cards to be produced to him).

TA 1988 s 566(2C) (penalties imposed on a person making payments under this section who makes inaccurate or incomplete statements concerning information on a registration card).

FA 1988 s 130(7)(*d*), (9) (company migration: provisions for securing payment by migrating company of tax under sub-s (4) above and F(No 2)A 1975 s 69).

IT (Employments) Regulations, SI 1993/744 reg 41(3)(*c*) (payment of tax quarterly by employer where average monthly total under this section is less than a certain amount).

Income and Corporation Taxes Act 1988, Section 559(4A), Order, SI 2000/921 (determination of relevant percentage for the purposes of sub-ss (4), (4A)).

Amendments—[1] Sub-s (6) repealed by the Insolvency (Northern Ireland) Order 1989, SI 1989/2405 Sch 9 para 61, Sch 10 with effect from 28 November 1988.

[2] Words in sub-s (1) substituted, and sub-s (1A) inserted, by FA 1998 s 55(2) with effect from 6 April 1998 in relation to any payments made on or after that date, other than made in respect of services rendered before that date, and any payments made before 6 April 1998 in respect of services to be rendered on or after that date.

[3] Words substituted by FA 1998 Sch 7 para 1 with effect from 31 July 1998.

[4] Sub-s (3) repealed by FA 1995 s 139(2), Sch 27 para 1(2), Sch 29 Pt VIII(21) with effect for payments made to a person in any case where that person's certificate under TA 1988 s 561 is one issued or renewed with respect to a period beginning after 31 July 1999 (by virtue of SI 1998/2620 art 3).

[5] Sub-s (3A) inserted by FA 1995 s 139(2), Sch 27 para 1(3) with effect for payments made after 31 July 1999 (by virtue of SI 1998/2620 art 3).

[6] Sub-s (5A) inserted by FA 1998 s 57, Sch 8 para 2(1) with effect for payments made after 31 July 1999 (by virtue of SI 1998/2620 art 3).

[7] Words "the relevant percentage" in sub-s (4) substituted, and sub-s (4A) inserted, by FA 1995 s 139(1), with effect for payments made after 5 April 2000 (by virtue of the Finance Act 1995, Section 139(3), (Appointed Day) Order, SI 2000/922 art 2). As to the relevant percentage, see Note above.

[8] Words in sub-s (4) repealed, and sub-ss (5), (5A), (8) repealed, by FA 2002 s 141, Sch 40 Pt 3(1) with effect for deductions made under this section after 5 April 2002.

[559A Treatment of sums deducted under s 559]

(1) A sum deducted under section 559 from a payment made by a contractor—

(*a*) shall be paid to the Board, and

(*b*) shall be treated for the purposes of income tax or, as the case may be, corporation tax as not diminishing the amount of the payment.

(2) If the sub-contractor is not a company a sum deducted under section 559 and paid to the Board shall be treated as being income tax paid in respect of the sub-contractor's relevant profits.

If the sum is more than sufficient to discharge his liability to income tax in respect of those profits, so much of the excess as is required to discharge any liability of his for Class 4 contributions shall be treated as being Class 4 contributions paid in respect of those profits.

(3) If the sub-contractor is a company—

(*a*) a sum deducted under section 559 and paid to the Board shall be treated, in accordance with regulations, as paid on account of any relevant liabilities of the sub-contractor;

(*b*) regulations shall provide for the sum to be applied in discharging relevant liabilities of the year of assessment in which the deduction is made;

(*c*) if the amount is more than sufficient to discharge the sub-contractor's relevant liabilities, the excess may be treated, in accordance with the regulations, as being corporation tax paid in respect of the sub-contractor's relevant profits; and

(*d*) regulations shall provide for the repayment to the sub-contractor of any amount not required for the purposes mentioned in paragraphs (*b*) and (*c*).

(4) For the purposes of subsection (3) the "relevant liabilities" of a sub-contractor are any liabilities of the sub-contractor, whether arising before or after the deduction is made, to make a payment to a collector of inland revenue in pursuance of an obligation as an employer or contractor.

(5) In this section—

(*a*) "the sub-contractor" means the person for whose labour (or for whose employees' or officers' labour) the payment is made;

(*b*) references to the sub-contractor's "relevant profits" are to the profits from the trade, profession or vocation carried on by him in the course of which the payment was received;

(*c*) "Class 4 contributions" means Class 4 contributions within the meaning of the Social Security Contributions and Benefits Act 1992 (c 4) or the Social Security Contributions and Benefits (Northern Ireland) Act 1992 (c 7).

(6) References in this section to regulations are to regulations made by the Board.

(7) Regulations under this section—

(*a*) may contain such supplementary, incidental or consequential provision as appears to the Board to be appropriate, and

(*b*) may make different provision for different cases.]¹

Cross reference—See FA 2002 s 40(4) (regulations under this section may be made so as to have effect for any such deductions made after 5 April 2002).

Amendments—¹ Inserted by FA 2002 s 40(1), (4) with effect for deductions made under TA 1988 s 559 after 5 April 2002.

560 Persons who are sub-contractors or contractors for purposes of Chapter IV

(1) For the purposes of this Chapter a party to a contract relating to construction operations is a sub-contractor if, under the contract—

(*a*) he is under a duty to the contractor to carry out the operations, or to furnish his own labour (that is to say, in the case of a company, the labour of employees or officers of the company) or the labour of others in the carrying out of the operations or to arrange for the labour of others to be furnished in the carrying out of the operations; or

(*b*) he is answerable to the contractor for the carrying out of the operations by others, whether under a contract or under other arrangements made or to be made by him.

(2) This subsection applies [(subject to subsection (2A) below)]⁵ to the following persons, that is to say—

(*a*) any person carrying on a business which includes construction operations;

[(*aa*) any public office or department of the Crown (including any Northern Ireland department [and any part of the Scottish Administration]⁶);]⁴

(*b*) any local authority;

(*c*) any development corporation or new town commission;

(*d*) the Commission for the New Towns;

[(*da*) the Secretary of State if the contract is made by him under section 89 of the Housing Associations Act 1985;]³

(*e*) the Housing Corporation, ...¹ a housing association, a housing trust, [Scottish Homes]², and the Northern Ireland Housing Executive;

[(*ea*) any such body, being a body (in addition to those falling within paragraphs (*aa*) to (*e*) above) which has been established for the purpose of carrying out functions conferred on it by or under any enactment, as may be designated as a body to which this subsection applies in regulations made by the Board;]⁴

(*f*) a person carrying on a business at any time if—

(i) his average annual expenditure on construction operations in the period of three years ending with the end of the last period of account before that time exceeds [£1,000,000]⁴, or

(ii) where he was not carrying on the business at the beginning of that period of three years, one-third of his total expenditure on construction operations for the part of that period during which he has been carrying on the business exceeds [£1,000,000]⁴;

...⁷

[(2A) Subject to subsection (2B) below, subsection (2) above does not apply at any time to an office, department or body falling within paragraph (*aa*), (*b*), (*c*), (*d*), (*e*) or (*ea*) of that subsection unless that office, department or body has, in the period of three years ending with the 31st March next before that time, had an average annual expenditure on construction operations of more than £1,000,000.]⁵

[(2B) Where the condition provided for in subsection (2A) above has been satisfied in the case of any office, department or body in relation to any period of three years, that subsection shall not prevent subsection (2) above from applying to that office, department or body until there have been three successive years after the end of that period in each of which the office, department or body has had expenditure on construction operations of less than £1,000,000.]⁵

(3) Where section 559(1)(*b*) begins to apply to any person in any period of account by virtue of his falling within subsection (2)(*f*) above, it shall continue to apply to him until he satisfies the Board that his expenditure on construction operations has been less than [£1,000,000]⁴ in each of three successive years beginning in or after that period of account.

(4) Where the whole or part of a trade is transferred by a company (''the transferor'') to another company (''the transferee'') and section 343 has effect in relation to the transfer, then in determining for the purposes of this section the amount of expenditure incurred by the transferee—

(*a*) the whole or, as the case may be, a proportionate part of any expenditure incurred by the transferor at a time before the transfer shall be treated as if it had been incurred at that time by the transferee; and

(*b*) where only a part of the trade is transferred the expenditure shall be apportioned in such manner as appears to the Board, or on appeal to the Commissioners, to be just and reasonable.

(5) In this section—

''development corporation'' has the same meaning as in the New Towns Act 1981 or the New Towns (Scotland) Act 1968;

''housing association'' has the same meaning as in the Housing Associations Act 1985 or the Housing (Northern Ireland) Order 1981;

"housing trust" has the same meaning as in the Housing Associations Act 1985; and
"new town commission" has the same meaning as in the New Towns Act (Northern Ireland) 1965.

Commentary—*Simon's Direct Tax Service* E5.503.
Concession B23—Payments of up to £250 made by the local managers of the bodies mentioned in sub-s (2)(*b*)–(*f*) above for minor repairs or maintenance are excluded from the tax deduction scheme within this Chapter.
Revenue & other press releases—IR 19-11-96 (reviews of employment status of construction industry workers must be completed by 5 April 1997).
IR Booklet IR 148/CA 69 (Are your workers employed or self-employed? A guide for tax and national insurance for contractors in the construction industry).
IR Booklet IR 157 (Workers in building and construction—help with tax for employees and the self-employed).
IR Tax Bulletin April 1997 p 405 (explains what contractors were expected to have done by 5 April 1997 in relation to the employment status of their workers and includes worked examples illustrating decisions on employment status for tax and NIC purposes).
Revenue Internal Guidance—Construction Industry Scheme manual CIS 1015 (sub-s (2): examples of businesses brought within the operation of the scheme although outside the mainstream construction industry).
CIS 1107 (sub-s (2)(*a*): meaning of "mainstream contractors"—a Revenue definition).
CIS 1109 (sub-s (2)(*aa*)–(*f*): meaning of "deemed contractors"—a Revenue definition).
CIS 1205–1225 (definition and obligations of a sub-contractor).
CIS 1307–1311 (outline of construction operations falling within the scope of the scheme).
Simon's Tax Cases—s 560(1)–(4), *Slater v Richardson Bottoms Ltd* [1979] STC 630*.
Definitions—"The Board", s 832(1); "company", s 832(1), (2); "construction operations", s 567; "local authority", s 519(4); "trade", s 832(1).
Cross references—See TA 1988 s 582A(6) (sub-s (2) above not to apply to designated international organisations).
FA 1998 Sch 8 para 2(2) (the reference in sub-s (2B) to a period of three years in relation to satisfying the condition provided for in sub-s (2A) does not include a reference to any such period ending more than a year before the day or first day mentioned in FA 1998 Sch 8 para 2(3)).
Income Tax (Sub-contractors in the Construction Industry) Regulations, SI 1993/743, Sch A1 (list of bodies to which sub-s (2) applies).
Amendments—[1] Words in sub-s (2)(*e*) repealed by the Government of Wales Act 1998 Sch 16 para 58 with effect from 1 November 1998, by virtue of the Government of Wales Act 1998 (Commencement No 1) Order 1998, SI 1998/2244.
[2] Words in sub-s (2)(*e*) substituted by the Housing (Scotland) Act 1988 Sch 2 para 1.
[3] Sub-s (2)(*da*) inserted by the Government of Wales Act 1998 Sch 16 para 58 with effect from 1 November 1998, by virtue of the Government of Wales Act 1998 (Commencement No 1) Order 1998, SI 1998/2244.
[4] Sub-s (2)(*aa*), (*ea*) inserted, and in sub-s (2)(*f*) and in sub-s (3) "£1,000,000" substituted for "£250,000", by FA 1995 s 139(2), Sch 27 para 2 with effect for payments made after 31 July 1999 (by virtue of the Finance Act 1995, Section 139(3), (Appointed Day) Order, SI 1998/2620 art 3).
[5] Sub-ss (2A), (2B), and words in sub-s (2), inserted by FA 1998 s 57, Sch 8 para 2(2) with effect for payments made after 31 July 1999 (by virtue of SI 1998/2620 art 3), subject to FA 1998 Sch 8 para 2(4).
[6] Words in sub-s (2)(*aa*) inserted by the Scotland Act 1998 (Consequential Modifications) (No 2) Order, SI 1999/1820 Sch 2 Pt I para 87(1), (3) with effect from 1 July 1999.
[7] The following words in sub-s (2) repealed by FA 2002 s 141, Sch 40 Pt 3(16) with effect from 24 July 2002—

"and in paragraph (*f*) "period of account" means a period for which an account is made up in relation to the business in question.".

561 Exceptions from section 559

(1) Subject to the provisions of regulations under ...[5] section 566(2), a person is excepted from section 559 in relation to payments made under a contract if a certificate under this section has been issued to that person and is in force when the payment is made, but—

(*a*) where the certificate has been issued to a person who becomes a partner in a firm, that person is not excepted in relation to payments made under contracts under which the firm or, where a person has nominated the firm to receive payments, the person who has nominated the firm is a sub-contractor; and

(*b*) where a certificate has been issued to a person as a partner in a firm, that person is excepted in relation only to payments made under contracts under which the firm or, where a person has nominated the firm to receive payments, the person who has nominated the firm, is a sub-contractor.

(2) If the Board are satisfied, on the application of an individual or a company, that—

(*a*) where the application is for the issue of a certificate to an individual (otherwise than as a partner in a firm), he satisfies the conditions set out in section 562;

(*b*) where the application is for the issue of a certificate to a person as a partner in a firm, that person satisfies the conditions set out in section [562][3] if he is an individual or, if a company, the conditions set out in section 565 and, in either case, the firm itself satisfies the conditions set out in section 564;

(*c*) where the application is for the issue of a certificate to a company, the company satisfies the conditions set out in section 565 and, if the Board have given a direction under [subsection (6)][1] below, each of the persons to whom any of the conditions set out in section 562 applies in accordance with the direction satisfies the conditions which so apply to him,

the Board shall issue to that individual or company a certificate excepting that individual or company (or, in a case falling within paragraph (*b*) above, that individual or company as a partner in the firm specified in the certificate) from section 559.

(3) References in subsection (2) above to an individual, a company or a firm satisfying conditions set out in section 562, ...[7] 564 or 565 include, in relation to a condition which may, by virtue of a provision of that section, be treated as being satisfied, references to that individual, company or firm being treated as satisfying that condition.

(4), (5) ...[5]

(6) Where it appears to the Board, on an application made under subsection (2) above by a company, that the company—

(a) was incorporated on a date within the period of three years ending with the date of the application; or

(b) has not carried on business continuously throughout that period; or

(c) has carried on business continuously throughout that period but the business has not at all times in that period consisted of or included the carrying out of construction operations; or

(d) does not at the date of the application hold a certificate which is then in force under this section;

the Board may direct that the conditions set out in section 562 or such of them as are specified in the direction shall apply to the directors of the company and, if the company is a close company, to the persons who are the beneficial owners of shares in the company or to such of those directors or persons as are so specified as if each of them were an applicant for a certificate under this section ...[7]

In this subsection "director" has the same meaning as in Chapter II of Part V.

(7) Where it appears to the Board that there has been a change in the control of a company holding or applying for a certificate, the Board may make any such direction as is referred to in subsection (6) above.

(8) The Board may at any time cancel a certificate which has been issued to a person and is in force under this section if it appears to them that—

(a) it was issued on information which was false;

(b) if an application for the issue of a certificate under this section to that person were made at that time, the Board would refuse to issue a certificate;

(c) that person has permitted the certificate to be misused; or

(d) in the case of a certificate issued to a company, there has been a change in the control of the company and information with respect to that change has not been furnished in accordance with regulations under section 566(2);

and may by notice require that person to deliver the certificate to the Board within the time specified in the notice.

Section 840 shall apply for the purposes of paragraph (d) above.

(9) A person aggrieved by the refusal of an application for a certificate under this section or the cancellation of such a certificate may, by notice given to the Board within 30 days after the refusal or, as the case may be, cancellation, appeal to the General Commissioners or, if he so elects in the notice, to the Special Commissioners; and the jurisdiction of the Commissioners on such an appeal shall include jurisdiction to review any relevant decision taken by the Board in the exercise of their functions under this section.

(10) If any person, for the purpose of obtaining a certificate under this section—

(a) makes any statement, or furnishes any document, which he knows to be false in a material particular; or

(b) recklessly makes any statement, or furnishes any document, which is false in a material particular,

he shall be liable [to a penalty not exceeding £3,000.][4]

(11) A person to whom a certificate is issued under this section or a voucher is given as required by regulations under section 566(2)(j) [or who is in possession of any form or other document supplied to him by the Board for use in connection with any regulations under this Chapter][2] shall take all reasonable steps to ensure its safety; and any person who, without lawful authority or lawful excuse—

(a) disposes of any such certificate or voucher or any form supplied by the Board in connection with regulations made by virtue of section 566(2)(e); or

(b) possesses such a certificate, voucher or form or any document purporting to be such a certificate, voucher or form,

shall be liable [to a penalty not exceeding £3,000.][4]

(12) ...[6]

(13) Without prejudice to section 843(3), this section shall come into force on 6th April 1988 to the exclusion of the provisions of section 70 of the Finance (No 2) Act 1975 which are re-enacted in this section, but any offence committed before that date shall not be punishable under this section and neither this subsection nor any other provision of this Act shall prevent any such offence from being punishable as if this Act had not been passed.

Commentary—*Simon's Direct Tax Service* E5.510.
Regulations—IT (Sub-Contractors in the Construction Industry) Regulations, SI 1993/743.
Revenue Internal Guidance—Construction Industry Scheme manual CIS 3005–3037, 3110–3117, 3135 (Revenue procedures for dealing with applications for certificates).
CIS 3410 (review of directors under sub-s (6)).
CIS 3615 (Revenue procedures where, in the course of an appeal meeting, the issue of confidentiality arises in respect of evidence presented about an individual director).
CIS 3719, 3721 (sub-s (8): Revenue policy on the cancellation of a certificate).
CIS 3905–3911 (Revenue procedures for dealing with applications for the renewal of a certificate).

CIS 8405 (sub-s (7): company change of control—Revenue procedures).
Simon's Tax Cases—*Kirvell v Guy* [1979] STC 312; *Slater v Richardson Bottoms Ltd* [1979] STC 630*; *R v Collector of Taxes, ex p Robert Goodall (Builders) Ltd* [1989] STC 206*.
s 561(2)(*b*), *T &C Hill v Gleig* [2000] STC (SCD) 64.
s 561(9), *Cooper v Sercombe* [1980] STC 76*; *Kington v Reilly* [1981] STC 121*.
Definitions—''The Board'', s 832(1); ''close company'', s 414(1); ''company'', s 832(1), (2); ''construction operations'', s 567; ''control'', s 840; ''notice'', s 832(1).
Cross references—See Finance Act 1995, Section 139(3), (Appointed Day) Order, SI 1998/2620 art 4 (certificates under this section for periods ending after 31 July 1999 cease to have effect at the end of 31 July 1999).
Amendments—[1] Words in sub-s (2)(*c*) substituted by FA 1994 Sch 17 para 5 and deemed always to have had effect.
[2] Words in sub-s (11) inserted by FA 1995 Sch 27 paras 3(3)(*a*), 8(2), with effect for forms and other documents in a person's possession at any time after 1 May 1995.
[3] In sub-s (2)(*b*) ''562'' substituted for ''563'' by FA 1995 s 139(2), Sch 27 para 3 (1) with effect for any application for the issue or renewal of a certificate under this section made after 31 July 1999 (by virtue of SI 1998/2620 art 3).
[4] Words in sub-ss (10), (11) substituted for words ''on summary conviction to a fine not exceeding £5,000'' by FA 1995 s 139(2), Sch 27 paras 3(2), (3)(*b*), 8(2) with effect for contraventions of sub-ss (10), (11) committed after 22 November 1998 (by virtue of SI 1998/2620 art 2).
[5] Sub-ss (4), (5), and words in sub-s (1), repealed by FA 1995 s 162, Sch 29 Pt VIII(21) with effect for payments made to a person in any case where that person's certificate under this section is one issued or renewed with respect to a period beginning after 5 August 1999 (by virtue of SI 1999/2156 art 2).
[6] Sub-s (12) repealed by FA 1995 s 162, Sch 29 Pt VIII(21) with effect for contraventions of sub-ss (10), (11) committed after 22 November 1998 (by virtue of SI 1998/2620 art 2)).
[7] Words in sub-ss (3), (6) repealed by FA 1995 s 162, Sch 29 Pt VIII(21) with effect for any application for the issue or renewal of a certificate under this section which is made with respect to a period beginning after 5 August 1999 (by virtue of SI 1999/2156 art 2).

562 Conditions to be satisfied by individuals

(1) In the case of an application for the issue of a certificate under section 561 to an individual ...[1] the following conditions are required to be satisfied by that individual [except that, where the application is for the issue of that certificate to that individual as a partner in a firm, this section shall have effect with the omission of subsections (2) to (2B)][2].

(2) The applicant must be carrying on a business in the United Kingdom which satisfies the following conditions, that is to say—

   (*a*) the business consists of or includes the carrying out of construction operations or the furnishing or arranging for the furnishing of labour in carrying out construction operations;
   (*b*) the business is, to a substantial extent, carried on by means of an account with a bank;
   (*c*) the business is carried on with proper records and in particular with records which are proper having regard to the obligations referred to in subsections (8) to (12) below; and
   (*d*) the business is carried on from proper premises and with proper equipment, stock and other facilities.

[(2A) The applicant must satisfy the Board, by such evidence as may be prescribed in regulations made by the Board, that the carrying on of the business mentioned in subsection (2) above is likely to involve the receipt, annually in the period to which the certificate would relate, of an aggregate amount by way of relevant payments which is not less than the amount specified in regulations made by the Board as the minimum turnover for the purposes of this subsection.][2]

[(2B) In subsection (2A) above ''relevant payments'' means payments under contracts relating to, or to the work of individuals participating in the carrying out of, any operations which—

   (*a*) are of a description specified in subsection (2) of section 567; but
   (*b*) are not of a description specified in subsection (3) of that section,

other than so much of the payments as represents the direct cost to the person receiving the payments of materials used or to be used in carrying out the operations in question.][4]
(3)–(7) ...[1]

(8) The applicant must, subject to subsection (10) below, have complied with all obligations imposed on him by or under the Tax Acts or the Management Act in respect of periods ending within the qualifying period and with all requests to supply to an inspector accounts of, or other information about, any business of his in respect of periods so ending.

(9) An applicant who at any time in the qualifying period had control of a company shall be taken not to satisfy the condition in subsection (8) above unless the company has satisfied that condition in relation to periods ending at a time within that period when he had control of it; and for this purpose ''control'' [shall be construed in accordance with section 416(2) to (6)][3].

(10) An applicant or company that has failed to comply with such an obligation or request as is referred to in subsection (8) above shall nevertheless be treated as satisfying that condition as regards that obligation or request if the Board are of the opinion that the failure is minor and technical and does not give reason to doubt that the conditions mentioned in subsection (13) below will be satisfied.

[(11) Where the applicant states, for the purpose of showing that he has complied with all obligations imposed on him as mentioned in subsection (8) above, that he was not subject to any of one or more obligations in respect of any period ending within the qualifying period—

   (*a*) he must satisfy the Board of that fact by such evidence as may be prescribed in regulations made by the Board; and
   (*b*) if for that purpose he states that he has been outside the United Kingdom for the whole or any part of the qualifying period, he must also satisfy them, by such evidence as may be so prescribed,][3]

that he has complied with any obligations imposed under the tax laws of any country in which he was living during that period which are comparable to the obligations mentioned in subsection (8) above.

(12) The applicant must, if any contribution has at any time during the qualifying period become due from him under Part I of the Social Security Act 1975 or Part I of the Social Security (Northern Ireland) Act 1975 have paid the contribution when it became due.

(13) There must be reason to expect that the applicant will, in respect of periods ending after the end of the qualifying period, comply with such obligations as are referred to in subsections (8) to (12) above and with such requests as are referred to in subsection (8) above.

[(13A) Subject to subsection (10) above, a person shall not be taken for the purposes of this section to have complied with any such obligation or request as is referred to in subsections (8) to (11) above if there has been a contravention of a requirement as to the time at which, or the period within which, the obligation or request was to be complied with.][3]

[(14) In this section "the qualifying period", in relation to an application for the issue of a certificate under section 561, means the period of three years ending with the date of the application.][3]

Commentary—*Simon's Direct Tax Service* E5.510–512.
Regulations—IT (Sub-contractors in the Construction Industry) Regulations, SI 1993/743.
Revenue & other press releases—IR Tax Bulletin December 1998 p 615 (guidance on turnover tests).
IR Tax Bulletin June 1999 p 667 (turnover tests and change in concern).
Revenue Internal Guidance—Construction Industry Scheme manual CIS 3019, 3021 (application for a certificate: the photographic evidence and identifying documents acceptable to the Revenue).
CIS 3241 (definition of "turnover").
CIS 3405 (compliance test as applied to individuals).
CIS 3413 (compliance test: failures substantial enough to justify the Revenue refusing a certificate).
CIS 3415 (compliance test: minor and technical failures that will not result in the refund of a certificate).
CIS 3417 (the operation of the three-year qualifying period).
CIS 3419 (the operation of the "reason to expect" test under sub-s (13)).
CIS 3423 (compliance test: what constitutes misuse of documents).
Note—SSA 1975 Pt I and SS (Northern Ireland) A 1975, Pt I referred to in sub-s (12) are re-enacted as Social Security Contributions and Benefits Act 1992 Pt I and Social Security Contributions and Benefits (Northern Ireland) Act 1992 Pt I respectively.
Simon's Tax Cases—*Kirvell v Guy* [1979] STC 312*.
s 562(2), *Jones v Lonnen* [1981] STC 337*
s 562(3), (5)–(7), (14), *Cooper v Sercombe* [1980] STC 76*; *Phelps v Moore* [1980] STC 568*; *Jones v Lonnen* [1981] STC 337*.
s 562(8), (9), (11), *Kington v Reilly* [1981] STC 121*.
s 562(8), (10), (13), (13A), *T &C Hill v Gleig* [2000] STC (SCD) 64.
s 562(10), *Cooper v Sercombe* [1980] STC 76*.
Definitions—"The Board", s 832(1); "company", s 832(1), (2); "construction operations", s 567; "inspector", s 832(1); "the Management Act", s 831(3); "the Tax Acts", s 831(2); "trade", s 832(1); "United Kingdom", s 830(1).
Cross references—See Finance Act 1995, Section 139(3), (Appointed Day) Order, SI 1998/2620 art 4 (certificates under TA 1988 s 561 for periods ending after 31 July 1999 cease to have effect at the end of 31 July 1999).
Amendments—[1] Sub-ss (3)–(7), and words in sub-s (1), repealed by FA 1995 ss 139(2), 162, Sch 27 para 4(2), (4), Sch 29 Pt VIII(21) with effect in relation to any application for the issue or renewal of a certificate with respect to any period beginning after 31 July 1999 (by virtue of SI 1998/2620 art 3).
[2] Sub-s (2A), and words in sub-s (1), inserted by FA 1995 s 139(2), Sch 27 para 4(2), (3) with effect in relation to any application for the issue or renewal of a certificate with respect to any period beginning after 31 July 1999 (by virtue of SI 1998/2620 art 3).
[3] Sub-ss (13A) inserted, and sub-s (14) and words in sub-ss (9), (11) substituted, by FA 1995 s 139(2), Sch 27 para 4(2), (3), (5)–(7) with effect in relation to any application for the issue or renewal of a certificate with respect to any period beginning after 31 July 1999 (by virtue of SI 1998/2620 art 3).
[4] Sub-s (2B) substituted by FA 1999 s 53 and deemed to always have had effect in relation to any application for the issue or renewal of a certificate under TA 1988 s 561 which is made with respect to a period beginning after 31 July 1999.

563 Conditions to be satisfied by partners who are individuals

Commentary—*Simon's Direct Tax Service* E5.512.
Amendments—This section repealed by FA 1995 s 139, Sch 27 paras 5, 8, Sch 29 Pt VIII(21) with effect for any application for the issue or renewal of a certificate under TA 1988 s 561 *ante* which is made with respect to a period beginning after 31 July 1999 by virtue of the Finance Act 1995, Section 139(3), (Appointed Day) Order, SI 1998/2620.

564 Conditions to be satisfied by firms

(1) In the case of an application for the issue of a certificate under section 561 to an individual or a company as a partner in a firm the following conditions are required to be satisfied by the firm.

(2) The firm's business must be carried on in the United Kingdom and must satisfy the conditions mentioned in section 562(2)(a) to (d).

[(2A) The partners must satisfy the Board, by such evidence as may be prescribed in regulations made by the Board, that the carrying on of the firm's business is likely to involve the receipt, annually in the period to which the certificate would relate, of an aggregate amount by way of relevant payments which is not less than whichever is the smaller of—

    (a) the sum specified in subsection (2B) below; and
    (b) the amount specified for the purposes of this paragraph in regulations made by the Board;

and in this subsection "relevant payments" has the meaning given by section 562(2B).][1]

[(2B) The sum referred to in subsection (2A)(a) above is the sum of the following amounts, that is to say—

(*a*) the amount obtained by multiplying the number of partners in the firm who are individuals by the amount specified in regulations as the minimum turnover for the purposes of section 562(2A); and

(*b*) in respect of each partner in the firm who is a company (other than one to which section 565(2A)(*b*) would apply), the amount equal to what would have been the minimum turnover for the purposes of section 565(2A) if the application had been for the issue of a certificate to that company.]¹

[(3) Subject to subsection (4) below, each of the persons who are partners at the time of the application must have complied, so far as any such charge to income tax or corporation tax is concerned as falls to be computed by reference to the profits or gains of the firm's business—

(*a*) with all obligations imposed on him by or under the Tax Acts or the Management Act in respect of periods ending within the qualifying period; and

(*b*) with all requests to him as such a partner to supply to an inspector accounts of, or other information about, the firm's business or his share of the profits or gains of that business.]¹

[(4) Where a person has failed to comply with such an obligation or request as is referred to in subsection (3) above the firm shall nevertheless be treated, in relation to that partner, as satisfying that condition as regards that obligation or request if the Board are of the opinion that the failure is minor and technical and does not give reason to doubt that the condition mentioned in subsection (5) below will be satisfied.]¹

[(5) There must be reason to expect that each of the persons who are from time to time partners in the firm will, in respect of periods ending after the end of the qualifying period, comply with such obligations and requests as are referred to in subsection (3) above.]¹

[(6) Subject to subsection (4) above, a person shall not be taken for the purposes of this section to have complied with any such obligation or request as is referred to in subsection (3) above if there has been a contravention of a requirement as to the time at which, or the period within which, the obligation or request was to be complied with.]¹

[(7) In this section "the qualifying period", in relation to an application for the issue of a certificate under section 561, means the period of three years ending with the date of the application.]¹

Commentary—*Simon's Direct Tax Service* E5.512.
Concession B52—Maximum number of partners in final six months of three year period may be used as multiplier for purpose of the multiple turnover test in sub-s (2B) above.
Revenue & other press releases—IR Tax Bulletin December 1998 p 615 (guidance on turnover tests).
IR Tax Bulletin June 1999 p 667 (turnover tests and change in concern).
Revenue Internal Guidance—Construction Industry Scheme manual CIS 3115 (circumstances under which Revenue will refuse to issue a certificate CIS5/CIS5(partner)).
CIS 3142–3145 (Revenue procedures for dealing with applications involving a change to or from a partnership).
CIS 3407 (compliance test as applied to partnerships).
Simon's Tax Cases—s 564(3), (4), (5), (6), *T & C Hill v Gleig* [2000] STC (SCD) 64.
Definitions—"The Board", s 832(1); "United Kingdom", s 830(1).
Note—The prospective amendments to this section which were due to be made by FA 1998 Sch 8 paras 3–5 were repealed by FA 1999 s 53(1) and do not therefore take effect.
Amendments—¹ Sub-ss (2A), (2B), (3), (4), (5), (6), (7) substituted for sub-ss (3)–(5) by FA 1995 s 139(2), Sch 27 para 6 with effect in relation to any application for the issue or renewal of a certificate under TA 1988 s 561 made for any period beginning after 31 July 1999 (by virtue of the Finance Act 1995, Section 139(3), (Appointed Day) Order, SI 1998/2620 art 3)

565 Conditions to be satisfied by companies

(1) In the case of an application for the issue of a certificate under section 561 to a company (whether as a partner in a firm or otherwise), the following conditions are required to be satisfied by the company.

(2) The company must be carrying on (whether or not in partnership) a business in the United Kingdom and that business must satisfy the conditions mentioned in section 562(2)(*a*) to (*d*).

[(2A) The company must either—

(*a*) satisfy the Board, by such evidence as may be prescribed in regulations made by them, that the carrying on of its business is likely to involve the receipt, annually in the period to which the certificate would relate, of an aggregate amount by way of relevant payments which is not less than the amount which is the minimum turnover for the purposes of this subsection; or

(*b*) satisfy the Board that the only persons with shares in the company are companies which are limited by shares and themselves excepted from section 559 by virtue of a certificate which is in force under section 561;

and in this subsection "relevant payments" has the meaning given by section 562(2B).

(2B) The minimum turnover for the purposes of subsection (2A) above is whichever is the smaller of—

(*a*) the amount obtained by multiplying the amount specified in regulations as the minimum turnover for the purposes of section 562(2A) by the number of persons who are relevant persons in relation to the company; and

(*b*) the amount specified for the purposes of this paragraph in regulations made by the Board.

(2C) For the purposes of subsection (2B) above a person is a relevant person in relation to the company—

(*a*) where the company is a close company, if he is a director of the company (within the meaning of Chapter II of Part V) or a beneficial owner of shares in the company; and

(*b*) in any other case, if he is such a director of the company.][6]

(3) The company must, subject to subsection (4) below, have complied with all obligations imposed on it by or under the Tax Acts or the Management Act in respect of periods ending within the qualifying period and with all requests to supply to an inspector accounts of, or other information about, the business of the company in respect of periods so ending.

(4) A company which has failed to comply with such an obligation or request as is referred to in subsection (3) above shall nevertheless be treated as satisfying this condition as regards that obligation or request if the Board are of the opinion that the failure is minor and technical and does not give reason to doubt that the conditions mentioned in subsection (8) below will be satisfied.

(5) The company must, if any contribution has at any time during the qualifying period become due from the company under Part I of the Social Security Act 1975 or Part I of the Social Security (Northern Ireland) Act 1975 have paid the contribution when it became due.

(6) The company must have complied with any obligations imposed on it by the following provisions of the Companies Act 1985 in so far as those obligations fell to be complied with within the qualifying period, that is to say—

(*a*) [sections 226, 241 and 242][1] (contents, laying and delivery of annual accounts);

(*b*) ...[3]

(*c*) section 288(2) (return of directors and secretary and notification of changes therein);

(*d*) [sections 363 to 365][2] (annual returns);

(*e*) section 691 (registration of constitutional documents and list of directors and secretary of oversea company);

(*f*) section 692 (notification of changes in constitution or directors or secretary of oversea company);

(*g*) section 693 (oversea company to state its name and country of incorporation);

(*h*) section 699 (obligations of companies incorporated in Channel Islands or Isle of Man);

(*j*) Chapter II of Part XXIII (accounts of oversea company).

(7) The company must have complied with any obligations imposed on it by the following provisions of the Companies (Northern Ireland) Order 1986, in so far as those obligations fell to be complied with within the qualifying period, that is to say—

[(*a*) Articles 234, 249 and 250 (contents, laying and delivery of annual accounts);][4]

(*b*) ...[5]

(*c*) Article 296(2) (return of directors and secretary and notification of changes therein);

(*d*) [Articles 371 to 373][5] (annual returns);

(*e*) Article 641 (registration of constitutional documents and list of directors and secretary of oversea company);

(*f*) Article 642 (notification of changes in constitution or directors or secretary of oversea company);

(*g*) Article 643 (oversea company to state its name and country of incorporation);

(*h*) Article 649 (accounts of oversea company).

(8) There must be reason to expect that the company will, in respect of periods ending after the end of the qualifying period, comply with all such obligations as are referred to in subsections (2) to (7) above and with such requests as are referred to in subsection (3) above.

[(8A) Subject to subsection (4) above, a company shall not be taken for the purposes of this section to have complied with any such obligation or request as is referred to in subsections (3) to (7) above if there has been a contravention of a requirement as to the time at which, or the period within which, the obligation or request was to be complied with.][6]

(9) In this section ''qualifying period'' means the period of three years ending with the date of the company's application for a certificate under section 561.

Commentary—*Simon's Direct Tax Service* E5.513.

Concession B52—Maximum number of directors etc in final six months of three year period may be used as multiplier for purpose of the multiple turnover test in sub-s (2B) above.

Revenue & other press releases—IR Tax Bulletin December 1998 p 615 (guidance on turnover tests).

IR Tax Bulletin June 1999 p 667 (turnover tests and change in concern).

Revenue Internal Guidance—Construction Industry Scheme manual CIS 3127–3132 (Revenue procedures for dealing with applications from companies where non-residence is a factor).

CIS 3148 (applications by companies acting as undisclosed agents).

CIS 3409 (compliance test as applied to companies).

Notes—SSA 1975 Pt I and SS (Northern Ireland) A 1975, Pt I referred to in sub-s (5) are re-enacted as Social Security Contributions and Benefits Act 1992 Pt I and Social Security Contributions and Benefits (Northern Ireland) Act 1992 Pt I respectively.

The prospective amendments to this section which were due to be made by FA 1998 Sch 8 paras 3–5 were repealed by FA 1999 s 53(1) and do not therefore take effect.

Simon's Tax Cases—*Gorge Fabrications Ltd v Wilson* [1999] STC (SCD) 293.

Definitions—''The Board'', s 832(1); ''company'', s 832(1), (2); ''inspector'', s 832(1); ''Management Act'', s 831(3); ''the Tax Acts'', s 831(2); ''United Kingdom'', s 830(1).

Cross references—See IT (Sub-Contractors in the Construction Industry) Regulations, SI 1988/636 reg 7 (information as to changes in control of close companies).

Amendments—[1] Words in sub-s (6)(*a*) substituted by the Companies Act 1989 Sch 10 para 38(1), (3) with effect from 1 April 1990 by virtue of the Companies Act 1989 (Commencement No 4) (Transitional and Savings Provisions) Order, SI 1990/355.

566 General powers to make regulations under Chapter IV

(1) The Board shall make regulations with respect to the collection and recovery, whether by assessment or otherwise, of sums required to be deducted from any payments under section 559 and for the giving of receipts by persons receiving the payments to persons making them; and those regulations may include any matters with respect to which regulations may be made under section 203.

(2) The Board may make regulations—

(*a*) prescribing the period for which certificates under section 561 are to be issued and the form of such certificates;

(*b*) providing for the renewal of such certificates;

(*c*) providing for the issue, renewal or cancellation of such certificates or the giving of directions under section 561(6) ...⁴ on behalf of the Board;

(*d*) requiring the furnishing of information with respect to changes in the control of a company holding or applying for such a certificate;

(*e*) requiring the production of such certificates to such persons and in such circumstances as may be specified in the regulations and providing for the completion and return to the Board of forms certifying such production;

(*f*) requiring the surrender to the Board of such certificates in such circumstances as may be specified in the regulations;

(*g*) requiring persons who make payments under contracts relating to construction operations to keep such records and to make to the Board such returns relating to payments so made by them as may be specified in the regulations, and requiring persons who hold such certificates to keep such records relating to payments so made to them as may be so specified;

(*h*) with respect to the production, copying and removal of, and the making of extracts from, any records kept by virtue of any such requirement as is referred to in paragraph (*g*) above and with respect to rights of access to or copies of any such records which are removed;

(*j*) requiring vouchers for payments made under contracts relating to construction operations to persons who hold such certificates to be obtained by the person making, and given by the person receiving, the payment, prescribing the form of the vouchers, and requiring their production or surrender to the Board in such circumstances as may be specified in the regulations; and

(*k*) excluding payments from the operation of section 561 where, in such circumstances as may be specified in the regulations, the requirements of regulations relating to the production of certificates or the obtaining, production or surrender of vouchers have not been complied with;

...²

Section 840 shall apply for the purposes of paragraph (*d*) above.

[(2A) The Board may by regulations make provision—

(*a*) for the issue of documents (to be known as ''registration cards'') to persons who are parties, as sub-contractors, to any contract relating to construction operations or who are likely to become such parties;

(*b*) for a registration card to contain all such information about the person to whom it is issued as may be required, for the purposes of any regulations under this section, by a person making payments under any such contract;

(*c*) for a registration card to take such form and to be valid for such period as may be prescribed by the regulations;

(*d*) for the renewal, replacement or cancellation of a registration card;

(*e*) for requiring the surrender of a registration card in such circumstances as may be specified in the regulations;

(*f*) for requiring the production of a registration card to such persons and in such circumstances as may be so specified;

(*g*) for requiring any person who—

(i) makes or is proposing to make payments to which section 559 applies, and

(ii) is a person to whom a registration card has to be produced under the regulations,

to take steps that ensure that it is produced to him and that he has an opportunity of inspecting it for the purpose of checking that it is a valid registration card issued to the person required to produce it.]³

[(2B) A person who fails to comply with an obligation imposed on him by virtue of subsection (2A)(*g*) above shall be liable to a penalty not exceeding £3,000.]³

[(2C) Subject to subsection (2D) below, where—

(*a*) a person who is a party to a contract relating to any construction operations ("the contractor") makes or is proposing to make payments to which section 559 applies,
(*b*) the contractor is required by regulations under this section to make statements about another party to the contract ("the sub-contractor") in any return, certificate or other document,
(*c*) a registration card containing the information to be stated should have been produced, in accordance with any such regulations, to the contractor, and
(*d*) the statements made in the return, certificate or other document, so far as relating to matters the information about which should have been obtainable from the card, are inaccurate or incomplete in any material respect,

the contractor shall be liable to a penalty not exceeding £3,000.]³

[(2D) A person shall not be liable to a penalty under subsection (2C) above if—

(*a*) a valid registration card issued to the sub-contractor, or a document which the contractor had reasonable grounds for believing to be such a card, was produced to the contractor and inspected by him before the statements in question were made; and
(*b*) the contractor took all such steps as were reasonable, in addition to the inspection of that card, for ensuring that the statements were accurate and complete.]³

[(2E) A person liable to a penalty under subsection (2C) above shall not, by reason only of the matters in respect of which he is liable to a penalty under that subsection, be liable to any further penalty under section 98 of the Management Act.]³

[(2F) Regulations under this section may make different provision for different cases.]³

[(3) Any power under this Chapter to make regulations prescribing the evidence required for establishing what is likely to happen at any time shall include power to provide for such matters to be presumed (whether conclusively or unless the contrary is shown in the manner provided for in the regulations) from evidence of what has previously happened.]¹

[(4) Any power under this Chapter to make regulations authorising or requiring a document (whether or not of a particular description), or any records or information, to be issued, given or requested or to be sent, produced, returned or surrendered to the Board shall include power—

(*a*) to authorise the Board to nominate a person who is not an officer of the Board to be the person who on behalf of the Board—

    (i) issues, gives or requests the document, records or information; or
    (ii) is the recipient of the document, records or information;

and

(*b*) to require the document, records or information, in cases prescribed by or determined under the regulations, to be sent, produced, returned or surrendered to the address (determined in accordance with the regulations) of the person nominated by the Board to receive it on their behalf.

(5) Any power under this Chapter to make regulations imposing requirements with respect to any description of document, with respect to documents generally or with respect to any records or information shall include power to make provision, subject to such conditions as may be prescribed by or determined in accordance with the regulations—

(*a*) for the documents, records or information to be allowed to take an electronic form so prescribed or determined;
(*b*) for the issue, completion, furnishing, production, keeping, cancellation, return, surrender or giving of the documents, records or information to be something that has to be or may be done by the electronic means so prescribed or determined; and
(*c*) for the manner of proving in any proceedings the contents or transmission of anything that, by virtue of any regulations under this Chapter, takes an electronic form or is transmitted to any person by electronic means.]⁴

Commentary—*Simon's Direct Tax Service* **E5.510, 520.**
Regulations—IT (Sub-Contractors in the Construction Industry) Regulations, SI 1993/743.
Revenue & other press releases—Code of Practice 3 (inspection of contractors' records).
Revenue Internal Guidance—Construction Industry Scheme manual CIS 2105–2141 (Revenue procedures for dealing with applications for registration cards).
CIS 2300–2317 (Revenue procedures for dealing with replacement registration cards).
Simon's Tax Cases—s 566(1), *Slater v Richardson Bottoms Ltd* [1979] STC 630*.
s 566(2), *Kirvell v Guy* [1979] STC 312*; *Slater v Richardson Bottoms Ltd* [1979] STC 630*.
Definitions—"the Board", s 832(1); "company", s 832(1), (2); "construction operations", s 567; "control", s 840; "inspector", s 832(1); the Management Act", s 831(3); "sub-contractor", s 560.
Cross references—See TMA 1970 ss 98, 98A(1) (special penalties in the case of matters under sub-ss (1), (2), (2A) of this section).
Amendments—¹ Sub-s (3) inserted by FA 1995 s 139, Sch 27 para 9.
² Words omitted in sub-s (2) repealed by FA 1996 Sch 41 Pt V(32).
³ Sub-ss (2A)–(2F) inserted by FA 1996 s 178(1).
⁴ Words in sub-s (2)(*c*) repealed and sub-ss (4)–(5) inserted by FA 1998 s 165, Sch 8 para 6, Sch 27 Part III (8) with effect from 31 July 1998.
Prospective amendment—Sub-s (5) will be repealed by FA 1999 s 139, Sch 20 Pt VII with effect on such day as the Treasury may by order appoint.

567 Meaning of "construction operations"

(1) In this Chapter "construction operations" means operations of any description specified in subsection (2) below, not being operations of any description specified in subsection (3) below; and references to construction operations shall be taken—

    (*a*) except where the context otherwise requires, as including references to the work of individuals participating in the carrying out of such operations; and
    (*b*) except in the case of offshore installations, as not including references to operations carried out or to be carried out otherwise than in the United Kingdom.

(2) The following operations are, subject to subsection (3) below, construction operations for the purposes of this Chapter—

    (*a*) construction, alteration, repair, extension, demolition or dismantling of buildings or structures (whether permanent or not), including offshore installations;
    (*b*) construction, alteration, repair, extension or demolition of any works forming, or to form, part of the land, including (without prejudice to the foregoing) walls, roadworks, power-lines, telecommunication apparatus, aircraft runways, docks and harbours, railways, inland waterways, pipe-lines, reservoirs, water-mains, wells, sewers, industrial plant and installations for purposes of land drainage, coast protection or defence;
    (*c*) installation in any building or structure of systems of heating, lighting, air-conditioning, ventilation, power supply, drainage, sanitation, water supply or fire protection;
    (*d*) internal cleaning of buildings and structures, so far as carried out in the course of their construction, alteration, repair, extension or restoration;
    (*e*) operations which form an integral part of, or are preparatory to, or are for rendering complete, such operations as are previously described in this subsection, including site clearance, earth-moving, excavation, tunnelling and boring, laying of foundations, erection of scaffolding, site restoration, landscaping and the provision of roadways and other access works;
    (*f*) painting or decorating the internal or external surfaces of any building or structure.

(3) The following operations are not construction operations for the purposes of this Chapter—

    (*a*) drilling for, or extraction of, oil or natural gas;
    (*b*) extraction (whether by underground or surface working) of minerals; tunnelling or boring, or construction of underground works, for this purpose;
    (*c*) manufacture of building or engineering components or equipment, materials, plant or machinery, or delivery of any of these things to site;
    (*d*) manufacture of components for systems of heating, lighting, air-conditioning, ventilation, power supply, drainage, sanitation, water supply or fire protection, or delivery of any of these things to site;
    (*e*) the professional work of architects or surveyors, or of consultants in building, engineering, interior or exterior decoration or in the laying-out of landscape;
    (*f*) the making, installation and repair of artistic works, being sculptures, murals and other works which are wholly artistic in nature;
    (*g*) signwriting and erecting, installing and repairing signboards and advertisements;
    (*h*) the installation of seating, blinds and shutters;
    (*j*) the installation of security systems, including burglar alarms, closed circuit television and public address systems.

(4) In this section "offshore installations" means installations which are maintained, or are intended to be established, for underwater exploitation or exploration to which the Mineral Workings (Offshore Installations) Act 1971 applies.

(5) The Treasury may by order—

    (*a*) include in subsection (2) above any description of operations as to which they are satisfied that it is a normal activity of the construction industry and that its inclusion in that subsection is necessary for achieving the object of section 559;
    (*b*) include in subsection (3) above any description of operations as to which they are satisfied that it cannot properly be considered a normal activity of the construction industry and ought to be excluded from subsection (2) above.

(6) An order under subsection (5) above shall not have effect unless a draft of the instrument containing it has been laid before and approved by a resolution of the House of Commons.

Commentary—*Simon's Direct Tax Service* **E5.502.**
Statement of Practice SP 12/81—Carpet fitting, even if included in a building contract, is not a construction operation.
Revenue Internal Guidance—Construction industry scheme manual CIS 1027 (meaning of "construction operations").
CIS 1313 (definition of territorial limits applying to the scheme).
CIS 1319–1380 (detailed examination of operations within or excluded from the construction industry scheme in accordance with sub-ss (2), (3)).
Definition—"United Kingdom", s 830(1).

CHAPTER V

SCHEMES FOR RATIONALISING INDUSTRY

Cross references—See TA 1988 s 572 (this Chapter to apply with necessary adaptations to statutory redundancy schemes).

568 Deductions from profits of contributions paid under certified schemes

(1) Notwithstanding anything contained in section 74 but subject to the following provisions of this Chapter, where a person pays, wholly and exclusively for the purposes of a trade in respect of which he is chargeable under Case I of Schedule D, a contribution in furtherance of a scheme which is for the time being certified by the Secretary of State under this section, the contribution shall, in so far as it is paid in furtherance of the primary object of the scheme, be allowed to be deducted as an expense in computing the [profits]¹ of that trade.

(2) The Secretary of State shall certify a scheme under this section if he is satisfied—

   (a) that the primary object of the scheme is the elimination of redundant works or machinery or plant from use in an industry in the United Kingdom; and
   (b) that the scheme is in the national interest and in the interests of that industry as a whole; and
   (c) that such number of persons engaged in that industry as are substantially representative of the industry are liable to pay contributions in furtherance of the primary object of the scheme by agreement between them and the body of persons carrying out the scheme.

References in this subsection to an industry in the United Kingdom shall include references to the business carried on by owners of ships or of a particular class of ships, wherever that business is carried on, and, in relation to that business, references in this subsection to works or machinery or plant shall include references to ships.

(3) The Secretary of State shall cancel any certificate granted under this section if he ceases to be satisfied as to any of the matters referred to in subsection (2) above.

(4) The Secretary of State may at any time require the body of persons carrying out a scheme certified under this section to produce any books or documents of whatever nature relating to the scheme and, if the requirement is not complied with, he may cancel the certificate.

(5) In this section and in section 569 "contribution", in relation to a scheme, does not include a sum paid by a person by way of loan or subscription of share capital, or in consideration of the transfer of assets to him, or by way of a penalty for contravening or failing to comply with the scheme.

Commentary—*Simon's Direct Tax Service* **B3.1472.**
Definitions—"Body of persons", s 832(1); "Schedule D", s 18(1); "trade", s 832(1); "United Kingdom", s 830(1).
Cross references—See TA 1988 s 571(1) (cancellation of a certificate granted under this section).
TA 1988 Sch 21, para 9 (determination of the amount of contribution to be allowed as deduction under sub-s (1) above).
Amendments—¹ Word in sub-s (1) substituted by FA 1998 Sch 7 para 1 with effect from 31 July 1998.

569 Repayment of contributions

(1) In the event of the repayment, whether directly or by way of distribution of assets on a winding up or otherwise, of a contribution or any part of a contribution which has been allowed to be deducted under section 568, the deduction of the contribution, or so much of it as has been repaid, shall be deemed to be an unauthorised deduction in respect of which an assessment shall be made, and, notwithstanding the provisions of the Tax Acts requiring assessments to be made within six years after the end of the chargeable period to which they relate, any such assessment and any consequential assessment may be made at any time within three years after the end of the chargeable period in which the repayment was made.

(2) For the purposes of this section, a sum received by any person by way of repayment of contributions shall be deemed to be by way of repayment of the last contribution paid by him, and, if the sum exceeds the amount of that contribution, by way of repayment of the penultimate contribution so paid, and so on.

Commentary—*Simon's Direct Tax Service* **B3.1472.**
Definitions—"Chargeable period", s 832(1); "contribution", s 568(5); "distribution", s 832(1); "the Tax Acts", s 831(2).

570 Payments under certified schemes which are not repayments of contributions

(1) Subject to the provisions of this section, where, under any scheme which is for the time being certified or has at any time been certified by the Secretary of State under section 568, any payment (not being a payment made by way of repayment of contributions) is made to a person carrying on a trade to which the scheme relates, that payment shall be treated for the purposes of the Tax Acts as a trading receipt of the trade, and shall accordingly be taken into account in computing the [profits]² of the trade for those purposes.

(2) Where ...¹ the payments which have been made under such a scheme in respect of a trade (not being payments made by way of repayment of contributions) have been made wholly or partly in respect of damage in respect of which no relief may be given under the Tax Acts [and a claim is made to that effect,]¹, then, subject to and in accordance with the provisions of [Schedule 21]¹—

   (a) relief shall be given in respect of those payments by reducing the amounts which are to be treated as trading receipts of the trade under subsection (1) above; but (*b*) where such relief is given, section 568 shall, in relation to contributions subsequently paid under the scheme in respect of the trade, have effect subject to the modifications specified in Part III of that Schedule

[and paragraph 6 of that Schedule applies for the purposes of this subsection as it applies for the purposes of that Schedule][1].

(3) The provisions of this section and Schedule 21 shall apply in relation to any payment made to a person who has ceased to carry on a trade to which any such scheme as is mentioned in subsection (1) above relates as they apply in relation to payments made to a person carrying on such a trade, subject to the modification that so much of that payment as falls to be treated as a trading receipt by virtue of those provisions shall be deemed for the purposes of those provisions to have been made to him on the last day on which he was engaged in carrying on the trade.

(4) In determining for the purposes of this section and of Schedule 21—

(*a*) whether any trade has ceased to be carried on; or

(*b*) whether any contribution is paid in respect of a trade in respect of which a payment has been made; or

(*c*) whether any payment is made in respect of a trade in respect of which a contribution has been paid,

no regard shall be had to any event which, by virtue of any of the provisions of section 113 or section 337(1), is to be treated as effecting a discontinuance of a trade.

Commentary—*Simon's Direct Tax Service* B3.1472, 1473, 1475.
Definitions—"the Tax Acts", s 831(2); "trade", s 832(1).
Amendments—[1] In sub-s (2): words "on a claim it is shown in accordance with the provisions of Part II of Schedule 21 that" repealed; words "and a claim is made to that effect," inserted; words "Schedule 21" substituted (for words "that Schedule") and words commencing "and paragraph 6" inserted by FA 1996 s 134, Sch 20 para 31, Sch 41 Pt V(10) with effect for the purposes of income tax from the year 1996–97, and for the purposes of corporation tax, as respects accounting periods ending after 30 June 1999 (by virtue of Finance Act 1994, Section 199, (Appointed Day) Order, SI 1998/3173 art 2).
[2] Word in sub-s (1) substituted by FA 1998 Sch 7 para 1 with effect from 31 July 1998.

571 Cancellation of certificates

(1) Where any certificate granted with respect to a scheme under section 568 is cancelled by the Secretary of State, and any deductible contributions paid in furtherance of the scheme have not been repaid at the expiration of one year from the cancellation, the body of persons carrying out the scheme shall, for the chargeable period in which that year expires, be charged to tax under Case VI of Schedule D upon the aggregate amount of the deductible contributions which have not been repaid at that time.

(2) The charge to tax under subsection (1) above shall not be made if the total amount of any contributions, other than deductible contributions, which have been paid under the scheme and have not been repaid before that time is greater than the available resources of the scheme, and shall not in any case be made upon an amount greater than the excess, if any, of those resources over that total amount.

(3) In subsection (2) above "the available resources", in relation to any scheme, means a sum representing the total funds held for the purposes of the scheme at the expiration of one year from the cancellation of the certificate plus a sum representing any funds held for the purposes of the scheme which, during that year, have been applied otherwise than in accordance with the provisions of the scheme as in force when the certificate was granted.

(4) Where the body of persons carrying out a scheme are charged to tax by virtue of subsection (1) above, and, after the expiration of one year from the cancellation of the certificate, any deductible contribution paid in furtherance of the scheme is repaid, the amount upon which the charge is made shall on the making of a claim be reduced by the amount repaid, and all such repayments of tax shall be made as are necessary to give effect to the provisions of this subsection.

(5) In this section "contribution" includes a part of a contribution, and "deductible contribution" means a contribution allowed to be deducted under section 568, any reduction under Part III of Schedule 21 being left out of account.

(6) For the purposes of this section, a sum received by any person by way of repayment of contributions shall be deemed to be by way of repayment of the last contribution paid by him, and, if the sum exceeds the amount of that contribution, by way of repayment of the penultimate contribution so paid, and so on.

Commentary—*Simon's Direct Tax Service* B3.1475.
Definitions—"Body of persons", s 832(1); "chargeable period", s 832(1); "Schedule D", s 18(1); "tax", s 832(3).

572 Application to statutory redundancy schemes

(1) Sections 569 to 571 and Schedule 21 shall, subject to the adaptations specified in subsection (2) below, apply in relation to a statutory redundancy scheme as they apply in relation to a scheme certified under section 568.

(2) The adaptations referred to above are as follows, that is to say—

(*a*) for any reference to a contribution allowed to be deducted under section 568 there shall be substituted a reference to a contribution allowed to be deducted under any provision of the Tax Acts other than that section;

(b) any provision that section 568 shall, in relation to contributions, have effect subject to modifications, shall be construed as a provision that so much of any provision of the Tax Acts other than that section as authorises the deduction of contributions shall, in relation to the contributions in question, have effect subject to the modifications in question;

(c) for any reference to the cancellation of a certificate with respect to a scheme there shall be substituted a reference to the scheme ceasing to have effect; and

(d) for any reference to the provisions of the scheme as in force when the certificate was granted there shall be substituted a reference to the provisions of the scheme as in force when the contributions were first paid thereunder.

(3) In this section ''statutory redundancy scheme'' means a scheme for the elimination or reduction of redundant works, machinery or plant, or for other similar purposes, to which effect is given by or under any Act, whether passed before or after this Act.

Commentary—*Simon's Direct Tax Service* **B3.1476.**
Definitions—''Act'', s 832(1); ''the Tax Acts'', s 831(2).

CHAPTER VI

OTHER PROVISIONS

Relief for losses on [unlisted]1 shares in trading companies

Concession D28—Claim for loss relief on shares becoming of negligible value: owner to be treated by concession as if the asset had been sold and reacquired on a particular date by virtue of TCGA 1992 s 24(2). Conditions for relief must be satisfied at the date of the claim and the date the owner is treated as having sold and reacquired the shares.
Amendments—[1] Reference in the heading to ''unquoted'' superseded by ''unlisted'' by virtue of s 576(4) as amended by FA 1996 Sch 38 para 6(1), 2(h), (9) with effect for relevant periods ending after 31 March 1996.

573 Relief for companies

(1) Subsection (2) below has effect where a company which has subscribed for shares in a qualifying trading company incurs an allowable loss (for the purpose of corporation tax on chargeable gains) on the disposal of the shares in any accounting period and the company disposing of the shares—

(a) is an investment company on the date of the disposal and either—

(i) has been an investment company for a continuous period of six years ending on that date; or

(ii) has been an investment company for a shorter continuous period ending on that date and has not before the beginning of that period been a trading company or an excluded company; and

(b) was not associated with, or a member of the same group as, the qualifying trading company at any time in the period beginning with the date when it subscribed for the shares and ending with the date of the disposal.

(2) The company disposing of the shares may, within two years after the end of the accounting period in which the loss was incurred, make a claim requiring that the loss be set off for the purposes of corporation tax against income—

(a) of that accounting period; and

(b) if the company was then an investment company and the claim so requires, of preceding accounting periods ending within the time specified in subsection (3) below;

and, subject to any relief for an earlier loss, the income of any of those periods shall then be treated as reduced by the amount of the loss or by so much of it as cannot be relieved under this subsection against income of a later accounting period.

(3) The time referred to in subsection (2) above is the period of 12 months ending immediately before the accounting period in which the loss is incurred; but the amount of the reduction which may be made under that subsection in the income of an accounting period falling partly before that time shall not exceed a part of that income proportionate to the part of the accounting period falling within that time.

(4) [Where relief is claimed under subsection (2) above, it must be claimed before any deduction is made for]1 charges on income, expenses of management or other amounts which can be deducted from or set against or treated as reducing profits of any description; and where relief [is obtained]1 under that subsection [for an amount]1 of a loss no deduction shall be made in respect of that amount for the purposes of corporation tax on chargeable gains. [This subsection is subject to subsection (4A) below.]2

[(4A) Paragraph 70 of Schedule 15 to the Finance Act 2000 (priority of loss relief) provides that where relief under Part VII of that Schedule (relief for losses on disposals of shares to which investment relief is attributable) is claimed it must be claimed in priority to relief under subsection (2) above.]2

(5) For the purposes of subsection (1)(b) above companies are associated with each other if one controls the other or both are under the control of the same person or persons; and section 416(2) to (6) shall apply for the purposes of this subsection.

(6) For the purposes of this section a company subscribes for shares in another company if they are issued to it by that other company in consideration of money or money's worth.

Commentary—*Simon's Direct Tax Service* D2.416.
Concession D46—Relief against income for capital losses on the disposal of unquoted shares in a trading company subject to certain conditions.
Revenue Internal Guidance—Capital gains tax manual CG 58320–58327 (conversion of loans into shares: base cost of shares may be restricted to market value on date of issue under TCGA 1992 s 122 (reorganisations), or s 251 (debts)).
CG 58372 (worked examples).
Definitions—"Accounting period", s 834(1); "allowable loss", s 834(1); "chargeable gain", s 832(1); "company", s 832(1), (2); "control", s 840; "excluded company", s 576(5); "group", s 576(5); "investment company", s 576(5); "qualifying trading company", s 576(4); "shares", s 576(5); "trading company", s 576(5).
Cross references—See TA 1988 s 242 (set–off of losses against surplus of franked investment income).
TA 1988 s 575 (exclusion of relief under this section).
TA 1988 s 576 (supplementary provisions).
FA 2000 Sch 15 para 70 (priority of loss relief in relation to the disposal of shares from a corporate venturing scheme).
Amendments—[1] Words in sub-s (4) substituted by FA 2000 s 63(2), (3), Sch 16 para 3(1), (2)(a)(i)–(iii) with effect for claims made under TA 1988 s 573, in respect of disposals after 31 March 2000, and for claims made under s 574 of that Act, in respect of disposals after 5 April 2000.
[2] Words in sub-s (4), and whole of sub-s (4A), inserted by FA 2000 s 63(2), (4), Sch 16 para 3(1), (2)(a)(iv), (b) with effect for shares issued after 31 March 2000 but before 1 April 2010.

574 Relief for individuals

[(1) Where an individual who has subscribed for shares in a qualifying trading company incurs an allowable loss (for capital gains tax purposes) on the disposal of the shares in any year of assessment, he may, by notice given within [twelve months from the 31st January next following][2] that year, make a claim for relief from income tax on—

(a) so much of his income for that year as is equal to the amount of the loss or, where it is less than that amount, the whole of that income; or
(b) so much of his income for the last preceding year as is equal to that amount or, where it is less than that amount, the whole of that income;

but relief shall not be given for the loss or the same part of the loss both under paragraph (a) and under paragraph (b) above.

Where such relief is given in respect of the loss or any part of it, no deduction shall be made in respect of the loss or (as the case may be) that part under the 1992 Act.][1]

[(2) Any relief claimed under paragraph (a) of subsection (1) above in respect of any income shall be given in priority to any relief claimed in respect of that income under paragraph (b) of that subsection; and any relief claimed under either paragraph in respect of any income shall be given in priority to any relief claimed in respect of that income under section 380 or 381.][1]

(3) For the purposes of this section—

(a) an individual subscribes for shares if they are issued to him by the company in consideration of money or money's worth; and
(b) an individual shall be treated as having subscribed for shares if his spouse did so and transferred them to him by a transaction inter vivos.

Commentary—*Simon's Direct Tax Service* E1.627.
Concession D46—Relief against income for capital losses on the disposal of unquoted shares in a trading company, subject to certain conditions. Loss relief under this section may include an appropriate amount of indexation loss.
Revenue Interpretation RI 14—Relief under this section for shareholders where a qualifying enterprise investment scheme company ceases to trade.
Revenue Internal Guidance—Capital gains tax manual CG 58320–58327 (conversion of loans into shares: base cost of shares may be restricted to market value on date of issue under TCGA 1992 s 122 (reorganisations), or s 251 (debts)).
CG 58372 (worked examples).
Simon's Tax Cases—s 574(2)(a), *Hobart v Williams* [1997] STC (SCD) 330.
Definitions—"The 1992 Act", s 831(3); "allowable loss", s 834(1); "company", s 832(1), (2); "earned income", s 833(4), (5); "notice", s 832(1); "qualifying trading company", s 576(4); "shares", s 576(5); "spouse", s 576(5); "year of assessment", s 832(4).
Cross references—See TA 1988 s 575 (exclusion of relief under this section).
TA 1988 s 576 (supplementary provisions).
Lloyd's Underwriters (Tax) (1992–93 to 1996–97) Regulations, SI 1995/352 regs 14, 15 and Sch (extension of time limit in sub-s (1) above where a claim falls to be made by a Lloyd's member, spouse, or both);
TCGA 1992 s 150 (shares qualifying for relief under business expansion scheme).
Amendments—[1] Sub-ss (1), (2) substituted by FA 1994 s 210 (as amended by FA 1995 s 119) and Sch 20 para 8 with effect in relation to losses incurred from the year 1994–95.
[2] Words in sub-s (1) substituted by FA 1994 s 210 and Sch 20 para 8 with effect from the year 1996–97.

575 Exclusion of relief under section 573 or 574 in certain cases

(1) Sections 573 and 574 do not apply unless the disposal is—

(a) by way of a bargain made at arm's length for full consideration; or
(b) by way of a distribution in the course of dissolving or winding up the company; or
[(ba) a disposal within section 24(1) of the 1992 Act (entire loss, destruction, dissipation or extinction of asset); or][2]
(c) a deemed disposal under section [24(2) of the 1992 Act][1] (claim that value of asset has become negligible).

(2) Where a person disposes of shares ("the new shares") which by virtue of section [127 of the 1992 Act][1] (reorganisation etc treated as not involving disposal) are identified with other shares ("the

old shares'') previously held by him, relief shall not be given under section 573 or 574 on the disposal of the new shares unless—

    (*a*) relief under section 573 or 574 could (or if this section had been in force could) have been given on a disposal of the old shares if he had incurred an allowable loss in disposing of them as mentioned in subsection (1)(*a*) above on the occasion of the disposal that would have occurred but for section [127 of the 1992 Act][1]; or

    (*b*) he gave new consideration for the new shares;

but in a case within paragraph (*b*) above the amount of relief under section 573 or 574 on the disposal of the new shares shall not exceed the amount or value of the new consideration taken into account as a deduction in computing the loss incurred on their disposal.

(3) Where the shares are the subject of an exchange or arrangement of the kind mentioned in section [135 or 136 of the 1992 Act][1] (company reconstructions etc) which by reason of section [137][1] of that Act involves a disposal of the shares, section 573 or 574 shall not apply to any allowable loss incurred on the disposal.

Commentary—*Simon's Direct Tax Service* **D2.416; E1.627.**
Revenue Internal Guidance—Capital gains tax manual CG 58400–58409 (sub-s (2) explanation with worked examples).
Definitions—"The 1992 Act", s 831(3); "allowable loss", s 834(1); "distribution", s 832(1); "shares", s 576(5).
Cross references—See TA 1988 s 576 (supplementary provisions).
Amendments—[1] Words in sub-ss (1)(*c*), (2), (2)(*a*), (3) substituted by TCGA 1992 Sch 10 para 14(1), (34).
[2] Sub-s (1)(*ba*) inserted by FA 2000 s 63(2), (3), Sch 16 para 3(1), (3) with effect for claims made under TA 1988 s 573, in respect of disposals after 31 March 2000, and for claims made under s 574 of that Act, in respect of disposals after 5 April 2000.

576 Provisions supplementary to sections 573 to 575

(1) [Subject to subsections (1A) [to (1C)][8] below,][6] where a person holds shares in a company which constitute a holding and comprise—

    (*a*) shares for which he has subscribed ("qualifying shares"); and

    (*b*) shares which he has acquired otherwise than by subscription,

any question whether a disposal by him of shares forming part of the holding is of qualifying shares shall be determined by treating that and any previous disposal by him out of the holding as relating to shares acquired later rather than earlier; and if a disposal by him is of qualifying shares forming part of a holding and he makes a claim under section 573 or 574 in respect of a loss incurred on their disposal, the amount of relief under that section on the disposal shall not exceed the sums that would be allowed as deductions in computing the loss if the shares had not been part of the holding.

[(1A) Subsection (1B) below applies where the holding mentioned in subsection (1) above comprises any of the following, namely—

    (*a*) shares issued before 1st January 1994 in respect of which relief has been given under Chapter III of Part VII and has not been withdrawn;

    (*b*) shares issued on or after that date to which relief under that Chapter is attributable; and

    (*c*) shares to which deferral relief (within the meaning of Schedule 5B to the 1992 Act) is attributable.

(1B) Any such question as is mentioned in subsection (1) above shall not be determined as provided by that subsection, but shall be determined instead—

    (*a*) in the case of shares issued before 1st January 1994, as provided by subsections (3) to (4C) of section 299 as it has effect in relation to such shares; and

    (*b*) in the case of shares issued on or after that date, as provided by subsections (6) to (6D) of that section as it has effect in relation to such shares.][6]

[(1C) Where the holding mentioned in subsection (1) above comprises any shares—

    (*a*) to which investment relief is attributable under Schedule 15 to the Finance Act 2000 (corporate venturing scheme), and

    (*b*) which have been held continuously (within the meaning of paragraph 97 of that Schedule) from the time they were issued until the disposal,

any such question as is mentioned in that subsection shall not be determined as provided by that subsection, but shall be determined instead as provided by paragraph 93 of that Schedule (identification of shares on a disposal of part of a holding where investment relief is attributable to any shares in the holding held continuously by the disposing company).

For this purpose paragraph 93 of that Schedule shall have effect as if the references in it to a disposal had the same meaning as in subsection (1) above.][8]

(2) Where a claim is made under section 573 or 574 in respect of a loss accruing on the disposal of shares, section [30 of the 1992 Act][2] (value-shifting) shall have effect in relation to the disposal as if for the references in subsections (1)(*b*) and [(5)][2] to a tax-free benefit there were substituted references to any benefit whether tax-free or not.

(3) There shall be made all such adjustments of corporation tax on chargeable gains or capital gains tax, whether by way of assessment or by way of discharge or repayment of tax, as may be required in consequence of relief being given under section 573 or 574 in respect of an allowable loss or in

consequence of the whole or part of such a loss in respect of which a claim is made not being relieved under that section.

[(4) For the purposes of sections 573 to 575 and this section a qualifying trading company is a company which ...⁹—

    (a) either—

        (i) is an eligible trading company on the date of the disposal; or
        (ii) has ceased to be an eligible trading company at a time which is not more than three years before that date and has not since that time been an excluded company, an investment company or a trading company that is not an eligible trading company; and

    (b) either—

        (i) has been an eligible trading company for a continuous period of six years ending on that date or at that time; or
        (ii) has been an eligible trading company for a shorter continuous period ending on that date or at that time and has not before the beginning of that period been an excluded company, an investment company or a trading company that is not an eligible trading company; and

    (c) has carried on its business wholly or mainly in the United Kingdom throughout the relevant period.

(4A) A company is an eligible trading company for the purposes of subsection (4) above at any time when, or in any period throughout which, it would comply with the requirements of section 293 if—

    (a) the provisions mentioned in subsection (4B) below were omitted;
    [(ab) the reference in subsection (1A) of section 293 to the beginning of the relevant period were a reference to the time at which the shares in respect of which relief is claimed under section 573 or 574 were issued;]⁹
    (b) the references in subsection (6) of section 293 to dissolution were omitted [and after paragraph (a) of that subsection there were inserted—

        "and
        (b) the company continues, during the winding up, to be a trading company within the meaning of section 576(5)."]¹⁰;

    (c) the reference in section 293(6A) to the eligible shares were a reference to the shares in respect of which relief is claimed under section 573 or 574;
    (d) any reference in section 293 [(except subsection (1A))]⁹, 297 or 308 to the relevant period were a reference to the time that is relevant for the purposes of subsection (4)(a) above or, as the case may require, the continuous period that is relevant for the purposes of subsection (4)(b) above;
    (e) the reference in section 304A(1)(e)(i) to eligible shares were a reference to shares in respect of which relief is claimed under section 573 or 574;
    (f) references in section 304A(3) to an individual were references to a person;
    (g) the reference in section 304A(4) to section 304 were a reference to section 574(3)(b); and
    (h) the reference in section 304A(6) to the expressions "eligible shares" and "subscriber shares" were a reference to the expression "subscriber shares".

(4B) The provisions are—

    (a) in section 293, the words "Subject to section 294," in subsection (1), the words ...¹¹ and subsections (8A) and (8B);
    (b) sections 294 to 296;
    (c) in section 298(5), the words "and section 312(1A)(b) shall apply to determine the relevant period for the purposes of that section";
    (d) in section 304A, subsections (1)(e)(ii) and (2)(b), in subsection (3), the words "to which relief becomes so attributable" and paragraphs (c) and (d), in subsection (4), the words "to which relief becomes so attributable" and paragraphs (c) and (d), and subsection (5); and
    (e) section 308(5A).]⁷

(5) In sections 573 to 575 and this section—

"excluded company" means a company—

    (a) which has a trade which consists wholly or mainly of [dealing in land, in commodities or futures or in shares, securities or other financial instruments,]⁷ or is not carried on a commercial basis and in such a way that profits in the trade can reasonably be expected to be realised; or
    (b) which is the holding company of a group other than a trading group; or
    (c) which is a building society or a registered industrial and provident society as defined in section 486(12);

"group" means a company which has one or more 51 per cent subsidiaries together with that or those subsidiaries;

["holding" means any number of shares of the same class held by one person in one capacity, growing or diminishing as shares of that class are acquired or disposed of, but shares shall not be treated as being of the same class unless they are so treated by the practice of a recognised stock exchange or would be so treated if dealt with on such a stock exchange, and subsection

(4) of section 104 of the 1992 Act shall apply for the purposes of this definition as it applies for the purposes of subsection (1) of that section;][3]

"holding company" means a company whose business consists wholly or mainly in the holding of shares or securities of one or more companies which are its 51 per cent subsidiaries;

"investment company" has the meaning given by section 130 except that it does not include the holding company of a trading group;

"new consideration" means consideration in money or money's worth other than consideration of the kind excluded by [paragraph (a) or (b) of section 128(2) [of the 1992 Act][4]][2];

"relevant period" means the period ending with the date on which the shares in question are disposed of and beginning with the incorporation of the company, or, if later, one year before the date on which the shares were [issued][7];

["shares"—

(a) except in subsections (1A) and (1B) above, includes stock; but

(b) except in the definition of "excluded company", does not include shares or stock not forming part of a company's ordinary share capital;";][7]

"spouse" refers to one of two spouses who are living together (construed in accordance with section [288(3) of the 1992 Act][2]);

"trading company" means a company other than an excluded company which is—

[(a) a company whose business consists wholly or mainly of the carrying on of a trade or trades;][1]

(b) the holding company of a trading group;

"trading group" means a group the business of whose members, taken together, consists wholly or mainly in the carrying on of a trade or trades, but for the purposes of this definition any trade carried on by a subsidiary which is an excluded company ...[7] shall be treated as not constituting a trade.

Commentary—*Simon's Direct Tax Service* **D2.416, E1.627.**
Definitions—"The 1992 Act", s 831(3); "allowable loss", s 834(1); "building society", s 832(1); "capital gains tax", s 831(5); "chargeable gain", s 832(1); "company", s 832(1), (2); "ordinary share capital", s 832(1); "51 per cent subsidiary", s 838; "tax", s 832(3); "trade", s 832(1); "United Kingdom", s 830(1).
Revenue & other press releases—IR 20-2-95 (shares listed on the Alternative Investment Market are not "quoted.").
Revenue Internal Guidance—Capital gains tax manual CG 58340 (sub-s (4): definition of a qualifying trading company where shares issued before 6 April 1998).
CG 58346–58347 (sub-ss (4), (4A), (4B): definition of a qualifying trading company where shares issued on or after 6 April 1998).
CG 58375–58384 (explanation with worked examples).
Amendments—[1] Para (a) in the definition of "trading company" substituted by FA 1989 Sch 12 para 14 in relation to disposals after 31 March 1989.
[2] Words in sub-s (2) and in the definitions of "new consideration" and "spouse" in sub-s (5) substituted by TCGA 1992 Sch 10 para 14(1), (35).
[3] Definition of "holding" in sub-s (5) substituted by TCGA 1992 Sch 10 para 14(1), (35).
[4] Words in the definition of "new consideration" in sub-s (5) inserted by FA 1994 Sch 17 para 6.
[5] Word in sub-s (4) substituted by FA 1996 Sch 38 para 6(1), (2)(h), (9) with effect for relevant periods ending after 31 March 1996.
[6] Words in sub-s (1), sub-ss (1A)–(1B) inserted by FA 1998 s 80(1)–(2) with effect in relation to disposals made after 5 April 1998.
[7] Sub-ss (4), (4A), (4B), and words in sub-s (5) substituted and words in sub-s (5) repealed by FA 1998 s 80(3)–(4) 165, Sch 27 Pt III(16) with effect in relation to shares issued after 5 April 1998.
[8] Words in sub-s (1) substituted for "and (1B)", and sub-s (1C) inserted, by FA 2000 s 63(2), (4), Sch 16 para 3(1), (4) with effect for shares issued after 31 March 2000 but before 1 April 2010.
[9] In sub-s (4), "the words at all times in the relevant period has been an unquoted company (within the meaning given by section 312) and which" repealed, sub-s (4A)(ab) inserted, and words inserted in sub-s (4A)(d), by FA 2001 ss 63, 110, Sch 15 para 38, Sch 33 Pt II(3) with effect—

(a) in relation to shares issued after 6 March 2001, and
(b) in relation to shares issued after 5 April 1998 but before 7 March 2001, in respect of any part of the relevant period which falls after 6 March 2001.

For these purposes, "relevant period" has the meaning given in TA 1988 s 576(5).
[10] In sub-s (4A)(b), words substituted for words "and the condition in paragraph (b) of that subsection were a condition that the company continue to be a trading company within the meaning of subsection (5) below" by FA 2001 s 63, Sch 15 para 38(3)(b) with effect for shares issued after 6 April 2001.
[11] Words "an unquoted company and be" in subsection (2)," in sub-s (4B)(a) repealed by FA 2001 s 110, Sch 33 Pt II(3) with effect—

(a) in relation to shares issued after 6 March 2001, and
(b) in relation to shares issued after 5 April 1998 but before 7 March 2001, in respect of any part of the relevant period which falls after 6 March 2001.

For these purposes, "relevant period" has the meaning given in TA 1988 s 576(5).

Miscellaneous

577 Business entertaining expenses

(1) Subject to the provisions of this section—

(a) no deduction shall be made in computing [profits][3] chargeable to tax under [...][2] Schedule D for any expenses incurred in providing business entertainment, and such expenses shall not be included in computing any expenses of management in respect of which relief may be given under the Tax Acts; [and][4]

(*b*) no deduction for expenses so incurred shall be made from emoluments chargeable to tax under Schedule E; ...[4]

(*c*) ...[4]

(2) ...[1]

(3) The expenses to which paragraph (*a*) of subsection (1) above applies include, in the case of any person, any sums paid by him to, or on behalf of, or placed by him at the disposal of a member of his staff exclusively for the purpose of defraying expenses incurred or to be incurred by him in providing business entertainment, but where—

(*a*) any such sum falls to be included in his emoluments chargeable to tax under Schedule E; and

(*b*) the deduction or inclusion of that sum as mentioned in that paragraph falls to be disallowed in whole or in part by virtue of this section;

paragraph (*b*) of that subsection shall not preclude the deduction of any expenses defrayed out of that sum.

(4) ...[1]

(5) For the purposes of this section "business entertainment" means entertainment (including hospitality of any kind) provided by a person, or by a member of his staff, in connection with a trade carried on by that person, but does not include anything provided by him for bona fide members of his staff unless its provision for them is incidental to its provision also for others.

(6) ...[1]

(7) In this section—

(*a*) any reference to expenses incurred in...[4] providing entertainment includes a reference to expenses incurred in...[4] providing anything incidental thereto;

(*b*) references to a trade include references to any business, profession or vocation; and

(*c*) references to the members of a person's staff are references to persons employed by that person, directors of a company or persons engaged in the management of a company being for this purpose deemed to be persons employed by it.

(8) This section shall apply in relation to the provision of a gift as it applies in relation to the provision of entertainment, except that it shall not by virtue of this subsection apply in relation to the provision for any person of a gift consisting of an article incorporating a conspicuous advertisement for the donor, being an article—

(*a*) which is not food, drink, tobacco or a token or voucher exchangeable for goods; and

(*b*) the cost of which to the donor, taken together with the cost to him of any other such articles given by him to that person in the same [relevant tax period][5], does not exceed [£50][5].

[(8A) In subsection (8)(*b*) "relevant tax period" means—

(*a*) for the purposes of corporation tax, an accounting period;

(*b*) for the purposes of income tax—

(i) for a year of assessment in relation to which sections 60 to 63 apply and give a basis period, that basis period;

(ii) in any other case, a year of assessment.][5]

(9) Subsection (8) above shall not preclude the deduction, in computing [profits][3] under [...][2] Case I or II of Schedule D, of expenditure incurred in making a gift to a body of persons or trust established for charitable purposes only; and for the purposes of this subsection the Historic Buildings and Monuments Commission for England and the Trustees of the National Heritage Memorial Fund shall each be treated as such a body of persons.

(10) Nothing in this section shall be taken as precluding the deduction of expenses incurred in...[4] the provision by any person of anything which it is his trade to provide, and which is provided by him in the ordinary course of that trade for payment or, with the object of advertising to the public generally, gratuitously.

Commentary—*Simon's Direct Tax Service* **B3.1438.**

Concession A70—Entertainment in the form of staff Christmas parties, annual dinner dance, etc is not taxed if the cost is limited to the specified amount.

B7—The cost of benevolent gifts to a trader's local trade or charitable associations are allowed as a deduction if specified conditions are satisfied.

Revenue Interpretation RI 151—Cost of trading stock donated to charity not disallowed under this section provided stock originally manufactured and/or purchased for sale in ordinary course of trade.

Revenue Internal Guidance—Schedule E manual SE 21840 (benefit and expenses payments: interaction with this section—liaison with accounts District).

SE 30077 (entertaining expenses and dispensations).

SE 32565 (table of contents relating to entertaining expenses covering references SE 32565–32650a).

SE 36580 (use of machinery or plant for business entertaining does not qualify for capital allowances).

SE 60046 (Ministers of religion: provision of reasonable entertainment on official occasions to visiting ministers, officers of the church or members of church organizations allowable, the provisions of this section do not normally apply because ministers do not normally hold office under a body carrying on a trade, profession or vocation).

Revenue & other press releases—IR Tax Bulletin August 1999 p 679 (Article to remove the confusion regarding the effect of this section on claims by employees to a deduction for the expenses of business entertaining).

Definitions—"The 1990 Act", s 831(3); "body of persons", s 832(1); "capital allowances", s 832(1); "company", s 832(1), (2); "emoluments", s 131(1); "inspector", s 832(1); "Schedule A", s 15(1); "Schedule D", s 18(1); "Schedule E", s 19(1); "the Tax Acts", s 831(1); "trade", s 832(1); "United Kingdom", s 830(1).

Amendments—[1] Sub-ss (2), (4), (6) repealed by FA 1988 s 72 and Sch 14 Pt IV in relation to entertainment provided after 14 March 1988 unless provided under a contract entered into before 15 March 1988.

[2] Words "Schedule A or" in sub-ss (1), (9) repealed by FA 1998 s 165, Sch 27 Part III(4) with effect for 1998–99 and subsequent years of assessment for income tax purposes, and from 1 April 1998 for corporation tax, subject to the transitional provisions in FA 1998 Sch 5 Part IV.
[3] Word in sub-ss (1), (9) substituted by FA 1998 Sch 7 para 1 with effect from 31 July 1998.
[4] Word "and" in sub-s (1)(a) added, words in sub-s (1)(b), (7)(a), and (10) repealed, sub-ss (1)(c) repealed, by CAA 2001 ss 578, 580, Sch 2 para 51, Sch 4 with effect for income tax purposes, as respects allowances and charges falling to be made for chargeable periods ending after 5 April 2001, and for corporation tax purposes, as respects allowances and charges falling to be made for chargeable periods ending after 31 March 2001.
[5] Words in sub-s (8)(b) substituted, and sub-s (8A) inserted, by FA 2001 s 73 with effect from the year 2001–02 or, in the case of companies, for accounting periods beginning after 31 March 2001.

[577A Expenditure involving crime

(1) In computing [profits][4] chargeable to tax under ...[5] Schedule D, no deduction shall be made for any expenditure incurred

[(a)][6] in making a payment the making of which constitutes the commission of a criminal offence [or

(b) in making a payment outside the United Kingdom where the making of a corresponding payment in any part of the United Kingdom would constitute a criminal offence there.][6]

[(1A) In computing [profits][4] chargeable to tax under ...[5] Schedule D, no deduction shall be made for any expenditure incurred in making a payment induced by a demand constituting—

(a) the commission in England or Wales of the offence of blackmail under section 21 of the Theft Act 1968
(b) the commission in Northern Ireland of the offence of blackmail under section 20 of the Theft Act (Northern Ireland) 1969, or
(c) the commission in Scotland of the offence of extortion.][2]

(2) [Any expenditure mentioned in subsection (1) or (1A) above][3] shall not be included in computing any expenses of management in respect of which relief may be given under the Tax Acts.][1]

Commentary—*Simon's Direct Tax Service* **A4.301A; B3.1202; D4.408.**
Amendments—[1] This section inserted by FA 1993 s 123 in relation to expenditure incurred after 10 June 1993.
[2] Sub-s (1A) inserted by FA 1994 s 141 in relation to expenditure incurred after 29 November 1993.
[3] Words in sub-s (2) substituted by FA 1994 s 141 in relation to expenditure incurred after 29 November 1993.
[4] Word in sub-ss (1), (1A) substituted by FA 1998 Sch 7 para 1 with effect from 31 July 1998.
[5] Words "Schedule A or" in sub-ss (1), (1A) repealed by FA 1998 s 165, Sch 27 Part III(4) with effect for 1998–99 and subsequent years of assessment for income tax purposes, and from 1 April 1998 for corporation tax, subject to the transitional provisions in FA 1998 Sch 5 Part IV.
[6] Words inserted by FA 2002 s 68 with effect for expenditure incurred after 31 March 2002.

578 Housing grants

(1) Where, under any enactment relating to the giving of financial assistance for the provision, maintenance or improvement of housing accommodation or other residential accommodation, a payment is made to a person by way of grant or other contribution towards expenses incurred, or to be incurred, by that or any other person, the payment shall not be treated as a receipt in computing income for any tax purpose.

(2) Subsection (1) above shall not apply to a payment in so far as it is made in respect of an expense giving rise to a deduction in computing income for any tax purpose.

Commentary—*Simon's Direct Tax Service* **D4.640.**

[578A Expenditure on car hire

(1) This section provides for a reduction in the amounts—

(a) allowable as deductions in computing profits chargeable to tax under Case I or II of Schedule D, [or][2]
(b) which can be included as expenses of management of an investment company (as defined by section 130), ...[2]
(c) ...[2]

for expenditure on the hiring of a car to which this section applies.

(2) This section applies to the hiring of a car—

(a) which is not a qualifying hire car, and
(b) the retail price of which when new exceeds £12,000.
"Car" and "qualifying hire car" are defined by section 578B.

[(2A) This section does not apply to the hiring of a car, other than a motorcycle, if—

(a) it is an electrically-propelled car, or
(b) it is a car with low CO_2 emissions.][3]

[(2B) In subsection (2A) above—

"car" has the meaning given by section 578B;
"car with low CO_2 emissions" has the meaning given by section 45D of the Capital Allowances Act 2001 (c 2) (expenditure on cars with low CO_2 emissions to be first-year qualifying expenditure);

"electrically-propelled car" has the meaning given by that section.][3]

(3) The amount which would, apart from this section, be allowable or capable of being included must be reduced by multiplying it by the fraction—

$$\frac{£12,000 + P}{2P}$$

where P is the retail price of the car when new.

(4) If an amount has been reduced under subsection (3) and subsequently—

(a) there is a rebate (however described) of the rentals, or

(b) there occurs in connection with the rentals a transaction that falls within section 94 (debts deducted and subsequently released),

the amount otherwise taxable in respect of the rebate or transaction must be reduced by multiplying it by the fraction in subsection (3) above.][1]

Modifications—Sub-ss (2), (3) modified by CAA 2001 Sch 3 para 113(1) so as to substitute "£8,000" for "£12,000" in relation to expenditure incurred under a contract entered into before 11 March 1992.
Sub-s (4) disapplied by CAA 2001 Sch 3 para 113(2) in relation to rebates made or transactions occurring before 29 April 1996.
Amendments—[1] This section inserted by CAA 2001 s 578, Sch 2 para 52 with effect for income tax purposes, as respects allowances and charges falling to be made for chargeable periods ending after 5 April 2001, and for corporation tax purposes, as respects allowances and charges falling to be made for chargeable periods ending after 31 March 2001.
[2] In sub-s (1), word inserted and repealed, and para (c) repealed by FA 2001 s 57(3), (4), Sch 12 Pt II para 11 with effect from the year 2002–03.
[3] Sub-ss (2A), (2B) inserted by FA 2002 s 60 with effect for expenditure—
(a) incurred after 16 April 2002 on the hiring of a car which is first registered after that date, and
(b) incurred on the hiring of a car, for a period of hire which begins before 1 April 2008, under a contract entered into before 1 April 2008.

[578B Expenditure on car hire: supplementary

(1) In section 578A "car" means a mechanically propelled road vehicle other than one—

(a) of a construction primarily suited for the conveyance of goods or burden of any description, or

(b) of a type not commonly used as a private vehicle and unsuitable for such use.

References to a car accordingly include a motor cycle.

(2) For the purposes of section 578A, a car is a qualifying hire car if—

(a) it is hired under a hire-purchase agreement (within the meaning of section 784(6)) under which there is an option to purchase exercisable on the payment of a sum equal to not more than 1 per cent. of the retail price of the car when new, or

(b) it is a qualifying hire car for the purposes of Part 2 of the Capital Allowances Act (under section 82 of that Act).

(3) In section 578A and this section "new" means unused and not second-hand.

(4) The power under section 74(4) of the Capital Allowances Act to increase or further increase the sums of money specified in Chapter 8 of Part 2 of that Act includes the power to increase or further increase the sum of money specified in section 578A(2)(b) or (3).][1]

Amendments—[1] This section inserted by CAA 2001 s 578, Sch 2 para 52 with effect for income tax purposes, as respects allowances and charges falling to be made for chargeable periods ending after 5 April 2001, and for corporation tax purposes, as respects allowances and charges falling to be made for chargeable periods ending after 31 March 2001.

579 Statutory redundancy payments

(1) Any redundancy payment, and the corresponding amount of any other employer's payment, shall be exempt from income tax under Schedule E.

(2) Where a redundancy payment or other employer's payment is made in respect of employment wholly in a trade, profession or vocation carried on by the employer, and within the charge to tax, the amount of the redundancy payment or the corresponding amount of the other employer's payment shall (if not otherwise so allowable) be allowable as a deduction in computing for the purposes of Schedule D the [profits][3] or losses of the trade, profession or vocation, but—

(a) ...[1]; and

(b) if the employer's payment was made after the discontinuance of the trade, profession or vocation the ...[1] amount so deductible shall be treated as if it were a payment made on the last day on which the trade, profession or vocation was carried on.

(3) Where a redundancy payment or other employer's payment is made in respect of employment wholly in a business carried on by the employer and expenses of management of the business are eligible for relief under section 75 or 76—

(a) the amount [of the redundancy payment, or the corresponding amount of the other employer's payment][1] shall (if not otherwise so allowable) be allowable as expenses of management eligible for relief under that section, and

(b) if the employer's payment was made after the discontinuance of the business the ...[1] amount so allowable shall be treated as if it were expenses of management incurred on the last day on which the business was carried on.

(4) ...[4]

(5) Relief shall not be given under subsections [(2) and (3)][4] above, or otherwise, more than once in respect of any employer's payment, and if the employee was being employed in such a way that different parts of his remuneration fell for tax purposes to be treated in different ways—

(a) the amount [of the redundancy payment or the corresponding amount of the other employer's payment][1] shall be apportioned to the different capacities in which the employee was employed; and

(b) subsections [(2) and (3)][4] above shall apply separately to the employment in those capacities, and by reference to the apportioned part of that amount, instead of by reference to the full amount of the employer's payment ...[1]

(6) Where the Minister pays a sum under [section 166 of the Employment Rights Act 1996][1] or [Article 201 of the Employment Rights (Northern Ireland) Order 1996][2] in respect of an employer's payment this section shall apply as if—

(a) that sum had been paid on account of that redundancy or other employer's payment, and
(b) so far as the employer has reimbursed the Minister, it had been so paid by the employer.

Commentary—*Simon's Direct Tax Service* B3.1477, E4.805B.
Statement of Practice SP 1/94—Extension of the exemption under this section to non-statutory redundancy payments, provided they are genuinely made to compensate for loss of employment through redundancy. Employers may submit proposed schemes to their inspector for advance clearance.
Revenue Interpretation RI 103—Timing of deductions for redundancy payments.
Revenue Internal Guidance—Schedule E manual SE 13760 (termination payments and benefits: statutory redundancy payments).
Simon's Tax Cases—s 579(1)(2)(4), *Vestey v IRC* [1977] STC 414*.
Definitions—"Corresponding amount", s 580; "employer's payment", s 580; "Minister", s 580; "rebate", s 580; "redundancy payment", s 580; "Schedule D", s 18(1); "Schedule E", s 19(1).
Cross references—See TA 1988 s 90 (references to redundancy payment and to the corresponding amount of an employer's payment shall be construed for the purposes of additional redundancy payments in accordance with references in this section and in s 580).
TA 1988 s 580 (supplementary provisions).
Amendments—[1] Words in sub-ss (3)(a), (4)(a), (5)(a), (6) substituted and words omitted in sub-ss (2)(b), (3)(b), (5)(b) repealed by the Employment Rights Act 1996 s 243, Sch 1 para 35(1), (2), Sch 3 with effect from 22 August 1996.
[2] Words in sub-s (6) substituted by the Employment Rights (Northern Ireland) Order, SI 1996/1919 Sch 1.
[3] Word in sub-s (2) substituted by FA 1998 Sch 7 para 1 with effect from 31 July 1998.
[4] Sub-s (4) repealed, and words in sub-s (5) substituted, by FA 1998 Sch 5 para 43 with effect for 1998–99 and subsequent years of assessment for income tax purposes, and from 1 April 1998 for corporation tax, subject to the transitional provisions in FA 1998 Sch 5 Part IV.

580 Provisions supplementary to section 579

(1) In section 579—

(a) "redundancy payment", [and "employer's payment"][1] have the same meaning as in Part XI of the Employment Rights Act 1996][1] or [part XII of the Employment Rights (Northern Ireland) Order 1996][2]
(b) references to the corresponding amount of an employer's payment (other than a redundancy payment) are references to the amount of that employer's payment so far as not in excess of the amount [which would have been payable as a redundancy payment had one been payable;][1]
(c) "the Minister" in relation to [the Employment Rights Act 1996][1] means the Secretary of State and in relation to [the Employment Rights (Northern Ireland) Order 1996][2] means the Department of Health and Social Services.

(2) ...[1]

(3) In section 579(1) the reference to tax under Schedule E does not include a reference to tax under section 148 and accordingly payments exempted by section 579(1) may be taken into account under section 148.

Commentary—*Simon's Direct Tax Service* B3.1477, E4.805B.
Statement of Practice SP 1/94—Extension of the exemption under this section to non-statutory redundancy payments, provided they are genuinely made to for loss of employment through redundancy. Employers may submit proposed schemes to their inspector for advance clearance.
Revenue Internal Guidance—Schedule E manual, SE 13760 (termination payments and benefits: statutory redundancy payments)
SE 13800 (meaning of "redundancy").
SE 13802 (redundancy: application of statutory definition, involves a reduction in need for employees in the business).
SE 13825 (redundancy: site agreements for short-service employees).
SE 68228 (sub-postmasters are not entitled to statutory redundancy payments but their contracts provide for similar payments to be made to them, should in practice be treated as statutory redundancy payments and charged only under s 148).
Definition—"Schedule E", s 19(1).
Amendments—[1] Words in sub-s (1)(a)–(c) substituted and sub-s (2) repealed by the Employment Rights Act 1996 243, Sch 1 para 35(1), (3), Sch 3 with effect from 22 August 1996.
[2] Words in sub-s (1)(a), (c) substituted by the Employment Rights (Northern Ireland) Order SI 1996/1919 Sch 1.

[580A Relief from tax on annual payments under certain insurance policies

(1) This section applies (subject to subsection (7)(b) below) in the case of any such annual payment under an insurance policy as—

(a) apart from this section, would be brought into charge under Case III of Schedule D; or (*b*) is equivalent to a description of payment brought into charge under Case III of that Schedule but (apart from this section) would be brought into charge under Case V of that Schedule.

(2) Subject to the following provisions of this section, the annual payment shall be exempt from income tax if—

(*a*) it constitutes a benefit provided under so much of an insurance policy as provides insurance against a qualifying risk;

(*b*) the provisions of the policy by which insurance is provided against that risk are self-contained (within the meaning of section 580B);

(*c*) the only annual payments relating to that risk for which provision is made by that policy are payments in respect of a period throughout which the relevant conditions of payment are satisfied; and

(*d*) at all times while the policy has contained provisions relating to that risk, those provisions have been of a qualifying type.

(3) For the purposes of this section and section 580B a qualifying risk is any risk falling within either of the following descriptions, that is to say—

(*a*) a risk that the insured will (or will in any specified way) become subject to, or to any deterioration in a condition resulting from, any physical or mental illness, disability, infirmity or defect;

(*b*) a risk that circumstances will arise as a result of which the insured will cease to be employed or will cease to carry on any trade, profession or vocation carried on by him.

(4) For the purposes of this section the relevant conditions of payment are satisfied in relation to payments under an insurance policy for so long as any of the following continues, that is to say—

(*a*) an illness, disability, infirmity or defect which is insured against by the relevant part of the policy, and any related period of convalescence or rehabilitation;

(*b*) any period during which the insured is, in circumstances insured against by the relevant part of the policy, either unemployed or not carrying on a trade, profession or vocation;

(*c*) any period during which the income of the insured (apart from any benefits under the policy) is less, in circumstances so insured against, than it would have been if those circumstances had not arisen; or

(*d*) any period immediately following the end, as a result of the death of the insured, of any period falling within any of paragraphs (*a*) to (*c*) above;

and in this subsection "the relevant part of the policy" means so much of it as relates to insurance against one or more risks mentioned in subsection (3) above.

(5) For the purposes of subsection (2)(*d*) above provisions relating to a qualifying risk are of a qualifying type if they are of such a description that their inclusion in any policy of insurance containing provisions relating only to a comparable risk would (apart from any reinsurance) involve the possibility for the insurer that a significant loss might be sustained on the amounts payable by way of premiums in respect of the risk, taken together with any return on the investment of those amounts.

(6) An annual payment shall not be exempt from income tax under this section if it is paid in accordance with a contract the whole or any part of any premiums under which have qualified for relief for the purposes of income tax by being deductible either—

(*a*) in the computation of the insured's income from any source; or

(*b*) from the insured's income.

(7) Where a person takes out any insurance policy wholly or partly for the benefit of another and that other person pays or contributes to the payment of the premiums under that policy, then to the extent only that the benefits under the policy are attributable, on a just and reasonable apportionment, to the payments or contributions made by that other person—

(*a*) that other person shall be treated for the purposes of this section and section 580B as the insured in relation to that policy;

(*b*) this section shall have effect in relation to those benefits, so far as comprised in payments to that other person or his spouse, as if the reference in subsection (1)(*a*) above to Case III of Schedule D included a reference to Schedule E; and

(*c*) subsection (6) above shall have effect as if the references to the premiums under the policy were references only to the payments or contributions made by that other person in respect of the premiums.

(8) Where—

(*a*) payments are made to or in respect of any person ("the beneficiary") under any insurance policy ("the individual policy"),

(*b*) the rights under the individual policy in accordance with which the payments are made superseded, with effect from the time when another policy ("the employer's policy") ceased to apply to that person, any rights conferred under that other policy,

(*c*) the employer's policy is or was a policy entered into wholly or partly for the benefit of persons holding office or employment under any person ("the employer") against risks falling within subsection (3)(*a*) above,

(d) the individual policy is one entered into in pursuance of, or in accordance with, any provisions contained in the employer's policy, and

(e) the beneficiary has ceased to hold office or employment under the employer as a consequence of the occurrence of anything insured against by so much of the employer's policy as related to risks falling within subsection (3)(a) above,

this section shall have effect as if the employer's policy and the individual policy were one policy.

(9) In the preceding provisions of this section references to the insured, in relation to any insurance policy, include references to—

(a) the insured's spouse; and

(b) in the case of a policy entered into wholly or partly for purposes connected with the meeting of liabilities arising from an actual or proposed transaction identified in the policy, any person on whom any of those liabilities will fall jointly with the insured or his spouse.

(10) References in this section and section 580B to insurance against a risk include references to any insurance for the provision (otherwise than by way of indemnity) of any benefits against that risk, and references to what is insured against by a policy shall be construed accordingly.]¹

Commentary—*Simon's Direct Tax Service* **B5.301.**
Revenue Interpretation RI 154—Benefits received under locum and fixed costs insurance policies fall within sub-s (6) and are thus *not* within the exemption.
Revenue & other press releases—Hansard 22-2-96 (sub-s (5) applies so as to exclude from exemption any investment or savings policies; the exemption is limited to real risk policies).
IR Booklet IR 153 (tax exemption for sickness or unemployment insurance payments).
IR Tax Bulletin December 1996 p 377 (explains circumstances in which insurance benefits may be paid without deduction of tax).
Revenue Internal Guidance—Schedule E manual, SE 06420 (sick pay and injury payments—sick pay funded by employees, application of this section).
SE 06460 (sick pay and injury payments—sick pay funded partly by the employer and partly by employees—examples).
Definitions—"Schedule D", s 18; "Schedule E", s 19; "trade", s 832(1).
Amendments—¹ Section inserted by FA 1996 s 143(1), (2) with effect from the year 1996–97 in relation to any payment which under the policy in question falls to be paid at any time after 5 April 1996. As to commencement for payments relating to earlier years of assessment, see further commencement provision in FA 1996 s 143(2)–(5).

[580B Meaning of "self-contained" for the purposes of s 580A

(1) For the purposes of section 580A the provisions of an insurance policy by which insurance is provided against a qualifying risk are self-contained unless subsection (2) or (3) below applies to the provisions of that policy so far as they relate to that risk; but, in determining whether either of those subsections so applies, regard shall be had to all the persons for whose benefit insurance is provided by that policy against that risk.

(2) This subsection applies to the provisions of an insurance policy so far as they relate to a qualifying risk if—

(a) that insurance policy contains provision for the payment of benefits other than those relating to that risk;

(b) the terms of the policy so far as they relate to that risk, or the manner in which effect is given to those terms, would have been significantly different if the only benefits under the policy had been those relating to that risk; and

(c) that difference is not one relating exclusively to the fact that the amount of benefits receivable by or in respect of any person under the policy is applied for reducing the amount of other benefits payable to or in respect of that person under the policy.

(3) This subsection applies to the provisions of an insurance policy ("the relevant policy") so far as they relate to a qualifying risk if—

(a) the insured under that policy is, or has been, the insured under one or more other policies;

(b) that other policy, or each of those other policies, is in force or has been in force at a time when the relevant policy was in force or at the time immediately before the relevant policy was entered into;

(c) the terms of the relevant policy so far as relating to that risk, or the manner in which effect is given to those terms, would have been significantly different if the other policy or policies had not been entered into; and

(d) that difference is not one relating exclusively to the fact that the amount of benefits receivable by or in respect of any person under the other policy, or any of the other policies, is applied for reducing the amount of benefits payable to or in respect of that person under the relevant policy.

(4) In subsections (2)(b) and (3)(c) above the references to the terms of a policy so far as they relate to a risk include references to the terms fixing any amount payable by way of premium or otherwise in respect of insurance against that risk.]¹

Commentary—*Simon's Direct Tax Service* **B5.301.**
Revenue & other press releases—Hansard 22-2-96 (sub-s (2)(b) the "significantly different" criterion applies to prevent the shifting of benefits between policies; sub-s (1) "self-contained" criterion prevents the shifting of benefit from investment-type policies to exempt policies).
Amendments—¹ Section inserted by FA 1996 s 143(1), (2) effect from the year 1996–97 in relation to any payment which under the policy in question falls to be paid at any time after 5 April 1996. As to commencement for payments relating to earlier years of assessment, see further commencement provision in FA 1996 s 143(2)–(5).

581 Borrowing in foreign currency by local authorities and statutory corporations

(1) If the Treasury direct that this section shall apply to any securities issued by a local authority and expressed in a currency other than sterling, interest on those securities—

(*a*) shall be paid without deduction of income tax, and

(*b*) so long as the beneficial owner is not resident in the United Kingdom, shall be exempt from income tax (but not corporation tax).

(2) Where for repayment of the principal amount due under the securities there is an option between sterling and one or more currencies other than sterling, that subsection shall be applicable to the securities if the option is exercisable only by the holder of the securities, and shall not be applicable to the securities in any other case.

(3) Where any income of any person is by virtue of any provision of the Income Tax Acts to be deemed to be income of any other person, that income shall not be exempt from tax by virtue of this section by reason of the first-mentioned person not being resident in the United Kingdom.

(4) This section shall have effect in relation to any securities issued by or loan made to a statutory corporation as it has effect in relation to any securities issued by a local authority, the references to the beneficial owner or holder of the securities being for this purpose read, in the case of such a loan, as references to the person for the time being entitled to repayment or eventual repayment of the loan.

(5) In subsection (4) above "statutory corporation" means—

(*a*) a corporation incorporated by an Act; or

(*b*) any other corporation, being a corporation to which functions in respect of the carrying on of an undertaking are entrusted by an Act or by an order made under or confirmed by an Act;

but, save as is provided by paragraph (*b*) above, does not include any company within the meaning of the Companies Act 1985 or the Companies (Northern Ireland) Order 1986.

(6) In relation to securities issued before 6th April 1982 subsections (1) and (2) above shall have effect with the substitution for references to sterling of references to a currency of a country which at the time of the issue was specified in Schedule 1 to the Exchange Control Act 1947.

Commentary—*Simon's Direct Tax Service* **B5.217, 218.**
Definitions—"Company", s 832(1), (2); "income tax", s 832(4); "the Income Tax Acts", s 831(1)(*b*); "local authority", s 519, by virtue of s 832(1).
Cross references—See Water Act 1989 s 95(11) (transfer of functions of water authorities to successor companies: the vesting in a successor company of any liability for a loan made to a water authority does not affect any direction made, or treated as made, under this section in respect of the loan).
Electricity Act 1989 s 90, Sch 11 para 10 (transfer of functions of Electricity Boards to successor companies: the vesting in a successor company of any liability for a loan made to an Electricity Board or the Electricity Council does not affect any direction made, or treated as made, under this section in respect of the loan).
FA 1994 Sch 24 para 26 (the vesting in a successor company of liability for a loan made to the British Railways Board, shall not affect a direction given by the Treasury under this section).

582 Funding bonds issued in respect of interest on certain debts

(1) Where any funding bonds are issued to a creditor in respect of any liability to pay interest on any debts to which this section applies—

(*a*) the issue of the bonds shall be treated for all the purposes of the Tax Acts as if it were the payment of an amount of that interest equal to the value of the bonds at the time of their issue, and

(*b*) the redemption of the bonds shall not be treated for those purposes as the payment of any amount of that interest.

(2) Where an issue of bonds is treated by virtue of subsection (1) above as if it were the payment of an amount of interest, and any person by or through whom the bonds are issued would be required by virtue of any provision of the Tax Acts to deduct income tax from that amount of interest if it had been actually paid by or through him, the following provisions shall have effect—

(*a*) subject to paragraph (*b*) below, any such person—

(i) shall retain bonds the value of which at the time of their issue is equal to income tax on that amount of interest at the [applicable][1] rate for the year of assessment in which the bonds are issued, and

(ii) shall be acquitted in respect of any such retention in the same way as if he had deducted such tax from the interest, and

(iii) shall be chargeable with that tax accordingly, but may tender the bonds retained in satisfaction thereof;

(*b*) where ...[2] it is impracticable to retain bonds on account of income tax under paragraph (*a*) above—

[(i) any such person shall be relieved from the obligation to retain bonds and account for income tax under that paragraph, on his furnishing to the Board][2] statement of the names and addresses of the persons to whom the bonds have been issued and the amount of the bonds issued to each such person; and

(ii) tax in respect of the amount of interest treated by virtue of this section as having been paid by the issue of the bonds shall be charged under Case VI of Schedule D for the chargeable period in which the bonds are issued on the persons receiving or entitled to the bonds.

[(2A) In subsection (2) above "the applicable rate", in relation to a year of assessment, means whichever of the basic rate and the lower rate for that year is the rate at which the person by or through whom the bonds are issued would have had to deduct income tax from the amount of interest in question if that amount had been actually paid by or through him.][1]

(3) This section applies to any debt incurred, whether in respect of any money borrowed or otherwise, by any government, public authority or public institution whatsoever, or by any body corporate whatsoever.

[(3A) Chapter 2 of Part 4 of the Finance Act 1996 has effect subject to and in accordance with this section, notwithstanding anything in section 80(5) of that Act (matters to be brought into account in the case of loan relationships only under Chapter 2 of Part 4 of that Act).][3]

(4) For the purposes of this section "funding bonds" includes any bonds, stocks, shares, securities or certificates of indebtedness.

Commentary—*Simon's Direct Tax Service* A3.425, A6.109.
Definitions—"Basic rate", s 832(1); "the Board", s 832(1); "chargeable period", s 832(1); "interest", s 832(1); "lower rate", s 832(1); "Schedule D", s 18(1); "the Tax Acts", s 831(2); "year of assessment", s 832(1).
Amendments—[1] Word in sub-s (2)(*a*)(i) substituted, and sub-s (2A) inserted, by FA 1996 Sch 6 paras 14, 32 with effect from the year 1996–97.
[2] Words omitted from sub-s (2)(*b*) repealed and words in sub-s (2)(*b*)(i) substituted by FA 1996 s 134, Sch 20 para 32, Sch 41 Pt V(10) with effect from the year 1996–97.
[3] Sub-s (3A) inserted by FA 2002 s 82, Sch 25 paras 43, 50 with effect for accounting periods beginning after 30 September 2002.

[582A Designated international organisations: miscellaneous exemptions

(1) The Treasury may by order designate for the purposes of any one or more of subsections [(2) and (4) to (6) below ...[4]][3] any international organisation of which the United Kingdom is a member; and in those subsections "designated" means designated under this subsection.

(2) Section 43 shall not apply in the case of payment made by an organisation designated for the purposes of this subsection.

(3) ...[2]

(4) Section 349 (1) shall not apply in the case of a payment of an amount payable by an organisation designated for the purposes of this subsection.

(5) Section 349 (2) shall not apply in the case of interest payable by—

    (*a*) an organisation designated for the purposes of this subsection, or
    (*b*) a partnership of which such an organisation is a member.

(6) An organisation designated for the purposes of this subsection shall not be a person to whom section 560(2) applies.][1]

Commentary—*Simon's Direct Tax Service* D4.339.
Regulations—The International Organisations (Miscellaneous Exemptions) Order 1997, SI 1997/168.
Definition—"United Kingdom", s 830(1).
Amendments—[1] This section inserted by FA 1991 s 118(1).
[2] Sub-s (3) repealed by FA 1996 Sch 7 paras 22, 32, Sch 41 Pt V(2) with effect from the year 1996–97 as respects income tax, and for the purposes of corporation tax for accounting periods ending after 31 March 1996.
[3] Words in sub-s (1) substituted by FA 1996 Sch 29 para 6.
[4] Words in sub-s (1) repealed by FA 2000 s 156, Sch 40 Pt II(17) with effect for relevant payments or receipts in relation to which the chargeable date for the purposes of Pt IV, Ch VIIA is after 31 March 2001.

583 Inter-American Development Bank

A person not resident in the United Kingdom shall not be liable to income tax in respect of income from any security issued by the Inter-American Development Bank if he would not be liable but for the fact that—

    (*a*) the security or income is issued, made payable or paid in the United Kingdom or in sterling; or
    (*b*) the Bank maintains an office or other place of business in the United Kingdom.

Commentary—*Simon's Direct Tax Service* D4.921.
Definition—"United Kingdom", s 830(1).

584 Relief for unremittable overseas income

(1) Where a person is chargeable to tax by reference to the amount of any income arising in a territory outside the United Kingdom ("overseas income"), then for the purposes of tax this section shall apply to the overseas income in so far as—

    (*a*) he is prevented from transferring the amount of the overseas income to the United Kingdom, either by the laws of that territory or any executive action of its government or by the impossibility of obtaining foreign currency in that territory; and
    (*b*) he has not realised the overseas income outside that territory for a consideration in sterling or a consideration in some other currency which he is not prevented from transferring to the United Kingdom.

Overseas income to which this section applies is referred to below as unremittable.

[(2) Subject to subsection (2A) below, where a person so chargeable makes a claim under this subsection in relation to any overseas income—

    (*a*) which is unremittable; and

    (*b*) to which subsection (1)(*a*) above will continue to apply notwithstanding any reasonable endeavours on his part,

then, in the first instance, account shall not be taken of that income, and tax shall be assessed, or, in the case of corporation tax, assessable, and shall be charged on all persons concerned and for all periods accordingly.][1]

(2A) If on any date paragraph (*a*) or (*b*) of subsection (2) above ceases to apply to any part of any overseas income in relation to which a claim has been made under that subsection—

    (*a*) that part of the income shall be treated as income arising on that date, and

    (*b*) account shall be taken of it, and of any tax payable in respect of it under the law of the territory where it arises, according to their value at that date.][1]

(4) Where [a person becomes chargeable to income tax or corporation tax in respect of income from any source by virtue of subsection (2) or (2A)][2] above after it has ceased to possess that source of income, the income shall be chargeable under Case VI of Schedule D.

(5) Where under an agreement entered into under arrangements made by the Secretary of State in pursuance of section 11 of the Export Guarantees and Overseas Investment Act 1978 any payment is made by the Export Credit Guarantee Department in respect of any income which cannot be transferred to the United Kingdom, then, to the extent of the payment, the income shall be treated as income [to which paragraphs (*a*) and (*b*) of subsection (2) above do not apply (and accordingly cannot cease to apply)].[2]

[(6) A claim under subsection (2) above—

    (*a*) for the purposes of income tax, shall be made on or before the first anniversary of the 31st January next following the year of assessment in which the income arises;

    (*b*) for the purposes of corporation tax, shall be made no later than two years after the end of the accounting period in which the income arises.][3]

(7) In the case of the death of a person who, if he had not died, would, under subsection (2) [or (2A)][2] above, have become chargeable to any income tax, the tax which would have been so chargeable shall be assessed and charged upon his executors or administrators, and shall be a debt due from and payable out of his estate.

(8) Subject to subsections (2) and [(2A)][2] above, the amount of any unremittable overseas income shall be determined by reference to the generally recognised market value in the United Kingdom (if any), or, in the absence of any such value, according to the official rate of exchange of the territory where the income arises.

(9) Any appeal against an assessment which involves a question as to the operation of this section shall be made to the Special Commissioners and not to the General Commissioners.

(10) This section shall have effect as respects any accounting period in which the conditions in subsection (2) above cease to be satisfied in relation to any income, being an accounting period ending on or before such day, not being earlier than 31st March 1992, as the Treasury may by order appoint for the purposes of this section, with the omission of subsections (3) and (4).

Commentary—*Simon's Direct Tax Service* **E1.326.**
Order—Corporation Tax Acts (Provisions for Payment of Tax and Returns) (Appointed Days) Order, SI 1992/3066 art 2(1), (2)(*b*) appoints 30 September 1993 for the purposes of this section by virtue of sub-s (10) above.
Concession B38—Tax concession on overseas debts: relief for trade receipts and trade debts the proceeds of which cannot be remitted to the UK.
Revenue Internal Guidance—Double taxation relief manual DT 920 (when payment is received from ECGD, the appropriate tax credit may be given for the income becoming assessable).
Inspector's manual IM 4152 (relief is withdrawn to the extent that the income is covered by ECGD payments).
Schedule E manual SE 40105 (emoluments that cannot be remitted to the United Kingdom: relief may be due under this section).
Definitions—"Accounting period", s 834(1); "company", s 832(1), (2); "notice", s 832(1); "Schedule D", s 18(1); "tax", s 832(3); "United Kingdom", s 830(1).
Cross references—See TA 1988 Sch 24 para 12 (certain assumptions to apply for the application of this section to the income of controlled foreign companies).
Amendments—[1] Sub-ss (2), (2A) substituted for sub-ss (2), (3) by FA 1996 s 134, Sch 20 para 33(2) with effect in relation to income tax from the year 1996–97 and, for the purposes of corporation tax, as respects accounting periods ending after 30 June 1999 (by virtue of Finance Act 1994, Section 199, (Appointed Day) Order, SI 1998/3173 art 2).
[2] Words in sub-ss (4), (5) substituted, words in sub-s (7) inserted and figure in sub-s (8) substituted by FA 1996 s 134, Sch 20 para 33(3), (4), (6), (7) respectively, with effect in relation to income tax from the year 1996–97 and, for the purposes of corporation tax, as respects accounting periods ending after 30 June 1999 (by virtue of Finance Act 1994, Section 199, (Appointed Day) Order, SI 1998/3173 art 2).
[3] Sub-s (6) substituted by FA 1996 s 134, Sch 20 para 33(5) with effect in relation to income tax from the year 1996–97 and, for the purposes of corporation tax, as respects accounting periods ending after 30 June 1999 (by virtue of SI 1998/3173 art 2).

585 Relief from tax on delayed remittances

(1) A person charged or chargeable for any year of assessment in respect of income from any source with tax which (apart from this section) falls to be computed under Case IV or V of Schedule D, or under Case III of Schedule E, on the amount of income received in the United Kingdom in the basis year for that year of assessment, may[, if the relevant conditions are satisfied, by making a claim

require that the following provisions of this section shall apply; and for this purpose the relevant conditions are—]¹

(*a*) that of the income so received all or part arose before the basis year but he was unable to transfer it to the United Kingdom before that year; and

(*b*) subject to subsection (2) below, that that inability was due to the laws of the territory where the income arose, or to executive action of its government, or to the impossibility of obtaining foreign currency in that territory; and

(*c*) that the inability was not due to any want of reasonable endeavours on his part.

(2) For the purposes of this section, where in any year of assessment a person is granted a pension or increase of pension retrospectively, the amount paid in respect of any previous year of assessment by virtue of the grant shall be treated as income arising in that previous year, whenever it is paid, and he shall be treated as having possessed the source of income from the time as from which the grant has effect; and subsection (1)(*b*) above shall not apply in relation to any amount so paid, except as respects the period after it becomes payable.

(3) Where a person claims that the provisions of this section shall apply for any year of assessment as respects the income from any source, then for the purposes of income tax—

(*a*) there shall be deducted from the income received in the United Kingdom in the basis year for that year the amount as respects which the conditions in paragraphs (*a*), (*b*) and (*c*) of subsection (1) above are satisfied, so far as applicable; but

(*b*) the part (if any) of that amount arising in each previous year of assessment shall be treated as if it were income received in the United Kingdom in the basis year for that previous year.

(4) Nothing in this section shall alter the year which is to be taken as the basis year for computing tax chargeable for any year of assessment under Case IV or V of Schedule D, and where under subsection (3)(*b*) above income is treated as received in the United Kingdom in a year which is the basis year for two years of assessment, it shall not by reason thereof be taken into account except in the year in which it arose.

(5) Where—

(*a*) a person makes a claim under this section for any year of assessment as respects income from any source chargeable under Case IV or V of Schedule D, and

(*b*) that year is the basis year for computing the tax with which he is chargeable on the income from that source both for that and for the succeeding year of assessment,

tax shall not be chargeable for either of those years of assessment on the amount referred to in paragraph (*a*) of subsection (3) above (without however being charged a second time by virtue of paragraph (*b*) of that subsection).

(6) No claim under this section shall be made in respect of any income [after the fifth anniversary of the 31st January next following]² the year of assessment in which the income is received in the United Kingdom.

(7) There shall be made all such adjustments, whether by way of repayment of tax, assessment or otherwise, as may be necessary to give effect to this section, and notwithstanding anything in the Income Tax Acts, any adjustment to give effect to a claim under this section may be made at any time.

(8) A person's executors or administrators may make any claim under this section which he might have made, if he had not died, and after a person's death—

(*a*) any tax paid by him and repayable by virtue of a claim under this section (whoever made the claim) shall be repaid to his executors or administrators; and

(*b*) any additional tax chargeable by virtue of such a claim shall be assessed and charged upon his executors or administrators and shall be a debt due from and payable out of his estate.

(9) In this section "basis year" means—

(*a*) in relation to tax chargeable for any year of assessment under Case IV or V of Schedule D in respect of income from any source, the year by reference to which the amount of the income chargeable finally falls to be computed; and

(*b*) in relation to tax chargeable for any year of assessment under Case III of Schedule E, that year of assessment;

and any reference in this section to a source of income includes a part of a source.

Commentary—*Simon's Direct Tax Service* E1.326, E4.723.
Revenue Internal Guidance—Inspector's manual IM 4153-4155 (explanation of this section).
Schedule E manual SE 40323 (Schedule E Case III: delayed remittances can be spread backwards under this section. Claims to be referred to Financial Institutions Division.).
Definitions—"Case III of Schedule E", s 19(2); "the Income Tax Acts", s 831(1)(*b*); "Schedule D", s 18(1); "United Kingdom", s 830(1); "year of assessment", s 832(1).
Amendments—¹ Words in sub-s (1) substituted by FA 1996 s 134, Sch 20 para 34 with effect from the year 1996–97.
² Words in sub-s (6) substituted by FA 1996 s 135, Sch 21 para 16 with effect from the year 1996–97.

586 Disallowance of deductions for war risk premiums

(1) In computing the amount of the profits or gains of any person for any tax purpose, no sum shall be deducted in respect of any payment made by him to which this section applies.

(2) No payment to which this section applies shall be included in computing the expenses of management in respect of which relief may be given under section 75 or 76.

(3) Subject to subsections (4) and (5) below, this section applies to any payment made by any person under any contract or arrangement under which that person is, in the event of war damage, entitled or eligible, either absolutely or conditionally, to or for any form of indemnification, whether total or partial, and whether by way of a money payment or not, in respect of that war damage.

(4) Where the payment is made in respect of the right or eligibility mentioned in sub-section (3) above and also in respect of other matters, the deduction or inclusion of so much of the payment as is properly attributable to the other matters shall not be disallowed by virtue only of subsection (1) or (2) above.

(5) This section shall not apply to any payment made under any contract of marine insurance, or any contract of insurance of an aircraft, or any contract of insurance of goods in transit.

(6) In this section "war damage" means loss or damage arising from action taken by an enemy of Her Majesty, or action taken in combating such an enemy or in repelling an imagined attack by such an enemy, or action taken in anticipation of or in consequence of an attack by such an enemy.

Commentary—*Simon's Direct Tax Service* **B3.1467.**
Definitions—"Profits or gains', s 833(1); "tax", s 832(3).

587 Disallowance of certain payments in respect of war injuries to employees

(1) In computing the amount of the profits or gains, or total income, of any person for any tax purpose, no sum shall be deducted in respect of any payment made by him to which this section applies.

(2) No payment to which this section applies shall be included in computing—

(*a*) the expenses of management in respect of which relief may be given under section 75 or 76; or

(*b*) the expenses of management or supervision in respect of which relief may be given under section 121.

(3) Subject to subsections (4) and (5) below, this section applies—

(*a*) to any payments by way of benefit made by any person to, or to the personal representatives or dependants of, any employees of his on account of their incapacity, retirement or death owing to war injuries, whether sustained in the United Kingdom or elsewhere; and

(*b*) to any payments made by any person by way of premium or contribution under any policy, agreement, scheme or arrangement providing for the payment of benefits to, or to the personal representatives or dependants of, any employees of his on account of their incapacity, retirement or death owing to such war injuries.

(4) This section shall not apply to any payment (whether by way of benefit or by way of premium or contribution) which is payable under any policy, agreement, scheme or arrangement made before 3rd September 1939, except to the extent that the amount of the payment is increased by any variation of the terms of that policy, agreement, scheme or arrangement made on or after that date.

(5) This section shall not apply to any payment by way of benefit if, in the opinion of the Board, that payment was made under an established practice which was such that the same or a greater payment would have been made if the incapacity, retirement or death had not been due to war injuries.

(6) Where a person makes a payment by way of benefit to which this section applies and, in the opinion of the Board, there is an established practice under which a smaller payment would have been made if the incapacity, retirement or death had not been due to war injuries, the deduction or inclusion of an amount equal to that smaller payment shall not be disallowed by virtue only of subsection (1) or (2) above.

(7) Where a person makes a payment to which this section applies by way of premium or contribution, and the policy, agreement, scheme or arrangement provides for the payment of any benefit in the event of incapacity, retirement or death not due to war injuries, the deduction or inclusion of so much of the payment of premium or contribution as, in the opinion of the Board, is properly attributable to benefit payable in the event of incapacity, retirement or death not due to war injuries shall not be disallowed by virtue only of subsection (1) or (2) above.

(8) In this section "war injuries" means physical injuries—

(*a*) caused by—

(i) the discharge of any missile (including liquids and gas);

(ii) the use of any weapon, explosive or other noxious thing; or

(iii) the doing of any other injurious act,

either by the enemy or in combating the enemy or in repelling an imagined attack by the enemy; or

(*b*) caused by the impact on any person or property of any enemy aircraft, or any aircraft belonging to, or held by any person on behalf of, or for the benefit of, Her Majesty or any allied power, or any part of, or anything dropped from, any such aircraft.

Commentary—*Simon's Direct Tax Service* **A4.301A; B3.1428.**
Definitions—''The Board'', s 832(1); ''profits or gains'', s 833(1); ''total income'', s 835(1); ''United Kingdom'', s 830(1).

[587A New issues of securities: extra return

(1) This section applies where—

(*a*) securities (old securities) of a particular kind are issued by way of the original issue of securities of that kind,

(*b*) on a later occasion securities (new securities) of the same kind are issued,

(*c*) a sum (the extra return) is payable in respect of the new securities, by the person issuing them, to reflect the fact that interest is accruing on the old securities,

(*d*) the issue price of the new securities includes an element (whether or not separately identified) representing payment for the extra return, and

(*e*) the extra return is equal to the amount of interest payable for the relevant period on so many old securities as there are new (or, if there are more new securities than old, the amount of interest which would be so payable if there were as many old securities as new).

[but this section shall not apply for the purposes of corporation tax, except where the issue of the new securities was before 1 April 1996.][2]

(2) Anything payable or paid by way of the extra return shall be treated for the purposes of the Tax Acts as payable or paid by way of interest (to the extent that it would not be so treated apart from this subsection).

(3) But as regards any payment by way of the extra return, relief shall not be given under any provision of the Tax Acts to the person by whom the new securities are issued; and ''relief'' here means relief by way of deduction in computing profits or gains or deduction or set off against income or total profits.

(4) For the purposes of this section securities are of the same kind if they are treated as being of the same kind by the practice of a recognised stock exchange or would be so treated if dealt with on such a stock exchange.

(5) For the purposes of this section the relevant period is the period beginning with the day following the relevant day and ending with the day on which the new securities are issued.

(6) For the purposes of this section the relevant day is—

(*a*) the last (or only) interest payment day to fall in respect of the old securities before the day on which the new securities are issued, or

(*b*) the day on which the old securities were issued, in a case where no interest payment day fell in respect of them before the day on which the new securities are issued;

and an interest payment day, in relation to the old securities, is a day on which interest is payable under them.][1]

Commentary—*Simon's Direct Tax Service* **A7.516.**
Definitions—''the Board, s 832(1); ''interest'', s 832(1); ''profits or gains'', s 833(1); ''the Tax Acts'', s 831(2).
Amendments—[1] This section inserted by FA 1991 Sch 12 paras 1, 5 and applies if the new securities are issued after 18 March 1991, whether the old securities are issued before or on or after that day.
[2] Words in sub-s (1) inserted by FA 1996 ss 104, 105, Sch 14 para 33 with effect for accounting periods ending after 31 March 1996, subject to transitional provisions in FA 1996 Sch 15.

[587B [Gifts of shares, securities and real property to charities etc][3]

(1) Subsections (2) and (3) below apply where, otherwise than by way of a bargain made at arm's length, an individual, or a company which is not itself a charity, disposes of the whole of the beneficial interest in a qualifying investment to a charity.

(2) On a claim made in that behalf to an officer of the Board—

(*a*) the relevant amount shall be allowed—

(i) in the case of a disposal by an individual, as a deduction in calculating his total income for the purposes of income tax for the year of assessment in which the disposal is made;

(ii) in the case of a disposal by a company, as a charge on income for the purposes of corporation tax for the accounting period in which the disposal is made; and

(*b*) no relief in respect of the disposal shall be given under section 83A or any other provision of the Income Tax Acts;

but paragraph (*a*)(i) above shall not apply for the purposes of any computation under section 550(2)(*a*) or (*b*).

(3) The consideration for which the charity's acquisition of the qualifying investment is treated by virtue of section 257(2) of the 1992 Act as having been made—

(*a*) shall be reduced by the relevant amount; or

(*b*) where that consideration is less than that amount, shall be reduced to nil.

(4) Subject to subsections (5) to (7) below, the relevant amount is an amount equal to—

(*a*) where the disposal is a gift, the market value of the qualifying investment at the time when the disposal is made;

(b) where the disposal is at an undervalue, the difference between that market value and the amount or value of the consideration for the disposal.

(5) Where there are one or more benefits received in consequence of making the disposal which are received by the person making the disposal or a person connected with him, the relevant amount shall be reduced by the value of that benefit or, as the case may be, the aggregate value of those benefits; and section 839 applies for the purposes of this subsection.

(6) Where the disposal is a gift, the relevant amount shall be increased by the amount of the incidental costs of making the disposal to the person making it.

(7) Where the disposal is at an undervalue—

(a) to the extent that the consideration for the disposal is less than that for which the disposal is treated as made by virtue of section 257(2)(a) of the 1992 Act, the relevant amount shall be increased by the amount of the incidental costs of making the disposal to the person making it; and

(b) section 48 of that Act (consideration due after time of disposal) shall apply in relation to the computation of the relevant amount as it applies in relation to the computation of a gain.

(8) In the case of a disposal by a company which is carrying on life assurance business—

(a) if the company is charged to tax under Case I of Schedule D in respect of such business, subsections (2) and (3) above shall not apply;

(b) if the company is not so charged to tax in respect of such business—

(i) subsection (2)(a)(ii) above shall have effect as if for "a charge on income" there were substituted "an expense of management"; and

(ii) the relevant amount given by subsection (4) above shall be reduced by so much (if any) of that amount as is not referable to basic life assurance and general annuity business;

and for the purpose of determining how much (if any) of that amount is not so referable, section 432A shall have effect as if that amount were a gain accruing on the disposal of the qualifying investment to the company.

(9) In this section—

"authorised unit trust" and "open-ended investment company" have the meanings given by section 468;

"charity" has the same meaning as in section 506 and includes each of the bodies mentioned in section 507(1);

"the incidental costs of making the disposal to the person making it" shall be construed in accordance with section 38(2) of the 1992 Act;

"life assurance business" and related expressions have the same meaning as in Chapter I of Part XII;

"offshore fund" means a collective investment scheme (within the meaning [given by section 235 of the Financial Services and Markets Act 2000][2]) which is constituted by any company, unit trust scheme or other arrangement falling within paragraph (a), (b) or (c) of section 759(1);

"qualifying investment" means any of the following—

(a) shares or securities which are listed or dealt in on a recognised stock exchange;

(b) units in an authorised unit trust;

(c) shares in an open-ended investment company; ...[3]

(d) an interest in an offshore fund[; and

(e) a qualifying interest in land][3]

[(9A) In this section a "qualifying interest in land" means—

(a) a freehold interest in land, or

(b) a leasehold interest in land which is a term of years absolute,

where the land in question is in the United Kingdom.

This subsection is subject to subsections (9B) to (9D) below.][3]

[(9B) Where a person makes a disposal to a charity of—

(a) the whole of his beneficial interest in such freehold or leasehold interest in land as is described in subsection (9A)(a) or (b) above, and

(b) any easement, servitude, right or privilege so far as benefiting that land,

the disposal falling within paragraph (b) above is to be regarded for the purposes of this section as a disposal by the person of the whole of his beneficial interest in a qualifying interest in land.][3]

[(9C) Where a person, who has a freehold or leasehold interest in land in the United Kingdom, grants a lease for a term of years absolute (or, in the case of land in Scotland, grants a lease) to a charity of the whole or part of that land, the grant of that lease is to be regarded for the purposes of this section as a disposal by the person of the whole of the beneficial interest in the leasehold interest so granted.][3]

[(9D) For the purposes of subsection (9A) above, an agreement to acquire a freehold interest and an agreement for a lease are not qualifying interests in land.][3]

[(9E) In the application of this section to Scotland—

(a) references to a freehold interest in land are references to the interest of the owner, (*b*) references to a leasehold interest in land which is a term of years absolute are references to a tenant's right over or interest in a property subject to a lease, and

(*c*) references to an agreement for a lease do not include references to missives of let that constitute an actual lease.][3]

(10) Subject to subsection (11) below, the market value of any qualifying investment shall be determined for the purposes of this section as for the purposes of the 1992 Act.

(11) In the case of an interest in an offshore fund for which there are separate published buying and selling prices, section 272(5) of the 1992 Act (meaning of "market value" in relation to rights of unit holders in a unit trust scheme) shall apply with any necessary modifications for determining the market value of the interest for the purposes of this section.][1]

[(12) This section is supplemented by section 587C below.][3]

Commentary—*Simon's Direct Tax Service* D2.234, E1.504C.
Cross referencesFA 2002 s 97(7), (8) (transitional provisions relating to the application of sub-s (9E) above).
Amendments—[1] This section inserted by FA 2000 s 43(1), (3) with effect for disposals made by individuals after 5 April 2000 and disposals made by companies after 31 March 2000.
[2] In sub-s (9), words in definition of "offshore fund" substituted by the Financial Services and Markets Act 2000 (Consequential Amendments) (Taxes) Order, SI 2001/3629 arts 13, 40 with effect from 1 December 2001, immediately after the coming into force of the Financial Services and Markets Act 2000 ss 411, 432(1), Sch 20.
[3] In sub-s (9), word repealed, para (*e*) inserted; sub-ss (9A)–(9E) inserted, sub-s (12) inserted, and Heading substituted; by FA 2002 ss 97(1)–(4), (6), 141, Sch 40 Pt 3(15) with effect for any disposal of a qualifying interest in land to a charity where the disposal is made—

(*a*) in the case of a disposal to the charity by an individual, after 5 April 2002, or
(*b*) in the case of a disposal to the charity by a company, after 31 March 2002.

[587C Supplementary provision for gifts of real property

(1) This section applies for the purposes of section 587B where a qualifying investment is a qualifying interest in land.

(2) Where two or more persons—

(*a*) are jointly beneficially entitled to the qualifying interest in land, or
(*b*) are, taken together, beneficially entitled in common to the qualifying interest in land,

section 587B applies only if each of those persons disposes of the whole of his beneficial interest in the qualifying interest in land to the charity.

(3) Relief under section 587B shall be available to each of the persons referred to in subsection (32) above, but the amount that may be allowed as respects any of them shall be only such share of the relevant amount as they may agree in the case of that person.

(4) No person may make a claim for a relief under subsection (2) of section 587B unless he has received a certificate given by or on behalf of the charity.

(5) The certificate must—

(*a*) specify the description of the qualifying interest in land which is the subject of the disposal,
(*b*) specify the date of the disposal, and
(*c*) contain a statement that the charity has acquired the qualifying interest in land.

(6) If, in the case of a disposal of a qualifying interest in land, a disqualifying event occurs at any time in the relevant period, the person (or each of the persons) who made the disposal to the charity shall be treated as never having been entitled to relief under section 587B in respect of the disposal.

(7) All such assessments and adjustments of assessments are to be made as are necessary to give effect to subsection (76) above.

(8) For the purposes of subsection (76) above a disqualifying event occurs if the person (or any one of the persons) who made the disposal or any person connected with him (or any one of them)—

(*a*) becomes entitled to an interest or right in relation to all or part of the land to which the disposal relates, or
(*b*) becomes party to an arrangement under which he enjoys some right in relation to all or part of that land,

otherwise than for full consideration in money or money's worth.

(9) A disqualifying event does not occur, for the purposes of subsection (76) above, if a person becomes entitled to an interest or right as mentioned in subsection (98)(*a*) above as a result of a disposition of property on death, whether the disposition is effected by will, under the law relating to intestacy or otherwise.

(10) For the purposes of subsection (76) above the relevant period is the period beginning with the date of the disposal of the qualifying interest in land and ending with—

(*a*) in the case of an individual, the fifth anniversary of the 31st January next following the end of the year of assessment in which the disposal was made, and
(*b*) in the case of a company, the sixth anniversary of the end of the accounting period in which the disposal was made.

(11) Section 839 (connected persons) applies for the purposes of this section.

(12) This section shall be construed as one with section 587B.][1]

Amendments—This section inserted inserted by FA 2002 s 97(5), (6) with effect for any disposal of a qualifying interest in land to a charity where the disposal is made—

   (*a*) in the case of a disposal to the charity by an individual, after 5 April 2002, or
   (*b*) in the case of a disposal to the charity by a company, after 31 March 2002.

588 Training courses for employees

(1) Where, on or after 6th April 1987, a person (in this section referred to as the "employer") incurs expenditure in paying or reimbursing relevant expenses incurred in connection with a qualifying course of training which—

   (*a*) is undertaken by a person (in this section referred to as the "employee") who is the holder or past holder of any office or employment under the employer; and
   (*b*) is undertaken with a view to retraining the employee,

the employee shall not thereby be regarded as receiving any emolument which forms part of his income for any purpose of Schedule E.

(2) Section 589 shall have effect to determine for the purposes of this section—

   (*a*) what is a qualifying course of training;
   (*b*) whether such a course is undertaken by an employee with a view to retraining; and
   (*c*) what are relevant expenses in relation to such a course.

(3) Subject to subsection (4) below, where—

   (*a*) an employer incurs expenditure in paying or reimbursing relevant expenses as mentioned in subsection (1) above; and
   (*b*) that subsection has effect in relation to the income of the employee for the purposes of Schedule E;

then, if and so far as that expenditure would not, apart from this subsection, be so deductible, it shall be deductible in computing for the purposes of Schedule D the [profits]² of the trade, profession or vocation of the employer for the purposes of which the employee is or was employed.

(4) If the employer carries on a business, the expenses of management of which are eligible for relief under section 75, subsection (3) above shall have effect as if for the words from "in computing" onwards there were substituted "as expenses of management for the purposes of section 75".

(4A) ...⁴

(5) In any case where—

   (*a*) an employee's liability to tax for any year of assessment is determined (by assessment or otherwise) on the assumption that subsection (1) above applies in his case and, subsequently, there is a failure to comply with any provision of section 589(3) and (4); or
   (*b*) an employer's liability to tax for any year is determined (by assessment or otherwise) on the assumption that, by virtue only of subsection (3) above (or subsections (3) and (4) above), he is entitled to a deduction on account of any expenditure and, subsequently, there is such a failure as is referred to in paragraph (*a*) above;

an assessment under [section 29(1)]¹ of the Management Act[, or paragraph 41 of Schedule 18 to the Finance Act 1998,]³ of an amount due in consequence of the failure referred to above may be made at any time not later than six years after the end of the chargeable period in which the failure occurred.

(6) Where an event occurs by reason of which there is a failure to comply with any provision of section 589(3) and (4), the employer of the employee concerned shall within 60 days of coming to know of the event give a notice to the inspector containing particulars of the event.

(7) If the inspector has reason to believe that an employer has not given a notice which he is required to give under subsection (6) above in respect of any event, the inspector may by notice require the employer to furnish him within such time (not less than 60 days) as may be specified in the notice with such information relating to the event as the inspector may reasonably require for the purposes of this section.

Commentary—*Simon's Direct Tax Service* **B3.1431; E4.422.**
Concession A63—Expenses in relation to further education or training in the UK are not charged to tax where they are paid for, or reimbursed, by the employer if certain conditions are met.
A64—Where expenses in relation to work-related training course are paid by the employee, relief is given if specified conditions are met.
Revenue Internal Guidance—Schedule E manual, SE 01290 (work-related training: inter-action of s 200B-D with these provisions).
SE 05000 (retraining expenses—exemption from Schedule E charge, table showing how the guidance on this subject is arranged).
SE 05030 (withdrawal of exemption—notification by employers of failure to comply with conditions for exemption and Inspector's power to obtain information, application of sub-s (5)(*a*), (6) and (7); failure to obtain a job etc or finding a job etc in an unconnected field does not invalidate the exemption).
SE 05040 (withdrawal of exemption—power of Inspector to make assessments, application of sub-s (5)).
Definitions—"Chargeable period", s 832(1); "emolument", s 131(1); "inspector", s 832(1); "the Management Act", s 831(3); "notice", s 832(1); "Schedule D", s 18(1); "Schedule E", s 19(1); "trade", s 832(1); "year of assessment", s 832(1).
Cross references—See TA 1988 s 200C(4) (TA 1988 s 200B (work-related training) to apply for the purposes of this section to the extent only that sub-s (1) above does not have effect).
Amendments—¹ Words in sub-s (5) substituted for words "section 29(3)" by FA 1996 Sch 18 paras 10, 17 with effect: for purposes of income tax from the year 1996–97; for purposes of corporation tax as respects accounting periods ending after 30 June 1999 (by virtue of Finance Act 1994, Section 199, (Appointed Day) Order, SI 1998/3173 art 2); and so far as relating to

partnerships whose trades, professions or businesses are set up and commenced before 6 April 1994, with effect from the year 1997–98.

[2] Word in sub-s (3) substituted by FA 1998 Sch 7 para 1 with effect from 31 July 1998.

[3] Words in sub-s (5) inserted by FA 1999 s 93, Sch 11 para 2 with effect for accounting periods ending after 30 June 1999.

[4] Sub-s (4A) (inserted for the purposes of income tax by FA 1995 s 39, Sch 6 para 24) repealed by FA 1998 s 165, Sch 27 Part III(4) with effect for 1998–99 and subsequent years of assessment.

589 Qualifying courses of training etc

(1) Subject to subsection (2) below, a course is a qualifying course of training if—

(a) it provides a course of training designed to impart or improve skills or knowledge relevant to, and intended to be used in the course of, gainful employment (including self-employment) of any description; and

(b) the course is entirely devoted to the teaching or practical application of the skills or knowledge (or to both such teaching and practical application); and

(c) the duration of the course does not exceed one year; and

(d) all teaching and practical application forming part of the course takes place within the United Kingdom.

(2) A course shall not be regarded as a qualifying course of training in relation to a particular employee unless—

(a) he attends the course on a full-time or substantially full-time basis; and

(b) he is employed by the employer full-time throughout the period of two years ending at the time when he begins to undertake the course or, if it is earlier, at the time he ceases to be employed by him; and

(c) the opportunity to undertake the course, on similar terms as to payment or reimbursement of relevant expenses, is available either generally to holders or past holders of offices or employment under the employer or to a particular class or classes of such holders or past holders.

(3) An employee shall not be regarded as undertaking a course with a view to retraining unless—

(a) he begins to undertake the course of training while he is employed by the employer or within the period of one year after he ceases to be so employed; and

(b) he ceases to be employed by the employer not later than the end of the period of two years beginning at the end of the qualifying course of training.

(4) An employee shall not be regarded as having undertaken a course with a view to retraining if, any time within the period of two years beginning at the time when he ceased to be employed as mentioned in subsection (3)(b) above, he is again employed by the employer.

(5) Where an employee undertakes a qualifying course of training, the relevant expenses consist of—

(a) fees for attendance at the course;

(b) fees for any examination which is taken during or at the conclusion of the course;

(c) the cost of any books which are essential for a person attending the course, and

(d) travelling expenses falling within subsection (6) below.

[(6) The travelling expenses referred to in subsection (5)(d) above are—

(a) those in respect of which, on the assumptions in subsection (6A) below, mileage allowance relief would be available if no mileage allowance payments (within the meaning of section 197AD(2)) had been made; or

(b) those which, on those assumptions, would be deductible under section 198.][1]

[(6A) The assumptions are—

(a) that attendance at the course is one of the duties of the employee's office or employment; and

(b) if the employee has in fact ceased to be employed by the employer, that he continues to be employed by him.][1]

(7) Any reference in this section to an employee being employed by an employer is a reference to the employee holding office or employment under the employer.

Commentary—*Simon's Direct Tax Service* B3.1431; E4.422.

Concession A63—Expenses in relation to further education or training in the UK are not charged to tax where they are paid for, or reimbursed, by the employer if certain conditions are met.

Statement of Practice SP 4/86—Circumstances in which payments made by employers to employees for periods of attendance on a full time education course, including ''sandwich'' courses are treated in practice as exempt from income tax.

Revenue Internal Guidance—Schedule E manual, SE 05010 (retraining expenses—conditions to be satisfied for exemption, application of sub-s (1)–(4)).

SE 05020 (retraining expenses qualifying for exemption , application of sub-ss (5) and (6)).

SE 05030 (withdrawal of exemption, application of sub-s 3 and failure to obtain a job etc or finding a job etc in an unconnected field does not invalidate the exemption).

Definition—''United Kingdom'', s 830(1).

Amendments—[1] Sub-ss (6), (6A) substituted for sub-s (6) by FA 2001 s 57(3), (4), Sch 12 Pt II para 12 with effect from the year 2002–03.

[589A Counselling services for employees

(1) This section applies where—

(a) qualifying counselling services are provided to a person (the employee) in connection with the termination of the holding by him of any office or employment, and (*b*) the termination takes place on or after 16th March 1993.

(2) This section also applies where—

(*a*) subsection (1)(*a*) above applies, and

(*b*) the termination takes place before 16th March 1993 but relevant expenditure is incurred on or after that date.

(3) Relevant expenditure is expenditure incurred in—

(*a*) providing the qualifying counselling services to the employee,

(*b*) paying or reimbursing fees for the provision to the employee of the qualifying counselling services, or

(*c*) paying or reimbursing any allowable travelling expenses incurred in connection with the provision of the qualifying counselling services to the employee.

(4) No charge to tax under Schedule E shall arise in respect of—

(*a*) the provision of the qualifying counselling services to the employee,

(*b*) the payment or reimbursement of fees for the provision to the employee of the qualifying counselling services, or

(*c*) the payment or reimbursement of any allowable travelling expenses incurred in connection with the provision of the qualifying counselling services to the employee.

(5) Where this section applies by virtue of subsection (2) above, subsection (4) above shall apply only to the extent that the expenditure incurred in providing the services or paying or reimbursing the fees or expenses is incurred on or after 16th March 1993.

(6) Subsection (4) above shall apply whether or not the person who provides the services or pays or reimburses the fees or expenses is the person under whom the employee holds or held the office or employment mentioned in subsection (1) above.

(7) Subsections (8) to (10) below apply where any relevant expenditure is incurred by the person under whom the employee holds or held the office or employment mentioned in subsection (1) above (the employer).

(8) If and so far as the expenditure would not, apart from this subsection, be so deductible, it shall be deductible in computing for the purposes of Schedule D the [profits][2] of the trade, profession or vocation of the employer for the purposes of which the employee is or was employed.

(9) If the employer carries on a business and the expenses of management of the business are eligible for relief under section 75, subsection (8) above shall have effect as if for the words from "in computing" onwards there were substituted "as expenses of management for the purposes of section 75".

[(9A) ...[3]]

(10) Where this section applies by virtue of subsection (2) above, subsections (8) and (9) above shall apply only to the extent that the expenditure is incurred on or after 16th March 1993.][1]

Commentary—*Simon's Direct Tax Service* **B3.1432.**
Revenue Internal Guidance—Schedule E manual SE 13745 (termination payments and benefits: payments for outplacement counselling, conditions for this exemption to apply).
Definitions—"qualifying counselling services", s 589B; "trade", s 832(1).
Amendments—[1] This section inserted by FA 1993 s 108.
[2] Word in sub-s (8) substituted by FA 1998 Sch 7 para 1 with effect from 31 July 1998.
[3] Sub-s (9A) (inserted for the purposes of income tax by FA 1995 s 39, Sch 6 para 24) repealed by FA 1998 s 165, Sch 27 Part III(4) with effect for 1998–99 and subsequent years of assessment.

[589B Qualifying counselling services etc

(1) Subsections (2) to (4) below apply for the purposes of section 589A.

(2) Subject to subsection (3) below, services are qualifying counselling services if—

(*a*) the purpose, or main purpose, of their provision is to enable the employee to adjust to the termination of his holding of the office or employment mentioned in section 589A(1) or is to enable him to find other gainful employment (including self-employment) or is to enable him to do both,

(*b*) the services consist wholly of any or all of the following, namely, giving advice and guidance, imparting or improving skills, and providing or making available the use of office equipment or similar facilities,

(*c*) the employee has been employed by the employer full-time throughout the period of two years ending at the time when the services begin to be provided to him or, if it is earlier, at the time he ceases to be employed by the employer,

(*d*) the opportunity to receive the services, on similar terms as to payment or reimbursement of any expenses incurred in connection with their provision, is available either generally to holders or past holders of offices or employment under the employer or to a particular class or classes of such holders or past holders, and

(*e*) the services are provided in the United Kingdom.

(3) Where paragraphs (*a*) to (*d*) of subsection (2) above are satisfied in relation to particular services but the services are provided partly in and partly outside the United Kingdom, the extent to which the services are qualifying counselling services shall be determined on a just and reasonable basis.

[(4) In relation to services, allowable travelling expenses are—

(*a*) those in respect of which, on the assumptions in subsection (4A) below, mileage allowance relief would be available if no mileage allowance payments (within the meaning of section 197AD(2)) had been made; or

(*b*) those which, on those assumptions, would be deductible under section 198.]²

[(4A) The assumptions are—

(*a*) that receipt of the services is one of the duties of the employee's office or employment; and

(*b*) if the employee has in fact ceased to be employed by the employer, that he continues to be employed by him.]²

(5) Any reference in this section or section 589A to an employee being employed by an employer is a reference to the employee holding office or employment under the employer.]¹

Commentary—*Simon's Direct Tax Service* B3.1432.
Revenue Internal Guidance—Schedule E manual SE 13745 (termination payments and benefits: payments for outplacement counselling, conditions for this exemption to apply).
Definitions—''the United Kingdom'', s 830(1).
Amendments—¹ This section inserted by FA 1993 s 108.
² Sub-ss (4), (4A) substituted for sub-s (4) by FA 2001 s 57(3), (4), Sch 12 Pt II para 13 with effect from the year 2002–03.

PART XIV
PENSION SCHEMES, SOCIAL SECURITY BENEFITS, LIFE ANNUITIES ETC

CHAPTER I
RETIREMENT BENEFIT SCHEMES

Statements of Practice SP D2—Concessionary exemption from CGT liability where a new scheme is established for obtaining approval under this Chapter by winding up an old scheme and transferring its funds to the new scheme.
SP 13/91—Ex gratia award made on termination of an office or employment by retirement or death.
Revenue Decision RD 6—Transactions in securities: contravention of tax advantages; director's pension scheme.
Cross references—See TA 1988 s 600(1) (charge to tax of unauthorised payments out of funds of schemes approved under this Chapter).
TA 1988 s 604 (procedure and form for application for approval under this Chapter).
TA 1988 s 612 (interpretative provisions and regulations for purposes of this Chapter).
TA 1988 s 660A(7) (irrevocable allocation of pension rights by one spouse to the other under terms of statutory scheme defined within this Chapter not a settlement).
TA 1988 Sch 23ZA (retirement benefits schemes which are being approved under this Chapter are eligible schemes for TA 1988 Sch 23ZA (conversion of certain retirement benefits schemes).
Occupational Pension Schemes (Additional Contributions) Regulations, SI 1987/1749 (extension of certain provisions of this Chapter to retirement benefits schemes to which employers do not contribute);
FA 1989 Sch 6, Pts II, III (new provisions in relation to retirement benefits schemes and additional voluntary contributions schemes approved before 27 July 1989);
FA 1990 Sch 10 para 22 (exemption from tax on transfer or redemption after 8 June 1989 of qualifying convertible securities held for the purposes of an exempt approved scheme within this Chapter);
TCGA 1992 Sch 1 para 2(8) (application of annual exempt amount of capital gains in cases of exempt approved schemes and statutory schemes defined in this Chapter);
Judicial Pensions and Retirement Act 1993 s 18 (continuity of tax treatment under this Chapter of judicial pensions falling under new arrangements enacted by the Judicial Pensions and Retirement Act 1993 Pt I),
Judicial Pensions and Retirement Act 1993 s 19(4) (pension or lump sum payable to a judicial officer in respect of his earnings in excess of pension-capped salary to be regarded as a separate and distinct statutory scheme not capable of being a relevant statutory scheme within the meaning of this Chapter).
FA 2000 Sch 8 para 83(2) (deduction of partnership share money from an employee's salary in accordance with a partnership share agreement to be disregarded for the purpose of ascertaining the amount of the employee's remuneration for the purposes of this Chapter).
FA 2000 Sch 13 para 28 (transitional provisions for personal pension schemes approved under this Chapter before 6 April 2001).

Approval of schemes

590 Conditions for approval of retirement benefit schemes

(1) Subject to section 591, the Board shall not approve any retirement benefits scheme for the purposes of this Chapter unless the scheme satisfies all of the conditions set out in subsection (2) below.

(2) The conditions are—

[(*a*) that the scheme is bona fide established for the sole purpose (subject to any enactment or Northern Ireland legislation requiring or allowing provision for the value of any rights to be transferred between schemes or between members of the same scheme) of providing relevant benefits in respect of service as an employee;]⁸

[(*aa*) that those benefits do not include any benefits payable to a person other than—

(i) the employee or a scheme member's ex-spouse,

(ii) a widow, widower, child, or dependant of the employee or of a scheme member's ex-spouse, or

(iii) the personal representatives of the employee or of a scheme member's ex-spouse;]⁸

(*b*) that the scheme is recognised by the employer and employees to whom it relates, and that every employee who is, or has a right to be, a member of the scheme has been given written particulars of all essential features of the scheme which concern him;

(*c*) that there is a person resident in the United Kingdom who will be responsible for the discharge of all duties imposed on the administrator of the scheme under this Chapter;

(*d*) that the employer is a contributor to the scheme;

(*e*) that the scheme is established in connection with some trade or undertaking carried on in the United Kingdom by a person resident in the United Kingdom;

(*f*) that in no circumstances, whether during the subsistence of the scheme or later, can any amount be paid by way of repayment of an employee's contributions under the scheme.

(3) Subject to subsection (1) above, the Board shall approve a retirement benefits scheme for the purposes of this Chapter if the scheme satisfies all the conditions of this subsection, that is to say—

(*a*) that any benefit for an employee is a pension on retirement at a specified age not earlier than 60 [and not later than 75]⁵, which does not exceed one-sixtieth of the employee's final remuneration for each year of service up to a maximum of 40;

(*b*) that any benefit for any widow [or widower,]⁴ of an employee is a pension payable on his death after retirement such that the amount payable to the widow [or widower]⁴ by way of pension does not exceed two-thirds of any pension or pensions payable to the employee;

[(*ba*) that any benefit for an ex-spouse, or for the widow or widower of an ex-spouse, is a benefit in relation to which the scheme satisfies the conditions set out in subsection (3A) below;

(*bb*) that the scheme does not allow any rights debited to a scheme member as a consequence of a pension sharing order or provision to be replaced with any rights which that scheme member would not have been able to acquire (in addition to the debited rights) had the order or provision not been made;

(*c*) that no benefits are payable under the scheme other than those mentioned in paragraphs (*a*), (*b*) and (*ba*) above;]⁸

(*d*) that no pension is capable in whole or in part of surrender, commutation or assignment, [except—

　(i) for the purpose of giving effect to a pension sharing order or provision, or

　(ii) in so far as the commutation of a benefit for an ex-spouse is allowed by virtue of subsection (3A) below, or

　(iii)]⁸ in so far as the scheme allows an employee on retirement to obtain, by commutation of [a pension provided for him]⁸, a lump sum or sums not exceeding in all three-eighths of his final remuneration ...¹ for each year of service up to a maximum of 40;

[(*da*) that, in a case in which—

　(i) a lump sum may be obtained by the commutation of a part of a pension provided for an employee, and

　(ii) the amount of that pension is affected by the making of a pension sharing order or provision,

the lump sum does not exceed the sum produced by multiplying by 2.25 the amount which (after effect has been given to the pension sharing order or provision) is the amount of that pension for the first year in which it is payable;]⁸

[(*e*) that, in the case of any employee who is a member of the scheme by virtue of two or more relevant associated employments, the amount payable by way of pension in respect of service in any one of them may not, when aggregated with any amount payable by way of pension in respect of service in the other or others, exceed the relevant amount;]²

[(*f*) that, in the case of any employee who is a member of the scheme by virtue of two or more relevant associated employments, the amount payable by way of commuted pension in respect of service in any one of them may not, when aggregated with any amount payable by way of commuted pension in respect of service in the other or others, exceed the relevant amount;]²

[(*g*) that, in the case of any employee in relation to whom the scheme is connected with another scheme which is (or other schemes each of which is) an approved scheme, the amount payable by way of pension under the scheme may not, when aggregated with any amount payable by way of pension under the other scheme or schemes, exceed the relevant amount;]²

[(*h*) that, in the case of any employee in relation to whom the scheme is connected with another scheme which is (or other schemes each of which is) an approved scheme, the amount payable by way of commuted pension may not, when aggregated with any amount payable by way of commuted pension under the other scheme or schemes, exceed the relevant amount.]²

[(3A) The conditions mentioned in subsection (3)(*ba*) above are—

(*a*) that any benefit for an ex-spouse takes the form of a pension (with or without an entitlement to commute a part of that pension);

(*b*) that any benefit for an ex-spouse is a pension payable only on the attainment by the ex-spouse of a specified age of not less than 60 and not more than 75;

(*c*) that any entitlement to commute a part of the pension is exercisable only on its becoming payable;

(*d*) that any benefit for the widow or widower of an ex-spouse is confined to a non-commutable pension payable on the death of the ex-spouse at a time when the ex-spouse is already entitled to receive a pension under the scheme;

(*e*) that any pension provided for the widow or widower of an ex-spouse is of an amount not exceeding two-thirds of the pension payable to the ex-spouse;

(*f*) that, in a case in which a lump sum may be obtained by the commutation of a part of a pension provided for an ex-spouse, the lump sum does not exceed the sum produced by multiplying the amount of the pension for the first year in which it is payable by 2·25.][8]

(4) The conditions set out in [subsections (2) to (3A)] above are in this Chapter referred to as "the prescribed conditions".

[(4A) In subsection (3)(*c*) above "benefits" does not include any benefits for whose payment the scheme makes provision in pursuance of any obligation imposed by legislation relating to social security.][6]

[(4B) For the purposes of this section a benefit provided under any scheme is provided for an ex-spouse or the widow or widower of an ex-spouse, and shall be treated as not provided for an employee or the widow or widower of an employee, to the extent (and to the extent only) that—

(*a*) it is provided for a person who is, or is the widow or widower of, either—

(i) an employee who is an ex-spouse; or
(ii) a scheme member's ex-spouse;

and

(*b*) it is as an ex-spouse, or as the widow or widower of an ex-spouse, that that person is the person for whom the benefit is provided.

(4C) For the purposes of this section a benefit provided for any person under any scheme is provided for that person as an ex-spouse, or as the widow or widower of an ex-spouse, to the extent (and to the extent only) that—

(*a*) the benefit is provided in respect of rights of an ex-spouse that are or represent rights conferred on the ex-spouse as a consequence of a pension sharing order or provision; and

(*b*) the scheme makes provision for the benefit to be treated as provided separately from any benefits which are provided under the scheme for the same person as an employee or as the widow or widower of an employee.

(4D) In this section "scheme member", in relation to a scheme, means—

(*a*) an employee; or
(*b*) a person entitled to any relevant benefits under the scheme as a consequence of a pension sharing order or provision.

(4E) The following rules shall apply in calculating for the purposes of subsection (3)(*da*) or (3A)(*f*) above the amount of a person's pension for the first year in which it is payable—

(*a*) if the pension payable for the year changes, the initial pension payable shall be taken;
(*b*) it shall be assumed that that person will survive for the year; and
(*c*) the effect of commutation shall be ignored.

(4F) A pension provided for an ex-spouse who is an employee, or for the widow or widower of such an ex-spouse, shall be disregarded in any determination of whether the conditions set out in subsection (3)(*e*) to (*h*) above are satisfied or continue to be satisfied in the case of that employee.][8]

(5), (6) ...[7]

[(7) Subsections (8) to (10) below apply where the Board are considering whether a retirement benefits scheme satisfies or continues to satisfy the prescribed conditions.][3]

[(8) For the purpose of determining whether the scheme, so far as it relates to a particular class or description of employees, satisfies or continues to satisfy the prescribed conditions, that scheme shall be considered in conjunction with—

(*a*) any other retirement benefits scheme (or schemes) which relates (or relate) to employees of that class or description and which is (or are) approved for the purposes of this Chapter,

(*b*) any other retirement benefits scheme (or schemes) which relates (or relate) to employees of that class or description and which is (or are) at the same time before the Board in order for them to decide whether to give approval for the purposes of this Chapter,

(*c*) any section 608 scheme or schemes relating to employees of that class or description, and

(*d*) any relevant statutory scheme or schemes relating to employees of that class or description.][3]

[(9) If those conditions are satisfied in the case of both or all of those schemes taken together, they shall be taken to be satisfied in the case of the scheme mentioned in subsection (7) above (as well as the other or others).][3]

[(10) If those conditions are not satisfied in the case of both or all of those schemes taken together, they shall not be taken to be satisfied in the case of the scheme mentioned in subsection (7) above.][3]

[(11) The reference in subsection (8)(*c*) above to a section 608 scheme is a reference to a fund to which section 608 applies.][3]

Commentary—*Simon's Direct Tax Service* E7.214, 217.
Revenue Decision RD 6—Refusal of clearance under s 707 from s 703 counteraction in connection with exempt schemes approved under this section.
Revenue & other press releases—IR12 Occupational pensions schemes practice notes (1979), IR12 (Supplement) and IR12 (1991) (explanation of the operation of approved pension schemes).
PSO 6-5-94 (SSAPs: deferment of annuity purchase until retiring member reaches age of 75).
Definitions—"The Board", s 832(1); "children", s 831(4), 832(5); "notice", s 832(1); "retirement benefits scheme", s 611; "trade", s 832(1); "United Kingdom", s 830(1).
Cross references—See TA 1988 s 590A (supplementary provisions).
TA 1988 s 590B (supplementary provisions).
TA 1988 s 590C (earnings cap).
TA 1988 s 591 (discretionary approval of schemes not satisfying conditions in sub-s (2) above).
FA 1991 s 36(4)(a) (FA 1970 s 19(3), (4) repealed and the repeal deemed always to have had effect);
Retirement Benefits Schemes (Restriction on Discretion to Approve) (Small Self-administered Schemes) Regulations, SI 1991/1614 (restriction on the Board's discretion to approve a small self-administered pension scheme).
Amendments—[1] Words in sub-s (3)(d) repealed by FA 1989 Sch 6 paras 3(1), (2), 18(2) and Sch 17, Pt IV in relation to a scheme not approved by the Board before 27 July 1989; but if the scheme came into existence before 14 March 1989, the repeal does not affect an employee who became a member of the scheme before 1 June 1989.
[2] Sub-s (3)(e)–(h) substituted by FA 1989 Sch 6 paras 3(1), (3), 18(2) in relation to a scheme not approved by the Board before 27 July 1989; but if the scheme came into existence before 14 March 1989, the substitution does not affect an employee who became a member of the scheme before 1 June 1989.
[3] Sub-ss (7)–(11) substituted for sub-s (7) by FA 1989 Sch 6 paras 3(1), (4), 18(3) and have effect where determination is made after 26 July 1989.
[4] Words in sub-ss (2)(a), (3)(b) inserted by FA 1988 Sch 3 para 18 with effect from 6 April 1990.
[5] Words in sub-s (3)(a) substituted for the words "or, if the employee is a woman, 55, and not later than 70" by FA 1991 s 34 in relation to a scheme not approved before 25 July 1991.
[6] Sub-s (4A) inserted by FA 1991 s 34 in relation to a scheme not approved before 25 July 1991.
[7] Sub-ss (5), (6) repealed by FA 1991 s 36(2), (3) and Sch 19 Pt V and the repeal is deemed always to have had effect.
[8] In sub-s (2), para (a) substituted, and para (aa) inserted, in sub-s (3) paras (ba)–(c) substituted for original para (c), words in para (d) substituted and para (da) inserted, sub-ss (3A), (4B)–(4F) inserted, and words in sub-s (4) substituted by FA 1999 s 79 Sch 10 para 2 with effect for the purposes of the grant or withdrawal at any time after 9 May 2000 of any approval of a retirement benefits scheme (whenever made or approved). Sub-ss (3)(bb) and (da) are to be disregarded for the purposes of determining whether any retirement benefits scheme approved before 10 May 2000 satisfies the prescribed conditions at any time before 1 December 2000 (by virtue of the Finance Act 1999, Schedule 10, Paragraph 18, (First and Second Appointed Days) Order, SI 2000/1093).

[590A Section 590: supplementary provisions

(1) For the purposes of section 590(3)(e) and (f) two or more employments are relevant associated employments if they are employments in the case of which—

(a) there is a period during which the employee has held both or all of them,

(b) the period counts under the scheme in the case of both or all of them as a period in respect of which benefits are payable, and

(c) the period is one during which both or all of the employers in question are associated.

(2) For the purposes of section 590(3)(g) and (h) the scheme is connected with another scheme in relation to an employee if—

(a) there is a period during which he has been the employee of two persons who are associated employers,

(b) the period counts under both schemes as a period in respect of which benefits are payable, and

(c) the period counts under one scheme by virtue of service with one employer and under the other scheme by virtue of service with the other employer.

(3) For the purposes of subsections (1) and (2) above, employers are associated if (directly or indirectly) one is controlled by the other or if both are controlled by a third person.

(4) In subsection (3) above the reference to control, in relation to a body corporate, shall be construed—

(a) where the body corporate is a close company, in accordance with section 416, and

(b) where it is not, in accordance with section 840.][1]

Commentary—*Simon's Direct Tax Service* E7.215.
Revenue Internal Guidance—Schedule E manual SE 15173 (non-approved "retirement benefits schemes": ex-gratia payments—small payments, definition of "associated employers").
Amendments—[1] This section inserted by FA 1989 Sch 6 paras 4, 18(2) in relation to a scheme not approved by the Board before 27 July 1989; but if the scheme came into existence before 14 March 1989, this section does not affect an employee who became a member of the scheme before 1 June 1989.

[590B Section 590: further supplementary provisions

(1) For the purposes of section 590(3)(e) the relevant amount, in relation to an employee, shall be found by applying the following formula—

$$\frac{A \times C}{60}$$

(2) For the purposes of section 590(3)(f) the relevant amount, in relation to an employee, shall be found by applying the following formula—

$$\frac{3 \times A \times C}{80}$$

(3) For the purposes of section 590(3)(g) the relevant amount, in relation to an employee, shall be found by applying the following formula—

$$\frac{B \times C}{60}$$

(4) For the purposes of section 590(3)(h) the relevant amount, in relation to an employee, shall be found by applying the following formula—

$$\frac{3 \times B \times C}{80}$$

(5) For the purposes of this section A is the aggregate number of years service (expressing parts of a year as a fraction), subject to a maximum of 40, which, in the case of the employee, count for the purposes of the scheme at the time the benefits in respect of service in the employment become payable.

(6) But where the same year (or part of a year) counts for the purposes of the scheme by virtue of more than one of the relevant associated employments it shall be counted only once in calculating the aggregate number of years service for the purposes of subsection (5) above.

(7) For the purposes of this section B is the aggregate number of years service (expressing parts of a year as a fraction), subject to a maximum of 40, which, in the case of the employee, count for the purposes of any of the following—

(a) the scheme, and
(b) the other scheme or schemes with which the scheme is connected in relation to him

at the time the benefits become payable.

(8) But where the same year (or part of a year) counts for the purposes of more than one scheme it shall be counted only once in calculating the aggregate number of years service for the purpose of subsection (7) above.

(9) For the purposes of this section C is the permitted maximum in relation to the year of assessment in which the benefits in question become payable, that is, the figure found for that year by virtue of subsections (10) and (11) below.

(10) For the years 1988–89 and 1989–90 the figure is £60,000.

(11) For any subsequent year of assessment the figure is the figure found for that year, for the purposes of section 590C, by virtue of section 590C(4) [to (5A)]².]¹

Commentary—*Simon's Direct Tax Service* E7.214.
Note—For the year 2000–01 the figure specified for the purpose of sub-s (11) by virtue of s 590C is £91,800 by virtue of the Retirement Benefits Schemes (Indexation of Earnings Cap) Order, SI 2000/807.
Amendments—¹ This section inserted by FA 1989 Sch 6 paras 4, 18(2) in relation to a scheme not approved by the Board before 27 July 1989; but if the scheme came into existence before 14 March 1989, this section does not affect an employee who became a member of the scheme before 1 June 1989.
² Words in sub-s (11) substituted by FA 1993 s 107(6), (8) with effect from the year 1994–95.

[590C Earnings cap

(1) In arriving at an employee's final remuneration for the purposes of section 590(3)(a) or (d), any excess of what would be his final remuneration (apart from this section) over the permitted maximum for the year of assessment in which his participation in the scheme ceases shall be disregarded.

(2) In subsection (1) above "the permitted maximum", in relation to a year of assessment, means the figure found for that year by virtue of subsections (3) and (4) below.

(3) For the years 1988–89 and 1989–90 the figure is £60,000.

(4) For any subsequent year of assessment the figure is also *£60,000,* subject to [subsections (5) and (5A)]² below.

(5) If the retail prices index for the month of [September]² preceding a year of assessment falling within subsection (4) above is higher than it was for the previous [September]², the figure for that year shall be an amount arrived at by—

(a) increasing the figure for the previous year of assessment by the same percentage as the percentage increase in the retail prices index, and
(b) if the result is not a multiple of £600, rounding it up to the nearest amount which is such a multiple.

[(5A) If the retail prices index for the month of September preceding a year of assessment falling within subsection (4) above is not higher than it was for the previous September, the figure for that year shall be the same as the figure for the previous year of assessment.]²

(6) The Treasury shall in the year of assessment 1989–90, and in each subsequent year of assessment, make an order specifying the figure which is by virtue of this section the figure for the following year of assessment.]¹

Commentary—*Simon's Direct Tax Service* E7.214.
Note—For the year 2000–01, the figure specified for the purposes of sub-s (4) above by virtue of sub-ss (5), (6) above is £91,800 by virtue of the Retirement Benefits Schemes (Indexation of Earnings Cap) Order, SI 2000/807. For the year 2001–02, the figure specified is £95,400 by virtue of the Retirement Benefits Schemes (Indexation of Earnings Cap) Order, SI 2001/637. For the year 2002–03, the figure specified is £97,200 by virtue of the Retirement Benefits Schemes (Indexation of Earnings Cap) Order, SI 2002/700.
Definitions—"Retail prices index", s 833(2); "year of assessment", s 832(1).

Amendments—¹ This section inserted by FA 1989 Sch 6 paras 4, 18(2) in relation to a scheme not approved by the Board before 27 July 1989; but if the scheme came into existence before 14 March 1989, this section does not affect an employee who became a member of the scheme before 1 June 1989.
² Words in sub-ss (4), (5) substituted and sub-s (5A) inserted by FA 1993 s 107(4), (5), (8) with effect from the year 1994–95.

591 Discretionary approval

(1) The Board may, if they think fit having regard to the facts of a particular case, and subject to such conditions, if any, as they think proper to attach to the approval, approve a retirement benefits scheme for the purposes of this Chapter notwithstanding that it does not satisfy one or more of the prescribed conditions; but this subsection has effect subject to subsection (5) below.

(2) The Board may in particular approve by virtue of this section a scheme—

(a) which exceeds the limits imposed by the prescribed conditions as respects benefits for less than 40 years; or

(b) which provides pensions for the widows [and widowers]⁴ of employees on death in service, or for the children or dependants of employees; or

[(ba) which provides pensions for the widows and widowers of ex-spouses dying before the age at which their pensions become payable and for the children or dependants of ex-spouses; or]⁴

(c) which provides on death in service a lump sum of up to four times the employee's final remuneration (exclusive of any refunds of contributions); or

(d) which allows benefits to be payable on retirement within ten years of the specified age, or on earlier incapacity; or

(e) which provides for the return in certain contingencies of employees' contributions; or

(f) which relates to a trade or undertaking carried on only partly in the United Kingdom and by a person not resident in the United Kingdom; or

(g) which provides in certain contingencies for securing relevant benefits [falling within subsection (2A) below]² (but no other benefits) by means of an annuity contract ...² made with an insurance company of the employee's choice; or

(h) to which the employer is not a contributor and which provides benefits additional to those provided by a scheme to which he is a contributor.

[(2A) Relevant benefits fall within this subsection if they correspond with benefits that could be provided by an approved scheme, and for this purpose—

(a) a hypothetical scheme (rather than any particular scheme) is to be taken, and

(b) benefits provided by a scheme directly (rather than by means of an annuity contract) are to be taken.]²

[(3) In subsection (2)(g) above "insurance company" has the meaning given by section 659B.]³

(4) In applying this section to a scheme which was in existence on 6th April 1980, the Board shall exercise their discretion, in such cases as appear to them to be appropriate, so as to preserve—

(a) benefits earned or rights arising out of service before 6th April 1980; and

(b) any rights to death-in-service benefits conferred by rules of the scheme in force on 26th February 1970.

(5) The Board shall not approve a scheme by virtue of this section if to do so would be inconsistent with regulations made [by the Board]¹ for the purposes of this section.

(6) Regulations made [by the Board]¹ for the purposes of this section may restrict the Board's discretion to approve a scheme by reference to the benefits provided by the scheme, the investments held for the purposes of the scheme, the manner in which the scheme is administered or any other circumstances whatever.

Commentary—*Simon's Direct Tax Service* E7.213–215.
Regulations—Retirement Benefits Schemes (Restriction on Discretion to Approve) (Small Self-administered Schemes) Regulations, SI 1991/1614; Retirement Benefits Schemes (Restriction on Discretion to Approve) (Additional Voluntary Contributions) Regulations, SI 1993/3016; Retirement Benefits Schemes (Restriction on Discretion to Approve) (Additional Voluntary Contributions) (Amendment) Regulations, SI 1999/1964.
Revenue & other press releases—Pension Schemes Office 23-8-95 (Update 7: trustees of SSAPS may defer purchase of annuities for widows, widowers and dependants in certain circumstances).
Revenue Internal Guidance—Inspector's manual IM 8210–8212 (contributions to schemes which are approved but not exempt-approved dealt with on general Case I principles).
Definitions—"The Board", s 832(1); "children", ss 831(4), 832(5); "retirement benefits scheme", s 611; "United Kingdom", s 830(1).
Cross references—See TA 1988 s 591A (effect on approved schemes of regulations under this section).
TA 1988 s 657(2)(da) (annuity purchased under a scheme approved by virtue of this section not to be treated as a purchased life annuity).
TA 1988 s 659B(1) (meaning of "insurance company" for purpose of sub-s (2)(g) above).
Retirement Benefits Schemes (Restriction on Discretion to Approve) (Additional Voluntary Contributions) Regulations, SI 1993/3016 regs 4, 5 (restriction on discretion to approve voluntary contributions schemes and other schemes unless certain conditions are complied with).
Amendments—¹ Words in sub-ss (5), (6) inserted by FA 1988 Sch 13 para 6.
² Words in sub-s (2)(g) and sub-s (2A) inserted, words in sub-s (2)(g) repealed by FA 1994 s 107, Sch 26, Pt V(12) in relation to a scheme not approved by virtue of this section before 1 July 1994.
³ Sub-s (3) substituted by FA 1995 ss 59(2), 60(1), in relation to a scheme not approved by virtue of this section before 1 May 1995.
⁴ Words in sub-s (2)(b), and whole of sub-s (2)(ba) inserted, by FA 1999 s 79 Sch 10 para 3 with effect in accordance with the commencement provisions contained in FA 1999 Sch 10 para 18. Sub-s (2)(ba) has effect for the purposes of the grant or withdrawal at any time after 9 May 2000 of any approval of a retirement benefits scheme (whenever made or approved). Sub-ss (3)(bb) and (da) are to be disregarded for the purposes of determining whether any retirement benefits scheme approved

before 10 May 2000 satisfies the prescribed conditions at any time before 1 December 2000 (by virtue of the Finance Act 1999, Schedule 10, Paragraph 18, (First and Second Appointed Days) Order, SI 2000/1093).

[591A Effect on approved schemes of regulations under section 591

(1) Subsection (2) below applies where on or after 17th April 1991 regulations are made for the purposes of section 591 ("section 591 regulations") which contain provisions restricting the Board's discretion to approve a retirement benefits scheme by reference to any circumstances other than the benefits provided by the scheme ("relevant provisions").

(2) Any retirement benefits scheme approved by the Board by virtue of section 591 before the day on which the section 591 regulations come into force shall cease to be approved by virtue of that section at the end of the period of 36 months beginning with that day if at the end of that period the scheme—

(*a*) contains a provision of a prohibited description, or

(*b*) does not contain a provision of a required description,

unless the description of provision is specified in regulations made by the Board for the purposes of this subsection.

(3) For the purposes of this section, a provision contained in a scheme shall not be treated as being of a prohibited description by reason only of the fact that it authorises the retention of an investment held immediately before the day on which the section 591 regulations are made.

(4) In determining for the purposes of this section whether any provision contained in a scheme is of a required description, the fact that it is framed so as not to require the disposal of an investment held immediately before the day on which the section 591 regulations are made shall be disregarded.

(5) In this section—

(*a*) references to a provision of a prohibited description are to a provision of a description specified in the relevant provisions of the section 591 regulations as a description of provision which, if contained in a retirement benefits scheme, would prevent the Board from approving the scheme by virtue of section 591;

(*b*) references to a provision of a required description are to a provision of a description specified in the relevant provisions of the section 591 regulations as a description of provision which must be contained in a retirement benefits scheme before the Board may approve the scheme by virtue of section 591.][1]

Commentary—*Simon's Direct Tax Service* E7.215, 217.
Regulations—Retirement Benefits Schemes (Restriction on Discretion to Approve) (Excepted Schemes) Regulations, SI 1996/1582; Retirement Benefits Schemes (Restriction on Discretion to Approve) (Excepted Provisions) Regulations 1998, SI 1998/729; Retirement Benefits Schemes (Restriction on Discretion to Approve) (Additional Voluntary Contributions) (Amendment) Regulations, SI 1999/1964; Retirement Benefits Schemes (Restriction on Discretion to Approve) (Excepted Provisions) Regulations, SI 2000/1087.
Definitions—"The Board", s 832(1); "retirement benefits scheme", s 611.
Cross references—See Retirement Benefits Schemes (Restriction on Discretion to Approve) (Additional Voluntary Contributions) (Amendment) Regulations, SI 1999/1964 reg 6 (disapplication of sub-s (2) above in relation to the amendments to SI 1993/3016 regs 4–6 made by SI 1999/1964 regs 3(2)–5).
Amendments—[1] This section inserted by FA 1991 s 35.

[591B Cessation of approval: general provisions

(1) If in the opinion of the Board the facts concerning any approved scheme or its administration cease to warrant the continuance of their approval of the scheme, they may at any time by notice to the administrator, withdraw their approval on such grounds, and from such date (which shall not be earlier than the date when those facts first ceased to warrant the continuance of their approval or 17th March 1987, whichever is the later), as may be specified in the notice.

(2) Where an alteration has been made in a retirement benefits scheme, no approval given by the Board as regards the scheme before the alteration shall apply after the date of the alteration unless—

(*a*) the alteration has been approved by the Board, or

(*b*) the scheme is of a class specified in regulations made by the Board for the purposes of this paragraph and the alteration is of a description so specified in relation to schemes of that class.][1]

Commentary—*Simon's Direct Tax Service* E7.250.
Revenue Internal Guidance—Inspector's manual IM 8041 (circumstances where inspector should make a report to PSO).
Simon's Tax Cases—*R v IRC, ex p Roux Waterside Inn Ltd* [1997] STC 781.
Definitions—"The Board", s 832(1); "notice", s 832(1); "retirement benefits scheme", s 611.
Cross references—See TA 1988 s 611AA(8) (appointment of an administrator in relation to a retirement benefits scheme: appointment made after a scheme is established is an alteration of the scheme for the purposes of sub-s (2) above).
FA 1991 s 36(4)(*b*) (FA 1970 to be deemed always to have had effect with the insertion of s 20A which is in the same form as this section with certain modifications).
Amendments—[1] This section inserted by FA 1991 s 36(1), (3) and deemed always to have had effect.

[591C Cessation of approval: tax on certain schemes

(1) Where an approval of a scheme to which this section applies ceases to have effect [otherwise than by virtue of paragraph 3(2)(*a*) of Schedule 23ZA][4], tax shall be charged in accordance with this section.

(2) The tax shall be charged under Case VI of Schedule D at the rate of 40 per cent on an amount equal to the value of the assets which immediately before the date of the cessation of the approval of the scheme are held for the purposes of the scheme (taking that value as it stands immediately before that date).

(3) Subject to section 591D(4), the person liable for the tax shall be the administrator of the scheme ...[2]

(4) This section applies to a retirement benefits scheme in respect of which [one or more][3] of the conditions set out below is satisfied.

(5) The first condition is satisfied in respect of a scheme if, immediately before the date of the cessation of the approval of the scheme, the number of individuals who are members of the scheme is less than twelve.

(6) The second condition is satisfied in respect of a scheme if at any time within the period of one year ending with the date of the cessation of the approval of the scheme, a person who is or has been a controlling director of a company which has contributed to the scheme is a member of the scheme.

[(6A) The third condition is satisfied in respect of a scheme if—

(a) at any time within the period of three years ending with the date of the cessation of the approval of the scheme, the scheme has received a transfer value in respect of any person;
(b) contributions made by or in respect of that person to any approved pension arrangements (whether or not those from which the transfer value was received) were represented in the transfer value; and
(c) the contributions so represented were made by or in respect of that person by reference to—

(i) any service by him with a company of which he is or has at any time been a controlling director;
(ii) any remuneration in respect of any such service; or
(iii) any income chargeable to tax under Schedule D and immediately derived by him from the carrying on or exercise by him (whether as an individual or in partnership with others) of a trade, profession or vocation.][3]

(7) For the purposes of [this section][3] a person is a controlling director of a company if he is a director of it and within section 417(5)(b) in relation to it.][1]

[(8) In subsection (6A) above—

(a) the references to the receipt of a transfer value by a scheme are references to the transfer, so as to become held for the purposes of the scheme, of any sum or asset held for the purposes of any other approved pension arrangements; and
(b) the references to contributions to approved pension arrangements include references to—

(i) any contributions made in accordance with, or for the purposes of, the arrangements; and
(ii) anything paid by way of premium or other consideration under an annuity contract for which the arrangements provide.

(9) In this section "approved pension arrangements" means—

(a) any scheme or arrangements approved for the purposes of this Chapter or Chapter IV of this Part or, in relation to a time before 6th April 1988, the corresponding provisions then in force;
(b) any scheme being considered for approval under this Chapter;
(c) any annuity contract entered into for the purposes of any scheme or arrangements falling within paragraph (a) or (b) above; or
(d) any contract or scheme approved for the purposes of Chapter III of this Part or, in relation to a time before 6th April 1988, the corresponding provisions then in force.][3]

Commentary—*Simon's Direct Tax Service* E7.241, 250.
Revenue & other press releases—Pension Schemes Office 23-8-95 (Update 6: trustees will be given the opportunity to bring the scheme within approval criteria before approval is withdrawn).
Simon's Tax Cases—*R v IRC, ex p Roux Waterside Inn Ltd* [1997] STC 781; *Lambert and ors (administrators of the CID Pension Fund) v Glover (Insp of Taxes)* [2001] STC(SCD) 250.
Definitions—"Member", s 591D(8); "tax", s 832(3); "Schedule D", s 18(1).
Cross references—See TA 1988 s 591D(4) (an approved independent trustee in relation to a scheme is not chargeable to tax by virtue of this section).
TCGA 1992 s 272 (meaning of "market value" in connection with this section).
Amendments—[1] Section inserted by FA 1995 s 61(1), (3), in relation to any approval of a retirement benefits scheme which ceases to have effect after 1 November 1994 other than an approval ceasing to have effect by virtue of a notice given on or before that day under s 591B(1) *ante*.
[2] Words in sub-s (3) repealed by FA 1998 Sch 27 Part III(20) with effect from 31 July 1998.
[3] Words in sub-ss (4), (7) substituted and sub-s (6A), (8), (9) inserted by FA 1998 Sch 15 para 1 with effect in relation to any case in which the date of the cessation of the approval is on or after 17 March 1998.
[4] Words in sub-s (1) inserted by FA 2000 s 61, Sch 13 paras 1, 3 with effect from 28 July 2000.

[591D Section 591C: supplementary

(1) For the purposes of section 591C(2) the value of an asset is, subject to subsection (2) below, its market value, construing "market value" in accordance with section 272 of the 1992 Act.

(2) Where an asset held for the purposes of a scheme is a right or interest in respect of any money lent (directly or indirectly) to any person mentioned in subsection (3) below, the value of the asset shall be treated as being the amount owing (including any unpaid interest) on the money lent.

(3)　The persons are—

    (*a*)　any employer who has at any time contributed to the scheme;

    (*b*)　any company connected with such an employer;

    [(*c*)　any person who has at any time (whether or not before the making of the loan) been a member of the scheme;

    (*d*)　any person connected, at the time of the making of the loan or subsequently, with a person falling within paragraph (*c*) above.][2]

(4)　Where the administrator of the scheme is constituted by persons who include a person who is an approved independent trustee in relation to a scheme, that person shall not be liable for tax chargeable by virtue of section 591C.

(5)　A person is an approved independent trustee in relation to a scheme only if he is—

    (*a*)　approved by the Board to act as a trustee of the scheme; and

    (*b*)　not connected with—

        (i)　a member of the scheme;

        (ii)　any other trustee of the scheme; or

        (iii)　an employer who has contributed to the scheme.

(6)　For the purposes of section 596A(9) income and gains accruing to a scheme shall not be regarded as brought into charge to tax merely because tax is charged in relation to the scheme in accordance with section 591C.

(7)　The reference in section 591C(1) to an approval of a scheme ceasing to have effect is a reference to—

    (*a*)　the scheme ceasing to be an approved scheme by virtue of section 591A(2);

    (*b*)　the approval of the scheme being withdrawn under section 591B(1); or

    (*c*)　the approval of the scheme no longer applying by virtue of section 591B(2);

and any reference in section 591C to the date of the cessation of the approval of the scheme shall be construed accordingly.

(8)　For the purposes of section 591C and this section a person is a member of a scheme at a particular time if at that time a benefit—

    (*a*)　is being provided under the scheme, or

    (*b*)　may be so provided,

in respect of any past or present employment of his.

(9)　Section 839 shall apply for the purposes of this section.][1]

Commentary—*Simon's Direct Tax Service* **E7.241.**
Simon's Tax Cases—*Lambert and ors (administrators of the CID Pension Fund) v Glover (Insp of Taxes)* [2001] STC(SCD) 250.
Definitions—"The Board", s 832(1); "tax", s 832(3).
Amendments—[1] Section inserted by FA 1995 s 61(1), (3), in relation to any approval of a retirement benefits scheme which ceases to have effect after 1 November 1994 other than an approval ceasing to have effect by virtue of a notice given on or before that day under s 591B(1) *ante*.
[2] Sub-s (3)(*c*), (*d*) substituted by FA 1998 Sch 15 para 2 with effect in relation to any case in which the date of the cessation of the approval of the scheme is on or after 17 March 1998.

Tax reliefs

592 Exempt approved schemes

(1)　This section has effect as respects—

    (*a*)　any approved scheme which is shown to the satisfaction of the Board to be established under irrevocable trusts; or

    (*b*)　any other approved scheme as respects which the Board, having regard to any special circumstances, direct that this section shall apply;

and any scheme which is for the time being within paragraph (*a*) or (*b*) above is in this Chapter referred to as an "exempt approved scheme".

(2)　Exemption from income tax shall, on a claim being made in that behalf, be allowed in respect of income derived from investments or deposits if, or to such extent as the Board are satisfied that, it is income from investments or deposits held for the purposes of the scheme.

(3)　Exemption from income tax shall, on a claim being made in that behalf, be allowed in respect of underwriting commissions if, or to such extent as the Board are satisfied that, the underwriting commissions are applied for the purposes of the schemes and would, but for this subsection, be chargeable to tax under Case VI of Schedule D.

(4)　Any sum paid by an employer by way of contribution under the scheme shall, for the purposes of Case I or II of Schedule D and of sections 75 and 76, be allowed to be deducted as an expense, or expense of management, incurred in the chargeable period in which the sum is paid [but no other sum shall for those purposes be allowed to be deducted as an expense, or expense of management, in respect of the making, or any provision for the making, of any contributions under the Scheme][3].

(5)　The amount of an employer's contributions which may be deducted under subsection (4) above shall not exceed the amount contributed by him under the scheme in respect of employees in a trade or undertaking in respect of the profits of which the employer is assessable to tax (that is to say, to United Kingdom income tax or corporation tax).

(6) A sum not paid by way of ordinary annual contribution shall for the purposes of subsection (4) above be treated, as the Board may direct, either as an expense incurred in the chargeable period in which the sum is paid, or as an expense to be spread over such period of years as the Board think proper.

[(6A) Where any sum is paid to the trustees of the scheme in or towards the discharge of any liability of an employer under section 58B of the Social Security Pensions Act 1975 or section 144 of the Pension Schemes Act 1993 (deficiencies in the assets of a scheme) or under Article 68B of the Social Security Pensions (Northern Ireland) Order 1975 or section 140 of the Pension Schemes (Northern Ireland) Act 1993 (which contain corresponding provision for Northern Ireland), the payment of that sum—

(a) shall be treated for the purposes of this section as an employer's contribution under the scheme; and

(b) notwithstanding (where it is the case) that the employer's trade, profession, vocation or business is permanently discontinued before the making of the payment, shall be allowed, in accordance with subsection (4) above, to be deducted as such a contribution to the same extent as it would have been allowed but for the discontinuance and as if it had been made on the last day on which the trade, profession, vocation or business was carried on.][4]

(7) Any contribution paid under the scheme by an employee shall, in assessing tax under Schedule E, be allowed to be deducted as an expense incurred in the year of assessment in which the contribution is paid.

(8) [Subject to subsection (8A) below,][1] the amount allowed to be deducted by virtue of subsection (7) above in respect of contributions paid by an employee in a year of assessment (whether under a single scheme or under two or more schemes) shall not exceed 15 per cent, or such higher percentage as the Board may in a particular case prescribe, of his remuneration for that year.

[(8A) Where an employee's remuneration for a year of assessment includes remuneration in respect of more than one employment, the amount allowed to be deducted by virtue of subsection (7) above in respect of contributions paid by the employee in that year by virtue of any employment (whether under a single scheme or under two or more schemes) shall not exceed 15 per cent, or such higher percentage as the Board may in a particular case prescribe, of his remuneration for the year in respect of that employment.][2]

[(8B) In arriving at an employee's remuneration for a year of assessment for the purposes of subsection (8) or (8A) above, any excess of what would be his remuneration (apart from this subsection) over the permitted maximum for that year shall be disregarded.][2]

[(8C) In subsection (8B) above "permitted maximum", in relation to a year of assessment, means the figure found for that year by virtue of subsections (8D) and (8E) below.][2]

[(8D) For the year of assessment 1989–90 the figure is £60,000.][2]

[(8E) For any subsequent year of assessment the figure is the figure found for that year, for the purposes of section 590C, by virtue of section 590C(4) [to (5A)][5].][2]

(9) Relief shall not be given under section 266 or 273 in respect of any payment in respect of which an allowance can be made under subsection (7) above.

(10) Subsection (2) of section 468 and subsection (3) of section 469 shall not apply to any authorised unit trust which is also an exempt approved scheme if the employer is not a contributor to the exempt approved scheme and that scheme provides benefits additional to those provided by another exempt approved scheme to which he is a contributor.

(11) Nothing in this section shall be construed as affording relief in respect of any sums to be brought into account under section 438.

(12) This section has effect only as respects income arising or contributions paid at a time when the scheme is an exempt approved scheme.

Commentary—*Simon's Direct Tax Service* E7.203, 216, 221, 231.
Note—For the year 2000–01 the figure specified for the purpose of sub-s (8E) by virtue of s 590C is £91,800 by virtue of the Retirement Benefits Schemes (Indexation of Earnings Cap) Order, SI 2000/807.
Simon's Tax Cases—s 592(3)(*c*), *Clarke v British Telecom Pension Scheme Trustees* [2000] STC 222.
s 592(4), (6), *Kelsall v Investment Chartwork Ltd* [1994] STC 33*.
Revenue Internal Guidance—Schedule E manual SE 42775 (contributions to an approved retirement benefits scheme. practical considerations, application of sub-ss (7) and (8)).
Definitions—"Authorised unit trust", s 832(1); "the Board", s 832(1); "chargeable period", s 832(1); "Schedule D", s 18(1); "Schedule E", s 19(1); "United Kingdom", s 830(1); "year of assessment", s 832(1).
Cross references—See TA 1988 s 129B (the income eligible for relief under sub-s (2) above includes stock lending fees payable in connection with approved arrangements relating to the relevant investments).
TA 1988 s 231A (tax credits not repayable in respect of qualifying distributions made after 1 July 1997 to pension funds — see sub-s (2) above).
TA 1988 s 593(1) (relief under sub-s (7) above to be given in accordance with s 593(2), (3)).
TA 1988 s 607 (this section to have effect with modifications in relation to pilots' benefit fund).
TA 1988 s 659A ("investments" and "income" for the purposes of sub-s (2) above to include futures and options and transactions relating to them).
TA 1988 s 659D(2) (the exemption within sub-s (2) above does not apply to income derived from investments, deposits or other property held as a member of a property investment LLP).

TA 1988 Sch 22, para 7(3), (4) (pension fund surpluses: curtailment under certain circumstances of tax exemption under sub-ss (2), (3) above).

TCGA 1992 s 271(1)(*j*) (an authorised unit trust to which sub-s (10) above applies exempt from tax in respect of gains on disposal of units);

FA 1993 s 112 (tax exemption for employer's contributions to occupational pension schemes; for accounting and basis periods ending after 5 April 1993, the exemption is limited to contributions actually paid).

Manufactured Payments and Transfer of Securities (Tax Relief) Regulations, SI 1995/3036 regs 3, 4 (manufactured payments and deemed interest payments on a sale and repurchase of securities for the benefit of a scheme referred to in sub-s (2) above to be treated as income of the person eligible for relief by virtue of that subsection).

Amendments—[1] Words in sub-s (8) inserted by FA 1989 Sch 6 para 5(1), (2).

[2] Sub-ss (8A) to (8E) inserted by FA 1989 Sch 6 paras 5(1), (3), (4), 18(4) with effect from the year 1989–90; sub-ss (8B)–(8E) (earnings cap) may be disapplied in circumstances prescribed by regulations: see SI 1990/586.

[3] Words in sub-s (4) inserted by FA 1993 s 112(1), (2) with effect in relation to accounting periods or basis periods (as defined in FA 1993 s 112(7)) ending after 5 April 1993.

[4] Sub-s (6A) inserted by FA 1993 s 112(6) in relation to payments made after 26 July 1993.

[5] Words in sub-s (8E) substituted by FA 1993 s 107(6), (8) with effect from the year 1994–95.

593 Relief by way of deductions from contributions

(1) Relief under section 592(7) shall be given in accordance with subsections (2) and (3) below in such cases and subject to such conditions as the Board may prescribe by regulations under section 612(3) in respect of schemes—

    (*a*) to which employees, but not their employers, are contributors; and

    (*b*) which provide benefits additional to benefits provided by schemes to which their employers are contributors.

(2) An employee who is entitled to relief under section 592(7) in respect of a contribution may deduct from the contribution when he pays it, and may retain, an amount equal to income tax at the basic rate on the contribution.

(3) The administrator of the scheme—

    (*a*) shall accept the amount paid after the deduction in discharge of the employee's liability to the same extent as if the deduction had not been made; and

    (*b*) may recover an amount equal to the deduction from the Board.

(4) Regulations under subsection (3) of section 612 may, without prejudice to the generality of that subsection—

    (*a*) provide for the manner in which claims for the recovery of a sum under subsection (3)(*b*) above may be made;

    (*b*) provide for the giving of such information, in such form, as may be prescribed by or under the regulations;

    (*c*) provide for the inspection by persons authorised by the Board of books, documents and other records.

Commentary—*Simon's Direct Tax Service* E7.205.

Regulations—Occupational Pension Schemes (Additional Voluntary Contributions) Regulations, SI 1987/1749. For continuity see Sch 30 para 21 of this Act.

Revenue Internal Guidance—Schedule E manual SE 20104 (notes on calculating whether an employment has emoluments of £8,500 a year or more, deductions under this section are made).

Definitions—''Administrator'', s 611AA; ''basic rate'', s 832(1); ''the Board'', s 832(1).

Cross references—See TA 1988 s 265(3), (4) (disallowance of the deduction on account of a payment under sub-s (2) above for calculating total income of a blind husband for determining any excess in blind person's allowance which may be transferred to wife).

594 Exempt statutory schemes

(1) Any contribution paid by any officer or employee under a [relevant][1] statutory scheme established under a public general Act shall, in assessing tax under Schedule E, be allowed to be deducted as an expense incurred in the year of assessment in which the contribution is paid; and relief shall not be given under section 266 or 273 in respect of any contribution allowable as a deduction under this section.

(2) [Subject to subsection (3) below,][2] the amount allowed to be deducted by virtue of subsection (1) above in respect of contributions paid by a person in a year of assessment (whether under a single scheme or under two or more schemes) shall not exceed 15 per cent, or such higher percentage as the Board may in a particular case prescribe, of his remuneration for that year.

[(3) Where a person's remuneration for a year of assessment includes remuneration in respect of more than one office or employment, the amount allowed to be deducted by virtue of subsection (1) above in respect of contributions paid by the person in that year by virtue of any office or employment (whether under a single scheme or under two or more schemes) shall not exceed 15 per cent, or such higher percentage as the Board may in a particular case prescribe, of his remuneration for the year in respect of that office or employment.

(4) In arriving at a person's remuneration for a year of assessment for the purposes of subsection (2) or (3) above, any excess of what would be his remuneration (apart from this subsection) over the permitted maximum for that year shall be disregarded.

(5) In subsection (4) above ''permitted maximum'', in relation to a year of assessment, means the figure found for that year by virtue of subsections (6) and (7) below.

(6) For the year 1989–90 the figure is £60,000.

(7) For any subsequent year of assessment the figure is the figure found for that year, for the purposes of section 590C, by virtue of section 590C(4) [to (5A)][4].][3]

Commentary—*Simon's Direct Tax Service* **E7.232, 261.**
Concession A9—This section extends to assessments under Schedule D Case II on the profits of a medical or dental practitioner. Concessionary relief is allowed on one of two bases specified in the Concession where a medical or dental practitioner makes superannuation contributions under NHS Acts and pays retirement annuity premiums under ss 619–624 of this Act.
Note—For the year 2000–01 the figure specified for the purpose of sub-s (7) by virtue of s 590C is £91,800 by virtue of the Retirement Benefits Schemes (Indexation of Earnings Cap) Order, SI 2000/807.
Revenue Internal Guidance—Schedule E manual SE 61025 (NHS contributions and payments under retirement annuity contracts—doctors, etc wholly in employment entitled under this section to a deduction for contributions to the National Health Service Superannuation Scheme).
Definitions—"Act", s 832(1); "the Board", s 832(1); "Schedule E", s 19(1); "year of assessment", s 832(1).
Amendments—[1] Word in sub-s (1) inserted by FA 1989 Sch 6 paras 6(1), (2), 18(1) with effect from 14 March 1989.
[2] Words in sub-s (2) inserted by FA 1989 Sch 6 paras 6(1), (3), 18(4).
[3] Sub-ss (3) to (7) inserted by FA 1989 Sch 6 paras 6(1), (4), (5), 18(4) with effect from the year 1989–90; sub-ss (4)–(7) (earnings cap) may be disapplied in circumstances prescribed by regulations: see SI 1990/586.
[4] Words in sub-s (7) substituted by FA 1993 s 107(6), (8) with effect from the year 1994–95.

Charge to tax in certain cases

595 Charge to tax in respect of certain sums paid by employer etc

(1) Subject to the provisions of this Chapter, where, pursuant to a retirement benefits scheme, the employer in any year of assessment pays a sum with a view to the provision of any relevant benefits for any employee of that employer, then (whether or not the accrual of the benefits is dependent on any contingency)—

  (*a*) the sum paid, if [(disregarding section 148) it is][3] not otherwise chargeable to income tax as income of the employee, shall be deemed for all purposes of the Income Tax Acts to be income of that employee for that year of assessment and assessable to tax under Schedule E; and
  (*b*) where the payment is made under such an insurance or contract as is mentioned in section 266, relief, if not otherwise allowable, shall be given to that employee under that section in respect of the payment to the extent, if any, to which such relief would have been allowable to him if the payment had been made by him and the insurance or contract under which the payment is made had been made with him.

(2), (3) ...[1]

(4) Where the employer pays any sum as mentioned in subsection (1) above in relation to more than one employee, the sum so paid shall, for the purpose of that subsection, be apportioned among those employees by reference to the separate sums which would have had to be paid to secure the separate benefits to be provided for them respectively, and the part of the sum apportioned to each of them shall be deemed for that purpose to have been paid separately in relation to that one of them.

(5) Any reference in this section to the provision for an employee of relevant benefits includes a reference to the provision of benefits payable to that employee's wife [or husband,][2] or widow [or widower or][2], children, dependants or personal representatives.

Commentary—*Simon's Direct Tax Service* **E7.205, 256, 257.**
Simon's Tax Cases—*Sports Club plc and others v Insp of Taxes* [2000] STC (SCD) 443.
Concession A72—Pension, annuity, gratuity, lump sum etc paid by an employer to his employee's family on employee's death or retirement is not taxed.
Revenue Internal Guidance—Schedule E manual SE 8005 (emoluments: transfer of real property to employees and directors—charge to tax under this section could arise where the transfer is part of an unapproved retirement benefits scheme).
SE 15000 (non-approved retirement benefits schemes: table of contents covering references SE 15010–15428).
SE 21800 (pension provisions: Schedule E charge under this section can arise where an employer makes contributions to a non-approved retirement benefits scheme).
Definitions—"Children", s 831(4), 832(5); "emoluments", s 131(1); "the Income Tax Acts", s 831(1)(*b*); "retirement benefits scheme", s 611; "Schedule E", s 19(1); "year of assessment", s 832(1).
Cross references—See TA 1988 s 189 (lump sum benefits on retirement).
TA 1988 s 596 (exceptions from this section).
TA 1988 Sch 14, para 5 (supplementary provisions as to relief under sub-s (1)(*b*) above).
Amendments—[1] Sub-ss (2), (3) repealed by FA 1989 Sch 6 paras 7, 18(5) and Sch 17, Pt IV with retrospective effect from the year 1988–89.
[2] In sub-s (5) words inserted by FA 1999 s 79 Sch 10 para 4 with effect in accordance with the commencement provisions contained in FA 1999 Sch 10 para 18.
[3] Words in sub-s (1)(*a*) inserted by FA 2002 s 37, Sch 6 para 6 with effect from the year 2002–03.

596 Exceptions from section 595

(1) [Section 595(1) shall not][1] apply where the retirement benefits scheme in question is—

  (*a*) an approved scheme, or
  (*b*) a [relevant][2] statutory scheme, or
  (*c*) a scheme set up by a government outside the United Kingdom for the benefit, or primarily for the benefit of, its employees.

(2) [Section 595(1) shall not][1] apply for any year of assessment—

  (*a*) where the employee performs the duties of his employment in such circumstances that no tax is chargeable under Case I or II of Schedule E in respect of the emoluments of his employment (or would be so chargeable were there such emoluments), or (*b*) where the emoluments from the employment are foreign emoluments within the meaning of section 192 and the Board are satisfied, on a claim made by the employee, that the retirement benefits scheme in question corresponds to such a scheme as is mentioned in paragraph (*a*), (*b*) or (*c*) of subsection (1) above.

(3) Where, in respect of the provision for an employee of any relevant benefits—

(*a*) a sum has been deemed to be income of his by virtue ...[3] of subsection (1) ...[3] of section 595, and

(*b*) subsequently, the employee proves to the satisfaction of the Board that—

(i) no payment in respect of, or in substitution for, the benefits has been made, and

(ii) some event has occurred by reason of which no such payment will be made,

and makes application for relief under this subsection within six years from the time when that event occurred,

the Board shall give relief in respect of tax on that sum by repayment or otherwise as may be appropriate; and if the employee satisfies the Board as mentioned above in relation to some particular part, but not the whole, of the benefits, the Board may give such relief as may seem to them just and reasonable.

[(4) Relief shall not be given under subsection (3) above in respect of tax on any sum if—

(*a*) the reason for there having been no payment in respect of, or in substitution for, the benefits, or part of the benefits, in question, or

(*b*) the event by reason of which there will be no such payment,

is a reduction or cancellation, as a consequence of any pension sharing order or provision, of the employee's rights in respect of the benefits.][4]

Commentary—*Simon's Direct Tax Service* **E4.802, E7.205.**
Concession B39—Contributions to overseas pension schemes.
Revenue Internal Guidance—Schedule E manual, SE 04800 (retirement lump sums exempt under this section).
SE 15030 (non-approved "retirement benefits schemes": identification).
SE 15050 (non-approved retirement benefits schemes: contributions made by employer excluded from charge, includes in practice where a 100% deduction is allowable against the emoluments).
SE 15070 (non-approved retirement benefits schemes: repayment claims, application of sub-s (3)).
Definitions—"The Board", s 832(1); "Case I of Schedule E", s 19(2); "Case II of Schedule E", s 19(2); "retirement benefits scheme", s 611; "United Kingdom", s 830(1).
Cross references—See TA 1988 s 189 (lump sum benefits on retirement).
TA 1988 s 596A (charge to tax of benefits under schemes other than the ones mentioned in sub-s (1) above).
Amendments—[1] Words in sub-ss (1), (2) substituted by FA 1989 Sch 6 paras 8(1), (2)(*a*), (3), 18(5) with retrospective effect from the year 1988–89.
[2] Words in sub-s (1)(*b*) inserted by FA 1989 Sch 6 paras 8(1), (2)(*b*), 18(1) with effect from 14 March 1989.
[3] Words in sub-s (3)(*a*) repealed by FA 1989 Sch 6 paras 8(1), (4), 18(6) and Sch 17, Pt IV except where a sum has been deemed to be income of a person by virtue of s 595(2) of this Act after 5 April 1988.
[4] Sub-s (4) inserted by FA 1999 s 79 Sch 10 para 5 with effect in accordance with the commencement provisions contained in FA 1999 Sch 10 para 18.

[596A Charge to tax: benefits under non-approved schemes

(1) Where in any year of assessment a person receives a benefit provided under a retirement benefits scheme which is not of a description mentioned in section 596(1)(*a*), (*b*) or (*c*), tax shall be charged in accordance with the provisions of this section.

(2) Where the benefit is received by an individual, he shall be charged to tax under Schedule E for that year.

(3) Where the benefit is received by a person other than an individual, the administrator of the scheme shall be charged to tax under Case VI of Schedule D for that year.

(4) [Subject to subsection (9) below][2] the amount to be charged to tax is—

(*a*) in the case of a cash benefit, the amount received, and

[(*b*) in the case of a non-cash benefit, whichever is the greater of—

(i) the amount which would be chargeable to tax under section 19(1) if the benefit were taxable as an emolument of the employment under Case I of Schedule E, or

(ii) the cash equivalent of the benefit determined in accordance with section 596B.][3]

(5) In the case of the charge under Case VI of Schedule D, the rate of tax is 40 per cent or such other rate (whether higher or lower) as may for the time being be specified by the Treasury by order.

[(6) Tax shall not be charged under this section in the case of—

(*a*) any pension or annuity which is chargeable to tax under Schedule E by virtue of section 19(1); or

(*b*) any pension or other benefit chargeable to tax under section 58.][2]

(7) But where the amount chargeable to tax [as mentioned in subsection (6)(*a*) above][2] is less than the amount which would be chargeable to tax under this section—

(*a*) [subsection (6)(*a*) above][2] shall not apply, and

(*b*) the amount chargeable to tax under this section shall be reduced by the amount chargeable to tax by virtue of [section 19(1)][2].

[(8) Subject to subsection (9) below, tax shall not be charged under this section (or section 19(1) or 148) in the case of a lump sum where—

(a) the employer has paid any sum or sums with a view to the provision of any relevant benefits under a retirement benefits scheme;

(b) an employee has been assessed to tax in respect of the sum or sums by virtue of section 595(1); and

(c) the lump sum is provided under the scheme to the employee, [an ex-spouse of the employee,][4] any person falling within section 595(5) in relation to the employee or any other individual designated by the employee.

(9) Where any of the income or gains accruing to the scheme under which the lump sum is provided is not brought into charge to tax, tax shall be charged under this section on the amount of the lump sum received less any deduction applicable under subsection (10) or (11) below.

(10) Subject to subsection (11) below, the deduction applicable is the aggregate of—

(a) any sum or sums in respect of which the employee has been assessed as mentioned in subsection (8)(b) above, and

(b) any sum or sums paid by the employee,

which in either case were paid by way of contribution to the provision of the lump sum.

(11) Where—

(a) the lump sum is provided under the scheme on the disposal of a part of any asset or the surrender of any part of or share in any rights in any asset, and

(b) the employee, any person falling within section 595(5) in relation to the employee or any person connected with the employee has any right to receive or any expectation of receiving a further lump sum (or further lump sums) under the scheme on a further disposal of any part of the asset or a further surrender of any part of or share in any rights in the asset,

the deduction applicable shall be determined in accordance with the formula in subsection (12) below.

(12) The formula is—

$$D = S \times \frac{A}{B}$$

(13) For the purposes of the formula in subsection (12) above—

D is the deduction applicable;

S is the aggregate amount of any sum or sums of a description mentioned in paragraphs (a) and (b) of subsection (10) above;

A is the amount of the lump sum received in relation to which the deduction applicable falls to be determined;

B is the market value of the asset in relation to which the disposal or surrender occurred, on the assumption that the valuation is made immediately before the disposal or surrender.

(14) An individual may not claim that a deduction is applicable in relation to a lump sum more than once.

(15) For the purposes of subsections (8) and (9) above, it shall be assumed unless the contrary is shown—

(a) that no sums have been paid, and the employee has not been assessed in respect of any sums paid, with a view to the provision of relevant benefits;

(b) that the income or gains accruing to a scheme under which the benefit is provided are not brought into charge to tax; and

(c) that no deduction is applicable under subsection (10) or (11) above.

(16) Section 839 shall apply for the purposes of subsection (11) above.

(17) In subsection (13) above "market value" shall be construed in accordance with section 272 of the 1992 Act.][2][1]

Commentary—*Simon's Direct Tax Service* E4.802, 805D, E7.256–258.
Concession A10—Lump sums paid under overseas pension schemes.
Statement of Practice SP13/91, para 9—Certain ex gratia award made on termination of an office or employment by retirement or death to be charged to tax under Schedule E.
Revenue & other press releases—IR booklet 3-9-91 "The Tax treatment of non-approved top-up pension schemes" (guidance, definitions and explanation of tax treatment, including employer's position and reporting requirements).
Revenue Internal Guidance—Schedule E manual SE 8005 (emoluments: transfer of real property to employees and directors—charge to tax under this section could arise where the transfer is part of an unapproved retirement benefits scheme).
SE 12805 and SE 12810 (termination payments and benefits: introduction and application of this section).
SE 13005 (termination payments and benefits: a gratuity given on or after retirement is taxed under this section; a payment to commute pensions from a non-approved retirement benefits scheme chargeable under this section).
SE 15000 (non-approved retirement benefits schemes: table of contents covering references SE 15010–15428).
SE 65870 (terminal gratuities for non-pensionable service made since 6 July 1995 under the Local Government Superannuation (Gratuities) Regulations 1995—lump sums from unapproved schemes chargeable under this section).
Definitions—"Administrator", s 611AA; "retirement benefits scheme", s 611; "year of assessment", s 832(1).
Cross references—See TA 1988 s 591D (income and gains accruing to a scheme shall not be regarded as chargeable to tax for the purposes of sub-s (9) merely because tax is charged in relation to the scheme in accordance with s 591C).
TA 1988 s 596B (supplementary provisions).

Amendments—[1] This section inserted by FA 1989 Sch 6 paras 9, 18(7) in relation to payments made and benefits provided after 26 July 1989.
[2] Words in sub-s (4) inserted, sub-s (6), sub-ss (8)–(17) (for sub-ss (8), (9)) and words in sub-s (7) substituted by FA 1994 s 108 in relation to retirement benefit schemes entered into after 30 November 1993 or entered into on or before that day if the scheme is varied on or after that day with a view to the provision of benefit.
[3] Sub-s (4)(b) substituted by FA 1998 s 93(1) with effect in relation to benefits received in the year 1998–99 and subsequent years of assessment.
[4] Words in sub-s (8) inserted by FA 1999 s 79 Sch 10 para 6 with effect in relation to a lump sum provided after 30 November 2000 (by virtue of the Finance Act 1999, Schedule 10, Paragraph 18, (First and Second Appointed Days) Order, SI 2000/1093).

[596B Section 596A: supplementary provisions

(1) For the purposes of section 596A the cash equivalent of a benefit in kind is—

(a) in the case of a benefit other than living accommodation, the amount which would be the cash equivalent of the benefit under Chapter II of Part V if it were chargeable under the appropriate provision of that Chapter (treating any sum made good by the recipient as made good by the employee), and

(b) in the case of living accommodation, an amount equal to the value of the accommodation to the recipient determined in accordance with the following provisions of this section less so much of any sum made good by him to those at whose cost the accommodation is provided as is properly attributable to the provision of the accommodation.

(2) Where the cost of providing the accommodation does not exceed £75,000, the value of the accommodation to the recipient in any period is the rent which would have been payable for the period if the premises had been let to him at an annual rent equal to their annual value as ascertained under section 837.

(3) But for a period in which those at whose cost the accommodation is provided pay rent at an annual rate greater than the annual value as so ascertained, the value of the accommodation to the recipient is an amount equal to the rent payable by them for the period.

(4) Where the cost of providing the accommodation does exceed £75,000, the value of the accommodation to the recipient shall be taken to be the aggregate of the value of the accommodation to him determined in accordance with subsections (2) and (3) above and the additional value of the accommodation to him determined in accordance with subsections (5) and (6) below.

(5) The additional value of the accommodation to the recipient in any period is the rent which would have been payable for that period if the premises had been let to him at an annual rent equal to the appropriate percentage of the amount by which the cost of providing the accommodation exceeds £75,000.

(6) Where throughout the period of six years ending with the date when the recipient first occupied the property any estate or interest in the property was held by a relevant person (whether or not it was the same estate, interest or person throughout), the additional value shall be calculated as if in subsection (7) below—

(a) the amount referred to in paragraph (a) were the market value of that property as at that date, and

(b) the amount referred to in paragraph (b) did not include expenditure on improvements made before that date.

(7) For the purposes of this section, the cost of providing any living accommodation shall be taken to be the aggregate of—

(a) the amount of any expenditure incurred in acquiring the estate or interest in the property held by a relevant person, and

(b) the amount of any expenditure incurred by a relevant person before the year of assessment in question on improvements to the property.

(8) The aggregate amount mentioned in subsection (7) above shall be reduced by the amount of any payment made by the recipient to a relevant person, so far as that amount represents a reimbursement of any such expenditure as is mentioned in paragraph (a) or (b) of that subsection or represents consideration for the grant to the recipient of a tenancy of the property.

(9) For the purposes of this section, any of the following persons is a relevant person—

(a) the person providing the accommodation;

[(b) the employer or former employer; or

(c) any person, other than the recipient, who is connected with a person falling within paragraph (a) or (b) above.][2]

(10) In this section—

"the appropriate percentage" means the rate applicable for the purposes of section 160 as at the beginning of the year of assessment in question;

"market value", in relation to any property, means the price which that property might reasonably be expected to fetch on a sale in the open market with vacant possession, no reduction being made, in estimating the market value, on account of any option in respect of the property held by the recipient, or a person connected with him, or by any of the persons mentioned in subsection (9) above;

"property", in relation to any living accommodation, means the property consisting of that living accommodation;

"tenancy" includes a sub-tenancy;

and section 839 shall apply for the purposes of this section.][1]

Commentary—*Simon's Direct Tax Service* E7.258.
Revenue Internal Guidance—Schedule E manual SE 13270 and SE 13280 (termination payments and benefits: valuation of non-cash benefits received on or after 6 April 1998, application of this section).
SE 13300 (calculating the "cash equivalent" for non-cash benefits other than living accommodation received after 6 April 1998)
SE 13310 (rules appropriate to particular benefits).
SE 13330 (calculating the "cash equivalent" for living accommodation received on or after 6 April 1998).
SE 13331 (living accommodation after 6 April 1998: "cash equivalent" list of definitions).
SE 13338 (example where "cost of providing" living accommodation is £75,000 or less).
SE 13340–13360 (examples where "cost of providing" living accommodation is more than £75,000).
SE 13934 (example of valuation of non-cash benefits received after 6 April 1998 using the "Section 19" value).
SE 14000 (example illustrating the calculation of "cost of providing living accommodation").
SE 15120 (non-approved retirement benefits schemes: non-cash benefits received, application of this section).
Amendments—[1] This section inserted by FA 1989 Sch 6 paras 9, 18(7) in relation to payments made and benefits provided after 26 July 1989.
[2] Sub-s (9)(*b*) substituted by FA 1998 s 93(2) with effect in relation to benefits received in the year 1998–99 and subsequent years of assessment.

[596C Notional interest treated as paid if amount charged in respect of beneficial loan

(1) This section applies where a person is chargeable to tax under section 596A in any year of assessment on an amount which consists of or includes an amount representing the cash equivalent of the benefit of a loan determined (by virtue of section 596B(1)(*a*)) in accordance with Part II of Schedule 7.

(2) Where this section applies, the person chargeable is treated as having paid interest on the loan of the same amount as the cash equivalent so determined.

(3) The interest is treated as paid for all the purposes of the Tax Acts (other than those relating to the charge under section 596A) but not so as to make it—

(*a*) income of the person making the loan, or
(*b*) relevant loan interest to which section 369 applies (mortgage interest payable under deduction of tax).

(4) The interest is treated as accruing during and paid at the end of the year of assessment or, if different, the period in that year during which the loan is outstanding.][1]

Commentary—*Simon's Direct Tax Service* E7.258.
Revenue Internal Guidance—Schedule E manual SE 15120 (non-approved retirement benefits schemes: non-cash benefits received, application of this section).
Amendments—[1] This section inserted by FA 1998 s 93(3) with effect in relation to benefits received in the year 1998–99 and subsequent years of assessment.

597 Charge to tax: pensions

(1) Subject to subsection (2) below, all pensions paid under any scheme which is approved or is being considered for approval under this Chapter shall be charged to tax under Schedule E, and section 203 shall apply accordingly.

(2) As respects any scheme which is approved or is being considered for approval under this Chapter, the Board may direct that, until such date as the Board may specify, pensions under the scheme shall be charged to tax as annual payments under Case III of Schedule D, and tax shall be deductible under sections 348 and 349 accordingly.

[(3) Without prejudice to subsection (1) above, where funds held for the purposes of any scheme which is approved or is being considered for approval under this Chapter are used to acquire an annuity—

(*a*) the annuity shall be charged to tax under Schedule E and section 203 shall apply accordingly;
(*b*) the annuity shall not be charged to tax under Case III of Schedule D.][1]

Commentary—*Simon's Direct Tax Service* E4.126; E7.234.
Simon's Tax Cases—*Esslemont v Estill* [1979] STC 624*.
Revenue Internal Guidance—Schedule E manual SE 74009 (pensions from superannuation funds—charge under this section).
Definitions—"The Board", s 832(1); "administrator", s 611AA; "Schedule D", s 18(1); "Schedule E", s 19(1).
Cross references—See TA 1988 s 607 (this section to have effect with modifications in relation to pilots' benefit fund).
FA 1989 s 41(1) (*d*) (a pension chargeable to income tax under this section to be charged in the year of assessment in which it accrues irrespective of when it is paid).
Amendments—[1] Sub-s (3) inserted by FA 1994 s 110 in relation to annuity payments made after 2 May 1994.

598 Charge to tax: repayment of employee's contributions

(1) Subject to the provisions of this section, tax shall be charged under this section on any repayment to an employee during his lifetime of any contributions (including interest on contributions, if any) if the payment is made under—

(*a*) a scheme which is or has at any time been an exempt approved scheme, or
(*b*) a [relevant][2] statutory scheme established under a public general Act.

(2) Where any payment is chargeable to tax under this section, the administrator of the scheme shall be charged to income tax under Case VI of Schedule D and, subject to subsection (3) below, the rate of tax shall be [20][1] per cent.

(3) The Treasury may by order from time to time increase or decrease the rate of tax under subsection (2) above.

(4) The tax shall be charged on the amount paid or, if the rules permit the administrator to deduct the tax before payment, on the amount before deduction of tax, and the amount so charged to tax shall not be treated as income for any other purpose of the Tax Acts.

(5) Subsection (1)(*a*) above shall not apply in relation to a contribution made after the scheme ceases to be an exempt approved scheme (unless it again becomes an exempt approved scheme).

(6) This section shall not apply where the employee's employment was carried on outside the United Kingdom.

(7) In relation to a statutory scheme, "employee" in this section includes any officer.

Commentary—*Simon's Direct Tax Service* **E4.802, E7.236.**
Definitions—"Act", s 832(1); "administrator", s 611AA; "Schedule D", s 18(1); "the Tax Acts", s 831(2); "United Kingdom", s 830(1).
Cross references—See TA 1988 s 599(3) (application of sub-s (2)-(4) above to tax chargeable on commutation of pension).
TA 1988 s 600(3) (charge to tax of unauthorised payments out of funds of schemes approved under this Chapter).
TA 1988 s 607 (this section to have effect with modifications in relation to pilots' benefit fund).
Amendments—[1] Rate mentioned in sub-s (2) increased from 10 per cent to 20 per cent by the Occupational Pension Schemes (Rate of Tax under Paragraph 2(2) of Part II of Schedule 5 to the Finance Act 1970) Order 1988, SI 1988/504 with effect from 6 April 1988.
[2] Word in sub-s (1)(*b*) inserted by FA 1989 Sch 6 paras 10, 18(1) with effect from 14 March 1989.

599 Charge to tax: commutation of entire pension in special circumstances

(1) [Subject to subsection (1A) below,][5] where a scheme to which this section applies contains a rule allowing, in special circumstances, a payment in commutation of an employee's entire pension, and any pension is commuted, whether wholly or not, under the rule, tax shall be charged on the amount by which the sum receivable exceeds—

(*a*) the largest sum which would have been receivable in commutation of any part of the pension if the scheme had secured that the aggregate value of the relevant benefits payable to an employee on or after retirement, excluding any pension which was not commutable, could not exceed three-eighteths of his final remuneration (disregarding any excess of that remuneration over the permitted maximum) for each year of service up to a maximum of 40; or
(*b*) the largest sum which would have been receivable in commutation of any part of the pension under any rule of the scheme authorising the commutation of part (but not the whole) of the pension, or which would have been so receivable but for those special circumstances;

whichever gives the lesser amount chargeable to tax.

[(1A) Subsection (1) above shall have effect in relation to the commutation of the whole or any part of a pension the amount of which has been affected by the making of any pension sharing order or provision as if paragraph (*a*) and the words after paragraph (*b*) were omitted.

(1B) Where—

(*a*) a scheme to which this section applies contains a rule allowing, in special circumstances, a payment in commutation of the entire pension provided under the scheme for an ex-spouse, and
(*b*) any pension is commuted, whether wholly or not, under the rule,

tax shall be charged on the amount by which the sum receivable exceeds the largest sum which would have been receivable in commutation of any part of the pension under any rule of the scheme authorising the commutation of a part (but not the whole) of the pension.

(1C) A pension provided for an ex-spouse shall be disregarded when applying subsection (1) above in relation to the commutation of any pension provided for an employee.

(1D) A pension provided for an employee shall be disregarded when applying subsection (1B) above in relation to the commutation of any pension provided for an ex-spouse.

(1E) Subsections (4B) and (4C) of section 590 apply for the purposes of subsections (1C) and (1D) above as they apply for the purposes of that section.][5]

(2) This section applies to—

(*a*) a scheme which is or has at any time been an approved scheme, or
(*b*) a [relevant][1] statutory scheme established under a public general Act.

(3) Where any amount is chargeable to tax under this section the administrator of the scheme shall be charged to income tax under Case VI of Schedule D on that amount, and section 598(2), (3) and (4) shall apply as they apply to tax chargeable under that section.

(4) This section shall not apply where the employee's employment was carried on outside the United Kingdom.

(5) In relation to a statutory scheme, "employee" in this section includes any officer.

(6) In applying paragraph (*a*) or (*b*) of subsection (1)[, or in applying subsection (1B) above][5] above—

(*a*) the same considerations shall be taken into account, including the provisions of any other relevant scheme, as would have been taken into account by the Board in applying section 590; and

(*b*) where the scheme has ceased to be an approved scheme, account shall only be taken of the rules in force when the scheme was last an approved scheme.

(7) Where the pension has been secured by means of an annuity contract with an insurance company and the sum receivable is payable under that contract by the insurance company, the references to the administrator of the scheme in subsection (3) above and in section 598(2) and (4) as applied by that subsection are to be read as references to the insurance company.

[(8) In subsection (7) above "insurance company" has the meaning given by section 659B.]³

(9) In relation to payments made under schemes approved or established before 17th March 1987 to employees who became members before that date, subsection (1)(*a*) above shall have effect with the omission of the words "(disregarding any excess of that remuneration over the permitted maximum)".

[(10) In subsection (1)(*a*) above "the permitted maximum" means, as regards a charge to tax arising under this section in a particular year of assessment, the figure found for that year by virtue of subsections (11) and (12) below.]²

[(11) For the years 1988–89 and 1989–90 the figure is £60,000.]²

[(12) For any subsequent year of assessment the figure is the figure found for that year, for the purposes of section 590C, by virtue of section 590C(4) [to (5A)]⁴.]²

Commentary—*Simon's Direct Tax Service* E7.235, 239.
Note—For the year 2000–01 the figure specified for the purpose of sub-s (12) by virtue of s 590C is £91,800 by virtue of the Retirement Benefits Schemes (Indexation of Earnings Cap) Order, SI 2000/807.
Definitions—"Act", s 832(1); "administrator", s 611AA; "branch or agency", s 834(1); "Schedule D", s 18(1); "tax", s 832(3); "United Kingdom", s 830(1).
Cross references—See TA 1988 s 600(3) (charge to tax of unauthorised payments out of funds of schemes approved under this Chapter).
TA 1988 s 607 (this section to have effect with modifications in relation to pilots' benefit fund).
TA 1988 s 659B(1) (meaning of "insurance company" for purpose of sub-s (7) above).
Amendments—¹ Word in sub-s (2)(*b*) inserted by FA 1989 Sch 6 paras 11(1), (2), 18(1) with effect from 14 March 1989.
² Sub-ss (10), (11), (12) inserted by FA 1989 Sch 6 paras 11(1), (3), 18(8) where the charge to tax under this section arises after 13 March 1989, but not where the scheme came into existence before 14 March 1989 and the employee became a member of it before 1 June 1989.
³ Sub-s (8) substituted by FA 1995 ss 59(3), 60(2), with effect where tax is charged under this section on or after 1 May 1995.
⁴ Words in sub-s (12) substituted by FA 1993 s 107(6), (8) with effect from the year 1994–95.
⁵ Words in sub-ss (1), (6) and whole of sub-ss (1A)–(1E) inserted by FA 1999 s 79 Sch 10 para 7 with effect in accordance with the commencement provisions contained in FA 1999 Sch 10 para 18.

[599A Charge to tax: payments out of surplus funds

(1) This subsection applies to any payment which is made to or for the benefit of an employee or to his personal representatives out of funds which are or have been held for the purposes of—

(*a*) a scheme which is or has at any time been an exempt approved scheme, or

(*b*) a relevant statutory scheme established under a public general Act,

and which is made in pursuance of duty to return surplus funds.

(2) On the making of a payment to which subsection (1) above applies, the administrator of the scheme shall be charged to income tax under Case VI of Schedule D at the relevant rate on such amount as, after deduction of tax at that rate, would equal the amount of the payment.

(3) Subject to subsection (4) below, the relevant rate shall be 35 per cent.

(4) The Treasury may by order from time to time increase or decrease the relevant rate.

(5) Where a payment made to or for the benefit of an employee is one to which subsection (1) applies, it shall be treated in computing the total income of the employee for the year in which it is made as income for that year which is—

(*a*) received by him after deduction of income tax at the basic rate from a corresponding gross amount, and

(*b*) chargeable to income tax under Case VI of Schedule D.

(6) But, ...² no repayment of income tax shall be made to, the employee.

(7) ...²

(8) Subsection (5) above applies whether or not the employee is the recipient of the payment.

(9) Any payment chargeable to tax under this section shall not be chargeable to tax under section 598, 599 or 600 or under the Regulations mentioned in paragraph 8 of Schedule 3 to the Finance Act 1971.

(10) In this section—

"employee", in relation to a relevant statutory scheme, includes any officer;

references to any payment include references to any transfer of assets or other transfer of money's worth.]¹

Commentary—*Simon's Direct Tax Service* E7.239.
Order—IT (Charge to Tax) (Payments out of Surplus Funds) (Relevant Rate) Order, SI 2000/600 (relevant rate under sub-s (2) is 32 per cent in relation to payments made after 5 April 2000).

Definitions—''Administrator'', s 611AA; ''basic rate'', s 832(1); ''total income'', s 835.
Amendments—[1] This section inserted by FA 1989 Sch 6 paras 12, 18(9) in relation to payments made after 26 July 1989.
[2] Words omitted from sub-s (6) and whole of sub-s (7) repealed by FA 1996 ss 121(8), 122(7)(*b*), (*c*), Sch 41 Pt V(6) with effect from the year 1996–97.

600 Charge to tax: unauthorised payments to or for employees

(1) This section applies to any payment to or for the benefit of an employee [or an ex-spouse][4], otherwise than in course of payment of a pension, being a payment made out of funds which are ...[1] held for the purposes of a scheme which is ...[2] approved for the purposes of—

    (*a*) this Chapter;
    (*b*) Chapter II of Part II of the Finance Act 1970; or
    (*c*) section 208 or Chapter II of Part IX of the 1970 Act.

(2) If the payment [is not expressly authorised by the rules of the scheme or by virtue of paragraph 33 of Schedule 6 to the Finance Act 1989][3] [the employee or, as the case may be, the ex-spouse shall (whether or not he is the recipient of the payment)][4] be chargeable to tax on the amount of the payment under Schedule E for the year of assessment in which the payment is made.

(3) Any payment chargeable to tax under this section shall not be chargeable to tax under section 598 or 599 or under the Regulations mentioned in paragraph 8 of Schedule 3 to the Finance Act 1971.

(4) References in this section to any payment include references to any transfer of assets or other transfer of money's worth.

Commentary—*Simon's Direct Tax Service* **E7.237.**
Revenue Internal Guidance—Schedule E manual SE 04800 (retirement lump sums: advise Pension Schemes Office before assessing a payment under this section).
Simon's Tax Cases—*Venables v Hornby (Inspector of Taxes)* [2001] STC 1221.
Definitions—''The 1970 Act'', s 831(3); ''Schedule E'', s 19(1); ''year of assessment'', s 832(1).
Cross references—See TA 1988 s 189 (lump sum benefits on retirement).
TA 1988 s 607 (this section to have effect with modifications in relation to pilots' benefit fund).
Amendments—[1] Words in sub-s (1) repealed by FA 1989 Sch 6 paras 13(1), (2), 18(9) and Sch 17, Pt IV in relation to payments made after 26 July 1989.
[2] Words in sub-s (1) repealed by FA 1989 Sch 6 paras 13(1), (2), 18(9) and Sch 17, Pt IV in relation to payments made after 26 July 1989.
[3] Words in sub-s (2) substituted for sub-s (2)(*a*), (*b*) by FA 1989 Sch 6 paras 13(1), (3), 18(9) in relation to payments made after 26 July 1989.
[4] Words in sub-s (1) inserted, and words in sub-s (2) substituted, by FA 1999 s 79 Sch 10 para 8 with effect in relation to any payment after 30 November 2000 (by virtue of the Finance Act 1999, Schedule 10, Paragraph 18, (First and Second Appointed Days) Order, SI 2000/1093). Words in sub-s (2) previously read ''the employee (whether or not he is the recipient of the payment) shall''.

601 Charge to tax: payments to employers

(1) Subsection (2) below applies where a payment is made to an employer out of funds which are or have been held for the purposes of a scheme which is or has at any time been an exempt approved scheme and whether or not the payment is made in pursuance of Schedule 22.

(2) An amount equal to [the relevant percentage of the payment][1] shall be recoverable by the Board from the employer.

[(2A) The relevant percentage is 35% or such other percentage (whether higher or lower) as may be prescribed.][1]

(3) Subsection (2) above does not apply to any payment—

    (*a*) to the extent that, if this section had not been enacted, the employer would have been exempt, or entitled to claim exemption, from income tax or corporation tax in respect of the payment; or
    (*b*) made before the scheme became an exempt approved scheme; or
    (*c*) of any prescribed description; or
    (*d*) made in pursuance of the winding-up of the scheme where the winding-up commenced on or before 18th March 1986; or
    (*e*) made in pursuance of an application which—

        (i) was made to the Board on or before that date and was not withdrawn before the making of the payment, and
        (ii) sought the Board's assurance that the payment would not lead to a withdrawal of approval under section 19(3) of the Finance Act 1970;

(4) Subsection (2) above does not apply where the employer is a charity (within the meaning of section 506).

(5) Where any payment is made or becomes due to an employer out of funds which are or have been held for the purposes of a scheme which is or has at any time been an exempt approved scheme then—

    (*a*) if the scheme relates to a trade, profession or vocation carried on by the employer, the payment shall be treated for the purposes of the Tax Acts as a receipt of that trade, profession or vocation receivable when the payment falls due or on the last day on which the trade, profession or vocation is carried on by the employer, whichever is the earlier;
    (*b*) if the scheme does not relate to such a trade, profession or vocation, the employer shall be charged to tax on the amount of the payment under Case VI of Schedule D.

TA 1988

This subsection shall not apply to a payment which fell due before the scheme became an exempt approved scheme or to a payment to which subsection (2) above applies or would apply but for subsection (3)(*a*) or (4) above.

(6) In this section—

(*a*) references to any payment include references to any transfer of assets or other transfer of money's worth; and

(*b*) "prescribed" means prescribed by regulations made by the Treasury.

Commentary—*Simon's Direct Tax Service* **E7.238.**
Regulations—Pension Scheme Surpluses (Administration) Regulations, SI 1987/352. For continuity see Sch 30, para 21 of this Act.
Revenue & other press releases—PSO Memorandum 117 13-1-94 (refund of contributions paid in error up to £1,000 can be made gross).
Simon's Tax Cases—*Hillsdown Holdings plc v IRC* [1999] STC 561.
Definitions—"The Board", s 832(1); "Schedule D", s 18(1); "the Tax Acts", s 831(2); "trade", s 832(1).
Cross references—See TA 1988 s 602 (regulations for the purposes of sub-s (2) above).
Amendments—¹ Words in sub-s (2) substituted and sub-s (2A) inserted by FA 2001 s 74 with effect for payments made to employers from 11 May 2001.

602 Regulations relating to pension fund surpluses

(1) In relation to an amount recoverable as mentioned in section 601(2), the Treasury may by regulations make any of the provisions mentioned in subsection (2) below; and for this purpose the amount shall be treated as if it were—

(*a*) an amount of income tax chargeable on the employer under Case VI of Schedule D for the year of assessment in which the payment is made; or

(*b*) where the employer is a company, an amount of corporation tax chargeable on the company for the accounting period in which the payment is made.

(2) The provisions are—

(*a*) provision requiring the administrator of the scheme or the employer (or both) to furnish to the Board, in respect of the amount recoverable and of the payment concerned, information of a prescribed kind;

(*b*) provision enabling the Board to serve a notice or notices requiring the administrator or employer (or both) to furnish to the Board, in respect of the amount and payment, particulars of a prescribed kind;

(*c*) provision requiring the administrator to deduct out of the payment the amount recoverable and to account to the Board for it;

(*d*) provision as to circumstances in which the employer may be assessed in respect of the amount recoverable;

(*e*) provision that, in a case where the employer has been assessed in respect of an amount recoverable but has not paid it (or part of it) within a prescribed period, the administrator may be assessed and charged (in the employer's name) in respect of the amount (or part unpaid);

(*f*) provision that, in a case where the amount recoverable (or part of it) has been recovered from the administrator by virtue of an assessment in the employer's name, the administrator is entitled to recover from the employer a sum equal to the amount (or part);

(*g*) provision enabling the employer or administrator (as the case may be) to appeal against an assessment made on him in respect of the amount recoverable;

(*h*) provision as to when any sum in respect of the amount recoverable is payable to the Board by the administrator or employer and provision requiring interest to be paid on any sum so payable;

(*j*) provision that an amount paid to the Board by the administrator shall be treated as paid on account of the employer's liability under section 601(2).

(3) For the purpose of giving effect to any provision mentioned in subsection (2)(*c*) to (*j*) above, regulations under this section may include provision applying (with or without modifications) provisions of the enactments relating to income tax and corporation tax.

(4) Subject to any provision of regulations under this section—

(*a*) a payment to which section 601(2) applies shall not be treated as a profit or gain brought into charge to income tax or corporation tax and shall not be treated as part of the employer's income for any purpose of this Act; and

(*b*) the amount recoverable shall not be subject to any exemption or reduction (by way of relief, set-off or otherwise) or be available for set-off against other tax.

(5) If the employer is a company and a payment to which section 601(1) and (2) applies is made at a time not otherwise within an accounting period of the company, an accounting period of the company shall for the purposes of subsection (1)(*b*) above be treated as beginning immediately before the payment is made.

Commentary—*Simon's Direct Tax Service* **E7.238.**
Regulations—Pension Scheme Surpluses (Administration) Regulations, SI 1987/352; Pension Scheme Surpluses (Valuation) Regulations, SI 1987/412. For continuity see Sch 30, para 21 of this Act.
Definitions—"Accounting period", s 834(1); "administrator", s 611AA; "the Board", s 832(1); "company", s 832(1), (2); "profit or gain", s 833(1); "Schedule D", s 18(1); "tax", s 832(3); "year of assessment", s 832(1).

603 Reduction of surpluses

Schedule 22 (which provides for the reduction of certain pension fund surpluses) shall have effect.

Regulations—Pension Scheme Surpluses (Administration) Regulations, SI 1987/352; Pension Scheme Surpluses (Valuation) Regulations, SI 1987/412. For continuity see Sch 30, para 21 of this Act.

Supplementary provisions

604 Application for approval of a scheme

(1) An application for the approval for the purposes of this Chapter of any retirement benefits scheme shall be made in writing by [the appropriate applicant][1] to the Board before the end of the first year of assessment for which approval is required, and shall be accompanied by—

(a) two copies of the instrument or other document constituting the scheme; and

(b) two copies of the rules of the scheme and, except where the application is being sought on the setting up of the scheme, two copies of the accounts of the scheme for the last year for which such accounts have been made up; and

(c) such other information and particulars (including copies of any actuarial report or advice given to the [appropriate applicant,][1] administrator or employer in connection with the setting up of the scheme) as the Board may consider relevant.

[(1A) In subsection (1) above "the appropriate applicant" means—

(a) in the case of a trust scheme, the trustee or trustees of the scheme; and

(b) in the case of a non-trust scheme, the scheme sponsor or scheme sponsors;

and subsection (9) of section 611AA applies for the purposes of this subsection as it applies for the purposes of that section.][1]

(2) The form in which an application for approval is to be made, or in which any information is to be given, in pursuance of this section may be prescribed by the Board.

Commentary—*Simon's Direct Tax Service* E7.246.
Definitions—"Administrator", s 611AA; "the Board", s 832(1); "employer", s 612(1); "retirement benefits scheme", s 611; "scheme", s 611(2); "year of assessment", s 832(1).
Cross references—See TA 1988 s 607 (this section to have effect with modifications in relation to pilots' benefit fund).
Amendments—[1] Words in sub-s (1) substituted and sub-s (1A) inserted by FA 1998 Sch 15 para 3 with effect in relation to any application made on or after 31 July 1998.

605 Information

(1) ...[3]

[(1A) The Board may by regulations make any of the following provisions—

(a) provision requiring prescribed persons to furnish to the Board at prescribed times information relating to any of the matters mentioned in subsection (1B) below;

(b) provision enabling the Board to serve a notice requiring prescribed persons to furnish to the Board, within a prescribed time, particulars relating to any of those matters;

(c) provision enabling the Board to serve a notice requiring prescribed persons to produce to the Board, within a prescribed time, documents relating to any of those matters;

(d) provision enabling the Board to serve a notice requiring prescribed persons to make available for inspection on behalf of the Board books, documents and other records, being books, documents and records which relate to any of those matters;

(e) provision requiring prescribed persons to preserve for a prescribed time books, documents and other records, being books, documents and records which relate to any of those matters.][2]

[(1B) The matters referred to in subsection (1A) above are—

[(a) a scheme which is or has been an approved scheme;][4]

(b) a relevant statutory scheme;

(c) an annuity contract by means of which benefits provided under an approved scheme or a relevant statutory scheme have been secured;

(d) a retirement benefits scheme which is not an approved scheme but in relation to which an application for approval for the purposes of this Chapter has been made.][2]

[(1C) A person who fails to comply with regulations made under subsection (1A)(e) above shall be liable to a penalty not exceeding £3,000.][2]

[(1D) Regulations under subsection (1A) above may make different provision for different descriptions of case.][2]

[(1E) In subsection (1A) above "prescribed" means prescribed by regulations made under that subsection.][2]

(2) ...[3]

(3) It shall be the duty of every employer—

(a) if there subsists in relation to any of his employees a retirement benefits scheme to which he contributes and which is neither an approved scheme nor a [relevant][1] statutory scheme, to deliver particulars of that scheme to the Board within three months beginning with the date on which the scheme first comes into operation in relation to any of his employees, and

(b) when required to do so by notice given by the Board, to furnish within the time limited by the notice such particulars as the Board may require with regard to—

    (i) any retirement benefits scheme relating to the employer which is neither an approved scheme nor a [relevant][1] statutory scheme; and

    (ii) the employees of his to whom any such scheme relates.

(4) It shall be the duty of the administrator of a retirement benefits scheme which is neither an approved scheme nor a [relevant][1] statutory scheme, when required to do so by notice given by the Board, to furnish within the time limited by the notice such particulars as the Board may require with regard to the scheme.

Commentary—*Simon's Direct Tax Service* A3.119; E7.247, 256.
Regulations—Retirement Benefits Schemes (Information Powers) Regulations, SI 1995/3103.
Revenue & other press releases—Pension Schemes Office 3-1-96 (summary of the new information powers under SI 1995/3103).
Revenue Internal Guidance—Schedule E manual SE 15200 (non-approved retirement benefits schemes: employer's responsibilities).
Definitions—"Administrator", s 611AA; "approved scheme", s 612(1); "the Board", s 832(1); "employee", s 612(1); "employer", s 612(1); "notice", s 832(1); "pension", s 612(1); "retirement benefits scheme", s 611; "scheme", s 611(2); "statutory scheme", s 612(1).
Cross references—See TA 1988 s 607 (this section to have effect with modifications in relation to pilots' benefit fund).
Amendments—[1] Word in sub-ss (3)(a), (b)(i), (4) inserted by FA 1989 Sch 6 paras 14, 18(1) with effect from 14 March 1989.
[2] Sub-ss (1A)–(1E) inserted by FA 1994 s 105(1), (2).
[3] Sub-ss (1), (2) repealed by FA 1994 s 105(3), (5) and Sch 26 Pt V(12) with effect from 1 January 1996 by virtue of the Finance Act 1994, section 105, (Appointed Day) Order, SI 1995/3125.
[4] Sub-s (1B)(a) substituted by FA 1998 Sch 15 para 4 with effect from 31 July 1998.

[605A False statements etc

(1) A person who fraudulently or negligently makes a false statement or false representation on making an application for the approval for the purposes of this Chapter of—

    (a) a retirement benefits scheme, or

    (b) an alteration in such a scheme,

shall be liable to a penalty not exceeding £3,000.

(2) In a case where—

    (a) a person fraudulently or negligently makes a false statement or false representation, and

    (b) in consequence that person, or any other person, obtains relief from or repayment of tax under this Chapter,

the person mentioned in paragraph (a) above shall be liable to a penalty not exceeding £3,000.][1]

Commentary—*Simon's Direct Tax Service* E7.247.
Amendments—[1] This section inserted by FA 1994 s 106 in relation to things done or omitted after 3 May 1994.

[606 Default of administrator etc

(1) This section applies in relation to a retirement benefits scheme if at any time—

    (a) there is no administrator of the scheme, or

    (b) the person who is, or all of the persons who are, the administrator of the scheme cannot be traced, or

    (c) the person who is, or all of the persons who are, the administrator of the scheme is or are in default for the purposes of this section.

(2) If the scheme is a trust scheme, then—

    (a) if subsection (1)(b) or (c) above applies and at the time in question the condition mentioned in subsection (3) below is fulfilled, the trustee or trustees shall at that time be responsible for the discharge of all duties imposed on the administrator under this Chapter (whenever arising) and liable for any tax due from the administrator in the administrator's capacity as such (whenever falling due);

    (b) if subsection (1)(a) above applies, or subsection (1)(b) or (c) above applies and at the time in question the condition mentioned in subsection (3) below is not fulfilled, the employer shall at that time be so responsible and liable;

and paragraph (b) above shall apply to a person in his capacity as the employer even if he is also the administrator, or a trustee, of the scheme.

(3) The condition is that there is at least one trustee of the scheme who—

    (a) can be traced,

    (b) is resident in the United Kingdom, and

    (c) is not in default for the purposes of this section.

(4) If the scheme is a non-trust scheme, then—

    (a) if subsection (1)(b) or (c) above applies and at the time in question the condition mentioned in subsection (5) below is fulfilled, the scheme sponsor or scheme sponsors shall at that time be responsible for the discharge of all duties imposed on the administrator under this Chapter (whenever arising) and liable for any tax due from the administrator in the administrator's capacity as such (whenever falling due);

(b) if subsection (1)(*a*) above applies, or subsection (1)(*b*) or (*c*) above applies and at the time in question the condition mentioned in subsection (5) below is not fulfilled, the employer shall at that time be so responsible and liable;

and paragraph (*b*) above shall apply to a person in his capacity as the employer even if he is also the administrator of the scheme, or a scheme sponsor.

(5) The condition is that there is at least one scheme sponsor who—

    (*a*) can be traced,

    (*b*) is resident in the United Kingdom, and

    (*c*) is not in default for the purposes of this section.

(6) Where at any time—

    (*a*) paragraph (*b*) or (*c*) of subsection (1) above applies in relation to a scheme, and

    (*b*) a person is by virtue of this section responsible for the discharge of any duties, or liable for any tax, in relation to the scheme,

then at that time the person or persons mentioned in paragraph (*b*) or (as the case may be) paragraph (*c*) of subsection (1) above shall not, by reason only of being the administrator of the scheme, be responsible for the discharge of those duties or liable for that tax.

(7) Where the scheme is a trust scheme and the employer is not a contributor to the scheme, subsection (2) above shall have effect as if—

    (*a*) for "the employer", in the first place where those words occur, there were substituted "the scheme sponsor or scheme sponsors", and

    (*b*) for "the employer", in the second place where those words occur, there were substituted "scheme sponsor".

(8) Where the scheme is a non-trust scheme and the employer is not a contributor to the scheme, subsection (4) above shall have effect as if paragraph (*b*) and the words after that paragraph were omitted.

(9) No liability incurred under this Chapter—

    (*a*) by the administrator of a scheme, or

    (*b*) by a person by virtue of this section,

shall be affected by the termination of a scheme or by its ceasing to be an approved scheme or to be an exempt approved scheme.

[(9A) Where by virtue of this section any person is the person, or one of the persons, responsible for the discharge of the duties of the administrator of a scheme, any power or duty by virtue of this Part to serve any notice on, or to do any other thing in relation to, the administrator may be exercised or performed, instead, by the service of that notice on that person or, as the case may be, by the doing of that other thing in relation to that person.][2]

(10) Where by virtue of this section a person becomes responsible for the discharge of any duties, or liable for any tax, the Board shall, as soon as is reasonably practicable, notify him of that fact; but any failure to give such notification shall not affect that person's being responsible or liable by virtue of this section.

(11) A person is in default for the purposes of this section if—

    (*a*) he has failed to discharge any duty imposed on him under this Chapter, or

    (*b*) he has failed to pay any tax due from him by virtue of this Chapter,

and (in either case) the Board consider the failure to be of a serious nature.

[(11A) In determining for the purposes of this section—

    (*a*) whether all of the persons who are the administrator of a scheme are at any time in default in respect of an amount of tax chargeable by virtue of section 591C, or

    (*b*) whether a trustee of a scheme is in default in respect of any amount of tax so chargeable,

the persons who at that time are trustees of the scheme or hold appointments in relation to the scheme under section 611AA(4) to (6) shall be deemed not to include any person who by virtue of section 591D(4) is not liable for that tax.][3]

(12) References in this section to a trust scheme, a non-trust scheme, trustees and scheme sponsors shall be construed in accordance with section 611AA.

(13) References in this section to the employer include, where the employer is resident outside the United Kingdom, references to any branch or agent of the employer in the United Kingdom, and in this subsection "branch or agent" has the meaning given by section 118(1) of the Management Act.

(14) This section does not apply for the purposes of sections 602 and 603 and Schedule 22.][1]

Commentary—*Simon's Direct Tax Service* E7.247.

Definitions—"Administrator", s 611AA; "approved scheme", s 612(1); "the Board", s 832(1); "employer", s 612(1); "exempt approved scheme", s 612(1); "the Management Act", s 831(3); "retirement benefits scheme", s 611; "scheme", s 611(2); "United Kingdom", s 830(1).

Cross references—See TA 1988 s 607 (this section to have effect with modifications in relation to pilots' benefit fund).

Amendments—[1] This section substituted by FA 1994 s 104(1), (3) and applies where the time in question falls after 2 May 1994.
[2] Sub-s (9A) inserted by FA 1998 Sch 15 para 5 with effect from 31 July 1998.
[3] Sub-s (11A) inserted by FA 1998 Sch 15 para 5 with effect for determinations made in relation to any time on or after 17 March 1998.

[606A Recourse to scheme members

(1) This section applies where—

    (*a*) an approval of a retirements benefits scheme has ceased to have effect;

    (*b*) a person (''the employer'') has become liable by virtue of section 606 to any tax chargeable on the administrator of the scheme under section 591C;

    (*c*) the employer has failed, either in whole or in part, to pay that tax; and

    (*d*) a person falling within subsection (2) below (''the relevant member'') was a member of the scheme at the time (''the relevant time'') immediately before the date of the cessation of its approval.

(2) A person falls within this subsection in relation to any tax chargeable under section 591C if—

    (*a*) at the relevant time or at any time before that time he was a controlling director of the employer; or

    (*b*) he is a person by or in respect of whom any contributions were made by reference to which the condition in subsection (6A) of that section has been satisfied for the purpose of the charge to that tax.

(3) Subject to subsection (4) below, if in a case where this section applies—

    (*a*) the employer has ceased to exist, or

    (*b*) the Board notify the relevant member that they consider the failure of the employer to pay the unpaid tax to be of a serious nature,

the relevant member shall be treated as included in the persons on whom the unpaid tax was charged and shall be assessable accordingly.

(4) The amount of tax for which the relevant member shall be taken to be assessable by virtue of this section shall not exceed the amount determined by—

    (*a*) taking the amount equal to 40 per cent of his share of the scheme; and

    (*b*) subtracting from that amount his share of any tax charged under section 591C that has already been paid otherwise than by another person on whom it is treated as charged in accordance with this section.

(5) For the purposes of this section the relevant member's share of the scheme is the amount equal to so much of the value of the assets held for the purposes of the scheme at the relevant time (taking the value at that time) as, on a just and reasonable apportionment, would have fallen to be treated as the value at that time of the assets then held for the purposes of the provision under the scheme of benefits to or in respect of the relevant member.

(6) For the purposes of this section the relevant member's share of an amount of tax already paid is such sum as bears the same proportion to the amount paid as is borne by his share of the scheme to the total value at the relevant time of the assets then held for the purposes of the scheme.

(7) The reference in subsection (5) above to the provision of benefits to or in respect of the relevant member includes a reference to the provision of a benefit to or in respect of a person connected with the relevant member.

(8) For the purposes of this section a person is a controlling director of a company if he is a director of the company and is within section 417(5)(*b*) in relation to the company.

(9) A notification given to any person for the purposes of subsection (3)(*b*) above may be included in any assessment on that person of the tax to which he becomes liable by virtue of the notification.

(10) An assessment to tax made by virtue of this section shall not be out of time if it is made within three years after the date on which the tax which the employer has failed to pay first became due from him.

(11) Subsections (1) to (3) of section 591D shall apply to the determination of the value at any time of an asset held for the purposes of a scheme as they apply for the purposes of section 591C(2).

(12) Subsections (7) and (8) of section 591D shall apply for the purposes of this section as they apply for the purposes of subsection (1) of section 591C and section 591C, respectively.

(13) Section 839 (connected persons) shall apply for the purposes of this section.]¹

Commentary—*Simon's Direct Tax Service* E7.247.
Amendments—¹ This section inserted by FA 1998 Sch 15 para 6 with effect in relation to any case in which the date of the cessation of the approval is on or after 17 March 1998.

607 Pilots' benefit fund

(1) The Board may, if they think fit, and subject to such conditions as they think proper to attach to the approval, approve a pilots' benefit fund for the purposes of this Chapter as if it were a retirement benefits scheme and notwithstanding that it does not satisfy one or more of the conditions set out in section 590(2) and (3).

(2) If a fund is approved by virtue of this section—

    (*a*) sections 592, 597 to 600 and 604 to 606 shall have effect in relation to the fund with the modifications specified in subsection (3) below;

    (*b*) pensions paid out of the fund and any sums chargeable to tax in connection with the fund under section 600 shall be treated for the purposes of the Income Tax Acts as earned income; and (*c*) Chapter III of this Part shall have effect as if a member of the fund were the holder of a pensionable office or employment and his earnings as a pilot (estimated in accordance with the provisions of Case II of Schedule D) were remuneration from such an office or employment.

(3) The modifications referred to in subsection (2)(*a*) above are as follows—

(*a*) in section 592, for the references in subsection (7) to an employee and Schedule E there shall be substituted respectively references to a member of the fund and Schedule D, and subsections (4) to (6), and in subsection (7) the words from "incurred" onwards, shall be omitted;

(*b*) in sections 597 to 606 (except sections 601 to 603)—

(i) for references to an employee there shall be substituted references to a member or former member of the fund;

(ii) in section 599(1)(*a*) for the reference to a year of service there shall be substituted a reference to a year as a pilot licensed by a pilotage authority or authorised by a competent harbour authority;

(iii) [section 606(2)(*b*), (4)(*b*), (7), (8) and (13)][1] and so much of any other provision as applies to an employer shall be omitted; and

(iv) in section 600, for references to Schedule E there shall be substituted references to Case VI of Schedule D.

(4) In this section "pilots' benefit fund" means a fund established under section 15(1)(i) of the Pilotage Act 1983 or any scheme supplementing or replacing any such fund.

Commentary—*Simon's Direct Tax Service* E7.264.
Definitions—"The Board", s 832(1); "earned income", s 833(4)–(6); "employee", s 612(1); "the Income Tax Acts", s 831(1)(*b*); "pensions", s 612(1); "remuneration", s 612(1); "retirement benefits scheme", s 611; "Schedule D", s 18(1); "Schedule E", s 19(1); "scheme", s 611(2).
Amendments—[1] Words in sub-s (3)(*b*)(iii) substituted by FA 1994 s 104(2), (3) with effect from 3 May 1994.

608 Superannuation funds approved before 6th April 1980

(1) This section applies to any fund which immediately before 6th April 1980 was an approved superannuation fund for the purposes of section 208 of the 1970 Act if—

(*a*) it has not been approved under this Chapter (or under Chapter II of Part II of the Finance Act 1970); and

(*b*) no sum has been paid to it by way of contribution since 5th April 1980.

(2) Subject to subsection (3) below, exemption from income tax shall, on a claim being made in that behalf, be allowed to a fund to which this section applies in respect of—

(*a*) income derived from investments or deposits of the fund;

(*b*) any underwriting commissions which apart from this subsection would be chargeable to tax under Case VI of Schedule D; and

(*c*) any profits or gains which (apart from this subsection) would be chargeable to tax under Case VI of Schedule D by virtue of section 56(1)(*a*) and (2);

if, or to such extent as the Board are satisfied that, the income, commissions, profits or gains are applied for the purposes of the fund.

(3) No claim under subsection (2) above shall be allowed unless the Board are satisfied that the terms on which benefits are payable from the fund have not been altered since 5th April 1980.

(4) An annuity paid out of a fund to which this section applies shall be charged to tax under Schedule E and section 203 shall apply accordingly.

Commentary—*Simon's Direct Tax Service* E7.271.
Concession B43—Tax exemption continues in respect of income, etc applied for the purposes of funds to which this section applies and to which alterations have been made if certain conditions are fulfilled.
Definitions—"The 1970 Act", s 831(3); "the Board", s 832(1); "profits or gains", s 833(1); "Schedule D", s 18(1); "Schedule E", s 19(1).
Cross references—See TA 1988 s 129B (exemption from income tax under sub-s (2)(*a*) above is extended to any stock lending fees payable in connection with approved arrangements relating to the relevant investments).
TA 1988 s 231A (tax credits not repayable in respect of qualifying distributions made after 1 July 1997 to pension funds — see sub-s (2)(*a*) above).
TA 1988 s 659A ("investments" and "income" for the purposes of sub-s (2) above to include futures and options and transactions relating to them).
TA 1988 s 659D(2) (the exemption within sub-s (2)(*a*) above does not apply to income derived from investments, deposits or other property held as a member of a property investment LLP).
TCGA 1992 s 271(2) (gains on disposal of investments held for the purposes of a fund under this section not to be chargeable gains).
Manufactured Payments and Transfer of Securities (Tax Relief) Regulations, SI 1995/3036 regs 3, 4 (manufactured payments and deemed interest payments arising on a sale and repurchase of securities falling to the benefit of a fund referred to in sub-s (2)(*a*) above to be treated as income of the person eligible for relief by virtue of that subsection).

609 Schemes approved before 23rd July 1987

Schedule 23 to this Act, which makes provision with respect to retirement benefit schemes approved before 23rd July 1987, shall have effect.

Commentary—*Simon's Direct Tax Service* E7.227.
Definition—"Retirement benefits scheme", s 611.

610 Amendments of schemes

(1) This section applies to any amendment of a retirement benefits scheme proposed in connection with an application for the Board's approval for the purposes of this Chapter which is needed in order to ensure that approval is so given, or designed to enhance the benefits under the scheme up to the limits suitable in a scheme for which approval is sought.

(2) A provision, however expressed, designed to preclude any amendment of a scheme which would have prejudiced its approval under section 208 or 222 of the 1970 Act shall not prevent any amendment to which this section applies.

(3) In the case of a scheme which contains no powers of amendment, the administrator of the scheme may, with the consent of all the members of the scheme, and of the employer (or of each of the employers), make any amendment to which this section applies.

Commentary—*Simon's Direct Tax Service* E7.217.
Definitions—''The 1970 Act'', s 831(3); ''administrator'', s 611AA; ''the Board'', s 832(1); ''employer'', s 612(1); ''retirement benefits scheme'', s 611; ''scheme'', s 611(2).

611 Definition of ''retirement benefits scheme''

(1) In this Chapter ''retirement benefits scheme'' means, subject to the provisions of this section, a scheme for the provision of benefits consisting of or including relevant benefits, but does not include—

[(*a*)]² any national scheme providing such benefits[; or
(*b*) any scheme providing such benefits which is an approved personal pension scheme under Chapter IV of this Part]².

(2) References in this Chapter to a scheme include references to a deed, agreement, series of agreements, or other arrangements providing for relevant benefits notwithstanding that it relates or they relate only to—

(*a*) a small number of employees, or to a single employee, or
(*b*) the payment of a pension starting immediately on the making of the arrangements.

(3) The Board may, if they think fit, treat a *retirement benefits*² scheme relating to [scheme members]¹ of two or more different classes or descriptions as being for the purposes of this Chapter [and Chapter IV of this Part]² two or more separate *retirement benefits*² schemes relating respectively to such one or more of those classes or descriptions of those [scheme members]¹ as the Board think fit.

(4) For the purposes of this section, and of any other provision of this Chapter—

(*a*) [scheme members]³ may be regarded as belonging to different classes or descriptions if they are employed by different employers; and
(*b*) a particular class or description of [scheme member]¹ may consist of a single [scheme member]¹, or any number of [scheme members]¹, however small.

(5) Without prejudice to subsections (3) and (4) above, the Board may continue to treat as two different schemes, for the purposes of this Chapter, any retirement benefits scheme which, in pursuance of paragraph 5 of Schedule 3 to the Finance Act 1971 (schemes in existence before 5th April 1973), they treated, immediately before the coming into force of this Chapter, as two separate schemes for the purposes of Chapter II of Part II of the Finance Act 1970.

[(6) In this section ''scheme member'', in relation to a scheme means—

(*a*) an employee; or
(*b*) a person whose rights under the scheme derive from a pension sharing order or provision.]¹ [;
or
(*c*) if the scheme is an approved personal pension scheme under Chapter IV of this Part, any other person who is a member of the scheme.]²

Commentary—*Simon's Direct Tax Service* E7.202.
Revenue Internal Guidance—Schedule E manual SE 15020 (non-approved ''retirement benefits schemes'': definition—''scheme'' does not have to be a formal document and non-approved schemes do not have to adopt any particular form). SE 15028 (meaning of ''scheme'', application of Statement of Practice SP 13/91).
Definitions—''The Board'', s 832(1); ''employee'', s 612(1); ''employers'', s 612(1); ''pension'', s 612(1); ''relevant benefits'', s 612(1).
Cross references—See TA 1988 s 189 (lump sum benefits on retirement).
Amendments—¹ Words in sub-ss (3), (4) substituted, and sub-s (6) inserted, by FA 1999 s 79 Sch 10 para 9 with effect in accordance with the commencement provisions contained in FA 1999 Sch 10 para 18. Words in sub-ss (3), (4) previously read ''employees'' and ''employee''.
² Words in sub-ss (1), (3), (6) inserted, words in sub-s (3) repealed by FA 2000 ss 61, 156, Sch 13 paras 1, 4, Sch 40 Pt II(4) with effect from 28 July 2000.
³ Words in sub-s (4)(*a*) substitued for word ''employees'' by FA 2000 ss 61, Sch 13 para 4 with effect from 28 July 2000.

[611AA Definition of the administrator

(1) In this Chapter references to the administrator, in relation to a retirement benefits scheme, are to the person who is, or the persons who are, for the time being the administrator of the scheme by virtue of the following provisions of this section.

(2) Subject to subsection (7) below, where—

(*a*) the scheme is a trust scheme, and

(*b*) at any time the trustee, or any of the trustees, is or are resident in the United Kingdom,

the administrator of the scheme at that time shall be the trustee or trustees of the scheme.

(3) Subject to subsection (7) below, where—

(*a*) the scheme is a non-trust scheme, and

(*b*) at any time the scheme sponsor, or any of the scheme sponsors, is or are resident in the United Kingdom,

the administrator of the scheme at that time shall be the scheme sponsor or scheme sponsors.

(4) At any time when the trustee of a trust scheme is not resident in the United Kingdom or (if there is more than one trustee) none of the trustees is so resident, the trustee or trustees shall ensure that there is a person, or there are persons—

(*a*) resident in the United Kingdom, and

(*b*) appointed by the trustee or trustees to be responsible for the discharge of all duties relating to the scheme which are imposed on the administrator under this Chapter.

(5) At any time when the scheme sponsor of a non-trust scheme is not resident in the United Kingdom or (if there is more than one scheme sponsor) none of the scheme sponsors is so resident, the scheme sponsor or scheme sponsors shall ensure that there is a person, or there are persons—

(*a*) resident in the United Kingdom, and

(*b*) appointed by the scheme sponsor or scheme sponsors to be responsible for the discharge of all duties relating to the scheme which are imposed on the administrator under this Chapter.

(6) Without prejudice to subsections (4) and (5) above—

(*a*) the trustee or trustees of a trust scheme, or

(*b*) the scheme sponsor or scheme sponsors of a non-trust scheme,

may at any time appoint a person who is, or persons who are, resident in the United Kingdom to be responsible for the discharge of all duties relating to the scheme which are imposed on the administrator under this Chapter.

(7) Where at any time there is or are a person or persons—

(*a*) for the time being appointed under subsection (4), (5) or (6) above as regards a scheme, and

(*b*) resident in the United Kingdom,

the administrator of the scheme at that time shall be that person or those persons (and no other person).

(8) Any appointment under subsection (4), (5) or (6) above—

(*a*) must be in writing, and

(*b*) if made after the time when the scheme is established, shall constitute an alteration of the scheme for the purposes of section 591B(2).

(9) In this section—

(*a*) references to a trust scheme are to a retirement benefits scheme established under a trust or trusts;

(*b*) references to the trustee or trustees, in relation to a trust scheme and to a particular time, are to the person who is the trustee, or the persons who are the trustees, of the scheme at that time;

(*c*) references to a non-trust scheme are to a retirement benefits scheme not established under a trust or trusts, and

(*d*) references to the scheme sponsor or scheme sponsors, in relation to a retirement benefits scheme and to a particular time, are references to any person who established the scheme and is in existence at that time or, if more than one, all such persons.]¹

Commentary—*Simon's Direct Tax Service* E7.247.
Revenue Internal Guidance—Schedule E manual SE 15036 (non-approved retirement benefits schemes: how to identify the administrator).
Amendments—¹ This section inserted by FA 1994 s 103(1), (3) and applies—
(*a*) so far as it relates to s 591B(1), in relation to notices given after 2 May 1994;
(*b*) so far as it relates to s 593(3), in relation to contributions paid after 2 May 1994;
(*c*) so far as it relates to s 596A(3), in relation to benefits received after 2 May 1994;
(*d*) so far as it relates to ss 598(2), (4), 599(3), 599A(2), in relation to payments made after 2 May 1994;
(*e*) so far as it relates to s 602(1), (2) and regulations made under s 602, in relation to amounts becoming recoverable after 2 May 1994;
(*f*) so far as it relates to s 604(1), in relation to applications made after 2 May 1994;
(*g*) so far as it relates to s 605(1), (4), in relation to notices given after 2 May 1994.

[611A Definition of relevant statutory scheme

[(1) In this Chapter any reference to a relevant statutory scheme is to—

(*a*) a statutory scheme established before 14th March 1989, or

(*b*) a statutory scheme established on or after that date and entered in the register maintained by the Board for the purposes of this section, or

(*c*) a parliamentary pension scheme.]²

(2) The Board shall maintain a register for the purposes of this section and shall enter in it the relevant particulars of any statutory scheme established on or after 14th March 1989 which is

reported to the Board by the authority responsible for establishing it as a scheme the provisions of which correspond with those of an approved scheme.

(3) The reference in subsection (2) above to the relevant particulars, in relation to a scheme, is a reference to—

(*a*) the identity of the scheme,

(*b*) the date on which it was established,

(*c*) the authority responsible for establishing it, and

(*d*) the date on which that authority reported the scheme to the Board.

(4) Where the Board enter the relevant particulars of a scheme in the register maintained by them for the purposes of this section, they shall inform the authority responsible for establishing the scheme of the date of the entry.

[(5) In subsection (1)(*c*) "parliamentary pension scheme" means—

(*a*) the Parliamentary pension scheme within the meaning of the Parliamentary and other Pensions Act 1987;

(*b*) any pension scheme established for members of the Scottish Parliament under section 81(4) of the Scotland Act 1998;

(*c*) any pension scheme established for members of the Welsh Assembly under section 18(2) of the Government of Wales Act 1998;

(*d*) any pension scheme established for members of the Northern Ireland Assembly under section 48(2) of the Northern Ireland Act 1998;

(*e*) the pension scheme established for members of the European Parliament under section 4 of the European Parliament (Pay and Pensions) Act 1979;

(*f*) the pension scheme established under section 3 of the Ministerial Salaries and Members' Pensions Act (Northern Ireland) 1965;

(*g*) the pension scheme established under the Assembly Pensions (Northern Ireland) Order 1976.]²]¹

Commentary—*Simon's Direct Tax Service* **E7.261.**
Statement of Practice SP13/91—Ex gratia lump sum payment made on termination of an office or employment on retirement or death.
Definitions—"The Board", s 832(1); "statutory scheme", s 612(1).
Amendments—¹ This section inserted by FA 1989 Sch 6 paras 15, 18(1) with effect from 14 March 1989.
² Words in sub-s (1) substituted and sub-s (5) inserted by FA 1999 s 52 Sch 5 para 5 with effect from the year 1999–00.

612 Other interpretative provisions, and regulations for purposes of this Chapter

(1) In this Chapter, except where the context otherwise requires—

...¹

"approved scheme" means a retirement benefits scheme for the time being approved by the Board for the purposes of this Chapter;

"director" in relation to a company includes—

(*a*) in the case of a company the affairs of which are managed by a board of directors or similar body, a member of that board or body,

(*b*) in the case of a company the affairs of which are managed by a single director or similar person, that director or person,

(*c*) in the case of a company the affairs of which are managed by the members themselves, a member of that company;

and includes a person who is to be or has been a director;

"employee"—

(*a*) in relation to a company, includes any officer of the company, any director of the company and any other person taking part in the management of the affairs of the company, and

(*b*) in relation to any employer, includes a person who is to be or has been an employee;

and "employer" and other cognate expressions shall be construed accordingly;

"exempt approved scheme" has the meaning given by section 592(1);

"final remuneration" means the average annual remuneration of the last three years' service;

"pension" includes annuity;

"the permitted maximum" has the meaning given by section 590(3);

"relevant benefits" means any pension, lump sum, gratuity or other like benefit given or to be given on retirement or on death[, or by virtue of a pension sharing order or provision]², or in anticipation of retirement, or, in connection with past service, after retirement or death, or to be given on or in anticipation of or in connection with any change in the nature of the service of the employee in question, except that it does not include any benefit which is to be afforded solely by reason of the disablement by accident of a person occurring during his service or of his death by accident so occurring and for no other reason;

"remuneration" does not include—

(*a*) anything in respect of which tax is chargeable under Schedule E and which arises from the acquisition or disposal of shares or an interest in shares or from a right to acquire shares; or

(*b*) anything in respect of which tax is chargeable by virtue of section 148;

"service" means service as an employee of the employer in question and other expressions, including "retirement", shall be construed accordingly; and

"statutory scheme" means a retirement benefits scheme established by or under any enactment—

(a) the particulars of which are set out in any enactment, or in any regulations made under any enactment, or

(b) which has been approved as an appropriate scheme by a Minister or government department (including the head of a Northern Ireland department or a Northern Ireland department).

(2) Any reference in this Chapter[, in relation to a scheme,][2] to the provision of relevant benefits, or of a pension, for employees [or ex-spouses][2] includes a reference to the provision of relevant benefits or a pension by means of a contract between the administrator or the employer or the employee [or ex-spouse][2] and a third person; and any reference to pensions or contributions paid, or payments made, under a scheme includes a reference to pensions or contributions paid, or payments made, under such a contract entered into for the purposes of the scheme.

[(2A) In subsection (2) above the reference to the employer is a reference to the person who is the employer in relation to the scheme.][2]

(3) The Board may make regulations generally for the purpose of carrying the preceding provisions of this Chapter into effect.

Commentary—*Simon's Direct Tax Service* E4.802, E7.202, 212, 214.
Regulations—Pension Scheme Surpluses (Administration) Regulations, SI 1987/352; Pension Scheme Surpluses (Valuation) Regulations, SI 1987/412; Occupational Pension Schemes (Additional Voluntary Contributions) Regulations, SI 1987/1749. For continuity see Sch 30, para 21 of this Act.
Statement of Practice SP13/91—Award of "relevant benefit" as defined in sub-s (1) above.
Revenue Internal Guidance—Schedule E manual SE 15020 (non-approved "retirement benefits schemes": definition of "relevant benefits").
SE 15022 (meaning of "retirement").
SE 15063 (overseas schemes and text of ESC A10: the term "relevant benefits" has the meaning given in this section).
SE 15120 (non-approved retirement benefits schemes: non-cash benefits received).
SE 15125 (payments other than on retirement or death can be "relevant benefits").
SE 15410 (example of payment on death).
SE 15415 (example of payment on death by accident).
Definitions—"The Board", s 832(1); "company", s 832(1), (2); "interest", s 832(1); "retirement benefits scheme", s 611(1); "Schedule E", s 19(1); "scheme", s 611(2).
Amendments—[1] Definition of "administrator" in sub-s (1) repealed by FA 1994 s 103(2) and Sch 26 Pt V(12).
[2] Words in sub-s (1), first and third words in sub-s (2), and whole of sub-s (2A) inserted, and second words in sub-s (2) substituted, by FA 1999 s 79 Sch 10 para 10 with effect in accordance with the commencement provisions contained in FA 1999 Sch 10 para 18. Words in sub-s (2) previously read "of an employer".

CHAPTER II
OTHER PENSION FUNDS AND SOCIAL SECURITY BENEFITS AND CONTRIBUTIONS

613 Parliamentary pension funds

(1) The salary of a Member of the House of Commons shall, for all the purposes of the Income Tax Acts, be treated as reduced by the amounts deducted in pursuance of section 1 of the House of Commons Members' Fund Act 1939; but a Member shall not by reason of any such deduction be entitled to relief under any other provision of the Income Tax Acts.

(2) In subsection (1) above the reference to salary shall be construed as mentioned in subsection (3) of section 1 of the House of Commons Members' Fund Act 1939 the reference to amounts deducted includes a reference to amounts required to be set aside under that subsection, and "deduction" shall be construed accordingly.

(3) Periodical payments granted out of the House of Commons Members' Fund (including periodical payments granted out of sums appropriated from that Fund or out of the income from those sums) shall be charged to income tax under Schedule E.

(4) The respective trustees of—

(a) the House of Commons Members' Fund established under section 1 of that Act of 1939;

(b) the Parliamentary Contributory Pension Fund;

[(bb) any fund maintained for the purposes of a pension scheme—

(i) established for members of the Scottish Parliament under section 81(4) of the Scotland Act 1998,

(ii) established for members of the Welsh Assembly under section 18(2) of the Government of Wales Act 1998, or

(iii) established for members of the Northern Ireland Assembly under section 48(2) of the Northern Ireland Act 1998;][1]

(c) the Members' Contributory Pension (Northern Ireland) Fund constituted under section 3(2) of the Ministerial Salaries and Members' Pensions Act (Northern Ireland) 1965; and

(d) the Assembly Contributory Pension Fund constituted under the Assembly Pensions (Northern Ireland) Order 1976;

shall be entitled to exemption from income tax in respect of all income derived from those [funds][1] or any investment of those [funds][1].

A claim under this subsection shall be made to the Board.

Commentary—*Simon's Direct Tax Service* **E7.262.**
Revenue Internal Guidance—Schedule E manual SE 74303 (pensions: particular occupations—Members of Parliament, periodical payments made out of the House of Commons Members' Fund are chargeable under Schedule E as pensions).
Definitions—''The Board'', s 832(1); ''the Income Tax Acts'', s 831(1)(*b*); ''Schedule E'', s 19(1).
Cross references—See TA 1988 s 129B (exemption from income tax under sub-s (4) above is extended to any stock lending fees payable in connection with approved arrangements relating to the relevant investments).
TA 1988 s 231A (tax credits not repayable in respect of qualifying distributions made after 1 July 1997 to pension funds — see sub-s (4) above).
TA 1988 s 659A (''investments'' and ''income'' for the purposes of sub-s (4) above to include futures and options and transactions relating to them).
TA 1988 s 659D(2) (the exemption within sub-s (4) above does not apply to income derived from investments, deposits or other property held as a member of a property investment LLP).
TCGA 1992 s 271(1)(*b*) (sub-s (4) exemption to apply also to capital gains tax).
Manufactured Payments and Transfer of Securities (Tax Relief) Regulations, SI 1995/3036 regs 3, 4 (manufactured payments and deemed interest payments arising on a sale and repurchase of securities falling to the benefit of a fund referred to in sub-s (4) above to be treated as income of the person eligible for relief by virtue of that subsection).
Amendments—¹ Sub-s (4)(*bb*) inserted, and word ''funds'' substituted for ''Funds'' twice in sub-s (4), by FA 1999 s 52, Sch 5 para 4 with effect from the year 1999–00.

614 Exemptions and reliefs in respect of income from investments etc of certain pension schemes

(1) ...¹.

(2) Any interest or dividends received by the person in whom is vested any of the Family Pension Funds mentioned in section 273 of the Government of India Act 1935 and having effect as a scheme made under section 2 of the Overseas Pensions Act 1973 on sums forming part of that fund shall be exempt from income tax.

[(2A) The reference in subsection (2) above to interest on sums forming part of a fund include references to any amount which is treated as income by virtue of paragraph 1 of Schedule 13 to the Finance Act 1996 (relevant discounted securities) and derives from any investment forming part of that fund.]²

(3) Income derived from investments or deposits of any fund referred to in paragraph (*b*), (*c*), (*d*) or (*f*) of subsection (2) of section 615 shall not be charged to income tax, and any income tax deducted from any such income shall be repaid by the Board to the persons entitled to receive the income.

(4) In respect of income derived from investments or deposits of the Overseas Service Pensions Fund established pursuant to section 7(1) of the Overseas Aid Act 1966 the Board shall give by way of repayment such relief from income tax as is necessary to secure that the income is exempt to the like extent (if any) as if it were income of a person not domiciled, ordinarily resident or resident in the United Kingdom.

(5) In respect of dividends and other income derived from investments, deposits or other property of a superannuation fund to which section 615(3) applies the Board shall give by way of repayment such relief from income tax as is necessary to secure that the income is exempt to the like extent (if any) as if it were income of a person not domiciled, ordinarily resident or resident in the United Kingdom.

(6) A claim under this section shall be made to the Board.

Commentary—*Simon's Direct Tax Service* **E4.314-316; E7.265–267.**
Definitions—''The Board'', s 832(1); ''interest'', s 832(1); ''United Kingdom'', s 830(1).
Cross references—TA 1988 s 129B (exemption from income tax under sub-s (3) above is extended to any stock lending fees payable in connection with approved arrangements relating to the relevant investments).
TA 1988 s 231A (tax credits not repayable in respect of qualifying distributions made after 1 July 1997 to pension funds—see sub-ss (2), (3)–(5) above).
TA 1988 s 659A (''investments'' and ''income'' for the purposes of sub-ss (3), (4) above to include futures and options and transactions relating to them).
TA 1988 s 659D(2) (the exemptions within sub-ss (3), (4), (5) above do not apply to income derived from investments, deposits or other property held as a member of a property investment LLP).
TCGA 1992 s 271(1)(*b*), (*c*) (sub-ss (1), (2) exemption to apply also to capital gains tax).
Manufactured Payments and Transfer of Securities (Tax Relief) Regulations, SI 1995/3036 regs 3, 4 (manufactured payments and deemed interest payments arising on a sale and repurchase of securities falling to the benefit of a fund referred to in sub-ss (2)–(4) above to be treated as income of the person eligible for relief by virtue of the relevant subsection).
Amendments—¹ Sub-s (1) repealed by FA 1994 Sch 26 Pt V(22).
² Sub-s (2A) inserted by FA 1996 ss 104, 105, Sch 14 para 34 with effect for the purposes of income tax from the year 1996–97 and for the purposes of corporation tax for accounting periods ending after 31 March 1996, subject to transitional provisions in FA 1996 Sch 15.

615 Exemption from tax in respect of certain pensions

(1) A pension to which this subsection applies shall not be liable to charge to income tax if it is the income of a person who satisfies the Board that he is not resident in the United Kingdom.

A claim under this subsection shall be made to the Board.

(2) Subsection (1) above applies to any of the following pensions—

(*a*) a pension paid under the authority of the Pensions (India, Pakistan and Burma) Act 1955 (which has effect, by virtue of subsection (3) of section 2 of the Overseas Pensions Act 1973 as a scheme made under that section);

(*b*) a pension paid out of any fund established in the United Kingdom by the government of any country which is, or forms part of, a country to which this paragraph applies, an associated state, a colony, a protectorate, a protected state or a United Kingdom trust territory, or by a government constituted for two or more such countries, if the fund was established for the sole purpose of providing pensions, whether contributory or not, payable in respect of service under that government;

(*c*) a pension paid out of the fund formed under the Overseas Superannuation Scheme (formerly known as the Colonial Superannuation scheme) [or which would have been so paid had section 2(2)(*e*) and (4A) of the Overseas Pensions Act 1973 not been enacted][1];

(*d*) a pension paid under section 1 of the Overseas Pensions Act 1973 whether or not paid out of a fund established under a scheme made under that section;

(*e*) so much of any pension paid to or in respect of any person—

    (i) under an order made under section 2 of the Overseas Service Act 1958 and having effect as if it were a scheme under section 2 of the Overseas Pensions Act 1973 or under a pension scheme originally provided and maintained under such an order and having such effect, or

    (ii) under section 4(2) of the Overseas Service Act 1958 which has effect as if it were a scheme under section 2 of the Overseas Pensions Act 1973

as may be certified by the Secretary of State to be attributable to the employment of that person in the public services of an overseas territory;

(*f*) a pension paid out of the fund established under the name "the Central African Pension Fund" by section 24 of the Federation of Rhodesia and Nyasaland (Dissolution) Order in Council 1963;

(*g*) a pension paid out of the Overseas Service Pensions Fund established under section 7(1) of the Overseas Aid Act 1966.

(3) Where an annuity is paid from a superannuation fund to which this subsection applies to a person who is not resident in the United Kingdom, income tax shall not be deducted from any payment of the annuity or accounted for under section 349(1) by the trustees or other persons having the control of the fund.

(4) Subsection (1) above shall not apply to so much of any pension falling within paragraph (*a*) or (*d*) of subsection (2) above as is paid by virtue of the application to the pension of the Pensions (Increase) Acts.

(5) Paragraph (*b*) of subsection (2) above applies to any country mentioned in Schedule 3 to the British Nationality Act 1981 except Australia, Canada, New Zealand, India, Sri Lanka and Cyprus.

(6) Subsection (3) above applies to any superannuation fund which—

(*a*) is bona fide established under irrevocable trusts in connection with some trade or undertaking carried on wholly or partly outside the United Kingdom;

(*b*) has for its sole purpose [(subject to any enactment or Northern Ireland legislation requiring or allowing provision for the value of any rights to be transferred between schemes or between members of the same scheme)][2] the provision of superannuation benefits in respect of persons' employment in the trade or undertaking wholly outside the United Kingdom; and

(*c*) is recognised by the employer and employed persons in the trade or undertaking;

and for the purposes of this subsection duties performed in the United Kingdom the performance of which is merely incidental to the performance of other duties outside the United Kingdom shall be treated as performed outside the United Kingdom.

(7) In this section—

"pension" includes a gratuity or any sum payable on or in respect of death or, in the case of a pension falling within subsection (2)(*g*) above, ill-health, and a return of contributions with or without interest thereon or any other addition thereto;

"overseas territory" means any territory or country outside the United Kingdom;

"the Pensions (Increase) Acts" means the Pensions (Increase) Act 1971 and any Act passed after that Act for purposes corresponding to the purposes of that Act;

"United Kingdom trust territory" means a territory administered by the government of the United Kingdom under the trusteeship system of the United Nations.

(8) In this section—

(*a*) ...[3]

(*b*) ...[3]

(*c*) any reference to an enactment or order having effect as if it were a scheme constituted under section 2 of the Overseas Pensions Act 1973 includes a reference to a scheme made under that section and certified by the Secretary of State for the purpose of the 1970 Act or this Act to correspond to that enactment or order.

[(9) For the purposes of this section, a person shall be taken to be employed in the public service of an overseas territory at any time when—

(*a*) he is employed in any capacity under the government of that territory, or under any municipal or other local authority in it,

(*b*) he is employed, in circumstances not falling within paragraph (a) above, by a body corporate established for any public purpose in that territory by an enactment of a legislature empowered to make laws for that territory, or (*c*) he is the holder of a public office in that territory in circumstances not falling within either paragraph (*a*) or (*b*).][3]

[(10) For the purposes of subsection (9), references to the government of an overseas territory include references to a government constituted for two or more overseas territories, and to any authority established for the purpose of providing or administering services which are common to, or relate to matters of common interest to, two or more such territories.][3]

Commentary—*Simon's Direct Tax Service* E4.314–316, E7.266, 267.
Concessions A10—Lump sums paid under overseas pension schemes.
B39—Contributions to overseas pension schemes.
Revenue Internal Guidance—Schedule E manual SE 15063 and SE 15064 (non-approved retirement benefits schemes: overseas schemes and text of ESC A10—income tax is not charged on lump sum relevant benefits receivable by an employee (or by his personal representatives or any dependant of his) from any superannuation fund accepted as being within this section; whether a fund is within this section is a matter for Pension Schemes Office).
SE 74402 (exemption of certain pensions paid to non-residents, application of this section).
Definitions—"The 1970 Act", s 831(3); "Act", s 832(1); "the Board", s 832(1); "trade", s 832(1); "United Kingdom", s 830(1).
Cross references—See TA 1988 s 232(2) (entitlement to a tax credit in respect of qualifying distribution which is income of a fund to which sub-s (2)(*b*) or (*c*) applies).
TA 1988 s 614(3), (5) (tax exemption in respect of investment income from pensions and superannuation funds mentioned in sub-ss (2)(*b*)–(*d*), (*f*), (3) above).
FA 1989 s 76(6A), (6B) (expenses of paying sums or providing benefits pursuant to a superannuation fund satisfying sub-s (6) above are not excluded from deduction in calculating profits nor prevented from being expenses of management).
TCGA 1992 s 271(1)(*c*) (capital gains tax exemption in respect of certain funds mentioned in sub-s (2) above);
TCGA 1992 Sch 1, para 2(8) (application of annual exempt amount of capital gains in cases of funds to which sub-s (3) above applies).
Amendments—[1] Words in sub-s (2)(*c*) added by the Overseas Superannuation Act 1991 s 2.
[2] Words in sub-s (6) inserted by FA 1999 s 79 Sch 10 para 11 with effect in accordance with the commencement provisions contained in FA 1999 Sch 10 para 18.
[3] In sub-ss (8), paras (*a*), (*b*) repealed, and sub-ss (9), (10) inserted, by the International Development Act 2002 s 19, Sch 3 para 9 with effect from 17 June 2002 (by virtue of SI 2002/1408). Sub-s (8)(*a*), (*b*) previously read as follows—

"(*a*) references to a government constituted for two or more countries include references to any authority established for the purpose of providing or administering services which are common to, or relate to matters of common interest to, two or more countries;

(*b*) any reference to employment in the public services of an overseas territory shall be construed as if it occurred in the Overseas Development and Co-operation Act 1980 and section 10(2) of that Act shall apply accordingly; and".

616 Other overseas pensions

(1) If and so long as provision is made by double taxation relief arrangements for a pension of a description specified in subsection (2) below to be exempt from tax in the United Kingdom and, by reason of Her Majesty's Government in the United Kingdom having assumed responsibility for the pension, payments in respect of it are made under section 1 of the Overseas Pensions Act 1973 then, to the extent that those payments are made to, or to the widow or widower of, an existing pensioner, the provision made under the arrangements shall apply in relation to the pension, exclusive of any statutory increases in it, as if it continued to be paid by the government which had responsibility for it before that responsibility was assumed by Her Majesty's Government in the United Kingdom.

(2) The pensions referred to in subsection (1) above are pensions paid by—

(*a*) the Government of Malawi for services rendered to that Government or to the Government of the Federation of Rhodesia and Nyasaland in the discharge of governmental functions;

(*b*) the Government of Trinidad and Tobago in respect of services rendered to that Government in the discharge of governmental functions;

(*c*) the Government of the Republic of Zambia for services rendered to that Government or to the Government of Northern Rhodesia or to the Government of the Federation of Rhodesia and Nyasaland in the discharge of governmental functions.

(3) If—

(*a*) immediately before 6th April 1973 a person resident in the United Kingdom was entitled to receive a pension as or as the widow or widower of an existing pensioner, and

(*b*) by reason of Her Majesty's Government in the United Kingdom having assumed responsibility for the pension, payments in respect of it are made under section 1 of the Overseas Pensions Act 1973

then, if and so long as the pension is received by that person or, where that person is an existing pensioner, by his or her widow or widower, the provisions of this Act shall apply in relation to it, exclusive of any statutory increases in it, as if it continued to be paid by the government or other body or fund which had responsibility for it before that responsibility was assumed by Her Majesty's Government in the United Kingdom.

(4) In this section—

"double taxation relief arrangements" means arrangements specified in an Order in Council making any such provisions as are referred to in section 788;

"existing pensioner", in relation to a pension, means a person by virtue of whose service the pension is payable and who retired from that service before 6th April 1973; and

"statutory increases", in relation to a pension, means so much (if any) of the pension as is paid by virtue of the application to it of any provision of the Pensions (Increase) Act 1971;

and in this subsection "pension" has the same meaning as in section 1 of the Overseas Pensions Act 1973.

Commentary—*Simon's Direct Tax Service* **E4.314.**
Concession A49—Extension of the exemption under this section to pensions paid to resident widows of Singapore nationality whose husbands were UK citizens employed in Singapore Government service.
Revenue Internal Guidance—Schedule E manual SE 74201 (pensions which before 6 April 1973 were paid by an overseas government but for which the UK now takes responsibility: by virtue of this section are treated as if they remained payable by an overseas government).
Definitions—"Tax", s 832(3); "United Kingdom", s 830(1).

617 Social security benefits and contributions

(1) Payments of benefit under [Parts II to IV of the Social Security Contributions and Benefits Act 1992][5], [or Parts II to IV of the Social Security Contributions and Benefits (Northern Ireland) Act 1992][5], except—

    (a) [short-term incapacity benefit at the lower rate][11], [short-term incapacity benefit at the higher rate or long-term incapacity benefit][12], attendance allowance, ...,[4] [disability living allowance,][2] severe disablement allowance, maternity allowance, [bereavement payments,][20] ...[19] child's special allowance and guardian's allowance; and

    (b) so much of any benefit as is attributable to an increase in respect of a child,

shall be charged to income tax under Schedule E.

(2) The following payments shall not be treated as income for any purpose of the Income Tax Acts—

    (a) payments of income support, [working families' tax credit][, disabled person's tax credits][3] or housing benefit under [Part VII of the Social Security Contributions and Benefits Act 1992][6] or [Part VII of the Social Security Contributions and Benefits (Northern Ireland) Act 1992][6] other than payments of income support which are taxable by virtue of section 151;

    [(aa) payments by way of an allowance under [paragraph 18 of Schedule 7 to the Social Security Contributions and Benefits Act 1992][7] and [paragraph 18 of Schedule 7 to the Social Security Contributions and Benefits (Northern Ireland) Act 1992][7];][1]

    [(ab) payments of a jobseeker's allowance, other than payments which are taxable by virtue of section 151A;][13]

    [(ac) payments of a back to work bonus;][13]

    [(ad) payments of a child maintenance bonus;][14]

    [(ae) compensation payments made under regulations under section 24 of the Child Support Act 1995 or under any corresponding enactment having effect with respect to Northern Ireland;][14]

    [(af) payments made under regulations under section 79 of the Welfare Reform and Pensions Act 1999 or under any corresponding enactment having effect with respect to Northern Ireland;][18]

    [(ag) payments of state pension credit under the State Pension Credit Act 2002 or under any corresponding enactment having effect with respect to Northern Ireland;][21]

    (b) payments of child benefit; and

    (c) payments excepted by subsection (1) above from the charge to tax imposed by that subsection.

(3) Subject to subsection (4) ...[16] below, no relief or deduction shall be given or allowed in respect of any contribution paid by any person under—

    (a) Part I of the Social Security [Contributions and Benefits Act 1992][8], or

    (b) Part I of the Social Security [Contributions and Benefits (Northern Ireland) Act 1992][9].

[(4) Subsection (3) above shall not apply to a contribution if it is a secondary Class 1 contribution[, a Class 1A contribution or a Class 1B contribution][17] (within the meaning of Part I of either of those Acts) and is allowable—

    (a) as a deduction in computing profits or gains;

    (b) as expenses of management deductible under section 75 or under that section as applied by section 76;

    (c) as expenses of management or supervision deductible under section 121;

    (d) as a deduction under section 198 from the emoluments of an office or employment; or

    (e) as a deduction under section 332(3)(a) from the profits, fees or emoluments of the profession or vocation of a clergyman or minister of any religious denomination.[10]]

(5) ...[15]

(6) ...[19]

Commentary—*Simon's Direct Tax Service* **E4.129, 328.**
Concession A24—Extension of the exemption under this section to social security payments, incapacity benefit and child benefits paid by foreign governments and which correspond to UK benefits.
A90—Payments made under the Employment Department's Jobmatch pilot scheme not chargeable to income tax.
A97—Income tax is not charged on payments made under the Jobmatch programme, nor in respect of training vouchers received by participants under the programme.
Revenue & other press releases—DSS 28-11-95 (list of taxable social security benefits for 1996–97).
Revenue Internal Guidance—Independent taxation handbook, In 110–114 (husband and wife situations: determination of taxable person).
Schedule E manual SE 74001 (state retirement pensions and war widows' pensions are chargeable under Schedule E by virtue of this section).
SE 76102 (treatment of dependency additions).
SE 76160 and SE 76161 (treatment of retirement pension).
SE 76171 (treatment of widow's payment).
SE 76172 (treatment of widowed mother's allowance).
SE 76173 (treatment of widow's pension).

SE 76210 (treatment of invalid care allowance).
Simon's Tax Cases—s 617(1), *Willows v Lewis* [1982] STC 141*.
Definitions—"Child", ss 831(4), 832(5); "the Income Tax Acts", s 831(1)(*b*); "profits or gains", s 833(1); "Schedule E", s 19(1); "year of assessment", s 832(1).
Cross references—See TA 1988 Sch 30 para 9 (modifications to this section applying for periods before 10 April 1988, the date on which the Income Support (General) Regulations, SI 1987/1967 came into force).
FA 1989 s 41(1)(*e*) (a benefit chargeable to income tax under sub-s (1) of this section to be charged in the year of assessment in which it accrues irrespective of when it is paid).
Amendments—[1] Sub-s (2)(*aa*) inserted by the Social Security Act 1988 Sch 4 para 1 with effect from 6 April 1988 by virtue of SI 1988/520.
[2] Words in sub-s (1)(*a*) inserted by the Disability Living Allowance and Disability Working Allowance Act 1991 Sch 2 para 18 with effect from 6 April 1992 by virtue of SI 1991/2617.
[3] Words in sub-s (2)(*a*) substituted for words "family credit" and ", disability working allowance" respectively by the Tax Credits Act 1999 ss 1(2), 20(2), Sch 1 paras 1, 6(*c*) with effect from 5 October 1999.
[4] Words omitted from sub-s (1)(*a*) repealed by the Disability Living Allowance and Disability Working Allowance (Northern Ireland Consequential Amendments) Order, SI 1991/2874 art 5.
[5] Words in sub-s (1) substituted by the Social Security (Consequential Provisions) Act 1992 Sch 2 para 93 and the Social Security (Consequential Provisions) (Northern Ireland) Act 1992 Sch 2 para 33 with effect from 1 July 1992.
[6] Words in sub-s (2)(*a*) substituted by the Social Security (Consequential Provisions) Act 1992 Sch 2 para 93 and the Social Security (Consequential Provisions) (Northern Ireland) Act 1992 Sch 2 para 33 with effect from 1 July 1992.
[7] Words in sub-s (2)(*aa*) substituted by the Social Security (Consequential Provisions) Act 1992 Sch 2 para 93 and the Social Security (Consequential Provisions) (Northern Ireland) Act 1992 Sch 2 para 33 with effect from 1 July 1992.
[8] Words in sub-s (3)(*a*) substituted by the Social Security (Consequential Provisions) Act 1992 Sch 2 para 93 with effect from 1 July 1992.
[9] Words in sub-s (3)(*b*) substituted by the Social Security (Consequential Provisions) (Northern Ireland) Act 1992 Sch 2 para 33 with effect from 1 July 1992.
[10] Sub-s (4) substituted by FA 1997 s 65(1), (3), (5) with effect in relation to contributions paid after 25 November 1996.
[11] Words in sub-s (1)(*a*) substituted by virtue of the Social Security (Incapacity for Work) Act 1994 s 13(2)(*a*), with effect from 13 April 1995 by virtue of SI 1994/2926.
[12] Words in sub-s (1)(*a*) substituted by virtue of the Social Security (Incapacity for Work) Act 1994 s 13(2)(*b*), with effect from 13 April 1995 by virtue of SI 1994/2926.
[13] Sub-s (2)(*ab*), (*ac*) inserted by the Jobseekers Act 1995 Sch 2 paras 11, 16 as from 7 October 1996 (by virtue of SI 1996/2208).
[14] Sub-s (2) (*ad*), (*ae*) inserted by the Child Support Act 1995 Sch 3 para 1 partly with effect from 1 October 1995 (by virtue of SI 1995/2302) and partly with effect from 14 October 1996 (by virtue of SI 1996/2630).
[15] Sub-s (5) repealed by FA 1996 s 147(1), (3), Sch 41 Pt V(15) with effect from the year 1996–97.
[16] Words in sub-s (3) repealed by FA 1997 s 65(1), (2), (4), Sch 18 Pt VI(5) with effect from the year 1996-97.
[17] Words in sub-s (4) substituted by FA 1999 s 61 with effect for contributions paid after 5 April 1999.
[18] Sub-s (2)(*af*) inserted by the Welfare Reform and Pensions Act 1999 s 84 Sch 12 paras 73, 75 with effect from 25 April 2000 (by virtue of SI 2000/1047).
[19] Words in sub-s (1)(*a*) and the whole of sub-s (6) repealed by the Welfare Reform and Pensions Act 1999, s 70, Sch 8 para 1, with effect from 9 April 2001 (by virtue of SI 2000/1047).
[20] Words in sub-s (1)(*a*) inserted by the Welfare Reform and Pensions Act 1999, s 70, Sch 8 para 1, with effect from 9 April 2001 (by virtue of SI 2000/1047).
[21] Sub-s (2)(*ag*) inserted by the State Pension Credit Act 2002 s 14, Sch 2 para 28 with effect from 2 July 2002 for the purpose only of exercising any power to make regulations or orders (by virtue of SI 2002/1691).
Prospective amendments—In sub-s (1)(*a*) words "severe disablement allowance," repealed by the Welfare Reform and Pensions Act 1999, s 88, Sch 13 Pt IV with effect from 3 November 2000 (for the purpose of authorising the making of regulations) and 6 April 2001 otherwise, subject to a saving (by virtue of SI 2000/2958).
In sub-s (2)(*ae*) for the words "section 24 of the Child Support Act 1995 or under any corresponding enactment" there shall be substituted "any enactment corresponding to section 24 of the Child Support Act 1995" by the Child Support, Pensions and Social Security Act 2000 ss 26, 86, Sch 3 para 8(1), (3) with effect from a day to be appointed.

CHAPTER III
RETIREMENT ANNUITIES

Statement of Practice SP 9/91—Investigation settlements; see annotation under s 625, *post*.
Cross references—See TA 1988 s 655 (transitional provisions for the purposes of this Chapter).
FA 2000 Sch 8 para 83(2) (deduction of partnership share money from an employee's salary in accordance with a partnership share agreement is disregarded for the purpose of ascertaining the amount of the employee's relevant earnings for the purposes of this Chapter).

618 Termination of relief under this Chapter, and transitional provisions

(1) Nothing in this Chapter shall apply in relation to—

(*a*) a contract made or trust scheme established on or after [1st July][1] 1988; or

(*b*) a person by whom contributions are first paid on or after that date under a trust scheme established before that date.

(2) Subject to subsection (4) below, the terms of a contract made, or the rules of a trust scheme established, on or after 17th March 1987 and before [1st July][1] 1988 and approved by the Board under section 620 shall have effect (notwithstanding anything in them to the contrary) as if they did not allow the payment to the individual by whom the contract is made, or an individual paying contributions under the scheme, of a lump sum exceeding £150,000 or such other sum as may for the time being be specified in an order under section 635(4).

(3) Subject to subsection (5) below, the rules of a trust scheme established before 17th March 1987 and approved by the Board under section 620 shall have effect (notwithstanding anything in them to the contrary) as if they did not allow the payment to any person first paying contributions under the scheme on or after 17th March 1987 of a lump sum such as is mentioned in subsection (2) above.

(4) Subsection (2) above shall not apply—

(*a*) to a contract if, before the end of January 1988, the persons by and to whom premiums are payable under it jointly give notice to the Board that subsection (2) is not to apply; or (*b*) to a scheme if, before the end of January 1988, the trustees or other persons having the management of the scheme give notice to the Board that subsection (2) is not to apply;

and where notice is given to the Board under this subsection, the contract or scheme shall, with effect from the date with effect from which it was approved, cease to be approved.

(5) Subsection (3) above shall not apply in the case of any person paying contributions under a scheme if, before the end of January 1988, he and the trustees or other persons having the management of the scheme jointly give notice to the Board that subsection (3) is not to apply; and where notice is given to the Board, the scheme shall cease to be approved in relation to the contributor with effect from the date on which he first paid a contribution under it or (if later) the date with effect from which it was approved.

Commentary—*Simon's Direct Tax Service* **E7.332.**
Definitions—"The Board", s 832(1); "notice", s 832(1).
Amendments—¹Date in sub-ss (1)(*a*), (2) substituted by FA 1988 s 54(2)(*a*)(i), (ii), (3) and deemed always to have had effect.

619 Exemption from tax in respect of qualifying premiums

(1) Where in any year of assessment an individual is (or would be but for an insufficiency of profits or gains be) chargeable to income tax in respect of relevant earnings from any trade, profession, vocation, office or employment carried on or held by him, and pays a qualifying premium, then—

(*a*) relief from income tax shall be given under this section in respect of that qualifying premium, but only on a claim made for the purpose, and where relief is to be so given, the amount of that premium shall, subject to the provisions of this section, be deducted from or set off against his relevant earnings for the year of assessment in which the premium is paid; and
(*b*) any annuity payable to the same or another individual shall be treated as earned income of the annuitant to the extent to which it is payable in return for any amount on which relief is so given.

Paragraph (*b*) above applies only in relation to the annuitant to whom the annuity is made payable by the terms of the annuity contract under which it is paid.

(2) Subject to the provisions of this section and section 626, the amount which may be deducted or set off in any year of assessment (whether in respect of one or more qualifying premiums, and whether or not including premiums in respect of a contract approved under section 621) shall not be more than 17½ per cent of the individual's net relevant earnings for that year.

(3) Subject to the provisions of this section, the amount which may be deducted or set off in any year of assessment in respect of qualifying premiums paid under a contract approved under section 621 (whether in respect of one or more such premiums) shall not be more than 5 per cent of the individual's net relevant earnings for that year.

(4) An individual who pays a qualifying premium in a year of assessment (whether or not a year for which he has relevant earnings) may [on or before the 31st January next following]² that year elect that the premium shall be treated as paid—

(*a*) in the last preceding year of assessment; or
(*b*) if he had no net relevant earnings in the year referred to in paragraph (*a*) above, in the last preceding year of assessment but one;

and where an election is made under this subsection in respect of a premium the other provisions of this Chapter shall have effect as if the premium had been paid in the year specified in the election and not in the year in which it was actually paid.

(5) Where relief under this section for any year of assessment is claimed and allowed (whether or not relief then falls to be given for that year), and afterwards there is made any assessment, alteration of an assessment, or other adjustment of the claimant's liability to tax, there shall be made also such adjustments, if any, as are consequential thereon in the relief allowed or given under this section for that or any subsequent year of assessment.

(6) Where relief under this section is claimed and allowed for any year of assessment in respect of any payment, relief shall not be given in respect of it under any other provision of the Income Tax Acts for the same or a later year of assessment nor (in the case of a payment under an annuity contract) in respect of any other premium or consideration for an annuity under the same contract; and references in the Income Tax Acts to relief in respect of life assurance premiums shall not be taken to include relief under this section.

(7) If any person, for the purpose of obtaining for himself or any other person any relief from or repayment of tax under this section, knowingly makes any false statement or false representation, he shall be liable to a penalty not exceeding [£3,000]¹.

Commentary—*Simon's Direct Tax Service* **E7.321.**
Concession A38—Retirement annuity relief interaction with employer's scheme for death or disability benefits paid in pension form.
Statement of Practice SP 9/91—Investigation settlements: utilisation by payment of contributions of unused retirement annuity relief arising from final and conclusive assessment to tax more than six years after the end of the year to which it relates.
Simon's Tax Cases—s 619(1), *Koenigsberger v Mellor* [1995] STC 547.
Definitions—"Earned income", s 833(4), (5); "net relevant earnings", s 623; "profits or gains", s 833(1); "qualifying premium", s 620; "relevant earnings", s 623; "trade", s 832(1); "year of assessment", s 832(1).
Cross references—See TMA 1970 Sch 1B para 2 (method of giving effect to claim where payment carried back to an earlier year of assessment).
TA 1988 s 266(1) (application of sub-s (6) above for the purposes of relief for life assurance premiums).

TA 1988 s 273 (relief for premiums paid to secure deferred annuity for widows, widowers and children).
TA 1988 s 625 (carry-forward of unused relief under this section).
TA 1988 s 626 (modification of this section in relation to persons over 50).
TA 1988 s 627 (provisions for Lloyd's underwriters in relation to election under sub-s (4) above).
TA 1988 s 657(2) (purchased life annuities).
Amendments—¹ Amount in sub-s (7) substituted by FA 1989 s 170(4)(*a*), (6) in relation to things done or omitted after 26 July 1989.
² Words in sub-s (4) substituted by FA 1996 s 135, Sch 21 para 17 with effect from the year 1996–97.

620 Qualifying premiums

(1) In this Chapter "qualifying premium" means, subject to subsection (5) below, a premium or other consideration paid by an individual—

(*a*) under an annuity contract for the time being approved by the Board under this section as having for its main object the provision for the individual of a life annuity in old age, or
(*b*) under a contract for the time being approved under section 621.

(2) Subject to subsection (3) and (4) below, the Board shall not approve a contract under this section unless it appears to them to satisfy the conditions that it is made by the individual with a person lawfully carrying on in the United Kingdom the business of granting annuities on human life, and that it does not—

(*a*) provide for the payment by that person during the life of the individual of any sum except sums payable by way of annuity to the individual; or
(*b*) provide for the annuity payable to the individual to commence before he attains the age of 60 or after he attains the age of 75; or
(*c*) provide for the payment by that person of any other sums except sums payable by way of annuity to the individual's widow or widower and any sums which, in the event of no annuity becoming payable either to the individual or to a widow or widower, are payable by way of return of premiums, by way of reasonable interest on premiums or by way of bonuses out of profits; or
(*d*) provide for the annuity, if any, payable to a widow or widower of the individual to be of a greater annual amount than that paid or payable to the individual; or
(*e*) provide for the payment of any annuity otherwise than for the life of the annuitant;

and that it does include provision securing that no annuity payable under it shall be capable in whole or in part of surrender, commutation or assignment.

(3) A contract shall not be treated as not satisfying the requirements of subsection (2) above by reason only that it—

(*a*) gives the individual the right to receive, by way of commutation of part of the annuity payable to him, a lump sum not exceeding three times the annual amount of the remaining part of the annuity, taking, where the annual amount is or may be different in different years, the initial annual amount, and
(*b*) makes any such right depend on the exercise by the individual of an election at or before the time when the annuity first becomes payable to him.

(4) The Board may, if they think fit, and subject to any conditions they think proper to impose, approve, under this section, a contract otherwise satisfying the preceding conditions, notwithstanding that the contract provides for one or more of the following matters—

(*a*) for the payment after the individual's death of an annuity to a dependant not the widow or widower of the individual;
(*b*) for the payment to the individual of an annuity commencing before he attains the age of 60, if the annuity is payable on his becoming incapable through infirmity of body or mind of carrying on his own occupation or any occupation of a similar nature for which he is trained or fitted;
(*c*) if the individual's occupation is one in which persons customarily retire before attaining the age of 60, for the annuity to commence before he attains that age;
(*d*) for the annuity payable to any person to continue for a term certain (not exceeding ten years), notwithstanding his death within that term, or for the annuity payable to any person to terminate, or be suspended, on marriage (or re-marriage) or in other circumstances;
(*e*) in the case of an annuity which is to continue for a term certain, for the annuity to be assignable by will, and in the event of any person dying entitled to it, for it to be assignable by his personal representatives in the distribution of the estate so as to give effect to a testamentary disposition, or to the rights of those entitled on intestacy, or to an appropriation of it to a legacy or to a share or interest in the estate.

(5) Subject to section 621(5), section 619 and subsections (1) to (4) above shall apply in relation to a contribution under a trust scheme approved by the Board as they apply in relation to a premium under an annuity contract so approved, with the modification that, for the condition as to the person with whom the contract is made, there shall be substituted a condition that the scheme—

(*a*) is established under the law of any part of, and administered in, the United Kingdom; and
(*b*) is established for the benefit of individuals engaged in or connected with a particular occupation (or one or other of a group of occupations), and for the purpose of providing retirement annuities for them, with or without subsidiary benefits for their families or dependants; and

(c) is so established under irrevocable trusts by a body of persons comprising or representing a substantial proportion of the individuals so engaged in the United Kingdom, or of those so engaged in England, Wales, Scotland or Northern Ireland;

and with the necessary adaptations of other references to the contract or the person with whom it is made.

(6) Exemption from income tax shall be allowed in respect of income derived from investments or deposits of any fund maintained for the purpose mentioned in subsection (5)(b) above under a scheme for the time being approved under that subsection.

(7) The Board may at any time, by notice given to the persons by and to whom premiums are payable under any contract for the time being approved under this section, or to the trustees or other persons having the management of any scheme so approved, withdraw that approval on such grounds and from such date as may be specified in the notice.

(8) Nothing in sections 4 and 6 of the Policies of Assurance Act 1867 (obligations of assurance companies in respect of notices of assignment of policies of life assurance) shall be taken to apply to any contract approved under this section.

(9) For the purposes of any provision applying this subsection "approved annuities" means—

(a) annuities under contracts approved by the Board under this section, being annuities payable wholly in return for premiums or other consideration paid by a person who (when the premiums or other consideration are or is payable) is, or would but for an insufficiency of profits or gains be, chargeable to tax in respect of relevant earnings from a trade, profession, vocation, office or employment carried on or held by him; and

(b) annuities or lump sums under approved personal pension arrangements within the meaning of Chapter IV of this Part.

Commentary—*Simon's Direct Tax Service* **E7.302, 311, 321.**
Definitions—"The Board", s 832(1); "body of persons", s 832(1); "distribution", s 209(2), 832(1); "income tax", s 832(4); "notice", s 832(1); "profits or gains", s 833(1); "relevant earnings", s 623; "trade", s 832(1); "United Kingdom", s 830(1).
Cross references—See TA 1988 s 129B (exemption from income tax under sub-s (6) above is extended to any stock lending fees payable in connection with arrangements relating to the relevant investments).
TA 1988 s 231A (tax credits not repayable in respect of qualifying distributions made after 1 July 1997 to pension funds—see sub-s (6) above).
TA 1988 s 622(1), (3) (approval of substituted retirement annuity contracts and treatment as earned income of annuities payable under them).
TA 1988 s 632(3) (retirement annuity schemes established before 1 July 1988 and approved under sub-s (5) above excluded from restrictions as to approvals).
TA 1988 s 657(2) (purchased life annuities).
TA 1988 s 659A ("investments" and "income" for the purposes of sub-s (6) above to include futures and options and transactions relating to them).
TA 1988 s 659D(2) (the exemption within sub-s (6) above does not apply to income derived from investments, deposits or other property held as a member of a property investment LLP).
TCGA 1992 s 271(1)(d) (capital gains tax exemption in respect of a fund maintained for the purpose mentioned in sub-s (5)(b) above),
TCGA 1992 Sch 1, para 2(8) (application of annual exempt amount of capital gains in cases of schemes and funds approved under this section).
Manufactured Payments and Transfer of Securities (Tax Relief) Regulations, SI 1995/3036 regs 3, 4 (manufactured payments and deemed interest payments arising on a sale and repurchase of securities falling to the benefit of a fund referred to in sub-s (6) above to be treated as income of the person eligible for relief by virtue of that subsection).

621 Other approved contracts

(1) The Board may approve under this section—

(a) a contract the main object of which is the provision of an annuity for the wife or husband of the individual, or for any one or more dependants of the individual,

(b) a contract the sole object of which is the provision of a lump sum on the death of the individual before he attains the age of 75.

(2) The Board shall not approve the contract unless it appears to them that it is made by the individual with a person lawfully carrying on in the United Kingdom the business of granting annuities on human life.

(3) The Board shall not approve a contract under subsection (1)(a) above unless it appears to them to satisfy all the following conditions, that is to say—

(a) that any annuity payable to the wife or husband or dependant of the individual commences on the death of the individual,

(b) that any annuity payable to the individual commences at a time after the individual attains the age of 60, and, unless the individual's annuity is one to commence on the death of a person to whom an annuity would be payable under the contract if that person survived the individual, cannot commence after the time when the individual attains the age of 75;

(c) that the contract does not provide for the payment by the person contracting with the individual of any sum, other than any annuity payable to the individual's wife or husband or dependant, or to the individual, except, in the event of no annuity becoming payable under the contract, any sums payable by way of return of premiums, by way of reasonable interest on premiums or by way of bonuses out of profits;

(d) that the contract does not provide for the payment of any annuity otherwise than for the life of the annuitant;

(*e*) that the contract does include provision securing that no annuity payable under it shall be capable in whole or in part of surrender, commutation or assignment.

(4) The Board may, if they think fit, and subject to any conditions that they think proper to impose, approve a contract under subsection (1)(*a*) above notwithstanding that, in one or more respects, they are not satisfied that the contract complies with the provisions of paragraphs (*a*) to (*e*) of subsection (3) above.

(5) The main purpose of a trust scheme, or part of a trust scheme, within section 620(5) may be to provide annuities for the wives, husbands and dependants of the individuals, or lump sums payable on death and in that case—

(*a*) approval of the trust scheme shall be subject to subsections (1) to (4) above with any necessary modifications, and not subject to section 620(2) to (4);
(*b*) the provisions of this Chapter shall apply to the scheme or part of the scheme when duly approved as they apply to a contract approved under this section; and
(*c*) section 620(6) shall apply to any duly approved trust scheme, or part of a trust scheme.

(6) Except as otherwise provided in this Chapter (and in particular except in section 620), any reference in the Tax Acts to a contract or scheme approved under that section shall include a reference to a contract or scheme approved under this section.

Commentary—*Simon's Direct Tax Service* E7.302, 312.
Definitions—"The Board", s 832(1); "the Tax Acts", s 831(2); "United Kingdom", s 830(1).
Cross references—See TA 1988 s 622(3) (treatment as earned income of annuity payable under a retirement annuity contract substituted for a contract approved under sub-s(1)(*a*) above).
TCGA 1992 s 271(1)(*d*) (capital gains tax exemption in respect of a fund maintained for the purpose mentioned in sub-s (5) above under an approved scheme),
TCGA 1992 Sch 1, para 2(8) (application of annual exempt amount of capital gains in cases of schemes and funds approved under this section).

622 Substituted retirement annuity contracts

(1) The Board may, if they think fit, and subject to any conditions they think proper to impose, approve an annuity contract under section 620 notwithstanding that the contract provides that the individual by whom it is made—

(*a*) may agree with the person with whom it is made that a sum representing the value of the individual's accrued rights under it should be applied as the premium or other consideration either under another annuity contract made between them and approved by the Board under section 620, or under personal pension arrangements made between them and approved by the Board under Chapter IV of this Part; or
(*b*) may require the person with whom it is made to pay such a sum to such other person as the individual may specify, to be applied by that other person as the premium or other consideration either under an annuity contract made between the individual and him and approved by the Board under section 620, or under personal pension arrangements made between the individual and him and approved by the Board under Chapter IV of this Part.

(2) References in subsection (1) above to the individual by whom the contract is made include references to any widow, widower or dependant having accrued rights under the contract.

(3) Where in pursuance of any such provision as is mentioned in subsection (1) above of an annuity contract approved under section 620, or of a corresponding provision of a contract approved under section 621(1)(*a*), a sum representing the value of accrued rights under one contract ("the original contract") is paid by way of premium or other consideration under another contract ("the substituted contract"), any annuity payable under the substituted contract shall be treated as earned income of the annuitant to the same extent that an annuity payable under the original contract would have been so treated.

Commentary—*Simon's Direct Tax Service* E7.302.
Definitions—"The Board", s 832(1); "earned income", s 833(4), (5).

623 Relevant earnings

(1) ...[3]

(2) ...[3] "relevant earnings", in relation to any individual, means, for the purposes of this Chapter, any income of his chargeable to tax for the year of assessment in question, being either—

(*a*) income arising in respect of remuneration from an office or employment held by him other than a pensionable office or employment; or
(*b*) income from any property which is attached to or forms part of the emoluments of any such office or employment held by him; or
(*c*) income which is chargeable under ...[1] Schedule D and is immediately derived by him from the carrying on or exercise by him of his trade, profession or vocation either as an individual or, in the case of a partnership, as a partner personally acting therein; or
(*d*) income treated as earned income by virtue of section 529;

but does not include any remuneration as director of a company whose income consists wholly or mainly of investment income [(that is to say, income which, if the company were an individual, would not be earned income)][2] being a company of which he is a controlling director.

(3) For the purposes of this Chapter, an office or employment is a pensionable office or employment if, and only if, service in it is service to which a sponsored superannuation scheme relates (not being a scheme under which the benefits provided in respect of that service are limited to a lump sum payable on the termination of the service through death or disability before the age of 75 or some lower age); but references to a pensionable office or employment apply whether or not the duties are performed wholly or partly in the United Kingdom or the holder is chargeable to tax in respect of it.

(4) Service in an office or employment shall not for the purposes of subsection (3) above be treated as service to which a sponsored superannuation scheme relates by reason only of the fact that the holder of the office or employment might (though he does not) participate in the scheme by exercising or refraining from exercising an option open to him by virtue of that service.

(5) For the purposes of relief under section 619, an individual's relevant earnings are those earnings before giving effect to any capital allowances, other than deductions allowable in computing profits or gains, but after taking into account the amounts on which charges fall to be made under [the Capital Allowances Act (including enactments which under this Act are to be treated as contained in that Act)][4]; and references to income in the following provisions of this section (other than references to total income) shall be construed similarly.

(6) Subject to the following provisions of this section "net relevant earnings" means, in relation to an individual, the amount of his relevant earnings for the year of assessment in question, less the amount of any deductions falling to be made from the relevant earnings in computing for the purposes of income tax his total income for that year, being—

(a) deductions which but for section 74(*m*), (*p*) or (*q*) could be made in computing his profits or gains; or

(b) deductions in respect of relief under Schedule 9 of the Finance Act 1981 (stock relief); or

(c) deductions in respect of losses or capital allowances arising from activities profits or gains of which would be included in computing relevant earnings of the individual ...[3].

(7) Where in any year of assessment for which an individual claims and is allowed relief under section 619—

(a) there falls to be made in computing the total income of the individual ...[3] a deduction in respect of any such loss or allowance of the individual as is mentioned in subsection (6)(*c*) above; and

(b) the deduction or part of it falls to be so made from income other than relevant earnings,

the amount of the deduction made from that other income shall be treated as reducing the individual's net relevant earnings for subsequent years of assessment (being deducted as far as may be from those of the immediately following year, whether or not he claims or is entitled to claim relief under this section for that year, and so far as it cannot be so deducted, then from those of the next year, and so on).

(8) An individual's net relevant earnings for any year of assessment are to be computed without regard to any relief which falls to be given for that year under section 619 ...[3] to that individual ...[3].

(9) An individual's relevant earnings, in the case of partnership profits, shall be taken to be his share of the partnership income, estimated in accordance with the Income Tax Acts, but the amount to be included in respect of those earnings in arriving at his net relevant earnings shall be his share of that income after making therefrom all such deductions (if any) in respect of payments made by the partnership or of relief given to the partnership under Schedule 9 of the Finance Act 1981 (stock relief) or in respect of capital allowances falling to be made to the partnership as would be made in computing the tax payable in respect of that income.

Commentary—*Simon's Direct Tax Service* **E7.322.**
Concession A95—Exception to sub-s (2)(*a*) in respect of benefits accrued under a "small" lump sum retirement benefits scheme.
Simon's Tax Cases—s 623(2)(*c*), *Koenigsberger v Mellor* [1995] STC 547.
Definitions—"Capital allowances", s 832(1); "the Capital Allowances Acts", s 832(1); "company", s 832(1), (2); "controlling director", s 624(3); "earned income", s 833(4), (5); "emoluments", s 131(1); "the Income Tax Acts", s 831(1)(*b*); "profits or gains", s 833(1); "Schedule D", s 18(1); "sponsored superannuation scheme", s 624; "trade", s 832(1); "United Kingdom", s 830(1); "year of assessment", s 832(1).
Note—In sub-s (6) words "section 74(*m*), (*p*) or (*q*)" should read "section 74(1)(*m*), (*p*) or (*q*)".
Cross references—See TA 1988 s 127(3) (sub-s (2)(*c*) above to include enterprise allowance).
TA 1988 s 503 (for the purposes of sub-s (2)(*c*) above, all lettings of furnished holiday accommodation treated as a single trade).
TCGA 1992 Sch 1 para 2(8) (application of annual exempt amount of capital gains in cases of sponsored superannuation schemes).
Amendments—[1] Words in sub-s (2)(*c*) repealed by FA 1988 Sch 14 Pt V.
[2] Words in sub-s (2) substituted by FA 1989 Sch 12 para 15 in relation to accounting periods beginning after 31 March 1989.
[3] Sub-s (1) and words in sub-ss (2), (6)(*c*), (7)(*a*), (8) repealed by FA 1988 Sch 14 Pt VIII with effect from the year 1990–91.
[4] Words in sub-s (5) substituted by CAA 2001 s 578, Sch 2 para 53 with effect for income tax purposes as respects allowances and charges falling to be made for chargeable periods ending after 5 April 2001.

624 Sponsored superannuation schemes and controlling directors

(1) In section 623 "a sponsored superannuation scheme" means a scheme or arrangement—

(a) relating to service in particular offices or employments, and

(b) having for its objects or one of its objects to make provision in respect of persons serving in those offices or employments against future retirement or partial retirement, against future termination of service through death or disability, or against similar matters, being a scheme or arrangement under which any part of the cost of the provision so made is or has been borne otherwise than by those persons by reason of their service (whether it is the cost or part of the cost of the benefits provided, or of paying premiums or other sums in order to provide those benefits, or of administering or instituting the scheme or arrangement).

(2) For the purposes of subsection (1) above a person shall be treated as bearing by reason of his service the cost of any payment made or agreed to be made in respect of his service, if that payment or the agreement to make it is treated under the Income Tax Acts as increasing his income, or would be so treated if he were chargeable to tax under Case I of Schedule E in respect of his emoluments from that service.

(3) In section 623 ''controlling director'' means a director of a company, the directors of which have a controlling interest in the company, who is the beneficial owner of, or able either directly or through the medium of other companies or by any other indirect means to control, more than 5 per cent of the ordinary share capital of the company; and for the purposes of this definition—

  ''company'' means one within the Companies Act 1985 or the Companies (Northern Ireland) Order 1986; and

  ''director'' means—

> (*a*) in relation to a body corporate the affairs of which are managed by a board of directors or similar body, a member of that board or similar body;
> (*b*) in relation to a body corporate the affairs of which are managed by a single director or similar person, that director or person;
> (*c*) in relation to a body corporate the affairs of which are managed by the members themselves, a member of the body corporate;

  and includes any person who is to be or has been a director.

Commentary—*Simon's Direct Tax Service* **E7.302.**
Definitions—''Case I of Schedule E'', s 19(2); ''control'', s 840; ''emoluments'', s 131(1); ''the Income Tax Acts'', s 831(1); ''ordinary share capital'', s 832(1).
Cross references—See TA 1988 s 657(2) (purchased life annuities).
TA 1988 TCGA 1992 Sch 1 para 2(8) (application of annual exempt amount of capital gains in cases of sponsored superannuation schemes).

625 Carry-forward of unused relief under section 619

(1) Where—

> (*a*) in any year of assessment an individual is (or would but for an insufficiency of profits or gains be) chargeable to income tax in respect of relevant earnings from any trade, profession, vocation, office or employment carried on or held by him, but
> (*b*) there is unused relief for that year, that is to say, an amount which would have been deducted from or set off against the individual's relevant earnings for that year under subsection (1) of section 619 if—
>> (i) he had paid a qualifying premium in that year; or
>> (ii) the qualifying premium or premiums paid by him in that year had been greater;

then, subject to section 655(1)(*b*), relief may be given under that section, up to the amount of the unused relief, in respect of so much of any qualifying premium or premiums paid by the individual in any of the next six years of assessment as exceeds the maximum applying for that year under subsection (2) of that section.

(2) Relief by virtue of this section shall be given for an earlier year rather than a later year, the unused relief taken into account in giving relief for any year being deducted from that available for giving relief in subsequent years and unused relief derived from an earlier year being exhausted before unused relief derived from a later year.

(3) Where a relevant assessment to tax in respect of a year of assessment becomes final and conclusive more than six years after the end of that year and there is an amount of unused relief for that year which results from the making of the assessment—

> (*a*) that amount shall not be available for giving relief by virtue of this section for any of the six years following that year, but
> (*b*) the individual may, within the period of six months beginning with the date on which the assessment becomes final and conclusive, elect that relief shall be given under section 619, up to that amount, in respect of so much of any qualifying premium or premiums paid by him within that period as exceeds the maximum applying under subsection (2) of that section for the year of assessment in which they were paid;

and to the extent to which relief in respect of any premium or premiums is given by virtue of this subsection it shall not be given by virtue of subsection (1) above.

(4) In this section ''a relevant assessment to tax'' means an assessment on the individual's relevant earnings or on the profits or gains of a partnership from which the individual derives relevant earnings.

Commentary—*Simon's Direct Tax Service* **E7.323.**
Statement of Practice SP 9/91—Investigation settlements: utilisation by payment of contributions of unused retirement annuity relief arising from final and conclusive assessment to tax more than six years after the end of the year to which it relates.
Definitions—''Profits or gains'', s 833(1); ''qualifying premium'', s 620; ''relevant earnings'', s 623; ''trade'', s 832(1); ''year of assessment'', s 832(1).

626 Modification of section 619 in relation to persons over 50

In the case of an individual whose age at the beginning of a year of assessment is within a range specified in the first column of the Table set out below, section 619(2) shall have effect for that year with the substitution for the reference to 17½ per cent of a reference to the relevant percentage specified in the second column of the Table.

TABLE

Age range	Percentage
51 to 55	20
56 to 60	22½
61 or more	27½

Commentary—*Simon's Direct Tax Service* E7.321.
Definition—"Year of assessment", s 832(1).

627 Lloyd's underwriters

Commentary—*Simon's Direct Tax Service* E5.653, E7.324, 410.
Amendments—This section repealed by FA 1994 s 228(2)(*a*), (4) and Sch 26 Pt V(25) with effect from the year 1997–98.

628 Partnership retirement annuities

(1) Where a person ("the former partner") has ceased to be a member of a partnership on retirement, because of age or ill-health or on death and, under—

(*a*) the partnership agreement; or
(*b*) an agreement replacing the partnership agreement or supplementing it or supplementing an agreement replacing it; or
(*c*) an agreement made with an individual who acquires the whole or part of the business carried on by the partnership;

annual payments are made for the benefit of the former partner or [a widow, widower or dependant of the former partner][1] and are for the purposes of income tax income of the person for whose benefit they are made, the payments shall be treated as earned income of that person, except to the extent that they exceed the limit specified in subsection (2) below.

(2) The limit mentioned in subsection (1) above is 50 per cent of the average of the amounts which, in the best three of the relevant years of assessment, were the former partner's shares of the relevant profits or gains; and for this purpose—

(*a*) the former partner's share in any year of the relevant profits or gains is, subject to subsection (3) below, so much of the relevant profits or gains as fell to be included in a return of his income for that year; and
(*b*) the relevant profits or gains are the profits or gains of any trade, profession or vocation on which the partnership or any other partnership of which the former partner was a member was assessed to income tax; and
(*c*) the relevant years of assessment are the last seven years of assessment in which he was required to devote substantially the whole of his time to acting as a partner in the partnership or those partnership; and
(*d*) the best three of the relevant years of assessment are those three of them in which the amounts of his shares of the relevant profits were highest;

but where, in any of the relevant years, the circumstances were such that any of the profits or gains of a partnership were not assessable to income tax, paragraphs (*a*), (*b*) and (*d*) above shall apply as they would apply had those profits or gains been so assessable.

(3) If the retail prices index for the month of December in the last of the seven years referred to in paragraph (*c*) of subsection (2) above is higher than it was for the month of December in any of the other years referred to in that paragraph, the amount which, for that other year, was the former partner's share of the relevant profits or gains shall be treated for the purposes of that subsection as increased by the same percentage as the percentage increase in that index.

(4) If the retail prices index for the month of December preceding a year of assessment after that in which the former partner ceased to be a member of the partnership is higher than it was for the month of December in the year of assessment in which he ceased to be such a member, the amount which under subsection (2) above is the limit for the first-mentioned year of assessment shall be treated as increased by the same percentage as the percentage increase in that index.

(5) Where the former partner ceased to be a member of the partnership before the year 1974–75, subsection (4) above shall have effect as if he had ceased to be a member in that year.

Commentary—*Simon's Direct Tax Service* E1.115.
Definitions—"Earned income", s 833(4), (5); "profits or gains", s 833(1); "retail prices index", s 833(2); "trade", s 832(1); "the year 1974–75", s 832(1); "years of assessment", s 832(1).
Amendments—[1] Words in sub-s (1) substituted by FA 1988 Sch 3 para 19 with effect from the year 1990–91.

629 Annuity premiums of Ministers and other officers

(1) For the purposes of this Chapter so much of any salary which—

(a) is payable to the holder of a qualifying office who is also a Member of the House of Commons, and

(b) is payable for a period in respect of which the holder is not a participant in relation to that office in arrangements contained in the Parliamentary pension scheme but is a participant in relation to his membership of the House of Commons in any such arrangements, or for any part of such a period,

as is equal to the difference between a Member's pensionable salary and the salary which (in accordance with any such resolution as is mentioned in subsection (3)(a) below) is payable to him as a Member holding that qualifying office shall be treated as remuneration from the office of Member and not from the qualifying office.

(2) In this section—

"Member's pensionable salary" means a Member's ordinary salary under any resolution of the House of Commons which, being framed otherwise than as an expression of opinion, is for the time being in force relating to the remuneration of Members or, if the resolution provides for a Member's ordinary salary thereunder to be treated for pension purposes as being at a higher rate, a notional yearly salary at that higher rate;

"qualifying office" means an office mentioned in section 2(2)(b), (c) or (d) of the Parliamentary and other Pensions Act 1987;

"the Parliamentary pension scheme" has the same meaning as in that Act;

and without prejudice to the power conferred by virtue of paragraph 13 of Schedule 1 to that Act, regulations under section 2 of that Act may make provision specifying the circumstances in which a person is to be regarded for the purposes of this section as being or not being a participant in relation to his Membership of the House of Commons, or in relation to any office, in arrangements contained in the Parliamentary pension scheme.

(3) In subsection (2) above "a Member's ordinary salary", in relation to any resolution of the House of Commons, means—

(a) if the resolution provides for salary to be paid to Members at different rates according to whether or not they are holders of particular offices, or are in receipt of salaries or pensions as the holders or former holders of particular offices, a Member's yearly salary at the higher or highest rate; and

(b) in any other case, a Member's yearly salary at the rate specified in or determined under the resolution.

Commentary—*Simon's Direct Tax Service* E7.321.
Cross references—See FA 1999 Sch 5 para 6 (circumstances in which this section applies in relation to pensions of members of the Scottish Executive).

CHAPTER IV
PERSONAL PENSION SCHEMES

Definitions—"Net relevant earnings", s 646; "relevant earnings", s 644.
Cross references—See TA 1988 s 622(1) (approval of retirement annuity contracts substituted for personal pension arrangements approved under this Chapter).
TA 1988 s 653 (penalty for misrepresentation to obtain relief under this Chapter).
TA 1988 s 655 (effect on premiums and relief allowed under this Chapter as a result of transitional provisions applying to retirement annuities under Ch III).
TA 1988 s 657(2) (purchased life annuities).
FA 1989 Sch 7, Pt II (new provisions in respect of personal pension schemes approved before 27 July 1989).
FA 2000 Sch 8 para 83(2) (deduction of partnership share money from an employee's salary in accordance with a partnership share agreementis disregarded for the purpose of ascertaining the amount of the employee's relevant earnings for the purposes of this Chapter).
FA 2000 Sch 13 para 28 (schemes approved before 6 April 2001 deemed to contain certain provisions).
Personal Pension Schemes (Restriction on Discretion to Approve) (Permitted Investments) Regulations, SI 2001/117 (restrictions on Revenue's discretion to approve personal pension schemes under this Chapter).

Preliminary

630 Interpretation

[(1)][3] In this Chapter—

"approved"—

(a) in relation to a scheme [(other than an approved retirement benefits scheme)][4], means approved by the Board under this Chapter; and

(b) in relation to arrangements, means—

[(i)][4] made in accordance with a scheme which is for the time being, and was when the arrangements were made, an approved scheme[; or

(ii) made in accordance with a scheme which is for the time being an approved converted scheme but which was, when the arrangements were made, an approved retirement benefits scheme;][4]

but does not refer to cases in which approval has been withdrawn;

[''approved converted scheme'' means an approved personal pension scheme which is such a scheme by virtue of paragraph 3(2)(b) of Schedule 23ZA;][4]

[''approved retirement benefits scheme'' means a retirement benefits scheme approved under Chapter I of this Part;][4]

[''authorised insurance company'' has the meaning given by section 659B.][2]

[''the earnings threshold'' for any year of assessment is £3,600;][6]

[''higher level contributions'', in the case of any year of assessment, means contributions in excess of the earnings threshold for the year;][6]

[''income withdrawal'' means a payment of income, under arrangements made in accordance with a personal pension scheme, otherwise than by way of an annuity;][3]

''member'', in relation to a personal pension scheme, means an individual who makes arrangements in accordance with the scheme;

[''pension date'', in relation to any personal pension arrangements, means [(subject to section 638ZA)][4] the date determined in accordance with the arrangements on which—

    (a) a annuity such as is mentioned in section 634 is first payable, or

    (b) the member elects to defer the purchase of such an annuity and to make income withdrawals in accordance with section 634A;][3]

''personal pension arrangements'' means arrangements made by an individual in accordance with a personal pension scheme;

''personal pension scheme'' means a scheme whose sole purpose is the provision of annuities[, income withdrawals][3] or lump sums under arrangements made by individuals in accordance with the scheme;

[''the personal pension fund'', in the case of any personal pension arrangement and an individual, means the accrued rights to which the individual is entitled conferring prospective entitlement to benefits under the arrangement;][4]

[''retirement benefits scheme'' has the same meaning as in Chapter I of this Part (see section 611);][4]

''scheme administrator'' means the person referred to in section 638(1);

[and references to an employee or to an employer include references to the holder of an office or to the person under whom an office is held.][1]

[(1A) The Treasury may by order amend the definition of ''the earnings threshold'' in subsection (1) above for any year of assessment by varying the amount there specified.][5]

[(2) For the purposes of this Chapter the annual amount of the annuity which would have been purchasable by a person on any date shall be calculated by reference to—

    (a) the value on that date, determined by or on behalf of the scheme administrator, of the [personal pension fund][5] under the arrangements in question, and

    (b) the current published tables of rates of annuities prepared for the purposes of this Chapter by the Government Actuary.][3]

[Where a lump sum falls to be paid on the date in question, the reference is to the value of the personal pension fund after allowing for that payment.][4]

(3) *The reference in subsection (2)(a) above to the value of the fund from which income withdrawals are to be or have been made under any personal pension arrangements is to the value of the accrued rights to which the person concerned is entitled conferring prospective entitlement to benefits under those arrangements.*

Where a lump sum falls to be paid on the date in question, the reference is to the value of the fund after allowing for that payment.[5]

[(4) The Board may make provision by regulations as to the basis on which the tables mentioned in subsection (2)(b) above are to be prepared and the manner in which they are to be applied.][3]

Commentary—*Simon's Direct Tax Service* **E7.406.**
Definition—''The Board'', s 832(1).
Amendments—[1] Words inserted by FA 1988 s 55(1), (4) with effect from 1 July 1988.
[2] Definition of ''authorised insurance company'' substituted by FA 1995 ss 59(4), 60(3), with effect in relation to a scheme not approved under this Chapter before 1 May 1995.
[3] Section as originally enacted renumbered as sub-s (1) thereof, definitions of ''income withdrawal'' and ''pension date'' inserted, words in definition of ''personal pension scheme'' inserted, and sub-ss (2)–(4) added, by FA 1995 Sch 11 paras 1, 2, with effect in relation to approvals, of schemes or amendments, given under this Chapter after 1 May 1995, but not so as to affect approvals previously given.
[4] In sub-s (1), words in definitions of ''approved'', ''pension date'' and definitions of ''approved converted scheme'', ''approved retirement benefits scheme'', ''the personal pension fund'' and ''retirement benefits scheme'', sub-s (1A) and words in sub-s (2) inserted by FA 2000 s 61, Sch 13 paras 1, 5(1)–(3), (4)(a), (b), (e), (f), (5), (6)(a) with effect from 28 July 2000.
[5] Words in sub-s (2)(a) substituted for words ''fund from which income withdrawals are to be or have been made by him'', and sub-s (3) repealed, by FA 2000 ss 61, 156, Sch 13 paras 1, 5(1), (6)(a), (7), Sch 40 Pt II(4) with effect from 28 July 2000.
[6] In sub-s (1) definitions ''the earnings threshold'' and ''higher level contributions'' inserted by FA 2000 s 61, Sch 13 paras 1, 5(4)(c), (d), (8) with effect from the year 2001–02.

631 Approval of schemes

(1) An application to the Board for their approval of a personal pension scheme shall be in such form, shall contain such information, and shall be accompanied by such documents, in such form, as the Board may prescribe.

(2) The Board may at their discretion grant or refuse an application for approval of a personal pension scheme, but their discretion shall be subject to the restrictions set out in sections 632 to [638A]¹ [(and, where applicable, Schedule 23ZA)]².

[(2A) An application for approval of a personal pension scheme may, if the Board think fit, be granted subject to conditions.]³

(3) The Board shall give notice to the applicant of the grant or refusal of an application; and

    [(*a*) in the case of a grant subject to conditions, the notice shall state that the grant is so subject and shall specify the conditions; and

    (*b*)]⁴ in the case of a refusal the notice shall state the grounds for the refusal.

(4) If an amendment is made to an approved scheme without being approved by the Board, their approval of the scheme shall cease to have effect.

Commentary—*Simon's Direct Tax Service* **E7.403.**
Definitions—"Approved", s 630(1); "The Board", s 832(1); "notice", s 832(1); "personal pension scheme", s 630(1).
Cross references—See TA 1988 s 651 (appeal against Board's refusal to approve a scheme under this section).
TA 1988 s 653 (penalty for misrepresentation to obtain approval under this section).
Personal Pension Scheme (Restriction on Discretion to Approve) (Establishment of Schemes under Trusts) Regulations, SI 2000/2314 (restriction on discretion to approve certain personal pension schemes).
Amendments—¹ Word in sub-s (2) substituted by FA 1998 s 94(2) with effect from 31 July 1998.
² Words in sub-s (2) inserted by FA 2000 s 61, Sch 13 paras 1, 6(1), (2) with effect from 28 July 2000.
³ Sub-s (2A) inserted and words in sub-s (3) to be amended by FA 2000 s 61, Sch 13 paras 1, 6(3)–(5) with effect for applications for approval granted after 5 April 2001.
⁴ Words in sub-s (3) inserted by FA 2000 s 61, Sch 13 paras 1, 6(3)–(5) with effect for applications for approval granted after 5 April 2001.

[631A Conversion of certain approved retirement benefits schemes

Schedule 23ZA to this Act (which makes provision for or in connection with the conversion of certain retirement benefits schemes approved under Chapter I of this Part into personal pension schemes approved under this Chapter) shall have effect.]¹

Amendments—¹ This section inserted by FA 2000 s 61, Sch 13 paras 1, 7 with effect from 28 July 2000.

Restrictions on approval

Cross references—See TA 1988 s 631(2) (Board's discretion to grant or refuse applications for approval of personal pension schemes subject to restrictions in ss 632–638).

632 Establishment of schemes

(1) [Subject to subsection (1A), the]⁴ Board shall not approve a personal pension scheme established by any person other than—

    (*a*) a person who [has permission under Part 4 of the Financial Services and Markets Act 2000 to effect or carry out contracts of long-term insurance or to manage unit trust schemes authorised under section 243 of that Act;]⁵

    [(*aa*) an EEA firm of the kind mentioned in paragraph 5(d) of Schedule 3 to the Financial Services and Markets Act 2000 which—

        (i) has permission under paragraph 15 of that Schedule (as a result of qualifying for authorisation under paragraph 12 of that Schedule) to effect or carry out contracts of long-term insurance; and

        (ii) fulfils any one of the requirements under subsections (5), (6) or (7) of section 659B;]⁵

    [(*ab*) a firm which has permission under paragraph 4 of Schedule 4 to the Financial Services and Markets Act 2000 (as a result of qualifying for authorisation under paragraph 2 of that Schedule) to manage unit trust schemes authorised under section 243 of that Act;]⁵

    [(*ac*) a person who qualifies for authorisation under Schedule 5 to the Financial Services and Markets Act 2000;]⁵

    (*b*) a building society within the meaning of the Building Societies Act 1986;

    (*bb*) ...⁵

    [(*c*) a person falling within section 840A(1)(*b*);]

    [(*cc*) a body corporate which is a subsidiary or holding company of [a person falling within section 840A(1)(*b*)]⁵ or is a subsidiary of the holding company of [such a person]⁵;]²

    (*d*) ...⁵

    [(*e*) an institution which—

        [(i) is an EEA firm of the kind mentioned in paragraph 5(*a*), (*b*) or (*c*) of Schedule 3 to the Financial Services and Markets Act 2000,

        (ii) qualifies for authorisation under paragraph 12(1) or (2) of that Schedule, and

        (iii) has permission under that Act to manage portfolios of investments.]⁵]³

[(1A) The Board may approve a personal pension scheme established by any person other than a person mentioned in subsection (1)(*a*) to (*e*) if the scheme is established under a trust or trusts.][4]

[(2) In subsection (1)(*a*) above "contracts of long-term insurance" means contracts which fall within Part II of Schedule 1 to the Financial Services and Markets Act 2000 (Regulated Activities) Order 2001.][5]

[(2A) In subsection (1)(*cc*) above "holding company" and "subsidiary" are to be construed in accordance with section 736 of the Companies Act 1985 or Article 4 of the Companies (Northern Ireland) Order 1986.][2]

(2B) ...[5]

(3) Subsection (1) above shall not apply in relation to a scheme approved by the Board by virtue of section 620(5) if it was established before [1st July][1] 1988.

(4) The Treasury may by order amend this section as it has effect for the time being.

Commentary—*Simon's Direct Tax Service* **E7.405.**
Definitions—"The Board", s 832(1); "building society", s 832(1); "personal pension scheme", s 630(1); "unit trust schemes",
   s 832(1).
Cross references—See the Personal Pension Schemes (Transfer Payments) Regulations, SI 2001/119 (provision for the making
   of, and acceptance of, transfer payments from one personal pension scheme to another).
Amendments—[1] Date in sub-s (3) substituted by FA 1988 s 54(2)(*a*)(iii), (3) and deemed always to have had effect.
[2] Sub-ss (1)(*bb*), (*cc*), (2A) inserted by the Personal Pension Schemes (Establishment of Schemes) Order, SI 1988/993 with effect
   from 1 July 1988.
[3] Sub-ss (1)(*aa*), (*e*), (2ZA), (2B) inserted by the Personal Pension Schemes (Establishment of Schemes) Order, SI 1997/2388
   with effect from 24 October 1997.
[4] Words in sub-s (1) substituted and sub-s (1A) inserted by the Personal Pension Schemes (Establishment of Schemes) Order
   SI 2000/2317 reg 2 with effect from 1 October 2000.
[5] In sub-s (1), words in paras (*a*) and (*cc*) substituted, paras (*aa*)–(*ac*) substituted for para (*aa*), paras (*bb*) and (*d*) repealed,
   paras (*c*) and para (*e*)(i)–(iii) substituted; sub-s (2) substituted for sub-ss (2), (2ZA) and sub-s (2B) repealed, by the Financial
   Services and Markets Act 2000 (Consequential Amendments) (Taxes) Order, SI 2001/3629 arts 13, 41 with effect from 1
   December 2001, immediately after the coming into force of the Financial Services and Markets Act 2000 ss 411, 432(1),
   Sch 20.

[632A Eligibility to make contributions

(1) The Board shall not approve a personal pension scheme if it permits, in relation to arrangements made by a member in accordance with the scheme, the acceptance of—

   (*a*) contributions by the member, or
   (*b*) contributions by an employer of the member,

at a time when the member is not eligible to make contributions.

(2) The Board shall not approve a personal pension scheme unless it makes provision for ensuring, in relation to any such arrangements, that any contributions accepted at a time when the member is not eligible to make contributions are repaid—

   (*a*) to the member, to the extent of his contributions; and
   (*b*) as to the remainder, to his employer.

(3) The following provisions of this section, and the provisions of section 632B, have effect for determining for the purposes of subsections (1) and (2) above the times at which a member is eligible to make contributions (and, for those purposes, a member is not eligible to make contributions at any other time).

(4) A member is eligible to make contributions at any time during a year of assessment for which he has actual net relevant earnings.

(5) A member who does not have actual net relevant earnings for a year of assessment ("the relevant year") is eligible to make contributions at any time during that year if—

   (*a*) for at least some part of the year he does not hold an office or employment to which section 645 applies; and
   (*b*) the condition in any of subsections (6) to (9) below is satisfied.

(6) Condition A is that at some time in the relevant year the member is resident and ordinarily resident in the United Kingdom.

(7) Condition B is that the member—

   (*a*) at some time during the five years of assessment preceding the relevant year, has been resident and ordinarily resident in the United Kingdom; and
   (*b*) was resident and ordinarily resident in the United Kingdom when he made the personal pension arrangements in question.

(8) Condition C is that at some time in the relevant year the member is a person who performs duties which, by virtue of section 132(4)(*a*), are treated as being performed in the United Kingdom.

(9) Condition D is that at some time in the relevant year the member is the spouse of a person who performs such duties as are mentioned in subsection (8) above.][1]

Amendments—[1] This section inserted by FA 2000 s 61, Sch 13 paras 1, 8 with effect after 5 April 2001.

[632B Eligibility to make contributions: concurrent membership

(1) A member who would not, apart from this section, be eligible to make contributions during a year of assessment shall be eligible to make contributions at any time during that year if—

    (a) throughout the year he holds an office or employment to which section 645 applies;

    (b) the condition in any of subsections (6) to (9) of section 632A is satisfied in his case as respects the year;

    (c) he is not, and has not been, a controlling director of a company at any time in the year or in any of the five years of assessment preceding it;

    (d) for at least one of the five years of assessment preceding the year, the aggregate of his grossed-up remuneration from each office and each employment held on 5th April in that preceding year does not exceed the remuneration limit for the relevant year; and

    (e) the total relevant contributions made in the year do not exceed the earnings threshold for the year.

(2) For the purposes of paragraphs (c) and (d) of subsection (1) above, no account shall be taken of any year of assessment earlier than the year 2000–01.

(3) For the purposes of paragraph (c) of subsection (1) above, a person is a controlling director of a company at any time if at that time—

    (a) he is a director, as defined by section 612(1); and

    (b) he is within paragraph (b) of section 417(5) in relation to the company.

(4) For the purposes of paragraph (d) of subsection (1) above—

    (a) ''grossed up'', in relation to a person's remuneration from an office or employment, means increased by being multiplied by a figure determined in accordance with an order made by the Treasury (or left unchanged, if that figure is unity);

    (b) ''remuneration'' shall be construed in accordance with an order made by the Treasury;

    (c) ''the remuneration limit'' for any year of assessment is £30,000;

    (d) ''the relevant year'' means the year of assessment first mentioned in subsection (1) above.

The Treasury may by order amend the definition of ''the remuneration limit'' in paragraph (c) above for any year of assessment by varying the amount there specified.

(5) For the purposes of paragraph (e) of subsection (1) above and the following provisions of this section, ''the total relevant contributions'', in the case of a year of assessment, means the aggregate amount of the contributions made in the year—

    (a) by the member in question, and

    (b) by any employer of his,

under arrangements made by the member under the scheme in question, together with the aggregate amounts of such contributions under other approved personal pension arrangements made by that member.

(6) If—

    (a) in the case of a member, the total relevant contributions in a year of assessment, apart from this subsection, exceed the earnings threshold for the year, and

    (b) but for that, the member would be eligible to make contributions by virtue of subsection (1) above at any time in that year,

the repayment required by subsection (2) of section 632A is repayment of the relevant excess contributions only (so that the condition in subsection (1)(e) above becomes satisfied).

(7) In subsection (6) above ''the relevant excess contributions'' means—

    (a) to the extent that a contribution is the first which caused the total relevant contributions in the year to exceed the earnings threshold for the year, that contribution; and

    (b) all subsequent contributions in the year.

(8) The Treasury may by order make provision requiring any person who claims to be eligible to make contributions by virtue of this section to provide to—

    (a) the Board,

    (b) an officer of the Board, or

    (c) the scheme administrator of the personal pension scheme concerned,

such declarations, certificates or other evidence in support of the claim as may be specified or described in, or determined in accordance with, the order.

(9) A person shall only be eligible to make contributions by virtue of this section in a year of assessment if he complies with any requirements imposed by order under subsection (8) above.]¹

Cross references—Personal Pension Schemes (Concurrent Membership) Order, SI 2000/2318 (provision to enable a member of both a personal pension scheme and an approved retirement benefits scheme to make contributions to both schemes in certain circumstances).

Amendments—¹ This section inserted by FA 2000 s 61, Sch 13 paras 1, 8 with effect after 5 April 2001.

633 Scope of benefits

(1) The Board shall not approve a personal pension scheme which makes provision for any benefit other than—

(a) the payment of an annuity satisfying the conditions in section 634 [or income withdrawals with respect to which the conditions in section 634A are satisfied][1];

(b) the payment to a member of a lump sum satisfying the conditions in section 635;

(c) the payment after the death of a member of an annuity satisfying the conditions in section 636 [or income withdrawals with respect to which the conditions in section 636A are satisfied][1];

(d) the payment on the death of a member of a lump sum satisfying [the conditions in section 637 (death benefit)][1];

[(e) the payment on or after the death of a member of a lump sum [with respect to which the conditions in section 637A (return of contributions) are satisfied][2]][1].

(2) ...[3]

Commentary—*Simon's Direct Tax Service* **E7.406.**
Definitions—''The Board'', s 832(1); ''income withdrawal'', s 632(1); ''member'', s 630(1); ''personal pension scheme'', s 630(1).
Amendments—[1] Words in sub-s (1)(a), (c), and sub-s (1)(e), inserted, and words in sub-s (1)(d) substituted by FA 1995 Sch 11 paras 1, 3, with effect for approvals, of schemes or amendments, given under this Chapter after 1 May 1995, but not so as to affect approvals previously given.
[2] Words in sub-s (1)(e) substituted by FA 1996 s 172(1), (3) with effect for approvals, of schemes or amendments, given under this Chapter after 29 April 1996 but not so as to affect approvals previously given.
[3] Sub-s (2) repealed by FA 2000 ss 61, 156, Sch 13 paras 1, 9, Sch 40 Pt II(4) with effect for insurance under a contract of insurance made after 5 April 2001.

634 Annuity to member

(1) The annuity must be payable by an authorised insurance company which may be chosen by the member.

(2) Subject to subsection (3) below, the annuity must not commence before the member attains the age of 50 or after he attains the age of 75.

(3) The annuity may commence before the member attains the age of 50 if—

(a) it is payable on his becoming incapable through infirmity of body or mind of carrying on his own occupation or any occupation of a similar nature for which he is trained or fitted; or

(b) the Board are satisfied that his occupation is one in which persons customarily retire before that age.

(4) Subject to subsection (5) below, the annuity must be payable to the member for his life.

(5) The annuity may continue for a term certain not exceeding ten years, notwithstanding the member's death within that term; and for this purpose an annuity shall be regarded as payable for a term certain notwithstanding that it may terminate, after the death of the member and before expiry of that term, on the happening of any of the following—

(a) the marriage of the annuitant;

(b) his attaining the age of 18;

(c) the later of his attaining that age and ceasing to be in full-time education.

(6) The annuity must not be capable of assignment or surrender, [except that—

(a) an annuity may be assigned or surrendered for the purpose of giving effect to a pension sharing order or provision; and

(b)][1] an annuity for a term certain may be assigned by will or by the annuitant's personal representatives in the distribution of his estate so as to give effect to a testamentary disposition, or to the rights of those entitled on an intestacy, or to an appropriation of it to a legacy or to a share or interest in the estate.

Commentary—*Simon's Direct Tax Service* **E7.406.**
Revenue & other press releases—Pension Schemes Office 23-8-95 paras 19–23 (Update 8: procedure where facility to defer annuity and withdraw income required).
Definitions—''Authorised insurance company'', s 630(1); ''the Board'', s 832(1); ''interest'', s 832(1); ''member'', s 630(1).
Cross references—See TA 1988 s 636(5) (deferred payment of an annuity to the surviving spouse under the age of 60 where it is payable for a term certain as mentioned in sub-s (5) above).
Amendments—[1] Words in sub-s (6) substituted by FA 1999 s 79 Sch 10 para 12(1), with effect in accordance with the commencement provisions contained in FA 1999 Sch 10 para 18. Words previously read ''except that''.

[634A Income withdrawals by member

(1) Where a member elects to defer the purchase of an annuity such as is mentioned in section 634, income withdrawals may be made by him during the period of deferral, subject as follows.

[(1A) The Board shall not refuse to approve a personal pension scheme by reason only that it makes provision for arrangements under the scheme which enable a member who makes such an election as is mentioned in subsection (1) above to apply different parts of the personal pension fund at different times in the purchase of different annuities satisfying the conditions in section 634 (whether commencing on the same day or on different days).][6]

(2) Income withdrawals must not be made before the member attains the age of 50, unless—

(a) they are available on his becoming incapable through infirmity of body or mind of carrying on his own occupation or any occupation of a similar nature for which he is trained or fitted, or

(b) the Board are satisfied that his occupation is one in which persons customarily retire before that age.

(3) Income withdrawals must not be made after the member attains the age of 75.

(4) The aggregate amount of income withdrawals by a member in each successive period of twelve months [in each valuation period]³ must be not less than 35 per cent or more than 100 per cent of the annual amount of the annuity which would have been purchasable by him—[

(*a*) in the case of the initial period, on the relevant reference date; and
(*b*) in the case of any subsequent valuation period,

[(i)]⁷ on a particular day in the period of sixty days ending with the relevant reference date]⁴[or
(ii) immediately after the last qualifying annuitisation,

whichever is the later.]⁷

[(4A) For the purposes of subsection (4) above—

(*a*) "annuitisation" means the application of part of the personal pension fund in the purchase of an annuity satisfying the conditions in section 634; and
(*b*) an annuitisation is a "qualifying annuitisation", in relation to any such period of twelve months as is mentioned in subsection (4) above, if it has taken place—

(i) in an earlier such period, but
(ii) since the relevant reference date.]⁶

[(5) For the purposes of this section, in the case of any arrangements the relevant reference date—

(*a*) for the period beginning with the member's pension date ("the initial period"), is that pension date; and
(*b*) for each succeeding period, is the first day of the period;

and, subject to subsection (5D) below, any period mentioned in paragraph (*a*) or (*b*) above (a "valuation period") is a period of three years.]⁴

[(5A) Where—

(*a*) a member has made an election under subsection (1) above in respect of two or more personal pension arrangements under the same personal pension scheme, and
(*b*) in the case of one or more of those arrangements, the relevant reference date for any valuation period after the initial period would not, apart from this subsection, coincide with a date which is (or, but for the ending of the period of deferral, would be) the relevant reference date for a valuation period in the case of the arrangements with the earliest pension date,

the relevant reference date for any valuation period other than the initial period, and the valuation period to which that date relates, shall, if the scheme or the arrangements so require, be determined in the case of all those arrangements on the assumption that the pension date is in each case the same as in the case of the arrangements with the earliest pension date.

(5B) In determining in accordance with subsection (5A) above the relevant reference date and the valuation period to which it relates, in the case of any arrangements ("the relevant arrangements"), there shall be left out of account any arrangements in whose case the period of deferral ended—

(*a*) before the actual pension date in the case of the relevant arrangements; or
(*b*) before the date on which the relevant arrangements first become subject to such a requirement as is mentioned in subsection (5A) above.

(5C) But where, in the case of any arrangements,—

(*a*) the relevant reference date for any valuation period falls to be determined, in accordance with the assumption in subsection (5A) above, by reference to the pension date for any other arrangements, and
(*b*) the period of deferral in the case of those other arrangements comes to an end,

the same pension date shall continue to be assumed under that subsection for that and any subsequent valuation period, notwithstanding the coming to an end of the period of deferral in the case of those other arrangements (and references in subsection (5A) to the arrangements with the earliest pension date shall be construed accordingly).

(5D) Where, in the case of any personal pension arrangements, in consequence of subsection (5A) above the relevant reference date for any valuation period ("the later date") falls less than three years after the relevant reference date for the previous valuation period ("the earlier date")—

(*a*) the valuation period beginning with the earlier date shall end with the day before the later date; and
(*b*) [subsections (4) and (4A)]⁷ above shall apply in relation to any portion of the period which remains after the completion of any successive periods of twelve months as if it were a period of twelve months.]⁵

(6) The right to income withdrawals must not be capable of assignment or surrender[, except for the purpose of giving effect to a pension sharing order or provision]².]¹

Commentary—*Simon's Direct Tax Service* E7.406.
Definitions—"The Board", s 832(1); "income withdrawals", s 630(1); "member", s 630(1); "pension date", s 630(1).
Amendments—¹ This section inserted by FA 1995 Sch 11 paras 1, 4, with effect in relation to approvals, of schemes or amendments, given under this Chapter after 1 May 1995, but not so as to affect approvals previously given.
² Words in sub-s (6) inserted by FA 1999 s 79 Sch 10 para 12(2) with effect for the purposes of the grant at any time after 9 May 2000 of any approval of a personal pension scheme (whenever made); or the withdrawal at any time after that day of approval

of any personal pension scheme or personal pension arrangements (whenever approved) (by virtue of the Finance Act 1999, Schedule 10, Paragraph 18, (First and Second Appointed Days) Order, SI 2000/1093)..
[3] Words in sub-s (4) substituted by FA 2000 s 61, Sch 13 paras 1, 10(1), (2)(*a*), (5) with effect after 30 September 2000. Words previously read "beginning with his pension date".
[4] Words in sub-s (4) substituted, and sub-ss (5A)–(5D) inserted, by FA 2000 s 61, Sch 13 paras 1, 10(1), (2)(*b*), (4), (6) with effect in relation to personal pensions arrangements—

(*a*) under any personal pension scheme to which approval under TA 1988 Pt XIV, Ch IV is given after 30 September 2000; or
(*b*) under any existing approved scheme (as defined by FA 2000 Sch 13 para 10(7)) amended after that date, with the approval of the Board under that Chapter, for the purpose of conforming to the amendment made by Sch 13 para 10(2)(*b*), or imposing such a requirement as is mentioned in sub-s (5A) (as inserted by sub-para (4)), as the case may be.
Words in sub-s (4) previously read "on the relevant reference date".
[5] Sub-s (5) substituted by FA 2000 s 61, Sch 13 para 10(1), (3), (5) with effect after 30 September 2000. Sub-s (5) previously read—

"(5) For the purposes of this section the relevant reference date for the first three years is the member's pension date, and for each succeeding period of three years is the first day of that period.".
[6] Sub-ss (1A), (4A) inserted by FA 2000 s 61, Sch 13 paras 1, 11 with effect after 5 April 2001.
[7] Words in sub-s (4) inserted, and in sub-s (5) substituted by FA 2000 s 61, Sch 13 paras 1, 11 with effect after 5 April 2001.

635 Lump sum to member

(1) The lump sum must be payable only if the member so elects on or before [his pension date under the arrangements in question][5]

(2) The lump sum must be payable [on the date which is his pension date under the arrangements in question.][5]

[(3) The lump sum must not exceed one quarter of the difference between—
(*a*) the total value, at the time when the lump sum is paid, of the benefits provided for by [the arrangements in question][5], and
(*b*) the value, at that time, of such of the member's rights [under those arrangements][5] as are protected rights for the purposes of the [Pension Schemes Act 1993][3] or the [Pension Schemes (Northern Ireland) Act 1993.][4]][1]

...[2]

(5) The right to payment of the lump sum must not be capable of assignment or surrender[, except for the purpose of giving effect to a pension sharing order or provision][6].

Commentary—*Simon's Direct Tax Service* **E7.406.**
Definition—"Member", s 630(1); "pension date", s 630(1).
Amendments—[1] Sub-s (3) substituted by FA 1989 Sch 7 paras 1, 2 in relation to the approval of a scheme after 26 July 1989 except as regards arrangements made by a member before 27 July 1989 in accordance with a scheme coming into existence before that date.
[2] Sub-s (4) repealed by FA 1989 Sch 7 paras 1, 2 and Sch 17 Pt IV in relation to the approval of a scheme after 26 July 1989 except as regards arrangements made by a member before 27 July 1989 in accordance with a scheme coming into existence before that date.
[3] Words in sub-s (3) substituted by the Pension Schemes Act 1993 s 190, Sch 8 para 20(2), with effect from 7 February 1994, by virtue of the Pension Schemes Act 1993 (Commencement No 1) Order, SI 1994/86.
[4] Words in sub-s (3) substituted by the Pension Schemes (Northern Ireland) Act 1993 s 184, Sch 7 para 22(1), with effect from 7 February 1994, by virtue of the Pension Schemes (1993 Act) (Commencement No 1) Order(NI) 1994, SR 1994/17.
[5] Words in sub-ss (1), (2), (3)(*a*), (*b*) substituted by FA 1995 Sch 11 paras 1, 5, with effect for approvals, of schemes or amendments, given under this Chapter after 1 May 1995, but not so as to affect approvals previously given.
[6] Words in sub-s (6) inserted by FA 1999 s 79, Sch 10 para 12(3) with effect for the purposes of the grant at any time after 9 May 2000 of any approval of a personal pension scheme (whenever made); or the withdrawal at any time after that day of approval of any personal pension scheme or personal pension arrangements (whenever approved) (by virtue of the Finance Act 1999, Schedule 10, Paragraph 18, (First and Second Appointed Days) Order, SI 2000/1093).

636 Annuity after death of member

(1) The annuity must be payable by an authorised insurance company which may be chosen by the member or by the annuitant.

(2) The annuity must be payable to the surviving spouse of the member, or to a person who was at the member's death a dependant of his.

(3) The aggregate annual amount (or, if that amount varies, the aggregate of the initial annual amounts) of all annuities to which this section applies and which are payable under the same personal pension arrangements shall not exceed—
(*a*) where before his death the member was in receipt of an annuity under the arrangements, the annual amount (or, if it varied, the highest annual amount) of that annuity; or
(*b*) where paragraph (*a*) does not apply, the highest annual amount of the annuity that would have been payable under the arrangements to the member (ignoring any entitlement of his to commute part of it for a lump sum) if it had [been purchased][1] on the day before his death.

[(3A) The references in subsection (3) above—
(*a*) to the annual amount or highest annual amount of an annuity of which the member was in receipt before his death, and
(*b*) to the highest annual amount of an annuity that would have been payable if it had been purchased on the day before the member's death,
shall each be construed in a case where payments of that annuity were or would have been affected by the making of any pension sharing order or provision as if the only payments of that annuity to be taken into account were those that have been or would have been so affected.][2]

(4) Subject to subsections (5) to (9) below, the annuity must be payable for the life of the annuitant.

(5) Where the annuity is payable to the surviving spouse of the member and at the time of the member's death the surviving spouse is under the age of 60, the annuity may be deferred to a time not later than—

   (*a*) the time when the surviving spouse attains that age; or

   (*b*) where the member's annuity is payable to the surviving spouse for a term certain as mentioned in section 634(5) and the surviving spouse attains the age of 60 before the time when the member's annuity terminates, that time.

(6) The annuity may cease to be payable on the marriage of the annuitant.

(7) Where the annuity is payable to the surviving spouse of the member, it may cease before the death of the surviving spouse if—

   (*a*) the member was survived by one or more dependants under the age of 18 and at the time of the member's death the surviving spouse was under the age of 45; and

   (*b*) at some time before the surviving spouse attains that age no such dependant remains under the age of 18.

(8) Where the annuity is payable to a person who is under the age of 18 when it is first payable, it must cease to be payable either—

   (*a*) on his attaining that age; or

   (*b*) on the later of his attaining that age and ceasing to be in full-time education,

unless he was a dependant of the member otherwise than by reason only that he was under the age of 18.

(9) The annuity may continue for a term certain not exceeding ten years, notwithstanding the original annuitant's death within that term; and for this purpose an annuity shall be regarded as payable for a term certain notwithstanding that it may terminate, after the death of the original annuitant and before the expiry of that term, on the happening of any of the following—

   (*a*) the marriage of the annuitant to whom it is payable;

   (*b*) his attaining the age of 18;

   (*c*) the later of his attaining that age and ceasing to be in full-time education.

(10) The annuity must not be capable of assignment or surrender, [except that—

   (*a*) an annuity may be assigned or surrendered for the purpose of giving effect to a pension sharing order or provision; and

   (*b*)]² an annuity for a term certain may be assigned by will or by the annuitant's personal representatives in the distribution of his estate so as to give effect to a testamentary disposition, or to the rights of those entitled on an intestacy, or to an appropriation of it to a legacy or to a share or interest in the estate.

Commentary—*Simon's Direct Tax Service* E7.406.
Definitions—"Authorised insurance company", s 630(1); "interest", s 832(1); "member", s 630(1); "personal pension arrangements", s 630(1).
Cross references—See the Personal Pension Schemes (Transfer Payments) Regulations, SI 1988/1014 reg 8 (where a personal pension scheme accepts a transfer payment from other specified schemes, the accumulated value may be applied under this section).
TA 1988 s 636A(2) (purchase of any annuity may not be deferred, or income withdrawals made where an election has been made under sub-s(5)(*a*) above).
TA 1988 s 637A(2) (contributions not returnable on death of member if election under sub-s(5)(*a*) has been made).
Amendments—¹ Words in sub-s (3) substituted by FA 1995 Sch 11 paras 1, 6, with effect in relation to approvals, of schemes or amendments, given under this Chapter after 1 May 1995, but not so as to affect any approval previously given.
² Sub-s (3A) inserted and words in sub-s (10) substituted by FA 1999 s 79 Sch 10 para 13 with effect for the purposes of the grant at any time after 9 May 2000 of any approval of a personal pension scheme (whenever made); or the withdrawal at any time after that day of approval of any personal pension scheme or personal pension arrangements (whenever approved) (by virtue of the Finance Act 1999, Schedule 10, Paragraph 18, (First and Second Appointed Days) Order, SI 2000/1093).

[636A Income withdrawals after death of member

(1) Where a person entitled to such an annuity as is mentioned in section 636 elects to defer the purchase of the annuity, income withdrawals may be made by him during the period of deferral, subject as follows.

[(1A)The Board shall not refuse to approve a personal pension scheme by reason only that it makes provision for arrangements under the scheme which enable a person who makes such an election as is mentioned in subsection (1) above to apply different parts of the personal pension fund at different times in the purchase of different annuities satisfying the conditions in section 636 (whether commencing on the same day or on different days).]⁴

(2) No such deferral may be made, and accordingly income withdrawals may not be made, if the person concerned elects in accordance with section 636(5)(*a*) to defer the purchase of an annuity.

(3) Income withdrawals must not be made after the person concerned if he had purchased such an annuity as is mentioned in section 636 would have ceased to be entitled to payments under it.

(4) Income withdrawals must not in any event be made after the member would have attained the age of 75 or, if earlier, after the person concerned attains the age of 75.

(5) The aggregate amount of income withdrawals by a person in each successive period of twelve months beginning with the date of the member's death must be not less than 35 per cent or more than 100 per cent of the annual amount of the annuity which would have been purchasable by him[—

  [(a) in the case of the first period of three years, on the relevant reference date; and
  (b) in the case of any succeeding period of three years,

    [(i)][5] on a particular day in the period of sixty days ending with the relevant reference date][3][,or
    (ii) immediately after the last qualifying annuitisation,

  whichever is the later.][5]

[(5A) For the purposes of subsection (5) above—

  (a) "annuitisation" means the application of part of the personal pension fund in the purchase of an annuity satisfying the conditions in section 636; and
  (b) an annuitisation is a "qualifying annuitisation", in relation to any such period of twelve months as is mentioned in subsection (5) above, if it has taken place—

    (i) in an earlier such period, but
    (ii) since the relevant reference date.][4]

(6) For the purposes of this section the relevant reference date for the first three years is the date of the member's death, and for each succeeding period of three years is the first day of that period.

(7) The right to income withdrawals must not be capable of assignment or surrender[, except for the purpose of giving effect to a pension sharing order or provision][2].][1]

Commentary—*Simon's Direct Tax Service* E7.406.
Definitions—"Income withdrawals", s 630(1); "member", s 630(1).
Amendments—[1] Section inserted by FA 1995 Sch 11 paras 1, 7, with effect in relation to approvals, of schemes or amendments, given under this Chapter after 1 May 1995, but not so as to affect any approval previously given.
[2] Words in sub-s (7) inserted by FA 1999 s 79 Sch 10 para 14 with effect for the purposes of the grant at any time after 9 May 2000 of any approval of a personal pension scheme (whenever made); or the withdrawal at any time after that day of approval of any personal pension scheme or personal pension arrangements (whenever approved) (by virtue of the Finance Act 1999, Schedule 10, Paragraph 18, (First and Second Appointed Days) Order, SI 2000/1093).
[3] Words in sub-s (5) substituted by FA 2000 s 61, Sch 13 paras 1, 12(1), (3), (6) with effect after 30 September 2000. Words previously read "on the relevant reference date".
[4] Sub-ss (1A), (5A) inserted by FA 2000 s 61, Sch 13 paras 1, 12(1), (2), (5), (7) with effect after 5 April 2001.
[5] Words in sub-s (5) inserted by FA 2000 s 61, Sch 13 paras 1, 12(1), (4), (7) with effect after 5 April 2001.

[637 Death benefit

The lump sum—

  (a) must be payable on the death of the member before he attains the age of 75, and
  (b) must be payable by an authorised insurance company.][1]

Commentary—*Simon's Direct Tax Service* E7.406.
Definitions—"Authorised insurance company", s 630(1); "member", s 630(1).
Cross references—See TA 1988 s 640(3), (5) (tax relief ceiling in respect of contributions paid to secure benefits satisfying conditions in sub-s (1) above).
Amendments—[1] This section and s 637A *post* substituted for s 637 as originally enacted by FA 1995 Sch 11 paras 1, 8, with effect for approvals of schemes or amendments, given under this Chapter after 1 May 1995, but not so as to affect any approval previously given.

[637A Return of contributions on or after death of member

(1) The lump sum payable under the arrangements in question (or, where two or more lump sums are so payable, those lump sums taken together) must represent no more than the return of contributions together with reasonable interest on contributions or bonuses out of profits, after allowing for—

  (a) any income withdrawals, and
  (b) any purchases of annuities such as are mentioned in section 636.

To the extent that contributions are invested in units under a unit trust scheme, the lump sum (or lump sums) may represent the sale or redemption price of the units.

(2) A lump sum must be payable only if, in the case of the arrangements in question—

  (a) no such annuity as is mentioned in section 634 has been purchased by the member;
  (b) no such annuity as is mentioned in section 636 has been purchased in respect of the relevant interest; and
  (c) no election in accordance with subsection (5)(a) of section 636 has been made in respect of the relevant interest.

(3) Where the member's death occurs after the date which is his pension date in relation to the arrangements in question, a lump sum must not be payable more than two years after the death unless, in the case of that lump sum, the person entitled to such an annuity as is mentioned in section 636 in respect of the relevant interest—

  (a) has elected in accordance with section 636A to defer the purchase of an annuity; and
  (b) has died during the period of deferral.

(4) In this section "the relevant interest" means the interest, under the arrangements in question, of the person to whom or at whose direction the payment in question is made, except where there are two or more such interests, in which case it means that one of them in respect of which the payment is made.

(5) Where, under the arrangements in question, there is a succession of interests, any reference in subsection (2) or (3) above to the relevant interest includes a reference to any interest (other than that of the member) in relation to which the relevant interest is a successive interest.][1]

Commentary—*Simon's Direct Tax Service* E7.406.
Definitions—"Income withdrawals", s 630(1); "interest", s 832(1); "member", s 630(1); "pension date", s 630(1); "unit trust scheme", s 832(1).
Amendments—[1] This section substituted by FA 1996 s 172(2), (3) with effect for approvals, of schemes or amendments, given under this Chapter after 29 April 1996 but not so as to affect approvals previously given, having previously been substituted by FA 1995 Sch 11 paras 1, 8 with effect in relation to approvals given after 1 May 1995).

638 Other restrictions on approval

(1) The Board shall not approve a personal pension scheme unless they are satisfied that there is a person resident in the United Kingdom who will be responsible for the management of the scheme.

(2) The Board shall not approve a personal pension scheme unless it makes such provision for the making, acceptance and application of transfer payments as satisfies any requirements imposed by or under regulations made by the Board.

(3) The Board shall not approve a personal pension scheme unless it makes provision, in relation to arrangements made in accordance with the scheme, for ensuring that—

(a) the aggregate amount of the contributions that may be made in a year of assessment by the member and an employer of his under the arrangements, together with the aggregate amounts of such contributions under other approved personal pension arrangements made by that member, does not exceed [the earnings threshold for that year or, if greater][8] the permitted maximum for that year; and

(b) any excess is repaid to the member to the extent of his contributions and otherwise to his employer.

(4) In subsection (3) above "the permitted maximum" for a year of assessment means an amount equal to...[9]—

(a) the relevant percentage of the member's net relevant earnings for the year; ...[9]

(b) ...[9]

and references in subsection (3) to contributions by the member do not include references to contributions treated by virtue of section 649(3) as paid by him.

(5) In subsection (4) above "the relevant percentage" means 17.5 per cent or, in a case where section 640(2) applies, the relevant percentage there specified.

(6) The Board shall not approve a personal pension scheme which permits the acceptance of contributions other than—

(a) contributions by members;

(b) contributions by employers of members;

(c) minimum contributions paid by the [Board][5] under [section 43 of the Pension Schemes Act 1993][2] or ...[6] under [section 39 of the Pension Schemes (Northern Ireland) Act 1993.][3]

[(7) The Board shall not approve a personal pension scheme which permits the acceptance of minimum contributions paid as mentioned in subsection (6)(c) above in respect of an individual's service as director of a company, if his emoluments as such are within section 644(5).][1]

[(7A) The Board shall not approve a personal pension scheme unless it prohibits, except in such cases as may be prescribed by regulations made by the Board—

(a) the acceptance of further contributions, and

(b) the making of transfer payments,

after the date which is the member's pension date in relation to the arrangements in question.][4]

[(7B) Subsection (7A) above shall have effect subject to and in accordance with section 638ZA.][7]

[(8) A personal pension scheme which permits the acceptance of minimum contributions paid as mentioned in subsection (6)(c) above in respect of an individual's service in an office or employment to which section 645 applies may be approved by the Board only if—

(a) the scheme does not permit the acceptance of contributions from the individual or from the person who is his employer in relation to that office or employment; or

(b) at the time when the minimum contributions are paid the individual is not serving in an office or employment to which section 645 applies.][1]

[(9) The Board may only approve a personal pension scheme if it prohibits the acceptance of contributions in any form other than—

(a) the payment of monetary sums; or

(b) the transfer, subject to the conditions in subsection (12) below, of eligible shares in a company;

and any reference in this Chapter to the payment of contributions includes a reference to the making of contributions in accordance with paragraph (b) above.][10]

[(10) For the purposes of this Chapter, the amount of a contribution made by way of a transfer of shares shall be the aggregate market value of the shares at the date of the transfer.][10]

[(11) For the purposes of subsection (9)(*b*) above, "eligible shares" means shares—

(*a*) which the member has exercised the right to acquire, or

(*b*) which have been appropriated to the member,

in accordance with the provisions of a savings-related share option scheme, an approved profit-sharing scheme or an employee share ownership plan.][10]

[(12) The conditions mentioned in subsection (9)(*b*) above are—

(*a*) in relation to shares which the member has exercised his right to acquire in accordance with the provisions of a savings-related share option scheme, that the transfer of the shares as contributions under the personal pension scheme takes place before the expiry of the period of 90 days following the exercise of that right;

(*b*) in relation to shares appropriated to the member in accordance with the provisions of an approved profit-sharing scheme or an employee share ownership plan, that the transfer of the shares as contributions under the personal pension scheme takes place before the expiry of the period of 90 days following the date when the member directed the trustees of the approved profit-sharing scheme or employee share ownership plan to transfer the ownership of the shares to him or, if earlier, the release date in relation to the shares.][10]

[(13) In this section—

"approved profit-sharing scheme" has the same meaning as in section 186;

"employee share ownership plan" has the same meaning as in Schedule 8 to the Finance Act 2000;

"market value" shall be construed in accordance with section 272 of the Taxation of Chargeable Gains Act 1992;

"savings-related share option scheme" has the same meaning as in Schedule 9 (see paragraph 1(1) of that Schedule).][10]

Commentary—*Simon's Direct Tax Service* E7.407, 412, 413, 416, 417.
Regulations—Personal Pension Schemes (Transfer Payments) Regulations, SI 2001/119.
Personal Pension Schemes (Deferred Annuity Purchase) (Acceptance of Contributions) Regulations, SI 1996/805.
Definitions—"Approved", s 630(1); "the Board", s 832(1); "member", s 630(1); "net relevant earnings", s 646; "personal pension arrangements", s 630(1); "pension date", s 630(1); "personal pension scheme", s 630(1); "United Kingdom", s 830(1); "year of assessment", s 832(1).
Cross references—See Personal Pension Schemes (Deferred Annuity Purchase) (Acceptance of Contributions) Regulations, SI 1996/805 reg 3(2) (personal pension scheme may be approved even though the scheme may accept minimum contributions from DSS under sub-s (6)(*c*) after the pension date where the member has elected to make income withdrawals).
Personal Pension Schemes (Transfer Payments) Regulations, SI 2001/119 reg 14 (provision for exceptions to sub-s (7A) with regards to the making of transfer payments).
Amendments—[1] Sub-ss (7), (8) substituted for sub-s (7) by FA 1988 s 55(2), (4) with effect from 1 July 1988.
[2] Words in sub-s (6)(*c*) substituted by the Pension Schemes Act 1993 s 190, Sch 8 para 20(3), with effect from 7 February 1994, by virtue of the Pension Schemes Act 1993 (Commencement No 1) Order, SI 1994/86.
[3] Words in sub-s (6)(*c*) substituted by the Pension Schemes (Northern Ireland) Act 1993 s 184, Sch 7 para 22(2), with effect from 7 February 1994, by virtue of the Pension Schemes (1993 Act) (Commencement No 1) Order (NI) 1994, SR 1994/17.
[4] Sub-s (7A) inserted by FA 1995 Sch 11 paras 1, 9, with effect for approvals, of schemes or amendments, given under this Chapter after 1 May 1995, but not so as to affect any approval previously given.
[5] Words in sub-s (6)(*c*) substituted by the Social Security Contributions (Transfer of Functions, etc) Act 1999 Sch 1 para 3 with effect from 1 April 1999 by virtue of the Social Security Contributions (Transfer of Functions, etc) Act 1999 (Commencement No 1 and Transitional Provisions) Order, SI 1999/527 art 2, Sch 2.
[6] Words in sub-s (6)(*c*) repealed by the Social Security Contributions (Transfer of Functions, etc) (Northern Ireland) Order, SI 1999/671 art 3(1) Sch 3, art 24(3) Sch 9, with effect from 1 April 1999 (by virtue of the Social Security Contributions (Transfer of Functions, etc) (1999 Order) (Commencement No 1 and Transitional Provisions) Order (Northern Ireland), SR 1999/149, art 2(*c*), Sch 2).
[7] Sub-s (7B) inserted by FA 2000 s 61, Sch 13 paras 1, 13(1), (4) with effect from 28 July 2000.
[8] Words in sub-s (3)(*a*) inserted by FA 2000 s 60, Sch 13 paras 1, 13(1), (2), (6) with effect from the year 2001–02.
[9] Words in sub-s (4), and the whole of sub-s (4)(*b*) repealed by FA 2000 ss 61, 156, Sch 13 paras 1, 13(1), (3), (7), Sch 40 Pt II(4) with effect for contributions paid from the year 2001–02.
[10] Sub-ss (9)–(13) added by FA 2000 s 61, Sch 13 paras 1, 13(1), (5), (8) with effect for contributions from the year 2001–02.

[638ZA Personal pension arrangements with more than one pension date etc

(1) This section applies where a personal pension scheme makes provision for a personal pension arrangement under the scheme to make provision—

(*a*) for the payment of more than one annuity satisfying the conditions in section 634 or 636 (a "qualifying annuity") and for different such annuities to commence, or be capable of commencing, on different days;

(*b*) for elections such as are mentioned in section 634A(1) or 636A(1) ("elections for deferral") to be capable of being made at different times in relation to different portions of the personal pension fund; and

(*c*) for a qualifying lump sum to be payable in connection with—

(i) each qualifying annuity (other than one purchased pursuant to section 634A, 636 or 636A); and

(ii) each election for deferral such as is mentioned in section 634A(1).

(2) The Board shall not refuse to approve a personal pension scheme by reason only that it makes such provision as is mentioned in subsection (1) above if they are satisfied that it makes provision in conformity with the provisions of this section.

(3) In this section—

"income withdrawal fund" means a portion of the personal pension fund which is specified or described in an election for deferral as the portion of that fund to which the election relates;

"qualifying lump sum" means a lump sum satisfying the conditions of section 635 (as that section has effect by virtue of and in accordance with this section);

"the relevant date", in relation to any qualifying annuity or election for deferral, means the date determined in accordance with the arrangement on which—

    (a) the qualifying annuity commences; or

    (b) the member makes the election for deferral.

(4) In the application of section 635 in relation to a qualifying lump sum, for the condition in subsection (3) there shall be substituted the conditions in subsections (5) and (6) below (as read with subsection (7) below).

(5) The first condition is that the lump sum must not exceed one-third of—

    (a) the difference between—

        (i) the value of the portion of the personal pension fund applied in the provision of the qualifying annuity in connection with which the lump sum is paid, determined as at the date on which that portion is so applied, and

        (ii) the value, determined as at that date, of so much of that portion as represents protected rights, or

    (b) the value, as at the relevant date, of the income withdrawal fund which relates to the election for deferral in connection with it is paid,

as the case may be.

(6) The second condition is that the lump sum must not represent any of the value, at the time when the lump sum is paid, of any protected rights.

(7) In subsections (5) and (6) above, "protected rights" means any of the member's rights under the personal pension arrangement which are protected rights for the purposes of the Pension Schemes Act 1993 or the Pension Schemes (Northern Ireland) Act 1993.

(8) Where a qualifying annuity commences, this Chapter and the personal pension scheme concerned shall have effect, as from the relevant date, as if there had been a separate personal pension arrangement and—

    (a) the annuity, and any qualifying lump sum payable in connection with it, were benefits provided for by that separate arrangement (instead of by the personal pension arrangement by which it was actually provided (in this subsection referred to as "the relevant arrangement"));

    (b) the portion of the personal pension fund applied in the provision of the annuity, together with the amount of any qualifying lump sum payable in connection with the annuity, had been the personal pension fund in the case of that separate arrangement (and were excluded from the personal pension fund in the case of the relevant arrangement);

    (c) any election for the annuity, or for such a qualifying lump sum, had been made under that separate arrangement (instead of under the relevant arrangement); and

    (d) except in the case of an annuity satisfying the conditions in section 636, the relevant date were the pension date in relation to that separate arrangement (and were not, by reference to that annuity, the pension date in relation to the relevant arrangement).

(9) Where, in the case of any personal pension arrangement (in this subsection referred to as "the relevant arrangement"), an election for deferral is made, this Chapter and the personal pension scheme concerned shall have effect, as from the relevant date, as if there had been, and continued to be, a separate personal pension arrangement and—

    (a) the income withdrawal fund which relates to the election, together with the amount of any qualifying lump sum payable in connection with the election, had been the personal pension fund in the case of that separate arrangement (and were excluded from the personal pension fund in the case of the relevant arrangement);

    (b) the election for deferral, and any election for such a qualifying lump sum, had been made under that separate arrangement (instead of under the relevant arrangement);

    (c) the election for deferral had been made in respect of the whole of the income withdrawal fund which relates to the election; and

    (d) except in the case of an election such as is mentioned in section 636A(1), the relevant date were the pension date in relation to that separate arrangement (and were not, by reference to that election, the pension date in relation to the relevant arrangement).]¹

Amendments—¹ This section inserted by FA 2000 s 61, Sch 13 paras 1, 14 with effect after 5 April 2001.

[638A Power to prescribe restrictions on approval

(1) The Board—

    (a) may by regulations restrict their discretion to approve a personal pension scheme; and

(b) shall not approve any such scheme if to do so would be inconsistent with any regulations under this section.

(2) The restrictions that may be imposed by regulations under this section may be imposed by reference to any one or more of the following, that is to say—

    (a) the benefits for which the scheme provides;
    (b) the investments held for the purposes of the scheme;
    (c) the manner in which the scheme is administered;
    (d) any other circumstances whatever.

(3) The following provisions of this section apply where—

    (a) any regulations are made under this section imposing a restriction (''the new restriction'') on the Board's discretion to approve a personal pension scheme;
    (b) the new restriction did not exist immediately before the making of the regulations; and
    (c) that restriction is one imposed by reference to circumstances other than the benefits for which the scheme provides.

(4) Subject to subsections (5) and (6) below, a personal pension scheme which is an approved scheme immediately before the day on which the regulations imposing the new restriction come into force shall cease to be approved at the end of the period of 36 months beginning with that day if, at the end of that period, the scheme—

    (a) contains a provision of a prohibited description, or
    (b) does not contain every provision which is a provision of a required description.

(5) The Board may by regulations provide that subsection (4) above is not to apply in the case of the inclusion of such provisions of a prohibited description, or in the case of the omission of such provisions of a required description, as may be specified in the regulations.

(6) For the purposes of subsection (4) above—

    (a) a provision contained in a scheme shall not be treated as being of a prohibited description to the extent that it authorises the retention of an investment held immediately before the day of the making of the new regulations; and
    (b) so much of any provision contained in a scheme as authorises the retention of an investment held immediately before that day shall be disregarded in determining if any provision of the scheme is of a required description.

(7) In this section—

    (a) references to a provision of a prohibited description are references to a provision of a description which, by virtue of the new restriction, is a description of provision which, if contained in a personal pension scheme, would prevent the Board from approving it; and
    (b) references to a provision of a required description are references to a provision of a description which, by virtue of the new restriction, is a description of provision which must be contained in a personal pension scheme before the Board may approve it.]¹

Commentary—*Simon's Direct Tax Service* **E7.407, 412, 413, 416, 417.**
Amendments—¹ This section inserted by FA 1998 s 94(1) with effect from 31 July 1998.

Tax reliefs

639 Member's contributions

[(1) An individual who pays a contribution under approved personal pension arrangements made by him shall be entitled to relief under this section in respect of the contribution.]¹

[(1A) Subsection (1) above is subject to the other provisions of this Chapter.]¹

[(1B) The total amount of contributions in respect of which relief may be given to an individual under this section for any year of assessment must not exceed—

    (a) the permitted maximum for the year, as defined in section 638(4), or
    (b) the earnings threshold for the year,

whichever is the greater.]¹

[(2) Any relief under this section shall be given in accordance with—

    (a) subsections (3) and (4) below, and
    (b) where applicable, subsection (5A) below.]¹

[(2A) Relief in accordance with subsections (3) and (4) below shall be subject to such conditions as the Board may prescribe in regulations.

(3) An individual who is entitled to relief under this section in respect of a contribution shall be entitled, on making the payment, to deduct and retain out of it a sum equal to income tax on the contribution at the basic rate for the year of assessment in which the payment is made.]²

[(4) Where a sum is deducted under subsection (3) above from a contribution—

    (a) the scheme administrator shall allow the deduction on receipt of the residue;
    (b) the individual paying the contribution shall be acquitted and discharged of so much money as is represented by the deduction as if the sum had been actually paid; and
    (c) the sum deducted shall be treated as income tax paid by the scheme administrator.]²

[(4A) Where payment of a contribution under approved personal pension arrangements is received—

(*a*) the scheme administrator shall be entitled to recover from the Board, in accordance with regulations, an amount which by virtue of subsection (4)(*c*) above is treated as income tax paid by him; and

(*b*) any amount so recovered shall be treated for the purposes of the Tax Acts in like manner as the payment of the contribution to which it relates.][2]

(5) Regulations under this section may make provision for carrying subsections [(3) to (4A)][3] above into effect and, without prejudice to the generality of that, may provide—

(*a*) for the manner in which claims for the recovery of a sum under subsection [(4A(*a*))][3] may be made;

(*b*) for the giving of such information, in such form, as may be prescribed by or under the regulations;

(*c*) for the inspection by persons authorised by the Board of books, documents and other records.

[(5A) Where—

(*a*) an individual is entitled to relief under this section in respect of contributions paid in any year of assessment, and

(*b*) apart from this subsection, income tax at the higher rate is chargeable in respect of any part of his total income for the year,

the basic rate limit for that year shall in his case be increased by the addition of the amount of the contributions in respect of which he is entitled to relief under this section.]

[(5B) Relief in accordance with subsection (5A) above shall be given only on a claim made for the purpose.][2]

(6) Where relief under this section for any year of assessment is claimed and allowed (whether or not it then falls to be given for that year), and afterwards an assessment, alteration of an assessment, or other adjustment of the claimant's liability to tax is made, there shall also be made such consequential adjustments in the relief allowed or given under this section for that or any subsequent year as are appropriate.

(7) Where relief [is given under this section][3] for any year of assessment in respect of a contribution, relief shall not be given in respect of it under any other provision of the Income Tax Acts for the same or any subsequent year, nor (in the case of a contribution under an annuity contract) in respect of any other premium or consideration for an annuity under the same contract.

(8) References in the Income Tax Acts to relief in respect of life assurance premiums shall not be taken to include relief under this section.

Commentary—*Simon's Direct Tax Service* E7.407, 417.
Regulations—Personal Pension Schemes (Relief at Source) Regulations, SI 1988/1013.
Statement of Practice SP 9/91—Investigation settlements: utilisation by payment of contributions of unused personal pension relief arising from final and conclusive assessment to tax more than six years after the end of the year to which it relates.
Revenue Interpretation RI 44—Personal pension contributions: treatment in computing profits for Class 4 national insurance contributions.
Concession A101—Sub-s (5A) above will also apply in respect of any member who is liable to capital gains tax at the higher rate on any chargeable gains for the tax year in which the payment in question is made; or would be so liable if the adjustment were not made.
A102—With effect from 6 April 2001, contributions to an approved personal pension scheme can reduce an individual's total income for the purposes only of determining the level of age-related allowances available under TA 1988 ss 257(5), 257A(5).
Definitions—"Approved", s 630(1); "basic rate", s 832(1); "the Board", s 832(1); "the Income Tax Acts", s 831(1)(*b*); "personal pension arrangements", s 630(1); "relevant earnings", s 644; "scheme administrator", s 630(1); "tax", s 832(3); "year of assessment", s 832(1).
Cross references—See TA 1988 s 257D(8) (disallowance of deduction under sub-s (3) above for calculating total income of a husband for determining any excess in married couple's allowance).
TA 1988 s 265(3), (4) (disallowance of deduction under sub-s (3) above for calculating total income of a blind husband for determining any excess in blind person's allowance which may be transferred to wife).
TA 1988 s 640(1), (2), (5) (maximum deductions allowed under sub-s (1) above).
TA 1988 s 642 (unused part of relief given by this section may be carried forward).
Amendments—[1] Sub-ss (1), (1A), (1B), (2), (2A) substituted for sub-ss (1), (2) by FA 2000 s 61, Sch 13 para 15 with effect for contributions paid from the year 2001–02.
[2] Sub-ss (3), (4) substituted, and sub-ss (4A), (5A), (5B) inserted by FA 2000 s 61, Sch 13 para 15 with effect for contributions paid from the year 2001–02.
[3] Words in sub-ss (5), (7) substituted by FA 2000 s 61, Sch 13 para 15 with effect for contributions paid from the year 2001–02.

640 Maximum amount of deductions

(1) The maximum amount [of contributions in respect of which relief may be given][3] in any year of assessment by virtue of section 639(1) shall be

[(*a*) an amount equal to the earnings threshold for that year; or
(*b*) if greater,][3] 17·5 per cent of the individual's net relevant earnings for that year.

(2) In the case of an individual whose age at the beginning of the year of assessment is within a range specified in the first column of the following table, subsection (1) above shall have effect with the substitution for 17·5 per cent of the relevant percentage specified in the second column.

[36 to 45	20 per cent
46 to 50	25 per cent
51 to 55	30 per cent
56 to 60	35 per cent
61 or more	40 per cent][1]

[(3) Without prejudice to subsection (1) above, where any contributions are paid in a year of assessment by an individual to secure benefits satisfying the conditions in section 637, the maximum amount of those contributions in respect of which relief may be given by virtue of section 639(1)][3] [shall be an amount equal to 10 per cent of the aggregate amount of the relevant pension contributions made in that year by the individual and an employer of his][4].

[(3A) In subsection (3) above "relevant pension contribution" means a contribution paid towards securing benefits falling within paragraph (a), (b) or (c) of section 633(1) under arrangements made under a personal pension scheme on or after 6th April 2001.][4]

(4) Where personal pension arrangements are made by an employee whose employer makes contributions under the arrangements, the maximum amount [of contributions in respect of which relief may be given by virtue of section 639(1)][3] in any year of assessment shall be reduced by the amount of the employer's contributions in the year.

(5) Any minimum contributions treated by virtue of section 649(3) as paid by the individual in respect of whom they are paid shall be disregarded for the purposes of this section.

Commentary—*Simon's Direct Tax Service* E7.407.
Statement of Practice SP 9/91—Investigation settlements: utilisation by payment of contributions of unused personal pension relief arising from final and conclusive assessment to tax more than six years after the end of the year to which it relates.
Definitions—"Net relevant earnings", s 646; "year of assessment", s 832(1).
Cross references—See TA 1988 s 640A (earning cap for the purposes of this section).
Amendments—[1] The Table in sub-s (2) substituted by FA 1989 Sch 7 paras 1, 3.
[2] Words in sub-s (3) substituted by FA 1995 Sch 11 paras 1, 10, with effect for approvals, of schemes or amendments, given under this Chapter after 1 May 1995, but not so as to affect any approval previously given.
[3] Words in sub-s (1) substituted and inserted, and in sub-ss (3), (4) substituted, by FA 2000 s 61, Sch 13 paras 1, 16(1)–(4), (7), (8) with effect for contributions paid from the year 2001–02.
[4] Words in sub-s (3) substituted, and sub-s (3A) inserted, by FA 2000 s 61, Sch 13 paras 1, 16(1), (3), (5), (6), (9) with effect for contributions paid to secure benefits satisfying the conditions in TA 1988 s 637 where the contract of life assurance concerned is made after 5 April 2001.

[640A Earnings cap

(1) In arriving at an individual's net relevant earnings for a year of assessment for the purposes of section 640 above, any excess of what would be his net relevant earnings for the year (apart from this subsection) over the allowable maximum for the year shall be disregarded.

(2) In subsection (1) above "the allowable maximum" means, as regards a particular year of assessment, the figure found for that year by virtue of subsections (3) and (4) below.

(3) For the year of assessment 1989–90 the figure is £60,000.

(4) For the year of assessment 1990–91 and any subsequent year of assessment the figure is the figure found for that year, for the purposes of section 590C, by virtue of section 590C(4) [to (5A)][2].][1]

Commentary—*Simon's Direct Tax Service* E7.407.
Note—For the year 2000–01 the figure specified for the purpose of sub-s (4) by virtue of s 590C is £91,800 by virtue of the Retirement Benefits Schemes (Indexation of Earnings Cap) Order, SI 2000/807.
Amendments—[1] This section inserted by FA 1989 Sch 7 paras 1, 4.
[2] Words in sub-s (4) substituted by FA 1993 s 107(6), (8) with effect from the year 1994–95.

641 Carry-back of contributions

Commentary—*Simon's Direct Tax Service* E7.410.
Amendments—This section repealed by FA 2000 s 156, Sch 40 Pt II(4) with effect for contributions paid after 5 April 2001.

[641A Election for contributions to be treated as paid in previous year

(1) A person who pays a contribution under approved personal pension arrangements on or before the 31st January in any year of assessment may, at or before the time when he pays the contribution, irrevocably elect that the contribution, or part of it, shall be treated as paid in the preceding year of assessment.

(2) Where an election is made under this section in respect of a contribution or part of a contribution, the other provisions of this Chapter shall have effect as if the contribution or part had been paid in the year specified in the election and not in the year in which it was actually paid.][1]

Amendment—[1] This section inserted by FA 2000 s 61, Sch 13 paras 1, 18 with effect for contributions paid from the year 2001–02.

642 Carry-forward of relief

Commentary—*Simon's Direct Tax Service* E7.411.
Amendment—This section repealed by FA 2000 s 156, Sch 40 Pt II(4) with effect from the year 2001–02.

643 Employer's contributions and personal pension income etc

(1) Where contributions are paid by an employer under approved personal pension arrangements made by his employee, those contributions shall not be regarded as emoluments of the employment chargeable to tax under Schedule E.

(2) Income derived by a person from investments or deposits held by him for the purposes of an approved personal pension scheme shall be exempt from income tax.

(3) An annuity payable under approved personal pension arrangements shall be treated as earned income of the annuitant.

(4) Subsection (3) above applies only in relation to the annuitant to whom the annuity is made payable by the terms of the arrangements.

[(5) Income withdrawals under approved personal pension arrangements shall be assessable to tax under Schedule E (and section 203 shall apply accordingly) and shall be treated as earned income of the recipient.][1]

Commentary—*Simon's Direct Tax Service* **E7.407, 414, 415.**
Definitions—"Approved", s 630(1); "earned income", s 833(4), (5); "emoluments", s 131(1); "income withdrawals", s 630(1); "personal pension arrangements", s 630(1); "Schedule E", s 19(1).
Cross references—See TA 1988 s 129B (exemption from income tax under sub-s (2) above is extended to stock lending fees payable in connection with approved arrangements relating to the relevant investments).
TA 1988 s 231A (tax credits not repayable in respect of qualifying distributions made after 1 July 1997 to pension funds — see sub-s (2) above).
TA 1988 s 438(8) (avoidance of double relief for an insurance company's pension business under sub-s (2) above and under s 438).
TA 1988 s 659A ("investments" and "income" for the purposes of sub-s (2) above to include futures and options and transactions relating to them).
TA 1988 s 659D(2) (the exemption within sub-s (2) above does not apply to income derived from investments, deposits or other property held as a member of a property investment LLP).
Manufactured Payments and Transfer of Securities (Tax Relief) Regulations, SI 1995/3036 regs 3, 4 (manufactured payments and deemed interest payments arising on a sale and repurchase of securities falling to the benefit of a scheme referred to in sub-s (2) above to be treated as income of the person eligible for relief by virtue of that subsection).
Amendments—[1] Sub-s (5) inserted by FA 1995 Sch 11 paras 1, 11, with effect for approvals, of schemes or amendments, given under this Chapter after 1 May 1995, but not so as to affect any approval previously given.

644 Meaning of "relevant earnings"

(1) In this Chapter, "relevant earnings", in relation to an individual, means any income of his which is chargeable to tax for the year of assessment in question and is within subsection (2) below.

(2) Subject to subsections (3) to [(6F)][1] below, income is within this subsection if it is—

    (a) emoluments chargeable under Schedule E from an office or employment held by the individual;
    (b) income from any property which is attached to or forms part of the emoluments of an office or employment held by him;
    (c) income which is chargeable under Schedule D and is immediately derived by him from the carrying on or exercise by him of his trade, profession or vocation (either as an individual or as a partner acting personally in a partnership);
    (d) income treated as earned income by virtue of section 529.

(3) Where section 645 applies to an office or employment held by the individual, neither emoluments from the office or employment nor income from any property which is attached to it or forms part of its emoluments are within subsection (2) above.

(4) The following are not income within subsection (2) above—

    (a) anything in respect of which tax is chargeable under Schedule E and which arises from the acquisition or disposal of shares or an interest in shares or from a right to acquire shares;
    (b) anything in respect of which tax is chargeable by virtue of section 148.

(5) Emoluments of an individual as director of a company are not income within subsection (2) above if—

    (a) the income of the company consists wholly or mainly of investment income; and
    (b) the individual, either alone or together with any other persons who are or have been at any time directors of the company, controls the company;

and section 840 shall apply for the purposes of this subsection.

(6) For the purposes of subsection (5) above—

"director" includes any person occupying the position of director by whatever name called; and
["investment income" means income which, if the company were an individual, would not be earned income.][3]

[(6A) Emoluments of an individual as an employee of a company are not income within subsection (2) above if—

    (a) he is a controlling director of the company at any time in the year of assessment in question or has been a controlling director of the company at any time in the ten years immediately preceding that year of assessment, and
    (b) any of subsections (6B) to (6E) below applies in his case.][2]

[(6B) This subsection applies in the case of the individual if—

(*a*) at any time in the year of assessment in question he is in receipt of benefits under a relevant superannuation scheme, and

(*b*) the benefits are payable in respect of past service with the company.][2]

[(6C) This subsection applies in the case of the individual if—

(*a*) at any time in the year of assessment in question he is in receipt of benefits under a personal pension scheme,

(*b*) the scheme has received a transfer payment relating to him from a relevant superannuation scheme, and

(*c*) the transfer payment is in respect of past service with the company.][2]

[(6D) This subsection applies in the case of the individual if—

(*a*) at any time in the year of assessment in question he is in receipt of benefits under a relevant superannuation scheme,

(*b*) the benefits are payable in respect of past service with another company,

(*c*) the emoluments are for a period during which the company mentioned in subsection (6A) above has carried on a trade or business previously carried on by the other company, and

(*d*) the other company carried on the trade or business at any time during the period of service in respect of which the benefits are payable.][2]

[(6E) This subsection applies in the case of the individual if—

(*a*) at any time in the year of assessment in question he is in receipt of benefits under a personal pension scheme,

(*b*) the scheme has received a transfer payment relating to him from a relevant superannuation scheme,

(*c*) the transfer payment is in respect of past service with another company,

(*d*) the emoluments are for a period during which the company mentioned in subsection (6A) above has carried on a trade or business previously carried on by the other company, and

(*e*) the other company carried on the trade or business at any time during the period of service in respect of which the transfer payment was made.][2]

[(6EA) Where—

(*a*) there is a time at which a person would be in receipt of any benefits under a scheme but for any debit to which any of his rights under that scheme became subject by virtue of any pension sharing order or provision, and

(*b*) the benefits he would be in receipt of are benefits payable in respect of past service with a company,

that person shall be deemed for the purposes of subsections (6A) to (6E) above to be in receipt at that time of benefits under that scheme and the benefits which he is deemed to be in receipt of shall be deemed to be benefits in respect of past service with that company.][5]

[(6F) For the purposes of subsections (6A) to [(6EA)][5] above—

(*a*) a person is a controlling director of a company if he is a director (as defined by section 612(1)), and he is within paragraph (*b*) of section 417(5), in relation to the company;

(*b*) ''relevant superannuation scheme'' has the same meaning as in section 645(1);

(*c*) references to benefits payable in respect of past service with a company include references to benefits payable partly in respect of past service with the company [but do not include references to benefits which (within the meaning of section 590) are provided for him as an ex-spouse][5]; and

(*d*) references to a transfer payment in respect of past service with a company include references to a transfer payment partly in respect of past service with the company [but do not include references to any transfer payment made for the purpose of giving effect to a pension sharing order or provision.][5].][2]

(7) ...[4]

Commentary—*Simon's Direct Tax Service* **E7.408.**
Concession A95—Exception to sub-s (3) in respect of benefits accrued under a ''small'' lump sum retirement benefits scheme.
Definitions—''Company'', s 832(1), (2); ''control'', s 840; ''earned income'', s 833(4), (5); ''emoluments'', s 131(1); ''interest'', s 832(1); ''Schedule D'', s 18(1); ''Schedule E'', s 19(1); ''trade'', s 832(1); ''year of assessment'', s 832(1).
Cross references—See TA 1988 s 503 (for the purposes of sub-s(2)(*c*) above, all lettings of furnished holiday accommodation treated as a single trade).
FA 2000 Sch 12 para 11 (provision of services through an intermediary: deemed Schedule E payment treated as relevant earnings of the worker for the purposes of this section).
Amendments—[1] Number in sub-s (2) substituted by FA 1989 Sch 7 paras 1, 5.
[2] Sub-ss (6A) to (6F) inserted by FA 1989 Sch 7 paras 1, 5.
[3] Definition of ''investment income'' in sub-s (6) substituted by FA 1989 Sch 12 para 16.
[4] Sub-s (7) repealed by FA 1988 Sch 14 Pt VIII with effect from 1990–91.
[5] Sub-s (6EA) and second and third words in sub-s (6F) inserted, and first words in sub-s (6F) substituted, by FA 1999 s 79 Sch 10 para 15 with effect in accordance with the commencement provisions contained in FA 1999 Sch 10 para 18. Words substituted in sub-s (6F) previously read ''(6E)''.

645 Earnings from pensionable employment

(1) This section applies to an office or employment held by an individual if—

(*a*) service in it is service to which a relevant superannuation scheme relates; and (*b*) the individual is a participant in the scheme; and

(*c*) [subsection (4) below does not apply]¹ to his participation in the scheme.

(2) This section applies whether or not the duties of the office or employment are performed wholly or partly in the United Kingdom or the individual is chargeable to tax in respect of it.

(3) In subsection (1) above "a relevant superannuation scheme" means a scheme or arrangement—

(*a*) the object or one of the objects of which is the provision, in respect of persons serving in particular offices or employments, of relevant benefits within the meaning of section 612; ...²

(*b*) which is established by a person other than the individual; [...⁵

(*c*) which is of a description mentioned in section 596(1)(*a*), (*b*) or (*c*)]³[; and

(*d*) which is not an approved converted scheme]⁵.

(4) This subsection applies to an individual's participation in a scheme if the scheme provides no benefits in relation to him other than—

(*a*) an annuity payable to his surviving spouse or a dependant of his;

(*b*) a lump sum payable on his death in service.

[(4A) Where the emoluments from an office or employment held by an individual are foreign emoluments within the meaning of section 192, this section shall have effect with the substitution of the following for paragraph (*c*) of subsection (3) above—

"(*c*) which corresponds to a scheme of a description mentioned in section 596(1)(*a*), (*b*) or (*c*)."]⁴

(5) ...²

Commentary—*Simon's Direct Tax Service* E7.408.
Definitions—"The Income Tax Acts", s 831(1)(*b*); "United Kingdom", s 830(1).
Cross references—See TA 1988 s 646A(1) (multiple earnings from pensionable and non-pensionable employments).
Amendments—¹ Words in sub-s (1)(*c*) substituted by FA 1989 Sch 7 paras 1, 6.
² Sub-s (5) and the word "and" in sub-s (3)(*a*) repealed by FA 1989 Sch 7 paras 1, 6 and Sch 17 Pt IV.
³ Sub-s (3)(*c*) and the preceding word "and" inserted by FA 1989 Sch 7 paras 1, 6.
⁴ Sub-s (4A) inserted by FA 1989 Sch 7 paras 1, 6.
⁵ Word in sub-s (3)(*b*) repealed, and sub-s (3)(*d*) and word preceding it inserted, by FA 2000 ss 61, 156, Sch 13 paras 1, 20, Sch 40 Pt II(4), with effect from 28 July 2000.

646 Meaning of "net relevant earnings"

(1) Subject to subsections (3) to (7) below [and section 646A]¹, in this Chapter "net relevant earnings", in relation to an individual, means the amount of his relevant earnings for the year of assessment in question, less the amount of any deductions within subsection (2) below which fall to be made from the relevant earnings in computing for the purposes of income tax his total income for that year.

(2) Deductions are within this subsection if they are—

(*a*) deductions which but for section 74(*m*), (*p*) or (*q*) could be made in computing the profits or gains of the individual;

(*b*) deductions made by virtue of section [197AG,]⁷ 198, 201 or 332(3);

(*c*) deductions in respect of relief under Schedule 9 to the Finance Act 1981 (stock relief);

(*d*) deductions in respect of losses or capital allowances, being losses or capital allowances arising from activities profits or gains of which would be included in computing relevant earnings of the individual ...².

(3) For the purposes of this section, an individual's relevant earnings shall be taken to be those earnings before giving effect to any capital allowances, other than deductions allowable in computing profits or gains, but after taking into account the amounts on which charges fall to be made [under [the Capital Allowances Act (including enactments which under this Act are to be treated as contained in that Act)]⁶]³; and in subsections (4) and (5) below, references to income (other than references to total income) shall be construed similarly.

(4) In the case of an individual's partnership profits, the amount to be included in arriving at his net relevant earnings shall be his share of the partnership income (estimated in accordance with the Income Tax Acts) after making from it any such deductions in respect of—

(*a*) payments made by the partnership;

(*b*) relief given to the partnership under Schedule 9 to the Finance Act 1981; or

(*c*) capital allowances falling to be made to the partnership,

as would be made in computing the tax payable in respect of that income.

(5) Where, in a year of assessment for which [the basic rate limit is increased in accordance with section 639(5A) in the case]⁴ of an individual—

(*a*) a deduction in respect of such a loss or allowance of the individual as is mentioned in subsection (2)(*d*) above falls to be made in computing the total income of the individual ...²; and

(*b*) the deduction or part of it falls to be so made from income other than relevant earnings;

the amount of the deduction made from that other income shall be treated as reducing the individual's net relevant earnings for subsequent years of assessment in accordance with subsection (6) below.

(6) The deduction shall be made so far as possible from the individual's net relevant earnings for the first of the subsequent years of assessment (whether or not he is entitled to relief [in accordance

with section 639(5A)][4] for that year), and than, so far as it cannot be so made, from those of the next year, and so on.

(7) ...[5]

Commentary—*Simon's Direct Tax Service* **E7.409.**
Definitions—"The 1968 Act", s 831(3); "the 1970 Act", s 831(3); "capital allowances", s 832(1); "the Income Tax Acts", s 831(1)(*b*); "profits or gains", s 833(1); "relevant earnings", s 644; "year of assessment", s 832(1).
Cross references—See TA 1988 s 646A(2) (modification of sub-s (1) above where an individual holds multiple pensionable and non–pensionable employments).
Amendments—[1] Words in sub-s (1) inserted by FA 1989 Sch 7 para 7.
[2] Words in sub-ss (2)(*d*), (5)(*a*), repealed by FA 1988 Sch 14 Pt VIII with effect from the year 1990–91.
[3] Words in sub-s (3) substituted by CAA 1990 Sch 1 para 8(1), (29).
[4] Words in sub-ss (5), (6) substituted by by FA 2000 ss 61, 156, Sch 13 paras 1, 21, Sch 40 Pt II(4) with effect from the year 2001–02.
[5] Sub-s (7) repealed by FA 2000 ss 61, 156, Sch 13 paras 1, 21, Sch 40 Pt II(4) with effect from the year 2001–02.
[6] Words in sub-s (3) substituted by CAA 2001 s 578, Sch 2 para 54 with effect for income tax purposes as respects allowances and charges falling to be made for chargeable periods ending after 5 April 2001.
[7] Word in sub-s (2)(*b*) inserted by FA 2001 s 57(3), (4), Sch 12 Pt II para 14 with effect from the year 2002–03.

[646A Earnings from associated employments

(1) This section applies where in the year of assessment in question—

(*a*) an individual holds two or more offices or employments which are associated in that year,

(*b*) one or more of them is an office or employment to which section 645 applies ("pensionable job"), and

(*c*) one or more of them is an office or employment to which that section does not apply ("non-pensionable job").

(2) Where the emoluments for that year from the pensionable job (or jobs) are equal to or exceed the allowable maximum for that year, section 646(1) shall have effect in the case of the individual as if the references to relevant earnings were references to relevant earnings not attributable to the non-pensionable job (or jobs).

(3) Where the allowable maximum for that year exceeds the emoluments for that year from the pensionable job (or jobs), the individual's net relevant earnings, so far as attributable to the non-pensionable job (or jobs), shall not be greater than the amount of the excess.

(4) For the purposes of this section two or more offices or employments held by an individual in a year of assessment are associated in that year if the employers in question are associated at any time during it.

(5) For the purposes of subsection (4) above, employers are associated if (directly or indirectly) one is controlled by the other or if both are controlled by a third person.

(6) In subsection (5) above the reference to control, in relation to a body corporate, shall be construed—

(*a*) where the body corporate is a close company, in accordance with section 416, and

(*b*) where it is not, in accordance with section 840.

(7) In this section "the allowable maximum" has the same meaning as in section 640A(1).][1]

Commentary—*Simon's Direct Tax Service* **E7.409A.**
Note—For the year 2000–01 the figure specified for the purpose of sub-s (7) by virtue of ss 590C, 640A is £91,800 by virtue of the Retirement Benefits Schemes (Indexation of Earnings Cap) Order, SI 2000/807.
Amendments—[1] This section inserted by FA 1989 Sch 7 para 8.

[646B Presumption of same level of relevant earnings etc for 5 years

(1) This section applies where an individual (the "relevant member") who is or becomes a member of a personal pension scheme provides to the scheme administrator the requisite evidence of the relevant amounts for any year of assessment (the "basis year").

(2) For the purposes of this section, the "relevant amounts" for any year of assessment are the amounts which need to be known in order to calculate the relevant member's net relevant earnings for that year.

(3) The basis year need not be a year of assessment in which the relevant member is a member of the personal pension scheme concerned.

(4) Where this section applies, it shall be presumed for the purposes of this Chapter in the case of the relevant member and the personal pension scheme concerned that, for each of the five years of assessment following the basis year, the relevant amounts (and, accordingly, the relevant member's net relevant earnings) are the same as for the basis year.

(5) Subsection (4) above is subject to—

(*a*) subsections (6) to (9) below; and

(*b*) such conditions or exceptions as may be prescribed.

(6) For the purposes of this section, the requisite evidence provided for a later basis year (the "later basis year") supersedes the requisite evidence provided for an earlier basis year (the "earlier basis year").

(7) Subsection (6) above has effect subject to, and in accordance with, subsections (8) and (9) below.

(8) If—

    (*a*) the actual net relevant earnings for the later basis year, exceed

    (*b*) the actual net relevant earnings for the earlier basis year,

the supersession effected by subsection (6) above has effect as respects the later basis year and subsequent years of assessment (and subsection (4) above applies accordingly).

(9) Where the condition in subsection (8) above is not satisfied, the supersession effected by subsection (6) above has effect only as respects years of assessment later than the last of the five years of assessment following the earlier basis year (and subsection (4) above applies accordingly).

(10) It is immaterial for the purposes of this section whether the requisite evidence for a later year of assessment is provided before or after, or at the same time as, the requisite evidence for an earlier year of assessment.

(11) This section is subject to section 646D.]¹

Amendments—¹ This section inserted by FA 2000 s 61, Sch 13 paras 1, 22 with effect for presumptions from the year 2001–02.

[646C Provisions supplementary to section 646B

(1) In this section and section 646B, ''requisite evidence'' means evidence—

    (*a*) of such a description as may be prescribed;

    (*b*) in such form as may be prescribed; and

    (*c*) satisfying such conditions as may be prescribed.

(2) Regulations may make further provision in connection with requisite evidence.

(3) The provision that may be made by regulations under subsection (2) above includes provision for or in connection with the provision, use, retention, production or inspection of, or of copies of—

    (*a*) requisite evidence;

    (*b*) books, documents or other records relating to any requisite evidence; or

    (*c*) extracts from requisite evidence or from such books, documents or other records.

(4) Any power to make regulations under this section or section 646B includes power to make different provision for different cases or different purposes.

(5) In this section and section 646B—

    ''prescribed'' means specified in or determined in accordance with regulations;

    ''regulations'' means regulations made by the Board.]¹

Amendments—¹ This section inserted by FA 2000 s 61, Sch 13 paras 1, 22 with effect for presumptions from the year 2001–02.

[646D Higher level contributions after cessation of actual relevant earnings: modification of section 646B

(1) This section applies where a member of a personal pension scheme—

    (*a*) has no actual relevant earnings in a year of assessment (the ''break year''); but

    (*b*) had actual relevant earnings in the preceding year of assessment (the ''cessation year''); and

    (*c*) was entitled to make higher level contributions under arrangements under the scheme in any one or more of the six years of assessment preceding the break year (the ''reference years'').

(2) In the application of the presumption in subsection (4) of section 646B for any qualifying post-cessation year, in a case where this section applies, the basis year may be any one of the reference years for which the member provides or has provided the requisite evidence—

    (*a*) notwithstanding anything in subsections (6) to (9) of that section; and

    (*b*) whether or not the qualifying post-cessation year is included among the five years of assessment following the basis year.

(3) If the member provides or has provided the requisite evidence for two or more of the reference years, he may by notice in writing to the scheme administrator nominate that one of those years which is to be the basis year by virtue of subsection (2) above.

(4) In this section ''post-cessation year'', in the case of the member concerned, means any of the five years of assessment following the cessation year.

(5) For the purposes of this section any post-cessation year is a ''qualifying'' post-cessation year unless—

    (*a*) it is a year for which the member has any actual relevant earnings;

    (*b*) it is a year throughout which the member holds an office or employment to which section 645 applies; or

    (*c*) it immediately follows a post-cessation year which is not a qualifying post-cessation year.

(6) Subsection (5) above is without prejudice to the further application of this section in relation to the member if the conditions in subsection (1) above are again fulfilled.

(7) In this section—

    ''the basis year'' shall be construed in accordance with section 646B;

    ''the requisite evidence'' has the same meaning as in that section]¹

Amendments—¹ This section inserted by FA 2000 s 61, Sch 13 paras 1, 23 with effect where the break year is any year from 2001–02.

Charge to tax

647 Unauthorised payments

(1) This section applies to any payment within subsection (2) below which is made—

(a) out of funds which are or have been held for the purposes of a personal pension scheme which is or has at any time been approved; and

(b) to or for the benefit of an individual who has made personal pension arrangements in accordance with the scheme.

(2) A payment is within this subsection if—

(a) it is not expressly authorised by the rules of the scheme; or

(b) it is made at a time when the scheme or the arrangements are not approved and it would not have been expressly authorised by the rules of the scheme or by the arrangements when the scheme, or as the case may be the arrangements, were last so approved.

(3) The individual referred to in subsection (1)(b) above, whether or not he is the recipient of the payment, shall be chargeable to tax under Schedule E on the amount of the payment for the year of assessment in which the payment is made.

(4) This section applies to a transfer of assets or other transfer of money's worth as it applies to a payment, and in relation to such a transfer the reference in subsection (3) above to the amount of the payment shall be read as a reference to the value of the transfer.

Commentary—*Simon's Direct Tax Service* E7.417.
Revenue Internal Guidance—Schedule E manual, SE 02900 (board and lodging—payments out of personal pension schemes that are taxable, application of this section).
Definitions—"Personal pension arrangements", s 630(1); "personal pension scheme", s 630(1); "year of assessment", s 832(1).

648 Contributions under unapproved arrangements

Where contributions are paid by an employer under personal pension arrangements made by his employee then, if those arrangements are not approved arrangements and the contributions are not otherwise chargeable to income tax as income of the employee, the contributions shall be regarded for all the purposes of the Income Tax Acts as emoluments of the employment chargeable to tax under Schedule E.

Commentary—*Simon's Direct Tax Service* E7.407, 415.
Definitions—"Approved", s 630(1); "emoluments", s 131(1); "the Income Tax Acts", s 831(1)(b); "personal pension arrangements", s 630(1); "Schedule E", s 19(1).

[...]¹

[648A Annuities: charge under Schedule E

(1) Subject to subsection (2) below, where funds held for the purposes of an approved personal pension scheme are used to acquire an annuity—

(a) the annuity shall be charged to tax under Schedule E and section 203 shall apply accordingly;

(b) the annuity shall not be charged to tax under Case III of Schedule D.

(2) As respects any approved personal pension scheme the Board may direct that, until such date as the Board may specify, annuities acquired with funds held for the purposes of the scheme shall be charged to tax as annual payments under Case III of Schedule D, and tax shall be deductible under sections 348 and 349 accordingly.]¹

Commentary—*Simon's Direct Tax Service* E7.406.
Definitions—"approved", s 630(1); "the Board", s 832(1); "personal pension scheme", s 630(1); "Schedule D Case III", s 18(3); "Schedule E", s 19(1).
Amendments—This section inserted by FA 1994 s 109 in relation to annuity payments made after 5 April 1995. The preceding heading (as so inserted, which read "*Annuities: charge to tax*") is repealed by FA 1995 Sch 11 paras 1, 12 (for commencement, see notes to s 648B).

[648B Return of contributions after pension date

(1) Tax shall be charged under this section on any payment to a person under approved personal pension arrangements of such a lump sum as is mentioned in section 637A in a case where the member's death occurred after his pension date in relation to the arrangement in question.

(2) Where a payment is chargeable to tax under this section, the scheme administrator shall be charged to income tax under Case VI of Schedule D and, subject to subsection (3) below, the rate of tax shall be 35 per cent.

(3) The Treasury may by order from time to time increase or decrease the rate of tax under subsection (2) above.

(4) The tax shall be charged on the amount paid or, if the rules of the scheme permit the scheme administrator to deduct the tax before payment, on the amount before deduction of tax; and the amount so charged to tax shall not be treated as income for any other purpose of the Tax Acts.]¹

Commentary—*Simon's Direct Tax Service* **E7.406, 415.**
Definitions—"approved", s 630(1); "pension date", s 630(1); "personal pension arrangements", s 630(1); "member", s 630;
  "Schedule D Case VI", s 18(3); "tax", s 832(2); "the Tax Acts", s 831(2).
Amendments—[1] Section inserted, and heading preceding s 648A omitted, by FA 1995 Sch 11 paras 1, 12, with effect for
  approvals, of schemes or amendments, given under this Chapter after 1 May 1995, but not so as to affect any approval
  previously given.

Miscellaneous

649 Minimum contributions under Social Security Act 1986

(1) Where under [section 43 of the Pension Schemes Act 1993][1] the [Board pays][5] minimum contributions for the purposes of approved personal pension arrangements, the amount of the employee's share of those contributions shall, instead of being the amount provided for in that Part, be the grossed-up equivalent of the amount so provided for.

(2) For the purposes of this section—

  ["the employee's share" of minimum contributions is the amount that would be the minimum contributions if, for the reference in section 45(1) of the Pension Schemes Act 1993 to the appropriate age-related percentage, there were substituted a reference to the percentage mentioned in section 41(1A)(*a*) of that Act][3];

  "the grossed-up equivalent" of an amount is such sum as, after deduction of income tax at the basic rate in force for the year of assessment for which the contributions are paid, is equal to that amount.

(3) The employee's share of minimum contributions paid for a year of assessment by the [Board][5] for the purposes of approved personal pension arrangements shall be treated for the purposes of income tax—

  (*a*) as the income for that year of the individual in respect of whom it is paid; and
  (*b*) as contributions paid in that year by that individual under those arrangements.

(4) The Board may make regulations—

  (*a*), (*b*) ...[5]
  (*c*) prescribing circumstances in which this section or any provision of it shall not apply;
  (*d*) making such provision as appears to the Board to be necessary or expedient for the purposes of supplementing the provisions of this section.

[(5) The Board shall pay into the National Insurance Fund out of money provided by Parliament the amount of any increase attributable to this section in the sums paid out of that Fund under the Pension Schemes Act 1993.][5]

(6) In relation to Northern Ireland, this section shall have effect as if—

  (*a*) ...[6] ;
  (*b*) references to [section 43, section 45(1) and section 41(1)(*a*) of the Pension Schemes Act 1993][1] were references to [sections 39, 41(1) and 37(1)(*a*) of the Pension Schemes (Northern Ireland) Act 1993 respectively;][2]
  [(*bb*) references to sections 45(1) and 41 (1A)(*a*) of the Pension Schemes Act 1993 were references to sections 41(1) and 37(1A)(*a*) of the Pension Schemes (Northern Ireland) Act 1993, respectively;][4] and
  (*c*) references to the National Insurance Fund were references to the Northern Ireland National Insurance Fund.

Commentary—*Simon's Direct Tax Service* **E7.413.**
Note—The provision heading should be read as "Minimum contributions under Pension Schemes Act 1993" to reflect the
  substitution of Pension Schemes Act 1993 for references to Social Security Act 1986 in this section.
Regulations—Personal Pension Schemes (Minimum Contributions under the Social Security Act 1986) Regulations, SI 1988/1012.
Definitions—"Approved", s 630(1); "basic rate", s 832(1); "the Board", s 832(1); "personal pension arrangements", s 630(1);
  "year of assessment", s 832(1).
Amendments—[1] Words in sub-ss (1), (6)(*b*) substituted by the Pension Schemes Act 1993 s 190, Sch 8 para 20(3), (5), with
  effect from 7 February 1994, by virtue of the Pension Schemes Act 1993 (Commencement No 1) Order, SI 1994/86.
[2] Words in sub-s (6)(*b*) substituted by the Pension Schemes (Northern Ireland) Act 1993 s 184, Sch 7 para 22(3), with effect from
  7 February 1994, by virtue of the Pension Schemes (1993 Act) (Commencement No 1) Order (NI) 1994, SR 1994/17.
[3] Definition of "the employee's share" in sub-s (2) substituted (but not as respects Northern Ireland) by the Pensions Act 1995,
  Sch 5 para 12, as from a day to be appointed. The existing definition (as amended by the Pension Schemes Act 1993, s 190,
  Sch 8 para 20(4)) reads: "'the employee's share' of minimum contributions is so much of the contributions as is attributable to
  [so much of the aggregate amount mentioned in section 45(1) of the Pension Schemes Act 1993 as is attributable to the
  reduction which would fall to be made under section 41(1)(*a*) of that Act]."
[4] Sub-s (6)(*bb*) inserted by the Pensions (Northern Ireland) Order, SI 1995/3213 Sch 3 para 8, as from a day to be appointed.
[5] Words in sub-ss (1), (3) substituted, sub-s (4)(*a*), (*b*) repealed and sub-s (5) inserted, by the Social Security Contributions
  (Transfer of Functions, etc) Act 1999 Sch 1 para 4, Sch 10 Pt I, with effect from 1 April 1999 by virtue of the Social Security
  Contributions (Transfer of Functions, etc) Act 1999 (Commencement No 1 and Transitional Provisions) Order, SI 1999/527
  art 2, Sch 2.
[6] Sub-s (6)(*a*) repealed by the Social Security Contributions (Transfer of Functions, etc) (Northern Ireland) Order, SI 1999/671
  art 3(1) Sch 1 para 4, with effect from 1 April 1999 (by virtue of the Social Security Contributions (Transfer of Functions, etc)
  (1999 Order) (Commencement No 1 and Transitional Provisions) Order (Northern Ireland), SR 1999/149, art 2(*c*), Sch 2).

650 Withdrawal of approval

(1) If in the opinion of the Board the facts concerning an approved personal pension scheme or its administration or arrangements made in accordance with it do not warrant the continuance of their

approval of the scheme, they may at any time by notice given to the scheme administrator withdraw their approval of the scheme.

(2) If in the opinion of the Board the facts concerning any approved personal pension arrangements do not warrant the continuance of their approval in relation to the arrangements, they may at any time by notice given to the individual who made them and to the scheme administrator withdraw their approval in relation to the arrangements.

(3) Without prejudice to the generality of subsection (2) above, the Board may withdraw their approval in relation to any personal pension arrangements if they are of the opinion that securing the provision of benefits under the arrangements was not the sole purpose of the individual in making them.

(4) A notice under subsection (1) or (2) above shall state the grounds on which, and the date from which, approval is withdrawn.

(5) The Board may not withdraw their approval from a date earlier than the date when the facts were first such that they did not warrant the continuance of their approval (so, however, that in a case within subsection (3) above their approval may be withdrawn from the day the arrangements in question were made).

[(6) The power of the Board under this section to withdraw their approval in relation to any arrangements made under a personal pension scheme shall be exercisable for the purposes of section 650A notwithstanding that the time from which the approval is withdrawn is a time from which, by virtue of section 631(4) or 638A(4), the whole scheme ceases to be an approved scheme.][1]

Commentary—*Simon's Direct Tax Service* **E7.404.**
Definitions—''Approved'', s 630(1); ''the Board'', s 832(1); ''notice'', s 832(1); ''personal pension arrangements'', s 630(1); ''personal pension scheme'', s 630(1); ''scheme administrator'', s 630(1).
Cross references—See TA 1988 s 651 (appeal against Board's decision to withdraw approval by virtue of this section).
Personal Pension Schemes (Relief at Source) Regulations, SI 1988/1013 reg 14(2) (information to be given to the Board where the approval of a scheme is withdrawn under this section).
Amendments—[1] Sub-s (6) inserted by FA 1998 s 95(2) with effect in relation to any case in which the date from which the Board's approval is withdrawn is a date on or after 17 March 1998, except a case where the notice under TA 1988 s 650(2) was given before that date.

[650A Charge on withdrawal of approval from arrangements

(1) Where any personal pension arrangements cease to be approved arrangements by virtue of the exercise by the Board of their power under section 650(2), tax shall be charged in accordance with this section.

(2) The tax shall be charged under Case VI of Schedule D at the rate of 40 per cent on an amount equal to the value (taking that value at the relevant time) of the appropriate part of the assets held at that time for the purposes of the relevant scheme.

(3) In subsection (2) above—

''the appropriate part'', in relation to the value of any assets, is so much of those assets as is properly attributable, in accordance with the provisions of the scheme and any just and reasonable apportionment, to the arrangements in question; and

''the relevant time'' means the time immediately before the date from which the Board's approval is withdrawn.

(4) Subject to subsection (5) below, the person liable for the tax charged under this section shall be the scheme administrator for the relevant scheme.

(5) If, in any case where an amount of tax has been charged under this section and has not been paid—

(a) there is at any time no person who, as the scheme administrator for the relevant scheme, may be assessed to that amount of tax, or is liable to pay it,
(b) the scheme administrator for that scheme cannot for the time being be traced,
(c) there has been such a failure by the scheme administrator for that scheme to meet a liability to pay that amount as the Board consider to be a failure of a serious nature, or
(d) it appears to the Board that a liability of the scheme administrator for that scheme to pay that amount of tax is a liability that he will be, or (were there an assessment) would be, unable to meet out of assets held in accordance with the scheme for the purposes of those arrangements,

the Board shall be entitled to assess the unpaid tax on the person who made the arrangements in question as if the tax charged under this section, to the extent that it is unpaid, were assessable under this section on that person, instead of on the scheme administrator.

(6) An assessment to tax made by virtue of subsection (5)(c) above shall not be out of time if it is made within three years after the date on which the tax which the scheme administrator has failed to pay first became due from him.

(7) For the purposes of this section the value of an asset is, subject to subsection (8) below, its market value, construing ''market value'' in accordance with section 272 of the 1992 Act.

(8) Where an asset held for the purposes of a scheme is a right or interest in respect of any money lent (directly or indirectly) to any person mentioned in subsection (9) below, the value of the asset shall be treated as being the amount owing (including any unpaid interest) on the money lent.

TA 1988

(9) Those persons are—

(*a*) the person who (whether or not before the making of the loan) made the arrangements in relation to which the Board's approval has been withdrawn;

(*b*) any other person who has at any time (whether or not before the making of the loan) made contributions under those arrangements; and

(*c*) any person connected, at the time of the making of the loan or subsequently, with a person falling within paragraph (*a*) or (*b*) above.

(10) In this section ''the relevant scheme'', in relation to any personal pension arrangements, means the scheme in accordance with which those arrangements were made.

(11) Section 839 shall apply for the purposes of this section.'']¹

Commentary—*Simon's Direct Tax Service* **E7.404.**
Amendments—¹ This section inserted by FA 1998 s 95(1) with effect in relation to any case in which the date from which the Board's approval is withdrawn is a date on or after 17 March 1998, except a case where the notice under TA 1988 s 650(2) was given before that date.

651 Appeals

(1) Where the Board—

(*a*) refuse an application by notice under section 631 [or paragraph 3 of Schedule 23ZA]¹; or

(*b*) withdraw an approval by notice under section 650;

the person to whom the notice is given may appeal to the Special Commissioners against the refusal or, as the case may be, the withdrawal.

(2) An appeal under this section shall be made by notice stating the grounds for the appeal and given to the Board before the end of the period of 30 days beginning with the day on which the notice of refusal or withdrawal was given to the appellant.

(3) On an appeal under this section against the withdrawal of an approval, the Special Commissioners may, instead of allowing or dismissing the appeal, order that the withdrawal shall have effect from a date other than that determined by the Board.

(4) The bringing of an appeal under this section shall not affect the validity of the decision appealed against pending the determination of the proceedings.

Commentary—*Simon's Direct Tax Service* **E7.403, 404.**
Definitions—''The Board'', s 832(1); ''notice'', s 832(1).
Amendments—¹ Words in sub-s (1)(*a*) inserted by FA 2000 s 61, Sch 13 paras 1, 24 with effect from 28 July 2000.

[651A Information powers

(1) The Board may by regulations make any of the following provisions—

(*a*) provision requiring prescribed persons to furnish to the Board, at prescribed times, information relating to any of the matters mentioned in subsection (2) below;

(*b*) provision enabling the Board to serve a notice requiring prescribed persons to furnish to the Board, within a prescribed time, particulars relating to any of those matters;

(*c*) provision enabling the Board to serve a notice requiring prescribed persons to produce to the Board, within a prescribed time, documents relating to any of those matters;

(*d*) provision enabling the Board to serve a notice requiring prescribed persons to make available for inspection on behalf of the Board books, documents and other records, being books, documents and records which relate to any of those matters;

(*e*) provision requiring prescribed persons to preserve for a prescribed time books, documents and other records, being books, documents and records which relate to any of those matters.

(2) The matters referred to in subsection (1) above are—

(*a*) any personal pension scheme which is or has been approved; and

(*b*) any personal pension arrangements which are or have been approved.

(3) A person who fails to comply with regulations made under subsection (1)(*e*) above shall be liable to a penalty not exceeding £3,000.

(4) Regulations under this section may make different provision for different descriptions of case.

(5) In this section ''prescribed'' means prescribed by regulations made under this section.]¹

Commentary—*Simon's Direct Tax Service* **E7.403, 404.**
Cross references—Personal Pension Schemes (Information Powers) Regulations, SI 2000/2316 (provision for the furnishing of information and documents to the Board of Inland Revenue).
Amendments—¹ This section inserted by FA 1998 s 96(1) with effect from 31 July 1998.

652 Information about payments

(1) An inspector may give a notice to a scheme administrator requiring him to provide the inspector with—

(a) such particulars as the notice may require relating to contributions paid under approved personal pension arrangements made in accordance with the scheme;

(b) such particulars as the notice may require relating to payments by way of return of contributions;

(c) copies of such accounts as the notice may require.

(2) A person to whom a notice is given under this section shall comply with the notice within the period of 30 days beginning with the day on which it is given.

Commentary—*Simon's Direct Tax Service* **E7.417.**
Definitions—"Approved", s 630(1); "inspector", s 832(1); "notice", s 832(1); "personal pension arrangements", s 630(1); "scheme administrator", s 630(1).
Amendments—This section is repealed by FA 1998 s 96(2), Sch 27 Part III(21) with effect from 1 October 2000 (by virtue of the Finance Act 1998, Section 96(4), (Appointed Day) Order, SI 2000/2319).

653 Information penalties

A person who knowingly makes a false statement or false representation on making an application under section 631 or for the purpose of obtaining for himself or any other person any relief from or repayment of tax under this Chapter shall be liable to a penalty not exceeding [£3,000][1].

Commentary—*Simon's Direct Tax Service* **A3.802; E7.403.**
Definition—"Tax", s 832(3).
Amendments—[1] Amount substituted by FA 1989 s 170(4)(b), (6) in relation to things done or omitted after 26 July 1989.

[653A Notices to be given to scheme administrator

(1) Where—

(a) the Board, or any officer of the Board, is authorised or required by or in consequence of any provision of this Chapter to give a notice to the person who is the scheme administrator of a personal pension scheme, but
(b) there is for the time being no scheme administrator for that scheme or the person who is the scheme administrator for that scheme cannot be traced,

that power or duty may be exercised or performed by giving that notice, instead, to the person specified in subsection (2) below.

(2) That person is—

(a) the person who established the scheme; or
(b) any person by whom that person has been directly or indirectly succeeded in relation to the provision of benefits under the scheme.

(3) The giving of a notice in accordance with this section shall have the same effect as the giving of that notice to the scheme administrator and, without prejudice to section 650A(5), shall not impose an additional obligation or liability on the person to whom the notice is actually given.][1]

Commentary—*Simon's Direct Tax Service* **A3.802; E7.403.**
Amendments—[1] This section inserted by FA 1998 s 97(1) with effect in relation to the giving of notices at any time on or after 31 July 1998.

654 Remuneration of Ministers and other officers

(1) This section applies to any salary—

(a) payable to the holder of a qualifying office who is also a Member of the House of Commons; and
(b) payable for a period in respect of which the holder is not a participant in relation to that office in arrangements contained in the Parliamentary pension scheme but is a participant in relation to his membership of the House of Commons in any such arrangements, or for any part of such a period.

(2) So much of any salary to which this section applies as is equal to the difference between a Member's pensionable salary and the salary which (in accordance with any such resolution as is mentioned in subsection (4)(a) below) is payable to him as a Member holding that qualifying office, shall be treated for the purposes of this Chapter as remuneration from the office of Member and not from the qualifying office.

(3) In this section—

"Member's pensionable salary" means a Member's ordinary salary under any resolution of the House of Commons which, being framed otherwise than as an expression of opinion, is for the time being in force relating to the remuneration of Members or, if the resolution provides for a Member's ordinary salary thereunder to be treated for pension purposes as being at a higher rate, a notional yearly salary at that higher rate;
"qualifying office" means an office mentioned in paragraph (b), (c) or (d) of subsection (2) of section 2 of the Parliamentary and other Pensions Act 1987;
"the Parliamentary pension scheme" has the same meaning as in that Act;

and, without prejudice to the power conferred by virtue of paragraph 13 of Schedule 1 to that Act, regulations under section 2 of that Act may make provision specifying the circumstances in which a person is to be regarded for the purposes of this section as being or not being a participant in relation to his membership of the House of Commons, or in relation to any office, in arrangements contained in the Parliamentary pension scheme.

(4) In subsection (3) above "a Member's ordinary salary", in relation to any resolution of the House of Commons, means—

(a) if the resolution provides for salary to be paid to Members at different rates according to whether or not they are holders of particular offices or are in receipt of salaries or pensions as the holders or former holders of particular offices, a Member's yearly salary at the higher or highest rate; and

(b) in any other case, a Member's yearly salary at the rate specified in or determined under the resolution.

Commentary—*Simon's Direct Tax Service* **E7.407.**
Definition—"Higher rate", s 832(1).
Cross references—See FA 1999 Sch 5 para 6 (circumstances in which this section applies in relation to pensions of members of the Scottish Executive).

655 Transitional provisions

(1) Where approved personal pension arrangements are made by an individual who pays qualifying premiums within the meaning of section 620(1)—

(a) the amount [of contributions in respect of which relief may be given][3] by virtue of section 639(1) in any year of assessment shall be reduced by the amount of any qualifying premiums which are paid in the year by the individual and in respect of which relief is given for the year under section 619(1)(a); and

(b) the relief which, by virtue of section 625, may be given under section 619 by reference to the individual's unused relief for any year shall be reduced by the amount of any contributions paid by him in that year under the approved personal pension arrangements.

(2) Where an individual elects under section 641 that a contribution or part of a contribution shall be treated as paid in the year of assessment [1985–86, 1986–87 or 1987–88][1], the payment shall be treated as the payment of a qualifying premium for the purposes of Chapter III of this Part; and in such a case references in section 641 to an amount of unused relief shall be construed in accordance with section 625.

(3) The references in section 642 to unused relief for any year are, for years of assessment before [1988–89][1], references to unused relief within the meaning of section 625.

(4) The Board shall not grant any application under section 631 so as to approve a scheme with effect from a date earlier than [1st July][1] 1988.

(5) The Board may by regulations make provisions for applications for approval of personal pension schemes to be granted provisionally ...[2], notwithstanding that the Board have not satisfied themselves that the schemes comply with the requirements of sections 632 to 638; and such regulations may, in particular, provide—

(a) for the contents and form of certificates or other documents which the Board may require the applicant to give them before they grant an application provisionally;

(b) for the making of such amendments of the rules of the scheme after the provisional grant of an application as are necessary to enable the scheme to comply with the requirements of sections 632 to 638, and for those amendments to have effect as from the date of approval of the scheme;

(c) for the withdrawal of approval of the scheme as from that date if it does not comply with the requirements of sections 632 to 638 and such amendments as are mentioned in paragraph (b) above are not made;

and may make such supplementary provision as appears to the Board to be necessary or expedient.

Commentary—*Simon's Direct Tax Service* **E7.403, 418.**
Simon's Tax Cases—s 655(1)(b), *Brock v O'Connor* [1997] STC (SCD) 157.
Definitions—"Approved", s 630(1); "the Board", s 832(1); "personal pension arrangements", s 630(1); "personal pension scheme", s 630(1); "year of assessment", s 832(1).
Amendments—[1] Dates in sub-ss (2), (3), (4) substituted by FA 1988 s 54(1), (2)(b), (c), (3) and deemed always to have had effect.
[2] Words in sub-s (5) repealed by FA 1989 Sch 7 paras 1, 9 and Sch 17 Pt IV.
[3] Words in sub-s (1)(a) substituted by FA 2000 s 61, Sch 13 paras 1, 25 with effect from the year 2001–02.

CHAPTER V
PURCHASED LIFE ANNUITIES

656 Purchased life annuities other than retirement annuities

(1) Subject to section 657, a purchased life annuity shall, for the purposes of the provisions of the Tax Acts relating to tax on annuities and other annual payments, be treated as containing a capital element and, to the extent of the capital element, as not being an annual payment or in the nature of an annual payment; but the capital element in such an annuity shall be taken into account in computing profits or gains or losses for other purposes of the Tax Acts in any circumstances in which a lump sum payment would be taken into account.

(2) Where, in the case of any purchased life annuity to which this section applies, the amount of any annuity payment (but not the term of the annuity) depends on any contingency other than the duration of a human life or lives—

(*a*) the capital element shall be determined by reference—

   (i) to the amount or value of the payments made or other consideration given for the grant of the annuity (''the purchase price''); and

   (ii) to the expected term of the annuity, as at the date when the first annuity payment began to accrue, expressed in years (and any odd fraction of a year), and determined by reference to the prescribed tables of mortality;

and in head (ii) above ''term'' means the period from the date when the first annuity payment begins to accrue to the date when the last payment becomes payable;

(*b*) the capital element in any annuity payment made in respect of a period of 12 months shall be a fraction—

$$\frac{1}{E}$$

of the purchase price, where E is the expected term referred to in paragraph (*a*)(ii) above;

(*c*) the capital element in any annuity payment made in respect of a period of less than, or more than, 12 months shall be the amount at (*b*) above reduced or, as the case may be, increased, in the same proportion as the length of that period bears to a period of 12 months;

(*d*) subsection (3) below shall not apply but paragraphs (*a*) and (*b*) of subsection (4) below shall apply as they apply to that subsection.

(3) Subject to subsection (2) above, in the case of any purchased life annuity to which this section applies—

(*a*) the capital element shall be determined by reference to the amount or value of the payments made or other consideration given for the grant of the annuity; and

(*b*) the proportion which the capital element in any annuity payment bears to the total amount of that payment shall be constant for all payments on account of the annuity; and

(*c*) where neither the term of the annuity nor the amount of any annuity payment depends on any contingency other than the duration of a human life or lives, that proportion shall be the same proportion which the total amount or value of the consideration for the grant of the annuity bears to the actuarial value of the annuity payments as determined in accordance with subsection (4) below; and

(*d*) where either the term of the annuity or the amount of any annuity payment (but not both) depends on any contingency other than the duration of a human life or lives, that proportion shall be such as may be just, having regard to paragraph (*c*) above and to the contingencies affecting the annuity; and

(*e*) where both the term of the annuity and the amount of any annuity payment depend on any contingency other than the duration of a human life or lives, that proportion shall be such as may be just, having regard to subsection (2) above and to the contingencies affecting the annuity.

(4) For the purposes of subsection (3) above—

(*a*) an entire consideration given for the grant of an annuity and for some other matter shall be apportioned as appears just (but so that a right to a return of premiums or other consideration for an annuity shall not be treated for this purpose as a distinct matter from the annuity);

(*b*) where it appears that the amount or value of the consideration purporting to be given for the grant of an annuity has affected, or has been affected by, the consideration given for some other matter, the aggregate amount or value of those considerations shall be treated as one entire consideration given for both and shall be apportioned under paragraph (*a*) above accordingly; and

(*c*) the actuarial value of any annuity payments shall be taken to be their value as at the date when the first of those payments begins to accrue, that value being determined by reference to the prescribed tables of mortality and without discounting any payment for the time to elapse between that date and the date it is to be made.

(5) Where a person making a payment on account of any life annuity has been notified in the prescribed manner of any decision as to its being or not being a purchased life annuity to which this section applies or as to the amount of the capital element (if any), and has not been notified of any alteration of that decision, the notice shall be conclusive as to those matters for the purpose of determining the amount of income tax which he is entitled or required to deduct from the payment, or for which he is chargeable in respect of it.

(6) Where a person making a payment on account of a purchased life annuity to which this section applies has not been notified in the prescribed manner of the amount of the capital element, the amount of income tax which he is entitled or required to deduct from the payment, or for which he is chargeable in respect of it, shall be the same as if the annuity were not a purchased life annuity to which this section applies.

[(7) In using the prescribed tables of mortality to determine—

(*a*) the expected term of an annuity for the purposes of subsection (2)(*a*) above, or

(*b*) the actuarial value of any annuity payments for the purposes of subsection (4)(*c*) above,

the age, as at the date when the first of the annuity payments begins to accrue, of a person during whose life the annuity is payable shall be taken to be the number of years of his age at his last birthday preceding that date.][1]

[(8) In any case where it is not possible to determine the expected term of an annuity for the purposes of subsection (2)(*a*) above by reference to the prescribed tables of mortality, that term shall for those purposes be such period as may be certified by the Government Actuary or the Deputy Government Actuary.]¹

[(9) In any case where it is not possible to determine the actuarial value of any annuity payments for the purposes of subsection (4)(*c*) above by reference to the prescribed tables of mortality, that value shall for those purposes be such amount as may be certified by the Government Actuary or the Deputy Government Actuary.]¹

Commentary—*Simon's Direct Tax Service* **B5.314.**
Concession A46—Variable purchased life annuities: carry forward of excess of capital element determined under this section over annuity payment made on a contingency other than the duration of a life or lives.
Definitions—"Life annuity", s 657; "notice", s 832(1); "profits or gains", s 833(1); "purchased life annuity", s 657; "the Tax Acts", s 831(2).
Cross references—See TA 1988 s 543(1) (capital element of annuity under this section taken into account in computing gain on the surrender of a life annuity contract).
TA 1988 s 658 (supplementary provisions).
FA 1991 s 76(2) (TA 1970 s 230 deemed always to have had effect with the insertion of provisions (with modifications) contained in sub-ss (7)–(9) above).
Amendments—¹ Sub-ss (7)–(9) added by FA 1991 s 76(1) and deemed always to have had effect.

657 Purchased life annuities to which section 656 applies

(1) For the purposes of section 656—

"life annuity" means an annuity payable for a term ending with (or at a time ascertainable only by reference to) the end of a human life, whether or not there is provision for the annuity to end during the life on the expiration of a fixed term or on the happening of any event or otherwise, or to continue after the end of the life in particular circumstances; and

"purchased life annuity" means a life annuity granted for consideration in money or money's worth in the ordinary course of a business of granting annuities on human life.

(2) Section 656 does not apply—

(*a*) to any annuity which would, apart from that section, be treated for the purposes of the provisions of the Tax Acts relating to tax on annuities and other annual payments as consisting to any extent in the payment or repayment of a capital sum;

(*b*) to any annuity where the whole or part of the consideration for the grant of the annuity consisted of sums satisfying the conditions for relief under section 266, 273 or 619 or to any annuity payable under a substituted contract within the meaning of section 622(3);

(*c*) to any annuity purchased in pursuance of any direction in a will, or to provide for an annuity payable by virtue of a will or settlement out of income of property disposed of by the will or settlement (whether with or without resort to capital);

(*d*) to any annuity purchased under or for the purposes of any sponsored superannuation scheme (as defined in section 624) or any scheme approved under section 620 or in pursuance of any obligation imposed, or offer or invitation made, under or in connection with any such scheme or to any other annuity purchased by any person in recognition of another's services (or past services) in any office or employment; [...

(*da*) to any annuity purchased under or for the purposes of a scheme approved by virtue of section 591 or in pursuance of any obligation imposed, or offer or invitation made, under or in connection with any such scheme;]¹

(*e*) to any annuity payable under approved personal pension arrangements within the meaning of Chapter IV of this Part[; or

(*f*) to any annuity purchased, for purposes connected with giving effect to any pension sharing order or provision, for consideration which derives from—

(i) a retirement benefits scheme (within the meaning of Chapter I of this Part) of a description mentioned in section 596(1);

(ii) sums satisfying the conditions for relief under section 619;

(iii) any such scheme or arrangements as are mentioned in paragraph (*d*) or (*e*) above; or

(iv) the surrender, in whole or in part, of an annuity falling within paragraph (*da*) above or this paragraph, or of a contract for such an annuity.]²

Commentary—*Simon's Direct Tax Service* **B5.314, E7.415.**
Definition—"The Tax Acts", s 831(2).
Amendments—¹ Para (2)(*da*) substituted for word "or" at end of para (*d*) by FA 1999 s 80 and deemed always to have had effect.
² Para (2)(*f*) and word "or" preceding it inserted, by FA 1999 s 79 Sch 10 para 16 with effect in accordance with the commencement provisions contained in FA 1999 Sch 10 para 18.

658 Supplementary

(1) Any question whether an annuity is a purchased life annuity to which section 656 applies, or what is the capital element in such an annuity, shall be determined by the inspector; but a person aggrieved by the inspector's decision on any such question may appeal within the prescribed time to the Special Commissioners.

(2) Save as otherwise provided in this Chapter, the procedure to be adopted in giving effect to this Chapter shall be such as may be prescribed.

(3) The Board may make regulations for prescribing anything which is to be prescribed under this Chapter, and the regulations may apply for the purposes of this Chapter or of the regulations any provision of the Income Tax Acts, with or without modifications.

(4) Regulations under subsection (3) above may in particular make provision as to the time limit for making any claim for relief from or repayment of tax under this Chapter and as to all or any of the following matters, that is to say—

(*a*) as to the information to be furnished in connection with the determination of any question whether an annuity is a purchased life annuity to which section 656 applies or what is the capital element in an annuity, and as to the persons who may be required to furnish any such information;

(*b*) as to the manner of giving effect to the decision on any such question, and (notwithstanding anything in section 348) as to the making of assessments for the purpose on the person entitled to the annuity; and

(*c*) as to the extent to which the decision on any such question is to be binding, and the circumstances in which it may be reviewed.

(5) If any person, for the purpose of obtaining for himself or for any other person any relief from or repayment of tax under this Chapter, knowingly makes any false statement or false representation, he shall be liable to a penalty not exceeding [£3,000][1].

Commentary—*Simon's Direct Tax Service* B5.314.
Regulations—IT (Purchased Life Annuities) Regulations, SI 1956/1230. For continuity see Sch 30, para 21 of this Act.
Definitions—"The Board", s 832(1); "the Income Tax Acts", s 831(1)(*b*); "inspector", s 832(1); "tax", s 832(3).
Amendments—[1] Amount in sub-s (5) substituted by FA 1989 s 170(4)(*c*), (6) in relation to things done or omitted after 26 July 1989.

CHAPTER VI
MISCELLANEOUS

[658A Charges and assessments on administrators

(1) Tax charged under Chapter I or IV of this Part on the administrator of a scheme—

(*a*) shall be treated as charged on every relevant person and be assessable by the Board in the name of the administrator of the scheme, but

(*b*) shall not be assessable on any relevant person who, at the time of the assessment, is no longer either the administrator of the scheme or included in the persons who are the administrator of the scheme.

(2) For the purposes of subsection (1) above a person is a relevant person in relation to any charge to tax on the administrator of a scheme if he is a person who at the time when the charge is treated as arising or any subsequent time is, or is included in the persons who are, the administrator of the scheme.

(3) Where tax charged under Chapter I of this Part on the administrator of a scheme is assessable by virtue of section 606 or 606A on a person who is not a relevant person for the purposes of subsection (1) above, the assessment shall be made by the Board.

(4) In this section "administrator", in relation to a scheme, means the person who is—

(*a*) the administrator of the scheme within the meaning given by section 611AA; or

(*b*) the scheme administrator, as defined in section 630.

(5) This section is without prejudice to section 591D(4).][1]

Amendments—[1] This section inserted by FA 1998 s 98(1) and deemed always to have had effect.

659 Financial futures and traded options

Amendments—This section repealed by FA 1990 s 81(4), (7), (8) and Sch 19 Pt IV in relation to income derived or disposal made after 25 July 1990.

[659A Futures and options

(1) For the purposes of sections 592(2), 608(2)(*a*), 613(4), 614(3) and (4), 620(6) and 643(2)—

(*a*) "investments" (or "investment") includes futures contracts and options contracts, and

(*b*) income derived from transactions relating to such contracts shall be regarded as income derived from (or income from) such contracts,

and paragraph 7(3)(*a*) of Schedule 22 to this Act shall be construed accordingly.

(2) For the purposes of subsection (1) above a contract is not prevented from being a futures contract or an options contract by the fact that any party is or may be entitled to receive or liable to make, or entitled to receive and liable to make, only a payment of a sum (as opposed to a transfer of assets other than money) in full settlement of all obligations.][1]

Commentary—*Simon's Direct Tax Service* C2.1012.
Simon's Tax Cases—*British Telecom Pension Scheme Trustees v Clarke* [1998] STC (SCD) 14.
Amendments—[1] This section inserted by FA 1990 s 81(2), (5) with effect in relation to income derived after 26 July 1990.

[659B Definition of insurance company

[(1) In sections 591(2)(g) and 599(7) "insurance company" means one of the following—

(a) a person who has permission under Part 4 of the Financial Services and Markets Act 2000 to effect or carry out contracts of long-term insurance;

(b) an EEA firm of the kind mentioned in paragraph 5(d) of Schedule 3 to that Act which—

(i) has permission under paragraph 15 of that Schedule (as a result of qualifying for authorisation under paragraph 12 of that Schedule) to effect or carry out contracts of long-term insurance; and

(ii) fulfils the requirement under subsection (5), (6) or (7) below. (1A) In subsection (1) above "contracts of long-term insurance" means contracts which fall within Part II of Schedule 1 to the Financial Services and Markets Act 2000 (Regulated Activities) Order 2001.]²

(2) In Chapter IV of this Part "authorised insurance company" means a company that is an insurance company within the meaning given by subsection (1) above.

(3) ...²

(4) ...²

(5) The requirement under this subsection is that—

(a) a person who falls within subsection (8) below is for the time being appointed by the company to be responsible for securing the discharge of the duties mentioned in subsection (9) below, and

(b) his identity and the fact of his appointment have been notified to the Board by the company.

(6) The requirement under this subsection is that there are for the time being other arrangements with the Board for a person other than the company to secure the discharge of those duties.

(7) The requirement under this subsection is that there are for the time being other arrangements with the Board designed to secure the discharge of those duties.

(8) A person falls within this subsection if—

(a) he is not an individual and has a business establishment in the United Kingdom, or

(b) he is an individual and is resident in the United Kingdom.

(9) The duties are the following duties that fall to be discharged by the company—

(a) any duty to pay by virtue of section 203 and regulations made under it tax charged under section 597(3);

(b) any duty to pay tax charged under section 599(3) and (7);

(c) any duty imposed by regulations made under section 605;

(d) any duty to pay by virtue of section 203 and regulations made under it tax charged under section 648A(1).

(10) ...²]¹

Commentary—*Simon's Direct Tax Service* E7.406A.
Definitions—"The Board", s 832(1); "the United Kingdom", s 830(1).
Amendments—¹ This section inserted by FA 1995 ss 59(5), 60 with effect: (i) so far as relating to s 591(2)(g), in relation to a scheme not approved by virtue of s 591 before 1 May 1995; (ii) so far as relating to s 599(7), where tax is charged under s 599 on or after 1 May 1995; (iii) so far as relating to Pt XIV, Chapter IV, in relation to a scheme not approved thereunder before 1 May 1995. (Note however for discretionary commencement, FA 1995 s 60(4), (5).)
² Sub-s (1) substituted, and sub-ss (3), (4), (10) repealed, by the Financial Services and Markets Act 2000 (Consequential Amendments) (Taxes) Order, SI 2001/3629 arts 12, 42 with effect from 1 December 2001, immediately after the coming into force of the Financial Services and Markets Act 2000 ss 411, 432(1), Sch 20.

[659C Effect of appointment or arrangements under section 659B

(1) This section shall have effect where—

(a) in accordance with section 659B(5) a person is for the time being appointed to be responsible for securing the discharge of duties, or

(b) in accordance with section 659B(6) there are for the time being arrangements for a person to secure the discharge of duties.

(2) In such a case the person concerned—

(a) shall be entitled to act on the company's behalf for any of the purposes of the provisions relating to the duties;

(b) shall secure (where appropriate by acting on the company's behalf) the company's compliance with and discharge of the duties;

(c) shall be personally liable in respect of any failure of the company to comply with or discharge any such duty as if the duties imposed on the company were imposed jointly and severally on the company and the person concerned.]¹

Commentary—*Simon's Direct Tax Service* E7.406A.
Amendments—¹ This section inserted by FA 1995 ss 59(5), 60. (As to commencement, see the notes to s 659B *ante*.)

[659D Interpretation of provisions about pension sharing

(1) In this Part 'ex-spouse' means a party to a marriage that has been dissolved or annulled and, in relation to any person, means the other party to a marriage with that person that has been dissolved or annulled.

(2) References in this Part to a pension sharing order or provision are references to any such order or provision as is mentioned in section [28(1)][2] of the Welfare Reform and Pensions Act 1999 (rights under pension sharing arrangements).][1]

Amendment—[1] This section inserted by FA 1999 s 79 Sch 10 para 17 with effect in accordance with the commencement provisions contained in FA 1999 Sch 10 para 18.
[2] Figure in sub-s (2) substituted by the Welfare Reform and Pensions Act 1999, s 84, Sch 12, para 13, with effect from 11 November 1999.

[659E Treatment of income from property investment LLPs

(1) The exemptions specified below do not apply to income derived from investments, deposits or other property held as a member of a property investment LLP.

(2) The exemptions are those provided by—

    section 592(2) (exempt approved schemes),
    section 608(2)(*a*) (former approved superannuation funds),
    section 613(4) (Parliamentary pension funds),
    section 614(3) (certain colonial, &c pension funds),
    section 614(4) (the Overseas Service Pension Fund),
    section 614(5) (other pension funds for overseas employees),
    section 620(6) (retirement annuity trust schemes), and
    section 643(2) (approved personal pension schemes).

(3) The income to which subsection (1) above applies includes relevant stock lending fees, in relation to any investments, to which any of the provisions listed in subsection (2) above would apply by virtue of section 129B.

(4) Section 659A (treatment of futures and options) applies for the purposes of subsection (1) above.][1]

Amendment—[1] This section inserted by FA 2001 s 76, Sch 25 para 2 with effect from 6 April 2001.

PART XV
SETTLEMENTS

Statement of Practice SP 5/92—Revenue's practice in applying the rules (contained in TCGA 1992 ss 80–98 and Sch 5) for capital gains of certain offshore trusts.
Revenue Internal Guidance—Trust manual gives detailed guidance on the identification of trusts and the Revenue procedures for dealing with them.
Amendments—Former Chapters I (ss 660–662), II (ss 663–670), III (in part: ss 671–676, 679–681) and ss 683–685 in former Chapter IV, repealed by FA 1995 Sch 29 Pt VIII(8), with effect from the year 1995–96, and replaced by new Chapter IA (ss 660A–660G) inserted by FA 1995 s 74, Sch 17 Pt I; and Chapter III, insofar as unrepealed, is renumbered as Chapter IB, by virtue of FA 1995 Sch 17 Pt II, para 8; and Chapter IV, insofar as unrepealed, is renumbered as Chapter IC, by virtue of FA 1995 Sch 17 para 12.

[CHAPTER IA
LIABILITY OF SETTLOR
Main provisions][1]

Cross references—See TMA 1970 s 46B(4) (any question as to the application of the chapter to be determined by the Special Commissioners).
TA 1988 s 660D(3) (provisions of this Chapter not to be construed as excluding a charge to tax on the trustees on any income received by them).
TA 1988 s 660E(1) (where there is more than one settlor, this Chapter to have effect in each as if he were the only settlor).
TA 1988 s 660F (power to obtain information under this Chapter).
FA 2000 s 44 (this Chapter does not apply to any qualifying income which arises under a trust (of which the trustees are resident in the UK) if it is given by the trustees to a charity in the year of assessment in which it arises or it is income to which a charity is entitled under the terms of the trust).
FA 2000 s 45 (''settlement'' in this Chapter does not include any arrangement so far as it consists of a loan of money made by an individual to a charity either for no consideration or for a consideration which only consists of interest).

[660A Income arising under settlement where settlor retains an interest

(1) Income arising under a settlement during the life of the settlor shall be treated for all purposes of the Income Tax Acts as the income of the settlor and not as the income of any other person unless the income arises from property in which the settlor has no interest.

(2) Subject to the following provisions of this section, a settlor shall be regarded as having an interest in property if that property or any derived property is, or will or may become, payable to or applicable for the benefit of the settlor or his spouse in any circumstances whatsoever.

(3) The reference in subsection (2) above to the spouse of the settlor does not include—

    (*a*) a person to whom the settlor is not for the time being married but may later marry, or
    (*b*) a spouse from whom the settlor is separated under an order of a court, or under a separation agreement or in such circumstances that the separation is likely to be permanent, or

(c) the widow or widower of the settlor.

(4) A settlor shall not be regarded as having an interest in property by virtue of subsection (2) above if and so long as none of that property, and no derived property, can become payable or applicable as mentioned in that subsection except in the event of—

(a) the bankruptcy of some person who is or may become beneficially entitled to the property or any derived property, or

(b) an assignment of or charge on the property or any derived property being made or given by some such person, or

(c) in the case of a marriage settlement, the death of both parties to the marriage and of all or any of the children of the marriage, or

(d) the death of a child of the settlor who had become beneficially entitled to the property or any derived property at an age not exceeding 25.

(5) A settlor shall not be regarded as having an interest in property by virtue of subsection (2) above if and so long as some person is alive and under the age of 25 during whose life that property, or any derived property, cannot become payable or applicable as mentioned in that subsection except in the event of that person becoming bankrupt or assigning or charging his interest in the property or any derived property.

(6) The reference in subsection (1) above to a settlement does not include an outright gift by one spouse to the other of property from which income arises, unless—

(a) the gift does not carry a right to the whole of that income, or

(b) the property given is wholly or substantially a right to income.

For this purpose a gift is not an outright gift if it is subject to conditions, or if the property given or any derived property is or will or may become, in any circumstances whatsoever, payable to or applicable for the benefit of the donor.

(7) ...[3]

(8) Subsection (1) above does not apply to income arising under a settlement made by one party to a marriage by way of provision for the other—

(a) after the dissolution or annulment of the marriage, or

(b) while they are separated under an order of a court, or under a separation agreement or in such circumstances that the separation is likely to be permanent,

being income payable to or applicable for the benefit of that other party.

(9) Subsection (1) above does not apply to income consisting of—

(a) annual payments made by an individual for bona fide commercial reasons in connection with his trade, profession or vocation; or

[(b) qualifying donations for the purposes of section 25 of the Finance Act 1990.][2] [; or

(c) a benefit under an approved pension arrangement][4]

(10) In this section "derived property", in relation to any property, means income from that property or any other property directly or indirectly representing proceeds of, or of income from, that property or income therefrom.][1]

[(11) In this section "approved pension arrangement" means—

(a) an approved scheme or exempt approved scheme;

(b) a relevant statutory scheme;

(c) a retirement benefits scheme set up by a government outside the United Kingdom for the benefit, or primarily for the benefit, of its employees;

(d) a contract or scheme which is approved under Chapter III of Part XIV (retirement annuities);

(e) a personal pension scheme which is approved under Chapter IV of that Part;

(f) an annuity purchased for the purpose of giving effect to rights under a scheme falling within any of paragraphs (a) to (c) and (e) above;

(g) any pension arrangements of any description which may be prescribed by regulations made by the Secretary of State.][4]

[(12) In subsection (11) above "approved scheme", "exempt approved scheme", "relevant statutory scheme" and "retirement benefits scheme" have the same meaning as in Chapter I of Part XIV.][4]

Commentary—*Simon's Direct Tax Service* C4.302, 303, 310.
Revenue Internal Guidance—Independent taxation handbook, In 202 (meaning of "outright gift" in sub-s (6)).
Definitions—"Income arising under a settlement", s 660G(3), (4); "Income Tax Acts", s 831(1)(b); "settlement", s 660G(1); "settlor", s 660G(1).
Cross references—See TA 1988 s 677 (capital sum paid by trustees to settlor not treated as settlor's income under TA 1988 s 677 if so treated under the above section; capital sum does not include a sum paid after 5 April 1995 in one of the events in sub-s (4) above or on the death under the age of 25 of a person in sub-s (5) above).
Amendments—[1] Chapter heading and this section inserted by FA 1995 s 74 Sch 17 para 1, with effect from the year 1995–96 (and applies to every settlement, wherever and whenever made or entered into).
[2] Sub-s (9)(b) substituted by FA 2000 s 41(6), (9) with effect for covenanted payments falling to be made by individuals after 5 April 2000 or made by companies after 31 March 2000.
[3] Sub-s (7) repealed by FA 2000 ss 61, 156, Sch 13 paras 1, 26, Sch 40 Pt II(4) with effect from the year 2001–02.
[4] Word "and", sub-ss (9)(c), (11), (12) added by FA 2000 ss 61, 156, Sch 13 paras 1, 26, Sch 40 Pt II(4) with effect from the year 2001–02.

[660B Payments to unmarried minor children of settlor

(1) Income arising under a settlement which does not fall to be treated as income of the settlor under section 660A but which during the life of the settlor

　[(*a*)]² is paid to or for the benefit of an unmarried minor child of the settlor[, or
　(*b*) would otherwise be treated (apart from this section) as income of an unmarried minor child of the settlor,]²

in any year of assessment shall be treated for all the purposes of the Income Tax Acts as the income of the settlor for that year and not as the income of any other person.

(2) Where income arising under a settlement is retained or accumulated by the trustees, any payment whatsoever made thereafter by virtue or in consequence of the settlement, or any enactment relating thereto, to or for the benefit of an unmarried minor child of the settlor shall be deemed for the purposes of subsection (1) above to be a payment of income if or to the extent that there is available retained or accumulated income.

(3) There shall be taken to be available retained or accumulated income at any time when the aggregate amount of the income which has arisen under the settlement since it was made or entered into exceeds the aggregate amount of income so arising which has been—

　[(*a*) treated as income of the settlor, or
　(*b*) paid (whether as income or capital) to or for the benefit of, or otherwise treated as the income of, a beneficiary other than an unmarried minor child of the settlor, or
　(*bb*) treated as the income of an unmarried minor child of the settlor, and subject to tax, in any of the years 1995–96, 1996–97 or 1997–98, or]³
　(*c*) applied in defraying expenses of the trustees which were properly chargeable to income (or would have been so chargeable but for any express provisions of the trust).

[(3A) For the purposes of subsection (3)(*bb*) above—

　(*a*) the amount of a child's income that is subject to tax in a year of assessment is the amount (''the taxable amount'') by which the child's total income for income tax purposes exceeds the aggregate amount of allowances that may be set against it; and
　(*b*) income arising under the settlement that is treated as income of the child is subject to tax to the extent that it does not exceed the taxable amount.

In this subsection ''allowance'' includes any deduction allowed against total income.]³

(4) Where an offshore income gain (within the meaning of Chapter V of Part XVII) accrues in respect of a disposal of assets made by a trustee holding them for a person who would be absolutely entitled as against the trustee but for being a minor, the income which by virtue of section 761(1) is treated as arising by reference to that gain shall for the purposes of this section be deemed to be paid to that person.

[(5) If in any year of assessment the aggregate amount of a child's relevant settlement income does not exceed £100, subsection (1) does not apply in relation to that income.

A child's ''relevant settlement income'' means income paid to or for the benefit of, or otherwise treated as income of, that child which apart from this subsection would be treated as income of the settlor under subsection (1).]³

(6) In this section—

　(*a*) ''child'' includes a stepchild and an illegitimate child;
　(*b*) ''minor'' means a person under the age of 18 years, and ''minor child'' shall be construed accordingly; and
　(*c*) references to payments include payments in money or money's worth.]¹

Commentary—*Simon's Direct Tax Service* C4.302, 315.
Concession A93—Settlor of a non-resident trust able to claim credit against his tax liability under this section for tax paid by trustees to the extent distribution made out of income which arose in six years before the end of the year of assessment.
Definitions—''Income arising under a settlement'', s 660G(3), (4); ''Income Tax Acts'', s 831(1)(*b*); ''settlement'', s 660G(1); ''settlor'', s 660G(1); ''year of assessment'', s 832(1).
Cross references—See TA 1988 s 660E(3) (certain income considered to be that of the settlor for the purpose of this section where paid to or for the benefit of a child of the settlor).
TA 1988 s 660E(3)(*b*) (modification of sub-s (2) above, payments under this sub-s deemed to be payments of income).
TA 1988 s 660E(4) (meaning of ''income arising under a settlement'' and ''payment made by virtue or in consequence of the settlement'' where there is more than one settlor).
TA 1988 s 677 (capital sum paid by trustees to settlor not treated as settlor's income under s 677 if so treated under this section above).
Amendments—¹ This section inserted by FA 1995 s 74 Sch 17 para 1, with effect from the year 1995–96 (and applies to every settlement, wherever and whenever made or entered into).
² Words in sub-s (1) inserted by FA 1999 s 64(1), (5) with effect for—
(*a*) income arising under a settlement made or entered into after 8 March 1999, and
(*b*) income arising under a settlement made or entered into before 9 March 1999 so far as it arises directly or indirectly from funds provided on or after that date
Any apportionment required for the purposes of (*b*) above shall be made on a just and reasonable basis (FA 1999 s 64(5)).
³ Sub-s (3)(*a*), (*b*), (*bb*), substituted for sub-s 3(*a*), (*b*), sub-s (5) substituted and sub-s (3A) inserted by FA 1999 s 64 with effect for any payment within sub-s (2) above after 8 March 1999.

[660C Nature of charge on settlor

(1) Tax chargeable by virtue of this Chapter shall be charged—

    [(a) in the case of income falling within subsection (1A) below, as if it were income to which section 1A applies by virtue of subsection (2)(b) of that section; and

    (b) in the case of any other income, under Case VI of Schedule D]².

[(1A) Income falls within this subsection if it is—

    (a) income chargeable under Schedule F;

    (b) income to which section 1A applies by virtue of its being equivalent foreign income falling within subsection (3)(b) of that section and chargeable under Case V of Schedule D;

    (c) a distribution in relation to which section 233(1) applies;

    (d) a qualifying distribution whose amount or value is determined in accordance with section 233(1A);

    (e) a non–qualifying distribution, within the meaning of section 233(1B);

    (f) income treated as arising by virtue of section 249;

    (g) income treated as received by virtue of section 421(1)(a).]²

(2) In computing the liability to income tax of a settlor chargeable by virtue of this Chapter the same deductions and reliefs shall be allowed as would have been allowed if the income treated as his by virtue of this Chapter had been received by him.

(3) Subject to section 833(3), income which is treated by virtue of this Chapter as income of a settlor shall be deemed for the purpose of this section to be the highest part of his income.]¹

Commentary—*Simon's Direct Tax Service* **C4.335.**
Definitions—"Schedule D", s 18(1); "settlor", s 660G(1).
Cross references—See FA 2000 s 46(2) (exemption under FA 2000 s 46(1) for income of a charity is not granted in respect of income chargeable to tax under Schedule D Case VI by virtue of this section).
Amendments—¹ This section inserted by FA 1995 s 74, Sch 17 para 1, with effect from the year 1995–96 (and applies to every settlement, wherever and whenever made or entered into).
² Words in sub-s (1) substituted for "under Case VI of Schedule D", and sub-s (1A) inserted by F(No 2)A 1997 s 34, Sch 4 para 14 with effect for the year 1999–00 and subsequent years of assessment.

[660D Adjustments between settlor and trustees, etc

(1) Where by virtue of this Chapter income tax becomes chargeable on and is paid by a settlor, he is entitled—

    (a) to recover from any trustee, or any other person to whom the income is payable by virtue of or in consequence of the settlement, the amount of the tax so paid; and

    (b) for that purpose to require an officer of the Board to furnish to him a certificate specifying the amount of income in respect of which he has so paid tax and the amount of tax so paid.

A certificate so furnished is conclusive evidence of the facts stated therein.

(2) Where a person obtains, in respect of an allowance or relief, a repayment of income tax in excess of the amount of the repayment to which he would, but for this Chapter, have been entitled, an amount equal to the excess shall be paid by him to the trustee, or other person to whom the income is payable by virtue or in consequence of the settlement, or, where there are two or more such persons, shall be apportioned among those persons as the case may require.

If any question arises as to the amount of a payment or as to an apportionment to be made under this subsection, that question shall be decided by the General Commissioners whose decision shall be final.

(3) Nothing in this Chapter shall be construed as excluding a charge to tax on the trustees as persons by whom any income is received.]¹

Commentary—*Simon's Direct Tax Service* **C4.336.**
Definitions—"The Board", s 832(1); "settlement", s 660G(1); "settlor", s 660G(1).
Amendments—¹ This section inserted by FA 1995 s 74 Sch 17 para 1, with effect from the year 1995–96 (and applies to every settlement, wherever and whenever made or entered into).

*[Supplementary provisions]*¹

[660E Application to settlements by two or more settlors

(1) In the case of a settlement where there is more than one settlor, this Chapter shall have effect in relation to each settlor as if he were the only settlor, as follows.

(2) In this Chapter, in relation to a settlor—

    (a) references to the property comprised in a settlement include only property originating from that settlor, and

    (b) references to income arising under the settlement include only income originating from that settlor.

(3) For the purposes of section 660B there shall be taken into account, [in relation to a child of the settlor]² only—

    (a) income originating from that settlor, and

(b) in a case in which section 660B(2) applies, payments which are under that provision (as adapted by subsection (4) below) to be deemed to be payments of income.

(4) In applying section 660B(2) to a settlor—

(a) the reference to income arising under the settlement includes only income originating from that settlor; and

(b) the reference to any payment made by virtue or in consequence of the settlement or any enactment relating thereto includes only a payment made out of property originating from that settlor or income originating from that settlor.

(5) References in this section to property originating from a settlor are references to—

(a) property which that settlor has provided directly or indirectly for the purposes of the settlement; and

(b) property representing that property; and

(c) so much of any property which represents both property so provided and other property as, on a just apportionment, represents the property so provided.

(6) References in this section to income originating from a settlor are references to—

(a) income from property originating from that settlor; and

(b) income provided directly or indirectly by that settlor.

(7) In subsections (5) and (6) above—

(a) references to property or income which a settlor has provided directly or indirectly include references to property or income which has been provided directly or indirectly by another person in pursuance of reciprocal arrangements with that settlor, but do not include references to property or income which that settlor has provided directly or indirectly in pursuance of reciprocal arrangements with another person; and

(b) references to property which represents other property include references to property which represents accumulated income from that other property.][1]

Commentary—*Simon's Direct Tax Service* **C4.304.**
Definitions—"Income arising under a settlement", s 660G(3), (4); "settlement", s 660G(1); "settlor", s 660G(1).
Amendments—[1] This section and preceding heading inserted by FA 1995 s 74 Sch 17 para 1, with effect from the year 1995–96 (and applies to every settlement, wherever and whenever made or entered into).
[2] Words in sub-s (3) substituted FA 1999 s 64(7).

[660F Power to obtain information

An officer of the Board may by notice require any party to a settlement to furnish him within such time as he may direct (not being less than 28 days) with such particulars as he thinks necessary for the purposes of this Chapter.][1]

Commentary—*Simon's Direct Tax Service* **C4.337.**
Definitions—"The Board", s 832(1); "settlement", s 660G(1).
Amendments—[1] This section inserted by FA 1995 s 74 Sch 17 para 1, with effect from the year 1995–96 (and applies to every settlement, wherever and whenever made or entered into).

[660G Meaning of "settlement" and related expressions

(1) In this Chapter—

"settlement" includes any disposition, trust, covenant, agreement, arrangement or transfer of assets, and

"settlor", in relation to a settlement, means any person by whom the settlement was made.

(2) A person shall be deemed for the purposes of this Chapter to have made a settlement if he has made or entered into the settlement directly or indirectly, and, in particular, but without prejudice to the generality of the preceding words, if he has provided or undertaken to provide funds directly or indirectly for the purpose of the settlement, or has made with any other person a reciprocal arrangement for that other person to make or enter into the settlement.

(3) References in this Chapter to income arising under a settlement include, subject to subsection (4) below, any income chargeable to income tax by deduction or otherwise, and any income which would have been so chargeable if it had been received in the United Kingdom by a person domiciled, resident and ordinarily resident in the United Kingdom.

(4) Where the settlor is not domiciled, or not resident, or not ordinarily resident, in the United Kingdom in a year of assessment, references in this Chapter to income arising under a settlement do not include income arising under the settlement in that year in respect of which the settlor, if he were actually entitled thereto, would not be chargeable to income tax by deduction or otherwise by reason of his not being so domiciled, resident or ordinarily resident.

But where such income is remitted to the United Kingdom in circumstances such that, if the settlor were actually entitled to that income when remitted, he would be chargeable to income tax by reason of his residence in the United Kingdom, it shall be treated for the purposes of this Chapter as arising under the settlement in the year in which it is remitted.][1]

Commentary—*Simon's Direct Tax Service* **C4.302.**
Amendments—[1] This section inserted by FA 1995 s 74 Sch 17 para 1, with effect from the year 1995–96 (and applies to every settlement, wherever and whenever made or entered into).

[CHAPTER IB

PROVISIONS AS TO CAPITAL SUMS PAID TO SETTLOR][1]

Cross references—See TMA 1970 s 46B(4) (any question as to the application of this chapter to be determined by the Special
Commissioners).
TA 1988 s 660E(1) (applied to this Chapter by s 682A(1)) (where there is more than one settlor, this Chapter to have effect on
each as if he were the only settlor).
TA 1988 s 660F (applied to this Chapter by s 682A(1)) (power to obtain information under this Chapter).
Amendments—[1] Heading inserted by FA 1995 s 74 Sch 17 para 8, with effect from the year 1995–96 (see, further, the
introductory notes to Part XV).

677 Sums paid to settlor otherwise than as income

(1) Any capital sum paid directly or indirectly in any year of assessment by the trustees of a
settlement to which this section applies to the settlor shall—

(a) to the extent to which the amount of that sum falls within the amount of income available up
to the end of that year, be treated for all the purposes of the Income Tax Acts as the income of the
settlor for that year;

(b) to the extent to which the amount of that sum is not by virtue of this subsection treated as his
income for that year and falls within the amount of the income available up to the end of the next
following year, be treated for those purposes as the income of the settlor for the next following
year;

and so on for each subsequent year up to a maximum of ten subsequent years, taking the reference
in paragraph (b) to the year mentioned in paragraph (a) as a reference to that and any other year
before the subsequent year in question.

(2) For the purposes of subsection (1) above, the amount of income available up to the end of any
year shall, in relation to any capital sum paid as mentioned in that subsection, be taken to be the
aggregate amount of income arising under the settlement in that year and any previous year which
has not been distributed, less—

(a) the amount of that income taken into account under that subsection in relation to that sum in
any previous year or years; and

(b) the amount of [that income taken into account under that subsection in relation to][3] any other
capital sums paid to the settlor in any year before that sum was paid; and

(c) so much of any income arising under the settlement in that year and any previous year which
has not been distributed as is shown to consist of income which has been treated as income of the
settlor by virtue of section 671, 672, 674, [674A][1] or 683; and

(d) any income arising under the settlement in that year and any previous year which has been
treated as the income of the settlor by virtue of section 673; and

(e) any sums paid by virtue or in consequence of the settlement, to the extent that they are not
allowable, by virtue of section 676, as deductions in computing the settlor's income for that year
or any previous year; and

(f) any sums paid by virtue or in consequence of the settlement in that year or any previous year
which have been treated as the income of the settlor by virtue of section 664(2)(b); and

[(fa) any income arising under the settlement in that year or any previous year which has been
treated as income of the settlor by virtue of section 660A or 660B; and][3]

(g) any sums included in the income arising under the settlement as amounts which have been or
could have been apportioned to a beneficiary as mentioned in section 681(1)(b); and

(h) an amount equal to [tax at the rate applicable to trusts][2] on—

(i) the aggregate amount of income arising under the settlement in that year and any previous
year which has not been distributed, less
(ii) the aggregate amount of the income and sums referred to in paragraphs (c), (d), (e), (f)
and (g) above.

(3) Where any amount is included in a person's income by virtue of section 421 in respect of any
loan or advance, there shall be a corresponding reduction in the amount (if any) afterwards falling to
be so included in respect of it by virtue of this section.

(4) Where the capital sum paid to the settlor is a sum paid by way of loan, then—

(a) if the whole of it is repaid, no part of that sum shall by virtue of subsection (1) above be
treated as the settlor's income for any year of assessment after that in which the repayment occurs;
and

(b) if one or more capital sums have previously been paid to him by way of loan and wholly
repaid, the amount of that capital sum shall be treated as equal to its excess, if any, over so much
of the sum or sums previously paid as has already fallen to be treated as his income by virtue of
that subsection.

(5) Where the capital sum paid to the settlor is a sum paid by way of complete repayment of a loan,
then, if an amount not less than that sum is thereafter lent by the settlor to the trustees of the
settlement, no part of that sum shall by virtue of subsection (1) above be treated as his income for
any year of assessment after that in which the further loan is made.

(6) Where the whole or any part of any sum is treated by virtue of this section as income of the settlor for any year, it shall be treated as income of such an amount as, after deduction of [tax at the rate applicable to trusts][2] for that year, would be equal to that sum or that part of that sum.

(7) Tax chargeable by virtue of this section shall be charged under Case VI of Schedule D; and there shall be set off against the tax charged on any amount treated by virtue of this section as income of the settlor for any year an amount equal to—

    (*a*) [tax at the rate applicable to trusts][2] for that year on the amount so treated as his income; or
    (*b*) so much of [the amount of tax at that rate][2] as is equal to the tax charged,

whichever is the less.

(8) In computing the liability to income tax of a settlor chargeable by virtue of this section, the same deductions and reliefs shall be allowed as would have been allowed if the amount treated as his income by virtue of this section had been received by him as income.

(9) This section applies to any settlement wherever made, and whether made before or after the passing of this Act, and in this section—

    (*a*) "capital sum" means, subject to subsection (10) below—

        (i) any sum paid by way of loan or repayment of a loan; and
        (ii) any other sum paid otherwise than as income, being a sum which is not paid for full consideration in money or money's worth,

    but does not include any sum which could not have become payable to the settlor except in one of the events specified in section 673(3) [or, in the case of a sum paid on or after 6th April 1995, in one of the events specified in section 660A(4) or on the death under the age of 25 of any such person as is mentioned in section 660A(5)][3]; and
    (*b*) references to sums paid to the settlor include references to sums paid to the wife or husband of the settlor or to the settlor (or the husband or wife of the settlor) jointly with another person.

(10) For the purposes of this section there shall be treated as a capital sum paid to the settlor by the trustees of the settlement any sum which—

    (*a*) is paid by them to a third party at the settlor's direction or by virtue of the assignment by him of his right to receive it where the direction or assignment was given or made on or after 6th April 1981; or
    (*b*) is otherwise paid or applied by them for the benefit of the settlor,

and which would not apart from this subsection be treated as a capital sum paid to him.

Commentary—*Simon's Direct Tax Service* **C4.321–324.**
Revenue Internal Guidance—Company Taxation Manual COT6643 (TA 1988 s 419 may apply to a loan to which s 677 applies by applying s 678: s 677 takes precedence over s 421 where such a loan is released).
Simon's Tax Cases—*Piratin v IRC* [1981] STC 441*.
Definitions—"Additional rate", s 832(1); "basic rate", s 832(1); "income arising under the settlement", s 660G(3), (4); "the Income Tax Acts", s 831(1)(*b*); "Schedule D", s 18(1); "settlement", s 660G(1); "settlor", s 660G(1); "tax", s 832(3); "year of assessment", s 832(1).
Cross references—See TA 1988 s 161(5) (release on termination of employment of a beneficial loan made to a director or higher-paid employees).
TA 1988 s 678 (extension of this section to capital sums paid to a settlor by a company connected with the settlement).
TA 1988 s 691(2) (election to exclude this section in respect of income from settlements for maintenance of historic and qualifying properties).
FA 2000 s 46(2) (exemption under FA 2000 s 46(1) for income of a charity is not granted in respect of income chargeable to tax under Schedule D Case VI by virtue of this section).
Amendments—[1] Number in sub-s (2)(*c*) inserted by FA 1989 s 109(4).
[2] Words in sub-ss (2)(*h*), (6), (7)(*a*), (*b*) substituted by FA 1993 Sch 6 paras 7, 25(1) with effect from the year 1993–94.
[3] Words in sub-s (2)(*b*), (9) inserted, and whole of sub-s (2)(*fa*) inserted, by FA 1995 s 74 Sch 17 para 9, with effect from the year 1995–96 (and apply to every settlement, wherever and whenever made or entered into).

678 Capital sums paid by body connected with settlement

(1) Where—

    (*a*) a capital sum is paid after 5th April 1981 to the settlor in a year of assessment by any body corporate connected with the settlement in that year; and
    (*b*) an associated payment has been or is made directly or indirectly to that body by the trustees of the settlement,

the capital sum shall, in accordance with subsection (2) below, be treated for the purposes of section 677 as having been paid to the settlor by the trustees of the settlement.

(2) A capital sum to which subsection (1) above applies shall—

    (*a*) to the extent to which the amount of that sum falls within the total of the associated payment or payments made up to the end of the year of assessment in which it is paid, be treated as having been paid to the settlor in that year;
    (*b*) to the extent to which the amount of that sum is not treated as paid to the settlor in that year and falls within the total of the associated payment or payments made up to the end of the next following year (less what was taken into account under this subsection in relation to that sum in the previous year), be treated as having been paid to the settlor in the next following year,

and so on for each subsequent year, taking the references in paragraph (*b*) to the year mentioned in paragraph (*a*) as references to that and any other year before the subsequent year in question.

(3) In this section "associated payment", in relation to any capital sum paid to the settlor by a body corporate, means—

(a) any capital sum paid to that body by the trustees of the settlement; and

(b) any other sum paid or asset transferred to that body by those trustees which is not paid or transferred for full consideration in money or money's worth,

being a sum paid or asset transferred in the five years ending or beginning with the date on which the capital sum is paid to the settlor.

(4) For the purposes of this section any capital sum paid by a body corporate, and any associated payment made to a body corporate, at a time when it is, within the meaning of section 416, associated with another body corporate may be treated as paid by or made to that other body corporate.

(5) In this section "capital sum" has the same meaning as in section 677; and any question whether a capital sum has been paid to the settlor by a body corporate or to a body corporate by the trustees shall be determined in the same way as any question under that section whether a capital sum has been paid to the settlor by the trustees.

(6) Subsection (1) above does not apply to any sum paid to the settlor by way of loan or repayment of a loan if—

(a) the whole of the loan is repaid within 12 months of the date on which it was made; and

(b) the period for which amounts are outstanding in respect of loans made to the settlor by that or any other body corporate connected with the settlement, or by him to that or any other such body, in any period of five years does not exceed 12 months.

(7) ...¹

Commentary—*Simon's Direct Tax Service* C4.322.
Revenue Internal Guidance—Company Taxation Manual COT6637 ("income" under sub-s(9)(a)(ii) is not confined to taxable income; the settlor's current account could be the source of capital payments; unpaid remuneration is regarded as the first source of withdrawals).
COT6638, 6639 (meaning of loans and repayment of loans).
Definitions—"Body corporate connected with settlement", s 682A(2); "settlement", s 660G(1); "settlor", s 660G(1); "year of assessment", s 832(1).
Amendments—¹ Sub-s (7) repealed by FA 1995 s 74 Sch 17 para 10, with effect from the year 1995–96 (and this amendment applies to every settlement, wherever and whenever made or entered into).

679 Application of Chapter III to settlements by two or more settlors

Commentary—*Simon's Direct Tax Service* C4.304, 324, 376.
Amendments—Section repealed by FA 1995 Sch 29 Pt VIII(8), with effect from the year 1995–96.

680 Power to obtain information for purposes of Chapter III

Commentary—*Simon's Direct Tax Service* C4.337.
Amendments—Section repealed by FA 1995 Sch 29 Pt VIII(8), with effect from the year 1995–96.

681 Interpretation of Chapter III

Commentary—*Simon's Direct Tax Service* C4.302, 303, 305.
Amendments—Section repealed by FA 1995 Sch 29 Pt VIII(8), with effect from the year 1995–96.

682 Ascertainment of undistributed income

(1) For the purposes of this Chapter, income arising under a settlement in any year of assessment shall be deemed not to have been distributed if and to the extent that it exceeds the aggregate amount of—

(a) the sums, excluding all payments of interest, paid in that year by the trustees of the settlement to any persons (not being a body corporate connected with the settlement and not being the trustees of another settlement made by the settlor or the trustees of the settlement) in such manner that they fall to be treated in that year, otherwise than by virtue of section 677, as the income of those persons for the purposes of income tax, or would fall to be so treated if those persons were domiciled, resident and ordinarily resident in the United Kingdom and the sums had been paid to them there, and

(b) subject to subsections (2) to (5) below, any expenses of the trustees of the settlement paid in that year which, in the absence of any express provision of the settlement, would be properly chargeable to income, in so far as such expenses are not included in the sums mentioned in paragraph (a) above, and

(c) in a case where the trustees of the settlement are trustees for charitable purposes, the amount by which any income arising under the settlement in that year in respect of which exemption from tax may be granted under section 505 exceeds the aggregate amount of any such sums or expenses as are mentioned in paragraphs (a) and (b) above paid in that year which are properly chargeable to that income.

(2) Subsection (1)(b) above shall apply to any interest paid by the trustees of the settlement subject to subsections (3) to (6) below.

(3) If no sums within subsection (1)(*a*) were paid to any person other than the settlor, or the wife or husband of the settlor, the whole of any interest paid by the trustees of the settlement shall be excluded from subsection (1)(*b*) above.

(4) If any sum was so paid, there shall be excluded from subsection (1)(*b*) above a fraction—

$$\frac{A - B}{A}$$

of any interest paid by the trustees of the settlement where—

A is the whole of the income arising under the settlement in the year of assessment, less the sums referred to in subsection (1)(*b*) above apart from subsections (2), (3) and (5) of this section; and

B is so much of the sums within subsection (1)(*a*) above as is paid to persons other than the settlor, or the wife or husband of the settlor.

(5) Subsections (2) to (4) above shall not apply to interest in respect of which relief from tax is allowable under any provision of the Income Tax Acts or to interest payable to the settlor or the wife or husband of the settlor if living with the settlor.

(6) Nothing in subsections (2) to (5) above shall be construed as affecting the liability to tax of the person receiving or entitled to the interest.

Commentary—*Simon's Direct Tax Service* **C4.324.**
Simon's Tax Cases—s 682(1)(*b*), *Piratin v IRC* [1981] STC 441*.
Definitions—"Body corporate connected with settlement", s 682A(2); "income arising under a settlement", s 660G(3), (4); "the Income Tax Acts", s 831(1)(*b*); "interest", s 832(1); "settlement", s 660G(1); "settlor", s 660G(1); "tax", s 832(3); "United Kingdom", s 830(1); "year of assessment", s 832(1).

[682A Supplementary provisions

(1) The provisions of sections 660E to 660G apply for the purposes of this Chapter as they apply for the purposes of Chapter IA.

(2) For the purposes of this Chapter, a body corporate shall be deemed to be connected with a settlement in any year of assessment if at any time in that year—

(*a*) it is a close company (or only not a close company because it is not resident in the United Kingdom) and the participators then include the trustees of the settlement; or

(*b*) it is controlled (within the meaning of section 840) by a company falling within paragraph (*a*) above.][1]

Definitions—"Settlement", s 660G(3), (4); "year of assessment", s 832(1).
Amendments—[1] Section inserted by FA 1995 s 74, Sch 17 para 11, with effect from the year 1995–96 (and applies to every settlement wherever and whenever made or entered into).

[CHAPTER IC
LIABILITY OF TRUSTEES][1]

Revenue Interpretation RI 199—
The taxation of Schedule F income received by trustees after 6 April 1999.
Amendments—[1] Heading substituted by FA 1995 s 74, Sch 17 para 12, with effect from the year 1995–96 (see further the introductory notes to Part XV).

683–685

Commentary—*Simon's Direct Tax Service* **C4.381, 382, 383, 384.**
Amendments—Sections repealed: see the introductory notes to Part XV.

686 [Accumulation and discretionary trusts: special rates of tax][12]

(1) So far as income arising to trustees is income to which this section applies it shall [be chargeable to income tax [at the rate applicable in accordance with subsection (1AA) below][4], instead of at the basic rate or, in accordance with [section 1A][7], at the lower rate [or the Schedule F ordinary rate][4].

[(1AA) The rate applicable in accordance with this subsection is—

(*a*) in the case of so much of any income to which this section applies as is Schedule F type income, the Schedule F trust rate; and

(*b*) in the case of any other income to which this section applies, the rate applicable to trusts.][11]

[(1A) [In relation to any year of assessment for which income tax is charged—

(*a*) the Schedule F trust rate shall be 25 per cent, and

(*b*) the rate applicable to trusts shall be 34 per cent,

or, in either case, such other rate as Parliament may determine.][4]

[For the purposes of assessments][4] for the year 1993–94 and in relation to years of assessment for which tax at the basic rate and the additional rate was separately chargeable, references to the charging of income with tax at the rate applicable to trusts shall be taken to include references to the charging of income with tax both at the basic rate and at the additional rate.][5]

(2) This section applies to income arising to trustees in any year of assessment so far as it—

(*a*) is income which is to be accumulated or which is payable at the discretion of the trustees or any other person (whether or not the trustees have power to accumulate it); and

[(*b*) is not, before being distributed, either—

(i) the income of any person other than the trustees, or

(ii) treated for any of the purposes of the Income Tax Acts as the income of a settlor; and]⁶

[(*c*) is not income arising under a trust established for charitable purposes only or[, subject to sub-s (6A) below,]¹³ income from investments, deposits or other property held—

(i) for the purposes of a fund or scheme established for the sole purpose of providing relevant benefits within the meaning of section 612; or

(ii) for the purposes of a personal pension scheme (within the meaning of section 630) which makes provision only for benefits such as are mentioned in section 633; and]¹

(*d*) ...¹⁰

[(2AA) The rate at which income tax is chargeable on so much of any income arising to trustees in any year of assessment as—

(*a*) is income to which this section applies, and

(*b*) is treated in accordance with section 689B as applied in defraying the expenses of the trustees in that year which are properly chargeable to income (or would be so chargeable but for any express provisions of the trust),

shall be the rate at which it would be chargeable on that income apart from this section, instead of the rate applicable to trusts [or the Schedule F trust rate (as the case may be)]¹¹.]¹⁰

[(2A) For the purposes of this section where—

(*a*) any trustees have expenses in any year of assessment (''management expenses'') which are properly chargeable to income or would be so chargeable but for any express provisions of the trust, and

(*b*) there is income arising to them in that year (''the untaxed income'') which does not bear income tax for that year by reason wholly or partly of the trustees not having been resident in the United Kingdom or being deemed under any arrangements under section 788, or any arrangements having effect by virtue of that section, to have been resident in a territory outside the United Kingdom,

there shall be disregarded for the purposes of [subsection (2AA)]¹⁰ above such part of the management expenses as bears the same proportion to all those expenses as the untaxed income bears to all the income arising to the trustees in that year.]⁵

[(2B) For the purposes of subsection (2A) above where the income tax borne by any income arising to trustees is limited in accordance with section 128 of the Finance Act 1995 (limit on income chargeable on non-residents), the income arising to the trustees which shall be taken not to bear tax by reason wholly or partly of their not having been resident in the United Kingdom shall include so much of any income arising to them as—

(*a*) is excluded income within the meaning of that section; and

(*b*) is not income which is treated for the purposes of subsection (1)(*b*) of that section as income the tax on which is deducted at source.]⁸

(3), (4) ...²

(5) ...³

[(5A) In this section ''Schedule F type income'', in relation to trustees, means—

(*a*) income chargeable under Schedule F;

(*b*) income to which section 1A applies by virtue of its being equivalent foreign income falling within subsection (3)(*b*) of that section and chargeable under Case V of Schedule D;

(*c*) a qualifying distribution whose amount or value is determined in accordance with section 233(1A);

(*d*) a non-qualifying distribution, within the meaning of section 233(1B);

(*e*) income treated as arising to the trustees by virtue of section 249(6)(*b*);

(*f*) income treated as received by the trustees by virtue of section 421(1)(*a*);

(*g*) any amount which, by virtue of section 686A, is treated for the purposes of the Tax Acts as if it were income to which this section applies.]¹¹

(6) In this section ''trustees'' does not include personal representatives; but where personal representatives, on or before the completion of the administration of the estate, pay to trustees any sum representing income which, if personal representatives were trustees within the meaning of this section, would be income to which this section applies, that sum shall be deemed to be paid to the trustees as income and to have borne income tax at the applicable rate.

This subsection shall be construed as if it were contained in Part XVI.

[(6A) The exemptions provided for by subsection (2)(*c*) above in relation to income from investments, deposits or other property held as mentioned in sub-paragraph (i) or (ii) of that paragraph do not apply to income derived from investments, deposits or other property held as a member of a property investment LLP.]¹³

Commentary—*Simon's Direct Tax Service* **C4.203.**
Concessions B18—Relief in respect of payment made by discretionary trustees to a beneficiary out of trust income arising from a foreign possession.
A93—Payments from offshore trusts to minor, unmarried child of settlor: claim by settlor for credit for tax paid by trustees. Trust returns must be supported by relevant certificates and details of payments to beneficiaries and tax paid at the applicable rate if claim to succeed.
Statement of Practice SP 4/93—Discretionary payments through trustees out of income of residuary estate: beneficiaries' entitlement to repayment of tax or liability to further tax: Revenue to open cases from the year 1986–87.
Revenue Interpretation RI 162—Exclusion from this section of income arising to a trust where a beneficiary has an indefeasibly vested interest in capital and no other person is entitled to receive the income.
RI 163—Capitalised income from mineral leases and from timber cropping is not an accumulation for purposes of this section and is thus not chargeable at rate applicable to trusts.
RI 199—Taxation of Schedule F income received by trustees from 6 April 1999.
Simon's Tax Cases—s 686(1), *IRC v Regent Trust Co Ltd* [1980] STC 140*.
s 686(2), *IRC v Berrill* [1981] STC 784*; *Carver v Duncan Bosanquet v Allen* [1985] STC 356*.
s 686(2)(*c*), *Clarke v British Telecom Pension Scheme Trustees* [2000] STC 222.
s 686(2)(*d*), *Carver v Duncan Bosanquet v Allen* [1984] STC 556*.
Definitions—"Basic rate", s 832(1); "the Income Tax Acts", s 831(1)(*b*); "lower rate", s 832(1); "rate applicable to trusts", s 832(1); "Schedule F ordinary rate", s 832(1); "Schedule F trust rate", s 832(1); "year of assessment", s 832(1).
Cross references—See TA 1988 s 186(11) (subject to specified conditions, this section not to apply to dividends received by the trustees of an approved profit sharing Scheme).
TA 1988 s 233(1A), (1B) (non-resident discretionary trusts: rates at which qualifying and non-qualifying distributions are chargeable to tax from the year of assessment 1993–94).
TA 1988 s 246D(4) (treatment of foreign income dividend received by trustees of discretionary trust).
TA 1988 s 249(6) (liability to additional rate tax of additional share capital issued to trustees in respect of shares in a company).
TA 1988 s 469(9) (this section not to apply to certain unit trust schemes).
TA 1988 Sch 5AA para 7 (with certain exceptions, income arising to trustees in accordance with that Schedule (certain disposals of futures or options to be charged as income under Schedule D Case VI) is to be treated as income to which this section applies).
TCGA 1992 s 5(2) (rate of capital gains tax in respect of gains accruing to trustees of discretionary trusts).
FA 1997 Sch 7 para 3 (relevant part of qualifying distribution to which FA 1997 Sch 7 applies (special treatment for certain distributions) to be treated as income to which this section applies).
Amendments—[1] Sub-s (2)(*c*) substituted by FA 1988 s 55(3), (4) with effect from 1 July 1988.
[2] Sub-ss (3), (4) repealed by FA 1989 Sch 17 Pt V in relation to accounting periods beginning after 31 March 1989.
[3] Sub-s (5) repealed by FA 1990 Sch 5 para 13 and Sch 19, Pt IV as regards a sum paid or credited after 5 April 1991.
[4] Sub-s (1), (1A) amended by F(No 2)A 1997 s 32(1)–(8), (10), (11). The substitution of words "For the purposes of assessments" in sub-s (1A) took effect from 6 April 1999; the other amendments took effect in relation to distributions made after 5 April 1999.
[5] Sub-ss (1A), (2A) inserted by FA 1993 Sch 6 paras 8, 25(1) with effect from the year 1993–94.
[6] Sub-s (2)(*b*) substituted by FA 1995 s 74, Sch 17 para 13, with effect from the year 1995–96, with effect for every settlement, wherever and whenever it was made or entered into.
[7] Words in sub-s (1) substituted by FA 1996 s 73(4), Sch 6 paras 13, 28 with effect from the year 1996–97.
[8] Sub-s (2B) inserted by FA 1996 s 73(4), Sch 6 paras 15, 28 with effect from the year 1996–97.
[9] Words in sub-s (1A) substituted by FA 1997 s 54(3), (4) with effect from the year 1997-98.
[10] Sub-s (2)(*d*) repealed, sub-s (2AA) inserted and words in sub-s (2A) substituted by FA 1997 Sch 7 paras 12(1), (2), (4), Sch 18 Pt VI(7) with effect from the year 1996-97.
[11] Sub-ss (1AA), (5A), and words in sub-s (2AA), inserted by F(No 2)A 1997 s 32(1)–(8), (10), (11) with effect in relation to distributions made after 5 April 1999.
[12] Headnote substituted by F(No 2)A 1997 s 32(1)–(8), (10), (11) with effect in relation to distributions made after 5 April 1999.
[13] Words in sub-s (2)(*c*), and sub-s (6A), inserted by FA 2001 s 76, Sch 25 para 3 with effect from 6 April 2001.

[686A Certain distributions to be treated as income to which section 686 applies

(1) This section applies where—

    (*a*) a qualifying distribution is made to trustees;
    (*b*) the trustees are not the trustees of a unit trust scheme; and
    (*c*) the qualifying distribution falls within subsection (2) below.

(2) A qualifying distribution falls within this subsection if it is a payment made by a company—

    (*a*) on the redemption, repayment or purchase of its own shares; or
    (*b*) on the purchase of rights to acquire its own shares.

(3) The relevant part of the distribution shall be treated for the purposes of the Tax Acts as if it were income to which section 686 applies.

(4) In subsection (3) above the reference to the relevant part of the distribution is a reference to so much (if any) of the distribution as—

    (*a*) is not income falling within paragraph (*a*) of section 686(2);
    (*b*) does not fall to be treated for the purposes of the Income Tax Acts as income of a settlor;
    (*c*) is not income arising under a trust established for charitable purposes; and
    (*d*) is not income from investments, deposits or other property held for any such purposes as are mentioned in sub-paragraph (i) or (ii) of section 686(2)(*c*).

(5) Subsection (6) of section 686 shall apply for the purposes of this section as it applies for the purposes of that section.][1]

Amendments—[1] This section inserted by F(No 2)A 1997 s 32(9), (11) with effect in relation to distributions made after 5 April 1999.

687 Payments under discretionary trusts

[(1) Where in any year of assessment trustees make a payment to any person in the exercise of a discretion, whether a discretion exercisable by them or by any other person, then if the payment—

(a) is for all the purposes of the Income Tax Acts income of the person to whom it is made (but would not be his income if it were not made to him), or

(b) is treated for those purposes as the income of the settlor by virtue of section 660B,

the following provisions of this section apply with respect to the payment in lieu of section 348 or 349(1).][10]

(2) The payment shall be treated as a net amount corresponding to a gross amount from which tax has been deducted at [the rate applicable to trusts][6] for the year in which the payment is made; and the sum treated as so deducted shall be treated—

(a) as income tax paid by the person to whom the payment is made [or, as the case may be, the settlor][10]; and

(b) so far as not set off under the following provisions of this section, as income tax assessable on the trustees.

(3) The following amounts, so far as not previously allowed, shall be set against the amount assessable (apart from this subsection) on the trustees in pursuance of subsection (2)(b) above—

[(a) the amount of any tax on income arising to trustees which (not being income the tax on which falls within paragraphs (a1) to (bc) below) is charged in pursuance of section 686 at the rate applicable to trusts or the Schedule F trust rate;][4]

[(a1) the amount of tax at a rate equal to the difference between the Schedule F ordinary rate and the Schedule F trust rate on any income of the trustees chargeable under Schedule F;][4]

[(a2) the amount of tax which, by virtue of section 233(1A), is charged, at a rate equal to the difference between the Schedule F ordinary rate and the Schedule F trust rate, on the amount or value of the whole or any part of any qualifying distribution included in the income arising to the trustees;][4]

[(aa) the amount of tax which, by virtue of section 233(1B), is charged, at a rate equal to the difference between the Schedule F ordinary rate and the Schedule F trust rate, on the amount or value of the whole or any part of any non–qualifying distribution included in the income arising to the trustees;][4]

[(aaa) ...][9]

[(b) the amount of tax at a rate equal to the difference between the Schedule F ordinary rate and the Schedule F trust rate on any sum treated, under section 249(6), as income of the trustees;][4]

[(bb) the amount of tax at a rate equal to the difference between the Schedule F ordinary rate and the Schedule F trust rate on any sum treated under section 421(1)(a) as income of the trustees;][4]

[(bc) the amount of tax at a rate equal to the difference between the Schedule F ordinary rate and the Schedule F trust rate on any sum treated under section 686A as income of the trustees;][4]

(c) ...[2]

(d) an amount of tax in respect of income found on a claim made by the trustees to have been available to them for distribution at the end of the year 1972–73, which shall be taken to be two-thirds of the net amount of that income;

(e) the amount of any tax on income arising to the trustees by virtue of section 761(1) and charged [at the rate applicable to trusts][8] by virtue of section 764; and

(f) the amount of any tax on annual profits or gains treated as received by trustees by virtue of section 714(2) or 716(3) of this Act or paragraph 2(2) or (3) of Schedule 22 to the Finance Act 1985 and charged [at the rate applicable to trusts][8] by virtue of section 720(5) of this Act or paragraph 8(1) of Schedule 23 to that Act;

(g) the amount of any tax on income which arose to the trustees by virtue of section 38(2) of the Finance Act 1974 (development gains) and charged at a rate equal to the basic rate and the additional rate in pursuance of section 43(1) of that Act;

[(h) the amount of any tax on an amount which is treated as income of the trustees by virtue of paragraph 4 of Schedule 4 and is charged to tax [at the rate applicable to trusts][8] by virtue of paragraph 17 of that Schedule;][1]

[(i) the amount of any tax on an amount which is treated as income of the trustees by virtue of paragraph 5 of Schedule 11 to the Finance Act 1989 and is charged to tax [at the rate applicable to trusts][8] by virtue of paragraph 11 of that Schedule;][1]

[(j) the amount of any tax on an amount which is treated as income of the trustees by virtue of paragraph 12 of Schedule 10 to the Finance Act 1990 and is charged to tax [at the rate applicable to trusts][8] by virtue of paragraph 19 of that Schedule;][5]

[(k) the amount of any tax on an amount which is treated as income of the trustees by virtue of paragraph 1 of Schedule 13 to the Finance Act 1996 and is charged to tax at the rate applicable to trusts by virtue of paragraph 6 of that Schedule.][7]

...[3]

(4) In this section "trustees" does not include personal representatives within the meaning of section 701(4).

[(5) References in this section to payments include payments in money or money's worth.][10]

Commentary—*Simon's Direct Tax Service* **C4.226.**
Concessions A68—Payments out of employee trusts which are taxed twice by reason of sub-s (2) above not applying to such payments; concessionary relief by way of repayment.
B18—Relief in respect of payment made by discretionary trustees to a beneficiary out of trust income arising from a foreign possession.

A93—Settlor of non-resident trust able to claim credit against his tax liability under this section for tax paid by trustees to the extent distribution made out of income which arose in six years before the end of the year of assessment.
Statement of Practice SP 3/86, para 7—Relief from UK tax under double taxation agreements in respect of payments made to non-residents from UK discretionary trusts or estates.
Definitions—"the Income Tax Acts", s 831(1)(*b*); "lower rate", s 832(1); "rate applicable to trusts", s 832(1); "Schedule F ordinary rate", s 832(1); "Schedule F trust rate", s 832(1); "tax", s 832(3); "year of assessment", s 832(1).
Cross references—See TA 1988 s 352 (payees right to obtain certificate of deduction where tax under this section is deducted).
TA 1988 s 469(9) (this section not to apply to certain unit trust schemes).
TA 1988 s 687A (additional provisions where payment made by a discretionary trust to a company after 1 July 1997; per s 687A(3), no repayment to be made of amount treated under sub-s (2) above as income tax paid by the company).
TA 1988 s 809 (double taxation relief in respect of payments under discretionary trusts).
Amendments—[1] Sub-s (3)(*h*), (*i*) inserted by FA 1989 s 96(2), (4) and apply where there is a disposal of a deep discount security or a transfer or a redemption of a deep gain security after 13 March 1989.
[2] Sub-s (3)(*c*) repealed by FA 1989 Sch 17 Pt V in relation to accounting periods beginning after 31 March 1989.
[3] Words following sub-s (3)(*i*) repealed by FA 1990 Sch 5 para 14 and Sch 19, Pt IV as regards an amount paid or credited after 5 April 1991.
[4] Sub-s (3)(*a*), (*aa*), (*b*) substituted, and sub-s (3)(*a1*), (*a2*), (*bb*)–(*bc*) inserted, by F(No 2)A 1997 s 34, Sch 4 para 15 with effect for the year 1999–00 and subsequent years of assessment.
[5] Sub-s (3)(*j*) inserted by virtue of FA 1993 s 79(2)(*b*) and Sch 6 para 9(2)(*d*) and has effect from the year 1993–94 by virtue of FA 1993 Sch 6 para 25(1).
[6] Words in sub- s (2) substituted by FA 1993 Sch 6 paras 9, 25(1) with effect from the year 1993–94.
[7] Sub-s (3)(*k*) inserted by FA 1996 ss 104, 105(1), Sch 14 para 35 with effect from the year 1996–97.
[8] Words in sub-s (3)(*e*) to (*j*) substituted by FA 1993 Sch 6 paras 9, 25(1) with effect from the year 1993–94.
[9] Sub-s (3)(*aaa*) repealed by F(No 2)A 1997 s 36(4), Sch 6 para 10, Sch 8 Pt II (11) with effect in relation to distributions made after 5 April 1999.
[10] Sub-s (1) substituted; words in sub-s (2)(*a*) inserted; and sub-s (5) inserted, by FA 1995 s 74, Sch 17 para 14, with effect from the year 1995–96 (and apply to every settlement wherever and whenever made or entered into).

[687A Payments to companies under section 687

(1) This section applies where —

    (*a*) trustees make a payment to a company;
    (*b*) section 687 applies to the payment; and
    (*c*) the company is chargeable to corporation tax and does not fall within subsection (2) below.

(2) A company falls within this subsection if it is —

    (*a*) a charity, as defined in section 506(1);
    (*b*) a body mentioned in section 507 (heritage bodies); or
    (*c*) an Association of a description specified in section 508 (scientific research organisations).

(3) Where this section applies —

    (*a*) none of the following provisions, namely —

        (i) section 7(2),
        (ii) section 11(3),
        (iii) paragraph 5(1) of Schedule 16,

    shall apply in the case of the payment;
    (*b*) the payment shall be left out of account in calculating the profits of the company for the purposes of corporation tax; and
    (*c*) no repayment shall be made of the amount treated under section 687(2) as income tax paid by the company in the case of repayment.

(4) If the company is not resident in the United Kingdom, this section applies only in relation to so much (if any) of the payment as is comprised in the company's chargeable profits for the purposes of corporation tax.][1]

Definitions— "Company", s 832(1), (2).
Amendments—[1] This section inserted by F(No 2)A 1997 s 27 with effect in relation to payments made by trustees to companies after 1 July 1997.

688 Schemes for employees and directors to acquire shares

Where under a scheme set up to comply with section 153(4)(*b*) of the Companies Act 1985 or Article 163(4)(*b*) of the Companies (Northern Ireland) Order 1986 (financial assistance for company employees and salaried directors acquiring shares) trustees receive interest from such employees or directors then, if and so far as the scheme requires an equivalent amount to be paid by way of interest by the trustees to the company, the trustees shall be exempt from tax under Case III of Schedule D on that interest received by them.

Commentary—*Simon's Direct Tax Service* B5.210.
Definitions—"Company", s 832(1), (2); "interest", s 832(1); "Schedule D", s 18(1); "tax", s 832(3).

689 Recovery from trustees of discretionary trusts of higher rate tax due from beneficiaries

Commentary—*Simon's Direct Tax Service* C4.203.
Amendments—This section repealed by FA 1995 s 74, Sch 17 para 15, Sch 29 Pt VIII(8), with effect from the year 1995–96.

[CHAPTER ID

TRUST MANAGEMENT EXPENSES][1]

Revenue Interpretation RI 199—The taxation of Schedule F income after 6 April 1999.
Revenue Internal Guidance—Trust manual TM 3260-3290 (trustees' expenses prior to enactment of this chapter).
Amendments—[1]Chapter I inserted by FA 1996 s 73(4), Sch 6 paras 16, 28 with effect from the year 1996–97.

[689A Disregard of expenses where beneficiary non-resident

(1) This section applies where—

(*a*) there is income ("the distributed income") arising to trustees in any year of assessment which (before being distributed) is income of a person ("the beneficiary") other than the trustees;

(*b*) the trustees have any expenses in that year ("the management expenses") which are properly chargeable to that income or would be so chargeable but for any express provisions of the trust; and

(*c*) the beneficiary is not liable to income tax on an amount of the distributed income ("the untaxed income") by reason wholly or partly of—

(i) his not having been resident in the United Kingdom, or

(ii) his being deemed under any arrangements under section 788, or any arrangements having effect by virtue of that section, to have been resident in a territory outside the United Kingdom.

(2) Where this section applies, there shall be disregarded in computing the income of the beneficiary for the purposes of the Income Tax Acts such part of the management expenses as bears the same proportion to all those expenses as the untaxed income bears to the distributed income.

(3) For the purpose of computing the proportion mentioned in subsection (2) above, the amounts of the distributed income and of the untaxed income shall not, in either case, include so much (if any) of the income as is equal to the amount of income tax, or of any foreign tax, chargeable on the trustees (by way of deduction or otherwise) in respect of that income.

(4) In subsection (3) above, "foreign tax" means any tax which is—

(*a*) of a similar character to income tax; and

(*b*) imposed by the laws of a territory outside the United Kingdom.

(5) For the purposes of this section, where the income tax chargeable on any person is limited in accordance with section 128 of the Finance Act 1995 (limit on income chargeable on non-residents), the income of that person on which he is not liable to tax by reason of not having been resident in the United Kingdom shall be taken to include so much of any income of his as—

(*a*) is excluded income within the meaning of that section; and

(*b*) is not income which is treated for the purposes of subsection (1)(*b*) of that section as income the tax on which is deducted at source.][1]

Commentary—*Simon's Direct Tax Service* **C4.203, 208.**
Definitions—"Income Tax Acts", s 831(1); "United Kingdom", s 830.
Amendments—[1]This section inserted by FA 1996 s 73(4), Sch 6 paras 16, 28 with effect from the year 1996–97.

[689B Order in which expenses to be set against income

(1) The expenses of any trustees in any year of assessment, so far as they are properly chargeable to income (or would be so chargeable but for any express provisions of the trust), shall be treated—

(*a*) as set against so much (if any) of any income as is income falling within subsection (2)[, (2A)][2] or (3) below before being set against other income; and

(*b*) as set against so much (if any) of any income as is income falling within subsection (2) [or (2A)][2] below before being set against income falling within subsection (3) below [and

(*c*) as set against so much (if any) of any income as is income falling within subsection (2) below before being set against income falling within subsection (2A) below][2].

(2) Income falls within this subsection if it is—

[(*za*) so much of the income of the trustees as is income chargeable under Schedule F;][2]

(*a*) so much of the income of the trustees as is income the amount or value of which is determined in accordance with section 233(1A);

[(*aa*) so much of the income of the trustees as is a non–qualifying distribution, within the meaning of section 233(1B);][2]

(*b*) income which is treated as having arisen to the trustees by virtue of section ...[3] 249(6); or

(*c*) income which is treated as received by the trustees by virtue of section 421(1)(*a*).

[(2A) Income falls within this subsection if it is income to which section 1A applies by virtue of its being equivalent foreign income falling within subsection (3)(*b*) of that section and chargeable under Case V of Schedule D.][2]

(3) Income falls within this subsection if it is income to which section 1A applies but which does not fall within subsection (2) [or (2A)][2] above.

(4) This section has effect—

(*a*) subject to sections 686(2A) and 689A, but

(*b*) notwithstanding anything in section 1A(5) and (6).][1]

Commentary—*Simon's Direct Tax Service* **C4.203, 208.**
Definitions—''Year of assessment'', s 832(1).
Amendments—¹ This section inserted by FA 1996 Sch 6 para 16, 28 with effect from the year 1996–97.
² Sub-s (2A), and words in sub-ss (1), (2), (3), inserted by F(No 2)A 1997 s 34, Sch 4 para 16 with effect for the year 1999–00
 and subsequent years of assessment,
³ Words in sub-s (2)(*b*) repealed by F(No 2)A 1997 s 36(4), Sch 6 para 11, Sch 8 Pt II (11) with effect in relation to distributions
 made after 5 April 1999.

CHAPTER V
MAINTENANCE FUNDS FOR HISTORIC BUILDINGS

Cross references—See TA 1988 s 693 (severance for purposes of this Chapter of a settlement which is partly for benefit of
maintenance of historic and qualifying properties and partly for benefit of other purposes).

690 Schedule 4 directions

In this Chapter ''a Schedule 4 direction'' means a direction under paragraph 1 of Schedule 4 to the
Inheritance Tax Act 1984 (maintenance funds for historic buildings); and any reference in this
Chapter to paragraph 1 or Schedule 4 is a reference to that paragraph or that Schedule, as the case
may be.

Commentary—*Simon's Direct Tax Service* **C1.419, C4.371; I7.542.**

691 Certain income not to be income of settlor etc

(1) This section applies to any settlement in relation to which a Schedule 4 direction has effect.

(2) The trustees of the settlement may elect that this subsection shall have effect in relation to any
year of assessment, and if they do so—

 (*a*) any income arising in that year from the property comprised in the settlement which, apart
 from this subsection, would be treated by virtue of this Part as income of the settlor shall not be so
 treated; and
 (*b*) no sum applied in that year out of the property for the purposes mentioned in paragraph
 3(1)(*a*)(i) of Schedule 4 (maintenance etc of qualifying property) shall be treated for any purposes
 of the Income Tax Acts as the income of any person—

  (i) by virtue of any interest of that person in, or his occupation of, the qualifying property in
  question; or
  (ii) by virtue of section 677.

(3) Where income arising from the property comprised in the settlement in a year of assessment for
which no election is made under subsection (2) above is treated by virtue of this Part as income of
the settlor, paragraph (*b*) of that subsection shall have effect in relation to any sums in excess of that
income which are applied in that year as mentioned in that paragraph.

(4) Any election under subsection (2) above shall be by notice to the Board in such form as the
Board may require and shall be made [on or before the first anniversary of the 31st January next
following]¹ the year of assessment to which it relates.

(5) Where—

 (*a*) for part of a year of assessment a Schedule 4 direction has effect and circumstances obtain by
 virtue of which income arising from property comprised in the settlement is treated as income of
 a settlor under this Part; and
 (*b*) for the remainder of that year either no such direction has effect, or no such circumstances
 obtain, or both,

subsections (1) to (4) above shall apply as if each of those parts were a separate year of assessment
and separate elections may be made accordingly.

Commentary—*Simon's Direct Tax Service* **C4.340; I7.541.**
Definitions—''The Board'', s 832(1); ''the Income Tax Acts'', s 831(1)(*b*); ''notice'', s 832(1); ''Schedule 4 direction'', s 690;
''year of assessment'', s 832(1).
Cross references—See TCGA 1992 s 79(8) (consequence of trustees' election under sub-s (2) above for purposes of tax on
chargeable gains).
Amendments—¹ Words in sub-s (4) substituted by FA 1996 s 135(1), (2), Sch 21 para 19 with effect from the year 1996–97.

692 Reimbursement of settlor

(1) This section applies to income arising from settled property in respect of which a Schedule 4
direction has effect if the income—

 (*a*) is treated by virtue of this Part as income of the settlor, and
 (*b*) is applied in reimbursing the settlor for expenditure incurred by him for a purpose within
 paragraph 3(1)(*a*)(i) of Schedule 4,

and if that expenditure is (or would apart from the reimbursement be) deductible in computing [either
the profits of a trade carried on by the settlor or the profits of a Schedule A business so carried on].¹

TA 1988

(2) Income to which this section applies shall not be treated as reducing the expenditure deductible in computing the profits referred to in subsection (1) above, and shall not be regarded as income of the settlor otherwise than by virtue of this Part.

Commentary—*Simon's Direct Tax Service* **C4.371, I7.541.**
Note—For the Inheritance Tax Act 1984 Sch 4, see Part II of this Handbook..
Definitions—''Schedule A business'', s 832(1); ''Schedule 4 direction'', s 690; ''trade'', s 832(1).
Amendments—¹ Words in sub-s (1) substituted by FA 1995 s 39, Sch 6 para 26, with effect from the year 1995–96, and so far as they relate to corporation tax, for accounting periods ending after 30 March 1995; however, this amendment does not apply in respect of certain sources of income which ceased during the year 1995–96: see FA 1995 s 39(5).

693 Severance of settled property for certain purposes

Where settled property in respect of which a Schedule 4 direction has effect constitutes part only of the property comprised in a settlement, it and the other property shall be treated as comprised in separate settlements for the purposes of sections 27 and 380 to 387 and this Part.

Commentary—*Simon's Direct Tax Service* **C4.340; I7.541.**
Note—For the Inheritance Tax Act 1984 Sch 4, see Part II of this Handbook.
Definition—''Schedule 4 direction'', s 690.

694 Trustees chargeable to income tax at 30 per cent in certain cases

(1) If in the case of a settlement in respect of which a Schedule 4 direction has effect—

  (a) any of the property comprised in the settlement (whether capital or income) is applied otherwise than as mentioned in paragraph 3(1)(a)(i) or (ii) of Schedule 4; or
  (b) any of that property on ceasing to be comprised in the settlement devolves otherwise than on any such body or charity as is mentioned in paragraph 3(1)(a)(ii) of that Schedule; or
  (c) the direction ceases to have effect;

then, unless subsection (6) below applies, income tax shall be charged under this section in respect of the settlement.

(2) Subject to subsection (3) below, tax chargeable under this section shall be charged ...¹ on the whole of the income which has arisen in the relevant period from the property comprised in the settlement and has not been applied (or accumulated and then applied) as mentioned in paragraph 3(1)(a)(i) or (ii) of Schedule 4.

In this subsection ''the relevant period'' means, if tax has become chargeable under this section in respect of the settlement on a previous occasion, the period since the last occasion and, in any other case, the period since the settlement took effect.

[(2A) The rate at which tax is charged under this section shall be equivalent to the higher rate of income tax for the year of assessment during which the charge arises, reduced by the [amount of the rate applicable to trusts]³ for that year.]²

(3) Tax shall not be chargeable under this section in respect of income which by virtue of [Chapter IA]⁴ of this Part is treated as income of the settlor; but where income arising in any year of assessment is exempted by this subsection any sums applied in that year as mentioned in paragraph 3(1)(a)(i) or (ii) of Schedule 4 shall be treated as paid primarily out of that income and only as to the excess, if any, out of income not so exempted.

(4) Tax charged under this section shall be in addition to any tax chargeable apart from this section and—

  (a) the persons assessable and chargeable with tax under this section shall be the trustees of the settlement; and
  (b) all the provisions of the Income Tax Acts relating to assessments and to the collection and recovery of income tax shall, so far as applicable, apply to the charge, assessment, collection and recovery of tax under this section.

(5) Tax shall also be chargeable in accordance with subsections (1) to (4) above if—

  (a) any of the property comprised in a settlement to which subsection (1) above applies, on ceasing at any time to be comprised in the settlement, devolves on any such body or charity as is referred to in paragraph (b) of that subsection, and
  (b) at or before that time an interest under the settlement is or has been acquired for a consideration in money or money's worth by that or another such body or charity;

but for the purposes of this subsection any acquisition from another such body or charity shall be disregarded.

(6) Tax shall not be chargeable under this section in respect of a settlement on an occasion when the whole of the property comprised in it is transferred tax-free into another settlement; but on the first occasion on which tax becomes chargeable under this section in respect of a settlement (''the current settlement'') comprising property which was previously comprised in another settlement or settlements and has become comprised in the current settlement as a result of, or of a series of, tax-free transfers, the relevant period for the purposes of subsection (2) above shall, as respects that property, be treated as having begun—

  (a) on the last occasion on which tax became chargeable under this section in respect of the other settlement or any of the other settlements; or (*b*) if there has been no such occasion, when the other settlement or the first of the other settlements took effect.

(7) For the purposes of subsection (6) above, property is transferred tax-free from one settlement into another if either—

(*a*) it ceases to be comprised in the first-mentioned settlement and becomes comprised in the other settlement in circumstances such that by virtue of paragraph 9(1) of Schedule 4 there is (or, but for paragraph 9(4), there would be) no charge to capital transfer tax or inheritance tax in respect of the property; or

(*b*) both immediately before and immediately after the transfer it is property in respect of which a Schedule 4 direction has effect.

Commentary—*Simon's Direct Tax Service* **C4.342; I7.546.**
Note—For the Inheritance Tax Act 1984 Sch 4, see Part II of this Handbook.
Definitions—"Higher rate", s 832(1); "the Income Tax Acts", s 831(1)(*b*); "rate applicable to trusts", s 832(1); "Schedule 4 direction", s 690; "tax", s 832(3).
Amendments—¹ Words in sub-s (2) repealed by FA 1988 s 24(3) and Sch 14 Pt IV.
² Sub-s (2A) inserted by FA 1988 s 24(3).
³ Words in sub-s (2A) substituted by FA 1993 Sch 6 paras 10, 25(1) with effect from the year 1993–94.
⁴ Words in sub-s (3) substituted by FA 1995 s 74, Sch 17 para 16, with effect from the year 1995–96 (and apply to every settlement wherever and whenever made or entered into).

PART XVI
ESTATES OF DECEASED PERSONS IN COURSE OF ADMINISTRATION

Cross references—See TMA 1970 s 46B(4) (any question as to the application of this Part to be determined by the Special Commissioners);
IT (Entertainers and Sportsmen) Regulations, SI 1987/530 reg 12(4) (Pt XIII, Ch III (ss 555–558)) of this Act to apply instead of this Part with regard to certain payments to entertainers.
TA 1988 s 246D(3) (foreign income dividend received by personal representatives of a deceased person to be treated as income of deceased).
TA 1988 s 249(5) (s 249(5) to be construed as if contained in this Part).
TA 1988 s 547(1) (a gain treated as arising in connection with life and capital redemption policies and life annuity contracts to form part of the aggregate income of deceased's estate for the purposes of this Part in certain circumstances).
TA 1988 s 686(6) (s 686(6) to be construed as if it were contained in this Part).
TA 1988 s 701 (interpretation of this Part).
TA 1988 s 702 (adaptation of this Part in its application to Scotland).

695 Limited interests in residue

(1) The following provisions of this section shall have effect in relation to a person who, during the period commencing on the death of a deceased person and ending on the completion of the administration of his estate ("the administration period") or during a part of that period, has a limited interest in the residue of the estate or in a part thereof.

(2) When any sum has been paid during the administration period in respect of that limited interest, the amount of that sum shall, ...², be deemed for all tax purposes to have been paid to that person as income for the year of assessment in which that sum was paid or, in the case of a sum paid in respect of an interest that has ceased, for the last year of assessment in which it was subsisting.

[(3) Where, on the completion of the administration of the estate, there is an amount which remains payable in respect of that limited interest, that amount shall be deemed for all tax purposes to have been paid to that person as income for the year of assessment in which the administration period ends or, in the case of a sum which is deemed to be paid in respect of an interest that ceased before the end of that period, for the last year of assessment in which that interest was subsisting.]²

(4) Any amount which is deemed to have been paid to that person as income for any year by virtue of this section shall—

(*a*) in the case of a United Kingdom estate, be deemed to be income of such an amount as would after deduction of income tax for that year be equal to the amount deemed to have been so paid, and to be income which has borne income tax at the [applicable rate]¹; and

(*b*) in the case of a foreign estate, be deemed to be income of the amount deemed to have been so paid, and shall be chargeable to income tax under Case IV of Schedule D as if it were income arising from securities in a place out of the United Kingdom.

(5) Where—

(*a*) a person has been charged to income tax for any year by virtue of this section in respect of an amount deemed to have been paid to him as income in respect of an interest in a foreign estate ("the deemed income"), and

(*b*) any part of the aggregate income of that estate for that year has borne United Kingdom income tax by deduction or otherwise ("the aggregate income"),

the tax so charged on him shall, on proof of the facts on a claim, be reduced by an amount bearing the same proportion thereto as the amount of the deemed income which has borne United Kingdom income tax, less the tax so borne, bears to the amount of the aggregate income, less the tax so borne.

(6) Where relief has been given under subsection (5) above, such part of the amount in respect of which he has been charged to income tax as corresponds to the proportion mentioned in that subsection shall, for the purpose of computing his total income, be deemed to represent income of such an amount as would after deduction of income tax be equal to that part of the amount charged.

Commentary—*Simon's Direct Tax Service* C4.115, 117.
Concession A14—Relief or exemption from tax in respect of residuary income which is deemed to be received during the administration period of a deceased person's estate by a non-resident beneficiary.
Statement of Practice SP 3/86, para 8—Relief from UK tax under double taxation agreements in respect of payments made to non-residents from UK discretionary trusts or estates.
Definitions—"Administration period", s 701(13); "aggregate income", s 701(8); "applicable rate", s 701(3A); "basic rate", s 832(1); "foreign estate", s 701(10); "limited interest", s 701(3); "Schedule D", s 18(1); "tax", s 832(3); "total income", s 835(1); "United Kingdom", s 830(1); "United Kingdom estate", s 701(9); "year of assessment", s 832(1).
Cross references—See TA 1988 s 698(3) (application of sub-s (4)–(6) above to income payable upon exercise of a discretion from a residuary estate).
TA 1988 s 699A(3) (notwithstanding sub-s (4)(b) above certain payments to foreign estates deemed to have borne income tax at basic or lower rate).
Amendments—[1] Words in sub-s (4)(a) substituted by FA 1993 Sch 6 paras 11(1), 25(1) with effect from the year 1993–94.
[2] Words omitted from sub-s (2) repealed and sub-s (3) substituted by FA 1995 s 75, Sch 18 para 2, Sch 29, Pt VIII(10) with effect for any estate the administration of which is completed after 5 April 1995.

696 Absolute interests in residue

(1) The following provisions of this section shall have effect in relation to a person who, during the administration period or during a part of that period, has an absolute interest in the residue of the estate of a deceased person or in a part thereof.

(2) There shall be ascertained in accordance with section 697 the amount of the residuary income of the estate for each whole year of assessment, and for each broken part of a year of assessment, during which—

(a) the administration period was current, and
(b) that person had that interest;

and the amount so ascertained in respect of any year or part of a year or, in the case of a person having an absolute interest in a part of a residue, a proportionate part of that amount, is in this Part referred to as the "residuary income" of that person for that year of assessment.

[(3) When any sum has been paid during the administration period in respect of that absolute interest, that sum, except so far as it is excluded from the operation of this subsection, shall be deemed for all tax purposes to have been paid to that person as income for the year of assessment in which it was actually paid.][2]

[(3A) A payment shall be excluded from the operation of subsection (3) above to the extent (if any) that the aggregate of that sum and all the sums which—

(a) have been paid previously during the administration period in respect of that absolute interest, and
(b) fall under this section to be treated as paid to that person as income,

exceeds the aggregated income entitlement of that person for the year of assessment in which the sum is paid.][2]

[(3B) For the purposes of this section the aggregated income entitlement of that person for any year of assessment is the amount which would be the aggregate of the amounts received for that year of assessment and all previous years of assessment in respect of the interest if that person had a right in each year to receive, and had received—

(a) in the case of a United Kingdom estate, his residuary income for that year less income tax at the applicable rate for that year; and
(b) in the case of a foreign estate, his residuary income for that year.][2]

(4) In the case of a United Kingdom estate, any amount which is deemed to have been paid to that person as income for any year by virtue of subsection (3) above shall be deemed to be income of such an amount as would, after deduction of income tax for that year, be equal to the amount deemed to have been so paid, and to be income that has borne income tax at the [applicable rate][1].

[(5) Where, on the completion of the administration of the estate, the aggregate of all the sums which, apart from this subsection—

(a) have been paid during the administration period in respect of that absolute interest, and
(b) fall under this section to be treated as paid to that person as income,

is exceeded by the aggregated income entitlement of that person for the year of assessment in which the administration of the estate is completed, then an amount equal to the amount of the excess shall be treated for the purposes of subsections (3) to (4) above as having been actually paid, immediately before the end of the administration period, in respect of that interest.][3]

(6) In the case of a foreign estate, any amount which is deemed to have been paid to that person as income for any year by virtue of this section shall be deemed to be income of that amount and shall be chargeable to income tax under Case IV of Schedule D as if it were income arising from securities in a place out of the United Kingdom.

(7) Where—

(*a*) a person has been charged to income tax for any year by virtue of this section in respect of an amount deemed to have been paid to him as income in respect of an interest in a foreign estate (''the deemed income''), and

(*b*) any part of the aggregate income of that estate for that year has borne United Kingdom income tax by deduction or otherwise (''the aggregate income''),

the tax so charged on him shall, on proof of the facts on a claim, be reduced by an amount bearing the same proportion thereto as the amount of the deemed income which has borne United Kingdom income tax bears to the amount of the aggregate income.

(8) For the purposes of any charge to corporation tax under this section, the residuary income of a company shall be computed in the first instance by reference to years of assessment, and the residuary income for any such year shall be apportioned between the accounting periods (if more than one) comprising that year.

Commentary—*Simon's Direct Tax Service* **C4.115, 118, 124.**
Concession A14—Relief or exemption from tax in respect of residuary income which is deemed to be received during the administration period of a deceased person's estate by a non-resident beneficiary.
Statement of Practice SP 3/86, para 8—Relief from UK tax under double taxation agreements in respect of payments made to non-residents from UK discretionary trusts or estates.
Revenue Interpretation RI 170—Explains the transition to the provisions of this section as amended by FA 1995 Sch 18 (see also Amendments notes below) and confirms that payment of ''a sum'' does not necessarily mean a cash sum (see also TA 1988 s 701(12) below).
Definitions—''Absolute interest'', s 701(2); ''accounting periods'', s 834(1); ''administration period'', s 701(13); ''aggregate income'', s 701(8); ''applicable rate'', s 701(3A); ''basic rate'', s 832(1); ''company'', s 832(1), (2); ''foreign estate'', s 701(10); ''Schedule D'', s 18(1); ''tax'', s 832(3); ''United Kingdom'', s 830(1); ''United Kingdom estate'', s 701(9); ''year of assessment'', s 832(1).
Cross references—See TA 1988 s 697 (supplementary provisions).
TA 1988 s 698(1B), (2) (different persons with successive interests during the administration period: application of special provisions in relation to certain interests for purpose of sub-ss (3A)–(5) above).
TA 1988 s 699A(3) notwithstanding sub-s (6) above payments to foreign estates deemed to have borne income tax at basic and lower rate).
Amendments—[1] Words in sub-s (4) substituted by FA 1993 Sch 6 paras 11(1), 25(1) with effect from the year 1993–94.
[2] Sub-ss (3)–(3B) substituted for sub-s (3) as originally enacted, by FA 1995 s 75, Sch 18 para 3(1), (3), (4) in relation to any payment made after 5 April 1995 (where any sum is deemed by virtue of sub-s (3) as so amended to have been paid to any person as income for the year 1994–95 or any previous year of assessment, that sum shall be treated for the purposes of sub-ss (3A) and (5) as amended by FA 1995 Sch 18 para 3 as a sum actually paid in respect of that person's absolute interest in that year of assessment).
[3] Sub-s (5) substituted by FA 1995 s 75, Sch 18 para 3(2), (3), with effect for any estate the administration of which is completed after 5 April 1995.

697 Supplementary provisions as to absolute interests in residue

(1) The amount of the residuary income of an estate for any year of assessment shall be ascertained by deducting from the aggregate income of the estate for that year—

(*a*) the amount of any annual interest, annuity or other annual payment for that year which is a charge on residue and the amount of any payment made in that year in respect of any such expenses incurred by the personal representatives as such in the management of the assets of the estate as, in the absence of any express provision in a will, would be properly chargeable to income, but excluding any such interest, annuity or payment allowed or allowable in computing the aggregate income of the estate; and

(*b*) the amount of any of the aggregate income of the estate for that year to which a person has on or after assent become entitled by virtue of a specific disposition either for a vested interest during the administration period or for a vested or contingent interest on the completion of the administration.

[(1A) For the purpose of ascertaining under subsection (1) above the residuary income of an estate for any year, where the amount of the deductions falling to be made from the aggregate income of the estate for that year (including any falling to be made by virtue of this subsection) exceeds the amount of that income, the excess shall be carried forward and treated for that purpose as an amount falling to be deducted from the aggregate income of the estate for the following year.][1]

(2) In the event of its appearing, on the completion of the administration of an estate in the residue of which, or in a part of the residue of which, a person had an absolute interest at the completion of the administration, that the aggregate of the benefits received in respect of that interest does not amount to as much as the aggregate for all years of the residuary income of the person having that interest, [section 696 shall have effect as if the amount of the deficiency were to be applied in reducing the amount taken to be his residuary income for the year in which the administration of the estate is completed and, in so far as the deficiency exceeds that income, in reducing the amount taken to be his residuary income for the previous year, and so on.][2]

(3) In subsection (2) above ''benefits received'' in respect of an absolute interest means the following amounts in respect of all sums paid before, or payable on, the completion of the administration in respect of that interest, that is to say—

(*a*) as regards a sum paid before the completion of the administration, in the case of a United Kingdom estate such an amount as would, after deduction of income tax for the year of assessment in which that sum was paid, be equal to that sum, or in the case of a foreign estate the amount of that sum; and (*b*) as regards a sum payable on the completion of the administration, in the case of a United Kingdom estate such an amount as would, after deduction of income tax for the year of assessment in which the administration is completed, be equal to that sum, or in the case of a foreign estate the amount of that sum.

(4) In the application of subsection (2) above to a residue or a part of a residue in which a person other than the person having an absolute interest at the completion of the administration had an absolute interest at any time during the administration period, the aggregates mentioned in that subsection shall be computed in relation to those interests taken together, and the residuary income of that other person also shall be subject to reduction under that subsection.

Commentary—*Simon's Direct Tax Service* **C4.107, 118.**
Concession A13—If the deductions under this section are greater than the gross income of the estate, the excess is allowed as a deduction in computing the net income of the preceding or succeeding years for higher rate tax.
Definitions—"Absolute interest", s 701(2); "administration period", s 701(13); "aggregate income", s 701(8); "charge on residue", s 701(6); "foreign estate", s 701(10); "personal representatives", s 701(4); "specific disposition", s 701(5); "United Kingdom estate", s 701(9); "year of assessment", s 832(1).
Amendments—[1] Sub-s (1A) inserted by FA 1995 s 75, Sch 18 para 4(1), (3), with effect for ascertaining the residuary income of an estate for the year 1995–96 or any subsequent year of assessment.
[2] Words in sub-s (2) substituted by FA 1995 s 75, Sch 18 para 4(2), (3), with effect for any estate the administration of which is completed after 5 April 1995.

698 Special provisions as to certain interests in residue

(1) Where the personal representatives of a deceased person have as such a right in relation to the estate of another deceased person such that, if that right were vested in them for their own benefit, they would have an absolute or limited interest in the residue of that estate or in a part of that residue, they shall be deemed to have that interest notwithstanding that that right is not vested in them for their own benefit, and any amount deemed to be paid to them as income by virtue of this Part shall be treated as part of the aggregate income of the estate of the person whose personal representatives they are.

[(1A) Subsection (1B) below applies where—

(*a*) successively during the administration period there are different persons with interests in the residue of the estate of a deceased person or in parts of such a residue;
(*b*) the later interest or, as the case may be, each of the later interests arises or is created on the cessation otherwise than by death of the interest that precedes it; and
(*c*) the earlier or, as the case may be, earliest interest is a limited interest.][1]

[(1B) Where this subsection applies, this Part shall have effect in relation to any payment made in respect of any of the interests referred to in subsection (1A) above—

(*a*) as if all those interests were the same interest so that none of them is to be treated as having ceased on being succeeded by any of the others;
(*b*) as if (subject to paragraph (*c*) below) the interest which is deemed to exist by virtue of paragraph (*a*) above ("the deemed single interest") were an interest of—

(i) except in a case to which sub-paragraph (ii) below applies, the person in respect of whose interest or previous interest the payment is made;
(ii) in a case where the person entitled to receive the payment is any other person who has or has had an interest which is deemed to be comprised in the deemed single interest, that other person; and

(*c*) in so far as any of the later interests is an absolute interest as if, for the purposes of section 696(3A) to (5)—

(i) the earlier interest or interests had never existed and the absolute interest had always existed;
(ii) the sums (if any) which were deemed in relation to the earlier interest or interests to have been paid as income for any year of assessment to any of the persons entitled thereto were sums previously paid during the administration period in respect of the absolute interest; and
(iii) those sums were sums falling to be treated as sums paid as income to the person entitled to the absolute interest.][1]

[(2) Where successively during the administration period there are different persons with absolute interests in the residue of the estate of a deceased person or in parts of such a residue, the aggregate payments and aggregated income entitlement referred to in subsections (3A) and (3B) of section 696 shall be computed for the purposes of that section in relation to an absolute interest subsisting at any time ("the subsequent interest")—

(*a*) as if the subsequent interest and any previous absolute interest corresponding to the subsequent interest, or relating to any part of the residue to which the subsequent interest relates, were the same interest; and
(*b*) as if the residuary income for any year of the person entitled to the previous interest were residuary income of the person entitled to the subsequent interest and any amount deemed to be paid as income to the person entitled to the previous interest were an amount deemed to have been paid to the person entitled to the subsequent interest.][1]

(3) Where, upon the exercise of a discretion, any of the income of the residue of the estate of a deceased person for any period (being the administration period or a part of the administration period) would, if the residue had been ascertained at the commencement of that period, be properly payable to any person, or to another in his right, for his benefit, whether directly by the personal representatives or indirectly through a trustee or other person—

    (*a*) the amount of any sum paid pursuant to an exercise of the discretion in favour of that person shall be deemed for all tax purposes to have been paid to that person as income for the year of assessment in which it was paid; and

    (*b*) section 695(4) to (6) shall have effect in relation to an amount which is deemed to have been paid as income by virtue of paragraph (*a*) above.

Commentary—*Simon's Direct Tax Service* **C4.119, 120.**
Statement of Practice SP 4/93—Revenue will apply sub-s (3) above to discretionary payments *whenever* made and to all open cases from the year 1986–87.
Definitions—"Absolute interest", s 701(2); "administration period", s 701(13); "aggregate income", s 701(8); "applicable rate", s 701(3A); "basic rate", s 832(1); "foreign estate", s 701(10); "limited interest", s 701(3); "personal representatives", s 701(4); "tax", s 832(3); "United Kingdom estate", s 701(9); "year of assessment", s 832(1);
Amendments—[1] Sub-ss (1A), (1B), (2) substituted for sub-s (2) as originally enacted by FA 1995 s 75, Sch 18 para 5, with effect for any payment made after 5 April 1995 and, in so far as relating to the operation of s 695(3) or 696(5) *ante*, in relation to the administration of any estate which is completed after 5 April 1995.

[698A Taxation of income of beneficiaries at lower rate or at rates applicable to Schedule F income

(1) Subject to subsection (3) below, in so far as any income of any person is treated under this Part as having borne income tax at the lower rate, section 1A shall have effect as if that income were income to which that section applies otherwise than by virtue of the income being income chargeable under Schedule F.

(2) Subject to subsection (3) below, in so far as any income of any person is treated under this Part as having borne income tax at the Schedule F ordinary rate, that income shall be treated as if it were income chargeable under Schedule F.

(3) Subsections (1) and (2) above shall not apply to income paid indirectly through a trustee and treated by virtue of section 698(3) as having borne income tax at the lower rate or the Schedule F ordinary rate; but, subject to section 686(1), section 1A shall have effect as if the payment made to the trustee were income of the trustee—

    (*a*) to which section 1A applies by virtue of the income being chargeable under Schedule F, in the case of income treated as having borne tax at the Schedule F ordinary rate; and

    (*b*) to which section 1A applies otherwise than by virtue of the income being chargeable under Schedule F, in any other case.][1]

Commentary—*Simon's Direct Tax Service* **C4.108.**
Definitions—"Lower rate", s 832(1); "Schedule F ordinary rate", s 832(1).
Amendments—[1] This section (originally inserted by FA 1993 Sch 6 paras 11(2), 25(1) with effect from the year 1993–94), and headnote of section, substituted by F(No 2)A 1997 s 33(1), (11) with effect for the year 1999–00 and subsequent years of assessment".

699 Relief from higher rate tax for inheritance tax on accrued income

(1) Where any income, having accrued before the death of any person, is taken into account both—

    (*a*) in determining the value of his estate for the purposes of any inheritance tax chargeable on his death; and

    (*b*) in ascertaining for the purposes of this Part the residuary income of his estate for any year of assessment;

then, in ascertaining the excess liability of any person having an absolute interest in the residue of that or any other estate or part thereof, that residuary income shall be treated as reduced by an amount calculated in accordance with the following provisions of this section.

(2) In subsection (1) above "excess liability" means the excess of liability to income tax over what it would be if all income tax [not chargeable][1] [[at the starting rate][5] were chargeable at the basic rate, or (so far as applicable in accordance with [section 1A][3]) the lower rate,][2] [or the Schedule F ordinary rate][4] to the exclusion of [the higher rate and the Schedule F upper rate][4].

(3) The amount of the reduction shall be an amount which, after deduction of income tax for the year of assessment in question, would be equal to the amount of inheritance tax attributable to so much of the income taken into account as mentioned in subsection (1) above as exceeds any liabilities so taken into account.

(4) The amount of any income accruing before the death of any person and taken into account in estimating the value of an estate shall (whether or not the income was valued separately or its amount known at the date of the death) be taken to be the actual amount so accruing less income tax at the basic rate for the year of assessment in which the death occurred.

(5) The amounts agreed between the persons liable for inheritance tax and the Board, or determined in the proceedings between them, as being respectively the value of an estate and the amount of any inheritance tax payable shall be conclusive for the purposes of this section; and evidence of those

amounts and of any facts relevant to their computation may be given by the production of a document purporting to be a certificate from the Board.

(6) In this section—

(a) references to liabilities taken into account in ascertaining the amount of the residuary income of an estate include references to liabilities allowed or allowable in computing its aggregate income; and

(b) references to inheritance tax include references to capital transfer tax.

Commentary—*Simon's Direct Tax Service* **C4.116, 118.**
Definitions—"Absolute interest", s 701(2); "aggregate income", s 701(8); "basic rate", s 832(1); "the Board", s 832(1); "higher rate", s 832(1); "lower rate", s 832(1); "Schedule F ordinary rate", s 832(1); "Schedule F upper rate", s 832(1); "starting rate" s 832(1); "year of assessment", s 832(1).
Cross references—See TCGA 1992 s 6(2)(c) (taxation of capital gains at income tax rates: sub-s (1) above to apply to capital gains as it applies to income).
Amendments—[1] Words in sub-s (2) inserted by F(No 2)A 1992 s 19(3), (7) with effect from the year 1992–93.
[2] Words in sub-s (2) substituted by FA 1993 Sch 6 paras 6, 25(1) with effect from the year 1993–94.
[3] Words in sub-s (2) substituted by FA 1996 s 73(4), Sch 6 paras 13, 28 with effect from the year 1996–97.
[4] Words in sub-s (2) inserted and substituted respectively by F(No 2)A 1997 s 34, Sch 4 para 17 with effect from the year 1999–00.
[5] Words in sub-s (2) substituted by FA 1999 s 22(8), (12) with effect from the year 1999–00.

[699A Untaxed sums comprised in the income of the estate

(1) In this section "a relevant amount" means so much of any amount which a person is deemed by virtue of this Part to receive or to have a right to receive as is or would be paid out of sums which—

(a) are included in the aggregate income of the estate of the deceased by virtue of any of sections ...[5] 249(5), 421(2) and 547(1)(c); and

(b) are sums in respect of which the personal representatives are not directly assessable to United Kingdom income tax.[or out of any sums included in the aggregate income of the estate of the deceased which fall within subsection (1A) below.][2]

[(1A) A sum falls within this subsection if it is a sum in respect of—

[(a) a distribution chargeable under Schedule F; or
(b)][3] a distribution to which section 233(1) applies.][2]

[(1B) Any reference in this Part to a sum to which subsection (1)(a) and (b) above applies includes a reference to a sum falling within subsection (1A) above which is included in the aggregate income of the estate of the deceased.][2]

(2) In determining for the purposes of this Part whether any amount is a relevant amount—

(a) such apportionments of any sums to which subsection (1)(a) and (b) above applies shall be made between different persons with interests in the residue of the estate as are just and reasonable in relation to their different interests; and

(b) subject to paragraph (a) above, the [assumptions][4] in section 701(3A)(b) shall apply, but (subject to that) it shall be assumed that payments are to be made out of other sums comprised in the aggregate income of the estate before they are made out of any sums to which subsection (1)(a) and (b) above applies.

(3) In the case of a foreign estate, and notwithstanding anything in section 695(4)(b) or 696(6), a relevant amount shall be deemed—

(a) to be income of such amount as would, after deduction of income tax for the year in which it is deemed to be paid, be equal to the relevant amount; and

(b) to be income that has borne tax at the applicable rate.

(4) Sums to which subsection (1)(a) and (b) above applies shall be assumed, for the purpose of determining the applicable rate in relation to any relevant amount, to bear tax—

(a) in the case of sums included by virtue of section ...[5] 249(5) or 421(2), at the [Schedule F ordinary rate][4], and

(b) in the case of sums included by virtue of section 547(1)(c), at the basic rate. [; and

(c) in the case of sums falling within subsection (1A) above, at the [Schedule F ordinary rate][4].][2]

(5) No repayment shall be made of any income tax which by virtue of this Part is treated as having been borne by the income that is represented by a relevant amount.

(6) For the purposes of sections 348 and 349(1) the income represented by a relevant amount shall be treated as not brought into charge to income tax [except to the extent that the relevant amount is or would be paid out of sums in respect of a distribution chargeable under Schedule F][4].][1]

Definitions—"Aggregate income", s 701(8); "applicable rate", s 701(3A); "basic rate", s 832(1); "distribution", s 209; "foreign estate", s 701(10); "Schedule F ordinary rate", s 832(1); "personal representatives", s 701(4); "United Kingdom", s 830(1).
Amendments—[1] Section inserted by FA 1995 s 76(4), (6), with effect from the year 1995–96.
[2] Words in sub-s (1), sub-ss (1A), (1B) and sub-s (4)(c) inserted by F(No 2)A 1997 s 21 with effect in relation to amounts which a person is deemed by virtue of this Part to receive, or to have a right to receive, after 1 July 1997.
[3] Words in sub-s (1A) inserted by F(No 2)A 1997 s 33(3), (10) with effect in relation to distributions made after 5 April 1999.
[4] Words in sub-ss (2)(b), (4)(a), (c) substituted, and words in sub-s (6) inserted, by F(No 2)A 1997 s 33(2), (4)–(6), (11) with effect from the year 1999–00.
[5] Words in sub-ss (1)(a), (4)(a) repealed by F(No 2)A 1997 s 36(4), Sch 6 para 12, Sch 8 Pt II(11) with effect for distributions made after 5 April 1999.

OFF.

700 Adjustments and information

(1) Where on the completion of the administration of an estate any amount is deemed by virtue of this Part to have been paid to any person as income for any year of assessment and—

    (*a*) that amount is greater than the amount that has previously been deemed to have been paid to him as income for that year by virtue of this Part; or

    (*b*) no amount has previously been so deemed to have been paid to him as income for that year;

an assessment may be made upon him for that year and tax charged accordingly or, on a claim being made for the purpose, any relief or additional relief to which he may be entitled shall be allowed accordingly.

(2) Where on the completion of the administration of an estate any amount is deemed by virtue of this Part to have been paid to any person as income for any year of assessment, and that amount is less than the amount that has previously been so deemed to have been paid to him, then—

    (*a*) if an assessment has already been made upon him for that year, such adjustments shall be made in that assessment as may be necessary for the purpose of giving effect to the provisions of this Part which take effect on the completion of the administration, and any tax overpaid shall be repaid; and

    (*b*) if—

       (i) any relief has been allowed to him by reference to the amount which has been previously deemed by virtue of this Part to have been paid to him as income for that year, and

       (ii) the amount of that relief exceeds the amount of relief which could have been given by reference to the amount which, on the completion of the administration, is deemed to have been paid to him as income for that year,

    the relief so given in excess may, if not otherwise made good, be charged under Case VI of Schedule D and recovered from that person accordingly.

(3) Notwithstanding anything in the Tax Acts, the time within which an assessment may be made for the purposes of this Part, or an assessment may be adjusted for those purposes, or a claim for relief may be made by virtue of this Part, shall not expire before the end of the [period of three years beginning with the 31st January next][2] following the year of assessment in which the administration of the estate in question was completed.

(4) An inspector may by notice require any person being or having been a personal representative of a deceased person, or having or having had an absolute or limited interest in the residue of the estate of a deceased person or in a part of such residue, to furnish him within such time as he may direct (not being less than 28 days) with such particulars as he thinks necessary for the purposes of this Part.

[(5) It shall be the duty of a personal representative of a deceased person, if a request to do so is made in writing by a person who has, or has had, an absolute or limited interest in the residue of the estate of the deceased or by a person to whom any of the income of the residue of that estate has been paid in the exercise of any discretion, to furnish the person making the request with a statement in writing setting out—

    (*a*) in respect of every amount which has been, or is treated as having been, actually paid to that person in respect of that interest or in the exercise of that discretion, the amount (if any) deemed under this Part to have been paid to him as income for a year of assessment; and

    (*b*) the amount of any tax at the applicable rate which any amount falling within paragraph (*a*) above is deemed to have borne;

and, where an amount deemed to have been paid as income to any person for any year of assessment is deemed for any of the purposes of this Part to have borne tax on different parts of it at different applicable rates, the matters to be set out in pursuance of paragraphs (*a*) and (*b*) above shall be set out separately as respects each part of that amount.][1]

[(6) The duty imposed by subsection (5) above shall be enforceable at the suit or instance of the person making the request.][1]

Commentary—*Simon's Direct Tax Service* **C4.117, 121.**
Definitions—"Absolute interest", s 701(2); "inspector", s 832(1); "limited interest", s 701(3); "notice", s 832(1); "personal representative", s 701(4); "Schedule D", s 18(1); "tax", s 832(3); "the Tax Acts", s 831(2); "year of assessment", s 832(1).
Amendments—[1] Sub-ss (5), (6) inserted by FA 1995 s 75, Sch 18 para 6.
[2] Words in sub-s (3) substituted by FA 1996 s 135(1), (2), Sch 21 para 20 with effect for the purposes of income tax from the year 1996–97, and, for the purposes of corporation tax, as respects accounting periods ending after 30 June 1999 (by virtue of Finance Act 1994, Section 199, (Appointed Day) Order, SI 1998/3173 art 2).

701 Interpretation

(1) The following provisions of this section shall have effect for the purpose of the interpretation of sections 695 to 700.

(2) A person shall be deemed to have an absolute interest in the residue of the estate of a deceased person, or in a part of such residue, if and so long as the capital of the residue or of that part would,

if the residue had been ascertained, be properly payable to him, or to another in his right, for his benefit, or is properly so payable, whether directly by the personal representatives or indirectly through a trustee or other person.

(3) A person shall be deemed to have a limited interest in the residue of the estate of a deceased person, or in a part of such residue, during any period, being a period during which he has not an absolute interest in the residue or in that part, where the income of the residue or of that part for that period would, if the residue had been ascertained at the commencement of that period, be properly payable to him, or to another in his right, for his benefit, whether directly by the personal representatives or indirectly through a trustee or other person.

[(3A) ''Applicable rate'', in relation to any amount which a person is deemed by virtue of this Part to receive or to have a right to receive, means the basic rate[, the lower rate or the Schedule F ordinary rate]⁶ according as the income of the residue of the estate out of which that amount is or would be paid bears tax at the basic rate[, the lower rate or the Schedule F ordinary rate]⁶; and in determining for the purposes of this Part whether or how much of any payment is or would be deemed to be made out of income that bears tax at one rate rather than another—

    (*a*) such apportionments of the amounts bearing tax at different rates shall be made between different persons with interests in the residue of the estate as are just and reasonable in relation to their different interests; and

    (*b*) subject to paragraph (*a*) above, it shall be assumed—

        [(*i*)]⁶ that payments are to be made out of income bearing tax at the basic rate before they are made out of income bearing tax at the lower rate [or the Schedule F ordinary rate; and

        (*ii*) that payments are to be made out of income bearing tax at the lower rate before they are made out of income bearing tax at the Schedule F ordinary rate]⁶.]²

(4) ''Personal representatives'' means, in relation to the estate of a deceased person, his personal representatives as defined in relation to England and Wales by section 55 of the Administration of Estates Act 1925 and persons having in relation to the deceased under the law of another country any functions corresponding to the functions for administration purposes under the law of England and Wales of personal representatives as so defined; and references to ''personal representatives as such'' shall be construed as references to personal representatives in their capacity as having such functions.

(5) ''Specific disposition'' means a specific devise or bequest made by a testator, and includes the disposition of personal chattels made by section 46 of the Administration of Estates Act 1925 and any disposition having, whether by virtue of any enactment or otherwise, under the law of another country an effect similar to that of a specific devise or bequest under the law of England and Wales.

Real estate included (either by a specific or general description) in a residuary gift made by the will of a testator shall be deemed to be a part of the residue of his estate and not to be the subject of a specific disposition.

(6) Subject to subsection (7) below, ''charges on residue'' means, in relation to the estate of a deceased person, the following liabilities, properly payable thereout and interest payable in respect of those liabilities, that is to say—

    (*a*) funeral, testamentary and administration expenses and debts, and

    (*b*) general legacies, demonstrative legacies, annuities and any sum payable out of residue to which a person is entitled under the law of intestacy of any part of the United Kingdom or any other country, and

    (*c*) any other liabilities of his personal representatives as such.

(7) Where, as between persons interested under a specific disposition or in a general or demonstrative legacy or in an annuity and persons interested in the residue of the estate, any such liabilities as are mentioned in subsection (6) above fall exclusively or primarily upon the property that is the subject of the specific disposition or upon the legacy or annuity, only such part (if any) of those liabilities as falls ultimately upon the residue shall be treated as charges on residue.

(8) References to the aggregate income of the estate of a deceased person for any year of assessment shall be construed as references to the aggregate income from all sources for that year of the personal representatives of the deceased as such, treated as consisting of—

    (*a*) any such income which is chargeable to United Kingdom income tax by deduction or otherwise, such income being computed at the amount on which that tax falls to be borne for that year; and

    (*b*) any such income which would have been so chargeable if it had arisen in the United Kingdom to a person resident and ordinarily resident there, such income being computed at the full amount thereof actually arising during that year, less such deductions as would have been allowable if it had been charged to United Kingdom income tax;

but excluding any income from property devolving on the personal representatives otherwise than as assets for payment of the debts of the deceased.

This subsection has effect subject to sections ...³249(5), 421(2), ...¹ and 547(1)(*c*).

(9) "United Kingdom estate" means, as regards any year of assessment, an estate the income of which comprises only income which either—

(*a*) has borne United Kingdom income tax by deduction, or
(*b*) in respect of which the personal representatives are directly assessable to United Kingdom income tax,

not being an estate any part of the income of which is income in respect of which the personal representatives are entitled to claim exemption from United Kingdom income tax by reference to the fact that they are not resident, or not ordinarily resident, in the United Kingdom.

(10) "Foreign estate" means, as regards any year of assessment, an estate which is not a United Kingdom estate.

[(10A) Amounts to which section 699A(1)(*a*) and (*b*) applies shall be disregarded in determining whether an estate is a United Kingdom estate or a foreign estate, except that any estate the aggregate income of which comprises only such amounts shall be a United Kingdom estate.]⁴

(11) In a case in which different parts of the estate of a deceased person are the subjects respectively of different residuary dispositions, this Part shall have effect in relation to each of those parts with the substitution—

(*a*) for references to the estate of references to that part of the estate; and
(*b*) for references to the personal representatives of the deceased as such of references to his personal representatives in their capacity as having the functions referred to in subsection (4) above in relation to that part of the estate.

(12) In this Part—

(*a*) references to sums paid include references to assets that are transferred or that are appropriated by a personal representative to himself, and to debts that are set off or released;
(*b*) references to sums payable include references to assets as to which an obligation to transfer or a right of a personal representative to appropriate to himself is subsisting on the completion of the administration and to debts as to which an obligation to release or set off, or a right of a personal representative so to do in his own favour, is then subsisting; and
(*c*) references to amount shall be construed, in relation to such assets as are referred to in paragraph (*a*) or (*b*) above, as references to their value at the date on which they were transferred or appropriated, or at the completion of the administration, as the case may require, and, in relation to such debts as are so referred to, as references to the amount thereof.

(13) In this Part references to the administration period shall be construed in accordance with section 695(1).

(14) ...⁵

Commentary—*Simon's Direct Tax Service* **C4.107, 115, 116.**
Definitions—"Additional rate", s 832(1); "basic rate", s 832(1); "lower rate", s 832(1); "Schedule F ordinary rate", s 832(1); "United Kingdom", s 830(1); "year of assessment", s 832(1).
Amendments—¹ Number in sub-s (8) repealed by FA 1989 Sch 17 Pt V.
² Sub-s (3A) inserted by FA 1993 Sch 6 paras 11(3), 25(1) with effect from the year 1993–94.
³ Words in sub-s (8) repealed by F(No 2)A 1997 s 36(4), Sch 6 para 13, Sch 8 Pt II (11) with effect for distributions made after 5 April 1999.
⁴ Sub-s (10A) inserted by FA 1995 s 76(5), (6), with effect from the year 1995–96.
⁵ Sub-s (14) repealed by FA 1995 s 75, Sch 18 para 7, Sch 29 Pt VIII(10).
⁶ Words in sub-s (3A) inserted by F(No 2)A 1997 s 33(7)–(9), (11) with effect from the year 1999–00.

702 Application to Scotland

For the purpose of the application of this Part to Scotland—

(*a*) any reference to the completion of the administration of an estate shall be construed as a reference to the date at which, after discharge of, or provision for, liabilities falling to be met out of the deceased's estate (including, without prejudice to the generality of the foregoing, debts, legacies immediately payable, prior rights of surviving spouse on intestacy and legal rights of surviving spouse or children), the free balance held in trust for behoof of the residuary legatees has been ascertained;
(*b*) for paragraph (*b*) of section 697(1) the following paragraph shall be substituted—

"(*b*) the amount of any of the aggregate income of the estate for that year to which a person has become entitled by virtue of a specific disposition";

(*c*) "real estate" means heritable estate, and
(*d*) "charge on residue" shall include, in addition to the liabilities specified in section 701(6), any sums required to meet claims in respect of prior rights by surviving spouse or in respect of legal rights by surviving spouse or children.

Commentary—*Simon's Direct Tax Service* **C4.107.**
Definition—"Children", ss 831(4), 832(5).

PART XVII
TAX AVOIDANCE

CHAPTER I
CANCELLATION OF TAX ADVANTAGES FROM CERTAIN TRANSACTIONS IN SECURITIES

Statement of Practice SP 3/80—Applications under s 707 below for clearance; where clearance is refused, reasons for refusal are given, if possible. Also, where application for clearance is made before the transaction is carried out, it is refused only if the circumstances are indicative of a counteraction under s 703 if the transaction were carried out.

703 Cancellation of tax advantage

(1) Where—

    (*a*) in any such circumstances as are mentioned in section 704, and

    (*b*) in consequence of a transaction in securities or of the combined effect of two or more such transactions,

a person is in a position to obtain, or has obtained, a tax advantage, then unless he shows that the transaction or transactions were carried out either for bona fide commercial reasons or in the ordinary course of making or managing investments, and that none of them had as their main object, or one of their main objects, to enable tax advantages to be obtained, this section shall apply to him in respect of that transaction or those transactions.

(2) For the purposes of this Chapter a tax advantage obtained or obtainable by a person shall be deemed to be obtained or obtainable by him in consequence of a transaction in securities or of the combined effect of two or more such transactions, if it is obtained or obtainable in consequence of the combined effect of the transaction or transactions and the liquidation of a company.

(3) Where this section applies to a person in respect of any transaction or transactions, the tax advantage obtained or obtainable by him in consequence thereof shall be counteracted by such of the following adjustments, that is to say an assessment, the nullifying of a right to repayment or the requiring of the return of a repayment already made (the amount to be returned being chargeable under Case VI of Schedule D and recoverable accordingly), or the computation or recomputation of profits or gains, or liability to tax, on such basis as the Board may specify by notice served on him as being requisite for counteracting the tax advantage so obtained or obtainable.

[(3A) The amount of income tax which may be specified in an assessment which is made under subsection (3) above to counteract a tax advantage—

    (*a*) obtained by a person in circumstances falling within paragraph D or paragraph E of section 704, and

    (*b*) consisting of the avoidance of a charge to income tax,

shall not exceed the amount of income tax for which that person would be liable in respect of the receipt, on the date on which the consideration mentioned in paragraph D or paragraph E of section 704 is received, of a qualifying distribution of an amount equal to the amount or value of that consideration.]²

(4)–(6) ...³

(7), (8) ...¹

(9) The Board shall not give a notice under subsection (3) above until they have notified the person in question that they have reason to believe that this section may apply to him in respect of a transaction or transactions specified in the notification; and if within 30 days of the issue of the notification that person, being of opinion that this section does not so apply to him, makes a statutory declaration to that effect stating the facts and circumstances upon which his opinion is based, and sends it to the Board, then subject to subsection (10) below, this section shall not apply to him in respect of the transaction or transactions.

(10) If, when a statutory declaration has been sent to the Board under subsection (9) above, they see reason to take further action in the matter—

    (*a*) the Board shall send to the tribunal a certificate to that effect, together with the statutory declaration, and may also send therewith a counter-statement with reference to the matter;

    (*b*) the tribunal shall take into consideration the declaration and the certificate, and the counter-statement, if any, and shall determine whether there is or is not a prima facie case for proceeding in the matter, and if they determine that there is no such case this section shall not apply to the person in question in respect of the transaction or transactions;

but any such determination shall not affect the operation of this section in respect of transactions which include that transaction or some or all of those transactions and also include another transaction or other transactions.

(11) Any notice or notification under subsection (3) or subsection (9) above, or under section 708, concerning the application of this section to a person who has died may be given or issued to his

personal representatives, and the provisions of this Chapter relating to the making of a statutory declaration, to rights of appeal and to the giving of information shall be construed accordingly.

(12) This section applies whether the tax advantage in question relates to a chargeable period ending before or after the commencement of this Act, but nothing in this section shall authorise the making of an assessment later than six years after the chargeable period to which the tax advantage relates; and no other provision contained in the Tax Acts shall be construed as limiting the powers conferred by this section.

Commentary—*Simon's Direct Tax Service* **A7.101, 128, 129**.
Revenue Decision RD 6—Refusal of clearance under s 707 from counteraction under this section in connection with exempt schemes approved under s 590.
Revenue & other press releases—IR Tax Bulletin November 1992 p 37 (application of this section to intra-group dividends).
IR Tax Bulletin April 2000 p 742 (Returning the proceeds of transactions in securities which have taken place either without any application being made for advance clearance under TA 1988 s 707 or where such an application was refused by the Board of Inland Revenue).
Revenue Internal Guidance—Inspector's manual IM 4524 (circumstances in which cases should be referred to head office).
Simon's Tax Cases—*IRC v Sheppard (Trustees of the Woodland Trust) (No 2)* [1993] STC 240*; *IRC v Universities Superannuation Scheme Ltd* [1997] STC 1; *Lewis (trustee of Redrow Staff Pension Scheme) v IRC* [1999] STC (SCD) 349; *Trustees of the Omega Group Pension Scheme v IRC* [2001] STC (SCD) 121; *IRC v Trustees of the Sema Group Pension Scheme* [2002] STC 276.
s 703(1), *IRC v Joiner* [1975] STC 657*; *IRC v Goodwin* [1976] STC 28*; *Clark v IRC* [1978] STC 614*; *IRC v Laird Group plc* [2002] STC 722.
s 703(2), *IRC v Joiner* [1975] STC 657*.
s 703(3), *Green v IRC* [1975] STC 633*.
s 703(9), (10)(a), *Balen v IRC* [1978] STC 420*.
s 703(10), *Howard v Borneman (No 2)* [1973] STC 506*.
Definitions—''Advance corporation tax'', s 14(1); ''basic rate'', s 832(1); ''the Board'', s 832(1); ''chargeable period'', s 832(1); ''company'', s 709(2); ''income tax'', s 832(4); ''lower rate'', s 832(1); ''notice'', s 832(1); ''profits or gains'', s 833(1); ''Schedule D'', s 18(1); ''tax'', s 832(3); ''the Tax Acts'', s 831(2); ''tax advantage'', s 709(1); ''tax credit'', s 832(1); ''transaction in securities'', s 709(2).
Cross references—See TA 1988 s 705 (appeal against Board's notices under this section).
TA 1988 s 707 (Procedure for obtaining Board's clearance in advance so as to exclude the application of this section to a transaction).
TA 1988 s 708 (Board's power to obtain information for the purposes of this section).
FA 1993 s 80(4) (special payments to charities, etc to compensate them for reduced tax repayments resulting from reduced tax credits in consequence of reduced ACT rate; Board's power to exclude a charity, etc, having regard to this section, from entitlement to the special payments).
FA 2000 s 46(2) (exemption under FA 2000 s 46(1) for income of a charity is not granted in respect of income chargeable to tax under Schedule D Case VI by virtue of this section).
Amendments—¹ Sub-ss (7), (8) repealed by FA 1988 Sch 14 Pt VIII with effect from the year 1990–91.
² Sub-s (3A) inserted by FA 1998 Sch 3 para 32 with effect in relation to assessments under sub-s (3) made after 5 April 1999
³ Sub-ss (4)–(6) repealed by FA 1998 Sch 3 para 32 with effect for the year 1999–00 and subsequent years of assessment. The prospective amendments to sub-s (5) which were to be made by F(No 2)A 1997 Sch 4 para 18 will therefore not take effect.

704 The prescribed circumstances

The circumstances mentioned in section 703(1) are—

A.—That in connection with the distribution of profits of a company, or in connection with the sale or purchase of securities being a sale or purchase followed by the purchase or sale of the same or other securities, the person in question receives an abnormal amount by way of dividend, and the amount so received is taken into account for any of the following purposes—

(a) any exemption from tax, or
(b) the setting-off of losses against profits or income, or
(c) the giving of group relief, or
(d) ...³
[(da) the application of franked investment income for the purpose of regulations made under section 32 of the Finance Act 1998, or]⁴
(e) ...² or
(f) the computation of profits or gains out of which are made payments falling within section 348 or 349(1), or
(g) the deduction from or set-off against income of interest under section 353.

OR

B.—(1) That in connection with the distribution of profits of a company, or in connection with the sale or purchase of securities being sale or purchase followed by the purchase or sale of the same or other securities, the person in question becomes entitled—

(a) in respect of securities held or sold by him, or
(b) in respect of securities formerly held by him (whether sold by him or not),

to a deduction in computing profits or gains by reason of a fall in the value of the securities resulting from the payment of a dividend thereon or from any other dealing with any assets of a company.

(2) Where a company in the circumstances mentioned in sub-paragraph (1) above becomes entitled to a deduction as there mentioned, section 703 shall apply in relation to any tax advantage obtained or obtainable in consequence of that deduction by another company by way of group relief as if obtained or obtainable by the other company in circumstances falling within sub-paragraph (1) above.

OR

C—(1) That the person in question receives, in consequence of a transaction whereby any other person—

(a) subsequently receives, or has received, an abnormal amount by way of dividend; or

(b) subsequently becomes entitled, or has become entitled, to a deduction as mentioned in paragraph B(1) above,

a consideration which either—

(i) is, or represents the value of, assets which are (or apart from anything done by the company in question would have been) available for distribution by way of dividend, or

(ii) is received in respect of future receipts of the company, or

(iii) is, or represents the value of, trading stock of the company,

and the person in question so receives the consideration that he does not pay or bear tax on it as income.

(2) The assets mentioned in sub-paragraph (1) above do not include assets which (while of a description which under the law of the country in which the company is incorporated is available for distribution by way of dividend) are shown to represent a return of sums paid by subscribers on the issue of securities.

OR

D—(1) That in connection with the distribution of profits of a company to which this paragraph applies, the person in question so receives as is mentioned in paragraph C(1) above such a consideration as is therein mentioned.

(2) The companies to which this paragraph applies are—

(a) any company under the control of not more than five persons, and

(b) any other company which does not satisfy the conditions that its shares or stocks or some class thereof (disregarding debenture stock, preferred shares or preferred stock), [are listed in the Official List of the Stock Exchange, and are dealt in on the Stock Exchange regularly or from time to time][1],

so, however, that this paragraph does not apply to a company under the control of one or more companies to which this paragraph does not apply.

(3) Subsections (2) to (6) of section 416 shall apply for the purposes of this paragraph.

OR

E—(1) That in connection with the transfer directly or indirectly of assets of a company to which paragraph D above applies to another such company, or in connection with any transaction in securities in which two or more companies to which paragraph D above applies are concerned, the person in question receives non-taxable consideration which is or represents the value of assets available for distribution by such a company, and which consists of any share capital or any security (as defined by section 254(1)) issued by such a company.

(2) So far as sub-paragraph (1) above relates to share capital other than redeemable share capital, it shall not apply unless and except to the extent that the share capital is repaid (in a winding-up or otherwise), and, where section 703 applies to a person by virtue of sub-paragraph (1) above on the repayment of any share capital, any assessment to tax under subsection (3) of that section shall be an assessment to tax for the year in which the share capital is repaid.

(3) In this paragraph—

"assets available for distribution" means assets which are, or apart from anything done by the company in question would have been, available for distribution by way of dividend, or trading stock of the company;

"non-taxable", in relation to a person receiving consideration, means that the recipient does not pay or bear tax on it as income (apart from the provisions of this Chapter);

"share" includes stock and any other interest of a member in a company;

and the reference in sub-paragraph (2) above to the repayment of share capital include references to any distribution made in respect of any shares in a winding-up or dissolution of the company.

Commentary—*Simon's Direct Tax Service* A7.111–115.

Revenue & other press releases—Hansard 27-2-96 (para 1(2)(b) alternative investment market companies are caught by this provision).

Revenue Internal Guidance—Inspector's manual IM 4514–4519 (explanation of the circumstances with examples).

IM 4520 (regarding circumstances C-E, the Board will invoke s 703 only if the tax on a potential assessment significantly exceeds the capital gains tax liability on the same consideration, e.g. where gain reduced by rebasing, indexation or retirement relief).

Simon's Tax Cases—*IRC v Garvin* [1981] STC 344*; *Bird v IRC* [1987] STC 168*; *IRC v Universities Superannuation Scheme Ltd* [1997] STC 1; *Marwood Homes Ltd v IRC* [1999] STC (SCD) 44; *Trustees of the Omega Group Pension Scheme v IRC* [2001] STC (SCD) 121; *IRC v Trustees of the Sema Group Pension Scheme* [2002] STC 276.

Definitions—"Abnormal (dividend)", s 709(4); "advance corporation tax", s 14(1); "company", s 709(2); "control", s 840; "distribution", s 709(3); "dividends", s 709(2); "franked investment income", s 832(1); "group relief", s 834(1); "profits", s 709(3); "profits or gains", s 833(1); "receipt of consideration", s 709(3); "securities", s 709(2); "tax", s 832(3); "tax advantage", s 709(1); "trading stock", s 709(2); "transaction in securities", s 709(2).

Cross references—See TA 1988 s 210(3) (repayment of share capital followed by issue of bonus shares to be treated as a distribution in relation to a company within paragraph D above).

TA 1988 s 211(2) (in relation to a company within paragraph D above, certain matters prevent a distribution being treated as repayment of share capital).

TA 1988 s 444B and Sch 19AC, para 12 (modification of this section in relation to overseas life insurance companies in accounting periods beginning after 31 December 1992).

TA 1988 s 709(4) (what constitutes abnormal dividend for the purposes of this section).

FA 1996 s 175(2), (3) (the reference in paragraphs D(2)(*b*) above to the Official List of the Stock Exchange is deemed to include a reference to the Unlisted Securities Market, except, to the extent that paragraph applies for the purposes of paragraphs D(1) and E above, in relation to transactions taking place after the date on which that the Unlisted Securities Market closes and, to the extent that paragraph applies for the purposes of TA 1988 ss 210(3) and 211(2), in relation to share capital issued or distributions made after that date).

Modification—This section has effect in relation to the rules concerning the treatment of unrelieved surplus ACT as if new para A(*da*) inserted: see Corporation Tax (Treatment of Unrelieved Surplus Advance Corporation Tax) Regulations, SI 1999/358 reg 23.

Amendments—[1] Words in para D(2)(*b*) substituted by FA 1996 s 175(1), (4) generally with effect as to relevant transactions, share capital issues distributions after 29 April 1996. Note for detailed application of this provision, FA 1996 s 175(2)–(5).
[2] Para A(*e*) repealed by F(No 2)A 1997 Sch 8 Pt II(4) with effect generally in relation to accounting periods beginning after 1 July 1997 but subject to the detailed provisions of F(No 2)A 1997 s 20(1)–(4).
[3] Para A(*d*) repealed by FA 1998 Sch 3 para 33 with effect in relation to distributions made after 5 April 1999.
[4] Para A(*da*) inserted by the Corporation Tax (Treatment of Unrelieved Surplus Advance Corporation Tax) Regulations, SI 1999/358 reg 23(2), with effect in relation from 6 April 1999.

705 Appeals against Board's notices under section 703

(1) Any person to whom notice has been given under section 703(3) may within 30 days by notice to the Board appeal to the Special Commissioners on the grounds that section 703 does not apply to him in respect of the transaction or transactions in question, or that the adjustments directed to be made are inappropriate.

(2) If he or the Board are dissatisfied with the determination of the Special Commissioners he or they may, on giving notice to the clerk to the Special Commissioners within 30 days after the determination, require the appeal to be re-heard by the tribunal, and the Special Commissioners shall transmit to the tribunal any document in their possession which was delivered to them for the purposes of the appeal.

(3) Where notice is given under subsection (2) above, the tribunal shall re-hear and determine the appeal and shall have and exercise the same powers and authorities in relation to the appeal as the Special Commissioners might have and exercise, and the determination of the tribunal thereon shall be final and conclusive.

(4) ...[1]

(5) On an appeal under subsections (1) to (3) above the Special Commissioners or the tribunal shall have power to cancel or vary a notice under subsection (3) of section 703 or to vary or quash an assessment made in accordance with such a notice, but the bringing of an appeal or the statement of a case shall not affect the validity of a notice given or of any other thing done in pursuance of that subsection pending the determination of the proceedings.

(6)–(8) ...[2]

Commentary—*Simon's Direct Tax Service* A7.130.
Simon's Tax Cases—s 705(1), *Balen v IRC* [1977] STC 148*.
s 705(2), *Marwood Homes Ltd v IRC* [1998] STC (SCD) 53.
s 705(4), *Anysz v IRC Manolescue v IRC* [1978] STC 296*.
Definitions—''Advance corporation tax'', s 14(1); ''the Board'', s 832(1); ''company'', s 709(2); ''the Management Act'', s 831(3); ''notice'', s 832(1).
Amendments—[1] Sub-s (4) repealed by the General and Special Commissioners (Amendment of Enactments) Regulations, SI 1994/1813 reg 2, Sch 1 paras 1, 23, Sch 2 Pt I, with effect from 1 September 1994 in relation to proceedings before the General Commissioners in respect of which the General Commissioners (Jurisdiction and Procedure) Regulations, SI 1994/1812 apply and in relation to proceedings before the Special Commissioners in respect of which the Special Commissioners (Jurisdiction and Procedure) Regulations, SI 1994/1811 apply.
[2] Sub-ss (6)–(8) repealed by FA 1998 Sch 3 para 34 with effect for the year 1999–00 and subsequent years of assessment.

[705A Statement of case by tribunal for opinion of High Court

(1) Immediately after the determination by the tribunal of an appeal re-heard by them under section 705 of this Act, the appellant or the Board, if dissatisfied with the determination as being erroneous in point of law, may declare his or their dissatisfaction to the tribunal.

(2) The appellant or the Board, as the case may be, having declared his or their dissatisfaction, may, within thirty days after the determination, by notice in writing require the tribunal to state and sign a case for the opinion of the High Court.

(3) The party requiring the case shall pay to the tribunal a fee of £25 for and in respect of the same, before he is entitled to have the case stated.

(4) The case shall set forth the facts and the determination of the tribunal, and the party requiring it shall transmit the case, when stated and signed, to the High Court, within thirty days after receiving the same.

(5) At or before the time when he transmits the case to the High Court, the party requiring it shall send notice in writing of the fact that the case has been stated on his application, together with a copy of the case, to the other party.

(6) The High Court shall hear and determine any question of law arising on the case, and may reverse, affirm or amend the determination in respect of which the case has been stated, or remit the matter to the tribunal with the Court's opinion on it, or make such other order in relation to the matter as the Court thinks fit.

(7) The High Court may cause the case to be sent back for amendment, and thereupon the case shall be amended accordingly, and judgement shall be delivered after it has been amended.

(8) Subject to subsection (9) below and to Part II of the Administration of Justice Act 1969 (appeal from High Court to House of Lords), an appeal shall, in England and Wales, lie from the decision of the High Court to the Court of Appeal and thence to the House of Lords.

(9) No appeal shall lie to the House of Lords from the Court of Appeal unless leave has been given under and in accordance with section 1 of the Administration of Justice (Appeals) Act 1934.

(10) Subject to subsection (11) below, where the determination of the tribunal is in respect of an assessment made in accordance with a notice under subsection (3) of section 703, then notwithstanding that a case has been required to be stated or is pending before the High Court in respect of the determination, tax shall be paid in accordance with the determination.

(11) If the amount charged by the assessment is altered by the order or judgement of the High Court, then—

(a) if too much tax has been paid the amount overpaid shall be refunded with such interest, if any, as the High Court may allow; or

(b) if too little tax has been charged, the amount undercharged shall be due and payable at the expiration of a period of thirty days beginning with the date on which the Board issue to the other party a notice of the total amount payable in accordance with the order or judgement of that Court.

(12) All matters within the jurisdiction of the High Court under this section shall be assigned in Scotland to the Court of Session sitting as the Court of Exchequer (references in this section to the High Court being construed accordingly); and an appeal shall lie from the decision under this section of the Court of Session, as the Court of Exchequer in Scotland, to the House of Lords.]¹

Commentary—*Simon's Direct Tax Service* A7.131.
Definitions—"Act", s 832(1); "the Board", s 832(1); "notice", s 832(1).
Cross references—See TA 1988 s 705B (application of this section in relation to proceedings in Northern Ireland).
Amendments—¹ This section inserted by the General and Special Commissioners (Amendment of Enactments) Regulations 1994, SI 1994/1813 reg 2, Sch 1 para 24, with effect from 1 September 1994 in relation to proceedings before the General Commissioners in respect of which the General Commissioners (Jurisdiction and Procedure) Regulations, SI 1994/1812 apply and in relation to proceedings before the Special Commissioners in respect of which the Special Commissioners (Jurisdiction and Procedure) Regulations, SI 1994/1811 apply.

[705B Proceedings in Northern Ireland

(1) A case which is stated by the tribunal under section 705A in proceedings in Northern Ireland shall be a case for the opinion of the Court of Appeal in Northern Ireland, and the Taxes Acts (as defined in section 118(1) of the Management Act shall have effect as if that section applied in relation to such proceedings—

(a) with the substitution for references to the High Court of references to the Court of Appeal in Northern Ireland;

(b) with the omission of subsections (4), (5), (8) and (9) of that section.

(2) The procedure relating to the transmission of the case to, and the hearing and determination of the case by, the Court of Appeal in Northern Ireland shall be that for the time being in force in Northern Ireland as respects cases stated by a county court in exercise of its general jurisdiction, and an appeal shall lie from the Court of Appeal to the House of Lords in accordance with section 42 of the Judicature (Northern Ireland) Act 1978.

(3) Where in proceedings in Northern Ireland an application is made for a case to be stated by the tribunal under this section, the case must be settled and sent to the applicant as soon after the application as is reasonably practicable.

(4) For the purposes of this section "proceedings in Northern Ireland" means proceedings as respects which the place given by the rules in Schedule 3 to the Management Act is in Northern Ireland.]¹

Commentary—*Simon's Direct Tax Service* A7.131.
Amendments—¹ This section inserted by the General and Special Commissioners (Amendment of Enactments) Regulations 1994, SI 1994/1813 reg 2, Sch 1 para 24, with effect from 1 September 1994 in relation to proceedings before the General Commissioners in respect of which the General Commissioners (Jurisdiction and Procedure) Regulations, SI 1994/1812 apply and in relation to proceedings before the Special Commissioners in respect of which the Special Commissioners (Jurisdiction and Procedure) Regulations, SI 1994/1811 apply.

706 The tribunal

[(1)]¹ For the purposes of this Chapter the tribunal shall consist of—

(a) a chairman, appointed by the Lord Chancellor, and

(b) two or more persons appointed by the Lord Chancellor as having special knowledge of and experience in financial or commercial matters.

[(2) A person appointed as chairman or other member of the tribunal shall vacate his office on the day on which he attains the age of 70; but this subsection is subject to section 26(4) to (6) of the Judicial Pensions and Retirement Act 1993 (power to authorise continuance in office up to the age of 75).]¹

Commentary—*Simon's Direct Tax Service* **A7.125**.
Simon's Tax Cases—*R v IRC, ex p Preston* [1983] STC 257*.
Cross references—See FA 1989 s 182(3)(*d*) (criminal liability of the tribunal appointed under this section for disclosure of information).
Amendments—¹ Numbering ''(1)'' and sub-s (2) inserted by the Judicial Pensions and Retirement Act 1993 Sch 6 para 44 with effect from 31 March 1995, by virtue of the Judicial Pensions and Retirement Act 1993 (Commencement) Order, SI 1995/631.

707 Procedure for clearance in advance

(1) The following provisions shall have effect where in pursuance of this section a person furnishes to the Board particulars of a transaction or transactions effected or to be effected by him, that is to say—

(*a*) if the Board are of opinion that the particulars, or any further information furnished in pursuance of this paragraph, are not sufficient for the purposes of this section, they shall within 30 days of the receipt thereof notify to that person what further information they require for those purposes, and unless that further information is furnished to the Board within 30 days from the notification, or such further time as the Board may allow, they shall not be required to proceed further under this section;

(*b*) subject to paragraph (*a*) above, the Board shall within 30 days of the receipt of the particulars, or, where that paragraph has effect, of all further information required, notify that person whether or not they are satisfied that the transaction or transactions as described in the particulars were or will be such that no notice under section 703(3) ought to be given in respect of it or them;

and, subject to the following provisions of this section, if the Board notify him that they are so satisfied, section 703 shall not apply to him in respect of that transaction or those transactions.

(2) If the particulars, and any further information given under this section with respect to any transaction or transactions, are not such as to make full and accurate disclosure of all facts and considerations relating thereto which are material to be known to the Board, any notification given by the Board under this section shall be void.

(3) In no event shall the giving of a notification under this section with respect to any transaction or transactions prevent section 703 applying to a person in respect of transactions which include that transaction or all or some of those transactions and also include another transaction or other transactions.

Commentary—*Simon's Direct Tax Service* **A7.120, 121**.
Statements of Practice SP 3/80—Applications under this section for clearance; where clearance is refused, reasons for refusal are given, if possible. Also, where application under this section for clearance is made before the transaction is carried out, it is refused only if the circumstances are indicative of a counteraction under s 703 if the transaction were carried out.
SP 13/80, Annex—Procedure for application for clearance under this section.
Revenue Decision RD 6—Refusal of clearance under this section from s 703 counteraction in connection with exempt schemes approved under s 590.
Revenue & other press releases—IR 9-9-89 (clearance application procedure under s 707).
Revenue Internal Guidance—Inspector's manual IM 4571 (where clearance is refused, but the transactions are effected notwithstanding the refusal, no associated relief, allowance etc will be given without authorisation from head office).
Definitions—''The Board'', s 832(1); ''notice'', s 832(1).

708 Power to obtain information

Where it appears to the Board that by reason of any transaction or transactions a person may be a person to whom section 703 applies, the Board may by notice served on him require him, within such time not less than 28 days as may be specified in the notice, to furnish information in his possession with respect to the transaction or any of the transactions, being information as to matters, specified in the notice, which are relevant to the question whether a notice under section 703(3) should be given in respect of him.

Commentary—*Simon's Direct Tax Service* **A7.126**.
Definitions—''The Board'', s 832(1); ''notice'', s 832(1).

709 Meaning of ''tax advantage'' and other expressions

(1) In this Chapter ''tax advantage'' means a relief or increased relief from, or repayment or increased repayment of, tax, or the avoidance or reduction of a charge to tax or an assessment to tax or the avoidance of a possible assessment thereto, whether the avoidance or reduction is effected by receipts accruing in such a way that the recipient does not pay or bear tax on them, or by a deduction in computing profits or gains.

(2) In this Chapter—

''company'' includes any body corporate;
''securities''—

(*a*) includes shares and stock, and
(*b*) in relation to a company not limited by shares (whether or not it has a share capital) includes also a reference to the interest of a member of the company as such, whatever the form of that interest;

''trading stock'' has the same meaning as in section 100(1);
''transaction in securities'' includes transactions, of whatever description, relating to securities, and in particular—

(i) the purchase, sale or exchange of securities;

(ii) the issuing or securing the issue of, or applying or subscribing for, new securities;

(iii) the altering, or securing the alteration of, the rights attached to securities;

and references to dividends include references to other qualifying distributions and to interest.

[(2A) In this Chapter references to a relief ...[2] include ...[2] references to a tax credit ...[2]][1]

(3) In section 704—

(*a*) references to profits include references to income, reserves or other assets;

(*b*) references to distribution include references to transfer or realisation (including application in discharge of liabilities); and

(*c*) references to the receipt of consideration include references to the receipt of any money or money's worth.

(4) For the purposes of section 704 an amount received by way of dividend shall be treated as abnormal if the Board, the Special Commissioners or the tribunal, as the case may be, are satisfied—

(*a*) in the case of a dividend at a fixed rate, that it substantially exceeds the amount which the recipient would have received if the dividend had accrued from day to day and he had been entitled only to so much of the dividend as accrued while he held the securities, so however that an amount shall not be treated as abnormal by virtue only of this paragraph if during the six months beginning with the purchase of the securities the recipient does not sell or otherwise dispose of, or acquire an option to sell, any of those securities or any securities similar to those securities; or

(*b*) in any case, that it substantially exceeds a normal return on the consideration provided by the recipient for the relevant securities, that is to say, the securities in respect of which the dividend was received and, if those securities are derived from securities previously acquired by the recipient, the securities which were previously acquired.

(5) For the purposes of subsection (4)(*a*) above securities shall be deemed to be similar if they entitle their holders to the same rights against the same persons as to capital and interest and the same remedies for the enforcement of those rights, notwithstanding any difference in the total nominal amounts of the respective securities or in the form in which they are held or the manner in which they can be transferred, and for those purposes rights guaranteed by the Treasury shall be treated as rights against the Treasury.

(6) For the purposes of subsection (4)(*b*) above—

(*a*) if the consideration provided by the recipient for any of the relevant securities was in excess of their market value at the time he acquired them, or if no consideration was provided by him for any of the relevant securities, the recipient shall be taken to have provided for those securities consideration equal to their market value at the time he acquired them; and

(*b*) in determining whether an amount received by way of dividend exceeds a normal return, regard shall be had to the length of time previous to the receipt of that amount that the recipient first acquired any of the relevant securities and to any dividends and other distributions made in respect of them during that time.

Commentary—*Simon's Direct Tax Service* **A7.103, 104.**
Revenue Internal Guidance—Inspector's manual IM 4513 (the avoidance of advance corporation tax is within the definition of tax advantage).
Simon's Tax Cases—*IRC v Universities Superannuation Scheme Ltd* [1997] STC 1; *Trustees of the Omega Group Pension Scheme v IRC* [2001] STC (SCD) 121; *IRC v Laird Group plc* [2002] STC 722.
s 709(1), *Emery v IRC* [1981] STC 150*; *Bird v IRC* [1988] STC 312*; *IRC v Sheppard (Trustees of the Woodland Trust) (No 2)* [1993] STC 240*; *IRC v Trustees of the Sema Group Pension Scheme* [2002] STC 276.
s 709(2), *IRC v Joiner* [1975] STC 657*; *IRC v Wiggins* [1979] STC 244*; *IRC v Williams* [1980] STC 535*.
s 709(4); *IRC v Trustees of the Sema Group Pension Scheme* [2002] STC 276.
Definitions—''The Board'', s 832(1); ''profits or gains'', s 833(1); ''qualifying distribution'', ss 14(2), 832(1); ''tax'', s 832(3) ''tax credit'', s 832(1).
Amendments—[1] Sub-s (2A) inserted by FA 1997 s 73 with effect for the purposes of the application of provisions of this Chapter in relation to chargeable periods ending at any time, including times before the passing of FA 1997, but without prejudice to the construction of this Chapter apart from FA 1997 s 73, does not apply in the case of a tax credit in respect of a distribution made before 8 October 1996.
[2] Words in sub-s (2A) repealed by F(No 2)A 1997 s 34, Sch 4 para 19, Sch 8 Pt II(9) with effect for the year 1999–00 and subsequent years of assessment.

CHAPTER II
TRANSFERS OF SECURITIES

Transfers with or without accrued interest: introductory

Cross references—See TA 1988 s 710(1A) (ss 711–728 do not apply for the purposes of corporation tax in relation to transfers of securities taking place after 31 March 1996).
TA 1988 s 722A (where gilt-edged securities are exchanged for strips of that security, or vice versa, the security is deemed to have been transferred with accrued interest for the purposes of ss 710–728).
TA 1988 s 726A(2) (new issues of securities).
TA 1988 s 728 (Board's power to obtain information and to make regulations for the purposes of ss 710–727).
FA 1993 s 176(4) (Lloyd's members' ancillary trust funds).
European Single Currency (Taxes) Regulations, SI 1998/3177 regs 31–35 (disapplication of the accrued income provisions in respect of an exchange or conversion of securities resulting from a euroconversion).
Revenue Internal Guidance—Inspector's manual IM 4230–4297 (description of scheme with worked examples).

710 Meaning of "securities", "transfer" etc for purposes of sections 711 to 728

(1) This section has effect for the interpretation of sections 711 to 728.

[(1A) Sections 711 to 728 shall not apply for the purposes of corporation tax except as respects transfers of securities taking place before 1st April 1996.][7]

(2) "Securities" does not[, except as provided by subsection (2A) below,][1] include shares in a company but, subject to subsection (3) below, includes any loan stock or similar security—

(*a*) whether of the government of the United Kingdom, any other government, any public or local authority in the United Kingdom or elsewhere, or any company or other body; and

(*b*) whether or not secured, whether or not carrying a right to interest of a fixed amount or at a fixed rate per cent of the nominal value of the securities, and whether or not in bearer form.

[(2A) "Securities" includes shares in a building society which are qualifying shares for the purposes of section [117(4) of the 1992 Act][3] (qualifying corporate bonds).][2]

(3) "Securities" does not include—

(*a*) securities on which the whole of the return is a distribution by virtue of [section 209(2)(*da*)][6];

(*b*) national savings certificates (including Ulster Savings Certificates);

(*c*) war savings certificates;

(*d*) certificates of deposit (within the meaning of section 56(5));

[(*da*) any security which fulfils the following conditions, namely, it is a right to receive an amount (with or without interest) in pursuance of a deposit of money, it subsists under an arrangement falling within section 56A, and no certificate of deposit (as defined in section 56(5)) has been issued in respect of it at the time of the transfer concerned;][4]

(*e*) any security which fulfils the following conditions, namely, it is redeemable, the amount payable on its redemption exceeds its issue price, and no return other than the amount of that excess is payable on it.

(4) Securities are to be taken to be of the same kind if they are treated as being of the same kind by the practice of a recognised stock exchange or would be so treated if dealt with on such a stock exchange.

(5) "Transfer", in relation to securities, means transfer by way of sale, exchange, gift or otherwise[, but—

(*a*) does not include the vesting of securities in a person's personal representatives on his death; and][8]

[(*b*) except as otherwise provided by subsections (1) and (3) of section 722A, does not include any transaction forming part of any such exchange as is mentioned in either of those subsections.][9]

(6) Where an agreement for the transfer of securities is made, they are transferred, and the person to whom they are agreed to be transferred becomes entitled to them, when the agreement is made and not on a later transfer made pursuant to the agreement; and "entitled", "transfer" and cognate expressions shall be construed accordingly.

(7) A person holds securities—

(*a*) at a particular time if he is entitled to them at the time;

(*b*) on a day if he is entitled to them throughout the day or he becomes and does not cease to be entitled to them on the day.

(8) A person acquires securities when he becomes entitled to them.

(9) Where—

(*a*) one individual holds securities at a particular time, and

(*b*) any interest on them would, if it became payable at that time, be treated for the purposes of the Tax Acts as part of another individual's income,

then, for the purposes of section 715(1)(*b*) and section 715(2)(*b*) so far as relating to section 715(1)(*b*), each of them shall be treated as holding at that time the securities which the other holds as well as those which he actually holds.

(10) Where in Scotland two or more persons carry on a trade or business in partnership, any partnership dealings shall be treated as dealings by the partners and not by the firm as such and the partners as being entitled to securities held by the firm.

(11) The nominal value of securities is—

(*a*) where the interest on them is expressed to be payable by reference to a given value, that value; and

(*b*) in any other case, the price of the securities when they were issued.

(12) Where apart from this subsection the nominal value of securities would be a value ("the foreign value") expressed in a currency other than sterling, then, for the purposes of section 715, their nominal value on a particular day is the sterling equivalent on that day of the foreign value.

For the purposes of this subsection the sterling equivalent of a value on a particular day is the sterling equivalent calculated by reference to the London closing rate of exchange for that day.

(13) Where there is a conversion of securities then,—

(*a*) the person who was entitled to them immediately before the conversion shall be treated as transferring them on the day of the conversion (if there is no actual transfer); and

(*b*) the interest period in which the conversion is made shall be treated as ending on the day on which it would have ended had the conversion not been made.

In this subsection "conversion" means a conversion within the meaning of section [132 of the 1992]³ Act.

[(13A) Where a security is deemed to have been transferred by virtue of section 722A(1), the interest period in which the exchange in question takes place shall be treated as ending on the day on which it would have ended had the exchange not taken place.]¹⁰

[(13B) Where a security is deemed to have been transferred by virtue of section 722A(3), the interest period in which the exchange in question takes place shall be treated as having begun on such day as shall for that purpose be specified in the security.]¹⁰

(14) ...⁵

Commentary—*Simon's Direct Tax Service* A7.502, 503.
Definitions—"The 1992 Act", s 831(3); "company", s 832(1), (2); "interest", s 711(7)–(9); "interest period", ss 711(3), (4), 725(9); "local authority", s 519(4); "recognised stock exchange", s 841; "the Tax Acts", s 831(2); "trade", s 832(1); "United Kingdom", s 830(1).
Cross references—See TCGA 1992 s 108 (identification for the purposes of tax on chargeable gains on disposals of securities within the meaning of this section).
TA 1988 s 119 (computation of gain for capital gains tax purposes where there is a transfer of securities within the meaning of this section).
Amendments—¹ Words in sub-s (2) inserted by FA 1991 Sch 10 para 2.
² Sub-s (2A) inserted by FA 1991 Sch 10 para 2 in relation to the application of ss 711–728 below to transfers of securities after 24 July 1991.
³ Words in sub-ss (2A), (13) substituted by TCGA 1992 Sch 10, para 14(1), (36).
⁴ Sub-s (3)(*da*) inserted by F(No 2)A 1992 Sch 8 paras 5, 6 in relation to arrangements made after 16 July 1992.
⁵ Sub-s (14) repealed by FA 1993 Sch 23, Pt III(12) with effect from 1 January 1994.
⁶ Words in sub-s (3)(*a*) substituted for the words "section 209(2)(*e*)(iv) or (v)" by FA 1995 s 87(5), with effect in relation to any interest or other distribution paid after 28 November 1994 (but note commencement provision in FA 1995 s 87(8)).
⁷ Sub-s (1A) inserted by FA 1996 ss 104, 105(1), Sch 14 para 36 with effect for accounting periods ending after 31 March 1996.
⁸ Words in sub-s (5) inserted by FA 1996 s 158(1), (5) with effect as respects deaths after 5 April 1996.
⁹ Words in sub-s (5) inserted by FA 1996 Sch 40 para 3(1).
¹⁰ Sub-ss (13A), (13B) inserted by FA 1996 Sch 40 para 3(2).

711 Meaning of "interest", "transfers with or without accrued interest" etc

(1) This section has effect for the interpretation of sections 710 and 712 to 728.

(2) An interest payment day, in relation to securities, is a day on which interest on them is payable; and, in a case where a particular payment of interest may be made on one of a number of days, the interest is for the purposes of this subsection payable on the first of those days.

(3) Subject to subsection (4) below, the following are interest periods in relation to securities—

(*a*) the period beginning with the day following that on which they are issued and ending with the first interest payment day to fall;

(*b*) the period beginning with the day following one interest payment day and ending with the next to fall.

(4) A period which would (apart from this subsection) be an interest period exceeding 12 months ("a long period") is not an interest period, but the following shall apply to it—

(*a*) the period of 12 months beginning with the day on which it begins is an interest period;

(*b*) each successive period (if any) of 12 months falling within it is an interest period;

(*c*) any period of it which remains after applying paragraphs (*a*) and (*b*) above is an interest period.

(5) Securities are transferred with accrued interest if they are transferred with the right to receive interest payable on—

(*a*) the settlement day, if that is an interest payment day; or

(*b*) the next (or first) interest payment day to fall after the settlement day, in any other case;

and they are transferred without accrued interest if they are transferred without that right.

(6) Where section 710(13), 715(3), 720(4), 721(1)[, 722(1) or (2) or 724(1A)]¹ applies, the transfer shall be treated as made with accrued interest if the person treated as making the transfer was entitled to receive in respect of the securities interest payable on—

(*a*) the settlement day, if that is an interest payment day; or

(*b*) the next (or first) interest payment day to fall after that day, in any other case;

and they shall be treated as transferred without accrued interest if he was not so entitled.

[(6A) In any case where section 722A(1) or (3) applies, the deemed transfer shall be treated as made—

(*a*) without accrued interest in any such case where the exchange in question is made at any time after the balance has been struck for a dividend on the security but before the day on which that dividend is payable;

(*b*) with accrued interest in any other such case.]³

(7) The interest applicable to securities for an interest period is, subject to subsection (8) below, the interest payable on them on the interest payment day with which the period ends.

(8) In the case of a period which is an interest period by virtue only of subsection (4) above ...[2]—

(a) the interest applicable to securities for the period is the interest payable on them on the interest payment day with which the long ...[2] period concerned ends; and

(b) section 713(6) shall have effect as if the references to the period were to the long ...[2] period concerned.

(9) "Interest" includes dividends and any other return (however described) except a return consisting of an amount by which the amount payable on a security's redemption exceeds its issue price.

Commentary—*Simon's Direct Tax Service* **A7.503.**
Definitions—"Securities", s 710; "settlement day", s 712.
Cross references—See TA s 710(1A) (this section does not apply for the purposes of corporation tax in relation to transfers of securities taking place after 31 March 1996).
TCGA 1992 s 119 (computation of gain for capital gains tax purposes where there is a transfer of securities with or without accrued interest within the meaning of this section).
Amendments—[1] Words in sub-s (6) substituted by FA 1990 Sch 6 paras 9(2), 11(1).
[2] Words in sub-s (8) repealed by FA 1993 Sch 23, Pt III(12) with effect from 1 January 1994.
[3] Sub-s (6A) inserted by FA 1996 Sch 40 para 4.

712 Meaning of "settlement day" for purposes of sections 711 to 728

(1) This section has effect to determine, for the purposes of sections 711 and 713 to 728, the settlement day in relation to a transfer of securities.

(2) Where the securities are transferred in accordance with the rules of a recognised market, the settlement day is the day on which the transferee agrees to settle or, if he may settle on one of a number of days, the day on which he settles; and, where they are transferred otherwise, subsections (3) to (5) below apply.

(3) Where the consideration for the transfer is money alone, and the transferee agrees to pay the whole of it on or before the next (or first) interest payment day to fall after an agreement for transfer is made, the settlement day is the day on which he agrees to make the payment or, if payment may be made on one of a number of days, or on a number of different days, the latest of them to fall.

(4) Where there is no consideration for the transfer, or the transfer is a transfer by virtue of sections 710(13), 715(3), 717(8), 720(4), 721[, 722[, 722A][2] and 724(1A)][1], the settlement day is the day on which the securities are transferred.

(5) In any other case, the settlement day is such day as an inspector decides; and the jurisdiction of the General Commissioners or the Special Commissioners on any appeal shall include jurisdiction to review such a decision of the inspector.

Commentary—*Simon's Direct Tax Service* **A7.503.**
Definitions—"Inspector", s 832(1); "interest payment day", s 711(2); "securities", s 710; "transfer", s 710.
Cross references—See TA s 710(1A) (this section does not apply for the purposes of corporation tax in relation to transfers of securities taking place after 31 March 1996).
TA 1988 s 726A(2)(d) (new issues of securities: "settlement day").
Amendments—[1] Words in sub-s (4) substituted by FA 1990 Sch 6 paras 9(3), 11(1).
[2] Words in sub-s (4) inserted by FA 1996 Sch 40 para 5.

Transfers with or without accrued interest: charge to tax and reliefs

713 Deemed sums and reliefs

(1) Subject to sections 714 to 728, this section applies whether the securities in question are transferred before, on or after 6th April 1988; and in this section references to a period are references to the interest period in which the settlement day falls.

(2) If securities are transferred with accrued interest—

(a) the transferor shall be treated as entitled to a sum on them in the period of an amount equal to the accrued amount; and

(b) the transferee shall be treated as entitled to relief on them in the period of the same amount.

(3) If securities are transferred without accrued interest—

(a) the transferor shall be treated as entitled to relief on them in the period of an amount equal to the rebate amount; and

(b) the transferee shall be treated as entitled to a sum on them in the period of the same amount.

(4) In subsection (2) above "the accrued amount" means—

(a) if the securities are transferred under an arrangement by virtue of which the transferee accounts to the transferor separately for the consideration for the securities and for gross interest accruing to the settlement day, an amount equal to the amount (if any) of gross interest so accounted for; and

(b) in any other case, an amount equal to the accrued proportion of the interest applicable to the securities for the period.

(5) In subsection (3) above "the rebate amount" means—

(*a*) if the securities are transferred under an arrangement by virtue of which the transferor accounts to the transferee for gross interest accruing from the settlement day to the next interest payment day, an amount equal to the amount (if any) of gross interest so accounted for; and

(*b*) in any other case, an amount equal to the rebate proportion of the interest applicable to the securities for the period.

(6) In this section—

(*a*) the accrued proportion is—

$$\frac{A}{B}$$

(*b*) the rebate proportion is—

$$\frac{B - A}{B}$$

where—

A is the number of days in the period up to (and including) the settlement day, and
B is the number of days in the period.

(7) For the purposes of subsection (2) above, in a case where the interest on the securities is payable in a currency other than sterling the accrued amount is to be determined as follows—

(*a*) if subsection (4)(*a*) above applies and the sterling equivalent of the amount of gross interest there mentioned is shown in an agreement for transfer, the accrued amount is the sterling equivalent so shown;

(*b*) if subsection (4)(*a*) applies but paragraph (*a*) above does not, or if subsection (4)(*b*) above applies, the accrued amount is the sterling equivalent on the settlement day of the amount found by virtue of subsection (4)(*a*) or (*b*) (as the case may be).

(8) For the purposes of subsection (3) above, in a case where the interest on the securities is payable in a currency other than sterling the rebate amount is to be determined as follows—

(*a*) if subsection (5)(*a*) above applies and the sterling equivalent of the amount of gross interest there mentioned is shown in an agreement for transfer, the rebate amount is the sterling equivalent so shown;

(*b*) if subsection (5)(*a*) applies but paragraph (*a*) above does not, or if subsection (5)(*b*) above applies, the rebate amount is the sterling equivalent on the settlement day of the amount found by virtue of subsection (5)(*a*) or (*b*) (as the case may be).

(9) For the purposes of subsections (7) and (8) above the sterling equivalent of an amount on a particular day is the sterling equivalent calculated by reference to the London closing rate of exchange for that day.

Commentary—*Simon's Direct Tax Service* **A7.510.**
Revenue Internal Guidance—Inspector's manual IM 4246 (worked examples illustrating this section).
Definitions—''Interest'', s 711(7)–(9); ''interest payment day'', s 711(2); ''interest period'', s 711(3), (4), 725(9); ''securities'', s 710; ''securities transferred with accrued interest'', s 711(5), (6); ''settlement day'', s 712.
Cross references—See TA 1988 s 710(1A) (this section does not apply for corporation tax purposes in relation to transfers of securities taking place after 31 March 1996).
TA 1988 s 722A (a deemed transfer upon an exchange of gilt-edged securities for strips of such securities, or vice versa, does not result in any person being treated as a transferor or transferee for the purposes of sub-s (2) above).
TA 1988 s 726A(3), (6) (new issues of securities).
TA 1988 s 727(2) (exclusion of sub-ss (2), (3) above in certain circumstances connected with transfer of securities by way of stock lending).
TA 1988 s 727A(1) (disapplication of sub-ss (2), TA 1988 (3) above in the case of agreements to sell and then repurchase securities).
TA 1988 Sch 22, para 7(6), (7) (pension fund surpluses).
TCGA 1992 s 119 (computation of gain for capital gains tax purposes where there is a transfer of securities and provisions of this section apply).

714 Treatment of deemed sums and reliefs

(1) Subsection (2) below applies if a person is treated as entitled under section 713 to a sum on securities of a particular kind in an interest period, and either—

(*a*) he is not treated as entitled under that section to relief on securities of that kind in the period; or

(*b*) the sum (or total sum) to which he is treated as entitled exceeds the amount (or total amount) of relief to which he is treated as entitled under that section on securities of that kind in the period.

(2) The person shall be treated as receiving on the day the period ends annual profits or gains whose amount is (depending on whether subsection (1)(*a*) or (1)(*b*) above applies) equal to the sum (or total sum) to which he is treated as entitled or equal to the amount of the excess; and the profits or gains shall be chargeable to tax under Case VI of Schedule D for the chargeable period in which they are treated as received.

(3) Subsection (4) below applies if a person is treated as entitled under section 713 to relief on securities of a particular kind in an interest period, and either—

(*a*) he is not treated as entitled under that section to a sum on securities of that kind in the period; or (*b*) the amount (or total amount) of relief to which he is treated as entitled exceeds the sum (or total sum) to which he is treated as entitled under that section on securities of that kind in the period.

(4) The person shall be entitled to an allowance whose amount is (depending on whether subsection (3)(*a*) or (3)(*b*) above applies) equal to the amount (or total amount) of relief to which he is treated as entitled or equal to the amount of the excess; and subsection (5) below shall apply.

(5) Any amount to which the person is entitled by way of interest which—

(*a*) falls due on the securities at the end of the interest period, and

(*b*) is taken into account in computing tax charged for the chargeable period in which the interest period ends,

shall for the purposes of the Tax Acts be treated as reduced by the amount of the allowance; but if the period is one which does not end with an interest payment day, he shall be treated as becoming, in the next interest period, entitled under section 713 to relief on the securities of an amount equal to the amount of the allowance.

(6) ...[1]

Commentary—*Simon's Direct Tax Service* A7.511.
Revenue Internal Guidance—Inspector's manual IM 4247 (worked examples illustrating this section).
Definitions—"Chargeable period", s 832(1); "interest", s 711(7)–(9); "interest payment day", s 711(2); "interest period", ss 711(3), (4), 725(9); "profits or gains", s 833(1); "Schedule D", s 18(1); "securities", s 710; "tax", s 832(3); "the Tax Acts", s 831(2).
Cross references—See TA 1988 s 328(2) (income from funds in court consisting of interest on securities to be calculated apart from sub-s (5) above).
TA 1988 s 710(1A) (this section does not apply for corporation tax purposes in relation to transfers of securities taking place after 31 March 1996).
TA 1988 s 742(4) (provisions applying where person mentioned in sub-s (2) above is resident or domiciled outside the UK).
TA 1988 s 807 (double taxation relief on sums treated as received under sub-s (2) above).
TA 1988 Sch 22, para 7(8) (pension fund surpluses).
Personal Equity Plan Regulations, SI 1989/469 reg 17(1) (exemption from tax for plan manager and plan investor in respect of annual profits or gains deemed to be received by them in respect of personal equity plan investments).
Amendments—[1] Sub-s (6) repealed by FA 1996 s 105, Sch 41 Pt V(3) with effect for accounting periods ending after 31 March 1996, subject to transitional provisions in FA 1996 Sch 15.

715 Exceptions from sections 713 and 714

(1) Section 713(2)(*a*) or (3)(*a*) (as the case may be) does not apply—

(*a*) if the transferor carries on a trade and the transfer falls to be taken into account for the purposes of the Tax Acts in computing the profits or losses of that trade;

(*b*) if the transferor is an individual and on no day in the year of assessment in which the interest period ends or the previous year of assessment the nominal value of securities held by him exceeded £5,000;

(*c*) if the securities transferred form part of the estate of a deceased person, the transferor is that person's personal representative and on no day in the year of assessment in which the interest period ends or the previous year of assessment the nominal value of securities held by him as the deceased's personal representative exceeded £5,000;

(*d*) where—

(i) if the transferor became entitled to any interest on the securities transferred and applied it for charitable purposes only, exemption could be granted under section 505(1)(*c*) in respect of the interest;

(ii) if the transferor became entitled to any interest on the securities transferred and applied it for the purposes mentioned in paragraph (*d*) of section 505(1), exemption could be granted under that paragraph in respect of the interest;

(*e*) if the securities transferred are held on a disabled person's trusts, the transferor is trustee of the settlement and on no day in the year of assessment in which the interest period ends or the previous year of assessment the nominal value of securities held by him as trustee of the settlement exceeded £5,000;

(*f*) if the transferor does not fulfil the residence requirement for the chargeable period in which the transfer is made and is not a non-resident United Kingdom trader in that period;

(*g*), (*h*) ...[3]

(*j*) if the transferor is an individual who, if he became entitled in the year of assessment in which the transfer occurs to any interest on the securities transferred, would be liable, in respect of the interest, to tax chargeable under Case IV or V of Schedule D and computed on the amount of sums received in the United Kingdom; or

(*k*) where, if the transferor became entitled to any interest on the securities transferred, exemption could be allowed under section 592(2) in respect of the interest.

(2) Section 713(2)(*b*) or (3)(*b*) (as the case may be) does not apply if—

(*a*) the transferee carries on a trade, and if at the time he acquired the securities he were to transfer them that transfer would fall to be taken into account for the purposes of the Tax Acts in computing the profits or losses of that trade; or

(*b*) any provision of subsection (1) above except paragraph (*a*) would apply if "transferor" read "transferee".

(3) If securities held on charitable trusts cease to be subject to charitable trusts the trustees shall be treated for the purposes of sections 710 to 728 as transferring the securities (in their capacity as charitable trustees) to themselves (in another capacity) at the time when the securities cease to be so subject.

(4) For the purposes of this section a person fulfils the residence requirement for a chargeable period if he is resident in the United Kingdom during any part of the period or is ordinarily resident in the United Kingdom during the period.

(5) For the purposes of this section a person is a non-resident United Kingdom trader in a chargeable period if during any part of it he is (though neither resident during any part of it nor ordinarily resident during it) carrying on a trade in the United Kingdom through a branch or agency and the securities transferred—

(a) were situated in the United Kingdom and used or held for the purposes of the branch or agency at or before the time of the transfer (where the person concerned is a transferor); or

(b) were so situated at the time of the transfer and were acquired for use by or for the purposes of the branch or agency (where the person concerned is a transferee);

but the provisions of this subsection relating to the situation of the securities in the United Kingdom do not apply where the person concerned is a company.

(6) In any case where securities are transferred without accrued interest to a person ("the seller") and a contract is made for the sale by the seller of securities of that kind ("the seller's contract") and the seller's contract or any contract under which the securities are transferred to the seller is one in the case of which ... [...⁴ paragraph 3 or 4 of Schedule 23A]² has effect and in relation to which the seller is the dividend manufacturer, then—

(a) where the nominal value of the securities subject to the seller's contract is greater than or equal to that of the securities transferred, the seller shall not be treated as entitled to any sum to which, but for this subsection, he would be treated as entitled under section 713(3)(b) on the securities transferred;

(b) where the nominal value of the securities subject to the seller's contract is less than that of the securities transferred, any sum (or the aggregate of any sums) to which he is treated as entitled under section 713(3)(b) on the securities transferred shall be reduced by the amount of any part of the sum (or aggregate) attributable to securities ("relevant securities") of a nominal value equal to that of the securities subject to the seller's contract;

and for the purposes of sections 710 to 728 the securities which the seller contracts to sell shall not be treated as transferred by him (though treated as transferred to the person to whom he contracts to sell).

(7) In determining for the purposes of subsection (6)(b) above which of the securities transferred are relevant securities, those transferred to the seller earlier must be chosen before those transferred to him later.

(8) For the purposes of this section—

"disabled person's trusts" means trusts falling within paragraph [1(1) of Schedule 1 to the 1992]¹ Act;

"branch or agency" has the meaning given by section [10(6) of the 1992]¹ Act;

...³

and the place where securities are situated shall be determined in accordance with section [275 of the 1992]¹ Act.

Commentary—*Simon's Direct Tax Service* **A7.505–508.**
Definitions—"the 1992 Act", s 831(3); "branch or agency", s 834(1); "chargeable period", s 832(1); "income tax", s 832(4); "interest", s 711(7)–(9); "interest period", ss 711(3), (4), 725(9); "nominal value (of securities)", s 710; "Schedule D", s 18(1); "securities", s 710; "tax", s 832(3); "the Tax Acts", s 831(2); "trade", s 832(1); "transfer", s 710; "United Kingdom", s 830(1); "year of assessment", s 832(1).
Cross references—See TA 1988 s 710(1A) (this section does not apply for corporation tax purposes in relation to transfers of securities taking place after 31 March 1996).
F(No 2)A 1992 s 65(2)(b) (life assurance business: I minus E basis: effect on I minus E basis where sub-ss (1)(a), (2)(a) above apply as regards a company.
Amendments—¹ Words in sub-s (8) substituted by TCGA 1992 Sch 10 para 14(1), (37).
² Words in sub-s (6) inserted by FA 1994 s 123(1), (6) and apply where any contract mentioned in sub-s (6) is made after 29 November 1993.
³ Sub-s (1)(g), (h) and definitions omitted from sub-s (8) repealed by FA 1996 s 154(9), Sch 41 Pt V(18) with effect from the year 1996–97.
⁴ Words in sub-s (6) repealed by FA 1997 Sch 18 Pt VI(10) with effect in relation to, and to transfers under, any arrangement made on or after 1 July 1997 by virtue of the Finance Act 1997 Schedule 10, (Appointed Day) Order, SI 1997/991.

716 Transfer of unrealised interest

(1) This section applies where securities are transferred (whether before or after 6th April 1988) with the right to receive interest ("unrealised interest") payable on them on an interest payment day falling before the settlement day.

(2) Where the settlement day falls within an interest period, section 714 shall (subject to subsection (5) below) apply as if the transferor were entitled under section 713 to a sum on them in the period of an amount equal to the unrealised interest (in addition to any other sum to which he may be treated as so entitled).

(3) Where the settlement day falls after the end of the last interest period in relation to the securities, the transferor shall be treated as receiving on the settlement day annual profits or gains of an amount equal to the unrealised interest; and the profits or gains shall be chargeable to tax under Case VI of Schedule D for the chargeable period in which they are treated as received.

(4) Where the transferee receives the unrealised interest, and but for this subsection it would be taken into account in computing tax charged for the chargeable period in which the interest is received, it shall for the purposes of the Tax Acts be left out of account.

(5) Section 715 shall apply for the purposes of this section as if—

(*a*) in subsection (1)—

(i) the reference to section 713(2)(*a*) or (3)(*a*) were a reference to subsection (2) or (3) above; and

(ii) references to the year of assessment in which the interest period ends were references to the year in which the settlement day falls; and

(*b*) in subsection (2) the reference to section 713(2)(*b*) or (3)(*b*) were a reference to subsection (4) above.

Paragraph (*b*) above does not apply where the securities in question were transferred before 19th March 1986.

(6) Where the unrealised interest is payable in a currency other than sterling its amount is for the purposes of this section the sterling equivalent on the settlement day of the amount it would be apart from this subsection; and for this purpose the sterling equivalent is to be calculated by reference to the London closing rate of exchange for the day.

Commentary—*Simon's Direct Tax Service* **A7.535.**
Definitions—"Chargeable period", s 832(1); "interest", s 711(7)–(9); "interest payment day", s 711(2); "interest period", ss 711(3), (4), 725(9); "profits or gains", s 833(1); "Schedule D", s 18(1); "securities", s 710; "settlement day", s 712; "tax", s 832(3); "the Tax Acts", s 831(2); "year of assessment", s 832(1).
Cross references—See TA 1988 s 710(1A) (this section does not apply for corporation tax purposes in relation to transfers of securities taking place after 31 March 1996).
TA 1988 s 727(2) (exclusion of this section in certain circumstances connected with transfer of securities by way of stock lending).
TA 1988 s 727A (disapplication of this section in the case of an agreement to sell and then repurchase securities).
TCGA 1992 s 119 (computation of gain for capital gains tax purposes where there is a transfer of securities and provisions of this section apply).

717 Variable interest rate

(1) This section applies to securities other than securities falling within subsection (2) ...[2] below.

(2) Securities fall within this subsection if their terms of issue provide that throughout the period from issue to redemption (whenever redemption might occur) they are to carry interest at a rate which falls into one, and one only, of the following categories—

(*a*) a fixed rate which is the same throughout the period;
(*b*) a rate which bears to a standard published base rate the same fixed relationship throughout the period;
(*c*) a rate which bears to a published index of prices the same fixed relationship throughout the period.

(3) In subsection (2)(*c*) above "published index of prices" means the retail prices index or any similar general index of prices which is published by, or by an agent of, the government of any territory outside the United Kingdom.

(4), (5) ...[2]

(6) Subsections (7) to (11) below apply if securities to which this section applies are transferred at any time between the time they are issued and the time they are redeemed.

(7) If the securities are transferred without accrued interest they shall be treated for the purposes of sections 710 to 728 as transferred with accrued interest.

(8) The person entitled to the securities immediately before they are redeemed shall be treated for the purposes of those sections as transferring them with accrued interest on the day they are redeemed.

(9) Where there is a transfer as mentioned in subsection (6) above or by virtue of subsection (8) above, section 713 shall have effect with the omission of subsection (2)(*b*) and with the substitution for subsections (3) to (6) of the following subsection—

"(3) In subsection (2) above "the accrued amount" means such amount (if any) as [is just and reasonable][1].".

(10) Subsection (11) below applies where there is a transfer by virtue of subsection (8) above and the settlement day in relation to the transfer falls after the end of a period which would (by virtue of section 711(3) and (4) and apart from this subsection) be the only or last interest period in relation to the securities.

(11) For the purposes of sections 710 to 728 the period beginning with the day following that interest period and ending with the settlement day shall be treated as an interest period in relation to the securities; and section 711(4) shall not apply to it.

Commentary—*Simon's Direct Tax Service* **A7.517.**
Revenue Internal Guidance—Inspector's manual IM 4273 (general description and guidance on application of this section).
Definitions—"Interest", s 711(7)–(9); "interest period", ss 711(3), (4), 725(9); "retail prices index", s 833(2); "securities", s 710; "securities transferred with accrued interest", s 711(5), (6); "settlement day", s 712; "transfer", s 710; "United Kingdom", s 830(1).
Cross references—See TA 1988 s 710(1A) (this section does not apply for corporation tax purposes in relation to transfers of securities taking place after 31 March 1996).
TA 1988 s 726A(7) (new issues of securities).
European Single Currency (Taxes) Regulations, SI 1998/3177 reg 33 (disapplication of the variable rate provision in respect of a euroconversion).
Amendments—[1] Words in sub-s (9) substituted by FA 1996 s 134(1), (2), Sch 20 para 35 with effect from the year 1996–97.
[2] Words in sub-s (1), and sub-ss (4)–(5) repealed by FA 1998 Sch 27 Part III(22) with effect from 31 July 1998.

718 Interest in default

(1) This section applies where, because of any failure to fulfil the obligation to pay interest on securities, the value (on a day mentioned in section 711(7) or (8)(*a*), as the case may be) of the right to receive the interest payable on them on that day is less than the interest so payable.

(2) Section 711(7) or (8)(*a*), as the case may be, shall be construed as if the reference to that interest were to an amount equal to that value.

Commentary—*Simon's Direct Tax Service* **A7.536.**
Definitions—"Interest", s 711(7)–(9); "securities", s 710.
Cross references—See TA 1988 s 710(1A) (this section does not apply for corporation tax purposes in relation to transfers of securities taking place after 31 March 1996).

719 Unrealised interest in default

(1) Where securities are transferred as mentioned in section 716(1) and, because of any failure to fulfil the obligation to pay interest on them, the value (on the day of the transfer) of the right to receive the unrealised interest is less than the amount of the unrealised interest, section 716 shall have effect as modified by subsections (2) to (4) below.

(2) In subsections (2) and (3) for "the unrealised interest" there shall be substituted "amount A".

(3) For subsection (4) there shall be substituted—

"(4) Where the transferee receives an amount by way of the unrealised interest (amount B) and that amount falls to be taken into account in computing tax charged for the chargeable period in which it is received, it shall for the purposes of the Tax Acts be treated as reduced by an amount (amount C) equal to—

(*a*) nil, if the amounts have been previously received by the transferee by way of the unrealised interest and their aggregate is equal to or greater than the value (on the day of the transfer to the transferee) of the right to receive the unrealised interest;

(*b*) amount B, if that value is equal to or greater than amount B (aggregated with other amounts previously so received, if any);

(*c*) that value, if no amount has been previously so received and that value is less than amount B; or

(*d*) so much of that value as exceeds the aggregate of amounts previously so received, in any other case.".

(4) The following shall be substituted for subsection (6)—

"(6) In this section "amount A" means, in a case where the transferor acquired the securities on or after 28th February 1986 with the right to receive unrealised interest—

(*a*) an amount equal to amount D less amount E; or

(*b*) if amount D is equal to or less than amount E, nil.

(7) In this section "amount A" means, in a case not falling within subsection (6) above, an amount equal to amount D.

(8) In this section "amount D" means an amount equal to the value (on the day of the transfer by the transferor) of the right to receive the unrealised interest.

(9) In this section "amount E" means, in a case where the transferor (as transferee) has received in respect of the securities an amount or amounts falling within subsection (4) above—

(*a*) an amount equal to amount F less the total received; or

(*b*) if amount F is equal to or less than the total received, nil.

(10) In this section "amount E" means, in any other case, an amount equal to amount F.

(11) In this section "amount F" means an amount equal to the value (on the day of the transfer to the transferor) of the right to receive the unrealised interest.

(12) In determining for the purposes of this section which securities of a particular kind a person has transferred, he is to be taken to have transferred securities of that kind which he acquired later before securities of that kind which he acquired earlier.

(13) Where the unrealised interest is payable in a currency other than sterling—

(*a*) any amount received by way of the interest is for the purposes of this section the sterling equivalent on the day it is received of the amount it would be apart from this subsection; and (*b*) the value (on the day of a transfer) of the right to receive the interest is for the purposes of this section the sterling equivalent (on that day) of the value it would be apart from this subsection;

and for this purpose the sterling equivalent is to be calculated by reference to the London closing rate of exchange for the day concerned.''

Commentary—*Simon's Direct Tax Service* A7.537.
Revenue Internal Guidance—Inspector's manual IM 4257 (guidance on application of this section).
Definitions—"Chargeable period", s 832(1); "interest", s 711(7)–(9); "securities", s 710; "tax", s 832(3); "the Tax Acts", s 831(2); "transfer", s 710.
Cross references—See TA 1988 s 710(1A) (this section does not apply for corporation tax purposes in relation to transfers of securities taking place after 31 March 1996).

Transfers with or without accrued interest: supplemental

720 Nominees, trustees etc

(1) Where securities are transferred by or to a person as nominee for another person, or as trustee for another person absolutely entitled as against the trustee, or for any person who would be so entitled but for being an infant or other person under disability, or for two or more persons who are or would be jointly so entitled, sections 713, 715 and 716 shall apply as if references to the transferor or the transferee (as the case may be) were to the person or persons for whom the nominee or trustee disposes or acquires.

(2) It is hereby declared that for the purposes of subsection (1) above—

(*a*) securities are transferred by a person as trustee for another person absolutely entitled as against the trustee if that other person has immediately before the transfer the exclusive right to direct how the securities shall be dealt with, subject only to satisfying any outstanding charge, lien or other right of the trustee to resort to the securities for payment of duty, taxes, costs or other outgoings; and
(*b*) securities are transferred to a person as trustee for another person so entitled if that other person has that right immediately after the transfer.

(3) ...[1]

(4) Where a person who is entitled to securities becomes trustee of them, he shall be treated for the purposes of sections 710 to 728 as transferring them (in a capacity other than trustee) to himself (in his capacity as trustee), or to himself and any other trustees, at the time he becomes trustee.

(5) Annual profits or gains which by virtue of 714(2) or 716(3) are treated as received in a year of assessment by trustees shall be chargeable to income tax [at the rate applicable to trusts][2] for that year.

... [4]

(6) In any case where—

(*a*) a trustee of a settlement is treated as receiving annual profits or gains under section 714(2), or
(*b*) a trustee of a settlement who is resident or domiciled outside the United Kingdom throughout any chargeable period in which an interest period (or part of it) falls would, at the end of the interest period, have been treated under section 714(2) as receiving annual profits or gains or annual profits or gains of a greater amount if he had been resident or domiciled in the United Kingdom during a part of each such chargeable period,

[Chapters IA, IB and IC][3] of Part XV shall have effect as if the amount which the trustee is or would be treated as receiving were income [arising under the settlement][3].

(7) In any case where income of a trustee of a settlement who is resident or domiciled outside the United Kingdom throughout any chargeable period in which an interest period (or part of it) falls consists of interest which—

(*a*) falls due at the end of the interest period; and
(*b*) would have been treated under section 714(5) as reduced by an allowance or an allowance of a greater amount if he had been resident or domiciled in the United Kingdom during a part of each such chargeable period;

then, for the purposes of [Chapters IA, IB and IC][3] of Part XV, the interest shall be treated as being reduced by the amount of the allowance or by the additional amount (as the case may be).

(8) In subsections (6) and (7) above—

(*a*) "settlement" means settlement within the meaning of [Chapter IA of Part XV (see section 660G(1) and (2))][3]; and
(*b*) references to a trustee of a settlement are, where there is no trustee of the settlement, to any person entitled to securities comprised in the settlement.

Commentary—*Simon's Direct Tax Service* A7.525.
Revenue Internal Guidance—Trust manual TM 3234-3235 (neither changes in beneficial interests nor changes in trustees involve transfers of trust securities).
Definitions—"Chargeable period", s 832(1); "interest period", ss 711(3), (4), 725(9); "profits or gains", s 833(1); "rate applicable to trusts", s 832(1); "securities", s 710; "United Kingdom", s 830(1); "year of assessment", s 832(1).
Cross references—See TA 1988 s 469(10) (sub-s (5) above not to apply to profits or gains of certain unit trust schemes).

TA 1988 s 710(1A) (this section does not apply for corporation tax purposes in relation to transfers of securities taking place after 31 March 1996).
Amendments—[1] Sub-s (3) repealed by FA 1993 Sch 23 Pt III(12) with effect from 1 January 1994.
[2] Words in sub-s (5) substituted by FA 1993 Sch 6 paras 13, 25(1) with effect from the year 1993–94.
[3] Words in sub-ss (6), (7), (8) substituted by FA 1995 s 74, Sch 17 para 17, with effect from the year 1995–96 (and apply to every settlement wherever and whenever made or entered into).
[4] Words in sub-s (5) repealed by FA 1999 s 139, Sch 20 Pt III(17) with effect for any income arising to a common investment fund after 5 April 1999, and any distribution made by such a fund for a distribution period beginning after that date.

721 Death

(1) ...[3]

[(2) Where—

(*a*) an individual who is entitled to securities dies, and

(*b*) in the interest period in which the individual died, the securities are transferred by his personal representatives to a legatee,

section 713 shall not apply to the transfer.][3]

(3) In subsection (2) above "legatee" includes any person taking (whether beneficially or as trustee) under a testamentary disposition or on an intestacy or partial intestacy, including any person taking by virtue of an appropriation by the personal representatives in or towards satisfaction of a legacy or other interest or share in the deceased's property.

(4) ...[3]

(5) ...[1]

(6) ...[2]

Commentary—*Simon's Direct Tax Service* A7.508.
Definitions—"Business", ss 457, 710; "interest", s 711(7)–(9); "interest period", ss 711(3), (4), 725(9); "securities transferred with accrued interest", s 711; "securities", s 710; "transfer", s 710(5).
Cross references—See TA 1988 s 710(1A) (this section does not apply for corporation tax purposes in relation to transfers of securities taking place after 31 March 1996).
FA 1993 s 176(3)(*a*) (sub-ss (1)–(4) above not to apply (with effect from the year 1992–93 by virtue of FA 1993 s 184(3)) where the deceased is a Lloyd's member and the securities to which he is entitled are part of his ancillary trust fund).
Amendments—[1] Sub-s (5) repealed by FA 1993 Sch 23 Pt III(12) with effect from 1 January 1994.
[2] Sub-s (6) repealed by FA 1993 Sch 23 Pt III(12) with effect from 1 January 1994.
[3] Sub-ss (1), (4) repealed and sub-s (2) substituted by FA 1996 s 158, Sch 41 Pt V(20) with effect as respects deaths after 5 April 1996.

722 Trading stock

(1) Where securities acquired by a person otherwise than as trading stock of a trade carried on by him are appropriated by him for the purposes of the trade as trading stock (whether on the commencement of the trade or otherwise), he shall be treated for the purposes of sections 710 to 728 as transferring them otherwise than in the course of the trade and re-acquiring them in the course of the trade on the day the appropriation is made.

(2) Where securities forming part of the trading stock of a person's trade are appropriated by him for any other purpose, or are retained by him on his ceasing to carry on the trade, he shall be treated for the purposes of sections 710 to 728 as transferring them in the course of the trade and re-acquiring them otherwise than in the course of the trade on the day the appropriation is made or (as the case may be) he ceases to carry on the trade.

Commentary—*Simon's Direct Tax Service* A7.519.
Cross references—See TA 1988 s 710(1A) (this section does not apply for corporation tax purposes in relation to transfers of securities taking place after 31 March 1996).
Definitions—"Securities", s 710; "trade", s 832(1).

[722A Gilt strips: deemed transfer

(1) For the purposes of sections 710 to 728, where a gilt-edged security is exchanged by any person for strips of that security the security shall be deemed to have been transferred by that person.

(2) Nothing in subsection (1) above shall have effect to cause any person to be treated as the transferee of any securities for the purposes of section 713(2)(*b*).

(3) For the purposes of sections 710 to 728, where strips of gilt-edged securities are exchanged by any person for a single gilt-edged security consolidating those strips, that security shall be deemed to have been transferred to that person.

(4) Nothing in subsection (3) above shall have effect to cause any person to be treated as the transferor of any securities for the purposes of section 713(2)(*a*).

(5) In this section—

"gilt-edged security" has the same meaning as in section [50][2]; and

"strip" means anything which, within the meaning of section 47 of the Finance Act 1942, is a strip of a gilt-edged security.][1]

Commentary—*Simon's Direct Tax Service* A7.522.
Definitions—"Interest", s 711(7)–(9).
Cross references—See TA 1988 s 710(1A) (this section does not apply for corporation tax purposes in relation to transfers of securities taking place after 31 March 1996).

TA 1988 s 710(13A), (13B) (determination of the relevant interest period for deemed transfers within sub-ss (1), (3) above).
TA 1988 s 711(6A) (deemed transfers within sub-ss (1), (3) above are treated as made with accrued interest only where the exchange is made after the balance has been struck for a dividend on the security but before it is payable).
Amendments—[1] Section inserted by FA 1996 Sch 40 para 6.
[2] Section number in sub-s (5) consequentially amended by F(No 2)A 1997 s 37(1), (7), (8) with effect in relation to payments of interest falling due after 5 April 1998.

723 Foreign securities: delayed remittances

(1) This section applies where in an interest period a person is treated as entitled to a sum or sums under section 713(2)(*a*) in respect of a transfer or transfers of securities of a particular kind which are situated outside the United Kingdom.

(2) Subject to subsection (3) below, the amount of any annual profits or gains which the person is treated under section 714 as receiving on the day the period ends in respect of securities of that kind shall be reduced—

(*a*) if the amount of the sum or aggregate of the sums exceeds the amount of the profits or gains, to nil; or

(*b*) in any other case, by the amount of the sum or aggregate.

(3) No reduction shall be made unless the person makes a claim and shows that the conditions in subsection (5) below are, so far as applicable, satisfied in the chargeable period in which the profits or gains are treated as received.

(4) The claimant (or his personal representatives) shall be charged to tax under Case VI of Schedule D on the amount of the reduction for the chargeable period in which the conditions in subsection (5) below cease to be satisfied.

(5) The conditions are—

(*a*) that the claimant was unable to remit the proceeds of the transfer or transfers to the United Kingdom;

(*b*) that the inability was due to the laws of the territory in which the securities are situated, or to the executive action of its government, or to the impossibility of obtaining foreign currency in that territory; and

(*c*) that the inability was not due to any want of reasonable endeavours on the part of the claimant.

(6) No claim under this section shall be made in respect of a transfer more than six years after the end of the interest period in which the transfer occurred.

(7) The personal representatives of a deceased person may make any claim which he might have made under this section if he had not died.

(8) For the purposes of this section the place where securities are situated shall be determined in accordance with section [275 of the 1992][1] Act.

Commentary—*Simon's Direct Tax Service* A7.515.
Revenue Internal Guidance—Inspector's manual IM 4269 (relief does not apply where person acquires foreign securities ex div.).
Definitions—"The 1992 Act", s 831(3); "chargeable period", s 832(1); "interest period", ss 711(3), (4), 725(9); "profits or gains", s 833(1); "Schedule D", s 18(1); "securities", s 710; "transfer", s 710; "United Kingdom", s 830(1).
Cross references—See TA 1988 s 710(1A) (this section does not apply for corporation tax purposes in relation to transfers of securities taking place after 31 March 1996).
Amendments—[1] Words in sub-s (8) substituted by TCGA 1992 Sch 10 para 14(1), (38).

724 Insurance companies

Commentary—*Simon's Direct Tax Service* A7.524.
Amendments—This section repealed by FA 1996 Sch 41 Pt V(3) with effect for accounting periods ending after 31 March 1996, subject to transitional provisions in FA 1996 Sch 15.

725 Lloyd's underwriters

Commentary—*Simon's Direct Tax Service* A7.528.
Amendments—This section repealed by FA 1993 Sch 23 Pt III(12) with effect from 1 January 1994.

726 Building societies

Amendments—This section repealed by FA 1991 Sch 19 Pt V with effect from the year 1991–92.

[726A New issues of securities

(1) This section applies where—

(*a*) securities (old securities) of a particular kind are issued by way of the original issue of securities of that kind,

(*b*) on a later occasion securities (new securities) of the same kind are issued,

(*c*) a sum (the extra return) is payable in respect of the new securities, by the person issuing them, to reflect the fact that interest is accruing on the old securities,

(*d*) the issue price of the new securities includes an element (whether or not separately identified) representing payment for the extra return, and

(e) the extra return is equal to the amount of interest payable for the relevant period on so many old securities as there are new (or, if there are more new securities than old, the amount of interest which would be so payable if there were as many old securities as new).

(2) For the purposes of sections 710 to 728—

(a) the new securities shall be treated as having been issued on the relevant day;

(b) they shall be treated as transferred to the person to whom they are in fact issued (though not treated as transferred by any person);

(c) the transfer shall be treated as a transfer with accrued interest and as made on the day on which the new securities are in fact issued;

(d) that day shall be treated as the settlement day (notwithstanding section 712);

but this subsection is subject to subsection (7) below.

(3) If the new securities are in fact issued under an arrangement by virtue of which the acquirer accounts to the issuer separately for the extra return mentioned in subsection (1) above and the rest of the issue price, in relation to the transfer mentioned in subsection (2)(b) above—

(a) section 713(4) shall not apply, and

(b) for the purposes of section 713(2) the accrued amount shall be the amount found under subsection (4) or(5) below (as the case may be);

and here "the acquirer" means the person to whom the new securities are in fact issued and "the issuer" means the person by whom they are in fact issued.

(4) Subject to subsection (5) below, the amount is one equal to the amount (if any) of the extra return separately accounted for.

(5) If the interest on the new securities is payable in a currency other than sterling, the amount is the sterling equivalent on the settlement day of the amount found under subsection (4) above; and for this purpose the sterling equivalent of an amount on the settlement day is the sterling equivalent calculated by reference to the London closing rate of exchange for that day.

(6) If the new securities are in fact issued otherwise than as mentioned in subsection (3) above, section 713(4)(b) shall apply in relation to the transfer mentioned in subsection (2)(b) above.

(7) If the new securities are securities to which section 717 applies (after applying subsection (2)(a) above) subsection (2)(b) to (d) above shall not apply.

(8) For the purposes of this section the relevant period is the period beginning with the day following the relevant day and ending with the day on which the new securities are in fact issued.

(9) For the purposes of this section the relevant day is—

(a) the last (or only) interest payment day to fall in respect of the old securities before the day on which the new securities are in fact issued, or

(b) the day on which the old securities were issued, in a case where no interest payment day fell in respect of them before the day on which the new securities are in fact issued.][1]

Commentary—*Simon's Direct Tax Service* A7.516.
Definitions—"Interest", s 711(7)–(9); "interest payment day", s 711(2); "securities", s 710; "settlement day", s 712; "transfer", s 710; "transfer with accrued interest", s 711(5), (6).
Cross references—See TA 1988 s 710(1A) (this section does not apply for corporation tax purposes in relation to transfers of securities taking place after 31 March 1996).
Amendments—[1] This section inserted by FA 1991 Sch 12 paras 2, 5 and applies if the new securities are issued after 18 March 1991, whether the old securities are issued before, on or after that day.

727 Stock lending

(1) ...[1]

(2) Where securities are transferred in circumstances such that by virtue of [section 263B(2) of the 1992 Act][1] (capital gains tax exemption) any disposal and acquisition are disregarded for the purposes of capital gains tax, sections 713(2) and (3) and 716 shall not apply.

Commentary—*Simon's Direct Tax Service* A7.508.
Definition—"The 1992 Act", s 831(3).
Cross references—See TA 1988 s 710(1A) (this section does not apply for corporation tax purposes in relation to transfers of securities taking place after 31 March 1996).
Amendments—[1] Sub-s (1) repealed and words in sub-s (2) substituted by FA 1997 Sch 10 paras 5(3), 7(1), Sch 18 Pt VI(10) with effect in relation to, and to transfers under, any arrangement made on or after 1 July 1997 by virtue of the Finance Act 1997, Schedule 10, (Appointed Day) Order, SI 1997/991.

[727A Exception for sale and repurchase of securities

(1) Where securities are transferred under an agreement to sell them, and under the same or any related agreement the transferor or a person connected with him—

(a) is required to buy back the securities, or

(b) acquires an option, which he subsequently exercises, to buy back the securities,

section 713(2) and (3) and section 716 do not apply to the transfer by the transferor or the transfer back.

(2) For the purposes of this section agreements are related if they are entered into in pursuance of the same arrangement (regardless of the date on which either agreement is entered into).

(3) Section 839 (connected persons) applies for the purposes of this section.

(4) References in this section to buying back securities include buying similar securities.

For this purpose securities are similar if they entitle their holders—

(a) to the same rights against the same persons as to capital and interest, and
(b) to the same remedies for the enforcement of those rights,

notwithstanding any difference in the total nominal amounts of the respective securities or in the form in which they are held or the manner in which they can be transferred.

(5) For the purposes of this section—

(a) a person connected with the transferor who is required to buy securities sold by the transferor shall be treated as being required to buy the securities back, and
(b) a person connected with the transferor who acquires an option to buy securities sold by the transferor shall be treated as acquiring an option to buy the securities back,

notwithstanding that it was not he who sold them.][1]

Commentary—*Simon's Direct Tax Service* A7.508.
Definitions—"Interest", s 832(1).
Cross references—See TA 1988 s 737E (Treasury may modify effect of this section by regulations).
Sale and Repurchase of Securities (Modification of Enactments) Regulations, SI 1995/3220 regs 3, 5 (modification of this section in relation to arrangements for the sale and redemption of securities or for the substitution of the original securities to be repurchased).
European Single Currency (Taxes) Regulations, SI 1998/3177 regs 13–19 (agreements for sale and repurchase of securities in relation to replacement of securities in a euroconversion).
Amendments—[1] This section inserted by FA 1995 s 79(1), with effect where the agreement to sell the securities is entered into on or after 1 May 1995. (Note, however, FA 1995 s 71(4).)

TA 1988

728 Information

(1) In order to obtain for the purposes of [sections 710 to 727A][1] particulars relating to securities, an inspector may by notice require a return under subsection (2) or (3) below.

(2) A member of the Stock Exchange, other than a market maker, may be required to make a return giving, in relation to any transactions effected by him in the course of his business in the period specified in the notice, such particulars as may be so specified.

In relation to transactions before 27th October 1986 this subsection shall have effect with the substitution of "jobber" for "market maker".

(3) A person (other than a member of the Stock Exchange), who acts as an agent or broker in the United Kingdom in transactions in securities, may be required to make a return giving, in relation to any such transactions effected by him in the period specified in the notice, such particulars as may be so specified.

(4) No person shall be required under subsection (2) or (3) above to include in a return particulars of any transaction effected more than three years before the service of the notice requiring him to make the return.

(5) In order to obtain for the purposes of [sections 710 to 727A][1] particulars relating to securities, the Board or an inspector may by notice require any person in whose name any securities are registered to state whether or not he is the beneficial owner of those securities and, if he is not the beneficial owner of them or any of them, to furnish the name and address of the person or persons on whose behalf the securities are registered in his name.

(6) In this section "market maker", in relation to securities, means a person who—

(a) holds himself out at all normal times in compliance with the rules of the Stock Exchange as willing to buy and sell securities of the kind concerned at a price specified by him; and
(b) is recognised as doing so by the Council of the Stock Exchange.

(7) The Board may by regulations provide that—

(a) subsections (2), (3) and (6)(a) above shall have effect as if references to the Stock Exchange were to any recognised investment exchange (within the meaning of the [Financial Services and Markets Act 2000][2]) or to any of those exchanges specified in the regulations; and
(b) subsection (6)(b) shall have effect as if the reference to the Council of the Stock Exchange were to the investment exchange concerned.

(8) Regulations under subsection (7) above shall apply in relation to transactions effected on or after such day as may be specified in the regulations.

Commentary—*Simon's Direct Tax Service* A7.504.
Definitions—"The Board", s 832(1); "business", ss 457, 710; "inspector", s 832(1); "notice", s 832(1); "United Kingdom", s 830(1).
Cross references—See TA 1988 s 737E (Treasury may modify effect of this section by regulations).
Amendments—[1] Words in sub-ss (1), (5) substituted by FA 1995 s 79(2), with effect where the agreement to sell the securities is entered into on or after 1 May 1995. (Note, however, FA 1995 s 79(4).)
[2] Words in sub-s (7)(a) substituted by the Financial Services and Markets Act 2000 s 432(1), Sch 20 para 4 with effect from 1 December 2001 (by virtue of SI 2001/3538).

Other transfers of securities

729 Sale and repurchase of securities

Commentary—*Simon's Direct Tax Service* **A7.201–205, 207.**
Amendments—This section repealed by FA 1996 s 159(1), Sch 41 Pt V(21) except in relation to cases where the initial agreement to sell or transfer securities or other property was made before 6 November 1996 (FA 1996 s 159 (Appointed Day) Order, SI 1996/2646).

730 Transfers of income arising from securities

(1) Where in any chargeable period the owner of any securities (''the owner'') sells or transfers the right to receive any interest payable (whether before or after the sale or transfer) in respect of the securities without selling or transferring the securities, then, for all the purposes of the Tax Acts, that interest, whether it would or would not be chargeable to tax apart from the provisions of this section—

    (*a*) shall be deemed to be the income of the owner or, in a case where the owner is not the beneficial owner of the securities and some other person (''a beneficiary'') is beneficially entitled to the income arising from the securities, the income of the beneficiary, and

    (*b*) shall be deemed to be the income of the owner or beneficiary for that chargeable period, and

    (*c*) shall not be deemed to be the income of any other person.

(2) For the purposes of subsection (1) above, in the case of a sale or other realisation the proceeds of which are chargeable to tax [by virtue of section 18(3B)][1] the interest so deemed to be the income of the owner or beneficiary shall be deemed to be equal in amount to the amount of those proceeds.

[(2A) This section does not have effect for the purposes of Chapter 2 of Part 4 of the Finance Act 1996 (loan relationships).][2]

(3) Nothing in subsection (1) above shall affect any provision of this Act authorising or requiring the deduction of income tax—

    (*a*) from any interest which, under that subsection, is deemed to be the income of the owner or beneficiary, or

    (*b*) from the proceeds of any subsequent sale or other realisation of the right to receive that interest;

but the proceeds of any such subsequent sale or other realisation shall not, for any of the purposes of the Tax Acts, be deemed to be the income of the seller or the person on whose behalf the right is otherwise realised.

(4) Where—

    (*a*) the securities are of such a character that the interest payable in respect thereof may be paid without deduction of income tax, and

    (*b*) the owner or beneficiary does not show that the proceeds of any sale or other realisation of the right to receive the interest which is deemed to be his income by virtue of this section have been charged to tax [by virtue of section 18(3B)][1],

then the owner or beneficiary shall be chargeable to tax under Case VI of Schedule D in respect of that interest, but shall be entitled to credit for any tax which that interest is shown to have borne.

(5) For the purposes of subsection (4) above, in any case where, if the interest had been chargeable under Case IV or Case V of Schedule D, the computation of tax would have been made by reference to the amount received in the United Kingdom, the tax under Case VI shall be computed on the full amount of the sums which have been or will be received in the United Kingdom in the year of assessment or any subsequent year in which the owner remains the owner of the securities.

(6) In relation to corporation tax, subsections (4) and (5) above shall not apply but, subject to the provisions of the Tax Acts about distributions, the owner or beneficiary shall, in respect of any interest which is deemed to be his income by virtue of this section, be chargeable to corporation tax under Case VI of Schedule D unless he shows that the proceeds of any sale or other realisation of the right to receive that interest have been charged to tax [by virtue of section 18(3B)][1].

(7) In this section—

    ''interest'' includes dividends, annuities and shares of annuities, and

    ''securities'' includes stocks and shares.

(8) The Board may by notice require any person to furnish them within such time as they may direct (not being less than 28 days), in respect of all securities of which he was the owner at any time during the period specified in the notice, with such particulars as they consider necessary for the purposes of this section and for the purpose of discovering whether—

    (*a*) tax has been borne in respect of the interest on all those securities; or

    (*b*) the proceeds of any sale or other realisation of the right to receive the interest on the securities have been charged to tax [by virtue of section 18(3B)][1].

Commentary—*Simon's Direct Tax Service* **A7.402–405; D2.525.**
Simon's Tax Cases—*McGuckian v IRC* [1994] STC 888*.
Definitions—''The Board'', s 832(1); ''chargeable period'', s 832(1); ''distributions'', ss 209(2), 832(1); ''income tax'', s 832(4); ''interest'', s 832(1); ''notice'', s 832(1); ''Schedule D'', s 18(1); ''tax'', s 832(3); ''the Tax Acts'', s 831(2); ''United Kingdom'', s 830(1); ''year of assessment'', s 832(1).

Amendments—¹ Words in sub-ss (2), (4)(*b*), (6), (8)(*b*) substituted by FA 1996 Sch 7 paras 23, 32 with effect as respects income tax from the year 1996–97 and as respects corporation tax for accounting periods ending after 31 March 1996.
² Sub-s (2A) inserted by FA 2002 s 82, Sch 25 paras 43, 51 with effect for accounting periods beginning after 30 September 2002.

[730A Treatment of price differential on sale and repurchase of securities

(1) Subject to subsection (8) below, this section applies where—

(*a*) a person (''the original owner'') has transferred any securities to another person (''the interim holder'') under an agreement to sell them;

(*b*) the original owner or a person connected with him is required to buy them back either—

(i) in pursuance of an obligation to do so imposed by that agreement or by any related agreement, or

(ii) in consequence of the exercise of an option acquired under that agreement or any related agreement;

and

(*c*) the sale price and the repurchase price are different.

(2) The difference between the sale price and the repurchase price shall be treated for the purposes of the Tax Acts—

(*a*) where the repurchase price is more than the sale price, as a payment of interest made by the repurchaser on a deemed loan from the interim holder of an amount equal to the sale price; and

(*b*) where the sale price is more than the repurchase price, as a payment of interest made by the interim holder on a deemed loan from the repurchaser of an amount equal to the repurchase price.

(3) Where any amount is deemed under subsection (2) above to be a payment of interest, that payment shall be deemed for the purposes of the Tax Acts to be one that becomes due at the time when the repurchase price becomes due and, accordingly, is treated as paid when that price is paid.

(4) Where any amount is deemed under subsection (2) above to be a payment of interest, the repurchase price shall be treated for the purposes of the Tax Acts (other than this section and sections 737A and 737C) and (in cases where section 263A of the 1992 Act does not apply) for the purposes of the 1992 Act—

(*a*) in a case falling within paragraph (*a*) of that subsection, as reduced by the amount of the deemed payment; and

(*b*) in a case falling within paragraph (*b*) of that subsection, as increased by the amount of the deemed payment.

(5) For the purposes of section 209(2)(*d*) and (*da*) any amount which is deemed under subsection (2)(*a*) above to be a payment of interest shall be deemed to be interest in respect of securities issued by the repurchaser and held by the interim holder.

[(5A) For the purposes of the Corporation Tax Acts, a company has a relationship to which this section applies in any case where—

(*a*) the circumstances are as set out in subsection (1) above; and

(*b*) interest on a deemed loan is deemed by virtue of subsection (2) above to be paid by or to the company;

and references to a relationship to which this section applies, and to a company's being party to such a relationship, shall be construed accordingly.]³

[(6) Where a company has a relationship to which this section applies—

(*a*) Chapter 2 of Part 4 of the Finance Act 1996 (loan relationships) shall, as respects that company, have effect in relation to the interest deemed by virtue of subsection (2) above to be paid or received by the company under that relationship as it would have effect if it were interest under a loan relationship to which the company is a party,

(*b*) the debits and credits falling to be brought into account for the purposes of that Chapter so far as they relate to the deemed interest shall be those given by the use in relation to the deemed interest of an authorised accruals basis of accounting, and

(*c*) the only debits or credits to be brought into account for the purposes of that Chapter by virtue of this subsection in respect of a relationship are those relating to that deemed interest,

and, subject to paragraphs (*b*) and (*c*) above, references in the Corporation Tax Acts to a loan relationship accordingly include a reference to a relationship to which this section applies.]³

[(6A) Any question whether debits or credits brought into account in accordance with subsection (6) above in relation to any company—

(*a*) are to be brought into account under section 82(2) of the Finance Act 1996 (trading loan relationships), or

(*b*) are to be treated as non-trading debits or credits,

shall be determined (subject to Schedule 11 to that Act (insurance companies)) according to the extent (if any) to which the company is a party to the repurchase in the course of activities forming an integral part of a trade carried on by the company.]²

[(6B) To the extent that debits or credits fall to be brought into account by a company under section 82(2) above in the case of a relationship to which this section applies, the company shall be regarded for the purposes of Chapter 2 of Part 4 of the Finance Act 1996 as being party to the relationship for the purposes of a trade carried on by the company.]³

(7) The Treasury may by regulations provide for any amount which is deemed under subsection (2) above to be received as a payment of interest to be treated, in such circumstances and to such extent as may be described in the regulations, as comprised in income that is eligible for relief from tax by virtue of section 438, 592(2), 608(2)(a), 613(4), 614(2), (3) or (4), 620(6) or 643(2).

(8) Except where regulations under section 737E otherwise provide, this section does not apply if—

(a) the agreement or agreements under which provision is made for the sale and repurchase are not such as would be entered into by persons dealing with each other at arm's length; or

(b) all of the benefits or risks arising from fluctuations, before the repurchase takes place, in the market value of the securities sold accrue to, or fall on, the interim holder.

(9) In this section references to the repurchase price are to be construed—

(a) in cases where section 737A applies, and

(b) in cases where section 737A would apply if it were in force in relation to the securities in question,

as references to the repurchase price which is or, as the case may be, would be applicable by virtue of section 737C(3)(b), (9) or (11)(c).]¹

Commentary—*Simon's Direct Tax Service* A7.206.
Regulations—Manufactured Payments and Transfers of Securities (Tax Relief) Regulations, SI 1995/3036.
Revenue & other press releases—IR Tax Bulletin December 1995 p 266 (guidance is given on when price differential should be regarded as annual interest).
Definitions—"Interest", s 832(1); "loan relationship", s 834(1), FA 1996 s 81; "securities", s 737B; "the Tax Acts", s 831(2); "the 1992 Act", s 831(3).
Cross references—TA 1988 s 730B (interpretation of this section).
TA 1988 s 737C(3) (repurchase price increased by gross amount of deemed manufactured dividend).
TA 1988 s 737C (9) (repurchase price increased by gross amount of deemed manufactured interest).
TA 1988 s 737C(11) (repurchase price increased by gross amount of deemed manufactured overseas dividend).
TA 1988 s 737E (power to modify the effect of this section by regulations).
TA 1988 s 839, by virtue of s 730B(5) (meaning of "connected persons").
Sale and Repurchase of Securities (Modification of Enactments) Regulations, SI 1995/3220 regs 3, 5 (modification of this section in relation to arrangements for the sale and redemption of securities or for the substitution of the original securities to be repurchased).
European Single Currency (Taxes) Regulations, SI 1998/3177 regs 13–19 (agreements for sale and repurchase of securities in relation to replacement of securities in a euroconversion).
Amendments—¹ Section inserted by FA 1995 s 80(1), with effect where the agreement to sell the securities is entered into on or after 1 May 1995.
² Sub-ss (6), (6A) substituted for sub-s (6) by FA 1996 ss 104, 105(1), Sch 14 para 37 with effect for accounting periods ending after 31 March 1996, subject to transitional provisions in FA 1996 Sch 15.
³ Sub-ss (5A), (6B) to be inserted, and sub-s (6) to be substituted, by FA 2002 s 82, Sch 25 paras 43, 52 with effect for accounting periods beginning after 30 September 2002. Sub-s (6) previously read as follows—

"(6) For the purposes of Chapter II of Part IV of the Finance Act 1996 (loan relationships)—

(a) interest deemed by virtue of subsection (2) above to be paid or received by any company shall be deemed to be interest under a loan relationship; and

(b) the debits and credits falling to be brought into account for the purposes of that Chapter so far as they relate to the deemed interest shall be those given by the use in relation to the deemed interest of an authorised accruals basis of accounting.".

[730B Interpretation of section 730A

(1) For the purposes of section 730A agreements are related if they are entered into in pursuance of the same arrangement (regardless of the date on which either agreement is entered into).

(2) References in section 730A to buying back securities—

(a) shall include references to buying similar securities; and

(b) in relation to a person connected with the original owner, shall include references to buying securities sold by the original owner or similar securities,

notwithstanding (in each case) that the securities bought have not previously been held by the purchaser; and references in that section to repurchase or to a repurchaser shall be construed accordingly.

(3) In section 730A and this section "securities" has the same meaning as in section 737A.

(4) For the purposes of this section securities are similar if they entitle their holders—

(a) to the same rights against the same persons as to capital, interest and dividends, and

(b) to the same remedies for the enforcement of those rights,

notwithstanding any difference in the total nominal amounts of the respective securities or in the form in which they are held or the manner in which they can be transferred.

(5) Section 839 (connected persons) applies for the purposes of section 730A.]¹

Commentary—*Simon's Direct Tax Service* A7.206.
Definitions—"Interest", s 832(1).
Cross references—See TA 1988 s 731(2F) (this section also to apply for the purposes of TA 1988 s 731(2B)–(2E)).
Amendments—¹ This section inserted by FA 1995 s 80(1), with effect where the agreement to sell the securities is entered into on or after 1 May 1995.

[730C Exchanges of gilts: traders etc

(1) This section has effect for the purposes of computing the [profits][3] arising from any trade, profession or vocation carried on by any person in so far as the computation is such as to require amounts in respect of the acquisition or redemption of a gilt-edged security (including any strip) to be brought into account.

(2) Where a gilt-edged security is exchanged by any person for strips of that security—

(*a*) the security shall be deemed to have been redeemed at the time of the exchange by the payment to that person of its market value; and

(*b*) that person shall be deemed to have acquired each strip for the amount which bears the same proportion to that market value as is borne by the market value of the strip to the aggregate of the market values of all the strips received in exchange for the security.

(3) Where strips of a gilt-edged security are consolidated into a single security by being exchanged by any person for that security—

(*a*) each of the strips shall be deemed to have been redeemed at the time of the exchange by the payment to that person of the amount equal to its market value; and

(*b*) that person shall be deemed to have acquired the security for the amount equal to the aggregate of the market values of the strips given in exchange for the security.

(4) References in this section to the market value of a security given or received in exchange for another are references to its market value at the time of the exchange.

(5) Subsections (3) and (4) of section 473 shall not apply in the case of any exchange to which subsection (2) or (3) above applies.

(6) Without prejudice to the generality of any power conferred by section 202 of the Finance Act 1996, the Treasury may by regulations make provision for the purposes of this section as to the manner of determining the market value at any time of any gilt-edged security (including any strip).

(7) Regulations under subsection (6) above may—

(*a*) make different provision for different cases; and

(*b*) contain such incidental, supplemental, consequential and transitional provision as the Treasury may think fit.

(8) This section does not apply for the purposes of corporation tax.

(9) In this section—

"gilt-edged security" has the same meaning as in section [50][2]; and

"strip" means anything which, within the meaning of section 47 of the Finance Act 1942, is a strip of a gilt-edged security.][1]

Commentary—*Simon's Direct Tax Service* A7.206.
Definitions—"trade", s 832(1).
Amendments—[1] This section inserted by FA 1996 s 202(8), Sch 40 para 7.
[2] Section number in sub-s (9) consequentially amended by F(No 2)A 1997 s 37(1), (7), (8) with effect in relation to payments of interest falling due after 5 April 1998.
[3] Word "profits" substituted for "profits and gains" in sub-s (1) by FA 1998 Sch 7 para 1 with effect from 31 July 1998.

Purchase and sale of securities

731 Application and interpretation of sections 732 to 734

(1) In this section "the relevant provisions" means sections 732, 733, 734 and this section.

(2) [Subject to subsections (2A) to (10) below][5], the relevant provisions [apply][5] to cases of a purchase by a person ("the first buyer") of any securities and their subsequent sale by him, the result of the transaction being that interest becoming payable in respect of the securities ("the interest") is receivable by the first buyer.

[(2A) The relevant provisions do not apply where the first buyer is required under the arrangements for the purchase of the securities to make to the person from whom he purchased the securities, not later than the date on which he subsequently sells the securities, a payment of an amount representative of the interest, or is treated by virtue of section 737A(5) as required to make such a payment.][6]

[(2B) Subject to subsection (2E) below, where there is a repo agreement in relation to any securities—

(*a*) neither—

(i) the purchase of the securities by the interim holder from the original owner, nor

(ii) the repurchase of the securities by the original owner,

shall be a purchase of those securities for the purposes of subsection (2) above; and

(*b*) neither—

(i) the sale of the securities by the original owner to the interim holder, nor

(ii) the sale by the interim holder under which the securities are bought back by the original owner, shall be taken for the purposes of subsection (2) above to be a subsequent sale of securities previously purchased by the seller.

(2C) Accordingly, where there is a repo agreement, the securities repurchased by the original owner shall be treated for the purposes of subsection (2) above (to the extent that that would not otherwise be the case) as if they were the same as, and were purchased by the original owner at the same time as, the securities sold by him to the interim holder.

(2D) For the purposes of subsections (2B) and (2C) above there is a repo agreement in relation to any securities if there is an agreement in pursuance of which a person (''the original owner'') sells the securities to another ('the interim holder') and, in pursuance of that agreement or a related agreement, the original owner—

(a) is required to buy back the securities;

(b) will be required to buy them back on the exercise by the interim holder of an option conferred by the agreement or related agreement; or

(c) is entitled, in pursuance of any obligation arising on a person's becoming entitled to receive an amount in respect of the redemption of those securities, to receive from the interim holder an amount equal to the amount of the entitlement.

(2E) Subsections (2B) and (2C) above do not apply if—

(a) the agreement or agreements under which the arrangements are made for the sale and repurchase of the securities are not such as would be entered into by persons dealing with each other at arm's length; or

(b) any of the benefits or risks arising from fluctuations, before the securities are repurchased, in the market value of the securities in question accrues to or falls on the interim holder.

(2F) Section 730B applies for the purposes of subsections (2B) to (2E) above as it applies for the purposes of section 730A.]⁸

(3) The relevant provisions do not [apply]⁵ where—

(a) the time elapsing between the purchase by the first buyer and his taking steps to dispose of the securities exceeded six months, or

(b) that time exceeded one month and [the purchase and sale were each effected at the current market price, and]⁷ the sale was not effected in pursuance of an agreement or arrangement made before or at the time of the purchase.

...⁷

(4) The reference in subsection (3) above to the first buyer taking steps to dispose of the securities shall be construed—

(a) if he sold them in the exercise of an option he had acquired, as a reference to his acquisition of the option,

(b) in any other case, as a reference to his selling them.

[(4A) For the purposes of subsection (3) above, where a purchase or sale is effected as a direct result of the exercise of a qualifying option, it shall be treated as effected at the current market price if the terms under which the first buyer acquired the option, or, as the case may be, became subject to it, were arm's length terms.]¹

[(4B) For the purposes of subsection (4A) above an option is a ''qualifying option'' if it would be a traded option or financial option as defined in subsection [(8) of section 144 of the 1992 Act]² were the reference in paragraph (b) of that subsection to the time of the abandonment or other disposal a reference to the time of exercise.]¹

[(4C) In subsection (4A) above the reference to arm's length terms is to terms—

(a) agreed between persons dealing at arm's length, or

(b) not so agreed, but nonetheless such as might reasonably be expected to have been agreed between persons so dealing.]¹

(5) For the purposes of the relevant provisions, a sale of securities similar to, and of the like nominal amount as, securities previously bought (''the original securities'') shall be equivalent to a sale of the original securities and subsection (4) above shall apply accordingly; and where the first buyer bought parcels of similar securities at different times a subsequent sale of any of the securities shall, so far as may be, be related to the last to be bought of the parcels, and then to the last but one, and so on.

(6) A person shall be under no greater liability to tax by virtue of subsection (5) above than he would have been under if instead of selling the similar securities he had sold the original securities.

(7) Where at the time when a trade is, or is deemed to be, set up and commenced any securities form part of the trading stock belonging to the trade, those securities shall be treated for the purposes of this section—

(a) as having been sold at that time in the open market by the person to whom they belonged immediately before that time, and

(b) as having been purchased at that time in the open market by the person thereafter engaged in carrying on the trade.

(8) Subject to subsection (7) above, where there is a change in the persons engaged in carrying on a trade which is not a change on which the trade is deemed to be discontinued, the provisions of this section shall apply in relation to the person so engaged after the change as if anything done to or by his predecessor had been done to or by him.

(9) For the purposes of the relevant provisions—

"interest" includes a qualifying distribution and any dividend which is not a qualifying distribution, ...[4];

"person" includes any body of persons, and references to a person entitled to any exemption from tax include, in a case of an exemption expressed to apply to income of a trust or fund, references to the persons entitled to make claims for the granting of that exemption;

"securities" includes stocks and shares, except securities which are securities for the purposes of sections 710 to 728.

[(9A) In applying references in the relevant provisions to interest in relation to a qualifying distribution ...[9]—

(a) "gross interest" means the qualifying distribution together with the tax credit to which the recipient of the distribution is entitled in respect of it, and

(b) "net interest" means the qualifying distribution exclusive of any such tax credit.][3]

[(9B)–(9D) ...][9]

(10) For the purposes of the relevant provisions, securities shall be deemed to be similar if they entitle their holders to the same rights against the same persons as to capital and interest and the same remedies for the enforcement of those rights, notwithstanding any difference in the total nominal amounts of the respective securities or in the form in which they are held or the manner in which they can be transferred; and for the purposes of this subsection, rights guaranteed by the Treasury shall be treated as rights against the Treasury.

Commentary—*Simon's Direct Tax Service* **A7.301, 302; D2.526.**
Revenue Internal Guidance—Inspector's manual IM 4330–4344 (explanation of section with examples).
Definitions—"the 1992 Act", s 831(3); "the Board", s 832(1); "body of persons", s 832(1); "interest", s 832(1); "qualifying distribution", ss 14(2), 832(1); "tax", s 831(2); "tax credit", s 832(1); "trade", s 832(1).
Amendments—[1] Sub-ss (4A)–(4C) inserted by FA 1991 s 55 and apply where the subsequent sale by the first buyer takes place after 24 July 1991.
[2] Words in sub-s (4B) substituted by TCGA 1992 Sch 10 para 14(1), (40).
[3] Sub-ss (9A)–(9D) inserted by FA 1994 Sch 16 para 17(1), (3).
[4] Words in the definition of "interest" in sub-s (9) repealed by FA 1994 Sch 16 para 17(1), (2) and Sch 26, Pt V(16).
[5] Words in sub-ss (2), (3), substituted by FA 1995 s 81(3), with effect where the date on which the payment referred to in sub-s (2A) is required to be made, or treated as required to be made, is after 1 May 1995.
[6] Sub-s (2A) inserted by FA 1995 s 81(2), with effect as noted to footnote 5 above.
[7] Words in sub-s (3)(b) substituted and words in sub-s (3) repealed, by FA 1996 s 134(1), (2), Sch 20 para 36, Sch 41 Pt V(10) with effect for the purposes of income tax from the year 1996–97 and as respects corporation tax for accounting periods ending after 30 June 1999 (by virtue of Finance Act 1994, Section 199, (Appointed Day) Order, SI 1998/3173 art 2).
[8] Sub-ss (2B)–(2F) inserted by FA 1997 s 77 with effect for cases in which the interest becomes payable after 18 March 1997.
[9] Sub-ss (9B)–(9D), and words in sub-s (9A), repealed by F(No 2)A 1997 s 36(4), Sch 6 para 14, Sch 8 Pt II(11) with effect for distributions made after 5 April 1999.

732 Dealers in securities

(1) Subject to the provisions of this section, if the first buyer is engaged in carrying on a trade which consists of or comprises dealings in securities, then, in computing for any of the purposes of the Tax Acts the profits arising from or loss sustained in the trade, the price paid by him for the securities shall be reduced by the appropriate amount in respect of the interest, as determined in accordance with section 735.

[(1A) Subsection (1) above shall not apply if the interest receivable by the first buyer falls to be taken into account by virtue of section 95(1) in computing profits of his which are chargeable to tax in accordance with the provisions of this Act applicable to Case I or II of Schedule D.][4]

(2), (2A) ...[3]

(3) ...[2]

(4) Subsection (1) above shall not apply if the securities are overseas securities bought by the first buyer ...[3] in the ordinary course of his trade as a dealer in securities and the following conditions are satisfied, namely—

(a) the interest is brought into account in computing for the purposes of the Tax Acts the profits arising from or loss sustained in the trade, and

(b) where credit against tax would fall to be allowed in respect of the interest under section 788 or 790, the first buyer elects that credit shall not be so allowed.

[In this subsection "overseas securities" means securities issued—

(a) by a government or public or local authority of a territory outside the United Kingdom; or

(b) by any other body of persons not resident in the United Kingdom.][3]

(5) ...[3]

[(5A) ...][1]

(6), (7) ...[3]

Commentary—*Simon's Direct Tax Service* A7.304; D2.526.
Regulations—IT (Dealers in Securities) Regulations, SI 1992/568.
IT (Dealers in Securities) (Tradepoint) Regulations, SI 1995/2050.
Definitions—"Body of persons", s 832(1); "income tax", s 832(4); "interest", s 731(9); "person", s 731(9); "Schedule D", s 18(1); "securities", ss 731(9), (10); "tax", s 832(3); "the Tax Acts", s 831(2); "trade", s 832(1); "United Kingdom", s 830(1).
Cross references—See TA 1988 s 95(1B) (treatment of transaction resulting in a qualifying distribution to which FA 1997 Sch 7 applies (special treatment for certain distributions) being receivable by a dealer).
TA 1988 s 731 (application and interpretation of this section).
TA 1988 s 734 (persons other than dealers in securities).
TA 1988 s 738 (Board's power to amend this section).
IT (Dealers in Securities) Regulations, SI 1992/568 regs 3, 4 (prescribed persons, date and circumstances for the purposes of sub-s (2A) above).
IT (Dealers in Securities) (Tradepoint) Regulations, SI 1995/2050 regs 3, 4 (prescribed persons, dates and circumstances for the purposes of sub-s (2A) above).
Amendments—[1] Sub-s (5A) inserted by FA 1990 s 53(1) and deemed always to have had effect, and repealed by F(No 2)A 1997 s 26(1), (6), (8), Sch 8 Pt II(8) with effect where, for the purposes of section 731(2) above, the interest receivable by the first buyer is paid after 1 July 1997.
[2] Sub-s (3) repealed by FA 1996 Sch 41 Pt V(21) except for cases where the initial agreement to sell or transfer securities or other property was made before 6 November 1996.
[3] Sub-ss (2), (2A), (5), (6), (7) and words in sub-s (4) repealed and words in sub-s (4) substituted by F(No 2)A 1997 s 26(1), (3)–(8), Sch 8 Pt II(8) with effect where, for the purposes of section 731(2) above, the interest receivable by the first buyer is paid after 1 July 1997 (sub-ss (2A), (7) previously inserted by FA 1991 s 56).
[4] Sub-s (1A) inserted by F(No 2)A 1997 s 26(1), (2), (8) with effect where, for the purposes of section 731(2) above, the interest receivable by the first buyer is paid after 1 July 1997.

733 Persons entitled to exemptions

(1) If the first buyer is entitled under any enactment to an exemption from tax which, apart from this subsection, would extend to the interest, then the exemption shall not extend to an amount equal to the appropriate amount in respect of the interest, as determined in accordance with section 735.

(2) If the first buyer is so entitled and any annual payment is payable by him out of the interest, the annual payment shall be deemed as to the whole thereof to be paid out of profits or gains not brought into charge to income tax, and section 349(1) shall apply accordingly.

Commentary—*Simon's Direct Tax Service* A7.307; D2.526.
Definitions—"Appropriate amount in respect of the interest", s 735; "income tax", s 832(4); "interest", s 731(9); "profits or gains", s 833(1); "tax", s 831(2).
Cross references—See TA 1988 s 731 (application and interpretation of this section).

734 Persons other than dealers in securities

(1) If the first buyer carries on a trade not falling within section 732, then in ascertaining whether any or what repayment of income tax is to be made to him under section 380 or 381 by reference to any loss sustained in the trade and the amount of his income for the year of assessment his income for which includes the interest, there shall be left out of account—

   (*a*) the appropriate amount in respect of the interest, as determined in accordance with section 735, and

   (*b*) any tax paid on that amount.

(2) Where the first buyer is a company which does not carry on a trade falling within section 732—

   (*a*) the appropriate amount in respect of the interest, as determined in accordance with section 735(2), and

   (*b*) any tax paid in respect of or deducted from that amount,

shall be disregarded except that, for the purposes of corporation tax on chargeable gains, the appropriate proportion of the net interest receivable by the first buyer as mentioned in section 735(2) shall be treated as if it were a capital distribution within the meaning of section [122(5)(*b*) of the 1992 Act][1] received in respect of the holding of the securities concerned.

(3) In applying references in this section to interest in relation to a qualifying distribution, references to any tax paid on or in respect of an amount shall be construed as references to so much of any related tax credit as is attributable to that amount; and for this purpose "related tax credit", in relation to an amount, means the tax credit to which the recipient of the distribution of which that amount is a proportion is entitled.

Commentary—*Simon's Direct Tax Service* A7.308; D2.526.
Definitions—"The 1992 Act", s 831(3); "appropriate amount in respect of the interest", s 735; "chargeable gains", s 832(1); "company", s 832(1), (2); "distribution", ss 209(2), 832(1); "income tax", s 832(4); "interest", s 731(9); "qualifying distribution", ss 14(2), 832(1); "tax", s 832(3); "tax credit", s 832(1); "trade", s 832(1); "year of assessment", s 832(1).
Cross references—See TA 1988 s 731 (application and interpretation of this section).
Amendments—[1] Words in sub-s (2) substituted by TCGA 1992 Sch 10 para 14(1), (41).

735 Meaning of "appropriate amount in respect of" interest

(1) For the purposes of section 732 the appropriate amount in respect of the interest is the appropriate proportion of the net interest receivable by the first buyer.

(2) For the purposes of sections 733 and 734 the appropriate amount in respect of the interest is the gross amount corresponding with the appropriate proportion of the net interest receivable by the first buyer.

(3) For the purposes of this section the appropriate proportion[, in relation to securities listed in the Official List of the Stock Exchange,]¹ is the proportion which—

    (*a*) the period beginning with the date on which the securities were[, in accordance with announcements made by The Stock Exchange, first to be dealt in without carrying rights to]¹ the interest payment last payable before the interest receivable by the first buyer, and ending with the day before the day on which the first buyer bought the securities,

bears to—

    (*b*) the period beginning with that date and ending with the day before the first date after the purchase by the first buyer on which the securities are[, in accordance with such announcements, first to be dealt in without carrying rights to]¹ the interest receivable by the first buyer.

(4) Where the interest receivable by the first buyer was the first interest payment payable in respect of the securities, paragraphs (*a*) and (*b*) of subsection (3) above shall have effect with the substitution, for references to the date on which the securities were first [to be dealt in]¹ as mentioned in paragraph (*a*), of the beginning of the period for which the interest was payable; except that where the capital amount of the securities was not fully paid at the beginning of that period and one or more instalments of capital were paid during that period—

    (*a*) the interest shall be treated as divided into parts, calculated by reference to the amount of the interest attributable to the capital paid at or before the beginning of that period and the amount thereof attributable to each such instalment, and

    (*b*) treating each of those parts as interest payable for that period or, where the part was calculated by reference to any such instalment, as interest payable for the part of that period beginning with the payment of the instalment, there shall be calculated, in accordance with the preceding provisions of this section, the amount constituting the appropriate proportion of each part, and

    (*c*) the appropriate proportion of the interest for the purposes of this section shall be the proportion thereof constituted by the sum of those amounts.

(5) In relation to securities not listed in the [Official List of The Stock Exchange]¹, subsection (3) above shall have effect [as it has effect in relation to securities which are so listed but]¹ with the substitution for the periods therein mentioned of such periods as in the opinion of the Commissioners having jurisdiction in the matter, correspond therewith in the case of the securities in question.

Commentary—*Simon's Direct Tax Service* A7.303; D2.526.
Definition—"Interest", ss 731(9), 832(1).
Cross references—See TA 1988 s 731(9C) (foreign income dividends).
TA 1988 s 738 (Board's power to amend this section).
Amendments—¹ Words in sub-ss (3), (4), (5) substituted and second words in sub-s (5) inserted by FA 1996 s 199, Sch 38 para 9(1), (2), (3), (4) with effect in relation to cases where the first buyer purchases securities after 31 March 1996.

Miscellaneous provisions relating to securities

736 Company dealing in securities: distribution materially reducing value of holding

(1) Subsection (2) below applies where a company has, as a dealing company, a holding in another company resident in the United Kingdom (being a body corporate), and—

    (*a*) the holding amounts to, or is an ingredient in a holding amounting to, 10 per cent of all holdings of the same class in that company, and

    (*b*) a distribution is, or two or more distributions are, made in respect of the holding, and

    (*c*) the value (at any accounting date or immediately before realisation or appropriation) of any security comprised in the holding is materially reduced below the value of the security at the time when it was acquired, and the whole or any part of this reduction is attributable to any distribution falling within paragraph (*b*) above;

and in relation to any security comprised in the holding, the company having the holding is in subsection (2) below referred to as "the dealing company" and so much of any reduction in the value of the security as is attributable to any distribution falling within paragraph (*b*) above is in that subsection referred to as "the relevant reduction".

(2) Where this subsection applies, an amount equal to the relevant reduction in the value of a security comprised in the holding—

    (*a*) shall, if and so long as the security is not realised or appropriated as mentioned below, be added to the value of the security for the purposes of any valuation;

    (*b*) shall be treated, on any realisation of the security in the course of trade, as a trading receipt of the dealing company or, in the event of a partial realisation, shall be so treated to an appropriate extent, and

    (*c*) shall be treated as a trading receipt of the dealing company if the security is appropriated in such circumstances that a profit on the sale of the security would no longer form part of the dealing company's trading profits.

(3) References in this section to a holding in a company refer to a holding of securities by virtue of which the holder may receive distributions made by the company, but so that—

    (*a*) a company's holdings of different classes in another company shall be treated as separate holdings, and (*b*) holdings of securities which differ in the entitlements or obligations they confer or impose shall be regarded as holdings of different classes.

(4) For the purposes of subsection (2) above—

(*a*) all a company's holdings of the same class in another company are to be treated as ingredients constituting a single holding, and

(*b*) a company's holding of a particular class shall be treated as an ingredient in a holding amounting to 10 per cent of all holdings of that class if the aggregate of that holding and other holdings of that class held by connected persons amounts to 10 per cent of all holdings of that class;

and section 839 shall have effect in relation to paragraph (*b*) above as if, in subsection (7) of that section, after the words "or exercise control of" in each place where they occur there were inserted the words "or to acquire a holding in".

(5) Where this section applies in relation to a distribution which consists of or includes interest to which section 732 applies, any reduction under that section in the price paid for the securities in respect of which the distribution is made shall be adjusted in such manner as seems appropriate to the Board to take account of subsection (2) above.

(6) For the purposes of this section "security" includes a share or other right and a company is a "dealing company" in relation to a holding if a profit on a sale of the holding would be taken into account in computing the company's trading profits.

Commentary—*Simon's Direct Tax Service* A7.1201.
Revenue Internal Guidance—Inspector's manual IM 4436 (inspectors will be looking for evidence of scheme, or persistence in, stripping operations rather than the odd fortuitous transaction).
Definitions—"The Board", s 832(1); "company", s 832(1), (2); "connected persons", s 839; "control", s 840; "distribution", ss 209(2), 832(1); "interest", s 832(1).

[736A Manufactured dividends and interest

Schedule 23A to this Act shall have effect in relation to certain cases where under a contract or other arrangements for the transfer of shares or other securities a person is required to pay to the other party an amount representative of a dividend or payment of interest on the securities.][1]

Commentary—*Simon's Direct Tax Service* Division A7.8.
Amendments—[1] This section inserted by FA 1991 s 58(1), (3). As regards commencement, see note at the beginning of Sch 23A.

[736B Deemed manufactured payments in the case of stock lending arrangements

(1) This section applies where—

(*a*) any interest on securities transferred by the lender under a stock lending arrangement is paid, as a consequence of the arrangement, to a person other than the lender; and

(*b*) no provision is made for securing that the lender receives payments representative of that interest.

(2) Where this section applies, Schedule 23A and the provisions for the time being contained in any regulations under that Schedule shall apply[, subject to subsection (2A) below][2] as if—

(*a*) the borrower were required under the stock lending arrangement to pay the lender an amount representative of the interest mentioned in subsection (1)(*a*) above;

(*b*) a payment were made by the borrower in discharge of that requirement; and

(*c*) that payment were made on the same date as the payment of the interest of which it is representative.

[(2A) The borrower is not entitled, by virtue of anything in Schedule 23A or any provision of regulations under that Schedule, or otherwise—

(*a*) to any deduction in computing profits or gains for the purposes of income tax or corporation tax, or

(*b*) to any deduction against total income or, as the case may be, total profits,

in respect of any such deemed requirement or payment as is provided for by subsection (2) above.

Where the borrower is a company, an amount may not be surrendered by way of group relief if a deduction in respect of it is prohibited by this subsection.][2]

(3) In this section—

"interest" includes dividends; and

"stock lending arrangement" and "securities" have the same meanings as in section 263B of the 1992 Act.][1]

Commentary—*Simon's Direct Tax Service* A7.802.
Amendments—[1] This section inserted by FA 1997 Sch 10 paras 3, 7(1) with effect in relation to, and to transfers under, any arrangement made on or after 1 July 1997 by virtue of the Finance Act 1997, Schedule 10, (Appointed Day) Order, SI 1997/991.
[2] Words in sub-s (2), and sub-s (2A), inserted by FA 2001 s 84 with effect for payments treated under the section above as made after 2 October 2000.

737 Manufactured dividends: treatment of tax deducted

Commentary—*Simon's Direct Tax Service* A7.802.
Amendments—Section repealed by FA 1997 Sch 10 paras 8, 16(1), Sch 18 Pt VI(10) with effect in relation to any payment of a manufactured dividend or manufactured interest which is a payment made on or after 1 July 1997 by virtue of the Finance Act 1997, Schedule 10, (Appointed Day) Order, SI 1997/991. The repeal of sub-s (8) has effect subject to FA 1997 Sch 10 para 16(3).

[737A Sale and repurchase of securities: deemed manufactured payments

(1) This section applies where on or after the appointed day a person (the transferor) agrees to sell any securities, and under the same or any related agreement the transferor or another person connected with him—

 (*a*) is required to buy back the securities, or

 (*b*) acquires an option, which he subsequently exercises, to buy back the securities;

but this section does not apply unless the conditions set out in subsection (2) below are fulfilled.

(2) The conditions are that—

 (*a*) as a result of the transaction, a dividend which becomes payable in respect of the securities is receivable otherwise than by the transferor,

 (*b*) ...²

 (*c*) there is no requirement under any agreement mentioned in subsection (1) above for a person to pay to the transferor on or before the relevant date an amount representative of the dividend, and

 (*d*) it is reasonable to assume that, in arriving at the repurchase price of the securities, account was taken of the fact that the dividend is receivable otherwise than by the transferor.

(3) For the purposes of subsection (2) above the relevant date is the date when the repurchase price of the securities becomes due.

(4) Where it is a person connected with the transferor who is required to buy back the securities, or who acquires the option to buy them back, references in the following provisions of this section to the transferor shall be construed as references to the connected person.

(5) Where this section applies, ...³ Schedule 23A and dividend manufacturing regulations shall apply as if—

 (*a*) the relevant person were required, under the arrangements for the transfer of the securities, to pay to the transferor an amount representative of the dividend mentioned in subsection (2)(*a*) above,

 (*b*) a payment were made by that person to the transferor in discharge of that requirement, and

 (*c*) the payment were made on the date when the repurchase price of the securities becomes due.

(6) In subsection (5) above "the relevant person" means—

 (*a*) where subsection (1)(*a*) above applies, the person from whom the transferor is required to buy back the securities;

 (*b*) where subsection (1)(*b*) above applies, the person from whom the transferor has the right to buy back the securities;

and in that subsection "dividend manufacturing regulations" means regulations under Schedule 23A (whenever made).]¹

Commentary—*Simon's Direct Tax Service* A7.1205.
Definitions—"the Tax Acts", s 831(2).
Cross references—See TA 1988 s 729 (sale and repurchase of securities: provisions of s 729 disregarded in determining whether the condition in sub-s(2)(*b*) above is fulfilled).
TA 1988 s 737B (interpretation and definitions).
TA 1988 s 737C (further provisions).
TA 1988 s 737E (power to modify the effect of this section).
Sale and Repurchase of Securities (Modification of Enactments) Regulations, SI 1995/3220 regs 3, 5 (modification of this section in relation to arrangements for the sale and redemption of securities or for the substitution of the original securities to be repurchased).
European Single Currency (Taxes) Regulations, SI 1998/3177 regs 13–19 (agreements for sale and repurchase of securities in relation to replacement of securities in a euroconversion).
Amendments—¹ This section (and ss 737B, 737C *post*) inserted by FA 1994 s 122 with effect for agreements to sell United Kingdom equities and United Kingdom securities (each with the same meaning as in Sch 23A para 1(1) to this Act *post*) entered into on or after 1 May 1995 (Income and Corporation Taxes Act 1988 s 737A, (Appointed Day) Order, SI 1995/1007 made under s 737B(9) *post*) and with effect for agreements to sell overseas securities (with the same meaning as in Sch 23A para 1(1) to this Act *post*) entered into on or after 6 November 1996 (Income and Corporation Taxes Act 1988, section 737A, (Appointed Day) Order, SI 1996/2645 made under s 737B(9) *post*).
² Sub-s (2)(*b*) repealed by FA 1996 s 159(1), Sch 41 Pt V(21) with effect except in relation to cases where the initial agreement to sell or transfer securities or other property was made before 6 November 1996 (FA 1996 s 159 (Appointed Day) Order, SI 1996/2646).
³ Words in sub-s (5) repealed by FA 1997 Sch 18 Pt VI(10) with effect in relation to payments made on or after 1 July 1997 by virtue of the Finance Act 1997, Schedule 10, (Appointed Day) Order, SI 1997/991

[737B Interpretation of section 737A

(1) In section 737A and this section "securities" means United Kingdom equities, United Kingdom securities or overseas securities; and—

(*a*) where the securities mentioned in section 737A(1) are United Kingdom securities, references in section 737A to a dividend shall be construed as references to a periodical payment of interest;
(*b*) where the securities mentioned in section 737A(1) are overseas securities, references in section 737A to a dividend shall be construed as references to an overseas dividend.

(2) In this section "United Kingdom equities", "United Kingdom securities", "overseas securities" and "overseas dividend" have the meanings given by paragraph 1(1) of Schedule 23A.

(3) For the purposes of section 737A agreements are related if each is entered into in pursuance of the same arrangement (regardless of the date on which either agreement is entered into).

(4) In section 737A "the repurchase price of the securities" means—

(*a*) where subsection (1)(*a*) of that section applies, the amount which, under any agreement mentioned in section 737A(1), the transferor or connected person is required to pay for the securities bought back, or
(*b*) where subsection (1)(*b*) of that section applies, the amount which under any such agreement the transferor or connected person is required, if he exercises the option, to pay for the securities bought back.

(5) In section 737A and subsection (4) above references to buying back securities include references to buying similar securities.

(6) For the purposes of subsection (5) above securities are similar if they entitle their holders to the same rights against the same persons as to capital and interest and the same remedies for the enforcement of those rights, notwithstanding any difference in the total nominal amounts of the respective securities or in the form in which they are held or the manner in which they can be transferred; and "interest" here includes dividends.

(7) For the purposes of section 737A and subsection (4) above—

(*a*) a person who is connected with the transferor and is required to buy securities sold by the transferor shall be treated as being required to buy the securities back notwithstanding that it was not he who sold them, and
(*b*) a person who is connected with the transferor and acquires an option to buy securities sold by the transferor shall be treated as acquiring an option to buy the securities back notwithstanding that it was not he who sold them.

(8) Section 839 shall apply for the purposes of section 737A and this section.

(9) In section 737A "the appointed day" means such day as the Treasury may by order appoint, and different days may be appointed in relation to—

(*a*) United Kingdom equities,
(*b*) United Kingdom securities, and
(*c*) overseas securities.][1]

Commentary—*Simon's Direct Tax Service* A7.1205.
Regulations—TA 1988 s 737A (Appointed Day) Order 1995, SI 1995/1007.
TA 1988 s 737A (Appointed Day) Order 1996 No 2645.
Definitions—"Interest", s 832(1); "United Kingdom", s 830.
Cross references—See TA 1988 s 737C (further provisions).
TA 1988 s 737E (power to modify the effect of this section by regulations).
Amendments—[1] This section inserted by FA 1994 s 122 and has effect as noted to s 737A *ante*.

[737C Deemed manufactured payments: further provisions

(1) This section applies where section 737A applies.

(2) Subsection (3) below applies where—

(*a*) the dividend mentioned in section 737A(2)(*a*) is a dividend on United Kingdom equities, and
(*b*) by virtue of section 737A(5), ...[3] paragraph 2 of Schedule 23A applies, in relation to the payment which is treated under section 737A(5) as having been made;
and in subsection (3) below "the deemed manufactured dividend" means that payment.

(3) Where this subsection applies—

(*a*) the amount of the deemed manufactured dividend shall be taken to be an amount equal to the amount of the dividend mentioned in section 737A(2)(*a*);
(*b*) the repurchase price of the securities shall be treated, for the purposes of [section 730A][2], as increased by an amount equal to the gross amount of the deemed manufactured dividend.

(4) In subsection (3) above the reference to the gross amount of the deemed manufactured dividend is to the aggregate of—

(*a*) the amount of the deemed manufactured dividend, and
(*b*) the amount of the tax credit that would have been issued in respect of the deemed manufactured dividend had the deemed manufactured dividend in fact been a dividend on the United Kingdom equities.

(5), (6) ...[3]

(7) Subsection (8) below applies where—

(*a*) the dividend mentioned in section 737A(2)(*a*) is a periodical payment of interest on United Kingdom securities, and (*b*) by virtue of section 737A(5), paragraph 3 of Schedule 23A applies in relation to the payment which is treated under section 737A(5) as having been made ...[3],

and in subsection (8) below "the deemed manufactured interest" means the payment referred to in paragraph (*b*) above.

(8) Where this subsection applies—

[(*a*) the amount which by virtue of section 737A(5) is taken to be the gross amount of the deemed manufactured payment for the purposes of paragraph 3 of Schedule 23A shall be taken to be the gross amount of the deemed manufactured interest for the purposes of this section;][3]
(*b*) any deduction which, by virtue of [that paragraph][3], is required to be made out of the gross amount of the deemed manufactured interest shall be deemed to have been made.

(9) Where ...[3] subsection (8) above applies, the repurchase price of the securities shall be treated, for the purposes of [section 730A][2], as increased by the gross amount of the deemed manufactured interest.

(10) Subsection (11) below applies where—

(*a*) the dividend mentioned in section 737A(2)(*a*) is an overseas dividend, and
(*b*) by virtue of section 737A(5), paragraph 4 of Schedule 23A applies in relation to the payment which is treated under section 737A(5) as having been made;

and in subsection (11) below "the deemed manufactured overseas dividend" means that payment.

(11) Where this subsection applies—

(*a*) the gross amount of the deemed manufactured overseas dividend shall be taken to be the amount found under paragraph 4(5)(*b*) and (*c*) of Schedule 23A;
(*b*) any deduction which, by virtue of paragraph 4 of Schedule 23A, is required to be made out of the gross amount of the deemed manufactured overseas dividend shall be deemed to have been made;
(*c*) the repurchase price of the securities shall be treated, for the purposes of [section 730A][2], as increased by the gross amount of the deemed manufactured overseas dividend.

[(11A) The deemed increase of the repurchase price which is made for the purposes of section 730A by subsection (3)(*b*), (9) or (11)(*c*) above shall also have effect—

(*a*) for all the purposes of the Tax Acts, other than section 737A,
(*b*) in cases where section 263A of the 1992 Act does not apply, for the purposes of the 1992 Act,

wherever in consequence of that increase there is for the purposes of section 730A no difference between the sale price and the repurchase price.][2]

[(11B) ...[3]]

(12) In this section—

(*a*) "United Kingdom equities", "United Kingdom securities" and "overseas dividend" have the meanings given by paragraph 1(1) of Schedule 23A;
(*b*) "the repurchase price of the securities" shall be construed in accordance with section 737B(4).][1]

Commentary—*Simon's Direct Tax Service* A7.1205.
Definitions—"the 1992 Act", s 831(3); "interest", s 832(1); "lower rate", s 832(1); "the Tax Acts", s 831(2); "tax credit", s 832(1); "United Kingdom", s 830; "year of assessment", s 832(1).
Cross references—TA 1988 s 737E (power to modify the effect of this section by regulations).
Sale and Repurchase of Securities (Modification of Enactments) Regulations, SI 1995/3220 reg 5 (modification of this section in relation to arrangements for the substitution of different securities for the securities to be repurchased).
Amendments—[1] This section inserted by FA 1994 s 122 and has effect as noted to s 737A *ante*.
[2] Words in sub-ss (3)(*b*), (9), (11)(*c*) substituted and sub-s (11A) inserted, by FA 1995 s 80(3), with effect where the agreement to sell the securities is entered into on or after 1 May 1995.
[3] Words in sub-ss (2)(*b*), (7)(*b*), (9) and whole of sub-ss (5), (6), (11B) repealed and sub-s (8)(*a*) and words in sub-s (8)(*b*) substituted by FA 1997 Sch 10 paras 11(2), 16(1), Sch 18 Pt VI(10) with effect in relation to any payment of a manufactured dividend or manufactured interest which is a payment made on or after 1 July 1997 by virtue of the Finance Act 1997, Schedule 10, (Appointed Day) Order, SI 1997/991.

Supplemental

[737D Power to provide for manufactured payments to be eligible for relief]

(1) The Treasury may by regulations provide for any manufactured payment made to any person to be treated, in such circumstances and to such extent as may be described in the regulations, as comprised in income of that person that is eligible for relief from tax by virtue of section 438, 592(2), 608(2)(*a*), 613(4), 614(2), (3) or (4), 620(6) or 643(2).

(2) In this section "manufactured payment" means any ...[2] manufactured interest or manufactured overseas dividend, within the meaning of Schedule 23A.][1]

Commentary—*Simon's Direct Tax Service* A7.830.
Cross references—TA 1988 s 828 (power of the Treasury to make regulations).
Amendments—[1] This section inserted by FA 1995 s 83(1).
[2] Words in sub-s (2) repealed by FA 1998 s 102(3), Sch 27 Pt III(24) with effect in relation to manufactured dividends paid (or treated for the purposes of TA 1988 Sch 23A as paid) after 5 April 1999.

[737E Power to modify sections 727A, 730A and 737A to 737C

(1) The Treasury may by regulations make provision for all or any of sections 727A, 730A and 737A to 737C to have effect with modifications in relation to cases involving any arrangement for the sale and repurchase of securities where—

(*a*) the obligation to make the repurchase is not performed or the option to repurchase is not exercised;

(*b*) provision is made by or under any agreement for different or additional securities to be treated as, or as included with, securities which, for the purposes of the repurchase, are to represent securities transferred in pursuance of the original sale;

(*c*) provision is made by or under any agreement for any securities to be treated as not included with securities which, for the purposes of the repurchase, are to represent securities transferred in pursuance of the original sale;

(*d*) provision is made by or under any agreement for the sale price or repurchase price to be determined or varied wholly or partly by reference to fluctuations, occurring in the period after the making of the agreement for the original sale, in the value of securities transferred in pursuance of that sale, or in the value of securities treated as representing those securities; or

(*e*) provision is made by or under any agreement for any person to be required, in a case where there are any such fluctuations, to make any payment in the course of that period and before the repurchase price becomes due.

(2) The Treasury may by regulations make provision for all or any of sections 727A, 730A and 737A to 737C to have effect with modifications in relation to cases where—

(*a*) arrangements, corresponding to those made in cases involving an arrangement for the sale and repurchase of securities, are made by any agreement, or by one or more related agreements, in relation to securities that are to be redeemed in the period after their sale; and

(*b*) those arrangements are such that the person making the sale or a person connected with him (instead of being required to repurchase the securities or acquiring an option to do so) is granted rights in respect of the benefits that will accrue from their redemption.

(3) The Treasury may by regulations provide that section 730A is to have effect with modifications in relation to cases involving any arrangement for the sale and repurchase of securities where there is an agreement relating to the sale or repurchase which is not such as would be entered into by persons dealing with each other at arm's length.

(4) The powers conferred by subsections (1) and (2) above shall be exercisable in relation to section 263A of the 1992 Act as they are exercisable in relation to section 730A of this Act.

(5) Regulations made for the purposes of this section may—

(*a*) make different provision for different cases; and

(*b*) contain such supplementary, incidental, consequential and transitional provision as appears to the Treasury to be appropriate.

(6) The supplementary, incidental and consequential provision that may be made by regulations under this section shall include—

(*a*) in the case of regulations relating to section 730A, provision modifying subsections (3)(*b*), (9), (11)(*c*) and (11A) of section 737C; and

(*b*) in the case of regulations relating to section 263A of the 1992 Act, provision modifying the operation of that Act in relation to cases where by virtue of the regulations any acquisition or disposal is excluded from those which are to be disregarded for the purposes of capital gains tax.

(7) In this section "modifications" includes exceptions and omissions; and any power under this section to provide for an enactment to have effect with modifications in any case shall include power to provide for it not to apply (if it otherwise would do) in that case.

(8) References in this section to a case involving an arrangement for the sale and repurchase of securities are references to any case where—

(*a*) a person makes a sale of any securities under any agreement ("the original sale"); and

(*b*) that person or a person connected with him either—

(i) is required under that agreement or any related agreement to buy them back; or

(ii) acquires, under that agreement or any related agreement, an option to buy them back.

(9) Section 730B shall apply for the purposes of this section as it applies for the purposes of section 730A.][1]

Commentary—*Simon's Direct Tax Service* **A7.1205**.
Regulations—Sale and Repurchase of Securities (Modification of Enactments) Regulations, SI 1995/3220.
Definitions—"Securities", s 737B; "the 1992 Act", s 831(3).
Cross references—TA 1988 s 828 (power of the Treasury to make regulations).
TA 1988 s 839, by virtue of s 730B(5) (meaning of connected persons).
Amendments—[1] This section inserted by FA 1995 s 83(1).

738 Power to amend sections 732, 735 and 737

(1) The Board may by regulations provide for all or any of the following—

(*a*), (*b*) ...[4]

(*c*) that for section 735(3) and (5) (which refer to the Stock Exchange Daily Official List) there shall be substituted such provisions as the Board think fit to take account of recognised investment exchanges.

Regulations under this subsection shall apply where the subsequent sale is carried out by the first buyer on or after such day as is specified in the regulations.

(2) ...[1]

(3), (4) ...[2]

(5) In this section "recognised investment exchange" [has the meaning given by section 285(1)(*a*) of the Financial Services and Markets Act 2000][4].

Commentary—*Simon's Direct Tax Service* A7.304.
Definition—"The Board", s 832(1).
Amendments—[1] Sub-s (2) repealed by FA 1991 Sch 13 para 4 and Sch 19, Pt V with effect from 30 June 1992 by virtue of FA 1991 s 58 (Commencement No 2) Regulations, SI 1992/1346.
[2] Sub-ss (3), (4) repealed by FA 1997 Sch 18 Pt VI(10) with effect in relation to payments made on or after 1 July 1997 by virtue of the Finance Act 1997, Schedule 10, (Appointed Day) Order, SI 1997/991
[3] Sub-s (1)(*a*), (*b*) repealed by F(No 2)A 1997 Sch 8 Pt II(8) with effect where, for the purposes of section 731(2) above, the interest receivable by the first buyer is paid after 1 July 1997.
[4] Words in sub-s (5) substituted by the Financial Services and Markets Act 2000 (Consequential Amendments) (Taxes) Order, SI 2001/3629 arts 13, 43 with effect from 1 December 2001, immediately after the coming into force of the Financial Services and Markets Act 2000 ss 411, 432(1), Sch 20.

CHAPTER III
TRANSFER OF ASSETS ABROAD

Revenue Interpretation RI 201—Revenue interpretation of provisions under this Chapter.

739 Prevention of avoidance of income tax

(1) Subject to section 747(4)(*b*), the following provisions of this section shall have effect for the purpose of preventing the avoiding by individuals ordinarily resident in the United Kingdom of liability to income tax by means of transfer of assets by virtue or in consequence of which, either alone or in conjunction with associated operations, income becomes payable to persons resident or domiciled outside the United Kingdom.

[(1A) Nothing in subsection (1) above shall be taken to imply that the provisions of subsections (2) and (3) apply only if —

    (*a*) the individual in question was ordinarily resident in the United Kingdom at the time when the transfer was made; or

    (*b*) the avoiding of liability to income tax is the purpose, or one of the purposes, for which the transfer was effected.][1]

(2) Where by virtue or in consequence of any such transfer, either alone or in conjunction with associated operations, such an individual has, within the meaning of this section, power to enjoy, whether forthwith or in the future, any income of a person resident or domiciled outside the United Kingdom which, if it were income of that individual received by him in the United Kingdom, would be chargeable to income tax by deduction or otherwise, that income shall, whether it would or would not have been chargeable to income tax apart from the provisions of this section, be deemed to be income of that individual for all purposes of the Income Tax Acts.

(3) Where, whether before or after any such transfer, such an individual receives or is entitled to receive any capital sum the payment of which is in any way connected with the transfer or any associated operation, any income which, by virtue or in consequence of the transfer, either alone or in conjunction with associated operations, has become the income of a person resident or domiciled outside the United Kingdom shall, whether it would or would not have been chargeable to income tax apart from the provisions of this section, be deemed to be income of that individual for all purposes of the Income Tax Acts.

(4) In subsection (3) above "capital sum" means, subject to subsection (5) below—

    (*a*) any sum paid or payable by way of loan or repayment of a loan, and
    (*b*) any other sum paid or payable otherwise than as income, being a sum which is not paid or payable for full consideration in money or money's worth.

(5) For the purposes of subsection (3) above, there shall be treated as a capital sum which an individual receives or is entitled to receive any sum which a third person receives or is entitled to receive at the individual's direction or by virtue of the assignment by him of his right to receive it.

(6) Income shall not by virtue of subsection (3) above be deemed to be that of an individual for any year of assessment by reason only of his having received a sum by way of loan if that sum has been wholly repaid before the beginning of that year.

Commentary—*Simon's Direct Tax Service* E1.721–743.
Statement of Practice SP 5/92—Revenue's practice in applying the rules (contained in TCGA 1992 ss 80–98 and Sch 5) for capital gains on transfers of certain offshore trusts.

Revenue Interpretation RI 201—Income of overseas person assessable only to the extent that it arose from the relevant transfer of assets and any associated operations; this section can apply to an individual who procured the transfer; where the same assets are transferred by several individuals, the transferors are assessed in proportion to their share of the assets.
Revenue Internal Guidance—Inspector's manual IM 4622 (circumstances in which cases will be referred to head office).
Simon's Tax Cases—*IRC v McGuckian* [1997] STC 908*; *IRC v Willoughby* [1997] STC 995; *Commercial Union Assurance Co plc v Shaw* [1998] STC 38; *IRC v Botnar* [1999] STC 711*.
s 739(2), *Lord Chetwode v IRC* [1977] STC 64*; *Vestey v IRC (No 2)* [1980] STC 10*; *IRC v Botnar* [1999] STC 711; *R v Dimsey; R v Allen* [1999] STC 846.
s 739(3), (4), *Vestey v IRC (Nos 1 and 2)* [1980] STC 10*.
Definitions—"Assets", s 742(9); "associated operation", s 742(1); "the Income Tax Acts", s 831(1)(b); "individual", s 742(9); "power to enjoy ... income", s 742; "resident ... outside the United Kingdom", s 742(8); "United Kingdom", s 830(1); "year of assessment", s 832(1).
Cross references—See TA 1988 s 741 (exemption from this section).
TA 1988 s 742 (interpretation).
TA 1988 s 743 (supplemental provisions).
TA 1988 s 744 (avoidance of double charge to tax and Board's discretion to choose the person chargeable and to apportion income).
TA 1988 s 746 (application of this section to residents of the Republic of Ireland).
TA 1988 s 762(5), (6) (this section to have effect with certain modification in relation to tax on offshore income gains).
TA 1988 Sch 5AA para 8 (treatment of purposes of this section of profits from disposals of futures and options producing a guaranteed return).
FA 1989 s 110(8) (residence of trustees).
FA 1989 s 111(7) (residence of personal representatives).
Amendments—[1] Sub-s (1A) inserted by FA 1997 s 81 and applied irrespective of when the transfer or associated operations took place, but applies only to income arising on or after 26 November 1996.

740 Liability of non-transferors

(1) This section has effect where—

(a) by virtue or in consequence of a transfer of assets, either alone or in conjunction with associated operations, income becomes payable to a person resident or domiciled outside the United Kingdom; and

(b) an individual ordinarily resident in the United Kingdom who is not liable to tax under section 739 by reference to the transfer receives a benefit provided out of assets which are available for the purpose by virtue or in consequence of the transfer or of any associated operations.

(2) Subject to the provisions of this section, the amount or value of any such benefit as is mentioned in subsection (1) above, if not otherwise chargeable to income tax in the hands of the recipient, shall—

(a) to the extent to which it falls within the amount of relevant income of years of assessment up to and including the year of assessment in which the benefit is received, be treated for all the purposes of the Income Tax Acts as the income of the individual for that year;

(b) to the extent to which it is not by virtue of this subsection treated as his income for that year and falls within the amount of relevant income of the next following year of assessment, be treated for those purposes as his income for the next following year,

and so on for subsequent years, taking the reference in paragraph (b) to the year mentioned in paragraph (a) as a reference to that and any other year before the subsequent year in question.

(3) Subject to subsection (7) below and section 744(1), the relevant income of a year of assessment, in relation to an individual, is any income which arises in that year to a person resident or domiciled outside the United Kingdom and which by virtue or in consequence of the transfer or associated operations referred to in subsection (1) above can directly or indirectly be used for providing a benefit for the individual or for enabling a benefit to be provided for him.

(4) Income tax chargeable by virtue of this section shall be charged under Case VI of Schedule D.

(5) An individual who is domiciled outside the United Kingdom shall not, in respect of any benefit not received in the United Kingdom, be chargeable to tax under this section by reference to relevant income which is such that if he had received it he would not, by reason of his being so domiciled, have been chargeable to income tax in respect of it; and subsections (6) to (9) of section 65 shall apply for the purposes of this subsection as they would apply for the purposes of subsection (5) of that section if the benefit were income arising from possessions outside the United Kingdom.

(6) Where—

(a) the whole or part of the benefit received by an individual in a year of assessment is a capital payment [to which section 87 or 89(2) of, or paragraph 8 of Schedule 4C to, the 1992 Act applies][1] (chargeable gains: [gains attributed to beneficiaries][1]) (because not falling within the amount of relevant income referred to in paragraph (a) of subsection (2) above); and

(b) chargeable gains are by reason of that payment treated under either of those sections[,or that paragraph,][1] as accruing to him in that or a subsequent year,

paragraph (b) of that subsection shall apply in relation to any year of assessment ("a year of charge") after one in which chargeable gains have been so treated as accruing to him as if a part of the amount or value of the benefit corresponding to the amount of those gains had been treated under that subsection as his income for a year of assessment before the year of charge.

(7) This section applies irrespective of when the transfer or associated operations referred to in subsection (1) above took place, but applies only to relevant income arising on or after 10th March 1981.

Commentary—*Simon's Direct Tax Service* E1.740, 741.
Statement of Practice SP 5/92—Revenue's practice in applying the rules (contained in TCGA 1992 ss 80–98 and Sch 5) for capital gains on transfers of certain offshore trusts.
Revenue Interpretation RI 201—A benefit within sub-s (1)(*b*) includes receipt of a loan at less than a commercial rate of interest, and the use of trust property at less than open market rental; once relevant income within sub-s (3) has arisen and continues to be available to provide a benefit, it must be carried forward year by year until extinguished by such a benefit.
Definitions—"the 1992 Act", s 831(3); "assets", s 742(9); "associated operations", s 742(1); "benefit", s 742(9); "chargeable gains", s 832(1); "the Income Tax Acts", s 831(2); "individual", s 742(9); "Schedule D", s 18(1); "tax", s 832(3); "United Kingdom", s 830(1); "year of assessment", s 832(1).
Cross references—See TMA 1970 s 46B(4) (any question as to the application of this section to be determined by the Special Commissioners).
TA 1988 s 741 (exemption from this section).
TA 1988 s 742 (interpretation).
TA 1988 s 744 (avoidance of double charge to tax and Board's discretion to choose the person chargeable and to apportion income).
TA 1988 s 762(5), (6) (this section to have effect with certain modification in relation to tax on offshore income gains).
TA 1988 Sch 5AA para 8 (treatment for purposes of this section of profits from disposals of futures and options producing a guaranteed return).
FA 1989 s 110(9) (residence of trustees),
FA 1989 s 111(8) (residence of personal representatives).
Amendments—[1] Words in sub-s (6)(*a*) substituted and words in sub-s (6)(*b*) inserted by FA 2000 s 92(4), (5), Sch 26 Pt II para 6 with effect for any transfer of value in relation to which the material time is after 20 March 2000.

741 Exemption from sections 739 and 740

Sections 739 and 740 shall not apply if the individual shows in writing or otherwise to the satisfaction of the Board either—

    (*a*) that the purpose of avoiding liability to taxation was not the purpose or one of the purposes for which the transfer or associated operations or any of them were effected; or
    (*b*) that the transfer and any associated operations were bona fide commercial transactions and were not designed for the purpose of avoiding liability to taxation.

The jurisdiction of the Special Commissioners on any appeal shall include jurisdiction to review any relevant decision taken by the Board in exercise of their functions under this section.

Commentary—*Simon's Direct Tax Service* E1.726.
Revenue Interpretation RI 201—Section 741(*b*) is not satisfied where there is a significant element of tax avoidance purpose in the design of the transfer and any associated operations.
Revenue Internal Guidance—Inspector's manual IM 4620 ("taxation" includes inheritance tax and capital gains tax as well as income tax).
IM 4622 (circumstances in which inspectors report cases to head office).
Simon's Tax Cases—*IRC v Brackett* [1986] STC 521*; *IRC v Willoughby* [1997] STC 995; *IRC v Botnar* [1999] STC 711*; *Carvill v IRC* [2000] STC (SCD) 143.
Definitions—"Associated operations", s 742(1); "the Board", s 832(1); "individual", s 742(9).
Cross references—See TA 1988 s 742 (interpretation).

742 Interpretation of sections 739 to 741

(1) For the purposes of sections 739 to 741 "an associated operation" means, in relation to any transfer, an operation of any kind effected by any person in relation to any of the assets transferred or any assets representing, whether directly or indirectly, any of the assets transferred, or to the income arising from any such assets, or to any assets representing, whether directly or indirectly, the accumulations of income arising from any such assets.

(2) An individual shall, for the purposes of section 739, be deemed to have power to enjoy income of a person resident or domiciled outside the United Kingdom if—

    (*a*) the income is in fact so dealt with by any person as to be calculated, at some point of time, and whether in the form of income or not, to enure for the benefit of the individual; or
    (*b*) the receipt or accrual of the income operates to increase the value to the individual of any assets held by him or for his benefit; or
    (*c*) the individual receives or is entitled to receive, at any time, any benefit provided or to be provided out of that income or out of moneys which are or will be available for the purpose by reason of the effect or successive effects of the associated operations on that income and on any assets which directly or indirectly represent that income; or
    (*d*) the individual may, in the event of the exercise or successive exercise of one or more powers, by whomsoever exercisable and whether with or without the consent of any other person, become entitled to the beneficial enjoyment of the income; or
    (*e*) the individual is able in any manner whatsoever, and whether directly or indirectly, to control the application of the income.

(3) In determining whether an individual has power to enjoy income within the meaning of subsection (2) above—

    (*a*) regard shall be had to the substantial result and effect of the transfer and any associated operations, and
    (*b*) all benefits which may at any time accrue to the individual (whether or not he has rights at law or in equity in or to those benefits) as a result of the transfer and any associated operations shall be taken into account irrespective of the nature or form of the benefits.

(4) Subsection (5) below applies where a person resident or domiciled outside the United Kingdom throughout any chargeable period in which an interest period (or part of it) falls would, at the end of

the interest period, have been treated under section 714(2) as receiving annual profits or gains or annual profits or gains of a greater amount if he had been resident or domiciled in the United Kingdom during a part of each such chargeable period.

(5) Sections 739 to 741 shall have effect as if the amount which the person would be treated as receiving or the additional amount (as the case may be) were income becoming payable to him; and, accordingly, any reference in those sections to income of (or payable or arising to) such a person shall be read as including a reference to such an amount.

(6) Where income of a person resident or domiciled outside the United Kingdom throughout any chargeable period in which an interest period (or part of it) falls consists of interest—

    (*a*) which falls due at the end of the interest period, and
    (*b*) which would have been treated under section 714(5) as reduced by an allowance or an allowance of a greater amount if he had been resident or domiciled in the United Kingdom during a part of each such chargeable period,

then for the purposes of sections 739 to 741, the interest shall be treated as being reduced by the amount of the allowance or by the additional amount (as the case may be).

(7) In subsections (4) to (6) above "interest period" has the meaning given by section 711.

(8) For the purposes of sections 739 to 741, any body corporate incorporated outside the United Kingdom ...[2] shall be treated as if it were resident outside the United Kingdom whether it is so resident or not.

(9) For the purposes of sections 739 to 741—

    (*a*) a reference to an individual shall be deemed to include the wife or husband of the individual;
    (*b*) "assets" includes property or rights of any kind and "transfer", in relation to rights, includes the creation of those rights;
    (*c*) "benefit" includes a payment of any kind;
    (*d*) ...[1]
    (*e*) references to assets representing any assets, income or accumulations of income include references to shares in or obligations of any company to which, or obligations of any other person to whom, those assets, that income or those accumulations are or have been transferred.

(10) ...[1]

Commentary—*Simon's Direct Tax Service* E1.721–743.
Revenue Interpretation RI 201—An "associated operation" within sub-s (1) can precede the transfer.
Simon's Tax Cases—*IRC v Botnar* [1999] STC 711*.
s 742(1)–(3), (8)–(10), *IRC v Pratt* [1982] STC 756*; *IRC v Brackett* [1986] STC 521*.
s 742(2)(c), *IRC v Botnar* [1999] STC 711.
s 742(2)(e), *IRC v Schroder* [1983] STC 480*.
s 742(9)(a), *Vestey v IRC* [1980] STC 10*.
Definitions—"Accounting period", s 834(1); "advance corporation tax", s 14(1); "apportionment", s 834(4); "chargeable period", s 832(1); "company", s 832(1), (2); "profits or gains", s 833(1); "United Kingdom", s 830(1).
Cross references—See TA 1988 s 743 (supplemental provisions).
TA 1988 s 746 (application of sub-ss (1)–(3) of this section to residents of the Republic of Ireland).
Amendments—[1] Sub-ss (9)(d), (10) repealed by FA 1989 Sch 17 Pt V in relation to accounting periods beginning after 31 March 1989.
[2] Words in sub-s (8) repealed by FA 1994 s 251(1)(a), (3)(a) and Sch 26 Pt VIII(1) in relation to transfers of assets and associated operations after 29 November 1993.

743 Supplemental provisions

(1) Income tax at the basic rate[, the lower rate or the Schedule F ordinary rate][2] shall not be charged by virtue of section 739 in respect of [any income to the extent that it has borne tax at that rate][1] by deduction or otherwise but, subject to that, income tax so chargeable shall be charged—

    [(*a*) in the case of income falling within subsection (1A) below, as if it were income to which section 1A applies by virtue of paragraph (2)(b) of that section; and
    (*b*) in the case of any other income, under Case VI of Schedule D.][2]

[(1A) Income falls within this subsection if it is—

    (*a*) income chargeable under Schedule F;
    (*b*) income to which section 1A applies by virtue of its being equivalent foreign income falling within subsection (3)(b) of that section and chargeable under Case V of Schedule D;
    (*c*) a distribution in relation to which section 233(1) applies;
    (*d*) a qualifying distribution whose amount or value is determined in accordance with section 233(1A);
    (*e*) a non–qualifying distribution, within the meaning of section 233(1B);
    (*f*) income treated as arising by virtue of section 249;
    (*g*) income treated as received by virtue of section 421(1)(a).][2]

(2) In computing the liability to income tax of an individual chargeable by virtue of section 739, the same deductions and reliefs shall be allowed as would have been allowed if the income deemed to be his by virtue of that section had actually been received by him.

(3) An individual who is domiciled outside the United Kingdom shall not be chargeable to tax in respect of any income deemed to be his by virtue of that section if he would not, by reason of his being so domiciled, have been chargeable to tax in respect of it if it had in fact been his income.

(4) Where an individual has been charged to income tax on any income deemed to be his by virtue of section 739 and that income is subsequently received by him, it shall be deemed not to form part of his income again for the purposes of the Income Tax Acts.

(5) In any case where an individual has for the purposes of that section power to enjoy income of a person abroad by reason of his receiving any such benefit as is referred to in section 742(2)(c), then notwithstanding anything in subsection (1) above, the individual shall be chargeable to income tax by virtue of section 739 for the year of assessment in which the benefit is received on the whole of the amount or value of that benefit except in so far as it is shown that the benefit derives directly or indirectly from income on which he has already been charged to tax for that or a previous year of assessment.

Commentary—*Simon's Direct Tax Service* **E1.731, 732, 736.**
Revenue Interpretation RI 201—Revenue practice in respect of sub-s (3).
Simon's Tax Cases—s 743(5), *IRC v Botnar* [1999] STC 711.
Definitions—"Basic rate", s 832(1); "income tax", s 832(4); "the Income Tax Acts", s 831(1)(b); "lower rate" s 832(1); "Schedule D", s 18(1); "Schedule F ordinary rate", s 832(1); "tax", s 832(3); "United Kingdom", s 830(1); "year of assessment", s 832(1).
Cross references—See TMA 1970 s 46B(4) (any question as to the application of sub-s (1) above to be determined by the Special Commissioners).
TA 1988 s 746 (application of this section to residents of the Republic of Ireland).
Amendments—[1] Words in sub-s (1) inserted and substituted, respectively, by FA 1996 s 73(4), Sch 6 paras 20, 28 with effect from the year 1996–97.
[2] Sub-s (1A) inserted, and words in sub-s (1) substituted, by F(No 2)A 1997 s 34, Sch 4 para 20 with effect for the year 1999–00 and subsequent years of assessment.

744 No duplication of charge

(1) No amount of income shall be taken into account more than once in charging tax under the provisions of sections 739 and 740; and where there is a choice as to the persons in relation to whom any amount of income can be so taken into account—

(a) it shall be so taken into account in relation to such of them, and if more than one in such proportions respectively, as appears to the Board to be just and reasonable; and
(b) the jurisdiction of the Special Commissioners on any appeal against an assessment charging tax under those provisions shall include jurisdiction to review any relevant decision taken by the Board under this subsection.

(2) In subsection (1) above references to an amount of income taken into account in charging tax are—

(a) in the case of tax which under section 739 is charged on income, to the amount of that income;
(b) in the case of tax charged under that section by virtue of section 743(5), to an amount of the income out of which the benefit is provided equal to the amount or value of the benefit charged;
(c) in the case of tax charged under section 740, to the amount of relevant income taken into account under subsection (2) of that section in charging the benefit.

Commentary—*Simon's Direct Tax Service* **E1.731.**
Revenue Interpretation RI 201—Where more than one person is potentially assessable under ss 739–740, the Revenue will seek to agree a just and reasonable division of liability.
Definitions—"The Board", s 832(1); "tax", s 832(3).

745 Power to obtain information

(1) The Board may by notice require any person to furnish them within such time as they may direct (not being less than 28 days) with such particulars as they think necessary for the purposes of this Chapter.

(2) The particulars which a person must furnish under this section, if he is required by such a notice so to do, include particulars—

(a) as to transactions with respect to which he is or was acting on behalf of others;
(b) as to transactions which in the opinion of the Board it is proper that they should investigate for the purposes of this Chapter notwithstanding that, in the opinion of the person to whom the notice is given, no liability to tax arises under this Chapter; and
(c) as to whether the person to whom the notice is given has taken or is taking any, and if so what, part in any, and if so what, transactions of a description specified in the notice.

(3) Notwithstanding anything in subsection (2) above, a solicitor shall not be deemed for the purposes of paragraph (c) of that subsection to have taken part in a transaction by reason only that he has given professional advice to a client in connection with that transaction, and shall not, in relation to anything done by him on behalf of his client, be compellable under this section, except with the consent of his client, to do more than state that he is or was acting on behalf of a client, and give the name and address of the client and also—

(a) in the case of anything done by the solicitor in connection with the transfer of any asset by or to an individual ordinarily resident in the United Kingdom or to or by any such body corporate as is mentioned in subsection (4) below, or in connection with any associated operation in relation to any such transfer, the names and addresses of the transferor and the transferee or of the persons concerned in the associated operations, as the case may be;

(*b*) in the case of anything done by the solicitor in connection with the formation or management of any such body corporate as is mentioned in subsection (4) below, the name and address of the body corporate;

(*c*) in the case of anything done by the solicitor in connection with the creation, or with the execution of the trusts, of any settlement by virtue or in consequence of which income becomes payable to a person resident or domiciled outside the United Kingdom, the names and addresses of the settlor and of that person.

(4) The bodies corporate mentioned in subsection (3) above are bodies corporate resident or incorporated outside the United Kingdom ...[2] which are, or if resident in the United Kingdom would be, close companies, but not [companies whose business consists wholly or mainly of the carrying on of a trade or trades][1].

(5) Nothing in this section shall impose on any bank the obligation to furnish any particulars of any ordinary banking transactions between the bank and a customer carried out in the ordinary course of banking business, unless the bank has acted or is acting on behalf of the customer in connection with the formation or management of any such body corporate as is mentioned in subsection (4) above or in connection with the creation, or with the execution of the trusts, of any such settlement as is mentioned in subsection (3)(*c*) above.

[(5A) In this section "bank" has the meaning given by section 840A.][4]

(6) In this section "settlement" and "settlor" have the meanings given by [section 660G(1) and (2)][3].

Commentary—*Simon's Direct Tax Service* E1.742.
Revenue Interpretation RI 201—Introducing a client to anyone responsible for establishing an overseas entity does not constitute "professional advice" within sub-s (3).
Simon's Tax Cases—s 745(1)(2), *Clinch v IRC* [1973] STC 155*.
Definitions—"The Board", s 832(1); "close companies", ss 414(1), 832(1); "notice", s 832(1); "tax", s 832(3); "United Kingdom", s 830(1).
Cross references—See TA 1988 s 746 (application of this section to residents of the Republic of Ireland).
TCGA 1992 s 98(2) (application of this section for the purposes of tax on chargeable gains of non-resident, dual resident and migrant settlements).
Amendments—[1] Words in sub-s (4) substituted by FA 1989 Sch 12 para 17.
[2] Words in sub-s (4) repealed by FA 1994 s 251(1)(a), (3)(b) and Sch 26 Pt VIII(1) with effect in relation to sub-ss (3)(b), (5) above from 30 November 1993 and in relation to the remaining provisions for transactions on or after that date.
[3] Words in sub-s (6) substituted by FA 1995 s 74, Sch 17 para 18, with effect from the year 1995–96 (and apply to every settlement wherever and whenever made or entered into).
[4] Sub-s (5A) inserted by FA 1996 s 198, Sch 37 paras 2(1), (2)(c), 9 with effect in relation to requirements imposed on or after 29 April 1996.

746 Persons resident in the Republic of Ireland

In relation to amounts which by virtue of any provision of section 34, 35 or 36 would, in the case of a person resident in the Republic of Ireland and not resident in the United Kingdom, be included in his income if he were not resident in the Republic of Ireland, sections 739, 742(1) to (3), 743 and 745 shall apply—

(*a*) as if his income included those amounts; and

(*b*) as if references to an individual included references to any person (and so that in accordance with section 9 those sections then apply for corporation tax as well as for income tax);

but section 741 shall not apply in any such case.

Commentary—*Simon's Direct Tax Service* E1.743.
Definitions—"Income tax", s 832(4); "United Kingdom", s 830(1).

CHAPTER IV
CONTROLLED FOREIGN COMPANIES

Revenue & other press releases—IR 5-10-93 (list of excluded countries for accounting periods ending before 1 July 1999).
IR 29–3–95 (controlled foreign companies—explanatory notes. These replace May 1990 edition).
IR 18–6–99 (controlled foreign companies—guidance notes).
Revenue Internal Guidance—Company Taxation Manual COT8211–8899 (detailed exposition of the CFC legislation).
Cross references—See TA 1988 s 756 (interpretation and construction of this Chapter).
See the Controlled Foreign Companies (Excluded Countries) Regulations, SI 1998/3081 (details of excluded countries in respect of accounting periods ending on or after 1 July 1999).
Modifications—Application of this Chapter in respect of UK companies which have a relevant interest in companies resident outside the UK carrying on general insurance business and drawing up accounts relating to that business on a non-annual basis: see Non-resident Companies (General Insurance Business) Regulations, SI 1999/1408 regs 3–6.

747 Imputation of chargeable profits and creditable tax of controlled foreign companies

(1) If ...[2] in any accounting period a company—

(*a*) is resident outside the United Kingdom, and

(*b*) is controlled by persons resident in the United Kingdom, and

(*c*) is subject to a lower level of taxation in the territory in which it is resident,

...[2] the provisions of this Chapter shall apply in relation to that accounting period.

[(1A) A company which would not, apart from this subsection, fall to be regarded as controlled by persons resident in the United Kingdom shall be taken for the purposes of this Chapter to be so controlled if—

    (*a*) there are two persons who, taken together, control the company;
    (*b*) one of those persons is resident in the United Kingdom and is a person in whose case the 40 per cent test in section 755D(3) is satisfied; and
    (*c*) the other is a person in whose case the 40 per cent test in section 755D(4) is satisfied.][3]

[(1B) In determining, for the purposes of any provision of this Chapter except subsection (1)(*a*) above, whether a company is a person resident in the United Kingdom, section 249 of the Finance Act 1994 (under which a company is treated as non-resident if it is so treated for double taxation relief purposes) shall be disregarded.][4]

(2) A company which falls within paragraphs (*a*) to (*c*) of subsection (1) above is in this Chapter referred to as a "controlled foreign company".

(3) [Subject to section 748, where][2] the provisions of this Chapter apply in relation to an accounting period of a controlled foreign company, the chargeable profits of that company for that period and its creditable tax (if any) for that period shall each be apportioned in accordance with section 752 among the persons (whether resident in the United Kingdom or not) who had an interest in that company at any time during that accounting period.

(4) Where, on such an apportionment of a controlled foreign company's chargeable profits for an accounting period as is referred to in subsection (3) above, an amount of those profits is apportioned to a company resident in the United Kingdom then, subject to subsection (5) below—

    (*a*) a sum equal to corporation tax at the appropriate rate on that apportioned amount of profits, less the portion of the controlled foreign company's creditable tax for that period (if any) which is apportioned to the resident company, shall be [chargeable on][2] the resident company as if it were an amount of corporation tax chargeable on that company; and
    (*b*) if, apart from this paragraph, section 739 would deem any sum forming part of the company's chargeable profits for that accounting period to be the income of an individual for the purposes of the Income Tax Acts, that section shall not apply to such portion of that sum as corresponds to the portion of those chargeable profits which is apportioned to companies which are resident in the United Kingdom and which, by virtue of paragraph (*a*) above, have a liability to tax in respect thereof;

and for the purposes of paragraph (*a*) above "the appropriate rate" means the rate of corporation tax applicable to profits of that accounting period of the resident company in which ends the accounting period of the controlled foreign company [which is mentioned in subsection (1) above][2] or, if there is more than one such rate, the average rate over the whole of that accounting period of the resident company.

[(4A) Where by virtue of section 747A a company's chargeable profits for an accounting period are to be computed and expressed in a currency other than sterling, for the purposes of subsection (4)(*a*) above the apportioned amount shall be taken to be the sterling equivalent of the apportioned amount found in the currency other than sterling.][1]

[(4B) The translation required by subsection (4A) above shall be made by reference to the London closing exchange rate for the two currencies concerned for the last day of the accounting period concerned.][1]

(5) Tax shall not, by virtue of subsection (4) above, be [chargeable on][2] a company resident in the United Kingdom unless, on the apportionment in question, the aggregate of—

    (*a*) the amount of the controlled foreign company's chargeable profits for the accounting period in question which is apportioned to the resident company, and
    (*b*) any amounts of those chargeable profits which are apportioned to persons who are connected or associated with the resident company,

is at least [25 per cent][2] of the total of those chargeable profits.

(6) In relation to a company resident outside the United Kingdom—

    (*a*) any reference in this Chapter to its chargeable profits for an accounting period is a reference to the amount which, on the assumptions in Schedule 24, would be the amount of the total profits of the company for that period on which, after allowing for any deductions available against those profits, corporation tax would be chargeable; and
    (*b*) any reference in this Chapter to profits does not include a reference to chargeable gains but otherwise (except as provided by paragraph (*a*) above) has the same meaning as it has for the purposes of corporation tax.

Commentary—*Simon's Direct Tax Service* D4.1201, 1202.
Regulations—European Single Currency (Taxes) Regulations, SI 1998/3177 reg 40 (Application of this section where accounts of a controlled foreign company are expressed in Euros).
Revenue Interpretation RI 113—(operation of transitional rules (under FA 1994 ss 153(4), 175) in relation to foreign exchange gains and losses on currency contracts where company has been, or may be, subject to a direction under this section).
Revenue Internal Guidance—Company Taxation Manual COT8302 (the "appropriate rate" in sub-s(4) is the main rate of corporation tax: the small companies' rate is not available: worked example).
COT8331 (a dual resident company cannot be a CFC unless it is treated as non-resident under a double taxation agreement, in which case FA 1994 s 249 applies).

COT8899 (flow chart for deciding whether a company is a CFC).

Simon's Tax Cases—s 747(4)(*a*), (6)(*a*), *Bricom Holdings Ltd v IRC* [1997] STC 1179.

Definitions—"Accounting period", s 751; "apportionment", s 834(4); "the Board", s 832(1); "company", s 832(1), (2); "the Income Tax Acts", s 831(1)(*b*); "tax", s 832(3); "United Kingdom", s 830(1).

Cross references—See TMA 1970 s 46B(4) (any question as to the application of sub-s (4)(*a*) above to be determined by the Special Commissioners).

TA 1970 s 55 (postponement of tax on appeals by UK controlled foreign companies against tax assessment and liability).

TA 1988 s 747A (apportionment under sub-s (3) above as regards computation of chargeable profits in currencies other than sterling).

TA 1988 s 748(1) (circumstances in which no apportionment to be given under sub-s (3) above with respect to an accounting period of a controlled foreign company).

TA 1988 s 751(4) (direction under sub-s (1) above specifying an accounting period in the case of a non–resident company whose accounting period is uncertain).

TA 1988 s 753(1) (notice of a direction given under sub-s (1) above to be given to resident companies having interest in controlled foreign companies).

TA 1988 s 754(1) (interpretation of sub-s (4)(*a*) above).

TA 1988 s 754(2) (notice of assessment relating to a sum assessable and recoverable under sub-s (4)(a) above).

TA 1988 s 754(3) (on an appeal against an assessment under sub-s (4)(a) above, the jurisdiction of the Special Commissioners extends to reviewing other relevant matters).

TA 1988 s 754(4) (appeal against assessment under sub-s (4)(*a*) not allowed on certain grounds).

TA 1988 Sch 26 para 1(1), (6) (losses or surplus allowances of a resident company in receipt of profits from a controlled foreign company: relief for losses or allowances by way of set-off against sub-s (4)(*a*) liability).

TA 1988 Sch 26 para 2 (set-off of surplus ACT against corporation tax liability under sub-s (4)(*a*) above of a resident company in receipt of profits from a controlled foreign company).

TA 1988 Sch 26 para 3 (gains on disposal of shares in controlled foreign company).

TA 1988 Sch 26 para 4 (dividends from foreign controlled company).

Corporation Tax (Treatment of Unrelieved Surplus Advance Corporation Tax) Regulations, SI 1999/358 reg 20 (set off of unrelieved surplus ACT against sub-s (4)(*a*) liability to corporation tax on profits of a controlled foreign company).

FA 2000 Sch 22 paras 54, 57 (operation of this section in relation to tonnage tax).

Amendments—[1] Sub-ss (4A), (4B) inserted by FA 1995 s 133, Sch 25 para 3.

[2] Words in sub-s (1) repealed and words in sub-ss (3), (4) and (5) substituted by FA 1998 Sch 17 para 1 with effect for accounting periods of companies resident in the United Kingdom ending after 30 June 1999 (by virtue of Finance Act 1994, Section 199, (Appointed Day) Order, SI 1998/3173 art 2).

[3] Sub-s (1A) inserted by FA 2000 s 104, Sch 31 paras 1, 2, 9(1) with effect after 20 March 2000.

[4] Sub-s (1B) inserted by FA 2002 s 90 and deemed to have come into force on 1 April 2002. This amendment does not apply to a company that—

    (i) by virtue of FA 1994 s 249 was treated as resident outside the United Kingdom, and not resident in the United Kingdom, immediately before that date, and

    (ii) has not subsequently ceased to be so treated.

[747A Special rule for computing chargeable profits

(1) Subsection (2) below applies where for the purposes of this Chapter a company's chargeable profits fall to be determined for—

    (*a*) the first relevant accounting period of the company, or

    (*b*) any subsequent accounting period of the company.

(2) Notwithstanding any other rule (whether statutory or otherwise) the chargeable profits for any such period shall be computed and expressed in the currency used in the accounts of the company for its first relevant accounting period.

(3) Subsection (4) below applies where for the purposes of this Chapter a company's chargeable profits fall to be determined for any accounting period of the company which—

    (*a*) begins on or after the appointed day, and

    (*b*) falls before the company's first relevant accounting period.

(4) Notwithstanding any other rule (whether statutory or otherwise) the chargeable profits for any such period shall be computed and expressed in the currency used in the accounts of the company for the accounting period concerned.

(5) For the purposes of this section the first relevant accounting period of the company shall be found in accordance with subsections (6) to (8) below.

(6) Where [an apportionment under section 747(3) has fallen to be made][3] as regards an accounting period of the company which begins before its commencement day, its first relevant accounting period is its accounting period which begins on its commencement day.

(7) ...[2]

(8) Where ...[2] subsection (6) above does not apply, [the company's][2] first relevant accounting period is its first accounting period which begins on or after its commencement day and as regards which—

    [(*a*) an apportionment under section 747(3) has fallen to be made, or

    (*b*) it can reasonably be assumed that such an apportionment would have fallen to be made, but for the fact that the company pursued, within the meaning of Part I of Schedule 25, an acceptable distribution policy,][3]

[unless the company is a trading company, in which case paragraph (*b*) above shall be disregarded in the case of its accounting periods beginning before 28th November 1995.][2]

(9) For the purposes of this section—

    (*a*) a company's commencement day is the first day of its first accounting period to begin after the day preceding the appointed day;

    [(*b*) "the appointed day" is 23rd March 1995.][4]

(10) References in this section to the accounts of a company—

    (*a*) are to the accounts which the company is required by the law of its home State to keep, or

    (*b*) if the company is not required by the law of its home State to keep accounts, are to the accounts of the company which most closely correspond to the individual accounts which companies formed and registered under the Companies Act 1985 are required by that Act to keep;

and for the purposes of this subsection the home State of a company is the country or territory under whose law the company is incorporated or formed.][1]

Commentary—*Simon's Direct Tax Service* **D4.1210.**
Definitions—"Accounting period", s 75(1)–(5); "company", s 832(1), (2); "profits", s 747(6).
Modification—This section shall have effect in accordance with the European Single Currency (Taxes) Regulations, SI 1998/3177 reg 40 in relation to the replacement of currency used in accounts of controlled foreign company by euro.
Amendments—[1] Section inserted by FA 1995 s 133, Sch 25 para 2.
[2] Sub-s (7) and words in sub-s (8) repealed and words in sub-s (8) substituted and inserted respectively by FA 1996 s 182, Sch 36 para 1(1), (2), (3), Sch 41 Pt V(34) with effect for accounting periods of a controlled foreign company, within the meaning of this Chapter, beginning after 27 November 1995.
[3] Words in sub-s (6) substituted, sub-s (8)(*a*), (*b*) substituted and words in sub-s (9) inserted by FA 1998 Sch 17 para 2 with effect in relation to accounting periods of companies resident in the United Kingdom ending after 30 June 1999 (by virtue of Finance Act 1994, Section 199, (Appointed Day) Order, SI 1998/3173 art 2).
[4] Sub-s (9)(*b*) substituted by FA 2002 s 79, Sch 123 para 19 with effect for accounting periods beginning after 30 September 2002. Sub-s (9)(*b*) previously read as follows—

    "(*b*) the appointed day (which, for ease of reference, is 23rd March 1995) is such day as may be appointed under section 165(7)(*b*) of the Finance Act 1993 (which relates to exchange gains and losses)."

748 [Cases where section 747(3) does not apply][3]

[(1) No apportionment under section 747(3) falls to be made as regards an accounting period of a controlled foreign company if—][3]

    (*a*) in respect of that period the company pursues, within the meaning of Part I of Schedule 25, an acceptable distribution policy; or

    (*b*) throughout that period the company is, within the meaning of Part II of that Schedule, engaged in exempt activities; or

    (*c*) the public quotation condition set out in Part III of that Schedule is fulfilled with respect to that period; or

    (*d*) the chargeable profits of the accounting period do not exceed [£50,000][3] or, if the accounting period is less than 12 months, a proportionately reduced amount [or

    (*e*) as respects the accounting period, the company is, within the meaning of regulations made by the Board for the purposes of this paragraph, resident in a territory specified in the regulations and satisfies—

        (i) such conditions with respect to its income or gains as may be so specified; and

        (ii) such other conditions (if any) as may be so specified.][3].

[(1A) Regulations under paragraph (e) of subsection (1) above may—

    (*a*) make different provision for different cases or with respect to different territories;

    (*b*) make provision having effect in relation to accounting periods of controlled foreign companies ending not more than one year before the date on which the regulations are made; and

    (*c*) contain such supplementary, incidental, consequential and transitional provision as the Board may think fit.][3]

(2) ...[3]

(3) Notwithstanding that none of paragraphs (*a*) to [(*e*)][3] of subsection (1) above applies to an accounting period of a controlled foreign company, [no apportionment under section 747(3) falls to be made as regards that accounting period if it is the case that]³—

    (*a*) in so far as any of the transactions the results of which are reflected in the profits arising in that accounting period, [or any two or more transactions taken together, the results of at least one of which are so reflected,][2] achieved a reduction in United Kingdom tax, either the reduction so achieved was minimal or it was not the main purpose or one of the main purposes of that transaction or, as the case may be, of those transactions taken together to achieve that reduction, and

    (*b*) it was not the main reason or, as the case may be, one of the main reasons for the company's existence in that accounting period to achieve a reduction in United Kingdom tax by a diversion of profits from the United Kingdom,

and Part IV of Schedule 25 shall have effect with respect to the preceding provisions of this subsection.

[(4) Where by virtue of section 747A a company's chargeable profits for an accounting period are to be computed and expressed in a currency other than sterling, for the purposes of subsection (1)(*d*) above its chargeable profits for the period shall be taken to be the sterling equivalent of its chargeable profits found in the currency other than sterling.][1]

[(5) The translation required by subsection (4) above shall be made by reference to the London closing exchange rate for the two currencies concerned for the last day of the accounting period concerned.][1]

[(6) This section is subject to section 748A.][4]

Commentary—*Simon's Direct Tax Service* **D4.1206**
Regulations—Controlled Foreign Company (Excluded Countries) Regulations, SI 1998/3081.
Revenue & other press releases—IR 9–11–94 (new clearance procedure for non-trading CFCs seeking to rely on the "exempt activities" test in sub-s (1)(b) above or, the "motive" test in sub-s (3) above).
Revenue Internal Guidance—Company Taxation Manual COT8520–8527 (discussion of the motive test).
COT8527 (whether holding company satisfies the motive test).
COT8899 (flow chart for deciding whether a company satisfies the motive test).
Definitions—"Accounting period", s 751(1)–(5); "the Board", s 832(1); "chargeable profits of the accounting period", s 747(6); "company", s 832(1), (2); "distribution", ss 209(2), 832(1); "profits", s 747(6); "tax", s 832(3); "United Kingdom", s 830(1).
Amendments—¹ Sub-ss (4), (5) inserted by FA 1995 s 133, Sch 25 para 4.
² Words in sub-s (3)(a) substituted by FA 1996 s 182, Sch 36 para 2 with effect for accounting periods of a controlled foreign company, within the meaning of this Chapter, beginning after 27 November 1995.
³ Words in sub-s (1), (3) and heading substituted, sub-ss (1)(e), (1A) inserted, sub-s (2) repealed by FA 1998 Sch 17 para 3 with effect in relation to accounting periods of companies resident in the United Kingdom ending after 30 June 1999 (by virtue of Finance Act 1994, Section 199, (Appointed Day) Order, SI 1998/3173 art 2).
⁴ Sub-s (6) inserted by FA 2002 s 89(1), (3) with effect for accounting periods of controlled foreign companies beginning after 23 July 2002.

[748A Territorial exclusions from exemption under section 748.

(1) Nothing in section 748 prevents an apportionment under section 747(3) falling to be made as regards an accounting period of a controlled foreign company if the company—

    (a) is a company incorporated in a territory to which this section applies as respects that accounting period; or

    (b) is at any time in that accounting period liable to tax in such a territory by reason of domicile, residence or place of management; or

    (c) at any time in that accounting period carries on business through a branch or agency in such a territory.

(2) The condition in subsection (1)(c) above is not satisfied as regards an accounting period of a controlled foreign company if the business carried on by the company in that period through branches or agencies in territories to which this section applies, taken as a whole, is only a minimal part of the whole of the business carried on by the company in that period.

(3) The territories to which this section applies as respects an accounting period of a controlled foreign company are those specified as such in regulations made by the Treasury.

(4) Regulations under subsection (3) above—

    (a) may make different provision for different cases or with respect to different territories; and

    (b) may contain such incidental, supplemental, consequential or transitional provision as the Treasury may think fit.

(5) A statutory instrument containing regulations under subsection (3) above shall not be made unless a draft of the instrument has been laid before, and approved by a resolution of, the House of Commons.]¹

Amendments—¹ This section inserted by FA 2002 s 89(2), (3) with effect for accounting periods of controlled foreign companies beginning after 23 July 2002.

[749 Residence

(1) Subject to subsections (2) to (4) and (6) below, in any accounting period in which a company is resident outside the United Kingdom, it shall be regarded for the purposes of this Chapter as resident in that territory in which, throughout that period, it is liable to tax by reason of domicile, residence or place of management.

(2) If, in the case of any company,—

    (a) there are in any accounting period two or more territories falling within subsection (1) above, and

    (b) no election or designation made under paragraph (d) or (e) of subsection (3) below in relation to an earlier accounting period of the company has effect by virtue of section 749A(1) in relation to that accounting period,

subsection (3) below shall apply with respect to that company and that accounting period.

(3) Where this subsection applies, the company shall in that accounting period be regarded for the purposes of this Chapter as resident in only one of those territories, namely—

    (a) if, throughout the accounting period, the company's place of effective management is situated in one of those territories only, in that territory;

    (b) if, throughout the accounting period, the company's place of effective management is situated in two or more of those territories, in that one of them in which, at the end of the accounting period, the greater amount of the company's assets is situated;

    (c) if neither paragraph (a) nor paragraph (b) above applies, in that one of the territories falling within subsection (1) above in which, at the end of the accounting period, the greater amount of the company's assets is situated;

    (d) if—

        (i) paragraph (a) above does not apply, and

(ii) neither paragraph (*b*) nor paragraph (*c*) above produces one, and only one, of those territories,

in that one of them (if any) which is specified in an election made in relation to that accounting period by any one or more persons who together have a majority assessable interest in the company in that accounting period; and

(*e*) if, in a case falling within paragraph (*d*) above, the time by which any election under that paragraph in relation to that accounting period must be made in accordance with section 749A(3)(*b*) expires without such an election having been made, in that one of those territories which the Board justly and reasonably designates in relation to that accounting period.

(4) If, in the case of any company,—

(*a*) there are in any accounting period two or more territories falling within subsection (1) above, and

(*b*) an election or designation made under paragraph (*d*) or (*e*) of subsection (3) above in relation to an earlier accounting period of the company has effect by virtue of section 749A(1) in relation to the accounting period mentioned in paragraph (*a*) above,

the company shall in that accounting period be regarded for the purposes of this Chapter as resident in that one of those territories which is the subject of the election or designation.

(5) If, in the case of any company, there is in any accounting period no territory falling within subsection (1) above, then, for the purposes of this Chapter, it shall be conclusively presumed that the company is in that accounting period resident in a territory in which it is subject to a lower level of taxation.

(6) In any case where it becomes necessary for the purposes of subsection (3) above to determine in which of two or more territories the greater amount of a company's assets is situated at the end of an accounting period—

(*a*) account shall be taken only of those assets which, immediately before the end of that period, are situated in those territories; and

(*b*) the amount of them shall be determined by reference to their market value at that time.

(7) This section is without prejudice to the provision that may be made in regulations under section 748(1)(*e*).

(8) For the purposes of this section, one or more persons together have a "majority assessable interest" in a controlled foreign company in an accounting period of the company if—

(*a*) each of them has an assessable interest in the company in that accounting period; and

(*b*) it is likely that, were an apportionment of the chargeable profits of the company for that accounting period made under section 747(3), the aggregate of the amounts which would be apportioned to them is greater than 50 per cent of the aggregate of the amounts which would be apportioned to all the persons who have an assessable interest in the company in that accounting period.

(9) For the purposes of subsection (8) above, a person has an "assessable interest" in a controlled foreign company in an accounting period of the company if he is one of the persons who it is likely would be chargeable to tax under section 747(4)(*a*) on an apportionment of the chargeable profits and creditable tax (if any) of the company for that accounting period under section 747(3).][1]

Commentary—*Simon's Direct Tax Service* **D4.1205.**
Amendments—[1] Substituted by FA 1998 Sch 17 para 4 with effect in relation to accounting periods of companies resident in the United Kingdom ending after 30 June 1999 (by virtue of Finance Act 1994, Section 199, (Appointed Day) Order, SI 1998/3173 art 2).

[749A Elections and designations under section 749: supplementary provisions

(1) An election under paragraph (*d*) or a designation under paragraph (*e*) of section 749(3) shall have effect in relation to—

(*a*) the accounting period in relation to which it is made ("the original accounting period"), and

(*b*) each successive accounting period of the controlled foreign company in question which precedes the next one in which the eligible territories are different,

and shall so have effect notwithstanding any change in the persons who have interests in the company or any change in the interests which those persons have in the company.

(2) For the purposes of subsection (1)(*b*) above, an accounting period of the controlled foreign company is one in which the eligible territories are different if in the case of that accounting period—

(*a*) at least one of the two or more territories which fell within subsection (1) of section 749 in the original accounting period does not fall within that subsection; or

(*b*) some other territory also falls within that subsection.

(3) Any election under section 749(3)(*d*)—

(*a*) must be made by notice given to an officer of the Board;

(*b*) must be made no later than twelve months after the end of the controlled foreign company's accounting period in relation to which it is made;

(*c*) must state, as respects each of the persons making it, the percentage of the chargeable profits and creditable tax (if any) of the controlled foreign company for that accounting period which it is likely would be apportioned to him on an apportionment under section 747(3) if one were made;

(d) must be signed by the persons making it; and

(e) is irrevocable.

(4) Nothing in—

(a) paragraph 10 of Schedule 18 to the Finance Act 1998 (claims or elections in company tax returns), or

(b) Schedule 1A to the Management Act (claims or elections not included in returns),

shall apply, whether by virtue of section 754 or otherwise, to an election under section 749(3)(d).

(5) A designation under section 749(3)(e) is irrevocable.

(6) Where the Board make a designation under section 749(3)(e), notice of the making of the designation shall be given to every company resident in the United Kingdom which appears to the Board to have had an assessable interest in the controlled foreign company at any time during the accounting period of the controlled foreign company in relation to which the designation is made.

(7) A notice under subsection (6) above shall specify—

(a) the date on which the designation was made;

(b) the controlled foreign company to which the designation relates;

(c) the accounting period of the controlled foreign company in relation to which the designation is made; and

(d) the territory designated.

(8) Subsection (9) of section 749 has effect for the purposes of subsection (6) above as it has effect for the purposes of subsection (8) of that section.]¹

Amendments—¹ This section inserted by FA 1998 Sch 17 para 4 with effect in relation to accounting periods of companies resident in the United Kingdom ending after 30 June 1999 (by virtue of Finance Act 1994, Section 199, (Appointed Day) Order, SI 1998/3173 art 2).

[749B Interests in companies

(1) For the purposes of this Chapter, the following persons have an interest in a company—

(a) any person who possesses, or is entitled to acquire, share capital or voting rights in the company;

(b) any person who possesses, or is entitled to acquire, a right to receive or participate in distributions of the company;

(c) any person who is entitled to secure that income or assets (whether present or future) of the company will be applied directly or indirectly for his benefit; and

(d) any other person who, either alone or together with other persons, has control of the company.

(2) Rights which a person has as a loan creditor of a company do not constitute an interest in the company for the purposes of this Chapter.

(3) For the purposes of subsection (1)(b) above, the definition of 'distribution' in Part VI shall be construed without any limitation to companies resident in the United Kingdom.

(4) References in subsection (1) above to being entitled to do anything apply where a person—

(a) is presently entitled to do it at a future date, or

(b) will at a future date be entitled to do it;

but a person whose entitlement to secure that any income or assets of the company will be applied as mentioned in paragraph (c) of that subsection is contingent upon a default of the company or any other person under any agreement shall not be treated as falling within that paragraph unless the default has occurred.

(5) Where a company has an interest in another company and a third person has, or two or more persons together have, an interest in the first company (as in a case where one company has a shareholding in a controlled foreign company and the first company is controlled by a third company or by two or more persons together) subsections (6) and (7) below apply.

(6) Where this subsection applies, the person who has, or each of the persons who together have, the interest in the first company shall be regarded for the purposes of this Chapter as thereby having an interest in the second company.

(7) In any case where this subsection applies, in construing references in this Chapter to one person having the same interest as another, the person or as the case may be, each of the persons who together have, the interest in the first company shall be treated as having, to the extent of that person's interest in that company, the same interest as the first company has in the second company.

(8) Where two or more persons jointly have an interest in a company otherwise than in a fiduciary or representative capacity, they shall be treated for the purposes of this Chapter as having the interest in equal shares.]¹

Amendments—¹ This section inserted by FA 1998 Sch 17 para 4 with effect in relation to accounting periods of companies resident in the United Kingdom ending after 30 June 1999 (by virtue of Finance Act 1994, Section 199, (Appointed Day) Order, SI 1998/3173 art 2).

750 Territories with a lower level of taxation

(1) Without prejudice to [subsection (5)]³ of section 749, a company which, by virtue of [any of subsections (1) to (4)]³ of that section, is to be regarded as resident in a particular territory outside

the United Kingdom shall be considered to be subject to a lower level of taxation in that territory if the amount of tax (''the local tax'') which is paid under the law of that territory in respect of the profits of the company which arise in any accounting period is less than [three-quarters][1] of the corresponding United Kingdom tax on those profits.

(2) For the purposes of this Chapter, the amount of the corresponding United Kingdom tax on the profits arising in an accounting period of a company resident outside the United Kingdom is the amount of corporation tax which, on the assumptions set out in Schedule 24 and subject to subsection (3) below, would be chargeable in respect of the chargeable profits of the company for that accounting period.

(3) In determining the amount of corporation tax which, in accordance with subsection (2) above, would be chargeable in respect of the chargeable profits of an accounting period of a company resident outside the United Kingdom—

[(*a*) it shall be assumed for the purposes of Schedule 24 that an apportionment under section 747(3) falls to be made as regards that period; and][3]
(*b*) there shall be disregarded so much of any relief from corporation tax in respect of income as would be attributable to the local tax and would fall to be given by virtue of any provision of Part XVIII ...[4]; and
(*c*) there shall be deducted from what would otherwise be the amount of that corporation tax—
(i) any amount which (on the assumptions set out in Schedule 24) would fall to be set off against corporation tax by virtue of section 7(2); and
(ii) any amount of income tax or corporation tax actually charged in respect of any of those chargeable profits.

(4) The references in subsection (3)(*c*) above to an amount falling to be set off or an amount actually charged do not include so much of any such amount as has been or falls to be repaid to the company whether on the making of a claim or otherwise.

[(5) Subsections (6) and (7) below apply where by virtue of section 747A a company's chargeable profits for an accounting period are to be computed and expressed in a currency other than sterling.][2]

[(6) For the purposes of subsection (2) above the company's chargeable profits for the period shall be taken to be the sterling equivalent of its chargeable profits found in the currency other than sterling.][2]

[(7) In applying section 13 for the purposes of making the determination mentioned in subsection (3) above, any reference in section 13 to the amount of the company's profits for the period on which corporation tax falls finally to be borne shall be construed as a reference to the sterling sum found under subsection (6) above.][2]

[(8) Any translation required by subsection (6) above shall be made by reference to the London closing exchange rate for the two currencies concerned for the last day of the accounting period concerned.][2]

Commentary—*Simon's Direct Tax Service* **D4.1205.**
Revenue & other press releases—IR 5-10-93 (list of excluded countries for the purposes of controlled foreign companies provisions TA 1988 ss 747–756 Schs 24–26 in respect of accounting periods ending before 1 July 1999).
IR 16-7-84 (clearance procedure: advice on technical points, group structures, treatment of other subsidiaries in group, sale of CFC).
Revenue Internal Guidance—Company Taxation Manual COT8353 (small companies' rate is potentially available in computing the UK tax which would be payable).
Definitions—''Accounting period'', s 751(1)–(5); ''the Board'', s 832(1); ''company'', s 832(1), (2); ''income tax'', s 832(4); ''notice'', s 832(1); ''profits'', s 747(6); ''resident'', s 749(1)–(4); ''tax'', s 832(3); ''United Kingdom'', s 830(1).
Amendments—[1] ''Three-quarters'' in sub-s (1) substituted for ''one-half'' by FA 1993 s 119(1), (2) in relation to accounting periods beginning after 15 March 1993. The ''three-quarters'' level also applies where an accounting period has begun before 16 March 1993 and ends on or after that date by virtue of FA 1993 s 119(3).
[2] Sub-ss (5)–(8) inserted by FA 1995 s 133, Sch 25 para 5.
[3] Words in sub-s (1) substituted and sub-s (3)(*a*) inserted by FA 1998 Sch 17 para 5 with effect in relation to accounting periods of companies resident in the United Kingdom ending after 30 June 1999 (by virtue of Finance Act 1994, Section 199, (Appointed Day) Order, SI 1998/3173 art 2).
[4] Words in sub-s (3)(*b*) repealed by FA 2000 s 156, Sch 40 Pt II(13) with effect for claims made after 31 March 2000.

[750A Deemed lower level of taxation: designer rate tax provisions

(1) Where—

(*a*) in any accounting period a company is to be regarded by virtue of any of subsections (1) to (4) of section 749 as resident in a particular territory outside the United Kingdom, and
(*b*) within the meaning of section 750(1), the local tax in respect of the profits arising to the company in that accounting period is equal to or greater than three-quarters of the corresponding United Kingdom tax on those profits, but
(*c*) that local tax is determined under designer rate tax provisions,

the company shall be taken for the purposes of this Chapter to be subject to a lower level of taxation in that territory in that accounting period.

(2) In subsection (1) above ''designer rate tax provisions'' means provisions—

(*a*) which appear to the Board to be designed to enable companies to exercise significant control over the amount of tax which they pay; and
(*b*) which are specified in regulations made by the Board.

(3) Regulations under subsection (2) above—

    (*a*) may make different provision for different cases or with respect to different territories; and

    (*b*) may contain such supplementary, incidental, consequential or transitional provision as the Board may think fit.

(4) The first regulations under subsection (2) above may make provision having effect in relation to accounting periods beginning not more than fifteen months before the date on which the regulations are made.]¹

Regulations—Controlled Foreign Companies (Designer Rate Tax Provisions) Regulations, SI 2000/3158 (provisions contained in the tax legislation of Guernsey, Jersey, the Isle of Man and Gibraltar are specified for the purposes of this section).
Amendments—¹ This section inserted by FA 2000 s 104, Sch 31 paras 1, 3, 9(2) with effect for any accounting period of a company resident outside the UK which begins after 5 October 1999.

751 Accounting periods and creditable tax

(1) For the purposes of this Chapter, an accounting period of a company resident outside the United Kingdom shall begin—

    (*a*) whenever the company comes under the control of [persons]¹ resident in the United Kingdom;

    (*b*) whenever the company [...]³ commences to carry on business [unless an accounting period of the company has previously begun as respects which an apportionment under section 747(3) falls or has fallen to be made]³; and

    (*c*) whenever an accounting period of the company ends without the company then ceasing either to carry on business or to have any source of income whatsoever.

(2) For the purposes of this Chapter, an accounting period of a company resident outside the United Kingdom shall end if and at the time when—

    (*a*) the company ceases to be under the control of persons resident in the United Kingdom; or

    (*b*) the company becomes, or ceases to be, liable to tax in a territory; or

    [(*bb*) ...²]

    (*c*) the company ceases to have any source of income whatsoever;

and for the purposes of paragraph (*b*) above "liable to tax" means liable to tax by reason of domicile, residence or place of management.

(3) Without prejudice to subsections (1) and (2) above, subsections (3), (5) and (7) of section 12 shall apply for the purposes of this Chapter as they apply for the purposes of corporation tax, but with the omission of so much of those provisions as relates to a company coming or ceasing to be within the charge to corporation tax.

(4) Where it appears to the Board that the beginning or end of any accounting period of a company resident outside the United Kingdom is uncertain, [the Board may by notice]³ specify as an accounting period of the company such period, not exceeding 12 months, as appears to the Board to be appropriate, and that period shall be treated for the purposes of this Chapter as an accounting period of the company unless [the notice]³ is subsequently amended under subsection (5) below.

(5) If, on further facts coming to the knowledge of the Board after the [giving of a notice under subsection (4) above]³, it appears to the Board that any accounting period specified in the [notice]³ is not the true accounting period, the Board shall amend the [notice]³ so as to specify the true period.

[(5A) Any notice under subsection (4) above, and notice of any amendment of such a notice under subsection (5) above, shall be given to every person who has an assessable interest, (as defined in section 749(9)) in the company in the accounting period in question.]³

(6) In this Chapter, in relation to an accounting period of a controlled foreign company [as regards which an apportionment under section 747(3) falls to be made]³, the creditable tax means the aggregate of—

    (*a*) the amount of any relief from corporation tax in respect of income which (on the assumptions set out in Schedule 24 and assuming the company to be liable for corporation tax on the chargeable profits of that accounting period) would fall to be given to the company by virtue of any provision of Part XVIII in respect of foreign tax attributable to any income which is brought into account in determining those chargeable profits; and

    (*b*) any amount which (on those assumptions) would fall to be set off against corporation tax on those chargeable profits by virtue of section 7(2); and

    (*c*) the amount of any income tax or corporation tax actually charged in respect of the chargeable profits of that accounting period, less any of that tax which has been or falls to be repaid to the company, whether on the making of a claim or otherwise.

Commentary—*Simon's Direct Tax Service* **D4.1203**.
Revenue Internal Guidance—Company Taxation Manual COT8356, 8371 (worked examples).
COT8372 (overseas tax "spared" is creditable tax).
COT8373 (foreign tax paid is converted into sterling at the rate applying on the date it becomes payable).
COT8420 (annual interest paid to loan creditor is apportioned on a just and reasonable basis where loan creditor is treated as having an interest in the CFC).
COT8420 (interest paid to non-resident out of UK source income received net: worked example).
Definitions—"The Board", s 832(1); "company", s 832(1), (2); "control", ss 416(2), 756(3); "income tax", s 832(4); "profits", s 747(6); "resident", s 749(1)–(4); "United Kingdom", s 830(1).
Cross references—See TA 1988 s 753(2), (3) (certain obligations imposed upon the Board in relation to amendment to direction made under sub-s (5) above).

FA 1993 s 168A (exchange gains or losses accruing to a non-resident company to be ignored if it subsequently becomes resident in the United Kingdom).

Amendments—¹ Word in sub-s (1)(*a*) substituted by FA 1990 Sch 14 paras 1, 9 and deemed always to have had effect.
² Sub-s (2)(*bb*) repealed by FA 1994 s 251(1)(*a*), (4) and Sch 26 Pt VIII(1) with effect from 30 November 1993.
³ Words in sub-s (1)(*b*) repealed, words in sub-s (1)(*b*) inserted, sub-s (5A) inserted and words in sub-s (4), (5) and (6) substituted by FA 1998 Sch 17 para 6 with effect in relation to accounting periods of companies resident in the United Kingdom ending after 30 June 1999 (by virtue of Finance Act 1994, Section 199, (Appointed Day) Order, SI 1998/3173 art 2).

[752 Apportionment of chargeable profits and creditable tax

(1) This section applies in any case where an apportionment under section 747(3) falls to be made as regards an accounting period of a controlled foreign company.

(2) Where—

  (*a*) the persons who have relevant interests in the controlled foreign company at any time in the relevant accounting period have those interests by virtue only of directly or indirectly holding ordinary shares of the company,
  (*b*) each of those persons satisfies the condition that he is either—
    (i) resident in the United Kingdom throughout that accounting period, or
    (ii) resident in the United Kingdom at no time in that accounting period, and
  (*c*) no company which has an intermediate interest in the controlled foreign company at any time in the relevant accounting period has that interest otherwise than by virtue of directly or indirectly holding ordinary shares of the controlled foreign company,

subsection (3) below shall apply.

(3) Where this subsection applies, the apportionment of the controlled foreign company's chargeable profits and creditable tax (if any) for the relevant accounting period shall be made among the persons who have relevant interests in the company at any time in that period in direct proportion to the percentage of the issued ordinary shares of the controlled foreign company which, in accordance with section 752B, each of those relevant interests represents.

(4) Where subsection (3) above does not apply, the apportionment of the controlled foreign company's chargeable profits and creditable tax (if any) for the relevant accounting period shall be made on a just and reasonable basis among the persons who have relevant interests in the company at any time in that period.]¹

Amendments—¹ This section inserted by FA 1998 Sch 17 para 7 with effect in relation to accounting periods of companies resident in the United Kingdom ending after 30 June 1999 (by virtue of Finance Act 1994, Section 199, (Appointed Day) Order, SI 1998/3173 art 2).

[752A Relevant interests

(1) This section has effect for the purpose of determining for the purposes of this Chapter who has a relevant interest in a controlled foreign company at any time; and references in this Chapter to relevant interests shall be construed accordingly.

(2) A UK resident company which has a direct or indirect interest in a controlled foreign company has a relevant interest in the company by virtue of that interest unless subsection (3) below otherwise provides.

(3) A UK resident company which has an indirect interest in a controlled foreign company does not have a relevant interest in the company by virtue of that interest if it has the interest by virtue of having a direct or indirect interest in another UK resident company.

(4) A related person who has a direct or indirect interest in a controlled foreign company has a relevant interest in the company by virtue of that interest unless subsection (5) or (6) below otherwise provides.

(5) A related person who has an indirect interest in a controlled foreign company does not have a relevant interest in the company by virtue of that interest if he has the interest by virtue of having a direct or indirect interest in—

  (*a*) a UK resident company; or
  (*b*) another related person.

(6) A related person who has a direct or indirect interest in a controlled foreign company does not have a relevant interest in the company by virtue of that interest to the extent that a UK resident company—

  (*a*) has the whole or any part of the same interest indirectly, by virtue of having a direct or indirect interest in the related person, and
  (*b*) by virtue of that indirect interest in the controlled foreign company, has a relevant interest in the company by virtue of subsection (2) above.

(7) A person who—

  (*a*) has a direct interest in a controlled foreign company, but
  (*b*) does not by virtue of subsections (2) to (6) above have a relevant interest in the company by virtue of that interest,

has a relevant interest in the company by virtue of that interest unless subsection (8) below otherwise provides.

(8) A person does not by virtue of subsection (7) above have a relevant interest in a controlled foreign company by virtue of having a direct interest in the company to the extent that another person—

(*a*) has the whole or any part of the same interest indirectly, and

(*b*) by virtue of that indirect interest, has a relevant interest in the company by virtue of subsections (2) to (6) above.

(9) No person has a relevant interest in a controlled foreign company otherwise than as provided by subsections (2) to (8) above.

(10) In this section—

"related person" means a person who—

(*a*) is not a UK resident company, but

(*b*) is connected or associated with a UK resident company which has by virtue of subsection (2) above a relevant interest in the controlled foreign company in question;

"UK resident company" means a company resident in the United Kingdom.]¹

Amendments—¹ This section inserted by FA 1998 Sch 17 para 7 with effect in relation to accounting periods of companies resident in the United Kingdom ending after 30 June 1999 (by virtue of Finance Act 1994, Section 199, (Appointed Day) Order, SI 1998/3173 art 2)

[752B Section 752(3): the percentage of shares which a relevant interest represents

(1) For the purposes of section 752(3) above, where a person has a relevant interest in a controlled foreign company by virtue of indirectly holding issued ordinary shares of the company, the percentage of the issued ordinary shares of the company which the relevant interest represents is equal to—

$$P \times S$$

where—

P is the product of the appropriate fractions of that person and each of the share-linked companies through which he indirectly holds the shares in question, other than the lowest share-linked company; and

S is the percentage of issued ordinary shares of the controlled foreign company which is held directly by the lowest share-linked company.

(2) In subsection (1) above and this subsection—

"the appropriate fraction", in the case of a person who directly holds ordinary shares of a share-linked company, means that fraction of the issued ordinary shares of that company which his holding represents;

"the lowest share-linked company", in relation to a person who indirectly holds ordinary shares of a controlled foreign company, means the share-linked company which directly holds the shares in question;

"share-linked company" means a company which is share-linked to the controlled foreign company in question.

(3) Where a person has different indirect holdings of shares of the controlled foreign company (as in a case where different shares are held through different companies which are share-linked to the controlled foreign company)—

(*a*) subsection (1) above shall apply separately in relation to the different holdings with any necessary modifications; and

(*b*) for the purposes of section 752(3) above the percentage of the issued ordinary shares of the company which the relevant interest represents is the aggregate of the percentages resulting from those separate applications.

(4) Where, for the purposes of subsection (3) of section 752, the percentage of the issued ordinary shares of the controlled foreign company which a person directly or indirectly holds varies during the relevant accounting period, he shall be treated for the purposes of that subsection as holding throughout that period that percentage of the issued ordinary shares of the company which is equal to the sum of the relevant percentages for each holding period in the relevant accounting period.

(5) For the purposes of subsection (4) above—

"holding period", in the case of any person, means a part of the relevant accounting period during which the percentage of the issued ordinary shares of the controlled foreign company which the person holds (whether directly or indirectly) remains the same;

"the relevant percentage", in the case of a holding period, means the percentage equal to—

$$\frac{P \times H}{A}$$

where—

P is the percentage of the issued ordinary shares of the controlled foreign company which the person in question directly or indirectly holds in the holding period, as calculated in accordance with subsections (1) to (3) above so far as applicable;

H is the number of days in the holding period; and

A is the number of days in the relevant accounting period.]'

Amendments—' This section inserted by FA 1998 Sch 17 para 7 with effect in relation to accounting periods of companies resident in the United Kingdom ending after 30 June 1999 (by virtue of Finance Act 1994, Section 199, (Appointed Day) Order, SI 1998/3173 art 2).

[752C Interpretation of apportionment provisions

(1) In this section "the relevant provisions" means sections 752 to 752B and this section.

(2) For the purposes of the relevant provisions—

(*a*) a person has a direct interest in a company if (and only if) he has an interest in the company otherwise than by virtue of having an interest in another company;

(*b*) a person has an indirect interest in a company if (and only if) he has an interest in the company by virtue of having an interest in another company;

(*c*) a person indirectly holds shares of a controlled foreign company if (and only if) he directly holds ordinary shares of a company which is share-linked to the controlled foreign company.

(3) For the purposes of the relevant provisions, a company is 'share-linked' to a controlled foreign company if it has an interest in the controlled foreign company only by virtue of directly holding ordinary shares—

(*a*) of the controlled foreign company, or

(*b*) of the controlled foreign company or of one or more companies which are share-linked to the controlled foreign company by virtue of paragraph (*a*) above, or

(*c*) of the controlled foreign company or of one or more companies which are share-linked to the controlled foreign company by virtue of paragraph (*a*) or (*b*) above,

and so on.

(4) For the purposes of the relevant provisions, a company ('company A') has an intermediate interest in a controlled foreign company if (and only if)—

(*a*) it has a direct or indirect interest in the controlled foreign company; and

(*b*) one or more other persons have relevant interests in the controlled foreign company by virtue of having a direct or indirect interest in company A.

(5) Any interest or shares held by a nominee or bare trustee shall be treated for the purposes of the relevant provisions as held by the person or persons for whom the nominee or bare trustee holds the interest or shares.

(6) Where—

(*a*) an interest in a controlled foreign company is held in a fiduciary or representative capacity, and

(*b*) subsection (5) above does not apply, but

(*c*) there are one or more identifiable beneficiaries,

the interest shall be treated for the purposes of the relevant provisions as held by that beneficiary or, as the case may be, as apportioned on a just and reasonable basis among those beneficiaries.

(7) In the relevant provisions—

"bare trustee" means a person acting as trustee—

(*a*) for a person absolutely entitled as against the trustee; or

(*b*) for any person who would be so entitled but for being a minor or otherwise under a disability; or

(*c*) for two or more persons who are or would, but for all or any of them being a minor or otherwise under a disability, be jointly so entitled;

"ordinary shares", in the case of any company, means shares of a single class, however described, which is the only class of shares issued by the company;

"the relevant accounting period" means the accounting period mentioned in section 752(1);

"share" includes a reference to a fraction of a share.]'

Amendments—' This section inserted by FA 1998 Sch 17 para 7 with effect in relation to accounting periods of companies resident in the United Kingdom ending after 30 June 1999 (by virtue of Finance Act 1994, Section 199, (Appointed Day) Order, SI 1998/3173 art 2).

753 Notices and appeals

Commentary—*Simon's Direct Tax Service* **D4.1255.**
Amendments—This section repealed by FA 1998 Sch 17 para 8 with effect in relation to accounting periods of companies resident in the United Kingdom ending after 30 June 1999 (by virtue of Finance Act 1994, Section 199, (Appointed Day) Order, SI 1998/3173 art 2).

754 Assessment, recovery and postponement of tax

(1) Subject to the following provisions of this section, the provisions of section 747(4)(*a*) relating to [the charging]' of a sum as if it were an amount of corporation tax shall be taken as applying, subject to the provisions of the Taxes Acts, and to any necessary modifications, all enactments applying

generally to corporation tax, including [those relating to company tax returns,][1] those relating to the assessing, collecting and receiving of corporation tax, those conferring or regulating a right of appeal and those concerning administration, penalties, interest on unpaid tax and priority of tax in cases of insolvency under the law of any part of the United Kingdom.

[(1A) Accordingly (but without prejudice to subsection (1) above) the Management Act shall have effect as if—

(a) any reference to corporation tax included a reference to a sum chargeable under section 747(4)(a) as if it were an amount of corporation tax; and

(b) any reference to profits of a company included a reference to an amount of chargeable profits of a controlled foreign company which falls to be apportioned to a company under section 747(3).][1]

[(2) For the purposes of the Taxes Acts, any sum chargeable on a company under section 747(4)(a) is chargeable for the accounting period of the company in which ends that one of the controlled foreign company's accounting periods the chargeable profits of which give rise to that sum.][1]

[(2A) Where—

(a) an apportionment under section 747(3) falls to be made as regards an accounting period of a controlled foreign company, and

(b) the apportionment falls to be made in accordance with section 752(4) on a just and reasonable basis, and

(c) a company tax return is made or amended using for the apportionment a particular basis adopted by the company making the return,

the Board may determine that another basis is to be used for the apportionment.

(2B) For the purposes of subsection (2A) above, the Board may by notice require the company making the return—

(a) to produce to them such documents in the company's power or possession, and

(b) to provide them with such information, in such form,

as they may reasonably require for the purpose of determining the basis which is to be used for making the apportionment.

(2C) The provisions of paragraphs 27 to 29 of Schedule 18 to the Finance Act 1998 (notice to produce documents etc for the purposes of enquiry: supplementary provisions and penalty) shall apply in relation to a notice under subsection (2B) above.

(2D) Once the Board have determined under subsection (2A) above the basis to be used for the apportionment, matters shall proceed as if that were the only basis allowed by the Tax Acts.

(2E) A determination under subsection (2A) above may be questioned on an appeal against an amendment, made under paragraph 30 or 34(2) of Schedule 18 to the Finance Act 1998, of the company's company tax return, but only on the ground that the basis of apportionment determined by the Board is not just and reasonable.][1]

[(3) Where any appeal—

(a) under paragraph 34(3) of Schedule 18 to the Finance Act 1998 against an amendment of a company tax return, or

(b) under paragraph 48 of that Schedule against a discovery assessment or discovery determination under paragraph 41 of that Schedule (including an assessment by virtue of paragraph 52 of that Schedule),

involves any question concerning the application of this Chapter in relation to any particular person, that appeal shall be to the Special Commissioners.

(3A) Where—

(a) any such question as is mentioned in subsection (3) above falls to be determined by the Special Commissioners for the purposes of any proceedings before them, and

(b) the question is one whose resolution is likely to affect the liability of more than one person under this Chapter in respect of the controlled foreign company concerned,

subsection (3B) below shall apply.

(3B) Where this subsection applies—

(a) each of the persons whose liability under this Chapter in respect of the controlled foreign company concerned is likely to be affected by the resolution of the question shall be entitled to appear and be heard by the Special Commissioners, or to make representations to them in writing;

(b) the Special Commissioners shall determine that question separately from any other questions in those proceedings; and

(c) their determination on that question shall have effect as if made in an appeal to which each of those persons was a party.][1]

(4) ...[1]

(5) Schedule 26 shall have effect with respect to the reliefs which may be claimed by a company resident in the United Kingdom which has a liability for tax in respect of an amount of chargeable profits; and no reliefs other than those provided for by that Schedule shall be allowed against any such liability.

(6) In any case where—

    (a) the whole or any part of the tax [chargeable][1] on a company ("the [chargeable][1] company") by virtue of section [747(4)(a)][1] is not paid before the date on which it is due and payable in accordance with this Act or, as the case may be, the Management Act; and

    (b) the Board serve a notice of liability to tax under this subsection on another company ("the responsible company") which is resident in the United Kingdom and holds or has held (whether directly or indirectly) [the whole or any part of][1] the same interest in the controlled foreign company as is or was held by the [chargeable][1] company,

[the whole or, as the case may be, the corresponding part of][1] the tax [chargeable][1] on the [chargeable][1] company or, as the case may be, so much of it as remains unpaid shall be payable by the responsible company upon service of the notice.

(7) Where a notice of liability is served under subsection (6) above—

    (a) [the whole, or (as the case may be) the corresponding part, of][1] any interest due on the tax [chargeable][1] on the [chargeable][1] company and not paid; and

    (b) any interest accruing due on that tax after the date of service [(so far as referable to tax payable by the responsible company by virtue of the notice)][1],

shall be payable by the responsible company.

(8) In any case where—

    (a) a notice of liability is served on the responsible company under subsection (6) above, and

    (b) the relevant tax and any interest payable by the responsible company under subsection (7) above is not paid by that company before the expiry of the period of three months beginning on the date of service of the notice,

that tax and interest may, without prejudice to the right of recovery from the responsible company, be recovered from the [chargeable][1] company.

(9) In this section "the Taxes Acts" has the same meaning as in the Management Act.

Commentary—*Simon's Direct Tax Service* **D4.1255**.
Revenue Internal Guidance—Assessed taxes manual AT 6.605 (Revenue collection procedures).
Simon's Tax Cases—*Bricom Holdings Ltd v IRC* [1996] STC (SCD) 228.
Definitions—"Accounting period", s 751(1)–(5); "apportionment", s 834(4); "the Board", s 832(1); "company", s 832(1), (2); "creditable tax", s 751(b); "interest", s 832(1); "the Management Act", s 831(3); "notice", s 832(1); "resident", s 749(1)–(4); "tax", s 832(3); "the Taxes Acts", s 831(2); "United Kingdom", s 830(1).
Amendments—[1] Words in sub-s (1), (6), (7), (8) and whole of sub-ss (2), (3) substituted, sub-s (1A), (2A)–(2E) and (3A), (3B) inserted and sub-s (4) repealed by FA 1998 Sch 17 para 9 with effect in relation to accounting periods of companies resident in the United Kingdom ending after 30 June 1999 (by virtue of Finance Act 1994, Section 199, (Appointed Day) Order, SI 1998/3173 art 2).

[754A Returns where it is not established whether acceptable distribution policy applies

(1) This section applies where—

    (a) a company resident in the United Kingdom ("the UK company") has an interest in a controlled foreign company at any time during an accounting period of the controlled foreign company;

    (b) the UK company delivers a company tax return; and

    (c) at the time when the UK company delivers the company tax return, it is not established whether or not the controlled foreign company has pursued an acceptable distribution policy in relation to the accounting period.

(2) If the UK company is of the opinion that the controlled foreign company is likely to pursue an acceptable distribution policy in relation to the accounting period, the UK company shall make the company tax return on the basis that the accounting period of the controlled foreign company is one in relation to which the controlled foreign company pursues such a policy.

(3) If the UK company is not of the opinion that the controlled foreign company is likely to pursue an acceptable distribution policy in relation to the accounting period, the UK company shall make the company tax return on the basis that the accounting period of the controlled foreign company is one in relation to which the controlled foreign company does not pursue such a policy.

(4) In any case where—

    (a) the UK company acts in pursuance of subsection (2) above, but

    (b) it becomes established that the controlled foreign company has not pursued an acceptable distribution policy in relation to the accounting period,

the UK company shall amend the company tax return on the basis that the accounting period is not one in relation to which the controlled foreign company pursues an acceptable distribution policy.

(5) In any case where—

    (a) the UK company acts in pursuance of subsection (3) above, but

    (b) it becomes established that the controlled foreign company has pursued an acceptable distribution policy in relation to the accounting period,

the UK company shall amend the company tax return on the basis that the accounting period is one in relation to which the controlled foreign company pursues an acceptable distribution policy.

(6) Any amendment required to be made to the company tax return by virtue of subsection (4) or (5) above ('an ADP amendment') shall be made by the UK company before the expiration of the period of 30 days next following the end of the period allowed for establishing an ADP in relation to the accounting period of the controlled foreign company.

(7) Subject to subsection (8) below, the making of any ADP amendment is subject to, and must be in accordance with, the other provisions of the Corporation Tax Acts as they apply for the purposes of this Chapter.

(8) The time limits otherwise applicable to amendment of a company tax return do not apply to an ADP amendment.

(9) A company which fails to make an ADP amendment required by subsection [(4)] above within the time allowed for doing so shall be liable to a tax-related penalty under paragraph 20 of Schedule 18 to the Finance Act 1998 (penalty, not exceeding amount of tax understated, for incorrect or uncorrected return).

(10) For the purposes of this section, if it has not previously been established whether or not the controlled foreign company has pursued an acceptable distribution policy in relation to the accounting period, it shall be taken to be established immediately after the end of the period allowed for establishing an ADP in relation to that accounting period.

(11) In this section, 'the period allowed for establishing an ADP' means, in relation to an accounting period of a controlled foreign company, the period ending with the expiration of—

  (*a*) subject to paragraph (*b*) below, the period of eighteen months next following the end of the accounting period; or
  (*b*) if the Board have, in the case of the accounting period, allowed further time under paragraph 2(1)(*b*) of Schedule 25, the further time so allowed.

(12) In this section any reference to a controlled foreign company pursuing an acceptable distribution policy in relation to an accounting period shall be construed in accordance with Part I of Schedule 25.]¹

Commentary—*Simon's Direct Tax Service* **D4.1257.**
Amendments—¹ This section inserted by FA 1998 Sch 17 para 10 with effect in relation to accounting periods of companies resident in the United Kingdom ending after 30 June 1999 (by virtue of Finance Act 1994, Section 199, (Appointed Day) Order, SI 1998/3173 art 2).

[754AA Returns where it is not established whether a non-resident company carrying on general insurance business is a controlled foreign company]

Modifications—This section treated as inserted in respect of UK companies which have a relevant interest in companies resident outside the UK carrying on general insurance business and drawing up accounts relating to that business on a non-annual basis: see Non-resident Companies (General Insurance Business) Regulations, SI 1999/1408 reg 4.

[754B Determinations requiring the sanction of the Board

(1) This section has effect where a determination requiring the Board's sanction is made for any of the following purposes, that is to say—

  (*a*) the giving of a closure notice; or
  (*b*) the making of a discovery assessment.

(2) If the closure notice or, as the case may be, notice of the discovery assessment is given to any person without—

  (*a*) the determination, so far as it is taken into account in the closure notice or the discovery assessment, having been approved by the Board, or
  (*b*) notification of the Board's approval having been served on that person at or before the time of the giving of the notice,

the closure notice or, as the case may be, the discovery assessment shall be deemed to have been given or made (and in the case of an assessment notified) in the terms (if any) in which it would have been given or made had that determination not been taken into account.

(3) A notification under subsection (2)(*b*) above—

  (*a*) must be in writing;
  (*b*) must state that the Board have given their approval on the basis that—
    (i) an amount of chargeable profits, and
    (ii) an amount of creditable tax (which may be nil),
  for the accounting period of the controlled foreign company in question fall to be apportioned under section 747(3) to the person in question;
  (*c*) must state the amounts mentioned in sub-paragraphs (i) and (ii) of paragraph (*b*) above; and
  (*d*) subject to paragraphs (*a*) to (*c*) above, may be in such form as the Board may determine.

(4) For the purposes of this section, the Board's approval of a determination requiring their sanction—

  (*a*) must be given specifically in relation to the case in question and must apply to the amount determined; but (*b*) subject to that, may be given by the Board (either before or after the making of the determination) in any such form or manner as they may determine.

(5) In this section references to a determination requiring the Board's sanction are references (subject to subsection (6) below) to any determination of the amount of chargeable profits or creditable tax for an accounting period of a controlled foreign company which falls to be apportioned to a particular person under section 747(3).

(6) For the purposes of this section, a determination shall be taken, in relation to a closure notice or a discovery assessment, not to be a determination requiring the Board's sanction if—

    (*a*) an agreement about the relevant amounts has been made between an officer of the Board and the person in whose case it is made;

    (*b*) that agreement is in force at the time of the giving of the closure notice or, as the case may be, notice of the assessment; and

    (*c*) the matters to which the agreement relates include the amount determined.

(7) In paragraph (*a*) of subsection (6) above, ''the relevant amounts'' means—

    (*a*) the amount of chargeable profits, and

    (*b*) the amount of creditable tax (which may be nil),

for the accounting period of the controlled foreign company in question which fall to be apportioned under section 747(3) to the person mentioned in that paragraph.

(8) For the purposes of subsection (6) above an agreement made between an officer of the Board and any person (''the taxpayer'') in relation to any matter shall be taken to be in force at any time if, and only if—

    (*a*) the agreement is one which has been made or confirmed in writing;

    (*b*) that time is after the end of the period of thirty days beginning—

        (i) in the case of an agreement made in writing, with the day of the making of the agreement, and

        (ii) in any other case, with the day of the agreement's confirmation in writing; and

    (*c*) the taxpayer has not, before the end of that period of thirty days, served a notice on an officer of the Board stating that he is repudiating or resiling from the agreement.

(9) The references in subsection (8) above to the confirmation in writing of an agreement are references to the service on the taxpayer by an officer of the Board of a notice—

    (*a*) stating that the agreement has been made; and

    (*b*) setting out the terms of the agreement.

(10) The matters that may be questioned on so much of any appeal by virtue of any provision of the Management Act or Schedule 18 to the Finance Act 1998 (company tax returns, assessments and related matters) as relates to a determination the making of which has been approved by the Board for the purposes of this section shall not include the Board's approval, except to the extent that the grounds for questioning the approval are the same as the grounds for questioning the determination itself.

(11) In this section—

    ''closure notice'' means a notice under paragraph 32 of Schedule 18 to the Finance Act 1998 (completion of enquiry and statement of conclusions);

    ''discovery assessment'' means a discovery assessment or discovery determination under paragraph 41 of that Schedule (including an assessment by virtue of paragraph 52 of that Schedule).]¹

Commentary—*Simon's Direct Tax Service* D4.1259B.
Amendments—¹ This section inserted by FA 1998 Sch 17 para 11 with effect in relation to accounting periods of companies resident in the United Kingdom ending after 30 June 1999 (by virtue of Finance Act 1994, Section 199, (Appointed Day) Order, SI 1998/3173 art 2).

755 Information relating to controlled foreign companies

Amendments—This section repealed by FA 1998 Sch 17 para 12 with effect in relation to accounting periods of companies resident in the United Kingdom ending after 30 June 1999 (by virtue of Finance Act 1994, Section 199, (Appointed Day) Order, SI 1998/3173 art 2).

[755A Treatment of chargeable profits and creditable tax apportioned to company carrying on life assurance business

(1) This section applies in any case where—

    (*a*) an amount (''the apportioned profit'') of a controlled foreign company's chargeable profits for an accounting period falls to be apportioned under section 747(3) to a company resident in the United Kingdom (''the UK company'');

    (*b*) the UK company carries on life assurance business in that one of its accounting periods (''the relevant accounting period'') in which ends the accounting period of the controlled foreign company; and

    (*c*) the property or rights which represent the UK company's relevant interest in the controlled foreign company constitute to any extent assets of the UK company's [long-term insurance fund]².

TA 1988

(2) Subsections (3) and (4) below apply if, in the case of the relevant accounting period, the UK company is not charged to tax under Case I of Schedule D in respect of its profits from life assurance business.

(3) Where this subsection applies, the 'appropriate rate' for the purposes of section 747(4)(*a*) and paragraph 1 of Schedule 26 in relation to the policy holders' part of any BLAGAB apportioned profit shall be—

(*a*) if a single rate of tax under section 88A(1) of the Finance Act 1989 (lower corporation tax rate on certain insurance company profits) is applicable in relation to the relevant accounting period, that rate; or

(*b*) if more than one such rate of tax is applicable in relation to the relevant accounting period, the average of those rates over the whole of that period.

(4) Where this subsection applies, the 'appropriate rate' for the purposes of section 747(4)(*a*) and paragraph 1 of Schedule 26 shall be nil in relation to so much of the apportioned profit as is referable to—

(*a*) pension business,

(*b*) life reinsurance business, or

(*c*) overseas life assurance business,

carried on by the UK company.

(5) If, in the case of the relevant accounting period, the UK company is charged to tax under Case I of Schedule D in respect of its profits from life assurance business, the "appropriate rate" for the purposes of—

(*a*) section 747(4)(*a*), and

(*b*) paragraph 1 of Schedule 26,

shall be nil in relation to so much of the apportioned profit as is referable to the UK company's relevant interest so far as represented by assets of its [long-term insurance fund][2].

(6) If, in the case of the relevant accounting period,—

(*a*) the UK company is not charged to tax under Case I of Schedule D in respect of its profits from life assurance business,

(*b*) any creditable tax of the controlled foreign company falls to be apportioned to the UK company, and

(*c*) the apportioned profit is to any extent referable to a category of business specified in paragraphs (*a*) to (*c*) of subsection (4) above,

so much of the creditable tax so apportioned as is attributable to the apportioned profit so far as so referable shall be left out of account for the purposes of this Chapter, other than section 747(3) and this section, and shall be treated as extinguished.

(7) If, in the case of the relevant accounting period,—

(*a*) the UK company is charged to tax under Case I of Schedule D in respect of its profits from life assurance business, and

(*b*) any creditable tax of the controlled foreign company falls to be apportioned to the UK company,

so much of the creditable tax so apportioned as is attributable to so much of the apportioned profit as is referable to the UK company's relevant interest so far as represented by assets of the UK company's [long-term insurance fund][2] shall be left out of account for the purposes of this Chapter, other than section 747(3) and this section, and shall be treated as extinguished.

(8) Any set off under paragraph 1 or 2 of Schedule 26 against the UK company's liability to tax under section 747(4)(*a*) in respect of the apportioned profit shall be made against only so much of that liability as is attributable to the eligible part of the apportioned profit.

(9) Accordingly, in the application of paragraph 2 of Schedule 26 in relation to the apportioned profit, in the definition of 'the relevant maximum' in sub-paragraph (3)—

(*a*) the reference to the liability to tax referred to in sub-paragraph (1) of that paragraph shall be taken as a reference to only so much of that liability as is attributable to the eligible part of the apportioned profit; and

(*b*) in paragraph (*a*), for the amount there described there shall be substituted a reference to the eligible part of the apportioned profit.

(10) For the purposes of this section, the "eligible part" of the apportioned profit is any BLAGAB apportioned profit, other than the policy holders' part.

(11) For the purposes of this section, the "policy holders' part" of any BLAGAB apportioned profit is—

(*a*) in a case where subsection (4) of section 88A of the Finance Act 1989 applies, the whole; and

(*b*) in any other case, the fraction described in subsection (5)(*b*) of that section.

(12) In this section—

"BLAGAB apportioned profit" means so much of the apportioned profit as is referable to basic life assurance and general annuity business carried on by the UK company;

"[long-term insurance fund][2]" has the meaning given by section 431(2).

(13) For the purposes of this section, the part of the apportioned profit which is referable to—

    (*a*) pension business,
    (*b*) life reinsurance business,
    (*c*) overseas life assurance business, or
    (*d*) basic life assurance and general annuity business,

carried on by the UK company is the part which would have been so referable under section 432A had the apportioned profit been a dividend paid to the UK company at the end of the accounting period mentioned in subsection (1)(a) above in respect of the property or rights which represent the UK company's relevant interest in the controlled foreign company.

(14) For the purposes of this section, any attribution of creditable tax to a particular part of the apportioned profit shall be made in the proportion which that part of the apportioned profit bears to the whole of the apportioned profit.][1]

Modifications—This section modified so far as it applies to the life or endowment business carried on by friendly societies with effect for accounting periods ending after 30 June 1999 by the Friendly Societies (Modification of the Corporation Tax Acts) Regulations, SI 1997/473 reg 30B (as inserted by SI 1999/2636).
New sub-ss (4)(*aa*) and (13)(*aa*) inserted in respect of individual savings account business of insurance companies by the Individual Savings Account Regulations 1998, SI 1998/1871 reg 18, with effect from 6 April 1999.
Amendments—[1] This section inserted by FA 1998 Sch 17 para 13 with effect in relation to accounting periods of companies resident in the United Kingdom ending after 30 June 1999 (by virtue of Finance Act 1994, Section 199, (Appointed Day) Order, SI 1998/3173 art 2).
[2] Words in sub-ss (1)(*c*), (5), (7) and (12) substituted by the Financial Services and Markets Act 2000 (Consequential Amendments) (Taxes) Order, SI 2001/3629 arts 13, 52(1)(*j*) with effect from 1 December 2001 (immediately after the coming into force of the Financial Services and Markets Act 2000 ss 411, 432(1), Sch 20).

[755B Amendment of return where general insurance business of foreign company accounted for on non-annual basis

(1) This section applies where—

    (*a*) a controlled foreign company carries on general insurance business in an accounting period;
    (*b*) an amount of the company's chargeable profits, and an amount of its creditable tax (if any), for that accounting period falls to be apportioned under section 747(3) to a company resident in the United Kingdom (''the UK company'');
    (*c*) the UK company delivers a company tax return for that one of its accounting periods in which the controlled foreign company's accounting period ends; and
    (*d*) in making or amending the return, the UK company has regard to accounts of the controlled foreign company drawn up using a method falling within subsection (2) below.

(2) The methods which fall within this subsection are—

    (*a*) the method described in paragraph 52 of Schedule 9A to the Companies Act 1985 (which provides for a technical provision to be made in the accounts which is later replaced by a provision for estimated claims outstanding); and
    (*b*) any method which would have fallen within paragraph (a) above, had final replacement of the technical provision, as described in sub-paragraph (4) of paragraph 52 of that Schedule, taken place, and been required to take place, no later than the end of the year referred to in that sub-paragraph as the third year following the underwriting year.

(3) Where this section applies—

    (*a*) the UK company may make any amendments of its company tax return arising from the replacement of the technical provision in the controlled foreign company's accounts at any time within twelve months from the date on which the provision was replaced; and
    (*b*) notice of intention to enquire into the return under paragraph 24 of Schedule 18 to the Finance Act 1998 may be given at any time up to two years from that date (or at any later time in accordance with the general rule in sub-paragraph (3) of that paragraph).

(4) If, in a case where this section applies, the accounts of the controlled foreign company are drawn up using a method falling within paragraph (*b*) of subsection (2) above—

    (*a*) the controlled foreign company, and
    (*b*) any person with an interest in the controlled foreign company,

shall be treated for the purposes of this section as if final replacement of the technical provision, as described in sub-paragraph (4) of paragraph 52 of Schedule 9A to the Companies Act 1985, had taken place at, and been required to take place no later than, the end of the year referred to in that sub-paragraph as the third year following the underwriting year.

(5) Regulations under section 755C may make provision with respect to the determination of the amount of the provision by which the technical provision is to be treated as replaced in cases falling within subsection (4) above.

[(6) In this section ''general insurance business'' means business which consists of the effecting or carrying out of contracts which fall within Part I of Schedule 1 to the Financial Services and Markets Act 2000 (Regulated Activities) Order 2001.][2]][1]

Regulations—Non-resident Companies (General Insurance Business) Regulations, SI 1999/1408.
Modifications—Sub-s (4A) treated as inserted in respect of UK companies which have a relevant interest in companies resident outside the UK carrying on general insurance business and drawing up accounts relating to that business on a non-annual basis: see Non-resident Companies (General Insurance Business) Regulations, SI 1999/1408 reg 5.

TA 1988

Amendments—¹ This section inserted by FA 1998 Sch 17 para 14 with effect in relation to accounting periods of companies resident in the United Kingdom ending after 30 June 1999 (by virtue of Finance Act 1994, Section 199, (Appointed Day) Order, SI 1998/3173 art 2).
² Sub-s (6) substituted by the Financial Services and Markets Act 2000 (Consequential Amendments) (Taxes) Order, SI 2001/3629 arts 13, 44 with effect from 1 December 2001, immediately after the coming into force of the Financial Services and Markets Act 2000 ss 411, 432(1), Sch 20.

[755C Application of Chapter where general insurance business of foreign company accounted for on non-annual basis

(1) The Treasury may by regulations provide for the provisions of this Chapter to have effect with prescribed modifications in any case where a non-resident company—

    (*a*) carries on general insurance business; and

    (*b*) draws up accounts relating to that business using a method falling within subsection (2) of section 755B.

(2) Regulations under subsection (1) above may—

    (*a*) make different provision for different cases;

    (*b*) make provision having effect in relation to accounting periods of non-resident companies ending not more than one year before the date on which the regulations are made; and

    (*c*) contain such supplementary, incidental, consequential and transitional provision as the Treasury may think fit.

(3) In this section—

    "general insurance business" has the same meaning as in section 755B;

    "non-resident company" means a company resident outside the United Kingdom;

    "prescribed" means prescribed in regulations under this section.]¹

Regulations—Non-resident Companies (General Insurance Business) Regulations, SI 1999/1408.
Amendments—¹ This section inserted by FA 1998 Sch 17 para 15 with effect in relation to accounting periods of companies resident in the United Kingdom ending after 30 June 1999 (by virtue of Finance Act 1994, Section 199, (Appointed Day) Order, SI 1998/3173 art 2).

[755D "Control" and the two "40 per cent" tests

(1) For the purposes of this Chapter "control", in relation to a company, means the power of a person to secure—

    (*a*) by means of the holding of shares or the possession of voting power in or in relation to the company or any other company, or

    (*b*) by virtue of any powers conferred by the articles of association or other document regulating the company or any other company,

that the affairs of the company are conducted in accordance with his wishes.

(2) Where two or more persons, taken together, have the power mentioned in subsection (1) above, they shall be taken for the purposes of this Chapter to control the company.

(3) The 40 per cent test in this subsection is satisfied in the case of one of two persons who, taken together, control a company if that one of them has interests, rights and powers representing at least 40 per cent of the holdings, rights and powers in respect of which the pair of them fall to be taken as controlling the company.

(4) The 40 per cent test in this subsection is satisfied in the case of one of two persons who, taken together, control a company if that one of them has interests, rights and powers representing—

    (*a*) at least 40 per cent, but

    (*b*) not more than 55 per cent,

of the holdings, rights and powers in respect of which the pair of them fall to be taken as controlling the company.

(5) For the purposes of this Chapter any question—

    (*a*) whether a company is controlled by a person, or by two or more persons taken together, or

    (*b*) whether, in the case of any company, the applicable 40 per cent test is satisfied in the case of each of two persons who, taken together, control the company,

shall be determined after attributing to each of the persons all the rights and powers mentioned in subsection (6) below that are not already attributed to that person for the purposes of subsections (1) to (4) above.

(6) The rights and powers referred to in subsection (5) above are—

    (*a*) rights and powers which the person is entitled to acquire at a future date or which he will, at a future date, become entitled to acquire;

    (*b*) rights and powers of other persons, to the extent that they are rights or powers falling within subsection (7) below;

    (*c*) if the person is resident in the United Kingdom, rights and powers of any person who is resident in the United Kingdom and connected with the person; and

    (*d*) if the person is resident in the United Kingdom, rights and powers which for the purposes of subsection (5) above would be attributed to a person who is resident in the United Kingdom and connected with the person (a "UK connected person") if the UK connected person were himself the person.

(7) Rights and powers fall within this subsection to the extent that they—

(a) are required, or may be required, to be exercised in any one or more of the following ways, that is to say—

(i) on behalf of the person;

(ii) under the direction of the person; or

(iii) for the benefit of the person; and

(b) are not confined, in a case where a loan has been made by one person to another, to rights and powers conferred in relation to property of the borrower by the terms of any security relating to the loan.

(8) In subsections (6)(b) to (d) and (7) above, the references to a person's rights and powers include references to any rights or powers which he either—

(a) is entitled to acquire at a future date, or

(b) will, at a future date, become entitled to acquire.

(9) In paragraph (d) of subsection (6) above, the reference to rights and powers which would be attributed to a UK connected person if he were the person includes a reference to rights and powers which, by applying that paragraph wherever one person resident in the United Kingdom is connected with another person, would be so attributed to him through a number of persons each of whom is resident in the United Kingdom and connected with at least one of the others.

(10) In determining for the purposes of this section whether one person is connected with another in relation to a company, subsection (7) of section 839 shall be disregarded.

(11) References in this section—

(a) to rights and powers of a person, or

(b) to rights and powers which a person is or will become entitled to acquire,

include references to rights or powers which are exercisable by that person, or (when acquired by that person) will be exercisable, only jointly with one or more other persons.]¹

Amendments—¹ This section inserted by FA 2000 s 104, Sch 31 paras 1, 4, 9(3) with effect for the purpose of determining whether at any time after 20 March 2000 a company resident outside the UK is to be regarded for the purposes of TA 1988 Pt XVII, Ch IV as controlled by persons resident in the UK, and for any accounting period of a company resident outside the UK which begins after 20 March 2000.

[756 Interpretation and construction of Chapter IV

(1) In this Chapter ["company tax return" means a return required to be made under Schedule 18 to the Finance Act 1998;]¹ "trading company" means a company whose business consists wholly or mainly of the carrying on of a trade or trades.

(2) For the purposes of this Chapter—

(a) section 839 applies; and

(b) subsection (10) of section 783 applies as it applies for the purposes of that section.

(3) The following provisions of Part XI apply for the purposes of this Chapter as they apply for the purposes of that Part—

(a) ...²

(b) section 417(7) to (9);

...²

Commentary—*Simon's Direct Tax Service* **D4.1202.**
Revenue Decision RD2—Controlled foreign company: acceptable distribution policy and standard for the purposes of definition of "trading company" in sub-s (1) above.
Definitions—"Company", s 832(1), (2); "resident", s 749(1)–(4); "trade", s 832(1); "United Kingdom", s 830(1).
Amendments—¹ Words in sub-s (1) inserted by FA 1998 Sch 17 para 16 with effect in relation to accounting periods of companies resident in the United Kingdom ending after 30 June 1999 (by virtue of Finance Act 1994, Section 199, (Appointed Day) Order, SI 1998/3173 art 2).
² Words in sub-s (3) repealed by FA 2000 ss 104, 156, Sch 31 paras 1, 4, 9(3), Sch 40 Pt II(14) with effect for the purpose of determining whether at any time after 20 March 2000 a company resident outside the UK is to be regarded for the purposes of TA 1988 Pt XVII, Ch IV as controlled by persons resident in the UK, and for any accounting period of a company resident outside the UK which begins after 20 March 2000.

CHAPTER V

OFFSHORE FUNDS

Material interests in non-qualifying offshore funds

Cross references—See TCGA 1992 s 108 (identification for purposes of tax on chargeable gains on disposals of securities which are material interests in non-qualifying offshore funds).

757 Disposal of material interests in non-qualifying offshore funds

(1) This Chapter applies to a disposal by any person of an asset if—

    (*a*) at the time of the disposal, the asset constitutes a material interest in an offshore fund which is or has at any material time been a non-qualifying offshore fund; or

    (*b*) at the time of the disposal, the asset constitutes an interest in a company resident in the United Kingdom or in a unit trust scheme, the trustees of which are at that time resident in the United Kingdom and at a material time after 31st December 1984 the company or unit trust scheme was a non-qualifying offshore fund and the asset constituted a material interest in that fund;

and for the purpose of determining whether the asset disposed of falls within paragraph (*b*) above, section [127 of the 1992][2] Act (equation of original shares and new holding) shall have effect as it has effect for the purposes of that Act.

(2) Subject to the following provisions of this section and section 758, there is a disposal of an asset for the purposes of this Chapter if there would be such a disposal for the purposes of the [1992][2] Act.

(3) Notwithstanding anything in paragraph (*b*) of subsection (1) of section [62 of the 1992][2] Act (general provisions applicable on death: no deemed disposal by the deceased) where a person dies and the assets of which he was competent to dispose include an asset which is or has at any time been a material interest in a non-qualifying offshore fund, then, for the purposes of this Chapter, other than section 758—

    (*a*) immediately before the acquisition referred to in paragraph (*a*) of that subsection, that interest shall be deemed to be disposed of by the deceased for such a consideration as is mentioned in that subsection; but

    (*b*) nothing in this subsection affects the determination, in accordance with subsection (1) above, of the question whether that deemed disposal is one to which this Chapter applies.

(4) Subject to subsection (3) above, section [62 of the 1992][2] Act applies for the purposes of this Chapter as it applies for the purposes of that Act, and the reference in that subsection to the assets of which a deceased person was competent to dispose shall be construed in accordance with subsection (10) of that section.

[(5) Section 135 of the 1992 Act (exchange of securities for those in another company treated as not involving a disposal) does not apply for the purposes of this Chapter if the company that is company A for the purposes of that section is or was at a material time a non-qualifying offshore fund and the company that is company B for those purposes is not such a fund.

In a case where that section would apply apart from this subsection, the exchange in question (of shares, debentures or other interests in or of an entity that is or was at a material time a non-qualifying offshore fund) shall for the purposes of this Chapter constitute a disposal of interests in the offshore fund for a consideration equal to their market value at the time of the exchange.][3]

[(6) Section 136 of the 1992 Act (scheme of reconstruction involving issue of securities treated as exchange not involving disposal) does not apply for the purposes of this Chapter so as to require persons to be treated as exchanging shares, debentures or other interests in or of an entity that is or was at a material time a non-qualifying offshore fund for assets that do not constitute interests in such a fund.

In a case where that section would apply apart from this subsection, the deemed exchange in question (of shares, debentures or other interests in or of an entity that is or was at a material time a non-qualifying offshore fund) shall for the purposes of this Chapter constitute a disposal of interests in the offshore fund for a consideration equal to their market value at the time of the deemed exchange.][3]

(7) For the purposes of this section—

    (*a*) a material time, in relation to the disposal of an asset, is [any time on or after][1] the earliest date on which any relevant consideration was given for the acquisition of the asset or, if that date is earlier than 1st January 1984, any time on or after 1st January 1984; and

    (*b*) "relevant consideration" means consideration which, assuming the application to the disposal of [Chapter III of Part II of the 1992][2] Act, would fall to be taken into account in determining the amount of the gain or loss accruing on the disposal, whether that consideration was given by or on behalf of the person making the disposal or by or on behalf of a predecessor in title of his whose acquisition cost represents, directly or indirectly, the whole or any part of the acquisition cost of the person making the disposal.

Commentary—*Simon's Direct Tax Service* **B7.420, 421.**
Definitions—"The 1992 Act", s 831(3); "company", s 832(1), (2); "market value", s 759(9); "material interest", s 759; "non-qualifying ... fund", s 760; "unit trust scheme", s 469, by virtue of s 832(1); "United Kingdom", s 830(1).
Cross references—See TA 1988 Sch 28 para 2 (calculation of offshore unindexed gain).
TCGA 1992 s 108 (identification for purposes of tax on chargeable gains on disposals of securities which are material interests in non-qualifying offshore funds).
Amendments—[1] Words in sub-s (7)(*a*) inserted by FA 1990 Sch 14 paras 1, 10 and deemed always to have had effect.
[2] Words in sub-ss (1)–(4), (7) substituted by TCGA 1992 Sch 10 para 14(1), (43).
[3] Sub-ss (5), (6) substituted by FA 2002 s 45, Sch 9 paras 4(1), (5), 7, 8(1) with effect for disposals after 16 April 2002. Sub-ss (5), (6) previously read as follows—

    "(5) Notwithstanding anything in section [135] of the [1992] Act (exchange of securities for those in another company) in any case where—

        (*a*) the company which is company B for the purposes of subsection (1) of that section is or was at a material time a non-qualifying offshore fund and the company which is company A for those purposes is not such a fund, or

(b) under section [136] of that Act (reconstruction or amalgamation involving issue of securities) persons are to be treated, in consequence of an arrangement, as exchanging shares, debentures or other interests in or of an entity which is or was at a material time a non-qualifying offshore fund for assets which do not constitute interests in such a fund;

then, subsection (3) of section [135] of that Act (which applies provisions of that Act treating transactions as not being disposals and equating original shares with a new holding in certain cases) shall not apply for the purposes of this Chapter.

(6) In any case where, apart from subsection (5) above, section [135(3) of the 1992] Act would apply, the exchange concerned of shares, debentures or other interests in or of a non-qualifying offshore fund shall for the purposes of this Chapter constitute a disposal of interests in the offshore fund for a consideration equal to their market value at the time of the exchange.''.

758 Offshore funds operating equalisation arrangements

(1) For the purposes of this Chapter, an offshore fund operates equalisation arrangements if, and at a time when, arrangements are in existence which have the result that where—

(a) a person acquires by way of initial purchase a material interest in the fund at some time during a period relevant to the arrangements; and

(b) the fund makes a distribution for a period which begins before the date of his acquisition of that interest;

the amount of that distribution which is paid to him (assuming him still to retain that interest) will include a payment of capital which is debited to an account maintained under the arrangements (''the equalisation account'') and which is determined by reference to the income which had accrued to the fund at the date of his acquisition.

(2) For the purposes of this section, a person acquires an interest in an offshore fund by way of initial purchase if—

(a) his acquisition is by way of subscription for or allotment of new shares, units or other interests issued or created by the fund; or

(b) his acquisition is by way of direct purchase from the persons concerned with the management of the fund and their sale to him is made in their capacity as managers of the fund.

(3) Without prejudice to section 757(1), this Chapter applies, subject to the following provisions of this section, to a disposal by any person of an asset if—

(a) at the time of the disposal, the asset constitutes a material interest in an offshore fund which at that time is operating equalisation arrangements; and

(b) the fund is not and has not at any material time (within the meaning of section 757(7)) been a non-qualifying offshore fund; and

(c) the proceeds of the disposal do not fall to be taken into account as a trading receipt.

(4) This Chapter does not, by virtue of subsection (3) above, apply to a disposal if—

(a) it takes place during such a period as is mentioned in subsection (1)(a) above; and

(b) throughout so much of that period as precedes the disposal, the income of the offshore fund concerned has been of such a nature as is referred to in paragraph 3(1) of Schedule 27.

(5) An event which, apart from section [127 of the 1992][2] Act (reorganisations etc), would constitute a disposal of an asset shall constitute such a disposal for the purpose of determining whether, by virtue of subsection (3) above, there is a disposal to which this Chapter applies.

(6) The reference in subsection (5) above to section [127 of the 1992][1] Act includes a reference to that section as applied by [any provision of Chapter 2 of Part 4 of that Act][2].

Commentary—*Simon's Direct Tax Service* **B7.424.**
Definitions—''The 1992 Act'', s 831(3); ''distribution'', s 209(2), by virtue of s 832(1); ''material interest'', s 759; ''non-qualifying ... fund'', s 760.
Cross references—See TA 1988 s 761 (charge to tax of offshore income gains arising under this section).
TA 1988 Sch 28, para 6(1) (a disposal to which sub-s (3) above applies gives rise to a gain equal to equalisation element relevant to the asset disposed of).
TA 1988 Sch 28, para 8(2) (sub-ss (5), (6) above to have effect with modification for the purposes of computation of offshore income gains on a disposal involving equalisation element).
Amendments—[1] Words in sub-ss (5), (6) substituted by TCGA 1992 Sch 10 para 14(1), (44).
[2] Words in sub-s (6) substituted for the words ''section 135 of that Act (exchange of securities) and a reference to section 127 as applied by section 132 of that Act (conversion of securities)'' by FA 2002 s 45, Sch 9 paras 4(1), (6), 7(1), 8(3) with effect for events occurring after 16 April 2002.

759 Material interests in offshore funds

(1) In this Chapter references to a material interest in an offshore fund are references to such an interest in any [collective investment scheme which is constituted by][2]—

(a) a company which is resident outside the United Kingdom;

(b) a unit trust scheme the trustees of which are not resident in the United Kingdom; [or][2]

(c) any arrangements which do not fall within paragraph (a) or (b) above, which take effect by virtue of the law of a territory outside the United Kingdom and which, under that law, create rights in the nature of co-ownership (without restricting that expression to its meaning in the law of any part of the United Kingdom);

and any reference in this Chapter to an offshore fund is a reference to any such [collective investment scheme][2] in which any person has an interest which is a material interest.

[(1A) In this section ''collective investment scheme'' has the [meaning given by section 235 of the Financial Services and Markets Act 2000][3].][2]

(2) Subject to the following provisions of this section, a person's interest in a company, unit trust scheme or arrangements is a material interest if, at the time when he acquired the interest, it could reasonably be expected that, at some time during the period of seven years beginning at the time of his acquisition, he would be able to realise the value of the interest (whether by transfer, surrender or in any other manner).

(3) For the purposes of subsection (2) above, a person is at any time able to realise the value of an interest if at that time he can realise an amount which is reasonably approximate to that portion which the interest represents (directly or indirectly) of the market value at that time of the assets of the company or, as the case may be, of the assets subject to the scheme or arrangements.

(4) For the purposes of subsections (2) and (3) above—

(a) a person is able to realise a particular amount if he is able to obtain that amount either in money or in the form of assets to the value of that amount; and
(b) if at any time an interest in an offshore fund has a market value which is substantially greater than the portion which the interest represents, as mentioned in subsection (3) above, of the market value at that time of the assets concerned, the ability to realise such a market value of the interest shall not be regarded as an ability to realise such an amount as is referred to in that subsection.

(5) An interest in a company, scheme or arrangements is not a material interest if—

(a) it is an interest in respect of any loan capital or debt issued or incurred for money which, in the ordinary course of a business of banking, is lent by a person carrying on that business; or
(b) it is a right arising under a policy of insurance.

(6) Shares in a company falling within subsection (1)(a) above (an "overseas company") do not constitute a material interest if—

(a) the shares are held by a company and the holding of them is necessary or desirable for the maintenance and development of a trade carried on by the company or a company associated with it; and
(b) the shares confer at least 10 per cent of the total voting rights in the overseas company and a right, in the event of a winding-up, to at least 10 per cent of the assets of that company remaining after the discharge of all liabilities having priority over the shares; and
(c) not more than ten persons hold shares in the overseas company and all the shares in that company confer both voting rights and a right to participate in the assets on a winding-up; and
(d) at the time of its acquisition of the shares, the company had such a reasonable expectation as is referred to in subsection (2) above by reason only of the existence of—

(i) an arrangement under which, at some time within the period of seven years beginning at the time of acquisition, that company may require the other participators to purchase its shares; or
(ii) provisions of either an agreement between the participators or the constitution of the overseas company under which the company will be wound up within a period which is, or is reasonably expected to be, shorter than the period referred to in subsection (2) above; or
(iii) both such an arrangement and such provisions;

and in this paragraph "participators" means the persons holding shares falling within paragraph (c) above.

(7) For the purposes of subsection (6)(a) above, a company is associated with another company if one of them has control of the other within the meaning of section 416 or both of them are under the control, within the meaning of that section, of the same person or persons.

(8) An interest in a company falling within subsection (1)(a) above is not a material interest at any time when the following conditions are satisfied, namely—

(a) that the holder of the interest has the right to have the company wound up; and
(b) that, in the event of a winding up, the holder is, by virtue of the interest and any other interest which he then holds in the same capacity, entitled to more than 50 per cent of the assets remaining after the discharge of all liabilities having priority over the interest or interests concerned.

(9) The market value of any asset for the purposes of this Chapter shall be determined in like manner as it would be determined for the purposes of the [1992][1] Act except that, in the case of an interest in an offshore fund for which there are separate published buying and selling prices, section [272(5)][1] of that Act (meaning of "market value" in relation to rights of unit holders in a unit trust scheme) shall apply with any necessary modifications for determining the market value of the interest for the purposes of this Chapter.

Commentary—*Simon's Direct Tax Service* B7.402.
Statement of Practice SP 2/86—This Statement sets out the Revenue's interpretation of the provisions in this section and Sch 27. The topics dealt with are—
(a) interpretation of the term "material interests" (b) conditions for distributor status (c) investment restrictions (d) computation of UK equivalent profits.
Definitions—"The 1992 Act", s 831(3); "company", s 832(1), (2); "control", s 840; "trade", s 832(1); "unit trust scheme", s 469, by virtue of s 832(1); "United Kingdom", s 830(1).
Cross references—See TA 1988 s 760(10) (end of account period of a company falling within sub-s (1)(a) above and of a unit trust scheme falling within sub-s (1)(b) above).
TA 1988 Sch 27, para 3 (certain income of an offshore fund falling within sub-s (1)(b) or (c) above taxable under Schedule D Case IV or V).

Amendments—[1] Numbers in sub-s (9) substituted by TCGA 1992 Sch 10 para 14(1), (45).
[2] Words in sub-s (1) substituted, and sub-s (1A) inserted, by FA 1995 s 134(1)–(3), (8) with effect where it falls to be decided (a) whether a material interest is, at any time after 28 November 1994, a material interest in an offshore fund; and (b) whether a company, unit trust scheme or arrangements in which any person has an interest which is a material interest is, at any time after that day, an offshore fund.
[3] Words in sub-s (1A) substituted by the Financial Services and Markets Act 2000 (Consequential Amendments) (Taxes) Order, SI 2001/3629 arts 13, 45 with effect from 1 December 2001, immediately after the coming into force of the Financial Services and Markets Act 2000 ss 411, 432(1), Sch 20.

760 Non-qualifying offshore funds

(1) For the purposes of this Chapter, an offshore fund is a non-qualifying fund except during an account period of the fund in respect of which the fund is certified by the Board as a distributing fund.

(2) An offshore fund shall not be certified as a distributing fund in respect of any account period unless, with respect to that period, the fund pursues a full distribution policy, within the meaning of Part I of Schedule 27.

(3) Subject to Part II of that Schedule, an offshore fund shall not be certified as a distributing fund in respect of any account period if, at any time in that period—

(a) more than 5 per cent by value of the assets of the fund consists of interests in other offshore funds; or

(b) subject to subsections (4) and (5) below, more than 10 per cent by value of the assets of the fund consists of interests in a single company; or

(c) the assets of the fund include more than 10 per cent of the issued share capital of any company or of any class of that share capital; or

(d) subject to subsection (6) below, there is more than one class of material interest in the offshore fund and they do not all receive proper distribution benefits, within the meaning of subsection (7) below.

(4) For the purposes of subsection (3)(b) above, in any account period the value, expressed as a percentage of the value of all the assets of an offshore fund, of that portion of the assets of the fund which consists of an interest in a single company shall be determined as at the most recent occasion (whether in that account period or an earlier one) on which the fund acquired an interest in that company for consideration in money or money's worth; but for this purpose there shall be disregarded any occasion—

(a) on which the interest acquired constituted the "new holding" for the purposes of section [127 of the 1992][1] Act (equation of original shares and new holding), including that section as applied by any later provision of Chapter II of Part IV of that Act (reorganisation of share capital etc); and

(b) on which no consideration fell to be given for the interest acquired, other than the interest which constituted the "original shares" for the purposes of that section.

(5) Except for the purpose of determining the total value of the assets of an offshore fund, an interest in a company shall be disregarded for the purposes of subsection (3)(b) above if—

(a) the company carries on (in the United Kingdom or elsewhere) a banking business providing current or deposit account facilities in any currency for members of the public and bodies corporate; and

(b) the interest consists of a current or deposit account provided in the normal course of the company's banking business.

(6) There shall be disregarded for the purposes of subsection (3)(d) above any interests in an offshore fund—

(a) which are held solely by persons employed or engaged in or about the management of the assets of the fund; and

(b) which carry no right or expectation to participate, directly or indirectly, in any of the profits of the fund; and

(c) which, on a winding up or on redemption, carry no right to receive anything other than the return of the price paid for the interests.

(7) If in any account period of an offshore fund there is more than one class of material interests in the fund, the classes of interest do not, for the purposes of subsection (3)(d) above, all receive proper distribution benefits unless, were each class of interests and the assets which that class represents interests in and assets of a separate offshore fund, each of those separate funds would, with respect to that period, pursue a full distribution policy, within the meaning of Part I of Schedule 27.

(8) For the purposes of this Chapter, an account period of an offshore fund shall begin—

(a) whenever the fund begins to carry on its activities; and

(b) whenever an account period of the funds ends without the fund then ceasing to carry on its activities.

(9) For the purposes of this Chapter, an account period of an offshore fund shall end on the first occurrence of any of the following—

(a) the expiration of 12 months from the beginning of the period;

(b) an accounting date of the fund or, if there is a period for which the fund does not make up accounts, the end of that period; and

(c) the fund ceasing to carry on its activities.

(10) For the purposes of this Chapter—

   (*a*) an account period of an offshore fund which is a company falling within section 759(1)(*a*) shall end if, and at the time when, the company ceases to be resident outside the United Kingdom; and

   (*b*) an account period of an offshore fund which is a unit trust scheme falling within section 759(1)(*b*) shall end if, and at the time when, the trustees of the scheme become resident in the United Kingdom.

(11) The provisions of Part III of Schedule 27 shall have effect with respect to the procedure for and in connection with the certification of an offshore fund as a distributing fund, and the supplementary provisions in Part IV of that Schedule shall have effect.

Commentary—*Simon's Direct Tax Service* B7.406, 408, 412, 413.
Revenue & other press releases—IR 31-7-84 (offshore funds application for certification as distributing fund: detailed information required).
Definitions—"The 1992 Act", s 831(3); "accounting date", s 834(1); "the Board", s 832(1); "company", s 832(1), (2); "material interest", s 759; "unit trust scheme", s 469, by virtue of s 832(1); "United Kingdom", s 830(1).
Amendments—¹ Words in sub-s (4)(*a*) substituted by TCGA 1992 Sch 10 para 14(1), (46).

Charge to tax of offshore income gains

761 Charge to income tax or corporation tax of offshore income gain

(1) If a disposal to which this Chapter applies gives rise in accordance with section 758 [or Schedule]¹28 to an offshore income gain, then, subject to the provisions of this section, the amount of that gain shall be treated for all the purposes of the Tax Acts as—

   (*a*) income arising at the time of the disposal to the person making the disposal, and

   (*b*) constituting profits or gains chargeable to tax under Case VI of Schedule D for the chargeable period in which the disposal is made.

(2) Subject to subsection (3) below, sections [2(1) and 10 of the 1992 Act]² (persons chargeable to tax in respect of chargeable gains) and section 11(2)(*b*) shall have effect in relation to income tax or corporation tax in respect of offshore income gains as they have effect in relation to capital gains tax or corporation tax in respect of chargeable gains.

(3) In the application of section [10 of the 1992 Act]² in accordance with subsection (2) above, paragraphs (*a*) and (*b*) of subsection (1) of that section (which define the assets on the disposal of which chargeable gains are taxable) shall have effect with the omission of the words "situated in the United Kingdom and" [and subsection (3) of that section (which makes similar provision in relation to corporation tax) shall have effect with the omission of the words "situated in the United Kingdom"]³.

(4) ...⁴

(5) In the case of individuals resident or ordinarily resident but not domiciled in the United Kingdom, section [12 of the 1992 Act]² (which provides for taxation on a remittance basis) shall have effect in relation to income tax chargeable by virtue of subsection (1) above on an offshore income gain as it has effect in relation to capital gains tax in respect of gains accruing to such individuals from the disposal of assets situated outside the United Kingdom.

(6) A charity shall be exempt from tax in respect of an offshore income gain if the gain is applicable and applied for charitable purposes; but if property held on charitable trusts ceases to be subject to charitable trusts and that property represents directly or indirectly an offshore income gain, the trustees shall be treated as if they had disposed of and immediately reacquired that property for a consideration equal to its market value, any gain (calculated in accordance with Schedule 28) accruing being treated as an offshore income gain not accruing to a charity.

In this subsection "charity" has the same meaning as in section 506 and "market value" has the same meaning as in the [1992]² Act.

(7) In any case where—

   (*a*) a disposal to which this Chapter applies is a disposal of settled property, within the meaning of the [1992]² Act, and

   (*b*) for the purposes of the [1992]² Act, the general administration of the trusts is ordinarily carried on outside the United Kingdom and the trustees or a majority of them for the time being are not resident or not ordinarily resident in the United Kingdom,

subsection (1) above shall not apply in relation to any offshore income gain to which the disposal gives rise.

Commentary—*Simon's Direct Tax Service* **B7.422.**
Definitions—"The 1992 Act", s 831(3); "capital gains tax", s 831(5); "chargeable gains", s 832(1); "chargeable period", s 832(1); "income tax", s 832(4); "market value", s 759(9); "profits or gains", s 833(1); "Schedule D", s 18(1); "the Tax Acts", s 831(2); "United Kingdom", s 830(1).
Cross references—See TA 1988 s 660B(4) (offshore income gain on disposal of assets by trustees, income arising by virtue of sub-s (1) above deemed to be paid out where beneficiary is absolutely entitled against the trustees but is under 18 years of age).
TA 1988 s 764 (tax rate for trustees in respect of gains under sub-s (1) above).
TCGA 1992 s 108 (identification for purposes of tax on chargeable gains on disposals of securities which are material interests in non-qualifying offshore funds).

Amendments—Words in sub-s (1) substituted by FA 1990 Sch 14 paras 1, 11 and deemed always to have had effect.
[2] Words in sub-ss (2), (3), (5)–(7) substituted by TCGA 1992 Sch 10 para 14(1), (47).
[3] Words in sub-s (3) added by TCGA 1992 Sch 10 para 14(1), (47).
[4] Sub-s (4) repealed by TCGA 1992 Sch 12.

762 Offshore income gains accruing to persons resident or domiciled abroad

(1) Section [13 of the 1992 Act][1] (chargeable gains accruing to certain non-resident companies) shall have effect in relation to offshore income gains subject to the following modifications—

    (*a*) for any reference to a chargeable gain there shall be substituted a reference to an offshore income gain;
    (*b*) for the reference in subsection (7) to capital gains tax there shall be substituted a reference to income tax or corporation tax; and
    (*c*) paragraphs (*b*) and (*c*) of subsection (5) and subsection (8) shall be omitted.

(2) Subject to subsections (3) and (4) below, sections [87 to 90 and 96 to 98 of the 1992 Act][1] (gains of non-resident settlements) shall have effect in relation to offshore income gains subject to the following modifications—

    (*a*) for any reference to chargeable gains, other than the reference in section [87(6)][1], there shall be substituted a reference to offshore income gains;
    (*b*) [in section 87(2) of the 1992 Act for the words "tax under section 2(2)"][1] there shall be substituted the words "income tax by virtue of section 761 of the Taxes Act";
    (*c*) in section [87(7)][1] the reference to tax shall be construed as a reference to income tax or corporation tax; and
    (*d*) sections [87(10) and 97(6)][1] shall be omitted.

(3) In section [87(6) of the 1992 Act][1], both as it applies apart from subsection (2) above and as applied by subsection (2) above, the reference to chargeable gains shall be construed as including a reference to offshore income gains.

(4) If, in any year of assessment—

    (*a*) under subsection (3) of section [87 of the 1992 Act][1], as it applies apart from subsection (2) above, a chargeable gain falls to be attributed to a beneficiary, and
    (*b*) under that subsection, as applied by subsection (2) above, an offshore income gain also falls to be attributed to him,

subsection (4) of that section (gains attributed in proportion to capital payments received) shall have effect as if it required offshore income gains to be attributed before chargeable gains.

(5) Subject to subsection (6) below, for the purpose of determining whether an individual ordinarily resident in the United Kingdom has a liability for income tax in respect of an offshore income gain which arises on a disposal to which this Chapter applies where the disposal is made by a person resident or domiciled outside the United Kingdom—

    (*a*) sections 739 and 740 shall apply as if the offshore income gain arising to the person resident or domiciled outside the United Kingdom constituted income becoming payable to him, and
    (*b*) any reference in those sections to income of (or payable or arising to) such a person accordingly includes a reference to the offshore income gain arising to him by reason of the disposal to which this Chapter applies.

(6) To the extent that an offshore income gain is treated, by virtue of subsection (1) or subsection (2) above, as having accrued to any person resident or ordinarily resident in the United Kingdom, that gain shall not be deemed to be the income of any individual for the purposes of section 739 or 740 or any provision of Part XV.

Commentary—*Simon's Direct Tax Service* **B7.422.**
Definitions—"The 1992 Act", s 831(3); "capital gains tax", s 831(5); "chargeable gain", s 832(1); "income tax", s 832(4); "year of assessment", s 832(1).
Amendments—[1] Words in sub-ss (1)–(4) substituted by TCGA 1992 Sch 10 para 14(1), (48).

763 Deduction of offshore income gain in determining capital gain

(1) The provisions of this section apply where a disposal to which this Chapter applies gives rise to an offshore income gain; and, if that disposal also constitutes the disposal of the interest concerned for the purposes of the [1992][1] Act, then that disposal is in the following provisions of this section referred to as "the [1992][1] Act disposal".

(2) So far as relates to an offshore income gain which arises on a material disposal (within the meaning of Part I of Schedule 28), subsections (3) and (4) below shall have effect in relation to the [1992][1] Act disposal in substitution for section [37(1)][1] of that Act (deduction of consideration chargeable to tax on income).

(3) Subject to the following provisions of this section, in the [computation of the gain][1] accruing on the [1992][1] Act disposal, a sum equal to the offshore income gain shall be deducted from the sum which would otherwise constitute the amount or value of the consideration for the disposal.

(4) Where the [1992][1] Act disposal is of such a nature that, by virtue of section [42][1] of that Act (part disposals) an apportionment falls to be made of certain expenditure, no deduction shall be made by

virtue of subsection (3) above in determining, for the purposes of the fraction in subsection (2) of that section, the amount or value of the consideration for the disposal.

(5) If the [1992]¹ Act disposal forms part of a transfer to which section [162]¹ of that Act applies (roll-over relief on transfer of business in exchange wholly or partly for shares) then, for the purposes of subsection (4) of that section (determination of the amount of the deduction from the gain on the old assets) "B" in the fraction in that subsection (the value of the whole of the consideration received by the transferor in exchange for the business) shall be taken to be what it would be if the value of the consideration other than shares so received by the transferor were reduced by a sum equal to the offshore income gain.

(6) Where the disposal to which this Chapter applies constitutes such a disposal by virtue of section 757(6) or 758(5), the [1992]¹ Act shall have effect as if an amount equal to the offshore income gain to which the disposal gives rise were given (by the person making the exchange concerned) as consideration for the new holding, within the meaning of section [128]¹ of that Act (consideration given or received for new holding on a reorganisation).

(7) In any case where—

  (a) a disposal to which this Chapter applies by virtue of subsection (3) of section 758 is made otherwise than to the offshore fund concerned or the persons referred to in subsection (2)(b) of that section; and

  (b) subsequently, a distribution which is referable to the asset disposed of is paid either to the person who made the disposal or to a person connected with him; and

  (c) the disposal gives rise (in accordance with Part II of Schedule 28) to an offshore income gain;

then, for the purposes of the Tax Acts, the amount of the first distribution falling within paragraph (b) above shall be taken to be reduced or, as the case may be, extinguished by deducting therefrom an amount equal to the offshore income gain referred to in paragraph (c) above and, if that amount exceeds the amount of that first distribution, the balance shall be set against the second and, where necessary, any later distribution falling within paragraph (b) above, until the balance is exhausted.

(8) Section 839 shall apply for the purposes of subsection (7)(b) above.

Commentary—*Simon's Direct Tax Service* **B7.425.**
Revenue Internal Guidance—Inspector's Manual IM 4107–4108 (explanation with worked example).
Definitions—"The 1992 Act", s 831(3); "the Tax Acts", s 831(2).
Amendments—¹ Words in sub-ss (1)–(6) substituted by virtue of TCGA 1992 Sch 10 para 14(1), (49).

764 Offshore income gains of trustees

Income arising in a year of assessment by virtue of section 761(1) to trustees shall be chargeable to income tax [at the rate applicable to trusts]¹ for that year.

Commentary—*Simon's Direct Tax Service* **C4.206.**
Definitions—"Rate applicable to trusts", s 832(1); 2(1); "year of assessment", s 832(1)
Amendments—¹ Words substituted by FA 1993 Sch 6 paras 13, 25(1) with effect from the year 1993–94.

CHAPTER VI
MISCELLANEOUS
Migration etc of company

765 Migration etc of companies

(1) Subject to the provisions of this section [and section 765A]², all transactions of the following classes shall be unlawful unless carried out with the consent of the Treasury, that is to say—

  (a), (b) ...¹

  (c) for a body corporate [resident in the United Kingdom]¹ to cause or permit a body corporate not [resident in the United Kingdom]¹ over which it has control to create or issue any shares or debentures; or

  (d) except for the purpose of enabling a person to be qualified to act as a director, for a body corporate so resident to transfer to any person, or cause or permit to be transferred to any person, any shares or debentures of a body corporate not so resident over which it has control, being shares or debentures which it owns or in which it has an interest.

(2) Nothing in subsection (1)(c) above shall apply to the giving to the bankers of the body corporate not resident in the United Kingdom of any security for the payment of any sum due or to become due from it to them by reason of any transaction entered into with it by them in the ordinary course of their business as bankers.

(3) Nothing in subsection (1)(c) above shall apply to the giving by the body corporate not resident in the United Kingdom to an insurance company of any security for the payment of any sum due or to become due from that body corporate to that company by reason of any transaction entered into with that body corporate by that company in the ordinary course of that company's business by way of investment of its funds.

(4) Any consent granted by the Treasury under this section—

(*a*) may be given either specially (that is to say, so as to apply only to specified transactions of or relating to a specified body corporate) or generally (that is to say, so as not only so to apply); and
(*b*) may, if given generally, be revoked by the Treasury; and
(*c*) may in any case be absolute or conditional; and
(*d*) shall be published in such a way as to give any person entitled to the benefit of it an adequate opportunity of getting to know of it, unless in the opinion of the Treasury publication is not necessary for that purpose.

Commentary—*Simon's Direct Tax Service* D2.537; D4.130.
Note—This section should be read in conjunction with the Treasury General Consents 1988 (Non-resident companies; general consents, procedures and Treasury guidance notes) which are reproduced in the Miscellaneous section of Part II of this Handbook, under Misc III.
Statement of Practice SP 2/92, para 5—Movement of capital between Gibraltar and UK.
SP 2/92, para 6—Difference between general and special consent transactions.
SP 2/92, paras 10–13—Issues and transfers of securities between residents of member States.
SP 2/92, paras 15–23—Revenue's approach to the question of ''residence'' for the purposes of this section.
Revenue Interpretation RI 221—Treasury consents under this section for transactions carried out after 27 July 2000, following changes to the definition of a group of companies made by FA 2000.
Revenue Internal Guidance—International tax handbook ITH 401–404 (background to the section).
Company Taxation Manual COT3442 (all applications for consent are referred to the Revenue for recommendations).
COT3444 (Treasury consent does not determine residence: this is a question of fact).
Simon's Tax Cases—*R v HM Treasury, ex p Daily Mail and General Trust plc* [1987] STC 157*.
Definitions—''Control'', s 767(5); ''debentures'', s 767(5); ''director'', s 767(5); ''funds'', s 767(5); ''insurance company'', s 767(5); ''resident'', s 767(1), (2), (5); ''shares'', s 767(5); ''trade'', s 832(1); ''transfer'', s 767(5); ''United Kingdom'', s 830(1).
Cross references—See TA 1988 s 765A (movements of capital between residents of member States).
TA 1988 s 766 (offences under this section).
TA 1988 s 767 (interpretation and commencement of this section).
Amendments—¹ Sub-s (1)(*a*), (*b*) repealed and words in sub-s (1)(*c*) substituted by FA 1988 s 105(6), (7) and Sch 14 Pt IV with effect from 15 March 1988 but the repeals do not affect an application for Treasury consent made before that date or a consent already granted.
² Words in sub-s (1) inserted by FA 1990 s 68(1).

[765A Movements of capital between residents of member States

(1) Section 765(1) shall not apply to a transaction which is a movement of capital to which Article 1 of the Directive of the Council of the European Communities dated 24th June 1988 No 88/361/EEC applies.

(2) Where if that Article did not apply to it a transaction would be unlawful under section 765(1), the body corporate in question (that is to say, the body corporate resident in the United Kingdom) shall—

(*a*) give to the Board within six months of the carrying out of the transaction such information relating to the transaction, or to persons connected with the transaction, as regulations made by the Board may require, and
(*b*) where notice is given to the body corporate by the Board, give to the Board within such period as is prescribed by regulations made by the Board (or such longer period as the Board may in the case allow) such further particulars relating to the transaction, to related transactions, or to persons connected with the transaction or related transactions, as the Board may require.]¹

Commentary—*Simon's Direct Tax Service* D2.537; D4.138.
Regulations—See the Movements of Capital (Required Information) Regulations, SI 1990/1671.
Statement of Practice SP 2/92, para 3—Revenue's views in respect of a transaction regarding which there is doubt as to whether it is movement of capital.
SP 2/92, para 4—Guidance on procedure to companies making a report under sub-s (2) above.
SP 2/92, para 5—Movement of capital between Gibraltar and UK.
SP 2/92, para 6—Difference between general and special consent transactions.
SP 2/92, paras 10–13—Issues and transfers of securities between residents of member States.
SP 2/92, paras 15–23—Revenue's approach to the question of ''residence'' for the purposes of this section.
SP 2/92, paras 24–26—Procedure for providing information under sub-s (2) above.
Definitions—''The Board'', s 832(1); ''notice'', s 832(1); ''resident'', s 767(1), (2), (5).
Cross references—See TMA 1970 s 98(5) (penalties for failure to comply with sub-s (2) above).
Amendments—¹ This section inserted by FA 1990 s 68(2), (4) and applies to transactions carried out after 30 June 1990.

766 Offences under section 765

(1) Any person who, whether within or outside the United Kingdom, does or is a party to the doing of any act which to his knowledge amounts to or results in, or forms part of a series of acts which together amount to or result in, or will amount to or result in, something which is unlawful under section 765(1) shall be guilty of an offence under this section.

(2) In any proceedings in respect of such an offence against a director of the body corporate in question (that is to say, the body corporate which is or was resident in the United Kingdom) or against any person who was purporting to act in that capacity—

(*a*) it shall be presumed that he was a party to every act of that body corporate unless he proves that it was done without his consent or connivance; and
(*b*) it shall, unless the contrary is proved, be presumed that any act which in fact amounted to or resulted in, or formed part of a series of acts which together amounted to or resulted in or would amount to or result in, something which is unlawful under section 765(1) was to his knowledge such an act.

(3) Any person who is guilty of an offence under this section shall be liable on conviction on indictment—

    (*a*) to imprisonment for not more than two years or to a fine, or to both; or

    (*b*) where the person in question is a body corporate which is or was resident in the United Kingdom, to a fine not exceeding an amount equal to three times the corporation tax, capital gains tax and income tax paid or payable which is attributable to the income, profits or gains (including chargeable gains) arising in the 36 months immediately preceding the commission of the offence, or £10,000, whichever is the greater;

and proceedings in respect of such an offence alleged to have been committed by a person may be taken before the appropriate court in the United Kingdom having jurisdiction in the place where that person is for the time being.

(4) No proceedings for an offence under this section shall be instituted, in England or Wales, except by or with the consent of the Attorney General, or in Northern Ireland, except by or with the consent of the Attorney General for Northern Ireland.

Commentary—*Simon's Direct Tax Service* **D4.142.**
Definitions—"Chargeable gains", s 832(1); "director", s 767(5); "profits or gains", s 833(1); "resident", s 767(1), (2), (5); "United Kingdom", s 830(1).
Cross references—See TA 1988 s 767 (interpretation and commencement of this section).

767 Interpretation and commencement of sections 765 and 766

(1)–(4) ...[1]

(5) In this section and in sections 765 and 766—

    "share", "debenture" and "director" have, in relation to any body corporate, the meanings respectively assigned to them by Part XXVI of the Companies Act 1985 in relation to a company;

    "control" (except in the expression "central management and control") has, in relation to a body corporate, the meaning given by section 840;

    "transfer", in relation to shares or debentures, includes a transfer of any beneficial interest therein;

    "insurance company" means a body corporate lawfully carrying on business as an insurer, whether in the United Kingdom or elsewhere; and

    "funds" in relation to an insurance company means the funds held by it in connection with that business;

...[1]

(6) This section and sections 765 and 766 shall come into force on 6th April 1988 to the exclusion of section 482 of the 1970 Act (which is re-enacted by those sections); but any offence committed before 6th April 1988 shall not be punishable under section 766 and neither this subsection nor any other provision of this Act shall prevent any such offence from being punishable as if this Act had not been passed.

Commentary—*Simon's Direct Tax Service* **D4.136.**
Simon's Tax Cases—s 767(1), (2), *R v HM Treasury and IRC, ex p Daily Mail and General Trust plc* [1988] STC 787*; *R v IRC, ex p Banque Internationale à Luxembourg SA [2000] STC 708.*
Definitions—"The 1970 Act", s 831(3); "control", s 840; "trade", s 832(1); "United Kingdom", s 830(1); "year of assessment", s 832(1).
Amendments—[1] Sub-ss (1)–(4) and words in sub-s (5) repealed by FA 1988 Sch 14 Pt IV with effect from 15 March 1988.

Change in ownership of company

[767A Change in company ownership: corporation tax

(1) Where it appears to the Board that—

    (*a*) there has been a change in the ownership of a company ("the taxpayer company"),

    (*b*) any corporation tax assessed on the taxpayer company for an accounting period beginning before the change remains unpaid at any time after the relevant date, and

    (*c*) any of the three conditions mentioned below is fulfilled,

any person mentioned in subsection (2) below may be assessed by the Board and charged (in the name of the taxpayer company) to an amount of corporation tax in accordance with this section.

(2) The persons are—

    (*a*) any person who at any time during the relevant period before the change in the ownership of the taxpayer company had control of it;

    (*b*) any company of which the person mentioned in paragraph (*a*) above has at any time had control within the period of three years before that change.

(3) In subsection (2) above, "the relevant period" means—

    (*a*) the period of three years before the change in the ownership of the taxpayer company; or

    (*b*) if during the period of three years before that change ("the later change") there was a change in the ownership of the taxpayer company ("the earlier change"), the period elapsing between the earlier change and the later change.

(4) The first condition is that—

(*a*) at any time during the period of three years before the change in the ownership of the taxpayer company the activities of a trade or business of that company cease or the scale of those activities become small or negligible; and

(*b*) there is no significant revival of those activities before that change occurs.

(5) The second condition is that at any time after the change in the ownership of the taxpayer company, but under arrangements made before that change, the activities of a trade or business of that company cease or the scale of those activities become small or negligible.

(6) The third condition is that—

(*a*) at any time during the period of six years beginning three years before the change in the ownership of the taxpayer company there is a major change in the nature or conduct of a trade or business of that company;

(*b*) there is a transfer or there are transfers of assets of the taxpayer company to a person mentioned in subsection (7) below or to any person under arrangements which enable any of those assets or any assets representing those assets to be transferred to a person mentioned in subsection (7) below;

(*c*) that transfer occurs or those transfers occur during the period of three years before the change in the ownership of the taxpayer company or after that change but under arrangements made before that change; and

(*d*) the major change mentioned in paragraph (*a*) above is attributable to that transfer or those transfers.

(7) The persons are—

(*a*) any person mentioned in subsection (2)(*a*) above; and

(*b*) any person connected with him.

(8) The amount of tax charged in an assessment made under this section must not exceed the amount of the tax which, at the time of that assessment, remains unpaid by the tax-payer company.

(9) For the purposes of this section the relevant date is the date six months from the date on which the corporation tax is assessed as mentioned in subsection (1)(*b*) above.

(10) Any assessment made under this section shall not be out of time if made within three years from the date on which the liability of the taxpayer company to corporation tax for the accounting period mentioned in subsection (1)(*b*) above is finally determined.]¹

Commentary—*Simon's Direct Tax Service* **D2.521; D4.136.**
Revenue Interpretation RI 107—Company purchase scheme: in certain circumstances no charge to tax on recipient of the payment under an indemnity or under s 767B(2).
Revenue & other press releases—IR 19-8-98 (Company purchase schemes: collection of outstanding tax—outcome of consultation).
Definitions—"Accounting period", s 834(1); "the Board", s 832(1); "change in the ownership of a company", s 769(1); "company", s 832(1), (2); "trade", ss 6(4), 834(2).
Cross references—See TA 1988 s 767B (supplementary provisions and definitions).
TA 1988 s 769 (rules for ascertaining change in ownership of company).
Amendments—¹ This section inserted by FA 1994 s 135(1), (6) in relation to any change in ownership occurring on or after 30 November 1993 other than any change occurring in pursuance of a contract entered into before that date.

[767AA Change in company ownership: postponed corporation tax]

(1) Where it appears to the Board that—

(*a*) there has been a change in the ownership of a company ("the transferred company"),

(*b*) any corporation tax relating to an accounting period ending on or after the change has been assessed on the transferred company or an associated company,

(*c*) that tax remains unpaid at any time more than six months after it was assessed, and

(*d*) the condition set out in subsection (2) below is fulfilled,

any person mentioned in subsection (4) below may be assessed by the Board and charged to an amount of corporation tax not exceeding the amount remaining unpaid.

(2) The condition is that it would be reasonable (apart from this section) to infer, from either or both of—

(*a*) the terms of any transactions entered into in connection with the change, and

(*b*) the other circumstances of the change and of any such transactions,

that at least one of those transactions was entered into by one or more of its parties on the assumption, as regards a potential tax liability, that that liability would be unlikely to be met, or met in full, if it were to arise.

(3) In subsection (2) above the reference to a potential tax liability is a reference to a liability to pay corporation tax which—

(*a*) in circumstances which were reasonably foreseeable at the time of the change in ownership, or

(*b*) in circumstances the occurrence of which is something of which there was at that time a reasonably foreseeable risk,

would or might arise from an assessment made, after the change in ownership, on the transferred company or an associated company (whether or not a particular associated company).

(4) The persons mentioned in subsection (1) above are—

(a) any person who at any time during the relevant period had control of the transferred company;
(b) any company of which the person mentioned in paragraph (a) above has at any time had control within the period of three years before the change in the ownership of the transferred company.

(5) In subsection (4) above, "the relevant period" means—

(a) the period of three years before the change in the ownership of the transferred company; or
(b) if during the period of three years before that change ("the later change") there was a change in the ownership of the transferred company ("the earlier change"), the period elapsing between the earlier change and the later change.

(6) For the purposes of this section a transaction is entered into in connection with a change in the ownership of a company if—

(a) it is the transaction, or one of the transactions, by which that change is effected; or
(b) it is entered into as part of a series of transactions, or scheme, of which transactions effecting the change in ownership have formed or will form a part.

(7) For the purposes of this section—

(a) references to a scheme are references to any scheme, arrangements or understanding of any kind whatever, whether or not legally enforceable, involving a single transaction or two or more transactions;
(b) it shall be immaterial in determining whether any transactions have formed or will form part of a series of transactions or scheme that the parties to any of the transactions are different from the parties to another of the transactions; and
(c) the cases in which any two or more transactions are to be taken as forming part of a series of transactions or scheme shall include any case in which it would be reasonable to assume that one or more of them—

(i) would not have been entered into independently of the other or others; or
(ii) if entered into independently of the other or others, would not have taken the same form or been on the same terms.

(8) In this section references, in relation to the transferred company and an assessment to tax, to an associated company are references to any company (whenever formed) which, at the time of the assessment or at an earlier time after the change in ownership—

(a) has control of the transferred company;
(b) is a company of which the transferred company has control; or
(c) is a company under the control of the same person or persons as the transferred company.

(9) A person assessed and charged to tax under this section shall be assessed and charged in the name of the company by whom the tax to which the assessment relates remains unpaid.

(10) Any assessment made under this section shall not be out of time if made within three years from the date of the final determination of the liability of the company by whom the tax remains unpaid to corporation tax for the accounting period for which that tax was assessed.][1]

Commentary—*Simon's Direct Tax Service* D2.521, 522.
Revenue & other press releases—IR 19-8-98 (Company purchase schemes: collection of outstanding tax—outcome of consultation).
Amendments—[1] This section inserted by FA 1998 s 114(1) with effect in relation to changes in ownership occurring after 1 July 1997, other than any change occurring in pursuance of a contract entered into before 2 July 1997.

[767B Change of company ownership: supplementary

(1) In relation to corporation tax assessed under section 767A—

(a) section 86 of the Management Act (interest on overdue tax), in so far as it has effect in relation to accounting periods ending on or before 30th September 1993, and
(b) section 87A of that Act (corresponding provision for corporation tax due for accounting periods ending after that date),

shall have effect as if the references in section 86 to the reckonable date and in section 87A to the date when the tax becomes due and payable were, respectively, references to the date which is the reckonable date in relation to the taxpayer company and the date when the tax became due and payable by the taxpayer company.

[(1A) In relation to corporation tax assessed under section 767AA, section 87A of the Management Act shall have effect as if the references to the date when the tax becomes due and payable were references to the date when the tax became due and payable by the transferred company or the associated company (as the case may be).][2]

(2) A payment in pursuance of an assessment under section 767A [or 767AA][2] shall not be allowed as a deduction in computing any income, profits or losses for any tax purposes; but any person making such a payment shall be entitled to recover an amount equal to the payment from the taxpayer company [or the transferred company or associated company (as the case may be)][2].

(3) In subsection (2) above the reference to a payment in pursuance of an assessment includes a reference to a payment of interest under section 86 or 87A of the Management Act (as they have effect by virtue of subsection (1) above).

(4) For the purposes of [sections 767A, 767AA and 767C][2], ''control'', in relation to a company, shall be construed in accordance with section 416 as modified by subsections (5) and (6) below.

(5) In subsection (2)(*a*) for ''the greater part of'' there shall be substituted ''50 per cent of''.

(6) For subsection (3) there shall be substituted—

''(3) Where two or more persons together satisfy any of the conditions in subsection (2) above and do so by reason of having acted together to put themselves in a position where they will in fact satisfy the condition in question, each of those persons shall be treated as having control of the company.''

(7) In section 767A(6) ''a major change in the nature or conduct of a trade or business'' includes any change mentioned in any of paragraphs (*a*) to (*d*) of section 245(4); and also includes a change falling within any of those paragraphs which is achieved gradually as the result of a series of transfers.

(8) In section 767A(6) ''transfer'', in relation to an asset, includes any disposal, letting or hiring of it, and any grant or transfer of any right, interest or licence in or over it, or the giving of any business facilities with respect to it.

(9) Section 839 shall apply for the purposes of section 767A(7).

(10) Subsection (9) of section 768 shall apply for the purposes of [sections 767A and 767AA][2] as it applies for the purposes of section 768.][1]

Commentary—*Simon's Direct Tax Service* **D2.521.**
Revenue Interpretation RI 107—Company purchase scheme: in certain circumstances no charge to tax on recipient of the payment under an indemnity or under s 767B(2).
Revenue & other press releases—IR 19-8-98 (Company purchase schemes: collection of outstanding tax—outcome of consultation).
Amendments—[1] This section inserted by FA 1994 s 135(1), (6) in relation to any change in ownership occurring on or after 30 November 1993 other than any change occurring in pursuance of a contract entered into before that date.
[2] Sub-s (1A), words in sub-s (2) inserted, and words in sub-ss (4), (10) substituted by FA 1998 s 116(1)–(4) with effect in relation to changes in ownership occurring after 1 July 1997 other than any change occurring in pursuance of a contract entered into before 2 July 1997.

[767C Change in company ownership: information

(1) This section applies where it appears to the Board that—

    (*a*) there has been a change in the ownership of a company (''the subject company''); and
    (*b*) in connection with that change a person (''the seller'') may be or become liable to be assessed and charged to corporation tax under section 767A or 767AA.

(2) The Board may by notice require any person to supply to them—

    (*a*) any document in the person's possession or power which appears to the Board to be relevant for determining any one or more of the matters referred to in subsection (3) below; or
    (*b*) any particulars which appear to them to be so relevant.

(3) Those matters are—

    (*a*) whether the seller is or may become liable as mentioned in subsection (1) above and the extent of the liability or potential liability; and
    (*b*) whether the subject company or an associated company is or may become liable to be assessed to any tax in respect of which the seller is or could become liable as mentioned in subsection (1) above, and the extent of the liability or potential liability of the subject company or associated company.

(4) Without prejudice to the following provisions of this section, the references in subsection (2) above to documents and particulars are references to the documents and particulars specified or described in the notice.

(5) A notice under subsection (2) above must specify the period, which must not be less than 30 days, within which the notice must be complied with.

(6) Any person to whom any documents are supplied under this section may take copies of them or of any extracts from them.

(7) A notice under subsection (2) above shall not oblige a person to supply any documents or particulars relating to the conduct of any pending appeal relating to tax.

(8) In relation to any notice under subsection (2) above—

    (*a*) subsection (4) of section 20B of the Taxes Management Act 1970 (rules relating to copies of documents) shall apply as it applies in relation to a notice under section 20(1) of that Act; and
    (*b*) subsections (8) to (14) of section 20B of that Act (rules about obtaining documents etc from professional advisers) shall apply as they apply in relation to a notice under section 20(3) of that Act but as if any reference to an inspector were a reference to the Board;

and subsection (8C) of section 20 of that Act (exclusion of personal records and journalistic material) shall apply for the purposes of this section as it applies for the purposes of that section.

(9) In this section references, in relation to the subject company and an assessment to tax, to an associated company are references to any company which, at the time of the assessment or at an earlier time after the change in ownership—

    (a) has control of the subject company;

    (b) is a company of which the subject company has control; or

    (c) is a company under the control of the same person or persons as the subject company.

(10) In this section "document" means anything in which information of any description is recorded.]¹

Commentary—*Simon's Direct Tax Service* **D2.521.**
Revenue & other press releases—IR 19-8-98 (Company purchase schemes: collection of outstanding tax—outcome of consultation).
Amendments—¹ This section inserted by FA 1998 s 115(1) with effect in relation to changes in ownership occurring after 1 July 1997 other than any change occurring in pursuance of a contract entered into before 2 July 1997.

768 Change in ownership of company: disallowance of trading losses

(1) If—

    (a) within any period of three years there is both a change in the ownership of a company and (either earlier or later in that period, or at the same time) a major change in the nature or conduct of a trade carried on by the company, or

    (b) at any time after the scale of the activities in a trade carried on by a company has become small or negligible, and before any considerable revival of the trade, there is a change in the ownership of the company,

no relief shall be given under section 393 by setting a loss incurred by the company in an accounting period beginning before the change of ownership against any income or other profits of an accounting period ending after the change of ownership.

(2) In applying this section to the accounting period in which the change of ownership occurs, the part ending with the change of ownership, and the part after, shall be treated as two separate accounting periods, and the profits or losses of the accounting period shall be apportioned to the two parts.

(3) The apportionment under subsection (2) above shall be on a time basis according to the respective lengths of those parts except that if it appears that that method would work unreasonably or unjustly such other method shall be used as appears just and reasonable.

(4) In subsection (1) above "major change in the nature or conduct of a trade" includes—

    (a) a major change in the type of property dealt in, or services or facilities provided, in the trade; or

    (b) a major change in customers, outlets or markets of the trade;

and this section applies even if the change is the result of a gradual process which began outside the period of three years mentioned in subsection (1)(a) above.

(5) In relation to any relief available under section 343 to a successor company, subsection (1) above shall apply as if any loss sustained by a predecessor company had been sustained by a successor company and as if the references to a trade included references to the trade as carried on by a predecessor company.

(6) Where relief in respect of a company's losses has been restricted under this section then, notwithstanding -section 577(3) of the Capital Allowances Act]¹, in applying the provisions of that Act about balancing charges to the company by reference to any event after the change of ownership of the company, any allowance or deduction falling to be made in taxing the company's trade for any chargeable period before the change of ownership shall be disregarded unless the profits or gains of that chargeable period or of any subsequent chargeable period before the change of ownership were sufficient to give effect to the allowance or deduction.

(7) In applying subsection (6) above it shall be assumed that any profits or gains are applied in giving effect to any such allowance or deduction in preference to being set off against any loss which is not attributable to such an allowance or deduction.

(8) Where the operation of this section depends on circumstances or events at a time after the change of ownership (but not more than three years after), an assessment to give effect to the provisions of this section shall not be out of time if made within six years from that time, or the latest of those times.

(9) Any person in whose name any shares, stock or securities of a company are registered shall, if required by notice by an inspector given for the purposes of this section, state whether or not he is the beneficial owner of those shares or securities and, if not the beneficial owner of those shares or securities of any of them, shall furnish the name and address of the person or persons on whose behalf those shares, stock or securities are registered in his name.

Commentary—*Simon's Direct Tax Service* **D2.410.**
Statements of Practice SP 13/80—Where there is a demerger of a company involving ownership passing to the shareholders and the purpose of the demerger is for efficient running of the business, the Revenue may disregard this section.
SP 10/91—Revenue's interpretation of the term "a major change in the nature or conduct of a trade or business".
Revenue Internal Guidance—Company Taxation Manual COT1201–1213 (identification of cases; meaning of "change of ownership"; meaning of "major change"; meaning of activities becoming "negligible").

Simon's Tax Cases—s 768(1)(*a*), (4)(*b*), *Willis v Peeters Picture Frames Ltd* [1983] STC 453*.
Definitions—"The 1990 Act", s 831(3); "accounting period", s 834(1); "apportionment", s 834(4); "change in the ownership of a company", s 769(1); "chargeable period", s 832(1); "company", s 832(1), (2); "inspector", s 832(1); "notice", s 832(1); "profits", ss 6(4), 834(2); "profits or gains", s 833(1); "trade", ss 6(4), 834(2).
Cross references—See TA 1988 s 245(7) (application of sub-ss (8) and (9) above for the purposes of restriction of relief for surplus ACT on change of ownership of a company).
TA 1988 s 245A(4) (application of sub-ss (8) and (9) above for the purposes of restriction of relief for surplus ACT on change of ownership of a subsidiary).
TA 1988 s 245B(5) (application of sub-ss (8) and (9) above where owing to change of ownership of company there is restriction on set–off of ACT against corporation tax on capital gains).
TA 1988 s 768A(2) (certain provisions of this section to apply for the purposes of s 768A).
TA 1988 s 768B(12), (13) (application of sub-ss (6)–(9) above and modification of sub-s (6) above to restrict deductions where there has been a change in the ownership of an investment company within sub-s (1)).
TA 1988 s 768C(11) (application of sub-s (8), (9) above where there is a change in ownership of an investment company and within 3 years a chargeable gain accrues on the disposal of an asset transferred intra group).
TA 1988 s 769 (rules for ascertaining change in ownership of company).
Corporation Tax (Treatment of Unrelieved Surplus Advance Corporation Tax) Regulations, SI 1999/358 reg 16 (application of sub-ss (8), (9) above and s 769 as if the reference to the benefit of losses in s 769(3) were a reference to the benefit of unrelieved surplus ACT).
Amendments—[1] Words in sub-s (6) substituted by CAA 2001 s 578, Sch 2 para 55 with effect for corporation tax purposes as respects allowances and charges falling to be made for chargeable periods ending after 31 March 2001.

[768A Change in ownership: disallowance of carry back of trading losses

(1) In any case where—

(*a*) within any period of three years there is both a change in the ownership of a company and (either earlier or later in that period, or at the same time) a major change in the nature or conduct of a trade carried on by the company, or

(*b*) at any time after the scale of the activities in a trade carried on by a company has become small or negligible, and before any considerable revival of the trade, there is a change in the ownership of the company,

no relief shall be given under section 393A(1) by setting a loss incurred by the company in an accounting period ending after the change in ownership against any profits of an accounting period beginning before the change in ownership.

(2) Subsections (2) to (4), (8) and (9) of section 768 shall apply for the purposes of this section as they apply for the purposes of that section.

(3) This section applies in relation to changes in ownership occurring on or after 14th June 1991.][1]

Commentary—*Simon's Direct Tax Service* **D2.410.**
Statement of Practice SP 10/91—Revenue's interpretation of the term "a major change in the nature or conduct of a trade or business".
Definitions—"Accounting period", s 834(1); "change in ownership of a company", s 769(1); "company", s 832(1), (2); "trade", s 832(1).
Cross references—See TA 1988 s 769 (rules for ascertaining change in ownership of company).
Amendments—[1] This section inserted by FA 1991 Sch 15 para 20(1).

[768B Change in ownership of investment company: deductions generally

(1) This section applies where there is a change in the ownership of an investment company and—

(*a*) after the change there is a significant increase in the amount of the company's capital; or

(*b*) within the period of six years beginning three years before the change there is a major change in the nature or conduct of the business carried on by the company; or

(*c*) the change in the ownership occurs at any time after the scale of the activities in the business carried on by the company has become small or negligible and before any considerable revival of the business.

(2) For the purposes of subsection (1)(*a*) above, whether there is a significant increase in the amount of a company's capital after a change in the ownership of the company shall be determined in accordance with the provisions of Part I of Schedule 28A.

(3) In paragraph (*b*) of subsection (1) above "major change in the nature or conduct of a business" includes a major change in the nature of the investments held by the company, even if the change is the result of a gradual process which began before the period of six years mentioned in that paragraph.

(4) For the purposes of this section—

(*a*) the accounting period of the company in which the change in the ownership occurs shall be divided into two parts, the first the part ending with the change, the second the part after;

(*b*) those parts shall be treated as two separate accounting periods; and

(*c*) the amounts in issue for the accounting period being divided shall be apportioned to those parts.

(5) In Schedule 28A—

(*a*) Part II shall have effect for identifying the amounts in issue for the accounting period being divided; and

(*b*) Part III shall have effect for the purpose of apportioning those amounts to the parts of that accounting period.

(6) Any sums which—

(*a*) are disbursed or treated as disbursed as expenses of management in the accounting period being divided, and

(*b*) under Part III of Schedule 28A are apportioned to either part of that period,

shall be treated for the purposes of section 75 as disbursed in that part.

(7) Any charges which under Part III of Schedule 28A are apportioned to either part of the accounting period being divided shall be treated for the purposes of sections 338 and 75 as paid in that part.

(8) Any allowances which under Part III of Schedule 28A are apportioned to either part of the accounting period being divided shall be treated for the purposes of [section 253 of the Capital Allowances Act][3] and section 75(4) as falling to be made in that part.

(9) In computing the total profits of the company for an accounting period ending after the change in the ownership, no deduction shall be made under section 75 by reference to—

(*a*) sums disbursed or allowances falling to be made for an accounting period beginning before the change; or

(*b*) charges paid in such an accounting period.

[(10) Part IV of Schedule 28A shall have effect for the purpose of restricting, in a case where this section applies, the debits to be brought into account for the purposes of Chapter II of Part IV of the Finance Act 1996 (loan relationships) in respect of the company's loan relationships [(including debits so brought into account by virtue of paragraph 14(3) of Schedule 26 to the Finance Act 2002)][4].][2]

(12) Subject to the modification in subsection (13) below, subsections (6) to (9) of section 768 shall apply for the purposes of this section as they apply for the purposes of that section.

(13) The modification is that in subsection (6) of section 768 for the words "relief in respect of a company's losses has been restricted" there shall be substituted "deductions from a company's total profits[, or the debits to be brought into account for the purposes of Chapter II of Part IV of the Finance Act 1996 in the case of a company in respect of its loan relationships [(or its derivative contracts by virtue of paragraph 14(3) of Schedule 26 to the Finance Act 2002)][4],][2] have been restricted".

(14) In this section "investment company" has the same meaning as in Part IV.][1]

Commentary—*Simon's Direct Tax Service* D4.409A, 409C, 409D.
Definitions—"Accounting period", s 834(1); "the 1992 Act", s 83(1); "apportionment", s 834(4); "change in ownership of a company", s 769(1); "company", s 832(1), (2); "loan relationships", s 834(1), FA 1996 s 81; "profits", ss 6(4), 834(2).
Cross references—See TA 1988 s 768C(5) (modification of the application of sub-ss (6)–(8) above where a chargeable gain arises on the disposal of an asset transferred intra group within 3 years of a change in ownership of an investment company; references to TA 1988 Sch 28A Part III to be read as references to Part IV of that Schedule).
TA 1988 s 769 (rules for ascertaining change in ownership of a company; sub-s (3) to apply as if "benefit of losses" were a reference to "benefit of deductions" by virtue of sub-s (3A)).
TA 1988 Sch 28A para 1 (determination of whether there is a significant increase in the amount of a company's capital after a change in the ownership of the company).
Amendments—[1] This section inserted by FA 1995 Sch 26 paras 2, 5, with effect for a change in ownership occurring on or after 29 November 1994 other than a change occurring in pursuance of a contract entered into on or before that date.
[2] Sub-s (10) substituted for sub-ss (10), (11), and words in sub-s (13) inserted, by FA 1996 ss 104, 105(1), Sch 14 para 39 with effect for accounting periods ending after 31 March 1996, subject to transitional provisions in FA 1996 Sch 15.
[3] Words in sub-s (8) substituted by CAA 2001 s 578, Sch 2 para 56 with effect for corporation tax purposes as respects allowances and charges falling to be made for chargeable periods ending after 31 March 2001.
[4] Words inserted in sub-ss (10), (13) by FA 2002 s 83(1)(*b*), (3) Sch 27 paras 1, 9 with effect for accounting periods beginning after 30 September 2002.

[768C Deductions: asset transferred within group

(1) This section applies where—

(*a*) there is a change in the ownership of an investment company ("the relevant company");

(*b*) none of paragraphs (*a*) to (*c*) of section 768B(1) applies;

(*c*) after the change in the ownership the relevant company acquires an asset from another company in circumstances such that section 171(1) of the 1992 Act applies to the acquisition; and

(*d*) a chargeable gain ("a relevant gain") accrues to the relevant company on a disposal of the asset within the period of three years beginning with the change in the ownership.

(2) For the purposes of subsection (1)(*d*) above an asset acquired by the relevant company as mentioned in subsection (1)(*c*) above shall be treated as the same as an asset owned at a later time by that company if the value of the second asset is derived in whole or in part from the first asset, and in particular where the second asset is a freehold and the first asset was a leasehold and the lessee has acquired the reversion.

(3) For the purposes of this section—

(*a*) the accounting period of the relevant company in which the change in the ownership occurs shall be divided into two parts, the first the part ending with the change, the second the part after;

(*b*) those parts shall be treated as two separate accounting periods; and

(*c*) the amounts in issue for the accounting period being divided shall be apportioned to those parts.

(4) In Schedule 28A—

(*a*) Part V shall have effect for identifying the amounts in issue for the accounting period being divided; and (*b*) Part VI shall have effect for the purpose of apportioning those amounts to the parts of that accounting period.

(5) Subsections (6) to (8) of section 768B shall apply in relation to the relevant company as they apply in relation to the company mentioned in subsection (1) of that section except that any reference in those subsections to Part III of Schedule 28A shall be read as a reference to Part VI of that Schedule.

(6) Subsections (7) and (9) below apply only where, in accordance with the relevant provisions of the 1992 Act and Part VI of Schedule 28A, an amount is included in respect of chargeable gains in the total profits for the accounting period of the relevant company in which the relevant gain accrues.

(7) In computing the total profits of the relevant company for the accounting period in which the relevant gain accrues, no deduction shall be made under section 75 by reference to—

(*a*) sums disbursed or allowances falling to be made for an accounting period of the relevant company beginning before the change in ownership, or
(*b*) charges paid in such an accounting period,

from an amount of the total profits equal to the amount which represents the relevant gain.

(8) For the purposes of this section, the amount of the total profits for an accounting period which represents the relevant gain is—

(*a*) where the amount of the relevant gain does not exceed the amount which is included in respect of chargeable gains for that period, an amount equal to the amount of the relevant gain;
(*b*) where the amount of the relevant gain exceeds the amount which is included in respect of chargeable gains for that period, the amount so included.

[(9) Part IV of Schedule 28A shall have effect for the purpose of restricting, in a case where this section applies, the debits to be brought into account for the purposes of Chapter II of Part IV of the Finance Act 1996 (loan relationships) in respect of the relevant company's loan relationships [(including debits so brought into account by virtue of paragraph 14(3) of Schedule 26 to the Finance Act 2002)]³.]²

(11) Subsections (8) and (9) of section 768 shall apply for the purposes of this section as they apply for the purposes of that section.

(12) In this section—

"the relevant provisions of the 1992 Act" means section 8(1) of and Schedule 7A to that Act; and "investment company" has the same meaning as in Part IV.]¹

[(13) This section applies in relation to an asset to which Schedule 29 to the Finance Act 2002 applies (intangible fixed assets), with the following adaptations—

(*a*) for the reference to section 171(1) of the 1992 Act substitute a reference to paragraph 55 of that Schedule;
(*b*) for any reference to a chargeable gain under that Act substitute a reference to a chargeable realisation gain within the meaning of that Schedule that is a credit within paragraph 34(1)(*a*) of that Schedule (non-trading credits);
(*c*) for any reference to a disposal of the asset substitute a reference to its realisation within the meaning of that Schedule;
(*d*) for the reference to the relevant provisions of the 1992 Act substitute a reference to Part 6 of that Schedule.]⁴

Commentary—*Simon's Direct Tax Service* **D4.409.**
Definitions—"Accounting period", s 834(1); "the 1992 Act", s 831(1); "change in ownership of an investment company", s 769(1); "company", s 832(1); "loan relationships", s 834(1), FA 1996 s 81; "profits", s 6(4), s 834(2).
Cross references—See TA 1988 s 769 (rules for ascertaining change in ownership of a company; sub-s (3) to apply as if "benefit of losses" were a reference to "benefit of deductions" by virtue of sub-s (3A)).
Amendments—¹ This section inserted by FA 1995 Sch 26 paras 2, 5, with effect in relation to a change in ownership occurring on or after 29 November 1994 other than a change occurring in pursuance of a contract entered into on or before that date.
² Sub-s (9) substituted for sub-ss (9), (10) by FA 1996 ss 104, 105(1), Sch 14 para 40 with effect for accounting periods ending after 31 March 1996, subject to transitional provisions in FA 1996 Sch 15.
³ Words in sub-s (9) inserted by FA 2002 s 83(1)(*b*), (3) Sch 27 paras 1, 10 with effect for accounting periods beginning after 30 September 2002.
⁴ Sub-s (13) inserted by FA 2002 s 84(2), Sch 30 para 4(1), (2) with effect from the 24 July 2002.

[768D Change in ownership of company carrying on property business

(1) This section applies where there is a change in the ownership of a company carrying on a Schedule A business and—

(*a*) in the case of an investment company, either—

(i) paragraph (*a*), (*b*) or (*c*) of section 768B(1) applies, or
(ii) section 768C applies;

(*b*) in the case of a company which is not an investment company, paragraph (*a*) or (*b*) of section 768(1) applies.

(2) Where this section applies the following provisions have effect to prevent relief being given under section 392A by setting a Schedule A loss incurred by the company before the change of ownership against profits arising after the change.

(3) The accounting period in which the change of ownership occurs is treated for that purpose as two separate accounting periods, the first ending with the change and the second consisting of the remainder of the period.

(4) The profits or losses of the period in which the change occurs are apportioned to those two periods—

    (a) in the case of an investment company—

        (i) where paragraph (a), (b) or (c) of section 768B(1) applies, in accordance with Parts II and III of Schedule 28A, or

        (ii) where section 768C applies, in accordance with Parts V and VI of that Schedule, and

    (b) in the case of a company which is not an investment company, according to the length of the periods,

unless in any case the specified method of apportionment would work unjustly or unreasonably in which case such other method shall be used as appears just and reasonable.

(5) Relief under section 392A(1) against total profits of the same accounting period is available only in relation to each of those periods considered separately.

(6) A loss made in any accounting period beginning before the change of ownership may not be set off under section 392A(2) against, or deducted by virtue of section 392A(3) from—

    (a) in the case of—

        (i) an investment company where paragraph (a), (b) or (c) of section 768B(1) applies, or

        (ii) a company which is not an investment company,

    profits of an accounting period ending after the change of ownership;

    (b) in the case of an investment company where section 768C applies, from so much of those profits as represents the relevant gain within the meaning of that section.

(7) Subsections (8) and (9) of section 768 (time limits for assessment; information powers) apply for the purposes of this section as they apply for the purposes of that section.

(8) In this section—

    (a) any reference to a case where paragraph (a) or (b) of section 768(1) applies includes the case where that paragraph would apply if the reference there to a trade carried on by the company were to a Schedule A business carried on by it;

    (b) "investment company" has the same meaning as in Part IV.

(9) The provisions of this section apply in relation to an overseas property business as they apply in relation to a Schedule A business.]¹

Amendments—¹ This section inserted by FA 1998 Sch 5 para 31 with effect from the year 1998–99 for income tax purposes, and from 1 April 1998 for corporation tax, subject to the transitional provisions in FA 1998 Sch 5 Part IV.

[768E Change in ownership of company with unused non-trading loss on intangible fixed assets

(1) Where there is a change in the ownership of an investment company and either—

    (a) paragraph (a), (b) or (c) of section 768B(1) applies, or

    (b) section 768C applies,

the following provisions have effect to prevent relief being given under paragraph 35 of Schedule 29 to the Finance Act 2002 by setting a non-trading loss on intangible fixed assets incurred by the company before the change of ownership against profits arising after the change.

(2) The accounting period in which the change of ownership occurs is treated for that purpose as two separate accounting periods, the first ending with the change and the second consisting of the remainder of the period.

(3) The profits or losses of the period in which the change occurs are apportioned to those two periods—

    (a) where paragraph (a), (b) or (c) of section 768B(1) applies, in accordance with Parts 2 and 3 of Schedule 28A, or

    (b) where section 768C applies, in accordance with Parts 5 and 6 of that Schedule,

unless in any case the specified method of apportionment would work unjustly or unreasonably in which case such other method shall be used as appears just and reasonable.

(4) Relief under paragraph 35 of Schedule 29 to the Finance Act 2002 against total profits of the same accounting period is available only in relation to each of those periods considered separately.

(5) A loss made in any accounting period beginning before the change of ownership may not be set off under paragraph 35(3) of Schedule 29 to the Finance Act 2002 against—

    (a) in a case where paragraph (a), (b) or (c) of section 768B(1) applies, profits of an accounting period ending after the change of ownership;

    (b) in a case where section 768C applies, so much of those profits as represents the relevant gain within the meaning of that section.

(6) Subsections (8) and (9) of section 768 (time limits for assessment; information powers) apply for the purposes of this section as they apply for the purposes of that section.

(7) In this section "investment company" has the same meaning as in Part 4.]¹

Amendments—¹ This section inserted by FA 2002 s 84(2), Sch 30 para 4(1), (3) with effect from the 24 July 2002.

769 Rules for ascertaining change in ownership of company

(1) For the purposes of [sections 767A, [sections 767AA, 767C][7] 768, 768A, 768B[, 768C and 768D][8]][5] there is a change in the ownership of a company—

(*a*) if a single person acquires more than half the ordinary share capital of the company; or
(*b*) if two or more persons each acquire a holding of 5 per cent or more of the ordinary share capital of the company, and those holdings together amount to more than half the ordinary share capital of the company; or
(*c*) if two or more persons each acquire a holding of the ordinary share capital of the company, and the holdings together amount to more than half the ordinary share capital of the company, but disregarding a holding of less than 5 per cent unless it is an addition to an existing holding and the two holdings together amount to 5 per cent or more of the ordinary share capital of the company.

(2) In applying subsection (1) above—

(*a*) the circumstances at any two points of time with not more than three years between may be compared, and a holder at the later time may be regarded as having acquired whatever he did not hold at the earlier time, irrespective of what he has acquired or disposed of in between;
(*b*) to allow for any issue of shares or other reorganisation of capital, the comparison may be made in terms of percentage holdings of the total ordinary share capital at the respective times, so that a person whose percentage holding is greater at the later time may be regarded as having acquired a percentage holding equal to the increase;
(*c*) to decide for the purposes of subsection (1)(*b*) or (*c*) above if any person has acquired a holding of at least 5 per cent, or a holding which makes at least 5 per cent when added to an existing holding, acquisitions by, and holdings of, two or more persons who are connected persons within the meaning of section 839 shall be aggregated as if they were acquisitions by, and holdings of, one and the same person;
(*d*) any acquisition of shares under the will or on the intestacy of a deceased person[, and any gift of shares which][6] is unsolicited and made without regard to the provisions of [sections 767A, [767AA,][7] 768, 768A, 768B[, 768C and 768D][8]][5], ...][6], shall be left out of account.

[(2A) Where—

(*a*) persons, whether company members or not, possess extraordinary rights or powers under the articles of association or under any other document regulating the company, and
(*b*) because of that fact ownership of the ordinary share capital may not be an appropriate test of whether there has been a change in the ownership of the company,

then, in considering whether there has been a change in the ownership of the company for the purposes of section 767A[, 767AA or 767C][7], holdings of all kinds of share capital, including preference shares, or of any particular category of share capital, or voting power or any other kind of special power may be taken into account instead of ordinary share capital.][4]

(3) Where, because persons, whether company members or not, possess extraordinary rights or powers under the articles of association or under any other document regulating the company, ownership of the ordinary share capital may not be an appropriate test of whether there has been a major change in the persons for whose benefit the losses may ultimately enure, then, in considering whether there has been a change in the ownership of the company for the purposes of section 768 [or [768A or 768D][8]][3], holdings of all kinds of share capital, including preference shares, or of any particular category of share capital, or voting power or any other special kind of power, may be taken into account instead of ordinary share capital.

[(3A) Subsection (3) above shall apply for the purposes of sections 768B and 768C as if the reference to the benefit of losses were a reference to the benefit of deductions.][5]

(4) Where [section 768, 768A, 768B[, 768C or 768D][8]][5] has operated to restrict relief by reference to a change of ownership taking place at any time, no transaction or circumstances before that time shall be taken into account in determining whether there is any subsequent change of ownership.

(5) A change in the ownership of a company shall be disregarded for the purposes of [sections 767A, [767AA, 767C,][7] 768, 768A, 768B[, 768C and 768D][8]][5] if—

(*a*) immediately before the change the company is the 75 per cent subsidiary of another company, and
(*b*) (although there is a change in the direct ownership of the company) that other company continues after the change to own the first-mentioned company as a 75 per cent subsidiary.

[(6) If there is a change in the ownership of a company, including a change occurring by virtue of the application of this subsection but not a change which is to be disregarded under subsection (5) above, then—

(*a*) in a case falling within subsection (1)(*a*) above, the person mentioned in subsection (1)(*a*) shall be taken for the purposes of this section to acquire at the time of the change any relevant assets owned by the company;

(b) in a case falling within subsection (1)(b) above but not within subsection (1)(a) above, each of the persons mentioned in subsection (1)(b) shall be taken for the purposes of this section to acquire at the time of the change the appropriate proportion of any relevant assets owned by the company; and

(c) in any other case, each of the persons mentioned in paragraph (c) of subsection (1) above (other than any whose holding is disregarded under that paragraph) shall be taken for the purposes of this section to acquire at the time of the change the appropriate proportion of any relevant assets owned by the company.][1]

[(6A) In subsection (6) above—

"the appropriate proportion", in relation to one of two or more persons mentioned in subsection (1)(b) or (c) above, means a proportion corresponding to the proportion which the percentage of the ordinary share capital acquired by him bears to the percentage of that capital acquired by all those persons taken together; and

"relevant assets", in relation to a company, means—

(a) any ordinary share capital of another company, and
(b) any property or rights which under subsection (3) above may be taken into account instead of ordinary share capital of another company.][1]

[(6B) Notwithstanding that at any time a company ("the subsidiary company") is a 75 per cent subsidiary of another company ("the parent company") it shall not be treated at that time as such a subsidiary for the purposes of this section unless, additionally, at that time—

(a) the parent company would be beneficially entitled to not less than 75 per cent of any profits available for distribution to equity holders of the subsidiary company; and
(b) the parent company would be beneficially entitled to not less than 75 per cent of any assets of the subsidiary company available for distribution to its equity holders on a winding-up.][1]

[(6C) Schedule 18 shall apply for the purposes of subsection (6B) above as it applies for the purposes of section 413(7).][1]

(7) For the purposes of this section—

(a) references to ownership shall be construed as references to beneficial ownership, and references to acquisition shall be construed accordingly;
(b), (c) ...[2]
(d) "shares" includes stock.

(8) If any acquisition of ordinary share capital or other property or rights taken into account in determining that there has been a change of ownership of a company was made in pursuance of a contract of sale or option or other contract, or the acquisition was made by a person holding such a contract, then the time when the change in the ownership of the company took place shall be determined as if the acquisition had been made when the contract was made with the holder or when the benefit of it was assigned to him so that, in the case of a person exercising an option to purchase shares, he shall be regarded as having purchased the shares when he acquired the option.

[(9) Subsection (8) above shall not apply in relation to section 767A[, 767AA or 767C][7].][4]

Commentary—*Simon's Direct Tax Service* D2.410.
Statement of Practice SP 10/91—Revenue's interpretation of the term "a major change in the nature or conduct of a trade or business".
Definitions—"Company", s 832(1), (2); "ordinary share capital", s 832(1); "75 per cent subsidiary", s 838.
Cross references—See TA 1988 s 245(7) (application of this section for the purposes of restriction of relief for surplus ACT on change of ownership of a company).
TA 1988 s 245A(4) (application of this section for the purposes of restriction of relief for surplus ACT on change of ownership of a subsidiary).
TA 1988 s 245B(5) (application of this section where owing to change of ownership of company there is restriction of set-off of ACT against corporation tax on capital gains).
Corporation Tax (Treatment of Unrelieved Surplus Advance Corporation Tax) Regulations, SI 1999/358 reg 16 (application of s 768(8), (9) and s 769 as if the reference to the benefit of losses in sub-s (3) above were a reference to the benefit of unrelieved surplus ACT).
Also see Taxline 1993/78—situation where a company is acquired by a new holding company and trade is transferred up to the parent is not covered by s 769(5) and thus there may be a change of ownership for the purposes of s 768 (not reproduced in this work).
Amendments—[1] Sub-ss (6) to (6C) substituted for sub-s (6) by FA 1989 s 100 where the change of ownership of a company would be treated as occurring after 13 March 1989.
[2] Sub-s (7)(b), (c) repealed by FA 1989 s 100 and Sch 17 Pt IV.
[3] Words in sub-s (3) inserted by FA 1991 Sch 15 para 20(2).
[4] Sub-ss (2A), (9) inserted by FA 1994 s 135(2), (4)–(6) in relation to any change in ownership occurring on or after 30 November 1993 other than a change occurring in pursuance of a contract entered into before that date.
[5] Words in sub-ss (1), (2)(d), (4), (5) substituted, and sub-s (3A) inserted, by FA 1995 Sch 26 paras 4, 5, with effect in relation to a change in ownership occurring on or after 29 November 1994 other than a change occurring in pursuance of a contract entered into on or before that date.
[6] Words in sub-ss (2)(d) substituted and repealed, by FA 1996 s 134(1), (2), Sch 20 para 37, Sch 41 Pt V(10) with effect as respects accounting periods ending after 30 June 1999 (by virtue of Finance Act 1994, Section 199, (Appointed Day) Order, SI 1998/3173 art 2).
[7] Words in sub-ss (1), (2)(d), (2A), (5) and (9) inserted by FA 1998 s 116(5) with effect in relation to changes in ownership occurring after 1 July 1997 other than any change occurring in pursuance of a contract entered into before 2 July 1997.
[8] Words in sub-ss (1), (2)(d), (3), (4) and (5) substituted by FA 1998 Sch 5 para 32 with effect for 1998–99 and subsequent years of assessment for income tax purposes, and from 1 April 1998 for corporation tax, subject to the transitional provisions in FA 1998 Sch 5 Part IV.

Transactions between associated persons

770 Sales etc at an undervalue or overvalue

Commentary—*Simon's Direct Tax Service* **B3.1827.**
Amendments—This section substituted by new s 770A as inserted by FA 1998 s 108(1) with effect (in relation to provision made or imposed at any time)—

(*a*) for the purposes of corporation tax, as respects accounting periods ending on or after the day appointed under FA 1994 s 199 (1 July 1999 by virtue of Finance Act 1994, Section 199, (Appointed Day) Order, SI 1998/3173 art 2); and
(*b*) for the purposes of income tax, as respects any year of assessment ending on or after that day.

[770A Provision not at arm's length

Schedule 28AA (which deals with provision made or imposed otherwise than at arm's length) shall have effect.][1]

Simon's Tax Cases—*Waterloo plc v IRC* [2002] STC(SCD) 95*.
Amendments—[1] This section inserted by FA 1998 s 108(1) with effect (in relation to provision made or imposed at any time)—

(*a*) for the purposes of corporation tax, as respects accounting periods ending on or after the day appointed under FA 1994 s 199 (1 July 1999 by virtue of Finance Act 1994, Section 199, (Appointed Day) Order, SI 1998/3173 art 2); and
(*b*) for the purposes of income tax, as respects any year of assessment ending on or after that day.

771 Transactions by petroleum companies

Commentary—*Simon's Direct Tax Service* **B3.1827.**
Amendments—This section substituted by new s 770A as inserted by FA 1998 s 108(1) with effect (in relation to provision made or imposed at any time)—

(*a*) for the purposes of corporation tax, as respects accounting periods ending on or after the day appointed under FA 1994 s 199 (1 July 1999 by virtue of Finance Act 1994, Section 199, (Appointed Day) Order, SI 1998/3173 art 2); and
(*b*) for the purposes of income tax, as respects any year of assessment ending on or after that day.

772 Information for purposes of section 770, and appeals

Commentary—*Simon's Direct Tax Service* **B3.1827.**
Amendments—This section substituted by new s 770A as inserted by FA 1998 s 108(1) with effect (in relation to provision made or imposed at any time)—

(*a*) for the purposes of corporation tax, as respects accounting periods ending on or after the day appointed under FA 1994 s 199 (1 July 1999 by virtue of Finance Act 1994, Section 199, (Appointed Day) Order, SI 1998/3173 art 2); and
(*b*) for the purposes of income tax, as respects any year of assessment ending on or after that day.

773 Interpretation of sections 770 and 771

Commentary—*Simon's Direct Tax Service* **B3.1827.**
Amendments—This section substituted by new s 770A as inserted by FA 1998 s 108(1) with effect (in relation to provision made or imposed at any time)—

(*a*) for the purposes of corporation tax, as respects accounting periods ending on or after the day appointed under FA 1994 s 199 (1 July 1999 by virtue of Finance Act 1994, Section 199, (Appointed Day) Order, SI 1998/3173 art 2); and
(*b*) for the purposes of income tax, as respects any year of assessment ending on or after that day.

774 Transactions between dealing company and associated company

(1) Subject to the provisions of this section, where—

(*a*) a dealing company becomes entitled to a deduction, in computing the profits or gains of the company for tax purposes for any period, in respect of the depreciation in the value of any right subsisting against an associated company, being a non-dealing company; or
(*b*) a dealing company makes any payment to such an associated company, being a payment in respect of which the dealing company is entitled to a deduction in computing its profits or gains for tax purposes for any period;

and the depreciation or payment is not brought into account in computing the profits or gains of the non-dealing company, that company shall be deemed to have received on the last day of the period income of an amount equal to the amount of the deduction and shall be chargeable in respect thereof under Case VI of Schedule D.

(2) Where the non-dealing company is carrying on a trade, the income referred to in subsection (1) above shall, if the company so elects, not be so chargeable but shall be deemed to have been a receipt of the trade, or, if the company is carrying on more than one trade, to have been a receipt of such one of the trades as the company may choose.

(3) Where the non-dealing company is carrying on, or was formed to carry on a trade, then if—

(*a*) either—
(i) the right subsisting against it was a right to the repayment of moneys lent for meeting expenditure which has proved (in whole or in part) abortive, or
(ii) the payment to the company was made for meeting such expenditure, and
(*b*) that expenditure is such that the company is not entitled in respect of it to any allowance or deduction in computing losses or gains,

subsection (1) above shall not apply in so far as the expenditure proved abortive.

(4) For the purposes of this section—

(a) "company" includes any body corporate;

(b) "dealing company" means a company dealing in securities, land or buildings and includes any company whose profits on the sale of securities, land or buildings are part of its trading profits;

(c) "non-dealing company" means any company which is not a dealing company;

(d) two or more companies shall be treated as associated companies if one has control of the other or others, or any person has control of both or all of them;

(e) references to a company ("the first company") having control of another company ("the second company") shall be construed as references to the first company having control of the second company either by itself or in conjunction with any person having control over the first company, and "control" has the meaning given by section 840;

(f) "securities" includes shares and stock.

(5) Where it appears to the Board that by reason of any transaction or transactions a person may by virtue of this section have incurred any liability to tax, the Board may by notice served on him require him, within such time not less than 28 days as may be specified in the notice, to furnish information in his possession with respect to the transaction or any of the transactions, being information as to matters, specified in the notice, which are relevant to the question whether he has incurred any such liability to tax.

Commentary—*Simon's Direct Tax Service* **D2.527.**
Revenue Internal Guidance—Inspector's manual IM 4670–4672 (background to legislation with example).
Definitions—"The Board", s 832(1); "control", s 840; "notice", s 832(1); "profits or gains", s 833(1); "Schedule D", s 18(1); "tax", s 832(3); "trade", s 832(1).

Other provisions

775 Sale by individual of income derived from his personal activities

(1) Subject to subsection (7) below, this section has effect where—

(a) transactions or arrangements are effected or made to exploit the earning capacity of an individual in any occupation by putting some other person in a position to enjoy all or any part of the profits or gains or other income, or of the receipts, derived from the individual's activities in that occupation, or anything derived directly or indirectly from any such income or receipts; and

(b) as part of, or in connection with, or in consequence of, the transactions or arrangements any capital amount is obtained by the individual for himself or for any other person; and

(c) the main object or one of the main objects of the transactions was the avoidance or reduction of liability to income tax.

(2) Any such capital amount shall for all the purposes of the Income Tax Acts be treated as being earned income of the individual which arises when the capital amount is receivable, and which is chargeable to tax under Case VI of Schedule D.

(3) In this section—

(a) references to any occupation are references to any activities of any of the kinds pursued in any profession or vocation, irrespective of whether the individual is engaged in a profession or vocation, or is employed by or holds office under some other person; and

(b) references in subsection (1) above to income or receipts include references to payments for any description of copyright or licence or franchise or other right deriving its value from the activities, including past activities, of the individual.

(4) This section shall not apply to a capital amount obtained from the disposal—

(a) of assets (including any goodwill) of a profession or vocation, or of a share in a partnership which is carrying on a profession or vocation, or

(b) of shares in a company,

in so far as the value of what is disposed of, at the time of disposal, is attributable to the value of the profession or vocation as a going concern, or as the case may be to the value of the company's business, as a going concern.

(5) If the value of the profession, vocation or business as a going concern is derived to a material extent from prospective income or receipts derived directly or indirectly from the individual's activities in the occupation, and for which, when all capital amounts are disregarded, the individual will not have received full consideration, whether as a partner in a partnership or as an employee or otherwise, subsection (4) above shall not exempt the part of the capital amount so derived.

(6) In subsections (4) and (5) above references to the company's business include references to the business of any other company in which it holds shares directly or indirectly.

(7) Where on any occasion an individual obtains a capital amount consisting of any property or right which derives substantially the whole of its value from the activities of the individual, or (as in the case where the individual acquires a stock option and subsequently exercises the stock option) there are two or more occasions on which an individual obtains a capital amount consisting of any such property or right, then—

(a) tax under this section shall not be charged on any such occasion, but (*b*) without prejudice to the generality of the provisions of this section or section 777, tax under this section shall be charged on the occasion when the capital amount, or any such capital amount, is sold or otherwise realised, and shall be so charged by reference to the proceeds of sale or the realised value.

(8) For the purposes of subsection (1)(*b*) above the cases where an individual obtains any capital amount for some other person include cases where the individual has put some other person in a position to receive the capital amount by providing that other person with something of value derived, directly or indirectly, from the individual's activities in the occupation.

(9) This section shall apply to all persons, whether resident in the United Kingdom or not, if the occupation of the individual is carried on wholly or partly in the United Kingdom.

Commentary—*Simon's Direct Tax Service* **E1.702–704.**
Revenue Internal Guidance—Inspector's manual IM 4688 (circumstances in which cases referred to Special Investigations Section).
Definitions—''Capital amount'', s 777(13); ''company'', s 777(13); ''the Income Tax Acts'', s 831(1)(*b*); ''profits or gains'', s 833(1); ''shares'', s 777(13); ''Schedule D'', s 18(1); ''tax'', s 832(3); ''United Kingdom'', s 830(1).
Cross references—See TA 1988 s 777 (supplementary provisions).
TA 1988 s 778 (Board's power to obtain information for the purposes of this section).

776 Transactions in land: taxation of capital gains

(1) This section is enacted to prevent the avoidance of tax by persons concerned with land or the development of land.

(2) This section applies wherever—

(*a*) land, or any property deriving its value from land, is acquired with the sole or main object of realising a gain from disposing of the land; or
(*b*) land is held as trading stock; or
(*c*) land is developed with the sole or main object of realising a gain from disposing of the land when developed;

and any gain of a capital nature is obtained from the disposal of the land—

(i) by the person acquiring, holding or developing the land, or by any connected person, or
(ii) where any arrangement or scheme is effected as respects the land which enables a gain to be realised by any indirect method, or by any series of transactions, by any person who is a party to, or concerned in, the arrangement or scheme;

and this subsection applies whether any such person obtains the gain for himself or for any other person.

(3) Where this section applies, the whole of any such gain shall for all the purposes of the Tax Acts be treated—

(*a*) as being income which arises when the gain is realised; and which constitutes profits or gains chargeable to tax under Case VI of Schedule D for the chargeable period in which the gain is realised; and ·
(*b*) subject to the following provisions of this section, as being income of the person by whom the gain is realised.

(4) For the purposes of this section—

(*a*) land is disposed of if, by any one or more transactions, or by any arrangement or scheme, whether concerning the land or property deriving its value from the land, the property in the land, or control over the land, is effectually disposed of; and
(*b*) references in subsection (2) above to the acquisition or development of property with the sole or main object of realising the gain from disposing of the land shall be construed accordingly.

(5) For those purposes—

(*a*) where, whether by a premature sale or otherwise, a person directly or indirectly transmits the opportunity of making a gain to another person, that other person's gain is obtained for him by the first-mentioned person; and
(*b*) any number of transactions may be regarded as constituting a single arrangement or scheme if a common purpose can be discerned in them, or if there is other sufficient evidence of a common purpose.

(6) For the purposes of this section, such method of computing a gain shall be adopted as is just and reasonable in the circumstances, taking into account the value of what is obtained for disposing of the land, and allowing only such expenses as are attributable to the land disposed of; and in applying this subsection—

(*a*) where a freehold is acquired and the reversion is retained on disposal, account may be taken of the way in which the [profits][2] under Case I of Schedule D of a person dealing in land are computed in such a case; or
(*b*) account may be taken of the adjustments to be made in computing such [profits][2] under subsections (2) and (3) of section 99.

In the application of this subsection to Scotland, ''freehold'' means the estate or interest of the proprietor of the *dominium utile* or, in the case of property other than feudal property, of the owner, and ''reversion'' means the interest of the landlord in property subject to a lease.

(7) Subsection (2)(*c*) above shall not apply to so much of any gain as is fairly attributable to the period, if any, before the intention to develop the land was formed, and which would not fall under paragraph (*a*) or (*b*) of that subsection; and in applying this subsection account shall be taken of the treatment under Case I of Schedule D of a person who appropriates land as trading stock.

(8) If all or any part of the gain accruing to any person is derived from value, or an opportunity of realising a gain, provided directly or indirectly by some other person, whether or not put at the disposal of the first-mentioned person, subsection (3)(*b*) above shall apply to the gain, or that part of it, with the substitution of that other person for the person by whom the gain was realised.

(9) This section shall not apply to a gain accruing to an individual which by virtue of sections [222 to 226 of the 1992][1] Act (private residences) is exempt from capital gains tax, or which would be so exempt but for the provisions of section [224(3)][1] of that Act (residences acquired partly with a view to making a gain).

(10) Where—

    (*a*) there is a disposal of shares in—

        (i) a company which holds land as trading stock; or

        (ii) a company which owns directly or indirectly 90 per cent or more of the ordinary share capital of another company which holds land as trading stock; and

    (*b*) all the land so held is disposed of—

        (i) in the normal course of its trade by the company which held it, and

        (ii) so as to procure that all opportunity of profit in respect of the land arises to that company,

then this section shall not by virtue of subsection (2)(i) above apply to any gain to the holder of shares as being a gain on property deriving value from that land (but without prejudice to any liability under subsection (2)(ii) above).

(11) Where a person who considers that paragraph (*a*) or (*c*) of subsection (2) above may apply as respects a gain of a capital nature which that person has obtained from the disposal of land, or which he would obtain from a proposed disposal of land, supplies to the inspector to whom he makes his return of income written particulars showing how the gain has arisen or would arise—

    (*a*) the inspector shall, within 30 days from his receipt of the particulars, notify that person whether or not he is satisfied that, in the circumstances as described in the particulars, the gain will not, or would not, be chargeable to tax on that person under this section; and

    (*b*) if the inspector notifies that person that he is so satisfied, the gain shall not be chargeable on that person under this section.

(12) If the particulars given under this section with respect to the gain are not such as to make full and accurate disclosure of all facts and considerations relating thereto which are material to be known to the inspector, any notification given by the inspector under subsection (11) above shall be void.

(13) In this section—

    (*a*) references to the land include references to all or any part of the land, and "land" includes buildings, and any estate or interest in land or buildings;

    (*b*) references to property deriving its value from land include—

        (i) any shareholding in a company, or any partnership interest, or any interest in settled property, deriving its value directly or indirectly from land, and

        (ii) any option, consent or embargo affecting the disposition of land;

and for the purposes of this section any question whether a person is connected with another shall be determined in accordance with section 839.

(14) This section shall apply to all persons, whether resident in the United Kingdom or not, if all or any part of the land in question is situated in the United Kingdom.

Commentary—*Simon's Direct Tax Service* **B3.636.**
Revenue Internal Guidance—Inspector's manual IM 4721 (section can apply to commercially motivated transaction and to transactions where land is traded indirectly eg, via share sales).
IM 4723 (section does not apply to simple purchase and sale of land which falls short of trading).
IM 4729 (the obtaining of planning consent does not, by itself, constitute development).
IM 4733–4735 ("slice of action" schemes caught).
IM 4736 ("diversion" schemes caught; eg transfer to intermediate non-resident purchaser and seller, or gift by a land dealer to connected individual).
IM 4740 (sub-s (6) Case I principles applied in computing gain).
IM 4748 (circumstances where cases must be submitted to head office).
Simon's Tax Cases—*Sugarwhite v Budd* [1988] STC 533*; *Lord Advocate v Mckenna* [1989] STC 485*.
s 776(1), *Page v Lowther* [1983] STC 799*.
s 776(2), *Yuill v Wilson* [1980] STC 460*; *Chilcott v IRC* [1982] STC 1*; *Page v Lowther* [1983] STC 799*; *Newman v Pepper, Newman v Morgan* [2000] STC (SCD) 345.
s 776(3), (8), *Yuill v Wilson* [1980] STC 460*; *Yuill v Fletcher* [1984] STC 401*.
s 776(4), (10), *Chilcott v IRC* [1982] STC 1*.
Definitions—"the 1992 Act", s 831(3); "capital gains tax", s 831(5); "chargeable period", s 832(1); "company", s 777(13); "connected person", s 839; "inspector", s 832(1); "ordinary share capital", s 832(1); "Schedule D", s 18(1); "shares", s 777(13); "tax", s 832(3); "the Tax Acts", s 831(2); "United Kingdom", s 830(1).
Cross references—See TA 1988 s 777 (supplementary provisions).
TA 1988 s 778 (Board's power to obtain information for the purposes of this section).
FA 2000 s 46(2) (exemption under FA 2000 s 46(1) for income of a charity is not granted in respect of income chargeable to tax under Schedule D Case VI by virtue of this section).
Amendments—[1] Words in sub-s (9) substituted by TCGA 1992 Sch 10 para 14(1), (50).

² Word "profits" substituted for "profits or gains" in sub-s (6)(a), (b) by FA 1998 Sch 7 para 1 with effect from 31 July 1998.
Prospective amendments—Words in sub-s (6) to be substituted by the Abolition of Feudal Tenure etc (Scotland) Act 2000 s 76(1), Sch 12 Pt I para 50(3), with effect from a day to be appointed.

777 Provisions supplementary to sections 775 and 776

(1) This section has effect to supplement sections 775 and 776, and those sections and this section are together referred to as the relevant provisions.

(2) In applying the relevant provisions account shall be taken of any method, however indirect, by which—

(a) any property or right is transferred or transmitted; or

(b) the value of any property or right is enhanced or diminished;

and accordingly the occasion of the transfer or transmission of any property or right, however indirect, and the occasion when the value of any property or right is enhanced, may be an occasion when, under sections 775 and 776, tax becomes chargeable.

(3) Subsection (2) above applies in particular—

(a) to sales, contracts and other transactions made otherwise than for full consideration or for more than full consideration; and

(b) to any method by which any property or right, or the control of any property or right, is transferred or transmitted by assigning share capital or other rights in a company or any partnership or interest in settled property; and

(c) to the creation of any option or consent or embargo affecting the disposition of any property or right, and to the consideration given for the option, or for the giving of the consent or the release of the embargo; and

(d) to the disposal of any property or right on the winding up, dissolution or termination of any company, partnership or trust.

(4) In ascertaining for the purposes of the relevant provisions the intentions of any person, the objects and powers of any company, partners or trustees, as set out in any memorandum, articles of association or other document, shall not be conclusive.

(5) In order to ascertain whether and to what extent the value of any property or right is derived from any other property or right, value may be traced through any number of companies, partnerships and trusts, and the property held by any company, partnership or trust shall be attributed to the shareholders, partners or beneficiaries at each stage in such manner as is appropriate in the circumstances.

(6) In applying the relevant provisions—

(a) any expenditure or receipt or consideration or other amount may be apportioned by such method as is just and reasonable in the circumstances;

(b) all such valuations shall be made as are appropriate to give effect to sections 775 and 776.

(7) For the purposes of the relevant provisions (and in particular for the purpose of the reference in section 775 to an individual putting some other person in a position to enjoy income or receipts) partners, or the trustees of settled property, or personal representatives, may be regarded as persons distinct from the individuals or other persons who are for the time being partners or trustees or personal representatives.

(8) Where a person is assessed to tax under the relevant provisions in respect of consideration receivable by another person—

(a) he shall be entitled to recover from that other person any part of that tax which he has paid; and

(b) if any part of that tax remains unpaid at the expiration of six months from the date when it became due and payable, it shall be recoverable from that other person as though he were the person assessed, but without prejudice to the right to recover it from the person actually assessed;

and for the purposes of paragraph (a) above the Board or an inspector shall on request furnish a certificate specifying the amount of income in respect of which tax has been paid, and the amount of tax so paid; and the certificate shall be conclusive evidence of any facts stated in it.

For the purposes of this subsection any income which a person is treated as having by virtue of sections 775 and 776 shall, subject to section 833(3), be treated as the highest part of his income.

(9) If it appears to the Board that any person entitled to any consideration or other amount taxable under section 775 and 776 is not resident in the United Kingdom, the Board may direct that section 349(1) shall apply to any payment forming part of that amount as if it were an annual payment charged with tax under Case III of Schedule D, but without prejudice to the final determination of the liability of that person, including any liability under subsection (8)(b) above.

(10) Sections 775 and 776 have effect subject to Part XV and to any other provision of the Tax Acts deeming income to belong to a particular person.

(11) Where under section 776(2)(c) any person is charged to tax on the realisation of a gain, and the computation of the gain proceeded on the footing that the land or some other property was appropriated at any time as trading stock, that land or other property shall be treated on that footing

also for the purposes of section [161 of the 1992][1] Act (property becoming or ceasing to be stock in trade).

(12) Where under section 775(1)(b) or 776(8) the person charged to tax is a person other than the person for whom the capital amount was obtained or the person by whom the gain was realised, and the tax has been paid, then, for the purposes of sections [37 and 39 of the 1992][1] Act (profits taxable as income excluded from tax on capital gains), the person for whom the capital amount was obtained or the person by whom the gain was realised shall be regarded as having been charged to that tax.

(13) For the purposes of the relevant provisions—

"capital amount" means any amount, in money or money's worth, which, apart from the sections 775 and 776, does not fall to be included in any computation of income for purposes of the Tax Acts, and other expressions including the word "capital" shall be construed accordingly;

"company" includes any body corporate; and

"share" includes stock;

and any amount in money or money's worth shall not be regarded as having become receivable by some person until that person can effectively enjoy or dispose of it.

Commentary—*Simon's Direct Tax Service* B3.636–646; E1.702–709.
Simon's Tax Cases— s 777(9), *Pardoe v Entergy Power Development Corp* [1999] STC 286.
s 777(13), *Yuill v Wilson* [1980] STC 460*; *Yuill v Fletcher* [1984] STC 401*; *Lord Advocate v Mckenna* [1989] STC 485*.
Definitions—"The 1992 Act", s 831(3); "the Board", s 832(1); "company", s 831(1), (2); "control", s 840; "inspector", s 832(1); "Schedule D", s 18(1); "tax", s 832(3); "the Tax Acts", s 831(2); "United Kingdom", s 830(1).
Amendments—[1] Words in sub-ss (11), (12) substituted by TCGA 1992 Sch 10 para 14(1), (51).

778 Power to obtain information

(1) The Board or an inspector may by notice require any person to furnish them within such time as the Board or the inspector may direct (not being less than 30 days) with such particulars as the Board or the inspector think necessary for the purposes of sections 775 and 776.

(2) The particulars which a person must furnish under this section, if he is required by a notice from the Board or the inspector so to do, include particulars—

(a) as to transactions or arrangements with respect to which he is or was acting on behalf of others;

(b) as to transactions or arrangements which in the opinion of the Board or the inspector should properly be investigated for the purposes of sections 775 and 776 notwithstanding that, in the opinion of the person to whom the notice is given, no liability to tax arises under those sections; and

(c) as to whether the person to whom the notice is given has taken or is taking any, and if so what, part in any, and if so what, transactions or arrangements of a description specified in the notice.

(3) Notwithstanding anything in subsection (2) above, a solicitor—

(a) shall not be deemed for the purposes of paragraph (c) of that subsection to have taken part in any transaction or arrangement by reason only that he has given professional advice to a client in connection with the transaction or arrangement, and

(b) shall not, in relation to anything done by him on behalf of a client, be compellable under this section, except with the consent of his client, to do more than state that he is or was acting on behalf of a client, and give the name and address of his client.

Commentary—*Simon's Direct Tax Service* B3.643; E1.709.
Simon's Tax Cases—s 778(1), (2), *Essex v IRC* [1980] STC 378*.
Definitions—"The Board", s 832(1); "inspector", s 832(1); "notice", s 832(1); "tax", s 832(3).

779 Sale and lease-back: limitation on tax reliefs

(1) If land or any estate or interest in land is transferred from one person to another and—

(a) as a result of a lease of the land or any part of the land granted at that time or subsequently by the transferee to the transferor, or

(b) as a result of any other transaction or series of transactions affecting the land or any estate or interest in the land,

the transferor, or any person who is associated with the transferor, becomes liable at the time of the transfer or subsequently to pay any rent under a lease of the land or any part of the land, this section shall apply to all rent due under the lease from the transferor, or from any person who is associated with the transferor.

(2) If—

(a) land or any estate or interest in land is transferred from one person to another, and

(b) as a result of any transaction or series of transactions affecting the land or any estate or interest in the land, the transferor, or any person who is associated with the transferor, becomes liable at the time of the transfer or subsequently to make any payment (other than rent under a lease) for which any relevant tax relief is available, being a payment by way of rentcharge on the land or any part of the land or a payment in any other way connected with the land,

then this section shall apply to all such payments under the rentcharge or other transaction due from the transferor, or from any person who is associated with the transferor.

(3) The references in subsections (1) and (2) above to the transfer of an estate or interest in land include references to—

    (*a*) the granting of a lease or any other transaction involving the creation of a new estate or interest in the land;

    (*b*) the transfer of the lessee's interest under a lease by surrender or forfeiture of the lease; and

    (*c*) any transaction or series of transactions affecting land or an estate or interest in land, such that some person is the owner, or one of the owners, before and after the carrying out of the transaction or transactions, but another person becomes or ceases to become one of the owners;

and in relation to any such transaction or series of transactions any person who is an owner before the carrying out of the transaction or transactions, and is not the sole owner thereafter, shall be regarded for the purposes of this section as a transferor.

(4) A deduction by way of any relevant tax relief, being a deduction in respect of rent or of any other payment to which this section applies, shall not exceed the commercial rent for the period for which the rent or other payment is made of the land in respect of which that payment is made.

(5) If—

    (*a*) under subsection (4) above part of a payment which would otherwise be allowable as a deduction by way of any relevant tax relief is not so allowable, and

    (*b*) one or more subsequent payments are made by the transferor, or a person who is associated with the transferor, under the lease or other transaction,

that part of the first-mentioned payment may be carried forward and treated for the purposes of any such deduction by way of tax relief as if it were made at the time when the next of those subsequent payments was made, and so made for the period for which that subsequent payment was made.

(6) For the purposes of subsection (4) above—

    (*a*) if more than one payment is made for the same period the payments shall be taken together;

    (*b*) if payments are made for periods which overlap, the payments shall be apportioned, and the apportioned payments which belong to the common part of the overlapping periods shall be taken together;

    (*c*) the preceding references to payments include references to parts of payments which under subsection (5) above are treated as if made at a time subsequent to that at which they were made, and to the extent that a part of a payment so carried forward under that subsection is not so allowable as a deduction by way of tax relief, it may again be carried forward under that subsection;

    (*d*) so much of any payment as is in respect of services or the use of assets or rates usually borne by the tenant shall be excluded, and in determining the amount to be so excluded provisions in any lease or agreement fixing the payments or parts of payments which are in respect of services or the use of assets may be overridden.

(7) A payment made for a period all of which falls more than one year after the payment is made shall be treated for the purposes of this section as made for that period of one year beginning with the date on which the payment was made, and a payment for a period part of which falls after the end of that year shall be treated for those purposes as if a corresponding part of the payment was made for that year (and no part for any later period).

(8) For the purpose of making a comparison under subsection (4) above between a payment consisting of rent under a lease ("the actual lease"), or such payments taken together, and the commercial rent of the land, "commercial rent" shall mean the rent which might be expected to be paid under a lease of the land negotiated in the open market at the time when the actual lease was created, being a lease which is of the same duration as the actual lease, which is, as respects liability for maintenance and repairs, subject to the terms and conditions of the actual lease and which provides for rent payable at uniform intervals and—

    (*a*) at a uniform rate, or

    (*b*) if the rent payable under the actual lease is rent at a progressive rate (and such that the amount of rent payable for any year is never less than the amount payable for any previous year), a rent which progresses by gradations proportionate to those provided by the actual lease.

(9) For the purpose of making a comparison under subsection (4) above between a payment which does not consist of rent under a lease (or such a payment taken together with other payments) and the commercial rent of the land, "commercial rent" shall mean the rent which might be expected to be paid under a tenant's repairing lease negotiated in the open market at the time when the transaction was effected under which the payment or payments became due, being—

    (*a*) where the period over which payments are to be made under that transaction is not less than 200 years, or the obligation to make such payments is perpetual, a lease for 200 years; and

    (*b*) where that period is less than 200 years, a lease which is of the same duration as that period.

(10) In this section references to rent under a lease include references to rent which the person entitled to the lease is under subsection (4), (5) or (6) of section 37 or under section 87 treated, for any purpose, as paying in respect of land comprised in the lease, and such rent shall be treated for the purposes of this section as having been paid from day to day as it has become due.

(11) For the purposes of this section the following persons shall be deemed to be associated with one another, that is—

(a) the transferor in any such transaction as is described in subsection (1) or (2) above, and the transferor in another such transaction, if those two persons are acting in concert, or if the two transactions are in any way reciprocal, and any person who is an associate of either of those associated transferors;

(b) any two or more bodies corporate participating in, or incorporated for the purposes of, a scheme for the reconstruction of any body or bodies corporate or for the amalgamation of any two or more bodies corporate;

(c) any persons who are associates as defined in section 783(10).

(12) In this section—

"asset" means any description of property or rights other than land or an interest in land;

"lease" includes an underlease, sublease or any tenancy or licence, and any agreement for a lease, underlease, sublease or tenancy or licence and, in the case of land outside the United Kingdom, any interest corresponding to a lease as so defined; and in relation to such land, expressions in this section relating to interests in land and their disposition shall be construed accordingly;

"rent" includes any payment made under a lease; and

"tenant's repairing lease" means a lease where the lessee is under an obligation to maintain and repair the whole, or substantially the whole, of the premises comprised in the lease.

(13) For the purposes of this section the following are deductions by way of relevant tax relief, that is to say—

(a) a deduction in computing profits or gains chargeable under Schedule A ...[1];

(b) a deduction in computing [profits][2] or losses of a trade, profession or vocation for the purposes of tax;

(c) a deduction in computing profits or gains chargeable under Case VI of Schedule D, or in computing any loss for which relief is allowable under section 392 or 396;

(d) allowance of a payment under section 75 or 76;

(e) a deduction from emoluments to be assessed under Schedule E made in pursuance of section 198(1) or allowable in computing losses in an employment for tax purposes;

(f) a deduction allowable for tax purposes in computing profits or gains or losses arising from woodlands.

(14) This section shall not apply if the transfer described in subsection (1) or (2) above was on or before 14th April 1964.

Commentary—*Simon's Direct Tax Service* B3.647.
Definitions—"Emoluments", s 131(1); "Schedule A", s 15(1); "Schedule D", s 18(1); "Schedule E", s 19(1); "tax", s 832(3); "trade", s 832(1); "United Kingdom", s 830(1).
Cross references—See TA 1988 s 780 (sale and lease–back of leases having not more than 50 years to run: taxation of consideration received on sale).
TA 1988 s 781 (sale and lease–back of assets other than land).
FA 1999 Sch 6 para 6 (sale and lease-back arrangements are excluded from provisions in FA 1999 Sch 6 concerning the tax treatment of receipts by way of reverse premiums).
Note—This section does not apply to any payment which falls to made under a public-private partnership agreement by virtue of the Greater London Authority Act 1999, s 419, Sch 33, para 13.
Amendments—[1] Words omitted from sub-s (13)(a) repealed by FA 1995 Sch 6 para 27, Sch 29 Pt VIII(1), with effect from the year 1995–96, and, so far as making provision having effect for the purposes of corporation tax, in relation to accounting periods ending after 30 March 1995 (this amendment did not apply in relation to certain sources of income which ceased during the year 1995–96; see FA 1995 s 39(5)).
[2] Word in sub-s (13)(b) substituted by FA 1998 Sch 7 para 1 with effect from 31 July 1998.

780 Sale and lease-back: taxation of consideration received

(1) If, in any case where a person ("the lessee") who is a lessee of land under a lease having not more than 50 years to run ("the original lease") is entitled in respect of the rent under the lease to a deduction by way of tax relief which is a relevant tax relief for the purposes of section 779—

(a) the lessee assigns the original lease to another person, or surrenders it to his landlord, for a consideration which apart from this section would not be taxable otherwise than as capital in the hands of the lessee, and

(b) there is granted or assigned to the lessee another lease ("the new lease") of or including the whole or any part of the land which was the subject of the original lease for a term not exceeding 15 years;

then, subject to the following provisions of this section, the provisions of this Act providing for deductions or allowances by way of tax relief in respect of payments of rent shall apply in relation to the rent under the new lease, and for the purposes of the Tax Acts a proportion of the consideration received by the lessee shall be treated not as a capital receipt but in accordance with subsection (3) below.

(2) For the purposes of this section—

(a) if the aggregate of the rent payable under the new lease in respect of any rental period ending on a date falling before the 15th anniversary of the date on which the term of the new lease begins is greater than the aggregate of the rent payable under the new lease in respect of the period of equal duration beginning on the day following that date, then unless the term of the new lease would be treated as ending on an earlier date by virtue of paragraph (*b*) below, that term shall be treated as ending on that date;

(*b*) if under the terms of the new lease—

(i) the lessor or the lessee has power to determine the new lease at a time before the expiry of the term for which it was granted, or

(ii) the lessee has power to vary his obligations under the new lease so as to reduce the rent which he would otherwise have to pay or in any other manner beneficial to him,

then, unless the term of the new lease would be treated as ending on an earlier date by virtue of paragraph (*a*) above, that term shall be treated as ending on the earliest date with effect from which, in exercise of that power, the lessor or the lessee could determine the new lease or, as the case may be, the lessee could so vary his obligations;

and in any case where a rentcharge payable by the lessee is secured on the whole or any part of the property which is the subject of the new lease, the rent payable under the new lease shall be treated for the purposes of paragraphs (*a*) and (*b*) above as equal to the aggregate of the rentcharge and the rent payable under the terms of that lease.

(3) Subject to the following provisions of this section, the proportion of the consideration received by the lessee as mentioned in subsection (1) above, or of any instalment of that consideration, which for the purposes of the Tax Acts is to be treated not as a capital receipt but in accordance with this subsection shall be determined by the formula—

$$\frac{16 - N}{15}$$

where N is the term of the new lease expressed in years or, if that term is less than a year, where N is 1; and that proportion shall be treated for the purposes of the Tax Acts—

(*a*) as a receipt of a trade, profession or vocation, if the rent payable by the lessee under the new lease is allowable as a deduction in computing [profits][2] or losses of a trade, profession or vocation for the purposes of tax and if the consideration is received by the lessee in the course of that trade, profession or vocation; and

(*b*) in any other case, as a profit or gain chargeable under Case VI of Schedule D.

(4) In any case where the property which is the subject of the new lease does not include the whole of the property which was the subject of the original lease, the consideration received by the lessee shall be treated for the purposes of subsection (3) above as reduced to that portion of the consideration which is reasonably attributable to such part of the property which was the subject of the original lease as consists of, or is included in, the property which is the subject of the new lease.

(5) ...[1]

(6) Where by agreement with his landlord, the lessee varies the terms of the original lease in such a manner that, in return for such a consideration as is specified in subsection (1)(*a*) above, the lessee undertakes to pay, during a period ending not later than 15 years after the date on which the consideration, or if the consideration is paid in instalments, the last such instalment, is paid to the lessee, a rent greater than that payable under the original lease, he shall be treated for the purposes of this section—

(*a*) as having surrendered the original lease for that consideration, and

(*b*) as having been granted a new lease for a term not exceeding 15 years but otherwise on the terms of the original lease as so varied.

(7) References in this section to the lessee (other than in subsection (1)(*a*) above) include references to a person who is a partner or associate of the lessee or an associate of a partner of the lessee; and for the purposes of this section the expression "associate" shall be construed in accordance with section 783(10).

(8) Subject to subsection (7) above, expressions used in this section have the meanings assigned to them by section 24, and in subsection (2)(*a*) above "rental period" means a period in respect of which a payment of rent falls to be made, and for the purposes of that subsection, in a case where the rental period is a quarter or a month, each such period shall be treated as of equal duration.

(9) The preceding provisions of this section shall not apply if the lessee had, before 22nd June 1971, a right enforceable at law or in equity to the grant of the new lease, but in any case where, apart from this subsection, those provisions would apply, no part of the rent paid under the new lease shall be treated as a payment of capital, and the provisions of this Act providing for deductions or allowances by way of tax relief in respect of payments of rent shall apply accordingly.

Commentary—*Simon's Direct Tax Service* **B3.648.**
Definitions—"Schedule D", s 18(1); "tax", s 832(3); "the Tax Acts", s 831(2); "trade", s 832(1); "year of assessment", s 832(1).
Cross references—See FA 1999 Sch 6 para 7 (sale and lease-back arrangements are excluded from provisions in FA 1999 Sch 6 concerning the tax treatment of receipts by way of reverse premiums).
Amendments—[1] Sub-s (5) repealed by FA 1988 s 75 and Sch 14 Pt IV.
[2] Word in sub-s (3)(a) substituted by FA 1998 Sch 7 para 1 with effect from 31 July 1998.

781 Assets leased to traders and others

(1) Subject to section 782, where—

(a) a deduction by way of tax relief which is one of the kinds listed in subsection (4) below is allowable in respect of a payment made under a lease of an asset of any description, and

(b) before, at or after the time when the payment is made, either—

(i) the person who made the payment has obtained or obtains a capital sum in respect of the lessee's interest in the lease, or

(ii) the lessor's interest in the lease, or any other interest in the asset, has belonged to an associate of the person who made the payment, and that associate has obtained a capital sum in respect of that interest,

the person obtaining that sum shall be charged under Case VI of Schedule D for the chargeable period in which the sum is obtained with tax on an amount equal to the amount of the payment in respect of which tax relief is so allowed.

(2) A person shall not be assessed to tax under subsection (1) above on any amount to the extent to which it exceeds the capital sum by reference to which he is so assessed.

(3) Subsection (1) above shall not apply to payments under a lease created on or before 14th April 1964.

(4) The kinds of deductions by way of tax relief to which subsection (1) above applies are as follows—

(a) a deduction in computing [profits][2] or losses of a trade, profession or vocation for the purposes of tax;

(b) a deduction in computing profits or gains chargeable under Case VI of Schedule D, or in computing any loss for which relief is allowable under section 392 or 396;

(c) allowance of a payment under section 75 or 76;

(d) a deduction from emoluments to be assessed under Schedule E made in pursuance of section 198(1) or allowable in computing losses in an employment for tax purposes;

(e) a deduction allowable for tax purposes in computing profits or gains or losses arising from woodlands.

(5) Where—

(a) the deduction by way of tax relief mentioned in subsection (1)(a) above is a deduction in computing, for income tax purposes, profits or gains or losses of a trade, profession or vocation, or arising from woodlands, and

(b) any part of the payments made under the lease by the person obtaining the capital sum is a payment in respect of which a deduction is not allowed for the reason that the whole or any part of the period in which the payment would fall to be allowed is not a period on the [profits][2] of which income tax falls to be computed in respect of the trade, profession or vocation,

for the reference in subsection (2) above to the amount of the capital sum there shall be substituted a reference to that amount after deducting the amount of the payment in respect of which a deduction is not allowed for that reason.

(6) So far as in respect of a capital sum any part of a payment allowed as a deduction by way of tax relief of a kind to which this section applies is taken into account in making an assessment under subsection (1) above, that part of the payment shall be left out of account in determining whether any and if so what amount should be assessed by reference to any other capital sum; and the order in which this subsection is applied shall be the order in which the capital sums are obtained.

(7) There shall be made all such adjustments of tax, whether by way of making assessments or by repayment of tax, as are required after the making of any such payment as is described in subsection (1) above to give effect to the charge under that subsection in respect of a sum obtained before the making of the payment.

(8) Notwithstanding anything in the Tax Acts limiting the time within which an assessment may be made or a claim for relief may be admitted any such adjustment may be made, by making an assessment or otherwise, at any time [within the period specified in subsection (8A) below][1].

[(8A) The period mentioned in subsection (8) above is—

(a) in the case of adjustments with respect to income tax, the period ending with the fifth anniversary of the 31st January next following the year of assessment in which the payment was made;

(b) in the case of adjustments with respect to corporation tax, the period of six years beginning at the end of the accounting period in which the payment was made.][1]

(9) This section shall not apply if the capital sum obtained in respect of the lessee's interest in a lease constituting a hire-purchase agreement for machinery or plant is a sum which is required to be brought into account as the whole or part of the disposal value of the machinery or plant under [section 68 of the Capital Allowances Act][3].

Commentary—*Simon's Direct Tax Service* B3.661, 662.
Revenue Internal Guidance—Inspector's manual IM 4808 (examples illustrating working of the section).

Definitions—''The 1990 Act'', s 831(3); ''asset'', s 785; ''associate'', s 783(10); ''capital sum'', s 785; ''chargeable period'', s 832(1); ''emoluments'', s 131(1); ''base'', s 785; ''Schedule D'', s 18(1); ''Schedule E'', s 19(1); ''tax'', s 832(3); ''the Tax Acts'', s 831(2); ''trade'', s 832(1).
Cross references—See TA 1988 s 783 (supplemental provisions).
TA 1988 s 784 (leased assets subject to hire–purchase agreements).
Note—This section does not apply to any payment, or by reason of any payment, which falls to made under a public-private partnership agreement by virtue of the Greater London Authority Act 1999, s 419, Sch 33, para 13.
Amendments—¹ Words in sub-s (8) substituted and sub-s (8A) inserted by FA 1996 s 135(1), (2), Sch 21 para 21 with effect for the purposes of income tax from the year 1996–97 and for the purposes of corporation tax as respects accounting periods ending after 30 June 1999 (by virtue of Finance Act 1994, Section 199, (Appointed Day) Order, SI 1998/3173 art 2).
² Word in sub-ss (4)(a), (5)(*b*) substituted by FA 1998 Sch 7 para 1 with effect from 31 July 1998.
³ Words in sub-s (9) substituted by CAA 2001 s 578, Sch 2 para 57 with effect for income tax purposes, as respects allowances and charges falling to be made for chargeable periods ending after 5 April 2001, and for corporation tax purposes, as respects allowances and charges falling to be made for chargeable periods ending after 31 March 2001.

782 Leased assets: special cases

(1) This section shall apply, and section 781 shall not apply, to payments—

    (*a*) which are allowable by way of deductions in computing the [profits]¹ or losses of a trade, and
    (*b*) which are made under a lease of an asset which at any time before the creation of the lease was used for the purposes—

        (i) of that trade; or
        (ii) of another trade carried on by the person who at that time or later was carrying on the first-mentioned trade;

    and when so used was owned by the person carrying on the trade in which it was being used.

(2) Subject to the following provisions of this section, the deduction allowable in computing the [profits]¹ or losses of the trade for the purposes of tax as respects any such payment shall not exceed the commercial rent of the asset for the period for which the payment was made.

(3) If under subsection (2) above part of a payment which would otherwise be allowable as a deduction is not so allowable, and one or more subsequent payments are made by the same person under the same lease, that part of the first-mentioned payment may be carried forward and treated for the purposes of computing the [profits]¹ or losses of the trade for the purposes of tax as if it were made at the time when the next of those subsequent payments was made, and so made for the period for which that subsequent payment was made.

(4) For the purposes of subsection (2) above—

    (*a*) if more than one payment is made for the same period the payments shall be taken together;
    (*b*) if the payments are made for periods which overlap, the payments shall be apportioned, and the apportioned payments which belong to the common part of the overlapping periods shall be taken together;
    (*c*) the preceding references to payments include references to parts of payments which under subsection (3) above are treated as if made at a time subsequent to that at which they were made;

and to the extent that a part of a payment carried forward under subsection (3) above is not allowable as a deduction it may again be carried forward under that subsection.

(5) A payment made for a period all of which falls more than one year after the payment is made shall be treated for the purposes of this section as made for that period of one year beginning with the date on which the payment is made, and a payment for a period part of which falls after the end of that year shall be treated for those purposes as if a corresponding part of the payment was made for that year (and no part for any later period).

(6) For the purpose of making a comparison under subsection (2) above between a payment, or payments taken together, and the commercial rent of the asset, ''commercial rent'' shall mean the rent which might at the relevant time be expected to be paid under a lease of the asset for the remainder of the anticipated normal working life of the asset, being a rent payable at uniform intervals and at a uniform rate which would afford a reasonable return for its market value at the relevant time, having regard to the terms and conditions of the lease; and in this subsection—

    ''anticipated normal working life'' means, in the case of any asset, the period which might be expected, when the asset is first put into use, to be going to elapse before it is finally put out of use as being unfit for further use, it being assumed that the asset is going to be used in the normal manner and to the normal extent, and is going to be so used throughout that period; and
    ''the relevant time'' means the time when the lease was created under which the payment was made with which the commercial rent is to be compared.

(7) If the asset is used at the same time partly for the purposes of the trade and partly for other purposes the commercial rent as defined in subsection (6) above shall be determined by reference to what would be paid for such a partial use of the asset.

(8) This section shall not apply in relation to payments made under a lease created on or before 14th April 1964.

(9) In this section references to the person carrying on a trade are references to the person carrying on the trade for the time being, and where at any time a person succeeds to a trade which until that time was carried on by another person, and by virtue of section 113 or 337(1) the trade is to be

treated as discontinued, the trade shall, nonetheless, be treated as the same trade for the purposes of this section.

(10) In this section references to a trade include references to a profession or vocation.

Commentary—*Simon's Direct Tax Service* B3.661, 664.
Revenue Internal Guidance—Inspector's manual IM 4814 (this section applied after other rules governing deductions are taken into account: see SP 3/91 regarding Case I principles).
Definitions—"Asset", s 785; "lease", s 785; "tax", s 832(3); "trade", s 832(1).
Note—This section does not apply to any payment which falls to made under a public-private partnership agreement by virtue of the Greater London Authority Act 1999, s 419, Sch 33, para 13.
Amendments—¹ Word in sub-ss (1)(a), (2), (3) substituted by FA 1998 Sch 7 para 1 with effect from 31 July 1998.

783 Leased assets: supplemental

(1) References in section 781 to a sum obtained in respect of the lessee's interest in a lease of an asset, or in respect of any other interest in an asset include—

(*a*) in the case of a lessee's interest, references to sums representing the consideration in money or money's worth obtained on a surrender of the rights to the lessor, or on an assignment of the lease, or on creating a sublease or any other interest out of the lease; and

(*b*) references to any insurance moneys payable in respect of the asset, so far as payable to the owner of the interest in the asset.

(2) Such references also include references to sums representing money or money's worth obtained by the person entitled to the interest by a transaction or series of transactions disposing of the asset, or of an interest in the asset, and in particular transactions which comprise arrangements under which the rights of the lessee under a lease of the asset are merged in any way with the rights of the lessor, or with any other rights as respects the asset, so far as the money or money's worth so obtained is attributable to the rights of the lessee under the lease.

(3) References in section 781 to sums obtained in respect of any interest in an asset include references to money or money's worth so obtained in any transaction (including a transaction of the kind described in subsection (1) or (2) above) by way of consideration received by a person who is an associate of the person entitled to the interest in the asset.

(4) If an interest in the asset is disposed of by any person to a person who is his associate, the person disposing of the interest shall (unless in fact he obtains a greater sum) be treated for the purposes of section 781 as having obtained in respect of the interest—

(*a*) the value of the interest in the open market; or

(*b*) the value of the interest to the person to whom it is, in effect, transferred;

whichever is the greater.

(5) For the purposes of subsections (3) and (4) above a disposition may be direct or indirect and may be effected by any such transaction as is described in subsection (2) above.

(6) For the purposes of sections 781 and 784 and this section any sum obtained by any persons carrying on a trade, profession or vocation in partnership in respect of an interest in an asset which is and continues to be used for the purposes of the trade, profession or vocation shall be regarded as apportionable between them in the shares in which they are then entitled to the profits of the trade, profession or vocation.

(7) Subject to subsection (6) above, for those purposes a sum obtained by persons jointly entitled to an interest in an asset shall be apportionable according to their respective interests in the rights.

(8) For those purposes, any payment in respect of which a deduction is allowable by way of tax relief which is made by persons carrying on a trade, profession or vocation in partnership shall be apportioned in such manner as may be just.

(9) Where under this section any sum or payment falls to be apportioned and, at the time of the apportionment, it appears that it is material as respects the liability to tax (for whatever period) of two or more persons, any question which arises as to the manner in which the sum or payment is to be apportioned shall be determined, for the purposes of tax of all those persons—

(*a*) in a case where the same body of General Commissioners have jurisdiction with respect to all those persons, by those Commissioners unless all those persons agree that it shall be determined by the Special Commissioners;

(*b*) in a case where different bodies of Commissioners have jurisdiction with respect to those persons, by such of those bodies as the Board may direct unless all those persons agree that it shall be determined by the Special Commissioners; and

(*c*) in any other case, by the Special Commissioners;

and any such Commissioners shall determine the question in like manner as if it were an appeal, except that all those persons shall be entitled to appear and be heard by the Commissioners who are to make the determination or to make representations to them in writing.

(10) For the purposes of this section and in construing the expressions "associate" and "associated" in section 781 and this section, the following persons shall be deemed to be associated with each other, that is to say—

(*a*) any individual and that individual's husband or wife, and any relative, or husband or wife of a relative, of that individual or that individual's husband or wife ("relative" meaning, for this purpose, brother, sister, ancestor or lineal descendant);

(*b*) any person in his capacity of trustee of a settlement and any individual who in relation to the settlement is a settlor, and any person associated with that individual ("settlement" and "settlor" having, for this purpose, the meanings given by [section 660G(1) and (2)]¹);

(*c*) any person and a body of persons of which that person, or persons associated with him, or that person and persons associated with him, has or have control;

(*d*) any two or more bodies of persons associated with the same person by virtue of paragraph (*c*) above;

(*e*) in relation to a disposal by joint owners, the joint owners and any person associated with any of them.

(11) In subsection (10) above "body of persons" includes a partnership and "control" has the meaning given by section 840.

Commentary—*Simon's Direct Tax Service* B3.663.
Definitions—"Apportionment", s 834(4); "asset", s 785; "the Board", s 832(1); "body of persons", s 832(1); "control", s 840; "lease", s 785; "tax", s 832(3); "trade", s 832(1).
Cross references—See TMA 1970 s 58(3)(b), FA 1988 s 134(4) (with effect from 3 April 1989, by virtue of FA 1988 (Commencement) Order 1989, SI 1989/473 proceedings under sub-s (9) above to be in Northern Ireland if the place given by certain rules in relation to the parties to the proceedings is in Northern Ireland).
TA 1988 s 756(2) (extension of the application of sub-s (10) above to Pt XVII Ch IV (taxation of controlled foreign companies).
Amendments—¹ Words in sub-s (10)(b) substituted by FA 1995 s 74, Sch 17 para 19, with effect from the year 1995–96 (and apply to every settlement wherever and whenever made or entered into).

784 Leased assets subject to hire-purchase agreements

(1) In the application of section 781 to a lease which constitutes a hire-purchase agreement, for the reference in subsection (2) of that section to the amount of the capital sum there shall, where that capital sum was obtained in respect of the lessee's interest in the lease constituting the hire-purchase agreement, be substituted references to the amount of the capital sum (adjusted, if necessary, under subsection (5) of that section) after deducting any capital expenditure which was incurred by the person obtaining the capital sum in providing the lessee's interest.

(2) In subsection (1) above "capital expenditure which was incurred by the person obtaining the capital sum in providing the lessee's interest" means—

(*a*) so much of any payment made under the lease by the person obtaining the capital sum (or, where the capital sum was obtained by the personal representatives of a deceased person, so made by that deceased person) as is not a payment in respect of which a deduction is allowable by way of tax relief which is one of the kinds listed in subsection (4) of section 781, plus

(*b*) where the lessee's interest was assigned to the person obtaining the capital sum, any capital payment made by that person as consideration for the assignment.

(3) If the amount to be deducted in pursuance of subsection (1) above exceeds the amount of the capital sum from which it is to be deducted, no charge shall arise under section 781(1) in respect of the capital sum.

(4) If the capital sum represents the consideration for part only of the lessee's interest in the lease which constitutes a hire-purchase agreement, the amount to be deducted under subsection (1) above shall be such proportion of the capital expenditure which is still unallowed as is reasonable having regard to the degree to which the capital expenditure has contributed to the value of what is disposed of in return for the capital sum.

(5) If more than one capital sum is, or is to be regarded as, obtained by the same person in respect of the lessee's interest in the lease which constitutes a hire-purchase agreement, then, so far as in respect of one of those capital sums any deduction is made in respect of capital expenditure in pursuance of subsection (1) above that capital expenditure shall be left out of account in applying subsections (1) and (3) above to any other such capital sum; and the order in which this subsection is applied shall be the order in which the capital sums are obtained.

(6) In this section—

"hire-purchase agreement" means an agreement, other than a conditional sale agreement, under which—

(*a*) goods are bailed or, in Scotland, hired in return for periodical payments by the person to whom they are bailed or hired, and

(*b*) the property in the goods will pass to that person if the terms of the agreement are complied with and one or more of the following occurs—

(i) the exercise of an option to purchase by that person;
(ii) the doing of any other specified act by any party to the agreement;
(iii) the happening of any other specified event; and

"conditional sale agreement" means an agreement for the sale of goods under which the purchase price or part of it is payable by instalments, and the property in the goods is to remain in the seller (notwithstanding that the buyer is to be in possession of the goods) until such conditions as to the payment of instalments or otherwise as may be specified in the agreement are fulfilled.

Commentary—*Simon's Direct Tax Service* **B3.665.**
Definitions—"Capital sum", s 785; "lease", s 785; "tax", s 832(3).
Cross references—See TA 1988 s 783(6) (apportionment of capital sums obtained by partners in respect of assets used for the partnership business).

785 Meaning of "asset", "capital sum" and "lease" for purposes of sections 781 to 784

In sections 781 to 784—

"asset" means any description of property or rights other than land or an interest in land;

"capital sum" means any sum of money, or any money's worth, except so far as it or any part of it is to be treated for the purposes of tax as a receipt to be taken into account in computing the [profits]¹ or losses of a trade, profession or vocation, or profits or gains or losses arising from woodlands, or is, apart from section 781, chargeable under Case VI of Schedule D; and

"lease", in relation to an asset, means any kind of agreement or arrangement under which payments are made for the use of, or otherwise in respect of, an asset, and includes, in particular, any agreement or arrangement all or any of the payments under which represent instalments of, or payments towards, a purchase price.

Commentary—*Simon's Direct Tax Service* **B3.661.**
Definitions—"Profits or gains", s 833(1); "Schedule D", s 18(1); "tax", s 832(3); "trade", s 832(1).
Amendments—¹ Word substituted by FA 1998 Sch 7 para 1 with effect from 31 July 1998.

786 Transactions associated with loans or credit

(1) This section applies as respects any transaction effected with reference to the lending of money or the giving of credit, or the varying of the terms on which money is lent or credit is given, or which is effected with a view to enabling or facilitating any such arrangement concerning the lending of money or the giving of credit.

(2) Subsection (1) above has effect whether the transaction is effected between the lender or creditor and the borrower or debtor, or between either of them and a person connected with the other or between a person connected with one and a person connected with the other.

(3) If the transaction provides for the payment of any annuity or other annual payment, not being interest, being a payment chargeable to tax under Case III of Schedule D, the payment shall be treated for all the purposes of the Tax Acts as if it were a payment of annual interest.

(4) ...¹

(5) If under the transaction a person assigns, surrenders or otherwise agrees to waive or forego income arising from any property (without a sale or transfer of the property) then, without prejudice to the liability of any other person, he shall be chargeable to tax under Case VI of Schedule D on a sum equal to the amount of income assigned, surrendered, waived or foregone.

(6) If credit is given for the purchase price of any property, and the rights attaching to the property are such that, during the subsistence of the debt, the purchaser's rights to income from the property are suspended or restricted, he shall be treated for the purposes of subsection (5) above as if he had surrendered a right to income of an amount equivalent to the income which he has in effect foregone by obtaining the credit.

(7) The amount of any income payable subject to deduction of income tax shall be taken for the purposes of subsection (5) above as the amount before deduction of tax.

(8) References in this section to connected persons shall be construed in accordance with section 839.

Revenue Internal Guidance—Inspector's manual IM 3943 (example of a transaction caught by this section).
Definitions—"Income tax", s 832(4); "interest", s 832(1); "person connected", see s 839; "Schedule D", s 18(1); "tax", s 832(3); "the Tax Acts", s 831(2).
Amendments—¹ Sub-s (4) repealed by FA 1996 s 159(1), Sch 41 Pt V(21) with effect except in relation to cases where the initial agreement to sell or transfer the securities or other property was made before 6 November 1996 (FA 1996 s 159 (Appointed Day) Order, SI 1996/2646).

787 Restriction of relief for payments of interest

(1) Relief shall not be given to any person under any provision of the Tax Acts in respect of any payment of interest if a scheme has been effected or arrangements have been made (whether before or after the time when the payment is made) such that the sole or main benefit that might be expected to accrue to that person from the transaction under which the interest is paid was the obtaining of a reduction in tax liability by means of any such relief.

[(1A) This section has effect in relation to Chapter 2 of Part 4 of the Finance Act 1996 (loan relationships) but taking the reference in subsection (1) above to giving relief to any person in respect of any payment of interest as including a reference to the bringing into account by any person in accordance with that Chapter of any debit in respect of interest (whether a payment or not); and other references in this section to relief shall be construed accordingly.]¹

(2) In this section "relief" means relief by way of deduction in computing profits or gains or deduction or set off against income or total profits.

[(3) Where the relief is claimed by virtue of section 403—

(*a*) in respect of a deficit to which section 83 of the Finance Act 1996 applies (non-trading deficit on loan relationships), or

(*b*) in respect of trading losses, in a case where in computing those losses debits in respect of loan relationships are treated under section 82(2)(*b*) of that Act as expenses of the trade which are deductible in computing the profits of the trade,

any question under this section as to what benefit might be expected to accrue from the transaction in question shall be determined by reference to the claimant company and the surrendering company taken together.]¹

Commentary—*Simon's Direct Tax Service* **E1.554.**
Simon's Tax Cases—*Westmoreland Investments Ltd v Macniven* [1998] STC 1131; *Lancaster v Inland Revenue Comrs* [2000] STC (SCD) 138.
Definitions—"Company", s 832(1), (2); "interest", s 832(1); "tax", s 832(3); "the Tax Acts", s 831(2).
Cross references—See TA 1988 s 338(1) (s 338 (allowances of charges on income and capital) to have effect subject to this section).
Amendments—¹ Sub-s (1A) inserted, and sub-s (3) substituted, by FA 2002 s 82, Sch 25 paras 43, 53 with effect for accounting periods beginning after 30 September 2002. Sub-s (3) previously read as follows—

"(3) Where the relief is claimed by virtue of [section 83(2)(*b*) of the Finance Act 1996 (claim to treat non-trading deficit as eligible for group relief)] any question under this section as to what benefit might be expected to accrue from the transaction in question shall be determined by reference to the claimant company and the surrendering company taken together.".

PART XVIII
DOUBLE TAXATION RELIEF

Revenue Internal Guidance—Double taxation relief manual DT 840 (where a claim to tax credit relief cannot be agreed, it is referred to International Division (Double Taxation) before a decision is made).
Cross references—See TA 1988 s 807A (for the purposes of corporation tax in relation to any company, this Part has effect as if foreign tax attributable to interest accruing under a loan relationship at a time when the company was not party to it were to be disregarded).
TA 1988 s 815A (foreign tax which would have been payable but for the Mergers Directive on the transfer of a non-UK trade falling within TA 1970 s 269C or TCGA 1992 s 140C is treated as payable for the purposes of this Part).
TA 1988 Sch 26 para 4(2) (dividends from foreign controlled company).
IT (Manufactured Overseas Dividends) Regulations, SI 1993/2004 reg 9(4A) (relief may not be claimed under this Part in respect of tax attributable to an overseas dividend which has been received by an overseas dividend manufacturer and either has been set off against tax attributable to manufactured overseas dividends paid or the relevant dividend has been matched against such a manufactured overseas dividend).
Lloyd's Underwriters (Double Taxation Relief) Regulations, SI 1997/405 reg 3 (method of taking into account, for the purposes of this Part, foreign tax paid in respect of profits or losses arising from the underwriting business of an individual member of Lloyd's).
Lloyd's Underwriters (Double Taxation Relief) Regulations, SI 1997/405 reg 9 (treatment of refunds of foreign tax to individual Lloyd's member where double taxation relief already given).

CHAPTER I
THE PRINCIPAL RELIEFS

788 Relief by agreement with other [territories]⁵

(1) If Her Majesty by Order in Council declares that arrangements specified in the Order have been [made in relation to any territory]³ outside the United Kingdom with a view to affording relief from double taxation in relation to—

(*a*) income tax,
(*b*) corporation tax in respect of income or chargeable gains, and
(*c*) any taxes of a similar character to those taxes imposed by the laws of that territory,

and that it is expedient that those arrangements should have effect, then those arrangements shall have effect in accordance with subsection (3) below.

(2) Without prejudice to the generality of subsection (1) above, if it appears to Her Majesty to be appropriate, the arrangements specified in an Order in Council under this section may include provisions with respect to the exchange of information necessary for carrying out the domestic laws of the United Kingdom and the laws of the territory to which the arrangements relate concerning taxes covered by the arrangements including, in particular, provisions about the prevention of fiscal evasion with respect to those taxes; and where arrangements do include any such provisions, the declaration in the Order in Council shall state that fact.

(3) Subject to the provisions of this Part, the arrangements shall, notwithstanding anything in any enactment, have effect in relation to income tax and corporation tax in so far as they provide—

(*a*) for relief from income tax, or from corporation tax in respect of income or chargeable gains; or

(*b*) for charging the income arising from sources, or chargeable gains accruing on the disposal of assets, in the United Kingdom to persons not resident in the United Kingdom; or

(*c*) for determining the income or chargeable gains to be attributed—

(i) to persons not resident in the United Kingdom and their agencies, branches or establishments in the United Kingdom; or

(ii) to persons resident in the United Kingdom who have special relationships with persons not so resident; or

(*d*) for conferring on persons not resident in the United Kingdom the right to a tax credit under section 231 in respect of qualifying distributions made to them by companies which are so resident.

(4) The provisions of Chapter II of this Part shall apply where arrangements which have effect by virtue of this section provide that tax payable under the laws of the territory concerned shall be allowed as a credit against tax payable in the United Kingdom.

(5) For the purposes of this section and, subject to section 795(3), Chapter II of this Part in its application to relief under this section, any amount of tax which would have been payable under the law of a territory outside the United Kingdom but for a relief to which this subsection applies given under the law of that territory shall be treated as having been payable; and references in this section and that Chapter to double taxation, to tax payable or chargeable, or to tax not chargeable directly or by deduction shall be construed accordingly.

This subsection applies—

(*a*) to any relief given with a view to promoting industrial, commercial, scientific, educational or other development in a territory outside the United Kingdom, being a relief with respect to which provision is made in the arrangements in question for double taxation relief; ...[1]
(*b*) ...[1]

[Relief does not fall to be given in accordance with section 801 by virtue of this subsection unless the arrangements in question make express provision for such relief (but this paragraph is without prejudice to section 790(10B)).][2]

(6) Except in the case of a claim for an allowance by way of credit in accordance with Chapter II of this Part, a claim for relief under subsection (3)(*a*) above shall be made to the Board.

(7) Where—

(*a*) under any arrangements which have effect by virtue of this section, relief may be given, either in the United Kingdom or in the territory [in relation to][4] which the arrangements are made, in respect of any income or chargeable gains, and
(*b*) it appears that the assessment to income tax or corporation tax made in respect of the income or chargeable gains is not made in respect of the full amount thereof, or is incorrect having regard to the credit, if any, which falls to be given under the arrangements,

any such assessments may be made as are necessary to ensure that the total amount of the income or chargeable gains is assessed, and the proper credit, if any, is given in respect thereof, and, where the income is, or the chargeable gains are, entrusted to any person in the United Kingdom for payment, any such assessment may be made on the recipient of the income or gains, and, in the case of an assessment in respect of income, may be assessed under Case VI of Schedule D.

(8) Any arrangements to which effect is given under this section may include provision for relief from tax for periods before the passing of this Act, or before the making of the arrangements, and provisions as to income or chargeable gains which is or are not subject to double taxation, and the preceding provisions of this section shall have effect accordingly.

(9) Any Order in Council made under this section revoking an earlier such Order in Council may contain such transitional provisions as appear to Her Majesty to be necessary or expedient.

(10) Before any Order in Council proposed to be made under this section is submitted to Her Majesty in Council, a draft of the Order shall be laid before the House of Commons, and the Order shall not be so submitted unless an Address is presented to Her Majesty by that House praying that the Order be made.

Commentary—*Simon's Direct Tax Service* F1.102, 111, 113.
Concessions B18—Payments out of a discretionary trust: entitlement to relief from UK tax under a double taxation agreement.
C1—Credit for underlying tax: dividends received by portfolio shareholders and insurance companies from trade investments in overseas companies.
Statements of Practice SP 3/86—Relief from UK tax under a double taxation agreement in respect of payments made to a non-resident from a UK discretionary trust or estate.
SP 6/88—This Statement sets out the circumstances which fall within the terms of this section.
SP 3/92—Double taxation convention of 31 July 1985 between the UK and the USSR regarded as in force between the UK and the Russian Federation.
Revenue & other press releases—IR 7-2-78 (US forces and civilian personnel serving in UK: UK/USA double taxation agreement Art.19, para.1, is without prejudice to the exemptions under TA 1988 ss 321, 323).
IR 2-3-78 and Hansard 2-3-78 (double taxation: exchange of information between UK and USA: text of working agreement).
CCAB TR508 June 1983 (residence test: days of arrival & departure, for the purpose of the 183 days present in the UK test, fractions of days of arrival & departure are counted).
IR 27-3-95 (new booklet IR 146 contains full list of admissible and inadmissible foreign taxes as at 31-12-94).
Revenue Internal Guidance—Double taxation relief manual DT 300–320 (determination of residence under double taxation agreements: tie-breaker rules: Revenue procedures).
DT 350–354 (exchange of information between Revenue authorities).
DT 701 (sub-s (5) relief for tax spared is given only where there is an agreement providing for a credit for such tax).
DT 802 (meaning of "subject to tax" in the UK for the purposes of double taxation agreements).
DT 955–975 (foreign dividends: basis of treaty relief).
Investigations handbook IH 421 (exchange of information is dealt with by London Special Compliance Office).
Simon's Tax Cases—*IRC v Commerzbank AG* [1990] STC 285*; *Getty Oil Co v Steele* [1990] STC 434*; [1996] STC (SCD) 228; *Memec plc v IRC* [1996] STC 1336.
s 788(1), *Union Texas Petroleum Corporation v Critchley* [1988] STC 691*.

s 788(3), *R v IRC, ex p Commerzbank AG* [1991] STC 271; *Padmore v IRC (No 2)* [2001] STC 280.
Definitions—"The Board", s 832(1); "chargeable gains", s 832(1); "income tax", s 832(4); "Schedule D", s 18(1); "tax", s 832(3); "United Kingdom", s 830(1).
Cross references—See TMA 1970 s 46C (any question in dispute concerning a claim under this Chapter on an appeal against an amendment to a self-assessment or partnership statement is to be determined by the Special Commissioners).
TA 1988 s 118G(8) (regulations may provide that a paying agent paying public revenue dividend on gilt-edged securities is relieved from deducting tax or may deduct tax at a reduced rate for the purpose of giving effect to arrangements under this section).
TA 1988 s 790 (unilateral relief).
TA 1988 s 791 (regulations for the purposes of this section).
TA 1988 s 807 (restriction on double taxation relief on income from securities purchased without accrued interest).
TA 1988 s 808A (double taxation arrangements in relation to interest where because of special relationship extra interest is paid).
TA 1988 s 815A(2), (3) (transfer of trade by a UK company trading in a member state through a branch or agency to a member state company; double tax relief).
TA 1988 s 816 (relaxation of the obligation as to secrecy of information).
TA 1988 Sch 15B para 1 (tax relief on qualifying investments in venture capital trusts is offset against tax liability for any year of assessment in priority to relief under this section).
TA 1988 Sch 26 para 5(1) (arrangements under this section for relief related to foreign dividends received by a resident company from a controlled foreign company: condition as regards degree of control of the paying company).
FA 1989 s 115 (double taxation: tax credits).
FA 1991 s 32(2B) (vocational training relief given in priority to relief under this section)
FA 1993 s 194 (double taxation relief in relation to petroleum revenue tax).
FA 2000 s 46(2) (exemption under FA 2000 s 46(1) for income of a charity is not granted in respect of income chargeable to tax under Schedule D Case VI by virtue of this section).
Amendments—[1] Sub-s (5)(*b*) and word "and" preceding it repealed by FA 2000 ss 103, 156, Sch 30 para 1, Sch 40 Pt II(13) with effect from 1 April 2000.
[2] Words in sub-s (5) inserted by FA 2000 s 103, Sch 30 para 2 with effect for any claim for credit in respect of underlying tax in relation to a dividend paid after 20 March 2000 by a company resident outside the UK to a company resident in the UK.
[3] In sub-s (1), words substituted for the words "made with the government of any territory" by FA 2002 s 88(1), (3) with effect on and after the date of the passing of FA 2002 (24 July 2002) in relation to arrangements made before that date (as well as in relation to arrangements made on or after that date).
[4] In sub-s (7)(*a*), words substituted for the words "with the government of" by FA 2002 s 88(2), (3) with effect on and after the date of the passing of FA 2002 (24 July 2002) in relation to arrangements made before that date (as well as in relation to arrangements made on or after that date).
[5] Words substituted for the words "countries" by FA 2002 s 88(2)(*b*), (3) with effect on and after the date of the passing of FA 2002 (24 July 2002) in relation to arrangements made before that date (as well as in relation to arrangements made on or after that date).

789 Arrangements made under old law

(1) Notwithstanding section 793(2), any arrangements made in relation to the profits tax under section 347 of the Income Tax Act 1952 or any earlier enactment corresponding to that section shall, except in so far as arrangements made after the passing of the Finance Act 1965 provide otherwise, have effect in relation to corporation tax and income and gains chargeable to corporation tax as they are expressed to have effect in relation to the profits tax and profits chargeable to the profits tax, with the substitution of accounting periods for chargeable accounting periods (and not as they had effect in relation to income tax).

(2) In so far as any arrangements made before 30th March 1971 provide for the exemption of any income from surtax they shall have effect, unless otherwise modified by subsequent arrangements, as if they provided for that income[—

(*a*) to bear income tax at the basic rate or, where that income is income to which section 1A applies, at the lower rate; and
(*b*)][1] to be disregarded for the purpose of computing total income, except in so far as the computation affects the matters mentioned in section 835(5).

(3) Any reference in the Tax Acts (including this Part) to arrangements under or by virtue of section 788 includes a reference to arrangements having effect by virtue of this section.

Commentary—*Simon's Direct Tax Service* **F1.102.**
Definitions—"Basic rate", s 832(1); "income tax", s 832(4); "lower rate", s 832(1); "the Tax Acts", s 831(2); "total income", s 835(1).
Cross references—See TMA 1970 s 46C (any question in dispute concerning a claim under this Chapter on an appeal against an amendment to a self-assessment or partnership statement is to be determined by the Special Commissioners).
Amendments—[1] Words in sub-s (2) substituted by FA 1996 s 73(4), Sch 6 paras 21, 28 with effect from the year 1996–97.

790 Unilateral relief

(1) To the extent appearing from the following provisions of this section, relief from income tax and corporation tax in respect of income and chargeable gains shall be given in respect of tax payable under the law of any territory outside the United Kingdom by allowing that tax as a credit against income tax or corporation tax, notwithstanding that there are not for the time being in force any arrangements under section 788 providing for such relief.

(2) Relief under subsection (1) above is referred to in this Part as "unilateral relief".

(3) Unilateral relief shall be such relief as would fall to be given under Chapter II of this Part if arrangements [in relation to][3] the territory in question containing the provisions specified in subsections (4) to [(10C)][1] below were in force by virtue of section 788, but subject to any particular provision made with respect to unilateral relief in that Chapter; and any expression in that Chapter which imports a reference to relief under arrangements for the time being having effect by virtue of that section shall be deemed to import also a reference to unilateral relief.

(4) Credit for tax paid under the law of the territory outside the United Kingdom and computed by reference to income arising or any chargeable gain accruing in that territory shall be allowed against any United Kingdom income tax or corporation tax computed by reference to that income or gain (profits from, or remuneration for, personal or professional services performed in that territory being deemed for this purpose to be income arising in that territory).

(5) Subsection (4) above shall have effect subject to the following modifications, that is to say—

(a) where the territory is the Isle of Man or any of the Channel Islands, the limitation to income or gains arising in the territory shall not apply;

(b) where arrangements [in relation to]³ the territory are for the time being in force by virtue of section 788, credit for tax paid under the law of the territory shall not be allowed by virtue of subsection (4) above in the case of any income or gains if any credit for that tax is allowable under those arrangements in respect of that income or those gains; and

(c) credit shall not be allowed by virtue of subsection (4) above for overseas tax on a dividend paid by a company resident in the territory unless—

(i) the overseas tax is directly charged on the dividend, whether by charge to tax, deduction of tax at source or otherwise, and the whole of it represents tax which neither the company nor the recipient would have borne if the dividend had not been paid; or

(ii) the dividend is paid to a company within subsection (6) below; or

(iii) the dividend is paid to a company to which section 802(1) applies and is a dividend of the kind described in that subsection.

(6) Where a dividend paid by a company resident in the territory is paid to a [company falling within subsection (6A) below]² which either directly or indirectly controls, or is a subsidiary of a company which directly or indirectly controls—

(a) not less than 10 per cent of the voting power in the company paying the dividend; or

(b) less than 10 per cent of the voting power in the company paying the dividend if—

(i) it has been reduced below that percentage on or after 1st April 1972; or

(ii) it has been acquired on or after that date in exchange for voting power in another company in respect of which relief under this subsection by virtue of paragraph (a) above was due prior to the exchange;

and the company receiving the dividend shows that the conditions specified in subsection (7) below are satisfied;

any tax in respect of its profits paid under the law of the territory by the company paying the dividend shall be taken into account in considering whether any, and if so what, credit is to be allowed in respect of the dividend.

In this subsection references to one company being a subsidiary of another are to be construed in accordance with section 792(2).

[(6A) A company falls within this subsection if—

(a) it is resident in the United Kingdom; or

(b) it is resident outside the United Kingdom but the dividend mentioned in subsection (6) above forms part of the profits of a branch or agency of the company's in the United Kingdom.]²

(7) The conditions referred to in subsection (6)(b) above are as follows—

(a) that the reduction below the 10 per cent limit (and any further reduction) or, as the case may be, the exchange (and any reduction thereafter) could not have been prevented by any reasonable endeavours on the part of the company receiving the dividend and was due to a cause or causes not reasonably foreseeable by it when control of the relevant voting power was acquired; and

(b) no reasonable endeavours on the part of that company could have restored or, as the case may be, increased the voting power to not less than 10 per cent.

(8) In subsection (7) above references to the company receiving the dividend include references—

(a) to any company of which it is a subsidiary within the meaning of section 792(2); and

(b) where prior to the reduction or exchange the voting power in question was controlled otherwise than directly by the company receiving the dividend, to each other company relevant for determining whether that voting power was controlled as required by subsection (6)(a) above.

(9) In subsection (7) above "the relevant voting power" means the voting power by virtue of which relief was due under subsection (6)(a) above prior to the reduction or exchange or, where control of the whole of that voting power was not acquired at the same time, that part of the voting power of which control was last acquired.

(10) In any case in which relief in respect of a dividend is due by virtue of subsection (6)(b) above, there shall be taken into account, as if it were tax payable under the law of the territory in which the company paying the dividend is resident, any tax that would be so taken into account under section 801 if the company paying the dividend and the company receiving it were related to each other within the meaning of section 801(5).

[(10A) In any case where—

(*a*) under the law of the territory outside the United Kingdom, an amount of tax ("the spared tax") would, but for a relief, have been payable by a company resident in that territory ("company A") in respect of any of its profits,

(*b*) company A pays a dividend out of those profits to another company resident in that territory ("company B"),

(*c*) company B, out of profits which consist of or include the whole or part of that dividend, pays a dividend to a company resident in the United Kingdom ("company C"), and

(*d*) the circumstances are such that, had company B been resident in the United Kingdom, it would have been entitled, under arrangements made [in relation to]³ the territory outside the United Kingdom and having effect by virtue of section 788, to a relief to which subsection (5) of that section applies in respect of the spared tax,

subsection (10B) below shall apply.

(10B) In any case falling within subsection (10A) above, the spared tax shall be taken into account for the purposes of—

(*a*) the other provisions of this section, and

(*b*) subject to section 795(3), Chapter II of this Part in its application to relief under this section in relation to the dividend paid to company C,

as if it had been payable and paid; and references in this section and that Chapter to double taxation, to tax payable or chargeable, or to tax not chargeable directly or by deduction shall be construed accordingly.

(10C) Except as provided by subsection (10B) above, in relation to any dividend paid—

(*a*) to a company resident in the United Kingdom,

(*b*) by a company resident in the territory outside the United Kingdom,

credit by virtue of section 801 does not fall to be given by virtue of this section in respect of tax which would have been payable under the law of that or any other territory outside the United Kingdom but for a relief (notwithstanding any arrangements made [in relation to]³ that or any other territory outside the United Kingdom which have effect by virtue of section 788 and provide for a relief to which subsection (5) of that section applies).]¹

(11) Where—

(*a*) unilateral relief may be given in respect of any income or chargeable gain, and

(*b*) it appears that the assessment to income tax or corporation tax made in respect of the income or chargeable gain is not made in respect of the full amount thereof, or is incorrect having regard to the credit, if any, which falls to be given by way of unilateral relief,

any such assessments may be made as are necessary to ensure that the total amount of the income or chargeable gain is assessed, and the proper credit, if any, is given in respect thereof, and, where the income is, or the chargeable gain is, entrusted to any person in the United Kingdom for payment, any such assessment may be made on the recipient of the income or gain, and, in the case of an assessment in respect of income, may be assessed under Case VI of Schedule D.

(12) In this section and in Chapter II of this Part in its application to unilateral relief, references to tax payable or paid under the law of a territory outside the United Kingdom include only references—

(*a*) to taxes which are charged on income and which correspond to United Kingdom income tax, and

(*b*) to taxes which are charged on income or chargeable gains and which correspond to United Kingdom corporation tax;

but for this purpose tax under the law of any such territory shall not be treated as not corresponding to income tax or corporation tax by reason only that it is payable under the law of a province, state or other part of a country, or is levied by or on behalf of a municipality or other local body.

Commentary—*Simon's Direct Tax Service* F1.103, 145–151.

Concession A12—Circumstances in which relief by way of credit for overseas tax is available on alimony or maintenance payments paid under a UK court order or agreement, notwithstanding that the source is a UK source in law.

B8—Payment made by non-resident to a resident trader who allows the use of any copyrights, patents, etc in a foreign country is income from a UK source; however relief by way of credit is allowed for such payments proportionately reduced if it includes consideration for any services rendered by the trader.

Statements of Practice SP 6/88—This Statement sets out the circumstances which fall within the terms of this section.

SP 7/91—Admissibility for unilateral relief of certain foreign taxes which were previously not admissible.

SP 12/93—

Rules for giving tax credit relief under this section.

Revenue Interpretation RI 125—South African secondary tax on companies qualifies for relief under sub-s (6) as underlying tax. The Revenue's change of view (in August 1995) applies to payments of secondary tax since its introduction in 1993.

R1 239—The additional tax charged in Chile qualifies for relief under sub-s (6) as underlying tax. The Revenue will not withdraw relief made in accordance with previous practice, which treated the tax as a withholding tax, for returns made before publication of this change of view (ie December 2001).

Revenue & other press releases—IR 27-3-95 (new booklet IR 146 contains full list of admissible and inadmissible foreign taxes as at 31-12-94).

IR Tax Bulletin October 1996 p 358 (admissibility for unilateral relief of certain foreign taxes not previously considered admissible).

Revenue Internal Guidance—Double taxation relief manual DT 507 (sub-s (4) relief given by reference to same income: foreign tax not necessarily borne by same person).

DT 842 (circumstances where a further assessment may be required under sub-s (11)).

DT 985 (where relief is denied under sub-s (5)(*c*), the tax may be deductible under TA 1988 s 811).

Simon's Tax Cases—*George Wimpey International Ltd v Rolfe* [1989] STC 609*.

s 790(1), (4), (12), *Yates v G C A International Ltd;* [1991] STC 157*.
s 790(6), *Memec plc v IRC* [1998] STC 754.
Definitions—''Chargeable gain'', s 832(1); ''company'', s 832(1), (2); ''control'', s 840; ''income tax'', s 832(4); ''Schedule D'', s 18(1); ''tax'', s 832(3).
Cross references—See TMA 1970 s 46C (any question in dispute concerning a claim under this Chapter on an appeal against an amendment to a self-assessment or partnership statement is to be determined by the Special Commissioners).
TA 1988 s 807 (restriction on tax credit under sub-s (4) above on income from securities purchased without accrued interest).
TA 1988 s 807A(3) (credit is allowed under sub-s (4) above for notional foreign tax where interest under a loan relationship is paid to a person other than the company in relation to which a non-trading credit is brought into account as a result of a disposal of rights or liabilities under the loan relationship).
TA 1988 Sch 15B, para 1 (tax relief on qualifying investments in a venture capital trusts is offset against tax liability, for any year of assessment, in priority to relief under sub-s (1)).
TA 1988 Sch 26, para 5(1) (arrangements under this section for relief related to foreign dividends received by a resident company from a controlled foreign company: condition as regards degree of control of the paying company).
FA 1991 s 32(2B) (vocational training relief given in priority to relief under this section)
FA 2000 s 46(2) (exemption under FA 2000 s 46(1) for income of a charity is not granted in respect of income chargeable to tax under Schedule D Case VI by virtue of this section).
Amendments—[1] Word in sub-s (3) substituted, and sub-ss (10A)–(10C) inserted, by FA 2000 s 103, Sch 30 para 3 with effect for any claim for credit, under any arrangements, in respect of underlying tax in relation to a dividend paid after 20 March 2000 by a company resident outside the UK to a company resident in the UK.
[2] Words in sub-s (6) substituted, and sub-s (6A) inserted, by FA 2000 s 103, Sch 30 para 4(1)–(3), (14) with effect for chargeable periods ending after 20 March 2000 by virtue of FA 2001 s 81, Sch 27 para 7.
[3] Words substituted for the words ''with the government of'' by FA 2002 s 88(2)(*a*), (3) with effect on and after the date of the passing of FA 2002 (24 July 2002) in relation to arrangements made before that date (as well as in relation to arrangements made on or after that date).

791 Power to make regulations for carrying out section 788

The Board may from time to time make regulations generally for carrying out the provisions of section 788 or any arrangements having effect thereunder, and may in particular by those regulations provide—

(*a*) for securing that relief from taxation imposed by the laws of the territory to which any such arrangements relate does not enure for the benefit of persons not entitled to such relief; and

(*b*) for authorising, in cases where tax deductible from any payment has, in order to comply with any such arrangements, not been deducted, and it is discovered that the arrangements did not apply to that payment, the recovery of the tax by assessment on the person entitled to the payment or by deduction from subsequent payments.

Commentary—*Simon's Direct Tax Service* F1.111.
Regulations—DTR (Taxes on Income) (General) Regulations, SI 1970/488; DTR (Taxes on Income) (General) (Dividend) Regulations, SI 1973/317; DTR (Taxes on Income) (General) (Manufactured Overseas Dividends) Regulations, SI 1993/1957, DTR (Taxes on Income) (Dividend) (Revocation) Regulations, SI 1999/1927 (revokes SI 1973/317). For continuity, see Sch 30, para 21 of this Act.
Revenue & other press releases—CCAB 19-10-79 (calculation of underlying tax rate for purposes of double tax relief).
Definitions—''The Board'', s 832(1); ''tax'', s 832(3).

CHAPTER II
RULES GOVERNING RELIEF BY WAY OF CREDIT
General

Revenue Internal Guidance—Double taxation relief manual DT 550-725 (detailed explanation of the rules governing relief by way of credit).
DT 825-828 (claims procedures).

792 Interpretation of credit code

(1) In this Chapter, except where the context otherwise requires—

''arrangements'' means any arrangements having effect by virtue of section 788;
''foreign tax'' means, in relation to any territory, arrangements [in relation to][1] which have effect by virtue of section 788, any tax chargeable under the laws of that territory for which credit may be allowed under the arrangements;
''the United Kingdom taxes'' means income tax and corporation tax;
''underlying tax'' means, in relation to any dividend, tax which is not chargeable in respect of that dividend directly or by deduction; and
''unilateral relief'' means relief under section 790.

(2) For the purposes of this Chapter one company is a subsidiary of another if the other company controls, directly or indirectly, not less than 50 per cent of the voting power in the first company.

(3) Any reference in this Chapter to foreign tax shall be construed in relation to credit to be allowed under any arrangements as a reference only to tax chargeable under the laws of the territory [in relation to][1] which the arrangements were made.

Commentary—*Simon's Direct Tax Service* F1.117; F2.106.
Revenue Internal Guidance—Double taxation relief manual DT 675 (the ''minimum foreign tax'' rule applies: the claimant is assumed to have claimed all available reliefs in computing foreign tax).
DT 845 (conversion of foreign tax into sterling is at the rate obtaining when that tax became payable).
DT 875 (meaning of ''income'').

Definitions—"Company", s 832(1), (2); "control", s 840; "income tax", s 832(4); "tax", s 832(3); "United Kingdom", s 830(1).
Amendments—¹ Words substituted for the words "with the government of" by FA 2002 s 88(2)(*a*), (3) with effect on and after the date of the passing of FA 2002 (24 July 2002) in relation to arrangements made before that date (as well as in relation to arrangements made on or after that date).

793 Reduction of United Kingdom taxes by amount of credit due

(1) Subject to the provisions of this Chapter, where under any arrangements credit is to be allowed against any of the United Kingdom taxes chargeable in respect of any income or chargeable gain, the amount of the United Kingdom taxes so chargeable shall be reduced by the amount of the credit.

(2) Nothing in subsection (1) above authorises the allowance of credit against any United Kingdom tax against which credit is not allowable under the arrangements.

Commentary—*Simon's Direct Tax Service* F1.117.
Revenue Internal Guidance—Double taxation relief manual DT 675 (the "minimum foreign tax" rule applies: the claimant is assumed to have claimed all available reliefs in computing foreign tax).
DT 845 (conversion of foreign tax into sterling is at the rate obtaining when that tax became payable).
DT 875 (meaning of "income").
Concessions A12—Although alimony or maintenance payments paid under a UK court order or agreement is income from a UK source, relief by way of credit is allowed if the conditions specified in the Concession are met.
B8—Payment made by a non-resident to a resident trader who allows the use of any copyright, patent, etc in a foreign country is income from a UK source; however, relief by way of credit is allowed for such payment proportionately reduced if it includes consideration for any services rendered by the trader.
Simon's Tax Cases—*Collard v Mining and Industrial Holdings Ltd* [1988] STC 15*.
Definitions—"Arrangements", s 792(1); "chargeable gain", s 832(1); "United Kingdom taxes", s 792(1).

[793A No double relief etc

(1) Where relief in respect of an amount of tax that would otherwise be payable under the law of a territory outside the United Kingdom may be allowed—

    (*a*) under arrangements made [in relation to]² that territory, or
    (*b*) under the law of that territory in consequence of any such arrangements,

credit may not be allowed in respect of that tax, whether the relief has been used or not.

(2) Where, under arrangements having effect by virtue of section 788, credit may be allowed in respect of an amount of tax, credit by way of unilateral relief may not be allowed in respect of that tax.

(3) Where arrangements made [in relation to]² a territory outside the United Kingdom contain express provision to the effect that relief by way of credit shall not be given under the arrangements in cases or circumstances specified or described in the arrangements, then neither shall credit by way of unilateral relief be allowed in those cases or circumstances.]¹

Amendments—¹ This section inserted by FA 2000 s 103, Sch 30 para 5. Sub-ss (1), (2) have effect for claims for credit made after 20 March 2000 and sub-s (3) has effect for arrangements made after 20 March 2000.
² Words substituted for the words "with the government of" by FA 2002 s 88(2)(*a*), (3) with effect on and after the date of the passing of FA 2002 (24 July 2002) in relation to arrangements made before that date (as well as in relation to arrangements made on or after that date).

794 Requirement as to residence

(1) Subject to subsection (2) below, credit shall not be allowed under any arrangements against any of the United Kingdom taxes for any chargeable period unless the person in respect of whose income or chargeable gains the United Kingdom tax is chargeable is resident in the United Kingdom for that period.

(2) Credit may be allowed by way of unilateral relief—

    (*a*) for tax paid under the law of the Isle of Man or any of the Channel Islands, if the person in question is, for the chargeable period in question, resident either in the United Kingdom or in the Isle of Man or any of the Channel Islands, as the case may be;
    (*b*) for tax paid under the law of any territory and computed by reference to income from an office or employment the duties of which are performed wholly or mainly in that territory, against income tax chargeable under Schedule E and computed by reference to that income, if the person in question is for the year of assessment in question resident either in the United Kingdom or that territory; and
    [(*bb*) for tax paid under the law of any territory outside the United Kingdom in respect of the income or chargeable gains of a branch or agency in the United Kingdom of a person who is not resident in the United Kingdom, where the following conditions are fulfilled, namely—

        (i) that the territory under whose law the tax was paid is not one in which the person is liable to tax by reason of domicile, residence or place of management; and
        (ii) that the amount of relief claimed does not exceed (or is by the claim expressly limited to) that which would have been available if the branch or agency had been a person resident in the United Kingdom and the income or gains in question had been income or gains of that person;]¹

    (*c*) ...¹

Commentary—*Simon's Direct Tax Service* **F1.118.**
Concession A11—This Concession allows a tax year to be split in relation to residence when an individual comes to the UK to take up residence for three years or more or to take up employment for two years or more or leaves the UK for permanent residence abroad.
Revenue Internal Guidance—Double taxation relief manual DT 625–628 (summary of this section).
Definitions—"Arrangements", s 792(2); "branch or agency", s 834(1); "chargeable gains", s 832(1); "chargeable period", s 832(1); "company", s 832(1), (2); "interest", s 832(1); "Schedule E", s 19(1); "tax", s 832(3); "United Kingdom", s 830(1); "United Kingdom taxes", s 792(1); "year of assessment", s 832(1).
Cross references—See TA 1988 s 444B and Sch 19AC para 13 (modification of this section in relation to overseas life insurance companies in chargeable periods beginning after 31 December 1992).
Amendments—¹ Sub-s (2)(*bb*) inserted, and sub-s (2)(*c*) repealed, by FA 2000 ss 103, 156, Sch 30 para 4(4)–(6), (14), Sch 40 Pt II(13) with effect for chargeable periods ending after 20 March 2000 by virtue of FA 2001 s 81, Sch 27 para 7.

795 Computation of income subject to foreign tax

(1) Where credit for foreign tax falls under any arrangements to be allowed in respect of any income and income tax is payable by reference to the amount received in the United Kingdom, the amount received shall be treated for the purposes of income tax as increased by the amount of the foreign tax in respect of the income, including in the case of a dividend any underlying tax which under the arrangements is to be taken into account in considering whether any and if so what credit is to be allowed in respect of the dividend.

(2) Where credit for foreign tax falls under any arrangements to be allowed in respect of any income or gain and subsection (1) above does not apply, then, in computing the amount of the income or gain for the purposes of income tax or corporation tax—

    (*a*) no deduction shall be made for foreign tax, whether in respect of the same or any other income or gain; and

    (*b*) the amount of the income shall, in the case of a dividend, be treated as increased by—

        [(i)]² any underlying tax which, under the arrangements, is to be taken into account in considering whether any and if so what credit is to be allowed in respect of the dividend[, and (ii) any underlying tax which, by virtue of section 799(1)(*b*) or section 799(1B)(*b*), does not fall to be so taken into account]².

(3) The amount of any income or gain shall not be treated as increased under this section by reference to any foreign tax which, although not payable, falls to be taken into account for the purposes of section 788(5).

[(3A) The amount of any income or gain shall not be increased under subsection (2)(*b*)(i) above by so much of any underlying tax—

    (*a*) as represents an increase under section 801(4B); or

    (*b*) as represents relievable underlying tax (within the meaning of sections 806A to 806J) arising in respect of another dividend and treated as underlying tax under those sections.]²

[(4) Subsections (2) and (3) above have effect for the purposes of corporation tax notwithstanding anything in—

    [(a)]³ section 80(5) of the Finance Act 1996 (matters to be brought into account in the case of loan relationships only under Chapter II of Part IV of that Act).]¹

[, or

    (*b*) paragraph 1(3) of Schedule 29 to the Finance Act 2002 (matters to be brought into account in respect of intangible fixed assets only under that Schedule).]³

Commentary—*Simon's Direct Tax Service* **D2.1139; F1.131, 133.**
Revenue Internal Guidance—Double taxation relief manual DT 750 (corresponding adjustment where profits of associated enterprises are adjusted on an arm's length basis).
DT 875 (meaning of "income").
DT 878–879 (computation of overseas branch profits).
DT 881 (computation of profit on long-term contracts).
DT 886 (computation of royalty income).
DT 887 (management and technical fees).
DT 888 (computation of dividend income).
DT 895 (computation of income from foreign partnership, with worked example).
DT 900–915 (other special cases).
DT 1110 (computation on arising basis or remittance basis).
Revenue Internal Guidance—Property Income Manual PIM4700 (worked example relating to the letting of property outside the UK).
Definitions—"Arrangements", s 792(1); "foreign tax", s 792(1), (3); "income tax", s 832(4); "underlying tax", s 792(1); "United Kingdom", s 830(1).
Cross references—See TA 1988 s 798 (limitation on double tax relief on income computed in accordance with this section).
TA 1988 s 804A(5) (disapplication of sub-s (2)(*a*) above in certain circumstances applicable to overseas life assurance business).
Amendments—¹ Sub-s (4) inserted by FA 1996 Sch 14 para 41 with effect for accounting periods ending after 31 March 1996, subject to transitional provisions in FA 1996 Sch 15.
² Words in sub-s (2), and sub-s (3A) inserted by FA 2001 s 81, Sch 27 para 1 with effect for dividends paid after 30 March 2001 by a company resident outside the UK to a company resident in the UK (whenever any such dividend as is mentioned in TA 1988 s 801(2) or (3) was paid).
³ In sub-s (4), "(*a*)" inserted, and para (*b*) added by FA 2002 s 84(2), Sch 30 para 5(1), (2) with effect from 24 July 2002.

[795A Limits on credit: minimisation of the foreign tax]

(1) The amount of credit for foreign tax which, under any arrangements, is to be allowed against tax in respect of any income or chargeable gain shall not exceed the credit which would be allowed had all reasonable steps been taken—

(a) under the law of the territory concerned, and

(b) under any arrangements made [in relation to][2] that territory,

to minimise the amount of tax payable in that territory.

(2) The steps mentioned in subsection (1) above include—

(a) claiming, or otherwise securing the benefit of, reliefs, deductions, reductions or allowances; and

(b) making elections for tax purposes.

(3) For the purposes of subsection (1) above, any question as to the steps which it would have been reasonable for a person to take shall be determined on the basis of what the person might reasonably be expected to have done in the absence of relief under this Part against tax in the United Kingdom.][1]

Amendments—[1] This section inserted by FA 2000 s 103, Sch 30 para 6 with effect for claims for credit made after 20 March 2000.

[2] Words substituted for the words "with the government of" by FA 2002 s 88(2)(a), (3) with effect on and after the date of the passing of FA 2002 (24 July 2002) in relation to arrangements made before that date (as well as in relation to arrangements made on or after that date).

796 Limits on credit: income tax

(1) The amount of the credit for foreign tax which, under any arrangements, is to be allowed to a person against income tax for any year of assessment shall not exceed the difference between the amounts of income tax which would be borne by him for the year (no credit being allowed for foreign tax [but allowing for the making of any other income tax reduction under the Income Tax Acts][1])—

(a) if he were charged to tax on his total income for the year, computed in accordance with section 795; and

(b) if he were charged to tax on the same income, computed in the same way, but excluding the income in respect of which the credit is to be allowed.

(2) Where credit for foreign tax is to be allowed in respect of income from more than one source, subsection (1) above shall be applied successively to the income from each source, but so that on each successive application, paragraph (a) shall apply to the total income exclusive of the income to which the subsection has already been applied.

(3) Without prejudice to subsections (1) and (2) above, the total credit for foreign tax to be allowed to a person against income tax for any year of assessment under all arrangements having effect by virtue of section 788 shall not exceed the total income tax payable by him for that year of assessment, less any income tax which he is entitled to charge against any other person.

Commentary—*Simon's Direct Tax Service* F1.121; F3.104.
Revenue Internal Guidance—Double taxation relief manual DT 1120–1125 (detailed explanation with worked example).
DT 11301–133 (transitional year 1996–97).
DT 11381–142 (other transitional matters).
DT 11501–165 (effect of loss relief claims).
Definitions—"Arrangements", s 792(1); "foreign tax", s 792(1), (3); "income tax", s 832(4); "Income Tax Acts", s 831(1)(b); "tax", s 832(3); "total income", s 835(1); "year of assessment", s 832(1).
Cross references—See TA 1988 Sch 26 para 4(4) (dividends from foreign controlled company).
FA 1990 s 25(6), (7) (where any gift made by an individual (a "donor") in a year of assessment is a qualifying donation, then for that year sub-s (3) above shall have effect in its application to him as if any reference to income tax which he is entitled to charge against any person included a reference to the tax treated as deducted from the gift).
Amendments—[1] Words in sub-s (1) inserted by FA 1994 s 77(7) and Sch 8 para 12 with effect from the year 1994–95.

797 Limits on credit: corporation tax

(1) The amount of the credit for foreign tax which under any arrangements is to be allowed against corporation tax in respect of any income or chargeable gain ("the relevant income or gain") shall not exceed the corporation tax attributable to the relevant income or gain, determined in accordance with subsections (2) and (3) below.

(2) Subject to subsection (3) below, the amount of corporation tax attributable to the relevant income or gain shall be treated as equal to such proportion of the amount of that income or gain as corresponds to the rate of corporation tax payable by the company (before any credit under this Part) on its income or chargeable gains for the accounting period in which the income arises or the gain accrues ("the relevant accounting period").

(3) Where in the relevant accounting period there is any deduction to be made for charges on income, expenses of management or other amounts which can be deducted from or set against or treated as reducing profits of more than one description—

(a) the company may for the purposes of this section allocate the deduction in such amounts and to such of its profits for that period as it thinks fit; and

(b) the amount of the relevant income or gain shall be treated for the purposes of subsection (2) above as reduced or, as the case may be, extinguished by so much (if any) of the deduction as is allocated to it.

[(3A) Where, in a case to which section 797A does not apply, a company has a non-trading deficit on its loan relationships for the relevant accounting period, then for the purposes of subsection (3) above that deficit shall be treated, to the extent that it is an amount to which a claim under—

(*a*) subsection (2)(*a*) of section 83 of the Finance Act 1996 (deficit set against current year profits), or

(*b*) paragraph 4(2) of Schedule 11 to that Act (set-off of deficits in the case of insurance companies),

relates, as an amount that can in that period be set against profits of any description but can be allocated in accordance with subsection (3) above only to the profits against which it is set off in pursuance of the claim.]¹

[(3B) For the purposes of subsection (3) above, where—

(*a*) section 797A does not apply in the case of any company, and

(*b*) any amount is carried forward to the relevant accounting period in pursuance of [subsection (3A) of]⁴ section 83 of the Finance Act 1996 [...]²,

then that amount must be allocated to non-trading profits of the company for that period (so far as they are sufficient for the purpose) and cannot be allocated to any other profits.]¹

(4), (5) ...³

[(6) In this section ''non-trading profits'' has the same meaning as in paragraph 4 of Schedule 8 to the Finance Act 1996.]¹

Commentary—*Simon's Direct Tax Service* F1.122, 123; F2.103.
Revenue & other press releases—IR Booklet IR6 (guidance on basis of relief and provisions of typical double taxation agreements).
Simon's Tax Cases—s 797(1), *Collard v Mining and Industrial Holdings Ltd* [1988] STC 15*.
s 797(3)(*a*), *Commercial Union Assurance Co plc v Shaw* [1999] STC 109.
s 797(4), *Collard v Mining and Industrial Holdings Ltd* [1989] STC 384*.
Definitions—''Accounting period'', s 834(1); ''advance corporation tax'', s 14(1); ''arrangements'', s 792(1); ''chargeable gain'', s 832(1); ''company'', s 832(1), (2); ''foreign tax'', s 792(1), (3); ''loan relationship'', s 834(1), FA 1996 s 81; ''non-trading deficit'', s 834(1), FA 1996 s 82.
Cross references—See TA 1988 s 727A(3), (7) (application of sub-s (3) above in relation to non-trading debits where foreign tax is available for credit against interest brought into account as a non-trading credit).
TA 1988 Sch 26 para 4(4) (dividends from foreign controlled company).
Manufactured Dividends (Tax) Regulations, SI 1997/993 reg 9(1) (sub-s (4) above to apply to a non-UK resident company is liable to account for those Regulations in relation to a manufactured dividend, as if that tax were advance corporation tax).
Corporation Tax (Treatment of Unrelieved Surplus Advance Corporation Tax) Regulations, SI 1999/358 reg 12 (application of this section in determining utilisation of shadow ACT).
Amendments—¹ Sub-ss (3A), (3B), (6) inserted by FA 1996 ss 104, 105(1), Sch 14 para 42(1) with effect for accounting periods ending after 31 March 1995, subject to transitional provisions in FA 1996 Sch 15.
² Words in sub-s (3B) repealed by FA 1998 s 82(2), Sch 27 Part III(17) and deemed always to have had effect.
³ Sub-ss (4), (5) repealed by FA 1998 s 31, Sch 3 para 35 with effect for accounting periods beginning after 5 April 1999.
⁴ In sub-s (3B)(*b*), words substituted for the words ''a claim under subsection (2)(*d*) of'' by FA 2002 s 82, Sch 25 paras 43, 54 with effect for accounting periods beginning after 30 September 2002.

[797A Foreign tax on [items giving rise to]³ a non-trading credit[: loan relationships]⁴

(1) This section applies for the purposes of any arrangements where, in the case of any company—

(*a*) any non-trading credit relating to an [item]³ is brought into account for the purposes of Chapter II of Part IV of the Finance Act 1996 (loan relationships) for any accounting period (''the applicable accounting period''); and

(*b*) there is in respect of [that item]³ an amount of foreign tax for which, under the arrangements, credit is allowable against United Kingdom tax computed by reference to [that item]³.

(2) It shall be assumed that tax chargeable under paragraph (*a*) of Case III of Schedule D on the profits and gains arising for the applicable accounting period from the company's loan relationships falls to be computed on the actual amount of its non-trading credits for that period, and without any deduction in respect of non-trading debits.

(3) Section 797(3) shall have effect (subject to subsection (7) below) as if—

(*a*) there were for the applicable accounting period an amount equal to the adjusted amount of the non-trading debits falling to be brought into account by being set against profits of the company for that period of any description; and

(*b*) different parts of that amount might be set against different profits.

(4) For the purposes of this section, the adjusted amount of a company's non-trading debits for any accounting period is the amount equal, in the case of that company, to the aggregate of the non-trading debits given for that period for the purposes of Chapter II of Part IV of the Finance Act 1996 (loan relationships) less the aggregate of the amounts specified in subsection (5) below.

(5) Those amounts are—

(*a*) so much of any non-trading deficit for the applicable accounting period as is an amount to which a claim under subsection [(2)(*c*)]⁵ of section 83 of the Finance Act 1996 or paragraph 4(3) of Schedule 11 to that Act [(deficit carried back and set against profits)]⁵ relates; and

[(*aa*) so much of any non-trading deficit for that period as is surrendered as group relief by virtue of section 403 of the Taxes Act 1988; and]⁵

(*b*) so much of any non-trading deficit for that period as falls to be carried forward to a subsequent period in accordance with subsection [(3A)]⁵ of that section or paragraph 4(4) of that Schedule.

(*c*) ...²

...⁶

(6) Section 797(3) shall have effect as if any amount [carried forward to the applicable accounting period [under section 83(3A)][5] of that Act][2] were an amount capable of being allocated only to any non-trading profits of the company.

(7) Where—

    (*a*) the company has a non-trading deficit for the applicable accounting period,

    (*b*) the amount of that deficit exceeds the aggregate of the amounts specified in subsection (5) above, and

    (*c*) in pursuance of a claim under—

        (i) subsection (2)(*a*) of section 83 of the Finance Act 1996 (deficit set against current year profits), or

        (ii) paragraph 4(2) of Schedule 11 to that Act (set-off of deficits in the case of insurance companies),

    the excess falls to be set off against profits of any description,

section 797(3) shall have effect as if non-trading debits of the company which in aggregate are equal to the amount of the excess were required to be allocated to the profits against which they are set off in pursuance of the claim.

...[6]

(8) In this section "non-trading profits" has the same meaning as in paragraph 4 of Schedule 8 to the Finance Act 1996.][1]

Commentary—*Simon's Direct Tax Service* **C1.618, F2.103.**
Definitions—"Accounting period", s 834(1); "arrangements", s 792(2); "company", s 832(1), (2); "foreign tax", s 792(1), (3); "interest", s 832(1); "loan relationship", s 834(1), FA 1996 s 81; "non-trading deficit", s 834(1), FA 1996 s 82; "profits and gains", s 833(1); "Schedule D", s 18; "United Kingdom tax", s 792(1).
Amendments—[1] This section inserted by FA 1996 ss 104, 105(1), Sch 14 para 43 with effect for accounting periods ending after 31 March 1996, subject to transitional provisions in FA 1996 Sch 15.
[2] Words in sub-ss (5), (7) inserted, words in sub-s (6) substituted, and sub-s (5)(*c*) repealed by FA 1998 s 82(2), Sch 27 Part III(17) and deemed always to have had effect.
[3] Words in section heading and sub-s (1) substituted by FA 2000 s 103, Sch 30 para 7 with effect for accounting periods ending after 20 March 2000.
[4] Words in section heading added by FA 2002 s 84(2), Sch 30 para 5(1), 3 with effect from the 24 July 2002.
[5] In sub-s (5), in para (*a*), words substituted for the words "(2)(*b*), (*c*) or (*d*)" and "(group relief and transfer to previous or subsequent period of deficits)"; para (*aa*) inserted, in para (*b*), "(3A)" substituted for "(3)", and in sub-s (6), words substituted for the words "in pursuance of a claim under section 83(2)(*d*)"; by FA 2002 s 82, Sch 25 paras 43, 55 with effect for accounting periods beginning after 30 September 2002.
[6] Words in sub-s (5) and sub-s (7) repealed by FA 2002 s 141, Sch 40 Pt 3(12) with effect for accounting periods beginning after 30 September 2002.
Repealed words in sub-s (5) read as follows—
    "An amount carried forward to the applicable accounting period under section 83(3) of that Act shall not be treated as a non-trading deficit for that period for the purposes of paragraphs (*a*) and (*b*).".
Repealed words in sub-s (7) read as follows—
    "An amount carried forward to the applicable accounting period under section 83(3) of the Finance Act 1996 shall be disregarded for the purposes of paragraphs (*a*) and (*b*).".

[797B Foreign tax on items giving rise to a non-trading credit: intangible fixed assets

(1) This section applies for the purposes of any arrangements where, in the case of a company—

    (*a*) a non-trading credit relating to an item is brought into account for the purposes of Schedule 29 to the Finance Act 2002 (intangible fixed assets) for an accounting period ("the applicable accounting period"), and

    (*b*) there is in respect of that item an amount of foreign tax for which, under the arrangements, credit is allowable against United Kingdom tax computed by reference to that item.

(2) It shall be assumed that tax chargeable under Case VI of Schedule D on the profits and gains arising for the applicable accounting period from the company's intangible fixed assets falls to be computed on the actual amount of its non-trading credits for that period, and without any deduction in respect of non-trading debits.

(3) Section 797(3) shall have effect as if—

    (*a*) there were for the applicable accounting period an amount equal to the adjusted amount of the non-trading debits falling to be brought into account by being set against profits of the company for that period of any description, and

    (*b*) different parts of that amount might be set against different profits.

(4) For this purpose the adjusted amount of a company's non-trading debits for an accounting period is given by:

$$\text{Total Debits} - \text{Amount Carried Forward}$$

where—

    Total Debits is the aggregate amount of the company's non-trading debits for that accounting period under Schedule 29 to the Finance Act 2002 (intangible fixed assets), and

Amount Carried Forward is the amount (if any) carried forward to the next accounting period of the company under paragraph 35(3) of that Schedule (carry-forward of non-trading loss in respect of which no claim is made for it to be set against total profits of current period).][1]

Commentary—*Simon's Direct Tax Service* **D1.701; D2.1139.**
Amendments—[1] This section inserted by FA 2002 s 84(2), Sch 30 para 5(1), (4) with effect from the 24 July 2002.

[798 Restriction of relief on certain interest and dividends

(1) This section applies where—

(*a*) in any chargeable period the profits of a trade carried on by a qualifying taxpayer include an amount computed in accordance with section 795 in respect of foreign interest or foreign dividends;

(*b*) the taxpayer is entitled in accordance with this Chapter to credit for foreign tax on the foreign interest or foreign dividends; and

(*c*) in the case of foreign dividends, the foreign tax mentioned in paragraph (*b*) above is or includes underlying tax.

(2) The amount of the credit for foreign tax referred to in subsection (1)(*b*) above which, in accordance with this Chapter, is to be allowed against income tax or corporation tax—

(*a*) shall be limited by treating the amount of the foreign interest or foreign dividends (as increased or reduced under section 798A) as reduced (or further reduced) for the purposes of this Chapter by an amount equal to the taxpayer's financial expenditure in relation to the interest or dividends (as determined in accordance with section 798B); and

(*b*) so far as the credit relates to foreign tax on interest or foreign tax on dividends which is not underlying tax, shall not exceed 15 per cent of the interest or dividends, computed without regard to paragraph (a) above or to any increase or reduction under section 798A.

(3) In this section and sections 798A and 798B—

"interest", in relation to a loan, includes any introductory or other fee or charge which is payable in accordance with the terms on which the loan is made or is otherwise payable in connection with the making of the loan;

"foreign dividends" means dividends payable out of or in respect of the stocks, funds, shares or securities of a body of persons not resident in the United Kingdom;

"foreign interest" means interest payable by a person not resident in the United Kingdom or by a government or public or local authority in a country outside the United Kingdom.

(4) In this section and section 798B "qualifying taxpayer" means, subject to subsection (5) below, a person carrying on a trade which includes the receipt of interest or dividends and is not an insurance business.

(5) Where a company which is connected or associated with a qualifying taxpayer is acting in accordance with a scheme or arrangement the purpose, or one of the main purposes, of which is to prevent or restrict the application of this section to the taxpayer—

(*a*) the company shall be treated for the purposes of this section as a qualifying taxpayer; and

(*b*) any foreign interest or foreign dividends received in pursuance of the scheme or arrangement shall be treated for those purposes as profits of a trade carried on by the company.

(6) For the purposes of this section and section 798B—

(*a*) section 839 applies; and

(*b*) subsection (10) of section 783 applies as it applies for the purposes of that section.][1]

Commentary—*Simon's Direct Tax Service* **D1.701; D2.1139.**
Revenue Internal Guidance—Double taxation relief manual DT1050 (paying agents, bankers etc are authorised to allow credit automatically for withholding tax on dividends and interest).
Amendments—[1] This section substituted by FA 1998 s 103(1) with effect in relation to foreign interest or foreign dividends paid out on or after 17 March 1998. Note that it does not have effect in relation to foreign interest or foreign dividends paid before 1 January 1999 in pursuance of arrangements which were entered into before, and are not altered on or after, 17 March 1998.

[798A Adjustments of interest and dividends for spared tax etc

(1) In a case where section 798 applies—

(*a*) subsection (2) below applies if the foreign tax referred to in subsection (1)(*b*) of that section is or includes an amount of spared tax; and

(*b*) subsection (3) below applies if the foreign tax so referred to is or includes an amount of tax which is not spared tax.

(2) For the purposes of income tax or corporation tax, the amount which apart from this subsection would be the amount of the foreign interest or foreign dividends shall be treated as increased by so much of the spared tax as does not exceed—

(*a*) the amount of the spared tax for which, in accordance with any arrangements applicable to the case in question, credit falls to be given as mentioned in section 798(1)(*b*); or

(*b*) if it is less, 15 per cent of the interest or dividends, computed without regard to any increase under this subsection.

(3) If the amount of tax which is not spared tax exceeds—

(*a*) the amount of the credit which, by virtue of this Chapter (but disregarding subsection (2) of section 798), is allowed for that tax against income tax or corporation tax; or (*b*) if it is less in the case of tax on foreign interest, 15 per cent of the interest, computed without regard to any increase or reduction under this section or that subsection,

then, for the purposes of income tax or corporation tax, the amount which, apart from this subsection, would be the amount of the foreign interest or foreign dividends shall be treated as reduced by a sum equal to the excess.

(4) Subsection (2) above has effect for the purposes of corporation tax notwithstanding anything in section 80(5) of the Finance Act 1996 (matters to be brought into account in the case of loan relationships only under Chapter II of Part IV of that Act).

(5) Nothing in subsection (2) above prejudices the operation of section 795 in relation to foreign tax which is not spared tax.

(6) In this section ''spared tax'' means foreign tax which although not payable falls to be taken into account for the purposes of credit by virtue of section 788(5).]¹

Commentary—*Simon's Direct Tax Service* **D1.701; D2.1139.**
Amendments—¹ This section inserted by FA 1998 s 104 with effect in relation to foreign interest or foreign dividends paid out on or after 17 March 1998. Note that it does not have effect in relation to foreign interest or foreign dividends paid before 1 January 1999 in pursuance of arrangements which were entered into before, and are not altered on or after, 17 March 1998.

[798B Meaning of ''financial expenditure''

(1) For the purposes of section 798 ''financial expenditure'', in relation to a qualifying taxpayer and any interest or dividends is, subject to the provisions of this section, the aggregate of—

(*a*) so much of the financial expenses (consisting of interest, discounts or similar sums or qualifying losses) incurred by the taxpayer or a person connected or associated with him as—

(i) is properly attributable to the earning of the interest or dividends; and
(ii) falls to be taken into account in computing the taxpayer's or person's liability to income tax or corporation tax; and

(*b*) so much of any other sum paid by the taxpayer or a person connected or associated with him which—

(i) falls to be taken into account as mentioned in paragraph (*a*) above; and
(ii) would not, apart from this paragraph, be taken into account in determining the amount of the interest or dividends,

as it is reasonable to regard as attributable to the earning of the interest or dividends (whether or not it would fall, in accordance with [generally accepted accounting practice]⁴, to be so treated).

(2) There shall be deducted from the aggregate given by subsection (1) above so much of the qualifying gains and profits accruing to the qualifying taxpayer or a person connected or associated with him as—

(*a*) is properly attributable to the earning of the interest or dividends; and
(*b*) falls to be taken into account in computing the taxpayer's or person's liability to income tax or corporation tax.

(3) In a case where the amount of a qualifying taxpayer's financial expenditure in relation to the earning of the interest or dividends is not readily ascertainable—

(*a*) that amount shall be taken, subject to subsection (4) below, to be such sum as it is just and reasonable to attribute to the earning of the interest or dividends; and
(*b*) in the case of interest, regard shall be had in particular to any market rates of interest by reference to which the rate of the interest is determined.

(4) The Board may by regulations supplement subsection (3) above—

(*a*) by specifying matters to be taken into account in determining such a just and reasonable attribution as is referred to in paragraph (*a*); and
(*b*) by making provision with respect to the determination of market rates of interest for the purposes of paragraph (*b*);

and any such regulations may make different provision for different cases.

(5) In this section ''qualifying losses'' means—

[(*a*) exchange losses falling to be brought into account as debits for the purposes of Chapter 2 of Part 4 of the Finance Act 1996 (loan relationships); and]²
[(*b*) the amount (if any) by which debits brought into account in respect of a derivative contract for the purposes of Schedule 26 to the Finance Act 2002 (derivative contracts) exceed credits so brought into account;]³

and ''qualifying gains'' and ''qualifying profits'' shall be construed accordingly.]¹

Commentary—*Simon's Direct Tax Service* **D1.701; D2.1139.**
Amendments—¹ This section substituted by FA 1998 s 105 with effect in relation to foreign interest or foreign dividends paid out on or after 17 March 1998. Note that it does not have effect in relation to foreign interest or foreign dividends paid before 1 January 1999 in pursuance of arrangements which were entered into before, and are not altered on or after, 17 March 1998.
² Sub-s (5)(*a*) substituted by FA 2002 s 79, Sch 23 para 20 with effect for accounting periods beginning after 30 September 2002. Sub-s (5)(*a*) previously read as follows—

''(*a*) losses falling to be brought into account for the purposes of Chapter II of Part II of the Finance Act 1993 (exchange gains and losses) in accordance with sections 125 to 127 of that Act; and''.

[3] Sub-s (5)(*b*) substituted by FA 2002 s 83(1)(*b*), (3) Sch 27 paras 1, 11 with effect for accounting periods beginning after 30 September 2002. Sub-s (5)(*b*) previously read as follows—

   ''(*b*) losses falling to be brought into account for the purposes of Chapter II of Part IV of the Finance Act 1994 (interest rate and currency contracts) in accordance with sections 155 to 158 of that Act;''.

[4] In sub-s (1), words substituted for the words ''normal accountancy practice'' by FA 2002 s 103(4)(*a*) with effect from the 24 July 2002.

Tax underlying dividends

799 Computation of underlying tax

(1) Where in the case of any dividend arrangements provide for underlying tax to be taken into account in considering whether any and if so what credit is to be allowed against the United Kingdom taxes in respect of the dividend, the tax to be taken into account by virtue of that provision shall be so much of the foreign tax borne on the relevant profits by the body corporate paying the dividend as

   [(*a*)]² is properly attributable to the proportion of the relevant profits represented by the dividend [, and

   (*b*) does not exceed the amount calculated by applying the formula set out in subsection (1A) below.]²

[''(1A) The formula is—

$$(D + U) \times M\%$$

where—

   D is the amount of the dividend;

   U is the amount of underlying tax that would fall to be taken into account as mentioned in subsection (1) above, apart from paragraph (*b*) of that subsection; and

   M% is the maximum relievable rate;

and for the purposes of this subsection the maximum relievable rate is the rate of corporation tax in force when the dividend was paid.

(1B) Where, under any arrangements, a company makes a claim for an allowance by way of credit in accordance with this Chapter—

   (*a*) the claim may be so framed as to exclude such amounts of underlying tax as may be specified for the purpose in the claim; and

   (*b*) any amounts of underlying tax so excluded shall be left out of account for the purposes of this section.]⁴

(2) Where under the foreign tax law the dividend has been increased for tax purposes by an amount to be set off against the recipient's own tax under that law or, to the extent that it exceeds his own tax thereunder, paid to him, then, from the amount of the underlying tax to be taken into account under subsection (1) above there is to be subtracted the amount of that increase.

(3) For the purposes of subsection (1) above the relevant profits, subject to subsection (4) below, are—

   (*a*) if the dividend is paid for a specified period, the profits of that period; [and]³

   (*b*) ...³

   (*c*) if the dividend is [not paid for a specified period]³, the profits of the last period for which accounts of the body corporate were made up which ended before the dividend became payable.

(4) If, in a case falling under paragraph (*a*) or (*c*) of subsection (3) above, the total dividend exceeds the profits available for distribution of the period mentioned in that paragraph the relevant profits shall be the profits of that period plus so much of the profits available for distribution of preceding periods (other than profits previously distributed or previously treated as relevant profits for the purposes of this section or section 506 of the 1970 Act) as is equal to the excess; and for the purposes of this subsection the profits of the most recent preceding period shall first be taken into account, then the profits of the next most recent preceding period, and so on.

[(5) For the purposes of paragraphs (*a*) and (*c*) of subsection (3) above, ''profits'', in the case of any period, means the profits available for distribution.

(6) In subsections (4) and (5) above, ''profits available for distribution'' means, in the case of any company, the profits available for distribution as shown in accounts relating to the company—

   (*a*) drawn up in accordance with the law of the company's home State, and

   (*b*) making no provision for reserves, bad debts or contingencies other than such as is required to be made under that law.

(7) In this section, ''home State'', in the case of any company, means the country or territory under whose law the company is incorporated or formed.]¹

Commentary—*Simon's Direct Tax Service* F1.134.

Revenue Internal Guidance—Company Taxation Manual COT8411 (meaning of ''relevant profits'' in sub-s(1)).

Definitions—''The 1970 Act'', s 831(3); ''arrangements'', s 792(1); ''distribution'', s 209(2), by virtue of s 832(1); ''dividend'', s 834(3); ''foreign tax'', s 792(1), (3); ''tax'', s 832(3); ''underlying tax'', s 792(1); ''United Kingdom taxes'', s 792(1).

Cross references—See TA 1988 Sch 25 paras 2(1)(1B), (3), 3 (controlled foreign company: acceptable distribution policy to exclude apportionment under s 747: application of this section in relating dividends to profits).

Amendments—¹ Sub-ss (5)–(7) inserted by FA 2000 s 103, Sch 30 para 9 with effect for any claim for credit, under any arrangements, in respect of underlying tax in relation to a dividend paid after 20 March 2000 by a company resident outside the UK to a company resident in the UK.

[2] In sub-s (1), words added and para (*b*) inserted by FA 2000 ss 103, 156, Sch 30 para 8, Sch 40 Pt II(13) with effect for any claim for an allowance by way of credit made after 30 March 2001 in respect of a dividend paid by a company resident outside the United Kingdom to a company resident in the United Kingdom, unless the dividend was paid before 31 March 2001.

[3] In sub-s (3), word in para (*a*) added, para (*b*) repealed, and words in para (*c*) substituted by FA 2000 ss 103, 156, Sch 30 para 8, Sch 40 Pt II(13) with effect for any claim for an allowance by way of credit made after 30 March 2001 in respect of a dividend paid by a company resident outside the UK to a company resident in the UK, unless the dividend was paid before 31 March 2001.

[4] Sub-s (1A) substituted, and sub-s (1B) inserted, by FA 2001 s 81, Sch 27 para 2 with effect for any claim for an allowance by way of credit made on or after 31 March 2001 in respect of a dividend paid by a company resident outside the UK to a company resident in the UK, unless the dividend was paid before that date. In determining, for the purpose of any such claim made after that date, the underlying tax of any such third, fourth or successive company as is mentioned in TA 1988 s 801(2) or (3), these amendments are taken to have had effect at the time the dividend paid by that company was paid

800 Dividends paid between related companies but not covered by arrangements

Where—

> (a) *arrangements provide, in relation to dividends of some classes but not in relation to dividends of other classes, that underlying tax is to be taken into account in considering whether any, and if so what, credit is to be allowed against the United Kingdom taxes in respect of the dividends; and*
> (b) *a dividend is paid which is not of a class in relation to which the arrangements so provide;*

then, if the dividend is paid to a company which controls directly or indirectly, or is a subsidiary of a company which controls directly or indirectly, not less than 10 per cent of the voting power in the company paying the dividend, credit shall be allowed as if the dividend were a dividend of a class in relation to which the arrangements so provide.[1]

Commentary—*Simon's Direct Tax Service* F2.107.
Definitions—"Arrangements", s 792(1); "company", s 832(1), (2); "control", s 840; "subsidiary", s 792(2); "underlying tax", s 792(1); "United Kingdom taxes", s 792(1).
Amendments—[1] This section repealed by FA 2000 ss 103, 156, Sch 30 para 10, Sch 40 Pt II(13) with effect for dividends paid after 31 March 2000.

801 Dividends paid between related companies: relief for UK and third country taxes

(1) Where a company resident outside the United Kingdom ("the overseas company") pays a dividend to a [company falling within subsection (1A) below ("the relevant company")][1] and the overseas company is related [to the relevant company][1], then for the purpose of allowing credit under any arrangements against corporation tax in respect of the dividend, there shall be taken into account, as if it were tax payable under the law of the territory in which the overseas company is resident—

> (a) any United Kingdom income tax or corporation tax payable by the overseas company in respect of its profits; and
> (b) any tax which, under the law of any other territory, is payable by the overseas company in respect of its profits.

[(1A) A company falls within this subsection if—

> (a) it is resident in the United Kingdom; or
> (b) it is resident outside the United Kingdom but the dividend mentioned in subsection (1) above forms part of the profits of a branch or agency of the company's in the United Kingdom.][1]

(2) Where the overseas company has received a dividend from a third company and the third company is related to the overseas company, then, [subject to subsections (4) to (4D)][3] below, there shall be treated for the purposes of subsection (1) above as tax paid by the overseas company in respect of its profits any underlying tax payable by the third company, to the extent that it would be taken into account under this Part if the dividend had been paid by a company resident outside the United Kingdom to a company resident in the United Kingdom and arrangements had provided for underlying tax to be taken into account.

[(2A) Section 799(1)(*b*) applies for the purposes of subsection (2) above only—

> (a) if the overseas company and the third company are not resident in the same territory; or
> (b) in such other cases as may be prescribed by regulations made by the Treasury.][2]

(3) Where the third company has received a dividend from a fourth company and the fourth company is related to the third company, then, subject to subsection (4) below, tax payable by the fourth company shall similarly be treated for the purposes of subsection (2) above as tax paid by the third company; and so on for successive companies each of which is related to the one before.

(4) Subsections (2) and (3) above are subject to the following limitations—

> (a) no tax shall be taken into account in respect of a dividend paid by a company resident in the United Kingdom except United Kingdom corporation tax and any tax for which that company is entitled to credit under this Part; and
> (b) no tax shall be taken into account in respect of a dividend paid by a company resident outside the United Kingdom to another such company unless it could have been taken into account under the other provisions of this Part had the other company been resident in the United Kingdom.

[(4A) If, in the application of section 799(1)(*b*) by subsection (2) or (3) above in relation to a dividend paid by a company resident in the United Kingdom—

> (a) the amount given by the formula in section 799(1A),

exceeds

    (*b*) the value of U in that formula,

subsection (4B) below shall apply.

(4B) Where this subsection applies, in the application (otherwise than by subsection (2) or (3) above) of subsection (1) of section 799 in relation to the dividend mentioned in that subsection (''the Case V dividend''), the amount of foreign tax which by virtue of the provision made by the arrangements mentioned in that subsection would fall to be taken into account under this Part in respect of the Case V dividend—

    (*a*) apart from this subsection, and
    (*b*) after applying paragraphs (*a*) and (*b*) of that subsection,

shall be increased by an amount of underlying tax equal to the appropriate portion of the amount of the excess described in subsection (4A) above in relation to the dividend paid by the company resident in the United Kingdom.

(4C) Subsection (6) of section 806B (meaning of ''appropriate portion''), as read with subsections (7) and (10) of that section, shall have effect for the purposes of subsection (4B) above as it has effect for the purposes of subsection (5) of that section (but taking the references in subsection (10) of that section to the Case V dividend as references to the Case V dividend within the meaning of subsection (4B) above).

(4D) Subsections (4A) to (4C) above shall be ignored in determining for the purposes of subsection (2) or (3) above the extent to which any underlying tax paid by a company would be taken into account under this Part if the dividend in question had been paid by a company resident outside the United Kingdom to a company resident in the United Kingdom.][3]

(5) For the purposes of this section a company is related to another company if that other company—

    (*a*) controls directly or indirectly, or
    (*b*) is a subsidiary of a company which controls directly or indirectly,

not less than 10 per cent of the voting power in the first-mentioned company.

Commentary—*Simon's Direct Tax Service* **F2.109.**
Regulations—Double Taxation Relief (Taxes on Income) (Underlying Tax on Dividends and Dual Resident Companies) Regulations, SI 2001/1156.
Revenue Internal Guidance—Double taxation relief manual DT 1015 (rates of underlying tax are determined by FICO (International)).
DT 1030–1031 (worked examples of relief for underlying tax).
Simon's Tax Cases—s 801(1), (2), *Memec plc v IRC* [1998] STC 754.
Definitions—''Company'', s 832(1), (2); ''control'', s 840; ''income tax'', s 832(4); ''subsidiary'', s 792(2); ''tax'', s 832(3); ''underlying tax'', s 792(1); ''United Kingdom'', s 830(1).
Amendments—[1] Words in sub-s (1) substituted and sub-s (1A) inserted by FA 2000 s 103, Sch 30 para 4(7)–(9), (14) with effect for chargeable periods ending after 20 March 2000 by virtue of FA 2001 s 81, Sch 27 para 7.
[2] Sub-s (2A) inserted by FA 2000 s 103, Sch 30 para 11 with effect for claims for allowances by way of credit made after 30 March 2001, in respect of a dividend paid by a company resident outside the UK to a company resident in the UK, unless the dividend was paid before 31 March 2001.
[3] Words in sub-s (2) substituted, and sub-ss (4A)–(4D) inserted, by FA 2001 s 81, Sch 27 para 3 with effect for any claim for an allowance by way of credit made on or after 31 March 2001 in respect of a dividend paid by a company resident outside the UK to a company resident in the UK, unless the dividend was paid before that date. In determining, for the purpose of any such claim made after that date, the underlying tax of any such third, fourth or successive company as is mentioned in TA 1988 s 801(2) or (3), these amendments are taken to have had effect at the time the dividend paid by that company was paid

[801A Restriction of relief for underlying tax

(1) This section applies where—

    (*a*) [a company (''the claimant company'')][2] makes a claim for an allowance by way of credit in accordance with this Part;
    (*b*) the claim relates to underlying tax on a dividend paid to that company by a company resident outside the United Kingdom (''the overseas company'');
    (*c*) that underlying tax is or includes an amount in respect of tax (''the high rate tax'') payable by—

        (i) the overseas company, or
        (ii) such a third, fourth or successive company as is mentioned in section 801,

    at a rate in excess of the relievable rate; and
    (*d*) the whole or any part of the amount in respect of the high rate tax which is or is included in the underlying tax would not be, or be included in, that underlying tax but for the existence of, or for there having been, an avoidance scheme.

(2) Where this section applies, the amount of the credit to which [the claimant company][2] is entitled on the claim shall be determined as if the high rate tax had been tax at the relievable rate, instead of at a rate in excess of that rate.

(3) For the purposes of this section tax shall be taken to be payable at a rate in excess of the relievable rate if, and to the extent that, the amount of that tax exceeds the amount that would represent tax on the relevant profits at the relievable rate.

(4) In subsection (3) above ''the relevant profits'' in relation to any tax, means the profits of the overseas company or, as the case may be, of the third, fourth or successive company which, for the purposes of this Part, are taken to bear that tax.

(5) In this section ''the relievable rate'' means the rate of corporation tax in force when the dividend mentioned in subsection (1)(*b*) above was paid.

(6) In this section ''an avoidance scheme'' means any scheme or arrangement which—

 (*a*) falls within subsection (7) below; and

 (*b*) is a scheme or arrangement the purpose, or one of the main purposes, of which is to have an amount of underlying tax taken into account on a claim for an allowance by way of credit in accordance with this Part.

(7) A scheme or arrangement falls within this subsection if the parties to it include both—

 (*a*) [the claimant company]², a company related to that company or a person connected with the United Kingdom company; and

 (*b*) a person who was not under the control of the United Kingdom company at any time before the doing of anything as part of, or in pursuance of, the scheme or arrangement.

(8) In this section ''arrangement'' means an arrangement of any kind, whether in writing or not.

(9) Section 839 (meaning of ''connected persons'') applies for the purposes of this section.

(10) Subsection (5) of section 801 (meaning of ''related company'') shall apply for the purposes of this section as it applies for the purposes of that section.

(11) For the purposes of this section a person who is a party to a scheme or arrangement shall be taken to have been under the control of [the claimant company]² at all the following times, namely—

 (*a*) any time when that company would have been taken (in accordance with section 416) to have had control of that person for the purposes of Part XI;

 (*b*) any time when that company would have been so taken if that section applied (with the necessary modifications) in the case of partnerships and unincorporated associations as it applies in the case of companies; and

 (*c*) any time when that person acted in relation to that scheme or arrangement, or any proposal for it, either directly or indirectly under the direction of that company.]¹

Commentary—*Simon's Direct Tax Service* F2.106–112.
Revenue Interpretation RI 171—Indicates circumstances in which the Revenue will or will not apply these provisions.
Revenue Internal Guidance—Double taxation relief manual DT972 (Revenue procedures regarding treatment of underlying tax paid on the pre-merger profits of an overseas company).
Definitions—''Company'', s 832(1), (2); ''tax'', s 832(3); ''underlying tax'', s 792(1); ''United Kingdom'', s 830(1).
Amendments—¹ This section inserted by FA 1997 s 90 with effect in relation to dividends paid to a company resident in the United Kingdom at any time after 25 November 1996.
² Words in sub-ss (1), (2), (7), (11) substituted by FA 2000 s 103, Sch 30 para 4(10)–(12), (14) with effect for chargeable periods ending after 20 March 2000 by virtue of FA 2001 s 81, Sch 27 para 7.

[801B Dividends paid out of transferred profits

(1) This section applies where—

 (*a*) a company (''company A'') resident outside the United Kingdom has paid tax under the law of a territory outside the United Kingdom in respect of any of its profits;

 (*b*) some or all of those profits become profits of another company resident outside the United Kingdom (''company B'') otherwise than by virtue of the payment of a dividend to company B; and

 (*c*) company B pays a dividend out of those profits to another company (''company C''), wherever resident.

(2) Where this section applies, this Part shall have effect, so far as relating to the determination of underlying tax in relation to any dividend paid—

 (*a*) by any company resident outside the United Kingdom (whether or not company B),

 (*b*) to a company resident in the United Kingdom,

as if company B had paid the tax paid by company A in respect of those profits of company A which have become profits of company B as mentioned in subsection (1)(*b*) above.

(3) But the amount of relief under this Part which is allowable to a company resident in the United Kingdom shall not exceed the amount which would have been allowable to that company had those profits become profits of company B by virtue of the payment of a dividend by company A to company B.]¹

Commentary—*Simon's Direct Tax Service* F1.122.
Amendments—¹ This section inserted by FA 2000 s 103, Sch 30 para 12 with effect for any claim for credit, under any arrangements, in respect of underlying tax in relation to a dividend paid after 20 March 2000 by a company resident outside the UK to a company resident in the UK.

[801C Separate streaming of dividend so far as representing an ADP dividend of a CFC

(1) This section applies in any case where—

 (*a*) by virtue only of section 748(1)(*a*), no apportionment under section 747(3) falls to be made as regards an accounting period of a controlled foreign company; and

 (*b*) one or more of the dividends paid by the controlled foreign company by virtue of which the condition in paragraph (*a*) above is satisfied are dividends falling within subsection (2) below.

(2) A dividend falls within this subsection if, for the purposes of Part I of Schedule 25, the whole or any part of it falls to be treated by virtue of paragraph 4 of that Schedule as paid by the controlled foreign company to a United Kingdom resident.

(3) If, in a case where this section applies,—

(a) an initial dividend is paid to a company resident outside the United Kingdom, and

(b) that company, or any other company which is related to it, pays an intermediate dividend which for the purposes of paragraph 4 of Schedule 25 to any extent represents that initial dividend,

subsection (4) below shall have effect in relation to the UK recipient concerned.

(4) Where this subsection has effect, it shall be assumed for the purposes of allowing credit relief under this Part to that UK recipient—

(a) that, instead of the intermediate dividend, the dividends described in subsection (5) below had been paid and the circumstances had been as described in subsection (6) or (7) below, as the case may be; and

(b) that any tax paid under the law of any territory in respect of the intermediate dividend, or which is underlying tax in relation to that dividend, had instead fallen to be borne accordingly (taking account of any reduction falling to be made under section 799(2)).

(5) The dividends mentioned in subsection (4)(a) above are—

(a) as respects each of the initial dividends which are, for the purposes of paragraph 4 of Schedule 25, to any extent represented by the intermediate dividend, a separate dividend (an "ADP dividend") representing, and of an amount equal to, so much of that initial dividend as is for those purposes represented by the intermediate dividend; and

(b) a further separate dividend (a "residual dividend") representing, and of an amount equal to, the remainder (if any) of the intermediate dividend.

(6) As respects each of the ADP dividends, the intermediate company is to be treated as if it were a separate company whose distributable profits are of a constitution corresponding to, and an amount equal to, that of the ADP dividend.

(7) As respects the residual dividend (if any), the relevant profits out of which it is to be regarded for the purposes of section 799(1) as paid by the intermediate company are, in consequence of subsection (6) above, to be treated as being of such constitution and amount as remains after excluding accordingly so much of those relevant profits as constitute the whole or any part of the distributable profits out of which the ADP dividends are paid.

(8) If, in a case where this section applies, an intermediate company also pays a dividend which is not an intermediate dividend (an "independent dividend") and either—

(a) that dividend is paid to a United Kingdom resident, or

(b) if it is not so paid, a dividend which to any extent represents it is paid by a company which is related to that company and resident outside the United Kingdom to a United Kingdom resident,

subsection (9) below shall have effect in relation to the United Kingdom resident.

(9) Where this subsection has effect, it shall be assumed for the purposes of allowing credit relief under this Part to the United Kingdom resident—

(a) that the relevant profits out of which the independent dividend is to be regarded for the purposes of section 799(1) as paid by the intermediate company are, in consequence of subsection (6) above, to be treated as being of such constitution and amount as remains after excluding so much of those relevant profits as constitute the whole or any part of the distributable profits out of which the ADP dividends are paid; and

(b) that any tax paid under the law of any territory in respect of the independent dividend, or which is underlying tax in relation to that dividend, had instead fallen to be borne accordingly (taking account of any reduction falling to be made under section 799(2)).

(10) For the purposes of this section—

(a) a controlled foreign company is an "ADP controlled foreign company" as respects any of its accounting periods if the condition in paragraph (a) of subsection (1) above is satisfied as respects that accounting period;

(b) an "initial dividend" (subject to subsection (14) below) is any of the dividends mentioned in paragraph (b) of subsection (1) above paid by an ADP controlled foreign company; and

(c) a "subsequent dividend" is any dividend which, in relation to one or more initial dividends, is the subsequent dividend for the purposes of paragraph 4 of Schedule 25.

(11) In this section—

"distributable profits" means a company's profits available for distribution, determined in accordance with section 799(6);

"intermediate company" means any company resident outside the United Kingdom which pays an intermediate dividend;

"intermediate dividend" means any dividend which is paid by a company resident outside the United Kingdom and which—

(a) for the purposes of paragraph 4 of Schedule 25, to any extent represents one or more initial dividends paid by other companies; and (*b*) either is the subsequent dividend in the case of those initial dividends or is itself to any extent represented for those purposes by a subsequent dividend;

"the UK recipient" means the United Kingdom resident to whom a subsequent dividend is paid.

(12) Where—

(*a*) one company pays a dividend ("dividend A") to another company, and
(*b*) that other company, or a company which is related to it, pays a dividend ("dividend B") to another company,

then, for the purposes of this section, dividend B represents dividend A, and dividend A is represented by dividend B, to the extent that dividend B is paid out of profits which are derived, directly or indirectly, from the whole or part of dividend A.

(13) Sub-paragraph (2) of paragraph 4 of Schedule 25 (related companies) shall apply for the purposes of this section as it applies for the purposes of that paragraph.

(14) Where an intermediate company which is an ADP controlled foreign company pays a dividend—

(*a*) by virtue of which (whether taken alone or with other dividends) the condition in subsection (1)(*a*) above is satisfied as regards an accounting period of the company, but
(*b*) which also for the purposes of paragraph 4 of Schedule 25 to any extent represents one or more initial dividends paid by other ADP controlled foreign companies,

the dividend shall not be regarded for the purposes of this section as an initial dividend paid by the company, to the extent that it so represents initial dividends paid by other ADP controlled foreign companies.][1]

Commentary—*Simon's Direct Tax Service* **F1.122.**
Amendments—[1] This section inserted by FA 2000 s 103, Sch 30 para 13 with effect for any claim for an allowance by way of credit made after 30 March 2001 in respect of a dividend paid by a company resident outside the UK to a company resident in the UK, unless the dividend was paid before 31 March 2001.

[802 UK insurance companies trading overseas

(1) Subject to subsection (2) below, where—

(a) a company resident in the United Kingdom is charged to tax under Case I of Schedule D in respect of any insurance business carried on by it, and
(b) that business or any part of it is carried on through a branch or agency in a territory outside the United Kingdom,

then, in respect of dividends referable to that business which are paid to the company by companies resident in that territory, any tax payable by those companies in respect of their profits under the law of that or any other territory outside the United Kingdom, and any United Kingdom income tax or corporation tax so payable, shall, in considering whether any and if so what credit is to be allowed under any arrangements, be taken into account as tax so payable under the law of the first-mentioned territory is taken into account in a case falling within section 799.

(2) Credit shall not be allowed to a company by virtue of subsection (1) above for any financial year in respect of a greater amount of dividends paid by companies resident in any overseas territory than is equal to any excess of—

(a) the relevant fraction of the company's total income in that year from investments (including franked investment income ...[1] ...[2]) so far as referable to the business referred to in subsection (1) above;

over

(b) the amount of the dividends so referable which are paid to it in the year by companies resident in that territory and in respect of which credit may, apart from subsection (1) above, be allowed to it for underlying tax.

(3) For the purposes of subsection (2) above the relevant fraction, in relation to any overseas territory, is—

$$\frac{A}{B}$$

where—

A is the company's local premium income in the financial year so far as referable to the business referred to in subsection (1) above;
B is the company's total premium income in the financial year so far as referable to that business;

and premium income shall be deemed to be local premium income in so far as it consists of premiums under contracts entered into at or through a branch or agency in that territory by persons not resident in the United Kingdom.

(4) ...[1]][3]

Commentary—*Simon's Direct Tax Service* **F2.113.**
Revenue Internal Guidance—Double taxation relief manual DT 1020-1022 (Revenue procedure regarding insurance companies).
Definitions—"Branch or agency", s 834(1); "company", s 832(1), (2); "financial year", s 834(1); "franked investment income", s 832(1); "income tax", s 832(4); "Schedule D", s 18(1); "tax", s 832(3); "total income", s 835(1); "underlying tax", s 792(1); "United Kingdom", s 830(1).

Cross references—See TA 1988 s 790(5) (unilateral relief for foreign tax paid in respect of dividends described in sub-s (1) above).
FA 1993 s 78(6) (reduction in the rate of tax credits from the financial year 1993: franked investment income for the purposes of this section to be calculated accordingly).
Amendments—[1] Sub-s (4), and words in sub-s (2)(a), (both originally inserted by FA 1994 Sch 16 para 8) repealed by F(No 2)A 1997 s 36 (4), Sch 6 para 15, Sch 8 Pt II (11) with effect for distributions made after 5 April 1999.
[2] Words in sub-s (2)(a) repealed by FA 1998 Sch 3 para 36 with effect for distributions made after 5 April 1999.
[3] This section repealed by FA 2000 ss 103, 156, Sch 30 para 14, Sch 40 Pt II(13) with effect for accounting periods beginning after 31 March 2000.

803 Underlying tax reflecting interest on loans

(1) This section applies in a case where—

(a) a bank or a company connected with a bank makes a claim for an allowance by way of credit in accordance with this Chapter; and

(b) the claim relates to underlying tax on a dividend [("the overseas dividend")][2] paid by the overseas company, within the meaning of section 801; and

(c) that underlying tax is or includes tax payable under the law of a territory outside the United Kingdom on or by reference to [interest or dividends earned or received][1] in the course of its business by that overseas company or by such third, fourth or successive company as is referred to in subsection (2) or (3) of that section; and

[(d) if the company which received the interest or dividends ("the company") had been resident in the United Kingdom, section 798 would apply in relation to that company.][3]

(2) In a case where this section applies, the amount of the credit for that part of the foreign tax which consists of the tax referred to in subsection (1)(c) above shall not exceed an amount determined under subsection (3) below.

(3) The amount referred to in subsection (2) above is a sum equal to corporation tax, at the rate in force at the time the foreign tax referred to in paragraph (c) of subsection (1) above was chargeable, [on so much of the interest or dividends as exceeds the amount of the company's relevant expenditure which is properly attributable to the earning of the interest or dividends.][1]

(4) In subsection (3) above—

(a) "interest", subject to subsection (5) below, has the meaning assigned to it by section [798(3)][1]; and

[(b) the company's relevant expenditure' means the amount which, if the company referred to in subsection (1)(d) above were resident in the United Kingdom and were a qualifying taxpayer for the purposes of section 798, would be its financial expenditure in relation to the earning of the interest or dividends, as determined in accordance with section 798B.][3]

(5) If, in accordance with subsection (6) or subsection (8) below, the amount of [the overseas dividend][1] would be treated for the purposes of corporation tax as increased or reduced by any amount, then the amount which, apart from this subsection, would be the amount of [the interest or dividends][1] referred to in subsection (3) above shall be taken to be increased or reduced by the same amount as [the overseas dividend][1] is so treated as increased or reduced.

(6) If, in a case where this section applies, the underlying tax is or includes an amount of spared tax, then, for the purposes of corporation tax, the amount which apart from this subsection would be the amount of [the overseas dividend][1] shall be treated as increased by an amount equal to so much of that spared tax as does not exceed—

[(a) the amount of the spared tax which under any arrangements is to be taken into account for the purpose of allowing credit against corporation tax in respect of the overseas dividend; or

(b) if it is less, 15 per cent of the interest or dividends;][3];

but nothing in this subsection prejudices the operation of section 795 in relation to foreign tax which is not spared tax.

[(7) In this section "spared tax" has the same meaning as in section 798A.][3]

(8) If, in a case where this section applies—

(a) the underlying tax is or includes an amount of tax which [is referable to interest and][2] is not spared tax, and

(b) that amount of tax exceeds 15 per cent of the interest to which it is referable,

then, for the purposes of corporation tax, the amount which would apart from this subsection be the amount of [the overseas dividend][1] shall be treated as reduced by a sum equal to the excess.

(9) Where this section applies, the amount of the credit referred to in paragraph (a) of subsection (1) above which is referable to the underlying tax payable as mentioned in paragraph (c) of that subsection shall not exceed 15 per cent of so much of [the interest or dividends][1] referred to in that paragraph as is included in the relevant profits of the company paying [the overseas dividend][1]; and for the purposes of this subsection—

(a) "relevant profits" has the same meaning as, by virtue of section 799, it has for the purposes of the computation of underlying tax; and

(b) the amount of [the interest or dividends][1] shall be determined without making any deduction in respect of any foreign tax.

[(10) In subsection (1) above "bank" means a company carrying on, in the United Kingdom or elsewhere, any trade which includes the receipt of interest or dividends, and section 839 applies for the purposes of that subsection.][3]

Commentary—*Simon's Direct Tax Service* **F1.123; F2.114.**
Revenue Internal Guidance—Banking manual BM 8.2.4.1–8.2.4.2 (banks: application of this section).
Definitions—"Arrangements", s 792(1); "company", s 832(1), (2); "foreign tax", s 792(1), (3); "interest", s 832(1); "tax", s 832(3); "underlying tax", s 792(1); "United Kingdom", s 830(1).
Amendments—[1] Words in sub-ss (1)(c), (3), (4)(a), (5), (6), (8), (9), substituted by FA 1998 s 106 with effect where the overseas dividend is paid on or after 17 March 1998, but does not apply where the overseas dividend is paid before 1 January 1999 in pursuance of arrangements which were entered into before, and are not altered on or after, 17 March 1998.
[2] Words in sub-ss (1)(b), (8) inserted by FA 1998 s 106 with effect where the overseas dividend is paid on or after 17 March 1998, but does not apply where the overseas dividend is paid before 1 January 1999 in pursuance of arrangements which were entered into before, and are not altered on or after, 17 March 1998.
[3] Sub-ss (1)(d), (4)(b), (6)(a), (b), (7), (10) substituted by FA 1998 s 106 with effect where the overseas dividend is paid on or after 17 March 1998, but does not apply where the overseas dividend is paid before 1 January 1999 in pursuance of arrangements which were entered into before, and are not altered on or after, 17 March 1998.

[803A Foreign taxation of group as a single entity

(1) This section applies in any case where, under the law of a territory outside the United Kingdom, tax is payable by any one company resident in that territory ("the responsible company") in respect of the aggregate profits, or aggregate profits and aggregate gains, of that company and one or more other companies so resident, taken together as a single taxable entity.

(2) Where this section applies, this Part shall have effect, so far as relating to the determination of underlying tax in relation to any dividend paid by any of the companies mentioned in subsection (1) above (the "non-resident companies") to another company ("the recipient company"), as if—

    (*a*) the non-resident companies, taken together, were a single company,
    (*b*) anything done by or in relation to any of the non-resident companies (including the payment of the dividend) were done by or in relation to that single company, and
    (*c*) that single company were related to the recipient company, if that one of the non-resident companies which actually pays the dividend is related to the recipient company,

(so that, in particular, the relevant profits for the purposes of section 799(1) is a single aggregate figure in respect of that single company and the foreign tax paid by the responsible company is foreign tax paid by that single company).

(3) For the purposes of this section a company is related to another company if that other company—

    (*a*) controls directly or indirectly, or
    (*b*) is a subsidiary of a company which controls directly or indirectly,

not less than 10 per cent of the voting power in the first-mentioned company.][1]

Revenue & other press releases—IR Tax Bulletin January 2002 p 911 (discussion of double taxation relief, specifically the tax consolidations falling within TA 1988 s 803A).
Amendments—[1] This section inserted by FA 2000 s 103, Sch 30 para 15 with effect for any claim for credit, under any arrangements, in respect of underlying tax in relation to a dividend paid after 20 March 2000 by a company resident outside the UK to a company resident in the UK.

Miscellaneous rules

804 Relief against income tax in respect of income arising in years of commencement

(1) Subject to the provisions of this section, credit for overseas tax paid in respect of [any income which is overlap profit][1] shall be allowed under this Part against United Kingdom income tax chargeable for any year of assessment in respect of that income if it would have been so allowed but for the fact that credit for that overseas tax had been allowed against the United Kingdom income tax chargeable in respect of that income for a previous year of assessment.

(2) The amount of credit to be allowed in respect of any income by virtue of this section for any year of assessment shall not exceed the difference between—

    (*a*) the total credit allowable against income tax in respect of that income under this Part (including this section) for all years of assessment for which credit is so allowable; and
    (*b*) the amount of credit which was in fact so allowed in respect of that income for any earlier year or years of assessment.

(3) The total credit so allowable in respect of any income for all those years of assessment shall be taken to be the amount of the overseas tax charged on that income, adjusted where the number of the United Kingdom periods of assessment exceeds the number of foreign periods of assessment, in the proportion which the former number bears to the latter, a period for which part only of the income is charged to tax being counted not as one period but as a fraction equal to the proportion which that part of the income bears to the whole of the income.

(4) Where the same income is charged to different overseas taxes for different foreign periods of assessment, subsection (3) above, so far as it relates to the adjustment of overseas tax, shall be applied separately to each of the overseas taxes, and the total credit allowable shall be the aggregate of those taxes after the making of any adjustments in accordance with that subsection as so applied.

[(5) Subsections (5A) and (5B) below apply where—

(*a*) credit against income tax for any year of assessment is allowed by virtue of subsection (1) above in respect of any income which is an overlap profit ("the original income"), and

(*b*) the original income or any part of it contributes to an amount which, by virtue of section 63A(1) or (3), is deducted in computing the profits or gains of a subsequent year of assessment ("the subsequent year").

(5A) The following shall be set off one against the other, namely—

(*a*) the difference between—

(i) the amount of the credit which, under this Part (including this section), has been allowed against income tax in respect of so much of the original income as contributes as mentioned in subsection (5) above, and

(ii) the amount of the credit which, apart from this section, would have been so allowed; and

(*b*) the amount of credit which, on the assumption that no amount were deducted by virtue of section 63A(1) or (3), would be allowable under this Part against income tax in respect of income arising in the subsequent year from the same source as the original income.

(5B) The person chargeable in respect of the income (if any) arising in the subsequent year from the same source as the original income shall—

(*a*) if the amount given by paragraph (*a*) of subsection (5A) above exceeds that given by paragraph (*b*) of that subsection, be treated as having received in that year a payment chargeable under Case VI of Schedule D of an amount such that income tax on it at the basic rate is equal to the excess; and

(*b*) if the amount given by paragraph (*b*) of subsection (5A) above exceeds that given by paragraph (*a*) of that subsection, be allowed for that year under this Part an amount of credit equal to the excess.

(5C) For the purposes of subsections (5) to (5B) above, it shall be assumed that, where an amount is deducted by virtue of section 63A(1), each of the overlap profits included in the aggregate of such profits contributes to that amount in the proportion which that overlap profit bears to that aggregate.]²

(6) Any payment which a person is treated by virtue of subsection (5) above as having received shall not on that account constitute income of his for any of the purposes of the Income Tax Acts other than that subsection and in particular no part thereof shall constitute profits or gains brought into charge to income tax for the purposes of section 348.

(7) Any claim for relief by way of credit under subsection (1) above against income tax for any year of assessment shall be made [on or before the fifth anniversary of the 31st January next following]³ that year or, where there is more than one year of assessment in respect of which such relief may be given, [on or before the fifth anniversary of the 31st January next following]³ the later of them.

(8) In this section—

["overlap profit" means an amount of profits or gains which, by virtue of sections 60 to 62, is included in the computations for two successive years of assessment;]²

"overseas tax" means tax under the law of a territory outside the United Kingdom;

...²

"United Kingdom period of assessment" and "foreign period of assessment", in relation to any income, mean respectively a year or other period for which under the relevant law the income falls to be charged to the relevant tax; and

...²

references to income arising in any year include, in relation to income the income tax on which is to be computed by reference to the amount of income received in the United Kingdom, references to income received in that year.

Commentary—*Simon's Direct Tax Service* F3.201–203.
Revenue Internal Guidance—Double taxation relief manual DT 1135–1137 (explanation with example).
DT 1143–1145 (trades etc commencing after 5 April 1994: recovery of credit where overlap relief is given).
Definitions—"Basic rate", s 832(1); "income tax", s 832(4); "the Income Tax Acts", s 831(1)(*b*); "profits or gains", s 833(1); "Schedule D", s 18(1); "tax", s 832(3); "United Kingdom", s 830(1); "year of assessment", s 832(1).
Cross references—See FA 2000 s 46(2) (exemption under FA 2000 s 46(1) for income of a charity is not granted in respect of income chargeable to tax under Schedule D Case VI by virtue of this section).
Amendments—¹ Words in sub-s (1) substituted for "any income arising in the years of commencement" by FA 1994 ss 217, 218, Sch 20 paras 10–13 with effect from the year 1994–95 in relation to trades etc commenced after 5 April 1994 and with effect from the year 1996–97 in relation to trades etc commenced before 6 April 1994. In the cases specified in FA 1994 Sch 20 para 12 this section has effect as if these amendments had not been made.
² Sub-ss (5), (5A)–(5C) substituted for sub-s (5) and in sub-s (8) definition of "overlap profit" inserted and words repealed by FA 1994 ss 217, 218, Sch 20 paras 10–13, Sch 26 Pt V(24) with effect from the year 1994–95 in relation to trades etc commenced after 5 April 1994 and with effect from the year 1996–97 in relation to trades etc commenced before 6 April 1994. In the cases specified in FA 1994 Sch 20 para 12 this section has effect as if these amendments had not been made.
³ Words in sub-s (7) substituted by FA 1996 s 135(1), (2), Sch 21 para 22 with effect from the year 1996–97.

[804A [Life assurance companies with overseas branches etc: restriction of credit]³

[(1) Subsection (2) below applies where credit for tax—

(*a*) which is payable under the laws of a territory outside the United Kingdom in respect of insurance business carried on by a company through a branch or agency in that territory, and

(*b*) which is computed otherwise than wholly by reference to profits arising in that territory, is to be allowed (in accordance with this Part) against corporation tax charged under Case I or Case VI of Schedule D in respect of the profits, computed in accordance with the provisions applicable to Case I of Schedule D, of life assurance business or any category of life assurance business carried on by the company in an accounting period (in this section referred to as "the relevant profits").

(1A) For the purposes of paragraph (b) of subsection (1) above, the cases where tax payable under the laws of a territory outside the United Kingdom is "computed otherwise than wholly by reference to profits arising in that territory" are those cases where the charge to tax in that territory falls within subsection (1B) below.

(1B) A charge to tax falls within this subsection if it is such a charge made otherwise than by reference to profits as (by disallowing their deduction in computing the amount chargeable) to require sums payable and other liabilities arising under policies to be treated as sums or liabilities falling to be met out of amounts subject to tax in the hands of the company.][4]

(2) Where this subsection applies, the amount of the credit shall not exceed the greater of—

    (a) any such part of the tax payable under the laws of the territory outside the United Kingdom as is charged by reference to profits arising in that territory, and

    (b) the shareholders' share of the tax so payable.

(3) For the purposes of subsection (2) above the shareholders' share of tax payable under the laws of a territory outside the United Kingdom is so much of that tax as is represented by the fraction

$$\frac{A}{B}$$

where—

    [A is an amount equal to the amount of the relevant profits before making any deduction authorised by subsection (5) below;][5]
    and
    B is an amount equal to the excess of—

        (a) the amount taken into account as receipts of the company in computing those profits, apart from premiums and sums received by virtue of a claim under a reinsurance contract, over

        (b) the amounts taken into account as expenses ...[2] in computing those profits.

(4) Where there is no such excess as is mentioned in subsection (3) above, or where the profits are greater than any excess, the whole of the tax payable under the laws of the territory outside the United Kingdom shall be the shareholders' share; and (subject to that) where there are no profits, none of it shall be the shareholders' share.

(5) Where, by virtue of this section, the credit for any tax payable under the laws of a territory outside the United Kingdom is less than it otherwise would be, section 795(2)(a) shall not prevent a deduction being made for the difference in computing [the relevant profits][6].][1]

Commentary—*Simon's Direct Tax Service* D4.512.
Revenue & other press releases—Inland Revenue Internal Guidance, Life Assurance Manual (paras 10.81–10.85: relief restricted on a country by country basis).
Revenue Internal Guidance—Life assurance manual LAM 10.81-10.85 (explanation of this section).
Definitions—"Accounting period", s 834(1); "company", s 832(1), (2); "interest", s 832(1); "overseas life assurance business", s 431(2).
Amendments—[1] This section inserted by FA 1990 Sch 7 paras 5, 10(1) with effect for accounting periods beginning after 31 December 1989.
[2] Words in sub-s (3) repealed by FA 1996 Sch 41 Pt V(3) with effect for accounting periods ending after 31 March 1996, subject to transitional provisions in FA 1996 Sch 15.
[3] Headnote substituted by FA 2000 s 103, Sch 30 para 16(5) with effect for accounting periods beginning after 31 March 2000. Previously headnote read "Overseas life assurance business: restriction of credit".
[4] Sub-s (1) substituted for new sub-ss (1), (1A), (1B) by FA 2000 s 103, Sch 30 para 16(2) with effect for accounting periods beginning after 31 March 2000.
[5] Definition of "A" in sub-s (3) substituted by FA 2000 s 103, Sch 30 para 16 with effect for accounting periods beginning after 31 March 2000.
[6] Words in sub-s (5) substituted for words "the profits of the overseas life assurance business" by FA 2000 s 103, Sch 30 para 16 with effect for accounting periods beginning after 31 March 2000.

[804B Insurance companies carrying on more than one category of business: restriction of credit

(1) Where—

    (a) an insurance company carries on more than one category of business in an accounting period, and

    (b) there arises to the company in that period any income or gain ("the relevant income") in respect of which credit for foreign tax falls to be allowed under any arrangements,

subsection (2) below shall have effect.

(2) In any such case, the amount of the credit for foreign tax which, under the arrangements, is allowable against corporation tax in respect of so much of the relevant income as is referable (in accordance with the provisions of sections 432ZA to 432E [or section 438B][2]) to a particular category of business must not exceed the fraction of the foreign tax which, in accordance with the following provisions of this section, is attributable to that category of business.

(3) Where the relevant income arises from an asset—

(*a*) which is linked solely to a category of business (other than overseas life assurance business), or

(*b*) which is an asset of the company's overseas life assurance fund,

the whole of the foreign tax is attributable to the category mentioned in paragraph (*a*) above or, as the case may be, to the company's overseas life assurance business, unless the case is one where subsection (7) below applies in relation to the category of business in question.

(4) Where subsection (3) above does not apply and the category of business in question is—

(*a*) basic life assurance and general annuity business, or

(*b*) [long-term][3] business which is not life assurance business,

the fraction of the foreign tax that is attributable to that category of business is the fraction whose numerator is the part of the relevant income which is referable to that category by virtue of any provision of section 432A [or 438B][2] and whose denominator is the whole of the relevant income.

(5) Subsections (6) and (7) below apply where the category of business in question is neither—

(*a*) basic life assurance and general annuity business; nor

(*b*) [long-term][3] business which is not life assurance business.

(6) Where—

(*a*) subsection (3) above does not apply, and

(*b*) some or all of the relevant income is taken into account in accordance with section 83 of the Finance Act 1989 in an account in relation to which the provisions of section 432C or 432D apply,

the fraction of the foreign tax that is attributable to the category of business in question is the fraction whose numerator is the part of the relevant income which is referable to that category by virtue of any provision of section 432C or 432D and whose denominator is the whole of the relevant income.

(7) Where some or all of the relevant income falls to be taken into account in determining in accordance with section 83(2) of the Finance Act 1989 the amount referred to in section 432E(1) as the net amount, the fraction of the foreign tax that is attributable to the category of business in question is the fraction—

(*a*) whose numerator is the part of that net amount which is referable by virtue of section 432E to that category; and

(*b*) whose denominator is the whole of that net amount.

(8) No part of the foreign tax is attributable to any category of business except as provided by subsections (3) to (7) above.

(9) Where for the purposes of this section an amount of foreign tax is attributable to a category of life assurance business other than basic life assurance and general annuity business, credit in respect of the foreign tax so attributable shall be allowed only against corporation tax in respect of profits chargeable under Case VI of Schedule D arising from carrying on that category of business.][1]

Amendments—[1] This section inserted by FA 2000 s 103, Sch 30 para 17 with effect for accounting periods beginning after 31 March 2000.
[2] Words in sub-ss (2), (4) inserted by FA 2001 s 76, Sch 25 para 6 with effect from 6 April 2001.
[3] Words in sub-ss (4)(*b*), (5)(*b*) substituted by the Financial Services and Markets Act 2000 (Consequential Amendments) (Taxes) Order, SI 2001/3629 arts 13 with effect from 1 December 2001 (immediately after the coming into force of the Financial Services and Markets Act 2000 ss 411, 432(1), Sch 20).

[804C Insurance companies: allocation of expenses etc in computations under Case I of Schedule D

(1) Where—

(*a*) an insurance company carries on any category of insurance business in a period of account,

(*b*) a computation in accordance with the provisions applicable to Case I of Schedule D falls to be made in relation to that category of business for that period, and

(*c*) there arises to the company in that period any income or gain in respect of which credit for foreign tax falls to be allowed under any arrangements,

subsection (2) below shall have effect.

(2) In any such case, the amount of the credit for foreign tax which, under the arrangements, is to be allowed against corporation tax in respect of so much of that income or gain as is referable to the category of business concerned ("the relevant income") shall be limited by treating the amount of the relevant income as reduced in accordance with subsections (3) and (4) below.

(3) The first limitation is to treat the amount of the relevant income as reduced (but not below nil) for the purposes of this Chapter by the amount of expenses (if any) attributable to the relevant income.

(4) If—

(*a*) the amount of the relevant income after any reduction under subsection (3) above,

exceeds

(*b*) the relevant fraction of the profits of the category of business concerned for the period of account in question which are chargeable to corporation tax, the second limitation is to treat the relevant amount as further reduced (but not below nil) for the purposes of this Chapter to an amount equal to that fraction of those profits.

In this subsection any reference to the profits of a category of business is a reference to those profits after the set off of any losses of that category of business which have arisen in any previous accounting period.

(5) In determining the amount of the credit for foreign tax which is to be allowed as mentioned in subsection (2) above, the relevant amount shall not be reduced except in accordance with that subsection.

(6) For the purposes of subsection (3) above, the amount of expenses attributable to the relevant income is the appropriate fraction of the total relevant expenses of the category of business concerned for the period of account in question.

(7) In subsection (6) above, the ''appropriate fraction'' means the fraction—

    (a) whose numerator is the amount of the relevant income before any reduction in accordance with subsection (2) above, and
    (b) whose denominator is the total income of the category of business concerned for the period of account in question,

unless the denominator so determined is nil, in which case the denominator shall instead be the amount described in subsection (8) below.

(8) That amount is so much in total of the income and gains—

    (a) which arise to the company in the period of account in question, and
    (b) in respect of which credit for foreign tax falls to be allowed under any arrangements,

as are referable to the category of business concerned (before any reduction in accordance with subsection (2) above).

(9) In subsection (4) above, the ''relevant fraction'' means the fraction—

    (a) whose numerator is the amount of the relevant income before any reduction in accordance with subsection (2) above; and
    (b) whose denominator is the amount described in subsection (8) above.

(10) Where a 75 per cent subsidiary of an insurance company is acting in accordance with a scheme or arrangement and—

    (a) the purpose, or one of the main purposes, of that scheme or arrangement is to prevent or restrict the application of subsection (2) above to the insurance company, and
    (b) the subsidiary does not carry on insurance business of any description,

the amount of corporation tax attributable (apart from this subsection) to any item of income or gain arising to the subsidiary shall be found by setting off against that item the amount of expenses that would be attributable to it under subsection (3) above if that item had arisen directly to the insurance company.

(11) Where the credit allowed for any tax payable under the laws of a territory outside the United Kingdom is, by virtue of subsection (2) above, less than it would be if the relevant income were not treated as reduced in accordance with that subsection, section 795(2)(a) shall not prevent a deduction being made for the difference in computing the profits of the category of business concerned.

(12) Where, by virtue of subsection (10) above, the credit allowed for any tax payable under the laws of a territory outside the United Kingdom is less than it would be apart from that subsection, section 795(2)(a) shall not prevent a deduction being made for the difference in computing the income of the 75 per cent subsidiary.

(13) Any reference in this section to any income or gain being to any extent referable to a category of insurance business shall, in the case of—

    (a) life assurance business or any category of life assurance business, or
    (b) [long-term][2] business which is not life assurance business,

be taken as a reference to the income or gain being to that extent referable to that category of business for the purposes of Chapter I of Part XII.

(14) This section shall be construed—

    (a) in accordance with section 804D, where the category of business concerned is life assurance business or a category of life assurance business; and
    (b) in accordance with section 804E, where the category of business concerned is not life assurance business or any category of life assurance business.][1]

Cross references—See TA 1988 s 804D (Interpretation of section 804C in relation to life assurance business)
TA 1988 s 804E (Interpretation of section 804C in relation to other insurance business
Amendments—[1] This section inserted, together with ss 804D, 804E by FA 2000 s 103, Sch 30 para 18 with effect for periods of account beginning after 31 March 2000.
[2] Words in sub-s (13)(b) substituted by the Financial Services and Markets Act 2000 (Consequential Amendments) (Taxes) Order, SI 2001/3629 arts 13, 52(2)(l) with effect from 1 December 2001 (immediately after the coming into force of the Financial Services and Markets Act 2000 ss 411, 432(1), Sch 20).

[804D Interpretation of section 804C in relation to life assurance business etc

(1) This section has effect for the interpretation of section 804C where the category of business concerned is life assurance business or a category of life assurance business.

(2) The "total income" of the category of business concerned for the period of account in question is the amount (if any) by which—

(*a*) so much of the total income shown in the revenue account in the periodical return of the company concerned for that period as is referable to that category of business,

exceeds

(*b*) so much of any commissions payable and any expenses of management incurred in connection with the acquisition of the business, as shown in that return, so far as referable to that category of business.

(3) Where any amounts fall to be brought into account in accordance with section 83 of the Finance Act 1989, the amounts that are referable to the category of business concerned shall be determined for the purposes of subsection (2) above in accordance with sections 432B to 432F.

(4) The "total relevant expenses" of the category of business concerned for any period of account is the amount of the claims incurred—

(*a*) increased by any increase in the liabilities of the company, or
(*b*) reduced (but not below nil) by any decrease in the liabilities of the company.

(5) For the purposes of subsection (4) above, the amounts to be taken into account in the case of any period of account are the amounts as shown in the company's periodical return for the period so far as referable to the category of business concerned.]¹

Amendments—¹ This section inserted, together with ss 804C, 804E by FA 2000 s 103, Sch 30 para 18 with effect for periods of account beginning after 31 March 2000.

[804E Interpretation of section 804C in relation to other insurance business

(1) This section has effect for the interpretation of section 804C where the category of business concerned is not life assurance business or any category of life assurance business.

(2) The "total income" of the category of business concerned for any period of account is the amount (if any) by which—

(*a*) the sum of the amounts specified in subsection (3) below,
exceeds
(*b*) the sum of the amounts specified in subsection (4) below.

(3) The amounts mentioned in subsection (2)(*a*) above are—

(*a*) earned premiums, net of reinsurance;
(*b*) investment income and gains;
(*c*) other technical income, net of reinsurance;
(*d*) any amount treated under section 107(2) of the Finance Act 2000 as a receipt of the company's trade.

(4) The amounts mentioned in subsection (2)(*b*) above are—

(*a*) acquisition costs;
(*b*) the change in deferred acquisition costs;
(*c*) losses on investments.

(5) The "total relevant expenses" of the category of business concerned for any period of account is the sum of—

(*a*) the claims incurred, net of reinsurance,
(*b*) the changes in other technical provisions, net of reinsurance,
(*c*) the change in the equalisation provision, and
(*d*) investment management expenses,

unless that sum is a negative amount, in which case the total relevant expenses shall be taken to be nil.

(6) The amounts to be taken into account for the purposes of the paragraphs of subsections (3) to (5) above are the amounts taken into account for the purposes of corporation tax.

(7) Expressions used—

(*a*) in the paragraphs of subsections (3) to (5) above, and
(*b*) in the provisions of section B of Schedule 9A to the Companies Act 1985 (form and content of accounts of insurance companies and groups) which relate to the profit and loss account format (within the meaning of paragraph 7(1) of that section),

have the same meaning in those paragraphs as they have in those provisions.]¹

Amendments—¹ This section inserted, together with ss 804C, 804D by FA 2000 s 103, Sch 30 para 18 with effect for periods of account beginning after 31 March 2000.

[804F Interpretation of sections 804A to 804E

Expressions used in sections 804A to 804E and in Chapter I of Part XII have the same meaning in those sections as in that Chapter.][1]

Amendments—[1] This section inserted by FA 2000 s 103, Sch 30 para 19 with effect so far as relating to sections 804A and 804B for accounting periods beginning after 31 March 2000 and so far as relating to sections 804C to 804E for periods of account beginning after 31 March 2000.

805 Elections against credit

Credit shall not be allowed under any arrangements against the United Kingdom taxes chargeable in respect of any income or chargeable gains of any person if he elects that credit shall not be allowed in respect of that income or those gains.

Commentary—*Simon's Direct Tax Service* **F1.113, 135.**
Definitions—"Arrangements", s 792(1); "chargeable gains", s 832(1); "United Kingdom taxes", s 792(1).

806 Time limit for claims etc

[(1) Subject to subsection (2) below and section 804(7), any claim for an allowance under any arrangements by way of credit for foreign tax in respect of any income or chargeable gain—

    (a) shall, in the case of any income or chargeable gain which falls to be charged to income tax for a year of assessment, be made on or before—

        (i) the fifth anniversary of the 31st January next following that year of assessment, or
        (ii) if later, the 31st January next following the year of assessment in which the foreign tax is paid;

    (b) shall, in the case of any income or chargeable gain which falls to be charged to corporation tax for an accounting period, be made not more than—

        (i) six years after the end of that accounting period, or
        (ii) if later, one year after the end of the accounting period in which the foreign tax is paid.][3]

(2) Where the amount of any credit given under the arrangements is rendered excessive or insufficient by reason of any adjustment of the amount of any tax payable either in the United Kingdom or under the laws of any other territory, nothing in the Tax Acts limiting the time for the making of assessments or claims for relief shall apply to any assessment or claim to which the adjustment gives rise, being an assessment or claim made not later than six years from the time when all such assessments, adjustments and other determinations have been made, whether in the United Kingdom or elsewhere, as are material in determining whether any and if so what credit falls to be given.

[(3) Subject to subsection (5) below, where—

    (a) any credit for foreign tax has been allowed to a person under any arrangements, and
    (b) the amount of that credit is subsequently rendered excessive by reason of an adjustment of the amount of any tax payable under the laws of a territory outside the United Kingdom,

that person shall give notice in writing to an officer of the Board that an adjustment has been made that has rendered the amount of the credit excessive.

(4) A notice under subsection (3) above must be given within one year from the time of the making of the adjustment.

(5) Subsections (3) and (4) above do not apply where the adjustment is one the consequences of which in relation to the credit fall to be given effect to in accordance with regulations made under—

    (a) section 182(1) of the Finance Act 1993 (regulations relating to individual members of Lloyd's); or
    (b) section 229 of the Finance Act 1994 (regulations relating to corporate members of Lloyd's).

(6) A person who fails to comply with the requirements imposed on him by subsections (3) and (4) above in relation to any adjustment shall be liable to a penalty of an amount not exceeding the amount by which the credit allowed has been rendered excessive by reason of the adjustment.][2]

Commentary—*Simon's Direct Tax Service* **F1.113, 135.**
Revenue Interpretation RI 206—An adjustment to the amount of foreign tax paid usually involves the foreign tax authority formally accepting that the amount of tax paid is excessive and agreeing to repay the excess either directly or indirectly by set-off. An adjustment is treated as made when the foreign tax authority issues a notification to the taxpayer (or adviser) or, if the tax authority does not issue such a notification, when the repayment is issued or the set-off is carried out.
Revenue Internal Guidance—Double taxation relief manual DT 836 (extended time limits apply only where credit has already been allowed and where there has been an adjustment of the tax payable).
Definitions—"Arrangements", s 792(1); "chargeable gain", s 832(1); "chargeable period", s 832(1); "foreign tax", s 792(1), (3); "income tax", s 832(4); "tax", s 832(3); "the Tax Acts", s 831(2); "United Kingdom", s 830(1).
Amendments—[1] Words in sub-s (1) substituted by FA 1996 s 135(1), (2), Sch 21 para 23 with effect for the purposes of income tax from the year 1996–97 and, for the purposes of corporation tax, as respects accounting periods ending after 30 June 1999 (by virtue of Finance Act 1994, Section 199, (Appointed Day) Order, SI 1998/3173 art 2).
[2] Sub-ss (3)–(6) inserted by FA 1998 s 107(1) and deemed to have effect from 17 March 1998 in relation to adjustments made on or after that date.
[3] Sub-s (1) substituted by FA 2000 s 103, Sch 30 para 20 with effect for claims for credit made after 20 March 2000.

[Foreign dividends: onshore pooling and utilisation of eligible unrelieved foreign tax

806A Eligible unrelieved foreign tax on dividends: introductory

(1) This section applies where, in any accounting period of a company resident in the United Kingdom, an amount of eligible unrelieved foreign tax arises in respect of a dividend falling within subsection (2) below paid to the company.

(2) The dividends that fall within this subsection are any dividends chargeable under Case V of Schedule D, other than—

   (*a*) any dividend which is trading income for the purposes of section 393;

   (*b*) any dividend which, in the circumstances described in paragraphs (*a*) and (*b*) of subsection (8) of section 393, would by virtue of that subsection fall to be treated as trading income for the purposes of subsection (1) of that section;

   (*c*) in a case where section 801A applies, the dividend mentioned in subsection (1)(*b*) of that section;

   (*d*) in a case where section 803 applies, the dividend mentioned in subsection (1)(*b*) of that section;

   (*e*) any dividend the amount of which is, under section 811, treated as reduced.

(3) For the purposes of this section—

   (*a*) the cases where an amount of eligible unrelieved foreign tax arises in respect of a dividend falling within subsection (2) above are the cases set out in subsections (4) and (5) below; and

   (*b*) the amounts of eligible unrelieved foreign tax which arise in any such case are those determined in accordance with section 806B.

(4) Case A is where—

   (*a*) the amount of the credit for foreign tax which under any arrangements would, apart from section 797, be allowable against corporation tax in respect of the dividend,

exceeds

   (*b*) the amount of the credit for foreign tax which under the arrangements is allowed against corporation tax in respect of the dividend.

(5) Case B is where the amount of tax which, by virtue of any provision of any arrangements, falls to be taken into account as mentioned in section 799(1) in the case of the dividend (whether or not by virtue of section 801(2) or (3)) is less than it would be apart from the mixer cap. [But if that is so in any case by reason only of the mixer cap restricting the amount of underlying tax that is treated as mentioned in subsection (2) or (3) of section 801 in the case of a dividend paid by a company resident in the United Kingdom, the case does not fall within Case B.][2]

(6) In determining whether the circumstances are as set out in subsection (4) or (5) above, sections 806C and 806D shall be disregarded.][1]

Amendments—[1] Inserted by FA 2000 s 103, Sch 30 para 21 with effect for dividends arising after 30 March 2001, and foreign tax in respect of such dividends, and accordingly the single related dividend or the single unrelated dividend which falls to be treated under those amendments as arising in any accounting period of a company shall not include any dividend arising on or before 30 March 2001.
[2] Words in sub-s (5) inserted by FA 2001 s 81, Sch 27 para 4 with effect for—

   (*a*) dividends arising after 30 March 2001 to companies resident in the UK from companies resident outside the UK, and
   (*b*) foreign tax in respect of such dividends,
(whenever the dividend mentioned in the amendment was paid).

[806B The amounts that are eligible unrelieved foreign tax

(1) This section has effect for determining the amounts of eligible unrelieved foreign tax which arise in the cases set out in section 806A(4) and (5).

(2) In Case A, the difference between—

   (*a*) the amount of the credit allowed as mentioned in section 806A(4)(*b*), and

   (*b*) the greater amount of the credit that would have been so allowed if, for the purposes of subsection (2) of section 797, the rate of corporation tax payable as mentioned in that subsection were the upper percentage,

shall be an amount of eligible unrelieved foreign tax.

[(3) In Case B, the amount (if any) by which—

   (*a*) the aggregate of the upper rate amounts falling to be brought into account for the purposes of this paragraph by virtue of subsection (4) or (5) below,

exceeds

   (*b*) the amount of tax to be taken into account as mentioned in section 799(1) in the case of the Case V dividend, before any increase under section 801(4B),

shall be an amount of eligible unrelieved foreign tax.

(4) In the case of the Case V dividend (but not any lower level dividend), the upper rate amount to be brought into account for the purposes of subsection (3)(*a*) above—

(*a*) in a case where the mixer cap does not restrict the amount of tax to be taken into account as mentioned in section 799(1) (before any increase under section 801(4B)) in the case of that dividend, is that amount of tax; or

(*b*) in a case where the mixer cap restricts the amount of tax to be so taken into account in the case of that dividend, is the greater amount that would have been so taken into account if, in the application of the formula in section 799(1A) in the case of that dividend (but not any lower level dividend) M% had, in relation to—

    (i) so much of D as does not represent any lower level dividend, and

    (ii) so much of U as is not underlying tax attributable to any lower level dividend,

been the upper percentage.

(5) In the case of any dividend (the ''relevant dividend'') received as mentioned in subsection (2) or (3) of section 801 which is a lower level dividend in relation to the Case V dividend, the upper rate amount to be brought into account for the purposes of subsection (3)(*a*) above—

(*a*) in a case where the mixer cap does not restrict the amount of underlying tax that is treated as mentioned in subsection (2) or (3), as the case may be, of section 801 in the case of the relevant dividend, is the appropriate portion of that amount of underlying tax;

(*b*) in a case where—

    (i) the relevant dividend was paid by a company resident in the United Kingdom, and

    (ii) the mixer cap restricts the amount of underlying tax that is treated as mentioned in subsection (2) or (3), as the case may be, of section 801 in the case of that dividend,

is the appropriate portion of that restricted amount of underlying tax; or

(*c*) in a case where—

    (i) the relevant dividend was paid by a company resident outside the United Kingdom, and

    (ii) the mixer cap restricts the amount of underlying tax that is treated as mentioned in subsection (2) or (3), as the case may be, of section 801 in the case of that dividend,

is the appropriate portion of the greater amount of tax that would have been so treated if, in the application of the formula in section 799(1A) in the case of that dividend (but not any other dividend) M% had, in relation to so much of D as does not represent any lower level dividend, and so much of U as is not underlying tax attributable to any lower level dividend, been the upper percentage.

(6) For the purposes of subsection (5) above, the ''appropriate portion'' of any amount there mentioned in the case of a dividend is found by multiplying that amount by the product of the reducing fractions for each of the higher level dividends.][2]

(7) For the purposes of subsection (6) above, the ''reducing fraction'' for any dividend is the fraction—

(*a*) whose numerator is the amount of the dividend; and

(*b*) whose denominator is the amount of the relevant profits (within the meaning of section 799(1)) out of which the dividend is paid.

(8) Any reference in this section to any tax being restricted by the mixer cap in the case of any dividend is a reference to that tax being so restricted otherwise than by virtue only of the application of the mixer cap in the case of one or more lower level dividends.

(9) For the purpose of determining the amount described in subsection (2)(*b*), [(4)(*b*) or (5)(*c*)][2] above, sections 806C and 806D shall be disregarded.

(10) In this section—

''the Case V dividend'' means the dividend mentioned in section 806A(1);

''higher level dividend'', in relation to another dividend, means any dividend—

    (*a*) by which that other dividend is to any extent represented; and

    (*b*) which either is the Case V dividend or is to any extent represented by the Case V dividend;

''lower level dividend'', in relation to another dividend, means any dividend which—

    (*a*) is received as mentioned in section 801(2) or (3); and

    (*b*) is to any extent represented by that other dividend;

''the relevant tax'' means—

    (*a*) in the case of the Case V dividend, the foreign tax to be taken into account as mentioned in section 799(1); and

    (*b*) in the case of any other dividend, the amount of underlying tax to be treated as mentioned in section 801(2) or (3) in the case of the dividend.][1]

Amendments—[1] This section inserted by FA 2000 s 103, Sch 30 para 21 with effect for dividends arising after 30 March 2001, and foreign tax in respect of such dividends, and accordingly the single related dividend or the single unrelated dividend which falls to be treated under those amendments as arising in any accounting period of a company shall not include any dividend arising on or before 30 March 2001.

[2] Sub-ss (3)–(6), and words in sub-s (9), substituted by FA 2001 s 81, Sch 27 para 5 with effect for—

    (*a*) dividends arising after 30 March 2001 to companies resident in the UK from companies resident outside the UK, and
    (*b*) foreign tax in respect of such dividends,

(whenever the dividend mentioned in TA 1988 s 801(2) or (3) was paid).

[806C Onshore pooling

(1) In this section "qualifying foreign dividend" means any dividend which falls within section 806A(2), other than—

(a) an ADP dividend paid by a controlled foreign company;

(b) so much of any dividend paid by any company as represents an ADP dividend paid by another company which is a controlled foreign company;

(c) a dividend in respect of which an amount of eligible unrelieved foreign tax arises.

(2) For the purposes of this section—

(a) a "related qualifying foreign dividend" is any qualifying foreign dividend paid to a company resident in the United Kingdom by a company which, at the time of payment of the dividend, is related to that company;

(b) an "unrelated qualifying foreign dividend" is any qualifying foreign dividend which is not a related qualifying foreign dividend.

(3) For the purposes of giving credit relief under this Part to a company resident in the United Kingdom—

(a) the related qualifying foreign dividends that arise to the company in an accounting period shall be aggregated;

(b) the unrelated qualifying foreign dividends that arise to the company in an accounting period shall be aggregated;

(c) the underlying tax in relation to the related qualifying foreign dividends that arise to the company in an accounting period shall be aggregated;

(d) so much of the foreign tax paid in respect of the qualifying foreign dividends that arise to the company in an accounting period as is not underlying tax shall be aggregated.

(4) Credit relief under this Part shall be given as if—

(a) the related qualifying foreign dividends aggregated under paragraph (a) of subsection (3) above in the case of any accounting period instead together constituted a single related qualifying foreign dividend arising in that accounting period ("the single related dividend" arising in that accounting period);

(b) the unrelated qualifying foreign dividends aggregated under paragraph (b) of that subsection in the case of any accounting period instead together constituted a single unrelated qualifying foreign dividend arising in that accounting period ("the single unrelated dividend" arising in that accounting period);

(c) the underlying tax aggregated under paragraph (c) of that subsection for any accounting period were instead underlying tax in relation to the single related dividend arising in that accounting period (the "aggregated underlying tax" in respect of the single related dividend);

(d) the tax aggregated under paragraph (d) of that subsection for any accounting period were instead foreign tax (other than underlying tax) paid in respect of, and computed by reference to,—

(i) the single related dividend arising in that accounting period,

(ii) the single unrelated dividend so arising, or

(iii) partly the one dividend and partly the other,

(that aggregated tax being referred to as the "aggregated withholding tax").

(5) For the purposes of this section, a dividend paid by a controlled foreign company is an "ADP dividend" if it is a dividend by virtue of which (whether in whole or in part and whether taken alone or with one or more other dividends) no apportionment under section 747(3) falls to be made as regards an accounting period of the controlled foreign company in a case where such an apportionment would fall to be made apart from section 748(1)(a).]¹

Amendments—¹ This section inserted by FA 2000 s 103, Sch 30 para 21 with effect for dividends arising after 30 March 2001, and foreign tax in respect of such dividends, and accordingly the single related dividend or the single unrelated dividend which falls to be treated under those amendments as arising in any accounting period of a company shall not include any dividend arising on or before 30 March 2001.

[806D Utilisation of eligible unrelieved foreign tax

(1) For the purposes of this section, where—

(a) any eligible unrelieved foreign tax arises in an accounting period of a company, and

(b) the dividend in relation to which it arises is paid by a company which, at the time of payment of the dividend, is related to that company,

that tax is "eligible underlying tax" to the extent that it consists of or represents underlying tax.

(2) To the extent that any eligible unrelieved foreign tax is not eligible underlying tax it is for the purposes of this section "eligible withholding tax".

(3) For the purposes of giving credit relief under this Part to a company resident in the United Kingdom—

(a) the amounts of eligible underlying tax that arise in an accounting period of the company shall be aggregated (that aggregate being referred to as the "relievable underlying tax" arising in that accounting period); and

(b) the amounts of eligible withholding tax that arise in an accounting period of the company shall be aggregated (that aggregate being referred to as the "relievable withholding tax" arising in that accounting period).

(4) The relievable underlying tax arising in an accounting period of the company shall be treated for the purposes of allowing credit relief under this Part as if it were—

(a) underlying tax in relation to the single related dividend that arises in the same accounting period,

(b) relievable underlying tax arising in the next accounting period (whether or not any related qualifying foreign dividend in fact arises to the company in that accounting period), or

(c) underlying tax in relation to the single related dividend that arises in such one or more preceding accounting periods as result from applying the rules in section 806E,

or partly in one of those ways and partly in each or either of the others.

(5) The relievable withholding tax arising in an accounting period of the company shall be treated for the purposes of allowing credit relief under this Part as if it were—

(a) foreign tax (other than underlying tax) paid in respect of, and computed by reference to, the single related dividend or the single unrelated dividend that arises in the same accounting period,

(b) relievable withholding tax arising in the next accounting period (whether or not any qualifying foreign dividend in fact arises to the company in that accounting period), or

(c) foreign tax (other than underlying tax) paid in respect of, and computed by reference to, the single related dividend or the single unrelated dividend that arises in such one or more preceding accounting periods as result from applying the rules in section 806E,

or partly in one of those ways and partly in any one or more of the others.

(6) The amount of relievable underlying tax or relievable withholding tax arising in an accounting period that is treated—

(a) under subsection (4)(a) or (c) above as underlying tax in relation to the single related dividend arising in the same or any earlier accounting period, or

(b) under subsection (5)(a) or (c) above as foreign tax paid in respect of, and computed by reference to, the single related dividend or the single unrelated dividend arising in the same or any earlier accounting period,

must not be such as would cause an amount of eligible unrelieved foreign tax to arise in respect of that dividend.]¹

Amendments—¹ This section inserted by FA 2000 s 103, Sch 30 para 21 with effect for dividends arising after 30 March 2001, and foreign tax in respect of such dividends, and accordingly the single related dividend or the single unrelated dividend which falls to be treated under those amendments as arising in any accounting period of a company shall not include any dividend arising on or before 30 March 2001.

[806E Rules for carry back of relievable tax under section 806D

(1) Where any relievable tax is to be treated as mentioned in section 806D(4)(c) or (5)(c), the rules for determining the accounting periods in question (and the amount of the relievable tax to be so treated in relation to each of them) are those set out in the following provisions of this section.

(2) Rule 1 is that the accounting periods in question must be accounting periods beginning not more than three years before the accounting period in which the relievable tax arises.

(3) Rule 2 is that the relievable tax must be so treated that—

(a) credit for, or for any remaining balance of, the relievable tax is allowed against corporation tax in respect of the single dividend arising in a later one of the accounting periods beginning as mentioned in rule 1 above,

before

(b) credit for any of the relievable tax is allowed against corporation tax in respect of the single dividend arising in any earlier such accounting period.

(4) Rule 3 is that the relievable tax must be so treated that, before allowing credit for any of the relievable tax against corporation tax in respect of the single dividend arising in any accounting period, credit for foreign tax is allowed—

(a) first for the aggregated foreign tax in respect of the single dividend arising in that accounting period, so far as not consisting of relievable tax arising in another accounting period; and

(b) then for relievable tax arising in any accounting period before that in which the relievable tax in question arises.

(5) The above rules are subject to sections 806D(6) and 806F.

(6) In this section—

"aggregated foreign tax" means aggregated underlying tax or aggregated withholding tax;

"relievable tax" means relievable underlying tax or relievable withholding tax;

"the single dividend" means—

(a) in relation to relievable underlying tax, the single related dividend; and

(b) in relation to relievable withholding tax, the single related dividend or the single unrelated dividend.]¹

Amendments—¹ This section inserted by FA 2000 s 103, Sch 30 para 21 with effect for dividends arising after 30 March 2001, and foreign tax in respect of such dividends, and accordingly the single related dividend or the single unrelated dividend which falls to be treated under those amendments as arising in any accounting period of a company shall not include any dividend arising on or before 30 March 2001.

[806F Credit to be given for underlying tax before other foreign tax etc

(1) For the purposes of this Part, credit in accordance with any arrangements shall, in the case of any dividend, be given so far as possible—

(a) for underlying tax (where allowable) before foreign tax other than underlying tax;

(b) for foreign tax other than underlying tax before amounts treated as underlying tax; and

(c) for amounts treated as underlying tax (where allowable) before amounts treated as foreign tax other than underlying tax.

(2) Accordingly, where the amount of foreign tax to be brought into account for the purposes of allowing credit relief under this Part is subject to any limitation or restriction, the limitation or restriction shall be taken to have the effect of excluding foreign tax other than underlying tax before excluding underlying tax.]¹

Amendments—¹ This section inserted by FA 2000 s 103, Sch 30 para 21 with effect for dividends arising after 30 March 2001, and foreign tax in respect of such dividends, and accordingly the single related dividend or the single unrelated dividend which falls to be treated under those amendments as arising in any accounting period of a company shall not include any dividend arising on or before 30 March 2001.

[806G Claims for the purposes of section 806D(4) or (5)

(1) The relievable underlying tax or relievable withholding tax arising in any accounting period shall only be treated as mentioned in subsection (4) or (5) of section 806D on a claim.

(2) Any such claim must specify the amount (if any) of that tax—

(a) which is to be treated as mentioned in paragraph (a) of the subsection in question;

(b) which is to be treated as mentioned in paragraph (b) of that subsection; and

(c) which is to be treated as mentioned in paragraph (c) of that subsection.

(3) A claim under subsection (1) above may only be made before the expiration of the period of—

(a) six years after the end of the accounting period mentioned in that subsection; or

(b) if later, one year after the end of the accounting period in which the foreign tax in question is paid.]¹

Amendments—¹ This section inserted by FA 2000 s 103, Sch 30 para 21 with effect for dividends arising after 30 March 2001, and foreign tax in respect of such dividends, and accordingly the single related dividend or the single unrelated dividend which falls to be treated under those amendments as arising in any accounting period of a company shall not include any dividend arising on or before 30 March 2001.

[806H Surrender of relievable tax by one company in a group to another

(1) The Board may by regulations make provision for, or in connection with, allowing a company which is a member of a group to surrender all or any part of the amount of the relievable tax arising to it in an accounting period to another company which is a member of that group at the time, or throughout the period, prescribed by the regulations.

(2) The provision that may be made under subsection (1) above includes provision—

(a) prescribing the conditions which must be satisfied if a surrender is to be made;

(b) determining the amount of relievable tax which may be surrendered in any accounting period;

(c) prescribing the conditions which must be satisfied if a claim to surrender is to be made;

(d) prescribing the consequences for tax purposes of a surrender having been made;

(e) allowing a claim to be withdrawn and prescribing the effect of such a withdrawal.

(3) Regulations under subsection (1) above—

(a) may make different provision for different cases; and

(b) may contain such supplementary, incidental, consequential or transitional provision as the Board may think fit.

(4) For the purposes of subsection (1) above a company is a member of a group if the conditions prescribed for that purpose in the regulations are satisfied.]¹

Regulations—Double Taxation Relief (Surrender of Relievable Tax Within a Group) Regulations, SI 2001/1163.
Amendments—¹ This section inserted by FA 2000 s 103, Sch 30 para 21 with effect for dividends arising after 30 March 2001, and foreign tax in respect of such dividends, and accordingly the single related dividend or the single unrelated dividend which falls to be treated under those amendments as arising in any accounting period of a company shall not include any dividend arising on or before 30 March 2001.

[806J Interpretation of foreign dividend provisions of this Chapter

(1) This section has effect for the interpretation of the foreign dividend provisions of this Chapter.

(2) In this section, "the foreign dividend provisions of this Chapter" means sections 806A to 806H and this section.

(3) For the purposes of the foreign dividend provisions of this Chapter, where—

(a) one company pays a dividend ("dividend A") to another company, and (*b*) that other company, or a company which is related to it, pays a dividend (''dividend B'') to another company,

dividend B represents dividend A, and dividend A is represented by dividend B, to the extent that dividend B is paid out of profits which are derived, directly or indirectly, from the whole or part of dividend A.

(4) Where—

    (*a*) one company is related to another, and

    (*b*) that other is related to a third company,

the first company shall be taken for the purposes of paragraph (*b*) of subsection (3) above to be related to the third, and so on where there is a chain of companies, each of which is related to the next.

(5) In any case where—

    (*a*) a company resident outside the United Kingdom pays a dividend to a company resident in the United Kingdom, and

    (*b*) the circumstances are such that subsection (6)(*b*) of section 790 has effect in relation to that dividend,

the foreign dividend provisions of this Chapter shall have effect as if the company resident outside the United Kingdom were related to the company resident in the United Kingdom (and subsection (10) of that section shall have effect accordingly).

(6) Subsection (5) of section 801 (related companies) shall apply for the purposes of the foreign dividend provisions of this Chapter as it applies for the purposes of that section.

(7) In the foreign dividend provisions of this Chapter—

    ''aggregated underlying tax'' shall be construed in accordance with section 806C(4)(*c*);

    ''aggregated withholding tax'' shall be construed in accordance with section 806C(4)(*d*);

    ''controlled foreign company'' has the same meaning as in Chapter IV of Part XVII;

    ''eligible unrelieved foreign tax'' shall be construed in accordance with sections 806A and 806B;

    ''the mixer cap'' means section 799(1)(*b*);

    ''qualifying foreign dividend'' has the meaning given by section 806C(1);

    ''related qualifying foreign dividend'' has the meaning given by section 806C(2)(*a*);

    ''relievable tax'' has the meaning given by section 806E(6);

    ''relievable underlying tax'' shall be construed in accordance with 806D(3)(*a*);

    ''relievable withholding tax'' shall be construed in accordance with 806D(3)(*b*);

    ''single related dividend'' shall be construed in accordance with section 806C(4)(*a*);

    ''single unrelated dividend'' shall be construed in accordance with section 806C(4)(*b*);

    ''the upper percentage'' is 45 per cent'']¹

Amendments—¹ This section inserted by FA 2000 s 103, Sch 30 para 21 with effect for dividends arising after 30 March 2001, and foreign tax in respect of such dividends, and accordingly the single related dividend or the single unrelated dividend which falls to be treated under those amendments as arising in any accounting period of a company shall not include any dividend arising on or before 30 March 2001.

[Application of foreign dividend provisions to branches or agencies in the UK of persons resident elsewhere

806K Application of foreign dividend provisions to branches or agencies in the UK of persons resident elsewhere

(1) Sections 806A to 806J shall apply in relation to an amount of eligible unrelieved foreign tax arising in a chargeable period in respect of any of the income of a branch or agency in the United Kingdom of a person resident outside the United Kingdom as they apply in relation to eligible unrelieved foreign tax arising in an accounting period of a company resident in the United Kingdom in respect of any of the company's income, but with the modifications specified in subsection (2) below.

(2) Those modifications are—

    (*a*) take any reference to an accounting period as a reference to a chargeable period;

    (*b*) take any reference to corporation tax as including a reference to income tax;

    (*c*) take the reference in section 806A(4)(*a*) to section 797 as a reference to sections 796 and 797;

    (*d*) in relation to income tax, for subsection (2) of section 806B substitute the subsection (2) set out in subsection (3) below.

(3) That subsection is—

    ''(2) In Case A, the difference between—

        (*a*) the amount of the credit allowed as mentioned in section 806A(4)(*b*), and

        (*b*) the greater amount of credit that would have been so allowed if, for the purposes of section 796, the amount of income tax borne on the dividend as computed under that section were charged at a rate equal to the upper percentage,

    shall be an amount of eligible unrelieved foreign tax.'']¹.

Amendments—¹ This section inserted by FA 2000 s 103, Sch 30 para 22 with effect for dividends arising after 30 March 2001, and foreign tax in respect of such dividends, and accordingly the single related dividend or the single unrelated dividend which falls to be treated under those amendments as arising in any chargeable period shall not include any dividend arising on or before 30 March 2001.

[Unrelieved foreign tax: profits of overseas branch or agency

806L Carry forward or carry back of unrelieved foreign tax

(1) This section applies where, in any accounting period of a company resident in the United Kingdom, an amount of unrelieved foreign tax arises in respect of any of the company's qualifying income from an overseas branch or agency of the company.

(2) The amount of the unrelieved foreign tax so arising shall be treated for the purposes of allowing credit relief under this Part as if it were foreign tax paid in respect of, and computed by reference to, the company's qualifying income from the same overseas branch or agency—

(*a*) in the next accounting period (whether or not the company in fact has any such income from that source in that accounting period), or

(*b*) in such one or more preceding accounting periods, beginning not more than three years before the accounting period in which the unrelieved foreign tax arises, as result from applying the rules in subsection (3) below,

or partly in the one way and partly in the other.

(3) Where any unrelieved foreign tax is to be treated as mentioned in paragraph (*b*) of subsection (2) above, the rules for determining the accounting periods in question (and the amount of the unrelieved foreign tax to be so treated in relation to each of them) are that the unrelieved foreign tax must be so treated under that paragraph—

1 that—

(*a*) credit for, or for any remaining balance of, the unrelieved foreign tax is allowed against corporation tax in respect of income of a later one of the accounting periods beginning as mentioned in that paragraph,

before

(*b*) credit for any of the unrelieved foreign tax is allowed against corporation tax in respect of income of any earlier such period;

2 that, before allowing credit for any of the unrelieved foreign tax against corporation tax in respect of income of any accounting period, credit for foreign tax is allowed—

(*a*) first for foreign tax in respect of the income of that accounting period, other than unrelieved foreign tax arising in another accounting period; and

(*b*) then for unrelieved foreign tax arising in any accounting period before that in which the unrelieved foreign tax in question arises.

(4) For the purposes of this section, the cases where an amount of unrelieved foreign tax arises in respect of any of a company's qualifying income from an overseas branch or agency in an accounting period are those cases where—

(*a*) the amount of the credit for foreign tax which under any arrangements would, apart from section 797, be allowable against corporation tax in respect of that income,

exceeds

(*b*) the amount of the credit for foreign tax which under the arrangements is allowed against corporation tax in respect of that income;

and in any such case that excess is the amount of the unrelieved foreign tax in respect of that income.

(5) For the purposes of this section, a company's qualifying income from an overseas branch or agency is the profits of the overseas branch or agency which are—

(*a*) chargeable under Case I of Schedule D; or

(*b*) included in the profits of life reinsurance business or overseas life assurance business chargeable under Case VI of Schedule D by virtue of section 439B or 441.

(6) Where (whether by virtue of this subsection or otherwise) an amount of unrelieved foreign tax arising in an accounting period falls to be treated under subsection (2) above for the purposes of allowing credit relief under this Part as foreign tax paid in respect of, and computed by reference to, qualifying income of an earlier accounting period, it shall not be so treated for the purpose of any further application of this section.

(7) In this section "overseas branch or agency", in relation to a company, means a branch or agency through which the company carries on a trade in a territory outside the United Kingdom.][1]

Amendments—[1] This section inserted by FA 2000 s 103, Sch 30 para 23 with effect for unrelieved foreign tax arising in any accounting period ending after 31 March 2000. No such tax shall be treated by virtue of this amendment as foreign tax in respect of income arising in any accounting period ending before 1 April 2000.

[806M Provisions supplemental to section 806L

(1) This section has effect for the purposes of section 806L and shall be construed as one with that section.

(2) If, in any accounting period, a company ceases to have a particular overseas branch or agency, the amount of any unrelieved foreign tax which arises in that accounting period in respect of the company's income from that overseas branch or agency shall, to the extent that it is not treated as mentioned in section 806L(2)(*b*), be reduced to nil (so that no amount arises which falls to be treated as mentioned in section 806L(2)(*a*)).

(3) If a company—

(*a*) at any time ceases to have a particular overseas branch or agency in a particular territory ("the old branch or agency"), but

(*b*) subsequently again has an overseas branch or agency in that territory ("the new branch or agency"),

the old branch or agency and the new branch or agency shall be regarded as different overseas branches or agencies.

(4) If, under the law of a territory outside the United Kingdom, tax is charged in the case of a company resident in the United Kingdom in respect of the profits of two or more of its overseas branches or agencies in that territory, taken together, then, for the purposes of—

(*a*) section 806L, and

(*b*) subsection (3) above,

those overseas branches or agencies shall be treated as if they together constituted a single overseas branch or agency of the company.

(5) Unrelieved foreign tax arising in respect of qualifying income from a particular overseas branch or agency in any accounting period shall only be treated as mentioned in subsection (2) of section 806L on a claim.

(6) Any such claim must specify the amount (if any) of the unrelieved foreign tax—

(*a*) which is to be treated as mentioned in paragraph (*a*) of that subsection; and

(*b*) which is to be treated as mentioned in paragraph (*b*) of that subsection.

(7) A claim under subsection (5) above may only be made before the expiration of the period of—

(*a*) six years after the end of the accounting period mentioned in that subsection, or

(*b*) if later, one year after the end of the accounting period in which the foreign tax in question is paid.]¹

Amendments—¹ This section inserted by FA 2000 s 103, Sch 30 para 23 with effect for unrelieved foreign tax arising in any accounting period ending after 31 March 2000. No such tax shall be treated by virtue of this amendment as foreign tax in respect of income arising in any accounting period ending before 1 April 2000.

CHAPTER III
MISCELLANEOUS PROVISIONS

807 Sale of securities with or without accrued interest

(1) In any case where—

(*a*) a person is treated under section 714(2) as receiving annual profits or gains on the day an interest period ends; and

(*b*) assuming that, in the chargeable period in which the day falls, he were to become entitled to any interest on the securities concerned, he would be liable in respect of the interest to tax chargeable under Case IV or V of Schedule D; and

(*c*) he is liable under the law of a territory outside the United Kingdom to tax in respect of interest payable on the securities at the end of the interest period or he would be so liable if he were entitled to that interest,

credit of an amount equal to the relevant proportion of the profits or gains shall be allowed against any United Kingdom income tax or corporation tax computed by reference to the profits or gains, and shall be treated as if it were allowed under section 790(4).

In this subsection the relevant proportion is the rate of tax to which the person is or would be liable as mentioned in paragraph (*c*) above.

(2) In any case where—

(*a*) a person is entitled to credit against United Kingdom tax under section 790(4) or any corresponding provision of arrangements under section 788; and

(*b*) the tax is computed by reference to income consisting of interest which falls due on securities at the end of an interest period and which is treated as reduced by virtue of section 714(5);

then the amount of that credit shall be a proportion of the amount it would be apart from this subsection, and the proportion is to be found by applying the formula—

$$\frac{I - R}{I}$$

where—

I is the amount of the interest; and

R is the amount by which it is treated as reduced.

(3) Where the person entitled to the credit is an individual, subsection (2) above does not apply unless the interest arises from securities to which the person either became or ceased to be entitled during the interest period.

(4) Where section 811(1) applies to any income and, if credit were allowable in respect of it the credit would be reduced by virtue of subsection (2) above, section 811(1) shall have effect in relation to the income as if the reference to any sum paid in respect of tax on it were a reference to the amount which would be the amount of the credit if it were allowable and subsection (2) above applied.

(5) Sections 710 and 711 shall apply for the interpretation of this section.

[(6) This section does not apply for the purposes of corporation tax.]¹

Commentary—*Simon's Direct Tax Service* A7.542.
Revenue Internal Guidance—Double taxation relief manual DT 884 (operation of this section with worked example).
Definitions—"Chargeable period", s 832(1); "income tax", s 832(4); "interest", s 832(1); "profits or gains", s 833(1); "Schedule D", s 18(1); "tax", s 832(3); "United Kingdom", s 830(1).
Amendments—¹ Sub-s (6) inserted by FA 1996 ss 104, 105(1), Sch 14 para 45 with effect from the year 1996–97.

[807A Disposals and acquisitions of company loan relationships with or without interest

(1) This Part shall have effect for the purposes of corporation tax in relation to any company as if tax falling within subsection (2) below were to be disregarded.

(2) [Subject to subsection (2A) below,]² tax falls within this subsection in relation to a company to the extent that it is—

(a) tax under the law of a territory outside the United Kingdom; and
(b) is attributable, on a just and reasonable apportionment,—

[(i)]⁵ to interest accruing under a loan relationship at a time when the company is not a party to the relationship[; or
(ii) to so much of a [relevant payment]⁶ as, on such an apportionment, is attributable to a time when the company is not a party to [the derivative contract concerned]⁶]⁵.

[(2A) Tax attributable to interest accruing to a company under a loan relationship does not fall within subsection (2) above if—

(a) at the time when the interest accrues, that company has ceased to be a party to that relationship by reason of having made the initial transfer under or in accordance with any repo or stock-lending arrangements relating to that relationship; and
(b) that time falls during the period for which those arrangements have effect.]²

(3) Subject to subsections (1), (4) and (5) of this section, where—

(a) any non-trading credit relating to an amount of interest under a loan relationship is brought into account for the purposes of Chapter II of Part IV of the Finance Act 1996 (loan relationships) in the case of any company,
(b) that amount falls, as a result of any related transaction [other than the initial transfer under or in accordance with any repo or stock-lending arrangements relating to that relationship]³, to be paid to a person other than the company, and
(c) had the company been entitled, at the time of that transaction, to receive a payment of an amount of interest equal to the amount of interest to which the non-trading credit relates, the company would have been liable in respect of the amount of interest received to an amount of tax under the law of a territory outside the United Kingdom,

credit for that amount of tax shall be allowable under section 790(4) as if that amount of tax were an amount of tax paid under the law of that territory in respect of the amount of interest to which the non-trading credit relates.

(4) Subsection (3) above does not apply in the case of a credit brought into account in accordance with paragraph 1(2) of Schedule 11 to the Finance Act 1996 (the I minus E basis).

(5) The Treasury may by regulations provide for subsection (3) above to apply—

(a) in the case of trading credits as well as in the case of non-trading credits;
(b) in the case of any credit ("an insurance credit") in the case of which, by virtue of subsection (4) above, it would not otherwise apply.

(6) Regulations under subsection (5) above may—

(a) provide for subsection (3) above to apply in the case of a trading credit or an insurance credit only if the circumstances are such as may be described in the regulations;
(b) provide for subsection (3) above to apply, in cases where it applies by virtue of any such regulations, subject to such exceptions, adaptations or other modifications as may be specified in the regulations;
(c) make different provision for different cases; and
(d) contain such incidental, supplemental, consequential and transitional provision as the Treasury think fit.

[(6A) In this section 'repo or stock-lending arrangements' has the same meaning as in paragraph 15 of Schedule 9 to the Finance Act 1996 (repo transactions and stock-lending); and, in relation to any such arrangements—

(*a*) a reference to the initial transfer is a reference to the transfer mentioned in sub-paragraph (3)(*a*) of that paragraph; and

(*b*) a reference to the period for which the arrangements have effect is a reference to the period from the making of the initial transfer until whichever is the earlier of the following—

    (i) the discharge of the obligations arising by virtue of the entitlement or requirement mentioned in sub-paragraph (3)(*b*) of that paragraph; and

    (ii) the time when it becomes apparent that the discharge mentioned in sub-paragraph (i) above will not take place.][4]

(7) In this section—

"related transaction" has the same meaning as in section 84 of the Finance Act 1996; and

["relevant payment" means a payment the amount of which falls to be determined (wholly or mainly) by applying to a notional principal amount specified in a derivative contract, for a period so specified, a rate the value of which at all times is the same as that of a rate of interest so specified;][6]

...[6]

"trading credit" means any credit falling to be brought into account for the purposes of Chapter II of Part IV of the Finance Act 1996 (loan relationships) in accordance with section 82(2) of that Act.][1]

Definitions—"Company", s 832(1), (2); "derivative contract", s 834(1); "interest", s 832(1); "loan relationship", s 834(1), FA 1996 s 81; "tax", s 832(3).
Amendments—[1] This section inserted by FA 1996 ss 104, 105(1), Sch 14 para 46 with effect for accounting periods ending after 31 March 1996, subject to transitional provisions in FA 1996 Sch 15.
[2] Words in sub-s (2), and sub-s (2A), inserted by FA 1997 s 91(1)–(3), (6) with effect in relation to interest accruing after 31 March 1996.
[3] Words in sub-s (3)(*b*) inserted by FA 1997 s 91(1), (4), (7) with effect in relation to transactions made after 25 November 1996.
[4] Sub-s (6A) inserted by FA 1997 s 91(1), (5).
[5] Words in sub-s (2) and definition of "relevant qualifying payment" in sub-s (7) inserted by FA 2000 s 103, Sch 30 para 24 with effect for accounting periods ending after 20 March 2000.
[6] In sub-s (2)(*b*)(ii), words substituted for the words "relevant qualifying payment" and the words "the interest rate or currency contract concerned", in sub-s (7), definition of "relevant payment" inserted, and definition of "relevant qualifying payment" repealed, by FA 2002 ss 83(1)(*b*), (3), 141, Sch 27 paras 1, 12, Sch 40 Pt 3(13) with effect for accounting periods beginning after 30 September 2002. The definition of "relevant qualifying payment" in sub-s (7) previously read as follows—

" 'relevant qualifying payment' means a qualifying payment, for the purposes of Chapter II of Part IV of the Finance Act 1994, falling within section 153(1)(*a*) or (*b*) of that Act;".

808 Restriction on deduction of interest or dividends from trading income

In the case of a person not resident in the United Kingdom who carries on in the United Kingdom [a business][2], receipts of interest[, dividend or royalties][2] which have been treated as tax-exempt under arrangements having effect by virtue of section 788 are not to be excluded from trading income or profits of the business so as to give rise to losses to be set off (under section 393 [393A(1)][1] or 436) against income or profits.

...[3]

Commentary—*Simon's Direct Tax Service* **D2.408; D4.410.**
Simon's Tax Cases—*Boote v Banco do Brasil SA* [1997] STC 327*.
Definitions—"Interest", s 832(1); "United Kingdom", s 830(1).
Amendments—[1] "393A(1)" inserted by FA 1991 Sch 15 para 21.
[2] Words substituted by FA 1994 s 140 where it is sought to exclude receipts from income or profits of an accounting period beginning after 29 November 1993.
[3] Words repealed by FA 1994 s 140 and Sch 26, Pt V(18).

[808A Interest: special relationship

(1) Subsection (2) below applies where any arrangements having effect by virtue of section 788—

(*a*) make provision, whether for relief or otherwise, in relation to interest (as defined in the arrangements), and

(*b*) make provision (the special relationship provision) that where owing to a special relationship the amount of the interest paid exceeds the amount which would have been paid in the absence of the relationship, the provision mentioned in paragraph (*a*) above shall apply only to the last-mentioned amount.

(2) The special relationship provision shall be construed as requiring account to be taken of all factors, including—

(*a*) the question whether the loan would have been made at all in the absence of the relationship,

(*b*) the amount which the loan would have been in the absence of the relationship, and

(*c*) the rate of interest and other terms which would have been agreed in the absence of the relationship.

(3) The special relationship provision shall be construed as requiring the taxpayer to show that there is no special relationship or (as the case may be) to show the amount of interest which would have been paid in the absence of the special relationship.

(4) In a case where—

(*a*) a company makes a loan to another company with which it has a special relationship, and (*b*) it is not part of the first company's business to make loans generally,

the fact that it is not part of the first company's business to make loans generally shall be disregarded in construing subsection (2) above.

(5) Subsection (2) above does not apply where the special relationship provision expressly requires regard to be had to the debt on which the interest is paid in determining the excess interest (and accordingly expressly limits the factors to be taken into account).][1]

Commentary—*Simon's Direct Tax Service* **F1.221.**
Revenue & other press releases—Law Society 15-2-93 (the absence of the normal group cross-guarantee provisions required by banks will not, by itself, be taken into account under s 808A(2). "Taxpayer" in s 808A(3) is the person making the claim under the double tax agreement).
ICAEW 19–3–93 TAX 5/93 (sub-s (5) does no more than take the treaties which use the OECD Model "special relationship provision; outside the scope of this section).
Revenue Internal Guidance—International tax handbook ITH 1200–1276 (background to this section; Delaware links; equity notes).
Oil Taxation Office ring fence corporation tax manual OTRF 9.1–9.11 (application to oil companies).
Definitions—"Company", s 832(1), (2).
Cross references—TA 1988 s 209(8A) (distributions between connected companies within sub-s(2)(*da*), modification of sub-ss (2), (4) where formal or informal arrangements exist).
Amendments—[1] This section inserted by F(No 2)A 1992 s 52 in relation to interest as defined in the arrangements paid after 14 May 1992.

[808B Royalties: special relationship

(1) Subsection (2) below applies where any arrangements having effect by virtue of section 788—

    (*a*) make provision, whether for relief or otherwise, in relation to royalties (as defined in the arrangements), and

    (*b*) make provision (the special relationship provision) that where owing to a special relationship the amount of the royalties paid exceeds the amount which would have been paid in the absence of the relationship, the provision mentioned in paragraph (*a*) above shall apply only to the last-mentioned amount.

(2) The special relationship provision shall be construed as requiring account to be taken of all factors, including—

    (*a*) the question whether the agreement under which the royalties are paid would have been made at all in the absence of the relationship,

    (*b*) the rate or amounts of royalties and other terms which would have been agreed in the absence of the relationship, and

    (*c*) where subsection (3) below applies, the factors specified in subsection (4) below.

(3) This subsection applies if the asset in respect of which the royalties are paid, or any asset which that asset represents or from which it is derived, has previously been in the beneficial ownership of—

    (*a*) the person who is liable to pay the royalties,

    (*b*) a person who is, or has at any time been, an associate of the person who is liable to pay the royalties,

    (*c*) a person who has at any time carried on a business which, at the time when the liability to pay the royalties arises, is being carried on in whole or in part by the person liable to pay those royalties, or

    (*d*) a person who is, or has at any time been, an associate of a person who has at any time carried on such a business as is mentioned in sub-paragraph (*c*) above.

(4) The factors mentioned in subsection (2)(*c*) above are—

    (*a*) the amounts which were paid under the transaction, or under each of the transactions in the series of transactions, as a result of which the asset has come to be an asset of the beneficial owner for the time being,

    (*b*) the amounts which would have been so paid in the absence of a special relationship, and

    (*c*) the question whether the transaction or series of transactions would have taken place in the absence of such a relationship.

(5) The special relationship provision shall be construed as requiring the taxpayer to show—

    (*a*) the absence of any special relationship, or

    (*b*) the rate or amount of royalties that would have been payable in the absence of the relationship,

as the case may be.

(6) The requirement on the taxpayer to show in accordance with subsection (5)(*a*) above the absence of any special relationship includes a requirement—

    (*a*) to show that no person of any of the descriptions in paragraphs (*a*) to (*d*) of subsection (3) above has previously been the beneficial owner of the asset in respect of which the royalties are paid, or of any asset which that asset represents or from which it is derived, or

    (*b*) to show the matters specified in subsection (7) below,

as the case may be.

(7) Those matters are—

    (*a*) that the transaction or series of transactions mentioned in subsection (4)(*a*) above would have taken place in the absence of a special relationship, and (*b*) the amounts which would have been paid under the transaction, or under each of the transactions in the series of transactions, in the absence of such a relationship.

(8) Subsection (2) above does not apply where the special relationship provision expressly requires regard to be had to the use, right or information for which royalties are paid in determining the excess royalties (and accordingly expressly limits the factors to be taken into account).

(9) For the purposes of this section one person (''person A'') is an associate of another person (''person B'') at a given time if—

(*a*) person A was, within the meaning of Schedule 28AA, directly or indirectly participating in the management, control or capital of person B at that time, or

(*b*) the same person was or same persons were, within the meaning of Schedule 28AA, directly or indirectly participating in the management, control or capital of person A and person B at that time.]¹

Amendments—¹ This section inserted by FA 2000 s 103, Sch 30 para 25 with effect for royalties (as defined in the arrangements) payable after 27 July 2000.

809 Relief in respect of discretionary trusts

(1) In any case where—

(*a*) a payment made by trustees falls to be treated as a net amount in accordance with section 687(2) and the income arising under the trust includes any taxed overseas income, and

(*b*) the trustees certify that—

(i) the income out of which the payment was made was or included taxed overseas income of an amount and from a source stated in the certificate, and

(ii) that amount arose to them not earlier than six years before the end of the year of assessment in which the payment was made;

then the person to whom the payment was made may claim that the payment, up to the amount so certified, shall be treated for the purposes of this Part as income received by him from that source and so received in the year in which the payment was made.

(2) In subsection (1) above ''taxed overseas income'', in relation to any trust, means income in respect of which the trustees are entitled to credit for overseas tax under this Part.

Commentary—*Simon's Direct Tax Service* C4.227.
Definition—''Year of assessment'', s 832(1).

810 Postponement of capital allowances to secure double taxation relief

Commentary—*Simon's Direct Tax Service* B2.113; F1.136.
Amendments—This section repealed by FA 2000 ss 103, 156, Sch 30 para 26, Sch 40 Pt II(13) with effect for claims made after 31 March 2000.

811 Deduction for foreign tax where no credit allowable

(1) For the purposes of the Tax Acts, the amount of any income arising in any place outside the United Kingdom shall, subject to subsection (2) below, be treated as reduced by any sum which has been paid in respect of tax on that income in the place where the income has arisen (that is to say, tax payable under the law of a territory outside the United Kingdom).

(2) Subsection (1) above—

(*a*) shall not apply to income the tax on which is to be computed by reference to the amount of income received in the United Kingdom; ...⁴

(*b*) shall not affect section 278(3); ...¹ [and]⁴

(*c*) ...¹

[(*d*) shall not require any income to be treated as reduced by an amount of underlying tax which, by virtue of section 799(1B)(*b*), falls to be left out of account for the purposes of section 799;'']⁴

and this section has effect subject to section 795(2).

[(3) This section has effect for the purposes of corporation tax notwithstanding anything in—

[(*a*)]⁵ section 80(5) of the Finance Act 1996 (matters to be brought into account in the case of loan relationships only under Chapter II of Part IV of that Act).]²

[, or

(*b*) paragraph 1(3) of Schedule 29 to the Finance Act 2002 (matters to be brought into account in respect of intangible fixed assets only under that Schedule).]⁵

[(4) Where the amount by which any income is treated under subsection (1) above as reduced is rendered excessive or insufficient by reason of any adjustment of the amount of any tax payable either—

(*a*) in the United Kingdom, or

(*b*) under the law of any other territory,

nothing in the Tax Acts limiting the time for the making of assessments or claims for relief shall apply to any assessment or claim to which the adjustment gives rise, being an assessment or claim made not later than six years from the time when all such assessments, adjustments and other determinations have been made, whether in the United Kingdom or elsewhere, as are material in determining whether any and if so what reduction under subsection (1) above falls to be treated as made.

(5) Subject to subsection (7) below, where—

(a) the amount of any income of a person is treated under subsection (1) above as reduced by any sum, and

(b) the amount of that reduction is subsequently rendered excessive by reason of an adjustment of the amount of any tax payable under the law of a territory outside the United Kingdom,

that person shall give notice in writing to an officer of the Board that an adjustment has been made that has rendered the amount of the reduction excessive.

(6) A notice under subsection (5) above must be given within one year from the time of the making of the adjustment.

(7) Subsections (5) and (6) above do not apply where the adjustment is one whose consequences in relation to the reduction fall to be given effect to in accordance with regulations made under—

(a) section 182(1) of the Finance Act 1993 (regulations relating to individual members of Lloyd's); or

(b) section 229 of the Finance Act 1994 (regulations relating to corporate members of Lloyd's).

(8) A person who fails to comply with the requirements imposed on him by subsections (5) and (6) above in relation to any adjustment shall be liable to a penalty of an amount not exceeding the amount of the difference specified in subsection (9) below.

(9) The difference is that between—

(a) the amount of tax payable by the person in question for the relevant chargeable period, after giving effect to the reduction that ought to be made under subsection (1) above; and

(b) the amount that would have been the tax so payable after giving effect instead to a reduction under that subsection of the amount rendered excessive as mentioned in subsection (5)(b) above.

(10) For the purposes of subsection (9) above "the relevant chargeable period" means the chargeable period as respects which the reduction was treated as made.]³

Commentary—*Simon's Direct Tax Service* **D2.1139; F1.113; F2.105.**
Revenue Internal Guidance—Double taxation relief manual DT 509–514 (effect of this section; example on 1996–97 at DT 510; it is not permissible to have relief partly as a credit and partly as a deduction).
Definitions—"Accounting period", s 834(1); "Schedule D", s 18(1); "tax", s 832(3); "the Tax Acts", s 831(2); "United Kingdom", s 830(1).
Cross references—See TA 1988 s 444B and Sch 19AC para 14 (modification of this section in relation to overseas life insurance companies in accounting periods beginning after 31 December 1992).
TA 1988 s 807 (restriction on relief on income from securities purchased without accrued interest).
Amendments—¹ Sub-s (2)(c) and the word "and" immediately preceding it repealed by FA 1993 s 103(2)(g), (3) and Sch 23 Pt III(9) in relation to accounting periods beginning after 31 December 1992.
² Sub-s (3) inserted by FA 1996 ss 104, 105(1), Sch 14 para 47 with effect for income tax from 1996–97 and for corporation tax for accounting periods ending after 31 March 1996, subject to transitional provisions in FA 1996 Sch 15.
³ Sub-ss (4)–(10) inserted by FA 2000 s 103, Sch 30 para 27 with effect for adjustments made after 20 March 2000.
⁴ Amendments in sub-s (2) made by FA 2001 ss 81, 110 Sch 27 para 6, Sch 33 Pt II(8) with effect for income arising after 30 March 2001.
⁵ In sub-s (3), "(a)" inserted, and para (b) inserted, by FA 2002 s 84(2), Sch 30 para 5(1), (5) with effect from the 24 July 2002.

812 Withdrawal of right to tax credit of certain non-resident companies connected with unitary states

(1) In any case where—

(a) a company has, or is an associated company of a company which has, a qualifying presence in a unitary state, and

(b) at any time when it or its associated company has such a qualifying presence, the company is entitled by virtue of arrangements having effect under section 788(1) to a tax credit in respect of qualifying distributions made to it by companies which are resident in the United Kingdom which is equal to one half of the tax credit to which an individual resident in the United Kingdom would be entitled in respect of such distributions,

then, notwithstanding anything to the contrary in the arrangements, the company shall not be entitled to claim under section 231(3) to have that tax credit set against the income tax chargeable on its income for the year of assessment in which the distribution is made or, where the credit exceeds that income tax, to have the excess paid to it.

(2) In this section and sections 813 and 814, "unitary state" means a province, state or other part of a territory outside the United Kingdom [in relation to]² which the arrangements referred to in subsection (1) above have been made which, in taxing the income or profits of companies from sources within that province, state or other part, takes into account, or is entitled to take into account, income, receipts, deductions, outgoings or assets of such companies, or associated companies of such companies, arising, expended or situated, as the case may be, outside that territory and which has been prescribed under subsection (6) below as a unitary state for the purposes of this subsection.

(3) A company shall be treated as having a qualifying presence in a unitary state if it is a member of a group and, in any period for which members of the group make up their accounts ending after the

relevant date, $7\frac{1}{2}$ per cent or more in value of the property, payroll or sales of such members situated in, attributable to or derived from the territory outside the United Kingdom, of which that state is a province, state or other part, are situated in, attributable to or derived from that state.

(4) For the purposes of subsection (3) above—

(a) ...[1]

(b) the value of the property, payroll or sales of a company shall be taken to be the value as shown in its accounts for the period in question and for this purpose the value of any property consisting of an interest in another member of the group or of any sales made to another such member shall be disregarded.

(5) Except where the context otherwise requires, in this section and sections 813 to 815—

(a) "arrangements" means the arrangements referred to in subsection (1) above;

(b) "group" and "member of a group" shall be construed in accordance with section 272(1) of the 1970 Act with the omission of the restriction in paragraph (a) of that subsection and the substitution of the words "51 per cent" for the words "75 per cent" wherever they occur;

(c) section 839 applies;

(d) section 416 applies with the substitution of the words "six years" for "one year" in subsection (1); and

(e) "the relevant date" means the earliest of the following dates—

(i) the date on which this section comes into force;

(ii) the earliest date on which a distribution could have been made in relation to which the provisions of this section and sections 813 and 814 are applied by an order under this section;

(iii) the earliest date on which a distribution could have been made in relation to which the provisions of section 54 of the Finance Act 1985 were applied by an order under that section.

(6) The Treasury may by order prescribe those provinces, states or other parts of a territory outside the United Kingdom which are to be treated as unitary states for the purposes of subsection (2) above, but no province, state or other part of such a territory shall be so prescribed which only takes into account such income, receipts, deductions, outgoings or assets as are mentioned in that subsection—

(a) if the associated company was incorporated under the law of the territory; or

(b) for the purpose of granting relief in taxing dividends received by companies.

(7) The Treasury may by order prescribe that for subsections (3) and (4) above (or for those subsections as they have effect at any time) there shall be substituted [either the following subsection—

"(3) A company shall be treated as having a qualifying presence in a unitary state if it is liable in such a state to a tax charged on its income or profits by whatever name called for any period ending after the relevant date for which that state charges tax.";

or the following subsections—

"(3) A company shall be treated as having a qualifying presence in a unitary state if it has its principal place of business in such a state at any time after the relevant date.

(4) For the purposes of subsection (3) above the principal place of business of a company shall include both the place where central management and control of the company is exercised and the place where the immediate day-to-day management of the company as a whole is exercised.".][2]

(8) The provisions of this section and sections 813 to 815 shall come into force on such date as the Treasury may by order appoint and the Treasury may in the order prescribe that those provisions shall apply in relation to distributions made, in accounting periods ending after 5th April 1988, before the date on which the order is made.

(9) No order shall be made under this section unless a draft of it has been laid before and approved by a resolution of the House of Commons.

Commentary—*Simon's Direct Tax Service* **F1.215.**
Definitions—"The 1970 Act", s 831(3); "the Board", s 832(1); "company", s 832(1), (2); "control", s 840; "distribution", s 209(2), by virtue of s 832(1); "income tax", s 832(4); "qualifying distribution", s 832(1); "tax", s 832(3); "tax credit", s 832(1); "United Kingdom", s 830(1); "year of assessment", s 832(1).
Cross references—See TA 1988 s 814 (arrangements to avoid this section).
TA 1988 s 815 (Board's power to inspect documents where this section may apply).
Amendments—[1] Sub-s (4)(a) repealed and words in sub-s (7) substituted by FA 1996 s 134(1), (2), Sch 20 para 38(2), Sch 41 Pt V(10) with effect from the year 1996–97.
[2] Words substituted for the words "with the government of" by FA 2002 s 88(2)(a), (3) with effect on and after the date of the passing of FA 2002 (24 July 2002) in relation to arrangements made before that date (as well as in relation to arrangements made on or after that date).

813 Recovery of tax credits incorrectly paid

(1) Where—

(a) section 812 applies so as to withdraw the entitlement of a company to claim to have a tax credit in respect of a qualifying distribution set against the income tax chargeable on its income and to have the excess of the credit over that income tax paid to it; and

(b) the company ("the recipient company") has either had that excess paid to it, or has received an additional amount in accordance with arrangements made under Regulation 2(1) of the Double Taxation Relief (Taxes on Income) (General) (Dividend) Regulations 1973;

the recipient company shall be liable to a fine for the violation of the provisions of section 812 equal to twice the amount of the excess or the additional amount, as the case may be.

(2) Any fine payable under subsection (1) above—

(a) shall be payable to the Board;

(b) shall be treated as having become payable at the date when the excess or additional amount was paid to the recipient company; and

(c) may be recovered in accordance with subsections (3) to (7) below;

and any such fine is referred to below as "the recoverable amount".

(3) The recoverable amount may be assessed and recovered as if it were unpaid tax and section 30 of the Management Act (recovery of overpayment of tax etc) shall apply accordingly.

(4) Any amount which may be assessed and recovered as if it were unpaid tax by virtue of this section shall carry interest at the rate of 9 per cent per annum from the date when it was payable in accordance with subsection (1) above until the date it is paid.

(5) It is hereby declared that this section applies to a recoverable amount which is paid without the making of an assessment (but is paid after it is due) and that, where the recoverable amount is charged by any assessment (whether or not any part of it has been paid when the assessment is made), this section applies in relation to interest running before, as well as after, the making of the assessment.

(6) Where the recoverable amount is not paid by the recipient company within six months from the date on which it became payable—

(a) the recoverable amount may at any time within six years from the date on which it became payable be assessed and recovered as if it were unpaid tax due from any person who—

(i) is or was at any time prior to the expiration of that six year period connected with the recipient company, or

(ii) would have been connected on the assumption that all the facts and circumstances relating to the recipient company at the time the excess or additional amount, as the case may be, was paid continued to apply for six years thereafter,

and section 30 of the Management Act shall apply accordingly; and

(b) ...¹

(7) Where a recoverable amount is assessed and recovered from a person connected with the recipient company in accordance with subsection (6)(a) above, that person shall be liable for the interest payable in accordance with subsection (4) above, and until the interest is so paid, subsection (6)(b) above shall apply as if the words "the interest due in accordance with subsection (4) above is paid" were substituted for the words "the recoverable amount is paid in accordance with the provisions of this section".

(8) Interest payable under this section shall be paid without any deduction of income tax and shall not be allowed as a deduction in computing any income, profits or losses for any tax purposes.

(9) Where under the law in force in a territory outside the United Kingdom interest is payable subject to a deduction in respect of taxation and such deduction applies to an amount of interest paid in accordance with subsection (4) above, the reference to the rate of 9 per cent per annum in that subsection shall be deemed to be a reference to such rate of interest as after such deduction shall be equal to the rate of 9 per cent per annum.

Commentary—*Simon's Direct Tax Service* **F1.215.**
Definitions—"Accounting period", s 834(1); "advance corporation tax", s 14(1); "arrangements", s 812(1), (5); "the Board", s 832(1); "company", s 832(1), (2); "income tax", s 832(4); "interest", s 832(1); "the Management Act", s 831(3); "person connected", see s 839; "qualifying distribution", s 14(2), by virtue of s 832(1); "tax", s 832(3); "tax credit", s 832(1); "United Kingdom", s 830(1).
Cross references—See TA 1988 s 815 (Board's power to inspect documents where this section may apply).
Amendments—¹ Sub-s (6)(b) repealed by FA 1998 Sch 3 para 37 with effect in relation to accounting periods beginning after 5 April 1999.

814 Arrangements to avoid section 812

(1) In any case where arrangements are made, whether before or after the coming into force of this section, as a result of which interest is paid or a discount is allowed by or through a person who is resident in the United Kingdom, or carries on business in the United Kingdom through a branch or agency, and it is reasonable to suppose that, if such payment or allowance had not been made, a qualifying distribution would have been made by that person, or by another company resident in the United Kingdom to a company which has, or is an associated company of a company which has, a qualifying presence in a unitary state at the time when the payment or allowance is made, then—

(a) no person who receives that payment or allowance shall be entitled to relief from income tax or corporation tax thereon by virtue of arrangements having effect under section 788(1); and

(b) the payment or allowance shall not be allowed as a deduction in computing any income, profits or losses for any tax purposes.

(2) Without prejudice to the generality of subsection (1) above, where a payment or allowance is not of itself a payment or allowance to which that subsection applies, but is made in conjunction with other payments of whatever nature and taken together with those payments has substantially similar effect to a distribution, then, for the purposes of subsection (1) above it shall be treated as a payment or allowance within that subsection.

(3) Any company which has received such a payment of interest as is referred to in subsection (1) above, from which income tax has not been deducted by the person making the payment, and has a qualifying presence in a unitary state at the time of the payment, shall be treated for the purposes of section 813 as a company—

(*a*) from which the entitlement to claim payment of the excess of a tax credit over the income tax chargeable on its income has been withdrawn by section 812(1), and
(*b*) which has had paid to it such an excess in an amount equal to the income tax which should have been deducted from the payment of interest.

Commentary—*Simon's Direct Tax Service* **F1.215.**
Definitions—"Arrangements", s 812(1), (5); "associated company", ss 416(1), 812(5); "branch or agency", s 834(1); "company", s 832(1), (2); "distribution", s 209(2), by virtue of s 832(1); "income tax", s 832(4); "interest", s 832(1); "qualifying distribution", s 14(2), by virtue of s 832(1); "tax", s 832(3); "tax credit", s 832(1); "unitary state", s 812(2); "United Kingdom", s 830(1).
Cross references—See TA 1988 s 815 (Board's power to inspect documents where this section may apply).

815 Power to inspect documents

Where it appears to the Board that the provisions of sections 812 to 814 may apply to a company resident outside the United Kingdom ("the foreign parent"), the Board may, by notice given to the foreign parent or any associated company of the foreign parent, require that company within such time (not being less than 30 days) as may be specified in the notice to make available for inspection any books, accounts or other documents or records whatsoever of that company where in the opinion of the Board it is proper that they should inspect such documents for the purposes of ascertaining whether those provisions apply to the foreign parent or such associated company notwithstanding that in the opinion of the person to whom the notice is given those provisions do not apply to that company or any associated company of that company.

Commentary—*Simon's Direct Tax Service* **F1.215.**
Definitions—"Associated company", ss 416(1), 812(5); "the Board", s 832(1); "company", s 832(1), (2); "notice", s 832(1); "United Kingdom", s 830(1).

[815A Transfer of a non-UK trade

(1) This section applies where section 269C of the 1970 Act or section 140C of the Taxation of Chargeable Gains Act 1992 applies; and references in this section to company A, the transfer and the trade shall be construed accordingly.

[(2) Where gains accruing to company A on the transfer would have been chargeable to tax under the law of the relevant member State but for the Mergers Directive, this Part, including any arrangements having effect by virtue of section 788, shall apply as if the amount of tax, calculated on the required basis, which would have been payable under that law in respect of the gains so accruing but for that Directive, were tax payable under that law.][2]

(5) For the purposes of this section, the required basis is that—

(*a*) so far as permitted under the law of the relevant member State, any losses arising on the transfer are set against any gains so arising, and
(*b*) any relief available to company A under that law has been duly claimed.

(6) In this section—

"the Mergers Directive" means the Directive of the Council of the European Communities dated 23rd July 1990 on the common system of taxation applicable to mergers, divisions, transfers of assets and exchanges of shares concerning companies of different member States (no 90/434/EEC);
"relevant member State" means the member State in which, immediately before the time of the transfer, company A carried on the trade through a branch or agency.][1]

Commentary—*Simon's Direct Tax Service* **D2.304B; F2.121.**
Notes—All provisions in TA 1970 relating to chargeable gains are consolidated in TCGA 1992. TA 1970 s 269C referred to in sub-s (1) and enacted by F(No 2)A 1992 s 48 contains the same provisions as TCGA 1992 s 149C reproduced *post*.
EC Directive 90/434/EEC is reproduced in Part II of this volume.
Amendments—[1] This section inserted by F(No 2)A 1992 s 50.
[2] Sub-s (2) substituted for sub-ss (2)–(4) by FA 1996 s 134(1), (2), Sch 20 para 39 with effect for income tax purposes from the year 1996–97 and, for the purposes of corporation tax, as respect accounting periods ending after 30 June 1999 (by virtue of Finance Act 1994, Section 199, (Appointed Day) Order, SI 1998/3173 art 2).

[815AA Mutual agreement procedure and presentation of cases under arrangements

(1) Where, under and for the purposes of arrangements made [in relation to][2] a territory outside the United Kingdom and having effect under section 788—

(*a*) a case is presented to the Board, or to an authority in that territory, by a person concerning his being taxed (whether in the United Kingdom or that territory) otherwise than in accordance with the arrangements; and

(*b*) the Board arrives at a solution to the case or makes a mutual agreement with an authority in that territory for the resolution of the case,

subsections (2) and (3) below have effect.

(2) The Board shall give effect to the solution or mutual agreement, notwithstanding anything in any enactment; and any such adjustment as is appropriate in consequence may be made (whether by way of discharge or repayment of tax, the allowance of credit against tax payable in the United Kingdom, the making of an assessment or otherwise).

(3) A claim for relief under any provision of the Tax Acts may be made in pursuance of the solution or mutual agreement at any time before the expiration of the period of 12 months following the notification of the solution or mutual agreement to the person affected, notwithstanding the expiration of the time limited by any other enactment for making the claim.

(4) Where arrangements having effect under section 788 include provision for a person to present a case to the Board concerning his being taxed otherwise than in accordance with the arrangements, subsections (5) and (6) below have effect.

(5) The presentation of any such case under and in accordance with the arrangements—

(*a*) does not constitute a claim for relief under the Tax Acts; and

(*b*) is accordingly not subject to section 42 of the Management Act or any other enactment relating to the making of such claims.

(6) Any such case must be presented before the expiration of—

(*a*) the period of 6 years following the end of the chargeable period to which the case relates; or

(*b*) such longer period as may be specified in the arrangements.][1]

Commentary—*Simon's Direct Tax Service* B3.1853.
Amendments—[1] This section inserted by FA 2000 s 103, Sch 30 para 28. In accordance with Sch 30 para 28(2), (3), sub-ss (1)–(3) have effect where the solution or mutual agreement is reached or made after 27 July 2000, and sub-s (6) (and sub-s (4) so far as relates to sub-s (6)) has effect for the first presentation of a case after 27 July 2000.
[2] Words substituted for the words "with the government of" by FA 2002 s 88(2)(*a*), (3) with effect on and after the date of the passing of FA 2002 (24 July 2002) in relation to arrangements made before that date (as well as in relation to arrangements made on or after that date).

[815B The Arbitration Convention

(1) Subsection (2) below applies if the Arbitration Convention requires the Board to give effect to—

(*a*) an agreement or decision, made under the Convention by the Board (or their authorised representative) and any other competent authority, on the elimination of double taxation, or

(*b*) an opinion, delivered by an advisory commission set up under the Convention, on the elimination of double taxation.

(2) The Board shall give effect to the agreement, decision or opinion notwithstanding anything in any enactment; and any such adjustment as is appropriate in consequence may be made (whether by way of discharge or repayment of tax, the making of an assessment or otherwise).

(3) Any enactment which limits the time within which claims for relief under any provision of the Tax Acts may be made shall not apply to a claim made in pursuance of an agreement, decision or opinion falling within subsection (1)(*a*) or (*b*) above.

(4) In this section "the Arbitration Convention" means the Convention on the elimination of double taxation in connection with the adjustment of profits of associated enterprises, concluded on 23rd July 1990 by the parties to the treaty establishing the European Economic Community (90/436/EEC).][1]

Commentary—*Simon's Direct Tax Service* F2.122.
Notes—EC Convention 90/436/EEC is reproduced in Part II of this publication.
Definitions—"the Board", s 832(1); "the Tax Acts", s 831(2).
Amendments—[1]This section inserted by F(No 2)A 1992 s 51(1).

[815C Exchange of information with other [territories][3]

(1) If Her Majesty by Order in Council declares that arrangements specified in the Order have been made [in relation to][2] f any territory outside the United Kingdom with a view to the exchange of information necessary for carrying out—

(*a*) the domestic laws of the United Kingdom concerning income tax, capital gains tax and corporation tax in respect of income and chargeable gains; and

(*b*) the laws of the territory to which the arrangements relate concerning any taxes of a similar character to those taxes imposed by the laws of that territory,

and that it is expedient that those arrangements shall have effect, then those arrangements shall have effect notwithstanding anything in any enactment.

(2) Any Order in Council made under this section revoking an earlier such Order in Council may contain such transitional provisions as appear to Her Majesty to be necessary or expedient.

(3) An Order under this section shall not be submitted to Her Majesty in Council unless a draft of the Order has been laid before and approved by a resolution of the House of Commons.][1]

Amendments—[1] This section inserted by FA 2000 s 146(1) with effect from 28 July 2000.
[2] Words substituted for the words "with the government of" by FA 2002 s 88(2)(*a*), (3) with effect on and after the date of the passing of FA 2002 (24 July 2002) in relation to arrangements made before that date (as well as in relation to arrangements made on or after that date).
[3] Words substituted for the words "countries" by FA 2002 s 88(2)(*b*), (3) with effect on and after the date of the passing of FA 2002 (24 July 2002) in relation to arrangements made before that date (as well as in relation to arrangements made on or after that date).

816 Disclosure of information

(1) Where under the law in force in any territory outside the United Kingdom provision is made for the allowance, in respect of the payment of United Kingdom income tax or corporation tax, of relief from tax payable under that law, the obligation as to secrecy imposed by the Tax Acts upon persons employed in relation to Inland Revenue shall not prevent the disclosure to the authorised officer of the [authorities][4] of the territory in question of such facts as may be necessary to enable the proper relief to be given under that law.

Section 790(12) shall apply for the interpretation of this subsection as it applies for the interpretation of that section.

(2) Where any arrangements have effect by virtue of section 788 [or 815C][3], the obligation as to secrecy imposed by any enactment shall not prevent the Board, or any authorised officer of the Board, from disclosing to any authorised officer of the [authorities of the territory in relation to][5] which the arrangements are made such information as is required to be disclosed under the arrangements.

[(2ZA) Neither the Board nor an authorised officer of the Board shall disclose any information in pursuance of any arrangements having effect by virtue of section 815C unless satisfied that the [authorities of the territory in relation to][5] which the arrangements are made [are bound][6] by, or [have undertaken][6] to observe, rules of confidentiality with respect to the information which are not less strict than those applying to it in the United Kingdom.][3]

[(2A) The obligation as to secrecy imposed by any enactment shall not prevent the Board, or any authorised officer of the Board, from disclosing information required to be disclosed under the Arbitration Convention in pursuance of a request made by an advisory commission set up under that Convention; and "the Arbitration Convention" here has the meaning given by section 815B(4).][1]

(3) Where a person beneficially entitled to income from any securities as defined by section 24 of the Management Act (information as to income from securities) is resident in a territory to which arrangements having effect under section 788 with respect to income tax or corporation tax relate, section 24(3) of that Act shall not exempt any bank from the duty of disclosing to the Board particulars relating to the income of that person.

[(3A) In this section "bank" has the meaning given by section 840A.][2]

(4) The obligation as to secrecy imposed by any enactments with regard to income tax or corporation tax shall not prevent the disclosure, to any authorised officer of any country to which a declaration made under section 514 of the 1970 Act (agreements about shipping etc) relates, of such facts as may be necessary to enable relief to be duly given in accordance with the arrangements specified in the declaration.

Commentary—*Simon's Direct Tax Service* **F1.111.**
Revenue Internal Guidance—Investigations handbook IH 421 (exchange of information is dealt with by London Special Compliance Office).
Notes—The Arbitration Convention 90/436/EEC is reproduced *post*.
Definitions—"The 1970 Act", s 831(3); "the Board", s 832(1); "income tax", s 832(4); "the Management Act", s 831(3); "tax", s 832(3); "the Tax Acts", s 831(2); "United Kingdom", s 830(1).
Cross references—See TCGA 1992 s 277(4) (this section to apply in relation to capital gains tax also).
Amendments—[1] Sub-s (2A) inserted by F(No 2)A 1992 s 51(2).
[2] Sub-s (3A) inserted by FA 1996 Sch 37 paras 2(1), (2)(*d*), 9 with effect in relation to requirements imposed on or after 29 April 1996.
[3] Words in sub-s (2) and whole of sub-s (2ZA) inserted by FA 2000 s 146(2) with effect from 28 July 2000.
[4] Word substituted for the words "government" by FA 2002 s 88(2)(*c*), (3) with effect on and after the date of the passing of FA 2002 (24 July 2002) in relation to arrangements made before that date (as well as in relation to arrangements made on or after that date).
[5] Word substituted for the words "government with" by FA 2002 s 88(2)(*d*), (*e*) (3) with effect on and after the date of the passing of FA 2002 (24 July 2002) in relation to arrangements made before that date (as well as in relation to arrangements made on or after that date).
[6] Words substituted for the words "is bound" and "has undertaken" by FA 2002 s 88(2)(*d*), (*e*) (3) with effect on and after the date of the passing of FA 2002 (24 July 2002) in relation to arrangements made before that date (as well as in relation to arrangements made on or after that date).

PART XIX
SUPPLEMENTAL
Miscellaneous

817 Deductions not to be allowed in computing profits or gains

(1) In arriving at the amount of profits or gains for tax purposes—

(*a*) no other deductions shall be made than such as are expressly enumerated in the Tax Acts; and (*b*) no deduction shall be made on account of any annuity or other annual payment (not being interest) to be paid out of such profits or gains in regard that a proportionate part of income tax is allowed to be deducted on making any such payment.

(2) In arriving at the amount of profits or gains from any property described in the Tax Acts, or from any office or employment, no deduction shall be made on account of diminution of capital employed, or of loss sustained, in any trade or in any profession, employment or vocation.

Commentary—*Simon's Direct Tax Service* **B3.1202, 1463.**
Definitions—"Income tax", s 832(4); "interest", s 832(1); "profits or gains", s 833(1); "tax", s 832(3); "the Tax Acts", s 831(2); "trade", s 832(1).

818 Arrangements for payments of interest less tax or of fixed net amount

(1) It is hereby declared that any provision made before or after the passing of this Act, whether orally or in writing, for the payment of interest "less tax", or using words to that effect, is to be construed, in relation to interest payable without deduction of tax, as if the words "less tax", or the equivalent words, were not included.

(2) In relation to interest on which the recipient is chargeable to tax under Case III of Schedule D, and which is payable without deduction of tax, any provision, made before or after the passing of this Act, whether orally or in writing, and however worded, for the payment of interest at such a rate ("the gross rate") as shall, after the deduction of income tax, be equal to a stated rate, shall be construed as if it were a provision requiring the payment of interest at the gross rate.

Commentary—*Simon's Direct Tax Service* **E1.424.**
Definitions—"Income tax", s 832(4); "interest", s 832(1); "Schedule D", s 18(1); "tax", s 832(3).

819 Old references to standard rate tax

(1) Where any provision, however worded, contained in an instrument (of whatever nature) made on or after 3rd September 1939 or in a will or codicil taking effect on or after that date provides for the payment, whether periodically or otherwise—

(*a*) of a stated amount free of income tax other than surtax; or
(*b*) of an amount which, after deduction of income tax at the standard rate, is equal to a stated amount;

it shall have effect as follows.

(2) If it is such a provision as is mentioned in subsection (1)(*a*) above it shall have effect as if it provided for the payment of the stated amount free of income tax other than such as exceeds the amount to which the person to whom the payment is made would be liable if all income tax [not chargeable]¹ [at the starting rate]⁵ [were charged at the basic rate, or (so far as applicable in accordance with [section 1A])³ the lower rate,]² [or the Schedule F ordinary rate]⁴ to the exclusion of [the higher rate and the Schedule F upper rate]⁴.

(3) If it is such a provision as is mentioned in subsection (1)(*b*) above it shall have effect as if it provided for the payment of an amount which after deduction of income tax at the basic rate is equal to the stated amount.

(4) Any instrument however worded conferring on any person a right to receive a dividend or interest the amount of which depends on the standard rate of income tax shall have effect as if instead of referring to the standard rate it referred to the basic rate.

(5) Any reference in a statutory instrument made under the Tax Acts to the standard rate of income tax shall have effect as if it were a reference to the basic rate.

Commentary—*Simon's Direct Tax Service* **E1.105.**
Definitions—"Basic rate", s 832(1); "higher rate", s 832(1); "income tax", s 832(4); "interest", s 832(1); "lower rate", s 832(1); "Schedule F ordinary rate", s 832(1); "Schedule F upper rate", s 832(1); "starting rate", s 831(1); "the Tax Acts", s 831(2).
Amendments—¹ Words in sub-s (2) inserted by F(No 2)A 1992 s 19(3), (7) with effect from the year 1992–93.
² Words in sub-s (2) substituted by FA 1993 Sch 6 paras 1, 25(1) with effect from the year 1993–94.
³ Words in sub-s (2) substituted by FA 1996 s 73(4), Sch 6 paras 13, 28 with effect from the year 1996–97.
⁴ Words in sub-s (2) inserted and substituted (for "any higher rate") respectively by F(No 2)A 1997 s 34, Sch 4 para 21 with effect for the year 1999–00 and subsequent years of assessment.
⁵ Words in sub-s (2) substituted by FA 1999 s 22(9), (12) with effect from the year 1999–00.

820 Application of Income Tax Acts from year to year

In order to ensure the collection in due time of income tax which may be granted for any year commencing on 6th April, all such provisions contained in the Income Tax Acts as were in force on the preceding day shall have full force and effect with respect to tax which may be so granted, in the same manner as if that tax had been actually granted by Act of Parliament and those provisions had been applied thereto by the Act.

Commentary—*Simon's Direct Tax Service* **A1.104.**
Definitions—"Act", s 832(1); "income tax", s 832(4); "the Income Tax Acts", s 831(1)(*b*); "tax", s 832(3).

821 Under-deductions from payments made before passing of annual Act

(1) Where, in any year of assessment, any half-yearly or quarterly payments have been made on account of any interest, dividends or other annual profits or gains, previously to the passing of the Act imposing income tax for that year, and tax has not been charged thereon or deducted therefrom or has not been charged thereon or deducted therefrom at the rate ultimately imposed for that year—

    (a) the amount not so charged or deducted shall be charged [under Case III of Schedule D in respect of those payments; and]³

    (b) the agents entrusted with the payment of the interest, dividends or other annual profits or gains shall furnish to the Board a list containing the names and addresses of the persons to whom payments have been made and the amount of those payments, upon a requisition made by the Board in that behalf.

(2) Any person liable to pay any rent, interest or annuity, or to make any other annual payment—

    (a) shall be authorised—

        (i) to make any deduction on account of income tax for any year of assessment which he has failed to make previously to the passing of the Act imposing the tax for that year, or

        (ii) to make up any deficiency in any such deduction which has been so made,

on the occasion of the next payment of the rent, interest or annuity or making of the other annual payment after the passing of the Act so imposing the tax, in addition to any other deduction which he may be by law authorised to make; and

    (b) shall also be entitled, if there is no future payment from which the deduction may be made, to recover the sum which might have been deducted as if it were a debt due from the person as against whom the deduction could originally have been made if the Act imposing the tax for the year had been in force.

(3) Subsection (2) above shall apply with respect to—

    (a) any payment for or in respect of copyright to which section 536 applies or of public lending right to which that section applies by virtue of section 537; and

    [(aa) any payment for or in respect of a right in a design to which section 537B applies; and]¹

    (b) any royalty or other sum paid in respect of the user of a patent; ...²

    (c) ...²

as it applies with respect to any rent, interest, annuity or other annual payment.

(4) In this section ''interest'' and ''dividends'' do not include any interest or dividend which is a distribution.

Commentary—*Simon's Direct Tax Service* A3.417; B7.216.
Definitions—''Act'', s 832(1); ''Board'', s 832(1); ''distribution'', s 209(2), by virtue of s 832(1); ''income tax'', s 832(4); ''interest'', s 832(1); ''profits or gains'', s 833(1); ''Schedule D'', s 18(1); ''tax'', s 832(3); ''year of assessment'', s 832(1).
Amendments—¹ Sub-s (3)(aa) inserted by the Copyright, Designs and Patents Act 1988 Sch 7 para 36(7) with effect from 1 August 1989 by virtue of the Copyright, Designs and Patents Act 1988 (Commencement No 1) Order 1989, SI 1989/816.
² Sub-s (3)(c) and preceding word ''and'' repealed by FA 1997 Sch 18 Pt VI(2) with effect in relation to payments made after 5 April 1997.
³ Words in sub-s (1)(a) substituted by FA 1996 s 73(4), Sch 6 paras 22, 28 with effect from the year 1996–97.

822 Over-deductions from interest on loan capital etc made before passing of annual Act

(1) If in any year of assessment (''the year'') a resolution having statutory effect under the Provisional Collection of Taxes Act 1968 provides for the charging of income tax at a [lower rate less]¹ than that charged for the previous year, the following provisions of this section shall have effect with respect to deductions in respect of income tax by any body corporate, from payments of interest (not being a distribution) on any of its securities.

(2) Any deduction which was made before the expiration of one month from the passing of the resolution and which would, if the tax had been renewed at the rate imposed for the previous year, have been a legal deduction, shall be deemed to be a deduction rendered legal by section 2 of the Provisional Collection of Taxes Act 1968 and that section shall, subject to this section, apply accordingly.

(3) Any over-deduction to be made good under that section may be made good by a reduction of the amount of tax deducted from the next payment of like nature made on the security in question after the passing of the Act imposing the tax for the year.

(4) Any amount made good under section 2 of the Provisional Collection of Taxes Act 1968 shall—

    (a) in the case of an over-deduction which is made good under subsection (3) above, enure to the benefit of the person entitled to the payment on the occasion of which the over-deduction is made good; and

    (b) in any other case, enure to the benefit of the person entitled to the security in question at the date when the amount is made good,

irrespective, in either case, of whether or not he is the person who was entitled to the payment, or to the security at the date when the original deduction was made.

(5) Subsection (3) above shall not authorise the retention of any part of the amount over-deducted for more than one year from the passing of the Act imposing the tax for the year.

Commentary—*Simon's Direct Tax Service* A3.417.
Definitions—"Act", s 832(1); "distribution", ss 209(2), 832(1); "income tax", s 832(4); "interest", s 832(1); "lower rate", s 832(1); "tax", s 832(3); "year of assessment", s 832(1).
Amendments—¹ Words in sub-s (1) substituted by FA 1996 s 73(4), Sch 6 paras 23, 28 with effect from the year 1996–97.

823 Adjustments of reliefs where given at different times

Where under the provisions of the Income Tax Acts an individual—

(a) is entitled to claim relief from income tax (other than relief in respect of life insurance premiums), by repayment or otherwise, in respect of—

(i) any amount which is paid or borne by him out of his income or which is allowable or may be deducted from his income; or

(ii) any reduction of an assessment relating to his income or any part of his income; or

(iii) any adjustment or set-off with regard to a loss; and

(b) claims that relief for any year of assessment,

any relief granted shall not extend so as to make the total income tax paid or payable by him for that year less than it would have been if the amount in respect of which relief is claimed had been deducted in computing his total income for the year and the amount of any other deductions or reliefs to which he is entitled for that year had been determined accordingly.

Commentary—*Simon's Direct Tax Service* E2.1106.
Definitions—"Income tax", s 832(4); "the Income Tax Acts", s 831(1)(b); "total income", s 835(1); "year of assessment", s 832(1).

824 Repayment supplements: individuals and others

[(1) Subject to the following provisions of this section, a repayment made by the Board or an officer of the Board of any of the following, namely—

(a) an amount paid on account of income tax under section 59A of the Management Act;

(b) any income tax paid by or on behalf of an individual for a year of assessment;

(c) a surcharge imposed under section 59C of that Act; and

(d) a penalty incurred by an individual under any of the provisions of that Act,

shall be increased under this section by an amount (a "repayment supplement") equal to interest on the amount repaid at the rate applicable under section 178 of the Finance Act 1989 for the period (if any) between the relevant time and the date on which the order for the repayment is issued]⁵.

[(1A) ...³]¹

(2) [Subsections (1) ...³]¹ above shall with the necessary modifications apply to a payment of the whole or part of a tax credit as [they apply to a repayment falling within subsection (1)]¹ of income tax paid in the year of assessment to which the tax credit relates.

[(2A) Subsection (1) above shall apply to a repayment made in consequence of a claim under section 228 of the Income Tax Act 1952 (relief in respect of income accumulated under trusts) as if the repayment were of income tax paid by the claimant for the year of assessment in which the contingency mentioned in that section happened.]¹

[(2B) Subsection (1) above shall apply to a payment made by the Board under section 375(8) (payment of amount which borrower would have been able to deduct from interest payment under section 369(1)) as if the payment were a repayment falling within that subsection.]⁷

[(2C) Subsection (1) above shall apply to a repayment made by the Board as a result of a claim for relief under—

(a) paragraph 2 of Schedule 1B to the Management Act (carry back of loss relief),

(b) paragraph 3 of that Schedule (relief for fluctuating profits of farming etc), or

(c) Schedule 4A to this Act (relief for fluctuating profits of creative artists etc),

as if it were a repayment falling within that subsection.]⁸

[(3) For the purposes of subsection (1) above—

[(aa) if the repayment is a payment made by the Board under section 375(8), the relevant time is—

(i) if the interest payment was made in the year 1996–97 or a subsequent year of assessment, the 31st January following that year;

(ii) if the interest payment was made in an earlier year of assessment, the 5th April next following that year;]⁷

[(ab) if the repayment is a repayment as a result of a claim for relief under any of the provisions mentioned in subsection (2C) above, the relevant time is the 31st January next following the year that is the later year in relation to the claim;]⁸

[(a) if the repayment is—

(i) the repayment of an amount paid in accordance with the requirements of section 59A of the Management Act on account of income tax for a year of assessment, or

(ii) the repayment of income tax for such a year which is not income tax deducted at source,

the relevant time is the date of the payment that is being repaid;

(b) if the repayment is of income tax deducted at source for a year of assessment, the relevant time is the 31st January next following that year; and]⁶ (*c*) if the repayment is of a penalty or surcharge, [the relevant time is the date on which the penalty or surcharge was paid]⁶]⁵

[(4) For the purposes of subsection (3) above, where a repayment in respect of income tax for a year of assessment is made to any person, that repayment—

    (*a*) shall be attributed first to so much of any payment made by him under section 59B of the Management Act as is a payment in respect of income tax for that year;
    (*b*) in so far as it exceeds the amount (if any) to which it is attributable under paragraph (*a*) above, shall be attributed in two equal parts to each of the payments made by him under section 59A of the Management Act on account of income tax for that year;
    (*c*) in so far as it exceeds the amounts (if any) to which it is attributable under paragraphs (*a*) and (*b*) above, shall be attributed to income tax deducted at source for that year; and
    (*d*) in so far as it is attributable to a payment made in instalments shall be attributed to a later instalment before being attributed to an earlier one.

(4A) In this section any reference to income tax deducted at source for a year of assessment is a reference to—

    (*a*) income tax deducted or treated as deducted from any income, or treated as paid on any income, in respect of that year, and
    (*b*) amounts which, in respect of that year, are tax credits to which section 231 applies,

but does not include a reference to amounts which, in that year, are deducted at source under section 203 in respect of previous years.]⁶

(5) ...⁵

(6) ...³ the Treasury may by order from time to time increase or decrease the rate of interest by reference to which—

    (*a*) repayment supplements are calculated under subsection (1) above; and
    (*b*) repayment supplements are calculated under section 47 of the Finance (No 2) Act 1975.

(7) A repayment supplement shall not be payable under this section in respect of a repayment or payment made in consequence of an order or judgment of a court having power to allow interest on the repayment or payment, or in respect of a repayment of a post-war credit within the meaning of the Income Tax (Repayment of Post-War Credits) Act 1959.

(8) A repayment supplement paid to any person under this section or under section [283 of the 1992 Act]⁴ shall not be income of that person for any tax purposes.

(9) Subsections (1) to (8) above shall apply in relation to ...⁵, [the trustees of a settlement]² [or personal representatives ...⁵]² as they apply in relation to an individual.

(10) ...⁵

Commentary—*Simon's Direct Tax Service* A3.614; 615.
Regulations—IT (Employments) Regulations, SI 1993/744.
Concession A51—Repayment supplement to apply to certain repayments of life assurance premium relief as if the payments were repayments of income tax.
A82—Repayment supplement will also be paid to individuals resident in other EC member States.
Statement of Practice SP A9—The Statement (not reproduced) gave examples indicating how the Regulations made by SI 1975/1283 (now SI 1993/744 regs 106, 107) worked for 1995–96 and earlier years.
Revenue & other press releases—IR 1-4-96 (details of when payments made to the Revenue are treated as received for the purpose of calculating repayment supplement).
Notes—FA 1989 s 178 and the Taxes (Interest Rate) Regulations 1989, SI 1989/1297 lay down the procedure and formula for calculating interest rate for the purposes of sub-s (1) above. Inland Revenue Press Releases announce the rate as and when it changes in accordance with the formula.
Definitions—"the 1992 Act", s 831(3); "the Board", s 832(1); "emoluments", s 131(1); "income tax", s 832(4); "inspector", s 832(1); "interest", s 832(1); "Schedule E", s 19(1); "tax", s 832(3); "tax credit", s 832(1); "United Kingdom", s 830(1); "year of assessment", s 832(1).
Cross references—See TMA 1970 s 70A (payments to the Board by cheque are treated as made when received provided paid on first presentation).
TA 1988 Sch 15B para 1 (where a repayment of tax arises on a claim for relief on qualifying shares in a venture capital trust, the period of 12 months in sub-ss (1)(*a*), (3)(*a*) shall be calculated with reference to the end of the year of assessment in which the shares were issued).
TA 1988 Sch 19A para 2A(4) (disapplication of this section for years 1988–89 to 1991–92 where tax deducted from syndicate investment income is repaid to a Lloyd's underwriting agent).
FA 1993 Sch 19 para 13(4) (disapplication of this section in respect of repayment of tax deducted from investment income of Lloyd's members).
Amendments—¹ Sub-ss (1A), (2A) inserted and words in sub-s (2) substituted by FA 1988 Sch 13 para 7.
² Words in sub-s (9) substituted by FA 1989 ss 110(5), 111(4).
³ Sub-s (1A) and words in sub-s (2), (6) repealed by FA 1989 Sch 17 Pt X with effect for periods beginning after 17 August 1989 by virtue of FA 1989 s 178(7) and FA 1989 s 178(1) (Appointed Day No 1) Order, SI 1989/1298.
⁴ Words in sub-s (8) substituted by TCGA 1992 Sch 10 para 14(1), (52).
⁵ Sub-ss (1), (3) substituted and sub-ss (5), (10) and the words omitted in sub-s (9) repealed by FA 1994 ss 196, 199(2)(*a*), Sch 19 para 41 and Sch 26 Pt V(23)—

    —in relation to individuals, with effect from the year 1996–97
    —in relation to partnerships commenced after 5 April 1994, with effect from the year 1996–97
    —in relation to partnerships commenced before 6 April 1994, with effect from the year 1997–98.
⁶ Sub-s (3)(*a*), (*b*), words in sub-s (3)(*c*) and sub-ss (4), (4A) substituted (for sub-s (4)) by FA 1997 s 92(1)–(4), (6) with effect from the year 1996–97.
⁷ Sub-s (2B), and sub-s (3)(*aa*), inserted by FA 1999 s 41(2), (3), (4) and deemed always to have had effect subject to FA 1999 s 41(5), (6).
⁸ Sub-ss (2C), (3)(*ab*) inserted by FA 2001 s 90 with effect for repayments made after the passing of FA 2001.

825 Repayment supplements: companies

(1) This section applies to the following payments made to a company in connection with any accounting period for which the company was resident in the United Kingdom ("the relevant accounting period"), that is to say—

(a) a repayment of corporation tax paid by the company for that accounting period (including advance corporation tax paid in respect of distributions made by the company in that accounting period ...[4]); or

(b) a repayment of income tax in respect of a payment received by the company in that accounting period on which the company bore income tax by deduction; or

(c) a payment of the whole or part of the tax credit comprised in any franked investment income received by the company in that accounting period.

(2) Subject to the following provisions of this section, where a payment ...[2] to which this section applies is made by the Board or an inspector after the end of the 12 months beginning with the material date, the payment shall be increased under this section by an amount (a "repayment supplement") equal to interest on the amount paid at the [rate applicable under section 178 of the Finance Act 1989][3] for each complete tax month contained in the period (if any) beginning with the relevant date and ending at the end of the tax month in which the order for the payment is issued.

[(2A) ...][1]

(3) For the purposes of subsection (2) above—

(a) if the payment is a repayment of corporation tax that was paid on or after the first anniversary of the material date, the relevant date is the anniversary of the material date that occurs next after the date on which that tax was paid;

(b) in any other case, the relevant date is the first anniversary of the material date;

and where a payment to which this section applies is a repayment of corporation tax paid by a company on different dates, the payment shall as far as possible be treated for the purposes of this subsection as a repayment of tax paid on a later rather than an earlier date among those dates.

(4) For the purposes of this section—

(a) a repayment of corporation tax made in consequence of a claim by a company under section 239(3) to have the whole or any part of an amount of surplus advance corporation tax arising in the case of any accounting period treated as if it were advance corporation tax paid in respect of distributions made by the company in any earlier accounting period shall be treated as a repayment of corporation tax paid for the accounting period in the case of which that amount of surplus advance corporation tax arose; and

(b) a repayment of income tax or corporation tax made on a claim under subsection (4) of section 419 shall be treated as if it were a repayment of corporation tax paid for the accounting period in which the repayment of, or of the part in question of, the loan or advance mentioned in that subsection was made; [and

(c) a repayment of corporation tax or income tax falling to be made as a result of a claim under section 393A (1) to have the whole or any part of a loss incurred in an accounting period set off against profits of an earlier accounting period ("the earlier period")—

(i) shall, in a case where the earlier period falls wholly within the period of twelve months immediately preceding the accounting period in which the loss was incurred, be treated as a repayment of tax paid for the earlier period; and

(ii) in any other case, shall be treated as a repayment of tax paid for the accounting period in which the loss is incurred; and][5]

(d) ...[5]

(5) ...[1] the Treasury may by order from time to time increase or decrease the rate of interest by reference to which repayment supplements are calculated under subsection (2) above.

(6) A repayment supplement shall not be payable under this section in respect of a payment made in consequence of an order or judgment of a court having power to allow interest on the payment.

(7) A repayment supplement paid under this section shall be disregarded for all purposes of income tax and corporation tax.

(8) In this section—

"tax month" means the period beginning with the 6th day of any calendar month and ending with the 5th day of the following calendar month;

"the material date" in relation to a payment to which this section applies, means the last date on which corporation tax on any of the profits of the company in question arising in the relevant accounting period could have been paid—

(a) in a case where section 10(1) applies, within the nine months there mentioned;

(b) in a case where section 478 applies, within the time limit imposed by subsection (2)(a) of that section, but subject to subsection (6) of that section.

(9) This section has effect subject to section 826(8).

Commentary—*Simon's Direct Tax Service* A3.617.
Revenue Interpretation RI 147—Explains relationship between s 825 and s 826 on transition to pay and file; the fact that repayment may result from relief carry-back is not relevant in deciding which of these two sections applies.

Revenue & other press releases—IR 23-7-93 (repayment supplement added to tax refunds made to EC resident companies).
IR 1-4-96 (details of when payments made to the Revenue are treated as received for the purpose of calculating repayment supplement).
Notes—FA 1989 s 178 and the Taxes (Interest Rate) Regulations 1989, SI 1989/1297 lay down the procedure and formula for calculating interest rate for the purposes of sub-s (2) above. Inland Revenue Press Releases announce the rate as and when it changes in accordance with the formula. For the rates in force for various periods, see Note under TMA 1970 s 89, *ante*.
Simon's Tax Cases—*R v IRC, ex p Commerzbank AG* [1993] STC 605.
s 825(4)(a), *Savacentre Ltd v IRC* [1995] STC 867.
Definitions—"Accounting period", s 834(1); "advance corporation tax", s 14(1); "the Board", s 832(1); "company", s 832(1), (2); "distributions", s 209(2), by virtue of s 832(1); "franked investment income", s 832(1); "income tax", s 832(4); "inspector", s 832(1); "interest", s 832(1); "tax", s 832(3); "tax credit", s 832(1); "United Kingdom", s 830(1).
Cross references—See TMA 1970 s 70A (payments to the Board by cheque are treated as made when received provided paid on first presentation).
Amendments—[1] Sub-s (2A) and words in sub-s (5) inserted by FA 1988 Sch 13 para 8 and repealed by FA 1989 Sch 17 Pt X with effect for periods beginning after 17 August 1989 by virtue of FA 1989 s 178(7) and FA 1989 s 178(1) (Appointed Day No 1) Order, SI 1989/1298.
[2] Words in sub-s (2) repealed by FA 1989 s 158(2), (5) and Sch 17 Pt VIII with effect from 6 April 1993 by virtue of FA 1989 s 158(1) and(2), (Appointed Days) Order, SI 1993/753 art 4.
[3] Words in sub-s (2) substituted by FA 1989 s 179(1)(a)(vii).
[4] Words in sub-s (1)(a) repealed by FA 1989 Sch 17 Pt V in relation to accounting periods beginning after 31 March 1989.
[5] Sub-s (4)(c) and the word "and" at the end of sub-s (4)(b) added by FA 1991 s 73(4), (5) and Sch 15 para 22 in relation to losses incurred in accounting periods ending after 31 March 1991 and in relation to losses so incurred this section to be deemed to have had effect at all times with this amendment.
[5] Sub-s (4)(d) repealed by F(No 2)A 1997 Sch 8 Pt II(4) with effect generally in relation to accounting periods beginning after 1 July 1997 but subject to the detailed provisions of F(No 2)A 1997 s 20(1)–(4) (originally inserted by FA 1991 s 73(4), (5), Sch 15 para 22).

826 Interest on tax overpaid

(1) In any case where—

(*a*) a repayment falls to be made of corporation tax paid by a company for an accounting period which ends after the appointed day; or

[(*aa*) a repayment falls to be made under sections 246N and 246Q of advance corporation tax paid by a company in respect of distributions made by it in such an accounting period; or][6]

(*b*) a repayment of income tax falls to be made in respect of a payment received by a company in such an accounting period; or

(*c*) a payment falls to be made to a company of the whole or part of the tax credit comprised in any franked investment income received by the company in such an accounting period[;or

(*d*) a payment of R&D tax credit falls to be made to a company under Schedule 20 to the Finance Act 2000 in respect of an accounting period,][22][; or

(*e*) a payment of land remediation tax credit or life assurance company tax credit falls to be made to a company under Schedule 22 to the Finance Act 2001 in respect of an accounting period,][24]

then, from the material date until [the order for repayment or payment is issued][2] the repayment or payment shall carry interest at the [rate applicable under section 178 of the Finance Act 1989][1].

(2) [Subject to section 826A(2),][14] in relation to corporation tax paid by a company for an accounting period, the material date for the purposes of this section is the date on which corporation tax was paid or, if it is later, the date on which corporation tax for that accounting period became (or, as the case may be, would have become) due and payable in accordance with [section 59D of the Management Act (payment of corporation tax)][8].

(2A) ...[20]

(3) In relation to a repayment of income tax falling within subsection (1)(*b*) above or a payment of the whole or part of a tax credit falling within subsection (1)(*c*) above, [the material date is the day after the end of the accounting period][17] in which the payment referred to in subsection (1)(*b*) above or, as the case may be, the franked investment income referred to in subsection (1)(*c*) above was received by the company.

[(3A) In relation to a payment of R&D tax credit falling within subsection (1)(*d*) above the material date is whichever is the later of—

(*a*) the filing date for the company's company tax return for the accounting period for which the R&D tax credit is claimed, and

(*b*) the date on which the company tax return or amended company tax return containing the claim for payment of the R&D tax credit is delivered to the Inland Revenue.

For this purpose "the filing date", in relation to a company tax return, has the same meaning as in Schedule 18 to the Finance Act 1998.][22]

[(3B) In relation to a payment of land remediation tax credit or life assurance company tax credit falling within subsection (1)(*e*) above the material date is whichever is the later of—

(*a*) the filing date for the company's company tax return for the accounting period for which the land remediation tax credit or the life assurance company tax credit is claimed, and

(*b*) the date on which the company tax return or amended company tax return containing the claim for payment of the land remediation tax credit or the life assurance company tax credit is delivered to the Inland Revenue.

For this purpose "the filing date", in relation to a company tax return, has the same meaning as in Schedule 18 to the Finance Act 1998.][24]

(4) For the purposes of this section a repayment of tax made on a claim under section 419(4) shall be treated as if it were a repayment of corporation tax for the accounting period in which [the event giving rise to entitlement to relief under section 419(4) occurred][21] but, in relation to such a repayment of tax, the material date for the purposes of this section is—

[(a) the date when the entitlement to relief in respect of the repayment accrued, that is to say—

(i) where the repayment[, or the release or writing off,][21] of the loan or advance (or part thereof) occurred on or after the day mentioned in section 419(4A), the date nine months after the end of that accounting period; and

(ii) in any other case, the date nine months after the end of the accounting period in which the loan or advance was made;

or][9]

(b) if it is later, the date on which the tax which is to be repaid was in fact paid.

(5) Interest paid under this section [—

(a) shall be paid without any deduction of income tax; and

(b) [subject to subsection (5A) below,][16] shall not be brought into account in computing any profits or income.][15]

[(5A) Paragraph (b) of subsection (5) above does not apply in relation to interest payable to a company within the charge to corporation tax.][16]

(6) Where a repayment of corporation tax is a repayment of tax paid by a company on different dates, the repayment shall so far as possible be treated for the purposes of this section as a repayment of tax paid on a later rather than an earlier date among those dates.

(7) ...[20]

[(7A) In any case where—

(a) a company carrying on a trade incurs a loss in the trade in an accounting period ("the later period"),

(b) as a result of a claim under section 393A(1), the whole or any part of that loss is set off for the purposes of corporation tax against profits (of whatever description) of an earlier accounting period ("the earlier period") which does not fall wholly within the period of twelve months immediately preceding the later period, and

(c) a repayment falls to be made of corporation tax paid for the earlier period or of income tax in respect of a payment received by the company in that accounting period,

then, in determining the amount of interest (if any) payable under this section on the repayment referred to in paragraph (c) above, no account shall be taken of [so much of the amount of that repayment as falls to be made][4] as a result of the claim under section 393A(1), except so far as concerns interest for any time after the date on which any corporation tax for the later period became (or, as the case may be, would have become) due and payable, [as mentioned in subsection (7D) below][19].][3]

[(7AA) ...[20]]

[(7B) ...][13]

[(7BB) Subject to subsection (7BC) below, in any case where—

(a) within the meaning of section 806D, any relievable underlying tax or relievable withholding tax arises in an accounting period of a company ("the later period"),

(b) pursuant to a claim under section 806G, the whole or any part of that tax is treated as mentioned in section 806D(4)(c) or (5)(c) in relation to the single related dividend or the single unrelated dividend arising in an earlier accounting period ("the earlier period"), and

(c) a repayment falls to be made of corporation tax paid for the earlier period or of income tax in respect of a payment received by the company in that period,

then, in determining the amount of interest (if any) payable under this section on the repayment referred to in paragraph (c) above, no account shall be taken of so much of the amount of the repayment as falls to be made as a result of the claim under section 806G, except so far as concerns interest for any time after the date on which any corporation tax for the later period became due and payable (as mentioned in subsection (7D) below).

(7BC) Where, in a case falling within subsection (7A)(a) and (b) above—

(a) as a result of the claim under section 393A(1), an amount or increased amount of eligible unrelieved foreign tax arises for the purposes of section 806A(1), and

(b) pursuant to a claim under section 806G, the whole or any part of an amount of relievable underlying tax or relievable withholding tax is treated as mentioned in section 806D(4)(c) or (5)(c) in relation to the single related dividend or the single unrelated dividend arising in an accounting period before the earlier period,

then subsection (7BB) above shall have effect in relation to the claim under section 806G as if the reference in the words after paragraph (c) to the later period within the meaning of that subsection were a reference to the period which, in relation to the claim under section 393A(1), would be the later period for the purposes of subsection (7A) above.][23]

[(7C) In a case where—

(*a*) there is for an accounting period of a company ("the later period") [a non-trading deficit on the company's loan relationships,][10]

(*b*) as a result of a claim under [section 83(2)(*c*) of the Finance Act 1996 or paragraph 4(3) of Schedule 11 to that Act the whole or part of the deficit the later period is set off against profits][11] of an earlier accounting period ("the earlier period"), and

(*c*) a repayment falls to be made of corporation tax for the earlier period [or of income tax in respect of a payment received by the company in that accounting period][7],

then, in determining the amount of interest (if any) payable under this section on the [repayment referred to in paragraph (*c*) above, no account shall be taken of so much of the amount of the repayment as falls to be made as a result of][7] the claim under [section 83(2)(*c*) of that Act or, as the case may be, paragraph 4(3) of Schedule 11 to that Act][12] except so far as concerns interest for any time after the date on which any corporation tax for the later period became (or, as the case may be, would have become) due and payable, [as mentioned in subsection (7D) below][19].][5]

[(7CA) ...][20]

[(7D) In subsections (7), (7A), (7B)[, (7BB)] and (7C) above, any reference to the date on which corporation tax for an accounting period became, or would have become, due and payable shall be construed on the basis that corporation tax for an accounting period becomes due and payable on the day following the expiry of nine months from the end of the accounting period.][19]

[(7E) The power conferred by section 59E of the Management Act (alteration of date on which corporation tax becomes due and payable) does not include power to make provision in relation to subsection (7), (7A), (7B), [(7BB),][23] (7C) or (7D) above the effect of which would be to change the meaning of references in subsection (7), (7A), (7B) [(7BB),][23] or (7C) above to the date on which corporation tax for an accounting period became, or would have become, due and payable (as mentioned in subsection (7D) above).][19]

(8) In consequence of the preceding provisions of this section, no repayment supplement (within the meaning of section 825) shall be paid in respect of any repayment of tax or payment of tax credit where the relevant accounting period (within the meaning of that section) ends after the appointed day.

[(8A) Where—

(*a*) interest has been paid to a company under subsection (1)(*a*) [or (*d*)][22] [or (*e*)][24] above,
[(*b*) there is—

(i) a change in the company's assessed liability to corporation tax, or
(ii) a change in the amount of the R&D tax credit[, land remediation tax credit or life assurance company tax credit][24] payable to the company (which does not result in a change falling within sub-paragraph (i)),

other than a change which in whole or in part corrects an error made by the Board or an officer of the Board, and][22]

(*c*) as a result only of that change (and, in particular, not as a result of any error in the calculation of the interest), it appears to an officer of the Board that the interest ought not to have been paid, either at all or to any extent,

the interest that ought not to have been paid may be recovered from the company as if it were interest charged under Part IX of the Management Act (interest on overdue tax).][18]

[(8B) For the purposes of subsection (8A) above, the cases where there is a change in a company's assessed liability to corporation tax are those cases where—

(*a*) an assessment, or an amendment of an assessment, of the amount of corporation tax payable by the company for the accounting period in question is made, or

(*b*) a determination of that amount is made under paragraph 36 or 37 of Schedule 18 to the Finance Act 1998 (which until superseded by a self-assessment under that Schedule has effect as if it were one),

whether or not any previous assessment or determination has been made.][18]

[(8BA) For the purposes of subsection (8A)(*b*) above, the cases where there is a change in the amount of the R&D tax credit[, land remediation tax credit or life assurance company tax credit][24] payable to the company are those cases where an assessment, or an amendment to an assessment, is made to recover an amount of R&D tax credit[, land remediation tax credit or life assurance company tax credit][24] paid to the company for the accounting period in question.][22]

[(8C) In subsection (8A)(*b*) above "error" includes—

(*a*) any computational error; and

(*b*) the allowance of a claim or election which ought not to have been allowed.][18]

(9) In this section "the appointed day" means such day or days, not being earlier than 31st March 1992, as the Treasury may by order appoint for the purposes of this section.

Commentary—*Simon's Direct Tax Service* D2.708, 845; 1417.
Note—The appointed day for this section is 30 September 1993 by virtue of Corporation Tax Acts (Provisions for Payment of Tax and Returns) (Appointed Days) Order, SI 1992/3066 art 2(1), (2)(*b*).
Regulations—Corporation Tax (Instalment Payments) Regulations, SI 1998/3175.
Revenue Interpretation RI 147—Explains relationship between s 825 and s 826 on transition to pay and file; the fact that repayment may result from relief carry-back is not relevant in deciding which of these two sections applies.

Revenue Internal Guidance—Pay & File manual, CT 10224, 10225 (worked examples in sub-ss (3), (7)–(7B)).

Revenue & other press releases—IR 1-4-96 (details of when payments made to the Revenue are treated as received for the purpose of calculating interest).

Definitions—"Accounting period", s 834(1); "advance corporation tax", s 14(1); "company", s 832(1), (2); "distribution", s 832(1); "franked investment income", s 832(1); "income tax", s 832(4); "interest", s 832(1); "loan relationship", s 834(1), FA 1996 s 81; "the Management Act", s 831(3); "non-trading deficit", s 834(1), FA 1996 s 82; "tax", s 832(3); "tax credit", s 832(1); "trade", s 832(1).

Cross references—See TMA 1970 s 70A (payments to the Board by cheque are treated as made when received provided paid on first presentation).

TA 1988 s 252(2) (rectification of excessive interest paid under this section on tax credit).

TA 1988 Sch 19AB, para 5(6) (pension business: interest on repayments on account of tax credits and deducted tax in an accounting period ending on or before the pay and file provisions are brought into force).

Taxes (Interest Rate) Regulations, SI 1989/1297 regs 3B, 3BA, 3BB (applicable rates of interest on tax overpaid).

Gilt-edged Securities (Tax on Interest) Regulations, SI 1995/3224 reg 20(2) (disapplication of this section to repayment of excessive payments on account of tax on excess gilt interest received).

Modifications—Modification of this section in relation to interest on overpaid amounts of a company's total liability for an accounting period with effect for accounting periods ending after 30 June 1999: the Corporation Tax (Instalment Payments) Regulations, SI 1998/3175 reg 8.

Amendments—[1] Words in sub-s (1) substituted by FA 1989 s 179(1)(c)(ii).

[2] Words in sub-s (1) substituted by FA 1989 s 180(6), (7) and deemed always to have had effect.

[3] Sub-s (7A) inserted by FA 1991 s 73(4), (5) and Sch 15 para 23 in relation to losses incurred in accounting periods ending after 31 March 1991 and in relation to losses so incurred this section to be deemed to have had effect at all times with this amendment.

[4] Words in sub-ss (7A), (7B) substituted by FA 1993 Sch 14 para 10(1)(b), (c), (2), (4).

[5] Sub-s (7C) inserted by FA 1993 Sch 18 para 5.

[6] Sub-s (1)(aa) inserted by FA 1994 Sch 16 para 20.

[7] In sub-s (7C)(c)words inserted and other words substituted by FA 1995 s 130, Sch 24 Pt II, paras 11, 12, generally with effect from 23 March 1995 (by virtue of FA 1995 Sch 24 Pt II, para 7, and the FA 1993 Section 165, (Appointed Day) Order 1994, SI 1994/3224), but note as to retrospective effect in relation to certain claims, FA 1995 Sch 24 para 12(4), (5).

[8] Words in sub-s (2) substituted for words "section 10" by FA 1994 ss 196, 199 and Sch 19 para 42 with effect for accounting periods ending after 30 June 1999 (by virtue of Finance Act 1994, Section 199, (Appointed Day) Order, SI 1998/3173 art 2).

[9] Sub-s (4)(a) substituted by FA 1996 s 173(5), (6) with effect in relation to any loan or advance made in an accounting period ending after 30 March 1996.

[10] Words in sub-s (7C)(a) substituted for "a relievable amount within the meaning of section 131 of the Finance Act 1993 (non-trading exchange gains and losses)" by FA 1996 ss 104, 105(1), Sch 14 para 48(1) with effect for accounting periods ending after 31 March 1996, subject to transitional provisions in FA 1996 Sch 15.

[11] Words in sub-s (7C)(b) substituted for "subsection (5) or (6) of that section the whole or part of the relievable amount for the later period is set off against the exchange profits (as defined in subsection (10) of that section)" by FA 1996 ss 104, 105(1), Sch 14 para 48(1) with effect for accounting periods ending after 31 March 1996, subject to transitional provisions in FA 1996 Sch 15.

[12] Words in sub-s (7C) substituted for "subsection (5) or (6) (as the case may be) of that section" by FA 1996 ss 104, 105(1), Sch 14 para 48(1) with effect for accounting periods ending after 31 March 1996, subject to transitional provisions in FA 1996 Sch 15.

[13] Sub-s (7B) (inserted by FA 1991 s 73(4), (5), Sch 15 para 23 in relation to losses incurred in accounting periods ending after 31 March 1991) repealed by F(No 2)A 1997 Sch 8 Pt II(4) with effect in accordance with the provisions of F(No 2)A 1997 s 20(1)–(4) and, accordingly, having effect only where the earlier periods mentioned in sub-s (7B) begins after 1 July 1997.

[14] Words in sub-s (2) inserted by FA 1998 Sch 4 para 1 with effect from 31 July 1998.

[15] Sub-s (5) amended by FA 1998 s 34(2) with effect from 31 July 1998.

[16] Words in sub-s (5)(b) and sub-s (5A) inserted by FA 1998 s 34(3), (4) with effect in relation to interest payable by virtue of any paragraph of TA 1988 s 826(1) if the accounting period mentioned in that paragraph is one which ends after 30 June 1999 by virtue of SI 1998/3173 art 2.

[17] Words in sub-s (3) substituted by FA 1998, Sch 4 para 2 with effect in relation to accounting periods ending after 30 June 1999 by virtue of SI 1998/3173 art 2.

[18] Sub-s (8A)–(8C) inserted by FA 1998, Sch 4 para 3 with effect in relation to accounting periods ending after 30 June 1999 by virtue of SI 1998/3173 art 2.

[19] Words in sub-ss (7), (7C) substituted, and sub-ss (7D), (7E) inserted, by FA 1998, Sch 4 para 5 with effect where the accounting period whose due and payable date falls to be determined is an accounting period ending after 30 June 1999 by virtue of SI 1998/3173 art 2. In this context, "due and payable date", in relation to an accounting period, means the date on which corporation tax for that period becomes, or (as the case may be) would become, due and payable.

[20] Sub-ss (2A), (7), (7AA) and (7CA) repealed by FA 1998 Sch 3 para 38 with effect where the relevant accounting period begins after 5 April 1999.

[21] Words in sub-s (4) substituted and words in sub-s (4)(a)(i) inserted by FA 1999 s 90 with effect in relation to the release or writing off of the whole or part of a debt after 5 April 1999.

[22] Sub-s (1)(d) and word "or" preceding it, sub-ss (3A), (8BA) and words in sub-s (8A) inserted and sub-s (8A)(b) substituted by FA 2000 s 69(2), Sch 21 para 1 with effect for accounting periods ending after 31 March 2000.

[23] Sub-s (7BB), (7BC) and words in sub-s (7D), (7E) inserted by FA 2000 s 103, Sch 30 para 29 with effect from 28 July 2000.

[24] Sub-s (1)(e) and preceding word "; or", sub-s (3B), and words in sub-ss (8A), (8BA) inserted by FA 2001 s 70(3), Sch 23 para 3 with effect for accounting periods ending after 31 March 2001.

Prospective amendments—Sub-ss (1)(da), (3AA) to be inserted; in sub-s (8A)(a), "(d), (da)" to be substituted for "or (d)"; in sub-ss (8)(b)(ii), (8BA), words ", tax credit under Schedule 13 to the Finance Act 2002" to be inserted (wherever occurring) after the words "R&D tax credit"; by FA 2002 s 54, Sch 14 paras 1, 5 with effect for tax credits payable under FA 2002 Sch 13 in respect of expenditure incurred on or after such day as the Treasury may appoint under FA 2002 Sch 13 para 28. Sub-ss (1)(da), (3AA) as inserted to read as follows—

"(da) a payment of a tax credit falls to be made to a company under Schedule 13 to the Finance Act 2002 in respect of an accounting period, or".

"(3AA) In relation to a payment of tax credit falling within subsection (1)(da) above, the material date is whichever is the later of—

(a) the filing date for the company's company tax return for the accounting period for which the tax credit is claimed, and

(b) the date on which the company tax return or amended company tax return containing the claim for payment of the tax credit is delivered to the Inland Revenue.

For this purpose "the filing date", in relation to a company tax return, has the same meaning as in Schedule 18 to the Finance Act 1998."

[826A Interest on payments in respect of corporation tax and meaning of "the material date"

(1) The Treasury may by regulations make provision applying section 826, with such modifications as may be prescribed, for the purpose of conferring on companies of such descriptions as may be prescribed a right to interest—

(*a*) on such payments made by them in respect of corporation tax as may be prescribed,
(*b*) at the rate applicable under section 178 of the Finance Act 1989, and
(*c*) for such period as may be prescribed,

and for treating any such interest for the purposes, or prescribed purposes, of the Tax Acts as interest under section 826(1)(a) on a repayment of corporation tax.

(2) The Treasury may by regulations make provision modifying section 826(2) in relation to companies of such description as may be prescribed.

(3) Subsections (1) and (2) above do not apply in relation to companies in relation to which section 826(2) is modified or otherwise affected by regulations under section 59E of the Management Act (alteration of date on which corporation tax becomes due and payable) in relation to the accounting period to which the corporation tax in question relates.

(4) Where the Treasury make regulations under subsection (2) above in relation to companies of any description, they may also make regulations modifying section 59DA(2) of the Management Act in relation to those companies, or any description of such companies, by varying the date before which the claim there mentioned may not be made.

(5) Regulations under this section—

(*a*) may make different provision in relation to different cases or circumstances or in relation to companies or accounting periods of different descriptions;
(*b*) may make such supplementary, incidental, consequential or transitional provision as appears to the Treasury to be necessary or expedient.

(6) Regulations under this section may not make provision in relation to accounting periods ending before the day appointed under section 199 of the Finance Act 1994 for the purposes of Chapter III of Part IV of that Act (corporation tax self-assessment).

(7) In this section "prescribed" means prescribed by regulations made under this section.]¹

Commentary—*Simon's Direct Tax Service* D2.845.
Regulations—Corporation Tax (Instalment Payments) Regulations, SI 1998/3175.
Amendments—¹ This section inserted by FA 1998 Sch 4 para 1 with effect from 31 July 1998.

827 VAT penalties etc

(1) Where, under [Part IV of the Value Added Tax Act 1994]² (value added tax), a person is liable to make a payment by way of—

(*a*) penalty under any of sections [60 to 70]²; or
(*b*) interest under section [74]²; or
(*c*) surcharge under section [59]²;

the payment shall not be allowed as a deduction in computing any income, profits or losses for any tax purposes.

[(1A) Where a person is liable to make a payment by way of a penalty under any of sections 8 to 11 of the Finance Act 1994 (penalties relating to excise), that payment shall not be allowed as a deduction in computing any income, profits or losses for any tax purposes.]³

[(1B) Where a person is liable to make a payment by way of—

(*a*) penalty under any of paragraphs 12 to 19 of Schedule 7 to the Finance Act 1994 (insurance premium tax), or
(*b*) interest under paragraph 21 of that Schedule,

the payment shall not be allowed as to deduction in computing any income, profits or losses for any tax purposes.]¹

[(1C) Where a person is liable to make a payment by way of—

(*a*) penalty under Part V of Schedule 5 to the Finance Act 1996 (landfill tax), or
(*b*) interest under paragraph 26 or 27 of that Schedule,

the payment shall not be allowed as a deduction in computing any income, profits or losses for any tax purposes.]⁴

[(1D) Where a person is liable to make a payment by way of—

(*a*) any penalty under any provision of Schedule 6 to the Finance Act 2000 (climate change levy),
(*b*) interest under paragraph 70 of that Schedule (interest on recoverable overpayments etc),
(*c*) interest under any of paragraphs 81 to 85 of that Schedule (interest on climate change levy due and on interest), or
(*d*) interest under paragraph 109 of that Schedule (interest on penalties),

the payment shall not be allowed as a deduction in computing any income, profits or losses for any tax purposes.]⁵

[(1E) Where a person is liable to make a payment by way of—

(*a*) any penalty under any provision of Part II of the Finance Act 2001 (aggregates levy),
(*b*) interest under any of paragraphs 5 to 9 of Schedule 5 to that Act (interest on aggregates levy due and on interest),

(*c*) interest under paragraph 6 of Schedule 8 to that Act (interest on recoverable overpayments etc), or

(*d*) interest under paragraph 5 of Schedule 10 to that Act (interest on penalties),

the payment shall not be allowed as a deduction in computing any income, profits or losses for any tax purposes.][6]

(2) A sum paid to any person by way of supplement under section [79 of that Act][2] (VAT repayment supplements) shall be disregarded for all purposes of corporation tax and income tax.

Commentary—*Simon's Direct Tax Service* B3.1454.
Revenue Interpretation RI 109—VAT repayments received by sports clubs and interest on the repayments: treatment for corporation tax purposes.
Definitions—''Income tax'', s 832(4); ''interest'', s 832(1); ''tax'', s 832(3).
Amendments—[1] Sub-s (1B) inserted by FA 1994 s 64, Sch 7 Pt VI, para 31 and applies when insurance premium tax is charged on the receipt of a premium by an insurer under a taxable insurance contract after 30 September 1994; see FA 1994 ss 48, 49.
[2] Words and figures in square brackets in sub-ss (1), (2) substituted by the Value Added Tax Act 1994 s 100(1), Sch 14 para 10(1), (2)(*a*)–(*d*).
[3] Sub-s (1A) inserted by FA 1994 ss 18(7), (8), 19 in relation to any chargeable period ending after 1 November 1994 (for purposes of air passenger duty) or 1 January 1995 (remaining purposes) (by virtue of the Finance Act 1994 Part I, (Appointed Day etc) Order 1994, SI 1994/2679 arts 2, 3).
[4] Sub-s (1C) inserted by FA 1996 Sch 5 para 40.
[5] Sub-s (1D) inserted by FA 2000 s 30(2), Sch 7 para 4 with effect from 28 July 2000.
[6] Sub-s (1E) inserted by FA 2001 s 49(3) with effect from 11 May 2001.

828 Orders and regulations made by the Treasury or the Board

(1) Subject to subsection (2) below, any power of the Treasury or the Board to make any order or regulations under this Act or under any other provision of the Tax Acts (including enactments passed after this Act) shall be exercisable by statutory instrument.

(2) Subsection (1) above shall not apply in relation to any power conferred by [section 841(1)(*b*) or 841A][7] [or section 178(5) of the Finance Act 1989][1].

(3) Subject to subsection (4) below and to any other provision to the contrary, any statutory instrument containing any order or regulations made by the Treasury or the Board under this Act or under any other provision of the Tax Acts (including enactments passed after this Act) shall be subject to annulment in pursuance of a resolution of the House of Commons.

(4) Subsection (3) above shall not apply in relation to an order or regulations made under section 1(6), [257C][4], 324, ...[6], ...[9] [582A(1),][5] [590C(6)][2], 658(3) [791 or 840A(1)(*d*)][8] or paragraph 7 of Schedule 14 [or [section 82(4)(*d*) of the Capital Allowances Act][10]][3] or—

(*a*) if any other Parliamentary procedure is expressly provided;
(*b*) if the order in question is an order appointing a day for the purposes of any provision of the Tax Acts, being a day as from which the provision will have effect, with or without amendments, or will cease to have effect.

Commentary—*Simon's Direct Tax Service* A1.106.
Simon's Tax Cases—*Kirvell v Guy* [1979] STC 312*; *Slater v Richardson Bottoms Ltd* [1979] STC 630*.
Definitions—''The 1990 Act'', s 831(3); ''the Board'', s 832(1); ''the Tax Acts'', s 831(2).
Amendments—[1] Words in sub-s (2) added by FA 1989 s 178(6).
[2] Number in sub-s (4) inserted by FA 1989 Sch 6 para 16.
[3] Words in sub-s (4) inserted by CAA 1990 Sch 1 para 8(1), (34).
[4] ''257C'' in sub-s (4) substituted by FA 1990 s 17(3).
[5] ''582A(1),'' in sub-s (4) inserted by FA 1991 s 118(2).
[6] ''376(5)'' in sub-s (4) repealed by FA 1994 Sch 26 Pt V(19).
[7] Words in sub-s (2) substituted by FA 1996 Sch 7 paras 24, 32 with effect as respects income tax from the year 1996–97, and for purposes of corporation tax, for accounting periods ending after 31 March 1996.
[8] Words in sub-s (4) substituted by FA 1996 Sch 37 para 1(2).
[9] Word in sub-s (4) repealed by FA 1999 s 139, Sch 20 Pt III(7) with effect for payments of interest made—
  –after 5 April 2000;
  –after 8 March 1999 and before 6 April 2000 in respect of interest falling due after 5 April 2000; or
  –after 8 March 1999 and before 6 April 2000 under a scheme made for a tax avoidance purpose after 8 March 1999.
[10] Words in sub-s (4) substituted by CAA 2001 s 578, Sch 2 para 58 with effect for income tax purposes, as respects allowances and charges falling to be made for chargeable periods ending after 5 April 2001, and for corporation tax purposes, as respects allowances and charges falling to be made for chargeable periods ending after 31 March 2001.

829 Application of Income Tax Acts to public departments and avoidance of exempting provisions

(1) Subject to subsections (2) and (3) below, all the provisions of the Income Tax Acts relating to the assessment, charge, deduction and payment of income tax shall apply in relation to public offices and departments of the Crown.

(2) Nothing in those provisions of the Income Tax Acts shall require the payment by any such office or department of any tax which would be ultimately borne by the Crown [unless it is tax which would not have been so borne but for a failure by a public office or department of the Crown to make a deduction required by virtue of subsection (1) above][1].

[(2A) Subsections (1) and (2) above have effect in relation to Chapter 4 of Part 13 of this Act (sub-contractors in the construction industry) as if the whole of any deduction required to be made under section 559 were in all cases a deduction of income tax.][2]

(3) Subsection (1) above shall not apply to public offices and departments of any country, state, province or colony within section 320(3)(b) or (c) and nothing in subsection (1) above shall exempt any government from taxation to which it is liable in connection with any office or department by virtue of section 25 of the Finance Act 1925 (liability in respect of trading operations of Dominion governments and others).

(4) No letters patent granted or to be granted by the Crown to any person, city, borough or town corporate of any liberty, privilege or exemption from subsidies, tolls, taxes, assessments or aids, and no statute which grants any salary, annuity or pension to any person free of any taxes, deductions or assessments, shall be construed or taken to exempt any person, city, borough or town corporate, or any inhabitant of any city, borough or town corporate, from income tax, and all non-obstantes in any such letters patent or statute made or to be made to the contrary effect shall be void.

Commentary—*Simon's Direct Tax Service* **A3.1101.**
Definitions—''Income tax'', s 832(4); ''the Income Tax Acts'', s 831(1)(b); ''tax'', s 832(3).
Cross references—See FA 1993 s 122(2) (interest and penalty provisions in TMA 1970 Pts IX and X to apply to public departments for their failure to collect tax as mentioned in sub-s (2) above).
Amendments—[1] Words in sub-s (2) inserted by FA 1993 s 122(1), (3) with effect from the year 1993–94.
[2] Sub-s (2A) inserted by FA 2002 s 40(2), (4) with effect for deductions made under TA 1988 s 559 after 5 April 2002.

830 Territorial sea and designated areas

(1) The territorial sea of the United Kingdom shall for all purposes of income tax and corporation tax (including the following provisions of this section) be deemed to be part of the United Kingdom.

(2) In this section—

    (a) ''exploration or exploitation activities'' means activities carried on in connection with the exploration or exploitation of so much of the seabed and subsoil and their natural resources as is situated in the United Kingdom or a designated area;

    (b) ''exploration or exploitation rights'' means rights to assets to be produced by exploration or exploitation activities or to interests in or to the benefit of such assets; and

    (c) ''designated area'' means an area designated by Order in Council under section 1(7) of the Continental Shelf Act 1964.

(3) Any profits or gains from exploration or exploitation activities carried on in a designated area or from exploration or exploitation rights shall be treated for the purposes of income tax or corporation tax as profits or gains from activities or property in the United Kingdom.

(4) Any profits or gains arising to any person not resident in the United Kingdom from exploration or exploitation activities or rights shall for the purposes of corporation tax be treated as [profits][1] of a trade carried on by that person in the United Kingdom through a branch or agency.

(5) Any emoluments from an office or employment in respect of duties performed in a designated area in connection with exploration or exploitation activities shall be treated for the purposes of income tax as emoluments in respect of duties performed in the United Kingdom.

Commentary—*Simon's Direct Tax Service* **A1.153.**
Statement of Practice SP 6/84—Where specified conditions are fulfilled, profits or gains accruing to a non-resident lessor of mobile machinery and vessels used in the territorial sea and designated areas are not charged to tax.
Revenue & other press releases—IR 3-3-89 (list of countries whose residents are not treated as exempt under the ''dependent personal services (employment)'' Article of the relevant Double Tax agreement, while working on UK continental shelf).
Revenue Internal Guidance—Oil Taxation Office section 830 manual gives a detailed exposition of Revenue practice in applying this section.
Schedule E manual SE 40032 (meaning of ''the United Kingdom'').
SE 40208 (Schedule E Cases I and II: location of duties for workers in the offshore oil and gas industry).
Simon's Tax Cases—s 830(5), *Clark v Oceanic Contractors Inc* [1983] STC 35*.
Definitions—''Branch or agency'', s 834(1); ''emoluments'', s 131(1); ''income tax'', s 832(4); ''profits or gains'', s 833(1); ''trade'', s 832(1).
Cross references—See TMA 1970 s 46B(5) (any question as to the application of this section to be determined by the Special Commissioners).
Amendments—[1] Word in sub-s (4) substituted by FA 1998 Sch 7 para 1 with effect from 31 July 1998.

Interpretation

831 Interpretation of this Act

(1) In this Act, except so far as the context otherwise requires—

    (a) ''the Corporation Tax Acts'' means the enactments relating to the taxation of the income and chargeable gains of companies and of company distributions (including provisions relating also to income tax); and

    (b) ''the Income Tax Acts'' means the enactments relating to income tax, including any provisions of the Corporation Tax Acts which relate to income tax.

(2) In this Act ''the Tax Acts'', except so far as the context otherwise requires, means this Act and all other provisions of the Income Tax Acts and the Corporation Tax Acts.

(3) In this Act—

    ''the Management Act'' means the Taxes Management Act 1970;
    ''the 1968 Act'' means the Capital Allowances Act 1968;
    ''the 1970 Act'' means the Income and Corporation Taxes Act 1970; and
    ''the 1979 Act'' means the Capital Gains Tax Act 1979;

["the 1990 Act" means the Capital Allowances Act 1990;][1]
["the 1992 Act" means the Taxation of Chargeable Gains Act 1992.][2]

(4) Section 1 of the Family Law Reform Act 1987 the paragraph inserted in Schedule 1 to the Interpretation Act 1978 by paragraph 73 of Schedule 2 to that Act and section 1(3) of the Law Reform (Parent and Child) (Scotland) Act 1986 (legal equality of illegitimate children) shall be disregarded in construing references in this Act to a child or to children (however expressed).

(5) This Act, so far as it relates to capital gains tax, shall be construed as one with the [1992][2] Act.

(6) Any reference in this Act to a section, Part or Schedule is a reference to that section, Part or Schedule of or to this Act, unless the context otherwise requires.

Commentary—*Simon's Direct Tax Service* A1.151.
Simon's Tax Cases—s 831(1)(b), *R v Dimsey* [1999] STC 846.
Definitions—"Chargeable gains", s 832(1); "company", s 832(1), (2); "distributions", s 209(2), by virtue of s 832(1); "income tax", s 832(4).
Modification—CAA 2001 Sch 2 para 59 (sub-s (3) continues to have effect with the addition of the definition of "the 1990 Act").
Amendments—[1] Words in sub-s (3) added by CAA 1990 Sch 1 para 8(1), (35).
[2] Words in sub-s (3) added and year in sub-s (5) substituted by TCGA 1992 Sch 10 para 14(1), (53).

832 Interpretation of the Tax Acts

(1) In the Tax Acts, except in so far as the context otherwise requires—

"Act" includes an Act of the Parliament of Northern Ireland and a Measure of the Northern Ireland Assembly;

...[1]

"authorised unit trust" has the meaning given by section 468(6);

"basic rate", in relation to the charging of income tax for any year of assessment, means the rate of income tax determined in pursuance of section 1(2)(a), and any reference to the basic rate limit shall be construed in accordance with section 1(3);

"the Board" means the Commissioners of Inland Revenue;

"body of persons" means any body politic, corporate or collegiate, and any company, fraternity, fellowship and society of persons whether corporate or not corporate;

"building society" means a building society within the meaning of the Building Societies Act 1986;

"capital allowance" means any allowance under [the Capital Allowances Act (including enactments which under this Act are to be treated as contained in that Act)][15];

["the Capital Allowances Act" means the Capital Allowances Act 2001;][15]

"chargeable gain" has the same meaning as in the [1992][4] Act;

"chargeable period" means an accounting period of a company or a year of assessment;

"close company" has the meaning given by sections 414 and 415;

"collector" means any collector of taxes;

"company" means, subject to subsection (2) below, any body corporate or unincorporated association but does not include a partnership, a local authority or a local authority association;

"distribution" has the meaning given by Part VI with section 418;

"farm land" means land in the United Kingdom wholly or mainly occupied for the purposes of husbandry, but excluding any dwelling or domestic offices, and excluding market garden land, and "farming" shall be construed accordingly;

["for accounting purposes" means for the purposes of accounts drawn up in accordance with generally accepted accounting practice;][18]

["franked investment income" means income of a company resident in the United Kingdom which consists of a distribution in respect of which the company is entitled to a tax credit (and which accordingly represents income equal to the aggregate of the amount or value of the distribution and the amount of that credit);][12]

...[12]
...[11]

[generally accepted accounting practice" has the meaning given by section 836A;][18]

"higher rate", in relation to the charging of income tax for any year of assessment, means any rate of income tax determined in pursuance of section 1(2)(b), ...[2]

"industrial assurance business" [means any such business carried on before the day appointed for the coming into force of section 167(4) of the Finance Act 1996 as was industrial business within][17] the meaning given by section 1(2) of the Industrial Assurance Act 1923 or Article 3(1) of the Industrial Assurance (Northern Ireland) Order 1979;

"inspector" means any inspector of taxes;

"interest" means both annual or yearly interest and interest other than annual or yearly interest;

["investment LLP" and "property investment LLP" have the meaning given by section 842B;][16]
["local authority association" has the meaning given by section 519;][3]
["lower rate", in relation to the charging of income tax for any year of assessment, means the rate of income tax specified in or determined in pursuance of section 1A(1B);][14]

"market garden land" means land in the United Kingdom occupied as a nursery or garden for the sale of the produce (other than land used for the growth of hops) and "market gardening" shall be construed accordingly;

"notice" means notice in writing [or in a form authorised (in relation to the case in question) by directions under section 116 of the Finance Act 1998][8];

"ordinary share capital", in relation to a company, means all the issued share capital (by whatever name called) of the company, other than capital the holders of which have a right to a dividend at a fixed rate but have no other right to share in the profits of the company;

["overseas property business" has the meaning given by section 65A(4) or 70A(4);][9]

["period of account"—

    (*a*) in relation to a person, means any period for which the person draws up accounts, and

    (*b*) in relation to a trade, profession, vocation or other business means any period for which accounts of the business are drawn up;][18]

"preference dividend" means a dividend payable on a preferred share or preferred stock at a fixed rate per cent or, where a dividend is payable on a preferred share or preferred stock partly at a fixed rate per cent and partly at a variable rate, such part of that dividend as is payable at a fixed rate per cent;

"qualifying distribution" has the meaning given by section 14(2);

"qualifying policy" means a policy of insurance which is a qualifying policy for the purposes of Chapter I of Part VII;

["the rate applicable to trusts" shall be construed in accordance with section 686(1A);][6]

...[11]

...[7]

["Schedule A business" means any business the profits or gains of which are chargeable to income tax under Schedule A, including the business in the course of which any transaction is by virtue of paragraph 1(2) of that Schedule to be treated as entered into;][6]

["starting rate", in relation to the charging of income tax for any year of assessment, means the rate of income tax determined in pursuance of section 1(2)(*aa*), and any reference to the starting rate limit shall be construed in accordance with section 1(2A);][14]

["the Schedule F ordinary rate" shall be construed in accordance with section 1B(2);][10]

["the Schedule F trust rate" shall be construed in accordance with section 686(1A);][10]

["the Schedule F upper rate" shall be construed in accordance with section 1B(2);][10]

...[12]

"tax credit" means a tax credit under section 231;

"trade" includes every trade, manufacture, adventure or concern in the nature of trade;

"Ulster Savings Certificates" means savings certificates issued or treated as issued under section 15 of the Exchequer and Financial Provisions Act (Northern Ireland) 1950;

"unit holder" has the meaning given by section 468(6);

"unit trust scheme" has the meaning given by section 469;

"year of assessment" means, with reference to any income tax, the year for which such tax was granted by any Act granting income tax;

"the year 1988–89" means the year of assessment beginning on 6th April 1988, and any corresponding expression in which two years are similarly mentioned means the year of assessment beginning on 6th April in the first-mentioned of those two years;

and a source of income is within the charge to corporation tax or income tax if that tax is chargeable on the income arising from it, or would be so chargeable if there were any such income, and references to a person, or to income, being within the charge to tax, shall be similarly construed.

(2) The definition of "company" is subject to section 468, and does not apply in the following provisions of this Act, that is to say—

    Chapter I of Part XVII;

        sections 774 to 777;

        section 839;

        paragraph 15 of Schedule 3;

(and also does not apply where the context otherwise requires because some other definition of "company" applies).

(3) Except so far as the context otherwise requires, in the Tax Acts, and in any enactment passed after 12th March 1970 which by any express provision is to be construed as one with the Tax Acts, the Corporation Tax Acts or the Income Tax Acts, "tax", where neither income tax nor corporation tax is specified, means either of those taxes.

(4) Subsection (3) above is without prejudice to the provisions of section 9 which apply income tax law for certain purposes of corporation tax, and accordingly the employment of "income tax" rather than "tax" in any provision of the Tax Acts is not a conclusive indication that that provision is not applied to corporation tax by that section.

[(4A) Any reference in the Tax Acts to franked investment income received by a company apply to any such income received by another person on behalf of or in trust for the company, but not to any such income received by the company on behalf of or in trust for another person.][13]

(5) In the Tax Acts any reference to a child, however expressed, shall be construed as including a reference to an adopted child.

This subsection does not apply for the purposes of paragraph 10 of Schedule 30.

Commentary—*Simon's Direct Tax Service* **A1.152–160.**
Concession C4—Where specified conditions are satisfied, tax is not charged on activities such as bazaars, jumble sales, carnivals, etc organised for charitable purposes although such activities may come within the definition of trade.
Simon's Tax Cases—s 832(1), *Ang v Parrish* [1980] STC 341*; *Walker v Centaur Clothes Group Ltd* [2000] STC 324; *South Shore Mutual Insurance Co Ltd v Blair* [1999] STC (SCD) 296.
s 832(1) ("company"), *Conservative and Unionist Central Office v Burrell* [1982] STC 317*.
s 832(1) ("ordinary share capital"), *Tilcon Ltd v Holland* [1981] STC 365*.
s 832(1) ("tax credit"), *Union Texas Petroleum Corporation v Critchley* [1988] STC 691*.
s 832(1) ("trade"), *Clark v Follett* [1973] STC 240*; *Taylor v Good* [1974] STC 148*; *Dickinson v Downes* [1974] STC 539*.
Definitions—"the 1992 Act", s 831(3); "basic rate limit", s 1(3); "higher rate band", s 1(3); "Schedule A", s 15(1); "the Tax Acts", s 831(2); "United Kingdom", s 830(1).
Modification—This section is modified, in relation to open-ended investment companies, by the Open-ended Investment Companies (Tax) Regulations, SI 1997/1154, regs 3, 14.
Amendments—[1] Definition of "additional rate" in sub-s (1) repealed by FA 1997 Sch 18 Pt VI(1) with effect from the year 1997-98.
[2] Words in the definition of "higher rate" in sub-s (1) repealed by FA 1988 Sch 14 Pt IV.
[3] The definition of "local authority association" in sub-s (1) substituted for the definition of "local authority" and "local authority association" by FA 1990 Sch 18 para 5(1), (3).
[4] Year in the definition of "chargeable gain" in sub-s (1) substituted by TCGA 1992 Sch 10 para 14(1), (54).
[5] Definition of "the rate applicable to trusts" in sub-s (1) inserted by FA 1993 Sch 6 paras 15, 25(1) with effect from the year 1993–94.
[6] Definition of "Schedule A business" in sub-s (1) inserted by FA 1995 s 39, Sch 6 para 28, with effect from the year 1995–96, and, so far as making provision having effect for the purposes of corporation tax, in relation to accounting periods ending after 30 March 1995; however, this amendment does not apply for certain sources of income which ceased during the year 1995–96 (see FA 1995 s 39(5)).
[7] Definition of "recognised clearing system" in sub-s (1) repealed by FA 1996 Sch 7 paras 25, 32, Sch 41 Pt V(2), with effect for the purposes of income tax from the year 1996–97 and, for the purposes of corporation tax, for accounting periods ending after 31 March 1996.
[8] Words in definition of "notice" inserted by FA 1998 s 118(10) with effect from 31 July 1998.
[9] Definition of "overseas property business" inserted by FA 1998 Sch 5 para 45 with effect for 1998–99 and subsequent years of assessment for income tax purposes, and from 1 April 1998 for corporation tax, subject to the transitional provisions in FA 1998 Sch 5 Part IV.
[10] New definitions inserted in sub-s (1) by F(No 2)A 1997 s 34, Sch 4 para 22 and FA 1998 Sch 3 para 39 with effect for the year 1999–00 and subsequent years of assessment.
[11] Definitions of "group income" and "the rate of advance corporation tax" in sub-s (1) repealed by FA 1998 Sch 3 para 39 with effect for distributions made after 5 April 1999.
[12] Definitions in sub-s (1) of "franked payment" and "surplus franked investment income" repealed; and definition of "franked investment income" substituted, by FA 1998 Sch 3 para 39 with effect for accounting periods beginning after 5 April 1999.
[13] Sub-s (4A) inserted by FA 1998 Sch 3 para 39 with effect for accounting periods beginning after 5 April 1999.
[14] Definition of "lower rate" substituted, and definition of "starting rate" inserted, in sub-s (1) by FA 1999 s 22(10), (12) with effect from the year 1999–00.
[15] Words in the definition of "capital allowance" substituted, and the definition of "Capital Allowances Act" substituted for the definition of "Capital Allowances Acts", by CAA 2001 s 578, Sch 2 para 60 with effect for income tax purposes, as respects allowances and charges falling to be made for chargeable periods ending after 5 April 2001, and for corporation tax purposes, as respects allowances and charges falling to be made for chargeable periods ending after 31 March 2001.
[16] Definitions of "investment LLP" and "property investment LLP" inserted by FA 2001 s 76, Sch 25 para 1(2) with effect from 6 April 2001.
[17] Words in definition of "industrial assurance business" in sub-s (1) substituted by FA 1996 s 167(4), (11) with effect from 1 December 2001 (by virtue of SI 2001/3643).
[18] Definitions of "for accounting purposes", "generally accepted accounting practice" and "period of account" inserted by FA 2002 s 103(1), (6) with effect for the purposes of provisions of FA 2002 using these definitions (including provisions inserted by amendment in other enactments) whenever those provisions are expressed to have effect or to come, or to have come, into force. This is without prejudice to the general effect of those amendments.
Prospective amendments—Definition of "estate in land" to be inserted in sub-s (1) by the Abolition of Feudal Tenure etc (Scotland) Act 2000 s 76(1), Sch 12 Pt I para 50(4) with effect from a day to be appointed.

833 Interpretation of Income Tax Acts

(1) In the Income Tax Acts references to profits or gains shall not include references to chargeable gains.

(2) References in the Income Tax Acts to the retail prices index are references to the general index of retail prices (for all items) published by the [Office for National Statistics][3], and if that index is not published for a month which is relevant for the purposes of any provision of those Acts that provision shall be construed as referring to any substituted index or index figures published by [that Office][3].

(3) For the purposes of any provision of the Income Tax Acts (other than section 550 ...[1]) requiring income of any description to be treated as the highest part of a person's income, his income shall be calculated without regard to—

(a) any payment [or other benefit][4] chargeable to tax by virtue of section 148; or
(b) any amount included in his total income by virtue of section 547(1)(a); ...[1]
(c) ...[1]

(4) Subject to subsections (5) and (6) below, in the Income Tax Acts "earned income" means, in relation to any individual—

(a) any income arising in respect of—

(i) any remuneration from any office or employment held by the individual, or
(ii) any pension, superannuation or other allowance, deferred pay or compensation for loss of office, given in respect of the past services of the individual or of the [spouse][2] or parent of the individual in any office or employment, or given to the individual in respect of past services of any deceased person, whether the individual or [spouse][2] or parent of the individual shall have contributed to such pension, superannuation allowance or deferred pay or not; and

(*b*) any income from any property which is attached to or forms part of the emoluments of any office or employment held by the individual; and

(*c*) any income which is charged under Schedule ...¹ or D and is immediately derived by the individual from the carrying on or exercise by him of his trade, profession or vocation, either as an individual or, in the case of a partnership, as a partner personally acting in the partnership.

...²

(5) Without prejudice to the generality of the provisions of subsection (4) above, in the Income Tax Acts, except so far as is otherwise expressly provided, "earned income" also includes, in relation to any individual—

(*a*) any income arising in respect of Civil List pensions granted under the Civil List Act 1837 as amended by any subsequent enactment; and

(*b*) any annuity, pension or annual payment to which section 58(2) or 133 applies; and

(*c*) any payments chargeable to income tax under Schedule E by virtue of section 150, 151 or 617;

(*d*) any sum payable by way of annuity to an individual by virtue of a scheme under section 27 of the Agriculture Act 1967 (grants for relinquishing occupation of uncommercial agricultural units), unless the annuity was granted to the individual by reason of his having relinquished occupation before attaining the age of 55; and

(*e*) income which is earned income by virtue of section 529.

(6) The provisions of this section are without prejudice to any other provision of the Income Tax Acts directing income to be treated as earned income.

Commentary—*Simon's Direct Tax Service* **A1.158; E1.112.**
Simon's Tax Cases—s 833(4), *Evans v Pearce* [1974] STC 46*.
s 833(4)(*c*), *Pegler v Abell* [1973] STC 23*; *Northend v White & Leonard and Corbin Greener (a firm)* [1975] STC 317*; *Lawrance v Hayman* [1976] STC 227*.
Definitions—"Chargeable gains", s 832(1); "emoluments", s 131(1); "income tax", s 832(4); "the Income Tax Acts", s 831(1)(*b*); "Schedule A", s 15(1); "Schedule B", s 16(1); "Schedule D", s 18(1); "Schedule E", s 19(1); "total income", s 835(1); "trade", s 832(1).
Cross references—See TA 1988 s 127(3) (sub-s (4)(*c*) above to include enterprise allowance).
TA 1988 s 503 (for the purposes of sub-s (4)(*c*) above, all lettings of furnished holiday accommodation treated as a single trade).
TA 1988 s 660C(3) (subject to sub-s (3) above income of settlor within Part XV Chapter IA deemed to be highest part of his income).
Amendments—¹ Words in sub-ss (3), (4)(*c*) repealed by FA 1988 Sch 14, Pts IV, V.
² Word in sub-s (4)(*a*)(ii) substituted and words in sub-s (4) repealed by FA 1988 Sch 3 para 21, Sch 14 Pt VIII with effect from the year 1990–91.
³ Words in sub-s (2) substituted by the Transfer of Functions (Registration and Statistics) Order 1996, SI 1996/273 Sch 2 para 22 with effect from 1 April 1996.
⁴ Words in sub-s (3)(a) inserted by FA 1998 Sch 9 Pt II para 4 with effect from 6 April 1998.

834 Interpretation of the Corporation Tax Acts

(1) For the purposes of the Corporation Tax Acts, except in so far as the context otherwise requires—

"accounting date" means the date to which a company makes up its accounts ...⁶

"accounting period" shall be construed in accordance with section 12;

"allowable loss" does not include, for the purposes of corporation tax in respect of chargeable gains, a loss accruing to a company in such circumstances that if a gain accrued the company would be exempt from corporation tax in respect of it;

"branch or agency" means any factorship, agency, receivership, branch or management;

"charges on income" has the meaning given by section [338A]⁵;

["derivative contract" has the same meaning as it has for the purpose of Schedule 26 to the Finance Act 2002;]⁴

"the financial year 1988" means the financial year beginning with April 1988, and similarly with references embodying other dates;

"group relief" has the meaning given by section 402.

["loan relationship" has the same meaning as it has for the purpose of Chapter II of Part IV of the Finance Act 1996;]²

["non-trading deficit", in relation to a company's loan relationships, shall be construed in accordance with section 82 of the Finance Act 1996.]²

(2) Section 6(4) shall also apply for the purposes of the following provisions of this Act, that is to say—

Chapter II of Part X except section 395;

sections 75 and 76;
section 490;
sections 768 and 769;

...³

(3) For all the purposes of the Corporation Tax Acts dividends shall be treated as paid on the date when they become due and payable, [except in so far as Chapter III of Part XII makes other provision for dividends treated as paid by virtue of that Chapter]¹.

(4) Except as otherwise provided by the Corporation Tax Acts, any apportionment to different periods which falls to be made under those Acts shall be made on a time basis according to the respective lengths of those periods.

Commentary—*Simon's Direct Tax Service* A1.152, 154, 158, 160.
Definitions—"The 1990 Act", s 831(3); "chargeable gains", s 832(1); "company", s 832(1), (2); "Corporation Tax Acts", s 831(1).
Amendments—¹ Words in sub-s (3) substituted by FA 1994 Sch 14 paras 6, 7(1) in relation to distribution periods beginning after 31 March 1994, but subject to FA 1994 Sch 14 para 7(2).
² In sub-s (1), definitions "loan relationship" and "non-trading deficit" inserted by FA 1996 ss 104, 105(1), Sch 14 para 49 with effect for accounting periods ending after 31 March 1996.
³ Words in sub-s (2) repealed by CAA 2001 ss 578, 580, Sch 2 para 61, Sch 4 with effect for corporation tax purposes as respects allowances and charges falling to be made for chargeable periods ending after 31 March 2001.
⁴ In sub-s (1), definition of "derivative contract" inserted by FA 2002 s 83(1)(b), (3) Sch 27 paras 1, 13 with effect for accounting periods beginning after 30 September 2002.
⁵ In sub-s (1), in the definition of "charges on income", "338A" substituted for "338" by FA 2002 s 84(2), Sch 30 para 1(4) with effect from 24 July 2002.
⁶ In sub-s (1), in the definition of "accounting date", words "and "period of account" means the period for which it does so;" repealed by FA 2002 s 141, Sch 40 Pt 3(16) with effect from 24 July 2002.

835 "Total income" in the Income Tax Acts

(1) In the Income Tax Acts "total income", in relation to any person, means the total income of that person from all sources estimated in accordance with the provisions of the Income Tax Acts.

(2) Any person who, on his own behalf or on behalf of another person, delivers a statement of the amount of his or that other person's total income shall observe the rules and directions contained in section 836.

(3) Where deductions reduce a person's total income and the order in which they are made or in which income of different descriptions is reduced thereby may affect his liability to income tax the deductions shall be made and treated as reducing income in accordance with subsections (4) and (5) below.

(4) Subject to any express provisions of the Income Tax Acts, any deductions allowable in computing a person's total income or to be made from a person's total income shall be treated as reducing income of different descriptions in the order which will result in the greatest reduction of his liability to income tax.

(5) Deductions from total income under Chapter I of Part VII shall be made after any other deductions and shall not affect the amount to be taken as a person's total income for the purposes of section 257(5)[, 257A(5)]² or 274 ...¹.

(6) In estimating the total income of any person—

(a) any income which is chargeable with income tax by way of deduction at the basic rate [or the lower rate]³ in force for any year or which for the purposes of Schedule F comprises an [amount which is equal to a tax credit calculated by reference to the tax credit fraction]⁴ shall be deemed to be income of that year; and

(b) any deductions which are allowable on account of sums payable under deduction of income tax at the basic rate in force for any year out of the property or profits of that person shall be allowed as deductions in respect of that year;

notwithstanding that the income or sums, as the case may be, accrued or will accrue in whole or in part before or after that year.

(7) Where an assessment has become final and conclusive for the purposes of income tax for any year of assessment—

(a) that assessment shall also be final and conclusive in estimating total income; and

(b) no allowance or adjustment of liability, on the ground of diminution of income or loss, shall be taken into account in estimating total income unless that allowance or adjustment has previously been made on an application under the special provisions of the Income Tax Acts relating thereto.

(8) Subsection (7) above shall apply in relation to—

(a) any relief under section 353;

(b) any relief by reason of the operation of an election for the herd basis under Schedule 5; and

[(c) any allowance given effect under section 258 or 479 of the Capital Allowances Act;]⁵

as it applies in relation to allowances or adjustments on the ground of diminution of income or loss.

Commentary—*Simon's Direct Tax Service* E1.401–403.
Revenue Internal Guidance—Relief manual RE 60–61 (meaning of "total income" and link with "net statutory income").
RE 70–73 (calculation of "total income"; no deduction for reliefs given in terms of tax).
RE 90–93 (treatment of payments made under deduction of income tax; set-off of reliefs against different sources of income; reliefs given in terms of tax).
RE 130–131 (charges allowable and not allowable in computing income liable at the higher rate).
Simon's Tax Cases—*IRC v Crawley* [1987] STC 147*.
s 835(1), *IRC v Addison* [1984] STC 540*.
s 835(7), *Aplin v White* [1973] STC 322*; *Nicholson v IRC* [1975] STC 245*.
Definitions—"The 1990 Act", s 831(3); "advance corporation tax", s 14(1); "basic rate", s 832(1); "income tax", s 832(4); "the Income Tax Acts", s 831(1)(b); "lower rate", s 832(1); "Schedule F", s 20(1); "tax", s 832(3); "tax credit", s 832(1); "year of assessment", s 832(1).
Amendments—¹ Words in sub-s (5) repealed by FA 1988 Sch 14 Pt IV.
² Section number in sub-s (5) inserted by FA 1988 Sch 3 para 22 with effect from the year 1990–91.

³ Words in sub-s (6)(*a*) inserted by FA 1996 s 73(4), Sch 6 paras 24, 28 with effect from the year 1996–97.
⁴ Words in sub-s (6)(*a*) substituted for words "amount which is or (apart from section 78(3) of the Finance Act 1993) would be equal to a tax credit calculated by reference to the rate of advance corporation tax in force for any year" by FA 1998 s 31(5), Sch 3 para 40 with effect for distributions made after 5 April 1999.
⁵ Sub-s (8)(*c*) substituted by CAA 2001 s 578, Sch 2 para 62 with effect for income tax purposes as respects allowances and charges falling to be made for chargeable periods ending after 5 April 2001.

836 Returns of total income

The following rules and directions shall be observed in delivering returns of total income under section 835(2)—

First—Declaration of the amount of profits or gains returned, or for which the person in question has been or is liable to be assessed.

Second—Declaration of the amount of rents, interest, annuities or other annual payments, in respect of which the person in question is liable to allow the tax, with the names of the respective persons by whom such payments are to be made, distinguishing the amount of each payment.

Third—Declaration of the amount of annuities or other annual payments (not being interest) to be made out of the property or profits or gains assessed on the person in question, distinguishing each source.

Fourth—Statement of the amount of income derived according to the three preceding declarations.

Fifth—Statement of any tax which the person in question may be entitled to deduct, retain or charge against any other person.

Commentary—*Simon's Direct Tax Service* E1.401.
Definitions—"Interest", s 832(1); "profits or gains", s 833(1); "tax", s 832(3); "total income", s 835(1).

[836A Generally accepted accounting practice

(1) In the Tax Acts, unless the context otherwise requires, "generally accepted accounting practice"—

(*a*) means generally accepted accounting practice with respect to accounts of UK companies that are intended to give a true and fair view, and

(*b*) has the same meaning in relation to—

    (i) individuals,
    (ii) entities other than companies, and
    (iii) companies that are not UK companies,

as it has in relation to UK companies.

(2) In subsection (1) "UK companies" means companies incorporated or formed under the law of a part of the United Kingdom.]¹

Amendments—¹ This section inserted by FA 2002 s 103(2), (6) with effect for the purposes of provisions of FA 2002 using these definitions (including provisions inserted by amendment in other enactments) whenever those provisions are expressed to have effect or to come, or to have come, into force. This is without prejudice to the general effect of those amendments.

837 "Annual value" of land

(1) For the purposes of, and subject to, the provisions of the Tax Acts which apply this section, the annual value of land shall be taken to be the rent which might reasonably be expected to be obtained on a letting from year to year if the tenant undertook to pay all usual tenant's rates and taxes, and if the landlord undertook to bear the costs of the repairs and insurance, and the other expenses, if any, necessary for maintaining the subject of the valuation in a state to command that rent.

(2) Section 23 of the General Rate Act 1967 (adjustment of gross value by reference to provision of or payment for services etc) shall apply for the purpose of subsection (1) above, and in relation to land in Scotland or Northern Ireland shall apply as if it extended to the whole of the United Kingdom.

(3) Where any question arises as to the annual value of land it shall be determined by the General Commissioners and those Commissioners shall hear and determine the question in like manner as an appeal.

Commentary—*Simon's Direct Tax Service* A4.311.
Concessions A56—Calculation of the "annual value" for the purposes of s 145 of this Act in respect of accommodation provided to employees in Scotland.
B30—The 1985 rating revaluation in Scotland is to be ignored for the purposes of this section.
Revenue & other press releases—IR 19-4-90 (valuation of properties built after the end of the rating system and provided to employees).
Revenue Internal Guidance—Schedule E manual SE 11434 (living accommodation: why annual value means gross rating value. UK properties).
SE 11440–11441 (living accommodation: meaning of annual value for properties outside the UK—description and detail).
SE 21618 (annual value of land or derated buildings).
Definitions—"The Tax Acts", s 831(2); "United Kingdom", s 830(1).

[837A Meaning of "research and development"

(1) The following provisions have effect for the purposes of, and subject to, the provisions of the Tax Acts which apply this section.

(2) "Research and development" means activities that fall to be treated as research and development in accordance with [generally accepted accounting practice][2].

This is subject to regulations under subsection (3) below.

(3) The Treasury may by regulations provide—

(a) that such activities as may be prescribed are not "research and development" for the purposes of this section, and

(b) that such other activities as may be prescribed are "research and development" for those purposes.

(4) Regulations under subsection (3) above may—

(a) make provision by reference to guidelines issued (whether before or after the coming into force of this section) by the Secretary of State, and

(b) make such supplementary, incidental, consequential or transitional provision as appears to the Treasury to be necessary or expedient.

(5) ...[3]

(6) Unless otherwise expressly provided, "research and development" does not include oil and gas exploration and appraisal.][1]

Commentary—*Simon's Direct Tax Service* B2.701.
Cross references—See Research and Development (Prescribed Activities) Regulations, SI 2000/2081 (prescription of activities for the purposes of this section by reference to the Guidelines on the Meaning of Research and Development (issued by the DTI on 28 July 2000—reproduced in the Miscellaneous section of Part II to this publication)).
Amendments—[1] This section inserted by FA 2000 s 68, Sch 19 Pt I para 1 with effect from 28 July 2000.
[2] In sub-s (2), words substituted for the words "normal accounting practice" by FA 2002 s 103(4)(a) with effect from 24 July 2002.
[3] Sub-s (5) repealed by FA 2002 s 141, Sch 40 Pt 3(16) with effect from 24 July 2002. Sub-s (5) previously read as follows—
    "(5) In subsection (2) above "normal accounting practice" means normal accounting practice in relation to the accounts of companies incorporated in a part of the United Kingdom.".

[837B Meaning of "oil and gas exploration and appraisal"

(1) References in the Tax Acts to "oil and gas exploration and appraisal" are to activities carried out for the purpose of—

(a) searching for petroleum anywhere in an area, or

(b) ascertaining—

(i) the extent or characteristics of any petroleum-bearing area, or

(ii) what the reserves of petroleum of any such area are,

so that it may be determined whether the petroleum is suitable for commercial exploitation.

(2) For this purpose "petroleum" has the meaning given in section 1 of the Petroleum Act 1998.][1]

Commentary—*Simon's Direct Tax Service* B2.711.
Amendments—[1] This section inserted by FA 2000 s 68, Sch 19 Pt I para 2 with effect from 28 July 2000.

838 Subsidiaries

(1) For the purposes of the Tax Acts a body corporate shall be deemed to be—

(a) a "51 per cent subsidiary" of another body corporate if and so long as more than 50 per cent of its ordinary share capital is owned directly or indirectly by that other body corporate;

(b) a "75 per cent subsidiary" of another body corporate if and so long as not less than 75 per cent of its ordinary share capital is owned directly or indirectly by that other body corporate;

(c) a "90 per cent subsidiary" of another body corporate if and so long as not less than 90 per cent of its ordinary share capital is owned directly by that other body corporate.

(2) In subsection (1)(a) and (b) above "owned directly or indirectly" by a body corporate means owned, whether directly or through another body corporate or other bodies corporate or partly directly and partly through another body corporate or other bodies corporate.

(3) In this section references to ownership shall be construed as references to beneficial ownership.

(4) For the purposes of this section the amount of ordinary share capital of one body corporate owned by a second body corporate through another body corporate or other bodies corporate, or partly directly and partly through another body corporate or other bodies corporate, shall be determined in accordance with the following provisions of this section.

(5) Where, in the case of a number of bodies corporate, the first directly owns ordinary share capital of the second and the second directly owns ordinary share capital of the third, then for the purposes of this section, the first shall be deemed to own ordinary share capital of the third through the second, and, if the third directly owns ordinary share capital of a fourth, the first shall be deemed to own ordinary share capital of the fourth through the second and third, and the second shall be deemed to own ordinary share capital of the fourth through the third and so on.

(6) In this section—

(a) any number of bodies corporate of which the first directly owns ordinary share capital of the next and the next directly owns ordinary share capital of the next but one, and so on, and, if they are more than three, any three or more of them, are referred to as "a series";

(b) in any series—

    (i) that body corporate which owns ordinary share capital of another through the remainder is referred to as the "first owner";

    (ii) that other body corporate the ordinary share capital of which is so owned is referred to as "the last owned body corporate";

    (iii) the remainder, if one only, is referred to as "an intermediary" and, if more than one, are referred to as "a chain of intermediaries";

(c) a body corporate in a series which directly owns ordinary share capital of another body corporate in the series is referred to as "an owner"; and

(d) any two bodies corporate in a series of which one owns ordinary share capital of the other directly, and not through one or more of the other bodies corporate in the series, are referred to as being directly related to one another.

(7) Where every owner in a series owns the whole of the ordinary share capital of the body corporate to which it is directly related, the first owner shall be deemed to own through the intermediary or chain of intermediaries the whole of the ordinary share capital of the last owned body corporate.

(8) Where one of the owners in a series owns a fraction of the ordinary share capital of the body corporate to which it is directly related, and every other owner in the series owns the whole of the ordinary share capital of the body corporate to which it is directly related, the first owner shall be deemed to own that fraction of the ordinary share capital of the last owned body corporate through the intermediary or chain of intermediaries.

(9) Where—

    (a) each of two or more of the owners in a series owns a fraction, and every other owner in the series owns the whole, of the ordinary share capital of the body corporate to which it is directly related; or

    (b) every owner in a series owns a fraction of the ordinary share capital of the body corporate to which it is directly related;

the first owner shall be deemed to own through the intermediary or chain of intermediaries such fraction of the ordinary share capital of the last owned body corporate as results from the multiplication of those fractions.

(10) Where the first owner in any series owns a fraction of the ordinary share capital of the last owned body corporate in that series through the intermediary or chain of intermediaries in that series, and also owns another fraction or other fractions of the ordinary share capital of the last owned body corporate, either—

    (a) directly, or

    (b) through an intermediary or intermediaries which is not a member or are not members of that series, or

    (c) through a chain or chains of intermediaries of which one or some or all are not members of that series, or

    (d) in a case where the series consists of more than three bodies corporate, through an intermediary or intermediaries which is a member or are members of the series, or through a chain or chains of intermediaries consisting of some but not all of the bodies corporate of which the chain of intermediaries in the series consists;

then, for the purpose of ascertaining the amount of the ordinary share capital of the last owned body corporate owned by the first owner, all those fractions shall be aggregated and the first owner shall be deemed to own the sum of those fractions.

Commentary—*Simon's Direct Tax Service* D2.604, 606.
Revenue Interpretation RI 224—If a Delaware Limited Liability Company (DLLC) issues "shares" under the Delaware Limited Liability Act s 18–702c, these may be regarded as "ordinary share capital" for the purposes of this section.
Simon's Tax Cases—*Burman v Hedges Butler Ltd* [1979] STC 136*.
Definitions—"Ordinary share capital", s 832(1); "the Tax Acts", s 831(2).
Cross references—See TCGA 1992 s 170(6)(d) (extension of sub-s(1)(a) of this section for the purposes of definition of groups of companies).

839 Connected persons

(1) For the purposes of, and subject to, the provisions of the Tax Acts which apply this section, any question whether a person is connected with another shall be determined in accordance with the following provisions of this section (any provision that one person is connected with another being taken to mean that they are connected with one another).

(2) A person is connected with an individual if that person is the individual's wife or husband, or is a relative, or the wife or husband of a relative, of the individual or of the individual's wife or husband.

[(3) A person, in his capacity as trustee of a settlement, is connected with—

    (a) any individual who in relation to the settlement is a settlor,

    (b) any person who is connected with such an individual, and

    (c) any body corporate which is connected with that settlement.

In this subsection "settlement" and "settlor" have the same meaning as in Chapter IA of Part XV (see section 660G(1) and (2)).][2]

[(3A) For the purpose of subsection (3) above a body corporate is connected with a settlement if—

(a) it is a close company (or only not a close company because it is not resident in the United Kingdom) and the participators include the trustees of the settlement; or

(b) it is controlled (within the meaning of section 840) by a company falling within paragraph (a) above.][2]

(4) Except in relation to acquisitions or disposals of partnership assets pursuant to bona fide commercial arrangements, a person is connected with any person with whom he is in partnership, and with the wife or husband or relative of any individual with whom he is in partnership.

(5) A company is connected with another company—

(a) if the same person has control of both, or a person has control of one and persons connected with him, or he and persons connected with him, have control of the other; or

(b) if a group of two or more persons has control of each company, and the groups either consist of the same persons or could be regarded as consisting of the same persons by treating (in one or more cases) a member of either group as replaced by a person with whom he is connected.

(6) A company is connected with another person if that person has control of it or if that person and persons connected with him together have control of it.

(7) Any two or more persons acting together to secure or exercise control of a company shall be treated in relation to that company as connected with one another and with any person acting on the directions of any of them to secure or exercise control of the company.

(8) In this section—

"company" includes any body corporate or unincorporated association, but does not include a partnership, and this section shall apply in relation to any unit trust scheme as if the scheme were a company and as if the rights of the unit holders were shares in the company;

"control" shall be construed in accordance with section 416; and

"relative" means brother, sister, ancestor or lineal descendant.

...[1]

Commentary—*Simon's Direct Tax Service* A1.157.
Concession C9—For the purposes of "small companies marginal relief", TA 1988 s 13, the Revenue will, by concession, not treat companies in certain circumstances as associated, and "relative" includes only a husband or wife or minor child where there is no substantial commercial interdependence.
Simon's Tax Cases—s 839(7), *Steele v European Vinyls Corp (Holdings) BV* [1996] STC 785.
Definitions—"Close company", s 832(1); "the Tax Acts", s 831(2); "unit holders", s 468(6), by virtue of s 832(1); "unit trust scheme", s 469, by virtue of s 832(1).
Cross references—See the Open-ended Investment Companies (Tax) Regulations, SI 1997/1154 regs 3, 15 (modification of sub-s (8) as it has effects in relation to open-ended investment companies).
FA 2000 Sch 14 para 71(2) (this section applies for the purposes of FA 2000 Sch 14 on enterprise management incentives).
FA 2002 s 55(5) (this section applies for the purposes of FA 2002 s 55(4) on gifts of medical supplies and equipment).
Modification—The definition of "company" in sub-s (8) is modified, in relation to open-ended investment companies, by the Open-ended Investment Companies (Tax) Regulations, SI 1997/1154, regs 5, 7, 15.
Amendments—[1] Words in sub-s (8) ceased to have effect on 29 April 1988 by virtue of TA 1988 (Appointed Day) Order, SI 1988/745.
[2] Sub-ss (3), (3A) substituted for sub-s (3) as originally enacted by FA 1995 s 74, Sch 17 para 20, with effect from the year 1995–96 (and apply to every settlement wherever and whenever made or entered into).

840 Meaning of "control" in certain contexts

For the purposes of, and subject to, the provisions of the Tax Acts which apply this section, "control", in relation to a body corporate, means the power of a person to secure—

(a) by means of the holding of shares or the possession of voting power in or in relation to that or any other body corporate; or

(b) by virtue of any powers conferred by the articles of association or other document regulating that or any other body corporate,

that the affairs of the first-mentioned body corporate are conducted in accordance with the wishes of that person, and, in relation to a partnership, means the right to a share of more than one-half of the assets, or of more than one-half of the income, of the partnership.

Commentary—*Simon's Direct Tax Service* A1.157.
Simon's Tax Cases—*Irving v Tesco Stores (Holdings) Ltd* [1982] STC 881*; *Cricket plc v Inspector of Taxes* [1998] STC (SCD) 101.
Definition—"The Tax Acts", s 831(2).

[840A Banks

(1) In any provision in relation to which it is provided that "bank" has the meaning given by this section "bank" means—

(a) the Bank of England;

[(b) a person who has permission under Part 4 of the Financial Services and Markets Act 2000 to accept deposits other than—

(i) a building society within the meaning of the Building Societies Act 1986, [(ii) a society registered within the meaning of the Friendly Societies Act 1974 or incorporated under the Friendly Societies Act 1992,][3]

(iii) a society registered as a credit union under the Industrial and Provident Societies Act 1965 or the Credit Unions (Northern Ireland) Order 1985, or

(iv) an insurance company within the meaning of section 659B(1);][2]

[(c) an EEA firm of the kind mentioned in paragraph 5(b) of Schedule 3 to the Financial Services and Markets Act 2000 which has permission under paragraph 15 of that Schedule (as a result of qualifying for authorisation under paragraph 12(1) of that Schedule) to accept deposits;][2]

(d) a relevant international organisation which is designated as a bank for the purposes of that provision by an order made by the Treasury.

(2) ...[2]

(3) For the purposes of subsection (1) above, a relevant international organisation is an international organisation of which the United Kingdom is a member.][1]

Commentary— *Simon's Direct Tax Service* **A7.902.**
Regulations—European Investment Bank (Designated International Organisation) Order, SI 1996/1179.
Revenue Internal Guidance—Banking manual BM 1.2.1–1.3.7 (meaning of "bank" and types of activity carried on by banks).
Definitions—"United Kingdom", s 830.
Amendments—[1] This section inserted by FA 1996 Sch 37 para 1(1).
[2] Sub-s (1)(b), (c) substituted, and sub-s (2) repealed, by the Financial Services and Markets Act 2000 (Consequential Amendments) (Taxes) Order, SI 2001/3629 arts 13, 46 with effect from 1 December 2001, immediately after the coming into force of the Financial Services and Markets Act 2000 ss 411, 432(1), Sch 20.
[3] Sub-s (1)(b)(ii) substituted by the Financial Services and Markets Act 2000 (Consequential Amendments) (Taxes) Order, SI 2002/1409 art 2(1), (2) with effect from 2 July 2002. Sub-s (1)(b)(ii) previously read as follows—

"(ii) a friendly society within the meaning of section 116 of the Friendly Societies Act 1992,".

841 Recognised stock exchange and recognised investment exchanges

(1) In the Tax Acts "recognised stock exchange" means—

(a) the Stock Exchange; and

(b) any such stock exchange outside the United Kingdom as is for the time being designated for the purposes of this section as a recognised stock exchange by order made by the Board.

(2) An order made by the Board under this section—

(a) may designate a stock exchange by name, or by reference to any class or description of stock exchanges including a class or description framed by reference to any authority or approval given in a country outside the United Kingdom;

(b) may contain such transitional and other supplemental provisions as appear to the Board to be necessary or expedient;

(c) may be varied or revoked by a subsequent order so made.

(3) The Board may by regulations make provision securing that enactments in the Tax Acts containing references to the Stock Exchange have effect, for such purposes and subject to such modifications as may be prescribed by the regulations, in relation to all other recognised investment exchanges (within the meaning of the [Financial Services and Markets Act 2000][1]), or in relation to such of those exchanges as may be prescribed.

Commentary—*Simon's Direct Tax Service* **A1.160.**
Note—Lists of recognised stock exchanges and recognised investment exchanges are provided in the *Miscellaneous* section of Part II to this Handbook (see Misc VIII and Misc X).
Statement of Practice SP 18/80—Securities dealt in on the Unlisted Securities Market are not "listed" or "quoted". They, however, are securities "authorised to be dealt in" and "dealt in" on a recognised stock exchange. Details of the bargains done around a given date are normally suggestive of the open market value of such securities on that date.
Definitions—"The Board", s 832(1); "the Tax Acts", s 831(2); "United Kingdom", s 830(1).
Amendments—[1] Words in sub-s (3) substituted by the Financial Services and Markets Act 2000 s 432(1), Sch 20 para 4 with effect from 1 December 2001 (by virtue of SI 2001/3538).

841A Recognised clearing systems

Commentary— *Simon's Direct Tax Service* **A7.902.**
Amendments—This section repealed by FA 2000 s 156, Sch 40 Pt II(17) with effect for payments of interest made after 31 March 2001.

842 Investment trusts

(1) In the Tax Acts "investment trust" means, as respects any accounting period, a company which is not a close company and which is approved for the purposes of this section for that accounting period by the Board, and the Board shall not approve any company unless it is shown to their satisfaction—

[(aa) that the company is resident in the United Kingdom; and][1]

(a) that the company's income [(as determined in accordance with subsection (1AB) below)][8] [consists wholly or mainly of eligible investment income [(as so determined)][8]][5]; and

(b) subject to subsection (2) below, that no holding in a company, other than an investment trust or a company which would qualify as an investment trust but for paragraph (c) below, represents more than 15 per cent by value of the investing company's investments; and [(*c*) that the shares making up the company's ordinary share capital (or, if there are such shares of more than one class, those of each class) are [listed in the Official List of]⁶ the Stock Exchange; and]¹

(*d*) that the distribution as dividend of surpluses arising from the realisation of investments is prohibited by the company's memorandum or articles of association; and

(*e*) that the company does not retain in respect of any accounting period [an amount which is greater than]⁸ 15 per cent of [its eligible investment income [(determined in accordance with subsection (1AB) below)]⁸]⁵.

[(1AA) Income is eligible investment income for the purposes of this section in so far as it is either—

(*a*) income deriving from shares or securities, or

(*b*) eligible rental income, within the meaning of section 508A.]⁵

[(1AB) In determining for the purposes of paragraph (*a*) or (*e*) of subsection (1) above (and accordingly of subsection (2A)(*b*) below)—

(*a*) the amount of a company's income, or

(*b*) the amount of income which a company derives from shares or securities,

the amounts to be brought into account under Chapter 2 of Part 4 of the Finance Act 1996 in respect of the company's loan relationships shall be determined without reference to any debtor relationships of the company.]⁸

[(1A) For the purposes of paragraph (*b*) of subsection (1) above and the other provisions of this section having effect in relation to that paragraph—

(*a*) holdings in companies which are members of a group (whether or not including the investing company) and are not excluded from that paragraph shall be treated as holdings in a single company; and

(*b*) where the investing company is a member of a group, money owed to it by another member of the group shall be treated as a security of the latter held by the investing company and accordingly as, or as part of, the holding of the investing company in the company owing the money;

and for the purposes of this subsection "group" means a company and all companies which are its 51 per cent subsidiaries.]¹

(2) Subsection (1)(*b*) above shall not apply—

(*a*) to a holding in a company acquired before 6th April 1965 which on that date represented not more than 25 per cent by value of the investing company's investments; or

(*b*) to a holding in a company which, when it was acquired, represented not more than 15 per cent by value of the investing company's investments;

so long as no addition is made to the holding.

[(2A) Subsection (1)(*e*) above shall not apply as regards an accounting period if—

(*a*) the company is required to retain income in respect of the period by virtue of a restriction imposed by law, and

(*b*) the amount of income the company is so required to retain in respect of the period exceeds an amount equal to 15 per cent of the income the company derives from shares and securities.

(2B) Subsection (2A) above shall not apply where—

(*a*) the amount of income the company retains in respect of the accounting period exceeds the amount of income it is required by virtue of a restriction imposed by law to retain in respect of the period, and

(*b*) the amount of the excess or, where the company distributes income in respect of the period, that amount together with the amount of income which the company so distributes is at least £10,000 or, where the period is less than 12 months, a proportionately reduced amount.

(2C) Paragraph (*e*) of subsection (1) above shall not apply as regards an accounting period if the amount which the company would be required to distribute in order to fall within that paragraph is less than £10,000 or, where the period is less than 12 months, a proportionately reduced amount.]²

(3) For the purposes of subsection (2) above—

(*a*) "holding" means the shares or securities (whether of one class or more than one class) held in any one company; and

(*b*) an addition is made to a holding whenever the investing company acquires shares or securities of that one company, otherwise than by being allotted shares or securities without becoming liable to give any consideration, and if an addition is made to a holding that holding is acquired when the addition or latest addition is made to the holding; and

(*c*) where in connection with a scheme of reconstruction ...⁹, a company issues shares or securities to persons holding shares or securities in a second company in respect of and in proportion to (or as nearly as may be in proportion to) their holdings in the second company, without those persons becoming liable to give any consideration, a holding of the shares or securities in the second company and a corresponding holding of the shares or securities so issued shall be regarded as the same holding.

(4) In this section "company" and "shares" shall be construed in accordance with sections [99 and 288 of [the 1992 Act]⁴]³ [and "scheme of reconstruction" has the same meaning as in section 136 of that Act]⁷.

Commentary—*Simon's Direct Tax Service* **D4.422.**
Statements of Practice SP 1/88, paras 7, 8—Profit of revenue nature on a forward currency transaction is not income within sub-s (1)(*a*) above, but the Revenue may regard it as such if certain conditions are satisfied.
SP 14/91, paras 17, 18—Revenue's views as regards approval of an investment trust under this section where profits or losses on financial futures and options are trading profits or losses.
SP 3/97—Investment trusts investing in authorised unit trusts: or open-ended investment companies tax implications.
Revenue Internal Guidance—Capital gains tax manual CG 41411 (sub-s (1)(*a*) "securities" includes Treasury Bills but not short term loans to local authorities; "income" means gross amount of statutory income, but interest received from deposit against reciprocal foreign currency loan may be set against interest paid on the loan; sub-s (1)(*a*): where accounts drawn up on accruals basis, income includes amount shown in accounts: however where securities are purchased cum div, the whole of the dividend must be included as income).
CG 41431 (applications for provisional approval dealt with by reference to declared intentions in the prospectus).
CG 41432–41438 (retained income: circular 25-10-73 issued by Association of Investment Trust Companies).
Definitions—"The 1992 Act", s 831(3); "accounting period", s 834(1); "the Board", s 832(1); "close company", ss 414, 415, by virtue of s 832(1); "company", s 832(1), (2); "securities", s 842AA(12); "the Tax Acts", s 831(2).
Cross references—See TA 1988 s 824AA(11) (this section to apply with certain modifications to venture capital trusts).
FA 1994 s 170 (non-trading profits of interest rate and currency contracts to be treated as income derived from shares or securities for the purpose of a company's approval under this section).
FA 2002 Sch 26 para 39 (collective investment schemes; excess of relevant credits over any relevant debits treated as income derived from shares or securities in determining whether a company may be approved for the purposes of this section).
Amendments—¹ Sub-s (1)(*aa*), (1A) inserted and sub-s (1)(*c*) substituted by FA 1988 s 117(1), (4) for companies' accounting periods ending after 5 April 1988.
² Sub-ss (2A)–(2C) inserted by FA 1990 s 55 with effect for accounting periods ending after 25 July 1990.
³ Words in sub-s (4) substituted by TCGA 1992 Sch 10 para 14(1), (55).
⁴ Words in sub-s (4) substituted by FA 1994 s 146, Sch 17 para 8 and deemed always to have had effect.
⁵ Words in sub-s (1)(*a*), (*e*) substituted, and sub-s (1AA) inserted, by FA 1996 Sch 30 paras 2, 3 with effect for accounting periods beginning after 28 April 1996.
⁶ Words in sub-s (1)(*c*) substituted by FA 1996 Sch 38 para 7(1), (2)(*b*), (4) with effect for accounting periods ending after 31 March 1996.
⁷ Words in sub-s (4) inserted by FA 2002 s 45, Sch 9 paras 4(1), (7), 7(1), 8(4) with effect for shares and securities (within the meaning of TA 1988 s 842) issued after 16 April 2002.
⁸ Words in sub-s (1)(*a*), (*e*) inserted, and in sub-s (1)(*e*), words substituted for the words "more than"; and sub-s (1AB) inserted; by FA 2002 s 82, Sch 25 paras 43, 56 with effect for accounting periods beginning after 30 September 2002.
⁹ Words "or amalgamation" repealed by FA 2002 s 141, Sch 40 Pt 3(2) with effect in accordance with FA 2002 Sch 9 paras 7, 8.

[842AA Venture capital trusts

(1) In the Tax Acts "venture capital trust" means a company which is not a close company and which is for the time being approved for the purposes of this section by the Board; and an approval for the purposes of this section shall have effect as from such time as may be specified in the approval, being a time which, if it falls before the time when the approval is given, is no earlier than—

(*a*) in the case of an approval given in the year 1995–96, 6th April 1995; or

(*b*) in any other case, the time when the application for approval was made.

(2) Subject to the following provisions of this section, the Board shall not approve a company for the purposes of this section unless it is shown to their satisfaction in relation to the most recent complete accounting period of the company—

(*a*) that the company's income in that period has been derived wholly or mainly from shares or securities;

(*b*) that at least 70 per cent by value of the company's investments has been represented throughout that period by shares or securities comprised in qualifying holdings of the company;

(*c*) that at least 30 per cent by value of the company's qualifying holdings has been represented throughout that period by holdings of eligible shares;

(*d*) that no holding in any company, other than a venture capital trust or a company which would qualify as a venture capital trust but for paragraph (*e*) below, has at any time during that period represented more than 15 per cent by value of the company's investments;

(*e*) that the shares making up the company's ordinary share capital (or, if there are such shares of more than one class, those of each class) have throughout that period been [listed in the Official List of]² the Stock Exchange; and

(*f*) that the company has not retained [an amount which is greater than]⁷15 per cent of the income it derived in that period from shares and securities.

(3) Where, in the case of any company, the Board are satisfied that the conditions specified in subsection (2) above are fulfilled in relation to the company's most recent complete accounting period, they shall not approve the company for the purposes of this section unless they are satisfied that the conditions will also be fulfilled in relation to the accounting period of the company which is current when the application for approval is made.

(4) The Board may approve a company for the purposes of this section notwithstanding that conditions specified in subsection (2) above are not fulfilled with respect to that company in relation to its most recent complete accounting period if they are satisfied—

(*a*) in the case of any of the conditions specified in paragraphs (*a*), (*d*), (*e*) and (*f*) of that subsection which are not fulfilled, that the conditions will be fulfilled in relation to the accounting period of the company which is current when the application for approval is made or in relation to its next accounting period;

(b) in the case of any of the conditions specified in paragraphs (b) and (c) of that subsection which are not fulfilled, that the conditions will be fulfilled in relation to an accounting period of the company beginning no more than three years after the time when they give their approval or, if earlier, when the approval takes effect; and

(c) in the case of every condition which is not fulfilled but with respect to which the Board are satisfied as mentioned in paragraph (a) or (b) above, that the condition will continue to be fulfilled in relation to accounting periods following the period in relation to which they are satisfied as so mentioned.

(5) For the purposes of subsection (2)(b) to (d) above the value of any holding of investments of any description shall be taken—

(a) unless—

(i) it is added to by a further holding of investments of the same description, or

(ii) any such payment is made in discharge, in whole or in part, of any obligation attached to the holding as (by discharging the whole or any part of that obligation) increases the value of the holding,

to be its value when acquired, and

(b) where it is so added to or such a payment is made, to be its value immediately after the most recent addition or payment.

[(5AA) For the purposes of subsection (2)(b) to (d) above where—

(a) any shares (''new shares'') are exchanged for other shares (''old shares'') under arrangements in relation to which paragraph 10C of Schedule 28B applies, and

(b) those arrangements have not ceased by virtue of sub-paragraph (13) of that paragraph to be arrangements by reference to which requirements of that Schedule are deemed to be satisfied,

the value of the new shares, both at the time of their acquisition and immediately after any subsequent addition to a holding of the new shares that is made under those arrangements, shall be taken to be the same as the value, when last valued in accordance with subsection (5) above, of the old shares for which they are exchanged.

(5AB) References in subsection (5AA) above to shares in a company include references to any securities of that company.

(5AC) For the purposes of subsection (2)(b) to (d) above, where—

(a) shares (''new shares'') are issued to a company by virtue of the exercise by that company of any right of conversion attached to other shares, or securities, held by that company (''convertibles''), and

(b) paragraph 10D of Schedule 28B applies in relation to the issue of the new shares,

the value of the new shares at the time of their acquisition shall be taken to be the same as the value, when last valued in accordance with subsection (5) above, of the convertibles for which they are exchanged.][5]

[(5AD) Regulations under paragraph 11B of Schedule 28B may make provision for the purposes of subsection (2)(b) to (d) above for securing that where—

(a) there is an exchange of shares to which regulations under that paragraph apply, and

(b) the new shares are treated by virtue of the regulations as meeting the requirements of that Schedule,

the value of the holding of new shares, and of any original shares that are retained under the exchange, shall be taken to be an amount such that the requirements of subsection (2)(b) to (d) above do not cease to be met by reason of the exchange.

(5AE) In subsection (5AD) above—

(a) ''shares'' includes securities; and

(b) ''exchange of shares'', ''new shares'' and ''original shares'' have the same meaning as in paragraph 11B of Schedule 28B.][6]

[(5A) Subsection (5B) below applies[, subject to any regulations under paragraph 11 of Schedule 33 to the Finance Act 2002,][8] where—

(a) there has been an issue of ordinary share capital of a company ('the first issue'),

(b) an approval of that company for the purposes of this section has taken effect on or before the day of the making of the first issue, and

(c) a further issue of ordinary share capital of that company has been made since the making of the first issue.][3]

[(5B) Where this subsection applies, the use to which the money raised by the further issue is put, and the use of any money deriving from that use, shall be disregarded in determining whether any of the conditions specified in subsection (2)(b) and (c) above are, have been or will be fulfilled in relation to—

(a) the accounting period in which the further issue is made; or

(b) any later accounting period ending no more than three years after the making of the further issue.]³

(6) The Board may withdraw their approval of a company for the purposes of this section wherever it at any time appears to them that there are reasonable grounds for believing—

(a) that the conditions for the approval of the company were not fulfilled at the time of the approval;

(b) in a case where the Board were satisfied for the purposes of subsection (3) or (4) above that a condition would be fulfilled in relation to any period, that that condition is one which will not be or, as the case may be, has not been fulfilled in relation to that period;

(c) in the case of a company approved in pursuance of subsection (4) above, that the company has not fulfilled such other conditions as may be prescribed by regulations made by the Board in relation to, or to any part of, the period of three years mentioned in subsection (4)(b) above;

[(ca) in a case where the use of any money falls to be disregarded for any accounting period in accordance with subsection (5B) above—

(i) that the first accounting period of the company for which the use of that money will not be disregarded will be a period in relation to which a condition specified in subsection (2) above will fail to be fulfilled; or

(ii) that the company has not fulfilled such other conditions as may be prescribed by regulations made by the Board in relation to, or to any part of, an accounting period for which the use of that money falls to be disregarded;]³

or

(d) that the company's most recent complete accounting period or its current one is a period in relation to which there has been or will be a failure of a condition specified in subsection (2) above to be fulfilled, not being a failure which, at the time of the approval, was allowed for in relation to that period by virtue of subsection (4) above.

(7) Subject to subsections (8) and (9) below, the withdrawal of the approval of any company for the purposes of this section shall have effect as from the time when the notice of the withdrawal is given to the company.

(8) If, in the case of a company approved for the purposes of this section in exercise of the power conferred by subsection (4) above, the approval is withdrawn at a time before all the conditions specified in subsection (2) above have been fulfilled with respect to that company in relation either—

(a) to a complete accounting period of twelve months, or

(b) to successive complete accounting periods constituting a continuous period of twelve months or more,

the withdrawal of the approval shall have the effect that the approval shall, for all purposes, be deemed never to have been given.

(9) A notice withdrawing the approval of a company for the purposes of this section may specify a time falling before the time mentioned in subsection (7) above as the time as from which the withdrawal is to be treated as having taken effect for the purposes of section 100 of the 1992 Act; but the time so specified shall be no earlier than the beginning of the accounting period in relation to which it appears to the Board that the condition by reference to which the approval is withdrawn has not been, or will not be, fulfilled.

(10) Notwithstanding any limitation on the time for making assessments, an assessment to any tax chargeable in consequence of the withdrawal of any approval given for the purposes of this section may be made at any time before the end of the period of three years beginning with the time when the notice of withdrawal is given.

(11) The following provisions of section 842 shall apply as follows for the purposes of this section as they apply for the purposes of that section, that is to say—

[(za) subsection (1AB) of that section shall apply in relation to subsection (2)(a) above as it applies in relation to subsection (1)(a) of that section;]⁷

(a) subsections (1A) and (2) of that section shall apply in relation to subsection (2)(d) above (but with the omission of subsection (2)(a) of that section) as they apply in relation to subsection (1)(b) of that section;

(b) subsections [(1AB) and]⁷ (2A) to (2C) of that section shall apply in relation to subsection (2)(f) above as they apply in relation to subsection (1)(e) of that section; and

(c) without prejudice to their application in relation to provisions applied by paragraph (a) or (b) above, subsections (3) and (4) of that section shall apply in relation to any reference in this section to a holding or an addition to a holding as they apply in relation to any such reference in that section.

(12) In this section, and in the provisions of section 842 as applied for the purposes of this section, "securities", in relation to any company—

(a) includes any liability of the company in respect of a loan (whether secured or not) which has been made to the company on terms that do not allow any person to require the loan to be repaid, or any stock or security relating to that loan to be re-purchased or redeemed, within the period of five years from the making of the loan or, as the case may be, the issue of the stock or security; but (*b*) does not include any stock or security relating to a loan which has been made to the company on terms which allow any person to require the loan to be repaid, or the stock or security to be re-purchased or redeemed, within that period.

(13) Schedule 28B shall have effect for construing the references in this section to a qualifying holding.

(14) In this section "eligible shares" means shares in a company which are comprised in the ordinary share capital of the company and carry no present or future preferential right to dividends or to the company's assets on its winding up and no present or future ...[4] right to be redeemed.][1]

Commentary—*Simon's Direct Tax Service* E3.610.
Statement of Practice SP 8/95—Revenue do not consider a standard event of default clause in a loan agreement as disqualifying the loan from being a security within the meaning of sub-s (2) provided the loan is made on normal commercial terms.
Revenue & other press releases—IR 20-2-95 (shares listed on the Alternative Investment Market are not "quoted").
Definitions—"The 1992 Act", s 831(3); "accounting period", s 834(1); "the Board", s 832(1); "close company", s 832(1); "company", s 832(1); "ordinary share capital", s 832(1); "Tax Acts", s 831(2).
Cross references—See FA 2002 Sch 26 para 40 (collective investment schemes; excess of relevant credits over any relevant debits treated as income derived from shares or securities in determining whether a company may be approved for the purpose of this section).
FA 2002 Sch 33 para 11 (regulations may make provision to disapply, or limit operation of, sub-s (5B) above).
FA 2002 Sch 33 para 12 (regulations may make provision for withdrawal of VCT approval for the purposes of this section in cases for which provision made under FA 2002 Sch 33 para 11).
Venture Capital Trust Regulations, SI 1995/1979 regs 3–8 (procedure for approval as a venture capital trust for the purposes of this section).
Amendments—[1] Section inserted by FA 1995 s 70(1).
[2] Words in sub-s (2)(*e*) substituted by FA 1996 Sch 38 para 7(1), (2)(*c*), (4) with effect for accounting periods ending after 31 March 1996.
[3] Sub-ss (5A), (5B) and sub-s (6)(*ca*) inserted by FA 1997 s 75 and deemed always to have had effect.
[4] Word in sub-s (14) repealed by FA 1998 s 73(1) with effect for the purpose of determining whether shares or securities are, at any time after 5 April 1998, to be regarded as comprised in a company's qualifying holdings.
[5] Sub-ss (5AA)–(5AC) inserted by FA 1999 s 69(4), (5) with effect for any arrangements made, and rights of conversion exercised, after 15 June 1999.
[6] Sub-ss (5AD), (5AE) inserted by TA 1988 Sch 28B, para 11B (as inserted by FA 2000 s 65, Sch 18 para 8(2), (4)) with effect for exchanges of shares or securities (within the meaning of TA 1988 Sch 28B, para 11B(1)) taking effect after 20 March 2000.
[7] In sub-s (2)(*f*), words substituted for the words "more than", sub-s (11)(*za*), and words in sub-s (11)(*b*) inserted, by FA 2002 s 82, Sch 25 paras 43, 57 with effect for accounting periods beginning after 30 September 2002.
[8] In sub-s (5A), words inserted by FA 2002 s 109, Sch 33 para 13 with effect from 24 July 2002.

[842A Local authorities

(1) Except so far as the context otherwise requires, in the Tax Acts "local authority" means—

(*a*) in relation to England and Wales, an authority of a description specified for the purposes of this paragraph ...[6]
(*b*) in relation to Scotland, an authority of a description specified for the purposes of this paragraph ...[6], and
(*c*) in relation to Northern Ireland, an authority of a description specified for the purposes of this paragraph ...[6].

(2) The following are the descriptions of authority specified for the purposes of paragraph (*a*) of subsection (1) above—

[(*a*) a billing authority as defined in section 69 of the Local Government Finance Act 1992;][2]
[(*b*) a precepting authority as defined in that section;][2]
[(*c*) a body having power by virtue of regulations under section 74 of the Local Government Finance Act 1988 to issue a levy;][2]
(*d*) a body having power by virtue of regulations under section 75 of that Act to issue a special levy;
(*e*) ...[3]
(*f*) a fire authority constituted by a combination scheme under the Fire Services Act 1947;
(*g*) an authority having power to make or determine a rate.
[(*h*) a residuary body established by order under section 22(1) of the Local Government Act 1992;][4]

(3) The following are the descriptions of authority specified for the purposes of paragraph (*b*) of subsection (1) above—

[(*a*) a council constituted under section 2 of the Local Government etc (Scotland) Act 1994;][5]
(*d*) a joint board or committee within the meaning of the Local Government (Scotland) Act 1973
(*e*) an authority having power to requisition any sum from an authority [such as is mentioned in paragraph (*a*) above][5]

(4) The following are the descriptions of authority specified for the purposes of paragraph (*c*) of subsection (1) above—

(*a*) an authority having power to make or determine a rate;
(*b*) an authority having power to issue a precept, requisition or other demand for the payment of money to be raised out of a rate.

(5) In this section "rate" means a rate the proceeds of which are applicable for public local purposes and which is leviable by reference to the value of land or other property.][1]

Commentary—*Simon's Direct Tax Service* **D4.301.**
Statement of Practice SP 8/95—Revenue do not consider a standard event of default clause in a loan agreement as disqualifying the loan from being a security within the meaning of sub-s (2)(*a*) provided the loan is made on normal commercial terms.
Definition—"The Tax Acts", s 831(2).
Amendments—[1] This section inserted by FA 1990 s 127(1), (4) with effect from 1 April 1990.
[2] Sub-s (2)(*a*)–(*c*) substituted by the Local Government Finance Act 1992 s 117(2)(*d*) and Sch 13 para 57 with effect from 1 April 1993 by virtue of the Local Government Finance Act 1992 (Commencement No 6 and Transitional Provisions) Order 1992, SI 1992/2454.
[3] Sub-s (2)(*e*) repealed by the Police and Magistrates' Courts Act 1994 s 93, Sch 9 Pt I as from 1 April 1995, by virtue of the Police and Magistrates' Courts Act 1994 (Commencement No 5 and Transitional Provisions) Order 1994, SI 1994/3262.
[4] Sub-s (2)(*h*) inserted by FA 1995 s 144, with effect from 29 November 1994.
[5] Sub-s (3)(*a*) substituted for former paras (*a*)–(*c*) and words in sub-s (3)(*e*) substituted by the Local Government (Scotland) Act 1994 Sch 13 para 155, as from 1 April 1996 (SI 1996/323).
[6] Words in sub-s (1)(*a*), (*b*) and (*c*) inserted by Police Act 1997 s 134(1) Sch 9 para 53 with effect from 1 April 1998 (SI 1998/354) and repealed by the Criminal Justice and Police Act 2001 s 128, Sch 6 Pt 3 para 71 with effect from 1 April 2002 (by virtue of SI 2002/344).

[842B Meaning of "investment LLP" and "property investment LLP"

(1) In this Act—

   (*a*) an "investment LLP" means a limited liability partnership whose business consists wholly or mainly in the making of investments and the principal part of whose income is derived therefrom; and

   (*b*) a "property investment LLP" means a limited liability partnership whose business consists wholly or mainly in the making of investments in land and the principal part of whose income is derived therefrom.

(2) Whether a limited liability partnership is an investment LLP or a property investment LLP is determined for each period of account of the partnership.

...[2]][1]

Amendments—[1] Section inserted by FA 2001 s 76, Sch 25 para 1(1) with effect from 6 April 2001.
[2] Words repealed by FA 2002 s 141, Sch 40 Pt 3(16) with effect from 24 July 2002. Words previously read as follows—
"A "period of account" means any period for which accounts of the partnership are drawn up.".

Commencement, savings, repeals etc

843 Commencement

(1) Except as otherwise provided by the following provisions of this section, this Act shall come into force in relation to tax for the year 1988–89 and subsequent years of assessment, and for companies' accounting periods ending after 5th April 1988.

(2) Except as otherwise provided by the following provisions of this section, such of the provisions of this Act as relate to capital gains tax (including the provisions of Part XVIII as applied to capital gains tax by section [277 of [the 1992 Act][3]][2]) shall come into force in relation to that tax for the year 1988–89 and subsequent years of assessment.

(3) The following provisions of this Act, that is to say—

   (*a*) so much of any provision as authorises the making of any Order in Council or regulations or other instrument;

   (*b*) so much of any provision as relates to the making of a return, the furnishing of a certificate or the giving of any other information, including any such provision which imposes a duty on the Board or an officer of the Board as well as any such provision which imposes a duty on any other person;

   (*c*) so much of any provision as imposes any penalty;

   (*d*) except where the tax concerned is all tax for years of assessment before the year 1988–89 or accounting periods ending before 6th April 1988, so much of any other provision as confers any power or imposes any duty the exercise or performance of which operates or may operate in relation to tax for more than one chargeable period,

shall come into force for all purposes on 6th April 1988 to the exclusion of the corresponding enactments repealed by this Act.

(4) This section has effect except as otherwise provided by any other provision of this Act, and in particular except as provided by sections 96, 380 to 384, 393, ...[1] 400, 703 and 812.

Definitions—"The 1992 Act", s 831(3); "accounting periods", s 834(1); "the Board", s 832(1); "chargeable period", s 832(1); "tax", s 832(3); "the year 1988–89", s 832(1); "years of assessment", s 832(1).
Amendments—[1] "394" in sub-s (4) repealed by FA 1991 Sch 15 para 24 and Sch 19 Pt V.
[2] Words in sub-s (2) substituted by TCGA 1992 Sch 10 para 14(1), (56).
[3] Words in sub-s (2) substituted by FA 1994 s 146, Sch 17 para 8, and deemed always to have had effect.

844 Savings, transitional provisions, consequential amendments and repeals

(1) Schedule 29, which makes amendments to other enactments consequential on the passing of this Act, shall have effect.

(2) Schedule 29, section 843 and this section are without prejudice to the provisions of the Interpretation Act 1978 as respects the effect of repeals.

(3) Schedule 30 which contains savings and transitional provisions shall have effect.

(4) The enactments mentioned in Schedule 31 are hereby repealed to the extent specified in the third column of that Schedule.

(5) Subject to subsection (6) below, section 843(3), Schedule 30 and to any other provision of this Act by which any provision is brought into force to the exclusion of the corresponding enactments repealed by this Act, those repeals shall come into force in accordance with subsections (1) and (2) of section 843.

(6) No provision mentioned in subsection (5) above shall be taken as bringing a repeal into force except to the extent that the repealed enactment is being superseded.

845 Short title

This Act may be cited as the Income and Corporation Taxes Act 1988.

SCHEDULES

SCHEDULE 1

RESTRICTIONS ON SCHEDULE A DEDUCTIONS

Section 31

Expenditure before 1964–65: deductions from rents

Commentary—*Simon's Direct Tax Service* **A4.323.**
Amendments—This Schedule repealed by FA 1998 s 165, Sch 27 Part III(4) with effect from 1998–99 for income tax purposes and from 1 April 1998 for corporation tax, subject to the transitional provisions in FA 1998 Sch 5 Part IV.

SCHEDULE 2

PREMIUMS ETC TAXABLE UNDER SCHEDULES A AND D: SPECIAL RELIEF FOR INDIVIDUALS

Section 39(3)

Amendments—This Schedule repealed by FA 1988 s 75 and Sch 14 Pt IV with effect from the year 1988–89.

SCHEDULE 3

MACHINERY FOR ASSESSMENT, CHARGE AND PAYMENT OF INCOME TAX UNDER SCHEDULE C AND, IN CERTAIN CASES, SCHEDULE D

Section 44(2)

Amendments—This Schedule repealed by FA 1996 Sch 7 paras 27, 32, Sch 41 Pt V(2) with effect from the year 1996–97 subject to savings and transitional provisions in FA 1996 Sch 7 paras 33, 35 in relation to the obligations of a person under this Schedule to set apart, retain or pay any amount of tax for the period between 6 April 1996 and 29 April 1996.

SCHEDULE 4

DEEP DISCOUNT SECURITIES

Section 57

Commentary—*Simon's Direct Tax Service* **D2.1165.**
Amendments—This Schedule repealed by FA 1996 ss 104, 105(1), Sch 14 para 50, Sch 41 Pt V(3) with effect so far as relating to income tax, for the year 1996–97, and for the purposes of corporation tax for accounting periods ending after 31 March 1996, subject to transitional provisions in FA 1996 Sch 15.

[SCHEDULE 4A

CREATIVE ARTISTS: RELIEF FOR FLUCTUATING PROFITS][1]

Section 95A

Amendments—[1] This Schedule inserted by FA 2001 s 71(2), Sch 24 para 1 with effect from 11 May 2001. The provisions in this Schedule apply for the year 2000–01 and subsequent years of assessment (so that the first years which may be the subject of a averaging claim are 2000–01 and 2001–02) by virtue of TA 1988 s 95A.

[Introduction

1 This Schedule enables an individual ("the taxpayer") to make a claim (an "averaging claim") if his profits from a qualifying trade, profession or vocation (his "relevant profits") fluctuate from one tax year to the next.][1]

Commentary—*Simon's Direct Tax Service* **B3.835**.
Amendments—[1] This Schedule inserted by FA 2001 s 71(2), Sch 24 para 1 with effect as stated in the note at the start of this Schedule.

[Qualifying trade, profession or vocation

2—(1) A trade, profession or vocation is a "qualifying trade, profession or vocation" if the taxpayer's profits from it—

(a) are derived wholly or mainly from qualifying creative works, and
(b) are chargeable to tax under Case I or II of Schedule D.

(2) In sub-paragraph (1) "qualifying creative works" means—

(a) literary, dramatic, musical or artistic works, or
(b) designs,

created by the taxpayer personally or, where the trade, profession or vocation is carried on by the taxpayer in partnership, by one or more of the partners personally.][1]

Commentary—*Simon's Direct Tax Service* **B3.835**.
Amendments—[1] This Schedule inserted by FA 2001 s 71(2), Sch 24 para 1 with effect as stated in the note at the start of this Schedule.

[Circumstances in which claim may be made

3—(1) An averaging claim may be made if the taxpayer has been carrying on the qualifying trade, profession or vocation in two consecutive tax years and either—

(a) his relevant profits for one of the tax years are less than 75% of his relevant profits for the other, or
(b) his relevant profits for one (but not both) of the tax years are nil.

(2) For the purposes of paragraph 4 (years in respect of which averaging claim may be made) an averaging claim relates to both of the years involved.][1]

Commentary—*Simon's Direct Tax Service* **B3.836**.
Amendments—[1] This Schedule inserted by FA 2001 s 71(2), Sch 24 para 1 with effect as stated in the note at the start of this Schedule.

[Years in respect of which claim may be made

4—(1) An averaging claim may not be made in relation to a tax year if an averaging claim in respect of the same qualifying trade, profession or vocation has already been made in relation to a later tax year.

(2) An averaging claim may not be made in relation to a tax year in which—

(a) the taxpayer starts, or permanently ceases, to carry on the trade, profession or vocation, or
(b) the trade, profession or vocation begins or ceases to be a qualifying trade, profession or vocation.

(3) An averaging claim may be made in relation to a tax year which was the later year on a previous averaging claim.][1]

Commentary—*Simon's Direct Tax Service* **B3.836**.
Amendments—[1] This Schedule inserted by FA 2001 s 71(2), Sch 24 para 1 with effect as stated in the note at the start of this Schedule.

[Time limit for claim

5 An averaging claim must be made not later than twelve months after the 31st January next following the end of the later of the tax years to which it relates.

This is subject to paragraph 10(2) (extended time limit where profits adjusted for some other reason).][1]

Commentary—*Simon's Direct Tax Service* **B3.836; E1.835**.
Amendments—[1] This Schedule inserted by FA 2001 s 71(2), Sch 24 para 1 with effect as stated in the note at the start of this Schedule.

[Adjustment of profits on averaging claim

6—(1) Where the taxpayer is entitled to make, and makes, an averaging claim, the amount taken to be his profits from the qualifying trade, profession or vocation for each of the tax years to which the claim relates is adjusted in accordance with this paragraph.

(2) If—

(*a*) the taxpayer's relevant profits for one of the years amount to 70% or less of his relevant profits for the other year, or

(*b*) the taxpayer's relevant profits for one (but not both) of the years are nil,

the amount of the adjusted profits for each of the years to which the claim relates is the average of the relevant profits for the two years.

(3) If the taxpayer's relevant profits for one of the years amount to more than 70%, but less than 75%, of his relevant profits for the other year, the amount of the profits in each of the years is calculated as follows, so as to reduce the variation between them.

Step 1 The amount of the adjustment is given by the formula—

where—

$$(D \times 3) - (P \times 0.75)$$

D is the difference between the taxpayer's relevant profits for the two tax years, and

P is the taxpayer's relevant profits for the year in which those profits are higher.

Step 2 Add the amount of the adjustment to the taxpayer's relevant profits for the year in which those profits are lower.

The result is the amount of the adjusted profits for that year.

Step 3 Subtract the amount of the adjustment from the taxpayer's relevant profits for the year in which those profits are higher.

The result is the amount of the adjusted profits for that year.

(4) Subject to the following provisions of this Schedule, the adjusted profits are taken to be the taxpayer's relevant profits for the years to which the claim relates for all the purposes of the Income Tax Acts, including the further application of this Schedule.]¹

Commentary—*Simon's Direct Tax Service* **B3.837**.
Amendments—¹ This Schedule inserted by FA 2001 s 71(2), Sch 24 para 1 with effect as stated in the note at the start of this Schedule.

[How averaging claim is given effect

7—(1) An averaging claim relating to two tax years (''the earlier year'' and ''the later year'') is given effect in the later year.

(2) In so far as the claim involves an adjustment to the profits for the earlier year it is treated as a claim for the amount of the difference between—

(*a*) the amount in which the taxpayer is chargeable to tax for the earlier year (''amount A''), and

(*b*) the amount in which he would be so chargeable if effect were given to the adjustment in that year (''amount B'').

(3) That claim is given effect in the later year by increasing the amount referred to in section 59B(1)(*b*) of the Management Act (aggregate amount of payments on account made by the taxpayer) or, as the case may require, by increasing the amount of tax payable.

(4) Where effect falls to be given to two or more associated claims, amounts A and B above shall each be determined on the assumption that effect could have been, and had been, given to the other claim or claims in relation to the earlier year.

(5) Where this paragraph applies twice in relation to the same tax year, the increase or reduction in the amount of tax payable for that year as a result of the earlier application shall be disregarded in determining amounts A and B above for the purposes of the later application.]¹

Commentary—*Simon's Direct Tax Service* **B3.837**.
Amendments—¹ This Schedule inserted by FA 2001 s 71(2), Sch 24 para 1 with effect as stated in the note at the start of this Schedule.

[Extension of time for making other claims

8—(1) A claim by the taxpayer for relief under any other provision of the Income Tax Acts for either of the years to which an averaging claim relates (''the other claim'')—

(*a*) is not out of time if made on or before the last date on which the averaging claim could have been made, and

(*b*) if already made, may be amended or revoked on or before that date.

(2) If the other claim is made by being included in a return, the reference in sub-paragraph (1)(*b*) to amending or revoking the claim shall be read as a reference to amending the return by amending or omitting the claim.]¹

Commentary—*Simon's Direct Tax Service* **B3.837; E1.835**.
Amendments—¹ This Schedule inserted by FA 2001 s 71(2), Sch 24 para 1 with effect as stated in the note at the start of this Schedule.

[Giving effect to late claim for other relief

9—(1) This paragraph applies where—

(*a*) the taxpayer makes or amends a claim for relief under any other provision of the Income Tax Acts for either of the years to which an averaging claim relates, and

(*b*) the making or amendment of the claim would be out of time but for paragraph 8.

(2) The claim or amendment is given effect in the later year.

(3) In so far as the claim or amendment relates to income of the earlier year, the amount claimed, or (as the case may be) the increase or reduction in the amount claimed, shall be equal to the difference between—

(a) the amount in which the taxpayer is chargeable to tax for the earlier year (''amount A''), and
(b) the amount in which he would be so chargeable on the assumption that effect could be, and was, given to the claim or amendment in relation to that year (''amount B'').

(4) That claim or amendment is given effect in the later year by increasing the amount referred to in section 59B(1)(b) of the Management Act (aggregate amount of payments on account made by the taxpayer) or, as the case may require, by increasing the amount of tax payable.

(5) Where effect falls to be given to two or more associated claims, amounts A and B above shall each be determined on the assumption that effect could have been, and had been, given to the other claim or claims in relation to the earlier year.

(6) In this paragraph ''amend'' includes revoke and ''amendment'' has a corresponding meaning.]¹

Commentary—*Simon's Direct Tax Service* **B3.837**.
Amendments—¹ This Schedule inserted by FA 2001 s 71(2), Sch 24 para 1 with effect as stated in the note at the start of this Schedule.

[Effect of later adjustment of profits

10—(1) If after the taxpayer has made an averaging claim, his relevant profits in either or both of the tax years to which the claim relates are adjusted for some other reason—

(a) the averaging claim shall be disregarded, and
(b) a further averaging claim may be made in relation to the taxpayer's relevant profits as adjusted.

(2) A further averaging claim is not out of time provided it is made not later than twelve months after the 31st January next following the tax year in which the adjustment for the other reason is made.]¹

Commentary—*Simon's Direct Tax Service* **B3.836; E1.835**.
Amendments—¹ This Schedule inserted by FA 2001 s 71(2), Sch 24 para 1 with effect as stated in the note at the start of this Schedule.

[Interpretation of references to profits

11—(1) References in this Schedule to the taxpayer's profits from a qualifying trade, profession or vocation are to profits before making deductions for losses sustained in any tax year.

(2) If the taxpayer sustains a loss in the qualifying trade, profession or vocation in any tax year, the profits of that year for the purposes of this Schedule are nil.

This shall not be read as preventing the taxpayer from obtaining relief under the Income Tax Acts for a loss sustained by him in that or any other tax year.]¹

Commentary—*Simon's Direct Tax Service* **B3.836**.
Amendments—¹ This Schedule inserted by FA 2001 s 71(2), Sch 24 para 1 with effect as stated in the note at the start of this Schedule.

[Interpretation of references to amount chargeable to tax

12 In this Schedule any reference to the amount in which a person is chargeable to tax is a reference to the amount in which he is so chargeable after taking into account any relief or allowance for which a claim is made.]¹

Amendments—¹ This Schedule inserted by FA 2001 s 71(2), Sch 24 para 1 with effect as stated in the note at the start of this Schedule.

[Meaning of ''claim'' and ''associated claim''

13—(1) In this Schedule any reference to a claim includes a reference to an election or notice.

(2) For the purposes of this Schedule, two or more claims made by the same person are associated with each other if each of them is any of the following—

(a) a claim to which this Schedule applies, or
(b) a claim to which Schedule 1B to the Management Act applies (other claims involving more than one year to be given effect in later year),

and the same tax year is the earlier year in relation to each of those claims.

(3) In sub-paragraph (2)—

(a) the reference to a claim to which this Schedule applies includes amendments and revocations to which paragraph 9 above applies;
(b) the reference to a claim to which Schedule 1B to the Management Act applies includes amendments and revocations to which paragraph 4 of that Schedule applies.]¹

Commentary—*Simon's Direct Tax Service* **B3.837**.
Amendments—¹ This Schedule inserted by FA 2001 s 71(2), Sch 24 para 1 with effect as stated in the note at the start of this Schedule.

[Meaning of "tax year"

14 In this Schedule a "tax year" means a year of assessment.][1]

Amendments—[1] This Schedule inserted by FA 2001 s 71(2), Sch 24 para 1 with effect as stated in the note at the start of this Schedule.

SCHEDULE 5

TREATMENT OF FARM ANIMALS ETC FOR PURPOSES OF CASE I OF SCHEDULE D

Section 97

Concession B37—Herd basis may be applied to a share in an animal and to shares in single production animals or animals forming part of a herd.
Concession B56—Slaughter of immature animals intended to be replacements. Farmers entitled to treat animals slaughtered as a result of the outbreak of foot and mouth disease in 2001 as if they had entered the herd before slaughter.
Revenue Interpretation RI 19—Fresh herd basis election is required after a change in the membership of a partnership if herd basis treatment is to continue.
RI 173—Confirms that the view expressed in the Revenue Interpretation RI 19 continues to apply under the self-assessment rules for partnerships, and gives details of the form of election required.
RI 235—Herd basis election does not lapse if a partnership converts to a Limited Liability Partnership (LLP) without a change in membership.
Revenue & other press releases—IR Tax Bulletin February 1997 p 396 (effect of BSE compensation payments where herd basis applies).

Farming: the general rule

1—(1) Subject to the provisions of this Schedule, in computing [profits][1] under Case I of Schedule D, animals kept by a farmer for the purposes of his farming shall be treated as trading stock.

(2) Animals forming part of production herds with respect to which an election under paragraph 2 below has effect shall not be so treated, but shall be treated instead in accordance with the rules set out in paragraph 3 below.

(3) An election under paragraph 2 below is referred to in this Schedule as "an election for the herd basis".

Commentary—*Simon's Direct Tax Service* B3.515.
Concession B11—Compensation for compulsory slaughter of animals treated as trading stock under sub-para (1) above may be spread over three years following the year of slaughter.
Revenue Interpretation 235—For cattle borne in the year of slaughter profit can be computed as compensation less 60%.
Definitions—"Profits or gains", s 833(1); "Schedule D", s 18(1).
Amendments—[1] Word in sub-para (1) substituted by FA 1998 Sch 7 para 1 with effect from 31 July 1998.

Farming: election for the herd basis

2—(1) An election for the herd basis shall apply to all production herds of a particular class kept by the farmer making the election, including herds which he has ceased to keep before, or first begins to keep after, the making of the election.

(2) An election for the herd basis must be made in writing to the inspector, and must specify the class of herds to which it relates.

(3) Subject to paragraphs 6 and 12 below, an election for the herd basis made by any farmer shall be valid only if it is made—

[(a) in the case of an election by a person chargeable to income tax, not later than twelve months from the 31st January next following the qualifying year of assessment;
(b) in the case of an election on behalf of persons in partnership, not later than twelve months from the 31st January next following the year of assessment in which the qualifying period of account ends; and
(c) in the case of an election by a person chargeable to corporation tax, not later than two years from the end of the qualifying accounting period.][1]

(4) An election for the herd basis made by any farmer shall be irrevocable and, subject to paragraph 6 below, shall have effect—

[(a) in a case falling within sub-paragraph (3)(a) above, for the qualifying year of assessment and all subsequent years;
(b) in a case falling within sub-paragraph (3)(b) above, for the qualifying period of account and all subsequent periods of account; and
(c) in a case falling within sub-paragraph (3)(c) above, for the qualifying accounting period and all subsequent accounting periods.][1]

[(5) Where, in a case falling within sub-paragraph (3)(a) above, the commencement year immediately precedes the qualifying year of assessment, sub-paragraph (4)(a) above shall have effect as if the reference to the qualifying year of assessment were a reference to the commencement year.][1]

[(6) In this paragraph—

"commencement year", in relation to a person chargeable to income tax, means the year of assessment in which his trade is set up and commenced;

...[3]

"qualifying accounting period", in relation to a person chargeable to corporation tax, means the first accounting period during the whole or part of which it kept a production herd of the class in question;

"qualifying period of account", in relation to persons in partnership, means the first period of account during the whole or part of which those persons kept such a herd;

"qualifying year of assessment", in relation to a person chargeable to income tax, means the first year of assessment after the commencement year for which the amount of [profits][2] or losses in respect of his farming is computed for tax purposes by reference to the facts of a period during the whole or part of which he kept such a herd.][1]

Commentary—*Simon's Direct Tax Service* B3.516; E1.835.
Revenue Interpretations RI 19—Fresh herd basis election is required after a change in the membership of a partnership if herd basis treatment is to continue.
RI 173—Confirms that the view expressed in the Revenue Interpretation RI 19 continues to apply under the self-assessment rules for partnerships, and gives details of the form of election required.
Definitions—"Accounting period", s 834(1); "chargeable period", s 832(1); "inspector", s 832(1); "profits or gains", s 833(1); "trade", s 832(1); "year of assessment", s 832(1).
Amendments—[1] Words in sub-paras (3), (4) substituted and sub-paras (5), (6) added by FA 1994 ss 196, 199(2)(a) and Sch 19 para 43 with effect from the year 1996–97.
[2] Word in sub-para (6) substituted by FA 1998 Sch 7 para 1 with effect from 31 July 1998.
[3] Definition of "period of account" repealed by FA 2002 s 141, Sch 40 Pt 3(16) with effect from 24 July 2002. Definition previously read thus—
   " 'period of account', in relation to persons in partnership, means any period for which accounts are drawn up;".

3—(1) Where an election for the herd basis has effect, the consequences for the purposes of computing [profits][1] under Case I of Schedule D shall be as provided by this paragraph.

(2) The initial cost of the herd and, subject to the provisions of this paragraph as to replacements, the cost of any animal added to the herd shall not be deducted as an expense and the value of the herd shall not be brought into account.

(3) Where an animal which has theretofore been treated as part of the farmer's trading stock is added to the herd otherwise than by way of replacement, there shall be included as a trading receipt—

(a) in the case of an animal bred by the farmer, a sum equal to the cost of breeding it and rearing it to maturity; and

(b) in any other case, a sum equal to the initial cost to the farmer of acquiring the animal, together with any cost incurred by him in rearing it to maturity.

(4) Where an animal (the "first animal") forming part of the herd dies, or ceases to form part of the herd, and is replaced in the herd by another animal (the "second animal")—

(a) any proceeds of sale of the first animal shall be included as a trading receipt; and

(b) the cost of the second animal, except in so far as that cost consists of such costs as are allowable apart from the provisions of this Schedule as deductions in computing [profits][1] of farming under Case I of Schedule D, shall, subject to sub-paragraphs (5) and (6) below, be deducted as an expense.

(5) Where the second animal is of better quality than the first animal, the amount deducted shall not exceed the amount which it would have been necessary to expend in order to acquire an animal of the same quality as the first animal.

(6) Where the first animal was slaughtered by the order of any Ministry, government department or local or public authority under the law relating to diseases of animals, and the second animal is of worse quality, the amount included as a trading receipt shall not exceed the amount allowable as a deduction.

(7) Where the herd is sold as a whole, and another production herd of the same class is acquired, sub-paragraphs (1) to (6) above shall apply as though there had been sold from, and replaced in, the original herd a number of animals equal to the number in the original herd or in the newly acquired herd, whichever is the less.

(8) Subject to sub-paragraph (9) below, if (either all at once or over a period not exceeding 12 months) either—

(a) the whole of a herd is sold in circumstances in which sub-paragraph (7) above does not apply, or

(b) a part of a herd is sold on a substantial reduction being made in the number of animals in the herd,

any profit or loss arising from the transaction shall not be taken into account.

(9) Where within five years of the sale the seller acquires or begins to acquire another production herd of the class in question or, as the case may be, acquires or begins to acquire animals to replace the part of the herd in question—

(a) sub-paragraphs (4) to (7) above shall apply to the acquisition or replacement, except that, if the sale was one which the seller was compelled to effect by causes wholly beyond his control, the amount included as a trading receipt in respect of any animal sold which is replaced by an animal of worse quality shall not exceed the amount allowable as a deduction in respect of that animal of worse quality; and

(*b*) for the purpose of the application of those sub-paragraphs, the proceeds of sale of the animals comprised in the original herd or part of a herd shall be brought into account as if they had been respectively received at the times of the corresponding acquisitions.

(10) If an animal forming part of the herd is sold, and none of sub-paragraphs (4) to (9) above applies, any profit or loss arising from the transaction shall be included or deducted, as the case may be; and for the purposes of this sub-paragraph, that profit or loss shall be computed by comparing with the proceeds of sale—

(*a*) in the case of an animal bred by the farmer, the cost of breeding it and rearing it to maturity; and

(*b*) in any other case, a sum equal to the initial cost to the farmer of acquiring the animal (or in the case of an animal acquired otherwise than for valuable consideration, its market value when the farmer acquired it) together, in both cases, with any cost incurred by him in rearing it to maturity.

(11) Where the herd is sold as a whole, and another production herd of the same class is acquired, and the number of animals in the newly acquired herd is less than the number in the original herd, then, if the difference is not substantial, sub-paragraphs (8) and (9) above shall not apply, and sub-paragraph (10) above shall apply to a number of animals in the original herd equal to the difference.

(12) The preceding provisions of this paragraph shall apply in relation to the death or destruction of animals as they apply in relation to their sale, as if any insurance or compensation moneys received by reason of the death or destruction were proceeds of sale, and any reference in this paragraph to the proceeds of sale of an animal includes a reference to any proceeds of sale of its carcass or any part of its carcass.

Commentary—*Simon's Direct Tax Service* **B3.518.**
Definitions—"Local ... authority", ss 519(4), 832(1); "profits or gains", s 833(1); "Schedule D", s 18(1).
Cross references—See TA 1988 Sch 6 para 3 (reduction of cash equivalent where car used mainly for business purposes).
Amendments—¹ Word in sub-paras 3(1) and (4)(*b*) substituted by FA 1998 Sch 7 para 1 with effect from 31 July 1998.

Farming: provisions applicable to special cases

4 A farmer who, having kept a production herd of a particular class, ceases altogether to keep herds of that class for a period of at least five years shall, as respects production herds kept by him after the end of that period, be treated as if he had never kept any production herds of that class before the end of that period.

Commentary—*Simon's Direct Tax Service* **B3.519.**

5—(1) Where a farmer transfers to another person all or any of the animals which form part of a production herd otherwise than by way of sale or by way of sale but for a price other than that which they would have fetched if sold in the open market, and either—

(*a*) the transferor is a body of persons over whom the transferee has control or the transferee is a body of persons over whom the transferor has control or both the transferor and the transferee are bodies of persons and some other person has control over both of them; or

(*b*) it appears with respect to the transfer, or with respect to transactions of which the transfer is one that the sole or main benefit, or one of the main benefits, which (apart from the provisions of this paragraph) might have been expected to accrue to the parties or any of them was a benefit resulting from—

(i) the obtaining of a right to make an election for the herd basis, or

(ii) such an election having effect or ceasing to have effect, or

(iii) such an election having a greater effect or a less effect;

the like consequences shall ensue, in relation to all persons concerned, for the purpose of computing [profits]¹ under Case I of Schedule D as would have ensued if the animals had been sold for the price which they would have fetched if sold in the open market.

(2) In this paragraph "body of persons" includes a partnership, and "control" has the meaning given by section 840.

Commentary—*Simon's Direct Tax Service* **B3.519.**
Definitions—"Profits or gains", s 833(1); "Schedule D", s 18(1).
Amendments—¹ Word in sub-para (1) substituted by FA 1998 Sch 7 para 1 with effect from 31 July 1998.

6—(1) Where the whole or a substantial part of a production herd kept by a farmer for the purposes of his farming is slaughtered by the order of any Ministry, government department or local or public authority under the law relating to the diseases of animals in such circumstances that compensation is payable in respect of it, an election for the herd basis thereupon made by the farmer in relation to that herd and any other production herds of the same class so kept by him shall, subject to sub-paragraph (2) below, be valid notwithstanding that it is not made within the time required by paragraph 2(3) above.

[(2) An election for the herd basis made by virtue of sub-paragraph (1) above shall only be valid if made—

(*a*) in the case of an election by a person chargeable to income tax, not later than twelve months from the 31st January next following the qualifying year of assessment;

(*b*) in the case of an election on behalf of persons in partnership, not later than twelve months from the 31st January next following the year of assessment in which the qualifying period of account ends; and

(*c*) in the case of an election by a person chargeable to corporation tax, not later than two years from the end of the qualifying accounting period.]¹

(3) An election for the herd basis made by virtue of sub-paragraph (1) above shall, notwithstanding paragraph 2(4) above, have effect—

(*a*) in a case falling within sub-paragraph (2)(*a*) above, for the qualifying year of assessment and all subsequent years;

(*b*) in a case falling within sub-paragraph (2)(*b*) above, for the qualifying period of account and all subsequent periods of account; and

(*c*) in a case falling within sub-paragraph (2)(*c*) above, for the qualifying accounting period and all subsequent accounting periods.]¹

[(4) In this paragraph—
...³

"qualifying accounting period", in relation to a person chargeable to corporation tax, means the first accounting period in which the compensation is relevant;

"qualifying period of account", in relation to persons in partnership, means the first period of account in which the compensation is relevant;

"qualifying year of assessment", in relation to a person chargeable to income tax, means the first year of assessment for which the amount of [profits]² or losses in respect of his farming falls to be computed for tax purposes by reference to the facts of a period in which the compensation is relevant.]¹

(5) For the purposes of this paragraph, compensation shall be deemed to be relevant in any period if, but only if, it falls (or would but for an election under this paragraph fall) to be taken into account as a trading receipt in computing the [profits]² or losses of that or an earlier period.

Commentary—*Simon's Direct Tax Service* **B3.517; E1.835.**
Definitions—"Accounting period", s 834(1); "chargeable period", s 832(1); "profits or gains", s 833(1); "tax", s 832(3); "year of assessment", s 832(1).
Amendments—¹ Sub-paras (2)–(4) substituted by FA 1994 ss 196, 199(2)(*a*) and Sch 19 para 43 with effect from the year 1996–97.
² Word in sub-paras (4) and (5) substituted by FA 1998 Sch 7 para 1 with effect from 31 July 1998.
³ Definition of "period of account" repealed by FA 2002 s 141, Sch 40 Pt 3(16) with effect from 24 July 2002. Definition previously read thus—

"'period of account', in relation to persons in partnership, means any period for which accounts are drawn up;".

Exclusion of working animals, and interpretation of preceding provisions

7 Nothing in this Schedule applies to any animals kept wholly or mainly for the work they do in connection with the carrying on of the farming.

Commentary—*Simon's Direct Tax Service* **B3.519.**

8—(1) In this Schedule "herd" includes a flock, and any other collection of animals however named.

(2) For the purposes of this Schedule, immature animals kept in a herd shall not be treated as forming part of the herd unless—

(*a*) the land on which the herd is kept is such that animals which die or cease to form part of the herd cannot be replaced except by animals bred and reared on that land; and

(*b*) the immature animals in question are bred in the herd, are maintained in the herd for the purpose of replacement, and are necessarily maintained for that purpose;

and references in this Schedule to herds shall be construed accordingly.

(3) References in this Schedule to an animal being added to a herd include references to an immature animal which is kept in the herd becoming a mature animal except that not more immature animals shall be treated as forming part of a herd than are required to prevent a fall in the numbers of the herd.

(4) Female animals shall be treated for the purposes of this Schedule as becoming mature when they produce their first young.

(5) In this Schedule "a production herd" means, in relation to a farmer, a herd of animals of the same species (irrespective of breed) kept by him wholly or mainly for the sake of the products which they produce for him to sell, being products obtainable from the living animal.

In this sub-paragraph "products obtainable from the living animal" means—

(*a*) the young of the animal, or

(*b*) any other product obtainable from the animal, not being a product obtainable only by slaughtering the animal itself.

(6) For the purposes of this Schedule, production herds kept by a farmer shall be deemed to be of the same class if, and only if, all the animals kept in the herds are of the same species (irrespective

of breed) and the products produced for him to sell for the sake of which (either wholly or mainly) the herds are kept by him are of the same kinds in the case of all the herds; and elections for the herd basis shall be framed accordingly.

(7) Any reference in this Schedule to [profits][1] chargeable to tax under Schedule D includes a reference to [profits][1] which would be so chargeable if there were any such [profits][1] for the chargeable period in question.

Commentary—*Simon's Direct Tax Service* **B3.516.**
Concession B56—Slaughter of immature animals intended to be replacements. Farmers entitled to treat animals slaughtered as a result of the outbreak of foot and mouth disease in 2001 as if they had entered the herd before the slaughter. Concession does not apply to animals intended to be additions to a herd.
RI 235—Herd basis election does not lapse if a partnership converts to a Limited Liability Partnership (LLP) without a change in membership.
Definitions—''Chargeable period'', s 832(1); ''profits or gains'', s 833(1); ''Schedule D'', s 18(1).
Amendments—[1] Word in sub-para (7) substituted by FA 1998 Sch 7 para 1 with effect from 31 July 1998.

Application of preceding provisions to trades other than farming, creatures other than animals, and animals and creatures kept singly

9—(1) The preceding provisions of this Schedule shall, with the necessary adaptations, apply in relation to trades other than farming, and trades consisting only in part of farming as they apply in relation to farming, and references to farmers shall be construed accordingly.

(2) Those provisions shall (both in relation to farming and in relation to other trades) apply in relation to living creatures other than animals as they apply in relation to animals.

(3) Laying birds shall be treated for the purposes of this Schedule as becoming mature when they first lay.

(4) The provisions of this Schedule shall (both in relation to farming and in relation to other trades) apply, with the necessary adaptations,—

　[(a) in relation to animals or other creatures kept singly as they apply in relation to herds; and
　(b) in relation to shares in animals or other creatures as they apply in relation to animals or other creatures themselves.][1]

(5) Nothing in this Schedule shall apply in relation to any animal or other creature kept wholly or mainly for public exhibition or for racing or other competitive purposes.

Commentary—*Simon's Direct Tax Service* **B3.515.**
Amendment—[1] Words in sub-para (4) substituted by FA 2000 s 76(2), (3) and deemed always to have had effect.

Supplemental and saving

10 Where an election for the herd basis is made, every person carrying on any farming or other trade affected by the election shall, if required to do so by notice from the inspector, make and deliver to the inspector, within the time specified in the notice, such returns as to, and as to the products of, the animals or other creatures kept by him for the purposes of the trade as may be required by the notice.

Commentary—*Simon's Direct Tax Service* **B3.521.**
Definitions—''Inspector'', s 832(1); ''notice'', s 832(1); ''trade'', s 832(1).

11 Where an election for the herd basis has effect for any chargeable period after an assessment for that period has become final and conclusive, any such assessment or, on a claim therefor, repayment of tax shall be made as may be necessary to give effect to the election.

Commentary—*Simon's Direct Tax Service* **B3.521.**
Definitions—''Chargeable period'', s 832(1); ''tax'', s 832(3).

12 The validity of an election for the herd basis in force immediately before the commencement of this Schedule and made in pursuance of—

　(a) section 35 of the Finance Act 1973 on or after 25th July 1973 and before 6th April 1976, or
　(b) section 48(6) to (9) of the Finance Act 1984

shall not be affected by the repeal of those sections by this Act.

[SCHEDULE 5AA

GUARANTEED RETURNS ON TRANSACTIONS IN FUTURES AND OPTIONS

Section 127A

Cross references—See TA 1988 s 399(1A) (relief for a loss arising from a transaction to which this Schedule applies is no precluded by section 399).
Amendments—[1] This Schedule inserted by FA 1997 s 80(2), (6), Sch 11, with effect for chargeable periods ending on or after 5 March 1997 in relation to profits and gains realised, and losses sustained, on or after that date. See also FA 1997 s 80(7) re commencement of the provisions of para 1(6), (7) of this Schedule.

[Charge to tax etc

1—(1) Subject to sub-paragraph (2) below, profits and gains arising from a transaction to which this Schedule applies (including those which, apart from this sub-paragraph, would be taken to be of a capital nature) shall be treated, when realised—

(a) as income of the person by whom they are realised; and

(b) as chargeable to tax under Case VI of Schedule D for the chargeable period in which they are realised.

(2) Sub-paragraph (1) above does not apply to—

(a) so much of any profits or gains arising to a person from a transaction as are charged to tax in his case under Case I or V of Schedule D;

(b) *any profits or gains arising to a company which is a qualifying company from a transaction which, as regards that company, is or is deemed to be a qualifying contract; or*[2]

(c) *any profits or gains arising to an authorised unit trust (within the meaning of section 468).*[2]

(3) *In sub-paragraph (2) above—*

"qualifying company" means a qualifying company for the purposes of Chapter II of Part IV of the Finance Act 1994 (interest rate, currency and debt contracts); and

"qualifying contract" means a qualifying contract for those purposes.[2]

(4) For the purposes of this Schedule the profits and gains arising from a transaction to which this Schedule applies are to be taken to be realised at the time when the disposal comprised in the transaction takes place.

(5) For the purposes of sections 392 ...[2] any loss in a transaction to which this Schedule applies is to be taken to be sustained at the time when, in accordance with sub-paragraph (4) above, any profits or gains arising from that transaction would have been realised.

(6) Subject to sub-paragraph (7) below, the following, namely—

(a) profits and gains to which sub-paragraph (1) above applies, and

(b) losses in transactions the profits and gains from which (if there were any) would be profits and gains to which that sub-paragraph applies,

shall not be brought into account for the purposes of income tax, *corporation tax*[2] or capital gains tax except by virtue of this Schedule and, in the case of losses, section 392 *or 396*[2].

(7) *Nothing in sub-paragraph (6) above shall prevent any amount from being brought into account in accordance with section 83 of the Finance Act 1989 (receipts to be brought into account in any Case I computation made in respect of life insurance).*[2]]^1

Commentary—*Simon's Direct Tax Service* **B7.204.**
Definitions—"Chargeable period", s 832(1); "company", s 832(1), (2); "profits or gains", s 833(1); "Schedule D", s 18; "tax", s 832(3).
Amendments—[1] This paragraph inserted by FA 1997 s 80(2), (6), Sch 11, with effect for chargeable periods ending on or after 5 March 1997 in relation to profits and gains realised, and losses sustained, on or after that date. See also FA 1997 s 80(7) re commencement of the provisions of sub-paras (6), (7) of this paragraph.
[2] Sub-paras (2)(b), (c), (3), (7) repealed, words "and 396" in sub-para (5), and ", corporation tax" and "or 396" in sub-para (6) repealed, by FA 2002 ss 83(1)(b), (3), 141, Sch 27 paras 1, 14(1), (2), Sch 40 Pt 3(13) with effect for accounting periods beginning after 30 September 2002.

[Transactions to which Schedule applies

2—(1) This Schedule applies to a transaction if—

(a) it is a disposal of futures or options;

(b) it is one of two or more related transactions designed to produce a guaranteed return; and

(c) the guaranteed return comprises the return from that disposal or from a number of disposals of futures or options, of which that disposal is one, taken together.

(2) For the purposes of this Schedule two or more related transactions are transactions designed to produce a guaranteed return if, taking the transactions together, it would be reasonable to assume, from either or both of—

(a) the likely effect of the transactions, and

(b) the circumstances in which the transactions are entered into, or in which any of them is entered into,

that their main purpose, or one of their main purposes, is or was the production of a guaranteed return from one or more disposals of futures or options.]^1

[(3) This Schedule also applies to a transaction if it is one of the disposals of futures or options to which section 93A of the Finance Act 1996 (loan relationships linked to the value of chargeable assets designed to produce guaranteed returns when taken together with disposals of options and futures) refers.][2]

Commentary—*Simon's Direct Tax Service* **B7.204.**
Definitions—"Disposal of futures or options", Sch 5AA para 4(1); "future", Sch 5AA para 4(6); guaranteed return", Sch 5AA para 3; "option", Sch 5AA para 4(6); "related transactions", Sch 5AA para 6.
Amendments—[1] This paragraph inserted by FA 1997 s 80(2), (6), Sch 11, with effect for chargeable periods ending on or after 5 March 1997 in relation to profits and gains realised, and losses sustained, on or after that date.

² Sub-para (3) inserted by FA 2002 s 78(1), (2), (6) with effect for accounting periods ending after 25 July 2001 in relation to profits and gains realised, and losses sustained, after that date. It is repealed by FA 2002 ss 83(1)(*a*), 141, Sch 27 paras 1, 14(1), (3), Sch 40 Pt 3(13) with effect for accounting periods beginning after 30 September 2002.

[Production of guaranteed return

3—(1) For the purposes of this Schedule a guaranteed return is produced from one or more disposals of futures or options wherever (taking all the disposals together where there is more than one) risks from fluctuations in the underlying subject matter are so eliminated or reduced as to produce a return from the disposal or disposals—

(*a*) the amount of which is not, to any significant extent, attributable (otherwise than incidentally) to any such fluctuations; and

(*b*) which equates, in substance, to the return on an investment of money at interest.

(2) For the purposes of sub-paragraph (1) above the cases where risks from fluctuations in the underlying subject matter are eliminated or reduced shall be deemed to include any case where the main reason, or one of the main reasons, for the choice of that subject matter is—

(*a*) that there appears to be no risk that it will fluctuate; or

(*b*) that the risk that it will fluctuate appears to be insignificant.

(3) In this paragraph the references, in relation to a disposal of futures or options, to the underlying subject matter are references to or to the value of the commodities, currencies, shares, stock or securities, interest rates, indices or other matters to which, or to the value of which, those futures or options are referable.]¹

Commentary—*Simon's Direct Tax Service* **B7.204.**
Definitions—"Disposal of futures options", Sch 5AA para 4(1); "future", Sch 5AA para 4(6); "interest", s 832(1); "option", Sch 5AA para 4(6).
Amendments—¹ This paragraph inserted by FA 1997 s 80(2), (6), Sch 11, with effect for chargeable periods ending on or after 5 March 1997 in relation to profits and gains realised, and losses sustained, on or after that date.

[Disposals of futures or options

4—(1) For the purposes of this Schedule a disposal is a disposal of futures or options if it consists in—

(*a*) the disposal of one or more futures;

(*b*) the disposal of one or more options; or

(*c*) the disposal of one or more futures together with one or more options.

(2) Subject to sub-paragraph (4) below, any question for the purposes of this Schedule as to whether there is a disposal falling within sub-paragraph (1)(*a*) to (*c*) above, or as to when such a disposal is made, shall be determined, on the assumptions specified in sub-paragraph (3) below, in accordance with—

(*a*) section 143(5) and (6), 144 and 144A of the 1992 Act (closing out and settlement of futures contracts and rules in relation to options); and

(*b*) the other provisions having effect for determining for the purposes of that Act whether or when an asset is disposed of;

and references in this Schedule to entering into a transaction are references, in relation to a transaction consisting in a disposal, to the making of the disposal.

(3) Those assumptions are—

(*a*) that all futures are assets for the purposes of the 1992 Act;

(*b*) that the words "in the course of dealing in commodity or financial futures" are omitted in each place where they occur in section 143(5) and (6) of that Act; and

(*c*) that any reference in that Act to a financial option within the meaning given by section 144(8) of that Act is a reference to any option that is not a traded option.

(4) Subject to sub-paragraph (5) below, where—

(*a*) one of a number of related transactions designed to produce a guaranteed return is the grant of an option,

(*b*) at least one of the other transactions is a transaction entered into after the grant of the option, and

(*c*) the transaction or transactions entered into after the grant of the option is or include a disposal which is not itself the grant of an option,

the disposal consisting in the grant of the option shall be deemed for the purposes of this Schedule to be a disposal made on the first occasion after the grant of the option when one of the other transactions which is a disposal but is not itself the grant of an option is entered into.

[(4A) *Where this paragraph has effect in relation to one of the associated transactions to which section 93A of the Finance Act 1996 (c 8) refers, sub-paragraph (4) shall have effect as if for paragraph (a) of that sub-paragraph there were substituted—*

*"(a) any one of the associated transactions to which section 93A of the Finance Act 1996 refers is the grant of an option,".*³

(5) Nothing in sub-paragraph (4) above affects so much of sub-paragraph (2) above as (by applying section 144(2) or 144A(2) of the 1992 Act (cases where options are exercised))—

(*a*) requires the grant of an option and the transaction entered into by the grantor in fulfilment of his obligations under that option to be treated for the purposes of this Schedule as a single transaction; or

(*b*) determines the time at which such a single transaction is to be treated for the purposes of this Schedule as entered into.

(6) In this paragraph—

"future" means outstanding rights and obligations under a commodity or financial futures contract;

"option" means a traded option or an option which is not a traded option but is an option relating to—

(*a*) currency, shares, stock, securities or an interest rate; or

(*b*) rights under a commodity or financial futures contract;

[and includes any liability or entitlement under an option.]²

"traded option" has the meaning given for the purposes of subsection (4) of section 144 of the 1992 Act by subsection (8) of that section.]¹

Commentary—*Simon's Direct Tax Service* B7.204.
Amendments—¹ This paragraph inserted by FA 1997 s 80(2), (6), Sch 11, with effect for chargeable periods ending on or after 5 March 1997 in relation to profits and gains realised, and losses sustained, on or after that date.
² Words in sub-para (6) inserted by FA 1998 s 99(4) with effect where the transaction consisting in the future running to delivery or the exercise of the option takes place on or after 6 February 1998.
³ Sub-para (4A) inserted by FA 2002 s 78(1), (3), (6) with effect for accounting periods ending after 25 July 2001 in relation to profits and gains realised, and losses sustained, after that date. It is repealed by FA 2002 ss 83(1)(*b*), (3), 141, Sch 27 paras 1, 14(1), (4), Sch 40 Pt 3(13) with effect for accounting periods beginning after 30 September 2002.

[Futures running to delivery and options exercised

4A—(1) This paragraph applies where for the purposes of this Schedule—

(*a*) there are or, apart from section 144(2) or (3) of the 1992 Act, would be two or more related transactions;

(*b*) one of those transactions is or would be the creation or acquisition (by the making or receiving of a grant or otherwise) of a future or option;

(*c*) the other transaction, or one of the other transactions, is or would be the running of the future to delivery or the exercise of the option; and

(*d*) the transaction mentioned in paragraph (c) above is not treated for those purposes as a disposal of a future or option.

(2) This Schedule shall have effect in relation to the parties to the future or option as if the transaction specified in sub-paragraph (3) below—

(*a*) were a transaction for which the scheme or arrangements by reference to which the transactions are related transactions provided; and

(*b*) were a transaction which in fact takes place at the time ("the relevant time") immediately before the future runs to delivery or, as the case may be, the option is exercised.

(3) That transaction is a disposal of the future or option which—

(*a*) in the case of a person whose rights and entitlements under the future or option have a market value at the relevant time, consists in a disposal for a consideration equal to that market value; and

(*b*) in the case of any other party to the future or option, consists in a disposal which—

(i) is made for a nil consideration; and

(ii) involves that person in incurring costs equal to the amount specified in sub-paragraph (4) below.

(4) That amount is the amount which that party to the future or option might reasonably have been expected to pay, in a transaction at arm's length entered into at the relevant time, for the release of his obligations and liabilities under the future or option.

(5) Where, in a case in which a transaction is deemed to take place by virtue of sub-paragraph (2)(*b*) above ("the deemed transaction")—

(*a*) any profits or gains arising from the deemed transaction are chargeable to tax under Case VI of Schedule D in accordance with paragraph 1(1) above, or

(*b*) any loss arising in the deemed transaction is brought into account for the purposes of section 392 *or* 396³ in accordance with paragraph 1(5) above,

amounts taken into account or allowable as deductions in computing those profits or gains, or that loss, shall not be excluded by virtue of section 37 or 39 of the 1992 Act (exclusion of amounts taken into account or allowable for the purposes of the taxation of income and profits) from any computation made for the purposes of that Act, but paragraph 1(6) above shall be given effect to in relation to the 1992 Act in accordance with sub-paragraphs (6) to (10) below.

(6) Where there are profits or gains arising to any person ("the taxpayer") from the deemed transaction, an increase equal to the amount of those profits or gains shall be made in the amount that would otherwise be taken for the purposes of the 1992 Act to be—

(*a*) the amount of the consideration for the acquisition of any asset acquired by the taxpayer by means of the future running to delivery or, as the case may be, by the exercise of the option; or

(*b*) the amount of the consideration for the acquisition by him of any asset disposed of by him by means of the future running to delivery or, as the case may be, in consequence of the exercise of the option;

but any increase made by virtue of paragraph (*b*) above in the amount of any consideration shall be disregarded in computing the amount of any indexation allowance.

(7) Where there is a loss for any person ("the taxpayer") in the deemed transaction—

(*a*) a reduction equal to the smaller of the amount of the loss and the amount to be reduced shall be made in the amount that would otherwise be taken for the purposes of the 1992 Act to be the amount of the consideration mentioned in sub-paragraph (6)(*a*) or (*b*) above; and

(*b*) the amount (if any) by which the amount of the loss exceeds the amount to be reduced shall be deemed to be a chargeable gain accruing to the taxpayer on the occasion specified in sub-paragraph (8) below.

(8) That occasion is—

(*a*) in a case where the consideration mentioned in paragraph (*a*) of sub-paragraph (6) above has been reduced to nil, the first occasion after the acquisition mentioned in that paragraph when there is a disposal of the asset in question; and

(*b*) in a case where it is the consideration mentioned in sub-paragraph (6)(*b*) above that has been reduced to nil, the occasion of the disposal made by the taxpayer by means of the future running to delivery or, as the case may be, in consequence of the exercise of the option.

(9) For the purposes of sub-paragraphs (6) and (7) above, where in any case there is a deemed disposal of an option by the person who granted it, any determination—

(*a*) of the profits arising to the grantor of the option from that disposal, or

(*b*) of the losses for the grantor in that disposal,

shall be made as if that disposal and the disposal by which the option was granted were a single transaction.

(10) In sub-paragraph (8) above—

(*a*) the reference in paragraph (*a*) to a disposal of the asset in question includes a reference to anything that would be such a disposal but for the provisions of section 116(10) or 127 of the 1992 Act; and

(*b*) the references in each of paragraphs (*a*) and (*b*) to a disposal include references to a disposal which, in accordance with the 1992 Act, would (apart from sub-paragraph (7)(*b*) above) be a disposal on which neither a gain nor a loss accrues.

[(10A) *Where this paragraph has effect in relation to one of the associated transactions to which section 93A of the Finance Act 1996 refers—*

(*a*) *sub-paragraph (1)(a) shall have effect as if for "two or more related transactions" there were substituted "two or more of the associated transactions to which section 93A of the Finance Act 1996 refers", and*

(*b*) *sub-paragraph (1)(c) shall have effect as if for "the other transaction, or one of the other transactions," there were substituted "one of the other transactions".]²*

(11) In this paragraph—

"future" and "option" have the same meanings as in paragraph 4 above;

"market value" has the same meaning as in the 1992 Act;

"party", in relation to a future or option, means one of the persons who has any right or entitlement comprised in or arising under the future or option or who is subject to any obligation or liability so comprised or arising;

and references in this paragraph to a future running to delivery are references to the discharge by performance of the obligations owed under the commodity or financial futures contract in question to the party to the future whose rights are in relation to its underlying subject matter.

(12) Sub-paragraph (3) of paragraph 3 above applies for the purposes of sub-paragraph (11) above as it applies for the purposes of that paragraph.]¹

Commentary—*Simon's Direct Tax Service* **B7.204.**
Amendments—¹ This paragraph inserted by FA 1998 s 99(1) with effect where the transaction consisting in the future running to delivery or the exercise of the option takes place on or after 6 February 1998.
² Sub-para (10A) inserted by FA 2002 s 78(1), (4), (6) with effect for accounting periods ending after 25 July 2001 in relation to profits and gains realised, and losses sustained, after that date. It is repealed by FA 2002 s 83(1)(*b*), (3) Sch 27 paras 1, 14(1), (5) with effect for accounting periods beginning after 30 September 2002.
³ In sub-para (5)(*b*), words "or 396" repealed by FA 2002 ss 83(1)(*b*), (3), 141, Sch 27 paras 1, 14(1), (5), Sch 40 Pt 3(13) with effect for accounting periods beginning after 30 September 2002.

[The return from one or more disposals

5—(1) In this Schedule references to the return from one or more disposals are references to the return on investment represented either—

(*a*) by the total net profits and gains arising from the disposal or disposals; or (*b*) by all but an insignificant part of those net profits and gains.

(2) For the purposes of the references in sub-paragraph (1) above to the total net profits and gains from any two or more disposals, it shall be assumed that profits and gains realised, and losses sustained, by persons who are associated with each other are all realised or sustained by the same person.

(3) For the purposes of sub-paragraph (2) above persons are associated with each other in relation to any two or more disposals made in pursuance of the same scheme or arrangements if—

(*a*) each of those persons shares or is to share, to an extent determined for the purposes of or in accordance with the scheme or arrangements, in the net return represented by the aggregate of all the profits, gains and losses realised or sustained on those disposals;
(*b*) those persons are associated companies at the time when the last of those disposals is made; or
(*c*) those persons have been associated companies at an earlier time falling after the first occasion on which a transaction was entered into in pursuance of the scheme or arrangements.

(4) In this paragraph—

"associated company" shall be construed in accordance with section 416; and
"scheme or arrangements" shall be construed in accordance with paragraph 6(4) below.]¹

Commentary—*Simon's Direct Tax Service* **B7.204.**
Amendments—¹ This paragraph inserted by FA 1997 s 80(2), (6), Sch 11, with effect for chargeable periods ending on or after 5 March 1997 in relation to profits and gains realised, and losses sustained, on or after that date.

[Related transactions

6—(1) For the purposes of this Schedule two or more transactions are related if all of them are entered into in pursuance of the same scheme or arrangements.

(2) Nothing in this Schedule shall be construed as preventing transactions with different parties, or transactions with parties different from the parties to the scheme or arrangements in pursuance of which they are entered into, from being related transactions.

(3) For the purposes of this paragraph the cases in which any two or more transactions are to be taken to be entered into in pursuance of the same scheme or arrangements shall include any case in which it would be reasonable to assume, from either or both of—

(*a*) the likely effect of the transactions, and
(*b*) the circumstances in which the transactions are entered into, or in which any of them is entered into,

that neither of them or, as the case may be, none of them would have been entered into independently of the other or others.

[(3A) Where this paragraph has effect in relation to one of the associated transactions to which section 93A of the Finance Act 1996 refers—

(*a*) *sub-paragraph (1) shall have effect as if for "two or more transactions are related" there were substituted "two or more transactions are associated transactions to which section 93A of the Finance Act 1996 refers", and*
(*b*) *sub-paragraph (2) shall have effect as if for "related transactions" there were substituted "associated transactions to which that section refers."]²*

(4) In this paragraph 'scheme or arrangements' includes schemes, arrangements and understandings of any kind, whether or not legally enforceable.]¹

Commentary—*Simon's Direct Tax Service* **B7.204.**
Amendments—¹ This paragraph inserted by FA 1997 s 80(2), (6), Sch 11, with effect for chargeable periods ending on or after 5 March 1997 in relation to profits and gains realised, and losses sustained, on or after that date.
² Sub-para (3A) inserted by FA 2002 s 78(1), (5), (6) with effect for accounting periods ending after 25 July 2001 in relation to profits and gains realised, and losses sustained, after that date. It is repealed by FA 2002 ss 83(1)(*b*), (3), 141, Sch 27 paras 1, 14(6), Sch 40 Pt 3(13) with effect for accounting periods beginning after 30 September 2002.

[Special rule for trusts

7—(1) Where any profits or gains are treated, in accordance with paragraph 1 above, as income arising to trustees for any year of assessment, the relevant part of that income shall be treated for the purposes of the Tax Acts as if it were income to which section 686 applies (income taxable at the rate applicable to trusts).

(2) In sub-paragraph (1) above the reference to the relevant part of any income is a reference to so much (if any) of that income as—

(*a*) does not fall to be treated for the purposes of the Income Tax Acts as income of a settlor;
(*b*) is not income arising under a trust established for charitable purposes; and
(*c*) is not income from investments, deposits or other property held for any such purposes as are mentioned in sub-paragraph (i) or (ii) of section 686(2)(*c*) (property held for pension purposes).

(3) Subsection (6) of section 686 (meaning of 'trustees' etc) shall apply for the purposes of this paragraph as it applies for the purposes of that section.]¹

Commentary—*Simon's Direct Tax Service* B7.204.
Amendments—¹ This paragraph inserted by FA 1997 s 80(2), (6), Sch 11, with effect for chargeable periods ending on or after 5 March 1997 in relation to profits and gains realised, and losses sustained, on or after that date.

[Transfer of assets abroad

8 For the purpose of determining whether an individual ordinarily resident in the United Kingdom has a liability for income tax in respect of any profit or gain which—

   (a) is realised by a person resident or domiciled outside the United Kingdom, and
   (b) arises from a transaction to which this Schedule applies,

sections 739 and 740 (transfer of assets abroad) shall have effect as if that profit or gain, when realised, constituted income becoming payable to the person resident or domiciled outside the United Kingdom.]¹

Commentary—*Simon's Direct Tax Service* B7.204.
Amendments—¹ This paragraph inserted by FA 1997 s 80(2), (6), Sch 11, with effect for chargeable periods ending on or after 5 March 1997 in relation to profits and gains realised, and losses sustained, on or after that date.

[Apportionment in the case of insurance companies

[9—(1) This paragraph applies where—

   (a) *any determination falls to be made under section 432A of the category of business to which any income or losses is or are referable; and*
   (b) *that income or those losses would all be chargeable or relievable by virtue of this Schedule but for the exemptions from tax and exclusions from the provisions of this Schedule that are applicable in respect of the category of business to which it or they are determined to be referable.*

(2) Section 432A shall have effect]² as if (where that would not otherwise be the case)—

   (a) *any such income were for the purposes of that section a gain accruing on the disposal of an asset; and*
   (b) *any such loss were for the purposes of that section a loss accruing on the disposal of an asset.*

[(3) Subject to sub-paragraphs (4) and (5) below, paragraph 4A above shall have effect as if the references in sub-paragraph (5) of that paragraph to—

   (a) *profits or gains arising from the deemed transaction that are chargeable to tax under Case VI of Schedule D in accordance with paragraph 1(1) above, or*
   (b) *any loss arising in the deemed transaction that is brought into account for the purposes of section 392 or 396 in accordance with paragraph 1(5) above,*

were references to all the income or losses in relation to which the determination mentioned in sub-paragraph (1) above falls to be made.

(4) Sub-paragraph (6) of paragraph 4A above shall not apply in relation to the amount of the consideration for the acquisition of any asset acquired by the taxpayer by means of the future running to delivery or, as the case may be, by the exercise of the option if—

   (a) *immediately before the time of the deemed transaction, the future or option is an asset within one of the categories set out in section 440(4); and*
   (b) *immediately after its acquisition, the asset acquired is within another of those categories.*

(5) Sub-paragraph (6) of paragraph 4A above shall not apply in relation to the amount of the consideration for the acquisition of any asset disposed of by the taxpayer by means of the future running to delivery or, as the case may be, by the exercise of the option if—

   (a) *immediately before the time of the deemed transaction, the future or option is an asset within one of the categories set out in section 440(4); and*
   (b) *immediately before its disposal, the asset disposed of is within another of those categories.*

(6) Where any future or option would not fall (apart from this sub-paragraph) to be treated as an asset for the purposes of section 440, any question for the purposes of this paragraph whether it is an asset within any of the categories set out in subsection (4) of that section shall be determined as if it were an asset.

(7) Expressions used in this paragraph and in paragraph 4A above have the same meanings in this paragraph as in that paragraph.]²

Note—This paragraph repealed by FA 2002 ss 83(1)(a), 141, Sch 27 paras 1, 14(7), Sch 40 Pt 3(13) with effect for accounting periods beginning after 30 September 2002.
Commentary—*Simon's Direct Tax Service* B7.204.
Amendments—¹ This paragraph inserted by FA 1997 s 80(2), (6), Sch 11, with effect for chargeable periods ending on or after 5 March 1997 in relation to profits and gains realised, and losses sustained, on or after that date.
² Sub-para (1) and words in sub-para (2) substituted, and sub-paras (3)–(7) inserted by FA 1998 s 99(2)–(3) with effect where the transaction consisting in the future running to delivery or the exercise of the option takes place on or after 6 February 1998.

[SCHEDULE 5A

STOCK LENDING: INTEREST ON CASH COLLATERAL][1]

Section 129A

Commentary—*Simon's Direct Tax Service* **B7.711.**
Amendments—[1] This schedule inserted by FA 1995 s 85(2), Sch 19, with effect for approved stock lending arrangements entered into after 1 May 1995 and repealed by FA 1997 Sch 10 paras 1(2), 7(1), Sch 18 Pt VI(10) with effect for, and transfers under, any arrangement made after 30 June 1997 by virtue of the Finance Act 1997, Schedule 10, (Appointed Day) Order, SI 1997/991.

[SCHEDULE 6

TAXATION OF DIRECTORS AND OTHERS IN RESPECT OF CARS][1]

Section 157

Revenue Internal Guidance—Schedule E manual SE 23300 (calculating the car benefit charge—general).
Amendments—[1] This Schedule substituted by FA 1993 Sch 3 paras 5, 7 with effect from the year 1994–95.

[[*Cash equivalent*

1—(1) The cash equivalent of the benefit is the appropriate percentage for the year of the price of the car as regards the year.

(2) This is subject to paragraphs 6 and 7 below (reductions for periods when car unavailable and payments for use of car).][1][2]

Commentary—*Simon's Direct Tax Service* **E4.626A.**
Revenue Internal Guidance—Schedule E manual SE 23100 (price of the car as regards the year—general).
Definitions—"Car", s 168(5)(*a*); "price", s 168(5)(*e*); "year", s 168(13).
Amendments—[1] This Schedule substituted by FA 1993 Sch 3 paras 5, 7 with effect from the year 1994–95.
[2] This paragraph substituted by FA 2000 s 59, Sch 11 para 1(1), (2) with effect from the year 2002–03.

[*The appropriate percentage*

2 The appropriate percentage for the year is determined in accordance with paragraphs 3 to 5G below.][1]

Commentary—*Simon's Direct Tax Service* **E4.626A.**
Amendments—[1] This Schedule substituted by FA 1993 Sch 3 paras 5, 7 with effect from the year 1994–95.
[2] This paragraph substituted by FA 2000 s 59, Sch 11 para 1(1), (2) with effect from the year 2002–03.

[[*Car with CO_2 emissions figure*

3—(1) This paragraph applies where—

   (*a*) the car—

      (i) is first registered on or after 1st January 1998 but before 1st October 1999, and
      (ii) when so registered conformed to a vehicle type with an EC type-approval certificate, or had a UK approval certificate, that specifies a CO_2 emissions figure in terms of grams per kilometre driven, or

   (*b*) the car—

      (i) is first registered on or after 1st October 1999, and
      (ii) is so registered on the basis of an EC certificate of conformity or UK approval certificate that specifies a CO_2 emissions figures in terms of grams per kilometre driven.

(2) In this paragraph references to "the applicable CO_2 emissions figure" are—

   (*a*) if the car is within sub-paragraph (1)(*a*) above, to the figure mentioned in paragraph (ii) of that sub-paragraph, and
   (*b*) if the car is within sub-paragraph (1)(*b*) above—

      (i) where the EC certificate of conformity or UK approval certificate specifies only one CO_2 emissions figure, that figure, and
      (ii) where it specifies more than one, the figure specified as the CO_2 emissions (combined) figure.

This is subject to paragraph 5 (bi-fuel cars) and paragraph 5A (disabled drivers).

(3) Where the applicable CO_2 emissions figure does not exceed the lower threshold for the year the appropriate percentage for the year is 15% ("the basic percentage").

(4) Where the applicable CO_2 emissions figure exceeds the lower threshold for the year, the appropriate percentage for the year is whichever is the smaller of—

   (*a*) the basic percentage increased by 1% for each 5 grams per kilometre by which the applicable CO_2 emissions figure exceeds the lower threshold for the year, and
   (*b*) 35%.

(5) This paragraph is subject to paragraph 5D (diesel car supplement) and any regulations under paragraph 5E (power to provide for discounts).][1][2]

Commentary—*Simon's Direct Tax Service* **E4.626A.**
Amendments—[1] This Schedule substituted by FA 1993 Sch 3 paras 5, 7 with effect from the year 1994–95.
[2] This paragraph substituted by FA 2000 s 59, Sch 11 para 1(1), (2) with effect from the year 2002–03.

[[The lower threshold

4—(1) For the purposes of paragraph 3 above the lower threshold is ascertained from the following Table—

TABLE

Year of assessment	Lower threshold (in g/km)
2002–03	165
2003–04	155
2004–05 and subsequent years of assessment	145

(2) The Treasury may by order provide for a lower threshold different from that provided for in the Table in sub-paragraph (1) above to apply for years of assessment beginning on or after 6th April 2005 or such later date as may be specified in the order.

(3) For the purposes of paragraph 3 above the applicable CO_2 emissions figure (if it is not a multiple of five) is rounded down to the nearest multiple of five.][1][2]

Commentary—*Simon's Direct Tax Service* **E4.626A.**
Simon's Tax Cases—*IRC v Quigley* [1995] STC 931[1].
Amendments—[1] This Schedule substituted by FA 1993 Sch 3 paras 5, 7 with effect from the year 1994–95.
[2] This paragraph substituted by FA 2000 s 59, Sch 11 para 1(1), (2) with effect from the year 2002–03.

[[Bi-fuel cars

5 Where the car—

(a) is first registered on or after 1st January 2000, and

(b) is so registered on the basis of an EC certificate of conformity, or UK approval certificate, that specifies separate CO_2 emissions figures in terms of grams per kilometre driven for different fuels,

then, for the purposes of paragraph 3 above, "the applicable CO_2 emissions figure" is the lowest figure specified or, if there is more than one figure specified in relation to each fuel, the lowest CO2 emissions (combined) figure specified.][2][1]

Commentary—*Simon's Direct Tax Service* **E4.626A.**
Amendments—[1] This Schedule substituted by FA 1993 Sch 3 paras 5, 7 with effect from the year 1994–95.
[2] This paragraph substituted by FA 2000 s 59, Sch 11 para 1(1), (2) with effect from the year 2002–03.

[[Automatic cars made available to disabled drivers

5A—(1) Sub-paragraph (2) below applies where—

(a) paragraph 3 above (car with CO_2 emissions figure) applies to the car,

(b) the car has automatic transmission,

(c) at any time in the year when the car is available to the employee, he holds a disabled person's badge, and

(d) by reason of his disability he must, if he wants to drive a car, drive a car that has automatic transmission.

For this purpose the car is not at any time available to the employee by reason only of its being made available to a member of his family or household.

(2) If the applicable CO_2 figure for the car ("the relevant car") is more than it would have been if the car had been an equivalent manual car, paragraph 3 above shall have effect as if the applicable CO_2 emissions figure in relation to the relevant car were the same as that in relation to an equivalent manual car.

(3) For this purpose "an equivalent manual car" means a car that—

(a) is first registered at or about the same time as the relevant car, and

(b) does not have automatic transmission, but otherwise is the closest variant available of the make and model of the relevant car.

(4) For the purposes of this paragraph a car has automatic transmission if—

(a) the driver of the car is not provided with any means whereby he may vary the gear ratio between the engine and the road wheels independently of the accelerator and the brakes, or

(b) he is provided with such means, but they do not include a clutch pedal or lever that he may operate manually.

(5) In this paragraph—

"the applicable CO_2 emissions figure" has the same meaning as in paragraph 3 above; and "disabled person's badge" has the meaning given in section 168AA(3).][1]

Commentary—*Simon's Direct Tax Service* **E4.626A**.
Amendments—[1] This paragraph inserted by FA 2000 s 59, Sch 11 para 1(1), (2) with effect from the year 2002–03.

["EC certificate of conformity", "EC type-approval certificate" and "UK approval certificate"

5B In this Schedule—

"EC certificate of conformity" means a certificate of conformity issued by a manufacturer under any provision of the law of a Member State implementing Article 6 of Council Directive 70/156/EEC, as amended;

"EC type-approval certificate" means a type-approval certificate issued under any provision of the law of a Member State implementing Council Directive 70/156/EEC, as amended; and

"UK approval certificate" means a certificate issued under—

    (a) section 58(1) or (4) of the Road Traffic Act 1988, or
    (b) Article 31A(4) or (5) of the Road Traffic (Northern Ireland) Order 1981.][1]

Amendments—[1] This paragraph inserted by FA 2000 s 59, Sch 11 para 1(1), (2) with effect from the year 2002–03.

[Car with no CO_2 emissions figure

5C—(1) This paragraph applies where—

    (a) the car is first registered on or after 1st January 1998, and
    (b) paragraph 3 above does not apply.

(2) If the car has an internal combustion engine with one or more reciprocating pistons, the appropriate percentage for the year is ascertained from the following Table—

TABLE

Cylinder capacity of car in cubic centimetres	Appropriate percentage
1,400 or less	15%
More than 1,400 but not more than 2,000	25%
More than 2,000	35%

For this purpose a car's cylinder capacity is the capacity of its engine calculated as for the purposes of the Vehicle Excise and Registration Act 1994.

(3) If sub-paragraph (2) above does not apply the appropriate percentage for the year is—

    (a) 15%, if the car is an electrically propelled vehicle, and
    (b) 35%, in any other case.

(4) This paragraph is subject to paragraph 5D (diesel car supplement) and any regulations under paragraph 5E (power to provide for discounts) below.][1]

Commentary—*Simon's Direct Tax Service* **E4.626A**.
Amendments—[1] This paragraph inserted by FA 2000 s 59, Sch 11 para 1(1), (2) with effect from the year 2002–03.

[Diesel car supplement

5D—(1) This paragraph applies where the car—

    (a) is propelled solely by diesel, and
    (b) is first registered on or after 1st January 1998.

(2) The appropriate percentage for the year is whichever is the smaller of—

    (a) the percentage which is 3% greater than the appropriate percentage for the year ascertained in accordance with paragraphs 2 to 5C above, and
    (b) 35%.

(3) In sub-paragraph (1) "diesel" means any diesel fuel within the definition in Article 2 of Directive 98/70/EC of the European Parliament and of the Council.

(4) This paragraph is subject to any regulations under paragraph 5E below (power to provide for discounts).][1]

Commentary—*Simon's Direct Tax Service* **E4.626A**.
Amendments—[1] This paragraph inserted by FA 2000 s 59, Sch 11 para 1(1), (2) with effect from the year 2002–03.

[Discounts

5E The Treasury may by regulations provide for the value of the appropriate percentage as determined in accordance with paragraphs 2 to 5D above to be reduced by such amount as may be prescribed in the regulations, in such circumstances and subject to such conditions as may be so prescribed.][1]

TA 1988

Commentary—*Simon's Direct Tax Service* **E4.626A**.
Regulations—See the Income Tax (Car Benefits) (Reduction of Value of Appropriate Percentage) Regulations, SI 2001/1123.
Amendments—[1] This paragraph inserted by FA 2000 s 59, Sch 11 para 1(1), (2) with effect from the year 2002–03.

[Car registered before 1st January 1998

5F—(1) This paragraph applies where the car was first registered before 1st January 1998.

(2) Where the car has an internal combustion engine with one or more reciprocating pistons, the appropriate percentage for the year is ascertained from the following Table—

TABLE

Cylinder capacity of car in cubic centimetres	Appropriate percentage
1,400 or less	15%
More than 1,400 but not more than 2,000	22%
More than 2,000	32%

For this purpose a car's cylinder capacity is the capacity of its engine calculated as for the purposes of the Vehicle Excise and Registration Act 1994.

(3) Where sub-paragraph (2) above does not apply, the appropriate percentage for the year is—

    (a) 15%, if the car is an electrically propelled vehicle, and

    (b) 32%, in any other case.][1]

Commentary—*Simon's Direct Tax Service* **E4.626A**.
Amendments—[1] This paragraph inserted by FA 2000 s 59, Sch 11 para 1(1), (2) with effect from the year 2002–03.

[Electrically propelled vehicle

5G For the purposes of this Schedule, a vehicle is not an electrically propelled vehicle unless—

    (a) it is propelled solely by electrical power, and

    (b) that power is derived from—

        (i) a source external to the vehicle, or

        (ii) an electrical storage battery which is not connected to any source of power when the vehicle is in motion.][1].

Commentary—*Simon's Direct Tax Service* **E4.626A**.
Amendments—[1] This paragraph inserted by FA 2000 s 59, Sch 11 para 1(1), (2) with effect from the year 2002–03.

Reduction for periods when car unavailable

[6 Subject to paragraph 7 below, where for any part of the year concerned the car is unavailable, the cash equivalent of the benefit is the amount ascertained under the preceding provisions of this Schedule [multiplied by the fraction—

$$\frac{A}{B}$$

where—

    A is the number of days in the year on which the car is available; and

    B is the number of days in the year.][2]][1]

Commentary—*Simon's Direct Tax Service* **E4.626A**.
Definitions—"Car", s 168(5)(a); "unavailable", Sch 6 para 9; "year", s 168(13).
Amendments—[1] This Schedule substituted by FA 1993 Sch 3 paras 5, 7 with effect from the year 1994–95.
[2] Words substituted by FA 2000 s 59, Sch 11 para 1(1), (3) with effect from the year 2002–03.

Reduction for payments for use of car

[7—(1) Where in the year concerned the employee is required, as a condition of the car being available for his private use, to pay any amount of money (whether by way of deduction from his emoluments or otherwise) for that use, then—

    (a) if the amount ascertained under the preceding provisions of this Schedule exceeds the relevant sum, the cash equivalent of the benefit is an amount equal to the excess;

    (b) if the relevant sum exceeds or is equal to the amount ascertained under the preceding provisions of this Schedule, the cash equivalent of the benefit is nil.

(2) In sub-paragraph (1) above—

    (a) "the relevant sum" means the amount paid by the employee, as there mentioned, in respect of the year concerned;

    (b) the reference to the car being available for the employee's private use includes a reference to the car being available for the private use of others being members of his family or household.][1]

Commentary—*Simon's Direct Tax Service* **E4.626.**
Revenue Decision RD 1—Deduction of monthly payments answered from the car benefit scale charge under this para where the payment was made by the employee to the employer, equal to the additional leasing costs of a more expensive car than that to which they were entitled.
Revenue Internal Guidance—Schedule E Manual SE 23530 (reduction for payments for private use of the car—general explanation).
SE 23531 (application of *CIR v Quigley* 67 TC 535, not all payments by an employee will necessarily qualify as private use payments to reduce the car benefit charge).
SE 23532 (payments for a more expensive car do not reduce the benefit charge).
SE 23533 (internal procedures where there is doubt about whether or not payments are admissible).
SE 23546 (worked example).
Definitions—"Available", Sch 6 para 10; "car", s 168(5)(*a*); "emoluments", s 131(1); "private use", s 168(5)(*f*); "year", s 168(13).
Amendments—[1] This Schedule substituted by FA 1993 Sch 3 paras 5, 7 with effect from the year 1994–95.

Replacement cars

[**8** The Treasury may by regulations provide that where—

(*a*) a car is normally available to the employee but for a period of less than 30 days it is not available to him,

(*b*) another car is made available to the employee in order to replace the car mentioned in paragraph (*a*) above for the whole or part of the period, and

(*c*) such other conditions as may be prescribed by the regulations are fulfilled,

this Schedule shall have effect in relation to the cars concerned subject to such modifications as are prescribed by the regulations.][1]

Commentary—*Simon's Direct Tax Service* **E4.626.**
Regulations—See the Income Tax (Car Benefits) (Reduction of Value of Appropriate Percentage) Regulations, SI 2001/1123.
Revenue Internal Guidance—Schedule E Manual SE 23502 (replacement cars—general).
SE 23503 (meaning of "similar quality").
SE 23504 (meaning of "arrangement").
SE 23513 and SE 23514 (examples where circumstances which do not count as "arrangements").
Definitions—"Available", Sch 6 para 10; "car", s 168(5)(*a*); "made available", s 168(6).
Amendments—[1] This Schedule substituted by FA 1993 Sch 3 paras 5, 7 with effect from the year 1994–95.

Meaning of "unavailable"

[**9** For the purposes of this Schedule a car is to be treated as being unavailable on any day if—

(*a*) the day falls before the first day on which the car is available to the employee,

(*b*) the day falls after the last day on which the car is available to the employee, or

(*c*) the day falls within a period, of 30 days or more, throughout which the car is not available to the employee.][1]

Commentary—*Simon's Direct Tax Service* **E4.626.**
Revenue Internal Guidance—Schedule E Manual SE 23501 (meaning of unavailability).
SE 23511 and SE 23512 (worked examples).
Definitions—"Available', Sch 6 para 10; "car", s 168(5)(*a*).
Amendments—[1] This Schedule substituted by FA 1993 Sch 3 paras 5, 7 with effect from the year 1994–95.

General

[**10** For the purposes of this Schedule a car is available to an employee at a particular time if it is then made available, by reason of his employment and without any transfer of the property in it, either to him or to others being members of his family or household.][1]

[This is subject to paragraph 5A(1) above.][2]

Commentary—*Simon's Direct Tax Service* **E4.626.**
Revenue Internal Guidance—Schedule E manual SE 23550 (transfer of ownership of the car to the employee: car benefit charge will cease to apply and the car benefit charge must be time apportioned up to that date).
Definitions—"Car", s 168(5)(*a*); "employment", s 168(2); "family or household", s 168(4).
Amendments—[1] This Schedule substituted by FA 1993 Sch 3 paras 5, 7 with effect from the year 1994–95.
[2] Words added by FA 2000 s 59, Sch 11 para 1(1), (4) with effect from the year 2002–03.

[SCHEDULE 6A

TAXATION OF DIRECTORS AND OTHERS IN RESPECT OF VANS][1]

Section 159AA

Revenue Internal Guidance—Schedule E manual SE 22051 (vans—general).
SE 22061 (exceptions to the charge).
Amendments—[1] This Schedule inserted by FA 1993 Sch 4 paras 7, 8 with effect from the year 1993–94.

PART I
BASIC CASE
Cash equivalent

[**1**—(1) This paragraph applies where the van mentioned in section 159AA(1)—

   (a) is not a van to which Part II of this Schedule applies for the year concerned, or

   (b) is a van to which that Part applies for the year concerned but is a shared van (within the meaning there given) for part only of the year.

(2) Subject to paragraphs 2 and 3 below, the cash equivalent of the benefit is—

   (a) £500, if the van is aged less than 4 years at the end of the year concerned;

   (b) £350, if the van is aged 4 years or more at the end of the year concerned.]¹

Commentary—*Simon's Direct Tax Service* E4.630A.
Revenue Internal Guidance—Schedule E manual SE 22067 (meaning of age of van).
SE 22068 (amount of van scale charges).
SE 22069 (amount of van scale charges—step-by-step calculation).
SE 22075 (charge for exclusive availability).
SE 22097 (shared van and exclusive use van both available in year—example).
Definitions—"Age of van", s 168(5A)(b); "van", s 168(5A)(a); "year", s 168(13).
Cross references—See TA 1988 Sch 6A para 10 (same van involved in calculation of benefit under this Part and under Part II).
Amendments—¹ This Schedule inserted by FA 1993 Sch 4 paras 7, 8 with effect from the year 1993–94.

Reductions for periods where van unavailable

[**2**—(1) Subject to paragraph 3 below, where paragraph 1 above applies and for any part of the year concerned—

   (a) the van is unavailable, or

   (b) the van is a shared van (within the meaning given by Part II of this Schedule),

the cash equivalent of the benefit is the amount ascertained under paragraph 1 above (the full amount) reduced by an amount which bears to the full amount the same proportion as the number of excluded days in the year bears to 365.

(2) For the purposes of sub-paragraph (1) above a van is to be treated as being unavailable on any day if—

   (a) the day falls before the first day on which the van is available to the employee,

   (b) the day falls after the last day on which the van is available to the employee, or

   (c) the day falls within a period, of 30 days or more, throughout which the van is not available to the employee.

(3) For the purposes of sub-paragraph (1) above an excluded day is a day on which the van falls within paragraph (a) or (b) of that sub-paragraph.]¹

Commentary—*Simon's Direct Tax Service* E4.630A.
Revenue Internal Guidance—Schedule E manual SE 22077 (meaning of "unavailable").
Definitions—"Van", s 168(5A)(a); "van is available", Sch 6A, para 11; "year", s 168(13).
Amendments—¹ This Schedule inserted by FA 1993 Sch 4 paras 7, 8 with effect from the year 1993–94.

Reduction for payments for use of van

[**3**—(1) Where paragraph 1 above applies and in the year concerned the employee is required, as a condition of the van being available for his private use, to pay any amount of money (whether by way of deduction from his emoluments or otherwise) for that use, then—

   (a) if the amount ascertained under paragraphs 1 and 2 above exceeds the relevant sum, the cash equivalent of the benefit is an amount equal to the excess;

   (b) if the relevant sum exceeds or is equal to the amount ascertained under paragraphs 1 and 2 above, the cash equivalent of the benefit is nil.

(2) In sub-paragraph (1) above—

   (a) "the relevant sum" means the amount paid by the employee, as there mentioned, in respect of the year concerned, and

   (b) the reference to the van being available for the employee's private use includes a reference to the van being available for the private use of others being members of his family or household.

(3) If the van is a shared van (within the meaning given by Part II of this Schedule) for part of the year concerned, the reference in sub-paragraph (2) above to the year shall be construed as a reference to the part of the year when the van is not a shared van.]¹

Commentary—*Simon's Direct Tax Service* E4.630A.
Revenue Internal Guidance—Schedule E manual SE 22080 (reduction for payments for use of van).
Definitions—"Available for private use", s 168(6)(c), (d); "emoluments", s 131(1); "family or household", s 168(4); "private use", s 168(5A)(f); "van", s 168(5A)(a); "van is available", Sch 6A para 11; "year", s 168(13).
Amendments—¹ This Schedule inserted by FA 1993 Sch 4 paras 7, 8 with effect from the year 1993–94.

PART II

SHARED VANS

Introduction

[**4**—(1) This Part of this Schedule applies to a van for a year if it is a shared van for any period in the year.

(2) A van is a shared van for a period if the period is one throughout which the van is available concurrently to more than one employee of the same employer.

(3) A van is also a shared van for a period if—

(a) the period is one throughout which the van is available to different employees of the same employer, but

(b) the circumstances are such that the employee or employees to whom the van is available at any given time in the period are not necessarily the same as the employee or employees to whom it is available at any other given time in the period.

(4) But if the van is available to one employee only for a period exceeding 30 days (an exclusive period)—

(a) the exclusive period shall not count towards any period that would otherwise fall within sub-paragraph (3) above;

(b) any period falling within sub-paragraph (3) above shall be treated as ending when the exclusive period begins (without prejudice to the start after the exclusive period of a further period falling within sub-paragraph (3) above).

(5) If a van would (apart from this sub-paragraph) be treated as shared during part of a day it shall be treated as shared throughout the day.]¹

Commentary—*Simon's Direct Tax Service* **E4.630A.**
Revenue Internal Guidance—Schedule E manual SE 22070 (what is a shared van?).
SE 22072 (meaning of exclusive period).
SE 22085 (charge for a shared van—general).
SE 22100 (shared vans—example).
Definitions—"Van", s 168(5A)(a); "van is available", Sch 6A para 11; "year", s 168(13).
Amendments—¹ This Schedule inserted by FA 1993 Sch 4 paras 7, 8 with effect from the year 1993–94.

Benefit to employee

[**5**—(1) This paragraph applies where for any year this Part of this Schedule—

(a) applies to a van, or

(b) applies to each of two or more vans made available by the same employer.

(2) For the purposes of this paragraph a participating employee is an employee to whom—

(a) the van is available for his private use while it is a shared van (where only one van is involved),

(b) one of the vans is available for his private use while it is a shared van (where more than one van is involved), or

(c) some or all of the vans are available for his private use while they are shared vans (where more than one van is involved);

but an employee is not a participating employee unless he makes private use of the van, or (if more than one is involved) he makes private use of at least one of them, at least once while it is a shared van.

(3) In sub-paragraph (2) above—

(a) any reference to a van being available for an employee's private use includes a reference to the van being available for the private use of others being members of his family or household, and

(b) any reference to an employee making private use of a van includes a reference to a member of his family or household making private use of it.

(4) This paragraph shall apply to each participating employee in the same way, irrespective of—

(a) the number available to a particular employee of the vans involved;

(b) the fact that a particular van involved is or is not available to him or used by him;

(c) the extent to which a particular van involved is available to him or used by him.

(5) Where this paragraph applies—

(a) find the basic value of the van for the year or (as the case may be) the basic value for the year of each van involved;

(b) take that basic value or (as the case may be) the aggregate of those basic values;

(c) find for each participating employee a portion of the figure taken under paragraph (b) above by dividing it equally among the participating employees.

(6) The figure found for a participating employee shall be taken to be the cash equivalent of the benefit to him in the year of—

(a) the van available to him while it is a shared van (where only one van is involved or only one of the vans involved is available to him), or (*b*) the vans available to him while they are shared vans (where more than one van is involved and more than one of them is available to him).][1]

Commentary—*Simon's Direct Tax Service* **E4.630A.**
Revenue Internal Guidance—Schedule E manual SE 22090 (meaning of 'participating employee').
Definitions—"Basic value", Sch 6A para 6; "family or household", s 168(4); "made available", s 168(6)(*c*), (*d*); "private use", s 168(5A)(*f*); "van", s 168(5A)(*a*); "van is available", Sch 6A para 11; "year", s 168(13).
Cross references—See TA 1988 Sch 6A para 7 (limit of benefit for a participating employee).
TA 1988 Sch 6A para 8 (alternative calculation of benefit for a participating employee).
TA 1988 Sch 6A para 9 (reduction in cash equivalent of benefit where employee contributes).
TA 1988 Sch 6A para 10 (same van involved in calculation of benefit under this Part and under Part I).
Amendments—[1] This Schedule inserted by FA 1993 Sch 4 paras 7, 8 with effect from the year 1993–94.

Basic value

[6—(1) Subject to sub-paragraph (2) below, the basic value of a van for a year is—

(*a*) £500, if the van is aged less than 4 years at the end of the year concerned;
(*b*) £350, if the van is aged 4 years or more at the end of the year concerned.

(2) Where for any part of the year—

(*a*) the van is not a shared van, or
(*b*) the van is incapable of use,

its basic value is the amount ascertained under sub-paragraph (1) above (the full value) reduced by an amount which bears to the full value the same proportion as the number of excluded days in the year bears to 365.

(3) For the purposes of sub-paragraph (2) above a van is to be treated as being incapable of use on any day if the day falls within a period, of 30 days or more, throughout which the van is incapable of being used at all.

(4) For the purposes of sub-paragraph (2) above an excluded day is a day on which the van falls within paragraph (*a*) or (*b*) of that sub-paragraph.][1]

Commentary—*Simon's Direct Tax Service* **E4.630A.**
Revenue Internal Guidance—Schedule E manual SE 22095 (scale charges for shared vans).
Definitions—"Age of van", s 168(5A)(*b*); "van", s 168(5A)(*a*); "year", s 168(13).
Amendments—[1] This Schedule inserted by FA 1993 Sch 4 paras 7, 8 with effect from the year 1993–94.

Limit of benefit

[7 Where (apart from this paragraph) the figure found under paragraph 5 above for a participating employee for a year would exceed £500, the figure for the employee for the year shall be taken to be £500.][1]

Commentary—*Simon's Direct Tax Service* **E4.630A.**
Revenue Internal Guidance—Schedule E manual SE 22110 (shared vans—overriding limit on charge).
Definitions—"Year", s 168(13).
Cross references—See TA 1988 Sch 6A para 8 (alternative calculation of benefit for a participating employee).
TA 1988 Sch 6A para 9 (reduction in cash equivalent of benefit where employee contributes).
Amendments—[1] This Schedule inserted by FA 1993 Sch 4 paras 7, 8 with effect from the year 1993–94.

Alternative calculation

[8—(1) In a case where—

(*a*) a figure is found under paragraph 5 or 7 above for a participating employee for a year, and
(*b*) the employee makes a claim for this paragraph to be applied,

the figure found for the employee for the year shall be taken to be the alternative figure found under this paragraph.

(2) The alternative figure is a figure found by—

(*a*) taking for each van involved the number of relevant days;
(*b*) aggregating the numbers found under paragraph (*a*) above where more than one van is involved;
(*c*) multiplying the number found under paragraph (*a*) (or paragraphs (*a*) and (*b*)) above by £5.

(3) For the purposes of sub-paragraph (2)(*a*) above a relevant day is a day which falls in the year and during which (or part of which) the employee, or a member of his family or household, makes private use of the van concerned while it is a shared van.

(4) For the purposes of section 95 of the Taxes Management Act 1970 (incorrect return etc) a claim under this paragraph shall be taken to be a claim for relief.][1]

Commentary—*Simon's Direct Tax Service* **E4.630A.**
Revenue Internal Guidance—Schedule E manual SE 22115 (shared vans—alternative daily basis of charge).
Definitions—"Family or household", s 168(4); "private use", s 168(5A)(*f*); "van", s 168(5A)(*a*); "year", s 168(13).
Cross references—See TA 1988 Sch 6A para 9 (reduction in cash equivalent of benefit where employee contributes).
Amendments—[1] This Schedule inserted by FA 1993 Sch 4 paras 7, 8 with effect from the year 1993–94.

Reduction for payments for use

[9—(1) Where this Part of this Schedule applies and in the year concerned a participating employee is required, as a condition of the van or vans being available for his private use, to pay any amount of money (whether by way of deduction from his emoluments or otherwise) for that use, then—

(a) if the figure found for the employee for the year under paragraph 5 or 7 or 8 above exceeds the relevant sum, the figure shall be taken to be a figure equal to the excess;

(b) if the relevant sum exceeds or is equal to the figure found for the employee for the year under paragraph 5 or 7 or 8 above, the figure shall be taken to be nil.

(2) For the purposes of this paragraph the relevant sum shall be found by—

(a) taking for any van involved the amount paid by the employee, as a condition of it being available for his private use, in respect of the period when the van is a shared van in the year concerned, and

(b) where more than one van is involved, aggregating the amounts found under paragraph (a) above.

(3) Any reference in this paragraph to a van being available for the employee's private use includes a reference to the van being available for the private use of others being members of his family or household.]¹

Commentary—*Simon's Direct Tax Service* **E4.630A.**
Revenue Internal Guidance—Schedule E manual SE 22120 (shared vans—payments for private use).
Definitions—"Emoluments", s 131(1); "family or household", s 168(4); "private use", s 168(5A)(f); "van", s 168(5A)(a); "van is available", Sch 6A para 11; "year", s 168(13).
Amendments—¹ This Schedule inserted by FA 1993 Sch 4 paras 7, 8 with effect from the year 1993–94.

PART III
GENERAL
Interaction of Parts I and II

[10—(1) This paragraph applies where—

(a) a cash equivalent of the benefit of a van to an employee in a year is found under Part I of this Schedule, and

(b) a cash equivalent of the benefit of the same van (or of vans including the same van) to the employee in the year is found under Part II of this Schedule.

(2) Once the different cash equivalents are so found, the employee shall be charged to tax as if the van concerned were different vans, one having a cash equivalent found under Part I of this Schedule and the other having (or counting towards) a cash equivalent found under Part II of this Schedule.]¹

Commentary—*Simon's Direct Tax Service* **E4.630A.**
Revenue Internal Guidance—Schedule E manual SE 22097 (shared van and exclusive use van both available in year—example).
Definitions—"Van", s 168(5A)(a); "year", s 168(13).
Amendments—¹ This Schedule inserted by FA 1993 Sch 4 paras 7, 8 with effect from the year 1993–94.

Limit of cash equivalent

[11 In a case where—

(a) the cash equivalent of the benefit of vans to an employee in a year would (apart from this paragraph) total more than £500, and

(b) no more than one of the vans is available to him for his private use, or the private use of others being members of his family or household, at any one time in the year,

the cash equivalent of the benefit of the vans to him in the year shall be £500.]¹

Commentary—*Simon's Direct Tax Service* **E4.630A.**
Revenue Internal Guidance—Schedule E manual SE 22125 (overriding limit where only one van available at a time).
Definitions—"Family or household", s 168(4); "private use", s 168(5A)(f); "van", s 168(5A)(a); "van is available", Sch 6A para 11; "year", s 168(13).
Amendments—¹ This Schedule inserted by FA 1993 Sch.4, paras 7, 8 with effect from the year 1993–94.

Interpretation

[12 For the purposes of this Schedule a van is available to an employee at a particular time if it is then made available, by reason of his employment and without any transfer of the property in it, either to him or to others being members of his family or household.]¹

Commentary—*Simon's Direct Tax Service* **E4.630.**
Definitions—"Employment", s 168(2); "family or household", s 168(4); "made available", s 168(6)(c), (d); "van", s 168(5A)(a).
Amendments—¹ This Schedule inserted by FA 1993 Sch 4 paras 7, 8 with effect from the year 1993–94.

SCHEDULE 7

TAXATION OF BENEFIT FROM LOANS OBTAINED BY REASON OF EMPLOYMENT

Section 160

Revenue Internal Guidance—Schedule E manual SE 26100 (index of guidance on beneficial loans, covering references 26101–26520).
Cross references—See TA 1988 s 191B (beneficial loan arrangements in relation to removal expenses on change of residence of an employee).

PART I

MEANING OF "OBTAINED BY REASON OF EMPLOYMENT"

1—(1) Subject to sub-paragraph (5) below, the benefit of a loan is obtained by reason of a person's employment if, in relation to that person, it is of a class described in sub-paragraphs (2), (3) or (4) below.

(2) A loan made by his employer.

(3) A loan made by a company—

    (*a*) over which his employer had control;
    (*b*) by which his employer (being a company) was controlled; or
    (*c*) which was controlled by a person by whom his employer (being a company) was controlled.

(4) A loan made in any case where—

    (*a*) his employer was, or had control over, or was controlled by, a close company; and
    (*b*) the loan was made by a person having a material interest in that close company or, that company being controlled by another company, in that other company.

(5) [Sub-paragraphs (2) and (4) above do][1] not apply to a loan made by ...[2] an individual, ...[3] in the normal course of his domestic, family or personal relationships.

Commentary—*Simon's Direct Tax Service* E4.631.
Revenue Internal Guidance—Schedule E manual SE 26113 (meaning of 'by reason of employment').
SE 26114 and SE 26115 ('by reason of employment': exception where loan made by an individual, application of sub-para (5)).
Definitions—"Close company", ss 414(1), 832(1); "company", s 832(1), (2); "control", ss 168(12), 840; "employment", s 168(2); "family", s 168(4); "loan", s 160(5), (7); "material interest", s 168(11). See also para 19 below.
Amendments—[1] Words in sub-para (5) substituted by FA 1994 s 88(4)(*a*), (6) with effect from the year 1994–95.
[2] Words in sub-para (5) repealed by FA 1994 s 88(4)(*a*), (6) and Sch 26 Pt V(5) from the year 1994–95.
[3] Words omitted from sub-para (5) repealed by FA 1996 s 134(1), (2), Sch 20 para 41, Sch 41 Pt V(10) with effect from the year 1996–97.

2 In paragraph 1 above—

    (*a*) references to a loan being made by any person include references to his assuming the rights and liabilities of the person who originally made the loan and to his arranging, guaranteeing or in any way facilitating the continuation of a loan already in existence;
    (*b*) "employer" includes a prospective employer; and
    (*c*) "company", except in the expression "close company", includes a partnership.

Commentary—*Simon's Direct Tax Service* E4.631.
Revenue Internal Guidance—Schedule E manual SE 26111 (loans taken over from another person).
Definitions—"Close company", ss 414(1), 832(1); "company", s 832(1), (2); "loan", s 160(5), (7). See also para 19 below.

PART II

CALCULATION OF CASH EQUIVALENT OF LOAN BENEFIT

General

3—(1) The cash equivalent for any year of the benefit obtained from a loan is—

    (*a*) the amount of interest (calculated in accordance with paragraph 4 or 5 below) which would have been payable for that year had interest at the official rate been payable on the loan, less
    (*b*) the amount of interest actually paid on the loan for that year

[and, in a case where there are two or more loans, the aggregate of the cash equivalents (if any) of the benefit of each of those loans shall be treated for the purposes of section 160 as the cash equivalent of the benefit of all of them.][1]

(2)–(3) ...[1]

Commentary—*Simon's Direct Tax Service* E4.633.
Revenue Internal Guidance—Schedule E Manual SE 26103 (explanation of the cash equivalent).
SE 26250–26261 (calculating the cash equivalent: what interest paid is taken into account).
Definitions—"Interest", s 832(1); "loan", s 160(5), (7); "official rate of interest", s 160(5), (7); "year", s 168(13).
Cross references—See TA 1988 s 160(1B) (certain loans between the same lender and borrower to be treated as a single loan for the purposes of this Part where the lender so elects).
Amendments—[1] Words in sub-para (1) added and sub-paras (2), (3) repealed by FA 1991 s 27(6), Sch 6 para 3, Sch 19 Pt V with effect from the year 1991–92.

Normal method of calculation (averaging)

4—[(1)][1] In the absence of a requirement or election that paragraph 5 below should apply, the amount of interest at the official rate payable on a loan for any year ("the relevant year") shall be ascertained as follows—

   (*a*) take half the aggregate of—

      (i) the maximum amount of the loan outstanding on 5th April preceding the relevant year or, if it was made in that year, on the date on which it was made, and
      (ii) the maximum amount of the loan outstanding on 5th April in the relevant year or, if the loan was discharged in that year, the date of discharge;

   (*b*) multiply that figure by the number of whole months during which the loan was outstanding in that year, and divide by 12;

   (*c*) multiply the result by the official rate of interest in force during the period when the loan was outstanding in that year or, if the official rate changed during that period, the average rate during that period ascertained by reference to the number of days in the period and the number of days for which each rate was in force.

For the purposes of this paragraph, months begin on the sixth day of the calendar month.

[(2) Where an employment-related loan is replaced, directly or indirectly—

   (*a*) by a further employment-related loan, or

   (*b*) by a non-employment-related loan which in turn is, in the same year of assessment or within 40 days thereafter, replaced, directly or indirectly, by a further employment- related loan,

sub-paragraph (1) above applies as if the replacement loan or, as the case may be, each of the replacement loans were the same loan as the first-mentioned employment-related loan.][1]

[(3) For the purposes of sub-paragraph (2) above "employment-related loan" means a loan the benefit of which is obtained by reason of a person's employment (and "non-employment-related loan" shall be construed accordingly).][1]

(4) The references in sub-paragraph (2) above to a further employment-related loan are to an employment-related loan the benefit of which is obtained by reason of—

   (*a*) the same or other employment with the person who is the employer in relation to the first-mentioned employment-related loan, or

   (*b*) employment with a person who is connected (within the meaning of section 839) with that employer.][1]

Commentary—*Simon's Direct Tax Service* **E4.633.**
Note—For the purposes of this Schedule, the official rate of interest is subject to frequent changes made by statutory instruments. The rates applicable at various periods may be obtained from *Simon's Direct Tax Services,* Binder 1, Rates of default interest.
Revenue Internal Guidance—Schedule E Manual SE 26200 (calculation of the cash equivalent: the 'averaging' and the 'precise' method, table summarizing methods).
SE 26210–26225 (calculation of the cash equivalent: the 'averaging' method, explanations and examples).
Definitions—"Interest", s 832(1); "loan", s 160(5), (7); "official rate of interest", s 160(5), (7); "year", s 168(13).
Cross references—See TA 1988 s 160(1B) (certain loans between the same lender and borrower to be treated as a single loan for the purposes of this Part where the lender so elects).
Amendments—[1] Provision as originally enacted numbered sub-para (1), and sub-paras (2)–(4) inserted, by FA 1995 s 45(4), (5), with effect from the year 1995–96 for loans whether made before or after 1 May 1995.

Election for alternative method of calculation

5—(1) For any year of assessment ("the relevant year") the alternative method of calculation set out in this paragraph applies if—

   (*a*) the inspector so requires, by notice given to the employee, [at a time allowed by sub-paragraph (2) below;][1]; or

   (*b*) the employee so elects, by notice given to the inspector [at such a time][1].

[(2) A notice containing a requirement or election for the purposes of sub-paragraph (1) above is allowed to be given at any time before the end of the period of 12 months beginning with the 31st January next following the relevant year.][1]

(3) The alternative method of calculating the amount of interest at the official rate payable on a loan for the relevant year is as follows—

   (*a*) take each period in the relevant year during which the official rate of interest remains the same;

   (*b*) for each such period take for each day in the period the maximum amount outstanding of the loan on that day, and add those amounts together;

   (*c*) multiply that sum by the official rate in force during the period divided by 365; and

   (*d*) add together the resulting figures for each period in the relevant year.

Commentary—*Simon's Direct Tax Service* **E4.633.**
Note—For the official rate of interest, see note under para 4, *ante.*
Revenue Internal Guidance—Schedule E Manual SE 26200 (calculation of the cash equivalent: the 'averaging' and the 'precise' method, table summarizing methods).
SE 26230–26245 (calculation of the cash equivalent: the precise method, explanations and details on elections).
Definitions—"Emoluments", s 131(1); "income tax", s 832(4); "inspector", s 832(1); "interest", s 832(1); "loan", s 160(5), (7); "notice", s 832(1); "official rate of interest", s 160(5), (7); "year of assessment", s 832(1).

Cross references—See TA 1988 s 160(1B) (certain loans between the same lender and borrower to be treated as a single loan for the purposes of this Part where the lender so elects).

Amendments—[1] Words in sub-paras (1)(*a*), (*b*) and whole of sub-para (2) substituted by FA 1996 s 107(2), (3), (4) with effect from the year 1996–97 and applying to loans wherever made.

[*Apportionment of cash equivalent in case of joint loan etc*

5A—(1) Where in any year there are two or more employees chargeable to tax in respect of the same loan—

    (*a*) the cash equivalent of the benefit of the loan (determined in accordance with this Schedule) shall be apportioned between them in a fair and reasonable manner, and

    (*b*) the portion allocated to each employee shall be treated as the cash equivalent of the benefit of the loan so far as he is concerned.

(2) For the purposes of determining the cash equivalent in such a case, the references in paragraph 5 above to the employee shall be construed as references to all the chargeable employees.][1]

Amendment—[1] This paragraph inserted by FA 2000 s 57, Sch 10 paras 1, 6 with effect from the year 2000–01.

PART III
EXCEPTIONS WHERE INTEREST ELIGIBLE FOR RELIEF

Amendments—This Part repealed by FA 1994 s 88(4)(*b*), (6) and Sch 26 Pt V(5) from the year 1994–95.

PART IV
INTEREST ELIGIBLE FOR RELIEF: CONSEQUENCES OF RESTRICTION OF RELIEF TO TAX AT THE BASIC RATE ONLY

Amendments—This Part repealed by FA 1994 s 88(4)(*b*), (6) and Sch 26 Pt V(5) from the year 1994–95.

PART V
INTERPRETATION

Amendments—This Part repealed by FA 1994 s 88(4)(*b*), (6) and Sch 26 Pt V(5) from the year 1994–95.

[SCHEDULE 7A
BENEFICIAL LOANS: LOANS ON ORDINARY COMMERCIAL TERMS][1]
Section 161B

Revenue Internal Guidance—Schedule E manual SE 26158–26165 (explanations of the rules relating to —exemption for 'commercial' loans).

Amendment—[1] This Schedule inserted by FA 2000 s 57, Sch 10 paras 1, 5(2) with effect from the year 2000–01.

[*Introduction*

1 For the purposes of section 161B(1) a loan ''on ordinary commercial terms'' means a loan—

    (*a*) made by a person (''the lender'') in the ordinary course of a business carried on by him which includes—

        (i) the lending of money, or

        (ii) the supplying of goods or services on credit, and

    (*b*) in relation to which the requirements of paragraph 2, 3 or 4 below are met.][1]

Amendment—[1] This Schedule inserted by FA 2000 s 57, Sch 10 paras 1, 5(2) with effect from the year 2000–01.

[*Requirements relating to original loan*

2—(1) This paragraph applies to any loan and the relevant time for the purposes of this paragraph is the time the loan was made.

(2) The requirements of this paragraph are—

    (*a*) that at the relevant time comparable loans were available to all those who might be expected to avail themselves of the services provided by the lender in the course of his business;

    (*b*) that a substantial proportion of the relevant loans were made to members of the public;

    (*c*) that the loan in question and comparable loans generally made by the lender at or about the relevant time to members of the public are held on the same terms; and

    (*d*) that if those terms differ from those applicable immediately after the relevant time they were imposed in the ordinary course of the lender's business.

(3) For the purposes of this paragraph a loan is comparable to another loan if it is made for the same or similar purposes and on the same terms and conditions.

(4) The relevant loans for the purposes of sub-paragraph (2)(*b*) are—

    (*a*) the loan in question, and
    (*b*) comparable loans made by the lender at or about the relevant time.

(5) In determining for the purposes of this paragraph whether any loans made by any person before 1st June 1994 are made on the same terms or conditions, or held on the same terms, there shall be left out of account any amounts, by way of fees, commission or other incidental expenses, incurred for the purpose of obtaining any of those loans by the persons to whom they are made.][1]

Amendment—[1] This Schedule inserted by FA 2000 s 57, Sch 10 paras 1, 5(2) with effect from the year 2000–01.

[Requirements relating to loan varied before 6th April 2000

3—(1) This paragraph applies to a loan that has been varied before 6th April 2000 and the relevant time for the purposes of this paragraph is the time of the variation.

(2) The requirements of this paragraph are—

    (*a*) that a substantial proportion of the relevant loans were made to members of the public;
    (*b*) that the loan in question and relevant loans generally made by the lender at or about the relevant time to members of the public are held on the same terms; and
    (*c*) that if those terms differ from those applicable immediately after the relevant time they were imposed in the ordinary course of the lender's business.

(3) The relevant loans for the purposes of sub-paragraph (2)(*a*) are—

    (*a*) the loan in question;
    (*b*) any existing loans which were varied at or about the time of the variation of the loan in question so as to be held on the same terms as that loan after it was varied;
    (*c*) any new loans made by the lender, at or about that time, which are held on those terms.][1]

Amendment—[1] This Schedule inserted by FA 2000 s 57, Sch 10 paras 1, 5(2) with effect from the year 2000–01.

[Requirements relating to loan varied on or after 6th April 2000

4—(1) The requirements of this paragraph apply to a loan that has been varied on or after 6th April 2000 and the relevant time for the purposes of this paragraph is the time of the variation.

(2) The first requirement is that at the relevant time members of the public that had loans from the lender for similar purposes had a right to vary their loans on the same terms and conditions as applied in relation to the variation of the loan in question.

(3) The second requirement is that any existing loans so varied and the loan in question as varied are held on the same terms.

(4) The third requirement is that if those terms differ from the terms applicable immediately after the relevant time, they were imposed in the ordinary course of the lender's business.

(5) The fourth requirement is that a substantial proportion of the relevant loans were made to members of the public.

(6) The relevant loans for the purposes of sub-paragraph (5) are—

    (*a*) the loan in question;
    (*b*) any existing loans which were varied at or about the time of the variation of the loan in question so as to be held on the same terms as that loan after it was varied;
    (*c*) any new loans made by the lender, at or about that time, which are held on those terms.][1]

Amendment—[1] This Schedule inserted by FA 2000 s 57, Sch 10 paras 1, 5(2) with effect from the year 2000–01.

[Disregard of certain penalties, fees, etc

5 Amounts incurred by the person to whom a loan is made—

    (*a*) on penalties or interest or similar amounts incurred as a result of varying the loan, and
    (*b*) on fees, commission or other incidental expenses, incurred for the purpose of obtaining the loan,

shall be left out of account in determining for the purposes of paragraph 3 or 4 whether rights to vary loans are exercisable on the same terms and conditions or loans are held on the same terms.][1]

Amendment—[1] This Schedule inserted by FA 2000 s 57, Sch 10 paras 1, 5(2) with effect from the year 2000–01.

[Meaning of "member of the public"

6 For the purposes of this Schedule a "member of the public" means a member of the public at large with whom the lender deals at arm's length.][1]

Amendment—[1] This Schedule inserted by FA 2000 s 57, Sch 10 paras 1, 5(2) with effect from the year 2000–01.

[SCHEDULE 8

PROFIT-RELATED PAY SCHEMES: CONDITIONS FOR REGISTRATION][1]

Section 176(9)

Revenue Internal Guidance—Profit-related pay manual PRP 3.100-3.666 (detailed explanation of the rules with worked examples).
Cross references—See TA 1988 s 177B (alteration in a registered Scheme).
TA 1988 s 178(2) (cancellation of a Scheme failing compliance with this Schedule at time of registration).
Amendments—[1] By FA 1997 s 61(2), Pt V, Chapter III (which includes this Schedule) shall not have effect in relation to any payment made by reference to a profit period beginning after 31 December 1999; and accordingly a scheme shall not be registered under this Chapter if the only payments for which it provides are payments by reference to profit periods beginning after 31 December 1999, and registration under this Chapter shall end on that date (s 61(3)). This Schedule is accordingly repealed by FA 1997 Sch 18 Pt VI(3) in accordance with s 61(2), (3), subject to the savings in Notes 2, 3 to Sch 18 Pt VI(3).

[Form

1 *The terms of the scheme must be set out in writing.]*[1]

Amendments—[1] This paragraph repealed by FA 1997 Sch 18 Pt VI(3); see the corresponding note at the beginning of this Schedule.

[Employer and employment unit

2 *The scheme must identify the scheme employer.]*[1]

Commentary—*Simon's Direct Tax Service* **E4.303.**
Definitions—"Employment unit", s 169(1); "scheme employer", s 169(1).
Amendments—[1] This paragraph repealed by FA 1997 Sch 18 Pt VI(3); see the corresponding note at the beginning of this Schedule.

3 If the scheme employer does not pay the emoluments of all the employees to whom the scheme relates, the scheme must identify each of the persons who pays the emoluments of any of those employees.

Commentary—*Simon's Direct Tax Service* **E4.303.**
Definitions—"Emoluments", s 131(1); "employees to whom scheme relates", s 169(2); "pay", s 169(1); "scheme employer", s 169(1).
Amendments—[1] This paragraph repealed by FA 1997 Sch 18 Pt VI(3); see the corresponding note at the beginning of this Schedule.

[4—*(1) The scheme must identify the undertaking to which the scheme relates and that undertaking must be one which is carried on with a view to profit.*

(2) The references in sub-paragraph (1) above to an undertaking include references to part of an undertaking; and the provisions of a scheme identifying part of an undertaking must do so in such a way as to distinguish it, otherwise than by name only, from other parts of the undertaking.][1]

Commentary—*Simon's Direct Tax Service* **E4.303.**
Definition—"profits", ss 169(1), 833(1).
Amendments—[1] This paragraph repealed by FA 1997 Sch 18 Pt VI(3); see the corresponding note at the beginning of this Schedule.

[Employees

5 *The scheme must contain provisions by reference to which the employees to whom the scheme relates may be identified.]*[1]

Commentary—*Simon's Direct Tax Service* **E4.304.**
Revenue Internal Guidance—Profit-related pay manual PRP 3.105 (extent of employer's discretion in setting the parameters for participation).
PRP 3.116-3.118 (employees joining and leaving a PRP scheme).
Definition—"Employees to whom scheme relates", s 169(2).
Amendments—[1] This paragraph repealed by FA 1997 Sch 18 Pt VI(3); see the corresponding note at the beginning of this Schedule.

[6 *The scheme must contain provisions ensuring that no payments are made under it by reference to a profit period if the employees to whom the scheme relates constitute less than 80 per cent of all the employees in the employment unit at the beginning of that profit period, but for this purpose any person who is at that time within paragraph 7 or 8 below shall not be counted.]*[1]

Commentary—*Simon's Direct Tax Service* **E4.304.**
Revenue Internal Guidance—Profit-related pay manual PRP 3.110-3.114 (operation of the 80% test).
Definitions—"Employees to whom scheme relates", s 169(2); "employment unit", s 169(1); "profit period", s 169(1).
Amendments—[1] This paragraph repealed by FA 1997 Sch 18 Pt VI(3); see the corresponding note at the beginning of this Schedule.

[7—*(1) The scheme must contain provisions ensuring that no payments are made under it to any person who is employed in the employment unit by a company and who has ...[1] a material interest in the company.*

(2) For the purposes of this paragraph a person shall be treated as having a material interest [in a company if he, either on his own or with one or more associates, or if any associate of his with or without such other associates,—

> *[(a) is the beneficial owner of, or able, directly or through the medium of other companies, or by any other indirect means to control, more than 25 per cent of the ordinary share capital of the company, or*
> *[(b) in the case of a close company, possesses, or is entitled to acquire, such rights as would, in the event of the winding-up of the company or in any other circumstances, give an entitlement to receive more than 25 per cent of the assets which would then be available for distribution among the participators.]*[4]

(3) In this paragraph—

> *"associate" has the same meaning as in section 417(3) and (4)[, but subject to sub-paragraph (4) below]*[2]*; ...*[5]
> *"control" has the meaning given by section 840; [and*
> *["participator" has the meaning given by section 417(1);]*[6]

and the definition of "control" in section 840 applies (with the necessary modifications) in relation to a company which is an unincorporated association as it applies in relation to one that is not.

[(4) For the purposes of this paragraph, where an employee of a company has an interest in shares or obligations of the company as a beneficiary of an employee benefit trust, the trustees shall not be regarded as associates of his by reason only of that interest unless sub-paragraph (8) below applies in relation to him.][3]

[(5) A trust is an employee benefit trust for the purposes of this paragraph if—

> *(a) all or most of the employees of the company are eligible to benefit under it, and*
> *(b) none of the property subject to it has been disposed of on or after 14th March 1989 (whether by sale, loan or otherwise) except in the ordinary course of management of the trust or in accordance with sub-paragraph (6) below.]*[3]

[(6) Property is disposed of in accordance with this sub-paragraph if—

> *(a) it is applied for the benefit of—*
>> *(i) individual employees or former employees of the company,*
>> *(ii) spouses, former spouses, widows or widowers of employees or former employees of the company,*
>> *(iii) relatives, or spouses of relatives, of persons within sub-paragraph (i) or (ii) above, or*
>> *(iv) dependants of persons within sub-paragraph (i) above,*
> *(b) it is applied for charitable purposes, or*
> *(c) it is transferred to the trustees of an approved profit sharing scheme (within the meaning of section 187), of another employee benefit trust, or of a qualifying employee share ownership trust (within the meaning of Schedule 5 to the Finance Act 1989),*

and the property applied or transferred consists of any of the ordinary share capital of the company or of money paid outright.][3]

[(7) In sub-paragraph (6)(a)(iii) above "relative" means parent or remoter forebear, child or remoter issue, brother, sister, uncle, aunt, nephew or niece.][3]

[(8) This sub-paragraph applies in relation to an employee if at any time on or after 14th March 1989—

> *(a) the employee, either on his own or with any one or more of his associates, or*
> *(b) any associate of his, with or without other such associates,*

has been the beneficial owner of, or able (directly or through the medium of other companies or by any other indirect means) to control, more than 25 per cent of the ordinary share capital of the company.][3]

[(9) Where—

> *(a) on or after 14th March 1989 an employee of a company, or an associate of his, receives a payment ("the relevant payment") from the trustees of an employee benefit trust, and*
> *(b) at any time during the period of three years ending with the day on which the relevant payment is received, the property subject to the trust consists of or includes any part of the ordinary share capital of the company,*

the employee or associate shall be treated for the purposes of sub-paragraph (8) above as if he were the beneficial owner of the appropriate percentage of the ordinary share capital of the company on the day on which the relevant payment is received (in addition to any percentage of that share capital of which he is actually the beneficial owner on that day).][3]

[(10) For the purposes of sub-paragraph (9) above, the appropriate percentage is—

$$\frac{A \times 100}{B}$$

where—
A is the smaller of—

(a) the aggregate of the relevant payment and any other payments received by the employee or associates of his from the trustees of the trust during the period of 12 months ending with the day on which the relevant payment is received, and

(b) the aggregate of the distributions made to the trustees of the trust by the company in respect of its ordinary share capital during the period of three years ending with the day on which the relevant payment is received; and

B is the aggregate of—

(a) any distributions made by the company in respect of its ordinary share capital during the period of 12 months ending with the day on which the relevant payment is received,

(b) any distributions so made during the period of 12 months immediately preceding that mentioned in paragraph (a) above, and

(c) any distributions so made during the period of 12 months immediately preceding that mentioned in paragraph (b) above,

divided by the number of the periods mentioned in paragraphs (a) to (c) above in which distributions were so made.]³

[(11) Where—

(a) an employee or associate is treated by sub-paragraph (9) above as if he were the beneficial owner of a percentage of the ordinary share capital of a company by reason of receiving the relevant payment from the trustees of a trust, and

(b) that employee, or an associate of his, has, during the period of 12 months ending with the day on which the relevant payment is received, received one or more payments from trustees of another employee benefit trust or trusts satisfying the requirement in paragraph (b) of sub-paragraph (9) above,

that sub-paragraph shall have effect in relation to the employee or associate mentioned in paragraph (a) above as if he had received the payment from the trustees of the trust or of each of the trusts mentioned in paragraph (b) above (or where more than one payment has been received from the trustees of a trust, the last of the payments) on the day on which the relevant payment is received.]³

[(12) In sub-paragraphs (8) to (11) above "associate", in relation to an employee, does not include the trustees of an employee benefit trust by reason only that the employee has an interest in shares or obligations of the trust.]³]⁷

Commentary—*Simon's Direct Tax Service* **E4.304.**
Revenue Internal Guidance—Profit-related pay manual PRP 3.119-3.134 (meaning of "material interest").
Definitions—"Close company", ss 414(1), 832(1); "company", s 832(1), (2); "control", s 840; "employment unit", s 169(1); "ordinary share capital", s 832(1); "total income", s 835(1).
Cross references—See TA 1988 Sch 9 para 40(4) (application of sub-paras (9)–(12) above to employee benefit trust).
FA 1989 Sch 5 para 16(6) (extension of the application of this paragraph to employee share ownership trusts).
Amendments—¹ Words in sub-para (1) repealed by FA 1989 Sch 4 para 9(1), (2) and Sch 17 Pt IV.
² Words in the definition of "associate" in sub-para (3) inserted by FA 1989 Sch 4 para 9(1), (3).
³ Sub-paras (4) to (12) added by FA 1989 Sch 4 para 9(1), (4).
⁴ Sub-para (2)(a), (b) and the preceding words substituted by FA 1989 Sch 12 para 18 in relation to accounting periods beginning after 31 March 1989.
⁵ Word "and" in sub-para (3) repealed by FA 1989 Sch 12 para 18 and Sch 17 Pt V.
⁶ Definition of "participator" in sub-para (3) inserted by FA 1989 Sch 12 para 18.
⁷ This paragraph repealed by FA 1997 Sch 18 Pt VI(3); see the corresponding note at the beginning of this Schedule.

[8 The persons within this paragraph are any of the following employees who are excluded by the scheme from receiving any payment of profit-related pay—

(a) ...¹

(b) those who have not been employed by a relevant employer for a minimum period (of not more than three years) specified in the scheme;

and for this purpose "relevant employer" means the scheme employer or any person who pays the emoluments of any of the employees to whom the scheme relates.]²

Commentary—*Simon's Direct Tax Service* **E4.304.**
Definitions—"Emoluments", s 131(1); "employees to whom scheme relates", s 169(2); "employment", s 169(1); "employment unit", s 169(1); "profit-related pay", s 169(1); "scheme employer", s 169(1).
Amendments—¹ Para 8(a) repealed by FA 1995 s 137(1), Sch 29 Pt VIII(20), with effect for any scheme not registered before 1 May 1995.
² This paragraph repealed by FA 1997 Sch 18 Pt VI(3); see the corresponding note at the beginning of this Schedule.

[Profit periods

9 The scheme must identify the accounting period or periods by reference to which any profit-related pay is to be calculated.]¹

Commentary—*Simon's Direct Tax Service* **E4.305.**
Definitions—"Accounting period", s 834(1); "profit period", s 169(1); "profit-related pay", s 169(1).
Amendments—¹ This paragraph repealed by FA 1997 Sch 18 Pt VI(3); see the corresponding note at the beginning of this Schedule.

[10—(1) Subject to sub-paragraphs (2) and (3) below, any such accounting period must be a period of 12 months.

(2) If the scheme is a replacement scheme, the first of two profit periods may be a period of less than 12 months, but the scheme may not provide for more than two profit periods.

(3) The scheme may make provision for a profit period to be abbreviated where registration of the scheme is cancelled with effect from a day after the beginning of the period; and a scheme making such provision may exclude the operation of all or any of the provisions of paragraph 13(4) and (5) or (as the case may be) paragraph 14(3)(b), (4) and (5) below in relation to the determination of the distributable pool for an abbreviated period.

(4) For the purposes of this paragraph, a scheme is a replacement scheme if—

(a) it succeeds another scheme (or two or more other schemes) registration of which was cancelled under section 178(1)(a) on the ground of a change in the employment unit or in the circumstances relating to the scheme; and

(b) that change occurred not more than three months before the beginning of the first (or only) profit period of the new scheme, and the Board are satisfied that it was not brought about with a view to the registration of the new scheme or in circumstances satisfying the conditions in section 177(1)(a), (b) and (c); and

(c) not less than one half of the employees to whom the new scheme relates were employees to whom the previous scheme (or any of the previous schemes) related at the time of that change.][1]

Commentary—*Simon's Direct Tax Service* **E4.305, 312.**
Definitions—''Accounting period'', s 834(1); ''Board, the'', s 832(1); ''employees to whom scheme relates'', s 169(2); ''employment unit'', s 169(1); ''profit period'', s 169(1).
Amendments—[1] This paragraph repealed by FA 1997 Sch 18 Pt VI(3); see the corresponding note at the beginning of this Schedule.

[Distributable pool

11 *The scheme must contain provisions by reference to which the aggregate sum that may be paid to employees in respect of a profit period (''the distributable pool'') may be determined.]*[1]

Commentary—*Simon's Direct Tax Service* **E4.306.**
Statement of Practice SP 7/92—Profit-related pay: use of pool determination formulae.
Definition—''Profit period'', s 169(1).
Amendments—[1] This paragraph repealed by FA 1997 Sch 18 Pt VI(3); see the corresponding note at the beginning of this Schedule.

*[***12** *Except where the scheme is a replacement scheme (within the meaning of paragraph 10 above), the provisions for the determination of the distributable pool must employ either the method specified in paragraph 13 below (''method A'') or the method specified in paragraph 14 below (''method B'').]*[1]

Commentary—*Simon's Direct Tax Service* **E4.306.**
Statement of Practice SP 7/92—Profit-related pay: use of pool determination formulae.
Amendments—[1] This paragraph repealed by FA 1997 Sch 18 Pt VI(3); see the corresponding note at the beginning of this Schedule.

*[***13**—*(1) Method A is that the distributable pool is equal to a ...*[1] *percentage of the profits of the employment unit in the profit period.*

[(1A) That percentage must be a fixed percentage specified in the scheme and, if the scheme relates to more than one period, must be the same for each period.][3]

(2), (3) ...[3]

(4) Notwithstanding sub-paragraph (1) above, a scheme employing method A may include provision for disregarding profits in the profit period so far as they exceed 160 per cent. (or such greater percentage as may be specified in the scheme) of—

(a) if the profit period is the first or only period to which the scheme relates, the profits for [a base year specified in the scheme][4]*;*

(b) in any other case, the profits for the previous profit period.

(5) Notwithstanding sub-paragraph (1) above, a scheme employing method A may include provision to the effect that there shall be no distributable pool if the profits in the profit period are less than an amount specified in, or ascertainable by reference to, the scheme; but that amount [must not exceed the profits for a base year specified in the scheme][4]*.*

[(6) The base year referred to in sub-paragraph (4)(a) and sub-paragraph (5) above must be a period of 12 months ending at a time within the period of two years immediately preceding the profit period, or the first of the profit periods, to which the scheme relates.][5]

[(7) Any provision included in a scheme by virtue of sub-paragraph (4) or (5) above may take effect either from the scheme's first profit period or from any later profit period determined in accordance with the scheme.][6]*]*[7]

Commentary—*Simon's Direct Tax Service* **E4.306.**
Statement of Practice SP 7/92—Profit-related pay: use of pool determination formulae.
Definitions—''Employees to whom scheme relates'', s 169(2); ''employment unit'', s 169(1); ''pay'', s 169(1); ''profits'', ss 169(1), 833(1); ''profit period'', s 169(1); ''scheme employer'', s 169(1).
Cross references—See TA 1988 Sch 8 para 10(3) (exclusion of sub-paras (4), (5) above in relation to the determination of distributable pool where because of cancellation of registration a profit period is abbreviated).
TA 1988 Sch 8 para 13A (accountancy treatment for a scheme under sub-paras (4), (5) above).

Amendments—[1] Word in sub-para (1) repealed by FA 1989 Sch 4 para 10(2)(*a*) and Sch 17 Pt IV.
[2] Sub-paras (2), (3) repealed by FA 1989 Sch 4 para 10(1), (2)(*a*) and Sch 17 Pt IV.
[3] Sub-para (1A) inserted by FA 1989 Sch 4 para 10(2)(*b*)(i).
[4] Words in sub-paras (4)(*a*), (5) substituted by FA 1989 Sch 4 para 10(2)(*b*)(ii), (iii).
[5] Sub-para (6) substituted by FA 1989 Sch 4 para 10(2)(*b*)(iv).
[6] Sub-para (7) added by FA 1989 Sch 4 para 11.
[7] This paragraph repealed by FA 1997 Sch 18 Pt VI(3); see the corresponding note at the beginning of this Schedule.

[13A—*(1) Where a scheme includes provision by virtue of paragraph 13(4) or (5) above the scheme must be so framed that in arriving at the profits for the base year or for the previous profit period any profit-related pay and any secondary Class I contributions in respect of it are accorded the same accountancy treatment as is accorded to any profit-related pay and any secondary Class I contributions in respect of it in arriving at the profits in the profit period.*

(2) In sub-paragraph (1) above—

(a) "profit-related pay" means profit-related pay under whatever scheme;

(b) "secondary Class I contributions" means secondary Class I contributions under Part I of the Social Security Act 1975 or Part I of the Social Security (Northern Ireland) Act 1975 or Part I of the Social Security Contributions and Benefits Act 1992 or Part I of the Social Security Contributions and Benefits (Northern Ireland) Act 1992.

(3) Sub-paragraph (1) above shall apply notwithstanding anything in paragraph 19 below.

(4) Where a scheme includes provision by virtue of paragraph 13(4) above the scheme must also include provision that if the pay for the profit period is less than the pay for the base year or for the previous profit period (as the case may be) the percentage to be applied for the purposes of the provision included by virtue of paragraph 13(4) above shall be the increased percentage (instead of any other percentage).

(5) The increased percentage must be one arrived at by—

(a) taking the percentage that would be applied for the purposes of the provision included by virtue of paragraph 13(4) above apart from the provision included by virtue of sub-paragraph (4) above, and

(b) adding the percentage found by expressing the difference in pay as a percentage of the profits for the base year or for the previous profit period (as the case may be).

(6) For the purposes of this paragraph—

(a) the pay for the profit period or for the previous profit period or for the base year is the pay paid to employees in respect of employment in the period or year concerned in the employment unit concerned;

(b) the difference in pay is the difference between the pay for the profit period and the pay for the previous profit period or for the base year (as the case may be);

and any profit-related pay shall be ignored in applying paragraph (a) above.][1]

Commentary—*Simon's Direct Tax Service* **E4.306.**
Definitions—"Base year", Sch 8 para 13(6); "employment", s 169(1); "employment unit", s 169(1); "pay", s 169(1); "profits", ss 169(1), 833(1); "profit period", s 169(1); "profit-related pay", s 169(1).
Amendments—[1] This paragraph inserted by FA 1994 s 98(1), (2), (4) in relation to any scheme not registered before 1 December 1993. It is repealed by FA 1997 Sch 18 Pt VI(3); see the corresponding note at the beginning of this Schedule.

[14—*(1) Method B is that the distributable pool is—*

(a) if the profit period is the first or only profit period to which the scheme relates, a percentage of a notional pool of an amount specified in the scheme;

(b) in any other case, a percentage of the distributable pool for the previous profit period.

(2) ...[1]

(3) The percentage referred to in sub-paragraph (1) above must be either—

(a) that arrived at by expressing the profits in the profit period as a percentage of the profits in the preceding period of 12 months; or

(b) the percentage mentioned in paragraph (a) above reduced (if it is more than 100) or increased (if it is less than 100) by a specified fraction of the difference between it and 100;

and the reference in paragraph (b) above to a specified fraction is a reference to a fraction of not more than one half specified in the scheme.

(4) Notwithstanding sub-paragraph (1) above, a scheme employing method B may include provision for disregarding profits in the profit period so far as they exceed 160 per cent. (or such greater percentage as may be specified in the scheme) of the profits in the preceding period of 12 months.

(5) Notwithstanding sub-paragraph (1) above, a scheme employing method B may include provision to the effect that there shall be no distributable pool if the profits in the profit period are less than an amount ...[3] *ascertainable by reference to, the scheme; but that amount [must not exceed the profits in the period of 12 months immediately preceding the first or only profit period to which the scheme relates]*[2]*.*

(6) Where by virtue of a provision of the kind described in sub-paragraph (5) above there is no distributable pool for a profit period, any comparison required in accordance with sub-paragraph (1)(b) to be made with the distributable pool for that period shall be made with what would have been the pool but for sub-paragraph (5).

(7) ...[1]

[(8) Any provision included in a scheme by virtue of sub-paragraph (3)(b), (4) or (5) above may take effect either from the scheme's first profit period or from any later profit period determined in accordance with the scheme.][4][5]

Commentary—*Simon's Direct Tax Service* **E4.306B.**
Statement of Practice SP 7/92—Profit-related pay: use of pool determination formulae.
Definitions—"Employment unit", s 169(1); "pay", s 169(1); "profits", ss 169(1), 833(1); "profit period", s 169(1).
Cross references—See TA 1988 s 178(1) (cancellation of a method B Scheme in consequence of losses).
TA 1988 Sch 8 para 10(3) (exclusion of sub-paras (3)(b), (4), (5) above in relation to the determination of distributable pool where because of cancellation of registration a profit period is abbreviated).
TA 1988 Sch 8 para 14A (accountancy treatment for a scheme under sub-paras (3)–(5) above).
Amendments—[1] Sub-paras (2), (7) repealed by FA 1989 Sch 4 para 10(1), (2)(a) and Sch 17 Pt IV.
[2] Words in sub-para (5) substituted by FA 1989 Sch 4 para 10(2)(c).
[3] Words in sub-para (5) repealed by FA 1989 Sch 4 para 12 and Sch 17 Pt IV.
[4] Sub-para (8) added by FA 1989 Sch 4 para 13.
[5] This paragraph repealed by FA 1997 Sch 18 Pt VI(3); see the corresponding note at the beginning of this Schedule.

[**14A**—(1) Where a scheme includes provision to give effect to paragraph 14(3) above or provision by virtue of paragraph 14(4) above the scheme must be so framed that in arriving at the profits in the preceding period of 12 months any profit-related pay and any secondary Class I contributions in respect of it are accorded the same accountancy treatment as is accorded to any profit-related pay and any secondary Class I contributions in respect of it in arriving at the profits in the profit period.

(2) Where a scheme includes provision by virtue of paragraph 14(5) above the scheme must be so framed that in arriving at the profits in the relevant period of 12 months any profit-related pay and any secondary Class I contributions in respect of it are accorded the same accountancy treatment as is accorded to any profit-related pay and any secondary Class I contributions in respect of it in arriving at the profits in the profit period; and for this purpose the relevant period of 12 months is the period of 12 months immediately preceding the first or only profit period to which the scheme relates.

(3) In sub-paragraphs (1) and (2) above—

(a) "profit-related pay" means profit-related pay under whatever scheme;
(b) "secondary Class I contributions" means secondary Class I contributions under Part I of the Social Security Contributions and Benefits Act 1992 or Part I of the Social Security Contributions and Benefits (Northern Ireland) Act 1992.

(4) Sub-paragraphs (1) and (2) above shall apply notwithstanding anything in paragraph 19 below.

(5) Where a scheme includes provision by virtue of paragraph 14(4) above the scheme must also include provision that if the pay for the profit period is less than the pay for the preceding period of 12 months the percentage to be applied for the purposes of the provision included by virtue of paragraph 14(4) above shall be the increased percentage (instead of any other percentage).

(6) The increased percentage must be one arrived at by—

(a) taking the percentage that would be applied for the purposes of the provision included by virtue of paragraph 14(4) above apart from the provision included by virtue of sub-paragraph (5) above, and
(b) adding the percentage found by expressing the difference in pay as a percentage of the profits in the preceding period of 12 months.

(7) For the purposes of this paragraph—

(a) the pay for the profit period or for the preceding period of 12 months is the pay paid to employees in respect of employment in the period concerned in the employment unit concerned;
(b) the difference in pay is the difference between the pay for the profit period and the pay for the preceding period of 12 months;

and any profit-related pay shall be ignored in applying paragraph (a) above.][1]

Commentary—*Simon's Direct Tax Service* **E4.305, 306.**
Definitions—"Employment", s 169(1); "employment unit", s 169(1); "pay", s 169(1); "profits", ss 169(1), 833(1); "profit period", s 169(1); "profit-related pay", s 169(1).
Amendments—[1] This paragraph inserted by FA 1994 s 98(1), (3), (4) in relation to any scheme not registered before 1 December 1993. It is repealed by FA 1997 Sch 18 Pt VI(3); see the corresponding note at the beginning of this Schedule.

[**15** If the scheme is a replacement scheme (within the meaning of paragraph 10 above), it must provide for the distributable pool for a profit period to be equal to a specified percentage of the profits for the period.][1]

Commentary—*Simon's Direct Tax Service* **E4.306, 312.**
Definitions—"Profits", ss 169(1), 833(1); "profit period", s 169(1).
Amendments—[1] This paragraph repealed by FA 1997 Sch 18 Pt VI(3); see the corresponding note at the beginning of this Schedule.

[Payment from distributable pool etc

16 *The scheme must provide for the whole of the distributable pool to be paid to employees in the employment unit.]*[1]

Commentary—*Simon's Direct Tax Service* **E4.307.**
Revenue Internal Guidance—Profit-related pay manual PRP 3.500–3.508 (the 80% rule in para 6 overrides para 16; PRP must not be topped up from a parallel bonus scheme; treatment of payments to excluded employees).
Definition—''Employment unit'', s 169(1).
Amendments—¹ This paragraph repealed by FA 1997 Sch 18 Pt VI(3); see the corresponding note at the beginning of this Schedule.

[17 *The scheme must make provision as to when payments will be made to employees.]*¹

Commentary—*Simon's Direct Tax Service* **E4.307.**
Revenue Internal Guidance—Profit-related pay manual PRP 3.509-3.519, 3.541-3.543 (timing of payments; problems with employees leaving; effect of interim payments).
Amendments—¹ This paragraph repealed by FA 1997 Sch 18 Pt VI(3); see the corresponding note at the beginning of this Schedule.

[18—*(1) The provisions of the scheme must be such that employees participate in the scheme on similar terms.*

*(2) For the purposes of sub-paragraph (1) above, the fact that the payments to employees vary according to the levels of their remuneration, the length of their service or similar factors shall not be regarded as meaning that they do not participate on similar terms.]*¹

Commentary—*Simon's Direct Tax Service* **E4.307.**
Revenue Internal Guidance—Profit-related pay manual PRP 3.520-3.540 (meaning of ''similar terms''; acceptable and unacceptable factors).
Amendments—¹ This paragraph repealed by FA 1997 Sch 18 Pt VI(3); see the corresponding note at the beginning of this Schedule.

[Ascertainment of profits

19—*(1) The scheme must provide for the preparation of a profit and loss account in respect of—*

　　(a) each profit period of the employment unit; and
　　(b) any other period the profits for which must be ascertained for the purposes of this Chapter.

(2) The profit and loss account must give a true and fair view of the profit or loss of the employment unit for the period to which it relates.

(3) Subject to sub-paragraph (2) above, the requirements of Schedule 4 to the Companies Act 1985 shall apply (with any necessary modifications) to a profit and loss account prepared for the purposes of the scheme as they apply to a profit and loss account of a company for a financial year.

(4) Notwithstanding the preceding provisions of this paragraph, a profit and loss account prepared for the purposes of the scheme must not make any deduction, in arriving at the profits or losses of the employment unit, for the remuneration of any person excluded from the scheme by virtue of paragraph 7 above.

*[(4A) In sub-paragraph (4) above ''remuneration'', in relation to a person, includes fees and percentages, any sums paid by way of expenses allowance (insofar as those sums are charged to income tax), any contributions paid in respect of him under any pension scheme and the estimated value of any other benefits received by him otherwise than in cash.]*¹

(5) Notwithstanding the preceding provisions of this paragraph, if the scheme so provides in relation to any of the items listed in sub-paragraph (6) below, a profit and loss account prepared for the purposes of the scheme may, in arriving at the profits or losses of the employment unit—

　　(a) leave the item out of account notwithstanding that Schedule 4 to the Companies Act 1985 requires it to be taken into account; or
　　*(b) take the item into account notwithstanding that Schedule 4 to the Companies Act 1985 [or section 3(3) of the Finance (No. 2) Act 1997]*⁴ *requires it to be left out of account.*

(6) The items referred to in sub-paragraph (5) above are—

　　(a) interest receivable and similar income;
　　(b) interest payable and similar charges;
　　(c) goodwill;
　　(d) tax on profit or loss on ordinary activities (but not any penalty under the Taxes Acts);
　　(e) research and development costs;
　　*[(f) profit-related pay payable under the scheme, and profit-related pay payable under any other registered scheme if it is one to which paragraph 21 below applies;]*²
　　*[(ff) secondary Class 1 contributions under Part I of the Social Security Act 1975 or Part I of the Social Security (Northern Ireland) Act 1975 in respect of profit-related pay payable under the scheme;]*²
　　*[(fg) windfall tax charged under Part I of the Finance (No 2) Act 1997;]*⁴
　　*(g)–(k) ... ,*³
　　*[(l) any exceptional items which fall within sub-paragraph (6A) below and should in accordance with any accounting practices regarded as standard be shown separately on the face of the profit and loss account.]*³

[(6A) The items are—

　　(a) profits or losses on the sale or termination of an operation;

(b) costs of a fundamental reorganisation or restructuring having a material effect on the nature and focus of the employment unit's operations;

(c) profits or losses on the disposal of fixed assets; and

(d) the effect on tax of any of the items mentioned in paragraphs (a) to (c) above.]³

(7) References in this paragraph to Schedule 4 to the Companies Act 1985 shall be construed, in relation to Northern Ireland, as references to Schedule 4 to the Companies (Northern Ireland) Order 1986.]⁵

Commentary—*Simon's Direct Tax Service* **E4.305.**
Note—SSA 1975 Pt I and SS (Northern Ireland) A 1975, Pt I mentioned in sub-s (6)(*ff*) are re-enacted as Social Security Contributions and Benefits Act 1992 Pt I and Social Security Contributions and Benefits (Northern Ireland) Act 1992 Pt I respectively.
Concession B44—Revenue will accept that items which might have been "extraordinary items", within SSAP 6 may continue to be taken into account, or left out, for the purpose of PRP, profit and loss accounts ending after 21 June 1993, where the scheme rules so permit. (This concession will cease to apply for profit periods beginning on or after 1 May 1995).
Revenue Internal Guidance—Profit related pay manual PRP 3.600-3.666 (detailed consideration of the requirement for accounts and ascertainment of distributable profits).
Definitions—"Company", s 832(1), (2); "employment unit", s 169(1); "interest", s 832(1); "losses", s 169(1); "profits", ss 169(1), 833(1); "profit period", s 169(1); "profit-related pay", s 169(1); "tax", s 832(3); "the Tax Acts", s 831(2).
Cross references—TA 1988 Sch 8 para 19A (Treasury may by order amend any of the items listed in sub-para (6) of this paragraph).
Amendments—¹ Sub-para (4A) inserted by FA 1989 Sch 4 para 14(1), (2).
² Sub-para (6)(*f*), (*ff*) substituted for sub-para (6)(*f*) by FA 1989 Sch 4 para 14(1), (3).
³ Sub-para (6)(*g*)–(*k*) repealed; sub-para (6)(*l*) and sub-para (6A) inserted by FA 1995 s 136(1), (2), (5), (6), Sch 29 Pt VIII(19) with effect for existing schemes (within FA 1995 s 136(11)) whose rules are altered to take account of FA 1995 s 136(2)–(4) within six months of 1 May 1995, and for new schemes, for profit and loss accounts for periods beginning after 1 May 1995.
⁴ Words in sub-para (5)(*b*), and sub-para (6)(*fg*), inserted by F(No 2)A 1997 s 4(1)–(3), (7) with effect in relation to the preparation, for the purpose of any scheme, of a profit and loss account for any period ending after 1 July 1997, but not so as to have effect in relation to an "existing scheme" unless, with in six months beginning with 31 July 1997, the scheme is altered, with effect for all periods ending after 1 July 1997, to take account of these amendments. See also F(No 2)A 1997 s (4)–(6).
⁵ This paragraph repealed by FA 1997 Sch 18 Pt VI(3); see the corresponding note at the beginning of this Schedule.

[19A—*(1) The Treasury may by order amend paragraph 19 above so as to add to, delete or vary any of the items mentioned in sub-paragraph (6) of that paragraph.*

(2) In this paragraph references to an order are references to an order under sub-paragraph (1) above.

(3) Subject to sub-paragraphs (4) to (8) below, any amendment or amendments made by virtue of an order shall have effect in relation to the preparation, for the purposes of a scheme, of a profit and loss account in respect of a period beginning on or after the day on which the order comes into force.

(4) Any amendment or amendments made by virtue of an order shall not have effect in relation to an existing scheme unless, before the end of the period of 6 months beginning with the day on which the order comes into force, the scheme is altered to take account of the amendment or amendments.

(5) Sub-paragraphs (6) to (8) below apply where, before the end of the period mentioned in sub-paragraph (4) above, an existing scheme is altered as mentioned in that sub-paragraph.

(6) The provision made by the scheme in compliance with paragraph 20(1) below shall not prevent a profit and loss account being prepared in accordance with the alteration.

(7) Where the distributable pool would but for this sub-paragraph be determined by reference—

(a) to an amount shown in a profit and loss account prepared in accordance with the altered scheme, and

(b) to an amount shown in a profit and loss account ("an earlier account") prepared in accordance with the scheme in a form in which it stood before the alteration,

then, for the purposes of the determination of the pool, the amount shown in the earlier account shall be recalculated using the same method as that used to calculate the amount mentioned in paragraph (a) above.

(8) The alteration of the existing scheme shall be treated as being within subsection (8) of section 177B.

(9) An order may include such supplementary, incidental or consequential provisions as appear to the Treasury to be necessary or expedient.

(10) In this paragraph "an existing scheme", in relation to an order, means a scheme which, immediately before the day on which the order comes into force, is a registered scheme.]¹

Commentary—*Simon's Direct Tax Service* **E4.305.**
Amendments—¹ This paragraph inserted by FA 1995 s 136(12), and repealed by FA 1997 Sch 18 Pt VI(3); see the corresponding note at the beginning of this Schedule.

[20—*(1) The scheme must provide that, in preparing a profit and loss account for the purposes of this Schedule, no changes may be made from the accounting policies used in preparing accounts for any earlier period relevant for those purposes, or in the methods of applying those policies, if the effect of the changes (either singly or taken together) would be that the amount of profits (or losses) differed by more than 5 per cent from what would be that amount if no changes were made.*

(2) Sub-paragraph (1) above has effect subject to paragraph 19(2) above.]¹

Commentary—*Simon's Direct Tax Service* **E4.305.**
Definitions—''Losses'', s 169(1); ''profits'', ss 169(1), 833(1).
Amendments—¹ This paragraph repealed by FA 1997 Sch 18 Pt VI(3); see the corresponding note at the beginning of this Schedule.

[Parts of undertakings

21—*(1) This paragraph shall apply to a scheme if the employment unit is a part of an undertaking, and the scheme states that the profits or losses of the unit are for the purposes of the scheme to be taken to be equivalent to those of the whole undertaking (which must be identified by the scheme).*

*(2) Where this paragraph applies to a scheme, this Schedule shall have effect as if any reference to the profits or losses of the employment unit were a reference to the profits or losses of the undertaking of which it forms part.]*¹

Commentary—*Simon's Direct Tax Service* **E4.303.**
Cross references—See TA 1988 Sch 8 para 22 (supplementary provisions).
TA 1988 Sch 8 para 23 (conditions to be complied with where this paragraph applies to a scheme and Method A is employed).
TA 1988 Sch 8 para 24 (conditions to be complied with where this paragraph applies to a scheme and Method B is employed).
Amendments—¹ This paragraph inserted by FA 1989 Sch 4 para 15, and repealed by FA 1997 Sch 18 Pt VI(3); see the corresponding note at the beginning of this Schedule.

[22—*(1) Where paragraph 21 above applies to a scheme, the scheme must contain provisions ensuring that no payments are made under it by reference to a profit period unless, at the beginning of that profit period,—*

(a) there is at least one other registered scheme which relates to employees employed in the same undertaking as that of which the employment unit forms part, and

(b) the number of the employees to whom the scheme relates does not exceed 33 per cent of the number of the employees to whom that other scheme relates (or if there is more than one other scheme, the aggregate number of the employees to whom they relate).

(2) Another registered scheme shall be disregarded for the purposes of sub-paragraph (1) above—

(a) if paragraph 21 above applies to it, or

(b) if, by virtue of provisions of the kind described in paragraph 6 above, no payments could be made under it by reference to the profit period concerned.

*(3) Where paragraph 21 above applies to two or more schemes relating to employment units which are parts of the same undertaking, an employee to whom another scheme relates shall not be counted for the purposes of sub-paragraph (1)(b) above in connection with more than one of those schemes.]*¹

Commentary—*Simon's Direct Tax Service* **E4.303.**
Definitions—''Employment unit'', s 169(1); ''profit period'', s 169(1).
Amendments—¹ This paragraph inserted by FA 1989 Sch 4 para 15 and repealed by FA 1997 Sch 18 Pt VI(3); see the corresponding note at the beginning of this Schedule.

[23—*(1) In a case where—*

(a) paragraph 21 above applies to a scheme, and

(b) method A (specified in paragraph 13 above) is employed for the purposes of the scheme,

the scheme must contain provisions which comply with this paragraph and which apply as regards each profit period to which the scheme relates.

(2) The scheme must ensure that no payments are made under it by reference to a given profit period if the percentage mentioned in paragraph 13(1) above exceeds the permitted percentage.

(3) The scheme must ensure that the permitted percentage is a percentage found by—

(a) taking the pay paid to employees in respect of employment in the relevant year in the employment unit to which the other scheme mentioned in paragraph 22(1)(a) above relates or (if there are two or more other schemes) the aggregate of the pay paid to employees in respect of employment in the relevant year in the employment units to which the other schemes relate;

(b) taking the profit-related pay paid to employees in respect of employment in the relevant year in the employment unit to which the other scheme mentioned in paragraph 22(1)(a) above relates or (if there are two or more other schemes) the aggregate of the profit-related pay paid to employees in respect of employment in the relevant year in the employment units to which the other schemes relate;

(c) taking the pay paid to employees in respect of employment in the relevant year in the employment unit to which the scheme mentioned in paragraph 21 above relates;

(d) taking the fraction whose denominator is equal to the number of whole pounds found under paragraph (a) above and whose numerator is equal to the number of whole pounds found under paragraph (b) above;

(e) multiplying the amount found under paragraph (c) above by the fraction found under paragraph (d) above;

(f) taking the profits for the relevant year of the undertaking mentioned in paragraph 21 above;

(g) expressing the amount found under paragraph (e) above as a percentage of the amount found under paragraph (f) above;

(h) taking the percentage found under paragraph (g) above as the permitted percentage.

(4) The scheme must ensure that the relevant year is a period of 12 months identified in the scheme and ending at a time within the period of two years immediately preceding the given profit period.][1]

Commentary—*Simon's Direct Tax Service* **E4.303,306.**
Definitions—"Employment", s 169(1); "employment unit", s 169(1); "pay", s 169(1); "profit period", s 169(1); "profit-related pay", s 169(1).
Amendments—[1] This paragraph inserted by FA 1994 s 99 in relation to any scheme not registered before 1 December 1993. It is repealed by FA 1997 Sch 18 Pt VI(3); see the corresponding note at the beginning of this Schedule.

[24—*(1) In a case where—*

   (a) paragraph 21 above applies to a scheme, and
   (b) method B (specified in paragraph 14 above) is employed for the purposes of the scheme,

the scheme must contain provisions which comply with this paragraph and which apply as regards each profit period to which the scheme relates.

(2) The scheme must ensure that no payments are made under it by reference to the first or only profit period to which the scheme relates if the notional pool mentioned in paragraph 14(1)(a) above exceeds the permitted limit.

(3) The scheme must also ensure that no payments are made under it by reference to a given profit period other than the first if the distributable pool for the previous profit period (mentioned in paragraph 14(1)(b) above) exceeds the permitted limit.

(4) The scheme must ensure that the permitted limit is a limit found by—

   (a) taking the pay paid to employees in respect of employment in the relevant year in the employment unit to which the other scheme mentioned in paragraph 22(1)(a) above relates or (if there are two or more other schemes) the aggregate of the pay paid to employees in respect of employment in the relevant year in the employment units to which the other schemes relate;
   (b) taking the profit-related pay paid to employees in respect of employment in the relevant year in the employment unit to which the other scheme mentioned in paragraph 22(1)(a) above relates or (if there are two or more other schemes) the aggregate of the profit-related pay paid to employees in respect of employment in the relevant year in the employment units to which the other schemes relate;
   (c) taking the pay paid to employees in respect of employment in the relevant year in the employment unit to which the scheme mentioned in paragraph 21 above relates;
   (d) taking the fraction whose denominator is equal to the number of whole pounds found under paragraph (a) above and whose numerator is equal to the number of whole pounds found under paragraph (b) above;
   (e) multiplying the amount found under paragraph (c) above by the fraction found under paragraph (d) above;
   (f) taking the amount found under paragraph (e) above as the permitted limit.

(5) The scheme must ensure that the relevant year is—

   (a) a period of 12 months identified in the scheme and ending at a time within the period of two years immediately preceding the first or only profit period to which the scheme relates (in the case of provisions contained in the scheme by virtue of sub-paragraph (2) above);
   (b) a period of 12 months identified in the scheme and ending at a time within the period of two years immediately preceding the given profit period (in the case of provisions contained in the scheme by virtue of sub-paragraph (3) above).][1]

Commentary—*Simon's Direct Tax Service* **E4.303, 306.**
Definitions—"Employment", s 169(1); "employment unit", s 169(1); "pay", s 169(1); "profit period", s 169(1); "profit-related pay", s 169(1).
Amendments—[1] This paragraph inserted by FA 1994 s 99 in relation to any scheme not registered before 1 December 1993. It is repealed by FA 1997 Sch 18 Pt VI(3); see the corresponding note at the beginning of this Schedule.

SCHEDULE 9

APPROVED SHARE OPTION SCHEMES AND PROFIT SHARING SCHEMES

Sections 185, 186, 187

Concession B27—If certain conditions are fulfilled, a jointly owned company and companies under the control of a jointly owned company are admitted as participating companies in an approved employee share scheme.
Revenue & other press releases—IR Booklet IR95 (Approved profit sharing schemes).
IR Booklet IR96 (Approved profit sharing schemes—explanatory notes).
IR Booklet IR97 (Approved SAYE share option schemes).
IR Booklet IR98 (Approved SAYE share option schemes—explanatory notes).
IR Booklet IR101 (Approved company share option plans).
IR Booklet IR102 (Approved company share option plans—explanatory notes).
Cross references—See TA 1988 s 84A(4) (relief for costs of establishing share option or profit sharing schemes).
TA 1988 s 187 (interpretation).
TA 1988 s 238(2) (computation of gains on disposal or part disposal of shares in schemes approved under this Schedule).
TCGA 1992 s 238(1) (notwithstanding anything in a profit sharing scheme approved under this Schedule, for the purposes of capital gains tax a participant in the scheme to be treated as absolutely entitled to his shares against the trustees).
FA 2000 s 49(1) (profit sharing schemes under this Schedule will not be approved by the Board unless the application for approval is received before 6 April 2000).

PART I

GENERAL

1—(1) Subject to the provisions of this Schedule, on the application of a body corporate ("the grantor") which has established a share option scheme or a profit sharing scheme, the Board shall approve the scheme if they are satisfied that it fulfils such requirements of Part II and this Part as apply in relation to the scheme in question, and the requirements of Part III, IV or V of this Schedule; and in this Schedule—

"the relevant requirements" means, in relation to any scheme, the requirements of this Schedule by reference to which the scheme is approved; and

"savings-related share option scheme" means a scheme in relation to which the relevant requirements include the requirements of Part III of this Schedule.

(2) An application under sub-paragraph (1) above shall be made in writing and contain such particulars and be supported by such evidence as the Board may require.

(3) Where the grantor has control of another company or companies, the scheme may be expressed to extend to all or any of the companies of which it has control and in this Schedule a scheme which is expressed so to extend is referred to as a "group scheme".

(4) In relation to a group scheme the expression "participating company" means the grantor or any other company to which for the time being the scheme is expressed to extend.

Commentary—*Simon's Direct Tax Service* **E4.553, 560, 574, 582.**
Concession B27—If certain conditions are fulfilled, a jointly owned company and companies under the control of a jointly owned company are admitted as participating companies in an approved employee share scheme.
Revenue Decision RD 5—Linkage between approved discretionary employee share option scheme and "phantom" share scheme.
Simon's Tax Cases—IRC v Reed International plc [1995] STC 889.
Definitions—"The Board", s 832(1); "company", s 832(1), (2); "control", ss 187(2), 839; "grantor", s 187(2); "scheme", s 187(2).
Cross references—See the CGT (Definition of Unit Trust Scheme) Regulations, SI 1988/266 reg 3(b) (a profit sharing scheme approved under this Part is treated as not being a unit trust scheme for the purposes of TCGA 1992).

2—(1) The Board shall not approve a scheme under this Schedule if it appears to them that it contains features which are neither essential nor reasonably incidental to the purpose of providing for employees and directors benefits in the nature of rights to acquire shares or, in the case of a profit sharing scheme, in the nature of interests in shares.

(2) A profit sharing scheme shall not be approved under paragraph 1 above unless the Board are satisfied that, whether under the terms of the scheme or otherwise, every participant in the scheme is bound in contract with the grantor—

(a) to permit his shares to remain in the hands of the trustees throughout the period of retention; and

(b) not to assign, charge or otherwise dispose of his beneficial interest in his shares during that period; and

(c) if he directs the trustees to transfer the ownership of his shares to him at any time before the release date, to pay to the trustees before the transfer takes place a sum equal to income tax at the basic rate on the appropriate percentage of the locked-in value of the shares at the time of the direction; and

(d) not to direct the trustees to dispose of his shares at any time before the release date in any other way except by sale for the best consideration in money that can reasonably be obtained at the time of the sale or, in the case of redeemable shares in a workers' co-operative, by redemption.

[(2A) The Board shall not approve a profit sharing scheme unless they are satisfied—

(a) that the arrangements for the scheme do not make any provision, and are not in any way associated with any provision made, for loans to some or all of the employees of—

(i) the company that established the scheme, or

(ii) in the case of a group scheme, any participating company, and

(b) that the operation of the scheme is not in any way associated with such loans.

(2B) For the purposes of sub-paragraph (2A) above "arrangements" includes any scheme, agreement or understanding, whether or not legally enforceable.][1]

(3) The Board must be satisfied in the case of a savings-related share option scheme or a profit sharing scheme—

(a) that there are no features of the scheme (other than any which are included to satisfy requirements of this Schedule) which have or would have the effect of discouraging any description of employees or former employees who fulfil the conditions in paragraph 26(1) or, as the case may be, 36(1) below from actually participating in the scheme; and

(b) where the grantor is a member of a group of companies, that the scheme does not and would not have the effect of conferring benefits wholly or mainly on directors of companies in the group or on those employees of companies in the group who are in receipt of the higher or highest levels of remuneration.

(4) For the purposes of sub-paragraph (3) above "a group of companies" means a company and any other companies of which it has control.

Commentary—*Simon's Direct Tax Service* **E4.553, 560, 574, 582.**
Simon's Tax Cases—Sub-para 2(1), *IRC v Burton Group plc* [1990] STC 242.
Definitions—"Basic rate", s 832(1); "the Board", s 832(1); "company", s 832(1), (2); "control", ss 187(2), 839; "grantor", s 187(2); "income tax", s 832(4); "locked-in value", s 187(2); "participant", s 187(2); "savings-related share option scheme", s 187(2); "scheme", s 187(2); "shares", s 187(2); "the trustees", s 187(2); "workers' co-operative", s 187(10).
Cross references—See TA 1988 Sch 9 para 3 (cancellation of approval of schemes for breach of obligations under this paragraph).
TA 1988 Sch 9 para 32(2) (prohibition against disposal of shares by trustees of a profit sharing scheme).
TA 1988 Sch 10 para 1 (limitations on contractual obligations of participants in a profit sharing scheme).
TA 1988 Sch 10 para 7(7) (treatment for purposes of Income Tax Acts of a sum referred to in sub-para 2(c) above).
TCGA 1992 s 238(1) (notwithstanding anything in sub-para (2) above, a participant in a profit sharing scheme to be treated as absolutely entitled to his shares as against the trustees).
Amendments—[1] Sub-paras (2A), (2B) inserted by FA 2000 s 53(1), (3) with effect from 21 March 2000.

3—(1) If, at any time after the Board have approved a share option scheme, any of the relevant requirements ceases to be satisfied or the grantor fails to provide information requested by the Board under paragraph 6 below, the Board may withdraw the approval with effect from that time or such later time as the Board may specify; but where rights obtained under a savings-related share option scheme before the withdrawal of approval from the scheme under this paragraph are exercised after the withdrawal, section 185(3) shall apply in respect of the exercise as if the scheme were still approved.

(2) If at any time after the Board have approved a profit sharing scheme—

(a) a participant is in breach of any of his obligations under paragraph 2(2)(a), (c) and (d) above; or

(b) there is, with respect to the operation of the scheme, any contravention of any of the relevant requirements, Schedule 10, the scheme itself or the terms of the trust referred to in paragraph 30(1)(c) below; or

(c) any shares of a class of which shares have been appropriated to the participants receive different treatment in any respect from the other shares of that class, in particular, different treatment in respect of—

    (i) the dividend payable;
    (ii) repayment;
    (iii) the restrictions attaching to the shares; or
    (iv) any offer of substituted or additional shares, securities or rights of any description in respect of the shares; or

[(ca) the Board—

    (i) cease to be satisfied of the matters mentioned in paragraph 2(2A) above, or
    (ii) in the case of a scheme approved before 21st March 2000, are not satisfied of those matters; or][2]

(d) the Board cease to be satisfied that the scheme complies with the requirements of paragraph 2(3) above or paragraph 36 below; or

(e) the trustees, the grantor or, in the case of a group scheme, a company which is or has been a participating company fail or fails to furnish any information which they are or it is required to furnish under paragraph 6 below[; or

(f) the trustees appropriate shares to participants, one or more of whom have had free shares appropriated to them, at an earlier time in the same year of assessment, under a relevant share plan][1],

the Board may, subject to sub-paragraph (3) below, withdraw the approval with effect from that time or from such later time as the Board may specify.

(3) It shall not be a ground for withdrawal of approval of a profit sharing scheme that shares which have been newly issued receive, in respect of dividends payable with respect to a period beginning before the date on which the shares were issued, treatment which is less favourable than that accorded to shares issued before that date.

[(4) For the purposes of sub-paragraph (2)(f) above the reference to persons having had free shares appropriated to them includes persons who would have had free shares appropriated to them but for their failure to obtain a performance allowance (within the meaning of paragraph 25 of Schedule 8 to the Finance Act 2000).

(5) In sub-paragraph (2)(f) and (4) above—

"free shares" has the same meaning as in Schedule 8 to the Finance Act 2000;
"relevant share plan", in relation to a profit sharing scheme, means an employee share ownership plan that—

    (a) was established by the grantor or a connected company, and
    (b) is approved under Schedule 8 to that Act.

(6) For the purposes of sub-paragraph (5) above "connected company" means—

    (a) a company which controls or is controlled by the grantor or which is controlled by a company which also controls the grantor, or
    (b) a company which is a member of a consortium owning the grantor or which is owned in part by the grantor as a member of a consortium.][1]

Commentary—*Simon's Direct Tax Service* E4.553, 574, 582.
Definitions—"The Board", s 832(1); "company", s 832(1), (2); "grantor", s 187(2); "group scheme", Sch 9 para 1(3); "participant", s 187(2); "participating company", Sch 9 para 1(4); "relevant requirements", s 187(2); "savings-related share option scheme", s 187(2); "scheme", s 187(2); "share", s 187(2); "the trustees", s 187(2).
Amendments—¹ Sub-para (2)(*f*), and words "; or" preceding it, and sub-paras (4)–(6), inserted by FA 2000 s 51 with effect from 28 July 2000.
² Sub-para (2)(*ca*) inserted by FA 2000 s 53(2), (3) with effect from 21 March 2000.

4 If an alteration is made in the scheme at any time after the Board have approved the scheme, the approval shall not have effect after the date of the alteration unless the Board have approved the alteration.

Commentary—*Simon's Direct Tax Service* E4.553, 582.
Definitions—"The Board", s 832(1); "scheme", s 187(2).

5 If aggrieved—

(*a*) in any case, by the failure of the Board to approve the scheme or to approve an alteration in the scheme or by the withdrawal of approval; or

(*b*) in the case of a savings-related share option scheme, by the failure of the Board to decide that a condition subject to which the approval has been given is satisfied; or

(*c*) in the case of a profit sharing scheme, by the failure of the Board to approve an alteration in the terms of the trust referred to in paragraph 30(1)(*c*) below;

the grantor may, by notice given to the Board within 30 days from the date on which it is notified of the Board's decision, require the matter to be determined by the Special Commissioners, and the Special Commissioners shall hear and determine the matter in like manner as an appeal.

Commentary—*Simon's Direct Tax Service* E4.553, 582.
Definitions—"The Board", s 832(1); "grantor", s 187(2); "notice", s 832(1); "savings-related share option scheme", s 187(2); "scheme", s 187(2).

6 The Board may by notice require any person to furnish them, within such time as the Board may direct (not being less than 30 days), with such information as the Board think necessary for the performance of their functions under the relevant provisions and as the person to whom the notice is addressed has or can reasonably obtain, including in particular information—

(*a*) to enable the Board to determine—

(i) whether to approve a scheme or withdraw an approval already given; or

(ii) the liability to tax, including capital gains tax, of any person who has participated in a scheme; and

(*b*) in relation to the administration of a scheme and any alteration of the terms of a scheme.

Commentary—*Simon's Direct Tax Service* E4.553, 554, 583.
Definitions—"The Board", s 832(1); "capital gains tax", s 831(5); "notice", s 832(1); "scheme", s 187(2); "tax", s 832(3).
Cross references—See TMA 1970 s 98 Table (failure to comply with notice under this paragraph).
TA 1988 Sch 9 para 3 (cancellation of approval of schemes where information under this paragraph is not furnished).

PART II
REQUIREMENTS GENERALLY APPLICABLE

7 The provisions of this Part apply in relation to all schemes unless otherwise stated.

8 The scheme must not provide for any person to be eligible to participate in it, that is to say, to obtain and exercise rights under it, or in the case of a profit sharing scheme to have shares appropriated to him, at any time when he has, or has within the preceding 12 months had, a material interest in a close company which is—

(*a*) a company shares in which, in the case of a profit sharing scheme, are to be appropriated or, in the case of a share option scheme, may be acquired pursuant to the exercise of rights obtained under the scheme; or

(*b*) a company which has control of such a company or is a member of a consortium which owns such a company.

In determining whether a company is a close company for the purposes of this paragraph, sections 414(1)(*a*) and 415 shall be disregarded.

Commentary—*Simon's Direct Tax Service* E4.576.
Definitions—"Close company", ss 414(1), 832(1); "company", s 832(1), (2); "control", ss 187(2), 839; "material interest", s 187(3); "scheme", s 187(2); "shares", s 187(2).
Cross references—See TA 1988 Sch 9 para 26(1) (requirement of eligibility of certain employees and directors to participate in the scheme).
TA 1988 Sch 9 para 36 (subject to this paragraph, every full-time director and employee to be eligible to participate in the scheme on similar terms).
TA 1988 Sch 10 para 6 (appropriation of profit sharing scheme shares to an ineligible individual).

[8A—(1) In the case of a savings-related share option scheme or a profit sharing scheme, the scheme must specify what age is to be the specified age for the purposes of the scheme.

(2) The age specified—

(*a*) must be the same for men and women, and

(*b*) must be not less than 60 and not more than 75.]¹

Commentary—*Simon's Direct Tax Service* **E4.560.**
Definitions—"Savings-related share option scheme", s 187(2); "specified age", s 187(2).
Amendments—¹ This paragraph inserted by FA 1991 s 38(1), (5), (6) in relation to a scheme not approved before 25 July 1991.

9—(1) A share option scheme must provide for directors and employees to obtain rights to acquire shares ("scheme shares") which satisfy the requirements of paragraphs 10 to 14 below [(disregarding paragraph 11A)]¹.

(2) In the case of a profit sharing scheme, the shares to be acquired by the trustees as mentioned in paragraph 30 below ("scheme shares") must satisfy the requirements of paragraphs 10 to 12 and 14 below.

Commentary—*Simon's Direct Tax Service* **E4.558.**
Definitions—"Scheme", s 187(2); "share", s 187(2); "the trustees", s 187(2).
Amendments—¹ Words in sub-para (1) inserted by FA 2000 s 52(1), (2), (5) with effect from 21 March 2000.

10 Scheme shares must form part of the ordinary share capital of—

  (*a*) the grantor; or
  (*b*) a company which has control of the grantor; or
  (*c*) a company which either is, or has control of, a company which—

    (i) is a member of a consortium owning either the grantor or a company having control of the grantor; ...¹
    (ii) ...¹

Commentary—*Simon's Direct Tax Service* **E4.558, 586.**
Definitions—"Company", s 832(1), (2); "control", ss 187(2), 839; "grantor", s 187(2); "ordinary share capital", s 832(1); "scheme", s 187(2); "shares", s 187(2).
Cross references—See TA 1988 Sch 9 para 9(1) (directors' and employees' right to acquire share option scheme shares).
TA 1988 Sch 9 para 9(2) (shares to be acquired by trustees of a profit sharing scheme must satisfy requirements of this paragraph).
TA 1988 Sch 9 para 30(1) (requirements applicable to profit sharing schemes).
TA 1988 Sch 10 para 5(4) (profit sharing scheme: replacement of old shares by new shares in company reconstruction; continuity of the conditions in this paragraph).
Amendments—¹ Para (*c*)(ii) and the preceding word "and" repealed by FA 1989 s 64 and Sch 17 Pt IV.

11 Scheme shares must be—

  (*a*) shares of a class [listed]¹ on a recognised stock exchange; or
  (*b*) shares in a company which is not under the control of another company; or
  (*c*) shares in a company which is under the control of a company (other than a company which is, or would if resident in the United Kingdom be, a close company), whose shares are [listed]¹ on a recognised stock exchange.

Commentary—*Simon's Direct Tax Service* **E4.558, 586.**
Definitions—"Close company", ss 414(1), 832(1); "company", s 832(1), (2); "control", ss 187(2), 839; "recognised stock exchange", s 841; "shares", s 187(2); "United Kingdom", s 830(1).
Cross references—See TA 1988 Sch 9 para 9(1) (directors' and employees' right to acquire share option scheme shares).
TA 1988 Sch 9 para 9(2) (shares to be acquired by trustees of a profit sharing scheme must satisfy requirements of this paragraph).
TA 1988 Sch 9 para 30(1) (requirements applicable to profit sharing schemes).
TA 1988 Sch 10 para 5(4) (profit sharing scheme: replacement of old shares by new shares in company reconstruction; continuity of the conditions in this paragraph).
Amendments—¹ Words in sub-paras (*a*), (*c*) substituted by FA 1996 Sch 38 para 6(1), (2)(*j*), (10) with effect in relation to any time falling after 31 March 1996.

[**11A**—(1) In the case of a profit sharing scheme, scheme shares must not be shares—

  (*a*) in an employer company, or
  (*b*) in a company that—

    (i) has control of an employer company, and
    (ii) is under the control of a person or persons within sub-paragraph (2)(*b*)(i) below in relation to an employer company.

(2) For the purposes of this paragraph a company is "an employer company" if—

  (*a*) the business carried on by it consists substantially in the provision of the services of the persons employed by it, and
  (*b*) the majority of those services are provided to—

    (i) a person who has, or two or more persons who together have, control of the company, or
    (ii) a company associated with the company.

(3) For the purposes of sub-paragraph (2)(*b*)(ii) above a company shall be treated as associated with another company if both companies are under the control of the same person or persons.

(4) For the purposes of sub-paragraphs (1) to (3) above—

  (*a*) references to a person include a partnership, and
  (*b*) where a partner, alone or together with others, has control of a company, the partnership shall be treated as having like control of that company.

(5) For the purposes of this paragraph the question whether a person controls a company shall be determined in accordance with section 416(2) to (6).]¹

Commentary—*Simon's Direct Tax Service* **E4.558, 575.**
Amendment—¹ This paragraph inserted by FA 2000 s 52(1), (3), (5), with effect from 21 March 2000. By virtue of FA 2000 s 52(6), this paragraph does not have effect for shares acquired before 21 March 2000 by the trustees of a profit sharing scheme approved under Sch 9 of this Act.

12—(1) Scheme shares must be—

   (*a*) fully paid up;

   (*b*) not redeemable; and

   (*c*) not subject to any restrictions [other than those permitted by sub-paragraph (1A) below.]¹

Sub-paragraph (*b*) above does not apply, in the case of a profit sharing scheme, in relation to shares in a workers' co-operative.

[(1A) Subject to sub-paragraph (1B) below, scheme shares may be subject to—

   (*a*) restrictions which attach to all shares of the same class, or

   (*b*) a restriction authorised by sub-paragraph (2) below.

(1B) In the case of a profit sharing scheme, scheme shares must not be subject to any restrictions affecting the rights attaching to those shares which relate to—

   (*a*) dividends, or

   (*b*) assets on a winding-up of the company,

other than restrictions which attach to all other ordinary shares in the same company.]¹

(2) Except as provided below, the shares may be subject to a restriction imposed by the company's articles of association—

   (*a*) requiring all shares held by directors or employees of the company or of any other company of which it has control to be disposed of on ceasing to be so held; and

   (*b*) requiring all shares acquired, in pursuance of rights or interests obtained by such directors or employees, by persons who are not (or have ceased to be) such directors or employees to be disposed of when they are acquired.

(3) A restriction is not authorised by sub-paragraph (2) above unless—

   (*a*) any disposal required by the restriction will be by way of sale for a consideration in money on terms specified in the articles of association; and

   (*b*) the articles also contain general provisions by virtue of which any person disposing of shares of the same class (whether or not held or acquired as mentioned in sub-paragraph (2) above) may be required to sell them on terms which are the same as those mentioned in paragraph (*a*) above.

(4) In the case of a profit sharing scheme, except in relation to redeemable shares in a workers' co-operative, nothing in sub-paragraph (2) above authorises a restriction which would require a person, before the release date, to dispose of his beneficial interest in shares the ownership of which has not been transferred to him.

Commentary—*Simon's Direct Tax Service* **E4.558, 575, 586.**
Revenue & other press releases—IR 11-6-85 (revised Revenue practice, some approved employee share option schemes: if company's Articles of Association authorise the directors to refuse to register a share transfer, then company is required to sign a declaration that this power will not be exercised to discriminate against the transfer of scheme shares; its existence should be made known to scheme participants.
Definitions—''Company'', s 832(1), (2); ''control'', ss 187(2), 839; ''scheme'', s 187(2); ''shares'', s 187(2); ''workers' co-operative'', s 187(10).
Cross references—See TA 1988 Sch 9 para 9(1) (directors' and employees' right to acquire share option scheme shares).
TA 1988 Sch 9 para 9(2) (shares to be acquired by trustees of a profit sharing scheme must satisfy requirements of this paragraph).
TA 1988 Sch 9 para 30(1) (requirements applicable to profit sharing schemes).
TA 1988 Sch 10 para 5(4) (profit sharing scheme: replacement of old shares by new shares in company reconstruction; continuity of the conditions in this paragraph).
Amendments—¹ Words in sub-para (1) substituted for words ''other than restrictions which attach to all shares of the same class or a restriction authorised by sub-paragraph (2) below'', and sub-paras (1A), (1B) inserted, by FA 2000 s 52(1), (4), (5) with effect from 21 March 2000. FA 2000 s 52(6) provides that these amendments do not have effect for shares acquired before 21 March 2000 by the trustees of a profit sharing scheme approved under Sch 9 of this Act.

13—(1) In determining, in the case of a share option scheme, for the purposes of paragraph 12(1)(*c*) above whether scheme shares which are or are to be acquired by any person are subject to any restrictions, there shall be regarded as a restriction attaching to the shares any contract, agreement, arrangement or condition by which his freedom to dispose of the shares or of any interest in them or of the proceeds of their sale or to exercise any right conferred by them is restricted or by which such a disposal or exercise may result in any disadvantage to him or to a person connected with him.

(2) Sub-paragraph (1) does not apply to so much of any contract, agreement, arrangement or condition as contains provisions similar in purpose and effect to any of the provisions of the Model Rules set out in the Model Code for Securities Transactions by Directors of Listed Companies issued by the Stock Exchange in November 1984.

[(3) In the case of schemes other than savings-related share option schemes, sub-paragraph (1) above does not apply in relation to any terms of a loan making provision about how it is to be repaid or the security to be given for it.]¹

14—(1) Except where scheme shares are shares in a company the ordinary share capital of which consists of shares of one class only, the majority of the issued shares of the same class either must be employee-control shares or must be held by persons other than—

(*a*) persons who acquired their shares in pursuance of a right conferred on them or an opportunity afforded to them as a director or employee of the grantor or any other company and not in pursuance of an offer to the public;

(*b*) trustees holding shares on behalf of persons who acquired their beneficial interests in the shares as mentioned in sub-paragraph (*a*) above; and

(*c*) in a case where the shares fall within sub-paragraph (*c*), but not within sub-paragraph (*a*), of paragraph 11 above, companies which have control of the company whose shares are in question or of which that company is an associated company.

(2) In its application to a profit sharing scheme, sub-paragraph (1) above shall have effect with the addition after the words ''ordinary share capital of which'' of the words ''at the time of the acquisition of the shares by the trustees''.

(3) For the purposes of this paragraph, shares in a company are employee-control shares if—

(*a*) the persons holding the shares are, by virtue of their holding, together able to control the company; and

(*b*) those persons are or have been employees or directors of the company or of another company which is under the control of the company.

15—(1) Except in the case of a profit sharing scheme, the scheme may provide that if any company (''the acquiring company'')—

(*a*) obtains control of a company whose shares are scheme shares as a result of making a general offer—

(i) to acquire the whole of the issued ordinary share capital of the company which is made on a condition such that if it is satisfied the person making the offer will have control of the company; or

(ii) to acquire all the shares in the company which are of the same class as the scheme shares;

(*b*) obtains control of a company whose shares are scheme shares in pursuance of a compromise or arrangement sanctioned by the court under section 425 of the Companies Act 1985 or Article 418 of the Companies (Northern Ireland) Order 1986; or

(*c*) becomes bound or entitled to acquire shares in a company whose shares are scheme shares under sections 428 to 430 of that Act or Articles 421 to 423 of that Order,

any participant in the scheme may at any time within the appropriate period, by agreement with the acquiring company, release his rights under the scheme (in this paragraph referred to as ''the old rights'') in consideration of the grant to him of rights (in this paragraph referred to as ''the new rights'') which are equivalent to the old rights but relate to shares in a different company (whether the acquiring company itself or some other company falling within paragraph 10(*b*) or (*c*) above).

(2) In sub-paragraph (1) above ''the appropriate period'' means—

(*a*) in a case falling within paragraph (*a*), the period of six months beginning with the time when the person making the offer has obtained control of the company and any condition subject to which the offer is made is satisfied;

(*b*) in a case falling within paragraph (*b*), the period of six months beginning with the time when the court sanctions the compromise or arrangement; and

(*c*) in a case falling within paragraph (*c*), the period during which the acquiring company remains bound or entitled as mentioned in that paragraph.

(3) The new rights shall not be regarded for the purposes of this paragraph as equivalent to the old rights unless—

(*a*) the shares to which they relate satisfy the conditions specified, in relation to scheme shares, in paragraphs 10 to 14 above; and

(*b*) the new rights will be exercisable in the same manner as the old rights and subject to the provisions of the scheme as it had effect immediately before the release of the old rights; and

(*c*) the total market value, immediately before the release, of the shares which were subject to the participant's old rights is equal to the total market value, immediately after the grant, of the shares in respect of which the new rights are granted to the participant; and (*d*) the total amount payable by the participant for the acquisition of shares in pursuance of the new rights is equal to the total amount that would have been payable for the acquisition of shares in pursuance of the old rights.

(4) Where any new rights are granted pursuant to a provision included in a scheme by virtue of this paragraph they shall be regarded—

(*a*) for the purpose of section 185 and this Schedule; and

(*b*) for the purposes of the subsequent application (by virtue of a condition complying with sub-paragraph (3)(*b*) above) of the provisions of the scheme,

as having been granted at the time when the corresponding old rights were granted.

(5) Where a scheme which was approved before 1st August 1987 is altered before 1st August 1989 so as to include such a provision as is mentioned above (''an exchange provision''), the scheme as altered may by virtue of this and the following sub-paragraphs apply that provision to rights obtained under the scheme before the date on which the alteration takes effect.

(6) If an exchange provision is applied as mentioned in sub-paragraph (5) above in a case where, on or after 17th March 1987 but before the date on which the alteration takes effect, an event has occurred by reason of which a person holding rights under the scheme would be able to take advantage of the exchange provision—

(*a*) the scheme may permit a person who held rights under the scheme immediately before that event to take advantage of the exchange provision; and

(*b*) in a case where rights then held would otherwise, by reason of the event, have ceased to be exercisable, the scheme may provide that the exchange provision shall apply as if the rights were still exercisable.

(7) The application of an exchange provision as mentioned in sub-paragraph (5) or (6) above shall not itself be regarded for the purposes of this Schedule as the acquisition of a right.

(8) Sub-paragraphs (5) and (6) above have effect subject to paragraph 4 above.

Commentary—*Simon's Direct Tax Service* E4.574, 585.
Definitions—''Company'', s 832(1), (2); ''control'', ss 187(2), 840; ''market value'', s 187(2); ''ordinary share capital'', s 832(1); ''participant'', s 187(2); ''scheme'', s 187(2); ''shares'', s 187(2).

PART III
REQUIREMENTS APPLICABLE TO SAVINGS-RELATED SHARE OPTION SCHEMES

16—(1) The scheme must provide for the scheme shares to be paid for with money not exceeding the amount of repayments made and any interest paid to them under a certified contractual savings scheme which has been approved by the Board for the purposes of this Schedule.

(2) Where the Board are satisfied that—

(*a*) a person has entered into a certified contractual savings scheme before 15th November 1980, and

(*b*) he has obtained rights under a scheme established before that date to acquire shares in a company of which he is an employee or director (or a company of which such a company has control) using repayments made under the certified contractual savings scheme;

then, repayments and interest paid under the certified contractual savings scheme shall be treated as repayments and interest paid, under a scheme approved by the Board for the purposes of this Schedule under sub-paragraph (1) above, and, accordingly, may be used for the purchase of shares under a savings-related share option scheme approved under this Schedule.

(3) The repayments and interest to which sub-paragraph (2) above applies shall not exceed the repayments and interest to which the participant would have been entitled if the terms of the scheme had corresponded to those of a certified contractual savings scheme approved by the Board under sub-paragraph (1) above.

Commentary—*Simon's Direct Tax Service* E4.574.
Definitions—''Approved'', s 187(2); ''the Board'', s 187(2); ''certified contractual savings scheme'', s 187(2); ''company'', s 832(1), (2); ''control'', ss 187(2), 839; ''interest'', s 832(1); ''participant'', s 187(2); ''savings-related share option scheme'', s 187(2); ''scheme'', s 187(2); ''shares'', s 187(2).

17 Subject to paragraphs 18 to 21 below, the rights obtained under the scheme must not be capable of being exercised before the bonus date, that is to say, the date on which repayments under the certified contractual savings scheme are due; and for the purposes of this paragraph and paragraph 16 above—

(*a*) repayments under a certified contractual savings scheme may be taken as including or as not including a bonus;

(*b*) the time when repayments are due shall be, where repayments are taken as including the maximum bonus, the earliest date on which the maximum bonus is payable and, in any other case, the earliest date on which a bonus is payable under the scheme; and

(*c*) the question what is to be taken as so included must be required to be determined at the time when rights under the scheme are obtained.

Commentary—*Simon's Direct Tax Service* E4.574.
Definitions—"Bonus date", s 187(2); "certified contractual savings scheme", s 187(2); "scheme", s 187(2).

18 The scheme must provide that if a person who has obtained rights under the scheme dies before the bonus date the rights must be exercised, if at all, within 12 months after the date of his death and if he dies within six months after the bonus date the rights may be exercised within 12 months after the bonus date.

Commentary—*Simon's Direct Tax Service* E4.574.
Definitions—"Bonus date", s 187(2); "scheme", s 187(2).
Cross references—See TA 1988 Sch 9 para 22 (time limit for the exercise of rights in other cases).

19 The scheme must provide that if a person who has obtained rights under it ceases to hold the office or employment by virtue of which he is eligible to participate in the scheme by reason of—

    (*a*) injury or disability or redundancy within the meaning of [the Employment Rights Act 1996][2] or

    (*b*) retirement on reaching [the specified age][1] or any other age at which he is bound to retire in accordance with the terms of his contract of employment,

then the rights must be exercised, if at all, within six months of his so ceasing and, if he so ceases for any other reason within three years of obtaining the rights, they may not be exercised at all except pursuant to such a provision of the scheme as is mentioned in paragraph 21(1)(*e*) below; and in relation to the case where he so ceases for any other reason more than three years after obtaining the rights the scheme must either provide that the rights may not be exercised or that they must be exercised, if at all, within six months of his so ceasing.

Commentary—*Simon's Direct Tax Service* E4.574.
Definitions—"Pensionable age", s 187(2); "scheme", s 187(2), "Specified age", s 187(2).
Cross references—See TA 1988 Sch 9 para 23 (time when a person ceases to hold an office or employment for the purposes of this paragraph).
TA 1988 Sch 9 para 26(3) (except as provided by this paragraph, no person other than a director or an employee must be eligible to participate in the scheme).
Amendments—[1] Words in para (*b*) substituted by FA 1991 s 38(1), (2), (6) in relation to a scheme not approved before 25 July 1991.
[2] Words in para (*a*) substituted by the Employment Rights Act 1996 s 243, Sch 1 para 35(1), (4) with effect from 22 August 1996.

20 The scheme must provide that where a person who has obtained rights under it continues to hold the office or employment by virtue of which he is eligible to participate in the scheme after the date on which he reaches [the specified age][1], he may exercise the rights within six months of that date.

Commentary—*Simon's Direct Tax Service* E4.574.
Definitions—"Pensionable age", s 187(2); "scheme", s 187(2); "specified age", s 187(2).
Amendments—[1] Words substituted by FA 1991 s 38(1), (2), (6) in relation to a scheme not approved before 25 July 1991.

21—(1) The scheme may provide that—

    (*a*) if any person obtains control of a company whose shares are scheme shares as a result of making a general offer falling within paragraph 15(*a*)(i) or (ii) above, rights obtained under the scheme to acquire shares in the company may be exercised within six months of the time when the person making the offer has obtained control of the company and any condition subject to which the offer is made has been satisfied;

    (*b*) if under section 425 of the Companies Act 1985 or Article 418 of the Companies (Northern Ireland) Order 1986 (power to compromise with creditors and members) the court sanctions a compromise or arrangement proposed for the purposes of or in connection with a scheme for the reconstruction of a company whose shares are scheme shares or its amalgamation with any other company or companies, rights obtained under the share option scheme to acquire shares in the company may be exercised within six months of the court sanctioning the compromise or arrangement;

    (*c*) if any person becomes bound or entitled, under sections 428 to 430 of that Act of 1985 or Articles 421 to 423 of that Order of 1986 (power to acquire shares of shareholders dissenting from schemes or contract approved by majority), to acquire shares in a company shares in which are scheme shares, rights obtained under the scheme to acquire shares in the company may be exercised at any time when that person remains so bound or entitled;

    (*d*) if a company whose shares are scheme shares passes a resolution for voluntary winding up, rights obtained under a scheme to acquire shares in the company may be exercised within six months of the passing of the resolution; ...[1]

    (*e*) if a person ceases to hold an office or employment by virtue of which he is eligible to participate in the scheme by reason only that—

        (i) that office or employment is in a company of which the grantor ceases to have control; or

        (ii) that office or employment relates to a business or part of a business which is transferred to a person who is neither an associated company of the grantor nor a company of which the grantor has control;

rights under the scheme held by that person may be exercised within six months of his so ceasing; [and][1]

[(*f*) if, at the bonus date, a person who has obtained rights under the scheme holds an office or employment in a company which is not a participating company but which is—

(i) an associated company of the grantor, or

(ii) a company of which the grantor has control,

those rights may be exercised within six months of that date.]¹

(2) For the purposes of this paragraph a person shall be deemed to have obtained control of a company if he and others acting in concert with him have together obtained control of it.

(3) Where a scheme which has been approved before 1st August 1986 has been or is altered before 1st August 1988 so as to include such a provision as is specified in sub-paragraph (1)(*e*) above, the scheme as altered may by virtue of this sub-paragraph apply that pro- vision to rights obtained under the scheme before the date on which the alteration takes effect, and where that provision is so applied in relation to such rights—

(*a*) the scheme may permit a person having such rights to take advantage of the provision notwithstanding that under the scheme he would otherwise be unable to exercise those rights after he has ceased to hold the office or employment in question; and

(*b*) if, before the date on which the alteration takes effect, a person who held such rights on 18th March 1986 ceases, in either of the circumstances set out in sub-paragraph (1)(*e*) above, to hold an office or employment by virtue of which he was eligible to participate in the scheme, then, so far as concerns the rights so held, the scheme may permit him to take advantage of the provision in question as if the alteration had been made immediately before he ceased to hold that office or employment; and

(*c*) the application of the provision shall not itself be regarded as the acquisition of a right for the purposes of this Schedule.

This sub-paragraph has effect subject to paragraph 4 above.

[(4) Where a scheme approved before the date of the passing of the Finance Act 1996 is altered before 5th May 1998 so as to include such a provision as is specified in sub-paragraph (1)(*f*) above, the scheme may apply the provision to rights obtained under the scheme before the alteration takes effect, whether the bonus date in relation to the rights occurred before or after the passing of that Act; and where the provision is applied to such rights by virtue of this sub-paragraph, its application to such rights shall not itself be regarded as the acquisition of a right for the purposes of this Schedule.]¹

This sub-paragraph has effect subject to paragraph 4 above.]¹

Commentary—*Simon's Direct Tax Service* **E4.574.**
Definitions—"Associated company", s 187(2); "company", s 832(1), (2); "control", ss 187(2), 839; "grantor", s 187(2); "participating company", Sch 9 para 1(4); "scheme", s 187(2); "shares", s 187(2).
Cross references—See TA 1988 Sch 9 para 23 (time when a person ceases to hold an office or employment for the purposes of sub-para (1)(*e*) above).
TA 1988 Sch 9 para 26(3) (except as provided in sub-paras 1(*e*) and 1(*f*) above, no person other than a director or an employee must be eligible to participate in the scheme).
Amendments—¹ Word omitted from sub-para (1)(*d*) repealed, sub-para (1)(*f*) and preceding word inserted and sub-para (4) added by FA 1996 s 113(1), (2), Sch 41 Pt V(5).

22 Except as provided in paragraph 18 above, rights obtained by a person under the scheme must not be capable—

(*a*) of being transferred by him, or

(*b*) of being exercised later than six months after the bonus date.

Commentary—*Simon's Direct Tax Service* **E4.574.**
Definitions—"Bonus date", s 187(2); "scheme", s 187(2).

23 No person shall be treated for the purposes of paragraph 19 or 21(1)(*e*) above as ceasing to hold an office or employment by virtue of which he is eligible to participate in the scheme until he ceases to hold an office or employment in the grantor or in any associated company or company of which the grantor has control.

Commentary—*Simon's Direct Tax Service* **E4.574.**
Definitions—"Associated company", s 187(2); "company", s 832(1), (2); "control", ss 187(2), 839; "grantor", s 187(2); "scheme", s 187(2).

24—(1) The scheme must provide for a person's contributions under the certified contractual savings scheme to be of such amount as to secure as nearly as may be repayment of an amount equal to that for which shares may be acquired in pursuance of rights obtained under the scheme; and for this purpose the amount of repayment under the certified contractual savings scheme shall be determined as mentioned in paragraph 17 above.

(2) The scheme must not—

(*a*) permit the aggregate amount of a person's contributions under certified contractual savings schemes linked to savings-related share option schemes approved under this Schedule to exceed [£250]¹ monthly, nor

(*b*) impose a minimum on the amount of a person's contributions which exceeds £10 monthly.

(3) The Treasury may by order amend sub-paragraph (2) above by substituting for any amount for the time being specified in that sub-paragraph such amount as may be specified in the order.

Commentary—*Simon's Direct Tax Service* **E4.574.**
Definitions—''Approved'', s 187(2); ''certified contractual savings scheme'', s 187(2); ''savings-related share option schemes'', s 187(2); ''scheme'', s 187(2); ''shares'', s 187(2).
Amendments—[1] Amount in sub-para (2)(a) substituted by FA 1991 s 40 with effect from 1 September 1991 by virtue of SI 1991/1741.

25 The price at which scheme shares may be acquired by the exercise of a right obtained under the scheme—

(a) must be stated at the time the right is obtained, and

(b) must not be manifestly less than [80 per cent.][1] of the market value of shares of the same class at that time or, if the Board and the grantor agree in writing, at such earlier time or times as may be provided in the agreement,

but the scheme may provide for such variation of the price as may be necessary to take account of any variation in the share capital of which the scheme shares form part.

Commentary—*Simon's Direct Tax Service* **E4.574.**
Simon's Tax Cases—*IRC v Reed International plc* [1995] STC 889.
Definitions—''The Board'', s 832(1); ''grantor'', s 187(2); ''market value'', s 187(2); ''scheme'', s 187(2); ''shares'', s 187(2).
Amendments—[1] Percentage in para (b) substituted by FA 1989 s 62(1), (3).

26—(1) Subject to paragraph 8 above, every person who—

(a) is [an employee][1] or a full time director of the grantor or, in the case of a group scheme, a participating company, and

(b) has been such an employee or director at all times during a qualifying period not exceeding five years, and

(c) is chargeable to tax in respect of his office or employment under Case I of Schedule E,

must be eligible to participate in the scheme, that is to say, to obtain and exercise rights under it, on similar terms, and those who do participate in the scheme must actually do so on similar terms.

(2) For the purposes of sub-paragraph (1) above, the fact that the rights to be obtained by the persons participating in a scheme vary according to the levels of their remuneration, the length of their service or similar factors shall not be regarded as meaning that they are not eligible to participate in the scheme on similar terms or do not actually do so.

(3) Except as provided by paragraph 19 above or pursuant to such a provision as is referred to in paragraph 21(1)(e) [or (f)][2] above, a person must not be eligible to participate in the scheme at any time unless he is at that time a director or employee of the grantor or, in the case of a group scheme, of a participating company.

Commentary—*Simon's Direct Tax Service* **E4.576.**
Simon's Tax Cases—*IRC v Reed International plc* [1995] STC 889
Definitions—''Case I of Schedule E'', s 19(2); ''grantor'', s 187(2); ''group scheme'', Sch 9 para 1(3); ''participating company'', Sch 9 para 1(4); ''scheme'', s 187(2).
Cross references—See TA 1988 Sch 9 para 2(3) (conditions for approval of schemes).
Amendments—[1] Words in sub-para (1)(a) substituted by FA 1995 s 137(2), with effect for any scheme not approved before 1 May 1995.
[2] Words in sub-para (3) inserted by FA 1996 s 113(3).

PART IV
REQUIREMENTS APPLICABLE TO OTHER SHARE OPTION SCHEMES

27—(1) A person must not be eligible to obtain rights under the scheme at any time unless he is at that time a full-time director or qualifying employee of the grantor or, in the case of a group scheme, of a participating company, but the scheme may provide that a person may exercise rights under it after he has ceased to be a full-time director or qualifying employee.

(2) The scheme must not permit any person obtaining rights under it to transfer any of them but may provide that, if a person who has obtained rights under it dies before exercising them, they may be exercised after, but not more than one year after, the date of his death.

(3) Where the scheme contains the provisions permitted by sub-paragraph (2) above and any rights are exercised—

(a) after the death of the person who obtained them; but

(b) before the expiry of the period of ten years beginning with his obtaining them;

subsection (3) of section 185 shall apply with the omission of the reference to subsection (5) of that section.

(4) In sub-paragraph (1) above ''qualifying employee'', in relation to a company, means an employee of the company (other than one who is a director of the company or, in the case of a group scheme, of a participating company) ...[1]

Commentary—*Simon's Direct Tax Service* **E4.585.**
Revenue & other press releases—ICAEW TR551 July 1984 (Revenue view, ''full time'' signifies working 25 or more hours per week. An employee who works requisite hours for a number of group companies, though not for one particular company accepted by Revenue as meeting criteria).

Definitions—"Company", s 832(1), (2); "grantor", s 187(2); "group scheme", Sch 9 para 1(3); "participating company", Sch 9 para 1(4); "scheme", s 187(2).
Amendments—[1] Words omitted from sub-para (4) repealed by FA 1995 s 137(3), Sch 29 Pt VIII(19), with effect for any scheme not approved before 1 May 1995 (but note FA 1995 s 137(8)).

28—(1) The scheme must provide that no person shall obtain rights under it which would, at the time they are obtained, cause the aggregate market value of the shares which he may acquire in pursuance of rights obtained under the scheme or under any other share option scheme, not being a savings-related share option scheme, approved under this Schedule and established by the grantor or by any associated company of the grantor (and not exercised) to exceed or further exceed [£30,000][1].

(2) ...[1]

(3) For the purposes of sub-paragraph (1) above, the market value of shares shall be calculated as at the time when the rights in relation to those shares were obtained or, in a case where an agreement relating to them has been made under paragraph 29 below, such earlier time or times as may be provided in the agreement.

(4) ...[1]

Commentary—*Simon's Direct Tax Service* E4.585.
Definitions—"Associated company", s 187(2); "grantor", s 187(2); "market value", s 187(2); "savings-related share option scheme", s 187(2); "scheme", s 187(2); "shares", s 187(2).
Amendments—[1] Sum in sub-para (1) substituted, and sub-paras (2), (4) repealed, by FA 1996 s 114(2), Sch 41 Pt V(5).

[29—[(1) The price at which scheme shares may be acquired by the exercise of a right obtained under the scheme—

(*a*) must be stated at the time the right is obtained, and
(*b*) must not be manifestly less than the market value of shares of the same class at that time or, if the Board and the grantor agree in writing, at such earlier time or times as may be provided in the agreement.][2]

(7) The scheme may provide for such variation of the price a which scheme shares may be acquired as may be necessary to take account of any variation in the share capital of which the scheme shares form part.

(8) ...[3]][1]

Commentary—*Simon's Direct Tax Service* E4.585.
Simon's Tax Cases—*IRC v Eurocopy plc* [1991] STC 707; *IRC v Reed International plc* [1995] STC 889.
Definitions—"The Board", s 832(1); "grantor", s 187(2); "market value", s 187(2); "scheme", s 187(2); "shares", s 187(2).
Cross references—See TA 1988 Sch 9 para 28(3) (market valuation of shares).
Amendments—[1] This paragraph substituted by FA 1991 s 39(1), (7) with effect from 1 January 1992.
[2] Sub-para (1) substituted for sub-paras (1)–(6) by FA 1996 s 113(3), (10) with effect in relation to rights obtained on or after 29 April 1996.
[3] Sub-para (8) repealed by FA 1996 Sch 41 Pt V(5) with effect in relation to rights obtained on or after 29 April 1996.

PART V
REQUIREMENTS APPLICABLE TO PROFIT SHARING SCHEMES

30—(1) The scheme must provide for the establishment of a body of persons resident in the United Kingdom ("the trustees")—

(*a*) who, out of moneys paid to them by the grantor or, in the case of a group scheme, a participating company, are required by the scheme to acquire shares in respect of which the conditions in paragraphs 10 to 12 and 14 above are fulfilled; and
(*b*) who are under a duty to appropriate shares acquired by them to individuals who participate in the scheme, not being individuals who are ineligible by virtue of paragraph 8 or 35 of this Schedule; and
(*c*) whose functions with respect to shares held by them are regulated by a trust which is constituted under the law of a part of the United Kingdom and the terms of which are embodied in an instrument which complies with the provisions of paragraphs 31 to 34 below.

(2) If at any time after the Board have approved the scheme, an alteration is made in the terms of the trust referred to in sub-paragraph (1)(*c*) above, the approval shall not have effect after the date of the alteration unless the Board have approved the alteration.

(3) The scheme must provide that the total of the initial market values of the shares appropriated to any one participant in a year of assessment will not exceed the relevant amount.

(4) In this Part of this Schedule "initial market value", in relation to a participant's shares, means the market value of those shares determined—

(*a*) except where paragraph (*b*) below applies, on the date on which the shares were appropriated to him; and
(*b*) if the Board and the trustees agree in writing, on or by reference to such earlier date or dates as may be provided for in the agreement.

Commentary—*Simon's Direct Tax Service* E4.555.
Definitions—"Approved", s 187(2); "the Board", s 832(1); "body of persons", s 832(1); "grantor", s 187(2); "group scheme", Sch 9 para 1(3); "market value", s 187(2); "participant", s 187(2); "participating company", Sch 9 para 1(4);

"scheme", s 187(2); "shares", s 187(2); "the trustees", s 187(2); "United Kingdom", s 830(1); "year of assessment", s 832(1).
Cross references—See TA 1988 Sch 9 para 3 (cancellation of approval of schemes for contravention of sub-para (1)(*c*) above).
TA 1988 Sch 9 para 5 (appeal to Special Commissioners where Board does not approve alterations of terms of trust referred to in sub-para (1)(*c*) above).

31 The trust instrument shall provide that, as soon as practicable after any shares have been appropriated to a participant, the trustees will give him notice of the appropriation—

  (*a*) specifying the number and description of those shares; and
  (*b*) stating their initial market value.

Commentary—*Simon's Direct Tax Service* E4.557.
Definitions—"Initial market value", s 187(2); "notice", s 832(1); "participant", s 187(2); "shares", s 187(2); "the trustees", s 187(2); "the trust instrument", s 187(2).

32—(1) The trust instrument must contain a provision prohibiting the trustees from disposing of any shares, except as mentioned in paragraph 1(1)(*a*), (*b*)[, (*c*) or (*cc*)]¹ of Schedule 10, during the period of retention (whether by transfer to the participant or otherwise).

(2) The trust instrument must contain a provision prohibiting the trustees from disposing of any shares after the end of the period of retention and before the release date except—

  (*a*) pursuant to a direction given by or on behalf of the participant or any person in whom the beneficial interest in his shares is for the time being vested; and
  (*b*) by a transaction which would not involve a breach of the participant's obligations under paragraph 2(2)(*c*) or (*d*) above.

Commentary—*Simon's Direct Tax Service* E4.557.
Definitions—"Participant", s 187(2); "period of retention", s 187(2); "shares", s 187(2); "the trustees", s 187(2); "the trust instrument", s 187(2).
Amendments—¹ Words in sub-para (1) substituted for the words "or (*c*)" by FA 1994 s 101(5), (9), (10) in relation to any scheme not approved before the day on which FA 1994 is passed (ie 3 May 1994) and in relation to any scheme approved before that day if it is altered on or after that day in accordance with FA 1994 s 101(10).

33 The trust instrument must contain a provision requiring the trustees—

  (*a*) subject to their obligations under paragraph 7 of Schedule 10 and to any such direction as is mentioned in paragraph 4(2) of that Schedule to pay over to the participant any money or money's worth received by them in respect of or by reference to any of his shares other than money's worth consisting of new shares within the meaning of paragraph 5 of that Schedule; and
  (*b*) to deal only pursuant to a direction given by or on behalf of the participant or any person in whom the beneficial interest in his shares is for the time being vested with any right conferred in respect of any of his shares to be allotted other shares, securities or rights of any description.

Commentary—*Simon's Direct Tax Service* E4.557.
Definitions—"Participant", s 187(2); "shares", s 187(2); "the trustees", s 187(2); "the trust instrument", s 187(2).
Cross references—See FA 1994 s 101(6), (11), (12), (14) (approved profit sharing schemes: acceptance by trustees of qualifying corporate bonds for shares of participants on mergers or reconstruction: exception in para (*a*) above in respect of new shares within Sch 10 para 5 extended to such qualifying corporate bonds).

34 The trust instrument must impose an obligation on the trustees—

  (*a*) to maintain such records as may be necessary to enable the trustees to carry out their obligations under paragraph 7 of Schedule 10; and
  (*b*) where the participant becomes liable to income tax under Schedule E by reason of the occurrence of any event, to inform him of any facts relevant to determining that liability.

Commentary—*Simon's Direct Tax Service* E4.557.
Definitions—"Participant", s 187(2); "Schedule E", s 19(1); "the trustees", s 187(2); "the trust instrument", s 187(2).

35—(1) An individual shall not be eligible to have shares appropriated to him under the scheme at any time unless he is at that time or was within the preceding 18 months a director or employee of the grantor or, in the case of a group scheme, of a participating company.

(2) An individual shall not be eligible to have shares appropriated to him under the scheme at any time if in that year of assessment shares have been appropriated to him under another approved scheme established by the grantor or by—

  (*a*) a company which controls or is controlled by the grantor or which is controlled by a company which also controls the grantor, or
  (*b*) a company which is a member of a consortium owning the grantor or which is owned in part by the grantor as a member of a consortium.

Commentary—*Simon's Direct Tax Service* E4.559.
Definitions—"Approved", s 187(2); "company", s 832(1), (2); "control", ss 187(2), 839; "grantor", s 187(2); "group scheme", Sch 9 para 1(3); "participating company", Sch 9 para 1(4); "scheme", s 187(2); "shares", s 187(2); "year of assessment", s 832(1).
Cross references—See TA 1988 Sch 9 para 36 (subject to this paragraph, every full–time director and employee to be eligible to participate in the scheme on similar terms).
TA 1988 Sch 10 para 6 (appropriation of profit sharing scheme shares to an ineligible individual).

36—(1) Subject to paragraphs 8 and 35 above, every person who at any time—

   (*a*) is [an employee]¹ or a full-time director of the grantor or, in the case of a group scheme, a participating company, and

   (*b*) has been such an employee or director at all times during a qualifying period, not exceeding five years, ending at that time, and

   (*c*) is chargeable to tax in respect of his office or employment under Case I of Schedule E,

must then be eligible (subject to paragraphs 8 and 35 of this Schedule) to participate in the scheme on similar terms and those who do participate must actually do so on similar terms.

(2) For the purposes of sub-paragraph (1) above, the fact that the number of shares to be appropriated to the participants in a scheme varies by reference to the levels of their remuneration, the length of their service or similar factors shall not be regarded as meaning that they are not eligible to participate in the scheme on similar terms or do not actually do so.

Commentary—*Simon's Direct Tax Service* **E4.555.**
Definitions—"Case I of Schedule E", s 19(2); "grantor", s 187(2); "group scheme", Sch 9 para 1(3); "participants", s 187(2); "participating company", Sch 9 para 1(4); "scheme", s 187(2); "shares", s 187(2).
Cross references—See TA 1988 Sch 9 para 2(3) (conditions for approval of schemes).
TA 1988 Sch 9 para 3 (cancellation of approval of schemes for breach of requirements of this paragraph).
Amendments—¹ Words in sub-para (1)(*a*) substituted by FA 1995 s 137(4), with effect for any scheme not approved before 1 May 1995.

PART VI
MATERIAL INTEREST TEST

Interests under trusts

37—(1) This paragraph applies in a case where—

   (*a*) the individual ("the beneficiary") was one of the objects of a discretionary trust; and

   (*b*) the property subject to the trust at any time consisted of or included any shares or obligations of the company.

(2) If neither the beneficiary nor any relevant associate of his had received any benefit under the discretionary trust before 14th November 1986, then, as respects any time before that date, the trustees of the settlement concerned shall not be regarded, by reason only of the matters referred to in sub-paragraph (1) above, as having been associates (as defined in section 417(3) and (4)) of the beneficiary.

(3) If, on or after 14th November 1986—

   (*a*) the beneficiary ceases to be eligible to benefit under the discretionary trust by reason of—

      (i) an irrevocable disclaimer or release executed by him under seal; or

      (ii) the irrevocable exercise by the trustees of a power to exclude him from the objects of the trust; and

   (*b*) immediately after he so ceases, no relevant associate of his is interested in the shares or obligations of the company which are subject to the trust; and

   (*c*) during the period of 12 months ending with the date when the beneficiary so ceases, neither the beneficiary nor any relevant associate of his received any benefit under the trust,

the beneficiary shall not be regarded, by reason only of the matters referred to in sub-paragraph (1) above, as having been interested in the shares or obligations of the company as mentioned in section 417(3)(*c*) at any time during the period of 12 months referred to in paragraph (*c*) above.

(4) In sub-paragraphs (2) and (3) above "relevant associate" has the meaning given to "associate" by subsection (3) or section 417 but with the omission of paragraph (*c*) of that subsection.

(5) Sub-paragraph (3)(*a*)(i) above, in its application to Scotland, shall be construed as if the words "under seal" were omitted.

Commentary—*Simon's Direct Tax Service* **E4.559, 587.**
Definitions—"Company", s 832(1), (2); "shares", s 187(2); "the trustees", s 187(2).

Options etc

38—(1) For the purposes of section 187(3)(*a*) a right to acquire shares (however arising) shall be taken to be a right to control them.

(2) Any reference in sub-paragraph (3) below to the shares attributed to an individual is a reference to the shares which, in accordance with section 187(3)(*a*), fall to be brought into account in his case to determine whether their number exceeds a particular percentage of the company's ordinary share capital.

(3) In any case where—

   (*a*) the shares attributed to an individual consist of or include shares which he or any other person has a right to acquire; and (*b*) the circumstances are such that, if that right were to be exercised, the shares acquired would be shares which were previously unissued and which the company is contractually bound to issue in the event of the exercise of the right;

then, in determining at any time prior to the exercise of that right whether the number of shares attributed to the individual exceeds a particular percentage of the ordinary share capital of the company, that ordinary share capital shall be taken to be increased by the number of unissued shares referred to in paragraph (*b*) above.

(4) This paragraph has effect as respects any time after 5th April 1987.

Commentary—*Simon's Direct Tax Service* **E4.559, 587.**
Definitions—''Company'', s 832(1), (2); ''control'', ss 187(2), 839; ''ordinary share capital'', s 832(1); ''shares'', s 187(2).

Shares held by trustees of approved profit sharing schemes

39 In applying section 187(3), as respects any time before or after the passing of this Act, there shall be disregarded—

(*a*) the interest of the trustees of an approved profit sharing scheme in any shares which are held by them in accordance with the scheme and have not yet been appropriated to an individual; and
(*b*) any rights exercisable by those trustees by virtue of that interest.

Commentary—*Simon's Direct Tax Service* **E4.559, 587.**
Definitions—''Approved'', s 187(2); ''scheme'', s 187(2); ''shares'', s 187(2); ''the trustees'', s 187(2).

[Shares subject to an employee benefit trust]1

[40—(1) Where an individual has an interest in shares or obligations of the company as a beneficiary of an employee benefit trust, the trustees shall not be regarded as associates of his by reason only of that interest unless sub-paragraph (3) below applies in relation to him.

(2) In this paragraph ''employee benefit trust'' has the same meaning as in paragraph 7 of Schedule 8.

(3) This sub-paragraph applies in relation to an individual if at any time on or after 14th March 1989—

(*a*) the individual, either on his own or with any one or more of his associates, or
(*b*) any associate of his, with or without other such associates,

has been the beneficial owner of, or able (directly or through the medium of other companies or by any other indirect means) to control, more than 25 per cent, or in the case of a share option scheme which is not a savings-related share option scheme more than 10 per cent, of the ordinary share capital of the company.

(4) Sub-paragraphs (9) to (12) of paragraph 7 of Schedule 8 shall apply for the purposes of this paragraph in relation to an individual as they apply for the purposes of that paragraph in relation to an employee.]1

Commentary—*Simon's Direct Tax Service* **E4.559, 587.**
Definitions—''Ordinary share capital'', s 832(1); ''savings-related share option scheme'', s 187(2); ''the trustees'', s 187(2).
Amendments—1 This paragraph inserted by FA 1989 s 65.

SCHEDULE 10

FURTHER PROVISIONS RELATING TO PROFIT SHARING SCHEMES

Section 186

Cross references—See TA 1988 s 187 (interpretation).
TA 1988 Sch 9 para 3 (cancellation of approval of schemes for contravention of provisions of this Schedule).
TCGA 1992 s 238(2) (computation of gains on disposal or part disposal of shares in a profit sharing scheme).

Limitations on contractual obligations of participants

1—(1) Any obligation placed on the participant by virtue of paragraph 2(2) of Schedule 9 shall not prevent the participant from—

(*a*) directing the trustees to accept an offer for any of his shares (''the original shares'') if the acceptance or agreement will result in a new holding being equated with the original shares for the purposes of capital gains tax; or
(*b*) directing the trustees to agree to a transaction affecting his shares or such of them as are of a particular class, if the transaction would be entered into pursuant to a compromise, arrangement or scheme applicable to or affecting—

(i) all the ordinary share capital of the company in question or, as the case may be, all the shares of the class in question; or
(ii) all the shares, or all the shares of the class in question, which are held by a class of shareholders identified otherwise than by reference to their employment or their participation in an approved scheme; or

(*c*) directing the trustees to accept an offer of cash, with or without other assets, for his shares if the offer forms part of a general offer which is made to holders of shares of the same class as his or of shares in the same company and which is made in the first instance on a condition such that if it is satisfied the person making the offer will have control of that company, within the meaning of section 416; or

[(*cc*) directing the trustees to accept an offer of a qualifying corporate bond, whether alone or with cash or other assets or both, for his shares if the offer forms part of a general offer which is made as mentioned in paragraph (*c*) above; or][1]

(*d*) agreeing after the expiry of the period of retention to sell the beneficial interest in his shares to the trustees for the same consideration as, in accordance with sub-paragraph (*d*) of paragraph 2(2) of Schedule 9, would be required to be obtained for the shares themselves.

(2) No obligation placed on the participant by virtue of paragraph 2(2)(*c*) of Schedule 9 shall be construed as binding his personal representatives to pay any sum to the trustees.

(3) If, in breach of his obligation under paragraph 2(2)(*b*) of Schedule 9 a participant assigns, charges or otherwise disposes of the beneficial interest in any of his shares, then, as respects those shares, he shall be treated for the purposes of the relevant provisions as if at the time they were appropriated to him he was ineligible to participate in the scheme; and paragraph 6 below shall apply accordingly.

[(4) In sub-paragraph (1)(*cc*) above "qualifying corporate bond" shall be construed in accordance with section 117 of the 1992 Act.][1]

Commentary—*Simon's Direct Tax Service* E4.560.
Revenue & other press releases—IR Booklet IR95 (Approved profit sharing schemes).
Definitions—"Approved (scheme)", s 187(2); "company", s 832(1), (2); "control", ss 187(2), 839; "new holding", s 187(2); "ordinary share capital", s 832(1); "participant", s 187(2); "period of retention", s 187(2); "relevant provisions", s 187(1); "scheme", s 187(2); "shares", s 187(2); "the trustees", s 187(2).
Cross references—See TA 1988 Sch 9 para 32(1) (prohibition against disposal of shares by trustees of a profit sharing scheme).
TCGA 1992 ss 126–137 (capital gains treatment on the reorganisation or reduction of share capital).
Amendments—[1] Sub-paras (1)(*cc*), (4) inserted by FA 1994 s 101(1)–(3), (7) and have effect where a direction is made on or after the date on which FA 1994 was passed (ie 3 May 1994).

The period of retention

2 For the purposes of any of the relevant provisions, "the period of retention", in relation to any of a participant's shares, means the period beginning on the date on which they are appropriated to him and ending on the second anniversary of that date or, if it is earlier—

(*a*) the date on which the participant ceases to be a director or employee of the grantor or, in the case of a group scheme, a participating company by reason of injury or disability or on account of his being dismissed by reason of redundancy, within the meaning of [the Employment Rights Act 1996][5] or the [Employment Rights (Northern Ireland) Order 1996][6]; or

(*b*) the date on which the participant reaches [the relevant age][2]; or

(*c*) the date of the participant's death; [or][1]

(*d*) in a case where the participant's shares are redeemable shares in a workers' cooperative, the date on which the participant ceases to be employed by, or by a subsidiary of, the cooperative.

For the purposes of sub-paragraph (*a*) above, in the case of a group scheme, the participant shall not be treated as ceasing to be a director or employee of a participating company until such times as he is no longer a director or employee of any of the participating companies.

[In this paragraph, the reference to the relevant age is a reference, in the case of a scheme approved before the day on which the Finance Act 1991 was passed, [in the case of a man, to the age of 65, and in the case of a woman, to the age of 60][4] and, in the case of a scheme approved on or after that day, to the specified age.][3]

Commentary—*Simon's Direct Tax Service* E4.560.
Note—FA 1991 was passed on 25 July 1991.
Definitions—"Grantor", s 187(2); "group scheme", s 187(2); "participant", s 187(2); "participant's shares", s 187(2); "participating company", s 187(2); "the relevant provisions", s 187(1); "specified age", s 187(2); "workers' co-operative", s 187(10).
Amendments—[1] Word in para (*c*) inserted by FA 1988 Sch 13 para 9.
[2] Words in para (*b*) substituted by FA 1991 s 38(3).
[3] Words inserted by FA 1991 s 38(3).
[4] Words substituted by Pensions Act 1995 Sch 4 para 12(*b*).
[5] Words in para (*a*) substituted by the Employment Rights Act 1996 s 243, Sch 1 para 35(1), (4) with effect from 22 August 1996.
[6] Words in para (*a*) substituted by the Employment Rights (Northern Ireland) Order, SI 1996/1919 Sch 1.

The appropriate percentage

[**3**—(1) For the purposes of any of the relevant provisions charging an individual to income tax under Schedule E by reason of the occurrence of an event relating to any of his shares, the "appropriate percentage" in relation to those shares is 100 per cent, unless sub-paragraph (2) below applies.

(2) Where the individual—

(*a*) ceases to be a director or employee of the grantor or, in the case of a group scheme, a participating company as mentioned in paragraph 2(*a*) above, or (*b*) reaches the relevant age,

before the event occurs, the "appropriate percentage" is 50 per cent, unless paragraph 6(4) below applies.]¹

Commentary—*Simon's Direct Tax Service* **E4.563.**
Definitions—"Grantor", s 187(2); "group scheme", s 187(2); "income tax", s 832(4); "participating company", s 187(2); "relevant age", Sch 10 para 3A; "Schedule E", s 19(1); "shares", s 187(2).
Cross references—See TA 1988 Sch 10 para 3A (interpretation of "relevant age").
Amendments—¹ Paragraph substituted by FA 1996 s 117(1), (3) with effect in relation to the occurrence on or after 29 April 1996 of events by reason of whose occurrence any provisions of ss 186, 187 of, and Schs 9, 10 to, this Act charges an individual to income tax under Schedule E.

[3A—(1) In paragraph 3 above the reference to the relevant age shall be construed as follows.

(2) Where the scheme is approved before 25th July 1991 and the event occurs before 30th November 1993, the relevant age is—

[(*a*) in the case of a man, 65, and
(*b*) in the case of a woman, 60.]²

(3) Where—

(*a*) the scheme is approved before 25th July 1991,
(*b*) the event occurs on or after 30th November 1993,
(*c*) the scheme defines the period of retention by reference to the age of 60 for both men and women, and
(*d*) the reference to that age is incorporated in the definition by virtue of an alteration approved by the Board under paragraph 4 of Schedule 9 before the event occurs,

the relevant age is 60.

(4) Where—

(*a*) the scheme is approved before 25th July 1991,
(*b*) the event occurs on or after 30th November 1993, and
(*c*) sub-paragraph (3) above does not apply,

the relevant age is [in the case of a man, 65, and in the case of a woman, 60]².

(5) Where the scheme is approved on or after 25th July 1991, the relevant age is the specified age.]¹

Commentary—*Simon's Direct Tax Service* **E4.563.**
Definitions—"Approved (scheme)", s 187(2); "the Board", s 832(1); "period of retention", s 187(2).
Amendments—¹ This paragraph inserted by FA 1994 s 100(1), (3).
² Words in sub-paras (2), (4) substituted by Pensions Act 1995 Sch 4 para 12(*c*), (*d*).

Capital receipts

4—(1) Money or money's worth is not a capital receipt for the purposes of section 186(3) if or, as the case may be, to the extent that—

(*a*) it constitutes income in the hands of the recipient for the purposes of income tax; or
(*b*) it consists of the proceeds of a disposal falling within section 186(4); or
(*c*) it consists of new shares within the meaning of paragraph 5 below.

(2) If, pursuant to a direction given by or on behalf of the participant or any person in whom the beneficial interest in the participant's shares is for the time being vested, the trustees—

(*a*) dispose of some of the rights arising under a rights issue, as defined in section 186(8), and
(*b*) use the proceeds of that disposal to exercise other such rights,

the money or money's worth which constitutes the proceeds of that disposal is not a capital receipt for the purposes of section 186(3).

(3) If, apart from this sub-paragraph, the amount or value of a capital receipt would exceed the sum which, immediately before the entitlement to the receipt arose, was the locked-in value of the shares to which the receipt is referable, section 186(3) shall have effect as if the amount or value of the receipt were equal to that locked-in value.

(4) Section 186(3) does not apply in relation to a capital receipt if the entitlement to it arises after the death of the participant to whose shares it is referable.

Commentary—*Simon's Direct Tax Service* **E4.563.**
Definitions—"Capital receipt", s 187(2); "income tax", s 832(4); "locked-in value", s 187(2); "participant", s 187(2); "participant's shares", s 187(2); "shares", s 187(2); "the trustees", s 187(2).
Cross references—See TA 1988 Sch 9 para 33 (obligation of trustees of a profit sharing scheme to pay over share dividends to participant).

Company reconstructions

5—(1) This paragraph applies where there occurs in relation to any of a participant's shares ("the original holding") a transaction which results in a new holding being equated with the original holding for the purposes of capital gains tax; and any such transaction is referred to below as a "company reconstruction".

(2) Where an issue of shares of any of the following descriptions (in respect of which a charge to income tax arises) is made as part of a company reconstruction, those shares shall be treated for the purposes of this paragraph as not forming part of the new holding, that is to say—

    (*a*) redeemable shares or securities issued as mentioned in section 209(2)(*c*);

    (*b*) share capital issued in circumstances such that section 210(1) applies; and

    (*c*) share capital to which section 249 applies.

(3) In this paragraph—

    "corresponding shares", in relation to any new shares, means those shares in respect of which the new shares are issued or which the new shares otherwise represent;

    "new shares" means shares comprised in the new holding which were issued in respect of, or otherwise represent, shares comprised in the original holding; and

    "original holding" has the meaning given by sub-paragraph (1) above.

(4) Subject to the following provisions of this paragraph, in relation to a profit sharing scheme, references in the relevant provisions to a participant's shares shall be construed, after the time of the company reconstruction, as being or, as the case may be, as including references to any new shares, and for the purposes of the relevant provisions—

    (*a*) a company reconstruction shall be treated as not involving a disposal of shares comprised in the original holding;

    (*b*) the date on which any new shares are to be treated as having been appropriated to the participant shall be that on which the corresponding shares were appropriated; and

    (*c*) the conditions in paragraphs 10 to 12 and 14 of Schedule 9 shall be treated as fulfilled with respect to any new shares if they were (or were treated as) fulfilled with respect to the corresponding shares.

(5) In relation to shares comprised in the new holding, section 186(5) shall apply as if the references in that subsection to the initial market value of the shares were references to their locked-in value immediately after the company reconstruction, which shall be determined as follows—

    (*a*) ascertain the aggregate amount of locked-in value immediately before the reconstruction of those shares comprised in the original holding which had at that time the same locked-in value; and

    (*b*) distribute that amount *pro rata* among—

        (i) such of those shares as remains in the new holding, and

        (ii) any new shares in relation to which those shares are the corresponding shares, according to their market value immediately after the date of their reconstruction;

and section 186(5)(*a*) shall apply only to capital receipts after the date of the reconstruction.

(6) For the purposes of the relevant provisions if, as part of a company reconstruction, trustees become entitled to a capital receipt, their entitlement to the capital receipt shall be taken to arise before the new holding comes into being and, for the purposes of sub-paragraph (5) above, before the date on which the locked-in value of any shares comprised in the original holding falls to be ascertained.

(7) In the context of a new holding, any reference in this paragraph to shares includes securities and rights of any description which form part of the new holding for the purposes of Chapter II of Part IV of the [1992][1] Act.

Commentary—*Simon's Direct Tax Service* **E4.64, 565.**
Definitions—"The 1992 Act", s 831(3); "capital receipt", s 187(2); "company", s 832(1), (2); "income tax", s 832(4); "initial market value", s 187(2); "locked-in value", s 187(2); "market value", s 187(2); "new holding", s 187(2); "participant", s 187(2); "participant's shares", s 187(2); "the relevant provisions", s 187(1); "shares", s 187(2); "the trustees", s 187(2).
Cross references—See TA 1988 Sch 10 para 5A (company mergers and reconstruction: acceptance by trustees of a profit sharing scheme of qualifying corporate bonds for participants' shares).
Amendments—[1] Year in sub-para (7) substituted by TCGA 1992 Sch 10 para 14(1), (58).

[**5A**—(1) Paragraph 5(2) to (6) above apply where there occurs in relation to any of a participant's shares ("the original holding") a relevant transaction which would result in a new holding being equated with the original holding for the purposes of capital gains tax, were it not for the fact that what would be the new holding consists of or includes a qualifying corporate bond; and "relevant transaction" here means a transaction mentioned in Chapter II of Part IV of the 1992 Act.

(2) In paragraph 5(2) to (6) above as applied by this paragraph—

    (*a*) references to a company reconstruction are to the transaction referred to in sub-paragraph (1) above;

    (*b*) references to the new holding are to what would be the new holding were it not for the fact mentioned in sub-paragraph (1) above;

    (*c*) references to the original holding shall be construed in accordance with sub-paragraph (1) above (and not paragraph 5(1));

    (*d*) references to shares, in the context of the new holding, include securities and rights of any description which form part of the new holding.

(3) In sub-paragraph (1) above "qualifying corporate bond" shall be construed in accordance with section 117 of the 1992 Act.][1]

Commentary—*Simon's Direct Tax Service* E4.565.
Definitions—"Participant", s 187(2); "shares", s 187(2).
Amendments—¹ This paragraph inserted by FA 1994 s 101(1), (4), (8), and has effect where the new holding referred to in sub-para (1) results on or after the date on which FA 1994 was passed (ie 3 May 1994). But see FA 1994 s 101(13) for conditions in which this paragraph does not apply.

Excess or unauthorised shares

6—(1) This paragraph applies in any case where—

(a) the total amount of the initial market value of all the shares which are appropriated to an individual in any one year of assessment (whether under a single approved profit sharing scheme or under two or more such schemes) exceeds the relevant amount; or

(b) the trustees of an approved profit sharing scheme appropriate shares to an individual at a time when he is ineligible to participate in the scheme by virtue of paragraph 8 or 35 of Schedule 9.

(2) In this paragraph—

"excess shares" means any share which caused the relevant amount to be exceeded and any share appropriated after that amount was exceeded; and
"unauthorised shares" means any share appropriated as mentioned in sub-paragraph (1)(b) above.

(3) For the purposes of sub-paragraph (1)(a) above, if a number of shares is appropriated to an individual at the same time under two or more approved profit sharing schemes, the same proportion of the shares appropriated at that time under each scheme shall be regarded as being appropriated before the relevant amount is exceeded.

(4) For the purposes of any of the relevant provisions charging an individual to income tax under Schedule E by reason of the occurrence of an event relating to any of his shares—

(a) the appropriate percentage in relation to excess or unauthorised shares shall in every case be 100 per cent; and

(b) without prejudice to section 187(8), the event shall be treated as relating to shares which are not excess or unauthorised shares before shares which are.

(5) Excess or unauthorised shares which have not been disposed of before the release date or, if it is earlier, the date of the death of the participant whose shares they are, shall be treated for the purposes of the relevant provisions as having been disposed of by the trustees immediately before the release date or, as the case may require, the date of the participant's death, for a consideration equal to their market value at that time.

(6) The locked-in value at any time of any excess or unauthorised shares shall be their market value at that time.

(7) Where there has been a company reconstruction to which paragraph 5 above applies, a new share (within the meaning of that paragraph) shall be treated as an excess or unauthorised share if the corresponding share (within the meaning of that paragraph) or, if there was more than one corresponding share, each of them was an excess or unauthorised share.

Commentary—*Simon's Direct Tax Service* E4.563, 566.
Definitions—"Appropriate percentage", s 187(2); "company", s 832(1), (2); "income tax", s 832(4); "initial market value", s 187(2); "locked-in value", s 187(2); "market value", s 187(2); "participant", s 187(2); "release date", s 187(2); "relevant amount", s 187(2); "the relevant provisions", s 187(1); "Schedule E", s 19(1); "scheme", s 187(2); "shares", s 187(2); "the trustees", s 187(2); "year of assessment", s 832(1).
Cross references—See TA 1988 Sch 10 para 1 (application of this paragraph where a participant in a profit sharing scheme deals with his shares in breach of his obligations).
TA 1988 Sch 10 para 3 (determination of "appropriate percentage").

PAYE deduction of tax

7—(1) Subject to sub-paragraphs (4) and (5) below, where the trustees of an approved profit sharing scheme receive a sum of money which constitutes (or forms part of)—

(a) the proceeds of a disposal of shares falling within section 186(4), or

(b) a capital receipt,

in respect of which a participant in the scheme is chargeable to income tax under Schedule E in accordance with section 186, the trustees shall pay out of that sum of money to the company specified in sub-paragraph (3) below an amount equal to that on which income tax is so payable; and the company shall then pay over that amount to the participant but in so doing shall make a PAYE deduction.

(2) Where a participant disposes of his beneficial interest in any of his shares to the trustees of the scheme and the trustees are deemed by virtue of section 186(9) to have disposed of the shares in question, this paragraph shall apply as if the consideration payable by the trustees to the participant on the disposal had been received by the trustees as the proceeds of disposal of shares falling within section 186(4).

(3) The company to which the payment mentioned in sub-paragraph (1) above is to be made is the company—

(a) of which the participant is an employee or director at the time the trustees receive the sum of money referred to in that sub-paragraph, and (*b*) whose employees are at that time eligible (subject to the terms of the scheme and Schedule 9) to be participants in the approved profit sharing scheme concerned,

and if there is more than one company which falls within paragraphs (*a*) and (*b*) above, such one of those companies as the Board may direct.

(4) Where the trustees of an approved profit sharing scheme receive a sum of money to which sub-paragraph (1) above applies but—

(*a*) there is no company which falls within paragraphs (*a*) and (*b*) of sub-paragraph (3) above, or

(*b*) the Board is of opinion that it is impracticable for the company which falls within those paragraphs (or, as the case may be, any of them) to make a PAYE deduction and accordingly direct that this sub-paragraph shall apply,

then, in paying over to the participant the proceeds of the disposal or the capital receipt, the trustees shall make a PAYE deduction in respect of an amount equal to that on which income tax is payable as mentioned in sub-paragraph (1) above as if the participant were a former employee of the trustees.

(5) Where the trustees of an approved profit sharing scheme receive a sum of money to which sub-paragraph (1) above applies and the Board direct that this sub-paragraph shall apply—

(*a*) the trustees shall make the payment mentioned in that sub-paragraph to the company specified in the Board's direction; and

(*b*) that company shall pay over that amount to the participant but in so doing shall make a PAYE deduction, and for that purpose if the participant is not an employee of that company he shall be treated as a former employee;

but no such direction shall be given except with the consent of the trustees, the company or companies (if any) specified in sub-paragraph (3) above and the company specified in the direction.

(6) Where, in accordance with this paragraph any person is required to make a PAYE deduction in respect of any amount, that amount shall be treated for the purposes of section 203 and any regulations made under that section as an amount of income payable to the recipient and assessable to income tax under Schedule E, and, accordingly, such deduction shall be made as is required by those regulations.

(7) Where, in connection with a transfer of a participant's shares to which sub-paragraph (*c*) of paragraph 2(2) of Schedule 9 applies, the trustees receive such a sum as is referred to in that sub-paragraph, that sum shall be treated for the purposes of the Income Tax Acts—

(*a*) as a sum deducted by the trustees pursuant to a requirement to make a PAYE. deduction under sub-paragraph (4) above; and

(*b*) as referable to the income tax to which, as a result of the transfer, the participant is chargeable by virtue of section 186(4).

(8) Unless the Board otherwise direct, in the application of this paragraph to a sum of money which constitutes or forms part of the proceeds of a disposal of, or a capital receipt referable to, excess or unauthorised shares (within the meaning of paragraph 6 above), the trustees shall determine the amount of the payment mentioned in sub-paragraph (1) above or, as the case may be, the amount of the PAYE deduction to be made under sub-paragraph (4) above as if the shares were not excess or unauthorised shares.

Commentary—*Simon's Direct Tax Service* **E4.567.**
Definitions—''The Board'', s 832(1); ''capital receipt'', s 187(2); ''company'', s 832(1), (2); ''income tax'', s 832(4); ''the Income Tax Acts'', s 831(1)(*b*); ''participant'', s 187(2); ''participant's shares'', s 187(2); ''scheme'', s 187(2); ''Schedule E'', s 19(1); ''shares'', s 187(2); ''the trustees'', s 187(2).
Cross references—See TA 1988 Sch 9 para 33 (obligation of trustees of a profit sharing scheme to pay over share dividends to participant).
TA 1988 Sch 9 para 34 (obligation of trustees of a profit sharing scheme to maintain records for the purposes of this paragraph).

[SCHEDULE 11

PAYMENTS AND OTHER BENEFITS IN CONNECTION WITH TERMINATION OF EMPLOYMENT, ETC

Section 148(6)

Revenue & other press releases—IR 17-3-97 (Revenue to apply special arrangements for employment termination agreements entered into from 6 April 1996).
IR Tax Bulletin June 1997 p 427 (gives information on the operation of the arrangements announced in IR press release 17-3-97 for taxing continuing non-cash benefits provided as part of an employment termination settlement).
IR 19-12-97 (Employment termination settlements – consultative document for legislative reform).
Revenue Internal Guidance—Schedule E manual SE 13500 (termination payments and benefits: exemptions and relief).
Cross references—See TA 1988 s 148 (Payments on retirement or removal from office or employment).
Amendments—¹ This Schedule substituted by FA 1998 Sch 9 Part I with effect in relation to payments or other benefits received after 5 April 1998, except where the payment or other benefit, or the right to receive it, has been brought into charge to tax before that date.

Introductory

1 The provisions of this Schedule supplement the provisions of section 148 with respect to the taxation of payments and other benefits received in connection with—

(*a*) the termination of a person's employment, or

(*b*) any change in the duties of or emoluments from a person's employment.

Commentary—*Simon's Direct Tax Service* **E4.805–807.**

Payments and other benefits to which section 148 applies

2—(1) Section 148 applies to all payments and other benefits received directly or indirectly in consideration or in consequence of, or otherwise in connection with, the termination or change—

(*a*) by the employee or former employee,

(*b*) by the spouse or any relative or dependant of the employee or former employee, or

(*c*) by the personal representatives of the former employee.

(2) For the purposes of section 148 a payment or other benefit which is provided on behalf of, or to the order of, the employee or former employee is treated as received by the employee or former employee.

Commentary—*Simon's Direct Tax Service* **E4.805G.**
Revenue Internal Guidance—Schedule E manual SE 13010 (termination payments and benefits: scope of the charge).
SE 13012 (this subpara expands the phrase "in connection with").
SE 13910 (examples involving "in connection with").
SE 13916 (examples of payment or benefit received by someone other than the employee).
SE 13918 (termination payments and benefits: example where payments or benefits provided on behalf of the employee or to the employee's order).

Payments and other benefits excluded from charge under section 148

3 Tax is not charged under section 148 on a payment or other benefit provided—

(*a*) in connection with the termination of the employment by the death of the employee, or

(*b*) on account of injury to or disability of the employee.

Commentary—*Simon's Direct Tax Service* **E4.806, 807.**
Revenue Internal Guidance—Schedule E manual SE 13600 (termination payments and benefits: exemption for payments on death).
SE 13610 (termination payments and benefits: exemption for payments on account of injury or disability: general).
SE 13620 (payments on account of injury or disability—meaning of "disability").
SE 13630 (meaning of "disability": application of *Hasted v Horner* (67 TC 439).
SE 13640 (payments on account of injury or disability: certain cases to be reported to Personal Tax Division).
SE 13650 (payments on account of injury or disability: interaction with Capital Gains Tax and retirement relief).

4—(1) Tax is not charged under section 148 on a payment or other benefit provided in pursuance of any such scheme or fund as was described in section 221(1) and (2) of the 1970 Act or as is described in section 596(1) (approved retirement benefits schemes, etc) in the following cases.

(2) The first case is where the payment or other benefit is by way of compensation for loss of employment or for loss or diminution of emoluments, and the loss or diminution is due to ill-health.

(3) The second case is where the payment or other benefits is properly regarded as earned by past service.

Commentary—*Simon's Direct Tax Service* **E4.805D, 824.**
Revenue Internal Guidance—Schedule E manual SE 13660 (termination payments and benefits: exemptions for lump sums from superannuation schemes).
SE 13670 (exemptions: lump sums from overseas schemes application of ESC A10).

5 Tax is not charged under section 148 on a payment or other benefit provided—

(*a*) under a Royal Warrant, Queen's Order or Order in Council relating to members of Her Majesty's forces, or

(*b*) by way of payment in commutation of annual or other periodical payments authorised by any such Warrant or Order.

Commentary—*Simon's Direct Tax Service* **E4.806.**

6—(1) Tax is not charged under section 148 on—

(*a*) any benefit provided under a superannuation scheme administered by the government of an overseas territory within the Commonwealth, or

(*b*) any payment of compensation for loss of career, interruption of service or disturbance made in connection with any change in the constitution of any such overseas territory to a person who, before the change, was employed in the public service of that territory.

(2) In sub-paragraph (1) references to an overseas territory, to the government of such a territory, and to employment in the public service of such a territory have the same meaning as in [section 615][1].

Commentary—*Simon's Direct Tax Service* **E4.806.**
Revenue Internal Guidance—Schedule E manual SE 13710 (termination payments and benefits: exemptions for benefits and other payments in respect of certain overseas territories).
SE 13720 (termination payments and benefits: exemptions for terminal grants to members of HM Forces).

Amendments—¹ Words substituted for the words "the Overseas Development and Cooperation Act 1980: see sections 10(2) and 13(1) and (2) of that Act" by the International Development Act 2002 s 19, Sch 3 para 10 with effect from 17 June 2002 (by virtue of SI 2002/1408).

Application of £30,000 threshold

7—(1) This paragraph specifies how the £30,000 threshold in section 148(1) applies.

(2) Tax is charged only on the excess over £30,000, but the threshold applies to the aggregate amount of payments and other benefits provided in respect of the same person—

(*a*) in respect of the same employment, or

(*b*) in respect of different employments with the same employer or associated employers (see paragraph 8).

(3) If payments and other benefits are received in different tax years, the £30,000 is set against the amount of payments and other benefits received in earlier years before those of later years.

(4) If more than one payment or other benefit is received in a tax year in which the threshold is exceeded—

(*a*) the £30,000 (or the balance of it) is set against the amounts of cash benefits as they are received, and

(*b*) any balance at the end of the year is set against the aggregate amount of non-cash benefits received in the year.

Commentary—*Simon's Direct Tax Service* E4.805, 805G.
Revenue Internal Guidance—Schedule E manual SE 13505 (£30,000 exemption: general).
SE 13520 (£30,000 exemption: payments and benefits received on or after 6 April 1998).
SE 13530 (£30,000 exemption: payments and benefits to be aggregated).
SE 13955 (example of £30,000 exemption and order of set-off: receipts on or after 6 April 1998)
SE 13960 (example of £30,000 exemption: receipts overlapping 6 April 1998).

8—(1) For the purposes of paragraph 7(2)(*b*) employers are associated if on the date which is the relevant date in relation to any of the payments or other benefits—

(*a*) one of them is under the control of the other, or

(*b*) one of them is under the control of a third person who controls or is under the control of the other on that or any other such date.

(2) In sub-paragraph (1)—

(*a*) "control" has the meaning given by section 840, and

(*b*) references to an employer, or to a person controlling or controlled by an employer, include the successors of the employer or person.

Commentary—*Simon's Direct Tax Service* E4.805G.
Revenue Internal Guidance—Schedule E manual SE 13540 (£30,000 exemption: meaning of "associated employers").

Exclusion or reduction of charge in case of foreign service

9—(1) If the employee's service in the employment in respect of which the payment or other benefit is received included foreign service, then—

(*a*) in certain cases, tax is not charged under section 148 (see paragraph 10);

(*b*) in other cases the amount charged to tax is reduced (see paragraph 11).

(2) "Foreign service" for this purpose means—

(*a*) service in or after the tax year 1974–75 such that—

(i) the emoluments from the employment were not chargeable under Case I of Schedule E (or would not have been so chargeable, had there been any), or

(ii) a deduction equal to the whole amount of the emoluments from the employment was or would have been allowable under paragraph 1 of Schedule 2 to the Finance Act 1974, paragraph 1 of Schedule 7 to the Finance Act 1977 or section 192A or 193(1) of this Act (foreign earnings deduction);

(*b*) service before the tax year 1974–75 such that tax was not chargeable in respect of the emoluments of the employment—

(i) in the tax year 1956–57 or later, under Case I of Schedule E;

(ii) in earlier tax years, under Schedule E.

Commentary—*Simon's Direct Tax Service* E4.806, 807.
Revenue Internal Guidance—Schedule E manual SE 13680 (termination payments and benefits: exemptions for "foreign service"—general).
SE 13690 (exemptions: definition of "foreign service").
SE 13970 (example of exemptions for "foreign service").
SE 13975 (example of exemptions for "foreign service" where group of companies involved).

10 Tax is not charged under section 148 if foreign service comprises—

(*a*) three-quarters or more of the whole period of service down to the relevant date, or

(*b*) if the period of service down to the relevant date exceeded ten years, the whole of the last ten years, or (*c*) if the period of service down to the relevant date exceeded 20 years, one-half or more of that period, including any ten of the last 20 years.

Commentary—*Simon's Direct Tax Service* **E4.806, 807.**

11—(1) Where there is foreign service and paragraph 10 does not apply, the person chargeable to tax under section 148 may claim relief in the form of a proportionate reduction of the amount charged to tax.

The amount charged to tax means the amount after any reduction under paragraph 7 (application of £30,000 threshold).

(2) The proportion is that which the length of the foreign service bears to the whole length of service in the employment before the relevant date.

(3) A person is not entitled to relief under this paragraph in so far as the relief, together with any personal relief allowed to him, would reduce the amount of income on which he is chargeable below the amount of income tax which he is entitled—

    (*a*) to charge against any other person, or
    (*b*) to deduct, retain or satisfy out of any payment which he is liable to make.

(4) For the purposes of sub-paragraph (3)—

    (*a*) "personal relief" means relief under Chapter I of Part VII; and
    (*b*) the amount of tax to which a person is or would be chargeable means the amount of tax to which he is or would be chargeable either by assessment or by deduction.

Commentary—*Simon's Direct Tax Service* **E4.806, 807.**
Revenue Internal Guidance—Schedule E manual SE 13700 (termination payments and benefits: "foreign service": reduction
  of charge).
SE 13980 (exemptions for "foreign service": example of reduction and interaction with £30,000 exemption).
SE 13985 (example of "foreign service" reduction).

Valuation of benefits

12—(1) For the purposes of section 148, the amount of a payment or other benefit is taken to be—

    (*a*) in the case of a cash benefit, the amount received, and
    (*b*) in the case of a non-cash benefit, the cash equivalent of the benefit.

(2) The cash equivalent of a non-cash benefit is whichever is the greater of—

    (*a*) the amount which would be chargeable to tax under section 19(1) if the benefit were an emolument of the employment chargeable to tax under Case I of Schedule E, or
    (*b*) the cash equivalent determined in accordance with the provisions of section 596B (cash equivalent of benefits in kind for purposes of charge to tax on benefits under non-approved retirement benefits scheme).

Commentary—*Simon's Direct Tax Service* **E4.805G.**
Simon's Tax Cases—*O'Brien v Williams* [2000] STC (SCD) 364.
Revenue Internal Guidance—Schedule E manual SE 13270 (termination payments and benefits: valuation of non-cash benefits
  received on or after 6 April 1998).
SE 13280 (usual application of "cash equivalent").
SE 13300 (non-cash benefits other than living accommodation received after 6 April 1998:"cash equivalent").
SE 13310 (non-cash benefits other than living accommodation received after 6 April 1998:"cash equivalent"—rules appropriate
  to particular benefits).
SE 13330 (benefit of living accommodation received on or after 6 April 1998:"cash equivalent").
SE 13340–13360 (examples where "cost of providing" living accommodation is more than £75,000).
SE 13905 (example of interaction with benefits received during employment).
SE 13934 (example of valuation of non-cash benefits received after 6 April 1998:"Section 19" value).
SE 14000 (example of living accommodation after 6 April 1998: cost of providing accommodation).

Notional interest treated as paid if amount charged in respect of beneficial loan

13—(1) This paragraph applies where a person is chargeable to tax under section 148 in any tax year on an amount which consists of or includes an amount representing the cash equivalent of the benefit of a loan determined in accordance with Part II of Schedule 7.

(2) Where this paragraph applies, the person chargeable is treated as having paid interest on the loan of the same amount as the cash equivalent so determined.

This is subject to application of the £30,000 threshold: see sub-paragraph (5) below.

(3) The interest is treated as paid for all the purposes of the Tax Acts (other than section 148 and this Schedule), but not so as to make it—

    (*a*) income of the person making the loan, or
    (*b*) relevant loan interest to which section 369 applies (mortgage interest payable under deduction of tax).

(4) The interest is treated as accruing during and paid at the end of the tax year or, if different, the period in the tax year during which the loan is outstanding.

(5) No amount of interest is treated as paid under this paragraph in a tax year in which, after applying the £30,000 threshold in section 148(1), no amount falls to be charged to tax.

If in any tax year the effect of the £30,000 threshold is that some but not all of the amount otherwise chargeable is charged to tax, the amount of interest treated as paid is limited to the amount charged to tax.

Commentary—*Simon's Direct Tax Service* E4.805G.
Revenue Internal Guidance—Schedule E manual SE 13320 (cash equivalent of beneficial loan treated as a payment of interest).

Giving effect to the charge to tax

14—(1) Tax under section 148 is charged on the employee or former employee, whether or not he is the recipient of the payment or other benefit.

(2) After the death of the employee or former employee, any amount chargeable to tax under section 148 shall be assessed and charged upon his personal representatives and is a debt due from and payable out of the estate.

Commentary—*Simon's Direct Tax Service* E4.805G.

Reporting requirements

15 Provision may be made by regulations under section 203(2) requiring an employer or former employer to provide such information as may be prescribed by the regulations, within such time as may be so prescribed, as to payments or other benefits provided or to be provided in connection with the termination of a person's employment or a change in the duties of or emoluments from a person's employment.

Commentary—*Simon's Direct Tax Service* E4.805J.
Regulations—IT (Employments) (Amendment) Regulations, SI 1999/70 (amends SI 1993/744). Revenue Internal Guidance—
Schedule E manual SE 13844 (termination payments and benefits: reports by employers of payments and benefits made on or
after 6 April 1998: general).
SE 13850 and SE 13855 (termination payments and benefits: reports by employers of payments and benefits made on or after 6
April 1998: content of initial and subsequent reports, application of SI 1999/70).

Interpretation

16 In this Schedule—

　　"the relevant date" means the date of the termination or change in question; and
　　"tax year" means a year of assessment.]¹

Commentary—*Simon's Direct Tax Service* E4.805.

[SCHEDULE 11A

REMOVAL EXPENSES AND BENEFITS]¹

Section 191A

Concessions A5—Benefits in kind: removal expenses and cheap or interest-free loans: concessionary treatment until 5 April
1993.
A67—Benefits in kind: payments to employees moved to higher cost housing areas: concessionary treatment until 5 April 1993.
Revenue & other press releases—IR leaflets 134 (guide for employees on taxation of relocation packages).
Revenue Internal Guidance—Schedule E manual SE 3101 (removal or transfer costs: expenses and benefits—general).
SE 3139 (removal or transfer costs: flat rate allowances).
Amendments—¹ This Schedule inserted by FA 1993 Sch 5 and has effect as provided in para 29 *post*.

PART I

TAX RELIEF

[1—(1) Where by reason of a person's employment—

　　(*a*) any sums are paid to that person (the employee) in respect of qualifying removal expenses,
　　(*b*) any sums are paid on behalf of the employee to another person in respect of qualifying
　　　　removal expenses, or
　　(*c*) any qualifying removal benefit is provided for the employee or for others being members of
　　　　his family or household,

the employee shall not thereby be regarded as receiving emoluments of the employment for any purpose of Case I or Case II of Schedule E.

(2) Sub-paragraph (1) above shall have effect subject to Part V of this Schedule.]¹

Commentary—*Simon's Direct Tax Service* E4.494.
Definitions—"Emoluments", s 131(1).
Cross references—See TA 1988 Sch 11A paras 25–28 (interpretation).
IT (Employments) Regulations, SI 1993/744 reg 46(2)(*b*) (requirement for employer to render a return of benefits exceeding the
limit in paragraph 24(9)).
Amendments—¹ This Schedule inserted by FA 1993 Sch 5 and has effect as provided in para 29 *post*.

[2—(1) This paragraph applies where—

(*a*) any payment or benefit would (apart from paragraph 1 above) constitute emoluments of an employment for any purpose of Case I or Case II of Schedule E, and

(*b*) by virtue of that paragraph it is treated as not being such emoluments.

(2) The payment or benefit shall be treated as not being emoluments of the employment for any purpose of Case III of Schedule E.][1]

Commentary—*Simon's Direct Tax Service* E4.494.
Definitions—''Emoluments'', s 131(1).
Cross references—See TA 1988 Sch 11A paras 25–28 (interpretation).
Amendments—[1]This Schedule inserted by FA 1993 Sch 5 and has effect as provided in para 29 *post*.

PART II
QUALIFYING EXPENSES AND QUALIFYING BENEFITS

Qualifying removal expenses

[**3**—(1) Expenses are not qualifying removal expenses unless they are eligible removal expenses and the conditions set out in this paragraph and paragraph 5 below are fulfilled.

(2) The expenses must be reasonably incurred by the employee in connection with a change of his residence.

(3) The expenses must be incurred on or before the relevant day.][1]

Commentary—*Simon's Direct Tax Service* E4.491.
Definitions—''Eligible removal expenses'', Sch 11A para 16; ''relevant day'', Sch 11A para 6; ''residence'', Sch 11A para 25.
Cross references—See TA 1988 Sch 11A paras 25–28 (interpretation).
Revenue Internal Guidance—Schedule E manual SE 3104 (removal or transfer costs: qualifying expenses and benefits—main conditions).
Amendments—[1]This Schedule inserted by FA 1993 Sch 5 and has effect as provided in para 29 *post*.

Qualifying removal benefits

[**4**—(1) A benefit is not a qualifying removal benefit unless it is an eligible removal benefit and the conditions set out in this paragraph and paragraph 5 below are fulfilled.

(2) The benefit must be reasonably provided in connection with a change of the employee's residence.

(3) The benefit must be provided on or before the relevant day.][1]

Commentary—*Simon's Direct Tax Service* E4.491.
Definitions—''Eligible removal benefits'', Sch 11A para 16; ''relevant day'', Sch 11A para 6; ''residence'', Sch 11A para 25.
Cross references—See TA 1988 Sch 11A paras 25–28 (interpretation).
Amendments—[1]This Schedule inserted by FA 1993 Sch 5 and has effect as provided in para 29 *post*.

Connection with employment

[**5**—(1) The change of residence mentioned in paragraphs 3(2) and 4(2) above must result from—

(*a*) the employee becoming employed by an employer,

(*b*) an alteration of the duties of the employee's employment (where his employer remains the same), or

(*c*) an alteration of the place where the employee is normally to perform the duties of his employment (where both his employer and the duties of his employment remain the same).

(2) The change must be made wholly or mainly to allow the employee to have his residence within a reasonable daily travelling distance of—

(*a*) the place where he performs, or is to perform, the duties of his employment (where sub-paragraph (1)(*a*) above applies);

(*b*) the place where he performs, or is to perform, the new duties of his employment (where sub-paragraph (1)(*b*) above applies);

(*c*) the new place where he performs, or is to perform, the duties of his employment (where sub-paragraph (1)(*c*) above applies);

and any reference in this sub-paragraph to the place where the employee performs, or is to perform, duties of his employment is to the place where he normally performs, or is normally to perform, those duties.

(3) The employee's former residence must not be within a reasonable daily travelling distance of the place mentioned in sub-paragraph (2) above.][1]

Commentary—*Simon's Direct Tax Service* E4.492.
Definitions—''Employment'', Sch 11A para 27; ''former residence'', Sch 11A para 25; ''residence'', Sch 11A para 25.
Cross references—See TA 1988 s 191B (beneficial loan arrangements as regards removal expenses).
TA 1988 Sch 11A paras 25–28 (interpretation).
Amendments—[1]This Schedule inserted by FA 1993 Sch 5 and has effect as provided in para 29 *post*.

The relevant day

[6—(1) Subject to sub-paragraph (2) below, the relevant day, in relation to a particular change of residence, is the day on which the relevant year ends; and for the purposes of this sub-paragraph the relevant year is the year of assessment next following the year of assessment in which—

  (*a*) the employee begins to perform the duties of his employment (where paragraph 5(1)(*a*) above applies);

  (*b*) the employee begins to perform the new duties of his employment (where paragraph 5(1)(*b*) above applies);

  (*c*) the employee begins to perform the duties of his employment at the new place (where paragraph 5(1)(*c*) above applies).

(2) If it appears reasonable to the Board to do so, having regard to all the circumstances of a particular change of residence, they may direct that in relation to that change the relevant day is a day which—

  (*a*) falls after the day mentioned in sub-paragraph (1) above, and

  (*b*) is a day on which a year of assessment ends.]¹

Commentary—*Simon's Direct Tax Service* E4.494.
Revenue Internal Guidance—Schedule E manual SE 3105–03107 (removal or transfer costs: qualifying expenses & benefits—extension of time limit including examples).
Definitions—"The Board", s 832(1); "employment", Sch 11A para 27; "residence", Sch 11A para 25; "year of assessment", s 832(1).
Cross references—See TA 1988 Sch 11A paras 25–28 (interpretation).
Amendments—¹ This Schedule inserted by FA 1993 Sch 5 and has effect as provided in para 29 *post*.

PART III
ELIGIBLE REMOVAL EXPENSES
Introduction

[7 Expenses are eligible removal expenses if they fall into one of the following categories—

  (*a*) expenses of disposal,
  (*b*) expenses of acquisition,
  (*c*) expenses of abortive acquisition,
  (*d*) expenses of transporting belongings,
  (*e*) travelling and subsistence expenses,
  (*f*) bridging loan expenses, and
  (*g*) duplicate expenses;

and paragraphs 8 to 14 below apply for the purpose of interpreting the preceding provisions of this paragraph.]¹

Commentary—*Simon's Direct Tax Service* E4.693.
Revenue Internal Guidance—Schedule E manual SE 3108 (removal or transfer costs: eligible expenses and benefits—general). SE 3126 (removal or transfer costs: non-eligible expenses and benefits—compensation payments for "loss on sale").
Definitions—"Subsistence", Sch 11A para 28.
Cross references—See TA 1988 Sch 11A paras 25–28 (interpretation).
Amendments—¹ This Schedule inserted by FA 1993 Sch 5 and has effect as provided in para 29 *post*.

Expenses of disposal

[8—(1) Expenses fall within paragraph 7(*a*) above if (and only if)—

  (*a*) the employee has an interest in his former residence,

  (*b*) that interest is disposed of, or is intended to be disposed of, in consequence of the change of residence, and

  (*c*) the expenses fall within sub-paragraph (2) below.

(2) Expenses fall within this sub-paragraph if they consist of one of the following—

  (*a*) legal expenses connected with the disposal or intended disposal of the employee's interest in his former residence (including legal expenses connected with the redemption of any loan relating to the residence),

  (*b*) any penalty for redeeming, for the purpose of the disposal or intended disposal, any loan relating to the residence,

  (*c*) fees of any estate agent or auctioneer engaged in the disposal or intended disposal,

  (*d*) expenses of advertising the disposal or intended disposal,

  (*e*) charges for disconnecting, for the purpose of the disposal or intended disposal, public utilities serving the residence,

  (*f*) expenses of maintaining, insuring, or preserving the security of the residence at any time when unoccupied pending the disposal or intended disposal, and

  (*g*) any rent paid in respect of the residence at any such time.

(3) The reference in this paragraph to the employee having an interest in his former residence includes a reference to—

  (*a*) one or more members of the employee's family or household having such an interest;

(*b*) the employee and one or more members of his family or household having such an interest;

and references to the disposal or intended disposal of the employee's interest in his former residence shall be construed accordingly.

(4) For the purposes of this paragraph a loan relates to a residence if the loan was raised to obtain an interest in the residence, or an interest in the residence forms security for the loan, or both.][1]

Commentary—*Simon's Direct Tax Service* **E4.493.**
Definitions—"Family or household", Sch 11A para 26; "former residence", Sch 11A para 25; "interest in a residence", Sch 11A para 25; "residence", Sch 11A para 25.
Cross references—See TA 1988 Sch 11A paras 25–28 (interpretation).
Revenue Internal Guidance—Schedule E manual SE 3109 (removal or transfer costs: eligible expenses and benefits—disposal of old residence).
SE 3127 (removal or transfer costs: sale of property to employer).
Amendments—[1] This Schedule inserted by FA 1993 Sch 5 and has effect as provided in para 29 *post*.

Expenses of acquisition

9—(1) Expenses fall within paragraph 7(*b*) above if (and only if) the employee acquires an interest in his new residence and the expenses consist of one of the following—

(*a*) legal expenses connected with the acquisition by the employee of the interest (including legal expenses connected with any loan raised to acquire the interest),
(*b*) any procurement fees connected with any such loan,
(*c*) the costs of any insurance effected to cover risks which are incurred by the maker of any such loan and which arise because the amount of the loan is equal to the whole, or a substantial part, of the value of the interest,
(*d*) fees relating to any survey or inspection of the residence undertaken in connection with the acquisition by the employee of the interest,
(*e*) fees payable to an appropriate registry or appropriate register in connection with the acquisition by the employee of the interest,
(*f*) stamp duty charged on the acquisition, and
(*g*) charges for connecting any public utility for use by the employee, if the utility serves the residence.

(2) References in this paragraph to the employee acquiring an interest in his new residence include references to—

(*a*) one or more members of the employee's family or household acquiring such an interest;
(*b*) the employee and one or more members of his family or household acquiring such an interest.

(3) References in this paragraph to a loan are to a loan raised by the employee, by one or more members of the employee's family or household or by the employee and one or more members of his family or household.

(4) The reference in this paragraph to a utility for use by the employee includes a reference to a utility for use by the employee and one or more members of his family or household.

(5) For the purposes of this paragraph an appropriate registry is any of the following—

(*a*) Her Majesty's Land Registry;
(*b*) the Land Registry in Northern Ireland;
(*c*) the Registry of Deeds for Northern Ireland;

and an appropriate register is any register under the management and control of the Keeper of the Registers of Scotland.][1]

Commentary—*Simon's Direct Tax Service* **E4.493.**
Definitions—"Family or household", Sch 11A para 26; "interest in a residence", Sch 11A para 25; "new residence", Sch 11A para 25; "residence", Sch 11A para 25.
Cross references—See TA 1988 Sch 11A paras 25–28 (interpretation).
Revenue Internal Guidance—Schedule E manual SE 3110 (removal or transfer costs: eligible expenses and benefits—acquisition of new residence).
Amendments—[1] This Schedule inserted by FA 1993 Sch 5 and has effect as provided in para 29 *post*.

Expenses of abortive acquisition

[**10** Expenses fall within paragraph 7(*c*) above if (and only if)—

(*a*) they are incurred with a view to the acquisition of an interest in a residence, the interest is not acquired, but (if it were) the residence would be the employee's new residence,
(*b*) they would fall within paragraph 7(*b*) above if the interest were acquired, and
(*c*) the interest is not acquired because of circumstances outside the control of the person seeking to acquire the interest, or because that person reasonably declines to proceed.][1]

Commentary—*Simon's Direct Tax Service* **E4.493.**
Definitions—"Interest in a residence", Sch 11A para 25; "new residence", Sch 11A para 25; "residence", Sch 11A para 25.
Cross references—See TA 1988 Sch 11A paras 25–28 (interpretation).
Revenue Internal Guidance—Schedule E manual SE 3110 (removal or transfer costs: eligible expenses and benefits—acquisition of new residence).
Amendments—[1] This Schedule inserted by FA 1993 Sch 5 and has effect as provided in para 29 *post*.

Expenses of transporting belongings

[11—(1) Expenses fall within paragraph 7(*d*) above if (and only if) they consist of one of the following—

(*a*) expenses connected with transporting domestic belongings from the employee's former residence to his new residence, and

(*b*) the costs of any insurance effected to cover such transporting.

(2) For the purposes of this paragraph transporting includes—

(*a*) packing and unpacking belongings,

(*b*) temporarily storing them if a direct move from the former to the new residence is not made,

(*c*) detaching domestic fittings from the former residence if they are to be taken to the new residence, and

(*d*) attaching domestic fittings to the new residence, and adapting them, if they are brought from the old residence.

(3) For the purposes of this paragraph domestic belongings are those of the employee and of members of his family or household.]¹

Commentary—*Simon's Direct Tax Service* E4.493.
Definitions—"Family or household", Sch 11A para 26; "former residence", Sch 11A para 25; "new residence", Sch 11A para 25.
Cross references—See TA 1988 Sch 11A paras 25–28 (interpretation).
Revenue Internal Guidance—Schedule E manual SE 3111 (removal or transfer costs: eligible expenses and benefits—transporting belongings).
Amendments—¹ This Schedule inserted by FA 1993 Sch 5 and has effect as provided in para 29 *post.*

Travelling and subsistence expenses

[12—(1) Expenses fall within paragraph 7(*e*) above if (and only if) they consist of one of the following—

(*a*) the costs of travelling and subsistence of the employee and members of his family or household while making temporary visits to the new area for purposes connected with the change,

(*b*) the employee's costs of travelling between his former residence and the place where he normally performs his new duties or (where paragraph 5(1)(*c*) above applies) between his former residence and the new place where he normally performs the duties of his employment,

(*c*) where paragraph 5(1)(*b*) or (*c*) above applies, the employee's costs of travelling, before the alteration mentioned in paragraph 5(1)(*b*) or (*c*), between his new residence and his original place of work,

(*d*) costs of the employee's subsistence (other than costs falling within paragraph (*a*) above),

(*e*) the employee's costs of travelling between his former residence and any temporary living accommodation of the employee,

(*f*) where paragraph 5(1)(*b*) or (*c*) above applies, the employee's costs of travelling, before the alteration mentioned in paragraph 5(1)(*b*) or (*c*), between his new residence and any temporary living accommodation of the employee,

(*g*) the costs of travelling of the employee and members of his family or household from the employee's former residence to his new residence in connection with the change,

(*h*) a relevant child's costs of subsistence while staying, for the purposes of securing the continuity of his education, in living accommodation in the old area after the change,

(*i*) a relevant child's costs of travelling between the accommodation mentioned in paragraph (*h*) above and the employee's new residence,

(*j*) a relevant child's costs of subsistence while staying, for the purposes of securing the continuity of his education, in living accommodation in the new area before the change, and

(*k*) a relevant child's costs of travelling between the accommodation mentioned in paragraph (*j*) above and the employee's former residence.

(2) For the purposes of this paragraph—

(*a*) the employee's new duties are the duties of his employment (where paragraph 5(1)(*a*) above applies) or the new duties of his employment (where paragraph 5(1)(*b*) above applies),

(*b*) the new area is the area round or near the place where the employee's new duties are, or are to be, normally performed, or (where paragraph 5(1)(*c*) above applies) the area round or near the new place where the duties of the employee's employment are, or are to be, normally performed,

(*c*) the employee's original place of work is the place where, before the alteration mentioned in paragraph 5(1)(*b*) or (*c*) above, the employee normally performs the duties of his employment,

(*d*) a relevant child is a person who is a member of the employee's family or household and who is aged under 19 at the material time, and

(*e*) the old area is the area round or near the former residence of the employee.

(3) For the purposes of this paragraph the material time is the beginning of the year of assessment in which—

(*a*) the employee becomes employed by an employer,

(*b*) the alteration of the duties of the employee's employment becomes effective, or

(*c*) the alteration of the place where the employee is normally to perform the duties of his employment becomes effective.

(4) In a case where—

    (*a*) expenses are incurred by the employee,

    (*b*) the expenses would, apart from this sub-paragraph, fall within paragraph 7(*e*) above, and

    (*c*) a deduction is allowable under any of sections 193 to 195 in respect of the whole or part of the expenses,

the expenses or, as the case may be, the part of them in respect of which the deduction is allowable shall be treated as not falling within paragraph 7(*e*) above.]¹

Commentary—*Simon's Direct Tax Service* **E4.493.**
Revenue Internal Guidance—Schedule E manual SE 3112 (removal or transfer costs: eligible expenses and benefits; travelling and subsistence—general).
SE 3113 (removal or transfer costs: eligible expenses and benefits; travelling and subsistence for the employee).
SE 3114 (travelling and subsistence for the family and household).
SE 3115 (travelling and subsistence—child's education).
SE 3116 (travelling and subsistence—international moves).
SE 3117 (travelling and subsistence—temporary living accommodation).
SE 3119 (travelling and subsistence—provided cars or vans).
Definitions—"Employment", Sch 11A para 27; "family or household", Sch 11A para 26; "former residence", Sch 11A para 25; "new residence", Sch 11A para 25; "subsistence", Sch 11A para 28; "year of assessment", s 832(1).
Cross references—See TA 1988 Sch 11A paras 25–28 (interpretation).
Amendments—¹ This Schedule inserted by FA 1993 Sch 5 and has effect as provided in para 29 *post*.

Bridging loan expenses

[**13**—(1) Expenses fall within paragraph 7(*f*) above if (and only if)—

    (*a*) the employee has an interest in his former residence,

    (*b*) he disposes of that interest in consequence of the change of residence,

    (*c*) he acquires an interest in his new residence, and

    (*d*) the expenses consist of interest falling within sub-paragraph (2) below.

(2) Interest falls within this sub-paragraph if it is payable by the employee in respect of a loan raised by him and the reason, or one of the reasons, for the loan being raised is that a period elapses between—

    (*a*) the date when expenditure is incurred in connection with the acquisition of the employee's interest in his new residence, and

    (*b*) the date when the proceeds of the disposal of the employee's interest in his former residence are available.

(3) Interest on so much of the loan as exceeds the market value of the employee's interest in his former residence (taken at the time his interest in his new residence is acquired) shall be regarded as not falling within sub-paragraph (2) above.

(4) Interest on so much of the loan as is not used for any of the following purposes shall also be regarded as not falling within sub-paragraph (2)—

    (*a*) the purpose of redeeming any loan relating to the employee's former residence and raised by him;

    (*b*) the purpose of acquiring the employee's interest in his new residence.

(5) For the purposes of this paragraph a loan relates to a residence if the loan was raised to obtain an interest in the residence, or an interest in the residence forms security for the loan, or both.

(6) References in this paragraph to an employee having, disposing of or acquiring an interest in a residence include references to—

    (*a*) one or more members of the employee's family or household having, disposing of or acquiring such an interest;

    (*b*) the employee and one or more members of his family or household having, disposing of or acquiring such an interest;

and references to the employee's interest shall be construed accordingly.

(7) The reference in this paragraph to interest payable by the employee includes a reference to interest payable by one or more members of the employee's family or household or by the employee and one or more members of his family or household.

(8) References in this paragraph to a loan raised by the employee include references to a loan raised by one or more members of the employee's family or household or by the employee and one or more members of his family or household.]¹

Commentary—*Simon's Direct Tax Service* **E4.493.**
Revenue Internal Guidance—Schedule E manual SE 3121–03122 (removal or transfer costs: eligible expenses and benefits—bridging loans—loans not provided by the employer, including example).
SE 3123–03125 (removal or transfer costs: eligible expenses and benefits—bridging loans—loans provided by the employer, background, procedure and example).
Definitions—"Family or household", Sch 11A para 26; "former residence", Sch 11A para 25; "interest", s 832(1); "interest in a residence", Sch 11A para 25; "new residence", Sch 11A para 25; "residence", Sch 11A para 25.
Cross references—See TA 1988 Sch 11A paras 25–28 (interpretation).
Amendments—¹ This Schedule inserted by FA 1993 Sch 5 and has effect as provided in para 29 *post*.

Duplicate expenses

[14—(1) Expenses fall within paragraph 7(*g*) above if (and only if)—

(*a*) the employee has an interest in his former residence,

(*b*) he disposes of that interest in consequence of the change of residence,

(*c*) he acquires an interest in his new residence,

(*d*) the expenses are incurred by the employee as a result of the change, and

(*e*) the expenses are incurred on the purchase of domestic goods intended to replace goods which were used at the employee's former residence but which are not suitable for use at his new residence.

(2) In arriving at the total of the expenses any amount mentioned in sub-paragraph (3) below shall be deducted from what would be the total apart from this sub-paragraph; and accordingly an amount equal to the aggregate of such amounts shall not be treated as eligible removal expenses.

(3) The amount is any amount obtained in respect of the sale of the replaced goods.

(4) References in this paragraph to the employee having, disposing of or acquiring an interest in a residence include references to—

(*a*) one or more members of the employee's family or household having, disposing of or acquiring such an interest;

(*b*) the employee and one or more members of his family or household having, disposing of or acquiring such an interest.]¹

Commentary—*Simon's Direct Tax Service* **E4.493.**
Revenue Internal Guidance—Schedule E manual SE 3120 (removal or transfer costs: eligible expenses and benefits; domestic goods for new residence).
Definitions—"Family or household", Sch 11A para 26; "former residence", Sch 11A para 25; "interest in a residence", Sch 11A para 25; "new residence", Sch 11A para 25; "residence", Sch 11A para 25.
Cross references—See TA 1988 Sch 11A paras 25–28 (interpretation).
Amendments—¹ This Schedule inserted by FA 1993 Sch 5 and has effect as provided in para 29 *post*.

Power to amend

[15—(1) The Treasury may make regulations amending the preceding provisions of this Part of this Schedule so as to secure that expenses that would not be eligible removal expenses (apart from the regulations) are such expenses.

(2) Any such regulations may include such supplementary, incidental or consequential provisions as appear to the Treasury to be necessary or expedient; and such provisions may be made by way of amendment to other Parts of this Schedule, or otherwise.

(3) Any such regulations shall have effect as regards any change of an employee's residence which results from—

(*a*) the employee becoming employed by an employer on or after the specified day;

(*b*) an alteration, with effect from a time falling on or after the specified day, of the duties of the employee's employment;

(*c*) an alteration, with effect from a time falling on or after the specified day, of the place where the employee is normally to perform the duties of his employment;

and in this sub-paragraph "the specified day" means the day specified in the regulations for the purposes of this sub-paragraph.]¹

Commentary—*Simon's Direct Tax Service* **E4.493.**
Definitions—"Eligible removal expenses", Sch 11A para 7; "employment", Sch 11A para 27; "residence", Sch 11A para 25.
Cross references—See TA 1988 Sch 11A paras 25–28 (interpretation).
Amendments—¹ This Schedule inserted by FA 1993 Sch 5 and has effect as provided in para 29 *post*.

PART IV
ELIGIBLE REMOVAL BENEFITS
Introduction

[16 Benefits are eligible removal benefits if they fall into one of the following categories—

(*a*) benefits in respect of disposal,

(*b*) benefits in respect of acquisition,

(*c*) benefits in respect of abortive acquisition,

(*d*) benefits in respect of the transporting of belongings,

(*e*) travelling and subsistence benefits, and

(*f*) benefits in respect of the new residence;

and paragraphs 17 to 22 below apply for the purpose of interpreting the preceding provisions of this paragraph.]¹

Commentary—*Simon's Direct Tax Service* **E4.493.**
Revenue Internal Guidance—Schedule E manual SE 3128–03129 (removal or transfer costs: relocation companies; treatment of management fees including example).
SE 3130–03137 (removal or transfer costs: relocation companies; guaranteed sale price schemes, different types of schemes with worked examples).

Definitions—''New residence'', Sch 11A para 25; ''subsistence'', Sch 11A para 28.
Cross references—See TA 1988 Sch 11A paras 25–28 (interpretation).
Amendments—¹ This Schedule inserted by FA 1993 Sch 5 and has effect as provided in para 29 *post*.

Benefits in respect of disposal

[17—(1) A benefit falls within paragraph 16(*a*) above if (and only if)—

(*a*) the employee has an interest in his former residence,
(*b*) that interest is disposed of, or is intended to be disposed of, in consequence of the change of residence, and
(*c*) the benefit falls within sub-paragraph (2) below.

(2) A benefit falls within this sub-paragraph if it consists of one of the following—

(*a*) legal services connected with the disposal or intended disposal of the employee's interest in his former residence (including legal services connected with the redemption of any loan relating to the residence),
(*b*) the waiving of any penalty for redeeming, for the purpose of the disposal or intended disposal, any loan relating to the residence,
(*c*) the services of an estate agent or auctioneer engaged in the disposal or intended disposal,
(*d*) services connected with the advertisement of the disposal or intended disposal,
(*e*) the disconnection, for the purpose of the disposal or intended disposal, of public utilities serving the residence, and
(*f*) services connected with the maintenance or insurance, or the preservation of the security, of the residence at any time when unoccupied pending the disposal or intended disposal.

(3) Sub-paragraphs (3) and (4) of paragraph 8 above apply for the purposes of this paragraph as they apply for the purposes of that.]¹

Commentary—*Simon's Direct Tax Service* **E4.493.**
Revenue Internal Guidance—Schedule E manual SE 3109 (removal or transfer costs: eligible expenses and benefits—disposal of old residence).
Definitions—''Former residence'', Sch 11A para 25; ''interest in a residence'', Sch 11A para 25; ''residence'', Sch 11A para 25.
Cross references—See TA 1988 Sch 11A paras 25–28 (interpretation).
Amendments—¹ This Schedule inserted by FA 1993 Sch 5 and has effect as provided in para 29 *post*.

Benefits in respect of acquisition

[18—(1) A benefit falls within paragraph 16(*b*) above if (and only if) the employee acquires an interest in his new residence and the benefit consists of one of the following—

(*a*) legal services connected with the acquisition by the employee of the interest (including legal services connected with any loan raised to acquire the interest),
(*b*) the waiving of any procurement fees connected with any such loan,
(*c*) the waiving of any amount payable in respect of insurance effected to cover risks which are incurred by the maker of any such loan and which arise because the amount of the loan is equal to the whole, or a substantial part, of the value of the interest,
(*d*) any survey or inspection of the residence undertaken in connection with the acquisition by the employee of the interest, and
(*e*) the connection of any public utility for use by the employee, if the utility serves the residence.

(2) Sub-paragraphs (2) to (4) of paragraph 9 above apply for the purposes of this paragraph as they apply for the purposes of that.]¹

Commentary—*Simon's Direct Tax Service* **E4.493.**
Revenue Internal Guidance—Schedule E manual SE 3110 (removal or transfer costs: eligible expenses and benefits—acquisition of new residence).
Definitions—''Interest in a residence'', Sch 11A para 25; ''new residence'', Sch 11A para 25; ''residence'', Sch 11A, para 25.
Cross references—See TA 1988 Sch 11A paras 25–28 (interpretation).
Amendments—¹ This Schedule inserted by FA 1993 Sch 5 and has effect as provided in para 29 *post*.

Benefits in respect of abortive acquisition

[19 A benefit falls within paragraph 16(*c*) above if (and only if)—

(*a*) it is provided with a view to the acquisition of an interest in a residence, the interest is not acquired, but (if it were) the residence would be the employee's new residence,
(*b*) it would fall within paragraph 16(*b*) above if the interest were acquired, and
(*c*) the interest is not acquired because of circumstances outside the control of the person seeking to acquire the interest, or because that person reasonably declines to proceed.]¹

Commentary—*Simon's Direct Tax Service* **E4.493.**
Revenue Internal Guidance—Schedule E manual SE 3110 (removal or transfer costs: eligible expenses and benefits—acquisition of new residence).
Definitions—''Interest in a residence'', Sch 11A para 25; ''new residence'', Sch 11A para 25; ''residence'', Sch 11A para 25.
Cross references—See TA 1988 Sch 11A paras 25–28 (interpretation).
Amendments—¹ This Schedule inserted by FA 1993 Sch 5 and has effect as provided in para 29 *post*.

Benefits in respect of the transporting of belongings

[20—(1) A benefit falls within paragraph 16(*d*) above if (and only if) it consists of one of the following—

(*a*) the transporting of domestic belongings from the employee's former residence to his new residence, and

(*b*) the effecting of insurance to cover such transporting.

(2) Sub-paragraphs (2) and (3) of paragraph 11 above apply for the purposes of this paragraph as they apply for the purposes of that.]¹

Commentary—*Simon's Direct Tax Service* **E4.493.**
Revenue Internal Guidance—Schedule E manual SE 3111 (removal or transfer costs: eligible expenses and benefits—transporting belongings).
SE 3120 (removal or transfer costs: eligible expenses and benefits; domestic goods for new residence).
Definitions—"Former residence", Sch 11A para 25; "new residence", Sch 11A para 25.
Cross references—See TA 1988 Sch 11A paras 25–28 (interpretation).
Amendments—¹ This Schedule inserted by FA 1993 Sch 5 and has effect as provided in para 29 *post*.

Travelling and subsistence benefits

[21—(1) A benefit falls within paragraph 16(*e*) above if (and only if) it consists of one of the following—

(*a*) subsistence, and facilities for travel, provided for the employee and members of his family or household while making temporary visits to the new area for purposes connected with the change

(*b*) facilities provided for the employee for travel between his former residence and the place where he normally performs his new duties or (where paragraph 5(1)(*c*) above applies) between his former residence and the new place where he normally performs the duties of his employment

(*c*) where paragraph 5(1)(*b*) or (*c*) above applies, facilities provided for the employee for travel before the alteration mentioned in paragraph 5(1)(*b*) or (*c*), between his new residence and his original place of work,

(*d*) subsistence provided for the employee (other than subsistence falling within paragraph (*a*) above),

(*e*) facilities provided for the employee for travel between his former residence and any temporary living accommodation of the employee,

(*f*) where paragraph 5(1)(*b*) or (*c*) above applies, facilities provided for the employee for travel before the alteration mentioned in paragraph 5(1)(*b*) or (*c*), between his new residence and any temporary living accommodation of the employee,

(*g*) facilities provided for the employee and members of his family or household for travel from the employee's former residence to his new residence in connection with the change,

(*h*) subsistence provided for a relevant child while staying, for the purposes of securing the continuity of his education, in living accommodation in the old area after the change,

(*i*) facilities provided for a relevant child for travel between the accommodation mentioned in paragraph (*h*) above and the employee's new residence,

(*j*) subsistence provided for a relevant child while staying, for the purposes of securing the continuity of his education, in living accommodation in the new area before the change, and

(*k*) facilities provided for a relevant child for travel between the accommodation mentioned in paragraph (*j*) above and the employee's former residence.

(2) Where (apart from this sub-paragraph) a car or van would constitute a facility for the purposes of sub-paragraph (1) above, it shall not do so if the car or van—

(*a*) is provided as mentioned in that sub-paragraph,

(*b*) is also available at any relevant time to the employee, or to others being members of his family or household, for his or their private use not falling within that sub-paragraph, and

(*c*) is so available by reason of the employee's employment and without any transfer of the property in it.

(3) Sub-paragraphs (2) and (3) of paragraph 12 above apply for the purposes of this paragraph as they apply for the purposes of that.

(4) In this paragraph "car", "van" and "private use" have the same meanings as in Chapter II of this Part of this Act.

(5) Section 168(6) applies for the purposes of this paragraph as it applies for the purposes of Chapter II of this Part of this Act.

(6) For the purposes of this paragraph a relevant time is any time falling on or before the day which is the relevant day (within the meaning given by paragraph 6 above) in relation to the change of residence concerned.

(7) In a case where—

(*a*) a benefit is provided for the employee or a member of his family or household,

(*b*) the benefit would, apart from this sub-paragraph, fall within paragraph 16(*e*) above, and

(*c*) a deduction is allowable under any of sections 193 to 195 in respect of the whole or part of the cost of the benefit, the benefit shall, subject to sub-paragraph (8) below, be treated as not falling within paragraph 16(*e*) above.

(8) Where a deduction is allowed as mentioned in sub-paragraph (7) above in respect of part only of the cost of the benefit, the extent to which the benefit is treated as falling within paragraph 16(*e*) above shall be determined on a just and reasonable basis.]¹

Commentary—*Simon's Direct Tax Service* **E4.493.**
Revenue Internal Guidance—Schedule E manual SE 3112 (removal or transfer costs: eligible expenses and benefits; travelling and subsistence—general).
SE 3113 (removal or transfer costs: eligible expenses and benefits; travelling and subsistence for the employee).
SE 3114 (travelling and subsistence for the family and household).
SE 3115 (travelling and subsistence—child's education).
SE 3116 (travelling and subsistence—international moves).
SE 3117 (travelling and subsistence—temporary living accommodation).
SE 3119 (travelling and subsistence—provided cars or vans).
Definitions—"Available", s 168(6); "car", s 168(5); "employment", Sch 11A para 27; "family or household", Sch 11A para 26; "former residence", Sch 11A para 25; "new residence", Sch 11A para 25; "private use", s 168(5); "residence", Sch 11A para 25; "subsistence", Sch 11A para 28; "van", s 168(5A).
Cross references—See TA 1988 Sch 11A paras 25–28 (interpretation).
Amendments—¹ This Schedule inserted by FA 1993 Sch 5 and has effect as provided in para 29 *post*.

Benefits in respect of new residence

[**22**—(1) A benefit falls within paragraph 16(*f*) above if (and only if)—

    (*a*) the employee has an interest in his former residence,
    (*b*) he disposes of that interest in consequence of the change of residence,
    (*c*) he acquires an interest in his new residence,
    (*d*) the benefit is provided as a result of the change, and
    (*e*) the benefit consists of domestic goods provided to replace goods which were used at the employee's former residence but which are not suitable for use at his new residence.

(2) Sub-paragraph (4) of paragraph 14 above applies for the purposes of this paragraph as it applies for the purposes of that.]¹

Commentary—*Simon's Direct Tax Service* **E4.493.**
Revenue Internal Guidance—Schedule E manual SE 1243f (this paragraph covers carpets and curtains which are the wrong size for the new residence, electric cooker to replace gas cooker; any sale proceeds from old goods are taken into account).
Definitions—"Former residence", Sch 11A para 25; "interest in a residence", Sch 11A para 25; "new residence", Sch 11A para 25; "residence", Sch 11A, para 25.
Cross references—See TA 1988 Sch 11A paras 25–28 (interpretation).
Amendments—¹ This Schedule inserted by FA 1993 Sch 5 and has effect as provided in para 29 *post*.

Power to amend

[**23**—(1) The Treasury may make regulations amending the preceding provisions of this Part of this Schedule so as to secure that a benefit that would not be an eligible removal benefit (apart from the regulations) is such a benefit.

(2) Any such regulations may include such supplementary, incidental or consequential provisions as appear to the Treasury to be necessary or expedient; and such provisions may be made by way of amendment to other Parts of this Schedule, or otherwise.

(3) Sub-paragraph (3) of paragraph 15 above applies to regulations made under this paragraph as it applies to regulations made under that.]¹

Commentary—*Simon's Direct Tax Service* **E4.493.**
Definitions—"Eligible removal benefit", Sch 11A para 16.
Cross references—See TA 1988 Sch 11A paras 25–28 (interpretation).
Amendments—¹ This Schedule inserted by FA 1993 Sch 5 and has effect as provided in para 29 *post*.

PART V

THE QUALIFYING LIMIT

[**24**—(1) In a case where, by reason of the employee's employment and in connection with a particular change of residence—

    (*a*) any sums are paid as mentioned in paragraph 1(1)(*a*) or (*b*) above, or
    (*b*) any qualifying removal benefit is provided as mentioned in paragraph 1(1)(*c*) above,

paragraph 1(1) above shall apply only to the extent that the total value to the employee, found under sub-paragraph (2) below, does not exceed the qualifying limit.

(2) The total value to the employee is the total of the following—

    (*a*) the aggregate of the amounts of any sums paid as mentioned in paragraph 1(1)(*a*) or (*b*) above in connection with the change of residence;
    (*b*) the aggregate of any amounts represented by qualifying removal benefits which are provided as mentioned in paragraph 1(1)(*c*) above in connection with the change.

(3) Subject to sub-paragraphs (4) to (8) below, for the purposes of sub-paragraph (2)(*b*) above the amount represented by a benefit is the amount which would be the cash equivalent of the benefit

under Chapter II of this Part of this Act if the benefit were chargeable under the appropriate provision of that Chapter.

(4) In the case of a benefit which—

(*a*) consists of living accommodation provided for a person, and

(*b*) is, or would be apart from this Schedule, chargeable under section 145 and not under section 146,

for the purposes of sub-paragraph (2)(*b*) above the amount represented by the benefit is the amount which, if the benefit were so chargeable, would be the value to the employee of the accommodation for the period in which the accommodation is provided, less the appropriate sum.

(5) For the purposes of sub-paragraph (4) above the value to the employee of accommodation in any period shall be determined in accordance with section 145, and the reference in that sub-paragraph to the appropriate sum is to the total of—

(*a*) so much of any sum made good by the employee to those at whose cost the accommodation is provided as is properly attributable to the provision of the accommodation, and

(*b*) any amounts which, if the benefit were chargeable under section 145, would be deductible by virtue of section 145(3) from the amount to be treated as emoluments under section 145(1) as regards the benefit.

(6) In the case of a benefit which—

(*a*) consists of living accommodation provided for a person, and

(*b*) is, or would be apart from this Schedule, chargeable under both section 145 and section 146,

for the purposes of sub-paragraph (2)(*b*) above the amount represented by the benefit is the total of the amounts mentioned in sub-paragraph (7) below.

(7) The amounts referred to in sub-paragraph (6) above are—

(*a*) the amount which would be found under sub-paragraph (4) above if the benefit were chargeable under section 145 and not under section 146, and

(*b*) the amount which, if the benefit were chargeable under section 146, would be the additional value to the employee of the accommodation for the period in which the accommodation is provided, less the appropriate sum.

(8) For the purposes of sub-paragraph (7) above the additional value to the employee of accommodation in any period shall be determined in accordance with section 146, and the reference in that sub-paragraph to the appropriate sum is to the total of—

(*a*) so much of any rent paid by the employee in respect of the accommodation to the person providing it as exceeds the value to the employee of the accommodation for the period (determined in accordance with section 145), and

(*b*) any amounts which, if the benefit were chargeable under section 146, would be deductible by virtue of subsection (9) of that section from the amount to be treated as emoluments under that section as regards the benefit.

(9) The qualifying limit, as regards any change of residence, is £8,000.

(10) The Treasury may by order substitute for the sum for the time being specified in sub-paragraph (9) above a sum of a greater amount.

(11) Any such substitution shall have effect as regards any change of an employee's residence which results from—

(*a*) the employee becoming employed by an employer on or after the specified day;

(*b*) an alteration, with effect from a time falling on or after the specified day, of the duties of the employee's employment;

(*c*) an alteration, with effect from a time falling on or after the specified day, of the place where the employee is normally to perform the duties of his employment;

and in this sub-paragraph "the specified day" means the day specified in the order for the purposes of this sub-paragraph.]¹

Commentary—*Simon's Direct Tax Service* **E4.494.**
Revenue Internal Guidance—Schedule E manual SE 3103 (removal or transfer costs: the exemption from charge).
Definitions—"Emoluments", s 131(1); "employment", Sch 11A para 27; "qualifying removal benefit", Sch 11A para 4; "residence", Sch 11A para 25.
Cross references—See TA 1988 s 191B (beneficial loan arrangements as regards removal expenses).
TA 1988 Sch 11A paras 25–28 (interpretation).
IT (Employments) Regulations, SI 1993/744 reg 46(2)(*b*) (requirement for employer to render a return of benefits exceeding the limit in paragraph 24(9)).
Amendments—¹ This Schedule inserted by FA 1993 Sch 5 and has effect as provided in para 29 *post.*

PART VI

GENERAL

Interpretation

[**25** In this Schedule—

(*a*) references to the residence of the employee are to his sole or main residence,

(*b*) references to the former residence of the employee are to his sole or main residence before the change,
(*c*) references to the new residence of the employee are to his sole or main residence after the change, and
(*d*) references to an interest in a residence are, in the case of a building, references to an estate or interest in the land concerned.]¹

Commentary—*Simon's Direct Tax Service* E4.492.
Amendments—¹ This Schedule inserted by FA 1993 Sch 5 and has effect as provided in para 29 *post*.

[**26** For the purposes of this Schedule a person is not a member of another person's family or household unless the former is—

(*a*) the latter's spouse, son, daughter, parent, servant, dependant or guest, or
(*b*) the spouse of a son or daughter of the latter.]¹

Commentary—*Simon's Direct Tax Service* E4.491.
Amendments—¹ This Schedule inserted by FA 1993 Sch 5 and has effect as provided in para 29 *post*.

[**27** In this Schedule references to employment include references to any office, and related expressions shall be construed accordingly.]¹

Commentary—*Simon's Direct Tax Service* E4.492.
Amendments—¹ This Schedule inserted by FA 1993 Sch 5 and has effect as provided in para 29 *post*.

[**28** References in this Schedule to subsistence are to food, drink and temporary living accommodation.]¹

Commentary—*Simon's Direct Tax Service* E4.493.
Revenue Internal Guidance—Schedule E manual SE 3118 (removal or transfer costs: eligible expenses and benefits—travelling and subsistence—meaning of "subsistence").
Amendments—¹ This Schedule inserted by FA 1993 Sch 5 and has effect as provided in para 29 *post*.

Commencement

[**29** This Schedule applies to any payment made, or any benefit provided, in connection with a change of an employee's residence which results from—

(*a*) the employee becoming employed by an employer on or after 6th April 1993,
(*b*) an alteration, with effect from a time falling on or after 6th April 1993, of the duties of the employee's employment, or
(*c*) an alteration, with effect from a time falling on or after 6th April 1993, of the place where the employee is normally to perform the duties of his employment.]¹

Commentary—*Simon's Direct Tax Service* E4.491.
Amendments—¹ This Schedule inserted by FA 1993 Sch 5.

SCHEDULE 12
FOREIGN EARNINGS
Section 193

1 This Schedule shall have effect for the purpose of supplementing the provisions of section [192A]¹.

Revenue Internal Guidance—Schedule E manual SE 33000 (Foreign Earnings Deduction (FED)—introduction and list of guidance covering references SE 33001–33301, mostly for periods up to 17 March 1998).
SE 70245 (Foreign Earnings Deduction—tax treatment of seafarers).
Amendments—¹ Section number substituted by FA 1998 s 63(3) with effect in relation to emoluments attributable to qualifying periods beginning on or after 17 March 1998, and emoluments attributable to qualifying periods beginning before 17 March 1998 which are received on or after that date.

[*Amount of emoluments*]1

[**1A** For the purposes of section [192A]² and this Schedule the amount of the emoluments for a year of assessment from any employment shall be taken to be the amount remaining after any capital allowance and after any deductions under section 192(3), 193(4), 194(1), 195(7), [197AG,]³ 198, 199, 201, 332, 592 or 594.]¹

Commentary—*Simon's Direct Tax Service* E4.115.
Revenue Internal Guidance—Schedule E manual SE 33002 (Foreign Earnings Deduction (FED): amount of the deduction).
Amendments—¹ This paragraph inserted by F(No 2)A 1992 s 54 with effect from the year 1992–93.
² Section number substituted by FA 1998 s 63(3) with effect in relation to emoluments attributable to qualifying periods beginning on or after 17 March 1998, and emoluments attributable to qualifying periods beginning before 17 March 1998 which are received on or after that date.
³ Word inserted by FA 2001 s 57(3), (4), Sch 12 Pt II para 15 with effect from the year 2002–03.

Emoluments eligible for relief

2—(1) This paragraph has effect where a deduction falls to be allowed under section [192A][3] in respect of the emoluments from an employment ("the relevant employment") for a year of assessment in which the duties of—

(*a*) the relevant employment; or

(*b*) any other employment or employments held by the person concerned which are associated with the relevant employment,

are not performed wholly outside the United Kingdom.

(2) The amount of the [emoluments for the year of assessment from the relevant employment in respect of which such a deduction is allowed][1] shall not exceed such proportion of the emoluments for that year from the relevant employment and the other employment or employments (if any) as is ...[2] reasonable having regard to the nature of and time devoted to the duties performed outside and in the United Kingdom respectively and to all other relevant circumstances.

(3) For the purposes of this paragraph an employment is associated with another if they are with the same person or with persons associated with each other and—

(*a*) a company is associated with another company if one of them has control of the other within the meaning of section 416 or both of them are under the control within the meaning of that section of the same persons or persons,

(*b*) an individual or partnership is associated with another person (whether or not a company) if one of them has control of the other within the meaning of section 840 or both are under the control within the meaning of that section of the same person or persons;

but paragraph (*b*) above shall not be construed as requiring an individual to be treated in any circumstances as under the control of another person.

Commentary—*Simon's Direct Tax Service* E4.115.
Revenue Internal Guidance—Schedule E manual SE 33070 (Foreign Earnings Deduction (FED): anti- avoidance legislation—case to be referred to Personal Tax Division before subpara 2 invoked).
SE 33071 (Foreign Earnings Deduction (FED): anti- avoidance legislation—meaning of associated employments).
SE 40103 and SE 40104(Foreign emoluments exception: dual contract arrangements—legislation permits the Inspector to reapportion the remuneration on a commercial basis, case to be submitted first to Personal Tax Division; example given).
Definitions—"Company", s 832(1), (2); "control", s 840; "emoluments", s 131(1); "United Kingdom", s 830(1); "year of assessment", s 832(1).
Cross references—See TA 1988 s 192(5) (sub-paras (2) and (3) above to apply with modifications for the purposes of s 192(2) (foreign emoluments)).
Amendments—[1] Words in sub-para (2) substituted by FA 1989 s 42(1), (5) with effect from the year 1989–90.
[2] Words omitted from sub-para (2) repealed by FA 1996 s 134(1), (2), Sch 20 para 42, Sch 41 Pt V(10) with effect from the year 1996–97.
[3] Section number in sub-para (1) substituted by FA 1998 s 63(3) with effect in relation to emoluments attributable to qualifying periods beginning on or after 17 March 1998, and emoluments attributable to qualifying periods beginning before 17 March 1998 which are received on or after that date.

Qualifying periods

3—(1) For the purposes of section [192A][1] a qualifying period is a period of consecutive days which either—

(*a*) consists entirely of days of absence from the United Kingdom; or

(*b*) consists partly of such days and partly of days included by virtue of sub-paragraph (2) below.

(2) Where, in the case of any person, a period consisting entirely of days of absence from the United Kingdom ("the relevant period") comes to an end and there have previously been one or more qualifying periods, the relevant period and the (or, if more than one, the last) qualifying period together with the intervening days between those periods shall be treated as a single qualifying period provided that—

(*a*) there are no more than [183][2] intervening days, and

(*b*) the number of days in the resulting period which are not days of absence from the United Kingdom does not exceed [one-half][2] of the total number of days in that period.

(2A) ...[3]

(3) For the purposes of section [192A][1] the emoluments from an employment attributable to a qualifying period include any emoluments from that employment for a period of leave immediately following that period but not so as to make any emoluments for one year of assessment emoluments for another.

Commentary—*Simon's Direct Tax Service* E4.113.
Statement of Practice SP 18/91—Foreign earnings deductions: interpretation of the term "qualifying period". Statement (not reproduced) classified obsolete by IR 131 Supplement (November 1998).
Simon's Tax Cases—*Carstairs (Inspector of Taxes) v Sykes* [2000] STC 1103.
Sub-para 3(2), *Robins v Durkin* [1988] STC 588*; *Massey v IRC* [1995] STC (SCD) 193.
Sub-para 3(2A)—s 193 *Lavery v Macleod* [2000] STC (SCD) 118; *Clark v Perks* [2001] STC 1254.
Revenue Internal Guidance—Schedule E manual SE 33301 (example of seafarer's calculation of qualifying period after 17 March 1998).
SE 33052 (Foreign Earnings Deduction (FED): attribution of emoluments—terminal leave pay).
Definitions—"Emoluments", s 131(1); "United Kingdom", s 830(1); "year of assessment", s 832(1).
Cross references—See TA 1988 s 132(3) (place of performance of duties of office or employment).

Amendments—[1] Section number in sub-paras (1), (3) substituted by FA 1998 s 63(3) with effect in relation to emoluments attributable to qualifying periods beginning on or after 17 March 1998, and emoluments attributable to qualifying periods beginning before 17 March 1998 which are received on or after that date.

[2] Number of days and fraction in sub-para (2) substituted by FA 1998 s 63(4) with effect in relation to emoluments attributable to qualifying periods beginning on or after 17 March 1998, and emoluments attributable to qualifying periods beginning before 17 March 1998 which are received on or after that date.

[3] Sub-para (2A) repealed by FA 1998 Sch 27 Part III(11) with effect in relation to emoluments attributable to qualifying periods beginning on or after 17 March 1998, and emoluments attributable to qualifying periods beginning before 17 March 1998 which are received on or after that date.

Supplementary

4 For the purposes of this Schedule a person shall not be regarded as absent from the United Kingdom on any day unless he is so absent at the end of it.

Commentary—*Simon's Direct Tax Service* E4.113.
Revenue & other press releases—IR 22-7-80 (passengers on board a ship leave the UK when the ship casts off from a UK berth and arrive when the ship berths in the UK).
Simon's Tax Cases—*Hoye v Forsdyke* [1981] STC 711*.
Definition—"United Kingdom", s 830(1).

5 Notwithstanding section 132(4)(*b*), there shall be treated for the purposes of section [192A][1] and this Schedule as performed outside the United Kingdom any duties which a person performs on a [ship (within the meaning of section 192A)][1] engaged on—

(*a*) a [voyage][1] beginning or ending outside the United Kingdom (but exclusive of any part of it which begins and ends in the United Kingdom); or

(*b*) any part beginning or ending outside the United Kingdom of a [voyage][1] which begins and ends in the United Kingdom;

and for the purposes of this paragraph any area designated under section 1(7) of the Continental Shelf Act 1964 shall be treated as part of the United Kingdom.

Commentary—*Simon's Direct Tax Service* E4.123.
Revenue & other press releases—IR 22-7-80 (Revenue view that a voyage from the UK to the UK not entailing a scheduled call at an overseas port is a voyage beginning and ending in the UK, no part ends or begins outside the UK).
Revenue Internal Guidance—Schedule E manual SE 33034 (Foreign Earnings Deduction (FED): location of duties; duties performed on ships and aircraft visiting oil and gas rigs).
Definition—"United Kingdom", s 830(1).
Amendments—[1] Section number and words in this sub-paragraph substituted by FA 1998 s 63(3)–(4)(*b*) with effect in relation to emoluments attributable to qualifying periods beginning on or after 17 March 1998, and emoluments attributable to qualifying periods beginning before 17 March 1998 which are received on or after that date.

6 Where an employment is in substance one the duties of which fall in the year of assessment to be performed in the United Kingdom, then, for the purposes of section [192A][1], there shall be treated as so performed any duties performed outside the United Kingdom the performance of which is merely incidental to the performance of other duties in the United Kingdom.

Commentary—*Simon's Direct Tax Service* E4.111.
Definitions—"United Kingdom", s 830(1); "year of assessment", s 832(1).
Cross references—See TA 1988 Sch 14 para 7(2) (regulations for carrying into effect the Board's powers under this paragraph).
Amendments—[1] Section number substituted by FA 1998 s 63(3) with effect in relation to emoluments attributable to qualifying periods beginning on or after 17 March 1998, and emoluments attributable to qualifying periods beginning before 17 March 1998 which are received on or after that date.

7 ...

Commentary—*Simon's Direct Tax Service* E4.111, 113.
Amendments—This paragraph repealed by FA 1998 Sch 27 Part III(11) with effect in relation to emoluments attributable to qualifying periods beginning on or after 17 March 1998, and emoluments attributable to qualifying periods beginning before 17 March 1998 which are received on or after that date.

[SCHEDULE 12AA

MILEAGE ALLOWANCES: INTERPRETATION][1]

Section 197AH

Commentary—*Simon's Direct Tax Service* E4.705.
Amendments—[1] This Schedule inserted by FA 2001 s 57(2), (4), Sch 12 Pt I with effect from the year 2002–03.

[Introduction

1—(1) The provisions of this Schedule apply for the purposes of sections 197AD to 197AG (Schedule E exemption for mileage allowance payments and passenger payments and mileage allowance relief).

(2) Expressions defined in this Schedule for those purposes have the same meaning for the purposes of this Schedule.

(3) In this Schedule "mileage allowance payments" has the meaning given by section 197AD(2) and "passenger payments" has the meaning given by section 197AE(2).][1]

Commentary—*Simon's Direct Tax Service* E4.705.
Amendments—[1] This Schedule inserted by FA 2001 s 57(2), (4), Sch 12 Pt I with effect from the year 2002–03.

[Business travel

2 "Business travel" means travelling the expenses of which, if incurred and defrayed by the employee in question out of the emoluments of his employment, would (in the absence of sections 197AD to 197AF) be deductible under section 198(1) (general relief for necessary expenses).][1]

Commentary—*Simon's Direct Tax Service* E4.705.
Amendments—[1] This Schedule inserted by FA 2001 s 57(2), (4), Sch 12 Pt I with effect from the year 2002–03.

[Qualifying vehicles

3—(1) "Qualifying vehicle" means a car, van, motor cycle or cycle.

(2) "Car" means a mechanically propelled road vehicle which is not—

    (*a*) a goods vehicle,

    (*b*) a motor cycle, or

    (*c*) a vehicle of a type not commonly used as a private vehicle and unsuitable to be so used.

(3) "Van" means a mechanically propelled road vehicle which—

    (*a*) is a goods vehicle, and

    (*b*) has a design weight not exceeding 3,500 kilograms,

and which is not a motor cycle.

(4) "Motor cycle" has the meaning given by section 185(1) of the Road Traffic Act 1988.

(5) "Cycle" has the meaning given by section 192(1) of that Act.

(6) In this paragraph—

    "design weight" means the weight which a vehicle is designed or adapted not to exceed when in normal use and travelling on a road laden; and

    "goods vehicle" means a vehicle of a construction primarily suited for the conveyance of goods or burden of any description.][1]

Commentary—*Simon's Direct Tax Service* E4.705.
Amendments—[1] This Schedule inserted by FA 2001 s 57(2), (4), Sch 12 Pt I with effect from the year 2002–03.

[The approved amount: mileage allowance payments

4—(1) The approved amount for mileage allowance payments that is applicable to a kind of vehicle is—

$$M \times R$$

where—

M is the number of miles of business travel by the employee (other than as a passenger), using that kind of vehicle, in the tax year in question; and

R is the rate applicable for that kind of vehicle.

(2) The rates applicable are as follows—

Kind of vehicle	Rate
Car or van	40p per mile for the first 10,000 miles; 25p per mile after that.
Motor cycle	24p per mile.
Cycle	20p per mile.

Note: The reference above to "the first 10,000 miles" is to the total number of miles of business travel in relation to the employment or any associated employment, by car or van, in the tax year in question.

One employment is associated with another if—

    (*a*) the employer is the same;

    (*b*) the employers are partnerships or bodies and an individual or another partnership or body has control over both of them; or

    (*c*) the employers are associated companies (as defined in section 416).

Section 168(12) (meaning of "control") applies for the purposes of paragraph (*b*).

(3) The Treasury may by regulations amend sub-paragraph (2) so as to alter the rates or rate bands.][1]

Commentary—*Simon's Direct Tax Service* E4.705.
Amendments—[1] This Schedule inserted by FA 2001 s 57(2), (4), Sch 12 Pt I with effect from the year 2002–03.

[The approved amount: passenger payments

5—(1) The approved amount for passenger payments is—

$$M \times R$$

where—

M is the number of miles of business travel by the employee, by car or van, for which the employee carries a qualifying passenger in the tax year in question and in respect of which passenger payments are made; and
R is 5p per mile.

(2) If the employee carries more than one qualifying passenger for all or part of a tax year, the approved amount for passenger payments is the total of the amounts calculated under sub-paragraph (1) in respect of each qualifying passenger.

(3) In this paragraph "qualifying passenger" means a passenger who is also an employee for whom the travel is business travel.

(4) The Treasury may by regulations amend sub-paragraph (1) so as to alter the rate.][1]

Commentary—*Simon's Direct Tax Service* **E4.705.**
Amendments—[1] This Schedule inserted by FA 2001 s 57(2), (4), Sch 12 Pt I with effect from the year 2002–03.

[Company vehicles

6—(1) A vehicle is a "company vehicle" in a tax year if in that year—

(*a*) the vehicle is made available to the employee by reason of his employment and is not available for his private use, or

(*b*) the employee is chargeable to tax in respect of the vehicle under section 154, 157 or 159AA (charge where benefit provided or car or van available for private use), or

(*c*) in the case of a car or van, the employee would be chargeable to tax in respect of it under section 157 or 159AA but for section 159 or 159AB (exception for pooled cars and vans), or

(*d*) in the case of a cycle, the employee would be chargeable to tax in respect of it under section 154 but for section 197AC(1)(*a*) (exception for cycles made available).

(2) Section 168(6) (when cars and vans are made available for private use and are made available by reason of employment) applies for the purposes of sub-paragraph (1).][1]

Commentary—*Simon's Direct Tax Service* **E4.705.**
Amendments—[1] This Schedule inserted by FA 2001 s 57(2), (4), Sch 12 Pt I with effect from the year 2002–03.

[Employment

7 "Employment" includes an office and "employee" includes an office-holder.][1]

Commentary—*Simon's Direct Tax Service* **E4.705.**
Amendments—[1] This Schedule inserted by FA 2001 s 57(2), (4), Sch 12 Pt I with effect from the year 2002–03.

[Tax year

8 "Tax year" means a year of assessment.][1]

Commentary—*Simon's Direct Tax Service* **E4.705.**
Amendments—[1] This Schedule inserted by FA 2001 s 57(2), (4), Sch 12 Pt I with effect from the year 2002–03.

[SCHEDULE 12A

ORDINARY COMMUTING AND PRIVATE TRAVEL][1]

Section 198(1A)

Commentary—*Simon's Direct Tax Service* **E4.708.**
Revenue & other press releases—IR Tax Bulletin December 1997 (The new tax rules on employee travel and subsistence—general scope).
IR Tax Bulletin February 1998 (The new tax rules on employee travel and subsistence—taxation of employees' travel expenses).
IR Tax Bulletin April 1998 (The new tax rules on employee travel and subsistence—explanation of the provision which denies relief for journeys that are substantially 'ordinary commuting', and practical examples).
IR Tax Bulletin December 2000 (Employees sent on secondment to work in the UK—How to identify "the employment" of an individual for the purposes of this Schedule).
Revenue Internal Guidance—Schedule E manual SE 32050 (travel expenses: 1998/99 and later years—definitions—introduction).
SE 32260 (introduction to safeguards against abuse).
Amendments—[1] This Schedule inserted by FA 1998 s 61(2), Sch 10 with effect from the year 1998–99.

Introduction

1—(1) The provisions of this Schedule apply for the purposes of section 198(1A)(*b*)(ii) (qualifying travelling expenses: exclusion of ordinary commuting and private travel).

(2) In this Schedule "employment" includes an office and "employee" includes an office-holder.

Commentary—*Simon's Direct Tax Service* **E4.708.**

Ordinary commuting and private travel

2—(1) "Ordinary commuting" means travel between—

   (*a*) the employee's home, or

   (*b*) a place that is not a workplace in relation to the employment,

and a place which is a permanent workplace in relation to the employment.

(2) "Private travel" means travel between—

   (*a*) the employee's home and a place that is not a workplace in relation to the employment, or

   (*b*) between two places neither of which is a workplace in relation to the employment.

(3) In sub-paragraphs (1)(*b*) and (2) "workplace" means a place at which the employee's attendance is necessary in the performance of the duties of the employment.

Commentary—*Simon's Direct Tax Service* **E4.708.**
Revenue Internal Guidance—Schedule E manual SE 32055 (definition of "ordinary commuting" and "workplace").
SE 32056 (attending permanent workplace outside normal working hours—no relief for extra costs)
SE 32060 (meaning of necessary journeys).
SE 32170–32173 (treatment of employees who work at home, including examples)
SE 32180 (definition of "private travel").
SE 32181–32182 (examples illustrating private travel).
SE 32240–32241 (emergency call-out: deduction will not be due just because the journey was made in response to an emergency, example given).
SE 32245–32246 (emergency call-out: exceptionally, where an employee is obliged to perform duties at home and while travelling to an emergency at a permanent workplace, the travel may be regarded as travel between two workplaces, example given).
SE 32250–32251 (stand-by: where an employee is on stand-by and can be called out at short notice he or she is not entitled to a deduction for the cost of a journey that is ordinary commuting, example given).
SE 32270–32272 (safeguards against abuse—the necessary attendance rule, explanation of sub-para (3) with examples).
Simon's Tax Cases—*Kirkwood (Inspector of Taxes) v Evans* [2001] STC (SCD) 231.

3 Travel between any two places that is for practical purposes substantially ordinary commuting or private travel is treated as ordinary commuting or private travel.

Commentary—*Simon's Direct Tax Service* **E4.708.**
Revenue Internal Guidance—Schedule E manual SE 32300 (safeguards against abuse—journeys treated as ordinary commuting).
SE 32301–32310 (series of examples illustrating safeguards against abuse—journeys treated as ordinary commuting).
SE 32320 (safeguards against abuse—journeys treated as private travel).
SE 32321–32325 (series of examples illustrating safeguards against abuse—journeys treated as private travel).

Permanent and temporary workplaces

4 For the purposes of paragraph 2, subject to the following provisions of this Schedule—

   "permanent workplace" means a place which the employee regularly attends in the performance of the duties of the employment and which is not a temporary workplace; and

   "temporary workplace" means a place which the employee attends in the performance of the duties of the employment for the purpose of performing a task of limited duration or for some other temporary purpose.

Commentary—*Simon's Direct Tax Service* **E4.708.**
Revenue Internal Guidance—Schedule E manual SE 32065 (definition of "permanent workplace").
SE 32070 (meaning of regular attendance).
SE 32075 (definition of "temporary workplace").
SE 32080 (meaning of limited duration).
SE 32081–32092 (series of examples illustrating temporary workplace).
SE 32140–32142 (treatment where more than one permanent workplace at the same time, including examples).
SE 32150 (meaning of temporary purpose).
SE 32151–32154 (examples of attendance for a temporary purpose).
SE 32220–32221 (when a workplace ceases to be a permanent workplace with example).
SE 32230–32231 (passing work on the way to somewhere else, classification of journeys with example).

The 24 month rule and fixed term appointments

5—(1) A place is not regarded as a temporary workplace if the employee's attendance is in the course of a period of continuous work at that place—

   (*a*) lasting more than 24 months, or

   (*b*) comprising all or almost all of the period for which the employee is likely to hold the employment,

or if the employee's attendance is at a time when it is reasonable to assume that it will be in the course of such a period.

(2) A "period of continuous work" at a place means a period over which, looking at the whole period and considering all the duties of the employment, the duties of the employment fall to be performed to a significant extent at that place.

(3) An actual or contemplated modification of the place at which the duties of the employment fall to be performed is disregarded for the purposes of this paragraph if it does not have, or would not have, any substantial effect on the employee's journey, or expenses of travelling, to and from the place where the duties fall to be performed.

Commentary—*Simon's Direct Tax Service* **E4.708.**
Revenue Internal Guidance—Schedule E manual SE 32080 (the 24 month rule; to a significant extent means 40% or more).

SE 32100 (the 24 month rule—how to find out the expected period of time at a workplace).
SE 32105–32108 (the 24 month rule—breaks in attendance and examples).
SE 32110–32111 (the 24 month rule—transitional rules with example).
SE 32115–32116 (the 24 month rule—transitional rules: no requirement to return to a permanent workplace with example).
SE 32125 (fixed term appointments: this rule not to be used to deny a deduction for travel to a workplace that would otherwise be a temporary workplace, that is the final posting for someone whose contract of employment has lasted for at least 5 years).
SE 32126–32127 (examples of fixed term appointment rules).
SE 32130–32134 (treatment of agency workers including examples).
SE 32280–32283 (safeguards against abuse—changes to a workplace, explanation of sub-para (3) with examples).
SE 32285–32286 (safeguards against abuse—changes to a workplace, a change in the journey with no change in cost with example).

Depots and bases

6 A place which the employee regularly attends in the performance of the duties of the employment—

    (*a*) which forms the base from which the duties of the employment are performed, or

    (*b*) is the place at which the tasks to be carried out in the performance of those duties are allocated,

is treated as a permanent, and not a temporary, workplace.

Commentary—*Simon's Direct Tax Service* **E4.708.**
Revenue Internal Guidance—Schedule E manual SE 32160–32164 (depots and similar bases: application of this para with examples).

Area-based employees

7—(1) An employee is treated as having a permanent workplace consisting of an area if the following conditions are met.

(2) The conditions are that—

    (*a*) the duties of the employment are defined by reference to an area (whether or not they also require attendance at places outside the area),

    (*b*) in the performance of the duties of the employment the employee attends different places within the area,

    (*c*) none of the places he attends in the performance of the duties of the employment is a permanent workplace, and

    (*d*) applying paragraphs 4 and 5 to the area as if it were a place, the area meets the conditions for being a permanent workplace.]

Commentary—*Simon's Direct Tax Service* **E4.708.**
Revenue Internal Guidance—Schedule E manual SE 32190–32207 (duties defined by reference to a particular area: application of this para with examples).

SCHEDULE 13

COLLECTION OF ADVANCE CORPORATION TAX

Sections 238(5), 241(4)

Commentary—*Simon's Direct Tax Service* **D1.602, 605, 606, 611, 706, 731, 732.**
Amendments—This Schedule repealed by FA 1998, ss 31, 165, Sch 3 para 41, Sch 27 Pt III(2) with effect for return periods and accounting periods beginning after 5 April 1999.

SCHEDULE 13A

SURRENDERS OF ADVANCE CORPORATION TAX

Section 240

Amendments—This Schedule, which was inserted by FA 1996 Sch 25 paras 2, 3 with effect where the accounting period of the surrendering company ends after 30 June 1999 (by virtue of Finance Act 1994, Section 199, (Appointed Day) Order, SI 1998/3173 art 2), is repealed by FA 1998 Sch 3 para 42 with effect for accounting periods of the surrendering company (as defined in TA 1988 s 240(1)) beginning after 5 April 1999.

[SCHEDULE 13B

CHILDREN'S TAX CREDIT][1]

Section 257AA

Amendments—[1] This Schedule inserted by FA 1999 s 30(2), (5), Sch 3 with effect from the year 2001–02.

Child living with more than one adult: married and unmarried couples

1—(1) Paragraphs 2 to 5 below apply where at any time in a year of assessment—

    (*a*) a husband and wife are living together or a man and a woman are living together as husband and wife, and

    (*b*) a relevant child is resident with them.

(2) In those paragraphs—

  (*a*) the husband and wife, or the man and the woman, are referred to as the partners,

  (*b*) "the higher-earning partner" means the partner who has the higher total income for the year of assessment,

  (*c*) "the lower-earning partner" means the partner who has the lower total income for the year of assessment, and

  (*d*) "relevant child" means a child who is a qualifying child in relation to both partners.

(3) If the partners have the same total income for the year—

  (*a*) they may elect that one of them be treated for the purposes of paragraphs 2 to 5 below as the lower-earning partner, and

  (*b*) if they do not make an election, neither shall be entitled to a children's tax credit for the year in respect of a relevant child.

2 Subject to paragraph 3 below, the lower-earning partner shall not be entitled to a children's tax credit for the year in respect of a relevant child.

3—(1) This paragraph applies if no part of either partner's income for the year falls within section 1(2)(*b*).

(2) If the lower-earning partner makes a claim for a children's tax credit for the year in respect of a relevant child—

  (*a*) paragraph 2 above shall not apply, and

  (*b*) in calculating the credit for each partner, the amount mentioned in section 257AA(2) shall be halved.

[(2A) If a relevant child is a qualifying baby the reference in sub-paragraph (2)(*b*) above to the amount mentioned in section 257AA(2) is to the higher amount applicable by virtue of subsection (2A) of that section.][1]

(3) If the partners make an election under this sub-paragraph—

  (*a*) paragraph 2 above shall not apply, and

  (*b*) the higher-earning partner shall not be entitled to a children's tax credit for the year in respect of a relevant child.

Amendments—[1] Sub-para (2A) inserted by FA 2001 s 53(5), (6), Sch 11 para 2 with effect from the year 2002–03.

4—(1) This paragraph applies where—

  (*a*) a partner is entitled to a children's tax credit for a year of assessment,

  (*b*) the amount by reference to which his credit falls to be calculated (Amount A) exceeds the amount which would be necessary, in accordance with section 256(2) [(read with section 25(6)(c))][1] of the Finance Act 1990 where applicable), to reduce his liability for the year to income tax on his total income to nil (Amount B), and

  (*c*) he gives notice to an officer of the Board under this paragraph.

(2) Where the other partner would not, by virtue of paragraph 2 or 3 above, be entitled to a children's tax credit for the year in respect of a relevant child—

  (*a*) he shall be entitled to a children's tax credit in respect of a relevant child notwithstanding that paragraph, and

  (*b*) the amount by reference to which his credit shall be calculated shall be the amount of the difference between Amount A and Amount B.

(3) In any other case, the difference between Amount A and Amount B shall be added to the amount by reference to which children's tax credit would otherwise be calculated for the other partner in respect of a relevant child.

(4) A notice under this paragraph—

  (*a*) must be given on or before the fifth anniversary of the 31st January next following the end of the year of assessment to which it relates,

  (*b*) shall be in such form as the Board may determine, and

  (*c*) shall be irrevocable.

Amendments—[1]Words in sub-para (1)(*b*) inserted by FA 2000 s 39(9), (10) with effect for gifts made after 5 April 2000 which are not covenanted payements and covenanted payments falling to be made after that date.

5—(1) This paragraph applies to elections under paragraph 3 above.

(2) An election—

  (*a*) shall be made by giving notice to an officer of the Board in such form as the Board may determine, and

  (*b*) may be made so as to have effect for a single year of assessment or for two or more consecutive years.

(3) Subject to sub-paragraph (4) below, an election must be made before the first year of assessment for which it is to have effect and on the basis of assumptions about the partners' incomes for that year.

(4) An election may be made, on the basis of such assumptions, at a time during the first year for which it is to have effect if—

  (a) the election is made within the first 30 days of that year and an officer of the Board has been given written notification before that year that the election will be made, or
  (b) the partners marry in that year, or
  (c) the partners start to live together as man and wife in that year, or
  [(ca) a relevant child is born in that year, or]¹
  (d) a relevant child becomes resident with the partners in that year and no relevant child has previously in that year been resident with the partners, or
  (e) it is assumed that the partner who was the higher-earning partner in the previous year will be the lower-earning partner in that year.

(5) An election may be withdrawn—

  (a) by the making of another election which supersedes the first, or
  (b) by notice given to an officer of the Board, in such form as the Board may determine, by either partner.

(6) A withdrawal shall have effect for the year of assessment in which it is given and subsequent years.

(7) If the higher-earning partner for one year of assessment (Year 1) is the lower-earning partner for the next year (Year 2), an election having effect for Year 1 shall not have effect for Year 2 or subsequent years.

Amendments—¹ Sub-para (4)(ca) inserted by FA 2001 s 53(5), (6), Sch 11 para 3 with effect from the year 2002–03.

Child living with more than one adult: other cases

6—(1) This paragraph applies to a child for a year of assessment if—

  (a) he is resident with two or more persons at the same time or at different times during the year,
  (b) he is a qualifying child in relation to two or more of those persons, and
  (c) paragraphs 2 to 5 above do not apply in relation to him in that year.

(2) The persons in relation to whom the child is a qualifying child are referred to in this paragraph as the taxpayers.

(3) None of the taxpayers shall be entitled to a children's tax credit for the year of assessment by virtue of the residence of any child to whom this paragraph applies except in accordance with the following provisions of this paragraph.

(4) If a taxpayer claims a children's tax credit for the year of assessment by virtue of the residence of any child to whom this paragraph applies, for the amount mentioned in section 257AA(2) (before any reduction) there shall be substituted his allotted proportion of that amount.

[(4A) If the child is a qualifying baby the reference in sub-paragraph (4) above to the amount mentioned in section 257AA(2) is to the higher amount applicable by virtue of subsection (2A) of that section.]¹

(5) A taxpayer's allotted proportion is—

  (a) such proportion as may be agreed between him and the other taxpayers, or
  (b) in default of agreement, a proportion which is assigned to him by the Commissioners.

(6) For the purposes of sub-paragraph (5) above—

  (a) a proportion may be 100 per cent,
  (b) the sum of the proportions shall not exceed 100 per cent, and
  (c) "the Commissioners" means such body of General Commissioners, being the General Commissioners for a division in which one of the taxpayers resides, as the Board may direct or, if none of the taxpayers resides in the United Kingdom, the Special Commissioners.

(7) Where a person—

  (a) is a member of more than one set of taxpayers in relation to whom this paragraph applies for a year of assessment,
  (b) has more than one allotted proportion under this paragraph for the year, and
  (c) claims a children's tax credit for the year,

for the amount mentioned in section 257AA(2) (before any reduction) there shall be substituted the aggregate of his allotted proportions of that amount (not exceeding 100 per cent).

[(7A) Where sub-paragraph (7) above applies in relation to a person, and any child in respect of which a proportion has been, or could have been, allotted to that person is a qualifying baby, the reference in that sub-paragraph to the amount mentioned in section 257AA(2) is to the higher amount applicable by virtue of subsection (2A) of that section.]¹

(8) Where—

  (a) a taxpayer makes a claim under section 257AA, and
  (b) it appears that an allotted proportion will need to be assigned to him under sub-paragraph (5)(b) above for that purpose,

the Board may direct that the claim shall be dealt with, and the assignment shall be made, by a specified body of Commissioners which could be directed under sub-paragraph (6)(*c*) above to make the assignment; and where a direction is given no other body of Commissioners shall have jurisdiction to determine the claim.

(9) For the purposes of any assignment to a taxpayer under sub-paragraph (5)(*b*) above—

    (*a*) the Commissioners shall hear and determine the case in the same manner as an appeal, and

    (*b*) any of the taxpayers shall be entitled to appear and be heard by the Commissioners or to make representations to them in writing.

Amendments—¹ Sub-paras (4A), (7A) inserted by FA 2001 s 53(5), (6), Sch 11 para 4 with effect from the year 2002–03.

Combined cases

7—(1) This paragraph applies where a child is a relevant child for the purposes of paragraphs 2 to 5 above in a year of assessment and—

    (*a*) he is a relevant child for the year in relation to more than one pair of partners, or

    (*b*) paragraph 6 above would apply to him for the year but for the fact that he is a relevant child for the purposes of paragraphs 2 to 5 above.

(2) Where this paragraph applies—

    (*a*) paragraph 6 above shall apply, but with each pair of partners for the purposes of paragraphs 2 to 5 above being treated as a single taxpayer, and

    (*b*) paragraphs 2 to 5 above shall apply in relation to each pair of partners, taking for the amount mentioned in section 257AA(2) (before any reduction) the amount substituted by virtue of paragraph 6 above.

[(3) Where paragraph 6(4A) or (7A) above applies, the reference in sub-paragraph (2) above to the amount mentioned in section 257AA(2) is to the higher amount applicable by virtue of subsection (2A) of that section.]¹

Amendments—¹ Sub-para (3) inserted by FA 2001 s 53(5), (6), Sch 11 para 5 with effect from the year 2002–03.

Change of circumstances

8—(1) For the purposes of this paragraph a change of circumstances occurs in relation to a child in a year of assessment if a relevant event takes place in that year and—

    (*a*) as a result of the event the child becomes a qualifying child in relation to any person or stops being a qualifying child in relation to any person, or

    (*b*) the child is, immediately before the event, a qualifying child in relation to both parties to the event.

(2) The following are relevant events—

    (*a*) a marriage or a man and a woman starting to live together as husband and wife;

    (*b*) a separation.

(3) A separation occurs when—

    (*a*) a husband and wife cease to live together, or

    (*b*) a man and a woman cease to live together as husband and wife, having been living together as husband and wife without being married.

(4) In a year of assessment in which a change of circumstances (or more than one) occurs in relation to a child, section 257AA [(except subsection (4A))]¹ and paragraphs 2 to 7 above shall apply in relation to the child's residence as if each of the following were a separate year of assessment—

    (*a*) the period ending with the day before the first (or only) change of circumstances,

    (*b*) the period starting with the day of the last (or only) change of circumstances, and

    (*c*) any period starting with the day of one change of circumstances and ending with the day before the next.

(5) For the purposes of sub-paragraph (4) above the amount specified in section 257AA(2) (before any reduction or substitution) shall be taken to be the result of the following formula—

$$\text{(Days during the period/365) x Amount in s 257AA(2)}$$

[(5A) If the child is a qualifying baby the references in sub-paragraph (5) above to the amount specified in section 257AA(2) are to the higher amount applicable by virtue of subsection (2A) of that section.]²

(6) In applying sub-paragraph (4) above a reference in section 257AA or this Schedule to a person's income for the year shall be taken as a reference to his income for the year and not his income for the period.]¹

Amendments—¹ Schedule 13B inserted by FA 1999 s 30(2), (5), Sch 3 with effect from the year 2001–02.
² Words in sub-para (4) inserted, and sub-para (5A) inserted by FA 2001 s 53(5), (6), Sch 11 para 6 with effect from the year 2002–03.

SCHEDULE 14

PROVISIONS ANCILLARY TO SECTION 266

Section 266(12)

PART I

MODIFICATION OF SECTION 266 IN CERTAIN CASES
Husband and wife

1—(1) The references in section 266 to an individual's spouse shall include any person who was that individual's spouse at the time the insurance or contract was made, unless the marriage was dissolved before 6th April 1979.

(2), (3) ...[1]

Commentary—*Simon's Direct Tax Service* E2.1043.
Concession A31—Relief to continue after divorce on premiums paid by one spouse on the life of the other if they were married when the policy was taken out and divorced after 5 April 1979. Relief is extended to premiums paid on a policy taken out before marriage.
Amendments—[1] Sub-paras (2), (3) repealed by FA 1988 Sch 14 Pt VIII with effect from the year 1990–91.

Premiums payable to friendly societies and industrial assurance companies

2—(1) This paragraph applies to—

(a) a policy issued in the course of an industrial assurance business; and
(b) a policy issued by a [friendly society][1] in the course of tax exempt life or endowment business (as defined in section 466).

(2) Subject to paragraph 3(2) below, if a policy to which this paragraph applies was issued before the passing of the Finance Act 1976 (29th July 1976), section 266 shall have effect in relation to it as if subsections (2)(b), (3)(a), (b) and (d) were omitted; and if a policy to which this paragraph applies was issued after the passing of that Act, subsection (2)(b) of that section shall have effect in relation to it as if it permitted the insurance to be on the life of the individual's parent or grandparent or, subject to sub-paragraph (3) below, on the life of the individual's child or grandchild.

(3) Relief may be given in respect of premiums under a policy of insurance on the life of an individual's child or grandchild which was or is issued after the passing of the Finance Act 1976 (29th July 1976), as if subsection (3)(d) of section 266 were omitted, but may be given only if the annual amount of the premiums, together with that of any relevant premiums, does not exceed £52 if the policy was issued in respect of an insurance made before 25th March 1982 or £64 in any other case.

(4) For the purposes of sub-paragraph (3) above, a relevant premium, in relation to an insurance made at any time on the life of an individual's child or grandchild, is any premium under a policy of insurance on the same life, where the insurance is made at the same time or earlier, whether it is made by the individual or any other person.

(5) In this paragraph "child" includes a step-child and an illegitimate child whose parents have married each other after his birth, and "grandchild", "parent" and "grandparent" have corresponding meanings.

Commentary—*Simon's Direct Tax Service* E2.1038, 1039.
Statement of Practice SP 11/79—Revenue practice for premium relief as it applies to policies on the lives of children under age 12.
Definitions—"Friendly society", s 266(13); "industrial assurance business", s 832(1).
Cross references—See TA 1988 Sch 14 para 3(1) (policy issued by a friendly society or industrial assurance company).
TA 1988 Sch 14 para 3(4) (increases in capital sums treated as made by virtue of para 3(3) to be disregarded for the purposes of sub-para (3) above).
Amendments—[1] Words in sub-para (1)(b) substituted by F(No 2)A 1992 Sch 9 paras 1, 18, 22 with effect from 19 February 1993 by virtue of F(No 2)A 1992 Sch 9 (Appointed Day) Order, SI 1993/236.

3—(1) Where a policy is issued or a contract is made by a [friendly society][3] or a policy to which paragraph 2 above applies is issued by an industrial assurance company, section 266(4), (5) and (8) shall apply in relation to premiums payable under the policy or contract subject to the following provisions of this paragraph.

(2) References to the deductions authorised under section 266(5) shall be construed as including references to any amount retained by or refunded to the person paying the premium under any scheme made by the society or company in accordance with regulations made under this paragraph.

(3) The appropriate authority may make regulations authorising—

(a) the adoption by [friendly societies][4] and industrial assurance companies of any prescribed scheme for securing that in the case of policies or contracts to which the scheme applies amounts equal to [12·5 per cent][1] of the premiums payable are retained by or refunded to the person paying the premiums or that, in the case of such policies or contracts issued or made before 6th April 1979, the amounts expressed as the amounts of the premiums payable are treated as amounts arrived at by deducting [12·5 per cent][1] from the amounts payable and that the amounts of the capital sums assured or guaranteed are treated as correspondingly increased; or

(b) the adoption by any such society or company of any special scheme for that purpose which may, in such circumstances as may be prescribed, be approved by the appropriate authority.

(4) Increases treated as made in pursuance of regulations under this paragraph shall not be treated as variations of a policy or contract and shall be disregarded for the purposes of paragraph 2(3) above, sections 268(6), 460, 461(1) and 464 of, and paragraph 7 of Schedule 15 to, this Act ...[2]

(5) The regulations may include such adaptations and modifications of the enactments relating to friendly societies or industrial assurance companies and such other incidental and supplementary provisions as appear to the appropriate authority necessary or expedient for the purpose of enabling such societies or companies to adopt the schemes authorised by the regulations.

(6) Subsections (4), (5) and (7) to (11) of section 6 of the Decimal Currency Act 1969 shall, with the necessary modifications, apply in relation to regulations made under this paragraph.

Commentary—*Simon's Direct Tax Service* **E2.1038, 1039.**
Regulations—Friendly Societies (Life Assurance Premium Relief) Regulations, SI 1977/1143 SI 1980/1947 SI 1984/323; Industrial Assurance (Life Assurance Premium Relief) Regulations, SI 1977/1144 SI 1984/322; Industrial Assurance (Life Assurance Premium Relief) (Change of Rate) Regulations, SI 1980/1948. For continuity see Sch 30 para 21 of this Act.
Definition—"Company", s 832(1), (2); "friendly society", s 266(13).
Amendments—[1] "12·5 per cent" in sub-para (3)(a) substituted by FA 1988 s 29 with effect from 6 April 1989.
[2] Words in sub-para (4) repealed by FA 1989 Sch 17 Pt IX.
[3] Words in sub-para (1) substituted by F(No 2)A 1992 Sch 9 paras 1, 18, 22 with effect from 19 February 1993 by virtue of F(No 2)A 1992 Sch 9 (Appointed Day) Order, SI 1993/236.
[4] Words in sub-para (3)(a) substituted by F(No 2)A 1992 Sch 9 paras 1, 18, 22.

PART II
SUPPLEMENTARY PROVISIONS AS TO RELIEF UNDER SECTION 266

4—(1) Where it appears to the Board that the relief (if any) to which a person is entitled under section 266 has been exceeded or might be exceeded unless the premiums payable by him under any policy or contract were paid in full, they may, by notice to that person and to the person to whom the payments are made, exclude the application of subsection (5) of that section in relation to any payments due or made after such date as may be specified in the notice and before such date as may be specified in a further notice to those persons.

(2) Where the application of section 266(5) is so excluded in relation to any payments, the relief (if any) to which the person by whom the payments are made is entitled under section 266 shall be given to him under paragraph 6 below.

Commentary—*Simon's Direct Tax Service* **E2.1035.**
Definitions—"The Board", s 832(1); "notice", s 832(1).
Cross references—See TA 1988 Sch 14 para 7(2) (regulations for carrying into effect the Board's powers under this paragraph).

5 Where a person is entitled to relief under section 266 in respect of a payment to which section 595 applies, section 266(5) shall not apply but the like relief shall be given to him under paragraph 6 below.

Commentary—*Simon's Direct Tax Service* **E2.1035.**

6—(1) Where in any year of assessment the relief to which a person is entitled under section 266, otherwise than in accordance with subsections (6) and (7) of that section, has not been fully given in accordance with that section and the preceding provisions of this Schedule, he may claim relief for the difference, and relief for the difference shall then be given by a payment made by the Board or by discharge or repayment of tax or partly in one such manner and partly in another; and where relief so given to any person exceeds that to which he is entitled under section 266, he shall be liable to make good the excess and an inspector may make such assessments as may in his judgment be required for recovering the excess.

(2) The Management Act shall apply to any assessment under this paragraph as if it were an assessment to tax for the year of assessment in which the relief was given ...[1]

Commentary—*Simon's Direct Tax Service* **E2.1044.**
Definitions—"The Board", s 832(1); "inspector", s 832(1); "the Management Act", s 831(3); "year of assessment", s 832(1).
Cross references—See TA 1988 Sch 14 para 4(2) (relief under this paragraph where the application of TA 1988 s 266(5) is excluded by para 4).
TA 1988 Sch 14 para 5 (relief under this paragraph where relief under TA 1988 s 266(5) is excluded by para 5 in respect of premiums paid by an employer for a retirement benefits scheme).
Amendments—[1] Words omitted from sub-para (2) repealed by FA 1996 Sch 18 paras 11(2), 17(5), Sch 41 Pt V(8) with effect from the year 1996–97; and in relation to any income or capital gains tax which is charged by an assessment after 5 April 1998 and is for the year 1995–96 or any earlier year of assessment subject to saving in FA 1996 Sch 18 para 17(5)(b), (7).

7—(1) The Board may make regulations for carrying into effect section 266(4), (5), (8) and (9) and the preceding provisions of this Schedule ...[1] ("the relevant provisions").

(2) Regulations under this paragraph may, without prejudice to the generality of sub-paragraph (1) above, provide—

(*a*) for the furnishing of such information by persons by whom premiums are payable as may be necessary for determining whether they are entitled to make deductions under section 266(5) and for excluding the operation of that subsection in relation to payments made by persons who fail to comply with the regulations;

(*b*) for rounding to a multiple of one penny any payment which, after a deduction authorised under section 266(5), is not such a multiple;

(*c*) for the manner in which claims for the recovery of any sum under section 266(5)(*b*) may be made;

(*d*) for the furnishing of such information by persons by or to whom premiums are payable as appears to the Board necessary for deciding such claims and for exercising their powers under paragraph 4 or 6 above; and

(*e*) for requiring persons to whom premiums are paid to make available for inspection by an officer authorised by the Board such books and other documents in their possession or under their control as may reasonably be required for the purposes of determining whether any information given by those persons for the purposes of the relevant provisions is correct and complete.

(3) The following provisions of the Management Act, that is to say—

[(*a*) section 29(1)(*c*) (excessive relief) as it has effect apart from section 29(2) to (10) of that Act.]²;

(*b*) section 30 (recovery of tax repaid in consequence of fraud or negligence etc) [apart from subsection (1B)]²;

(*c*) [section 86]³ (interest); and

(*d*) section 95 (incorrect return or accounts);

[shall apply in relation to an amount which is paid to any person by the Board as an amount recoverable by virtue of section 266(5)(*b*) but to which that person is not entitled as if it were income tax which ought not to have been repaid and, where that amount was claimed by that person, as if it had been repaid as respects a chargeable period as a relief which was not due.]⁴

[(4) In the application of section 86 of the Management Act by virtue of sub-paragraph (3) above in relation to sums due and payable by virtue of an assessment made for the whole or part of a year of assessment ("the relevant year of assessment") under section 29(1)(*c*) or 30 of that Act, as applied by that sub-paragraph, the relevant date—

(*a*) is 1st January in the relevant year of assessment in a case where the person falling within section 266(5)(*b*) has made a relevant interim claim; and

(*b*) in any other case, is the later of the following dates, that is to say—

    (i) 1st January in the relevant year of assessment; or

    (ii) the date of the making of the payment by the Board which gives rise to the assessment.]³

[(5) In this paragraph—

"financial year", in relation to any person, means a financial year of that person for the purposes of the relevant regulations;

"interim claim" means an interim claim within the meaning of the relevant regulations;

"relevant interim claim" means, in relation to an assessment made for a period coterminous with, or falling wholly within, a person's financial year, an interim claim made for a period falling wholly or partly within that financial year;

"the relevant regulations" means regulations made under sub-paragraph (1) above.]3

Commentary—*Simon's Direct Tax Service* E2.1044.
Regulations—IT (Life Assurance Premium Relief) Regulations, SI 1978/1159. For continuity see Sch 30 para 21 of this Act.
Simon's Tax Cases—Sub-para 7(3), *United Friendly Insurance plc v IRC* [1998] STC 621.
Definitions—"The Board", s 832(1); "financial year", s 834(1); "the Management Act", s 831(3); "year of assessment", s 832(1).
Amendments—¹ The words "and paragraphs 9 and 10 of Schedule 15" in sub-para (1) repealed by FA 1995 Sch 29 Pt VIII(7), with effect from a date to be appointed in accordance with FA 1995 s 55(1)–(5) as amended by FA 1996 s 162.
² Sub-para (3)(*a*) substituted and words in sub-para (3)(*b*) inserted by FA 1996 Sch 18 paras 11(3)(*a*), (*b*), 17(1), (2) with effect: as respects income and capital gains tax from the year 1996–97 and, for purposes of corporation tax as respects accounting periods ending after 30 June 1999 (by virtue of Finance Act 1994, Section 199, (Appointed Day) Order, SI 1998/3173 art 2); and so far as relating to partnerships whose trades, professions or businesses were set up and commenced before 6 April 1994, with effect as respects the year 1997–98 and subsequent years of assessment (see FA 1996 Sch 18 para 17(1), (2)).
³ Words in sub-para (3)(*c*) substituted (for words "section 88") and sub-paras (4), (5) inserted by FA 1996 Sch 18 paras 11(3)(*c*), (4), 17(3), (4) with effect: (i) from the year 1996–97 (ii) in relation to any income or capital gains tax which is charged by an assessment made after 5 April 1998 and is for the year 1995–96 or any earlier year of assessment (but in the case of sub-para (4) with the substitution of words "section 29(3)(*c*)" for "section 29(1)(*c*)" in this instance) (see FA 1996 Sch 18 para 17(3)); and (iii) so far as relating to partnerships whose trades, professions or businesses were set up and commenced before 6 April 1994 as respects the year 1997–98 and subsequent years of assessment and in relation to income tax which is charged by an assessment made after 5 April 1998 and is for the year 1995–96 or any earlier year of assessment (FA 1996 Sch 18 para 17(4)).
⁴ Words in sub-para (3) substituted by FA 1996 Sch 18 paras 11(3)(*d*), 17(8) except in relation to any payment where the payment itself, or claim on which it is made, was made before 29 April 1996.

8—(1) A policy of life insurance issued in respect of an insurance made on or before 19th March 1968 shall be treated for the purposes of section 266(3)(*b*) as issued in respect of one made after that date if varied after that date so as to increase the benefits secured or to extend the term of the insurance.

(2) A variation effected before the end of the year 1968 shall be disregarded for the purposes of sub-paragraph (1) above if its only effect was to bring into conformity with paragraph 2 of Schedule 9 to the Finance Act 1968 (qualifying conditions for endowment policies, and now re-enacted as paragraph 2 of Schedule 15 to this Act) a policy previously conforming therewith except as respects the amount guaranteed on death, and no increase was made in the premiums payable under the policy.

(3) A policy which was issued in the course of industrial assurance business in respect of an insurance made after 13th March 1984 shall be treated for the purposes of section 266(3)(*c*) and this paragraph as issued in respect of an insurance made on or before that date if—

(*a*) the proposal form for the policy was completed on or before that date; and

(*b*) on or before 31st March 1984 the policy was prepared for issue by the company or society concerned; and

(*c*) on or before 31st March 1984 and in accordance with the normal business practice of the company or society a permanent record of the preparation of the policy was made in any book or by any other means kept or instituted by the company or society for the purpose.

(4) [Subject to sub-paragraph (8) below,][1] for the purposes of section 266(3)(*c*) a policy of life insurance which was issued in respect of an insurance made on or before 13th March 1984 shall be treated as issued in respect of an insurance made after that date if the policy is varied after that date so as to increase the benefits secured or to extend the term of the insurance.

(5) If a policy of life insurance which was issued as mentioned in sub-paragraph (4) above confers on the person to whom it was issued an option to have another policy substituted for it or to have any of its terms changed, then, for the purposes of that sub-paragraph and section 266(3)(*c*), any change in the terms of the policy which is made in pursuance of the option shall be deemed to be a variation of the policy.

(6) In any case where—

(*a*) one policy is replaced by another in such circumstances that the provisions of paragraph 20 of Schedule 15 apply; and

(*b*) the earlier policy was issued in respect of an insurance made on or before 13th March 1984; and

(*c*) the later policy confers on the life or lives assured thereby benefits which are substantially equivalent to those which would have been enjoyed by the life or lives assured under the earlier policy, if that policy had continued in force;

then, for the purposes of section 266(3)(*c*), the insurance in respect of which the later policy is issued shall be deemed to have been made before 13th March 1984; and in this sub-paragraph "the earlier policy" and "the later policy" have the same meaning as in paragraph 20 of Schedule 15.

(7) In any case where—

(*a*) there is a substitution of policies falling within paragraph 25(1) or (3) of Schedule 15; and

(*b*) the old policy was issued in respect of an insurance made on or before 13th March 1984;

then, for the purposes of section 266(3)(*c*), the insurance in respect of which the new policy is issued shall be deemed to have been made before 13th March 1984; and in this sub-paragraph "the old policy" and "the new policy" have the same meaning as in paragraph 17 of Schedule 15.

[(8) Sub-paragraph (4) above does not apply in the case of a variation so as to increase the benefits secured, if the variation is made—

(*a*) on or after such day as the Board may by order appoint, and

(*b*) in consideration of a change in the method of payment of premiums from collection by a person collecting premiums from house to house to payment by a different method.][1]

Commentary—*Simon's Direct Tax Service* E2.1047.
Definitions—"The Board", s 832(1); "company", s 832(1), (2); "industrial assurance business", s 832(1).
Cross reference—Finance Act 1996, Section 167, (Appointed Day) Order, SI 2001/3643. The appointed day for the purpose of sub-para (8)(*a*) above is 1 December 2001.
Amendments—[1] Words in sub-para (4) and whole of sub-para (8) inserted by FA 1996 s 167(5), (6).

SCHEDULE 15

QUALIFYING POLICIES

Section 267

Concession A96—(IR 4-2-97)—For the purposes of this Schedule, no account will be taken of an alteration to the terms of a policy if a number of specified conditions are satisfied.
Simon's Tax Cases—*Legal & General Assurance Society Ltd v IRC* [1996] STC (SCD) 419*.
Cross references—See TA 1988 s 266(2) (application of this Schedule for the purposes of relief for life assurance premiums).

PART I

QUALIFYING CONDITIONS

Concession B42—Free gifts not exceeding specified amount in value made by insurance companies in connection with insurance policies are not regarded as contravening qualifying conditions.

Cross references—See TA 1988 Sch 15 para 27 (treatment for the purposes of this Part of non–resident policies issued on or before 17 November 1983).

General rules applicable to whole life and term assurances

1—(1) Subject to the following provisions of this Part of this Schedule, if a policy secures a capital sum which is payable only on death, or one payable either on death or on earlier disability, it is a qualifying policy if—

(*a*) it satisfies the conditions appropriate to it under sub-paragraphs (2) to (5) below, and

(*b*) except to the extent permitted by sub-paragraph (7) below, it does not secure any other benefits.

(2) If the capital sum referred to in sub-paragraph (1) above is payable whenever the event in question happens, or if it happens at any time during the life of a specified person—

(*a*) the premiums under the policy must be payable at yearly or shorter intervals, and either—

(i) until the happening of the event or, as the case may require, until the happening of the event or the earlier death of the specified person, or

(ii) until the time referred to in sub-paragraph (i) above or the earlier expiry of a specified period ending not earlier than ten years after the making of the insurance; and

(*b*) the total premiums payable in any period of 12 months must not exceed—

(i) twice the amount of the total premiums payable in any other such period, or

(ii) one-eighth of the total premiums which would be payable if the policy were to continue in force for a period of ten years from the making of the insurance, or, in a case falling within sub-paragraph (ii) of paragraph (*a*) above, until the end of the period referred to in that sub-paragraph.

(3) If the capital sum referred to in sub-paragraph (1) above is payable only if the event in question happens before the expiry of a specified term ending more than ten years after the making of the insurance, or only if it happens both before the expiry of such a term and during the life of a specified person—

(*a*) the premiums under the policy must be payable at yearly or shorter intervals, and either—

(i) until the happening of the event or the earlier expiry of that term or, as the case may require, until the happening of the event or, if earlier, the expiry of the term or the death of the specified person, or

(ii) as in sub-paragraph (i) above, but with the substitution for references to the term of references to a specified shorter period being one ending not earlier than ten years after the making of the insurance or, if sooner, the expiry of three-quarters of that term; and

(*b*) the total premiums payable in any period of 12 months must not exceed—

(i) twice the amount of the total premiums payable in any other such period, or

(ii) one-eighth of the total premiums which would be payable if the policy were to continue in force for the term referred to in sub-paragraph (i) of paragraph (*a*) above, or, as the case may require, for the shorter period referred to in sub-paragraph (ii) of that paragraph.

(4) If the capital sum referred to in sub-paragraph (1) above is payable only if the event in question happens before the expiry of a specified term ending not more than ten years after the making of the insurance, or only if it happens both before the expiry of such a term and during the life of a specified person, the policy must provide that any payment made by reason of its surrender during the period is not to exceed the total premiums previously paid under the policy.

(5) Except where—

(*a*) the capital sum referred to in sub-paragraph (1) above is payable only in the circumstances mentioned in sub-paragraph (3) or (4) above; and

(*b*) the policy does not provide for any payment on the surrender in whole or in part of the rights conferred by it; and

(*c*) the specified term mentioned in sub-paragraph (3) or, as the case may be, (4) above ends at or before the time when the person whose life is insured attains the age of 75 years;

the capital sum, so far as payable on death, must not be less than 75 per cent of the total premiums that would be payable if the death occurred at the age of 75 years, the age being, if the sum is payable on the death of the first to die of two persons, that of the older of them, if on the death of the survivor of them, that of the younger of them, and in any other case, that of the person on whose death it is payable; and if the policy does not secure a capital sum in the event of death occurring before the age of 16 or some lower age, it must not provide for the payment in that event of an amount exceeding the total premiums previously paid under it.

(6) In determining for the purposes of sub-paragraph (5) above whether a capital sum is less than 75 per cent of the total premiums, any amount included in the premiums by reason of their being payable otherwise than annually shall be disregarded, [and if the policy provides for payment otherwise than annually without providing for the amount of the premiums if they are paid annually,][1] 10 per cent of the premiums payable under the policy shall be treated as so included.

(7) Notwithstanding sub-paragraph (1)(*b*) above, if a policy secures a capital sum payable only on death, it may also secure benefits (including benefits of a capital nature) to be provided in the event

of a person's disability; and no policy is to be regarded for the purposes of that provision as securing other benefits by reason only of the fact that—

(*a*) it confers a right to participate in profits, or

(*b*) it provides for a payment on the surrender in whole or in part of the rights conferred by the policy, or

(*c*) it gives an option to receive payments by way of annuity, or

(*d*) it makes provision for the waiver of premiums by reason of a person's disability, or for the effecting of a further insurance or insurances without the production of evidence of insurability.

(8) In applying sub-paragraph (2) or (3) above to any policy—

(*a*) no account shall be taken of any provision for the waiver of premiums by reason of a person's disability, and

(*b*) if the term of the policy runs from a date earlier, but not more than three months earlier, than the making of the insurance, the insurance shall be treated as having been made on that date, and any premium paid in respect of the period before the making of the insurance, or in respect of that period and a subsequent period, as having been payable on that date.

(9) References in this paragraph to a capital sum payable on any event include references to any capital sum, or series of capital sums, payable by reason of that event but where what is so payable is either an amount consisting of one sum or an amount made up of two or more sums, the 75 per cent mentioned in sub-paragraph (5) above shall be compared with the smaller or smallest amount so payable; and a policy secures a capital sum payable either on death or on disability notwithstanding that the amount payable may vary with the event.

(10) In relation to any policy issued in respect of an insurance made before 1st April 1976 this paragraph shall have effect—

(*a*) with the omission of sub-paragraphs (5) and (6) and in sub-paragraph (9) the words "but where what is so payable is either an amount consisting of one sum or an amount made up of two or more sums, the 75 per cent mentioned in sub-paragraph (5) above shall be compared with the smaller or smallest amount so payable"; and

(*b*) with the substitution, for sub-paragraph (7)(*b*), of—

"(*b*) it carries a guaranteed surrender value;".

Commentary—*Simon's Direct Tax Service* E2.1036.
Concession A41—Concessions for minor infringement of qualifying conditions; where, under sub-para (8) above the commencement date of a policy is back-dated by not more than three months, the earlier date is treated as the date on which the assurance is made.
Simon's Tax Cases—Para 1(1)(*b*), (7), *R (on the application of Monarch Assurance plc) v IRC*, CA [2001] STC 1639.
Definitions—"Qualifying policy", s 832(1).
Cross references—See TA 1988 Sch 15 para 2(3) (application of sub-paras (8), (9) above to endowment assurances).
TA 1988 Sch 15 para 3(1) (this paragraph not to apply to friendly society policy issued after 18 March 1985).
TA 1988 Sch 15 para 6(1) (certain friendly society policies to be qualifying policies notwithstanding non-compliance with this paragraph).
TA 1988 Sch 15 para 7(1) (certain industrial assurance policies not qualifying under this paragraph to qualify under para 7).
TA 1988 Sch 15 para 8 (industrial assurance policies issued after 1 April 1976).
TA 1988 Sch 15 para 15 (single premium policy; premium payment discharged from money payable on maturity of a previous policy).
TA 1988 Sch 15 para 17(2)(*c*) (conditions for qualification of a substituted policy not qualifying under this paragraph).
TA 1988 Sch 15 para 18(2) (adaptation of this paragraph in its application to policies which are varied).
Amendments—[1] Words substituted by FA 1996 s 167(7)(*a*), (12) with effect in relation to policies issued after 30 November 2001 (by virtue of SI 2001/3643).

General rules applicable to endowment assurances

2—(1) Subject to the following provisions of this Part of this Schedule, a policy which secures a capital sum payable either on survival for a specified term or on earlier death, or earlier death or disability, including a policy securing the sum on death only if occurring after the attainment of a specified age not exceeding 16, is a qualifying policy if it satisfies the following conditions—

(*a*) the term must be one ending not earlier than ten years after the making of the insurance;

(*b*) premiums must be payable under the policy at yearly or shorter intervals, and—

(i) until the happening of the event in question; or

(ii) until the happening of that event, or the earlier expiry of a specified period shorter than the term but also ending not earlier than ten years after the making of the insurance; or

(iii) if the policy is to lapse on the death of a specified person, until one of those times or the policy's earlier lapse;

(*c*) the total premiums payable under the policy in any period of 12 months must not exceed—

(i) twice the amount of the total premiums payable in any other such period, or

(ii) one-eighth of the total premiums which would be payable if the policy were to run for the specified term;

(*d*) the policy—

(i) must guarantee that the capital sum payable on death, or on death occurring after the attainment of a specified age not exceeding 16, will, whenever that event may happen, be equal to 75 per cent at least of the total premiums which would be payable if the policy were to run for that term, disregarding any amounts included in those premiums by reason of their being payable otherwise than annually, except that if, at the beginning of that term, the age of the person concerned exceeds 55 years, the capital sum so guaranteed may, for each year of the excess, be less by 2 per cent of that total than 75 per cent thereof, the person concerned being, if the capital sum is payable on the death of the first to die of two persons, the older of them, if on the death of the survivor of them, the younger of them and in any other case the person on whose death it is payable; and

(ii) if it is a policy which does not secure a capital sum in the event of death before the attainment of a specified age not exceeding 16, must not provide for the payment in that event of an amount exceeding the total premiums previously paid thereunder; and

(e) the policy must not secure the provision (except by surrender in whole or in part of the rights conferred by the policy) at any time before the happening of the event in question of any benefit of a capital nature other than a payment falling within paragraph (d)(ii) above, or benefits attributable to a right to participate in profits or arising by reason of a person's disability.

(2) For the purposes of sub-paragraph (1)(d)(i) above, 10 per cent of the premiums payable under any policy [that provides for the payment of premiums otherwise than annually without providing for the amount of the premiums if they are paid annually][1] shall be treated as attributable to the fact that they are not paid annually.

(3) Sub-paragraphs (8) and (9) of paragraph 1 above shall, with any necessary modifications, have effect for the purposes of this paragraph as they have effect for the purposes of that paragraph.

(4) In relation to any policy issued in respect of an insurance made before 1st April 1976 this paragraph shall have effect with the omission in sub-paragraph (1)(d)(i) of the words from "except that if" to the end, and in sub-paragraph (1)(e) of the words "in whole or in part of the rights conferred by the policy".

Commentary—*Simon's Direct Tax Service* E2.1037.
Definitions—"Qualifying policy", s 832(1).
Cross references—See TA 1988 Sch 14 para 8(2) (variations made before the end of the year 1968 to a life insurance policy so that it conforms with this paragraph).
TA 1988 Sch 15 para 3(1) (this paragraph not to apply to friendly society policy issued after 18 March 1985).
TA 1988 Sch 15 para 6(1) (certain friendly society policies to be qualifying policies notwithstanding non-compliance with this paragraph).
TA 1988 Sch 15 para 7(1) (certain industrial assurance policies not qualifying under this paragraph to qualify under para 7).
TA 1988 Sch 15 para 8 (industrial assurance policies issued after 1 April 1976).
TA 1988 Sch 15 para 15 (single premium policy; premium payment discharged from money payable on maturity of a previous policy).
TA 1988 Sch 15 para 17(2)(c) (conditions for qualification of a substituted policy not qualifying under this paragraph).
TA 1988 Sch 15 para 18(2) (adaptation of this paragraph in its application to policies which are varied).
Amendments—[1] Words substituted by FA 1996 s 167(7)(b), (12) with effect in relation to policies issued after 30 November 2001 (by virtue of SI 2001/3643).

Special types of policy

(i) Friendly Society policies

3—(1) Paragraphs 1 and 2 above do not apply to a policy issued by a [friendly society][3] in the course of tax exempt life or endowment business in respect of an insurance made or varied on or after 19th March 1985, but such a policy shall not be a qualifying policy unless—

(a) in the case of a policy for the assurance of a gross sum or annuity, the conditions in sub-paragraph (2) are fulfilled with respect to it; and

(b) in the case of a policy for the assurance of a gross sum, the conditions in sub-paragraphs (5) to (11) below are fulfilled with respect to it; ...[2]

(c) ...[2]

(2) The conditions referred to in sub-paragraph (1) above are as follows—

(a) subject to sub-paragraph (3) below, the period (the "term" of the policy) between—

(i) the making of the insurance or, where the contract provides for the term to begin on a date not more than three months earlier than the making of the insurance, that date, and

(ii) the time when the gross sum assured is payable (or, as the case may be, when the first instalment of the annuity is payable),

shall be not less than ten years, and must not, on any contingency other than the death, or retirement on grounds of ill health, of the person liable to pay the premiums or whose life is insured, become less than ten years;

(b) subject to sub-paragraph (4) below, the premiums payable under the policy shall be premiums of equal or rateable amounts payable at yearly or shorter intervals over the whole term of the policy of assurance, or over the whole term of the policy of assurance apart from any period after the person liable to pay the premiums or whose life is insured attains a specified age, being an age which he will attain at a time not less than ten years after the beginning of the term of the policy of assurance;

(c) ...[5]

(3) Notwithstanding sub-paragraph (2)(a) above, the policy—

(*a*) may provide for a payment to a person of an age not exceeding 18 years at any time not less than five years from the beginning of the term of the policy if the premium or premiums payable in any period of 12 months in the term of the policy do not exceed £13;

(*b*) may provide for a payment at any time not less than five years from the beginning of the term of the policy, if it is one of a series of payments falling due at intervals of not less than five years, and the amount of any payment, other than the final payment, does not exceed four-fifths of the premiums paid in the interval before its payment.

For the purposes of paragraph (*a*) above, if the term begins on a date earlier than the making of the insurance, any premium paid in respect of a period before the making of the insurance, or in respect of that period and a subsequent period, shall be treated as having been payable on that date.

(4) Notwithstanding sub-paragraph (2)(*b*) above, the policy—

(*a*) may allow a payment at any time after the expiration of one-half of the term of the policy of assurance, or of ten years from the beginning of the term, whichever is the earlier, being a payment in commutation of the liability to pay premiums falling due after that time;

(*b*) may allow the person liable to pay the premiums to commute any liability for premiums where he ceases to reside in the United Kingdom or gives satisfactory proof of intention to emigrate;

(*c*) may allow any liability for premiums to be discharged in consideration of surrendering a sum which has become payable on the maturity of any other policy of assurance issued by the same friendly society [(or any predecessor of it)][4] to the person liable to pay the premiums, or to his parent, where that other policy of assurance is issued as part of the friendly society's tax exempt life or endowment business; and

(*d*) may make provision for the waiver of premiums by reason of a person's disability.

[(4A) For the purposes of sub-paragraphs (2) and (4) above—

(*a*) a friendly society formed on the amalgamation of two or more friendly societies is the successor of each of those societies (and each of those societies was a predecessor of the society so formed), and

(*b*) an incorporated friendly society that was a registered friendly society before its incorporation is the successor of the registered friendly society (and the registered friendly society was the predecessor of the incorporated friendly society).][4]

(5) Where the policy secures a capital sum which is payable only on death or only on death occurring after the attainment of a specified age not exceeding 16, that capital sum must be not less than 75 per cent of the total premiums which would be payable if the death of the relevant beneficiary occurred at the age of 75.

(6) Where the policy secures a capital sum which is payable only on survival for a specified term, that capital sum must be not less than 75 per cent of the total premiums which would be payable if the policy were to run for that term.

(7) Where the policy secures a capital sum which is payable on survival for a specified term or on earlier death, or on earlier death or disability (including a policy securing the sum on death only if occurring after the attainment of a specified age not exceeding 16), the capital sum payable on death, whenever that event occurs, must be not less than 75 per cent of the total premiums which would be payable if the policy were to run for that term, except that if, at the beginning of that term, the age of the relevant beneficiary exceeds 55, that capital sum may, for each year of the excess, be less by 2 per cent of that total than 75 per cent thereof.

(8) For the purposes of sub-paragraphs (5) to (7) above—

(*a*) "the relevant beneficiary" means—

(i) if the capital sum concerned is payable on the death of the first to die of two persons, the older of them;

(ii) if that capital sum is payable on the death of the survivor of two persons, the younger of them; and

(iii) in any other case, the person on whose death that capital sum is payable; and

(*b*) in determining the total premiums payable in any circumstances—

(i) where those premiums are payable otherwise than annually, and the policy is issued by a new society, there shall be disregarded an amount equal to 10 per cent of those premiums;

(ii) where the policy is issued by a society other than a new society, there shall be disregarded an amount equal to £10 for each year for which account is taken of those premiums [or, where those premiums are payable otherwise than annually, an amount equal to 10 per cent of those premiums if that is greater][1]; and

(iii) so much of any premium as is charged on the ground that an exceptional risk of death is involved shall be disregarded; and

(*c*) in determining the capital sum payable on any event, there shall be disregarded any provision of the policy under which, on the ground referred to in paragraph (*b*)(iii) above, any sum may become chargeable as a debt against that capital sum.

(9) If the policy does not secure a capital sum in the event of death occurring before the age of 16 or some lower age, it must not provide for the payment in that event of an amount exceeding the total premiums previously paid under it.

(10) References in this paragraph to a capital sum payable on any event include references to a capital sum or series of capital sums payable by reason of that event, but where what is so payable is either an amount consisting of one sum or an amount made up to two or more sums, any reference in sub-paragraphs (5) to (7) above to 75 per cent of the total premiums payable in any circumstances shall be compared with the smaller or smallest amount so payable; and for the purposes of those sub-paragraphs a policy secures a capital sum payable either on death or on disability notwithstanding that the amount may vary with the event.

(11) For the purposes of sub-paragraphs (5) to (7) and (10) above, in the case of a policy which provides for any such payments as are referred to in sub-paragraph (3) above ("interim payments"), the amount of the capital sum which is payable on any event shall be taken to be increased—

(a) in the case of a policy which secures such a capital sum as is referred to in sub-paragraph (5) above, by the total of the interim payments which would be payable if the death of the relevant beneficiary (within the meaning of that sub-paragraph) occurred at the age of 75; and

(b) in the case of a policy which secures such a capital sum as is referred to in sub-paragraph (6) or (7) above, by the total of the interim payments which would be payable if the policy were to run for the specified term referred to in that sub-paragraph.

Commentary—*Simon's Direct Tax Service* **D4.613; E2.1038.**
Definitions—"Friendly society", s 466(2); "incorporated friendly society", s 466(2); "qualifying policy", s 832(1); "registered friendly society", s 466(2); "United Kingdom", s 830(1).
Cross references—See TA 1988 s 462(3) (extension of sub-paras (2)–(11) above to registered friendly societies).
TA 1988 s 465(3) (extension of restrictions in sub-para (1)(b), (c) above to old friendly societies).
TA 1988 Sch 15 para 4(1) (para 4 to have effect notwithstanding anything in this paragraph).
TA 1988 Sch 15 para 6(2) (friendly society member in breach in s 464 after 18 March 1985).
TA 1988 Sch 15 para 18(2) (adaptation of this paragraph in its application to policies which are varied).
Amendments—[1] Words in sub-para (8)(b)(ii) inserted by FA 1990 s 49(5).
[2] Sub-para (1)(c) and the preceding word "and" repealed by FA 1991 Sch 9 para 4 and Sch 19 Pt V in relation to policies issued in pursuance of contracts made after 24 July 1991.
[3] Words in sub-para (1) substituted by F(No 2)A 1992 Sch 9 paras 1, 19, 22 with effect from 19 February 1993 by virtue of F(No 2)A 1992 Sch 9 (Appointed Day) Order, SI 1993/236.
[4] Words in sub-para (4)(c) and sub-para (4A) inserted by F(No 2)A 1992 Sch 9 paras 1, 19, 22.
[5] Sub-para (2)(c) repealed by FA 1995 Sch 10 para 3, Sch 29, Pt VIII(6).

4—(1) The provisions of this paragraph have effect notwithstanding anything in paragraph 3 above.

(2) In determining whether a policy—

(a) which affords provision for sickness or other infirmity (whether bodily or mental), and

(b) which also affords assurance for a gross sum independent of sickness or other infirmity, and

(c) under which not less than 60 per cent of the amount of the premiums is attributable to the provision referred to in paragraph (a) above,

is a qualifying policy, the conditions referred to in paragraph 3(1)(b) above shall be deemed to be fulfilled with respect to it.

(3) A policy shall cease to be a qualifying policy—

(a) if it falls within sub-paragraph (1) of paragraph 3 above and there is such a variation of its terms that any of the conditions referred to in that sub-paragraph ceases to be fulfilled; or

(b) if—

[(i) it was effected in the course of [the business of effecting or carrying out contracts of insurance which fall within paragraph 1 of Part I or paragraph VI of Part II of Schedule 1 to the Financial Services and Markets Act 2000 (Regulated Activities) Order 2001][2]][1]

(ii) it was issued by a new society, and

(iii) the rights conferred by it are surrendered in whole or in part.

Commentary—*Simon's Direct Tax Service* **D4.613; E2.1039.**
Definition—"Qualifying policy", s 832(1).
Cross references—See TA 1988 s 465(3) (extension of restrictions in sub-para.(3)(b) above to old friendly societies).
TA 1988 Sch 15 para 6(2) (friendly society member in breach of limits in s 464 after 18 March 1985).
TA 1988 Sch 15 para 18(2) (adaptation of this paragraph in its application to policies which are varied).
FA 1991 Sch 9 para 5 (sub-para (3)(a) above not to apply to a policy effected by a contract made after 31 August 1987 and before 25 July 1991 and the premium in respect of which is increased without contravening the limits in s 464 above on or after 25 July 1991 and before 1 August 1992).
FA 1995 Sch 10 para 4(2) (disapplication of sub-para (3)(a) above in relation to policies effected by contract made after 31 August 1987 but before 1 May 1995 the premium in respect of which is increased without contravening the limits in s 464 on or after 1 May 1995 and before 1 April 1996).
Amendments—[1] Sub-para (3)(b)(i) substituted by F(No 2)A 1992 Sch 9 paras 1, 19(6), 22 with effect from 19 February 1993 by virtue of F(No 2)A 1992 Sch 9 (Appointed Day) Order, SI 1993/236.
[2] Words in sub-para (3)(b)(i) substituted by the Financial Services and Markets Act 2000 (Consequential Amendments) (Taxes) Order, SI 2001/3629 arts 13, 47(1), (2) with effect from 1 December 2001, immediately after the coming into force of the Financial Services and Markets Act 2000 ss 411, 432(1), Sch 20.

5 Section 466 shall apply for the interpretation of paragraphs 3 and 4 above as it applies for the interpretation of sections 460 to 465.

Commentary—*Simon's Direct Tax Service* **D4.613; E2.1039.**
Cross references—See TA 1988 Sch 15 para 6(2) (friendly society member in breach of limits in s 464 after 18 March 1985).
TA 1988 Sch 15 para 18(2) (adaptation of this paragraph in its application to policies which are varied).

6—(1) A policy which was issued by [any registered friendly society (as defined in section 466)][1], or branch of [such a society][2], in the course of tax exempt life or endowment business (as defined in section 466) in respect of insurances made before 19th March 1985 and which has not been varied on or after that date is a qualifying policy notwithstanding that it does not comply with the conditions specified in paragraph 1 or 2 above.

(2) Notwithstanding paragraphs 3 to 5 or sub-paragraph (1) above, if, on or after 19th March 1985, a person becomes in breach of the limits in section 464, the policy effected by that contract which causes those limits to be exceeded shall not be a qualifying policy; and in any case where—

(*a*) the limits in that section are exceeded as a result of the aggregation of the sums assured or premiums payable under two or more contracts, and

(*b*) at a time immediately before one of those contracts was entered into (but not immediately after it was entered into) the sums assured by or, as the case may be, the premiums payable under the contract or contracts which were then in existence did not exceed the limits in that section,

only those policies effected by contracts made after that time shall be treated as causing the limits to be exceeded.

Definition—"Qualifying policy", s 832(1).
Cross references—See TA 1988 s 462(1) (extension of sub-para (2) above to registered friendly societies).
TA 1988 Sch 15 para 18(2) (adaptation of this paragraph in its application to policies which are varied).
Amendments—[1] Words in sub-para (1) substituted by F(No 2)A 1992 Sch 9 paras 1, 19(7), 22 with effect from 19 February 1993 by virtue of F(No 2)A 1992 Sch 9 (Appointed Day) Order, SI 1993/236.
[2] Words in sub-para (1) substituted by F(No 2)A 1992 Sch 9 paras 1, 19(7), 22.

(ii) Industrial assurance policies

7—(1) A policy issued in the course of an industrial assurance business, and not constituting a qualifying policy by virtue of paragraph 1 or 2 above, is nevertheless a qualifying policy if—

(*a*) the sums guaranteed by the policy, together with those guaranteed at the time the assurance is made by all other policies issued in the course of such a business to the same person and not constituting qualifying policies apart from this paragraph, do not exceed £1,000;

(*b*) it satisfies the conditions with respect to premiums specified in paragraph 1(2) above;

(*c*) except by reason of death or surrender, no capital sum other than one falling within paragraph (*d*) below can become payable under the policy earlier than ten years after the making of the assurance; and

(*d*) where the policy provides for the making of a series of payments during its term—

(i) the first such payment is due not earlier than five years after the making of the assurance, and the others, except the final payment, at intervals of not less than five years, and

(ii) the amount of any payment, other than the final payment, does not exceed four-fifths of the premiums paid in the interval before its payment; or

(*e*) the policy was issued before 6th April 1976, or was issued before 6th April 1979 and is in substantially the same form as policies so issued before 6th April 1976.

(2) For the purposes of this paragraph, the sums guaranteed by a policy do not include any bonuses, or in the case of a policy providing for a series of payments during its term, any of those payments except the first, or any sum payable on death during the term by reference to one or more of those payments except so far as that sum is referable to the first such payment.

Commentary—*Simon's Direct Tax Service* E2.1039.
Definitions—"Industrial assurance business", s 832(1); "qualifying policy", s 832(1).
Cross references—See TA 1988 Sch 14 para 3(4) (increases in capital sums treated as made by virtue of Sch 14 para 3(3) to be disregarded for the purposes of this paragraph).
TA 1988 Sch 15, para 8 (industrial assurance policies issued after 1 April 1976).
TA 1988 Sch 15 para 8A (modification of the construction of references to the issue of policies in the course of industrial assurance business after an appointed day).
TA 1988 Sch 15 para 18(2) (adaptation of this paragraph in its application to policies which are varied).

8 Where a policy issued in respect of an insurance made after 1st April 1976 in the course of an industrial assurance business is not a qualifying policy by virtue of paragraph 1 or 2 above but is a policy with respect to which the conditions in paragraph 7(1)(*b*) and (*c*) above are satisfied, it shall be a qualifying policy whether or not the condition in paragraph 7(1)(*a*) above is satisfied with respect to it; but where that condition is not satisfied, relief under section 266 in respect of premiums paid under the policy shall be given only on such amount (if any) as would have been the amount of those premiums had that condition been satisfied.

Commentary—*Simon's Direct Tax Service* E2.1039.
Definitions—"Industrial assurance business", s 832(1); "qualifying policy", s 832(1).
Cross references—See TA 1988 Sch 15 para 8A (modification of the construction of references to the issue of policies in the course of industrial assurance business from an appointed day).
TA 1988 Sch 15 para 18(2) (adaptation of this paragraph in its application to policies which are varied).

[**8A**—(1) Paragraphs 7 and 8 above shall have effect in relation to any policy issued on or after the appointed day as if the references to the issue of a policy in the course of an industrial assurance business were references to the issue of a policy by any company in a case in which—

(*a*) the company, before that day and in the course of such a business, issued any policy which was a qualifying policy by virtue of either of those paragraphs; and

(*b*) the policies which on 28th November 1995 were being offered by the company as available to be issued included policies of the same description as the policy issued on or after the appointed day.

(2) In this paragraph "the appointed day" means such day as the Board may by order appoint.]¹

Commentary—*Simon's Direct Tax Service* **E2.1039.**
Cross reference—Finance Act 1996, Section 167, (Appointed Day) Order, SI 2001/3643. The appointed day for the purposes of this paragraph is 1 December 2001.
Definitions—"Company", s 832(1), (2); "industrial assurance business", s 832(1); "qualifying policy", s 832(1).
Amendments—¹ This paragraph inserted by FA 1996 s 167(8).

(iii) Family income policies and mortgage protection policies

9—(1) The following provisions apply to any policy which is not a qualifying policy apart from those provisions, and the benefits secured by which consist of or include the payment on or after a person's death of—

(*a*) one capital sum which does not vary according to the date of death, plus a series of capital sums payable if the death occurs during a specified period, or

(*b*) a capital sum, the amount of which is less if the death occurs in a later part of a specified period than if it occurs in an earlier part of that period.

(2) A policy falling within sub-paragraph (1)(*a*) above is a qualifying policy if—

(*a*) it would be one if it did not secure the series of capital sums there referred to, and the premiums payable under the policy were such as would be chargeable if that were in fact the case, and

(*b*) it would also be one if it secured only that series of sums, and the premiums thereunder were the balance of those actually so payable.

(3) A policy falling within sub-paragraph (1)(*b*) above is a qualifying policy if—

(*a*) it would be one if the amount of the capital sum there referred to were equal throughout the period to its smallest amount, and the premiums payable under the policy were such as would be chargeable if that were in fact the case, and

(*b*) it would also be one if it secured only that capital sum so far as it from time to time exceeds its smallest amount, and the premiums payable thereunder were the balance of those actually so payable.

Commentary—*Simon's Direct Tax Service* **E2.1040.**
Definition—"Qualifying policy", s 832(1).
Cross references—See TA 1988 Sch 14 para 7 (regulations for carrying into effect this paragraph).
TA 1988 Sch 15 para 18(2) (adaptation of this paragraph in its application to policies which are varied).

Other special provisions

(i) Short-term assurances

10 A policy which secures a capital sum payable only on death or payable either on death or on earlier disability shall not be a qualifying policy if the capital sum is payable only if the event in question happens before the expiry of a specified term ending less than one year after the making of the insurance.

Commentary—*Simon's Direct Tax Service* **E2.1032.**
Definition—"Qualifying policy", s 832(1).
Cross references—See TA 1988 Sch 14 para 7 (regulations for carrying into effect this paragraph).

(ii) Personal accident insurance

11—(1) A policy which evidences a contract of insurance to which sub-paragraph (3) below applies shall not be a qualifying policy unless it also evidences [—

(*a*) a contract of insurance on human life; or

(*b*) a contract to pay annuities on human life.]¹

(2) A policy which evidences a contract of insurance to which sub-paragraph (4) below applies shall not be a qualifying policy unless it also evidences a contract falling within section 83(2)(*a*) of the Insurance Companies Act 1974.

(3) This sub-paragraph applies to contracts of insurance issued in respect of insurances made on or after 25th March 1982 against risks of persons dying as a result of an accident or an accident of a specified class, not being contracts which—

(*a*) are expressed to be in effect for a period of not less than five years or without limit of time; and

(*b*) either are not expressed to be terminable by the insurer before the expiration of five years from their taking effect or are expressed to be so terminable before the expiration of that period only in special circumstances therein mentioned.

(4) This sub-paragraph applies to contracts of insurance issued in respect of insurances made before 25th March 1982 against risks of persons dying as a result of an accident or an accident of a specified class, not being contracts falling within section 83(2)(b) of the Insurance Companies Act 1974.

Commentary—*Simon's Direct Tax Service* **E2.1032.**
Definition—"Qualifying policy", s 832(1).
Amendments—[1] Words in sub-para (1) substituted by the Financial Services and Markets Act 2000 (Consequential Amendments) (Taxes) Order, SI 2001/3629 arts 13, 47(1), (3) with effect from 1 December 2001, immediately after the coming into force of the Financial Services and Markets Act 2000 ss 411, 432(1), Sch 20.

(iii) Exceptional mortality risk

12 For the purpose of determining whether any policy is a qualifying policy, there shall be disregarded—

(a) so much of any premium thereunder as is charged on the grounds that an exceptional risk of death is involved; and

(b) any provision under which, on those grounds, any sum may become chargeable as a debt against the capital sum guaranteed by the policy on death.

Commentary—*Simon's Direct Tax Service* **E2.1041.**
Definition—"Qualifying policy", s 832(1).
Cross references—See TA 1988 Sch 15 para 18(2) (adaptation of this paragraph in its application to policies which are varied).

(iv) Connected policies

13 Subject to paragraph 14 below, where the terms of any policy provide that it is to continue in force only so long as another policy does so, neither policy is a qualifying policy unless, if they had constituted together a single policy issued in respect of an insurance made at the time of the insurance in respect of which the first-mentioned policy was issued, that single policy would have been a qualifying policy.

Commentary—*Simon's Direct Tax Service* **E2.1041.**
Definition—"Qualifying policy", s 832(1).
Cross references—See TA 1988 Sch 15 para 18(2) (adaptation of this paragraph in its application to policies which are varied).

14—(1) A policy shall not be a qualifying policy if the policy is connected with another policy and the terms of either policy provide benefits which are greater than would reasonably be expected if any policy connected with it were disregarded.

(2) For the purposes of this paragraph a policy is connected with another policy if they are at any time simultaneously in force and either of them is issued with reference to the other, or with a view to enabling the other to be issued on particular terms or facilitating its being issued on those terms.

(3) In this paragraph "policy" means a policy [evidencing a contract of long-term insurance][1] and includes any such policy issued outside the United Kingdom.

[(3A) In sub-paragraph (3) "contract of long-term insurance" means a contract which falls within Part II of Schedule 1 to the Financial Services and Markets Act 2000 (Regulated Activities) Order 2001.][1]

(4) Where any person issues a policy—

(a) which by virtue of this paragraph is not a qualifying policy, or

(b) the issue of which causes another policy to cease by virtue of this paragraph to be a qualifying policy,

he shall within three months of issuing the policy give notice of that fact to the Board.

(5) The Board may, by notice, require any person who is, or appears to them to be, concerned in the issue of any such policy as is mentioned in sub-paragraph (4) above, to furnish them within such time (not being less than 30 days) as may be specified in the notice with such particulars as they think necessary for the purposes of this paragraph and as the person to whom the notice is addressed has or can reasonably obtain; but no solicitor shall be deemed for the purposes of this sub-paragraph to have been concerned in the issue of a policy by reason only that he has given professional advice to a client in connection with that policy.

(6) This paragraph shall apply to policies issued in respect of insurances made before 23rd August 1983 in accordance with sub-paragraphs (7) and (8) below.

(7) Where—

(a) a policy is issued in respect of an insurance made before 23rd August 1983, and

(b) a policy is issued in respect of an insurance made on or after that date which is connected with it within the meaning of this paragraph,

sub-paragraphs (1) to (6) above shall apply to the policy issued in respect of an insurance made before that date.

(8) Sub-paragraphs (1) to (7) above shall apply to policies issued in respect of insurances made before 23rd August 1983 (other than policies which, disregarding this paragraph, fall within sub-paragraph (7)) with the substitution—

(*a*) in sub-paragraph (1) for the words "and the terms of either policy" of the words "the terms of which";

(*b*) in sub-paragraph (3) for the words from "long term business" to "1982" of the words "ordinary long-term insurance business within the meaning of section 83(2) of the Insurance Companies Act 1974 (as enacted) or, in relation to a policy made after 25th March 1982, section 96(1) of the Insurance Companies Act 1982"; and

(*c*) in sub-paragraphs (6) and (7) for the words "23rd August 1983" of the words "26th March 1980".

(9) In any case where payments made—

(*a*) after 22nd August 1983, and

(*b*) by way of premium or other consideration in respect of a policy issued in respect of an insurance made before that date,

exceed £5 in any period of 12 months, the policy shall be treated for the purposes of this paragraph as if it were issued in respect of an insurance made after 22nd August 1983; but nothing in this paragraph shall apply with respect to any premium paid in respect of it before that date.

(10) Sub-paragraphs (8) and (9) above do not apply in relation to policies issued in the course of industrial assurance business.

Commentary—*Simon's Direct Tax Service* **E2.1041.**
Statement of Practice SP E4—Life assurance policies and annuities not affected by the associated operation rules if the assurance policy was issued on full medical evidence and, it would have been issued in the same terms if the annuity had not been bought.
Definitions—"The Board", s 832(1); "industrial assurance business", s 832(1); "notice", s 832(1); "qualifying policy", s 832(1).
Amendments—[1] Words in sub-para (3) substituted, and sub-para (3A) inserted, by the Financial Services and Markets Act 2000 (Consequential Amendments) (Taxes) Order, SI 2001/3629 arts 13, 47(1), (4), (5) with effect from 1 December 2001, immediately after the coming into force of the Financial Services and Markets Act 2000 ss 411, 432(1), Sch 20.

(v) Premiums paid out of sums due under previous policies

15—(1) Where, in the case of a policy under which a single premium only is payable, liability for the payment of that premium is discharged in accordance with sub-paragraph (2) below, the policy is a qualifying policy notwithstanding anything in paragraph 1(2) or (3) or paragraph 2(1)(*b*) or (*c*) above; and where, in the case of any other policy, liability for the payment of the first premium thereunder, or of any part of that premium, is so discharged, the premium or part shall be disregarded for the purposes of paragraphs 1(2)(*b*) and (3)(*b*) and 2(1)(*c*) above.

(2) Liability for the payment of a premium is discharged in accordance with this sub-paragraph if it is discharged by the retention by the company with which the insurance is made of the whole or a part of any sum which has become payable on the maturity of, or on the surrender more than ten years after its issue of the rights conferred by, a policy—

(*a*) previously issued by the company to the person making the insurance, or, if it is made by trustees, to them or any predecessors in office; or

(*b*) issued by the company when the person making the insurance was an infant, and securing a capital sum payable either on a specified date falling not more than one month after his attaining 25, or on the anniversary of the policy immediately following his attainment of that age,

being, unless it is a policy falling within paragraph (*b*) above and the premium in question is a first premium only, a policy which was itself a qualifying policy, or which would have been a qualifying policy had it been issued in respect of an insurance made after 19th March 1968.

Commentary—*Simon's Direct Tax Service* **E2.1041.**
Definitions—"Company", s 832(1), (2); "qualifying policy", s 832(1).

(vi) Additional premiums under section 72(9) of the Finance Act 1984

16 In determining whether a policy is a qualifying policy, no account shall be taken of any amount recovered, as if it were an additional premium, in pursuance of section 72(9) of the Finance Act 1984.

Commentary—*Simon's Direct Tax Service* **E2.1049.**
Definition—"Qualifying policy", s 832(1).

(vii) Substitutions and variations

17—(1) Subject to paragraph 19 below, where one policy ("the new policy") is issued in substitution for, or on the maturity of and in consequence of an option conferred by, another policy ("the old policy"), the question whether the new policy is a qualifying policy shall, to the extent provided by the rules in sub-paragraph (2) below, be determined by reference to both policies.

(2) The rules (for the purposes of which, the question whether the old policy was a qualifying policy shall be determined in accordance with this Part of this Schedule, whatever the date of the insurance in respect of which it was issued), are as follows—

(*a*) if the new policy would apart from this paragraph be a qualifying policy but the old policy was [not][1], the new policy is not a qualifying policy unless the person making the insurance in respect of which it is issued was an infant when the old policy was issued, and the old policy was one securing a capital sum payable either on a specified date falling not later than one month after his attaining 25 or on the anniversary of the policy immediately following his attainment of that age;

(*b*) if the new policy would apart from this paragraph be a qualifying policy, and the old policy was also a qualifying policy, the new policy is a qualifying policy unless—

(i) it takes effect before the expiry of ten years from the making of the insurance in respect of which the old policy was issued, and

(ii) subject to sub-paragraph (4) below, the highest total of premiums payable thereunder for any period of 12 months expiring before that time is less than one half of the highest total paid for any period of 12 months under the old policy, or under any related policy issued less than ten years before the issue of the new policy (''related policy'' meaning any policy in relation to which the old policy was a new policy within the meaning of this paragraph, any policy in relation to which that policy was such a policy, and so on);

(*c*) if the new policy would not apart from this paragraph be a qualifying policy, and would fail to be so by reason only of paragraph 1(2) or (3) or 2(1)(*a*), (*b*) or (*c*) above, it is nevertheless a qualifying policy if the old policy was a qualifying policy and—

(i) the old policy was issued in respect of an insurance made more than ten years before the taking effect of the new policy, and, subject to sub-paragraph (4) below, the premiums payable for any period of 12 months under the new policy do not exceed the smallest total paid for any such period under the old policy; or

(ii) the old policy was issued outside the United Kingdom, and the circumstances are as specified in sub-paragraph (3) below.

(3) The circumstances are—

(*a*) where the new policy referred to in sub-paragraph (2)(*c*) above is issued after 22nd February 1984, that the policy holder under the new policy became resident in the United Kingdom during the 12 months ending with the date of its issue;

(*b*) where paragraph (*a*) above does not apply, that the person in respect of whom the new insurance is made became resident in the United Kingdom during the 12 months ending with the date of its issue;

(*c*) that the issuing company certify that the new policy is in substitution for the old, and that the old was issued either by a branch or agency of theirs outside the United Kingdom or by a company outside the United Kingdom with whom they have arrangements for the issue of policies in substitution for ones held by persons coming to the United Kingdom; and

(*d*) that the new policy confers on the holder benefits which are substantially equivalent to those which he would have enjoyed if the old policy had continued in force.

(4) Where the new policy is one issued on or after 1st April 1976 then, in determining under sub-paragraph (2) above whether that policy would or would not (apart from sub-paragraphs (1) to (3) above) be a qualifying policy, there shall be left out of account so much of the first premium payable thereunder as is accounted for by the value of the old policy.

Commentary—*Simon's Direct Tax Service* **E2.1041, 1048.**
Concessions A41—Concessions for minor infringements of qualifying conditions; where the commencement date of a policy is back-dated by not more than three months for the purposes of sub-para (2) above, the earlier date is treated as the date on which the assurance is made.
A45—Term assurance of 10 years or less: reduction of sum assured by more than half or extension of term to 10 years: where in consequence of those variations, the premium is reduced by more than half, the policy is not disqualified notwithstanding sub-para (2)(*b*) above.
Definitions—''Branch or agency'', s 834(1); ''company'', s 832(1), (2); ''qualifying policy'', s 832(1); ''United Kingdom'', s 830(1).
Cross references—See TA 1988 Sch 15 para 18 (qualifications rules of this paragraph to apply to policies which are varied).
TA 1988 Sch 15 para 25 (modified application of this paragraph where a new non-resident policy is issued for an old policy issued on, before or after 17 November 1983).
Amendments—¹ Word in sub-para (2)(*a*) inserted by FA 1988 Sch 13 para 10.

18—(1) Subject to paragraph 19 below and to the provisions of this paragraph, where the terms of a policy are varied, the question whether the policy after the variation is a qualifying policy shall be determined in accordance with the rules in paragraph 17 above, with references in those rules to the new policy and the old policy construed for that purpose as references respectively to the policy after the variation and the policy before the variation, and with any other necessary modifications.

(2) In applying any of those rules by virtue of this paragraph, the question whether a policy after a variation would be a qualifying policy apart from the rule shall be determined as if any reference in paragraphs [1, 2, 3(5) to (11), 4 to 9]¹, 12 and 13 above to the making of an insurance, or to a policy's term, were a reference to the taking effect of the variation or, as the case may be, to the term of the policy as from the variation.

(3) This paragraph does not apply by reason of—

(*a*) any variation which, whether or not of a purely formal character, does not affect the terms of a policy in any significant respect, or (*b*) any variation effected before the end of the year 1968 for the sole purpose of converting into a qualifying policy any policy issued (but not one treated, by virtue of paragraph 8(1) and (2) of Schedule 14, as issued) in respect of an insurance made after 19th March 1968. [or]²

[(*c*) any variation so as to increase the benefits secured or reduce the premiums payable which is effected—

    (i) on or after such day as the Board may by order appoint, and

    (ii) in consideration of a change in the method of payment of premiums from collection by a person collecting premiums from house to house to payment by a different method.]²

Commentary—*Simon's Direct Tax Service* **E2.1041.**
Concession A45—Term assurance of 10 years or less: reduction of sum assured by more than half or extension of term to 10 years: where in consequence of those variations, the premium is reduced by more than half, the policy is not disqualified notwithstanding sub-para (2)(b) above.
Cross reference—Finance Act 1996, Section 167, (Appointed Day) Order, SI 2001/3643. The appointed day for the purposes of sub-para (3)(*c*) is 1 December 2001.
Definitions—"The Board", s 832(1); "the new policy", see para 17(1); "the old policy", see para 17(1); "qualifying policy", s 832(1).
Modifications—FA 1991 Sch 9 para 5 (modification of sub-para (2) above in its application to a policy effected by a contract made after 31 August 1987 and before 25 July 1991 and the premium in respect of which is increased without contravening the limits in s 464 above on or after 25 July 1991 and before 1 August 1992).
FA 1995 Sch 10 para 4(3) (modification of sub-para (2) above as it applies to policies effected by contract after 31 August 1987 but before 1 May 1995 the premium in respect of which is increased without contravening the limits in s 464 on or after 1 May 1995 and before 1 April 1996).
Amendments—¹ Numbers in sub-para (2) substituted by FA 1988 Sch 13 para 11.
² Sub-para (3)(*c*) and word "or" preceding it inserted by FA 1996 s 167(9).

19—(1) The following provisions of this paragraph shall have effect for determining for the purposes of this Schedule whether a policy has been varied or whether a policy which confers on the person to whom it is issued an option to have another policy substituted for it or to have any of its terms changed is a qualifying policy.

(2) If the policy is one issued in respect of an insurance made before 1st April 1976—

    (*a*) any such option shall, until it is exercised, be disregarded in determining whether the policy is a qualifying policy; and

    (*b*) any change in the terms of the policy which is made in pursuance of such an option shall be deemed to be a variation of the policy.

(3) If the policy is one issued in respect of an insurance made on or after 1st April 1976, the policy shall not be a qualifying policy unless it satisfies the conditions applicable to it under this Schedule before any such option is exercised and—

    (*a*) each policy that might be substituted for it in pursuance of such an option would satisfy those conditions under the rules of paragraph 17 above; and

    (*b*) the policy would continue to satisfy those conditions under the rules of that paragraph as applied by paragraph 18 above if each or any of the changes capable of being made in pursuance of such an option had been made and were treated as a variation;

and it shall not be treated as being varied by reason only of any change made in pursuance of such an option.

Commentary—*Simon's Direct Tax Service* **E2.1041.**
Definition—"Qualifying policy", s 832(1).

20—(1) Where, as a result of a variation in the life or lives for the time being assured, a qualifying policy ("the earlier policy") is replaced by a new policy ("the later policy") which in accordance with the rules in paragraph 17 above is also a qualifying policy, then, subject to sub-paragraph (2) below, for the purposes of—

    (*a*) sections 268 to 270 and 540 and 541; and

    (*b*) any second or subsequent application of this paragraph;

the later policy and the earlier policy shall be treated as a single policy issued in respect of an insurance made at the time of the making of the insurance in respect of which the earlier policy was issued; and, accordingly, so long as the later policy continues to be a qualifying policy, the single policy shall also be treated as a qualifying policy for those purposes.

(2) Sub-paragraph (1) above does not apply unless—

    (*a*) any sum which would otherwise become payable by the insurer on or in connection with the coming to an end of the earlier policy is retained by the insurer and applied in the discharge of some or all of the liability for any premium becoming due under the later policy; and

    (*b*) no consideration in money or money's worth (other than the benefits for which provision is made by the later policy) is receivable by any person on or in connection with the coming to an end of the earlier policy or the coming into existence of the later policy.

(3) Any sum which is applied as mentioned in sub-paragraph (2)(*a*) above—

    (*a*) shall be left out of account in determining, for the purposes of sections 268 to 270 and 540 and 541, the total amount which at any time has been paid by way of premiums under the single policy referred to in sub-paragraph (1) above; and

    (*b*) shall not be regarded, in relation to that single policy, as a relevant capital payment, within the meaning of section 541.

(4) This paragraph applies where the later policy comes into existence on or after 25th March 1982.

Commentary—*Simon's Direct Tax Service* **E2.1051, 1052.**
Definition—''Qualifying policy'', s 832(1).
Cross references—See TA 1988 Sch 14 para 8(6) (certain ''later policies'' (as defined in this paragraph) to be deemed to have been made before 13 March 1984).

PART II
CERTIFICATION OF QUALIFYING POLICIES

Policies issued in respect of insurances made on or after 1st April 1976 or varied on or after that date

21—*(1) A policy of life insurance issued in respect of an insurance made on or after 1st April 1976 or varied on or after that date (other than one to which paragraph 22(2)(c) below applies) shall not be a qualifying policy unless—*

(a) it is certified by the Board as being a qualifying policy; or
(b) it conforms with a form which at the time the policy is issued or varied is either—

(i) a standard form certified by the Board as a standard form of qualifying policy; or
(ii) a form varying from a standard form so certified in no other respect than by making such additions thereto as are, at the time the policy is issued, certified by the Board as compatible with a qualifying policy when made to that standard form and satisfy any conditions subject to which they are so certified;

and any certificate issued in pursuance of paragraph (a) above shall be conclusive evidence that the policy is a qualifying policy.

(2) In issuing a certificate in pursuance of sub-paragraph (1) above the Board may disregard any provision of the policy, standard form or addition which appears to them insignificant.

(3) Where the Board refuse to certify a policy as being a qualifying policy, the person to whom it is issued may appeal to the General Commissioners or, if he so elects, to the Special Commissioners.

(4) Sub-paragraphs (1) to (3) above do not apply in relation to such a policy as is mentioned in paragraphs 3 to 6 above.[1]

Commentary—*Simon's Direct Tax Service* **E2.1032, 1042.**
Concession A41—A policy capable of being certified, but which has not been certified, may be certified from the date when the assurance was made and any premium relief already given is not normally recovered.
Simon's Tax Cases—*R (on the application of Monarch Assurance plc) v IRC*, CA [2001] STC 1639.
Definitions—''The Board'', s 832(1); ''qualifying policy'', s 832(1).
Cross references—See TA 1988 s 462A(3)(b) (election as to tax exempt business by a registered friendly society).
Prospective amendments—This paragraph repealed with savings with effect from a date to be appointed; see FA 1995 s 55(1)–(3) as amended by FA 1996 s 162, Sch 29 Pt VIII(7).

22—*(1) A body which issues or which, after 5th April 1979, has issued any policy of life insurance (other than one to which sub-paragraph (2)(c) below applies)—*

(a) which is certified by the Board as being a qualifying policy; or
(b) which conforms with such a form as is mentioned in paragraph 21(1)(b) above, and is in the opinion of the body issuing it a qualifying policy,

shall, within three months of receipt of a request in writing by the policy holder, give to the policy holder a duly authenticated certificate to that effect, specifying in the certificate the name of the policy holder, the name of the person whose life is assured, the reference number or other means of identification allocated to the policy, the reference number of the relevant Inland Revenue certificate (if any), the capital sum or sums assured and the amounts and dates for payment of the premiums.

(2) Subject to sub-paragraph (3) below, where a policy of life insurance is varied after 5th April 1979, and, after the variation—

(a) it is certified by the Board as a qualifying policy, or
(b) it conforms with such a form as is referred to in sub-paragraph (1) above and is in the opinion of the body by whom it was issued a qualifying policy, or
(c) in the case of a policy issued in respect of an insurance made before 1st April 1976, it is in the opinion of the body by whom it was issued a qualifying policy,

that body shall, within three months of receipt of a request in writing by the policy holder, give to the policy holder a like certificate with respect to the policy as varied.

(3) Sub-paragraph (2) above shall not apply by reason of—

(a) any variation which, whether or not of a purely formal character, does not affect the terms of a policy in any significant respect; or
(b) any variation of a policy issued in respect of an insurance made on or before 19th March 1968, other than a variation by virtue of which the policy falls, under paragraph 8(1) and (2) of Schedule 14, to be treated as issued in respect of an insurance made after that date.[1]

Commentary—*Simon's Direct Tax Service* **E2.1042.**
Revenue & other press releases—IR 22-1-88 (variations which fundamentally restructure a qualifying life assurance policy may cause Revenue to refuse to certify the policy as varied).
Definitions—''The Board'', s 832(1); ''qualifying policy'', s 832(1).

Prospective amendments—This paragraph repealed in relation to any time on or after a date to be appointed by FA 1995 s 55(4) as amended by FA 1996 s 162, Sch 29 Pt VIII(7).

PART III
POLICIES ISSUED BY NON-RESIDENT COMPANIES

23 In this Part—

    (*a*) any reference to a paragraph is a reference to that paragraph of this Schedule; and

    (*b*) ''the old policy'' and ''the new policy'' have the same meanings as in paragraph 17.

24—(1) This paragraph applies to a policy of life insurance—

    (*a*) which is issued in respect of an insurance made after 17th November 1983; and

    (*b*) which is so issued by a company resident outside the United Kingdom;

and in the following provisions of this paragraph such a policy is referred to as ''a new non-resident policy'' and the company by which it is issued is referred to as ''the issuing company''.

(2) Notwithstanding anything in paragraph 21—

    (*a*) a new non-resident policy shall not be certified under sub-paragraph (1)(*a*) of that paragraph, and

    (*b*) a new non-resident policy which conforms with such a form as is mentioned in sub-paragraph (1)(*b*) of that paragraph shall not be a qualifying policy,

until such time as the conditions in either sub-paragraph (3) or sub-paragraph (4) below are fulfilled with respect to it.

(3) The conditions first referred to in sub-paragraph (2) above are—

    (*a*) that the issuing company is lawfully carrying on in the United Kingdom life assurance business (as defined in section 431(2)); and

    (*b*) that the premiums under the policy are payable to a branch in the United Kingdom of the issuing company, being a branch through which the issuing company carries on its life assurance business; and

    (*c*) the premiums under the policy form part of those business receipts of the issuing company which arise through that branch.

(4) The conditions secondly referred to in sub-paragraph (2) above are—

    (*a*) that the policy holder is resident in the United Kingdom; and

    (*b*) that the income of the issuing company from the investments of its life assurance fund is, by virtue of section 445, charged to corporation tax under Case III of Schedule D;

and expressions used in paragraph (*b*) above have the same meaning as in section 445(1).

Commentary—*Simon's Direct Tax Service* **E2.1032, 1042.**
Definitions—''Branch'', s 832(1); ''company'', s 832(1), (2); ''qualifying policy'', s 832(1); ''Schedule D'', s 18(1); ''United Kingdom'', s 830(1).
Cross references—See TA 1988 s 553(2), (7) (new non-resident policies and new off-shore capital redemption policies).
TA 1988 Sch 15 para 25 (modified application of this paragraph where a new non-resident policy is issued for an old policy issued on, before or after 17 November 1983).
Prospective amendments—Sub-paras (2), (2A) to be substituted for sub-para (2), word ''first'' in sub-para (3), and sub-para (4), to be repealed in relation to any time on or after a date to be appointed, by FA 1995 s 55(5) as amended by FA 1996 s 162, Sch 29 Pt VIII(7). Sub-paras (2), (2A) to read as follows—

''(2) Subject to section 55(3) of the Finance Act 1995 (transitional provision for the certification of certain policies), a new non-resident policy that falls outside sub-paragraph (2A) below shall not be a qualifying policy until such time as the conditions in sub-paragraph (3) are fulfilled with respect to it.

(2A) A policy falls outside this sub-paragraph unless, at the time immediately before [the appointed date for the purposes of section 55 of the Finance Act 1995 (removal of certification requirements)] it was a qualifying policy by virtue of sub-paragraphs (2)(*b*) and (4) of this paragraph, as they had effect in relation to that time.''.

25—(1) In the application of paragraph 17 in any case where—

    (*a*) the old policy was issued in respect of an insurance made after 17th November 1983 and could not be a qualifying policy by virtue of paragraph 24, and

    (*b*) the new policy is not a new non-resident policy as defined in that paragraph,

the rules for the determination of the question whether the new policy is a qualifying policy shall apply with the modifications in sub-paragraph (2) below.

[(2) The modifications are the following—

    (*a*) if, apart from paragraph 24, the old policy or any related policy (within the meaning of paragraph 17(2)(*b*)) of which account falls to be taken would have been a qualifying policy, that policy shall be assumed to have been a qualifying policy for the purposes of paragraph 17(2); and

    (*b*) if, apart from this paragraph, the new policy would be a qualifying policy, it shall not be such a policy unless the circumstances are as specified in paragraph 17(3); and

    (*c*) in paragraph 17(3)(*c*) the words ''either by a branch or agency of theirs outside the United Kingdom or'' shall be omitted;

and references in this sub-paragraph to being a qualifying policy shall have effect, in relation to any time before [the appointed date for the purposes of section 55 of the Finance Act 1995 (removal of certification requirements)]² as including a reference to being capable of being certified as such a policy.]¹

(3) In the application of paragraph 17 in any case where—

(*a*) the old policy is a qualifying policy which was issued in respect of an insurance made on or before 17th November 1983 but, if the insurance had been made after that date, the policy could not have been a qualifying policy by virtue of paragraph 24, and

(*b*) the new policy is issued after that date and is not a new non-resident policy, as defined in paragraph 24,

the rules for the determination of the question whether the new policy is a qualifying policy shall apply with the modification in sub-paragraph (2)(*c*) above.

Commentary—*Simon's Direct Tax Service* E2.1048.
Definitions—"The new policy", para 17(1), by virtue of para 23; "the old policy", para 17(1), by virtue of para 23; "qualifying policy", s 832(1).
Cross references—See TA 1988 s 553 (where the new policy referred to in sub-paras(1), (3) above is qualifying policy, s 540 (life policies: chargeable events) applies with modifications).
TA 1988 Sch 14 para 8(7) (certain "new policies" (as defined in this paragraph) to be deemed to have been made before 13 March 1984).
Amendments—¹ Sub-para (2) substituted by FA 1995 s 55(6) with effect from 1 May 1995.
² Words in sub-para (2) substituted for "5th May 1996" by FA 1996 s 162(2) with effect from 29 April 1996.

26 If, in the case of a substitution of policies falling within paragraph 25(1) or (3), the new policy confers such an option as results in the application to it of paragraph 19(3), the new policy shall be treated for the purposes of paragraph 19(3) as having been issued in respect of an insurance made on the same day as that on which was made the insurance in respect of which the old policy was issued.

Commentary—*Simon's Direct Tax Service* E2.1048.
Definitions—"The new policy", para 17(1), by virtue of para 23; "the old policy", para 17(1), by virtue of para 23.
Cross references—See TA 1988 Sch 15 para 25 (modified application of this paragraph where a new non-resident policy is issued for an old policy issued on, before or after 17 November 1983).

27—(1) For the purposes of Part I and [paragraph]¹ 24, a policy of life insurance which was issued—

(*a*) in respect of an insurance made on or before 17th November 1983, and

(*b*) by a company resident outside the United Kingdom,

shall be treated as issued in respect of an insurance made after that date if the policy is varied after that date so as to increase the benefits secured or to extend the term of the insurance.

(2) If a policy of life insurance which was issued as mentioned in sub-paragraph (1)(*a*) and (*b*) above confers on the person to whom it is issued an option to have another policy substituted for it or to have any of its terms changed, then for the purposes of that sub-paragraph any change in the terms of the policy which is made in pursuance of the option shall be deemed to be a variation of the policy.

Commentary—*Simon's Direct Tax Service* E2.1048.
Definitions—"Company", s 832(1), (2); "United Kingdom", s 830(1).
Amendments—¹ Word in sub-para (1) substituted for the words "paragraphs 21 and", by FA 1995 s 55(7), with effect from 1 May 1995, except so far as it has effect for the purposes of any case to which para 21 of this Schedule applies by virtue of FA 1995 s 55(1)–(3).

[SCHEDULE 15A

CONTRACTUAL SAVINGS SCHEMES]¹

Section 326(9)

Commentary—*Simon's Direct Tax Service* D4.733, E4.588.
Amendments—¹ This Schedule inserted by FA 1995 s 65, Sch 12 para 6(2).

Introduction

[1 This Schedule shall have effect for the purposes of section 326.]¹

Amendments—¹ This Schedule inserted by FA 1995 s 65, Sch 12 para 6(2).

Share option linked schemes

[2—(1) A share option linked scheme is a scheme under which periodical contributions are to be made by an individual—

(*a*) who is eligible to participate in (that is, to obtain and exercise rights under) an approved savings-related share option scheme, and

(*b*) who is to make the contributions for the purpose of enabling him to participate in that approved scheme.

(2) In sub-paragraph (1) above—

(*a*) "savings-related share option scheme" has the meaning given by paragraph 1 of Schedule 9, and (*b*) "approved" means approved under that Schedule.][1]

Amendments—[1] This Schedule inserted by FA 1995 s 65, Sch 12 para 6(2).

Relevant European institutions

[3 A relevant European institution is [an EEA firm of the kind mentioned in paragraph 5(*b*) of Schedule 3 to the Financial Services and Markets Act 2000 which has permission under paragraph 15 of that Schedule (as a result of qualifying for authorisation under paragraph 12 of that Schedule) to accept deposits.][2]][1]

Definitions—"United Kingdom", s 830(1).
Amendments—[1] This Schedule inserted by FA 1995 s 65, Sch 12 para 6(2).
[2] Words substituted by the Financial Services and Markets Act 2000 (Consequential Amendments) (Taxes) Order, SI 2001/3629 arts 13, 48 with effect from 1 December 2001, immediately after the coming into force of the Financial Services and Markets Act 2000 ss 411, 432(1), Sch 20.

Treasury specifications

[4—(1) The requirements which may be specified under section 326(3)(*b*), (4)(*b*) or (5)(*b*) are such requirements as the Treasury think fit.

(2) In particular, the requirements may relate to—

(*a*) the descriptions of individuals who may enter into contracts under a scheme;
(*b*) the contributions to be paid by individuals;
(*c*) the sums to be paid or repaid to individuals.

(3) The requirements which may be specified under any of the relevant provisions may be different from those specified under any of the other relevant provisions; and the relevant provisions are section 326(3)(*b*), (4)(*b*) and (5)(*b*).][1]

Amendments—[1] This Schedule inserted by FA 1995 s 65, Sch 12 para 6(2).

[5—(1) Where a specification has been made under section 326(3)(*b*), (4)(*b*) or (5)(*b*) the Treasury may—

(*a*) withdraw the specification and any certification made by reference to the specification, and
(*b*) stipulate the date on which the withdrawal is to become effective.

(2) No withdrawal under this paragraph shall affect—

(*a*) the operation of the scheme before the stipulated date, or
(*b*) any contract entered into before that date.

(3) No withdrawal under this paragraph shall be effective unless the Treasury—

(*a*) send a notice by post to each relevant body informing it of the withdrawal, and
(*b*) do so not less than 28 days before the stipulated date;

and a relevant body is a society or institution authorised (whether unconditionally or subject to conditions being met) to enter into contracts under the scheme concerned.][1]

Amendments—[1] This Schedule inserted by FA 1995 s 65, Sch 12 para 6(2).

[6—(1) Where a specification has been made under section 326(3)(*b*), (4)(*b*) or (5)(*b*) the Treasury may—

(*a*) vary the specification,
(*b*) withdraw any certification made by reference to the specification obtaining before the variation, and
(*c*) stipulate the date on which the variation and withdrawal are to become effective;

and the Treasury may at any time certify a scheme as fulfilling the requirements obtaining after the variation.

(2) No variation and withdrawal under this paragraph shall affect—

(*a*) the operation of the scheme before the stipulated date, or
(*b*) any contract entered into before that date.

(3) No variation and withdrawal under this paragraph shall be effective unless the Treasury—

(*a*) send a notice by post to each relevant body informing it of the variation and withdrawal, and
(*b*) do so not less than 28 days before the stipulated date;

and a relevant body is a society or institution authorised (whether unconditionally or subject to conditions being met) to enter into contracts under the scheme concerned.][1]

Amendments—[1] This Schedule inserted by FA 1995 s 65, Sch 12 para 6(2).

Treasury authorisation

[7—(1) The Treasury may authorise a society or institution under section 326(7) or (8) as regards schemes generally or as regards a particular scheme or particular schemes.

(2) More than one authorisation may be given to the same society or institution.][1]

Amendments—¹ This Schedule inserted by FA 1995 s 65, Sch 12 para 6(2).

[8—(1) Where an authorisation has been given under section 326(7) or (8) the Treasury may withdraw the authorisation and stipulate the date on which the withdrawal is to become effective; and the withdrawal shall have effect as regards any contract not entered into before the stipulated date.

(2) No withdrawal under this paragraph shall be effective unless the Treasury—

   (*a*) send a notice by post to the society or institution concerned informing it of the withdrawal, and

   (*b*) do so not less than 28 days before the stipulated date.

(3) A withdrawal of an authorisation shall not affect the Treasury's power to give another authorisation or other authorisations.]¹

Amendments—¹ This Schedule inserted by FA 1995 s 65, Sch 12 para 6(2).

[9—(1) Where an authorisation has been given under section 326(7) the Treasury may—

   (*a*) stipulate that the authorisation is to be varied by being treated as given subject to specified conditions being met, and

   (*b*) stipulate the date on which the variation is to become effective.

(2) As regards any contract entered into on or after the stipulated date the authorisation shall be treated as having been given under section 326(8) subject to the conditions being met.

(3) No variation under this paragraph shall be effective unless the Treasury—

   (*a*) send a notice by post to the society or institution concerned informing it of the variation, and

   (*b*) do so not less than 28 days before the stipulated date.]¹

Amendments—¹ This Schedule inserted by FA 1995 s 65, Sch 12 para 6(2).

[10—(1) Where an authorisation has been given under section 326(8) the Treasury may withdraw the conditions and stipulate the date on which the withdrawal is to become effective.

(2) As regards any contract entered into on or after the stipulated date the authorisation shall be treated as having been given under section 326(7) without any conditions being imposed.]¹

Amendments—¹ This Schedule inserted by FA 1995 s 65, Sch 12 para 6(2).

[11—(1) Where an authorisation has been given under section 326(8) the Treasury may vary the conditions and stipulate the date on which the variation is to become effective; and the variation shall have effect as regards any contract entered into on or after the stipulated date.

(2) No variation under this paragraph shall be effective unless the Treasury—

   (*a*) send a notice by post to the society or institution concerned informing it of the variation, and

   (*b*) do so not less than 28 days before the stipulated date.]¹

Amendments—¹ This Schedule inserted by FA 1995 s 65, Sch 12 para 6(2).

[12—(1) If the Treasury act as regards an authorisation under a relevant paragraph, the paragraph concerned shall have effect subject to their power to act later, as regards the same authorisation, under the same or (as the case may be) another relevant paragraph.

(2) If the Treasury act later as mentioned in sub-paragraph (1) above that sub-paragraph shall apply again, and so on however many times they act as regards an authorisation.

(3) If the Treasury act as regards an authorisation under a relevant paragraph the paragraph concerned shall have effect subject to their power to act later, as regards the same authorisation, under paragraph 8 above.

(4) For the purposes of this paragraph the relevant paragraphs are paragraphs 9 to 11 above.]¹

Amendments—¹ This Schedule inserted by FA 1995 s 65, Sch 12 para 6(2).

[SCHEDULE 15B

VENTURE CAPITAL TRUSTS: RELIEF FROM INCOME TAX]¹

Section 332A

Amendments—¹ This Schedule inserted by FA 1995 s 71(2) with effect from the year 1995–96.

PART I

RELIEF ON INVESTMENT

Entitlement to claim relief

[1—(1) Subject to the following provisions of this Schedule, an individual shall, for any year of assessment, be entitled under this Part of this Schedule to claim relief in respect of an amount equal to the aggregate of the amounts (if any) which, by reference to eligible shares issued to him by venture capital trusts in the course of that year, are amounts on which he is eligible for relief in accordance with sub-paragraph (2) below.

(2) The amounts on which an individual shall be taken for the purposes of sub-paragraph (1) above to be eligible for relief shall be any amounts subscribed by him on his own behalf for eligible shares issued by a venture capital trust for raising money.

(3) An individual shall not be entitled under this Part of this Schedule to claim relief for any given year of assessment in respect of an amount of more than £100,000.

(4) An individual shall not be entitled under this Schedule to claim any relief to which he is eligible by reference to any shares unless he had attained the age of eighteen years before those shares were issued.

(5) Where an individual makes a claim for any relief to which he is entitled under this Part of this Schedule for any year of assessment, the amount of his liability for that year to income tax on his total income shall be equal to the amount to which he would be so liable apart from this Part of this Schedule less whichever is the smaller of—

    (*a*) an amount equal to tax at the lower rate for that year on the amount in respect of which he is entitled to claim relief for that year, and

    (*b*) the amount which reduces his liability to nil.

(6) In determining for the purposes of sub-paragraph (5) above the amount of income tax to which a person would be liable apart from this Part of this Schedule, no account shall be taken of—

    (*a*) any income tax reduction under section 289A;

    (*b*) any income tax reduction under Chapter I of Part VII or under section 347B,

    (*c*) any income tax reduction under section 353(1A),

    (*d*) any income tax reduction under section 54(3A) of the Finance Act 1989

    (*e*) any relief by way of a reduction of liability to tax which is given in accordance with any arrangements having effect by virtue of section 788 or by way of a credit under section 790(1), or

    (*f*) any tax at the basic rate on so much of that person's income as is income the income tax on which he is entitled to charge against any other person or to deduct, retain or satisfy out of any payment.

(7) ...[2]

(8) A person shall not be entitled to be given any relief under this Part of this Schedule by reference to any shares if circumstances have arisen which would have resulted, had that relief already been given, in the withdrawal or reduction of the relief.

(9) A person shall not under this Part of this Schedule be eligible for any relief on any amount by reference to any shares unless the shares are both subscribed for and issued for bona fide commercial purposes and not as part of a scheme or arrangement the main purpose of which, or one of the main purposes of which, is the avoidance of tax.][1]

Commentary—*Simon's Direct Tax Service* **E3.641.**
Definitions—''Basic rate'', s 832(1); ''eligible shares'', Sch 15B para 6(1); ''lower rate'', s 832(1); ''tax'', s 832(3); ''venture capital trusts'', s 842AA(1); ''year of assessment'', s 832(1).
Cross references—See FA 1990 s 25(6), (7) (where any gift made by an individual (a ''donor'') in a year of assessment is a qualifying donation, then for that year sub-s (3) above shall have effect in its application to him as if any reference to income tax which he is entitled to charge against any person included a reference to the tax treated as deducted from the gift).
Amendments—[1] This Schedule inserted by FA 1995 s 71(2) with effect from the year 1995–96.
[2] Sub-para 7 repealed by FA 2001 ss 64, 110, Sch 16 para 3, Sch 33 Pt II(3) with effect for repayments of tax after 6 March 2001.
Prospective amendments—Sub-para (6)(*da*) to be inserted by FA 2002 s 57, Sch 17 para 3 with effect from such day as the Treasury may by order appoint. This amendment shall have effect for years of assessment ending on or after the appointed day. Sub-para (6)(*da*) as inserted to read as follows—

    ''(*da*) any income tax reduction under paragraph 19(2) of Schedule 16 to the Finance Act 2002 (community investment tax relief),''.

Loan-linked investments

[2—(1) An individual shall not be entitled to relief under this Part of this Schedule in respect of any shares if—

    (*a*) there is a loan made by any person, at any time in the relevant period, to that individual or any associate of his; and

    (*b*) the loan is one which would not have been made, or would not have been made on the same terms, if that individual had not subscribed for those shares or had not been proposing to do so.

(2) References in this paragraph to the making by any person of a loan to any individual or an associate of his include references—

    (*a*) to the giving by that person of any credit to that individual or any associate of his; and

    (*b*) to the assignment or assignation to that person of any debt due from that individual or any associate of his.

(3) In this paragraph—

    ''associate'' has the meaning given in subsections (3) and (4) of section 417, except that in those subsections (as applied for the purposes of this paragraph) ''relative'' shall not include a brother or sister; and "the relevant period", in relation to relief under this Part of this Schedule in respect of any shares in a company which is a venture capital trust, means the period beginning with the incorporation of the company (or, if the company was incorporated more than two years before the date on which the shares were issued, beginning two years before that date) and [ending immediately before the third anniversary of the date on which the shares were issued][2].][1]

Commentary—*Simon's Direct Tax Service* E3.641.
Definitions—"Venture capital trust", s 842AA(1).
Statements of Practice SP 3/94—For holdings of shares issued before 6 April 1998, loans made to acquire shares and available to other borrowers on the same terms do not necessarily preclude relief, but "eligible shares" or associated rights specified as security for the loan would.
SP 6/98—For holdings of shares issued after 5 April 1998, loans made to acquire shares do not necessarily preclude relief; the test is whether the lender makes the loan on terms which are influenced by the fact that the borrower, or an associate of the borrower, has acquired, or is proposing to acquire, the shares.
Amendments—[1] This Schedule inserted by FA 1995 s 71(2) with effect from the year 1995–96.
[2] Words in sub-para (3) substituted for words "ending five years after the issue of the shares" by FA 2000 s 65, Sch 18 para 1(1), (2) with effect for shares issued after 5 April 2000.

Loss of investment relief

[3—(1) This paragraph applies, subject to sub-paragraph (5) below, where—

(a) an individual who has made any claim for relief under this Part of this Schedule makes any disposal of eligible shares in a venture capital trust, and

(b) that disposal takes place before the end of the period of [three years beginning with the date on which those shares were issued to that individual][2].

(2) If the disposal is made otherwise than by way of a bargain made at arm's length, any relief given under this Part of this Schedule by reference to the shares which are disposed of shall be withdrawn.

(3) Where the disposal was made by way of a bargain made at arm's length—

(a) if, apart from this sub-paragraph, the relief given by reference to the shares that are disposed of is greater than the amount mentioned in sub-paragraph (4) below, it shall be reduced by that amount, and

(b) if paragraph (a) above does not apply, any relief given by reference to those shares shall be withdrawn.

(4) The amount referred to in sub-paragraph (3) above is an amount equal to tax at the lower rate for the year of assessment for which the relief was given on the amount or value of the consideration which the individual receives for the shares.

(5) This paragraph shall not apply in the case of any disposal of shares which is made by a married man to his wife or by a married woman to her husband if it is made, in either case, at a time when they are living together.

(6) Where any eligible shares issued to any individual ("the transferor"), being shares by reference to which any amount of relief under this Part of this Schedule has been given, are transferred to the transferor's spouse ("the transferee") by a disposal such as is mentioned in sub-paragraph (5) above, this paragraph shall have effect, in relation to any subsequent disposal or other event, as if—

(a) the transferee were the person who had subscribed for the shares,

(b) the shares had been issued to the transferee at the time when they were issued to the transferor,

(c) there had been, in respect of the transferred shares, such a reduction under this Part of this Schedule in the transferee's liability to income tax as is equal to the actual reduction in respect of those shares of the transferor's liability, and

(d) that deemed reduction were (notwithstanding the transfer) to be treated for the purposes of this paragraph as an amount of relief given by reference to the shares transferred.

(7) Any assessment for withdrawing or reducing relief by reason of a disposal or other event falling within sub-paragraph (6) above shall be made on the transferee.

(8) In determining for the purposes of this paragraph any question whether any disposal relates to shares by reference to which any relief under this Part of this Schedule has been given, it shall be assumed, in relation to any disposal by any person of any eligible shares in a venture capital trust, that—

(a) as between eligible shares acquired by the same person on different days, those acquired on an earlier day are disposed of by that person before those acquired on a later day; and

(b) as between eligible shares acquired by the same person on the same day, those by reference to which relief under this Part of this Schedule has been given are disposed of by that person only after he has disposed of any other eligible shares acquired by him on that day.

(9) Where—

(a) the approval of any company as a venture capital trust is withdrawn, and

(b) the withdrawal of the approval is not one to which section 842AA(8) applies,

any person who, at the time when the withdrawal takes effect, is holding any shares by reference to which relief under this Part of this Schedule has been given shall be deemed for the purposes of this paragraph to have disposed of those shares immediately before that time and otherwise than by way of a bargain made at arm's length.][1]

Assessment on withdrawal or reduction of relief

[**4**—(1) Any relief given under this Part of this Schedule which is subsequently found not to have been due shall be withdrawn by the making of an assessment to tax under Case VI of Schedule D for the year of assessment for which the relief was given.

(2) An assessment for withdrawing or reducing relief in pursuance of paragraph 3 above shall also be made as an assessment to tax under Case VI of Schedule D for the year of assessment for which the relief was given.

(3) No assessment for withdrawing or reducing relief given by reference to shares issued to any person shall be made by reason of any event occurring after his death.][1]

Provision of information

[**5**—(1) Where an event occurs by reason of which any relief under this Part of this Schedule falls to be withdrawn or reduced, the individual to whom the relief was given shall, within 60 days of his coming to know of the event, give a notice to the inspector containing particulars of the event.

(2) If the inspector has reason to believe that a person has not given a notice which he is required to give under sub-paragraph (1) above in respect of any event, the inspector may by notice require that person to furnish him within such time (not being less than 60 days) as may be specified in the notice with such information relating to the event as the inspector may reasonably require for the purposes of this Part of this Schedule.

(3) No obligation as to secrecy imposed by statute or otherwise shall preclude the inspector from disclosing to a venture capital trust that relief given by reference to a particular number or proportion of its shares has been given or claimed under this Part of this Schedule.][1]

Interpretation of Part I

[**6**—(1) In this Part of this Schedule "eligible shares", in relation to a company which is a venture capital trust, means new ordinary shares in that trust which, throughout the period of [three][3] years beginning with the date on which they are issued, carry no present or future preferential right to dividends or to a company's assets on its winding up and no present or future ...[2] right to be redeemed.

(2) In this Part of this Schedule "ordinary shares", in relation to a company, means shares forming part of a company's ordinary share capital.

(3) In this Part of this Schedule references to a disposal of shares shall include references to a disposal of an interest or right in or over the shares.][1]

PART II

RELIEF ON DISTRIBUTIONS

[**7**—(1) A relevant distribution of a venture capital trust shall not be regarded as income for any income tax purposes if the person beneficially entitled to it is a qualifying investor.

(2) For the purposes of this paragraph a person is a qualifying investor, in relation to any distribution, if he is an individual who has attained the age of eighteen years and is beneficially entitled to the distribution—

(*a*) as the person who himself holds the shares in respect of which the distribution is made, or
(*b*) as a person with such a beneficial entitlement to the shares as derives from their being held for him, or for his benefit, by a nominee of his.

(3) In this paragraph "relevant distribution", in relation to a company which is a venture capital trust, means any distribution which—

(a) consists in a dividend (including a capital dividend) which is paid in respect of any ordinary shares in that company which—

(i) were acquired by the person to whom the distribution is made at a time when the company was such a trust,

[(ia) were so acquired for bona fide commercial purposes and not as part of a scheme or arrangement the main purpose of which, or one of the main purposes of which, is the avoidance of tax,]² and

(ii) are not shares acquired in excess of the permitted maximum for any year of assessment; and

(b) is not a dividend paid in respect of profits or gains arising or accruing in any accounting period ending at a time when the company was not such a trust.]¹

Commentary—*Simon's Direct Tax Service* E3.643.
Definitions—"Accounting date", s 834(1); "nominee", Sch 15B para 9; "permitted maximum", Sch 15B para 8; "profits or gains", s 833(1); "venture capital trust", s 842AA(1); "year of assessment", s 832(1).
Cross references—Venture Capital Trust Regulations, SI 1995/1979 regs 10–15 (requirement for an enduring declaration in respect of relevant shares for relief from income tax on distributions by a trust company on those shares).
Venture Capital Trust Regulations, SI 1995/1979 regs 10, 16–18 (relief from income tax on distributions by a trust company to be dependent on appropriate claims being made by the company).
Amendments—¹ This Schedule inserted by FA 1995 s 71(2) with effect from the year 1995–96.
² Words in sub-para 3(a) inserted by FA 1999 s 70 with effect for shares acquired after 8 March 1999.

Meaning of "permitted maximum"

[8—(1) For the purposes of this Part of this Schedule shares in a venture capital trust shall be treated, in relation to any individual, as acquired in excess of the permitted maximum for any year of assessment to the extent that the value of the shares comprised in the relevant acquisitions of that individual for that year exceeds £100,000.

(2) The reference in sub-paragraph (1) above to the relevant acquisitions of an individual for a year of assessment is a reference to all shares which—

(a) are acquired in that year of assessment by that individual or any nominee of his;

(b) are ordinary shares in a company which is a venture capital trust at the time of their acquisition; and

(c) are shares so acquired for bona fide commercial purposes and not as part of a scheme or arrangement the main purpose of which, or one of the main purposes of which, is the avoidance of tax.

(3) Sub-paragraph (4) below applies where—

(a) any ordinary shares in a venture capital trust ("the new shares") are acquired by any individual in circumstances in which they are required for the purposes of the 1992 Act to be treated as the same assets as any other shares; and

(b) the other shares consist of or include any ordinary shares in a venture capital trust that were, or are treated as, acquired otherwise than in excess of the permitted maximum for any year of assessment.

(4) Where this sub-paragraph applies—

(a) the value of the new shares shall be disregarded in determining whether any other shares acquired in the same year of assessment as the new shares are acquired in excess of the permitted maximum for that year; and

(b) the new shares or, as the case may be, an appropriate proportion of them shall be treated as themselves acquired otherwise than in excess of the permitted maximum.

(5) For the purposes of this paragraph the value of any shares acquired by or on behalf of any individual shall be taken to be their market value (within the meaning of the 1992 Act) at the time of their acquisition.

(6) Where any shares in a venture capital trust are acquired in excess of the permitted maximum for any year of assessment, the shares representing the excess shall be identified for the purposes of this Part of this Schedule—

(a) by treating shares acquired later in the year as comprised in the excess before those acquired earlier in the year;

(b) by treating shares of different descriptions acquired on the same day as acquired within the permitted maximum in the same proportions as are borne by the respective values of the shares comprised in the acquisitions of each description to the total value of all the shares in the trust acquired on that day; and

(c) by applying the rules in section 151A(4) and (5) of the 1992 Act for determining the shares to which any disposal of shares in the trust relates (even one which is not a disposal for the purposes of that Act).]¹

Commentary—*Simon's Direct Tax Service* E3.643.
Definitions—"The 1992 Act", s 831(3); "ordinary shares", Sch 15B para 9; "permitted maximum", Sch 15B para 8; "venture capital trust", s 842AA(1); "year of assessment", s 832(1); "tax", s 832(3).
Amendments—¹ This Schedule inserted by FA 1995 s 71(2) with effect from the year 1995–96.

Interpretation of Part II

[**9**—(1) In this Part of this Schedule "ordinary shares", in relation to a company, means shares forming part of the company's ordinary share capital.

(2) In this Part of this Schedule "nominee", in relation to any individual, includes the trustees of a bare trust of which that individual is the only beneficiary.]¹

Commentary—*Simon's Direct Tax Service* E3.643.
Amendments—¹ This Schedule inserted by FA 1995 s 71(2) with effect from the year 1995–96.

SCHEDULE 16

COLLECTION OF INCOME TAX ON COMPANY PAYMENTS WHICH ARE NOT DISTRIBUTIONS

Section 350(4)

Cross references—See TMA 1970 s 55 (postponement of tax pending an appeal against an assessment under this Schedule, other than an assessment for tax the time for payment of which is given by paras 4(1) or 9).
TA 1988 s 339(4), (7) ("relevant payment" for the purposes of this Schedule includes qualifying donation to charity).
TA 1988 s 480A (application of this Schedule with modifications in relation to interest payments by deposit–takers).
TA 1988 s 737(1), (1A), (2), (7A) (manufactured dividends: treatment of tax deemed to be deducted at the lower rate).
TA 1988 Sch 16 para 11 (Board's powers for recovery of tax under this Schedule).
TA 1988 Sch 23A para 3(7) (manufactured interest on UK securities).
IT (Building Societies) (Dividends and Interest) Regulations, SI 1990/2231 reg 10 (modification of this Schedule in relation to certain payments by building societies).
Gilt-edged Securities (Tax on Interest) Regulations, SI 1995/3224 reg 4(2) (a return made by a person receiving payments of interest on gilt-edged securities without deduction of tax may be combined with a return under this Schedule).
Manufactured Interest (Tax) Regulation, SI 1997/992 reg 3 (this Schedule to apply with appropriate modification to payments interest in relation to which recipient must account for tax under TA 1988 Sch 23A para 3(5)).

Interpretation

1 In this Schedule "relevant payment" means any payment to which section 350(4)(*a*) applies.

Commentary—*Simon's Direct Tax Service* D1.615.

Duty to make returns

2—(1) A company shall for each of its accounting periods make, in accordance with this Schedule, returns to the collector of the relevant payments made by it in that period and of the income tax for which it is accountable in respect of those payments.

(2) A return shall be made for—

(*a*) each complete quarter falling within the accounting period, that is to say, each of the periods of three months ending with 31st March, 30th June, 30th September and 31st December which falls within that period;

(*b*) each part of the accounting period which is not a complete quarter and ends on the first (or only), or begins immediately after the last (or only), of those dates which falls within the accounting period;

(*c*) if none of those dates falls within the accounting period, the whole accounting period.

(3) A return for any period for which a return is required to be made under this paragraph shall be made within 14 days from the end of that period.

Commentary—*Simon's Direct Tax Service* D1.615.
Definitions—"Accounting period", s 834(1); "company", s 832(1), (2).
Cross references—See TA 1988 Sch 16 para 5 (claim for set-off of tax deducted at source against tax under this Schedule to be included in a return under this paragraph).
IT (Building Societies) (Dividends and Interest) Regulations, SI 1990/2231 reg 10 (modifications of sub-para (2) above for the purpose of its application to building societies);
IT (Building Societies) (Annual Payments) Regulations, SI 1991/512 reg 3(2)(*b*) (modifications of sub-para (2) above for the purpose of its application to building societies);
FA 1991 Sch 11 para 3(1) (modifications of sub-para (2) above for the purpose of its application to building societies).

Contents of returns

3 The return made by a company for any period shall show—

(*a*) the amount of any relevant payments made by the company in that period; and

(*b*) the income tax in respect of those payments for which the company is accountable.

Commentary—*Simon's Direct Tax Service* D1.615.
Definitions—"Company", s 832(1), (2); "income tax", s 832(4).
Cross references—See the IT (Manufactured Interest) Regulations, SI 1992/2074 regs 3(*b*), (*d*), 7, 13, 14(1), (4), (5)(*a*) (revoked) (modifications of this paragraph where a return includes information relating to manufactured interest in respect of UK securities).

Payment of tax

4—(1) . . .² income tax in respect of any payment required to be included in a return under this Schedule shall be due at the time by which the return is to be made, and income tax so due—

(a) shall be payable by the company without the making of any assessment; and

(b) may be assessed on the company (whether or not it has been paid when the assessment is made) if it, or any part of it, is not paid on or before the due date.

(2) If it appears to [an officer of the Board]¹ that there is a relevant payment which ought to have been and has not been included in a return, [or if an officer of the Board is of the opinion that a return is incorrect, any such officer may]¹ make an assessment on the company to the best of his judgment; and any income tax due under an assessment made by virtue of this sub-paragraph shall be treated for the purposes of interest on unpaid tax as having been payable at the time when it would have been payable if a correct return had been made.

[(3) . . .²

Commentary—*Simon's Direct Tax Service* **D1.616.**
Definitions—"The Board", s 832(1); "company", s 832(1), (2); "interest", s 832(1); "qualifying distribution", ss 14(2), 832(1).
Cross references—See TA 1988 Sch 16 para 10 (assessments, appeals and due date for payment of tax under this Schedule).
Gilt-edged Securities (Tax on Interest) Regulations, SI 1995/3224 reg 10 (subject to any claim under para 5 below, excess gilt interest received may be set against a liability to pay income tax under this Schedule).
Amendments—¹ Words in sub-para (2) substituted for words "the inspector" and "or if the inspector is dissatisfied with any return, he may" by FA 1996 s 137, Sch 23 para 11 with effect as respects return periods (as defined in FA 1996 s 137(3)) ending on or after the appointed day under FA 1994 s 199 (1 July 1999 by virtue of the Finance Act 1994, Section 199, (Appointed Day) Order, SI 1998/3173).
² Words in sub-para (1), and sub-para (3), repealed by FA 1999 ss 91(2), (5), 139, Sch 20 Pt III(19) with effect for periods for which a return is required under TA 1988 Sch 16 para 2 beginning after 5 April 1999; and for accounting periods beginning after that date.

Set-off of income tax borne on company income against tax payable

5—(1) Where in any accounting period a company receives any payment on which it bears income tax by deduction the company may claim to have the income tax thereon set against any income tax which it is liable to pay under this Schedule in respect of payments made by it in that period.

(2) Any such claim shall be included in a return made under paragraph 2 above for the accounting period in question and (where necessary) income tax paid by the company under this Schedule for that accounting period and before the claim is allowed shall be repaid accordingly.

Commentary—*Simon's Direct Tax Service* **D1.616.**
Definitions—"Accounting period", s 834(1); "company", s 832(1), (2).
Cross references—See TA 1988 s 480A(3), (4) (modification of this paragraph in its application to deposits received by deposit–takers).
TA 1988 s 687A(3)(a) (sub-para (1) above not to apply in the case of a payment by a discretionary trust to a company after 1 July 1997).
TA 1988 Sch 16 para 6 (effect of a claim under this paragraph on proceedings for collecting tax).
TA 1988 Sch 16 para 7 (avoidance of double relief under this paragraph and s 7(2)).
IT (Building Societies) (Dividends and Interest) Regulations, SI 1990/2231 reg 10 (collection of income tax from building societies);
IT (Building Societies) (Annual Payments) Regulations, SI 1991/512 reg 3(2)(c) (this paragraph to have effect in relation to certain payments received by building societies);
FA 1991 Sch 11 para 4 (avoidance of double claims to relief in respect of the same deduction by a building society).
IT (Manufactured Interest) Regulations, SI 1992/2074 reg 14 (revoked) (modification of this para in relation to certain payments of manufactured dividends by non-resident corporate market makers).

6—(1) Where a claim has been made under paragraph 5 above no proceedings for collecting tax which would fall to be discharged if the claim were allowed shall be instituted pending the final determination of the claim, but this sub-paragraph shall not affect the date when the tax is due.

(2) When the claim is finally determined any tax underpaid in consequence of sub-paragraph (1) above shall be paid.

(3) Where proceedings are instituted for collecting tax assessed, or interest on tax assessed, under any provision of paragraph 4 above, effect shall not be given to any claim made after the institution of the proceedings so as to affect or delay the collection or recovery of the tax charged by the assessment or of interest thereon, until the claim has been finally determined.

(4) When the claim is finally determined any tax overpaid in consequence of sub-paragraph (3) above shall be repaid.

(5) References in this paragraph to proceedings for the collection of tax include references to proceedings by way of distraint or poinding for tax.

Commentary—*Simon's Direct Tax Service* **D1.618.**
Definition—"Interest", s 832(1).
Prospective amendments—In sub-s (5) words "or poinding" repealed by the Abolition of Poindings and Warrant Sales Act 2001 s 3(1), Schedule, Pt 2 with effect from 31 December 2002 or such earlier date as the Scottish Ministers may by statutory instrument appoint.

7 Income tax set against other tax under paragraph 5 above shall be treated as paid or repaid, as the case may be, and the same tax shall not be taken into account both under this Schedule and under section 7(2).

Commentary—*Simon's Direct Tax Service* **D1.616.**
Cross references—See TA 1988 s 480A(3) (modification of this paragraph in its application to interest payments by deposit–takers).
IT (Manufactured Interest) Regulations, SI 1992/2074 reg 14 (revoked) (modification of this para in relation to certain payments of manufactured dividends by non-resident corporate market makers).

[Amended return where company becomes aware of an error]1

[7A—(1) If a company becomes aware—

(a) that anything which ought to have been included in a return made by it under this Schedule for any period has not been so included,

(b) that anything which ought not to have been included in a return made by it under this Schedule for any period has been so included, or

(c) that any other error has occurred in a return made by it under this Schedule for any period,

it shall forthwith supply to the collector an amended return for that period.

(2) The duty imposed by sub-paragraph (1) above is without prejudice to any duty that may also arise under paragraph 7A of Schedule 13.

(3) Where an amended return is supplied under this paragraph, all such assessments, adjustments, set-offs or payments or repayments of tax shall be made as may be required for securing that the resulting liabilities to tax (including interest on unpaid or overpaid tax) whether of the company or of any other person are the same as they would have been if a correct return had been made.]1

Definitions—"Collector", s 832(1); "company", s 832(1), (2); "tax", s 832(3).
Amendments—1 This paragraph inserted by FA 1996 s 137, Sch 23 para 12 with effect as respects return periods (as defined in FA 1996 s 137(3)) ending on or after the appointed day under FA 1994 s 199 (1 July 1999 by virtue of the Finance Act 1994, Section 199, (Appointed Day) Order, SI 1998/3173).

Items included in error

8 Where any item has been included in a return or claim under this Schedule as a relevant payment but [should not have been so included]2, [an officer of the Board]1 may make such assessments, adjustments or set-offs as may be required for securing that the resulting liabilities to tax (including interest on unpaid tax) whether of the company or of any other person are the same as they would have been if the item had [not been included in the return or claim in question]2.

Commentary—*Simon's Direct Tax Service* **D1.618.**
Definitions—"The Board", s 832(1); "company", s 832(1), (2); "interest", s 832(1).
Amendments—1 Words substituted for words "the inspector" by FA 1996 s 137, Sch 23 para 13 with effect as respects return periods (as defined in FA 1996 s 137(3)) ending on or after the appointed day under FA 1994 s 199 (1 July 1999 by virtue of the Finance Act 1994, Section 199, (Appointed Day) Order, SI 1998/3173).
2Words in para 8 substituted for words "should have been included in a return under Schedule 13" and "been included in the right return" respectively by FA 1999 s 91 (3), (5) with effect for periods for which a return is required under TA 1988 Sch 16 para 2 beginning after 5 April 1999; and for accounting periods beginning after that date

Relevant payment made otherwise than in accounting period

9 Where a company makes a relevant payment on a date which does not fall within an accounting period the company shall make a return of that payment within 14 days from that date, and the income tax for which the company is accountable in respect of that payment shall be due at the time by which the return is to be made.

Commentary—*Simon's Direct Tax Service* **D1.602.**
Definitions—"Accounting period", s 834(1); "company", s 832(1), (2).
Cross references—See TA 1988 Sch 16 para 10 (assessments, appeals and due date for payment of tax under this Schedule).
TA 1988 Sch 16 para 11 (treatment of an assessment under this paragraph for the purposes of para 10(1)).

Assessments and due date of tax

10—(1) All the provisions of the Income Tax Acts as to the time within which an assessment may be made, so far as they refer or relate to the year of assessment for which an assessment is made, or the year to which an assessment relates, shall apply in relation to any assessment under this Schedule notwithstanding that, under this Schedule, the assessment may be said to relate to a quarter or other period which is not a year of assessment, and the provisions of [section 36]1 of the Management Act as to the circumstances in which an assessment may be made out of time shall apply accordingly on the footing that any such assessment relates to the year of assessment in which the quarter or other period ends.

(2) Income tax assessed on a company under this Schedule shall be due within 14 days after the issue of the notice of assessment (unless due earlier under paragraph 4(1) or 9 above).

(3) Sub-paragraph (2) above has effect subject to any appeal against the assessment, but no such appeal shall affect the date when tax is due under paragraph 4(1) or 9 above.

(4) On the determination of an appeal against an assessment under this Schedule any tax overpaid shall be repaid.

(5) Any tax assessable under any one or more of the provisions of this Schedule may be included in one assessment if the tax so included is all due on the same date.

Commentary—*Simon's Direct Tax Service* **D1.616, 618.**
Definitions—''The Income Tax Acts'', s 831(1)(*b*); ''the Management Act'', s 831(3); ''notice'', s 832(1); ''year of assessment'', s 832(1).
Amendments—¹ Words in sub-para (1) substituted by FA 1989 s 149(3)(*d*).

Saving

11 Nothing in paragraphs 1 to 10 above shall be taken to prejudice any powers conferred by the Income Tax Acts for the recovery of income tax by means of an assessment or otherwise; and any assessment in respect of tax payable under paragraph 9 above shall be treated for the purposes of the provisions mentioned in paragraph 10(1) above as relating to the year of assessment in which the payment is made.

Commentary—*Simon's Direct Tax Service* **D1.618.**
Definitions—''The Income Tax Acts'', s 831(1)(*b*); ''year of assessment'', s 832(1).

SCHEDULE 17

DUAL RESIDENT INVESTING COMPANIES

Section 404

Commentary—*Simon's Direct Tax Service* **D4.133.**
Cross references—See TA 1988 Sch 17 para 8(2) (references in this Schedule to ''this Chapter'' not to include any provision of this Schedule).

PART I

DIVISION OF ACCOUNTING PERIODS COVERING 1ST APRIL 1987

Cross references—See TA 1988 Sch 17 para 8(1) (this Part to have priority over s 409).

1—(1) This Part of this Schedule has effect in the circumstances set out in section 404(3)(*a*).

(2) In this Part of this Schedule—

    (*a*) ''the straddling period'' means the accounting period of the dual resident investing company which begins before and ends on or after 1st April 1987; and

    (*b*) ''dual resident investing company'' has the same meaning as in section 404.

(3) It shall be assumed for the purposes of this Chapter (except section 404(3) to (6)) and Part II of this Schedule—

    (*a*) that an accounting period of the company ends on 31st March 1987; and

    (*b*) that a new accounting period begins on 1st April 1987, the new accounting period to end with the end of the straddling period.

(4) In this Part of this Schedule ''the component accounting periods'' means the two accounting periods referred to in sub-paragraph (3) above.

Definitions—''Accounting period'', s 834(1); ''company'', s 413(5).
Cross references—See TA 1988 Sch 17 para 2 (apportionment for the purposes of sub-para (3) above of losses etc of the straddling period).
TA 1988 Sch 17 para 3 (apportionment for the purposes of sub-para (3) above of excess of charges on income paid in the straddling period).

2 Subject to paragraph 5 below, for the purposes referred to in paragraph 1(3) above, the losses and other amounts of the straddling period of a dual resident investing company, excluding any such excess of charges on income as is referred to in section 403(7), shall be apportioned to the component accounting periods on a time basis according to their lengths.

Definitions—''Accounting period'', s 834(1); ''company'', s 413(5).

3 If, in the straddling period of a dual resident investing company, the company has paid any amount by way of charges on income, then, for the purposes referred to in paragraph 1(3) above, the excess of that amount referred to in section 403(7) shall be apportioned to the component accounting periods—

    (*a*) according to the dates on which, subject to paragraph 6 below, the interest or other payments giving rise to those charges were paid (or were treated as paid for the purposes of section 338); and

    (*b*) in proportion to the amounts of interest or other payments paid (or treated as paid) on those dates.

Definitions—''Accounting period'', s 834(1); ''company'', s 413(5); ''interest'', s 832(1).

PART II
EARLY PAYMENTS OF INTEREST ETC AND CHARGES ON INCOME

Cross references—See TA 1988 Sch 17 paras 1(3), 2 (for the purposes of this Part, certain assumptions apply as respects a company's accounting period).
TA 1988 Sch 17 para 8(1) (this Part to have priority over s 409).

Interpretation

4 In this Part of this Schedule—

    (*a*) a "1986 accounting period" means an accounting period which begins or ends (or begins and ends) in the financial year 1986;

    (*b*) a "post-1986 accounting period" means an accounting period which begins on or after 1st April 1987; and

    (*c*) "dual resident investing company" has the same meaning as in section 404.

Definitions—"Accounting period", s 834(1); "the financial year 1986", s 834(1).

Early payment of interest etc

5—(1) If the conditions in sub-paragraph (2) or (3) below are fulfilled and if the Board so direct, this paragraph applies in relation to a 1986 accounting period of a dual resident investing company.

(2) The conditions in this sub-paragraph are applicable only if the company is carrying on a trade in the 1986 accounting period, and those conditions are—

    (*a*) that in that accounting period the company has incurred a loss, computed as for the purposes of section 393(2), in carrying on that trade; and

    (*b*) that in that period the company has made a payment falling within section 404(6)(*a*)(iii); and

    (*c*) that the payment referred to in paragraph (*b*) above either did not fall due in that period or would not have fallen due in that period but for the making, on or after 5th December 1986, of arrangements varying the due date for payment.

(3) The conditions in this sub-paragraph are applicable only if the company is an investment company in the 1986 accounting period, and those conditions are—

    (*a*) that for that accounting period the company has (apart from this paragraph) such an excess as is referred to in section 403(4); and

    (*b*) that one or more of the sums which for that accounting period may be deducted as expenses of management under section 75(1) either did not fall due in that period or would not have fallen due in that period but for the making, on or after 5th December 1986, of arrangements varying the due date for payment.

(4) The Board shall not give a direction under this paragraph with respect to a 1986 accounting period of a dual resident investing company unless it appears to the Board that the sole or main benefit that might be expected to accrue from the early payment or, as the case may be, from the arrangements was that (apart from this paragraph) the company would, for that period, have an amount or, as the case may be, a larger amount available for surrender by way of group relief.

(5) If this paragraph applies in relation to a 1986 accounting period of a dual resident investing company which is carrying on a trade then, for the purposes of this Chapter and, where appropriate, any apportionment under paragraph 2 above—

    (*a*) the loss (if any) of the company for that period shall be computed (as mentioned in section 403(1)) as if any payment falling within sub-paragraph (2)(*b*) above had not been made in that period; and

    (*b*) the loss (if any) of the company for its first post-1986 accounting period shall be computed as if any such payment were made in that period.

(6) If this paragraph applies in relation to a 1986 accounting period of a dual resident investing company which is an investment company, then, for the purposes referred to in sub-paragraph (5) above—

    (*a*) the amount which may be deducted as expenses of management for that period, as mentioned in section 403(4), shall be computed as if any sum falling within sub-paragraph (3)(*b*) above had not been disbursed; and

    (*b*) the amount which may be so deducted as expenses of management for the first of the company's post-1986 accounting periods shall be computed as if any such sum were disbursed in that period.

Definitions—"Accounting period", s 834(1); "apportionment", s 834(4); "the Board", s 832(1); "company", s 413(5); "group relief", ss 402(1), 413(2); "trade", s 6(4).
Cross references—See TA 1988 Sch 17 para 7 (company's rights to a notice of a direction given under this paragraph and appeal against such direction).

Early payment of charges on income

6—(1) If, in the case of a dual resident investing company, either of the following conditions is fulfilled—

(*a*) that any interest or other payment which is, or is treated as, a charge on income falls due in a post-1986 accounting period but is paid (or treated for the purposes of section 338 as paid) in a 1986 accounting period, or

(*b*) that, on or after 5th December 1986, arrangements have been made such that any such interest or other payment which, but for the arrangements, would have fallen due in a post-1986 accounting period, fell due in a 1986 accounting period,

the interest or other payment shall, if the Board so direct, be treated for the purposes of this Chapter and, where appropriate, paragraph 3 above as paid in the post-1986 accounting period referred to in paragraph (*a*) or, as the case may be, paragraph (*b*) above.

(2) The Board shall not give a direction under this paragraph unless it appears to them that the sole or main benefit that might be expected to accrue from the early payment or, as the case may be, from the arrangements was that (apart from the direction) the interest or other payment would be attributed or apportioned to a 1986 accounting period rather than a post-1986 accounting period, so that, for the 1986 accounting period, the dual resident investing company would have an amount or, as the case may be, a larger amount available for surrender by way of group relief.

Definitions—"Accounting period", s 834(1); "the Board", s 832(1); "company", s 413(5); "group relief", ss 402(1), 413(2); "interest", s 832(1).
Cross references—See TA 1988 Sch 17 para 7 (company's rights to a notice of a direction given under this paragraph and appeal against such direction).

Appeals

7 Notice of the giving of a direction under paragraph 5 or 6 above shall be given to the dual resident investing company concerned; and any company to which such a notice is given may, by giving notice of appeal to the Board within 60 days of the date of the notice given to the company, appeal to the Special Commissioners against the direction on either or both of the following grounds—

(*a*) that the conditions applicable to the company under paragraph 5(2) or (3) above are not fulfilled or, as the case may be, that neither of the conditions in paragraph 6(1) above is fulfilled;

(*b*) that the sole or main benefit that might be expected to accrue from the early payment or, as the case may be, the arrangements was not that stated in paragraph 5(4) or, as the case may be, paragraph 6(2) above.

Definitions—"The Board", s 832(1); "company", s 413(5); "notice", s 832(1).

PART III
GENERAL

8—(1) Parts I and II of this Schedule have effect in priority to section 409 and, accordingly, each of the component accounting periods resulting from the operation of Part I of this Schedule shall be regarded as a true accounting period for the purposes of that section.

(2) References in this Schedule to this Chapter do not include any provision of this Schedule.

Definition—"Accounting period", s 834(1).

[SCHEDULE 17A

GROUP RELIEF: CLAIMS][1]

Section 412

Commentary—*Simon's Direct Tax Service* **D2.629, 631.**
Amendments—[1] This Schedule repealed by FA 1998 s 165, Sch 27 Part III(28) with effect in relation to accounting periods ending after 30 June 1999 (by virtue of Finance Act 1994, Section 199, (Appointed Day) Order, SI 1998/3173 art 2). For the text of this Schedule, see *Butterworths Yellow Tax Handbook*, 1998–99, 38th edition.

SCHEDULE 18

GROUP RELIEF: EQUITY HOLDERS AND PROFITS OR ASSETS AVAILABLE FOR DISTRIBUTION

Section 413(10)

Commentary—*Simon's Direct Tax Service* **D2.635.**
Revenue Internal Guidance—Company Taxation Manual COT2730–2750 (explanation of Sch 18 with worked examples).
Cross references—See TA 1988 s 240(13) (application of this Schedule with modifications for determining whether a company is a subsidiary for the purposes of set–off of surplus ACT).
TA 1988 s 247(9A) (extension of the application of this Schedule to s 247 (dividends, etc paid by one member of a group to another).
TA 1988 s 769(6C) (this Schedule to apply also for the purposes of s 769(6B) (change in ownership of company)).
TCGA 1992 s 170(8) (this Schedule to apply with certain modifications for the purposes of TCGA 1992 s 170(6), (7) (definitions of groups of companies));
TCGA 1992 s 228(10) (this Schedule to apply with modifications in respect of roll-over relief for dispersal after 19 March 1990 of shares to trustees of employee share ownership trusts).

Corporation Tax (Treatment of Unrelieved Surplus Advance Corporation Tax) Regulations, SI 1999/358 reg 6(7) (this Schedule to apply with modifications for the purposes of defining ''group'' in relation to the shadow ACT rules).

1—(1) For the purposes of [sections 403C and 413(7)]⁵ and this Schedule, an equity holder of a company is any person who—

   (*a*) holds ordinary shares in the company, or

   (*b*) is a loan creditor of the company in respect of a loan which is not a normal commercial loan,

and any reference in that section to profits or assets available for distribution to a company's equity holders does not include a reference to any profits or assets available for distribution to any equity holder otherwise than as an equity holder.

(2) For the purposes of sub-paragraph (1)(*a*) above ''ordinary shares'' means all shares other than fixed-rate preference shares.

(3) In this Schedule ''fixed-rate preference shares'' means shares which—

   (*a*) are issued for consideration which is or includes new consideration; and

   [(*b*) do not carry any right either to conversion into shares or securities of any other description except—

      (i) shares to which sub-paragraph (5A) below applies,

      (ii) securities to which sub-paragraph (5B) below applies, or

      (iii) shares or securities in the company's quoted parent company,

or to the acquisition of any additional shares or securities;]¹

   (*c*) do not carry any right to dividends other than dividends which—

      (i) are of a fixed amount or at a fixed rate per cent of the nominal value of the shares, and

      (ii) represent no more than a reasonable commercial return on the new consideration received by the company in respect of the issue of the shares; and

   (*d*) on repayment do not carry any rights to an amount exceeding that new consideration except in so far as those rights are reasonably comparable with those general for fixed dividend shares listed [on a recognised stock exchange]⁸.

(4) Subsection (7) of section 417 shall apply for the purposes of sub-paragraph (1)(*b*) above as it applies for the purposes of Part XI, but with the omission of the reference to subsection (9) of that section.

(5) In sub-paragraph (1)(*b*) above ''normal commercial loan'' means a loan of or including new consideration and—

   [(*a*) which does not carry any right either to conversion into shares or securities of any other description except—

      (i) shares to which sub-paragraph (5A) below applies,

      (ii) securities to which sub-paragraph (5B) below applies, or

      (iii) shares or securities in the company's quoted parent company,

or to the acquisition of any additional shares or securities;]¹

   (*b*) which does not entitle that loan creditor to any amount by way of interest which depends to any extent on the results of the company's business or any part of it or on the value of any of the company's assets or which exceeds a reasonable commercial return on the new consideration lent; and

   (*c*) in respect of which the loan creditor is entitled, on repayment, to an amount which either does not exceed the new consideration lent or is reasonably comparable with the amount generally repayable (in respect of an equal amount of new consideration) under the terms of issue of securities listed [on a recognised stock exchange]⁸.

[(5A) This sub-paragraph applies to any shares which—

   (*a*) satisfy the requirements of sub-paragraph (3)(*a*), (*c*) and (*d*) above, and

   (*b*) do not carry any rights either to conversion into shares or securities of any other description, except shares or securities in the company's quoted parent company, or to the acquisition of any additional shares or securities.

(5B) This sub-paragraph applies to any securities representing a loan of or including new consideration and—

   (*a*) which satisfies the requirements of sub-paragraph (5)(*b*) and (*c*) above, and

   (*b*) which does not carry any such rights as are mentioned in sub-paragraph (5A)(*b*) above.

(5C) For the purposes of sub-paragraphs (3) and (5) to (5B) above a company (''the parent company'') is another company's ''quoted parent company'' if and only if—

   (*a*) the other company is a 75 per cent. subsidiary of the parent company,

   (*b*) the parent company is not a 75 per cent. subsidiary of any company, and

   (*c*) the parent company's ordinary shares (or, if its ordinary share capital is divided into two or more classes, its ordinary shares of each class) are [listed]⁴ on a recognised stock exchange or dealt in on the Unlisted Securities Market;

and in this sub-paragraph ''ordinary shares'' means shares forming part of ordinary share capital.

(5D) In the application of sub-paragraphs (3) and (5) to (5B) above in determining for the purposes of sub-paragraph (5C)(*a*) above who are the equity holders of the other company (and, accordingly, whether section 413(7) prevents the other company from being treated as a 75 per cent. subsidiary of the parent company for the purposes of sub-paragraph (5C)(*a*)), it shall be assumed that the parent company is for the purposes of sub-paragraphs (3) and (5) to (5B) above the other company's quoted parent company.]²

[(5E) For the purposes of sub-paragraph (5)(*b*) above, the amount to which the loan creditor is entitled by way of interest—

(*a*) shall not be treated as depending to any extent on the results of the company's business or any part of it by reason only of the fact that the terms of the loan provide for the rate of interest to be reduced in the event of the results of the company's business or any part of it improving[, or for the rate of interest to be increased in the event of the results of the company's business or any part of it deteriorating]⁶, and

(*b*) shall not be treated as depending to any extent on the value of any of the company's assets by reason only of the fact that the terms of the loan provide for the rate of interest to be reduced in the event of the value of any of the company's assets increasing[, or for the rate of interest to be increased in the event of the value of any of the company's assets diminishing]⁶.

(5F) Sub-paragraph (5H) below applies where—

(*a*) a person makes a loan to a company on the basis mentioned in sub-paragraph (5G) below for the purpose of facilitating the acquisition of land, and

(*b*) none of the land which the loan is used to acquire is acquired with a view to resale at a profit.

(5G) The basis referred to above is that—

(*a*) the whole of the loan is to be applied in the acquisition of land by the company or in meeting the incidental costs of obtaining the loan,

(*b*) the payment of any amount due in connection with the loan to the person making it is to be secured on the land which the loan is to be used to acquire, and

(*c*) no other security is to be required for the payment of any such amount.

(5H) For the purposes of sub-paragraph (5)(*b*) above, the amount to which the loan creditor is entitled by way of interest shall not be treated as depending to any extent on the value of any of the company's assets by reason only of the fact that the terms of the loan are such that the only way the loan creditor can enforce payment of an amount due is by exercising rights granted by way of security over the land which the loan is used to acquire.

(5I) In sub-paragraph (5G)(*a*) above the reference to the incidental costs of obtaining the loan is to any expenditure on fees, commissions, advertising, printing or other incidental matters wholly and exclusively incurred for the purpose of obtaining the loan or of providing security for it.]³

(6) Notwithstanding anything in sub-paragraphs (1) [to (5D)]² above but subject to sub-paragraph (7) below, where—

(*a*) any person has, directly or indirectly, provided new consideration for any shares or securities in the company, and

(*b*) that person, or any person connected with him, uses for the purposes of his trade assets which belong to the company and in respect of which there is made to the company—

(i) a first-year allowance within the meaning of [Part 2 of the Capital Allowances Act]⁹ in respect of expenditure incurred by the company on the provision of [plant or machinery]⁹;

(ii) a writing-down allowance within the meaning of [Part 2 of the Capital Allowances Act]⁹ in respect of expenditure incurred by the company on the provision of [plant or machinery]⁹; or

(iii) an allowance under [Chapter 3 of Part 6 of the Capital Allowances Act]⁹ in respect of expenditure incurred by the company on [research and development (within the meaning of [Part 6]⁹of that Act)]⁷;

then, for the purposes of this Schedule, that person, and no other, shall be treated as being an equity holder in respect of those shares or securities and as being beneficially entitled to any distribution of profits or assets attributable to those shares or securities.

(7) In any case where sub-paragraph (6) above applies in relation to a bank in such circumstances that—

(*a*) the only new consideration provided by the bank as mentioned in paragraph (*a*) of that sub-paragraph is provided in the normal course of its banking business by way of a normal commercial loan as defined in sub-paragraph (5) above; and

(*b*) the cost to the company concerned of assets falling within paragraph (*b*) of that sub-paragraph which are used as mentioned in that paragraph by the bank or a person connected with the bank is less than the amount of that new consideration,

references in sub-paragraph (6) above, other than the reference in paragraph (*a*), to shares or securities in the company shall be construed as references to so much only of the loan referred to paragraph (*a*) above as is equal to the cost referred to in paragraph (*b*) above.

(8) In this paragraph "new consideration" has the same meaning as in section 254 and any question whether one person is connected with another shall be determined in accordance with section 839.

Commentary—*Simon's Direct Tax Service* **D2.635.**
Definitions—"The 1990 Act", s 831(3); "company", s 413(5); "distribution", ss 209(2), 832(1); "profits", s 6(4); "research and development", s 837A; "trade", s 6(4).
Cross references—See TA 1988 Sch 18 para 5 (determination of an equity holder's percentage of profits in a distribution or assets in a notional winding–up where his rights in future periods are different to those in the current period).
TA 1988 Sch 18 paras 5A–5E (new definition with effect from 15 November 1991 of share arrangements for group relief).
TA 1988 Sch 18 paras 5A–5E (options to buy and sell shares treated as exercised in certain circumstances).
TCGA 1992 s 170(8) (modification of sub-para (4) above in its application for the purposes of TCGA 1992 s 170 (definitions of groups of companies)),
TCGA 1992 s 228(10) modification of this paragraph in its application to roll-over relief for disposals after 19 March 1990 of shares to trustees of employee share ownership trusts);
TCGA 1992 Sch 11, para 16(4) (in relation to a disposal or exchange after 5 April 1992, the amendments to this paragraph by FA 1991 s 77 to be regarded as always having had effect).
Amendments—[1] Sub-paras (3)(*b*), (5)(*a*) substituted by FA 1989 s 101 and in their application (by virtue of FA 1989 s 138 (now TCGA 1992 s 170) for the purposes of TA 1970 s 272(1D), (1E) (now TCGA 1992 s 170(6), (7)) are deemed to have come into force on 14 March 1989.
[2] Sub-paras (5A)–(5D) inserted, and words in sub-para (6) substituted, by FA 1989 s 101.
[3] Sub-paras (5E)–(5I) inserted by FA 1991 s 77 and are deemed to have come into force on 1 April 1991.
[4] Word in sub-para (5C) substituted by FA 1996 Sch 38 para 6(1), (2)(*k*), (10) with effect in relation to any time falling after 31 March 1996.
[5] Words in sub-para (1) substituted by FA 2000 s 100(4)(*a*), (5) and deemed always to have had effect.
[6] Words in sub-para (5E) inserted by FA 2000 s 86(2) with effect for the purposes of determining whether, at any time after 20 March 2000, a loan is a normal commercial loan for the purposes of TA 1988 Sch 18 para 1(1)(*b*).
[7] Words in sub-para (6)(*b*)(iii) substituted by FA 2000 s 68, Sch 19 para 6 with effect for the purposes of income tax and capital gains tax from the year 2000–01 and for the purposes of corporation tax, for accounting periods ending after 31 March 2000.
[8] Words in sub-paras (3)(*d*) and (5)(*c*) substituted by FA 2000 s 97, Sch 27 paras 5(1), (2), 6(1), (3) with effect for the application of TA 1988 Sch 18, for any purpose, after 31 March 2000. This amendment does not have effect for any determination as to whether the qualifying conditions for the purposes of TA 1988 s 403A(9) were met at any time before 1 April 2000.
[9] Words in sub-para (6) substituted by CAA 2001 s 578, Sch 2 para 63 with effect for income tax purposes, as respects allowances and charges falling to be made for chargeable periods ending after 5 April 2001, and for corporation tax purposes, as respects allowances and charges falling to be made for chargeable periods ending after 31 March 2001.

2—(1) Subject to the following provisions of this Schedule, for the purposes of [sections 403C and 413(7)][1] the percentage to which one company is beneficially entitled of any profits available for distribution to the equity holders of another company means the percentage to which the first company would be so entitled in the relevant accounting period on a distribution in money to those equity holders of—

(*a*) an amount of profits equal to the total profits of the other company which arise in that accounting period (whether or not any of those profits are in fact distributed); or

(*b*) if there are no profits of the other company in that accounting period, profits of £100;

and in the following provisions of this Schedule that distribution is referred to as "the profit distribution".

[(1A) The total profits of a non-resident company arising in an accounting period shall be determined for the purposes of sub-paragraph (1)(*a*) above as if it were resident in the United Kingdom in that accounting period.][2]

(2) For the purposes of the profit distribution, it shall be assumed that no payment is made by way of repayment of share capital or of the principal secured by any loan unless that payment is a distribution.

(3) Subject to sub-paragraph (2) above, where an equity holder is entitled to such a payment of any description which, apart from this sub-paragraph, would not be treated as a distribution, it shall nevertheless be treated as an amount to which he is entitled on the profit distribution.

Commentary—*Simon's Direct Tax Service* **D2.635.**
Definitions—"Accounting period", s 834(1); "company", s 413(5); "distribution", ss 209(2), 832(1); "profits", s 6(4); "relevant accounting period", s 413(2).
Cross references—See TA 1988 Sch 18 para 5 (determination of an equity holder's percentage of profits in a distribution or assets in a notional winding–up where his rights in future periods are different to those in the current period).
TA 1988 Sch 18 paras 5A–5E (new definition with effect from 15 November 1991 of share arrangements for group relief).
TA 1988 Sch 18 paras 5A–5E (options to buy and sell shares treated as exercised in certain circumstances).
TCGA 1992 s 228(10) (modification of this paragraph in its application to roll-over relief for disposals after 19 March 1990 of shares to trustees of employee share ownership trusts).
Amendments—[1] Words in sub-para (1) substituted by FA 2000 s 100(4)(*a*), (5) and deemed always to have had effect.
[2] Sub-para (1A) inserted by FA 2000 s 97, Sch 27 paras 5(1), (3), 6(1), (3) with effect for the application of TA 1988 Sch 18, for any purpose, after 31 March 2000. This amendment does not have effect for any determination as to whether the qualifying conditions for the purposes of TA 1988 s 403A(9) were met at any time before 1 April 2000.

3—(1) Subject to the following provisions of this Schedule, for the purposes of [sections 403C and 413(7)][1] the percentage to which one company would be beneficially entitled of any assets of another company available for distribution to its equity holders on a winding-up means the percentage to which the first company would be so entitled if the other company were to be wound up and on that winding-up the value of the assets available for distribution to its equity holders (that is to say, after deducting any liabilities to other persons) were equal to—

(*a*) the excess, if any, of the total amount of the assets of the company, as shown in the balance sheet relating to its affairs as at the end of the relevant accounting period, over the total amount of those of its liabilities as so shown which are not liabilities to equity holders as such; or

(*b*) if there is no such excess or if the company's balance sheet is prepared to a date other than the end of the relevant accounting period, £100.

(2) In the following provisions of this Schedule a winding-up on the basis specified in sub-paragraph (1) above is referred to as "the notional winding-up".

(3) If, on the notional winding-up, an equity holder would be entitled as such to an amount of assets of any description which, apart from this sub-paragraph, would not be treated as a distribution of assets, it shall nevertheless be treated, subject to sub-paragraph (4) below, as an amount to which the equity holder is entitled on the distribution of assets on the notional winding up.

(4) If an amount ("the returned amount") which corresponds to the whole or any part of the new consideration provided by an equity holder of a company for any shares or securities in respect of which he is an equity holder is applied by the company, directly or indirectly, in the making of a loan to, or in the acquisition of any shares or securities in, the equity holder or any person connected with him, then, for the purposes of this Schedule—

(a) the total amount referred to in sub-paragraph (1)(a) above shall be taken to be reduced by a sum equal to the returned amount; and

(b) the amount of assets to which the equity holder is beneficially entitled on the notional winding-up shall be taken to be reduced by a sum equal to the returned amount.

(5) In sub-paragraph (4) above "new consideration" has the same meaning as in section 254 and any question whether one person is connected with another shall be determined in accordance with section 839.

Commentary—*Simon's Direct Tax Service* **D2.635.**
Definitions—"Company", s 413(5); "distribution", ss 209(2), 832(1); "relevant accounting period", s 413(2).
Cross references—See TA 1988 Sch 18, para 5 (determination of an equity holder's percentage of profits in a distribution or assets in a notional winding–up where his rights in future periods are different to those in the current period).
TA 1988 Sch 18 paras 5A–5E (new definition with effect from 15 November 1991 of share arrangements for group relief).
TA 1988 Sch 18 paras 5A–5E (options to buy and sell shares treated as exercised in certain circumstances).
TCGA 1992 s 228(10) (modification of this paragraph in its application to roll-over relief for disposals after 19 March 1990 of shares to trustees of employee share ownership trusts).
Amendments—[1] Words in sub-para (1) substituted by FA 2000 s 100(4)(a), (5) and deemed always to have had effect.

4—(1) This paragraph applies if any of the equity holders—

(a) to whom the profit distribution is made, or

(b) who is entitled to participate in the notional winding-up,

holds, as such an equity holder, any shares or securities which carry rights in respect of dividend or interest or assets on a winding-up which are wholly or partly limited by reference to a specified amount or amounts (whether the limitation takes the form of the capital by reference to which a distribution is calculated or operates by reference to an amount of profits or otherwise).

(2) Where this paragraph applies there shall be determined—

(a) the percentage of profits to which, on the profit distribution, the first company referred to in paragraph 2(1) above would be entitled, and

(b) the percentage of assets to which, on the notional winding-up, the first company referred to in paragraph 3(1) above would be entitled,

if, to the extent that they are limited as mentioned in sub-paragraph (1) above, the rights of every equity holder falling within that sub-paragraph (including the first company concerned if it is such an equity holder) had been waived.

(3) If, on the profit distribution, the percentage of profits determined as mentioned in sub-paragraph (2)(a) above is less than the percentage of profits determined under paragraph 2(1) above without regard to that sub-paragraph, the lesser percentage shall be taken for the purposes of [sections 403C and 413(7)][1] to be the percentage of profits to which, on the profit distribution, the first company referred to in paragraph 2(1) above would be entitled as mentioned in that paragraph.

(4) If, on the notional winding-up, the percentage of assets determined as mentioned in sub-paragraph (2)(b) above is less than the percentage of assets determined under paragraph 3(1) above without regard to that sub-paragraph, the lesser percentage shall be taken for the purposes of [sections 403C and 413(7)][1] to be the percentage to which, on the notional winding-up, the first company mentioned in paragraph 3(1) above would be entitled of any assets of the other company available for distribution to its equity holders on a winding-up.

[(5) In determining in a case in which paragraph 5F below applies whether any rights in respect of dividend or interest or assets on a winding-up are limited as mentioned in sub-paragraph (1) above, the limitations so mentioned shall be treated as not including so much of any limitation as has effect as mentioned in sub-paragraph (2) of that paragraph.][2]

Commentary—*Simon's Direct Tax Service* **D2.636.**
Definitions—"Company", s 413(5); "distribution", ss 209(2), 832(1); "interest", s 832(1); "profits", s 6(4).
Cross references—See TA 1988 Sch 18 para 5 (determination of an equity holder's percentage of profits in a distribution or assets in a notional winding–up where his rights in future periods are different to those in the current period).
TA 1988 Sch 18 paras 5A–5E (new definition with effect from 15 November 1991 of share arrangements for group relief).
TA 1988 Sch 18 paras 5A–5E (options to buy and sell shares treated as exercised in certain circumstances).
TCGA 1992 s 228(10) (modification of this paragraph in its application to roll-over relief for disposals after 19 March 1990 of shares to trustees of employee share ownership trusts).
Amendments—[1] Words in sub-paras (3), (4) substituted by FA 2000 s 100(4)(a), (5) and deemed always to have had effect.
[2] Sub-para (5) inserted by FA 2000 s 97, Sch 27 paras 5(1), (4), 6(1), (3) with effect for the application of TA 1988 Sch 18, for any purpose, after 31 March 2000. This amendment does not have effect for any determination as to whether the qualifying conditions for the purposes of TA 1988 s 403A(9) were met at any time before 1 April 2000.

5—(1) This paragraph applies if, at any time in the relevant accounting period, any of the equity holders—

(*a*) to whom the profit distribution is made, or

(*b*) who is entitled to participate in the notional winding-up,

holds, as such an equity holder, any shares or securities which carry rights in respect of dividend or interest or assets on a winding-up which are of such a nature, (as, for example, if any shares will cease to carry a right to a dividend at a future time) that if the profit distribution or the notional winding-up were to take place in a different accounting period the percentage to which, in accordance with paragraphs 1 to 4 above, that equity holder would be entitled of profits on the profit distribution or of assets on the notional winding-up would be different from the percentage determined in the relevant accounting period.

(2) Where this paragraph applies, there shall be determined—

(*a*) the percentage of profits to which, on the profit distribution, the first company referred to in paragraph 2(1) above would be entitled, and

(*b*) the percentage of assets to which, on the notional winding-up, the first company referred to in paragraph 3(1) above would be entitled,

if the rights of the equity holders in the relevant accounting period were the same as they would be in the different accounting period referred to in sub-paragraph (1) above.

(3) If in the relevant accounting period an equity holder holds, as such, any shares or securities in respect of which arrangements exist by virtue of which, in that or any subsequent accounting period, the equity holder's entitlement to profits on the profit distribution or to assets on the notional winding-up could be different as compared with his entitlement if effect were not given to the arrangements, then for the purposes of this paragraph—

(*a*) it shall be assumed that effect would be given to those arrangements in a later accounting period, and

(*b*) those shares or securities shall be treated as though any variation in the equity holder's entitlement to profits or assets resulting from giving effect to the arrangements were the result of the operation of such rights attaching to the share or securities as are referred to in sub-paragraph (1) above.

In this sub-paragraph ''arrangements'' means arrangements of any kind whether in writing or not.

(4) Sub-paragraphs (3) and (4) of paragraph 4 above shall apply for the purposes of this paragraph as they apply for the purposes of that paragraph and, accordingly, references therein to sub-paragraphs (2)(*a*) and (2)(*b*) of that paragraph shall be construed as references to sub-paragraphs (2)(*a*) and (2)(*b*) of this paragraph.

(5) ...[1]

Commentary—*Simon's Direct Tax Service* **D2.636.**
Simon's Tax Cases—*J Sainsbury plc v O'Connor* [1991] STC 318*.
Definitions—''Accounting period'', s 834(1); ''company'', s 413(5); ''distribution'', ss 209(2), 832(1); ''interest'', s 832(1); ''profits'', s 6(4); ''relevant accounting period'', s 413(2).
Cross references—See TA 1988 Sch 18 paras 5A–5E (new definition with effect from 15 November 1991 of share arrangements for group relief).
TA 1988 Sch 18 paras 5A–5E (options to buy and sell shares treated as exercised in certain circumstances).
TCGA 1992 s 170(8) (omission of sub-para (3) of this paragraph in its application for the purposes of TCGA 1992 s 170 (definitions of groups of companies)).
Amendments—[1] Para 5A below substituted for sub-para (5) of this paragraph by F(No 2)A 1992 Sch 6 para 1.

[5A—(1) In a case where paragraphs 4 and 5 above apply, each of the following percentages, namely—

(*a*) the percentage of profits to which, on the profit distribution, the first company referred to in paragraph 2(1) above would be entitled, and

(*b*) the percentage of assets to which, on the notional winding-up, the first company referred to in paragraph 3(1) above would be entitled,

shall be determined on each of the different bases set out in sub-paragraph (2) below.

(2) The bases are—

(*a*) the basis specified in paragraph 4(2) above;

(*b*) the basis specified in paragraph 5(2) above;

(*c*) the basis specified in paragraph 4(2) above and the basis specified in paragraph 5(2) above taken together;

(*d*) the basis specified in paragraph 2(1) or 3(1) above (according to the percentage concerned) without regard to paragraphs 4(2) and 5(2) above.

(3) The lowest of the four percentages of profits so determined shall be taken for the purposes of [sections 403C and 413(7)][2] to be the percentage of profits to which, on the profit distribution, the first company referred to in paragraph 2(1) above would be entitled as mentioned in that paragraph.

(4) The lowest of the four percentages of assets so determined shall be taken for the purposes of [sections 403C and 413(7)][2] to be the percentage to which, on the notional winding-up, the first company mentioned in paragraph 3(1) above would be entitled of any assets of the other company available for distribution to its equity holders on a winding-up.][1]

Commentary—*Simon's Direct Tax Service* **D2.636.**
Definitions—"Company", s 413(5); "distribution", ss 209(2), 832(1); "profits", s 413(5).
Amendments—[1] This paragraph substituted for para 5(5) above by F(No 2)A 1992 Sch 6 para 1 in relation to an accounting period in which a certain event occurs after 14 November 1991; see F(No 2)A 1992 Sch 6 para 6.
[2] Words in sub-paras (3), (4) substituted by FA 2000 s 100(4)(a), (5) and deemed always to have had effect.

[5B—(1) This paragraph applies if, at any time in the relevant accounting period, option arrangements exist; and option arrangements are arrangements of any kind (whether in writing or not) as regards which the two conditions set out below are fulfilled.

(2) The first condition is that the arrangements are ones by virtue of which there could be a variation in—

(*a*) the percentage of profits to which any of the equity holders is entitled on the profit distribution, or

(*b*) the percentage of assets to which any of the equity holders is entitled on the notional winding-up.

(3) The second condition is that, under the arrangements, the variation could result from the exercise of any of the following rights (option rights)—

(*a*) a right to acquire shares or securities in the second company referred to in paragraphs 2(1) and 3(1) above;

(*b*) a right to require a person to acquire shares or securities in that company.

(4) For the purposes of sub-paragraph (3) above—

(*a*) it is immaterial whether or not the shares or securities were issued before the arrangements came into existence;

(*b*) "shares" does not include fixed-rate preference shares;

(*c*) "securities" does not include normal commercial loans (within the meaning given by paragraph 1(5) above);

(*d*) "right" does not include a right of an individual to acquire shares, if the right was obtained by reason of his office or employment as a director or employee of the company and in accordance with the provisions of a share option scheme approved under Schedule 9 at the time it was obtained.

(5) As regards each point in time when option arrangements exist in the relevant accounting period—

(*a*) there shall be taken each possible state of affairs that could then subsist if the outstanding option rights, or any of them or any combination of them, became effective at that point, and

(*b*) taking each such state of affairs, it shall be assumed that the rights and duties of the equity holders in the relevant accounting period were to be found accordingly.

(6) The following rules shall have effect—

(*a*) for the purposes of sub-paragraph (5) above outstanding option rights are all such option rights under the arrangements (or sets of arrangements if more than one) as exist at the point in time concerned but have not become effective at or before that point;

(*b*) for the purpose of applying sub-paragraph (5) above it is immaterial whether or not the rights are exercisable at or before the point in time concerned and it is immaterial whether or not they are capable of becoming effective at or before that point;

(*c*) for the purposes of sub-paragraph (5) above and this sub-paragraph an option right becomes effective when the shares or securities to which it relates are acquired in pursuance of it.

(7) The determination mentioned in sub-paragraph (8) below shall be made as regards each point in time when option arrangements exist in the relevant accounting period; and for each such point in time a separate determination shall be made for each of the possible states of affairs mentioned in sub-paragraph (5) above.

(8) The determination is a determination of—

(*a*) the percentage of profits to which, on the profit distribution, the first company referred to in paragraph 2(1) above would be entitled, and

(*b*) the percentage of assets to which, on the notional winding-up, the first company referred to in paragraph 3(1) above would be entitled,

if the rights and duties of the equity holders in the relevant accounting period were found as mentioned in sub-paragraph (5) above.

(9) Where different determinations yield different percentages of profits and different percentages of assets, only one determination of each percentage (yielding the lowest figure) shall be treated as having been made.

(10) Sub-paragraphs (3) and (4) of paragraph 4 above shall apply for the purposes of this paragraph as they apply for the purposes of that paragraph and, accordingly, references there to sub-paragraphs (2)(*a*) and (2)(*b*) of that paragraph shall be construed as references to sub-paragraphs (8)(*a*) and (8)(*b*) of this paragraph.]¹

Commentary—*Simon's Direct Tax Service* **D2.636.**
Concession C10—Groups of companies: arrangements.
Statement of Practice SP 3/93—Interpretation of the word "arrangements" used in this paragraph.
Definitions—"Company", s 413(5); "distribution", ss 209(2), 832(1); "profits", s 413(5); "relevant accounting period", s 413(2).

Cross references—See TA 1988 Sch 18 paras 5C–5E (determination of percentage of profits and assets where this paragraph and other paragraphs of this Schedule apply).
Amendments—¹ This paragraph inserted by F(No 2)A 1992 Sch 6 paras 2, 7 and applies where option arrangements are made after 14 November 1991.

[5C—(1) In a case where paragraphs 4 and 5B above apply, each of the following percentages, namely—

    (a) the percentage of profits to which, on the profit distribution, the first company referred to in paragraph 2(1) above would be entitled, and
    (b) the percentage of assets to which, on the notional winding-up, the first company referred to in paragraph 3(1) above would be entitled,

shall be determined on each of the different bases set out in sub-paragraph (2) below.

(2) The bases are—

    (a) the basis specified in paragraph 4(2) above;
    (b) the basis specified in paragraph 5B(8) above;
    (c) the basis specified in paragraph 4(2) above and the basis specified in paragraph 5B(8) above taken together;
    (d) the basis specified in paragraph 2(1) or 3(1) above (according to the percentage concerned) without regard to paragraphs 4(2) and 5B(8) above.

(3) The lowest of the four percentages of profits so determined shall be taken for the purposes of [sections 403C and 413(7)]² to be the percentage of profits to which, on the profit distribution, the first company referred to in paragraph 2(1) above would be entitled as mentioned in that paragraph.

(4) The lowest of the four percentages of assets so determined shall be taken for the purposes of [sections 403C and 413(7)]² to be the percentage to which, on the notional winding-up, the first company mentioned in paragraph 3(1) above would be entitled of any assets of the other company available for distribution to its equity holders on a winding-up.

(5) For the purposes of this paragraph the basis specified in paragraph 5B(8) above is such basis as gives the percentage of profits arrived at by virtue of paragraph 5B(9) above or (as the case may be) such basis as gives the percentage of assets arrived at by virtue of paragraph 5B(9) above.]¹

Commentary—*Simon's Direct Tax Service* **D2.636.**
Definitions—"Company", s 413(5); "distribution", ss 209(2), 832(1); "profits", s 413(5).
Amendments—¹ This paragraph inserted by F(No 2)A 1992 Sch 6 paras 2, 7 and applies where option arrangements are made after 14 November 1991.
² Words in sub-paras (3), (4) substituted by FA 2000 s 100(4)(a), (5) and deemed always to have had effect.

[5D—(1) In a case where paragraphs 5 and 5B above apply, each of the following percentages, namely—

    (a) the percentage of profits to which, on the profit distribution, the first company referred to in paragraph 2(1) above would be entitled, and
    (b) the percentage of assets to which, on the notional winding-up, the first company referred to in paragraph 3(1) above would be entitled,

shall be determined on each of the different bases set out in sub-paragraph (2) below.

(2) The bases are—

    (a) the basis specified in paragraph 5(2) above;
    (b) the basis specified in paragraph 5B(8) above;
    (c) the basis specified in paragraph 5(2) above and the basis specified in paragraph 5B(8) above taken together;
    (d) the basis specified in paragraph 2(1) or 3(1) above (according to the percentage concerned) without regard to paragraphs 5(2) and 5B(8) above.

(3) The lowest of the four percentages of profits so determined shall be taken for the purposes of [sections 403C and 413(7)]² to be the percentage of profits to which, on the profit distribution, the first company referred to in paragraph 2(1) above would be entitled as mentioned in that paragraph.

(4) The lowest of the four percentages of assets so determined shall be taken for the purposes of [sections 403C and 413(7)]² to be the percentage to which, on the notional winding-up, the first company mentioned in paragraph 3(1) above would be entitled of any assets of the other company available for distribution to its equity holders on a winding-up.

(5) For the purposes of this paragraph the basis specified in paragraph 5B(8) above is such basis as gives the percentage of profits arrived at by virtue of paragraph 5B(9) above or (as the case may be) such basis as gives the percentage of assets arrived at by virtue of paragraph 5B(9) above.]¹

Commentary—*Simon's Direct Tax Service* **D2.636.**
Definitions—"Company", s 413(5); "distribution", ss 209(2), 832(1); "profits", s 413(5).
Amendments—¹ This paragraph inserted by F(No 2)A 1992 Sch 6 paras 2, 7 and applies where option arrangements are made after 14 November 1991.
² Words in sub-paras (3), (4) substituted by FA 2000 s 100(4)(a), (5) and deemed always to have had effect.

[5E—(1) In a case where paragraphs 4 and 5 and 5B above apply, each of the following percentages, namely—

(*a*) the percentage of profits to which, on the profit distribution, the first company referred to in paragraph 2(1) above would be entitled, and

(*b*) the percentage of assets to which, on the notional winding-up, the first company referred to in paragraph 3(1) above would be entitled,

shall be determined on each of the different bases set out in sub-paragraph (2) below.

(2) The bases are—

(*a*) the basis specified in paragraph 4(2) above;

(*b*) the basis specified in paragraph 5(2) above;

(*c*) the basis specified in paragraph 5B(8) above;

(*d*) the basis specified in paragraph 4(2) above and the basis specified in paragraph 5(2) above taken together;

(*e*) the basis specified in paragraph 4(2) above and the basis specified in paragraph 5B(8) above taken together;

(*f*) the basis specified in paragraph 5(2) above and the basis specified in paragraph 5B(8) above taken together;

(*g*) the basis specified in paragraph 4(2) above and the basis specified in paragraph 5(2) above and the basis specified in paragraph 5B(8) above all taken together;

(*h*) the basis specified in paragraphs 2(1) or 3(1) above (according to the percentage concerned) without regard to paragraphs 4(2), 5(2) and 5B(8) above.

(3) The lowest of the eight percentages of profits so determined shall be taken for the purposes of [sections 403C and 413(7)][2] to be the percentage of profits to which, on the profit distribution, the first company referred to in paragraph 2(1) above would be entitled as mentioned in that paragraph.

(4) The lowest of the eight percentages of assets so determined shall be taken for the purposes of [sections 403C and 413(7)][2] to be the percentage to which, on the notional winding-up, the first company mentioned in paragraph 3(1) above would be entitled of any assets of the other company available for distribution to its equity holders on a winding-up.

(5) For the purposes of this paragraph the basis specified in paragraph 5B(8) above is such basis as gives the percentage of profits arrived at by virtue of paragraph 5B(9) above or (as the case may be) such basis as gives the percentage of assets arrived at by virtue of paragraph 5B(9) above.][1]

Commentary—*Simon's Direct Tax Service* **D2.636.**
Definitions—"Company", s 413(5); "distribution", ss 209(2), 832(1); "profits", s 413(5).
Amendments—[1] This paragraph inserted by F(No 2)A 1992 Sch 6 paras 2, 7 and applies where option arrangements are made after 14 November 1991.
[2] Words in sub-paras (3), (4) substituted by FA 2000 s 100(4)(*a*), (5) and deemed always to have had effect.

[**5F**—(1) This paragraph has effect, in the cases specified in sub-paragraphs (2) and (3) below, for the following purposes ("the relevant purposes")—

(*a*) the determination, in a case where the surrendering company or the claimant company is a non-resident company, of whether that company is a 75 per cent or a 90 per cent subsidiary of another company;

(*b*) the determination of a member's share in a consortium in any case where the surrendering company or the claimant company is a non-resident company owned by the consortium.

(2) The first case in which this paragraph applies is where any of the equity holders—

(*a*) to whom the profit distribution is made, or

(*b*) who is entitled to participate in the notional winding-up of that company,

holds, as such an equity holder of the non-resident company, any shares or securities which carry rights in respect of dividend or interest or assets on a winding-up which have effect wholly or partly by reference to whether or not, or to what extent, the profits or assets distributed are referable to the non-resident company's UK trade.

(3) The second case in which this paragraph applies is where—

(*a*) option arrangements (within the meaning of paragraph 5B above) exist at any time in the relevant accounting period; and

(*b*) the percentage which, in any of the states of affairs referred to in sub-paragraph (5) of that paragraph, is—

(i) the percentage of profits to which any of the equity holders of the non-resident company would be entitled on the profit distribution, or

(ii) the percentage of assets to which any of the equity holders of that company would be entitled on the notional winding-up,

would differ, at any of the times so referred to, according to whether or not, or to what extent, the profits or assets distributed are referable to the non-resident company's UK trade.

(4) If the percentage of profits to which, on the profit distribution, a particular equity holder would be taken for the relevant purposes to be entitled would be less if the determination under paragraph 2(1) above were made on the basis specified in sub-paragraph (7) below, then that shall be the basis used for the relevant purposes in the case of that equity holder.

(5) If the percentage of assets to which, on the notional winding-up, a particular equity holder would be taken for the relevant purposes to be entitled would be less if the determination under paragraph

3(1) above were made on the basis specified in sub-paragraph (7) below, then that shall be the basis used for the relevant purposes in the case of that equity holder.

(6) If the percentage that falls to be taken for any of the purposes of section 403C or section 413(7) would, under any of paragraphs 4 to 5E above, be the lower or lowest of a number of percentages determined on different bases—

(*a*) each of the percentages falling to be compared for the purposes of that paragraph shall be determined both—

(i) on the basis specified in sub-paragraph (7) below, and
(ii) without making the assumption required for a determination on that basis;

and

(*b*) the comparison required by that paragraph, so far as made for the relevant purposes, shall be made using, in the case of each of the percentages to be compared, only the lower of the percentages determined under paragraph (*a*) above.

(7) That basis is the assumption—

(*a*) that the profit distribution or the distribution on the notional winding-up is confined to a distribution of profits or assets that are referable to the non-resident company's UK trade; and
(*b*) that the amount of the distribution does not exceed whichever is the greater of £100 and the following amount—

(i) in the case of a profit distribution, the amount (if any) of so much of the company's chargeable profits for the relevant accounting period as is referable to its UK trade; and
(ii) in the case of a distribution on a notional winding-up, its net UK assets;

and

(*c*) that none of the ordinary equity holders has an entitlement to a proportion of the profits or assets mentioned in paragraph (*a*) above that is any greater than the proportion of the distribution to which he would be entitled if—

(i) the assumptions specified in paragraphs (*a*) and (*b*) above were disregarded; but
(ii) it were assumed, where it is less, that the distribution is equal to £100.

(8) In sub-paragraph (7) above—

''net UK assets'', in relation to a non-resident company, means the excess, if any, of the total amount of the assets of the company that are referable to its UK trade (as shown in the relevant balance sheet), over the total amount of those of its liabilities (as so shown) which are so referable and are not liabilities to equity holders as such; and
''ordinary equity holder'' means any equity holder whose entitlement on the profit distribution or the distribution on the notional winding-up does not differ according to whether or not, or the extent to which, the profits or assets distributed are referable to the non-resident company's UK trade.

(9) In sub-paragraph (8) above ''relevant balance sheet'', in relation to a company, means any balance sheet relating to its affairs as at the end of the relevant accounting period.

(10) For the purposes of this paragraph profits, assets or liabilities of a non-resident company shall be taken to be referable to its UK trade to the extent only that they—

(*a*) are attributable to, or used for the purposes of, activities the income and gains from which are, or (were there any) would be, brought into account in computing the company's chargeable profits for any accounting period, and
(*b*) are not attributable to, or used for the purposes of, any activities which (within the meaning of section 403D) are made exempt from corporation tax for any accounting period by any double taxation arrangements.][1]

Commentary—*Simon's Direct Tax Service* D2.636.
Amendments—[1] This paragraph inserted by FA 2000 s 97, Sch 27 Pt I paras 5(1), (5), 6(1), (3) with effect for the application of TA 1988 Sch 18, for any purpose, after 31 March 2000. This amendment does not have effect for any determination as to whether the qualifying conditions for the purposes of TA 1988 s 403A(9) were met at any time before 1 April 2000.

6 For the purposes of [sections 403C and 413(7)][1] and paragraphs 2 to [5F][2] above—

(*a*) the percentage to which one company is beneficially entitled of any profits available for distribution to the equity holders of another company, and
(*b*) the percentage to which one company would be beneficially entitled of any assets of another company on a winding-up,

means the percentage to which the first company is, or would be, so entitled either directly or through another body corporate or other bodies corporate or partly directly and partly through another body corporate or other bodies corporate.

Commentary—*Simon's Direct Tax Service* D2.635.
Definitions—''Company'', s 413(5); ''distribution'', ss 209(2), 832(1); ''profits'', s 6(4).
Amendments—[1] Words substituted by FA 2000 s 100(4)(*a*), (5) and deemed always to have had effect.
[2] ''5F'' substituted for ''5E'' by FA 2000 s 97, Sch 27 paras 5(1), (6), 6(1), (3) with effect for accounting periods ending after 31 March 2000. This amendment does not have effect for any determination as to whether the qualifying conditions for the purposes of TA 1988 s 403A(9) were met at any time before 1 April 2000.

7—(1) In this Schedule "the relevant accounting period" means—

    (*a*) in a case falling within subsection (7) of section 413, the accounting period current at the time in question; and

    (*b*) in a case falling within [section 403C][1], the accounting period in relation to which the share in the consortium falls to be determined.

(2) For the purposes of this Schedule, a loan to a company shall be treated as a security, whether or not it is a secured loan, and, if it is a secured loan, regardless of the nature of the security.

Commentary—*Simon's Direct Tax Service* **D2.635.**
Definitions—"Accounting period", s 834(1); "company", s 413(5).
Cross references—See TCGA 1992 s 170(8) (omission of sub-para(1)(*b*) of this paragraph in its application for the purposes of TCGA 1992 s 170 (definitions of groups of companies)),
TA 1988 s 228(10) (modification of this paragraph in its application to roll-over relief for disposals after 19 March 1990 of shares to trustees of employee share ownership trusts).
Amendment—[1] Words in sub-para (1)(*b*) substituted by FA 2000 s 100(4)(*b*), (5) and deemed always to have had effect.

SCHEDULE 19

APPORTIONMENT OF INCOME OF CLOSE COMPANIES

Section 423

PART I

DETERMINATION OF RELEVANT INCOME AND DISTRIBUTIONS

Amendments—This Schedule repealed by FA 1989 s 103 and Sch 17 Pt V in relation to accounting periods beginning after 31 March 1989 except that Part I of the Schedule continues to have effect in any case where the subsequent distribution referred to in s 427(4) of this Act is made before 1 April 1992. The text of this Schedule was reproduced in *Butterworths Yellow Tax Handbook 1994–95.*

PART II

PROCEDURE

Amendments—This Part of this Schedule repealed by FA 1989 s 103 and Sch 17 Pt V in relation to accounting periods beginning after 31 March 1989.

[SCHEDULE 19AA][1]

OVERSEAS LIFE ASSURANCE FUND

Section 431

Commentary—*Simon's Direct Tax Service* **D4.525.**
Revenue Internal Guidance—Life assurance manual LAM 10.31-10.58 (explanation of this Schedule).
Amendments—[1] This Schedule inserted by FA 1990 Sch 7 paras 6, 10(1) with effect for accounting periods beginning after 31 December 1989, subject to the provisions of para 10(2) in relation to first accounting period beginning after 31 December 1989.

[1—(1) This Schedule shall have effect for determining for the purposes of this Chapter the assets of a company which are the assets of its overseas life assurance fund.

(2) The Treasury may by order amend any of the following provisions of this Schedule [(including any modification of any of those provisions made by paragraph 14A of Schedule 19AC)][2].]

Commentary—*Simon's Direct Tax Service* **D4.525.**
Definitions—"Company", s 832(1); "overseas life assurance fund", s 431(2).
Amendments—[1] This Schedule inserted by FA 1990 Sch 7 paras 6, 10(1) with effect for accounting periods beginning after 31 December 1989, subject to the provisions of para 10(2) in relation to first accounting period beginning after 31 December 1989.
[2] Words in sub-para (2) inserted by FA 1995 Sch 8 paras 33, 55 with effect in relation to accounting periods beginning after 31 October 1994 (but note FA 1995 Sch 8 para 55(2)).

[2—(1) Assets of a company at the end of a period of account which—

    (*a*) were assets of the overseas life assurance fund at the end of the immediately preceding period of account, and

    (*b*) are assets of the [long-term insurance fund][3] of the company throughout the period,

shall be assets of the overseas life assurance fund throughout the period.

(2) Where in a period of account assets of a company which were assets of the overseas life assurance fund at the end of the immediately preceding period of account are disposed of by the company, or otherwise cease to be assets of the [long-term insurance fund][3] of the company, they shall be assets of the overseas life assurance fund from the beginning of the period until they are disposed of or, as the case may be, they cease to be assets of the [long-term insurance fund][3].

(3) Where—

(*a*) in any period of account assets are acquired by a company as assets of the [long-term insurance fund][3], or otherwise become assets of that fund,

(*b*) the assets are disposed of by the company, or otherwise cease to be assets of that fund, later in the same period,

(*c*) throughout the part of the period during which the assets are assets of the [long-term insurance fund][3] they are [assets within paragraph 5(5)(*a*) or][2] 5(5)(*c*) below, and

(*d*) it is appropriate having regard to all the circumstances (including a comparison between the relationship of the value of the assets of the overseas life assurance fund and the liabilities of the overseas life assurance business and that of the value of the assets of the long term business fund and the liabilities of the company's [long-term][4] business) that they be assets of the overseas life assurance fund,

they shall be assets of the overseas life assurance fund for the part of the period during which they are assets of the [long-term insurance fund][3].][1]

Commentary—*Simon's Direct Tax Service* D4.525.
Definitions—"Company", s 832(1); "liabilities", s 431(2); "long term business fund", s 431(2); "overseas life assurance business", s 431(2); "overseas life assurance fund", s 431(2); "value", s 431(2).
Cross references—See TA 1988 Sch 19AA para 3 (circumstances under which assets mentioned in sub-para (1) above become or cease to be assets of overseas life assurance fund).
FA 1990 Sch 7 para 10(2) (in relation to first period of account beginning after 31 December 1989, certain assets to be treated for the purposes of sub-paras (1) and(2) above as assets of overseas life assurance fund at the end of the immediately preceding period of account).
Amendments—[1] This Schedule inserted by FA 1990 Sch 7 paras 6, 10(1) with effect for accounting periods beginning after 31 December 1989, subject to the provisions of para 10(2) in relation to first accounting period beginning after 31 December 1989.
[2] Words in sub-para (3)(*c*) substituted by Overseas Life Assurance Fund (Amendment) Order 1994, SI 1994/3278 art 3, with effect from 10 January 1995 (but applies in relation to periods of account of a company beginning after 31 October 1994 and ending on or after that date).
[3] Words in sub-paras (1)(*b*), (2), (3) substituted by the Financial Services and Markets Act 2000 (Consequential Amendments) (Taxes) Order, SI 2001/3629 arts 13, 52(1)(*k*)(i) with effect from 1 December 2001, immediately after the coming into force of the Financial Services and Markets Act 2000 ss 411, 432(1), Sch 20.
[4] Words in sub-para (3)(*d*) substituted by the Financial Services and Markets Act 2000 (Consequential Amendments) (Taxes) Order, SI 2001/3629 arts 13, 52(2)(*m*)(i) with effect from 1 December 2001, immediately after the coming into force of the Financial Services and Markets Act 2000 ss 411, 432(1), Sch 20.

[**3**—(1) Where the value of the assets mentioned in paragraph 2(1) above at the end of the period is less than the amount mentioned in paragraph 4 below (or where there are no assets within paragraph 2(1)), assets which—

(*a*) are assets of the [long-term insurance fund][2] of the company at the end of the period,

(*b*) have a value at that time equal to the difference (or to that amount), and

(*c*) are designated in accordance with paragraph 5 below,

shall become assets of the overseas life assurance fund at the relevant time.

(2) In sub-paragraph (1) above "the relevant time" means—

(*a*) where the asset is not an asset of the [long-term insurance fund][2] of the company throughout the period, the time when it became such an asset, and

(*b*) in any other case, the end of the period.

(3) Where the value of the assets mentioned in paragraph 2(1) above at the end of the period is greater than the amount mentioned in paragraph 4 below, assets which—

(*a*) are assets of the [long-term insurance fund][2] of the company at the end of the period,

(*b*) have a value at that time equal to the difference, and

(*c*) are designated in accordance with paragraph 5 below,

shall cease to be assets of the overseas life assurance fund at the end of the period.][1]

Commentary—*Simon's Direct Tax Service* D4.525.
Definitions—"Company", s 832(1); "long term business fund", s 431(2); "overseas life assurance fund", s 431(2); "value", s 431(2).
Amendments—[1] This Schedule inserted by FA 1990 Sch 7 paras 6, 10(1) with effect for accounting periods beginning after 31 December 1989, subject to the provisions of para 10(2) in relation to first accounting period beginning after 31 December 1989.
[2] Words in sub-paras (1)(*a*), (2)(*a*), (3)(*a*) substituted by the Financial Services and Markets Act 2000 (Consequential Amendments) (Taxes) Order, SI 2001/3629 arts 13, 52(1)(*k*)(ii) with effect from 1 December 2001, immediately after the coming into force of the Financial Services and Markets Act 2000 ss 411, 432(1), Sch 20.

[**4**—[(1) The amount referred to in paragraph 3 above shall be determined by the formula—

$$A + B - C - D$$

where—

A is the liabilities of the company's overseas life assurance business at the end of the period of account,

[B is the aggregate of—

(*a*) the appropriate part of the investment reserve at that time, and

(*b*) the appropriate part of any liabilities of the company's [long-term insurance fund][4] at that time which represent a money debt,]

C is the value, at that time, of any land in the United Kingdom which is an asset linked solely to the company's overseas life assurance business, and
D is the relevant fraction of the value, at that time, of any land in the United Kingdom which is an asset linked both to the company's overseas life assurance business and to some other category of business.][2]

[(2) In sub-paragraph (1) above, in B, the "appropriate part" of the company's investment reserve at the end of the period of account, or of any liabilities of its [long-term insurance fund][4] at that time which represent a money debt, is—

(a) where none (or none but an insignificant proportion) of the liabilities of the company's [long-term][5] business at that time are with-profits liabilities, the part which bears to the whole the proportion A/B; and
(b) in any other case, the part which bears to the whole the proportion C/D.
For this purpose—

A is the amount of the liabilities of the company's overseas life assurance business at the end of the period of account,
B is the whole amount of the liabilities of the company's [long-term][5] business at that time,
C is the amount of the with-profits liabilities of the company's overseas life assurance business at that time, and
D is the whole amount of the with-profits liabilities of the company's long-term business at that time.][3]

[(3) In this Schedule "land" includes buildings and other structures, land covered with water, and any estate, interest, easement, servitude, right or licence in or over land.][2]

[(4) In sub-paragraph (1) above, in D, "the relevant fraction" is the fraction of which—

(a) the numerator is the value, at the end of the period of account, of such of the liabilities of the company's overseas life assurance business as were liabilities in respect of benefits to be determined by references to the value of the asset; and
(b) the denominator is the value, at that time, of all the liabilities of the company's [long-term][5] business which were liabilities in respect of benefits to be so determined.][2]][1]

[(5) In this paragraph—

"investment reserve", in relation to an insurance company, means the excess of the value of the assets of the company's [long-term][5] business over the aggregate of—

(a) the liabilities of that business, and
(b) any liabilities of the [long-term insurance fund][4] which represent a money debt;

"money debt" has the same meaning as in Chapter II of Part IV of the Finance Act 1996.][3]

Commentary—*Simon's Direct Tax Service* D4.525.
Definitions—"Investment reserve", s 431(2); "liabilities", s 431(2); "listed assets", s 431(2); "long term business", s 431(2); "overseas life assurance business", s 431(2); "United Kingdom", s 830(1); "with-profits liabilities", s 431(2).
Cross references—See FA 1990 Sch 7 para 10(2) (assets having *inter alia* a value equal to the amount mentioned in this paragraph in the first period of account beginning after 31 December 1989 to be treated for the purposes of para 2(1) and(2) above as assets of overseas life assurance fund at the end of the immediately preceding period of account).
Amendments—[1] This Schedule inserted by FA 1990 Sch 7 paras 6, 10(1) with effect for accounting periods beginning after 31 December 1989, subject to the provisions of para 10(2) in relation to first accounting period beginning after 31 December 1989.
[2] Sub-para (1) substituted and sub-paras (3), (4) added, by Overseas Life Assurance Fund (Amendment) Order 1994, SI 1994/3278 art 4, with effect from 10 January 1995 (but applies in relation to periods of account of a company beginning after 31 October 1994 and ending on or after that date).
[3] Definition of B and sub-para (2) substituted and sub-para (5) added by the Overseas Life Assurance Fund (Amendment) Order, SI 2000/2188 art 3 with effect for accounting periods beginning after 31 December 1999 and ending after 31 August 2000. Definition of "B" in sub-para (1) and sub-para (2) previously read as—

"B the appropriate part of the investment reserve at that time,", and

"(2) In sub-paragraph (1) above, in B, the "appropriate part", in relation to the investment reserve (within the meaning of section 432A), means—

(a) where all of the liabilities of the long term business are linked liabilities, the part of that reserve which bears to the whole the same proportion as the amount of the liabilities of the overseas life assurance business bears to the whole amount of the liabilities of the long term business,
(b) where any of the liabilities of the long term business are not linked liabilities but none (or none but an insignificant proportion) are with-profits liabilities, the part of that reserve which bears to the whole the same proportion as the amount of the liabilities of the overseas life assurance business which are not linked liabilities bears to the whole amount of the liabilities of the long term business which are not linked liabilities, and
(c) in any other case, the part of that reserve which bears to the whole the same proportion as the amount of the with-profits liabilities of the overseas life assurance business bears to the whole amount of the with-profits liabilities of the long term business;

and in this sub-paragraph "linked liabilities" means liabilities in respect of benefits to be determined by reference to the value of linked assets.".
[4] Words in sub-paras (1), (2), (5) substituted by the Financial Services and Markets Act 2000 (Consequential Amendments) (Taxes) Order, SI 2001/3629 arts 13, 52(1)(k)(iii) with effect from 1 December 2001, immediately after the coming into force of the Financial Services and Markets Act 2000 ss 411, 432(1), Sch 20.
[5] Words in sub-paras (2)(a), (b), (4)(b), (5) (3) substituted by the Financial Services and Markets Act 2000 (Consequential Amendments) (Taxes) Order, SI 2001/3629 arts 13, 52(2)(m)(ii) with effect from 1 December 2001, immediately after the coming into force of the Financial Services and Markets Act 2000 ss 411, 432(1), Sch 20.

[5—(1) Any designation of assets required for the purposes of paragraph 3 above shall be made by a company in accordance with the following provisions of this paragraph.

(2) When designating assets for the purposes of paragraph 3(1) above, a company shall not designate an asset falling within any paragraph of sub-paragraph (5) below unless it designates all assets falling within each of the preceding paragraphs of that sub-paragraph.

(3) When designating assets for the purposes of paragraph 3(3) above, a company shall not designate an asset falling within any paragraph of sub-paragraph (5) below unless it designates all assets falling within each of the succeeding paragraphs of that sub-paragraph.

(4) When an asset falls within more than one paragraph of sub-paragraph (5) below, it shall be taken for the purposes of this paragraph to fall only within the first of them.

(5) The categories of assets referred to in sub-paragraphs (2) and (3) above are—

(*a*) assets[, other than land in the United Kingdom,]³ linked solely to overseas life assurance business;

(*b*) so many of any assets denominated in an overseas currency, other than any non-overseas linked assets, as have a value at the end of the period not exceeding the amount of the company's [non-linked liabilities]⁴ in respect of benefits expressed in that currency so far as referable to overseas life assurance business;

[(*c*) assets, other than land in the United Kingdom, which—

(i) are shown in the books of the company as being held as assets of a fund where all, or all but an insignificant part, of the liabilities of the fund are in respect of overseas life assurance business carried on by the company at or through a branch or agency outside the United Kingdom; or

(ii) are managed under the control of a person whose normal place of work is at a branch or agency outside the United Kingdom at or through which the company carries on overseas life assurance business;

(*d*) assets other than land in the United Kingdom;

(*e*) land in the United Kingdom;]⁴

but assets linked solely to [pension business, life reinsurance or basic life assurance and general annuity business]² are not within any paragraph of this sub-paragraph (and may not be designated for the purposes of paragraph 3 above).

(6) For the purposes of sub-paragraph (5)(*b*) above assets are "non-overseas linked assets" if they are linked assets and none of the policies or contracts providing for the benefits concerned are policies or contracts the effecting of which constitutes the carrying on of overseas life assurance business.

[(6A) For the purposes of sub-paragraph (5)(*b*) above 'non-linked liabilities' means liabilities other than liabilities in respect of benefits to be determined by reference to the value of linked assets.]⁴

(7) ...⁴]¹

Commentary—*Simon's Direct Tax Service* D4.525.
Definitions—"Basic life assurance business", s 431(2); "branch or agency", s 834(1); "company", s 832(1); "liabilities", s 431(2); "life reinsurance business", s 431(2); "linked assets", s 431(2); "overseas life assurance business", s 431(2); "pension business", s 431(2); "United Kingdom", s 830(1); "value", s 431(2).
Cross references—See TA 1988 Sch 19AA para 2 (assets described in sub-para(5)(*c*) above to be assets of overseas life assurance fund in certain circumstances).
FA 1990 Sch 7 para 10(2) (in relation to first period of account beginning after 31 December 1989, assets which *inter alia* are designated in accordance with this paragraph on the same basis as a designation under para 3(1) above to be treated for the purposes of para 2(1) and(2) above as assets of overseas life assurance fund at the end of the immediately preceding period of account).
Modifications—Sub-para (5) modified so far as it applies to the life or endowment business carried on by friendly societies by the Friendly Societies (Modification of the Corporation Tax Acts) Regulations, SI 1997/473 reg 31.
Words inserted in sub-para (5) in respect of individual savings account business carried on by insurance companies by the Individual Savings Account Regulations, SI 1998/1871 reg 19, with effect from 6 April 1999.
Amendments—¹ This Schedule inserted by FA 1990 Sch 7 paras 6, 10(1) with effect for accounting periods beginning after 31 December 1989, subject to the provisions of para 10(2) in relation to first accounting period beginning after 31 December 1989.
² Words in sub-para (5) substituted by FA 1995 Sch 8 paras 8, 57 with effect for accounting periods beginning after 31 December 1994.
³ Words in sub-para (5)(*a*) added by the Overseas Life Assurance Fund (Amendment) Order 1994, SI 1994/3278 art 5, with effect from 10 January 1995 (but applies in relation to periods of account of a company beginning after 31 October 1994 and ending on or after that date).
⁴ In sub-para (*b*) words in para (*b*) substituted for word "liabilities" and whole of paras (*c*)–(*e*) substituted (for original paras (*c*)– (*g*)), sub-para (6A) inserted and sub-para (7) repealed by the Overseas Life Assurance Fund (Amendment) Order, SI 2000/2188 art 4 with effect for accounting periods beginning after 31 December 1999 and ending after 31 August 2000. Sub-paras (5)(*c*)– (*g*) and (7) previously read as—

"(*c*) assets, other than land in the United Kingdom, the management of which is under the control of a person whose normal place of work is at a branch or agency outside the United Kingdom at or through which the company carries on overseas life assurance business;
(*d*) securities issued by the Treasury with a FOTRA condition and securities to which section 581 of this Act applies;
(*e*) assets not within any of paragraphs (*ea*), (*f*) and (*g*) below;
(*ea*) interests in authorised unit trusts;
(*f*) shares in companies resident in the United Kingdom;
(*g*) land in the United Kingdom;", and

"(7) For the purposes of sub-paragraph (5)(*d*) above, the reference to securities issued with a FOTRA condition is a reference to any FOTRA security within the meaning of section 154 of the Finance Act 1996."

[[SCHEDULE 19AB

PENSION BUSINESS: PAYMENTS ON ACCOUNT OF TAX CREDITS AND DEDUCTED TAX][1]

Section 438A

Revenue Internal Guidance—Life assurance manual paras 15.31–15.94 (description of provisional repayment rules).

Modifications—See FA 1993 s 121 (modifications of and exceptions in this Schedule may be made by statutory instrument in relation to certain business of a friendly society). For distributions made before 6 April 1999, this Schedule is deemed to have effect, for the purposes of FA 1993 s 121 *without* the amendments made by F(No 2)A 1997 Sch 3 paras 10, 11 (per F(No 2)A 1997 Sch 3 para 12).

Individual Savings Account (Insurance Companies) Regulations 1998, SI 1998/1871 (as amended by the Individual Savings Accounts (Insurance Companies) (Amendment) Regulations, SI 2001/3974) (this Schedule, other than paras 3 and 4, shall apply in relation to individual savings account business of insurance companies as it applies in relation to pension business of such companies, with the modifications specified in SI 1998/1871 regs 20 and 21). The modified text of TA 1988 Sch 19AB is reproduced in SI 2001/3974, Schedule).

Friendly Societies (Provisional Repayments for Exempt Business) Regulations, SI 1999/622 reg 3 (as amended by the Friendly Societies (Provisional Repayments for Exempt Business) (Amendment) Regulations, SI 2001/3973 (application of this Schedule with effect for exempt business of a friendly society for accounting periods beginning after 31 December 2001). The modified text of TA 1988 Sch 19AB is reproduced in SI 2001/3973, Schedule).

Insurance Companies (Gilt-edged Securities) (Periodic Accounting for Tax on Interest) Regulations, SI 1999/623 regs 4–9 (application of this Schedule, with modifications, in cases where payments of interest on certain gilt-edged securities are made without deduction of tax to insurance companies carrying on pension business with effect for accounting periods beginning before 1 April 1999 and ending after 30 June 1999).

Amendments—[1] This Schedule (inserted by FA 1991 s 49(2), (3) and Sch 8 in relation to accounting periods beginning after 1 October 1992 by virtue of FA 1991 s 49 (Appointed Day) Order, SI 1992/1746) repealed by FA 2001 ss 87, 110, Sch 33 Pt II(12) with effect in accordance with FA 2001 s 87.

Entitlement to certain payments on account

[[**1**—(1) An insurance company carrying on pension business shall for each provisional repayment period in an accounting period be entitled on a claim made in that behalf to a payment (in this Schedule referred to as a "provisional repayment") of an amount equal[, subject to paragraph 2 below,][6] ...[4]—

(a) the appropriate portion of any income tax borne by deduction on any payment received by the company in that provisional repayment period and referable to its pension business, ...

(b) ...[4]

or of such lesser amount as may be specified in the claim.

(2) For the purposes of this paragraph, a "provisional repayment period" of a company—

(a) shall begin whenever—

(i) the company begins to carry on pension business;

(ii) an accounting period of the company begins, at a time when the company is carrying on such business; or

(iii) a provisional repayment period of the company ends, at a time when the company is carrying on such business; and

(b) shall end on the first occurrence of either of the following—

(i) the expiration of three months from the beginning of the provisional repayment period; or

(ii) the end of an accounting period of the company.

[(3) In the application of subsections (5) to (9) of section 432A for the purpose of determining the amounts to which a company is entitled by way of provisional repayments in the case of any accounting period of the company, the reference in subsection (5) to "the relevant fraction" shall be taken as a reference to the provisional fraction for that accounting period.][6]

[(4) For the purposes of this paragraph—

(a) the provisional fraction for an accounting period of a company is the fraction which would, on the basis of the company's latest [company tax return]', be the relevant fraction for the purposes of section 432A(5) for the accounting period to which that return relates; but

(b) if there is no section 11 return on the basis of which that fraction can be ascertained, the provisional fraction shall be taken to be nil;

but this sub-paragraph is subject to paragraph 2 below.][6]

(5) In sub-paragraph (1) above "the appropriate portion" means—

(a) in the case of an insurance company carrying on pension business and no other category of [long-term][9] business, the whole; and

(b) in the case of an insurance company carrying on more than one category of [long-term][9] business—

(i) where the payment or distribution in question is income arising from an asset [linked][3] to pension business, the whole; ...[6]

[(ii) if and to the extent that the payment or distribution in question is income which is not referable to a category of business by virtue of subsection (3) or (4) of section 432A, the provisional fraction; and][6]

[(iii) except as provided by sub-paragraph (i) or (ii) above, none.][6]

[(6) Paragraphs 57 to 60 of Schedule 18 to the Finance Act 1998 (general provisions as to procedure on claims and elections) do not apply to a claim for a provisional repayment.]⁷

[(6A) A claim for a provisional repayment shall be in such form as the Board may determine and the form of claim shall provide for a declaration to the effect that all the particulars given in the form are correctly stated to the best of the knowledge and belief of the person making the claim.]⁶

[(7) A provisional repayment for a provisional repayment period shall be regarded as a payment on account of the amounts (if any) which the company would, apart from this Schedule, be entitled to be ...⁵ repaid in respect of its pension business for the accounting period in which that provisional repayment period falls, in respect of—

(a) income tax borne by deduction on payments received by the company in that accounting period and referable to its pension business, ...⁵

(b) ...⁵

on a claim such as is mentioned in [paragraph 9(2) of Schedule 18 to the Finance Act 1998]⁷ ...⁵ in respect of that accounting period.]⁶

(8) ...⁶

(9) ...²

[(10) In this paragraph—

"latest company tax return", in the case of an accounting period of a company ("the current accounting period"), means, subject to sub-paragraph (11) below, the company tax return for the latest preceding accounting period of the company for which such a return has been delivered before the making of the first claim for a provisional repayment for the current accounting period; and

"self-assessment" means an assessment included in a company tax return, and includes a reference to such an assessment as amended.

(11) In any case where—

(a) there is a company tax return which would, apart from this sub-paragraph, be the latest such return in the case of an accounting period of a company,

(b) the self-assessment required to be included in that return has been amended, and

(c) that amendment was made before the making of the first claim for a provisional repayment for the accounting period mentioned in paragraph (a) above,

the return which is to be regarded as the latest company tax return in the case of that accounting period shall be that return as it stands amended immediately after the making of that amendment of the self-assessment (or, if the self-assessment has been so amended more than once, that return as it stands amended immediately after the making of the last such amendment) but ignoring amendments which do not give rise to any change in the fraction which, on the basis of the return as it has effect from time to time, would be the relevant fraction for the purposes of section 432A(5) for the accounting period to which the return relates.]⁷]¹]⁸

Commentary—*Simon's Direct Tax Service* **D4.534.**
Definitions—"Accounting period", s 834(1); "the Board", s 832(1); "the Management Act", s 831(3); "provisional fraction", para 6(1); "provisional repayment", para 6(1), (2); "provisional repayment period", para 6(1); "tax credits", s 832(1).
Cross references—See TA 1988 Sch 19AB para 2(1) (changes in the provisional fraction mentioned in sub-para (3) above).
TA 1988 Sch 19AB para 2(4) (meaning of expressions used in this paragraph).
TA 1988 Sch 19AB para 5(5) (transitional application of pay and file provisions).
TA 1988 Sch 19AB para 6(5) (modification of the provisions calculating the provisional fraction for provisional payment claims for accounting periods ending after the appointed date for self-assessment but made before the company has delivered its first return under TMA 1970 s 11 for such an accounting period).
TA 1988 Sch 19AC para 15 (modification of sub-para (8) above in the case of application of this paragraph to overseas life insurance companies).
FA 1993 s 78(6) (calculation of franked investment income for the purposes of sub-para (8) above in accordance with change in tax credit rate from the financial year 1993);
Modifications—Individual Savings Account (Insurance Companies) Regulations, SI 1998/1871, regs 20 and 21 (application from 6 April 1999 in relation to pension business and individual savings account business taken together, so that references to repayments are references to the aggregate of amounts relating to pension business and individual savings account business; the amendments made by F(No2)A 1997 Sch 3 paras 10 and 11(see amendment notes ⁴,⁵,⁷ below) cease to apply with effect from 6 April 1999, but this does not apply to the amendment made by F(No2)A 1997 Sch 3 para 10(4); and, words in sub-para (3) and new sub-paras (4A)-(4C) inserted with effect from 6 April 1999).
Friendly Societies (Provisional Repayments for Exempt Business) Regulations, SI 1999/622 regs 3–8 (modification of this paragraph in applying this Schedule (as amended by F(No 2)A 1997 Sch 3 in relation to distributions made to friendly societies after 5 April 2004 and as unamended by F(No 2)A 1997 Sch 3 in relation to distributions made to friendly societies before 6 April 2004) to exempt business of a friendly society for accounting periods ending after 30 June 1999).
Amendments—¹ This Schedule inserted by FA 1991 s 49(2), (3) and Sch 8 in relation to accounting periods beginning after 1 October 1992 by virtue of FA 1991 s 49 (Appointed Day) Order, SI 1992/1746.
Sub-para (9) repealed by FA 1993 s 103(2)(h), (3) and Sch 23 Pt III(9) in relation to accounting periods beginning after 31 December 1992.
Word in sub-para (5)(b)(i) substituted by FA 1995 Sch 8 paras 12(1)(b), 57 with effect for accounting periods beginning after 31 December 1994.
Words in sub-para (1), and sub-para (1)(b), repealed by F(No 2)A 1997 s 23, Sch 3 para 10(1), (2), (6), Sch 8 Pt II(6) with effect in relation to distributions made after 2 July 1997.
Words in sub-para (7) (as substituted with effect from an appointed day–see footnote 6 below) repealed by F(No 2)A 1997 s 23, Sch 3 para 11(1), (2), Sch 8 Pt II(7).
Words in sub-para (1) inserted, sub-paras (3), (4) substituted, words in sub-para (5) substituted, word omitted from sub-para (5)(b) repealed, sub-paras (6), (6A) substituted for sub-para (6), sub-para (7) substituted, sub-para (8) repealed and sub-paras (10), (11) substituted for sub-para (10) by FA 1996 s 169, Sch 34 para 1, Sch 41 Pt V(27), with effect in relation to

provisional repayment periods, within the meaning of this Schedule, falling in accounting periods ending after 30 June 1999 (by virtue of Finance Act 1994, Section 199, (Appointed Day) Order, SI 1998/3173 art 2).
[7] Sub-paras (6), (10) and (11) and words in sub-paras (4), (7) substituted by FA 1998 Sch 19 para 51 with effect in relation to accounting periods ending on or after the "self-assessment appointed day" (1 July 1999 by virtue of SI 1998/3173).
[8] This paragraph repealed by FA 2001 ss 87, 110, Sch 33 Pt II(12) with effect in accordance with FA 2001 s 87.
[9] Words in sub-paras (5)(*a*), (*b*) substituted for the words "long term" by the Financial Services and Markets Act 2000 (Consequential Amendments) (Taxes) Order, SI 2002/1409 art 2(1), (3) with effect from 2 July 2002.

[Entitlement to certain notional payments on account]

[1A ...]

Note—This paragraph is treated as inserted as a modification of this Schedule in relation to cases where payments of interest on relevant gilt-edged securities are made without deduction of tax to insurance companies carrying on pension business for accounting periods beginning before 1 April 1999 and ending after 30 June 1999: see the Insurance Companies (Gilt-edged Securities) (Periodic Accounting for Tax on Interest) Regulations, SI 1999/623 regs 4, 6.
Amendments—This paragraph repealed by FA 2001 ss 87, 110, Sch 33 Pt II(12) with effect in accordance with FA 2001 s 87.

Changes in the provisional fraction

[[2—*[(1) This paragraph applies in any case where—*

(a) a claim has been made for a provisional repayment for at least one provisional repayment period in an accounting period of a company;
(b) subsequently, a further such claim is made for a provisional repayment period falling within that accounting period; and
(c) had that further claim been the first claim made for a provisional repayment for that accounting period, the provisional fraction for the accounting period would have been a different fraction (whether in consequence of the delivery of a [company tax return]4 for a later preceding accounting period or the application of paragraph 1(11) above);

and in this paragraph the "substituted provisional fraction" means the different fraction mentioned in paragraph (c) above.]2

[(2) Where this paragraph applies—

(a) the amount of any provisional repayment to which the company is entitled for the provisional repayment period mentioned in sub-paragraph (1)(b) above shall be an amount determined in accordance with sub-paragraph (3) below or such lesser amount as may be specified in the claim; and

(b) in relation to any later provisional repayment period in the same accounting period, the substituted provisional fraction shall, subject to any further application of this paragraph, be treated as the provisional fraction for the accounting period.]2

(3) The amount referred to in sub-paragraph (2) above is the amount (if any) by which total entitlement exceeds total past payments, and for this purpose—

"total entitlement" means the aggregate of the provisional repayments to which the company would have been entitled (apart from this paragraph) for—

(a) the provisional repayment period to which the claim relates, and
(b) any earlier provisional repayment period in the same accounting period,

[had the substituted provisional fraction been the provisional fraction for the accounting period as from the beginning of that period; and]3
"total past payments" means the aggregate of any amounts already paid by way of provisional repayments for provisional repayment periods falling within that accounting period.

(4) Expressions used in this paragraph and in paragraph 1 above have the same meaning in this paragraph as they have in that paragraph.]1]5

Commentary—*Simon's Direct Tax Service* **D4.534.**
Definitions—"Accounting period", s 834(1); "provisional fraction", para 6(1); "provisional repayment", para 6(1), (2) "provisional repayment period", para 6(1).
Cross references—See TA 1988 Sch 19AB para 6(5) (this section applies as originally enacted in relation to an accounting period ending after 30 June 1999 where a claim for a provisional repayment is made for that period before a return under TMA 1970 s 11 is made for it).
Modifications—Friendly Societies (Provisional Repayments for Exempt Business) Regulations, SI 1999/622 regs 3, 9 (modification of this paragraph in applying this Schedule (as amended by F(No 2)A 1997 Sch 3 in relation to distribution made to friendly societies after 5 April 2004 and as unamended by F(No 2)A 1997 Sch 3 in relation to distributions made to friendly societies before 6 April 2004) to exempt business of a friendly society for accounting periods ending after 30 June 1999).
Insurance Companies (Gilt-edged Securities) (Periodic Accounting for Tax on Interest) Regulations, SI 1999/623 regs 4, 7 (application of this paragraph, with modifications, in cases where payments of interest on certain gilt-edged securities are made without deduction of tax to insurance companies carrying on pension business with effect for accounting periods beginning before 1 April 1999 and ending after 30 June 1999).
Amendments—[1] This Schedule inserted by FA 1991 s 49(2), (3) and Sch 8 in relation to accounting periods beginning after 1 October 1992 by virtue of FA 1991 s 49 (Appointed Day) Order, SI 1992/1746.
[2] Sub-paras (1), (2) substituted by FA 1996 s 169, Sch 34 para 2(1), (2) with effect in relation to provisional repayment periods within the meaning of this Schedule, falling in accounting periods ending on or after the appointed day under FA 1994 s 199 (1 July 1999 by virtue of Finance Act 1994, Section 199 (Appointed Day) Order, SI 1998/3173).
[3] Words in sub-para (3) substituted for "had the later or, as the case may be, latest provisional fraction applicable in relation to that accounting period been so applicable as from the beginning of that period; and" by FA 1996 s 169, Sch 34 para 2(1), (3) with effect in relation to provisional repayment periods, within the meaning of this Schedule, falling in accounting periods ending on or after the appointed day under FA 1994 s 199 (1 July 1999 by virtue of SI 1998/3173). For the *continued*

application of this para as originally enacted for accounting periods ending on or after the appointed day in certain circumstances, see Sch 19AB para 5(6).
[4] Words in sub-para (1)(c) substituted by FA 1998 Sch 19 para 51 with effect in relation to accounting periods ending on or after the "self-assessment appointed day" (1 July 1999 by virtue of SI 1998/3173).
[5] This paragraph repealed by FA 2001 ss 87, 110, Sch 33 Pt II(12) with effect in accordance with FA 2001 s 87.

Repayment, with interest, of excessive provisional repayments

[[3—(1) In any case where—

[(a) an insurance company's self-assessment for an accounting period becomes final, and][2]
[(b) the aggregate amount of the provisional repayments made to the company for that accounting period exceeds the appropriate amount,][2]

the excess, together with the amount of any relevant interest, shall be treated for the purposes of [paragraph 52 of Schedule 18 to the Finance Act 1998][7] as if it were an amount of corporation tax for that accounting period which had been repaid to the insurance company and which ought not to have been so repaid.

[(1ZA) In its application by sub-paragraph (1) above, section 30 of the Management Act shall have effect as if, instead of the provision made by subsection (5), it provided that an assessment under that section by virtue of sub-paragraph (1) above is not out of time under section 34 of that Act if it is made no later than the end of the accounting period following that in which the assessment mentioned in paragraph (a) of that sub-paragraph is finally determined.][4]

[(1A) For the purposes of sub-paragraph (1)(b) above, the appropriate amount for an accounting period of a company is the amount (if any) which, on the assumptions in sub-paragraphs (1B) and (1C) below and disregarding any provisional repayments, the company would be entitled to be ...[3] repaid, when its self-assessment for the period becomes final, in respect of its pension business for that accounting period on a claim such as is mentioned in [paragraph 9(2) of Schedule 18 to the Finance Act 1998][7] ...[3] in respect of—

(a) income tax borne by deduction on payments received by the company in that accounting period and referable to its pension business, ...[3]
(b) ...[3]][2]

[(1B) The first assumption is that no ...[3] repayments have been made to the company in respect of—

(a) income tax such as is mentioned in paragraph (a) of sub-paragraph (1A) above, ...[3]
(b) ...[3]

before the company's self-assessment for the accounting period in question becomes final.][2]

[(1C) The second assumption is that in making any set off under—

(a) section 7(2), [or][5]
(b) paragraph 5 of Schedule 16, [or
(c) regulations made by virtue of section 51B,][6]

income tax borne by deduction on income which is not referable to pension business is set off before income tax so borne on income which is referable to pension business.][2]

[(1D) Paragraph 53 of Schedule 18 to the Finance Act 1998 (time limit for recovery of excessive repayments etc) does not apply to an assessment under paragraph 52 of that Schedule made by virtue of this paragraph.

But such an assessment is not out of time under paragraph 46 of that Schedule (general six year time limit for assessments) if it is made not later than the end of the accounting period following that in which the self-assessment mentioned in sub-paragraph (1)(a) above becomes final.][7]

(2) In this paragraph, "relevant interest" means interest—

(a) on so much of the excess referred to in sub-paragraph (1) above as is or was from time to time outstanding,
(b) for any period for which it is or was so outstanding, and
(c) at the rate applicable under section 178 of the Finance Act 1989 for the purposes of section 87A of the Management Act (interest on overdue corporation tax).

(3) In the application of section 87A of the Management Act in relation to an amount assessed to corporation tax under [paragraph 52 of Schedule 18 to the Finance Act 1998][7] by virtue of this paragraph—

(a) the amount so assessed shall be taken to have become due and payable on the date on which that assessment was made; and
(b) the words ["(in accordance with section 59D of this Act)"][2] in subsection (1) shall accordingly be disregarded.

(4) In determining the amount of any relevant interest, any question whether the excess mentioned in sub-paragraph (1) above (in the following provisions of this paragraph referred to as "the principal") or any part of it is or was "outstanding" at any time shall be determined in accordance with sub-paragraphs (5) to [(8)][2] below.

(5) So much of the principal as does not exceed the amount of the last provisional repayment made to the company for the accounting period in question shall be taken to have become outstanding on the date on which that provisional repayment was made.

(6) So much (if any) of the principal as—

(a) exceeds the amount of the provisional repayment referred to in sub-paragraph (5) above, but

(b) does not exceed the amount of the preceding provisional repayment for that accounting period,

shall be taken to have become outstanding on the date on which that preceding provisional repayment was made; and so on with any remaining portion of the principal and any preceding provisional repayments for that accounting period.

(7) So much (if any) of the principal as has become outstanding as mentioned in sub-paragraph (5) or (6) above and has at any time neither been repaid to the Board nor been assessed to corporation tax under [paragraph 52 of Schedule 18 to the Finance Act 1998]7 by virtue of this paragraph shall be taken to remain outstanding at that time (and an amount shall accordingly be taken to cease being outstanding only when it is repaid to the Board or when it is so assessed).

[(8) For the purposes of sub-paragraph (7) above, any repayment made by the company in respect of an amount ...[3] repaid to it in respect of—

(a) income tax such as is mentioned in paragraph (a) of sub-paragraph (1A) above, ...[3]

(b) ...[3]

shall be treated as a repayment in respect of the principal, taking an earlier such repayment by the company before a later.][2]

[(9) In this paragraph "self-assessment" means an assessment included in a [company tax return]7 and includes a reference to such an assessment as amended.][2][1][8]

Commentary—*Simon's Direct Tax Service* D4.534.
Definitions—"Accounting period", s 834(1); "the Management Act", s 831(3); "provisional fraction", para 6(1); "provisional repayment", para 6(1), (2); "provisional repayment period", para 6(1).
Cross references—See TA 1988 Sch 19AC para 15(3) (modification of sub-para (1C)(a) above in its application to overseas life insurance companies).
Modifications—Individual Savings Account (Insurance Companies) Regulations 1998, SI 1998/1871, regs 20 and 21 (application from 6 April 1999 in relation to pension business and individual savings account business taken together, so that references to repayments are references to the aggregate of amounts relating to pension business and individual savings account business; words inserted in sub-paras (1A) and (1C) with effect from 6 April 1999; and, the repeals made by F(No2)A 1997 Sch 3 para 11 (see amendment note [3] below) cease to apply by virtue of SI 1998/1871 reg 21 with effect from 6 April 1999).
Friendly Societies (Provisional Repayments for Exempt Business) Regulations, SI 1999/622 regs 3, 10 (modification of this paragraph in applying this Schedule (as amended by F(No 2)A 1997 Sch 3 in relation to distributions made to friendly societies after 5 April 2004 and as unamended by F(No 2)A 1997 Sch 3 in relation to distributions made to friendly societies before 6 April 2004) to exempt business of a friendly society for accounting periods ending after 30 June 1999).
Insurance Companies (Gilt-edged Securities) (Periodic Accounting for Tax on Interest) Regulations, SI 1999/623 regs 4, 8 (application of this paragraph, with modifications, in cases where payments of interest on certain gilt-edged securities are made without deduction of tax to insurance companies carrying on pension business with effect for accounting periods beginning before 1 April 1999 and ending after 30 June 1999).
Amendments—[1] This Schedule inserted by FA 1991 s 49(2), (3) and Sch 8 in relation to accounting periods beginning after 1 October 1992 by virtue of FA 1991 s 49 (Appointed Day) Order, SI 1992/1746.
[2] Sub-para (1)(a), (b) substituted, sub-paras (1A)–(1D) inserted, words in sub-para (3)(b) substituted for "(in accordance with section 10 of the principal Act)", word in sub-para (4) substituted for "(7)", and sub-paras (8), (9) inserted by FA 1996 s 169, Sch 34 para 3 with effect in relation to provisional repayment periods, within the meaning of this Schedule, falling in accounting periods ending on or after the appointed day under FA 1994 s 199 (1 July 1999 by virtue of Finance Act 1994, Section 199 (Appointed Day) Order, SI 1998/3173).
[3] Words in sub-paras (1A), (1B), (8) (as those sub-paras have effect for accounting periods ending on or after the appointed day in footnote 2 above) repealed by F(No 2)A 1997 s 23, Sch 3 para 11(1), (3)–(5), Sch 8 Pt II(7).
[4] Sub-paragraph (1ZA) inserted by FA 1998 s 91(1) with effect in relation to accounting periods beginning at any time after 1 October 1992 and ending before the day appointed under FA 1994 s 199 (1 July 1999 by virtue of SI 1998/3173).
[5] Word substituted by FA 1998 s 37(2) with effect in relation only to payments of interest falling after 31 March 1999 by virtue of Finance Act 1998, Section 37, (Appointed Day) Order, SI 1999/619.
[6] Words in sub-para (1C)(c) and preceding word "or" deleted by FA 1998, s 37(2) with effect in relation only to payments of interest falling after 31 March 1999 by virtue of SI 1999/619.
[7] Sub-para (1D) and words in sub-paras (1), (1A), (3), (7) and (9) substituted by FA 1998 Sch 19 para 51 with effect in relation to accounting periods ending on or after the "self-assessment appointed day" (1 July 1999 by virtue of SI 1998/3173).
[8] This paragraph repealed by FA 2001 ss 87, 110, Sch 33 Pt II(12) with effect in accordance with FA 2001 s 87.

Reduced entitlement during transitional period

[[4—(1) The Board may by regulations make provision for the amount of any provisional repayment to which a company would otherwise be entitled for any accounting period ending after the opening transitional date and before the closing transitional date to be reduced by a prescribed percentage.

(2) The regulations may require a company claiming a provisional repayment for a provisional repayment period falling within such an accounting period to specify in the claim—

(a) the maximum amount to which it could have been entitled by way of provisional repayment for that provisional repayment period apart from the regulations;

(b) the maximum reduced entitlement for that provisional repayment period; and

(c) the amount of the provisional repayment claimed for that provisional repayment period.

(3) The regulations may make provision—

(a) for the charging of interest in any case where an insurance company claims, and is paid, by way of provisional repayment an amount in excess of the maximum reduced entitlement for the provisional repayment period to which the claim relates;

(b) for the period for which, and the rate at which, any such amount is to carry interest under the regulations;

(c) *for any such interest to be treated for the purposes of section 30 of the Management Act as if it were an amount of corporation tax which had been repaid and which ought not to have been repaid; and*

(d) *for section 87A of that Act to apply in relation to an amount assessed to corporation tax under section 30 of that Act by virtue of the regulations with modifications corresponding to those specified in paragraph 3(3) above.*

(4) *The regulations may prescribe for the purposes of sub-paragraph (1) above different percentages for accounting periods ending after different dates.*

(5) *Sub-paragraphs (2) to (4) above are without prejudice to the generality of sub-paragraph (1) above.*

(6) *In this paragraph—*

"*the maximum reduced entitlement*", *in relation to an insurance company and a provisional repayment period, means the maximum amount (as reduced in accordance with the regulations) to which the company could have been entitled by way of provisional repayment for that provisional repayment period;*

"*the opening transitional date*" *and* "*the closing transitional date*" *mean respectively such date as the Board may specify for the purpose in the first regulations made under this paragraph;*

"*prescribed*" *means specified in the regulations;*

"*the regulations*" *means any regulations under this paragraph.]*[1]][2]

Commentary—*Simon's Direct Tax Service* **D4.534.**
Regulations—Insurance Companies (Pensions Business) (Transitional Provisions) Regulations, SI 1992/2326.
Definitions—"Provisional fraction", para 6(1); "provisional repayment", para 6(1), (2); "provisional repayment period", para 6(1).
Cross references—See Insurance Companies (Pensions Business) (Transitional Provisions) Regulations, SI 1992/2326 reg 3 ("the opening transitional date" and "the closing transitional date" for the purposes of this paragraph is 2 October 1992 and 1 January 1999 respectively),
Insurance Companies (Pensions Business) (Transitional Provisions) Regulations, SI 1992/2326 reg 4 (prescribed percentage for the purposes of sub-para (1) above),
Insurance Companies (Pensions Business) (Transitional Provisions) Regulations, SI 1992/2326 reg 6 (provisions for charging interest under sub-para (3) above);
Modifications—Friendly Societies (Provisional Repayments for Exempt Business) Regulations, SI 1999/622 regs 3, 11 (disapplication of this paragraph in applying this Schedule (as amended by F(No 2)A 1997 Sch 3 in relation to distributions made to friendly societies after 5 April 2004 and as unamended by F(No 2)A 1997 Sch 3 in relation to distributions made to friendly societies before 6 April 2004) to exempt business of a friendly society for accounting periods ending after 30 June 1999).
Amendments—[1] This Schedule inserted by FA 1991 s 49(2), (3) and Sch 8 in relation to accounting periods beginning after 1 October 1992 by virtue of FA 1991 s 49 (Appointed Day) Order, SI 1992/1746.
[2] This paragraph repealed by FA 2001 ss 87, 110, Sch 33 Pt II(12) with effect in accordance with FA 2001 s 87.

Transitional application of pay and file provisions

[[5—(1) *This paragraph applies in relation to an accounting period of an insurance company if—*

(a) *the accounting period—*

   (i) *begins on or after the commencement day; and*

   (ii) *ends on or before the day appointed for the purposes of section 10;*

(b) *the company carries on pension business for the whole or part of the accounting period; and*

(c) *the company makes a claim for a provisional repayment for the accounting period;*

and in this paragraph "*transitional accounting period*" *means an accounting period in relation to which this paragraph applies.*

(2) *An insurance company shall be entitled—*

(a) *to make a claim for payment of a tax credit in respect of any income of a transitional accounting period, and*

(b) *to make a claim for the purposes of section 7(5), so far as relating to section 7(2) or 11(3), in respect of any income tax falling to be set off against corporation tax for a transitional accounting period,*

and may do so whether or not the income in question is referable to the company's pension business).

(3) *For the purposes of sub-paragraph (2) above, sections 7(2) and 11(3) shall have effect in relation to a transitional accounting period as if the words from* "*and accordingly*" *to the end, in each provision, were omitted.*

(4) *A claim under sub-paragraph (2) above may only be made at such time or within such period as the Board may by regulations provide.*

(5) *In the application of this Schedule in relation to a transitional accounting period, paragraph 1 above shall have effect as if the reference in each of sub-paragraphs (7) and (10) to a claim such as is mentioned in section 7(6) or in section 42(5A) of the Management Act were a reference to a claim under paragraph (a) or (b) of sub-paragraph (2) above.*

(6) *If and to the extent that the provisions of section 826, or of section 87A of the Management Act, would not, apart from this sub-paragraph, have effect in relation to a transitional accounting period, they shall be treated as having effect for all purposes in relation to that accounting period; and—*

(a) in the application of section 826 by virtue of this sub-paragraph, the reference in subsection (1)(a) of that section to an accounting period which ends after the appointed day shall be treated as a reference to a transitional accounting period; and

(b) in the application of section 87A of the Management Act by virtue of this sub-paragraph, corporation tax shall be taken to become due and payable on the day following the expiration of the period within which it is required under section 10(1)(b) to be paid.

(7) If and to the extent that the amendments of section 30 of the Management Act specified in subsections (1) to (4) of section 88 of the Finance (No 2) Act 1987 would not, apart from this sub-paragraph, have effect in relation to a transitional accounting period, they shall be treated as having effect for all purposes in relation to that transitional accounting period.

(8) Subsection (7) of section 88 of the Finance (No 2) Act 1987 shall have effect for the purposes of sub-paragraph (7) above as if the reference in paragraph (a) of that subsection to accounting periods ending after the appointed day were a reference to transitional accounting periods.

(9) In this paragraph "the commencement day" means the day appointed under section 49 of the Finance Act 1991.]¹]²

Commentary—*Simon's Direct Tax Service* **D4.534.**
Regulations—Insurance Companies (Pensions Business) (Transitional Provisions) Regulations, SI 1992/2326.
Notes—The "commencement day" for the purposes of sub-paras (1)(a)(i), (9) above is 1 October 1992 by virtue of FA 1991 s 49 (Appointed Day) Order, SI 1992/1746; and the day appointed for the purposes of sub-para (1)(a)(ii) above is 30 September 1993 by virtue of Corporation Tax Acts (Provisions for Payment of Tax and Returns) (Appointed Days) Order, SI 1992/3066 art 2(1), (2)(b).
Definitions—"Provisional fraction", para 6(1); "provisional repayment", para 6(1), (2); "provisional repayment period", para 6(1).
Cross references—See Insurance Companies (Pensions Business) (Transitional Provisions) Regulations, SI 1992/2326 reg 7 (a claim under sub-paras (2), (4) to be made for the accounting period to which it relates at the time when a return is made under TMA 1970 s 11);
Modifications—Friendly Societies (Provisional Repayments for Exempt Business) Regulations, SI 1999/622 regs 3, 11 (disapplication of this paragraph in applying this Schedule (as amended by F(No 2)A 1997 Sch 3 in relation to distributions made to friendly societies after 5 April 2004 and as unamended by F(No 2)A 1997 Sch 3 in relation to distributions made to friendly societies before 6 April 2004) to exempt business of a friendly society for accounting periods ending after 30 June 1999).
Amendments—¹ This Schedule inserted by FA 1991 s 49(2), (3) and Sch 8 in relation to accounting periods beginning after 1 October 1992 by virtue of FA 1991 s 49 (Appointed Day) Order, SI 1992/1746.
² This paragraph repealed by FA 2001 ss 87, 110, Sch 33 Pt II(12) with effect in accordance with FA 2001 s 87.

Interpretation

[6—(1) In this Schedule—

["provisional fraction" shall be construed in accordance with paragraphs 1(4) and 2 above;]²
"provisional repayment" means a provisional repayment under paragraph 1 above;
"provisional repayment period" shall be construed in accordance with paragraph 1 above.

(2) Any reference in this Schedule to a provisional repayment for an accounting period is a reference to a provisional repayment for a provisional repayment period falling within that accounting period.

(3) ...³

[(4) Sub-paragraph (5) below applies in any case where an insurance company—

(a) which has delivered a return under section 11 of the Management Act for an accounting period ending before the self-assessment appointed day, but
(b) which has not delivered its first [company tax return]⁵ for an accounting period ending on or after that day,

makes the first claim for a provisional repayment for a particular accounting period ending on or after that day.]⁴

[(5) Where this sub-paragraph applies—

(a) the provisional fraction for the accounting period to which the claim mentioned in sub-paragraph (4) above relates shall be determined in accordance with paragraph 1(3), (4), and (6) and sub-paragraph (3) above, as they have effect in relation to accounting periods ending before that day; and
(b) paragraph 2 above, as originally enacted, shall have effect in relation to that accounting period as it has effect in relation to accounting periods ending before that day.]⁴

[(6) In this paragraph "the self-assessment appointed day" means the day appointed under section 199 of the Finance Act 1994 for the purposes of Chapter III of Part IV of that Act (self-assessment management provisions).]⁴]¹]⁶

Commentary—*Simon's Direct Tax Service* **D4.534.**
Note—The amendments to TMA 1970 s 11 made by F(No 2)A 1987 s 82 have effect where a notice to deliver a return is served after 31 December 1993 by virtue of Corporation Tax Act (Provisions for Payment of Tax and Returns) (Appointed Days) Order, SI 1992/3066 art 3.
Definitions—"Accounting period", s 834(1); "the Management Act", s 831(3).
Modifications—Friendly Societies (Provisional Repayments for Exempt Business) Regulations, SI 1999/622 regs 3, 12 (modification of this paragraph in applying this Schedule (as amended by F(No 2)A 1997 Sch 3 in relation to distributions made to friendly societies after 5 April 2004 and as unamended by F(No 2)A 1997 Sch 3 in relation to distributions made to friendly societies before 6 April 2004) to exempt business of a friendly society for accounting periods ending after 30 June 1999).

Insurance Companies (Gilt-edged Securities) (Periodic Accounting for Tax on Interest) Regulations, SI 1999/623 regs 4, 9 (application of this paragraph, with modifications, in cases where payments of interest on certain gilt-edged securities are made without deduction of tax to insurance companies carrying on pension business with effect for accounting periods beginning before 1 April 1999 and ending after 30 June 1999).

Amendments—[1] This Schedule inserted by FA 1991 s 49(2), (3) and Sch 8 in relation to accounting periods beginning after 1 October 1992 by virtue of FA 1991 s 49 (Appointed Day) Order, SI 1992/1746.

[2] In sub-para (1) definition "provisional fraction" substituted for former words "'provisional fraction' shall be construed in accordance with paragraphs 1(3), (4)(b) and 2 above;" by FA 1996 s 169, Sch 34 para 4(1), (2) with effect in relation to provisional repayment periods (as defined in sub-para (1) above) falling in accounting periods ending on or after the appointed day under FA 1994 s 199 (1 July 1999).

[3] Sub-para (3) repealed by FA 1996 s 169, Sch 34 para 4(1), (3), Sch 41 Pt V(27) with effect in relation to provisional repayment periods (as defined in sub-para (1) above) falling in accounting periods ending on or after the appointed day under FA 1994 s 199 (1 July 1999). [4] Sub-paras (4)–(6) inserted by FA 1996 s 169, Sch 34 para 4(1), (4) with effect in relation to provisional repayment periods (as defined in sub-para (1) above) falling in accounting periods ending on or after the appointed day under FA 1994 s 199 (1 July 1999).

[5] Words in sub-para (4)(b) substituted by FA 1998 Sch 19 para 51 with effect in relation to accounting periods ending on or after the "self-assessment appointed day" (1 July 1999).

[6] This paragraph repealed by FA 2001 ss 87, 110, Sch 33 Pt II(12) with effect in accordance with FA 2001 s 87.

[SCHEDULE 19AC

MODIFICATION OF ACT IN RELATION TO OVERSEAS LIFE INSURANCE COMPANIES][1]

Section 444B

Regulations—Insurance Companies (Capital Redemption Business) (Modification of the Corporation Tax Acts) Regulations, SI 1999/498.
Revenue Internal Guidance—Life assurance manual Chapter 17 (Revenue interpretation of this Schedule).
Amendments—[1] This Schedule inserted by FA 1993 Sch 9 para 1.

[1 In its application to an overseas life insurance company this Act shall have effect with the following modifications.][1]

Commentary—*Simon's Direct Tax Service* **D4.537.**
Definitions—"Insurance company", s 431(2); "overseas life insurance company", s 431(2).
Amendments—[1] This Schedule inserted by FA 1993 Sch 9 para 1.

[2 ...]

Commentary—*Simon's Direct Tax Service* **D4.537.**
Amendments—This paragraph repealed by F(No 2)A 1997 s 23, Sch 3 para 13(1), (2), (14), Sch 8 Pt II(6) with effect for accounting periods beginning after 1 July 1997.

[3—(1) In subsection (2) of section 11, the following paragraphs shall be treated as inserted after paragraph (*a*)—

"(*aa*) where section 11B applies for an accounting period, any trading or other income arising in that period from assets which by virtue of that section are attributed to the branch or agency at the time the income arises (but so that this paragraph shall not include distributions received from companies resident in the United Kingdom); and
(*ab*) where section 11C applies for an accounting period, any trading or other income falling within section 11C(2) in that period (but so that this paragraph shall not include distributions received from companies resident in the United Kingdom); and".

(2) The following shall be treated as inserted after paragraph (*b*) of that subsection
"and
(*c*) chargeable gains accruing to the company on the disposal of assets of the company's [long-term insurance fund][3] situated outside the United Kingdom and used or held for the purposes of the branch or agency immediately before the disposal; and
(*d*) where section 11B applies for an accounting period, chargeable gains accruing to the company in that period on the disposal of assets which by virtue of that section are attributed to the branch or agency immediately before the disposal; and
(*e*) where section 11C applies for an accounting period, chargeable gains accruing to the company in that period by virtue of section 11C(3)."

(3) The following subsection shall be treated as inserted after that subsection—
"(2A) For the purposes of subsection (2)(*c*) above—
(*a*) section 275 of the 1992 Act (location of assets) shall apply as it applies for the purposes of that Act;
(*b*) "[long-term insurance fund][3]" has the meaning given by section 431(2)."

(4) ...][1]

Commentary—*Simon's Direct Tax Service* **D4.537**
Definitions—"Accounting period", s 834(1); "the 1992 Act", s 831(3); "branch or agency", s 834(1); "chargeable gains", s 832(1); "company", s 832(1); "distribution", s 832(1); "trade", s 832(1).
Cross references—See TA 1988 s 444D (qualifying distributions, tax credits, etc).
Amendments—[1] This Schedule inserted by FA 1993 Sch 9 para 1.
Sub-para (4) repealed by FA 1995 Sch 29 Pt VIII(5), with effect for accounting periods beginning after 31 December 1994.

³ Words in sub-paras (2), (3) substituted by the Financial Services and Markets Act 2000 (Consequential Amendments) (Taxes) Order, SI 2001/3629 arts 13, 52(1)(*l*)(i) with effect from 1 December 2001, immediately after the coming into force of the Financial Services and Markets Act 2000 ss 411, 432(1), Sch 20.

[**4**—(1) The following sections shall be treated as inserted after section 11—

"11A Overseas life insurance companies: interpretation of sections 11B and 11C

(1) For the purposes of this section and sections 11B and 11C—

(*a*) an asset is at any time a section 11(2)(*b*) asset if, were it to be disposed of at that time, any chargeable gains accruing to the company on the disposal would form part of its chargeable profits for corporation tax purposes by virtue of section 11(2)(*b*);

(*b*) an asset is at any time a section 11(2)(*c*) asset if, were it to be disposed of at that time, any chargeable gains accruing to the company on the disposal would form part of its chargeable profits for corporation tax purposes by virtue of section 11(2)(*c*);

(*c*) relevant contracts and policies are contracts and policies the effecting of which constitutes the carrying on of life assurance business;

and in this section and those sections any expression to which a meaning is given by section 431(2) has that meaning.

(2) For the purposes only of subsection (1)(*a*) and (*b*) above any enactment which—

(*a*) limits any chargeable gain on the disposal of an asset;

(*b*) treats any gain on the disposal of an asset as not being a chargeable gain; or

(*c*) treats any disposal of an asset as not giving rise to a chargeable gain,

shall be disregarded.

(3) For the purposes of sections 11B and 11C—

(*a*) the notional value at any time is the value at that time of the assets which the branch or agency would reasonably be expected to hold at that time in consequence of any relevant contracts, and any relevant policies, which at that time are carried out at the branch or agency;

(*b*) the section 11B value at any time is the value at that time of such of the section 11(2)(*b*) and section 11(2)(*c*) assets as are assets held at that time in consequence of any relevant contracts, and any relevant policies, which at that time are carried out at the branch or agency;

(*c*) the section 11C value at any time is the value at that time of—

(i) such of the section 11(2)(*b*) and section 11(2)(*c*) assets as are assets held at that time in consequence of any relevant contracts, and any relevant policies, which at that time are carried out at the branch or agency; and

(ii) the assets which by virtue of section 11B are attributed to the branch or agency at that time;

(*d*) a relevant fund is a fund of assets of the company (wherever those assets may be situated) any part of which is held in consequence of any relevant contracts, and any relevant policies, which at any time in the accounting period concerned are carried out at the branch or agency.

(4) In applying subsection (3)(*a*) above as regards a particular time, it shall be assumed that—

(*a*) at that time the branch or agency is a company resident in the United Kingdom undertaking the activities it then actually undertakes;

(*b*) the terms of any dealings between the branch or agency and another part of the company are not (or not necessarily) their actual terms but are such as would be the terms if the branch or agency and the other part of the company were independent persons dealing at arm's length

11B Overseas life insurance companies: attribution of assets

(1) This section applies for an accounting period where the mean of the notional value at the beginning and end of the accounting period exceeds the mean of the section 11B value at those times.

(2) Where this section applies for an accounting period, assets shall be attributed to the branch or agency in that period in accordance with the following provisions of this section.

(3) There shall be attributed to the branch or agency in the accounting period such of the qualifying assets of the company as (having regard to the excess mentioned in subsection (1 above) it is just and reasonable to attribute to the branch or agency.

(4) For the purposes of subsection (3) above—

(*a*) where an asset is a qualifying asset for the whole of the accounting period it may, subject to paragraphs (*c*) and (*d*) below, be attributed to the branch or the agency for the whole or any part or parts of that period;

(*b*) where an asset is a qualifying asset for any portion of the accounting period it may, subject to paragraphs (*c*) and (*d*) below, be attributed to the branch or agency for the whole or any part or parts of that portion;

(*c*) an asset shall not be attributed to the branch or agency for any period of time during which it is a section 11(2)(*b*) or section 11(2)(*c*) asset;

(*d*) an asset shall not be attributed to the branch or agency at any particular time unless it is held in consequence of any relevant contracts, and any relevant policies, which at that time are carried out at the branch or agency.

(5) An asset of the company is a qualifying asset at any time if it is an asset of one or more of the following descriptions, that is to say—

(*a*) an asset which, in relation to any relevant contracts and any relevant policies which at that time are carried out at the branch or agency, is a linked asset within the meaning given by section 431(2);

(*b*) an asset which at that time is maintained in the United Kingdom as a result of a requirement imposed under section [43 of the Financial Services and Markets Act 2000 other than an asset not treated as so maintained under that requirement;][3]

(*c*) an asset which at that time is treated for the purposes of any such requirement as is mentioned in paragraph (*b*) above as maintained in the United Kingdom [under that requirement;][1]

(*d*) an asset which at that time is held in respect of the business carried on by the branch or agency as a result of a condition of [a direction under section 148 of the Financial Services and Markets Act 2000][1];

(*e*) an asset which at that time is held in a fund which the company is required to maintain under the prudential legislation of a territory outside the United Kingdom in respect of the business carried on by the branch or agency;

(*f*) an asset which is identified in tax returns submitted to a taxing authority of a territory outside the United Kingdom as an asset which at that time is wholly referable to the business carried on by the branch or agency.

11C Overseas life insurance companies: additional income and gains

(1) This section applies for an accounting period where the mean of the notional value at the beginning and end of the accounting period exceeds the mean of the section 11C value at those times.

(2) Where this section applies for an accounting period, the income which falls within this subsection in that period shall be the specified amount of each item of relevant income arising in that period from any assets of the relevant fund.

(3) Where this section applies for an accounting period, the chargeable gains accruing to the company in that period by virtue of this subsection shall be the specified amount of each relevant gain accruing to the company in that period on the disposal of any assets of the relevant fund.

(4) For the purposes of this section—

(*a*) relevant income is income other than income which falls within section 11(2)(*a*) or (*aa*);

(*b*) a relevant gain is a gain (other than a chargeable gain which falls within section 11(2)(*b*),

(*c*) or (*d*)) which would be a chargeable gain if the company were resident in the United Kingdom.

(5) For the purposes of this section the specified amount of an item of relevant income arising in the accounting period from any assets of the relevant fund shall be determined by the formula—

$$SI = I \times \frac{(NV - CV)}{RF}$$

(6) For the purposes of this section the specified amount of a relevant gain accruing to the company in the accounting period on the disposal of any assets of the relevant fund shall be determined by the formula—

$$SG = G \times \frac{(NV - CV)}{RF}$$

(7) In subsections (5) and (6) above—

SI is the specified amount of an item of relevant income arising in the accounting period from any assets of the relevant fund;

I is an item of relevant income arising in that period from any assets of the relevant fund;

NV is the mean of the notional value at the beginning and end of that period;

CV is the mean of the section 11C value at the beginning and end of that period;

RF (subject to subsection (8) below) is the mean of the value of the relevant fund at the beginning and end of that period;

SG is the specified amount of a relevant gain accruing to the company in that period on the disposal of any assets of the relevant fund;

G is a relevant gain accruing to the company in that period on the disposal of any assets of the relevant fund.

(8) Where the assets of the relevant fund at the beginning or end of the accounting period include—

(*a*) section 11(2)(*b*) or section 11(2)(*c*) assets; or

(*b*) assets which by virtue of section 11B are attributed to the branch or agency, the value at that time of the relevant fund for the purposes of the definition of RF in subsection (7) above shall be reduced by the value at that time of those assets.

(9) Where in the accounting period the company has more than one relevant fund—

(*a*) in the definition of RF in subsection (7) above, the reference to the value of the relevant fund shall be treated as a reference to the value of the relevant funds; and

(*b*) any other reference in this section to the relevant fund shall be treated as a reference to the relevant funds.''

(2) ...²]¹

Commentary—*Simon's Direct Tax Service* **D4.537.**
Definitions—''Accounting period'', s 834(1); ''branch or agency'', s 834(1); ''chargeable gain'', s 832(1); ''company'', s 832(1).
Amendments—¹ This Schedule inserted by FA 1993 Sch 9 para 1.
² Sub-para (2) repealed by FA 1995 Sch 29 Pt VIII(5), with effect in relation to accounting periods beginning after 31 December 1994.
³ Words substituted by the Financial Services and Markets Act 2000 (Consequential Amendments) (Taxes) Order, SI 2001/3629 arts 13, 49(1), (2) with effect for the purposes of determining whether an asset is a qualifying asset at any time after 30 November 2001.

[4A—(1) In section 12(7A), the reference to [an insurance business transfer scheme]² shall be treated as including a reference to a qualifying overseas transfer.

(2) In this paragraph 'a qualifying overseas transfer' means so much of any transfer of the whole or any part of the business of an overseas life insurance company carried on through a branch or agency in the United Kingdom as takes place in accordance with any authorisation granted outside the United Kingdom for the purposes of Article 11 of the third [life insurance]² Directive.

[(3) In sub-paragraph (2) above, ''the third life insurance directive'' means the Council Directive of 10th November 1992 on the co-ordination of laws, regulations and administrative provisions relating to direct life assurance and amending Directives 79/267/EEC and 90/619/EEC (No.92/96/EEC).]²]¹

Commentary—*Simon's Direct Tax Service* **D4.501.**
Definitions—''Branch or agency'', s 834(1); ''overseas life insurance company'', s 431(2); ''United Kingdom'', s 830(1).
Amendments—¹ This paragraph inserted by FA 1995 s 53(2), Sch 9 para 2(2) with effect for any transfers sanctioned or authorised after 30 June 1994.
² Words in sub-paras (1), (2) substituted, and sub-para (3) substituted, by the Financial Services and Markets Act 2000 (Consequential Amendments) (Taxes) Order, SI 2001/3629 arts 13, 49(1), (3) with effect from 1 December 2001, immediately after the coming into force of the Financial Services and Markets Act 2000 ss 411, 432(1), Sch 20.

[5—(1) In section 76, the following subsections shall be treated as inserted after subsection (6)—

''(6A) In its application to an overseas life insurance company this section shall have effect as if—

(*a*) the reference in subsection (1)(*ca*) to any reinsurance commission were to any such reinsurance commission concerned as is attributable to the branch or agency in the United Kingdom through which the company carries on life assurance business [or capital redemption business]⁵;

(*b*) the references in subsection (1) to income and gains were to such income and gains concerned as are so attributable.

(6B) ...⁶''

[(1A)In section 76 references to franked investment income shall be treated as being references to UK distribution income within the meaning of paragraph 5B of this Schedule.]⁴

(2) ...³]¹

Commentary—*Simon's Direct Tax Service* **D4.537.**
Definitions—''Branch or agency'', s 834(1); ''insurance company'', s 431(2); ''life assurance business'', s 431(2); ''overseas life insurance company'', s 431(2).
Modifications—The words ''or capital redemption business'' in sub-para (1) omitted in applying life assurance provisions of the Corporation Tax Acts to insurance companies carrying on capital redemption business with effect for accounting periods ending after 30 June 1999: see Insurance Companies (Capital Redemption Business) (Modification of the Corporation Tax Acts) Regulations, SI 1999/498 reg 8.
Amendments—¹ This Schedule inserted by FA 1993 Sch 9 para 1.
² Words in sub-para (1) substituted by FA 1995 Sch 8 paras 36, 57 with effect for accounting periods beginning after 31 December 1994.
³ Sub-para (2) repealed by FA 1995 Sch 29 Pt VIII(5), with effect for accounting periods beginning after 31 December 1994.
⁴ Word in sub-para (1) substituted, words omitted therein repealed, and sub-para (1A) inserted by FA 1996 s 164(3), (5), Sch 41 Pt V(24) with effect for accounting periods beginning after 31 December 1995.
⁵ Words in sub-para (1) inserted by FA 1996 Sch 33 paras 3, 4 with effect as respects accounting periods ending on or after the appointed day under FA 1994 s 199 (1 July 1999).
⁶ In sub-para (1), the notionally inserted sub-s (6B) repealed by F(No 2)A 1997 s 23, Sch 3 para 13(1), (3), (14), Sch 8 Pt II(6) with effect for accounting periods beginning after 1 July 1997.

[5A—(1) Where an overseas life insurance company receives a qualifying distribution made by a company resident in the United Kingdom and the distribution (or part of the distribution)—

(*a*) would fall within paragraph (*a*), (*aa*) or (*ab*) of section 11(2) but for the exclusion contained in that paragraph, and

(*b*) is referable to life assurance business, but not to overseas life assurance business,

then the recipient shall be treated for the purposes of the Corporation Tax Acts as entitled to such a tax credit in respect of the distribution (or part of the distribution) as it would be entitled to under section 231 if it were resident in the United Kingdom.

(2) Where part only of a qualifying distribution would fall within paragraph (*ab*) of section 11(2) but for the exclusion contained in that paragraph, the tax credit to which the recipient shall be treated as entitled by virtue of sub-paragraph (1) above is the proportionate part of the tax credit to which the recipient would be so treated as entitled in respect of the whole of the distribution.][1]

[(3) Nothing in this paragraph shall be taken to confer on an overseas life insurance company any entitlement to make a claim under section 231(3).][2]

Commentary—*Simon's Direct Tax Service* **D4.501.**
Definitions—"The Corporation Tax Acts", s 831(3); "distribution", s 832(1); "life insurance business", s 431(2); "overseas life insurance company", s 431(2); "tax credit", s 832(1); "United Kingdom", s 830(1).
Amendments—[1] Para 5A inserted by FA 1995 Sch 8 paras 35(1), 57 with effect for accounting periods beginning after 31 December 1994.
[2] Sub-para (3) inserted by F(No 2)A 1997 s 23, Sch 3 para 13(1), (4), (15) with effect in relation to distributions made after 1 July 1997.

[5B—(1)–(3) ...[2]

(4) In this paragraph "UK distribution income" means income of an overseas life insurance company which consists of a distribution (or part of a distribution) in respect of which the company is entitled to a tax credit (and which accordingly represents income equal to the aggregate of the amount or value of the distribution (or part) and the amount of that credit).][1]

Commentary—*Simon's Direct Tax Service* **D4.501.**
Definitions—"Distribution", s 832(1); "overseas life insurance company", s 431(2); "tax credits", s 832(1); "United Kingdom", s 830(1).
Amendments—[1] Para 5B inserted by FA 1995 Sch 8 paras 35(1), 57 with effect for accounting periods beginning after 31 December 1994.
[2] Sub-paras (1)–(3) repealed by F(No 2)A 1997 s 23, Sch 3 para 13(1), (5), (14), Sch 8 Pt II(6) with effect for accounting periods beginning after 1 July 1997, and see F(No 2)A 1997 Sch 3 para 13(16) as regards the position for accounting periods straddling that date.

[5C—(1) This paragraph applies to income from the investments of an overseas life insurance company attributable to the basic life assurance and general annuity business of the branch or agency in the United Kingdom through which the company carries on life assurance business.

[(2) Where, in computing the income to which this paragraph applies, any profits and gains arising from a FOTRA security, or from any loan relationship represented by it, are excluded by virtue of the tax exemption condition of that security, the amount which by virtue of section 76 is to be deductible by way of management expenses shall be reduced in accordance with sub-paragraph (3) below.][2]

[(3) That amount shall be reduced so that it bears to the amount which would be deductible apart from this sub-paragraph the same proportion as the amount of the income to which this paragraph applies (after applying the provisions of section 154(2) to (7) of the Finance Act 1996) bears to what would be the amount of that income if the tax exemption condition were disregarded.][2]

[(4) Subsection (8) of section 154 of the Finance Act 1996 (meaning of "FOTRA security" and "tax exemption condition") shall apply for the purposes of this paragraph as it applies for the purposes of that section.][2]][1]

Commentary—*Simon's Direct Tax Service* **D4.501.**
Definitions—"Basic life assurance and general annuity business", s 431(2); "branch or agency", s 834(1); "life insurance business", s 431(2); "loan relationship", FA 1996 s 81; "overseas life insurance company", s 431(2); "tax", s 832(3); "United Kingdom", s 830(1).
Amendments—[1] Para 5C inserted by FA 1995 Sch 8 paras 35(1), 57 with effect for accounting periods beginning after 31 December 1994.
[2] Sub-paras (2)–(4) substituted for sub-para (2) by FA 1996 s 154(7), (9), Sch 28 para 5 with effect for accounting periods ending after 31 March 1996.

[6—(1) In subsection (2) of section 431, the following definition shall be treated as substituted for the definition of "investment reserve"—

"'investment reserve', in relation to an overseas life insurance company, means the excess of the value of the relevant assets over the relevant liabilities, and for the purposes of this definition—

   (*a*) relevant assets are such assets of the company's [long-term insurance fund][5] as are—

      (i) section 11(2)(*b*) assets;
      (ii) section 11(2)(*c*) assets; or
      (iii) assets which by virtue of section 11B are attributed to the branch or agency in the United Kingdom through which the company carries on life assurance business; and

   (*b*) relevant liabilities are such liabilities of the [long-term][6] business as are attributable to the branch or agency;

and in a case where section 11C applies, the value of the relevant assets shall be increased by the amount by which the notional value exceeds the section 11C value; and any expression used in this definition to which a meaning is given by section 11A has that meaning;".

(2) In that subsection, the following definition shall be treated as substituted for the definition of "liabilities"—

"'liabilities', where the company concerned is an overseas life insurance company, does not include excluded liabilities and (subject to that) means—

(*a*) liabilities as estimated for the purposes of the company's periodical return, or

(*b*) in the case of liabilities not estimated for the purposes of such a periodical return, liabilities as estimated for the purposes of any return equivalent to a periodical return and required to be made by the company under the law of the territory in which the company is resident, or

(*c*) in the case of liabilities not estimated for the purposes of such a periodical return or equivalent return, liabilities as found from the company's records;

and excluded liabilities are any liabilities that have fallen due or been reinsured and any not arising under or in connection with policies or contracts effected as part of the company's insurance business;''.

(3) , (4) ...[2]

[(4A) In that subsection the following definition shall be inserted at the appropriate place—

"UK distribution income" has the meaning given by paragraph 5B(4) of Schedule 19AC;''.][4]

(5) In that subsection, the following definition shall be treated as substituted for the definition of '''value'—

'''"value", in relation to assets and where the company concerned is an overseas life insurance company, means—

(*a*) their value as taken into account for the purposes of the company's periodical return, or

(*b*) where their value is not taken into account for the purposes of such a periodical return, their value as taken into account for the purposes of any return equivalent to a periodical return and required to be made by the company under the law of the territory in which the company is resident, or

(*c*) where their value is not taken into account for the purposes of such a periodical return or equivalent return, their value as found from the company's records;

and the reference in paragraph (*c*) above to the value of assets as found from the company's records is a reference to the market value as so found or, where applicable, the current value (within the meaning of the Directive of the Council of the European Communities dated 19th December 1991 No 91/674/EEC (directive on the annual accounts and consolidated accounts of insurance undertakings)) as so found;''.

(6) ...][3][1]

Commentary—*Simon's Direct Tax Service* **D4.537.**
Amendments—[1] This Schedule inserted by FA 1993 Sch 9 para 1.
[2] Sub-paras (3), (4) repealed by FA 1995 Sch 8 paras 37, 55, Sch 29 Pt VIII(5), with effect in relation to accounting periods beginning after 31 October 1994 (subject to FA 1995 Sch 8 para 55(2)).
[3] Sub-para (6) repealed by FA 1995 Sch 29 Pt VIII(5), with effect for accounting periods beginning after 31 December 1994.
[4] Sub-para (4A) inserted by FA 1995 Sch 8 paras 35(3), 57 with effect for accounting periods beginning after 31 December 1994.
[5] Words in sub-para (1) substituted by the Financial Services and Markets Act 2000 (Consequential Amendments) (Taxes) Order, SI 2001/3629 arts 13, 52(1)(*l*)(ii) with effect from 1 December 2001, immediately after the coming into force of the Financial Services and Markets Act 2000 ss 411, 432(1), Sch 20.
[6] Word "long-term" in sub-para (1) substituted by the Financial Services and Markets Act 2000 (Consequential Amendments) (Taxes) Order, SI 2001/3629 arts 13, 52(2)(*o*)(i) with effect from 1 December 2001, immediately after the coming into force of the Financial Services and Markets Act 2000 ss 411, 432(1), Sch 20.

[**6A**—In section 431D(1), the words "carried on through a branch or agency in the United Kingdom by an overseas life insurance company" shall be treated as inserted after the words "means life assurance business".][1]

Commentary—*Simon's Direct Tax Service* **D4.501.**
Definitions—"Branch or agency", s 834(1); "overseas life insurance company", s 431(2); "United Kingdom", s 830(1).
Amendments—[1] Para 6A inserted by FA 1995 Sch 8 paras 38, 55 with effect in relation to accounting periods beginning after 31 October 1994 (subject to FA 1995 Sch 8 para 55(2)).

[**7**—(1) Section 432A has effect as if the references in subsections (3), (6) and (8) to assets were to such of the assets concerned as are—

(*a*) section 11(2)(*b*) assets,

(*b*) section 11(2)(*c*) assets, or

(*c*) assets which by virtue of section 11B are attributed to the branch or agency in the United Kingdom through which the company carries on life assurance business;

and as if the references in subsections (6) and (8) to liabilities were to such of the liabilities concerned as are attributable to the branch or agency.

Expressions used in this sub-paragraph to which a meaning is given by section 11A have that meaning.

(2) For the purposes of section 432A as it applies in relation to an overseas life insurance company, income which falls within section 11(2)(*aa*) or (*ab*), and chargeable gains or allowable losses which fall within section 11(2)(*d*) or (*e*)—

(*a*) shall not be referable to [long-term][4] business other than life assurance business; and

(*b*) shall be apportioned under subsections (5) and (6) of that section separately from other income, gains and losses.

(3) For the purposes of the application of section 432A(6) in relation to such income, gains or losses as are mentioned in sub-paragraph (2) above—

(*a*) "liabilities" does not include liabilities of the [long-term][4] business other than life assurance business;

(*b*) the [net value][3] of assets directly referable to any category of business does not include assets directly referable to [long-term][4] business other than life assurance business; and

(*c*) ...[3].[2]][1]

Commentary—*Simon's Direct Tax Service* **D4.503.**
Definitions—"Allowable loss", s 834(1); "branch or agency", s 834(1); "chargeable gain", s 832(1); "life assurance business", s 431(2); "long term business", s 431(2); "overseas life insurance company", s 431(2); "United Kingdom", s 830(1).
Amendments—[1] This Schedule inserted by FA 1995 Sch 9 para 1.
[2] Para 7 substituted by FA 1995 Sch 8 paras 39, 57 with effect for accounting periods beginning after 31 December 1994.
[3] Words in sub-para (3)(*b*) substituted for word "value", and sub-para (3)(*c*) repealed, by FA 2000 ss 109(9)(*c*), 156, Sch 40 Pt II(16) with effect for accounting periods beginning after 31 December 1999 and ending after 20 March 2000.
[4] Words in sub-paras (2)(*a*), (3)(*a*), (*b*) substituted by the Financial Services and Markets Act 2000 (Consequential Amendments) (Taxes) Order, SI 2001/3629 arts 13, 52(2)(*o*)(ii) with effect from 1 December 2001, immediately after the coming into force of the Financial Services and Markets Act 2000 ss 411, 432(1), Sch 20.

[8—(1) In subsection (1) of section 432B, the words "or treated as brought into account by virtue of [paragraph 1C][2] of Schedule 8A to the Finance Act 1989" shall be treated as inserted after [the words "brought into account, within the meaning of that section,"][2].

(2) The following words shall be treated as inserted at the end of subsection (2) of that section "; but this subsection shall not apply for a period of account in relation to which [any provision of paragraph 1C][3] of Schedule 8A to the Finance Act 1989 applies."

[(3) Subsection (3) of section 432B shall have effect as if after the words "with which an account is concerned" there were inserted the words "or in respect of which items are treated as brought into account by virtue of paragraph 1C of Schedule 8A to the Finance Act 1989"; and that subsection and sections 432C to 432E shall have effect as if the reference to relevant business were to relevant business of the branch or agency in the United Kingdom through which the company carries on life assurance business.][4]

(4) ...[5]][1]

Commentary—*Simon's Direct Tax Service* **D4.537.**
Definitions—"Branch or agency", s 834(1); "insurance company", s 431(2); "life assurance business", s 432(1); "overseas life insurance company", s 431(2); "United Kingdom", s 830(1).
Amendments—[1] This Schedule inserted by FA 1993 Sch 9 para 1.
[2] Words in sub-para (1), substituted by FA 1995 Sch 8 paras 40(2), 57 with effect for accounting periods beginning after 31 December 1994.
[3] Words in sub-para (2) substituted by FA 1995 Sch 8 paras 40(3), 57 with effect for accounting periods beginning after 31 December 1994.
[4] Sub-para (3) substituted by FA 1995 Sch 8 paras 40(4), 57 with effect for accounting periods beginning after 31 December 1994.
[5] Sub-para (4) repealed by FA 1995 Sch 29 Pt VIII(5), with effect for accounting periods beginning after 31 December 1994.

[9—[(1) In section 434, the following subsection shall be treated as inserted after subsection (1B)—

"(1C) The exclusion from section 11(2)(*a*), (*aa*) or (*ab*) of distributions received from companies resident in the United Kingdom shall not apply in relation to—

(*a*) the charge to corporation tax on the life assurance profits of an overseas life insurance company computed in accordance with the provisions of this Act applicable to Case I of Schedule D; or

(*b*) any computation of such profits in accordance with those provisions.

(1D) Paragraph 2 of Schedule F shall not have effect for the purposes of subsection (1C)(*a*) or (*b*) above, ...[4].

(1E) The reference in subsection (1C) above to the life assurance profits of an overseas life insurance company is a reference to the profits of the company—

(*a*) in respect of its life assurance business; or

(*b*) in respect of any category of life assurance business which it carries on."][3]

(2), (3) ...[2]][1]

Commentary—*Simon's Direct Tax Service* **D4.537.**
Definitions— "Distribution", s 209; "life assurance business", s 431(2); "overseas life insurance company", s 431(2); "Schedule D", s 18(1); "Schedule F", s 20(1); "tax credit", s 832(1).
Cross references—See F(No 2)A 1992 s 65(2), (5) (the application of the notionally inserted sub-ss (1C), (1D) does not prevent the application of the I minus E basis to a company's life assurance business).
Amendments—[1] This Schedule inserted by FA 1993 Sch 9 para 1.
[2] Sub-paras (2), (3) repealed by FA 1995 Sch 29 Pt VIII(5), with effect for accounting periods beginning after 31 December 1994.
[3] Sub-s (1) substituted by F(No 2)A 1997 s 23, Sch 3 para 13(1), (6), (15) with effect in relation to distributions made after 1 July 1997.
[4] In sub-para (1), words in the notionally inserted sub-s (1D) repealed by F(No 2)A 1997 s 34, Sch 4 para 29(1), (2), (4), Sch 8 Pt II(10) with effect in relation to distributions made after 5 April 1999.

[9A ...]

Commentary—*Simon's Direct Tax Service* **D4.501.**
Amendments—This paragraph inserted by FA 1995 Sch 8 paras 42, 57 with effect for accounting periods beginning after 31 December 1994 and repealed by F(No 2)A 1997 s 23, Sch 3 para 13(1), (7), (14), Sch 8 Pt II(6) with effect for accounting periods beginning after 1 July 1997.

[9B [The following section shall be treated as inserted after section 434A—

"434AA Treatment of annuities

An][2] overseas life insurance company shall not be entitled to treat as paid out of profits or gains brought into charge to income tax any part of the annuities paid by the company which is referable to its life assurance business.".][1]

Commentary—*Simon's Direct Tax Service* **D4.501.**
Definitions—"Life assurance business", s 432(1); "overseas life insurance company", s 431(2); "profits or gains", s 833(1).
Amendments—[1] Para 9B inserted by FA 1995 Sch 8 paras 42, 57 with effect for accounting periods beginning after 31 December 1994.
[2] Words substituted by FA 1997 s 67(5) with effect in relation to accounting periods beginning after 5 March 1997.

9C ...

Amendments—Para 9C repealed by CAA 2001 ss 578, 580, Sch 2 para 64, Sch 4 with effect for corporation tax purposes, as respects allowances and charges falling to be made for chargeable periods ending after 31 March 2001.

[10—(1) ...][2]
(2) ...[3]
(3) ...[1]

Amendments—[1] Sub-para (3) repealed by FA 1995 Sch 29 Pt VIII(5) with effect for accounting periods beginning after 31 December 1994.
[2] Sub-para (1) repealed by F(No 2)A 1997 s 23, Sch 3 para 13(1), (8), (15), Sch 8 Pt II(6) with effect in relation to distributions made after 1 July 1997.
[3] Sub-para (2) repealed by F(No 2)A 1997 s 23, Sch 3 para 13(1), (9), (14), Sch 8 Pt II(6) with effect for accounting periods beginning after 1 July 1997, see F(No 2)A 1997 Sch 3 para 13(17) as regards the position for accounting periods straddling that date.

[10A ...]

Amendments—This paragraph repealed by F(No 2)A 1997s 23, Sch 3 para 13(1), (10), (15), Sch 8 Pt II(6) with effect in relation to distributions made after 1 July 1997 (previously inserted by FA 1995 Sch 8 paras 44, 57 with effect for accounting periods beginning after 31 December 1994).

[10AA In section 440(2)(a), the reference to [an insurance business transfer scheme][2] shall be treated as including a reference to a qualifying overseas transfer (within the meaning of paragraph 4A above).][1]

Definitions—"Long term business", s 431(2).
Amendments—[1] This paragraph inserted by FA 1995 s 53(2), Sch 9 para 2(3), with effect for any transfers sanctioned or authorised after 30 June 1994.
[2] Words substituted by the Financial Services and Markets Act 2000 (Consequential Amendments) (Taxes) Order, SI 2001/3629 arts 13, 49(4) with effect from 1 December 2001, immediately after the coming into force of the Financial Services and Markets Act 2000 ss 411, 432(1), Sch 20.

[10B—(1) Where the company mentioned in section 440(1) is an overseas life insurance company, section 440 has effect with the following modifications.

(2) Subsection (4) shall be treated as if—

(a) in paragraphs (a), (b), (d), (e) and (f) the words "UK assets" were substituted for the words "assets"; and
(b) at the end there were inserted—

"(g) section 11C assets;
(h) non-UK assets.".

[(2A) The following subsection shall be treated as inserted after subsection (4)—

"(4AA) [Section 13 of the Capital Allowances Act (use for qualifying activity of plant or machinery provided for other purposes)][3] shall apply in relation to any case in which an asset or part of an asset held by an overseas life insurance company—

(a) ceases to be within the category set out in paragraph (h) of subsection (4) above; and
(b) at the same time comes within another of the categories set out in that subsection.".][2]

(3) The following subsection shall be treated as inserted at the end of the section—

"(7) For the purposes of this section—

(a) UK assets are—
(i) section 11(2)(b) assets;
(ii) section 11(2)(c) assets; or
(iii) assets which by virtue of section 11B are attributed to the branch or agency in the United Kingdom through which the company carries on life assurance business;

(b) section 11C assets are assets—
(i) (in a case where section 11C (other than subsection (9)) applies) of the relevant fund, other than UK assets; or
(ii) (in a case where that section including that subsection applies) of the relevant funds, other than UK assets;

(c) non-UK assets are assets which are not UK assets or section 11C assets;

and any expression used in this subsection to which a meaning is given by section 11A has that meaning.''.

(4) Where one of the companies mentioned in section 440(2) is an overseas life insurance company, section 440(2)(b) shall have effect as if for the words ''is within another of those categories'' there were substituted ''is not within the corresponding category''.

(5) Where the transferor company mentioned in section 440(2) is an overseas life insurance company, section 440 shall have effect, as regards the time immediately before the acquisition, with the modifications in sub-paragraphs (2) and (3) above.

(6) Where the acquiring company mentioned in section 440(2) is an overseas life insurance company, section 440 shall have effect, as regard the time immediately after the acquisition, with the modifications in sub-paragraphs (2) and (3) above.]¹

Commentary—*Simon's Direct Tax Service* **D4.501.**
Definitions—''Branch or agency'', s 834(1); ''life assurance company'', s 431(2); ''overseas life insurance company'', s 431(2); ''United Kingdom'', s 830(1).
Amendments—¹ Para 10B inserted by FA 1995 Sch 8 paras 44, 57 with effect for accounting periods beginning after 31 December 1994.
² Sub-para (2A) inserted by FA 2000 s 75(4), (6)(a) with effect for chargeable periods ending after 20 March 2000.
³ Words substituted by CAA 2001 s 578, Sch 2 para 64(2) with effect for corporation tax purposes as respects allowances and charges falling to be made for chargeable periods ending after 31 March 2001.

[10C—(1) In section 440B the following subsection shall be treated as substituted for subsection (3)—

''(3) Section 440(1) and (2) have effect as if the only categories specified in subsection (4) of that section were—

   (a) UK assets of the [long-term insurance fund]²,
   (b) other UK assets,
   (c) section 11C assets, and
   (d) non-UK assets,

(those expressions having the meanings given by section 440(7)).''.

(2) The following subsection shall be treated as substituted for subsection (4) of that section—

''(4) Section 440A applies as if for paragraphs (a) to (e) of subsection (2) there were substituted—

   ''(a) so many of the UK securities as are identified in the company's records as securities by reference to the value of which there are to be determined benefits provided for under policies or contracts the effecting of all (or all but an insignificant proportion) of which constitutes the carrying on of [long-term]³ business, shall be treated for the purposes of corporation tax as a separate holding linked solely to that business,
   (b) any remaining UK securities shall be treated for those purposes as a separate holding which is not of the description mentioned in the preceding paragraph,
   (c) the section 11C securities shall be treated for those purposes as a separate holding which is not of any of the descriptions mentioned in the preceding paragraphs; and
   (d) the non-UK securities shall be treated for those purposes as a separate holding which is not of any of the descriptions mentioned in the preceding paragraphs.''.]¹

Commentary—*Simon's Direct Tax Service* **D4.501.**
Definitions—''Long term business'', s 431(2); ''United Kingdom'', s 830(1).
Amendments—¹ Para 10C inserted by FA 1995 Sch 8 paras 44, 57 with effect for accounting periods beginning after 31 December 1994.
² Words in sub-para (1) substituted by the Financial Services and Markets Act 2000 (Consequential Amendments) (Taxes) Order, SI 2001/3629 arts 13, 52(1)(l)(iii) with effect from 1 December 2001, immediately after the coming into force of the Financial Services and Markets Act 2000 ss 411, 432(1), Sch 20.
³ Word in sub-para (2) substituted by the Financial Services and Markets Act 2000 (Consequential Amendments) (Taxes) Order, SI 2001/3629 arts 13, 52(2)(o)(iii) with effect from 1 December 2001, immediately after the coming into force of the Financial Services and Markets Act 2000 ss 411, 432(1), Sch 20.

[11—[(1) In section 440A(2), in paragraph (a) the words ''UK securities'' shall be treated as substituted for the word ''securities'' in the first place where it occurs.]²

(2) ...³

(3) In paragraphs (d) and (e) of that subsection, the words ''UK securities'' shall be treated as substituted for the word ''securities''.

(4) The following paragraphs shall be treated as inserted at the end of that subsection—

   ''(f) the section 11C securities shall be treated for those purposes as a separate holding which is not of any of the descriptions mentioned in the preceding paragraphs; and
   (g) the non-UK securities shall be treated for those purposes as a separate holding which is not of any of the descriptions mentioned in the preceding paragraphs.''

(5) The following subsection shall be treated as inserted after subsection (6) of that section—

''[(6A)]⁴ For the purposes of this section—

   (a) UK securities are such securities as are—
      (i) section 11(2)(b) assets;
      (ii) section 11(2)(c) assets; or

        (iii) assets which by virtue of section 11B are attributed to the branch or agency in the United Kingdom through which the company carries on life assurance business;

    (*b*) section 11C securities are securities—

        (i) (in a case where section 11C (other than subsection (9)) applies) which are assets of the relevant fund, other than UK securities; or

        (ii) (in a case where that section including that subsection applies) which are assets of the relevant funds, other than UK securities;

    (*c*) non-UK securities are securities which are not UK securities or section 11C securities;

and any expression used in this subsection to which a meaning is given by section 11A has that meaning.''

(6) ...[5]]''[1]

Commentary—*Simon's Direct Tax Service* D4.537.
Amendments—[1] This Schedule inserted by FA 1993 Sch 9 para 1.
[2] Sub-para (1) substituted by FA 1995 Sch 8 paras 45(2), 57 with effect for accounting periods beginning after 31 December 1994.
[3] Sub-para (2) repealed by FA 1995 Sch 8 paras 45(3), 55 Sch 29 Pt VIII(5), with effect for accounting periods beginning after 31 October 1994 (subject to FA 1995 Sch 8 para 55(2)).
[4] Word in sub-para (5) substituted by FA 1995 Sch 8 paras 45(4), 57 with effect for accounting periods beginning after 31 December 1994.
[5] Sub-para (6) repealed by FA 1995 Sch 29 Pt VIII(5), with effect for accounting periods beginning after 31 December 1994.

[11A—(1) ...[1]

(2) ...[2]

Commentary—*Simon's Direct Tax Service* D4.501.
Amendments—[1] Sub-para (1) repealed by F(No 2)A 1997 s 23, Sch 3 para 13(1), (11), (15), Sch 8 Pt II(6) with effect in relation to distributions made after 1 July 1997.
[2] Sub-para (2) repealed by F(No 2)A 1997 s 34, Sch 4 para 29(3), (4), Sch 8 Pt II(10) with effect in relation to distributions made after 5 April 1999.

[11B In section 442A the following subsection shall be treated as inserted after subsection (6)—

    ''(7) In the case of an overseas life insurance company, the investment return treated as accruing under this section in any accounting period in relation to a policy or contract shall be treated as chargeable profits within section 11(2) of the Taxes Act 1988 where the policy or contract is one which in that accounting period gives rise, or but for the reinsurance arrangement would give rise, to such profits.''.][1]

Commentary—*Simon's Direct Tax Service* D4.501.
Amendments—[1] Para 11B inserted by FA 1995 Sch 8 paras 46, 57 with effect for accounting periods beginning after 31 December 1994.

[11C In sections 444A(1) and 460(10A), the references to [an insurance business transfer scheme][2] shall be treated as including references to a qualifying overseas transfer (within the meaning of paragraph 4A above).][1]

Commentary—*Simon's Direct Tax Service* D4.501.
Amendments—[1] Para 11C inserted by FA 1995 s 53(2), Sch 9 para 2(4), with effect for any transfers sanctioned or authorised after 30 June 1994.
2 Words substituted by the Financial Services and Markets Act 2000 (Consequential Amendments) (Taxes) Order, SI 2001/3629 arts 13, 49(4) with effect from 1 December 2001, immediately after the coming into force of the Financial Services and Markets Act 2000 ss 411, 432(1), Sch 20.

[12—(1) ...[2]

(2) ...[1]]

Amendments—[1] Sub-para (2) repealed by FA 1995 Sch 29 Pt VIII(5), with effect for accounting periods beginning after 31 December 1994.
[2] Sub-para (1) repealed by F(No 2)A 1997 s 23, Sch 3 para 13(1), (12), (14), Sch 8 Pt II(6) with effect for accounting periods beginning after 1 July 1997.

[13—(1) ...[3]

(2) The following [subsection shall be treated as inserted after subsection (2) of section 794][3]—

    ''(3) ...[3]

    (4) In relation to any item of income falling within section 11(2)(*ab*), or any chargeable gain falling within section 11(2)(*e*), the reference in [subsection (2)(*bb*)][3] above to tax paid shall be construed as a reference to that part of the tax paid which bears to the whole of the tax paid the same proportion as that item of income, or that chargeable gain, bears to the relevant income, or relevant gain, by reference to which that item of income, or that chargeable gain, is, by virtue of section 11C, calculated; and, in relation to any such item of income or any such chargeable gain, the reference in section 790(4) to tax paid shall be construed accordingly.''

(3) ...[2]][1]

Commentary—*Simon's Direct Tax Service* **D4.537.**
Definitions—''Branch or agency'', s 834(1); ''chargeable gain'', s 832(1); ''chargeable period'', s 832(1); ''insurance company'', s 431(2); ''overseas life insurance company'', s 431(2).
Amendments—[1] This Schedule inserted by FA 1993 Sch 9 para 1.
[2] Sub-para (3) repealed by FA 1995 Sch 29 Pt VIII(5), with effect for accounting periods beginning after 31 December 1994.
[3] Sub-paras (1) and sub-s (3) as notionally inserted by sub-para (2) repealed, and words in notionally inserted sub-s (4) substituted, by FA 2000 ss 103, 156, Sch 30 para 4(13), (14), Sch 40 Pt II(13) with effect for chargeable periods ending after 20 March 2000 by virtue of FA 2001 s 81, Sch 27 para 7.

[14—(1) In subsection (1) of section 811, the words ''subsections (1A) and (2)'' shall be treated as substituted for the words ''subsection (2)''.

(2) The following subsection shall be treated as inserted after that subsection—

''(1A) In relation to any item of income falling within section 11(2)(*ab*), the reference in subsection (1) above to any sum which has been paid in respect of tax on that income shall be construed as a reference to the part of that sum which bears to the whole of that sum the same proportion as that item of income bears to the relevant income by reference to which that item of income is, by virtue of section 11C, calculated.''

(3) ...[2]]¹

Commentary—*Simon's Direct Tax Service* **D4.537.**
Amendments—[1] This Schedule inserted by FA 1993 Sch 9 para 1.
[2] Sub-para (3) repealed by FA 1995 Sch 29 Pt VIII(5), with effect in relation to accounting periods beginning after 31 December 1994.

[14A—(1) In Schedule 19AA, paragraph 5(5)(*c*) (and the reference to it in paragraph 2(3) of that Schedule) shall be treated as omitted.

(2) The following paragraph shall be treated as inserted at the end of that Schedule—

''**6** In its application to an overseas life insurance company this Schedule shall have effect as if—

    (*a*) the references in paragraphs 2 and 3 to assets of the [long-term insurance fund]³ were to such of the assets as are—

        (i) section 11(2)(*b*) assets;
        (ii) section 11(2)(*c*) assets; or
        (iii) assets which by virtue of section 11B are attributed to the branch or agency in the United Kingdom through which the company carries on life assurance business; ...²

    (*b*) the references in paragraphs 2 and 4 to the liabilities of the company's [long-term]⁴ business were to such of those liabilities as are attributable to the branch or agency; [and
    (*c*) the references in paragraph 4 to any liabilities of the company's [long-term insurance fund]³ which represent a money debt were to any such of those liabilities as are attributable to the branch or agency;]²

and any expression used in this paragraph to which a meaning is given by section 11A has that meaning.''.]¹

Commentary—*Simon's Direct Tax Service* **D4.501.**
Definitions—''Branch or agency'', s 834(1); ''life assurance business'', s 431(2); ''overseas life insurance company'', s 431(2); ''United Kingdom'', s 830(1).
Amendments—[1] Para 14A inserted by FA 1995 Sch 8 paras 48, 55 with effect for accounting periods beginning after 31 October 1994 (subject to FA 1995 Sch 8 para 55(2)).
[2] In para 6 treated as inserted by this paragraph, word ''and'' in sub-para (2)(*a*) repealed and sub-para (2)(*c*) inserted by the Overseas Life Assurance Fund (Amendment) Order, SI 2000/2188 art 5 with effect for accounting periods beginning after 31 December 1999 and ending after 31 August 2000.
[3] Words in sub-para (2) substituted by the Financial Services and Markets Act 2000 (Consequential Amendments) (Taxes) Order, SI 2001/3629 arts 13, 52(1)(*l*)(iv) with effect from 1 December 2001, immediately after the coming into force of the Financial Services and Markets Act 2000 ss 411, 432(1), Sch 20.
[4] Word in sub-para (2) substituted by the Financial Services and Markets Act 2000 (Consequential Amendments) (Taxes) Order, SI 2001/3629 arts 13, 52(2)(*o*)(iv) with effect from 1 December 2001, immediately after the coming into force of the Financial Services and Markets Act 2000 ss 411, 432(1), Sch 20.

[[15—*(1)* ...⁴

(2) ...²

[(3) In paragraph 3(1C) of Schedule 19AB, for paragraph (a) there shall be substituted—

    ''(a) section 11(3),''.]³]¹]⁵

Amendments—[1] This Schedule inserted by FA 1993 Sch 9 para 1.
[2] Sub-para (2) repealed by FA 1995 Sch 29 Pt VIII(5), with effect for accounting periods beginning after 31 December 1994.
[3] Sub-para (3) inserted by FA 1996 s 169, Sch 34 para 5, Sch 41 Pt V(27) with effect in relation to provisional repayment periods, within the meaning of Sch 19AB *ante*, falling in accounting periods ending on or after the appointed day (1 July 1999 by virtue of Finance Act 1994, Section 199, (Appointed Day) Order, SI 1998/3173).
[4] Sub-para (1) repealed by F(No 2)A 1997 s 23, Sch 3 para 13(1), (13), (14), Sch 8 Pt II(6) with effect for accounting periods beginning after 1 July 1997.
[5] This paragraph repealed by FA 2001 s 110, Sch 33 Pt II(12) with effect in accordance with FA 2001 s 87.

[SCHEDULE 19A]

UNDERWRITERS: ASSESSMENT AND COLLECTION OF TAX

Section 450(2A)

Amendments—This Schedule inserted by FA 1988 s 58(4)(*a*), (5) and Sch 5.
This Schedule repealed by FA 1993 Sch 23 Pt III(12) with effect from the year 1992–93. It is superseded with effect from that year by FA 1993 s 173(2) and Sch 19.

SCHEDULE 20

CHARITIES: QUALIFYING INVESTMENTS AND LOANS

Section 506

Modifications—See the Open-ended Investment Companies (Tax) Regulations, SI 1997/1154 regs 3, 5, 7, 16 (modification of this Schedule as it has effect in relation to open-ended investment companies).

PART I

QUALIFYING INVESTMENTS

1 Investments specified in any of the following paragraphs of this Part of this Schedule are qualifying investments for the purposes of section 506.

Commentary—*Simon's Direct Tax Service* **C4.528.**

2 Any investment falling within Part I, Part II, apart from paragraph 13 (mortgages etc) or Part III of Schedule 1 to the Trustee Investments Act 1961.

Commentary—*Simon's Direct Tax Service* **C4.528.**

3 Any investment in a common investment fund established under section 22 of the Charities Act 1960[, section 24 of the Charities Act 1993][1] or section 25 of the Charities Act (Northern Ireland) 1964 or in any similar fund established for the exclusive benefit of charities by or under any enactment relating to any particular charities or class of charities.

Commentary—*Simon's Direct Tax Service* **C4.528.**
Definition—"Charities", s 506(1).
Amendments—[1] Words inserted by the Charities Act 1993 Sch 6 para 25(*a*) with effect from 1 August 1993.

[3A Any investment in a common deposit fund established under section 22A of the Charities Act 1960 [or section 25 of the Charities Act 1993][2] or in any similar fund established for the exclusive benefit of charities by or under any enactment relating to any particular charities or class of charities.][1]

Commentary—*Simon's Direct Tax Service* **C4.528.**
Definition—"Charities", s 506(1).
Amendments—[1] This paragraph inserted by the Charities Act 1992 Sch 6 para 17 with effect from 1 September 1992 by virtue of Charities Act 1992 (Commencement No 1 and Transitional Provisions) Order, SI 1992 No 1900.
[2] Words inserted by the Charities Act 1993 Sch 6 para 25(*b*) with effect from 1 August 1993.

4 Any interest in land, other than an interest held as security for a debt of any description.

Commentary—*Simon's Direct Tax Service* **C4.528.**

5 Shares in, or securities of, a company which are [listed][1] on a recognised stock exchange, or which are dealt in on the Unlisted Securities Market.

Commentary—*Simon's Direct Tax Service* **C4.528.**
Definitions—"Company", s 832(1), (2); "recognised stock exchange", s 841.
Amendments—[1] Word substituted by FA 1996 Sch 38 para 6(1), (2)(*l*), (11) with effect in relation to chargeable periods ending after 31 March 1996.

6 Units, or other shares of the investments subject to the trusts, of a unit trust scheme within the meaning [given by section 237(1) of the Financial Services and Markets Act 2000][1].

Commentary—*Simon's Direct Tax Service* **C4.528.**
Definitions—"Unit trust scheme", s 469, by virtue of s 832(1).
Amendments—[1] Words substituted by the Financial Services and Markets Act 2000 (Consequential Amendments) (Taxes) Order, SI 2001/3629 arts 13, 50 with effect from 1 December 2001, immediately after the coming into force of the Financial Services and Markets Act 2000 ss 411, 432(1), Sch 20.

7—(1) Deposits with [a bank][1] in respect of which interest is payable at a commercial rate.

(2) A deposit mentioned in sub-paragraph (1) above is not a qualifying investment if it is made as part of an arrangement under which a loan is made by the authorised institution to some other person.

[(3) In this paragraph "bank" has the meaning given by section 840A.][1]

Commentary—*Simon's Direct Tax Service* **C4.528.**
Definition—"Interest", s 832(1).

Amendments—[1] Words in sub-para (1) substituted and sub-para (3) inserted by FA 1996 Sch 37 paras 2(3), 5, 10 with effect in relation to deposits made or, as the case may be, money placed on or after 29 April 1996.

8 Certificates of deposit as defined in section 56(5).

Commentary—*Simon's Direct Tax Service* **C4.528.**

9—(1) Any loan or other investment as to which the Board are satisfied, on a claim made to them in that behalf, that the loan or other investment is made for the benefit of the charity and not for the avoidance of tax (whether by the charity or any other person).

(2) The reference in sub-paragraph (1) above to a loan includes a loan which is secured by a mortgage or charge of any kind over land.

Commentary—*Simon's Direct Tax Service* **C4.528.**
Definitions—"The Board", s 832(1); "charity", s 506(1).

PART II
QUALIFYING LOANS

10—[(1)][1] For the purposes of section 506, a loan which is not made by way of investment is a qualifying loan if it consists of—

(*a*) a loan made to another charity for charitable purposes only; or
(*b*) a loan to a beneficiary of the charity which is made in the course of carrying out the purposes of the charity; or
(*c*) money placed on current account with [a bank][1] otherwise than as part of such an arrangement as is mentioned in paragraph 7(2) above; or
(*d*) any other loan as to which the Board are satisfied, on a claim made to them in that behalf, that the loan is made for the benefit of the charity and not for the avoidance of tax (whether by the charity or by some other person).

[(2) In this paragraph "bank" has the meaning given by section 840A.][1]

Commentary—*Simon's Direct Tax Service* **C4.528.**
Definitions—"The Board", s 832(1); "charity", s 506(1).
Amendments—[1] Existing provision re-numbered as sub-para (1), words therein substituted and sub-para (2) added by FA 1996 Sch 37 paras 2(4), 5, 10 with effect in relation to deposits made or, as the case may be, money placed on or after 29 April 1996.

PART III
ATTRIBUTION OF EXCESS NON-QUALIFYING EXPENDITURE TO EARLIER CHARGEABLE PERIODS

11 This Part of this Schedule applies in the circumstances specified in subsection (6) of section 506 and in this Part—

(*a*) "the primary period" means the chargeable period of the charity concerned in which there is such an excess as is mentioned in that subsection;
(*b*) "unapplied non-qualifying expenditure" means so much of the excess referred to in that subsection as does not exceed the non-qualifying expenditure of the primary period; and
(*c*) "earlier period", in relation to an amount of unapplied non-qualifying expenditure, means any chargeable period of the charity concerned which ended not more than six years before the end of the primary period.

Commentary—*Simon's Direct Tax Service* **C4.527.**
Definitions—"Chargeable period", s 832(1); "charity", s 506(1).

12—(1) So much of the unapplied non-qualifying expenditure as is not shown by the charity to be the expenditure of non-taxable sums received by the charity in the primary period shall be treated in accordance with paragraph 13 below as non-qualifying expenditure of earlier periods.

(2) In sub-paragraph (1) above "non-taxable sums" means donations, legacies and other sums of a similar nature which, apart from section 505(1) of this Act and section [256 of the 1992][1] Act, are not within the charge to tax.

Commentary—*Simon's Direct Tax Service* **C4.527.**
Definitions—"The 1992 Act", s 831(3); "charity", s 506(1).
Amendments—[1] Words in sub-para (2) substituted by TCGA 1992 Sch 10 para 14(1), (59).

13—(1) Where, in accordance with paragraph 12 above, an amount of unapplied non-qualifying expenditure ("the excess expenditure") falls to be treated as non-qualifying expenditure of earlier periods—

(*a*) it shall be attributed only to those earlier periods (if any) which, apart from the attribution, (but taking account of any previous operation of this paragraph) the relevant income and gains exceed the aggregate of the qualifying and non-qualifying expenditure incurred in that period; and
(*b*) the amount to be attributed to any such earlier period shall not be greater than the excess of that period referred to in paragraph (*a*) above.

(2) Where there is more than one earlier period to which the excess expenditure can be attributed in accordance with sub-paragraph (1) above, it shall be attributed to later periods in priority to earlier periods.

(3) In so far as any of the excess expenditure cannot be attributed to earlier periods in accordance with this paragraph, it shall be disregarded for the purposes of section 506(6) (and this Part of this Schedule).

Commentary—*Simon's Direct Tax Service* **C4.527.**
Definition—"Qualifying expenditure", s 506(1).

14 All such adjustments shall be made, whether by way of the making of assessments or otherwise, as may be required in consequence of the provisions of this Part of this Schedule.

SCHEDULE 21

TAX RELIEF IN CONNECTION WITH SCHEMES FOR RATIONALISING INDUSTRY AND OTHER REDUNDANCY SCHEMES

Sections 570 and 572

PART I
PRELIMINARY

1—(1) In this Schedule—

"scheme" means a scheme which is for the time being certified or has at any time been certified by the Secretary of State under section 568;

"payment" means a payment made under a scheme, being a payment made to a person carrying on a trade to which the scheme relates and not being a payment made by way of repayment of contributions;

"the person chargeable" means, in relation to any such payment, the person liable to pay any tax which may fall to be paid by reason of the receipt of the payment;

"damage" includes any loss, liability, expense or other burden, and references to the amount of any damage are references to the sum which would be fair compensation for that damage;

"contribution" includes part of a contribution, and "deductible contribution" means a contribution allowed to be deducted under section 568, any reduction under Part III of this Schedule being left out of account; and

"asset" includes part of an asset.

(2) For the purposes of this Schedule, a sum received by any person by way of repayment of contributions shall be deemed to be by way of repayment of the last contribution paid by him, and, if the sum exceeds the amount of that contribution, by way of repayment of the penultimate contribution so paid, and so on.

Commentary—*Simon's Direct Tax Service* **B3.1473.**
Definition—"Trade", s 832(1).

PART II
RELIEF IN RESPECT OF CERTAIN PAYMENTS

2 The question whether any, and if so, what, relief is to be given shall be determined separately in relation to each payment made under the scheme in respect of the trade, but for the purpose of determining that question regard shall be had, as provided by the following provisions of this Part of this Schedule, to the sum ("the total payment") produced by adding the amount of the payment to the amount of any payments previously so made.

Commentary—*Simon's Direct Tax Service* **B3.1473.**
Definitions—"Payment", see para 1(1); "scheme", see para 1(1); "trade", s 832(1).

3 ...

Commentary—*Simon's Direct Tax Service* **B3.1473.**
Amendments—[1] This paragraph repealed by FA 1996 s 134(1), (2), Sch 20 para 43, Sch 41 Pt V(10) with effect for the purposes of income tax from the year 1996–97 and, for the purposes of corporation tax, as respects accounting periods ending after 30 June 1999 (by virtue of Finance Act 1994, Section 199, (Appointed Day) Order, SI 1998/3173 art 2).

4 No relief shall be given in respect of the payment unless the total payment, or the amount of the damage in respect of which the total payment has been made, whichever is the smaller, exceeds the aggregate amount of the deductible contributions which have been paid in furtherance of the scheme in respect of the trade in question before the payment is made, exclusive of any contributions which have been repaid before the payment is made.

Commentary—*Simon's Direct Tax Service* **B3.1473.**
Definitions—"Contributions", see para 1(1); "damage", see para 1(1); "payment", see para 1(1); "scheme", see para 1(1); "trade", s 832(1).

5 The amount of the reduction to be made in respect of the payment shall be arrived at by—

   (*a*) ascertaining the sum which bears to the excess mentioned in paragraph 4 above the same proportion that the amount mentioned in paragraph 3(*b*) above bears to the amount mentioned in paragraph 3(*a*); and

   (*b*) deducting from that sum the total amount of any reductions which have been or fall to be made under this Schedule in respect of payments previously made under the scheme in respect of the trade.

Commentary—*Simon's Direct Tax Service* **B3.1473.**
Definitions—"Payment", see para 1(1); "scheme", see para 1(1); "trade", s 832(1).

6—(1) For the purposes of this Schedule, and subject to sub-paragraph (2) below, damage shall be deemed to be damage in respect of which relief may be given under the Tax Acts if and only if—

   (*a*) the damage is attributable to any of the following events, that is to say, the demolition, destruction or putting out of use of any asset, or the disposition or termination of an interest in any asset, and, by reason of that event, an allowance falls to be made under [Part 2 or 3 of the Capital Allowances Act in calculating the profits of a trade][3] in taxing the trade; or

   (*b*) the damage consists of any loss, liability, expense or other burden in respect of which an allowance may be made in computing the [profits][2] of the trade for the purposes of the Tax Acts.

(2) ...[1]

(3) Where any event occurs which would give rise to an allowance under the Tax Acts in respect of any asset in taxing, or computing the [profits][2] of, a trade but for any of the following matters, that is to say—

   (*a*) that there are no [profits][2] against which the allowance could be made, or

   (*b*) that account is required to be taken of allowances previously made or deemed to have been made in respect of the asset; or

   (*c*) that account is required to be taken of any sum which falls to be written off the expenditure incurred on the asset for the purpose of determining whether any and if so what allowance may be given by reason of the event; or

   (*d*) that account is required to be taken of any sum falling to be taken into account as sale, insurance, salvage or compensation moneys, the like consequences shall ensue under this Schedule as if an allowance had fallen to be made by reason of that event.

(4) Where any damage is attributable to a permanent change in the purposes for which an asset is used, or the temporary or permanent putting out of use of an asset, the question whether the damage is damage in respect of which relief may be given under the Tax Acts shall be determined as if the damage had been attributable to a sale of the asset on the date upon which the change or putting out of use took place.

Commentary—*Simon's Direct Tax Service* **B3.1473.**
Definitions—"The 1990 Act", s 831(3); "asset", see para 1(1); "damage", see para 1(1); "interest", s 832(1); "profits or gains", s 833(1); "the Tax Acts", s 831(2); "trade", s 832(1).
Amendments—[1] Sub-para (2) repealed by CAA 1990 Sch 2.
[2] Word substituted in sub-paras (1)(*b*), (3) by FA 1998 Sch 7 para 1 with effect from 31 July 1998.
[3] Words in para (1)(*a*) substituted by CAA 2001 s 578, Sch 2 para 65 with effect for income tax purposes, as respects allowances and charges falling to be made for chargeable periods ending after 5 April 2001, and for corporation tax purposes, as respects allowances and charges falling to be made for chargeable periods ending after 31 March 2001.

PART III

EXCLUSION OF RELIEF IN RESPECT OF CONTRIBUTIONS PAID AFTER RELIEF HAS BEEN GIVEN UNDER PART II

7 The provisions of this Part of this Schedule shall have effect where—

   (*a*) a contribution is paid under a scheme in respect of a trade; and

   (*b*) before the contribution is paid, payments have been made under the scheme to the person carrying on the trade; and

   (*c*) reductions have been made, under Part II of this Schedule, in the amounts which, by reason of those payments, are to be treated as trading receipts of the trade.

Commentary—*Simon's Direct Tax Service* **B3.1474.**

8 There shall be ascertained—

   (*a*) the total amount of those reductions; and

   (*b*) the sum by which that total would have been decreased if the contribution, and any previous contributions to which this Part of this Schedule applies, had been paid before any of the payments were made.

Commentary—*Simon's Direct Tax Service* **B3.1474.**
Definitions—"Contribution", see para 1(1); "payments", see para 1(1).

9 For the purpose of determining what deduction is to be made in respect of the contribution under section 568, the contribution shall be deemed to be reduced by the sum specified in paragraph 8(*b*) above, but—

(*a*) for the purpose of the application of paragraph 8 above in relation to contributions subsequently paid under the scheme in respect of the trade, the total amount of the reductions referred to in that paragraph shall be treated as decreased by that sum; and

(*b*) for the purpose of the application of paragraph 5 above in relation to payments subsequently made under the scheme in respect of the trade, the total amount of the reductions referred to in that paragraph shall be treated as decreased by that sum.

Commentary—*Simon's Direct Tax Service* B3.1474.
Definitions—"Contribution", see para 1(1); "scheme", see para 1(1); "trade", s 832(1).

10 When two or more contributions are paid at the same time, the provisions of this Part of this Schedule shall have effect as if they were a single contribution.

Commentary—*Simon's Direct Tax Service* B3.1474.
Definition—"Contribution", see para 1(1).

SCHEDULE 22

REDUCTION OF PENSION FUND SURPLUSES

Section 603

1—(1) The Board may make regulations providing for this Schedule to apply, as from a prescribed date, in relation to any exempt approved scheme which is of a prescribed kind.

(2) The Board may make regulations providing for prescribed provisions of this Schedule to apply, as from a prescribed date, in prescribed circumstances, and subject to any prescribed omissions or modifications, in relation to any exempt approved scheme of another prescribed kind.

(3) In this Schedule "prescribed" means prescribed by regulations made by the Board.

Commentary—*Simon's Direct Tax Service* E7.233.
Regulations—Pension Scheme Surpluses (Administration) Regulations, SI 1987/352; Pension Scheme Surpluses (Valuation) Regulations, SI 1987/412. For continuity see Sch 30, para 21 of this Act.
Definitions—"The Board", s 832(1); "exempt approved scheme", s 612(1).

2—(1) The administrator of a scheme in relation to which this Schedule applies shall, in prescribed circumstances and at a prescribed time, either produce to the Board a written valuation such as is mentioned in sub-paragraph (2) below or give to the Board a certificate such as is mentioned in sub-paragraph (3) below.

(2) The valuation must be a valuation of the assets held for the purposes of the scheme and the liabilities of the scheme, must be determined in accordance with prescribed principles and fulfil prescribed requirements, and must be signed by a person with qualifications of a prescribed kind.

(3) The certificate must state whether or not the value of the assets (as determined in accordance with prescribed principles) exceeds the value of the liabilities (as so determined) by a percentage which is more than a prescribed maximum, must be in a prescribed form, and must be signed by a person with qualifications of a prescribed kind.

Commentary—*Simon's Direct Tax Service* E7.248.
Definitions—"Administrator", s 612(1); "the Board", s 832(1); "prescribed", see para 1(3); "scheme", s 611(2).
Cross references—See TA 1988 Sch 22 para 3 (proposals required to be submitted where valuation under this paragraph shows assets exceed liabilities by more than prescribed maximum).
TA 1988 Sch 22 para 4 (particulars to be furnished as respects valuation or certificate under this paragraph).
Pension Scheme Surpluses (Valuation) Regulations, SI 1987/412 reg 4 (regulations in accordance with which valuation and liabilities are to be determined).
SI 1987/412 reg 9 (prescribed circumstances and time for the purposes of sub-para (1) above),
SI 1987/412 reg 10(4) (prescribed maximum for the purposes of sub-para (3) above),
SI 1987/412 reg 12 (special provisions in respect of self-administered and insured schemes),
SI 1987/412 reg 13 (prescribed period for the purposes of sub-para (1) above),
SI 1987/412 reg 15 (prescribed form of certificate for the purposes of sub-para (3) above).

3—(1) Subject to paragraph 4(4) below, where a valuation produced under paragraph 2 shows, or a certificate given under that paragraph states, that the value of the assets exceeds the value of the liabilities by a percentage which is more than the prescribed maximum, the administrator of the scheme shall within a prescribed period submit to the Board for their approval proposals which comply with sub-paragraph (2) below.

(2) The proposals must be proposals for reducing (or, subject to paragraph (*b*) below, eliminating) the excess in a way or ways set out in the proposals and falling within sub-paragraph (3) below; and they must be such as to secure that—

(*a*) by the end of a prescribed period the percentage (if any) by which the value of the assets exceeds the value of the liabilities is no more than the prescribed maximum; and

(*b*) if the way, or one of the ways, set out in the proposals falls within sub-paragraph (3)(*a*) below, there remains an excess which is of a level not less than the prescribed minimum.

(3) Subject to sub-paragraph (4) below, the permitted ways of reducing or eliminating the excess are—

(*a*) making payments to an employer;

(b) suspending for a period (of five years or less) set out in the proposals an employer's obligation to pay contributions under the scheme or reducing for such a period the amount of an employer's contributions under the scheme;

(c) suspending for a period (of five years or less) set out in the proposals the obligation of employees to pay contributions under the scheme or reducing for such a period the amount of employees' contributions under the scheme;

(d) improving existing benefits provided under the scheme;

(e) providing new benefits under the scheme;

(f) such other ways as may be prescribed.

(4) In prescribed circumstances sub-paragraph (3) above shall apply subject to such omissions or modifications as may be prescribed.

(5) Subject to paragraph 4(4) below, if the administrator of the scheme fails to submit proposals to the Board within the period mentioned in sub-paragraph (1) above, or if the proposals submitted to them within that period are not approved by the Board within a further prescribed period, paragraph 7 below shall apply.

Commentary—*Simon's Direct Tax Service* **E7.249.**
Definitions—''Administrator'', s 612(1); ''the Board'', s 832(1); ''employees'', s 612(1); ''employer'', s 612(1); ''prescribed'', see para 1(3); ''scheme'', s 611(2).
Cross references—See TA 1988 Sch 22 para 5(3) (proposals required to be submitted in compliance with sub-paras (2)–(4) above where assets exceed liabilities by more than the prescribed maximum).
TA 1988 Sch 22 para 6(1) (administrator's obligation to carry out proposals within time limit).
Pension Scheme Surpluses (Valuation) Regulations, SI 1987/412 reg 10 (prescribed periods, prescribed excess and prescribed maximum for the purposes of sub-paras(1), (2)(a), (b) above),
SI 1987/412 reg 11 (prescribed modifications for the purposes of sub-para (4) above),
SI 1987/412 reg 13 (prescribed period for the purposes of sub-para (5) above).

4—(1) Where a valuation has been produced under paragraph 2 above, the Board may serve on the administrator of the scheme a notice requiring him to furnish the Board, within a prescribed period, with such particulars relating to the valuation as may be specified in the notice.

(2) Where a certificate has been given under paragraph 2 above, the Board may serve on the administrator of the scheme a notice requiring him to produce to the Board, within a prescribed period, a written valuation such as is mentioned in paragraph 2(2) above.

(3) Where a valuation has been produced in compliance with a notice served under sub-paragraph (2) above, the Board may serve on the administrator of the scheme a further notice requiring him to furnish the Board, within a prescribed period, with such particulars relating to the valuation as may be specified in the notice.

(4) Where a notice is served on the administrator of a scheme under sub-paragraph (1) or (2) above, paragraph 3(1) and (5) above shall cease to apply.

Commentary—*Simon's Direct Tax Service* **E7.248, 249.**
Definitions—''Administrator'', s 612(1); ''the Board'', s 832(1); ''notice'', s 832(1); ''prescribed'', see para 1(3); ''scheme'', s 611(2).
Cross references—See TA 1988 Sch 22 para 5 (further provisions as respects particulars furnished under this paragraph).
Pension Scheme Surpluses (Valuation) Regulations, SI 1987/412 reg 12 (special provisions in respect of self-administered and insured schemes),
SI 1987/412 reg 13 (prescribed period for the purposes of sub-paras (1), (2), (3) above).

5—(1) Where particulars have been furnished under paragraph 4 above, or a valuation has been produced under that paragraph, the Board shall, within a prescribed period, serve on the administrator of the scheme a notice—

(a) stating that they accept the valuation produced under paragraph 2 or, as the case may be, 4 above; or

(b) stating that they do not accept the valuation so produced, and specifying their estimate of the value of the liabilities of the scheme at the relevant time and their estimate of the value of the assets held for the purposes of the scheme at that time.

(2) For the purposes of sub-paragraph (1)(b) above, the relevant time is the time specified in the valuation produced under paragraph 2 or 4 above as the time by reference to which the values of the assets and liabilities are determined.

(3) Where—

(a) in a case falling within sub-paragraph (1)(a) above, the valuation shows that the value of the assets exceeds the value of the liabilities by a percentage which is more than the prescribed maximum; or

(b) in a case falling within sub-paragraph (1)(b) above, the value of the assets as estimated by the Board exceeds the value of the liabilities as so estimated by a percentage which is more than the prescribed maximum;

the administrator of the scheme shall within a prescribed period submit to the Board for their approval proposals which comply with paragraph 3(2) to (4) above.

(4) If the administrator of the scheme fails to submit proposals to the Board within the period mentioned in sub-paragraph (3) above, or if proposals submitted to them within that period are not approved by the Board within a further prescribed period, paragraph 7 below shall apply.

Commentary—*Simon's Direct Tax Service* **E7.249.**
Definitions—"Administrator", s 612(1); "the Board", s 832(1); "notice", s 832(1); "prescribed", see para 1(3); "scheme", s 611(2).
Cross references—See TA 1988 Sch 22 para 6(1) (administrator's obligation to carry out proposals within time limit).
TA 1988 Sch 22 para 8 (regulations as regards appeals against notices under sub-para (1)(*b*) above).
Pension Scheme Surpluses (Valuation) Regulations, SI 1987/412 reg 12 (special provisions in respect of self-administered and insured schemes).
SI 1987/412 reg 13 (prescribed period for the purposes of sub-paras (1), (3), (4) above).

6—(1) Where proposals are submitted to the Board under paragraph 3(1) or 5(3) above and they approve them within the further prescribed period mentioned in paragraph 3(5) or 5(4) above, the administrator of the scheme shall carry out the proposals within the period mentioned in paragraph 3(2) above.

(2) If the administrator fails to carry out the proposals within that period, paragraph 7 below shall apply.

Commentary—*Simon's Direct Tax Service* **E7.249.**
Definitions—"Administrator", s 612(1); "the Board", s 832(1); "scheme", s 611(2).

7—(1) Where this paragraph applies the Board may specify a percentage equivalent to the fraction—

$$\frac{A}{B}$$

where—

A represents their estimate of the value of the liabilities of the scheme at the relevant time increased by a prescribed percentage; and
B represents their estimate of the value of the assets held for the purposes of the scheme at that time.

(2) For the purposes of this paragraph the relevant time is the time specified—

(*a*) in the valuation produced or certificate given under paragraph 2 above; or
(*b*) where a valuation has been produced under paragraph 4 above, in that valuation,

as the time by reference to which the values of the assets and liabilities are determined.

(3) Where a percentage has been so specified—

(*a*) section 592(2) shall apply only to that percentage of any income derived in the relevant period from the assets held for the purposes of the scheme;
(*b*) section 592(3) shall apply only to that percentage of any underwriting commissions applied in the relevant period for the purposes of the scheme;
(*c*) section 56 shall by virtue of subsection (3)(*b*) of that section not apply only to that percentage of any profits or gains arising to the scheme in the relevant period; and
(*d*) section [271(1)(*g*) of the 1992][1] Act (capital gains tax exemption) shall apply only to that percentage of any gain accruing on the disposal in the relevant period of any of those assets.

(4) Sub-paragraphs (5) to (8) below shall apply where a percentage has been so specified, securities are transferred in the relevant period, and the transferor or transferee is such that, if he became entitled to any interest on them, exemption could be allowed under section 592(2).

(5) Section 715(1)(*k*) shall not apply.

(6) Where, in consequence of sub-paragraph (5) above, section 713(2)(*a*) or (3)(*b*) applies, the sum concerned shall be treated as reduced by an amount equal to the specified percentage of itself.

(7) Where, in consequence of sub-paragraph (5) above, section 713(2)(*b*) or (3)(*a*) applies, the relief concerned shall be treated as reduced by an amount equal to the specified percentage of itself.

(8) For the purposes of section 714(5), the amount of interest falling to be reduced by the amount of the allowance shall be treated as the amount found after applying section 592(2).

(9) In sub-paragraphs (4) to (8) above expressions which also appear in sections 710 to 728 have the same meanings as in those sections.

(10) In this paragraph "the relevant period" means the period beginning at the relevant time and ending when it is proved to the satisfaction of the Board that the value of the assets (as determined in accordance with prescribed principles) exceeds the value of the liabilities (as so determined) by a percentage which is no more than the prescribed maximum.

Commentary—*Simon's Direct Tax Service* **E7.249.**
Definitions—"The 1992 Act", s 831(3); "the Board", s 832(1); "interest", s 832(1); "prescribed", see para 1(3); "profits or gains", s 833(1); "scheme", s 611(2).
Cross references—See TA 1988 s 659A ("income" in para 3(*a*) above to include income from transactions relating to futures and options contracts).
TA 1988 Sch 22 para 3(5) (this paragraph to apply where proposals required to be submitted under para 3 are not submitted or not approved).
TA 1988 Sch 22 para 5(4) (this paragraph to apply where proposals required to be submitted under para 5 are not submitted or not approved).
TA 1988 Sch 22 para 6(2) (this paragraph to apply where proposals are not carried out within time limit).
Pension Scheme Surpluses (Valuation) Regulations, SI 1987/412 reg 10(4), (5) (prescribed percentage and prescribed maximum for the purposes of sub-paras(1), (10) above).
TCGA 1992 s 271(10) (sub-para (3)(*d*) above to be construed as if s 271(1)(*g*), (*h*), (2) included futures and options contracts).
Amendments—[1] Words in sub-para (3)(*d*) substituted by TCGA 1992 Sch 10 para 14(1), (60).

8—(1) The Board may make regulations providing that an appeal may be brought against a notice under paragraph 5(1)(*b*) above as if it were notice of the decision of the Board on a claim made by the administrator of the scheme concerned.

(2) Regulations under this paragraph may include—

(*a*) provision that bringing an appeal shall suspend the operation of paragraph 5(3) and (4) above; and

(*b*) other provisions consequential on the provision that an appeal may be brought (including provisions modifying this Schedule).

Commentary—*Simon's Direct Tax Service* E7.249.
Definitions—"Administrator", s 612(1); "the Board", s 832(1); "notice", s 832(1); "scheme", s 611(2).
Cross references—See Pension Scheme Surpluses (Valuation) Regulations, SI 1987/412 reg 14 (appeals procedure and consequences of appeal).

SCHEDULE 23

OCCUPATIONAL PENSION SCHEMES:

SCHEMES APPROVED BEFORE 23RD JULY 1987

Section 609

Cross references—See FA 1989 Sch 6 para 20(2) (notwithstanding the effect of anything in this Schedule, certain rules to apply in arriving at relevant annual remuneration for the purposes of calculating benefits of an employee joining after 31 May 1989 a retirement benefits scheme coming into existence before 14 March 1989);
Retirement Benefits Schemes (Continuation of Rights of Members of Approved Schemes) Regulations, SI 1990/2101 reg 5(1) (notwithstanding the effect of anything in this Schedule, certain rules to apply in arriving at relevant annual remuneration for the purposes of calculating benefits of an employee who is treated as having additional years of service by the rules of a scheme to which a transfer payment has been made.

Preliminary

1—(1) This Schedule shall be deemed to have come into force on 17th March 1987 and, subject to sub-paragraphs (2) and (3) below, applies in relation to any retirement benefits scheme approved by the Board before the passing of the Finance (No 2) Act 1987 (23rd July 1987).

[(2) The Board may by regulations provide that, in circumstances prescribed in the regulations, this Schedule or any provision of it shall not apply or shall apply with such modifications as may be so prescribed.][1]

[(2A) Regulations under sub-paragraph (2) above—

(*a*) may include provision authorising the Board to direct that this Schedule or any provision of it shall not apply in any particular case where in the opinion of the Board the facts are such that its application would not be appropriate;

(*b*) may take effect (and may authorise any direction given under them to take effect) as from 17th March 1987 or any later date;

(*c*) may make such supplementary provision as appears to the Board to be necessary or expedient.][1]

(3) This Schedule shall not apply to a retirement benefits scheme if, before the end of 1987, the administrator of the scheme gave notice to the Board that it is not to apply.

(4) Where a notice is given to the Board under sub-paragraph (3) above, the scheme shall, with effect from 17th March 1987 or (if later) the date with effect from which it was approved, cease to be approved.

Commentary—*Simon's Direct Tax Service* E7.214.
Regulations—Occupational Pension Schemes (Transitional Provisions) Regulations, SI 1988/1436, made under sub-para (2) above which contain regulations disapplying or applying with modifications certain paragraphs of this Schedule.
Definitions—"Administrator", s 612(1); "the Board", s 832(1); "notice", s 832(1); "retirement benefits scheme", s 611(1); "scheme", s 611(2).
Amendments—[1] Sub-paras (2), (2A) substituted for sub-para (2) by FA 1988 s 56.

Accelerated accrual

2—(1) This paragraph applies where an employee becomes a member of the scheme on or after 17th March 1987.

(2) Notwithstanding anything to the contrary in the rules of the scheme, they shall have effect as if they did not allow the provision for the employee of a pension exceeding one-thirtieth of his relevant annual remuneration for each year of service up to a maximum of 20.

Commentary—*Simon's Direct Tax Service* E7.214, 227.
Definitions—"Employee", s 612(1); "pension", s 612(1); "scheme", s 611(2); "service", s 612(1).
Cross references—See Occupational Pension Schemes (Transitional Provisions) Regulations, SI 1988/1436 reg 3 (disapplication of this paragraph),
Occupational Pension Schemes (Transitional Provisions) Regulations, SI 1988/1436 reg 4A (modification of this paragraph in circumstances where an employee retires early because of physical incapacity),
Occupational Pension Schemes (Transitional Provisions) Regulations, SI 1988/1436 reg 5 (modification of this paragraph),
Occupational Pension Schemes (Transitional Provisions) Regulations, SI 1988/1436 reg 5A (modification of this paragraph in circumstances where an employee retires with an immediate pension),

Occupational Pension Schemes (Transitional Provisions) Regulations, SI 1988/1436 reg 5B (modification of this paragraph in circumstances where an employee retires with a pension payable from a future date),

Occupational Pension Schemes (Transitional Provisions) Regulations, SI 1988/1436 reg 5C (modification of this paragraph in circumstances where an employee continues in service after normal retirement age),

Occupational Pension Schemes (Transitional Provisions) Regulations, SI 1988/1436 reg 5D (modification of this paragraph in circumstances where an employee has pension rights transferred from a previous employment to his pension rights in the present employment).

3—(1) This paragraph applies where an employee becomes a member of the scheme on or after 17th March 1987 and the scheme allows him to commute his pension or part of it for a lump sum or sums.

(2) If the employee's full pension (that is, the pension before any commutation) is equal to or less than a basic rate commutable pension, the rules of the scheme shall have effect (notwithstanding anything in them to the contrary) as if they did not allow him to obtain by way of commutation a lump sum or sums exceeding in all a basic rate lump sum.

(3) If the employee's full pension is greater than a basic rate commutable pension but less than a maximum rate commutable pension, the rules of the scheme shall have effect (notwithstanding anything in them to the contrary) as if they did not allow him to obtain by way of commutation a lump sum or sums exceeding in all the aggregate of—

    (*a*) a basic rate lump sum, and

    (*b*) an amount equal to the relevant percentage of the difference between a basic rate lump sum and a maximum rate lump sum.

(4) In this paragraph, as it applies in relation to an employee—

    (*a*) a "basic rate commutable pension" means a pension of one-sixtieth of his relevant annual remuneration for each year of service up to a maximum of 40;

    (*b*) a "maximum rate commutable pension" means a pension of one-thirtieth of his relevant annual remuneration for each year of service up to a maximum of 20;

    (*c*) a "basic rate lump sum" means a lump sum of three-eightieths of his relevant annual remuneration for each year of service up to a maximum of 40;

    (*d*) a "maximum rate lump sum" means a lump sum of such amount as may be determined by or under regulations made by the Board for the purposes of this paragraph and paragraph 4 below;

    (*e*) "the relevant percentage" means the difference between a basic rate commutable pension and the employee's full pension expressed as a percentage of the difference between a basic rate commutable pension and a maximum rate commutable pension.

Commentary—*Simon's Direct Tax Service* E7.214, 227.
Regulations—Occupational Pension Schemes (Maximum Rate Lump Sum) Regulations, SI 1987/1513. For continuity see Sch 30, para 21 of this Act.
Definitions—"The Board", s 832(1); "employee", s 612(1); "pension", s 612(1); "scheme", s 611(2); "service", s 612(1).
Cross references—See Occupational Pension Schemes (Transitional Provisions) Regulations, SI 1988/1436 regs 3, 6 (disapplication of this paragraph);
FA 1989 Sch 6 para 23(2) (new rules for commutation of pension for a lump sum).

4—(1) This paragraph applies where an employee becomes a member of the scheme on or after 17th March 1987 and the scheme provides a lump sum or sums for him otherwise than by commutation of his pension or part of it.

(2) If the employee's pension is equal to or less than a basic rate non-commutable pension, the rules of the scheme shall have effect (notwithstanding anything in them to the contrary) as if they did not allow the payment to him, otherwise than by way of commutation, of a lump sum or sums exceeding in all a basic rate lump sum.

(3) If the employee's pension is greater than a basic rate non-commutable pension but less than a maximum rate non-commutable pension the rules of the scheme shall have effect (notwithstanding anything in them to the contrary) as if they did not allow the payment to him, otherwise than by way of commutation, of a lump sum or sums exceeding in all the aggregate of—

    (*a*) a basic rate lump sum, and

    (*b*) an amount equal to the relevant percentage of the difference between a basic rate lump sum and a maximum rate lump sum.

(4) In this paragraph, as it applies in relation to an employee—

    (*a*) a "basic rate non-commutable pension" means a pension of one-eightieth of his relevant annual remuneration for each year of service up to a maximum of 40,

    (*b*) a "maximum rate non-commutable pension" means a pension of one-fortieth of his relevant annual remuneration for each year of service up to a maximum of 20,

    (*c*) "basic rate lump sum" and "maximum rate lump sum" have the same meanings as in paragraph 3 above, and

    (*d*) "the relevant percentage" means the difference between a basic rate non-commutable pension and the employee's actual pension expressed as a percentage of the difference between a basic rate non-commutable pension and a maximum rate non-commutable pension.

Commentary—*Simon's Direct Tax Service* E7.214, 227.
Regulations—Occupational Pension Schemes (Maximum Rate Lump Sum) Regulations, SI 1987/1513. For continuity see TA 1988 Sch 30 para 21.
Definitions—"Basic rate lump sum", see para 3(4)(*c*); "employee", s 612(1); "pension", s 612(1); "scheme", s 611(2).

Cross references—See Occupational Pension Schemes (Transitional Provisions) Regulations, SI 1988/1436 regs 3, 6 (disapplication of this paragraph);
FA 1989 Sch 6 para 24(2) (new rules for accelerated accrual of lump sum benefits).

Final remuneration

5—(1) This paragraph applies where an employee who is a member of the scheme retires on or after 17th March 1987.

(2) The rules of the scheme shall have effect as if they provided that in determining the employee's relevant annual remuneration for the purpose of calculating benefits, no account should be taken of anything excluded from the definition of "remuneration" in section 612(1).

(3) In the case of an employee—

(a) whose employer is a company and who at any time in the last ten years of his service is a controlling director of the company, or

(b) whose relevant annual remuneration for the purpose of calculating benefits, so far as the remuneration is ascertained by reference to years beginning on or after 6th April 1987, would (apart from this Schedule) exceed the permitted maximum,

the rules of the scheme shall have effect as if they provided that his relevant annual remuneration must not exceed his highest average annual remuneration for any period of three or more years ending within the period of ten years which ends with the date on which his service ends.

(4) In the case of an employee within paragraph (b) of sub-paragraph (3) above who retires before 6th April 1991, the rules of the scheme shall have effect as if they provided that his relevant annual remuneration must not exceed the higher of—

(a) the average annual remuneration referred to in that sub-paragraph, and

(b) his remuneration (within the meaning given by section 612(1)) assessable to income tax under Schedule E for the year of assessment 1986–87.

(5) For the purposes of this paragraph a person is a controlling director of a company if—

(a) he is a director (as defined in section 612), and

(b) he is within paragraph (b) of section 417(5),

in relation to the company.

Commentary—*Simon's Direct Tax Service* **E7.214, 227.**
Definitions—"Company", s 832(1), (2); "director", s 612(1); "employee", s 612(1); "employer", s 612(1); "the permitted maximum", s 612(1); "Schedule E", s 19(1); "scheme", s 611(2); "service", s 612(1).
Cross references—See Occupational Pension Schemes (Transitional Provisions) Regulations, SI 1988/1436 regs 7, 8, 9 (disapplication of sub-paras (2), (3) and modification of sub-paras (3), (4)).

Lump sums

6—(1) This paragraph applies where an employee becomes a member of the scheme on or after 17th March 1987.

(2) If the rules of the scheme allow the employee to obtain, (by commutation of his pension or otherwise), a lump sum or sums calculated by reference to his relevant annual remuneration, they shall have effect as if they included a rule that in calculating a lump sum any excess of that remuneration over the permitted maximum should be disregarded.

Commentary—*Simon's Direct Tax Service* **E7.214, 227.**
Definitions—"Employee", s 612(1); "scheme", s 611(2).
Cross references—See Occupational Pension Schemes (Transitional Provisions) Regulations, SI 1988/1436 regs 3, 6 (disapplication of this paragraph).

Additional voluntary contributions

7—(1) This paragraph applies where—

(a) the rules of the scheme make provision for the payment by employees of voluntary contributions, and

(b) on or after 8th April 1987 an employee enters into arrangements to pay such contributions.

(2) Notwithstanding anything in the rules of the scheme, they shall have effect as if they did not allow the payment to the employee of a lump sum in commutation of a pension if or to the extent that the pension is secured by the voluntary contributions.

Commentary—*Simon's Direct Tax Service* **E7.222, 227.**
Definitions—"Employee", s 612(1); "pension", s 612(1); "scheme", s 611(2).
Cross references—See Occupational Pension Schemes (Transitional Provisions) Regulations, SI 1988/1436 regs 6, 10 (disapplication of this paragraph).

8 ...

Commentary—*Simon's Direct Tax Service* **E7.222.**
Definitions—"Approved scheme", s 612(1); "employee", s 612(1); "employer", s 612(1); "scheme", s 611(2).
Amendments—This paragraph repealed by FA 1989 Sch 6 paras 17, 18(10) and Sch 17, Pt IV in relation to benefits provided after 26 July 1989.

Supplementary

9 In this Schedule "relevant annual remuneration" means final remuneration or, if the scheme provides for benefits to be calculated by reference to some other annual remuneration, that other annual remuneration.

Commentary—*Simon's Direct Tax Service* **E7.214, 227.**
Definition—"'Final remuneration'', s 612(1).
Cross references—See Occupational Pension Schemes (Transitional Provisions) Regulations, SI 1988/1436 reg 4A (final remuneration of an employee retiring early because of physical incapacity).

[SCHEDULE 23ZA

CONVERSION OF CERTAIN APPROVED RETIREMENT BENEFITS SCHEMES][1]

Section 631A

Cross references—See the Personal Pension Schemes (Conversion of Retirement Benefits Schemes) Regulations, SI 2001/118 (provision for way in which retirement benefit schemes (which are money-purchase schemes) may apply to the Revenue for approval as personal pension schemes).
Amendments—[1] This Schedule inserted by FA 2000 s 61, Sch 13 para 27 with effect from 28 July 2000.

[Interpretation

1—(1) In this Schedule—
　　"the date of the change" shall be construed in accordance with paragraph 3(2) below;
　　"eligible scheme" shall be construed in accordance with paragraph 2(4) below;
　　"the personal pension provisions of this Act" means this Schedule and the other provisions of Chapter IV of Part XIV;
　　"prescribed" (except in paragraph 2(3)(*c*)) means specified in, or determined in accordance with, regulations;
　　"regulations" means regulations made by the Board.
(2) Any power conferred by this Schedule to make regulations includes power to make different provision for different cases or different purposes.][1]

Amendments—[1] This Schedule inserted by FA 2000 s 61, Sch 13 para 27 with effect from 28 July 2000.

[Eligible schemes

2—(1) This Schedule applies to any retirement benefits scheme which is for the time being approved under Chapter I of Part XIV.
(2) Sub-paragraph (1) above is subject to the following provisions of this paragraph.
(3) This Schedule applies to a retirement benefits scheme only if—
　　(*a*) it is an occupational pension scheme, as defined in section 1 of the Pension Schemes Act 1993 or section 1 of the Pensions Schemes (Northern Ireland) Act 1993;
　　(*b*) it is a money-purchase scheme, as defined in section 181 of the Pension Schemes Act 1993 or section 176 of the Pensions Schemes (Northern Ireland) Act 1993;
　　(*c*) any documents relating to the scheme which are prescribed under section 631(1) are such that, subject to approval under paragraph 3 below, the scheme is capable of being an approved personal pension scheme for the purposes of Chapter IV of Part XIV as from the date of the change; and
　　(*d*) such other conditions as may be prescribed are satisfied in the case of the scheme.
(4) Any retirement benefits scheme to which this Schedule applies is referred to in this Schedule as an "eligible scheme".][1]

Amendments—[1] This Schedule inserted by FA 2000 s 61, Sch 13 para 27 with effect from 28 July 2000.

[Approval of eligible schemes as approved personal pension schemes

3—(1) The trustees of an eligible scheme may at any time on or after 1st October 2000 apply to the Board for approval of the scheme under this paragraph.
(2) If an application under sub-paragraph (1) above is granted, the eligible scheme shall, as from such date as the Board may specify in granting the application (the "date of the change"),—
　　(*a*) irrevocably cease to be approved, and to be capable of approval, under Chapter I of Part XIV; and
　　(*b*) become an approved personal pension scheme (and subject accordingly to section 631(4) and the other provisions of Chapter IV of Part XIV).
(3) The date of the change must not be earlier than 6th April 2001.
(4) An application under sub-paragraph (1) above shall be in such form, shall contain such information, and shall be accompanied by such documents, in such form, and prepared as at such time, as the Board may prescribe.
(5) The Board may at their discretion grant or refuse an application under sub-paragraph (1) above.

(6) The Board's discretion under sub-paragraph (5) above shall be subject to the restrictions set out in sections 632 to 638A and this Schedule.

(7) The Board shall give notice to the applicant of the grant or refusal of an application.

(8) A notice under sub-paragraph (7) above shall, in the case of a refusal, state the grounds for the refusal.

(9) If, at any time after the making of an application under sub-paragraph (1) above, the eligible scheme concerned ceases to be approved under Chapter I of Part XIV otherwise than by virtue of the operation of sub-paragraph (2)(*a*) above, the scheme shall not, by virtue of that application, become an approved personal pension scheme.]¹

Amendments—¹ This Schedule inserted by FA 2000 s 61, Sch 13 para 27 with effect from 28 July 2000.

[Excessive funding of certain individual members

4—(1) The Board may refuse or withhold approval under paragraph 3 above in the case of an eligible scheme of a prescribed description if or so long as they are not satisfied that prescribed requirements will be fulfilled with respect to—

    (*a*) the value of any prescribed benefits which may be provided for or in respect of an individual member of a prescribed description, and

    (*b*) the value of the assets held for the purpose of providing benefits for or in respect of that member,

if approval under paragraph 3 above is granted.

(2) Regulations may make provision for or in connection with cases where the value mentioned in paragraph (*b*) of sub-paragraph (1) above exceeds, or exceeds by more than a prescribed percentage, the value mentioned in paragraph (*a*) of that sub-paragraph.

(3) The provision that may be made by virtue of sub-paragraph (2) above includes provision for or in connection with eliminating or reducing any such excess within a prescribed period by one or more prescribed methods.

(4) Regulations may make provision for the purposes of this paragraph for or in connection with—

    (*a*) the valuation of benefits; or

    (*b*) the valuation of assets.

(5) The provision that may be made by virtue of sub-paragraph (4)(*a*) or (*b*) above includes provision with respect to, or in connection with,—

    (*a*) the person by whom any such valuation is to be made;

    (*b*) the method or principles of valuation to be used;

    (*c*) certification of any such valuations and of any prescribed matters relating to or connected with them;

    (*d*) any facts, matters or assumptions by reference to which any such valuation is to be made;

    (*e*) any tables to be used for the purpose of making any such valuation;

    (*f*) the basis on which any such tables are to be prepared;

    (*g*) the manner in which any such tables are to be applied.

(6) The methods or principles of valuation and the tables that may be prescribed by virtue of sub-paragraph (5) above include methods or principles or, as the case may be, tables published by the Government Actuary for any purposes of the personal pension provisions of this Act.]¹

Amendments—¹ This Schedule inserted by FA 2000 s 61, Sch 13 para 27 with effect from 28 July 2000.

[Directions as to contributions between valuation and date of change etc

5—(1) The Board may give directions for or in connection with—

    (*a*) prohibiting the making of contributions during the post-valuation period, or

    (*b*) restricting the amount of the contributions that may be made during that period,

by or in respect of members of a converting scheme.

(2) Directions under sub-paragraph (1) above—

    (*a*) may be given in respect of schemes generally, schemes of a particular description or any particular scheme or schemes; and

    (*b*) may make different provision in relation to different schemes or different members.

(3) Any directions under sub-paragraph (1) above must be complied with by—

    (*a*) the trustees and managers, or administrators, of any scheme to which the directions relate;

    (*b*) any member of such a scheme to whom the directions relate; and

    (*c*) any person who is the employer of such a member.

(4) If there is any contravention of, or failure to comply with, directions under sub-paragraph (1) above, the Board may—

    (*a*) refuse or withhold approval of the conversion application in question; or

    (*b*) revoke or vary any approval granted or any conditions pending the satisfaction of which approval is withheld.

(5) Sub-paragraph (4) above is without prejudice to any other powers of the Board.

(6) In this paragraph—

"conversion application", in the case of a converting scheme, means the application under paragraph 3(1) above in respect of the scheme;

"converting scheme" means a scheme in respect of which an application under paragraph 3(1) above has been made and not withdrawn or finally refused;

"the post-valuation period", in the case of a converting scheme, means the period which—

(*a*) begins with the day as at which any valuation for the purposes of paragraph 4 above is made in connection with the conversion application; and

(*b*) ends with the day preceding the date of the change (or, if earlier, the date on which the conversion application is withdrawn or finally refused).

(7) For the purposes of this paragraph, an application is "finally refused" when it has been refused by the Board and—

(*a*) the time for appealing under section 651 against the refusal has expired without such an appeal being made; or

(*b*) an appeal under that section against the refusal has been withdrawn or finally disposed of in a way which affirms refusal of the application.

(8) Any directions under this paragraph must be given in writing.]¹

Amendments—¹ This Schedule inserted by FA 2000 s 61, Sch 13 para 27 with effect from 28 July 2000.

[Scheme rules to allow changes for purpose of conversion

6 An approved retirement benefits scheme shall be taken to include provisions allowing the making of changes to any provisions of the scheme for the purpose of enabling the scheme to become an eligible scheme, notwithstanding anything to the contrary in any provision of the scheme.]¹

Amendments—¹ This Schedule inserted by FA 2000 s 61, Sch 13 para 27 with effect from 28 July 2000.

[SCHEDULE 23A

MANUFACTURED DIVIDENDS AND INTEREST]¹

Section 736A

Revenue Internal Guidance—Inspectors manual IM4330–4358 (Revenue procedures in relation to manufactured payments).
Cross references—See TMA 1970 s 21(5A) (Board's power to require information from a person who may have incurred a tax liability under this Schedule).
TA 1988 s 736B (deemed manufactured payments in the case of stock lending arrangements).
TA 1988 s 737A(5) (sale and repurchase of securities: provisions to counter tax avoidance: application of this Schedule).
FA 1997 Sch 7 para 7 (manufactured dividend not to be taken to be a qualifying distribution to which that Schedule applies (special treatment for certain distributions), except to the extent stated).
IT (Dividend Manufacturing) Regulations, SI 1992/569 Pt IV (revoked) (administrative arrangements relating to this Schedule);
IT (Manufactured Interest) Regulations, SI 1992/2074 Pt III (revoked) (administrative arrangements relating to this Schedule);
Double Taxation Relief (Taxes on Income) (General) (Manufactured Overseas Dividends) Regulations, SI 1993/1957 (payment of manufactured overseas dividends without deduction of tax to a non-resident under a double tax relief agreement);
IT (Manufactured Overseas Dividends) Regulations, SI 1993/2004 (substantive regulations relating to manufactured dividends on overseas securities).
Manufactured Interest (Tax) Regulations, SI 1997/992 (provides detailed rules about how the tax due each quarter from those involved is to be accounted for).
Manufactured Dividends (Tax) Regulations, SI 1997/993 (provides detailed rules about how the tax due each quarter from those involved is to be accounted for, and also set out the way in which tax accounted for on manufactured dividends on UK equities by UK branches of non-resident companies can be set off against corporation tax).
Amendments—¹ This Schedule inserted by FA 1991 s 58(2), (3) and Sch 13 and has effect (*a*) in relation to manufactured dividends on UK equities paid or payable after 25 February 1992 by virtue of FA 1991 (s 58) (Commencement No 1) Regulations, SI 1992/173 and (*b*) in relation to manufactured interest on UK securities paid or payable after 29 June 1992 by virtue of FA 1991 (s 58) (Commencement No 2) Regulations, SI 1992/1346. As regards manufactured dividends on overseas securities, FA 1991 (s 58) (Commencement No 3) Regulations, SI 1993/933 were made on 29 March 1993 and came into force on 21 April 1993. However, in IR Press Release 31.3.93 and IR (Financial Institutions Division) letter to Bank of England 30.4.93 the Revenue stated that the provisions of this Schedule would not be operated in respect of overseas dividends until substantive regulations were in force. The substantive regulations (SI 1993/2004) have been made and are in force from 1 October 1993.

Interpretation

1—(1) In this Schedule—

...²

"dividend manufacturer" has the meaning given by paragraph 2(1) below;

"dividend manufacturing regulations" means regulations made by the Treasury under this Schedule;

...¹

"interest manufacturer" has the meaning given by paragraph 3(1) below;

"manufactured dividend", "manufactured interest" and "manufactured overseas dividend" shall be construed respectively in accordance with paragraphs 2, 3 and 4 below, as shall references to the gross amount thereof;

...²

"overseas dividend" means any interest, dividend or other annual payment payable in respect of any overseas securities;

"overseas dividend manufacturer" has the meaning given by paragraph 4(1) below;

"overseas securities" means—

     (a) shares, stock or other securities issued by a government or public or local authority of a territory outside the United Kingdom or by any other body of persons not resident in the United Kingdom; ...³

     (b) ...³

"overseas tax" means tax under the law of a territory outside the United Kingdom;

"overseas tax credit" means any such credit under the law of a territory outside the United Kingdom in respect of overseas tax as corresponds to a tax credit;

"prescribed" means prescribed in dividend manufacturing regulations;

...²

"securities" includes any loan stock or similar security;

"transfer" includes any sale or other disposal;

...²

"United Kingdom equities" means shares of any company resident in the United Kingdom;

"United Kingdom securities" means securities of the government of the United Kingdom, of any public or local authority in the United Kingdom or of any company or other body resident in the United Kingdom, but does not include ...³ United Kingdom equities.

(2) ...²

Commentary—*Simon's Direct Tax Service* **A7.801.**
Regulations—IT (Dividend Manufacturing) Regulations, SI 1992/569 (revoked).
IT (Manufactured Interest) Regulations, SI 1992/2074 (revoked).
IT (Manufactured Overseas Dividends) Regulations, SI 1993/2004.
IT (Manufactured Dividends) (Tradepoint) Regulations, SI 1995/2052 (revoked).
Manufactured Overseas Dividends (French Indemnity Payments) Regulations, SI 1996/1826.
Manufactured Interest (Tax) Regulations, SI 1997/992.
Manufactured Dividends (Tax) Regulations, SI 1997/993.
Definitions—"Company", s 832(1), (2); "interest", s 832(1); "recognised clearing system", s 841A; "resident in the United Kingdom", FA 1988 s 66; "tax", s 832(3); "United Kingdom", s 830(1).
Cross references—See IT (Dividend Manufacturing) Regulations, SI 1992/569 reg 3 and Pt II (revoked) (prescription of matters for the purposes of the definition of "unapproved manufactured payment" in sub-para (1) above).
IT (Manufactured Dividends) (Tradepoint) Regulations, SI 1995/2052 regs 3, 4 (revoked) (prescribed persons and circumstances for sub-para (ii) of the definition of "unapproved manufactured payment"; prescription of The London Clearing House as a recognised clearing house within sub-para (iii) of that definition).
Amendments—¹ Definition of "foreign income dividend" in sub-para (1) repealed by F(No 2)A 1997 s 36(4), Sch 6 para 17(1), (2), (5), Sch 8 Pt II(11) with effect in relation to manufactured dividends which are representative of dividends paid after 5 April 1999.
² Definitions of "approved stock lending arrangement", "market maker", "recognised clearing house", "recognised investment exchange", "unapproved manufactured payment" and "unapproved stock lending arrangement" in sub-para (1), and sub-para (2), repealed by FA 1997 Sch 18 Pt VI(10) with effect, in relation to the repeals of the definitions of "unapproved manufactured payment" and "unapproved stock lending arrangement.", and of sub-para (2)(b), in relation to manufactured payments made on or after 1 July 1997 by virtue of the Finance Act 1997, Schedule 10, (Appointed Day) Order, SI 1997/991 and in relation to the repeals of the remaining definitions in sub-para (1) with effect in relation to, and to transfers under, any arrangement made on or after 1 July 1997 by virtue of the Finance Act 1997, Schedule 10, (Appointed Day) Order, SI 1997/991.
³ Words revoked by FA 2000 s 156, Sch 40 Pt II(17) with effect for payments of interest made after 31 March 2001.

[*Manufactured dividends on UK equities: general*]1

[2—(1) This paragraph applies in any case where, under a contract or other arrangements for the transfer of United Kingdom equities, one of the parties (a "dividend manufacturer") is required to pay to the other ("the recipient") an amount (a "manufactured dividend") which is representative of a dividend on the equities.

[(2) Where a manufactured dividend is paid by a dividend manufacturer who is a company resident in the United Kingdom, the Tax Acts shall have effect—

     (a) in relation to the recipient, and persons claiming title through or under him, as if the manufactured dividend were a dividend on the UK equities in question; and

     (b) in relation to the dividend manufacturer, as if the amount paid were a dividend of his.]³

(3) Where a manufactured dividend to which sub-paragraph (2) above does not apply is paid by any person—

     (a) ...⁴

     (b) the Tax Acts shall have effect in relation to the recipient, and persons claiming title through or under him, as if the manufactured dividend were a dividend on the United Kingdom equities in question; and

     (c) the Tax Acts shall have effect in relation to the dividend manufacturer subject to the provisions of paragraph 2A below.

(4), (5) ...⁴

(6) ...² where—

(*a*) a dividend manufacturer pays a manufactured dividend [to which sub-paragraph (3) above applies]⁴, ...⁴

(*b*) ...⁴

the dividend manufacturer shall, on paying the manufactured dividend, provide the recipient with a statement in writing setting out the matters specified in sub-paragraph (7) below.

(7) Those matters are—

(*a*) the amount of the manufactured dividend;

(*b*) the date of the payment of the manufactured dividend; and

(*c*) the amount of the tax credit to which, by virtue of sub-paragraph (3)(*b*) above, the recipient or a person claiming title through or under him either—

(i) is entitled in respect of the manufactured dividend, or

(ii) would be so entitled were all the conditions of a right to a tax credit satisfied, in the case of the recipient or that person, as respects the dividend which the recipient is deemed to receive.

(8) The duty imposed by sub-paragraph (6) above shall be enforceable at the suit or instance of the recipient.]¹

Commentary—*Simon's Direct Tax Service* A7.805–807.
Regulations—Manufactured Dividends (Tax) Regulations, SI 1997/993.
Definitions—"Advance corporation tax", s 14(1); "branch or agency", s 834(1); "company", s 832(1)(2); "dividend manufacturing regulations", para 1(1); "tax", s 832(3); "Tax Acts", s 831(2); "tax credit", s 832(1); "trade", s 832(1); "transfer", para 1(1); "United Kingdom", s 830(1); "United Kingdom equities", para 1(1).
Cross references.—See TA 1988 Sch 23A para 2B (where manufactured dividend is representative of a foreign income dividend, there is no requirement to account for tax by virtue of sub-para (3)(*a*) above).
TA 1988 Sch 23A para 7 (irregular manufactured payments).
TA 1988 Sch 23A para 8 (regulations to modify this paragraph).
Manufactured Dividends (Tax) Regulations, SI 1997/993 reg 4 (criteria for determining whether the payer or the recipient of a manufactured dividend is liable to account for tax as mentioned in sub-para (3) above).
SI 1997/993 reg 5 (liability for tax where the dividend manufacturer receives the dividend of which the manufactured interest is representative).
SI 1997/993 reg 6 (makes provision for accounting for tax by recipients of manufactured dividends that are UK resident companies).
SI 1997/993 regs 7–9 (make provision for the accounting for tax, the making of returns and the set-off of tax by payers or recipients of manufactured dividends that are not UK resident companies).
Corporation Tax (Treatment of Unrelieved Surplus Advance Corporation Tax) Regulations, SI 1999/358 reg 11 (provides for the computation of shadow ACT in respect of distributions made by a company, including manufactured dividends to which sub-para 2 above applies).
Amendments—¹ Paras 2, 2A, 2B substituted for para 2 by FA 1997 Sch 10 paras 10(1), 16(1) with effect in relation to any payment of a manufactured dividend or manufactured interest which is a payment made after 30 June 1997 by virtue of the Finance Act 1997, Schedule 10, (Appointed Day) Order, SI 1997/991.
² Words in sub-para (6) repealed by F(No 2)A 1997 s 36(4), Sch 6 para 17(1), (3), (5), Sch 8 Pt II(11) with effect in relation to manufactured dividends which are representative of dividends paid after 5 April 1999.
³ Sub-para (2) substituted by FA 1998 s 102(5)–(8), Sch 27 Part III(24), with effect in relation to manufactured dividends paid (or treated for the purposes of TA 1988 Sch 23A as paid) after 5 April 1999.
⁴ Sub-paras (3)(*a*), (4), (5), (6)(*b*) repealed, and words in sub-para (6)(*a*) inserted, by FA 1998 s 102(5)–(8), Sch 27 Part III(24), with effect in relation to manufactured dividends paid (or treated for the purposes of TA 1988 Sch 23A as paid) after 5 April 1999.

*[Deductibility of manufactured payment in the case of the manufacturer]*¹

[2A—(1) Where, in the case of a manufactured dividend, the dividend manufacturer—

(*a*) is resident in the United Kingdom, but

(*b*) is not a company,

the amount of the manufactured dividend actually paid (so far as is it is not otherwise deductible), ...³ shall be allowable for the purposes of income tax as a deduction against the total income of the dividend manufacturer[, subject to sub-paragraph (1A) below]⁴.

[(1A) An amount shall be allowable under sub-paragraph (1) above as a deduction against total income only to the extent that—

(*a*) the dividend manufacturer receives the dividend on the equities which is represented by the manufactured dividend, or receives a payment which is representative of that dividend, and is chargeable to income tax on the dividend or other payment so received;

(*b*) the dividend manufacturer is treated under section 730A (repos) as receiving a payment of interest in respect of the equities and is chargeable to income tax on that payment; or

(*c*) a chargeable gain accrues to the dividend manufacturer as a result of a transaction whose nature is such as to give rise to the payment of a manufactured dividend by him,

but the amount allowable by virtue of paragraph (*c*) above is limited to so much of the chargeable gain as does not exceed the manufactured dividend paid as a result of the transaction.]⁴

[(1B) Where an amount is allowable under sub-paragraph (1) above by reference to the whole or any part of—

(*a*) a dividend or other payment falling within paragraph (*a*) of sub-paragraph (1A) above,

(*b*) a payment of interest which a person is treated as receiving, as mentioned in paragraph (*b*) of that sub-paragraph, or

(*c*) a chargeable gain falling within paragraph (*c*) of that sub-paragraph, (the "utilised portion" of the dividend, other payment or chargeable gain) no other amount shall be allowable under sub-paragraph (1) above by reference to all or any of the utilised portion of the dividend, other payment or chargeable gain.][4]

(2) ...[2]

(3) ...[3]

(4) The references in this paragraph to an amount being deductible are references to its being either—

(a) deductible in computing the amount of any of the dividend manufacturer's profits or gains for the purposes of income tax or corporation tax; or

(b) deductible for those purposes from the total income or, as the case may be, total profits of the dividend manufacturer.][1]

Commentary—*Simon's Direct Tax Service* **A7.806.**
Definitions—"Advance corporation tax", s 14(1); "company", s 832(1), (2); "distribution", s 832(1); "dividend manufacturer", para 2(1); "manufactured dividend", para 2(1); "profits or gains", s 833(1); "total income", s 835; "United Kingdom", s 830(1).
Cross references.—See TA 1988 s 95(1A) (treatment of qualifying distribution to which FA 1997 Sch 7 applies (special treatment for certain distributions) received by a dealer).
TA 1988 Sch 23A para 2B (where manufactured dividend is representative of a foreign income dividend, any deduction made under sub-para (1) above is not to include notional ACT).
Amendments—[1] Paras 2, 2A, 2B substituted for para 2 by FA 1997 Sch 10 paras 10(1), 16(1) with effect in relation to any payment of a manufactured dividend or manufactured interest which is a payment made on or after 1 July 1997 by virtue of the Finance Act 1997, Schedule 10, (Appointed Day) Order, SI 1997/991.
[2] Sub-para (2) repealed by F(No 2)A 1997 s 24(13), (15), Sch 8 Pt II(8) with effect in relation to any distribution made after 1 July 1997 and any payment which is representative of such a distribution, and accordingly para 2(3)(c) of this Schedule has effect instead.
[3] Sub-para (3), and words in sub-para (1) repealed by FA 1998 s 102(8), Sch 27 Part III(24), with effect in relation to manufactured dividends paid (or treated for the purposes of TA 1988 Sch 23A as paid) after 5 April 1999.
[4] Words in sub-para (1) inserted, and sub-paras (1A), (1B) inserted, by FA 2002 s 108(1)–(3), (6) with effect for manufactured dividends paid after 16 April 2002.

Manufactured dividends representative of foreign income dividends

[2B ...]

Commentary—*Simon's Direct Tax Service* **A7.806.**
Definitions—"dividend manufacturer", para 2(1); "foreign income dividend", para 1(1); "manufactured dividend", para 2(1); "tax", s 832(3); "Tax Acts", s 831(2); "tax credit", s 832(1); "United Kingdom equities", para 1(1).
Amendments—[1] This paragraph repealed by F(No 2)A 1997 s 36(4), Sch 6 para 17(1), (4), (5), Sch 8 Pt II(11) with effect in relation to manufactured dividends which are representative of dividends paid after 5 April 1999 (previously paras 2, 2A, 2B substituted for para 2 by FA 1997 Sch 10 paras 10(1), 16(1)).

[*Manufactured interest on UK securities: general*]1

[3—(1) This paragraph applies (subject to paragraph 3A below) in any case where, under a contract or other arrangements for the transfer of United Kingdom securities, one of the parties (an "interest manufacturer") is required to pay to the other ("the recipient") an amount ("the manufactured interest") which is representative of a periodical payment of interest on the securities.

(2) For the relevant purposes of the Tax Acts, in their application in relation to the interest manufacturer—

(a) the manufactured interest shall be treated, except in determining whether it is deductible, as if it—

(i) were an annual payment to the recipient, but

(ii) were neither yearly interest nor an amount payable wholly out of profits or gains brought into charge for income tax;

(b) the gross amount of that deemed annual payment shall be taken—

(i) to be equal to the gross amount of the interest of which the manufactured interest is representative; and

(ii) to constitute income of the recipient falling within section 1A; and

(c) an amount equal to so much of the gross amount of the manufactured interest as is not otherwise deductible shall be allowable as a deduction against the total income or, as the case may be, total profits of the interest manufacturer[, but only to the extent that—

(i) it would be so allowable if it were interest, or

(ii) so far as not falling within sub-paragraph (i) above, it falls within sub-paragraph (2A) below][2].

[(2A) An amount of manufactured interest falls within this sub-paragraph if and to the extent that the interest manufacturer—

(a) receives the periodical payment of interest on the securities which is represented by the manufactured interest, or receives a payment which is representative of that periodical payment of interest, and is chargeable to income tax on the periodical payment or representative payment so received;

(b) is treated under section 713(2)(a) or (3)(b) (accrued income scheme) as entitled to a sum in respect of a transfer of the securities and is chargeable to income tax on that sum; or (*c*) is treated under section 730A (repos) as receiving a payment of interest in respect of the securities and is chargeable to income tax on that payment.]²

[(2B) Where an amount is allowable under sub-paragraph (2)(*c*) above by reference to the whole or any part of—

(*a*) a periodical payment of interest, or a payment representative of such a payment, falling within paragraph (*a*) of sub-paragraph (2A) above,

(*b*) a sum falling within paragraph (*b*) of that sub-paragraph, or

(*c*) a payment of interest which a person is treated as receiving, as mentioned in paragraph (*c*) of that sub-paragraph,

(the "utilised portion" of the interest, sum or other payment) no other amount shall be allowable under sub-paragraph (2)(*c*) above by reference to all or any of the utilised portion of the interest, sum or other payment.]²

(3) For the relevant purposes of the Tax Acts, in their application in relation to the recipient and any persons claiming title through or under him—

(*a*) the manufactured interest shall be treated as if it were a periodical payment of interest on the securities in question; and

(*b*) the gross amount of that deemed periodical payment of interest shall be taken to be equal to the gross amount of the interest of which the manufactured interest is representative.

(4) Sub-paragraph (2) above shall not require any deduction of tax to be made by the interest manufacturer if—

(*a*) the interest manufacturer is not resident in the United Kingdom, and

(*b*) the manufactured interest is paid otherwise than in the course of a trade carried on by the interest manufacturer in the United Kingdom through a branch or agency.

(5) Where, in a case falling within sub-paragraph (4)(*a*) and (*b*) above, the recipient—

(*a*) is resident in the United Kingdom, or

(*b*) (without being so resident) receives the manufactured interest for the purposes of a trade carried on by him in the United Kingdom through a branch or agency,

the recipient shall be liable to account for income tax in respect of the manufactured interest.

(6) The amount of the income tax for which the recipient is liable to account under sub-paragraph (5) above is the amount equal to the income tax which the interest manufacturer, had he been resident in the United Kingdom, would have been required, in respect of the manufactured interest, to account for and pay by virtue of sub-paragraph (2) above.

(7) For the purposes of sub-paragraph (2) above, if the interest manufacturer is a company which—

(*a*) is not resident in the United Kingdom, but

(*b*) carries on a trade in the United Kingdom through a branch or agency, Schedule 16 shall have effect in relation to the manufactured interest as it has effect in the case of a company which is resident in the United Kingdom but as if, in paragraph 7, the words "section 11(3)" were substituted for the words "section 7(2)".

(8) Where sub-paragraph (2) above has effect in the case of any manufactured interest so as to require any amount to be deducted by way of tax from the gross amount of the manufactured interest, the interest manufacturer shall, on paying the manufactured interest, provide the recipient with a statement in writing setting out—

(*a*) the gross amount of the manufactured interest;

(*b*) the amount deducted by way of tax by the interest manufacturer;

(*c*) the amount actually paid by the interest manufacturer; and

(*d*) the date of the payment by the interest manufacturer.

(9) The duty imposed by sub-paragraph (8) above shall be enforceable at the suit or instance of the recipient.

(10) The references in this paragraph to an amount being deductible are references to its being either—

(*a*) deductible in computing the amount of any of the interest manufacturer's profits or gains for the purposes of income tax or corporation tax; or

(*b*) deductible for those purposes from the total income or, as the case may be, total profits of the interest manufacturer.

(11) For the purposes of this paragraph "the relevant purposes of the Tax Acts" means all the purposes of those Acts except the purposes of Chapter II of Part IV of the Finance Act 1996 (loan relationships).

(12) Without prejudice to the generality of section 80(5) of the Finance Act 1996 (matters to be brought into account only under that Chapter), this paragraph does not have effect for determining how any manufactured interest falls to be treated for any purpose in relation to a company in relation to which that interest falls to be treated in accordance with section 97 of that Act.

(13) For the purposes of this paragraph references to the gross amount of any interest or payment are references to the amount of the interest or payment before the making of any deduction of income tax that is required to be deducted from it on its being paid or made.]¹

Commentary—*Simon's Direct Tax Service* **A7.810, 811; D2.1128.**
Definitions—"Branch or agency", s 834(1); "company", s 832(1)(2); "income tax", s 832(4); "profits or gains", s 833(1); "tax", s 832(3); "Tax Acts", s 831(2); "total income", s 835; "trade", s 832(1); "transfer", para 1(1); "United Kingdom", s 830(1); "United Kingdom securities", para 1(1).
Cross references.—See TA 1988 s 715(6) (exceptions from provisions about deemed sums and reliefs under the accrued income scheme).
TA 1988 Sch 23A para 3A (where manufactured interest is representative of interest on securities specified in that para, sub-para (2) above does not require any deduction of tax to be made on payment and sub-para (5) above does not require the recipient to account for income tax).
TA 1988 Sch 23A para 7 (irregular manufactured payments).
TA 1988 Sch 23A para 8 (regulations to modify this paragraph).
Manufactured Interest (Tax) Regulations, SI 1997/992 reg 3 (TA 1988 Sch 16 to apply with appropriate modification to payments of manufactured interest in relation to which recipient must account for tax under sub-para (5) above).
SI 1997/992 reg 4 (liability for tax where the interest manufacturer is in receipt of real interest of which the manufactured interest is representative).
Amendments—[1] Para 3 substituted by FA 1997 Sch 10 paras 11(1), 16(1) with effect in relation to any payment of a manufactured dividend or manufactured interest which is a payment made on or after 1 July 1997 by virtue of the Finance Act 1997, Schedule 10, (Appointed Day) Order, SI 1997/991.
[2] Words in sub-para (2)(c) inserted, and sub-paras (2A), (2B) inserted, by FA 2002 s 108(1), (4), (5), (7) with effect for manufactured interest paid after 16 April 2002.

[Manufactured interest on gilt-edged securities etc]1

[3A—(1) Where any manufactured interest is representative of interest on securities to which this paragraph applies—

(*a*) paragraph 3(2) above shall not require any deduction of tax to be made on the payment of that manufactured interest; and

(*b*) without prejudice to any other liability of his to income tax in respect of the manufactured interest, the recipient shall not by virtue of paragraph 3(5) above be liable to account for any income tax in respect of that manufactured interest.

(2) This paragraph applies to—

(*a*) gilt-edged securities (within the meaning of section [50]2); and

(*b*) securities not falling within paragraph (*a*) above on which the interest is payable without deduction of tax.]1

Commentary—*Simon's Direct Tax Service* **A7.802, 1101.**
Definitions—"Income tax", s 832(4); "manufactured interest", para 3(1); "securities", para 1(1).
Amendments—[1] Para 3A substituted by FA 1997 Sch 10 paras 11(1), 16(1) with effect in relation to any payment of a manufactured dividend or manufactured interest which is a payment made on or after 1 July 1997 by virtue of the Finance Act 1997, Schedule 10, (Appointed Day) Order, SI 1997/991.
[2] In sub-para (2)(a) "50" substituted for "51A" by F(No 2)A 1997 s 37(1), (7), (8) with effect in relation to payments of interest falling due after 5 April 1998.

Manufactured overseas dividends

4—(1) This paragraph applies in any case where, under a contract or other arrangements for the transfer of overseas securities, one of the parties (the "overseas dividend manufacturer") is required to pay to the other ("the recipient") an amount representative of an overseas dividend on the overseas securities; and in this Schedule the "manufactured overseas dividend" means any payment which the overseas dividend manufacturer makes in discharge of that requirement.

(2) Subject to sub-paragraph (3) below, where this paragraph applies the gross amount of the manufactured overseas dividend shall be treated for all purposes of the Tax Acts as an annual payment, within section 349, but—

(*a*) the amount which is to be deducted from that gross amount on account of income tax shall be an amount equal to the relevant withholding tax on that gross amount; and

(*b*) in the application of sections [338B(4)(*a*)]6 and 350(4) in relation to manufactured overseas dividends the references to Schedule 16 shall be taken as references to dividend manufacturing regulations;

and paragraph (*a*) above is without prejudice to any further amount required to be deducted under dividend manufacturing regulations by virtue of sub-paragraph (8) below.

(3) If, in a case where this paragraph applies, the overseas dividend manufacturer is not resident in the United Kingdom and the manufactured overseas dividend is paid by him otherwise than in the course of a trade which he carries on through a branch or agency in the United Kingdom, sub-paragraph (2) above shall not apply; but if the manufactured overseas dividend is received by [a United Kingdom recipient, that recipient shall]2 account for and pay an amount of tax in respect of the manufactured overseas dividend equal to that which the overseas dividend manufacturer would have been required to account for and pay had he been resident in the United Kingdom; and any reference in this Schedule to an amount deducted under sub-paragraph (2) above includes a reference to an amount of tax accounted for and paid under this sub-paragraph.

[(3A) For the purposes of sub-paragraph (3) above a person who receives a manufactured overseas dividend is a United Kingdom recipient if—

(*a*) he is resident in the United Kingdom; or

(*b*) he is not so resident but receives that dividend for the purposes of a trade carried on through a branch or agency in the United Kingdom.]2

[(3B) Dividend manufacturing regulations may make provision, in relation to cases falling within sub-paragraph (3) above, for the amount of tax required under that sub-paragraph to be taken to be reduced, to such extent and for such purposes as may be determined under the regulations, by reference to amounts of overseas tax charged on, or in respect of—

(*a*) the making of the manufactured overseas dividend; or

(*b*) the overseas dividend of which the manufactured overseas dividend is representative.]²

(4) Where a manufactured overseas dividend is paid after deduction of the amount required by sub-paragraph (2) above, or where the amount of tax required under sub-paragraph (3) above in respect of such a dividend has been accounted for and paid, then for all purposes of the Tax Acts as they apply in relation to persons resident in the United Kingdom or to persons not so resident but carrying on business through a branch or agency in the United Kingdom—

(*a*) the manufactured overseas dividend shall be treated in relation to the recipient, and all persons claiming title through or under him, as if it were an overseas dividend of an amount equal to the gross amount of the manufactured overseas dividend, but paid after the withholding therefrom, on account of overseas tax, of the amount deducted under sub-paragraph (2) above; and

(*b*) the amount so deducted shall accordingly be treated in relation to the recipient, and all persons claiming title through or under him, as an amount so withheld instead of as an amount on account of income tax.

(5) For the purposes of this paragraph—

(*a*) "relevant withholding tax", in relation to the gross amount of a manufactured overseas dividend, means an amount of tax representative of—

(i) the amount (if any) that would have been deducted by way of overseas tax from an overseas dividend on the overseas securities of the same gross amount as the manufactured overseas dividend; and

(ii) the amount of the overseas tax credit (if any) in respect of such an overseas dividend;

(*b*) the gross amount of a manufactured overseas dividend is an amount equal to the gross amount of that overseas dividend of which the manufactured overseas dividend is representative, as mentioned in sub-paragraph (1) above; and

(*c*) the gross amount of an overseas dividend is an amount equal to the aggregate of—

(i) so much of the overseas dividend as remains after the deduction of the overseas tax (if any) chargeable on it;

(ii) the amount of the overseas tax (if any) so deducted; and

(iii) the amount of the overseas tax credit (if any) in respect of the overseas dividend.

(6) Dividend manufacturing regulations may make provision with respect to the rates of relevant withholding tax which are to apply in relation to manufactured overseas dividends in relation to different overseas territories, but in prescribing those rates the Treasury shall have regard to—

(*a*) the rates at which overseas tax would have fallen to be deducted, and

(*b*) the rates of overseas tax credits,

in overseas territories, or in the particular overseas territory, in respect of payments of overseas dividends on overseas securities.

(7) Dividend manufacturing regulations may make provision for a person who, in any chargeable period, is an overseas dividend manufacturer to be entitled in prescribed circumstances to set off [in accordance with the regulations and to the prescribed extent, amounts falling within paragraph (*a*) of sub-paragraph (7AA) below against the sums falling within paragraph (*b*) of that sub-paragraph, and to account]² to the Board for, or as the case may be, claim credit in respect of, the balance.

[(7AA) Those amounts and sums are—

(*a*) amounts of overseas tax in respect of overseas dividends received by him in that chargeable period, amounts of overseas tax charged on, or in respect of, the making of manufactured overseas dividends so received by him and amounts deducted under sub-paragraph (2) above from any such manufactured overseas dividends; and

(*b*) the sums due from him on account of the amounts deducted by him under sub-paragraph (2) above from the manufactured overseas dividends paid by him in that chargeable period.]²

[(7A) ...]¹

(8) ...⁵

[(9) Without prejudice to section 97 of the Finance Act 1996 (manufactured interest), the references in this paragraph to all the purposes of the Tax Acts do not include the purposes of Chapter II of Part IV of that Act (loan relationships).]⁴

Commentary—*Simon's Direct Tax Service* **A7.815.**
Regulations—See IT (Manufactured Overseas Dividends) Regulations, SI 1993/2004.
Definitions—"The Board", s 832(1); "branch or agency", s 834(1); "dividend manufacturing regulations", para 1(1); "manufactured dividend" and "manufactured overseas dividend", para 1(1); "overseas dividend", para 1(1); "overseas dividend manufacturer", para 1(1); "overseas securities", para 1(1); "overseas tax", para 1(1); "overseas tax credit", para 1(1); "prescribed", para 1(1); "recognised clearing system", s 841A; "Tax Acts", s 831(2); "trade", s 832(1).
Cross references—See TA 1988 s 715(6) (exceptions from provisions about deemed sums and reliefs under the accrued income scheme).
TA 1988 s 737C(11B) (this paragraph continues to apply for the purposes of s 737C in cases where it is otherwise disapplied by Sch 23A para 5).

TA 1988 Sch 23A para 5(1)–(4) (this paragraph not to apply in relation to manufactured payment or subsequent manufactured payment in certain circumstances).
TA 1988 Sch 23A para 7 (irregular manufactured payments).
TA 1988 Sch 23A para 8(1) (regulations to modify this paragraph).
IT (Manufactured Overseas Dividends) Regulations, SI 1993/2004 regs 4, 8 (tax treatment of approved manufactured overseas dividends paid to approved UK intermediaries and collecting agents),
IT (Manufactured Overseas Dividends) Regulations, SI 1993/2004 regs 5, 8 (tax treatment of approved manufactured overseas dividends paid to non-residents),
IT (Manufactured Overseas Dividends) Regulations, SI 1993/2004 regs 7, 8 (disapplication of sub-para (3) above in prescribed circumstances),
IT (Manufactured Overseas Dividends) Regulations, SI 1993/2004 reg 11 (accounting for tax payable under this paragraph),
IT (Manufactured Overseas Dividends) Regulations, SI 1993/2004 reg 15 (issue of vouchers in respect of tax deducted from manufactured overseas dividends in accordance with this paragraph).
Amendments—[1] Sub-para (7A) (inserted by FA 1994 s 124) repealed by FA 1996 Sch 41 Pt V(21) with effect from 29 April 1996.
[2] Words in sub-para (3) substituted and sub-paras (3A), (3B) inserted by FA 1996 s 159(4), (5), (9) with effect for the purposes of corporation tax for accounting periods ending after 31 March 1996 and for the purposes of income tax from the year 1996–97.
[3] Words in sub-para (7) substituted and sub-para (7AA) inserted by FA 1996 s 159(6).
[4] Sub-para (9) inserted by FA 1996 ss 104, 105(1), Sch 14 para 52(4) with effect for the purposes of income tax from the year 1996–97 and for the purposes of corporation tax for accounting periods ending after 31 March 1996, subject to transitional provisions in FA 1996 Sch 15.
[5] Sub-para (8) repealed by FA 2000 s 156, Sch 40 Pt II(17) with effect for payments of interest made after 31 March 2001.
[6] In sub-para (2)(b), reference substituted for ''338(4)(a)'' by FA 2002 s 84(2), Sch 30 para 1(5) with effect from 24 July 2002.

Dividends and interest passing through the market

5 ...

Commentary—*Simon's Direct Tax Service* **A7.832; D2.1128.**
Amendments—This paragraph repealed by FA 1997 Sch 10 para 12, 16(1), Sch 18 Pt V1(10) with effect in relation to any payment of a manufactured dividend on manufactured interest which is a payment made on or after 1 July 1997 by virtue of the Finance Act 1997, Schedule 10, (Appointed Day) Order, SI 1997/991.

Unapproved manufactured payments

6 ...

Commentary—*Simon's Direct Tax Service* **A7.805.**
Amendments—This paragraph repealed by FA 1997 Sch 10 paras 4(a), 7(2), Sch 18 Pt VI(10) with effect in relation to any manufactured payment made on or after 1 July 1997 by virtue of the Finance Act 1997, Schedule 10, (Appointed Day) Order, SI 1997/991.

Irregular manufactured payments

7—(1) ...[3] in any case where (apart from this paragraph)—

(*a*) an amount paid by way of manufactured dividend would exceed the amount of the dividend of which it is representative, or
(*b*) the aggregate of—

    (i) an amount paid by way of manufactured interest or manufactured overseas dividend, and
    (ii) the tax required to be accounted for in connection with the making of that payment,

would exceed the gross amount (as determined in accordance with paragraph 3 or 4 above) of the interest or overseas dividend of which it is representative, as the case may be,

the payment shall, to the extent of an amount equal to the excess, not be regarded for the purposes of this Schedule as made in discharge of the requirement referred to in paragraph 2(1), 3(1) or 4(1) above, as the case may be, but shall instead to that extent be taken for all purposes of the Tax Acts to constitute a separate fee for entering into the contract or other arrangements under which it was made, notwithstanding anything in paragraphs 2 to 4 above.

[(1A) Sub-paragraph (1) above does not apply in the case of the amount of any manufactured interest or manufactured overseas dividend which falls in accordance with section 97 of the Finance Act 1996 to be treated for the purposes of Chapter II of Part IV of that Act as interest under a loan relationship.][1]

(2) ...[3]

(3) For the purpose of giving relief under any provision of the Tax Acts in a case falling within paragraph 3(1) or 4(1) above where (apart from this paragraph) the aggregate referred to in sub-paragraph (1)(b) above would be less than the gross amount there mentioned—

(*a*) the gross amount of the manufactured interest or manufactured overseas dividend shall be taken to be an amount equal to the aggregate referred to in sub-paragraph (1)(b) above, ...[2]
(*b*) ...[2]

notwithstanding anything in paragraph [3 or 4][2] above.

(4) In this paragraph ''relief'' means relief by way of—

(*a*) deduction in computing profits or gains, or
(*b*) deduction or set off against income or total profits.

Commentary—*Simon's Direct Tax Service* A7.830.
Definitions—''Dividend manufacturing regulations'', para 1(1); ''loan relationship'', FA 1996 s 81; ''manufactured dividend'', ''manufactured interest'' and ''manufactured overseas dividend'', para 1(1); ''prescribed'', para 1(1); ''profits or gains'', s 833(1); ''Tax Acts'', s 831(2).
Amendments—[1] Sub-para (1A) inserted by FA 1996 ss 104, 105(1), Sch 14 para 52(7) with effect for the purposes of income tax from the year 1996–97 and for the purposes of corporation tax for accounting periods ending after 31 March 1996, subject to transitional provisions in FA 1996 Sch 15.
[2] Words in sub-para (3)(*a*), and whole of sub-para (3)(*b*) repealed, and words substituted by FA 1997 Sch 10 paras 4(*b*), 7(2), Sch 18 Pt VI(10) with effect in relation to any manufactured payment made on or after 1 July 1997 by virtue of the Finance Act 1997, Schedule 10, (Appointed Day) Order, SI 1997/991.
[3] Words in sub-para (1) and whole of sub-para (2), repealed by FA 1997 Sch 18 Pt VI(10) with effect in relation to payments made on or after 1 July 1997 by virtue of the Finance Act 1997, Schedule 10, (Appointed Day) Order, SI 1997/991.

Dividend manufacturing regulations: general

8—(1) Dividend manufacturing regulations may make provision for—

(*a*) such manufactured dividends, manufactured interest or manufactured overseas dividends as may be prescribed,

[(*aa*) such persons who receive, or become entitled to receive, manufactured dividends, manufactured interest or manufactured overseas dividends as may be prescribed,][1] or

(*b*) such dividend manufacturers, interest manufacturers or overseas dividend manufacturers as may be prescribed,

to be treated in prescribed circumstances otherwise than as mentioned in [paragraphs 2 to 4 above][2] for the purposes of such provisions of the Tax Acts as may be prescribed.

[(1A) Dividend manufacturing regulations may provide, in relation to prescribed cases where a person makes or receives the payment of any amount representative of an overseas dividend, or is treated for any purposes of this Schedule or such regulations as a person making or receiving such a payment—

(*a*) for any entitlement of that person to claim relief under Part XVIII to be extinguished or reduced to such extent as may be found under the regulations; and

(*b*) for the adjustment, by reference to any provision having effect under the law of a territory outside the United Kingdom, of any amount falling to be taken, for any prescribed purposes of the Tax Acts or the 1992 Act, to be the amount paid or payable by or to any person in respect of any sale, repurchase or other transfer of the overseas securities to which the payment relates.][1]

(2) Dividend manufacturing regulations may make provision with respect to—

(*a*) the accounts and other records which are to be kept,

(*b*) the vouchers which are to be issued or produced,

(*c*) the returns which are to be made,

(*d*) the manner in which amounts required to be deducted or accounted for under or by virtue of this Schedule on account of tax are to be accounted for and paid,

[by persons by or to whom manufactured dividends, manufactured interest or manufactured overseas dividends are paid.][2]

[(2A) Dividend manufacturing regulations with respect to any liability to account for tax may contain any of the following, that is to say—

(*a*) provision for computing the amounts to be accounted for;

(*b*) provision, in relation to the determination of the amount to be paid on any occasion, for setting other amounts against the amounts to be accounted for;

(*c*) provision as to the liabilities against which amounts accounted for are to be, or are not to be, set for the purposes of income tax or corporation tax;

(*d*) provision modifying, or applying (with or without modifications), any enactments contained in the Tax Acts.][2]

(3) Dividend manufacturing regulations may—

(*a*) make provision for prescribed provisions of the Management Act to apply in relation to manufactured dividends, manufactured interest or manufactured overseas dividends with such modifications, specified in the regulations, as the Treasury think fit;

(*b*) make such further provision with respect to the administration, assessment, collection and recovery of amounts required to be deducted or accounted for under or by virtue of this Schedule on account of tax as the Treasury think fit.

(4) Dividend manufacturing regulations may make different provision for different cases.

Commentary—*Simon's Direct Tax Service* A7.802.
Regulations—IT (Dividend Manufacturing) Regulations, SI 1992/569 (revoked).
IT (Manufactured Interest) Regulations, SI 1992/2074 (revoked).
IT (Manufactured Overseas Dividends) Regulations, SI 1993/2004.
IT (Manufactured Dividends) (Tradepoint) Regulations, SI 1995/2052 (revoked).
Manufactured Overseas Dividends (French Indemnity Payments) Regulations, SI 1996/1826.
Manufactured Interest (Tax) Regulations, SI 1997/992.
Manufactured Dividends (Tax) Regulations SI 1997/993.
Definitions—''The 1992 Act'', s 831(3); ''dividend manufacturer'', para 1(1); ''dividend manufacturing regulations'', para 1(1); ''interest manufacturer'', para 1(1); ''the Management Act'', s 831(3); ''manufactured dividend'', ''manufactured interest'' and ''manufactured overseas dividend'', para 1(1); ''overseas dividend'', para 1(1); ''overseas dividend manufacturer'', para 1(1); ''prescribed'', para 1(1); ''the Tax Acts'', s 831(2).

Amendments—[1] Sub-paras (1)(*aa*), (1A) inserted by FA 1996 s 159(7), (8).
[2] Words in sub-paras (1), (2) substituted and sub-para (2A) inserted by FA 1997 Sch 10 paras 13, 16(1) with effect in relation to any payment of a manufactured dividend or manufactured interest which is a payment made on or after 1 July 1997 by virtue of the Finance Act 1997, Schedule 10, (Appointed Day) Order, SI 1997/991.

SCHEDULE 24

ASSUMPTIONS FOR CALCULATING CHARGEABLE PROFITS, CREDITABLE TAX AND CORRESPONDING UNITED KINGDOM TAX OF FOREIGN COMPANIES

Section 747(6)

Commentary—*Simon's Direct Tax Service* **D4.1211, 1213-1215.**
Revenue & other press releases—IR 12.11.97 (Controlled foreign companies (CFCs)—Inland Revenue publish draft legislation on assessment and returns).
Cross references—See TA 1988 s 750(2)–(4) (Territories with a lower level of taxation).
Exchange gains and losses (Alternative Method of Calculation of Gain or Loss) Regulations 1994, SI 1994/3227.
FA 2000 Sch 22 para 54 (operation of this Schedule in relation to tonnage tax).

General

1—(1) The company shall be assumed to be resident in the United Kingdom.

(2) Nothing in sub-paragraph (1) above requires it to be assumed that there is any change in the place or places at which the company carries on its activities.

(3) For the avoidance of doubt, it is hereby declared that, if any sums forming part of the company's profits for an accounting period have been received by the company without any deduction of or charge to tax [and have been so received by virtue of section 154(2) of the Finance Act 1996][1] the effect of the assumption in sub-paragraph (1) above is that those sums are to be brought within the charge to tax for the purposes of calculating the company's chargeable profits or corresponding United Kingdom tax.

[(3A) In any case where—

    (*a*) it is at any time necessary for any purpose of Chapter IV of Part XVII to determine [in the case of any person][3] the chargeable profits of the company for an accounting period, and

    (*b*) at that time—

        [(i) it has not been established in the case of that person that that or any earlier accounting period of the company is an accounting period in respect of which an apportionment under section 747(3) falls to be made, and][3]

        (ii) it has not been established [in the case of that person][3] that that or any earlier accounting period of the company is an ADP exempt period,

[in determining the chargeable profits of the company for the accounting period mentioned in paragraph (a) above, it shall be assumed, for the purposes of those provisions of paragraphs 2 and 10 below which refer to the first accounting period in respect of which an apportionment under section 747(3) falls to be made or which is an ADP exempt period, that that period (but not any earlier period) is an accounting period in respect of which such an apportionment falls to be made or which is an ADP exempt period.][3][2]

(4) In any case where—

    (*a*) it is at any time necessary for any purpose of Chapter IV of Part XVII to determine [in the case of any person][3] the chargeable profits of the company for an accounting period, and

    [(*b*) at that time it has not been established in the case of that person that that or any earlier accounting period of the company is an accounting period in respect of which an apportionment under section 747(3) falls to be made,][3]

[in determining the chargeable profits of the company for the accounting period mentioned in paragraph (a) above, it shall be assumed, for the purposes of those provisions of paragraph 9 below which refer to the first accounting period in respect of which an apportionment under section 747(3) falls to be made, that such an apportionment falls to be made in respect of that period (but not in respect of any earlier period).][3]

(5) Nothing in this Schedule affects any liability for, or the computation of, corporation tax in respect of a trade which is carried on by a company resident outside the United Kingdom through a branch or agency in the United Kingdom.

[(6) Any reference in this Schedule to an "ADP exempt period", in the case of any company, is a reference to an accounting period of the company—

    (*a*) which begins on or after 28th November 1995; and

    (*b*) in respect of which the company pursued, within the meaning of Part I of Schedule 25, an acceptable distribution policy.][3]

Commentary—*Simon's Direct Tax Service* **D4.1211.**
Revenue Internal Guidance—Company Taxation Manual COT8603 (UK residence in preceding period not assumed unless the CFC legislation applied to that period; example given).

COT8604 (on a deemed change of residence during an accounting period, profits are apportioned by reference to the transactions in the period rather than on a time basis).

COT9605 (place of trade remains actual place: therefore Case V rules apply).

COT8606 (the provisions of TA 1988 s 209 apply for the purposes of computing the chargeable profits, but the over-riding provisions of any double taxation agreement do not apply, with the result that the disallowance of interest could be greater than for a UK resident company).

COT8607 (example dealing with lump sum for patent rights).

Simon's Tax Cases—Sub-para (1), *Bricom Holdings Ltd v IRC* [1997] STC 1179.

Definitions—"Accounting period", s 834(1); "branch or agency", s 834(1); "company", s 832(1), (2); "tax", s 832(3); "trade", s 832(1); "United Kingdom", s 830(1).

Amendments—[1] Words in sub-para (3) inserted by FA 1996 s 154(7), (9), Sch 28 para 6 with effect for the purposes of income tax from the year 1996–97 and for the purposes of corporation tax for accounting periods ending after 31 March 1996.
[2] Sub-paras (3A), (6) inserted by FA 1996 s 182, Sch 36 para 3(2), (3) with effect for accounting periods of a controlled foreign company beginning after 27 November 1995.
[3] Sub-paras (3)(b)(i) and (4)(b)(i) and words following sub-paras (3)(b) and (4)(b) substituted, words inserted in sub-paras (3)(a), (3)(b)(ii), (4)(a) by FA 1998 Sch 17 para 17 with effect in relation to accounting periods of companies resident in the United Kingdom ending after 30 June 1999 (by virtue of Finance Act 1994, Section 199, (Appointed Day) Order, SI 1998/3173 art 2). See FA 1998 Sch 17 para 37 for details of the commencement and transitional provisions.

2—(1) The company shall be assumed to have become resident in the United Kingdom (and, accordingly, within the charge to corporation tax) at the beginning of the first accounting period—

[(a) in respect of which [an apportionment under section 747(3) falls to be made][2] or
(b) which is an ADP exempt period,

and][1] that United Kingdom residence shall be assumed to continue throughout subsequent accounting periods of the company (whether or not [an apportionment falls to be made][2] in respect of all or any of them) until the company ceases to be controlled by persons resident in the United Kingdom.

(2) Except in so far as the following provisions of this Schedule otherwise provide, for the purposes of calculating a company's chargeable profits or corresponding United Kingdom tax for any accounting period which is not the first such period referred to in sub-paragraph (1) above (and, in particular, for the purpose of applying any relief which is relevant to two or more accounting periods), it shall be assumed that a calculation of chargeable profits or, as the case may be, corresponding United Kingdom tax has been made for every previous accounting period throughout which the company was, by virtue of sub-paragraph (1) above, assumed to have been resident in the United Kingdom.

Commentary—*Simon's Direct Tax Service* **D4.1211.**
Definitions—"Accounting period", s 834(1); "company", s 832(1), (2); "tax", s 832(3); "United Kingdom", s 830(1).
Amendments—[1] Words in sub-para (1) substituted by FA 1996 s 182, Sch 36 para 3(4) with effect in relation to accounting periods of a controlled foreign company beginning after 27 November 1995.
[2] Words substituted in sub-para (1) by FA 1998 Sch 17 para 18 with effect in relation to accounting periods of companies resident in the United Kingdom ending after 30 June 1999 (by virtue of Finance Act 1994, Section 199, (Appointed Day) Order, SI 1998/3173 art 2). See FA 1998 Sch 17 para 37 for details of the commencement and transitional provisions.

3 The company shall be assumed not to be a close company.

Commentary—*Simon's Direct Tax Service* **D4.1211.**
Definitions—"Close company", ss 414(1), 832(1); "company", s 832(1), (2).

4—(1) Subject to sub-paragraph (2) below, where any relief under the Corporation Tax Acts is dependent upon the making of a claim or election, the company shall be assumed to have made that claim or election which would give the maximum amount of relief and to have made that claim or election within any time limit applicable to it.

[(1A) Sub-paragraph (2) below applies to any accounting period of the company—

(a) in respect of which [an apportionment under section 747(3) falls to be made][2]; or
(b) which is an ADP exempt period.][1]

(2) [Where this sub-paragraph applies to an accounting period of the company, then][1] if, by notice [given to an officer of the Board][2] at any time not later than the expiry of [the period of twenty months following the end of the accounting period][2] or within such longer period as the Board may in any particular case allow, the United Kingdom resident company which has or, as the case may be, any two or more United Kingdom resident companies which together have, a majority interest in the company so request, the company shall be assumed—

(a) not to have made any claim or election specified in the notice; or
(b) to have made a claim or election so specified, being different from one assumed by sub-paragraph (1) above but being one which (subject to compliance with any time limit) could have been made in the case of a company within the charge to corporation tax; or
(c) to have disclaimed or required the postponement, in whole or in part, of an allowance if (subject to compliance with any time limit) a company within the charge to corporation tax could have disclaimed the allowance or, as the case may be, required such postponement.

[(2A) ...][1]

(3) For the purposes of this paragraph, a United Kingdom resident company has, or two or more United Kingdom resident companies together have, a majority interest in the company if on the apportionment of the company's chargeable profits for the relevant accounting period under section 747(3) more than half of the amount of those profits—

(a) which are apportioned to all United Kingdom resident companies, and (*b*) which give rise to [any liability][2] on any such companies under subsection (4)(*a*) of that section,

are apportioned to the United Kingdom resident company or companies concerned.

[(3A) Sub-paragraph (3) above shall apply in relation to an accounting period which is an ADP exempt period as it would apply if—

    (*a*) that accounting period had instead been one in respect of which [an apportionment under section 747(3) had fallen to be made][2], and

    [(*b*) such apportionments as are mentioned in sub-paragraph (3) above had been made and such liabilities as are mentioned in that sub-paragraph had arisen.][2]][1]

(4) In sub-paragraph (3) above, "the relevant accounting period" means the accounting period or, as the case may be, the first accounting period in which the relief in question is or would be available in accordance with sub-paragraph (1) above.

Commentary—*Simon's Direct Tax Service* D4.1213.
Regulations—See General Insurance Reserve (Tax) Regulations, SI 2001/1757 reg 8.
Revenue Internal Guidance—Company Taxation Manual COT8622 (no special form for disclaimer under sub-para (2): notice should be sent to International Division, Room 311, Melbourne House).
COT8624 (circumstances in which late notice of disclaimer accepted).
Definitions—"Accounting period", s 834(1); "the Board", s 832(1); "company", s 832(1), (2); "notice", s 832(1); "United Kingdom", s 830(1).
Cross references—See TA 1988 s 753 (notice by the Board to a resident company and the company's right of appeal in relation to a direction under s 747(1)).
Amendments—[1] Sub-paras (1A), (2A), (3A), and words in sub-para (2) inserted by FA 1996 s 182, Sch 36 para 3(5), (6)(*a*), (7), (8) with effect for accounting periods of a controlled foreign company beginning after 27 November 1995.
[2] Sub-para (3A)(*b*) substituted and words in sub-paras (1A), (2), (2A), (3)(*b*) and (3A)(*a*) substituted by FA 1998 Sch 17 para 19, Sch 27 Part III(27), with effect in relation to accounting periods of companies resident in the United Kingdom ending after 30 June 1999 (by virtue of Finance Act 1994, Section 199, (Appointed Day) Order, SI 1998/3173 art 2). See FA 1998 Sch 17 para 37 for details of the commencement and transitional provisions.

4A ...

Amendments—This paragraph was inserted by FA 1993 s 96, which is deemed never to have been enacted and accordingly this paragraph is deemed never to have been inserted; see FA 1995 Sch 25 para 6(3), Sch 29 Pt VIII(18).

Group relief etc

5—[(1)][1] The company shall be assumed to be neither a member of a group of companies nor a member of a consortium for the purposes of any provision of the Tax Acts.

[(2) Where, under Chapter IV of Part X, any relief is in fact surrendered by the company and allowed to another company by way of group relief, it shall be assumed that the chargeable profits of the company, apart from this paragraph, are to be increased by an amount of additional profits equal to the amount of the relief so surrendered and allowed.][1]

Commentary—*Simon's Direct Tax Service* D4.1211.
Definitions—"Company", s 832(1), (2); "the Tax Acts", s 831(2).
Amendments—[1] Sub-para (1) numbered as such, and sub-para (2) inserted, by FA 2000 s 97, Sch 27 paras 10, 12(1) with effect for accounting periods ending after 31 March 2000.

[**6**—*(1) In relation to section 247 it shall be assumed—*

    (a) ...[1]
    (b) that the conditions for the making of an election under subsection (4) are not fulfilled with respect to payments made or received by the company.

(2) References in sub-paragraph (1) above to ...[1] payments received by the company apply to any received by another person on behalf of or in trust for the company, but not to any received by the company on behalf of or in trust for another person][2].

Commentary—*Simon's Direct Tax Service* D4.1211.
Definition—"Company", s 832(1), (2).
Amendments—[1] Sub-para (1)(*a*), and words in sub-para (2) repealed by FA 1998 Sch 3 para 42 with effect for accounting periods of companies resident outside the United Kingdom which begin after 5 April 1999.
[2] This paragraph repealed by FA 2001 s 110, Sch 33 Pt II(10) with effect for payments made after 11 May 2001.

7 ...

Commentary—*Simon's Direct Tax Service* D4.1211.
Definitions—"Advance corporation tax", s 14(1); "company", s 832(1), (2).
Amendments—This paragraph repealed by FA 1998 Sch 3 para 43 with effect for accounting periods of companies resident outside the United Kingdom which begin after 5 April 1999.

Company reconstructions

8 Without prejudice to the operation of section 343 in a case where the company is the predecessor, within the meaning of that section, and a company resident in the United Kingdom is the successor, within the meaning of that section—

    (*a*) the assumption that the company is resident in the United Kingdom shall not be regarded as requiring it also to be assumed that the company is within the charge to tax in respect of a trade for the purposes of that section, and (*b*) except in so far as the company is actually within that charge (by carrying on the trade through a branch or agency in the United Kingdom), it shall accordingly be assumed that the company can never be the successor, within the meaning of that section, to another company (whether resident in the United Kingdom or not).

Commentary—*Simon's Direct Tax Service* **D4.1211.**
Definitions—"Branch or agency", s 834(1); "company", s 832(1), (2); "tax", s 832(3); "trade", s 832(1); "United Kingdom", s 830(1).

Losses in pre-direction accounting periods

9—(1) ...[2] This paragraph applies in any case where the company incurred a loss in trade in an accounting period—

(*a*) which precedes the first accounting period in respect of which [an apportionment under section 747(3) falls to be made][2] ("the starting period"); and

(*b*) which ended less than six years before the beginning of the starting period; and

(*c*) in which the company was not resident[, and is not to be assumed by virtue of paragraph 2(1)(*b*) above to have been resident,][1] in the United Kingdom;

and in this paragraph any such accounting period is referred to as a "[pre-apportionment][2] period".

(2) ...[2]

(3) If a claim is made for the purpose by the United Kingdom resident company or companies referred to in paragraph 4(2) above, the chargeable profits (if any) of the company for accounting periods beginning with that [pre-apportionment][2] period which is specified in the claim and in which a loss is incurred as mentioned in sub-paragraph (1) above shall be determined (in accordance with the provisions of this Schedule other than this paragraph) on the assumption that that [pre-apportionment][2] period was the first accounting period in respect of which [an apportionment under section 747(3) fell to be made][2].

[(4) A claim under sub-paragraph (3) above shall be made by notice given to an officer of the Board within the period of twenty months following the end of the starting period or within such longer period as the Board may in any particular case allow.][2]

(5), (6) ...[2]

[(7) Nothing in—

(*a*) paragraph 10 of Schedule 18 to the Finance Act 1998 (claims or elections in company tax returns), or

(*b*) Schedule 1A to the Management Act (claims or elections not included in returns),

shall apply, whether by virtue of section 754 or otherwise, to a claim under sub-paragraph (3) above.][2]

Commentary—*Simon's Direct Tax Service* **D4.1215.**
Definitions—"Accounting period", s 834(1); "the Board", s 832(1); "company", s 832(1), (2); "notice", s 832(1); "trade", s 832(1); "United Kingdom", s 830(1).
Cross references—See TA 1988 Sch 24 para 11(2) (where a claim is made under sub-para (3) above no account to be taken for the purposes of capital allowances of the effect of sub-para (3) in determining which accounting period is the starting period).
Amendments—[1] Words in sub-para (1)(*c*) inserted by FA 1996 s 182, Sch 36 para 3(9) with effect for accounting periods of a controlled foreign company beginning after 27 November 1995.
[2] Sub-paras (2), (5) and (6) and words in sub-para (1) repealed, sub-para (4) and words in sub-paras (1) and (3) substituted and sub-para (7) inserted by FA 1998 Sch 17 para 20, Sch 27 Part III(27), with effect for accounting periods of companies resident in the United Kingdom ending after 30 June 1999 (by virtue of Finance Act 1994, Section 199, (Appointed Day) Order, SI 1998/3173 art 2). See FA 1998 Sch 17 para 37 for details of the commencement and transitional provisions.

Capital allowances

10—(1) [Subject to paragraph 12 below,][2] if, in an accounting period falling before the beginning of the first accounting period—

[(*a*) in respect of which [an apportionment under section 747(3) falls to be made][2], or

(*b*) which is an ADP exempt period,

the][1] company incurred any capital expenditure on the provision of [plant or machinery for the purposes of its trade, that plant or machinery shall be assumed, for the purposes of Part 2 of the Capital Allowances Act][3], to have been provided for purposes wholly other than those of the trade and not to have been brought into use for the purposes of that trade until the beginning of that first accounting period, and [section 13 of that Act (use for qualifying activity of plant or machinery provided for other purposes)][3] shall apply accordingly.

(2) This paragraph shall be construed as one with [Part 2 of the Capital Allowances Act][3].

Commentary—*Simon's Direct Tax Service* **D4.1214.**
Definitions—"The 1990 Act", s 831(3); "accounting period", s 834(1); "company", s 832(1), (2); "trade", s 832(1).
Amendments—[1] Words in sub-para (1) substituted by FA 1996 s 182, Sch 36 para 3(10) with effect for accounting periods of a controlled foreign company beginning after 27 November 1995.
[2] Words in sub-para (1) substituted by FA 1998 Sch 17 para 21 with effect for accounting periods of companies resident in the United Kingdom ending after 30 June 1999 (by virtue of Finance Act 1994, Section 199, (Appointed Day) Order, SI 1998/3173 art 2). See FA 1998 Sch 17 para 37 for details of the commencement and transitional provisions.
[3] Words substituted by CAA 2001 s 578, Sch 2 para 66(1), (2) with effect for corporation tax purposes, as respects allowances and charges falling to be made for chargeable periods ending after 31 March 2001.

11 ...

Commentary—*Simon's Direct Tax Service* **D4.1214.**
Amendments—This paragraph repealed by FA 1998 Sch 17 para 22, Sch 27 Part III(27), with effect for accounting periods of companies resident in the United Kingdom ending after 30 June 1999 (by virtue of Finance Act 1994, Section 199, (Appointed Day) Order, SI 1998/3173 art 2). See FA 1998 Sch 17 para 37 for details of the commencement and transitional provisions.

11A—(1) This paragraph applies where by virtue of section 747A the company's chargeable profits for an accounting period (the period in question) are to be computed and expressed in a currency (the relevant foreign currency) other than sterling.

(2) For the purposes of making in relation to the period in question any calculation which—

(*a*) falls to be made under the enactments relating to capital allowances, and
(*b*) takes account of amounts arrived at under those enactments in relation to accounting periods falling before the company's commencement day (within the meaning given by section 747A(9)),

it shall be assumed that any such amount is the equivalent, expressed in the relevant foreign currency, of the amount expressed in sterling.

[(3) ...]²

(4) For the purposes of the application of [section 578A or 578B or section 74(2), 75(1), 76(2), (3) or (4) or 511(3) of the Capital Allowances Act]³ (motor cars and dwelling-houses) in relation to expenditure incurred in the period in question, it shall be assumed that any sterling sum mentioned in any of those sections is the equivalent, expressed in the relevant foreign currency, of the amount expressed in sterling.

(5) The translation required by sub-paragraph (2) above shall be made by reference to the London closing exchange rate for the two currencies concerned for the first day of the period in question.

[(6) ...]²

(7) The translation required by sub-paragraph (4) above shall be made by reference to the London closing exchange rate for the two currencies concerned for the day on which the expenditure concerned was incurred.¹

Commentary —*Simon's Direct Tax Service* **D4.1214.**
Definitions—"Accounting period, s 834(1); "capital allowance", s 832(1); "company", s 832(1), (2); "profits", s 6(4).
Amendments—¹ Para 11A inserted by FA 1995 s 133, Sch 25 para 6(4).
² Sub-paras (3), (6) repealed by FA 1998 Sch 17 para 23, Sch 27 Part III(27), with effect for accounting periods of companies resident in the United Kingdom ending after 30 June 1999 (by virtue of Finance Act 1994, Section 199, (Appointed Day) Order, SI 1998/3173 art 2). See FA 1998 Sch 17 para 37 for details of the commencement and transitional provisions.
³ Words in sub-para (4) substituted by CAA 2001 s 578, Sch 2 para 66(3) with effect for corporation tax purposes, as respects allowances and charges falling to be made for chargeable periods ending after 31 March 2001.

Unremittable overseas income

12 For the purposes of the application of section 584 to the company's income it shall be assumed—

(*a*) that any reference in paragraph (*a*) or paragraph (*b*) of subsection (1) of that section to the United Kingdom is a reference to both the United Kingdom and the territory in which the company is in fact resident; and
(*b*) that a notice under subsection (2) of that section (expressing a wish to be assessed in accordance with that subsection) may be given on behalf of the company by the United Kingdom resident company or companies referred to in paragraph 4(2) above.

Commentary—*Simon's Direct Tax Service* **D4.1211.**
Definitions—"Company", s 832(1), (2); "notice", s 832(1); "United Kingdom", s 830(1).
Cross references—See TA 1988 s 753 (notice by the Board to a resident company and the company's right of appeal for a direction under s 747(1)).

[Exchange gains and losses]1

[13 *Paragraphs 14 to 19 below apply for the purposes of the application of Chapter II of Part II of the Finance Act 1993.]*¹

Note—This paragraph repealed by FA 2002 s 141, Sch 40 Pt 3(10) with effect for accounting periods beginning after 30 September 2002.
Amendments—¹ Para 13 and preceding heading inserted by FA 1995 s 133, Sch 25 para 6(5).

[14—*(1) This paragraph applies where—*

(a) by virtue of section 747A the company's chargeable profits for an accounting period are to be computed and expressed in a particular currency (the relevant currency),
(b) in an accrual period an asset or contract was held, or a liability was owed, by the company, and
(c) the accrual period falls within or constitutes the accounting period concerned.

(2) It shall be assumed that—

(a) the local currency for the purposes of sections 125 to 127 of the Finance Act 1993 is the relevant currency, and

(b) section 149 of that Act (local currency to be used) does not apply as regards the accrual period concerned.][1]

Note—This paragraph repealed by FA 2002 s 141, Sch 40 Pt 3(10) with effect for accounting periods beginning after 30 September 2002.
Definitions—"Accounting period", s 834(1); "profits", s 6(4).
Amendments—[1] Para 14 inserted by FA 1995 s 133, Sch 25 para 6(5).

[15 Where the accounting period mentioned in section 139(1) of the Finance Act 1993 is one for which, by virtue of section 747A, the company's chargeable profits are to be computed and expressed in a currency other than sterling—

(a) section 142(1) to (4) of that Act shall be assumed not to apply as regards that period;
(b) section 142(5) and (6) of that Act shall be assumed not to apply as regards the next accounting period of the company.][1]

Note—This paragraph repealed by FA 2002 s 141, Sch 40 Pt 3(10) with effect for accounting periods beginning after 30 September 2002.
Definitions—"Accounting period", s 834(1); "profits", s 6(4).
Amendments—[1] Para 15 inserted by FA 1995 s 133, Sch 25 para 6(5).

[16—(1) This paragraph applies where the last relevant accounting period for the purposes of section 146 of the Finance Act 1993 is one for which by virtue of section 747A the company's chargeable profits are to be computed and expressed in a particular currency (the relevant currency).
(2) Subsections (10), (11) and (14) of section 146 of the Finance Act 1993 shall be assumed not to apply.][1]

Note—This paragraph repealed by FA 2002 s 141, Sch 40 Pt 3(10) with effect for accounting periods beginning after 30 September 2002.
Definitions—"Accounting period", s 834(1); "profits", s 6(4).
Amendments—[1] Para 16 inserted by FA 1995 s 133, Sch 25 para 6(5).

[17 Where by virtue of section 747A the company's chargeable profits for an accounting period are to be computed and expressed in a particular currency, the references in section 148(9) of the Finance Act 1993 to sterling shall be assumed to be references to that particular currency.][1]

Note—This paragraph repealed by FA 2002 s 141, Sch 40 Pt 3(10) with effect for accounting periods beginning after 30 September 2002.
Definitions—"Accounting period", s 834(1); "profits", s 6(4).
Amendments—[1] Para 17 inserted by FA 1995 s 133, Sch 25 para 6(5).

[18—(1) This paragraph applies where the accounting period mentioned in paragraph (b) of subsection (11) of section 153 of the Finance Act 1993 is one for which, by virtue of section 747A, the company's chargeable profits are to be computed and expressed in a particular currency (the relevant currency).
(2) That subsection shall have effect as if the reference to the local currency of the trade for the accounting period were a reference to the relevant currency.][1]

Note—This paragraph repealed by FA 2002 s 141, Sch 40 Pt 3(10) with effect for accounting periods beginning after 30 September 2002.
Definitions—"Accounting period", s 834(1); "profits", s 6(4).
Amendments—[1] Para 18 inserted by FA 1995 s 133, Sch 25 para 6(5).

[19—(1) This paragraph applies where—

(a) Chapter II of Part II of the Finance Act 1993 falls to be applied as regards an accounting period of the company;
(b) under that Chapter, an exchange gain or an exchange loss accrued to the company for an accrual period constituting or falling within an earlier accounting period of the company, and
(c) the accounting period mentioned in paragraph (b) above falls before the company's first relevant accounting period.

(2) It shall be assumed, for the purposes of applying Chapter II of Part II of the Finance Act 1993 as respects the accounting period mentioned in sub-paragraph (1)(a) above, that the exchange gain or loss mentioned in sub-paragraph (1)(b) above never existed.

(3) In sub-paragraph (1) above—

(a) references to an exchange gain are to an exchange gain of a trade or an exchange gain of part of a trade or a non-trading exchange gain;
(b) references to an exchange loss are to an exchange loss of a trade or an exchange loss of part of a trade or a non-trading exchange loss;
(c) the reference in sub-paragraph (1)(b) to an exchange gain or an exchange loss accruing is to the gain or loss accruing before the application of any of sections 131, 136, 137 and 140 of the Finance Act 1993 in relation to the accounting period mentioned in sub-paragraph (1)(b);
(d) references to the first relevant accounting period of the company shall be construed in accordance with section 747A.][1]

Note—This paragraph repealed by FA 2002 s 141, Sch 40 Pt 3(10) with effect for accounting periods beginning after 30 September 2002.

Definitions—"Accounting period", s 834(1); "company", s 832(1), (2).
Amendments—[1] Para 19 inserted by FA 1995 s 133, Sch 25 para 6(5).

Transfer pricing

20—(1) Sub-paragraph (2) of paragraph 5 of Schedule 28AA (no potential UK tax advantage where both parties are within charge to income or corporation tax etc) shall be assumed not to apply in any case where, apart from that sub-paragraph (and on the assumption in paragraph 1(1) above),—

(a) paragraph 6 of that Schedule would apply; and

(b) the company would be the disadvantaged person for the purposes of that paragraph.

(2) Schedule 28AA (transfer pricing etc: provision not at arm's length) shall be assumed not to apply in any case where, apart from this sub-paragraph,—

(a) the actual provision would (on the assumption in paragraph 1(1) above) confer a potential advantage in relation to United Kingdom taxation on the company;

(b) the other affected person would be a company resident outside the United Kingdom; and

(c) each accounting period of that company which falls wholly or partly within the accounting period in question is one as regards which—

(i) an apportionment under section 747(3) falls to be made; or

(ii) no such apportionment falls to be made by virtue of the period being an ADP exempt period.

(3) In any case where—

(a) by virtue of sub-paragraph (2) above, Schedule 28AA is assumed not to apply, and

(b) the actual provision mentioned in paragraph (a) of that sub-paragraph involves (on the assumption in paragraph 1(1) above) any such interest or other distribution out of assets as would constitute a distribution for the purposes of the Corporation Tax Acts by virtue of paragraph (da) of section 209(2),

that interest or distribution out of assets shall be assumed not to constitute such a distribution by virtue of that paragraph.][1]

Amendments—[1] Inserted by FA 1998 Sch 17 para 24 with effect for accounting periods of companies resident in the United Kingdom ending after 30 June 1999 (by virtue of Finance Act 1994, Section 199, (Appointed Day) Order, SI 1998/3173 art 2). See FA 1998 Sch 17 para 37 for details of the commencement and transitional provisions.

SCHEDULE 25

[CASES WHERE SECTION 747(3) DOES NOT APPLY][1]

Section 748

Commentary—*Simon's Direct Tax Service* **D4.1220–1226, 11231–1237, 1240, 1242.**
Revenue & other press releases—IR 12-11-97 (Controlled foreign companies (CFCs) – Inland Revenue publish draft legislation on assessment and returns).
Amendments—[1] Heading to this Schedule substituted by FA 1998 Sch 17 para 25 with effect for accounting periods of companies resident in the United Kingdom ending after 30 June 1999 (by virtue of Finance Act 1994, Section 199, (Appointed Day) Order, SI 1998/3173 art 2). See FA 1998 Sch 17 para 37 for details of the commencement and transitional provisions.

PART I

ACCEPTABLE DISTRIBUTION POLICY

1 The provisions of this Part of this Schedule have effect for the purposes of paragraph (a) of subsection (1) of section 748 [and the other provisions of Chapter IV of Part XVII which refer to a company pursuing an acceptable distribution policy][1].

Commentary—*Simon's Direct Tax Service* **D4.1220.**
Revenue Internal Guidance—Company Taxation Manual COT8899 (flow chart for deciding whether a company pursues an acceptable distribution policy).
Amendments—[1] Words inserted by FA 1998 Sch 17 para 26 with effect for accounting periods of companies resident in the United Kingdom ending after 30 June 1999 (by virtue of Finance Act 1994, Section 199, (Appointed Day) Order, SI 1998/3173 art 2). See FA 1998 Sch 17 para 37 for details of the commencement and transitional provisions.

2—(1) Subject to [paragraph 2A][2] below, a controlled foreign company pursues an acceptable distribution policy in respect of a particular accounting period if, and only if—

(a) a dividend which is not paid out of specified profits is paid for that accounting period ...[2]; and

(b) the dividend is paid during, or not more than eighteen months after the expiry of, [that period][2] or at such later time as the Board may, in any particular case, allow; and

(c) ...[1]

(d) the [amount][2] of the dividend or, if there is more than one, of the aggregate of those dividends which is paid to persons resident in the United Kingdom [is not less than][2] [90 per cent of the company's net chargeable profits][3] for the accounting period referred to in paragraph (a) above or, where sub-paragraph (4) or (5) below applies, of the appropriate portion of those profits;

...[2].

[(1A) A payment of dividend to a company shall not fall within sub-paragraph (1)(*d*) above unless it is taken into account in computing the company's income for corporation tax][1][and—

(*a*) it is chargeable neither under Case I of Schedule D nor under Case VI of that Schedule in circumstances where by virtue of section 436, 439B or 441 profits are computed in accordance with the provisions of this Act applicable to Case I; or

(*b*) if it is chargeable under Case I, or under Case VI in the circumstances described in paragraph (*a*) above, it is not involved in a UK tax avoidance scheme;

and paragraph 2B below has effect for the purposes of paragraph (*b*) above.][5]

[(1B) A dividend paid by a company shall not fall within sub-paragraph (1)(*d*) above if, and to the extent that, the profits which are the relevant profits in relation to the dividend derive from dividends or other distributions paid to the company at any time which are dividends or other distributions—

(*a*) to which section 208 applied; or

(*b*) to which that section would have applied if the company had been resident in the United Kingdom at that time.

Subsections (3) and (4) of section 799 (double taxation relief: computation of underlying tax) apply for the purposes of this sub-paragraph as they apply for the purposes of subsection (1) of that section.][4]

(2) ...[2]

[(3) For the purposes of this paragraph and paragraph 2A below, a dividend which is not paid for the period or periods the profits of which are, in relation to the dividend, the relevant profits for the purposes of section 799 shall be treated (subject to sub-paragraph (3A) below) as so paid.

(3A) For the purposes of this paragraph and paragraph 2A below—

(*a*) where a dividend is paid for a period which is not an accounting period but falls wholly within an accounting period, it shall be treated as paid for that accounting period, and

(*b*) where a dividend (''the actual dividend'') is paid for a period which falls within two or more accounting periods—

(i) it shall be treated as if it were a number of separate dividends each of which is paid for so much of the period as falls wholly within an accounting period, and

(ii) the necessary apportionment of the amount of the actual dividend shall be made to determine the amount of the separate dividends.][2]

(4) This sub-paragraph applies where—

(*a*) throughout the accounting period in question all the issued shares of the controlled foreign company are of a single class, and

(*b*) at the end of that accounting period some of those shares are held by persons resident outside the United Kingdom, and

(*c*) at no time during that accounting period does any person have an interest in the company other than an interest derived from the issued shares of the company;

and in a case where this sub-paragraph applies the appropriate portion for the purposes of sub-paragraph (1)(*d*) above is the fraction of which the denominator is the total number of the issued shares of the company at the end of the accounting period in question and, subject to sub-paragraph 8 below, the numerator is the number of those issued shares by virtue of which persons resident in the United Kingdom have interests in the company at that time.

(5) This sub-paragraph applies where—

(*a*) throughout the accounting period in question there are only two classes of issued shares of the controlled foreign company and, of those classes, one (''non-voting shares'') consists of non-voting fixed-rate preference shares and the other (''voting shares'') consists of shares which carry the right to vote in all circumstances at general meetings of the company; and

(*b*) at the end of that accounting period some of the issued shares of the company are held by persons resident outside the United Kingdom; and

(*c*) at no time during that accounting period does any person have an interest in the company other than an interest derived from non-voting or voting shares;

and in a case where this sub-paragraph applies the appropriate portion of the profits referred to in sub-paragraph (1)(*d*) above is the amount determined in accordance with sub-paragraph (6) below.

(6) The amount referred to in sub-paragraph (5) above is that given by the formula—

$$\frac{P \times Q}{R} + \frac{(X - P) \times Y}{Z}$$

where—

P is the amount of any dividend falling within (*a*) and (*b*) of sub-paragraph (1) above which is paid in respect of the non-voting shares or, if there is more than one such dividend, of the aggregate of them;

Q is, subject to sub-paragraph (8) below, the number of the non-voting shares by virtue of which persons resident in the United Kingdom have interests in the company at the end of the accounting period in question;

R is the total number at that time of the issued non-voting shares;

X is the [net chargeable profits][3] for the accounting period in question;

Y is, subject to sub-paragraph (8) below, the number of voting shares by virtue of which persons resident in the United Kingdom have interests in the company at the end of that accounting period; and

Z is the total number at that time of the issued voting shares.

(7) For the purposes of sub-paragraph (5)(*a*) above, non-voting fixed-rate preference shares are shares—

    (*a*) which are fixed-rate preference shares as defined in paragraph 1 of Schedule 18; and

    (*b*) which either carry no right to vote at a general meeting of the company or carry such a right which is contingent upon the non-payment of a dividend on the shares and which has not in fact become exercisable at any time prior to the payment of a dividend for the accounting period in question.

(8) In any case where the immediate interests held by persons resident in the United Kingdom who have indirect interests in a controlled foreign company at the end of a particular accounting period do not reflect the proportion of the shares or, as the case may be, shares of a particular class in the company by virtue of which they have those interests (as in the case where they hold, directly or indirectly, part of the shares in a company which itself holds, directly or indirectly, some or all of the shares in the controlled foreign company) the number of those shares shall be treated as reduced for the purposes of sub-paragraph (4) or (6) above, as the case may be, to such number as may be appropriate having regard to—

    (*a*) the immediate interests held by the persons resident in the United Kingdom; and

    (*b*) any intermediate shareholdings between those interests and the shares in the controlled foreign company.

(9) The definition of "profits" in section 747(6)(*b*) does not apply to any reference in this paragraph to specified profits or to relevant profits for the purposes of section 799.

Commentary—*Simon's Direct Tax Service* D4.1220, 1221.

Revenue Decision RD 2—Controlled foreign company: acceptable distribution policy and standard for the purposes of definition of "trading company" in s 756(1).

Revenue Internal Guidance—Company Taxation Manual COT8401 (attribution of dividends to accounting periods, with worked example).

COT8414 (net chargeable profits may be increased by TA 1988 s 770 adjustment (transfer pricing)).

COT8242 (worked example on sub-para (5)).

Definitions—"Accounting period", s 834(1); "the Board", s 832(1); "company", s 832(1), (2); "distribution", ss 209(2), 832(1); "United Kingdom", s 830(1).

Modifications—Sub-paras (1AA), (1AB) treated as inserted, and sub-para (1) treated as amended, in respect of UK companies which have a relevant interest in companies resident outside the UK carrying on general insurance business and drawing up accounts relating to that business on a non-annual basis: see Non-resident Companies (General Insurance Business) Regulations, SI 1999/1408 reg 6.

Amendments—[1] Sub-para (1)(*c*) repealed and sub-para (1A) inserted by FA 1990 s 67(3), (4), Sch 19 Pt IV with effect for dividends paid after 19 March 1990.

[2] Words in sub-para (1) and whole of sub-paras (3), (3A) substituted, and words in sub-para (1) and whole of sub-para (2) repealed, by FA 1994 s 134(1), (2), (5) and apply as regards determination of acceptable distribution policy for accounting periods ending after 29 November 1993.

[3] Words in sub-paras (1)(*d*), (6) substituted by FA 1996 s 182, Sch 36 para 4(2) with effect for accounting periods of a controlled foreign company beginning after 27 November 1995.

[4] Sub-para (1B) inserted by FA 1999 s 88 with effect in determining whether dividends paid after 8 March 1999 for accounting periods ending after that date fall within sub-paragraph (1)(*d*) above.

[5] Words in sub-para (1A) inserted by FA 2001 s 82(2), (8) with effect for dividends paid after 6 March 2001 by a controlled foreign company for any accounting period of that controlled foreign company which ends after that date. For these purposes "accounting period" and "controlled foreign company" have the same meaning as they have in TA 1988 Part XVII Chapter IV by virtue of FA 2001 s 82(9).

[2A—(1) Paragraph 2 above shall have effect in accordance with this paragraph to determine whether a controlled foreign company ...[2] pursues an acceptable distribution policy in respect of a particular accounting period ("the relevant accounting period").

(2) Subject to sub-paragraph (4) below, where the distribution condition is satisfied in relation to the relevant accounting period, then, in addition to any dividend which falls within paragraph 2(1)(*a*) above apart from this paragraph—

    (*a*) any dividend which is paid for the accounting period ("the preceding period") [immediately preceding][3] the relevant accounting period and [which is not an excluded dividend][3] shall be treated as falling within that paragraph, and

    (*b*) if the distribution condition is satisfied in relation to the preceding period, any dividend which is paid for the accounting period [immediately preceding][3] the preceding period and [which is not an excluded dividend][3] shall be treated as falling within that paragraph,

and so on; and in this sub-paragraph "dividend" means a dividend not paid out of specified profits.

(3) For the purposes of this paragraph, the distribution condition is satisfied in relation to any accounting period if—

    (*a*) a dividend or dividends are paid for the period to persons resident in the United Kingdom,

    (*b*) the amount or, as the case may be, aggregate amount of any dividends falling within paragraph (*a*) above is not less than—

       (i) the relevant profits for that period, or

(ii) where paragraph 2(4) or (5) above applies (with the modifications of paragraph 2 made by sub-paragraph (5) below), the appropriate portion of those profits, and

(*c*) any dividends falling within that paragraph are paid not later than the time by which any dividend paid for the relevant accounting period is required by paragraph 2(1)(*b*) above to be paid;

or if there are no relevant profits for the period.

(4) Where, by reason only of the fact that a company pursued an acceptable distribution policy in respect of any accounting period ("the earlier period") earlier than the relevant accounting period, [no apportionment under section 747(3) fell to be made in respect of the earlier period][3], sub-paragraph (2) above shall apply to any dividend required to be taken into account for the purpose of showing that the company pursued an acceptable distribution policy in respect of the earlier period only to the extent (if any) to which that dividend was not required to be taken into account for that purpose.

(5) The modifications of paragraph 2 above referred to in sub-paragraph (3)(*b*) above are that—

(*a*) the references in sub-paragraphs (4) and (5) to the accounting period in question are to be read as references to the accounting period for which the dividend or dividends are paid,

(*b*) the references in those sub-paragraphs to sub-paragraph (1)(*d*) are to be read as references to sub-paragraph (3)(*b*) above, and

(*c*) the reference in the definition of "X" in sub-paragraph (6) to [net chargeable profits][2] is to be read as a reference to relevant profits.

(6), (7) ...[2]

(8) For the purposes of this paragraph—

[(*aa*) a dividend is an excluded dividend if it is paid, in whole or in part, out of the total profits from which (in accordance with section 747(6)(a)) the chargeable profits for an excluded period are derived,][3]

(*a*) a period is an excluded period if it is an accounting period in respect of which [an apportionment under section 747(3) falls to be made][3], and

(*b*) relevant profits for any accounting period are the profits which would be the relevant profits of that period for the purposes of section 799 if a dividend were actually paid for that period.][1]

Commentary—*Simon's Direct Tax Service* **D4.1221.**
Revenue & other press releases—IR Tax Bulletin August 1994 p 138 (Revenue's interpretation of this paragraph).
Revenue Internal Guidance—Company Taxation Manual COT8416, 8417 (worked examples).
Definitions—"Accounting period", s 834(1); "company", s 832(1), (2); "distribution", ss 209(2), 832(1); "net chargeable profits", Sch 25 para 3(4A); "United Kingdom", s 830(1).
Amendments—[1] This paragraph inserted by FA 1994 s 134(1), (3), (5) and applies as regards determination of acceptable distribution policy for accounting periods ending after 29 November 1993.
[2] Words omitted in sub-para (1) repealed, words in sub-para (5)(c) substituted and sub-paras (6), (7) repealed by FA 1996 s 182, Sch 36 para 4(3), Sch 41 Pt V(34) with effect for accounting periods of a controlled foreign company beginning after 27 November 1995.
[3] Words in sub-paras (2), (4), and (8)(a) substituted and sub-para (8)(aa) inserted by FA 1998 Sch 17 para 27 with effect for accounting periods of companies resident in the United Kingdom ending after 30 June 1999 (by virtue of Finance Act 1994, Section 199, (Appointed Day) Order, SI 1998/3173 art 2). See FA 1998 Sch 17 para 37 for details of the commencement and transitional provisions.

[**2B**—(1) This paragraph has effect for the purposes of paragraph 2(1A)(*b*) above.

(2) No payment of dividend by a controlled foreign company for an accounting period shall be regarded as involved in a UK tax avoidance scheme by reason only that there is no charge to tax under section 747(4)(*a*) if the controlled foreign company pursues an acceptable distribution policy for that accounting period.

(3) "UK tax avoidance scheme" means a scheme or arrangement the purpose, or one of the main purposes, of which is to achieve a reduction in United Kingdom tax.

(4) A scheme or arrangement achieves a reduction in United Kingdom tax if, apart from the scheme or arrangement, any company—

(*a*) would have been liable for any such tax or for a greater amount of any such tax; or

(*b*) would not have been entitled to a relief from or repayment of any such tax or would have been entitled to a smaller relief from or repayment of any such tax.

(5) In this paragraph—

"arrangement" means an arrangement of any kind, whether in writing or not;

"United Kingdom tax" means corporation tax or any tax chargeable as if it were corporation tax..][1]

Commentary—*Simon's Direct Tax Service* **D4.1221.**
Amendments—[1] This paragraph inserted by FA 2001 s 82(3), (8) with effect for dividends paid after 6 March 2001 by a controlled foreign company for any accounting period of that controlled foreign company which ends after that date. For these purposes "accounting period" and "controlled foreign company" have the same meaning as they have in TA 1988 Part XVII Chapter IV by virtue of FA 2001 s 82(9).

3—(1)–(4) ...[2]

[(4A) Subject to sub-paragraph (5) below, for the purposes of this Part of this Schedule, the net chargeable profits of a controlled foreign company for any accounting period are—

(*a*) its chargeable profits for that period, less

(b) the amount (if any) which, if [an apportionment under section 747(3) fell to be made][3] in respect of the period, would be the company's unrestricted creditable tax for that period;

and for the purposes of this sub-paragraph "unrestricted creditable tax" in relation to a company's accounting period means the amount which would be its creditable tax for that period if the reference in section 751(6)(a) to Part XVIII did not include section 797.][1]

(5) In any case where—

(a) a controlled foreign company pays a dividend for any period out of specified profits, and

(b) those profits represent dividends received by the company, directly or indirectly, from another controlled foreign company,

so much of those specified profits as is equal to the dividend referred to in paragraph (a) above shall be left out of account in determining, for the purposes of this Part of this Schedule, ...[2] [...[2] the chargeable profits][1] of the controlled foreign company referred to in that paragraph for any accounting period.

Commentary—*Simon's Direct Tax Service* **D4.1222.**
Revenue Internal Guidance—Company Taxation Manual COT8421, 8428 (dividends received from other CFCs: worked examples).
COT8422 (background to para 3(2)).
Definitions—"Accounting period", s 834(1); "the Board", s 832(1); "company", s 832(1), (2); "the Income Tax Acts", s 831(1)(b).
Cross references—See TA 1988 s 753 (notice by the Board to a resident company and the company's right of appeal in relation to a direction under s 747(1)).
Amendments—[1] Sub-para (4A) and words in sub-para (5) inserted by FA 1994 s 134(1), (4), (5) and applies as regards determination of acceptable distribution policy for accounting periods ending after 29 November 1993.
[2] Sub-paras (1)–(4) and words omitted in sub-para (5) repealed by FA 1996 s 182, Sch 36 para 4(4), Sch 41 Pt V(34) with effect for accounting periods of a controlled foreign company beginning after 27 November 1995.
[3] Words in sub-para (4A) substituted by FA 1998 Sch 17 para 28 with effect for accounting periods of companies resident in the United Kingdom ending after 30 June 1999 (by virtue of Finance Act 1994, Section 199, (Appointed Day) Order, SI 1998/3173 art 2). See FA 1998 Sch 17 para 37 for details of the commencement and transitional provisions.

4—(1) For the purposes of this Part of this Schedule, where—

(a) a controlled foreign company pays a dividend ("the initial dividend") to another company which is also not resident in the United Kingdom, and

(b) that other company or another company which is related to it pays a dividend ("the subsequent dividend") to a United Kingdom resident, and

(c) ...[1]

(d) the subsequent dividend is paid out of profits which are derived, directly or indirectly, from the whole or part of the initial dividend,

so much of the initial dividend as is represented by the subsequent dividend shall be regarded as paid to the United Kingdom resident[and shall be taken to satisfy the conditions in paragraph 2(1A) above][2].

[(1A) A payment to a company shall not be a subsequent dividend within the meaning of sub-paragraph (1)(b) above unless it is taken into account in computing the company's income for corporation tax][and—

(a) it is chargeable neither under Case I of Schedule D nor under Case VI of that Schedule in circumstances where by virtue of section 436, 439B or 441 profits are computed in accordance with the provisions of this Act applicable to Case I; or

(b) if it is chargeable under Case I, or under Case VI in the circumstances described in paragraph (a) above, it is not involved in a UK tax avoidance scheme;

and paragraph 4A below has effect for the purposes of paragraph (b) above.][2]

(2) For the purposes of this paragraph, one company is related to another if [neither is resident in the United Kingdom and][2] the other—

(a) controls directly or indirectly, or

(b) is a subsidiary of a company which controls directly or indirectly,

at least 10 per cent of the voting power in the first-mentioned company; and where one company is so related to another and that other is so related to a third company, the first company is for the purposes of this paragraph related to the third, and so on where there is a chain of companies, each of which is related to the next.

Commentary—*Simon's Direct Tax Service* **D4.1220.**
Revenue Internal Guidance—Company Taxation Manual COT8427 (worked examples).
Definitions—"Company", s 832(1), (2); "controls", s 840; "United Kingdom", s 830(1).
Amendments—[1] Sub-para (1)(c) repealed and sub-para (1A) inserted by FA 1990 s 67(3)(a), (4) and Sch 19 Pt IV with effect for dividends paid after 19 March 1990.
[2] Words in sub-paras (1), (1A), (2) inserted by FA 2001 s 82(4)–(6), (8) with effect for dividends paid after 6 March 2001 by a controlled foreign company for any accounting period of that controlled foreign company which ends after that date. For these purposes "accounting period" and "controlled foreign company" have the same meaning as they have in TA 1988 Part XVII Chapter IV by virtue of FA 2001 s 82(9).

[4A—(1) This paragraph has effect for the purposes of paragraph 4(1A)(b) above.

(2) No payment to a company resident in the United Kingdom which represents the whole or part of a dividend paid by a controlled foreign company for an accounting period shall be regarded as involved in a UK tax avoidance scheme by reason only that—

(a) there is no charge to tax under section 747(4)(a) if the controlled foreign company pursues an acceptable distribution policy for that accounting period, and

(b) so much of the dividend as is represented by that payment will (if paragraph 4(1) above has effect) fall to be brought into account in determining whether the controlled foreign company has done so.

(3) "UK tax avoidance scheme" means a scheme or arrangement the purpose, or one of the main purposes, of which is to achieve a reduction in United Kingdom tax.

(4) A scheme or arrangement achieves a reduction in United Kingdom tax if, apart from the scheme or arrangement, any company—

(a) would have been liable for any such tax or for a greater amount of any such tax; or

(b) would not have been entitled to a relief from or repayment of any such tax or would have been entitled to a smaller relief from or repayment of any such tax.

(5) In this paragraph—

"arrangement" means an arrangement of any kind, whether in writing or not;

"United Kingdom tax" means corporation tax or any tax chargeable as if it were corporation tax.][1]

Commentary—*Simon's Direct Tax Service* **D4.1220.**
Definitions—"Company", s 832(1), (2); "United Kingdom", s 830(1).
Amendments—[1] This paragraph inserted by FA 2001 s 82(7), (8) with effect for dividends paid after 6 March 2001 by a controlled foreign company for any accounting period of that controlled foreign company which ends after that date. For these purposes "accounting period" and "controlled foreign company" have the same meaning as they have in TA 1988 Part XVII Chapter IV by virtue of FA 2001 s 82(9).

PART II
EXEMPT ACTIVITIES

5—(1) The provisions of this Part of this Schedule have effect for the purposes of paragraph (b) of subsection (1) of section 748.

(2) In the case of a controlled foreign company—

(a) which is, by virtue of section [749(5)][1], presumed to be resident in a territory in which it is subject to a lower level of taxation, and

(b) the business affairs of which are, throughout the accounting period in question, effectively managed in a territory outside the United Kingdom other than one in which companies are liable to tax by reason of domicile, residence or place of management,

references in the following provisions of this Part of this Schedule to the territory in which that company is resident shall be construed as references to the territory falling within paragraph (b) above, or, if there is more than one, to that one of them which may be notified to the Board by the United Kingdom resident company or companies referred to in paragraph 4(2) of Schedule 24.

Commentary—*Simon's Direct Tax Service* **D4.1230.**
Definitions—"Accounting period", s 834(1); "the Board", s 832(1); "company", s 832(1), (2); "United Kingdom", s 830(1).
Amendments—[1] Word in sub-para (2)(a) substituted by FA 1998 Sch 17 para 29 with effect for accounting periods of companies resident in the United Kingdom ending after 30 June 1999 (by virtue of Finance Act 1994, Section 199, (Appointed Day) Order, SI 1998/3173 art 2). See FA 1998 Sch 17 para 37 for details of the commencement and transitional provisions.

6—(1) Throughout an accounting period a controlled foreign company is engaged in exempt activities if, and only if, each of the following conditions is fulfilled—

(a) that, throughout that accounting period, the company has a business establishment in the territory in which it is resident; and

(b) that, throughout that accounting period, its business affairs in that territory are effectively managed there; and

(c) that any of sub-paragraphs (2) to [(4A)][2] below applies to the company.

(2) This sub-paragraph applies to a company if—

(a) at no time during the accounting period in question does the main business of the company consist of either—

(i) investment business, or

(ii) dealing in goods for delivery to or from the United Kingdom or to or from connected or associated persons; and

(b) in the case of a company which is mainly engaged in wholesale, distributive [financial or service][3] business in that accounting period, less than 50 per cent of its gross trading receipts from that business is derived directly or indirectly from [persons falling within sub-paragraph (2A) below][5].

[(2A) Those persons are—

(a) persons who are connected or associated with the company;

(*b*) persons who have a 25 per cent assessable interest in the company in the case of the accounting period in question; and

(*c*) if the company is a controlled foreign company in that accounting period by virtue of subsection (1A) of section 747, persons who are connected or associated with either or both of the two persons mentioned in that subsection.][5]

(3) This sub-paragraph applies to a company which is a holding company if at least 90 per cent of its gross income during the accounting period in question [is received by it in the territory in which it is resident and][5] is derived directly from companies which it controls and which, throughout that period—

    (*a*) are resident in the territory in which the holding company is resident; and

    (*b*) are not themselves holding companies [or superior holding companies][2], but otherwise are, in terms of this Schedule, engaged in exempt activities [or are, in terms of sub-paragraph (5A) below, exempt trading companies][2];

and a holding company to which this sub-paragraph applies is in this Part of this Schedule referred to as a "local holding company".

(4) This sub-paragraph applies to a company which is a holding company, but not a local holding company, if at least 90 per cent of its gross income during the accounting period in question [falls within sub-paragraph (4ZA) below and][5] is derived directly from companies which it controls and which, throughout that period—

    (*a*) are local holding companies; or

    (*b*) are not themselves holding companies (whether local or not) [or superior holding companies][2], but otherwise are, in terms of this Schedule, engaged in exempt activities [or are, in terms of sub-paragraph (5A) below, exempt trading companies][2].

[(4ZA) For the purposes of sub-paragraph (4) above, income of the holding company falls within this sub-paragraph if—

    (*a*) the company from which the holding company directly derives the income is, throughout the accounting period in question, resident in the territory in which the holding company is resident and the income is received by the holding company in that territory; or

    (*b*) the income consists of qualifying dividends.][5]

[(4A) This sub-paragraph applies to a company which is a superior holding company if at least 90 per cent of its gross income during the accounting period in question—

    (*a*) represents qualifying exempt activity income of its subsidiaries; and

    (*b*) is derived directly from companies which it controls and which fall within sub-paragraph (4B) below[; and

    (*c*) falls within sub-paragraph (4AA) below.][5]

[(4AA) For the purposes of sub-paragraph (4A) above, income of the superior holding company falls within this sub-paragraph if—

    (*a*) the company from which the superior holding company directly derives the income is, throughout the accounting period in question, resident in the territory in which the superior holding company is resident and the income is received by the superior holding company in that territory; or

    (*b*) the income consists of qualifying dividends.][5]

(4B) For the purposes of paragraph (*b*) of sub-paragraph (4A) above, a company falls within this sub-paragraph if—

    (*a*) throughout the accounting period mentioned in that sub-paragraph, it is not itself a superior holding company but otherwise is, in terms of this Schedule, engaged in exempt activities or is, in terms of sub-paragraph (5A) below, an exempt trading company; or

    (*b*) it is itself a superior holding company throughout that period and at least 90 per cent of its gross income during that period—

        (i) represents qualifying exempt activity income of its subsidiaries, and

        (ii) is derived directly from companies which it controls and which themselves fall within this paragraph or paragraph (a) above][2][, and

        (iii) falls within sub-paragraph (4BB) below][5].

[(4BB) For the purposes of sub-paragraph (4B)(*b*) above, income of the superior holding company there mentioned falls within this sub-paragraph if—

    (*a*) the company from which that superior holding company directly derives the income is, throughout the accounting period in question, resident in the territory in which that superior holding company is resident and the income is received by that superior holding company in that territory; or

    (*b*) the income consists of qualifying dividends.][5]

[(4C) For the purposes of sub-paragraph (2)(*b*) above, a person has a 25 per cent assessable interest in a controlled foreign company in the case of an accounting period of the company if, on an apportionment of the chargeable profits and creditable tax (if any) of the company for that accounting period under section 747(3), at least 25 per cent of the controlled foreign company's chargeable profits for the accounting period would be apportioned to that person.][2]

(5) Any reference in [sub-paragraphs (3) to (4B)][2] above to a company which a holding company [or superior holding company][2] controls includes a reference to a trading company [to which sub-paragraph (5ZA) or (5ZB) below applies.

(5ZA) This sub-paragraph applies to a trading company][5] in which the holding company [or superior holding company][2] holds the maximum amount of ordinary share capital which is permitted under the law of the territory—

    (*a*) in which the trading company is resident; and

    (*b*) from whose laws the trading company derives its status as a company.

[(5ZB) This sub-paragraph applies to a trading company if—

    (*a*) it is a controlled foreign company by virtue of subsection (1A) of section 747; and

    (*b*) the person who satisfies the requirement in paragraph (*b*) of that subsection in relation to the company also controls the holding company or superior holding company.][5]

[(5A) For the purposes of sub-paragraphs (3) to (4B) above, a company is an exempt trading company throughout any period if—

    (*a*) it is a trading company throughout each of its accounting periods which falls wholly or partly within that period; and

    (*b*) each of those accounting periods is one as regards which—

        (i) the condition in section 747(1)(*c*) is not satisfied; or

        (ii) the conditions in section 748(1)(*e*) are satisfied; or

        (iii) the conditions in section 748(3)(*a*) and (*b*) are satisfied.][2]

[(5B) In this paragraph "qualifying dividend" means any dividend other than one for which the company paying the dividend is entitled to a deduction against its profits for tax purposes under the law of the territory in which it is resident.][5]

(6) The following provisions of this Part of this Schedule have effect in relation to sub-paragraphs (1) to [(4BB)][4] above.

Commentary—*Simon's Direct Tax Service* **D4.1230–1236.**
Revenue & other press releases—Hansard 27-2-96 (sub-para (2)(*b*): the final words designed to prevent two or more parties getting together to run a controlled foreign company: "interest" should be taken to mean holders of at least 10 per cent interest).
Revenue Internal Guidance—Company Taxation Manual COT8443 (meaning of "effectively managed").
COT8445 (meaning of "main business").
COT8447 ("dealing" usually implies buying and selling: the subjection of goods to a process is not usually regarded as dealing).
COT8448 (meaning of "wholesale, distributive or financial" business).
COT8899 (flow chart for deciding whether a company is an exempt holding company).
Definitions—"Accounting period", s 834(1); "company", s 832(1), (2); "connected persons", s 839; "controls", ss 416, 756; "ordinary share capital", s 832(1); "United Kingdom", s 830(1).
Cross references—See TA 1988 Sch 25 para 8 (rules to fulfil condition in sub-para(1)(*b*) above).
TA 1988 Sch 25 para 9 (activities which constitute investment business for the purposes of sub-para (2)(*a*)(i) above).
TA 1988 Sch 25 para 10 (goods not taken into account for the purposes of sub-para (2)(*a*)(ii) above).
TA 1988 Sch 25 para 11 (activities which constitute wholesale, distributive or financial business for the purposes of sub-para (2)(*b*) above).
Amendments—[1] Words in sub-para (2)(*b*) inserted by FA 1996 s 182, Sch 36 para 4(5) with effect for accounting periods of a controlled foreign company beginning after 27 November 1995.
[2] Words substituted in sub-paras (1)(*c*), (2)(*b*) and (5) new sub-paras (4A)–(4C) and (5A) and words in sub-paras (3) and (4) inserted by FA 1998 Sch 17 para 30 with effect for accounting periods of companies resident in the United Kingdom ending after 30 June 1999 (by virtue of Finance Act 1994, Section 199, (Appointed Day) Order, SI 1998/3173 art 2). See FA 1998 Sch 17 para 37 for details of the commencement and transitional provisions.
[3] Words in sub-para (2)(*b*) substituted by FA 2000 s 104, Sch 31 paras 1, 5, 9(4) with effect for any accounting period of a controlled foreign company which begins after 20 March 2000. Sub-para (2)(*b*) previously read—

    "(*b*) in the case of a company which is mainly engaged in wholesale, distributive or financial business in that accounting period, less than 50 per cent of its gross trading receipts from that business is derived directly or indirectly from connected or associated persons or persons who have a 25 per cent assessable interest in the company in the case of that accounting period."

[4] Words in sub-para (6) substituted for word "(4)" by FA 2000 s 104, Sch 31 paras 1,7(11), 9(4) with effect for any accounting period of a controlled foreign company which begins after 20 March 2000.
[5] Sub-paras (2A), (4ZA), (4AA), (4BB), (5ZA), (5ZB), (5B) and words in sub-paras (3), (4), (4A), (4B), (5) inserted by FA 2000 s 104, Sch 31 paras 1, 5–7, 9(4) with effect for any accounting period of a controlled foreign company which begins after 20 March 2000.

7—(1) For the purposes of paragraph 6(1)(*a*) above, a "business establishment", in relation to a controlled foreign company, means premises—

    (*a*) which are, or are intended to be, occupied and used with a reasonable degree of permanence; and

    (*b*) from which the company's business in the territory in which it is resident is wholly or mainly carried on.

(2) For the purposes of sub-paragraph (1) above the following shall be regarded as premises—

    (*a*) an office, shop, factory or other building or part of a building; or

    (*b*) a mine, an oil or gas well, a quarry or any other place of extraction of natural resources; or

    (*c*) a building site or the site of a construction or installation project;

but such a site as is referred to in paragraph (*c*) above shall not be regarded as premises unless the building work or the project, as the case may be, has a duration of at least twelve months.

Commentary—*Simon's Direct Tax Service* **D4.1231.**
Revenue Internal Guidance—Company Taxation Manual COT8442 (meaning of "business establishment").
Definition—"Company", s 832(1), (2).

8—(1) Subject to sub-paragraph (4) below, the condition in paragraph 6(1)(*b*) above shall not be regarded as fulfilled unless—

(*a*) the number of persons employed by the company in the territory in which it is resident is adequate to deal with the volume of the company's business; and

(*b*) any services provided by the company for persons resident outside that territory are not in fact performed in the United Kingdom.

(2) For the purposes of sub-paragraph (1)(*a*) above, persons who are engaged wholly or mainly in the business of the company and whose remuneration is paid by a person connected with, and resident in the same territory as, the company shall be treated as employed by the company.

(3) In the case of a holding company [or superior holding company]¹, sub-paragraph (2) above shall apply with the omission of the words "wholly or mainly".

(4) For the purposes of sub-paragraph (1)(*b*) above, no account shall be taken of services—

(*a*) provided through a branch or agency of the controlled foreign company if the profits or gains of the business carried on through the branch or agency are within the charge to tax in the United Kingdom; or

(*b*) provided through any other person whose profits or gains from the provision of the services are within the charge to tax in the United Kingdom and who provides the services for a consideration which is, or which is not dissimilar from what might reasonably be expected to be, determined under a contract entered into at arm's length; or

(*c*) which are no more than incidental to services provided outside the United Kingdom.

Commentary—*Simon's Direct Tax Service* **D4.1232.**
Definitions—"Branch or agency", s 834(1); "company", s 832(1), (2); "profits or gains", s 833(1); "United Kingdom", s 830(1).
Amendments—¹ Words in sub-para (3) substituted by FA 1998 Sch 17 para 31 with effect for accounting periods of companies resident in the United Kingdom ending after 30 June 1999 (by virtue of Finance Act 1994, Section 199, (Appointed Day) Order, SI 1998/3173 art 2). See FA 1998 Sch 17 para 37 for details of the commencement and transitional provisions.

9—(1) Subject to sub-paragraph (3) below, for the purposes of paragraph 6(2)(*a*)(i) above, each of the following activities constitutes investment business—

(*a*) the holding of securities, [or intellectual property]¹;

(*b*) dealing in securities, other than in the capacity of a broker;

(*c*) the leasing of any description of property or rights; and

(*d*) the investment in any manner of funds which would otherwise be available, directly or indirectly, for investment by or on behalf of any person (whether resident in the United Kingdom or not) who has, or is connected or associated with a person who has, control, either alone or together with other persons, of the controlled foreign company in question.

[(1A) In sub-paragraph (1)(*a*) above "intellectual property" includes (in particular)—

(*a*) any industrial, commercial or scientific information, knowledge or expertise;

(*b*) any patent, trade mark, registered design, copyright or design right;

(*c*) any licence or other right in respect of intellectual property;

(*d*) any rights under the law of a country outside the United Kingdom which correspond or are similar to those falling within paragraph (*b*) or (*c*) above.]²

(2) In sub-paragraph (1)(*b*) above "broker" includes any person offering to sell securities to, or purchase securities from, members of the public generally.

(3) For the purposes of paragraph 6(2) above, in the case of a company which is mainly engaged in [business]³ falling within paragraph 11(1)(*c*) below, nothing in sub-paragraph (1) above shall require the main business of the company to be regarded as investment business.

Commentary—*Simon's Direct Tax Service* **D4.1234.**
Definitions—"Company", s 832(1), (2); "United Kingdom", s 830(1).
Amendments—¹ Words in sub-para (1)(*a*) substituted by the Copyright, Designs and Patents Act 1988 Sch 7 para 36(9) with effect from 1 August 1989 by virtue of the Copyright, Designs and Patents Act 1988 (Commencement No 1) Order 1989, SI 1989/816.
² Sub-para (1A) inserted by the Copyright, Designs and Patents Act 1988 Sch 7 para 36(9).
³ Sub-para (1A) and word in sub-para (3) substituted by FA 1998 s 112 (2), (4) with effect for accounting periods of a controlled foreign company, within the meaning of TA 1988 Part XVII Chapter IV, beginning on or after 17 March 1998.

10 Goods which are actually delivered into the territory in which the controlled foreign company is resident shall not be taken into account for the purposes of paragraph 6(2)(*a*)(ii) above.

Commentary—*Simon's Direct Tax Service* **D4.1235.**
Definition—"Company", s 832(1), (2).

11—(1) For the purposes of paragraph 6(2)(*b*) above, each of the following activities constitutes wholesale, distributive [financial or service]² business—

(*a*) dealing in any description of goods wholesale rather than retail;

(*b*) the business of shipping or air transport, that is to say, the business carried on by an owner of ships or the business carried on by an owner of aircraft ("owner" including, for this purpose, any charterer);

[(*c*) banking, deposit-taking, money-lending or debt-factoring, or any business similar to banking, deposit-taking, money-lending or debt-factoring;]¹

(*d*) the administration of trusts;

(*e*) dealing in securities in the capacity of a broker, as defined in paragraph 9(2) above;

(*f*) dealing in commodity or financial futures; ...²

[(*g*) the effecting or carrying out of contracts of insurance; and]³

[(*h*) the provision of services not falling within any of the preceding paragraphs.]²

[(1A) For the purposes of sub-paragraph (1)(*g*) above "contract of insurance" has the meaning given by Article 3(1) of the Financial Services and Markets Act 2000 (Regulated Activities) Order 2001.]³

(2) In a case where the gross trading receipts of a company include an amount in respect of the proceeds of sale of any description of property or rights, the cost to the company of the purchase of that property or those rights shall be a deduction in calculating the company's gross trading receipts for the purposes of paragraph 6(2)(*b*) above.

(3) In the case of a controlled foreign company engaged in a [business]¹ falling within sub-paragraph (1)(*c*) above—

(*a*) no payment of interest received from a company resident in the United Kingdom shall be regarded for the purposes of paragraph 6(2)(*b*) above as a receipt derived directly or indirectly from connected or associated persons, but

(*b*) it shall be conclusively presumed that the condition in paragraph 6(2)(*b*) above is not fulfilled if, at any time during the accounting period in question, the amount by which the aggregate value of the capital interests in the company held directly or indirectly by—

(i) the persons who have control of the company, and

(ii) any person connected or associated with those persons,

exceeds the value of the company's fixed assets is 15 per cent or more of the amount by which the company's outstanding capital exceeds that value.

(4) For the purposes of this paragraph, in relation to a controlled foreign company—

(*a*) "capital interest" means an interest in the issued share capital or reserves of the company or in a loan to or deposit with the company or the liability of a guarantor under a guarantee given to or for the benefit of the company;

(*b*) except in the case of the liability of a guarantor, the value of a capital interest is its value as shown in the company's accounts;

(*c*) in the case of the liability of a guarantor, the value shall be taken to be the market value of the benefit which the controlled foreign company derives from the provision of the guarantee;

(*d*) the value of the company's fixed assets means the value, as shown in the company's accounts, of the plant, premises and trade investments employed in the company's business; and

(*e*) "outstanding capital" means the total value of all the capital interests in the company, less the value, as shown in the company's accounts, of any advances made by the company to persons resident outside the United Kingdom and falling within paragraph (i) or paragraph (ii) of sub-paragraph (3)(*b*) above.

(5) For the purposes of sub-paragraph (4) above—

(*a*) "trade investments", in relation to a controlled foreign company, means securities any profit on the sale of which would not be brought into account as a trading receipt in computing the chargeable profits of an accounting period in which that profit arose; and

(*b*) the reference in paragraph (*e*) to advances made to a person by the controlled foreign company includes, in the case of a company which is a person resident outside the United Kingdom and falling within paragraph (i) or paragraph (ii) of sub-paragraph (3)(*b*) above, any securities of that company which are held by the controlled foreign company but are not trade investments, as defined in paragraph (*a*) above;

and in this sub-paragraph "securities" includes stocks and shares.

(6) In the application of paragraph 6(2)(*b*) above in the case of a controlled foreign company engaged in insurance business of any kind—

(*a*) the reference to gross trading receipts which are derived directly or indirectly from connected or associated persons is a reference to those which, subject to sub-paragraph (7) below, are attributable, directly or indirectly, to liabilities undertaken in relation to any of those persons or their property;

(*b*) the only receipts to be taken into account are commissions and premiums received under insurance contracts;

(*c*) so much of any such commission or premium as is returned is not to be taken into account; and

(*d*) when a liability under an insurance contract is reinsured, in whole or in part, the amount of the premium which is attributable, directly or indirectly, to that liability shall be treated as reduced by so much of the premium under the reinsurance contract as is attributable to that liability.

(7) In determining, in relation to a controlled foreign company to which sub-paragraph (6) above applies, the gross trading receipts referred to in paragraph (*a*) of that sub-paragraph, there shall be left out of account any receipts under a local reinsurance contract which are attributable to liabilities which—

(a) are undertaken under an insurance contract made in the territory in which the company is resident; and

(b) are not reinsured under any contract other than a local reinsurance contract; and

(c) relate either to persons who are resident in that territory and are neither connected nor associated with the company or to property which is situated there and belongs to persons who are not so connected or associated;

and in paragraph (a) above "insurance contract" does not include a reinsurance contract.

(8) In sub-paragraph (7) above "local reinsurance contract" means a reinsurance contract—

(a) which is made in the territory in which the controlled foreign company is resident; and

(b) the parties to which are companies which are resident in that territory.

(9) For the purposes of sub-paragraphs (7) and (8) above, any question as to the territory in which a company is resident shall be determined in accordance with section 749 and, where appropriate, paragraph 5(2) above; and, for the purpose of the application of those provisions in accordance with this sub-paragraph, the company shall be assumed to be a controlled foreign company.

Commentary—*Simon's Direct Tax Service* **D4.1236.**
Revenue Internal Guidance—Company Taxation Manual COT8449 (worked examples).
Definitions—"Accounting period", s 834(1); "company", s 832(1), (2); "connected ... persons", s 839; "control", ss 416, 756; "interest", s 832(1); "trade", s 832(1); "United Kingdom", s 830(1).
Amendments—[1] Sub-para (1)(c) and word in sub-para (3) substituted by FA 1998 s 112(3)–(4) with effect for accounting periods of a controlled foreign company, within the meaning of TA 1988 Part XVII Chapter IV, beginning on or after 17 March 1998.
[2] In sub-para (1), words substituted for words "or financial", word "and" in sub-para (1)(f) repealed, and whole of sub-para (1)(h) inserted, by FA 2000 ss 104, 156, Sch 31 paras 8, 9(4), Sch 40 Pt II(14) with effect for any accounting period of a controlled foreign company which begins after 20 March 2000.
[3] Sub-para (1)(g) substituted, and sub-para (1A) inserted, by the Financial Services and Markets Act 2000 (Consequential Amendments) (Taxes) Order, SI 2001/3629 arts 13, 51 with effect from 1 December 2001, immediately after the coming into force of the Financial Services and Markets Act 2000 ss 411, 432(1), Sch 20.

12—(1) Subject to sub-paragraph (2) below, in paragraphs 6 and 8(3) above and [paragraph 12A below and in][1] sub-paragraphs (4) and (5) below "holding company" means—

(a) a company the business of which consists wholly or mainly in the holding of shares or securities of companies which are either local holding companies and its 90 per cent subsidiaries or trading companies and either its 51 per cent subsidiaries or companies falling within paragraph 6(5) above; or

(b) a company which would fall within paragraph (a) above if there were disregarded so much of its business as consists in the holding of property or rights of any description for use wholly or mainly by companies which it controls and which are resident in the territory in which it is resident.

(2) In determining whether a company is a holding company for the purposes of paragraph 6(3) above (and, accordingly, whether the company is or may be a local holding company), sub-paragraph (1) above shall have effect with the omission from paragraph (a) thereof of the words "either local holding companies and its 90 per cent subsidiaries or".

(3) In its application for the purposes of this paragraph, section 838 shall have effect with the omission of—

(a) in subsection (1)(a), the words "or indirectly"; and

(b) subsection (2).

(4) For the purposes of sub-paragraph (3) or (4), as the case may be, of paragraph 6 above, as it applies in relation to a holding company part of whose business consists of activities other than the holding of shares or securities or the holding of property or rights as mentioned in paragraph (a) or (b) of sub-paragraph (1) above, the company's gross income during any accounting period shall be determined as follows—

(a) there shall be left out of account so much of what would otherwise be the company's gross income as is derived from any activity which, if it were the business in which the company is mainly engaged, would be such that paragraph 6(2) above would apply to the company; and

(b) to the extent that the receipts of the company from any other activity include receipts from the proceeds of sale of any description of property or rights, the cost to the company of the purchase of that property or those rights shall (to the extent that the cost does not exceed the receipts) be a deduction in calculating the company's gross income, and no other deduction shall be made in respect of that activity.

(5) For the purposes of sub-paragraphs (3) and (4) of paragraph 6 above, so much of the income of a holding company as—

(a) is derived directly from another company which it controls and which is not a holding company [or superior holding company][1] but otherwise is, in terms of this Schedule, engaged in exempt activities [or, in terms of sub-paragraph (5A) of that paragraph, is an exempt trading company][1], and

(b) was or could have been paid out of any non-trading income of that other company which is derived directly or indirectly from a third company connected or associated with it,

shall be treated, in relation to the holding company, as if it were not derived directly from companies which it controls.

(6) The reference in sub-paragraph (5) above to the non-trading income of a company is a reference to so much of its trade in the United Kingdom, would not be within the charge to corporation tax under Case I of Schedule D.

Commentary—*Simon's Direct Tax Service* **D4.1237.**
Revenue Internal Guidance—Company Taxation Manual COT8455 (worked example).
Definitions—"Accounting period", s 834(1); "company", s 832(1), (2); "controls", ss 416, 756; "Schedule D", s 18(1); "51 per cent subsidiaries", s 838; "90 per cent subsidiaries", s 838; "trade", s 832(1); "United Kingdom", s 830(1).
Amendments—¹ Words inserted in sub-para (1) and (5) by FA 1998 Sch 17 para 32 with effect for accounting periods of companies resident in the United Kingdom ending after 30 June 1999 (by virtue of Finance Act 1994, Section 199, (Appointed Day) Order, SI 1998/3173 art 2). See FA 1998 Sch 17 para 37 for details of the commencement and transitional provisions.

[12A—(1) In paragraphs 6, 8(3) and 12(5) above and this paragraph, "superior holding company" means—

(*a*) a company whose business consists wholly or mainly in the holding of shares or securities of companies which—

(i) are holding companies or local holding companies; or

(ii) are themselves superior holding companies; or

(*b*) a company which would fall within paragraph (*a*) above if there were disregarded so much of its business as consists in the holding of property or rights of any description for use wholly or mainly by companies which it controls and which are resident in the territory in which it is resident.

(2) For the purposes of sub-paragraphs (4A) and (4B) of paragraph 6 above, the income of a company during any period which "represents qualifying exempt activity income of its subsidiaries" is any income of the company during that period which is directly or indirectly derived from companies—

(*a*) which it controls, and

(*b*) which, throughout that period, fall within sub-paragraph (4B)(a) of that paragraph, but

(*c*) which are not holding companies other than local holding companies.

(3) In determining for the purposes of sub-paragraph (4A) or (4B) of paragraph 6 above the companies from which, and the proportions in which, different descriptions of income of a company are derived (whether directly or indirectly), any dividend shall be taken to be paid out of the appropriate profits.

(4) Subsections (3) and (4) of section 799 (which provide rules for determining the profits out of which a dividend is to be regarded as paid for the purpose of subsection (1) of that section) shall apply for determining the appropriate profits for the purposes of subsection (3) above as they apply for determining the relevant profits for the purposes of subsection (1) of that section.

(5) Sub-paragraphs (4) to (6) of paragraph 12 above shall apply in relation to sub-paragraph (4A) or (4B) of paragraph 6 above and a superior holding company as they apply in relation to sub-paragraph (3) or (4) of paragraph 6 above and a holding company, but taking the reference in sub-paragraph (4) of paragraph 12 above to paragraph (*a*) or (*b*) of sub-paragraph (1) of that paragraph as a reference to paragraph (*a*) or (*b*) of sub-paragraph (1) above.]¹

Amendments—¹ This paragraph inserted by FA 1998 Sch 17 para 33 with effect for accounting periods of companies resident in the United Kingdom ending after 30 June 1999 (by virtue of Finance Act 1994, Section 199, (Appointed Day) Order, SI 1998/3173 art 2). See FA 1998 Sch 17 para 37 for details of the commencement and transitional provisions.

PART III
THE PUBLIC QUOTATION CONDITION

13—(1) The provisions of this Part of this Schedule have effect for the purposes of section 748(1)(*c*).

(2) Subject to paragraph 14 below, a controlled foreign company fulfils the public quotation condition with respect to a particular accounting period if—

(*a*) shares in the company carrying not less than 35 per cent of the voting power in the company (and not being shares entitled to a fixed rate of dividend, whether with or without a further right to participate in profits) have been allotted unconditionally to, or acquired unconditionally by, the public and, throughout that accounting period, are beneficially held by the public; and

(*b*) within the period of 12 months ending at the end of the accounting period, any such shares have been the subject of dealings on a recognised stock exchange situated in the territory in which the company is resident; and

(*c*) within that period of 12 months the shares have been [listed]¹ in the official list of such a recognised stock exchange.

Commentary—*Simon's Direct Tax Service* **D4.1240.**
Definitions—"Accounting period", s 834(1); "company", s 832(1), (2); "recognised stock exchange", s 841.
Amendments—¹ Word in sub-para (2)(c) substituted by FA 1996 Sch 38 para 6(1), (2)(*m*), (5) with effect for accounting periods ending after 31 March 1996.

14—(1) The condition in paragraph 13(2) above is not fulfilled with respect to an accounting period of a controlled foreign company if at any time in that period the total percentage of the voting power in the company possessed by all of the company's principal members exceeds 85 per cent.

(2) For the purposes of paragraph 13(2) above shares in a controlled foreign company shall be deemed to be beneficially held by the public if they are held by any person other than—

    (*a*) a person connected or associated with the company; or

    (*b*) a principal member of the company;

and a corresponding construction shall be given to the reference to shares which have been allotted unconditionally to, or acquired unconditionally by, the public.

Commentary—*Simon's Direct Tax Service* **D4.1240.**
Definitions—"Accounting period", s 834(1); "company", s 832(1), (2); "a person connected ... with the company", see s 839.

15—(1) References in this Part of this Schedule to shares held by any person include references to any shares the rights or powers attached to which could, for the purposes of section 416, be attributed to that person under subsection (5) of that section.

(2) For the purposes of this Part of this Schedule—

    (*a*) a person is a principal member of a controlled foreign company if he possesses a percentage of the voting power in the company of more than 5 per cent. and—

        (i) where there are more than five such persons, if he is one of the five persons who possess the greatest percentages, or

        (ii) if, because two or more persons possess equal percentages of the voting power in the company, there are no such five persons, he is one of six or more persons (so as to include those two or more who possess the equal percentages) who possess the greatest percentages; and

    (*b*) a principal member's holding consists of the shares which carry the voting power possessed by him.

(3) In arriving at the voting power which a person possesses, there shall be attributed to him any voting power which, for the purposes of section 416, would be attributed to him under subsection (5) or (6) of that section.

(4) In this Part of this Schedule "shares" include "stock".

Commentary—*Simon's Direct Tax Service* **D4.1240.**
Definition—"Company", s 832(1), (2).

PART IV

REDUCTIONS IN UNITED KINGDOM TAX AND DIVERSION OF PROFITS

16—(1) The provisions of this Part of this Schedule have effect for the purposes of section 748(3).

(2) Any reference in paragraphs 17 and 18 below to a transaction—

    (*a*) is a reference to a transaction [the results of which are][1] reflected in the profits arising in an accounting period of a controlled foreign company; and

    (*b*) includes a reference to [two or more transactions taken together, the results of at least one of which are so reflected][2].

Definitions—"Accounting period", s 834(1); "company", s 832(1), (2).
Amendments—[1] Words in sub-para (2) inserted by FA 1996 s 182, Sch 36 para 4(6)(*a*) with effect for accounting periods of a controlled foreign company beginning after 27 November 1995.
[2] Words in sub-para (2) substituted by FA 1996 s 182, Sch 36 para 4(6)(*b*) with effect for accounting periods of a controlled foreign company beginning after 27 November 1995.

17—(1) A transaction achieves a reduction in United Kingdom tax if, had the transaction not been effected, any person—

    (*a*) would have been liable for any such tax or for a greater amount of any such tax; or

    (*b*) would not have been entitled to a relief from or repayment of any such tax or would have been entitled to a smaller relief from or repayment of any such tax.

(2) In this Part of this Schedule and section 748(3) "United Kingdom tax" means income tax, corporation tax or capital gains tax.

Commentary—*Simon's Direct Tax Service* **D4.1242.**
Definition—"Transaction", para 16(2); "United Kingdom", s 830(1).

18 It is the main purpose or one of the main purposes of a transaction to achieve a reduction in United Kingdom tax if this is the purpose or one of the main purposes—

    (*a*) of the controlled foreign company concerned; or

    (*b*) of a person who has an interest in that company at any time during the accounting period concerned.

Commentary—*Simon's Direct Tax Service* **D4.1242.**
Revenue Internal Guidance—Company Taxation Manual COT8522 (meaning of "main purpose").
Definitions—"Accounting period", s 834(1); "company", s 832(1), (2); "transaction", para 16(2); "United Kingdom", s 830(1).

19—(1) The existence of a controlled foreign company achieves a reduction in United Kingdom tax by a diversion of profits from the United Kingdom in an accounting period if it is reasonable to suppose that, had neither the company nor any company related to it been in existence—

(a) the whole or a substantial part of the receipts which are reflected in the controlled foreign company's profits in that accounting period would have been received by a company or individual resident in the United Kingdom; and

(b) that company or individual or any other person resident in the United Kingdom either—

(i) would have been liable for any United Kingdom tax or for a greater amount of any such tax; or

(ii) would not have been entitled to a relief from or repayment of any such tax or would have been entitled to a smaller relief from or repayment of any such tax.

(2) For the purposes of sub-paragraph (1) above, a company is related to a controlled foreign company if—

(a) it is resident outside the United Kingdom; and

(b) it is connected or associated with the controlled foreign company; and

(c) in relation to any company or companies resident in the United Kingdom, it fulfils or could fulfil, directly or indirectly, substantially the same functions as the controlled foreign company.

(3) Any reference in sub-paragraph (1) above to a company resident in the United Kingdom includes a reference to such a company which, if the controlled foreign company in question were not in existence, it is reasonable to suppose would have been established.

Commentary—*Simon's Direct Tax Service* **D4.1242.**
Revenue Internal Guidance—Company Taxation Manual COT8523 (criteria for deciding whether diversion of profits has occurred).
COT8525 (consideration of newly established overseas business).
COT8526 (whether incorporation of foreign branch causes diversion of profits).
Definitions—"Accounting period", s 834(1); "company", s 832(1), (2); "United Kingdom", s 830(1).

SCHEDULE 26

RELIEFS AGAINST LIABILITY FOR TAX IN RESPECT OF CHARGEABLE PROFITS

Section 754(5)

Trading losses and group relief etc

1—(1) In any case where—

(a) an amount of chargeable profits is apportioned to a company resident in the United Kingdom, and

(b) the company is entitled, or would on the making of a claim be entitled, in computing its profits for the appropriate accounting period, to a deduction in respect of any relevant allowance, and

(c) ...[4]

then, on the making of a claim, a sum equal to corporation tax at the appropriate rate on so much of the relevant allowance ...[4] as is specified in the claim shall be set off against the company's liability to tax under section 747(4)(a) in respect of the chargeable profits apportioned to it.

(2) In this paragraph—

(a) "the appropriate accounting period" means the accounting period for which, by virtue of section 754(2), the company is [chargeable to tax by virtue of this Chapter][4] in respect of the chargeable profits concerned; and

(b) "the appropriate rate" means the rate of corporation tax applicable to profits of the appropriate accounting period or, if there is more than one such rate, the average rate over the whole accounting period.

(3) In this paragraph "relevant allowance" means—

(a) any loss to which [section 392A(1) or 393A(1)][3] applies;

(b) any charge on income to which section 338(1) applies;

(c) any expenses of management to which section 75(1) applies;

(d) so much of any allowance to which section 74 of the 1968 Act applies as falls within subsection (3) of that section; ...[2]

(e) any amount available to the company by way of group relief [and][1]

[(f) any non-trading deficit on its loan relationships.][1]

(4) ...[4]

(5) Where, by virtue of sub-paragraph (1) above, a sum is set off against a liability to tax, so much of the relevant allowance as gives rise to the amount set off shall be regarded for the purposes of the Tax Acts as having been allowed as a deduction against the company's profits in accordance with the appropriate provisions of those Acts.

(6) ...[4]

Commentary—*Simon's Direct Tax Service* **D4.1260.**
Revenue Internal Guidance—Company Taxation Manual COT8801, 8802, 8806 (worked examples).
Definitions—"Accounting period", s 834(1); "charges on income", s 338(2); "company", s 832(1), (2); "group relief", s 834(1); "income tax", s 832(4); "loan relationship", s 834(1); "the Management Act", s 831(3); "non-trading deficit", s 834(1); "profits", s 747(6); "resident", s 749(1)–(4); "tax", s 832(3); "the Tax Acts", s 831(2); "United Kingdom", s 830(1); "year of assessment", s 832(1).
Cross references—See TA 1988 Sch 26 para 2 (relief for corporation tax liability not relieved under this paragraph).
Amendments—¹ Word in sub-para (3)(e) and sub-para (3)(f) inserted by FA 1996 ss 104, 105(1), Sch 14 para 53 with effect for accounting periods ending after 31 March 1996, subject to transitional provisions in FA 1996 Sch 15.
² Word at end of sub-para (3)(d) repealed by FA 1996 Sch 41 Pt V(3) with effect for accounting periods ending after 31 March 1996, subject to transitional provisions in FA 1996 Sch 15.
³ Words in sub-para (3)(a) substituted by FA 1998 Sch 5 para 46 with effect from the year 1998–99 for income tax purposes, and from 1 April 1998 for corporation tax, subject to the transitional provisions in FA 1998 Sch 5 Part IV.
⁴ Sub-paras (4) and (6) and words in sub-para (1) repealed, words substituted in sub-para (2) by FA 1998 Sch 17 para 34, Sch 27 Part III(27), with effect for accounting periods of companies resident in the United Kingdom ending after 30 June 1999 (by virtue of Finance Act 1994, Section 199, (Appointed Day) Order, SI 1998/3173 art 2). See FA 1998 Sch 17 para 37 for details of the commencement and transitional provisions.

Advance corporation tax

2 ...

Commentary—*Simon's Direct Tax Service* **D4.1261.**
Amendments—This paragraph repealed by FA 1998 Sch 3 para 44 with effect for accounting periods beginning after 5 April 1999.

Gains on disposal of shares in controlled foreign companies

3—(1) This paragraph applies in any case where—

[(a) an accounting period of a controlled foreign company ('the apportionment period') is one in respect of which an apportionment under section 747(3) falls to be made; and]²

(b) the company's chargeable profits for [the apportionment period]² have been apportioned among the persons in subsection (3) of that section; and

(c) a company resident in the United Kingdom ("the claimant company") disposes of—

  (i) shares in the controlled foreign company, or

  (ii) shares in another company which, in whole or in part, give rise to the claimant company's interest in the controlled foreign company,

being, in either case, shares acquired before the end of [the apportionment period]²; and

(d) by virtue of the apportionment referred to in paragraph (b) above, a sum is, under section 747(4)(a), [chargeable on]² the claimant company as if it were an amount of corporation tax; and

(e) the claimant company makes a claim for relief under this paragraph;

and in this paragraph the disposal mentioned in paragraph (c) above is referred to as "the relevant disposal".

(2) Subject to the following provisions of this paragraph, in the computation under Chapter [III of Part II of the 1992]¹ Act of the gain accruing on the relevant disposal, the appropriate fraction of the sum referred to in sub-paragraph (1)(d) above shall be allowable as a deduction; but to the extent that any sum has been allowed as a deduction under this sub-paragraph it shall not again be allowed as a deduction on any claim under this paragraph (whether made by the claimant company or another company).

(3) In relation to the relevant disposal, the appropriate fraction is—

$$\frac{A}{B}$$

where—

A is the average market value in [the apportionment period]² of the shares disposed of, and
B is the average market value in that period of the interest in the controlled foreign company which, in the case of the claimant company, was taken into account in the apportionment referred to in sub-paragraph (1)(b) above.

(4) Where, before the relevant disposal—

(a) a dividend is paid by the controlled foreign company, and

(b) the profits out of which the dividend is paid are those from which the chargeable profits referred to in sub-paragraph (1)(b) above are derived, and

(c) at least one of the two conditions in sub-paragraph (5) below is fulfilled,

this paragraph does not apply in relation to a sum [chargeable under section 747(4)(a)]² in respect of so much of the chargeable profits as corresponds to the profits which the dividend represents.

(5) The conditions referred to in sub-paragraph (4) above are—

(a) that the effect of the payment of the dividend is such that the value of the shares disposed of by the relevant disposal is less after the payment than it was before it; and

(b) that, in respect of a dividend paid or payable on the shares disposed of by the relevant disposal, the claimant company is, by virtue of paragraph 4(2) below, entitled under Part XVIII to relief (by way of underlying tax) by reference to sums which include the sum referred to in sub-paragraph (1)(d) above.

(6) A claim for relief under this paragraph shall be made before the expiry of the period of three months beginning—

(a) at the end of the accounting period in which the relevant disposal occurs; or

(b) if it is later, on the date on which the assessment to tax for which the claimant company is liable by virtue of section 747(4)(a) becomes final and conclusive.

[(6A) Nothing in—

(a) paragraph 10 of Schedule 18 to the Finance Act 1998 (claims or elections in company tax returns), or

(b) Schedule 1A to the Management Act (claims or elections not included in returns),

shall apply, whether by virtue of section 754 or otherwise, to a claim under sub-paragraph (6) above.]²

(7) In identifying for the purposes of this paragraph shares in a company with shares of the same class which are disposed of by the relevant disposal, shares acquired at an earlier time shall be deemed to be disposed of before shares acquired at a later time.

Commentary—*Simon's Direct Tax Service* **D4.1263.**
Revenue Internal Guidance—Company Taxation Manual COT8832 (worked example).
Definitions—"Accounting period", s 834(1); "accounting period (of a non-resident company)", s 751(1)–(5); "chargeable profits for an accounting period", s 747(6); "company", s 832(1), (2); "control", ss 416(2), 756(3), 840; "interest in a controlled foreign company", s 749(5)–(7); "market value", s 759(9); "profits", s 747(6); "resident", s 749(1)–(4); "tax", s 832(3); "United Kingdom", s 830(1).
Amendments—¹ Words in sub-para (2) substituted by TCGA 1992 Sch 10 para 14(1), (62).
² Sub-para (1)(a) substituted and words substituted in sub-paras (1)(b)–(d), (3) and (4), and sub-para (6A) inserted by FA 1998 Sch 17 para 35 with effect for accounting periods of companies resident in the United Kingdom ending after 30 June 1999 (by virtue of Finance Act 1994, Section 199, (Appointed Day) Order, SI 1998/3173 art 2). See FA 1998 Sch 17 para 37 for details of the commencement and transitional provisions.

Dividends from the controlled foreign company

4—(1) This paragraph applies in any case where—

[(a) an accounting period of a controlled foreign company is one in respect of which an apportionment under subsection (3) of section 747 falls to be made; and]¹

(b) the company's chargeable profits for that period have been apportioned among the persons referred to in [that subsection]¹, and

(c) the controlled foreign company pays a dividend in whole or in part out of the total profits from which (in accordance with subsection (6)(a) of that section) those chargeable profits are derived.

(2) Subject to paragraphs 5 and 6 below, where this paragraph applies, the aggregate of the sums [chargeable on]¹ companies resident in the United Kingdom in accordance with section 747(4)(a) in respect of the chargeable profits referred to in sub-paragraph (1)(b) above shall be treated for the purposes of Part XVIII as if it were an amount of tax paid in respect of the profits concerned under the law of the territory in which the controlled foreign company was resident and, accordingly, as underlying tax for the purposes of Chapter II of that Part.

(3) In the following provisions of this paragraph and in paragraphs 5 and 6 below, the aggregate of the sums which, under sub-paragraph (2) above, fall to be treated as underlying tax is referred to as the "gross attributed tax".

(4) If, in the case of a person who receives the dividend, section 796 or section 797 has the effect of reducing the amount which (apart from that section) would have been the amount of the credit for foreign tax which is to be allowed to that person, then, for the purposes of sub-paragraph (5) below, the amount of that reduction shall be determined and so much of it as does not exceed the amount of the foreign tax, exclusive of underlying tax, for which credit is to be allowed in respect of the dividend is in that sub-paragraph referred to as "the wasted relief".

(5) Except for the purpose of determining the amount of the wasted relief, the gross attributed tax shall be treated as reduced by the aggregate of the wasted relief arising in the case of all the persons falling within sub-paragraph (4) above and, on the making of a claim by any of the companies referred to in sub-paragraph (2) above—

(a) the amount of tax [chargeable on]¹ the company in accordance with section 747(4)(a) in respect of the chargeable profits referred to in sub-paragraph (1)(b) above shall, where appropriate, be reduced; and

(b) all such adjustments (whether by repayment of tax or otherwise) shall be made as are appropriate to give effect to any reduction under paragraph (a) above.

Commentary—*Simon's Direct Tax Service* **D4.1262.**
Revenue Internal Guidance—Company Taxation Manual COT8852 (worked example).
COT8855 (wasted relief: qualifying and non-qualifying relief).
Definitions—"Accounting period", s 834(1); "company", s 832(1), (2); "control", s 840; "tax", s 832(3); "United Kingdom", s 830(1).
Amendments—¹ Sub-para (1)(a) inserted and words substituted in sub-paras (1)(b), (2) and (5)(a) by FA 1998 Sch 17 para 36 with effect for accounting periods of companies resident in the United Kingdom ending after 30 June 1999 (by virtue of Finance Act 1994, Section 199, (Appointed Day) Order, SI 1998/3173 art 2). See FA 1998 Sch 17 para 37 for details of the commencement and transitional provisions.

5—(1) In so far as any provision of—

(*a*) arrangements having effect by virtue of section 788, or

(*b*) section 790,

makes relief which is related to foreign dividends received by a company resident in the United Kingdom conditional upon that company either having a particular degree of control of the company paying the dividend or being a subsidiary of another company which has that degree of control, that condition shall be treated as fulfilled in considering whether any such company is by virtue of paragraph 4(2) above entitled to relief under Part XVIII in respect of any of the gross attributed tax.

(2) Notwithstanding anything in paragraph 4(2) above, in section 795(2)(*b*) the expression "underlying tax" does not include gross attributed tax.

(3) In a case where the controlled foreign company pays a dividend otherwise than out of specified profits and, on the apportionment referred to in paragraph 4(1) above, less than the whole of the chargeable profits of the controlled foreign company concerned is apportioned to companies which are resident in the United Kingdom and liable for tax thereon as mentioned in section 747(4)(*a*)—

(*a*) the gross attributed tax shall be regarded as attributable to a corresponding proportion of the profits in question, and in this sub-paragraph the profits making up that proportion are referred to as "taxed profits";

(*b*) so much of the dividend as is received by, or by a successor in title of, any such company shall be regarded as paid primarily out of taxed profits; and

(*c*) so much of the dividend as is received by any other person shall be regarded as paid primarily out of profits which are not taxed profits.

(4) The reference in sub-paragraph (3)(*b*) above to a successor in title of a company resident in the United Kingdom is a reference to a person who is such a successor in respect of the whole or any part of that interest in the controlled foreign company by virtue of which an amount of its chargeable profits was apportioned to that company.

Commentary—*Simon's Direct Tax Service* **D4.1262.**
Definitions—"Apportionment", s 834(4); "company", s 832(1), (2); "control", s 840; "tax", s 832(3); "United Kingdom", s 830(1).

6—(1) In any case where—

(*a*) on a claim for relief under paragraph 3 above, the whole or any part of any sum has been allowed as a deduction on a disposal of shares in any company; and

(*b*) that sum forms part of the gross attributed tax in relation to a dividend paid by that company; and

(*c*) a person receiving the dividend in respect of the shares referred to in paragraph (*a*) above ("the primary dividend") or any other relevant dividend is, by virtue of paragraph 4(2) above, entitled under Part XVIII to relief (by way of underlying tax) by reference to the whole or any part of the gross attributed tax;

the amount which, apart from this paragraph, would be available by way of any such relief to the person referred to in paragraph (*c*) above shall be reduced or, as the case may be, extinguished by deducting therefrom the amount allowed by way of relief as mentioned in paragraph (*a*) above.

(2) For the purposes of sub-paragraph (1)(*c*) above, in relation to the primary dividend, another dividend is a relevant dividend if—

(*a*) it is a dividend in respect of shares in a company which is resident outside the United Kingdom; and

(*b*) it represents profits which, directly or indirectly, consist of or include the primary dividend.

Commentary—*Simon's Direct Tax Service* **D4.1264.**
Revenue Internal Guidance—Company Taxation Manual COT8857 (background and scope of restriction).
Definitions—"Company", s 832(1), (2); "tax", s 832(3); "United Kingdom", s 830(1).

SCHEDULE 27

DISTRIBUTING FUNDS

Section 760

Statement of Practice SP 2/86—This statement sets out the Revenue's interpretation of the provisions in this Schedule and s 759.

The topics dealt with are: (*a*) interpretation of the term "material interests" (*b*) conditions for distributor status (*c*) investment restrictions (*d*) computation of UK equivalent profits.

PART I

THE DISTRIBUTION TEST

Cross references—See TA 1988 Sch 27 para 11 (modification of this Part for its application to offshore funds with wholly-owned subsidiaries).

Requirements as to distributions

1—(1) For the purposes of this Chapter, an offshore fund pursues a full distribution policy with respect to an account period if—

(*a*) a distribution is made for that account period or for some other period which, in whole or in part, falls within that account period; and

(*b*) subject to Part II of this Schedule, the amount of the distribution which is paid to the holders of material and other interests in the fund—

(i) represents at least 85 per cent of the income of the fund for that period, and

(ii) is not less than 85 per cent of the fund's United Kingdom equivalent profits for that period; and

(*c*) the distribution is made during that account period or not more than six months, or such longer period as the Board may in any particular case allow, after the expiry of it; and

(*d*) the form of the distribution is such that, if any sum forming part of it were received in the United Kingdom by a person resident there and did not form part of the profits of a trade, profession or vocation, that sum would fall to be chargeable to tax under Case IV or V of Schedule D;

and any reference in this sub-paragraph to a distribution made for an account period includes a reference to any two or more distributions so made or, in the case of paragraph (*b*), the aggregate of them.

(2) Subject to sub-paragraph (3) below, with respect to any account period for which—

[(*a*) there is no income of the fund and there are no United Kingdom equivalent profits of the fund, or

(*b*) the amount of the gross income of the fund does not exceed 1 per cent of the average value of the fund's assets held during the account period,]¹

the fund shall be treated as pursuing a full distribution policy notwithstanding that no distribution is made as mentioned in sub-paragraph (1) above.

(3) For the purposes of this Chapter, an offshore fund shall be regarded as not pursuing a full distribution policy with respect to an account period for which the fund does not make up accounts.

(4) For the purposes of this paragraph—

(*a*) where a period for which an offshore fund makes up accounts includes the whole or part of two or more account periods of the fund, then, subject to paragraph (*c*) below, income shown in those accounts shall be apportioned between those account periods on a time basis according to the number of days in each period which are comprised in the period for which the accounts are made up;

(*b*) where a distribution is made for a period which includes the whole or part of two or more account periods of the fund, then, subject to sub-paragraph (5) below, the distribution shall be apportioned between those account periods on a time basis according to the number of days in each period which are comprised in the period for which the distribution is made;

(*c*) where a distribution is made out of specified income but is not made for a specified period, that income shall be attributed to the account period of the fund in which it in fact arose and the distribution shall be treated as made for that account period; and

(*d*) where a distribution is made neither for a specified period nor out of specified income, then, subject to sub-paragraph (5) below, it shall be treated as made for the last account period of the fund which ended before the distribution was made.

(5) If, apart from this sub-paragraph, the amount of a distribution made, or treated by virtue of sub-paragraph (4) above as made, for an account period would exceed the income of that period, then, for the purposes of this paragraph—

(*a*) if the amount of the distribution was determined by apportionment under sub-paragraph (4)(*b*) above, the excess shall be re-apportioned, as may be just and reasonable, to any other account period which, in whole or in part, falls within the period for which the distribution was made or, if there is more than one such period, between those periods; and

(*b*) subject to paragraph (*a*) above, the excess shall be treated as an additional distribution or series of additional distributions made for preceding account periods in respect of which the distribution or, as the case may be, the aggregate distributions would otherwise be less than the income of the period, applying the excess to later account periods before earlier ones, until it is exhausted.

(6) In any case where—

(*a*) for a period which is or includes an account period, an offshore fund is subject to any restriction as regards the making of distributions, being a restriction imposed by the law of any territory outside the United Kingdom; and

(*b*) the fund is subject to that restriction by reason of an excess of losses over profits (applying the concepts of ''profits'' and ''losses'' in the sense in which and to the extent to which they are relevant for the purposes of the law in question);

then in determining for the purposes of the preceding provisions of this paragraph the amount of the fund's income for that account period, there shall be allowed as a deduction any amount which, apart from this sub-paragraph, would form part of the income of the fund for that account period and which cannot be distributed by virtue of the restriction.

Commentary—*Simon's Direct Tax Service* **B7.405.**
Definitions—"Apportionment", s 834(4); "the Board", s 832(1); "distribution", ss 209(2), 832(1); "profits", s 747(6); "resident", s 749(1)–(4); "Schedule D", s 18(1); "trade", s 832(1); "United Kingdom", s 830(1).
Cross references—See TA 1988 Sch 27 para 3(2) (treatment for the purposes of Pt I of this Schedule of income of an offshore fund not actually forming part of a distribution complying with sub-para (1)(c), (d) above).
TA 1988 Sch 27 para 4 (treatment for the purposes of sub-para (1)(b) above of commodity income of an offshore fund).
Amendments—¹ Sub-para (2)(a), (b) substituted by FA 1995 s 134(4), (9), with effect for account periods ending after 28 November 1994.

TA 1988

Funds operating equalisation arrangements

2—(1) In the case of an offshore fund which throughout any account period operates equalisation arrangements, on any occasion in that period when there is a disposal to which this sub-paragraph applies, the fund shall be treated for the purposes of this Part of this Schedule as making a distribution of an amount equal to so much of the consideration for the disposal as, in accordance with this paragraph, represents income accrued to the date of the disposal.

(2) Sub-paragraph (1) above applies to a disposal—

(a) which is a disposal of a material interest in the offshore fund concerned; and
(b) which is a disposal to which this Chapter applies (whether by virtue of section 758(3) or otherwise) or is one to which this Chapter would apply if subsections (5) and (6) of that section applied generally and not only for the purpose of determining whether, by virtue of subsection (3) of that section, there is a disposal to which this Chapter applies; and
(c) which is not a disposal with respect to which the conditions in subsection (4) of that section are fulfilled; and
(d) which is a disposal to the fund itself or to the persons concerned in the management of the fund ("the managers") in their capacity as such.

(3) On a disposal to which sub-paragraph (1) above applies, the part of the consideration which represents income accrued to the date of the disposal is, subject to sub-paragraph (4) and paragraph 4(4) below, the amount which would be credited to the equalisation account of the offshore fund concerned in respect of accrued income if, on the date of the disposal, the material interest which is disposed of were acquired by another person by way of initial purchase.

(4) If, after the beginning of the period by reference to which the accrued income referred to in sub-paragraph (3) above is calculated, the material interest disposed of by a disposal to which sub-paragraph (1) above applies was acquired by way of initial purchase (whether or not by the person making the disposal)—

(a) there shall be deducted from the amount which, in accordance with sub-paragraph (3) above, would represent income accrued to the date of the disposal, the amount which on that acquisition was credited to the equalisation account of the fund in respect of accrued income; and
(b) if in that period there has been more than one such acquisition of that material interest by way of initial purchase, the deduction to be made under this sub-paragraph shall be the amount so credited to the equalisation account on the latest such acquisition prior to the disposal in question.

(5) Where, by virtue of this paragraph, an offshore fund is treated for the purposes of this Part of this Schedule as making a distribution on the occasion of a disposal, the distribution shall be treated for those purposes—

(a) as complying with paragraph 1(1)(d) above; and
(b) as made out of the income of the fund for the account period in which the disposal occurs; and
(c) as paid, immediately before the disposal, to the person who was then the holder of the interest disposed of.

(6) In any case where—

(a) a distribution in respect of an interest in an offshore fund is made to the managers of the fund, and
(b) their holding of that interest is in their capacity as such, and
(c) at the time of the distribution, the fund is operating equalisation arrangements,

the distribution shall not be taken into account for the purposes of paragraph 1(1) above except to the extent that the distribution is properly referable to that part of the period for which the distribution is made during which that interest has been held by the managers of the fund in their capacity as such.

(7) Subsection (2) of section 758 applies for the purposes of this paragraph as it applies for the purposes of that section.

Commentary—*Simon's Direct Tax Service* **B2.408.**
Definition—"Distribution", ss 209(2), 832(1).
Cross references—See TA 1988 Sch 27 para 4(4) (treatment of commodity income for the purposes of this paragraph).

Income taxable under Case IV or Case V of Schedule D

3—(1) Sub-paragraph (2) below applies if any sums which form part of the income of an offshore fund falling within section 759(1)(*b*) or (*c*) are of such a nature that—

(*a*) the holders of interests in the fund who are either companies resident in the United Kingdom or individuals domiciled and resident there—

(i) are chargeable to tax under Case IV or Case V of Schedule D in respect of such of those sums as are referable to their interests; or

(ii) if any of that income is derived from assets within the United Kingdom, would be so chargeable had the assets been outside the United Kingdom; and

(*b*) the holders of interests who are not such companies or individuals would be chargeable as mentioned in sub-paragraph (i) or (ii) above if they were resident in the United Kingdom or, in the case of individuals, if they were domiciled and both resident and ordinarily resident there.

(2) To the extent that sums falling within sub-paragraph (1) above do not actually form part of a distribution complying with paragraphs 1(1)(*c*) and (*d*) above, they shall be treated for the purposes of this Part of this Schedule—

(*a*) as a distribution complying with those paragraphs and made out of the income of which they form part; and

(*b*) as paid to the holders of the interests to which they are referable.

Commentary—*Simon's Direct Tax Service* **B7.405.**
Definitions—''Distribution'', ss 209(2), 832(1); ''resident'', s 749(1)–(4); ''Schedule D'', s 18(1); ''United Kingdom'', s 830(1).

Commodity income

4—(1) To the extent that the income of an offshore fund for any account period includes profits from dealing in commodities, one half of those profits shall be left out of account in determining for the purposes of paragraphs 1(1)(*b*) and 5 below—

(*a*) the income of the fund for that period; and

(*b*) the fund's United Kingdom equivalent profits for that period;

but in any account period in which an offshore fund incurs a loss in dealing in commodities the amount of that loss shall not be varied by virtue of this paragraph.

(2) In this paragraph ''dealing in commodities'' shall be construed as follows—

(*a*) ''commodities'' does not include currency, securities, debts or other assets of a financial nature but, subject to that, means tangible assets which are dealt with on a commodity exchange in any part of the world; and

(*b*) ''dealing'' includes dealing by way of futures contracts and traded options.

(3) Where the income of an offshore fund for any account period consists of profits from dealing in commodities and other income, then—

(*a*) in determining whether the condition in paragraph 1(1)(*b*) above is fulfilled with respect to that account period, the expenditure of the fund shall be apportioned in such manner as is just and reasonable between the profits from dealing in commodities and the other income; and

(*b*) in determining whether, and to what extent, any expenditure is deductible under section [75][1] in computing the fund's United Kingdom equivalent profits for that period, so much of the business of the fund as does not consist of dealing in commodities shall be treated as a business carried on by a separate company.

(4) Where there is a disposal to which paragraph 2(1) above applies, then, to the extent that any amount which was or would be credited to the equalisation account in respect of accrued income, as mentioned in sub-paragraph (3) or (4) of that paragraph, represents profits from dealing in commodities, one half of that accrued income shall be left out of account in determining under those sub-paragraphs the part of the consideration for the disposal which represents income accrued to the date of the disposal.

Commentary—*Simon's Direct Tax Service* **B7.405.**
Definitions—''Company'', s 832(1), (2); ''profits'', s 747(6); ''United Kingdom'', s 830(1).
Amendments—[1] Number in sub-para (3)(*b*) substituted by FA 1988 Sch 13 para 12.

United Kingdom equivalent profits

5—(1) Any reference in this Schedule to the United Kingdom equivalent profits of an offshore fund for an account period is a reference to the amount which, on the assumptions in sub-paragraph (3) below, would be the total profits of the fund for that period on which, after allowing for any deductions available against those profits, corporation tax would be chargeable.

(2) In this paragraph the expression ''profits'' does not include chargeable gains.

[(2A) *In applying sub-paragraph (1) above the effect of the following shall be ignored, namely—*

(*a*) *sections 125 to 133 of the Finance Act 1993 (exchange gains and losses), and*[3]

(*b*) *sections 159 and 160 of, and paragraph 1 of Schedule 18 to, the Finance Act 1994 (treatmen of profits and losses on interest rate and currency contracts).*][1]

(3) The assumptions referred to in sub-paragraph (1) above are—

(*a*) that the offshore fund is a company which, in the account period in question, but not in any other account period, is resident in the United Kingdom; and

(*b*) that the account period is an accounting period of that company; and

(*c*) that any dividends or distributions which, by virtue of section 208, should be left out of account in computing income for corporation tax purposes are nevertheless to be brought into account in that computation in like manner as if they were dividends or distributions of a company resident outside the United Kingdom.

(4) Without prejudice to any deductions available apart from this sub-paragraph, the deductions referred to in sub-paragraph (1) above include—

(*a*) a deduction equal to any amount which, by virtue of paragraph 1(6) above, is allowed as a deduction in determining the income of the fund for the account period in question; and

(*b*) a deduction equal to any amount of tax (paid under the law of a territory outside the United Kingdom) which was taken into account as a deduction in determining the income of the fund for the account period in question but which, because it is referable to capital rather than income, does not fall to be taken into account by virtue of section 811.

(5) For the avoidance of doubt it is hereby declared that, if any sums forming part of the offshore fund's income for any period have been received by the fund without any deduction of or charge to tax [and have been so received by virtue of section 154(2) of the Finance Act 1996][2], the effect of the assumption in sub-paragraph (3)(*a*) above is that those sums are to be brought into account in determining the total profits referred to in sub-paragraph (1) above.

Commentary—*Simon's Direct Tax Service* **B7.407.**
Definitions—"Chargeable gains", s 832(1); "company", s 832(1), (2); "distributions", ss 209(2), 832(1); "profits", s 747(6); "resident", s 749(1)–(4); "tax", s 832(3); "United Kingdom", s 830(1).
Cross references—See TA 1988 Sch 27 para 4 (treatment for the purposes of this paragraph of commodity income of an offshore fund).
FA 1996 Sch 10 para 3 (treatment for purposes of this paragraph of profits, gains and losses arising from "creditor relationships" of an offshore fund—see FA 1996 s 103(1) for definition of "creditor relationship").
Amendments—[1]Sub-para (2A) inserted by FA 1993 Sch 18 para 6 and substituted by FA 1994 s 176(2).
[2] Words in sub-para (5) inserted by FA 1996 s 154(7), (9), Sch 28 para 6 with effect for the purposes of income tax from the year 1996–97 and for the purposes of corporation tax for accounting periods ending after 31 March 1996.
[3] Sub-s (2A), so far as relating to FA 1993 ss 125–133 and FA 1994 ss 159, 160, Sch 18 para 1, repealed by FA 2002 s 141, Sch 40 Pt 3(10), (13) with effect for accounting periods beginning after 30 September 2002.

PART II
MODIFICATIONS OF CONDITIONS FOR CERTIFICATION IN CERTAIN CASES
Exclusion of investments in distributing offshore funds

6—(1) In any case where—

(*a*) in an account period of an offshore fund (in this Part of this Schedule referred to as the "primary fund"), the assets of the fund consist of or include interests in another offshore fund; and

(*b*) those interests (together with other interests which the primary fund may have) are such that, by virtue of subsection (3)(*a*) or, if the other fund concerned is a company, subsection (3)(*b*) or (*c*) of section 760, the primary fund could not, apart from this paragraph, be certified as a distributing fund in respect of that account period; and

(*c*) without regard to the provisions of this paragraph, that other fund could be certified as a distributing fund in respect of its account period or, as the case may be, each of its account periods which comprises the whole or any part of the account period of the primary fund;

then, in determining whether anything in section 760(3)(*a*) to (*c*) prevents the primary fund being certified as mentioned in paragraph (*b*) above, the interests of the primary fund in that other fund shall be left out of account except for the purposes of determining the total value of the assets of the primary fund.

(2) In this Part of this Schedule an offshore fund falling within sub-paragraph (1)(*c*) above is referred to as a "qualifying fund".

(3) In a case falling within sub-paragraph (1) above—

(*a*) section 760(3)(*a*) to (*c*) shall have effect in relation to the primary fund with the modification in paragraph 7 below (in addition to that provided for by sub-paragraph (1) above); and

(*b*) Part I of this Schedule shall have effect in relation to the primary fund with the modification in paragraph 8 below.

Commentary—*Simon's Direct Tax Service* **B7.411.**
Definition—"Company", s 832(1), (2).

7 The modification referred to in paragraph 6(3)(*a*) above is that, in any case where—

(*a*) at any time in the account period referred to in paragraph 6(1) above, the assets of the primary fund include an interest in an offshore fund or in any company (whether an offshore fund or not); and (*b*) that interest falls to be taken into account in determining whether anything in section 760(3)(*a*) to (*c*) prevents the primary fund being certified as a distributing fund in respect of that account period; and

(*c*) at any time in that account period the assets of the qualifying fund include an interest in the offshore fund or company referred to in paragraph (*a*) above;

for the purposes of the application in relation to the primary fund of section 760(3)(*a*) to (*c*), at any time when the assets of the qualifying fund include the interest referred to in paragraph (*c*) above, the primary fund's share of that interest shall be treated as an additional asset of the primary fund.

Commentary—*Simon's Direct Tax Service* **B7.411.**
Definition—''Company'', s 832(1), (2).
Cross references—See TA 1988 Sch 27 para 9 (construction of certain references in this paragraph).

8—(1) The modification referred to in paragraph 6(3)(*b*) above is that, in determining whether the condition in paragraph 1(1)(*b*)(ii) above is fulfilled with respect to the account period of the primary fund referred to in paragraph 6(1) above, the United Kingdom equivalent profits of the primary fund for that period shall be treated as increased by the primary fund's share of the excess income (if any) of the qualifying fund which is attributable to that period.

(2) For the purposes of this paragraph, the excess income of the qualifying fund for any account period of that fund is the amount (if any) by which its United Kingdom equivalent profits for that account period exceed the amount of the distributions made for that period, as determined for the purposes of the application of paragraph 1(1) above to the qualifying fund.

(3) If an account period of the qualifying fund coincides with an account period of the primary fund, then the excess income (if any) of the qualifying fund for that period is the excess income which is attributable to that period of the primary fund.

(4) In a case where sub-paragraph (3) above does not apply, the excess income of the qualifying fund which is attributable to an account period of the primary fund is the appropriate fraction of the excess income (if any) of the qualifying fund for any of its account periods which comprises the whole or any part of the account period of the primary fund and, if there is more than one such account period of the qualifying fund, the aggregate of the excess income (if any) of each of them.

(5) For the purposes of sub-paragraph (4) above, the appropriate fraction is—

$$\frac{A}{B}$$

where—

A is the number of days in the account period of the primary fund which are also days in an account period of the qualifying fund; and

B is the number of days in that account period of the qualifying fund or, as the case may be, in each of those account periods of that fund which comprises the whole or any part of the account period of the primary fund.

Commentary—*Simon's Direct Tax Service* **B7.411.**
Definitions—''Distributions'', ss 209(2), 832(1); ''profits'', s 747(6); ''United Kingdom'', s 830(1).
Cross references—See TA 1988 Sch 27 para 9 (construction of certain references in sub-para (1) above).

9—(1) The references in paragraphs 7 and 8(1) above to the primary fund's share of—

(*a*) an interest forming part of the assets of the qualifying fund, or

(*b*) the excess income (as defined in paragraph 8 above) of the qualifying fund,

shall be construed as references to the fraction specified in sub-paragraph (2) below of that interest or excess income.

(2) In relation to any account period of the primary fund, the fraction referred to in sub-paragraph (1) above is—

$$\frac{C}{D}$$

where—

C is the average value of the primary fund's holding of interests in the qualifying fund during that period; and

D is the average value of all the interests in the qualifying fund held by any persons during that period.

Commentary—*Simon's Direct Tax Service* **B7.411.**

Offshore funds investing in trading companies

10—(1) In any case where the assets of an offshore fund for the time being include an interest in a trading company, as defined in sub-paragraph (2) below, the provisions of section 760(3) have effect subject to the modifications in sub-paragraphs (3) and (4) below.

(2) In this paragraph ''trading company'' means a company whose business consists wholly of the carrying on of a trade or trades and does not to any extent consist of—

(*a*) dealing in commodities, as defined in paragraph 4(2) above, or dealing, as so defined, in currency, securities, debts or other assets of a financial nature; or

(*b*) banking or money-lending.

(3) In the application of section 760(3)(*b*) to so much of the assets of an offshore fund as for the time being consists of interests in a single trading company, for the words ''10 per cent'' there shall be substituted the words ''20 per cent''.

(4) In the application of section 760(3)(*c*) to an offshore fund the assets of which for the time being include any issued share capital of a trading company or any class of that share capital, for the words ''more than 10 per cent'' there shall be substituted the words ''50 per cent or more''.

Commentary—*Simon's Direct Tax Service* **B7.412**.

Offshore funds with wholly-owned subsidiaries

11—(1) In relation to an offshore fund which has a wholly-owned subsidiary which is a company the provisions of section 760(3) and Part I of this Schedule shall have effect subject to the modifications in sub-paragraph (3) below.

(2) Subject to sub-paragraph (3) below, for the purposes of this paragraph, a company is a wholly-owned subsidiary of an offshore fund if and so long as the whole of the issued share capital of the company is—

(*a*) in the case of an offshore fund falling within section 759(1)(*a*), directly and beneficially owned by the fund; and

(*b*) in the case of an offshore fund falling within section 759(1)(*b*), directly owned by the trustees of the fund for the benefit of the fund; and

(*c*) in the case of an offshore fund falling within section 759(1)(*c*), owned in a manner which, as near as may be, corresponds either to paragraph (*a*) or paragraph (*b*) above.

(3) In the case of a company which has only one class of issued share capital, the reference in sub-paragraph (2) above to the whole of the issued share capital shall be construed as a reference to at least 95 per cent of that share capital.

(4) The modifications referred to in sub-paragraph (1) above are that, for the purposes of section 760(3) and Part I of this Schedule—

(*a*) that percentage of the receipts, expenditure, assets and liabilities of the subsidiary which is equal to the percentage of the issued share capital of the company concerned which is owned as mentioned in sub-paragraph (2) above shall be regarded as the receipts, expenditure, assets and liabilities of the fund; and

(*b*) there shall be left out of account the interest of the fund in the subsidiary and any distributions or other payments made by the subsidiary to the fund or by the fund to the subsidiary.

Commentary—*Simon's Direct Tax Service* **B7.412**.
Definition—''Company'', s 832(1), (2).

Offshore funds with interests in dealing and management companies

12—(1) Section 760(3)(*c*) shall not apply to so much of the assets of an offshore fund as consists of issued share capital of a company which is either—

(*a*) a wholly-owned subsidiary of the fund which falls within sub-paragraph (2) below; or

(*b*) a subsidiary management company of the fund, as defined in sub-paragraph (3) below.

(2) A company which is a wholly-owned subsidiary of an offshore fund is one to which sub-paragraph (1)(*a*) above applies if—

(*a*) the business of the company consists wholly of dealing in material interests in the offshore fund for the purposes of and in connection with the management and administration of the business of the fund; and

(*b*) the company is not entitled to any distribution in respect of any material interest for the time being held by it;

and paragraph 11(2) above shall apply to determine whether a company is, for the purposes of this paragraph, a wholly-owned subsidiary of an offshore fund.

(3) A company in which an offshore fund has an interest is for the purposes of sub-paragraph (1)(*b*) above a subsidiary management company of the fund if—

(*a*) the company carries on no business other than providing services falling within sub-paragraph (4) below either for the fund alone or for the fund and for any other offshore fund which has an interest in the company; and

(*b*) the company's remuneration for the services which it provides to the fund is not greater than it would be if it were determined at arm's length between the fund and a company in which the fund has no interest.

(4) The services referred to in sub-paragraph (3) above are—

(*a*) holding property (of any description) which is occupied or used in connection with the management or administration of the fund; and

(*b*) providing administrative, management and advisory services to the fund.

(5) In determining, in accordance with sub-paragraph (3) above, whether a company in which an offshore fund has an interest is a subsidiary management company of that fund—

(a) every business carried on by a wholly-owned subsidiary of the company shall be treated as carried on by the company; and

(b) no account shall be taken of so much of the company's business as consists of holding its interests in a wholly-owned subsidiary; and

(c) any reference in sub-paragraph (3)(b) above to the company shall be taken to include a reference to a wholly-owned subsidiary of the company.

(6) Any reference in sub-paragraph (5) above to a wholly-owned subsidiary of a company is a reference to another company the whole of the issued share capital of which is for the time being directly and beneficially owned by the first company.

Commentary—*Simon's Direct Tax Service* **B7.414.**
Definition—"Company", s 832(1), (2).

Disregard of certain investments forming less than 5 per cent of a fund

13—(1) In any case where—

(a) in any account period of an offshore fund, the assets of the fund include a holding of issued share capital (or any class of issued share capital) of a company; and

(b) that holding is such that by virtue of section 760(3)(c) the fund could not (apart from this paragraph) be certified as a distributing fund in respect of that account period;

then, if the condition in sub-paragraph (3) below is fulfilled, that holding shall be disregarded for the purposes of section 760(3)(c).

(2) In this paragraph any holding falling within sub-paragraph (1) above is referred to as an "excess holding".

(3) The condition referred to in sub-paragraph (1) above is that at no time in the account period in question does that portion of the fund which consists of—

(a) excess holdings, and

(b) interests in other offshore funds which are not qualifying funds,

exceed 5 per cent by value of all the assets of the fund.

Commentary—*Simon's Direct Tax Service* **B7.412.**
Definition—"Company", s 832(1), (2).

Power of Board to disregard certain breaches of conditions

14 If, in the case of any account period of an offshore fund ending after the passing of the Finance (No 2) Act 1987 (23rd July 1987), it appears to the Board that there has been a failure to comply with any of the conditions in paragraphs (a) to (c) of section 760(3) (as modified, where appropriate, by the preceding provisions of this Part of this Schedule) but the Board are satisfied—

(a) that the failure occurred inadvertently; and

(b) that the failure was remedied without unreasonable delay,

the Board may disregard the failure in determining whether to certify the fund as a distributing fund in respect of that account period.

Commentary—*Simon's Direct Tax Service* **B7.410.**
Definition—"The Board", s 832(1).

PART III
CERTIFICATION PROCEDURE
Application for certification

15—(1) The Board shall, in such manner as they think appropriate, certify an offshore fund as a distributing fund in respect of an account period if—

(a) an application in respect of that period is made under this paragraph; and

(b) the application is accompanied by the accounts of the fund for, or for a period which includes, the account period to which the application relates; and

(c) there is furnished to the Board such information as they may reasonably require for the purposes of determining whether the fund should be so certified; and

(d) they are satisfied that nothing in section 760(2) or (3) prevents the fund being so certified.

(2) An application under this paragraph shall be made to the Board by the fund or by a trustee or officer thereof on behalf of the fund and may be so made—

(a) before the expiry of the period of six months beginning at the end of the account period to which the application relates; or

(b) at such later time as the Board may in any particular case allow.

(3) In any case where, on an application under this paragraph, the Board determine that the offshore fund concerned should not be certified as a distributing fund in respect of the account period to which the application relates, they shall give notice of that fact to the fund.

(4) If at any time it appears to the Board that the accounts accompanying an application under this paragraph in respect of any account period of an offshore fund or any information furnished to the Board in connection with such an application is or are not such as to make full and accurate disclosure of all facts and considerations relevant to the application, they shall give notice to the fund accordingly, specifying the period concerned.

(5) Where a notice is given by the Board under sub-paragraph (4) above, any certification by them in respect of the account period in question shall be void.

Commentary—*Simon's Direct Tax Service* **B7.408.**
Revenue & other press releases—IR 31-7-84 (procedure for application for certification as distributing fund).
Definitions—''The Board'', s 832(1); ''notice'', s 832(1).
Cross references—See TA 1988 Sch 27, para 16 (appeals against determination or notification).
TA 1988 Sch 27 para 18 (procedure for application and certification where no application is made under this paragraph).
TA 1988 Sch 27 para 19 (postponement of tax pending certification under this paragraph).
TA 1988 Sch 27 para 20 (no obligation as to secrecy of notice under sub-para (4) above).

Appeals

16—(1) An appeal to the Special Commissioners—

(a) against such a determination as is referred to in paragraph 15(3) above, or

(b) against a notification under paragraph 15(4) above,

may be made by the offshore fund or by a trustee or officer thereof on behalf of the fund, and shall be so made by notice specifying the grounds of appeal and given to the Board within 90 days of the date of the notice under paragraph 15(3) or (4), as the case may be.

(2) The jurisdiction of the Special Commissioners on an appeal under this paragraph shall include jurisdiction to review any decision of the Board which is relevant to a ground of the appeal.

Commentary—*Simon's Direct Tax Service* **B7.408.**
Definitions—''The Board'', s 832(1); ''notice'', s 832(1).
Cross references—See TA 1988 Sch 27 para 18(8) (no right of appeal under this paragraph against a determination under para 18).

PART IV
SUPPLEMENTARY
Assessment: effect of non-certification

17 No appeal may be brought against an assessment to tax on the ground that an offshore fund should have been certified as a distributing fund in respect of an account period of the fund.

Commentary—*Simon's Direct Tax Service* **B7.426.**
Definition—''Tax'', s 832(3).

18—(1) Without prejudice to paragraph 17 above, in any case where no application has been made under paragraph 15 above in respect of an account period of an offshore fund, any person who is assessed to tax for which he would not be liable if the offshore fund were certified as a distributing fund in respect of that period may by notice in writing require the Board to take action under this paragraph with a view to determining whether the fund should be so certified.

(2) Subject to sub-paragraphs (3) and (5) below, if the Board receive a notice under sub-paragraph (1) above, they shall by notice invite the offshore fund concerned to make an application under paragraph 15 above in respect of the period in question.

(3) Where sub-paragraph (2) above applies, the Board shall not be required to give notice under that sub-paragraph before the expiry of the account period to which the notice is to relate nor if an application under paragraph 15 above has already been made; but where notice is given under that sub-paragraph, an application under paragraph 15 above shall not be out of time under paragraph 15(2)(a) above if it is made within 90 days of the date of that notice.

(4) If an offshore fund to which notice is given under sub-paragraph (2) above does not, within the time allowed by sub-paragraph (3) above or, as the case may be, paragraph 15(2)(a) above, make an application under paragraph 15 above in respect of the account period in question, the Board shall proceed to determine the question of certification in respect of that period as if such an application had been made.

(5) Where the Board receive more than one notice under sub-paragraph (1) above with respect to the same account period of the same offshore fund, their obligations under sub-paragraphs (2) and (4) above shall be taken to be fulfilled with respect to each of those notices if they are fulfilled with respect to any one of them.

(6) Notwithstanding anything in sub-paragraph (5) above, for the purpose of a determination under sub-paragraph (4) above with respect to an account period of an offshore fund, the Board shall have regard to accounts and other information furnished by all persons who have given notice under sub-

paragraph (1) above with respect to that account period; and paragraph 15 above shall apply as if accounts and information so furnished had been furnished in compliance with sub-paragraph (1) of that paragraph.

(7) Without prejudice to sub-paragraph (5) above, in any case where—

(a) at a time after the Board have made a determination under sub-paragraph (4) above that an offshore fund should not be certified as a distributing fund in respect of an account period, notice is given under sub-paragraph (1) above with respect to that period; and

(b) the person giving that notice furnishes the Board with accounts or information which had not been furnished to the Board at the time of the earlier determination;

the Board shall reconsider their previous determination in the light of the new accounts or information and, if they consider it appropriate, may determine to certify the fund accordingly.

(8) Where any person has given notice to the Board under sub-paragraph (1) above with respect to an account period of an offshore fund and no application has been made under paragraph 15 above with respect to that period—

(a) the Board shall notify that person of their determination with respect to certification under sub-paragraph (4) above; and

(b) paragraph 16 above shall not apply in relation to that determination.

Commentary—*Simon's Direct Tax Service* **B7.426.**
Definitions—"The Board", s 832(1); "notice", s 832(1); "tax", s 832(3).
Cross references—See TA 1988 Sch 27 para 19 (postponement of tax pending determination under this paragraph).

Postponement of tax pending determination of question as to certification

19—(1) In any case where—

(a) an application has been made under paragraph 15 above with respect to an account period of an offshore fund and that application has not been finally determined; or

(b) paragraph (a) above does not apply but notice has been given under paragraph 18(1) above in respect of an account period of an offshore fund and the Board have not yet given notice of their decision as to certification under paragraph 18(4) above;

any person who has been assessed to tax and considers that, if the offshore fund were to be certified as a distributing fund in respect of the account period in question, he would be overcharged to tax by the assessment may, by notice given to the inspector within 30 days after the date of the issue of the notice of assessment, apply to the General Commissioners for a determination of the amount of tax the payment of which should be postponed pending the determination of the question whether the fund should be so certified.

(2) A notice of application under sub-paragraph (1) above shall state the amount in which the applicant believes that he is over-charged to tax and his grounds for that belief.

(3) Subsections (3A) onwards of section 55 of the Management Act (recovery of tax not postponed) shall apply with any necessary modifications in relation to an application under sub-paragraph (1) above as if it were an application under subsection (3) of that section and as if the determination of the question as to certification (whether by the Board or on appeal) were the determination of an appeal.

Commentary—*Simon's Direct Tax Service* **B7.408.**
Definitions—"The Board", s 832(1); "inspector", s 832(1); "the Management Act", s 831(3); "notice", s 832(1); "tax", s 832(3).

Information as to decisions on certification etc

20 No obligation as to secrecy imposed by statute or otherwise shall preclude the Board or an inspector from disclosing to any person appearing to have an interest in the matter—

(a) any determination of the Board or (on appeal) the Special Commissioners whether an offshore fund should or should not be certified as a distributing fund in respect of any account period; or

(b) the content and effect of any notice given by the Board under paragraph 15(4) above.

Commentary—*Simon's Direct Tax Service* **B7.426.**
Definitions—"The Board", s 832(1); "inspector", s 832(1).

SCHEDULE 28

COMPUTATION OF OFFSHORE INCOME GAINS

Section 761(1)

PART I

DISPOSALS OF INTERESTS IN NON-QUALIFYING FUNDS

Cross references—See TA 1988 Sch 28 paras 7, 8 (determination of Part I gain on disposal involving equalisation element).

Interpretation

1 In this Part of this Schedule "material disposal" means a disposal to which this Chapter applies, otherwise than by virtue of section 758.

Calculation of unindexed gain

2—(1) Where there is a material disposal, there shall first be determined for the purposes of this Part of this Schedule the amount (if any) which, in accordance with the provisions of this paragraph, is the unindexed gain accruing to the person making the disposal.

(2) Subject to section 757(3) to (6) and paragraph 3 below, the unindexed gain accruing on a material disposal is the amount which would be the gain on that disposal for the purposes of the [1992][1] Act if it were computed—

    (*a*) without regard to any charge to income tax or corporation tax by virtue of section 761; and

    (*b*) without regard to any indexation allowance on the disposal under [the 1992 Act][1].

Commentary—*Simon's Direct Tax Service* **B7.423.**
Revenue Internal Guidance—Inspector's manual IM 4096 (worked example).
Definitions—"The 1992 Act", s 831(3); "income tax", s 832(4); "material disposal", see para 1.
Cross references—See TA 1988 Sch 28 para 4 (calculation of unindexed gain where gain arises from offshore fund acquired before 1 January 1984).
TCGA 1992 s 108 (identification rules applicable on disposals of securities in a non-qualifying offshore fund).
Amendments—[1] Year and words in sub-para (2) substituted by TCGA 1992 Sch 10 para 14(1), (63)(*a*).

3—(1) If the amount of any chargeable gain or allowable loss which (apart from section 763) would accrue on the material disposal would fall to be determined in a way which, in whole or in part, would take account of the indexation allowance on an earlier disposal to which [section 56(2) of the 1992 Act][3] (disposals on a no gain/no loss basis) applies, the unindexed gain on the material disposal shall be computed as if—

    (*a*) no indexation allowance had been available on any such earlier disposal; and

    (*b*) subject to that, neither a gain nor a loss had accrued to the person making such an earlier disposal.

(2) If the material disposal forms part of a transfer to which section [162 of the 1992 Act][3] (roll-over relief on transfer of business) applies, the unindexed gain accruing on the disposal shall be computed without regard to any deduction which falls to be made under that section in computing a chargeable gain.

(3) If the material disposal is made otherwise than under a bargain at arm's length and a claim for relief is made in respect of that disposal under [section 165 or 260 of the 1992 Act (relief for gifts) the claim shall][3] not affect the computation of the unindexed gain accruing on the disposal.

(4) ...[4]

(5) Notwithstanding section [16 of the 1992 Act][3] (losses determined in like manner as gains) if, apart from this sub-paragraph, the effect of any computation under the preceding provisions of this Part of this Schedule would be to produce a loss, the unindexed gain on the material disposal shall be treated as nil; and accordingly for the purposes of this Part of this Schedule no loss shall be treated as accruing on a material disposal.

(6) Section 431 has effect in relation to sub-paragraph (4) above as if it were included in Chapter I of Part XII.

Commentary—*Simon's Direct Tax Service* **B7.423.**
Definitions—"Allowable loss", s 834(1); "chargeable gain", s 832(1); "company", s 832(1), (2); "material disposal", see para 1.
Cross references—See TA 1988 Sch 28 para 4 (calculation of unindexed gain where gain arises from offshore fund acquired before 1 January 1984).
Amendments—[1] Words in sub-para (4) substituted by FA 1990 Sch 7 paras 7, 10 with effect for accounting periods beginning after 31 December 1989.
[2] Sub-para (4)(*a*) repealed by FA 1991 Sch 7 para 10, Sch 19 Pt V with effect for accounting periods beginning after 31 December 1991.
[3] Words in sub-paras (1)–(3), (5) substituted by TCGA 1992 Sch 10 para 14(1), 63(*b*).
[4] Sub-para (4) repealed by FA 1995 Sch 8 para 55, Sch 29 Pt VIII(5), with effect for accounting periods beginning after 31 October 1994, but this repeal does not have effect for the purposes of determining whether policies or contracts for life assurance business made before 1 November 1994 constitute overseas life insurance business.

Gains since 1st January 1984

4—(1) This paragraph applies where—

    (*a*) the interest in the offshore fund which is disposed of by the person making a material disposal was acquired by him before 1st January 1984; or

    (*b*) he is treated by virtue of any provision of sub-paragraphs (3) and (4) below as having acquired the interest before that date.

(2) Where this paragraph applies, there shall be determined for the purposes of this Part of this Schedule the amount which would have been the gain on the material disposal—

    (*a*) on the assumption that, on 1st January 1984, the interest was disposed of and immediately reacquired for a consideration equal to its market value at that time; and (*b*) subject to that, on the basis that the gain is computed in like manner as, under paragraphs 2 and 3 above, the unindexed gain on the material disposal is determined;

and that amount is in paragraph 5 below referred to as the "post-1983 gain" on the material disposal.

(3) Where the person making the material disposal acquired the interest disposed of—

    (*a*) on or after 1st January 1984, and

    (*b*) in such circumstances that, by virtue of any enactment other than section [56, 57, 131 or 145 of the 1992 Act][1] (indexation provisions), he and the person from whom he acquired it ("the previous owner") fell to be treated for the purposes of the [1992][1] Act as if his acquisition were for a consideration of such an amount as would secure that, on the disposal under which he acquired it, neither a gain nor a loss accrued to the previous owner,

the previous owner's acquisition of the interest shall be treated as his acquisition of it.

(4) If the previous owner acquired the interest disposed of on or after 1st January 1984 and in circumstances similar to those referred to in sub-paragraph (3) above, his predecessor's acquisition of the interest shall be treated for the purposes of this paragraph as the previous owner's acquisition, and so on back through previous acquisitions in similar circumstances until the first such acquisition before 1st January 1984 or, as the case may be, until an acquisition on a material disposal on or after that date.

Commentary—*Simon's Direct Tax Service* B7.423.
Definitions—"The 1992 Act", s 831(3); "material disposal", see para 1.
Cross references—See TCGA 1992 s 108 (identification rules applicable on disposals of securities in a non-qualifying offshore fund).
Amendments—[1] Words in sub-para (3)(*b*) substituted by TCGA 1992 Sch 10 para 14(1), (63)(*c*).

The offshore income gain

5—(1) Subject to sub-paragraph (2) below, a material disposal gives rise to an offshore income gain of an amount equal to the unindexed gain on that disposal.

(2) In any case where—

    (*a*) paragraph 4 above applies, and

    (*b*) the post-1983 gain on the material disposal is less than the unindexed gain on the disposal,

the offshore income gain to which the disposal gives rise is an amount equal to the post-1983 gain.

Commentary—*Simon's Direct Tax Service* B7.423.
Revenue Internal Guidance—Inspector's manual IM 4367 (overseas dividends: original tax voucher required as evidence of valid tax credit).
Definition—"Material disposal", see para 1.
Cross references—See TCGA 1992 s 108 (identification rules applicable on disposals of securities in a non-qualifying offshore fund).

PART II

DISPOSALS INVOLVING AN EQUALISATION ELEMENT

6—(1) Subject to paragraph 7 below, a disposal to which this Chapter applies by virtue of section 758(3) gives rise to an offshore income gain of an amount equal to the equalisation element relevant to the asset disposed of.

(2) Subject to sub-paragraphs (4) to (6) below, the equalisation element relevant to the asset disposed of by a disposal falling within sub-paragraph (1) above is the amount which would be credited to the equalisation account of the offshore fund concerned in respect of accrued income if, on the date of the disposal, the asset which is disposed of were acquired by another person by way of initial purchase.

(3) In the following provisions of this Part of this Schedule, a disposal falling within sub-paragraph (1) above is referred to as a "disposal involving an equalisation element".

(4) Where the asset disposed of by a disposal involving an equalisation element was acquired by the person making the disposal after the beginning of the period by reference to which the accrued income referred to in sub-paragraph (2) above is calculated, the amount which, apart from this sub-paragraph, would be the equalisation element relevant to that asset shall be reduced by the following amount, that is to say—

    (*a*) if that acquisition took place on or after 1st January 1984, the amount which, on that acquisition, was credited to the equalisation account of the offshore fund concerned in respect of accrued income or, as the case may be, would have been so credited if that acquisition had been an acquisition by way of initial purchase; and

    (*b*) in any other case, the amount which would have been credited to that account in respect of accrued income if that acquisition had been an acquisition by way of initial purchase taking place on 1st January 1984.

(5) In any case where—

    (*a*) the asset disposed of by a disposal involving an equalisation element was acquired by the person making the disposal at or before the beginning of the period by reference to which the accrued income referred to in sub-paragraph (2) above is calculated, and (*b*) that period began before 1st January 1984 and ends after that date,

the amount which, apart from this sub-paragraph, would be the equalisation element relevant to that asset shall be reduced by the amount which would have been credited to the equalisation account of the offshore fund concerned in respect of accrued income if the acquisition referred to in paragraph (*a*) above had been an acquisition by way of initial purchase taking place on 1st January 1984.

(6) Where there is a disposal involving an equalisation element, then, to the extent that any amount which was or would be credited to the equalisation account of the offshore fund in respect of accrued income, as mentioned in any of sub-paragraphs (2) to (5) above, represents profits from dealing in commodities, within the meaning of paragraph 4 of Schedule 27, one half of that accrued income shall be left out of account in determining under those sub-paragraphs the equalisation element relevant to the asset disposed of by that disposal.

Commentary—*Simon's Direct Tax Service* **B7.424.**
Definition—"Profits", s 747(6).

7—(1) For the purposes of this Part of this Schedule, there shall be determined, in accordance with paragraph 8 below, the Part I gain (if any) on any disposal involving an equalisation element.

(2) Notwithstanding anything in paragraph 6 above—

    (*a*) if there is no Part I gain on a disposal involving an equalisation element, that disposal shall not give rise to an offshore income gain; and

    (*b*) if, apart from this paragraph, the offshore income gain on a disposal involving an equalisation element would exceed the Part I gain on that disposal, the offshore income gain to which that disposal gives rise shall be reduced to an amount equal to that Part I gain.

Commentary—*Simon's Direct Tax Service* **B7.424.**

8—(1) On a disposal involving an equalisation element, the Part I gain is the amount (if any) which, by virtue of Part I of this Schedule (as modified by sub-paragraphs (2) to (5) below), would be the offshore income gain on that disposal if it were a material disposal within the meaning of that Part.

(2) For the purposes only of the application of Part I of this Schedule to determine the Part I gain (if any) on a disposal involving an equalisation element, subsections (5) and (6) of section 758 shall have effect as if, in subsection (5), the words "by virtue of subsection (3) above" were omitted.

(3) If a disposal involving an equalisation element is one which, by virtue of any enactment other than section [56, 57, 131 or 145 of the 1992 Act][1], is treated for the purposes of the [1992][1] Act as one on which neither a gain nor a loss accrues to the person making the disposal, then, for the purpose only of determining the Part I gain (if any) on the disposal, that enactment shall be deemed not to apply to it (but without prejudice to the application of that enactment to any earlier disposal).

(4)–(5) ...[2]

Commentary—*Simon's Direct Tax Service* **B7.424.**
Revenue Internal Guidance—Inspector's manual IM 4097 (explanation with worked example).
Definitions—"The 1992 Act", s 831(3); "company", s 832(1), (2); "material disposal", see para 1.
Amendments—[1] Words in sub-para (3) substituted by TCGA 1992 Sch 10 para 14(1), (63)(*c*).
[2] Sub-paras (4), (5) repealed by TCGA 1992 Sch 12.

[SCHEDULE 28A

CHANGE IN OWNERSHIP OF INVESTMENT COMPANY: DEDUCTIONS][1]

Sections 768B, 768C

Amendments—[1] This Schedule inserted by FA 1995 s 135, Sch 26 paras 3, 5, with effect for changes of ownership occurring after 28 November 1994 other than a change occurring in pursuance of a contract entered into before that date.

PART I

SIGNIFICANT INCREASE IN COMPANY CAPITAL

General

[**1** The provisions referred to in section 768B(2) for determining whether there is a significant increase in the amount of a company's capital after a change in the ownership of the company are as follows.][1]

Definitions—"Company", s 832(1).
Amendments—[1] This Schedule inserted by FA 1995 s 135, Sch 26 paras 3, 5, with effect for changes of ownership occurring after 28 November 1994 other than a change occurring in pursuance of a contract entered into before that date.

The basic rule

[**2** There is a significant increase in the amount of a company's capital if amount B—

    (*a*) exceeds amount A by at least £1 million; or

    (*b*) is at least twice amount A.][1]

Commentary—*Simon's Direct Tax Service* **D4.409B.**
Definitions—"Company", s 832(1).
Amendments—¹ This Schedule inserted by FA 1995 s 135, Sch 26 paras 3, 5, with effect for changes of ownership occurring after 28 November 1994 other than a change occurring in pursuance of a contract entered into before that date.

Amount A

[**3**—(1) Amount A is the lower of—

(*a*) the amount of the company's capital immediately before the change in the ownership; and
(*b*) the highest 60 day minimum amount for the pre-change year, found in accordance with sub-paragraphs (2) to (6) below.

(2) Find the daily amounts of the company's capital over the pre-change year.

(3) Take the highest of the daily amounts.

(4) Find out whether there was in the pre-change year a period of 60 days or more in which there was no daily amount lower than the amount taken.

(5) If there was, the amount taken is the highest 60 day minimum amount for the pre-change year.

(6) If there was not, take the next highest of the daily amounts and repeat the process in sub-paragraph (4) above; and so on, until the highest 60 day minimum amount for the pre-change year is found.

(7) In this Part of this Schedule "the pre-change year" means the period of one year ending immediately before the change in the ownership of the company in question.]¹

Commentary—*Simon's Direct Tax Service* **D4.409B.**
Definitions—"Company", s 832(1).
Amendments—¹ This Schedule inserted by FA 1995 s 135, Sch 26 paras 3, 5, with effect for changes of ownership occurring after 28 November 1994 other than a change occurring in pursuance of a contract entered into before that date.

Amount B

[**4**—(1) Amount B is the highest 60 day minimum amount for the post-change period (finding that amount for that period in the same way as the highest 60 day minimum amount for the pre-change year is found).

(2) In this paragraph "the post-change period" means the period of three years beginning with the change in the ownership of the company in question.]¹

Commentary—*Simon's Direct Tax Service* **D4.409B.**
Definitions—"Company", s 832(1); "pre-change year", Sch 28A, para 3(7).
Amendments—¹ This Schedule inserted by FA 1995 s 135, Sch 26 paras 3, 5, with effect for changes of ownership occurring after 28 November 1994 other than a change occurring in pursuance of a contract entered into before that date.

Capital and amounts of capital

[**5**—(1) The capital of a company consists of the aggregate of—

(*a*) the amount of the paid up share capital of the company;
(*b*) the amount outstanding of any debts incurred by the company which are of a description mentioned in any of paragraphs (*a*) to (*c*) of section 417(7); and
(*c*) the amount outstanding of any redeemable loan capital issued by the company.

(2) For the purposes of sub-paragraph (1) above—

(*a*) the amount of the paid up share capital includes any amount in the share premium account of the company (construing "share premium account" in the same way as in section 130 of the Companies Act 1985); and
(*b*) the amount outstanding of any debts includes any interest due on the debts.

(3) Amounts of capital shall be expressed in sterling and rounded up to the nearest pound.]¹

Commentary—*Simon's Direct Tax Service* **D4.409B.**
Definitions—"Company", s 832(1).
Amendments—¹ This Schedule inserted by FA 1995 s 135, Sch 26 paras 3, 5, with effect for changes of ownership occurring after 28 November 1994 other than a change occurring in pursuance of a contract entered into before that date.

PART II
AMOUNTS IN ISSUE FOR PURPOSES OF SECTION 768B

[**6** The amounts in issue referred to in section 768B(4)(*c*) are—

(*a*) the amount of any sums (including commissions) actually disbursed as expenses of management for the accounting period being divided, except any such expenses as would (apart from section 768B) be deductible in computing profits otherwise than under section 75;
(*b*) the amount of any charges which are paid in that accounting period wholly and exclusively for the purposes of the company's business;
(*c*) the amount of any excess carried forward under section 75(3) to the accounting period being divided;

(*d*) the amount of any allowances falling to be made for that accounting period by virtue of [section 253 of the Capital Allowances Act][4] which would (apart from section 768B) be added to the expenses of management for that accounting period by virtue of section 75(4);

[(*da*) the amount (if any) of the adjusted Case III profits and gains or non-trading deficit of the company for that accounting period [(other than one within sub-paragraph (*dc*) *below*)[3];][2]

[(*db*) the amount of any non-trading debit (other than one within sub-paragraph ...[3] (*dd*) below) that falls to be brought into account for that accounting period for the purposes of Chapter II of Part IV of the Finance Act 1996 (loan relationships) in respect of any debtor relationship of the company;][2]

[(*dc*) the amount of any non-trading [deficit carried forward to that accounting period under][3] section [83(3A)][6] of the Finance Act 1996 (carried forward deficit not set off against profits);][2]

[(*dd*) the amount of any non-trading debit given for that accounting period by paragraph 13 of Schedule 15 to the Finance Act 1996 (transitional adjustment for past interest) in respect of any debtor relationship of the company;][2]

[(*de*) the amount of any non-trading credits or debits in respect of intangible fixed assets that fall to be brought into account for that period under paragraph 34 of Schedule 29 to the Finance Act 2002;]

[(*df*) the amount of any non-trading loss on intangible fixed assets carried forward to that accounting period under paragraph 35(3) of that Schedule;][5]

(*e*) any other amounts by reference to which the profits or losses of that accounting period would (apart from section 768B) be calculated.][1]

Commentary—*Simon's Direct Tax Service* **D4.409C.**
Definitions—''Accounting period'', s 834(1); ''company'', s 832(1); ''non-trading deficit'', s 834(1); ''profits'', s 6(4).
TA 1988 Sch 28A para 6A (meaning of ''adjusted Case III profits'' for the purposes of sub-paragraph (*da*) above).
Amendments—[1] This Schedule inserted by FA 1995 s 135, Sch 26 paras 3, 5, with effect for changes of ownership occurring after 28 November 1994 other than a change occurring in pursuance of a contract entered into before that date.
[2] Sub-paras (*da*)–(*dd*) inserted by FA 1996 ss 104, 105(1), Sch 14 para 54(1) with effect for accounting periods ending after 31 March 1996, subject to transitional provisions in FA 1996 Sch 15.
[3] Words in sub-para (*da*) inserted, in (*db*) repealed, and in sub-para (*dc*) substituted, by FA 1998 s 82(3) and these amendments are deemed always to have had effect.
[4] Words in sub-para (*d*) substituted by CAA 2001 s 578, Sch 2 para 67(1) with effect for corporation tax purposes, as respects allowances and charges falling to be made for chargeable periods ending after 31 March 2001.
[5] Sub-paras (*dd*), (*de*) inserted by FA 2002 s 84(2), Sch 30 para 4(1), (4) with effect from 24 July 2002.
[6] Figure substituted for ''83(3)'' by FA 2002 s 82, Sch 25 paras 43, 58(1), (2) with effect for accounting periods beginning after 30 September 2002.

[**6A** For the purposes of paragraph 6(*da*) above, the amount for any accounting period of the adjusted Case III profits and gains or non-trading deficit of a company is the amount which, as the case may be, would be—

 (*a*) the amount of the profits and gains chargeable under Case III of Schedule D as profits and gains arising from the company's loan relationships, or

 (*b*) the amount of the company's non-trading deficit on those relationships for that period,

if, in computing that amount, amounts for that period falling within paragraph 6(*db*) to (*dd*) above were disregarded.][1]

Commentary—*Simon's Direct Tax Service* **D4.409C.**
Definitions—''Accounting period'', s 834(1); ''company'', s 832(1), (2); ''loan relationship'', s 834(1); ''non-trading deficit'', s 834(1); ''Schedule D'', s 18.
Amendments—[1] This paragraph inserted by FA 1996 ss 104, 105(1), Sch 14 para 54(2) with effect for accounting periods ending after 31 March 1996, subject to transitional provisions in FA 1996 Sch 15.

PART III
APPORTIONMENT FOR PURPOSES OF SECTION 768B

[**7**—(1) Subject to paragraph 8 below, the apportionment required by section 768B(4)(*c*) shall be made—

 (*a*) in the case of the sums and charges mentioned in paragraph 6(*a*) and (*b*) above, by reference to the time when the sum or charge is due to be paid;

 (*b*) in the case of the excess mentioned in paragraph 6(*c*) above, [or in the case of the non-trading [deficit][3] mentioned in paragraph 6(*dc*) above,][2] by apportioning the whole amount of the excess to the first part of the accounting period being divided;

 (*c*) in the case of the amounts mentioned in paragraph 6(*d*)[, (*da*)][2] and (*e*) above, by reference to the respective lengths of the parts of the accounting period being divided.

 [(*d*) in the case of any such debit as—

  (i) is mentioned in paragraph 6(*db*) above,

  (ii) falls to be brought into account for the purposes of Chapter II of Part IV of the Finance Act 1996 in accordance with an authorised accruals basis of accounting, ...[5]

  (iii) so falls to be brought into account otherwise than on the assumption, specified in paragraph 2(2) of Schedule 9 to that Act, that the interest to which it relates does not accrue until it is paid[, and

  (iv) so falls to be brought into account without any adjustment under paragraph 17 or 18 of that Schedule (debit relating to amount of discount referable to the relevant accounting period to be brought into account instead for the accounting period in which the security is redeemed),][5]

by reference to the time of accrual of the amount to which the debit relates;][2]

[(*e*) in the case of any such debit as—

(i) is mentioned in paragraph 6(*db*) above,

(ii) falls to be brought into account for the purposes of Chapter II of Part IV of the Finance Act 1996 in accordance with an authorised accruals basis of accounting, ...[5]

(iii) so falls to be brought into account on the assumption mentioned in paragraph (*d*)(iii) above[, and

(iv) so falls to be brought into account with such an adjustment as is mentioned in paragraph (*d*)(iv) above,][5]

by apportioning the whole amount of the debit to the first part of the accounting period being divided;][2]

[(*f*) in the case of any such debit as is mentioned in paragraph 6(*dd*) above, by apportioning the whole amount of the debit to the first part of the accounting period being divided.][2]

[(*g*) in the case of any such credit or debit as is mentioned in paragraph 6(*de*), by apportioning to each accounting period the credits or debits that would fall to be brought into account in that period if it were a period of account for which accounts were drawn up in accordance with generally accepted accounting practice;][4]

[(*h*) in the case of any such loss as is mentioned in paragraph 6(*df*) above, by apportioning the whole amount of the loss to the first part of the accounting period being divided.][4]

(2) ...[5]][1]

Commentary—*Simon's Direct Tax Service* **D4.409C.**
Amendments—[1] This Schedule inserted by FA 1995 s 135, Sch 26 paras 3, 5, with effect for changes of ownership occurring after 28 November 1994 other than a change occurring in pursuance of a contract entered into before that date.
[2] Words in sub-paras (1)(*b*), (*c*), and whole of sub-paras (1)(*d*)–(*f*), inserted by FA 1996 ss 104, 105(1), Sch 14 para 54(3) with effect for accounting periods ending after 31 March 1996, subject to transitional provisions in FA 1996 Sch 15.
[3] Word substituted in sub-para (1)(*b*) by FA 1998 s 82(3) and deemed always to have had effect.
[4] Sub-paras (1)(*g*), (*h*) added by FA 2002 s 84(2), Sch 30 para 4(1), (5) with effect from 24 July 2002.
[5] Words "and", and sub-para (2) repealed, and sub-paras (1)(*d*)(iv), (1)(*e*)(iv) inserted, by FA 2002 ss 82, 141, Sch 25 paras 43, 58(1)–(5), Sch 40 Pt 3(12) with effect for accounting periods beginning after 30 September 2002. Sub-para (2) previously read as follows—

"(2) For the purposes of sub-paragraph (1)(*a*) above, in the case of any charge consisting of interest, the interest shall be assumed to become due on a day to day basis as it arises.".

[8 If it appears that any method of apportionment given by paragraph 7 above would work unreasonably or unjustly for any case for which it is given, such other method shall be used for that case as appears just and reasonable.][1]

Commentary—*Simon's Direct Tax Service* **D4.409C.**
Amendments—[1] This Schedule inserted by FA 1995 s 135, Sch 26 paras 3, 5, with effect for changes of ownership occurring after 28 November 1994 other than a change occurring in pursuance of a contract entered into before that date.

[PART IV
DISALLOWED DEBITS][1]

[9—(1) This paragraph has effect in a case to which section 768B applies for determining the debits to be brought into account for the purposes of Chapter II of Part IV of the Finance Act 1996 (loan relationships) for—

(*a*) the accounting period beginning immediately after the change in the ownership of the company; and

(*b*) any subsequent accounting period.

(2) The debits so brought into account shall not include the debits falling within paragraph 11 below to the extent (if at all) that the aggregate of—

(*a*) the amount of those debits, and

(*b*) the amount of any debits falling within that paragraph which have been brought into account for the purposes of that Chapter for any previous accounting period ending after the change in the ownership,

exceeds the profits for the accounting period ending with the change in the ownership.

(3) The reference in sub-paragraph (2) above to the profits is a reference to profits after making all deductions and giving all reliefs that for the purposes of corporation tax are made or given against the profits, including deductions and reliefs which under any provision are treated as reducing them for those purposes.][1]

Commentary—*Simon's Direct Tax Service* **D4.409C.**
Definitions—"Accounting period", s 834(1); "change in ownership", s 769(1); "company", s 832(1), (2).
Amendments—[1] Pt IV of this Schedule substituted by FA 1996 ss 104, 105(1), Sch 14 para 54(4) with effect for accounting periods ending after 31 March 1996, subject to transitional provisions in FA 1996 Sch 15.

[10—(1) This paragraph has effect in a case to which section 768C applies for determining the debits to be brought into account for the purposes of Chapter II of Part IV of the Finance Act 1996 (loan relationships) for—

   (*a*) the accounting period beginning immediately after the change in the ownership of the relevant company; and

   (*b*) any subsequent accounting period.

(2) The debits so brought into account for any such accounting period shall not include the debits falling within paragraph 11 below to the extent (if at all) that the amount of those debits exceeds the modified total profits for the accounting period.

(3) The reference in sub-paragraph (2) above to the modified total profits for an accounting period is a reference to the total profits for that period—

   (*a*) reduced, if that period is the period in which the relevant gain accrues, by an amount equal to the amount of the total profits for that period which represents the relevant gain; and

   (*b*) after making all deductions and giving all reliefs that for the purposes of corporation tax are made or given against the profits, including deductions and reliefs which under any provision are treated as reducing them for those purposes, other than any reduction by virtue of paragraph 1(2) of Schedule 8 to the Finance Act 1996.

(4) Where by virtue of sub-paragraph (2) above a debit is to any extent not brought into account for an accounting period, that debit may (to that extent) be brought into account for the next accounting period, but this is subject to the application of sub-paragraphs (1) to (3) above to that next accounting period.]¹

Commentary—*Simon's Direct Tax Service* **D4.409C, 409D.**
Definitions—''Accounting period'', s 834(1); ''change in ownership'', s 769(1); ''company'', s 832(1), (2).
Amendments—¹ Pt IV of this Schedule substituted by FA 1996 ss 104, 105(1), Sch 14 para 54(4) with effect for accounting periods ending after 31 March 1996, subject to transitional provisions in FA 1996 Sch 15.

[11—(1) A debit falls within this paragraph if it is a non-trading debit which—

   (*a*) falls to be brought into account for the purposes of Chapter II of Part IV of the Finance Act 1996 in accordance with an authorised accruals basis of accounting;

   (*b*) so falls to be brought into account on the assumption, specified in sub-paragraph (2) of paragraph 2 of Schedule 9 to that Act, that the interest to which it relates does not accrue until it is paid; ...³

   [(*bb*) so falls to be brought into account with an adjustment under paragraph 17 or 18 of that Schedule (debit relating to amount of discount referable to the relevant accounting period to be brought into account instead for the accounting period in which the security is redeemed); and]³

   (*c*) [apart from paragraphs 2(2), 17 and 18 of that Schedule,]³ would have fallen to be brought into account for those purposes for an accounting period ending before or with the change in the ownership of the company or, as the case may be, the relevant company.

(2) The debits that fall within this paragraph also include—

   (*a*) ...²

   (*b*) any non-trading debit given by paragraph 13 of Schedule 15 to the Finance Act 1996 (transitional adjustment for past interest) in respect of any debtor relationship of the company or, as the case may be, the relevant company.

(3) The debits that fall within this paragraph also include any non-trading debit which—

   (*a*) is not such a debit as is mentioned in sub-paragraph (1) or (2) above;

   (*b*) is a debit in respect of a debtor relationship of the company or, as the case may be, the relevant company;

   (*c*) falls to be brought into account for the purposes of Chapter II of Part IV of the Finance Act 1996 in accordance with an authorised accruals basis of accounting; and

   (*d*) relates to an amount that accrued before the change in the ownership of that company.

(4) In this paragraph ''post-change accounting period'' means the accounting period beginning immediately after the change in the ownership of the company or, as the case may be, the relevant company.]¹

Commentary—*Simon's Direct Tax Service* **D4.409C, 409D.**
Definitions—''Accounting period'', s 834(1); ''authorised accruals basis of accounting'', FA 1996 s 103(1); ''change in ownership'', s 769; ''company'', s 832(1), (2); ''debtor relationship'', FA 1996 s 103(1); ''non-trading debit'', FA 1996 s 103(1).
Amendments—¹ Pt IV of this Schedule substituted by FA 1996 ss 104, 105(1), Sch 14 para 54(4) with effect for accounting periods ending after 31 March 1996, subject to transitional provisions in FA 1996 Sch 15.
² Sub-para (2)(a) is repealed by FA 1998 s 82(3), Sch 27 Part III(17) and this amendment is deemed always to have had effect.
³ Word ''and'' repealed, and sub-para (1)(*bb*) inserted, and in sub-para (1)(*c*), words substituted for the words ''apart from that sub-paragraph'', by FA 2002 s 82, Sch 25 paras 43, 58(1), (6) with effect for accounting periods beginning after 30 September 2002.

[12 Expressions used both in this Part of this Schedule and in Chapter II of Part IV of the Finance Act 1996 have the same meanings in this Part of this Schedule as in that Chapter.]¹

Commentary—*Simon's Direct Tax Service* **D4.409C.**
Amendments—¹ Pt IV of this Schedule substituted by FA 1996 ss 104, 105(1), Sch 14 para 54(4) with effect for accounting periods ending after 31 March 1996, subject to transitional provisions in FA 1996 Sch 15.

PART V

AMOUNTS IN ISSUE FOR PURPOSES OF SECTION 768C

[13—(1) The amounts in issue referred to in section 768C(3)(c) are—

(a) the amount which would in accordance with the relevant provisions of the 1992 Act (and apart from section 768C) be included in respect of chargeable gains in the total profits for the accounting period being divided;

(b) the amount of any sums (including commissions) actually disbursed as expenses of management for the accounting period being divided except any such expenses as would (apart from section 768C) be deductible in computing total profits otherwise than under section 75;

(c) the amount of any charges which are paid in that accounting period wholly and exclusively for the purposes of the company's business;

(d) the amount of any excess carried forward under section 75(3) to the accounting period being divided;

(e) the amount of any allowances falling to be made for that accounting period by virtue of [section 253 of the Capital Allowances Act][4] which would (apart from section 768C) be added to the expenses of management for that accounting period by virtue of section 75(4); and

[(ea) the amount (if any) of the adjusted Case III profits and gains or non-trading deficit of the company for that accounting period [(other than one within paragraph (ec) below)][3];][2]

[(eb) the amount of any non-trading debit (other than one within paragraph ...[3] (ed) below) that falls to be brought into account for that accounting period for the purposes of Chapter II of Part IV of the Finance Act 1996 (loan relationships) in respect of any debtor relationship of the company;][2]

[(ec) the amount of any non-trading [deficit carried forward to that accounting period under][3] by section [83(3A)][6] of the Finance Act 1996 (carried forward deficit not set off against profits);][2]

[(ed) the amount of any non-trading debit given for that accounting period by paragraph 13 of Schedule 15 to the Finance Act 1996 (transitional adjustment for past interest) in respect of any debtor relationship of the company;][2]

[(ee) the amount of any non-trading credits or debits in respect of intangible fixed assets that fall to be brought into account for that period under paragraph 34 of Schedule 29 to the Finance Act 2002;][5]

[(ef) the amount of any non-trading loss on intangible fixed assets carried forward to that accounting period under paragraph 35(3) of that Schedule;][5]

(f) any other amounts by reference to which the profits or losses of the accounting period being divided would (apart from section 768C) be calculated.

(2) In sub-paragraph (1)(a) above "the relevant provisions of the 1992 Act" means section 8(1) of and Schedule 7A to that Act.][1]

Commentary—*Simon's Direct Tax Service* D4.409D.
Definitions—"The 1992 Act", s 831(3); "accounting period", s 834(1); "chargeable gain", s 832(1); "non-trading deficit", s 834(1); "profits", s 6(4).
Amendments—[1] This Schedule inserted by FA 1995 s 135, Sch 26 paras 3, 5, with effect for changes of ownership occurring after 28 November 1994 other than a change occurring in pursuance of a contract entered into before that date.
[2] Sub-paras (1)(ea)–(ed) inserted by FA 1996 ss 104, 105(1), Sch 14 para 54(5) with effect for accounting periods ending after 31 March 1996.
[3] Words in sub-para (1)(ea) inserted, in (eb) repealed, and in (ec) substituted, by FA 1998 s 82(3) and deemed always to have had effect.
[4] Words in sub-para (1)(e) substituted by CAA 2001 s 578, Sch 2 para 67(2) with effect for corporation tax purposes, as respects allowances and charges falling to be made for chargeable periods ending after 31 March 2001.
[5] Sub-paras (1)(ee), (ef) inserted by FA 2002 s 84(2), Sch 30 para 4(1), (6) with effect from 24 July 2002.
[6] Figure substituted for "83(3)" by FA 2002 s 82, Sch 25 paras 43, 58(7) with effect for accounting periods beginning after 30 September 2002.

[13A Paragraph 6A above shall apply for the purposes of paragraph 13(1)(ea) above as it applies for the purposes of paragraph 6(da) above.][1]

Commentary—*Simon's Direct Tax Service* D4.409D.
Amendments—[1] This paragraph inserted by FA 1996 ss 104, 105(1), Sch 14 para 54(6) with effect for accounting periods ending after 31 March 1996, subject to transitional provisions in FA 1996 Sch 15.

PART VI

APPORTIONMENT FOR PURPOSES OF SECTION 768C

[14 The apportionment required by section 768C(3)(c) shall be made as follows.][1]

Commentary—*Simon's Direct Tax Service* D4.409D.
Amendments—[1] This Schedule inserted by FA 1995 s 135, Sch 26 para 3, with effect for changes of ownership occurring after 28 November 1994 other than a change occurring in pursuance of a contract entered into before that date.

[15 In the case of the amount mentioned in paragraph 13(1)(a) above—

(a) if it does not exceed the amount of the relevant gain, the whole of it shall be apportioned to the second part of the accounting period being divided;

(*b*) if it exceeds the amount of the relevant gain, the excess shall be apportioned to the first part of the accounting period being divided and the relevant gain shall be apportioned to the second part.]¹

Commentary—*Simon's Direct Tax Service* **D4.409D.**
Definitions—''Accounting period'', s 834(1).
Amendments—¹ This Schedule inserted by FA 1995 s 135, Sch 26 paras 3, 5, with effect for changes of ownership occurring after 28 November 1994 other than a change occurring in pursuance of a contract entered into before that date.

[16—(1) Subject to paragraph 17 below, the apportionment shall be made—

(*a*) in the case of the sums and charges mentioned in paragraph 13(1)(*b*) and (*c*) above, by reference to the time when the sum or charge is due to be paid;
(*b*) in the case of the excess mentioned in paragraph 13(1)(*d*) above, [or in the case of the non-trading [deficit]³ mentioned in paragraph 13(1)(*ec*) above,]² by apportioning the whole amount of the excess to the first part of the accounting period being divided;
(*c*) in the case of the amounts mentioned in paragraph 13(1)(*e*)[, (*ea*)]² and (*f*) above, by reference to the respective lengths of the parts of the accounting period being divided.
[(*d*) in the case of any such debit as—

    (i) is mentioned in paragraph 13(1)(*eb*) above,
    (ii) falls to be brought into account for the purposes of Chapter II of Part IV of the Finance Act 1996 in accordance with an authorised accruals basis of accounting, ...⁵
    (iii) so falls to be brought into account otherwise than on the assumption, specified in paragraph 2(2) of Schedule 9 to that Act, that the interest to which it relates does not accrue until it is paid[, and
    (iv) so falls to be brought into account without any adjustment under paragraph 17 or 18 of that Schedule (debit relating to amount of discount referable to the relevant accounting period to be brought into account instead for the accounting period in which the security is redeemed),]⁵

by reference to the time of accrual of the amount to which the debit relates;]²
[(*e*) in the case of any such debit as—

    (i) is mentioned in paragraph 13(1)(*eb*) above,
    (ii) falls to be brought into account for the purposes of Chapter II of Part IV of the Finance Act 1996 in accordance with an authorised accruals basis of accounting, ...⁵
    (iii) so falls to be brought into account on the assumption mentioned in paragraph (*d*)(iii) above[, and
    (iv) so falls to be brought into account with such an adjustment as is mentioned in paragraph (*d*)(iv) above,]⁵

by apportioning the whole amount of the debit to the first part of the accounting period being divided;]²
[(*f*) in the case of any such debit as is mentioned in paragraph 13(1)(*ed*) above, by apportioning the whole amount of the debit to the first part of the accounting period being divided.]²
[(*g*) in the case of any such credit or debit as is mentioned in paragraph 13(*ee*), by apportioning to each accounting period the credits or debits that would fall to be brought into account in that period if it were a period of account for which accounts were drawn up in accordance with generally accepted accounting practice;]⁴
[(*h*) in the case of any such loss as is mentioned in paragraph 13(*ef*), by apportioning the whole amount of the loss to the first part of the accounting period being divided.]⁴

(2) ...⁵]¹

Commentary—*Simon's Direct Tax Service* **D4.409D.**
Amendments—¹ This Schedule inserted by FA 1995 s 135, Sch 26 paras 3, 5, with effect for changes in ownership after 28 November 1994 other than a change occurring in pursuance of a contract entered into before that date.
² Words in sub-para (1)(*b*), (*c*) and whole of sub-paras (1)(*d*)–(*f*), inserted by FA 1996 ss 104, 105(1), Sch 14 para 54(7) with effect for accounting periods ending after 31 March 1996, subject to transitional provisions in FA 1996 Sch 15.
³ Word in sub-para (1)(*b*) substituted by FA 1998 s 82(3) and deemed always to have had effect.
⁴ Sub-paras (1)(*g*), (*h*) added by FA 2002 s 84(2), Sch 30 para 4(1), (7) with effect from 24 July 2002.
⁵ Word ''and'' in sub-paras (1)(*d*), (1)(*e*) repealed; sub-paras (1)(*d*)(iv), (1)(*e*)(iv) inserted, and sub-para (2) repealed, by FA 2002 ss 82, 141, Sch 25 paras 43, 58(1), (8)–(10), Sch 40 Pt 3(12) with effect for accounting periods beginning after 30 September 2002. Sub-para (2) previously read as follows—

''(2) For the purposes of sub-paragraph (1)(*a*) above, in the case of any charge consisting of interest, the interest shall be assumed to become due on a day to day basis as it arises.''.

[17 If it appears that any method of apportionment given by paragraph 16 above would work unreasonably or unjustly for any case for which it is given, such other method shall be used for that case as appears just and reasonable.]¹

Commentary—*Simon's Direct Tax Service* **D4.409D.**
Amendments—¹ This Schedule inserted by FA 1995 s 135, Sch 26 paras 3, 5, with effect for changes in ownership occurring after 28 November 1994 other than a change occurring in pursuance of a contract entered into before that date.

[SCHEDULE 28AA

PROVISION NOT AT ARM'S LENGTH][1]

Section 770A

Revenue & other press releases—IR Tax Bulletin October 1998 p 579 (guidance on transfer pricing).
IR Tax Bulletin December 1998 p 603 (penalties and transfer pricing).
IR Tax Bulletin April 2000 p 740 (Non-resident landlords—practical implications of new transfer pricing legislation in TA 1988 Sch 28AA).
Cross references—See FA 1999 ss 85–88 (operation of this Schedule in relation to advance pricing agreements).
FA 2000 Sch 22 paras 58–60 (operation of this Schedule in relation to tonnage tax).
Amendments—[1] This Schedule inserted by FA 1998 s 108(2), Sch 16 with effect (in relation to provision made or imposed at any time)—

   (a) for the purposes of corporation tax, as respects accounting periods ending after 30 June 1999 (by virtue of Finance Act 1994, Section 199, (Appointed Day) Order, SI 1998/3173 art 2); and
   (b) for the purposes of income tax, as respects any year of assessment ending after that date.
This Schedule shall not, in the case of any potentially advantaged person, apply as respects the consequences at any time of the difference between the actual provision and the arm's length provision if—

   (a) that time falls before 17 March 2001;
   (b) the actual provision is a provision made or imposed by means of contractual arrangements entered into by that person before 17 March 1998;
   (c) the requirements of paragraph 1(1)(b) of Schedule 28AA to that Act (control requirements) are satisfied in the case of the actual provision and that person by reference only to paragraph 4(2)(b) of that Schedule (joint ventures etc);
   (d) the rights and obligations of that person by virtue of the actual provision are not ones that have been varied or continued in pursuance of any transaction entered into by that person in the period between 17 March 1998 and that time; and
   (e) that person is not a party, and has not been a party, to any transaction by virtue of which he could during that period have secured the variation or termination of those rights and obligations.

[Basic rule on transfer pricing etc

1—(1) This Schedule applies where—

   (a) provision ("the actual provision") has been made or imposed as between any two persons ("the affected persons") by means of a transaction or series of transactions, and
   (b) at the time of the making or imposition of the actual provision—

      (i) one of the affected persons was directly or indirectly participating in the management, control or capital of the other; or
      (ii) the same person or persons was or were directly or indirectly participating in the management, control or capital of each of the affected persons.

(2) Subject to paragraphs 8, 10 and 13 below, if the actual provision—

   (a) differs from the provision ("the arm's length provision") which would have been made as between independent enterprises, and
   (b) confers a potential advantage in relation to United Kingdom taxation on one of the affected persons, or (whether or not the same advantage) on each of them,

the profits and losses of the potentially advantaged person or, as the case may be, of each of the potentially advantaged persons shall be computed for tax purposes as if the arm's length provision had been made or imposed instead of the actual provision.

(3) For the purposes of this Schedule the cases in which provision made or imposed as between any two persons is to be taken to differ from the provision that would have been made as between independent enterprises shall include the case in which provision is made or imposed as between any two persons but no provision would have been made as between independent enterprises; and references in this Schedule to the arm's length provision shall be construed accordingly.][1]

Commentary—*Simon's Direct Tax Service* B3.1812, 1814.
Amendments—[1] This Schedule inserted by FA 1998 s 108(2), Sch 16 with effect (in relation to provision made or imposed at any time)—

   (a) for the purposes of corporation tax, as respects accounting periods ending after 30 June 1999 (by virtue of Finance Act 1994, Section 199, (Appointed Day) Order, SI 1998/3173 art 2); and
   (b) for the purposes of income tax, as respects any year of assessment ending after that date.

[Principles for construing rules in accordance with OECD principles

2—(1) This Schedule shall be construed (subject to paragraphs 8 to 11 below) in such manner as best secures consistency between—

   (a) the effect given to paragraph 1 above; and
   (b) the effect which, in accordance with the transfer pricing guidelines, is to be given, in cases where double taxation arrangements incorporate the whole or any part of the OECD model, to so much of the arrangements as does so.

(2) In this paragraph "the OECD model" means—

   (a) the rules which, at the passing of this Act, were contained in Article 9 of the Model Tax Convention on Income and on Capital published by the Organisation for Economic Co-operation and Development; or
   (b) any rules in the same or equivalent terms.

(3) In this paragraph "the transfer pricing guidelines" means—

(*a*) all the documents published by the Organisation for Economic Co-operation and Development, at any time before 1st May 1998, as part of their Transfer Pricing Guidelines for Multinational Enterprises and Tax Administrations; and

(*b*) such documents published by that Organisation on or after that date as may for the purposes of this Schedule be designated, by an order made by the Treasury, as comprised in the transfer pricing guidelines.][1]

Amendments—[1] This Schedule inserted by FA 1998 s 108(2), Sch 16 with effect (in relation to provision made or imposed at any time)—
(*a*) for the purposes of corporation tax, as respects accounting periods ending after 30 June 1999 (by virtue of Finance Act 1994, Section 199, (Appointed Day) Order, SI 1998/3173 art 2); and
(*b*) for the purposes of income tax, as respects any year of assessment ending after that date.

[Meaning of "transaction" and "series of transactions"

3—(1) In this Schedule "transaction" includes arrangements, understandings and mutual practices (whether or not they are, or are intended to be, legally enforceable).

(2) References in this Schedule to a series of transactions include references to a number of transactions each entered into (whether or not one after the other) in pursuance of, or in relation to, the same arrangement.

(3) A series of transactions shall not be prevented by reason only of one or more of the matters mentioned in sub-paragraph (4) below from being regarded for the purposes of this Schedule as a series of transactions by means of which provision has been made or imposed as between any two persons.

(4) Those matters are—

(*a*) that there is no transaction in the series to which both those persons are parties;

(*b*) that the parties to any arrangement in pursuance of which the transactions in the series are entered into do not include one or both of those persons; and

(*c*) that there is one or more transactions in the series to which neither of those persons is a party.

(5) In this paragraph, "arrangement" means any scheme or arrangement of any kind (whether or not it is, or is intended to be, legally enforceable).][1]

Commentary—*Simon's Direct Tax Service* B3.1813.
Amendments—[1] This Schedule inserted by FA 1998 s 108(2), Sch 16 with effect (in relation to provision made or imposed at any time)—

(*a*) for the purposes of corporation tax, as respects accounting periods ending after 30 June 1999 (by virtue of Finance Act 1994, Section 199, (Appointed Day) Order, SI 1998/3173 art 2); and
(*b*) for the purposes of income tax, as respects any year of assessment ending after that date.

[Participation in the management, control or capital of a person

4—(1) For the purposes of this Schedule a person is directly participating in the management, control or capital of another person at a particular time if, and only if, that other person is at that time—

(*a*) a body corporate or a partnership; and

(*b*) controlled by the first person.

(2) For the purposes of this Schedule a person ("the potential participant") is indirectly participating in the management, control or capital of another person at a particular time if, and only if—

(*a*) he would be taken to be directly so participating at that time if the rights and powers attributed to him included all the rights and powers mentioned in sub-paragraph (3) below that are not already attributed to him for the purposes of sub-paragraph (1) above; or

(*b*) he is, at that time, one of a number of major participants in that other person's enterprise.

(3) The rights and powers referred to in sub-paragraph (2)(*a*) above are—

(*a*) rights and powers which the potential participant is entitled to acquire at a future date or which he will, at a future date, become entitled to acquire;

(*b*) rights and powers of persons other than the potential participant to the extent that they are rights or powers falling within sub-paragraph (4) below;

(*c*) rights and powers of any person with whom the potential participant is connected; and

(*d*) rights and powers which for the purposes of sub-paragraph (2)(*a*) above would be attributed to a person with whom the potential participant is connected if that connected person were himself the potential participant.

(4) Rights and powers fall within this sub-paragraph to the extent that they—

(*a*) are required, or may be required, to be exercised in any one or more of the following ways, that is to say—

(i) on behalf of the potential participant;

(ii) under the direction of the potential participant; or

(iii) for the benefit of the potential participant;

and

(*b*) are not confined, in a case where a loan has been made by one person to another, to rights and powers conferred in relation to property of the borrower by the terms of any security relating to the loan.

(5) In sub-paragraphs (3)(*b*) to (*d*) and (4) above, the references to a person's rights and powers include references to any rights or powers which he either—

    (*a*) is entitled to acquire at a future date, or

    (*b*) will, at a future date, become entitled to acquire.

(6) In paragraph (*d*) of sub-paragraph (3) above, the reference to rights and powers which would be attributed to a connected person if he were the potential participant includes a reference to rights and powers which, by applying that paragraph wherever one person is connected with another, would be so attributed to him through a number of persons each of whom is connected with at least one of the others.

(7) For the purposes of this paragraph a person ("the potential major participant") is a major participant in another person's enterprise at a particular time if at that time—

    (*a*) that other person ("the subordinate") is a body corporate or partnership; and

    (*b*) the 40 per cent test is satisfied in the case of each of two persons who, taken together, control the subordinate and of whom one is the potential major participant.

(8) For the purposes of this paragraph the 40 per cent test is satisfied in the case of each of two persons wherever each of them has interests, rights and powers representing at least 40 per cent of the holdings, rights and powers in respect of which the pair of them fall to be taken as controlling the subordinate.

(9) For the purposes of this paragraph—

    (*a*) the question whether a person is controlled by any two or more persons taken together, and

    (*b*) any question whether the 40 per cent test is satisfied in the case of a person who is one of two persons,

shall be determined after attributing to each of the persons all the rights and powers attributed to a potential participant for the purposes of sub-paragraph (2)(a) above.

(10) References in this paragraph—

    (*a*) to rights and powers of a person, or

    (*b*) to rights and powers which a person is or will become entitled to acquire,

include references to rights or powers which are exercisable by that person, or (when acquired by that person) will be exercisable, only jointly with one or more other persons.

(11) For the purposes of this paragraph two persons are connected with each other if—

    (*a*) one of them is an individual and the other is his spouse, a relative of his or of his spouse, or the spouse of such a relative; or

    (*b*) one of them is a trustee of a settlement and the other is—

        (i) a person who in relation to that settlement is a settlor; or

        (ii) a person who is connected with a person falling within sub-paragraph (i) above.

(12) In sub-paragraph (11) above—

"relative" means brother, sister, ancestor or lineal descendant; and

"settlement" and "settlor" have the same meanings as in Chapter IA of Part XV.]¹

Commentary—*Simon's Direct Tax Service* B3.1815.
Amendments—¹ This Schedule inserted by FA 1998 s 108(2), Sch 16 with effect (in relation to provision made or imposed at any time)—

    (*a*) for the purposes of corporation tax, as respects accounting periods ending after 30 June 1999 (by virtue of Finance Act 1994, Section 199, (Appointed Day) Order, SI 1998/3173 art 2); and

    (*b*) for the purposes of income tax, as respects any year of assessment ending after that date.

[Advantage in relation to United Kingdom taxation

5—(1) For the purposes of this Schedule (but subject to sub-paragraph (2) below) the actual provision confers a potential advantage on a person in relation to United Kingdom taxation wherever, disregarding this Schedule, the effect of making or imposing the actual provision, instead of the arm's length provision, would be one or both of the following, that is to say—

    (*a*) that a smaller amount (which may be nil) would be taken for tax purposes to be the amount of that person's profits for any chargeable period; or

    (*b*) that a larger amount (or, if there would not otherwise have been losses, any amount of more than nil) would be taken for tax purposes to be the amount for any chargeable period of any losses of that person.

(2) Subject to paragraph 11(2) below, the actual provision shall not be taken for the purposes of this Schedule to confer a potential advantage in relation to United Kingdom taxation on either of the persons as between whom it is made or imposed if—

    (*a*) the three conditions set out in sub-paragraphs (3) to (5) below are all satisfied in the case of each of those two persons; and

    (*b*) the further condition set out in sub-paragraph (6) below is satisfied in the case of each of those persons who is an insurance company.

(3) The first condition is satisfied in the case of any person if—

(*a*) that person is within the charge to income tax or corporation tax in respect of profits arising from the relevant activities;

(*b*) that person is not entitled to any exemption from income tax or corporation tax in respect of, or of a part of, the income or profits arising from the relevant activities in respect of which he is within that charge; and

(*c*) where that person is within the charge to income tax in respect of profits arising from those activities, he is resident in the United Kingdom in the chargeable periods in which he is so within that charge.

(4) The second condition is satisfied in the case of any person if he is neither—

(*a*) a person with an entitlement, in pursuance of any double taxation arrangements or under section 790(1), to be given credit in any chargeable period for any foreign tax on or in respect of profits arising from the relevant activities; nor

(*b*) a person who would have such an entitlement in any such period if there were any such profits or if they exceeded a certain amount.

(5) The third condition is satisfied in the case of any person if the amounts taken into account in computing the profits or losses arising from the relevant activities to that person in any chargeable period in which he is within the charge to income tax or corporation tax in respect of profits arising from those activities do not include any income the amount of which is reduced in accordance with section 811(1) (deduction for foreign tax where no credit allowable).

(6) The further condition is satisfied in the case of an insurance company if the profits arising from the relevant activities in respect of which the company is within the charge to corporation tax do not include—

(*a*) any profits in the computation of which acquisition expenses have been brought into account in accordance with section 86 of the Finance Act 1989 (expenses of acquiring insurance business); or

(*b*) any profits in relation to which the rate of corporation tax is fixed by section 88 or 88A of that Act (lower rate on certain profits of insurance companies).][1]

Commentary—*Simon's Direct Tax Service* **B3.1816.**
Amendments—[1] This Schedule inserted by FA 1998 s 108(2), Sch 16 with effect (in relation to provision made or imposed at any time)—

(*a*) for the purposes of corporation tax, as respects accounting periods ending after 30 June 1999 (by virtue of Finance Act 1994, Section 199, (Appointed Day) Order, SI 1998/3173 art 2); and
(*b*) for the purposes of income tax, as respects any year of assessment ending after that date.

[Elimination of double counting

6—(1) This paragraph applies where—

(*a*) only one of the affected persons ("the advantaged person") is a person on whom a potential advantage in relation to United Kingdom taxation is conferred by the actual provision; but

(*b*) the other affected person ("the disadvantaged person") is a person in relation to whom the condition set out in sub-paragraph (3) of paragraph 5 above either--

(i) is satisfied, or

(ii) were any such exemption as is mentioned in paragraph (*b*) of that sub-paragraph to be disregarded, would be satisfied..

(2) Subject to sub-paragraphs (3) to (6) and paragraph 7 below, on the making of a claim by the disadvantaged person for the purposes of this paragraph—

(*a*) the disadvantaged person shall be entitled to have his profits and losses computed for tax purposes as if the arm's length provision had been made or imposed instead of the actual provision; and

(*b*) notwithstanding any limit in the Tax Acts on the time within which any adjustment may be made, all such adjustments shall be made in his case as may be required to give effect to the assumption that the arm's length provision was made or imposed instead of the actual provision.

(3) A claim made by the disadvantaged person for the purposes of this paragraph—

(*a*) shall not be made unless a computation has been made in the case of the advantaged person on the basis that the arm's length provision was made or imposed instead of the actual provision; and

(*b*) must be consistent with the computation made on that basis in the case of the advantaged person.

(4) For the purposes of sub-paragraph (3) above a computation shall be taken to have been made in the case of the advantaged person on the basis that the arm's length provision was made or imposed instead of the actual provision if, and only if—

(*a*) the computations made for the purposes of any return by the advantaged person have been made on that basis by virtue of this Schedule; or

(*b*) a relevant notice given to the advantaged person takes account of a determination in pursuance of this Schedule of an amount falling to be brought into account for tax purposes on that basis.

(5) Subject to section 109(3)(*b*) of the Finance Act 1998 (which provides for the extension of the period for making a claim), a claim for the purposes of this paragraph shall not be made except within one of the following periods—

(*a*) in a case where a return has been made by the advantaged person on the basis mentioned in sub-paragraph (3)(a) above, the period of two years beginning with the day of the making of the return; and

(*b*) in any case where a relevant notice taking account of such a determination as is mentioned in sub-paragraph (4)(*b*) above has been given to the advantaged person, the period of two years beginning with the day on which that notice was given.

(6) Subject to section 109(3)(*b*) of the Finance Act 1998, where—

(*a*) a claim for the purposes of this paragraph is made by the disadvantaged person in relation to a return made on the basis mentioned in sub-paragraph (3)(a) above, and

(*b*) a relevant notice taking account of such a determination as is mentioned in sub-paragraph (4)(*b*) above is subsequently given to the advantaged person,

the disadvantaged person shall be entitled, within the period mentioned in sub-paragraph (5)(*b*) above, to make any such amendment of the claim as may be appropriate in consequence of the determination contained in that notice.

(7) In this paragraph—

"relevant notice" means—

[(*a*) a closure notice under section 28A(1) or 28B(1) of the Management Act in relation to an enquiry into a return under section 8 or 8A of that Act or into a partnership return;]²

(*b*) a closure notice under paragraph 32 of Schedule 18 to the Finance Act 1998 in relation to an enquiry into a company tax return;

(*c*) a notice of an assessment under section 29 of the Management Act;

(*d*) a notice of any discovery assessment or discovery determination under paragraph 41 of Schedule 18 to the Finance Act 1998 (including any notice of an assessment by virtue of paragraph 52 of that Schedule);

(*e*) a notice under section 30B(1) of the Management Act amending a [partnership return]²;

"return" means any return required to be made under the Management Act or Schedule 18 to the Finance Act 1998 for income tax or corporation tax purposes or any voluntary amendment of such a return; and

"voluntary amendment", in relation to a return, means [—

(*a*) an amendment under section 9ZA or 12ABA of the Management Act (amendment of personal, trustee or partnership return by taxpayer), or

(*b*) an amendment under Schedule 18 to the Finance Act 1998 other than one made in response to the giving of a relevant notice.]²]¹

Commentary—*Simon's Direct Tax Service* **B3.1817.**
Cross references—See FA 1999 s 87(2) (application of this paragraph in determining the effect of advance pricing agreements on non-parties).
Amendments—¹ This Schedule inserted by FA 1998 s 108(2), Sch 16 with effect (in relation to provision made or imposed at any time)—

(*a*) for the purposes of corporation tax, as respects accounting periods ending after 30 June 1999 (by virtue of Finance Act 1994, Section 199, (Appointed Day) Order, SI 1998/3173 art 2); and

(*b*) for the purposes of income tax, as respects any year of assessment ending after that date.

² In sub-para 6(7), in the definition of "relevant notice", sub-para (*a*) substituted, words in sub-para (*e*) substituted for the words "partnership statement"; and words in the definition of "voluntary amendment", substituted for the words "any amendment in accordance with the Management Act or Schedule 18 to the Finance Act 1998, other than one made in response to the giving of a relevant notice." by FA 2001 s 88, Sch 29(35) with effect from the passing of FA 2001 in relation to returns whether made before or after the passing of FA 2001, and whether relating to periods before or after the passing of FA 2001. Sub-para (*a*) in the definition of "relevant notice" previously read as follows—

(*a*) a notice under section 28A(5) or 28B(5) of the Management Act stating the conclusions of an officer of the Board in relation to any self-assessment, partnership statement, claim or election;".

[Adjustment of disadvantaged person's double taxation relief

7—(1) Subject to sub-paragraph (4) below, where—

(*a*) a claim is made for the purposes of paragraph 6 above, and

(*b*) the disadvantaged person is entitled, on that claim, to make a computation, or to have an adjustment made in his case, on the basis that the arm's length provision was made or imposed instead of the actual provision,

the assumptions specified in sub-paragraph (2) below shall apply, in the disadvantaged person's case, as respects any credit for foreign tax which the disadvantaged person has been or may be given in pursuance of any double taxation arrangements or under section 790(1).

(2) Those assumptions are—

(*a*) that the foreign tax paid or payable by the disadvantaged person does not include any amount of foreign tax which would not be or have become payable were it to be assumed for the purposes of that tax that the arm's length provision had been made or imposed instead of the actual provision; and (*b*) that the amount of the relevant profits of the disadvantaged person in respect of which he is given credit for foreign tax does not include the amount (if any) by which his relevant profits are treated as reduced in accordance with paragraph 6 above.

(3) Sub-paragraph (4) below applies if—

(*a*) a claim is made for the purposes of paragraph 6 above;

(*b*) the disadvantaged person is entitled, on that claim, to make a computation, or to have an adjustment made in his case, on the basis that the arm's length provision was made or imposed instead of the actual provision;

(*c*) the application of that basis in the computation of the disadvantaged person's profits or losses for any chargeable period involves a reduction in the amount of any income; and

(*d*) that income is also income that falls to be treated as reduced in accordance with section 811(1).

(4) Where this sub-paragraph applies—

(*a*) the reduction mentioned in sub-paragraph (3)(*c*) above shall be treated as made before any reduction under section 811(1); and

(*b*) tax paid, in the place in which any income arises, on so much of that income as is represented by the amount of the reduction mentioned in sub-paragraph (3)(*c*) above shall be disregarded for the purposes of section 811(1).

(5) Where, in a case in which a claim has been made for the purposes of paragraph 6 above, any adjustment is required to be made for the purpose of giving effect to any of the preceding provisions of this paragraph—

(*a*) it may be made in any case by setting the amount of the adjustment against any relief or repayment to which the disadvantaged person is entitled in pursuance of that claim; and

(*b*) nothing in the Tax Acts limiting the time within which any assessment is to be or may be made or amended shall prevent that adjustment from being so made.

(6) References in this paragraph to relevant profits of the disadvantaged person are references to profits arising to the disadvantaged person from the carrying on of the relevant activities.]¹

Cross references—See FA 1999 s 86(2) (application of this paragraph in determining the effect of advance pricing agreements on non-parties).

Amendments—¹ This Schedule inserted by FA 1998 s 108(2), Sch 16 with effect (in relation to provision made or imposed at any time)—

(*a*) for the purposes of corporation tax, as respects accounting periods ending after 30 June 1999 (by virtue of Finance Act 1994, Section 199, (Appointed Day) Order, SI 1998/3173 art 2); and

(*b*) for the purposes of income tax, as respects any year of assessment ending after that date.

[*Foreign exchange gains and losses and financial instruments*

8—(1) [Subject to sub-paragraph (3)]² [and sub-paragraph (4)]³ below, this Schedule shall not require the amounts brought into account in any person's case under—

[(*a*) Chapter 2 of Part 4 of the Finance Act 1996 (loan relationships) in respect of exchange gains or losses from loan relationships (as defined in section 103(1A) and (1B) of that Act), or]²

[(*b*) Schedule 26 to the Finance Act 2002 (derivative contracts) in respect of exchange gains and losses (as defined in paragraph 54 of that Schedule),]³

to be computed in that person's case on the assumption that the arm's length provision had been made or imposed instead of the actual provision.

[(2) Sub-paragraph (1) above—

(a) shall not affect so much of sections 136 and 136A of the Finance Act 1993 (application of arm's length test) as has effect by reference to whether the whole or any part of a loan falls to be treated in accordance with this Schedule as an amount on which interest has been charged or, as the case may be, has been charged at a higher rate; and

*(b) accordingly, shall not prevent the assumption mentioned in that sub-paragraph from determining for the purposes of sections 136(8) and (9) and 136A(6) and (7) of that Act how much (if any) of any loan falls to be so treated.]*²

[(3) Sub-paragraph (1) above shall not affect so much of paragraph 11A of Schedule 9 to the Finance Act 1996 (loan relationships: exchange gains or losses where loan not on arm's length terms) as has effect by reference to whether profits or losses fall to be computed by virtue of this Schedule as if the whole or any part of a loan had not been made.]²

[(4) Sub-paragraph (1) above shall not affect so much of paragraph 27 of Schedule 26 to the Finance Act 2002 (derivative contracts: exchange gains or losses where derivative contract not on arm's length terms) as has effect by reference to whether profits or losses fall to be computed by virtue of this Schedule as if a company were not party to a derivative contract or as if the terms of the contract to which it is party were different.]³]¹

Commentary—*Simon's Direct Tax Service* B3.1819.

Amendments—¹ This Schedule inserted by FA 1998 s 108(2), Sch 16 with effect (in relation to provision made or imposed at any time)—

(*a*) for the purposes of corporation tax, as respects accounting periods ending after 30 June 1999 (by virtue of Finance Act 1994, Section 199, (Appointed Day) Order, SI 1998/3173 art 2); and

(*b*) for the purposes of income tax, as respects any year of assessment ending after that date.

² In sub-para (1), words substituted for the words "Subject to sub-paragraph (2)", sub-para (1)(*a*) substituted, and sub-para (3) substituted for sub-para (2), by FA 2002 s 79, Sch 23 para 21 with effect for accounting periods beginning after 30 September 2002.
Sub-paras (1)(*a*) previously read as follows—

"(*a*) Chapter II of Part II of the Finance Act 1993 (foreign exchange gains and losses), or".

³ Words in sub-para (1) inserted, sub-para (1)(*b*) substituted, and sub-para (4) inserted, by FA 2002 s 83(1)(*b*), (3) Sch 27 paras 1, 15 with effect for accounting periods beginning after 30 September 2002. Sub-para (1)(*b*) previously read as follows—

"(*b*) Chapter II of Part IV of the Finance Act 1994 (financial instruments),".

[Special rules for sales etc of oil

9—(1) Subject to paragraph 10 below, this paragraph applies to provision made or imposed by or in relation to the terms of a sale of oil if—

(*a*) the oil sold is oil which has been, or is to be, extracted under rights exercisable by a company ("the producer") which (although it may be the seller) is not the buyer; and

(*b*) at the time of the sale not less than 20 per cent of the producer's ordinary share capital is owned directly or indirectly by one or more of the following, that is to say, the buyer and the companies (if any) that are linked to the buyer.

(2) Where this paragraph applies to provision made or imposed by or in relation to the terms of a sale of oil, this Schedule shall have effect as respects that provision as if the buyer, the seller and (if it is not the seller) the producer were all controlled by the same person at the time of the making or imposition of that provision.

(3) For the purposes of this paragraph two companies are linked if—

(*a*) one is under the control of the other; or

(*b*) both are under the control of the same person or persons.

(4) For the purposes of this paragraph—

(*a*) any question whether ordinary share capital is owned directly or indirectly by a company shall be determined as for section 838;

(*b*) rights to extract oil shall be taken to be exercisable by a company even if they are exercisable by that company only jointly with one or more other companies; and

(*c*) a sale of oil shall be deemed to take place at the time of the completion of the sale or when possession of the oil passes, whichever is the earlier.

(5) In this paragraph "oil" includes any mineral oil or relative hydrocarbon, as well as natural gas.]¹

Commentary—*Simon's Direct Tax Service* B3.1820.
Amendments—¹ This Schedule inserted by FA 1998 s 108(2), Sch 16 with effect (in relation to provision made or imposed at any time)—

(*a*) for the purposes of corporation tax, as respects accounting periods ending after 30 June 1999 (by virtue of Finance Act 1994, Section 199, (Appointed Day) Order, SI 1998/3173 art 2); and

(*b*) for the purposes of income tax, as respects any year of assessment ending after that date.

[Transactions and deemed transactions involving oil

10 This Schedule does not apply in relation to provision made or imposed by means of any transaction or deemed transaction in the case of which the price or consideration is determined in accordance with any of subsections (1) to (4) of section 493 (transactions and deemed transactions involving oil treated as made at market value).]¹

Amendments—¹ This Schedule inserted by FA 1998 s 108(2), Sch 16 with effect (in relation to provision made or imposed at any time)—

(*a*) for the purposes of corporation tax, as respects accounting periods ending after 30 June 1999 (by virtue of Finance Act 1994, Section 199, (Appointed Day) Order, SI 1998/3173 art 2); and

(*b*) for the purposes of income tax, as respects any year of assessment ending after that date.

[Special provision for companies carrying on ring fence trades

11—(1) This paragraph applies where any person ("the taxpayer") carries on as, or as part of, a trade any activities ("the ring fence trade") which, in accordance with section 492(1) either—

(*a*) fall to be treated for any tax purposes as a separate trade, distinct from all other activities carried on by him as part of the trade; or

(*b*) would so fall if the taxpayer did carry on any other activities as part of that trade.

(2) Subject to paragraph 10 above and sub-paragraph (4) below, where provision made or imposed as between the taxpayer and another person by means of a transaction or series of transactions—

(*a*) falls, in relation to the taxpayer, to be regarded as made or imposed in the course of, or with respect to, the ring fence trade; but

(*b*) falls, in relation to the other person, to be regarded as made or imposed in the course of, or with respect to, activities of that other person which do not fall within section 492(1),

this Schedule shall have effect in relation to that provision with the omission of paragraph 5(2) above.

(3) Subject to paragraph 10 above and sub-paragraph (4) below, this Schedule shall have effect as respects any provision made or imposed by the taxpayer as between the ring fence trade and any other activities carried on by him as if—

    (*a*) that trade and those activities were carried on by two different persons;

    (*b*) that provision were made or imposed as between those two persons by means of a transaction;

    (*c*) a potential advantage in relation to United Kingdom taxation were conferred by that provision on each of those two persons;

    (*d*) those two persons were both controlled by the same person at the time of the making or imposition of that provision; and

    (*e*) paragraphs 5 to 7 above were omitted.

(4) This Schedule shall apply in accordance with this paragraph in relation to any provision mentioned in sub-paragraph (2) or (3) above only where the effect of its application in relation to that provision is either—

    (*a*) that a larger amount (including, if there would not otherwise have been profits, an amount of more than nil) is taken for tax purposes to be the amount of the profits of the ring fence trade for any chargeable period; or

    (*b*) that a smaller amount (including nil) is taken for tax purposes to be the amount for any chargeable period of any losses of that trade.]¹

Amendments—¹ This Schedule inserted by FA 1998 s 108(2), Sch 16 with effect (in relation to provision made or imposed at any time)—

(*a*) for the purposes of corporation tax, as respects accounting periods ending after 30 June 1999 (by virtue of Finance Act 1994, Section 199, (Appointed Day) Order, SI 1998/3173 art 2); and

(*b*) for the purposes of income tax, as respects any year of assessment ending after that date.

[Appeals

12—(1) In so far as the question in dispute on any appeal falling within sub-paragraph (2) below—

    (*a*) is or involves a determination of whether this Schedule has effect as respects any provision made or imposed as between any two persons, or of how it so has effect, and

    (*b*) is not a question that would fall to be determined by the Special Commissioners apart from this sub-paragraph,

that question shall be determined by them.

(2) The appeals falling within this sub-paragraph are—

    (*a*) any appeal under section 31 of, or Schedule 1A to, the Management Act;

    (*b*) any appeal under paragraph 34(3) of Schedule 18 to the Finance Act 1998 against an amendment of a company's return; and

    (*c*) any appeal under paragraph 48 of that Schedule against a discovery assessment or a discovery determination.

(3) Sub-paragraph (4) below applies where—

    (*a*) any such question as is mentioned in sub-paragraph (1) above falls to be determined by the Special Commissioners for the purposes of any proceedings before them; and

    (*b*) that question relates to any provision made or imposed as between two persons each of whom is a person in relation to whom the condition set out in paragraph 5(3) above is satisfied.

(4) Where this sub-paragraph applies—

    (*a*) each of the persons as between whom the actual provision was made or imposed shall be entitled to appear and be heard by the Special Commissioners, or to make representations to them in writing;

    (*b*) the Special Commissioners shall determine that question separately from any other questions in those proceedings; and

    (*c*) their determination on that question shall have effect as if made in an appeal to which each of those persons was a party.

(5) In this paragraph—

    "discovery assessment" means a discovery assessment under paragraph 41 of Schedule 18 to the Finance Act 1998 (including one by virtue of paragraph 52 of that Schedule); and

    "discovery determination" means a discovery determination under paragraph 41 of that Schedule.]¹

Commentary—*Simon's Direct Tax Service* **B3.1821.**

Amendments—¹ This Schedule inserted by FA 1998 s 108(2), Sch 16 with effect (in relation to provision made or imposed at any time)—

(*a*) for the purposes of corporation tax, as respects accounting periods ending after 30 June 1999 (by virtue of Finance Act 1994, Section 199, (Appointed Day) Order, SI 1998/3173 art 2); and

(*b*) for the purposes of income tax, as respects any year of assessment ending after that date.

[Saving for the provisions relating to capital allowances and capital gains

13 Nothing in this Schedule shall be construed as affecting—

    (*a*) the computation of the amount of any capital allowance or balancing charge made under [the Capital Allowances Act]²; or (*b*) the computation in accordance with the 1992 Act of the amount of any chargeable gain or allowable loss;

and nothing in this Schedule shall require the profits or losses of any person to be computed for tax purposes as if, in his case, instead of income or losses falling to be brought into account in connection with the taxation of income, there were gains or losses falling to be brought into account in accordance with the 1992 Act.]¹

Commentary—*Simon's Direct Tax Service* **B3.1824.**
Amendments—¹ This Schedule inserted by FA 1998 s 108(2), Sch 16 with effect (in relation to provision made or imposed at any time)—

(*a*) for the purposes of corporation tax, as respects accounting periods ending after 30 June 1999 (by virtue of Finance Act 1994, Section 199, (Appointed Day) Order, SI 1998/3173 art 2); and
(*b*) for the purposes of income tax, as respects any year of assessment ending after that date.
² Words in sub-para (*a*) substituted by CAA 2001 s 578, Sch 2 para 68 with effect for income tax purposes, as respects allowances and charges falling to be made for chargeable periods ending after 5 April 2001, and for corporation tax purposes, as respects allowances and charges falling to be made for chargeable periods ending after 31 March 2001.

[General interpretation etc

14—(1) In this Schedule—

"the actual provision" and "the affected persons" shall be construed in accordance with paragraph 1(1) above;
"the arm's length provision" shall be construed in accordance with paragraph 1(2) and (3) above;
"double taxation arrangements" means arrangements having effect by virtue of section 788;
"foreign tax" means any tax under the law of a territory outside the United Kingdom or any amount which falls for the purposes of any double taxation arrangements to be treated as if it were such tax;
"insurance company" has the same meaning as in Chapter I of Part XII;
"losses" includes amounts which are not losses but in respect of which relief may be given in accordance with any of the following enactments—

(*a*) section 75(3) (excess of management expenses);
(*b*) section 468L(5) (allowance for interest distributions of a unit trust);
(*c*) Part X (loss relief and group relief);
(*d*) section 83 of and Schedule 8 to the Finance Act 1996 or paragraph 4 of Schedule 11 to that Act (deficits on loan relationships);

"profits" includes income;
"the relevant activities", in relation to a person who is one of the persons as between whom any provision is made or imposed, means such of his activities as—

(i) comprise the activities in the course of which, or with respect to which, that provision is made or imposed; and
(ii) are not activities carried on either separately from those activities or for the purposes of a different part of that person's business;

"transaction" and "series of transactions" shall be construed in accordance with paragraph 3 above.

(2) Without prejudice to paragraphs 9(2) and 11(3) above, references in this Schedule to a person controlling a body corporate or a partnership shall be construed in accordance with section 840.

(3) In determining for the purposes of this Schedule whether a person has an entitlement, in pursuance of any double taxation arrangements or under section 790(1), to be given credit for foreign tax, any requirement that a claim is made before such a credit is given shall be disregarded.

(4) Any adjustments required to be made by virtue of this Schedule may be made by way of discharge or repayment of tax, by the modification of any assessment or otherwise.

(5) This Schedule shall have effect as if—

(*a*) a unit trust scheme were a company that is a body corporate;
(*b*) the rights of the unit holders under such a scheme were shares in the company that the scheme is deemed to be;
(*c*) rights and powers of a person in the capacity of a person entitled to act for the purposes of the scheme were rights and powers of the scheme; and
(*d*) provision made or imposed as between any person in such a capacity and another person were made or imposed as between the scheme and that other person.]¹

Amendments—¹ This Schedule inserted by FA 1998 s 108(2), Sch 16 with effect (in relation to provision made or imposed at any time)—

(*a*) for the purposes of corporation tax, as respects accounting periods ending after 30 June 1999 (by virtue of Finance Act 1994, Section 199, (Appointed Day) Order, SI 1998/3173 art 2); and
(*b*) for the purposes of income tax, as respects any year of assessment ending after that date.

[SCHEDULE 28B

VENTURE CAPITAL TRUSTS: MEANING OF "QUALIFYING HOLDINGS"][1]

Section 842AA(13)

Cross references—See TA 1988 s 824AA(13) (this Schedule to have effect for purpose of construing references to qualifying holding under that section).
Amendments—[1] This Schedule inserted by FA 1995 s 70(2), Sch 14.

Introductory

[**1**—(1) This Schedule applies, where any shares in or securities of any company ("the relevant company") are at any time held by another company ("the trust company"), for determining whether and to what extent those shares or securities ("the relevant holding") are, for the purposes of section 842AA, to be regarded as at that time comprised in the trust company's qualifying holdings.

(2) The relevant holding shall be regarded as comprised in the trust company's qualifying holdings at any time if—

    (*a*) all the requirements of the following provisions of this Schedule are satisfied at that time in relation to the relevant company and the relevant holding; and

    (*b*) the relevant holding consists of shares or securities which were first issued by the relevant company to the trust company and have been held by the trust company ever since.

(3) Subject to paragraph 6(3) below, where the requirements of paragraph 6 or 7 below would be satisfied as to only part of the money raised by the issue of the relevant holding and that holding is not otherwise capable of being treated as comprising separate holdings, this Schedule shall have effect in relation to that holding as if it were two holdings consisting of—

    (*a*) a holding from which that part of the money was raised; and

    (*b*) a holding from which the remainder was raised;

and section 842AA shall have effect as if the value of the holding were to be apportioned accordingly between the two holdings which are deemed to exist in pursuance of this sub-paragraph.][1]

Commentary—*Simon's Direct Tax Service* **E3.620.**
Revenue Interpretation RI 124—Circumstances in which an acquisition of shares or securities in a company, which is to be used for a management buy-out, may give rise to a qualifying holding.
Definitions—"Recognised stock exchange", s 841(1); "securities", Sch 28B para 13(1); "United Kingdom", s 830(1).
Amendments—[1] This Schedule inserted by FA 1995 s 70(2), Sch 14.

Requirement that company must be unquoted company

[**2**—(1) The requirement of this paragraph is that the relevant company (whether or not it is resident in the United Kingdom) must be an unquoted company.

(2) In this paragraph "unquoted company" means a company none of whose shares, stocks, debentures or other securities is marketed to the general public.

(3) For the purposes of this paragraph shares, stocks, debentures or other securities are marketed to the general public if they are—

    (*a*) listed on a recognised stock exchange,

    (*b*) listed on a designated exchange in a country outside the United Kingdom, or

    (*c*) dealt in on the Unlisted Securities Market or dealt in outside the United Kingdom by such means as may be designated.

(4) In sub-paragraph (3) above "designated" means designated by an order made by the Board for the purposes of that sub-paragraph; and an order made for the purposes of paragraph (*b*) of that sub-paragraph may designate an exchange by name, or by reference to any class or description of exchanges, including a class or description framed by reference to any authority or approval given in a country outside the United Kingdom.

(5) Section 828(1) does not apply to an order made for the purposes of sub-paragraph (3) above.

(6) Where a company any shares in or securities of which are included in the qualifying holdings of the trust company ceases at any time while the trust company is approved as a venture capital trust to be an unquoted company, the requirements of this paragraph shall be deemed, in relation to shares or securities acquired by the trust company before that time, to continue to be satisfied for a period of five years after that time.][1]

Commentary—*Simon's Direct Tax Service* **E3.621.**
Amendments—[1] This Schedule inserted by FA 1995 s 70(2), Sch 14.

Requirements as to company's business

[**3**—(1) The requirements of this paragraph are as follows.

(2) The relevant company must be one of the following, that is to say—

(*a*) a company which exists wholly for the purpose of carrying on one or more qualifying trades or which so exists apart from purposes capable of having no significant effect (other than in relation to incidental matters) on the extent of the company's activities; [or][2]

[(*aa*) the parent company of a trading group.][2]

(3) Subject to sub-paragraph (4) below, the relevant company or a [relevant qualifying subsidiary][3] of that company must, when the relevant holding was issued and at all times since, have been either—

(*a*) carrying on a qualifying trade wholly or mainly in the United Kingdom; or

(*b*) preparing to carry on a qualifying trade which at the time when the relevant holding was issued it intended to carry on wholly or mainly in the United Kingdom

[and for the purposes of this sub-paragraph a company is a relevant qualifying subsidiary of another company at any time when it would be a qualifying subsidiary of that company if "90" were substituted for "75" in every place where "75" occurs in paragraph 10(3) below][3].

(4) The requirements of sub-paragraph (3) above shall not be capable of being satisfied by virtue of paragraph (*b*) of that sub-paragraph at any time after the end of the period of two years beginning with the issue of the relevant holding unless—

(*a*) the relevant company or the subsidiary in question began to carry on the intended trade before the end of that period, and

(*b*) that company or subsidiary has, at all times since the end of that period, been carrying on a qualifying trade wholly or mainly in the United Kingdom.

(5) The requirements of that sub-paragraph shall also be incapable of being so satisfied at any time after the abandonment, within the period mentioned in sub-paragraph (4) above, of the intention in question.][1]

[(6) For the purposes of this paragraph a company is the parent company of a trading group if—

(*a*) it has one or more subsidiaries;

(*b*) each of its subsidiaries is a qualifying subsidiary of the company; and

(*c*) the requirements of sub-paragraph (7) below are fulfilled by what would be the business of the company and its qualifying subsidiaries if all the activities, taken together, of the company and its qualifying subsidiaries were regarded as one business.][2]

[(7) A business fulfils the requirements of this sub-paragraph if neither the business nor a substantial part of it consists in, or in either of, the following, that is to say—

(*a*) activities falling within paragraph 4(2)(*a*) to (*f*) below but not within sub-paragraph (8) below; and

(*b*) activities carried on otherwise than in the course of a trade.][2]

[(8) The activities falling within this sub-paragraph are—

(*a*) the receiving of royalties or licence fees in circumstances where [the requirement mentioned in paragraph 4(5) below is][4] satisfied in relation to the company receiving them;

(*b*) the letting of ships, other than oil rigs or pleasure craft, on charter in circumstances where the requirements mentioned in paragraphs (*a*) to (*d*) of paragraph 4(7) below are satisfied in relation to the company so letting them.][2]

[(9) Activities of a company or of any of its qualifying subsidiaries shall be disregarded for the purposes of sub-paragraphs (6) to (8) above to the extent that they consist in—

(*a*) the holding of shares in or securities of, or the making of loans to, one or more of the company's qualifying subsidiaries; or

(*b*) the holding and managing of property used by the company or any of its qualifying subsidiaries for the purposes of—

(i) research and development from which it is intended that a qualifying trade to be carried on by the company or any of its qualifying subsidiaries will be derived; or

(ii) one or more qualifying trades so carried on.][2]

[(10) Activities of a qualifying subsidiary of a company shall also be disregarded for the purposes of sub-paragraphs (6) to (8) above to the extent that they consist in—

(*a*) the making of loans to the company; or

(*b*) in the case of a mainly trading subsidiary, activities carried on in pursuance of its insignificant purposes (within the meaning given by sub-paragraph (11) below).][2]

[(11) In sub-paragraph (10) above "mainly trading subsidiary" means a qualifying subsidiary which, apart from purposes ("its insignificant purposes") which are capable of having no significant effect (other than in relation to incidental matters) on the extent of its activities, exists wholly for the purpose of carrying on one or more qualifying trades.][2]

Commentary—*Simon's Direct Tax Service* E3.622.

Statements of Practice SP 2/94—Interpretation of sub-para (3) "qualifying trade" for holdings of shares issued before 6 April 1998—Revenue look at totality of activities, location of capital assets at which business processes are performed and where employees customarily carry out their duties. No one factor is decisive but over half of the aggregate activities must take place in the UK.

SP 3/00—Venture Capital Trusts—location of activity.

Revenue Interpretation RI 124—Circumstances in which an acquisition of shares or securities in a company, which is to be used for a management buy-out, may give rise to a qualifying holding.

Definitions—''Qualifying subsidiary'', Sch 28B para 10; ''qualifying trade'', Sch 28B para 4; ''securities'', Sch 28B para 13(1); ''United Kingdom'', s 830(1).
Amendments—¹ This Schedule inserted by FA 1995 s 70(2), Sch 14.
² Sub-para (2)(*aa*) and word ''or'' preceding it substituted for sub-paras (2)(*b*), (*c*) and sub-paras (6)–(11) inserted, by FA 1997 Sch 9 paras 2, 6 with effect for the purposes of determining whether shares or securities are, as at any time after 26 November 1996, to be regarded as comprised in a company's qualifying holdings.
³ Sub-para (3) amended by FA 1998 s 73(3) with effect for the purpose of determining whether shares or securities are, as at any time after 5 April 1998, to be regarded as comprised in a company's qualifying holdings.
⁴ Words in sub-para 8(*a*) substituted for the words ''the requirements mentioned in paragraphs (*a*) and (*b*) of paragraph 4(5) or (6) below are'' by FA 2001 s 64, Sch 16 para 1. This amendment shall be deemed always to have had effect, for the purpose of determining whether shares or securities issued after 5 April 2000 are, for the purposes of TA 1988 s 842AA (venture capital trusts), to be regarded as comprised in a company's qualifying holdings.

Meaning of ''qualifying trade''

[4—(1) For the purposes of this Schedule—

    (*a*) a trade is a qualifying trade if it is a trade complying with this paragraph; and
    (*b*) the carrying on of any activities of research and development from which it is intended that there will be derived a trade that—

        (i) will comply with this paragraph and
        (ii) will be carried on wholly or mainly in the United Kingdom,

shall be treated as the carrying on of a qualifying trade.

(2) Subject to sub-paragraphs (3) to (9) below, a trade complies with this paragraph if neither that trade nor a substantial part of it consists in one or more of the following activities, that is to say—

    (*a*) dealing in land, in commodities or futures or in shares, securities or other financial instruments;
    (*b*) dealing in goods otherwise than in the course of an ordinary trade of wholesale or retail distribution;
    (*c*) banking, insurance, money-lending, debt-factoring hire purchase financing or other financial activities;
    (*d*) leasing (including letting ships on charter or other assets on hire) or receiving royalties or licence fees;
    (*e*) providing legal or accountancy services;
    [(*ea*) property development;
    (*eb*) farming or market gardening;
    (*ec*) holding, managing or occupying woodlands, any other forestry activities or timber production;
    (*ed*) operating or managing hotels or comparable establishments, or managing property used as an hotel or comparable establishment;
    (*ee*) operating or managing nursing homes or residential care homes, or managing property used as a nursing home or residential care home;]³
    (*f*) providing services or facilities for any such trade carried on by another person (not being a company of which the company providing the services or facilities is a subsidiary) as—

        (i) consists, to a substantial extent, in activities within any of paragraphs (*a*) to (*ee*) above; and
        (ii) is a trade in which a controlling interest is held by a person who also has a controlling interest in the trade carried on by the company providing the services or facilities.

(3) For the purposes of sub-paragraph (2)(*b*) above—

    (*a*) a trade of wholesale distribution is one in which the goods are offered for sale and sold to persons for resale by them, or for processing and resale by them, to members of the general public for their use or consumption;
    (*b*) a trade of retail distribution is one in which the goods are offered for sale and sold to members of the general public for their use or consumption; and
    (*c*) a trade is not an ordinary trade of wholesale or retail distribution if—

        (i) it consists, to a substantial extent, in dealing in goods of a kind which are collected or held as an investment, or in that activity and any other activity of a kind falling within sub-paragraph (2)(*a*) to (*f*) above, taken together; and
        (ii) a substantial proportion of those goods are held by the company for a period which is significantly longer than the period for which a vendor would reasonably be expected to hold them while endeavouring to dispose of them at their market value.

[(3A) For the purposes of this Schedule the activities of a person shall not be taken to fall within paragraph (*ed*) or (*ee*) of sub-paragraph (2) above except where that person has an estate or interest in, or is in occupation of, the hotels or comparable establishments or, as the case may be, the nursing homes or residential care homes.]³

(4) In determining for the purposes of this paragraph whether a trade carried on by any person is an ordinary trade of wholesale or retail distribution, regard shall be had to the extent to which it has the following features, that is to say—

    (*a*) the goods are bought by that person in quantities larger than those in which he sells them;
    (*b*) the goods are bought and sold by that person in different markets;

(c) that person employs staff and incurs expenses in the trade in addition to the cost of the goods and, in the case of a trade carried on by a company, to any remuneration paid to any person connected with it;

(d) there are purchases or sales from or to persons who are connected with that person;

(e) purchases are matched with forward sales or vice versa;

(f) the goods are held by that person for longer than is normal for goods of the kind in question;

(g) the trade is carried on otherwise than at a place or places commonly used for wholesale or retail trade;

(h) that person does not take physical possession of the goods;

and for the purposes of this sub-paragraph the features specified in paragraphs (a) to (c) above shall be regarded as indications that the trade is such an ordinary trade and those in paragraphs (d) to (h) above shall be regarded as indications of the contrary.

[(5) A trade shall not be treated as failing to comply with this paragraph by reason only that it consists to a substantial extent in the receiving of royalties or licence fees if the royalties and licence fees (or all but for a part that is not a substantial part in terms of value) are attributable to the exploitation of relevant intangible assets.

(6) For this purpose an intangible asset is a "relevant intangible asset" if the whole or greater part (in terms of value) of it has been created—

(a) by the company carrying on the trade, or

(b) by a company which at all times during which it created the intangible asset was—

(i) the parent company of the company carrying on the trade, or

(ii) a qualifying subsidiary of that parent company.

(6A) In the case of a relevant asset that is intellectual property, references in sub-paragraph (6) above to the creation of the asset by a company are to its creation in circumstances in which the right to exploit it vests in the company (whether alone or jointly with others).

(6B) For the purposes of sub-paragraphs (5) to (6A) above "intangible asset" means any asset which falls to be treated as an intangible asset in accordance with [generally accepted accounting practice]⁵.

...⁶

(6C) For the purposes of sub-paragraph (6) above

(a) "parent company" means a company that—

(i) has one or more 51% subsidiaries, but

(ii) is not itself a 51% subsidiary of another company; and

(b) paragraph 10 below (meaning of "qualifying subsidiary") shall apply as if the references in that paragraph to the relevant company were references to the parent company referred to in sub-paragraph (6)(b) above.

(6D) For the purposes of sub-paragraph (6A) above "intellectual property" means—

(a) any patent, trade mark, registered design, copyright, design right, performer's right or plant breeder's right; and

(b) any rights under the law of a country or territory outside the United Kingdom which correspond or are similar to those falling within paragraph (a) above.]⁴

(7) A trade shall not be treated as failing to comply with this paragraph by reason only of its consisting in letting ships, other than oil rigs or pleasure craft, on charter if—

(a) every ship let on charter by the company carrying on the trade is beneficially owned by the company;

(b) every ship beneficially owned by the company is registered in the United Kingdom;

(c) the company is solely responsible for arranging the marketing of the services of its ships; and

(d) the conditions mentioned in sub-paragraph (8) below are satisfied in relation to every letting of a ship on charter by the company;

but where any of the requirements mentioned in paragraphs (a) to (d) above are not satisfied in relation to any lettings, the trade shall not thereby be treated as failing to comply with this paragraph if those lettings and any other activity of a kind falling within sub-paragraph [(2)(a) to (f)]² above do not, when taken together, amount to a substantial part of the trade.

(8) The conditions are that—

(a) the letting is for a period not exceeding 12 months and no provision is made at any time (whether in the charterparty or otherwise) for extending it beyond that period otherwise than at the option of the charterer;

(b) during the period of the letting there is no provision in force (whether by virtue of being contained in the charterparty or otherwise) for the grant of a new letting to end, otherwise than at the option of the charterer, more than 12 months after that provision is made;

(c) the letting is by way of a bargain made at arm's length between the company and a person who is not connected with it; and

(d) under the terms of the charter the company is responsible as principal—

(i) for taking, throughout the period of the charter, management decisions in relation to the ship, other than those of a kind generally regarded by persons engaged in trade of the kind in question as matters of husbandry; and

(ii) for defraying all expenses in connection with the ship throughout that period, or substantially all such expenses, other than those directly incidental to a particular voyage or to the employment of the ship during that period;

and

(*e*) no arrangements exist by virtue of which a person other than the company may be appointed to be responsible for the matters mentioned in paragraph (*d*) above on behalf of the company;

but this sub-paragraph shall have effect, in relation to any letting between one company and another where one of those companies is the relevant company and the other is a qualifying subsidiary of that company, or where both companies are qualifying subsidiaries of the relevant company, as if paragraph (*c*) were omitted.

(9) A trade shall not comply with this paragraph unless it is conducted on a commercial basis and with a view to the realisation of profits.]¹

Commentary—*Simon's Direct Tax Service* E3.623–626.
Revenue Interpretation RI 120—Consideration of the kinds of "non-qualifying activities" under sub-s (2)(*d*)—leasing, receiving royalties and receiving licence fees.
Definitions—"Film", Sch 28B para 5(1); "oil rig", Sch 28B para 5(1); "pleasure craft", Sch 28B para 5(1); "research and development", Sch 28B para 5(1); "securities", Sch 28B para 13(1); "sound recording", Sch 28B para 5(1); "United Kingdom", s 830(1).
Amendments—¹ This Schedule inserted by FA 1995 s 70(2), Sch 14.
² Words in sub-para (7) substituted by FA 1997 Sch 9 paras 3, 6 with effect for the purposes of determining whether shares or securities are, as at any time after 26 November 1996, to be regarded as comprised in a company's qualifying holdings.
³ Sub-paras (2)(*ea*)–(*ee*) and (3A) inserted by FA 1998 Sch 12 para 3 with effect for the purpose of determining whether any shares or securities are, as at any time on or after 17 March 1998, to be regarded as comprised in the qualifying holdings of any company ("the trust company"). The amendments shall not have effect for the purpose of making such a determination in relation to any shares or securities acquired by the trust company by means of the investment of—

(*a*) money raised by the issue before 17 March 1998 of shares in or securities of the trust company, or

(*b*) money derived from the investment by that company of any such money.

⁴ Sub-paras (5)–(6D) substituted for original sub-paras (5), (6), by FA 2000 s 65, Sch 18 paras 4, 5 with effect for the purpose of determining whether shares or securities issued after 5 April 2000 are, for the purpose of TA 1988 s 842AA, to be regarded as comprised in a company's qualifying holdings. Sub-paras (5), (6) previously read—

"(5) A trade shall not be treated as failing to comply with this paragraph by reason only of its consisting, to a substantial extent, in the receiving of royalties or licence fees if—

(*a*) the company carrying on the trade is engaged in—

(i) the production of films; or

(ii) the production of films and the distribution of films produced by it since the issue of the relevant holding;

and

(*b*) all royalties and licence fees received by it are in respect of films produced by it since the issue of the relevant holding, in respect of sound recordings in relation to such films or in respect of other products arising from such films.

(6) A trade shall not be treated as failing to comply with this paragraph by reason only of its consisting, to a substantial extent, in the receiving of royalties or licence fees if—

(*a*) the company carrying on the trade is engaged in research and development; and

(*b*) all royalties and licence fees received by it are attributable to research and development which it has carried out."

⁵ In sub-para (6B), words substituted for the words "normal accounting practice" by FA 2002 s 103(4)(*a*) with effect from 24 July 2002.

⁶ The following words in sub-para (6B) repealed by FA 2002 s 141, Sch 40 Pt 3(16) with effect from 24 July 2002—

"For this purpose "normal accounting practice" means normal accounting practice in relation to the accounts of companies incorporated in any part of the United Kingdom.".

Provisions supplemental to paragraph 4

[5—(1) In paragraph 4 above—

"film" means an original master negative of a film, an original master film disc or an original master film tape;

["nursing home" means any establishment which exists wholly or mainly for the provision of nursing care for persons suffering from sickness, injury or infirmity or for women who are pregnant or have given birth to children;]²

"oil rig" means any ship which is an offshore installation for the purposes of the Mineral Workings (Offshore Installations) Act 1971;

"pleasure craft" means any ship of a kind primarily used for sport or recreation;

["property development" means the development of land—

(*a*) by a company which has, or at any time has had, an interest in the land, and

(*b*) with the sole or main object of realising a gain from the disposal of an interest in the land when it is developed;]²

["research and development" has the meaning given by section 837A;]³

["residential care home" means any establishment which exists wholly or mainly for the provision of residential accommodation, together with board and personal care, for persons in need of personal care by reason of old age, mental or physical disabilities, past or present dependence on alcohol or drugs or any past illnesses or past or present mental disorders;]² and

"sound recording", in relation to a film, means its sound track, original master audio disc or original master audio tape.

(2) For the purposes of paragraph 4 above, in the case of a trade carried on by a company, a person has a controlling interest in that trade if—

(*a*) he controls the company;

(*b*) the company is a close company and he or an associate of his, being a director of the company, either—

(i) is the beneficial owner of more than 30 per cent of the ordinary share capital of the company, or

(ii) is able, directly or through the medium of other companies or by any other indirect means, to control more than 30 per cent of that share capital;

or

(*c*) not less than half of the trade could, in accordance with section 344(2), be regarded as belonging to him for the purposes of section 343;

and, in any other case, a person has a controlling interest in a trade if he is entitled to not less than half of the assets used for, or of the income arising from, the trade.

(3) For the purposes of sub-paragraph (2) above there shall be attributed to any person any rights or powers of any other person who is an associate of his.

(4) References in paragraph 4 above or this paragraph to a trade, except the references in paragraph 4(2)(*f*) to the trade for which services or facilities are provided, shall be construed without reference to so much of the definition of trade in section 832(1) as relates to adventures or concerns in the nature of trade; and those references in paragraph 4(2)(*f*) above to a trade, shall have effect, in relation to cases in which what is carried on is carried on by a person other than a company, as including references to any business, profession or vocation.

(5) In this paragraph—

"associate" has the meaning given in subsections (3) and (4) of section 417, except that in those subsections, as applied for the purposes of this paragraph, "relative" shall not include a brother or sister;

"director" shall be construed in accordance with subsection (5) of that section.]¹

["interest in land" means (subject to sub-paragraph (6) below)—

(*a*) any estate, interest or right in or over land, including any right affecting the use or disposition of land; or

(*b*) any right to obtain such an estate, interest or right from another which is conditional on the other's ability to grant the estate, interest or right.]²

[(6) References in paragraph 4 above, in relation to an hotel, to a comparable establishment are references to a guest house, hostel or other establishment the main purpose of maintaining which is the provision of facilities for overnight accommodation (whether with or without catering services).

(7) References in this paragraph to an interest in land do not include references to—

(*a*) the interest of a creditor (other than a creditor in respect of a rentcharge) whose debt is secured by way of mortgage, an agreement for a mortgage or a charge of any kind over land; or

(*b*) in the case of land in Scotland, the interest of a creditor in a charge or security of any kind over land.]²

Commentary—*Simon's Direct Tax Service* E3.621.
Amendments—¹ This Schedule inserted by FA 1995 s 70(2), Sch 14.
² Definitions in sub-paras (1), (5), and sub-paras (6)–(7) inserted by FA 1998 Sch 12 para 4 with effect for the purpose of determining whether any shares or securities are, as at any time after 16 March 1998, to be regarded as comprised in the qualifying holdings of any company ("the trust company").
These amendments shall not have effect for the purpose of making such a determination in relation to any shares or securities acquired by the trust company by means of the investment of—
(*a*) money raised by the issue before 17 March 1998 of shares in or securities of the trust company, or
(*b*) money derived from the investment by that company of any such money.
³ Definition of "research and development" substituted by FA 2000 s 65, Sch 18 paras 4, 6 with effect for the purpose of determining whether shares or securities issued after 5 April 2000 are, for the purpose of TA 1988 s 842AA, to be regarded as comprised in a company's qualifying holdings. Definition previously read—
"research and development" means any activity which is intended to result in a patentable invention (within the meaning of the Patents Act 1977) or in a computer program;"
By virtue of FA 2000 Sch 18 para 6(3), this amendment does not affect the operation of TA 1988 Sch 28B as it has effect for the purpose of determining whether shares or securities issued before that date are, for the purposes of s 842AA of that Act, to be regarded as comprised in a company's qualifying holdings.

Requirements as to the money raised by the investment in question

[6—[(1) The requirements of this paragraph are that either—

(*a*) at least 80% of the money raised by the issue of the relevant holding must—

(i) have been employed wholly for the purposes of the trade by reference to which the requirements of paragraph 3(3) above are satisfied; or

(ii) be money which the relevant company or a relevant qualifying subsidiary of that company is intending to employ wholly for the purposes of that trade; or

(*b*) all of the money so raised must have been employed as mentioned in paragraph (*a*)(i) above.]⁴

[(2) For the purposes of this Schedule—

(*a*) the requirements of sub-paragraph (1) above shall not be capable of being satisfied by virtue of paragraph (*a*)(ii) of that sub-paragraph at any time after 12 months have expired from the trading time, and

(*b*) the requirements of that sub-paragraph shall not be capable of being satisfied by virtue of paragraph (*a*)(i) of that sub-paragraph at any time after 24 months have expired from the trading time.][4]

[(2AA) In sub-paragraph (2) above, "the trading time" means whichever is applicable of the following—

(*a*) in a case where the requirements of sub-paragraph (3) of paragraph 3 above were satisfied in relation to the time when the relevant holding was issued by virtue of paragraph (*a*) of that sub-paragraph, that time; and

(*b*) in a case where they were satisfied in relation to that time by virtue of paragraph (*b*) of that sub-paragraph, the time when the relevant company or, as the case may be, the subsidiary in question began to carry on the intended trade.][4]

[(2A) Where the relevant company is a company falling within paragraph 3(2)(*aa*) above, the requirements of this paragraph are not satisfied unless—

(*a*) the trader company is a company in relation to which the requirements of paragraph 3(2)(*a*) above are satisfied, or

(*b*) the trader company is a company in relation to which those requirements would be satisfied if its purposes were disregarded to the extent that they consist in the carrying on of activities such as are mentioned in paragraph 3(9)(*a*) and (*b*) and (10)(*a*) above, or

(*c*) the trader company is a [relevant qualifying subsidiary][3] of the relevant company and falls within sub-paragraph (2B) below.][2]

[(2B) A [relevant qualifying subsidiary][3] of the relevant company falls within this sub-paragraph if—

(*a*) apart from purposes capable of having no significant effect (other than in relation to incidental matters) on the extent of its activities, it exists wholly for the purpose of carrying on activities such as are mentioned in paragraph 3(9)(*b*) above; or

(*b*) it has no profits for the purposes of corporation tax and no part of its business consists in the making of investments.][2]

[(2C) In sub-paragraph (2A) above "the trader company" means the company (whether the relevant company or a qualifying subsidiary of the relevant company) carrying on, or preparing to carry on, the trade by reference to which the requirements of paragraph 3(3) above are satisfied.][2]

(3) For the purposes of this paragraph money shall not be treated as employed otherwise than wholly for the purposes of a trade if the only amount employed for other purposes is an amount which is not a significant amount; and nothing in paragraph 1(3) above shall require any money whose use is disregarded by virtue of this sub-paragraph to be treated as raised by a different holding.

(4) References in this paragraph to employing money for the purposes of a trade shall include references to employing it for the purpose of preparing for the carrying on of the trade.][1]

[(5) For the purposes of this paragraph a company is a relevant qualifying subsidiary of another company at any time when it would be a qualifying subsidiary of that company if "90" were substituted for "75" in every place where "75" occurs in paragraph 10(3) below.][3]

Commentary—*Simon's Direct Tax Service* E3.629.
Revenue Interpretation RI 124—Circumstances in which an acquisition of shares or securities in a company, which is to be used for a management buy-out, may give rise to a qualifying holding.
Definition—"Qualifying subsidiary", Sch 28B para 10.
Amendments—[1] This Schedule inserted by FA 1995 s 70(2), Sch.14.
[2] Sub-paras (2A)-(2C) inserted by FA 1997 Sch 9 paras 4, 6 with effect for the purposes of determining whether shares or securities are, as at any time after 26 November 1996, to be regarded as comprised in a company's qualifying holdings.
[3] Words in sub-paras (2A), (2B) substituted, and sub-para (5) inserted by FA 1998 s 73(4) with effect for the purpose of determining whether shares or securities are, as at any time after 5 April 1998, to be regarded as comprised in a company's qualifying holdings.
[4] Sub-paras (1)–(2AA) substituted for sub-paras (1), (2) by FA 2001 s 64, Sch 16 para 2 with effect for the purpose of determining whether shares or securities held by the trust company (within the meaning of TA 1988 Schedule 28B) after 6 March 2001 are, for the purposes of that Schedule, to be regarded as comprised in that company's qualifying holdings.

Requirement imposing a maximum on qualifying investments in the relevant company

[7—(1) The requirement of this paragraph is that the relevant holding did not, when it was issued, represent an investment in excess of the maximum qualifying investment for the relevant period.

(2) Subject to sub-paragraph (4) below, the maximum qualifying investment for any period is exceeded to the extent that the aggregate amount of money raised in that period by the issue to the trust company during that period of shares in or securities of the relevant company exceeds £1 million.

(3) Any question for the purposes of this paragraph as to whether any shares in or securities of the relevant company which are for the time being held by the trust company represent an investment in excess of the maximum qualifying investment for any period shall be determined on the assumption, in relation to disposals by the trust company, that, as between shares or securities of the same description, those representing the whole or any part of the excess are disposed of before those which do not.

(4) Where—

    (*a*) at the time of the issue of the relevant holding the relevant company or any of its qualifying subsidiaries was a member of a partnership or a party to a joint venture,

    (*b*) the trade by virtue of which the requirements of paragraph 3(3) above are satisfied was at that time being carried on, or to be carried on, by those partners in partnership or by the parties to the joint venture as such, and

    (*c*) the other partners or parties to the joint venture include at least one other company,

this paragraph shall have effect in relation to the relevant company as if the sum of money for the time being specified in sub-paragraph (2) above were to be divided by the number of companies (including the relevant company) which, at the time when the relevant holding was issued, were members of the partnership or, as the case may be, parties to the joint venture.

(5) For the purposes of this paragraph the relevant period is the period beginning with whichever is the earlier of—

    (*a*) the time six months before the issue of the relevant holding; and

    (*b*) the beginning of the year of assessment in which the issue of that holding took place.]¹

Commentary—*Simon's Direct Tax Service* E3.630.
Definitions—"Qualifying subsidiary", Sch 28B para 10; "securities", Sch 28B, para 13(1).
Amendments—¹ This Schedule inserted by FA 1995 s 70(2), Sch 14.

Requirement as to the assets of the relevant company

[8—(1)The requirement of this paragraph is that the value of the relevant assets—

    (*a*) did not exceed [£15]² million immediately before the issue of the relevant holding; and

    (*b*) did not exceed [£16]² million immediately afterwards.

(2) Subject to sub-paragraph (3) below, the reference in sub-paragraph (1) above to the value of the relevant assets is a reference—

    (*a*) in relation to a time when the relevant company did not have any qualifying subsidiaries, to the value of the gross assets of that company at that time; and

    (*b*) in relation to any other time, to the aggregate value at that time of the gross assets of all the companies in the relevant company's group.

(3) For the purposes of this paragraph assets of any member of the relevant company's group that consist in rights against, or in shares in or securities of, another member of the group shall be disregarded.

(4) In this paragraph references, in relation to any time, to the relevant company's group are references to the relevant company and its qualifying subsidiaries at that time.]¹

Commentary—*Simon's Direct Tax Service* E3.628.
Statements of Practice SP 7/95—Revenue approach to the calculation of a company's gross assets in respect of holdings of shares issued before 6 April 1998.
SP 2/00—Venture Capital Trusts—value of "gross assets".
Definitions—"Qualifying subsidiary", Sch 28B para 10; "securities", Sch 28B, para 13(1).
Amendments—¹ This Schedule inserted by FA 1995 s 70(2), Sch 14.
² Amounts in sub-para (1) substituted by FA 1998 s 73(5) with effect for relevant holdings issued after 5 April 1998.

Requirements as to the subsidiaries etc of the relevant company

[9—(1) The requirements of this paragraph are that ...² the relevant company must not be—

    (*a*) a company which controls (whether on its own or together with any person connected with it) any company that is not a qualifying subsidiary of the relevant company; or

    (*b*) a company which is under the control of another company (or of another company and a person connected with the other company);

and arrangements must not be in existence by virtue of which the relevant company could fall within paragraph (*a*) or (*b*) above.

(2) ...²]¹

Commentary—*Simon's Direct Tax Service* E3.627.
Definitions—"Venture capital trust", s 842AA.
Amendments—¹ This Schedule inserted by FA 1995 s 70(2), Sch 14.
² Words omitted from sub-para (1) and sub-para (2) repealed by FA 1996 s 161(1), (2), Sch 41 Pt V(22) and these amendments deemed always to have had effect.

Meaning of "qualifying subsidiary"

[10—(1) Subject to the following provisions of this paragraph, a company is a qualifying subsidiary of the relevant company for the purposes of this Schedule if—

    (*a*) the company in question ("the subsidiary"), and

    (*b*) where the relevant company has more than one subsidiary, every other subsidiary of the relevant company,

is a company falling within [sub-paragraph]² (3) below.

(2) ...²

(3) The subsidiary falls within this sub-paragraph if—

(a) the relevant company, or another of its subsidiaries, possesses not less than [75]³ per cent of the issued share capital of, and not less than [75]³ per cent of the voting power in, the subsidiary;

(b) the relevant company, or another of its subsidiaries, would in the event of a winding up of the subsidiary or in any other circumstances be beneficially entitled to receive not less than [75]³ per cent of the assets of the subsidiary which would then be available for distribution to the equity holders of the subsidiary;

(c) the relevant company, or another of its subsidiaries, is beneficially entitled to not less than [75]³ per cent of any profits of the subsidiary which are available for distribution to the equity holders of the subsidiary;

(d) no person other than the relevant company or another of its subsidiaries has control of the subsidiary within the meaning of section 840; and

(e) no arrangements are in existence by virtue of which the relevant company could cease to fall within this sub-paragraph.

(4) The subsidiary shall not be regarded, at a time when it is being wound up, as having ceased on that account to be a company falling within [sub-paragraph]² (3) above if it is shown—

(a) that it would fall within [that sub-paragraph]² apart from the winding up; and

(b) that the winding up is for bona fide commercial reasons and not part of a scheme or arrangement the main purpose of which, or one of the main purposes of which, is the avoidance of tax.

(5) The subsidiary shall not be regarded, at any time when arrangements are in existence for the disposal by the relevant company, or (as the case may be) by another subsidiary of that company, of all its interest in the subsidiary in question, as having ceased on that account to be a company falling within [sub-paragraph]² (3) above if it is shown that the disposal is to be for bona fide commercial reasons and not part of a scheme or arrangement the main purpose of which, or one of the main purposes of which, is the avoidance of tax.

(6) For the purposes of this paragraph the persons who are equity holders of the subsidiary and the percentage of the assets of the subsidiary to which an equity holder would be entitled shall be determined in accordance with paragraphs 1 and 3 of Schedule 18, taking references in paragraph 3 to the first company as references to an equity holder, and references to a winding up as including references to any other circumstances in which assets of the subsidiary are available for distribution to its equity holders.]¹

Commentary—*Simon's Direct Tax Service* E3.631.
Definitions—"Qualifying trade", Sch 28B para 4; "tax", s 832(3).
Amendments—¹ This Schedule inserted by FA 1995 s 70(2), Sch 14.
² Words in sub-paras (1), (4), (5) substituted and sub-para (2) repealed by FA 1997 Sch 9 paras 5, 6, Sch 18 Pt VI(9) with effect for the purposes of determining whether shares or securities are, as at any time after 26 November 1996, to be regarded as comprised in a company's qualifying holdings.
³ Percentage in sub-para (3) substituted by FA 1998 s 73(2) with effect for the purpose of determining whether shares or securities are, as at any time after 5 April 1998, to be regarded as comprised in a company's qualifying holdings.

[Requirement that securities should not relate to a guaranteed loan

10A—(1) The requirement of this paragraph is that there are no securities relating to a guaranteed loan in the relevant holding.

(2) For the purposes of this paragraph a security relates to a guaranteed loan if (and only if) there are arrangements for the trust company to be or become entitled, in the event of a failure by any person to comply with—

(a) the terms of the loan to which the security relates, or

(b) the terms of the security,

to receive anything (whether directly or indirectly) from a third party.

(3) For the purposes of sub-paragraph (2) above it shall be immaterial whether the arrangements apply in all cases of a failure to comply or only in certain such cases.

(4) For the purposes of this paragraph "third party" means any person except—

(a) the relevant company; and

(b) if the relevant company is the parent company of a trading group for the purposes of paragraph 3 above, the subsidiaries of the relevant company.]¹

Amendments—¹ This paragraph inserted by FA 1998 s 72(1) with effect for accounting periods ending after 1 July 1997, subject to the provisions in FA 1998 s 72(4).

[Requirement that a proportion of the holding in each company must be eligible shares

10B—(1) The requirement of this paragraph is that eligible shares represent at least 10 per cent by value of the totality of the shares in or securities of the relevant company (including the relevant holding) which are held by the trust company.

(2) For the purposes of this paragraph the value at any time of any shares in or securities of a company shall be taken (subject to sub-paragraph (4) below) to be their value immediately after—

(a) any relevant event occurring at that time; or

(*b*) where no relevant event occurs at that time, the last relevant event to occur before that time.

(3) In sub-paragraph (2) above "relevant event", in relation to any shares in or securities of the relevant company, means—

(*a*) the acquisition by the trust company of those shares or securities;

(*b*) the acquisition by the trust company of any other shares in or securities of the relevant company which—

(i) are of the same description as those shares or securities, and

(ii) are acquired otherwise than by virtue of being allotted to the trust company without that company's becoming liable to give any consideration;

or

(*c*) the making of any such payment in discharge, in whole or in part, of any obligation attached to any shares in or securities of the relevant company held by the trust company as (by discharging that obligation) increases the value of any such shares or securities.

(4) If at any time the value of any shares or securities held by the trust company is less than the amount of the consideration given by the trust company for those shares or securities, it shall be assumed for the purposes of this paragraph that the value of those shares or securities at that time is equal to the amount of that consideration.

(5) In this paragraph "eligible shares" has the same meaning as in section 842AA.]¹

Commentary—*Simon's Direct Tax Service* **E3.622.**
Amendments—¹ This paragraph inserted by FA 1998 s 72(2) with effect for accounting periods ending after 1 July 1997, subject to the provisions in FA 1998 s 72(5)–(6).

[Acquisitions for restructuring purpose

10C—(1) This paragraph applies where—

(*a*) arrangements are made for a company ("the new company") to acquire all the shares ("old shares") in another company ("the old company");

(*b*) the acquisition provided for by the arrangements falls within sub-paragraph (2) below; and

(*c*) the Board have, before any exchange of shares takes place under the arrangements, given an approval notification.

(2) An acquisition of shares falls within this sub-paragraph if—

(*a*) the consideration for the old shares consists wholly of the issue of shares ("new shares") in the new company;

(*b*) new shares are issued in consideration of old shares only at times when there are no issued shares in the new company other than subscriber shares and new shares previously issued in consideration of old shares;

(*c*) the consideration for new shares of each description consists wholly of old shares of the corresponding description; and

(*d*) new shares of each description are issued to the holders of old shares of the corresponding description in respect of, and in proportion to, their holdings.

(3) For the purposes of sub-paragraph (1)(*c*) above an approval notification is one which, on an application by either the old company or the new company, is given to the applicant company and states that the Board are satisfied that the exchange of shares under the arrangements—

(*a*) will be effected for bona fide commercial reasons; and

(*b*) will not form part of any such scheme or arrangements as are mentioned in section 137(1) of the 1992 Act.

(4) If the requirements of paragraph 3 above were satisfied in relation to the old company and any old shares immediately before the beginning of the period for giving effect to the arrangements, then (to the extent that it would not otherwise be the case) those requirements shall be deemed to be satisfied in relation to the new company and the matching new shares at all times which—

(*a*) fall in that period; and

(*b*) do not fall after a time when (apart from the arrangements) those requirements would have ceased by virtue of—

(i) sub-paragraph (4) or (5) of that paragraph, or

(ii) any cessation of a trade by any company,

to be satisfied in relation to the old company and the matching old shares.

(5) For the purposes of paragraph 3 above the period of two years mentioned in sub-paragraph (4) of that paragraph shall be deemed, in the case of any new shares, to expire at the same time as it would have expired (or by virtue of this sub-paragraph would have been deemed to expire) in the case of the matching old shares.

(6) Subject to sub-paragraph (7) below, where—

(*a*) there is an exchange under the arrangements of any new shares for any old shares, and

(*b*) those old shares are shares in relation to which the requirements of paragraphs 6 and 8 above were (or were deemed to be) satisfied to any extent immediately before the exchange, those requirements shall be deemed, at all times after that time, to be satisfied to the same extent in relation to the matching new shares.

(7) Where there is a time following any exchange under the arrangements of any new shares for any old shares when (apart from the arrangements) the requirements of paragraph 6 above would have ceased under—

(a) sub-paragraph (2) of that paragraph, or
(b) this sub-paragraph,

to be satisfied in relation to those old shares, those requirements shall cease at that time to be satisfied in relation to the matching new shares.

(8) For the purposes of paragraph 7 above any new shares acquired under the arrangements shall be deemed to represent an investment which—

(a) raised the same amount of money as was raised (or, by virtue of this sub-paragraph, is deemed to have been raised) by the issue of the matching old shares, and
(b) raised that amount by an issue of shares in the new company made at the time when the issue of the matching old shares took place (or, as the case may be, is deemed to have taken place).

(9) In determining whether the requirements of paragraph 9 above are satisfied in relation to the old company or the new company at a time in the period for giving effect to the arrangements, both—

(a) the arrangements themselves, and
(b) any exchange of new shares for old shares that has already taken place under the arrangements,

shall be disregarded.

(10) For the purposes of paragraph 10B above the value of the new shares, both immediately after the time of their acquisition and immediately after the time of any subsequent relevant event occurring by virtue of the arrangements, shall be taken to be the same as the value, when last valued in accordance with that paragraph, of the old shares for which they are exchanged.

(11) Nothing in this paragraph shall deem any of the requirements of this Schedule to be satisfied in relation to any new shares unless the matching old shares were first issued to the trust company and have been held by that company from the time when they were issued until they are acquired by the new company.

(12) References in this paragraph to the period for giving effect to the arrangements are references to the period which—

(a) begins with the time when those arrangements first came into existence; and
(b) ends with the time when the new company completes its acquisition under the arrangements of all the old shares.

(13) If, at any time after the arrangements first came into existence and before the new company has acquired all the old shares, the arrangements—

(a) cease to be arrangements for the acquisition of all the old shares by the new company, or
(b) cease to be arrangements for an acquisition falling within sub-paragraph (2) above,

this paragraph shall not deem any requirement of this Schedule to be satisfied, and sub-paragraph (10) above shall not apply, in the case of any new shares at any time after the arrangements have so ceased.

(14) Subject to sub-paragraph (15) below, references in this paragraph, except in the expression "subscriber shares", to shares in a company include references to any securities of that company.

(15) For the purposes of this paragraph, a relevant security of the old company shall not be treated as a security of that company if—

(a) the arrangements do not provide for the acquisition of the security by the new company; or
(b) such treatment prevents sub-paragraph (1)(b) above from being satisfied in connection with the arrangements.

(16) In sub-paragraph (15) above "relevant security" means an instrument which is a security for the purposes of this Schedule by reason only of section 842AA(12).

(17) For the purposes of this paragraph—

(a) old shares and new shares are of a corresponding description if, were they shares in the same company, they would be of the same description; and
(b) old shares and new shares are matching shares in relation to each other if the old shares are the shares for which those new shares are exchanged under the arrangements.][1]

Commentary—*Simon's Direct Tax Service* E3.633.
Amendments—[1] This paragraph inserted by FA 1999 s 69(2), (5) with effect for any arrangements made, and rights of conversion exercised, after 15 June 1999.

[Conversion of convertible shares and securities

10D—(1) This paragraph applies where—

(a) shares have been issued to the trust company by virtue of the exercise by that company of any right of conversion attached to other shares, or securities, held by that company ("the convertibles");

(*b*) the shares so issued are in the same company as the convertibles to which the right was attached;

(*c*) the convertibles to which the right was attached were first issued to the trust company and were held by that company from the time they were issued until converted; and

(*d*) the right was attached to the convertibles when they were first so issued and was not varied before it was exercised.

(2) Sub-paragraphs (5) to (8) of paragraph 10C above shall apply in relation to the exchange of convertibles for shares by virtue of the exercise of the right of conversion as if—

(*a*) that exchange were an exchange under any such arrangements as are mentioned in that paragraph of new shares for old shares; and

(*b*) the references in those sub-paragraphs and sub-paragraph (17)(*b*) of that paragraph to the arrangements were references to the provision conferring the right of conversion.

(3) For the purposes of paragraph 10B above the value of the new shares immediately after the time of their acquisition by the trust company shall be taken to be the same as the value, when last valued in accordance with that paragraph, of the convertibles for which they are exchanged.][1]

Commentary—*Simon's Direct Tax Service* E3.634.
Amendments—[1] This paragraph inserted by FA 1999 s 69(2), (5) with effect for any arrangements made, and rights of conversion exercised, after 15 June 1999.

Winding up of the relevant company

[11 None of the requirements of this Schedule shall be regarded, at a time when the relevant company is being wound up, as being, on that account, a requirement that is not satisfied in relation to that company if it is shown—

(*a*) that the requirements of this Schedule would be satisfied in relation to that company apart from the winding up; and

(*b*) that the winding up is for bona fide commercial reasons and not part of a scheme or arrangement the main purpose of which, or one of the main purposes of which, is the avoidance of tax.][1]

Commentary—*Simon's Direct Tax Service* E3.625.
Definitions—"Tax", s 832(3).
Amendments—[1] This Schedule inserted by FA 1995 s 70(2), Sch 14.

[Company in administration or receivership

11A—(1) A company which is in administration or receivership shall not be regarded as ceasing to comply with paragraph 3(2) or (3) by reason of anything done as a consequence of its being in administration or receivership.

(2) For this purpose—

(*a*) a company is "in administration" if there is in force in relation to it—

(i) an administration order under Part II of the Insolvency Act 1986 or Part III of the Insolvency (Northern Ireland) Order 1989, or

(ii) any corresponding order under the law of a country or territory outside the United Kingdom; and

(*b*) a company is "in receivership" if there is in force in relation to it—

(i) an order for the appointment of an administrative receiver, a receiver and manager or a receiver under Chapter I or II of Part III of the Insolvency Act 1986 or Part IV of the Insolvency (Northern Ireland) Order 1989, or

(ii) any corresponding order under the law of a country or territory outside the United Kingdom.

(3) This paragraph applies only if—

(*a*) the making of the order in question, and

(*b*) everything done as a consequence of the company being in administration or receivership,

is for bona fide commercial reasons and is not part of a scheme or arrangement the main purpose or one of the main purposes of which is the avoidance of tax.".][1]

Commentary—*Simon's Direct Tax Service* E3.635.
Amendments—[1] This paragraph inserted by FA 2000 s 65, Sch 18 paras 4, 7 with effect for the purposes of determining whether shares or securities are, as at any time after 20 March 2000, to be regarded as comprised in a company's qualifying holdings.

[Company reorganisations etc involving exchange of shares

11B—(1) The Treasury may by regulations make provision for cases where—

(*a*) a holding of shares or securities that meets the requirements of this Schedule is exchanged for other shares or securities,

(*b*) the exchange is made for bona fide commercial reasons and does not form part of a scheme or arrangements of which the main purpose, or one of the main purposes, is the avoidance of tax, and

(*c*) the new shares or securities do not meet some or all the requirements of this Schedule, providing that the new shares or securities shall be treated as meeting those requirements.

(2) The references in sub-paragraph (1) to an exchange of shares or securities include any form of company reorganisation or other arrangement which involves a holder of shares or securities in a company receiving other shares or securities—

  (*a*) whether the original shares or securities are transferred, cancelled or retained, and
  (*b*) whether the new shares or securities are in the same or another company.

(3) The regulations shall specify—

  (*a*) the cases in which, and conditions subject to which, they apply,
  (*b*) which requirements of this Schedule are to be treated as met, and
  (*c*) the period for which those requirements are to be treated as met.

(4) The regulations may contain such administrative provisions (including provision for advance clearances) as appear to the Treasury to be necessary or expedient.

(5) The regulations may authorise the Board to give notice to any person requiring him to provide such information, specified in the notice, as they may reasonably require in order to determine whether any conditions imposed by the regulations are met.

(6) Regulations under this paragraph—

  (*a*) may make different provision for different cases,
  (*b*) may include such supplementary, incidental and transitional provisions as appear to the Treasury to be appropriate, and
  (*c*) may include provision having retrospective effect.]¹

Commentary—*Simon's Direct Tax Service* **E3.628, 630.**
Amendments—¹ This paragraph inserted by FA 2000 s 65, Sch 18 paras 4, 8(1), (4) with effect for exchanges of shares or securities (within the meaning sub-para (1) above) taking effect after 20 March 2000.

Power to amend Schedule

[12 The Treasury may by order amend this Schedule for any or all of the following purposes, that is to say—

  (*a*) to make such modifications of paragraphs [3 to 5]² above as they may consider expedient;
  (*b*) to substitute different sums for the sums of money for the time being specified in paragraphs 7(2) and 8 above.]¹

Commentary—*Simon's Direct Tax Service* **E3.633.**
Amendments—¹ This Schedule inserted by FA 1995 s 70(2), Sch 14.
² Words substituted by FA 1998 s 70(3) with effect from 31 July 1998.

General interpretation

[13—(1) [Subject to paragraph 10C(15) above,]⁴ in this Schedule—

  "debenture" has the meaning given by section 744 of the Companies Act 1985; and
  "securities" has the same meaning as in section 842AA;

and references in this Schedule to the issue of any securities, in relation to any security consisting in a liability in respect of an unsecured loan, shall have effect as references to the making of the loan.

[(2) For the purposes of paragraphs 5(2) and 9 above, the question whether a person controls a company shall be determined in accordance with subsections (2) to (6) of section 416 with the modification given by sub-paragraph (3) below.]²

[(3) The modification is that, in determining whether a person controls a company, there shall be disregarded—

  (*a*) his or any other person's possession of, or entitlement to acquire, relevant fixed-rate preference shares of the company; and
  (*b*) his or any other person's possession of, or entitlement to acquire, rights as a loan creditor of the company.]²

[(4) Section 839 shall apply for the purposes of this Schedule, but as if the reference in subsection (8) to section 416 were a reference to subsections (2) to (6) of section 416 with the modification given by sub-paragraph (3) above.]²

[(5) For the purposes of sub-paragraph (3) above—

  (*a*) relevant fixed-rate preference shares are fixed-rate preference shares that do not for the time being carry any voting rights; ...³
  (*b*) ...³]²]¹

[(6) In this paragraph "fixed-rate preference shares" means shares which—

  (*a*) were issued wholly for new consideration;
  (*b*) do not carry any right either to conversion into shares or securities of any other description or to the acquisition of any additional shares or securities; and
  (*c*) do not carry any right to dividends other than dividends which—

    (i) are of a fixed amount or at a fixed rate per cent of the nominal value of the shares, and

(ii) together with any sum paid on a redemption, represent no more than a reasonable commercial return on the consideration for which the shares were issued;

and in paragraph (*a*) above "new consideration" has the meaning given by section 254.]³

Definition—"Company", s 832(1), (2).
Amendments—¹ This Schedule inserted by FA 1995 s 70(2), Sch 14.
² Sub-paras (2)–(5) substituted for sub-paras (2), (3) by FA 1996 s 161(1), (3) and deemed always to have had effect.
³ Sub-para (5)(*b*) repealed, and sub-para (6) inserted, by F(No 2)A 1997 s 25(2)–(4), Sch 8 Pt II(6) with effect on and after 2 July 1997.
⁴ Words in sub-para (1) inserted by FA 1999 s 69(3), (5) with effect for any arrangements made, and rights of conversion exercised, after 15 June 1999.

SCHEDULE 29

CONSEQUENTIAL AMENDMENTS

Section 844

1, 2 Repealed by CAA 1990 Sch 2

3 The Taxes Management Act 1970 shall have effect subject to the amendments made by paragraphs 4 to 10 below.

4 Repealed by FA 1990 Sch 19 Pt V.

5 Repealed by the Copyright, Designs and Patents Act 1988 s 303(2), Sch 8.

6 Inserts TMA 1970 s 16A.

7 Amends TMA 1970 s 18.

8 Amends TMA 1970 s 55; amended by FA 1988 Sch 13 para 13.

9 Amends TMA 1970 s 98.

10 Amends TMA ss 11, 30, 87A, 89, 91, 94, 109.

11 Repealed by the Friendly Societies Act 1992 s 120(2), Sch 22 Pt I.

12 Repealed by TCGA 1992 s 290(3), Sch 12.

13 Amends the Friendly Societies Act 1974 s 7.

14 Repealed by the Social Security (Consequential Provisions) Act 1992 Sch 1 and Social Security (Consequential Provisions) (Northern Ireland) Act 1992 Sch 1.

15–28 Repealed by TCGA 1992 s 290(3), Sch 12.

29 Amends FA 1982 s 134.

30 Amends the Administration of Justice Act 1985 Sch 2 para 36(3).

31 Amends the Law Reform (Miscellaneous Provisions) (Scotland) Act 1985 Sch 1 para 41.

Translation of references to enactments repealed and re-enacted

32 In the enactments specified in Column 1 of the following Table for the words set out or referred to in Column 2 there shall be substituted the words set out in the corresponding entry in Column 3.

Note—The Table has been repealed in part by several enactments, or is in part superseded on the repeal of the legislation affected by it. The effect of those provisions still extant has been noted to the legislation concerned.

SCHEDULE 30

TRANSITIONAL PROVISIONS AND SAVINGS

Section 844

Corporation tax payment dates

1—(1) In this paragraph, an "old company" means a company to which section 244 of the 1970 Act applied in respect of the last accounting period ending before 17th March 1987.

(2) In relation to an old company—

(*a*) "the company's section 244 interval" means the interval after the end of an accounting period of the company which, in accordance with section 244 of the 1970 Act, was the period within which corporation tax assessed for that period was required to be paid; and

(*b*) "the period of reduction" means the number of whole days which are comprised in a period equal to one-third of the difference between nine months and the company's section 244 interval.

(3) Subject to sub-paragraph (6) below, with respect to the first accounting period of an old company beginning on or after 17th March 1987, section 243(4) of the 1970 Act and section 10(1) of this Act (time for payment of corporation tax) shall have effect as if for the reference to nine months there were substituted a reference to a period which is equal to the company's section 244 interval less the period of reduction.

(4) Subject to sub-paragraph (6) below, with respect to any accounting period of an old company which begins—

    (*a*) after the accounting period referred to in sub-paragraph (3) above, but
    (*b*) before the second anniversary of the beginning of that period,

section 10(1) of this Act shall have effect as if for the reference to nine months there were substituted a reference to a period equal to the previous payment interval less the period of reduction.

(5) In relation to any accounting period of an old company falling within sub-paragraph (4) above, "the previous payment interval" means the interval after the end of the immediately preceding accounting period within which corporation tax for that preceding period is required to be paid by virtue of section 243(4) of the 1970 Act or section 10(1) of this Act, as modified by this paragraph.

(6) If the accounting period referred to in sub-paragraph (3) above or any accounting period falling within sub-paragraph (4) above is less than 12 months, the sub-paragraph in question shall have effect in relation to that accounting period as if for the reference in that sub-paragraph to the period of reduction there were substituted a reference to the number of whole days comprised in a period which bears to the period of reduction the same proportion as that accounting period bears to 12 months.

(7) With respect to any accounting period of an old company which falls within sub-paragraph (3) or (4) above, section 86(4) of the Management Act (interest on overdue tax) shall have effect as if, in paragraph 5(*a*) of the Table (the reckonable date in relation to corporation tax), the reference to the nine months mentioned in section 243(4) of the 1970 Act or section 10(1) of this Act were a reference to the period which, under sub-paragraphs (3) to (6) above, is substituted for those nine months.

(8) In section 88(5)(*e*) of the Management Act (the date when corporation tax ought to have been paid) for the words from "where section 244(1)" to "the interval" there shall be substituted "in the case of an accounting period in respect of which section 10(1) of the principal Act applies as modified by sub-paragraph 1(3) or (4) of Schedule 30 to that Act, at the end of the period which, under that sub-paragraph, is substituted for the period of nine months".

(9) With respect to any accounting period of an old company which falls within sub-paragraph (3) or (4) above, section 825 shall have effect as if, in subsection (8) in paragraph (*a*) of the definition of "the material date", the reference to the nine months mentioned in section 10(1) were a reference to the period which, under sub-paragraphs (1) to (8) above is substituted for those nine months.

Commentary—*Simon's Direct Tax Service* **D2.111.**

Duration of leases

2—(1) Subject to sub-paragraph (2) and paragraph 3 below, section 38 has effect—

    (*a*) as respects a lease granted after 12th June 1969; and
    (*b*) so far as it relates to section 34(5), as respects a variation or waiver the contract for which is entered into after that date.

(2) So far as relates to relief under—

    (*a*) section 385 ...[1] 393 [or 393A(1)][1]; or
    (*b*) section 380(1) as applied by subsection (2) of that section; or
    (*c*) section 25(1);

given by setting a loss against, or making a deduction from, income of—

    (i) the year 1988–89 or any subsequent year of assessment, or
    (ii) a company's accounting period ending after 5th April 1988,

section 38 shall be deemed to have had effect as from the passing of the Finance Act 1963 and as respects leases granted at any time.

(3) Notwithstanding section 31 or any other enactment governing the order in which reliefs are given, in applying sub-paragraph (2) above it shall be assumed that all relief which could not be affected by the operation of that sub-paragraph was given (for all years of assessment and accounting periods before or after the passing of this Act) before relief which could be affected by the operation of that sub-paragraph.

(4) All such adjustments shall be made, whether by way of assessment or discharge of repayment of tax, as are required to give effect to section 38 with this paragraph.

Commentary—*Simon's Direct Tax Service* **A4.203.**
Note—FA 1963 referred to in sub-para (2) above was passed on 31 July 1963.
Amendments—[1] Words in sub-para (2)(*a*) inserted and repealed by FA 1991 Sch 15 para 27(1), Sch 19 Pt V.

3—(1) Sections 24 and 38 shall have effect subject to the modifications set out in sub-paragraphs (2) to (4) below in relation to any lease granted after 12th June 1969 and before 25th August 1971 and, so far as section 38 relates to section 34(5), in relation to any variation or waiver the contract for which was entered into between those dates, except to the extent that section 38 affects the computation of the profits or gains or losses of a trade, profession or vocation or relates to relief under—

(a) section 25(1);

(b) section 385 ...[1] 393 [or 393A(1)][1];

(c) subsection (1) of section 380 as applied by subsection (2) of that section; or

(d) section 779(5).

(2) In section 24, in subsection (1), in the definition of "premium", the words from "or to" to "landlord", and subsections (3) and (4) shall be omitted.

(3) In subsection (1) of section 38 the following paragraph shall be inserted before paragraph (a)—

"(aa) where the terms of the lease include provision for the determination of the lease by notice given by the landlord, the lease shall not be treated as granted for a term longer than one ending at the earliest date on which it could be determined by notice so given;";

and sub-paragraph (ii) of paragraph (a) and paragraph (c) shall be omitted.

(4) In subsection (2) of that section for the words "Subsection (1)" there shall be substituted the words "Subsection (1)(a)", and subsection (4) of that section shall be omitted.

Commentary—*Simon's Direct Tax Service* A4.203; B3.647.

Amendments—[1] Words in sub-para (1)(b) inserted and repealed by FA 1991 Sch 15 para 27(2), Sch 19 Pt V.

4—(1) Where section 38 does not have effect, the following provisions of this paragraph shall apply in ascertaining the duration of a lease for the purposes of sections 34 to 36.

(2) Subject to sub-paragraph (4) below, where the terms of the lease include provision for the determination of the lease by notice given either by the landlord or by the tenant, the lease shall not be treated as granted for a term longer than one ending at the earliest date on which it could be determined by notice.

(3) Subject to sub-paragraph (4) below, where any of the terms of the lease (whether relating to forfeiture or to any other matter) or any other circumstances render it unlikely that the lease will continue beyond a date falling before the expiration of the term of the lease, the lease shall not be treated as having been granted for a term longer than one ending on that date.

(4) Where the duration of a lease falls to be ascertained after the date on which the lease has for any reason come to an end, the duration shall be taken to have extended from its commencement to that date, and where the duration falls to be ascertained at a time when the lease is subsisting the preceding provisions of this paragraph shall be applied in accordance with circumstances prevailing at that time.

(5) In relation to Scotland, "term" in this paragraph, where referring to the duration of a lease, means "period".

(6) This paragraph shall be construed as one with Part II.

Commentary—*Simon's Direct Tax Service* A4.203.

Repeal of section 136 of the Income Tax Act 1952: allowance of annual value of land as a business expense

5—(1) This paragraph has effect for allowing deductions by reference to those which would have fallen to be made if section 136 of the Income Tax Act 1952 had applied for the years 1963–64 and 1964–65.

(2) Subject to the provisions of this paragraph, an allowance under this paragraph shall be made to the person ("the occupier") carrying on a trade where land which was occupied by him at any time before the end of the year 1962–63 for the purposes of the trade permanently ceases to be occupied by him for those purposes.

(3) The amount of the allowance shall be the excess of—

(a) the aggregate of any deductions in respect of the annual value of the land which, by virtue of section 136, would have been made in computing the profits or gains of the trade for the years 1963–64 and 1964–65 but for section 29(1) of the Finance Act 1963 and the repeal by that Act of section 136;

over

(b) the aggregate of any deductions relating to the land made in computing the profits or gains of the trade for those years, being—

(i) deductions permitted by section 29(2) of the Finance Act 1963 so far as made in respect of the period in respect of which the deductions mentioned in paragraph(a) above would have been made; or

(ii) deductions in respect of rent from which an amount representing tax was deducted under section 173 of the Income Tax Act 1952 so far as made in respect of that period.

(4) The allowance shall be made by—

(a) treating the amount of it as rent paid for the land by the occupier (in addition to any actual rent), becoming due from day to day during the period defined in sub-paragraph (5) below; and

(b) allowing deductions accordingly in computing the profits or gains of the trade chargeable under Case I of Schedule D for any chargeable period the profits or gains for which fall to be computed by reference to a period including the period defined in sub-paragraph (5) below or any part thereof.

(5) The period referred to in sub-paragraph (4) above is that ending when the land permanently ceases to be occupied by the occupier for the purposes of the trade, and of a duration, equal to the aggregate of—

(a) the number of months and fractions of months during which the land was occupied by him for the purposes of the trade in so much of the period by reference to which the profits or gains of the trade for the year 1963–64 fell to be computed as fell before the beginning of that year; and
(b) the number of months and fractions of months during which the land was so occupied in so much of the period by reference to which the profits or gains of the trade for the year 1964–65 fell to be computed as fell before the beginning of the year 1963–64.

(6) No allowance shall be made under this paragraph where the date on which the land permanently ceases to be occupied by the occupier for the purposes of the trade—

(a) falls within a chargeable period in which he permanently ceases to carry on the trade; or
(b) where the occupier is not a company, falls within a year of assessment and also within a period by reference to which the profits or gains of the trade for that year of assessment fall to be computed.

(7) Where, by reason of a change in the persons carrying on the trade, the trade falls to be treated for any of the purposes of the Income Tax Acts as permanently discontinued, a person engaged in carrying on the trade immediately before the change occurred who continues to be so engaged immediately after it occurred shall be treated for the purposes of this paragraph as not having been in occupation of the land at any time before it occurred.

(8) Where there has been a change in the persons carrying on the trade, but by virtue of section 113 of this Act or section 17(1) of the Finance Act 1954 (company reconstructions before introduction of corporation tax), the trade does not by reason of the change fall to be treated for any of the purposes of the Income Tax Acts as permanently discontinued, this paragraph (including this sub-paragraph) shall apply as if any occupation of the land before the change occurred by the persons carrying on the trade immediately before it occurred were occupation by the persons carrying on the trade immediately after it occurred.

(9) Where section 343(1) applies, then for the purposes of this paragraph any occupation of land for the purposes of the trade by the predecessor shall be treated as having been the occupation of the successor.

Subsection (6) of that section shall apply to this sub-paragraph as it applies to subsections (2) to (5) of that section, and in this paragraph ''predecessor'' and ''successor'' have the same meaning as in that section.

(10) Where section 518 has effect, then for the purposes of this paragraph any occupation of land for the purposes of the trade by the transferor shall be treated as having been the occupation of the transferee.

This sub-paragraph shall be construed as one with section 518.

(11) Sub-paragraph 1 to 10 above shall apply in relation to a profession or vocation as they apply in relation to a trade, but as if the reference in sub-paragraph (4) to Case I of Schedule D were a reference to Case II of that Schedule.

(12) For the purposes of this paragraph, any occupation of land by the London Transport Board which was by virtue of paragraph 6 of Schedule 3 to the Finance Act 1970 immediately before the commencement of this Act treated as occupation by another body, shall continue to be so treated by virtue of this sub-paragraph.

Commentary—*Simon's Direct Tax Service* B3.1342.

Loss relief etc

6—(1) The substitution of this Act for the corresponding enactments repealed by this Act shall not alter the effect of any provision enacted before this Act (whether or not there is a corresponding provision in this Act) so far as it determines whether and to what extent—

(a) losses or expenditure incurred in, or other amounts referable to, a chargeable period earlier than those to which this Act applies may be taken into account for any tax purposes in a chargeable period to which this Act applies; or
(b) losses or expenditure incurred in, or other amounts referable to, a chargeable period to which this Act applies may be taken into account for any tax purposes in a chargeable period earlier than those to which this Act applies.

(2) Without prejudice to sub-paragraph (1) above, the repeals made by this Act shall not affect the following enactments (which are not re-enacted)—

(a) section 27(4) of the Finance Act 1952 (restrictions on removal of six year time limit on carry forward of trading losses);
(b) section 29(3) of the Finance Act 1953 (Isles of Scilly);

(c) section 17 of, and Schedule 3 to, the Finance Act 1954 (company reconstructions before corporation tax) so far as in force by virtue of the saving in Part IV of Schedule 22 to the Finance Act 1965 and section 80(8) of the Finance Act 1965 (which amends Schedule 3 to the Finance Act 1954);

(d) section 82(4) of the Finance Act 1965 (losses allowable against chargeable gains);

(e) section 85 of the Finance Act 1965 (carry forward of surplus of franked investment income: dividends paid out of pre-1966–67 profits) and the enactments amending that section;

(f) paragraph 25 of Schedule 15 to the Finance Act 1965 (continuity of elections for purposes of corporation tax);

(g) paragraph 7 of Schedule 16 to the Finance Act 1965 (overseas trade corporations);

in so far as those enactments may be relevant to tax for any chargeable period to which this Act applies.

7—(1) This paragraph shall apply with respect to claims for group relief in respect of any amount which is attributable—

(a) to writing-down allowances, within the meaning of Chapter II of Part I of the 1968 Act, or, as the case may require, Chapter I of Part III of the Finance Act 1971 in respect of expenditure incurred by the surrendering company on the provision of machinery or plant; or

(b) to initial allowances under section 56 of the 1968 Act (expenditure in connection with mines etc) in respect of expenditure incurred by the surrendering company and falling within section 52(1) of that Act of 1971 (works in a development area or in Northern Ireland); or

(c) to allowances under section 91 of the 1968 Act in respect of expenditure incurred by the surrendering company on scientific research;

where the expenditure is incurred under a contract entered into by the surrendering company before 6th March 1973.

(2) Notwithstanding anything in section 410(1) to (6) or 413(7) to (10) or in Schedule 18 but subject to sub-paragraph (5) below, group relief may be claimed in respect of any such amount as is referred to in sub-paragraph (1) above if—

(a) immediately before 6th March 1973—

(i) the surrendering company and the company claiming relief were members of a group of companies, and

(ii) throughout the period beginning on that date and ending at the end of the accounting period in respect of which the claim is made, there is no reduction in the rights of the parent company with respect to the matters specified in section 413(7)(a) and (b); or

(b) immediately before 6th March 1973 the company claiming relief was a member of a consortium and, throughout the period beginning on that date and ending at the end of the accounting period in respect of which the claim is made, there is—

(i) no variation in the percentage of the ordinary share capital of the company owned by that member, and

(ii) no reduction in the rights of that member (in respect of the company owned by the consortium) with respect to the matters specified in section 413(7)(a) and (b);

and in either case no such arrangements as are specified in section 410(1) or (2) have come into existence after 5th March 1973 with respect to any of the companies concerned and no variation is made in any such arrangements which are in existence on that date with respect to any of those companies.

(3) For the purposes of sub-paragraph (2)(a) above, "the parent company" means the company of which another member of the group referred to in that sub-paragraph was, immediately before 6th March 1973, a 75 per cent. subsidiary, and the rights of the parent company referred to in that paragraph are—

(a) if the parent company is either the surrendering company or the company claiming relief, its rights in the other company; and

(b) in any other case, its rights in both the surrendering company and the company claiming relief.

(4) For the purposes of this paragraph an amount which the claimant company claims by way of group relief shall be treated as attributable to an allowance falling within any of paragraphs (a) to (c) of sub-paragraph (1) above to the extent that that amount would not have been available for surrender by the surrendering company if no such allowance had been available to the surrendering company in respect of the expenditure concerned.

(5) Sub-paragraph (2) above shall not apply if, during the period referred to in that sub-paragraph—

(a) there is a major change in the nature or conduct of a trade or business carried on by the relevant company; or

(b) the relevant company sets up and commences a trade or business which it did not carry on immediately before 6th March 1973.

(6) In sub-paragraph (5) above—

"a major change in the nature or conduct of a trade or business" has the same meaning as in section 245(1); and "the relevant company" means, if the machinery or plant to which the allowance relates was brought into use on or before 6th March 1978, the company claiming group relief and in any other case either that company or the company which if sub-paragraph (5) did not apply would be the surrendering company.

(7) This paragraph shall be construed as if it were contained in Chapter IV of Part X.

Capital allowances

8 Without prejudice to paragraphs 6 and 7 above, where a person is, immediately before the commencement of this Act, entitled to a capital allowance by virtue of any enactment repealed by this Act, he shall not cease to be so entitled by reason only of that repeal, notwithstanding that the enactment in question is not re-enacted by this Act; and accordingly the provisions of this Act shall apply, with any necessary modifications, so far as may be necessary to give effect to any such entitlement.

Social security benefits

9 (*Spent.*)

Commentary—*Simon's Direct Tax Service* E4.129, 328.

10–12 (Repealed by FA 1995 Sch 29 Pt VIII(8).)

Commentary—*Simon's Direct Tax Service* C4.346, 349, 362, 373.

General powers of amendment in Acts relating to overseas countries

13 Where under any Act passed before this Act and relating to a country or territory outside the United Kingdom there is a power to affect Acts passed or in force before a particular time, or instruments made or having effect under such Acts, and the power would but for the passing of this Act, have included power to change the law which is reproduced in, or is made or has effect under, this Act, then that power shall include power to make such provision as will secure the like change in the law reproduced in, or made or having effect under, this Act notwithstanding that it is not an Act passed or in force before that time.

Double taxation agreements

14 The repeal by this Act of section 16 of the Finance (No 2) Act 1979 shall not prejudice the effect of any Order in Council which gives effect to arrangements contained in the Convention mentioned in that section and is made under section 497 of the 1970 Act.

Securities

15 The repeal by this Act of Schedule 22 to the Finance Act 1985 shall not affect the continued operation of paragraph 6 of that Schedule in relation to the holding of securities by any person at any time during the year (within the meaning of that Schedule).

Building societies

16 Any enactment relating to building societies contained in this Act which re-enacts an enactment which was an existing enactment for the purposes of section 121 of the Building Societies Act 1986 shall continue to be an existing enactment for those purposes.

Pension business

17 Any reference to pension business in any enactment (other than an enactment repealed by this Act) which immediately before the commencement of this Act was such a reference by virtue of paragraph 11(3) of Part III of Schedule 5 to the Finance Act 1970 shall not be affected by the repeal by this Act of that paragraph and accordingly the business in question shall continue to be known as pension business.

Stock relief

18 Schedule 9 to the Finance Act 1981 shall continue to have effect in relation to any relief to which paragraph 9 or 17(1) of that Schedule applied immediately before the commencement of this Act notwithstanding the repeal by this Act of that Schedule.

[18A—(1) This paragraph applies in any case where a person is entitled to a relief to which Part II of Schedule 9 to the Finance Act 1981 applies (income tax: stock relief) for a year of assessment and—

(*a*) he and the inspector have come to an agreement, in writing, as to the extent to which the relief is to be given effect in that year (whether by deduction from profits or gains or by discharge or repayment of tax, or both); and

(*b*) no assessment giving effect to the relief is made for that year.

(2) In a case to which this paragraph applies the relief shall be taken to have been given effect in the year of assessment in question, as if an assessment had been made, to the extent set out in the agreement mentioned in subsection (1) above.]¹

Cross reference—See CAA 2001 Sch 3 para 114 (this paragraph continues to have effect in relation to any relief to which it applied before the commencement of CAA 2001 despite the repeal by CAA 2001 of CAA 1990 Sch 1 para 8(43)).
Amendments—¹ This paragraph inserted by CAA 1990 Sch 1 para 8(1), (43).

Schedule E emoluments

19 The repeal by this Act of section 21 of the Finance Act 1974 shall not affect the taxation of emoluments which if that section had been in force before 1973–74 would have fallen within Case I or Case II of Schedule E, and, accordingly, any such emoluments shall not be chargeable under Case III of Schedule E.

Unitary states

20 The repeal by this Act of section 54 of and Schedule 13 to the Finance Act 1985 shall not prevent the Treasury making an order under subsection (7) of section 54 exercising the powers conferred on the Treasury by that subsection in relation to distributions made in chargeable periods ending before 6th April 1988 and, accordingly, subsections (7) and (8) of section 54 shall continue to have effect in later chargeable periods for that purpose.

Continuity and construction of references to old and new law

21—(1) The continuity of the operation of the Tax Acts and of the law relating to chargeable gains shall not be affected by the substitution of this Act for the enactments repealed by this Act and earlier enactments repealed by and corresponding to any of those enactments ("the repealed enactments").

(2) Any reference, whether express or implied, in any enactment, instrument or document (including this Act and any Act amended by this Act) to, or to things done or falling to be done under or for the purposes of, any provision of this Act shall, if and so far as the nature of the reference permits, be construed as including, in relation to the times, years or periods, circumstances or purposes in relation to which the corresponding provision in the repealed enactments has or had effect, a reference to, or as the case may be to things done or falling to be done under or for the purposes of, that corresponding provision.

(3) Any reference, whether express or implied, in any enactment, instrument or document (including the repealed enactments and enactments, instruments and documents passed or made after the passing of this Act) to, or to things done or falling to be done under or for the purposes of, any of the repealed enactments shall, if and so far as the nature of the reference permits, be construed as including, in relation to the times, years or periods, circumstances or purposes in relation to which the corresponding provision in this Act has effect, a reference to, or as the case may be to things done or falling to be done under or for the purposes of, that corresponding provision.

(4) Any reference to Case VIII of Schedule D, whether a specific reference or one imported by more general words, in any enactment, instrument or document shall, in relation to the chargeable periods to which section 843(1) applies, be construed as a reference to Schedule A, and for the purposes of sub-paragraph (2) above, Schedule A in this Act shall be treated as corresponding to Case VIII of Schedule D in the repealed enactments, and any provision of this Act or of any Act passed after 12th March 1970 and before this Act referring to Schedule A shall be construed accordingly.

FINANCE ACT 1988

(1988 Chapter 39)

ARRANGEMENT OF SECTIONS

PART III

INCOME TAX, CORPORATION TAX AND CAPITAL GAINS TAX

CHAPTER I

GENERAL

PART IV
MISCELLANEOUS AND GENERAL

Inheritance tax

Sections 136–137 *(see Yellow Tax Handbook Part II, IHT)*

Petroleum revenue tax

Sections 138–139 (not printed)

Stamp duty and stamp duty reserve tax

Sections 140–144 *(see Orange Tax Handbook: Stamp duty)*

Miscellaneous

SCHEDULES:

An Act to grant certain duties, to alter other duties, and to amend the law relating to the National Debt and the Public Revenue, and to make further provision in connection with Finance.

[29th July 1988]

PART III
INCOME TAX, CORPORATION TAX AND CAPITAL GAINS TAX

CHAPTER I
GENERAL

23 Charge and basic rate of income tax for 1988–89

(spent).

Commentary—*Simon's Direct Tax Service* **E1.102; E2.105.**

24 Higher and additional rates of income tax

(1) (specifies the higher rate of income tax for the year 1988–89).

(2) (amends TA 1988 s 1(2),(3), (4), (6) (note, however, FA 1992 s 9(1), (6), (7), (10))).

(3) (amends TA 1988 s 694(2) and inserts s 694(2A)).

(4) (repealed by FA 1997 Sch 18 Pt VI(1) with effect from the year 1997–98).

Commentary—*Simon's Direct Tax Service* **E1.102.**

25 Personal reliefs

(1) (*amends* TA 1988 s 257(1), (2), (3), (5), *the amendment now being superseded*).

(2) (*disapplies* TA 1988 s 257(9) for the year 1988–89).

(3) (*repeals* TA 1988 ss 258, 263, 264 from the year 1988–89).

26 Charge and rate of corporation tax for financial year 1988

(*spent*).

Commentary—*Simon's Direct Tax Service* **D2.108.**

27 Corporation tax: small companies

(*Spent.*)

Commentary—*Simon's Direct Tax Service* **D2.109.**

28 Deduction rate for sub-contractors in construction industry

(*Amends TA* 1988 s 559(4), *the amendment now superseded*).

Amendments—This section repealed by FA 1995 Sch 29, Pt VIII(21), with effect in relation to payments made after 5 August 1999 (by virtue of Finance Act 1995, Section 139(3), (Appointed Day) Order, SI 1999/2156 art 2).

29 Life assurance premium relief

(1) (*amends* TA 1988 ss 266(5)(*a*), 274(3)(*a*) and Sch 14 para 3(3)(*a*)).

(2) This section shall have effect on and after 6th April 1989.

30 Additional relief in respect of children

(*Amended TA* 1988 s 259(2) *and inserted* s 259(4A); *repealed* by FA 1999 s 139, Sch 20 Pt III(4) with effect from the year 2000–01).

31 Non-residents' personal reliefs

(*Amends TA* 1988 s 278).

32 Abolition of aggregation of income

(*Repeals TA* 1988 s 279 *with effect from the year 1990–91*).

33 Personal allowance and married couple's allowance

(*Substitutes TA* 1988 ss 257–257F for the old s 257).

34 Jointly held property

(*Inserts TA* 1988 ss 282A, 282B).

35 Minor and consequential provisions

Schedule 3 to this Act (which makes provision consequential on sections 32 and 33 above and other minor amendments relating to the treatment for income tax purposes of husbands, wives, widowers and widows) shall have effect.

36 Annual payments

(1) (*inserts* TA 1988 ss 347A, 347B).

(2) (*inserts* TA 1970 ss 51A, 51B (*now repealed*)).

(3) This section shall have effect in relation to any payment falling due on or after 15th March 1988 unless it is made in pursuance of an existing obligation.

(4) In subsection (3) above "existing obligation" means a binding obligation—

    (*a*) under an order made by a court (whether in the United Kingdom or elsewhere) before 15th March 1988, or before the end of June 1988 on an application made on or before 15th March 1988;

    (*b*) under a deed executed or written agreement made before 15th March 1988 and received by an inspector before the end of June 1988;

    (*c*) under an oral agreement made before 15th March 1988, written particulars of which have been received by an inspector before the end of June 1988; or

    (*d*) under an order made by a court (whether in the United Kingdom or elsewhere) on or after 15th March 1988, or under a written agreement made on or after that date, where the order or agreement replaces, varies or supplements an order or agreement within this subsection;

but subject to subsection (5) below.

(5) An obligation within subsection (4)(*d*) above is an existing obligation only if—

    (*a*) it is an obligation to make periodical payments (not being instalments of a lump sum) which are made by a person—

        (i) as one of the parties to a marriage (including a marriage which has been dissolved or annulled) to or for the benefit of the other party to the marriage and for the maintenance of the other party, or

        (ii) to any person under 21 years of age for his own benefit, maintenance or education, or

(iii) to any person for the benefit, maintenance or education of a person under 21 years of age, and

(b) the order or agreement replaced, varied or supplemented provided for such payments to be made for the benefit, maintenance or, as the case may be, education of the same person.

[(5A) The reference in subsection (4)(d) above to an order made by a court, and the reference in subsection (5)(b) above to an order, in each case includes a reference to a maintenance assessment made under the Child Support Act 1991 or the Child Support (Northern Ireland) Order 1991.][1]

(6) Section 351 of the Taxes Act 1988 and section 65 of the Taxes Act 1970 shall not apply to any payment in relation to which this section has effect.

Commentary—*Simon's Direct Tax Service* A3.403; B5.301–303; E1.501–503.
Concession A52—Relief for maintenance payments made under this section and under existing regulations.
Revenue & other press releases—IR 9-2-94 (EEA Agreement extends relief to payments made after 31 December 1993 under court orders or written agreements).
Cross references—See TA 1988 s 347B(5) (relief for periodical maintenance payments becoming due after 5 April 1994); FA 1988 Sch 3 para 32 (application of this section to payments made after 5 April 1990 between spouses living together). FA 1994 s 79(2) (restriction on relief for maintenance payments, falling within sub-s (4)(a)–(c) above, becoming due after 5 April 1994).
Amendments—[1] Sub-s (5A) inserted by F(No 2)A 1992 s 62(2), (4) with effect from 6 April 1993 by virtue of F(No 2)A 1992 s 62 (Commencement) Order, SI 1992/2642.
Prospective amendments—In sub-s (5A) for the words "maintenance assessment made" there shall be substituted "maintenance calculation or maintenance assessment made respectively" by the Child Support, Pensions and Social Security Act 2000 ss 26, 86, Sch 3 para 9 with effect from a day to be appointed.

37 Maintenance payments under existing obligations: 1988–89

(*Spent.*)

38 Maintenance payments under existing obligations: 1989–90 onwards

(1) This section applies to any annual payment due in the year 1989–90 or any subsequent year of assessment which—

(a) is made in pursuance of an existing obligation under an order made by a court (whether in the United Kingdom or elsewhere) or under a written or oral agreement,

(b) is made by an individual—

(i) as one of the parties to a marriage (including a marriage which has been dissolved or annulled) to or for the benefit of the other party to the marriage and for the maintenance of the other party, or

(ii) to any person under 21 years of age for his own benefit, maintenance or education, or

(iii) to any person for the benefit, maintenance or education of a person under 21 years of age, and

(c) is (apart from this section) within the charge to tax under Case III or Case V of Schedule D, and is not by virtue of Part XV of the Taxes Act 1988 treated for any purpose as the income of the person making it.

(2) A payment to which this section applies shall not be a charge on the income of the person liable to make it ...[6]

(3)–(6) ...[6]

(7) A payment to which this section applies shall be made without deduction of income tax.

(8) ...[6]

[(8A) The reference in subsection (1)(a) above to an order made by a court includes a reference to a maintenance assessment made under the Child Support Act 1991 or under the Child Support (Northern Ireland) Order 1991.][2]

(9) No deduction shall be made under section 65(1)(b)[, 68(1)(b) or 192(3)][1] of the Taxes Act 1988 on account of a payment to which this section applies.

Commentary—*Simon's Direct Tax Service* E5.108.
Concessions A12—Although maintenance payments paid by a non-resident under a UK court order or agreement is income from a UK source, relief by way of credit under TA 1988 s 793 is allowed if the conditions specified in the concession are met.
Statements of Practice SP 15/80—The payer of maintenance payments which include school fees paid directly to the child's school is allowed tax relief on the fees if specified conditions are satisfied.
Revenue Interpretation RI 100—Revenue practice of granting relief for 1989–90 and subsequent years of assessment, on the payments due and made in 1988–89 even where the payer's income for that year was insufficient to give him entitlement to relief, to be withdrawn with effect for new claims made from February 1995. Claimants who already receive relief on this basis will not be affected.
Revenue & other press releases—IR 9-2-94 (EEA Agreement extends relief to payments made after 31 December 1993 under court orders or written agreements).
Amendments—[1] Words in sub-s (9) inserted by F(No 2)A 1992 s 60 with effect from the year 1992–93.
[2] Sub-s (8A) inserted by F(No 2)A 1992 s 62(3), (4) with effect from 6 April 1993 by virtue of F(No 2)A 1992 s 62 (Commencement) Order, SI 1992/2642.
[3] Words in sub-s (2), and sub-ss (3)–(6), (8), repealed by FA 1999 s 139, Sch 20 Pt III(6) with effect for any payment falling due after 5 April 2000.
Prospective amendments—In sub-s (8A) for the words "maintenance assessment made" there shall be substituted "maintenance calculation or maintenance assessment made respectively" by the Child Support, Pensions and Social Security Act 2000 ss 26, 86, Sch 3 para 9 with effect from a day to be appointed.

39 Maintenance payments under existing obligations: election for new rules

Commentary—*Simon's Direct Tax Service* **E5.109.**
Amendments—This section repealed by FA 1999 s 139, Sch 20 Pt III(6) with effect for any payment falling due after 5 April 2000.

40 Provisions supplementary to sections 37 to 39

(1) In sections 37 to 39 above—

...²

"existing obligation" has the same meaning as in section 36(3) above.

(2) ...²

(3) ...¹

Commentary—*Simon's Direct Tax Service* **E5.108.**
Amendments—¹ Sub-s (3) repealed by FA 1988 Sch 14 Pt VIII with effect from the year 1990–91.
² Definition of "child of the family" in sub-s (1), and whole of sub-s (2), repealed by FA 1999 s 139, Sch 20 Pt III(6) with effect for any payment falling due after 5 April 2000.

Relief for interest

41 Qualifying maximum for loans

(*Enacts* TA 1988 s 367(5) *qualifying maximum for the year 1988–89*).

Commentary—*Simon's Direct Tax Service* **A3.431; E1.538, 539.**

42 Home loans: restriction of relief

Amendments—¹ This section repealed by FA 1999 s 139, Sch 20 Pt III(7) with effect for payments of interest made—
 –after 5 April 2000;
 –after 8 March 1999 and before 6 April 2000 in respect of interest falling due after 5 April 2000; or
 –after 8 March 1999 and before 6 April 2000 under a scheme made for a tax avoidance purpose after 8 March 1999.

43 Home improvement loans

Commentary—*Simon's Direct Tax Service* **A3.431; E1.536.**
Amendments—¹ This section repealed by FA 1999 s 139, Sch 20 Pt III(7) with effect for payments of interest made—
 –after 5 April 2000;
 –after 8 March 1999 and before 6 April 2000 in respect of interest falling due after 5 April 2000; or
 –after 8 March 1999 and before 6 April 2000 under a scheme made for a tax avoidance purpose after 8 March 1999.

44 Loans for residence of dependent relative etc

Commentary—*Simon's Direct Tax Service* **A3.431; E1.537.**
Amendments—¹ This section repealed by FA 1999 s 139, Sch 20 Pt III(7) with effect for payments of interest made—
 –after 5 April 2000;
 –after 8 March 1999 and before 6 April 2000 in respect of interest falling due after 5 April 2000; or
 –after 8 March 1999 and before 6 April 2000 under a scheme made for a tax avoidance purpose after 8 March 1999.

Benefits in kind

45 Car benefits

(*substituted* TA 1988 Sch 6 Pt I, *with effect from 1988–89, and is now superseded*).

46 Car parking facilities

(1)–(4) (*amend* TA 1988 s 141(6) and *insert* s 141(6A), 142(3A), 155(1A), 197A)).

(5) This section shall have effect for the year 1988–89 and subsequent years of assessment.

47 Entertainment: non-cash vouchers

(1) (*insert* TA 1988 s 141(6B)).

(2)–(4) (*amend* F(No 2)A 1975, s 36 (now repealed)).

48 Entertainment: credit tokens

(1) (*insert* TA 1988 s 142(3B)).

(2), (3) (*insert* F(No 2)A 1975, s 36A(3A) (now repealed)).

49 Entertainment of directors and higher-paid employees

(1) (*add* TA 1988 s 155(7)).

(2), (3) (*add* FA 1976 s 62(9) (now repealed)).

Business expansion scheme

50 Private rented housing

(*repealed by* FA 1994 Sch 26 Pt V(17) *in relation to shares issued after 31 December 1993*).

Commentary—*Simon's Direct Tax Service* E3.225.

51 Restriction of relief

(1) (*amends* TA 1988 s 289(12)(*b*) and inserts TA 1988 s 290A).

(2) (*amends* FA 1983 Sch 5 para 2(7) and *inserts* para 3A (*now repealed*)).

52 Valuation of interests in land

(1) (*inserts* TA 1988 s 294(5A)).

(2) This section shall have effect in relation to valuations which fall to be made after the passing of this Act.

53 Approved investment funds

(1) (*substitutes* TA 1988 s 311(2A), (2B), (3) for sub-s (3)).

(2) This section shall have effect in relation to approved funds closing after 15th March 1988.

Pensions etc

54 Personal pension schemes: commencement

(1) (*amends* TA 1988 s 655(4)).

(2) (*amends* TA 1988 s 618(1), (2), 632(3), 655(2), (3), (5)).

(3) The amendments made by this section shall be deemed always to have had effect.

55 Personal pension schemes: other amendments

(1) (*amends* TA 1988 s 630).

(2) (*substitutes* TA 1988 s 638(7), (8) for sub-s (7)).

(3) (*substitutes* TA 1988 s 686(2)(*c*)).

(4) The amendments made by this section shall be deemed to have come into force on 1st July 1988.

56 Occupational pension schemes

(*substitutes* TA 1988 Sch 23 para 1(2), (2A) for sub-para (2)).

57 Lump sum benefits paid otherwise than on retirement

(*amends* TA 1988 s 189 and FA 1973 s 14).

Underwriters

58 Assessment and collection

(1) (*substitutes* TA 1988 s 450(2)).

(2)–(4) (*spent*).

(5) Subsections (1) ... shall have effect for the year 1988–89 and subsequent years of assessment ...

59 Reinsurance: general

(1) (*substitutes* TA 1988 s 450(4)(*b*)).

(2) (*spent*).

(5) Subsection (1) above shall have effect for the year 1988–89 and subsequent years of assessment ...

60 Reinsurance to close

(1) (*substitutes* TA 1988 s 450(5)).

(2) (*spent*).

(3) ...

61 Minor and consequential amendments

(1) (*amends* TA 1988 ss 20, 451, 452).

(2)–(4) (*spent*).

(5) Subsection (1) above shall have effect for the year 1988–89 and subsequent years of assessment ...

Miscellaneous

65 Commercial woodlands

Schedule 6 to this Act (which abolishes the charge to tax under Schedule B and makes other provision with respect to the occupation of commercial woodlands) shall have effect.

66 Company residence

(1) Subject to the provisions of Schedule 7 to this Act, a company which is incorporated in the United Kingdom shall be regarded for the purposes of the Taxes Acts as resident there; and accordingly, if a different place of residence is given by any rule of law, that place shall no longer be taken into account for those purposes.

(2) For the purposes of the Taxes Acts, a company which—

(a) is no longer carrying on any business; or
(b) is being wound up outside the United Kingdom,

shall be regarded as continuing to be resident in the United Kingdom if it was so regarded for those purposes immediately before it ceased to carry on business or, as the case may be, before any of its activities came under the control of a person exercising functions which, in the United Kingdom, would be exercisable by a liquidator.

(3) In this section "the Taxes Acts" has the same meaning as in the Taxes Management Act 1970.

(4) This section and Schedule 7 to this Act shall be deemed to have come into force on 15th March 1988.

Commentary—*Simon's Direct Tax Service* **D4.101, 102.**
Statement of Practice SP 1/90—This Statement interprets (a) various terms used in Sch 7 of this Act (b) the case law where the
incorporation rule enacted in this section does not have relevance and (c) the effect of double taxation agreements where a
company is regarded as resident in the UK and also in other countries.
SP2/90—Guidance notes for migrating companies: notice and arrangements for payment of tax.
Revenue & other press releases—IR 24-2-93 (Helpline for companies becoming resident in the UK).
Revenue Internal Guidance—International Tax Handbook ITH 300–371 (the law of company residence).
Company Taxation Manual COT3373 (flow chart for determining company residence).
COT3378–3381 (shelf companies, dormant companies and "nowhere" companies).
COT3383 (central management and control test relevant only to companies incorporated abroad).
COT3385–3387 (circumstances when Revenue will question residence).
COT3388–3391 (discussion of the central management and control test).
Cross references—See FA 1994 s 249(3) (certain companies to be regarded as non-resident even if incorporated in the UK).

67 Seafarers: foreign earnings

Amendments—This section repealed by FA 1998 Sch 27 Part III(11) with effect in relation to emoluments attributable to
qualifying periods beginning on or after 17 March 1998 and to qualifying periods beginning before 17 March 1998 which are
received on or after that date. Sub-s (1) inserted TA 1988 Sch 12 para 3(2A) (now repealed).

68 Priority share allocations for employees etc

(1) Where—

(a) there is [a bona fide offer]⁵ to the public of shares in a company at a fixed price or by tender, and
(b) a director or employee (whether of that company or of any other company or person) is entitled by reason of his office or employment to an allocation of the shares, in priority to members of the public, ...³, and
(c) the conditions set out in subsection (2) below are satisfied,

any benefit derived by the director or employee from his entitlement shall not be treated as an emolument of his office or employment.

[(1ZA) A case falls within this subsection if—

(a) there is a bona fide offer to the public of a combination of shares in two or more companies at a fixed price or by tender ("the public offer");
(b) there is at the same time an offer ("the employee offer") of shares, or of a combination of shares, in any one or more, but not all, of those companies—
(i) to directors or employees, or
(ii) to directors or employees and to other persons,
(whether the directors or employees are directors or employees of any of those companies, or of any other company or person); and
(c) any of those directors or employees is entitled, by reason of his office or employment, to an allocation of shares under the employee offer in priority to any allocation to members of the public under the public offer.]⁶

[(1ZB) In any case falling within subsection (IZA) above—

(a) the public offer and the employee offer shall be regarded for the purposes of subsection (1) above as together constituting a single offer of shares to the public, notwithstanding the difference in the shares to which each offer relates;

(b) the reference to "the shares" in paragraph (b) of that subsection shall be taken as a reference to any of the shares which, in consequence of paragraph (a) above, are to be regarded as subject to that single offer; and

(c) in the following provisions of this section references to the offer or to shares subject to the offer shall be construed accordingly.]⁶

[(1A) Where, disregarding the amount or value of any registrant discount made to the director or employee in respect of the shares of the company (or, in a case falling within subsection (1ZA) above, of the company in question), the price payable by him for the shares of that company which are allocated to him under the offer—

(a) in a case not falling within subsection (1ZA) above, is less than the fixed price or the lowest price successfully tendered, or

(b) in a case falling within that subsection, is not the same as, or as near as reasonably practicable to, the appropriate notional price for the shares of that company,

subsection (1) above shall not apply to the benefit (if any) represented by the difference in price.]⁷

(2) The conditions referred to in subsection (1) above are—

[(a) that the aggregate number of shares subject to the offer that may be allocated as mentioned in subsection (1)(b) above does not exceed the limit specified in subsection (2A) below or, as the case may be, either of the limits specified in subsection (2B) below]²;

(b) that all the persons entitled to such an allocation are entitled to it on similar terms;

(c) that those persons are not restricted wholly or mainly to persons who are directors or whose remuneration exceeds a particular level.

[(2A) Except where subsection (2B) below applies, the limit relevant for the purposes of subsection (2)(a) above is 10 per cent of the shares subject to the offer (including the shares that may be allocated as mentioned in subsection (1)(b) above).]¹

(2B) Where the offer is part of arrangements which include one or more other offers to the public of shares of the same class, the limits relevant for the purposes of subsection (2)(a) above are—

(a) 40 per cent of the shares subject to the offer (including the shares that may be allocated as mentioned in subsection (1)(b) above), and

(b) 10 per cent of all the shares of the class in question (including the shares that may be so allocated) that are subject to any of the offers forming part of the arrangements.]¹

[(2C) In a case falling within subsection (1ZA) above, the condition in paragraph (a) of subsection (2) above shall be taken to be satisfied in relation to the offer if, and only if, it is separately satisfied with respect to the shares in each one of the companies which are subject to that offer; and for this purpose only, any reference in that paragraph or in subsection (2A) or (2B) above to shares is a reference to shares in the particular company in question.]⁶

(3) For the purposes of subsection (2)(b) above the fact that different provision is made for persons according to the levels of their remuneration, the length of their service or similar factors shall not be regarded as meaning that they are not entitled to an allocation on similar terms.

[(3A) The fact that the allocations of shares in the company [(or, in a case falling within subsection (1ZA) above, any one or more of the companies to which the offer relates)]⁸ to which persons who are not directors or employees of the company are entitled are smaller than those to which directors or employees of the company are entitled shall not be regarded for the purposes of subsection (2)(b) above as meaning that they are not entitled on similar terms if—

(a) each of the first-mentioned persons is also entitled, by reason of his office or employment and in priority to members of the public, to an allocation of shares in another company or companies which are offered to the public (at a fixed price or by tender) at the same time as the shares in the company, and

(b) in the case of each of those persons the aggregate value (measured by reference to the fixed price or the lowest price successfully tendered) of all the shares included in the allocations to which he is entitled is the same, or as nearly the same as is reasonably practicable, as that of the shares in the company included in the entitlement of a comparable director or employee of the company.]⁴

(4) Section [17(1) of the Taxation of Chargeable Gains Act 1992]¹⁰ (assets deemed to be acquired at market value) shall not apply to any acquisition in relation to which sub-section (1) above applies.

(5) In this section "director" includes a person who is to be, or has ceased to be, a director and "employee" includes a person who is to be, or has ceased to be, an employee; ["the public offer" and "the employee offer" have the meaning given by paragraphs (a) and (b) of subsection (1ZA) above.]⁹

[(5A) For the purposes of this section, there is a "registrant discount" in respect of the shares of a company in any case where—

(a) in connection with the offer, members of the public who comply with such requirements as may be imposed in that behalf are, or may become, entitled to a discount in respect of the whole or some part of the shares of that company which are allocated to them; and

(b) at least 40 per cent of the shares of that company which are allocated to members of the public other than employees and directors are allocated to individuals who are or become entitled either to that discount or to some other benefit of similar value for which they may elect as an alternative to the discount; and

(c) directors or employees who either—

(i) subscribe for shares under the offer (or, in a case falling within subsection (1ZA) above, under the public offer) as members of the public, or

(ii) subscribe for shares under the employee offer, as directors or employees,

and who comply (or, in the case of a requirement to register, are taken under the terms of the offer to comply) with the same requirements as are mentioned in paragraph (a) above, are, or may become, entitled to the same discount in respect of the shares of the company as any other members of the public to whom shares of that company are allocated under the offer;

and any reference in this section to the amount or value of the registrant discount made to a director or employee is a reference to the amount of any such discount made to him as is mentioned in paragraph (c) above or, as the case may be, the value of any such other benefit as is mentioned in paragraph (b) above which is conferred upon him as an alternative to the discount.

(5B) For the purposes of this section, in a case falling within subsection (1ZA) above "the appropriate notional price" for the shares of any of the companies subject to the offer is such price as—

(a) had the shares of that company, and of each of the other companies, instead of being subject to the offer, been subject to separate offers to the public in respect of each company at fixed prices, and

(b) had those separate offers been made at the time at which the public offer was in fact made,

might reasonably have been expected to be the fixed price for the shares of that company under the separate offer of those shares; but where subsection (5C) below applies, the amount determined in accordance with this subsection as the notional price for the shares of any company shall be varied in accordance with that subsection.

(5C) If the amounts determined in accordance with subsection (5B) above as the appropriate notional prices for the shares of each of the companies subject to the public offer are such that, had the price for the combination of shares subject to the public offer been determined by aggregating the appropriate notional price (as so determined) for each one of the shares comprised in the combination, the price for the combination would have been different from the actual fixed price or (as the case may be) lowest successfully tendered price, then those amounts shall each be varied by multiplying them by the fraction of which—

(a) the numerator is the actual fixed or lowest successfully tendered price for the combination of shares subject to the public offer; and

(b) the denominator is the different price mentioned above;

and those amounts, as so varied, shall be the appropriate notional prices for the purposes of this section.]⁶

(6) This section shall apply to offers made on or after 23rd September 1987.

Commentary—*Simon's Direct Tax Service* E4.506.
Revenue Internal Guidance—Share Schemes Manual SSM 6.3–6.9 (application of this section).
Amendments—¹ Sub-ss (2A), (2B) inserted by FA 1989 s 66 in relation to offers made after 10 October 1988.
² Sub-s (2)(a) substituted by FA 1989 s 66.
³ Words in sub-s (1) repealed by FA 1989 s 66and Sch 17, Pt IV in relation to offers made after 10 October 1988.
⁴ Sub-s (3A) inserted by FA 1990 s 79 in relation to offers made after 25 July 1990.
⁵ Words in sub-s (1)(a) substituted by FA 1991 s 44(1), (2) in relation to offers made after 15 January 1991.
⁶ Sub-ss (1ZA), (1ZB), (2C), (5A), (5B), (5C) inserted by FA 1991 s 44(1), (3), (5), (8) in relation to offers made after 15 January 1991.
⁷ Sub-s (1A) substituted by FA 1991 s 44(1), (4) in relation to offers made after 15 January 1991.
⁸ Words in sub-s (3A) inserted by FA 1991 s 44(1), (6).
⁹ Definitions of "the public offer" and "the employee offer" in sub-s (5) inserted by FA 1991 s 44(1), (7).
¹⁰ Words in sub-s (4) substituted by TCGA 1992 Sch 10 para 16(1), (3).

69 Share options: loans

(1) (amends TA 1988 Sch 9 para 13).

(2) (inserted FA 1984 Sch 10 para 10(3) (now repealed).

70 Charities: payroll deduction scheme

(1) (amends TA 1988 s 202(7) (which provision, as amended, is now superseded)).

(2) This section shall have effect from the year 1988–89.

71 Unit trusts: relief on certain payments

(inserts TA 1988 s 469(5A)–(5D)).

72 Entertainment of overseas customers

(1) Subsection (2) of section 577 of the Taxes Act 1988 (which excepts the entertainment of overseas customers from the general rule that entertainment expenses are not deductible for tax purposes) shall not have effect in relation to entertainment provided on or after 15th March 1988.

(2) Subsection (1) above shall not apply where the expenses incurred or the assets used in providing the entertainment were incurred or used under a contract entered into before 15th March 1988.

73 Consideration for certain restrictive undertakings

(1) (*amends* TA 1988 s 313).

(2) Notwithstanding anything in section 74 of the Taxes Act 1988, any sum to which section 313 of that Act applies, and which is paid or treated as paid by a person carrying on a trade, profession or vocation, may be deducted as an expense in computing the [profits][1] of the trade, profession or vocation for the purposes of tax.

(3) Any sum to which section 313 of the Taxes Act 1988 applies, and which is paid or treated as paid by an investment company, shall for the purposes of section 75 of that Act be treated as an expense of management.

(4) This section has effect in relation to sums paid or treated as paid in respect of the giving of, or the total or partial fulfilment of, undertakings given on or after 9th June 1988.

Commentary—*Simon's Direct Tax Service* B3.1429; E4.481.
Amendments—[1] Words substituted by FA 1998 Sch 7 para 2 with effect from 31 July 1998.

74 Payments on termination of office or employment etc

Amendments—Repealed by FA 1998 s 165, Sch 27 Part III(9) in relation to payments or other benefits received after 5 April 1998, except where the payment or other benefit or the right to receive it has been brought into charge to tax before 6 April 1998 (FA 1998 s 58(4)).

75 Premiums for leases etc

(*Repeals TA* 1988 ss 39(3), 780(5) and Sch 2).

76 Foreign dividends etc, quoted Eurobonds and recognised clearing systems

(1)–(6) ...[1], [2]

Amendments—[1] Sub-ss (1)–(3), (5) repealed by FA 1996 Sch 7 para 32, Sch 41 Pt V(2) with effect for income tax from the year 1996–97 and for corporation tax for accounting periods ending after 31 March 1996.
[2] Sub-ss (4), (6) repealed by FA 1996 Sch 41 Pt V(19) with effect from 29 April 1996.

CHAPTER II
UNAPPROVED EMPLOYEE SHARE SCHEMES

Construction—TCGA 1992 s 120(1) to be construed as if it were contained in this Chapter; see TCGA 1992 s 120(1).
Revenue Internal Guidance—Share Schemes Manual SSM 5.2–5.56 (Revenue interpretation of this Chapter).
Cross references—See TCGA 1992 s 120(1) (increase in expenditure for the purposes of capital gains tax by reference to tax charged in relation to shares, etc under this Chapter).

Preliminary

77 Scope of Chapter

(1) [Subject to [section 140A of the Taxes Act 1988 and][3] subsections (2) to (4) below][1], this Chapter shall apply where, on or after 26th October 1987, a person acquires shares or an interest in shares in a company in pursuance of a right conferred on him or an opportunity offered to him by reason of his office as a director of, or his employment by, that or any other company.

(2) This Chapter shall not apply in relation to an acquisition by a person who is not chargeable to tax under Case I of Schedule E in respect of the office or employment in question.

(3) This Chapter shall not apply where the acquisition is made in pursuance of an offer to the public.

[(4) Where, in a case falling within subsection (1ZA) of section 68 above, subsection (1) of that section—

(a) applies or applied in relation to such a benefit as is there mentioned, or
(b) would so apply or have applied, had there been any such benefit,

any acquisition made on or after 16th January 1991 in pursuance of any of the offers which, in that case, fall to be regarded by virtue of subsection (1ZB) of that section as together constituting a single offer of shares to the public for the purposes of subsection (1) of that section shall be regarded for the purposes of subsection (3) above as an acquisition made in pursuance of an offer to the public.][2]

Commentary—*Simon's Direct Tax Service* E4.517.
Revenue & other press releases—ICAEW TR739 February 1989 (Revenue confirmation that an option to acquire shares is not an "interest in shares").
Amendments—[1] Words in sub-s (1) substituted by FA 1991 s 44(9), (10).
[2] Sub-s (4) added by FA 1991 s 44(9), (10).
[3] Words in sub-s (1) inserted by FA 1998 s 50(2) with effect in relation to interests acquired on or after 17 March 1998.

Charges to tax

78 Charge where restrictions removed etc

(1) The person acquiring the shares or interest in shares shall be chargeable to tax if—

(*a*) a chargeable event occurs in relation to the shares at a time when he has not ceased to have a beneficial interest in them, and

(*b*) the shares are shares in a company which was not a dependent subsidiary at the time of the acquisition and is not a dependent subsidiary at the time of the chargeable event.

(2) Subject to subsections (4) and (5) below, any of the following events is a chargeable event in relation to shares in a company for the purposes of this section if it increases, or but for the occurrence of some other event would increase, the value of the shares—

(*a*) the removal or variation of a restriction to which the shares are subject;

(*b*) the creation or variation of a right relating to the shares;

(*c*) the imposition of a restriction on other shares in the company or the variation of a restriction to which such other shares are subject;

(*d*) the removal or variation of a right relating to other shares in the company.

(3) A charge by virtue of this section shall be a charge under Schedule E, for the year of assessment in which the chargeable event occurs, on the amount by which the value of the shares is increased by the chargeable event or the amount by which it would be increased but for the occurrence of some other event (or, if the interest of the person chargeable is less than full beneficial ownership, on an appropriate part of that amount).

(4) An event is not a chargeable event in relation to shares in a company for the purposes of this section unless the person who acquired the shares or interest has been a director or employee of—

(*a*) that company, or

(*b*) (if it is different) the company as a director or employee of which he acquired the shares or interest, or

(*c*) an associated company of a company within paragraph (*a*) or (*b*) above,

at some time during the period of seven years ending with the date on which the event occurs.

(5) An event is not a chargeable event for the purposes of this section if it consists of—

(*a*) the removal of a restriction to which all shares of a class are subject from all those shares,

(*b*) the variation of such a restriction in the case of all those shares,

(*c*) the creation of a right relating to all shares of a class,

(*d*) the variation of such a right in the case of all those shares,

(*e*) the imposition of a restriction on all shares of a class, or

(*f*) the removal of a right relating to all shares of a class from all those shares,

and any of the conditions in subsection (6) below is satisfied.

(6) The conditions referred to in subsection (5) above are—

(*a*) that at the time of the event the majority of the company's shares of the same class as those which, or an interest in which, the person acquired are held otherwise than by or for the benefit of—

    (i) directors or employees of the company,

    (ii) an associated company of the company, or

    (iii) directors or employees of any such associated company;

(*b*) that at the time of the event the company is employee-controlled by virtue of holdings of shares of that class;

(*c*) that at the time of the event the company is a subsidiary which is not a dependent subsidiary and its shares are of a single class.

(7) References in this section to restrictions to which shares are subject, or to rights relating to shares, include references to restrictions imposed or rights conferred by any contract or arrangement or in any other way.

Commentary—*Simon's Direct Tax Service* **E4.518**
Revenue Internal Guidance—Share Schemes Manual SSM 7.21 (definition of value as applied in these sections).
Cross references—See FA 2000 Sch 8 para 80(1), (2) (exclusions of certain charges under this section in relation shares of a participant in an employee share ownership plan).
FA 2000 Sch 14 para 55 (a charge under this section applies in respect of shares acquired under an enterprise management incentive option).
Revenue & other press releases—IR 14-4-88 (Management buy-outs: where the proportion of equity represented by managers' shares is increased on a pre-determined basis in line with the company's performance, and rights are attached to the shares from the outset, this section does not apply).

79 Charge for shares in dependent subsidiaries

(1) The person acquiring the shares or interest in shares shall be chargeable to tax if the shares are shares in a company which—

(*a*) was a dependent subsidiary at the time of the acquisition, or

(*b*) was not a dependent subsidiary at that time but becomes a dependent subsidiary before the person making the acquisition ceases to have any beneficial interest in the shares,

and there is a chargeable increase in the value of the shares.

(2) There is a chargeable increase in the value of shares in a case within subsection (1)(*a*) above if the value of the shares at the earlier of—

(*a*) the expiration of seven years from the time of the acquisition, and

(*b*) the time when the person making the acquisition ceases to have any beneficial interest in the shares,

exceeds their value at the time of the acquisition.

(3) Subject to subsection (7) below, there is a chargeable increase in the value of shares in a case within subsection (1)(*b*) above if the value of the shares at the earlier or earliest of—

(*a*) the expiration of seven years from the time when the company becomes a dependent subsidiary, and

(*b*) the time when the person making the acquisition ceases to have any beneficial interest in the shares, and

(*c*) if the company ceases to be a dependent subsidiary, the time when it does so,

exceeds their value at the time when the company becomes a dependent subsidiary.

(4) A charge by virtue of this section shall be a charge under Schedule E, for the year of assessment which includes the end of the period for which the chargeable increase is determined, on an amount equal to that increase (or, if the interest of the person chargeable is less than full beneficial ownership, on an appropriate part of that amount).

(5) Where, in accordance with the terms on which the acquisition was made, the consideration for the acquisition is subsequently increased, the amount chargeable to tax by virtue of this section shall be reduced by an amount equal to the increase in the consideration.

(6) Where, in accordance with those terms, the person making the acquisition subsequently ceases to have a beneficial interest in the shares by a disposal made for a consideration which is less than the value of the shares or his interest in them at the time of the disposal, the amount on which tax is chargeable by virtue of this section shall be reduced so as to be equal to the excess of that consideration over the value of the shares or interest at the time of the acquisition.

[(6A) If, before the time by reference to which the chargeable increase is determined, an event occurs by virtue of which the person making the acquisition becomes chargeable to tax under section 140A(4) of the Taxes Act 1988 (employee's interest in shares ceasing to be only conditional) on any amount ("the charged amount") in respect of the shares, the amount on which tax is chargeable by virtue of this section shall be reduced by the charged amount.][1]

[(6B) If, before the time by reference to which the chargeable increase is determined, an event occurs by virtue of which the person making the acquisition becomes chargeable to tax under section 140D(3) of the Taxes Act 1988 (charge on conversion of convertible shares) on any amount ("the charged amount") in respect of the shares, the amount on which tax is chargeable by virtue of this section shall be reduced by the charged amount.][2]

(7) In a case within subsection (1)(*b*) above there is no chargeable increase in the value of shares in a company unless the person who acquired the shares or interest has been a director or employee of—

(*a*) that company, or

(*b*) (if it is different) the company as a director or employee of which he acquired the shares or interest, or

(*c*) an associated company of a company within paragraph (*a*) or (*b*) above,

at some time during the period of seven years ending with the time when the company becomes a dependent subsidiary.

Commentary—*Simon's Direct Tax Service* **E4.519.**
Revenue Internal Guidance—Share Schemes Manual SSM 7.21 (definition of value as applied in these sections).
Cross references—See TCGA 1992 s 120(1) (increase in expenditure for the purposes of capital gains tax charged in relation to shares, etc under this Chapter).
FA 2000 Sch 8 para 80(3) (no charge to income tax under this section for any shares that are subject to an approved employee share ownership plan at the end of the period for which the chargeable increase is determined).
FA 2000 Sch 14 para 55 (a charge under this section applies in respect of shares acquired under an enterprise management incentive option).
Amendments—[1] Sub-s (6A) inserted by FA 1998 s 50(3) with effect in relation to interests acquired on or after 17 March 1998.
[2] Sub-s (6B) inserted by FA 1998 s 51(2) with effect in relation to shares acquired on or after 17 March 1998.

80 Charge on special benefits

(1) Subject to subsections (5) and (6) below, the person acquiring the shares or interest in shares shall be chargeable to tax if he receives a special benefit by virtue of his ownership of or interest in the shares.

[(1A) If when a benefit is received the company is a dependent subsidiary and its shares are of a single class, the benefit is a special benefit for the purposes of subsection (1) above.][1]

[(2) A benefit which does not fall within subsection (1A) above is a special benefit for the purposes of subsection (1) above unless—

(*a*) when it becomes available it is available to at least ninety per cent of the persons who then hold shares of the same class as those which, or an interest in which, the person acquired, and

(*b*) any of the conditions in subsection (3) below is satisfied.][1]

(3) The conditions referred to in subsection (2) above are—

(*a*) that when the benefit is received the majority of the company's shares [in respect of which the benefit is received][2] are held otherwise than by or for the benefit of—

    (i) directors or employees of the company,
    (ii) an associated company of the company, or
    (iii) directors or employees of any such associated company;

(*b*) that when the benefit is received the company is employee-controlled by virtue of holdings of shares of the class concerned;

(*c*) that when the benefit is received the company is a subsidiary which is not a dependent subsidiary and [the majority of its shares in respect of which the benefit is received are held otherwise than by or for the benefit of—

    (i) directors or employees of the company,
    (ii) a company which is an associated company of the company but is not its parent company, or
    (iii) directors or employees of a company which is an associated company of the company][2].

[(3A) For the purposes of subsection (3)(*c*)(ii) above a company is another company's parent company if the second company is a subsidiary of the first.][2]

(4) A charge by virtue of this section shall be a charge under Schedule E, for the year of assessment in which the benefit is received, on an amount equal to the value of the benefit.

(5) Subsection (1) above shall apply only if the person receiving the benefit has been a director or employee of—

(*a*) the company referred to in that subsection, or
(*b*) (if it is different) the company as a director or employee of which he acquired the shares or interest, or
(*c*) an associated company of a company within paragraph (*a*) or (*b*) above,

at some time during the period of seven years ending with the date on which the benefit is received.

(6) A benefit shall not be chargeable by virtue of this section if it is chargeable to income tax apart from this section.

Commentary—*Simon's Direct Tax Service* E4.520.
Revenue Internal Guidance—Share Schemes Manual SSM 7.21 (definition of value as applied in these sections).
Cross references—See TCGA 1992 s 120(1) (increase in expenditure for the purposes of capital gains by reference to tax charged in relation to shares, etc under this Chapter).
FA 2000 Sch 14 para 55 (a charge under this section applies in respect of shares acquired under an enterprise management incentive option).
Amendments—[1] Sub-ss (1A), (2) substituted for sub-s (2) by F(No 2)A 1992 s 37 in relation to benefits received after 11 November 1991.
[2] Words in sub-s (3)(*a*), (*c*) substituted and sub-s (3A) inserted by F(No 2)A 1992 s 37.

Miscellaneous

81 Changes in interest

Where a person's interest in shares is increased or reduced he shall be treated for the purposes of this Chapter as acquiring or disposing of a separate interest proportionate to the increase or reduction.

Commentary—*Simon's Direct Tax Service* E4.521.

82 Company reorganisations etc

(1) Subsection (2) below applies where—

(*a*) a person has acquired shares or an interest in shares as mentioned in section 77 above (those shares being referred to in subsection (2) below as "the originally-acquired shares"); and
(*b*) by virtue of his holding of those shares or the interest in them he acquires (whether or not for consideration) additional shares or an interest in additional shares (those shares being referred to in subsection (2) below as "the additional shares").

(2) Where this subsection applies—

(*a*) the additional shares or the interest in them shall be treated for the purposes of this Chapter as having been acquired as mentioned in section 77 above and as having been acquired at the same time as the originally-acquired shares or the interest in them;
(*b*) for the purposes of section 79 above, the additional shares and the originally-acquired shares shall be treated as one holding of shares and the value of the shares comprised in that holding at any time shall be determined accordingly (the value of the originally-acquired shares at the time of acquisition being attributed proportionately to all the shares in the holding); and
(*c*) for the purposes of that section, any consideration given for the acquisition of the additional shares or the interest in them shall be taken to be an increase falling within subsection (5) of that section in the consideration for the original acquisition.

(3) If, on a person ceasing to have a beneficial interest in any shares, he acquires other shares or an interest in other shares and the circumstances are such that, for the purposes of sections [127 to 130 of the Taxation of Chargeable Gains Tax 1992][1] (reorganisations etc) the shares in which he ceases

to have a beneficial interest constitute "original shares" and the other shares constitute a "new holding"—

    (a) section [127][1] of that Act (which equates the original shares and the new holding) shall apply for the purposes of this Chapter; and

    (b) if any such consideration is given for the new holding as is mentioned in section [128(1) and (2)][1] of that Act, it shall be treated for the purposes of this Chapter as an increase falling within section 79(5) above in the consideration for the shares; and

    (c) if any such consideration is received for the disposal of the original shares as is mentioned in section [128(3)][1] of that Act, the consideration shall be apportioned among the shares comprised in the new holding and the amount which, apart from this paragraph, would at any subsequent time be the value of any of those shares shall be taken to be increased by the amount of the consideration apportioned to them.

Commentary—*Simon's Direct Tax Service* **E4.521.**
Amendments—[1] Words and numbers in sub-s (3) substituted by TCGA 1992 Sch 10 para 16(1), (4).

83 Connected persons etc

(1) For the purposes of this Chapter, where a person acquires shares or an interest in shares in a company in pursuance of a right conferred on him or opportunity offered to him as a person connected with a director or employee of that or any other company, the shares or interest shall be deemed to be acquired by the director or employee.

(2) For the purposes of this Chapter, where a person who acquires shares or an interest in shares disposes of the shares or interest otherwise than by a bargain at arm's length with a person who is not connected with him, he shall be deemed to continue to have a beneficial interest in the shares until there is a disposal of the shares or interest by such a bargain.

(3) Subsection (2) above shall not apply where shares, or an interest in shares, in a company are disposed of to the company in accordance with the terms on which the acquisition was made.

(4) Where a person who has made an acquisition as mentioned in subsection (1) above receives a benefit in the circumstances described in section 80 above, the benefit shall be treated for the purposes of that section as received by the person deemed by that subsection to have made the acquisition; and where at a time when a person is deemed by subsection (2) above to continue to have a beneficial interest in shares another person receives a benefit in such circumstances, the benefit shall be treated for those purposes as received by him.

Commentary—*Simon's Direct Tax Service* **E4.521.**
Cross references—See TCGA 1992 s 120(1) (increase in expenditure for the purposes of capital gains tax by reference to tax charged in relation to shares, etc under this Chapter).

84 Capital gains tax

Where an amount is chargeable to tax under this Chapter on a person who acquires shares or an interest in shares, then on the first disposal of the shares (whether by him or another person) after his acquisition, section [38(1)(a)][1] of the Taxation of Chargeable Gains Act 1992[1] (expenditure allowable in computation of chargeable gains) shall apply as if a sum equal to the amount chargeable had formed part of the consideration given by the person making the disposal for his acquisition of the shares; and this section shall apply with the appropriate modifications in a case to which section 83 above applies.

Commentary—*Simon's Direct Tax Service* **E4.522.**
Amendments—[1] Words substituted by TCGA 1992 Sch 10 para 16(1), (5).

85 Information

(1) Where in any year of assessment a person acquires shares, or an interest in shares, in a company in the circumstances described in section 77(1) above, that company and (if it is different) the company as a director or employee of which he acquires the shares or interest shall give written particulars of the acquisition to the inspector within [92 days][1] of the end of the year.

(2) Where—

    (a) there occurs in relation to shares in a company an event which is a chargeable event for the purposes of section 78 above, or

    (b) a person receives a special benefit (within the meaning given for the purposes of section 80(1) above) in respect of shares, or an interest in shares, in a company,

the company, and (if it is different) the company as a director or employee of which the person who acquired the shares or an interest in the shares made the acquisition, shall within 60 days give to the inspector written particulars of the event or benefit and of the shares concerned.

(3) (*amends* TMA 1970 s 98).

Commentary—*Simon's Direct Tax Service* **E4.524.**
Amendments—[1] Words in sub-s (1) substituted by FA 2000 s 56(3) with effect where the event giving rise to the duty to deliver particulars occurs after 5 April 2000.

Supplementary

86 Meaning of "dependent subsidiary"

(1) For the purposes of this Chapter a company which is a subsidiary is a dependent subsidiary throughout a period of account of the company unless—

(*a*) the whole or substantially the whole of the company's business during the period of account (taken as a whole) is business carried on with persons who are not members of the same group as the company,

(*b*) during the period of account either there is no increase in the value of the company as a result of intra-group transactions, or any such increase in value does not exceed 5 per cent of the value of the company at the beginning of the period (or a proportionately greater or smaller percentage in the case of a period which is longer or shorter than a year),

(*c*) the directors of the principal company of the group give to the inspector, not later than two years after the end of the period of account, a certificate that in their opinion the conditions mentioned in paragraphs (*a*) and (*b*) above are satisfied in relation to the period of account, and

(*d*) there is attached to the certificate a report addressed to those directors by the auditors of the subsidiary that the auditors—

(i) have enquired into the state of affairs of the company with particular reference to the conditions mentioned in paragraphs (*a*) and (*b*) above, and

(ii) are not aware of anything to indicate that the opinion expressed by the directors in their certificate is unreasonable in all the circumstances.

(2) For the purposes of subsection (1)(*a*) above business carried on with any subsidiary of the company concerned shall be treated as carried on with a person who is not a member of the same group as the company unless the whole or substantially the whole of the business of that or any other subsidiary of the company during the company's period of account (taken as a whole) is carried on with members of the group other than the company and its subsidiaries.

(3) In this section—

"group" means a principal company and all its subsidiaries;

"intra-group transactions" means transactions between companies which are members of the same group on terms which are not such as might be expected to be agreed between persons acting at arm's length (other than any payment for group relief, within the meaning given in section 402(6) of the Taxes Act 1988);

...¹

"principal company" means a company of which another company is a subsidiary and which is not itself a subsidiary of another company.

Commentary—*Simon's Direct Tax Service* **E4.519.**
Amendments—¹ In sub-s (3), the following definition of "period of account" repealed by FA 2002 s 141, Sch 40 Pt 3(16) with effect from 24 July 2002—

" 'period of account', in relation to a company, means the period for which it makes up its accounts;".

87 Other interpretation provisions

(1) In this Chapter, except where the context otherwise requires,—

"associated company" has the same meaning as, by virtue of section 416 of the Taxes Act 1988, it has for the purposes of Part XI of that Act;

"director" includes a person who is to be, or who has ceased to be, a director;

"employee" includes a person who is to be, or who has ceased to be, an employee;

"shares" includes stock and also includes securities as defined in section 254(1) of the Taxes Act 1988;

"subsidiary" means 51 per cent. subsidiary;

"value", in relation to shares or a benefit, means the amount which the person holding the shares or receiving the benefit might reasonably expect to obtain from a sale in the open market;

and references to an interest in any shares include references to an interest in the proceeds of sale of part of the shares.

(2) For the purposes of this Chapter a company is "employee-controlled" by virtue of shares of a class if—

(*a*) the majority of the company's shares of that class (other than any held by or for the benefit of an associated company) are held by or for the benefit of employees or directors of the company or a company controlled by the company, and

(*b*) those directors and employees are together able as holders of the shares to control the company.

(3) Sections 839 (connected persons) and 840 (control) of the Taxes Act 1988 shall apply for the purposes of this Chapter.

(4) Where a right to acquire shares or an interest in shares in a company is assigned to a person and the right was conferred on some other person by reason of the assignee's office as a director of, or his employment by, that or any other company, the assignee shall be treated for the purposes of this

Chapter as acquiring the shares or interest in pursuance of a right conferred on him by reason of that office or employment.

Commentary—*Simon's Direct Tax Service* E4.517, 518.

88 Transitional provisions

(1) Section 138 of the Taxes Act 1988 and section 79 of the Finance Act 1972 shall not apply to an acquisition of shares, or of an interest in shares, made on or after 26th October 1987.

(2) Where—

(a) tax is chargeable by virtue of section 138(1)(a) of the Taxes Act 1988 or section 79(4) of the Finance Act 1972 by reference to the market value, after 26th October 1987, of shares in a company which is not a dependent subsidiary on that date, and

(b) that market value is greater than the market value of the shares on 26th October 1987,

the amount on which tax is chargeable (and the question whether any tax is chargeable) shall be determined by reference to the market value on 26th October 1987 (and for this purpose "market value" has the same meaning as in section 138 of the Taxes Act 1988).

(3) Subject to subsection (4) below, this Chapter, with the omission of sections 79 and 80, shall have effect where shares, or an interest in shares, in a company which is not a dependent subsidiary on 26th October 1987 have been acquired before that date as it has effect (apart from this section) where shares or an interest in shares are acquired on or after that date.

(4) In relation to shares which were, or an interest in which was, acquired before 26th October 1987 the removal or variation of a restriction to which the shares are subject shall not be a chargeable event for the purposes of section 78 above if, because of paragraph 7 of Schedule 8 to the Finance Act 1973, the restriction would not have been regarded as one to which the shares were subject for the purposes of section 79(2)(c) of the Finance Act 1972.

Commentary—*Simon's Direct Tax Service* E4.523.

89 Consequential amendments

(a) (*amends* TA 1988 ss 185(3)(a), 186(2)(b)).

(b) (*amends* FA 1978 s 53(3)(b); FA 1980 s 47(1)(b); FA 1984 s 38(3)(a) (all of which are now repealed).

CHAPTER III
CAPITAL ALLOWANCES

90 Buildings or structures sold by exempt bodies
(*Repealed by* CAA 1990 Sch 2).

91 Sales without change of control
(*Repealed by* CAA 1990 Sch 2).

92 Successions to trades between connected persons
(*Repealed by* CAA 1990 Sch 2).

93 Safety at sports grounds
(*Repealed by* CAA 1990 Sch 2).

94 Quarantine premises
(*Repealed by* CAA 1990 Sch 2).

95 Dwelling-houses let on assured tenancies
(*Repealed by* CAA 1990 Sch 2).

Commentary—*Simon's Direct Tax Service* B2.902.

CHAPTER IV
CAPITAL GAINS
Re-basing to 1982

96 Assets held on 31st March 1982
(*Repealed by* TCGA 1992 Sch 12).

Commentary—*Simon's Direct Tax Service* C2.601, 603, 604; C2.705.

97 Deferred charges on gains before 31st March 1982

(Repealed by TCGA 1992 Sch 12).

Unification of rates of tax on income and capital gains

98 Rates of capital gains tax

(Repealed by TCGA 1992 Sch 12).

Commentary—*Simon's Direct Tax Service* **C1.107.**

99 Husband and wife

(Repealed by TCGA 1992 Sch 12).

Commentary—*Simon's Direct Tax Service* **C1.202.**

100 Accumulation and discretionary settlements

(Repealed by TCGA 1992 Sch 12).

Commentary—*Simon's Direct Tax Service* **C1.107.**

101 Underwriters

(Repealed by TCGA 1992 Sch 12).

102 Other special cases

(Repealed by TCGA 1992 Sch 12).

Commentary—*Simon's Direct Tax Service* **C1.107.**

103 Commencement of sections 98 to 102

(Repealed by TCGA 1992 Sch 12).

Married couples

104 Married couples

(Repealed by TCGA 1992 Sch 12).

Commentary—*Simon's Direct Tax Service* **C1.605.**

Company migration

105 Deemed disposal of assets on company ceasing to be resident in UK

(1)–(5) ...[1]

(6) ...[2]

(7) This section and sections 106 and 107 below shall be deemed to have come into force on 15th March 1988.

Amendments—[1] Sub-ss (1)–(5) repealed by TCGA 1992 Sch 12.
[2] Sub-s (6) repeals TA 1988 s 765(1)(*a*), (*b*) and amends s 765(1)(*c*).

106 Deemed disposal of assets on company ceasing to be liable to UK tax

(Repealed by TCGA 1992 Sch 12).

Commentary—*Simon's Direct Tax Service* **D4.108.**

107 Postponement of charge on deemed disposal

(Repealed by TCGA 1992 Sch 12).

Commentary—*Simon's Direct Tax Service* **D4.108, 113.**

Miscellaneous

108 Annual exempt amount for 1988–89

(Repealed by TCGA 1992 Sch 12).

Commentary—*Simon's Direct Tax Service* **C1.401, 402.**

109 Gains arising from certain settled property

(Repealed by TCGA 1992 Sch 12).

110 Retirement relief

(Repealed by TCGA 1992 Sch 12).

111 Dependent relative's residence

(*Repealed by* TCGA 1992 Sch 12).

Commentary—*Simon's Direct Tax Service* **C2.1311.**

112 Roll-over relief

(*Repealed by* TCGA 1992 Sch 12).

113 Indexation: building societies etc

(*Repealed by* TCGA 1992 Sch 12).

Commentary—*Simon's Direct Tax Service* **C2.303; D4.773.**

114 Indexation: groups and associated companies

(*Repealed by* TCGA 1992 Sch 12).

115 Transfers within a group

(*Repealed by* TCGA 1992 Sch 12).

116 Personal equity plans

(*Repealed by* TCGA 1992 Sch 12).

117 Definition of "investment trust"

(1) (*amends* TA 1988 s 842).

(2) The repeal by the Finance (No 2) Act 1987 of section 93 of the Finance Act 1972 shall be treated as not having extended to subsection (6) of that section (amendment of definition of "investment trust" in section 359 of the Taxes Act 1970).

(3) (*amends the* Companies Act 1985 s 266 *and the* Companies (Northern Ireland) Order 1986, SI 1986—1032, art 274).

(4) Subsections (1) and (3) above shall have effect for companies' accounting periods ending after 5th April 1988 and subsection (2) above shall have effect for companies' accounting periods ending on or before that date.

Commentary—*Simon's Direct Tax Service* **D4.422.**

118 Amendments of Finance Act 1985 s 68

(*Repealed by* TCGA 1992 Sch 12).

CHAPTER V
MANAGEMENT
Assessment

119 Current year assessments

(*Inserts TMA* 1970 s 29(1)(*c*), (1A)).

Returns of income and gains

120 Notice of liability to income tax

(1) (*substitutes* TMA 1970 s 7 and is now superseded).

(2) This section has effect with respect to notices required to be given for the year 1988–89 or any subsequent year of assessment.

121 Notice of liability to corporation tax

Amendments—This section repealed by FA 1998 s 165, Sch 27 Part III(28) with effect in relation to accounting periods ending after 30 June 1999 (by virtue of Finance Act 1994, Section 199, (Appointed Day) Order, SI 1998/3173 art 2).

122 Notice of liability to capital gains tax

(1) (*inserted* TMA 1970 s 11A (now repealed)).

(2) (*substituted* TMA 1970 s 12(1) (now repealed)).

(3) This section has effect with respect to notices required to be given for the year 1988–89 or any subsequent year of assessment.

Other returns and information

123 Three year time limit

(1)–(4) (*add* TMA 1970 ss 13(3), 19(4), *amend* TMA 1970 s 17(1) and *insert* TMA 1970 s 18(3A) thereof).

(5) This section has effect with respect to notices given after the passing of this Act.

124 Returns of fees, commissions etc

(1) (*adds* TMA 1970 s 16(8)).

(2) This section has effect with respect to payments made in the year 1988–89 or any subsequent year of assessment.

125 Other payments and licences etc

(*Inserts* TMA 1970 s 18A).

Production of accounts, books etc

126 Production of documents relating to a person's tax liability

(1) (*amended* TMA 1970 s 20(4)(*b*), *repealed by* FA 1989 s 187(1), Sch 17 Pt VIII, *with respect to notices given, or warrant issued, after 26 July 1989*).

(2)–(4) (*amend* TMA 1970 ss 20(7), 20B(1), (2), (4), (8), (9) and *insert* TMA 1970 s 20(8A), (8B)).

(5) (*amends* National Savings Bank Act 1971 s 12(3)).

(6) The amendments made by this section have effect with respect to notices given after the passing of this Act.

127 Production of computer records etc

(1) Any provision made by or under the Taxes Acts which requires a person—

    (*a*) to produce, furnish or deliver any document or cause any document to be produced, furnished or delivered; or

    (*b*) to permit the Board, or an inspector or other officer of the Board—

        (i) to inspect any document, or

        (ii) to make or take extracts from or copies of or remove any document,

shall have effect as if any reference in that provision to a document [were a reference to anything in which information of any description is recorded and any reference to a copy of a document were a reference to anything onto which information recorded in the document has been copied, by whatever means and whether directly or indirectly].[1]

(2) In connection with tax, a person authorised by the Board to exercise the powers conferred by this subsection—

    (*a*) shall be entitled at any reasonable time to have access to, and inspect and check the operation of, any computer and any associated apparatus or material which is or has been in use in connection with any document to which this subsection applies; and

    (*b*) may require—

        (i) the person by whom or on whose behalf the computer is or has been so used, or

        (ii) any person having charge of, or otherwise concerned with the operation of, the computer, apparatus, or material,

to afford him such reasonable assistance as he may require for the purposes of paragraph (*a*) above.

(3) Subsection (2) above applies to any document[, within the meaning given by subsection (1) above,][1] which a person is or may be required by or under any provision of the Taxes Acts—

    (*a*) to produce, furnish or deliver, or cause to be produced, furnished or delivered; or

    (*b*) to permit the Board, or an inspector or other officer of the Board, to inspect, make or take extracts from or copies of or remove.

(4) Any person who—

    (*a*) obstructs a person authorised under subsection (2) above in the exercise of his powers under paragraph (*a*) of that subsection, or

    (*b*) fails to comply within a reasonable time with a requirement under paragraph (*b*) of that subsection,

shall be liable to a penalty not exceeding £500.

(5) ...[2]

(6) This section shall be construed as if it were contained in the Taxes Management Act 1970.

Commentary—*Simon's Direct Tax Service* A3.150.

Amendments—[1] Words in sub-ss (1), (3) substituted by the Civil Evidence Act 1995, Sch 1 para 13, with effect from 31 January 1997.
[2] Sub-s (5) repealed by the Civil Evidence Act 1995 Sch 2 with effect from 31 January 1997.

Interest and penalties

128 Interest on overdue or overpaid PAYE

(*Substitutes* TA 1988 s 203(2)(*d*), (*dd*) for s 203(2)(*d*), *adds* sub-s (9)).

129 Two or more tax-geared penalties in respect of same tax

(1) (*inserts* TMA 1970 s 97A).

(2) Section 97A(*a*) of that Act has effect with respect to the year 1988–89 or any subsequent year of assessment; and section 97A(*b*) has effect with respect to accounting periods ending after 31st March 1989.

Company migration

130 Provisions for securing payment by company of outstanding tax

(1) The requirements of subsections (2) and (3) below must be satisfied before a company ceases to be resident in the United Kingdom otherwise than in pursuance of a Treasury consent.

(2) The requirements of this subsection are satisfied if the company gives to the Board—

(*a*) notice of its intention to cease to be resident in the United Kingdom, specifying the time ("the relevant time") when it intends so to cease;

(*b*) a statement of the amount which, in its opinion, is the amount of the tax which is or will be payable by it in respect of periods beginning before that time; and

(*c*) particulars of the arrangements which it proposes to make for securing the payment of that tax.

(3) The requirements of this subsection are satisfied if—

(*a*) arrangements are made by the company for securing the payment of the tax which is or will be payable by it in respect of periods beginning before the relevant time; and

(*b*) those arrangements as so made are approved by the Board for the purposes of this subsection.

(4) If any question arises as to the amount which should be regarded for the purposes of subsection (3) above as the amount of the tax which is or will be payable by the company in respect of periods beginning before the relevant time, that question shall be referred to the Special Commissioners, whose decision shall be final.

(5) If any information furnished by the company for the purpose of securing the approval of the Board under subsection (3) above does not fully and accurately disclose all facts and considerations material for the decision of the Board under that subsection, any resulting approval of the Board shall be void.

(6) In this section "Treasury consent" means a consent under section 765 of the Taxes Act 1988 (restrictions on the migration etc of companies) given for the purposes of subsection (1)(*a*) of that section.

(7) In this section and sections 131 and 132 below any reference to the tax payable by a company includes a reference to—

(*a*) any amount of tax which it is liable to pay under regulations made under section 203 of the Taxes Act 1988 (PAYE);

(*b*) any income tax which it is liable to pay in respect of payments to which section 350(4)(*a*) of that Act (company payments which are not distributions) applies;

(*c*) any amount representing income tax which it is liable to pay under—

(i) regulations made under section 476(1) of that Act (building societies);

(ii) section 479 of that Act (interest paid on deposits with banks etc); or

(iii) section 555 of that Act (entertainers and sportsmen);

(*d*) any amount which it is liable to pay under section 559(4) of that Act (sub-contractors in the construction industry); and

(*e*) any amount which it is liable to pay under paragraph 4 of Schedule 15 to Finance Act 1973 (territorial extension of charge of tax).

(8) In this section and section 132 below any reference to the tax payable by a company in respect of periods beginning before any particular time includes a reference to any interest on the tax so payable, or on tax paid by it in respect of such periods, which it is liable to pay in respect of periods beginning before or after that time.

(9) In this section and sections 131 and 132 below any reference to a provision of the Taxes Act 1988 shall be construed, in relation to any time before 6th April 1988, as a reference to the corresponding enactment repealed by that Act.

(10) This section and sections 131 and 132 below shall be deemed to have come into force on 15th March 1988.

Commentary—*Simon's Direct Tax Service* **D4.131.**
Statement of Practice SP1/90—Company residence.
SP 2/90—This Statement explains the procedure to be followed by migrating companies in respect of their obligations under this section.

Cross references—See FA 1994 s 250(1) (certain companies treated as non-resident by virtue of FA 1994 s 249 even if they would otherwise be regarded as resident; sub-ss (1)–(6) above not to apply to such companies ceasing to be treated as resident on 30 November 1993).

131 Penalties for failure to comply with section 130

(1) If a company fails to comply with section 130 above at any time, it shall be liable to a penalty not exceeding the amount of tax which is or will be payable by it in respect of periods beginning before that time and which has not been paid at that time.

(2) If, in relation to a company ("the migrating company"), any person does or is party to the doing of any act which to his knowledge amounts to or results in, or forms part of a series of acts which together amount to or result in, or will amount to or result in, the migrating company failing to comply with section 130 above at any time and either—

(a) that person is a person to whom subsection (3) below applies; or
(b) the act in question is a direction or instruction given (otherwise than by way of advice given by a person acting in a professional capacity) to persons to whom that subsection applies,

that person shall be liable to a penalty not exceeding the amount of tax which is or will be payable by the migrating company in respect of periods beginning before that time and which has not been paid at that time.

(3) This subsection applies to the following persons, namely—

(a) any company which has control of the migrating company; and
(b) any person who is a director of the migrating company or of a company which has control of the migrating company.

(4) In any proceedings against any person to whom subsection (3) above applies for the recovery of a penalty under subsection (2) above—

(a) it shall be presumed that he was party to every act of the migrating company unless he proves that it was done without his consent or connivance; and
(b) it shall, unless the contrary is proved, be presumed that any act which in fact amounted to or resulted in, or formed part of a series of acts which together amounted to or resulted in, or would amount to or result in, the migrating company failing to comply with section 130 above was to his knowledge such an act.

(5) References in this section to a company failing to comply with section 130 above are references to the requirements of subsections (2) and (3) of that section not being satisfied before the company ceases to be resident in the United Kingdom otherwise than in pursuance of a Treasury consent; and in this subsection "Treasury consent" has the same meaning as in that section.

(6) In this section and section 132 below "director", in relation to a company—

(a) has the meaning given by subsection (8) of section 168 of the Taxes Act 1988 (read with subsection (9) of that section); and
(b) includes any person falling within subsection (5) of section 417 of that Act (read with subsection (6) of that section);

and any reference to a person having control of a company shall be construed in accordance with section 416 of that Act.

Commentary—*Simon's Direct Tax Service* **D4.131.**
Cross references—See FA 1994 s 250(1) (certain companies treated as non-resident by virtue of FA 1994 s 249 even if they would otherwise be regarded as resident; sub-ss (1)–(5) above not to apply to such companies ceasing to be treated as resident on 30 November 1993).

132 Liability of other persons for unpaid tax

(1) This section applies where—

(a) a company ("the migrating company") ceases to be resident in the United Kingdom at any time; and
(b) any tax which is payable by the migrating company in respect of periods beginning before that time is not paid within six months from the time when it becomes payable.

(2) The Board may, at any time before the end of the period of three years beginning with the time when the amount of the tax is finally determined, serve on any person to whom subsection (3) below applies a notice—

(a) stating particulars of the tax payable, the amount remaining unpaid and the date when it became payable; and
(b) requiring that person to pay that amount within thirty days of the service of the notice.

(3) This subsection applies to the following persons, namely—

(a) any company which is, or within the relevant period was, a member of the same group as the migrating company; and
(b) any person who is, or within the relevant period was, a controlling director of the migrating company or of a company which has, or within that period had, control over the migrating company.

(4) Any amount which a person is required to pay by a notice under this section may be recovered from him as if it were tax due and duly demanded of him; and he may recover any such amount paid by him from the migrating company.

(5) A payment in pursuance of a notice under this section shall not be allowed as a deduction in computing any income, profits or losses for any tax purposes.

(6) In this section—

"controlling director", in relation to a company, means a director of the company who has control of it;

"group" has the meaning which would be given by section [170 of the Taxation of Chargeable Gains Act 1992][1] if in that section ...[2]for references to 75 per cent. subsidiaries there were substituted references to 51 per cent. subsidiaries;

"the relevant period" means—

(a) where the time when the migrating company ceases to be resident in the United Kingdom is less than twelve months after 15th March 1988, the period beginning with that date and ending with that time;

(b) in any other case, the period of twelve months ending with that time.

Commentary—*Simon's Direct Tax Service* D4.131.
Revenue Internal Guidance—Company Taxation Manual COT3419 (s 132 applies whether or not arrangements have been made under s 130 or penalties have been incurred).
Statement of Practice SP1/90—Company residence.
Cross references—See FA 2000 Sch 29 para 15(2) (the main amendments made to TCGA 1992 s 170 by FA 2000 Sch 29 para 1 have effect for the purposes of this section with effect for cases in which the migrating company ceases to be resident in the UK after 31 March 2000).
FA 2000 Sch 29 para 15(3) (any question as to whether a company was a member of a group during the period of twelve months ending when the migrating company ceased to be resident in the UK after 31 March 2000 is determined in accordance with TCGA 1992 s 170 as amended by FA 2000 Sch 29, para 1).
Amendments—[1] Words in the definition of "group" in sub-s (6) substituted by TCGA 1992 Sch 10 para 16(1), (6).
[2] Words in sub-s (6) repealed by FA 2000 ss 102, 156, Sch 29 para 15(1), (2), Sch 40 Pt II(12) with effect in relation to cases in which the migrating company ceases to be resident in the UK after 31 March 2000.

Appeals etc

133 Jurisdiction of General Commissioners

(1) ...[1]

(2) (*substitutes* TMA 1970 s 44(2)).

(3) The amendment made by subsection (1) above shall have effect in relation to proceedings instituted on or after 1st January 1989; and the amendment made by subsection (2) above shall have effect in relation to proceedings instituted after the passing of this Act.

Amendments—[1] Sub-s (1) (which inserted TMA 1970 s 44(1A), (1B)) repealed by FA 1996 Sch 41 Pt V(12) with effect for any proceedings from the year 1996–97 and any proceedings relating to an accounting period ending after 30 June 1999 (by virtue of Finance Act 1994, Section 199, (Appointed Day) Order, SI 1998/3173 art 2).

134 General Commissioners for Northern Ireland

(1), (2) (*amend* TMA 1970 s 2 and *repeal* TMA 1970 ss 58(1), 59).

(3) ...[1]

(4) This section and section 135 below shall come into force on such day as the Lord Chancellor may by order made by statutory instrument appoint.

(5) Subject to the following provisions of this section, the preceding provisions of this section and section 135(2) below shall not affect any proceedings instituted before the day appointed under subsection (4) above.

(6) Subject to subsection (8) below, where—

(a) before the day appointed under subsection (4) above proceedings in Northern Ireland have been instituted before the Special Commissioners but not determined by them, and

(b) the proceedings might have been instituted before the General Commissioners if they had been proceedings in Great Britain,

they shall be transferred to the General Commissioners; and subsection (3) of section 58 of the Taxes Management Act 1970 shall apply for the purposes of this subsection as for those of that section (the reference to proceedings in Great Britain being construed accordingly).

(7) Section 44 of that Act shall apply in relation to proceedings transferred to the General Commissioners under subsection (6) above as it applies to proceedings instituted before them; and in the case of an appeal so transferred a notice of election under rule 3 or 5 of Schedule 3 to that Act may be given at any time before the end of the period of thirty days beginning with the day appointed under subsection (4) above.

(8) Subsection (6) above shall not apply in relation to proceedings if—

(a) before the end of that period an election that the proceedings be not transferred is made by any of the parties to the proceedings and written notice of the election is given to the other parties to the proceedings, or (*b*) they are proceedings under section 100 of the Taxes Management Act 1970 (recovery of penalties);

but subsections (5A) to (5E) of section 31 of that Act shall apply in relation to an election under paragraph (*a*) of this subsection in respect of an appeal against an assessment or the decision of an inspector on a claim as they apply in relation to an election under subsection (4) of that section.

(9) The Lord Chancellor may by order made by statutory instrument make provision supplementing or modifying the effect of subsections (5) to (8) above; and an order under this subsection shall be subject to annulment in pursuance of a resolution of either House of Parliament.

Commentary—*Simon's Direct Tax Service* **A2.507.**
Amendment—¹ Sub-s (3) repealed by FA 1999 s 139, Sch 20 Pt III(4) with effect from the year 2000–01.

135 Cases stated in Northern Ireland

(1) (*repealed by* General and Special Commissioners (Amendment of Enactments) Regulations 1994, SI 1994—1813 reg 2(2), Sch 2 Pt I).

(2) (*substitutes* TMA 1970 s 58(3)).

PART IV
MISCELLANEOUS AND GENERAL
Miscellaneous

145 Building societies: change of status

Schedule 12 to this Act (which makes provision in connection with the transfer of a building society's business to a company in accordance with the Building Societies Act 1986) shall have effect.

146 Post-consolidation amendments

The enactments specified in Schedule 13 to this Act shall have effect subject to the amendments specified in that Schedule (being amendments to correct errors in the Taxes Act 1988 and in the amendments made by the Finance Act 1987 for the purposes of the consolidation effected by the Taxes Act 1988).

147 Interpretation etc

(1) In this Act "the Taxes Act 1970" means the Income and Corporation Taxes Act 1970 and "the Taxes Act 1988" means the Income and Corporation Taxes Act 1988.

(2) (*not relevant to this publication*).

(3) Part III of this Act, so far as it relates to income tax, shall be construed as one with the Income Tax Acts, so far as it relates to corporation tax, shall be construed as one with the Corporation Tax Acts and, so far as it relates to capital gains tax, shall be construed as one with the Capital Gains Tax Act 1979.

149 Short title

This Act may be cited as the Finance Act 1988.

SCHEDULES

Section 35

SCHEDULE 3

MARRIED COUPLES: MINOR AND CONSEQUENTIAL PROVISIONS

PART I

AMENDMENTS OF THE TAXES ACT 1988
Introductory

1 The Taxes Act 1988 shall have effect subject to the following amendments.

Commencement of trade etc

2 (*inserts* TA 1988 s 62(2A)).

Discontinuance of trade etc

3 (*amends* TA 1988 s 63(1)(*b*), (2)).

Underpayments

4 (*inserts* TA 1988 s 203(3A)).

Additional relief in respect of children

5, 6 (*Repealed* by FA 1999 s 139, Sch 20 Pt III(4) with effect from the year 2000–01).

Widow's bereavement allowance

7 (Sub-paras (1), (2) *lapsed* on repeal of TA 1988, s 262 by FA 1999 ss 34, 139, Sch 20 Pt III(5) with effect for deaths occurring after 5 April 2000; sub-para (3) *repealed* by FA 1999 s 139, Sch 20 Pt III(5) with effect for deaths occurring after 5 April 2000.)

Blind person's allowance

8 (*Amends* TA 1988 s 265).

Life assurance premiums

9 (*Amends* TA 1988 s 266).

Payments securing annuities

10 (*Substitutes* TA 1988 s 273).

Married couples living together

11 (*Amends* TA 1988 s 282).

Business expansion scheme

12 (*Spent*).

Commentary—*Simon's Direct Tax Service* E3.213, 240.

Qualifying maintenance payments

13 (*amends* TA 1988 s 347B(3)).

Home loans

14 (*substitutes* TA 1988 s 356B).

Amendments—This paragraph repealed by FA 1999 s 139, Sch 20 Pt III(7) with effect for payments of interest within FA 1999 s 38(3), (4).

Loans for shares in employee-controlled company

15—(1) (*Amends* TA 1988 s 361).

(2) Sub-paragraph (1) above shall have effect in relation to payments of interest made on or after 6th April 1990 unless the proceeds of the loan were used before that date to defray money applied as mentioned in section 361(3).

(3) Interest paid on a loan made on or after 6th April 1990 to defray money applied in paying off another loan shall not be eligible for relief by virtue of paragraph (*b*) of subsection (3) of section 361 unless—

(*a*) the proceeds of the loan paid off were used on or after 6th April 1990 to defray money applied as mentioned in that subsection, or

(*b*) those proceeds were so used before that date but interest on the loan paid off would have been eligible for relief had they been so used on or after that date.

Close company loans

16—(1) (*amends* TA 1988 s 420(2)(*a*)(i)).

(2) This paragraph shall apply where the loan first mentioned in section 420(2) is made on or after 6th April 1990.

Trade unions and employers' associations

17—(1) (*amends* TA 1988 s 467(2)).

(2) This paragraph shall apply for any chargeable period beginning on or after 6th April 1990.

Retirement benefit schemes

18—(1) (*Amends* TA 1988 s 590).

(2) This paragraph shall have effect on and after 6th April 1990.

Partnership retirement annuities

19 (*amends* TA 1988 s 628(1)).

20 (*repealed by* FA 1995 Sch 29 Pt VIII (8) *with effect from the year 1995–96*).

Earned income

21 (*amends* TA 1988 s 833(4)(*a*)).

Total income

22 (*amends* TA 1988 s 835(5)).

PART II
OTHER PROVISIONS
Capital allowances

23, 24 (*repealed* by CAA 1990 Sch 2).

The transition

25 The operation of section 279(1) of the Taxes Act 1988 for a year of assessment earlier than the year 1990–91 in the case of a married woman shall not affect the question whether there is any income of hers chargeable to income tax for the year 1990–91 or any subsequent year of assessment or, if there is, what is to be taken to be its amount for income tax purposes.

Commentary—*Simon's Direct Tax Service* E5.103.

Returns

26–28 (*Spent*).

Commentary—*Simon's Direct Tax Service* A3.107; E5.103.

Time limits for assessments

29 (*repealed by* FA 1989 Sch 17 Pt VIII, subject to FA 1989 s 149(7) (ie not affecting the making of assessments for years of assessments before 1983–84 or for accounting periods which ended before 3 April 1983).).

Commentary—*Simon's Direct Tax Service* A3.228.

Transfers of allowances

30 (*Inserts* TMA 1970 s 37A from the year 1990–91).

Class 4 social security contributions

31 (*repealed in part by the* Social Security (Consequential Provisions) Act 1992 s 3(1), Sch 1, *and fully by the* Social Security (Consequential Provisions) (Northern Ireland) Act 1992 s 3(1), Sch1).

Annual payments

32 Section 36 of this Act shall have effect in relation to a payment which is due from a husband to his wife or from a wife to her husband at a time after 5th April 1990 when they are living together, notwithstanding that the payment is made in pursuance of an obligation which is an existing obligation for the purposes of subsection (3) of that section.

Commentary—*Simon's Direct Tax Service* E5.103.

Maintenance payments

33 (*Repealed by* FA 1994 Sch 26 Pt V(1) *in relation to payments becoming due after 5 April 1994*).

SCHEDULE 4

BUSINESS EXPANSION SCHEME: PRIVATE RENTED HOUSING

Section 50

Amendments—This Schedule repealed by FA 1994 Sch 26 Pt V(17) in relation to shares issued after 31 December 1993.

SCHEDULE 5

UNDERWRITERS: ASSESSMENT AND COLLECTION OF TAX

Section 58

Note—This Schedule inserts FA 1973 Sch 16A and TA 1988 Sch 19A, both Schedules being identical. FA 1973 Sch 16A is now spent and TA 1988 Sch 19A is now repealed.

SCHEDULE 6

COMMERCIAL WOODLANDS

Section 65

Commentary—*Simon's Direct Tax Service* **Divisions A5.1, A5.2; B3.506.**

Preliminary

1 In this Schedule "commercial woodlands" means woodlands in the United Kingdom which are managed on a commercial basis and with a view to the realisation of profits.

Abolition of charge under Schedule B

2—(1) The charge to tax under Schedule B in respect of the occupation of commercial woodlands is hereby abolished.

(2) In any case where, as respects an accounting period of a company which begins before and ends on or after 6th April 1988, the charge to tax under Schedule B has effect in relation to one part of that period but does not have effect in relation to the other part—

(*a*) the income deemed to arise to the company for that period from the occupation of the woodlands concerned shall be apportioned between those parts; and

(*b*) so much of that income as is apportioned to the part beginning on 6th April 1988 shall not be regarded as income arising to the company for that period.

(3) This paragraph shall be deemed to have come into force on 6th April 1988.

Abolition of Schedule D election etc

3—(1) (*repeals* TA 1988 s 54 and TA 1970 s 111).

(2) Subject to paragraph 5(1) below, profits or gains or losses which arise to a person from the occupation of commercial woodlands on or after 15th March 1988 shall not be regarded for any purposes as profits or gains or losses chargeable under Schedule D.

(3) Subject to paragraph 5(1) below—

(*a*) *interest which is paid by a company on or after 15th March 1988 shall not be treated as a charge on income for the purposes of corporation tax; and*[1]

(*b*) interest which is paid by any person on or after that date and—

(i) is stated in section 360(1), 361(3) or 362 of the Taxes Act 1988 (loans to buy interest in close company, interest in employee-controlled company or into partnership) to be eligible for relief under section 353 of that Act; or

(ii) is stated in any of the corresponding enactments repealed by that Act to be eligible for relief under section 75 of the Finance Act 1972,

shall not be so eligible,

if the relevant business consists of the occupation of commercial woodlands.

(4) Where part only of the relevant business consists of the occupation of commercial woodlands—

(*a*) *interest falling within paragraph (a) of sub-paragraph (3) above shall not be treated as a charge on income for the purposes of corporation tax; and*[1]

(*b*) interest falling within paragraph (*b*) of that sub-paragraph shall not be eligible for relief under section 353 of the Taxes Act 1988 or section 75 of the Finance Act 1972,

to such extent as may be just and reasonable having regard to all the circumstances of the case and, in particular, to the proportion which that part of that business bears to the whole.

(5) In this paragraph "the relevant business" means—

(*a*) *in relation to interest paid on or after 15th March 1988 by a company which is not a member of a group, the business carried on by the company;*

(*b*) *in relation to interest paid on or after that date by a company which is a member of a group, the business carried on by the group; and*[1]

(*c*) in relation to interest falling within paragraph (*b*) of sub-paragraph (3) above, the business carried on by the close company, employee-controlled company or partnership concerned;

and for the purposes of this paragraph two or more businesses carried on by a company, *group*[1] or partnership shall be regarded as a single business.

(6) *For the purposes of this paragraph a company shall be deemed to be a member of a group with one or more other companies if the relationship between that company and the other company or, as the case may be, each of the other companies is as mentioned in section 341(2) of the Taxes Act 1988 or section 60(2) of the Finance (No 2) Act 1987 (payments of interest between related companies).*

(7) This paragraph shall be deemed to have come into force on 15th March 1988.

Amendments—¹ Sub-paras (3)(*a*), (4)(*a*), (5)(*a*), (5)(*b*), (6) and in sub-para (5), the words "group", repealed by FA 2002 ss 82, 141, Sch 25 para 59, Sch 40 Pt 3(12), with effect for accounting periods beginning after 30 September 2002.

Transitional provisions

4 (*repealed by* FA 1988 Sch 6 para 4 (9), Sch 14 Pt V with effect from 6 April 1993).

5 (sub-para (1) *repealed by* FA 1988 Sch 6 para 5(5), Sch 14 Pt V; sub-paras (2)–(4) *spent*).

Consequential amendments

6—(1) (*repealed by* CAA 1990 Sch 2).

(2)–(4) (*spent*).

(5) (*repealed by* TCGA 1992 s 290(3), Sch 12).

(6) (*amends* TA 1988 s 15).

(7) (*substitutes* TA 1988 s 53(4)).

(8) (*amends* TA 1988 ss 380, 383, 385).

(9) Sub-paragraphs (1), (4) and (8) above shall be deemed to have come into force on 15th March 1988; and sub-paragraphs (2), (3) and (5) to (7) above shall be deemed to have come into force on 6th April 1988.

SCHEDULE 7

EXCEPTIONS TO RULE IN SECTION 66(1)

Section 66

Commentary—*Simon's Direct Tax Service* **D4.102.**

Cases where rule does not apply

1—(1) Subject to sub-paragraphs (2) and (3) below, section 66(1) of this Act shall not apply in relation to a company which, immediately before the commencement date—

(*a*) was carrying on business;

(*b*) was not resident in the United Kingdom, having ceased to be so resident in pursuance of a Treasury consent; and

(*c*) where that consent was a general consent, was taxable in a territory outside the United Kingdom.

(2) If at any time on or after the commencement date a company falling within sub-paragraph (1) above—

(*a*) ceases to carry on business; or

(*b*) where the Treasury consent there referred to was a general consent, ceases to be taxable in a territory outside the United Kingdom,

section 66(1) of this Act shall apply in relation to the company after that time or after the end of the transitional period, whichever is the later.

(3) If at any time on or after the commencement date a company falling within sub-paragraph (1) above becomes resident in the United Kingdom, section 66(1) of this Act shall apply in relation to the company after that time.

Statement of Practice SP 1/90—This Statement interprets (*a*) various terms used in this Schedule (*b*) the case law where the incorporation rule enacted by s 66 of this Act does not have relevance and (*c*) the effect of double taxation agreements where a company is regarded as resident in the UK and also in other countries.

2—(1) Subject to sub-paragraphs (2) and (3) below, section 66(1) of this Act shall not apply in relation to a company which—

(*a*) carried on business at any time before the commencement date;

(*b*) ceases to be resident in the United Kingdom at any time on or after that date in pursuance of a Treasury consent; and

(*c*) is carrying on business immediately after that time.

(2) If at any time after it ceases to be resident in the United Kingdom a company falling within sub-paragraph (1) above ceases to carry on business, section 66(1) of this Act shall apply in relation to the company after that time or after the end of the transitional period, whichever is the later.

(3) If at any time after it ceases to be resident in the United Kingdom a company falling within sub-paragraph (1) above becomes resident in the United Kingdom, section 66(1) of this Act shall apply in relation to the company after that time.

Statement of Practice SP 1/90—This Statement interprets (*a*) various terms used in this Schedule (*b*) the case law where the incorporation rule enacted by s 66 of this Act does not have relevance and (*c*) the effect of double taxation agreements where a company is regarded as resident in the UK and also in other countries.

Cases where rule does not apply until end of transitional period

3—(1) Subject to sub-paragraph (2) below, in relation to a company which—

(*a*) carried on business at any time before the commencement date;

(*b*) was not resident in the United Kingdom immediately before that date; and

(*c*) is not a company falling within paragraph 1(1) above,

section 66(1) of this Act shall not apply until after the end of the transitional period.

(2) If at any time on or after the commencement date a company falling within sub-paragraph (1) above becomes resident in the United Kingdom, section 66(1) of this Act shall apply in relation to the company after that time.

Statement of Practice SP 1/90—This Statement interprets (*a*) various terms used in this Schedule (*b*) the case law where the incorporation rule enacted by s 66 of this Act does not have relevance and (*c*) the effect of double taxation agreements where a company is regarded as resident in the UK and also in other countries.

4—(1) Subject to sub-paragraph (2) below, in relation to a company which—

(*a*) carried on business at any time before the commencement date;

(*b*) ceases to be resident in the United Kingdom at any time on or after that date in pursuance of a Treasury consent; and

(*c*) is not a company falling within paragraph 2(1) above,

section 66(1) of this Act shall not apply until after the end of the transitional period.

(2) If at any time after it ceases to be resident in the United Kingdom a company falling within sub-paragraph (1) above becomes resident in the United Kingdom, section 66(1) of this Act shall apply in relation to the company after that time.

Statement of Practice SP 1/90—This Statement interprets (*a*) various terms used in this Schedule (*b*) the case law where the incorporation rule enacted by s 66 of this Act does not have relevance and (*c*) the effect of double taxation agreements where a company is regarded as resident in the UK and also in other countries.
Note—The transitional period ended on 15 March 1993.

Supplemental

5—(1) In this Schedule—

"the commencement date" means the date of the coming into force of this Schedule;

"general consent" means a consent under any section to which sub-paragraph (2) below applies given generally within the meaning of subsection (4) of that section;

"taxable" means liable to tax on income by reason of domicile, residence or place of management;

"the transitional period" means the period of five years beginning with the commencement date;

"Treasury consent" means a consent under any section to which sub-paragraph (2) below applies given for the purposes of subsection (1)(*a*) of that section.

(2) This sub-paragraph applies to the following sections (restrictions on the migration etc of companies), namely—

section 765 of the Taxes Act 1988;

section 482 of the Taxes Act 1970;

section 468 of the Income Tax Act 1952; and

section 36 of the Finance Act 1951.

(3) Any question which arises under any of the provisions of this Schedule shall be determined without regard to the provision made by section 66(1) of this Act.

Statement of Practice SP 1/90—This Statement interprets (*a*) various terms used in this Schedule (*b*) the case law where the incorporation rule enacted by s 66 of this Act does not have relevance and (*c*) the effect of double taxation agreements where a company is regarded as resident in the UK and also in other countries.
Note—The transitional period ended on 15 March 1993.

SCHEDULE 8

CAPITAL GAINS: ASSETS HELD ON 31st MARCH 1982

Section 96

(*Repealed by* TCGA 1992 Sch 12).

SCHEDULE 9

DEFERRED CHARGES ON GAINS BEFORE 31st MARCH 1982

Section 97

(*Repealed by* TCGA 1992 Sch 12).

SCHEDULE 10

GAINS ARISING FROM CERTAIN SETTLED PROPERTY

Section 109

(*Repealed by* TCGA 1992 Sch 12).

SCHEDULE 11

CAPITAL GAINS INDEXATION: GROUPS AND ASSOCIATED COMPANIES

Section 114

(*Repealed by* TCGA 1992 Sch 12).

SCHEDULE 12

BUILDING SOCIETIES: CHANGE OF STATUS

Section 145

Introductory

1 Paragraphs [3][1] to 7 below apply where there is a transfer of the whole of a building society's business to a company ("the successor company") in accordance with section 97 and the other applicable provisions of the Building Societies Act 1986.

Commentary—*Simon's Direct Tax Service* **D4.771–773.**
Amendments—[1] Figure substituted for "2" by FA 2002 s 105(2)(*a*) with effect from 24 July 2002.

Gilt-edged securities and other financial trading stock

...

Commentary—*Simon's Direct Tax Service* **D4.772.**
Amendment—This paragraph repealed by FA 2002 ss 105(2)(*b*), 141, Sch 40 Pt 3(17) with effect from 24 July 2002. This paragraph previously read as follows—

"Gilt-edged securities and other financial trading stock

2—(1) For the purposes of section 100(1) of the Taxes Act 1988 (valuation of trading stock on discontinuance of trade) the society's financial trading stock shall be valued at an amount equal to its cost to the society.

(2) In computing for any corporation tax purpose the [profits] of a trade carried on by the successor company, such of the assets comprised in the transfer as constituted the society's financial trading stock shall be regarded as acquired by the company at their cost to the society.

(3) In this paragraph "financial trading stock", in relation to a building society, means [those assets held by the society that—

(*a*) are of such proportion and composition as will enable it at all times to meet its liabilities as they arise, and
(*b*) constitute trading stock for the purposes of section 100 of the Taxes Act 1988.]".

Capital allowances

3—(1) For the purposes of the allowances and charges provided for by [the Capital Allowances Act 2001][1] the trade of the society shall not be treated as permanently discontinued and the trade of the successor company shall not be treated as a new trade set up and commenced by the successor company.

(2) There shall be made to or on the successor company in accordance with those Acts all such allowances and charges as would, if the society had continued to carry on the trade, have fallen to be made to or on it, and the amount of any such allowance or charge shall be computed as if the successor company had been carrying on the trade since the society began to do so and as if everything done to or by the society had been done to or by the successor company.

(3) No transfer of assets from the society to the successor company effected by section 97 of the Building Societies Act 1986 shall be treated as giving rise to any such allowance or charge.

Commentary—*Simon's Direct Tax Service* **D4.772.**
Amendments—[1] Words in sub-para (1) substituted by CAA 2001 s 578, Sch 2 para 69 with effect for income tax purposes, as respects allowances and charges falling to be made for chargeable periods ending after 5 April 2001, and for corporation tax purposes, as respects allowances and charges falling to be made for chargeable periods ending after 31 March 2001.

Capital gains: assets acquired from society, etc

4 (*Repealed by* TCGA 1992 Sch 12).

Capital gains: shares, and rights to shares, in successor company

5 (*Repealed by* TCGA 1992 Sch 12).

Distributions

6—(1) Where, in connection with the transfer, qualifying benefits are conferred by the society or the successor company on members of the society, the conferring of those benefits shall not be regarded as either—

   (*a*) the making of a distribution, within the meaning of the Corporation Tax Acts; or
   (*b*) the payment or crediting of a dividend for the purposes of [section 477A][1] of the Taxes Act 1988 or any regulations under that section (building society interest etc).

(2) Sub-paragraph (1) above does not preclude any qualifying benefit (and, in particular, any qualifying benefit which in the hands of the recipient would, apart from that sub-paragraph, constitute income for the purposes of income tax) from being a capital distribution for the purposes of section [122 of the Taxation of Chargeable Gains Act 1992][2], and in that section "distribution" shall be construed accordingly.

(3) In this paragraph "qualifying benefits" means—

   (*a*) any such rights as are mentioned in paragraph 5(1)(*a*), (*b*) or (*c*) above, and any property obtained by the exercise of those rights;
   (*b*) any shares issued or disposed of as mentioned in paragraph 5(2) above;
   (*c*) any shares issued or disposed of, or to which a member becomes entitled, as mentioned in paragraph 5(3) or (4) above, and any interest in the settled property constituted by those shares;
   (*d*) any payment in lieu of a qualifying benefit falling within paragraphs (*a*) to (*c*) above;
   (*e*) any distribution made in pursuance of section 100(2)(*b*) of the Building Societies Act 1986.

(4) "Member" has the same meaning in this paragraph as in paragraph 5 above.

Commentary—*Simon's Direct Tax Service* **D4.773.**
Amendments—[1] Words in sub-para (1)(*b*) substituted by FA 1991 s 79 and sub-para (1)(*b*) as so amended applies where qualifying benefits are conferred after 5 April 1991.
[2] Words in sub-para (2) substituted by TCGA 1992 Sch 10 para 16(1), (7).

Contractual savings schemes

7 The following provisions, namely—

   (*a*) section 326 of the Taxes Act 1988 (certain sums to be disregarded for income tax purposes), and
   (*b*) ...[1]

shall have effect in relation to any terminal bonus, or interest or other sum, payable after the transfer under a savings scheme which immediately before the transfer was a certified contractual savings scheme (within the meaning of section 326) in relation to the society notwithstanding that it ceased to be such a scheme by reason of the transfer.

Commentary—*Simon's Direct Tax Service* **D4.771.**
Amendments—[1] Para (*b*) repealed by TCGA 1992 s 290(3), Sch 12.

Stamp duty

8 (See *Orange Tax Handbook*).

SCHEDULE 13

POST-CONSOLIDATION AMENDMENTS
Section 146

Note—This Schedule made retrospective amendments to TA 1988, CGTA 1979, FA 1980, FA 1981, FA 1984, FA 1986 and FA 1987. The effect of these provisions still extant has been noted to the legislation concerned.

HOUSING ACT 1988

(1988 Chapter 50)

Note—This Act received Royal Assent on 15 November 1988.

PART II
HOUSING ASSOCIATIONS
Grants: functions of Secretary of State

54 Tax relief grants

(1) If a housing association makes a claim to the Secretary of State in respect of a period and satisfies him that throughout the period it was a housing association to which this section applies and its functions either—

(a) consisted exclusively of the function of providing or maintaining housing accommodation for letting or hostels and activities incidental to that function, or
(b) included that function and activities incidental to that function,

the Secretary of State may make grants to the association for affording relief from tax chargeable on the association.

(2) This section applies to a housing association at any time if, at that time—

(a) it is [a registered social landlord][1];
(b) it does not trade for profit; and
(c) it is not approved for the purposes of section 488 of the Income and Corporation Taxes Act 1988 (tax treatment of co-operative housing associations).

(3) References in this section to tax chargeable on an association are to income tax (other than income tax which the association is entitled to deduct on making any payment) and corporation tax.

(4) A grant under this section may be made—

(a) in a case falling within subsection (1)(a) above, for affording relief from any tax chargeable on the association for the period in respect of which the claim is made; and
(b) in a case falling within subsection (1)(b) above, for affording relief from such part of any tax so chargeable as the Secretary of State considers appropriate having regard to the other functions of the association;

and in any case shall be of such amount, shall be made at such times and shall be subject to such conditions as the Secretary of State thinks fit.

(5) The conditions may include conditions for securing the repayment in whole or in part of a grant made to an association—

(a) in the event of tax in respect of which it was made being found not to be chargeable; or
(b) in such other events (including the association beginning to trade for profit) as the Secretary of State may determine.

(6) A claim under this section shall be made in such manner and shall be supported by such evidence as the Secretary of State may direct.

(7) The Commissioners of Inland Revenue and their officers may disclose to the Secretary of State such particulars as he may reasonably require for determining whether a grant should be made on a claim or whether a grant should be repaid or the amount of such grant or repayment.

(8) In this section "letting" includes—

(a) in England and Wales, the grant of a shared ownership lease or a licence to occupy;
(b) in Scotland, disposal under a shared ownership agreement or the grant of a right or permission to occupy.

Notes—This section has effect from 1 April 1989 by virtue of SI 1989/404.
The Housing (Northern Ireland) Order, SI 1992/1725 art 22 contains identical provisions (with necessary modifications) for Northern Ireland which came into force on 15 September 1992 by virtue of art 1(2). The modifications are that "the Department" (ie the Department of the Environment) and "the article" replaces "the Secretary of State" and "the section" respectively where they appear in this section, and sub-s (8) is replaced as follows—

"(8) In this Article "letting" includes the grant of an equity-sharing lease or a licence to occupy."

Amendments—[1] Words in sub-s (2)(a) substituted by the Housing Act 1996 (Consequential Provisions) Order, SI 1996/2325 Sch 2 para 18(1), (7) with effect from 1 October 1996.
Prospective amendments—This section to be repealed by the Housing (Scotland) Act 2001 ss 112, 113(1), Sch 10 para 15(5) with effect from such day as the Scottish Ministers may by order appoint.

FINANCE ACT 1989

(1989 Chapter 26)

ARRANGEMENT OF SECTIONS

PART II
INCOME TAX, CORPORATION TAX AND CAPITAL GAINS TAX

CHAPTER I
GENERAL

Part I—Administrative provisions.
Part II—Amendments connected with repeal of Chapter III of Part XI of Taxes Act 1988.
Schedule 13—Capital allowances: miscellaneous amendments.
Schedule 14—*Capital gains tax: gifts etc.* (repealed)
Schedule 15—*Capital gains: re-basing to 1982 etc.* (repealed)
Schedule 16—*Broadcasting: additional payments by programme contractors.* (not printed)
Schedule 17—*Repeals* (not printed).

An Act to grant certain duties, to alter other duties, and to amend the law relating to the National Debt and the Public Revenue, and to make further provision in connection with Finance.

[27th July 1989]

PART II
INCOME TAX, CORPORATION TAX AND CAPITAL GAINS TAX

CHAPTER I
GENERAL

Income tax rates and allowances

30 Charge and rates of income tax for 1989–90

(*spent*).

Commentary—*Simon's Direct Tax Service* E1.102.

31 Age allowance

(*Amends TA* 1988 s 257(3), (5) with effect for the year 1989–90).

32 Operative date for PAYE

(*Amends TA* 1988 ss 1(5), 257(10) with effect for the year 1989–90).

33 Married couples

(1) Sections 257 to 257F and 265 of the Taxes Act 1988, as inserted for the year 1990–91 and subsequent years by the Finance Act 1988, shall be amended as follows.

(2)–(13) (*amend* TA 1988 s 257(1)–(3), (5), 257A(1)–(3), (5), 257B(2), 257D(8), 265(3), 257E(1), (2)).

Amendments—This section repealed in part by F (No 2) Act 1992 s 82, Sch 18 Pt VII and partly superseded. Sub-ss (6), (11)–(13), and words in sub-s (10), repealed by FA 1999 s 139, Sch 20 Pt III(3) with effect from the year 2000–01.

Corporation tax rates etc

34 Charge and rate of corporation tax for financial year 1989

(*spent*).

Commentary—*Simon's Direct Tax Service* D2.108.

35 Corporation tax: small companies

(1) (*enacts* the small companies' rate and TA 1988 s 13(2) fraction for the year 1989).

(2) (*amends* TA 1988 s 13(3) (now superseded)).

(3) Subsection (2) above shall have effect for the financial year 1989 and subsequent financial years; and where by virtue of that subsection section 13 of the Taxes Act 1988 has effect with different relevant maximum amounts in relation to different parts of a company's accounting period, then for the purposes of that section those parts shall be treated as if they were separate accounting periods and the profits and basic profits of the company for that period shall be apportioned between those parts.

Commentary—*Simon's Direct Tax Service* D2.109.

Receipts basis etc

36 Schedule E: revised Cases

(1) The Taxes Act 1988 shall be amended as follows.

(2) (*amends* TA 1988 s 19(1), para 1).

(3) (*inserts* TA 1988 s 19(1) para 4A).

(4) Subsection (2) above shall apply where the year of assessment mentioned in the substituted Case I, II or III is 1989–90 or a subsequent year of assessment.

(5) Subsection (3) above shall apply where each of the years mentioned in the new paragraph 4A(*a*) or (*b*) (as the case may be) is 1989–90 or a subsequent year of assessment.

37 Schedule E: assessment on receipts basis

(1) (*inserts TA 1988 ss 202A, 202B*).

(2) This section shall apply where the year of assessment mentioned in the new section 202A(1) is 1989–90 or a subsequent year of assessment, even if the emoluments concerned are for a year of assessment before 1989–90.

(3) This section shall not apply in the case of emoluments of an office or employment held by a person who died before 6th April 1989.

38 Schedule E: unpaid emoluments

(1) This section applies to emoluments of an office or employment if—

    (*a*) they are emoluments for a year of assessment (a relevant year) before 1989–90,
    (*b*) they fall within Case I or II of Schedule E as the Case applies for years before 1989–90,
    (*c*) they have not been paid before 6th April 1989, and
    (*d*) they have been received on or after 6th April 1989 and before 6th April 1991;

and section 202B of the Taxes Act 1988 shall apply for the purposes of paragraph (*d*) above as it applies for the purposes of section 202A(1)(*a*) of that Act.

(2) The emoluments shall be charged to income tax only by reference to the year of assessment in which they are received.

(3) Any adjustments consequential on this section (such as the amendment of assessments or the repayment or setting–off of tax paid) shall be made.

(4) This section shall not apply to emoluments of an office or employment held by a person who died before 6th April 1989.

(5) This section shall not apply if the only emoluments of the office or employment not paid before 6th April 1989 are emoluments for a period consisting of or falling within the period beginning with 5th March 1989 and ending with 5th April 1989.

(6) This section shall not apply unless—

    (*a*) written notice that it is to apply is given to the inspector before 6th April 1991,
    (*b*) the notice is given by or on behalf of the person who holds or held the office or employment concerned, and
    (*c*) the notice states the amount of the emoluments falling within subsection (1) above.

(7) Subsection (8) below applies where emoluments of an office or employment have been or fall to be computed by reference to the accounts basis as regards the year 1987–88 or years of assessment including that year.

(8) In deciding for the purposes of subsection (1)(*a*) above whether emoluments are emoluments for a particular year, the emoluments of the office or employment for the year or (as the case may be) years mentioned in subsection (7) above, and for the year 1988–89, shall be computed by reference to that basis.

(9) In deciding whether subsection (8) above applies in a particular case, any request to revoke the application of the accounts basis shall be ignored if—

    (*a*) it is made after 5th April 1989, or
    (*b*) it is made before 6th April 1989 otherwise than in writing.

(10) In the application of this section to emoluments of an office or employment under or with a person carrying on business as an authorised Lloyd's underwriting agent, the references in subsections (1)(*d*) and (6)(*a*) above to 6th April 1991 shall be construed as references to 6th April 1994.

(11) Subsection (10) above shall not apply unless the duties of the office or employment relate wholly or mainly to the underwriting agency business.

(12) The reference in subsection (10) above to an authorised Lloyd's underwriting agent is to a person permitted by the Council of Lloyd's to act as an underwriting agent at Lloyd's.

(13) If in a particular case it appears to the Board reasonable to do so they may direct that subsections (1)(*d*) and (6)(*a*) above shall have effect in relation to that case as if for the references to 6th April 1991 or (as the case may be) 6th April 1994 there were substituted references to such later date as they may specify in the direction.

(14) In this section "the accounts basis" means the basis commonly so called (under which emoluments for a year of assessment are computed by reference to the emoluments for a period other than the year of assessment).

Commentary—*Simon's Direct Tax Service* E4.106.
Statement of Practice SP 1/92—Directors' and employees' emoluments: extension of the 6 April 1991 time limit for relief on transition to receipts basis of assessment. Statement (not reproduced) classified obsolete by IR 131 Supplement (November 1998).
Simon's Tax Cases—s 38(8), *Malone v Quinn (Inspector of Taxes)* [2001] STC (SCD) 63.

39 Schedule E: unremitted emoluments

(1) This section applies to emoluments of an office or employment if—

  (a) they are emoluments for a year of assessment (a relevant year) before 1989–90,
  (b) they are received in the United Kingdom after 5th April 1989, and
  (c) had this Act not been passed they would have fallen within Case III of Schedule E.

(2) The emoluments shall be treated as if they were not emoluments for the relevant year.

(3) But they shall be treated as if they were emoluments for the year of assessment in which they are received in the United Kingdom and as if they fell within Case III as substituted by section 36 above; and accordingly income tax shall be charged, in accordance with section 202A of the Taxes Act 1988, by reference to the year of assessment in which the emoluments are received in the United Kingdom.

Commentary—*Simon's Direct Tax Service* **E4.106.**

40 Schedule E: emoluments already paid

(1) Subsection (2) below applies to emoluments of an office or employment if—

  (a) they are emoluments for a year of assessment after 1988–89,
  (b) they have been paid before 6th April 1989, and
  (c) they fall within Case I or II of Schedule E as substituted by section 36 above.

(2) The emoluments shall be treated as if they were received, within the meaning of section 202B of the Taxes Act 1988, on 6th April 1989; and accordingly income tax shall be charged, in accordance with section 202A of that Act, by reference to the year 1989–90.

(3) Subsection (4) below applies to emoluments of an office or employment if—

  (a) they are emoluments for a year of assessment after 1988–89,
  (b) they have been received in the United Kingdom before 6th April 1989, and
  (c) they fall within Case III of Schedule E as substituted by section 36 above.

(4) The emoluments shall be treated as if they were received in the United Kingdom on 6th April 1989; and accordingly income tax shall be charged, in accordance with section 202A of the Taxes Act 1988 by reference to the year 1989–90.

Commentary—*Simon's Direct Tax Service* **E4.106.**

41 Schedule E: pensions etc

(1) This section applies in relation to the following pensions and other benefits—

  (a) a pension, stipend or annuity chargeable to income tax under Schedule E by virtue of paragraph 2, 3 or 4 of section 19(1) of the Taxes Act 1988;
  (b) a pension or annual payment chargeable to income tax under Schedule E by virtue of section 133 of that Act (voluntary pensions);
  (c) income support chargeable to income tax under Schedule E by virtue of section 151 of that Act;
  (d) a pension chargeable to income tax under Schedule E by virtue of section 597 of that Act (retirement benefit schemes);
  (e) a benefit chargeable to income tax under Schedule E by virtue of section 617(1) of that Act (social security benefits).

(2) As regards any particular year of assessment income tax shall be charged on the amount of the pension or other benefit accruing in respect of the year; and this shall apply irrespective of when any amount is actually paid in respect of the pension or other benefit.

(3) This section shall apply where the year of assessment mentioned in subsection (2) above is 1989–90 or a subsequent year of assessment.

Commentary—*Simon's Direct Tax Service* **E4.126.**
Cross references—See FA 1994 s 139(3) (taxation of incapacity benefit as respects 1995–96 and subsequent years of assessment; amount of benefit to be charged).

42 Schedule E: supplementary

(1) The Taxes Act 1988 shall be amended as follows.

(2), (3) (*amend* TA 1988 s 131(2), 149(1)).

(4) (*repeals* TA 1988 s 170)[1].

(5) (*amends* TA 1988 Sch 12 para 2(2)).

(6) This section shall apply for the year 1989–90 and subsequent years of assessment.

Amendments—[1] Sub-s (4) repealed by FA 1997 Sch 18 Pt VI(3) with effect for any payment made by reference to a profit period beginning after 31 December 1999 in accordance with FA 1997 s 61(2), (3), but subject to FA 1997 Sch 18 Pt VI(3) note 2.

43 Schedule D: computation

(1) Subsection (2) below applies where—

(*a*) a calculation is made of profits or gains which are to be charged under Schedule D and are for a period of account ending after 5th April 1989,

(*b*) relevant emoluments would (apart from that subsection) be deducted in making the calculation, and

(*c*) the emoluments are not paid before the end of the period of nine months beginning with the end of that period of account.

(2) The emoluments—

(*a*) shall not be deducted in making the calculation mentioned in subsection (1)(*a*) above, but

(*b*) shall be deducted in calculating profits or gains which are to be charged under Schedule D and are for the period of account in which the emoluments are paid.

(3) Subsections (4) and (5) below apply where—

(*a*) a calculation such as is mentioned in subsection (1)(*a*) above is made,

(*b*) the calculation is made before the end of the period of nine months beginning with the end of the period of account concerned,

(*c*) relevant emoluments would (apart from subsection (2) above) be deducted in making the calculation, and

(*d*) the emoluments have not been paid when the calculation is made.

(4) It shall be assumed for the purpose of making the calculation that the emoluments will not be paid before the end of that period of nine months.

(5) But the calculation shall be adjusted if—

(*a*) the emoluments are paid after the calculation is made but before the end of that period of nine months,

(*b*) a claim to adjust the calculation is made to the inspector, and

(*c*) the claim is made before the end of the period of two years beginning with the end of the period of account concerned.

(6), (7) ...¹

(8) In a case where the period of account mentioned in subsection (1)(*a*) above begins before 6th April 1989 and ends before 6th April 1990, the references in subsections (1)(*c*), (3)(*b*), (4) and (5)(*a*) above to nine months shall be construed as references to eighteen months.

(9) ...²

(10) For the purposes of this section ''relevant emoluments'' are emoluments for a period after 5th April 1989 allocated either—

(*a*) in respect of particular offices or employments (or both), or

(*b*) generally in respect of offices or employments (or both).

(11) This section applies in relation to potential emoluments as it applies in relation to relevant emoluments, and for this purpose—

(*a*) potential emoluments are amounts or benefits reserved in the accounts of an employer, or held by an intermediary, with a view to their becoming relevant emoluments;

(*b*) potential emoluments are paid when they become relevant emoluments which are paid.

(12) In deciding for the purposes of this section whether emoluments are paid at any time after 5th April 1989, section 202B of the Taxes Act 1988 (time when emoluments are treated as received) shall apply as it applies for the purposes of section 202A(1)(*a*) of that Act, but reading ''paid'' for ''received'' throughout.

(13) In section 436(1)(*b*) of the Taxes Act 1988 (profits to be computed in accordance with provisions of that Act applicable to Case I of Schedule D) the reference to that Act shall be deemed to include a reference to this section.

Commentary—*Simon's Direct Tax Service* **B3.1425.**
Revenue Interpretation RI 103—Redundancy payments and provisions—Schedule D Cases I and II.
Cross references—TMA 1970 s 42 ''(income tax and capital gains tax version)'' (procedure for making claims under self-assessment).
Amendments—¹ Sub-ss (6), (7) repealed by FA 1993 s 181 and Sch 23 Pt III(12) with effect in relation to periods of account ending after 29 June 1993.
² Sub-s (9) repealed by FA 2002 s 141, Sch 40 Pt 3(16) with effect from 24 July 2002. Sub-s (9) previously read—
  ''(9) In this section ''period of account'' means a period for which an account is made up.''.

44 Investment and insurance companies: computation

(1) Subsection (2) below applies where—

(*a*) a calculation is made for the purposes of corporation tax of the profits of an investment company for an accounting period ending after 5th April 1989,

(*b*) relevant emoluments would (apart from that subsection) be deducted in making the calculation, and

(*c*) the emoluments are not paid before the end of the period of nine months beginning with the end of the relevant period of account.

(2) The emoluments—

(*a*) shall not be deducted in making the calculation mentioned in subsection (1)(*a*) above, but

(*b*) shall be deducted in calculating for the purposes of corporation tax the profits of the company concerned for the accounting period in which the emoluments are paid.

(3) Subsections (4) and (5) below apply where—

(*a*) a calculation such as is mentioned in subsection (1)(*a*) above is made,

(*b*) the calculation is made before the end of the period of nine months beginning with the end of the relevant period of account,

(*c*) relevant emoluments would (apart from subsection (2) above) be deducted in making the calculation, and

(*d*) the emoluments have not been paid when the calculation is made.

(4) It shall be assumed for the purpose of making the calculation that the emoluments will not be paid before the end of that period of nine months.

(5) But the calculation shall be adjusted if—

(*a*) the emoluments are paid after the calculation is made but before the end of that period of nine months,

(*b*) a claim to adjust the calculation is made to the inspector by or on behalf of the company concerned, and

(*c*) the claim is made before the end of the period of two years beginning with the end of the period of account concerned.

(6) In a case where the accounting period mentioned in subsection (1)(*a*) above begins before 6th April 1989 and ends before 6th April 1990, the references in subsections (1)(*c*), (3)(*b*), (4) and (5)(*a*) above to nine months shall be construed as references to eighteen months.

(7) In this section "investment company" has the same meaning as in Part IV of the Taxes Act 1988.

(8) For the purposes of this section "relevant emoluments" are emoluments for a period after 5th April 1989 allocated either—

(*a*) in respect of particular offices or employments (or both), or

(*b*) generally in respect of offices or employments (or both).

(9) This section applies in relation to potential emoluments as it applies in relation to relevant emoluments, and for this purpose—

(*a*) potential emoluments are amounts or benefits reserved in the accounts of an employer, or held by an intermediary, with a view to their becoming relevant emoluments;

(*b*) potential emoluments are paid when they become relevant emoluments which are paid.

(10) For the purpose of this section the relevant period of account is the period of account which—

(*a*) includes the accounting period concerned, or

(*b*) begins when the accounting period concerned begins and ends when the accounting period concerned ends.

(11) In deciding for the purposes of this section whether emoluments are paid at any time after 5th April 1989, section 202B of the Taxes Act 1988 (time when emoluments are treated as received) shall apply as it applies for the purposes of section 202A(1)(*a*) of that Act, but reading "paid" for "received" throughout.

(12) Where the profits of a company carrying on life assurance business are not charged under Case I of Schedule D, this section shall apply in calculating the profits as it applies in calculating the profits of an investment company; but the effect of section 86 below shall be ignored in construing subsection (1)(*b*) above.

(13) In a case where, apart from this subsection and by virtue of subsection (2)(*b*) above as it applies by virtue of subsection (12) above, emoluments fall to be deducted in calculating profits for a particular accounting period—

(*a*) subsection (2)(*b*) above shall have effect subject to section 86 below;

(*b*) in construing section 86 the emoluments shall be treated as expenses for that accounting period.

Commentary—*Simon's Direct Tax Service* **D4.406, 504.**
Modification—Sub-s (12A) treated as inserted in applying life assurance provisions of the Corporation Tax Acts to insurance companies carrying on capital redemption business with effect for accounting periods ending after 30 June 1999: see Insurance Companies (Capital Redemption Business) (Modification of the Corporation Tax Acts) Regulations, SI 1999/498 reg 9.

45 PAYE: meaning of payment

(1) The Taxes Act 1988 shall be amended as follows.

(2), (3) (*insert* TA 1988 s 203A and *repeal* s 203(4)).

(4) Subsection (2) above shall have effect to determine whether anything occurring on or after the day on which this Act is passed constitutes a payment for the purposes mentioned in the new section 203A.

(5) But if an event occurring before the day on which this Act is passed constituted a payment of or on account of income for the purposes mentioned in the new section 203A, nothing occurring on or after that day shall constitute a payment of or on account of the same income for those purposes.

Interest

46 Relief for interest

(*Enacts* TA 1988 s 367(5) qualifying maximum for the year 1989–90).

Commentary—*Simon's Direct Tax Service* A3.431; E1.538, 539.

47 Close company loans: business expansion scheme

(*Inserts* TA 1988 s 360(3A)).

48 Close company loans: material interest

(1) (*substitutes* TA 1988 s 360(4)).

(2) (*inserts* TA 1988 s 360A).

Benefits in kind

49 Car benefits

(*Substituted* TA 1988 Sch 6, Part I from the year 1989–90 and is now superseded).

50 Security assets and services

(1) For the purposes of this section a security asset is an asset which improves personal security, and a security service is a service which improves personal security.

(2) In a case where—

(*a*) a security asset or security service is provided for an employee by reason of his employment, or is used by an employee, and

(*b*) the cost is wholly or partly borne by or on behalf of a person (the provider) other than the employee,

in charging tax under Schedule E on the emoluments from the employment a deduction shall be allowed of an amount equal to so much of the cost so borne as falls to be included in the emoluments of the employment.

(3) In a case where—

(*a*) a security asset or security service is provided for or used by an employee,

(*b*) expenses in connection with the provision or use are incurred out of the emoluments of the employment, and

(*c*) the expenses are reimbursed by or on behalf of a person (the provider) other than the employee,

in charging tax under Schedule E on the emoluments from the employment a deduction shall be allowed of an amount equal to the amount of the expenses.

(4) Subsection (2) or (3) above shall not apply unless the asset or service is provided for or used by the employee to meet a threat which—

(*a*) is a special threat to his personal physical security, and

(*b*) arises wholly or mainly by virtue of the particular employment concerned.

(5) Subsection (2) or (3) above shall not apply unless the provider has the meeting of that threat as his sole object in wholly or partly bearing the cost or reimbursing the expenses (as the case may be).

(6) Subsection (2) or (3) above shall not apply in the case of a service unless the benefit resulting to the employee consists wholly or mainly of an improvement of his personal physical security.

(7) Subsection (2) or (3) above shall not apply in the case of an asset unless the provider intends the asset to be used solely to improve personal physical security.

Commentary—*Simon's Direct Tax Service* E4.622.
Revenue Internal Guidance—Schedule E manual SE 21811 (no deduction for security measures against general criminal threat, expenditure to meet threat to property or security measures unconnected with employment).

51 Assets used partly for security

(1) In a case where—

(*a*) apart from section 50(7) above, section 50(2) above would apply in the case of an asset, and

(*b*) the provider intends the asset to be used partly to improve personal physical security,

section 50(2) shall nevertheless apply, but only so as to allow a deduction of the appropriate proportion of the amount there mentioned.

(2) For the purposes of subsection (1) above the appropriate proportion of the amount mentioned in section 50(2) above is such proportion of that amount as is attributable to the provider's intention that the asset be used to improve personal physical security.

(3) In a case where—

(*a*) apart from section 50(7) above, section 50(3) above would apply in the case of an asset, and

(*b*) the provider intends the asset to be used partly to improve personal physical security,

section 50(3) shall nevertheless apply, but only so as to allow a deduction of the appropriate proportion of the amount there mentioned.

(4) For the purposes of subsection (3) above the appropriate proportion of the amount mentioned in section 50(3) above is such proportion of that amount as is attributable to the provider's intention that the asset be used to improve personal physical security.

Commentary—*Simon's Direct Tax Service* E4.622.

52 Security: supplementary

(1) If the provider intends the asset to be used solely to improve personal physical security, but there is another use for the asset which is incidental to improving personal physical security, that other use shall be ignored in construing section 50(7) above.

(2) The fact that an asset or service improves the personal physical security of any member of the employee's family or household, as well as that of the employee, shall not prevent section 50(2) or (3) above from applying.

(3) In sections 50 and 51 above and this section—

(*a*) references to an asset do not include references to a car, a ship or an aircraft,

(*b*) references to an asset or service do not include references to a dwelling, grounds appurtenant to a dwelling, or living accommodation,

(*c*) references to an asset include references to equipment and a structure (such as a wall),

(*d*) references to an employee are to a person who holds an employment, and

(*e*) references to an employment include references to an office.

(4) For the purposes of sections 50 and 51 above and this section in their application to an asset, it is immaterial whether or not the asset becomes affixed to land (whether constituting a dwelling or otherwise).

(5) For the purposes of sections 50 and 51 above and this section in their application to an asset, it is immaterial whether or not the employee is or becomes entitled to the property in the asset or (in the case of a fixture) an estate or interest in the land concerned.

(6) Sections 50 and 51 above and this section apply where expenditure is incurred on or after 6th April 1989 in or towards bearing a cost or in reimbursing expenses (as the case may be).

Commentary—*Simon's Direct Tax Service* E4.622.
Revenue Internal Guidance—Schedule E manual SE 3256 (sub-s (3)(*b*): dwelling includes flat used as residence, but not block of flats; grounds appurtenant to dwelling similar to "garden or grounds").

53 Employees earning £8,500 or more and directors

(1) (*substitutes* TA 1988 s 167),

(2) (*a*) (*substitutes* the heading to TA 1988 Pt V, Ch II).

(*b*)–(*f*) (*substitute* TA 1988 s 160(3) and *amend* TA 1988 ss 153(1), 154(1), 157(1), 158(1), 160(1), (2), 162(1), (5), (7), 163(1), 165(6)(*b*), 332(2)(*c*), 418(3)(*a*)).

(*g*) (*amends* TMA 1970 s 15(3)(*a*) and is now superseded).

Medical insurance

54 Relief

Commentary—*Simon's Direct Tax Service* E2.901–903.
Amendments—This section repealed by F(No 2)A 1997 s 17(1), (5), Sch 8 Pt II(2) with effect for 1997–98 and subsequent years of assessment where either the premium is a premium under a contract entered into on or after 2 July 1997 or the payment is received by the insurer after 5 April 1999, subject to F(No 2)A 1997 s 17(2)–(4) re certain contracts entered into before 1 August 1997.

55 Eligible contracts

Commentary—*Simon's Direct Tax Service* E2.904.
Amendments—This section repealed by F(No 2)A 1997 Sch 8 Pt II(2) with effect for 1997–98 and subsequent years of assessment except in relation to cases in which relief due under FA 1989 s 54 in respect of any payment is unaffected by the provisions of F(No 2)A 1997 s 17(1) (see the Amendments note to section 54 above).

56 Certification of contracts

Commentary—*Simon's Direct Tax Service* E2.904, 906.
Simon's Tax Cases—s 56, *Sturgeon v Matthews* [1995] STC (SCD) 284.
Amendments—This section repealed by F(No 2)A 1997 Sch 8 Pt II(2) with effect for 1997–98 and subsequent years of assessment except in relation to cases in which relief due under FA 1989 s 54 in respect of any payment is unaffected by the provisions of F(No 2)A 1997 s 17(1) (see the Amendments note to section 54 above).

57 Medical insurance: supplementary

Commentary—*Simon's Direct Tax Service* E2.901, 906.
Amendments—This section repealed by F(No 2)A 1997 Sch 8 Pt II(2) with effect for 1997–98 and subsequent years of
  assessment except in relation to cases in which relief due under FA 1989 s 54 in respect of any payment is unaffected by the
  provisions of F(No 2)A 1997 s 17(1) (see the Amendments note to section 54 above).

Charities

58 Payroll deduction scheme

Note—Amends TA 1988 s 202(7) from the year 1989–90 and is now superseded.

59 Covenanted subscriptions

Commentary—*Simon's Direct Tax Service* C4.520; E1.503.
Amendments—This section repealed by FA 2000 ss 41(7), (9), 156, Sch 40 Pt II(1) with effect for covenanted payments falling
  to be made by individuals after 5 April 2000 or made by companies after 31 March 2000.

60 British Museum and Natural History Museum

(1), (2) ...

(3) ...[1]

(4) Subsection (1) above shall apply in relation to accounting periods ending on or after 14th March
1989, and [subsection (2)][2] above shall apply to payments due on or after that day.

Notes—Sub-s (1) inserts TA 1988 s 507(1)(c), (d) and repeals s 507(2).
Sub-s (2) amends TA 1988 s 339(9).
Amendments—[1] Sub-s (3) repealed by FA 1995 Sch 17 para 25, Sch 29 Pt VIII(8), with effect from the year 1995–96.
[2] Words in sub-s (4) substituted by FA 1995 Sch 17 para 25, with effect from the year 1995–96 and apply to every settlement,
  wherever and whenever made or entered into.

Profit-related pay, share schemes etc

[61 Profit-related pay

*Schedule 4 to this Act (which amends the provisions of the Taxes Act 1988 relating to profit-related
pay) shall have effect.]*[1]

Amendments—[1] This section repealed by FA 1997 Sch 18 Pt VI(3) with effect for any payment made by reference to a profit
  period beginning after 31 December 1999 in accordance with FA 1997 s 61(2), (3), but subject to FA 1997 Sch 18 Pt VI(3)
  note 2.

62 Savings-related share option schemes

(1) Part III of Schedule 9 to the Taxes Act 1988 (requirements applicable to savings-related share
option schemes) shall be amended as follows.

(2) (*amended* TA 1988 Sch 9 para 24(2)(a), *repealed by* FA 1991 Sch 19 Pt V).

(3) (*amends* TA 1988 Sch 9, para 25(b)).

(4) Subsection (2) above shall come into force on such day as the Treasury may by order made by
statutory instrument appoint.

Notes—The day appointed under sub-s (4) is 1 September 1989 by FA 1989 (Savings-Related Share Option Schemes) (Appointed
  Day) Order, SI 1989/1520.

63 Profit sharing schemes

(*amended* TA 1988 s 187(2) *repealed by* FA 1991 Sch 19 Pt V).

64 Share option and profit sharing schemes: shares of consortium member

(*Repeals* TA 1988 Sch 9, para 10(c)(ii)).

65 Employee share schemes: material interest

(*Inserts* TA 1988 Sch 9 para 40).

66 Priority share allocations for employees etc

(1) In relation to offers made on or after 11th October 1988, section 68 of the Finance Act 1988
(which provides for the benefits derived from priority rights in share offers to be disregarded in
certain circumstances) shall have effect with the following amendments.

(2)–(5) (*amend* FA 1988 s 68(1), *insert* s 68(1A), (2A), (2B) and *substitute* FA 1988 s 68(2)(a)).

Employee share ownership trusts

67 Tax relief

(1) This section applies where—

(*a*) a company expends a sum in making a payment by way of contribution to the trustees of a trust which is a qualifying employee share ownership trust at the time the sum is expended,

(*b*) at that time, the company or a company which it then controls has employees who are eligible to benefit under the terms of the trust deed,

(*c*) at that time the company is resident in the United Kingdom,

(*d*) before the expiry of the expenditure period the sum is expended by the trustees for one or more of the qualifying purposes, and

(*e*) before the end of the claim period a claim for relief under this section is made.

(2) In such a case the sum—

(*a*) shall be deducted in computing for the purposes of Schedule D the [profits]¹ of a trade carried on by the company, or

(*b*) if the company is an investment company or a company in the case of which section 75 of the Taxes Act 1988 applies by virtue of section 76 of that Act, shall be treated as expenses of management.

(3) For the purposes of subsection (1)(*b*) above, the question whether one company is controlled by another shall be construed in accordance with section 840 of the Taxes Act 1988.

(4) For the purposes of subsection (1)(*d*) above each of the following is a qualifying purpose—

(*a*) the acquisition of shares in the company which established the trust;

(*b*) the repayment of sums borrowed;

(*c*) the payment of interest on sums borrowed;

(*d*) the payment of any sum to a person who is a beneficiary under the terms of the trust deed;

(*e*) the meeting of expenses.

(5) For the purposes of subsection (1)(*d*) above the expenditure period is the period of nine months beginning with the day following the end of the period of account in which the sum is charged as an expense of the company, or such longer period as the Board may allow by notice given to the company.

(6) For the purposes of subsection (1)(*e*) above the claim period is the period of two years beginning with the day following the end of the period of account in which the sum is charged as an expense of the company.

(7) For the purposes of this section the trustees of an employee share ownership trust shall be taken to expend sums paid to them in the order in which the sums are received by them (irrespective of the number of companies making payments).

Commentary—*Simon's Direct Tax Service* D2.227.
Amendment—¹ Words substituted by FA 1998 Sch 7 para 3 with effect from 31 July 1998.

68 Principal charges to tax

(1) This section applies where a chargeable event (within the meaning of section 69 below) occurs in relation to the trustees of an employee share ownership trust.

(2) In such a case—

(*a*) the trustees shall be treated as receiving, when the event occurs, annual profits or gains whose amount is equal to the chargeable amount (within the meaning of section 70 below),

(*b*) the profits or gains shall be chargeable to tax under Case VI of Schedule D for the year of assessment in which the event occurs, and

(*c*) the rate at which the tax is chargeable shall be [the rate applicable to trusts]¹ for the year of assessment in which the event occurs.

(3) If the whole or any part of the tax assessed on the trustees is not paid before the expiry of the period of six months beginning with the day on which the assessment becomes final and conclusive, a notice of liability to tax under this subsection may be served on a qualifying company and the tax or the part unpaid (as the case may be) shall be payable by the company on service of the notice.

(4) Where a notice of liability is served under subsection (3) above—

(*a*) any interest which is due on the tax or the part (as the case may be) and has not been paid by the trustees, and

(*b*) any interest accruing due on the tax or the part (as the case may be) after the date of service,

shall be payable by the company.

(5) Where a notice of liability is served under subsection (3) above and any amount payable by the company (whether on account of tax or interest) is not paid by the company before the expiry of the period of three months beginning with the date of service, the amount unpaid may be recovered from the trustees (without prejudice to the right to recover it instead from the company).

(6) For the purposes of this section each of the following is a qualifying company—

(*a*) the company which established the employee share ownership trust;

(b) any company falling within subsection (7) below.

(7) A company falls within this subsection if, before it is sought to serve a notice of liability on it under subsection (3) above—

(a) it has paid a sum to the trustees, and
(b) the sum has been deducted as mentioned in section 67(2)(a) above or treated as mentioned in section 67(2)(b) above.

Commentary—*Simon's Direct Tax Service* D2.229; E4.598.
Amendments—¹ Words in sub-s (2)(c) substituted by FA 1993 Sch 6 paras 20, 25(1) with effect from the year 1993–94.

69 Chargeable events

(1) For the purposes of section 68 above each of the following is a chargeable event in relation to the trustees of an employee share ownership trust—

(a) the transfer of securities by the trustees, if the transfer is not a qualifying transfer;
(b) the transfer of securities by the trustees to persons who are at the time of the transfer beneficiaries under the terms of the trust deed, if the terms on which the transfer is made are not qualifying terms;
(c) the retention of securities by the trustees at the expiry of the [qualifying period]³ beginning with the date on which they acquired them;
(d) the expenditure of a sum by the trustees for a purpose other than a qualifying purpose.
[(e) where—

(i) the trustees make a qualifying transfer within subsection (3AA) below for a consideration, and
(ii) they do not, during the period specified in subsection (5A) below, expend a sum of not less than the amount of that consideration for one or more qualifying purposes,

the expiry of that period.]⁶

(2) For the purposes of subsection (1)(a) above a transfer is a qualifying transfer if it is made to a person who at the time of the transfer is a beneficiary under the terms of the trust deed.

(3) For the purposes of subsection (1)(a) above a transfer is also a qualifying transfer if—

(a) it is made to the trustees of a scheme which at the time of the transfer is a profit sharing scheme approved under Schedule 9 to the Taxes Act 1988, and
(b) it is made for a consideration which is not less than the price the securities might reasonably be expected to fetch on a sale in the open market.

[(3AA) For the purposes of subsection (1)(a) above a transfer is also a qualifying transfer if—

(a) it is a transfer of relevant shares made to the trustees of the plan trust of an employee share ownership plan,
(b) the plan is approved under Schedule 8 to the Finance Act 2000 when the transfer is made, and
(c) the consideration (if any) for which the transfer is made does not exceed the market value of the shares.

(3AB) For the purpose of determining whether a transfer by the trustees is a qualifying transfer within subsection (3AA) above, where on or after 21st March 2000—

(a) the trustees transfer or dispose of part of a holding of shares (whether by way of a qualifying transfer or otherwise), and
(b) the holding includes any relevant shares,

the relevant shares shall be treated as transferred or disposed of before any other shares included in that holding.

For this purpose "holding" means any number of shares of the same class held by the trustees, growing or diminishing as shares of that class are acquired or disposed of.

(3AC) For the purposes of subsections (3AA) and (3AB) above—

"market value" has the same meaning as in Schedule 8 to the Finance Act 2000; and
"relevant shares" means—

(i) shares that are held by the trustees of the employee share ownership trust at midnight on 20th March 2000, and
(ii) shares purchased by those trustees with original funds after that time.

(3AD) For the purposes of subsection (3AC) above—

(a) "original funds" means any money held by the trustees of the employee share ownership trust in a bank or building society account at midnight on 20th March 2000, and
(b) any payment made by the trustees after that time (whether to acquire shares or otherwise) shall be treated as made out of original funds (and not out of money received after that time) until those funds are exhausted.]⁶

[(3A) For the purposes of subsection (1)(a) above a transfer is also a qualifying transfer if it is made by way of exchange in circumstances mentioned in section 85(1) of the Capital Gains Tax Act 1979 or section 135(1) of the Taxation of Chargeable Gains Act 1992.]²

(4) For the purposes of subsection (1)(*b*) above a transfer of securities is made on qualifying terms if—

    (*a*) all the securities transferred at the same time [other than those transferred on a transfer such as is mentioned in subsection (4ZA) below]⁵ are transferred on similar terms,

    (*b*) securities have been offered to all the persons who are beneficiaries under the terms of the trust deed [by virtue of a rule which conforms with paragraph 4(2), (3) or (4) of Schedule 5 to this Act]⁵ when the transfer is made, and

    (*c*) securities are transferred to all such [persons]⁵ who have accepted.

[(4ZA) For the purposes of subsection (1)(*b*) above a transfer of securities is also made on qualifying terms if—

    (*a*) it is made to a person exercising a right to acquire shares, and

    (*b*) that right was obtained in accordance with the provisions of a savings-related share option scheme within the meaning of Schedule 9 to the Taxes Act 1988—

        (i) which was established by, or by a company controlled by, the company which established the trust, and

        (ii) which is approved under that Schedule, and

    (*c*) that right is being exercised in accordance with the provisions of that scheme, and

    (*d*) the consideration for the transfer is payable to the trustees.]⁵

[(4A) For the purposes of subsection (1)(*c*) above the qualifying period is—

    (*a*) seven years, in the case of trusts established on or before the day on which the Finance Act 1994 was passed;

    (*b*) twenty years, in the case of other trusts;

and for this purpose a trust is established when the deed under which it is established is executed.]⁴

(5) For the purposes of subsection (1)(*d*) [or (*e*)]⁶ above each of the following is a qualifying purpose—

    (*a*) the acquisition of shares in the company which established the trust;

    (*b*) the repayment of sums borrowed;

    (*c*) the payment of interest on sums borrowed;

    (*d*) the payment of any sum to a person who is a beneficiary under the terms of the trust deed;

    (*e*) the meeting of expenses.

[(5A) The period referred to in paragraph (*e*) of subsection (1) above is the period—

    (*a*) beginning with the qualifying transfer mentioned in that paragraph, and

    (*b*) ending nine months after the end of the period of account in which that qualifying transfer took place.

For this purpose the period of account means the period of account of the company that established the employee share ownership trust.]⁶

(6) For the purposes of subsection (4) above, the fact that terms vary according to the levels of remuneration of beneficiaries, the length of their service, or similar factors, shall not be regarded as meaning that the terms are not similar.

(7) In ascertaining for the purposes of this section whether particular securities are retained, securities acquired earlier by the trustees shall be treated as transferred by them before securities acquired by them later.

(8) For the purposes of this section trustees—

    (*a*) acquire securities when they become entitled to them (subject to the exceptions in subsection (9) below);

    (*b*) transfer securities to another person when that other becomes entitled to them;

    (*c*) retain securities if they remain entitled to them.

(9) The exceptions are these—

    (*a*) if securities are issued to trustees in exchange in circumstances mentioned in section [135(1) of the Taxation of Chargeable Gains Act 1992]¹, they shall be treated as having acquired them when they became entitled to the securities for which they are exchanged;

    (*b*) if trustees become entitled to securities as a result of a reorganisation, they shall be treated as having acquired them when they became entitled to the original shares which those securities represent (construing ''reorganisation'' and ''original shares'' in accordance with section [126]¹ of that Act).

(10) If trustees agree to take a transfer of securities, for the purposes of this section they shall be treated as becoming entitled to them when the agreement is made and not on a later transfer made pursuant to the agreement.

(11) If trustees agree to transfer securities to another person, for the purposes of this section the other person shall be treated as becoming entitled to them when the agreement is made and not on a later transfer made pursuant to the agreement.

(12) For the purposes of this section the following are securities—

    (*a*) shares;

    (*b*) debentures.

Commentary—*Simon's Direct Tax Service* **E4.594, 597.**
Amendments—[1] Words and number in sub-s (9) substituted by TCGA 1992 Sch 10 para 19(1).
[2] Sub-s (3A) inserted by F(No 2)A 1992 s 36 in relation to exchanges made after 31 December 1991.
[3] Words in sub-s (1)(c) substituted by FA 1994 Sch 13 para 6.
[4] Sub-s (4A) inserted by FA 1994 Sch 13 para 6.
[5] Words in sub-s (4)(a), (b) inserted, word in sub-s (4)(c) substituted and sub-s (4ZA) inserted by FA 1996 s 120(3), (4), (12) with effect in relation to trusts established after 28 April 1996.
[6] Sub-ss (1)(e), (3AA)–(3AD), (5A), and words in sub-s (5), inserted by FA 2000 s 55(1)–(5) with effect from 28 July 2000.

70 Chargeable amounts

(1) This section has effect to determine the chargeable amount for the purposes of section 68 above.

(2) If the chargeable event falls within section 69(1)(a), (b) or (c) above the following rules shall apply—

   (a) if the event constitutes a disposal of the securities by the trustees for the purposes of the [Taxation of Chargeable Gains Act 1992][1], the chargeable amount is an amount equal to the sums allowable under section [38(1)(a)][1] and (b) of that Act;

   (b) if the event does not constitute such a disposal, the chargeable amount is an amount equal to the sums which would be so allowable had the trustees made a disposal of the securities for the purposes of that Act at the time the chargeable event occurs.

(3) If the chargeable event falls within section 69(1)(d) above the chargeable amount is an amount equal to the sum concerned.

[(4) If the chargeable event falls within section 69(1)(e) above the chargeable amount is an amount equal to—

   (a) the amount of the consideration received for the qualifying transfer mentioned in section 69(1)(e) above, less

   (b) the amount of any expenditure by the trustees for a qualifying purpose during the period mentioned in section 69(5A) above.][2]

Commentary—*Simon's Direct Tax Service* **E4.594.**
Amendments—[1] Words and number in sub-s (2)(a) substituted by TCGA 1992 Sch 10 para 19(2).
[2] Sub-s (4) inserted by FA 2000 s 55(6) with effect from 28 July 2000.

71 Further charges to tax: borrowing

(1) This section applies where—

   (a) a chargeable event (within the meaning of section 69 above) occurs in relation to the trustees of an employee share ownership trust,

   (b) at the time the event occurs anything is outstanding in respect of the principal of an amount or amounts borrowed at any time by the trustees, and

   (c) the chargeable event is one as regards which section 72(2)(b) below applies.

(2) In the following provisions of this section—

   (a) "the initial chargeable event" means the event referred to in subsection (1)(a) above, and

   (b) "the total outstanding amount" means the total amount outstanding, at the time the initial chargeable event occurs, in respect of the principal of an amount or amounts borrowed at any time by the trustees.

(3) If any of the total outstanding amount is repaid after the initial chargeable event occurs, a further chargeable event shall occur in relation to the trustees at the end of the year of assessment in which the repayment is made.

(4) In such a case—

   (a) the trustees shall be treated as receiving, when the further event occurs, annual profits or gains whose amount is equal to the chargeable amount,

   (b) the profits or gains shall be chargeable to tax under Case VI of Schedule D for the year of assessment at the end of which the further event occurs, and

   (c) the rate at which the tax is chargeable shall be [the rate applicable to trusts][1] for the year of assessment at the end of which the further event occurs.

(5) Subject to subsection (6) below, for the purposes of subsection (4) above the chargeable amount is an amount equal to the aggregate of the total outstanding amount repaid in the year of assessment.

(6) In a case where section 72(2)(b) below had effect in the case of the initial chargeable event, for the purposes of subsection (4) above the chargeable amount is an amount equal to the smaller of—

   (a) the aggregate of the total outstanding amount repaid in the year of assessment, and

   (b) an amount found by applying the formula A–B–C.

(7) For the purposes of subsection (6) above—

   (a) A is the amount which would be the chargeable amount for the initial chargeable event apart from section 72(2) below,

   (b) B is the chargeable amount for the initial chargeable event, and

   (c) C is the amount (if any) found under subsection (8) below.

(8) If, before the further chargeable event occurs, one or more prior chargeable events have occurred in relation to the trustees by virtue of the prior repayment of any of the total outstanding amount

found for the time the initial chargeable event occurs, the amount found under this subsection is an amount equal to the chargeable amount for the prior chargeable event or to the aggregate of the chargeable amounts for the prior chargeable events (as the case may be).

(9) In a case where—

(a) a chargeable event (within the meaning of section 69 above) occurs in relation to the trustees in circumstances mentioned in subsection (1) above,

(b) a sum falls to be included in the total outstanding amount found for the time the event occurs,

(c) another chargeable event (within the meaning of that section) occurs in relation to the trustees in circumstances mentioned in subsection (1) above, and

(d) the same sum or a part of it would (apart from this subsection) fall to be included in the total outstanding amount found for the time the event occurs,

the sum or part (as the case may be) shall not be included in the total outstanding amount found for the time the other chargeable event occurs.

(10) In ascertaining for the purposes of this section whether a repayment is in respect of a particular amount, amounts borrowed earlier shall be taken to be repaid before amounts borrowed later.

(11) Subsections (3) to (7) of section 68 above shall apply where tax is assessed by virtue of this section as they apply where tax is assessed by virtue of that section.

Commentary—*Simon's Direct Tax Service* **E4.597.**
Amendments—¹ Words in sub-s (4)(c) substituted by FA 1993 Sch 6 paras 20, 25(1) with effect from the year 1993–94.

72 Limit on chargeable amount

(1) For the purposes of this section each of the following is a chargeable event in relation to the trustees of an employee share ownership trust—

(a) an event which is a chargeable event by virtue of section 69 above;

(b) an event which is a chargeable event by virtue of section 71 above.

(2) If a chargeable event (the event in question) occurs in relation to the trustees of an employee share ownership trust, the following rules shall apply—

(a) the amount which would (apart from this subsection) be the chargeable amount for the event in question shall be aggregated, for the purposes of paragraph (b) below, with the chargeable amounts for other chargeable events (if any) occurring in relation to the trustees before the event in question,

(b) if the amount which would (apart from this subsection) be the chargeable amount for the event in question (or the aggregate found under paragraph (a) above, if there is one) exceeds the deductible amount, the chargeable amount for the event in question shall be the amount it would be apart from this subsection less an amount equal to the excess, and

(c) section 70(2) and (3) and section 71(5) above shall have effect subject to paragraph (b) above.

(3) For the purposes of subsection (2) above the deductible amount (as regards the event in question) is an amount equal to the total of the sums falling within subsection (4) below.

(4) A sum falls within this subsection if it has been received by the trustees before the occurrence of the event in question and—

(a) it has been deducted as mentioned in section 67(2)(a) above, or treated as mentioned in section 67(2)(b) above, before the occurrence of that event, or

(b) it would fall to be so deducted or treated if a claim for relief under section 67 above had been made immediately before the occurrence of that event.

Commentary—*Simon's Direct Tax Service* **E4.597.**

73 Information

(1) An inspector may by notice in writing require a return to be made by the trustees of an employee share ownership trust if they have at any time received a sum which has been deducted as mentioned in section 67(2)(a) above or treated as mentioned in section 67(2)(b) above.

(2) Where he requires such a return to be made the inspector shall specify the information to be contained in it.

(3) The information which may be specified is information the inspector needs for the purposes of sections 68 to 72 above, and may include information about—

(a) sums received (including sums borrowed) by the trustees;

(b) expenditure incurred by them;

(c) assets acquired by them;

(d) transfers of assets made by them.

(4) The information which may be required under subsection (3)(a) above may include the persons from whom the sums were received.

(5) The information which may be required under subsection (3)(b) above may include the purpose of the expenditure and the persons receiving any sums.

(6) The information which may be specified under subsection (3)(c) above may include the persons from whom the assets were acquired and the consideration furnished by the trustees.

(7) The information which may be included under subsection (3)(*d*) above may include the persons to whom assets were transferred and the consideration furnished by them.

(8) In a case where a sum has been deducted as mentioned in section 67(2)(*a*) above, or treated as mentioned in section 67(2)(*b*) above, the inspector shall send to the trustees to whom the payment was made a certificate stating—

(*a*) that a sum has been so deducted or so treated, and

(*b*) what sum has been so deducted or so treated.

(9) (*inserts an entry in TMA 1970 s 98 Table*).

Commentary—*Simon's Direct Tax Service* **D2.230; E4.599.**

74 Interpretation

Schedule 5 to this Act shall have effect to determine whether, for the purposes of sections 67 to 73 above, a trust is at a particular time—

(*a*) an employee share ownership trust;

(*b*) a qualifying employee share ownership trust.

Pensions etc

75 Retirement benefits schemes

Schedule 6 to this Act (which relates to retirement benefits schemes) shall have effect.

76 Non-approved retirement benefits schemes

(1) In computing the amount of the [profits]² to be charged under Case I or Case II of Schedule D, no sum shall be deducted in respect of any expenses falling within subsection (2) or (3) below; and no expenses falling within either of those subsections shall be treated for the purposes of section 75 of the Taxes Act 1988 (investment companies) as expenses of management.

(2) [Subject to subsection (6A) below, expenses]¹ fall within this subsection if—

(*a*) they are expenses of providing benefits pursuant to a relevant retirement benefits scheme, and

(*b*) the benefits are not ones in respect of which a person is on receipt chargeable to income tax.

(3) [Subject to subsection (6A) below, expenses]¹ fall within this subsection if—

(*a*) they are expenses of paying any sum pursuant to a relevant retirement benefits scheme with a view to the provision of any benefits, and

(*b*) the sum is not one which when paid is treated as the income of a person by virtue of section 595(1) of the Taxes Act 1988 (sum paid with a view to the provision of any relevant benefits for an employee).

(4) No sum shall be deducted in respect of any expenses falling within subsection (5) or (6) below—

(*a*) in computing the amount of the [profits]² to be charged under Case I or Case II of Schedule D, or

(*b*) by virtue of section 75 of the Taxes Act 1988,

unless the sum has actually been expended.

(5) [Subject to subsection (6A) below, expenses]¹ fall within this subsection if—

(*a*) they are expenses of providing benefits pursuant to a relevant retirement benefits scheme, and

(*b*) the benefits are ones in respect of which a person is on receipt chargeable to income tax.

(6) [Subject to subsection (6A) below, expenses]¹ fall within this subsection if—

(*a*) they are expenses of paying any sum pursuant to a relevant retirement benefits scheme with a view to the provision of any benefits, and

(*b*) the sum is one which when paid is treated as the income of a person by virtue of section 595(1) of the Taxes Act 1988.

[(6A) Expenses to which subsection (6B) or (6C) below applies shall be treated as not falling within any of subsections (2), (3), (5) or (6) above.]¹

[(6B) This subsection applies to expenses of paying any sum, or of providing benefits, pursuant to a superannuation fund which satisfies the requirements of section 615(6) of the Taxes Act 1988.]¹

[(6C) This subsection applies to expenses of paying any sum, or of providing benefits, pursuant to a retirement benefits scheme which is established outside the United Kingdom and which the Board are satisfied corresponds to such a scheme as is mentioned in paragraphs (*a*), (*b*) or (*c*) of section 596(1) of the Taxes Act 1988, where the expenses are incurred for the benefit of:

(*a*) employees whose emoluments are foreign emoluments within the meaning of section 192 of the Taxes Act 1988; or

(*b*) employees who are not resident in the United Kingdom and whose duties are performed wholly outside the United Kingdom (and for this purpose duties performed in the United Kingdom the performance of which is merely incidental to the performance of other duties outside the United Kingdom shall be treated as performed outside the United Kingdom).]¹

(7) In this section—

"retirement benefits scheme" has the same meaning as in Chapter I of Part XIV of the Taxes Act 1988, and

references to a relevant retirement benefits scheme are references to a retirement benefits scheme which is not of a description mentioned in section 596(1)(a), (b) or (c) of the Taxes Act 1988.

(8) This section has effect in relation to expenses incurred on or after the day on which this Act is passed.

Commentary—*Simon's Direct Tax Service* B3.1430; E7.226.
Concession B39—
Contributions to overseas pension schemes.
Revenue Interpretation RI 118—The Revenue consider that relief under sub-s (4) should not be given to an employer before the period in which the expense is actually incurred, based on the Financial Secretary to the Treasury's statement in introducing the Bill, there is no ambiguity.
Revenue Internal Guidance—Inspector's manual IM 8420–8425 (income chargeable to income tax at basic rate and possibly additional rate under TA 1988 s 686; "set-off assessment" arrangement available where benefits take form of annual payments under deduction of tax).
Amendments—¹ Words in sub-ss (2), (3), (5), (6) substituted, and sub-ss (6A)–(6C) inserted, by FA 1996 Sch 39 para 2 with effect for expenses incurred after 28 April 1996.
² Words substituted by FA 1998 Sch 7 para 3 with effect from 31 July 1998.

77 Personal pension schemes

Schedule 7 to this Act (which relates to personal pension schemes) shall have effect.

Unit trusts etc

78 Certified unit trusts

(*Inserted* TA 1988 ss 468A–468C and is repealed by FA 1990 s 132, Sch 19 Pt IV).

79 Funds of funds

(*Inserted* TA 1988 s 468D and is repealed by FA 1990 s 132, Sch 19 Pt IV).

80 Gilt unit trusts

Amendment—Repealed by FA 1998 s 165, Sch 27 Part III(23) with effect from 31 July 1998.

81 Offshore funds operating equalisation arrangements

(1) (*amends* TA 1988 s 758(6)).

(2) This section shall apply where a conversion of securities occurs on or after 14th March 1989; and "conversion of securities" here has the same meaning as in section 82 of the Capital Gains Tax Act 1979.

Note—As regards the meaning of "conversion of securities" see TCGA 1992 s 132.

Life assurance

82 Calculation of profits

(1) Where the profits of an insurance company in respect of its life assurance business are, for the purposes of the Taxes Act 1988, computed in accordance with the provisions of that Act applicable to Case I of Schedule D, then, in calculating the profits for any period of account,—

(a) there shall be taken into account as an expense (so far as not so taken into account apart from this section) any amounts which [are allocated to, and any amounts of tax *or foreign tax*² which are expended on behalf of, policy holders or annuitants in respect of the period]¹; and

(b) if, at the end of the period, the company has an unappropriated surplus on valuation, as shown in [the return deposited with the Financial Services Authority under section 9.6 of the Prudential Sourcebook (Insurers)]³, then, subject to subsection(3) below, the closing liabilities of the period may include such amount, forming part of that surplus, as is required to meet the reasonable expectations of policy holders or annuitants with regard to bonuses or other additions to benefit of a discretionary nature.

[(1A) In subsection (1)(b) above "the Prudential Sourcebook (Insurers)" means the Interim Prudential Sourcebook for Insurers made by the Financial Services Authority under the Financial Services and Markets Act 2000.]³

(2) For the purposes of this section an amount is allocated to policy holders or annuitants if, and only if,—

(a) bonus payments are made to them; or

(b) reversionary bonuses are declared in their favour or a reduction is made in the premiums payable by them;

and the amount of the allocation is, in a case within paragraph (a) above, the amount of the payments and, in a case within paragraph (b) above, the amount of the liabilities assumed by the company in consequence of the declaration or reduction.

(3) The amount which, apart from this subsection, would be included in the closing liabilities of a period of account by virtue of subsection (1)(*b*) above shall be reduced or, as the case may be, extinguished by deducting therefrom the total of the amounts which,—

 (*a*) for periods of account ending before 14th March 1989 have been excluded, by virtue of section 433 of the Taxes Act 1988, as being reserved for policy holders or annuitants, and

 (*b*) have not before that date either been allocated to or expended on behalf of policy holders or annuitants or been treated as profits of an accounting period on ceasing to be so reserved.

(4) Where the closing liabilities of a period of account include an amount by virtue of subsection (1)(*b*) above, the like amount shall be included in the opening liabilities of the next following period of account.

(5) This section has effect with respect to periods of account ending on or after 14th March 1989; and the following provisions of this section shall apply for the purposes of the application of this section to any such period which begins before that date (in this section referred to as a "straddling period").

(6) For the purposes referred to in subsection (5) above, it shall be assumed that the straddling period consists of two separate periods of account,—

 (*a*) the first beginning at the beginning of the straddling period and ending on 13th March 1989 (in this section referred to as "the first notional period"); and

 (*b*) the second beginning on 14th March 1989 and ending at the end of the straddling period (in this section referred to as "the second notional period");

and any reference in subsection (7) or subsection (8) below to a time apportionment is a reference to an apportionment made by reference to the respective lengths of the two notional periods.

(7) To determine the profits of the first notional period and the amount excluded from the profits of that period by virtue of section 433 of the Taxes Act 1988, as being reserved for policy holders or annuitants,—

 (*a*) in the first instance the profits of the straddling period and the amount so excluded from those profits shall be computed as if subsections (1) to (4) above did not apply with respect to any part of the straddling period; and

 (*b*) there shall then be determined that part of the profits and the amount computed under paragraph (*a*) above which, on a time apportionment, is properly attributable to the first notional period.

(8) To determine the profits of the second notional period,—

 (*a*) in the first instance the profits of the straddling period shall be computed as if subsections (1) to (4) above applied to the whole of the straddling period; and

 (*b*) there shall then be determined that part of the profits computed under paragraph (*a*) above which, on a time apportionment, is properly attributable to the second notional period.

Commentary—*Simon's Direct Tax Service* D4.513.
Statement of Practice SP4/95—Computation for tax purposes of profits from long term insurance business.
Revenue Internal Guidance—Life assurance manual LAM 6.31–6.54 (deductions allowable under sub-ss (1), (2) LAM 7.1–7.57 (explanation of the new basis of Case I computation with worked examples).
Cross references—See TA 1988 s 439B (application of this section with modification of sub-s (1)(*a*) by omission of the words "tax or", and sub-ss (2), (4) in computing the profits from life re-insurance business).
TA 1988 s 441(4)(*a*) (application of this section with necessary modifications in computing the profits from overseas life assurance business);
Modifications—This section modified so far as it applies to the life of endowment business carried on by friendly societies and by non-directive societies by the Friendly Societies (Modification of the Corporation Tax Acts) Regulations, SI 1997/473 reg 32.
Sub-s (9) treated as inserted in applying life assurance provisions of the Corporation Tax Acts to insurance companies carrying on capital redemption business with effect for accounting periods ending after 30 June 1999: see Insurance Companies (Capital Redemption Business) (Modification of the Corporation Tax Acts) Regulations, SI 1999/498 reg 9.
Amendments—[1] Words in sub-s (1)(*a*) substituted by FA 1990 s 43(1), (3) and deemed always to have had effect.
[2] Words in sub-s (1)(*a*) repealed by FA 2000 ss 103, 156, Sch 30 para 18(2), (4), Sch 40 Pt II(13) with effect for periods of account beginning after 31 March 2000.
[3] Words in sub-s (1)(*b*) substituted, and sub-s (1A) inserted, by the Financial Services and Markets Act 2000 (Consequential Amendments) (Taxes) Order, SI 2001/3629 arts 54, 55 with effect for periods of account ending after 30 November 2001.

[83 Receipts to be brought into account

(1) The following provisions of this section have effect where the profits of an insurance company in respect of its life assurance business are, for the purposes of the Taxes Act 1988, computed in accordance with the provisions of that Act applicable to Case I of Schedule D.

(2) So far as referable to that business, the following items, as brought into account for a period of account (and not otherwise), shall be taken into account as receipts of the period—

 (*a*) the company's investment income from the assets of its [long-term insurance][4] fund, and

 (*b*) any increase in value (whether realised or not) of those assets.

If for any period of account there is a reduction in the value referred to in paragraph (*b*) above (as brought into account for the period), that reduction shall be taken into account as an expense of that period.

[(3) In ascertaining whether or to what extent a company has incurred a loss in respect of that business in a case where an amount is added to the company's [long-term insurance]⁴ fund as part of or in connection with—

(*a*) a transfer of business to the company, or

(*b*) a demutualisation of the company not involving a transfer of business,

that amount shall (subject to subsection (4) below) be taken into account, for the period for which it is brought into account, as an increase in value of the assets of that fund within subsection (2)(*b*) above.]²

[(4) Subsection (3) above does not apply where, or to the extent that, the amount concerned—

(*a*) would fall to be taken into account as a receipt apart from this section,

(*b*) is taken into account under subsection (2) above otherwise than by virtue of subsection (3) above, or

(*c*) is specifically exempted from tax.]²

[(5) Any amount which is to be taken into account pursuant to subsection (3) above for a period of account shall be so taken into account—

(*a*) after the making of any reduction under subsection (6) of section 83AA below in relation to that period, but

(*b*) before the making of any reduction under subsection (3) of that section in relation to an accounting period of the company ending in or with that period.]²

[(6) In subsection (3) above "transfer of business" means—

[(*a*) a transfer, under an insurance business transfer scheme, of business which consists of the effecting or carrying out of contracts of long-term insurance;]³

(*b*) a qualifying overseas transfer, within the meaning of paragraph 4A of Schedule 19AC to the Taxes Act 1988; or

(*c*) the making of a contract of reinsurance which, in whole or in part, constitutes or forms part of a total reinsurance by the reinsured, unless the reinsurer under the contract falls within section 439A of the Taxes Act 1988 (pure reinsurance).]²

[(6A) In subsection (6)(*a*) above—

"insurance business transfer scheme" means a scheme falling within section 105 of the Financial Services and Markets Act 2000, including an excluded scheme falling within Case 2, 3 or 4 of subsection (3) of that section;

"contracts of long-term insurance" means contracts which fall within Part II of Schedule 1 to the Financial Services and Markets Act 2000 (Regulated Activities) Order 2001.]³

[(7) For the purposes of subsection (3)(*a*) above, a transfer of business falling within subsection (6)(*c*) above shall be treated as a transfer of business to the company which is the reinsurer under the contract of reinsurance.]²

[(8) In this section—

"add", in relation to an amount and a company's [long-term insurance]⁴ fund, includes transfer (whether from other assets of the company or otherwise);

"demutualisation" means the conversion, under the law of any territory, of a company which has been carrying on insurance business without having a share capital into a company with a share capital, without any change of legal personality;

"total reinsurance" means the reinsurance (whether effected by a single contract of reinsurance or by two or more such contracts, taken together, whether or not made with the same reinsurer) of the whole, or substantially the whole, of the reinsured's risk—

(*a*) under policies of a particular description issued in respect of insurances made in the course of carrying on life assurance business before the making of the contract of reinsurance (or, in a case where there are two or more contracts of reinsurance, the last of them); or

(*b*) under contracts of a particular description so made.]²]¹

Commentary—*Simon's Direct Tax Service* **D4.513.**
Revenue Internal Guidance—Life assurance manual LAM 6.1–6.19 (income within this section)
LAM 6.21–6.23 (Case I income not within this section).
LAM 6.61–6.66 (fiscal adjustments under this section).
Definitions—"Brought into account", s 83A; "company", TA 1988 s 832(1); "tax", TA 1988 s 832(3).
Cross reference—See TA 1988 s 436(3)(*aa*) (application of this section with necessary modification in computing the profits from pension business).
TA 1988 s 439B (application of this section with necessary modification in computing the profits from life reinsurance business).
TA 1988 s 441(4) (application of this section with necessary modification in computing the profits from overseas life assurance business).
FA 1989 Sch 8A paras 1A–1C (modifications of this section in its application to an overseas life insurance company).
FA 1999 Sch 6 para 4(2) (application of this section notwithstanding provisions in FA 1999 Sch 6 paras 2, 3 concerning tax treatment of receipts by way of reverse premium).
Modifications—This section modified so far as it applies to the life of endowment business carried on by directive societies, by non-directive societies, and in relation to specified transactions, by the Friendly Societies (Modification of the Corporation Tax Acts) Regulations, SI 1997/473 regs 32–35.
Amendments—¹ This section and s 83A substituted for s 83 as originally enacted, by FA 1995 Sch 8 para 16(1), with effect for accounting periods beginning after 31 December 1994.
² Sub-ss (3)–(8) substituted for sub-s (3) by FA 1996 Sch 31 para 4 with effect for periods of account beginning after 31 December 1995.

[83AA Amounts added to [long-term insurance]² fund of a company in excess of that company's loss

(1) If one or more relevant amounts are brought into account for a period of account of a company and either—

  (*a*) the aggregate of those amounts exceeds the loss which, after the making of any reduction under subsection (6) below but before any application of section 83(3) above in relation to that period, would have arisen to the company in that period in respect of its life assurance business, or

  (*b*) no such loss would have so arisen,

the surplus for that period shall be applied in accordance with the following provisions of this section and section 83AB below.

(2) In this section—

  "relevant amount" means so much of any amount which is added to the [long-term insurance]² fund of a company as mentioned in subsection (3) of section 83 above as does not fall within any of the paragraphs of subsection (4) of that section;

  "surplus", in relation to a period of account of a company, means (subject to section 83AB(2) below)—

    (*a*) if the aggregate of the relevant amounts brought into account for that period exceeds the amount of any loss which, after the making of any reduction under subsection (6) below but before any application of section 83(3) above in relation to that period, would have arisen to the company in that period in respect of its life assurance business, the amount of the excess; or

    (*b*) if no such loss would have so arisen, the aggregate of the relevant amounts brought into account for that period.

(3) Where, apart from section 83AB(2) below, there is a surplus for a period of account of a company for which there are brought into account one or more relevant amounts which were added to the company's [long-term insurance]² fund as part of, or in connection with, a particular transfer of business, the appropriate portion of the surplus for that period shall be treated as reducing (but not below nil) so much of any loss arising to the transferor company in the relevant accounting period as, on a just and reasonable apportionment of the loss, is referable to the business which is the subject of that particular transfer.

(4) For the purposes of subsection (3) above, the appropriate portion of the surplus for a period of account of a company is, in the case of any particular transfer of business, the amount which bears to that surplus (apart from any additions by virtue of section 83AB(2) below) the proportion which A bears to B, where—

  A is the aggregate of such of the relevant amounts added to the company's [long-term insurance]² fund as part of, or in connection with, that particular transfer of business as are brought into account for that period, and
  B is the aggregate of the relevant amounts brought into account for that period.

(5) Any reduction pursuant to subsection (3) above of the loss arising to the transferor company in the relevant accounting period shall be made after—

  (*a*) the making of any reduction under subsection (6) below, and
  (*b*) any application of section 83(3) above,

in relation to the period of account of that company in which falls the date of the particular transfer of business in question.

(6) Any loss arising to a company in respect of its life assurance business in a period of account subsequent to one for which there is a surplus shall be reduced (but not below nil) by so much of that surplus as cannot be applied—

  (*a*) under subsection (3) above;
  (*b*) under this subsection, in the reduction of a loss arising to the company in an earlier period of account; or
  (*c*) under section 83AB below, in relation to a transfer of business from the company in that or any earlier period of account.

(7) Any reduction pursuant to subsection (6) above of a loss arising to a company in a period of account shall be made—

  (*a*) before any application of section 83(3) above in relation to that period, and (*b*) if the company is also the transferor company in relation to a particular transfer of business, before the making of any reduction under subsection (3) above in relation to that one of its accounting periods which is the relevant accounting period in relation to that transfer.

(8) A surplus in respect of an earlier period of account shall be applied under subsection (6) above before a surplus in respect of a later period of account.

(9) All such adjustments to the liability to tax of any person shall be made, whether by assessment or otherwise, as may be required to give effect to this section.

(10) In this section—

"add" has the same meaning as in section 83 above;

"the relevant accounting period" means that accounting period of the transferor company which—

(*a*) ends on the date of the transfer of business mentioned in subsection (3) above, or

(*b*) if that transfer of business falls within section 83(6)(*c*) above and no accounting period of the transferor company ends on that date, ends next after that date;

"transfer of business" has the same meaning as in section 83(3) above;

"the transferor company" means the company from which the transfer of business mentioned in subsection (3) above is effected.

(11) A transfer of business falling within section 83(6)(*c*) above shall be treated for the purposes of this section as a transfer of business from the company which is the reinsured under the contract of reinsurance.]¹

Commentary—*Simon's Direct Tax Service* **D4.513**.
Cross reference—See FA 1989 Sch 8A para 1A(5) (for purposes of sub-ss (2), (3), (4) amount being added to relevant company's long term business fund to be construed in accordance with sub-para (4)).
Amendments—¹ Section inserted by FA 1996 Sch 31 para 5 with effect for periods of account beginning after 31 December 1995, but subject to transitional provisions in para 9 thereof.
² Words in Heading and sub-ss (2), (3), (4) substituted by the Financial Services and Markets Act 2000 (Consequential Amendments) (Taxes) Order, SI 2001/3629 arts 54, 60(1)(*b*) with effect from 1 December 2001, immediately after the coming into force of the Financial Services and Markets Act 2000 ss 411, 432(1), Sch 20.

[83AB Treatment of surplus where there is a subsequent transfer of business from the company etc

(1) If an amount is added to the [long-term insurance]² fund of a company as part of or in connection with a transfer of business to the company, or a demutualisation of the company not involving a transfer of business, and—

(*a*) there is a surplus for the period of account of the company for which that amount is brought into account,

(*b*) at any time after the transfer of business or demutualisation, there is a transfer of business from the company (the "subsequent transfer"), and

(*c*) at the end of the relevant period of account there remains at least some of the surplus mentioned in paragraph (*a*) above which cannot be applied—

(i) under subsection (3) of section 83AA above,

(ii) under subsection (6) of that section, in the reduction of a loss arising to the company in an earlier period of account, or

(iii) under this section, in relation to an earlier subsequent transfer,

so much of the surplus falling within paragraph (*c*) above as, on a just and reasonable apportionment, is referable to business which is the subject of the subsequent transfer shall be applied under this section.

(2) An amount of surplus which is to be applied under this section shall be so applied by being treated as an amount of surplus (additional to any other amounts of surplus) for the period of account of the transferee company which last precedes the period of account of that company in which the subsequent transfer is effected, whether or not there is in fact any such preceding period of account.

(3) If, in a case where an amount is treated under subsection (2) above as an amount of surplus for a period of account of a company, the period is not one for which there is brought into account an amount added to the company's [long-term insurance]² fund in connection with the subsequent transfer, subsection (1) above shall have effect in relation to any transfer of business from the company subsequent to that transfer as if an amount had been so added and had been brought into account for that period.

(4) Any question as to what is a just and reasonable apportionment in any case for the purposes of subsection (1) above shall be determined by the Special Commissioners who shall determine the question in the same manner as they determine appeals; but any person affected by the apportionment shall be entitled to appear and be heard or make representations in writing.

(5) A surplus in respect of an earlier period of account shall be applied under this section before a surplus in respect of a later period of account.

(6) All such adjustments to the liability to tax of any person shall be made, whether by assessment or otherwise, as may be required to give effect to this section.

(7) In this section—

"add" has the same meaning as in section 83 above;

"demutualisation" has the same meaning as in section 83 above;

"the relevant period of account" means the period of account of the company from which the subsequent transfer is effected which consists of or includes the accounting period of that company which—

(*a*) ends with the day on which the subsequent transfer is effected; or

(*b*) if the subsequent transfer is a transfer of business falling within section 83(6)(*c*) above and no accounting period of the company ends on that day, ends next after that day;

"surplus" has the same meaning as in section 83AA above;

"transfer of business" has the same meaning as in section 83(3) above;

"transferee company" means the company to which the subsequent transfer of business is effected.

(8) Where it is necessary for any purpose of this section to identify the time at which a demutualisation of a company takes place, that time shall be taken to be the time when the company first issues shares.

(9) A transfer of business falling within section 83(6)(*c*) above shall be treated for the purposes of this section as a transfer of business from the company which is the reinsured under the contract of reinsurance to the company which is the reinsurer under that contract.]¹

Commentary—*Simon's Direct Tax Service* D4.513.
Cross reference—See FA 1989 Sch 8A para 1A(5) (for purpose of sub-ss (1), (3) amount being added to relevant company's long term business fund to be construed in accordance with sub-para (4)).
Amendments—¹ Section inserted by FA 1996 Sch 31 para 5 with effect for periods of account beginning after 31 December 1995, but subject to transitional provisions in para 9 thereof.
² Words in sub-ss (1), (3) substituted by the Financial Services and Markets Act 2000 (Consequential Amendments) (Taxes) Order, SI 2001/3629 arts 54, 60(1)(*c*) with effect from 1 December 2001, immediately after the coming into force of the Financial Services and Markets Act 2000 ss 411, 432(1), Sch 20.

[83A Meaning of "brought into account"

(1) [In sections 83 to 83AB]³ "brought into account" means brought into account in an account which is recognised for the purposes of [those sections]³.

(2) Subject to the following provisions of this section and to any regulations made by the Treasury, the accounts recognised for the purposes of [those sections]³ are—

(*a*) a revenue account prepared for the purposes of [Chapter 9 of the Prudential Sourcebook (Insurers)]⁴ in respect of the whole of the company's [long-term]⁵ business;

(*b*) any separate revenue account required to be prepared [under that Chapter]⁴ in respect of a part of that business.

[In paragraph (*a*) [above]⁶ "the Prudential Sourcebook (Insurers)" means the Interim Prudential Sourcebook for Insurers made by the Financial Services Authority under the Financial Services and Markets Act 2000.]⁴

[Paragraph (*b*) above does not include accounts required in respect of internal linked funds.]⁶

(3) Where there are prepared any such separate accounts as are mentioned in subsection (2)(*b*) above, reference shall be made to those accounts rather than to the account for the whole of the business.

(4) If in any such case the total of the items brought into account in the separate accounts is not equal to the total amount brought into account in the account prepared for the whole business, there shall be treated as having been required and prepared a further separate revenue account covering the balance.

(5) ...2]1

Commentary—*Simon's Direct Tax Service* D4.513.
Statement of Practice SP4/95—Computation for tax purposes of profits from long term insurance business.
Revenue Internal Guidance—Life assurance manual LAM 8.26A–8.26D (application of this section).
Modifications— This section is modified in its application to an overseas life insurance company by FA 1989 Sch 8A paras 1A–1C.
This section is modified so far as it applies to the life of endowment business carried on by directive societies and by non-directive societies by the Friendly Societies (Modification of the Corporation Tax Acts) Regulations, SI 1997/473 regs 36, 37.
Amendments—¹ This section and s 83 *ante*. substituted for s 83 as originally enacted, by FA 1995 Sch 8 para 16(1), with effect for accounting periods beginning after 31 December 1994.
² Sub-s (5) repealed by FA 1996 Sch 41 Pt V(26) with effect for accounting periods beginning after 31 December 1995.
³ Words in sub-ss (1), (2) substituted by FA 1996 Sch 31 para 6 with effect for periods of account beginning after 31 December 1995.
⁴ Words in sub-s (2) substituted by the Financial Services and Markets Act 2000 (Consequential Amendments) (Taxes) Order, SI 2001/3629 arts 54, 57 with effect for periods of account ending after 30 November 2001.
⁵ Word in sub-s (2)(*a*) substituted by SI 2001/3629 arts 54, 60(2)(*a*) with effect from 1 December 2001, immediately after the coming into force of the Financial Services and Markets Act 2000 ss 411, 432(1), Sch 20.
⁶ In sub-s (2), words inserted by the Financial Services and Markets Act 2000 (Consequential Amendments) (Taxes) Order, SI 2002/1409 art 3 with effect from 2 July 2002.

84 Interpretation of sections 85 to 89 and further provisions about insurance companies

[(1) In sections 85 to 89 below "basic life assurance and general annuity business" has the same meaning as in Chapter I of Part XII of the Taxes Act 1988.]¹

(2) Any reference in the sections referred to in subsection (1) above or the following provisions of this section to a straddling period is a reference to an accounting period which begins before 1st January 1990 and ends on or after that date.

(3) For the purposes of the sections referred to in subsection (1) above and for the purposes of subsection (5)(*b*) below it shall be assumed that a straddling period consists of two separate accounting periods—

(*a*) the first beginning at the beginning of the straddling period and ending on 31st December 1989; and

(*b*) the second beginning on 1st January 1990 and ending at the end of the straddling period;

and in those sections and subsection (5)(*b*) below the first of those two notional accounting periods is referred to as ''the 1989 component period'' and the second is referred to as ''the 1990 component period''.

(4) Chapter I of Part XII of the Taxes Act 1988 (insurance companies) shall have effect subject to the amendments in Schedule 8 to this Act, being—

(*a*) amendments relating to franked investment income, loss relief and group relief; and

(*b*) amendments consequential on or supplemental to sections 82 and 83 above and sections 85 to 89 below.

(5) Subject to subsection (6) below, in Schedule 8 to this Act,—

(*a*) paragraphs 2 and 6 shall be deemed to have come into force on 14th March 1989; and

(*b*) the remainder shall have effect with respect to accounting periods beginning on or after 1st January 1990 (including the 1990 component period).

(6) Nothing in subsection (5) above affects the operation, by virtue of any provision of sections 82 and 83 above and sections 85 to 89 below, of any enactment repealed or amended by Schedule 8 to this Act and, so long as the provisions of that Schedule do not have effect in relation to sections 434 and 435 of the Taxes Act 1988 nothing in subsection (5)(*a*) above affects the continuing operation of section 433 of that Act for the purpose only of determining the fraction of the profits referred to in subsection (6) of section 434 and subsection (1)(*b*) of section 435.

Commentary—*Simon's Direct Tax Service* **D4.504.**
Amendments—[1] Sub-s (1) substituted by FA 1991 Sch 7 paras 11, 18 with respect to accounting periods beginning after 31 December 1991.

85 Charge of certain receipts of basic life assurance business

(1) Subject to subsection (2) below, where the profits of an insurance company in respect of its life assurance business are not charged under Case I of Schedule D, there shall be chargeable under Case VI of that Schedule any receipts referable to the company's [basic life assurance and general annuity business][2]—

(*a*) which, if those profits were charged under Case I of Schedule D, would be taken into account in computing those profits; and

(*b*) which would not be within the charge to tax (except under Case I of Schedule D) apart from this section;

and for the purposes of paragraph (*a*) above, the provisions of section 83 above as to the manner in which any item is to be taken into account shall be disregarded.

(2) The receipts referred to in subsection (1) above do not include—

(*a*) any premium; or

(*b*) any sum received by virtue of a claim under an insurance contract (including a reinsurance contract); or

(*c*) any repayment or refund (in whole or in part) of a sum disbursed by the company as acquisition expenses falling within paragraphs (*a*) to (*c*) of subsection (1) of section 86 below; or

[(*ca*) any reinsurance commission; or][1]

(*d*) any sum which is taken into account under section 76(1)(*a*) of the Taxes Act 1988 as a deduction from the amount treated as expenses of management of the company; or

(*e*) any sum which is not within the charge to tax (except under Case I of Schedule D) because of an exemption from tax.

(3) This section has effect with respect to the receipts of accounting periods beginning on or after 1st January 1990 (including the 1990 component period).

Commentary—*Simon's Direct Tax Service* **D4.510.**
Modification—Sub-s (1) is modified so far as it applies to the life or endowment business carried on by friendly societies by the Friendly Societies (Modification of the Corporation Tax Acts) Regulations, SI 1997/473 reg 38.
Amendments—[1] Sub-s (2)(*ca*) inserted by FA 1990 s 44(1), (4) and deemed always to have had effect.
[2] Words in sub-s (1) substituted by FA 1991 Sch 7 paras 12, 18 with respect to accounting periods beginning after 31 December 1991.

86 Spreading of relief for acquisition expenses

(1) For the purposes of this section, the acquisition expenses for any period of an insurance company carrying on life assurance business are such of the following expenses of management as are for that period attributable to the company's [basic life assurance and general annuity business][2],—

(*a*) commissions (however described), other than commissions [for persons who collect premiums from house to house]⁵,

(*b*) any other expenses of management which are disbursed solely for the purpose of the acquisition of business, and

(*c*) so much of any other expenses of management which are disbursed partly for the purpose of the acquisition of business and partly for other purposes as are properly attributable to the acquisition of business,

[reduced by the items specified in subsection (1A) below]¹.

[(1A) Those items are—

(*a*) the appropriate portion of any deduction falling to be made under paragraph (*aa*) of subsection (1) of section 76 of the Taxes Act 1988 for the period in question;

(*b*) any such repayments or refunds falling within paragraph (*c*) of that subsection as are received in that period;

(*c*) any reinsurance commissions falling within paragraph (*ca*) of that subsection.]¹

[(1B) For the purposes of paragraph (*a*) of subsection (1A) above, ''the appropriate portion'' of the deduction there mentioned is the amount which bears to the whole of that deduction the proportion which the acquisition expenses, without making the reduction required by subsection (1) above, would bear to the whole of the expenses of management, without making the deductions required by paragraphs (*aa*), (*a*), (*c*) and (*ca*) of section 76(1) of the Taxes Act 1988.]¹

(2) The exclusion from paragraph (*a*) of subsection (1) above of commissions [for persons who collect premiums from house to house]⁵ shall not prevent such commissions constituting expenses of management for the purposes of paragraph (*b*) or paragraph (*c*) of that subsection.

(3) Nothing in subsections (1) and (2) above applies to commissions (however described) in respect of insurances made before 14th March 1989, but without prejudice to the application of those subsections to any commission attributable to a variation on or after that date in a policy issued in respect of an insurance made before that date; and, for this purpose, the exercise of any rights conferred by a policy shall be regarded as a variation of it.

[(3A) Nothing in subsection (1), (2) or (3) above applies to commissions (however described) in respect of annuity contracts made in accounting periods beginning before 1st January 1992, but without prejudice to the application of subsections (1) and (2) above to any commission attributable to a variation, in an accounting period beginning on or after that date, of an annuity contract so made; and for this purpose the exercise of any rights conferred by an annuity contract shall be regarded as a variation of it.]³

(4) In subsection (1) above ''the acquisition of business'' includes—

[(*a*)]³ the securing on or after 14th March 1989 of the payment of increased or additional premiums in respect of a policy of insurance issued in respect of an insurance already made (whether before, on or after that date) [and]³

[(*b*) the securing, in an accounting period beginning on or after 1st January 1992, of the payment of increased or additional consideration in respect of an annuity contract already made (whether in an accounting period beginning before, or on or after, that date).]³

(5) In relation to any period, the expenses of management attributable to a company's [basic life assurance and general annuity business]² are expenses—

(*a*) which are disbursed for that period (disregarding any treated as so disbursed by section 75(3) of the Taxes Act 1988); and

(*b*) which, disregarding subsection (6) below, are deductible as expenses of management in accordance with sections 75 and 76 of the Taxes Act 1988.

[(5A) References in this section to expenses of management do not include any amounts treated as additional expenses of management [under section 256(2)(*a*) of the Capital Allowances Act (giving effect to capital allowances referable to basic life assurance and general annuity business of company carrying on life assurance business)]⁶.]⁴

(6) Notwithstanding anything in sections 75 and 76 of the Taxes Act 1988 but subject to subsection (7) below, only one-seventh of the acquisition expenses for any accounting period (in this section referred to as ''the base period'') shall be treated as deductible under those sections for the base period, and in subsections (8) and (9) below any reference to the full amount of the acquisition expenses for the base period is a reference to the amount of those expenses which would be deductible for that period apart from this subsection.

(7) In the case of the acquisition expenses for an accounting period or part of an accounting period falling wholly within 1990, subsection (6) above shall have effect as if for ''one-seventh'' there were substituted ''five-sevenths''; and, in the case of the acquisition expenses for an accounting period or part of an accounting period falling wholly within 1991, 1992 or 1993, the corresponding substitution shall be ''four-sevenths'', ''three-sevenths'' or ''two-sevenths'' respectively.

(8) Where, by virtue of subsection (6) (and, where appropriate, subsection (7)) above, only a fraction of the full amount of the acquisition expenses for the base period is deductible under sections 75 and 76 of the Taxes Act 1988 for that period, then, subject to subsection (9) below, a further one-seventh of the full amount shall be so deductible for each succeeding accounting period after the base period

until the whole of the full amount has become so deductible, except that, for any accounting period of less than a year, the fraction of one-seventh shall be proportionately reduced.

(9) For any accounting period for which the fraction of the full amount of the acquisition expenses for the base period which would otherwise be deductible in accordance with subsection (8) above exceeds the balance of those expenses which has not become deductible for earlier accounting periods, only that balance shall be deductible.

(10) This section has effect for accounting periods beginning on or after 1st January 1990 (including the 1990 component period).

Commentary—*Simon's Direct Tax Service* **D4.505.**
Modification—This section is modified so far as it applies to the life or endowment business carried on by friendly societies by the Friendly Societies (Modification of the Corporation Tax Acts) Regulations, SI 1997/473 reg 39.
Amendments—[1] Words in sub-s (1) substituted, and sub-ss (1A), (1B), inserted by FA 1996 Sch 31 para 3(1), (2) with effect for accounting periods beginning after 31 December 1995.
[2] Words in sub-ss (1), (5) substituted by FA 1991 Sch 7 paras 13, 18 with respect to accounting periods beginning after 31 December 1991.
[3] Sub-s (3A) and words in sub-s (4) inserted by FA 1991 Sch 7 paras 13, 18.
[4] Sub-s (5A) inserted by FA 1995 Sch 8 para 23(3), with effect for accounting periods beginning after 31 December 1994.
[5] Words in sub-s (1)(a), (2) substituted by FA 1996 s 167(3), (10) with effect for accounting periods beginning after 31 December 1995.
[6] Words in sub-s (5A) substituted by CAA 2001 s 578, Sch 2 para 70 with effect for corporation tax purposes as respects allowances and charges falling to be made for chargeable periods ending after 31 March 2001.

87 Management expenses

(1) Section 76 of the Taxes Act 1988 shall be amended in accordance with subsections (2) and (3) below.

(2) (*inserts* TA 1988 s 76(1)(c)–(e)).

(3) (*substituted* TA 1988 s 76(8) repealed by FA 1991 Sch 19 Pt V).

(4) (*repeals* TA 1988 s 436(3)(b)).

(5) This section has effect with respect to accounting periods beginning on or after 1st January 1990; and, in relation to a straddling period, sections 75, 76 and 436 of the Taxes Act 1988—

　(a) shall have effect in relation to the 1989 component period without regard to the amendments made by subsections (2) to (4) above; and
　(b) shall have effect in relation to the 1990 component period as amended by those subsections.

(6) If, for the 1989 component period, there is an amount of expenses of management available to be carried forward to the 1990 component period under section 75(3)(a) of the Taxes Act 1988 (as applied by section 76 thereof),—

　(a) that amount shall form a pool to which the following provisions of this section shall apply and to which section 75(3)(b) of that Act (in this subsection referred to as "the carry-forward provision") shall apply only to the extent specified in paragraph (c) below;
　(b) if, for the 1990 component period or any subsequent accounting period, the amount which (disregarding the pool) may be deducted in respect of expenses of management is less than the amount of the profits from which, disregarding section 76(1)(e) of that Act (as set out in subsection (2) above), the expenses of management are deductible, paragraph (c) below shall apply for that period; and in that paragraph the difference between the amount which may be so deducted and that amount of profits is referred to as "the potential deficiency" for the period;
　(c) where this paragraph applies for an accounting period (including the 1990 component period) the carry-forward provision shall be taken to have had effect to carry forward to the accounting period (as if disbursed as expenses for that period) so much of the pool as does not exceed the potential deficiency for the period and is permitted under section 76(2) of the Taxes Act 1988; and the amount of the pool shall be reduced accordingly.

(7) In the case of a company which has an accounting period beginning on 1st January 1990, subsection (6) above shall apply as if—

　(a) any reference therein to the 1989 component period were a reference to the accounting period ending on 31st December 1989; and
　(b) any reference therein to the 1990 component period were a reference to the accounting period beginning on 1st January 1990.

Commentary—*Simon's Direct Tax Service* **D4.504.**

88 Corporation tax: policy holders' fraction of profits

(1) Subject to subsection (2) [and section 88A below][4] below, in the case of a company carrying on life assurance business, the rate of corporation tax chargeable for any financial year on—

　[(a) the policy holders' share of the relevant profits for any accounting period, or
　(b) where the business is mutual business, the whole of those profits,

shall][1] be deemed to be the rate at which income tax at the basic rate is charged for the year of assessment which begins on 6th April in the financial year concerned.

(2) Subsection (1) above does not apply in relation to profits charged under Case I of Schedule D.

[(3) For the purposes of subsection (1) above, the relevant profits of a company for an accounting period are the income and gains of the company's life assurance business reduced by the aggregate amount of—

[(*aa*) amounts falling in respect of any non-trading deficits on the company's loan relationships to be brought into account in that period in accordance with paragraph 4 of Schedule 11 to the Finance Act 1996,][5]

(*a*) expenses of management falling to be deducted under section 76 of the Taxes Act 1988, and

(*b*) charges on income,

so far as referable to the company's life assurance business.][3]

(4) In determining for the purposes of section 13 of the Taxes Act 1988 (small companies' relief) the profits and basic profits (within the meaning of that section) of an accounting period of a company carrying on life assurance business, the policy holders' [share][1] of the company's relevant profits for that period [, or where the business is mutual business the whole of those profits,][2] shall be left out of account.

(5) This section has effect with respect to the profits of a company for accounting periods beginning on or after 1st January 1990 (including the 1990 component period); and, for this purpose, the profits of the 1990 component period shall be taken to be that portion of the profits of the straddling period which the length of the 1990 component period bears to the length of the straddling period.

Commentary—*Simon's Direct Tax Service* **D4.509, 514.**
Simon's Tax Cases—s 88(3), *Prudential Assurance Co Ltd v Bibby* [1999] STC (SCD) 108; *Prudential Assurance Co Ltd v Bibby* [1999] STC 952.
Cross reference—See FA 1988 s 89(9) (application of s 89 for the purpose of construing references to the policy holders' share of the relevant profits for an accounting period of a company carrying on life assurance business).
Amendments—[1] Words in sub-ss (1), (4) substituted by FA 1990 s 45(1), (2), (10) and deemed always to have had effect.
[2] Words in sub-s (4) inserted by FA 1990 s 45(1), (2), (10).
[3] Sub-s (3) substituted by FA 1995 Sch 8 para 21(2), with effect for accounting periods beginning after 31 December 1994.
[4] Words in sub-s (1) inserted by FA 1996 Sch 6 para 26(1), (4) with effect for the financial year 1996 and subsequent years.
[5] Sub-s (3)(*aa*) inserted by FA 1996 s 104, Sch 14 para 56 with effect for accounting periods ending after 31 March 1996, subject to transitional provisions in FA 1996 Sch 15.

[88A Lower corporation tax rate on certain insurance company profits

(1) Subject to subsection (2) below, in the case of a company carrying on basic life assurance and general annuity business, the rate of corporation tax chargeable for any financial year on so much of the company's BLAGAB profits for any accounting period as represents the company's lower rate income for the period shall be deemed to be the rate at which income tax at the lower rate is charged for the year of assessment which begins on 6th April in the financial year concerned.

(2) Subsection (1) above does not apply in relation to profits charged under Case I of Schedule D.

(3) In this section, references to a company's lower rate income for any accounting period are references to so much of the income and gains of its basic life assurance and general annuity business for the period as consists in income of any of the following descriptions—

(*a*) income falling within paragraph (*a*) of Case III of Schedule D, as that Case applies for the purposes of corporation tax;

(*b*) purchased life annuities to which section 656 of the Taxes Act 1988 applies or to which that section would apply but for section 657(2)(*a*) of that Act;

(*c*) any such dividends or other distributions of a company not resident in the United Kingdom as would be chargeable under Schedule F if the company were resident in the United Kingdom;

(*d*) so much of—

(i) any dividend distribution (within the meaning of section 468J of the Taxes Act 1988), ...[2]

(ii) ...[2]

as is deemed by subsection (2) of section 468Q of that Act ...[2] to be an annual payment.

(4) Where for any period—

(*a*) an insurance company's basic life assurance and general annuity business is mutual business,

(*b*) the policy holders' share of the company's relevant profits is equal to all those profits, or

(*c*) the policy holders' share of the company's relevant profits is more than the company's BLAGAB profits,

the amount to be taken for the purposes of this section as the amount of the company's BLAGAB profits for that period representing its lower rate income for that period shall be the amount equal to the applicable proportion of its BLAGAB profits.

(5) Where subsection (4) above does not apply in the case of an insurance company for any period, the amount to be taken for the purposes of this section as the amount of the company's BLAGAB profits for the period representing its lower rate income for that period shall be the amount produced by multiplying the following, that is to say—

(*a*) the applicable proportion of those profits; and

(*b*) the fraction given by dividing the policy holders' share of the relevant profits of the company for the period by its BLAGAB profits for that period.

(6) For the purposes of this section the applicable proportion of a company's BLAGAB profits for any period is the amount which bears the same proportion to those profits as the aggregate amount

of the company's lower rate income for that period bears to the total income and gains for that period of the company's basic life assurance and general annuity business.

(7) For the purposes of this section, the BLAGAB profits of a company for an accounting period are the income and gains of the company's basic life assurance and general annuity business reduced by the aggregate amount of—

(a) any non-trading deficit on the company's loan relationships,

(b) expenses of management falling to be deducted under section 76 of the Taxes Act 1988, and

(c) charges on income,

so far as referable to the company's basic life assurance and general annuity business.

(8) Section 88(3) above applies for the purposes of this section as it applies for the purposes of section 88(1) above.]¹

Commentary—*Simon's Direct Tax Service* **D4.509.**
Cross references—See FA 1989 s 89(9) (application of s 89 for the purpose of construing references to the policy holders' share of the BLAGAB profits for an accounting period of a company carrying on basic life assurance and general annuity business).
Modification—This section is modified so far as it applies to the life or endowment business carried on by friendly societies by the Friendly Societies (Modification of the Corporation Tax Acts) Regulations, SI 1997/473 reg 40.
Amendments—¹ This section inserted by FA 1996 Sch 6 para 26(2), (4) with effect for the financial year 1996 and subsequent years.
² Words in sub-s (3) repealed by F(No 2)A 1997 s 36(4), Sch 6 para 18, Sch 8 Pt II(11) with effect in relation to distributions made after 5 April 1999.

[89 Policy holders' share of profits

(1) The references in [sections 88 and 88A]³ above to the policy holders' share of the relevant profits for an accounting period of a company carrying on life assurance business [or, as the case may be, basic life assurance and general annuity business]³ are references to the amount arrived at by deducting from those profits the Case I profits of the company for the period in respect of [its life assurance business]³, reduced in accordance with subsection (2) below.

(2) For the purposes of subsection (1) above, the Case I profits for a period shall be reduced by—

(a) ...⁴

(b) the shareholders' share of any ...⁴ franked investment income arising in the period [which is referable to the company's basic life assurance and general annuity business]⁵ ...²

(c) ...²

[(2A) ...]²

(3) For the purposes of this section "the shareholders' share" in relation to any income is so much of the income as is represented by the fraction

$$\frac{A}{B}$$

where—

A is an amount equal to the Case I profits of the company for the period in question in respect of its life assurance business, and

B is an amount equal to the excess of the company's relevant non-premium income and relevant gains over its relevant expenses and relevant interest for the period.

(4) Where there is no such excess as is mentioned in subsection (3) above, or where the Case I profits are greater than any excess, the whole of the income shall be the shareholders' share; and (subject to that) where there are no Case I profits, none of the income shall be the shareholders' share.

(5) In subsection (3) above the references to the relevant non-premium income, relevant gains, relevant expenses and relevant interest of a company for an accounting period are references respectively to the following items as brought into account for the period, so far as referable to the company's life assurance business,—

(a) the company's investment income from the assets of its long-term [insurance]⁷ fund together with its other income, apart from premiums;

(b) any increase in the value (whether realised or not) of those assets;

(c) expenses payable by the company;

(d) interest payable by the company;

and if for any period there is a reduction in the value referred to in paragraph (b) above (as brought into account for the period), that reduction shall be taken into account as an expense of the period.

(6) Except in so far as regulations made by the Treasury otherwise provide, in this section "brought into account" means brought into account in the revenue account prepared for the purposes of [Chapter 9 of the Prudential Sourcebook (Insurers)]⁶; and where the company's period of account does not coincide with the accounting period, any reference to an amount brought into account for the accounting period is a reference to the corresponding amount brought into account for the period of account in which the accounting period is comprised, proportionately reduced to reflect the length of the accounting period as compared with the length of the period of account.

[(7) In this section—

"Case I profits" means profits computed in accordance with the provisions of the Taxes Act 1988 applicable to Case I of Schedule D;

"the Prudential Sourcebook (Insurers)" means the Interim Prudential Sourcebook for Insurers made by the Financial Services Authority under the Financial Services and Markets Act 2000.][6]

(8) ...[4][1]

Commentary—*Simon's Direct Tax Service* **D4.514.**
Revenue Internal Guidance—Life Assurance manual 14.1–14.9 (explanation and example of computation of policyholder's share of income and profits).
Cross references—See TA 1988 s 434(1) (franked investment income and foreign income dividends to be taken into account in any computation of profit for the purposes of sub-s (7) above notwithstanding anything in TA 1988 s 208).
FA 1989 s 89A and Sch 8A (modification of this section in relation to overseas life insurance companies for periods of account beginning after 31 December 1992).
FA 1993 s 78(6), (7) (rate of ACT for distributions made after 5 April 1993 for the purpose of computations under this section).
Amendments—[1] This section substituted by FA 1990 s 45(3), (10) and deemed always to have had effect.
[2] Sub-s (2)(c) and the preceding word "and" and sub-s (2A) (originally inserted by FA 1994 Sch 16 para 9) repealed by F(No 2)A 1997 s 36(4), Sch 6 para 19, Sch 8 Pt II(11) with effect in relation to distributions made after 5 April 1999.
[3] Words in sub-s (1) substituted by FA 1996 Sch 6 para 26(3), (4) with effect for financial year 1996 and subsequent financial years.
[4] Sub-s (2)(a), words in sub-s (2)(b), and sub-s (8) repealed by F(No 2)A 1997 s 23, Sch 3 para 14, Sch 8 Pt II(6) with effect in relation to distributions made on or after 2 July 1997.
[5] Words in sub-s (2)(b) substituted, for the words "from investments held in connection with [the company's life assurance business]" (as amended by FA 1996 Sch 6 para 26(3), (4) for financial year 1996 onwards), by F(No 2)A 1997 s 23, Sch 3 para 14(1), (2)(b), (4) with effect as in note 4 above.
[6] Words in sub-s (6), and sub-s (7) substituted, by the Financial Services and Markets Act 2000 (Consequential Amendments) (Taxes) Order, SI 2001/3629 arts 54, 58 with effect for periods of account ending after 30 November 2001.
[7] Word in sub-s (5)(a) substituted by SI 2001/3629 arts 54, 60(3) with effect from 1 December 2001, immediately after the coming into force of the Financial Services and Markets Act 2000 ss 411, 432(1), Sch 20.

[89A Modification of sections 83 and 89 in relation to overseas life insurance companies

Schedule 8A to this Act (which makes modifications of sections 83 and 89 in relation to overseas life insurance companies) shall have effect.][1]

Commentary—*Simon's Direct Tax Service* **D4.537.**
Amendments—[1] This section inserted by FA 1993 s 101(1).

90 Life policies etc held by companies

Schedule 9 to this Act (which imposes tax on certain benefits relating to life policies, life annuities and capital redemption policies held by companies, and makes related provision) shall have effect.

Underwriters

91 Premiums trust funds: stock lending

(1) *(inserts TA 1988 s 725(10), (11). (repealed))*

(2) *(inserts CGTA 1979 s 142A(4A), (4B) and is repealed by TCGA 1992 Sch 12).*

(3) This section applies where the transfer by the trustees of a premiums trust fund is made after the date specified as mentioned in section 129(6) of the Taxes Act 1988.

92 Regulations about underwriters etc

(1) *(amends TA 1988 s 451(1A). (repealed))*

(2) *(inserts TA 1988 s 451(1B). (repealed))*

(3) *(repeals CGTA 1979 s 142A(5)(c), inserts sub-ss (6), (7) and is repealed by TCGA 1992 s 290, Sch 12).*

(4)–(7) ...[1]

Commentary—*Simon's Direct Tax Service* **E5.604, 613.**
Regulations—Lloyd's Underwriters (Tax) (1991–92) Regulations, SI 1994/728. For the continuity of the operation of these Regulations, see FA 1993 s 182(5)(b).
Amendments—[1] Sub-ss (4)–(7) repealed by FA 1993 Sch 23, Part III(12) with effect from the year 1992–93.

Securities

93 Deep discount securities: amendments

Amendments—This section repealed by FA 1996 s 105, Sch 41 Pt V(3) with effect for income tax from the year 1996–97 and for corporation tax for accounting periods ending after 31 March 1996, subject to transitional provisions in FA 1996 Sch 15.

94 Deep gain securities

Amendments—This section repealed by FA 1996 s 105, Sch 41 Pt V(3) with effect for income tax from the year 1996–97 and for corporation tax for accounting periods ending after 31 March 1996, subject to transitional provisions in FA 1996 Sch 15.

95 Treasury securities issued at a discount

Amendments—This section repealed by FA 1996 s 105, Sch 41 Pt V(3) with effect for income tax from the year 1996–97 and for corporation tax for accounting periods ending after 31 March 1996, subject to transitional provisions in FA 1996 Sch 15.

96 Securities: miscellaneous

(1) (*amends* TA 1988 s 452(8). (repealed))

(2) (*inserts* TA 1988 s 687(3)(*h*), (*i*)).

(3) (*inserts* CGTA 1979 s 132A(5), (6) and is repealed by TCGA 1992 s 290, Sch 12).

(4) The new paragraphs (*b*) and (*c*) inserted by subsection (1) above, and subsection (2) above, shall apply—

    (*a*) in the case of a deep discount security, where there is a disposal (within the meaning of Schedule 4 to the Taxes Act 1988) on or after 14th March 1989;

    (*b*) in the case of a deep gain security, where there is a transfer within the meaning of Schedule 11 to this Act, or a redemption, on or after 14th March 1989.

Groups of companies

97 Set-off of ACT where companies remain in same group

Amendments—This section repealed by FA 1998 Sch 27 Part III(2) in relation to accounting periods of the surrendering company beginning after 5 April 1999.

98 Restriction on set-off of ACT

Amendments—This section repealed by FA 1998 Sch 27 Part III(2) for TA 1988 s 245A in relation to changes of ownership occurring after 5 April 1999, and for TA 1988 s 245B in relation to disposals after 5 April 1999.

99 Dividends etc paid by one member of a group to another

(1) *Section 247 of the Taxes Act 1988 (dividends etc paid by one member of a group to another) shall be amended in accordance with this section.*

(2) (*repealed* by FA 1998 Sch 27 Part III(2) for distributions made after 5 April 1999).

(3)–(6) (*insert* TA 1988 s 247(1A), (8A), (9A) and *substitute* TA 1988 s 247(9)(*c*)).

(7) *This section shall have effect in relation to dividends and other sums paid on or after the day on which this Act is passed.*

Amendments—This section repealed by FA 2001 s 110, Sch 33 Pt II(10) with effect for payments made after 11 May 2001.

100 Change in ownership of company

(1) Section 769 of the Taxes Act 1988 (which contains rules for determining whether for the purposes of sections 245 and 768 of that Act there is a change in the ownership of a company) shall be amended in accordance with this section.

(2) (*substitutes* TA 1988 s 769(6)–(6C) for sub-s (6)).

(3) (*repeals* TA 1988 s 769(7)(*b*), (*c*)).

(4) This section shall have effect where the change of ownership of a company would be treated as occurring on or after 14th March 1989.

101 Treatment of convertible shares or securities for purposes relating to group relief etc

(1) Paragraph 1 of Schedule 18 to the Taxes Act 1988 (which contains definitions relating to group relief) shall be amended in accordance with this section.

(2)–(5) (*substitute* TA 1988 Sch 18 para 1(3)(*b*), (5)(*a*), *insert* Sch 18 para 1(5A)–(5D) and *amend* Sch 18 para 1(6)).

(6) This section, so far as relating to Schedule 18 of the Taxes Act 1988 in its application (by virtue of section 138 below) for the purposes of subsections (1D) and (1E) of section 272 of the Taxes Act 1970, shall be deemed to have come into force on 14th March 1989.

102 Surrender of company tax refund etc within group

(1) Subsection (2) below applies where—

    (*a*) there falls to be made to a company (''the surrendering company'') which is a member of a group throughout the appropriate period a tax refund relating to an accounting period of the company (''the relevant accounting period''), and

    (*b*) another company (''the recipient company'') which is a member of the same group throughout the appropriate period also has the relevant accounting period as an accounting period.

(2) Where this subsection applies the two companies may, at any time before the refund is made to the surrendering company, jointly give notice to the inspector in such form as the Board may require that subsection (4) below is to have effect in relation to the refund or to any part of the refund specified in the notice.

(3) In subsection (1) above—

''appropriate period'' means the period beginning with the relevant accounting period and ending on the day on which the notice under subsection (2) above is given, and "tax refund relating to an accounting period" means, in relation to a company—

   (*a*) a repayment of corporation tax paid by the company for the period,

   (*b*) a repayment of income tax in respect of a payment received by the company in the period, or

   (*c*) a payment of the whole or part of the tax credit comprised in any franked investment income received by the company in the period.

(4) Subject to subsection (6) below, where this subsection has effect in relation to any refund or part of a refund—

   (*a*) the recipient company shall be treated for all purposes of the Tax Acts as having paid on the relevant date an amount of corporation tax for the relevant accounting period equal to the amount of the refund or part, and

   (*b*) there shall be treated for all those purposes as having been made to the surrendering company on the relevant date a repayment of corporation tax or income tax or a payment of tax credit (as the case may be) equal to the amount of the refund or part;

and where the refund is a repayment of corporation tax, any interest relating to it which has been paid by the surrendering company shall be treated as having been paid by the recipient company.

[(4A) Where subsection (4) above has effect in relation to any amount and there is, by virtue of any of subsections (7) to [(7CA)][2] of section 826 of the Taxes Act 1988, a period for which the whole or any part of that amount would not, had the refund been made to the surrendering company, have carried interest under that section, that period shall be treated as excluded—

   (*a*) from any period for which any refund made by virtue of subsection (4) above to the recipient company in respect of some or all of that amount or, as the case may be, that part of it is to carry interest under that section; and

   (*b*) from any period for which a sum representing some or all of that amount or part would (apart from this subsection) be treated by virtue of subsection (4) above as not carrying interest under section 87A of the Taxes Management Act 1970;

and in determining for the purposes of this subsection which part of any amount is applied in discharging a liability of the recipient company to pay any corporation tax and which part is represented by a refund to the recipient company, it shall be assumed that the part in relation to which there is a period which would not have carried interest under section 826 of the Taxes Act 1988 is applied in preference to any other part of that amount in or towards discharging the liability.][1]

(5) In subsection (4) above "relevant date", in relation to a refund, means—

   (*a*) in so far as it consists of a repayment of corporation tax paid by the surrendering company after the date on which it became due and payable under [section 59D or 59E of the Taxes Management Act 1970][3], the day on which it was paid by that company, and

   (*b*) otherwise, the date on which corporation tax for the relevant accounting period became due and payable.

(6) For the purpose of ascertaining the amount of any penalty to which the recipient company is liable under [paragraph 18 of Schedule 18 to the Finance Act 1998][4], the corporation tax which the company is treated as having paid by subsection(4)(*a*) above shall be treated as paid on the day on which the notice under subsection (2) above is given (and not on the relevant date).

(7) A payment for a transferred tax refund—

   (*a*) shall not be taken into account in computing profits or losses of either company for corporation tax purposes, and

   (*b*) shall not for any of the purposes of the Corporation Tax Acts be regarded as a distribution or a charge on income;

and in this subsection "a payment for a transferred tax refund" means a payment made by the receiving company to the surrendering company in pursuance of an agreement between them as respects the giving of a notice under this section, being a payment not exceeding the amount of the refund in question.

(8) For the purposes of this section two companies are members of the same group if and only if they would be for the purposes of Chapter IV of Part X of the Taxes Act 1988.

(9) This section shall not apply unless the relevant accounting period ends after such day, not being earlier than 31st March 1992, as the Treasury may by order made by statutory instrument appoint.

Commentary—*Simon's Direct Tax Service* **D2.706.**
Regulations—Corporation Tax (Instalment Payments) Regulations, SI 1998/3175.
Revenue Internal Guidance—Corporation tax manual CT 10227 (no prescribed form under sub-s (2); notice must state names and tax references of companies, type and amount of tax surrendered, and must be signed on behalf of each company).
Revenue and other press releases—
IR Tax Bulletin April 2001 p 831 (the effect of a Group Payment Arrangement (GPA) on the operation of this section and SI 1998/3175 reg 9).
Notes—The appointed day as mentioned in sub-s (9) above is 30 September 1993 by virtue of Corporation Tax Acts (Provisions for Payment of Tax and Returns) (Appointed Days) Order, SI 1992/3066 art 2(1),(2)(*c*).
Modifications—Sub-ss (3), (5) amended, and sub-ss (5A)–(5F) inserted, to include surrender of an excess amount paid by a large company in respect of its tax liability with effect for accounting periods ending after 30 June 1999: Corporation Tax (Instalment Payments) Regulations, SI 1998/3175 reg 9.
Amendments—[1] Sub-s (4A) inserted by FA 1993 Sch 14 para 11.
[2] Word in sub-s (4A) substituted by FA 1995 Sch 24 para 12(3), with effect from 23 March 1995.

[3] Words in sub-s (5)(*a*) substituted by FA 1999 s 89(2), (3) with effect for accounting periods ending after 30 June 1999.
[4] Words in sub-s (6) substituted by FA 1999 s 93, Sch 11 para 3 with effect for accounting periods ending after 30 June 1999.

Close companies

103 Repeal of apportionment provisions

(1) Except as provided by subsection (2) below, Chapter III of Part XI of the Taxes Act 1988 (apportionment of undistributed income etc of close companies) shall not have effect in relation to accounting periods beginning after 31st March 1989.

(2) Section 427(4) of the Taxes Act 1988 (which gives relief to an individual where income apportioned to him in an earlier accounting period of a close company is included in a distribution received by him in a later accounting period), and section 427(5) of, and Part I of Schedule 19 to, that Act so far as they relate to section 427(4), shall continue to have effect in any case where the subsequent distribution referred to in section 427(4) is made before 1st April 1992.

104 Meaning of "close company"

(1) (*substitutes* TA 1988 s 414(2)–(2D) for sub-s (2)).

(2) (*repeals* TA 1988 s 414(3)).

(3) (*amends* TA 1988 s 414(5)(*b*)).

(4) This section shall be deemed to have come into force on 1st April 1989.

105 Small companies' rate not available to certain close companies

(1) (*amends* TA 1988 s 13(1)).

(2) (*inserts* TA 1988 s 13A).

(3) This section shall have effect in relation to accounting periods beginning after 31st March 1989.

106 Restriction on payment of tax credits

Amendments—This section repealed by F(No 2)A 1997 Sch 8 Pt II(9) with effect in relation to distributions made after 5 April 1999.

107 Close companies: consequential amendments

Schedule 12 to this Act (in which Part I contains administrative provisions relating to close companies and Part II makes amendments connected with section 103 above) shall have effect.

Settlements etc

108 Outright gifts etc between husband and wife

Amendments—This section repealed by FA 1995 Sch 29 Pt VIII(8) with effect from the year 1995–96.

109 Settlements where settlor retains interest in settled property

(1)–(3) ...[1]

(4) (*amends* TA 1988 s 677(2)(*c*)).

Amendments—[1] Sub-ss (1)–(3) repealed by FA 1995 Sch 29 Pt VIII(8), with effect from the year 1995–96.

110 Residence of trustees

(1) Where the trustees of a settlement include at least one who is not resident in the United Kingdom as well as at least one who is, then for all the purposes of the Income Tax Acts—

(a) if the condition in subsection (2) below is satisfied, the trustee or trustees not resident in the United Kingdom shall be treated as resident there, and

(b) otherwise, the trustee or trustees resident in the United Kingdom shall be treated as not resident there (but as resident outside the United Kingdom).

(2) The condition referred to in subsection (1) above is that the settlor or, where there is more than one, any of them is at any relevant time—

(a) resident in the United Kingdom,

(b) ordinarily resident there, or

(c) domiciled there.

(3) For the purposes of subsection (2) above the following are relevant times in relation to a settlor—

(a) in the case of a settlement arising under a testamentary disposition of the settlor or on his intestacy, the time of his death, and

(b) in the case of any other settlement, the time or, where there is more than one, each of the times when he has provided funds directly or indirectly for the purposes of the settlement.

(4) For the purposes of this section "settlor", in relation to a settlement, includes any person who has provided or undertaken to provide funds directly or indirectly for the purposes of the settlement.

(5) (*amends* TA 1988 s 824(9)).

(6) Subject to subsections (7) to (9) below, this section shall apply for the year 1989–90 and subsequent years of assessment.

(7) For the purpose of determining the residence of trustees at any time during the year 1989–90, the condition in subsection (2) above shall be regarded as not having been satisfied if none of the trustees of the settlement is resident in the United Kingdom at any time during the period beginning with 1st October 1989 and ending with 5th April 1990.

(8) This section shall not apply for any of the purposes of section 739 of the Taxes Act 1988 in relation to income payable before 15th June 1989, or for the purposes of subsection (3) of that section in relation to income payable on or after that date if—

    (*a*) the capital sum there referred to is received, or the right to receive it is acquired, before that date, and

    (*b*) that sum is wholly repaid, or the right to it waived, before 1st October 1989.

(9) This section shall not apply for any of the purposes of section 740 of the Taxes Act 1988 in relation to benefits received before 15th June 1989; and, in relation to benefits received on or after that date, "relevant income" for those purposes shall include income arising to trustees before 6th April 1989 notwithstanding that one or more of them was not resident outside the United Kingdom, unless they have been charged to tax in respect of it.

Commentary—*Simon's Direct Tax Service* **C4.403.**
Concession A11—This Concession allows a tax year to be split in relation to residence where an individual comes to the UK to take up residence for three years or more or to take up employment for two years or more or leaves the UK for permanent residence abroad.

111 Residence of personal representatives

(1) Where the personal representatives of a deceased person include at least one who is not resident in the United Kingdom as well as at least one who is, then for all the purposes of the Income Tax Acts—

    (*a*) if the condition in subsection (2) below is satisfied, the personal representative or representatives not resident in the United Kingdom shall be treated as resident there, and

    (*b*) otherwise, the personal representative or representatives resident in the United Kingdom shall be treated as not resident there (but as resident outside the United Kingdom).

(2) The condition referred to in subsection (1) above is that the deceased person is at his death—

    (*a*) resident in the United Kingdom,

    (*b*) ordinarily resident there, or

    (*c*) domiciled there.

(3) In this section "personal representatives" means—

    (*a*) in relation to England and Wales, the deceased person's personal representatives as defined by section 55 of the Administration of Estates Act 1925;

    (*b*) in relation to Scotland, his executor or the judicial factor on his estate;

    (*c*) in relation to Northern Ireland, his personal representatives as defined by section 45(1) of the Administration of Estates Act (Northern Ireland) 1955; and

    (*d*) in relation to another country or territory, the persons having in relation to him under its law any functions corresponding to the functions for administration purposes of personal representatives under the law of England and Wales.

(4) (*amends* TA 1988 s 824(9)).

(5) Subject to subsections (6) to (8) below, this section shall apply for the year 1989–90 and subsequent years of assessment.

(6) For the purpose of determining the residence of personal representatives at any time during the year 1989–90, the condition in subsection (2) above shall be regarded as not having been satisfied if none of the personal representatives is resident in the United Kingdom at any time during the period beginning with 1st October 1989 and ending with 5th April 1990.

(7) This section shall not apply for any of the purposes of section 739 of the Taxes Act 1988 in relation to income payable before 15th June 1989, or for the purposes of subsection (3) of that section in relation to income payable on or after that date if—

    (*a*) the capital sum there referred to is received, or the right to receive it is acquired, before that date, and

    (*b*) that sum is wholly repaid, or the right to it waived, before 1st October 1989.

(8) This section shall not apply for any of the purposes of section 740 of the Taxes Act 1988 in relation to benefits received before 15th June 1989 and, in relation to benefits received on or after that date, "relevant income" for those purposes shall include income arising to personal representatives before 6th April 1989 notwithstanding that one or more of them was not resident outside the United Kingdom, unless they have been charged to tax in respect of it.

Commentary—*Simon's Direct Tax Service* C4.117.
Concession A11—This Concession allows a tax year to be split in relation to residence where an individual comes to the UK to take up residence for three years or more or to take up employment for two years or more or leaves the UK for permanent residence abroad.

Miscellaneous

112 Security: trades etc

(1) This section applies in computing, for the purposes of Case I or Case II of Schedule D, the [profits]¹ of a trade, profession or vocation carried on by an individual or by a partnership of individuals.

(2) In a case where this section applies, nothing in section 74(a) or (b) of the Taxes Act 1988 (deductions limited by reference to purposes of trade etc) shall prevent the deduction of a sum in respect of expenditure incurred in connection with the provision for or use by the individual, or any of the individuals, of a security asset or security service.

(3) Subsection (2) above shall not apply unless the asset or service is provided or used to meet a threat which—

    (a) is a special threat to the individual's personal physical security, and
    (b) arises wholly or mainly by virtue of the particular trade, profession or vocation concerned.

(4) Subsection (2) above shall not apply unless the person incurring the expenditure has as his sole object in doing so the meeting of that threat.

(5) Subsection (2) above shall not apply in the case of a service unless the benefit resulting to the individual consists wholly or mainly of an improvement of his personal physical security.

(6) Subsection (2) above shall not apply in the case of an asset unless the person incurring the expenditure intends the asset to be used solely to improve personal physical security.

(7) But in a case where—

    (a) apart from subsection (6) above, subsection (2) above would apply in the case of an asset, and
    (b) the person incurring the expenditure intends the asset to be used partly to improve personal physical security,

subsection (2) shall nevertheless apply, but only as regards the appropriate proportion of the expenditure there mentioned.

(8) For the purposes of subsection (7) above the appropriate proportion of the expenditure mentioned in subsection (2) above is such proportion of that expenditure as is attributable to the intention of the person incurring it that the asset be used to improve personal physical security.

Commentary—*Simon's Direct Tax Service* B3.1436.
Amendment—¹ Words substituted by FA 1998 Sch 7 para 3 with effect from 31 July 1998.

113 Security: trades etc (supplementary)

(1) For the purposes of section 112 above—

    (a) a security asset is an asset which improves personal security,
    (b) a security service is a service which improves personal security,
    (c) references to an asset do not include references to a car, a ship or an aircraft,
    (d) references to an asset or service do not include references to a dwelling or grounds appurtenant to a dwelling, and
    (e) references to an asset include references to equipment and a structure (such as a wall).

(2) If the person incurring the expenditure intends the asset to be used solely to improve personal physical security, but there is another use for the asset which is incidental to improving personal physical security, that other use shall be ignored in construing section 112(6) above.

(3) The fact that an asset or service improves the personal physical security of any member of the family or household of the individual concerned, as well as that of the individual, shall not prevent section 112(2) above from applying.

(4) For the purposes of section 112 above in its application to an asset, it is immaterial whether or not the asset becomes affixed to land (whether constituting a dwelling or otherwise).

(5) For the purposes of section 112 above in its application to an asset, it is immaterial whether or not the individual concerned is or becomes entitled to the property in the asset or (in the case of a fixture) an estate or interest in the land concerned.

(6) Section 112 above applies where expenditure is incurred on or after 6th April 1989.

Commentary—*Simon's Direct Tax Service* B3.1436.

114 Relief for pre-trading expenditure

(*Amended TA* 1988 s 401(1) and is now superseded).

115 Double taxation: tax credits

(1) Where any arrangements having effect by virtue of section 788 of the Taxes Act 1988 provide—

(*a*) for persons who are resident outside the United Kingdom and who receive distributions from companies resident in the United Kingdom to be entitled to tax credits, and

(*b*) for the amount paid to such a person by way of tax credit to be determined by reference to the amount to which an individual resident in the United Kingdom would have been entitled, subject to a deduction calculated by reference to the aggregate of the amount or value of the distribution and the amount of the tax credit paid,

the arrangements shall be construed as providing for that deduction to be calculated by reference to the gross amount or value of the distribution and tax credit, without any allowance for the deduction itself.

(2) This section shall have effect in relation to payments made before the passing of this Act as well as those made after that time, except that it shall not affect—

(*a*) the judgment of any court given before 25th October 1988, or

(*b*) the law to be applied in proceedings on appeal to the Court of Appeal or the House of Lords where the judgment of the High Court or the Court of Session which is in issue was given before that date.

Commentary—*Simon's Direct Tax Service* **F1.215.**
Simon's Tax Cases—*Getty Oil Co v Steele* [1990] STC 434.

116 Interest payments to Netherlands Antilles subsidiaries

Commentary—*Simon's Direct Tax Service* **F4.102; F4.5** .
Amendments—[1] This section repealed by FA 1996 s 105, Sch 41 Pt V(3) with effect for income tax from the year 1996–97 and for corporation tax for accounting periods ending after 31 March 1996, subject to transitional provisions in FA 1996 Sch 15.

CHAPTER II
CAPITAL ALLOWANCES

117 Security

Commentary—*Simon's Direct Tax Service* **B2.312.**
Amendments—This section repealed by CAA 1990 Sch 2; and consolidated in CAA 1990 s 71.

118 Security: supplementary

Commentary—*Simon's Direct Tax Service* **B2.312.**
Amendments—This section repealed by CAA 1990 Sch 2; and consolidated in CAA 1990 s 72.

119 Expenditure on stands at sports grounds

Commentary—*Simon's Direct Tax Service* **B2.310.**
Amendments—This section repealed by CAA 1990 Sch 2; and consolidated in CAA 1990 s 70(1), (5).

120 Forestry land: abolition of agricultural buildings allowances

Commentary—*Simon's Direct Tax Service* **B2.515**.
Amendments—This section repealed by CAA 1990 Sch 2; and consolidated in CAA 1990 s 131.

121 Miscellaneous amendments

Amendment—This section repealed by the Capital Allowances Act 2001 s 580, Sch 4 with effect for income tax purposes, as respects allowances and charges falling to be made for chargeable periods ending on or after 6 April 2001, and for corporation tax purposes, as respects allowances and charges falling to be made for chargeable periods ending on or after 1 April 2001.

CHAPTER III
CAPITAL GAINS
Exemptions

122 Annual exempt amount for 1989–90

Commentary—*Simon's Direct Tax Service* **CI.401, 402.**
Amendments—This section repealed by TCGA 1992 Sch 12.

123 Increase of chattel exemption

(1)(*a*) (*amends* CGTA 1979 s 128 and is repealed by TCGA 1992 Sch 12).

(*b*) (*amends* TMA 1970 s 12(2)(*b*)).

(*c*) (*amends* TMA 1970 s 25(7)).

(2) (specifies commencement date for amendments made by sub-s (1)).

Gifts

124 Relief for gifts

Commentary—*Simon's Direct Tax Service* C1.425, 429.
Amendments—This section repealed by TCGA 1992 Sch 12.

125 Gifts to housing associations

Amendments—This section repealed by TCGA 1992 Sch 12.

Non-residents etc

126 Non-resident carrying on profession or vocation in the United Kingdom

Commentary—*Simon's Direct Tax Service* C1.602.
Amendments—This section repealed by TCGA 1992 Sch 12.

127 Non-residents: deemed disposals

Commentary—*Simon's Direct Tax Service* D2.314.
Amendments—This section repealed by TCGA 1992 Sch 12.

128 Non-residents: post-cessation disposals

Amendments—This section repealed by TCGA 1992 Sch 12.

129 Non-residents: roll-over relief

Commentary—*Simon's Direct Tax Service* C3.318.
Amendments—This section repealed by TCGA 1992 Sch 12.

130 Exploration or exploitation assets: definition

Amendments—This section repealed by TCGA 1992 Sch 12.

131 Exploration or exploitation assets: deemed disposals

Commentary—*Simon's Direct Tax Service* D4.1024.
Amendments—This section repealed by TCGA 1992 Sch 12.

132 Dual resident companies: deemed disposal

Commentary—*Simon's Direct Tax Service* D4.108.
Amendments—This section repealed by TCGA 1992 Sch 12.

133 Dual resident companies: roll-over relief

(*Repealed by* TCGA 1992 Sch 12).

Commentary—*Simon's Direct Tax Service* D4.108.
Amendments—This section repealed by TCGA 1992 Sch 12.

134 Non-payment of tax by non-resident companies

(*Repealed by* TCGA 1992 Sch 12).

Commentary—*Simon's Direct Tax Service* D4.122, 123.
Amendments—This section repealed by TCGA 1992 Sch 12.

Value shifting and groups of companies

135 Value shifting

Commentary—*Simon's Direct Tax Service* D4.122, 123.

136 Value shifting: reductions attributable to distributions within a group

Commentary—*Simon's Direct Tax Service* D2.635.
Amendments—This section repealed by TCGA 1992 Sch 12.

137 Value shifting: transactions treated as a reorganisation of share capital

Commentary—*Simon's Direct Tax Service* D2.635.
Amendments—This section repealed by TCGA 1992 Sch 12.

138 Groups of companies

Commentary—*Simon's Direct Tax Service* D2.622, 630.
Amendments—This section repealed by TCGA 1992 Sch 12.

139 Corporate bonds

Amendments—This section repealed by TCGA 1992 Sch 12.

140 Collective investment schemes

Commentary—*Simon's Direct Tax Service* C1.621; C2.735.
Amendments—This section repealed by TCGA 1992 Sch 12.

141 Re-basing to 1982 etc

Amendments—This section repealed by TCGA 1992 Sch 12.

CHAPTER IV
MANAGEMENT
Information

142 Power to call for documents and information

(1) Section 20 of the Taxes Management Act 1970 (power to call for documents of taxpayer and others) shall be amended in accordance with subsections (2) to (8) below.

(2)–(8) (*amend* TMA 1970 s 20(1), (2), (3), (6), *substitute* s 20(8) and *insert* s 20(8C), (8D)).

(9) (*amends* the National Savings Bank Act 1971 s 12(3)).

(10) This section shall apply with respect to notices given on or after the day on which this Act is passed.

143 Power to call for papers of tax accountant

(1) (*substitutes* TMA 1970 s 20A(1A), (1B) for the last sentence of sub-s (1)).

(2) This section shall apply with respect to notices given on or after the day on which this Act is passed.

144 Restrictions on powers under TMA ss 20 and 20A

(1) Section 20B of the Taxes Management Act 1970 (restrictions on powers under sections 20 and 20A) shall be amended as follows.

(2)–(7) (*amend* TMA 1970 s 20B(1), (2), (5), (7), *insert* s 20B(1A), (1B) and *substitute* s 20B(9)–(14) for sub-s (9)).

(8) This section shall apply with respect to notices given on or after the day on which this Act is passed.

145 Falsification etc of documents

(1) (*inserts* TMA 1970 s 20BB).

(2) This section shall apply to any falsification, concealment, destruction or disposal of a document occurring on or after the day on which this Act is passed.

146 Entry with warrant to obtain documents

(1) Section 20C of the Taxes Management Act 1970 (entry with warrant to obtain documents) shall be amended as follows.

(2)–(4) (*amend* TMA 1970 s 20C(1) *insert* s 20C(1A), (1B) and *substitute* s 20C(3)–(8) for sub-ss (3)–(5)).

(5) This section shall apply with respect to warrants issued on or after the day on which this Act is passed.

147 Procedure where documents etc are removed

(1) (*inserts* TMA 1970 s 20CC).

(2) This section shall apply with respect to warrants issued on or after the day on which this Act is passed.

148 Interpretation

(1) Section 20D of the Taxes Management Act 1970 shall be amended as follows.

(2), (3) (*amend* TMA 1970 s 20D(2) and *substitute* TMA 1970 s 20D(3)).

(4) Subsection (3) above shall not affect the meaning of ''business'' in sections 20 and 20C of the Taxes Management Act 1970 before the coming into force of sections 142 and 146 above.

Assessments, claims etc

149 Assessments founded on fraudulent or negligent conduct

(1), (2) (*substitute* TMA 1970 s 36 and *repeal* ss 37–39).

(3)(*a*), (*b*) (*amend* TMA 1970 s 30(6), 118(3)).

(*c*) (*repealed by FA 1998 Sch 27 Pt III(2) in relation to to return periods and accounting periods beginning after 5 April 1999*).
(*d*) (*amends* TA 1988 Sch 16 para 10(1)).

(4)(*a*)(i) (*amends* TMA 1970 s 37A).

a(ii) (*amends* TMA 1970 s 40(2)).

a(iii) (*amends* FA 1973 Sch 16A para 9 and TA 1988 Sch 19A para 9 (now repealed)).
(*b*) (*amends* TA 1988 s 307(5)).

(5) (*amends* TMA 1970 s 105).

(6) (*amends* FA 1973 Sch 16A para 9 and TA 1988 Sch 19A para 9).

(7) Nothing in this section shall affect the making of assessments—

(*a*) for years of assessment before the year 1983–84, or
(*b*) for accounting periods which ended before 1st April 1983.

150 Further assessments: claims etc

(1) (*inserts* TMA 1970 ss 43A, 43B).

(2) This section shall apply in relation to any assessment notice of which is issued on or after the day on which this Act is passed.

151 Assessment of trustees etc

(1) Income tax chargeable in respect of income arising to the trustees of a settlement, or to the personal representatives of a deceased person, may be assessed and charged on and in the name of any one or more of the relevant trustees or, as the case may be, the relevant personal representatives.

[(2) In this section ''the relevant trustees''—

(*a*) in relation to any income, other than gains treated as arising under Chapter II of Part XIII of the Taxes Act 1988, means the trustees to whom the income arises and any subsequent trustees of the settlement; and
(*b*) in relation to gains treated as arising under Chapter II of Part XIII of the Taxes Act 1988, means the trustees in the year of assessment in which the gains arise and any subsequent trustees of the settlement;

and ''the relevant personal representatives'' has a corresponding meaning.]¹

(3) In this section ''personal representatives'' has the same meaning as in section 111 of this Act.

(4) This section shall be deemed always to have had effect.

Commentary—*Simon's Direct Tax Service* **A3.323, 329.**
Amendment—¹ Sub-s (2) substituted by FA 1998 Sch 14 para 6 with effect in relation to income arising on or after 6 April 1998.

Distress and poinding etc

152 Distress for non-payment of tax

(1) Section 61 of the Taxes Management Act 1970 (distress) shall be amended as follows.

(2)–(5) (*amend* TMA 1970 s 61(1), (2), (4), (5)).

(6) (*adds* TMA 1970 s 61(6)).

(7) This section shall come into force on such day as the Treasury may by order made by statutory instrument appoint.

Commentary—*Simon's Direct Tax Service* **A3.1411.**
Notes—The appointed day for the purpose of sub-s (7) is 1 February 1994, by virtue of FA 1989, s 152 (Appointed Day) Order 1994, SI 1994/87.

153 Priority in cases of distraint by others

(*amends* TMA 1970 s 62).

154 Recovery of tax from debtor in Scotland

(*amends* TMA 1970 s 63).

155 Priority in cases of poinding etc by others in Scotland

(*amends* TMA 1970 s 64).

Interest etc

156 Interest on overdue tax

(1) (*substitutes* TMA 1970 s 86(3), (3A) for sub-s (3) and amends sub-s (4)).

(2), (3) (*amend* TMA 1970 s 55(2), 56(9) and *substitute* s 55(6)(*a*), (*b*), (9)).

(4) This section shall apply to tax charged by any assessment notice of which is issued after 30th July 1982.

157 Effect of certain claims on interest

(ceased to have effect on 30 September 1993).

Commentary—*Simon's Direct Tax Service* A3.1321; D2.655.

158 Small amounts of interest

(1) (*a*) (*repeals* TMA 1970 s 86(6),

(*b*) (*repeals* TMA 1970 s 87(4)).

(2) (*amends* TCGA 1992 s 283(1) and TA 1988 s 824(1), (5)).

(3) Paragraph (*a*) of subsection (1) above shall have effect—

(*a*) in relation to income tax under Schedule E, where the demand for the tax is made on or after the appointed day, and

(*b*) in any other case, where the tax is charged by an assessment notice of which is issued on or after the appointed day.

(4) Paragraph (*b*) of that subsection shall have effect where the tax is charged by an assessment relating to an accounting period beginning on or after the appointed day.

(5) Subsection (2) above shall have effect in relation to repayments of tax made on or after the appointed day.

(6) In this section ''the appointed day'' means such day as the Treasury may by order made by statutory instrument appoint; and different days may be appointed for different enactments or for different purposes of the same enactment.

159 Interest on tax in case of failure or error

Amendments—This section repealed by FA 1996 Sch 18 paras 17(3), (4) and Sch 41 Pt V(8) with effect from the year 1996–97, and in relation to income tax or capital gains tax which is charged by an assessment made after 5 April 1998 which is for 1995–96 or any earlier year of assessment, and so far as it relates to partnerships whose trades, professions or businesses were set up and commenced before 6 April 1994 with effect from the year 1997–98 in relation to income tax which is charged by an assessment made after 5 April 1998 which is for 1995–96 or any earlier year of assessment.

160 Determinations under TMA s 88

(1), (2) ...[1]

(3) (*substitutes* TMA 1970 s 70(3)).

(4) ...[1]

(5) (*amends* TMA 1970 s 114).

(6) ...[2]

Amendments—[1] Sub-ss (1), (2), (4) repealed by FA 1996 Sch 18 paras 17(3), (4) and Sch 41 Pt V(8) with effect from the year 1996–97, and in relation to income tax or capital gains tax which is charged by an assessment made after 5 April 1998 which is for 1995–96 or any earlier year of assessment, and so far as it relates to partnerships whose trades, professions or businesses were set up and commenced before 6 April 1994 with effect from the year 1997–98 in relation to income tax which is charged by an assessment made after 5 April 1998 which is for 1995–96 or any earlier year of assessment.
[2] Sub-s (6) repealed by FA 1996 Sch 22 para 12 and Sch 41 Pt V(12) with effect for any proceedings relating to 1996–97 or any subsequent year of assessment and any proceedings relating to an accounting period ending on or after the appointed day (1 July 1999 by virtue of Finance Act 1994, Section 199, (Appointed Day) Order, SI 1998/3173).

161 Tax carrying interest under TMA ss 86 and 88

Amendments—This section repealed by FA 1996 Sch 18 paras 17(3), (4) and Sch 41 Pt V(8) with effect from the year 1996–97, and in relation to income tax or capital gains tax which is charged by an assessment made after 5 April 1998 which is for 1995–96 or any earlier year of assessment, and so far as it relates to partnerships whose trades, professions or businesses were set up and commenced before 6 April 1994 with effect from the year 1997–98 in relation to income tax which is charged by an assessment made after 5 April 1998 which is for 1995–96 or any earlier year of assessment.

Penalties

162 Failure to make return

(1–5) (*substitute* TMA 1970 s 93(1)(*a*), (*b*), (2), (5), (7) (now *superseded*)).

(6) This section shall apply in relation to any failure to comply with a notice served on or after 6th April 1989.

163 Incorrect return, accounts etc

(1) (*amends* TMA 1970 ss 95(1), 96(1)).

(2) This section shall apply in relation to returns, statements, declarations or accounts delivered, made or submitted on or after the day on which this Act is passed.

164 Special returns, information etc

(1) Section 98 of the Taxes Management Act 1970 (special returns, information etc) shall be amended as follows.

(2)–(6) (*amend* TMA 1970 s 98(1), (2), Table, *substitute* s 98(3), (4) for sub-s (3) and *repeal* s 16(6)).

(7) This section shall apply in relation to—

(*a*) any failure to comply with a notice or to furnish information, give a certificate or produce a document or record beginning on or after the day on which this Act is passed, and

(*b*) the furnishing, giving, producing or making of any incorrect information, certificate, document, record or declaration on or after that day.

165 Special penalties in the case of certain returns

(1) (*inserts* TMA 1970 s 98A).

(2) ...¹

Commentary—*Simon's Direct Tax Service* A3.801; E4.965.
Amendment—¹ Sub-s (2) repealed by FA 1989 s 187 and Sch 17 Part VIII, with effect from 20 May 1995 by virtue of SI 1994/2508.

166 Assisting in preparation of incorrect return etc

(1) (*substitutes* TMA 1970 s 99).

(2) This section shall apply in relation to assistance and inducements occurring on or after the day on which this Act is passed.

167 Determination of penalties

(*Substitutes* TMA 1970 ss 100, 100A–100D for s 100).

168 Amendments consequential on section 167

(1) In consequence of the amendment made by section 167 above the Taxes Management Act 1970 shall be amended in accordance with subsections (2) to (8) below.

(2) (*amends* TMA 1970 s 20A(1), (2), (4)).

(3) (*repealed* by the General and Special Commissioners (Amendment of Enactments) Regulations, SI 1994/1813 reg 2(2), Sch 2 Pt I).

(4)–(7) (*amend* TMA 1970 ss 102, 105(1), (2), 113(3), *add* s 112(3) and *insert* s 113(1D)).

(8) ...¹

(9) (*inserts* DLTA 1976 s 41(1A) (which is now repealed except in relation to disposals, etc taking place before 19 March 1985)).

Amendments—¹ Sub-s (8) repealed by FA 1996 Sch 22 para 12 and Sch 41 Pt V(12) with effect for any proceedings relating to 1996–97 or any subsequent year of assessment and any proceedings relating to an accounting period ending after 30 June 1999 (by virtue of Finance Act 1994, Section 199, (Appointed Day) Order, SI 1998/3173 art 2).

169 Time limits

(1) (*substitutes* TMA 1970 s 103).

(2) The amendment made by subsection (1) above shall not affect the application of section 103(4) of the Taxes Management Act 1970 to proceedings under section 100 of that Act as it has effect before the amendment made by section 167 above.

170 Up-rating of certain penalties

(1) (*repealed* by FA 1995 Sch 29 Pt VIII(1), with effect from the year 1995–96 and so far as relating to corporation tax, for accounting periods ending after 30 March 1995).

(2) (*repealed* by F(No 2)A 1992 s 82, Sch 18 Pt VII.).

(3) (*amends* TA 1988 s 306(6)).

(4) (*amends* TA 1988 ss 619(7), 653, 658(5)).

(5) (*amends* TA 1988 Sch 19A para 2(4) (now repealed) and FA 1973 Sch 16A para 2(4) (now spent)).

(6) This section shall apply in relation to things done or omitted on or after the day on which this Act is passed.

PART III
MISCELLANEOUS AND GENERAL
Interest etc

178 Setting of rates of interest

(1) The rate of interest applicable for the purposes of an enactment to which this section applies shall be the rate which for the purposes of that enactment is provided for by regulations made by the Treasury under this section.

(2) This section applies to—

[(*aa*) section 15A of the Stamp Act 1891;][12]
(*a*) section 8(9) of the Finance Act 1894,
(*b*) section 18 of the Finance Act 1896,
(*c*) section 61(5) of the Finance (1909–10) Act 1910,
(*d*) section 17(3) of the Law of Property Act 1925,
(*e*) *section 73(6) of the Land Registration Act 1925,*
(*f*) [sections [59C][11], 86, 86A, 87, 87A, ...][9] and [103A][10]][8] of the Taxes Management Act 1970,
(*g*) paragraph 3 of Schedule 16A to the Finance Act 1973,
[(*gg*) [paragraph 6 of Schedule 1 to the Social Security Contributions and Benefits Act 1992][4],][1]
[(*gh*) section 71(8A) of the Social Security Administration Act 1992, and section 69(8A) of the Social Security Administration (Northern Ireland) Act 1992, as they have effect in any case where the overpayment was made in respect of working families' tax credit or disabled person's tax credit;][15]
(*h*) paragraphs 15 and 16 of Schedule 2, and paragraph 8 of Schedule 5, to the Oil Taxation Act 1975,
[(*i*) section 283 of the Taxation of Chargeable Gains Act 1992;][5]
(*j*) paragraph 59 of Schedule 8 to the Development Land Tax Act 1976,
(*k*) sections 233 and 236(3) and (4) of the Inheritance Tax Act 1984,
(*l*) section 92 of the Finance Act 1986, and
(*m*) sections ...[16] 160, 824, 825 [826 and 826A(1)(*b*)][11] of, [....,][7] and paragraph 3 of Schedule 19A to, the Taxes Act 1988 [and][2].
[(*n*) ...][6] [and][3]
[(*o*) section 14(4) of the Ports Act 1991][3]
[(*p*) paragraph 8 of Schedule 4 to the Tax Credits Act 1999][13] [, and
(*p*) section 110 of the Finance Act][14].

(3) Regulations under this section may—

(*a*) make different provision for different enactments or for different purposes of the same enactment,
(*b*) either themselves specify a rate of interest for the purposes of an enactment or make provision for any such rate to be determined by reference to such rate or the average of such rates as may be referred to in the regulations,
(*c*) provide for rates to be reduced below, or increased above, what they otherwise would be by specified amounts or by reference to specified formulae,
(*d*) provide for rates arrived at by reference to averages to be rounded up or down,
(*e*) provide for circumstances in which alteration of a rate of interest is or is not to take place, and
(*f*) provide that alterations of rates are to have effect for periods beginning on or after a day determined in accordance with the regulations in relation to interest running from before that day as well as from or from after that day.

(4) The power to make regulations under this section shall be exercisable by statutory instrument which shall be subject to annulment in pursuance of a resolution of the House of Commons.

(5) Where—

(*a*) the rate provided for by regulations under this section as the rate applicable for the purposes of any enactment is changed, and
(*b*) the new rate is not specified in the regulations,

the Board shall by order specify the new rate and the day from which it has effect.

(6) (*amends* TA 1988 s 828(2)).

(7) Subsection (1) shall have effect for periods beginning on or after such day as the Treasury may by order made by statutory instrument appoint and shall have effect in relation to interest running

from before that day as well as from or from after that day; and different days may be appointed for different enactments.

Commentary—*Simon's Direct Tax Service* A3.1322.

Regulations—Taxes (Interest Rate) Regulations, SI 1989/1297; Finance Act 1989, section 178(1), (Appointed Day) Order 1997, SI 1997/2708; Finance Act 1989, section 178(1), (Appointed Day) Order 1998, SI 1998/311; Taxes (Interest Rate) (Amendment No 2) Regulations, SI 1998/3176; Taxes (Interest Rate) (Amendment No 2) Regulations, SI 1999/1928; Finance Act 1989, Section 178(1), (Appointed Day) Order, SI 2001/253.

Note—The appointed day for the purposes of all the enactments mentioned in sub-s (2) above (with such exceptions as mentioned in the **Amendments** note below) and appointed under sub-s (7) above is 18 August 1989; FA 1989 s 178(1) (Appointed Day No 1) Order, SI 1989/1298.

Amendments—[1] Sub-s (2)(*gg*) inserted by the Social Security Act 1990 s 17(10) with effect from 6 April 1992.
[2] Word "and" added by FA 1990 s 118(8) with effect from 26 July 1990.
[3] Sub-s (2)(*o*) and preceding word "and" added by the Ports Act 1991 s 14(5) with effect from 15 July 1991.
[4] Words in sub-s (2)(*gg*) substituted by the Social Security (Consequential Provisions) Act 1992 s 4, Sch 2 para 107 with effect from 1 July 1992.
[5] Sub-s (2)(*i*) substituted by TCGA 1992 Sch 10 para 19(4) with effect from the year 1992–93.
[6] Sub-s (2)(*n*) (inserted by FA 1990 s 118(8)) repealed by FA 1995 Sch 29 Pt XII.
[7] Words in sub-s (2)(*m*) repealed by FA 1996 Sch 7 para 30 and Sch 41 Pt V(2) with effect for income tax for the year 1996–97 and for corporation tax for accounting periods ending after 31 March 1996.
[8] Words in sub-s (2)(*f*) substituted by FA 1994 ss 196, 199 and Sch 19 para 44 with effect from the year 1996–97 in relation to income tax and capital gains tax and, in relation to corporation tax, for accounting periods ending after 30 June 1999 (by virtue of Finance Act 1994, Section 199, (Appointed Day) Order, SI 1998/3173 art 2).
[9] Word "88" in sub-s (2)(*f*) repealed by FA 1996 Sch 18 para 13 and Sch 41 Pt V(8) with effect for the year 1996–97, and in relation to any income tax or capital gains tax which is charged by an assessment made after 5 April 1998 which is for the year 1995–96 or any earlier year of assessment, and so far as relating to partnerships whose trades, professions or businesses were set up and commenced before 6 April 1994 from the year 1997–98 in relation to any income tax which is charged by an assessment made after 5 April 1998 which is for the year 1995–96 or any earlier year of assessment.
[10] The appointed day for the purposes of TMA 1970 ss 59C and 103A and appointed under sub-s (7) above is 9 March 1998; Finance Act 1989, section 178(1), (Appointed Day) Order 1998, SI 1998/311.
[11] Words substituted by FA 1998 Sch 4 para 1(3) with effect for accounting periods ending on or after 1 July 1999 (the date appointed under FA 1994 s 199, by virtue of SI 1998/3173, for the purposes of corporation tax self-assessment).
[12] Sub-s (2)(*aa*) inserted by FA 1999 s 109(2), (4) with effect for instruments executed after 30 September 1999.
[13] Sub-s (2)(*p*) inserted by Tax Credits Act 1999 Sch 4 para 8(1) with effect from 7 March 2001 (by virtue of SI 2001/253).
[14] Sub-s (2)(*p*) and preceding word "", and" inserted by FA 1999 s 110(8), (9) with effect for instruments executed after 30 September 1999. It would appear that this paragraph has been incorrectly numbered.
[15] Sub-s (2)(*gh*) inserted in relation to the transfer of functions concerning the working families' tax credit and the disabled person's tax credit by Tax Credits Act 1999 s 2(3), Sch 2 para 10(2) with effect from 5 October 1999.
[16] Words in sub-s (2)(*m*) repealed by FA 2000 s 156, Sch 40 Pt II(17) with effect for relevant payments or receipts in relation to which the chargeable date for the purposes of TA 1988 Pt IV, Ch VIIA is after 31 March 2001.

Prospective amendments—Sub-s (2)(*e*) to be repealed by the Land Registration Act 2002 ss 135, 136(2), Sch 13 with effect from a date to be appointed.

179 Provisions consequential on section 178

(1)(*a*)(i)–(v) (not relevant to this publication).

    (vi) (*amends* F(No 2)A 1975 s 47(1) and is repealed by TCGA 1992 s 290, Sch 12).

    (vii) (*amends* TA 1988 ss 824(1), 825(2)").

  (*b*)(i) (*amends* TMA 1970 ss 86(1), 86A(1), 87A(1), (5), 88(1) and is repealed in part by FA 1996 Sch 41 Pt V(8)).

    (ii) (*amends* FA 1973 Sch 16A para 3(4), which is now spent).

    (iii) (*amends* TA 1988 Sch 19A para 3(4), which is now repealed).

  (*c*)(i) (not relevant to this publication).

    (ii) (*amends* TA 1988 s 826(1)).

  (*d*)–(*f*) (not relevant to this publication).

  (*g*) (*amends* TA 1988 s 160(5)(*d*)).

(2), (3) (not relevant to this publication).

(4) Any amendment made by subsection (1), (2) or (3) above shall have effect in relation to any period for which section 178(1) above has effect for the purposes of the enactment concerned.

(5) (*amends* TA 1988 s 146(11)).

180 Repayment interest: period of accrual

(1)–(5) (not relevant to this publication).

(6) (*amends* TA 1988 s 826(1)).

(7) The amendments made by this section shall be deemed always to have had effect.

Miscellaneous

182 Disclosure of information

(1) A person who discloses any information which he holds or has held in the exercise of tax functions[, tax credit functions][4] [or social security functions][3] is guilty of an offence if it is information about any matter relevant, for the purposes of [any of those functions—

  (*a*) to tax or duty in the case of any identifiable person,

  [(*aa*) to working families' tax credit or disabled person's tax credit in respect of any identifiable person][4] (*b*) to contributions payable by or in respect of any identifiable person, or

(*c*) to statutory sick pay or statutory maternity pay in respect of any identifiable person.]³

(2) In this section "tax functions" means functions relating to tax ...—

(*a*) of ... the Board and their officers,

(*b*) of any person carrying out the administrative work of any tribunal mentioned in subsection (3) below, and

(*c*) of any other person providing, or employed in the provision of, services to any person mentioned in paragraph (*a*) or (*b*) above.

[(2AA) In this section "tax credit functions" means the functions relating to working families' tax credit or disabled person's tax credit—

(*a*) of the Board and their officers,

(*b*) of any person carrying out the administrative work of the General Commissioners or the Special Commissioners, and

(*c*) of any other person providing, or employed in the provision of, services to any person mentioned in paragraph (*a*) or (*b*) above.]⁴

[(2A) In this section "social security functions" means—

(*a*) the functions relating to contributions, statutory sick pay or statutory maternity pay—

(i) of the Board and their officers,

(ii) of any person carrying out the administrative work of the General Commissioners or the Special Commissioners, and

(iii) of any other person providing, or employed in the provision of, services to any person mentioned in sub-paragraph (i) or (ii) above, and

(*b*) the functions under Part III of the Pension Schemes Act 1993 or Part III of the Pension Schemes (Northern Ireland) Act 1993 of the Board and their officers and any other person providing, or employed in the provision of, services to the Board or their officers.]³

(3) The tribunals referred to in subsection (2)(*b*) above are—

(*a*) the General Commissioners and the Special Commissioners,

(*b*) ...

(*c*) any referee or board of referees appointed ...¹ under section 26(7) of the Capital Allowances Act 1968, and

(*d*) any tribunal established under section 463 of the Taxes Act 1970 or section 706 of the Taxes Act 1988.

(4) A person who discloses any information which—

(*a*) he holds or has held in the exercise of functions—

(i) of the Comptroller and Auditor General and any member of the staff of the National Audit Office,

(ii) of the Parliamentary Commissioner for Administration and his officers,

[(iii) of the Auditor General for Wales and any member of his staff, or

(iv) of the Welsh Administration Ombudsman and any member of his staff,]²

(*b*) is, or is derived from, information which was held by any person in the exercise of tax functions[, tax credit functions]⁴ [or social security functions]³, and

(*c*) is information about any matter relevant, for the purposes of [tax functions[, tax credit functions]⁴ or social security functions—

(i) to tax or duty in the case of any identifiable person,

[(ia) to working families' tax credit or disabled person's tax credit in respect of any identifiable person,]⁴

(ii) to contributions payable by or in respect of any identifiable person, or

(iii) to statutory sick pay or statutory maternity pay in respect of any identifiable person,]³

is guilty of an offence.

(5) Subsections (1) and (4) above do not apply to any disclosure of information—

(*a*) with lawful authority,

(*b*) with the consent of any person in whose case the information is about a matter relevant to tax or duty[, to working families' tax credit or disabled person's tax credit]⁴, or

(*c*) which has been lawfully made available to the public before the disclosure is made.

(6) For the purposes of this section a disclosure of any information is made with lawful authority if, and only if, it is made—

(*a*) by a Crown servant in accordance with his official duty,

(*b*) by any other person for the purposes of the function in the exercise of which he holds the information and without contravening any restriction duly imposed by the person responsible,

(*c*) to, or in accordance with an authorisation duly given by, the person responsible,

(*d*) in pursuance of any enactment or of any order of a court, or

(*e*) in connection with the institution of or otherwise for the purposes of any proceedings relating to any matter within the general responsibility of the Commissioners or, as the case requires, the Board, and in this subsection "the person responsible" means ... the Board, the Comptroller, [the Parliamentary Commissioner, the Auditor General for Wales or the Welsh Administration Ombudsman][2] as the case requires.

(7) It is a defence for a person charged with an offence under this section to prove that at the time of the alleged offence—

(a) he believed that he had lawful authority to make the disclosure in question and had no reasonable cause to believe otherwise, or

(b) he believed that the information in question had been lawfully made available to the public before the disclosure was made and had no reasonable cause to believe otherwise.

(8) A person guilty of an offence under this section is liable—

(a) on conviction on indictment, to imprisonment for a term not exceeding two years or a fine or both, and

(b) on summary conviction, to imprisonment for a term not exceeding six months or a fine not exceeding the statutory maximum or both.

(9) No prosecution for an offence under this section shall be instituted in England and Wales or in Northern Ireland except—

(a) by ... the Board ... or

(b) by or with the consent of the Director of Public Prosecutions or, in Northern Ireland, the Director of Public Prosecutions for Northern Ireland.

(10) In this section—

"the Board" means the Commissioners of Inland Revenue,

...

["contributions" means contributions under Part I of the Social Security Contributions and Benefits Act 1992 or Part I of the Social Security Contributions and Benefits (Northern Ireland) Act 1992;][3]

"Crown servant" has the same meaning as in the Official Secrets Act 1989, and

"tax ..." means any tax ... within the general responsibility of ... the Board.

(11) In this section—

(a) references to the Comptroller and Auditor General include the Comptroller and Auditor General for Northern Ireland,

(b) references to the National Audit Office include the Northern Ireland Audit Office, and

(c) references to the Parliamentary Commissioner for Administration include the Health Service Commissioner for England, the Health Service Commissioner for Wales, the Health Service Commissioner for Scotland, the Northern Ireland Parliamentary Commissioner for Administration and the Northern Ireland Commissioner for Complaints.

(12) This section shall come into force on the repeal of section 2 of the Official Secrets Act 1911.

Commentary—*Simon's Direct Tax Service* **A2.803.**
Notes—This section came into force on 1 March 1990 when the repeal of the Official Secrets Act 1911 came into effect by virtue of the Official Secrets Act Order, SI 1990/199.
Words omitted from this section are not relevant for the purposes of this publication.
Amendments—[1] Words in sub-s (3)(c) repealed by FA 1995 Sch 29 Pt VIII(16), with effect from the year 1996–97 in relation to income and capital gains tax, and in relation to corporation tax for accounting periods beginning after 31 March 1996.
[2] Sub-s (4)(a)(iii) and (iv) inserted by, and words in sub-s (6) substituted by, the Government of Wales Act 1998 with effect from 1 February 1999 (by virtue of the Government of Wales Act 1998 (Commencement No 3) Order, SI 1999/118 art 2).
[3] Sub-ss (1), (4), (5), (10) amended, and sub-s (2A) inserted, by the Social Security Contributions (Transfer of Functions, etc) Act 1999 Sch 6 para 9 with effect from 1 April 1999 by virtue of the Social Security Contributions (Transfer of Functions, etc) Act 1999 (Commencement No 1 and Transitional Provisions) Order, SI 1999/527 art 2, Sch 2.
[4] Sub-s (2AA), and words in sub-ss (1), (4), (5), inserted by Tax Credits Act 1999 ss 12(1)–(5), 20(2) with effect from 5 October 1999.

[182A Double taxation: disclosure of information

(1) A person who discloses any information acquired by him in the exercise of his functions as a member of an advisory commission set up under the Arbitration Convention is guilty of an offence.

(2) Subsection (1) above does not apply to any disclosure of information—

(a) with the consent of the person who supplied the information to the commission, or

(b) which has been lawfully made available to the public before the disclosure is made.

(3) It is a defence for a person charged with an offence under this section to prove that at the time of the alleged offence he believed that the information in question had been lawfully made available to the public before the disclosure was made and had no reasonable cause to believe otherwise.

(4) A person guilty of an offence under this section is liable—

(a) on conviction on indictment, to imprisonment for a term not exceeding two years or a fine or both;

(b) on summary conviction, to imprisonment for a term not exceeding six months or a fine not exceeding the statutory maximum or both.

(5) No prosecution for an offence under this section shall be instituted in England and Wales or in Northern Ireland except—

(a) by the Board, or

(b) by or with the consent of the Director of Public Prosecutions or, in Northern Ireland, the Director of Public Prosecutions for Northern Ireland.

(6) In this section—

"the Arbitration Convention" has the meaning given by section 815B(4) of the Taxes Act 1988; "the Board" means the Commissioners of Inland Revenue.][1]

Commentary—*Simon's Direct Tax Service* **A2.803.**
Revenue Internal Guidance—Investigations Handbook IH 421 (exchange of information is dealt with by London Special Compliance Office).
Note—The Arbitration Convention 90/436/EEC is reproduced in EC legislation division.
Amendments—[1] This section inserted by F(No 2)A 1992 s 51(3).

General

186 Interpretation etc

(1) In this Act "the Taxes Act 1970" means the Income and Corporation Taxes Act 1970 and "the Taxes Act 1988" means the Income and Corporation Taxes Act 1988.

(2) (not relevant to this publication).

(3) Part II of this Act, so far as it relates to capital gains tax, shall be construed as one with the Capital Gains Tax Act 1979.

188 Short title

This Act may be cited as the Finance Act 1989.

SCHEDULES

[SCHEDULE 4

PROFIT-RELATED PAY][1]

Section 61

Amendments—[1] Schedule repealed by FA 1997 Sch 18 Pt VI(3) with effect for any payment made by reference to a profit period beginning after 31 December 1999 in accordance with FA 1997 s 61(2), (3), but subject to FA 1997 Sch 18 Pt VI(3) note 2.

1 *The Taxes Act 1988 shall be amended in accordance with the following provisions of this Schedule.*

2—(1) (*amended* TA 1988 s 171(4)).

(2) *This paragraph shall have effect in relation to profit-related pay paid by reference to profit periods beginning on or after 1st April 1989.*

3 (*inserted* TA 1988 ss 177A, 177B).

4—(1) *Section 178 (cancellation of registration) shall be amended as follows.*

(2) (*amended* sub-s (1)).

(3) (*inserted* sub-ss (3A), (3B)).

(4) (*inserted* sub-s (5A)).

5 (*inserted* s 179(3), (4)).

6 (*inserted* s 180(5)).

7 (*inserted* s 181(4)).

8—(1) *Section 182 (appeals) shall be amended as follows.*

(2) (*inserted* sub-s (1)(bb)).

(3) (*inserted* sub-s (1A)).

(4) (*amended* sub-s (2)).

9—(1) *Paragraph 7 of Schedule 8 (no payments for employees with material interest in company) shall be amended as follows.*

(2) (*amended* sub-para (1)).

(3) (*amended* sub-para (3)).

(4) (*inserted* sub-paras (4)–(12)).

10—(1) (*repealed* Sch 8, paras 13(2), 14(2)).

(2) *In consequence of sub-paragraph (1) above—*

    (a) (*repealed* ss 175(3), 178(2)(b), Sch 8 paras 13(3), 14(2), (7) and *amended* s 176(1), Sch 8, para 13(1)).

    (b) *in paragraph 13 of Schedule 8—*

        (i) (*inserted* sub-para (1A)).

      (ii) (*amended* sub-para (4)(*a*)).
      (iii) (*amended* sub-para (5)).
      (iv) (*substituted* sub-para (6)).
   (*c*) (*amended* Sch 8, para 14(5)).

11 (*inserted* Sch 8, para 13(7)).

12 (*amended* Sch 8, para 14(5)).

13 (*inserted* Sch 8, para 14(8)).

14—(1) *Paragraph 19 of Schedule 8 (profit and loss account for purposes of profit-related pay scheme) shall be amended as follows.*

(2) (*inserted* sub-para (4A)).

(3) (*substituted* sub-para (6)(*f*), (*ff*) for sub-para (6)(*f*)).

15 (*inserted* Sch 8, para 21, 22).

SCHEDULE 5

EMPLOYEE SHARE OWNERSHIP TRUSTS

Section 74

Cross references—See TA 1988 s 85A(4) (relief for costs of establishing employee share ownership trusts);
TCGA 1992 ss 227–236 (rollover relief where certain shares are disposed of after 19 March 1990 to trustees of a qualifying employee share ownership trust).

Qualifying trusts

1 A trust is a qualifying employee share ownership trust at the time it is established if the conditions set out in paragraphs 2 to 11 below are satisfied in relation to the trust at that time.

Commentary—*Simon's Direct Tax Service* **D2.221–226.**
Revenue & other press releases—IR 9-5-90 (introduction of clearance procedure for trust deeds).
IR 14-12-90 (clearance procedure: Revenue will examine and comment on draft trust deeds).

General

2—(1) The trust must be established under a deed (the trust deed).

(2) The trust must be established by a company (the founding company) which, at the time the trust is established, is resident in the United Kingdom and not controlled by another company.

Commentary—*Simon's Direct Tax Service* **E4.592.**

Trustees

3—(1) The trust deed must provide for the establishment of a body of trustees.

(2) The trust deed must—
   (*a*) appoint the initial trustees;
   (*b*) contain rules for the retirement and removal of trustees;
   (*c*) contain rules for the appointment of replacement and additional trustees.

(3) The trust deed must provide that at any time while the trust subsists (the relevant time)—
   (*a*) the number of trustees must not be less than three;
   (*b*) all the trustees must be resident in the United Kingdom;
   (*c*) the trustees must include one person who is a trust corporation, a solicitor, or a member of such other professional body as the Board may from time to time allow for the purposes of this paragraph;
   (*d*) most of the trustees must be persons who are not and have never been directors of any company which falls within the founding company's group at the relevant time;
   (*e*) most of the trustees must be persons who are employees of companies which fall within the founding company's group at the relevant time, and who do not have and have never had a material interest in any such company;
   (*f*) the trustees falling within paragraph (*e*) above must, before being appointed as trustees, have been selected by a majority of the employees of the companies falling within the founding company's group at the time of the selection or by persons elected to represent those employees.

(4) For the purposes of sub-paragraph (3) above a company falls within the founding company's group at a particular time if—
   (*a*) it is the founding company, or
   (*b*) it is at that time resident in the United Kingdom and controlled by the founding company.

[(5) This paragraph applies in relation to trusts established on or before the day on which the Finance Act 1994 was passed.][1]

Commentary—*Simon's Direct Tax Service* **E4.592.**
Amendments—[1] Sub-para (5) inserted by FA 1994 Sch 13 paras 1, 2.

[3A Where a trust is established after the day on which the Finance Act 1994 was passed, the trust deed must make provision as mentioned in one of paragraphs (*a*) to (*c*) below—

    (*a*) provision for the establishment of a body of trustees and complying with paragraph 3(2) to (4) above;

    (*b*) provision for the establishment of a body of trustees and complying with paragraph 3B(2) to (9) below;

    (*c*) provision that at any time while the trust subsists there must be a single trustee.]¹

Commentary—*Simon's Direct Tax Service* **E4.592.**
Amendments—¹ This paragraph inserted by FA 1994 Sch 13 paras 1, 3.

[3B—(1) The following are the provisions that must be complied with under paragraph 3A(*b*) above.

(2) The trust deed must—

    (*a*) appoint the initial trustees;

    (*b*) contain rules for the retirement and removal of trustees;

    (*c*) contain rules for the appointment of replacement and additional trustees.

(3) The trust deed must be so framed that at any time while the trust subsists the conditions set out in sub-paragraph (4) below are fulfilled as regards the persons who are then trustees; and in that sub-paragraph ''the relevant time'' means that time.

(4) The conditions are that—

    (*a*) the number of trustees is not less than three;

    (*b*) all the trustees are resident in the United Kingdom;

    (*c*) the trustees include at least one person who is a professional trustee and at least two persons who are non-professional trustees;

    (*d*) at least half of the non-professional trustees were, before being appointed as trustees, selected in accordance with sub-paragraph (7) or (8) below;

    (*e*) all the trustees so selected are persons who are employees of companies which fall within the founding company's group at the relevant time, and who do not have and have never had a material interest in any such company.

(5) For the purposes of this paragraph a trustee is a professional trustee at a particular time if—

    (*a*) the trustee is then a trust corporation, a solicitor, or a member of such other professional body as the Board may at that time allow for the purposes of this sub-paragraph,

    (*b*) the trustee is not then an employee or director of any company then falling within the founding company's group, and

    (*c*) the trustee meets the requirements of sub-paragraph (6) below;

and for the purposes of this paragraph a trustee is a non-professional trustee at a particular time if the trustee is not then a professional trustee for those purposes.

(6) A trustee meets the requirements of this sub-paragraph if—

    (*a*) he was appointed as an initial trustee and, before being appointed as trustee, was selected by (and only by) the persons who later became the non-professional initial trustees, or

    (*b*) he was appointed as a replacement or additional trustee and, before being appointed as trustee, was selected by (and only by) the persons who were the non-professional trustees at the time of the selection.

(7) Trustees are selected in accordance with this sub-paragraph if the process of selection is one under which—

    (*a*) all the persons who are employees of the companies which fall within the founding company's group at the time of the selection, and who do not have and have never had a material interest in any such company, are (so far as is reasonably practicable) given the opportunity to stand for selection,

    (*b*) all the employees of the companies falling within the founding company's group at the time of the selection are (so far as is reasonably practicable) given the opportunity to vote, and

    (*c*) persons gaining more votes are preferred to those gaining less.

(8) Trustees are selected in accordance with this sub-paragraph if they are selected by persons elected to represent the employees of the companies falling within the founding company's group at the time of the selection.

(9) For the purposes of this paragraph a company falls within the founding company's group at a particular time if—

    (*a*) it is at that time resident in the United Kingdom, and

    (*b*) it is the founding company or it is at that time controlled by the founding company.]¹

Commentary—*Simon's Direct Tax Service* **E4.592.**
Amendments—¹ This paragraph inserted by FA 1994 Sch 13 paras 1, 3.

[3C—(1) This paragraph applies where the trust deed provides that at any time while the trust subsists there must be a single trustee.

(2) The trust deed must—

(*a*) be so framed that at any time while the trust subsists the trustee is a company which at that time is resident in the United Kingdom and controlled by the founding company;

(*b*) appoint the initial trustee;

(*c*) contain rules for the removal of any trustee and for the appointment of a replacement trustee.

(3) The trust deed must be so framed that at any time while the trust subsists the company which is then the trustee is a company so constituted that the conditions set out in sub-paragraph (4) below are then fulfilled as regards the persons who are then directors of the company; and in that sub-paragraph "the relevant time" is that time and "the trust company" is that company.

(4) The conditions are that—

(*a*) the number of directors is not less than three;

(*b*) all the directors are resident in the United Kingdom;

(*c*) the directors include at least one person who is a professional director and at least two persons who are non-professional directors;

(*d*) at least half of the non-professional directors were, before being appointed as directors, selected in accordance with sub-paragraph (7) or (8) below;

(*e*) all the directors so selected are persons who are employees of companies which fall within the founding company's group at the relevant time, and who do not have and have never had a material interest in any such company.

(5) For the purposes of this paragraph a director is a professional director at a particular time if—

(*a*) the director is then a solicitor or a member of such other professional body as the Board may at that time allow for the purposes of this sub-paragraph,

(*b*) the director is not then an employee of any company then falling within the founding company's group,

(*c*) the director is not then a director of any such company (other than the trust company), and

(*d*) the director meets the requirements of sub-paragraph (6) below;

and for the purposes of this paragraph a director is a non-professional director at a particular time if the director is not then a professional director for those purposes.

(6) A director meets the requirements of this sub-paragraph if—

(*a*) he was appointed as an initial director and, before being appointed as director, was selected by (and only by) the persons who later became the non-professional initial directors, or

(*b*) he was appointed as a replacement or additional director and, before being appointed as director, was selected by (and only by) the persons who were the non-professional directors at the time of the selection.

(7) Directors are selected in accordance with this sub-paragraph if the process of selection is one under which—

(*a*) all the persons who are employees of the companies which fall within the founding company's group at the time of the selection, and who do not have and have never had a material interest in any such company, are (so far as is reasonably practicable) given the opportunity to stand for selection,

(*b*) all the employees of the companies falling within the founding company's group at the time of the selection are (so far as is reasonably practicable) given the opportunity to vote, and

(*c*) persons gaining more votes are preferred to those gaining less.

(8) Directors are selected in accordance with this sub-paragraph if they are selected by persons elected to represent the employees of the companies falling within the founding company's group at the time of the selection.

(9) For the purposes of this paragraph a company falls within the founding company's group at a particular time if—

(*a*) it is at that time resident in the United Kingdom, and

(*b*) it is the founding company or it is at that time controlled by the founding company.]¹

Commentary—*Simon's Direct Tax Service* **E4.592.**
Amendments—¹ This paragraph inserted by FA 1994 Sch 13 paras 1, 3.

Beneficiaries

4—(1) The trust deed must contain provision as to the beneficiaries under the trust, in accordance with the following rules.

(2) The trust deed must provide that a person is a beneficiary at a particular time (the relevant time) if—

(*a*) he is at the relevant time an employee or director of a company which at that time falls within the founding company's group,

(*b*) at each given time in a qualifying period he was an employee or director of a company falling within the founding company's group at that given time, and

(*c*) [in the case of a director, at that given time he worked as a]¹ director of the company concerned at the rate of at least 20 hours a week (ignoring such matters as holidays and sickness).

[(2A) The trust deed may provide that a person is a beneficiary at a given time if at that time he is eligible to participate in a savings-related share option scheme within the meaning of Schedule 9 to the Taxes Act 1988—

    (*a*) which was established by a company within the founding company's group, and
    (*b*) which is approved under that Schedule.]³

[(2B) Where a trust deed contains a rule conforming with sub-paragraph (2A) above it must provide that the only powers and duties which the trustees may exercise in relation to persons who are beneficiaries by virtue only of that rule are those which may be exercised in accordance with the provisions of a scheme such as is mentioned in that sub-paragraph.]³

(3) The trust deed may provide that a person is a beneficiary at a particular time (the relevant time) if—

    (*a*) he has at each given time in a qualifying period been an employee or director of a company falling within the founding company's group at that given time,
    (*b*) he has ceased to be an employee or director of the company or the company has ceased to fall within that group, and
    (*c*) at the relevant time a period of not more than eighteen months has elapsed since he so ceased or the company so ceased (as the case may be).

(4) The trust deed may provide for a person to be a beneficiary if the person is a charity and the circumstances are such that—

    (*a*) there is no person who is a beneficiary within any rule which is included in the deed and conforms with sub-paragraph (2) [, (2A)]³ or (3) above, and
    (*b*) the trust is in consequence being wound up.

(5) For the purposes of sub-paragraph (2) above a qualifying period is a period—

    (*a*) whose length is [*not less than one year*]² and not more than five years,
    (*b*) whose length is specified in the trust deed, and
    (*c*) which ends with the relevant time (within the meaning of that sub-paragraph).

(6) For the purposes of sub-paragraph (3) above a qualifying period is a period—

    (*a*) whose length is equal to that of the period specified in the trust deed for the purposes of a rule which conforms with sub-paragraph (2) above, and
    (*b*) which ends when the person or company (as the case may be) ceased as mentioned in sub-paragraph (3)(*b*) above.

(7) The trust deed must not provide for a person to be a beneficiary unless he falls within any rule which is included in the deed and conforms with sub-paragraph (2) [, (2A)]³, (3) or (4) above.

(8) The trust deed must provide that, notwithstanding any other rule which is included in it, a person cannot be a beneficiary at a particular time (the relevant time) [by virtue of a rule which conforms with sub-paragraph (2), (3) or (4) above]³ if—

    (*a*) at that time he has a material interest in the founding company, or
    (*b*) at any time in the period of one year preceding the relevant time he has had a material interest in that company.

(9) For the purposes of this paragraph a company falls within the founding company's group at a particular time if—

    (*a*) it is at that time resident in the United Kingdom, and
    (*b*) it is the founding company or it is at that time controlled by the founding company.

(10) For the purposes of this paragraph a charity is a body of persons established for charitable purposes only.

Commentary—*Simon's Direct Tax Service* **D2.225; E4.595.**
Cross references—See FA 1989 Sch 5 para 17 (when a trust is established).
Amendments—¹ Words in sub-para (2)(*c*) substituted by FA 1995 s 137(5), with effect for trusts established after 30 April 1995.
² Words omitted from sub-para (5)(*a*) repealed by FA 1996 s 119, Sch 41 Pt V(5) with effect for trusts established on or after 29 April 1996.
³ Sub-paras (2A), (2B) and words in sub-paras (4)(*a*), (7), (8) inserted by FA 1996 s 120(1), (5)–(7), (12) with effect for trusts established after 28 April 1996.

Trustees' functions

5—(1) The trust deed must contain provision as to the functions of the trustees.

(2) The functions of the trustees must be so expressed that it is apparent that their general functions are—

    (*a*) to receive sums from the founding company and other sums (by way of loan or otherwise);
    (*b*) to acquire securities;
    (*c*) to transfer securities or sums (or both) to persons who are beneficiaries under the terms of the trust deed;
    [(*cc*) to grant rights to acquire shares to persons who are beneficiaries under the terms of the trust deed;]¹

(*d*) to transfer securities to the trustees of profit sharing schemes approved under Schedule 9 to the Taxes Act 1988, for a price not less than the price the securities might reasonably be expected to fetch on a sale in the open market;

(*e*) pending transfer, to retain the securities and to manage them (whether by exercising voting rights or otherwise).

Commentary—*Simon's Direct Tax Service* **D2.223.**
Amendments—[1] Sub-para (2)(*cc*) inserted by FA 1996 s 120(8), (12) with effect for trusts established after 28 April 1996.

Sums

6—(1) The trust deed must require that any sum received by the trustees—

(*a*) must be expended within the relevant period,

(*b*) may be expended only for one or more of the qualifying purposes, and

(*c*) must, while it is retained by them, be kept as cash or be kept in an account with a bank or building society.

(2) For the purposes of sub-paragraph (1) above the relevant period is the period of nine months beginning with the day found as follows—

(*a*) in a case where the sum is received from the founding company, or a company which is controlled by that company at the time the sum is received, the day following the end of the period of account in which the sum is charged as an expense of the company from which it is received;

(*b*) in any other case, the day the sum is received.

(3) For the purposes of sub-paragraph (1) above each of the following is a qualifying purpose—

(*a*) the acquisition of shares in the founding company;

(*b*) the repayment of sums borrowed;

(*c*) the payment of interest on sums borrowed;

(*d*) the payment of any sum to a person who is a beneficiary under the terms of the trust deed;

(*e*) the meeting of expenses.

(4) The trust deed must provide that, in ascertaining for the purposes of a relevant rule whether a particular sum has been expended, sums received earlier by the trustees shall be treated as expended before sums received by them later; and a relevant rule is one which is included in the trust deed and conforms with sub-paragraph (1) above.

(5) The trust deed must provide that, where the trustees pay sums to different beneficiaries at the same time, all the sums must be paid on similar terms.

(6) For the purposes of sub-paragraph (5) above, the fact that terms vary according to the levels of remuneration of beneficiaries, the length of their service, or similar factors, shall not be regarded as meaning that the terms are not similar.

Commentary—*Simon's Direct Tax Service* **E4.594.**

Securities

7—(1) Subject to paragraph 8 below, the trust deed must provide that securities acquired by the trustees must be shares in the founding company which—

(*a*) form part of the ordinary share capital of the company,

(*b*) are fully paid up,

(*c*) are not redeemable, and

(*d*) are not subject to any restrictions other than restrictions which attach to all shares of the same class or a restriction authorised by sub-paragraph (2) below.

(2) Subject to sub-paragraph (3) below, a restriction is authorised by this sub-paragraph if—

(*a*) it is imposed by the founding company's articles of association,

(*b*) it requires all shares held by directors or employees of the founding company, or of any other company which it controls for the time being, to be disposed of on ceasing to be so held, and

(*c*) it requires all shares acquired, in pursuance of rights or interests obtained by such directors or employees, by persons who are not (or have ceased to be) such directors or employees to be disposed of when they are acquired.

(3) A restriction is not authorised by sub-paragraph (2) above unless—

(*a*) any disposal required by the restriction will be by way of sale for a consideration in money on terms specified in the articles of association, and

(*b*) the articles also contain general provisions by virtue of which any person disposing of shares of the same class (whether or not held or acquired as mentioned in sub-paragraph (2) above) may be required to sell them on terms which are the same as those mentioned in paragraph (*a*) above.

(4) The trust deed must provide that shares in the founding company may not be acquired by the trustees at a price exceeding the price they might reasonably be expected to fetch on a sale in the open market.

(5) The trust deed must provide that shares in the founding company may not be acquired by the trustees at a time when that company is controlled by another company.

Commentary—*Simon's Direct Tax Service* **D2.226; E4.596.**
Cross references—See TCGA 1992 s 227(3)(*e*) (description of shares for the purposes of rollover relief on their disposal after 19 March 1990 to employee share ownership trusts),
TCGA 1992 s 228(5)(*a*) (conditions for rollover relief on disposal after 19 March 1990 of certain shares to employee share ownership trusts).

8 The trust deed may provide that the trustees may acquire securities other than shares in the founding company—

(*a*) if they are securities issued to the trustees in exchange in circumstances mentioned in section [135(1) of the Taxation of Chargeable Gains Act 1992][1], or

(*b*) if they are securities acquired by the trustees as a result of a reorganisation, and the original shares the securities represent are shares in the founding company (construing "reorganisation" and "original shares" in accordance with section [126][1] of that Act).

Commentary—*Simon's Direct Tax Service* **D2.226.**
Amendments—[1] Words and number in paras (*a*), (*b*) substituted by TCGA 1992 Sch 10 para 19(5).

9—(1) The trust deed must provide that—

(*a*) where the trustees transfer securities to a beneficiary, they must do so on qualifying terms;

(*b*) the trustees must transfer securities before the expiry of the [qualifying period][1] beginning with the date on which they acquired them.

(2) For the purposes of sub-paragraph (1) above a transfer of securities is made on qualifying terms if—

(*a*) all the securities transferred at the same time [other than those transferred on a transfer such as is mentioned in sub-paragraph (2ZA) below][3] are transferred on similar terms,

(*b*) securities have been offered to all the persons who are beneficiaries under the terms of the trust deed [by virtue of a rule which conforms with paragraph 4(2), (3) or (4) above][3] when the transfer is made, and

(*c*) securities are transferred to all such [persons][3] who have accepted.

[(2ZA) For the purposes of sub-paragraph (1) above a transfer of securities is also made on qualifying terms if—

(*a*) it is made to a person exercising a right to acquire shares, and

(*b*) that right was obtained in accordance with the provisions of a savings-related share option scheme within the meaning of Schedule 9 to the Taxes Act 1988—

(i) which was established by, or by a company controlled by, the founding company, and

(ii) which is approved under that Schedule, and

(*c*) that right is being exercised in accordance with the provisions of that scheme, and

(*d*) the consideration for the transfer is payable to the trustees.][4]

[(2A) For the purposes of sub-paragraph (1) above the qualifying period is—

(*a*) seven years, in the case of trusts established on or before the day on which the Finance Act 1994 was passed;

(*b*) twenty years, in the case of other trusts.][2]

(3) For the purposes of sub-paragraph (2) above, the fact that terms vary according to the levels of remuneration of beneficiaries, the length of their service, or similar factors, shall not be regarded as meaning that the terms are not similar.

(4) The trust deed must provide that, in ascertaining for the purposes of a relevant rule whether particular securities are transferred, securities acquired earlier by the trustees shall be treated as transferred by them before securities acquired by them later; and a relevant rule is one which is included in the trust deed and conforms with sub-paragraph (1) above.

Commentary—*Simon's Direct Tax Service* **D2.226.**
Amendments—[1] Words substituted by FA 1994 Sch 13 paras 1, 7.
[2] Sub-para (2A) inserted by FA 1994 Sch 13 paras 1, 7.
[3] Words in sub-paras (2)(*a*), (*b*) inserted, word in sub-para (2)(*c*) substituted by FA 1996 s 120(9), (10), (12) with effect for trusts established after 28 April 1996.
[4] Sub-s (2ZA) inserted by FA 1996 s 120(9), (10), (12) with effect for trusts established after 28 April 1996.

Other features

10 The trust deed must not contain features which are not essential or reasonably incidental to the purpose of acquiring sums and securities, [granting rights to acquire shares to persons who are eligible to participate in savings-related share option schemes approved under Schedule 9 to the Taxes Act 1988, transferring shares to such persons,][1] transferring sums and securities to employees and directors, and transferring securities to the trustees of profit sharing schemes approved under [that Schedule][2].

Commentary—*Simon's Direct Tax Service* **D2.223.**
Amendments—[1] Words inserted by FA 1996 s 120(11), (12) with effect for trusts established after 28 April 1996.
[2] Words substituted by FA 1996 s 120(11), (12) with effect for trusts established after 28 April 1996.

Rules about acquisition etc

11—(1) The trust deed must provide that, for the purposes of the deed, the trustees—

(*a*) acquire securities when they become entitled to them;

(*b*) transfer securities to another person when that other becomes entitled to them;

(*c*) retain securities if they remain entitled to them.

(2) But if the deed provides as mentioned in paragraph 8 above, it must provide for the following exceptions to any rule which is included in it and conforms with sub-paragraph (1)(*a*) above, namely, that—

(*a*) if securities are issued to the trustees in exchange in circumstances mentioned in section [135(1) of the Taxation of Chargeable Gains Act 1992][1], they shall be treated as having acquired them when they became entitled to the securities for which they are exchanged;

(*b*) if the trustees become entitled to securities as a result of a reorganisation, they shall be treated as having acquired them when they became entitled to the original shares which those securities represent (construing "reorganisation" and "original shares" in accordance with section [126][1] of that Act).

(3) The trust deed must provide that—

(*a*) if the trustees agree to take a transfer of securities, for the purposes of the deed they become entitled to them when the agreement is made and not on a later transfer made pursuant to the agreement;

(*b*) if the trustees agree to transfer securities to another person, for the purposes of the deed the other person becomes entitled to them when the agreement is made and not on a later transfer made pursuant to the agreement.

Commentary—*Simon's Direct Tax Service* D2.226.
Amendments—[1] Words and number in sub-para 2(*a*), (*b*) substituted by TCGA 1992 Sch 10 para 19(5).

Position after trust's establishment

12 A trust which was at the time it was established a qualifying employee share ownership trust shall continue to be one, except that it shall not be such a trust at any time when the requirements mentioned in paragraph 3(3)(*a*) to (*f*) above are not satisfied.

[This paragraph applies in relation to trusts established on or before the day on which the Finance Act 1994 was passed.][1]

Commentary—*Simon's Direct Tax Service* D2.221; E4.591.
Amendments—[1] Words inserted by FA 1994 Sch 13 paras 1, 4.

[**12A**—(1) Subject to sub-paragraphs (2) and (3) below, a trust which was at the time it was established a qualifying employee share ownership trust shall continue to be one.

(2) If the trust deed makes provision under paragraph 3A(*a*) above, the trust shall not be a qualifying employee share ownership trust at any time when the requirements mentioned in paragraph 3(3)(*a*) to (*f*) above are not satisfied.

(3) If the trust deed makes provision under paragraph 3A(*b*) above, the trust shall not be a qualifying employee share ownership trust at any time when the conditions mentioned in paragraph 3B(4)(*a*) to (*e*) above are not satisfied.

(4) If the trust deed makes provision under paragraph 3A(*c*) above, the trust shall not be a qualifying employee share ownership trust at any time when—

(*a*) there is not a single trustee,

(*b*) the trustee is not a company which is resident in the United Kingdom and controlled by the founding company, or

(*c*) the conditions mentioned in paragraph 3C(4)(*a*) to (*e*) above are not satisfied as regards the directors of the trustee.

(5) This paragraph applies in relation to trusts established after the day on which the Finance Act 1994 was passed.][1]

Commentary—*Simon's Direct Tax Service* E4.591.
Amendments—[1] This paragraph inserted by FA 1994 Sch 13 paras 1, 5.

13 A trust is an employee share ownership trust at a particular time (the relevant time) if it was a qualifying employee share ownership trust at the time it was established; and it is immaterial whether or not it is a qualifying employee share ownership trust at the relevant time.

Commentary—*Simon's Direct Tax Service* D2.221; E4.591.

Interpretation

14 For the purposes of this Schedule the following are securities—

(*a*) shares;

(*b*) debentures.

Commentary—*Simon's Direct Tax Service* D2.226.

15 For the purposes of this Schedule, the question whether one company is controlled by another shall be construed in accordance with section 840 of the Taxes Act 1988.

Commentary—*Simon's Direct Tax Service* E4.592.

16—(1) For the purposes of this Schedule a person shall be treated as having a material interest in a company if he, either on his own or with one or more of his associates, or if any associate of his with or without other such associates,—

(*a*) is the beneficial owner of, or able (directly or through the medium of other companies or by any other indirect means) to control, more than 5 per cent of the ordinary share capital of the company, or

(*b*) possesses, or is entitled to acquire, such rights as would, in the event of the winding-up of the company or in any other circumstances, give an entitlement to receive more than 5 per cent of the assets which would then be available for distribution among the participators.

(2) In this paragraph—

(*a*) "associate" has the same meaning as in section 417(3) and (4) of the Taxes Act 1988, but subject to sub-paragraph (3) below,

(*b*) "control" has the meaning given by section 840 of that Act, and

(*c*) "participator" has the same meaning as in Part XI of that Act.

(3) Where a person has an interest in shares or obligations of the company as a beneficiary of an employee benefit trust, the trustees shall not be regarded as associates of his by reason only of that interest unless sub-paragraph (5) below applies in relation to him.

(4) In sub-paragraph (3) above "employee benefit trust" has the same meaning as in paragraph 7 of Schedule 8 to the Taxes Act 1988, except that in its application for this purpose paragraph 7(5)(*b*) of that Schedule shall have effect as if it referred to the day on which this Act was passed instead of to 14th March 1989.

(5) This sub-paragraph applies in relation to a person if at any time on or after the day on which this Act was passed—

(*a*) he, either on his own or with any one or more of his associates, or

(*b*) any associate of his, with or without other such associates,

has been the beneficial owner of, or able (directly or through the medium of other companies or by any other indirect means) to control, more than 5 per cent of the ordinary share capital of the company.

(6) Sub-paragraphs (9) to (12) of paragraph 7 of Schedule 8 to the Taxes Act 1988 shall apply for the purposes of sub-paragraph (5) above as they apply for the purposes of that paragraph.

Commentary—*Simon's Direct Tax Service* E4.592.

[**17** For the purposes of this Schedule a trust is established when the deed under which it is established is executed.][1]

Commentary—*Simon's Direct Tax Service* E4.592.
Amendments—[1] Paragraph 17 inserted by FA 1994 Sch 13 paras 1, 8.

SCHEDULE 6

RETIREMENT BENEFITS SCHEMES

Section 75

PART I

AMENDMENTS OF TAXES ACT

Preliminary

1 The Taxes Act 1988 shall be amended as mentioned in the following provisions of this Part of this Schedule.

Amendments

2 (*repealed by FA 1995 Sch 29 Pt VIII(5), with effect for accounting periods beginning after 31 December 1994*).

3 (*amends s 590*).

4 (*inserts ss 590A–590C*).

5 (*amends s 590*).

6 (*amends s 594*).

7 (*repeals s 595(2), (3)*).

8 (*amends s 596*).

9 (*inserts ss 596A, 596B*).

10 (*amends* s 598(1)(*b*)).

11 (*amends* s 599)

12 (*inserts* s 599A).

13 (*amends* TA 1988 s 600)

14 (*amends* s 605(2), (3)(*a*), (*b*)(i), (4)).

15 (*inserts* s 611A).

16 (*amends* s 828(4)).

17 (*repeals* Sch 23, para 8).

Effect of amendments

18—(1) Paragraphs 2, 6(2), 8(2)(*b*), 10, 11(2), 14 and 15 above shall be deemed to have come into force on 14th March 1989.

(2) Paragraphs 3(2) and (3) and 4 above shall have effect in relation to a scheme not approved by the Board before the day on which this Act is passed; but if the scheme came into existence before 14th March 1989 those provisions shall not have effect as regards an employee who became a member of the scheme before 1st June 1989.

(3) Paragraph 3(4) above shall have effect where a determination is made on or after the day on which this Act is passed.

(4) Paragraphs 5 and 6(3), (4) and (5) above shall have effect for the year 1989–90 and subsequent years of assessment, but paragraphs 5(4) and 6(5) above shall not have effect as regards a person's remuneration in respect of an office or employment in such circumstances as the Board may by regulations prescribe for the purposes of this sub-paragraph.

(5) Paragraphs 7 and 8(2)(*a*) and (3) above shall have effect for the year 1988–89 and subsequent years of assessment.

(6) Paragraph 8(4) above shall not have effect where a sum has been deemed to be income of a person by virtue of section 595(2) before 6th April 1988.

(7) Paragraph 9 above shall have effect in relation to payments made and benefits provided on or after the day on which this Act is passed.

(8) Paragraph 11(3) above shall have effect where the charge to tax under section 599 arises on or after 14th March 1989, but not where the scheme came into existence before that date and the employee became a member of it before 1st June 1989.

(9) Paragraphs 12 and 13 above shall have effect in relation to payments made on or after the day on which this Act is passed.

(10) Paragraph 17 above shall have effect in relation to benefits provided on or after the day on which this Act is passed.

Regulations—Retirement Benefits Schemes (Tax Relief on Contributions) (Disapplication of Earnings Cap) Regulations, SI 1990/586.

PART II
APPROVED SCHEMES: GENERAL

Statement of Practice D2—Concessionary exemption from CGT liability where a new scheme is established for obtaining approval under this Part and Part III by winding up an old scheme and transferring its funds to the new scheme.

Preliminary

19—(1) This Part of this Schedule shall be deemed to have come into force on 14th March 1989 and, subject to sub-paragraphs (2) to (4) below, applies in relation to any retirement benefits scheme (within the meaning of Chapter I of Part XIV of the Taxes Act 1988) approved by the Board before the day on which this Act is passed.

(2) The Board may by regulations provide that, in circumstances prescribed in the regulations, this Part of this Schedule or any provision of it shall not apply or shall apply with such modifications as may be so prescribed.

(3) Regulations under sub-paragraph (2) above—

(a) may include provision authorising the Board to direct that this Part of this Schedule or any provision of it shall not apply in any particular case where in the opinion of the Board the facts are such that its application would not be appropriate;

(b) may take effect (and may authorise any direction given under them to take effect) as from 14th March 1989 or any later date;

(c) may make such supplementary provision as appears to the Board to be necessary or expedient.

(4) This Part of this Schedule shall not apply to a scheme if, before the end of 1989, the administrator of the scheme gives written notice to the Board that it is not to apply.

(5) Where a notice is given to the Board under sub-paragraph (4) above, the scheme shall cease to be approved—

(a) if it came into existence before 14th March 1989, with effect from 1st June 1989 or (if later) the date with effect from which it was approved;

(b) if it came into existence on or after 14th March 1989, with effect from the date with effect from which it was approved.

Commentary—*Simon's Direct Tax Service* **E7.215A.**
Regulations—Retirement Benefits Schemes (Continuation of Rights of Members of Approved Schemes) Regulations, SI 1990/2101; Retirement Benefits Schemes (Continuation of Rights of Members of Approved Schemes) (Amendment) Regulations, SI 1999/1963.

Remuneration

20—(1) This paragraph applies—

(a) where the scheme came into existence before 14th March 1989, as regards an employee who became a member of the scheme on or after 1st June 1989;

(b) where the scheme came into existence on or after 14th March 1989, as regards any employee who is a member of the scheme (whenever he became a member).

(2) The rules of the scheme shall have effect (notwithstanding anything in them to the contrary and notwithstanding the effect of anything in Schedule 23 to the Taxes Act 1988) as if, in arriving at the employee's relevant annual remuneration for the purposes of calculating benefits, any excess of what would be his relevant annual remuneration (apart from this paragraph) over the permitted maximum for the year of assessment in which his participation in the scheme ceases shall be disregarded.

(3) The rules of the scheme shall have effect (notwithstanding anything in them to the contrary) as if, in arriving at the employee's remuneration for the year 1988–89 or any subsequent year of assessment for the purposes of any restriction on the aggregate amount of contributions payable under the scheme by the employee and the employer, there were disregarded any excess of what would be his remuneration for the year (apart from this paragraph) over the permitted maximum for the year.

(4) In this paragraph "the permitted maximum", in relation to a year of assessment, means the figure found for that year by virtue of sub-paragraphs (5) and (6) below.

(5) For the years 1988–89 and 1989–90 the figure is £60,000.

(6) For any subsequent year of assessment the figure is the figure found for that year, for the purposes of section 590C of the Taxes Act 1988, by virtue of section 590C(4) [to(5A)][1].

Commentary—*Simon's Direct Tax Service* **E7.215A.**
Note—For the year 1999–00 the figure specified for the purpose of s 590C is £90,600 by virtue of the Retirement Benefits Schemes (Indexation of Earnings Cap) Order, SI 1999/592.
Cross references—See the Retirement Benefits Schemes (Continuation of Rights of Members of Approved Schemes) Regulations, SI 1990/2101 reg 3 (disapplication of this paragraph in prescribed circumstances),
SI 1990/2101 reg 5 (modification of this paragraph in prescribed circumstances).
Amendments—[1] Words in sub-para (6) substituted by FA 1993 s 107(7), (8) with effect from the year 1994–95.

21—(1) The rules of the scheme shall have effect (notwithstanding anything in them to the contrary) as if the amount of contributions payable under the scheme by an employee in the year 1989–90 or any subsequent year of assessment were limited to 15 per cent of his remuneration for the year in respect of the employment.

(2) Where in relation to any year of assessment a percentage higher than 15 per cent. applies for the purposes of section 592(8) or (8A) of the Taxes Act 1988 (relief in respect of contributions) as regards any employee, sub-paragraph (1) above, as regards him, shall have effect in relation to that year with the substitution for 15 per cent of that higher percentage.

Commentary—*Simon's Direct Tax Service* **E7.215A.**
Cross references—See the Retirement Benefits Schemes (Continuation of Rights of Members of Approved Schemes) Regulations, SI 1990/2101 reg 6 (modification of sub-para (1) above in prescribed circumstances),
SI 1990/2101 reg 6A (modification of this paragraph where an employee is temporarily absent from his employment and is not paid or is paid at a reduced rate for the period of his absence).

22—(1) This paragraph applies—

(a) where the scheme came into existence before 14th March 1989, as regards an employee who became a member of the scheme on or after 1st June 1989;

(b) where the scheme came into existence on or after 14th March 1989, as regards any employee who is a member of the scheme (whenever he became a member).

(2) For the purposes of paragraph 21(1) above, in arriving at the employee's remuneration for the year any excess of what would be his remuneration for the year (apart from this sub-paragraph) over the permitted maximum for the year shall be disregarded.

(3) In sub-paragraph (2) above "the permitted maximum", in relation to a year of assessment, means the figure found for that year by virtue of sub-paragraphs (4) and (5) below.

(4) For the year 1989–90 the figure is £60,000.

(5) For any subsequent year of assessment the figure is the figure found for that year, for the purposes of section 590C of the Taxes Act 1988, by virtue of section 590C(4) [to(5A)][1].

Commentary—*Simon's Direct Tax Service* E7.215A.
Note—For the year 1999–00 the figure specified for the purpose of s 590C is £90,600 by virtue of the Retirement Benefits Schemes (Indexation of Earnings Cap) Order, SI 1999/592.
Cross references—See the Retirement Benefits Schemes (Continuation of Rights of Members of Approved Schemes) Regulations, SI 1990/2101 reg 3 (disapplication of this paragraph in prescribed circumstances).
Amendments—[1] Words in sub-para (5) substituted by FA 1993 s 107(7), (8) with effect from the year 1994–95.

Accelerated accrual

23—(1) This paragraph applies where the scheme allows a member to commute his pension or part of it for a lump sum or sums and—

   (a) where the scheme came into existence before 14th March 1989, applies as regards an employee who became a member of the scheme on or after 1st June 1989, and
   (b) where the scheme came into existence on or after 14th March 1989, applies as regards any employee who is a member of the scheme (whenever he became a member).

(2) The rules of the scheme shall have effect (notwithstanding anything in them to the contrary and notwithstanding the effect of paragraph 3 of Schedule 23 to the Taxes Act 1988) as if they did not allow the employee to obtain by way of commutation a lump sum or sums exceeding in all the greater of the following sums—

   (a) a sum of three-eighths of his relevant annual remuneration for each year of service up to a maximum of 40;
   (b) a sum of the pension payable under the scheme to the employee for the first year in which it is payable multiplied by 2.25.

(3) The following rules shall apply in calculating, for the purposes of sub-paragraph (2) above, the pension payable under the scheme to the employee for the first year in which it is payable—

   (a) if the pension payable for the year changes, the initial pension payable shall be taken;
   (b) it shall be assumed that the employee will survive for the year;
   (c) the effect of commutation, and of any allocation of pension to provide benefits for survivors, shall be ignored.

Commentary—*Simon's Direct Tax Service* E7.215A.
Cross references—See the Retirement Benefits Schemes (Continuation of Rights of Members of Approved Schemes) Regulations, SI 1990/2101 regs 3, 4 (disapplication of this paragraph in prescribed circumstances),
SI 1990/2101 reg 7 (modification of sub-para (2)(b) above in prescribed circumstances),
SI 1990/2101 reg 7AA (modification of this para in certain circumstances where a pension commences to be paid from funds provided by additional voluntary contributions made by the employee before benefits become payable under the provisions of the scheme).
SI 1990/2101 reg 7A (modification of this paragraph where an employee retires early owing to incapacity).

24—(1) This paragraph applies where the scheme provides a lump sum or sums for a member otherwise than by commutation of his pension or part of it and—

   (a) where the scheme came into existence before 14th March 1989, applies as regards an employee who became a member of the scheme on or after 1st June 1989, and
   (b) where the scheme came into existence on or after 14th March 1989, applies as regards any employee who is a member of the scheme (whenever he became a member).

(2) The rules of the scheme shall have effect (notwithstanding anything in them to the contrary and notwithstanding the effect of paragraph 4 of Schedule 23 to the Taxes Act 1988) as if they did not allow the payment to the employee, otherwise than by way of commutation, of a lump sum or sums exceeding in all the greater of the following sums—

   (a) a sum of three-eighths of his relevant annual remuneration for each year of service up to a maximum of 40;
   (b) a sum of the relevant number of eighths of his relevant annual remuneration.

(3) For the purposes of sub-paragraph (2) above the relevant number shall be found by taking the number of eighths (of relevant annual remuneration) by reference to which the pension payable under the scheme to the employee is calculated, multiplying that number by three, and treating the resulting number as 120 if it would otherwise exceed 120.

Commentary—*Simon's Direct Tax Service* E7.215A.
Cross references—See the Retirement Benefits Schemes (Continuation of Rights of Members of Approved Schemes) Regulations, SI 1990/2101 regs 3, 4 (disapplication of this paragraph in prescribed circumstances),
SI 1990/2101 reg 7A (modification of this paragraph where an employee retires early owing to incapacity).

Associated employments

25—(1) This paragraph applies—

   (a) where the scheme came into existence before 14th March 1989, as regards an employee who became a member of the scheme on or after 1st June 1989;
   (b) where the scheme came into existence on or after 14th March 1989, as regards any employee who is a member of the scheme (whenever he became a member).

(2) Where the employee is a member of the scheme by virtue of two or more relevant associated employments, the rules of the scheme shall have effect as mentioned in sub-paragraph (3) below.

(3) The rules of the scheme shall have effect (notwithstanding anything in them to the contrary) as if they prohibited the amount payable by way of pension in respect of service in any of the relevant associated employments, when aggregated with any amount payable by way of pension in respect of service in the other such employment or employments, from exceeding the relevant amount.

(4) For the purposes of sub-paragraph (3) above the relevant amount, in relation to the employee, shall be found by applying the following formula—

$$\frac{A \times C}{30}$$

(5) For the purposes of this paragraph—

   (a) section 590B(5) and (6) of the Taxes Act 1988 shall apply for the purpose of defining A, and
   (b) section 590B(9) to (11) of that Act shall apply for the purpose of defining C,

as they apply for the purposes of section 590B of that Act, except that for the purposes of this paragraph A shall not exceed 20.

(6) The reference to two or more relevant associated employments shall be construed in accordance with section 590A of the Taxes Act 1988.

Commentary—*Simon's Direct Tax Service* E7.215A.
Cross references—See the Retirement Benefits Schemes (Continuation of Rights of Members of Approved Schemes) Regulations, SI 1990/2101 reg 3 (disapplication of this paragraph in prescribed circumstances).

Connected schemes

26—(1) This paragraph applies—

   (a) where the scheme came into existence before 14th March 1989, as regards an employee who became a member of the scheme on or after 1st June 1989;
   (b) where the scheme came into existence on or after 14th March 1989, as regards any employee who is a member of the scheme (whenever he became a member).

(2) Where in relation to the employee the scheme is connected with another scheme which is (or other schemes each of which is) an approved scheme, the rules of the scheme shall have effect as mentioned in sub-paragraph (3) below.

(3) The rules of the scheme shall have effect (notwithstanding anything in them to the contrary) as if they prohibited the amount payable by way of pension under the scheme, when aggregated with any amount payable by way of pension under the other scheme or schemes, from exceeding the relevant amount.

(4) For the purposes of sub-paragraph (3) above the relevant amount, in relation to the employee, shall be found by applying the following formula—

$$\frac{B \times C}{30}$$

(5) For the purposes of this paragraph—

   (a) section 590B(7) and (8) of the Taxes Act 1988 shall apply for the purpose of defining B, and
   (b) section 590B(9) to (11) of that Act shall apply for the purpose of defining C,

as they apply for the purposes of section 590B of that Act, except that for the purposes of this paragraph B shall not exceed 20.

(6) References in this paragraph to the scheme being connected with another scheme in relation to the employee shall be construed in accordance with section 590A of the Taxes Act 1988.

Commentary—*Simon's Direct Tax Service* E7.215A.
Cross references—See the Retirement Benefits Schemes (Continuation of Rights of Members of Approved Schemes) Regulations, SI 1990/2101 reg 3 (disapplication of this paragraph in prescribed circumstances).

Augmentation

27—(1) This paragraph applies—

   (a) where the scheme came into existence before 14th March 1989, as regards an employee who became a member of the scheme on or after 1st June 1989;
   (b) where the scheme came into existence on or after 14th March 1989, as regards any employee who is a member of the scheme (whenever he became a member).

(2) Where in addition to being a member of the scheme (the main scheme) the employee is also a member of an approved scheme (the voluntary scheme) which provides additional benefits to supplement those provided by the main scheme and to which no contributions are made by any employer of his, sub-paragraph (3) below shall apply in relation to any augmentation of the benefits provided for him by the main scheme after he has ceased to participate in it.

(3) Any rules of the main scheme imposing a limit on the amount of a benefit provided for the employee shall have effect (notwithstanding anything in them to the contrary) as if they provided for

the limit to be reduced by the amount of any like benefit provided for the employee by the voluntary scheme.

Commentary—*Simon's Direct Tax Service* **E7.215A.**

Centralised schemes

28—(1) Where the scheme is a centralised scheme, sub-paragraph (1)(*a*) and (*b*) of each of paragraphs 20 and 22 to 27 above shall have effect with the substitution for the reference to the coming into existence of the scheme of a reference to the commencement of the employer's participation in the scheme.

(2) For the purposes of this paragraph a centralised scheme is a retirement benefits scheme (within the meaning of Chapter I of Part XIV of the Taxes Act 1988) established for the purpose of enabling any employer, other than an employer associated with the person by whom the scheme is established, to participate in it as regards his employees.

(3) For the purposes of sub-paragraph (2) above one person is associated with another if (directly or indirectly) one is controlled by the other or if both are controlled by a third person.

(4) In sub-paragraph (3) above the reference to control, in relation to a body corporate, shall be construed—

    (*a*) where the body corporate is a close company, in accordance with section 416 of the Taxes Act 1988, and

    (*b*) where it is not, in accordance with section 840 of that Act.

Commentary—*Simon's Direct Tax Service* **E7.215A.**

Election

29—(1) In a case where—

    (*a*) an employee became a member of the scheme on or after 17th March 1987 and before 1st June 1989, and

    (*b*) he gives written notice to the administrator of the scheme that this Part of this Schedule is to apply in his case,

he shall be deemed for the purposes of this Part of this Schedule to have become a member of the scheme on 1st June 1989.

(2) A notice under this paragraph shall be given in such form as the Board may prescribe.

Commentary—*Simon's Direct Tax Service* **E7.215A.**

Supplementary

30 In this Part of this Schedule "relevant annual remuneration" means final remuneration or, if the scheme provides for benefits to be calculated by reference to some other annual remuneration, that other annual remuneration.

Commentary—*Simon's Direct Tax Service* **E7.215A.**

PART III
APPROVED SCHEMES: ADDITIONAL VOLUNTARY CONTRIBUTIONS

Statement of Practice D2—Concessionary exemption from CGT liability where a new scheme is established for obtaining approval under this Part and Part II by winding up an old scheme and transferring its funds to the new scheme.

Preliminary

31—(1) Subject to sub-paragraphs (2) to (4) below, this Part of this Schedule applies in relation to any retirement benefits scheme which was approved by the Board before the day on which this Act is passed and which makes provision for the payment by an employee of voluntary contributions.

(2) Paragraph 32 below only applies where—

    (*a*) the provision for the payment of voluntary contributions is freestanding, and

    (*b*) the scheme is not one to which contributions are made by any employer of the employee.

(3) The Board may by regulations provide that, in circumstances prescribed in the regulations, this Part of this Schedule or any provision of it shall not apply or shall apply with such modifications as may be so prescribed.

(4) Regulations under sub-paragraph (3) above—

    (*a*) may include provision authorising the Board to direct that this Part of this Schedule or any provision of it shall not apply in any particular case where in the opinion of the Board the facts are such that its application would not be appropriate;

    (*b*) may make such supplementary provision as appears to the Board to be necessary or expedient.

Commentary—*Simon's Direct Tax Service* **E7.222.**

Abatement of benefits

32—(1) The scheme shall have effect (notwithstanding anything in it to the contrary) as if its rules included a rule imposing, in the case of each benefit provided for the employee, such a limit on the amount of the benefit as is mentioned in sub-paragraph (2) below.

(2) The limit referred to above is a limit of such an amount as is found by—

  (*a*) taking the amount of the limit imposed by the main scheme on the provision of any like benefit for the employee by that scheme, and

  (*b*) subtracting from that amount an amount equal to the relevant amount.

(3) For the purposes of sub-paragraph (2) above the relevant amount is—

  (*a*) where the employee is not a member of any other relevant scheme, the amount of any like benefit provided for the employee by the main scheme, and

  (*b*) where the employee is a member of another relevant scheme or schemes, an amount equal to the aggregate of the amount mentioned in paragraph (*a*) above and the amount of any like benefit provided for the employee by the other relevant scheme or schemes.

(4) In sub-paragraph (3) above, references to the employee being a member of another relevant scheme are references to his being a member of any approved scheme, other than the scheme, which provides additional benefits for him to supplement those provided by the main scheme.

(5) This paragraph shall have effect in relation to benefits provided on or after the day on which this Act is passed.

Commentary—*Simon's Direct Tax Service* **E7.222.**

Return of surplus funds

33—(1) The scheme shall have effect (notwithstanding anything in it to the contrary) as if its rules included a rule requiring the administrator, in the circumstances mentioned in sub-paragraph (2) or (3) below, as the case may be, to make to the employee or his personal representatives a payment of an amount equal to the prescribed amount out of funds which are or have been held for the purposes of the scheme.

(2) Where the provision for the payment of voluntary contributions is freestanding, the circumstances referred to above are that the amount of any benefit provided for the employee by the scheme would have been greater had the amount of any like benefit provided for him by the main scheme, or any other relevant scheme of which he is a member, been less.

(3) Where the provision for the payment of voluntary contributions is not freestanding, the circumstances referred to above are that the amount of any benefit provided for the employee by virtue of the voluntary contributions would have been greater had the amount of any like benefit provided for him by the principal provisions of the scheme, or any other relevant scheme of which he is a member, been less.

(4) In sub-paragraph (1) above, the reference to the prescribed amount is to an amount calculated in accordance with the method for the time being specified in regulations made for the purposes of section 591 of the Taxes Act 1988 as the method to be used for calculating the amount of any surplus funds.

(5) In sub-paragraph (2) above, the reference to the employee being a member of another relevant scheme is a reference to his being a member of any approved scheme, other than the scheme, which provides additional benefits for him to supplement those provided by the main scheme.

(6) In sub-paragraph (3) above, the reference to the employee being a member of another relevant scheme is a reference to his being a member of any approved scheme, other than the scheme, which provides additional benefits for him to supplement those provided by the principal provisions of the scheme.

Commentary—*Simon's Direct Tax Service* **E7.218.**
Cross references—See TA 1988 s 600(2) (unauthorised payments from pension schemes etc).

34 The scheme shall have effect (notwithstanding anything in it to the contrary) as if its rules included a rule enabling the administrator, before making any payment by virtue of paragraph 33 above, to deduct the amount of any tax to which he is charged by section 599A of the Taxes Act 1988 by virtue of making the payment.

Commentary—*Simon's Direct Tax Service* **E7.222.**

Supplementary

35 In this Part of this Schedule—

  (*a*) "administrator", "approved scheme", "employee" and "retirement benefits scheme" have the same meanings as in Chapter I of Part XIV of the Taxes Act 1988,

  (*b*) "freestanding", in relation to provision for the payment of voluntary contributions, means provision which is contained in a retirement benefits scheme other than the one which provides the benefits which the voluntary contributions are intended to supplement, (*c*) "the main scheme", in relation to provision for the payment of voluntary contributions which is freestanding, means the retirement benefits scheme which provides the benefits which the voluntary contributions are intended to supplement,

(*d*) "principal provisions", in relation to a retirement benefits scheme which makes provision for the payment of voluntary contributions which is not freestanding, means the provisions of the scheme concerning the provision of the benefits which the voluntary contributions are intended to supplement,

(*e*) references to the provision of a benefit for an employee shall, in relation to a deceased employee, be construed as references to the provision of a benefit in respect of him, and

(*f*) references to an employee being (or not being) a member of a scheme shall, in relation to a deceased employee, be construed as references to his having been (or not having been) a member of a scheme immediately before the time of his death.

Commentary—*Simon's Direct Tax Service* **E7.222.**

SCHEDULE 7

PERSONAL PENSION SCHEMES

Section 77

PART I

AMENDMENTS OF TAXES ACT

1 Chapter IV of Part XIV of the Taxes Act 1988 (personal pension schemes) shall be amended as mentioned in the following provisions of this Part of this Schedule.

2—(1) Section 635 (lump sum to member) shall be amended as follows.

(2) (*substitutes* sub-s (3)).

(3) (*repeals* sub-s (4)).

(4) This paragraph shall have effect in relation to the approval of a scheme on or after the day on which this Act is passed; but if the scheme came into existence before that day sub-paragraph (2) above shall not have effect as regards arrangements made by a member in accordance with the scheme before that day.

3—(1) (*substitutes* s 640(2) Table).

(2) This paragraph shall have effect for the year 1989–90 and subsequent years of assessment.

4—(1) (*inserts* s 640A).

(2) This paragraph shall have effect for the year 1989–90 and subsequent years of assessment.

5—(1)–(3) (*amend* s 644(2) and *insert* s 644(6A)–(6F)).

(4) This paragraph shall be deemed to have come into force on 6th April 1989.

6—(1)–(5) (*amend* s 645(1)(*c*), (3), *insert* sub-s (4A) and *repeal* sub-s (5)).

(6) This paragraph shall be deemed to have come into force on 6th April 1989.

7—(1) (*amends* s 646(1)).

(2) This paragraph shall have effect for the year 1989–90 and subsequent years of assessment.

8—(1) (*inserts* s 646A).

(2) This paragraph shall have effect for the year 1989–90 and subsequent years of assessment.

9 (*amends* s 655(5)).

PART II

SCHEMES APPROVED BEFORE PASSING OF THIS ACT

Interpretation

10 In this Part of this Schedule—

(*a*) "personal pension scheme" has the same meaning as in Chapter IV of Part XIV of the Taxes Act 1988, and

(*b*) references to approval of such a scheme do not include references to provisional approval under regulations made under section 655(5) of that Act.

Commentary—*Simon's Direct Tax Service* **E7.406.**

Lump sum to member

11—(1) This paragraph applies as regards arrangements made by a member of a personal pension scheme approved by the Board before the day on which this Act is passed, if the arrangements are made by the member in accordance with the scheme on or after that day.

(2) The rules of the scheme shall have effect (notwithstanding anything in them to the contrary) as if any limitation imposed on the maximum amount payable to the member by way of lump sum, and imposed by reference to a fraction of the total value of the benefits for him provided for by the arrangements, were imposed by reference to the same fraction of the difference between—

    (*a*) the total value, at the time when the lump sum is paid, of the benefits provided for by the arrangements, and

    (*b*) the value, at that time, of such of his rights under the scheme as are protected rights for the purposes of the [Pension Schemes Act 1993][1] or the [Pension Schemes (Northern Ireland) Act 1993][2].

Commentary—*Simon's Direct Tax Service* **E7.406.**
Amendments—[1] Words in para 11(2)(*b*) substituted by the Pension Schemes Act 1993 s 190, Sch 8 para 22 with effect from 7 February 1994 by virtue of the Pension Schemes Act 1993 (Commencement No 1) Order 1994, SI 1994/86.
[2] Words in para 11(2)(*b*) substituted by the Pension Schemes (Northern Ireland) Act 1993 s 184, Sch 7 para 24.

12—(1) This paragraph applies where on or after the day on which this Act is passed a lump sum becomes payable under a personal pension scheme approved by the Board before that day.

(2) The rules of the scheme shall have effect (notwithstanding anything in them to the contrary) as if any limitation imposed on the maximum amount payable to a member by way of lump sum, and imposed by reference to a figure, did not apply.

(3) The reference in sub-paragraph (2) above to a limitation imposed on the maximum amount payable to a member by way of lump sum does not include a reference to a limitation imposed on the maximum amount so payable out of a transfer payment.

Commentary—*Simon's Direct Tax Service* **E7.406.**

SCHEDULE 8

AMENDMENTS OF CHAPTER I Of PART XII OF TAXES ACT 1988 (INSURANCE COMPANIES)

Section 84

1 ...[1]

2 (*repeals* s 433).

3—(1) (*substitutes* s 434(3), (3A) for sub-s (3)).

    (2) (*repeals* s 434(4), (5)).

    (3) ...[1]

    (4) (*amends* s 434(7))(now repealed).

4 ...[2]

5 (*repeals* s 435).

6 (*amends* s 436(3)(*a*)).

7 ...[1]

Amendments—[1] Paras 1, 3(3), 7 repealed by FA 1990 ss 45(11), 132, Sch 19 Pt IV.
[2] Para 4 repealed by FA 1995 Sch 29 Pt VIII(5), with effect for accounting periods beginning after 31 December 1994.

[SCHEDULE 8A

MODIFICATION OF SECTIONS 83 [TO 83A][2] AND 89 IN RELATION TO OVERSEAS LIFE INSURANCE COMPANIES][1]

Section 89A

Amendments—[1] This Schedule inserted by FA 1993 s 101 and Sch 10.
[2] Words in heading inserted by FA 1996 Sch 31 para 8(2) with effect for periods of account beginning after 31 December 1995.

[1—(1) In their application to an overseas life insurance company [sections 83 to 83A][2] of this Act shall have effect with the modifications specified in paragraphs 1A to 1C below.

(2) In those paragraphs—

    (*a*) any reference to the Taxes Act 1988 is a reference to that Act as it has effect in relation to such a company by virtue of Schedule 19AC to that Act; and

    (*b*) any expression to which a meaning is given by section 11A of that Act has that meaning.][1]

Commentary—*Simon's Direct Tax Service* **D4.537.**
Amendments—[1] Paras 1, 1A–1C, substituted for para 1, by FA 1995 Sch 8 para 49(2), with effect for accounting periods beginning after 31 December 1994.
[2] Words in sub-para (1) substituted by FA 1996 Sch 31 para 8(3) with effect for periods of account beginning after 31 December 1995.

[1A—(1) The reference in section 83(2)(*a*) to investment income shall be construed as a reference to such of the income concerned as is attributable to the branch or agency in the United Kingdom through which the company carries on life assurance business.

(2) The reference to assets in section 83(2)(*b*) (as it applies apart from subsection (3) of that section) shall be construed as a reference to such of the assets concerned—

(*a*) as are—

(i) section 11(2)(*b*) assets;

(ii) section 11(2)(*c*) assets; or

(iii) assets which by virtue of section 11B of the Taxes Act 1988 are attributed to the branch or agency; or

(*b*) as are assets—

(i) (in a case where section 11C of that Act (other than subsection (9)) applies) of the relevant fund, or

(ii) (in a case where that section including that subsection applies) of the relevant funds,

other than assets which fall within paragraph (*a*) above.

(3) In determining for the purposes of section 83(2) (as it applies apart from subsection (3) of that section) whether there has been any increase or reduction in the value (whether realised or not) of assets—

(*a*) no regard shall be had to any period of time during which an asset held by the company does not fall within paragraph (*a*) or (*b*) of sub-paragraph (2) above; and

(*b*) in the case of an asset which falls within paragraph (*b*) of that sub-paragraph, only the specified portion of any increase or reduction in the value of the asset shall be taken into account.

For the purposes of paragraph (*b*) above the specified portion of any increase or reduction in the value of an asset is found by applying to that increase or reduction the same fraction as would, by virtue of section 11C of the Taxes Act 1988 be applied to any relevant gain accruing to the company on the disposal of the asset.

(4) For the reference in section 83(3) to any amount [being added to the company's [long-term insurance]³ fund]², there shall be substituted a reference to assets becoming assets of the [long-term insurance]³ fund used or held for the purposes of the company's United Kingdom branch or agency, having immediately previously been held by the company otherwise than as assets of that fund or used or held otherwise than for those purposes.

The amount of the increase in value under section 83(2)(*b*), as it applies in relation to such [an addition]², shall be taken to be an amount equal to the value of the assets [added]².]¹

[(5) Any reference in section 83AA(2), (3) or (4) or 83AB(1) or (3) to an amount being added to the relevant company's [long-term insurance]³ fund shall be construed in accordance with sub-paragraph (4) above.]²

Commentary—*Simon's Direct Tax Service* **D4.537.**
Cross references—See TA 1988 Sch 19AC para 4(1) (meaning of "section 11(2)(*b*) assets", "section 11(2)(*c*) assets" and provisions of TA 1988 ss 11A–11C).
Amendments—¹ Para 1A substituted with para 1 *ante* and paras 1B, 1C *post*, for para 1, by FA 1995 Sch 8 para 49(2), with effect for accounting periods beginning after 31 December 1994.
² Words in sub-para (4) substituted and sub-para (5) inserted by FA 1996 Sch 31 para 8(4), (5) with effect for periods of account beginning after 31 December 1995.
³ Words in sub-paras (4) and (5) substituted by the Financial Services and Markets Act 2000 (Consequential Amendments) (Taxes) Order, SI 2001/3629 arts 54, 60(1)(*d*) with effect from 1 December 2001, immediately after the coming into force of the Financial Services and Markets Act 2000 ss 411, 432(1), Sch 20.

[1B[—(1)]² The references in section 83A to the company's [long-term]³ business shall be construed as references to the whole of that business or to the whole of that business other than business in respect of which preparation of a revenue account for the purposes of [Chapter 9 of the Prudential Sourcebook (Insurers)]² is not required.]¹

[(2) In sub-paragraph (1) "the Prudential Sourcebook (Insurers)" means the Interim Prudential Sourcebook for Insurers made by the Financial Services Authority under the Financial Services and Markets Act 2000.]²

Commentary—*Simon's Direct Tax Service* **D4.537.**
Amendments—¹ Para 1B substituted, for para 1, by FA 1995 Sch 8 para 49(2), with effect for accounting periods beginning after 31 December 1994.
² Words substituted, sub-para (1) numbered as such, and sub-para (2) added, by the Financial Services and Markets Act 2000 (Consequential Amendments) (Taxes) Order, SI 2001/3629 arts 54, 58 with effect for periods of account ending after 30 November 2001.
³ Word in sub-para (1) substituted by SI 2001/3629 arts 54, 60(2)(*b*) with effect from 1 December 2001, immediately after the coming into force of the Financial Services and Markets Act 2000 ss 411, 432(1), Sch 20.

[1C—(1) Where for a period of account any investment income referred to in section 83(2)(*a*) is not otherwise brought into account within the meaning of that section, it shall be treated as brought into account for the period if it arises in the period.

(2) Where for a period of account any increase in value referred to in section 83(2)(*b*) (as it applies apart from subsection (3) of that section) is not otherwise brought into account within the meaning of that section, it shall be treated as brought into account for the period if it is shown in the company's

records as available to fund one or both of the following for the period, namely, bonuses to policy holders and dividends to shareholders.

(3) Where for a period of account any reduction in value referred to in section 83(2) (as it applies apart from subsection (3) of that section) is not otherwise brought into account within the meaning of that section, it shall be treated as brought into account for the period if it is shown in the company's records as reducing sums available to fund one or both of the following for the period, namely, bonuses to policy holders and dividends to shareholders.

(4) Where in any period of account any such [addition]² is made as is mentioned in section 83(3) which is not otherwise brought into account within the meaning of that section, it shall be treated as brought into account for the period in which it is made.]¹

Commentary—*Simon's Direct Tax Service* **D4.537.**
Amendments—¹ Para 1C substituted for para 1, by FA 1995 Sch 8 para 49(2), with effect for accounting periods beginning after 31 December 1994.
² Word in sub-para (4) substituted by FA 1996 Sch 31 para 8(6) with effect for periods of account beginning after 31 December 1995.

[**2**—(1) In its application to an overseas life insurance company section 89 of this Act shall have effect with the following modifications; and in those modifications any reference to the Taxes Act 1988 is a reference to that Act as it has effect in relation to such a company by virtue of Schedule 19AC to that Act.

(2) Any reference to franked investment income shall be treated as a reference to UK distribution income (as defined by [paragraph 5B(4) of that Schedule]²).

(3) Any reference in subsection (5)(*a*) to income shall be construed as a reference to such of the income concerned as is attributable to the branch or agency in the United Kingdom through which the company carries on life assurance business.

(4) The reference in subsection (5)(*b*) to assets shall be construed as a reference to such of the assets concerned—

    (*a*) as are—

        (i) section 11(2)(*b*) assets;
        (ii) section 11(2)(*c*) assets; or
        (iii) assets which by virtue of section 11B of the Taxes Act 1988 are attributed to the branch or agency; or

    (*b*) as are assets—

        (i) (in a case where section 11C of that Act (other than subsection (9)) applies) of the relevant fund, or
        (ii) (in a case where that section including that subsection applies) of the relevant funds,

other than assets which fall within paragraph (*a*) above.

(5) In subsection (5)(*c*) the reference to expenses shall be construed as a reference to such of the expenses concerned as are attributable to the branch or agency.

(6) In subsection (5)(*d*) the reference to interest shall be construed as a reference to such of the interest concerned as is so attributable.

(7) In determining for the purposes of subsection (5) whether there has been any increase or reduction in the value (whether realised or not) of assets—

    (*a*) no regard shall be had to any period of time during which an asset does not fall within paragraph (*a*) or (*b*) of sub-paragraph (4) above; and
    (*b*) in the case of an asset which falls within paragraph (*b*) of that sub-paragraph, only the specified portion of any increase or reduction in the value of the asset shall be taken into account;

[and in paragraph (*b*) above "the specified portion" has the same meaning as in paragraph 1A(3)(*b*) above.]⁴

[(7A) For the purposes of this paragraph any expression to which a meaning is given by section 11A of the Taxes Act 1988 has that meaning.]⁴

(8) Where for a period of account any item consisting of income, expenses or interest referred to in subsection (5) is not brought into account within the meaning given by subsection (6) it shall be treated as brought into account for the period if it arises in the period.

(9) Where for a period of account any increase in value referred to in subsection (5) is not brought into account within the meaning given by subsection (6) it shall be treated as brought into account for the period if it is shown in the company's records as available to fund one or both of the following for the period, namely, bonuses to policy holders and dividends to shareholders.

(10) Where for a period of account any reduction in value referred to in subsection (5) is not brought into account within the meaning given by subsection (6) it shall be treated as brought into account for the period if it is shown in the company's records as reducing sums available to fund one or both of the following for the period, namely, bonuses to policy holders and dividends to shareholders.

(11) ...³]¹

Commentary—*Simon's Direct Tax Service* **D4.537.**
Cross references—See TA 1988 Sch 19AC para 4(1) (meaning of "section 11(2)(*b*) assets", "section 11(2)(*c*) assets" and provisions of TA 1988 ss 11A–11C).
Amendments—¹ This Schedule inserted by FA 1993 s 101 and Sch 10.
² Words in para 2(2) substituted by FA 1995 Sch 8 para 35(5), with effect for accounting periods beginning after 31 December 1994.
³ Para 2(11) repealed by FA 1995 Sch 29 Pt VIII(5), with effect for accounting periods beginning after 31 December 1994.
⁴ Words in para 2(7) substituted, and para 2(7A) inserted, by FA 1995 Sch 8 para 49(3),(4), with effect for accounting periods beginning after 31 December 1994.

SCHEDULE 9

LIFE POLICIES ETC HELD BY COMPANIES

Section 90

1 Chapter II of Part XIII of the Taxes Act 1988 shall be amended as follows.

2 (*adds* s 539(9)).

3—(1) Section 540 shall be amended as follows.

(2) (*amends* sub-s (4)).

(3) (*inserts* sub-s (5A)).

4—(1) Section 541 shall be amended as follows.

(2) (*inserts* sub-s (4A)–(4D)).

(3) (*inserts* sub-s (5)(*c*)).

5—(1) Section 547 shall be amended as follows.

(2) (*substitutes* sub-s (1)(*b*)).

(3) (*inserts* sub-s (8)).

6—(1) Section 548 shall be amended as follows.

(2) (*amends* sub-s (1)).

(3) (*inserts* sub-s (3A)).

7 (*inserts* s 552(2)(*c*)).

8 Paragraph 5 above shall have effect in relation to chargeable events happening in any accounting period of the company concerned which begins after 31st March 1989; but subject to that this Schedule shall have effect as from 14th March 1989.

SCHEDULE 10

DEEP DISCOUNT SECURITIES: AMENDMENTS

Section 93

Amendments—This Schedule repealed by FA 1996 s 105 Sch 41 Pt V(3) with effect for income tax from the year 1996–97 and for corporation tax for accounting periods ending after 31 March 1996, subject to the transitional provisions in FA 1996 Sch 15.

SCHEDULE 11

DEEP GAIN SECURITIES

Section 94

Commentary—*Simon's Direct Tax Service* **B5.421–423, C2.805, D2.246.**
Amendments—This Schedule repealed by FA 1996 s 105 Sch 14 para 57, Sch 41 Pt V(3) with effect for income tax from the year 1996–97 and for corporation tax for accounting periods ending after 31 March 1996, subject to the transitional provisions in FA 1996 Sch 15.

SCHEDULE 12

CLOSE COMPANIES

Section 107

PART I

ADMINISTRATIVE PROVISIONS

Interpretation

1 In this Part of this Schedule "the relevant provisions" means—

(*a*) sections [13 to 13A]¹, 231 and 419 to 422 of the Taxes Act 1988, and (*b*) Chapter III of Part XI of that Act (as it has effect in relation to accounting periods beginning before 1st April 1989).

Amendments—[1] Words in sub-para (*a*) substituted by FA 1999 s 28(4), (6) with effect for corporation tax from the financial year 2000, subject to FA 1999 s 28(7) (concerning accounting periods straddling 1 April 2000).

Provision of information by company

2 The inspector may, by notice, require any company which is, or appears to him to be, a close company to furnish him within such time (not being less than 30 days) as may be specified in the notice with such particulars as he thinks necessary for the purposes of the relevant provisions.

Commentary—*Simon's Direct Tax Service* **D3.116.**

Provision of information by shareholders

3—(1) If for the purposes of the relevant provisions any person in whose name any shares are registered is so required by notice by the inspector, he shall state whether or not he is the beneficial owner of the shares and, if not the beneficial owner of the shares, shall furnish the name and address of the person or persons on whose behalf the shares are registered in his name.

(2) This paragraph shall apply in relation to loan capital as it applies in relation to shares.

Commentary—*Simon's Direct Tax Service* **D3.116.**

Information about bearer securities

4—(1) The inspector may, for the purposes of the relevant provisions, by notice require—

    (*a*) any company which appears to him to be a close company to furnish him with particulars of any bearer securities issued by the company, and the names and addresses of the persons to whom the securities were issued and the respective amounts issued to each person, and

    (*b*) any person to whom bearer securities were issued by the company, or to or through whom such securities were subsequently sold or transferred, to furnish him with such further information as he may require with a view to enabling him to ascertain the names and addresses of the persons beneficially interested in the securities.

(2) In this paragraph—

    "loan creditor" has the same meaning as in Part XI of the Taxes Act 1988, and

    "securities" includes shares, stocks, bonds, debentures and debenture stock and also any promissory note or other instrument evidencing indebtedness to a loan creditor of the company.

Commentary—*Simon's Direct Tax Service* **D3.116.**

PART II
AMENDMENTS CONNECTED WITH REPEAL OF CHAPTER III OF PART XI OF TAXES ACT 1988
The Taxes Management Act 1970 (c 9)

5 (*amends* s 98 Table).

Commentary—*Simon's Direct Tax Service* **B2.112.**

The Capital Gains Tax Act 1979 (c 14)

6 (*repealed by* TCGA 1992 Sch 12).

The Income and Corporation Taxes Act 1988 (c 1)

7 (*amends* s 13(9)).

8—(1) *amends* s 168(11).

(2) This paragraph shall have effect in relation to accounting periods beginning after 31st March 1989.

Commentary—*Simon's Direct Tax Service* **B2.708.**

9—(1) (*amends* s 187(3)).

(2) This paragraph shall have effect in relation to accounting periods beginning after 31st March 1989.

10—(1) (*amends* s 214(1)(*c*)).

(2) This paragraph shall have effect in relation to accounting periods beginning after 31st March 1989, except in any case where section 427(4) of the Taxes Act 1988 has effect by virtue of section 103(2) of this Act.

11 (*amends* s 234(9)).

12—(1) Section 360 of the Taxes Act 1988 (loan to buy interest in a close company) shall be amended in accordance with this paragraph.

(2), (3) (*amend* sub-s (1)(*a*), (2)(*a*), (3)(*a*)).

(4) This paragraph shall have effect in relation to interest paid on or after the day on which this Act is passed (and, accordingly, the conditions of section 424(4) of the Taxes Act 1988 shall continue to have effect for the purposes of section 360 of that Act in relation to interest paid before that day).

13—(1) Section 360A of the Taxes Act 1988 (cases in which a person has a material interest in a company for the purposes of section 360(2)(*a*)) shall be amended in accordance with this paragraph.

(2), (3) (*amend* sub-ss (1), (10)).

(4) This paragraph shall have effect in relation to accounting periods beginning after 31st March 1989.

14—(1) (*substitutes* para (*a*) of the definition of "trading company" in s 576(5)).

(2) This paragraph shall have effect in relation to disposals made after 31st March 1989.

15—(1) (*amends* s 623(2)).

(2) This paragraph shall have effect in relation to accounting periods beginning after 31st March 1989.

16—(1) (*substitutes* definition of "investment income" in s 644(6)).

(2) This paragraph shall have effect in relation to accounting periods beginning after 31st March 1989.

17 (*amends* s 745(4)).

[18—(1) *Paragraph 7 of Schedule 8 to the Taxes Act 1988 (cases in which a person has a material interest in a company for the purposes of a profit-related pay scheme) shall be amended in accordance with this paragraph.*

(2), (3) (*amended* sub-paras (2), (3)).

(4) *This paragraph shall have effect in relation to accounting periods beginning after 31st March 1989.*][1]

Amendments—[1] Para 18 repealed by FA 1997 Sch 18 Pt VI(3) with effect for any payment made by reference to a profit period beginning after 31 December 1999 in accordance with FA 1997 s 61(2), (3), but subject to FA 1997 Sch 18 Pt VI(3) note 2.

SCHEDULE 13

CAPITAL ALLOWANCES: MISCELLANEOUS AMENDMENTS
Section 121

Amendment—Paras 1–26 of this Schedule repealed by CAA 1990 Sch 2.

Patent rights

Amendment—Para 27 of this Schedule repealed by CAA 2001 s 580, Sch 4 with effect in accordance with CAA 2001 s 579. Paras 28–30 of this Schedule repealed by CAA 1990 Sch 2.

SCHEDULE 14

CAPITAL GAINS TAX: GIFTS ETC
Section 124

Amendment—This Schedule repealed by TCGA 1992 Sch 12.

SCHEDULE 15

CAPITAL GAINS: RE-BASING TO 1982 ETC
Section 141

Amendment—This Schedule repealed by TCGA 1992 Sch 12.

FINANCE ACT 1990

(1990 Chapter 29)

ARRANGEMENT OF SECTIONS

PART II

INCOME TAX, CORPORATION TAX AND CAPITAL GAINS TAX

CHAPTER I

GENERAL

CHAPTER II
MANAGEMENT

PART IV
MISCELLANEOUS AND GENERAL
Ports levy

An Act to grant certain duties, to alter other duties, and to amend the law relating to the National Debt and the Public Revenue, and to make further provision in connection with Finance.

[26th July 1990]

PART II
INCOME TAX, CORPORATION TAX AND CAPITAL GAINS TAX

CHAPTER I
GENERAL
Income tax rates and allowances

17 Rates and main allowances

(1) *(spent).*

(2) *(amended* TA 1988 ss 1(5), 257C(2), *repealed by* FA 1993 s 213, Sch 23 Pt III(10) *with effect from the year 1994–95).*

(3) *(amends* TA 1988 s 828(4)).

(4) *(spent).*

Commentary—*Simon's Direct Tax Service* E1.102, 104.

18 Relief for blind persons

(amends TA 1988 s 265(1)).

Corporation tax rates

19 Charge and rate of corporation tax for 1990

(spent).

Commentary—*Simon's Direct Tax Service* D2.108.

20 Small companies

(spent).

Commentary—*Simon's Direct Tax Service* D2.109.

Benefits in kind

21 Care for children

(1) *(inserts* TA 1988 s 155A).

(2) *(amends* TA 1988 s 154(2)).

(3) This section applies for the year 1990–91 and subsequent years of assessment.

22 Car benefits

(substituted TA 1988 Sch 6 Pt I *from the year 1990–91 and is now superseded).*

Mileage allowances

23 Limit on chargeable mileage profit

...

Amendment—This section repealed by FA 2001 s 110, Sch 33 Pt II(1) with effect from the year 2002–03.

Charities

24 Payroll deduction scheme

(repealed by FA 1993 Sch 23, Pt III(2) with effect from the year 1993–94).

25 Donations to charity by individuals

(1) For the purposes of this section, a gift to a charity by an individual (''the donor'') is a qualifying donation if—

  (*a*) it is made on or after 1st October 1990,

  (*b*) it satisfies the requirements of subsection (2) below, and

  (*c*) the donor gives [an appropriate declaration][2] in relation to it to the charity.

(2) A gift satisfies the requirements of this subsection if—

  (*a*) it takes the form of a payment of a sum of money;

  (*b*) it is not subject to a condition as to repayment;

  (*c*) ...[2]

  (*d*) it does not constitute a sum falling within section 202(2) of the Taxes Act 1988 (payroll deduction scheme);

(*e*) neither the donor nor any person connected with him receives a benefit in consequence of making it or, where the donor or a person connected with him does receive a benefit in consequence of making it, the relevant value in relation to the gift does not exceed [the limit imposed by subsection (5A) below][2] and the amount to be taken into account for the purposes of this paragraph in relation to the gift does not exceed £250;

(*f*) it is not conditional on or associated with, or part of an arrangement involving, the acquisition of property by the charity, otherwise than by way of gift, from the donor or a person connected with him;

(*g*) ...[2]

(*h*) ...[1]; and

[(*i*) either—

(i) at the time the gift is made, the donor is resident in the United Kingdom or performs duties which by virtue of section 132(4)(*a*) of the Taxes Act 1988 (Crown employees serving overseas) are treated as being performed in the United Kingdom; or

(ii) the grossed up amount of the gift would, if in fact made, be payable out of profits or gains brought into charge to income tax or capital gains tax.][2]

[(3) The reference in subsection (1)(*c*) above to an appropriate declaration is a reference to a declaration which—

(*a*) is given in such manner as may be prescribed by regulations made by the Board; and

(*b*) contains such information and such statements as may be so prescribed.

(3A) Regulations made for the purposes of subsection (3) above may—

(*a*) provide for declarations to have effect, to cease to have effect or to be deemed never to have had effect in such circumstances and for such purposes as may be prescribed by the regulations;

(*b*) require charities to keep records with respect to declarations given to them by donors; and

(*c*) make different provision for declarations made in a different manner.][2]

(4) For the purposes of subsections (2)(*e*) above and (5) below, the relevant value in relation to a gift is—

(*a*) where there is one benefit received in consequence of making it which is received by the donor or a person connected with him, the value of that benefit;

(*b*) where there is more than one benefit received in consequence of making it which is received by the donor or a person connected with him, the aggregate value of all the benefits received in consequence of making it which are received by the donor or a person connected with him.

(5) The amount to be taken into account for the purposes of subsection (2)(*e*) above in relation to a gift to a charity is an amount equal to the aggregate of—

(*a*) the relevant value in relation to the gift, and

(*b*) the relevant value in relation to each gift already made to the charity by the donor in the relevant year of assessment which is a qualifying donation for the purposes of this section.

[(5A) The limit imposed by this subsection is—

(*a*) where the amount of the gift does not exceed £100, 25 per cent of the amount of the gift;

(*b*) where the amount of the gift exceeds £100 but does not exceed £1,000, £25;

(*c*) where the amount of the gift exceeds £1,000, 2.5 per cent of the amount of the gift.

(5B) Where a benefit received in consequence of making a gift—

(*a*) consists of the right to receive benefits at intervals over a period of less than twelve months;

(*b*) relates to a period of less than twelve months; or

(*c*) is one of a series of benefits received at intervals in consequence of making a series of gifts at intervals of less than twelve months,

the value of the benefit shall be adjusted for the purposes of subsection (4) above and the amount of the gift shall be adjusted for the purposes of subsection (5A) above.

(5C) Where a benefit, other than a benefit which is one of a series of benefits received at intervals, is received in consequence of making a gift which is one of a series of gifts made at intervals of less than twelve months, the amount of the gift shall be adjusted for the purposes of subsection (5A) above.

(5D) Where the value of a benefit, or the amount of a gift, falls to be adjusted under subsection (5B) or (5C) above, the value or amount shall be multiplied by 365 and the result shall be divided by—

(*a*) in a case falling within subsection (5B)(*a*) or (*b*) above, the number of days in the period of less than twelve months;

(*b*) in a case falling within subsection (5B)(*c*) or (5C) above, the average number of days in the intervals of less than twelve months;

and the reference in subsection (5B) above to subsection (4) above is a reference to that subsection as it applies for the purposes of subsection (2)(*e*) above.

(5E) In determining whether a gift to a charity falling within subsection (5F) below is a qualifying donation, there shall be disregarded the benefit of any right of admission received in consequence of the making of the gift—

(*a*) to view property the preservation of which is the sole or main purpose of the charity; or (*b*) to observe wildlife the conservation of which is the sole or main purpose of the charity;

but this subsection shall not apply unless the opportunity to make gifts which attract such a right is available to members of the public.

(5F) A charity falls within this subsection if its sole or main purpose is the preservation of property, or the conservation of wildlife, for the public benefit.

(5G) In subsection (5E) above "right of admission" refers to admission of the person making the gift (or any member of his family who may be admitted because of the gift) either free of the charges normally payable for admission by members of the public, or on payment of a reduced charge.]²

[(6) Where any gift made by the donor in a year of assessment is a qualifying donation, then, for that year—

(*a*) the Income Tax Acts and the Taxation of Chargeable Gains Act 1992 shall have effect, in their application to him, as if—

(i) the gift had been made after deduction of income tax at the basic rate; and

(ii) the basic rate limit were increased by an amount equal to the grossed up amount of the gift;

(*b*) the provisions mentioned in subsection (7) below shall have effect, in their application to him, as if any reference to income tax which he is entitled to charge against any person included a reference to the tax treated as deducted from the gift; and

(*c*) to the extent, if any, necessary to ensure that he is charged to an amount of income tax and capital gains tax equal to the tax treated as deducted from the gift, he shall not be entitled to relief under Chapter I of Part VII of the Taxes Act 1988;

but paragraph (*a*)(ii) above shall not apply for the purposes of any computation under section 550(2)(*a*) or (*b*) of that Act (relief where gain charged at a higher rate).

(7) The provisions referred to in subsection (6)(*b*) above are—

(*a*) section 289A(5)(*e*) of the Taxes Act 1988 (relief under enterprise investment scheme);

(*b*) section 796(3) of that Act (credit for foreign tax); and

(*c*) paragraph 1(6)(*f*) of Schedule 15B to that Act (venture capital trusts).

(8) Where the tax treated as deducted from a gift by virtue of subsection (6) above exceeds the amount of income tax and capital gains tax with which the donor is charged for the year of assessment, the donor shall be assessable and chargeable with income tax at the basic rate on so much of the gift as is necessary to recover an amount of tax equal to the excess.

(9) In determining for the purposes of subsection (8) above the total amount of income tax and capital gains tax with which the donor is charged for the year of assessment, there shall be disregarded—

(*a*) any tax charged at the basic rate by virtue of—

(i) section 348 of the Taxes Act 1988 (read with section 3 of that Act); or

(ii) section 349 of that Act (read with section 350 of that Act);

(*b*) any tax treated as having been paid under—

(i) section 233(1)(*a*) of that Act (taxation of certain recipients of distributions);

(ii) section 249(4)(*a*) of that Act (stock dividends treated as income); or

(iii) section 547(5)(*a*) of that Act (method of charging life policy gain to tax);

(*c*) any relief to which section 256(2) of that Act applies (relief by way of income tax reduction);

(*d*) any relief under—

(i) section 347B of that Act (relief for maintenance payments);

(ii) section 788 of that Act (relief by agreement with other countries); or

(iii) section 790(1) of that Act (unilateral relief);

(*e*) any set off of tax deducted, or treated as deducted, from income other than—

(i) tax treated as deducted from income by virtue of section 421(1)(*a*) of that Act (taxation of borrower when loan released etc); or

(ii) tax treated as deducted from a relevant amount within the meaning of section 699A of that Act (untaxed sums comprised in the income of an estate) except to the extent that the relevant amount is or would be paid in respect of a distribution chargeable under Schedule F; and

(*f*) any set off of tax credits.

(9A) For the purposes of sections 257(5) and 257A(5) of the Taxes Act 1988 (age related allowances), the donor's total income shall be treated as reduced by the aggregate amount of gifts from which tax is treated as deducted by virtue of subsection (6) above.]²

(10) The receipt by a charity of a gift which is a qualifying donation shall be treated for the purposes of the Tax Acts, in their application to the charity, as the receipt, under deduction of income tax at the basic rate for the relevant year of assessment, of an annual payment of an amount equal to the grossed up amount of the gift.

(11) Section 839 of the Taxes Act 1988 applies for the purposes of subsections (2) and (4) above.

(12) For the purposes of this section—

(*a*) "charity" has the same meaning as in section 506 of the Taxes Act 1988 and includes each of the bodies mentioned in section 507 of that Act;

(*b*) ...[2]

(*c*) "relevant year of assessment", in relation to a gift, means the year of assessment in which the gift is made;

(*d*) references, in relation to a gift, to the grossed up amount are to the amount which after deducting income tax at the basic rate for the relevant year of assessment leaves the amount of the gift; ...[2]

(*e*) ...[2]

Commentary—*Simon's Direct Tax Service* E1.504A.
Note—Any regulations made under sub-s (3) above before 28 October 2000 may be so made as to apply to any payments in relation to which FA 2000 s 39 has effect (FA 2000 s 39(10)).
Revenue and other press releases—IR 17-3-98 (millennium gift aid: details and list of eligible countries).
Cross references—See FA 2002 s 98 (donor who makes a qualifying donation after 5 April 2003 may elect to be treated for the purposes of this section as if the qualifying donation was made in the previous year of assessment).
FA 2002 Sch 18 para 9 (relief for donors in relation to community amateur sports clubs. This section has effect as if a registered club were a charity. For the purposes of this section, membership fees are not gifts).
Donations to Charity by Individuals (Appropriate Declarations) Regulations, SI 2000/2074 (requirements relating to the declaration required to be given under sub-s (1)(*c*) above).
Amendments—[1] Sub-s (2)(*h*) repealed by FA 1991 s 71(5), (6) and Sch 19 Pt V in relation to gifts made after 18 March 1991.
[2] Words in sub-ss (1)(*c*), (2)(*e*) and whole of sub-ss (2)(*i*), (3), (3A), (6)–(9A) substituted, sub-ss (2)(*c*), (*g*), (12)(*b*), (*e*) and word "and" in sub-s (12)(*d*) repealed, and sub-ss (5A)–(5G) inserted, by FA 2000 ss 39(1)–(7), (10), 156, Sch 40 Pt II(1) with effect for gifts made after 5 April 2000 which are not covenanted payments and covenanted payments falling to be made after that date.
Prospective amendments—In sub-s (7), word "and" at end of para (*b*) repealed, and words inserted after para (*c*), by FA 2002 ss 57, 141, Sch 17 para 4, Sch 40 Pt 3(6) with effect from such day as the Treasury may by order appoint. This amendment shall have effect for years of assessment ending on or after the appointed day. Words inserted to read as follows—
"and
(*d*) paragraph 19(6)(*d*) of Schedule 16 to the Finance Act 2002."

26 Company donations to charity

(1)–(5) (*amend* TA 1988 s 339).

(6) This section applies in relation to payments made on or after 1st October 1990.

27 Maximum qualifying company donations

(1) (*repealed by* FA 1991 Sch 19 Pt V *in relation to accounting periods beginning after 18 March 1991*).

(2) (*amends* TA 1988 s 339).

(3) (*repealed by* FA 1991 Sch 19 Pt V *in relation to accounting periods beginning after 18 March 1991*).

(4) This section applies in relation to accounting periods ending on or after 1st October 1990.

Savings

28 Tax-exempt special savings accounts

(1) (*inserts* TA 1988 ss 326A–326C).

(2) (*amends* TMA 1970 s 98 Table).

(3) (*amends* CGTA 1979 s 149B and is repealed by TCGA 1992 s 290, Sch 12).

29 Extension of SAYE

(*amends* TA 1988 s 326).

30 Building societies and deposit-takers

Schedule 5 to this Act (which contains provisions relating to building societies, deposit-takers and investors) shall have effect.

Employee share ownership trusts

31 Conditions for roll-over relief

Commentary—*Simon's Direct Tax Service* C1.431.
Amendments—This section repealed by TCGA 1992 Sch 12.

32 Conditions for relief: supplementary

Commentary—*Simon's Direct Tax Service* C1.431.
Amendments—This section repealed by TCGA 1992 Sch 12.

33 The relief

Commentary—*Simon's Direct Tax Service* C1.431.
Amendments—This section repealed by TCGA 1992 Sch 12.

34 Dwelling-houses: special provision

Commentary—*Simon's Direct Tax Service* C1.432.
Amendments—This section repealed by TCGA 1992 Sch 12.

35 Shares: special provision

Commentary—*Simon's Direct Tax Service* C1.432.
Amendments—This section repealed by TCGA 1992 Sch 12.

36 Chargeable event when replacement assets owned

Commentary—*Simon's Direct Tax Service* C1.433.
Amendments—This section repealed by TCGA 1992 Sch 12.

37 Chargeable event when replacement property owned

Commentary—*Simon's Direct Tax Service* C1.433.
Amendments—This section repealed by TCGA 1992 Sch 12.

38 Chargeable event when bonds owned

Commentary—*Simon's Direct Tax Service* C1.433.
Amendments—This section repealed by TCGA 1992 Sch 12.

39 Information

Commentary—*Simon's Direct Tax Service* C1.431.
Amendments—This section repealed by TCGA 1992 Sch 12.

40 Other enactments

Commentary—*Simon's Direct Tax Service* C1.433; C3.311.
Amendments—This section repealed by TCGA 1992 Sch 12.

Insurance companies and friendly societies

41 Apportionment of income etc

Schedule 6 to this Act (which makes provision about the apportionment of income etc and related provision) shall have effect.

42 Overseas life assurance business

Schedule 7 to this Act (which makes provision about the taxation of overseas life assurance business) shall have effect.

43 Deduction for policy holders' tax

(1) (*amends* FA 1989 s 82(1)(*a*)).

(2) (*amends* TA 1988 s 436(3)).

(3) The Finance Act 1989 shall be deemed always to have had effect with the amendment made by subsection (1) above, and the amendment made by subsection (2) above shall have the same effect as, by virtue of section 84(5)(*b*) of that Act, it would have had if it had been made by Schedule 8 to that Act.

44 Reinsurance commissions

(1) (*amends* FA 1989 s 85(2)).

(2) (*amended* FA 1989 s 86(1) *and is now superseded*).

(3) (*amends* TA 1988 s 76(1)).

(4) Sections 85 and 86 of the Finance Act 1989 shall be deemed always to have had effect with the amendments made by subsections (1) and (2) above, and section 76 of the Taxes Act 1988 shall have effect as if the amendment made by subsection (3) above had been included among those made by section 87 of the Finance Act 1989.

(5) Nothing in subsection (2) above applies to commissions in respect of the reinsurance of liabilities assumed by the recipient company in respect of insurances made before 14th March 1989, but without prejudice to the application of that subsection to any reinsurance commission attributable to a variation on or after that date in a policy issued in respect of such an insurance; and for this purpose the exercise of any rights conferred by a policy shall be regarded as a variation of it.

Commentary—*Simon's Direct Tax Service* D4.505.

45 Policy holders' share of profits etc

(1), (2) (*amend* FA 1989 s 88(1), (4)).

(3) (*substitutes* FA 1989 s 89).

(4)–(7) (*amend* TA 1988 s 434; sub-s (6) repealed by FA 1998 Sch 27 Part III(2)).

(8) (repealed by FA 1995 s 162, Sch 29 Pt VIII(5)).

(9) (*amends* TA 1988 s 438 *and is repealed by* F(No 2)A 1997 Sch 8 Pt II (6)).

(10) The Finance Act 1989 shall be deemed always to have had effect with the amendments made by subsections (1) to (3) above, and the amendments made by subsections (4) to (9) above shall have the same effect as, by virtue of section 84(5)(*b*) of that Act, they would have had if they had been made by Schedule 8 to that Act.

(11) Paragraphs 1 and 3(3) of Schedule 8 to the Finance Act 1989 shall be deemed never to have had effect.

46 Annual deemed disposal of holdings of unit trusts etc

Commentary—*Simon's Direct Tax Service* **D4.527.**
Amendments—This section repealed by TCGA 1992 Sch 12.

47 Spreading of gains and losses under section 46

Commentary—*Simon's Direct Tax Service* **D4.527.**
Amendments—This section repealed by TCGA 1992 Sch 12.

48 Transfers of long term business

Schedule 9 to this Act (which makes provision about the tax consequences of certain transfers of long term business by insurance companies) shall have effect.

49 Friendly societies: increased tax exemption

(*amends* TA 1988 ss 460, 464, Sch 15 para 3(8)).

50 Friendly societies: application of enactments

(*amends* TA 1988 s 463).

Unit and investment trusts etc

51 Authorised unit trusts

(*repealed by* FA 1996 Sch 41 Pt V(1) with effect from the year 1996–97).

52 Unit trusts: repeals

(1) The Taxes Act 1988 shall have effect subject to the following provisions of this section.

(2) (*repeals* TA 1988 s 468(5)).

(3) Where a particular distribution period is by virtue of subsection (2) above the last distribution period as regards which section 468(5) applies in the case of a trust, the trustees' liability to income tax in respect of any source of income chargeable under Case III of Schedule D shall be assessed as if they had ceased to possess the source of income on the last day of that distribution period.

(4) But where section 67 of the Taxes Act 1988 applies by virtue of subsection (3) above, it shall apply with the omission from subsection (1)(*b*) of the words from ''and shall'' to ''this provision''.

(5)–(7) (*repeal* TA 1988 ss 468B–468D).

(8) In this section ''distribution period'' has the same meaning as in section 468 of the Taxes Act 1988.

Commentary—*Simon's Direct Tax Service* **D4.414–418.**

53 Unit trust managers: exemption from bond-washing provisions

(1) (*inserts* TA 1988 s 732(5A) and is repealed by F(No 2)A 1997 Sch 8 Pt II (8)).

(2) (*inserts* TA 1970 s 472(5A)).

54 Indexation: collective investment schemes

Amendments—This section repealed by TCGA 1992 Sch 12.

55 Investment trusts

(1) (*inserts* TA 1988 s 842(2A)–(2C)).

(2) This section applies in relation to accounting periods ending on or after the day on which this Act is passed.

Securities

56 Convertible securities

Amendments—This section repealed by FA 1996 Sch 41 Pt V(3) with effect for income tax from the year 1996–97 and for corporation tax for accounting periods ending after 31 March 1996, subject to transitional provisions in FA 1996 Sch 15.

57 Deep gain securities

Amendments—This section repealed by F(No 2)A 1992 s 82, Sch 18 Pt VII.

58 Qualifying indexed securities

Amendments—This section, repealed in part by F(No 2)A 1992 s 82, Sch 18 Pt VII, repealed by FA 1996 Sch 41 Pt V(3) with effect for income tax from the year 1996–97 and for corporation tax for accounting periods ending after 31 March 1996, subject to transitional provisions in FA 1996 Sch 15.

59 Deep discount securities

Amendments—This section repealed by FA 1996 Sch 41 Pt V(3) with effect for income tax from the year 1996–97 and for corporation tax for accounting periods ending after 31 March 1996, subject to transitional provisions in FA 1996 Sch 15.

International

65 Dual resident companies: capital gains

Amendments—This section repealed by TCGA 1992 Sch 12.

66 Dual resident companies: transfers of assets abroad

Amendments—This section repealed by FA 1994 Sch 26 Pt VIII(1)).

67 Dual resident companies: controlled foreign companies

(1), (2) (*amended* TA 1988 ss 749(4A), 751(2)(*bb*), *repealed by* FA 1994 Sch 26 Pt VIII(1)).

(3), (4) (*amend* TA 1988 Sch 25 para 2).

68 Movements of capital between residents of member States

(1) (*amends* TA 1988 s 765(1)).

(2) (*inserts* TA 1988 s 765A).

(3) (*amends* TMA 1970 s 98).

(4) This section shall apply to transactions carried out on or after 1st July 1990.

69 European Economic Interest Groupings

Schedule 11 to this Act (which makes provision about the taxation of income and gains in the case of European Economic Interest Groupings) shall have effect.

70 Transfer of United Kingdom branch or agency

Amendments—This section repealed by TCGA 1992 Sch 12.

Miscellaneous

71 Relief for interest

(*spent*).

Commentary—*Simon's Direct Tax Service* A3.431; E1.539.

72 Capital gains: annual exempt amount for 1990–91

Commentary—*Simon's Direct Tax Service* C1.401, 402.
Amendments—This section repealed by TCGA 1992 s 290, Sch 12.

73 Business expansion scheme: abolition of "locality rule"

Amendments—This section repealed by FA 1994 Sch 26 Pt V(17).

74 Debts of overseas governments etc

Amendments—This section repealed by FA 1996 Sch 41 Pt V(3).

75 Local enterprise agencies

Amendments—This section repealed by FA 1994 Sch 26 Pt V(21).

76 Training and enterprise councils and local enterprise companies

(*inserts* TA 1988 s 79A).

77 Expenses of entertainers

(*inserts* TA 1988 s 201A).

78 Waste disposal

(*inserts* TA 1988 ss 91A, 91B).

79 Priority share allocations for employees etc

(1) (*inserts* FA 1988 s 68(3A)).

(2) This section applies to offers made on or after the day on which this Act is passed.

80 Broadcasting: transfer of undertakings of Independent Broadcasting Authority and Cable Authority

Schedule 12 to this Act shall have effect.

81 Futures and options: exemptions

(1) (*inserted* TA 1988 s 468AA; *repealed by* FA 2002 s 141, Sch 40 Pt 3(13) with effect for accounting periods beginning after 30 September 2002).

(2) (*inserts* TA 1988 s 659A).

(3) (*inserted* CGTA 1979 s 149B(10), (11), *repealed by* TCGA 1992 Sch 12).

(4) (*repeals* TA 1988 s 659).

(5) Subsections (1) and (2) above apply in relation to income derived after the day on which this Act is passed.

(6) (*repealed* by TCGA 1992 Sch 12).

(7) Insofar as section 659 of the Taxes Act 1988 relates to provisions of that Act, subsection (4) above applies in relation to income derived after the day on which this Act is passed.

(8) Insofar as section 659 of the Taxes Act 1988 relates to section 149B of the Capital Gains Tax Act 1979 subsection(4) above applies in relation to disposals made after the day on which this Act is passed.

82 Settlements: child's income

Amendments—This section repealed by FA 1995 Sch 29 Pt VIII(8).

83 Loans to traders

(*repealed by* TCGA 1992 Sch 12).

84 Qualifying corporate bonds: relief

Amendments—This section repealed by TCGA 1992 Sch 12.

85 Qualifying corporate bonds: reorganisations etc

Amendments—This section repealed by TCGA 1992 Sch 12.

86 Groups of companies

Commentary—*Simon's Direct Tax Service* **D2.622.**
Amendments—This section repealed by TCGA 1992 Sch 12.

87 Capital allowances: vehicles provided by employees

Commentary—*Simon's Direct Tax Service* **E4.711.**
Amendment—This section repealed by the Capital Allowances Act 2001 s 580, Sch 4 with effect for income tax purposes, as respects allowances and charges falling to be made for chargeable periods ending after 5 April 2001, and for corporation tax purposes, as respects allowances and charges falling to be made for chargeable periods ending after 31 March 2001.

88 Capital allowances: miscellaneous amendments

Schedule 13 to this Act shall have effect.

89 Correction of errors in Taxes Act 1988

Schedule 14 to this Act shall have effect.

CHAPTER II

MANAGEMENT

Returns and information

90 Income tax returns

(1) (*substitutes* TMA 1970 ss 8, 8A, 9 for ss 8, 9).

(2)–(4) (*amend* TMA 1970 ss 12, 93, 95).

(5) This section applies where a notice to deliver a return was, or falls to be, given after 5th April 1990.

91 Corporation tax returns

Amendment—This section repealed by FA 1998 s 165, Sch 27 Part III(28) with effect in relation to accounting periods ending after 30 June 1999 (by virtue of Finance Act 1994, Section 199, (Appointed Day) Order, SI 1998/3173 art 2).

92 Information powers relating to interest

(1)–(6) (*amend* TMA 1970 ss 17, 18).

(7) Subsections (1) to (3) above shall have effect as regards a case where interest is paid or credited in the year 1991–92 or a subsequent year of assessment.

(8) Subsections (4) to (6) above shall have effect as regards a case where interest is paid in the year 1991–92 or a subsequent year of assessment.

93 Restrictions on Board's power to call for information

(1) (*inserts* TMA 1970 s 20(7A)).

(2) This section shall apply with respect to notices given on or after the day on which this Act is passed.

94 Donations to charity: inspection powers

Commentary—*Simon's Direct Tax Service* C4.540.
Amendments—This section repealed by F(No 2)A 1992 s 28(5), (6) and Sch 18 Pt VII(2) in relation to claims made after 16 July 1992.

Corporation tax determinations

95 Determinations

Amendments—This section repealed by FA 1998 s 165, Sch 27 Part III(28) with effect in relation to accounting periods ending after 30 June 1999 (by virtue of Finance Act 1994, Section 199, (Appointed Day) Order, SI 1998/3173 art 2).

96 Consequential group relief adjustments

Commentary—*Simon's Direct Tax Service* D2.649.
Amendments—This section repealed by FA 1999 ss 92(6), (7), 139, Sch 20 Pt III(20) with effect for accounting periods ending after 30 June 1999.

Claims by companies

97 Payment of tax credits

Amendment—This section repealed by F(No 2)A 1997 Sch 8 Pt II (9) with effect in relation to tax credits in respect of distributions made after 5 April 1999.

98 Repayment of income tax deducted at source

(1) The Taxes Act 1988 shall be amended as follows.

(2)–(4) (*amend* TA 1988 ss 7, 11(3)).

(5) This section applies in relation to income tax falling to be set off against corporation tax for accounting periods ending after the day appointed for the purposes section 10 of the Taxes Act 1988 (pay and file).

Note—The appointed day as mentioned in sub-s (5) is 30 September 1993 by virtue of SI 1992/3066.
Amendment—Sub-s (3) repealed by FA 1998 Sch 27 Part III(28) with effect in relation to accounting periods ending after 30 June 1999 (by virtue of Finance Act 1994, Section 199, (Appointed Day) Order, SI 1998/3173 art 2).

99 Loss relief

(1) The Taxes Act 1988 shall be amended as follows.

(2), (3) (*amend* TA 1988 ss 393, 396).

(4) This section applies in relation to accounting periods ending after the day appointed for the purposes of section 10 of the Taxes Act 1988 (pay and file).

Notes—The appointed day as mentioned in sub-s (4) above is 30 September 1993 by virtue of SI 1992/3066.

100 Group relief: general

Amendment—This section repealed by FA 1998 Sch 27 Part III(28) with effect in relation to accounting periods ending after 30 June 1999 (by virtue of Finance Act 1994, Section 199, (Appointed Day) Order, SI 1998/3173 art 2).

101 Group relief: relieved losses

Amendment—This section repealed by FA 1999 s 139, Sch 20 Pt III(21) with effect for accounting periods ending after 30 June 1999.

102 Capital allowances: general

Amendment—This section repealed by FA 1998 Sch 27 Part III(28) with effect in relation to accounting periods ending after 30 June 1999 (by virtue of Finance Act 1994, Section 199, (Appointed Day) Order, SI 1998/3173 art 2).

103 Capital allowances: assimilation to claims by individuals

Amendment—This section repealed by the Capital Allowances Act 2001 s 580, Sch 4 with effect for income tax purposes, as respects allowances and charges falling to be made for chargeable periods ending after 5 April 2001, and for corporation tax purposes, as respects allowances and charges falling to be made for chargeable periods ending after 31 March 2001.

Miscellaneous

104 Officers

(1) (*inserts* TMA 1970 s 1(2A), (2B)).

(2) (*amends* TMA 1970 s 55, *part repealed* by FA 2001 s 110, Sch 33 Pt II(13) with effect in accordance with FA 2001 s 88, Sch 29).

(3) The amendment made by subsection (1) above shall be deemed always to have had effect.

(4) The amendments made by subsection (2) above shall apply where notice of appeal is given on or after the day on which this Act is passed.

105 Recovery of excessive repayments of tax

(1) (*inserts* TMA 1970 s 30(1A)).

(2) This section applies in relation to amounts of tax repaid on or after the day on which this Act is passed.

106 Corporation tax: collection

(*Substitutes* TA 1988 s 10(2)).

PART IV
MISCELLANEOUS AND GENERAL

Miscellaneous

125 Information for tax authorities in other member States

(1) Subsections (1) to (8) and (8C) to (9) of section 20 of the Taxes Management Act 1970 (powers to call for information relevant to liability to income tax, corporation tax or capital gains tax) shall have effect as if the references in those provisions to tax liability included a reference to liability to a tax of a member State other than the United Kingdom which is a tax on income or on capital for the purposes of the Directive of the Council of the European Communities dated 19th December 1977 No 77/799/EEC.

(2) In their application by virtue of subsection (1) above those provisions shall have effect as if—

(*a*) the reference in section 20(7A) to any provision of the Taxes Acts were a reference to any provision of the law of the member State in accordance with which the tax in question is charged,

(*b*) the references in subsection (2) of section 20B to an appeal relating to tax were references to an appeal, review or similar proceedings under the law of the member State relating to the tax in question, and

(*c*) the reference in subsection (6) of that section to believing that tax has or may have been lost to the Crown were a reference to believing that the tax in question has or may have been lost to the member State.

(3), (4) (*not relevant to this work*).

(5) In section 77 of the Finance Act 1978 (disclosure of information to tax authorities of member States: obligation of secrecy) references to the Directive mentioned in subsection (1) above shall include a reference to that Directive as extended by any other Directive of the Council (whether adopted before or after the passing of this Act) to any taxes of a character similar to that of inheritance tax or chargeable on or by reference to death or gifts inter vivos.

(6) Subsections (1) and (2) above shall apply with respect to notices given on or after the day on which this Act is passed, subsections (3) and (4) above shall apply with respect to notices given on or after such day as the Treasury may by order made by statutory instrument appoint and subsection (5) above shall come into force on that day.

Commentary—*Simon's Direct Tax Service* **A3.154.**
Revenue Internal Guidance—Investigations Handbook IH 421 (exchange of information is dealt with by London Special Compliance Office).

126 Pools payments for football ground improvements

(1) This section applies to any payment (including a payment made before the passing of this Act) which, in consequence of the reduction in pool betting duty effected by section 4 above, is made by a person liable to pay that duty in order to meet, directly or indirectly, capital expenditure incurred (whether by the person to whom it is made or any other person) in improving the safety or comfort of spectators at a ground to be used for the playing of association football.

(2) Where a person carrying on a trade makes a payment to which this section applies, the payment may be deducted in computing for tax purposes the [profits][1] of the trade.

(3) A payment to which this section applies shall not be regarded as an annual payment.

(4) [Section 532 of the Capital Allowances Act 2001][2] shall not apply to expenditure of the kind mentioned in subsection (1) above in so far as it has been or is to be met, directly or indirectly, out of a payment to which this section applies.

(5) Where a payment to which this section applies is made to trustees, the sum received by them and any assets representing it (but not any income or gains arising from them) shall not be relevant property for the purposes of Chapter III of Part III of the Inheritance Tax Act 1984.

Commentary—*Simon's Direct Tax Service* **B3.1446.**
Amendments—[1] Words substituted by FA 1998 Sch 7 para 5 with effect from 31 July 1998.
[2] Words in sub-s (4) substituted by CAA 2001 s 578, Sch 2 para 72 with effect for income tax purposes, as respects allowances and charges falling to be made for chargeable periods ending after 5 April 2001, and for corporation tax purposes, as respects allowances and charges falling to be made for chargeable periods ending after 31 March 2001.

127 Definition of "local authority" for certain tax purposes

(1) (*inserts* TA 1988 s 842A).

(2) (*amended* CGTA 1979 s 155(1), *repealed by* TCGA 1992 Sch 12).

(3) Schedule 18 to this Act (consequential amendments) shall have effect.

(4) This section shall be deemed to have come into force on 1st April 1990.

General

131 Interpretation etc

(1) In this Act "the Taxes Act 1970" means the Income and Corporation Taxes Act 1970 and "the Taxes Act 1988" means the Income and Corporation Taxes Act 1988.

(2) (*not relevant to this work*).

(3) Part II of this Act, so far as it relates to capital gains tax, shall be construed as one with the Capital Gains Tax Act 1979.

133 Short title

This Act may be cited as the Finance Act 1990.

SCHEDULES

SCHEDULE 4

LIMIT ON CHARGEABLE MILEAGE PROFIT

Section 23

(*Inserted* TA 1988 ss 197B–197F and *repealed from 2002–03 by* FA 2001 s 110, Sch 33 Part II(1)).

SCHEDULE 5

BUILDING SOCIETIES AND DEPOSIT-TAKERS

Section 30

Introduction

1 The Taxes Act 1988 shall be amended as mentioned in paragraphs 2 to 14 below.

Building societies

2—(1) (*repeals* TA 1988 s 476).
(2) This paragraph shall apply as regards the year 1991–92 and subsequent years of assessment.
3—(1) (*repeals* TA 1988 s 477).
(2) This paragraph shall apply as regards any time falling on or after 6th April 1991.
4—(1) (*inserts* TA 1988 s 477A).
(2) This paragraph shall apply as regards the year 1991–92 and subsequent years of assessment.

Deposit-takers

5—(1) (*repeals* TA 1988 s 479).
(2) This paragraph shall apply as regards interest paid or credited on or after 6th April 1991.
6—(1) (*repeals* TA 1988 s 480).
(2) This paragraph shall apply as regards any time falling on or after 6th April 1991.
7—(1) (*inserts* TA 1988 ss 480A–480C).
(2) This paragraph shall apply as regards interest paid or credited on or after 6th April 1991.
8, 9 (*amend* TA 1988 ss 481, 482).

General

10—(1)–(3) (*amends* TA 1988 s 349).
(4) This paragraph shall apply as regards a payment made on or after 6th April 1991.
11—(1) (*amends* TA 1988 s 352).
(2) This paragraph shall apply as regards a payment made on or after 6th April 1991.
12—(1) (*amends* TA 1988 s 483).
(2) This paragraph shall apply where the first year of assessment mentioned in section 483(1) is 1990–91 or a subsequent year of assessment.
13—(1) (*amends* TA 1988 s 686).
(2) This paragraph shall apply as regards a sum paid or credited on or after 6th April 1991.
14—(1) (*amends* TA 1988 s 687).
(2) This paragraph shall apply as regards an amount paid or credited on or after 6th April 1991.

Management

15 (*amends* TMA 1970 s 98 Table).

Transitional provision

16 (*spent*).
Commentary—*Simon's Direct Tax Service* **D4.732.**

SCHEDULE 6

LIFE ASSURANCE: APPORTIONMENT OF INCOME ETC

Section 41

1—(1)–(4) (*amends* TA 1988 s 431; *repealed in part* by FA 1995 s 162, Sch 29 Pt VIII(5), with effect partly for accounting periods beginning after 31 October 1994, and partly for such periods beginning after 31 December 1994.)
2 (*inserts* TA 1988 s 431A).
3 (*repealed by* FA 1996 Sch 41 Pt V(26) with effect for accounting periods beginning after 31 December 1995).
4 (*inserts* TA 1988 s 432A–432E).
5 (*repealed by* F(No 2)A 1997 Sch 8 Pt II (6)).

6 (*repealed by* FA 1991 Sch 19 Pt V).

7 (*amends* TA 1988 s 439).

8 (*substitutes* TA 1988 s 440, 440A for s 440).

9—(1)–(3) (*amend* TA 1988 ss 711, 712, 724).

10 (*repealed by* TCGA 1992 Sch 12).

11—(1) Paragraph 9 above shall be deemed to have come into force on 24th May 1990 but, subject to that,—

(*a*) in so far as it relates to determinations of profits in accordance with section 83 of the Finance Act 1989 this Schedule shall apply in relation to any period for which such a determination falls to be made, other than a period for which it falls to be made only by virtue of an election under section 83(5) of the Finance Act 1989 and

(*b*) in so far as it relates to section 432A of the Taxes Act 1988 this Schedule shall apply to income arising, and disposals occurring, on or after 1st January 1990.

(2) Subject to sub-paragraph (1) above, this Schedule shall be deemed to have come into force on 1st January 1990.

(3) The preceding provisions of this paragraph shall have effect subject to paragraph 12 below.

12—(1) Where at the end of 1989 the assets of an insurance company include securities of a class some of which are regarded as a single 1982 holding, and the rest of which are regarded as a single new holding, for the purposes of corporation tax on chargeable gains—

(*a*) at the beginning of 1990 there shall be both a 1982 holding and a new holding of the description mentioned in any paragraph of section 440A(2) of the Taxes Act 1988 within which any of the securities fall at that time (whether or not there would be apart from this sub-paragraph), and

(*b*) the 1982 holding and the new holding of the description mentioned in any such paragraph shall at that time bear to one another the same proportions as the single 1982 holding and the single new holding at the end of 1989.

(2) For the period beginning with 1st January 1990 and ending with 19th March 1990, section 440(4) of the Taxes Act 1988 (as substituted by paragraph 8 of this Schedule) and section 440A(2) of that Act shall have effect with the omission of paragraph (*d*) (so that all assets not within paragraphs (*a*) to (*c*) fall within paragraph (*e*)).

(3) Sub-paragraph (4) below applies where—

(*a*) at the end of 19th March 1990 the assets of an insurance company include securities of a class some of which are regarded as a relevant 1982 holding, and others of which are regarded as a relevant new holding, for the purposes of corporation tax on chargeable gains, and

(*b*) some of the securities are included in the company's long term business fund but others are not;

and for the purposes of this sub-paragraph a holding is a "relevant" holding if it is not linked to pension business or basic life assurance business and is not an asset of the overseas life assurance fund.

(4) Where this sub-paragraph applies—

(*a*) at the beginning of 20th March 1990 there shall be both a 1982 holding and a new holding of each of the descriptions mentioned in paragraphs (*d*) and (*e*) of section 440A(2) of the Taxes Act 1988 (whether or not there would be apart from this sub-paragraph), and

(*b*) the 1982 holding and the new holding of each of those descriptions shall at that time bear to one another the same proportions as the 1982 holding and the new holding mentioned in sub-paragraph (3)(*a*) above at the end of 19th March 1990.

(5) Except for the purposes of determining the assets of a company which are linked solely to basic life assurance business, the amendments made by this Schedule shall have effect in relation to a company with the omission of references to overseas life assurance business as respects any time before the provisions of Schedule 7 to this Act have effect in relation to the company.

(6) Sub-paragraph (7) below applies where—

(*a*) the first accounting period of an insurance company beginning on or after 1st January 1990 begins after 20th March 1990,

(*b*) at some time during the accounting period the company carries on overseas life assurance business, and

(*c*) immediately before the beginning of the accounting period the assets of the long term business fund of the company include both a relevant 1982 holding and a relevant new holding of securities of the same class;

and for the purposes of this sub-paragraph a holding is a "relevant" holding if it is not linked to pension business or basic life assurance business.

(7) Where this sub-paragraph applies—

(*a*) at the beginning of the accounting period there shall be both a 1982 holding and a new holding of each of the descriptions mentioned in paragraphs (*c*) and (*d*) of section 440A(2) of the Taxes Act 1988 (whether or not there would be apart from this sub-paragraph), and (*b*) the 1982 holding and the new holding of each of those descriptions shall at that time bear to one another the same proportions as the 1982 holding and the new holding mentioned in sub-paragraph (6)(*c*) above immediately before the beginning of the period.

(8) No disposal or re-acquisition shall be deemed to occur by virtue of section 440 of the Taxes Act 1988 (as substituted by paragraph 8 of this Schedule) by reason only of the coming into force (in accordance with the provisions of paragraph 11 of this Schedule and this paragraph) of any provision of section 440A of that Act.

(9) The substitution made by paragraph 8 of this Schedule shall not affect—

(*a*) the operation of section 440 of the Taxes Act 1988 (as it has effect before the substitution) before 20th March 1990, or

(*b*) the operation of subsections (6) and (7) of that section (as they have effect before the substitution) in relation to the disposal of an asset which has not been deemed to be disposed of by virtue of section 440 (as it has effect after the substitution) before the time of the disposal.

(10) In this paragraph—

"1982 holding" has the meaning given by Part II of Schedule 19 to the Finance Act 1985;
"new holding" has the meaning given by Part III of that Schedule; and
"securities" has the same meaning as in section 65 of the Capital Gains Tax Act 1979.

Cross references—See TA 1988 s 440A(4)(*b*) (an insurance company's securities of a class all of which are regarded as constituting one holding).

SCHEDULE 7

OVERSEAS LIFE ASSURANCE BUSINESS

Section 42

1, 2 (*amend* TA 1988 ss 76, 231).

3 (*substitutes* TA 1988 ss 441, 441A for s 441).

4 (*amends* TA 1988 s 724).

5 (*inserts* TA 1988 s 804A).

6 (*inserts* TA 1988 Sch 19AA).

7 (*amended* TA 1988 Sch 28 para 3(4); *repealed* by FA 1995 s 162, Sch 29 Pt VIII(5), with effect for accounting periods beginning after 31 October 1994).

8 (*repealed by* FA 1991 Sch 19 Pt V).

9 (*amended* CAA 1990 s 28, *repealed by* CAA 2001 s 580, Sch 4 with effect in accordance with CAA 2001 s 579).

10—(1) This Schedule shall apply for accounting periods beginning on or after 1st January 1990; and paragraph 9 above shall apply for accounting periods beginning on or after that date and ending on or before 5th April 1990 as well as for later accounting periods.

(2) In relation to the first period of account of an insurance company beginning on or after 1st January 1990, the assets of the company which—

(*a*) are assets of the long term business fund of the company at the beginning of the period,

(*b*) have a value at that time equal to the amount mentioned in paragraph 4 of Schedule 19AA to the Taxes Act 1988, and

(*c*) are designated in accordance with paragraph 5 of that Schedule (on the same basis as a designation required for the purposes of paragraph 3(1) of that Schedule),

shall be treated for the purposes of sub-paragraphs (1) and (2) of paragraph 2 of that Schedule as if they were the assets of the overseas life assurance fund at the end of the immediately preceding period of account.

SCHEDULE 8

INSURANCE COMPANIES: HOLDINGS OF UNIT TRUSTS ETC

Section 46

(*repealed by* TCGA 1992 Sch 12).

SCHEDULE 9

INSURANCE COMPANIES: TRANSFERS OF LONG TERM BUSINESS

Section 48

Commentary—*Simon's Direct Tax Service* **D4.527.**

Capital gains

1, 2 (*repealed by* TCGA 1992 Sch 12).

Accounting periods

3 (*inserts* TA 1988 s 12(7A)).

Expenses of management and losses

4 (*inserts* TA 1988 s 444A).

Capital allowances

5 (*inserted* CAA 1990 s 152A, *repealed by* CAA 2001 s 580, Sch 4 with effect in accordance with CAA 2001 s 579).

Transfer to friendly society

6 (*inserts* TA 1988 s 460(10A)).

Commencement

7 This Schedule shall apply to transfers of business taking place on or after 1st January 1990; and (subject to that) the amendment made by paragraph 5 of this Schedule shall apply in relation to accounting periods ending on or after 5th April 1990 as well as in relation to later accounting periods.

SCHEDULE 10

CONVERTIBLE SECURITIES

Section 56

Commentary—*Simon's Direct Tax Service* **B5.425–429, D2.216; 1167.**
Amendments—This Schedule repealed by FA 1996 ss 104, 105(1), Sch 14 para 58, Sch 41 Pt V(3) with effect for the purposes of corporation tax for accounting periods ending after 31 March 1996 and as respects income tax from the year 1996–97, subject to transitional provisions in FA 1996 Sch 15

SCHEDULE 11

EUROPEAN ECONOMIC INTEREST GROUPINGS

Section 69

Taxation

1 (*inserts* TA 1988 s 510A).

Management

2–4 (*insert* TMA 1970 ss 12A, 36(4), 40(3), 98B, and *amend* TMA 1970 s 100).

Commencement

5 This Schedule shall be deemed to have come into force on 1st July 1989.

SCHEDULE 12

BROADCASTING: TRANSFER OF UNDERTAKINGS OF INDEPENDENT BROADCASTING AUTHORITY AND CABLE AUTHORITY

Section 80

Transfer of IBA's transmission activities to nominated company: corporation tax

1—(1) Subject to sub-paragraph (2), the following provisions shall apply for the purposes of the Corporation Tax Acts, namely—

(*a*) the part of the trade carried on by the IBA which is transferred to the nominated company under the Broadcasting Act 1990 (''the principal Act'') shall be treated as having been, at the time when it began to be carried on by the IBA and at all times since that time, a separate trade carried on by that company;

(*b*) the trade carried on by that company after the transfer date shall be treated as the same trade as that which, by virtue of paragraph (*a*) above, it is treated as having carried on before that date;

(*c*) all property, rights and liabilities of the IBA which are transferred under the principal Act to that company shall be treated as having been, at the time when they became vested in the IBA and at all times since that time, property, rights and liabilities of that company; and

(*d*) anything done by the IBA in relation to any such property, rights and liabilities as are mentioned in paragraph (*c*) above shall be deemed to have been done by that company.

(2) There shall be apportioned between the IBA and the nominated company—

(*a*) the unallowed tax losses of the IBA, and

(*b*) any expenditure which they have incurred before the transfer date and by reference to which capital allowances may be made,

in such manner as is just and reasonable having regard—

(i) to the extent to which such losses and expenditure are attributable to the part of the trade carried on by them which is transferred to that company under the principal Act, and

(ii) as respects the apportionment of such expenditure, to the division of their assets between the relevant transferees which is effected under that Act.

(3) In this paragraph—

"the IBA's final accounting period" means the last complete accounting period of the IBA ending before the transfer date;

"unallowed tax losses" means losses, allowances or amounts which, as at the end of the IBA's final accounting period, are tax losses within the meaning given by section 400(2) of the Taxes Act 1988 excluding losses which are allowable capital losses within the meaning of paragraph 6 below.

(4) This paragraph shall have effect in relation to accounting periods beginning after the IBA's final accounting period.

Transfer of IBA's assets to Commission and Radio Authority: chargeable gains

2—(1) For the purposes of [the Taxation of Chargeable Gains Act 1992 ("the 1992 Act")][1] the transfer under the principal Act of any asset from the IBA to the Commission or the Radio Authority shall be deemed to be for a consideration such that no gain or loss accrues to the IBA; and Schedule [2][1] to that Act (assets held on 6th April 1965) shall have effect in relation to an asset so transferred as if the acquisition or provision of it by the IBA had been the acquisition or provision of it by the Commission or (as the case may be) by the Authority.

(2) ...[2]

(3) Where the benefit of any debt in relation to which the IBA are, for the purposes of section [251 of the 1992][1] Act (debts), the original creditor is transferred under the principal Act to the Commission or the Radio Authority, the Commission or (as the case may be) the Radio Authority shall be treated for those purposes as the original creditor in relation to the debt in place of the IBA.

Cross references—See TCGA 1992 s 55(5) (modification of indexation allowance for the purposes of sub-para (1) above with respect to disposals of assets after 31 March or 5 April).
Amendments—[1] Words in sub-paras (1), (3) substituted by TCGA 1992 Sch 10 para 22(1), (5)(*a*).
[2] Sub-para (2) repealed by TCGA 1992 Sch 12.

Disposal by IBA of DBS assets to DBS programme contractor: chargeable gains

3—(1) For the purposes of the 1979 Act the disposal under the principal Act of any relevant asset by the IBA to a DBS programme contractor shall be deemed to be for a consideration such that no gain or loss accrues to the IBA.

(2) In this paragraph—

(*a*) "relevant asset" means any equipment or other asset (of whatever description) which has been used or held by the IBA in connection with the transmission of DBS services; and

(*b*) "DBS programme contractor" and "DBS service" have the meaning given by section 37(3) of the Cable and Broadcasting Act 1984.

Transfer of Cable Authority's assets to Commission: chargeable gains

4 For the purposes of the [1992][1] Act the transfer by the principal Act of any asset from the Cable Authority to the Commission shall be deemed to be for a consideration such that no gain or loss accrues to that Authority.

Amendments—[1] Year substituted by TCGA 1992 Sch 10 para 22(1), (5)(*b*).

Transfer of shares from Commission to Channel 4 company: chargeable gains

5—(1) For the purposes of the [1992][1] Act the transfer by the principal Act of shares in the Channel 4 company from the Commission to the Channel Four Television Corporation shall be deemed to be for a consideration such that no gain or loss accrues to the Commission.

(2) In sub-paragraph (1) "the Channel 4 company" means the body corporate referred to in section 12(2) of the Broadcasting Act 1981.

Amendments—[1] Year substituted by TCGA 1992 Sch 10 para 22(1), (5)(*b*).

Apportionment of unallowed capital losses between relevant transferees

6—(1) The unallowed capital losses of the IBA shall be apportioned between the relevant transferees in such manner as is just and reasonable having regard to the purposes, or principal purposes, for which the relevant assets were respectively used or held by the IBA and the activities which are to be carried on by those transferees respectively as from the transfer date.

(2) Any unallowed capital losses of the IBA which are apportioned to one of the relevant transferees under sub-paragraph (1) shall be treated as allowable capital losses accruing to that transferee on the disposal of an asset on the transfer date.

(3) In this paragraph—

"allowable capital losses" means losses which are allowable for the purposes of the [1992][1] Act;

"relevant assets", in relation to unallowed capital losses of the IBA, means the assets on whose disposal by the IBA those losses accrued;

"unallowed capital losses", in relation to the IBA, means allowable capital losses which have accrued to the IBA before the transfer date, in so far as they have not been allowed as deductions from chargeable gains.

Amendments—[1] Year substituted by TCGA 1992 Sch 10 para 22(1), (5)(*b*).

Roll-over relief in connection with nominated company

7 Where the IBA have before the transfer date disposed of (or of their interest in) any assets used, throughout the period of ownership, wholly or partly for the purposes of the part of their trade transferred to the nominated company under the principal Act, sections [152 to 156 of the 1992][1] Act (roll-over relief on replacement of business assets) shall have effect in relation to that disposal as if the IBA and the nominated company were the same person.

Amendments—[1] Words substituted by TCGA 1992 Sch 10 para 22(1), (5)(*c*).

Disputes as to apportionments etc

8—(1) This paragraph applies where any apportionment or other matter arising under the foregoing provisions of this Schedule appears to be material as respects the liability to tax (for whatever period) of two or more relevant transferees.

(2) Any question which arises as to the manner in which the apportionment is to be made or the matter is to be dealt with shall be determined, for the purposes of the tax of both or all of the relevant transferees concerned—

(*a*) in a case where the same body of General Commissioners have jurisdiction with respect to both or all of those transferees, by those Commissioners, unless those transferees agree that it shall be determined by the Special Commissioners;

(*b*) in a case where different bodies of Commissioners have jurisdiction with respect to those transferees, by such of those bodies as the Board may direct, unless those transferees agree that it shall be determined by the Special Commissioners; and

(*c*) in any other case, by the Special Commissioners.

(3) The Commissioners by whom the question falls to be determined shall make the determination in like manner as if it were an appeal except that both or all of the relevant transferees concerned shall be entitled to appear and be heard by the Commissioners or to make representations to them in writing.

Securities of nominated company

9—(1) Any share issued by the nominated company to the Secretary of State in pursuance of the principal Act shall be treated for the purposes of the Corporation Tax Acts as if it had been issued wholly in consideration of a subscription paid to that company of an amount equal to the nominal value of the share.

(2) Any debenture issued by the nominated company to the Secretary of State in pursuance of the principal Act shall be treated for the purposes of the Corporation Tax Acts as if it had been issued—

(*a*) wholly in consideration of a loan made to that company of an amount equal to the principal sum payable under the debenture; and

(*b*) wholly and exclusively for the purposes of the trade carried on by that company.

Interpretation

10—(1) In this Schedule—

["the 1992 Act" means the Taxation of Chargeable Gains Act 1992;][1]

"the Commission" means the Independent Television Commission;

"the IBA" means the Independent Broadcasting Authority;

"the nominated company" and "the transfer date" have the same meaning as in the provisions of the principal Act relating to the transfer of the undertakings of the IBA and the Cable Authority;

"the principal Act" means the Broadcasting Act 1990;

"the relevant transferees" means the Commission, the Radio Authority and the nominated company.

(2) References in this Schedule to things transferred under the principal Act are references to things transferred in accordance with a scheme made under that Act.

Note—The Broadcasting (Transfer Date and Nominated Company) Order 1990, SI 1990/2540 nominates the National Transcommunications Limited as "the nominated company" and appoints 1 January 1991 as "the transfer date".
Amendments—[1] Definition in sub-para (1) substituted by TCGA 1992 Sch 10 para 22(1), (5)(*d*).

SCHEDULE 13

CAPITAL ALLOWANCES: MISCELLANEOUS AMENDMENTS

Section 88

Hotels in enterprise zones: initial allowances

1–6 (*amended* CAA 1990 ss 1, 7, 8, 78, 149, 154, 161, *repealed by* CAA 2001 s 580, Sch 4 with effect in accordance with CAA 2001 s 579).

Assured tenancies allowance

7—(1) (*amends* TA 1988 s 832).
(2) This paragraph shall apply for chargeable periods beginning on or after 6th April 1990.

SCHEDULE 14

AMENDMENTS CORRECTING ERRORS IN THE TAXES ACT 1988

Section 89

PART I

AMENDMENTS OF THE TAXES ACT 1988

1 The Taxes Act 1988 shall have effect, and shall be deemed always to have had effect, subject to the amendments made by this Part of this Schedule.
2 (*amends* TA 1988 s 37).[1]

Amendments—[1] Paragraph 2(*a*), (*b*) repealed by FA 1998 Sch 27 Part III(4) for income tax with effect for the year 1998–99 and subsequent years of assessment, and for corporation tax from 1 April 1998 subject to transitional provisions in FA 1998 Sch 5 Part IV.

3–6 (*amends* TA 1988 ss 213, 322, 323, 326, 377).

Amendment—This paragraph repealed by FA 1999 s 139, Sch 20 Pt III(7) with effect for payments of interest made—
–after 5 April 2000;
–after 8 March 1999 and before 6 April 2000 in respect of interest falling due after 5 April 2000; or
–after 8 March 1999 and before 6 April 2000 under a scheme made for a tax avoidance purpose after 8 March 1999.

7 (*repealed* by FA 1991 Sch 19 Pt V).
8–11 (*amend* TA 1988 s 478, 751, 757, 761).
12 (*amended* TA 1988 s 773; *repealed* by FA 1998 Sch 27 Part III(25) with effect for accounting periods ending after 30 June 1999 (by virtue of Finance Act 1994, Section 199, (Appointed Day) Order, SI 1998/3173 art 2)).
13 (*amended* TA 1988 Sch 16 para 4; *repealed* by FA 1999 s 139, Sch 20 Pt III(19) with effect for periods for which a return is required under TA 88 Sch 16 para 2 beginning after 5 April 1999; and in relation to accounting periods beginning on or after that date).

PART II

AMENDMENTS OF OTHER ENACTMENTS

The Taxes Management Act 1970 (c 9)

14, 15 (*amend* TMA 1970 ss 31, 98, Table).

The Oil Taxation Act 1975 (c 22)

16 (*amends* OTA 1975 Sch 3 para 5).

The Capital Gains Tax Act 1979 (c 14)

17 (*repealed by* TCGA 1992 Sch 12).

The Finance Act 1981 (c 35)

18 (*repealed by* TCGA 1992 Sch 12).

Commencement

19—(1) Subject to the following provisions of this paragraph, the amendments made by this Part of this Schedule shall be treated for the purposes of their commencement as if they had been made by the Taxes Act 1988.

(2)–(4) (*repealed* by TCGA 1992 Sch 12).

SCHEDULE 15

CLAIMS FOR GROUP RELIEF

Section 100

Amendment—This Schedule repealed by FA 1998 Sch 27 Part III(28) with effect in relation to accounting periods ending after 30 June 1999 (by virtue of Finance Act 1994, Section 199, (Appointed Day) Order, SI 1998/3173 art 2).

SCHEDULE 16

CAPITAL ALLOWANCES: CLAIMS BY COMPANIES

Section 102

Amendment—This Schedule repealed by FA 1998 Sch 27 Part III(28) with effect in relation to accounting periods ending after 30 June 1999 (by virtue of Finance Act 1994, Section 199, (Appointed Day) Order, SI 1998/3173 art 2).

SCHEDULE 17

CAPITAL ALLOWANCES: ASSIMILATION OF CLAIMS BY COMPANIES TO CLAIMS BY INDIVIDUALS

Section 103

Amendment—This Schedule repealed by the Capital Allowances Act 2001 s 580, Sch 4 with effect for income tax purposes, as respects allowances and charges falling to be made for chargeable periods ending after 5 April 2001, and for corporation tax purposes, as respects allowances and charges falling to be made for chargeable periods ending after 31 March 2001.

SCHEDULE 18

DEFINITION OF "LOCAL AUTHORITY"

Section 127

1 (*amends* FA 1952 s 74).

2 (*repeals* FA 1974 s 52).

3 (*repealed by* TCGA 1992 Sch 12).

4 (*amends* IHTA 1984 s 272).

5—(1) The Taxes Act 1988 shall be amended as follows.

(2) (*repeals* TA 1988 s 519(4)).

(3) (*amends* TA 1988 s 832).

FINANCE ACT 1991

(1991 Chapter 31)

ARRANGEMENT OF SECTIONS

PART II

INCOME TAX, CORPORATION TAX AND CAPITAL GAINS TAX

CHAPTER I

GENERAL

123   *Repeals.* (not printed)
124   Short title.

SCHEDULES:

Schedule 6—Restriction of higher rate relief: beneficial loans etc.
Schedule 7—Basic life assurance and general annuity business.
Schedule 8—Pension business: payments on account of tax credits and deducted tax.
Schedule 9—Friendly societies.
Schedule 10—Building societies: qualifying shares.
Schedule 11—Building societies: marketable securities.
Schedule 12—Securities: new issues.
Schedule 13—Manufactured dividends and interest.
Schedule 14—*Capital allowances: VAT capital goods scheme.* (repealed)
Schedule 15—Relief for company trading losses.
Schedule 16—*Settlements: settlors.* (repealed)
Schedule 17—*Settlements: beneficiaries.* (repealed)
Schedule 18—*Settlements: beneficiaries (miscellaneous).* (repealed)
Schedule 19—*Repeals* (not printed)

An Act to grant certain duties, to alter other duties, and to amend the law relating to the National Debt and the Public Revenue, and to make further provision in connection with Finance.

[25th July 1991]

PART II
INCOME TAX, CORPORATION TAX AND CAPITAL GAINS TAX

CHAPTER I
GENERAL
Income tax rates and allowances

21 Charge and rates of income tax for 1991–92

(Spent).

Commentary—*Simon's Direct Tax Service* E1.102, 104.

22 Married couple's allowance

(Spent).

Commentary—*Simon's Direct Tax Service* E2.202.

Corporation tax rates

23 Rate of corporation tax for 1990

(Spent).

Commentary—*Simon's Direct Tax Service* D2.108, 109.

24 Charge and rate of corporation tax for 1991

(Spent).

Commentary—*Simon's Direct Tax Service* D2.108.

25 Small companies

(1) *(spent).*

(2) *(amends* TA 1988 s 13(3)).

(3) Subsection (2) above shall have effect for the financial year 1991 and subsequent financial years; and where by virtue of that subsection section 13 of the Taxes Act 1988 has effect with different relevant maximum amounts in relation to different parts of a company's accounting period, then for the purposes of that section those parts shall be treated as if they were separate accounting periods and the profits and basic profits of the company for that period shall be apportioned between those parts.

Commentary—*Simon's Direct Tax Service* D2.109.

Interest

26 Relief for interest

(*Spent*).

Commentary—*Simon's Direct Tax Service* **A3.431; E1.539.**

27 Abolition of higher rate relief on certain mortgage interest etc

(1)–(5) (*amended* TA 1988 ss 353, 369 repealed by FA 1994 Sch 26 Pt V(2).

(6) The enactments mentioned in Schedule 6 to this Act shall have effect for the year 1991–92 and subsequent years of assessment with the amendments there specified.

(7) (*amended* TA 1988 ss 353, 369 repealed by FA 1994 Sch 26 Pt V(2).

Commentary—*Simon's Direct Tax Service* **A3.430; E1.531, 539**.

28 Mortgage interest relief: caravans

(*Spent*).

Commentary—*Simon's Direct Tax Service* **E2.1301–1303.**

Benefits in kind

29 Car benefits

(*Amends TA* 1988 Sch 6 Pt I and is now superseded).

30 Mobile telephones

Amendment—This section repealed by FA 1999 s 139, Sch 20 Pt III(9) with effect from the year 1999–00.

31 Beneficial loans: increase of de minimis limit

(*Amends TA* 1988 s 161(1); repealed by FA 1994 Sch 26 Pt V(5)).

Vocational training

32 Relief

(1) This section applies where—

    (a) on or after 6th April 1992 an individual resident in the United Kingdom makes a payment in respect of a qualifying course of vocational training,

    (b) the payment is made in respect of an allowable expense,

    (c) the payment is made in connection with the individual's own training,

    [(ca) at the time the payment is made, the individual—

        (i) in a case where the qualifying course of vocational training is such a course by virtue only of paragraph (b) of subsection (10) below, has attained the age of thirty, or

        (ii) in any other case, has attained school-leaving age and, if under the age of nineteen, is not a person who is being provided with full-time education at a school,]²

    [(cb) the individual undertakes the course neither wholly nor mainly for recreational purposes or as a leisure activity,]¹

    (d) at the time the payment is made, the individual has not received in relation to the course, and is not entitled to receive in relation to it, any public financial assistance of a description specified in regulations made by the Treasury for the purposes of this paragraph, and

    (e) the individual is not entitled to claim any relief or deduction in respect of the payment under any other provision of the Income Tax Acts.

[(2) The individual shall be entitled to relief under this subsection in respect of the payment for the year of assessment in which it is made; but relief under this subsection shall be given only on a claim made for the purpose, except where subsections (3) to (5) below apply.]⁵

[(2A) Where an individual is entitled to relief under subsection (2) above in respect of any payment made in a year of assessment, the amount of his liability for that year to income tax on his total income shall be the amount to which he would be liable apart from this section less whichever is the smaller of—

    (a) the amount which is equal to such percentage of the amount of the payment as is the basic rate for the year; and

    (b) the amount which reduces his liability to nil.]⁵

[(2B) In determining for the purposes of subsection (2A) above the amount of income tax to which a person would be liable apart from this section, no account shall be taken of—

    (a) any income tax reduction under Chapter I of Part VII of the Taxes Act 1988 or under section 347B of that Act;

    (b) any income tax reduction under section 353(1A) of the Taxes Act 1988;

(c) *any relief by way of a reduction of liability to tax which is given in accordance with any arrangements having effect by virtue of section 788 of the Taxes Act 1988 or by way of a credit under section 790(1) of that Act;*

(d) *any tax at the basic rate on so much of that person's income as is income the income tax on which he is entitled to charge against any other person or to deduct, retain or satisfy out of any payment.]*[5]

(3) *In such cases and subject to such conditions as the Board may specify in regulations, relief under subsection (2) above shall be given in accordance with subsections (4) and (5) below.*

(4) *An individual who is entitled to such relief in respect of a payment may deduct and retain out of it an amount equal to income tax on it at the basic rate for the year of assessment in which it is made.*

(5) *The person to whom the payment is made—*

(a) *shall accept the amount paid after deduction in discharge of the individual's liability to the same extent as if the deduction had not been made, and*

(b) *may, on making a claim [in accordance with regulations]*[3], *recover from the Board an amount equal to the amount deducted.*

(6) *The Treasury may make regulations providing that in circumstances prescribed in the regulations—*

(a) *an individual who makes, in respect of a qualifying course of vocational training, a payment in respect of an allowable expense shall cease to be and be treated as not having been entitled to relief under subsection (2) above in respect of the payment or such part of it as may be determined in accordance with the regulations; and*

(b) *he or the person to whom the payment was made (depending on the terms of the regulations) shall account to the Board for tax from which relief has been given on the basis that the individual was so entitled.*

(7) *Regulations under subsection (6) above may include provision adapting or modifying the effect of any enactment relating to income tax in order to secure the performance of any obligation imposed under paragraph (b) of that subsection.*

(8) *In subsection (1)(a) above, the reference to an individual resident in the United Kingdom includes an individual performing duties which are treated by virtue of section 132(4)(a) of the Taxes Act 1988 as performed in the United Kingdom.*

(9) *For the purposes of this section, a payment made in respect of a qualifying course of vocational training is made in respect of an allowable expense if—*

(a) *it is made in respect of fees payable in connection with undertaking the course, including fees payable for assessment purposes, or*

(b) *it is made in respect of fees payable in connection with the making, as a result of having undertaken the course, of any entry in an official register or any award.*

[(10) *In this section "qualifying course of vocational training" means—*

(a) *any programme of activity capable of counting towards a qualification—*

[(i) *accredited as a National Vocational Qualification by the Qualifications and Curriculum Authority or by the Qualifications, Curriculum and Assessment Authority for Wales, or]*[4]
(ii) *accredited as a Scottish Vocational Qualification by the Scottish Vocational Education Council; or*

(b) *any course of training which—*

(i) *satisfies the conditions set out in the paragraphs of section 589(1) of the Taxes Act 1988 (qualifying courses of training etc),*
(ii) *requires participation on a full-time or substantially full-time basis, and*
(iii) *extends for a period which consists of or includes four consecutive weeks,*

but treating any time devoted to study in connection with the course as time devoted to the practical application of skills or knowledge.][2]

[(11) *In this section—*

"school" means any institution at which full-time education is provided to persons at least some of whom are under school-leaving age; and
"school-leaving age" means the age of sixteen.][1, 6]

Commentary—*Simon's Direct Tax Service* **E2.1301–1303.**
Regulations—Vocational Training (Public Financial Assistance and Disentitlement to Tax Relief) Regulations, SI 1992/734.
Vocational Training (Tax Relief) Regulations, SI 1992/746.
Revenue & other press releases— IR Booklet IR 119 (Tax relief for vocational training).
Cross references—See Vocational Training (Tax Relief) Regulations, SI 1992/746 reg 3 (cases and conditions for relief at source under sub-s (2) above),
SI 1992/746 reg 4 (information in a notice of entitlement to relief at source about amount deducted and retained under sub-s (4) above),
SI 1992/746 reg 5 (recovery of amount paid to training provider on a claim under sub-s (5)(*b*) above),
SI 1992/746 reg 6 (regulations governing claims by training provider).
TA 1988 s 200C(5) (TA 1988 s 200B (work-related training) not to apply in the case of any payment in respect of which there is entitlement to relief under this section).

FA 1996 s 129(1)(*b*), (6) (disapplication of TMA 1970 s 42, procedure for making claims etc, in relation to claims under sub-
s 5(*b*) of this section for vocational training relief).
Amendments—¹ Sub-ss (1)(*cb*), (11) inserted by FA 1994 s 84 in relation to payments made after 31 December 1993.
² Sub-ss (1)(*ca*)(inserted by FA 1994 s 84), (10) substituted by FA 1996 s 144 with effect in relation to payments made after 5
May 1996.
³ Words in sub-s (5)(*b*) inserted by FA 1996 s 129(2).
⁴ Sub-s (10)(*a*)(i) substituted by the Education Act 1997 Sch 7 para 6 with effect from 1 October 1997 (by virtue of the Education
Act 1997 (Commencement No 2 and Transitional Provisions) Order, SI 1997/1468).
⁵ Sub-s (2) substituted, and sub-ss (2A), (2B) inserted, by FA 1999 s 59(1), (3) with effect for payments made after 5 April 1999.
⁶ This section repealed by FA 1999 ss 59(2), (3)(*b*), 139, Sch 20 Pt III(15) with effect for payments made after 31 August 2000
(by virtue of the Finance Act 1999, Section 59(3)(*b*), (Appointed Day) Order, SI 2000/2004).

33 Section 32: supplementary

(1) The Board may by regulations—

(a) provide that a claim under section 32(2) or (5) (b) above shall be made in such form and manner, shall be made at such time, and shall be accompanied by such documents, as may be prescribed;

[(aa) make provision for and with respect to appeals against a decision of [an officer of the Board or the Board with respect to a claim under section 32(5)(b) above;]¹

(b) make provision, in relation to payments in respect of which a person is entitled to relief under section 32 above, for persons who provide vocational training courses to give, in such circumstances as may be prescribed, certificates of payment in such form as may be prescribed to such persons as may be prescribed;

(c) provide that a person who provides (or has at any time provided) training courses which are (or were) qualifying courses of vocational training for the purposes of section 32 above shall comply with any notice which is served on him by the Board and which requires him within a prescribed period to make available for the Board's inspection documents (of a prescribed kind) relating to such courses;

(d) provide that persons of such description as may be prescribed shall, within a prescribed period of being required to do so by the Board, furnish to the Board information (of a prescribed kind) about training courses which are qualifying courses of vocational training for the purposes of section 32 above;

(e) make provision generally as to administration in connection with section 32 above.

(2) (amends TMA 1970 s 98 Table).

(3) The following provisions of the Taxes Management Act 1970 namely—

[(a) section 29(1)(c) (excessive relief) as it has effect apart from section 29(2) to (10) of that Act;]²,

(b) section 30 (tax repaid in error etc) [apart from subsection (1B)]²,

(c) [section 86]³ (interest), and

(d) section 95 (incorrect return or accounts),

[shall apply in relation to an amount which is paid to any person by the Board as an amount recoverable by virtue of section 32(5)(b) above but to which that person is not entitled as if it were income tax which ought not to have been repaid and, where that amount was claimed by that person, as if it had been repaid as respects a chargeable period as a relief which was not due.]⁵

[(3A) In the application of section 86 of the Taxes Management Act 1970 by virtue of subsection (3) above in relation to sums due and payable by virtue of an assessment made under section 29(1)(c) or 30 of that Act, as applied by that subsection, the relevant date—

(a) in a case where the person falling within section 32(5) above has made any interim claim, within the meaning of regulations made under subsection (1) above, as respects some part of the year of assessment for which the assessment is made, is 1st January in that year of assessment; and

(b) in any other case, is the later of the following dates, that is to say—

(i) 1st January in the year of assessment for which the assessment is made; or

(ii) the date of the making of the payment by the Board which gives rise to the assessment.]⁴

(4) (amends TA 1988 ss 257B(2), 257D(8), 265(3); remainder repealed by F(No 2)A 1992 s 82, Sch 18, Pt VII (from the year 1994–95)).

(5) In subsection (1) above, ''prescribed'' means prescribed by or, in relation to form, under the regulations.⁶

Commentary—*Simon's Direct Tax Service* E2.1304, 1305.
Regulations—Vocational Training (Tax Relief) Regulations, SI 1992/746.
Amendments—¹ Sub-s (1)(*aa*) inserted by FA 1996 s 129(4).
² Sub-s (3)(*a*) substituted for the words ''(*a*) section 29(3)(*c*) (excessive relief);'' and words in sub-s (3)(*b*) inserted by FA 1996
Sch 18 paras 14(2)(*a*), (*b*), 17(1), (2) with effect for the purposes of income tax and capital gains tax, from the year 1996–97
and for purposes of corporation tax as respects accounting periods ending on or after the appointed day, being not earlier than
1 April 1996; and so far as relating to partnerships whose trades, professions or businesses were set up and commenced before
6 April 1994 from the year 1997–98.
³ Words in sub-s (3)(*c*) substituted for the words ''section 88'', by FA 1996 Sch 18 paras 14(2)(*c*), 17(3), (4) with effect from the
year 1996–97 (except so far as relating to partnerships whose trades, professions or businesses were set up and commenced
before 6 April 1994 when it has effect from the year 1997–98) and in relation to any income tax which is charged by an
assessment made after 5 April 1998 which is for the year 1995–96 or any earlier year of assessment.

[4] Sub-s (3A) inserted by FA 1996 Sch 18 paras 14(3), 17(3), (4) with effect from the year 1996–97 (except so far as relating to partnerships whose trades, professions or businesses were set up and commenced before 6 April 1994 when it has effect from the year 1997–98) and in relation to any income tax which is charged by an assessment made after 5 April 1998 which is for all the year 1995–96 or any earlier year of assessment (when it applies, except in relation to partnerships whose trades etc were set up and commenced before 6 April 1994, as modified by FA 1996 Sch 18 para 17(3)).
[5] Words in sub-s (3) substituted by FA 1996 Sch 18 paras 14(2)(*d*), 17(8) but not in relation to any payment if the payment, or the claim on which it is made, was made before 29 April 1996.
[6] This section repealed by FA 1999 ss 59(2), (3)(*b*), 139, Sch 20 Pt III(15) with effect for payments made after 31 August 2000 (by virtue of the Finance Act 1999, Section 59(3)(*b*), (Appointed Day) Order, SI 2000/2004).

Retirement benefits schemes

34 Conditions for approval: amendments

(1)–(3) (*amend* TA 1988 s 590).

(4) This section shall have effect in relation to a scheme not approved by the Board before the day on which this Act is passed.

35 Cessation of approval

(*Inserts* TA 1988 s 591A).

36 Cessation of approval: general provisions

(1) (*inserts* TA 1988 s 591B).

(2) (*repeals* TA 1988 s 590(5), (6)).

(3) The amendments made by subsections (1) and (2) above shall be deemed always to have had effect.

(4) The Finance Act 1970 shall be deemed always to have had effect—

    (*a*) with the omission of section 19(3) and (4), and

    (*b*) with the insertion after section 20 of a section 20A in the same form as section 591B of the Taxes Act 1988 (with the omission before 17th March 1987 of the words from "(which shall not" to "whichever is the later)").

Profit-related pay, share schemes etc

37 Profit-related pay: increased relief

Amendments—This section repealed by FA 1997 Sch 18 Pt VI(3) with effect for any payment made by reference to a profit period beginning after 31 December 1999 in accordance with FA 1997 s 61(2), (3), but subject to FA 1997 Sch 18 Pt VI(3) note 2.

38 Employee share schemes: non-discrimination

(1) The Taxes Act 1988 shall be amended as follows.

(2) (amends TA 1988 Sch 9, paras 19(b), 20).

(3) (amends TA 1988 Sch 10, paras 2(b), 3(c)).

(4) (amends TA 1988 s 187(2)).

(5) (inserts TA 1988 Sch 9 para 8A).

(6) Subsections (2) and (5) above shall have effect in relation to a scheme not approved before the day on which this Act is passed.

39 Approved share option schemes: price at which shares may be acquired

(1) (substitutes TA 1988 Sch 9 para 29).

(2)—(6) (amend TA 1988 s 185).

(7) Subsections (1), (5) and (6) above shall come into force on 1st January 1992.

(8) Subsections (3) and (4) above shall apply in relation to rights obtained on or after 1st January 1992.

40 Savings-related share option schemes

(1) (amends TA 1988 Sch 9 para 24(2)(a)).

(2) This section shall come into force on such day as the Treasury may by order made by statutory instrument appoint.

41 Profit sharing schemes

(Amends TA 1988 s 187(2)).

42 Costs of establishing share option or profit sharing schemes: relief

(Inserts TA 1988 s 84A).

43 Costs of establishing employee share ownership trusts: relief
(Inserts TA 1988 s 85A).

44 Priority share allocations for employees etc

(1) In relation to offers made on or after 16th January 1991, section 68 of the Finance Act 1988 (which provides for the benefits derived from priority rights in share offers to be disregarded in certain circumstances) shall have effect, and be deemed at all times on and after that date to have had effect, with the amendments specified in subsections (2) to (8) below.

(2)–(9) (amend FA 1988 s 68, 77).

(9) (amends FA 1988 s 77).

(10) The amendments made by subsection (9) above shall be deemed to have come into force on 16th January 1991.

Foreign earnings

45 Seafarers

Amendments—This section repealed by FA 1998 Sch 27 Part III with effect in relation to emoluments attributable to qualifying periods beginning on or after 17 March 1998 and to qualifying periods beginning before 17 March 1998 which are received on or after that date.

46 Workers in Kuwait or Iraq

(Spent).

Insurance companies and friendly societies

47 Investor protection schemes

(1)–(3) (amend TA 1988 s 76).

(4) The amendments made by subsection (1) above shall have effect in relation to levies imposed, and sums paid, before or after the coming into force of that subsection.

Prospective amendments—This section to be amended by the Financial Services and Markets Act 2000 s 432(1), Sch 20 para 5 with effect from a day to be appointed.

48 Assimilation of basic life assurance business and general annuity business
Schedule 7 to this Act shall have effect.

49 Pension business: payments on account of tax credits and deducted tax

(*Inserted TA* 1988 s 438A and Sch 19AB; *repealed by* FA 2001 s 110, Sch 33 Pt II(12) with effect in accordance with FA 2001 s 87.).

50 Friendly societies
Schedule 9 to this Act (which makes provision about friendly societies) shall have effect.

Building societies

51 Qualifying shares
Schedule 10 to this Act (which makes provision about certain kinds of building society share) shall have effect.

52 Marketable securities

(1) Schedule 11 to this Act (which makes provision about the deduction of income tax in the case of marketable securities issued by building societies) shall have effect.

(2), (3) ...[1]

Commentary—*Simon's Direct Tax Service* D4.732.
Amendments—[1] Sub-ss (2), (3) repealed by FA 1996 Sch 41 Pt V(3) with effect for income tax from the year 1996–97 and so far as relating to corporation tax for accounting periods ending after 31 March 1996, subject to transitional provisions in FA 1996 Sch 15.

53 Income Tax (Building Societies) Regulations 1986

(1) Section 343(1A) of the Income and Corporation Taxes Act 1970 (building societies) shall be deemed to have conferred power to make all the provisions in fact contained in the Income Tax (Building Societies) Regulations 1986 (the regulations).

(2) Where a provision of the regulations requires a building society to pay to the Board a sum calculated by reference to the reduced rate and the basic rate, subsection (3) below shall apply to the extent that the sum is one in respect of payments or credits made in the period beginning with 1st March in any year and ending with 5th April in the same year.

(3) The provision shall be deemed always to have had effect as if the reduced and basic rates concerned were those for the year of assessment in which the period falls.

(4) In relation to a building society which commenced proceedings to challenge the validity of the regulations before 18th July 1986, this section shall not have effect to the extent that the regulations apply (or purport to apply) to payments or credits made before 6th April 1986.

Commentary—*Simon's Direct Tax Service* **D4.721.**
Simon's Tax Cases—*National & Provincial Building Society v United Kingdom* [1997] STC 1466.

Securities

54 New issues

Schedule 12 to this Act (which contains provisions about securities issued after an issue of securities of the same kind) shall have effect.

55 Purchase and sale of securities: options

(1) (*inserts* TA 1988 s 731(4A)–(4C)).

(2) This section shall apply where the subsequent sale by the first buyer takes place on or after the day on which this Act is passed.

56 Bondwashing

(1) (*inserts* TA 1988 s 732(2A) and is repealed by F(No 2)A 1997 Sch 8 Pt II (8)).

(2) (*adds* TA 1988 s 732(7) and is repealed by F(No 2)A 1997 Sch 8 Pt II (8)).

57 Stock lending

(1)–(3) (amend TA 1988 s 129).

(4) (repealed by TCGA 1992 s 290, Sch 12).

(5) This section shall apply to transfers made after such date as is specified for this purpose by regulations under section 129 of the Taxes Act 1988.[1]

Amendments—[1] Section repealed by FA 1997 Sch 18 Pt VI(10) with effect in relation to, and to transfers under, any arrangement made on or after 1 July 1997 by virtue of the Finance Act 1997, Schedule 10, (Appointed Day) Order, SI 1997/991.

58 Manufactured dividends and interest

(1) (*inserts* TA 1988 s 736A).

(2) The enactments mentioned in Schedule 13 to this Act shall have effect with the amendments there specified.

(3) This section shall have effect in relation to payments made on or after such day as the Treasury may specify for this purpose by regulations made by statutory instrument and different days may be so appointed for different provisions or different purposes.

Capital allowances

59 Interaction with VAT capital goods scheme

Amendments—This section repealed by the Capital Allowances Act 2001 s 580, Sch 4 with effect for income tax purposes, as respects allowances and charges falling to be made for chargeable periods ending on or after 6 April 2001, and for corporation tax purposes, as respects allowances and charges falling to be made for chargeable periods ending on or after 1 April 2001.

60 Toll roads

Amendments—This section repealed by the Capital Allowances Act 2001 s 580, Sch 4 with effect for income tax purposes, as respects allowances and charges falling to be made for chargeable periods ending on or after 6 April 2001, and for corporation tax purposes, as respects allowances and charges falling to be made for chargeable periods ending on or after 1 April 2001.

61 Hiring motor cars

Amendments—This section repealed by the Capital Allowances Act 2001 s 580, Sch 4 with effect for income tax purposes, as respects allowances and charges falling to be made for chargeable periods ending on or after 6 April 2001, and for corporation tax purposes, as respects allowances and charges falling to be made for chargeable periods ending on or after 1 April 2001.

Oil industry

62 Expenditure on and under abandonment guarantees

(1) To the extent that, by virtue of paragraph (*hh*) of subsection (1) of section 3 of the Oil Taxation Act 1975 (as set out in section 103(2) of this Act), expenditure incurred on or after 19th March 1991 by a participator in an oil field is allowable for the purposes of petroleum revenue tax under the said section 3, that expenditure shall be allowed as a deduction in computing the participator's ring fence income.

(2) Expressions used in subsection (1) above and the following provisions of this section have the same meaning as in Chapter V of Part XII of the Taxes Act 1988 (petroleum extraction activities).

(3) If, under an abandonment guarantee, a payment is made by the guarantor on or after 19th March 1991, then, to the extent that any expenditure for which the relevant participator is liable is met, directly or indirectly, out of the payment, that expenditure shall not be regarded for any purposes of tax as having been incurred by the relevant participator or any other participator in the oil field concerned.

(4) In any case where—

(a) a payment made by the guarantor under the abandonment guarantee is not immediately applied in meeting any expenditure, and
(b) the payment is for any period invested (either specifically or together with payments made by persons other than the guarantor) so as to be represented by, or by part of, the assets of a fund or account, and
(c) at a subsequent time, any expenditure for which the relevant participator is liable is met out of the assets of the fund or account,

any reference in subsection (3) above or section 63 below to expenditure which is met, directly or indirectly, out of the payment shall be construed as a reference to so much of the expenditure for which the relevant participator is liable as is met out of those assets of the fund or account which, at the subsequent time referred to in paragraph (c) above, it is just and reasonable to attribute to the payment.

(5) In subsections (3) and (4) above—

(a) "abandonment guarantee" has the same meaning as, by virtue of section 104 of this Act, it has for the purposes of section 105 of this Act; and
(b) "the guarantor" and "the relevant participator" have the same meaning as in subsection (1) of section 104 of this Act.

Commentary—*Simon's Direct Tax Service* **D4.1012.**

63 Relief for reimbursement expenditure under abandonment guarantees

(1) This section applies in any case where—

(a) on or after 19th March 1991 a payment (in this section referred to as "the guarantee payment") is made by the guarantor under an abandonment guarantee; and
(b) by virtue of the making of the guarantee payment, the relevant participator becomes liable under the terms of the abandonment guarantee to pay any sum or sums to the guarantor; and
(c) expenditure is incurred, or consideration in money's worth is given, by the relevant participator in or towards meeting that liability.

(2) In any case where the whole of the guarantee payment or, as the case may require, of the assets which, under section 62(4) above, are attributed to the guarantee payment is not applied in meeting liabilities of the relevant participator which fall within paragraphs (a) and (b) of subsection (1) of section 104 of this Act and a sum representing the unapplied part of the guarantee payment or of those assets is repaid, directly or indirectly, to the guarantor,—

(a) any liability of the relevant participator to repay that sum shall be excluded in determining the total liability of the relevant participator which falls within subsection (1)(b) above; and
(b) the repayment to the guarantor of that sum shall not be regarded as expenditure incurred by the relevant participator as mentioned in subsection (1)(c) above.

(3) In the following provisions of this section "reimbursement expenditure" means expenditure incurred as mentioned in subsection (1)(c) above or consideration (or, as the case may require, the value of consideration) given as so mentioned; and any reference to the incurring of reimbursement expenditure shall be construed accordingly.

(4) So much of any reimbursement expenditure as, in accordance with subsection (5) below, is qualifying expenditure shall, by virtue of this section, be allowed as a deduction in computing the relevant participator's ring fence income; and no part of the expenditure which is so allowed shall be otherwise deductible or allowable by way of relief for any purposes of tax.

(5) Subject to subsection (6) below, of the reimbursement expenditure incurred in any accounting period by the relevant participator, the amount which constitutes qualifying expenditure shall be determined by the formula—

$$A \times \frac{B}{C}$$

where—

"A" is the reimbursement expenditure incurred in the accounting period;
"B" is so much of the expenditure represented by the guarantee payment as, if it had been incurred by the relevant participator, would have been taken into account (by way of capital allowance or a deduction) in computing his ring fence income; and

"C" is the total of the sums which, at or before the end of the accounting period, the relevant participator is or has become liable to pay to the guarantor as mentioned in subsection (1)(*b*) above.

(6) In relation to the guarantee payment, the total of the reimbursement expenditure (whenever incurred) which constitutes qualifying expenditure shall not exceed whichever is the less of "B" and "C" in the formula in subsection (5) above; and any limitation on qualifying expenditure arising by virtue of this subsection shall be applied to the expenditure of a later in preference to an earlier accounting period.

(7) For the purposes of this section, the expenditure represented by the guarantee payment is any expenditure—

    (*a*) for which the relevant participator is liable; and

    (*b*) which is met, directly or indirectly, out of the guarantee payment (and which, accordingly, by virtue of section 62 (3) above is not to be regarded as expenditure incurred by the relevant participator).

(8) In this section—

    (*a*) "abandonment guarantee" has the same meaning as, by virtue of section 104 of this Act, it has for the purposes of section 3 of the 1975 Act;

    (*b*) "the guarantor" and "the relevant participator" have the same meaning as in subsection (1) of section 104 of this Act; and

    (*c*) other expressions have the same meaning as in Chapter V of Part XII of the Taxes Act 1988 (petroleum extraction activities).

Commentary—Simon's Direct Tax Service **D4.1012.**

64 Relief for expenditure incurred by a participator in meeting defaulter's abandonment expenditure

(1) This section applies in any case where—

    (*a*) paragraph 2A of Schedule 5 to the 1975 Act (as set out in section 107 of this Act) applies or would apply if a claim were made as mentioned in sub-paragraph (1) (*a*) of that paragraph; and

    (*b*) under sub-paragraph (4) of that paragraph the default payment falls, in whole or in part, to be attributed to the qualifying participator (as an addition to his share of the abandonment expenditure).

(2) In this section "default payment", "the defaulter" and "qualifying participator" have the same meaning as in paragraph 2A of Schedule 5 to the 1975 Act and other expressions have the same meaning as in Chapter V of Part XII of the Taxes Act 1988 (petroleum extraction activities).

(3) In this section, the amount which is attributed to the qualifying participator as mentioned in subsection (1)(*b*) above (whether representing the whole or only a part of the default payment) is referred to as the additional abandonment expenditure.

(4) Relief by way of capital allowance or, as the case may be, a deduction in computing ring fence income shall be available to the qualifying participator by virtue of this section in respect of the additional abandonment expenditure in any case where any such relief or deduction would have been available to the defaulter if—

    (*a*) the defaulter had incurred the additional abandonment expenditure; and

    (*b*) at the time that that expenditure was incurred the defaulter continued to carry on a ring fence trade.

(5) The basis of qualification for or entitlement to any relief or deduction which is available to the qualifying participator by virtue of this section shall be determined on the assumption that the conditions in paragraphs (*a*) and (*b*) of subsection (4) above are fulfilled but, subject to that, any such relief or deduction shall be available in like manner as if the additional abandonment expenditure had been incurred by the qualifying participator for the purposes of the ring fence trade carried on by him.

Commentary—Simon's Direct Tax Service **D4.1013.**

65 Reimbursement by defaulter in respect of certain abandonment expenditure

(1) This section applies in any case where—

    (*a*) paragraph 2A of Schedule 5 to the 1975 Act (as set out in section 107 of this Act) applies or would apply if a claim were made as mentioned in sub-paragraph (1) (*a*) of that paragraph; and

    (*b*) under sub-paragraph (4) of that paragraph the default payment falls, in whole or in part, to be attributed to the qualifying participator (as an addition to his share of the abandonment expenditure); and

    (*c*) expenditure is incurred, or consideration in money's worth is given, by the defaulter in reimbursing the qualifying participator in respect of, or otherwise making good to him, the whole or any part of the default payment;

and in this section "default payment", "the defaulter" and "qualifying participator" have the same meaning as in the said paragraph 2A and other expressions have the same meaning as in Chapter V of Part XII of the Taxes Act 1988 (petroleum extraction activities).

(2) In the following provisions of this section "reimbursement expenditure" means expenditure incurred as mentioned in subsection (1)(c) above or consideration (or, as the case may require, the value of consideration) given as so mentioned; and any reference to the incurring of reimbursement expenditure shall be construed accordingly.

(3) Subject to subsection (7) below, reimbursement expenditure shall be allowed as a deduction in computing the defaulter's ring fence income.

(4) Subject to subsection (7) below, reimbursement expenditure received by the qualifying participator shall be treated as a receipt (in the nature of income) of his ring fence trade for the relevant accounting period.

(5) For the purposes of subsection (4) above, the relevant accounting period is the accounting period in which the reimbursement expenditure is received by the qualifying participator or, if the qualifying participator's ring fence trade is permanently discontinued before the receipt of the reimbursement expenditure, the last accounting period of that trade.

(6) Any additional assessment to corporation tax required in order to take account of the receipt of reimbursement expenditure by the qualifying participator may be made at any time not later than six years after the end of the calendar year in which the reimbursement expenditure is so received.

(7) In relation to a particular default payment, reimbursement expenditure incurred at any time—

(a) shall be allowed as mentioned in subsection (3) above, and

(b) shall be taken into account in computing the qualifying participator's ring fence income by virtue of subsection (4) above,

only to the extent that, when aggregated with any reimbursement expenditure previously incurred in respect of that default payment, it does not exceed so much of the default payment as falls to be attributed to the qualifying participator as mentioned in subsection (1) (b) above.

(8) The incurring of reimbursement expenditure shall not be regarded, by virtue of [section 532 of the Capital Allowances Act (the general rule excluding contributions)][1], as the meeting of the expenditure of the qualifying participator in making the default payment.

Commentary—*Simon's Direct Tax Service* **D4.1913.**
Amendments—[1] Words in sub-s 8 substituted by CAA 2001 s 578, Sch 2 para 73 with effect for income tax purposes, as respects allowances and charges falling to be made for chargeable periods ending after 5 April 2001, and for corporation tax purposes, as respects allowances and charges falling to be made for chargeable periods ending after 31 March 2001.

66 Restriction on setting ACT against liability to corporation tax on profits from oil extraction activities etc

(Amends TA 1988 s 497).

67 Oil licences

(Repealed by TCGA 1992 s 290, Sch 12).

Miscellaneous

68 Gifts to educational establishments

(1) *(amend* TA 1988 s 84).

(2) The amendment made by subsection (1) above shall have effect with respect to gifts made on or after 19th March 1991.

69 Expenses of entertainers

(1)–(5) (amend TA 1988 s 201A).

(6) The amendments made by this section shall apply for the year 1990–91 and subsequent years of assessment.

(7) Any such adjustment (whether by way of discharge or repayment of tax, the making of an assessment or otherwise) as is appropriate in consequence of this section may be made.

70 Personal equity plans

(Amends TA 1988, s 333).

71 Donations to charity

(1) (repeals TA 1988 s 339A).

(2) (amends TA 1988 s 338(2)).

(3) Subsections (1) and (2) above shall apply in relation to accounting periods beginning on or after 19th March 1991.

(4) In its application to accounting periods beginning before 19th March 1991 and ending on or after that date, section 339A of the Taxes Act 1988 shall have effect as if—

(a) in subsections (1) and (2), after the words "in that period", in the first place where they occur, there were inserted "and before 19th March 1991"; and

(b) in subsection (3)(b), after "that section" there were inserted "in respect of payments made before 19th March 1991".

(5) (repeals FA 1990 s 25(2)(h)).

(6) Subsection (5) above shall apply in relation to gifts made on or after 19th March 1991.

72 Deduction of trading losses

(1) Where under section 380 of the Taxes Act 1988 (set-off of trading losses against general income) a person makes a claim for relief for a year of assessment in respect of an amount ("the trading loss") which is available for relief under that section, he may in the notice by which the claim is made make a claim under this subsection for the relevant amount for the year to be determined.

(2) The relevant amount for the year is so much of the trading loss as—

    (a) cannot be set off against the claimant's income for the year, and

    (b) has not already been taken into account for the purpose of giving relief (under section 380 or this section or otherwise) for any other year.

(3) Where the claim under subsection (1) above is finally determined, the relevant amount for the year shall be treated for the purposes of capital gains tax as an allowable loss accruing to the claimant in the year; but the preceding provisions of this subsection shall not apply to so much of the relevant amount as exceeds the maximum amount.

(4) The maximum amount is the amount on which the claimant would be chargeable to capital gains tax for the year, disregarding section [3(1) of the Taxation of Chargeable Gains Act 1992]¹ and the effect of this section.

(5) In ascertaining the maximum amount, no account shall be taken of any event—

    (a) occurring after the date on which the claim under subsection (1) above is finally determined, and

    (b) in consequence of which the amount referred to in subsection (4) above is reduced by virtue of any enactment relating to capital gains tax.

(6) An amount treated as an allowable loss by virtue of this section shall not be allowed as a deduction from chargeable gains accruing to a person in any year of assessment beginning after he has ceased to carry on the trade, profession, vocation or employment in which the relevant trading loss was sustained.

(7) For the purposes of this section, the claim under subsection (1) above shall not be deemed to be finally determined until the relevant amount for the year can no longer be varied, whether by the Commissioners on appeal or on the order of any court.

(8) References in sections 382(3),...² and 385 (1) of the Taxes Act 1988 to relief under section 380 of that Act shall be construed as including references to relief under this section.

(9) This section shall apply in relation to losses sustained in the year 1991–92 and subsequent years of assessment.

Commentary—*Simon's Direct Tax Service* E1.603.
Revenue Interpretation RI 47—Claims for relief under this section and under TA 1988 s 380 (trading losses set against income) may be made separately subject to certain conditions.
Revenue Internal Guidance—Inspector's manual IM 3515–3520 (detailed explanation with worked examples).
Cross references—See TCGA 1992 s 16(1) (this section to have effect in relation to computation of losses for the purposes of computation of chargeable gains);
Lloyd's Underwriters (Tax) (1992–93 to 1996–97) Regulations, SI 1995/352 reg 14 and Sch (extension of time limit under sub-s (1) above where an election falls to be made by Lloyd's member, spouse, or both).
FA 2002 s 48(3), (5) (election for prospective amendments made by FA 2002 s 48(1) to apply in respect of trading losses sustained in 2002–03).
FA 2002 s 48(4), (5) (election for prospective amendments made by FA 2002 s 48(1) to apply in respect of trading losses sustained in 2003–04).
Amendments—¹ Words in sub-s (4) substituted by TCGA 1992 Sch 10 para 23.
² Words in sub-s (8) repealed by FA 1994 ss 211(2), 218, Sch 26, Pt V(24) with effect from the year 1994–95 as regards trades, etc commenced after 5 April 1994 and with effect from the year 1997–98 as regards trades, etc commenced before 6 April 1994.
Prospective amendments—In sub-s (4), words "disregarding sections 2A (taper relief) and 3(1) (annual exempt amount)" to be substituted for the words "disregarding section 3(1)" by FA 2002 s 48(1), (2) with effect for claims under this section in respect of trading losses sustained in the year 2004–05 or subsequent years of assessment, subject to FA 2002 s 48(3)–(5).

73 Relief for company trading losses

(1) (*inserts* TA 1988 s 393A).

(2) (*repeals* TA 1988 ss 393(2)–(6), 394).

(3) Schedule 15 to this Act shall have effect.

(4) This section shall have effect only in relation to losses incurred in accounting periods ending on or after 1st April 1991.

(5) Any enactment amended by this section or that Schedule shall, in its application in relation to losses so incurred, be deemed to have had effect at all times with that amendment; and where any such enactment is the re-enactment of a repealed enactment, the repealed enactment shall, in its application in relation to losses so incurred, be deemed to have had effect at all times with a corresponding amendment.

Commentary—*Simon's Direct Tax Service* D2.405.

74 Trade unions and employers' associations

(1) Section 467 of the Taxes Act 1988 (trade unions and employers' associations) shall be amended as follows.

(2)–(5) (*amend* TA 1988 s 467(1), (3), (4) and *insert* TA 1988, s 467(3A)).

(6) Subsections (2) and (3) above shall have effect in relation to income or gains which are applicable and applied as mentioned in section 467 of the Taxes Act 1988 on or after 1st April 1991.

(7) Subsection (5) above shall be deemed always to have had effect.

75 Audit powers in relation to non-residents

(*Inserts* TA 1988 s 482A).

76 Capital element in annuities

(1) Section 656 of the Taxes Act 1988 (purchased life annuities other than retirement annuities) shall have effect, and be deemed always to have had effect, with the addition of the following subsections—

(*inserts* TA 1988 s 656(7)–(9)).

(2) Section 230 of the Income and Corporation Taxes Act 1970 (from which section 656 of the Taxes Act 1988 is derived) shall be deemed always to have had effect as if the subsections (7) to (9) set out in subsection (1) above had been contained in that section as subsections (8) to (10) respectively, but with the substitution for "(2) (*a*)" and "(4) (*c*)", in each place where they occur, of "(2A) (*a*)" and "(3) (*c*)" respectively.

(3) Section 27 of the Finance Act 1956 (from which section 230 of the Income and Corporation Taxes Act 1970 was derived) shall be deemed always to have had effect as if the subsections (7) and (9) set out in subsection (1) above had been contained in that section as subsections (8A) and (8B) respectively, but with the omission in subsection (7) of paragraph (*a*) and with the substitution of "(3) (*c*)" for "(4) (*c*)" in both places where it occurs.

77 Definition of "normal commercial loan"

(1) (*inserts* TA 1988 Sch 18 para 1(5E)–(5I)).

(2) ...¹

(3) Except as provided by subsection (2) above, this section shall be deemed to have come into force on 1st April 1991.

Amendments—¹ Sub-s (2) repealed by TCGA 1992 Sch 12.

78 Sharing of transmission facilities

(1) This section applies to any agreement relating to the sharing of transmission facilities—
  (*a*) to which the parties are national broadcasting companies,
  (*b*) which is entered into on or after the day on which this Act is passed and before 1st January 1992 or such later date as may be specified for the purposes of this paragraph by the Secretary of State, and
  (*c*) in relation to which the Secretary of State has certified that it is expedient that this section should apply.

(2), (3) ...¹

(4) Where under an agreement to which this section applies one party to the agreement disposes of [plant or machinery]² to another party to the agreement, the [Capital Allowances Act]² shall apply—
  (*a*) in the case of the party making the disposal, as if the disposal value of the [plant or machinery]² for the purposes of [section 60 of that Act]² were equal to the capital expenditure incurred by that party on its provision, and
  (*b*) in the case of the party to whom the disposal is made, as if the amount expended by that party in acquiring the [plant or machinery]² were equal to the capital expenditure so incurred.

(5) In subsection (4) above, references to [plant or machinery] include a share in [plant or machinery]².

(6), (7) ...¹

(8) In this section, "national broadcasting company" means a body corporate engaged in the broadcasting for general reception by means of wireless telegraphy of radio or television services or both on a national basis.

Commentary—*Simon's Direct Tax Service* B3.246; C1.421.
Amendments—¹ Sub-ss (2), (3), (6), (7) repealed by TCGA 1992 Sch 12.
² Words in sub-ss (4), (5) substituted by CAA 2001 s 578, Sch 2 para 74 with effect for corporation tax purposes as respects allowances and charges falling to be made for chargeable periods ending after 31 March 2001.

79 Abolition of CRT: consequential amendment

(*Amends* FA 1988 Sch 12 para 6(1)(*b*)).

80 Interest on certain debentures

(*Amends Electricity* Act 1989 Sch 11 para 8(2)).

81 Agents acting for non-residents

Amendments—This section is repealed by FA 1995 s 162, Sch 29 Pt VIII(16), for the purposes of income and capital gains tax from the year 1996–97, and for the purposes of corporation tax for accounting periods beginning after 31 March 1996.

82 Certificates of non-liability to tax

(1) (*inserts* TMA 1970 s 99A).

(2) So far as relating to the giving of a certificate, this section shall apply in relation to certificates given on or after the day on which this Act is passed.

(3) So far as relating to failure to comply with an undertaking contained in a certificate, this section shall apply in relation to certificates whenever given, but not so as to impose liability for a failure occurring before the day on which this Act is passed.

CHAPTER II
CAPITAL GAINS

Amendments—This Chapter (ie ss 83–102) repealed by TCGA 1992 Sch 12.

PART V
MISCELLANEOUS AND GENERAL
Miscellaneous

118 Designated international organisations: miscellaneous exemptions

(1), (2) (*insert* TA 1988 s 582A and *amend* TA 1988, s 828(4)).

121 Pools payments to support games etc

(1) This section applies to any payment which, in consequence of the reduction in pool betting duty effected by section 5 above, is made—

    (*a*) by a person liable to pay that duty, and
    (*b*) to trustees established mainly for the support of athletic sports or athletic games but with power to support the arts.

(2) Where a person carrying on a trade makes a payment to which this section applies, the payment may be deducted in computing for tax purposes the [profits]¹ of the trade.

(3) A payment to which this section applies shall not be regarded as an annual payment.

(4) Where a payment to which this section applies is made, the sum received by the trustees and any assets representing it (but not any income or gains arising from them) shall not be relevant property for the purposes of Chapter III of Part III of the Inheritance Tax Act 1984.

Commentary—*Simon's Direct Tax Service* **B3.1446.**
Amendments—¹ Words substituted by FA 1998 Sch 7 para 6 with effect from 31 July 1998.

General

122 Interpretation etc

(1) In this Act "the Taxes Act 1988" means the Income and Corporation Taxes Act 1988.

(2) Part II of this Act, so far as it relates to capital gains tax, shall be construed as one with the Capital Gains Tax Act 1979.

(3) Part III of this Act shall be construed as one with Part I of the Oil Taxation Act 1975 and in that Part of this Act "the principal Act" means that Act.

124 Short title

This Act may be cited as the Finance Act 1991.

SCHEDULES

SCHEDULE 6

RESTRICTION OF HIGHER RATE RELIEF: BENEFICIAL LOANS ETC

Section 27

Taxation of beneficial loan arrangements

1 (*amends* TA 1988 s 160).

2 (*amended* TA 1988 s 167; *repealed* by FA 1994 Sch 26 Pt V(5)).

3 (*amends* TA 1988 Sch 7 para 3).

4 (*repeals* TA 1988 Sch 7 para 6).

5 (*inserted* TA 1988 Sch 7 para 13, Pt IV (ie paras 14–18) and Pt V (ie para 19); *repealed* by FA 1994 Sch 26 Pt V(5)).

Applicable rates of capital gains tax

6 (*amended* FA 1988 s 102; *repealed* by TCGA 1992 s 290, Sch 12).

SCHEDULE 7

BASIC LIFE ASSURANCE AND GENERAL ANNUITY BUSINESS

Section 48

Management expenses

1 (*amends* TA 1988 s 76).

Interpretation of Chapter I of Part XII

2 (*amended* TA 1988 s 431; *repealed* by FA 1995 s 162, Sch 29 Pt VIII(5), with effect for accounting periods beginning after 31 December 1994).

Apportionment of income and gains

3 (*amended* TA 1988 ss 432A, 432C, 432D; *repealed* by FA 1995 s 162, Sch 29 Pt VIII(5), with effect for accounting periods beginning after 31 December 1994).

Computation of trading profit

4 (*amends* TA 1988 ss 436, 437).

Deduction for annuities referable to basic life assurance and general annuity business

5 (*substitutes* TA 1988 s 437(1A)–(1F) for s 437(1)).

Transfer of assets between classes of business

6 (*amended* TA 1988 ss 440, 440A; *repealed* by FA 1995 s 162, Sch 29 Pt VIII(5), with effect for accounting periods beginning after 31 December 1994).

Commentary—*Simon's Direct Tax Service* **D4.532.**

United Kingdom branches of overseas life assurance companies

7—(1) (*amends* TA 1988 s 446; *repealed in part* by FA 1993 s 213, Sch 23, Pt III(9)).

(2)–(4) (*amended* TA 1988 s 447; *repealed* by FA 1993 s 213, Sch 23, Pt III(9)).

(5) (*amended* TA 1988 s 448; *repealed* by FA 1993 s 213, Sch 23, Pt III(9)).

Treatment of tax-free income

8 (*amends* TA 1988 s 474).

Life annuity contracts; taxation of gain on chargeable event

9—(1)–(3) (*amend* TA 1988 s 547).

(4) (*amends* TA 1988 s 549).

Computation of offshore income gains

10 (*repealed* TA 1988 Sch 28 para 3(4)(*a*); *repealed* by FA 1995 s 162, Sch 29 Pt VIII(5), with effect for accounting periods beginning after 31 October 1994).

Interpretation of sections 85 to 89 of Finance Act 1989

11 (*amends* FA 1989 s 84).

Miscellaneous receipts

12 (*amends* FA 1989 s 85).

Spreading of relief for acquisition expenses

13 (*amends* FA 1989 s 86).

Deemed disposal of unit trusts etc

14 (*amended* FA 1990 s 46; *repealed* by TCGA 1992 s 290, Sch 12).

Exemptions and exclusions from charges by virtue of section 46

15 (*amended* FA 1990 Sch 8 paras 1, 3; *repealed* by TCGA 1992 s 290, Sch 12).

Transitional relief for old general annuity contracts

16—(1) [In the computation, otherwise than in accordance with the provisions applicable to Case I of Schedule D, of the profits for any accounting period of an insurance company's life assurance business, an amount equal to the lesser of the following amounts shall be treated (if it is not nil) as a sum disbursed as expenses of management of the company for that period, that is to say—][1]

    (*a*) A, and

    (*b*) $A - (R1 - R2 + C - SV - DB)$,

and if the result of the formula in paragraph (*b*) above is a negative amount, it shall be taken to be nil.

(2) For the purposes of sub-paragraph (1) above—

    A is the gross amount of any annuities paid in the accounting period so far as referable to old annuity contracts;

    R1 is the amount of the company's opening liabilities for the accounting period in respect of old annuity contracts;

    R2 is the amount of the company's closing liabilities for the accounting period in respect of old annuity contracts;

    C is the amount of any consideration received in the accounting period in respect of old annuity contracts;

    SV is the amount of any sums paid in the accounting period by reason of the surrender of rights conferred by old annuity contracts;

    DB is the amount of any death benefits paid in the accounting period in respect of old annuity contracts.

(3), (4) ...[2]

(5) If, in the case of an annuity under a group annuity contract made by an insurance company in an accounting period beginning before 1st January 1992—

    (*a*) the company's liabilities first include an amount in respect of that annuity in an accounting period beginning on or after that date, and

    (*b*) the company's liability in respect of that annuity is referable to its basic life assurance and general annuity business,

the group annuity contract, so far as relating to that annuity, shall be treated for the purposes of this paragraph, other than this sub-paragraph, as if it had been made in an accounting period beginning on or after 1st January 1992 (and were, accordingly, not an old annuity contract).

(6) If, in the case of an annuity which is subject to a reinsurance treaty made by the reinsurer in an accounting period beginning before 1st January 1992—

    (*a*) the reinsurer's liabilities first include an amount in respect of that annuity in an accounting period beginning on or after that date, and

    (*b*) the reinsurer's liability in respect of that annuity is referable to its basic life assurance and general annuity business,

the reinsurance treaty, as respects the reinsurer and so far as relating to that annuity, shall be treated for the purposes of this paragraph, other than this sub-paragraph, as if it had been made in an accounting period beginning on or after 1st January 1992 (and were, accordingly, not an old annuity contract).

(7) In this paragraph—

"general annuity contract" means an annuity contract so far as referable to general annuity
business;

"group annuity contract" means a contract between an insurance company and some other person
under which the company undertakes to become liable to pay annuities to or in respect of such
persons as may subsequently be specified or otherwise ascertained under or in accordance with
the contract (whether or not annuities under the contract are also payable to or in respect of
persons who are specified or ascertained at the time the contract is made);

"old annuity contract" means a general annuity contract made by an insurance company in an
accounting period beginning before 1st January 1992;

"reinsurance treaty" means a contract under which one insurance company is obliged to cede,
and another (in this paragraph referred to as a "reinsurer") to accept, the whole or part of a risk
of a class or description to which the contract relates;

and, subject to that, expressions used in this paragraph and in Chapter I of Part XII of the Taxes Act
1988 have the same meaning in this paragraph as they have in that Chapter.

Commentary—*Simon's Direct Tax Service* **D4.520A.**
Modification—Sub-para (7) is modified so far as it applies to the life or endowment business carried on by friendly societies by
the Friendly Societies (Modification of the Corporation Tax Acts) Regulations, SI 1997/473 reg 42.
Amendments—¹ Words in sub-para (1) substituted by FA 1997 s 67(6), (7), with effect in relation to accounting periods
beginning after 5 March 1997.
² Sub-paras (3), (4) repealed by FA 1997 s 67(6), (7), Sch 18 Pt VI(6) with effect in relation to accounting periods beginning after
5 March 1997.

Transitional provisions for chargeable gains and unrelieved general annuity losses

17—(1) An insurance company's unrelieved general annuity losses shall be relieved under this
paragraph by setting them against the relevant part of any chargeable gains arising to the company
in accounting periods beginning on or after 1st January 1992.

(2) Any relief under this paragraph shall be given as far as possible for the first accounting period of
the company beginning on or after 1st January 1992 and, so far as it cannot be so given, for the next
accounting period, and so on.

(3) For the purposes of this paragraph an insurance company's "unrelieved general annuity losses"
are so much of any losses—

(*a*) arising from the company's general annuity business in an accounting period or year of
assessment beginning before 1st January 1992, and
(*b*) computed as mentioned in paragraph (*c*) of subsection (3) of section 436 of the Taxes Act
1988 as it applied in relation to such accounting periods,

as, by virtue only of an insufficiency of profits, cannot be relieved under that subsection (or any
previous enactment which it re-enacts) by setting them off against the profits of such an accounting
period or year of assessment.

(4) For the purposes of this paragraph the relevant part of the chargeable gains arising to a company
in an accounting period shall be determined by the application of the following formula—

$$X \times \frac{Y}{Z}$$

where—

X is so much of the chargeable gains arising to the company in the accounting period as are
referable to its basic life assurance and general annuity business;
Y is the mean of the company's opening and closing liabilities for the accounting period in respect
of old annuity contracts; and
Z is the mean of the company's opening and closing liabilities for the accounting period in respect
of its basic life assurance and general annuity business.

(5) Sub-paragraphs (5) to (7) of paragraph 16 above shall apply for the purposes of this paragraph
as they apply for the purposes of that paragraph.

Commentary—*Simon's Direct Tax Service* **D4.520A.**
Concession C29—Unrelieved losses may be treated as losses of transferee where long-term business is transferred to another
company.
Modification—Sub-para (4) is modified so far as it applies to the life or endowment business carried on by friendly societies by
the Friendly Societies (Modification of the Corporation Tax Acts) Regulations, SI 1997/473 reg 43.

Application of this Schedule

18 Paragraphs 1, 3, 4, 5, 6 (1) and (2), 7, 8, 10 to 14, 16 and 17 above have effect with respect only
to accounting periods beginning on or after 1st January 1992.

SCHEDULE 8

PENSION BUSINESS: PAYMENTS ON ACCOUNT OF TAX CREDITS AND DEDUCTED TAX

Section 49

(*inserted* TA 1988 Sch 19AB; *repealed by* FA 2001 s 110, Sch 33 Pt II(12) with effect in accordance with FA 2001 s 87.).

SCHEDULE 9

FRIENDLY SOCIETIES

Section 50

Tax exempt life or endowment business

1 (*amends* TA 1988 s 460).

2 (*inserts* TA 1988 s 462A).

Maximum benefits payable to members

3 (*amends* TA 1988 s 464).

Qualifying policies

4—(1) (*repeals* TA 1988 Sch 15 para 3(1)(c)).

(2) This paragraph shall apply in relation to policies issued in pursuance of contracts made on or after the day on which this Act is passed.

5—(1) This paragraph applies to any policy—

    (a) issued by a friendly society, or branch of a friendly society, in the course of tax exempt life or endowment business (as defined in section 466 of the Taxes Act 1988), and
    (b) effected by a contract made after 31st August 1987 and before the day on which this Act is passed.

(2) Where—

    (a) the amount payable by way of premium under a policy to which this paragraph applies is increased by virtue of a variation made in the period beginning with the day on which this Act is passed and ending with 31st July 1992, and
    (b) the variation is not such as to cause a person to become in breach of the limits in section 464 of the Taxes Act 1988

Schedule 15 to that Act, in its application to the policy, shall have effect, in relation to that variation, with the modifications mentioned in sub-paragraph (3) below.

(3) The modifications are the omission of paragraph 4 (3) (a) and the insertion at the end of paragraph 18(2) of ''and as if for paragraph 3 (2) (b) above there were substituted—

    ''(b) subject to sub-paragraph (4) below, the premiums payable under the policy shall be premiums of equal or rateable amounts payable at yearly or shorter intervals over the whole of the term of the policy as from the variation, or, where premiums are not payable for any period after the person liable to pay them or whose life is insured has attained a specified age, being an age attained at a time not less than ten years after the beginning of the term of the policy, over the whole of the remainder of the period for which premiums are payable.'' ''

Commentary—*Simon's Direct Tax Service* **D4.604.**

SCHEDULE 10

BUILDING SOCIETIES: QUALIFYING SHARES

Section 51

Capital gains: exemption

1 (*repealed by* TCGA 1992 Sch 12).

Accrued income scheme: inclusion

2—(1)–(2) (*amend* TA 1988 s 710).

(4) This paragraph shall have effect in relation to the application of sections 711 to 728 of the Taxes Act 1988 to transfers of securities on or after the day on which this Act is passed.

Incidental costs of issue

3—(1) (*inserts* TA 1988 s 477B).

(2) This paragraph shall apply in relation to costs incurred on or after the day on which this Act is passed.

Preferential rights of acquisition

4 (*repealed by* TCGA 1992 Sch 12).

Commentary—*Simon's Direct Tax Service* **C2.1008; D4.739.**

SCHEDULE 11

BUILDING SOCIETIES: MARKETABLE SECURITIES

Section 52

Deduction of income tax

1, 2 (*amend* TA 1988 ss 349, 477A).

Collection

3—(1) Schedule 16 to the Taxes Act 1988 (collection of income tax on company payments which are not distributions), in its application to building societies by virtue of section 350(4) of that Act, shall have effect as if for paragraph 2 (2) (*a*) there were substituted—

"(*a*) each complete quarter falling within the accounting period, that is to say, each of the periods of three months ending with the last day of February, May, August and November;".

(2) In section 350(4) of that Act, the second reference to regulations shall be treated as including a reference to sub-paragraph (1) above.

(3) Regulations under section 350(4) of that Act (power to modify Schedule 16) may repeal sub-paragraphs (1) and (2) above.

Commentary—*Simon's Direct Tax Service* **D4.731.**

4—(1) A building society may not make more than one claim to relief under paragraph 5 of Schedule 16 to the Taxes Act 1988 (set-off of income tax borne on company income against tax payable) in respect of the same deduction.

(2) In sub-paragraph (1) above, the reference to a claim under paragraph 5 of Schedule 16 to the Taxes Act 1988 includes a reference to a claim under that paragraph as applied by regulations under section 477A (1) of that Act.

Commentary—*Simon's Direct Tax Service* **D4.739.**

Information

5—(1) (*inserts* TMA 1970 s 18(3D)).

(2) This paragraph shall have effect as regards a case where the payment is made on or after the day on which this Act is passed.

SCHEDULE 12

SECURITIES: NEW ISSUES

Section 54

General treatment of extra return

1 (*inserts* TA 1988 s 587A).

Accrued income scheme

2 (*inserts* TA 1988 s 726A).

Deep discount securities

3 (*repealed by* FA 1996 Sch 41 Pt V(3) with effect for the purposes of income tax from the year 1996–97 and for the purposes of corporation tax in relation to accounting periods ending after 31 March 1996 subject to transitional provisions in FA 1996 Sch 15.)

Deep gain securities

4 (*repealed* by FA 1996 Sch 41 Pt V(3) with effect for the purposes of income tax from the year 1996–97 and for the purposes of corporation tax in relation to accounting periods ending after 31 March 1996 subject to transitional provisions in FA 1996 Sch 15.)

General

5 This Schedule applies if the new securities are issued on or after 19th March 1991 (whether the old securities are issued before or on or after that day).

SCHEDULE 13

MANUFACTURED DIVIDENDS AND INTEREST

Section 58

Note—This Schedule inserts TA 1988 Sch 23A, amends ss 737, 738 of that Act and FA 1986 Sch 18 para 9(1)(*b*); insofar as it amends TA 1988 ss 737, 738 and FA 1986 Sch 18 para 9(1)(*b*) it is repealed by FA 1997 Sch 18 Pt VI (10) with effect so far as relating to ss 737, 738 in relation to payments made on or after 1 July 1997 by virtue of the Finance Act 1997, Schedule 10, (Appointed Day) Order, SI 1997/991, and with effect so far as relating to Sch 18 para 9(1)(*b*) in accordance with FA 1997 Sch 10 paras 16(2), (3) (for which the day appointed is also 1 July 1997 by virtue of the Finance Act 1997, Schedule 10, (Appointed Day) Order, SI 1997/991).

SCHEDULE 14

CAPITAL ALLOWANCES: VAT CAPITAL GOODS SCHEME

Section 59

Amendments—This Schedule repealed by the Capital Allowances Act 2001 s 580, Sch 4 with effect for income tax purposes, as respects allowances and charges falling to be made for chargeable periods ending on or after 6 April 2001, and for corporation tax purposes, as respects allowances and charges falling to be made for chargeable periods ending on or after 1 April 2001.

SCHEDULE 15

RELIEF FOR COMPANY TRADING LOSSES

Section 73

The Taxes Management Act 1970 (c 9)

1—(1) (*inserts* TMA 1970 s 86(2A)).

(2) The subsection (2A) inserted by sub-paragraph (1) above shall be omitted where the accounting period referred to in that subsection as the earlier period ends after the appointed day for the purposes of section 86 of the Finance (No 2) Act 1987 so far as relating to the omission of section 86 (2) (*d*) of the Taxes Management Act 1970.

Commentary—*Simon's Direct Tax Service* **A3.1321.**
Note—The appointed day mentioned in sub-para (2) above is 30 September 1993 by virtue of Corporation Tax Acts (Provisions for Payment of Tax and Returns) (Appointed Days) Order, SI 1992/3066 art 2(1), (2)(*a*).

2 (*inserted* TMA 1970 s 87A(6); *repealed by* FA 1993 ss 120, 213, Sch 14 para 8(1),(5), Sch 23 Pt III(11)).

The Income and Corporation Taxes Act 1988 (c 1)

3, 4 (*repeal* TA 1988 s 114(3)(*c*) and *amend* TA 1988, ss 118).

5 (*amends* TA 1988 s 242; *repealed by* F(No 2)A 1997 Sch 8 Pt II (4)).

6 (*amends* TA 1988 s 243; *repealed by* F(No 2)A 1997 Sch 8 Pt II (4)).

7, 8 (*amend* TA 1988 ss 343, 393).

9 (*amended* TA 1988 s 395; *repealed by* FA 1993 ss 120, 213, Sch 14 para 8(1), (5), Sch 23 Pt III(11)).

10–12 (*amend* TA 1988 ss 397, 399, 400).

13 ...[1]

Amendments—This paragraph repealed by FA 1998 Sch 27 Part III(4) with effect in relation to income tax for the year 1998–99 and subsequent years of assessment and for corporation tax from 1 April 1998 subject to transitional provisions in FA 1998 Sch 5 Part IV.

14–17 (*amend* TA 1988 ss 407, 434, 458, 492).

18 (*amends* TA 1988 s 503; *repealed by* FA 1995 s 162, Sch 29 Pt VIII(1), with effect generally from the year 1995–96 (but see FA 1995 s 39(4), (5))).

19–25 (*amend* TA 1988 ss 518, 769, 808, 843, Sch 5, para 2 and *insert* TA 1988 ss 768A, 825(4)(*c*), (*d*), 826(7A), (7B)).

26 ...[1]

Amendments—[1] This paragraph repealed by FA 1998 Sch 27 Part III(4) with effect in relation to income tax for the year 1998–99 and subsequent years of assessment and for corporation tax from 1 April 1998 subject to transitional provisions in FA 1998 Sch 5 Part IV.

27 (*amends* TA 1988 Sch 30 paras 2, 3).

The Capital Allowances Act 1990 (c 1)

28 (*amended* CAA 1990 s 17; *repealed by* CAA 2001 s 580, Sch 4 with effect in accordance with CAA 2001 s 579).

SCHEDULE 16

SETTLEMENTS: SETTLORS

Section 89

Amendments—This Schedule repealed by TCGA 1992 Sch 12.

SCHEDULE 17

SETTLEMENTS: BENEFICIARIES

Section 90

Commentary—*Simon's Direct Tax Service* **C4.443.**
Amendments—This Schedule repealed by TCGA 1992 Sch 12.

SCHEDULE 18

SETTLEMENTS: BENEFICIARIES (MISCELLANEOUS)

Section 91

Amendments—This Schedule repealed by TCGA 1992 Sch 12.

TAXATION OF CHARGEABLE GAINS ACT 1992

(1992 Chapter 12)

ARRANGEMENT OF SECTIONS

PART I

CAPITAL GAINS TAX AND CORPORATION TAX ON CHARGEABLE GAINS

General

PART II

GENERAL PROVISIONS RELATING TO COMPUTATION OF GAINS AND ACQUISITIONS AND DISPOSALS OF ASSETS

CHAPTER I

INTRODUCTORY

CHAPTER II

ASSETS AND DISPOSALS OF ASSETS

General provisions

CHAPTER II

SETTLEMENTS

General provisions

Migration of settlements, non-resident settlements and dual resident settlements

CHAPTER III

COLLECTIVE INVESTMENT SCHEMES AND INVESTMENT TRUSTS

PART IV

SHARES, SECURITIES, OPTIONS ETC

CHAPTER I

GENERAL

Share pooling, identification of securities, and indexation

CHAPTER III

MISCELLANEOUS PROVISIONS RELATING TO COMMODITIES, FUTURES, OPTIONS AND OTHER SECURITIES

PART V

TRANSFER OF BUSINESS ASSETS

CHAPTER I

GENERAL PROVISIONS

Replacement of business assets

Stock in trade

Transfer of business to a company

Retirement relief

CHAPTER IA

ROLL-OVER RELIEF ON RE-INVESTMENT

CHAPTER II

GIFTS OF BUSINESS ASSETS

PART VI

COMPANIES, OIL, INSURANCE ETC

CHAPTER I

COMPANIES

Groups of companies

Transactions within groups

Losses attributable to depreciatory transactions

Companies leaving groups

Restriction on indexation allowance for groups and associated companies

Non-resident and dual resident companies

PART VIII

SUPPLEMENTAL

SCHEDULES:

An Act to consolidate certain enactments relating to the taxation of chargeable gains.

[6th March 1992]

Revenue & other press releases—IR booklet CGT 14 (Capital gains tax: an introduction—includes *inter alia* a list of available helpsheets about particular CGT provisions).
Definitions—"Asset", s 21(1); "chargeable gain", s 15(2); "the Taxes Act", s 288(1).
Cross references—See TMA 1970 s 11(2)(*b*) (return of profits required to be made by a company);
TMA 1970 s 27(1) (settlor, trustee or beneficiary of settled property may be required to give necessary particulars for capital gains tax purposes);
TMA 1970 s 47(1) (appeal against capital gains tax assessment on land to be referred to Lands Tribunal);
TMA 1970 s 57(1)(*a*) (regulations about appeals on capital gains tax);
TMA 1970 s 111(1) (inspector of taxes to be permitted to inspect property for ascertainment of market value for capital gains tax purposes);
TMA 1970 s 119(4) (TMA 1970 so far as it relates to chargeable gains, to be construed as one with this Act);
TA 1970 s 278(3) (charge to capital gains tax when a company ceases to be a member of a group);
TA 1988 s 122(1), (2) (taxation of mineral royalties);
TA 1988 s 345(4) (computation of companies' capital gains);
TA 1988 s 442(3) (insurance companies' overseas business; treatment of profit or loss for the purposes of capital gains tax);
FA 1990 Sch 12 (transfers of undertakings of Independent Broadcasting Authority and Cable Authority).
F(No 2)A 1992 Sch 17 para 1(2) (F(No 2)A 1992 Sch 17 (transfer of the undertaking of Northern Ireland Electricity), so far as it relates to corporation tax on chargeable gains to be construed as one with this Act).
FA 1997 Sch 12 paras 12, 17 (computation of chargeable gain on disposal of certain leased assets or of lessor's interest).

PART I

CAPITAL GAINS TAX AND CORPORATION TAX ON CHARGEABLE GAINS

General

1 The charge to tax

(1) Tax shall be charged in accordance with this Act in respect of capital gains, that is to say chargeable gains computed in accordance with this Act and accruing to a person on the disposal of assets.

(2) Companies shall be chargeable to corporation tax in respect of chargeable gains accruing to them in accordance with section 6 of the Taxes Act and the other provisions of the Corporation Tax Acts.

(3) Without prejudice to subsection (2), capital gains tax shall be charged for all years of assessment in accordance with the following provisions of this Act.

Commentary—*Simon's Direct Tax Service* **C1.101.**
Simon's Tax Cases—*Turner v Follett* [1973] STC 148*.

Capital gains tax

2 Persons and gains chargeable to capital gains tax, and allowable losses

(1) Subject to any exceptions provided by this Act, and without prejudice to sections 10 and 276, a person shall be chargeable to capital gains tax in respect of chargeable gains accruing to him in a year of assessment during any part of which he is resident in the United Kingdom, or during which he is ordinarily resident in the United Kingdom.

(2) Capital gains tax shall be charged on the total amount of chargeable gains accruing to the person chargeable in the year of assessment, after deducting—

  (a) any allowable losses accruing to that person in that year of assessment, and
  (b) so far as they have not been allowed as a deduction from chargeable gains accruing in any previous year of assessment, any allowable losses accruing to that person in any previous year of assessment (not earlier than the year 1965–66).

(3) Except as provided by section 62, an allowable loss accruing in a year of assessment shall not be allowable as a deduction from chargeable gains accruing in any earlier year of assessment, and relief shall not be given under this Act more than once in respect of any loss or part of a loss, and shall not be given under this Act if and so far as relief has been or may be given in respect of it under the Income Tax Acts.

[(4) Where any amount is treated by virtue of any of sections 77, 86, 87 and 89(2) (read, where applicable, with section 10A) as an amount of chargeable gains accruing to any person in any year of assessment—

  (a) that amount shall be disregarded for the purposes of subsection (2) above; and
  (b) the amount on which that person shall be charged to capital gains tax for that year (instead of being the amount given by that subsection) shall be the sum of the amounts specified in subsection (5) below.

(5) Those amounts are—

  (a) the amount which after—

    (i) making any deductions for which subsection (2) provides, and
    (ii) applying any reduction in respect of taper relief under section 2A,

is the amount given for the year of assessment by the application of that subsection in accordance with subsection (4)(a) above; and
  (b) every amount which is treated by virtue of sections 77, 86, 87 and 89(2) (read, where applicable, with section 10A) as an amount of chargeable gains accruing to the person in question in that year.][1]

Commentary—*Simon's Direct Tax Service* **C1.101, 102.**
Concession A11—Residence in the UK: year of commencement or cessation of residence.
D2—Residence in the UK: year of commencement or cessation of residence.
Statements of Practice D7—Treatment of VAT.
SP 3/81—Individuals coming to the UK: ordinary residence.
Simon's Tax Cases—s 2(2), *Ritchie v Mckay* [1984] STC 422*.
Definitions—"Allowable loss", ss 8(2), 16, 288(1); "chargeable gain", s 15(2); "ordinarily resident", s 9(1); "resident", s 9(1); "year of assessment", s 288(1).
Cross references—See TA 1988 s 761(2) (application of this section to offshore income gains).
TCGA 1992 Sch 5 para 1(2) (construction of certain provisions of s 86 (which attaches tax charge to settlor of a non-resident settlement) by reference to sub-s (2) above).
FA 2002 Sch 11 para 8 (election for prospective amendments made by FA 2002 ss 51, 141, Sch 11, Sch 40 Pt 3(4) to apply with effect for chargeable gains treated as accruing to a person by virtue of TCGA 1992 s 77 or 86 (read, where appropriate, with TCGA s 10A) in any or all of the tax years 2000–01, 2001–02, and 2002–03).
Amendments—[1] Sub-ss (4), (5) inserted by FA 1998 Sch 21 para 2 with effect from the year 1998–99.
Prospective amendments—In sub-s (5), para (aa) to be substituted for the word "and" at the end of para (a), in para (b), figures "77, 86" to be repealed; and sub-ss (6)–(8) to be inserted, by FA 2002 ss 51, 141, Sch 11 paras 1, 2, 7, Sch 40 Pt 3(4), with effect for chargeable gains treated as accruing to a person by virtue of TCGA 1992 s 77 or 86 (read, where appropriate, with TCGA 1992 s 10A) from 2003–04. Para (aa) as substituted to read as follows—

"(aa) every amount which is treated by virtue of sections 77 and 86 as an amount of chargeable gains accruing to the person in question for that year, reduced as follows—

  (i) first, by making the deductions for which subsection (2) provides in respect of any allowable losses accruing to that person;
  (ii) then, where taper relief would be deductible by the trustees of the settlement in question but for section 77(1)(b)(i) or 86(1)(e)(ii), by applying reductions in respect of taper relief under section 2A at the rates that would be applicable in the case of the trustees;

and".

Sub-ss (6)–(8) as inserted to read as follows—

"(6) Allowable losses must (notwithstanding section 2A(6)) be deducted under paragraph (a)(i) of subsection (5) above before any may be deducted under paragraph (aa)(i) of that subsection.

(7) Where in any year of assessment—

(a) there are amounts treated as accruing to a person by virtue of section 77 or 86,
(b) two or more of those amounts, or elements of them—

(i) relate to different settlements, and
(ii) attract taper relief (by virtue of subsection (5)(aa)(ii) above) at the same rate, or are not eligible for taper relief, and

(c) losses are deductible from the amounts or elements mentioned in paragraph (b) above (''the equal-tapered amounts'') but are not enough to exhaust them all,
the deduction applicable to each of the equal-tapered amounts shall be the appropriate proportion of the aggregate of those losses.

The ''appropriate proportion'' is that given by dividing the equal-tapered amount in question by the total of the equal-tapered amounts.

(8) The references to section 86 in subsection (5)(aa) above (in the opening words) and subsection (7)(a) above include references to that section read with section 10A.''.

[2A Taper relief

(1) This section applies where, for any year of assessment—

(a) there is, in any person's case, an excess of the total amount referred to in subsection (2) of section 2 over the amounts falling to be deducted from that amount in accordance with that subsection; and
(b) the excess is or includes an amount representing the whole or a part of any chargeable gain that is eligible for taper relief.

(2) The amount on which capital gains tax is taken to be charged by virtue of section 2(2) shall be reduced to the amount computed by—

(a) applying taper relief to so much of every chargeable gain eligible for that relief as is represented in the excess;
(b) aggregating the results; and
(c) adding to the aggregate of the results so much of every chargeable gain not eligible for taper relief as is represented in the excess.

(3) Subject to the following provisions of this Act, a chargeable gain is eligible for taper relief if—

(a) it is a gain on the disposal of a business asset with a qualifying holding period of at least one year; or
(b) it is a gain on the disposal of a non-business asset with a qualifying holding period of at least three years.

(4) Where taper relief falls to be applied to the whole or any part of a gain on the disposal of a business or non-business asset, that relief shall be applied by multiplying the amount of that gain or part of a gain by the percentage given by the table in subsection (5) below for the number of whole years in the qualifying holding period of that asset.

(5) That table is as follows—

[Gains on disposals of business assets		Gains on disposals of non-business assets	
[Number of whole years in qualifying holding period	Percentage of gain chargeable	Number of whole years in qualifying holding period	Percentage of gain chargeable
1	50	—	—
2 or more	25]⁴	—	—
		3	95
		4	90
		5	85
		6	80
		7	75
		8	70
		9	65
		10 or more	60

(6) The extent to which the whole or any part of a gain on the disposal of a business or non-business asset is to be treated as represented in the excess mentioned in subsection (1) above shall be determined by treating deductions made in accordance with section 2(2)(a) and (b) as set against chargeable gains in such order as results in the largest reduction under this section of the amount charged to capital gains tax under section 2.

(7) Schedule A1 shall have effect for the purposes of this section.

[(8) The qualifying holding period of an asset for the purposes of this section is—

(a) in the case of a business asset, the period after 5th April 1998 for which the asset had been held at the time of its disposal;
(b) in the case of a non-business asset where—

(i) the time which, for the purposes of paragraph 2 of Schedule A1, is the time when the asset is taken to have been acquired by the person making the disposal is a time before 17th March 1998, and

(ii) there is no period which by virtue of paragraph ...[5] 12 of that Schedule does not count for the purposes of taper relief,

the period mentioned in paragraph (*a*) plus one year;

(*c*) in the case of any other non-business asset, the period mentioned in paragraph (*a*).

This subsection is subject to paragraph 2(4) of Schedule A1 and paragraph 3 of Schedule 5BA.][3]

Commentary—*Simon's Direct Tax Service* C1.403; C2.1401.
Revenue Internal Guidance—Capital gains manual CG 17897 (sub-s (8): outlines modifications to the basic rule governing the qualifying holding period).
CG 17902 (meaning of "bonus year" and example).
CG 17903 (example illustrating how taper relief is given).
CG 17976 (allowable losses are to be relieved in the most beneficial way: worked examples).
CG 27626, CG 27627, CG 27628 (worked examples where an individual partner disposes of all or part of their fractional share in a partnership asset on or after 6 April 1998).
Cross references—TCGA 1992 Sch 5BA (application of taper relief on the disposal of shares to which EIS deferral relief or income tax relief is attributable).
Amendments—[1] This section inserted by FA 1998 s 121(1) with effect from the year 1998–99.
[2] Words in sub-s (8) inserted by FA 1999 s 72(3).
[3] Sub-s (8) substituted for original sub-ss (8), (9) by FA 2000 s 66 with effect for disposals after 5 April 2000.
[4] First two columns in table in sub-s (5) substituted by FA 2002 s 46 with effect for disposals after 5 April 2002.
[5] In sub-s (8)(*b*), words "11 or" repealed by FA 2002 s 141, Sch 40 Pt 3(3) with effect for disposals after 17 April 2002. This amendment has effect for periods of ownership after that date: FA 2002 Sch 10 paras 2, 4, 7.

3 Annual exempt amount

(1) An individual shall not be chargeable to capital gains tax in respect of so much of his taxable amount for any year of assessment as does not exceed the exempt amount for the year.

(2) Subject to subsection (3) below, the exempt amount for any year of assessment shall be [£7,700][1].

(3) If the retail prices index for the month of [September][2] preceding a year of assessment is higher than it was for the previous [September][2], then, unless Parliament otherwise determines, subsection (2) above shall have effect for that year as if for the amount specified in that subsection as it applied for the previous year (whether by virtue of this subsection or otherwise) there were substituted an amount arrived at by increasing the amount for the previous year by the same percentage as the percentage increase in the retail prices index and, if the result is not a multiple of £100, rounding it up to the nearest amount which is such a multiple.

(4) The Treasury shall, before each year of assessment, make an order specifying the amount which by virtue of this section is the exempt amount for that year.

[(5) For the purposes of this section an individual's taxable amount for any year of assessment is the amount which, after—

(*a*) making every deduction for which section 2(2) provides,
(*b*) applying any reduction in respect of taper relief under section 2A, and
(*c*) adding any amounts falling to be added by virtue of section 2(5)(*b*),

is (apart from this section) the amount for that year on which that individual is chargeable to capital gains tax in accordance with section 2.

(5A) Where, in the case of any individual, the amount of the adjusted net gains for any year of assessment is equal to or less than the exempt amount for that year, no deduction shall be made for that year in respect of—

(*a*) any allowable losses carried forward from a previous year; or
(*b*) any allowable losses carried back from a subsequent year in which the individual dies.

(5B) Where, in the case of any individual, the amount of the adjusted net gains for any year of assessment exceeds the exempt amount for the year, the deductions made for that year in respect of allowable losses falling within subsection (5A)(*a*) or (*b*) above shall not be greater than the excess.

(5C) In subsections (5A) and (5B) above the references, in relation to any individual's case, to the adjusted net gains for any year are references to the amount given in his case by—

(*a*) taking the amount for that year from which the deductions for which section 2(2)(*a*) and (*b*) provides are to be made;
(*b*) deducting only the amounts falling to be deducted in accordance with section 2(2)(*a*); and
(*c*) in a year in which any amount falls to be brought into account by virtue of section 2(5)(*b*), adding whichever is the smaller of the exempt amount for that year and the amount falling to be so brought into account.][3]

(6) Where in a year of assessment—

(*a*) the amount of chargeable gains accruing to an individual does not exceed the exempt amount for the year, and
(*b*) the aggregate amount or value of the consideration for all the disposals of assets made by him (other than disposals gains accruing on which are not chargeable gains) does not exceed an amount equal to twice the exempt amount for the year,

a statement to the effect of paragraphs (*a*) and (*b*) above shall, unless the inspector otherwise requires, be sufficient compliance with any notice under section 8 of the Management Act requiring the individual to make a return of the chargeable gains accruing to him in that year.

(7) For the year of assessment in which an individual dies and for the next 2 following years, subsections (1) to (6) above shall apply to his personal representatives as they apply to an individual.

(8) Schedule 1 shall have effect as respects the application of this section to trustees.

Commentary—*Simon's Direct Tax Service* **C1.401, 503; C2.1403.**
Revenue Internal Guidance—Capital gains manual CG 18031 (Revenue procedures for annual exemption and losses 1998–99 onwards).
CG 18199–18207 (worked examples).
Definitions—"Allowable loss", ss 8(2), 16, 288(1); "asset", s 21(1); "chargeable gain", s 15(2); "inspector", s 288(1); "the Management Act", s 288(1); "notice", s 288(1); "personal representatives", s 288(1), TA 1988 s 701(4); "retail prices index", s 288(2), TA 1988 s 833(2); "year of assessment", s 288(1).
Cross references—See TCGA 1992 s 287(4) (exception for the purposes of sub-s (4) above to the general rule of orders being subject to annulment by Parliament).
TCGA 1992 Sch 5 para 1(1) (effect of this section to be ignored for certain provisions of s 86 which attaches tax charge to settlor of a non-resident settlement).
Amendments—[1] Amount in sub-s (2) specified for the year 2002–03 by virtue of the CGT (Annual Exempt Amount) Order, SI 2002/702 art 2.
[2] "September" in sub-s (3) substituted by FA 1993 s 83 with effect from the year 1994–95.
[3] Sub-ss (5), (5A)–(5C), substituted by FA 1998 Sch 21 para 3 with effect from the year 1998–99.

4 Rates of capital gains tax

(1) Subject to the provisions of this section ...[1], the rate of capital gains tax in respect of gains accruing to a person in a year of assessment shall be equivalent to the [lower rate][4] of income tax for the year.

[(1AA) The rate of capital gains tax in respect of gains accruing to—

    (*a*) the trustees of a settlement, or

    (*b*) the personal representatives of a deceased person,

in a year of assessment shall be equivalent to the rate which for that year is [the rate applicable to trusts under section 686 of the Taxes Act][4].][2]

[(1AB) If (after allowing for any deductions in accordance with the Income Tax Acts) an individual has no income for a year of assessment or his total income for the year is less than the starting rate limit, then—

    (*a*) if the amount on which he is chargeable to capital gains tax does not exceed the unused part of his starting rate band, the rate of capital gains tax in respect of gains accruing to him in the year shall be equivalent to the starting rate;

    (*b*) if the amount on which he is chargeable to capital gains tax exceeds the unused part of his starting rate band, the rate of capital gains tax in respect of such gains accruing to him in the year as correspond to the unused part shall be equivalent to the starting rate.

(1AC) The references in subsection (1AB) above to the unused part of an individual's starting rate band are to the amount by which the starting rate limit exceeds his total income (as reduced by any deductions made in accordance with the Income Tax Acts).][6]

(1A), (1B) ...[5]

(2) If income tax is chargeable at the higher rate [or the Schedule F upper rate][3] in respect of any part of the income of an individual for a year of assessment, the rate of capital gains tax in respect of gains accruing to him in the year shall be equivalent to the higher rate.

(3) If no income tax is chargeable at the higher rate [or the Schedule F upper rate][3] in respect of the income of an individual for a year of assessment, but the amount on which he is chargeable to capital gains tax exceeds the unused part of his basic rate band, the rate of capital gains tax on the excess shall be equivalent to the higher rate of income tax for the year.

(3A), (3B) ...[5]

(4) The reference in subsection (3) above to the unused part of an individual's basic rate band is a reference to the amount by which ...[5] the basic rate limit exceeds his total income (as reduced by any deductions made in accordance with the Income Tax Acts).

Commentary—*Simon's Direct Tax Service* **C1.107.**
Revenue Interpretation RI 48—Repayment of overpaid CGT resulting from retrospective reduction(s) in CGT rate(s) applicable to individuals caused, for example, by terminal loss relief.
Definitions—"Basic rate limit", TA 1988 s 832(1); "higher rate", s 6 and TA 1988 s 832(1); "Income Tax Acts", TA 1988 s 831(1); "lower rate", TA 1988 s 832(1); "lower rate limit", TA 1988 s 1(2A); "total income", TA 1988 s 835; "year of assessment" s 288(1).
Cross references—See TA 1988 s 1A(1B) (lower rate for the year 2000–01 is 20%)
Amendments—[1] Words in sub-s (1) repealed by FA 1998 s 165, Sch 27 Pt III(29) with effect from the year 1998–99.
[2] Sub-s (1AA) inserted by FA 1998 s 120(1) with effect from the year 1998–99.
[3] Words in sub-ss (2), (3), (4) inserted by F(No 2)A 1997 s 34, Sch 4 para 24 with effect from the year 1999–00.
[4] Words in sub-ss (1), (1AA) substituted by FA 1999 s 26(2), (3), (6) with effect from the year 1999–00.
[5] Sub-ss (1A), (1B), (3A), (3B), and words in sub-s (4), repealed by FA 1999 s 26(4), (5), (6), Sch 20 Pt III(1) with effect from the year 1999–00.
[6] Sub-ss (1AB), (1AC) inserted by FA 2000 s 37 with effect from the year 2000–01.

5 Accumulation and discretionary settlements

Amendments—This section repealed by FA 1998 s 165, Sch 27 Part III(29) with effect from the year 1998–99.

6 Other special cases

(1) ...[1]

(2) Where for any year of assessment—

(a) by virtue of section 549(2) of the Taxes Act (gains under life policy or life annuity contract) a deduction of an amount is made from a person's total income for the purposes of excess liability, or

(b) ...[1]

(c) by virtue of section 699(1) of that Act (income accruing before death) the residuary income of an estate is treated as reduced so as to reduce a person's income by any amount for those purposes,

section 4(4) shall have effect as if his income for the year were reduced by that amount.

(3) Where by virtue of section 547(1)(a) of the Taxes Act (gains from insurance policies etc) a person's total income for a year of assessment is deemed to include any amount or amounts—

(a) section 4(4) shall have effect as if his total income included not the whole of the amount or amounts concerned but only the appropriate fraction within the meaning of section 550(3) of that Act, and

(b) if relief is given under section 550 of that Act and the calculation required by section 550(2)(b) does not involve the higher rate of income tax, section 4(2) and (3) shall have effect as if no income tax were chargeable at the higher rate [or the Schedule F upper rate][2] in respect of his income.

(4) Nothing in subsection (1) above shall be taken to reduce, and nothing in subsections (2) and (3) above shall be taken to increase, the amount of the deduction which a person is entitled to make from his total income by virtue of any provision of Chapter I of Part VII of the Taxes Act which limits any allowance by reference to the level of his total income.

Commentary—*Simon's Direct Tax Service* C1.107.
Definitions—"Basic rate", TA 1988 s 832(1); "lower rate", TA 1988 s 832(1); "the Taxes Act", s 288(1); "year of assessment", s 288(1).
Amendments—[1] Sub-ss (1), (2)(b), repealed by FA 1995 s 162, Sch 29 Pt VIII(8), with effect from the year 1995–96.
[2] Words in sub-s (3)(b) inserted by F(No 2)A 1997 s 34, Sch 4 para 25 from the year 1999–00.

7 Time for payment of tax

Commentary—*Simon's Direct Tax Service* C1.108.
Amendments—This section repealed by FA 1995 s 103(7), 115(12) Sch 29 Pt VIII(14) with effect from the year 1996–97.

Corporation tax

8 Company's total profits to include chargeable gains

(1) Subject to the provisions of this section and section 400 of the Taxes Act, the amount to be included in respect of chargeable gains in a company's total profits for any accounting period shall be the total amount of chargeable gains accruing to the company in the accounting period after deducting—

(a) any allowable losses accruing to the company in the period, and

(b) so far as they have not been allowed as a deduction from chargeable gains accruing in any previous accounting period, any allowable losses previously accruing to the company while it has been within the charge to corporation tax.

(2) For the purposes of corporation tax in respect of chargeable gains, "allowable loss" does not include a loss accruing to a company in such circumstances that if a gain accrued the company would be exempt from corporation tax in respect of it.

(3) Except as otherwise provided by this Act or any other provision of the Corporation Tax Acts, the total amount of the chargeable gains to be included in respect of chargeable gains in a company's total profits for any accounting period shall for purposes of corporation tax be computed in accordance with the principles applying for capital gains tax, all questions—

(a) as to the amounts which are or are not to be taken into account as chargeable gains or as allowable losses, or in computing gains or losses, or charged to tax as a person's gain; or

(b) as to the time when any such amount is to be treated as accruing,

being determined in accordance with the provisions relating to capital gains tax as if accounting periods were years of assessment.

(4) Subject to subsection (5) below, where the enactments relating to capital gains tax contain any reference to income tax or to the Income Tax Acts the reference shall, in relation to a company, be construed as a reference to corporation tax or to the Corporation Tax Acts; but—

(a) this subsection shall not affect the references to income tax in section 39(2); and

(b) in so far as those enactments operate by reference to matters of any specified description, account shall for corporation tax be taken of matters of that description which are confined to companies, but not of any which are confined to individuals.

(5) This Act as it has effect in accordance with this section shall not be affected in its operation by the fact that capital gains tax and corporation tax are distinct taxes but, so far as is consistent with

the Corporation Tax Acts, shall apply in relation to capital gains tax and corporation tax on chargeable gains as if they were one tax, so that, in particular, a matter which in a case involving 2 individuals is relevant for both of them in relation to capital gains tax shall in a like case involving an individual and a company be relevant for him in relation to that tax and for it in relation to corporation tax.

(6) Where assets of a company are vested in a liquidator under section 145 of the Insolvency Act 1986 or Article 123 of the Insolvency (Northern Ireland) Order 1989 or otherwise, this section and the enactments applied by this section shall apply as if the assets were vested in, and the acts of the liquidator in relation to the assets were the acts of, the company (acquisitions from or disposals to him by the company being disregarded accordingly).

Commentary—*Simon's Direct Tax Service* **D2.301.**
Revenue Internal Guidance—Company Taxation Manual COT3432 (there is no rebasing of cost where a non-resident company becomes resident in the UK).
Definitions—"Allowable loss", ss 8(2), 16, 288(1); "asset", s 21(1); "chargeable gain", s 15(2); "company", ss 99, 288(1); "the Taxes Act", s 288(1).
Cross references—See Exchange Gains and Losses (Transitional Provisions) Regulations, SI 1994/3226 reg 16(12) (no deduction under this section for allowable losses within an election to set off pre-commencement losses against exchange gains).

Residence etc

9 Residence, including temporary residence

(1) In this Act "resident" and "ordinarily resident" have the same meanings as in the Income Tax Acts.

(2) Section 207 of the Taxes Act (disputes as to domicile or ordinary residence) shall apply in relation to capital gains tax as it applies for the purposes mentioned in that section.

(3) Subject to [sections 10(1) and 10A]², an individual who is in the United Kingdom for some temporary purpose only and not with any view or intent to establish his residence in the United Kingdom shall be charged to capital gains tax on chargeable gains accruing in any year of assessment if and only if the period (or the sum of the periods) for which he is resident in the United Kingdom in that year of assessment exceeds 6 months.

[(4) The question whether for the purposes of subsection (3) above an individual is in the United Kingdom for some temporary purpose only and not with any view or intent to establish his residence there shall be decided without regard to any living accommodation available in the United Kingdom for his use.]¹

Commentary—*Simon's Direct Tax Service* **C1.201, 601.**
Concession A11—Residence in the UK: year of commencement or cessation of residence.
D2—Residence in the UK: year of commencement or cessation of residence.
Statement of Practice SP 3/81—Individuals coming to the UK: ordinary residence.
Definitions—"Chargeable gain", s 15(2); "ordinarily resident", s 9(1); "resident", s 9(1); "the Taxes Act", s 288(1); "year of assessment", s 288(1).
Amendments—¹ Sub-s (4) inserted by FA 1993 s 208(2), (4) with effect from the year 1993–94.
² Words in sub-s (3) substituted by FA 1998 s 127(2) with effect in any case in which the year of departure is the year 1998–99 or a subsequent year of assessment; and in any case in which the year of departure is the year 1997–98 and the taxpayer was resident or ordinarily resident in the United Kingdom at a time in that year on or after 17 March 1998.

10 Non-resident with United Kingdom branch or agency

(1) Subject to any exceptions provided by this Act, a person shall be chargeable to capital gains tax in respect of chargeable gains accruing to him in a year of assessment in which he is not resident and not ordinarily resident in the United Kingdom but is carrying on a trade in the United Kingdom through a branch or agency, and shall be so chargeable on chargeable gains accruing on the disposal—

   (*a*) of assets situated in the United Kingdom and used in or for the purposes of the trade at or before the time when the capital gain accrued, or

   (*b*) of assets situated in the United Kingdom and used or held for the purposes of the branch or agency at or before that time, or assets acquired for use by or for the purposes of the branch or agency.

(2) Subsection (1) above does not apply unless the disposal is made at a time when the person is carrying on the trade in the United Kingdom through a branch or agency.

(3) For the purposes of corporation tax the chargeable profits of a company not resident in the United Kingdom but carrying on a trade or vocation there through a branch or agency shall be, or include, such chargeable gains accruing on the disposal of assets situated in the United Kingdom as are by this section made chargeable to capital gains tax in the case of an individual not resident or ordinarily resident in the United Kingdom.

(4) This section shall not apply to a person who, by virtue of Part XVIII of the Taxes Act (double taxation relief agreements), is exempt from income tax or corporation tax chargeable for the chargeable period in respect of the profits or gains of the branch or agency.

(5) This section shall apply as if references in subsections (1) and (2) above to a trade included references to a profession or vocation, but subsection (1) shall not apply in respect of chargeable gains accruing on the disposal of assets only used in or for the purposes of the profession or vocation

before 14th March 1989 or only used or held for the purposes of the branch or agency before that date.

(6) In this Act, unless the context otherwise requires, "branch or agency" means any factorship, agency, receivership, branch or management, but does not include any person within the exemptions in section 82 of the Management Act (general agents and brokers).

Commentary—*Simon's Direct Tax Service* **C1.602.**
Statement of Practice SP 4/92—Capital gains rebasing elections.
Revenue Internal Guidance—Capital gains tax manual CG 42161–42170 (gain based on actual cost: no allowance for period before branch trading started: worked example—see CG 42170).
Simon's Tax Cases—s 10(6), *Young v Phillips* [1984] STC 520*.
Definitions—"Asset", s 21(1); "branch or agency", s 10(6); "chargeable gain", s 15(2); "chargeable period", s 288(1); "company", ss 99, 288(1); "the Management Act", s 288(1); "ordinarily resident", s 9(1); "resident", s 9(1); "the Taxes Act", s 288(1); "trade", s 288(1), TA 1988 s 832(1); "year of assessment", s 288(1).
Cross references—See TA 1988 s 11(2)(*b*) (gains chargeable to capital gains tax under this section are chargeable to corporation tax if they accrue to a non-resident company);
TA 1988 s 761(2)–(4) (modification of this section in its application to offshore income gains).
TCGA 1992 s 9(3) (exception to sub-s (1) above in the case of an individual temporarily present in the UK).
TCGA 1992 s 13(5)(*d*) (taxation of gains of non-resident "close" company; avoidance of charge under s 13 where gains are chargeable under sub-s (3) above).
TCGA 1992 s 16(3) (treatment of losses incurred by a non-resident).
TCGA 1992 s 140A(2) (transfer of a UK trade by one member State company to another member State company).
FA 1995 s 126(2)(*c*) (UK representatives of non-residents).
FA 2000 Sch 15 para 79(5) (a chargeable gain accruing on a chargeable event for the purposes of para 79 is treated as accruing on the disposal of an asset to which sub-s (3) above applies).
Note—TMA 1970 s 82 (as referred to in sub-s (6)) repealed by FA 1995 s 162, Sch 29 Pt VIII(16); see now FA 1995 s 126(2)(*c*) (UK representatives of non-residents).

[10A Temporary non-residents

(1) This section applies in the case of any individual ("the taxpayer") if—

   (*a*) he satisfies the residence requirements for any year of assessment ("the year of return");
   (*b*) he did not satisfy those requirements for one or more years of assessment immediately preceding the year of return but there are years of assessment before that year for which he did satisfy those requirements;
   (*c*) there are fewer than five years of assessment falling between the year of departure and the year of return; and
   (*d*) four out of the seven years of assessment immediately preceding the year of departure are also years of assessment for each of which he satisfied those requirements.

(2) Subject to the following provisions of this section and section 86A, the taxpayer shall be chargeable to capital gains tax as if—

   (*a*) all the chargeable gains and losses which (apart from this subsection) would have accrued to him in an intervening year,
   (*b*) all the chargeable gains which under section 13 or 86 would be treated as having accrued to him in an intervening year if he had been resident in the United Kingdom throughout that intervening year, and
   (*c*) any losses which by virtue of section 13(8) would have been allowable in his case in any intervening year if he had been resident in the United Kingdom throughout that intervening year,

were gains or, as the case may be, losses accruing to the taxpayer in the year of return.

(3) Subject to subsection (4) below, the gains and losses which by virtue of subsection (2) above are to be treated as accruing to the taxpayer in the year of return shall not include any gain or loss accruing on the disposal by the taxpayer of any asset if—

   (*a*) that asset was acquired by the taxpayer at a time in the year of departure or any intervening year when he was neither resident nor ordinarily resident in the United Kingdom;
   (*b*) that asset was so acquired otherwise than by means of a relevant disposal which by virtue of section 58, 73 or 258(4) is treated as having been a disposal on which neither a gain nor a loss accrued;
   (*c*) that asset is not an interest created by or arising under a settlement; and
   (*d*) the amount or value of the consideration for the acquisition of that asset by the taxpayer does not fall, by reference to any relevant disposal, to be treated as reduced under section 23(4)(*b*) or (5)(*b*), 152(1)(*b*), 162(3)(*b*) or 247(2)(*b*) or (3)(*b*).

(4) Where—

   (*a*) any chargeable gain that has accrued or would have accrued on the disposal of any asset ("the first asset") is a gain falling (apart from this section) to be treated by virtue of section 116(10) or (11), 134 or 154(2) or (4) as accruing on the disposal of the whole or any part of another asset, and
   (*b*) the other asset is an asset falling within paragraphs (*a*) to (*d*) of subsection (3) above but the first asset is not,

subsection (3) above shall not exclude that gain from the gains which by virtue of subsection (2) above are to be treated as accruing to the taxpayer in the year of return.

(5) The gains and losses which by virtue of subsection (2) above are to be treated as accruing to the taxpayer in the year of return shall not include any chargeable gain or allowable loss accruing to the

taxpayer in an intervening year which, in the taxpayer's case, has fallen to be brought into account for that year by virtue of section 10 or 16(3).

(6) The reference in subsection (2)(c) above to losses allowable in an individual's case in an intervening year is a reference to only so much of the aggregate of the losses that would have been available in accordance with subsection (8) of section 13 for reducing gains accruing by virtue of that section to that individual in that year as does not exceed the amount of the gains that would have accrued to him in that year if it had been a year throughout which he was resident in the United Kingdom.

(7) Where this section applies in the case of any individual, nothing in any enactment imposing any limit on the time within which an assessment to capital gains tax may be made shall prevent any such assessment for the year of departure from being made in the taxpayer's case at any time before the end of two years after the 31st January next following the year of return.

(8) In this section—

"intervening year" means any year of assessment which, in a case where the conditions in paragraphs (a) to (d) of subsection (1) above are satisfied, falls between the year of departure and the year of return;

"relevant disposal", means a disposal of an asset acquired by the person making the disposal at a time when that person was resident or ordinarily resident in the United Kingdom; and

"the year of departure" means the last year of assessment before the year of return for which the taxpayer satisfied the residence requirements.

(9) For the purposes of this section an individual satisfies the residence requirements for a year of assessment if that year of assessment is one during any part of which he is resident in the United Kingdom or during which he is ordinarily resident in the United Kingdom.

(10) This section is without prejudice to any right to claim relief in accordance with any double taxation relief arrangements.][1]

Commentary—*Simon's Direct Tax Service* **C1.601.**
Revenue Internal Guidance—Capital gains manual CG 26100–26999 (explanation of this section and Revenue procedures).
Amendments—[1] This section inserted by FA 1998 s 127(1) with effect in any case in which the year of departure is the year 1998–99 or a subsequent year of assessment; and in any case in which the year of departure is the year 1997–98 and the taxpayer was resident or ordinarily resident in the United Kingdom at a time in that year on or after 17 March 1998.

11 Visiting forces, agents-general etc

(1) A period during which a member of a visiting force to whom section 323(1) of the Taxes Act applies is in the United Kingdom by reason solely of his being a member of that force shall not be treated for the purposes of capital gains tax either as a period of residence in the United Kingdom or as creating a change in his residence or domicile.

This subsection shall be construed as one with subsection (2) of section 323 and subsections (4) to (8) of that section shall apply accordingly.

(2) An Agent-General who is resident in the United Kingdom shall be entitled to the same immunity from capital gains tax as that to which the head of a mission so resident is entitled under the Diplomatic Privileges Act 1964.

(3) Any person having or exercising any employment to which section 320(2) of the Taxes Act (staff of Agents-General etc) applies (not being a person employed in any trade, business or other undertaking carried on for the purposes of profit) shall be entitled to the same immunity from capital gains tax as that to which a member of the staff of a mission is entitled under the Diplomatic Privileges Act 1964.

(4) Subsections (2) and (3) above shall be construed as one with section 320 of the Taxes Act.

Commentary—*Simon's Direct Tax Service* **C1.221.**
Concession A11—Residence in the UK: year of commencement or cessation of residence.
D2—Residence in the UK: year of commencement or cessation of residence.
Statement of Practice SP 3/81—Individuals coming to the UK: ordinary residence.
Definitions—"Resident", s 9(1); "the Taxes Act", s 288(1); trade", s 288(1), TA 1988 s 832(1).
Cross references—Visiting Forces and Allied Headquarters (Income Tax and Capital Gains Tax) (Designation) Order 1998, SI 1998/1513 and Visiting Forces (Income Tax and Capital Gains Tax) (Designation) Order 1998, SI 1998/1514.

12 Foreign assets of person with foreign domicile

(1) In the case of individuals resident or ordinarily resident but not domiciled in the United Kingdom, capital gains tax shall not be charged in respect of gains accruing to them from the disposal of assets situated outside the United Kingdom (that is, chargeable gains accruing in the year 1965–66 or a later year of assessment) except that the tax shall be charged on the amounts (if any) received in the United Kingdom in respect of those chargeable gains, any such amounts being treated as gains accruing when they are received in the United Kingdom.

(2) For the purposes of this section there shall be treated as received in the United Kingdom in respect of any gain all amounts paid, used or enjoyed in or in any manner or form transmitted or brought to the United Kingdom, and subsections (6) to (9) of section 65 of the Taxes Act (under which income applied outside the United Kingdom in payment of debts is, in certain cases, treated

as received in the United Kingdom) shall apply as they would apply for the purposes of subsection (5) of that section if the gain were income arising from possessions out of the United Kingdom.

Commentary—*Simon's Direct Tax Service* C1.603.
Revenue Internal Guidance—Capital gains manual CG 25310 (gains arising when resident abroad are ignored).
CG 25311–25312 (gains arising when domicile abroad remain chargeable if remitted after the acquisition of United Kingdom domicile).
CG 25320 (indexation relief is given only up to the date of disposal).
CG 25331–25332 (gains arising from gifts for no consideration and other deemed disposals cannot be remitted and are not chargeable).
CG 25350–25440 (meaning of "received in the United Kingdom", with worked example).
Simon's Tax Cases—s 12(1), *Young v Phillips* [1984] STC 520*; *White (Paul) v Carline* [1995] STC (SCD) 186*; *Puddu v Doleman* [1995] STC (SCD) 236*.
Definitions—"Asset", s 21(1); "chargeable gain", s 15(2); "ordinarily resident", s 9(1); "resident", s 9(1); "the Taxes Act", s 288(1); "year of assessment", s 288(1).
Cross references—See TA 1988 s 761(5) (application of this section to offshore income gains);
FA 1988 s 104(3) (claim by husband under this section in respect of chargeable gains accruing to wife before 6 April 1990).
TCGA 1992 s 16(4) (treatment of losses incurred by a person resident but not domiciled in the UK).

13 Attribution of gains to members of non-resident companies

(1) This section applies as respects chargeable gains accruing to a company—

   (*a*) which is not resident in the United Kingdom, and
   (*b*) which would be a close company if it were resident in the United Kingdom.

(2) Subject to this section, every person who at the time when the chargeable gain accrues to the company is resident or ordinarily resident in the United Kingdom, who, if an individual, is domiciled in the United Kingdom, and who [is a participator][1] in the company, shall be treated for the purposes of this Act as if a part of the chargeable gain had accrued to him.

[(3) That part shall be equal to the proportion of the gain that corresponds to the extent of the participator's interest as a participator in the company.][1]

[(4) Subsection (2) above shall not apply in the case of any participator in the company to which the gain accrues where the aggregate amount falling under that subsection to be apportioned to him and to persons connected with him does not exceed [one tenth][4] of the gain.][1]

(5) This section shall not apply in relation to—

   (*a*) ...[1]
   [(*b*) a chargeable gain accruing on the disposal of an asset used, and used only—

      (i) for the purposes of a trade carried on by the company wholly outside the United Kingdom, or
      (ii) for the purposes of the part carried on outside the United Kingdom of a trade carried on by the company partly within and partly outside the United Kingdom,][4] or

   (*c*) a chargeable gain accruing on the disposal of currency or of a debt within section 252(1), where the currency or debt is or represents money in use for the purposes of a trade carried on by the company wholly outside the United Kingdom, or
   (*d*) to a chargeable gain in respect of which the company is chargeable to tax by virtue of section 10(3).

[(5A) Where—

   (*a*) an amount of tax is paid by a person in pursuance of subsection (2) above, and
   (*b*) an amount in respect of the chargeable gain is distributed (either by way of dividend or distribution of capital or on the dissolution of the company) before the end of the period specified in subsection (5B) below,

the amount of tax (so far as neither reimbursed by the company nor applied as a deduction under subsection (7) below) shall be applied for reducing or extinguishing any liability of that person to income tax, capital gains tax or corporation tax in respect of the distribution.

(5B) The period referred to in subsection (5A)(*b*) above is the period of three years from—

   (*a*) the end of the period of account of the company in which the chargeable gain accrued, or
   (*b*) the end of the period of twelve months beginning with the date on which the chargeable gain accrued,

whichever is earlier.

...[5][4]

(6) ...[1]

(7) The amount of capital gains tax paid by a person in pursuance of subsection (2) above (so far as [neither reimbursed by the company nor applied under subsection (5A) above for reducing any liability to tax)][1] shall be allowable as a deduction in the computation under this Act of a gain accruing on the disposal by him of [any asset representing his interest as a participator in the company.][1]

[(7A) In ascertaining for the purposes of subsection (5A) or (7) above the amount of capital gains tax or income tax chargeable on any person for any year on or in respect of any chargeable gain or distribution—

(*a*) any such distribution as is mentioned in subsection (5A)(*b*) above and falls to be treated as income of that person for that year shall be regarded as forming the highest part of the income on which he is chargeable to tax for the year;

(*b*) any gain accruing in that year on the disposal by that person of any asset representing his interest as a participator in the company shall be regarded as forming the highest part of the gains on which he is chargeable to tax for that year;

(*c*) where any such distribution as is mentioned in subsection (5A)(*b*) above falls to be treated as a disposal on which a gain accrues on which that person is so chargeable, that gain shall be regarded as forming the next highest part of the gains on which he is so chargeable, after any gains falling within paragraph (*b*) above; and

(*d*) any gain treated as accruing to that person in that year by virtue of subsection (2) above shall be regarded as the next highest part of the gains on which he is so chargeable, after any gains falling within paragraph (*c*) above.][1]

(8) So far as it would go to reduce or extinguish chargeable gains accruing by virtue of this section to a person in a year of assessment this section shall apply in relation to a loss accruing to the company on the disposal of an asset in that year of assessment as it would apply if a gain instead of a loss had accrued to the company on the disposal, but shall only so apply in relation to that person; and subject to the preceding provisions of this subsection this section shall not apply in relation to a loss accruing to the company.

(9) If [a person who is a participator in the company][1] at the time when the chargeable gain accrues to the company is itself a company which is not resident in the United Kingdom but which would be a close company if it were resident in the United Kingdom, an amount equal to the amount apportioned under subsection (3) above out of the chargeable gain [to the participating company's interest as a participator in the company to which the gain accrues shall be further apportioned among the participators in the participating company according to the extent of their respective interests as participators, and subsection (2) above shall apply to them accordingly in relation to the amounts further apportioned, and so on through any number of companies.][1]

(10) The persons treated by this section as if a part of a chargeable gain accruing to a company had accrued to them shall include trustees [who are participators in the company, or in any company amongst the participators in which the gain is apportioned under subsection (9) above,][1] if when the gain accrues to the company the trustees are neither resident nor ordinarily resident in the United Kingdom.

[(10A) A gain which is treated as accruing to any person by virtue of this section shall not be eligible for taper relief.][2]

[(10B) A chargeable gain that would be treated as accruing to a person under subsection (2) above shall not be so treated if—

(*a*) it would be so treated only if assets that are assets of a pension scheme were taken into account in ascertaining that person's interest as a participator in the company, and

(*b*) at the time the gain accrues a gain arising on a disposal of those assets would be exempt from tax by virtue of section 271(1)(*b*), (*c*), (*d*), (*g*) or (*h*) or (2).

In paragraph (*a*) above "assets of a pension scheme" means assets held for the purposes of a fund or scheme to which any of the provisions mentioned in paragraph (*b*) above applies.][4]

(11) If any tax payable by any person by virtue of subsection (2) above is paid by the company to which the chargeable gain accrues, or in a case under subsection (9) above is paid by any such other company, the amount so paid shall not for the purposes of income tax, capital gains tax or corporation tax be regarded as a payment to the person by whom the tax was originally payable.

[(11A) For the purposes of this section the amount of the gain or loss accruing at any time to a company that is not resident in the United Kingdom shall be computed (where it is not the case) as if that company were within the charge to corporation tax on capital gains.][3]

[(12) In this section "participator", in relation to a company, has the meaning given by section 417(1) of the Taxes Act for the purposes of Part XI of that Act (close companies).][1]

[(13) In this section—

(*a*) references to a person's interest as a participator in a company are references to the interest in the company which is represented by all the factors by reference to which he falls to be treated as such a participator; and

(*b*) references to the extent of such an interest are references to the proportion of the interests as participators of all the participators in the company (including any who are not resident or ordinarily resident in the United Kingdom) which on a just and reasonable apportionment is represented by that interest.][1]

[(14) For the purposes of this section, where—

(*a*) the interest of any person in a company is wholly or partly represented by an interest which he has under any settlement ("his beneficial interest"), and

(*b*) his beneficial interest is the factor, or one of the factors, by reference to which that person would be treated (apart from this subsection) as having an interest as a participator in that company, the interest as a participator in that company which would be that person's shall be deemed, to the extent that it is represented by his beneficial interest, to be an interest of the trustees of the settlement (and not of that person), and references in this section, in relation to a company, to a participator shall be construed accordingly.]¹

[(15) Any appeal under section 31 of the Management Act involving any question as to the extent for the purposes of this section of a person's interest as a participator in a company shall be to the Special Commissioners.]¹

Commentary—*Simon's Direct Tax Service* **C2.1455; D2.316.**
Revenue & other press releases—CCAB June 1969 (where a non-resident company (which would be a close company if resident in the UK) is liable for overseas tax on a capital gain; a UK shareholder may claim relief for his apportioned share of the tax paid as a deduction under s 278 or as a credit under s 277).
CCAB TR500 10-3-83 (gains of overseas subsidiary are not apportioned to its UK parent company if the overseas subsidiary is resident in a territory with which UK has a double taxation agreement which contains an article exempting residents of that territory from UK tax on capital gains).
Revenue Internal Guidance—Capital gains tax manual CG 25420–25440 (worked examples).
CG 57300–57312 (summarises exemptions, tax adjustments and reliefs relating to this section).
Simon's Tax Cases—*Van-Arkadie v Plunket* [1983] STC 54*.
s 13(10), *Marshall v Kerr* [1991] STC 686*.
Definitions—''Asset'', s 21(1); ''chargeable gain'', s 15(2); ''close company'', s 288(1), TA 1988 ss 414, 415; ''company'', ss 99, 288(1); ''issued'', s 288(5); ''lease'', Sch 8 para 10(1); ''the Management Act'', s 288(1); ''ordinarily resident'', s 9(1); ''resident'', s 9(1); ''shares'', s 288(1); ''the Taxes Act'', s 288(1); ''trade'', s 288(1), TA 1988 s 832(1); ''year of assessment'', s 288(1).
Cross references—See TMA 1970 s 28(1) (non-resident companies and trusts);
TA 1988 s 762(1) (offshore income gains).
TCGA 1992 s 14 (attribution of gains of members of non-resident groups of companies).
TCGA 1992 Sch 5 para 1(3) (construction of certain provisions of s 86 (which attaches tax charge to settlor of a non-resident settlement) by reference to this section).
TCGA 1992 Sch 7B paras 1, 2 (modification of sub-s (5)(*d*) above in the case of application of this section to an overseas life insurance company in relation to chargeable gains accruing in accounting periods beginning after 31 December 1992).
Amendments—¹ Words in sub-ss (2), (7), (9), (10) substituted or inserted, sub-ss (3), (4) substituted, sub-s (7A), (12)–(15) inserted and sub-ss (5)(*a*), (6) repealed by FA 1996 s 174(1)–(9), (11), Sch 41 Pt V(30) with effect in relation to gains accruing after 27 November 1995.
² Sub-s (10A) inserted by FA 1998 Sch 21 para 4 with effect from the year 1998–99.
³ Sub-s (11A) inserted by FA 1998 s 122(4) with effect in relation to disposals on or after 6 April 1998, subject to FA 1998 s 122(7).
⁴ Words in sub-s (4) substituted, sub-s (5)(*b*) substituted, sub-ss (5A), (5B) substituted for old sub-s (5A), and sub-s (10B) inserted by FA 2001 s 80 with effect for chargeable gains accruing as mentioned in sub-s (1) above after 6 March 2001.
⁵ In sub-s (5B), the following words repealed by FA 2002 s 141, Sch 40 Pt 3(16) with effect from 24 July 2002—
''and in paragraph (*a*) above ''period of account'' means a period for which the accounts of the trade are made up''.

14 Non-resident groups of companies

(1) This section has effect for the purposes of section 13.

[(2) The following provisions—

    (*a*) section 41(8),

    (*b*) section 171 (except subsections (1)(*b*) and (1A)),

    (*c*) section 173 (with the omission of the words ''to which this section applies'' in subsections (1)(*a*) and (2)(*a*) and ''such'' in subsections (1)(*c*) and (2)(*c*) and with the omission of subsection (3)),

    (*d*) section 174(4) (with the substitution of ''at a time when both were members of the group'' for ''in a transfer to which section 171(1) applied''), and

    (*e*) section 175(1) (with the omission of the words ''to which this section applies''),

shall apply in relation to non-resident companies which are members of a non-resident group of companies as they apply in relation to companies which are members of a group of companies.]¹

(3) [Section 179 (except subsections (1)(*b*) and (1A))]¹ shall apply for the purposes of section 13 as if for any reference therein to a group of companies there were substituted a reference to a non-resident group of companies, and as if references to companies were references to companies not resident in the United Kingdom.

(4) For the purposes of this section—

    (*a*) a ''non-resident group'' of companies—

        (i) in the case of a group, none of the members of which are resident in the United Kingdom, means that group, and

        (ii) in the case of a group, 2 or more members of which are not resident in the United Kingdom, means the members which are not resident in the United Kingdom;

    (*b*) ''group'' shall be construed in accordance with section 170 ...¹.

Commentary—*Simon's Direct Tax Service* **D2.317.**
Revenue Interpretation RI 43—Intra-group transfers by members of non-resident group of companies.
Revenue Internal Guidance—Capital Gains Manual CG 45231 (where a transfer between a member of a non-resident group and any UK resident company takes place the no gain/no loss treatment does not apply).
Definition—''Resident'', s 9(1).
Cross references—See FA 2000 Sch 29 para 16(5) (the main amendments made to TCGA 1992 s 170 by FA 2000 Sch 29 para 1 have effect for the purposes of this section with effect in cases in which ss 41, 171, 173, 174(4), 175(1) or 179, as the case may be, have effect as amended by FA 2000 Sch 29).
Amendments—¹ Sub-s (2) and words in sub-s (3) substituted, and words in sub-s (4) repealed, by FA 2000 ss 102, 156, Sch 29 para 16, Sch 40 Pt II(12) with effect in cases in which ss 41, 171, 173, 174(4), 175(1) or 179, as the case may be, have effect as amended by FA 2000 Sch 29.

PART II

GENERAL PROVISIONS RELATING TO COMPUTATION OF GAINS AND ACQUISITIONS AND DISPOSALS OF ASSETS

Concession D18—Default on mortgage granted by vendor.
Cross references—See TA 1988 s 763(3) (deduction of offshore income gains from the disposal value in computing the gains under this Part);
TA 1988 Sch 26 para 3(2) (computation under this Part of gains on disposal of shares in UK controlled foreign company).

CHAPTER I
INTRODUCTORY

15 Computation of gains

(1) The amount of the gains accruing on the disposal of assets shall be computed in accordance with this Part, subject to the other provisions of this Act.

(2) Every gain shall, except as otherwise expressly provided, be a chargeable gain.

Commentary—*Simon's Direct Tax Service* **C1.101.**
Statement of Practice D7—Treatment of VAT.
SP 8/79—Compensation for acquisition of property under compulsory powers.
Definitions—"Asset", s 21(1); "chargeable gain", s 15(2).
Cross reference—See TMA 1970 s 28(1) (non-resident companies and trusts).

16 Computation of losses

(1) Subject to section 72 of the Finance Act 1991 and except as otherwise expressly provided, the amount of a loss accruing on a disposal of an asset shall be computed in the same way as the amount of a gain accruing on a disposal is computed.

(2) Except as otherwise expressly provided, all the provisions of this Act which distinguish gains which are chargeable gains from those which are not, or which make part of a gain a chargeable gain, and part not, shall apply also to distinguish losses which are allowable losses from those which are not, and to make part of a loss an allowable loss, and part not; and references in this Act to an allowable loss shall be construed accordingly.

[(2A) A loss accruing to a person in a year of assessment shall not be an allowable loss for the purposes of this Act unless, in relation to that year, he gives a notice to an officer of the Board quantifying the amount of that loss; and sections 42 and 43 of the Management Act shall apply in relation to such a notice as if it were a claim for relief.][1]

(3) A loss accruing to a person in a year of assessment during no part of which he is resident or ordinarily resident in the United Kingdom shall not be an allowable loss for the purposes of this Act unless, under section 10, he would be chargeable to tax in respect of a chargeable gain if there had been a gain instead of a loss on that occasion.

(4) In accordance with section 12(1), losses accruing on the disposal of assets situated outside the United Kingdom to an individual resident or ordinarily resident but not domiciled in the United Kingdom shall not be allowable losses.

Commentary—*Simon's Direct Tax Service* **C1.501.**
Revenue Internal Guidance—Capital gains tax manual CG 13350–13372 (bed and breakfast transactions: conditions for accepting allowable loss: transfer of beneficial ownership (CG 13361); exposure to price movements (CG 13362); transactions at arm's length).
Inspector's manual IM 1833 ("bed and breakfast" transactions, information required to substantiate a loss claim and stamp duty implications).
Simon's Tax Cases—s 16(3), *Ritchie v Mckay* [1984] STC 422*.
Definitions—"Allowable loss", ss 8(2), 16, 288(1); "asset", s 21(1); "the Board", s 288(1); "chargeable gain", s 15(2); "the Management Act", s 288(1); "ordinarily resident", s 9(1); "resident", s 9(1); "year of assessment", s 288(1).
Cross references—See TA 1988 Sch 28 para 3(5) (offshore income gains).
TCGA 1992 s 97(6) (sub-s (3) above not to affect relief for losses accruing to non-resident settlements).
TCGA 1992 s 150A(2) (sub-s (3) not to apply to a disposal of enterprise investment scheme shares on which a loss accrues notwithstanding sub-s (2) above).
TCGA 1992 Sch 5 para 1(2) (construction of certain provisions of s 86 (which attaches tax charge to settlor of a non-resident settlement) by reference to sub-s (3) above).
TCGA 1992 Sch 7B paras 1, 3 (modification of sub-s (3) above in the case of application of this section to an overseas life insurance company in relation to accounting periods beginning after 31 December 1992).
FA 1995 s 113(2) "allowable losses" deduction of losses for 1996–97 or a subsequent year in preference to those accruing for earlier years, and for companies, losses accruing in an accounting period ending on or after the appointed day for the purpose of FA 1994 Chapter III Pt IV deductible in preference to those for earlier accounting periods. The appointed day is (1 July 1999).
Amendments—[1] Sub-s (2A) inserted by FA 1995 s 113(1) with effect from the year 1996–97 in relation to income tax and capital gains tax, and in relation to corporation tax with effect for accounting periods ending after 30 June 1999 (by virtue of Finance Act 1994, Section 199, (Appointed Day) Order, SI 1998/3173 art 2).

17 Disposals and acquisitions treated as made at market value

(1) Subject to the provisions of this Act, a person's acquisition or disposal of an asset shall for the purposes of this Act be deemed to be for a consideration equal to the market value of the asset—

(*a*) where he acquires or, as the case may be, disposes of the asset otherwise than by way of a bargain made at arm's length, and in particular where he acquires or disposes of it by way of gift or on a transfer into settlement by a settlor or by way of distribution from a company in respect of shares in the company, or

(*b*) where he acquires or, as the case may be, disposes of the asset wholly or partly for a consideration that cannot be valued, or in connection with his own or another's loss of office or employment or diminution of emoluments, or otherwise in consideration for or recognition of his or another's services or past services in any office or employment or of any other service rendered or to be rendered by him or another.

(2) Subsection (1) shall not apply to the acquisition of an asset if—

(*a*) there is no corresponding disposal of it, and

(*b*) there is no consideration in money or money's worth or the consideration is of an amount or value lower than the market value of the asset.

Commentary—*Simon's Direct Tax Service* **C2.109.**
Revenue Interpretation RI 93—Transfer of assets at under value to employees or directors: disposal consideration to be on statutory market value basis for transfer after 5 April 1995.
RI 152—Principle in *Gray v IRC* [1994] STC 360 (two or more assets can be valued as single unit in certain circumstances) *not* to be applied in determining market value under this section.
RI 210—Application of sub-s (2) as regards acquisition costs of bookmakers' pitches.
Revenue Internal Guidance—Capital gains manual CG 3094 (Example: exchange of assets between connected persons); CG 13095, CG 13097 (Examples: exchange of assets between unconnected persons).
CG 16280 (sub-s (1)(*b*) from 6-4-95, this covers transfer of asset to employee at undervalue; actual loss to employer is allowable as Case I deduction (CG 16293); actual consideration includes amount of unpaid remuneration discharged by transfer of asset—(CG 16277–16279).
CG 70823 (the section applies *inter alia* to the grant of a lease, the tenant being deemed to have paid the appropriate premium).
Simon's Tax Cases—s 17(1), *Whitehouse v Ellam* [1995] STC 503*; *Director v Inspector of Taxes* [1998] STC (SCD) 172. s 17(1)(*a*), [1997] STC (SCD) 249; *Bullivant Holdings Ltd v IRC* [1998] STC 905*.
Definitions—"Asset", s 21(1); "company", ss 99, 288(1); "market value", ss 272–274, Sch 11; shares", s 288(1).
Cross references—See TA 1988 s 185(3) (exclusion of sub-s (1) of this section in relation to approved share option schemes); FA 1988 s 68(4) (exclusion of sub-s (1) of this section in relation to certain priority share allocations to employees).
TCGA 1992 s 18(2) (transactions between connected persons);
TCGA 1992 s 62(5) (sub-s (1) of this section not to apply to disposals by way of donatio mortis causa);
TCGA 1992 s 142(3) (deemed acquisition value of stock dividends issued in respect of shares held by a bare trustee);
TCGA 1992 s 149A (this section not to apply for calculating consideration for an option granted after 15 March 1993 in relation to share option scheme).
TCGA 1992 s 239(2) (sub-s (1) of this section not to apply to disposal of assets by close company or individual to trustees of employee trust);
TCGA 1992 s 257(2) (sub-s (1) of this section not to apply to certain gifts to charities);
TCGA 1992 s 259(2) (sub-s (1) of this section not to apply to certain gifts to housing associations).

18 Transactions between connected persons

(1) This section shall apply where a person acquires an asset and the person making the disposal is connected with him.

(2) Without prejudice to the generality of section 17(1) the person acquiring the asset and the person making the disposal shall be treated as parties to a transaction otherwise than by way of a bargain made at arm's length.

(3) Subject to subsection (4) below, if on the disposal a loss accrues to the person making the disposal, it shall not be deductible except from a chargeable gain accruing to him on some other disposal of an asset to the person acquiring the asset mentioned in subsection (1) above, being a disposal made at a time when they are connected persons.

(4) Subsection (3) above shall not apply to a disposal by way of gift in settlement if the gift and the income from it is wholly or primarily applicable for educational, cultural or recreational purposes, and the persons benefiting from the application for those purposes are confined to members of an association of persons for whose benefit the gift was made, not being persons all or most of whom are connected persons.

(5) Where the asset mentioned in subsection (1) above is an option to enter into a sale or other transaction given by the person making the disposal a loss accruing to the person acquiring the asset shall not be an allowable loss unless it accrues on a disposal of the option at arm's length to a person who is not connected with him.

(6) Subject to subsection (7) below, in a case where the asset mentioned in subsection (1) above is subject to any right or restriction enforceable by the person making the disposal, or by a person connected with him, then (where the amount of the consideration for the acquisition is, in accordance with subsection (2) above, deemed to be equal to the market value of the asset) that market value shall be—

(*a*) what its market value would be if not subject to the right or restriction, minus—

(*b*) the market value of the right or restriction or the amount by which its extinction would enhance the value of the asset to its owner, whichever is the less.

(7) If the right or restriction is of such a nature that its enforcement would or might effectively destroy or substantially impair the value of the asset without bringing any countervailing advantage either to the person making the disposal or a person connected with him or is an option or other right to acquire the asset or, in the case of incorporeal property, is a right to extinguish the asset in the

hands of the person giving the consideration by forfeiture or merger or otherwise, the market value of the asset shall be determined, and the amount of the gain accruing on the disposal shall be computed, as if the right or restriction did not exist.

(8) Subsections (6) and (7) above shall not apply to a right of forfeiture or other right exercisable on breach of a covenant contained in a lease of land or other property, and shall not apply to any right or restriction under a mortgage or other charge.

Commentary—*Simon's Direct Tax Service* C1.508; C2.113.
Revenue Interpretation RI 38—For the purposes of this section, are settlor and trustees connected at the time of settlement and are trustees and beneficiaries connected after settlor's death and are trustees and beneficiaries connected when beneficiaries become absolutely entitled.
Simon's Tax Cases—s 18(2), *Berry v Warnett* [1978] STC 504*; *Aspden v Hildesley* [1982] STC 206*.
s 18(3), *News International plc v Shepherd* [1989] STC 617*.
Definitions—"Allowable loss", ss 8(2), 16, 288(1); "asset", s 21(1); "chargeable gain", s 15(2); "connected", s 286; "land", s 288(1); "lease", Sch 8 para 10(1); "market value", ss 272–274, Sch 11.
Cross references—See TCGA 1992 s 58(2) (this section not to apply to disposals between spouses living together);
TCGA 1992 s 197(6), (7) (modification of this section in its application to losses incurred on ring fence transactions between connected persons).

19 Deemed consideration in certain cases where assets disposed of in a series of transactions

(1) For the purposes of this Act, in any case where—

(a) by way of 2 or more material transactions which are linked (a series of linked transactions), one person disposes of assets to another person with whom he is connected or to 2 or more other persons with each of whom he is connected, and

(b) the original market value of the assets disposed of by any of the transactions in the series, as determined under section 20, is less than the appropriate portion of the aggregate market value of the assets disposed of by all the transactions in the series, as so determined,

then, subject to subsection (2) below, the disposal effected by any linked transaction in the series in respect of which the condition in paragraph (b) above is fulfilled shall be deemed to be for a consideration equal to the appropriate portion referred to in that paragraph.

(2) Where the disposal effected by a material transaction is one to which section 58 applies, nothing in subsection (1) above shall affect the amount which, for the purposes of this Act, is the consideration for that disposal.

(3) Subject to subsection (5) below, any reference in this section to a material transaction is a reference to a transaction by way of gift or otherwise; and, for the purposes of this section, 2 or more material transactions are linked if they occur within the period of 6 years ending on the date of the last of them.

(4) This section shall apply or, as the case may be, shall again apply—

(a) when a second material transaction causes a series of linked transactions to come into being; and

(b) whenever, on the occurrence of a further material transaction, an existing series is extended by the inclusion of that transaction (whether or not an earlier transaction ceases to form part of the series);

and all such assessments and adjustments of assessments shall be made as may be necessary to give effect to this section on each such occasion.

(5) Where a member of a group of companies disposes of an asset to another member of the group in circumstances such that, by virtue of section 171, both companies are treated, so far as relates to corporation tax on chargeable gains, as if the consideration for the disposal were of such an amount as would secure that neither a gain nor a loss would accrue, the transaction by which that disposal is effected is not a material transaction; and a disposal in these circumstances is in this section referred to as an "inter-group transfer".

(6) In any case where—

(a) a company ("company A") disposes of an asset by way of a material transaction, and

(b) company A acquired the asset after 19th March 1985 by way of an inter-group transfer, and

(c) the disposal by company A is to a person who is connected with another company ("company B") which at some time after 19th March 1985 disposed of the asset by way of an inter-group transfer, and

(d) either the disposal by way of inter-group transfer which is referred to in paragraph (c) above was the occasion of the acquisition referred to in paragraph (b) above or, between that disposal and that acquisition, there has been no disposal of the asset which was not an inter-group transfer,

then, for the purpose of determining whether subsection (1) above applies in relation to a series of linked transactions, the disposal by company A shall be treated as having been made by company B; but any increase in the consideration for that disposal resulting from the application of subsection (1) above shall have effect with respect to company A.

Commentary—*Simon's Direct Tax Service* C2.114.
Definitions—"Asset", s 21(1); "chargeable gain", s 15(2); "company", ss 99, 288(1); "connected", s 286; "market value", ss 272–274, Sch 11.
Cross references—See TCGA 1992 Sch 11 para 2 (gifts and series of transactions between connected persons before 20 March 1985).

20 Original market value and aggregate market value for purposes of section 19

(1) This section has effect for determining the original market value of assets and the aggregate market value of assets as mentioned in subsection (1)(*b*) of section 19.

(2) Expressions used in this section have the same meaning as in that section.

(3) Where there is a series of linked transactions, the original market value of the assets disposed of by each transaction in the series shall be determined as follows—

    (*a*) if at the time in question the transaction is the most recent in the series, the original market value of the assets disposed of by that transaction is the market value which, apart from section 19, would be deemed to be the consideration for that transaction for the purposes of this Act; and

    (*b*) in the case of any other transaction in the series, the original market value of the assets disposed of by that transaction is the value which, prior to the occurrence of the most recent transaction in the series, was or would have been deemed for the purposes of this Act to be the consideration for the transaction concerned (whether by virtue of the previous operation of section 19, or by virtue of any other provision of this Act).

(4) Subject to subsections (6) to (9) below, in relation to any transaction in a series of linked transactions—

    (*a*) any reference in this section or section 19 to the aggregate market value of the assets disposed of by all the transactions in the series is a reference to what would have been the market value of all those assets for the purposes of this Act if, considering all the assets together, they had been disposed of by one disposal occurring at the time of the transaction concerned; and

    (*b*) any reference in section 19 to the appropriate portion of the aggregate market value of the assets disposed of by all the transactions in the series is a reference to that portion of the market value determined in accordance with paragraph (*a*) above which it is reasonable to apportion to those of the assets which were actually disposed of by the transaction concerned.

(5) The reference in subsection (4)(*a*) above to considering all the assets together includes a reference not only to considering them as a group or holding or collection of assets retaining their separate identities but also (if it gives a higher market value) to considering them as brought together, physically or in law, so as to constitute either a single asset or a number of assets which are distinct from those which were comprised in each of the transactions concerned.

(6) If any of the assets disposed of by all the transactions in a series of linked transactions were acquired after the time of the first of those transactions, then, in the application of subsections (4) and (5) above in relation to each of the transactions in the series—

    (*a*) no account shall be taken of any assets which were acquired after the time of that transaction unless they were acquired by way of an inter-group transfer; and

    (*b*) subject to subsection (7) below, the number of assets of which account is to be taken shall be limited to the maximum number which were held by the person making the disposal at any time in the period beginning immediately before the first of the transactions in the series and ending immediately before the last.

(7) If, before the first of the transactions referred to in paragraph (*b*) of subsection (6) above, the person concerned (being a company) disposed of any assets by way of an inter-group transfer, the maximum number of assets referred to in that paragraph shall be determined as if the inter-group transfer had occurred after that first transaction.

(8) In the application of subsection (6) above in a case where the assets disposed of are securities, the assets disposed of by any of the transactions in a series of linked transactions shall be identified with assets acquired on an earlier date rather than with assets acquired on a later date.

(9) In subsection (8) above "securities" includes any assets which are of a nature to be dealt in without identifying the particular assets disposed of or acquired.

Commentary—*Simon's Direct Tax Service* C2.114.
Definitions—"Asset", s 21(1); "company", ss 99, 288(1); "market value", ss 272–274, Sch 11.

CHAPTER II
ASSETS AND DISPOSALS OF ASSETS
General provisions

21 Assets and disposals

(1) All forms of property shall be assets for the purposes of this Act, whether situated in the United Kingdom or not, including—

    (*a*) options, debts and incorporeal property generally, and

    (*b*) any currency other than sterling, and

    (*c*) any form of property created by the person disposing of it, or otherwise coming to be owned without being acquired.

(2) For the purposes of this Act—

    (*a*) references to a disposal of an asset include, except where the context otherwise requires, references to a part disposal of an asset, and (*b*) there is a part disposal of an asset where an interest or right in or over the asset is created by the disposal, as well as where it subsists before the disposal, and generally, there is a part disposal of an asset where, on a person making a disposal, any description of property derived from the asset remains undisposed of.

Commentary—*Simon's Direct Tax Service* **C1.301, 315.**
Regulations—European Single Currency (Taxes) Regulations, SI 1998/3177 reg 36.
Statement of Practice SP 4/92—Capital gains rebasing elections.
Revenue Interpretation RI 11—Rollover relief in respect of gain arising on grant of option over land.
RI 210—The right of a bookmaker to occupy a particular pitch at a particular racecourse is an asset for capital gains purposes.
Revenue Internal Guidance—Capital gains manual, CG 11710 (list of assets that can be disposed of without a capital gains charge).
CG 53400–53530 (treatment of debts).
CG 77520–77640 (found objects and treasure trove; ownership of objects CG 77520–77547; compensation received from owner not taxable CG 77570; disposal of object; worked example CG 77640).
CG 77800–77983 (treatment of various EC agricultural quotas).
CG 78050–78095 (capital gains tax treatment of land which has been "set aside").
CG 78110–78118 (capital gains tax treatment of land which has been "grubbed-up").
CG 78204 (copyright is a single asset, not a collection of rights, each being a single asset. An assignment of a particular right is therefore a part disposal).
CG 78300–78407 (treatment of foreign currency).
Simon's Tax Cases—*Golding v Kaufman* [1985] STC 152*; *Chaloner v Pellipar Investments Ltd* [1996] STC 234*; *Watton v Tippett* [1997] STC 893*; *Joseph Carter and Sons Ltd v Baird* [1999] STC 120*.
s 21(1), *Strange v Openshaw* [1983] STC 416*; *Davenport v Chilver* [1983] STC 426*; *Procter v Zim Properties Ltd* [1985] STC 90*; *Kirby v Thorn EMI plc* [1987] STC 621*.
s 21(2) *Berry v Warnett* [1982] STC 396*; *Strange v Openshaw* [1983] STC 416*; *Anders Utkilens Rederi A/S v O/Y Lovisa Stevedoring Co A/Band Keller BryantTransport Co Ltd* [1985] STC 301*; *Kirby v Thorn EMI plc* [1987] STC 621*.
Definition—"Part disposal", s 21(2).
Cross references—TMA 1970 s 12(2) (information about chargeable gains).
TCGA 1992 s 144 (grant of certain options to be treated as part of larger transactions).

22 Disposal where capital sums derived from assets

(1) Subject to sections 23 and 26(1), and to any other exceptions in this Act, there is for the purposes of this Act a disposal of assets by their owner where any capital sum is derived from assets notwithstanding that no asset is acquired by the person paying the capital sum, and this subsection applies in particular to—

(*a*) capital sums received by way of compensation for any kind of damage or injury to assets or for the loss, destruction or dissipation of assets or for any depreciation or risk of depreciation of an asset,

(*b*) capital sums received under a policy of insurance of the risk of any kind of damage or injury to, or the loss or depreciation of, assets,

(*c*) capital sums received in return for forfeiture or surrender of rights, or for refraining from exercising rights, and

(*d*) capital sums received as consideration for use or exploitation of assets.

(2) In the case of a disposal within paragraph (*a*), (*b*), (*c*) or (*d*) of subsection (1) above, the time of the disposal shall be the time when the capital sum is received as described in that subsection.

(3) In this section "capital sum" means any money or money's worth which is not excluded from the consideration taken into account in the computation of the gain.

Commentary—*Simon's Direct Tax Service* **C1.319.**
Concession D1—Insurance recoveries: short leases.
D33—Capital gains tax on compensation and damages. This Concession has been revised.
D50—Capital gains tax treatment of compensation deriving from an overseas government.
Revenue Interpretation RI 77—Compensation for permanent units in milk quota.
RI 225—Capital gains tax treatment where the receipt for the grant of an indefeasible right to use is a capital receipt.
RI 227—A lump sum payable under the Matrimonial Causes Act 1973 s 31(7B) is not a capital payment derived from an asset.
Revenue Internal Guidance—Capital gains tax manual, CG 12940–13024 (detailed explanation of the provisions; examples of capital sums CG 12942–12944; meaning of "capital sums" CG 12950–12954; meaning of "derived from other assets" CG 12960–12966; meaning of "notwithstanding that no asset is acquired" CG 12970–12971; meaning of "owner" CG 12975–12976; interaction with TCGA 1992 s 24 CG 12980–12983; concurrent rights over an asset CG 12984–12998; damages treated as arising from underlying asset CG 13010–13024 and ESC D33).
CG 13030–13078 (sub-s (1)(a) specific types of compensation considered; personal injury CG 13030–13034; warranty and indemnity payments CG 13040–13045; termination of building society agencies CG 13050–13053; taking up employment or not CG 13064–13069).
CG 13090–13099 (sub-s (3) exchanges of assets; market value rule: worked example given).
CG 72300–72501, (compensation payments to displaced tenants; CG 72300–72316; business tenancies CG 72328–72361; agricultural tenancies CG 72380–72430; tenancies of licensed premises CG 72450–72499).
CG 77750–77754 (fishing vessels, decommissioning grants).
CG 77800–78866 (compensation for confiscated property).
Simon's Tax Cases—s 22, *Cottle v Coldicott* [1995] STC (SCD) 239*; *Chaloner v Pellipar Investments Ltd* [1996] STC 234*.
s 22(1), *Kirby v Thorn EMI plc* [1987] STC 621*; *Welbeck Securities Ltd v Powlson* [1987] STC 468*; *Pennine Raceway Ltd v Kirklees Metropolitan Council (No 2)* [1989] STC 122*.
s 22(1)(a), *Neely v Ward* [1991] STC 656*.
s 22(1)(c), *Davis v Powell* [1977] STC 32*; *O'Brien v Benson's Hosiery (Holdings) Ltd* [1979] STC 735*.
Definition—"Asset", s 21(1).
Cross references—See TCGA 1992 s 28 (time of disposal and acquisition where asset disposed of under contract).
TCGA 1992 s 204(2) (sums received under insurance policies are for the purposes of this section sums derived from insured assets).
TCGA 1992 s 245(1) (treatment for the purposes of this section of compensation paid on compulsory acquisition of land).
TCGA 1992 s 250(3) (exemption for insurance compensation for certain insured risks to woodlands notwithstanding sub-s (2) above).

TCGA 1992 Sch 2 para 10(8) (computation of gain on part disposal resulting under sub-s (1) above of land reflecting development value).

23 Receipt of compensation and insurance money not treated as a disposal

(1) If the recipient so claims, receipt of a capital sum within paragraph (*a*), (*b*), (*c*) or (*d*) of section 22(1) derived from an asset which is not lost or destroyed shall not be treated for the purposes of this Act as a disposal of the asset if—

(*a*) the capital sum is wholly applied in restoring the asset, or

(*b*) (subject to subsection (2) below), the capital sum is applied in restoring the asset except for a part of the capital sum which is not reasonably required for the purpose and which is small as compared with the whole capital sum, or

(*c*) (subject to subsection (2) below), the amount of the capital sum is small, as compared with the value of the asset,

but, if the receipt is not treated as a disposal, all sums which would, if the receipt had been so treated, have been brought into account as consideration for that disposal in the computation of the gain shall be deducted from any expenditure allowable under Chapter III of this Part as a deduction in computing a gain on the subsequent disposal of the asset.

(2) If the allowable expenditure is less than the consideration for the disposal constituted by the receipt of the capital sum (or is nil)—

(*a*) paragraphs (*b*) and (*c*) of subsection (1) above shall not apply, and

(*b*) if the recipient so elects (and there is any allowable expenditure)—

(i) the amount of the consideration for the disposal shall be reduced by the amount of the allowable expenditure, and

(ii) none of that expenditure shall be allowable as a deduction in computing a gain accruing on the occasion of the disposal or any subsequent occasion.

In this subsection ''allowable expenditure'' means expenditure which, immediately before the disposal, was attributable to the asset under paragraphs (*a*) and (*b*) of section 38(1).

(3) If, in a case not falling within subsection (1)(*b*) above, a part of a capital sum within paragraph (*a*) or paragraph (*b*) of section 22(1) derived from an asset which is not lost or destroyed is applied in restoring the asset, then if the recipient so claims, that part of the capital sum shall not be treated as consideration for the disposal deemed to be effected on receipt of the capital sum but shall be deducted from any expenditure allowable under Chapter III of this Part as a deduction in computing a gain on the subsequent disposal of the asset.

(4) If an asset is lost or destroyed and a capital sum received by way of compensation for the loss or destruction, or under a policy of insurance of the risk of the loss or destruction, is within one year of receipt, or such longer period as the inspector may allow, applied in acquiring an asset in replacement of the asset lost or destroyed the owner shall if he so claims be treated for the purposes of this Act—

(*a*) as if the consideration for the disposal of the old asset were (if otherwise of a greater amount) of such amount as would secure that on the disposal neither a gain nor a loss accrues to him, and

(*b*) as if the amount of the consideration for the acquisition of the new asset were reduced by the excess of the amount of the capital sum received by way of compensation or under the policy of insurance, together with any residual or scrap value, over the amount of the consideration which he is treated as receiving under paragraph (*a*) above.

(5) A claim shall not be made under subsection (4) above if part only of the capital sum is applied in acquiring the new asset but if all of that capital sum except for a part which is less than the amount of the gain (whether all chargeable gain or not) accruing on the disposal of the old asset is so applied, then the owner shall if he so claims be treated for the purposes of this Act—

(*a*) as if the amount of the gain so accruing were reduced to the amount of the said part (and, if not all chargeable gain, with a proportionate reduction in the amount of the chargeable gain), and

(*b*) as if the amount of the consideration for the acquisition of the new asset were reduced by the amount by which the gain is reduced under paragraph (*a*) of this subsection.

[(6) If a building (''the old building'') is destroyed or irreparably damaged, and all or part of a capital sum received by way of compensation for the destruction or damage, or under a policy of insurance of the risk of the destruction or damage, is applied by the recipient in constructing or otherwise acquiring a replacement building situated on other land (''the new building''), then for the purposes of subsections (4) and (5) above each of the old building and the new building shall be regarded as an asset separate from the land on which it is or was situated and the old building shall be treated as lost or destroyed.][1]

[(7) For the purposes of subsection (6) above:

(*a*) references to a building include references to any permanent or semi-permanent structure in the nature of a building; and

(*b*) the reference to a sum applied in acquiring the new building does not include a reference to a sum applied in acquiring the land on which the new building is situated; and

(*c*) all necessary apportionments shall be made of any expenditure, compensation or consideration, and the method of apportionment shall be such as is just and reasonable.][1]

[(8) This section shall apply in relation to a wasting asset with the following modifications:

(*a*) paragraphs (*b*) and (*c*) of subsection (1) above, and subsection (2) above, shall not apply; and

(*b*) in subsections (1) and (3) above, the amount of the expenditure from which the deduction is to be made shall be the amount which would have been allowable under Chapter III of this Part if the asset had been disposed of immediately after the application of the capital sum.]¹

Commentary—*Simon's Direct Tax Service* C1.325, 326; C2.502, 1106.
Concession D19—Replacement of buildings destroyed.
D33—Capital gains tax on compensation and damages. This Concession has been revised.
Revenue Interpretation RI 164—From 24 February 1997, the Revenue regard a receipt as "small" wherever its amount or value is £3,000 or less, whether or not it would also meet the 5% test (see Revenue & other press releases below).
Revenue & other press releases—CCAB June 1965 ("small" is regarded by Revenue as not exceeding 5 per cent of the relevant amount. See now also Revenue Interpretation RI 164 above.
Definitions—"Asset", s 21(1); "chargeable gain", s 15(2); "inspector", s 288(1); "wasting asset", ss 44, 288(1), Sch 8 para 1.
Cross references—See TCGA 1992 Sch 2 para 23 (where sub-s (4)(*a*) above applies to exclude a gain which in consequence of Sch 2 is not all chargeable gain, the reduction under sub-s (4)(*b*) above is equal to the chargeable gain, not the whole gain).
TCGA 1992 Sch 3 para 4(2) (application of sub-s (2) of this section where TCGA 1992 s 35(2) (rebasing) applies in relation to the disposal of an asset).
TCGA 1992 Sch 4 para 2(1), (5) (deferred charges on gains before 31 March 1992).
Amendments—¹ Sub-ss (6)–(8) substituted for sub-s (6) by FA 1996 Sch 39 para 3 with effect for capital sums received after 5 April 1996.

24 Disposals where assets lost or destroyed, or become of negligible value

(1) Subject to the provisions of this Act and, in particular to section 144, the occasion of the entire loss, destruction, dissipation or extinction of an asset shall, for the purposes of this Act, constitute a disposal of the asset whether or not any capital sum by way of compensation or otherwise is received in respect of the destruction, dissipation or extinction of the asset.

[(2) Where the owner of an asset which has become of negligible value makes a claim to that effect:

(*a*) this Act shall apply as if the claimant had sold, and immediately reacquired, the asset at the time of the claim or (subject to paragraphs (*b*) and (*c*) below) at any earlier time specified in the claim, for a consideration of an amount equal to the value specified in the claim.

(*b*) An earlier time may be specified in the claim if:

(i) the claimant owned the asset at the earlier time; and

(ii) the asset had become of negligible value at the earlier time; and either

(iii) for capital gains tax purposes the earlier time is not more than two years before the beginning of the year of assessment in which the claim is made; or

(iv) for corporation tax purposes the earlier time is on or after the first day of the earliest accounting period ending not more than two years before the time of the claim.

(*c*) Section 93 of and Schedule 12 to the Finance Act 1994 (indexation losses and transitional relief) shall have effect in relation to an asset to which this section applies as if the sale and reacquisition occurred at the time of the claim and not at any earlier time.]¹

(3) For the purposes of subsections (1) and (2) above, a building and any permanent or semi-permanent structure in the nature of a building may be regarded as an asset separate from the land on which it is situated, but where either of those subsections applies in accordance with this subsection, the person deemed to make the disposal of the building or structure shall be treated as if he had also sold, and immediately reacquired, the site of the building or structure (including in the site any land occupied for purposes ancillary to the use of the building or structure) for a consideration equal to its market value at that time.

Commentary—*Simon's Direct Tax Service* C1.320, 321, 505, 506; C2.1107.
Concession D33—Capital gains tax on compensation and damages. This Concession has been revised.
D46—Relief against income for capital losses on the disposal of unquoted shares in a trading company.
Revenue Interpretation RI 14—Relief under sub-s (2) above for shareholders where a qualifying EIS company ceases to trade.

Revenue Internal Guidance—Capital gains tax manual, CG 13119 (Compensation received for the loss of an asset may give rise to a capital gains charge).
CG 13124 (sub-s (2) "negligible" means considerably less than 5 per cent of the original cost or March 1982 value).
CG 13128 (sub-s (2): a negligible value claim should specify the date of the deemed disposal: no separate claim form is provided).
CG 13129, 13130 (sub-s (2): Revenue's approach to dealing with negligible value claims).
CG 13131 (unquoted shares of negligible value if company registered in UK but not as a plc, claim is less than £10,000 and company is in liquidation or has ceased trading).
CG 13139–13146 (involuntary transfers, eg, theft: owner's interest in the asset may have become of negligible value even though asset not destroyed).
CG 27720–27733 (application of sub-s (2) to partnership goodwill).
CG 68760–68764 (Revenue do not consider the existence, or otherwise of a market for a firm's goodwill to be a relevant factor, following a decision to write off goodwill and claim under sub-s (2)).
CG 68780–68781 (a claim under sub-s (2) is not valid at the date a business ceases. A claim under sub-s (1) that goodwill has become "lost" or "destroyed" may succeed see CG 68800).
Revenue & other press releases—CCAB June 1971 ("small" is interpreted as 5 per cent "negligible" is considerably less).
Simon's Tax Cases—s 24(1), *Golding v Kaufman* [1985] STC 152*; *Director v Inspector of Taxes* [1998] STC (SCD) 172.
s 24(2), *Cleveleys Investment Trust Co v IRC* [1975] STC 457*; *Williams v Bullivant* [1983] STC 107*; *Larner v Warrington* [1985] STC 442*, *Little v George Little Sebire & Co* [2001] STC 1065.
Definitions—"Accounting period", TA 1988 s 834(1); "asset", s 21(1); "land", s 288(1); "market value", ss 272–274, Sch 11.
Cross references—See TA 1988 s 575(1)(*c*) (income tax relief for losses on unquoted shares in certain trading companies).
TCGA 1992 s 176(8) (effect on a claim under sub-s (2) above where the value of securities for which the claim is made was reduced by a depreciatory transaction).
FA 1999 s 82(9) (sub-s (1) above applies in respect of the extinction of rights in a Lloyd's members' agent pooling arrangement).
Amendments—¹ Sub-s (2) substituted by FA 1996 Sch 39 para 4 with effect for claims made after 5 April 1996.

25 Non-residents: deemed disposals

(1) Where an asset ceases by virtue of becoming situated outside the United Kingdom to be a chargeable asset in relation to a person, he shall be deemed for all purposes of this Act—

    (a) to have disposed of the asset immediately before the time when it became situated outside the United Kingdom, and

    (b) immediately to have reacquired it,

at its market value at that time.

(2) Subsection (1) above does not apply—

    (a) where the asset becomes situated outside the United Kingdom contemporaneously with the person there mentioned ceasing to carry on a trade in the United Kingdom through a branch or agency, or

    (b) where the asset is an exploration or exploitation asset.

(3) Where an asset ceases to be a chargeable asset in relation to a person by virtue of his ceasing to carry on a trade in the United Kingdom through a branch or agency, he shall be deemed for all purposes of this Act—

    (a) to have disposed of the asset immediately before the time when he ceased to carry on the trade in the United Kingdom through a branch or agency, and

    (b) immediately to have reacquired it,

at its market value at that time.

[(3A) Subsection (3) above shall not apply if—

    (a) the person ceasing to carry on the trade is a company, and

    (b) the trade is transferred to another company in circumstances in which section 139 or 171 applies in relation to the assets transferred.][1]

(4) ...[2]

(5) Subsection (3) above does not apply to an asset which is a chargeable asset in relation to the person there mentioned at any time after he ceases to carry on the trade in the United Kingdom through a branch or agency and before the end of the chargeable period in which he does so.

(6) In this section—

    "exploration or exploitation asset" means an asset used in connection with exploration or exploitation activities carried on in the United Kingdom or a designated area, and

    "designated area" and "exploration or exploitation activities" have the same meanings as in section 276.

(7) For the purposes of this section an asset is at any time a chargeable asset in relation to a person if, were it to be disposed of at that time, any chargeable gains accruing to him on the disposal—

    (a) would be gains in respect of which he would be chargeable to capital gains tax under section 10(1), or

    (b) would form part of his chargeable profits for corporation tax purposes by virtue of section 10(3).

(8) This section shall apply as if references to a trade included references to a profession or vocation.

Commentary—*Simon's Direct Tax Service* **C1.602.**
Revenue Internal Guidance—Capital gains tax manual 13630 (outlines the effect of Concession D2).
CG 42240 (worked example).
CG 45711 (sub-s (3) where relief is given under s 140A, there is no charge under sub-s (3)).
Definitions—"Asset", s 21(1); "branch or agency", s 10(6); "chargeable gain", s 15(2); "chargeable period", s 288(1); "company", ss 99, 288(1); "market value", ss 272–274, Sch 11; "resident", s 9(1); "trade", s 288(1), TA 1988 s 832(1).
Cross references—See TCGA 1992 s 140A(4) (transfer of a UK trade by one member State company to another member State company).
TCGA 1992 s 172(2) (disapplication of sub-s (3) of this section in respect of disposals of assets on the transfer of the trade of a UK branch or agency to a UK resident company).
TCGA 1992 Sch 7B paras 1, 4 (substitution of sub-s (7) above in the case of application of this section to an overseas life insurance company in relation to accounting periods beginning after 31 December 1992).
Amendments—[1] Sub-s (3A) inserted by FA 2000 s 102, Sch 29 para 6(1), (2), (4) with effect for cases where s 139, or as the case may be, s 171 has effect as amended by FA 2000 Sch 29.
[2] Sub-s (4) repealed by FA 2000 ss 102, 156, Sch 29 para 6(1), (3), (5), Sch 40 Pt II(12) with effect for cases where s 139 has effect as amended by FA 2000 Sch 29.

26 Mortgages and charges not to be treated as disposals

(1) The conveyance or transfer by way of security of an asset or of an interest or right in or over it, or transfer of a subsisting interest or right by way of security in or over an asset (including a retransfer on redemption of the security), shall not be treated for the purposes of this Act as involving any acquisition or disposal of the asset.

(2) Where a person entitled to an asset by way of security or to the benefit of a charge or incumbrance on an asset deals with the asset for the purpose of enforcing or giving effect to the security, charge or incumbrance, his dealings with it shall be treated for the purposes of this Act as if they were done through him as nominee by the person entitled to it subject to the security, charge or incumbrance; and this subsection shall apply to the dealings of any person appointed to enforce or give effect to

the security, charge or incumbrance as receiver and manager or judicial factor as it applies to the dealings of the person entitled as aforesaid.

(3) An asset shall be treated as having been acquired free of any interest or right by way of security subsisting at the time of any acquisition of it, and as being disposed of free of any such interest or right subsisting at the time of the disposal; and where an asset is acquired subject to any such interest or right the full amount of the liability thereby assumed by the person acquiring the asset shall form part of the consideration for the acquisition and disposal in addition to any other consideration.

Commentary—*Simon's Direct Tax Service* **C1.309; C2.1113.**
Simon's Tax Cases—s 26(1), *Aspden v Hildesley* [1982] STC 206*.
s 26(3), *Passant v Jackson* [1985] STC 133*.
Definition—''Asset'', s 21(1).

27 Disposals in cases of hire-purchase and similar transactions

A hire-purchase or other transaction under which the use and enjoyment of an asset is obtained by a person for a period at the end of which the property in the asset will or may pass to that person shall be treated for the purposes of this Act, both in relation to that person and in relation to the person from whom he obtains the use and enjoyment of the asset, as if it amounted to an entire disposal of the asset to that person at the beginning of the period for which he obtains the use and enjoyment of the asset, but subject to such adjustments of tax, whether by way of repayment or discharge of tax or otherwise, as may be required where the period for which that person has the use and enjoyment of the asset terminates without the property in the asset passing to him.

Commentary—*Simon's Direct Tax Service* **C1.310, 322.**
Revenue Internal Guidance—Capital gains tax manual CG 12850–12898 (full description of the provisions; multiple agreements CG 12880–12885; obtaining a tax advantage CG 12890–12898).
Simon's Tax Cases—*Lyon v Pettigrew* [1985] STC 369*.
Definition—''Asset'', s 21(1).

28 Time of disposal and acquisition where asset disposed of under contract

(1) Subject to section 22(2), and subsection (2) below, where an asset is disposed of and acquired under a contract the time at which the disposal and acquisition is made is the time the contract is made (and not, if different, the time at which the asset is conveyed or transferred).

(2) If the contract is conditional (and in particular if it is conditional on the exercise of an option) the time at which the disposal and acquisition is made is the time when the condition is satisfied.

Commentary—*Simon's Direct Tax Service* **C1.322.**
Revenue Interpretation RI 210—The date of disposal when a bookmaker's pitch is auctioned is the date on which the purchaser's bid is accepted.
Revenue Internal Guidance—Capital gains manual CG 12850–12809 (treatment of hire purchase contracts).
CG 14261–14275 (General principles concerning contracts).
CG 25820–26061 (deferral of date of disposal where taxpayer emigrates; oral contract pre-dating written contract CG 25910–25943; use of options CG 26040–26050; transfer to spouse who is emigrating CG 26060–26061).
Simon's Tax Cases—*Chaney v Watkis* [1986] STC 89*; *Magnavox Electronics Co Ltd (in liquidation) v Hall* [1986] STC 561*; *Pellipar Investments Ltd v Chaloner (Inspector of Taxes)* [1995] STC (SCD) 304.
s 28(2), *Lyon v Pettigrew* [1985] STC 369*; [1999] STC (SCD) 171; *Hatt v Newman* [2000] STC 113; *Jerome v Kelly (Inpector of Taxes)* [2001] STC (SCD) 170*.
Definition—''Asset'', s 21(1).

Value shifting

29 General provisions

(1) Without prejudice to the generality of the provisions of this Act as to the transactions which are disposals of assets, any transaction which under the following subsections is to be treated as a disposal of an asset—

  (*a*) shall be so treated (with a corresponding acquisition of an interest in the asset) notwithstanding that there is no consideration, and
  (*b*) so far as, on the assumption that the parties to the transaction were at arm's length, the party making the disposal could have obtained consideration, or additional consideration, for the disposal, shall be treated as not being at arm's length and the consideration so obtainable, or the additional consideration so obtainable added to the consideration actually passing, shall be treated as the market value of what is acquired.

(2) If a person having control of a company exercises his control so that value passes out of shares in the company owned by him or a person with whom he is connected, or out of rights over the company exercisable by him or by a person with whom he is connected, and passes into other shares in or rights over the company, that shall be a disposal of the shares or rights out of which the value passes by the person by whom they are owned or exercisable.

(3) A loss on the disposal of an asset shall not be an allowable loss to the extent to which it is attributable to value having passed out of other assets, being shares in or rights over a company which by virtue of the passing of value are treated as disposed of under subsection (2) above.

(4) If, after a transaction which results in the owner of land or of any other description of property becoming the lessee of the property there is any adjustment of the rights and liabilities under the

lease, whether or not involving the grant of a new lease, which is as a whole favourable to the lessor, that shall be a disposal by the lessee of an interest in the property.

(5) If an asset is subject to any description of right or restriction the extinction or abrogation, in whole or in part, of the right or restriction by the person entitled to enforce it shall be a disposal by him of the right or restriction.

Commentary—*Simon's Direct Tax Service* **C1.335, 336; C2.115.**
Simon's Tax Cases—s 29(2), *Floor v Davis* [1979] STC 379*.
Definitions—"Allowable loss", ss 8(2), 16, 288(1); "asset", s 21(1); "company", ss 99, 288(1); "connected", s 286; "control", s 288(1), TA 1988 s 416; "land", s 288(1); "lease", Sch 8 para 10(1); "lessee", Sch 8 para 10(1); "lessor", Sch 8 para 10(1); "market value", ss 272–274, Sch 11; "shares", s 288(1).

30 Tax-free benefits

(1) This section has effect as respects the disposal of an asset if a scheme has been effected or arrangements have been made (whether before or after the disposal) whereby—

  (*a*) the value of the asset or a relevant asset has been materially reduced, and
  (*b*) a tax-free benefit has been or will be conferred—

    (i) on the person making the disposal or a person with whom he is connected, or
    (ii) subject to subsection (4) below, on any other person.

(2) For the purposes of this section, where the asset disposed of by a company ("the disposing company") consists of shares in, or securities of, another company, another asset is a relevant asset if, at the time of the disposal, it is owned by a company associated with the disposing company; but no account shall be taken of any reduction in the value of a relevant asset except in a case where—

  (*a*) during the period beginning with the reduction in value and ending immediately before the disposal by the disposing company, there is no disposal of the asset to any person, other than a disposal falling within section 171(1),
  (*b*) no disposal of the asset is treated as having occurred during that period by virtue of section ...[2] 179, and
  (*c*) if the reduction had not taken place but any consideration given for the relevant asset and any other material circumstances (including any consideration given before the disposal for the asset disposed of) were unchanged, the value of the asset disposed of would, at the time of the disposal, have been materially greater;

and in this subsection "securities" has the same meaning as in section 132.

(3) For the purposes of subsection (1)(*b*) above a benefit is conferred on a person if he becomes entitled to any money or money's worth or the value of any asset in which he has an interest is increased or he is wholly or partly relieved from any liability to which he is subject; and a benefit is tax-free unless it is required, on the occasion on which it is conferred on the person in question, to be brought into account in computing his income, profits or gains for the purposes of income tax, capital gains tax or corporation tax.

(4) This section shall not apply by virtue of subsection (1)(*b*)(ii) above [in a case where][1] avoidance of tax was not the main purpose or one of the main purposes of the scheme or arrangements in question.

(5) Where this section has effect in relation to any disposal, any allowable loss or chargeable gain accruing on the disposal shall be calculated as if the consideration for the disposal were increased by such amount as [is][1] just and reasonable having regard to the scheme or arrangements and the tax-free benefit in question.

(6) Where—

  (*a*) by virtue of subsection (5) above the consideration for the disposal of an asset has been treated as increased, and
  (*b*) the benefit taken into account under subsection (1)(*b*) above was an increase in the value of another asset,

any allowable loss or chargeable gain accruing on the first disposal of the other asset after the increase in its value shall be calculated as if the consideration for that disposal were reduced by such amount as [is][1] just and reasonable having regard to the scheme or arrangements in question and the increase made in relation to the disposal mentioned in paragraph (*a*) above.

(7) References in this section to a disposal do not include references to any disposal falling within section 58(1), 62(4) or 171(1).

(8) References in this section, in relation to any disposal, to a reduction in the value of an asset, where the asset consists of shares owned by a company in another company, shall be interpreted in accordance with sections 31 to 33 and, in those sections, the disposal, the asset and those companies are referred to respectively as "the section 30 disposal", "the principal asset", "the first company" and "the second company".

(9) In relation to a case in which the disposal of an asset precedes its acquisition the references in subsections (1)(*a*) and (2) above to a reduction shall be read as including a reference to an increase.

Commentary—*Simon's Direct Tax Service* **D2.669.**
Statement of Practice D18—Value shifting: TCGA 1992 s 30, Sch 11 para 10(1).

Revenue & other press releases—IR 3-2-81 (surrender of losses by way of group relief without payment, or where payment is less than the value of group relief is not caught under s 30).
Revenue Internal Guidance—Capital gains manual CG 46903 (if a loss remains after any value shifting adjustment, a further adjustment under s 176 or s 177 may be in point).
Definitions—"Allowable loss", ss 8(2), 16, 288(1); "asset", s 21(1); "chargeable gain", s 15(2); "company", ss 99, 288(1); "shares", s 288(1).
Modifications—See TCGA 1992 s 33A (modification of this section in relation to chargeable intangible asset).
Cross references—See TA 1988 s 576(2) (modification of sub-ss (1)(*b*), (4) of this section where income tax relief is claimed for losses under TA 1988 s 576).
TCGA 1992 s 33 (supplementary provisions).
TCGA 1992 s 34 (transactions treated as reorganisation of share capital).
TCGA 1992 Sch 11 para 10(1) (transitory provision where reduction or increase in value mentioned in sub-s (1) or (8) above is after 29 March 1977).
FA 2000 Sch 15 para 71 (modification of this section in relation to a disposal of shares (in respect of corporate venturing scheme) under FA 2000 Sch 15 Pt VII (relief for losses on disposal of shares)).
FA 2000 Sch 29 para 17(4) (the main amendments made to TCGA 1992 s 170 by FA 2000 Sch 29 para 1 have effect for the purposes of this section with effect for disposals after 31 March 2000).
Amendments—[1] Words in sub-ss (4), (5), (6) substituted by FA 1996 s 134(1), (2), Sch 20 paras 46, 47(*a*) with effect for capital gains tax from the year 1996–97 and, for purposes of corporation tax, as respects accounting periods ending after 30 June 1999 (by virtue of Finance Act 1994, Section 199, (Appointed Day) Order, SI 1998/3173 art 2).
[2] Words "178 or" in sub-s (2)(*b*) repealed by FA 2000 s 156, Sch 40 Pt II(12) with effect from 28 July 2000.

31 Distributions within a group followed by a disposal of shares

(1) The references in section 30 to a reduction in the value of an asset, in the case mentioned in subsection (8) of that section, do not include a reduction attributable to the payment of a dividend by the second company at a time when it and the first company are associated, except to the extent (if any) that the dividend is attributable to chargeable profits of the second company and, in such a case, the tax-free benefit shall be ascertained without regard to any part of the dividend that is not attributable to such profits.

(2) Subsections (3) to (11) below apply for the interpretation of subsection (1) above.

(3) Chargeable profits shall be ascertained as follows—

(*a*) the distributable profits of any company are chargeable profits of that company to the extent that they are profits arising on a transaction caught by this section, and
(*b*) where any company makes a distribution attributable wholly or partly to chargeable profits (including any profits that are chargeable profits by virtue of this paragraph) to another company, the distributable profits of the other company, so far as they represent that distribution or so much of it as was attributable to chargeable profits, are chargeable profits of the other company,

and for this purpose any loss or other amount to be set against the profits of a company in determining the distributable profits shall be set first against profits other than the profits so arising or, as the case may be, representing so much of the distribution as was attributable to chargeable profits.

(4) The distributable profits of a company are such profits computed on a commercial basis as, after allowing for any provision properly made for tax, the company is empowered, assuming sufficient funds, to distribute to persons entitled to participate in the profits of the company.

(5) Profits of a company ("company A") are profits arising on a transaction caught by this section where each of the following 3 conditions is satisfied.

(6) The first condition is that the transaction is—

(*a*) a disposal of an asset by company A to another company in circumstances such that company A and the other company are treated as mentioned in section 171(1), or
[(*b*) an exchange, or deemed exchange, of shares in or debentures of a company held by company A for shares in or debentures of another company, being a company associated with company A immediately after the transaction, that is treated by virtue of section 135 or 136 as a reorganisation of share capital within the meaning of section 126 to which sections 127 to 131 apply with the necessary adaptations, or][2]
(*c*) a revaluation of an asset in the accounting records of company A.

In the following conditions the "asset with enhanced value" means (subject to section 33), in the paragraph (*a*) case, the asset acquired by the person to whom the disposal is made, in the paragraph (*b*) case, the shares in or debentures of the other company and, in the paragraph (*c*) case, the revalued asset.

(7) The second condition is that—

(*a*) during the period beginning with the transaction referred to in subsection (6) above and ending immediately before the section 30 disposal, there is no disposal of the asset with enhanced value to any person, other than a disposal falling within section 171(1), and
(*b*) no disposal of the asset with enhanced value is treated as having occurred during that period by virtue of section ...[1] 179.

(8) The third condition is that, immediately after the section 30 disposal, the asset with enhanced value is owned by a person other than the company making that disposal or a company associated with it.

(9) The conditions in subsections (6) to (8) above are not satisfied if—

  (*a*) at the time of the transaction referred to in subsection (6) above, company A carries on a trade and a profit on a disposal of the asset with enhanced value would form part of the trading profits, or

  (*b*) by reason of the nature of the asset with enhanced value, a disposal of it could give rise neither to a chargeable gain nor to an allowable loss, or

  (*c*) immediately before the section 30 disposal, the company owning the asset with enhanced value carries on a trade and a profit on a disposal of the asset would form part of the trading profits.

(10) The amount of chargeable profits of a company to be attributed to any distribution made by the company at any time in respect of any class of shares, securities or rights shall be ascertained by—

  (*a*) determining the total of distributable profits, and the total of chargeable profits, that remains after allowing for earlier distributions made in respect of that or any other class of shares, securities or rights, and for distributions made at or to be made after that time in respect of other classes of shares, securities or rights, and

  (*b*) attributing first to that distribution distributable profits other than chargeable profits.

(11) The amount of chargeable profits of a company to be attributed to any part of a distribution made at any time to which a person is entitled by virtue of any part of his holding of any class of shares, securities or rights, shall be such proportion of the chargeable profits as are attributable under subsection (10) above to the distributions made at that time in respect of that class as corresponds to that part of his holding.

Commentary—*Simon's Direct Tax Service* D2.669.
Revenue Internal Guidance—Capital gains manual CG 46805, 46820–46853 (explanation of this section with examples).
Definitions—"Allowable loss", ss 8(2), 16, 288(1); "asset", s 21(1); "chargeable gain", s 15(2); "class", s 288(1); "company", ss 99, 288(1); "shares", s 288(1); "trade", s 288(1), TA 1988 s 832(1).
Modifications—See TCGA 1992 s 33A (modification of this section in relation to chargeable intangible asset).
Cross references—See TCGA 1992 s 30(8) ("reduction in the value of an asset" in s 30 to be interpreted in accordance with this section).
TCGA 1992 s 31A (application of s 31A to cases where sub-s (8) above not satisfied).
TCGA 1992 s 33 (supplementary provisions).
TCGA 1992 Sch 11 para 10(2) (no account to be taken, by virtue of this section, of any reduction in the value of an asset attributable to the payment of a dividend before 14 March 1989).
FA 2000 Sch 29 para 17(4) (the main amendments made to TCGA 1992 s 170 by FA 2000 Sch 29 para 1 have effect for the purposes of this section with effect for disposals after 31 March 2000).
Amendments—[1] Words "178 or" in sub-s (7)(*b*) repealed by FA 2000 s 156, Sch 40 Pt II(12) with effect from 28 July 2000.
[2] Sub-s (6)(*b*) substituted by FA 2002 s 45, Sch 9 paras 5(1), (2), 7 with effect for shares or debentures issued after 16 April 2002. The reference to shares or debentures includes any interests falling to be treated as shares or debentures for the purposes of TCGA 1992 s 135 or 136 as substituted by FA 2002 Sch 9. Sub-s (6)(*b*) previously read as follows—

"(*b*) an exchange, or a transaction treated for the purposes of section 135(2) and (3) as an exchange, of shares in or debentures of a company held by company A for shares in or debentures of another company, being a company associated with company A immediately after the transaction, and is treated by virtue of section 135(3) as a reorganisation of share capital, or".

[31A Asset-holding company leaving the group

(1) This section applies where profits of a company would be profits arising on a transaction caught by section 31 but for the fact that the condition in section 31(8) is not satisfied.

(2) The profits shall be treated as profits arising on a transaction caught by section 31 if—

  (*a*) subsection (4) or (5) below is satisfied, and
  (*b*) subsection (6) below is satisfied.

(3) In the following provisions of this section—

  "the asset-holding company" means, in relation to any particular time, the company which holds the asset with enhanced value at that time,

  "the disposal group" means the group of companies of which the company which made the section 30 disposal was a member at the time of the disposal (or a group which, by virtue of section 170(10), is treated as the same as that group), and

  "the six-year period" means the period of six years starting with the date of the section 30 disposal.

(4) This subsection is satisfied if at any time during the six-year period an event occurs which consists in the asset-holding company ceasing to be a member of the disposal group otherwise than by reason of the fact that the principal company of that group becomes a member of another group.

(5) This subsection is satisfied if—

  (*a*) at any time during the six-year period the asset-holding company ceases to be a member of the disposal group by reason only of the fact that the principal company of that group becomes a member of another group, and

  (*b*) at any time during that period an event occurs as a result of which there is no member of the disposal group of which the asset-holding company is a 75 per cent subsidiary or there is no member of that group of which the asset-holding company is an effective 51 per cent subsidiary.

(6) This subsection is satisfied if no disposal of the asset with enhanced value is treated as having occurred by virtue of section 179 during the period—

  (*a*) beginning with the time of the section 30 disposal, and
  (*b*) ending immediately before the event referred to in subsection (4) or (5)(*b*) above.

(7) Where section 30 has effect by virtue of this section in relation to a disposal—

(*a*) a chargeable gain of the differential amount shall be treated as accruing to the chargeable company immediately before the event referred to in subsection (4) or (5)(*b*) above, and

(*b*) subsection (5) of section 30 shall not apply.

(8) The "differential amount" is A minus B where—

(*a*) A is the amount of the allowable loss or chargeable gain which would have accrued on the section 30 disposal if the consideration for the disposal had been increased in accordance with section 30(5),

(*b*) B is the amount of the allowable loss or chargeable gain which accrued on the section 30 disposal,

(*c*) an allowable loss is treated as a negative amount, and

(*d*) a negative result is treated as a result of nil.

(9) The "chargeable company" is—

(*a*) the company which made the section 30 disposal, or

(*b*) if that company is no longer a member of the disposal group immediately before the event referred to in subsection (4) or (5)(*b*) above, [any other company which—

(i) is a member of that group immediately before that event, and

(ii) is designated as the chargeable company for the purposes of this section in a notice served on the company by an officer of the Board.][2]

(10) A gain which is treated as accruing by virtue of subsection (7) above shall, for the purposes of section 18(3), be treated as a gain accruing on a disposal between the parties to the section 30 disposal made at a time when they are connected persons.][1]

[(11) Where a notice is served on a company under subsection (9)(*b*) above, the Inland Revenue may make an assessment to tax in the amount which in their opinion ought to be charged under this section.][2]

Commentary—*Simon's Direct Tax Service* **D2.669.**
Modifications—See TCGA 1992 s 33A (modification of this section in relation to chargeable intangible asset).
Cross references—See TCGA 1992 s 33 (supplementary provisions).
TCGA 1992 s 34(1A)–(1C) (application of this section where the reorganisation provisions of TCGA 1992 ss 127, 135(3) prevent a share exchange being a disposal for capital gains purposes).
FA 2000 Sch 29 para 17(4) (the main amendments made to TCGA 1992 s 170 by FA 2000 Sch 29 para 1 have effect for the purposes of this section with effect for disposals after 31 March 2000).
Amendment—[1] This section inserted by FA 1999 s 74, Sch 9 paras 2, 5 with effect for any disposal of an asset after 8 March 1999.
[2] Words in sub-s (9)(*b*) substituted, and sub-s (11) added, by FA 2000 s 102, Sch 29 para 17 with effect for disposals after 31 March 2000.

32 Disposals within a group followed by a disposal of shares

(1) The references in section 30 to a reduction in the value of an asset, in the case mentioned in subsection (8) of that section, do not include a reduction attributable to the disposal of any asset ("the underlying asset") by the second company at a time when it and the first company are associated, being a disposal falling within section 171(1), except in a case within subsection (2) below.

(2) A case is within this subsection if the amount or value of the actual consideration for the disposal of the underlying asset—

(*a*) is less than the market value of the underlying asset, and

(*b*) is less than the cost of the underlying asset,

unless the disposal is effected for bona fide commercial reasons and does not form part of a scheme or arrangements of which the main purpose, or one of the main purposes, is avoidance of liability to corporation tax.

(3) For the purposes of subsection (2) above, the cost of an asset owned by a company is the aggregate of—

(*a*) any capital expenditure incurred by the company in acquiring or providing the asset, and

(*b*) any other capital expenditure incurred by the company in respect of the asset while owned by that company.

(4) For the purposes of this section, where the disposal of the underlying asset is a part disposal, the reference in subsection (2)(*a*) above to the market value of the underlying asset is to the market value of the asset acquired by the person to whom the disposal is made and the amounts to be attributed to the underlying asset under paragraphs (*a*) and (*b*) of subsection (3) above shall be reduced to the appropriate proportion of those amounts, that is—

(*a*) the proportion of capital expenditure in respect of the underlying asset properly attributed in the accounting records of the company to the asset acquired by the person to whom the disposal is made, or

(*b*) where paragraph (*a*) above does not apply, such proportion as [is][1] just and reasonable.

(5) Where by virtue of a distribution in the course of dissolving or winding up the second company the first company is treated as disposing of an interest in the principal asset, the exception mentioned in subsection (1) above does not apply.

Commentary—*Simon's Direct Tax Service* **D2.669.**
Revenue Internal Guidance—Capital gains manual CG 46880–46885 (general outline of this section).
Definitions—''Asset'', s 21(1); ''company'', ss 99, 288(1); ''market value'', ss 272–274, Sch 11; ''part disposal'', s 21(2); ''shares'', s 288(1).
Modifications—See TCGA 1992 s 33A (modification of this section in relation to chargeable intangible asset).
Cross references—See TCGA 1992 s 30(8) (''reduction in the value of an asset'' in s 30 to be interpreted in accordance with this section).
TCGA 1992 s 33 (supplementary provisions).
TCGA 1992 Sch 11 para 10(3) (no account to be taken, by virtue of this section, of any reduction in the value of an asset attributable to the disposal of another asset before 14 March 1989).
FA 2000 Sch 29 para 17(4) (the main amendments made to TCGA 1992 s 170 by FA 2000 Sch 29 para 1 have effect for the purposes of this section with effect for disposals after 31 March 2000).
Amendments—[1] Word in sub-s (4)(*b*) substituted by FA 1996 s 134(1), (2), Sch 20 para 47(*b*) with effect for capital gains tax from the year 1996–97 and, so far as relating to corporation tax, as respects accounting periods ending after 30 June 1999 (by virtue of Finance Act 1994, Section 199, (Appointed Day) Order, SI 1998/3173 art 2).

33 Provisions supplementary to sections 30 to 32

(1) For the purposes of sections 30(2) and 31(7) to (9), subsections (2) to (6) below apply for the purpose of determining in the case of any asset (''the original asset'') whether it is subsequently disposed of or treated as disposed of or owned or any other condition is satisfied in respect of it.

[(1A) For the purposes of section 31A, subsections (2) to (6) below apply for the purpose of determining any question in relation to the asset with enhanced value.][2]

(2) References in sections 30(2)(*a*) and (*b*)[,31(7) and 31A(6)][3] to a disposal are to a disposal other than a part disposal.

(3) [For the purposes of sections 30(2) and 31(7) to (9),][4] references to an asset are to the original asset or, where at a later time one or more assets are treated by virtue of subsections (5) or (6) below as the same as the original asset—

    (*a*) if no disposal falling within paragraph (*a*) or (*b*) of section 30(2) or, as the case may be, of 31(7) has occurred, those references are to the asset so treated or, as the case may be, all the assets so treated, and

    (*b*) in any other case, those references are to an asset or, as the case may be, all the assets representing that part of the value of the original asset that remains after allowing for earlier disposals falling within the paragraphs concerned,

references in this subsection to a disposal including a disposal which would fall within the paragraphs concerned but for subsection (2) above.

[(3A) Subsections (3B) and (3C) below apply (instead of subsection (3) above) for the purposes of section 31A where one or more assets are treated by virtue of subsection (5) or (6) below as the same as the asset with enhanced value.][2]

[(3B) If in the period beginning with the time of the transaction referred to in section 31(6) and ending immediately before the event referred to in section 31A(4) or (5)(*b*)—

    (*a*) there is no disposal of the asset with enhanced value to any person other than a disposal falling with section 171(1), and

    (*b*) no disposal of the asset with enhanced value is treated as having occurred by virtue of section 179,

then references to the asset with enhanced value are to the asset which is treated by virtue of subsection (5) or (6) below as the same as that asset or, as the case may be, all the assets so treated.][2]

[(3C) In any other case, references to the asset with enhanced value are to an asset or, as the case may be, all the assets representing that part of the value of the asset with enhanced value that remains after allowing for disposals of a kind mentioned in subsection (3B)(*a*) or (*b*).][2]

(4) [Where by virtue of subsection (3), (3B) or (3C) above references to an asset are taken as references to two or more assets][3]—

    (*a*) those assets shall be treated as if they were a single asset,

    (*b*) any disposal of any one of them is to be treated as a part disposal, and

    (*c*) the reference in section 30(2) to the asset owned at the time of the disposal by a company associated with the disposing company and [a reference in section 31(8) or 31A(3)][3] to the asset with enhanced value is to all or any of those assets.

(5) Where there is a part disposal of an asset, that asset and the asset acquired by the person to whom the disposal is made are to be treated as the same.

(6) Where the value of an asset is derived from any other asset in the ownership of the same or an associated company, in a case where assets have been merged or divided or have changed their nature or rights or interests in or over assets have been created or extinguished, the first asset is to be treated as the same as the second.

(7) For the purposes of section 30(2), where account is to be taken under that subsection of a reduction in the value of a relevant asset and at the time of the disposal by the disposing company referred to in that subsection—

    (*a*) references to the relevant asset are by virtue of this section references to 2 or more assets treated as a single asset, and (*b*) one or more but not all of those assets are owned by a company associated with the disposing company,

the amount of the reduction in the value of the relevant asset to be taken into account by virtue of that subsection shall be reduced to such amount as [is][1] just and reasonable.

(8) For the purposes of section 31, where—

(*a*) a dividend paid by the second company is attributable to chargeable profits of that company, and

(*b*) the condition in subsection (7), (8) or (9)(*c*) of that section is satisfied by reference to an asset, or assets treated as a single asset, treated by virtue of subsection (3)(*b*) above as the same as the asset with enhanced value,

the amount of the reduction in value of the principal asset shall be reduced to such amount as [is][1] just and reasonable.

[(8A) In a case where—

(*a*) profits are treated as profits arising on a transaction caught by section 31 by virtue of section 31A, and

(*b*) the condition in section 31(7) or a condition in section 31A is satisfied by reference to an asset, or assets treated as a single asset, treated by virtue of subsection (3C) above as the same as the asset with enhanced value,

the amount of the reduction in value of the principal asset shall be reduced to such amount as is just and reasonable.][2]

(9) For the purposes of sections 30 to 32 and this section, companies are associated if they are members of the same group.

(10) Section 170(2) to (11) applies for the purposes of sections 30 to 32 and this section as it applies for the purposes of that section.

Commentary—*Simon's Direct Tax Service* D2.669.
Definitions—"Asset", s 21(1); "company", ss 99, 288(1); "part disposal", s 21(2).
Modifications—See TCGA 1992 s 33A (modification of this section in relation to chargeable intangible asset).
Cross references—See TCGA 1992 s 30(8) ("reduction in the value of an asset" in s 30 to be interpreted in accordance with this section).
FA 2000 Sch 29 para 17(4) (the main amendments made to TCGA 1992 s 170 by FA 2000 Sch 29 para 1 have effect for the purposes of this section with effect for disposals after 31 March 2000).
Amendments—[1] Words in sub-ss (7), (8) substituted by FA 1996 s 134(1), (2), Sch 20 para 47(*c*) with effect for capital gains tax from the year 1996–97 and, for the purposes of corporation tax, for accounting periods ending after 30 June 1999 (by virtue of Finance Act 1994, Section 199, (Appointed Day) Order, SI 1998/3173 art 2).
[2] Sub-ss (1A). (3A), (3B), (3C), (8A) inserted by FA 1999 s 74, Sch 9 paras 3, 5 with effect for any disposal of an asset after 8 March 1999.
[3] Words in sub-s (2), (4) substituted by FA 1999 s 74, Sch 9 paras 3, 5 with effect for any disposal of an asset after 8 March 1999.
[4] Words in sub-s (3) inserted by FA 1999 s 74, Sch 9 paras 3, 5 with effect for any disposal of an asset after 8 March 1999.

[33A Modification of sections 30 to 33 in relation to chargeable intangible asset

(1) Sections 30 to 33 have effect in relation to a chargeable intangible asset subject to the following modifications.

In this section "chargeable intangible asset" has the same meaning as in Schedule 29 to the Finance Act 2002.

(2) Any reference in those sections—

(*a*) to a disposal or part disposal of the asset shall be read as a reference to its realisation or part realisation within the meaning of that Schedule (see paragraph 19 of that Schedule);

(*b*) to an disposal of the asset under section 171(1) shall be read as a reference to its transfer under paragraph 55 of that Schedule (transfers within a group);

(*c*) to a disposal of the asset under section 179 shall be read as a reference to its realisation under paragraph 58 or 60 of that Schedule (degrouping).

(3) In section 31(6), paragraph (*c*) shall not apply to a revaluation where the profit on the revaluation is wholly taken into account as a credit under that Schedule (see paragraph 15 of that Schedule).

(4) None of the conditions in section 31(9) shall be treated as satisfied if the asset with enhanced value is a chargeable intangible asset within the meaning of that Schedule.

(5) The reference in section 32(2)(*b*) to the cost of the underlying asset shall be read, in the case of a chargeable intangible asset, as a reference to the capitalised value of the asset recognised for accounting purposes.][1]

Amendments—This section inserted by FA 2002 s 84(2), Sch 30 para 6 with effect from 24 July 2002.

34 Transactions treated as a reorganisation of share capital

(1) Where—

(*a*) but for [section 135 or 136][2], section 30 would have effect as respects the disposal by a company ("the disposing company") of an asset consisting of shares in or debentures of another company ("the original holding") in exchange for shares in or debentures of a further company which, immediately after the disposal, is not a member of the same group as the disposing company, and

(*b*) if section 30 had effect as respects that disposal, any allowable loss or chargeable gain accruing on the disposal would be calculated as if the consideration for the disposal were increased by an amount,

the disposing company shall be treated for the purposes of section 128(3) as receiving, on the reorganisation of share capital that is treated as occurring by virtue of [section 135 or 136]², that amount for the disposal of the original holding.

[(1A) Subsection (1B) below applies where, but for [section 135 or 136]², section 30 would have effect, by virtue of section 31A, as respects the disposal by a company (''the disposing company'') of an asset consisting of shares in or debentures of another company (''the original holding'') in exchange for shares in or debentures of a further company which, immediately after the disposal, is not a member of the same group as the disposing company.]¹

[(1B) Section 31A shall apply as if [section 135 or 136]² did not apply.]¹

[(1C) In applying section 31A(7) and (8)—

(*a*) the reference in section 31A(8) to an allowable loss or chargeable gain which accrued on the section 30 disposal shall be taken as a reference to the allowable loss or chargeable gain which would have accrued had [section 135 or 136]² not applied, and

(*b*) an allowable loss shall be treated as a chargeable gain of nil.]¹

(2) [In subsections (1) to (1C)]² ''group'' has the same meaning as in sections 30 to 33.

Commentary—*Simon's Direct Tax Service* **D2.669.**
Revenue Internal Guidance—Capital gains manual CG 46900–46901 (the effect of this section is that there is a deemed part disposal).
Definitions—''Allowable loss'', ss 8(2), 16, 288(1); ''asset'', s 21(1); ''chargeable gain'', s 15(2); ''company'', ss 99, 288(1); ''shares'', s 288(1).
Cross references—See TCGA 1992 Sch 11 para 10(4) (this section not to apply where the reduction in value occurred before 14 March 1989).
FA 2000 Sch 29 para 17(4) (the main amendments made to TCGA 1992 s 170 by FA 2000 Sch 29 para 1 have effect for the purposes of this section with effect for disposals after 31 March 2000).
Amendments—¹ Sub-ss (1A). (1B), (1C), inserted by FA 1999 s 74, Sch 9 paras 4, 5 with effect for any disposal of an asset after 8 March 1999.
² In sub-ss (1)(*a*), (1A), (1B) and (1C)(*a*), words substituted for the words ''sections 127 and 135(3)'', words in sub-s (1) substituted for the words ''section 135(3)'', and words and in sub-s (2), words substituted; by FA 2002 s 45, Sch 9 paras 5(1), (3), 7 with effect for shares or debentures issued after 16 April 2002. The reference to shares or debentures includes any interests falling to be treated as shares or debentures for the purposes of TCGA 1992 s 135 or 136 as substituted by FA 2002 Sch 9. Sub-s (2) previously read as follows—

''For the purposes of subsections (1) to (1C) above it shall be assumed that section 136 has effect generally for the purposes of this Act, and in those subsections,''group'' has the same meaning as in sections 30 to 33.''

CHAPTER III
COMPUTATION OF GAINS: GENERAL PROVISIONS

Cross references—See TA 1988 s 763(3) (treatment of offshore income gains in capital gains tax computation); TA 1988 Sch 26 para 3 (controlled foreign companies).

Re-basing to 1982, and assets held on 6th April 1965

35 Assets held on 31st March 1982 (including assets held on 6th April 1965)

(1) This section applies to a disposal of an asset which was held on 31st March 1982 by the person making the disposal.

(2) Subject to the following provisions of this section, in computing for the purpose of this Act the gain or loss accruing on the disposal it shall be assumed that the asset was on 31st March 1982 sold by the person making the disposal, and immediately reacquired by him, at its market value on that date.

(3) Subject to subsection (5) below, subsection (2) above shall not apply to a disposal—

(*a*) where a gain would accrue on the disposal to the person making the disposal if that subsection did apply, and either a smaller gain or a loss would so accrue if it did not,

(*b*) where a loss would so accrue if that subsection did apply, and either a smaller loss or a gain would accrue if it did not,

(*c*) where, either on the facts of the case or by virtue of Schedule 2, neither a gain nor a loss would accrue if that subsection did not apply, or

(*d*) where neither a gain nor a loss would accrue by virtue of any of—

(i) sections 58, 73, 139, [140A,]¹ 171, ...¹¹ 215, 216, [217A,]² 218 to 221, 257(3), 258(4), 264 and 267(2) of this Act;

(ii) section 148 of the 1979 Act;

(iii) section 148 of the Finance Act 1982;

(iv) paragraph 2 of Schedule 2 to the Trustee Savings Banks Act 1985;

(*v*) section 130(3) of the Transport Act 1985;

(vi) section 486(8) of the Taxes Act; ...⁴

(vii) paragraph 2(1) of Schedule 12 to the Finance Act 1990 ...[6];

[(viii) paragraph 5(3) of Schedule 17 to the Finance (No 2) Act 1992;][3]

[(ix) paragraphs 2(1), 7(2), 11(3) and (4) and 25(2) of Schedule 24 to the Finance Act 1994][5].

[(x) paragraph 4(2) of Schedule 25 to the Finance Act 1994][7]

[(xi) paragraph 2(1) of Schedule 4 to the Coal Industry Act 1994;][8]

[(xii) paragraph 2(1) of Schedule 7 to the Broadcasting Act 1996;][10]

[(xiii) paragraph 2(1) of Schedule 7 to the Transport Act 2000;][13]

[(xiv) paragraphs 3 and 9 of Schedule 26 to the Transport Act 2000;][12]

(4) Where in the case of a disposal of an asset—

(*a*) the effect of subsection (2) above would be to substitute a loss for a gain or a gain for a loss, but

(*b*) the application of subsection (2) is excluded by subsection (3),

it shall be assumed in relation to the disposal that the asset was acquired by the person making the disposal for a consideration such that, on the disposal, neither a gain nor a loss accrues to him.

(5) If a person so elects, disposals made by him (including any made by him before the election) shall fall outside subsection (3) above (so that subsection (2) above is not excluded by that subsection).

(6) An election by a person under subsection (5) above shall be irrevocable and shall be made by notice to [an officer of the Board][9] at any time before 6th April 1990 or at any time during the period beginning with the day of the first relevant disposal and ending—

[(*a*) in the case of an election for the purposes of capital gains tax, with the first anniversary of the 31st January next following the year of assessment in which the disposal is made;][9]

[(*aa*) in the case of an election for the purposes of corporation tax, 2 years after the end of the accounting period in which the disposal is made; or][9]

[(*b*) in either case, at such later time as the Board may allow;][9]

and "the first relevant disposal" means the first disposal to which this section applies which is made by the person making the election.

(7) An election made by a person under subsection (5) above in one capacity does not cover disposals made by him in another capacity.

(8) All such adjustments shall be made, whether by way of discharge or repayment of tax, the making of assessments or otherwise, as are required to give effect to an election under subsection (5) above.

(9) Schedule 2 shall have effect in relation to disposals of assets owned on 6th April 1965 in cases where neither subsection (2) nor subsection (4) above applies.

(10) Schedule 3, which contains provisions supplementary to subsections (1) to (8) above, shall have effect.

Commentary—*Simon's Direct Tax Service* C2.601, 603, 604.

Concession D34—Calculation of cost or indexation allowance on a disposal of shares or securities where some but not all are valued at 31 March 1982 to be based on the proportion that the shares or securities disposed of bears to the total holding at 31 March 1982.

Statement of Practice SP 4/92—Extension of time limit for an election in sub-s (6) above in respect of certain disposals.

Revenue Interpretation RI 9—Procedure for rebasing elections where they are made by the same person in different capacities.

RI 152—Principle in *Gray v IRC* [1994] STC 360 (two or more assets can be valued as single unit in certain circumstances) *not* to be applied in determining market value under this section.

RI 210—Determination of market value of bookmaker's pitches.

Revenue & other press releases—IR 18-11-91 (Shares Valuation Division (SVD) will begin valuing unquoted shares in advance of a formal request from the inspector of taxes, where shareholders with similar holdings agree and approach SVD before submitting their tax returns).

Law Society 18-3-92 (valuation of agricultural tenancies: principles to be applied).

IR Tax Bulletin, February 1993 (Revenue view quota and land are separate assets for CGT purposes. The cost of milk quota acquired by allotment in 1984 is nil TCGA s 17(2)).

Revenue Internal Guidance—Capital Gains Manual CG 16820–16822 (sub-s (5): outlines the circumstances in which a late election may be accepted).

Definitions—"The 1979 Act", s 288(1); "accounting period", TA 1988 s 834(1); "asset", s 21(1); "the Board", s 288(1); "market value", ss 272–274, Sch 11; "notice", s 288(1); "the Taxes Acts", s 288(1); "year of assessment", s 288(1).

Cross references—See TCGA 1992 s 55(2), (7) (indexation allowance on assets owned or deemed to be owned on 31 March 1982).

TCGA 1992 s 267(3) (disposal of assets between national broadcasting companies under agreements relating to the sharing of transmission facilities).

TCGA 1992 Sch 3 para 4(2) (deduction from deemed reacquisition cost for purposes of sub-s (2) of this section where certain small part disposals took place between 31 March 1982 and 5 April 1988).

TCGA 1992 Sch 3 para 7 (disposals excluded from rebasing election).

Amendments—[1] Number in sub-s (3)(*d*)(i) inserted by F(No 2)A 1992 s 46(1), (2) and deemed always to have had effect.

[2] Number in sub-s (3)(*d*)(i) inserted by F(No 2)A 1992 Sch 9 paras 21(1), (2), 22 with effect from 19 February 1993 by virtue of F(No 2)A 1992 Sch 9 (Appointed Day) Order, SI 1992/236.

[3] Sub-s (3)(*d*)(viii) and the preceding word "and" inserted by F(No 2)A 1992 Sch 17 para 5(9) and deemed always to have had effect.

[4] Word "and" in sub-s (3)(*d*)(vi) repealed by F(No 2)A 1992 Sch 17 para 5(9) and Sch 18 Pt X.

[5] Sub-s (3)(*d*)(ix) inserted by FA 1994 Sch 24 para 2(2).

[6] Word "and" in sub-s (3)(*d*)(vii) repealed by FA 1994 Sch 24 para 2(2) and Sch 26 Pt VIII(2).

[7] Sub-s (3)(*d*))(x) inserted by FA 1994 s 253, Sch 25 para 4(3).

[8] Sub-s (3)(*d*)(xi) inserted by the Coal Industry Act 1994 s 21, Sch 4 para 2(3) with effect from 19 September 1994.

[9] Words "an officer of the Board" in sub-s (6) and sub-s (6)(*a*), (*aa*), (*b*) substituted by FA 1996 s 135(1), (2), Sch 21 para 35 with effect in relation to capital gains tax from the year 1996–97 and, for the purposes of corporation tax, as respects accounting periods ending after 30 June 1999 (by virtue of Finance Act 1994, Section 199, (Appointed Day) Order, SI 1998/3173 art 2).
[10] Sub-s (3)(*d*)(xii) inserted by the Broadcasting Act 1996 Sch 7 para 3 with effect from 24 July 1996.
[11] Word "172" in sub-s (3)(*d*)(i) repealed by FA 2000 s 156, Sch 40 Pt II(12) with effect for disposals after 31 March 2000.
[12] Sub-s (3)(*d*)(xiv) inserted by the Transport Act 2000 s 250, Sch 26 para 37 with effect from 15 Jnauary 2001 (by virtue of SI 2000/3376).
[13] Sub-s (3)(*d*)(xiii) inserted by the Transport Act 2000 s 64, Sch 7 para 2 with effect from 1 February 2001 (by virtue of SI 2001/57).

36 Deferred charges on gains before 31st March 1982

Schedule 4, which provides for the reduction of a deferred charge to tax where the charge is wholly or partly attributable to an increase in the value of an asset before 31st March 1982, shall have effect.

Commentary—*Simon's Direct Tax Service* C2.605.
Definition—"Asset", s 21(1).

Allowable deductions

37 Consideration chargeable to tax on income

(1) There shall be excluded from the consideration for a disposal of assets taken into account in the computation of the gain any money or money's worth charged to income tax as income of, or taken into account as a receipt in computing income or profits or gains or losses of, the person making the disposal for the purposes of the Income Tax Acts.

(2) Subsection (1) above shall not be taken as excluding from the consideration so taken into account any money or money's worth which is—

[(*a*) taken into account in the making of a balancing charge under the Capital Allowances Act but excluding Part 10 of that Act,][1]

[(*b*) brought into account as the disposal value of plant or machinery under Part 2 of that Act, or][1]

[(*c*) brought into account as the disposal value of an asset representing qualifying expenditure under Part 6 of that Act.][1]

(3) This section shall not preclude the taking into account in a computation of the gain, as consideration for the disposal of an asset, of the capitalised value of a rentcharge (as in a case where a rentcharge is exchanged for some other asset) or of the capitalised value of a ground annual or feu duty, or of a right of any other description to income or to payments in the nature of income over a period, or to a series of payments in the nature of income.

(4) The reference in subsection (1) above to computing income or profits or gains or losses shall not be taken as applying to a computation of a company's income for the purposes of subsection (2) of section 76 of the Taxes Act (expenses of management of insurance companies).

Commentary—*Simon's Direct Tax Service* C2.102.
Statements of Practice D12—Partnerships.
SP 8/79—Compensation for acquisition of property under compulsory powers.
SP 8/89—Independent taxation: mortgage interest relief time limit for allocation of married couples' allocation of interest elections.
Simon's Tax Cases—*Bye v Coren* [1985] STC 113*.
s 37(1), (2), *Hirsch v Crowthers Cloth Ltd* [1990] STC 174*.
Definitions—"The 1990 Act", s 288(1); "asset", s 21(1); "company", ss 99, 288(1); "income or profits chargeable to tax", s 52(3); "sum taken into account in computing profits or losses", s 52(2); "the Taxes Acts", s 288(1).
Cross references—See TA 1988 s 763(2) (exclusion of this section in relation to offshore income gains);
TCGA 1992 s 118(1)–(3) (disapplication of this section in computing gains on disposal or conversion of deep discount securities).
TCGA 1992 s 119(1)(*a*) (disapplication of this section in computing gains accruing on disposal of securities within accrued income scheme).
TCGA 1992 s 119(4)(*a*) (disapplication of this section in computing certain gains accruing on disposal of securities with the right to receive unrealised interest).
TCGA 1992 s 195(5) (application of this section to receipts on the disposal of oil licences).
TCGA 1992 Sch 8 para 5(6) (premiums taxed under Schedule A etc: this section not to authorise any deduction by reference to an amount chargeable under TA 1988 s 348 or 349).
TCGA 1992 Sch 8 para 6(2) (assignment of lease granted at undervalue: this section not to apply to amounts taxed under TA 1988 s 35).
F(No 2)A 1992 s 65(2)(*e*) (life assurance business: I minus E basis: effect on I minus E basis of the application of this section as regards a company);
FA 1993 s 176(2) (Lloyd's underwriters: consideration for disposal of ancillary trust fund assets not to be excluded under this section for computation of gain).
FA 1997 Sch 12 paras 12, 17 (application of this section to disposals of certain leased assets or of lessor's interest).
Amendments—[1] Sub-ss (2)(*a*)–(*c*) substituted for sub-ss (2)(*a*), (*b*) by CAA 2001 s 578, Sch 2 para 77 with effect for income tax purposes, as respects allowances and charges falling to be made for chargeable periods ending after 5 April 2001, and for corporation tax purposes, as respects allowances and charges falling to be made for chargeable periods ending after 31 March 2001.

38 Acquisition and disposal costs etc

(1) Except as otherwise expressly provided, the sums allowable as a deduction from the consideration in the computation of the gain accruing to a person on the disposal of an asset shall be restricted to—

(*a*) the amount or value of the consideration, in money or money's worth, given by him or on his behalf wholly and exclusively for the acquisition of the asset, together with the incidental costs to him of the acquisition or, if the asset was not acquired by him, any expenditure wholly and exclusively incurred by him in providing the asset,

(b) the amount of any expenditure wholly and exclusively incurred on the asset by him or on his behalf for the purpose of enhancing the value of the asset, being expenditure reflected in the state or nature of the asset at the time of the disposal, and any expenditure wholly and exclusively incurred by him in establishing, preserving or defending his title to, or to a right over, the asset,

(c) the incidental costs to him of making the disposal.

(2) For the purposes of this section and for the purposes of all other provisions of this Act, the incidental costs to the person making the disposal of the acquisition of the asset or of its disposal shall consist of expenditure wholly and exclusively incurred by him for the purposes of the acquisition or, as the case may be, the disposal, being fees, commission or remuneration paid for the professional services of any surveyor or valuer, or auctioneer, or accountant, or agent or legal adviser and costs of transfer or conveyance (including stamp duty) together—

(a) in the case of the acquisition of an asset, with costs of advertising to find a seller, and

(b) in the case of a disposal, with costs of advertising to find a buyer and costs reasonably incurred in making any valuation or apportionment required for the purposes of the computation of the gain, including in particular expenses reasonably incurred in ascertaining market value where required by this Act.

(3) Except as provided by section 40, no payment of interest shall be allowable under this section.

(4) Any provision in this Act introducing the assumption that assets are sold and immediately reacquired shall not imply that any expenditure is incurred as incidental to the sale or reacquisition.

Commentary—*Simon's Direct Tax Service* C2.202.
Concession D52—Incidental costs of acquisition and warranty payments attributable to new holding of shares or debentures following a share exchange, company amalgamation or reconstruction may be treated as consideration given for the shares etc.

Statements of Practice D24—Capital gains tax: initial repairs to property.
SP 8/94—Capital gains tax: expenses incurred by personal representatives and corporate trustees.
Revenue Interpretation RI 63—Valuation costs for ascertaining gains allowable; subsequent valuation costs not allowable.
Revenue & other press releases—ICAEW TR713 26-8-88 (capital contributions made to a company by shareholders without an issue of shares rank as part of the acquisition cost of the shares if paid at the time of their acquisition and may be in the nature of a share premium; otherwise not treated as "money expended on shares").
IR 3–10–91 (compulsory acquisition of property: scale of fees for valuation services, new Ryde's scale of charges effective from 1-10-91).
IR Tax bulletin February 1993 (Revenue view quota and land are separate assets for CGT purposes. The cost of milk quota acquired by allotment in 1984 is nil TCGA s 17(2)).
Revenue Internal Guidance—Capital gains manual CG 15250–15295 (sub-s (2): treatment of incidental costs of acquisition and disposal).
CG 68061–68062 (sub-s (1)(a): the cost of a purchased goodwill is an allowable acquisition cost when acquired on or after 6 April 1998).
70850–70852 (circumstances in which a reverse premium is deductible under sub-s (1)(b)).
Simon's Tax Cases—*Capcount Trading v Evans* [1993] STC 11*; *Clark (executor of Clark, decd) v Green*, [1995] STC (SCD) 99*; *Quinn v Cooper* [1998] STC 772; *Garner v Pounds Shipowners and Shipbreakers Ltd* [1999] STC 19*.
s 38(1), *Chaney v Watkis* [1986] STC 89*; *Passant v Jackson* [1986] STC 164*.
s 38(1)(a), *Eilbeck v Rawling* [1979] STC 16*; *Stanton v Drayton Commercial Investment Co Ltd* [1982] STC 585*.
s 38(1)(b), *Emmerson v Computer Time International Ltd (in liquidation)* [1976] STC 111*; *C & E Comrs v Little Spain Club Ltd* [1979] STC 170*, 302; *Oram v Johnson* [1980] STC 222*; *Nuttall v Barrett* [1992] STC 112*; *Lee v Jewitt (Inspector of Taxes)* [2000] STC (SCD) 517.
s 38(2)(b), *Administrators of the Estate of Caton (decd) v Couch* [1997] STC 970*.
Definitions—"Asset", s 21(1); "market value", ss 272–274, Sch 11.
Cross references—See TA 1988 s 185(7) (computation of chargeable gains accruing on shares in a share option scheme);
FA 1988 s 84 (application of sub-s (1)(a) of this section on the first disposal of shares acquired under unapproved employee share schemes).
TCGA 1992 s 39 (allowable expenditure).
TCGA 1992 s 40 (relief for interest on money borrowed to defray capital expenditure on construction of a building, etc).
TCGA 1992 s 42 (apportionment of expenditure on part disposals).
TCGA 1992 s 43 (assets derived from other assets: allowable expenditure).
TCGA 1992 s 46 (straightline restriction of allowable expenditure on wasting assets).
TCGA 1992 ss 53, 54 (calculation of indexation allowance on allowable expenditure).
TCGA 1992 s 64 (relief for expenditure incurred transferring assets to legatee or trust beneficiary).
TCGA 1992 s 109(6) (indexation allowance for relevant allowable expenditure attributable to securities).
TCGA 1992 s 118 (deep discount securities).
TCGA 1992 s 120(2) (disposal of shares acquired under unapproved employee share scheme: allowable expenditure on construction of a building, etc).
TCGA 1992 s 195 (allowance of drilling expenditure on disposal of oil licence).
TCGA 1992 s 237A(2) (acquisition cost of a right to acquire shares obtained upon release of rights under a share option scheme).

39 Exclusion of expenditure by reference to tax on income

(1) There shall be excluded from the sums allowable under section 38 as a deduction in the computation of the gain any expenditure allowable as a deduction in computing the [profits][1] or losses of a trade, profession or vocation for the purposes of income tax or allowable as a deduction in computing any other income or profits or gains or losses for the purposes of the Income Tax Acts and any expenditure which, although not so allowable as a deduction in computing any losses, would be so allowable but for an insufficiency of income or profits or gains; and this subsection applies irrespective of whether effect is or would be given to the deduction in computing the amount of tax chargeable or by discharge or repayment of tax or in any other way.

(2) Without prejudice to the provisions of subsection (1) above, there shall be excluded from the sums allowable under section 38 as a deduction in the computation of the gain any expenditure which, if the assets, or all the assets to which the computation relates, were, and had at all times been, held or used as part of the fixed capital of a trade the [profits][1] of which were (irrespective of whether the person making the disposal is a company or not) chargeable to income tax would be allowable as a deduction in computing the [profits][1] or losses of the trade for the purposes of income tax.

(3) No account shall be taken of any relief under Chapter II of Part IV of the Finance Act 1981 or under Schedule 5 to the Finance Act 1983 in so far as it is not withdrawn and relates to shares issued before 19th March 1986, in determining whether any sums are excluded by virtue of subsection(1) or(2) above from the sums allowable as a deduction in the computation of gains or losses for the purposes of this Act.

Commentary—*Simon's Direct Tax Service* **C2.216.**
Simon's Tax Cases—s 39(2), *Emmerson v Computer Time International Ltd (in liquidation)* [1976] STC 111*.
Definitions—"Asset", s 21(1); "company", ss 99, 288(1); "income or profits chargeable to tax", s 52(3); "issued", s 288(5); "shares", s 288(1); "trade", s 288(1), TA 1988 s 832(1).
Cross references—See TA 1988 s 777(12) (sales of income from personal activities and transactions in land);
TCGA 1992 s 8(4) (sub-s (2) above not affected by s 8(4) which, in relation to a company, construes references to income tax as references to corporation tax).
TCGA 1992 s 41(1) (treatment of expenditure in respect of which capital or renewals allowance is made).
TCGA 1992 s 41(1) (allowances not to be excluded under this section).
TCGA 1992 s 119(1)(*b*) (disapplication of this section in computing certain gains accruing on disposal of securities within the accrued income scheme).
TCGA 1992 s 119(4)(*b*) (disapplication of this section in computing certain gains accruing on disposal of securities with the right to receive unrealised interest).
FA 1993 s 176(2) (Lloyd's underwriters: cost of acquisition of ancillary trust fund assets not to be excluded under this section for computation of gain).
Amendments—[1] Word "profits" in sub-ss (1), (2), substituted by FA 1998 Sch 7 para 7 with effect from 31 July 1998.

40 Interest charged to capital

(1) Where—

     (*a*) a company incurs expenditure on the construction of any building, structure or works, being expenditure allowable as a deduction under section 38 in computing a gain accruing to the company on the disposal of the building, structure or work, or of any asset comprising it, and
     (*b*) that expenditure was defrayed out of borrowed money,

the sums so allowable under section 38 shall, subject to subsection (2) below, include the amount of any interest on that borrowed money which is referable to a period or part of a period ending on or before the disposal.

(2) Subsection (1) above has effect subject to section 39 and does not apply to interest which is a charge on income.

(3) In relation to interest paid in any accounting period ending before 1st April 1981 subsection (1) above shall have effect with the substitution for all following paragraph (*b*) of—

     "and

         (*c*) the company charged to capital all or any of the interest on that borrowed money referable to a period or part of a period ending on or before the disposal,

     and the sums so allowable under section 38 shall include the amount of that interest charged to capital.";

and subsection (2) above shall not apply.

[(4) In consequence of Chapter 2 of Part 4 of the Finance Act 1996 (loan relationships) this section does not have effect in relation to interest referable to an accounting period ending on or after 1st April 1996.][1]

Commentary—*Simon's Direct Tax Service* **C2.219.**
Definitions—"Asset", s 21(1); "company", ss 99, 288(1).
Amendments—[1] Sub-s (4) inserted by FA 2002 s 82, Sch 25 para 60 with effect for accounting periods beginning after 30 September 2002.

41 Restriction of losses by reference to capital allowances and renewals allowances

(1) Section 39 shall not require the exclusion from the sums allowable as a deduction in the computation of the gain of any expenditure as being expenditure in respect of which a capital allowance or renewals allowance is made, but the amount of any losses accruing on the disposal of an asset shall be restricted by reference to capital allowances and renewals allowances as follows.

(2) In the computation of the amount of a loss accruing to the person making the disposal, there shall be excluded from the sums allowable as a deduction any expenditure to the extent to which any capital allowance or renewals allowance has been or may be made in respect of it.

(3) If the person making the disposal acquired the asset—

     [(*a*) by a transfer by way of sale in relation to which an election under section 569 of the Capital Allowances Act was made, or][3]
     [(*b*) by a transfer to which section 268 of that Act applies,][3]

(being enactments under which a transfer is treated for the purposes of capital allowances as being made at written down value), the preceding provisions of this section shall apply as if any capital allowance made to the transferor in respect of the asset had (except so far as any loss to the transferor was restricted under those provisions) been made to the person making the disposal (that is the transferee); and where the transferor acquired the asset by such a transfer, capital allowances which by virtue of this subsection can be taken into account in relation to the transferor shall also be taken into account in relation to the transferee (that is the person making the disposal), and so on for any series of transfers before the disposal.

(4) In this section "capital allowance" means—

   [(*a*) any allowance under the Capital Allowances Act,]³

   (*b*) any relief given under section 30 of the Taxes Act (expenditure on sea walls), and

   (*c*) any deduction in computing [profits]¹ allowable under section 91 of the Taxes Act (cemeteries).

(5) In this section "renewals allowance" means a deduction allowable in computing the [profits]¹ of a trade, profession or vocation for the purpose of income tax by reference to the cost of acquiring an asset for the purposes of the trade, profession or vocation in replacement of another asset, and for the purposes of this Chapter a renewals allowance shall be regarded as a deduction allowable in respect of the expenditure incurred on the asset which is being replaced.

(6) The amount of capital allowances to be taken into account under this section in relation to a disposal include any allowances falling to be made by reference to the event which is the disposal, and there shall be deducted from the amount of the allowances the amount of any balancing charge to which effect has been or is to be given by reference to the event which is the disposal, or any earlier event.

(7) Where the disposal is of [plant or machinery]³ in relation to expenditure on which allowances or charges have been made under [Part 2 of the Capital Allowances Act, and neither Chapter 15 (assets provided or used only partly for qualifying activity) nor Chapter 16 (partial depreciation subsidies) of that Part]³ applies, the capital allowances to be taken into account under this section are to be regarded as equal to the difference between the [qualifying expenditure]³ incurred, or treated as incurred, under that Part on the provision of the [plant or machinery]³ by the person making the disposal and the disposal value required to be brought into account in respect of the [plant or machinery]³.

[(8) Where there is a disposal of an asset acquired in circumstances in which—

   (*a*) section 140A applies, or

   (*b*) section 171 applies or would apply but for subsection (2) of that section,

this section has effect in relation to capital allowances made to the person from which it was acquired (so far as not taken into account in relation to a disposal of the asset by that person), and so on as respects previous transfers of the asset in such circumstances.

This does not affect the consideration for which an asset is deemed under section 140A or 171 to be acquired.]²

Commentary—*Simon's Direct Tax Service* C2.217.
Revenue Internal Guidance—Capital gains manual CG 17430–17460 (explanation of this section with worked example).
Definitions—"The 1990 Act", s 288(1); "asset", s 21(1); "income or profits chargeable to tax", s 52(3); "land", s 288(1); "the Taxes Acts", s 288(1); "trade", s 288(1), TA 1988 s 832(1).
Cross references—See TCGA 1992 s 14(2) (application of sub-s (8) to non-resident groups of companies which are members of a non-resident group as it applies to companies which are members of a group of companies).
TCGA 1992 s 42(3) (apportionment of expenditure on part disposals to be made before applying this section).
TCGA 1992 s 55(3) (indexation allowance on assets owned or deemed to be owned on 31 March 1982).
TCGA 1992 s 174(1) (disposals or acquisitions outside a group of companies).
TCGA 1992 s 195(5) (disposals of oil licences).
TCGA 1992 s 217C (application of this section on disposal of assets acquired from a registered friendly society by an incorporated friendly society at the time of incorporation).
TCGA 1992 s 276(8) (modification of sub-s (8) in its application to disposals of continental shelf exploration and exploitation rights and assets by a non-resident company to a company resident in the same territory, by a resident company to another resident company, or by a non-resident company to a resident company).
TCGA 1992 Sch 2 para 20 (capital allowances made in respect of assets for which an election for market value at 6 April 1965 is made).
TCGA 1992 Sch 3 para 3 (capital allowances made in respect of assets for which an election for market value at 31 March 1982 is made).
F(No 2)A 1992 Sch 17 para 6(2), (5) (privatisation of Northern Ireland Electricity: restriction of losses by reference to capital allowances).
Amendments—¹ Word "profits" in sub-ss (4), (5), substituted by FA 1998 Sch 7 para 7 with effect from 31 July 1998.
² Sub-s (7) inserted by FA 2000 s 102, Sch 29 para 12 with effect for cases where the disposal first referred to in sub-s (8) is after 31 March 2000.
³ Sub-ss (3)(*a*), (*b*), (4)(*a*) and words in (7) substituted by CAA 2001 s 578, Sch 2 para 78 with effect for income tax purposes, as respects allowances and charges falling to be made for chargeable periods ending after 5 April 2001, and for corporation tax purposes, as respects allowances and charges falling to be made for chargeable periods ending after 31 March 2001.

42 Part disposals

(1) Where a person disposes of an interest or right in or over an asset, and generally wherever on the disposal of an asset any description of property derived from that asset remains undisposed of, the sums which under paragraphs (*a*) and (*b*) of section 38(1) are attributable to the asset shall, both for the purposes of the computation of the gain accruing on the disposal and for the purpose of applying this Part in relation to the property which remains undisposed of, be apportioned.

(2) The apportionment shall be made by reference—

(*a*) to the amount or value of the consideration for the disposal on the one hand (call that amount or value A), and

(*b*) to the market value of the property which remains undisposed of on the other hand (call that market value B),

and accordingly the fraction of the said sums allowable as a deduction in the computation of the gain accruing on the disposal shall be—

$$\frac{A}{A + B}$$

and the remainder shall be attributed to the property which remains undisposed of.

(3) Any apportionment to be made in pursuance of this section shall be made before operating the provisions of section 41 and if, after a part disposal, there is a subsequent disposal of an asset the capital allowances or renewals allowances to be taken into account in pursuance of that section in relation to the subsequent disposal shall, subject to subsection (4) below, be those referable to the sums which under paragraphs (*a*) and (*b*) of section 38(1) are attributable to the asset whether before or after the part disposal, but those allowances shall be reduced by the amount (if any) by which the loss on the earlier disposal was restricted under the provisions of section 41.

(4) This section shall not be taken as requiring the apportionment of any expenditure which, on the facts, is wholly attributable to what is disposed of, or wholly attributable to what remains undisposed of.

(5) It is hereby declared that this section, and all other provisions for apportioning on a part disposal expenditure which is deductible in computing a gain, are to be operated before the operation of, and without regard to, section 58(1), sections 152 to 158 (but without prejudice to section 152(10)), section 171(1) or any other enactment making an adjustment to secure that neither a gain nor a loss occurs on a disposal.

Commentary—*Simon's Direct Tax Service* C2.402.
Statement of Practice SP 4/92—Capital gains rebasing elections.
Revenue Internal Guidance—Capital gains tax manual, CG 76720–76749 (consideration of different kinds of wasting assets).
Revenue & other press releases—CCAB June 1968 (part disposals—explanation of circumstances in which a ''single asset'' or ''multiple asset'', land and buildings are acquired for purposes of s 42).
IR Tax bulletin February 1993 (Revenue view quota and land are separate assets for CGT purposes. Disposal of milk quota therefore is not a disposal of an interest in land, but a disposal of a separate asset).
Simon's Tax Cases—*Watton v Tippett* [1997] STC 893*.
Definitions—''Asset'', s 21(1); ''capital allowance'', ss 41(4), 52(5); ''market value'', ss 272–274, Sch 11; ''part disposal'', s 21(2); ''renewals allowance'', ss 41(5), 52(5).
Cross references—See TA 1988 s 763(4) (offshore income gains).
TCGA 1992 s 56(1) (apportionment under this section to be made before determining indexation allowance).
TCGA 1992 s 194(4), (5) (application of this section to part disposals of oil licences relating to undeveloped areas).
TCGA 1992 s 195(7) (part disposals of oil licences).
TCGA 1992 s 242(6) (small part disposals of land).
TCGA 1992 s 243(3) (part disposals of land to authority with compulsory acquisition powers).
TCGA 1992 s 267(3) (modification of this section in its application to certain disposals between national broadcasting companies).
TCGA 1992 Sch 2 para 16(7), (8) (computation of chargeable gain on part disposals of certain assets held before 6 April 1965).
TCGA 1992 Sch 2 para 17(5) (restriction on election for valuation of certain assets at 6 April 1965 value where market value of the assets is to be ascertained according to this section).
TCGA 1992 Sch 3 para 4(1) (assets held on 31 March 1982).
TCGA 1992 Sch 8 para 2(2) (part disposal of land consequent on payment of premium for lease of land).
TCGA 1992 Sch 8 para 4(1) (provisions for apportionment of gains accruing on part disposal of a lease which is a wasting asset).
FA 1997 Sch 12 para 12, 17 (computation of chargeable gain on part disposal of certain leased assets or of lessor's interest).

43 Assets derived from other assets

If and so far as, in a case where assets have been merged or divided or have changed their nature or rights or interests in or over assets have been created or extinguished, the value of an asset is derived from any other asset in the same ownership, an appropriate proportion of the sums allowable as a deduction in the computation of a gain in respect of the other asset under paragraphs (*a*) and (*b*) of section 38(1) shall, both for the purpose of the computation of a gain accruing on the disposal of the first-mentioned asset and, if the other asset remains in existence, on a disposal of that other asset, be attributed to the first-mentioned asset.

Commentary—*Simon's Direct Tax Service* C2.209.
Concession D42—Mergers of leases: rules for calculating indexation allowance where a lease is merged with a superior lease or the freehold reversion.
Revenue Internal Guidance—Capital gains manual CG 17370–17372 (explanation of this section).
Simon's Tax Cases—*Aberdeen Construction Group Ltd v IRC* [1978] STC 127*; *Bayley v Rogers* [1980] STC 544*; [1995] STC (SCD) 239*.
Definition—''Asset'', s 21(1).
Cross references—See TCGA 1992 s 55(4) (modification of indexation allowance in respect of assets derived after 31 March 1982 from assets held on that date).
TCGA 1992 Sch 2 para 16(9) (apportionment of chargeable gains accruing on disposal of certain assets held before 6 April 1965 where disposed assets were derived from other assets).
TCGA 1992 Sch 2 para 17(1) (election for 6 April 1965 market value of certain assets held on 6 April 1965 which were derived from other assets).
TCGA 1992 Sch 3 para 5 (rebasing to 1982 where assets derived after 31 March 1982).
TCGA 1992 Sch 4 para 8 (deferred charges on gains before 31 March 1982 where assets derived on or after that date).

Wasting assets

44 Meaning of "wasting asset"

(1) In this Chapter "wasting asset" means an asset with a predictable life not exceeding 50 years but so that—

(a) freehold land shall not be a wasting asset whatever its nature, and whatever the nature of the buildings or works on it;

(b) "life", in relation to any tangible movable property, means useful life, having regard to the purpose for which the tangible assets were acquired or provided by the person making the disposal;

(c) plant and machinery shall in every case be regarded as having a predictable life of less than 50 years, and in estimating that life it shall be assumed that its life will end when it is finally put out of use as being unfit for further use, and that it is going to be used in the normal manner and to the normal extent and is going to be so used throughout its life as so estimated;

(d) a life interest in settled property shall not be a wasting asset until the predictable expectation of life of the life tenant is 50 years or less, and the predictable life of life interests in settled property and of annuities shall be ascertained from actuarial tables approved by the Board.

(2) In this Chapter "the residual or scrap value", in relation to a wasting asset, means the predictable value, if any, which the wasting asset will have at the end of its predictable life as estimated in accordance with this section.

(3) The question what is the predictable life of an asset, and the question what is its predictable residual or scrap value at the end of that life, if any, shall, so far as those questions are not immediately answered by the nature of the asset, be taken, in relation to any disposal of the asset, as they were known or ascertainable at the time when the asset was acquired or provided by the person making the disposal.

Commentary—*Simon's Direct Tax Service* C2.221, 901.
Revenue Interpretation RI 208—A fine wine that not unusually is kept for over 50 years is not a wasting asset.
Revenue Internal Guidance—Capital gains manual CG 17381 (indexation based on 31 March 1982 value is restricted as if an actual cost was incurred on that date).
Ring fence corporation tax manual 10.12.4 (wasting assets—oil licences; contains text of a recent paper issued by the Oil Taxation Office following consultation with UKOITC).
Definitions—"Asset", s 21(1); "the Board", s 288(1); "land", s 288(1); "settled property", s 68; "wasting asset", ss 44, 288(1), Sch 8 para 1.
Cross references—See TCGA 1992 s 146 (provisions instead of this section applying to quoted, traded and financial options and options to acquire business assets).
TCGA 1992 s 146(3) (wasting assets rules for traded, quoted and financial options and options to acquire assets for trade).

45 Exemption for certain wasting assets

(1) Subject to the provisions of this section, no chargeable gain shall accrue on the disposal of, or of an interest in, an asset which is tangible movable property and which is a wasting asset.

(2) Subsection (1) above shall not apply to a disposal of, or of an interest in, an asset—

(a) if, from the beginning of the period of ownership of the person making the disposal to the time when the disposal is made, the asset has been used and used solely for the purposes of a trade, profession or vocation and if that person has claimed or could have claimed any capital allowance in respect of any expenditure attributable to the asset or interest under paragraph (a) or paragraph (b) of section 38(1); or

(b) if the person making the disposal has incurred any expenditure on the asset or interest which has otherwise qualified in full for any capital allowance.

(3) In the case of the disposal of, or of an interest in, an asset which, in the period of ownership of the person making the disposal, has been used partly for the purposes of a trade, profession or vocation and partly for other purposes, or has been used for the purposes of a trade, profession or vocation for part of that period, or which has otherwise qualified in part only for capital allowances—

(a) the consideration for the disposal, and any expenditure attributable to the asset or interest by virtue of section 38(1)(a) and (b), shall be apportioned by reference to the extent to which that expenditure qualified for capital allowances, and

(b) the computation of the gain shall be made separately in relation to the apportioned parts of the expenditure and consideration, and

(c) subsection (1) above shall not apply to any gain accruing by reference to the computation in relation to the part of the consideration apportioned to use for the purposes of the trade, profession or vocation, or to the expenditure qualifying for capital allowances.

(4) Subsection (1) above shall not apply to a disposal of commodities of any description by a person dealing on a terminal market or dealing with or through a person ordinarily engaged in dealing on a terminal market.

Commentary—*Simon's Direct Tax Service* C1.407; C2.905.
Statement of Practice SP 4/92—Capital gains rebasing elections.
Simon's Tax Cases—*Burman v Westminster Press Ltd* [1987] STC 669*.
Definitions—"Asset", s 21(1); "capital allowance", ss 41(4), 52(5); "chargeable gain", s 15(2); "trade", s 288(1), TA 1988 s 832(1); "wasting asset", ss 44, 288(1), Sch 8 para 1.
Cross references—See TCGA 1992 s 146(3) (wasting assets rules for traded, quoted and financial options and options to acquire assets for trade).

46 Straightline restriction of allowable expenditure

(1) In the computation of the gain accruing on the disposal of a wasting asset it shall be assumed—

(a) that any expenditure attributable to the asset under section 38(1)(a) after deducting the residual or scrap value, if any, of the asset, is written off at a uniform rate from its full amount at the time when the asset is acquired or provided to nothing at the end of its life, and

(b) that any expenditure attributable to the asset under section 38(1)(b) is written off from the full amount of that expenditure at the time when that expenditure is first reflected in the state or nature of the asset to nothing at the end of its life,

so that an equal daily amount is written off day by day.

(2) Thus, calling the predictable life of a wasting asset at the time when it was acquired or provided by the person making the disposal L, the period from that time to the time of disposal T(1), and, in relation to any expenditure attributable to the asset under section 38(1)(b), the period from the time when that expenditure is first reflected in the state or nature of the asset to the said time of disposal T(2), there shall be excluded from the computation of the gain—

(a) out of the expenditure attributable to the asset under section 38(1)(a) a fraction—

$$\frac{T(1)}{L}$$

of an amount equal to the amount of that expenditure minus the residual or scrap value, if any, of the asset, and

(b) out of the expenditure attributable to the asset under section 38(1)(b) a fraction—

$$\frac{T(2)}{L-(T(1)-T(2))}$$

of the amount of the expenditure.

(3) If any expenditure attributable to the asset under section 38(1)(b) creates or increases a residual or scrap value of the asset, the provisions of subsection (1)(a) above shall be applied so as to take that into account.

Commentary—*Simon's Direct Tax Service* **C2.902, 903.**
Revenue Internal Guidance—Capital gains tax manual, CG 76770–76792 (explanation of formulae and worked examples).
Ring fence corporation tax manual 10.12.4 (wasting assets—oil licences; contains text of a recent paper issued by the Oil Taxation Office following consultation with UKOITC).
Definitions—"Asset", s 21(1); "residual or scrap value, s 44(2); "wasting asset", ss 44, 288(1), Sch 8, para 1.
Cross references—See TCGA 1992 s 47 (disapplication of this section in relation to wasting assets qualifying for capital allowances).
TCGA 1992 s 146 (provisions instead of this section applying to quoted, traded and financial options and options to acquire business assets).
TCGA 1992 s 146(3) (wasting assets rules for quoted, traded and financial options and option to acquire assets for trade).
TCGA 1992 Sch 8 para 1(3) (rate at which expenditure to be written off in the case of wasting asset which is lease of land).

47 Wasting assets qualifying for capital allowances

(1) Section 46 shall not apply in relation to a disposal of an asset—

(a) which, from the beginning of the period of ownership of the person making the disposal to the time when the disposal is made, is used and used solely for the purposes of a trade, profession or vocation and in respect of which that person has claimed or could have claimed any capital allowance in respect of any expenditure attributable to the asset under paragraph (a) or paragraph (b) of section 38(1), or

(b) on which the person making the disposal has incurred any expenditure which has otherwise qualified in full for any capital allowance.

(2) In the case of the disposal of an asset which, in the period of ownership of the person making the disposal, has been used partly for the purposes of a trade, profession or vocation and partly for other purposes, or has been used for the purposes of a trade, profession or vocation for part of that period, or which has otherwise qualified in part only for capital allowances—

(a) the consideration for the disposal, and any expenditure attributable to the asset by paragraph (a) or paragraph (b) of section 38(1) shall be apportioned by reference to the extent to which that expenditure qualified for capital allowances, and

(b) the computation of the gain shall be made separately in relation to the apportioned parts of the expenditure and consideration, and

(c) section 46 shall not apply for the purposes of the computation in relation to the part of the consideration apportioned to use for the purposes of the trade, profession or vocation, or to the expenditure qualifying for capital allowances, and

(d) if an apportionment of the consideration for the disposal has been made for the purposes of making any capital allowance to the person making the disposal or for the purpose of making any balancing charge on him, that apportionment shall be employed for the purposes of this section, and

(e) subject to paragraph (d) above, the consideration for the disposal shall be apportioned for the purposes of this section in the same proportions as the expenditure attributable to the asset is apportioned under paragraph (a) above.

Commentary—*Simon's Direct Tax Service* C2.906.
Definitions—''Asset'', s 21(1); ''capital allowance'', ss 41(4), 52(5); ''trade'', s 288(1), TA 1988 s 832(1); ''wasting asset'', ss 44, 288(1), Sch 8 para 1.
Cross references—See TCGA 1992 s 55(3) (indexation allowance on assets owned or deemed to be owned on 31 March 1982).
TCGA 1992 s 146 (provisions instead of this section applying to quoted, traded and financial options and options to acquire business assets).
TCGA 1992 s 146(3) (wasting assets rules for traded, quoted and financial options and options to acquire assets for trade).
TCGA 1992 Sch 2 para 20 (capital allowances made in respect of assets for which an election for market value at 6 April 1965 is made).
TCGA 1992 Sch 3 para 3 (capital allowances made in respect of assets for which an election for market value at 31 March 1982 is made).
TCGA 1992 Sch 8 para 1(6) (application of this section to short leases).

Miscellaneous provisions

48 Consideration due after time of disposal

In the computation of the gain consideration for the disposal shall be brought into account without any discount for postponement of the right to receive any part of it and, in the first instance, without regard to a risk of any part of the consideration being irrecoverable or to the right to receive any part of the consideration being contingent; and if any part of the consideration so brought into account [subsequently proves to be irrecoverable, there shall be made, on a claim being made to that effect, such adjustment, whether by way of discharge or repayment of tax or otherwise, as is required in consequence.]¹

Commentary—*Simon's Direct Tax Service* C2.106.
Revenue Internal Guidance—Capital gains manual CG 14910–14922 (Payment of tax by instalments where consideration for an asset is paid by instalments).
CG 14931 (circumstances in which an irrecoverable consideration does not arise where consideration for a disposal is in foreign currency or takes the form of money's worth).
CG 14933 (under self-assessment the vendor only has to be able to demonstrate as a fact that some part of the consideration has become irrecoverable).
Simon's Tax Cases—*Randall v Plumb* [1975] STC 191*; *Marson v Marriage* [1980] STC 177*; *Lyon v Pettigrew* [1985] STC 369*; *Goodbrand v Loffland Bros North Sea Inc* [1998] STC 930*.
s 48(2), *Loffland Bros North Sea Inc v Goodbrand* [1997] STC 102*; *Garner v Pounds Shipowners and Shipbreakers Ltd* [1999] STC 19*.
Amendments—¹ Words substituted by FA 1996 s 134(1), (2), Sch 20 para 48 with effect for capital gains tax from the year 1996–97 and, as respects corporation tax, for accounting periods ending after 30 June 1999 (by virtue of Finance Act 1994, Section 199, (Appointed Day) Order, SI 1998/3173 art 2).

49 Contingent liabilities

(1) In the first instance no allowance shall be made in the computation of the gain—

(a) in the case of a disposal by way of assigning a lease of land or other property, for any liability remaining with, or assumed by, the person making the disposal by way of assigning the lease which is contingent on a default in respect of liabilities thereby or subsequently assumed by the assignee under the terms and conditions of the lease,
(b) for any contingent liability of the person making the disposal in respect of any covenant for quiet enjoyment or other obligation assumed as vendor of land, or of any estate or interest in land, or as a lessor,
(c) for any contingent liability in respect of a warranty or representation made on a disposal by way of sale or lease of any property other than land.

[(2) If any such contingent liability subsequently becomes enforceable and is being or has been enforced, there shall be made, on a claim being made to that effect, such adjustment, whether by way of discharge or repayment of tax or otherwise, as is required in consequence.]¹

(3) Subsection (2) above also applies where the disposal in question was before the commencement of this section.

Commentary—*Simon's Direct Tax Service* C2.108.
Concession D52—Treatment of contingent liabilities following share exchange or company reconstruction or amalgamation.
Simon's Tax Cases—*Randall v Plumb* [1975] STC 191*.
Revenue Internal Guidance—Capital Gains Manual CG 14800–14827 (Treatment of contingent liabilities).
Definitions—''Land'', s 288(1); ''lease'', Sch 8 para 10(1); ''lessor'', Sch 8 para 10(1).
Amendments—¹ Sub-s (2) substituted by FA 1996 s 134(1), (2), Sch 20 para 49 with effect for capital gains tax from the year 1996–97 and, as respects corporation tax, for accounting periods ending after 30 June 1999 (by virtue of Finance Act 1994, Section 199, (Appointed Day) Order, SI 1998/3173 art 2).

50 Expenditure reimbursed out of public money

There shall be excluded from the computation of a gain any expenditure which has been or is to be met directly or indirectly by the Crown or by any Government, public or local authority whether in the United Kingdom or elsewhere.

Commentary—*Simon's Direct Tax Service* C2.218.
Concession D53—Where grant subsequently repaid, amount repaid treated as reducing consideration on disposal of the asset.
Definition—''Local authority'', s 288(1), TA 1988 s 842A.
Cross reference—See TA 1988 s 400(6) (writing-off of government investment in a company not to be treated as expenditure by the Crown).

51 Exemption for winnings and damages, etc

(1) It is hereby declared that winnings from betting, including pool betting, or lotteries or games with prizes are not chargeable gains, and no chargeable gain or allowable loss shall accrue on the disposal of rights to winnings obtained by participating in any pool betting or lottery or game with prizes.

(2) It is hereby declared that sums obtained by way of compensation or damages for any wrong or injury suffered by an individual in his person or in his profession or vocation are not chargeable gains.

Commentary—*Simon's Direct Tax Service* **C1.405.**
Concession D33—Capital gains tax on compensation and damages. This Concession has been revised.
Statement of Practice SP 4/92—Capital gains rebasing elections.
Definitions—''Allowable loss'', ss 8(2), 16, 288(1); ''chargeable gain'', s 15(2).

52 Supplemental

(1) No deduction shall be allowable in a computation of the gain more than once from any sum or from more than one sum.

(2) References in this Chapter to sums taken into account as receipts or as expenditure in computing profits or gains or losses for the purposes of income tax shall include references to sums which would be so taken into account but for the fact that any profits or gains of a trade, profession, employment or vocation are not chargeable to income tax or that losses are not allowable for those purposes.

(3) In this Chapter references to income or profits charged or chargeable to tax include references to income or profits taxed or as the case may be taxable by deduction at source.

(4) For the purposes of any computation of the gain any necessary apportionments shall be made of any consideration or of any expenditure and the method of apportionment adopted shall, subject to the express provisions of this Chapter, be ...[1] just and reasonable.

(5) In this Chapter ''capital allowance'' and ''renewals allowance'' have the meanings given by subsections (4) and (5) of section 41.

Commentary—*Simon's Direct Tax Service* **C2.101; C2.202.**
Statement of Practice SP 4/92—Capital gains rebasing elections.
Simon's Tax Cases—s 52(4), *Aberdeen Construction Group Ltd v IRC* [1978] STC 127*.
Definitions—''Inspector'', s 288(1); ''trade'', s 288(1), TA 1988 s 832(1).
Cross references—See TCGA 1992 s 152(11) (apportionment of rollover relief for business assets as is just and reasonable, but without prejudice to sub-s (4) above).
TCGA 1992 s 245(1) (compensation paid on compulsory acquisition of land may be regarded as paid not exclusively for land but for land and other factors such as goodwill).
TCGA 1992 Sch 11 para 11(3), (4) (apportionment of consideration or expenditure in relation to disposals chargeable under Schedule D Case VII).
Amendments—[1] Words repealed by FA 1996 s 134(1), (2), Sch 20 para 50, Sch 41 Pt V(10) with effect for capital gains tax from the year 1996–97 and, for the purposes of corporation tax, as respects accounting periods ending after 30 June 1999 (by virtue of Finance Act 1994, Section 199, (Appointed Day) Order, SI 1998/3173 art 2).

CHAPTER IV
COMPUTATION OF GAINS: THE INDEXATION ALLOWANCE

53 The indexation allowance and interpretative provisions

(1) Subject to any provision to the contrary, [if on the disposal of an asset there is an unindexed gain, an allowance (''the indexation allowance'') shall be allowed against the unindexed gain—

    (*a*) so as to give the gain for the purposes of this Act, or

    (*b*) if the indexation allowance equals or exceeds the unindexed gain, so as to extinguish it (in which case the disposal shall be one on which, after taking account of the indexation allowance, neither a gain nor a loss accrues)][1]

and any reference in this Act to an indexation allowance or to the making of an indexation allowance shall be construed accordingly.

[(1A) Indexation allowance in respect of changes shown by the retail prices indices for months after April 1998 shall be allowed only for the purposes of corporation tax.][2]

(2) For the purposes of [this Chapter][1], in relation to any disposal of an asset—

    [(*a*) ''unindexed gain'' means the amount of the gain on the disposal computed in accordance with this Part][2];

    (*b*) ''relevant allowable expenditure'' means, subject to subsection (3) below, any sum which, in the computation of the unindexed [gain][2] was taken into account by virtue of paragraph (*a*) or paragraph (*b*) of section 38(1).

[(2A) Notwithstanding anything in section 16 of this Act, this section shall not apply to a disposal on which a loss accrues.][1]

(3) In determining what sum (if any) was taken into account as mentioned in subsection (2)(*b*) above, account shall be taken of any provision of any enactment which, for the purpose of the computation of the gain, increases, excludes or reduces the whole or any part of any item of expenditure falling within section 38 or provides for it to be written down.

(4) Sections 54 and 108 and this section have effect subject to sections 56, 57, 109, 110[, 110A][3], 113, 131 and 145.

Commentary—*Simon's Direct Tax Service* **C2.301, 302.**
Statement of Practice SP 3/82—Capital gains tax indexation.
Revenue Internal Guidance—Capital gains manual CG 17700–17835 (restriction of indexation relief so as not to create or augment a loss, with worked examples).
Simon's Tax Cases—*Smith v Schofield* [1993] STC 268*; *X plc v Roe* [1996] STC (SCD) 139; *Tesco plc v Crimmin* [1997] STC 981*.
s 53(3), *Quinn v Cooper* [1998] STC 772.
Definition—''Asset'', s 21(1).
Cross references—See TCGA 1992 s 55(7) (restriction of indexation allowance for disposals on or after 30 November 1993; ''rolled-up indexation'' to prevent loss of indexation for disposals before that date).
TCGA 1992 s 113 (computation of indexation allowance where part of purchase price of shares is paid more than 12 months after acquisition of the shares).
TCGA 1992 s 131(2) (computation of indexation allowance where on a reorganisation new consideration is payable for conversion of old shares into new shares).
TCGA 1992 s 145 (computation of indexation allowance on disposal of options).
Amendments—[1] Words in sub-ss (1), (2) substituted and sub-s (2A) inserted by FA 1994 s 93(1)–(3), (11) in relation to disposals after 29 November 1993, subject to transitional provisions in FA 1994 Sch 12.
[2] Sub-s (1A) inserted by FA 1998 s 122(1) with effect in relation to disposals on or after 6 April 1998, subject to FA 1998 s 122(7).
[3] Section number in sub-s (4) inserted by FA 1998 s 125(3) with effect in relation to disposals on or after 6 April 1998.

54 Calculation of indexation allowance

(1) Subject to any provision to the contrary, the indexation allowance is the aggregate of the indexed rise in each item of relevant allowable expenditure; and, in relation to any such item of expenditure, the indexed rise is a sum produced by multiplying the amount of that item by a figure expressed as a decimal and determined, subject to subsections (2) and (3) below, by the formula—

$$\frac{(RD - RI)}{RI}$$

where—

RD is the retail prices index for [the relevant month][1]; and
RI is the retail prices index for March 1982 or the month in which the expenditure was incurred, whichever is the later.

[(1A) In subsection (1) above—

(a) the references to an item of relevant allowable expenditure shall not, except for the purposes of corporation tax, include any item of expenditure incurred on or after 1st April 1998; and
(b) the reference to the relevant month is a reference—

(i) where that subsection has effect for the purposes of capital gains tax, to April 1998; and
(ii) where that subsection has effect for the purposes of corporation tax, to the month in which the disposal occurs.][1]

(2) If, in relation to any item of expenditure—

(a) the expenditure is attributable to the acquisition of relevant securities, within the meaning of section 108, which are disposed of within the period of 10 days beginning on the day on which the expenditure was incurred, or
(b) RD, as defined in subsection (1) above, is equal to or less than RI, as so defined,

the indexed rise in that item is nil.

(3) If, in relation to any item of expenditure, the figure determined in accordance with the formula in subsection (1) above would, apart from this subsection, be a figure having more than 3 decimal places, it shall be rounded to the nearest third decimal place.

(4) For the purposes of this section—

(a) relevant allowable expenditure falling within paragraph (a) of subsection (1) of section 38 shall be assumed to have been incurred at the time when the asset in question was acquired or provided; and
(b) relevant allowable expenditure falling within paragraph (b) of that subsection shall be assumed to have been incurred at the time when that expenditure became due and payable.

Commentary—*Simon's Direct Tax Service* **C2.302.**
Revenue & other press releases—Retail Prices Index: See *BDO Stoy Hayward* App. 22.
Simon's Tax Cases—*Smith v Schofield* [1993] STC 268*.
Definitions—''Asset'', s 21(1); ''indexation allowance'', s 53; ''retail prices index'', s 288(2), TA 1988 s 833(2).
Cross references—See TCGA 1992 s 53(4) (this section to have effect subject to the following provisions—
TCGA 1992 s 56 (part disposals and no gain/no loss disposals);
TCGA 1992 s 107(6) (identification of securities disposed of within 10 days of acquisition);
TCGA 1992 s 109 (pre-April 1982 share pools);
TCGA 1992 s 110 (indexation allowance on share holdings);
TCGA 1992 s 113 (calls on shares);
TCGA 1992 s 131 (share reorganisations: indexation allowance);
TCGA 1992 s 145 (call options: indexation allowance)).
Amendments—[1] Words in sub-s (1) substituted, and sub-s (1A) inserted by FA 1998 s 122 with effect in relation to disposals on or after 6 April 1998, subject to FA 1998 s 122(7).

55 Assets owned on 31st March 1982 or acquired on a no gain/no loss disposal

(1) For the purpose of computing the indexation allowance on a disposal of an asset where, on 31st March 1982, the asset was held by the person making the disposal, it shall be assumed that on that date the asset was sold by the person making the disposal and immediately reacquired by him at its market value on that date.

(2) Except where an election under section 35(5) has effect, neither subsection (1) above nor section 35(2) shall apply for the purpose of computing the indexation allowance in a case where that allowance would be greater if they did not apply.

(3) If under subsection (1) above it is to be assumed that any asset was on 31st March 1982 sold by the person making the disposal and immediately reacquired by him, sections 41 and 47 shall apply in relation to any capital allowance or renewals allowance made in respect of the expenditure actually incurred by him in providing the asset as if it were made in respect of expenditure which, on that assumption, was incurred by him in reacquiring the asset on 31st March 1982.

(4) Where, after 31st March 1982, an asset which was held on that date has been merged or divided or has changed its nature or rights in or over the asset have been created, then, subject to subsection (2) above, subsection (1) above shall have effect to determine for the purposes of section 43 the amount of the consideration for the acquisition of the asset which was so held.

(5) Subsection (6) below applies to a disposal of an asset which is not a no gain/no loss disposal if—

    (a) the person making the disposal acquired the asset after 31st March 1982; and

    (b) the disposal by which he acquired the asset and any previous disposal of the asset after 31st March 1982 was a no gain/no loss disposal;

and for the purposes of this subsection a no gain/no loss disposal is one on which, by virtue of section 257(2) or 259(2) or any of the enactments specified in section 35(3)(d), neither a gain nor a loss accrues (or accrued) to the person making the disposal.

(6) Where this subsection applies to a disposal of an asset—

    (a) the person making the disposal shall be treated for the purpose of computing the indexation allowance on the disposal as having held the asset on 31st March 1982; and

    (b) for the purpose of determining any gain or loss on the disposal, the consideration which, apart from this subsection, that person would be treated as having given for the asset shall be taken to be reduced by deducting therefrom any indexation allowance brought into account by virtue of section 56(2) on any disposal falling within subsection (5)(b) above.

[(7) The rules in subsection (8) below apply (after the application of section 53 but before the application of section 35(3) or (4)) to give the gain or loss for the purposes of this Act where—

    (a) subsection (6) above applies to the disposal (the "disposal in question") of an asset by any person (the "transferor"), and

    (b) but for paragraph (b) of that subsection, the consideration the transferor would be treated as having given for the asset would include an amount or amounts of indexation allowance brought into account by virtue of section 56(2) on any disposal made before 30th November 1993.][1]

[(8) The rules are as follows—

    (a) where (apart from this subsection) there would be a loss, an amount equal to the rolled-up indexation shall be added to it so as to increase it;

    (b) where (apart from this subsection) the unindexed gain or loss would be nil, there shall be a loss of an amount equal to the rolled-up indexation, and

    (c) where (apart from this subsection)—

        (i) there would be an unindexed gain, and

        (ii) the gain or loss would be nil but the amount of the indexation allowance used to extinguish the gain would be less than the rolled-up indexation,

    the difference shall constitute a loss.][1]

[(9) In this section the "rolled-up indexation" means, subject to subsections (10) and (11) below, the amount or, as the case may be, the aggregate of the amounts referred to in subsection (7)(b) above; and subsections (10) and (11) below shall, as well as applying on the disposal in question, be treated as having applied on any previous part disposal by the transferor.][1]

[(10) Where, for the purposes of any disposal of the asset by the transferor, any amount falling within any, or any combination of, paragraphs (a) to (c) of section 38(1) is required by any enactment to be excluded, reduced or written down, the amount or aggregate referred to in subsection (9) above (or so much of it as remains after the application of this subsection and subsection (11) below on a previous part disposal) shall be reduced in proportion to any reduction made in the amount falling within the paragraph, or the combination of paragraphs, in question.][1]

[(11) Where the transferor makes a part disposal of the asset at any time, then, for the purposes of that and any subsequent disposal, the amount or aggregate referred to in subsection (9) above (or so much of it as remains after the application of this subsection and subsection (10) above on a previous part disposal by him or after the application of subsection (10) above on the part disposal) shall be apportioned between the property disposed of and the property which remains in the same proportions as the sums falling within section 38(1)(a) and (b).][1]

TCGA 1992

Commentary—*Simon's Direct Tax Service* **C2.607.**
Regulations—CGT (Parallel Pooling) Regulations, SI 1986/387.
Concession D44—Rebasing and indexation: shares derived from larger holdings held at 31 March 1982.
D34—Calculation of cost or indexation allowance on a disposal of shares or securities where some but not all are valued at 31 March 1982 to be based on the proportion that the shares or securities disposed of bears to the total holding at 31 March 1982.

Statements of Practice D12—Partnerships.
SP 1/89—Capital gains tax—partnerships: further extension of statement of practice.
Revenue Interpretation RI 26—Indexation: treatment of enhancement expenditure incurred after 31 March 1982 by a previous owner of an asset deemed to be held on that date by the person making the disposal.
Simon's Tax Cases—*Smith v Schofield* [1993] STC 268*.
Definitions—"Asset", s 21(1); "indexation allowance", s 53; "market value", ss 272–274, Sch 11.
Cross references—See TCGA 1992 Sch 7A para 2(8A) (restriction on set-off of pre-entry losses).
Amendments—[1] Sub-ss (7)–(11) inserted by FA 1994 s 93(4), (11) in relation to disposals after 29 November 1993.

56 Part disposals and disposals on a no-gain/no-loss basis

(1) For the purpose of determining the indexation allowance (if any) on the occasion of a part disposal of an asset, the apportionment under section 42 of the sums which make up the relevant allowable expenditure shall be effected before the application of section 54 and, accordingly, in relation to a part disposal—

(a) references in section 54 to an item of expenditure shall be construed as references to that part of that item which is so apportioned for the purposes of the computation of the unindexed gain ...[3] on the part disposal; and

(b) no indexation allowance shall be determined by reference to the part of each item of relevant allowable expenditure which is apportioned to the property which remains undisposed of.

(2) [On a no gain/no loss disposal by any person ("the transferor")][2]—

(a) the amount of the consideration shall be calculated for the purposes of this Act on the assumption that, on the disposal, an unindexed gain accrues to the transferor which is equal to the indexation allowance on the disposal, and

(b) the disposal shall accordingly be one on which, after taking account of the indexation allowance, neither a gain nor a loss accrues;

and for the purposes of the application of sections 53 and 54 there shall be disregarded so much of any enactment as provides that, on the subsequent disposal of the asset by the person acquiring the asset on the disposal ("the transferee"), the transferor's acquisition of the asset is to be treated as the transferee's acquisition of it.

[(3) Where apart from this subsection—

(a) a loss would accrue on the disposal of an asset, and

(b) the sums allowable as a deduction in computing that loss would include an amount attributable to the application of the assumption in subsection (2) above on any no gain/no loss disposal made on or after 30th November 1993,

those sums shall be determined as if that subsection had not applied on any such disposal made on or after that date and the loss shall be reduced accordingly or, if those sums are then equal to or less than the consideration for the disposal, the disposal shall be one on which neither a gain nor a loss accrues.][1]

[(4) For the purposes of this section a no gain/no loss disposal is one which, by virtue of any enactment other than section 35(4), 53(1) or this section, is treated as a disposal on which neither a gain nor a loss accrues to the person making the disposal.][1]

Commentary—*Simon's Direct Tax Service* **C2.304.**
Revenue Internal Guidance—Capital gains manual CG 17400–17401 (operation of sub-s (2); main examples are intra-group transfers and transfers between spouses).
CG 17745–17747 (sub-s (3): worked examples of no gain/no loss transfers before and after 30 November 1993).
Definitions—"Asset", s 21(1); "indexation allowance", s 53; "part disposal", s 21(2).
Cross references—See TA 1988 Sch 28 para 3(1) (computation of offshore income gains: calculation of unindexed gain).
TCGA 1992 s 55(6) (computation of indexation allowance where assets acquired on a no gain/no loss disposal are disposed of on a no gain/no loss disposal).
TCGA 1992 s 110(6A) (indexation allowance for share pools: disapplication of sub-s (2) above for a no gain/no loss disposal after 29 November 1993).
TCGA 1992 Sch 7A para 2(6A), (8B) (restriction on set-off of pre-entry losses).
Amendments—[1] Sub-ss (3), (4) added by FA 1994 s 93(5), (11) in relation to disposals after 29 November 1993, subject to transitional provisions in FA 1994 Sch 12.
[2] Words in sub-s (2) substituted by FA 1994 s 93(5), (11).
[3] Words in sub-s (1)(a) repealed by FA 1994 Sch 26 Pt V(8) in relation to disposals after 29 November 1993, subject to transitional provisions in FA 1994 Sch 12.

57 Receipts etc which are not treated as disposals but affect relevant allowable expenditure

(1) This section applies where, in determining the relevant allowable expenditure in relation to a disposal of an asset, account is required to be taken, as mentioned in section 53(3), of any provision of any enactment which, by reference to a relevant event, reduces the whole or any part of an item of expenditure as mentioned in that subsection.

(2) For the purpose of determining, in a case where this section applies, the indexation allowance (if any) to which the person making the disposal is entitled, no account shall in the first instance be taken of the provision referred to in subsection (1) above in calculating the indexed rise in the item

of expenditure to which that provision applies but, from that indexed rise as so calculated, there shall be deducted a sum equal to the indexed rise (determined as for the purposes of the actual disposal) in a notional item of expenditure which—

    (*a*) is equal to the amount of the reduction effected by the provision concerned; and
    (*b*) was incurred on the date of the relevant event referred to in subsection (1) above.

(3) In this section "relevant event" means any event which does not fall to be treated as a disposal for the purposes of this Act.

Commentary—*Simon's Direct Tax Service* **C2.302, 1007.**
Revenue Internal Guidance—Capital gains manual CG 17360–17363 (interaction with indexation relief; cases where this section applies; worked examples at CG 17482).
Definitions—"Asset", s 21(1); "indexation allowance", s 53.

PART III

INDIVIDUALS, PARTNERSHIPS, TRUSTS AND COLLECTIVE INVESTMENT SCHEMES

CHAPTER I
MISCELLANEOUS PROVISIONS

58 Husband and wife

(1) If, in any year of assessment, and in the case of a woman who in that year of assessment is a married woman living with her husband, the man disposes of an asset to the wife, or the wife disposes of an asset to the man, both shall be treated as if the asset was acquired from the one making the disposal for a consideration of such amount as would secure that on the disposal neither a gain nor a loss would accrue to the one making the disposal.

(2) This section shall not apply—

    (*a*) if until the disposal the asset formed part of trading stock of a trade carried on by the one making the disposal, or if the asset is acquired as trading stock for the purposes of a trade carried on by the one acquiring the asset, or
    (*b*) if the disposal is by way of donatio mortis causa,

but this section shall have effect notwithstanding the provisions of section 18 or 161, or of any other provisions of this Act fixing the amount of the consideration deemed to be given on a disposal or acquisition.

Commentary—*Simon's Direct Tax Service* **C1.202; C2.112.**
Concession D44—CGT: rebasing and indexation: shares derived from larger holdings held at 31 March 1982.
Revenue Interpretation RI 233—(guidance on how the matching rules work where shares are transferred between spouses, and sub-s (1) above applies, so that the transfer is treated as being made at no gain/no loss to the transferor).
Revenue & other press releases—IR 21-11-90 (independent taxation CGT on jointly held assets. Revenue normally accept that husband and wife hold the asset in equal parts in absence of evidence to the contrary).
Revenue Internal Guidance—Capital gains manual CG 22070–22076 (definition of terms).
CG 22400–22509 (transfer of assets following separation or divorce: date of disposal and consideration for the disposal).
Relief Manual RE 1040–1045 (Revenue practice in dealing with differences of opinion).
RE 1050–1065 (treatment where couples separate).
RE 1080 (reconciliation after period of separation).
RE 1090–1091 (divorce).
Simon's Tax Cases—s 58(1), *Gubay v Kington* [1984] STC 99*.
Definitions—"Asset", s 21(1); "married woman living with her husband, s 288(3), TA 1988 s 282; "trade", s 288(1), TA 1988 s 832(1); "trading stock", s 288(1), TA 1988 s 100(2); "year of assessment", s 288(1).
Cross references—See the CGT Regulations, SI 1967/149 reg 13(4) (where this section applies, a determination or agreement relating to market value of an asset is conclusive for both the spouse disposing of and the spouse acquiring the asset).
TCGA 1992 s 19(2) (disposals between spouses forming part of a series of linked transactions).
TCGA 1992 s 35(3)(*d*) (assets held on 31 March 1982 and disposed of under this section are excluded from the re-basing to 31 March 1982 valuation rule unless the disponer elects).
TCGA 1992 s 42(5) (apportionment of expenditure on part disposals to be made without regard to sub-s (1) above).
TCGA 1992 s 55(5) (indexation allowance on a non-no gain/no loss disposal after 31 March 1982 of assets acquired on a no gain/no loss acquisition under this section).
TCGA 1992 s 116(11) (treatment of gain or loss on inter-spouse disposal on reorganisations, etc involving qualifying corporate bonds).
TCGA 1992 s 134(4) (treatment of gain or loss on inter-spouse disposal of gilt-edged securities issued in exchange for shares on nationalisation).
TCGA 1992 s 137(4) (anti-avoidance provisions in relation to reconstructions, etc: recovery of tax not paid within 6 months from person who acquired shares on an inter-spouse transfer).
TCGA 1992 s 150 (business expansion schemes).
TCGA 1992 s 150(7) (inter-spouse disposal of business expansion scheme shares).
TCGA 1992 Sch 2 para 4(9) (election for pooling of quoted securities held on 6 April 1965 and disposed of after 19 March 1968 by a disposal to which this section applies).
TCGA 1992 Sch 2 para 22 (transfers between spouses of assets held on 6 April 1965).
TCGA 1992 Sch 3 para 2 (inter-spouse disposal after 5 April 1988 followed by disposal by transferee spouse to third party: effect on an election under s 35(5) for 31 March 1982 valuation by the spouses).
TCGA 1992 Sch 4 para 7 (deferred charges on gains accruing on disposal by a spouse of assets acquired after 31 March 1982 from the other spouse who acquired the assets before that date).

TCGA 1992

59 Partnerships

Where 2 or more persons carry on a trade or business in partnership—

(a) tax in respect of chargeable gains accruing to them on the disposal of any partnership assets shall, in Scotland as well as elsewhere in the United Kingdom, be assessed and charged on them separately, and

(b) any partnership dealings shall be treated as dealings by the partners and not by the firm as such,...[1]

(c) ...[1].

Commentary—*Simon's Direct Tax Service* **C3.201.**
Statement of Practice D12—Partnerships.
Revenue Interpretation RI 9—Procedure for rebasing elections where they are made by the same person in different capacities.

Simon's Tax Cases—*West Somerset Railway plc v Chivers* [1995] STC (SCD) 1*.
Revenue Internal Guidance—Capital Gains Manual CG 27780–27786 (worked examples illustrating various situations involving acquisitions and disposals of partnership assets).
Definitions—"Asset", s 21(1); "chargeable gain", s 15(2); the Taxes Acts", s 288(1); "trade", s 288(1), TA 1988 s 832(1).
Amendments—[1] Para (c) and the word "and" immediately preceding it repealed by FA 1995 s 162, Sch 29 Pt VIII(16) with effect for any cases in relation to which TA 1988 s 112 has effect as amended by FA 1995 s 125 (ie partly as from the year 1997–98 and partly as respects 1995–96 and 1996–97; see further the notes to TA 1988 s 112).

[59A Limited liability partnerships

(1) Where a limited liability partnership carries on a trade or business with a view to profit—

(a) assets held by the limited liability partnership are treated for the purposes of tax in respect of chargeable gains as held by its members as partners, and

(b) any dealings by the limited liability partnership are treated for those purposes as dealings by its members in partnership (and not by the limited liability partnership as such);

and tax in respect of chargeable gains accruing to the members of the limited liability partnership on the disposal of any of its assets shall be assessed and charged on them separately.

(2) For all purposes, except as otherwise provided, in the enactments relating to tax in respect of chargeable gains—

(a) references to a partnership include a limited liability partnership in relation to which subsection (1) above applies,

(b) references to members of a partnership include members of such a limited liability partnership,

(c) references to a company do not include such a limited liability partnership, and

(d) references to members of a company do not include members of such a limited liability partnership.

(3) Subsection (1) above continues to apply in relation to a limited liability partnership which no longer carries on any trade or business with a view to profit—

(a) if the cessation is only temporary, or

(b) during a period of winding up following a permanent cessation, provided—

(i) the winding up is not for reasons connected in whole or in part with the avoidance of tax, and

(ii) the period of winding up is not unreasonably prolonged,

but subject to subsection (4) below.

(4) Subsection (1) above ceases to apply in relation to a limited liability partnership—

(a) on the appointment of a liquidator or (if earlier) the making of a winding-up order by the court, or

(b) on the occurrence of any event under the law of a country or territory outside the United Kingdom corresponding to an event specified in paragraph (a) above.

(5) Where subsection (1) above ceases to apply in relation to a limited liability partnership with the effect that tax is assessed and charged—

(a) on the limited liability partnership (as a company) in respect of chargeable gains accruing on the disposal of any of its assets, and

(b) on the members in respect of chargeable gains accruing on the disposal of any of their capital interests in the limited liability partnership,

it shall be assessed and charged on the limited liability partnership as if subsection (1) above had never applied in relation to it.

(6) Neither the commencement of the application of subsection (1) above nor the cessation of its application in relation to a limited liability partnership shall be taken as giving rise to the disposal of any assets by it or any of its members.][1]

Commentary—*Simon's Direct Tax Service* **C3.231.**
Revenue Internal Guidance—Capital Gains Manual CG 28000–28025 (general outline of this section).
Amendments—[1] This section (originally inserted by the Limited Liability Partnerships Act 2000 s 10(3)) substituted by FA 2001 s 75(2), (6) with effect from 6 April 2001.

60 Nominees and bare trustees

(1) In relation to assets held by a person as nominee for another person, or as trustee for another person absolutely entitled as against the trustee, or for any person who would be so entitled but for being an infant or other person under disability (or for 2 or more persons who are or would be jointly so entitled), this Act shall apply as if the property were vested in, and the acts of the nominee or trustee in relation to the assets were the acts of, the person or persons for whom he is the nominee or trustee (acquisitions from or disposals to him by that person or persons being disregarded accordingly).

(2) It is hereby declared that references in this Act to any asset held by a person as trustee for another person absolutely entitled as against the trustee are references to a case where that other person has the exclusive right, subject only to satisfying any outstanding charge, lien or other right of the trustees to resort to the asset for payment of duty, taxes, costs or other outgoings, to direct how that asset shall be dealt with.

Commentary—*Simon's Direct Tax Service* **C1.203; C4.208.**
Revenue interpretation RI 222—Transfer of shares and securities in the case of a bare trust.
Revenue & other press releases—IR 20–1–97 (tax obligations of trustees and certain beneficiaries of bare trusts).
Revenue Internal Guidance—Capital gains manual CG 20600–20690 (investment clubs).
Simon's Tax Cases—s 60(1), *Passant v Jackson* [1985] STC 133*; *Frampton (Trustees of the Worthing Rugby Football Club) v IRC* [1985] STC 186*; *Anders Utkilens Rederi A/S v O/Y Lovisa Stevedoring Co A/Band Keller BryantTransport Co Ltd* [1985] STC 301*; *Jenkins v Brown* [1989] STC 577*.
s 60(2), *Jenkins v Brown* [1974] STC 325*.
s 60(5), *Harthan v Mason* [1980] STC 94*.
Definition—"Asset", s 21(1).
Cross references—See TCGA 1992 s 61(1) (funds in court held by Accountant General).
TCGA 1992 s 65 (liability for CGT of trustees and personal representatives).
TCGA 1992 s 97 (2) (for the purposes of ss 87–96 (non-resident, dual, migrant, etc settlements), "capital payment" includes transfers under this section).

61 Funds in court

(1) For the purposes of section 60, funds in court held by the Accountant General shall be regarded as held by him as nominee for the persons entitled to or interested in the funds, or as the case may be for their trustees.

(2) Where funds in court standing to an account are invested or, after investment, are realised, the method by which the Accountant General effects the investment or the realisation of investments shall not affect the question whether there is for the purposes of this Act an acquisition, or as the case may be a disposal, of an asset representing funds in court standing to the account, and in particular there shall for those purposes be an acquisition or disposal of shares in a court investment fund notwithstanding that the investment in such shares of funds in court standing to an account, or the realisation of funds which have been so invested, is effected by setting off, in the Accountant General's accounts, investment in one account against realisation of investments in another.

(3) In this section "funds in court" means—

(*a*) money in the Supreme Court, money in county courts and statutory deposits described in section 40 of the Administration of Justice Act 1982 and
(*b*) money in the Supreme Court of Judicature of Northern Ireland and money in a county court in Northern Ireland,

and investments representing such money; and references in this section to the Accountant General are references to the Accountant General of the Supreme Court of Judicature in England and, in relation to money within paragraph (*b*) above and investments representing such money, include references to the Accountant General of the Supreme Court of Judicature of Northern Ireland or any other person by whom such funds are held.

Commentary—*Simon's Direct Tax Service* **C1.210.**
Definitions—"Asset", s 21(1); "court investment fund", s 100; "shares", s 288(1).

62 Death: general provisions

(1) For the purposes of this Act the assets of which a deceased person was competent to dispose—

(*a*) shall be deemed to be acquired on his death by the personal representatives or other person on whom they devolve for a consideration equal to their market value at the date of the death, but
(*b*) shall not be deemed to be disposed of by him on his death (whether or not they were the subject of a testamentary disposition).

(2) Allowable losses sustained by an individual in the year of assessment in which he dies may, so far as they cannot be deducted from chargeable gains accruing in that year, be deducted from chargeable gains accruing to the deceased in the 3 years of assessment preceding the year of assessment in which the death occurs, taking chargeable gains accruing in a later year before those accruing in an earlier year.

[(2A) Amounts deductible from chargeable gains for any year in accordance with subsection (2) above shall not be so deductible from any such gains so far as they are gains that are brought into account for that year by virtue of section 2(5)(*b*).

(2B) Where deductions under subsection (2) above fall to be made from the chargeable gains for any year, the provisions of this Act relating to taper relief shall have effect as if those deductions were deductions under section 2(2)(a) and (b) and, accordingly, as if—

(a) those deductions were to be made (before the application of the relief) in computing for that year the excess (if any) mentioned in section 2A(1); and

(b) for the purpose of determining the gains represented in that excess, the gains for that year from which those deductions are treated as made were to be ascertained in accordance with section 2A(6).][1]

(3) In relation to property forming part of the estate of a deceased person the personal representatives shall for the purposes of this Act be treated as being a single and continuing body of persons (distinct from the persons who may from time to time be the personal representatives), and that body shall be treated as having the deceased's residence, ordinary residence, and domicile at the date of death.

(4) On a person acquiring any asset as legatee (as defined in section 64)—

(a) no chargeable gain shall accrue to the personal representatives, and

(b) the legatee shall be treated as if the personal representatives' acquisition of the asset had been his acquisition of it.

(5) Notwithstanding section 17(1) no chargeable gain shall accrue to any person on his making a disposal by way of donatio mortis causa.

(6) Subject to subsections (7) and (8) below, where within the period of 2 years after a person's death any of the dispositions (whether effected by will, under the law relating to intestacy or otherwise) of the property of which he was competent to dispose are varied, or the benefit conferred by any of those dispositions is disclaimed, by an instrument in writing made by the persons or any of the persons who benefit or would benefit under the dispositions—

(a) the variation or disclaimer shall not constitute a disposal for the purposes of this Act, and

(b) this section shall apply as if the variation had been effected by the deceased or, as the case may be, the disclaimed benefit had never been conferred.

(7) Subsection (6) above does not apply to a variation [unless the instrument contains a statement by the persons making the instrument to the effect that they intend the subsection to apply to the variation.][2]

(8) Subsection (6) above does not apply to a variation or disclaimer made for any consideration in money or money's worth other than consideration consisting of the making of a variation or disclaimer in respect of another of the dispositions.

(9) Subsection (6) above applies whether or not the administration of the estate is complete or the property has been distributed in accordance with the original dispositions.

(10) In this section references to assets of which a deceased person was competent to dispose are references to assets of the deceased which (otherwise than in right of a power of appointment or of the testamentary power conferred by statute to dispose of entailed interests) he could, if of full age and capacity, have disposed of by his will, assuming that all the assets were situated in England and, if he was not domiciled in the United Kingdom, that he was domiciled in England, and include references to his severable share in any assets to which, immediately before his death, he was beneficially entitled as a joint tenant.

Commentary—*Simon's Direct Tax Service* **C1.206.**
Revenue Interpretation RI 36—Devolution on death of qualifying corporate bonds with a held over gain: circumstances in which the held over gain becomes chargeable.
RI 152—Valuation of two or more assets acquired by personal representatives or legatees may in certain circumstances be made as if those assets comprised a single unit of property.
RI 210—Bookmaker's pitch acquired by inheritance after October 1998 falls within sub-s (1).
Revenue & other press releases—CCAB June 1967 (''legatee'' includes a person who acquires assets as a result of an appointment or appropriation by the deceased's personal representatives, where the recipient's consent is required to the appropriation).
Revenue Internal Guidance—Capital gains manual CG 30435 (the normal procedures and time limits relating to claims apply to claims to carry back losses of the year of death).
CG 68970–68976 (deceased's transfer of a business as a going concern).
Simon's Tax Cases—*Lake v Lake* [1989] STC 865*; *Administrators of the Estate of Caton, (decd) v Couch* [1995] STC (SCD) 34*; *Clark (executor of Clark, decd) v Green,* [1995] STC (SCD) 99*.
s 62(1), *Passant v Jackson* [1985] STC 133*; *Marshall v Kerr* [1994] STC 638*.
s 62(4), (6), *Marshall v Kerr* [1994] STC 638*.
Definitions—''Allowable loss'', ss 8(2), 16, 288(1); ''asset'', s 21(1); ''the Board'', s 288(1); ''chargeable gain'', s 15(2); ''legatee'', s 64(2), (3); ''market value'', ss 272–274, Sch 11; ''notice'', s 288(1); ''personal representatives'', s 288(1), TA 1988 s 282 ''year of assessment'', s 288(1).
Cross references—See TA 1988 s 757(4) (partial exclusion of this section in relation to offshore income gains);
TCGA 1992 s 2(3) (restriction of carrying back losses).
TCGA 1992 s 66(2)(b) (modification of sub-s (1) above in its application to assets passing on insolvent's death).
TCGA 1992 s 116(11) (treatment of gain or loss on disposals by personal representatives to legatees on reorganisations, etc involving qualifying corporate bonds).
TCGA 1992 s 134(4) (treatment of gain or loss on an acquisition by a legatee of gilt-edged securities acquired by the deceased on nationalisation in exchange for other securities).
Amendments—[1] Sub-ss (2A), (2B) inserted by FA 1998 Sch 21 para 5 with effect from the year 1998–99.
[2] Words in sub-s (7) substituted by FA 2002 s 52 with effect for instruments made after 31 July 2002. Sub-s (7) previously read as follows—

''(7) Subsection (6) above does not apply to a variation unless the person or persons making the instrument so elect by notice given to the Board within 6 months after the date of the instrument or such longer time as the Board may allow.''.

63 Death: application of law in Scotland

(1) The provisions of this Act, so far as relating to the consequences of the death of an heir of entail in possession of any property in Scotland subject to an entail, whether sui juris or not, or of a proper liferenter of any property, shall have effect subject to the provisions of this section.

(2) For the purposes of this Act, on the death of any such heir or liferenter the heir of entail next entitled to the entailed property under the entail or, as the case may be, the person (if any) who, on the death of the liferenter, becomes entitled to possession of the property as heir shall be deemed to have acquired all the assets forming part of the property at the date of the deceased's death for a consideration equal to their market value at that date.

Commentary—*Simon's Direct Tax Service* **C4.209.**
Definitions—''Asset'', s 21(1); ''market value'', ss 272–274, Sch 11.

64 Expenses in administration of estates and trusts

(1) In the case of a gain accruing to a person on the disposal of, or of a right or interest in or over, an asset to which he became absolutely entitled as legatee or as against the trustees of settled property—

    (*a*) any expenditure within section 38(2) incurred by him in relation to the transfer of the asset to him by the personal representatives or trustees, and

    (*b*) any such expenditure incurred in relation to the transfer of the asset by the personal representatives or trustees,

shall be allowable as a deduction in the computation of the gain accruing to that person on the disposal.

(2) In this Act, unless the context otherwise requires, ''legatee'' includes any person taking under a testamentary disposition or on an intestacy or partial intestacy, whether he takes beneficially or as trustee, and a person taking under a donatio mortis causa shall be treated (except for the purposes of section 62) as a legatee and his acquisition as made at the time of the donor's death.

(3) For the purposes of the definition of ''legatee'' above, and of any reference in this Act to a person acquiring an asset ''as legatee'', property taken under a testamentary disposition or on an intestacy or partial intestacy includes any asset appropriated by the personal representatives in or towards satisfaction of a pecuniary legacy or any other interest or share in the property devolving under the disposition or intestacy.

Commentary—*Simon's Direct Tax Service* **C1.206; C4.208.**
Statement of Practice SP 8/94—Capital gains tax: allowable expenses: expenses incurred by personal representatives and corporate trustees.
Definitions—''Absolutely entitled as against trustee'', s 60(2); ''asset'', s 21(1); ''personal representatives'', s 288(1), TA 1988 s 282; ''settled property'', s 68.

65 Liability for tax of trustees or personal representatives

[(1) Subject to subsection (3) below, capital gains tax chargeable in respect of chargeable gains accruing to the trustees of a settlement or capital gains tax due from the personal representatives of a deceased person may be assessed and charged on and in the name of any one or more of the relevant trustees or the relevant personal representatives.][1]

(2) Subject to section 60 and any other express provision to the contrary, chargeable gains accruing to the trustees of a settlement or to the personal representatives of a deceased person, and capital gains tax chargeable on or in the name of such trustees or personal representatives, shall not be regarded for the purposes of this Act as accruing to, or chargeable on, any other person, nor shall any trustee or personal representative be regarded for the purposes of this Act as an individual.

[(3) Where section 80 applies as regards the trustees of a settlement (''the migrating trustees''), nothing in subsection (1) above shall enable any person—

    (*a*) who ceased to be a trustee of the settlement before the end of the relevant period, and

    (*b*) who shows that, when he ceased to be a trustee of the settlement, there was no proposal that the trustees might become neither resident nor ordinarily resident in the United Kingdom,

to be assessed and charged to any capital gains tax which is payable by the migrating trustees by virtue of section 80(2).][1]

[(4) In this section—

    ''the relevant period'' has the same meaning as in section 82;

    ''the relevant trustees'', in relation to any chargeable gains, means the trustees in the year of assessment in which the chargeable gains accrue and any subsequent trustees of the settlement, and ''the relevant personal representatives'' has a corresponding meaning.][1]

Commentary—*Simon's Direct Tax Service* **C1.206; C4.209.**
Simon's Tax Cases—*Roome v Edwards* [1981] STC 96*.
s 65(1), *Roome v Edwards* [1980] STC 99*.
Definitions—''Chargeable gain'', s 15(2); ''ordinarily resident'', s 9(1); ''personal representatives'', s 288(1), TA 1988 s 282; ''resident'', s 9(1).
Amendments—[1] Sub-s (1) substituted, and sub-ss (3), (4) added, by FA 1995 ss 103(7)(*a*), 114 with effect from the year 1996–97.

TCGA 1992

66 Insolvents' assets

(1) In relation to assets held by a person as trustee or assignee in bankruptcy or under a deed of arrangement this Act shall apply as if the assets were vested in, and the acts of the trustee or assignee in relation to the assets were the acts of, the bankrupt or debtor (acquisitions from or disposals to him by the bankrupt or debtor being disregarded accordingly), and tax in respect of any chargeable gains which accrue to any such trustee or assignee shall be assessable on and recoverable from him.

(2) Assets held by a trustee or assignee in bankruptcy or under a deed of arrangement at the death of the bankrupt or debtor shall for the purposes of this Act be regarded as held by a personal representative of the deceased and—

    (*a*) subsection (1) above shall not apply after the death, and

    (*b*) section 62(1) shall apply as if any assets held by a trustee or assignee in bankruptcy or under a deed of arrangement at the death of the bankrupt or debtor were assets of which the deceased was competent to dispose and which then devolved on the trustee or assignee as if he were a personal representative.

(3) Assets vesting in a trustee in bankruptcy after the death of the bankrupt or debtor shall for the purposes of this Act be regarded as held by a personal representative of the deceased, and subsection (1) above shall not apply.

(4) The definition of "settled property" in section 68 shall not include any property as being property held by a trustee or assignee in bankruptcy or under a deed of arrangement.

(5) In this section—

    "deed of arrangement" means a deed of arrangement to which the Deeds of Arrangement Act 1914 or any corresponding enactment forming part of the law of Scotland or Northern Ireland applies and,

    "trustee in bankruptcy" includes a permanent trustee within the meaning of the Bankruptcy (Scotland) Act 1985.

Commentary—*Simon's Direct Tax Service* **C1.213.**
Simon's Tax Cases—*Re McMeekin (a bankrupt)* [1974] STC 429*.
Definitions—"Asset", s 21(1); "chargeable gain", s 15(2); "settled property", s 68.

67 Provisions applicable where section 79 of the Finance Act 1980 has applied

(1) In this section "a claim" means a claim under section 79 of the Finance Act 1980 ("section 79") and "relief" means relief under that section (which provided general relief for gifts).

(2) Where a disposal in respect of which a claim is or has been made is or proves to be a chargeable transfer for inheritance tax purposes, there shall be allowed as a deduction in computing (for capital gains tax purposes) the chargeable gain accruing to the transferee on the disposal of the asset in question an amount equal to whichever is the lesser of—

    (*a*) the inheritance tax attributable to the value of the asset; and

    (*b*) the amount of the chargeable gain as computed apart from this subsection;

and in the case of a disposal which, being a potentially exempt transfer, proves to be a chargeable transfer, all necessary adjustments shall be made, whether by the discharge or repayment of capital gains tax or otherwise.

(3) Where an amount of inheritance tax—

    (*a*) falls to be redetermined in consequence of the transferor's death within 7 years of making the chargeable transfer in question; or

    (*b*) is otherwise varied,

after it has been taken into account under subsection (2) above (or under section 79(5)), all necessary adjustments shall be made, whether by the making of an assessment to capital gains tax or by the discharge or repayment of such tax.

(4) Where—

    (*a*) a claim for relief has been made in respect of the disposal of an asset to a trustee, and

    (*b*) the trustee is deemed to have disposed of the asset, or part of it, by virtue of section 71(1) or 72(1)(*a*),

sections 72(1)(*b*) and 73(1)(*a*) shall not apply to the disposal of the asset, or part by the trustee, but any chargeable gain accruing to the trustee on the disposal shall be restricted to the amount of the held-over gain (or a corresponding part of it) on the disposal of the asset to him.

(5) Subsection (4) above shall not have effect in a case within section 73(2) but in such a case the reduction provided for by section 73(2) shall be diminished by an amount equal to the proportion there mentioned of the held-over gain.

(6) Section 168 shall apply where relief has been given—

    (*a*) with the substitution for subsection (1) of the following—

    "(1) If—

        (*a*) relief has been given under section 79 of the Finance Act 1980 in respect of a disposal made after 5th April 1981 to an individual ("the relevant disposal"); and

(b) at a time when he has not disposed of the asset in question, the transferee becomes neither resident nor ordinarily resident in the United Kingdom,

then, subject to the following provisions of this section, a chargeable gain shall be deemed to have accrued to the transferee immediately before that time, and its amount shall be equal to the held-over gain (within the meaning of section 67) on the relevant disposal.'';

and

(b) with the substitution in subsections (2), (6) and (10) for the references to section 165(4)(b) of references to section 79(1)(b).

(7) In this section ''held-over gain'', in relation to a disposal, means the chargeable gain which would have accrued on that disposal apart from section 79, reduced where applicable in accordance with subsection (3) of that section, and references to inheritance tax include references to capital transfer tax.

Commentary—*Simon's Direct Tax Service* C1.429.
Definitions—''Asset'', s 21(1); ''chargeable gain'', s 15(2); ''ordinarily resident'', s 9(1); ''resident'', s 9(1).
Note—Text of FA 1980 s 79—

79 General relief for gifts

(1) If after 5th April 1980 an individual (in this section referred to as ''the transferor'') makes a disposal, otherwise than under a bargain at arm's length, to an individual resident or ordinarily resident in the United Kingdom (in this section referred to as ''the transferee'') and the transferor and transferee make a claim for relief under this section—
  (a) the amount of any chargeable gain which, apart from this section, would accrue to the transferor on the disposal; and
  (b) the amount of the consideration for which, apart from this section, the transferee would be regarded for the purposes of capital gains tax as having acquired the asset in question,

shall each be reduced by an amount equal to the held-over gain on the disposal.

(2) Subject to subsection (3) below, the reference in subsection (1) above to the held-over gain on a disposal is a reference to the chargeable gain which would have accrued on that disposal apart from this section.
(3) In any case where—
  (a) there is actual consideration (as opposed to the consideration equal to the market value which is deemed to be given by virtue of section 19(3) of the Capital Gains Tax Act 1979) for a disposal in respect of which a claim for relief is made under this section; and
  (b) that actual consideration exceeds the sums allowable as a deduction under section 32 of that Act,

the held-over gain on the disposal shall be reduced by the excess referred to in paragraph (b) above or, if part of the gain on the disposal is relieved under section 124 of the said Act of 1979 (retirement relief), by so much, if any, of that excess as exceeds the part so relieved.

(4) Section 126 of the said Act of 1979 (relief for gifts of business assets) shall not apply to a disposal to an individual; but this subsection shall not be construed as affecting the operation of that section in a case where by virtue of section 46(1) of that Act an individual is treated as acquiring an asset on a disposal under section 54(1) of that Act.
(5) Where a disposal in respect of which a claim is made under this section is a chargeable transfer (for capital transfer tax purposes) there shall be allowed as a deduction in computing (for capital gains tax purposes) the chargeable gain accruing to the transferee on the disposal of the asset in question an amount equal to whichever is the lesser of—
  (a) the capital transfer tax chargeable on the value transferred which is attributable to the value of the asset as ascertained for capital transfer tax purposes; and
  (b) the amount of the chargeable gain as computed apart from this subsection;

and where the capital transfer tax chargeable on the value transferred which is attributable to the value of the asset is paid by the transferor the reference in paragraph (a) above to the value transferred which is so attributable includes a reference to the value transferred which is attributable to that tax.

(6) Where an amount of capital transfer tax—
  (a) falls to be re-determined in consequence of the transferor's death within three years of making the chargeable transfer in question; or
  (b) is otherwise varied,

after it has been taken into account under subsection (5) above, all necessary adjustments shall be made, whether by the making of an assessment to capital gains tax or by the discharge or repayment of such tax.

CHAPTER II
SETTLEMENTS
General provisions

68 Meaning of ''settled property''

In this Act, unless the context otherwise requires, ''settled property'' means any property held in trust other than property to which section 60 applies.

Commentary—*Simon's Direct Tax Service* C4.206.
Simon's Tax Cases—*Kidson v Macdonald* [1974] STC 54*; *Crowe v Appleby* [1975] STC 502*.
Cross references—See TCGA 1992 s 66(4) (meaning of ''settled property'' in this section).

69 Trustees of settlements

(1) In relation to settled property, the trustees of the settlement shall for the purposes of this Act be treated as being a single and continuing body of persons (distinct from the persons who may from time to time be the trustees), and that body shall be treated as being resident and ordinarily resident in the United Kingdom unless the general administration of the trusts is ordinarily carried on outside the United Kingdom and the trustees or a majority of them for the time being are not resident or not ordinarily resident in the United Kingdom.

(2) Notwithstanding subsection (1) above, a person carrying on a business which consists of or includes the management of trusts, and acting as trustee of a trust in the course of that business, shall

be treated in relation to that trust as not resident in the United Kingdom if the whole of the settled property consists of or derives from property provided by a person not at the time (or, in the case of a trust arising under a testamentary disposition or on an intestacy or partial intestacy, at his death) domiciled, resident or ordinarily resident in the United Kingdom, and if in such a case the trustees or a majority of them are or are treated in relation to that trust as not resident in the United Kingdom, the general administration of the trust shall be treated as ordinarily carried on outside the United Kingdom.

(3) For the purposes of this section, and of sections 71(1) and 72(1), where part of the property comprised in a settlement is vested in one trustee or set of trustees and part in another (and in particular where settled land within the meaning of the Settled Land Act 1925 is vested in the tenant for life and investments representing capital money are vested in the trustees of the settlement), they shall be treated as together constituting and, in so far as they act separately, as acting on behalf of a single body of trustees.

(4) If tax assessed on the trustees, or any one trustee, of a settlement in respect of a chargeable gain accruing to the trustees is not paid within 6 months from the date when it becomes payable by the trustees or trustee, and before or after the expiration of that period of 6 months the asset in respect of which the chargeable gain accrued, or any part of the proceeds of sale of that asset, is transferred by the trustees to a person who as against the trustees is absolutely entitled to it, that person may at any time within 2 years from the time when the tax became payable be assessed and charged (in the name of the trustees) to an amount of capital gains tax not exceeding tax chargeable on an amount equal to the amount of the chargeable gain and, where part only of the asset or of the proceeds was transferred, not exceeding a proportionate part of that amount.

Commentary—*Simon's Direct Tax Service* **C4.206.**
Revenue Interpretation RI 9—Procedure for rebasing elections where they are made by the same person in different capacities.

Simon's Tax Cases—s 69(1), (3), *Roome v Edwards* [1981] STC 96*
Definitions—"Absolutely entitled as against trustee", s 60(2); "asset", s 21(1); "chargeable gain", s 15(2); "land", s 288(1); "ordinarily resident", s 9(1); "resident", s 9(1); "settled property", s 68.
Cross references—See TCGA 1992 s 169(3) (relief for gifts of business assets into dual resident settlements: restriction on relief in cases where this section applies to the trustees of such settlements).

70 Transfers into settlement

A transfer into settlement, whether revocable or irrevocable, is a disposal of the entire property thereby becoming settled property notwithstanding that the transferor has some interest as a beneficiary under the settlement and notwithstanding that he is a trustee, or the sole trustee, of the settlement.

Commentary—*Simon's Direct Tax Service* **C4.206.**
Statement of Practice D10—Termination of life interest in settled property.
Simon's Tax Cases—*Berry v Warnett* [1982] STC 396*.
Definition—"Settled property", s 68.

71 Person becoming absolutely entitled to settled property

(1) On the occasion when a person becomes absolutely entitled to any settled property as against the trustee all the assets forming part of the settled property to which he becomes so entitled shall be deemed to have been disposed of by the trustee, and immediately reacquired by him in his capacity as a trustee within section 60(1), for a consideration equal to their market value.

[(2) Where, in any case in which a person ("the beneficiary") becomes absolutely entitled to any settled property as against the trustee, an allowable loss would (apart from this subsection) have accrued to the trustee on the deemed disposal under subsection (1) above of an asset comprised in that property—

    (*a*) that loss shall be treated, to the extent only that it cannot be deducted from pre-entitlement gains of the trustee, as an allowable loss accruing to the beneficiary (instead of to the trustee); but
    (*b*) any allowable loss treated as accruing to the beneficiary under this subsection shall be deductible under this Act from chargeable gains accruing to the beneficiary to the extent only that it can be deducted from gains accruing to the beneficiary on the disposal by him of—
        (i) the asset on the deemed disposal of which the loss accrued; or
        (ii) where that asset is an estate, interest or right in or over land, that asset or any asset deriving from that asset.][1]

[(2A) In subsection (2) above "pre-entitlement gain", in relation to an allowable loss accruing to a trustee on the deemed disposal of any asset comprised in any settled property, means a chargeable gain accruing to that trustee on—

    (*a*) a disposal which, on the occasion on which the beneficiary becomes absolutely entitled as against the trustee to that property, is deemed under subsection (1) above to have taken place; or
    (*b*) any other disposal taking place before that occasion but in the same year of assessment.][1]

[(2B) For the purposes of subsection (2)(*b*)(ii) above an asset ("the relevant asset") derives from another if, in a case where—

    (*a*) assets have merged,

(*b*) an asset has divided or otherwise changed its nature, or

(*c*) different rights or interests in or over any asset have been created or extinguished at different times,

the value of the relevant asset is wholly or partly derived (through one or more successive events falling within paragraphs (*a*) to (*c*) above but not otherwise) from the other asset.][1]

[(2C) The rules set out in subsection (2D) below shall apply (notwithstanding any other rules contained in this Act or in section 113(2) of the Finance Act 1995 (order of deduction))—

(*a*) for determining for the purposes of this section whether an allowable loss accruing to the trustee, or treated as accruing to the beneficiary, can be deducted from particular chargeable gains for any year of assessment; and

(*b*) for the making of deductions of allowable losses from chargeable gains in cases where it has been determined that such an allowable loss can be deducted from particular chargeable gains.][1]

[(2D) Those rules are as follows—

(*a*) allowable losses accruing to the trustee on a deemed disposal under subsection (1) above shall be deducted before any deduction is made in respect of any other allowable losses accruing to the trustee in that year;

(*b*) allowable losses treated as accruing to the beneficiary under this section, so far as they cannot be deducted in a year of assessment as mentioned in subsection (2)(*b*) above, may be carried forward from year to year until they can be so deducted; and

(*c*) allowable losses treated as accruing to the beneficiary for any year of assessment under this section, and allowable losses carried forward to any year of assessment under paragraph (*b*) above—

    (i) shall be deducted before any deduction is made in respect of any allowable losses accruing to the beneficiary in that year otherwise than by virtue of this section; and

    (ii) in the case of losses carried forward to any year, shall be deductible as if they were losses actually accruing in that year.][1]

(3) References in this section to the case where a person becomes absolutely entitled to settled property as against the trustee shall be taken to include references to the case where a person would become so entitled but for being an infant or other person under disability.

Commentary—*Simon's Direct Tax Service* **C4.208, 229.**
Statement of Practice SP 7/84—Capital gains tax: exercise of a power of appointment or advancement over settled property.
Revenue Interpretation RI 38—
Where a beneficiary becomes absolutely entitled under sub-s (1) above, unused losses are transferred to beneficiary under sub-s (2) above.
RI 152—Valuation required by sub-s (1) of two or more assets may in certain circumstances be made as if those assets comprised a single unit of property.
Simon's Tax Cases—s 71(1), *Bond v Pickford* [1983] STC 517*; *Swires v Renton* [1991] STC 490*; *Figg v Clarke* [1997] STC 247*.
Revenue Internal Guidance—Capital Gains Manual CG 37200–37250 (explanation and illustration of specific situations).
Definitions—"Absolutely entitled as against trustee", s 60(2); "allowable loss", ss 8(2), 16, 288(1); "asset", s 21(1); "chargeable gain", s 15(2); "market value", ss 272–274, Sch 11; "settled property", s 68; "year of assessment", s 288(1).
Cross references—See TCGA 1992 s 69(3) (settled property vested in different trustees).
TCGA 1992 s 73 (CGT exemption where the occasion referred to in sub-s (1) above is life tenant's death).
TCGA 1992 s 217 (exclusion of this section in relation to shares acquired in connection with the transfer of a building society's business to a company).
TCGA 1992 s 257(3) (gifts to charities).
TCGA 1992 s 281(1), (7) (payment by instalments of tax chargeable on gains from deemed disposals under sub-s (1) above).
Amendments—[1] Sub-ss (2)–(2D) substituted for sub-s (2) by FA 1999 s 75 with effect for any occasion after 15 June 1999 on which a person becomes absolutely entitled to settlor property as against the trustee. Sub-s (2) previously read—

"(2) On the occasion when a person becomes absolutely entitled to any settled property as against the trustee, any allowable loss which has accrued to the trustee in respect of property which is, or is represented by, the property to which that person so becomes entitled (including any allowable loss carried forward to the year of assessment in which that occasion falls), being a loss which cannot be deducted from chargeable gains accruing to the trustee in that year, but before that occasion, shall be treated as if it were an allowable loss accruing at that time to the person becoming so entitled, instead of to the trustee."

72 Termination of life interest on death of person entitled

(1) On the termination, on the death of the person entitled to it, of [an][1] interest in possession in all or any part of settled property—

(*a*) the whole or a corresponding part of each of the assets forming part of the settled property and not ceasing at that time to be settled property shall be deemed for the purposes of this Act at that time to be disposed of and immediately reacquired by the trustee for a consideration equal to the whole or a corresponding part of the market value of the asset; but

(*b*) no chargeable gain shall accrue on that disposal.

For the purposes of this subsection [an][1] interest which is a right to part of the income of settled property shall be treated as [an][1] interest in a corresponding part of the settled property.

(2) Subsection (1) above shall apply where the person entitled to [an][1] interest in possession in all or any part of settled property dies (although the interest does not then terminate) as it applies on the termination of such [an][1] interest.

[(3) This section shall apply on the death of the person entitled to any annuity payable out of, or charged on, settled property or the income of settled property as it applies on the death of a person whose interest in possession in the whole or any part of settled property terminates on his death.][1]

[(4) Where, in the case of any entitlement to an annuity created by a settlement some of the settled property is appropriated by the trustees as a fund out of which the annuity is payable, and there is no right of recourse to, or to the income of, settled property not so appropriated, then without prejudice to subsection (5) below, the settled property so appropriated shall, while the annuity is payable, and on the occasion of the death of the person entitled to the annuity, be treated for the purposes of this section as being settled property under a separate settlement.][1]

(5) If there is [an][1] interest in a part of the settled property and, where that is [an][1] interest in income, there is no right of recourse to, or to the income of, the remainder of the settled property, the part of the settled property in which the ...[1] interest subsists shall while it subsists be treated for the purposes of this section as being settled property under a separate settlement.

Commentary—*Simon's Direct Tax Service* **C4.209, 210.**
Statements of Practice D10—Termination of life interest in settled property.
Revenue & other press releases—IR 14-2-80 ("corresponding part" TCGA 1992 s 72(1)(a) is normally taken to be the proportion which the annuity bears to the income of the fund).
Revenue Internal Guidance—Capital gains manual CG 36450–36513 (application of this section with worked examples).
Simon's Tax Cases—s 72(1), (5), *Pexton v Bell* [1975] STC 84*; *Crowe v Appleby* [1976] STC 301*.
Definitions—"Asset", s 21(1); "chargeable gain", s 15(2); "market value", ss 272–274, Sch 11; "settled property", s 68.
Cross references—See TCGA 1992 s 69(3) (settled property vested in different trustees).
TCGA 1992 s 74 (modification of sub-s (1) of this section where holdover relief has been claimed).
TCGA 1992 s 281(1), (7) (payment by instalments of tax chargeable on gains from deemed disposals under sub-s (1) above).
Amendments—[1] Words in sub-ss (1), (2), (5) substituted, sub-ss (3), (4) substituted and word omitted from sub-s (5) repealed, by FA 1996 Sch 39 para 5, Sch 41 Pt VIII(4), with effect in relation to deaths occurring after 5 April 1996.

73 Death of life tenant: exclusion of chargeable gain

(1) Where, by virtue of section 71(1), the assets forming part of any settled property are deemed to be disposed of and reacquired by the trustee on the occasion when a person becomes (or would but for a disability become) absolutely entitled thereto as against the trustee, then, if that occasion is the [death of a person entitled to an interest in possession in the settled property][1]—

    (a) no chargeable gain shall accrue on the disposal, and
    (b) if on the death the property reverts to the disponer, the disposal and reacquisition under that subsection shall be deemed to be for such consideration as to secure that neither a gain nor a loss accrues to the trustee, and shall, if the trustee had first acquired the property at a date earlier than 6th April 1965, be deemed to be at that earlier date.

(2) Where the ...[1] interest referred to in subsection (1) above is an interest in part only of the settled property to which section 71 applies, subsection (1)(a) above shall not apply but any chargeable gain accruing on the disposal shall be reduced by a proportion corresponding to that represented by the part.

(3) The last sentence of subsection (1) of section 72 and [subsections (3) to (5) of that section shall apply for the purposes of this section][1] as they apply for the purposes of section 72(1).

Commentary—*Simon's Direct Tax Service* **C4.210.**
Definitions—"Absolutely entitled as against trustee", s 60(2); "asset", s 21(1); "chargeable gain", s 15(2); "settled property", s 68.
Cross references—See TCGA 1992 s 35(3)(d) (application of rebasing provisions).
TCGA 1992 s 55(5) (indexation allowance by reference to market value on 31 March 1982).
TCGA 1992 s 74 (modification of sub-s (1) of this section where holdover relief has been claimed).
TCGA 1992 Sch 3 para 1 (assets treated as held on 31 March 1982).
TCGA 1992 Sch 4 para 7 (reduction of deferred charges on gains accruing on disposals after 31 March 1982 where the disposed assets were acquired before that date on a no gain/no loss disposal in accordance with this section).
Amendments—[1] Words in sub-ss (1), (3) substituted and word omitted from sub-s (2) repealed by FA 1996 Sch 39 para 6, Sch 41 Pt VIII(4) with effect in relation to deaths occurring after 5 April 1996.

74 Effect on sections 72 and 73 of relief under section 165 or 260

(1) This section applies where—

    (a) a claim for relief was made under section 165 or 260 in respect of the disposal of an asset to a trustee, and
    (b) the trustee is deemed to have disposed of the asset, or part of it, by virtue of section 71(1) or 72(1)(a).

(2) Sections 72(1)(b) and 73(1)(a) shall not apply to the disposal of the asset or part by the trustee, but any chargeable gain accruing to the trustee on the disposal shall be restricted to the amount of the held-over gain (or a corresponding part of it) on the disposal of the asset to him.

(3) Subsection (2) above shall not have effect in a case within section 73(2) but in such a case the reduction provided for by section 73(2) shall be diminished by an amount equal to the proportion there mentioned of the held-over gain.

(4) In this section "held-over gain" has the same meaning as in section 165 or, as the case may be, 260.

Commentary—*Simon's Direct Tax Service* **C4.210.**
Definitions—"Asset", s 21(1); "chargeable gain", s 15(2).

75 Death of annuitant

Commentary—*Simon's Direct Tax Service* **C4.210.**
Amendments—This section repealed by FA 1996 Sch 41 Pt VIII(4) with effect in relation to deaths occurring after 5 April 1996.

76 Disposal of interests in settled property

(1) [Subject to subsection (1A) below][1] no chargeable gain shall accrue on the disposal of an interest created by or arising under a settlement (including, in particular, an annuity or life interest, and the reversion to an annuity or life interest) by the person for whose benefit the interest was created by the terms of the settlement or by any other person except one who acquired, or derives his title from one who acquired, the interest for a consideration in money or money's worth, other than consideration consisting of another interest under the settlement.

[(1A) Subject to subsection (3) below, subsection (1) above does not apply if—

    (*a*) the settlement falls within subsection (1B) below; or
    (*b*) the property comprised in the settlement is or includes property deriving directly or indirectly from a settlement falling within that subsection.

(1B) A settlement falls within this subsection if there has been a time when the trustees of that settlement—

    (*a*) were not resident or ordinarily resident in the United Kingdom; or
    (*b*) fell to be regarded for the purposes of any double taxation relief arrangements as resident in a territory outside the United Kingdom.][1]

(2) Subject to subsection (1) above, where a person who has acquired an interest in settled property (including in particular the reversion to an annuity or life interest) becomes, as the holder of that interest, absolutely entitled as against the trustee to any settled property, he shall be treated as disposing of the interest in consideration of obtaining that settled property (but without prejudice to any gain accruing to the trustee on the disposal of that property deemed to be effected by him under section 71(1)).

[(3) Subsection (1A) above shall not prevent subsection (1) above from applying where the disposal in question is a disposal in consideration of obtaining settled property that is treated as made under subsection (2) above.][1]

Commentary—*Simon's Direct Tax Service* **C4.228.**
Simon's Tax Cases—*Harthan v Mason* [1980] STC 94*,
s 76(1), *Kidson v Macdonald* [1974] STC 54*; *Eilbeck v Rawling* [1981] STC 174*.
Definitions—"Absolutely entitled as against trustee", s 60(2); "chargeable gain", s 15(2); "settled property", s 68.
Cross references—See TCGA 1992 s 85 (restriction of the application of sub-s (1) of this section in respect of disposals of interests in non-resident settlements).
TCGA 1992 s 217(4) (exclusion of sub-s (1) of this section in relation to shares acquired in connection with the transfer of a building society's business to a company).
Amendments—[1] Words in sub-s (1) and sub-ss (1A), (1B), (3) inserted by FA 1998 s 128 with effect in relation to any disposal on or after 6 March 1998.

[76A Disposal of interest in settled property: deemed disposal of underlying assets

Schedule 4A to this Act has effect with respect to disposals for consideration of an interest in settled property.][1]

Amendments—[1] This section inserted by FA 2000 s 91(1), (3) with effect for any disposal of an interest in settled property made, or the effective completion of which falls, after 20 March 2000.

[76B Transfers of value by trustees linked with trustee borrowing

Schedule 4B to this Act has effect with respect to transfers of value by trustees that are, in accordance with the Schedule, treated as linked with trustee borrowing.][1]

Amendments—[1] This section inserted by FA 2000 s 92(1), (5) with effect for any transfer of value in relation to which the material time is after 20 March 2000.

[77 Charge on settlor with interest in settlement

(1) Where in a year of assessment—

    (*a*) chargeable gains accrue to the trustees of a settlement from the disposal of any or all of the settled property,
    (*b*) after making any deduction provided for by section 2(2) in respect of disposals of the settled property there remains an amount on which the trustees would, disregarding section 3, be chargeable to tax for the year in respect of those gains, and
    (*c*) at any time during the year the settlor has an interest in the settlement,

the trustees shall not be chargeable to tax in respect of those but instead chargeable gains of an amount equal to that referred to in paragraph (*b*) shall be treated as accruing to the settlor in that year.

(2) Subject to the following provisions of this section, a settlor shall be regarded as having an interest in a settlement if—

(*a*) any property which may at any time be comprised in the settlement, or any derived property is, or will or may become, payable to or applicable for the benefit of the settlor or his spouse in any circumstances whatsoever, or

(*b*) the settlor or his spouse enjoys a benefit deriving directly or indirectly from any property which is comprised in the settlement or any derived property.

(3) The references in subsection (2)(*a*) and (*b*) above to the spouse of the settlor do not include—

(*a*) a person to whom the settlor is not for the time being married but may later marry, or

(*b*) a spouse from whom the settlor is separated under an order of a court, or under a separation agreement or in such circumstances that the separation is likely to be permanent, or

(*c*) the widow or widower of the settlor.

(4) A settlor shall not be regarded as having an interest in a settlement by virtue of subsection (2)(*a*) above if and so long as none of the property which may at any time be comprised in the settlement, and no derived property, can become payable or applicable as mentioned in that provision except in the event of—

(*a*) the bankruptcy of some person who is or may become beneficially entitled to the property or any derived property, or

(*b*) an assignment of or charge on the property or any derived property being made or given by some such person, or

(*c*) in the case of a marriage settlement, the death of both parties to the marriage and of all or any of the children of the marriage, or

(*d*) the death of a child of the settlor who had become beneficially entitled to the property or any derived property at an age not exceeding 25.

(5) A settlor shall not be regarded as having an interest in a settlement by virtue of subsection (2)(*a*) above if and so long as some person is alive and under the age of 25 during whose life the property or any derived property cannot become payable or applicable as mentioned in that provision except in the event of that person becoming bankrupt or assigning or charging his interest in that property.

(6) This section does not apply—

(*a*) where the settlor dies during the year; or

(*b*) in a case where the settlor is regarded as having an interest in the settlement by reason only of—

(i) the fact that property is, or will or may become, payable to or applicable for the benefit of his spouse, or

(ii) the fact that a benefit is enjoyed by his spouse,

where the spouse dies, or the settlor and the spouse cease to be married, during the year.

[(6A) Without prejudice to so much of this section as requires section [2A to be applied in the computation of any amount that is treated under this section as an amount of chargeable gains accruing to the settlor, chargeable gains that are treated as accruing to the settlor under this section shall not be eligible for taper relief.]²

(7) This section does not apply unless the settlor is, and the trustees are, either resident in the United Kingdom during any part of the year or ordinarily resident in the United Kingdom during the year.

(8) In this section ''derived property'', in relation to any property, means income from that property or any other property directly or indirectly representing proceeds of, or of income from, that property or income therefrom.]¹

Commentary—*Simon's Direct Tax Service* **C4.330.**
Simon's Tax Cases—*de Rothschild v Lawrenson* [1995] STC 623*.
Definitions—''Chargeable gain'', s 15(2); ''ordinarily resident'', s 9(1); ''resident'', s 9(1); ''settled property'', s 68; ''year of assessment'', s 288(1).
Cross references—See TCGA 1992 s 78 (right of recovery from trustees of tax paid by settlor under sub-s (1) above).
TCGA 1992 s 79 (supplementary provisions).
TCGA 1992 s 87(8) (this section to be ignored in computing gains attributable to beneficiaries of certain non-resident settlements).
TCGA 1992 s 88(6) (this section to be ignored in computing gains attributable to certain dual resident settlements).
TCGA 1992 Sch 5 para 1(1) (this section to be ignored in computing gains attributable to settlor of certain non-resident trusts).
FA 2002 Sch 11 para 8 (election for prospective amendments made by FA 2002 ss 51, 141, Sch 11, Sch 40 Pt 3(4) to apply with effect for chargeable gains treated as accruing to a person by virtue of TCGA 1992 s 77 or 86 (read, where appropriate, with TCGA s 10A) in any or all of the tax years 2000–01, 2001–02, and 2002–03).
Amendments—¹ This section substituted by FA 1995 s 74, Sch 17 para 27 with effect from the year 1995–96 and applies to every settlement, wherever and whenever it was made or entered into.
² Sub-s (6A) inserted by FA 1998 Sch 21 para 6 with effect from the year 1998–99.
Prospective amendments—In sub-s (1)(*b*), words to be substituted for the words from ''would'' to the end, by FA 2002 s 51, Sch 11 paras 1, 3, 7 with effect for chargeable gains treated as accruing to a person by virtue of TCGA 1992 s 77 or 86 (read, where appropriate, with TCGA 1992 s 10A) from 2003–04. Words to be substituted to read as follows—

''would be chargeable to tax for the year in respect of those gains if—

(i) the gains were not eligible for taper relief, but section 2(2) applied as if they were (so that the order of deducting losses provided for by section 2A(6) applied), and
(ii) section 3 were disregarded,
and''.
Sub-s (6A) to be repealed by FA 2002 s 141, Sch 40 Pt 3(4) with effect for chargeable gains treated as accruing to a person by virtue of TCGA 1992 s 77 or 86 (read, where appropriate, with TCGA 1992 s 10A) for 2003–04 and subsequent years of assessment.

78 Right of recovery

(1) Where any tax becomes chargeable on and is paid by a person in respect of gains treated as accruing to him under [section 77][1] he shall be entitled—

    (*a*) to recover the amount of the tax from any trustee of the settlement, and

    (*b*) for that purpose to require an inspector to give him a certificate specifying—

        (i) the amount of the gains accruing to the trustees in respect of which he has paid tax; and

        (ii) the amount of tax paid;

and any such certificate shall be conclusive evidence of the facts stated in it.

(2) In order to ascertain for the purposes of subsection (1) above the amount of tax chargeable for any year by virtue of [section 77][1] in respect of gains treated as accruing to any person, those gains shall be regarded as forming the highest part of the amount on which he is chargeable to capital gains tax for the year.

(3) In a case where—

    (*a*) gains are treated as accruing to a person in a year under section 86(4), and

    (*b*) gains are treated as accruing to the same person under [section 77][1] in the same year,

subsection (2) above shall have effect subject to section 86(4)(*b*).

Commentary—*Simon's Direct Tax Service* **C4.330, 336.**
Definition—''Inspector'', s 288(1).
Cross references—See TCGA 1992 s 79 (supplemental provisions).
TCGA 1992 s 87(8) (this section to be ignored in computing gains attributable to beneficiaries of certain non-resident settlements).
TCGA 1992 s 88(6) (this section to be ignored in computing chargeable amount attributable to certain dual resident settlements).
TCGA 1992 Sch 5 para 1(1) (this section to be ignored in computing gains attributable to settlors of certain non-resident trusts).
Amendments—[1] Words in sub-ss (1)–(3) substituted by FA 1995 s 74, Sch 17 para 28 with effect from the year 1995–96 and apply to every settlement, wherever and whenever it was made or entered into.

79 Provisions supplemental to sections 77 and 78

(1) For the purposes of this section and sections 77 and 78 a person is a settlor in relation to a settlement if the settled property consists of or includes property originating from him.

(2) In this section and sections 77 and 78—

    (*a*) references to settled property (and to property comprised in a settlement), in relation to any settlor, are references only to property originating from that settlor, ...[1]

    (*b*) ...[1]

(3) References in this section to property originating from a settlor are references to—

    (*a*) property which that settlor has provided directly or indirectly for the purposes of the settlement,

    (*b*) property representing that property, and

    (*c*) so much of any property which represents both property so provided and other property as, on a just apportionment, represents the property so provided.

(4) ...[1]

(5) In [subsection (3)][2]

    (*a*) references to property ...[1] which a settlor has provided directly or indirectly include references to property ...[1] which has been provided directly or indirectly by another person in pursuance of reciprocal arrangements with that settlor, but do not include references to property ...[1] which that settlor has provided directly or indirectly in pursuance of reciprocal arrangements with another person, and

    (*b*) references to property which represents other property include references to property which represents accumulated income from that other property.

(6) An inspector may by notice require any person who is or has been a trustee of, a beneficiary under, or a settlor in relation to, a settlement to give him within such time as he may direct, not being less than 28 days, such particulars as he thinks necessary for the purposes of this section and sections 77 and 78.

(7) The reference in section 77(1)(*a*) to gains accruing to trustees from the disposal of settled property includes a reference to gains treated as accruing to them under section 13 and the reference in section 77(1)(*b*) to deductions in respect of disposals of the settled property includes a reference to deductions on account of losses treated under section 13 as accruing to the trustees.

(8) Where the trustees of a settlement have elected that section 691(2) of the Taxes Act (certain income of maintenance funds for historic buildings not to be income of settlor etc) shall have effect in the case of any settlement or part of a settlement in relation to a year of assessment, sections 77 and 78 and subsections (1) to (7) above shall not apply in relation to the settlement or part for the year.

Commentary—*Simon's Direct Tax Service* **C4.330.**
Definitions—''Inspector'', s 288(1); ''notice'', s 288(1); ''settled property'', s 68; ''the Taxes Act'', s 288(1); ''year of assessment'', s 288(1).
Cross references—See TCGA 1992 s 87(8) (this section to be ignored in computing gains attributable to beneficiaries of certain non-resident settlements).
TCGA 1992 s 88(6) (this section to be ignored in computing chargeable amount attributable to certain dual resident settlements).
TCGA 1992 Sch 5 para 1(1) (this section to be ignored in computing gains attributable to settlors of certain non-resident trusts).

Amendments—¹ Sub-ss (2)(*b*) (and word immediately preceding it), (4) and words omitted from sub-s (5)(*a*), repealed by FA 1995 s 74, Sch 17 para 29(2), (3), (4)(*b*), Sch 29 Pt VIII(8), with effect from the year 1995–96.
² Words in sub-s (5) substituted by FA 1995 s 74, Sch 17 para 29(4)(*a*) with effect from the year 1995–96 and apply to every settlement, wherever and whenever it was made or entered into.

[79A Restriction on set-off of trust losses

(1) This section applies to a chargeable gain accruing to the trustees of a settlement where—

(*a*) in computing the gain, the allowable expenditure is reduced in consequence, directly or indirectly, of a claim to gifts relief in relation to an earlier disposal to the trustees;
(*b*) the transferor on that earlier disposal, or any person connected with the transferor, has at any time—

(i) acquired an interest in the settled property, or
(ii) entered into an arrangement to acquire such an interest; and

(*c*) in connection with that acquisition or arrangement any person has at any time received, or become entitled to receive, any consideration.

(2) Where this section applies to a chargeable gain, no allowable losses accruing to the trustees (in the year in which the gain accrues or any earlier year) may be set against the gain.

This applies to the whole of the chargeable gain (and not just the element deferred as a result of the claim to gifts relief).

(3) In this section—

(*a*) "gifts relief" means relief under section 165 or 260; and
(*b*) references to losses not being allowed to be set against a chargeable gain are to the losses not being allowed as a deduction against chargeable gains to the extent that they include that gain.

(4) The references in subsection (1)(*b*) above to an interest in settled property have the same meaning as in Schedule 4A.]¹

Commentary—*Simon's Direct Tax Service* **C4.332**.
Revenue Internal Guidance—Capital Gains Manual CG 33553 (general outline of this section).
Amendment—¹ This section inserted by FA 2000 s 93 with effect for gains accruing after 20 March 2000.

[79B Attribution to trustees of gains of non-resident companies

(1) This section applies where trustees of a settlement are participators—

(*a*) in a close company, or
(*b*) in a company that is not resident in the United Kingdom but would be a close company if it were resident in the United Kingdom.

For this purpose "participator" has the same meaning as in section 13.

(2) Where this section applies, nothing in any double taxation relief arrangements shall be read as preventing a charge to tax arising by virtue of the attribution to the trustees under section 13, by reason of their participation in the company mentioned in subsection (1) above, of any part of a chargeable gain accruing to a company that is not resident in the United Kingdom.

(3) Where this section applies and—

(*a*) a chargeable gain accrues to a company that is not resident in the United Kingdom but would be a close company if it were resident in the United Kingdom, and
(*b*) all or part of the chargeable gain is treated under section 13(2) as accruing to a close company which is not chargeable to corporation tax in respect of the gain by reason of double taxation arrangements, and
(*c*) had the company mentioned in paragraph (*b*) (and any other relevant company) not been resident in the United Kingdom, all or part of the chargeable gain would have been attributed to the trustees by reason of their participation in the company mentioned in subsection (1) above,

section 13(9) shall apply as if the company mentioned in paragraph (*b*) above (and any other relevant company) were not resident in the United Kingdom.

(4) The references in subsection (3) above to "any other relevant company" are to any other company which if it were not resident in the United Kingdom would be a company in relation to which section 13(9) applied with the result that all or part of the chargeable gain was attributed to the trustees as mentioned in that subsection.]¹

Commentary—*Simon's Direct Tax Service* **C4.442**.
Amendment—¹ This section inserted by FA 2000 s 94 with effect where a chargeable gain accrues after 20 March 2000 to a company that is not resident in the UK.

Migration of settlements, non-resident settlements and dual resident settlements

Statement of Practice SP 5/92—Revenue's practice in applying the rules (contained in ss 80–98 and Sch 5 of this Act) for capital gains of certain offshore trusts.

80 Trustees ceasing to be resident in UK

(1) This section applies if the trustees of a settlement become at any time ("the relevant time") neither resident nor ordinarily resident in the United Kingdom.

(2) The trustees shall be deemed for all purposes of this Act—

    (*a*) to have disposed of the defined assets immediately before the relevant time, and
    (*b*) immediately to have reacquired them,

at their market value at that time.

(3) Subject to subsections (4) and (5) below, the defined assets are all assets constituting settled property of the settlement immediately before the relevant time.

(4) If immediately after the relevant time—

    (*a*) the trustees carry on a trade in the United Kingdom through a branch or agency, and
    (*b*) any assets are situated in the United Kingdom and either used in or for the purposes of the trade or used or held for the purposes of the branch or agency,

the assets falling within paragraph (*b*) above shall not be defined assets.

(5) Assets shall not be defined assets if—

    (*a*) they are of a description specified in any double taxation relief arrangements, and
    (*b*) were the trustees to dispose of them immediately before the relevant time, the trustees would fall to be regarded for the purposes of the arrangements as not liable in the United Kingdom to tax on gains accruing to them on the disposal.

(6) Section 152 shall not apply where the trustees—

    (*a*) have disposed of the old assets, or their interest in them, before the relevant time, and
    (*b*) acquire the new assets, or their interest in them, after that time, unless the new assets are excepted from this subsection by subsection (7) below.

(7) If at the time when the new assets are acquired—

    (*a*) the trustees carry on a trade in the United Kingdom through a branch or agency, and
    (*b*) any new assets are situated in the United Kingdom and either used in or for the purposes of the trade or used or held for the purposes of the branch or agency,

the assets falling within paragraph (*b*) above shall be excepted from subsection (6) above.

(8) In this section "the old assets" and "the new assets" have the same meanings as in section 152.

Commentary—*Simon's Direct Tax Service* **C4.434.**
Definitions—"Asset", s 21(1); "branch or agency", s 10(6); "double taxation relief arrangements", s 288(1); "market value", ss 272–274, Sch 11; "ordinarily resident", s 9(1); "resident", s 9(1); "settled property", s 68; "trade", s 288(1), TA 1988 s 832(1).
Cross references—See TCGA 1992 s 81 (change in residence status of trusts in consequence of death of trustee).
TCGA 1992 s 82 (liability for tax of certain past trustees where tax payable by migrating trustees to whom this section applies is not paid within six months).
TCGA 1992 s 85(2), (5) (disposals from non-resident settlements).

81 Death of trustee: special rules

(1) Subsection (2) below applies where—

    (*a*) section 80 applies as a result of the death of a trustee of the settlement, and
    (*b*) within the period of 6 months beginning with the death, the trustees of the settlement become resident and ordinarily resident in the United Kingdom.

(2) That section shall apply as if the defined assets were restricted to such assets (if any) as—

    (*a*) would be defined assets apart from this section, and
    (*b*) fall within subsection (3) or (4) below.

(3) Assets fall within this subsection if they were disposed of by the trustees in the period which—

    (*a*) begins with the death, and
    (*b*) ends when the trustees become resident and ordinarily resident in the United Kingdom.

(4) Assets fall within this subsection if—

    (*a*) they are of a description specified in any double taxation relief arrangements,
    (*b*) they constitute settled property of the settlement at the time immediately after the trustees become resident and ordinarily resident in the United Kingdom, and
    (*c*) were the trustees to dispose of them at that time, the trustees would fall to be regarded for the purposes of the arrangements as not liable in the United Kingdom to tax on gains accruing to them on the disposal.

(5) Subsection (6) below applies where—

    (*a*) at any time the trustees of a settlement become resident and ordinarily resident in the United Kingdom as a result of the death of a trustee of the settlement, and
    (*b*) section 80 applies as regards the trustees of the settlement in circumstances where the relevant time (within the meaning of that section) falls within the period of 6 months beginning with the death.

(6) That section shall apply as if the defined assets were restricted to such assets (if any) as—

(*a*) would be defined assets apart from this section, and

(*b*) fall within subsection (7) below.

(7) Assets fall within this subsection if—

(*a*) the trustees acquired them in the period beginning with the death and ending with the relevant time, and

(*b*) they acquired them as a result of a disposal in respect of which relief is given under section 165 or in relation to which section 260(3) applies.

Commentary—*Simon's Direct Tax Service* **C4.435.**
Definitions—''Asset'', s 21(1); ''double taxation relief arrangements'', s 288(1); ''ordinarily resident'', s 9(1); ''resident'', s 9(1); ''settled property'', s 68.

82 Past trustees: liability for tax

(1) This section applies where—

(*a*) section 80 applies as regards the trustees of a settlement (''the migrating trustees''), and

(*b*) any capital gains tax which is payable by the migrating trustees by virtue of section 80(2) is not paid within 6 months from the time when it became payable.

(2) The Board may, at any time before the end of the period of 3 years beginning with the time when the amount of the tax is finally determined, serve on any person to whom subsection (3) below applies a notice—

(*a*) stating particulars of the tax payable, the amount remaining unpaid and the date when it became payable;

(*b*) stating particulars of any interest payable on the tax, any amount remaining unpaid and the date when it became payable;

(*c*) requiring that person to pay the amount of the unpaid tax, or the aggregate amount of the unpaid tax and the unpaid interest, within 30 days of the service of the notice.

(3) This subsection applies to any person who, at any time within the relevant period, was a trustee of the settlement, except that it does not apply to any such person if—

(*a*) he ceased to be a trustee of the settlement before the end of the relevant period, and

(*b*) he shows that, when he ceased to be a trustee of the settlement, there was no proposal that the trustees might become neither resident nor ordinarily resident in the United Kingdom.

(4) Any amount which a person is required to pay by a notice under this section may be recovered from him as if it were tax due and duly demanded of him; and he may recover any such amount paid by him from the migrating trustees.

(5) A payment in pursuance of a notice under this section shall not be allowed as a deduction in computing any income, profits or losses for any tax purposes.

(6) For the purposes of this section—

(*a*) where the relevant time (within the meaning of section 80) falls within the period of 12 months beginning with 19th March 1991, the relevant period is the period beginning with that date and ending with that time;

(*b*) in any other case, the relevant period is the period of 12 months ending with the relevant time.

Commentary—*Simon's Direct Tax Service* **C4.434.**
Revenue Internal Guidance—Assessed taxes manual AT 6.608 (Revenue procedure where this section is to be applied).
Definitions—''The Board'', s 288(1); ''notice'', s 288(1); ''ordinarily resident'', s 9(1); ''resident'', s 9(1).

83 Trustees ceasing to be liable to UK tax

(1) This section applies if the trustees of a settlement, while continuing to be resident and ordinarily resident in the United Kingdom, become at any time (''the time concerned'') trustees who fall to be regarded for the purposes of any double taxation relief arrangements—

(*a*) as resident in a territory outside the United Kingdom, and

(*b*) as not liable in the United Kingdom to tax on gains accruing on disposals of assets (''relevant assets'') which constitute settled property of the settlement and fall within descriptions specified in the arrangements.

(2) The trustees shall be deemed for all purposes of this Act—

(*a*) to have disposed of their relevant assets immediately before the time concerned, and

(*b*) immediately to have reacquired them,

at their market value at that time.

Commentary—*Simon's Direct Tax Service* **C4.447.**
Definitions—''Asset'', s 21(1); ''double taxation relief arrangements'', s 288(1); ''market value'', ss 272–274, Sch 11; ''ordinarily resident'', s 9(1); ''resident'', s 9(1); ''settled property'', s 68.
Cross references—See TCGA 1992 s 85(5), (8) (disposals from non-resident settlements).

84 Acquisition by dual resident trustees

(1) Section 152 shall not apply where—

(*a*) the new assets are, or the interest in them is, acquired by the trustees of a settlement, (*b*) at the time of the acquisition the trustees are resident and ordinarily resident in the United Kingdom and fall to be regarded for the purposes of any double taxation relief arrangements as resident in a territory outside the United Kingdom,

(*c*) the assets are of a description specified in the arrangements, and

(*d*) were the trustees to dispose of the assets immediately after the acquisition, the trustees would fall to be regarded for the purposes of the arrangements as not liable in the United Kingdom to tax on gains accruing to them on the disposal.

(2) In this section "the new assets" has the same meaning as in section 152.

Commentary—*Simon's Direct Tax Service* **C4.447.**
Definitions—"Asset", s 21(1); "double taxation relief arrangements", s 288(1); "ordinarily resident", s 9(1); "resident", s 9(1).

85 Disposal of interests in non-resident settlements

(1) Subsection (1) of section 76 shall not apply to the disposal of an interest in settled property, other than one treated under subsection (2) of that section as made in consideration of obtaining the settled property, if at the time of the disposal the trustees are neither resident nor ordinarily resident in the United Kingdom.

(2) [Subject to subsections (4), (9) and (10) below,]¹ subsection (3) below applies where—

(*a*) section 80 applies as regards the trustees of a settlement,

(*b*) after the relevant time (within the meaning of that section) a person disposes of an interest created by or arising under the settlement and the circumstances are such that subsection (1) above prevents section 76(1) applying, and

(*c*) the interest was created for his benefit, or he otherwise acquired it, before the relevant time.

(3) For the purpose of calculating any chargeable gain accruing on the disposal of the interest, the person disposing of it shall be treated as having—

(*a*) disposed of it immediately before the relevant time, and

(*b*) immediately reacquired it,

at its market value at that time.

(4) Subsection (3) above shall not apply if section 83 applied as regards the trustees in circumstances where the time concerned (within the meaning of that section) fell before the time when the interest was created for the benefit of the person disposing of it or when he otherwise acquired it.

(5) [Subject to subsection (10) below,]¹ subsection (7) below applies where—

(*a*) section 80 applies as regards the trustees of a settlement,

(*b*) after the relevant time (within the meaning of that section) a person disposes of an interest created by or arising under the settlement and the circumstances are such that subsection (1) above prevents section 76(1) applying,

(*c*) the interest was created for his benefit, or he otherwise acquired it, before the relevant time, and

(*d*) section 83 applied as regards the trustees in circumstances where the time concerned (within the meaning of that section) fell in the relevant period.

(6) The relevant period is the period which—

(*a*) begins when the interest was created for the benefit of the person disposing of it or when he otherwise acquired it, and

(*b*) ends with the relevant time.

(7) For the purpose of calculating any chargeable gain accruing on the disposal of the interest, the person disposing of it shall be treated as having—

(*a*) disposed of it immediately before the time found under subsection (8) below, and

(*b*) immediately reacquired it,

at its market value at that time.

(8) The time is—

(*a*) the time concerned (where there is only one such time), or

(*b*) the earliest time concerned (where there is more than one because section 83 applied more than once).

(9) Subsection (3) above shall not apply where subsection (7) above applies.

[(10) Subsection (3) or (7) above does not apply to the disposal of an interest created by or arising under a settlement which has relevant offshore gains at the material time.

The material time is—

(*a*) in relation to subsection (3) above, the relevant time within the meaning of section 80;

(*b*) in relation to subsection (7) above, the time found under subsection (8) above.

(11) For the purposes of subsection (10) above, a settlement has relevant offshore gains at any time if, were the year of assessment to end at that time, there would be an amount of trust gains which by virtue of section 89(2) or paragraph 8(3) of Schedule 4C would be available to be treated as chargeable gains accruing to any beneficiaries of the settlement receiving capital payments in the following year of assessment.]¹

Commentary—*Simon's Direct Tax Service* **C4.436.**
Definitions—"Chargeable gain", s 15(2); "market value", ss 272–274, Sch 11; "ordinarily resident", s 9(1); "resident", s 9(1); "settled property", s 68.
Amendment—¹ Words in sub-s (2) substituted and words in sub-ss (5) and whole of sub-ss (10), (11) inserted, by FA 2000 s 95 with effect where the material time (within the meaning of sub-s (10) above) falls after 20 March 2000.

[85A Transfers of value: attribution of gains to beneficiaries

Schedule 4C to this Act has effect with respect to the attribution to beneficiaries of gains accruing under Schedule 4B.]¹

Amendment—¹ This section inserted by FA 2000 s 92(3), (5) with effect for any transfer of value in relation to which the material time is after 20 March 2000.

86 Attribution of gains to settlors with interest in non-resident or dual resident settlements

(1) This section applies where the following conditions are fulfilled as regards a settlement in a particular year of assessment—

(*a*) the settlement is a qualifying settlement in the year;

(*b*) the trustees of the settlement fulfil the condition as to residence specified in subsection (2) below;

(*c*) a person who is a settlor in relation to the settlement ("the settlor") is domiciled in the United Kingdom at some time in the year and is either resident in the United Kingdom during any part of the year or ordinarily resident in the United Kingdom during the year;

(*d*) at any time during the year the settlor has an interest in the settlement;

(*e*) by virtue of disposals of any of the settled property originating from the settlor, there is an amount on which the trustees would be chargeable to tax for the year under section 2(2) if the assumption as to residence specified in subsection (3) below were made;

(*f*) paragraph 3, 4 or 5 of Schedule 5 does not prevent this section applying.

(2) The condition as to residence is that—

(*a*) the trustees are not resident or ordinarily resident in the United Kingdom during any part of the year, or

(*b*) the trustees are resident in the United Kingdom during any part of the year or ordinarily resident in the United Kingdom during the year, but at any time of such residence or ordinary residence they fall to be regarded for the purposes of any double taxation relief arrangements as resident in a territory outside the United Kingdom.

(3) Where subsection (2)(*a*) above applies, the assumption as to residence is that the trustees are resident or ordinarily resident in the United Kingdom throughout the year; and where subsection (2)(*b*) above applies, the assumption as to residence is that the double taxation relief arrangements do not apply.

(4) Where this section applies—

(*a*) chargeable gains of an amount equal to that referred to in subsection (1)(*e*) above shall be treated as accruing to the settlor in the year, and

(*b*) those gains shall be treated as forming the highest part of the amount on which he is chargeable to capital gains tax for the year.

[(4A) Without prejudice to so much of this section as requires section 2A to be applied in the computation of any amount that is treated under this section as an amount of chargeable gains accruing to the settlor, chargeable gains that are treated as accruing to the settlor under this section shall not be eligible for taper relief.]¹

(5) Schedule 5 (which contains provisions supplementary to this section) shall have effect.

Commentary—*Simon's Direct Tax Service* **C4.437–439.**
Concession D40—Non-resident trusts: definition of "participator".
Revenue Interpretation RI 232—Change of interpretation: Non-resident trusts—gains and losses accruing in the transitional period to trusts brought within the settlor charge by FA 1988—treatment for tax year 1999/2000.
Revenue & other press releases—Law Society 29-1-92 (if a foreign pension scheme is part of the normal arrangements for remunerating employees, Revenue do not regard either the employer or employee as settlors s 86, Sch 5).
ICAEW TAX 20/92 14-12-92 (in computing the amount under sub-s (1)(*e*), the trustees are entitled to make all normal claims and elections available to UK taxpayers).
Definitions—"Chargeable gain", s 15(2); "double taxation relief arrangements", s 288(1); "ordinarily resident", s 9(1); "property originating from a person", Sch 5 para 8(1); "qualifying settlement", Sch 5 para 9; "resident", s 9(1); "settled property", s 68; "settlor", Sch 5 para 7; "year of assessment", s 288(1).
Cross references—See TCGA 1992 s 78(3) (attribution of gains to settlors with interest in resident settlements).
TCGA 1992 s 87(3) (attribution of gains to beneficiaries of a non-resident settlement made by a resident settlor).
FA 1998 s 132(5) (no account taken of disposals made before 6 April 1999 when construing sub-s (1)(*e*) in relation to a pre-19 March 1991 settlement which is a qualifying settlement in 1999–00 but was not a qualifying settlement in any earlier year of assessment).
FA 1998 Sch 23 (transitional provisions for gains of pre-19 March 1991 non-resident settlements realised between 17 March 1998 and 5 April 1999).
FA 2002 Sch 11 para 8 (election for prospective amendments made by FA 2002 ss 51, 141, Sch 11, Sch 40 Pt 3(4) to apply with effect for chargeable gains treated as accruing to a person by virtue of TCGA 1992 s 77 or 86 (read, where appropriate, with TCGA s 10A) in any or all of the tax years 2000–01, 2001–02, and 2002–03).
Amendments—¹ Sub-s (4A) inserted by FA 1998 Sch 21 para 6 with effect from the year 1998–99.
Prospective amendments—In sub-s (1)(*e*), words to be substituted for the words from "if" to the end by FA 2002 s 51, Sch 11 paras 1, 4, 7 with effect for chargeable gains treated as accruing to a person by virtue of TCGA 1992 s 77 or 86 (read, where appropriate, with TCGA 1992 s 10A) from 2003–04. Words to be substituted to read as follows—

''if—

    (i) the assumption as to residence specified in subsection (3) below were made, and

    (ii) any chargeable gains on the disposals were not eligible for taper relief, but section 2(2) applied as if they were (so that the order of deducting losses provided for by section 2A(6) applied);''.

Sub-s (4A) to be repealed by FA 2002 s 141, Sch 40 Pt 3(4) with effect for chargeable gains treated as accruing to a person by virtue of TCGA 1992 s 77 or 86 (read, where appropriate, with TCGA 1992 s 10A) from 2003–04.

[86A Attribution of gains to settlor in section 10A cases

(1) Subsection (2) below applies in the case of a person who is a settlor in relation to any settlement (''the relevant settlement'') where—

    (a) by virtue of section 10A, amounts falling within section 86(1)(e) for any intervening year or years would (apart from this section) be treated as accruing to the settlor in the year of return; and

    (b) there is an excess of the relevant chargeable amounts for the non-residence period over the amount of the section 87 pool at the end of the year of departure.

(2) Only so much (if any) of—

    (a) the amount falling within section 86(1)(e) for the intervening year, or

    (b) if there is more than one intervening year, the aggregate of the amounts falling within section 86(1)(e) for those years,

as exceeds the amount of the excess mentioned in subsection (1)(b) above shall fall in accordance with section 10A to be attributed to the settlor for the year of return.

(3) In subsection (1) above, the reference to the relevant chargeable amounts for the non-residence period is (subject to subsection (5) below) a reference to the aggregate of the amounts on which beneficiaries of the relevant settlement are charged to tax under section 87 or 89(2) for the intervening year or years in respect of any capital payments received by them.

(4) In subsection (1) above, the reference to the section 87 pool at the end of the year of departure is (subject to subsection (5) below) a reference to the amount (if any) which, in accordance with subsection (2) of that section, fell in relation to the relevant settlement to be carried forward from the year of departure to be included in the amount of the trust gains for the year of assessment immediately following the year of departure.

(5) Where the property comprised in the relevant settlement has at any time included property not originating from the settlor, only so much (if any) of any capital payment or amount carried forward in accordance with section 87(2) as, on a just and reasonable apportionment, is properly referable to property originating from the settlor shall be taken into account for the purposes of subsections (3) and (4) above.

(6) Where any reduction falls to be made by virtue of subsection (2) above in any amount to be attributed in accordance with section 10A to any settlor for any year of assessment, the reduction to be treated as made for that year in accordance with section 87(3) in the case of the settlement in question shall not be made until-

    (a) the reduction (if any) falling to be made by virtue of that subsection has been made in the case of every settlor to whom any amount is so attributed; and

    (b) effect has been given to any reduction required to be made under subsection (7) below.

(7) Where in the case of any settlement there is (after the making of any reduction or reductions in accordance with subsection (2) above) any amount or amounts falling in accordance with section 10A to be attributed for any year of assessment to settlors of the settlement, the amount or (as the case may be) aggregate amount falling in accordance with that section to be so attributed shall be] applied in reducing the amount carried forward to that year in accordance with section 87(2).

(8) Where an amount or aggregate amount has been applied, in accordance with subsection (7)) above, in reducing the amount which in the case of any settlement is carried forward to any year in accordance with section 87(2), that amount (or, as the case may be, so much of it as does not exceed the amount which it is applied in reducing) shall be deducted from the amount used for that year for making the reduction under section 87(3) in the case of that settlement.

(9) Expressions used in this section and section 10A have the same meanings in this section as in that section; and paragraph 8 of Schedule 5 shall apply for the construction of the references in subsection (5) above to property originating from the settlor as it applies for the purposes of that Schedule.][1]

Commentary—*Simon's Direct Tax Service* **C1.607.**

Cross references—FA 2002 Sch 11 para 8 (election for prospective amendments made by FA 2002 ss 51, 141, Sch 11, Sch 40 Pt 3(4) to apply with effect for chargeable gains treated as accruing to a person by virtue of TCGA 1992 s 77 or 86 (read, where appropriate, with TCGA s 10A) in any or all of the tax years 2000–01, 2001–02, 2002–03).

Amendments—[1] This section inserted by FA 1998 s 129(1) with effect where the year of departure is the year 1997–98 or any subsequent year of assessment.

Prospective amendments—In sub-s (2)(a) words ''the tapered section 86(1)(e) amount'' to be substituted for the words ''the amount falling within section 86(1)(e)''; in sub-s (2)(b), words ''the tapered section 86(1)(e) amounts'' to be substituted for the words ''the amounts falling within section 86(1)(e)''; sub-ss (2A), (2B), (7A) to be inserted, and in sub-s (7), words ''the tapered section 10A amount'' to be substituted for words from ''the amount'' to ''so attributed''; by FA 2002 s 51, Sch 11 paras 1, 5, 7 with effect for chargeable gains treated as accruing to a person by virtue of TCGA 1992 s 77 or 86 (read, where appropriate, with TCGA 1992 s 10A) from 2003–04. Sub-ss (2A), (2B), (7A) as inserted to read as follows—

''(2A) In subsection (2) above ''tapered section 86(1)(e) amount'' means an amount falling within section 86(1)(e) as it would apply with the omission of sub-paragraph (ii).

(2B) Where subsection (2) above has effect to reduce an amount that is treated by virtue of section 86 as accruing to the settlor for a year of assessment—

(*a*) the reduced amount shall be treated as falling within paragraph (*b*) of section 2(5) and not paragraph (*aa*);

(*b*) section 86(1)(*e*) shall have effect in relation to that amount with the omission of sub-paragraph (ii).

(7A) In subsection (7) above ''the tapered section 10A amount'' means the amount, or aggregate of the amounts, falling to be attributed as mentioned in that subsection, minus the total amount of any taper relief that would be deductible from that amount or aggregate by the trustees of the settlement but for section 86(1)(*e*)(ii).

Where section 86A(2) has effect to reduce that amount or aggregate, the words from ''minus'' to ''section 86(1)(*e*)(ii)'' above do not apply.''.

In sub-s (8), words ''or aggregate amount'' repealed by FA 2002 s 141, Sch 40 Pt 3(4) with effect for chargeable gains treated as accruing to a person by virtue of TCGA 1992 s 77 or 86 (read, where appropriate, with TCGA 1992 s 10A) from 2003–04.

87 Attribution of gains to beneficiaries

(1) This section applies to a settlement for any year of assessment during which the trustees are at no time resident or ordinarily resident in the United Kingdom ...[1].

(2) There shall be computed in respect of every year of assessment for which this section applies the amount on which the trustees would have been chargeable to tax under section 2(2) if they had been resident or ordinarily resident in the United Kingdom in the year; and that amount, together with the corresponding amount in respect of any earlier such year so far as not already treated under subsection (4) below or section 89(2) as chargeable gains accruing to beneficiaries under the settlement, is in this section and sections 89 and 90 referred to as the trust gains for the year.

(3) Where as regards the same settlement and for the same year of assessment—

(*a*) chargeable gains, whether of one amount or of 2 or more amounts, are treated as accruing by virtue of section 86(4), and

(*b*) an amount falls to be computed under subsection (2) above,

the amount so computed shall be treated as reduced by the amount, or aggregate of the amounts, mentioned in paragraph (*a*) above.

(4) Subject to the following provisions of this section, the trust gains for a year of assessment shall be treated as chargeable gains accruing in that year to beneficiaries of the settlement who receive capital payments from the trustees in that year or have received such payments in any earlier year.

(5) The attribution of chargeable gains to beneficiaries under subsection (4) above shall be made in proportion to, but shall not exceed, the amounts of the capital payments received by them.

(6) A capital payment shall be left out of account for the purposes of subsections (4) and (5) above to the extent that chargeable gains have by reason of the payment been treated as accruing to the recipient in an earlier year.

[(6A) Without prejudice to so much of this section as requires section 2A to be applied in the computation of the amount of the trust gains for any year of assessment, chargeable gains that are treated as accruing to beneficiaries under this section shall not be eligible for taper relief.][2]

(7) A beneficiary shall not be charged to tax on chargeable gains treated by virtue of subsection (4) above as accruing to him in any year unless he is domiciled in the United Kingdom at some time in that year.

(8) In computing an amount under subsection (2) above in respect of the year 1991–92 or a subsequent year of assessment, the effect of sections 77 to 79 shall be ignored.

(9) For the purposes of this section a settlement arising under a will or intestacy shall be treated as made by the testator or intestate at the time of his death.

(10) Subsection (1) above does not apply in relation to any year beginning before 6th April 1981; and the reference in subsections (4) and (5) to capital payments received by beneficiaries do not include references to any payment received before 10th March 1981 or any payment received on or after that date and before 6th April 1984 so far as it represents a chargeable gain which accrued to the trustees before 6th April 1981.

Commentary—*Simon's Direct Tax Service* C4.442.

Revenue Interpretation RI 189—Gains otherwise chargeable on UK charities under this section to be exempted by TCGA 1992 s 256.

Revenue & other press releases—Law Society 29-1-92 (lump sums paid under foreign pension schemes which would be chargeable to income tax under TA 1988 s 596A, but for Concession A10, are not regarded as capital payments under s 87(4)).

Simon's Tax Cases—s 87, *Leedale v Lewis* [1982] STC 835*.

s 87(1), *Marshall v Kerr* [1994] STC 638*.

s 87(2), *de Rothschild v Lawrenson* [1995] STC 623*.

s 87(4), *Billingham v Cooper, Edwards v Fisher* [2001] STC 1177.

Definitions—''Capital payment'', s 97(1); ''chargeable gain'', s 15(2); ''ordinarily resident'', s 9(1); ''resident'', s 9(1); ''settlement'', s 97(7), TA 1988 s 681(4); ''settlor'', s 97(7), TA 1988 s 681(4); ''year of assessment'', s 288(1).

Cross references—See TA 1988 s 762(2), (3) (modification of this section in its application to offshore income gains).

TCGA 1992 s 88 (application of this section to gains of certain dual resident settlements).

TCGA 1992 s 89(1) (capital payment received by a beneficiary in a resident period to which this section does not apply to be disregarded for the purposes of this section in certain circumstances).

TCGA 1992 s 90 (provisions to prevent circumvention of this section by transfers of assets between settlements).

TCGA 1992 s 91(1) (increase in tax payable under this section where a capital payment is made from a settlement after 5 April 1992).

TCGA 1992 s 92 (provisions to ascertain qualifying amount and matching it with capital payment made after 5 April 1991 where this section applies to a settlement for the year 1992–93 and subsequently).

TCGA 1992 s 93 (matching: capital payment from a settlement paid after 5 April 1992 in respect of which tax is levied on beneficiary under this section).

TCGA 1992 s 94(5) (transfer of settled property into another settlement in the year 1990–91 and subsequently: qualifying amounts not matched with capital payments: apportionment).

TCGA 1992 s 96 (supplementary provisions).

TCGA 1992 s 96(1) (capital payment to be treated as received from trustees of settlement where it is received from a qualifying company controlled by the trustees).

TCGA 1992 s 96(2) (for the purposes of this section, s 96(3)–(6) to apply where capital payment is made by trustees of a settlement to a non-resident qualifying company).

TCGA 1992 s 97 (supplementary provisions).

TCGA 1992 s 98 (Board's power to obtain information for the purposes of this section).

FA 1998 Sch 23 para 4 (transitional provisions for gains of pre-19 March 1991 non-resident settlements realised between 17 March 1998 and 5 April 1999: rules to prevent a double charge).

FA 2002 Sch 11 para 8 (election for prospective amendments made by FA 2002 s 51, Sch 11 to apply with effect for chargeable gains treated as accruing to a person by virtue of TCGA 1992 s 77 or 86 (read, where appropriate, with TCGA s 10A) in any or all of the tax years 2000–01, 2001–02, and 2002–03).

Amendments—[1] Words in sub-s (1) repealed by FA 1998 ss 130(1), 165, Sch 27 Part III(30) from the year 1998–99, and shall be deemed to have applied for the year 1997–98.

[2] Sub-s (6A) inserted by FA 1998 Sch 21 para 6 with effect from the year 1998–99.

Prospective amendments—In sub-s (3), words "reduced by the tapered section 86(4) amount" to be substituted for the words from "reduced by the amount" to the end, and sub-s (3A) to be inserted by FA 2002 s 51, Sch 11 paras 1, 6, 7 with effect for chargeable gains treated as accruing to a person by virtue of TCGA 1992 s 77 or 86 (read, where appropriate, with TCGA 1992 s 10A) from 2003–04. Sub-s (3A) as inserted to read as follows—

"(3A) In subsection (3) above "the tapered section 86(4) amount" means the amount, or aggregate of the amounts, treated as accruing as mentioned in subsection (3)(*a*) above, minus the total amount of any taper relief that would be deductible from that amount or aggregate by the trustees of the settlement but for section 86(1)(*e*)(ii)."

88 Gains of dual resident settlements

(1) Section 87 also applies to a settlement for any year of assessment beginning on or after 6th April 1991 if—

(*a*) the trustees are resident in the United Kingdom during any part of the year or ordinarily resident in the United Kingdom during the year, [and][1]

(*b*) at any time of such residence or ordinary residence they fall to be regarded for the purposes of any double taxation relief arrangements as resident in a territory outside the United Kingdom. [...][1]

[(*c*) ...][1]

(2) In respect of every year of assessment for which section 87 applies by virtue of this section, section 87 shall have effect as if the amount to be computed under section 87(2) were the assumed chargeable amount; and the reference in section 87(2) to the corresponding amount in respect of an earlier year shall be construed as a reference to the amount computed under section 87(2) apart from this section or (as the case may be) the amount computed under section 87(2) by virtue of this section.

(3) For the purposes of subsection (2) above the assumed chargeable amount in respect of a year of assessment is the lesser of the following 2 amounts—

(*a*) the amount on which the trustees would be chargeable to tax for the year under section 2(2) on the assumption that the double taxation relief arrangements did not apply;

(*b*) the amount on which, by virtue of disposals of protected assets, the trustees would be chargeable to tax for the year under section 2(2) on the assumption that those arrangements did not apply.

(4) For the purposes of subsection (3)(*b*) above assets are protected assets if—

(*a*) they are of a description specified in the double taxation relief arrangements, and

(*b*) were the trustees to dispose of them at any relevant time, the trustees would fall to be regarded for the purposes of the arrangements as not liable in the United Kingdom to tax on gains accruing to them on the disposal.

(5) For the purposes of subsection (4) above—

(*a*) the assumption specified in subsection (3)(*b*) above shall be ignored;

(*b*) a relevant time is any time, in the year of assessment concerned, when the trustees fall to be regarded for the purposes of the arrangements as resident in a territory outside the United Kingdom;

(*c*) if different assets are identified by reference to different relevant times, all of them are protected assets.

(6) In computing the assumed chargeable amount in respect of a particular year of assessment, the effect of sections 77 to 79 shall be ignored.

(7) For the purposes of section 87 as it applies by virtue of this section, capital payments received before 6th April 1991 shall be disregarded.

Commentary—*Simon's Direct Tax Service* **C4.447.**

Definitions—"Asset", s 21(1); "capital payment", s 97(1); "double taxation relief arrangements", s 288(1); "ordinarily resident", s 9(1); "resident", s 9(1); "settlement", s 97(7), TA 1988 s 681(4); "settlor", s 97(7), TA 1988 s 681(4); "year of assessment", s 288(1).

Cross references—See TA 1988 s 762(2) (modification of this section in its application to offshore income gains).

TCGA 1992 s 96 (supplementary provisions).

TCGA 1992 s 96(1) (capital payment to be treated as received from trustees of settlement where it is received from a qualifying company controlled by the trustees).

TCGA 1992 s 96(2) (for the purposes of this section, s 96(3)–(6) to apply where capital payment is made by trustees of a settlement to a non-resident qualifying company).

TCGA 1992 s 97 (supplementary provisions).
TCGA 1992 s 98 (Board's power to obtain information for the purposes of this section).
Amendments—¹ Word in sub-s (1)(*a*) inserted, and (1)(*c*) and preceding word "and" repealed, by FA 1998 ss 130(2), 165, Sch 27 Part III(30) from the year 1998–99, and shall be deemed to have applied for the year 1997–98.

89 Migrant settlements etc

(1) Where a period of one or more years of assessment for which section 87 applies to a settlement ("a non-resident period") succeeds a period of one or more years of assessment for each of which section 87 does not apply to the settlement ("a resident period"), a capital payment received by a beneficiary in the resident period shall be disregarded for the purposes of section 87 if it was not made in anticipation of a disposal made by the trustees in the non-resident period.

(2) Where—

(*a*) a non-resident period is succeeded by a resident period, and
(*b*) the trust gains for the last year of the non-resident period are not (or not wholly) treated as chargeable gains accruing in that year to beneficiaries,

then, subject to subsection (3) below, those trust gains (or the outstanding part of them) shall be treated as chargeable gains accruing in the first year of the resident period to beneficiaries of the settlement who receive capital payments from the trustees in that year; and so on for the second and subsequent years until the amount treated as accruing to beneficiaries is equal to the amount of the trust gains for the last year of the non-resident period.

(3) Subsections (5)[, (6A)]¹ and (7) of section 87 shall apply in relation to subsection (2) above as they apply in relation to subsection (4) of that section.

Commentary—*Simon's Direct Tax Service* **C4.442.**
Simon's Tax Cases—*Marshall v Kerr* [1991] STC 686*.
Definitions—"Capital payment", s 97(1); "chargeable gain", s 15(2); "resident", s 9(1); "settlement", s 97(7), TA 1988 s 681(4); "year of assessment", s 288(1).
Cross references—See TA 1988 s 762(2) (modification of this section in its application to offshore income gains).
TCGA 1992 s 90 (transfer of settled property to another settlement).
TCGA 1992 s 91(1) (increase in tax payable under sub-s (2) above where a capital payment is made from a settlement after 5 April 1992).
TCGA 1992 s 92 (provisions to ascertain qualifying amount and matching it with capital payment from a settlement paid after 5 April 1991 where sub-s (2) above treats chargeable gains as accruing in respect of the capital payment).
TCGA 1992 s 93 (matching: capital payment from a settlement paid after 5 April 1992 in respect of which tax is levied on beneficiary under sub-s (2) above).
TCGA 1992 s 96 (supplementary provisions).
TCGA 1992 s 96(1) (capital payment to be treated as received from trustees of settlement where it is received from a qualifying company controlled by the trustees).
TCGA 1992 s 96(2) (for the purposes of this section, s 96(3)–(6) to apply where capital payment is made by trustees of a settlement to a non-resident qualifying company).
TCGA 1992 s 97 (supplementary provisions).
TCGA 1992 s 98 (Board's power to obtain information for the purposes of this section).
Amendments—¹ Number in sub-s (3) inserted by FA 1998 Sch 21 para 6 with effect from the year 1998–99.

90 Transfers between settlements

(1) If in a year of assessment for which section 87 or 89(2) applies to a settlement ("the transferor settlement") the trustees transfer all or part of the settled property to the trustees of another settlement ("the transferee settlement") then, subject to the following provisions—

(*a*) if section 87 applies to the transferee settlement for the year, its trust gains for the year shall be treated as increased by an amount equal to the outstanding trust gains for the year of the transferor settlement or, where part only of the settled property is transferred, to a proportionate part of those trust gains;
(*b*) if subsection (2) of section 89 applies to the transferee settlement for the year (otherwise than by virtue of paragraph (*c*) below), the trust gains referred to in that subsection shall be treated as increased by the amount mentioned in paragraph (*a*) above;
(*c*) if (apart from this paragraph) neither section 87 nor section 89(2) applies to the transferee settlement for the year, subsection (2) of section 89 shall apply to it as if the year were the first year of a resident period succeeding a non-resident period and the trust gains referred to in that subsection were equal to the amount mentioned in paragraph (*a*) above.

(2) Subject to subsection (3) below, the reference in subsection (1)(*a*) above to the outstanding trust gains for the year of the transferor settlement is a reference to the amount of its trust gains for the year so far as they are not treated under section 87(4) as chargeable gains accruing to beneficiaries in that year.

(3) Where section 89(2) applies to the transferor settlement for the year, the reference in subsection (1)(*a*) above to the outstanding trust gains of the settlement is a reference to the trust gains referred to in section 89(2) so far as not treated as chargeable gains accruing to beneficiaries in that or an earlier year.

(4) This section shall not apply to a transfer so far as it is made for consideration in money or money's worth.

[(5) This section shall not apply—

(*a*) to a transfer to the extent that it is in accordance with Schedule 4B treated as linked with trustee borrowing; or

(*b*) to any chargeable gains arising by virtue of that Schedule.]¹

Commentary—*Simon's Direct Tax Service* **C4.444.**
Simon's Tax Cases—*Marshall v Kerr* [1991] STC 686*.
Definitions—''Chargeable gain'', s 15(2); ''resident'', s 9(1); ''settled property'', s 97(7), TA 1988 s 681(4); ''settlement'', s 97(7), TA 1988 s 681(4); ''year of assessment'', s 288(1).
Cross references—See TA 1988 s 762(2) (modification of this section in its application to offshore income gains).
TCGA 1992 s 96 (supplementary provisions).
TCGA 1992 s 96(1) (capital payment to be treated as received from trustees of settlement where it is received from a qualifying company controlled by the trustees).
TCGA 1992 s 96(2) (for the purposes of this section, s 96(3)–(6) to apply where capital payment is made by trustees of a settlement to a non-resident qualifying company).
TCGA 1992 s 97 (supplementary provisions).
TCGA 1992 s 98 (Board's power to obtain information for the purposes of this section).
Amendment—¹ Sub-s (5) added by FA 2000 s 92(4), (5), Sch 26 Pt II para 2 with effect for any transfer of value in relation to which the material time is after 20 March 2000.

91 Increase in tax payable under section 87 or 89(2)

(1) This section applies where—

(*a*) a capital payment is made by the trustees of a settlement on or after 6th April 1992,

(*b*) the payment is made in a year of assessment for which section 87 applies to the settlement or in circumstances where section 89(2) treats chargeable gains as accruing in respect of the payment,

(*c*) the whole payment is, in accordance with sections 92 to 95, matched with a qualifying amount of the settlement for a year of assessment falling at some time before that immediately preceding the one in which the payment is made, and

(*d*) a beneficiary is charged to tax in respect of the payment by virtue of section 87 or 89(2).

(2) The tax payable by the beneficiary in respect of the payment shall be increased by the amount found under subsection (3) below, except that it shall not be increased beyond the amount of the payment; and an assessment may charge tax accordingly.

(3) The amount is one equal to the interest that would be yielded if an amount equal to the tax which would be payable by the beneficiary in respect of the payment (apart from this section) carried interest for the chargeable period at the rate of 10 per cent per annum.

(4) The chargeable period is the period which—

(*a*) begins with the later of the 2 days specified in subsection (5) below, and

(*b*) ends with 30th November in the year of assessment following that in which the capital payment is made.

(5) The 2 days are—

(*a*) 1st December in the year of assessment following that for which the qualifying amount mentioned in subsection (1)(*c*) above is the qualifying amount, and

(*b*) 1st December falling 6 years before 1st December in the year of assessment following that in which the capital payment is made.

(6) The Treasury may by order substitute for the percentage specified in subsection (3) above (whether as originally enacted or as amended at any time under this subsection) such other percentage as they think fit.

(7) An order under subsection (6) above may provide that an alteration of the percentage is to have effect for periods beginning on or after a day specified in the order in relation to interest running for chargeable periods beginning before that day (as well as interest running for chargeable periods beginning on or after that day).

(8) Sections 92 to 95 have effect for the purpose of supplementing subsections (1) to (5) above.

Commentary—*Simon's Direct Tax Service* **C4.443.**
Definitions—''Capital payment'', s 97(1); ''chargeable gain'', s 15(2); ''chargeable period'', s 288(1); ''settlement'', s 97(7), TA 1988 s 660G(1); ''year of assessment'', s 288(1).
Cross references—See TCGA 1992 s 93 (matching of capital payment from a settlement paid after 5 April 1992 with qualifying amount for the preceding year of assessment).
TCGA 1992 s 96 (supplementary provisions).
TCGA 1992 s 97 (supplementary provisions).

92 Qualifying amounts and matching

(1) If section 87 applies to a settlement for the year 1992–93 or a subsequent year of assessment the settlement shall have a qualifying amount for the year, and the amount shall be the amount computed for the settlement in respect of the year concerned under section 87(2).

(2) The settlement shall continue to have the same qualifying amount (if any) for the year 1990–91 or 1991–92 as it had for that year by virtue of paragraph 2 of Schedule 17 to the Finance Act 1991 (subject to subsection (3) below).

(3) Where—

(*a*) capital payments are made by the trustees of a settlement on or after 6th April 1991, and (*b*) the payments are made in a year or years of assessment for which section 87 applies to the settlement or in circumstances where section 89(2) treats chargeable gains as accruing in respect of the payments,

the payments shall be matched with qualifying amounts of the settlement for the year 1990–91 and subsequent years of assessment (so far as the amounts are not already matched with payments by virtue of this subsection).

(4) In applying subsection (3) above—

(*a*) earlier payments shall be matched with earlier amounts;

(*b*) payments shall be carried forward to be matched with future amounts (so far as not matched with past amounts);

(*c*) a payment which is less than an unmatched amount (or part) shall be matched to the extent of the payment;

(*d*) a payment which is more than an unmatched amount (or part) shall be matched, as to the excess, with other unmatched amounts.

(5) Where part only of a capital payment is taxable, the part which is not taxable shall not fall to be matched until taxable parts of other capital payments (if any) made in the same year of assessment have been matched; and subsections (3) and (4) above shall have effect accordingly.

(6) For the purposes of subsection (5) above a part of a capital payment is taxable if the part results in chargeable gains accruing under section 87 or 89(2).

Commentary—*Simon's Direct Tax Service* **C4.443.**
Definitions—''Capital payment'', s 97(1); ''chargeable gain'', s 15(2); ''settlement'', s 97(7), TA 1988 s 660G(1); ''year of assessment'', s 288(1).
Cross references—See TCGA 1992 s 95 (matching after transfer in a case where this section applies).
TCGA 1992 s 96 (supplementary provisions).
TCGA 1992 s 97 (supplementary provisions).

93 Matching: special cases

(1) Subsection (2) or (3) below applies (if the case permits) where—

(*a*) a capital payment is made by the trustees of a settlement on or after 6th April 1992,

(*b*) the payment is made in a year of assessment for which section 87 applies to the settlement or in circumstances where section 89(2) treats chargeable gains as accruing in respect of the payment, and

(*c*) a beneficiary is charged to tax in respect of the payment by virtue of section 87 or 89(2).

(2) If the whole payment is matched with qualifying amounts of the settlement for different years of assessment, each falling at some time before that immediately preceding the one in which the payment is made, then—

(*a*) the capital payment (''the main payment'') shall be treated as being as many payments (''subsidiary payments'') as there are qualifying amounts,

(*b*) a qualifying amount shall be attributed to each subsidiary payment and each payment shall be quantified accordingly, and

(*c*) the tax in respect of the main payment shall be divided up and attributed to the subsidiary payments on the basis of a just and reasonable apportionment,

and section 91 shall apply in the case of each subsidiary payment, the qualifying amount attributed to it and the tax attributed to it.

(3) If part of the payment is matched with a qualifying amount of the settlement for a year of assessment falling at some time before that immediately preceding the one in which the payment is made, or with qualifying amounts of the settlement for different years of assessment each so falling, then—

(*a*) only tax in respect of so much of the payment as is so matched shall be taken into account, and references below to the tax shall be construed accordingly,

(*b*) the capital payment shall be divided into 2, the first part representing so much as is matched as mentioned above and the second so much as is not,

(*c*) the second part shall be ignored, and

(*d*) the first part shall be treated as a capital payment, the whole of which is matched with the qualifying amount or amounts mentioned above, and the whole of which is charged to the tax,

and section 91, or that section and subsections (1) and (2) above (as the case may be), shall apply in the case of the capital payment arrived at under this subsection, the qualifying amount or amounts, and the tax.

(4) Section 91 and subsections (1) to (3) above shall apply (with appropriate modifications) where a payment or part of a payment is to any extent matched with part of an amount.

Commentary—*Simon's Direct Tax Service* **C4.443.**
Definitions—''Capital payment'', s 97(1); ''chargeable gain'', s 15(2); ''settlement'', s 97(7), TA 1988 s 660G(1); ''year of assessment'', s 288(1).
Cross references—See TCGA 1992 s 96 (supplementary provisions).
TCGA 1992 s 97 (supplementary provisions).

94 Transfers of settled property where qualifying amounts not wholly matched

(1) This section applies if—

(*a*) in the year 1990–91 or a subsequent year of assessment the trustees of a settlement ("the transferor settlement") transfer all or part of the settled property to the trustees of another settlement ("the transferee settlement"), and

(*b*) looking at the state of affairs at the end of the year of assessment in which the transfer is made, there is a qualifying amount of the transferor settlement for a particular year of assessment ("the year concerned") and the amount is not (or not wholly) matched with capital payments.

(2) If the whole of the settled property is transferred—

(*a*) the transferor settlement's qualifying amount for the year concerned shall be treated as reduced by so much of it as is not matched, and

(*b*) so much of that amount as is not matched shall be treated as (or as an addition to) the transferee settlement's qualifying amount for the year concerned.

(3) If part of the settled property is transferred—

(*a*) so much of the transferor settlement's qualifying amount for the year concerned as is not matched shall be apportioned on such basis as is just and reasonable, part being attributed to the transferred property and part to the property not transferred,

(*b*) the transferor settlement's qualifying amount for the year concerned shall be treated as reduced by the part attributed to the transferred property, and

(*c*) that part shall be treated as (or as an addition to) the transferee settlement's qualifying amount for the year concerned.

(4) If the transferee settlement did not in fact exist in the year concerned, it shall be treated as having been made at the beginning of that year.

(5) If the transferee settlement did in fact exist in the year concerned, this section shall apply whether or not section 87 applies to the settlement for that year or for any year of assessment falling before that year.

Commentary—*Simon's Direct Tax Service* **C4.443.**
Definitions—"Capital payment", s 97(1); "settled property", s 97(7), TA 1988 s 681(4); "settlement", s 97(7), TA 1988 s 660G(1); "year of assessment", s 288(1).
Cross references—See TCGA 1992 s 95 (matching after transfer in a case where this section applies).
TCGA 1992 s 96 (supplementary provisions).
TCGA 1992 s 97 (supplementary provisions).

95 Matching after transfer

(1) This section applies as regards the transferee settlement in a case where section 94 applies.

(2) Matching shall be made under section 92 by reference to the state of affairs existing immediately before the beginning of the year of assessment in which the transfer is made, and the transfer shall not affect matching so made.

(3) Subject to subsection (2) above, payments shall be matched with amounts in accordance with section 92 and by reference to amounts arrived at under section 94.

Commentary—*Simon's Direct Tax Service* **C4.443.**
Definitions—"Settlement", s 97(7), TA 1988 s 660G(1); "year of assessment", s 288(1).
Cross references—See TCGA 1992 s 96 (supplementary provisions).
TCGA 1992 s 97 (supplementary provisions).

96 Payments by and to companies

(1) Where a capital payment is received from a qualifying company which is controlled by the trustees of a settlement at the time it is received, for the purposes of sections 87 to 90 [and Schedule 4C][3] it shall be treated as received from the trustees.

(2) Where a capital payment is received from the trustees of a settlement (or treated as so received by virtue of subsection (1) above) and it is received by a non-resident qualifying company, the rules in subsections (3) to (6) below shall apply for the purposes of sections 87 to 90 [and Schedule 4C][3].

(3) If the company is controlled by one person alone at the time the payment is received, and that person is then resident or ordinarily resident in the United Kingdom, it shall be treated as a capital payment received by that person.

(4) If the company is controlled by 2 or more persons (taking each one separately) at the time the payment is received, then—

(*a*) if one of them is then resident or ordinarily resident in the United Kingdom, it shall be treated as a capital payment received by that person;

(*b*) if 2 or more of them are then resident or ordinarily resident in the United Kingdom ("the residents") it shall be treated as being as many equal capital payments as there are residents and each of them shall be treated as receiving one of the payments.

(5) If the company is controlled by 2 or more persons (taking them together) at the time the payment is received ...[2]—

(a) it shall be treated as being as many capital payments as there are participators in the company at the time it is received, and

(b) each such participator (whatever his residence or ordinary residence) shall be treated as receiving one of the payments, quantified on the basis of a just and reasonable apportionment,

but where (by virtue of the preceding provisions of this subsection and apart from this provision) a participator would be treated as receiving less than one-twentieth of the payment actually received by the company, he shall not be treated as receiving anything by virtue of this subsection.

(6) For the purposes of subsection (1) above a qualifying company is a close company or a company which would be a close company if it were resident in the United Kingdom.

(7) For the purposes of subsection (1) above a company is controlled by the trustees of a settlement if it is controlled by the trustees alone or by the trustees together with a person who (or persons each of whom) falls within subsection (8) below.

(8) A person falls within this subsection if—

(a) he is a settlor in relation to the settlement, or

(b) he is connected with a person falling within paragraph (a) above.

(9) For the purposes of subsection (2) above a non-resident qualifying company is a company which is not resident in the United Kingdom and would be a close company if it were so resident.

[(9A) For the purposes of this section an individual shall be deemed to have been resident in the United Kingdom at any time in any year of assessment which in his case is an intervening year for the purposes of section 10A.

(9B) If—

(a) it appears after the end of any year of assessment that any individual is to be treated by virtue of subsection (9A) above as having been resident in the United Kingdom at any time in that year, and

(b) as a consequence, any adjustments fall to be made to the amounts of tax taken to have been chargeable by virtue of this section on any person,

nothing in any enactment limiting the time for the making of any claim or assessment shall prevent the making of those adjustments (whether by means of an assessment, an amendment of an assessment, a repayment of tax or otherwise).][1]

(10) For the purposes of this section—

(a) the question whether a company is controlled by a person or persons shall be construed in accordance with section 416 of the Taxes Act, but in deciding that question for those purposes no rights or powers of (or attributed to) an associate or associates of a person shall be attributed to him under section 416(6) if he is not a participator in the company;

(b) "participator" has the meaning given by section 417(1) of the Taxes Act.

(11) This section shall apply to payments received on or after 19th March 1991.

Commentary—*Simon's Direct Tax Service* **C4.445.**
Concession D34—Calculation of cost or indexation allowance on a disposal of shares or securities where some but not all are valued at 31 March 1982 to be based on the proportion that the shares or securities disposed of bears to the total holding at 31 March 1982.
Definitions—"Capital payment", s 97(1); "close company", s 288(1); TA 1988 ss 414, 415; "company", ss 99, s 288(1); "connected", s 286; "control", s 288, TA 1988 s 416; "ordinarily resident", s 9(1); "resident", s 9(1); "settlement", s 97(7), TA 1988 s 660G(1); "settlor", s 97(7), TA 1988 s 681(4); "the Taxes Act", s 288(1).
Cross references—See TA 1988 s 762(2) (modification of this section in its application to offshore income gains).
TCGA 1992 s 96 (supplementary provisions).
TCGA 1992 s 97 (supplementary provisions).
Amendments—[1] Sub-ss (9A), (9B) inserted by FA 1998 s 127(3) with effect in any case in which the year of departure is the year 1998–99 or a subsequent year of assessment; and in any case in which the year of departure is the year 1997–98 and the taxpayer was resident or ordinarily resident in the United Kingdom at a time in that year on or after 17 March 1998.
[2] Words in sub-s (5) repealed by FA 2000 s 96 with effect for payments received after 20 March 2000.
[3] Words in sub-ss (1), (2) inserted by FA 2000 s 92(4), (5), Sch 26 Pt II para 3 with effect for any transfer of value in relation to which the material time is after 20 March 2000.

97 Supplementary provisions

(1) In sections [86A][2] to 96 [and Schedule 4C][3] and this section "capital payment"—

(a) means any payment which is not chargeable to income tax on the recipient or, in the case of a recipient who is neither resident nor ordinarily resident in the United Kingdom, any payment received otherwise than as income, but

(b) does not include a payment under a transaction entered into at arm's length if it is received on or after 19th March 1991.

(2) In subsection (1) above references to a payment include references to the transfer of an asset and the conferring of any other benefit, and to any occasion on which settled property becomes property to which section 60 applies.

(3) The fact that the whole or part of a benefit is by virtue of section 740(2)(b) of the Taxes Act treated as the recipient's income for a year of assessment after that in which it is received—

(a) shall not prevent the benefit or that part of it being treated for the purposes of sections [86A][2] to 96 [and Schedule 4C][3] as a capital payment in relation to any year of assessment earlier than that in which it is treated as his income; but

(b) shall preclude its being treated for those purposes as a capital payment in relation to that or any later year of assessment.

(4) For the purposes of sections [86A][2] to 96 [and Schedule 4C][3] the amount of a capital payment made by way of loan, and of any other capital payment which is not an outright payment of money, shall be taken to be equal to the value of the benefit conferred by it.

(5) For the purposes of sections [86A][2] to 90 [and Schedule 4C][3] a capital payment shall be regarded as received by a beneficiary from the trustees of a settlement if—

(a) he receives it from them directly or indirectly, or

(b) it is directly or indirectly applied by them in payment of any debt of his or is otherwise paid or applied for his benefit, or

(c) it is received by a third person at the beneficiary's direction.

(6) Section 16(3) shall not prevent losses accruing to trustees in a year of assessment for which section 87 of this Act or section 17 of the 1979 Act applied to the settlement from being allowed as a deduction from chargeable gains accruing in any later year (so far as they have not previously been set against gains for the purposes of a computation under either of those sections or otherwise).

(7) In sections [86A][2] to 96 [and Schedule 4C][3] and in the preceding provisions of this section—

"settlement" and

"settlor" have the meaning given by [section 660G(1) and (2)][1] of the Taxes Act and "settlor" includes, in the case of a settlement arising under a will or intestacy, the testator or intestate, and

"settled property" shall be construed accordingly.

(8) In a case where—

(a) at any time on or after 19th March 1991 a capital payment is received from the trustees of a settlement or is treated as so received by virtue of section 96(1),

(b) it is received by a person, or treated as received by a person by virtue of section 96(2) to (5),

(c) at the time it is received or treated as received, the person is not (apart from this subsection) a beneficiary of the settlement, and

(d) subsection (9) or (10) below does not prevent this subsection applying,

for the purposes of sections [86A][2] to 90 [and Schedule 4C][3] the person shall be treated as a beneficiary of the settlement as regards events occurring at or after that time.

(9) Subsection (8) above shall not apply where a payment mentioned in paragraph (a) is made in circumstances where it is treated (otherwise than by subsection (8) above) as received by a beneficiary.

(10) Subsection (8) above shall not apply so as to treat—

(a) the trustees of the settlement referred to in that subsection, or

(b) the trustees of any other settlement,

as beneficiaries of the settlement referred to in that subsection.

Commentary—*Simon's Direct Tax Service* **C4.442.**
Simon's Tax Cases—*Marshall v Kerr* [1991] STC 686*.
s 97(1), (2), (4), *Billingham v Cooper, Edwards v Fisher* [2001] STC 1177.
Definitions—"The 1979 Act", s 288(1); "asset", s 21(1); "chargeable gain", s 15(2); "ordinarily resident", s 9(1); "resident", s 9(1); "settled property", s 68; "the Taxes Act", s 288(1); "year of assessment", s 288(1).
Cross references—See FA 1984 Sch 14 para 1(2) (application of this section in relation to the postponement of a beneficiary's CGT liability on the gains of non-resident settlement);
TA 1988 s 762(2) (modification of this section in its application to offshore income gains).
Amendments—[1] Words in sub-s (7) substituted by FA 1995 s 74, Sch 17 para 30 with effect from the year 1995–96 and apply to every settlement, wherever and whenever it was made or entered into.
[2] Section number substituted in sub-ss (1), (3)–(5), (7)–(8) by FA 1998 s 129(2) with effect where the year of departure is 1997–98 or any subsequent year of assessment.
[3] Words in sub-ss (1), (3)(a), (4), (5), (7), (8) inserted by FA 2000 s 92(4), (5), Sch 26 Pt II para 4 with effect for any transfer of value in relation to which the material time is after 20 March 2000.

98 Power to obtain information for purposes of sections 87 to 90

(1) The Board may by notice require any person to furnish them within such time as they may direct, not being less than 28 days, with such particulars as they think necessary for the purposes of sections 87 to 90.

(2) Subsections (2) to (5) of section 745 of the Taxes Act shall have effect in relation to subsection (1) above as they have effect in relation to section 745(1), but in their application by virtue of this subsection—

(a) references to Chapter III of Part XVII of the Taxes Act shall be construed as references to sections 87 to 90; and

(b) the expressions "settlement" and "settlor" have the same meanings as in those sections.

[(3) The provisions of subsections (1) and (2) above have effect as if the references to sections 87 to 90 included references to Schedule 4C.][1]

Commentary—*Simon's Direct Tax Service* **C4.446.**
Simon's Tax Cases—*Marshall v Kerr* [1991] STC 686*.
Definitions—"The Board", s 288(1); "notice", s 288(1); "the Taxes Act", s 288(1).
Cross references—See TA 1988 s 762(2) (modification of this section in its application to offshore income gains).
¹ Sub-s (3) added by FA 2000 s 92(4), (5) Sch 26 Pt II para 5 with effect for any transfer of value in relation to which the material time is after 20 March 2000.

[98A Settlements with foreign element: information

Schedule 5A to this Act (which contains general provisions about information relating to settlements with a foreign element) shall have effect.]¹

Commentary—*Simon's Direct Tax Service* **C4.441.**
Amendments—¹ This section inserted by FA 1994 s 97(1), (2).

CHAPTER III
COLLECTIVE INVESTMENT SCHEMES AND INVESTMENT TRUSTS

Statement of Practice SP 2/99—Authorised unit trusts, approved investment trusts, and open-ended investment companies: monthly savings schemes: explains where the Revenue will accept simplified capital gains computations from individuals investing regular sums.

99 Application of Act to unit trust schemes

(1) This Act shall apply in relation to any unit trust scheme as if—

    (*a*) the scheme were a company,
    (*b*) the rights of the unit holders were shares in the company, and
    (*c*) in the case of an authorised unit trust, the company were resident and ordinarily resident in the United Kingdom,

except that nothing in this section shall be taken to bring a unit trust scheme within the charge to corporation tax on chargeable gains.

(2) Subject to subsection (3) below, in this Act—

    (*a*) "unit trust scheme" has the [meaning given by section 237(1) of the Financial Services and Markets Act 2000]¹
    (*b*) "authorised unit trust" has the meaning given by section 468(6) of the Taxes Act.

(3) The Treasury may by regulations provide that any scheme of a description specified in the regulations shall be treated as not being a unit trust scheme for the purposes of this Act; and regulations under this section may contain such supplementary and transitional provisions as appear to the Treasury to be necessary or expedient.

Commentary—*Simon's Direct Tax Service* **C1.209; C2.705.**
Regulations—CGT (Definition of Unit Trust Scheme) Regulations, SI 1988/266.
CGT (Pension Funds Pooling Schemes) Regulations, SI 1996/1583.
Revenue Interpretation RI 169—Explains the way in which this section applies to an umbrella scheme which is an authorised unit trust.
Definitions—"Chargeable gain", s 15(2); "ordinarily resident", s 9(1); "resident", s 9(1); "shares", s 288(1); "the Taxes Act", s 288(1).
Modification—This section is modified, in relation to open-ended investment companies, by the Open-ended Investment Companies (Tax) Regulations 1997, SI 1997/1154, regs 3, 20.
Amendments—¹ Words in sub-s (2)(*a*) substituted by the Financial Services and Markets Act 2000 (Consequential Amendments) (Taxes) Order, SI 2001/3629 arts 61, 62(1) with effect from 1 December 2001 immediately after the coming into force of the Financial Services and Markets Act 2000 ss 411, 432(1), Sch 20.

100 Exemption for authorised unit trusts etc

(1) Gains accruing to an authorised unit trust, an investment trust [a venture capital trust]¹ or a court investment fund shall not be chargeable gains.

(2) If throughout a year of assessment all the issued units in a unit trust scheme (other than an authorised unit trust) are assets such that any gain accruing if they were disposed of by the unit holder would be wholly exempt from capital gains tax or corporation tax (otherwise than by reason of residence) gains accruing to the unit trust scheme in that year of assessment shall not be chargeable gains.

(3) In this Act "court investment fund" means a fund established under section 42 of the Administration of Justice Act 1982.

Commentary—*Simon's Direct Tax Service* **C1.209.**
Concession D17—Unit trusts for exempt unit holders.
Definitions—"Asset", s 21(1); "authorised unit trust", s 99; "chargeable gain", s 15(2); "investment trust", s 288(1), TA 1988 s 842; "issued", s 288(5); "unit trust scheme", s 99; "venture capital trust", s 288(1); "year of assessment", s 288(1).
Modification—This section is modified, in relation to open-ended investment companies, by the Open-ended Investment Companies (Tax) Regulations, SI 1997/1154, reg 3.
Amendments—¹ Words in sub-s (1) inserted by FA 1995 s 72(2), in relation to gains accruing after 5 April 1995.

101 Transfer of company's assets to investment trust

(1) Where section 139 has applied on the transfer of a company's business (in whole or in part) to a company which at the time of the transfer was not an investment trust, then if—

(a) at any time after the transfer the company becomes for an accounting period an investment trust, and

(b) at the beginning of that accounting period the company still owns any of the assets of the business transferred,

the company shall be treated for all the purposes of this Act as if immediately after the transfer it had sold, and immediately reacquired, the assets referred to in paragraph (b) above at their market value at that time.

[(1A) Any chargeable gain or allowable loss which, apart from this subsection, would accrue to the company on the sale referred to in subsection (1) above shall be treated as accruing to the company immediately before the end of the last accounting period to end before the beginning of the accounting period mentioned in that subsection.][1]

[(1B) This section does not apply if at the time at which the company becomes an investment trust there has been an event by virtue of which it falls by virtue of section 101B(1) to be treated as having sold, and immediately reacquired, the assets immediately after the transfer referred to in subsection (1) above.][2]

(2) Notwithstanding any limitation on the time for making assessments, an assessment to corporation tax chargeable in consequence of subsection (1) above may be made at any time within 6 years after the end of the accounting period referred to in subsection (1) above, and where under this section a company is to be treated as having disposed of, and reacquired, an asset of a business, all such recomputations of liability in respect of other disposals and all such adjustments of tax, whether by way of assessment or by way of discharge or repayment of tax, as may be required in consequence of the provisions of this section shall be carried out.

Commentary—*Simon's Direct Tax Service* **C1.621; C2.735.**
Definitions—"Accounting period", TA 1988 s 834(1); "allowable loss", ss 8(2), 16, 288(1); "asset", s 21(1); "chargeable gain", s 15(2); "company", ss 99, 288(1); "investment trust", s 288(1), TA 1988 s 842; "market value", ss 272–274, Sch 11.
Amendments—[1] Sub-s (1A) inserted by FA 1996 s 140 with effect for accounting periods ending after 30 June 1999 (by virtue of Finance Act 1994, Section 199, (Appointed Day) Order, SI 1998/3173 art 2).
[2] Sub-s (1B) inserted by FA 1998 s 134(3) with effect for a company in respect of which an approval for the purposes of TA 1988 s 842AA (venture capital trusts) has effect as from a time falling on or after 17 March 1998.

[101A Transfer within group to investment trust

(1) This section applies where—

(a) an asset has been disposed of to a company (the "acquiring company") and the disposal has been treated by virtue of section 171(1) as giving rise to neither a gain nor a loss,

(b) at the time of the disposal the acquiring company was not an investment trust, and

(c) the conditions set out in subsection (2) below are satisfied by the acquiring company.

(2) Those conditions are satisfied by the acquiring company if—

(a) it becomes an investment trust for an accounting period beginning not more than 6 years after the time of the disposal,

(b) at the beginning of that accounting period, it owns, otherwise than as trading stock—

(i) the asset, or

(ii) property to which a chargeable gain has been carried forward from the asset on a replacement of business assets,

(c) it has not been an investment trust for any earlier accounting period beginning after the time of the disposal, and

(d) at the time at which it becomes an investment trust, there has not been an event by virtue of which it falls by virtue of section 179(3) or 101C(3) to be treated as having sold, and immediately reacquired, the asset at the time specified in subsection (3) below.

(3) The acquiring company shall be treated for all the purposes of this Act as if immediately after the disposal it had sold, and immediately reacquired, the asset at its market value at that time.

(4) Any chargeable gain or allowable loss which, apart from this subsection, would accrue to the acquiring company on the sale referred to in subsection (3) above shall be treated as accruing to it immediately before the end of the last accounting period to end before the beginning of the accounting period for which the acquiring company becomes an investment trust.

(5) For the purposes of this section a chargeable gain is carried forward from an asset to other property on a replacement of business assets if—

(a) by one or more claims under sections 152 to 158, the chargeable gain accruing on a disposal of the asset is reduced, and

(b) as a result an amount falls to be deducted from the expenditure allowable in computing a gain accruing on the disposal of the other property.

(6) For the purposes of this section an asset acquired by the acquiring company shall be treated as the same as an asset owned by it at a later time if the value of the second asset is derived in whole or in part from the first asset; and, in particular, assets shall be so treated where—

(*a*) the second asset is a freehold and the first asset was a leasehold; and

(*b*) the lessee has acquired the reversion.

(7) Where under this section a company is to be treated as having disposed of and reacquired an asset—

(*a*) all such recomputations of liability in respect of other disposals, and

(*b*) all such adjustments of tax, whether by way of assessment or by way of discharge or repayment of tax,

as may be required in consequence of the provisions of this section shall be carried out.

(8) Notwithstanding any limitation on the time for making assessments, any assessment to corporation tax chargeable in consequence of this section may be made at any time within 6 years after the end of the accounting period referred to in subsection (2)(*a*) above.]¹

Commentary—*Simon's Direct Tax Service* **D2.653.**
Amendments—¹ This section inserted by FA 1998 s 133(1) with effect for any company which becomes an investment trust for an accounting period beginning on or after 17 March 1998.

[101B Transfer of company's assets to venture capital trust

(1) Where section 139 has applied on the transfer of a company's business (in whole or in part) to a company which at the time of the transfer was not a venture capital trust, then if—

(*a*) at any time after the transfer the company becomes a venture capital trust by virtue of an approval for the purposes of section 842AA of the Taxes Act; and

(*b*) at the time as from which the approval has effect the company still owns any of the assets of the business transferred,

the company shall be treated for all the purposes of this Act as if immediately after the transfer it had sold, and immediately reacquired, the assets referred to in paragraph (*b*) above at their market value at that time.

(2) Any chargeable gain or allowable loss which, apart from this subsection, would accrue to the company on the sale referred to in subsection (1) above shall be treated as accruing to the company immediately before the time mentioned in subsection (1)(*b*) above.

(3) This section does not apply if at the time mentioned in subsection (1)(*b*) above there has been an event by virtue of which the company falls by virtue of section 101(1) to be treated as having sold, and immediately reacquired, the assets immediately after the transfer referred to in subsection (1) above.

(4) Notwithstanding any limitation on the time for making assessments, any assessment to corporation tax chargeable in consequence of this section may, in a case in which the approval mentioned in subsection (1)(*a*) above has effect as from the beginning of an accounting period, be made at any time within 6 years after the end of that accounting period.

(5) Where under this section a company is to be treated as having disposed of, and reacquired, an asset of a business, all such recomputations of liability in respect of other disposals and all such adjustments of tax, whether by way of assessment or by way of discharge or repayment of tax, as may be required in consequence of the provisions of this section shall be carried out.]¹

Commentary—*Simon's Direct Tax Service* **D2.303.**
Amendments—¹ This section inserted by FA 1998 s 134(2) with effect for a company in respect of which an approval for the purposes of TA 1988 s 842AA (venture capital trusts) has effect as from a time falling on or after 17 March 1998.

[101C Transfer within group to venture capital trust

(1) This section applies where—

(*a*) an asset has been disposed of to a company (the ''acquiring company'') and the disposal has been treated by virtue of section 171(1) as giving rise to neither a gain nor a loss,

(*b*) at the time of the disposal the acquiring company was not a venture capital trust, and

(*c*) the conditions set out in subsection (2) below are satisfied by the acquiring company.

(2) Those conditions are satisfied by the acquiring company if—

(*a*) it becomes a venture capital trust by virtue of an approval having effect as from a time (the ''time of approval'') not more than 6 years after the time of the disposal,

(*b*) at the time of approval the company owns, otherwise than as trading stock—

(i) the asset, or

(ii) property to which a chargeable gain has been carried forward from the asset on a replacement of business assets,

(*c*) it has not been a venture capital trust at any earlier time since the time of the disposal, and

(*d*) at the time of approval, there has not been an event by virtue of which it falls by virtue of section 179(3) or 101A(3) to be treated as having sold, and immediately reacquired, the asset at the time specified in subsection (3) below.

(3) The acquiring company shall be treated for all the purposes of this Act as if immediately after the disposal it had sold, and immediately reacquired, the asset at its market value at that time.

(4) Any chargeable gain or allowable loss which, apart from this subsection, would accrue to the acquiring company on the sale referred to in subsection (3) above shall be treated as accruing to it immediately before the time of approval.

(5) Subsections (5) to (7) of section 101A apply for the purposes of this section as they apply for the purposes of that section.

(6) Notwithstanding any limitation on the time for making assessments, any assessment to corporation tax chargeable in consequence of this section may, in a case in which the time of approval is the time at which an accounting period of the company begins, be made at any time within 6 years after the end of that accounting period.

(7) Any reference in this section to an approval is a reference to an approval for the purposes of section 842AA of the Taxes Act.][1]

Commentary—*Simon's Direct Tax Service* **D2.655.**
Revenue Internal Guidance—*Capital gains manual CG 41520–24 (explanation of this section and Revenue procedures).*
Amendments—[1] This section inserted by FA 1998 s 135(2) with effect for a company in respect of which an approval for the purposes of TA 1988 s 842AA (venture capital trusts) has effect as from a time falling on or after 17 March 1998.

102 Collective investment schemes with property divided into separate parts

(1) Subsection (2) below applies in the case of arrangements which constitute a collective investment scheme and under which—

(a) the contributions of the participants, and the profits or income out of which payments are to be made to them, are pooled in relation to separate parts of the property in question, and
(b) the participants are entitled to exchange rights in one part for rights in another.

(2) If a participant exchanges rights in one such part for rights in another, section 127 shall not prevent the exchange constituting a disposal and acquisition for the purposes of this Act.

(3) The reference in subsection (2) above to section 127—

(a) includes a reference to that section as applied by section 132, but
(b) does not include a reference to section 127 as applied by section 135 [or 136][2];

and in this section "participant" shall be construed in accordance with [section 235 of the Financial Services and Markets Act 2000][1].

Commentary—*Simon's Direct Tax Service* **C1.621.**
Revenue Interpretation RI 169—This section not to apply where investor switches between income units and accumulation units in the same sub-fund of an authorised unit trust umbrella scheme.
Definition—"Collective investment scheme", s 288(1).
Amendments—[1] Words in subs-s (3) substituted by the Financial Services and Markets Act 2000 (Consequential Amendments) (Taxes) Order, SI 2001/3629 arts 61, 62(2) with effect from 1 December 2001 immediately after the coming into force of the Financial Services and Markets Act 2000 ss 411, 432(1), Sch 20.
[2] Words in sub-s (3)(b) added by FA 2002 s 45, Sch 9 paras 5(1), (4), 7 with effect for shares or debentures issued after 16 April 2002. The reference to shares or debentures includes any interests falling to be treated as shares or debentures for the purposes of TCGA 1992 s 135 or 136 as substituted by FA 2002 Sch 9.

103 Restriction on availability of indexation allowance

Amendment—This section repealed by FA 1994 s 93(7), (11) and Sch 26 Pt V(8) in relation to disposals after 29 November 1993, subject to transitional provisions in FA 1994 Sch 12.

PART IV

SHARES, SECURITIES, OPTIONS ETC

Statement of Practice SP 18/80—Securities dealt in on the Stock Exchange Unlisted Securities Market: status and valuation for tax purposes.
Cross references—See TCGA 1992 Sch 11 para 16 (this Part to have effect subject to Sch 11 para 16).

CHAPTER I

GENERAL

Cross references—See FA 2000 Sch 8 para 100 (a participant's employee share ownership plan shares are treated as of a different class from any other shares for the purposes of this Chapter).
FA 2000 Sch 15 para 93(5) (this Chapter has effect subject to FA 2000 Sch 15 para 93 in identifiying shares on a disposal under the corporate venturing scheme).

Share pooling, identification of securities, and indexation

104 Share pooling: general interpretative provisions

(1) Any number of securities of the same class acquired by the same person in the same capacity shall for the purposes of this Act be regarded as indistinguishable parts of a single asset growing or diminishing on the occasions on which additional securities of the same class are acquired or some of the securities of that class are disposed of.

(2) Subsection (1) above—

(*a*) does not apply to any securities which were acquired before 6th April 1982 or in the case of a company 1st April 1982;

[(*aa*) does not apply, except for the purposes of corporation tax, to any securities acquired on or after 6th April 1998;][1] and

(*b*) has effect subject to sections 105, 106 and 107.

[(2A) Subsection (2)(*aa*) above shall not prevent the application of subsection (1) above to any securities that would be treated as acquired on or after 6th April 1998 but for their falling by virtue of section 127 to be treated as the same as securities acquired before that date.][1]

(3) For the purposes of this section and sections 105, 107, 110[, 110A][2] and 114—

["a section 104 holding" is][1] a holding of securities which, by virtue of subsection (1) above, is to be regarded as a single asset;

"securities" does not include relevant securities as defined in section 108 but, subject to that, means—

(i) shares or securities of a company; and

(ii) any other assets where they are of a nature to be dealt in without identifying the particular assets disposed of or acquired; and

"relevant allowable expenditure" has the meaning assigned to it by section 53(2)(*b*) and (3);

but shares or securities of a company shall not be treated as being of the same class unless they are so treated by the practice of a recognised stock exchange or would be so treated if dealt with on a recognised stock exchange.

[(4) For the purposes of this Chapter securities of a company which are held—

(*a*) by a person who acquired them as an employee of the company or of any other person, and

(*b*) on terms which for the time being restrict his right to dispose of them,

shall (notwithstanding that they would otherwise fall to be treated as of the same class) be treated as of a different class from any securities acquired by him otherwise than as an employee of the company or of any other person and also from any shares that are not held subject to restrictions, or the same restrictions, on disposal or in the case of which the restrictions are no longer in force.][1]

(5) Nothing in this section or sections 110[, 110A][2] and 114 shall be taken as affecting the manner in which the market value of any securities is to be ascertained.

(6) Without prejudice to the generality of subsections (1) and (2) above, a disposal of securities in a [section 104 holding][1], other than a disposal of the whole of it, is a disposal of part of an asset and the provisions of this Act relating to the computation of a gain accruing on a disposal of part of an asset shall apply accordingly.

Commentary—*Simon's Direct Tax Service* C2.703.
Revenue Internal Guidance—Capital gains manual CG 50575 (Revenue interpretation of sub-s (4)).
CG 78316 (currency is subject to the same rules of identification).
Definitions—"Asset", s 21(1); "class", s 288(1); "company", ss 99, 288(1); "issued", s 288(5); "market value", ss 272–274, Sch 11; "recognised stock exchange", s 288(1), TA 1988 s 841; "shares", s 288(1).
Cross references—See TCGA 1992 s 150(5) (this section not to apply to shares in respect of which business expansion scheme relief has been given and not withdrawn).
TCGA 1992 s 151B(1) (this section not to apply to shares in a venture capital trust eligible for relief under s 151A).
TCGA 1992 s 208 (application of this section to assets forming part of a premiums trust fund).
FA 2000 Sch 15 para 93 (this section does not to shares from a corporate venturing scheme to which investment relief is attributable).
Modifications—Personal Equity Plan Regulations, SI 1989/469 reg 27 (application of this section in relation to the pooling of investments under a personal equity plan).
Individual Savings Accounts Regulations, SI 1998/1870 reg 34(2)(*a*) (modification of TCGA 1992 ss 104–114 in relation to the pooling and identifying account investments).
Amendments—[1] Sub-ss (2)(aa) and (2A) inserted, sub-s (4) substituted and words in sub-ss (3) and (6) substituted by FA 1998 s 123 with effect in relation to any disposal on or after 6 April 1998 of any securities (whenever acquired).
[2] Section numbers in sub-ss (3), (5) inserted by FA 1998 s 125(3) with effect in relation to disposals on or after 6 April 1998.

105 Disposal on or before day of acquisition of shares and other unidentified assets

(1) [Paragraphs (*a*) and (*b*) below][1] shall apply where securities of the same class are acquired or disposed of by the same person on the same day and in the same capacity—

(*a*) all the securities so acquired shall be treated as acquired by a single transaction and all the securities so disposed of shall be treated as disposed of by a single transaction, and

(*b*) all the securities so acquired shall, so far as their quantity does not exceed that of the securities so disposed of, be identified with those securities.

[(2) Where the quantity of securities disposed of by any person exceeds the aggregate quantity of—

(*a*) the securities (if any) which are required by subsection (1) above to be identified with securities acquired on the day of the disposal,

(*b*) the securities (if any) which are required by any of the provisions of section 106 or 106A(5) to be identified with securities acquired after the day of the disposal, and

(*c*) the securities (if any) which are required by any of the provisions of sections 104, 106, 106A or 107, or of Schedule 2, to be identified with securities acquired before the day of the disposal,

the disposal shall be treated as diminishing a quantity of securities subsequently acquired, and as so diminishing any quantity so acquired at an earlier date, rather than one so acquired at a later date.][1]

Commentary—*Simon's Direct Tax Service* **C2.701A, 701B.**
Revenue Interpretation RI 226—The same day rule does not apply in any case where a particular shareholding is deemed to be disposed of and the same asset reacquired.
Definitions—"Same class", s 104(3); "class", s 288(1); "securities", s 104(3).
Cross references—See TA 1988 s 440A(5) (this section to have effect in relation to certain securities of an insurance company).
TCGA 1992 s 106(9) (sub-s (1) above to apply for the purposes of s 106 (disposal of shares and securities by company within prescribed period of acquisitions)).
TCGA 1992 s 107(3) (identification of securities disposed of within 10 days of acquisition).
TCGA 1992 s 110(1) (s 110 (new holdings: indexation allowance) and s 114 (options) to have effect subject to this section).
TCGA 1992 s 150(5) (this section not to apply to shares in respect of which business expansion scheme relief has been given and not withdrawn).
TCGA 1992 s 151B(1) (this section not to apply to shares in a venture capital trust eligible for relief under s 151A).
TCGA 1992 Sch 2 para 2(3) (restriction of gain or loss by reference to actual cost of securities held on 6 April 1965).
TCGA 1992 Sch 2 para 4(3) (election for pooling for securities held on 6 April 1965).
FA 2000 Sch 15 para 93 (this section does not apply to shares from a corporate venturing scheme to which investment relief is attributable).
Modifications—Individual Savings Accounts Regulations, SI 1998/1870 reg 34(2)(*a*) (modification of TCGA 1992 ss 104–114 in relation to the pooling and identifying account investments).
Amendments—[1] Words in sub-s (1) and sub-s (2) substituted by FA 1998 s 124(2) with effect in relation to any disposal on or after 6 April 1998, subject to FA 1998 s 124(8).

[105A Shares acquired on same day: election for alternative treatment

(1) Subsection (2) below applies where an individual—

(*a*) acquires shares ("the relevant shares") of the same class, on the same day and in the same capacity, and
(*b*) some of the relevant shares ("the approved-scheme shares") are shares acquired by him as a result of—

    (i) the exercise of a qualifying option within the meaning of paragraph 1(1) of Schedule 14 to the Finance Act 2000 (enterprise management incentives) in circumstances where paragraph 44, 45 or 46 of that Schedule (exercise of option to acquire shares) applies, or
    (ii) the exercise of an option to which subsection (1) of section 185 of the Taxes Act (approved share option schemes) applies in circumstances where paragraphs (*a*) and (*b*) of subsection (3) of that section apply.

(2) Where the individual first makes a disposal of any of the relevant shares, he may elect for subsections (3) to (5) below to have effect in relation to that disposal and all subsequent disposals of any of those shares.

(3) In circumstances where section 105 applies, that section shall have effect as if—

(*a*) paragraph (*a*) of subsection (1) of that section required the approved-scheme shares to be treated as acquired by the individual by a single transaction separate from the remainder of the relevant shares (which shall also be treated by virtue of that paragraph as acquired by the individual by a single transaction), and
(*b*) subsection (1) of that section required the approved-scheme shares to be treated as disposed of after the remainder of the relevant shares.

(4) If the relevant shares include shares to which relief under Chapter 3 of Part 7 of the Taxes Act or deferral relief (within the meaning of Schedule 5B to this Act) is attributable—

(*a*) paragraph 4(4) of that Schedule has effect as if it required the approved-scheme shares falling within paragraph (*a*), (*b*), (*c*) or (*d*) of that provision to be treated as disposed of after the remainder of the relevant shares falling within the paragraph in question, and
(*b*) section 299 of the Taxes Act has effect for the purposes of section 150A(4) below as if it required—

    (i) the approved-scheme shares falling within paragraph (*a*), (*b*), (*c*) or (*d*) of subsection (6A) of section 299 of that Act to be treated as disposed of after the remainder of the relevant shares falling within the paragraph in question, and
    (ii) the approved-scheme shares to which subsection (6B) of that section applies to be treated as disposed of after the remainder of the relevant shares to which that subsection applies.

(5) Where section 127 applies in relation to any of the relevant shares ("the reorganisation shares"), that section shall apply separately to such of those shares as are approved-scheme shares and to the remainder of the reorganisation shares (so that those approved-scheme shares and the remainder of the reorganisation shares are treated as comprised in separate holdings of original shares and identified with separate new holdings).

(6) In subsection (5)—

(*a*) the reference to section 127 includes a reference to that section as it is applied by virtue of any enactment relating to chargeable gains, and
(*b*) "original shares" and "new holding" have the same meaning as in section 127 or (as the case may be) that section as applied by virtue of the enactment in question.

(7) For the purposes of subsection (1) above—

(*a*) any shares to which relief under Chapter 3 of Part 7 of the Taxes Act is attributable and which were transferred to an individual as mentioned in section 304 of that Act, and (*b*) any shares to which deferral relief (within the meaning of Schedule 5B to this Act), but not relief under that Chapter, is attributable and which were acquired by an individual on a disposal to which section 58 above applies,

shall be treated as acquired by the individual on the day on which they were issued.

(8) In this section the references to Chapter 3 of Part 7, section 299 and section 304 of the Taxes Act shall be read as references to those provisions as they apply to shares issued after 31st December 1993 (enterprise investment scheme).][1]

Amendments—[1] This section inserted by FA 2002 s 50(1), (2) with effect for shares acquired by an individual after 5 April 2002. For this purpose—

(*a*) any shares to which relief under TA 1988 Pt 7 Chapter 3 is attributable, and which were transferred to an individual as mentioned in TA 1988 s 304 (as these provisions apply to shares issued after 31 December 1993), and

(*b*) any shares to which deferral relief (within the meaning of TCGA 1992 Sch 5B), but not relief under TA 1988 Pt 7 Chapter 3, is attributable, and which were acquired by an individual on a disposal to which TCGA 1992 s 58 applies

shall be treated as acquired by the individual on the day on which they were issued: FA 2002 s 50(3), (4).

[105B Provision supplementary to section 105A

(1) The provisions of section 105A have effect in the case of any disposal notwithstanding that some or all of the securities disposed of are otherwise identified—

(*a*) by the disposal, or

(*b*) by a transfer or delivery giving effect to it.

(2) An election must be made, by a notice given to an officer of the Board, on or before the first anniversary of the 31st January next following the year of assessment in which the individual first makes a disposal of any of the relevant shares.

(3) Where—

(*a*) an election is made in respect of the relevant shares, and

(*b*) any shares ("the other shares") acquired by the individual on the same day and in the same capacity as the relevant shares cease to be treated under section 104(4) as shares of a different class from the relevant shares,

the election shall have effect in respect of the other shares from the time they cease to be so treated.

(4) In determining for the purposes of section 105A(2) and subsection (2) above whether the individual has made a disposal of any of the relevant shares, sections 122(1) and 128(3) shall be disregarded.

(5) No election may be made in respect of ordinary shares in a venture capital trust.

For this purpose "ordinary shares" has the meaning given in section 151A(7).

(6) For the purposes of section 105A, shares in a company shall not be treated as being of the same class unless they are so treated by the practice of a recognised stock exchange, or would be so treated if dealt with on that recognised stock exchange.

(7) In section 105A(2) to (5) and subsections (2) to (4) above, any reference to the relevant shares or to the approved-scheme shares includes a reference to the securities (if any) directly or indirectly derived from the shares in question by virtue of one or more applications of section 127 (including that section as applied by virtue of any enactment relating to chargeable gains).

(8) In this section—

"the approved-scheme shares" has the same meaning as in section 105A;

"election" means an election under that section;

"the relevant shares" has the same meaning as in that section; and

"securities" has the meaning given in section 104(3);

and in subsection (4) the reference to section 128(3) includes a reference to that provision as it is applied by virtue of any enactment relating to chargeable gains.][1]

Amendments—[1] This section inserted by FA 2002 s 50(1), (2) with effect for shares acquired by an individual after 5 April 2002. For this purpose—

(*a*) any shares to which relief under TA 1988 Pt 7 Chapter 3 is attributable, and which were transferred to an individual as mentioned in TA 1988 s 304 (as these provisions apply to shares issued after 31 December 1993), and

(*b*) any shares to which deferral relief (within the meaning of TCGA 1992 Sch 5B), but not relief under TA 1988 Pt 7 Chapter 3, is attributable, and which were acquired by an individual on a disposal to which TCGA 1992 s 58 applies

shall be treated as acquired by the individual on the day on which they were issued: FA 2002 s 50(3), (4).

106 Disposal of shares and securities by company within prescribed period of acquisition

(1) For the purposes of corporation tax on chargeable gains, shares disposed of by a company shall be identified in accordance with the following provisions where—

(*a*) the number of shares of that class held by the company at any time during the prescribed period before the disposal amounted to not less than 2 per cent of the number of issued shares of that class; and

(*b*) shares of that class have been or are acquired by the company within the prescribed period before or after the disposal.

[(2) Subsections (2A) to (2C) below apply where the company making the disposal is a member of a group.

(2A) Where—

    (*a*) shares of the class in question are held by another member of the group, and

    (*b*) at any time during the prescribed period before the disposal, the condition in subsection (2D) below is met,

those shares shall be treated for the purposes of paragraph (*a*) of subsection (1) above as held by the company making the disposal.

(2B) Where—

    (*a*) shares of the class in question are acquired by another member of the group, and

    (*b*) at the time of the acquisition, the condition in subsection (2D) below is met,

those shares shall be treated for the purposes of paragraph (*b*) of subsection (1) above as acquired by the company making the disposal.

(2C) Where—

    (*a*) shares of the class in question are acquired by the company making the disposal from another company which was a member of the group throughout the prescribed period before and after the disposal, and

    (*b*) throughout the part of the prescribed period before or after the disposal for which the other member of the group held the shares, the condition in subsection (2D) below is met,

those shares shall be disregarded for the purposes of paragraph (*b*) of subsection (1) above.

(2D) The condition referred to in subsections (2A) to (2C) above is—

    (*a*) that the other member of the group is resident in the United Kingdom, or

    (*b*) that the shares are chargeable shares in relation to that other member.]¹

(3) References in subsection (1) above to a company's disposing, holding and acquiring shares are references to its doing so in the same capacity; and references in that subsection to the holding or acquisition of shares do not include references to the holding or acquisition of shares as trading stock.

(4) The shares disposed of shall be identified—

    (*a*) with shares acquired as mentioned in subsection (1)(*b*) above (''available shares'') rather than other shares; and

    (*b*) with available shares acquired by the company making the disposal rather than other available shares.

(5) The shares disposed of shall be identified with available shares acquired before the disposal rather than available shares acquired after the disposal and—

    (*a*) in the case of available shares acquired before the disposal, with those acquired later rather than those acquired earlier;

    (*b*) in the case of available shares acquired after the disposal, with those acquired earlier rather than those acquired later.

(6) Where available shares could be identified—

    (*a*) with shares disposed of either by the company that acquired them or by another company; or

    (*b*) with shares disposed of either at an earlier date or at a later date,

they shall in each case be identified with the former rather than the latter; and the identification of any available shares with shares disposed of by a company on any occasion shall preclude their identification with shares comprised in a later disposal by that company or in a disposal by another company.

(7) Where a company disposes of shares which have been identified with shares disposed of by another company, the shares disposed of by the first-mentioned company shall be identified with the shares that would, apart from this section, have been comprised in the disposal by the other company or, if those shares have themselves been identified with shares disposed of by a third company, with the shares that would, apart from this section, have been comprised in the disposal by the third company and so on.

(8) Where shares disposed of by one company are identified with shares acquired by another, the sums allowable to the company making the disposal under section 38 shall be—

    (*a*) the sums allowable under subsection (1)(*c*) of that section; and

    (*b*) the sums that would have been allowable under subsection (1)(*a*) and (*b*) of that section to the company that acquired the shares if they have been disposed of by that company.

(9) This section shall have effect subject to section 105(1).

(10) In this section—

    ''group'' has the meaning given in section 170(2) to (14);

    ''the prescribed period'' means—

        (*a*) in the case of a disposal through a stock exchange or Automated Real-Time Investments Exchange Limited, one month;

        (*b*) in any other case, 6 months

[and for the purposes of this section shares are ''chargeable shares'' in relation to a company at any time if, were the shares to be disposed of by the company at that time, any gain accruing to the company would be a chargeable gain and would by virtue of section 10(3) form part of its chargeable profits for corporation tax purposes.]²

(11) Shares shall not be treated for the purpose of this section as being of the same class unless they are so treated by the practice of a recognised stock exchange or would be so treated if dealt with on such a stock exchange.

(12) This section applies to securities as defined in section 132 as it applies to shares.

Commentary—*Simon's Direct Tax Service* **C2.702.**
Revenue Internal Guidance—Life assurance manual LAM 2.54, 2.55 (application to life assurance companies).
Definitions—''Chargeable gain'', s 15(2); ''class'', s 288(1); ''company'', ss 99, 288(1); ''issued'', s 288(5); ''recognised stock exchange'', s 288(1), TA 1988 s 841; ''shares'', s 288(1); ''trading stock'', s 288(1), TA 1988 s 832(1).
Cross references—See TCGA 1992 s 110(1) (s 110 (new holdings: indexation allowance) and s 114 (options) to have effect subject to this section).
FA 2000 Sch 15 para 93 (this section does not to shares from a corporate venturing scheme to which investment relief is attributable).
FA 2000 Sch 29 para 18(4) (the main amendments made to TCGA 1992 s 170 by FA 2000 Sch 29 para 1 have effect for the purposes of this section with effect for cases in which the prescribed period before the disposal (within the meaning of that section) begins after 31 March 2000).
Modifications—Individual Savings Accounts Regulations, SI 1998/1870 reg 34(2)(a) (modification of TCGA 1992 ss 104–114 in relation to the pooling and identifying account investments).
Amendment—¹ Sub-ss (2)–(2D) substituted for original sub-s (2), and words in sub-s (10) inserted, by FA 2000 s 102, Sch 29 para 18 with effect for cases in which the prescribed period before the disposal (within the meaning of this section) begins after 31 March 2000.

[106A Identification of securities: general rules for capital gains tax

(1) This section has effect for the purposes of capital gains tax (but not corporation tax) where any securities are disposed of by any person.

(2) The securities disposed of shall be identified in accordance with the following provisions of this section with securities of the same class that have been acquired by the person making the disposal.

(3) The provisions of this section have effect in the case of any disposal notwithstanding that some or all of the securities disposed of are otherwise identified—

  (*a*) by the disposal, or
  (*b*) by a transfer or delivery giving effect to it;

but where a person disposes of securities in one capacity, they shall not be identified under those provisions with any securities which he holds, or can dispose of, only in some other capacity.

(4) Securities disposed of on an earlier date shall be identified before securities disposed of on a later date; and, accordingly, securities disposed of by a later disposal shall not be identified with securities already identified as disposed of by an earlier disposal.

(5) Subject to subsection (4) above, if within the period of thirty days after the disposal the person making it acquires securities of the same class, the securities disposed of shall be identified—

  (*a*) with securities acquired by him within that period, rather than with other securities; and
  (*b*) with securities acquired at an earlier time within that period, rather than with securities acquired at a later time within that period.

(6) Subject to subsections (4) and (5) above, securities disposed of shall be identified with securities acquired at a later time, rather than with securities acquired at an earlier time.

(7) Subsection (6) above shall not require securities to be identified with particular securities comprised in a section 104 holding or a 1982 holding.

(8) Accordingly, that subsection shall have effect for determining whether, and to what extent, any securities should be identified with the whole or any part of a section 104 holding or a 1982 holding—

  (*a*) as if the time of the acquisition of a section 104 holding were the time when it first came into being; and
  (*b*) as if 31st March 1982 were the time of the acquisition of a 1982 holding.

(9) The identification rules set out in the preceding provisions of this section have effect subject to subsection (1) of section 105, and securities disposed of shall not be identified with securities acquired after the disposal except in accordance with that section or subsection (5) above.

(10) In this section—

  ''1982 holding'' has the same meaning as in section 109;
  ''securities'' means any securities within the meaning of section 104 or any relevant securities within the meaning of section 108.

(11) For the purposes of this section securities of a company shall not be treated as being of the same class unless they are so treated by the practice of a recognised stock exchange, or would be so treated if dealt with on that recognised stock exchange.]¹

Commentary—*Simon's Direct Tax Service* **C2.701A, 701B, 702.**
RI 226—Guidance on ''bed and breakfast'' transactions.
Revenue Internal Guidance—Capital gains manual CG 50579 (examples illustrating sub-s (6)).
CG 51089 (example illustrating sub-s (7)).
Cross references—See TCGA 1992 s 150(5) (this section not to apply to shares in respect of which business expansion scheme relief has been given and not withdrawn).
TCGA 1992 s 151B(1) (this section not to apply to shares in a venture capital trust eligible for relief under s 151A).

Modifications—Personal Equity Plan Regulations, SI 1989/469 reg 27 (modification of this section in relation to the pooling and identification of investments under a personal equity plan), as amended by SI 1998/1869 regs 12 and 13.
Individual Savings Accounts Regulations, SI 1998/1870 reg 34(2)(*a*) (modification of TCGA 1992 ss 104–114 in relation to the pooling and identifying account investments).
Individual Savings Accounts Regulations, SI 1998/1870 reg 34(3) (modification of this section for the purposes of identifying securities which are eligible to become account investments).
Amendments—[1] This section inserted by FA 1998 s 124(1) with effect in relation to any disposal on or after 6 April 1998, subject to FA 1998 s 124(8).

107 Identification of securities etc: general rules

[(1) This section has effect for the purposes of corporation tax where any securities are disposed of by a company.

(1A) The securities disposed of shall be identified in accordance with the following provisions of this section with securities of the same class that have been acquired by the company making the disposal and could be comprised in that disposal.

(2) The provisions of this section have effect in the case of any disposal notwithstanding that some or all of the securities disposed of are otherwise identified—

(*a*) by the disposal, or
(*b*) by a transfer or delivery giving effect to it;

but where a company disposes of securities in one capacity, they shall not be identified with securities which it holds, or can dispose of, only in some other capacity.][1]

(3) Without prejudice to section 105 if, within a period of 10 days, a number of securities are acquired and subsequently a number of securities are disposed of and, apart from this subsection—

(*a*) the securities acquired would increase the size of, or constitute a [section 104 holding][2], and
(*b*) the securities disposed of would decrease the size of, or extinguish, the same [section 104 holding][2],

then, subject to subsections (4) and (5) below, the securities disposed of shall be identified with the securities acquired and none of them shall be regarded as forming part of an existing [section 104 holding][2] or constituting a [section 104 holding][2].

(4) If, in a case falling within subsection (3) above, the number of securities acquired exceeds the number disposed of—

(*a*) the excess shall be regarded as forming part of an existing [section 104 holding][2] or, as the case may be, as constituting a [section 104 holding][2]; and
(*b*) if the securities acquired were acquired at different times (within the 10 days referred to in subsection (3) above) the securities disposed of shall be identified with securities acquired at an earlier time rather than with securities acquired at a later time.

(5) If, in a case falling within subsection (3) above, the number of securities disposed of exceeds the number acquired, the excess shall not be identified in accordance with that subsection.

(6) Securities which, by virtue of subsection (3) above, do not form part of or constitute a [section 104 holding][2] shall be treated for the purposes of section 54(2) as relevant securities within the meaning of section 108.

(7) The identification rules set out in subsections (8) and (9) below have effect subject to section 105 but, subject to that, have priority according to the order in which they are so set out.

(8) Securities disposed of shall be identified with securities forming part of a [section 104 holding][2] rather than with other securities.

(9) Securities disposed of shall be identified with securities forming part of a 1982 holding, within the meaning of section 109, rather than with other securities and, subject to that, shall be identified with securities acquired at a later time rather than with securities acquired at an earlier time.

Commentary—*Simon's Direct Tax Service* C2.701B, 703.
Definitions—"Class", s 288(1); "new holding", s 104(3); "securities", s 104(3); "shares", s 288(1).
FA 2000 Sch 15 para 93 (this section does not to shares from a corporate venturing scheme to which investment relief is attributable).
Modifications—Personal Equity Plan Regulations, SI 1989/469 reg 27(2A) (modification of this section by the addition of sub-ss (10), (11) for the purposes of identifying securities until 5 April 1998 which are eligible to become investments in a personal equity plan).
Individual Savings Accounts Regulations, SI 1998/1870 reg 34(2)(*a*) (modification of TCGA 1992 ss 104–114 in relation to the pooling and identifying account investments).
Amendments—[1] Sub-s (1), (1A), (2) substituted by FA 1998 s 124(3) with effect in relation to any disposal on or after 6 April 1998, subject to FA 1998 s 124(8).
[2] Words in sub-ss (3)–(4), (6), (8) substituted by FA 1998 s 123(5) with effect in relation to any disposal on or after 6 April 1998 of any securities (whenever acquired).

108 Identification of relevant securities

[(A1) This section has effect for the purposes of corporation tax where any relevant securities are disposed of by a company.][3]

(1) In this section "relevant securities" means—

(*a*) securities, within the meaning of section 710 of the Taxes Act;
[(*aa*) qualifying corporate bonds;][1]

TCGA 1992

(*b*) deep discount securities, within the meaning of Schedule 4 to that Act; and[2]

(*c*) securities which are, or have at any time been, material interests in a non-qualifying offshore fund, within the meaning of Chapter V of Part XVII of that Act;

and shares or securities of a company shall not be treated for the purposes of this section as being of the same class unless they are so treated by the practice of a recognised stock exchange or would be so treated if dealt with on a recognised stock exchange.

(2) Where a [company][3] disposes of relevant securities, the securities disposed of shall be identified in accordance with the rules contained in this section with the securities of the same class acquired by [the company][3] which could be comprised in that disposal, and shall be so identified notwithstanding that they are otherwise identified by the disposal or by a transfer or delivery giving effect to it (but so that where a [company][3] disposes of securities in one capacity, they shall not be identified with securities which [it][3] holds or can dispose of only in some other capacity).

(3) Relevant securities disposed of on an earlier date shall be identified before securities disposed of on a later date, and the identification of the securities first disposed of shall accordingly determine the securities which could be comprised in the later disposal.

(4) Relevant securities disposed of for transfer or delivery on a particular date or in a particular period—

(*a*) shall not be identified with securities acquired for transfer or delivery on a later date or in a later period; and

(*b*) shall be identified with securities acquired for transfer or delivery on or before that date or in or before that period, but on or after the date of the disposal, rather than with securities not so acquired.

(5) The relevant securities disposed of shall be identified—

(*a*) with securities acquired within the 12 months preceding the disposal rather than with securities not so acquired, and with securities so acquired on an earlier date rather than with securities so acquired on a later date, and

(*b*) subject to paragraph (*a*) above, with securities acquired on a later date rather than with securities acquired on an earlier date; and

(*c*) with securities acquired at different times on any one day in as nearly as may be equal proportions.

(6) The rules contained in the preceding subsections shall have priority according to the order in which they are so contained.

(7) Notwithstanding anything in subsections (3) to (5) above, where, under arrangements designed to postpone the transfer or delivery of relevant securities disposed of, a [company][3] by a single bargain acquires securities for transfer or delivery on a particular date or in a particular period and disposes of them for transfer or delivery on a later date or in a later period, then—

(*a*) the securities disposed of by that bargain shall be identified with the securities thereby acquired; and

(*b*) securities previously disposed of which, but for the operation of paragraph (*a*) above in relation to acquisitions for transfer or delivery on the earlier date or in the earlier period, would have been identified with the securities acquired by that bargain—

(i) shall, subject to subsection (3) above, be identified with any available securities acquired for such transfer or delivery (that is to say, any securities so acquired other than securities to which paragraph (*a*) above applies and other than securities with which securities disposed of for such transfer or delivery would be identified apart from this subsection); and

(ii) in so far as they cannot be so identified shall be treated as disposed of for transfer or delivery on the later date, or in the later period, mentioned above.

(8) This section shall have effect subject to section 106 but shall not apply—

(*a*) where the disposal is of quoted securities (within the meaning of paragraph 8 of Schedule 2), unless an election has been made with respect to the securities under paragraph 4 of that Schedule or under section 109(4), or

(*b*) where the disposal is of securities as respects which paragraph 17 or 18 of Schedule 2 has effect.

Commentary—*Simon's Direct Tax Service* **C2.810.**
Revenue Internal Guidance—Inspector's manual IM 4120–4122 (sub-s (1)–(9) composite holdings of shares etc acquired pre and post distributor status may be dealt with on LIFO basis).
Definitions—''Class'', s 288(1); ''company'', ss 99, 288(1); ''quoted on UK stock exchange'', s 288(4); ''recognised stock exchange'', s 288(1), TA 1988 s 841; ''shares'', s 288(1); ''the Taxes Act'', s 288(1).
Cross references—See TCGA 1992 s 53(4) (this section to have effect subject to the following provisions—
TCGA 1992 s 56 (part disposals and no gain/no loss disposals);
TCGA 1992 s 57 (receipts affecting allowable expenditure);
TCGA 1992 s 109 (pre-April 1982 share pools);
TCGA 1992 s 110 (indexation allowance on share holdings);
TCGA 1992 s 113 (calls on shares);
TCGA 1992 s 131 (share reorganisations: indexation allowance);
TCGA 1992 s 145 (call options: indexation allowance)).
TCGA 1992 Sch 2 para 4 (election for pooling of relevant securities within the meaning of this section held on 6 April 1965).
Modifications—Individual Savings Accounts Regulations, SI 1998/1870 reg 34(2)(*a*) (modification of TCGA 1992 ss 104–114 in relation to the pooling and identifying account investments).

Amendments—[1] Sub-s (1)(*aa*) inserted by FA 1996 ss 104, 105(1), Sch 14 para 59 with effect for capital gains tax purposes from the year 1996–97 and, for the purposes of corporation tax, for accounting periods ending after 31 March 1996, subject to transitional provisions in FA 1996 Sch 15.
[2] Sub-s (1)(*b*) repealed by FA 1996 Sch 41 Pt V(3) with effect for capital gains tax purposes from the year 1996–97 and, for the purposes of corporation tax, for accounting periods ending after 31 March 1996, subject to transitional provisions in FA 1996 Sch 15.
[3] Sub-s (A1) and words in sub-ss (2), (7) substituted by FA 1998 s 124(4) with effect in relation to any disposal on or after 6 April 1998, subject to FA 1998 s 124(8).

109 Pre-April 1982 share pools

(1) This section has effect in relation to any 1982 holding, and in this section "1982 holding" means a holding which, immediately before the coming into force of this section, was a 1982 holding for the purposes of Part II of Schedule 19 to the Finance Act 1985.

(2) Subject to subsections (3) to (5) below—

(*a*) the holding shall continue to be regarded as a single asset for the purposes of this Act, but one which cannot grow by the acquisition of additional securities of the same class, and

(*b*) every sum, which on a disposal of the holding, would be an item of relevant allowable expenditure shall be regarded for the purposes of section 54 as having been incurred at such a time that the month which determines RI in the formula in subsection (1) of that section is March 1982.

Securities of a company shall not be treated for the purposes of this section as being of the same class unless they are so treated by the practice of a recognised stock exchange or would be so treated if dealt with on a recognised stock exchange.

(3) Nothing in subsection (2) above affects the operation of section 127 in relation to the holding, but without prejudice to section 131.

(4) If a person so elects, quoted securities, as defined in paragraph 8 of Schedule 2 which are covered by the election—

(*a*) shall be treated as an accretion to an existing 1982 holding or, as the case may be, as constituting a new 1982 holding; and

(*b*) shall be excluded from paragraph 2 of that Schedule;

and the relevant allowable expenditure which is attributable to that 1982 holding shall be adjusted or determined accordingly.

(5) Paragraphs 4(8) to (13) and 5 to 8 of Schedule 2 shall apply in relation to an election under subsection (4) above as they apply in relation to an election under paragraph 4(2) of that Schedule, but with the substitution for any reference to 19th March 1968 of a reference to 31st March 1985 in the case of holdings or disposals by companies and 5th April 1985 in any other case.

(6) For the purpose of computing the indexation allowance (if any) on a disposal of a 1982 holding, the relevant allowable expenditure attributable to the holding on the coming into force of this section shall be the amount which, if the holding had been disposed of immediately before the coming into force of this section, would have been the relevant allowable expenditure in relation to that holding on that disposal, and for the purposes of section 54(4) relevant allowable expenditure attributable to a 1982 holding shall be deemed to be expenditure falling within section 38(1)(*a*).

Commentary—*Simon's Direct Tax Service* C2.704.
Statement of Practice SP 3/82—CGT indexation.
Definitions—"Asset", s 21(1); "class", s 288(1); "company", ss 99, 288(1); "indexation allowance", s 53; "quoted on UK stock exchange", s 288(4); "recognised stock exchange", s 288(1), TA 1988 s 841; "shares", s 288(1).
Cross references—See TCGA 1992 s 108(8) (application of s 108 (identification of relevant securities) to apply where an election has been made under sub-s (4) above).
Modifications—Individual Savings Accounts Regulations, SI 1998/1870 reg 34(2)(*a*) (modification of TCGA 1992 ss 104–114 in relation to the pooling and identifying account investments).

110 [Section 104 holdings][2]: indexation allowance

(1) [For the purposes of corporation tax this][3] section and section 114—

(*a*) apply in place of section 54 in relation to a disposal of a [section 104 holding][2] for the purpose of computing the indexation allowance;

(*b*) have effect subject to sections 105 and 106.

(2) On any disposal of a [section 104 holding][2], other than a disposal of the whole of it—

(*a*) the qualifying expenditure and the indexed pool of expenditure shall each be apportioned between the part disposed of and the remainder in the same proportions as, under this Act, the relevant allowable expenditure is apportioned; and

(*b*) the indexation allowance is the amount by which the portion of the indexed pool which is attributed to the part disposed of exceeds the portion of the qualifying expenditure which is attributed to that part.

(3) On a disposal of the whole of a [section 104 holding][2], the indexation allowance is the amount by which the indexed pool of expenditure at the time of the disposal exceeds the qualifying expenditure at that time.

(4) In relation to a [section 104 holding][2], the qualifying expenditure is at any time the amount which would be the aggregate of the relevant allowable expenditure in relation to a disposal of the whole of the holding occurring at that time.

(5) Subject to subsection (6) below and section 114 the indexed pool of expenditure shall come into being at the time that the holding comes into being or, if it is earlier, when any of the qualifying expenditure is incurred and shall at the time it comes into being be the same as the qualifying expenditure at that time.

(6) In relation to a [section 104 holding][2] which was in existence immediately before the coming into force of this section, the indexed pool of expenditure on the coming into force of this section shall be the same as it was for the purposes of Part III of Schedule 19 to the Finance Act 1985 immediately before then.

[(6A) Where a disposal to a person acquiring or adding to a [section 104 holding][2] is treated by virtue of any enactment as one on which neither a gain nor a loss accrues to the person making the disposal—

   (a) section 56(2) shall not apply to the disposal (and, accordingly, the amount of the consideration shall not be calculated on the assumption that a gain of an amount equal to the indexation allowance accrues to the person making the disposal), but

   (b) an amount equal to the indexation allowance on the disposal shall be added to the indexed pool of expenditure for the holding acquired or, as the case may be, held by the person to whom the disposal is made (and, where it is added to the indexed pool of expenditure for a holding so held, it shall be added after any increase required by subsection (8)(a) below).][1]

(7) Any reference below to an operative event is a reference to any event (whether a disposal or otherwise) which has the effect of reducing or increasing the qualifying expenditure referable to the [section 104 holding][2].

(8) Whenever an operative event occurs—

   (a) there shall be added to the indexed pool of expenditure the indexed rise, as calculated under subsection (10) or (11) below, in the value of the pool since the last operative event or, if there has been no previous operative event, since the pool came into being; and

   (b) if the operative event results in an increase in the qualifying expenditure then, in addition to any increase under paragraph (a) above, the same increase shall be made to the indexed pool of expenditure; and

   (c) if the operative event is a disposal resulting in a reduction in the qualifying expenditure, the indexed pool of expenditure shall be reduced in the same proportion as the qualifying expenditure is reduced; and

   (d) if the operative event results in a reduction in the qualifying expenditure but is not a disposal, the same reduction shall be made to the indexed pool of expenditure.

(9) Where the operative event is a disposal—

   (a) any addition under subsection (8)(a) above shall be made before the calculation of the indexation allowance under subsection (2) above; and

   (b) the reduction under subsection (8)(c) above shall be made after that calculation.

(10) At the time of any operative event, the indexed rise in the indexed pool of expenditure is a sum produced by multiplying the value of the pool immediately before the event by a figure expressed as a decimal and determined, subject to subsection (11) below, by the formula—

$$\frac{RE - RL}{RL}$$

where—

RE is the retail prices index for the month in which the operative event occurs; and
RL is the retail prices index for the month in which occurred the immediately preceding operative event or, if there has been no such event, in which the indexed pool of expenditure came into being.

(11) If RE, as defined in subsection (10) above, is equal to or less than RL, as so defined, the indexed rise is nil.

Commentary—*Simon's Direct Tax Service* C2.703.
Revenue Internal Guidance—Capital gains manual CG 50607–50608 (explanation of this section and examples).
Definitions—"Indexation allowance", s 53; "relevant allowable expenditure", s 104(3); "retail prices index", s 288(2), TA 1988 s 833(2).
Cross references—See TCGA 1992 s 104(4) (shares acquired under employee share schemes).
TCGA 1992 s 104(5) (this section not to affect the method of ascertaining the market value of securities).
TCGA 1992 s 114(1) (option binding grantor to sell: increase in indexed pool of expenditure in addition to the increase under sub-s (8)(a) or (b) by indexed consideration for the option).
Modifications—Personal Equity Plan Regulations, SI 1989/469 reg 27(2) (application of this section in its application to pooling investments in a personal equity plan).
Individual Savings Accounts Regulations, SI 1998/1870 reg 34(2)(a) (modification of TCGA 1992 ss 104–114 in relation to the pooling and identifying account investments).
Amendments—[1] Sub-s (6A) inserted by FA 1994 s 93(6), (11) in relation to disposals after 29 November 1993.
[2] Words in section title, and in sub-ss (1)–(4), (6)–(6A), (7) inserted by FA 1998 s 123(5) with effect in relation to any disposal on or after 6 April 1998 of any securities (whenever acquired).
[3] Words in sub-s (1) substituted by FA 1998 s 125(1) with effect in relation to disposals on or after 6 April 1998, subject to FA 1998 s 125(5).

[110A Indexation for section 104 holdings: capital gains tax

(1) For the purposes of capital gains tax (but not corporation tax) where—

    (*a*) there is a disposal on or after 6th April 1998 of a section 104 holding, and

    (*b*) any of the relevant allowable expenditure was incurred before 6th April 1998,

this section applies, in place of section 54 and subject to section 105, for computing the indexation allowance.

(2) There shall be an indexed pool of expenditure and subsection (2) or, as the case may be, subsection (3) of section 110 shall apply by reference to that pool in relation to the disposal as it would apply (by reference to the pool for which that section provides) for the purposes of corporation tax.

(3) The amount at any time of the indexed pool of expenditure shall be determined by—

    (*a*) taking the amount which would, under section 110 and section 114, have been the amount of the indexed pool of expenditure for the purposes of a disposal of the whole of the holding at the end of 5th April 1998; and

    (*b*) making any adjustments by way of increase or reduction that would be required to be made by virtue of subsection (8) of section 110 on the assumptions set out in subsection (4) below.

(4) Those assumptions are—

    (*a*) that the indexed pool of expenditure is an indexed pool of expenditure for the purposes of section 110;

    (*b*) that no increase or reduction is to be made except for an operative event on or after 6th April 1998; and

    (*c*) that paragraph (*a*) of section 110(8) and section 114 are to be disregarded.

(5) For the purposes of making any adjustment in accordance with subsection (3)(*b*) above, subsection (9) of section 110 shall be assumed to provide only that, where the operative event is a disposal, the calculation of the indexation allowance under subsection (2) of that section, as applied by subsection (2) above, is to be made before the reduction under subsection (8)(*c*) of that section.][1]

Commentary—*Simon's Direct Tax Service* **C2.703.**
Modifications—Personal Equity Plan Regulations, SI 1989/469 reg 27 (modification of this section in relation to the pooling of investments under a personal equity plan), as amended by SI 1998/1869 reg 13.
Individual Savings Accounts Regulations, SI 1998/1870 reg 34(2)(*a*) (modification of TCGA 1992 ss 104–114 in relation to the pooling and identifying account investments).
Amendments—[1] This section inserted by FA 1998 s 125(2) with effect in relation to disposals on or after 6 April 1998, subject to FA 1998 s 125(5).

111 Indexation: building society etc shares

Commentary—*Simon's Direct Tax Service* **C2.303.**
Amendment—This section repealed by FA 1994 s 93(7), (11) and Sch 26 Pt V(8) in relation to disposals after 29 November 1993, subject to transitional provisions in FA 1994 Sch 12.

112 Parallel pooling regulations

(1) The Capital Gains Tax (Parallel Pooling) Regulations 1986 made by the Treasury under paragraph 21 of Schedule 19 to the Finance Act 1985 shall continue to have effect notwithstanding the repeal by this Act of that Schedule, and for the purposes of section 14 of the Interpretation Act 1978 that paragraph shall be deemed not to have been repealed.

(2) An election under Schedule 6 to the Finance Act 1983 which has not been revoked before 6th April 1992 shall not have effect in relation to any disposal after 5th April 1992 and may, if the Board allow, be revoked by notice to the inspector.

(3) All such adjustments shall be made, whether by way of discharge or repayment of tax, or the making of assessments or otherwise, as are required in consequence of a revocation under subsection (2) above.

Commentary—*Simon's Direct Tax Service* **C2.713.**
Regulations—CGT (Parallel Pooling) Regulations, SI 1986/387.
Definitions—''The Board'', s 288(1); ''inspector'', s 288(1); ''notice'', s 288(1).
Modifications—Individual Savings Accounts Regulations, SI 1998/1870 reg 34(2)(*a*) (modification of TCGA 1992 ss 104–114 in relation to the pooling and identifying account investments).

113 Calls on shares

(1) Subsection (2) below applies where—

    (*a*) on a disposal to which section 53 applies, the relevant allowable expenditure is or includes the amount or value of the consideration given for the issue of shares or securities in, or debentures of, a company; and

    (*b*) the whole or some part of that consideration was given after the expiry of the period of 12 months beginning on the date of the issue of the shares, securities or debentures.

(2) For the purpose of computing the indexation allowance (if any) on the disposal referred to in subsection (1)(*a*) above—

(a) so much of the consideration as was given after the expiry of the period referred to in subsection (1)(b) above shall be regarded as an item of expenditure separate from any consideration given during that period; and

(b) section 54(4) shall not apply to that separate item of expenditure which, accordingly, shall be regarded as incurred at the time the consideration in question was actually given.

Commentary—*Simon's Direct Tax Service* C2.702.
Definitions—"Company", ss 99, 288(1); "indexation allowance", s 53; "shares", s 288(1).
Modifications—Individual Savings Accounts Regulations, SI 1998/1870 reg 34(2)(a) (modification of TCGA 1992 ss 104–114 in relation to the pooling and identifying account investments).

114 Consideration for options

(1) If, in a case where section 110(8)(b) applies, the increase in the qualifying expenditure is, in whole or in part, attributable to the cost of acquiring an option binding the grantor to sell ("the option consideration"), then, in addition to any increase under section 110(8)(a) or (b), the indexed pool of expenditure shall be increased by an amount equal to the indexed rise in the option consideration, as determined under subsection (2) below.

(2) The indexed rise in the option consideration is a sum produced by multiplying the consideration by a figure expressed as a decimal and determined, subject to subsection (3) below, by the formula—

$$\frac{RO - RA}{RA}$$

where—

RO is the retail prices index for the month in which falls the date on which the option is exercised; and

RA is the retail prices index for the month in which falls the date in which the option was acquired or, if it is later, March 1982.

(3) If RO, as defined in subsection (2) above, is equal to or less than RA, as so defined, the indexed rise is nil.

Commentary—*Simon's Direct Tax Service* C2.1008.
Definition—"Retail prices index", s 288(2), TA 1988 s 833(2).
Cross references—See Personal Equity Plan Regulations, SI 1989/469 reg 27(2) (application of this section for the purposes of pooling investments in a personal equity plan).
TCGA 1992 s 104(4) (shares acquired under employee share schemes).
TCGA 1992 s 104(5) (this section not to affect the method of ascertaining the market value of securities).
TCGA 1992 s 110(1) (s 110 and this section to apply in place of s 54 for the purpose of calculating indexation allowance on disposal of new holding of securities as defined in s 104(3)).
TCGA 1992 s 145(1) (indexation allowance on call options).
Modifications—Personal Equity Plan Regulations, SI 1989/469 reg 27 (application of this section in relation to the pooling of investments under a personal equity plan).
Individual Savings Accounts Regulations, SI 1998/1870 reg 34(2)(a) (modification of TCGA 1992 ss 104–114 in relation to the pooling and identifying account investments).

Gilt-edged securities and qualifying corporate bonds

115 Exemptions for gilt-edged securities and qualifying corporate bonds etc

(1) A gain which accrues on the disposal by any person of—

(a) gilt-edged securities or qualifying corporate bonds, or

(b) any option or contract to acquire or dispose of gilt-edged securities or qualifying corporate bonds,

shall not be a chargeable gain.

(2) In subsection (1) above the reference to the disposal of a contract to acquire or dispose of gilt-edged securities or qualifying corporate bonds is a reference to the disposal of the outstanding obligations under such a contract.

(3) Without prejudice to section 143(5), where a person who has entered into any such contract as is referred to in subsection (1)(b) above closes out that contract by entering into another contract with obligations which are reciprocal to those of the first-mentioned contract, that transaction shall for the purposes of this section constitute the disposal of an asset, namely, his outstanding obligations under the first-mentioned contract.

Commentary—*Simon's Direct Tax Service* C2.803, 806.
Statement of Practice SP 4/92—Capital gains rebasing elections.
Definitions—"Asset", s 21(1); "chargeable gain", s 15(2); "gilt-edged securities", Sch 9 para 1, Sch 11 para 15; "qualifying corporate bond", s 117.
Cross references—TA 1988 s 126A (charge to tax on appropriation of gilt-edged securities and qualifying corporate bonds);
TCGA 1992 s 116(10)(c) (reorganisations, etc involving transactions whereby qualifying corporate bonds are exchanged for other securities; this section to have effect in relation to actual gain or loss).
TCGA 1992 s 134(2) (gilt-edged securities issued in exchange for original securities on nationalisation).

116 Reorganisations, conversions and reconstructions

(1) This section shall have effect in any case where a transaction occurs of such a description that, apart from the provisions of this section—

(*a*) sections 127 to 130 would apply by virtue of any provision of Chapter II of this Part; and

(*b*) either the original shares would consist of or include a qualifying corporate bond and the new holding would not, or the original shares would not and the new holding would consist of or include such a bond;

and in paragraph (*b*) above "the original shares" and "the new holding" have the same meaning as they have for the purposes of sections 127 to 130.

(2) In this section [references to a transaction include references to any conversion of securities (whether or not effected by a transaction) within the meaning of section 132 and]⁴"relevant transaction" means a reorganisation, conversion of securities or other transaction such as is mentioned in subsection (1) above, and, in addition to its application where the transaction takes place after the coming into force of this section, subsection (10) below applies where the relevant transaction took place before the coming into force of this section so far as may be necessary to enable any gain or loss deferred under paragraph 10 of Schedule 13 to the Finance Act 1984 to be taken into account on a subsequent disposal.

(3) Where the qualifying corporate bond referred to in subsection (1)(*b*) above would constitute the original shares for the purposes of sections 127 to 130, it is in this section referred to as "the old asset" and the shares or securities which would constitute the new holding for those purposes are referred to as "the new asset".

(4) Where the qualifying corporate bond referred to in subsection (1)(*b*) above would constitute the new holding for the purposes of sections 127 to 130, it is in this section referred to as "the new asset" and the shares or securities which would constitute the original shares for those purposes are referred to as "the old asset".

[(4A) In determining for the purposes of subsections (1) to (4) above, as they apply for the purposes of corporation tax—

(*a*) whether sections 127 to 130 would apply in any case, and

(*b*) what, in a case where they would apply, would constitute the original shares and the new holding,

it shall be assumed that every asset representing a loan relationship of a company is a security within the meaning of section 132.]²

(5) So far as the relevant transaction relates to the old asset and the new asset, sections 127 to 130 shall not apply in relation to it.

(6) In accordance with subsection (5) above, the new asset shall not be treated as having been acquired on any date other than the date of the relevant transaction or, subject to subsections (7) and (8) below, for any consideration other than the market value of the old asset as determined immediately before that transaction.

(7) If, on the relevant transaction, the person concerned receives, or becomes entitled to receive, any sum of money which, in addition to the new asset, is by way of consideration for the old asset, that sum shall be deducted from the consideration referred to in subsection (6) above.

(8) If, on the relevant transaction, the person concerned gives any sum of money which, in addition to the old asset, is by way of consideration for the new asset, that sum shall be added to the consideration referred to in subsection (6) above.

[(8A) Where subsection (6) above applies for the purposes of corporation tax in a case where the old asset consists of a qualifying corporate bond, Chapter II of Part IV of the Finance Act 1996 (loan relationships) shall have effect so as to require such debits and credits to be brought into account for the purposes of that Chapter in relation to the relevant transaction as would have been brought into account if the transaction had been a disposal of the old asset at the market value mentioned in that subsection.]²

(9) In any case where the old asset consists of a qualifying corporate bond, then, so far as it relates to the old asset and the new asset, the relevant transaction shall be treated for the purposes of this Act as a disposal of the old asset and an acquisition of the new asset.

(10) Except in a case falling within subsection (9) above, so far as it relates to the old asset and the new asset, the relevant transaction shall be treated for the purposes of this Act as not involving any disposal of the old asset but—

(*a*) there shall be calculated the chargeable gain or allowable loss that would have accrued if, at the time of the relevant transaction, the old asset had been disposed of for a consideration equal to its market value immediately before that transaction; and

(*b*) subject to subsections (12) to (14) below, the whole or a corresponding part of the chargeable gain or allowable loss mentioned in paragraph (*a*) above shall be deemed to accrue on a subsequent disposal of the whole or part of the new asset (in addition to any gain or loss that actually accrues on that disposal); and

(*c*) on that subsequent disposal, section 115 shall have effect only in relation to any gain or loss that actually accrues and not in relation to any gain or loss which is deemed to accrue by virtue of paragraph (*b*) above.

(11) Subsection (10)(*b*) and (*c*) above shall not apply to any disposal falling within section 58(1), 62(4), 139, [140A,]¹ [or 171(1)]⁵, but a person who has acquired the new asset on a disposal falling

within any of those sections (and without there having been a previous disposal not falling within any of those sections or a devolution on death) shall be treated for the purposes of subsection (10)(*b*) and (*c*) above as if the new asset had been acquired by him at the same time and for the same consideration as, having regard to subsections (5) to (8) above, it was acquired by the person making the disposal.

(12) In any case where—

    (*a*) on the calculation under subsection (10)(*a*) above, a chargeable gain would have accrued, and

    (*b*) the consideration for the old asset includes such a sum of money as is referred to in subsection (7) above,

then, subject to subsection (13) below, the proportion of that chargeable gain which that sum of money bears to the market value of the old asset immediately before the relevant transaction shall be deemed to accrue at the time of that transaction.

(13) If ...[3] the sum of money referred to in subsection (12)(*b*) above is small, as compared with the market value of the old asset immediately before the relevant transaction, ...[3] subsection (12) above shall not apply.

(14) In a case where subsection (12) above applies, the chargeable gain which, apart from that subsection, would by virtue of subsection (10)(*b*) above be deemed to accrue on a subsequent disposal of the whole or part of the new asset shall be reduced or, as the case may be, extinguished by deducting therefrom the amount of the chargeable gain which, by virtue of subsection (12) above, is deemed to accrue at the time of the relevant transaction.

(15) In any case where—

    (*a*) the new asset mentioned in subsections (10) and (11) above is a qualifying corporate bond in respect of which an allowable loss is treated as accruing under section 254(2), and

    (*b*) the loss is treated as accruing at a time falling after the relevant transaction but before any actual disposal of the new asset subsequent to the relevant transaction,

then for the purposes of subsections (10) and (11) above a subsequent disposal of the new asset shall be treated as occurring at (and only at) the time the loss is treated as accruing.

[(16) This section has effect for the purposes of corporation tax notwithstanding anything in section 80(5) of the Finance Act 1996 (matters to be brought into account in the case of loan relationships only under Chapter II of Part IV of that Act).][2]

Commentary—*Simon's Direct Tax Service* C2.726, 727, 804; D2.1162.

Concession D38—Qualifying corporate bonds.

Revenue Interpretation RI 23—Gift of qualifying corporate bonds to a charity.

RI 36—Devolution on death of qualifying corporate bonds with a held over gain: circumstances in which the held over gain becomes chargeable.

RI 39—Where consideration on a share exchange is partly made up of qualifying corporate bonds and other securities, the base cost of the original shares is apportioned between qualifying corporate bonds and new shares according to their market values at the time of the exchange.

RI 69—Reinvestment relief: extent available on disposal of a qualifying corporate bond.

RI 159—Where shares transferred between group companies in exchange for qualifying corporate bonds, no gain/no loss rule in TCGA 1992 s 171(1) does not apply to transferee company's acquisition.

RI 133—Reinvestment relief and qualifying corporate bonds.

RI 164—From 24 February 1997, the Revenue regard a receipt as "small" (see sub-s (13) above) wherever its amount or value is £3,000 or less, whether or not it would also meet the 5% test (see Revenue Internal Guidance below).

Revenue Internal Guidance—Capital gains manual CG 53857 (for purposes of sub-s (13) above, the Revenue regard "small" as meaning 5% or less of the market value of the old asset). See now also Revenue Interpretation RI 164 above.

Definitions—"Allowable loss", ss 8(2), 16, 288(1); "asset", s 21(1); "chargeable gain", s 15(2); "inspector", s 288(1); "loan relationship", TA 1988 s 834(1), FA 1996 s 81; "market value", ss 272–274, Sch 11; "qualifying corporate bond", s 117; "shares", s 288(1).

Cross references—See TCGA 1992 s 164A(2A), (2B) (reinvestment relief on disposals of qualifying corporate bonds acquired on an exchange: reduction in the consideration mentioned in sub-s (10) above).

TCGA 1992 s 164F(2) (roll-over relief on re-investment of consideration received from disposal of shares and securities: carry-forward of relief into replacement shares: conditions for carry-forward).

TCGA 1992 s 234 (roll-over relief for employee share ownership trust).

TCGA 1992 Sch 4 para 4 (reduction of deferred charge to tax in respect of a gain accruing on the disposal before 6 April 1988 of an asset acquired before 31 March 1982 where the gain crystallises after 5 April 1988).

TCGA 1992 Sch 7A paras 1(7), 2(8) (restriction on set-off of losses under sub-s (10)(*b*) above suffered by a company before becoming a member of a group).

Exchange Gains and Losses (Alternative Method of Calculation of Gain or Loss) Regulations, SI 1994/3227 reg 9 (treatment of deferred gain or loss following a matching election).

FA 1996 Sch 15 para 30 (transitional provisions for relevant discounted securities acquired as a result of a reorganisation and held on and immediately after 5 April 1996).

FA 1999 s 66(2) (application of this section for "relevant transactions" (to which TCGA 1992 ss 127–130 apply) made before 15 February 1999 where the new asset includes something which is treated as being a qualifying corporate bond by virtue of FA 1999 s 65).

FA 2000 Sch 15 para 88 (this section applies to the company restructuring provisions under the corporate venturing scheme in FA 2000 Sch 15 Pt IX subject to FA 2000 Sch 15 paras 80–82, 84).

Amendments—[1] Number in sub-s (11) inserted by F(No 2)A 1992 s 46(1), (3) and deemed always to have had effect.

[2] Sub-ss (4A), (8A), (16) inserted by FA 1996 ss 104, 105(1), Sch 14 para 60 with effect for accounting periods ending after 31 March 1996, subject to transitional provisions in FA 1996 Sch 15.

[3] Words in sub-s (13) repealed by FA 1996 s 134(1), (2), Sch 20 para 51, Sch 41 Pt V(10) with effect from the year 1996–97 and, for the purposes of corporation tax, as respects accounting periods ending after 30 June 1999 (by virtue of Finance Act 1994, Section 199, (Appointed Day) Order, SI 1998/3173 art 2).

[4] Words in sub-s (2) inserted by FA 1997 s 88(4), (6) with effect for the purposes of the application of this Act in relation to any disposal after 25 November 1996 and so have effect, where a conversion took place at a time before 26 November 1996, as if they had come into force before that time.

[5] Words in sub-s (11) substituted by FA 2000 s 102, Sch 29 para 19 with effect for disposals after 31 March 2000.

117 Meaning of "qualifying corporate bond"

[(A1) For the purposes of corporation tax "qualifying corporate bond" means ...⁵ any asset representing a loan relationship of a company; and for purposes other than those of corporation tax references to a qualifying corporate bond shall be construed in accordance with the following provisions of this section.]³

(1) For the purposes of this section, a "corporate bond" is a security, as defined in section 132(3)(*b*)—

    (*a*) the debt on which represents and has at all times represented a normal commercial loan; and
    (*b*) which is expressed in sterling and in respect of which no provision is made for conversion into, or redemption in, a currency other than sterling,

and in paragraph (*a*) above "normal commercial loan" has the meaning which would be given by sub-paragraph (5) of paragraph 1 of Schedule 18 to the Taxes Act if for paragraph (*a*)(i) to (iii) of that sub-paragraph there were substituted the words "corporate bonds (within the meaning of section 117 of the 1992 Act)".

(2) For the purposes of subsection (1)(*b*) above—

    (*a*) a security shall not be regarded as expressed in sterling if the amount of sterling falls to be determined by reference to the value at any time of any other currency or asset; and
    (*b*) a provision for redemption in a currency other than sterling but at the rate of exchange prevailing at redemption shall be disregarded.

[(2AA) For the purposes of this section "corporate bond" also includes any asset which is not included in the definition in subsection (1) above and which is a relevant discounted security for the purposes of Schedule 13 to the Finance Act 1996.]³

(2A) ...²

(3) ...²

(4) For the purposes of this section "corporate bond" also includes a share in a building society—

    (*a*) which is a qualifying share,
    (*b*) which is expressed in sterling, and
    (*c*) in respect of which no provision is made for conversion into, or redemption in, a currency other than sterling.

(5) For the purposes of subsection (4) above, a share in a building society is a qualifying share if—

    (*a*) it is a permanent interest bearing share, or
    (*b*) it is of a description specified in regulations made by the Treasury for the purposes of this paragraph.

(6) Subsection (2) above applies for the purposes of subsection (4) above as it applies for the purposes of subsection (1)(*b*) above, treating the reference to a security as a reference to a share.

[(6A) For the purposes of this section "corporate bond" also includes, except in relation to a person who acquires it on or after a disposal in relation to which section 115 has or has had effect in accordance with section 116(10)(*c*), any debenture issued on or after 16th March 1993 which is not a security (as defined in section 132) but—

    (*a*) is issued in circumstances such that it would fall by virtue of section 251(6) to be treated for the purposes of section 251 as such a security; and
    (*b*) would be a corporate bond if it were a security as so defined.]¹

[(6B) An excluded indexed security issued on or after 6th April 1996 is not a corporate bond for the purposes of this section; and an excluded indexed security issued before that date shall be taken to be such a bond for the purposes of this section only if—

    (*a*) it would be so taken apart from this subsection; and
    (*b*) the question whether it should be so taken arises for the purposes of section 116(10)]³

[(6C) In subsection (6B) above "excluded indexed security" has the same meaning as in Schedule 13 to the Finance Act 1996 (relevant discounted securities).]³

(7) Subject to subsections (9) and (10) below, for the purposes of this Act, a corporate bond—

    (*a*) is a "qualifying" corporate bond if it is issued after 13th March 1984; and
    (*b*) becomes a "qualifying" corporate bond if, having been issued on or before that date, it is acquired by any person after that date and that acquisition is not as a result of a disposal which is excluded for the purposes of this subsection, or which was excluded for the purposes of section 64(4) of the Finance Act 1984.

(8) Where a person disposes of a corporate bond which was issued on or before 13th March 1984 and, before the disposal, the bond had not become a qualifying corporate bond, the disposal is excluded for the purposes of subsection (7) above if, by virtue of any enactment—

    (*a*) the disposal is treated for the purposes of this Act as one on which neither a gain nor a loss accrues to the person making the disposal; or
    (*b*) the consideration for the disposal is treated for the purposes of this Act as reduced by an amount equal to the held-over gain on that disposal, as defined for the purposes of section 165 or 260.

[(8A) A corporate bond falling within subsection (2AA) above is a qualifying corporate bond whatever its date of issue.][3]

(9) ...[2]

(10) ...[2]

(11) For the purposes of this section—

(*a*) where a security is comprised in a letter of allotment or similar instrument and the right to the security thereby conferred remains provisional until accepted, the security shall not be treated as issued until there has been acceptance; and

[(*b*) "permanent interest bearing share" means a share which is a permanent interest bearing share within the meaning of, and is eligible for inclusion in the calculation for capital adequacy in accordance with, the Prudential Sourcebook (Building Societies) as that Sourcebook applies in relation to shares issued on the date that the share is issued,

and in paragraph (*b*) above "the Prudential Sourcebook (Building Societies)" means the Interim Prudential Sourcebook for Building Societies made by the Financial Services Authority under the Financial Services and Markets Act 2000.][4].

(12) The Treasury may by regulations provide that for the definition of the expression "permanent interest bearing share" in subsection (11) above (as it has effect for the time being) there shall be substituted a different definition of that expression, and regulations under this subsection or subsection (5)(*b*) above may contain such supplementary, incidental, consequential or transitional provision as the Treasury thinks fit.

(13) This section shall have effect for the purposes of section 254 with the omission of subsections (4) to (6), (11) and (12).

Commentary—*Simon's Direct Tax Service* C2.802; D2.1162.
Definitions—"Asset", s 21(1); "building society", s 288(1); "company", ss 99, 288(1); "issued", s 288(5); "loan relationship", TA 1988 s 834(1), FA 1996 s 81; "shares", s 288(1); "the Taxes Act", s 288(1).
Cross references—See TCGA 1992 s 117A (certain foreign currency debts involving companies are not qualifying corporate bonds).
TCGA 1992 s 117B (certain foreign currency denominated holdings in unit trusts and offshore funds held by companies are not qualifying corporate bonds).
FA 1993 s 165 and Sch 17 para 5 (foreign exchange gains and losses: foreign currency debts on securities may be treated as qualifying corporate bonds),
FA 1993 s 165 and Sch 17 para 6 (foreign exchange gains and losses: relief for foreign currency debts on securities).
FA 1996 Sch 13 paras 3(1), (1A), 10(3), 13(9) (application of these sub-paras (as inserted by FA 1999 s 65) concerning the meaning of "relevant discounted securities" for the purposes of sub-s (2AA) above with effect for any disposal, in whole or in part of an asset after 14 February 1999: FA 1999 s 65(11)).
Amendments—[1] Sub-s (6A) inserted by FA 1993 s 84(1), (3) in relation to any chargeable period ending after 15 March 1993.
[2] Sub-ss (2A), (3), (9), (10) repealed by FA 1996 Sch 41 Pt V(3) with effect for accounting periods ending after 31 March 1996, subject to transitional provisions in FA 1996 Sch 15.
[3] Sub-ss (A1), (2AA), (6B), (6C), (8A) inserted by FA 1996 ss 104, 105(1), Sch 14 para 61 with effect for accounting periods ending after 31 March 1996, subject to transitional provisions in FA 1996 Sch 15.
[4] Sub-s (11)(*b*) substituted, and words in sub-s (11) added, by the Financial Services and Markets Act 2000 (Consequential Amendments) (Taxes) Order, SI 2001/3629 arts 61, 63 with effect for shares in a building society issued after 30 November 2001.
[5] Words "subject to section 117A and 117B below)" repealed by FA 2002 s 141, Sch 40 Pt 3(10) with effect for accounting periods beginning after 30 September 2002.

[117A Assets that are not qualifying corporate bonds for corporation tax purposes

(1) An asset to which this section applies is not a qualifying corporate bond for the purposes of corporation tax in relation to any disposal of that asset.

(2) This section applies to any asset representing a loan relationship of a company where—

(a) subsection (3) or (4) below applies to the asset; and

(b) it is held in exempt circumstances.

(3) This subsection applies to an asset if—

(a) the settlement currency of the debt to which it relates is a currency other than sterling; and

(b) that debt is not a debt on a security.

(4) This subsection applies to an asset if the debt to which it relates is a debt on a security and is in a foreign currency.

(5) For the purposes of subsection (4) above a debt is a debt in a foreign currency if it is—

(a) a debt expressed in a currency other than sterling;

(b) a debt the amount of which in sterling falls at any time to be determined by reference to the value at that time of a currency other than sterling; or

(c) subject to subsection (6) below, a debt as respects which provision is made for its conversion into, or redemption in, a currency other than sterling.

(6) A debt is not a debt in a foreign currency for those purposes by reason only that provision is made for its redemption on payment of an amount in a currency other than sterling equal, at the rate prevailing at the date of redemption, to a specified amount in sterling.

(7) The provisions specified in subsection (8) below, so far as they require a disposal to be treated as a disposal on which neither a gain nor a loss accrues, shall not apply to any disposal of an asset to which this section applies.

(8) The provisions referred to in subsection (7) above are—

    (a) sections 139, 140A, [and 171]² of this Act; and

    (b) section 486(8) of the Taxes Act.

(9) Paragraph 3 of Schedule 17 to the Finance Act 1993 shall have effect for construing the reference in subsection (2)(b) above to exempt circumstances as if references to a currency were references to the debt to which the relationship relates.

(10) In this section "security" includes a debenture that is deemed to be a security for the purposes of section 251, by virtue of subsection (6) of that section.]¹

Note—This section repealed by FA 2002 s 141, Sch 40 Pt 3(10) with effect for accounting periods beginning after 30 September 2002.
Commentary—*Simon's Direct Tax Service* **C2.802**.
Definitions—"Asset", s 21(1); "company", ss 99, 288(1); "loan relationship", TA 1988 s 834(1), FA 1996 s 81; "the Taxes Act", s 288(1).
Cross reference—See Exchange Gains and Losses (Insurance Companies) Regulations, SI 1994/3231 reg 8A (insurance company may elect to disapply this section on the disposal of assets falling within SI 1994 Bo 3231 reg 7).
Amendments—¹ This section inserted by FA 1996 ss 104, 105(1), Sch 14 para 62 with effect for accounting periods ending after 31 March 1996, subject to transitional provisions in FA 1996 Sch 15.
² Words in sub-s (8)(a) substituted by FA 2000 s 102, Sch 29 para 20 with effect for disposals after 31 March 2000.

[117B Holdings in unit trusts and offshore funds excluded from treatment as qualifying corporate bonds

(1) For the purposes of corporation tax an asset to which this section applies is not a qualifying corporate bond in relation to any disposal of that asset in an accounting period for which that asset falls, under paragraph 4 of Schedule 10 to the Finance Act 1996 (holdings in unit trusts and offshore funds), to be treated as a right under a creditor relationship of a company.

(2) This section applies to an asset which is comprised in a relevant holding (within the meaning of paragraph 4 of Schedule 10 to the Finance Act 1996) if—

    (a) it is denominated in a currency other than sterling; and

    (b) it is held in exempt circumstances.

(3) For the purposes of this section—

    (a) a unit in a unit trust scheme, or

    (b) a right (other than a share in a company) which constitutes a relevant interest in an offshore fund,

shall be taken to be denominated in a currency other than sterling if the price at which it may be acquired from, or disposed of to, persons concerned in the management of the trust or fund is fixed by those persons in a currency other than sterling.

(4) For the purposes of this section shares constituting a relevant interest in an offshore fund shall be taken to be denominated in a currency other than sterling if their nominal value is expressed in such a currency.

(5) The provisions specified in subsection (6) below, so far as they require a disposal to be treated as a disposal on which neither a gain nor a loss accrues, shall not apply to any disposal in relation to which this section applies.

(6) The provisions referred to in subsection (5) above are—

    (a) sections 139, 140A, [and 171]² of this Act; and

    (b) section 486(8) of the Taxes Act.

(7) Paragraph 3 of Schedule 17 to the Finance Act 1993 shall have effect for construing the reference in subsection (2)(b) above to exempt circumstances as if references to a currency were references to the asset in question.

(8) Paragraph 7 of Schedule 10 to the Finance Act 1996 shall apply for construing any reference in this section to a relevant interest in an offshore fund as it applies for the purposes of paragraph 4 of that Schedule.]¹

Note—This section repealed by FA 2002 s 141, Sch 40 Pt 3(1) with effect for accounting periods beginning after 30 September 2002.
Commentary—*Simon's Direct Tax Service* **C2.802**.
Simon's Tax Cases—*Jenks v Dickinson* [1997] STC 853*.
Definitions—"Accounting period", TA 1988 s 834(1); "asset", s 21(1); "company", ss 99, 288(1); "qualifying corporate bond", s 117; "share", s 288(1); "the Taxes Act", s 288(1).
Cross reference—See Exchange Gains and Losses (Insurance Companies) Regulations, SI 1994/3231 reg 8A (insurance company may elect to disapply this section on the disposal of assets falling within SI 1994/3231 reg 7).
Modification—This section is modified, in relation to open-ended investment companies, by the Open-ended Investment Companies (Tax) Regulations, SI 1997/1154, regs 3, 21.
Amendments—¹ This section inserted by FA 1996 ss 104, 105(1), Sch 14 para 62 with effect for accounting periods ending after 31 March 1996, subject to transitional provisions in FA 1996 Sch 15.
² Words in sub-s (6)(a) substituted by FA 2000 s 102, Sch 29 para 21 with effect for disposals after 31 March 2000.

Deep discount securities, the accrued income scheme etc

118 Amount to be treated as consideration on disposal of deep discount securities etc

Commentary—*Simon's Direct Tax Service* **C2.812**.
Amendment—This section repealed by FA 1996 Sch 41 Pt V(3) with effect for income tax from the year 1996-97 and for corporation tax for accounting periods ending after 31 March 1996, subject to transitional provisions in FA 1996 Sch 15.

119 Transfers of securities subject to the accrued income scheme

(1) Where there is a transfer of securities within the meaning of section 710 of the Taxes Act (accrued income scheme)—

(a) if section 713(2)(a) or (3)(a) of that Act applies, section 37 shall be disregarded in computing the gain accruing on the disposal concerned;

(b) if section 713(2)(b) or (3)(b) of that Act applies, section 39 shall be disregarded in computing the gain accruing to the transferee if he disposes of the securities;

but subsections (2) and (3) below shall apply.

(2) Where the securities are transferred with accrued interest (within the meaning of section 711 of the Taxes Act)—

(a) if section 713(2)(a) of that Act applies, an amount equal to the accrued amount (determined under that section) shall be excluded from the consideration mentioned in subsection (8) below;

(b) if section 713(2)(b) of that Act applies, an amount equal to that amount shall be excluded from the sums mentioned in subsection (9) below.

(3) Where the securities are transferred without accrued interest (within the meaning of section 711 of the Taxes Act)—

(a) if section 713(3)(a) of that Act applies, an amount equal to the rebate amount (determined under that section) shall be added to the consideration mentioned in subsection (8) below;

(b) if section 713(3)(b) of that Act applies, an amount equal to that amount shall be added to the sums mentioned in subsection (9) below.

(4) Where section 716 of the Taxes Act applies—

(a) if subsection (2) or (3) of that section applies, section 37 shall be disregarded in computing the gain accruing on the disposal concerned, but the relevant amount shall be excluded from the consideration mentioned in subsection (8) below; and

(b) if subsection (4) of that section applies, section 39 shall be disregarded in computing the gain accruing on the disposal concerned, but the relevant amount shall be excluded from the sums mentioned in subsection (9) below.

(5) In subsection (4) above "the relevant amount" means an amount equal to—

(a) if paragraph (b) below does not apply, the amount of the unrealised interest in question (within the meaning of section 716 of the Taxes Act);

(b) if section 719 of the Taxes Act applies—

(i) in a case falling within subsection (4)(a) above, amount A (within the meaning of section 719);

(ii) in a case falling within subsection (4)(b) above, amount C (within the meaning of section 719).

(6) In relation to any securities which by virtue of subsection (7) below are treated for the purposes of this subsection as having been transferred, subsections (2) and (3) above shall have effect as if for "applies" (in each place where it occurs) there were substituted "would apply if the disposal were a transfer".

(7) Where there is a disposal of securities for the purposes of this Act which is not a transfer for the purposes of section 710 of the Taxes Act but, if it were such a transfer, one or more of the following paragraphs would apply, namely, paragraphs (a) and (b) of section 713(2) and paragraphs (a) and (b) of section 713(3) of that Act, the securities shall be treated—

(a) for the purposes of subsection (6) above, as transferred on the day of the disposal, and

(b) for the purposes of subsections (2) and (3) above, as transferred with accrued interest if, had the disposal been a transfer for the purposes of section 710, it would have been a transfer with accrued interest and as transferred without accrued interest if, had the disposal been such a transfer, it would have been a transfer without accrued interest.

(8) The consideration is the consideration for the disposal of the securities transferred which is taken into account in the computation of the gain accruing on the disposal.

(9) The sums are the sums allowable to the transferee as a deduction from the consideration in the computation of the gain accruing to him if he disposes of the securities.

(10) Where on a conversion or exchange of securities a person is treated as entitled to a sum under subsection (2)(a) of section 713 of the Taxes Act an amount equal to the accrued amount (determined under that section) shall, for the purposes of this Act, be treated as follows—

(a) to the extent that it does not exceed the amount of any consideration which the person receives (or is deemed to receive) or becomes entitled to receive on the conversion or exchange (other than his new holding), it shall be treated as reducing that consideration; and

(b) to the extent that it does exceed that amount, it shall be treated as consideration which the person gives on the conversion or exchange;

and where on a conversion or exchange of securities a person is treated as entitled to relief under subsection (3)(a) of that section an amount equal to the rebate amount (determined under that section) shall, for the purposes of the computation of the gain, be treated as consideration which the person receives on the conversion or exchange.

(11) In subsection (10) above "conversion" means conversion within the meaning of section 132 and "exchange" means an exchange which by virtue of Chapter II of this Part does not involve a disposal.

Commentary—*Simon's Direct Tax Service* **C2.811.**
Definition—"The Taxes Act", s 288(1).

120 Increase in expenditure by reference to tax charged in relation to shares, etc

(1) Where an amount is chargeable to tax under Chapter II of Part III of the Finance Act 1988 on a person who acquires shares or an interest in shares, then on the first disposal of the shares (whether by him or by another person) after his acquisition, section 38(1)(a) shall apply as if a sum equal to the amount chargeable had formed part of the consideration given by the person making the disposal for his acquisition of the shares; and this subsection shall apply with the appropriate modifications in a case to which section 83 of that Act applies.

This subsection shall be construed as if it were contained in Chapter II of Part III of the Finance Act 1988.

(2) Section 38(1)(a) applies as if the relevant amount as defined in the following provisions of this section in the cases there specified had formed part of the consideration given by the person making the disposal for his acquisition of the assets in question.

(3) Where an amount is chargeable to tax by virtue of section 162(5) of the Taxes Act in respect of shares or an interest in shares, then—

    (a) on a disposal of the shares or interest, where that is the event giving rise to the charge; or
    (b) in any case, on the first disposal of the shares or interest after the event,

the relevant amount is a sum equal to the amount so chargeable.

(4) If a gain chargeable to tax under section 135(1) or (6) of the Taxes Act is realised by the exercise of a right to acquire shares, the relevant amount is a sum equal to the amount of the gain so chargeable to tax.

(5) Where an amount is chargeable to tax under section 138 of the Taxes Act on a person acquiring any shares or interest in shares, then on the first disposal (whether by him or another person) of the shares after his acquisition, the relevant amount is an amount equal to the amount so chargeable.

[(5A) Where an amount is chargeable to tax under section 140A of the Taxes Act in respect of—

    (a) the acquisition or disposal of any interest in shares, or
    (b) any interest in shares ceasing to be only conditional,

the relevant amount is a sum equal to the amount so chargeable.

(5B) Where an amount is chargeable to tax under section 140D of the Taxes Act in respect of the conversion of shares, the relevant amount is a sum equal to the amount so chargeable.][4]

(6) Where an amount was chargeable to tax under [the applicable provision][1] of the Taxes Act in respect of shares acquired in exercise of any such right as is mentioned in section 185(1) of that Act, the relevant sum in relation to those shares is an amount equal to the amount so chargeable [; and in this subsection "the applicable provision" means—

    (a) subsection (6) of section 185 of the Taxes Act (as that subsection had effect before the coming into force of section 39(5) of the Finance Act 1991), or
    [(b) subsection (6A) of that section (as that subsection has effect in relation to rights obtained before the day on which the Finance Act 1996 was passed), or][3]
    [(c) subsection (6) of that section (as that subsection has effect in relation to rights obtained after that day);][3]][2]

(7) Subsections (3), (4), (5)[, (5A), (5B)][4] and (6) above shall be construed as one with sections 162, 135, 138[, 140A, 140D][4] and 185 of the Taxes Act respectively.

[(8) For the purposes of subsection (5A) above this section shall have effect as if references in this section to shares included anything referred to as shares in section 140A of the Taxes Act.][4]

Commentary—*Simon's Direct Tax Service* **E4.590, 599, 621.**
Revenue Internal Guidance—Capital Gains Manual CG 56391 (worked example showing how the acquisition cost of shares is
    increased where an additional amount is charged to income tax under Schedule E).
Definitions—"Asset", s 21(1); "shares", s 288(1); "the Taxes Act", s 288(1).
Amendments—[1] Words in sub-s (6) substituted by FA 1993 s 105(1), (2) and deemed always to have had effect.
[2] Words in sub-s (6) inserted by FA 1993 s 105(1), (2).
[3] Sub-s (6)(b), (c) substituted for sub-s (6)(b) by FA 1996 s 114(8).
[4] Sub-ss (5A), (5B), (8), and words in sub-s (7) inserted by FA 1998 s 54 with effect in relation to disposals on or after 17 March
    1998 of interests and shares acquired after that date.

Savings certificates etc

121 Exemption for government non-marketable securities

(1) Savings certificates and non-marketable securities issued under the National Loans Act 1968 or the National Loans Act 1939 or any corresponding enactment forming part of the law of Northern Ireland, shall not be chargeable assets, and accordingly no chargeable gain shall accrue on their disposal.

(2) In this section—

  (a) ''savings certificates'' means savings certificates issued under section 12 of the National Loans Act 1968 or section 7 of the National Debt Act 1958 or section 59 of the Finance Act 1920 and any war savings certificates as defined in section 9(3) of the National Debt Act 1972 together with any savings certificates issued under any enactment forming part of the law of Northern Ireland and corresponding to the said enactments, and

  (b) ''non-marketable securities'' means securities which are not transferable, or which are transferable only with the consent of some Minister of the Crown, or the consent of a department of the Government of Northern Ireland, or only with the consent of the National Debt Commissioners.

Commentary—*Simon's Direct Tax Service* **C1.405.**
Statement of Practice SP 4/92—Capital gains rebasing elections.
Definitions—''Asset'', s 21(1); ''chargeable gain'', s 15(2); ''issued'', s 288(5).

Capital distribution in respect of shares etc

122 Distribution which is not a new holding within Chapter II

(1) Where a person receives or becomes entitled to receive in respect of shares in a company any capital distribution from the company (other than a new holding as defined in section 126) he shall be treated as if he had in consideration of that capital distribution disposed of an interest in the shares.

(2) If ...[1] the amount distributed is small, as compared with the value of the shares in respect of which it is distributed, ...[1]—

  (a) the occasion of the capital distribution shall not be treated for the purposes of this Act as a disposal of the asset, and

  (b) the amount distributed shall be deducted from any expenditure allowable under this Act as a deduction in computing a gain or loss on the disposal of the shares by the person receiving or becoming entitled to receive the distribution of capital.

(3) ...[1]

(4) Where the allowable expenditure is less than the amount distributed (or is nil)—

  (a) [subsection (2)][1] above shall not apply, and

  (b) if the recipient so elects (and there is any allowable expenditure)—

    (i) the amount distributed shall be reduced by the amount of the allowable expenditure, and

    (ii) none of that expenditure shall be allowable as a deduction in computing a gain accruing on the occasion of the capital distribution, or on any subsequent occasion.

In this subsection ''allowable expenditure'' means the expenditure which immediately before the occasion of the capital distribution was attributable to the shares under paragraphs (a) and (b) of section 38(1).

(5) In this section—

  (a) the ''amount distributed'' means the amount or value of the capital distribution,

  (b) ''capital distribution'' means any distribution from a company, including a distribution in the course of dissolving or winding up the company, in money or money's worth except a distribution which in the hands of the recipient constitutes income for the purposes of income tax.

Commentary—*Simon's Direct Tax Service* **C2.720, E4.568.**
Revenue Interpretation RI 34—The Revenue will not insist on applying sub-s (2) above if it is advantageous to the recipient of a small capital distribution to treat it as a disposal.
RI 164—From 24 February 1997, the Revenue regard a receipt as ''small'' wherever its amount or value is £3,000 or less, whether or not it would also meet the 5% test (see Revenue and other press releases below).
Revenue & other press releases—CCAB June 1965 (''small'' is regarded by Revenue as not exceeding 5 per cent of the relevant amount). See now also Revenue Interpretation RI 164 above.
Simon's Tax Cases—s 122(2), (4), *O'Rourke v Binks* [1992] STC 703*.
Definitions—''Asset'', s 21(1); ''company'', ss 99, 288(1); ''shares'', s 288(1).
Cross reference—See FA 1988 Sch 12 para 6(2) (distributions in connection with the transfer of a building society's business to a company).
TCGA 1992 s 123(1) (application of this section where a right to acquire securities is disposed of).
TCGA 1992 s 128(3) (reorganisation: consideration for disposal of old shares being other than new holding).
TCGA 1992 s 163(2) (retirement relief on deemed disposal of an interest in shares under this section).
TCGA 1992 s 164(4) (retirement relief on deemed disposal of an interest in shares under this section).
TCGA 1992 s 171(2) (disposal of securities by one member of a group of companies to another member in consideration for a capital distribution).
TCGA 1992 s 192(2) (certain distributions made on company demergers not to be capital distributions for the purposes of this section).
TCGA 1992 Sch 3 para 4(2) (application of this section where TCGA 1992 s 35(2) (rebasing) applies in relation to the disposal of an asset).
TCGA 1992 Sch 6 para 11(1) (restriction of retirement relief where there is disposal of business assets treated under this section as made in consideration of a capital distribution).
TCGA 1992 Sch 6 para 12(5) (disposals qualifying for retirement relief and treated as made by virtue of this section in consideration of a capital distribution; election to preserve retirement relief).
Amendments—[1] Words in sub-s (2) and whole of sub-s (3) repealed, and words in sub-s (4)(a) substituted by FA 1996 s 134(1), (2), Sch 20 para 52, Sch 41 Pt V(10) with effect from the year 1996–97 and, for the purposes of corporation tax, as respects accounting periods ending after 30 June 1999 (by virtue of Finance Act 1994, Section 199, (Appointed Day) Order, SI 1998/3173 art 2).

123 Disposal of right to acquire shares or debentures

(1) Where a person receives or becomes entitled to receive in respect of any shares in a company a provisional allotment of shares in or debentures of the company and he disposes of his rights, section 122 shall apply as if the amount of the consideration for the disposal were a capital distribution received by him from the company in respect of the first-mentioned shares, and as if that person had, instead of disposing of the rights, disposed of an interest in those shares.

(2) This section shall apply in relation to rights obtained in respect of debentures of a company as it applies in relation to rights obtained in respect of shares in a company.

Commentary—*Simon's Direct Tax Service* C2.719.
Definitions—''Company'', ss 99, 288(1); ''shares'', s 288(1).

Close companies

124 Disposal of shares: relief in respect of income tax consequent on shortfall in distributions

(1) If in pursuance of section 426 of the Taxes Act (consequences for income tax of apportionment of income etc of close company) a person is assessed to income tax, then, in the computation of the gain accruing on a disposal by him of any shares forming part of his interest in the company to which the relevant apportionment relates, the amount of the income tax paid by him, so far as attributable to those shares, shall be allowable as a deduction.

(2) Subsection (1) above shall not apply in relation to tax charged in respect of undistributed income which has, before the disposal, been subsequently distributed and is then exempt from tax by virtue of section 427(4) of the Taxes Act or in relation to tax treated as having been paid by virtue of section 426(2)(*b*) of that Act.

(3) For the purposes of this section the income assessed to tax shall be the highest part of the individual's income for the year of assessment in question, but so that if the highest part of the said income is taken into account under this section in relation to an assessment to tax the next highest part shall be taken into account in relation to any other relevant assessment, and so on.

(4) For the purpose of identifying shares forming part of an interest in a company with shares subsequently disposed of which are of the same class, shares bought at an earlier time shall be deemed to have been disposed of before shares bought at a later time.

Commentary—*Simon's Direct Tax Service* C2.225.
Definitions—''Class'' (of shares), s 288(1); ''close company'', s 288(1), TA 1988 ss 414, 415; ''company'', ss 99, 288(1);
   ''shares'', s 288(1); ''the Taxes Act'', s 288(1); ''year of assessment'', s 288(1).
Cross reference—TA 1988 ss 426, 427 (since repealed).

125 Shares in close company transferring assets at an undervalue

(1) If a company which is a close company transfers, or has after 31st March 1982 transferred, an asset to any person otherwise than by way of a bargain made at arm's length and for a consideration of an amount or value less than the market value of the asset, an amount equal to the difference shall be apportioned among the issued shares of the company, and the holders of those shares shall be treated in accordance with the following provisions of this section.

(2) For the purposes of the computation of the gain accruing on the disposal of any of those shares by the person owning them on the date of transfer, an amount equal to the amount so apportioned to that share shall be excluded from the expenditure allowable as a deduction under section 38(1)(*a*) from the consideration for the disposal.

(3) If the person owning any of the shares at the date of transfer is itself a close company an amount equal to the amount apportioned to the shares so owned under subsection (1) above to that close company shall be apportioned among the issued shares of that close company, and the holders of those shares shall be treated in accordance with subsection (2) above, and so on through any number of close companies.

(4) This section shall not apply where the transfer of the asset is a disposal to which section 171(1) applies.

(5) In relation to a disposal to which section 35(2) does not apply, subsection (1) above shall have effect with the substitution of ''6th April 1965'' for ''31st March 1982''.

Commentary—*Simon's Direct Tax Service* D2.318.
Concession D51—Revenue do not seek to apply this section where a transfer at under value is made other than at arm's length to
  a (*a*) participator (or an associate of his) which is an income distribution or capital distribution, or (*b*) to an employee who is
  assessed on the market value of the asset less any amount paid.
Revenue & other press releases—CCAB June 1967 (the acquisition cost of shares in a close company is not reduced where an
  amount is apportioned as a result of a distribution made under TA 1988 s 209(4)).
Definitions—''Asset'', s 21(1); ''close company'', s 288(1), TA 1988 ss 414, 415; ''company'', ss 99, 288(1); ''issued'',
  s 288(5); ''market value'', ss 272–274, Sch 11; ''shares'', s 288(1).
Cross references—See TCGA 1992 s 239(3) (application of sub-s (1) of this section to disposals by a close company to trustees
  of an employee trust).

CHAPTER II
REORGANISATION OF SHARE CAPITAL, CONVERSION OF SECURITIES
ETC

Concession D27—Earn outs.
Cross references—FA 2000 Sch 15 para 88 (this Chapter applies subject to FA 2000 Sch 15 paras 80–82, 84 in respect of the corporate venturing scheme).

Reorganisation or reduction of share capital

126 Application of sections 127 to 131

(1) For the purposes of this section and sections 127 to 131 ''reorganisation'' means a reorganisation or reduction of a company's share capital, and in relation to the reorganisation—

(a) ''original shares'' means shares held before and concerned in the reorganisation,

(b) ''new holding'' means, in relation to any original shares, the shares in and debentures of the company which as a result of the reorganisation represent the original shares (including such, if any, of the original shares as remain).

(2) The reference in subsection (1) above to the reorganisation of a company's share capital includes—

(a) any case where persons are, whether for payment or not, allotted shares in or debentures of the company in respect of and in proportion to (or as nearly as may be in proportion to) their holdings of shares in the company or of any class of shares in the company, and

(b) any case where there are more than one class of share and the rights attached to shares of any class are altered.

(3) The reference in subsection (1) above to a reduction of share capital does not include the paying off of redeemable share capital, and where shares in a company are redeemed by the company otherwise than by the issue of shares or debentures (with or without other consideration) and otherwise than in a liquidation, the shareholder shall be treated as disposing of the shares at the time of the redemption.

Commentary—*Simon's Direct Tax Service* C2.716.
Statement of Practice SP 4/94—Enhanced stock dividends received by trustees of interest in possession trusts.
Revenue Interpretation RI 74—Open offer treated as a share reorganisation.
Revenue Internal Guidance—Capital gains manual CG 51760–51766 (Revenue procedures relating to open offers and vendor placings).
Simon's Tax Cases—*Unilever (UK) Holdings Ltd v Smith (Inspector of Taxes)* [2002] STC 113.
s 126(1), *IRC v Burmah Oil Co Ltd* [1980] STC 731*; *Dunstan v Young Austen Young Ltd* [1989] STC 69*.
Definitions—''Class'' (of shares), s 288(1); ''company'', ss 99, 288(1); ''shares'', s 288(1).
Cross references—See TA 1988 s 305 (enterprise investment scheme: reorganisation of share capital);
TA 1988 s 473(2)(a) (conversion of securities held as trading stock by banks, insurance companies and dealers in securities);
Personal Equity Plan Regulations, SI 1989/469 reg 27(3) (ss 127–131 of this Act not to apply in relation to certain securities held under a PEP if there is by virtue of an allotment for payment within sub-s (2) above a reorganisation affecting those securities).
TCGA 1992 s 142 (certain issues of stock dividends in respect of shares held by bare trustees not to constitute a reorganisation for the purposes of this section).
TCGA 1992 s 150 (business expansion schemes).
TCGA 1992 s 150A (enterprise investment schemes).
TCGA 1992 s 192(2) (application of this section to company demergers).
FA 2000 Sch 8 para 116 (disapplication of ss 127–130—treatment of shares held in an employee share ownership plan acquired under certain circumstances under a rights issue).
FA 2000 Sch 15 para 81 (disapplication of ss 127–130 in relation to rights issues of shares qualifying for investment relief under the corporate venturing scheme).

127 Equation of original shares and new holding

Subject to sections 128 to 130, a reorganisation shall not be treated as involving any disposal of the original shares or any acquisition of the new holding or any part of it, but the original shares (taken as a single asset) and the new holding (taken as a single asset) shall be treated as the same asset acquired as the original shares were acquired.

Commentary—*Simon's Direct Tax Service* C2.715.
Statement of Practice SP 4/92—Capital gains rebasing elections.
Revenue Interpretation RI 36—Devolution on death of qualifying corporate bonds with a held over gain: circumstances in which the held over gain becomes chargeable.
Simon's Tax Cases—*Westcott v Woolcombers Ltd* [1987] STC 600*; *NAP Holdings UK Ltd v Whittles* [1994] STC 979*.
Definitions—''Asset'', s 21(1); ''new holding'', s 126(1); ''original shares'', s 126(1); ''reorganisation'', s 126(1); ''shares'', s 288(1).
Cross references—See TA 1988 s 305 (enterprise investment scheme: reorganisation of share capital);
TA 1988 s 473(2)(a) (conversion of securities held as trading stock by banks, insurance companies and dealers in securities);
TA 1988 s 757(1) (application of this section to disposals of material interest in offshore funds);
FA 1988 s 82(3) (unapproved employee share schemes).
Personal Equity Plan Regulations, SI 1989/469 reg 27(4) (disapplication of this section in relation to certain securities held under a PEP if there is by virtue of an allotment for payment within s 126(2) a reorganisation affecting those securities).
TCGA 1992 s 34 (transactions treated as a reorganisation of share capital).
TCGA 1992 s 102(2), (3) (collective investment schemes: exchange of rights by participants to constitute disposal and acquisition notwithstanding this section).
TCGA 1992 s 116 (modification of this section in relation to reorganisations, etc where the original holding consists of qualifying corporate bonds and the new holding does not or vice versa).

TCGA 1992 s 128(3) (reorganisations; disposal of original shares for consideration other than new holding; disposal treated as made by virtue of this section in consideration of a capital distribution; treatment of the capital distribution in relation to new holding).

TCGA 1992 s 131 (indexation allowance on a reorganisation).

TCGA 1992 s 132(1) (application of this section to conversions of securities).

TCGA 1992 s 135(3) (application of this section to certain share exchanges).

TCGA 1992 s 142 (certain issues of stock dividends in respect of shares held by bare trustees not to constitute a reorganisation for the purposes of this section).

TCGA 1992 s 150 (business expansion schemes).

TCGA 1992 s 150A (enterprise investment schemes).

TCGA 1992 s 150(6), (9) (business expansion scheme shares).

TCGA 1992 s 151B(2) (venture capital trust relief: where there is a share reorganisation within s 126, this section to apply separately to the shares (if any), so that there are separate holdings of different kinds of shares which are identified with new holdings).

TCGA 1992 s 151B(4) (disapplication of this section: venture capital trusts: reorganisation of share capital).

TCGA 1992 s 164F(7) (roll-over relief on re-investment of consideration received from disposal of shares and securities: carry-forward of relief into replacement shares: conditions for carry-forward).

TCGA 1992 s 171(3) (transfers within a group of companies after 14 March 1988).

TCGA 1992 s 192(2) (application of this section to company demergers).

TCGA 1992 Sch 6 para 2 (retirement relief on shares disposed of in reorganisation: election to disapply this section).

Exchange Gains and Losses (Alternative Method of Calculation of Gain or Loss) Regulations, SI 1994/3227 reg 9 (treatment of deferred gain or loss following a matching election).

FA 2000 Sch 8 para 116 (this section does not apply in certain circumstances where shares acquired under a rights issue conferred in respect of an employee share ownership plan).

FA 2000 Sch 14 para 58 (ss 127–130 do not apply to rights issues in respect of enterprise management incentive shares).

FA 2000 Sch 15 paras 80, 81, 93 (application/disapplication of this section in relation to the corporate venturing scheme).

128 Consideration given or received by holder

(1) Subject to subsection (2) below, where, on a reorganisation, a person gives or becomes liable to give any consideration for his new holding or any part of it, that consideration shall in relation to any disposal of the new holding or any part of it be treated as having been given for the original shares, and if the new holding or part of it is disposed of with a liability attaching to it in respect of that consideration, the consideration given for the disposal shall be adjusted accordingly.

(2) There shall not be treated as consideration given for the new holding or any part of it—

(*a*) any surrender, cancellation or other alteration of the original shares or of the rights attached thereto, or

(*b*) any consideration consisting of any application, in paying up the new holding or any part of it, of assets of the company or of any dividend or other distribution declared out of those assets but not made,

and, in the case of a reorganisation on or after 10th March 1981, any consideration given for the new holding or any part of it otherwise than by way of a bargain made at arm's length shall be disregarded to the extent that its amount or value exceeds the relevant increase in value; and for this purpose "the relevant increase in value" means the amount by which the market value of the new holding immediately after the reorganisation exceeds the market value of the original shares immediately before the reorganisation.

(3) Where on a reorganisation a person receives (or is deemed to receive), or becomes entitled to receive, any consideration, other than the new holding, for the disposal of an interest in the original shares, and in particular—

(*a*) where under section 122 he is to be treated as if he had in consideration of a capital distribution disposed of an interest in the original shares, or

(*b*) where he receives (or is deemed to receive) consideration from other shareholders in respect of a surrender of rights derived from the original shares,

he shall be treated as if the new holding resulted from his having for that consideration disposed of an interest in the original shares (but without prejudice to the original shares and the new holding being treated in accordance with section 127 as the same asset).

(4) Where for the purpose of subsection (3) above it is necessary in computing the gain or loss accruing on the disposal of the interest in the original shares mentioned in that subsection to apportion the cost of acquisition of the original shares between what is disposed of and what is retained, the apportionment shall be made in the like manner as under section 129.

Commentary—*Simon's Direct Tax Service* **C2.718.**

Revenue Interpretation RI 36—Devolution on death of qualifying corporate bonds with a held over gain: circumstances in which the held over gain becomes chargeable.

Revenue Internal Guidance—Capital gains manual CG 52042–52044 (Revenue procedures and example illustrating this section).

Simon's Tax Cases—*Unilever (UK) Holdings Ltd v Smith (Inspector of Taxes)* [2002] STC 113.

s 128(1), *IRC v Burmah Oil Co Ltd* [1982] STC 30*.

Definitions—"Asset", s 21(1); "company", ss 99, 288(1); "market value", ss 272–274, Sch 11; "new holding", s 126(1); "original shares", s 126(1); "reorganisation", s 126(1); "shares", s 288(1).

Cross references—TA 1988 s 305 (business expansion scheme: reorganisation of share capital; this section not to apply in relation to reorganisation after 18 March 1986 affecting ordinary shares if certain conditions exist);

TA 1988 s 473(2)(*a*) (conversion of securities held as trading stock by banks, insurance companies and dealers in securities);

TA 1988 s 763(6) (offshore income gains);

Personal Equity Plan Regulations, SI 1989/469 reg 27(4) (disapplication of this section in relation to certain securities held under a PEP if there is by virtue of an allotment for payment within s 126(2) a reorganisation affecting those securities).

TCGA 1992 s 34 (transactions treated as a reorganisation of share capital).

TCGA 1992 s 116 (modification of this section in relation to reorganisations, etc where the original holding consists of qualifying corporate bonds and the new holding does not or vice versa).
TCGA 1992 s 127 (in a reorganisation new shares exchanged for original shares to be treated as the same asset as the original shares).
TCGA 1992 s 132(1) (application of this section to conversions of securities).
TCGA 1992 s 135(3) (application of this section to certain share exchanges).
TCGA 1992 s 141 (application of this section to issues of stock dividends).
TCGA 1992 s 142 (certain issues of stock dividends in respect of shares held by bare trustees not to constitute a reorganisation for the purposes of this section).
TCGA 1992 s 150(9) (business expansion scheme shares).
TCGA 1992 s 150A (enterprise investment schemes).
TCGA 1992 s 151B(4) (disapplication of this section: venture capital trust: reorganisation of share capital).
TCGA 1992 s 192(2) (application of this section to company demergers).
FA 2000 Sch 8 para 116 (this section does not apply in certain circumstances where shares acquired under a rights issue conferred in respect of an employee share ownership plan).
FA 2000 Sch 14 para 58 (ss 127–130 do not apply to rights issues in respect of enterprise management incentive shares).
FA 2000 Sch 15 para 81 (ss 127–130 do not apply for an allotment of shares under a rights issues when the original holding, or the allotted shares, qualify for investment relief under the corporate venturing scheme).

129 Part disposal of new holding

Subject to section 130(2), where for the purpose of computing the gain or loss accruing to a person from the acquisition and disposal of any part of the new holding it is necessary to apportion the cost of acquisition of any of the original shares between what is disposed of and what is retained, the apportionment shall be made by reference to market value at the date of the disposal (with such adjustment of the market value of any part of the new holding as may be required to offset any liability attaching thereto but forming part of the cost to be apportioned).

Commentary—*Simon's Direct Tax Service* C2.722.
Revenue Interpretation RI 36—Devolution on death of qualifying corporate bonds with a held over gain: circumstances in which the held over gain becomes chargeable.
Revenue Internal Guidance—Capital gains manual CG 51892–51895 (Revenue procedures and example illustrating this section).
Definitions—"Market value", ss 272–274, Sch 11; "new holding", s 126(1); "original shares", s 126(1); "part disposal", s 21(2); "shares", s 288(1).
Cross references—TA 1988 s 305 (business expansion scheme: reorganisation of share capital; this section not to apply in relation to reorganisation after 18 March 1986 affecting ordinary shares if certain conditions exist);
TA 1988 s 473(2)(a) (conversion of securities held as trading stock by banks, insurance companies and dealers in securities);
Personal Equity Plan Regulations, SI 1989/469 reg 27(4) (disapplication of this section in relation to certain securities held under a PEP if there is by virtue of an allotment for payment within s 126(2) a reorganisation affecting those securities).
TCGA 1992 s 116 (modification of this section in relation to reorganisations, etc where the original holding consists of qualifying corporate bonds and the new holding does not or vice versa).
TCGA 1992 s 127 (in a reorganisation new shares exchanged for original shares to be treated as the same asset as the original shares).
TCGA 1992 s 132(1) (application of this section to conversions of securities).
TCGA 1992 s 135(3) (application of this section to certain share exchanges).
TCGA 1992 s 150 (business expansion schemes).
TCGA 1992 s 150(9) (business expansion scheme shares).
TCGA 1992 s 150A (enterprise investment schemes).
TCGA 1992 s 151B(4) (disapplication of this section: venture capital trust: reorganisation of share capital).
TCGA 1992 s 192(2) (application of this section to company demergers).
FA 2000 Sch 8 para 116 (this section does not apply in certain circumstances where shares acquired under a rights issue conferred in respect of an employee share ownership plan).
FA 2000 Sch 14 para 58 (ss 127–130 do not apply to rights issues in respect of enterprise management incentive shares).
FA 2000 Sch 15 para 81 (ss 127–130 do not apply for an allotment of shares under a rights issues when the original holding, or the allotted shares, qualify for investment relief under the corporate venturing scheme).

130 Composite new holdings

(1) This section shall apply to a new holding—

(a) if it consists of more than one class of shares in or debentures of the company and one or more of those classes is of shares or debentures which, at any time not later than the end of the period of 3 months beginning with the date on which the reorganisation took effect, or of such longer period as the Board may by notice allow, had quoted market values on a recognised stock exchange in the United Kingdom or elsewhere, or

(b) if it consists of more than one class of rights of unit holders and one or more of those classes is of rights the prices of which were published daily by the managers of the scheme at any time not later than the end of that period of 3 months (or longer if so allowed).

(2) Where for the purpose of computing the gain or loss accruing to a person from the acquisition and disposal of the whole or any part of any class of shares or debentures or rights of unit holders forming part of a new holding to which this section applies it is necessary to apportion costs of acquisition between what is disposed of and what is retained, the cost of acquisition of the new holding shall first be apportioned between the entire classes of shares or debentures or rights of which it consists by reference to market value on the first day (whether that day fell before the reorganisation took effect or later) on which market values or prices were quoted or published for the shares, debentures or rights as mentioned in subsection (1)(a) or (1)(b) above (with such adjustment of the market value of any class as may be required to offset any liability attaching thereto but forming part of the cost to be apportioned).

(3) For the purposes of this section the day on which a reorganisation involving the allotment of shares or debentures or unit holders' rights takes effect is the day following the day on which the right to renounce any allotment expires.

Commentary—*Simon's Direct Tax Service* **C2.722**.
Statement of Practice SP 4/92—Capital gains rebasing elections.
Revenue Interpretation RI 36—Devolution on death of qualifying corporate bonds with a held over gain: circumstances in which the held over gain becomes chargeable.
Definitions—"The Board", s 288(1); "class" (of shares), s 288(1); "company", ss 99, 288(1); "market value", ss 272–274, Sch 11; "new holding", s 126(1); "notice", s 288(1); "quoted on UK stock exchange", s 288(4); "recognised stock exchange", s 288(1), TA 1988 s 841; "reorganisation", s 126(1); "shares", s 288(1).
Cross references—TA 1988 s 305 (business expansion scheme; reorganisation of share capital; this section not to apply in relation to reorganisation after 18 March 1986 affecting ordinary shares if certain conditions exist);
TA 1988 s 473(2)(a) (conversion of securities held as trading stock by banks, insurance companies and dealers in securities);
Personal Equity Plan Regulations, SI 1989/469 reg 27(4) (disapplication of this section in relation to certain securities held under a PEP if there is by virtue of an allotment for payment within s 126(2) a reorganisation affecting those securities).
TCGA 1992 s 116 (modification of this section in relation to reorganisations, etc where the original holding consists of qualifying corporate bonds and the new holding does not or vice versa).
TCGA 1992 s 127 (in a reorganisation new shares exchanged for original shares to be treated as the same asset as the original shares).
TCGA 1992 s 132(1) (application of this section to conversions of securities).
TCGA 1992 s 135(3) (application of this section to certain share exchanges).
TCGA 1992 s 150 (business expansion schemes).
TCGA 1992 s 150(9) (business expansion scheme shares).
TCGA 1992 s 150A (enterprise investment schemes).
TCGA 1992 s 151B(4) (disapplication of this section: venture capital trust: reorganisation of share capital).
TCGA 1992 s 192(2) (application of this section to company demergers).
FA 2000 Sch 8 para 116 (this section does not apply in certain circumstances where shares acquired under a rights issue conferred in respect of an employee share ownership plan).
FA 2000 Sch 14 para 58 (ss 127–130 do not apply to rights issues in respect of enterprise management incentive shares).
FA 2000 Sch 15 para 81 (ss 127–130 do not apply for an allotment of shares under a rights issues when the original holding, or the allotted shares, qualify for investment relief under the corporate venturing scheme).

131 Indexation allowance

(1) This section applies where—

(a) by virtue of section 127, on a reorganisation the original shares (taken as a single asset) and the new holding (taken as a single asset) fall to be treated as the same asset acquired as the original shares were acquired; and

(b) on the reorganisation, a person gives or becomes liable to give any consideration for his new holding or any part of it.

(2) Where this section applies, so much of the consideration referred to in subsection (1)(b) above as, on a disposal to which section 53 applies of the new holding, will, by virtue of section 128(1), be treated as having been given for the original shares, shall be treated for the purposes of section 54 as an item of relevant allowable expenditure incurred not at the time the original shares were acquired but at the time the person concerned gave or became liable to give the consideration (and, accordingly, section 54(4) shall not apply in relation to that item of expenditure).

Commentary— *Simon's Direct Tax Service* **C2.718**.
Definitions—"Asset", s 21(1); "indexation allowance", s 53; "new holding", s 126(1); "original shares", s 126(1); "reorganisation", s 126(1); "shares", s 288(1).
Cross references—See Personal Equity Plan Regulations, SI 1989/469 reg 27(4) (disapplication of this section in relation to certain securities held under a PEP if there is by virtue of an allotment for payment within s 126(2) a reorganisation affecting those securities).
TCGA 1992 s 132(1) (this section to apply with necessary adaptation in relation to conversion of securities).
TCGA 1992 s 135(3) (this section to apply with necessary adaptations in relation to company reconstructions and amalgamations).

Conversion of securities

Cross reference—See the European Single Currency (Taxes) Regulations, SI 1998/3177 regs 36–38 (a euroconversion of currency is not treated as involving any disposal of the original currency or any acquisition of the new euro holding).

132 Equation of converted securities and new holding

(1) Sections 127 to 131 shall apply with any necessary adaptations in relation to the conversion of securities as they apply in relation to a reorganisation (that is to say, a reorganisation or reduction of a company's share capital).

(2) This section has effect subject to sections 133 and 134.

(3) For the purposes of this section and section 133—

(a) "conversion of securities" includes [any of the following, whether effected by a transaction or occurring in consequence of the operation of the terms of any security or of any debenture which is not a security, that is to say][1]—

(i) a conversion of securities of a company into shares in the company, and
[(ia) a conversion of a security which is not a qualifying corporate bond into a security of the same company which is such a bond, and
(ib) a conversion of a qualifying corporate bond into a security which is a security of the same company but is not such a bond, and][1].

(ii) a conversion at the option of the holder of the securities converted as an alternative to the redemption of those securities for cash, and

(iii) any exchange of securities effected in pursuance of any enactment (including an enactment passed after this Act) which provides for the compulsory acquisition of any shares or securities and the issue of securities or other securities instead,

(b) ''security'' includes any loan stock or similar security whether of the Government of the United Kingdom or of any other government, or of any public or local authority in the United Kingdom or elsewhere, or of any company, and whether secured or unsecured.

[(4) In subsection (3)(a)(ia) above the reference to the conversion of a security of a company into a qualifying corporate bond includes a reference to—

(a) any such conversion of a debenture of that company that is deemed to be a security for the purposes of section 251 as produces a security of that company which is a qualifying corporate bond; and

(b) any such conversion of a security of that company, or of a debenture that is deemed to be a security for those purposes, as produces a debenture of that company which, when deemed to be a security for those purposes, is such a bond.]¹

[(5) In subsection (3)(a)(ib) above the reference to the conversion of a qualifying corporate bond into a security of the same company which is not such a bond includes a reference to any conversion of a qualifying corporate bond which produces a debenture which—

(a) is not a security; and

(b) when deemed to be a security for the purposes of section 251, is not such a bond.]¹

Commentary—*Simon's Direct Tax Service* **C2.724.**
Revenue & other press releases—CCAB June 1969 (definition of ''security'' is regarded as exhaustive, TCGA 1992 s 132(3)(b); ''loan stock'' implies a general class of debt the holdings in which are transferable by purchase or sale).
Simon's Tax Cases—*Tarmac Roadstone Holdings Ltd v Williams* [1996] STC (SCD) 409*; *Taylor Clark International Ltd v Lewis* [1998] STC 1259*.
s 132(3)(b), *W T Ramsay Ltd v IRC* [1981] STC 174*.
Definitions—''Company'', ss 99, 288(1); ''local authority'' s 288(1), TA 1988 s 842A; ''qualifying corporate bond'', s 117; ''shares'', s 288(1).
Cross references—TA 1988 s 473(2)(a) (conversion of securities held as trading stock by banks, insurance companies and dealers in securities);
TCGA 1992 s 106(12) (s 106 (disposal of shares and securities by company within prescribed period of acquisitions) to apply to securities defined in this section).
TCGA 1992 s 118(2) (provisions which apply where securities to which this section applies include deep discount securities).
TCGA 1992 s 134(2) (gilt-edged securities issued in exchange for original securities on nationalisation).
TCGA 1992 s 251(2) (subject to this section, satisfaction of a debt to be treated as disposal of it by the creditor at the time when it is satisfied).
Amendments—¹ Words in sub-s (3)(a), and sub-ss (3)(a)(ia), (ib), (4), (5), inserted by FA 1997 s 88(1), (2), (3), (6) with effect for the purposes of the application of this Act in relation to any disposal after 25 November 1996 and so as to have effect, where a conversion took place at a time before 26 November 1996, as if they had come into force before that time.

133 Premiums on conversion of securities

(1) This section applies where, on a conversion of securities, a person receives, or becomes entitled to receive, any sum of money (''the premium'') which is by way of consideration (in addition to his new holding) for the disposal of the converted securities.

(2) If ...¹ the premium is small, as compared with the value of the converted securities, ...¹—

(a) receipt of the premium shall not be treated for the purposes of this Act as a disposal of part of the converted securities, and

(b) the premium shall be deducted from any expenditure allowable under this Act as a deduction in computing a gain or loss on the disposal of the new holding by the person receiving or becoming entitled to receive the premium.

(3) ...¹

(4) Where the allowable expenditure is less than the premium (or is nil)—

(a) [subsection (2)]¹ above shall not apply, and

(b) if the recipient so elects (and there is any allowable expenditure)—

(i) the amount of the premium shall be reduced by the amount of the allowable expenditure, and

(ii) none of that expenditure shall be allowable as a deduction in computing a gain accruing on the occasion of the conversion, or on any subsequent occasion.

(5) In subsection (4) above ''allowable expenditure'' means expenditure which immediately before the conversion was attributable to the converted securities under paragraphs (a) and (b) of section 38(1).

Commentary—*Simon's Direct Tax Service* **C2.724.**
Revenue Interpretation RI 164—From 24 February 1997, the Revenue regard a receipt as ''small'' wherever its amount or value is £3,000 or less, whether or not it would also meet the 5% test (see Revenue Internal Guidance below).
Revenue Internal Guidance—Capital gains manual CG 55031 (the Revenue regard ''small'' as meaning 5% or less of the value of the converted securities before the conversions). See now also Revenue Interpretation RI 164 above.
Definitions—''Conversion of securities'', s 132; ''securities'', s 132.
Cross references—See TA 1988 s 473(2)(a) (conversion of securities held as trading stock by banks, insurance companies and dealers in securities).

TCGA 1992 Sch 3 para 4(2) (application of this section where TCGA 1992 s 35(2) (rebasing) applies in relation to the disposal of an asset).

Amendments—[1] Words in italics in sub-s (2) repealed, whole of sub-s (3) repealed and words in sub-s (4)(*a*) substituted by FA 1996 s 134(1), (2), Sch 20 para 53, Sch 41 Pt V(10) with effect from the year 1996–97 and, for the purposes of corporation tax, as respects accounting periods ending after 30 June 1999 (by virtue of Finance Act 1994, Section 199, (Appointed Day) Order, SI 1998/3173 art 2).

[133A Cash payments received on euroconversion of securities

(1) This section applies where, under a euroconversion of a security that does not involve a disposal of the security and accordingly is not a conversion of securities within section 132(3)(*a*), a person receives, or becomes entitled to receive, any sum of money (''the cash payment'').

(2) If the cash payment is small, as compared with the value of the security concerned—

(*a*) receipt of the cash payment shall not be treated for the purposes of this Act as a disposal of part of the security, and

(*b*) the cash payment shall be deducted from any expenditure allowable under this Act as a deduction in computing a gain or a loss on a disposal of the security by the person receiving or becoming entitled to receive the cash payment.

(3) Where the allowable expenditure is less than the cash payment (or is nil)—

(*a*) subsection (2) above shall not apply, and

(*b*) if the recipient so elects (and there is any allowable expenditure)—

    (i) the amount of the cash payment shall be reduced by the amount of the allowable expenditure, and

    (ii) none of that expenditure shall be allowable as a deduction in computing a gain accruing on the occasion of the euroconversion or on any subsequent occasion.

(4) In this section—

(*a*) ''allowable expenditure'' means expenditure which immediately before the euroconversion was attributable to the security under paragraphs (*a*) and (*b*) of section 38(1);

(*b*) ''euroconversion'' has the meaning given by regulation 3 of the European Single Currency (Taxes) Regulations 1998.][1]

Commentary—*Simon's Direct Tax Service* C2.724.
Regulations—European Single Currency (Taxes) Regulations SI 1998/3177.
Amendment—[1]This section inserted by the European Single Currency (Taxes) Regulations, SI 1998/3177 reg 39 with effect from 1 January 1999.

134 Compensation stock

(1) This section has effect where gilt-edged securities are exchanged for shares in pursuance of any enactment (including an enactment passed after this Act) which provides for the compulsory acquisition of any shares and the issue of gilt-edged securities instead.

(2) The exchange shall not constitute a conversion of securities within section 132 and shall be treated as not involving any disposal of the shares by the person from whom they were compulsorily acquired but—

(*a*) there shall be calculated the gain or loss that would have accrued to him if he had then disposed of the shares for a consideration equal to the value of the shares as determined for the purpose of the exchange, and

(*b*) on a subsequent disposal of the whole or part of the gilt-edged securities by the person to whom they were issued—

    (i) there shall be deemed to accrue to him the whole or a corresponding part of the gain or loss mentioned in paragraph (*a*) above, and

    (ii) section 115(1) shall not have effect in relation to any gain or loss that is deemed to accrue as aforesaid.

(3) Where a person to whom gilt-edged securities of any kind were issued as mentioned in subsection (1) above disposes of securities of that kind, the securities of which he disposes—

(*a*) shall, so far as possible, be identified with securities which were issued to him as mentioned in subsection (1) above rather than with other securities of that kind, and

(*b*) subject to paragraph (*a*) above, shall be identified with securities issued at an earlier time rather than those issued at a later time.

(4) Subsection (2)(*b*) above shall not apply to any disposal falling within the provisions of section 58(1), 62(4) or 171(1) but a person who has acquired the securities on a disposal falling within those provisions (and without there having been a previous disposal not falling within those provisions or a devolution on death) shall be treated for the purposes of subsections (2)(*b*) and (3) above as if the securities had been issued to him.

(5) Where the gilt-edged securities to be exchanged for any shares are not issued until after the date on which the shares are compulsorily acquired but on that date a right to the securities is granted, this section shall have effect as if the exchange had taken place on that date, as if references to the issue of the securities and the person to whom they were issued were references to the grant of the

right and the person to whom it was granted and references to the disposal of the securities included references to disposals of the rights.

(6) In this section "shares" includes securities within the meaning of section 132.

(7) This section does not apply where the compulsory acquisition took place before 7th April 1976.

Commentary—*Simon's Direct Tax Service* C2.807.
Definitions—"Gilt-edged securities", Sch 9 para 1, Sch 11 para 15; "issued", s 288(5); "shares", s 288(1).
Cross references—See TA 1988 s 473(2)(*b*) (conversion of securities held as trading stock by banks, insurance companies and dealers in securities).
TCGA 1992 Sch 4 para 4 (reduction of deferred charge to tax in respect of a gain accruing on the disposal before 6 April 1988 of an asset acquired before 31 March 1982 where the gain crystallises after 5 April 1988).

Company reconstructions ...[1]

Amendments—[1] Words "and amalgamations" repealed by FA 2002 s 141, Sch 40 Pt 3(2) with effect in accordance with FA 2002 Sch 9 paras 7, 8.

[135 Exchange of securities for those in another company

(1) This section applies in the following circumstances where a company ("company B") issues shares or debentures to a person in exchange for shares in or debentures of another company ("company A").

(2) The circumstances are:

Case 1

Where company B holds, or in consequence of the exchange will hold, more than 25% of the ordinary share capital of company A.

Case 2

Where company B issues the shares or debentures in exchange for shares as the result of a general offer—

(*c*) made to members of company A or any class of them (with or without exceptions for persons connected with company B), and
(*d*) made in the first instance on a condition such that if it were satisfied company B would have control of company A.

Case 3

Where company B holds, or in consequence of the exchange will hold, the greater part of the voting power in company A.

(3) Where this section applies, sections 127 to 131 (share reorganisations etc) apply with the necessary adaptations as if company A and company B were the same company and the exchange were a reorganisation of its share capital.

(4) In this section "ordinary share capital" has the meaning given by section 832(1) of the Taxes Act and also includes—

(*a*) in relation to a unit trust scheme, any rights that are treated by section 99(1)(*b*) of this Act (application of Act to unit trust schemes) as shares in a company, and
(*b*) in relation to a company that has no share capital, any interests in the company possessed by members of the company.

(5) This section applies in relation to a company that has no share capital as if references to shares in or debentures of the company included any interests in the company possessed by members of the company.

(6) This section has effect subject to section 137(1) (exchange must be for bona fide commercial reasons and not part of tax avoidance scheme).][1]

Commentary—*Simon's Direct Tax Service* C2.726, 727.
Concession D52—Incidental costs of acquisition and warranty payments attributable to new holding of shares or debentures following a share exchange, company amalgamation or reconstruction may be treated as consideration given for the shares etc.
Revenue Interpretation RI 224—Circumstances in which Delaware Limited Liability Companies (DLLCs) can be regarded as issuing "ordinary share capital" for the purposes of TCGA 1992 ss 135, 136.
Revenue & other press releases—ICAEW TR657 10-4-87 (applications for clearance under s 138 include consideration of whether the tests in s 137(1) are satisfied, but not the applicability of s 135. Revenue may indicate cases in which it is apparent that s 135 will not apply).
Revenue Internal Guidance—Capital gains manual CG 45550–45570 (interaction with s 171; discussion of the *Woolcombers* case and the *NAP Holdings* case.)
Simon's Tax Cases—*Floor v Davis* [1978] STC 436*; *NAP Holdings UK Ltd v Whittles* [1994] STC 979*.
s 135(1), *Floor v Davis* [1976] STC 475*; *Furniss v Dawson* [1982] STC 267*.
s 135(3), *Furniss v Dawson* [1982] STC 267*; *Westcott v Woolcombers Ltd* [1987] STC 600*.
Definitions—"Company", ss 99, 288(1); "connected", s 286; "shares", s 288(1); "the Taxes Act", s 288(1).
Cross references—See TA 1988 s 473(2)(*a*) (conversion of securities held as trading stock by banks, insurance companies and dealers in securities);
TA 1988 s 757(5) (disposals of material interest in offshore funds);
FA 1989 s 69(3A) (chargeable events as regards employee share ownership trusts).

TCGA 1992 s 31(6)(*b*) (exchange of securities under this section may constitute chargeable profits for the purposes of s 31 (value shifting)).
TCGA 1992 s 34 (transactions treated as a reorganisation of share capital).
TCGA 1992 s 118(2) (provisions which apply where securities including deep discount securities are exchanged in circumstances in which sub-s (3) above applies).
TCGA 1992 s 137 (restrictions on application of this section).
TCGA 1992 s 138(1) (advance clearance).
TCGA 1992 s 138A (use of earn-out rights for exchange of securities).
TCGA 1992 s 150(8)–(8C) (business expansion scheme shares).
TCGA 1992 s 150A (enterprise investment schemes).
TCGA 1992 s 151B(5) (this section not to apply where shares in a venture capital trust, eligible for relief under s 151A(1), are exchanged, or treated as exchanged, for shares other than ordinary shares in a venture capital trust).
TCGA 1992 s 171(3) (transfers within a group of companies after 14 March 1988).
TCGA 1992 s 251(2) (subject to this section, satisfaction of a debt to be treated as disposal of it by the creditor at the time when it is satisfied).
TCGA 1992 Sch 6 para 2(2) (retirement relief entitlement on company reorganisation within the meaning of sub-s (3) above).
FA 2000 Sch 15 para 82 (this section does not apply in respect of shares to which investment relief under the corporate venturing scheme is attributable, subject to FA 2000 Sch 15 para 84 (no disposal on certain exchanges of shares)).
Amendments—¹ Section substituted by FA 2002 s 45, Sch 9 paras 1, 7 with effect for shares or debentures issued after 16 April 2002. The reference to shares or debentures includes any interests falling to be treated as shares or debentures for the purposes of TCGA 1992 s 135 or 136 as substituted by FA 2002 Sch 9 paras 1, 2. Section 135 previously read as follows—

"135 Exchange of securities for those in another company

(1) Subsection (3) below has effect where a company ("company A") issues shares or debentures to a person in exchange for shares in or debentures of another company ("company B") and—

(*a*) company A holds, or in consequence of the exchange will hold, more than one-quarter of the ordinary share capital (as defined in section 832(1) of the Taxes Act) of company B, or
(*b*) company A issues the shares or debentures in exchange for shares as the result of a general offer—

  (i) which is made to members of company B or any class of them (with or without exceptions for persons connected with company A), and
  (ii) which is made in the first instance on a condition such that if it were satisfied company A would have control of company B,
  or

(*c*) company A holds, or in consequence of the exchange will hold, the greater part of the voting power in company B.
(2) Subsection (3) below also has effect where under section 136 persons are to be treated as exchanging shares or debentures held by them in consequence of the arrangement there mentioned.

(3) Subject to sections 137 and 138, sections 127 to 131 shall apply with any necessary adaptations as if the 2 companies mentioned in subsection (1) above or, as the case may be, in section 136 were the same company and the exchange were a reorganisation of its share capital."

[136 Scheme of reconstruction involving issue of securities

(1) This section applies where—

(*a*) an arrangement between a company ("company A") and—

  (i) the persons holding shares in or debentures of the company, or
  (ii) where there are different classes of shares in or debentures of the company, the persons holding any class of those shares or debentures,

is entered into for the purposes of, or in connection with, a scheme of reconstruction, and
(*b*) under the arrangement—

  (i) another company ("company B") issues shares or debentures to those persons in respect of and in proportion to (or as nearly as may be in proportion to) their relevant holdings in company A, and
  (ii) the shares in or debentures of company A comprised in relevant holdings are retained by those persons or are cancelled or otherwise extinguished.

(2) Where this section applies—

(*a*) those persons are treated as exchanging their relevant holdings in company A for the shares or debentures held by them in consequence of the arrangement, and
(*b*) sections 127 to 131 (share reorganisations etc) apply with the necessary adaptations as if company A and company B were the same company and the exchange were a reorganisation of its share capital.

For this purpose shares in or debentures of company A comprised in relevant holdings that are retained are treated as if they had been cancelled and replaced by a new issue.

(3) Where a reorganisation of the share capital of company A is carried out for the purposes of the scheme of reconstruction, the provisions of subsections (1) and (2) apply in relation to the position after the reorganisation.

(4) In this section—

(*a*) "scheme of reconstruction" has the meaning given by Schedule 5AA to this Act;
(*b*) references to "relevant holdings" of shares in or debentures of company A are—

  (i) where there is only one class of shares in or debentures of the company, to holdings of shares in or debentures of the company, and
  (ii) where there are different classes of shares in or debentures of the company, to holdings of a class of shares or debentures that is involved in the scheme of reconstruction (within the meaning of paragraph 2 of Schedule 5AA);

(*c*) references to shares or debentures being retained include their being retained with altered rights or in an altered form, whether as the result of reduction, consolidation, division or otherwise; and

(*d*) any reference to a reorganisation of a company's share capital is to a reorganisation within the meaning of section 126.

(5) This section applies in relation to a company that has no share capital as if references to shares in or debentures of the company included any interests in the company possessed by members of the company.

(6) This section has effect subject to section 137(1) (scheme of reconstruction must be for bona fide commercial reasons and not part of tax avoidance scheme).]¹

Commentary—*Simon's Direct Tax Service* C2.726, 727.
Concession D52—Incidental costs of acquisition and warranty payments attributable to new holding of shares or debentures following a share exchange, company amalgamation or reconstruction may be treated as consideration given for the shares etc.

Statement of Practice SP2/99—Application of this section in respect of disposals of shares or units in investment funds acquired before 6 April 1999 through monthly savings schemes with an AUT, AIT or OEID whose business is transferred to or merged with another trust or company.
Revenue Interpretation RI 35—Relief under this section is available for reconstruction schemes under the Companies Act 1985 s 425.
RI 39—New holding of securities on reconstruction or amalgamation consisting partly of qualifying corporate bonds.
RI 224—Circumstances in which Delaware Limited Liability Companies (DLLCs) can be regarded as issuing "ordinary share capital" for the purposes of TCGA 1992 ss 135, 136.
Simon's Tax Cases—*Fallon and anor (executors of Morgan, decd) v Fellows (Inspector of Taxes)* [2001] STC 1409*.
Definitions—"Company", ss 99, 288(1); "shares", s 288(1); "scheme of reconstruction", Sch 5AA.
Cross references—See TA 1988 s 473(2)(*a*) (conversion of securities held as trading stock by banks, insurance companies and dealers in securities);
TA 1988 s 757(5) (reconstruction etc after 31 December 1984 involving transactions whereby interests in non-qualifying offshore funds are exchanged for assets which are not non-qualifying offshore funds);
TCGA 1992 s 34 (transactions treated as a reorganisation of share capital).
TCGA 1992 s 118(2) (provisions which apply where securities including deep discount securities are by virtue of sub-s (1) above treated as exchanged in certain circumstances).
TCGA 1992 s 137 (restrictions on application of this section).
TCGA 1992 s 138(1) (advance clearance).
TCGA 1992 s 150(8)–(8C) (business expansion scheme shares).
TCGA 1992 s 150A (enterprise investment schemes).
TCGA 1992 s 151B(5) (this section not to apply where shares in a venture capital trust eligible for relief under s 151A(1) are exchanged, or treated as exchanged, for shares other than ordinary shares in a venture capital trust).
FA 2000 Sch 15 para 82 (this section does not apply in respect of shares to which investment relief under corporate venturing scheme is attributable, subject to FA 2000 Sch 15 para 84 (no disposal on certain exchanges of shares)).
Amendments—¹ Section substituted by FA 2002 s 45, Sch 9 paras 2, 7 with effect for shares or debentures issued after 16 April 2002. The reference to shares or debentures includes any interests falling to be treated as shares or debentures for the purposes of TCGA 1992 s 135 or 136 as substituted by FA 2002 Sch 9 paras 1, 2. Section 136 previously read as follows—

"136 Reconstruction or amalgamation involving issue of securities

(1) Where—

(*a*) an arrangement between a company and the persons holding shares in or debentures of the company, or any class of such shares or debentures, is entered into for the purposes of or in connection with a scheme of reconstruction or amalgamation, and
(*b*) under the arrangement another company issues shares or debentures to those persons in respect of and in proportion to (or as nearly as may be in proportion to) their holdings of shares in or debentures of the first-mentioned company, but the shares in or debentures of the first-mentioned company are either retained by those persons or cancelled,

then those persons shall be treated as exchanging the first-mentioned shares or debentures for those held by them in consequence of the arrangement (any shares or debentures retained being for this purpose regarded as if they had been cancelled and replaced by a new issue), and subsections (2) and (3) of section 135 shall apply accordingly.

(2) In this section "scheme of reconstruction or amalgamation" means a scheme for the reconstruction of any company or companies or the amalgamation of any 2 or more companies, and references to shares or debentures being retained include their being retained with altered rights or in an altered form whether as the result of reduction, consolidation, division or otherwise.

(3) This section, and section 135(2), shall apply in relation to a company which has no share capital as if references to shares in or debentures of a company included references to any interests in the company possessed by members of the company."

137 Restriction on application of sections 135 and 136

(1) Subject to subsection (2) below, and section 138, neither section 135 nor section 136 shall apply to any issue by a company of shares in or debentures of that company in exchange for or in respect of shares in or debentures of another company unless the exchange [or scheme of reconstruction]³ in question is effected for bona fide commercial reasons and does not form part of a scheme or arrangements of which the main purpose, or one of the main purposes, is avoidance of liability to capital gains tax or corporation tax.

(2) Subsection (1) above shall not affect the operation of section 135 or 136 in any case where the person to whom the shares or debentures are issued does not hold more than 5 per cent of, or of any class of, the shares in or debentures of the second company mentioned in subsection (1) above.

(3) For the purposes of subsection (2) above shares or debentures held by persons connected with the person there mentioned shall be treated as held by him.

(4) If any tax assessed on a person (the chargeable person) by virtue of subsection (1) above is not paid within 6 months from [the date determined under subsection (4A) below]¹, any other person who—

(*a*) holds all or any part of the shares or debentures that were issued to the chargeable person, and (*b*) has acquired them without there having been, since their acquisition by the chargeable person, any disposal of them not falling within section 58(1) or 171,

may, at any time within 2 years from [that date][1], be assessed and charged (in the name of the chargeable person) to all or, as the case may be, a corresponding part of the unpaid tax; and a person paying any amount of tax under this subsection shall be entitled to recover [from the chargeable person a sum equal to that amount together with any interest paid by him under section 87A of the Management Act on that amount][1].

[(4A) The date referred to in subsection (4) above is whichever is the later of—

   (*a*) the date when the tax becomes due and payable by the chargeable person; and

   (*b*) the date when the assessment was made on the chargeable person.][2]

(5) (*amends* sub-s (4) and *inserts* sub-s (4A))

(6) In this section references to shares or debentures include references to any interests or options to which this Chapter applies by virtue of [section 135(5), 136(5)][3] or 147.

Commentary—*Simon's Direct Tax Service* **C2.726, 727.**
Revenue & other press releases—ICAEW TR657 10-4-87 (applications for clearance under s 138 include consideration of whether the tests in s 137(1) are satisfied, but not the applicability of s 135. Revenue may indicate cases in which it is apparent that s 135 will not apply).
Simon's Tax Cases—s 137(1), *Young v Phillips* [1984] STC 520*.
Definitions—"Chargeable gain", s 15(2); "chargeable period", s 288(1); "class" (of shares), s 288(1); "company", ss 99, 288(1); "connected", s 286; "issued", s 288(5); "the Management Act", s 288(1); "shares", s 288(1).
Cross references—See TA 1988 s 473(7) (reference in sub-s (1) of this section to capital gains tax to be construed as a reference to income tax for determining whether conversion of certain securities would result in the original holding being equated with a new holding).
Amendments—[1] Words in sub-s (4) substituted by virtue of sub-s (5) with respect to chargeable gains accruing in chargeable periods ending after 30 September 1993 by virtue of Corporation Tax Acts (Provisions for Payment of Tax and Returns) (Appointed Days) Order, SI 1992/3066 art 2(1), (2)(*d*).
[2] Sub-s (4A) inserted by virtue of sub-s (5) with respect to chargeable gains accruing in chargeable periods ending after 30 September 1993 by virtue of Corporation Tax Acts (Provisions for Payment of Tax and Returns) (Appointed Days) Order, SI 1992/3066 art 2(1), (2)(*d*).
[3] In sub-s (1), words substituted for the words ", reconstruction and amalgamation", and in sub-s (6), words substituted for the words "section 136(3)", by FA 2002 s 45, Sch 9 paras 5(1), (5), 7 with effect for shares or debentures issued after 16 April 2002. The reference to shares or debentures includes any interests falling to be treated as shares or debentures for the purposes of TCGA 1992 s 135 or 136 as substituted by FA 2002 Sch 9.

138 Procedure for clearance in advance

(1) Section 137 shall not affect the operation of section 135 or 136 in any case where, before the issue is made, the Board have, on the application of either company mentioned in section 137(1), notified the company that the Board are satisfied that the exchange [or scheme of reconstruction][1] will be effected for bona fide commercial reasons and will not form part of any such scheme or arrangements as are mentioned in section 137(1).

(2) Any application under subsection (1) above shall be in writing and shall contain particulars of the operations that are to be effected and the Board may, within 30 days of the receipt of the application or of any further particulars previously required under this subsection, by notice require the applicant to furnish further particulars for the purpose of enabling the Board to make their decision; and if any such notice is not complied with within 30 days or such longer period as the Board may allow, the Board need not proceed further on the application.

(3) The Board shall notify their decision to the applicant within 30 days of receiving the application or, if they give a notice under subsection (2) above, within 30 days of the notice being complied with.

(4) If the Board notify the applicant that they are not satisfied as mentioned in subsection (1) above or do not notify their decision to the applicant within the time required by subsection (3) above, the applicant may within 30 days of the notification or of that time require the Board to transmit the application, together with any notice given and further particulars furnished under subsection (2) above, to the Special Commissioners; and in that event any notification by the Special Commissioners shall have effect for the purposes of subsection (1) above as if it were a notification by the Board.

(5) If any particulars furnished under this section do not fully and accurately disclose all facts and considerations material for the decision of the Board or the Special Commissioners, any resulting notification that the Board or Commissioners are satisfied as mentioned in subsection (1) above shall be void.

Commentary—*Simon's Direct Tax Service* **C2.726, 727.**
Statement of Practice SP 13/80 Annex—Demergers: TA 1988 ss 213–218.
Revenue & other press releases—ICAEW TR 657 10-4-87 (Revenue considers applications for clearance under s 138 where consideration is in the form of short-dated stock on their merits, but does not normally refuse clearance in the case of short-dated stock with a life of more than six months. Applications for clearance include consideration of whether tests in s 137(1) are satisfied, but not the applicability of s 135. Revenue may indicate cases in which it is apparent s 135 will not apply).
Law Society 27-3-91 (clearance is normally sent by letter, but in cases of genuine urgency Revenue will consider faxing a copy to Somerset House for collection, or where the application is made from outside London, direct to the applicant).
Definitions—"The Board", s 288(1); "company", ss 99, 288(1); "notice", s 288(1).
Cross references—See TA 1988 s 444A(8) (transfer of long term business of an insurance company to another company in accordance with a scheme under the Insurance Companies Act 1982 Sch 2C Part I);
TCGA 1992 s 139(5) (procedural rules in this section to apply also in the case of an application for clearance that company reconstruction or amalgamation is for *bona fide* commercial reasons).

TCGA 1992 s 140B(3) (application of sub-ss (2)–(5) above for the purposes of s 140B(2) (transfer of UK trade by one member State company to another member State company)).

TCGA 1992 s 140D(3) (application of sub-ss (2)–(5) above for the purposes of s 140D(2) (transfer of non-UK trade by one member State company to another member State company)).

Amendments—[1] Words in sub-s (1) substituted for the words '', reconstruction or amalgamation'' in sub-s (1) by FA 2002 s 45, Sch 9 paras 5(1), (6), 7 with effect for shares or debentures issued after 16 April 2002. The reference to shares or debentures includes any interests falling to be treated as shares or debentures for the purposes of TCGA 1992 s 135 or 136 as substituted by FA 2002 Sch 9.

[138A Use of earn-out rights for exchange of securities.

(1) For the purposes of this section an earn-out right is so much of any right conferred on any person (''the seller'') as—

(a) constitutes the whole or any part of the consideration for the transfer by him of shares in or debentures of a company (''the old securities'');

(b) consists in a right to be issued with shares in or debentures of another company (''the new company'');

(c) is such that the value or quantity of the shares or debentures to be issued in pursuance of the right (''the new securities'') is unascertainable at the time when the right is conferred; and

(d) is not capable of being discharged in accordance with its terms otherwise than by the issue of the new securities.

(2) Where—

(a) there is an earn-out right,

(b) the exchange of the old securities for the earn-out right is an exchange to which section 135 would apply, in a manner unaffected by section 137, if the earn-out right were an ascertainable amount of shares in or debentures of the new company, and

(c) the seller elects under this section for the earn-out right to be treated as a security of the new company,

this Act shall have effect, in the case of the seller and every other person who from time to time has the earn-out right, in accordance with the assumptions specified in subsection (3) below.

(3) Those assumptions are—

(a) that the earn-out right is a security within the definition in section 132;

(b) that the security consisting in the earn-out right is a security of the new company and is incapable of being a qualifying corporate bond for the purposes of this Act;

(c) that references in this Act (including those in this section) to a debenture include references to a right that is assumed to be a security in accordance with paragraph (a) above; and

(d) that the issue of shares or debentures in pursuance of such a right constitutes the conversion of the right, in so far as it is discharged by the issue, into the shares or debentures that are issued.

(4) For the purposes of this section where—

(a) any right which is assumed, in accordance with this section, to be a security of a company ('the old right') is extinguished,

(b) the whole of the consideration for the extinguishment of the old right consists in another right ('the new right') to be issued with shares in or debentures of that company,

(c) the new right is such that the value or quantity of the shares or debentures to be issued in pursuance of the right ('the replacement securities') is unascertainable at the time when the old right is extinguished,

(d) the new right is not capable of being discharged in accordance with its terms otherwise than by the issue of the replacement securities, and

(e) the person on whom the new right is conferred elects under this section for it to be treated as a security of that company,

the assumptions specified in subsection (3) above shall have effect in relation to the new right, in the case of that person and every other person who from time to time has the new right, as they had effect in relation to the old right.

(5) An election under this section in respect of any right must be made, by a notice given to an officer of the Board—

(a) in the case of an election by a company within the charge to corporation tax, within the period of two years from the end of the accounting period in which the right is conferred; and

(b) in any other case, on or before the first anniversary of the 31st January next following the year of assessment in which that right is conferred.

(6) An election under this section shall be irrevocable.

(7) Subject to subsections (8) to (10) below, where any right to be issued with shares in or debentures of a company is conferred on any person, the value or quantity of the shares or debentures to be issued in pursuance of that right shall be taken for the purposes of this section to be unascertainable at a particular time if, and only if—

(a) it is made referable to matters relating to any business or assets of one or more relevant companies; and

(b) those matters are uncertain at that time on account of future business or future assets being included in the business or assets to which they relate.

(8) Where a right to be issued with shares or debentures is conferred wholly or partly in consideration for the transfer of other shares or debentures or the extinguishment of any right, the value and quantity of the shares or debentures to be issued shall not be taken for the purposes of this section to be unascertainable in any case where, if—

    (*a*) the transfer or extinguishment were a disposal, and

    (*b*) a gain on that disposal fell to be computed in accordance with this Act,

the shares or debentures to be issued would, in pursuance of section 48, be themselves regarded as, or as included in, the consideration for the disposal.

(9) Where any right to be issued with shares in or debentures of a company comprises an option to choose between shares in that company and debentures of that company, the existence of that option shall not, by itself, be taken for the purposes of this section either—

    (*a*) to make unascertainable the value or quantity of the shares or debentures to be issued; or

    (*b*) to prevent the requirements of subsection (1)(*b*) and (*d*) or (4)(*b*) and (*d*) above from being satisfied in relation to that right.

(10) For the purposes of this section the value or quantity of shares or debentures shall not be taken to be unascertainable by reason only that it has not been fixed if it will be fixed by reference to the other and the other is ascertainable.

(11) In subsection (7) above ''relevant company'', in relation to any right to be issued with shares in or debentures of a company, means—

    (*a*) that company or any company which is in the same group of companies as that company; or

    (*b*) the company for whose shares or debentures that right was or was part of the consideration, or any company in the same group of companies as that company;

and in this subsection the reference to a group of companies shall be construed in accordance with section 170(2) to (14).][1]

Commentary—*Simon's Direct Tax Service* **C2.727.**
Note—This section replaces extra-statutory concession D27.
Revenue Internal Guidance—Capital gains manual CG 58000–58206 (Revenue procedures and illustrative examples).
Definitions—''Accounting period'', TA 1988 s 834(1); ''the Board'', s 288(1); ''company'', s 288(1); ''notice'', s 288(1); ''qualifying corporate bond'', s 117; ''shares'', s 288(1); ''year of assessment'', s 288(1).
Cross references—See FA 2000 Sch 29 para 22 (the main amendments made to TCGA 1992 s 170 by FA 2000 Sch 29 para 1 have effect for the purposes of this section with effect for rights conferred after 31 March 2000).
Amendments—[1] This section inserted by FA 1997 s 89(1), (2) and is deemed always to have had effect, subject to FA 1997 s 87(3)–(8).

139 Reconstruction ...[6] involving transfer of business

(1) Subject to the provisions of this section, where—

    (*a*) any scheme of reconstruction ...[6] involves the transfer of the whole or part of a company's business to another company, and

    [(*b*) the conditions in subsection (1A) below are met in relation to the assets included in the transfer, and][4]

    (*c*) the first-mentioned company receives no part of the consideration for the transfer (otherwise than by the other company taking over the whole or part of the liabilities of the business),

then, so far as relates to corporation tax on chargeable gains, the 2 companies shall be treated as if any assets included in the transfer were acquired by the one company from the other company for a consideration of such amount as would secure that on the disposal by way of transfer neither a gain nor a loss would accrue to the company making the disposal, and for the purposes of Schedule 2 the acquiring company shall be treated as if the respective acquisitions of the assets by the other company had been the acquiring company's acquisition of them.

[(1A) The conditions referred to in subsection (1)(*b*) above are—

    (*a*) that the company acquiring the assets is resident in the United Kingdom at the time of the acquisition, or the assets are chargeable assets in relation to that company immediately after that time, and

    (*b*) that the company from which the assets are acquired is resident in the United Kingdom at the time of the acquisition, or the assets are chargeable assets in relation to that company immediately before that time.

For this purpose an asset is a ''chargeable asset'' in relation to a company at any time if, were the asset to be disposed of by the company at that time, any gain accruing to the company would be a chargeable gain and would by virtue of section 10(3) form part of its chargeable profits for corporation tax purposes.][4]

(2) This section does not apply in relation to an asset which, until the transfer, formed part of trading stock of a trade carried on by the company making the disposal, or in relation to an asset which is acquired as trading stock for the purposes of a trade carried on by the company acquiring the asset.

Section 170(1) applies for the purposes of this subsection.

(3) ...[2]

(4) This section does not apply in the case of a transfer of the whole or part of a company's business to a unit trust scheme to which section 100(2) applies or which is an authorised unit trust or to an investment trust [or a venture capital trust][3].

(5) This section does not apply unless the reconstruction ...[6] is effected for bona fide commercial reasons and does not form part of a scheme or arrangements of which the main purpose, or one of the main purposes, is avoidance of liability to corporation tax, capital gains tax or income tax; but the foregoing provisions of this subsection shall not affect the operation of this section in any case where, before the transfer, the Board have, on the application of the acquiring company, notified the company that the Board are satisfied that the reconstruction ...[6] will be effected for bona fide commercial reasons and will not form part of any such scheme or arrangements as aforesaid.

Subsections (2) to (5) of section 138 shall have effect in relation to this subsection as they have effect in relation to subsection (1) of that section.

(6) Where, if the company making the disposal had not been wound up, tax could have been assessed on it by virtue of subsection (5) above, that tax may be assessed and charged (in the name of the company making the disposal) on the company to which the disposal is made.

(7) If any tax assessed on a company ("the chargeable company") by virtue of subsection (5) or (6) above is not paid within 6 months from the date [when it is due and payable or, if later, the date when the assessment is made on the company][1], any other person who—

(a) holds all or any part of the assets in respect of which the tax is charged; and

(b) either is the company to which the disposal was made or has acquired the assets without there having been any subsequent disposal not falling within this section or section 171,

may, within 2 years from [the later of those dates][1], assessed and charged (in the name of the chargeable company) to all or, as the case may be, a corresponding part of the unpaid tax; and a person paying any amount of tax under this section shall be entitled to recover [from the chargeable company a sum equal to that amount together with any interest paid by him under section 87A of the Management Act on that amount][1].

(8) (*amends* sub-s (7)).

[(9) In this section "scheme of reconstruction" has the same meaning as in section 136.][5]

Commentary—*Simon's Direct Tax Service* C2.727; D2.303.
Statements of Practice SP 13/80 Annex—Demergers: TA 1988 ss 213–218.
SP 5/85—Capital gains: division of a company on a share for share basis.
SP 7/93—Revenue's interpretation of provisions allowing deferral of corporation tax when a life insurance company transfers the whole or part of its long term business to another company.
Revenue Internal Guidance—Life assurance manual LAM 16.11–16.16 (application to life assurance companies).
Definitions—"Asset", s 21(1); "authorised unit trust", s 99; "the Board", s 288(1); "chargeable gain", s 15(2); "chargeable period", s 288(1); "company", ss 99, 288(1); "double taxation relief arrangements", s 288(1); "investment trust", s 288(1), TA 1988 s 842; "the Management Act", s 288(1); "resident", s 9(1); "trade", s 288(1), TA 1988 s 832(1); "trading stock", s 288(1), TA 1988 s 100(2); "unit trust scheme", s 99.
Cross references—See TCGA 1992 s 25(4) (deemed disposal provisions not to apply where this section has effect in relation to assets of a non-resident insurance company transferring abroad its long term business carried on through UK branch or agency).
TCGA 1992 s 35(3)(*d*) (application of rebasing provisions).
TCGA 1992 s 55(5) (indexation allowance on a non-no gain/no loss disposal after 31 March 1982 of assets acquired on a no gain/no loss acquisition under this section).
TCGA 1992 s 101 (transfer of company's business to investment trust).
TCGA 1992 s 116(11) (treatment of gain or loss accruing on a reorganisation, etc where the old or the new shares include qualifying corporate bonds).
TCGA 1992 s 117A(7), (8) (to the extent that this section treats disposals as made on a no gain/no loss basis, it does not apply to disposals of certain foreign currency debts involving companies).
TCGA 1992 s 117B(5), (6) (to the extent that this section treats disposals as made on a no gain/no loss basis, it does not apply to disposals of certain foreign currency denominated holdings in unit trusts and offshore funds treated as a right under a creditor relationship of a company).
TCGA 1992 s 211 (transfer of long term business of an insurance company).
TCGA 1992 Sch 4 para 7 (reduction of deferred charges on gains accruing on disposal of assets not held by the vendor on 31 March 1982 but acquired by him from a person who acquired them before that date on a no gain/no loss disposal in accordance with this section).
FA 1993 s 165 and Sch 17 para 7 (reconstructions of long term or mutual insurance businesses involving disposals and acquisitions of foreign currency, foreign debts and foreign securities; disapplication of this section in certain circumstances).
Amendments—[1] Words in sub-s (7) substituted by virtue of sub-s (8) with respect to chargeable gains accruing in chargeable periods ending after 30 September 1993 by virtue of Corporation Tax Acts (Provisions for Payment of Tax and Returns) (Appointed Days) Order, SI 1992/3066 art 2(1), (2)(*d*).
[2] Sub-s (3) repealed by FA 1994 s 251(1), (5) and Sch 26 Pt VIII(1) in relation to acquisitions after 29 November 1993.
[3] Words in sub-s (1) inserted by FA 1998 s 134(1) with effect in relation to transfers made on or after 17 March 1998.
[4] Sub-s (1)(*b*) substituted, and sub-s (1A) inserted, by FA 2000 s 102, Sch 29 para 5 with effect for disposals made after 31 March 2000.
[5] Sub-s (9) substituted by FA 2002 s 45, Sch 9 paras 5(1), (7), 7 with effect for shares or debentures issued after 16 April 2002. The reference to shares or debentures includes any interests falling to be treated as shares or debentures for the purposes of TCGA 1992 s 135 or 136 as substituted by FA 2002 Sch 9. Sub-s (9) previously read as follows—

"(9) In this section "scheme of reconstruction or amalgamation" means a scheme for the reconstruction of any company or companies or the amalgamation of any 2 or more companies.".

[6] Words "or amalgamation" repealed by FA 2002 s 141, Sch 40 Pt 3(2) with effect in accordance with FA 2002 Sch 9 paras 7, 8.

140 Postponement of charge on transfer of assets to non-resident company

(1) This section applies where a company resident in the United Kingdom carries on a trade outside the United Kingdom through a branch or agency and—

(a) that trade, or part of it, together with the whole assets of the company used for the purposes of the trade or part (or together with the whole of those assets other than cash) is transferred to a company not resident in the United Kingdom;

(b) the trade or part is so transferred wholly or partly in exchange for securities consisting of shares, or of shares and loan stock, issued by the transferee company to the transferor company;

(c) the shares so issued, either alone or taken together with any other shares in the transferee company already held by the transferor company, amount in all to not less than one quarter of the ordinary share capital of the transferee company; and

(d) either no allowable losses accrue to the transferor company on the transfer or the aggregate of the chargeable gains so accruing exceeds the aggregate of the allowable losses so accruing;

and also applies in any case where section 268A of the Income and Corporation Taxes Act 1970 applied unless the deferred gain had been wholly taken into account in accordance with that section before the coming into force of this section.

Section 170(1) shall apply for the purposes of this section.

(2) In any case to which this section applies the transferor company may claim that this Act shall have effect in accordance with the following provisions.

(3) Any allowable losses accruing to the transferor company on the transfer shall be set off against the chargeable gains so accruing and the transfer shall be treated as giving rise to a single chargeable gain equal to the aggregate of those gains after deducting the aggregate of those losses and—

(a) if the securities are the whole consideration for the transfer, the whole of that gain shall be treated as not accruing to the transferor company on the transfer but an equivalent amount (''the deferred gain'') shall be brought into account in accordance with subsections (4) and (5) below;

(b) if the securities are not the whole of that consideration—

(i) paragraph (a) above shall apply to the appropriate proportion of that gain; and

(ii) the remainder shall be treated as accruing to the transferor company on the transfer.

In paragraph (b)(i) above ''the appropriate proportion'' means the proportion that the market value of the securities at the time of the transfer bears to the market value of the whole of the consideration at that time.

(4) If at any time after the transfer the transferor company disposes of the whole or part of the securities held by it immediately before that time, the consideration received by it on the disposal shall be treated as increased by the whole or the appropriate proportion of the deferred gain so far as not already taken into account under this subsection or subsection (5) below.

In this subsection ''the appropriate proportion'' means the proportion that the market value of the part of the securities disposed of bears to the market value of the securities held immediately before the disposal.

(5) If at any time within 6 years after the transfer the transferee company disposes of the whole or part of the relevant assets held by it immediately before that time there shall be deemed to accrue to the transferor company as a chargeable gain on that occasion the whole or the appropriate proportion of the deferred gain so far as not already taken into account under this subsection or subsection (4) above.

In this subsection ''relevant assets'' means assets the chargeable gains on which were taken into account in arriving at the deferred gain and ''the appropriate proportion'' means the proportion which the chargeable gain so taken into account in respect of the part of the relevant assets disposed of bears to the aggregate of the chargeable gains so taken into account in respect of the relevant assets held immediately before the time of the disposal.

(6) There shall be disregarded—

(a) for the purposes of subsection (4) above any disposal to which section 171 applies; and

(b) for the purposes of subsection (5) above any disposal to which that section would apply [if subsections (1)(b) and (1A) of that section and section 170(9) were disregarded][2];

and where a person acquires securities or an asset on a disposal disregarded for the purposes of subsection (4) or (5) above (and without there having been a previous disposal not so disregarded) a disposal of the securities or asset by that person shall be treated as a disposal by the transferor or, as the case may be, transferee company.

[(6A) No claim may be made under this section as regards a transfer in relation to which a claim is made under section 140C.][1]

(7) If in the case of any such transfer as was mentioned in section 268(1) of the Income and Corporation Taxes Act 1970 there were immediately before the coming into force of this section chargeable gains which by virtue of section 268(2) and 268A(8) of that Act were treated as not having accrued to the transferor company, subsection (4) above shall (without any claim in that behalf) apply to the aggregate of those gains as if references to the deferred gain were references to that aggregate and as if references to the transfer and the securities were references to the transfer and the shares, or shares and loan stock, mentioned in section 268(1).

(8) If in the case of any such transfer as was mentioned in section 268A(1) of the Income and Corporation Taxes Act 1970 there were immediately before the coming into force of this section deferred gains which by virtue of section 268A(3) were treated as not having accrued to the transferor

company, subsections (4) and (5) above shall (without any claim in that behalf) apply to those deferred gains as they apply to gains deferred by virtue of subsection (3) above (as if the references to the transfer and the securities were references to the transfer and securities mentioned in section 268A(1)).

Commentary—*Simon's Direct Tax Service* D2.305.
Statement of Practice SP 6/88 para 4(iii)—Double taxation relief: CGT.
Definitions—"Asset", s 21(1); "allowable loss", ss 8(2), 16, 288(1); "branch or agency", s 10(6); "chargeable gain", s 15(2); "company", ss 99, 288(1); "issued", s 288(5); "market value", ss 272–274, Sch 11; "resident", s 9(1); "shares", s 288(1); "trade", s 288(1), TA 1988 s 832(1).
Cross references—See TCGA 1992 s 140C(4) (loss relief on transfer of a non-UK trade to one member State company by another member State company; avoidance of double claims for relief).
TCGA 1992 Sch 4 para 4 (reduction of deferred charge to tax in respect of a gain accruing on the disposal before 6 April 1988 of an asset acquired before 31 March 1982 where the gain crystallises after 5 April 1988).
Amendments—¹ Sub-s (6A) inserted by F(No 2)A 1992 s 46(1), (4) and deemed always to have had effect.
² Words in sub-s (6)(b) substituted by FA 2000 s 102, Sch 29 para 23 with effect for disposals after 31 March 2000.

[Transfers concerning companies of different member States]¹

[140A Transfer of a UK trade

(1) This section applies where—

(a) a qualifying company resident in one member State (company A) transfers the whole or part of a trade carried on by it in the United Kingdom to a qualifying company resident in another member State (company B),
(b) the transfer is wholly in exchange for securities issued by company B to company A,
(c) a claim is made under this section by company A and company B,
(d) section 140B does not prevent this section applying, and
(e) the appropriate condition is met in relation to company B immediately after the time of the transfer.

(2) Where immediately after the time of the transfer company B is not resident in the United Kingdom, the appropriate condition is that were it to dispose of the assets included in the transfer any chargeable gains accruing to it on the disposal would form part of its chargeable profits for corporation tax purposes by virtue of section 10(3).

(3) Where immediately after the time of the transfer company B is resident in the United Kingdom, the appropriate condition is that none of the assets included in the transfer is one in respect of which, by virtue of the asset being of a description specified in double taxation relief arrangements, the company falls to be regarded for the purposes of the arrangements as not liable in the United Kingdom to tax on gains accruing to it on a disposal.

(4) Where this section applies—

(a) the two companies shall be treated, so far as relates to corporation tax on chargeable gains, as if any assets included in the transfer were acquired by company B from company A for a consideration of such amount as would secure that on the disposal by way of transfer neither a gain nor a loss would accrue to company A;
(b) section 25(3) shall not apply to any such assets by reason of the transfer (if it would apply apart from this paragraph).

(5) For the purposes of subsection (1)(a) above, a company shall be regarded as resident in a member State if it is within a charge to tax under the law of the State because it is regarded as resident for the purposes of the charge.

(6) For the purposes of subsection (5) above, a company shall be treated as not within a charge to tax under the law of a member State if it falls to be regarded for the purposes of any double taxation relief arrangements to which the State is a party as resident in a territory which is not within any of the member States.

(7) In this section—

"qualifying company" means a body incorporated under the law of a member State; "securities" includes shares.]¹

Commentary—*Simon's Direct Tax Service* D2.304A, D4.128.
Definitions—"Chargeable gain", s 15(2); "trade", s 288(1), TA 1988 s 832(1).
Cross references—See TCGA 1992 s 35(3)(d)(i) (re-basing to 31 March 1982 value of assets held on that date).
TCGA 1992 s 116(11) (reorganisations, etc where assets transferred include qualifying corporate bonds).
TCGA 1992 s 117A(7), (8) (to the extent that this section treats disposals as made on a no gain/no loss basis, it does not apply to disposals of certain foreign currency debts involving companies).
TCGA 1992 s 117B(5), (6) (to the extent that this section treats disposals as made on a no gain/no loss basis, it does not apply to disposals of certain foreign currency denominated holdings in unit trusts and offshore funds treated as a right under a creditor relationship of a company).
TCGA 1992 s 174(2), (3) (disposals or acquisitions outside a group).
TCGA 1992 s 177(2) (dividend stripping).
TCGA 1992 Sch 7B paras 1, 5 (modification of sub-s (2) above in the case of application of this section to an overseas life insurance company in relation to transfers taking place in accounting periods of company B beginning after 31 December 1992).
Amendments—¹ This section inserted by F(No 2)A 1992 s 44 and deemed always to have had effect.

[140B Section 140A: anti-avoidance

(1) Section 140A shall not apply unless the transfer of the trade or part is effected for bona fide commercial reasons and does not form part of a scheme or arrangements of which the main purpose, or one of the main purposes, is avoidance of liability to income tax, corporation tax or capital gains tax.

(2) Subsection (1) above shall not apply where, before the transfer, the Board have on the application of company A and company B notified those companies that the Board are satisfied that the transfer will be effected for bona fide commercial reasons and will not form part of any such scheme or arrangements as are mentioned in that subsection.

(3) Subsections (2) to (5) of section 138 shall have effect in relation to subsection (2) above as they have effect in relation to subsection (1) of that section.][1]

Commentary—*Simon's Direct Tax Service* **D2.304A.**
Definitions—''the Board'', s 288(1); ''trade'', s 288(1), TA 1988 s 832(1).
Amendments—[1]This section inserted by F(No 2)A 1992 s 44 and deemed always to have had effect.

[140C Transfer of a non-UK trade

(1) This section applies where—

    (*a*) a qualifying company resident in the United Kingdom (company A) transfers to a qualifying company resident in another member State (company B) the whole or part of a trade which, immediately before the time of the transfer, company A carried on in a member State other than the United Kingdom through a branch or agency,
    (*b*) the transfer includes the whole of the assets of company A used for the purposes of the trade or part (or the whole of those assets other than cash),
    (*c*) the transfer is wholly or partly in exchange for securities issued by company B to company A,
    (*d*) the aggregate of the chargeable gains accruing to company A on the transfer exceeds the aggregate of the allowable losses so accruing,
    (*e*) a claim is made under this section by company A, and
    (*f*) section 140D does not prevent this section applying.

(2) In a case where this section applies, this Act shall have effect in accordance with subsection (3) below.

(3) The allowable losses accruing to company A on the transfer shall be set off against the chargeable gains so accruing and the transfer shall be treated as giving rise to a single chargeable gain equal to the aggregate of those gains after deducting the aggregate of those losses.

(4) No claim may be made under this section as regards a transfer in relation to which a claim is made under section 140.

(5) In a case where this section applies, section 815A of the Taxes Act shall also apply.

(6) For the purposes of subsection (1)(*a*) above—

    (*a*) a company shall not be regarded as resident in the United Kingdom if it falls to be regarded for the purposes of any double taxation relief arrangements to which the United Kingdom is a party as resident in a territory which is not within any of the member States;
    (*b*) a company shall be regarded as resident in another member State if it is within a charge to tax under the law of the State because it is regarded as resident for the purposes of the charge.

(7) For the purposes of subsection (6)(*b*) above, a company shall be treated as not within a charge to tax under the law of a member State if it falls to be regarded for the purposes of any double taxation relief arrangements to which the State is a party as resident in a territory which is not within any of the member States.

(8) Section 442(3) of the Taxes Act (overseas business of UK insurance companies) shall be ignored in arriving at the chargeable gains accruing to company A on the transfer, and the allowable losses so accruing, for the purposes of subsections (1)(*d*) and (3) above.

(9) In this section—

    ''qualifying company'' means a body incorporated under the law of a member State;
    ''securities'' includes shares.][1]

Commentary—*Simon's Direct Tax Service* **D2.304B; F2.121.**
Definitions—''Allowable loss'', s 288(1); ''branch or agency'', s 10(6); ''chargeable gain'', s 15(2); ''trade'', s 288(1), TA 1988 s 832(1).
Amendments—[1] This section inserted by F(No 2)A 1992 s 45 and deemed always to have had effect.

[140D Section 140C: anti-avoidance

(1) Section 140C shall not apply unless the transfer of the trade or part is effected for bona fide commercial reasons and does not form part of a scheme or arrangements of which the main purpose, or one of the main purposes, is avoidance of liability to income tax, corporation tax or capital gains tax.

(2) Subsection (1) above shall not apply where, before the transfer, the Board have on the application of company A notified that company that the Board are satisfied that the transfer will be effected for

bona fide commercial reasons and will not form part of any such scheme or arrangements as are mentioned in that subsection.

(3) Subsections (2) to (5) of section 138 shall have effect in relation to subsection (2) above as they have effect in relation to subsection (1) of that section.]¹

Commentary—*Simon's Direct Tax Service* D2.304B; F2.121.
Definitions—"the Board", s 288(1); "trade", s 288(1), TA 1988 s 832(1).
Amendments—¹ This section inserted by F(No 2)A 1992 s 45 and deemed always to have had effect.

CHAPTER III
MISCELLANEOUS PROVISIONS RELATING TO COMMODITIES, FUTURES, OPTIONS AND OTHER SECURITIES

141 Stock dividends: consideration for new holding

Commentary—*Simon's Direct Tax Service* C2.721.
Definitions—"Company", ss 99, 288(1); "issued", s 288(5); "the Taxes Act", s 288(1).
Amendments—¹ This section substituted by new section 142 below by virtue of FA 1998 s 126, with effect in relation to any share capital issued after 5 April 1998. The text previously read as follows—

"(1) In applying section 128(1) in relation to the issue of any share capital to which section 249 of the Taxes Act (stock dividends) applies as involving a reorganisation of the company's share capital, there shall be allowed, as consideration given for so much of the new holding as was issued as mentioned in subsection (4), (5) or (6) of section 249 (read in each case with subsection (3) of that section) an amount equal to what is, for that much of the new holding, the appropriate amount in cash within the meaning of section 251(2) of the Taxes Act.
(2) This section shall have effect notwithstanding section 128(2)."

[142 Capital gains on stock dividends

(1) This section applies where any share capital to which section 249 of the Taxes Act applies is issued as mentioned in subsection (4), (5) or (6) of that section in respect of shares in the company held by any person.

(2) The case shall not constitute a reorganisation of the company's share capital for the purposes of sections 126 to 128.

(3) The person who acquires the share capital by means of its issue shall (notwithstanding section 17(1)) be treated for the purposes of section 38(1)(a) as having acquired that asset for a consideration equal to the appropriate amount in cash (within the meaning of section 251(2) to (4) of the Taxes Act).]¹

Commentary—*Simon's Direct Tax Service* C2.721.
Revenue Internal Guidance—Capital Gains Manual CG 57763 (stock dividends: worked example).
Amendments—¹ This section substituted by FA 1998 s 126 with effect in relation to any share capital issued after 5 April 1998. The text previously read as follows—

"(1) This section applies where a company issues any share capital to which section 249 of the Taxes Act applies in respect of shares in the company held by a person as trustee, and another person is at the time of the issue absolutely entitled thereto as against the trustee or would be so entitled but for being an infant or other person under disability (or 2 or more other persons are or would be jointly so entitled thereto).
(2) Notwithstanding paragraph (a) of section 126(2) the case shall not constitute a reorganisation of the company's share capital for the purposes of sections 126 to 128.
(3) Notwithstanding section 17(1), the person who is or would be so entitled to the share capital (or each of the persons who are or would be jointly so entitled thereto) shall be treated for the purposes of section 38(1)(a) as having acquired that share capital, or his interest in it, for a consideration equal to the appropriate amount in cash within the meaning of section 251(2) to (4) of the Taxes Act."

143 Commodity and financial futures and qualifying options

(1) If, apart from section 128 of the Taxes Act, gains arising to any person in the course of dealing in commodity or financial futures or in qualifying options would constitute, for the purposes of the Tax Acts, profits or gains chargeable to tax under Schedule D otherwise than as the profits of a trade, then his outstanding obligations under any futures contract entered into in the course of that dealing and any qualifying option granted or acquired in the course of that dealing shall be regarded as assets to the disposal of which this Act applies.

(2) In subsection (1) above—

(a) "commodity or financial futures" means commodity futures or financial futures which are for the time being dealt in on a recognised futures exchange; and
(b) "qualifying option" means a traded option or financial option as defined in section 144(8).

(3) Notwithstanding the provisions of subsection (2)(a) above, where, otherwise than in the course of dealing on a recognised futures exchange—

(a) an authorised person ...³ enters into a commodity or financial futures contract with another person, or
(b) the outstanding obligations under a commodity or financial futures contract to which an authorised person ...³ is a party are brought to an end by a further contract between the parties to the futures contract,

then, except in so far as any gain or loss arising to any person from that transaction arises in the course of a trade, that gain or loss shall be regarded for the purposes of subsection (1) above as arising to him in the course of dealing in commodity or financial futures.

(4) ...²

(5) For the purposes of this Act, where, in the course of dealing in commodity or financial futures, a person who has entered into a futures contract closes out that contract by entering into another futures contract with obligations which are reciprocal to those of the first-mentioned contract, that transaction shall constitute the disposal of an asset (namely, his outstanding obligations under the first-mentioned contract) and, accordingly—

(a) any money or money's worth received by him on that transaction shall constitute consideration for the disposal; and
(b) any money or money's worth paid or given by him on that transaction shall be treated as incidental costs to him of making the disposal.

[(6) In any case where, in the course of dealing in commodity or financial futures, a person has entered into a futures contract and—

(a) he has not closed out the contract (as mentioned in subsection (5) above), and
(b) he becomes entitled to receive or liable to make a payment, whether under the contract or otherwise, in full or partial settlement of any obligations under the contract,

then, for the purposes of this Act, he shall be treated as having disposed of an asset (namely, that entitlement or liability) and the payment received or made by him shall be treated as consideration for the disposal or, as the case may be, as incidental costs to him of making the disposal.]¹

[(7) Section 46 shall not apply to obligations under—

(a) a commodity or financial futures contract which is entered into by a person in the course of dealing in such futures on a recognised futures exchange; or
(b) a commodity or financial futures contract to which an authorised person ...³ is a party.]¹

[(8) In this section "authorised person" means a person who—

(a) falls within section 31(1)(a), (b) or (c) of the Financial Services and Markets Act 2000, and
(b) has permission under that Act to carry on one or more of the activities specified in Article 14 and, in so far as it applies to that Article, Article 64 of the Financial Services and Markets Act 2000 (Regulated Activities) Order 2001.]³

Commentary—*Simon's Direct Tax Service* **C2.1012.**
Statement of Practice SP 14/91—Tax treatment of transactions in financial futures and options.
Revenue Internal Guidance—Capital gains manual CG56000–56092 (detailed explanation of the treatment of futures contracts).
Simon's Tax Cases—s 143(2), *Griffin (Inspector of Taxes) v Citibank Investments* [2000] STC 1010; *HSBC Life (UK) Ltd v Stubbs (Insp of Taxes), Nationwide Life Ltd v Crisp (Insp of Taxes), Abbey Life Assurance Co Ltd v Colclough (Insp of Taxes), TSB Life Ltd v Colclough (Insp of Taxes), Lloyds TSB Life Assurance Co Ltd v Colclough (Insp of Taxes)* [2002] STC (SCD) 9.
Definitions—"Asset", s 21(1); "recognised futures exchange", s 288(6); "the Taxes Act", s 288(1); "trade", s 288(1), TA 1988 s 832(1).
Cross references—See TCGA 1992 s 115(3) (transaction mentioned in sub-s (5) above relating to gilt-edged securities and qualifying corporate bonds).
Amendments—¹ Sub-ss (6), (7), and original sub-s (8) substituted for sub-s (6) by FA 1994 s 95 in relation to contracts entered into after 29 November 1993.
² Sub-s (4) repealed by FA 1994 s 95 and Sch 26 Pt V(9).
³ Words in sub-ss (3)(a), (b), (7)(b) revoked, and sub-s (8) substituted, by the Financial Services and Markets Act 2000 (Consequential Amendments) (Taxes) Order, SI 2001/3629 arts 61, 64 with effect from 1 December 2001 immediately after the coming into force of the Financial Services and Markets Act 2000 ss 411, 432(1), Sch 20.

144 Options and forfeited deposits

(1) Without prejudice to section 21, the grant of an option, and in particular—

(a) the grant of an option in a case where the grantor binds himself to sell what he does not own, and because the option is abandoned, never has occasion to own, and
(b) the grant of an option in a case where the grantor binds himself to buy what, because the option is abandoned, he does not acquire,

is the disposal of an asset (namely of the option), but subject to the following provisions of this section as to treating the grant of an option as part of a larger transaction.

(2) If an option is exercised, the grant of the option and the transaction entered into by the grantor in fulfilment of his obligations under the option shall be treated as a single transaction and accordingly—

(a) if the option binds the grantor to sell, the consideration for the option is part of the consideration for the sale, and
(b) if the option binds the grantor to buy, the consideration for the option shall be deducted from the cost of acquisition incurred by the grantor in buying in pursuance of his obligations under the option.

(3) The exercise of an option by the person for the time being entitled to exercise it shall not constitute the disposal of an asset by that person, but, if an option is exercised then the acquisition of the option (whether directly from the grantor or not) and the transaction entered into by the person

exercising the option in exercise of his rights under the option shall be treated as a single transaction and accordingly—

    (*a*) if the option binds the grantor to sell, the cost of acquiring the option shall be part of the cost of acquiring what is sold, and

    (*b*) if the option binds the grantor to buy, the cost of the option shall be treated as a cost incidental to the disposal of what is bought by the grantor of the option.

(4) The abandonment of—

    (*a*) a quoted option to subscribe for shares in a company, or

    (*b*) a traded option or financial option, or

    (*c*) an option to acquire assets exercisable by a person intending to use them, if acquired, for the purpose of a trade carried on by him,

shall constitute the disposal of an asset (namely of the option); but the abandonment of any other option by the person for the time being entitled to exercise it shall not constitute the disposal of an asset by that person.

(5) This section shall apply in relation to an option binding the grantor both to sell and to buy as if it were 2 separate options with half the consideration attributed to each.

(6) In this section references to an option include references to an option binding the grantor to grant a lease for a premium, or enter into any other transaction which is not a sale, and references to buying and selling in pursuance of an option shall be construed accordingly.

(7) This section shall apply in relation to a forfeited deposit of purchase money or other consideration money for a prospective purchase or other transaction which is abandoned as it applies in relation to the consideration for an option which binds the grantor to sell and which is not exercised.

(8) In subsection (4) above and sections 146 and 147—

    (*a*) ''quoted option'' means an option which, at the time of the abandonment or other disposal, is quoted on a recognised stock exchange;

    (*b*) ''traded option'' means an option which, at the time of the abandonment or other disposal, is [listed][1] on a recognised stock exchange or a recognised futures exchange; and

    (*c*) ''financial option'' means an option which is not a traded option, as defined in paragraph (*b*) above, but which, subject to subsection (9) below—

        (i) relates to currency, shares, securities or an interest rate and is granted (otherwise than as agent) by a member of a recognised stock exchange, by an [authorised person within the meaning given by section 143(8)][2]; or

        (ii) relates to shares or securities which are dealt in on a recognised stock exchange and is granted by a member of such an exchange, acting as agent; or

        (iii) relates to currency, shares, securities or an interest rate and is granted to such an authorised person ...[2] as is referred to in sub-paragraph (i) above and concurrently and in association with an option falling within that sub-paragraph which is granted by that authorised person ...[2] to the grantor of the first-mentioned option; or

        (iv) relates to shares or securities which are dealt in on a recognised stock exchange and is granted to a member of such an exchange, including such a member acting as agent.

(9) If the Treasury by order so provide, an option of a description specified in the order shall be taken to be within the definition of ''financial option'' in subsection (8)(*c*) above.

Commentary—*Simon's Direct Tax Service* **C2.1009, 1010.**
Revenue Interpretation RI 11—Rollover relief in respect of gain arising on grant of option over land.
Revenue Internal Guidance—Capital gains manual CG55400–55603 (detailed explanation of the treatment of options).
Simon's Tax Cases—*Golding v Kaufman* [1985] STC 152*; *Welbeck Securities Ltd v Powlson* [1987] STC 468*.
s 144(1), *Strange v Openshaw and related appeals* [1983] STC 416*.
s 144(8) *Griffin (Inspector of Taxes) v Citibank Investments* [2000] STC 1010.
Definitions—''Asset'', s 21(1); ''company'', ss 99, 288(1); ''lease'', Sch 8 para 10(1); ''recognised futures exchange'', s 288(6); ''recognised stock exchange'', s 288(1), TA 1988 s 841; ''shares'', s 288(1); ''trade'', s 288(1), TA 1988 s 832(1).
Cross references—See TCGA 1992 s 24(1) (loss, destruction, etc of assets to constitute disposal).
TCGA 1992 s 144A(1), (4) (disapplication and modifications of sub-ss (2), (3) above for cash-settled options).
TCGA 1992 s 145(3) effect of this section on s 145 (call options: indexation allowance)).
TCGA 1992 s 146(2) (sub-ss (5), (6) above to apply to quoted, traded and financial options and option to acquire assets for trade).
TCGA 1992 s 217(1) (rights of members to shares in company on transfer of building society's business).
Amendments—[1] Word in sub-s (8)(*b*) substituted by FA 1996 Sch 38 para 10(1), (2)(*a*), (3) with effect in relation to disposals after 31 March 1996.
[2] In sub-s (8)(*c*), words in para (i) substituted, and words in para (iii) revoked, by the Financial Services and Markets Act 2000 (Consequential Amendments) (Taxes) Order, SI 2001/3629 arts 61, 65 with effect from 1 December 2001 immediately after the coming into force of the Financial Services and Markets Act 2000 ss 411, 432(1), Sch 20.

[144A Cash-settled options

(1) In any case where—

    (*a*) an option is exercised; and

    (*b*) the nature of the option (or its exercise) is such that the grantor of the option is liable to make, and the person exercising it is entitled to receive, a payment in full settlement of all obligations under the option,

subsections (2) and (3) below shall apply in place of subsections (2) and (3) of section 144.

(2) As regards the grantor of the option—

(*a*) he shall be treated as having disposed of an asset (namely, his liability to make the payment) and the payment made by him shall be treated as incidental costs to him of making the disposal; and

(*b*) the grant of the option and the disposal shall be treated as a single transaction and the consideration for the option shall be treated as the consideration for the disposal.

(3) As regards the person exercising the option—

(*a*) he shall be treated as having disposed of an asset (namely, his entitlement to receive the payment) and the payment received by him shall be treated as the consideration for the disposal;

(*b*) the acquisition of the option (whether directly from the grantor or not) and the disposal shall be treated as a single transaction and the cost of acquiring the option shall be treated as expenditure allowable as a deduction under section 38(1)(*a*) from the consideration for the disposal; and

(*c*) for the purpose of computing the indexation allowance (if any) on the disposal, the cost of the option shall be treated (notwithstanding paragraph (*b*) above) as incurred when the option was acquired.

(4) In any case where subsections (2) and (3) above would apply as mentioned in subsection (1) above if the reference in that subsection to full settlement included a reference to partial settlement, those subsections and subsections (2) and (3) of section 144 shall both apply but with the following modifications—

(*a*) for any reference to the grant or acquisition of the option there shall be substituted a reference to the grant or acquisition of so much of the option as relates to the making and receipt of the payment or, as the case may be, the sale or purchase by the grantor; and

(*b*) for any reference to the consideration for, or the cost of or of acquiring, the option there shall be substituted a reference to the appropriate proportion of that consideration or cost.

(5) In this section ''appropriate proportion'' means such proportion as may be just and reasonable in all the circumstances.]¹

Commentary—*Simon's Direct Tax Service* **C1.318.**
Definitions—''Indexation allowance'', s 53.
Amendment—¹ This section inserted by FA 1994 s 96 in relation to options granted after 29 November 1993.

145 Call options: indexation allowance

(1) This section applies [(subject to subsection (1A) below)]¹ where, on a disposal to which section 53 applies, the relevant allowable expenditure includes both—

(*a*) the cost of acquiring an option binding the grantor to sell (''the option consideration''); and

(*b*) the cost of acquiring what was sold as a result of the exercise of the option (''the sale consideration''),

but does not apply in any case where section 114 applies.

[(1A) In a case where the whole of the expenditure comprised in the option consideration was incurred on or after 1st April 1998, this section applies for the purposes of corporation tax only.]¹

(2) For the purpose of computing the indexation allowance (if any) on the disposal referred to in subsection (1) above—

(*a*) the option consideration and the sale consideration shall be regarded as separate items of expenditure; and

(*b*) subsection (4) of section 54 shall apply to neither of those items and, accordingly, they shall be regarded as incurred when the option was acquired and when the sale took place, respectively.

(3) This section has effect notwithstanding section 144, but expressions used in this section have the same meaning as in that section and subsection (5) of that section applies for the purpose of determining the cost of acquiring an option binding the grantor to sell.

Commentary—*Simon's Direct Tax Service* **C2.302.**
Definition—''Indexation allowance'', s 53.
Amendments—¹ Words in sub-s (1), and sub-s (1A) inserted by FA 1998 s 122(5) with effect in relation to disposals on or after 6 April 1998, subject to FA 1998 s 122(7).

146 Options: application of rules as to wasting assets

(1) Section 46 shall not apply—

(*a*) to a quoted option to subscribe for shares in a company, or

(*b*) to a traded option, or financial option, or

(*c*) to an option to acquire assets exercisable by a person intending to use them, if acquired, for the purpose of a trade carried on by him.

(2) In relation to the disposal by way of transfer of an option (other than an option falling within subsection (1)(*a*) or (*b*) above) binding the grantor to sell or buy quoted shares or securities, the option shall be regarded as a wasting asset the life of which ends when the right to exercise the option ends, or when the option becomes valueless, whichever is the earlier.

Subsections (5) and (6) of section 144 shall apply in relation to this subsection as they apply in relation to that section.

(3) The preceding provisions of this section are without prejudice to the application of sections 44 to 47 to options not within those provisions.

(4) In this section—

(a) "financial option", "quoted option" and "traded option" have the meanings given by section 144(8), and

(b) "quoted shares or securities" means shares or securities which [are listed][1] on a recognised stock exchange in the United Kingdom or elsewhere.

Commentary—*Simon's Direct Tax Service* **C2.1003.**
Definitions—"Asset", s 21(1); "company", ss 99, 288(1); "financial option", s 144(8); "market value", ss 272–274, Sch 11; "quoted option", s 144(8); "recognised stock exchange", s 288(1), TA 1988 s 841; "shares", s 288(1); "trade", s 288(1), TA 1988 s 832(1); "traded option", s 144(8); "wasting asset", ss 44, 288(1), Sch 8 para 1.
Amendments—[1] Words in sub-s (4)(b) substituted by FA 1996 Sch 38 para 11 with effect in relation to disposals of options after 31 March 1996.

147 Quoted options treated as part of new holdings

(1) If a quoted option to subscribe for shares in a company is dealt in (on the stock exchange where it is quoted) within 3 months after the taking effect, with respect to the company granting the option, of any reorganisation, reduction, conversion[, exchange or scheme of reconstruction][1] to which Chapter II of this Part applies, or within such longer period as the Board may by notice allow—

(a) the option shall, for the purposes of that Chapter be regarded as the shares which could be acquired by exercising the option, and

(b) section 272(3) shall apply for determining its market value.

(2) In this section "quoted option" has the meaning given by section 144(8) [and "scheme of reconstruction" has the same meaning as in section 136][1].

Commentary—*Simon's Direct Tax Service* **C2.738.**
Definitions—"The Board", s 288(1); "company", ss 99, 288(1); "market value", ss 272–274, Sch 11; "notice", s 288(1); "quoted option", s 144(8); "shares", s 288(1).
Cross references—See TCGA 1992 s 137(6) (restriction on relief for company reconstruction or amalgamation which is not for *bona fide* commercial reasons).
Amendments—[1] In sub-s (1), words substituted for the words "or amalgamation", and in sub-s (2), words inserted, by FA 2002 s 45, Sch 9 paras 5(1), (8), 7 with effect for shares or debentures issued after 16 April 2002. The reference to shares or debentures includes any interests falling to be treated as shares or debentures for the purposes of TCGA 1992 s 135 or 136 as substituted by FA 2002 Sch 9.

148 Traded options: closing purchases

(1) This section applies where a person ("the grantor") who has granted a traded option ("the original option") closes it out by acquiring a traded option of the same description ("the second option").

(2) Any disposal by the grantor involved in closing out the original option shall be disregarded for the purposes of capital gains tax or, as the case may be, corporation tax on chargeable gains.

(3) The incidental costs to the grantor of making the disposal constituted by the grant of the original option shall be treated for the purposes of the computation of the gain as increased by an amount equal to the aggregate of—

(a) the amount or value of the consideration, in money or money's worth, given by him or on his behalf wholly and exclusively for the acquisition of the second option, and

(b) the incidental costs to him of that acquisition.

(4) In this section "traded option" has the meaning given by section 144(8).

Commentary—*Simon's Direct Tax Service* **C2.1012.**
Definition—"Chargeable gain", s 15(2).

149 Rights to acquire qualifying shares

(1) This section applies where on or after 25th July 1991 (the day on which the Finance Act 1991 was passed) a building society confers—

(a) on its members, or

(b) on any particular class or description of its members,

any rights to acquire, in priority to other persons, shares in the society which are qualifying shares.

(2) Any such right so conferred shall be regarded for the purposes of capital gains tax as an option granted to, and acquired by, the member concerned for no consideration and having no value at the time of that grant and acquisition.

(3) In this section—

"member" includes a former member, and

"qualifying share" has the same meaning as in section 117(4).

Commentary—*Simon's Direct Tax Service* **C2.1008.**
Definitions—"Building society", s 288(1); "shares", s 288(1).

[149A [Share option schemes][2]

(1) This section applies where—

(*a*) an option is granted on or after 16th March 1993,

(*b*) the option consists of a right to acquire shares in a body corporate and is obtained [by an individual by reason of his office or employment as a director or employee of that or any other body corporate][2], and

(*c*) section 17(1) would (apart from this section) apply for the purposes of calculating the consideration for the grant of the option.

(2) [Both the grantor of the option and the person to whom the option is granted][2] shall be treated for the purposes of this Act as if section 17(1) did not apply for the purposes of calculating the consideration and, accordingly, as if the amount or value of the consideration was its actual amount or value.

(3) Where the option is granted wholly or partly in recognition of services or past services in any office or employment, the value of those services shall not be taken into account in calculating the actual amount or value of the consideration.

(4) ...][2]][1]

Commentary—*Simon's Direct Tax Service* **E4.516, 579.**
Definitions—''Shares'', s 288(1).
Amendments—[1] This section inserted by FA 1993 s 104.
[2] Section heading and words in sub-ss (1)(*b*), (2) substituted and sub-s (4) repealed by FA 1996 s 111, Sch 41 Pt V(5) with effect in relation to any right to acquire shares in a body corporate obtained after 27 November 1995 by an individual by reason of his office or employment as a director or employee of a body corporate.

[149B Employee incentive schemes: conditional interests in shares

(1) Where—

(*a*) an individual has acquired an interest in any shares or securities which is only conditional,

(*b*) that interest is one which for the purposes of section 140A of the Taxes Act is taken to have been acquired by him as a director or employee of a company, and

(*c*) by virtue of section 17(1)(*b*) the acquisition of that interest would, apart from this section, be an acquisition for a consideration equal to the market value of the interest,

section 17 shall not apply for calculating the consideration.

(2) Instead, the consideration for the acquisition shall be taken (subject to section 120) to be equal to the actual amount or value of the consideration given for that interest as computed in accordance with section 140B of the Taxes Act.

(3) This section shall apply in relation only to the individual making the acquisition and, accordingly, shall be disregarded in calculating the consideration received by the person from whom the interest is acquired.

(4) Expressions used in this section and in section 140A of the Taxes Act have the same meanings in this section as in that section.][1]

Commentary—*Simon's Direct Tax Service* **C2.731.**
Revenue Internal Guidance—Capital Gains Manual CG 56353 (operation of this section).
Amendments—[1] This section inserted by FA 1998 s 54(5) with effect in relation to disposals on or after 17 March 1998 of interests and shares acquired on or after that date.

150 Business expansion schemes

(1) In this section ''relief'' means relief under Chapter III of Part VII of the Taxes Act, Schedule 5 to the Finance Act 1983 (''the 1983 Act'') or Chapter II of Part IV of the Finance Act 1981 (''the 1981 Act'') and ''eligible shares'' has the meaning given by section 289(4) of the Taxes Act [and references in this section to Chapter III of Part VII of the Taxes Act or any provision of that Chapter are to that Chapter or provision as it applies in relation to shares issued before 1st January 1994][1].

(2) A gain or loss which accrues to an individual on the disposal of any shares issued after 18th March 1986 in respect of which relief has been given to him and not withdrawn shall not be a chargeable gain or allowable loss for the purposes of capital gains tax.

(3) The sums allowable as deductions from the consideration in the computation for the purposes of capital gains tax of the gain or loss accruing to an individual on the disposal of shares issued before 19th March 1986 in respect of which relief has been given and not withdrawn shall be determined without regard to that relief, except that where those sums exceed the consideration they shall be reduced by an amount equal to—

(*a*) the amount of that relief; or

(*b*) the excess,

whichever is the less, but the foregoing provisions of this subsection shall not apply to a disposal falling within section 58(1).

(4) Any question—

(*a*) as to which of any shares [acquired by an individual][4] at different times, being shares in respect of which relief has been given and not withdrawn, a disposal relates [to][4], or

(b) whether a disposal relates to shares in respect of which relief has been given and not withdrawn or to other shares,

shall for the purposes of capital gains tax be determined as for the purposes of section 299 of the Taxes Act, or section 57 of the Finance Act 1981 if the relief has only been given under that Act; and Chapter I of this Part shall have effect subject to the foregoing provisions of this subsection.

(5) [Sections 104, 105 and 106A do not apply]⁴ to shares in respect of which relief has been given and not withdrawn.

(6) Where an individual holds shares which form part of the ordinary share capital of a company and the relief has been given (and not withdrawn) in respect of some but not others, then, if there is within the meaning of section 126 a reorganisation affecting those shares, section 127 shall apply separately to the shares in respect of which the relief has been given (and not withdrawn) and to the other shares (so that shares of each kind are treated as a separate holding of original shares and identified with a separate new holding).

(7) Where section 58 has applied to any [shares in respect of which relief has been given and not withdrawn]⁴ disposed of by an individual to his or her spouse ("the transferee"), subsection (2) above shall apply in relation to the subsequent disposal of the shares by the transferee to a third party.

(8) Where section 135 or 136 would, but for this subsection, apply in relation to ...⁵ shares issued after 18th March 1986 in respect of which an individual has been given relief, that section shall apply only if the relief is withdrawn.

[(8A) Subsection (8) above shall not have effect to disapply section 135 or 136 where—

(a) the new holding consists of new ordinary shares carrying no present or future preferential right to dividends or to a company's assets on its winding up and no present or future ...⁶ right to be redeemed,

(b) the new shares are issued on or after 29th November 1994 and after the end of the relevant period, and

(c) the condition in subsection (8B) below is fulfilled.]²

[(8B) The condition is that at some time before the issue of the new shares—

(a) the company issuing them issued eligible shares, and

(b) a certificate in relation to those eligible shares was issued by the company for the purposes of subsection (2) of section 306 of the Taxes Act and in accordance with that section.]²

[(8C) In subsection (8A) above—

(a) "new holding" shall be construed in accordance with sections 126, 127, 135 and 136;

(b) "relevant period" means the period found by applying section 289(12)(a) of the Taxes Act by reference to the company issuing the shares referred to in subsection (8) above and by reference to those shares.]²

[(8D) Where shares in respect of which relief has been given and not withdrawn are exchanged for other shares in circumstances such that section 304A of the Taxes Act (acquisition of share capital by new company) applies—

(a) subsection (8) above shall not have effect to disapply section 135; and

(b) subsections (2)(b), (3) and (4) of section 304A of the Taxes Act, and subsection (5) of that section so far as relating to section 306(2) of that Act, shall apply for the purposes of this section as they apply for the purposes of Chapter III of Part VII of that Act.]⁷

(9) Sections 127 to 130 shall not apply in relation to any shares in respect of which relief (other than relief under the 1981 Act) has been given and which form part of a company's ordinary share capital if—

(a) there is, by virtue of any such allotment for payment as is mentioned in section 126(2)(a), a reorganisation occurring after 18th March 1986 affecting those shares; and

(b) immediately following the reorganisation, the relief has not been withdrawn in respect of those shares or relief has been given in respect of the allotted shares and not withdrawn.

(10) Where relief is reduced by virtue of subsection (2) of section 305 of the Taxes Act—

(a) the sums allowable as deductions from the consideration in the computation, for the purposes of capital gains tax, of the gain or loss accruing to an individual on the disposal, after 18th March 1986, of any of the allotted shares or debentures shall be taken to include the amount of the reduction apportioned between the allotted shares or (as the case may be) debentures in [a way which is]³ just and reasonable; and

(b) the sums so allowable on the disposal (in circumstances in which subsections (2) to (8) above do not apply) of any of the shares referred to in section 305(2)(a) shall be taken to be reduced by the amount mentioned in paragraph (a) above, similarly apportioned between those shares.

(11) There shall be made all such adjustments of capital gains tax, whether by way of assessment or by way of discharge or repayment of tax, as may be required in consequence of the relief being given or withdrawn.

[(12) In this section—

"ordinary share capital" has the same meaning as in the Taxes Act;

"ordinary shares", in relation to a company, means shares forming part of its ordinary share capital.][8]

Commentary—*Simon's Direct Tax Service* **E3.202.**
Statement of Practice SP 4/92—Capital gains rebasing elections.
Note—For Pt VII Ch III as it applies in relation to shares issued before 1 January 1994, see *Yellow Tax Handbook*, 1993–94, 32nd edition.
Simon's Tax Cases—s 150(3), [1998] STC (SCD) 6; *Quinn v Cooper* [1998] STC 772.
Definitions—"Allowable loss", ss 8(2), 16, 288(1); "chargeable gain", s 15(2); "company", ss 99, 288(1); "issued", s 288(5); "shares", s 288(1); "the Taxes Act", s 288(1).
Amendments—[1] Words in sub-s (1) inserted by FA 1994 Sch 15 paras 28, 29.
[2] Sub-ss (8A)–(8C) inserted by FA 1995 s 69.
[3] Words in sub-s (10)(a) substituted by FA 1996 s 134(1), (2), Sch 20 para 54 with effect from the year 1996–97.
[4] Words in sub-ss (4), (5), (7) substituted and word in sub-s (4) inserted by FA 1998 Sch 13 para 42 with effect in relation to disposals made after 5 April 1998.
[5] Word in sub-s (8) repealed by FA 1998 Sch 13 para 42, Sch 27 Part III(14) with effect in relation to events occurring after 5 April 1998.
[6] Word in sub-s (8A)(a) repealed by FA 1998 Sch 13 para 42, Sch 27 Part III(14) with effect in relation to new shares (within the meaning of TCGA 1992 s 150(8A)) issued after 5 April 1998.
[7] Sub-s (8D) inserted by FA 1998 Sch 13 para 42 with effect in relation to new shares (within the meaning of TA 1988 s 304A) issued after 5 April 1998.
[8] Sub-s (12) inserted by FA 1998 Sch 13 para 42 with effect in relation to events occurring after 5 April 1998.

[150A Enterprise investment schemes

(1) For the purpose of determining the gain or loss on any disposal of ...[5] shares by an individual where—

    (a) an amount of relief is attributable to the shares, and
    (b) apart from this subsection there would be a loss,

the consideration given by him for the shares shall be treated as reduced by the amount of the relief.

(2) Subject to subsection (3) below, if on any disposal of ...[5] shares by an individual after the end of the period referred to in section 312(1A)(a) of the Taxes Act where an amount of relief is attributable to the shares, there would (apart from this subsection) be a gain, the gain shall not be a chargeable gain.

[(2A) Notwithstanding anything in section 16(2), subsection (2) above shall not apply to a disposal on which a loss accrues.][2]

(3) Where—

    (a) an individual's liability to income tax has been reduced (or treated by virtue of section 304 of the Taxes Act (husband and wife) as reduced) for any year of assessment under section 289A of that Act in respect of any issue of shares, and
    [(aa) the amount of the reduction is not found under section 289A(2)(b) of that Act, and][2]
    (b) the amount of the reduction ("A") is less than the amount ("B") which is equal to tax at the lower rate for that year on the amount subscribed for the issue,

then, if there is a disposal of the shares on which there is a gain, subsection (2) above shall apply only to so much of the gain as is found by multiplying it by the fraction—

$$\frac{A}{B}$$

(4) Any question as to—

    (a) which of any shares [acquired by an individual at different times a disposal relates to][5], being shares to which relief is attributable, or
    (b) whether a disposal relates to shares to which relief is attributable or to other shares,

shall for the purposes of capital gains tax be determined as for the purposes of section 299 of the Taxes Act; and Chapter I of this Part shall have effect subject to the foregoing provisions of this subsection.

(5) Sections 104, 105 and [106A][5] shall not apply to shares to which relief is attributable.

[(6) Where an individual holds shares which form part of the ordinary share capital of a company and include shares of more than one of the following kinds, namely—

    (a) shares to which relief is attributable and to which subsection (6A) below applies;
    (b) shares to which relief is attributable and to which that subsection does not apply; and
    (c) shares to which relief is not attributable,

then, if there is within the meaning of section 126 a reorganisation affecting those shares, section 127 shall apply (subject to the following provisions of this section) separately to shares falling within paragraph (a), (b) or (c) above (so that shares of each kind are treated as a separate holding of original shares and identified with a separate new holding).

(6A) This subsection applies to any shares if—

    (a) expenditure on the shares has been set under Schedule 5B to this Act against the whole or part of any gain; and
    (b) in relation to the shares there has been no chargeable event for the purposes of that Schedule.][6]

(7) Where—

(*a*) an individual holds shares ("the existing holding") which form part of the ordinary share capital of a company,

(*b*) there is, by virtue of any such allotment for payment as is mentioned in section 126(2)(*a*), a reorganisation affecting the existing holding, and

(*c*) immediately following the reorganisation, relief is attributable to the existing holding or the allotted shares,

sections 127 to 130 shall not apply in relation to the existing holding.

(8) Sections 135 and 136 shall not apply in respect of shares to which relief is attributable.

[(8A) Subsection (8) above shall not have effect to disapply section 135 or 136 where—

(*a*) the new holding consists of new ordinary shares carrying no present or future preferential right to dividends or to a company's assets on its winding up and no present or future ...[7] right to be redeemed,

(*b*) the new shares are issued on or after 29th November 1994 and after the end of the relevant period, and

(*c*) the condition in subsection (8B) below is satisfied.][3]

[(8B) The condition is that at some time before the issue of the new shares—

(*a*) the company issuing them issued eligible shares, and

(*b*) a certificate in relation to those eligible shares was issued by the company for the purposes of subsection (2) of section 306 of the Taxes Act and in accordance with that section.][3]

[(8C) In subsection (8A) above—

(*a*) "new holding" shall be construed in accordance with sections 126, 127, 135 and 136;

(*b*) "relevant period" means the period found by applying section 312(1A)(*a*) of the Taxes Act by reference to the company issuing the shares referred to in subsection (8) above and by reference to those shares.][3]

[(8D) Where shares to which relief is attributable are exchanged for other shares in circumstances such that section 304A of the Taxes Act (acquisition of share capital by new company) applies—

(*a*) subsection (8) above shall not have effect to disapply section 135; and

(*b*) subsections (2)(*b*), (3) and (4) of section 304A of the Taxes Act, and subsection (5) of that section so far as relating to section 306(2) of that Act, shall apply for the purposes of this section as they apply for the purposes of Chapter III of Part VII of that Act.][8]

(9) Where the relief attributable to any shares is reduced by virtue of section 305(2) of the Taxes Act—

(*a*) the sums allowable as deductions from the consideration in the computation, for the purposes of capital gains tax, of the gain or loss accruing to an individual on the disposal of any of the allotted shares or debentures shall be taken to include the amount of the reduction apportioned between the allotted shares or (as the case may be) debentures in [a way which is][4] just and reasonable, and

(*b*) the sums so allowable on the disposal (in circumstances in which the preceding provisions of this section do not apply) of any of the shares referred to in section 305(1)(*a*) shall be taken to be reduced by the amount mentioned in paragraph (*a*) above, similarly apportioned between those shares.

(10) There shall be made all such adjustments of capital gains tax, whether by way of assessment or by way of discharge or repayment of tax, as may be required in consequence of the relief being given or withdrawn.

[(10A) In this section—

"ordinary share capital" has the same meaning as in the Taxes Act;

"ordinary shares", in relation to a company, means shares forming part of its ordinary share capital.][9]

(11) Chapter III of Part VII of the Taxes Act (enterprise investment scheme) applies for the purposes of this section to determine whether relief is attributable to any shares and, if so, the amount of relief so attributable; and "eligible shares" has the same meaning as in that Chapter.

(12) References in this section to Chapter III of Part VII of the Taxes Act or any provision of that Chapter are to that Chapter or provision as it applies in relation to shares issued on or after 1st January 1994.][1]

Commentary—*Simon's Direct Tax Service* **C3.1005–1008.**
Revenue Internal Guidance—Capital gains manual CG 62810, 62815 (example illustrating sub-s (3)).
CG 62818 (example illustrating sub-s (1) where an allowable loss arises).
CG 62826 (example illustrating sub-ss (4) and (5)).
CG 62940–62942 (sub-s (8D): sets out and illustrates the circumstances where a share exchange is not treated as a disposal and the deferred gain does not come back into charge).
Definitions—"Chargeable gains", s 15(2); "company", ss 99, 288(1); "lower rate", TA 1988 s 832(1); "new holding", s 126(1); "ordinary share capital", TA 1988 s 832(1); "original shares", s 126(1); "relief", TA 1988 s 312(1); "shares", s 288(1); "year of assessment", s 288(1).
Cross references—See TCGA 1992 s 150 (business enterprise schemes).
TCGA 1992 s 150B (enterprise investment scheme: reduction of relief).
Amendments—[1] This section inserted by FA 1994 Sch 15 paras 28, 30 and has effect in relation to shares issued after 31 December 1993 and in relation to such shares from the year 1993–94 by virtue of FA 1994 s 137.

[2] Sub-ss (2A), (3)(*aa*) inserted by FA 1995 s 67, Sch 13 para 2(2), (3), with effect in relation to shares issued after 31 December 1993.
[3] Sub-ss (8A)–(8C) inserted by FA 1995 Sch 13 para 2(4).
[4] Words in sub-s (9)(*a*) substituted by FA 1996 s 134(1), (2), Sch 20 para 54 with effect from the year 1996–97.
[5] Word "eligible" in sub-ss (1) and (2) repealed, and words in sub-s (4)(*a*) and (5) substituted by FA 1998 Sch 13 para 24 with effect in relation to disposals made after 5 April 1998.
[6] Sub-ss (6), (6A) substituted by FA 1998 Sch 13 para 24 with effect in relation to reorganisations taking effect after 5 April 1998.
[7] Word in sub-s (8A)(a) repealed by FA 1998 Sch 13 para 24 with effect in relation to new shares (within the meaning of TCGA 1992 s 150A(8A)) issued after 5 April 1998.
[8] Sub-s (8D) inserted by FA 1998 Sch 13 para 24 with effect in relation to new shares (within the meaning of TA 1988 s 304A)) issued after 5 April 1998.
[9] Sub-s (10A) inserted by FA 1998 Sch 13 para 24 with effect in relation to events occurring after 5 April 1998.

[150B Enterprise investment scheme: reduction of relief

(1) This section has effect where section 150A(2) applies on a disposal of ...[2] shares, and before the disposal but on or after 29th November 1994—

    (*a*) value is received in circumstances where relief attributable to the shares is reduced by an amount under section 300(1A)(*a*) of the Taxes Act,
    (*b*) there is a repayment, redemption, repurchase or payment in circumstances where relief attributable to the shares is reduced by an amount under section 303(1A)(*a*) of that Act, or
    (*c*) paragraphs (*a*) and (*b*) above apply.

(2) If section 150A(2) applies on the disposal but section 150A(3) does not, section 150A(2) shall apply only to so much of the gain as remains after deducting so much of it as is found by multiplying it by the fraction—

    (*a*) whose numerator is equal to the amount by which the relief attributable to the shares is reduced as mentioned in subsection (1) above, and
    (*b*) whose denominator is equal to the amount of the relief attributable to the shares.

(3) If section 150A(2) and (3) apply on the disposal, section 150A(2) shall apply only to so much of the gain as is found by—

    (*a*) taking the part of the gain found under section 150A(3), and
    (*b*) deducting from that part so much of it as is found by multiplying it by the fraction mentioned in subsection (2) above.

(4) Where the relief attributable to the shares is reduced as mentioned in subsection (1) above by more than one amount, the numerator mentioned in subsection (2) above shall be taken to be equal to the aggregate of the amounts.

(5) The denominator mentioned in subsection (2) above shall be found without regard to any reduction mentioned in subsection (1) above.

(6) Subsections (11) and (12) of section 150A apply for the purposes of this section as they apply for the purposes of that section.][1]

Commentary—*Simon's Direct Tax Service* E3.140, 142.
Definitions—"Eligible shares", TA 1988 s 289(7); "relief attributable to the shares", TA 1988 s 289B(1); "shares", s 288(1); "value received", TA 1988 ss 300, 303.
Amendments—[1] This section inserted by FA 1995 s 67, Sch 13 para 3.
[2] Word "eligible" in sub-s (1) repealed by FA 1998 Sch 13 para 25 with effect in relation to disposals made after 5 April 1998.

[150C Enterprise investment scheme: re-investment

Schedule 5B to this Act (which provides relief in respect of re-investment under the enterprise investment scheme) shall have effect.][1]

Commentary—*Simon's Direct Tax Service* E3.145–148.
Amendments—[1] This section inserted by FA 1995 s 67, Sch 13 para 4(1), with effect in relation to gains accruing and events occurring after 28 November 1994.

[150D Enterprise investment scheme: application of taper relief

Schedule 5BA to this Act (which provides for the application of taper relief in cases where relief under Schedule 5B, or Chapter III of Part VII of the Taxes Act, applies) shall have effect.][1]

Amendment—[1] This section inserted by FA 1999 s 72(1) with effect from 27 July 1999.

151 Personal equity plans

(1) The Treasury may make regulations providing that an individual who invests under a plan shall be entitled to relief from capital gains tax in respect of the investments.

(2) Subsections [(1A)][4] to (5) of section 333 of the Taxes Act ...[3] shall apply in relation to regulations under subsection (1) above as they apply in relation to regulations under subsection (1) of that section but with the substitution for any reference to income tax of a reference to capital gains tax.

[(2A) Section 333A of the Taxes Act (...[3] tax representatives) shall apply in relation to regulations under subsection (1) above as it applies in relation to regulations under section 333 of that Act.][2]

(3) Regulations under this section may include provision securing that losses are disregarded for the purposes of capital gains tax where they accrue on the disposal of investments on or after 18th January 1988.

[(4) Regulations under this section may include provision which, for cases where a person subscribes to a plan by transferring or renouncing shares or rights to shares—

   (*a*) modifies the effect of this Act in relation to their acquisition and their transfer or renunciation; and

   (*b*) makes consequential modifications of the effect of this Act in relation to anything which (apart from the regulations) would have been regarded on or after their acquisition as an indistinguishable part of the same asset.]¹

Commentary—*Simon's Direct Tax Service* **C1.103**.
Regulations—Personal Equity Plan Regulations, SI 1989/469.
Individual Savings Account Regulations, SI 1998/1870.
Individual Savings Account (Amendment) Regulations, SI 1998/3174.
Revenue & other press releases—IR Tax Bulletin April 1997 p 418 (explains the rules whereby certain shares received when a building society or insurance company transfers its business to a company may be transferred into a PEP).
Definition—''The Taxes Act'', s 288(1).
Amendments—¹ Sub-s (4) inserted by FA 1993 s 85.
² Sub-s (2A) inserted by FA 1995 s 64(2).
³ Words in sub-ss (2), (2A) repealed by FA 1998 s 165, Sch 27 Part III(15) with effect from 31 July 1998.
⁴ Words in sub-s (2) substituted by FA 1998 s 75(6) with effect from 31 July 1998.

[151A Venture capital trusts: reliefs

(1) A gain or loss accruing to an individual on a qualifying disposal of any ordinary shares in a company which—

   (*a*) was a venture capital trust at the time when he acquired the shares, and

   (*b*) is still such a trust at the time of the disposal,

shall not be a chargeable gain or, as the case may be, an allowable loss.

(2) For the purposes of this section a disposal of shares is a qualifying disposal in so far as—

   (*a*) it is made by an individual who has attained the age of eighteen years;

   (*b*) the shares disposed of were not acquired in excess of the permitted maximum for any year of assessment; and

   (*c*) that individual acquired those shares for bona fide commercial purposes and not as part of a scheme or arrangement the main purpose of which, or one of the main purposes of which, is the avoidance of tax.

(3) Schedule 5C shall have effect for providing relief in respect of gains invested in venture capital trusts.

(4) In determining for the purposes of this section whether a disposal by any person of shares in a venture capital trust relates to shares acquired in excess of the permitted maximum for any year of assessment, it shall be assumed (subject to subsection (5) below)—

   (*a*) as between shares acquired by the same person on different days, that those acquired on a earlier day are disposed of by that person before those acquired on a later day; and

   (*b*) as between shares acquired by the same person on the same day, that those acquired in excess of the permitted maximum are disposed of by that person before he disposes of any other shares acquired on that day.

(5) It shall be assumed for the purposes of subsection (1) above that a person who disposes of shares in a venture capital trust disposes of shares acquired at a time when it was not such a trust before he disposes of any other shares in that trust.

(6) References in this section to shares in a venture capital trust acquired in excess of the permitted maximum for any year of assessment shall be construed in accordance with the provisions of Part II of Schedule 15B to the Taxes Act; and the provisions of that Part of that Schedule shall apply (with subsections (4) and (5) above) for identifying the shares which are, in any case, to be treated as representing shares acquired in excess of the permitted maximum.

(7) In this section and section 151B ''ordinary shares'' in relation to a company, means any shares forming part of the company's ordinary share capital (within the meaning of the Taxes Act).]¹

Commentary—*Simon's Direct Tax Service* **C3.1103**.
Amendment—¹ This section inserted by FA 1995 s 72(3), with effect from the year 1995–96.

[151B Venture capital trusts: supplementary

(1) Sections 104, 105 and [106A]² shall not apply to any shares in a venture capital trust which are eligible for relief under section 151A(1).

(2) Subject to the following provisions of this section, where—

   (*a*) an individual holds any ordinary shares in a venture capital trust,

   (*b*) some of those shares fall within one of the paragraphs of subsection (3) below, and

   (*c*) others of those shares fall within at least one other of those paragraphs, then, if there is within the meaning of section 126 reorganisation affecting those shares, section 127 shall apply separately in relation to the shares (if any) falling within each of the paragraphs of that subsection (so that shares of each kind are treated as a separate holding of original shares and identified with a separate new holding).

(3) The kinds of shares referred to in subsection (2) above are—

(a) any shares in a venture capital trust which are eligible for relief under section 151A(1) and by reference to which any person has been given or is entitled to claim relief under Part I of Schedule 15B to the Taxes Act;

(b) any shares in a venture capital trust which are eligible for relief under section 151A(1) but by reference to which no person has been given, or is entitled to claim, any relief under that Part of that Schedule;

(c) any shares in a venture capital trust by reference to which any person has been given, or is entitled to claim, any relief under that Part of that Schedule but which are not shares that are eligible for relief under section 151A(1); and

(d) any shares in a venture capital trust that do not fall within any of paragraphs (a) to (c) above.

(4) Where—

(a) an individual holds ordinary shares in a company ("the existing holding"),

(b) there is, by virtue of any such allotment for payment as is mentioned in section 126(2)(a), a reorganisation affecting the existing holding, and

(c) immediately following the reorganisation, the shares or the allotted holding are shares falling within any of paragraphs (a) to (c) of subsection (3) above,

sections 127 to 130 shall not apply in relation to the existing holding.

(5) Sections 135 and 136 shall not apply where—

(a) the exchanged holding consists of shares falling within paragraph (a) or (b) of subsection (3) above; and

(b) that for which the exchanged holding is or is treated as exchanged does not consist of ordinary shares in a venture capital trust.

(6) Where—

(a) the approval of any company as a venture capital trust is withdrawn, and

(b) the withdrawal of the approval is not one to which section 842AA(8) of the Taxes Act applies,

any person who at the time when the withdrawal takes effect is holding shares in that company which (apart from the withdrawal) would be eligible for relief under section 151A(1) shall be deemed for the purposes of this Act, at that time, to have disposed of and immediately reacquired those shares for a consideration equal to their market value at that time.

(7) The disposal that is deemed to take place by virtue of subsection (6) above shall be deemed for the purposes of section 151A to take place while the company is still a venture capital trust; but, for the purpose of applying sections 104, 105 and [106A][2] to the shares that are deemed to be re-acquired, it shall be assumed that the re-acquisition for which that subsection provides takes place immediately after the company ceases to be such a trust.

(8) For the purposes of this section—

(a) shares are eligible for relief under section 151A(1) at any time when they are held by an individual whose disposal of the shares at that time would (on the assumption, where it is not the case, that the individual attained the age of eighteen years before that time) be a disposal to which section 151A(1) would apply; and

(b) shares shall not, in relation to any time, be treated as shares by reference to which relief has been given under Part I of Schedule 15B to the Taxes Act if that time falls after—

(i) any relief given by reference to those shares has been reduced or withdrawn,

(ii) any chargeable event (within the meaning of Schedule 5C) has occurred in relation to those shares, or

(iii) the death of a person who held those shares immediately before his death;

and

[(c) a reference to the exchanged holding is, in relation to section 135 or 136, to the shares in the company referred to in that section as company A.][3][1]

Commentary—*Simon's Direct Tax Service* **C3.1103.**
Amendments—[1] This section inserted by FA 1995 s 72(3), with effect from the year 1995–96.
[2] Section number in sub-ss (1), (7) substituted by FA 1998 s 124(6) with effect in relation to any disposal on or after 6 April 1998, subject to FA 1998 s 124(8).
[3] Sub-s 8(c) substituted by FA 2002 s 45, Sch 9 paras 5(1), (9), 7 with effect for shares or debentures issued after 16 April 2002. The reference to shares or debentures includes any interests falling to be treated as shares or debentures for the purposes of TCGA 1992 s 135 or 136 as substituted by FA 2002 Sch 9. Sub-s (8)(c) previously read as follows—

"(c) the references, in relation to sections 135 and 136, to the exchanged holding is a reference to the shares in company B or, as the case may be, to the shares or debentures in respect of which shares or debentures are issued under the arrangement in question."

PART V
TRANSFER OF BUSINESS ASSETS

CHAPTER I
GENERAL PROVISIONS

Concession D16—Relief for the replacement of business assets: repurchase of the same asset.
D22—Relief for the replacement of business assets: expenditure on improvements to existing assets.
D23—Relief for the replacement of business assets: partition of land on the dissolution of a partnership.
D24—Relief for the replacement of business assets: assets not brought immediately into trading use.
D25—Relief for the replacement of business assets: acquisition of an interest in an asset already used for the purposes of a trade.

D33—CGT on compensation and damages. This Concession has been revised.
Statement of Practice D6—Rollover relief: extension of time limit for acquisition of development land where land acquired under compulsory purchase powers is leased back to the vendor.
D11—A partner may claim relief in respect of the disposal of a qualifying asset owned by him which is used for the trade etc carried on by the partnership of which he is a member.
Cross references—See FA 1990 Sch 12 para 7 (transfer of undertakings of Independent Broadcasting Authority and Cable Authority).
TCGA 1992 s 236 (restriction of relief under TCGA 1992 ss 152–158 where relief has been given under TCGA 1992 s 229 (sale of shares to employee share ownership trust) and a chargeable event under TCGA 1992 s 232 or 233 has occurred).

Replacement of business assets

152 Roll-over relief

(1) If the consideration which a person carrying on a trade obtains for the disposal of, or of his interest in, assets (''the old assets'') used, and used only, for the purposes of the trade throughout the period of ownership is applied by him in acquiring other assets, or an interest in other assets (''the new assets'') which on the acquisition are taken into use, and used only, for the purposes of the trade, and the old assets and new assets are within the classes of assets listed in section 155, then the person carrying on the trade shall, on making a claim as respects the consideration which has been so applied, be treated for the purposes of this Act—

(*a*) as if the consideration for the disposal of, or of the interest in, the old assets were (if otherwise of a greater amount or value) of such amount as would secure that on the disposal neither a gain nor a loss accrues to him, and

(*b*) as if the amount or value of the consideration for the acquisition of, or of the interest in, the new assets were reduced by the excess of the amount or value of the actual consideration for the disposal of, or of the interest in, the old assets over the amount of the consideration which he is treated as receiving under paragraph (*a*) above,

but neither paragraph (*a*) nor paragraph (*b*) above shall affect the treatment for the purposes of this Act of the other party to the transaction involving the old assets, or of the other party to the transaction involving the new assets.

(2) Where subsection (1)(*a*) above applies to exclude a gain which, in consequence of Schedule 2, is not all chargeable gain, the amount of the reduction to be made under subsection (1)(*b*) above shall be the amount of the chargeable gain, and not the whole amount of the gain.

(3) Subject to subsection (4) below, this section shall only apply if the acquisition of, or of the interest in, the new assets takes place, or an unconditional contract for the acquisition is entered into, in the period beginning 12 months before and ending 3 years after the disposal of, or of the interest in, the old assets, or at such earlier or later time as the Board may by notice allow.

(4) Where an unconditional contract for the acquisition is so entered into, this section may be applied on a provisional basis without waiting to ascertain whether the new assets, or the interest in the new assets, is acquired in pursuance of the contract, and, when that fact is ascertained, all necessary adjustments shall be made by making [or amending]¹ assessments or by repayment or discharge of tax, and shall be so made notwithstanding any limitation on the time within which assessments [or amendments]¹ may be made.

(5) This section shall not apply unless the acquisition of, or of the interest in, the new assets was made for the purpose of their use in the trade, and not wholly or partly for the purpose of realising a gain from the disposal of, or of the interest in, the new assets.

(6) If, over the period of ownership or any substantial part of the period of ownership, part of a building or structure is, and part is not, used for the purposes of a trade, this section shall apply as if the part so used, with any land occupied for purposes ancillary to the occupation and use of that part of the building or structure, were a separate asset, and subject to any necessary apportionments of consideration for an acquisition or disposal of, or of an interest in, the building or structure and other land.

(7) If the old assets were not used for the purposes of the trade throughout the period of ownership this section shall apply as if a part of the asset representing its use for the purposes of the trade having regard to the time and extent to which it was, and was not, used for those purposes, were a separate asset which had been wholly used for the purposes of the trade, and this subsection shall

apply in relation to that part subject to any necessary apportionment of consideration for an acquisition or disposal of, or of the interest in, the asset.

(8) This section shall apply in relation to a person who, either successively or at the same time, carries on 2 or more trades as if both or all of them were a single trade.

(9) In this section "period of ownership" does not include any period before 31st March 1982.

(10) The provisions of this Act fixing the amount of the consideration deemed to be given for the acquisition or disposal of assets shall be applied before this section is applied.

(11) Without prejudice to section 52(4), where consideration is given for the acquisition or disposal of assets some or part of which are assets in relation to which a claim under this section applies, and some or part of which are not, the consideration shall be apportioned in such manner as is just and reasonable.

Commentary—*Simon's Direct Tax Service* **C3.301–305.**
Concession D16—Rollover relief allowed where same asset reacquired for purely commercial reasons.
D24—Assets not immediately taken into trade use, but enhanced, may qualify for rollover relief.
Statement of Practice D6—Extension of time limit in cases of compulsory acquisition.
SP 8/81, paras 1, 2—CGT rollover relief for replacement of business assets: trades carried on successively. Revenue will accept separate trades carried on within 3 years of one another as "successively".
Revenue Interpretation RI 5—Circumstances in which the Revenue may allow extension of time beyond the limit in sub-s (3) above.
RI 7—Interpretation of the words "on the acquisition" in sub-s (1) above.
RI 11—Rollover relief in respect of gain arising on grant of option over land.
RI 28—Rollover relief: commercial letting of furnished holiday accommodation in excess of 30 days.
Revenue & other press releases—ICAEW TR 588 25-9-85 (limited application of Furniss v Dawson principle where wife owns assets which have been used in business carried on by husband and transferred beneficial ownership to husband prior to sale of business. Revenue will not question most transactions, but nature and consequences of transaction will be considered and Revenue may seek to restrict relief to the amount which would have been due to wife).
Country Landowners' Association 19-12-91 (share farming: both parties to a share farming agreement are considered to be carrying on a farming business for tax purposes).
Revenue Internal Guidance—Capital gains manual Capital Gains Manual CG 60640–60644 (sub-s (3): circumstances governing extension of time limit for re-investment).
CG 60670–60673 (determination of claims for relief under s 152).
CG 60750–60756 (requirements as to ownership of assets).
CG 60770–60777 (application of the disposal consideration and allocation of relief between several new assets).
CG 60791 (relief is not available on deemed disposals under s 178(3) or s 179(3)).
CG 60810 (husbands and wives are treated as separate persons for rollover relief purposes).
CG 60830–60834 (meaning of " on the acquisition are taken into use" in sub-s (1)—see also Concession D24).
CG 60870 (no relief is normally available on a deemed disposal and acquisition of the same asset—but see Concession D16).
CG 60873 (no rollover relief is available on the acquisition of a freehold reversion by a tenant followed by the sale of part of the freehold of the same land).
CG 61020–61021 (rollover relief is available on the grant of an option over a qualifying asset).
CG 61030–61031 (application to licensed premises).
CG 61150–61173 (treatment of partnerships).
Simon's Tax Cases—*Campbell Connelly & Co Ltd v Barnett* [1994] STC 50*; *Milton v Chivers* [1996] STC (SCD) 36*; *Victoria and Albert Museum Trustees v C & E Comrs* [1996] STC 101*; *Watton v Tippett* [1997] STC 893*.
s 152(1), (3), (8), *Steibelt v Paling* [1999] STC 594.
s 152(7), *Richart v J Lyons & Co Ltd* [1989] STC 665*.
Definitions—"Asset", s 21(1); "the Board", s 288(1); "chargeable gain", s 15(2); "land", s 288(1); "notice", s 288(1); "trade", ss 158(2), 288(1), TA 1988 s 832(1).
Cross references—See TA 1988 s 503 (treatment of the commercial letting of furnished holiday accommodation for the purposes of this section);
TCGA 1992 s 42(5) (apportionment of expenditure on part disposals).
TCGA 1992 s 80(6) (restriction of relief where trustees become non-resident before acquiring new asset).
TCGA 1992 s 84 (restriction of relief where new assets acquired by dual resident trustees).
TCGA 1992 s 153 (assets only partly replaced).
TCGA 1992 s 153A (provisional application of this section upon declaration of intention to acquire new assets).
TCGA 1992 s 154 (new assets which are depreciating assets).
TCGA 1992 s 157 (assets owned by an individual and used in a trade carried on by his family company).
TCGA 1992 s 158 (application of this section to activities other than trades).
TCGA 1992 s 159(1) (restriction of relief for non-residents and dual resident persons).
TCGA 1992 s 175 (application of this section to replacement of business assets by members of a group).
TCGA 1992 s 185(3) (restriction of relief where company becomes non-resident before acquiring new asset).
TCGA 1992 s 198 (restriction of relief in respect of assets used in oil industry ring fence trade).
TCGA 1992 s 236 (prevention of double charge under this section and ss 232–233).
TCGA 1992 s 241(3) (commercial letting of furnished holiday accommodation to be treated as a trade for the purposes of this section).
TCGA 1992 s 247(5), (5A) (rollover relief on compulsory acquisition of land; this section to apply on an intra-group disposal as if both companies were the same person and by virtue of sub-s (5A) as if the reference in sub-s (2C) above to the new asset was a reference to new land).
TCGA 1992 Sch 4 para 2 (deferred charges on gains accruing before 31 March 1982).
F(No 2)A 1992 Sch 17 para 3 (privatisation of Northern Ireland Electricity; rollover relief).
FA 2000 Sch 22 para 67 (this section does not apply if or to the extent that new assets are tonnage assets).
Modifications—TCGA 1992 Sch 7AB paras 1, 2 (modification of this section for the purposes of TCGA 1992 s 179B (as inserted by FA 2002 s 43) which relates to roll-over of degrouping charge on business assets).
Amendments—Words in sub-s (4) inserted by FA 1996 ss 121(8), 141(1) with effect from the year 1996–97 and, so far as relating to corporation tax, with effect as respects accounting periods ending after 30 June 1999 (by virtue of Finance Act 1994, Section 199, (Appointed Day) Order, SI 1998/3173 art 2).

153 Assets only partly replaced

(1) Section 152(1) shall not apply if part only of the amount or value of the consideration for the disposal of, or of the interest in, the old assets is applied as described in that subsection, but if all of the amount or value of the consideration except for a part which is less than the amount of the gain (whether all chargeable gain or not) accruing on the disposal of, or of the interest in, the old assets is

so applied, then the person carrying on the trade, on making a claim as respects the consideration which has been so applied, shall be treated for the purposes of this Act—

(a) as if the amount of the gain so accruing were reduced to the amount of the said part (and, if not all chargeable gain, with a proportionate reduction in the amount of the chargeable gain), and

(b) as if the amount or value of the consideration for the acquisition of, or of the interest in, the new assets were reduced by the amount by which the gain is reduced (or as the case may be the amount by which the chargeable gain is proportionately reduced) under paragraph (a) of this subsection,

but neither paragraph (a) nor paragraph (b) above shall affect the treatment for the purposes of this Act of the other party to the transaction involving the old assets, or of the other party to the transaction involving the new assets.

(2) Subsections (3) to (11) of 152 shall apply as if this section formed part of that section.

Commentary—*Simon's Direct Tax Service* **C3.309, 321.**
Definitions—''Asset'', s 21(1); ''chargeable gain'', s 15(2); ''trade'', ss 158(2), 288(1), TA 1988 s 832(1).
Cross references—TA 1988 s 503 (treatment of the commercial letting of furnished holiday accommodation for the purposes of this section);
TCGA 1992 s 42(5) (apportionment of expenditure on part disposals).
TCGA 1992 s 153A (provisional application of this section upon declaration of intention to acquire new assets).
TCGA 1992 s 154 (new assets which are depreciating assets).
TCGA 1992 s 157 (assets owned by an individual and used in a trade carried on by his family company).
TCGA 1992 s 158 (application of this section to activities other than trades).
TCGA 1992 s 175 (application of this section to replacement of business assets by members of a group).
TCGA 1992 s 198 (restriction of relief in respect of assets used in oil industry ring fence trade).
TCGA 1992 s 236 (prevention of double charge under this section and ss 232–238).
TCGA 1992 s 241(3) (commercial letting of furnished holiday accommodation to be treated as a trade for the purposes of this section).
F(No 2)A 1992 Sch 17 para 3 (privatisation of Northern Ireland Electricity; rollover relief).
FA 2000 Sch 22 para 67 (this section does not apply if or to the extent that new assets are tonnage assets).
Modifications—TCGA 1992 Sch 7AB paras 1, 3 (modification of this section for the purposes of TCGA 1992 s 179B (as inserted by FA 2002) which relates to roll-over of degrouping charge on business assets).

[153A Provisional application of sections 152 and 153

(1) This section applies where a person carrying on a trade who for a consideration disposes of, or of his interest in, any assets (''the old assets'') declares, in his return for the chargeable period in which the disposal takes place—

(a) that the whole or any specified part of the consideration will be applied in the acquisition of, or of an interest in, other assets (''the new assets'') which on the acquisition will be taken into use, and used only, for the purposes of the trade;

(b) that the acquisition will take place as mentioned in subsection (3) of section 152; and

(c) that the new assets will be within the classes listed in section 155.

(2) Until the declaration ceases to have effect, section 152 or, as the case may be, section 153 shall apply as if the acquisition had taken place and the person had made a claim under that section.

(3) The declaration shall cease to have effect as follows—

(a) if and to the extent that it is withdrawn before the relevant day, or is superseded before that day by a valid claim made under section 152 or 153, on the day on which it is so withdrawn or superseded; and

(b) if and to the extent that it is not so withdrawn or superseded, on the relevant day.

(4) On the declaration ceasing to have effect in whole or in part, all necessary adjustments—

(a) shall be made by making or amending assessments or by repayment or discharge of tax; and

(b) shall be so made notwithstanding any limitation on the time within which assessments or amendments may be made.

(5) In this section ''the relevant day'' means—

(a) in relation to capital gains tax, the third anniversary of the 31st January next following the year of assessment in which the disposal of, or of the interest in, the old assets took place;

(b) in relation to corporation tax, the fourth anniversary of the last day of the accounting period in which that disposal took place.

(6) Subsections (6), (8), (10) and (11) of section 152 shall apply for the purposes of this section as they apply for the purposes of that section.][1]

Commentary—*Simon's Direct Tax Service* **C3.306; E1.837.**
Definitions—''Accounting period'', TA 1988 s 834(1); ''asset'', s 21(1); ''chargeable period'', s 288(1); ''trade'', s 288(1).
Modifications—TCGA 1992 Sch 7AB paras 1, 4 (modification of this section for the purposes of TCGA 1992 s 179B (as inserted by FA 2002 s 43) which relates to roll-over of degrouping charge on business assets).
Amendments—[1] This section inserted by FA 1996 ss 121(8), 141(2) with effect as respects capital gains tax from the year 1996–97 and, so far as relating to corporation tax, as respects accounting periods ending after 30 June 1999 (by virtue of Finance Act 1994, Section 199, (Appointed Day) Order, SI 1998/3173 art 2).

154 New assets which are depreciating assets

(1) Sections 152, 153 and 229 shall have effect subject to the provisions of this section in which—

(a) the ''held-over gain'' means the amount by which, under those sections, and apart from the provisions of this section, any chargeable gain on one asset (''asset No 1'') is reduced, with a corresponding reduction of the expenditure allowable in respect of another asset (''asset No 2''), and

(b) any reference to a gain of any amount being carried forward to any asset is a reference to a reduction of that amount in a chargeable gain coupled with a reduction of the same amount in expenditure allowable in respect of that asset.

(2) If asset No 2 is a depreciating asset, the held-over gain shall not be carried forward, but the claimant shall be treated as if so much of the chargeable gain on asset No 1 as is equal to the held-over gain did not accrue until—

    (a) the claimant disposes of asset No 2, or

    (b) he ceases to use asset No 2 for the purposes of a trade carried on by him, or

    (c) the expiration of a period of 10 years beginning with the acquisition of asset No 2,

whichever event comes first.

(3) Where section 229 has effect subject to the provisions of this section, subsection (2)(b) above shall have effect as if it read—

    "(b) section 232(3) applies as regards asset No 2 (whether or not by virtue of section 232(5)), or".

(4) If, in the circumstances specified in subsection (5) below, the claimant acquires an asset ("asset No 3") which is not a depreciating asset, and claims under section 152 or 153—

    (a) the gain held-over from asset No 1 shall be carried forward to asset No 3, and

    (b) the claim which applies to asset No 2 shall be treated as withdrawn (so that subsection (2) above does not apply).

(5) The circumstances are that asset No 3 is acquired not later than the time when the chargeable gain postponed under subsection (2) above would accrue and, assuming—

    (a) that the consideration for asset No 1 was applied in acquiring asset No 3, and

    (b) that the time between the disposal of asset No 1 and the acquisition of asset No 3 was within the time limited by section 152(3),

the whole amount of the postponed gain could be carried forward from asset No 1 to asset No 3; and the claim under subsection (4) above shall be accepted as if those assumptions were true.

(6) If part only of the postponed gain could be carried forward from asset No 1 to asset No 3, and the claimant so requires, that and the other part of the postponed gain shall be treated as derived from 2 separate assets, so that, on that claim—

    (a) subsection (4) above applies to the first-mentioned part, and

    (b) the other part remains subject to subsection (2) above.

(7) For the purposes of this section, an asset is a depreciating asset at any time if—

    (a) at that time it is a wasting asset, as defined in section 44, or

    (b) within the period of 10 years beginning at that time it will become a wasting asset (so defined).

Commentary—*Simon's Direct Tax Service* **C3.311.**
Concession D45—CGT charge does not arise where the cessation mentioned in sub-s (2)(b) above occurs on death of claimant.
Revenue Interpretation RI 42—Whether a building constricted on leasehold land where the lease has 60 years or less to run and whether an item of fixed plant or machinery which has become part of a building are depreciating assets.
Definitions—"Asset", s 21(1); "chargeable gain", s 15(2); "trade", ss 158(2), 288(1), TA 1988 s 832(1); "wasting asset", ss 44, 288(1), Sch 8 para 1.
Revenue & other press releases—IR 30-10-79 ("asset no. 3" must be acquired not later than the earliest of events in s 154(2)).
Cross references—TA 1988 s 503 (treatment of the commercial letting of furnished holiday accommodation for the purposes of this section);
TCGA 1992 s 42(5) (apportionment of expenditure on part disposals).
TCGA 1992 s 157 (assets owned by an individual and used in a trade carried on by his family company).
TCGA 1992 s 158 (application of this section to activities other than trades).
TCGA 1992 s 175(1), (3) (trades carried on by members of a group of companies to be treated as a single trade for the purposes of this section; application of sub-s (2) above to claims by group members).
TCGA 1992 s 198 (restriction of relief in respect of assets used in oil industry ring fence trade).
TCGA 1992 s 236 (prevention of double charge under this section and ss 232–233).
TCGA 1992 s 241(3) (commercial letting of furnished holiday accommodation to be treated as a trade for the purposes of this section).
TCGA 1992 s 248(3) (roll-over relief on compulsory acquisition of land where new land is a depreciating asset).
TCGA 1992 Sch 4 para 2(4) (rebasing provisions where relief for assets acquired after 18 March 1991 is claimed under Sch 4 following deferral under this section).
TCGA 1992 Sch 4 para 3 (reduction of charge to tax deferred under this section).
TCGA 1992 Sch 4 para 4 (deferred charges on gains accruing before 31 March 1982).
F(No 2)A 1992 Sch 17 para 3 (privatisation of Northern Ireland Electricity; rollover relief).

155 Relevant classes of assets

The classes of assets for the purposes of section 152(1) are as follows.

CLASS 1

Assets within heads A and B below.

Head A

1. Any building or part of a building and any permanent or semi-permanent structure in the nature of a building, occupied (as well as used) only for the purposes of the trade.

2. Any land occupied (as well as used) only for the purposes of the trade.

Head A has effect subject to section 156.

Head B

Fixed plant or machinery which does not form part of a building or of a permanent or semi-permanent structure in the nature of a building.

CLASS 2

Ships, aircraft and hovercraft ("hovercraft" having the same meaning as in the Hovercraft Act 1968).

CLASS 3

Satellites, space stations and spacecraft (including launch vehicles).

CLASS 4

Goodwill.

CLASS 5

Milk quotas (that is, rights to sell dairy produce without being liable to pay milk levy or to deliver dairy produce without being liable to pay a contribution to milk levy) and potato quotas (that is, rights to produce potatoes without being liable to pay more than the ordinary contribution to the Potato Marketing Board's fund).

[CLASS 6

Ewe and suckler cow premium quotas (that is, rights in respect of any ewes or suckler cows to receive payments by way of any subsidy entitlement to which is determined by reference to limits contained in a Community instrument).][1]

[CLASS 7

Fish quota (that is, an allocation of quota to catch fish stocks, which derives from the Total Allowable Catches set in pursuance of Article 8(4) of Council Regulation (EEC) No 3760/92 and under annual Council Regulations made in accordance with that Article, or under any replacement Community Instruments).][2]

[CLASS 8

Assets within heads A and B below.

Head A

Rights of a member of Lloyd's under a syndicate within the meaning of Chapter III of Part II of the Finance Act 1993.

Head B

An asset which a member of Lloyd's is treated as having acquired by virtue of section 82 of the Finance Act 1999.][3]

Commentary—*Simon's Direct Tax Service* **C3.303.**
Revenue Interpretation RI 11—Rollover relief in respect of gain arising on grant of option over land.
RI 42—Whether a building constricted on leasehold land where the lease has 60 years or less to run and whether an item of fixed plant or machinery which has become part of a building are depreciating assets.
RI 210—A bookmaker's pitch does not comprise land nor an interest in land within class 1 head A. Furthermore, the Revenue resist any argument that it represents goodwill within class 4.
Revenue Internal Guidance—Capital gains manual CG 60970–60975 (meaning of "fixed plant or machinery").
CG 60990–61002 (land and buildings qualifying for rollover relief).
CG 61080–61083 (various EC agricultural quotas now included as qualifying assets).
CG 68000–68062 (goodwill: meaning and circumstances in which it arises CG 68000–68083; franchises, dealerships and licences CG 68100–68132; restrictive covenants CG 68150–68204; procedures CG 68250–68414 including advice from Shares Valuation Division, appeals etc; valuation of goodwill CG 68540–68681; negligible value claims CG 68760–68765; disposal of part of business involves part disposal of goodwill of whole business CG 68850–68862).
Simon's Tax Cases—*Temperley v Visibell Ltd* [1974] STC 64*; *Anderton v Lamb* [1981] STC 43*; *Williams v Evans* [1982] STC 498*.
Definitions—"Asset", s 21(1); "control", s 288(1), TA 1988 s 416; "land", s 288(1); "trade", ss 158(2), 288(1), TA 1988 s 832(1).
Cross references—TA 1988 s 503 (treatment of the commercial letting of furnished holiday accommodation for the purposes of this section);
TCGA 1992 s 42(5) (apportionment of expenditure on part disposals).
TCGA 1992 s 157 (assets owned by an individual and used in a trade carried on by his family company).
TCGA 1992 s 158 (application of this section to activities other than trades).
TCGA 1992 s 175 (trades carried on by members of a group of companies to be treated as a single trade for the purposes of this section).
TCGA 1992 s 236 (prevention of double charge under this section and ss 232–233).
TCGA 1992 s 241(3) (commercial letting of furnished holiday accommodation to be treated as a trade for the purposes of this section).
F(No 2)A 1992 Sch 17 para 3 (privatisation of Northern Ireland Electricity; rollover relief);
FA 1993 s 86(2), (3) (Treasury may add further classes of assets in this section).
Modifications—TCGA 1992 Sch 7AB paras 1, 5 (modification of this section for the purposes of TCGA 1992 s 179B (as inserted by FA 2002) which relates to roll-over of degrouping charge on business assets).
Amendments—[1] Class 6 inserted by FA 1993 s 86(1), (4) where disposal of old assets or acquisition of new assets is after 31 December 1992.
[2] Class 7 inserted by Finance Act 1993, Section 86(2), (Fish Quota) Order, SI 1999/564 art 3 where disposal of old assets or acquisition of new assets is after 28 March 1999.
[3] Class 8 inserted by FA 1999 s 84 with effect for assets (or interests in them) acquired, or disposed of, after 5 April 1999.

156 Assets of Class 1

(1) This section has effect as respects head A of Class 1 in section 155.

(2) Head A shall not apply where the trade is a trade—

(*a*) of dealing in or developing land, or

(b) of providing services for the occupier of land in which the person carrying on the trade has an estate or interest.

(3) Where the trade is a trade of dealing in or developing land, but a profit on the sale of any land held for the purposes of the trade would not form part of the trading profits, then, as regards that land, the trade shall be treated for the purposes of subsection (2)(a) above as if it were not a trade of dealing in or developing land.

[(4) Where section 98 of the Taxes Act applies (tied premises: receipts and expenses treated as those of trade) the trader shall be treated, to the extent that the conditions in subsection (1) of that section are met in relation to premises, as occupying as well as using the premises for the purposes of the trade.]¹

Commentary—*Simon's Direct Tax Service* **C3.303.**
Definitions—"Asset", s 21(1); "land", s 288(1); "lessor", Sch 8 para 10(1); "the Taxes Act", s 288(1); "trade", ss 158(2), 288(1), TA 1988 s 832(1).
Cross references—TA 1988 s 503 (treatment of the commercial letting of furnished holiday accommodation for the purposes of this section);
TCGA 1992 s 42(5) (apportionment of expenditure on part disposals).
TCGA 1992 s 157 (assets owned by an individual and used in a trade carried on by his family company).
TCGA 1992 s 158 (application of this section to activities other than trades).
TCGA 1992 s 175 (trades carried on by members of a group of companies to be treated as a single trade for the purposes of this section).
TCGA 1992 s 236 (prevention of double charge under this section and ss 232–233).
TCGA 1992 s 241(3) (commercial letting of furnished holiday accommodation to be treated as a trade for the purposes of this section).
F(No 2)A 1992 Sch 17 para 3 (privatisation of Northern Ireland Electricity; rollover relief).
Amendments—¹ Sub-s (4) substituted by FA 1998 s 41(2) with effect from 17 March 1998, subject to the transitional provisions in FA 1998 s 41 sub-ss (3)–(7).

[156A Cessation of trade by limited liability partnership

(1) Where, immediately before the time of cessation of trade, a member of a limited liability partnership holds an asset, or an interest in an asset, acquired by him for a consideration treated as reduced under section 152 or 153, he shall be treated as if a chargeable gain equal to the amount of the reduction accrued to him immediately before that time.

(2) Where, as a result of section 154(2), a chargeable gain on the disposal of an asset, or an interest in an asset, by a member of a limited liability partnership has not accrued before the time of cessation of trade, the member shall be treated as if the chargeable gain accrued immediately before that time.

(3) In this section "the time of cessation of trade", in relation to a limited liability partnership, means the time when section 59A(1) ceases to apply in relation to the limited liability partnership.]¹

Amendments—¹ This section inserted by the Limited Liability Partnerships Act 2000 s 10(4) with effect from 6 April 2001 (by virtue of SI 2000/3316 art 2). For the full text of that Act, see *Halsbury's Statutes* (4th edn) PARTNERSHIP.

157 Trade carried on by [personal company]¹: business assets dealt with by individual

In relation to a case where—

(a) the person disposing of, or of his interest in, the old assets and acquiring the new assets, or an interest in them, is an individual, and
(b) the trade or trades in question are carried on not by that individual but by a company which, both at the time of the disposal and at the time of the acquisition referred to in paragraph (a) above, is his [personal company]¹, within the meaning of Schedule 6,

any reference in sections 152 to 156 to the person carrying on the trade (or the 2 or more trades) includes a reference to that individual.

Commentary—*Simon's Direct Tax Service* **C3.316.**
Revenue & other press releases—IR 10-11-81 (as regards an asset used by a family company, payment of rent by the company to an individual does not preclude a claim. Revenue view "a company" does not include the plural "companies").
Definitions—"Asset", s 21(1); "company", ss 99, 288(1); "personal company", Sch 6 para 1(2); "trade", s 288(1), TA 1988 s 832(1).
Cross references—TA 1988 s 503 (treatment of the commercial letting of furnished holiday accommodation for the purposes of this section);
TCGA 1992 s 42(5) (apportionment of expenditure on part disposals).
TCGA 1992 s 158 (application of this section to activities other than trades).
TCGA 1992 s 175 (trades carried on by members of a group of companies to be treated as a single trade for the purposes of this section).
TCGA 1992 s 236 (prevention of double charge under this section and ss 232–233).
TCGA 1992 s 241(3) (commercial letting of furnished holiday accommodation to be treated as a trade for the purposes of this section).
F(No 2)A 1992 Sch 17 para 3 (privatisation of Northern Ireland Electricity; rollover relief).
Amendments—¹ Words in heading and para (b) substituted by FA 1993 s 87 and Sch 7 para 1(1) in relation to disposals made after 15 March 1993.
Prospective amendment—Words in (b) will be substituted by FA 1998 s 140(3) with effect in relation to the year 2003–04 and subsequent years of assessment.

158 Activities other than trades, and interpretation

(1) Sections 152 to 157 shall apply with the necessary modifications—

(a) in relation to the discharge of the functions of a public authority, and (*b*) in relation to the occupation of woodlands where the woodlands are managed by the occupier on a commercial basis and with a view to the realisation of profits, and

(*c*) in relation to a profession, vocation, office or employment, and

(*d*) in relation to such of the activities of a body of persons whose activities are carried on otherwise than for profit and are wholly or mainly directed to the protection or promotion of the interests of its members in the carrying on of their trade or profession as are so directed, and

(*e*) in relation to the activities of an unincorporated association or other body chargeable to corporation tax, being a body not established for profit whose activities are wholly or mainly carried on otherwise than for profit, but in the case of assets within head A of class 1 only if they are both occupied and used by the body, and in the case of other assets only if they are used by the body,

as they apply in relation to a trade.

(2) In sections 152 to 157 and this section the expressions "trade", "profession", "vocation", "office" and "employment" have the same meanings as in the Income Tax Acts, but not so as to apply the provisions of the Income Tax Acts as to the circumstances in which, on a change in the persons carrying on a trade, a trade is to be regarded as discontinued, or as set up and commenced.

(3) Sections 152 to 157 and this section shall be construed as one.

Commentary—*Simon's Direct Tax Service* **C3.302.**
Concession D15—Relief for the replacement of business assets: unincorporated associations.
Statement of Practice SP 5/86—CGT: relief for replacement of business assets: employees and office-holders.
Revenue Internal Guidance—Capital gains tax manual, CG 67600–67603 (registered trade unions may benefit where gains not wholly exempt under TA 1988 s 467; worked examples).
Revenue & other press releases—CCAB TR489 December 1982 (qualifying unincorporated associations owning property through a company the shares in which are held by the association or its members, roll-over relief s 152 can be claimed subject to usual conditions).
Definitions—"Asset", s 21(1); "trade", ss 158(2), 288(1), TA 1988 s 832(1).
Cross references—See TCGA 1992 s 42(5) (apportionment of expenditure on part disposals).
TCGA 1992 s 175 (trades carried on by members of a group of companies to be treated as a single trade for the purposes of this section).
TCGA 1992 s 236 (prevention of double charge under this section and ss 232–233).

159 Non-residents: roll-over relief

(1) Section 152 shall not apply in the case of a person if the old assets are chargeable assets in relation to him at the time they are disposed of, unless the new assets are chargeable assets in relation to him immediately after the time they are acquired.

(2) Subsection (1) above shall not apply where—

(*a*) the person acquires the new assets after he has disposed of the old assets, and

(*b*) immediately after the time they are acquired the person is resident or ordinarily resident in the United Kingdom.

(3) Subsection (2) above shall not apply where immediately after the time the new assets are acquired—

(*a*) the person is a dual resident, and

(*b*) the new assets are prescribed assets.

(4) For the purposes of this section an asset is at any time a chargeable asset in relation to a person if, were it to be disposed of at that time, any chargeable gains accruing to him on the disposal—

(*a*) would be gains in respect of which he would be chargeable to capital gains tax under section 10(1), or

(*b*) would form part of his chargeable profits for corporation tax purposes by virtue of section 10(3).

(5) In this section—

"dual resident" means a person who is resident or ordinarily resident in the United Kingdom and falls to be regarded for the purposes of any double taxation relief arrangements as resident in a territory outside the United Kingdom; and

"prescribed asset", in relation to a dual resident, means an asset in respect of which, by virtue of the asset being of a description specified in any double taxation relief arrangements, he falls to be regarded for the purposes of the arrangements as not liable in the United Kingdom to tax on gains accruing to him on a disposal.

(6) In this section—

(*a*) "the old assets" and "the new assets" have the same meanings as in section 152,

(*b*) references to disposal of the old assets include references to disposal of an interest in them, and

(*c*) references to acquisition of the new assets include references to acquisition of an interest in them or to entering into an unconditional contract for the acquisition of them.

(7) Where the acquisition of the new assets took place before 14th March 1989 and the disposal of the old assets took place, or takes place, on or after that date, this section shall not apply if the disposal of the old assets took place, or takes place, within 12 months of the acquisition of the new assets or such longer period as the Board may by notice allow.

Commentary—*Simon's Direct Tax Service* **C3.318.**
Definitions—"Asset", s 21(1); "the Board", s 288(1); "chargeable gain", s 15(2); "double taxation relief arrangements", s 288(1); "notice", s 288(1); "ordinarily resident", s 9(1); "resident", s 9(1).
Cross references—See TCGA 1992 Sch 7B paras 1, 6 (modification of sub-s (4)(*b*) above in the application of this section to an overseas life insurance company).
Modifications—TCGA 1992 Sch 7AB paras 1, 6 (modification of this section for the purposes of TCGA 1992 s 179B (as inserted by FA 2002 s 43) which relates to roll-over of degrouping charge on business assets).

160 Dual resident companies: roll-over relief

Commentary—*Simon's Direct Tax Service* **D4.108.**
Amendment—This section repealed by FA 1994 s 251(1), (6) and Sch 26 Pt VIII(1) where old assets are disposed of after 29 November 1993 or new assets are acquired (or contract for their acquisition is entered into) after 29 November 1993.

Stock in trade

161 Appropriations to and from stock

(1) Subject to subsection (3) below, where an asset acquired by a person otherwise than as trading stock of a trade carried on by him is appropriated by him for the purposes of the trade as trading stock (whether on the commencement of the trade or otherwise) and, if he had then sold the asset for its market value, a chargeable gain or allowable loss would have accrued to him, he shall be treated as having thereby disposed of the asset by selling it for its then market value.

(2) If at any time an asset forming part of the trading stock of a person's trade is appropriated by him for any other purpose, or is retained by him on his ceasing to carry on the trade, he shall be treated as having acquired it at that time for a consideration equal to the amount brought into the accounts of the trade in respect of it for tax purposes on the appropriation or on his ceasing to carry on the trade, as the case may be.

(3) Subject to subsection (4) below, subsection (1) above shall not apply in relation to a person's appropriation of an asset for the purposes of a trade if he is chargeable to income tax in respect of the profits of the trade under Case I of Schedule D, and elects that instead the market value of the asset at the time of the appropriation shall, in computing the profits of the trade for purposes of tax, be treated as reduced by the amount of the chargeable gain or increased by the amount of the allowable loss referred to in subsection (1), and where that subsection does not apply by reason of such an election, the profits of the trade shall be computed accordingly.

[(3A) An election under subsection (3) above shall be made-

    (*a*) for the purposes of capital gains tax, on or before the first anniversary of the 31st January next following the year of assessment in which ends the period of account in which the asset is appropriated for the purposes of the trade as trading stock;
    (*b*) for the purposes of corporation tax, within 2 years after the end of the accounting period in which the asset is appropriated for the purposes of the trade as trading stock;
...²]¹

(4) If a person making an election under subsection (3) is at the time of the appropriation carrying on the trade in partnership with others, the election shall not have effect unless concurred in by the others.

Commentary—*Simon's Direct Tax Service* **C3.801, 802.**
Simon's Tax Cases—*Coates v Arndale Properties Ltd* [1982] STC 573*: *Reed v Nova Securities Ltd* [1985] STC 124*.
s 161(1), (3), *Reed v Nova Securities Ltd* [1984] STC 124*; *N Ltd v Inspector of Taxes* [1996] STC (SCD) 346*.
s 161(3), *Coates v Arndale Properties Ltd* [1984] STC 637*.
Definitions—"Accounting period", TA 1988 s 834(1); "asset", s 21(1); "allowable loss", ss 8(2), 16, 288(1); "chargeable gain", s 15(2); "market value", ss 272–274, Sch 11; "trade", s 288(1), TA 1988 s 832(1); "trading stock", s 288(1), TA 1988 s 100(2).
Cross references—TA 1988 s 777(11) (transactions in land);
TCGA 1992 s 58(2) (no gain/no loss consideration for disposals between spouses living together not affected by this section).
TCGA 1992 s 173 (assets transferred between members of groups of companies).
FA 1994 Sch 12 para 3 (indexation losses: transitional relief).
Amendments—¹ Sub-s (3A) inserted by FA 1996 s 135(1), (2), Sch 21 para 36 with effect for the purposes of capital gains tax from the year 1996–97 and, for the purposes of corporation tax, as respects accounting periods ending after 30 June 1999 (by virtue of Finance Act 1994, Section 199, (Appointed Day) Order, SI 1998/3173 art 2).
² In sub-s (3A), the following words repealed by FA 2002 s 141, Sch 40 Pt 316) with effect from 24 July 2002—
    "and in paragraph (*a*) above "period of account" means a period for which the accounts of the trade are made up".

Transfer of business to a company

162 Roll-over relief on transfer of business

(1) This section shall apply for the purposes of this Act where a person who is not a company transfers to a company a business as a going concern, together with the whole assets of the business, or together with the whole of those assets other than cash, and the business is so transferred wholly or partly in exchange for shares issued by the company to the person transferring the business.

Any shares so received by the transferor in exchange for the business are referred to below as "the new assets".

(2) The amount determined under subsection (4) below shall be deducted from the aggregate of the chargeable gains less allowable losses ("the amount of the gain on the old assets").

(3) For the purpose of computing any chargeable gain accruing on the disposal of any new asset—

(*a*) the amount determined under subsection (4) below shall be apportioned between the new assets as a whole, and

(*b*) the sums allowable as a deduction under section 38(1)(*a*) shall be reduced by the amount apportioned to the new asset under paragraph (*a*) above;

and if the shares which comprise the new assets are not all of the same class, the apportionment between the shares under paragraph (*a*) above shall be in accordance with their market values at the time they were acquired by the transferor.

(4) The amount referred to in subsections (2) and (3)(*a*) above shall not exceed the cost of the new assets but, subject to that, it shall be the fraction—

$$\frac{A}{B}$$

of the amount of the gain on the old assets where—

"A" is the cost of the new assets, and

"B" is the value of the whole of the consideration received by the transferor in exchange for the business;

and for the purposes of this subsection "the cost of the new assets" means any sums which would be allowable as a deduction under section 38(1)(*a*) if the new assets were disposed of as a whole in circumstances giving rise to a chargeable gain.

(5) References in this section to the business, in relation to shares or consideration received in exchange for the business, include references to such assets of the business as are referred to in subsection (1) above.

Commentary—*Simon's Direct Tax Service* **C3.401–403.**
Concession D32—Transfer of a business to a company.
Revenue Internal Guidance—Capital gains tax manual, CG 65712–65715 (meaning of "business").
CG 65716–65717 (meaning of "going concern").
CG 65742–65756 (summary of provisions applicable where consideration is other than shares).
CG 65780–65784 (worked examples).
CG 65800–65848 (provisions applicable where a transfer takes place on or after 6 April 1998).
CG 68000–68862 (goodwill: meaning and circumstances in which it arises CG 68000–68083; franchises, dealerships and licences CG 68100–68132; restrictive covenants CG 68150–68204; procedures CG 68250–68414; including advice from Shares Valuation Division, appeals etc; valuation of goodwill CG 68540–68681; negligible value claims CG 68760–68765; disposal of part of business involves part disposal of goodwill of whole business CG 68850–68862).
Revenue & other press releases—ICAEW Tax 7/95 20-2-95 (Section C: incorporation of partnership business; company assuming liability for annuities payable to retired partners; relief not restricted under s 165. Relief is available under this section even if partnership contains corporate partners).
Simon's Tax Cases—s 162(1), *Gordon v IRC* [1991] STC 174*.
Definitions—"Asset", s 21(1); "allowable loss", ss 8(2), 16, 288(1); "chargeable gain", s 15(2); "company", ss 99, 288(1); "issued", s 288(5); "market value", ss 272–274, Sch 11; "shares", s 288(1).
Cross references—See TA 1988 s 763(5) (disposal constituting disposal for capital gains tax purposes and also giving rise to an offshore income gain; deduction of the offshore income gain in determining fraction "B" in sub-s (4) above);
TA 1988 Sch 28 para 3(2) (offshore income gains).
TCGA 1992 Sch 4 para 2 (deferred charges on gains accruing before 31 March 1982).

[162A Election for section 162 not to apply

(1) Section 162 shall not apply where the transferor makes an election under this section.

(2) An election under this section must be made by a notice given to an officer of the Board no later than the relevant date.

(3) Except where subsection (4) below applies, the relevant date is the second anniversary of the 31st January next following the year of assessment in which the transfer of the business took place.

(4) Where, by the end of the year of assessment following the one in which the transfer of the business took place, the transferor has disposed of all the new assets, the relevant date is the first anniversary of the 31st January next following the year of assessment in which the transfer of the business took place.

(5) For the purposes of subsection (4) above—

(*a*) a disposal of any of the new assets by the transferor shall be disregarded if it falls within section 58(1) (transfers between husband and wife); but

(*b*) where a disposal of any assets to a person is disregarded by virtue of paragraph (*a*) above, a subsequent disposal by that person of any of those assets (other than a disposal to the transferor) shall be regarded as a disposal by the transferor.

(6) All such adjustments shall be made, whether by way of discharge or repayment of tax, the making of assessments or otherwise, as are required to give effect to an election under this section.

(7) Where, immediately before it was transferred, the business was owned by two or more persons—

(*a*) each of them has a separate entitlement to make an election under this section;

(*b*) an election made by a person by virtue of paragraph (*a*) above shall apply only to—

(i) the share of the amount of the gain on the old assets, and

(ii) the share of the new assets, that is attributable to that person for the purposes of this Act.

(8) The reference in subsection (7) above to ownership by two or more persons includes, in Scotland as well as elsewhere in the United Kingdom, a reference to ownership by a partnership consisting of two or more persons.

(9) Expressions used in this section and in section 162 have the same meaning in this section as in that one.

But references in this section to new assets also include any shares or debentures that are treated by virtue of one or more applications of section 127 (including that section as applied by virtue of any enactment relating to chargeable gains) as the same asset as the new assets.][1]

Amendments—[1] This section inserted by FA 2002 s 49 with effect for a transfer of a business after 5 April 2002.

Retirement relief

Revenue Internal Guidance—Capital gains tax manual CG 63500–63921 (description of relief with examples).

163 Relief for disposals by individuals on retirement from family business

(1) Relief from capital gains tax shall be given, subject to and in accordance with Schedule 6, in any case where a material disposal of business assets is made by an individual who, at the time of the disposal—

    (*a*) has attained [the age of 50][2], or
    (*b*) has retired on ill-health grounds below [the age of 50][2].

(2) For the purposes of this section and Schedule 6, a disposal of business assets is—

    (*a*) a disposal of the whole or part of a business, or
    (*b*) a disposal of one or more assets which, at the time at which a business ceased to be carried on, were in use for the purposes of that business, or
    (*c*) a disposal of shares or securities of a company (including a disposal of an interest in shares which a person is treated as making by virtue of section 122),

and the question whether such a disposal is a material disposal shall be determined in accordance with the following provisions of this section.

(3) A disposal of the whole or part of a business is a material disposal if, throughout a period of at least one year ending with the date of the disposal, the relevant conditions are fulfilled and, in relation to such a disposal, those conditions are fulfilled at any time if at that time the business is owned by the individual making the disposal or—

    (*a*) the business is owned by a company—

        (i) which is a trading company, and
        (ii) which is either that individual's [personal company][1] or a member of a trading group of which the holding company is that individual's [personal company][1]; and

    (*b*) that individual is a [full-time working officer or employee][1] of that company or, if that company is a member of a group or commercial association of companies, of one or more companies which are members of the group or association.

(4) A disposal of assets such as is mentioned in subsection (2)(*b*) above is a material disposal if—

    (*a*) throughout a period of at least one year ending with the date on which the business ceased to be carried on the relevant conditions are fulfilled and, in relation to such a disposal, those conditions are fulfilled at any time if at that time either the business was owned by the individual making the disposal or paragraphs (*a*) and (*b*) of subsection (3) above apply; and
    (*b*) on or before the date on which the business ceased to be carried on, the individual making the disposal had either attained [the age of 50][2] or retired on ill-health grounds below that age; and
    (*c*) the date on which the business ceased to be carried on falls within the permitted period before the date of the disposal.

(5) A disposal of shares or securities of a company (including such a disposal of an interest in shares as is mentioned in subsection (2)(*c*) above) is a material disposal if, throughout a period of at least one year ending with the operative date, the relevant conditions are fulfilled and, in relation to such a disposal, those conditions are fulfilled at any time if at that time—

    (*a*) the individual making the disposal owns the business which, at the date of the disposal, is owned by the company or, if the company is the holding company of a trading group, by any member of the group; or
    (*b*) the company is the individual's [personal company][1] and is either a trading company or the holding company of a trading group and the individual is a [full-time working officer or employee][1] of the company or, if the company is a member of a group or commercial association of companies, of one or more companies which are members of the group or association;

and, except where subsection (6) or subsection (7) below applies, the operative date for the purposes of this subsection is the date of the disposal.

(6) In any case where—

    (*a*) within the permitted period before the date of the disposal referred to in subsection (5) above, the company concerned either ceased to be a trading company without continuing to be or becoming a member of a trading group or ceased to be a member of a trading group without continuing to be or becoming a trading company, and

(b) on or before the date of that cessation, the individual making the disposal attained [the age of 50][2] or retired on ill-health grounds below that age,

then, subject to subsection (7) below, the operative date for the purposes of subsection (5) above is the date of the cessation referred to in paragraph (a) above; and, where this subsection applies, the reference in subsection (5)(a) above to the date of the disposal shall also be construed as a reference to the date of that cessation.

(7) If, throughout a period which ends on the date of the disposal referred to in subsection (5) above or, if subsection (6) above applies, on the date of the cessation referred to in paragraph (a) of that subsection and which begins when the individual concerned ceased to be a [full-time working officer or employee][1] of the company or, if that company is a member of a group or commercial association of companies, of one or more companies which are members of the group or association—

(a) the company concerned was his [personal company][1] and either a trading company or the holding company of a trading group, and

(b) he was [an officer or employee][1] of the company concerned or, as the case may be, of one or more members of the group or association and, in that capacity, devoted at least 10 hours per week (averaged over the period) to the service of the company or companies in a technical or managerial capacity,

the operative date for the purposes of subsection (5) above is the date on which the individual ceased to be a [full-time working officer or employee][1] as mentioned above.

(8) For the purposes of this section—

(a) any reference to the disposal of the whole or part of a business by an individual includes a reference to the disposal by him of his interest in the assets of a partnership carrying on the business; and

(b) subject to paragraph (a) above, at any time when a business is carried on by a partnership, the business shall be treated as owned by each individual who is at that time a member of the partnership.

(9) Part I of Schedule 6 shall have effect for the interpretation of this section as well as of that Schedule.

Commentary—*Simon's Direct Tax Service* **C3.601, 606, 608.**
Concession D31—Retirement relief: date of disposal.
Revenue Interpretations RI 6—Disallowance of retirement relief on account of ill-health where it is claimed by a person affected by the ill-health of another person.
RI 202—Meaning of full-time working officer; examples of disallowance of retirement relief for disposals after 5 April 2003.
Revenue & other press releases—Country Landowners' Association 19-12-91 (share farming: both parties to a share farming agreement are considered to be carrying on a farming business for tax purposes).
Revenue Internal Guidance—Capital gains manual CG 63380–63407 (qualifying conditions for a claim to relief on the grounds of ill-health).
CG 63530–63536 (meaning of ''part of a business'' in sub-s (3))
CG 63540–63541 (meaning of ''business'').
CG 63570–63586 (qualifying conditions where assets disposed of after cessation of a business).
CG 63600–63685 (qualifying conditions for a disposal of shares in a company).
Simon's Tax Cases—*Clarke v Mayo* [1994] STC 570*; *Marriott v Lane* [1996] STC 704*; *Mayes v Woods* [1997] STC (SCD) 206*; *Plumbly (personal representatives of the estate of Harbour (decd)) v Spencer* [1999] STC 677*.
s 163(4)(c), *Hatt v Newman* [2000] STC 113.
s 163(5)(b), *Palmer v Moloney* [1999] STC 890.
Definitions—''Asset'', s 21(1); ''commercial association of companies'', Sch 6 para 1(2); ''company'', ss 99, 288(1); ''full-time working officer or employee'', Sch 6 para 1(2); ''group of companies'', Sch 6 para 1(2); ''holding company'', Sch 6 para 1(2); ''permitted period'', Sch 6 para 1(2); ''personal company'', Sch 6 para 1(2); ''shares'', s 288(1); ''trading company'', Sch 6 para 1(2); ''trading group'', Sch 6 para 1(2).
Cross references—See TCGA 1992 s 164 (retirement relief on disposals by employees and trustees of family trusts).
Amendments—[1] Words in sub-ss (3)(a), (b), (5)(b), (7) substituted by FA 1993 s 87 and Sch 7 paras 1(1), 2(1), (2) in relation to disposals made after 15 March 1993.
[2] Words in sub-ss (1)(a), (b), (4)(b), (6)(b) substituted by FA 1996 s 176 with effect in relation to disposals after 27 November 1995.
Prospective amendment—This section will be repealed by FA 1998 s 140, Sch 27 Part III(31) with effect for disposals in the year 2003–04 and subsequent years of assessment.

164 Other retirement relief

(1) Relief from capital gains tax shall be given, subject to and in accordance with Schedule 6, in any case where an individual—

(a) who has attained [the age of 50][2], or

(b) who has retired on ill-health grounds below [the age of 50][2],

makes a relevant disposal of the whole or part of the assets provided or held for the purposes of an office or employment exercised by him; and, if he ceases to exercise that office or employment before the date of the relevant disposal, the date on which he ceased to exercise it is in subsection (2) below referred to as the ''prior cessation date''.

(2) For the purposes of subsection (1) above, a disposal of the whole or part of the assets provided or held as mentioned in that subsection is a relevant disposal if—

(*a*) throughout a period of at least one year ending with the date of the disposal or, where applicable, the prior cessation date, the office or employment was the full-time occupation of the individual making the disposal; and

(*b*) that office or employment is other than that of [officer or employee]¹ of a company which is either the [personal company]¹ of the individual concerned or is a member of a trading group of which the holding company is his [personal company]¹; and

(*c*) where there is a prior cessation date, the individual either had attained [the age of 50]² on or before that date or on that date retired on ill-health grounds below that age; and

(*d*) where there is a prior cessation date, the disposal takes place within the permitted period after the cessation date.

(3) Relief from capital gains tax shall be given, subject to and in accordance with Schedule 6, where—

    (*a*) the trustees of a settlement dispose of—

        (i) shares or securities of a company, or

        (ii) an asset used or previously used for the purposes of a business,

being, in either case, part of the settled property; and

    (*b*) the conditions in subsection (4) or, as the case may be, subsection (5) below are fulfilled with respect to a beneficiary who, under the settlement, has an interest in possession in the whole of the settled property or, as the case may be, in a part of it which consists of or includes the shares or securities or the asset referred to in paragraph (*a*) above, but excluding, for this purpose, an interest for a fixed term; and in those subsections that beneficiary is referred to as "the qualifying beneficiary".

(4) In relation to a disposal of shares or securities of a company (including such a disposal of an interest in shares as is mentioned in section 163(2)(*c*)), the conditions referred to in subsection (3)(*b*) above are—

    (*a*) that, throughout a period of at least one year ending not earlier than the permitted period before the disposal, the company was the qualifying beneficiary's [personal company]¹ and either a trading company or the holding company of a trading group; and

    (*b*) that, throughout a period of at least one year ending as mentioned in paragraph (*a*) above, the qualifying beneficiary was a [full-time working officer or employee]¹ of the company or, if the company is a member of a group or commercial association of companies, of one or more companies which are members of the group or association; and

    (*c*) that, on the date of the disposal or within the permitted period before that date, the qualifying beneficiary ceased to be a [full-time working officer or employee]¹ as mentioned in paragraph (*b*) above, having attained [the age of 50]² or retired on ill-health grounds below that age.

(5) In relation to a disposal of an asset, the conditions referred to in subsection (3)(*b*) above are—

    (*a*) that, throughout a period of at least one year ending not earlier than the permitted period before the disposal, the asset was used for the purposes of a business carried on by the qualifying beneficiary; and

    (*b*) that, on the date of the disposal or within the permitted period before that date, the qualifying beneficiary ceased to carry on the business referred to in paragraph (*a*) above; and

    (*c*) that, on or before the date of the disposal or, if it was earlier, the date on which the qualifying beneficiary ceased to carry on that business, he attained [the age of 50]² or retired on ill-health grounds below that age.

(6) In any case where—

    (*a*) by virtue of section 163, relief falls to be given, in accordance with Schedule 6, in respect of a material disposal of business assets which either consists of the disposal by an individual of his interest in the assets of a partnership or is of a description falling within subsection (5) of that section, and

    (*b*) the individual making that material disposal makes an associated disposal of assets, as defined in subsection (7) below,

relief from capital gains tax shall also be given, subject to and in accordance with that Schedule in respect of the associated disposal.

(7) In relation to a material disposal of business assets, a disposal of an asset is an associated disposal if—

    (*a*) it takes place as part of a withdrawal of the individual concerned from participation in the business carried on by the partnership referred to in subsection (6)(*a*) above or, as the case may be, by the company which owns the business as mentioned in section 163(5)(*a*); and

    (*b*) immediately before the material disposal or, if it was earlier, the cessation of the business mentioned in paragraph (*a*) above, the asset was in use for the purposes of that business; and

    (*c*) during the whole or part of the period in which the asset has been in the ownership of the individual making the disposal the asset has been used—

        (i) for the purposes of the business mentioned in paragraph (*a*) above (whether or not carried on by the partnership or company there referred to); or

        (ii) for the purposes of another business carried on by the individual or by a partnership of which the individual concerned was a member; or

(iii) for the purposes of another business in respect of which the conditions in paragraphs (*a*) and (*b*) of subsection (3) of section 163 were fulfilled.

(8) In subsections (6) and (7) above "material disposal of business assets" has the same meaning as in section 163 and Part I of Schedule 6 shall have effect for the interpretation of this section as well as of that Schedule.

Commentary—*Simon's Direct Tax Service* **C3.604, 605.**
Concession D31—Retirement relief: date of disposal.
Revenue Interpretation RI 202—Meaning of full-time working officer; disallowance of retirement relief for disposals after 5 April 2003.
Revenue Internal Guidance—Capital gains manual CG 63640–63641 (share disposals by trustees: summary of sub-s (4)).
CG 63700–63706 (disposals of assets by employees).
CG 63720–63737 (associated disposals: operation of sub-s (7)).
Simon's Tax Cases—*Clarke v Mayo* [1994] STC 570*.
Definitions—"Asset", s 21(1); "commercial association of companies", Sch 6 para 1(2); "company", ss 99, 288(1); "employment", Sch 6 para 1(2); "full-time working officer or employee", Sch 6 para 1(2); "holding company", Sch 6 para 1(2); "office", Sch 6 para 1(2); "permitted period", Sch 6 para 1(2); "personal company", Sch 6 para 1(2); "settled property", s 68; "shares", s 288(1); "trading company", Sch 6 para 1(2); "trading group", Sch 6 para 1(2).
Amendments—[1] Words in sub-ss (2)(*b*), (4)(*a*), (*b*), (*c*) substituted by FA 1993 s 87 and Sch 7 paras 1(1), 2(1), (3) in relation to disposals made after 15 March 1993.
[2] Words in sub-ss (1)(*a*), (*b*), (2)(*c*), (4)(*c*), (5)(*c*) substituted by FA 1996 s 176 with effect in relation to disposals after 27 November 1995.
Prospective amendment—This section will be repealed by FA 1998 s 140(2), Sch 27 Part III(31) with effect for disposals in the year 2003–04 and subsequent years of assessment.

[CHAPTER IA
ROLL-OVER RELIEF ON RE-INVESTMENT][1]

Amendments—[1] This Chapter inserted by FA 1993 s 87 and Sch 7 para 3 in relation to disposals made after 15 March 1993.
[1] This Chapter is repealed by FA 1998 s 165, Sch 27 Part III(32) with effect in relation to acquisitions made after 5 April 1998.

[164A Relief on re-investment for individuals

(1) Subject to the following provisions of this Chapter, roll-over relief under this section shall be available where—

(a) a chargeable gain would (apart from this section) accrue to any individual ("the re-investor") [on any disposal by him of any asset ("the asset disposed of"); and][3]

(b) that individual acquires a qualifying investment at any time in the qualifying period.

(2) ...[4], where roll-over relief under this section is available, the re-investor shall, on making a claim as respects the qualifying investment, be treated—

(a) as if the consideration for the disposal of the [asset disposed of][3], were reduced by whichever is the smallest of the following, that is to say—

(i) the amount of the chargeable gain which apart from this subsection would accrue on the disposal of the [asset disposed of][3], so far as that amount has not already been held over by way of reductions under this subsection,

(ii) the actual amount or value of the consideration for the acquisition of the qualifying investment,

(iii) in the case of a qualifying investment acquired otherwise than by a transaction at arm's length, the market value of that investment at the time of its acquisition, and

(iv) the amount specified for the purposes of this subsection in the claim;

and

(b) as if the amount or value of the consideration for the acquisition of the qualifying investment were reduced by the amount of the reduction made under paragraph (a) above,

but neither paragraph (a) nor paragraph (b) above shall affect the treatment for the purposes of this Act of the other party to the transaction involving the [asset disposed of][3] or of the other party to the transaction involving the qualifying investment.

[(2A) Where the chargeable gain referred to in subsection (1)(a) above is one which (apart from this section) would be deemed to accrue by virtue of section 116(10)(b)—

(a) any reduction falling to be made by virtue of subsection (2)(a) above shall be treated as one made in the consideration mentioned in section 116(10)(a), instead of in the consideration for the disposal of the asset disposed of; but

(b) if the disposal on which that gain is deemed to accrue is a disposal of only part of the new asset, it shall be assumed, for the purpose only of making a reduction affecting the amount of that gain—

(i) that the disposal is a disposal of the whole of a new asset,

(ii) that the gain accruing on that disposal relates to an old asset consisting in the corresponding part of what was in fact the old asset, and

(iii) that the corresponding part of the consideration deemed to be given for what was in fact the old asset is taken to be the consideration by reference to which the amount of that gain is computed;

and in this subsection "new asset" and "old asset" have the same meanings as in section 116.][9]

[(2B) Where a chargeable gain accrues in accordance with subsection (12) of section 116, this Chapter shall have effect—

    (a) as if that gain were a gain accruing on the disposal of an asset; and
    (b) in relation to that deemed disposal, as if references in this Chapter to the consideration for the disposal were references to the sum of money falling, apart from this Chapter, to be used in computing the gain accruing under that subsection.]⁹

(3)–(7) ...⁴

[(8) For the purposes of this section, a person who acquires any eligible shares in a qualifying company shall[, subject to subsection (8A) below,]¹⁰ be regarded as acquiring a qualifying investment unless, where the asset disposed of consisted of shares in or other securities of any company ("the initial holding"), the qualifying company—

    (a) is the company in which the initial holding subsisted, or
    (b) is a company that was, at the time of the disposal of the initial holding, or is, at the time of the acquisition of the qualifying investment, a member of the same group of companies as the company in which the initial holding subsisted.]⁵

[(8A) Where the eligible shares acquired by any person in a qualifying company are shares which he acquires by their being issued to him, his acquisition of the shares shall not be regarded as the acquisition of a qualifying investment unless the qualifying company, or a qualifying subsidiary of that company, is intending to employ the money raised by the issue of the shares wholly for the purposes of a qualifying trade carried on by it.]¹⁰

[(8B) For the purposes of subsection (8A) above—

    (a) the purposes of a trade include the purpose of preparing for the carrying on of the trade; and
    (b) "qualifying subsidiary" has the same meaning as in section 164G.]¹⁰

(9) For the purposes of this section the acquisition of a qualifying investment shall be taken to be in the qualifying period if, and only if, it takes place—

    (a) at any time in the period beginning 12 months before and ending 3 years after the disposal of the [asset disposed of]³, or
    (b) at such time before the beginning of that period or after it ends as the Board may by notice allow.

(10) The provisions of this Act fixing the amount of the consideration deemed to be given for the acquisition or disposal of assets shall be applied before this section is applied; and, without prejudice to the generality of this subsection, section 42(5) shall apply in relation to an adjustment under this section of the consideration for the acquisition of any shares as it applies in relation to an adjustment under any enactment to secure that neither a gain nor a loss accrues on a disposal.

(11) ...⁶.

[(12) Without prejudice to section 52(4), where consideration is given for the acquisition of any assets some of which are shares to the acquisition of which a claim under this section relates and some of which are not, the consideration shall be apportioned in such manner as is just and reasonable]2.]¹

[(13) Where an acquisition is made on or after 29th November 1994 section 164H shall be ignored in deciding whether it is an acquisition of a qualifying investment for the purposes of this section.]⁷

[(14) This section is subject to sections 164FF and 164FG.]⁸

Commentary—*Simon's Direct Tax Service* C3.901–903.
Revenue Interpretation RI 69—Reinvestment relief; meaning of "actual amount or value of the consideration".
RI 133—Reinvestment relief and qualifying corporate bonds.
Definitions—"Asset", s 21(1); "the Board", s 288(1); "chargeable gain", s 15(2); "company", s 288(1); "eligible shares", s 164N(1); "group of companies", Sch 6 para 1(2); "qualifying company", s 164G; "shares", s 288(1).
Cross references—See TCGA 1992 s 164B (roll-over relief on re-investment by trustees).
TCGA 1992 s 164F (failure of conditions of relief).
TCGA 1992 s 164L (anti-avoidance provisions).
Amendments—¹ This Chapter inserted by FA 1993 s 87 and Sch 7 para 3 in relation to disposals made after 15 March 1993, and repealed by FA 1998 s 165, Sch 27 Part III(32) with effect for acquisitions made after 5 April 1998.
² Sub-s (12) substituted by FA 1994 s 91 and Sch 11 paras 1, 2 in relation to disposals after 29 November 1993.
³ Words in sub-ss (1), (2), (9) substituted by FA 1994 s 91 and Sch 11 paras 1, 2.
⁴ Sub-ss (3)–(7) and words in sub-s (2) repealed by FA 1994 s 91 and Sch 11 paras 1, 2 and Sch 26 Pt V(7).
⁵ Sub-s (8) substituted by FA 1994 s 91 and Sch 11 paras 1, 7 in relation to disposals after 29 November 1993.
⁶ Sub-s (11) repealed by FA 1994 s 91 and Sch 11 paras 1, 8 and Sch 26 Pt V(7) in relation to disposals after 29 November 1993.
⁷ Sub-s (13) added by FA 1995 s 46(2).
⁸ Sub-s (14) added by FA 1995 s 47(2) generally with effect from 20 June 1994 (for detailed commencement provision, see FA 1995 s 47(6), (7)).
⁹ Sub-ss (2A), (2B) inserted, and deemed always to have had effect, by FA 1996 s 177.
¹⁰ Words in sub-s (8), and sub-ss (8A), (8B), inserted by FA 1997 Sch 17, paras 1, 2, 7(1) with effect in relation to shares acquired after 26 November 1996 and , subject to FA 1997 Sch 17 para 7(3), with effect after that date in relation to shares acquired on or before that date and falling within FA 1997 Sch 17 para 7(2).

[164B Roll-over relief on re-investment by trustees

(1) Subject to the following provisions of this section, section 164A shall apply, as it applies in such a case as is mentioned in subsection (1) of that section, where there is—

(a) a disposal by the trustees of a settlement of any asset comprised in any settled property to which this section applies, and

(b) such an acquisition by those trustees of eligible shares in a qualifying company as would for the purposes of that section be an acquisition of a qualifying investment at a time in the qualifying period.

(2) This section applies—

(a) to any settled property in which the interests of the beneficiaries are not interests in possession, if all the beneficiaries are individuals, and

(b) to any settled property in which the interests of the beneficiaries are interests in possession, if any of the beneficiaries are individuals,

and references in this section to individuals include any charity.

(3) If, at the time of the disposal of the asset mentioned in subsection (1)(a) above, the settled property comprising that asset is property to which this section applies by virtue of subsection (2)(b) above but not all the beneficiaries are individuals, then—

(a) only the relevant proportion of the gain which would accrue to the trustees on the disposal shall be taken into account for the purposes of section 164A(2)(a)(i), and

(b) no reduction under section 164A(2) shall be made in respect of the whole or any part of the balance of the gain.

(4) Section 164A shall not apply by virtue of this section in a case where, at the time of the disposal of the asset mentioned in subsection (1)(a) above, the settled property which comprises that asset is property to which this section applies by virtue of subsection (2)(a) above unless, immediately after the acquisition of shares mentioned in subsection (1)(b) above, the settled property comprising the shares is also property to which this section applies by virtue of subsection (2)(a) above.

(5) Section 164A shall not apply by virtue of this section in a case where, at the time of the disposal of the asset mentioned in subsection (1)(a) above, the settled property which comprises that asset is property to which this section applies by virtue of subsection (2)(b) above unless, immediately after the acquisition of shares mentioned in subsection (1)(b) above—

(a) the settled property comprising the shares is also property to which this section applies by virtue of subsection (2)(b) above, and

(b) if not all the beneficiaries are individuals, the relevant proportion is not less than the proportion which was the relevant proportion at the time of the disposal of the asset mentioned in subsection (1)(a) above.

(6) If, at any time, in the case of settled property to which this section applies by virtue of subsection (2)(b) above, both individuals and others have interests in possession, the relevant proportion at that time is the proportion which the amount specified in paragraph (a) below bears to the amount specified in paragraph (b) below, that is—

(a) the total amount of the income of the settled property, being income the interests in which are held by beneficiaries who are individuals, and

(b) the total amount of all the income of the settled property.

(7) Where, in the case of any settled property in which any beneficiary holds an interest in possession, one or more beneficiaries (''the relevant beneficiaries'') hold interests not in possession, this section shall apply as if—

(a) the interests of the relevant beneficiaries were a single interest in possession, and

(b) that interest were held, where all the relevant beneficiaries are individuals, by an individual and, in any other case, by a person who is not an individual.

(8) In this section references to interests in possession do not include interests for a fixed term.]²]¹

Commentary—*Simon's Direct Tax Service* C3.966, 967.
Definitions—''Company'', s 288(1); ''eligible shares'', s 164N(1); ''qualifying company'', s 164G; ''shares'', s 288(1).
Amendments—¹ This Chapter inserted by FA 1993 s 87 and Sch 7 para 3 in relation to disposals made after 15 March 1993, and repealed by FA 1998 s 165, Sch 27 Part III(32) with effect for acquisitions made after 5 April 1998.
² This section substituted by FA 1994 s 91 and Sch 11 paras 1, 3 in relation to disposals after 29 November 1993.

[164BA Interaction with retirement relief

(1) The provisions of section 164A for making any reduction shall apply before any provisions for calculating the amount of, or giving effect to, any relief under section 163 or 164; and references in that section and this to a chargeable gain (except the second reference in subsection (4)(a) below) shall be construed accordingly.

(2) Subsection (3) below applies where—

(a) any claim for relief is made under section 164A in respect of any chargeable gain, and

(b) apart from this Chapter, the whole or any part of that gain would be relieved under section 163 or 164.

(3) For the purpose of giving relief under section 163 or 164, any reduction under section 164A shall be treated as having been made first against the unrelieved part of the chargeable gain; and only the amount (if any) which is equal to the unrelieved part of the chargeable gain after that reduction shall be treated as exceeding the amount available for relief.

(4) For the purposes of this section—

(a) the unrelieved part of a chargeable gain is so much of that gain as, apart from this Chapter, would constitute a chargeable gain after the application of the appropriate paragraph of Schedule 6,

(b) "amount available for relief" has the same meaning as in the appropriate paragraph of that Schedule, and

(c) the "appropriate paragraph" means, as the case may be, paragraph 6, 7(1)(b) or 8(1)(b).]¹

Commentary—*Simon's Direct Tax Service* **C3.936.**
Definitions—"Chargeable gain", s 15(2); "reduction", s 164N(4).
Cross references—See TCGA 1992 s 164L (anti-avoidance provisions).
Amendments—¹ This section inserted by FA 1994 s 91 and Sch 11 paras 1, 8 in relation to disposals after 29 November 1993, and repealed by FA 1998 s 165, Sch 27 Part III(32) with effect for acquisitions made after 5 April 1998.

[164C Restriction applying to retirement relief and roll-over relief on re-investment]¹

...²

Commentary—*Simon's Direct Tax Service* **C3.931.**
Amendments—¹ This Chapter inserted by FA 1993 s 87 and Sch 7 para 3 in relation to disposals made after 15 March 1993.
² This section repealed by FA 1994 s 91, Sch 11 paras 1, 4 and Sch 26 Pt V(7) in relation to disposals after 29 November 1993.

[164D Relief carried forward into replacement shares

(1) This section shall apply where a person has acquired any eligible shares in a qualifying company ("the acquired holding") for a consideration which is treated as reduced, under section 164A or the following provisions of this section, by any amount ("the held-over gain").

(2) If—

(a) the person who acquired the acquired holding disposes of eligible shares in the company in question ("the acquired shares"),

(b) that person at any time in the relevant period acquires other eligible shares ("the replacement shares") in a qualifying company which is not a relevant company;

(c) the acquisition of the replacement shares would, in relation to the disposal of the acquired shares, be treated (were the disposal a material disposal) as an acquisition of a qualifying investment for the purposes of section 164A, and

(d) roll-over relief is not available under section 164A in relation to the acquisition of the replacement shares,

that person shall, on making a claim as respects the acquisition of the replacement shares, be treated in relation to that acquisition in accordance with subsection (3) below.

(3) Where a person falls to be treated in accordance with this subsection in relation to the acquisition of the replacement shares, he shall be treated—

(a) as if the consideration for the disposal of the acquired shares were reduced by whichever is the smallest of the following, that is to say—

(i) the amount of the held-over gain on the acquisition of the acquired holding, so far as that amount has not already been carried forward under this section from any disposal of eligible shares in the company in question or been charged on a disposal or under section 164F,

(ii) the actual amount or value of the consideration for the acquisition of the replacement shares,

(iii) in the case of replacement shares acquired otherwise than by a transaction at arm's length, the market value of the replacement shares at the time of their acquisition, and

(iv) the amount specified for the purposes of this subsection in the claim;

and

(b) as if the amount or value of the consideration for the acquisition of the replacement shares were reduced by the amount of the reduction made under paragraph (a) above,

but neither paragraph (a) nor paragraph (b) above shall affect the treatment for the purposes of this Act of the other party to the transaction involving the acquired shares or of the other party to the transaction involving the replacement shares.

(4) For the purposes of this section the whole or a part of any held-over gain on the acquisition of the acquired holding shall be treated—

(a) in accordance with subsection (5) below as charged on any disposal in relation to which the whole or any part of the held-over gain falls to be taken into account in determining the chargeable gain or allowable loss accruing on the disposal; and

(b) as charged under section 164F so far as it falls to be disregarded in accordance with subsection (11) of that section.

(5) In the case of any such disposal as is mentioned in subsection (4)(a) above, the amount of the held-over gain charged on that disposal—

(a) shall, except in the case of a part disposal, be so much of the amount taken into account as so mentioned as is not carried forward under this section from the disposal in question; and

(b) in the case of a part disposal, shall be calculated by multiplying the following, that is to say—

(i) so much of the amount of the held-over gain as is not carried forward under this section from the disposal in question and has not already been either charged on a previous disposal or carried forward under this section from a previous disposal; and

(ii) the fraction used in accordance with section 42(2) for determining, subject to any deductions in pursuance of this Chapter, the amount allowable as a deduction in the computation of the gain accruing on the disposal in question.

(6) Where section 58 applies to any disposal of the whole or any part of the acquired holding to any individual—

(a) that individual shall not be treated for the purposes of subsection (1) above as a person who has acquired eligible shares for a consideration which is treated as reduced under section 164A or this section; and

(b) the amount of the held-over gain which for the purposes of this section shall be treated as charged on the disposal shall be the amount that would have been charged on the disposal if it had been a disposal at market value.

(7) References in this section to an amount being carried forward from a disposal are references, in relation to the disposal of any shares, to the reduction by that amount, in accordance with subsection (3)(a) above, of the amount of the consideration for the disposal of those shares.

(8) Subsections (10) to (12) of section 164A shall apply in the case of any claim under this section as they apply in the case of a claim under that section.

(9) For the purposes of this section a company is a relevant company if it is—

(a) the company in which the acquired holding has subsisted or a company which was a member of the same group of companies as that company at the time of the disposal of the acquired holding or of the acquisition of the replacement shares;

(b) a company in relation to the disposal of any shares in which there has been a claim under this Chapter such that without that or an equivalent claim there would be no held-over gain in relation to the acquired holding; or

(c) a company which, at the time of the disposal or acquisition to which the claim relates, was a member of the same group of companies as a company falling within paragraph (b) above.

(10) In this section "the relevant period" means the period (not including any period before the acquisition of the acquired holding) which begins 12 months before and ends 3 years after the disposal of the acquired shares, together with any such further period after the disposal as the Board may by notice allow.][1]

Commentary—*Simon's Direct Tax Service* **C3.953, 961–963.**
Amendments—[1] This Chapter inserted by FA 1993 s 87 and Sch 7 para 3 in relation to disposals made after 15 March 1993.
This section repealed by FA 1994 s 91, Sch 11 paras 1, 4 and Sch 26 Pt V(7) in relation to disposals after 29 November 1993.
  The text is retained here for the purpose of s 164F.

[164E Application of Chapter in cases of an exchange of shares][1]

...[2]

Commentary—*Simon's Direct Tax Service* **C3.963.**
Amendments—[1] This Chapter inserted by FA 1993 s 87 and Sch 7 para 3 in relation to disposals made after 15 March 1993.
[2] This section repealed by FA 1994 s 91, Sch 11 paras 1, 4 and Sch 26 Pt V(7) in relation to disposals after 29 November 1993.

[164F Failure of conditions of relief

[(1) This section shall apply where a person has acquired any eligible shares in a qualifying company ("the acquired holding") for a consideration which is treated as reduced, under section 164A or this section [or section 164FA][10], by any amount ("the held-over gain").][2]

(2) Subject to the following provisions of this section, if at any time in the relevant period—

(a) the shares comprised in the acquired holding cease to be eligible shares,

(b) the company in which the acquired holding subsists ceases to be a qualifying company,

(c) the person who acquired the acquired holding becomes neither resident nor ordinarily resident in the United Kingdom, or

(d) any of the shares comprised in the acquired holding are included in the original shares (within the meaning of sections 127 to 130) in the case of any transaction with respect to which section 116 has effect,

a chargeable gain equal to the appropriate proportion of the held-over gain shall be treated as accruing to that person immediately before that time or, in a case falling within paragraph (d) above, immediately before the disposal assumed for the purposes of section 116(10)(a).

[(2A) In deciding for the purposes of subsection (2)(b) above whether a company is a qualifying company at a time falling on or after 29th November 1994 section 164H shall be ignored.][7]

(3) For the purposes of this section the appropriate proportion of the held-over gain is so much, if any, of that gain as has not already been [charged on any disposal or under this section]5 or, in a case to which subsection (2) above applies by virtue of paragraph (d) of that subsection or in accordance with subsection (7) below, such part of that proportion of that gain as is just and reasonable having regard to the extent to which the acquired holding comprises the original shares.

[(4) For the purposes of this section the whole or a part of any held-over gain on the acquisition of the acquired holding shall be treated—

(a) in accordance with subsection (4A) below as charged on any disposal in relation to which the whole or any part of the held-over gain falls to be taken into account in determining the chargeable gain or allowable loss accruing on the disposal, and

(b) as charged under this section so far as it falls to be disregarded in accordance with subsection (11) below.]³

[(4A) In the case of any such disposal as is mentioned in subsection (4)(a) above, the amount of the held-over gain charged on that disposal—

(a) shall, except in the case of a part disposal, be the amount taken into account as so mentioned, and

(b) in the case of a part disposal, shall be calculated by multiplying the following, that is to say—

(i) so much of the amount of the held-over gain as has not already been charged on a previous disposal, and

(ii) the fraction used in accordance with section 42(2) for determining, subject to any deductions in pursuance of this Chapter, the amount allowable as a deduction in the computation of the gain accruing on the disposal in question.]³

(5) Where the acquired holding or any asset treated as comprised in a single asset with the whole or any part of that holding has been disposed of under section 58 by the individual who acquired that holding to another person (''the spouse'')—

(a) the spouse shall not (subject to the following provisions of this subsection) be treated for the purposes of this section as a person who has acquired eligible shares for a consideration which is treated as reduced under section 164A ...⁶;

(b) the disposal shall not be included in the disposals on which the whole or any part of the held-over gain may be treated as charged for the purposes of this section;

(c) disposals by the spouse, as well as disposals by that individual, shall be taken into account for the purposes of [subsections (4) and (4A) above]⁵;

(d) any charge under subsection (2) above (other than one by virtue of paragraph (c) of that subsection) shall be apportioned between that individual and the spouse according to the extent to which the appropriate proportion of the held-over gain would be charged on the disposal by each of them of their respective holdings (if any);

(e) paragraph (c) of that subsection shall have effect as if the reference in that paragraph to that individual included a reference to the spouse;

(f) a charge by virtue of that paragraph shall be imposed only on a person who becomes neither resident nor ordinarily resident in the United Kingdom; and

(g) the amount of the charge imposed on any person by virtue of that paragraph shall be that part of the charge on the appropriate proportion of the held-over gain which would be apportioned to that person in a case to which paragraph (d) above applies.

(6) Subject to subsection (7) below, where the qualifying company in which the acquired holding subsists ceases to be an unquoted company this section shall have effect as if the relevant period ended immediately before it so ceased.

(7) Where there is a transaction by virtue of which any shares in a company are to be regarded under section 127 as the same asset as the acquired holding or the whole or any part of an asset comprising that holding, this section shall not apply by virtue of subsection (2)(a) or (b) above except where—

(a) those shares are not, or cease to be, eligible shares in that company;

(b) neither that company nor (if different) the company in which the acquired holding subsisted—

(i) is or continues to be a qualifying company; or

(ii) would be or continue to be a qualifying company if it were an unquoted company;

(c) the transaction is one by virtue of which the shares comprised in the acquired holding cease to be eligible shares in pursuance of section 164L; or

(d) there is a transaction by virtue of which any shares at any time comprised in the acquired holding would have so ceased in pursuance of that section.

(8) This section shall not apply by virtue of subsection (2)(a) or (b) above where the company in which the acquired holding subsists is wound up or dissolved without winding up and—

(a) ...⁹ the winding up or dissolution is for bona fide commercial reasons and not part of a scheme or arrangement the main purpose of which, or one of the main purposes of which, is the avoidance of tax; and

(b) the company's net assets (if any) are distributed to its members or dealt with as bona vacantia before the end of the period of 3 years from the commencement of the winding up or, as the case may be, from the dissolution.

(9) This section shall not apply by virtue of subsection (2)(c) above in relation to any person if—

(a) the reason for his becoming neither resident nor ordinarily resident in the United Kingdom is that he works in an employment or office all the duties of which are performed outside the United Kingdom, and

(b) he again becomes resident or ordinarily resident in the United Kingdom within the period of 3 years from the time when he ceases to be so, without having meanwhile disposed of any eligible shares in the company in question;

and, accordingly, no assessment shall be made by virtue of subsection (2)(c) above before the end of that period in any case where the condition in paragraph (a) above is satisfied and the condition in paragraph (b) above may be satisfied.

(10) For the purposes of subsection (9) above a person shall be taken to have disposed of an asset if there has been such a disposal as would, if the person making the disposal had been resident in the United Kingdom, have been a disposal on which ...[6] the whole or any part of the held-over gain would have been charged.

[(10A) Where (apart from this subsection) a chargeable gain of any amount would by virtue of subsection (2) above accrue to the person who acquired the acquired holding but, within the period mentioned in subsection (10B) below, that person acquires a qualifying investment (within the meaning of section 164A), that person shall, on making a claim as respects the qualifying investment, be treated—

(a) as if the amount of the gain were reduced by whichever is the smallest of the following—

(i) the actual amount or value of the consideration for the acquisition of the qualifying investment,
(ii) in the case of a qualifying investment acquired otherwise than by a transaction at arm's length, the market value of that investment at the time of its acquisition,
(iii) the amount specified for the purposes of this subsection in the claim, and

(b) as if the amount or value of the consideration for the acquisition of the qualifying investment were reduced by the amount of the reduction made under paragraph (a) above;

but paragraph (b) above shall not affect the treatment for the purposes of this Act of the other party to the transaction involving the qualifying investment.][4]

[(10B) The period referred to in subsection (10A) above is the period (not including any period before the acquisition of the acquired holding) which begins 12 months before and ends 3 years after the time when the chargeable gain accrues or would but for that subsection accrue, together with any such further period after the disposal as the Board may by notice allow.][4]

[(10C) Subsection (10A) above is subject to sections 164FF and 164FG.][8]

(11) Gains on disposals made after a chargeable gain has under this section been deemed to accrue in respect of the acquired holding to any person shall be computed as if so much of the held-over gain as is equal to the amount of the chargeable gain were to be disregarded.

(12) In this section "the relevant period" means (subject to subsection (6) above) the period of 3 years after the acquisition of the acquired holding.][1]

Commentary—*Simon's Direct Tax Service* **C3.917–919.**
Definitions—"Asset", s 21(1); "the Board", s 288(1); "chargeable gain", s 15(2); "company", s 288(1); "eligible shares", s 164N(1); "ordinarily resident", s 9(1); "qualifying company", s 164G; "reduction", s 164N(4); "resident", s 9(1); "shares", s 288(1); "unquoted company", s 164N(1).
Amendments—[1] This Chapter inserted by FA 1993 s 87 and Sch 7 para 3 in relation to disposals made after 15 March 1993, and repealed by FA 1998 s 165, Sch 27 Part III(32) with effect for acquisitions made after 5 April 1998.
[2] Sub-s (1) substituted by FA 1994 s 91 and Sch 11 paras 1, 9 in relation to disposals after 29 November 1993, subject to, Sch 11 para 9(2), (3); see below.
[3] Sub-ss (4), (4A) substituted for sub-s (4) by FA 1994 s 91 and Sch 11 paras 1, 9, subject to Sch 11 para 9(2), (3); see below.
[4] Sub-ss (10A), (10B) inserted by FA 1994 s 91 and Sch 11 paras 1, 9.
[5] Words in sub-ss (3), (5)(c) substituted by FA 1994 s 91 and Sch 11 paras 1, 9, subject to Sch 11 para 9(2), (3); see below.
[6] Words in sub-ss (5)(a), (10) repealed by FA 1994 s 91 and Sch 11 paras 1, 9 and Sch 26 Pt V(7).
[7] Sub-s (2A) inserted by FA 1995 s 46(3).
[8] Sub-s (10C) inserted by FA 1995 s 47(3) generally with effect from 20 June 1994 (for detailed commencement provision, see FA 1995 s 47(6), (7)).
[9] Words in sub-s (8)(a) repealed by FA 1996 s 134(1), (2), Sch 20 para 55, Sch 41 Pt V(10) with effect from the year 1996–97.
[10] Words in sub-s (1) inserted by FA 1997 Sch 17 paras 1, 3(1), 7(1) with effect in relation to shares acquired after 26 November 1996 and, subject to FA 1997 Sch 17 para 7(3), with effect after that date in relation to shares acquired on or before that date and falling within FA 1997 Sch 17 para 7(2).

[164FA Loss of relief in cases where shares acquired on being issued.

(1) Subsection (5) below applies in any case falling within any of subsections (2) to (4) below which is a case where—

(a) a person has acquired any eligible shares in a qualifying company ("the acquired holding") for a consideration which is treated as reduced, under section 164A or 164F or this section, by any amount ("the held-over gain"); and
(b) that person acquired those shares by their being issued to him.

(2) A case falls within this subsection if—

(a) the money raised by the issue of the shares comprised in the acquired holding was, at the time when those shares were acquired, intended to be employed for the purposes of a qualifying trade then being carried on; and
(b) that money has not been wholly employed for permissible purposes by the end of the initial utilisation period.

(3) A case falls within this subsection if—

(a) the money raised by the issue of the shares comprised in the acquired holding was, at the time when those shares were acquired, intended to be employed for the purposes of a qualifying trade not then being carried on;

(b) that trade begins to be carried on before the end of the period of 2 years from that time; and

(c) that money (apart from any part of it wholly employed for permissible purposes within the initial utilisation period) has not been wholly employed for the purposes of that trade by the end of the period of 1 year from the time when that trade begins to be carried on (''the first trading year'').

(4) A case falls within this subsection if—

(a) the money raised by the issue of the shares comprised in the acquired holding was, at the time when those shares were acquired, intended to be employed for the purposes of a qualifying trade not then being carried on;

(b) that trade does not begin to be carried on before the end of the period of 2 years from that time; and

(c) that money has not been wholly employed for permissible purposes by the end of the initial utilisation period.

(5) In a case in which this subsection applies, but subject to the following provisions of this section, a chargeable gain equal to the appropriate portion of the held-over gain shall be treated as accruing to the person mentioned in subsection (1) above immediately before the utilisation time; and in this subsection ''the utilisation time'' means—

(a) in relation to a case falling within subsection (2) above, the end of the initial utilisation period;

(b) in relation to a case falling within subsection (3) above, the end of the first trading year; and

(c) in relation to a case falling within subsection (4) above, the end of the period of 2 years mentioned in that subsection.

(6) If, in a case in which subsection (5) above applies, part (but only part) of the money raised by the issue of the shares comprised in the acquired holding has been permissibly employed, this Chapter shall have effect in relation to that holding—

(a) as if it were two separate holdings consisting of—

(i) a holding from which that part of the money was raised; and
(ii) a holding from which the remainder was raised;
and

(b) as if its value were to be apportioned accordingly between those two holdings;

but nothing in this subsection shall require any money whose use is disregarded by virtue of subsection (8)(e) below to be treated as raised by a different holding.

(7) For the purposes of subsection (6) above a part of the money raised by the issue of the shares comprised in the acquired holding shall be taken to have been permissibly employed if—

(a) in a case falling within subsection (2) or (4) above, that part has been wholly employed for permissible purposes within the initial utilisation period; or

(b) in a case falling within subsection (3) above that part has been wholly employed—

(i) for permissible purposes within the initial utilisation period, or
(ii) for the purposes of the trade mentioned in that subsection before the end of the first trading year.

(8) For the purposes of this section—

(a) the appropriate portion of the held-over gain is so much, if any, of that gain as has not already been charged on any disposal or under section 164F or this section;

(b) ''the initial utilisation period'' means the period of 1 year from the time when the acquired holding was acquired;

(c) ''permissible purposes'', in relation to a company, means the purposes of any qualifying trade carried on by it or by any of its qualifying subsidiaries;

(d) ''qualifying subsidiary'' has the same meaning as in section 164G;

(e) money shall not be treated as employed otherwise than wholly for particular purposes if the only amount employed for other purposes is an amount which is not a significant amount; and

(f) the purposes of a qualifying trade shall be taken to include the purpose of preparing for the carrying on of the trade.

(9) Subsections (4) to (5) and (10A) to (11) of section 164F shall apply for the purposes of this section as they apply for the purposes of that section, but—

(a) subsection (5) of that section shall so apply—

(i) with the omission of paragraphs (e) to (g), and
(ii) as if the reference in paragraph (d) to any charge under subsection (2) of that section were a reference to any charge under subsection (5) of this section; and

(b) subsection (10A) of that section shall so apply as if the reference to subsection (2) of that section were a reference to subsection (5) of this section.]'

Commentary—*Simon's Direct Tax Service* **C3.917.**
Definitions—"Chargeable gain", s 15(2); "eligible shares", s 164N(1); "qualifying company", s 164G.
Amendments—[1] This section inserted by FA 1997 Sch 17 paras 1, 3(2), 7(1) with effect in relation to shares acquired after 26 November 1996 and subject to FA 1997 Sch 17 para 7(3), with effect after that date in relation to shares acquired on or before that date and falling within FA 1997 Sch 17 para 7(2). Section repealed by FA 1998 s 165, Sch 27 Part III(32) with effect for acquisitions made after 5 April 1998.

[164FF Qualifying investment acquired from husband or wife

(1) This section applies where—

(a) *a claim is made under subsection (2) of section 164A or subsection (10A) of section 164F; and*

(b) *the qualifying investment as respects which the claim is made is acquired by a disposal to which section 58 applies.*

(2) The amounts by reference to which the reduction is determined shall be treated as including the amount of the consideration which the claimant would under this Act be treated as having given for the qualifying investment if he had, immediately upon acquiring the qualifying investment, disposed of it on a disposal which was not a no gain/no loss disposal.

(3) Where—

(a) *the claimant makes a disposal, which is not a no gain/no loss disposal, of the qualifying investment, and*

(b) *any disposal after 31st March 1982 and before he acquired the qualifying investment was a no gain/no loss disposal,*

nothing in paragraph 1 of Schedule 3, section 35 or section 55 shall operate to defeat the reduction falling to be made under section 164A(2)(b) or, as the case may be, section 164F(10A)(b) in the consideration for the acquisition of the qualifying investment.

(4) Where—

(a) *the claimant makes a disposal of the qualifying investment and that disposal is a disposal to which section 58 applies, and*

(b) *any disposal after 31st March 1982 and before the claimant acquired the qualifying investment was a no gain/no loss disposal,*

nothing in the application of paragraph 1 of Schedule 3, section 35 or section 55 to the person to whom the claimant makes the disposal of the qualifying investment shall operate to defeat the reduction made under section 164A(2)(b) or, as the case may be, section 164F(10A)(b).

(5) For the purposes of this section a no gain/no loss disposal is one on which by virtue of any of the enactments specified in section 35(3)(d) neither a gain nor a loss accrues.][1]

Commentary—*Simon's Direct Tax Service* **C3.920.**
Cross references—See TCGA 1992 s 164A(14) (relief on reinvestment for individuals).
TCGA 1992 s 164F(10C) (failure of conditions for relief).
Amendments—[1] This section inserted by FA 1995 s 47(4) generally with effect from 20 June 1994 (for detailed commencement provision, see FA 1995 s 47(6)), and repealed by FA 1998 s 165, Sch 27 Part III(32) with effect for acquisitions made after 5 April 1998.

[164FG Multiple claims

(1) This section applies where—

(a) *a reduction is claimed by a person as respects a qualifying investment under subsection (2) of section 164A or subsection (10A) of section 164F; and*

(b) *any other reduction has been or is being claimed by that person under either subsection as respects that investment.*

(2) Subject to subsection (5) below, the reductions shall be treated as claimed separately in such sequence as the claimant elects ...[2]

(3) In relation to a later claim as respects the qualifying investment under either subsection, the subsection shall have effect as if each of the relevant amounts were reduced by the aggregate of any reductions made in the amount or value of the consideration for the acquisition of that investment by virtue of any earlier claims as respects that investment.

(4) In subsection (3) above "the relevant amounts" means—

(a) *if the claim is under section 164A(2), the amounts referred to in subsection (2)(a)(ii) and (iii) and any amount required to be included by virtue of section 164FF(2); and*

(b) *if the claim is under section 164F(10A), the amounts referred to in subsection (10A)(a)(i) and (ii) and any amount required to be included by virtue of section 164FF(2).*

(5) A claim that has become final shall be treated as made earlier than any claim that has not become final.

(6) For the purposes of subsection (5) above, a claim becomes final when—

(a) *it may no longer be amended, or*

(b) *it is finally determined,*

whichever occurs first.][1]

Commentary—*Simon's Direct Tax Service* **C3.905.**
Cross references—See TCGA 1992 s 164A(14) (relief on reinvestment for individuals).
TCGA 1992 s 164F(10C) (failure of conditions for relief).

Amendments—[1] This section inserted by FA 1995 s 47(5), generally with effect from 20 June 1994 (for detailed commencement provision, see FA 1995 s 47(7)), and repealed by FA 1998 s 165, Sch 27 Part III(32) with effect for acquisitions made after 5 April 1998.
[2] Words in sub-s (2) repealed by FA 1996 s 134(1), (2), Sch 20 para 56, Sch 41 Pt V(10) with effect from the year 1996–97.

[164G Meaning of "qualifying company"]

(1) Subject to section 164H, a company is a qualifying company for the purposes of this Chapter if it complies with this section.

(2) Subject to the following provisions of this section, a company complies with this section if it is—

(a) an unquoted company which exists wholly for the purpose of carrying on one or more qualifying trades or which so exists apart from purposes capable of having no significant effect (other than in relation to incidental matters) on the extent of the company's activities; [or]²

[(aa) an unquoted company which is the parent company of a trading group.]²

(3) A company does not comply with this section if—

(a) it controls (whether on its own or together with any person connected with it) any company which is not a qualifying subsidiary or, without controlling it, has a 51 per cent subsidiary which is not a qualifying subsidiary;

(b) it is under the control of another company (or of another company and a person connected with the other company) or, without being controlled by it, is a 51 per cent subsidiary of another company; or

(c) arrangements are in existence by virtue of which the company could fall within paragraph (a) or (b) above;

and in this subsection "51 per cent subsidiary" has the meaning given by section 838 of the Taxes Act.

[(4) In this section "qualifying subsidiary", in relation to a company ("the holding company"), means any company which is a member of a group of companies of which the holding company is the principal company.]²

[(4A) For the purposes of this section a company is the parent company of a trading group if—

(a) it is the principal company of a group of companies; and

(b) the requirements of subsection (4B) below are fulfilled by what would be the business of the company and its qualifying subsidiaries if all the activities, taken together, of the company and its qualifying subsidiaries were regarded as one business.]²

(4B) A business fulfils the requirements of this subsection if—

(a) it is carried on wholly or mainly in the United Kingdom; and

(b) neither the business nor a substantial part of it consists in, or in either of, the following, that is to say—

(i) activities falling within section 164I(2) but not within subsection (4C) below; and

(ii) activities carried on otherwise than in the course of a trade.]²

[(4C) The activities falling within this subsection are—

(a) the receiving of royalties or licence fees in circumstances where the requirements mentioned in paragraphs (a) and (b) of section 164I(5) or (6) are satisfied in relation to the company receiving them;

(b) the letting of ships, other than oil rigs or pleasure craft, on charter in circumstances where the requirements mentioned in paragraphs (a) to (d) of section 164I(7) are satisfied in relation to the company so letting them.]²

[(4D) Activities of a company or of any of its qualifying subsidiaries shall be disregarded for the purposes of subsections (4A) to (4C) above to the extent that they consist in—

(a) the holding of shares in or securities of, or the making of loans to, one or more of the company's qualifying subsidiaries; or

(b) the holding and managing of property used by the company or any of its qualifying subsidiaries for the purposes of—

(i) research and development from which it is intended that a qualifying trade to be carried on by the company or any of its qualifying subsidiaries will be derived; or

(ii) one or more qualifying trades so carried on.]²

[(4E) Activities of a qualifying subsidiary of a company shall also be disregarded for the purposes of subsections (4A) to (4C) above to the extent that they consist in—

(a) the making of loans to the company; or

(b) in the case of a mainly trading subsidiary, activities carried on in pursuance of its insignificant purposes (within the meaning given by subsection (4F) below)]².

[(4F) In subsection (4E) above "mainly trading subsidiary" means a qualifying subsidiary which, apart from purposes ("its insignificant purposes") capable of having no significant effect (other than in relation to incidental matters) on the extent of its activities, exists wholly for the purpose of carrying on one or more qualifying trades.]²

(6) Without prejudice to the generality of subsection (2) above or to section 164F(8), a company ceases to comply with this section if—

(a) a resolution is passed, or an order is made, for the winding up of the company;
(b) in the case of a winding up otherwise than under the Insolvency Act 1986 or the Insolvency (Northern Ireland) Order 1989, any other act is done for the like purpose; or
(c) the company is dissolved without winding up.]¹

Commentary—*Simon's Direct Tax Service* **C3.917–919, 921.**
Revenue & other press releases—IR 2-12-96 (Revenue clearance is available to a company as to whether it has qualifying status).
Definitions—''Company'', s 288(1); ''control'', s 288(1); ''group of companies'', s 164N(2); ''oil rig'', s 164N(1); ''pleasure craft'', s 164N(1); ''qualifying trade'', ss 164I, 164J; ''research and development'', s 164N(1); ''shares'', s 288(1); ''unquoted company'', s 164N(1).
Cross references—See TCGA 1992 s 164N(2) (interpretation of this section).
Amendments—¹ This Chapter inserted by FA 1993 s 87 and Sch 7 para 3 in relation to disposals made after 15 March 1993, and repealed by FA 1998 s 165, Sch 27 Part III(32) with effect for acquisitions made after 5 April 1998.
² Sub-s (2)(*aa*) and preceding word ''or'' substituted for sub-s (2)(*b*), (*c*) and sub-ss (4), (4A)–(4F) by FA 1997 Sch 17 paras 1, 4, 7(1) with effect in relation to shares acquired after 26 November 1996 and, subject to FA 1997 Sch 17 para 7(3), with effect after that date in relation to shares required on or before that date and falling within FA 1997 Sch 17 para 7(2).

[164H Property companies etc not to be qualifying companies

(1) For the purposes of this Chapter a company is not a qualifying company at any time when the value of the interests in land held by the company [exceeds]⁴ half the value of the company's chargeable assets ...² [or half the value of the company's assets as a whole (whichever is the greater); and section 294(3) and (4) of the Taxes Act (meaning of value of company's assets as a whole) applies for the purposes of this subsection as it applies for the purposes of section 294 of that Act]³.

(2) For the purposes of this section the value of the interests in land held by a company at any time shall be arrived at by first aggregating the market value at that time of each of those interests and then deducting—

(a) the amount of any debts of the company which are secured on any of those interests (including any debt secured by a floating charge on property which comprises any of those interests);
(b) the amount of any unsecured debts of the company which do not fall due for payment before the end of the period of 12 months beginning with that time; and
(c) the amount paid up in respect of those shares of the company (if any) which carry a present or future preferential right to the company's assets on its winding up.

(3) In this section ''interest in land'' means any estate or interest in land, any right in or over land or affecting the use or disposition of land, and any right to obtain such an estate, interest or right from another which is conditional on that other's ability to grant the estate, interest or right in question, except that it does not include—

(a) the interest of a creditor (other than a creditor in respect of a rentcharge) whose debt is secured by way of a mortgage, an agreement for a mortgage or a charge of any kind over land; or
(b) in the case of land in Scotland, the interest of a creditor in a charge or security of any kind over land.

(4) For the purposes of this section, the value of an interest in any building or other land shall be adjusted by deducting the market value of any machinery or plant which is so installed or otherwise fixed in or to the building or other land as, in law, to become part of it.

(5) In arriving at the value of any interest in land for the purposes of this section—

(a) it shall be assumed that there is no source of mineral deposits in the land of a kind which it would be practicable to exploit by extracting them from underground otherwise than by means of opencast mining or quarrying; and
(b) any borehole on the land shall be disregarded if it was made in the course of oil exploration.

(6) Where a company is a member of a partnership which holds any interest in land—

(a) that interest shall, for the purposes of this section, be treated as an interest in land held by the company; but
(b) its value at any time shall, for those purposes, be taken to be such fraction of its value (apart from this subsection) as is equal to the fraction of the assets of the partnership to which the company would be entitled if the partnership were dissolved at that time.

(7) Where a company is a member of a group of companies all the members of the group shall be treated as a single company for the purposes of this section; but any debt owed by, or liability of, one member of the group to another shall be disregarded for those purposes.]¹

Commentary—*Simon's Direct Tax Service* **C3.919, 921.**
Definitions—''Company'', s 288(1); ''group of companies'', Sch 6 para 1(2); ''land'', s 288(1); ''market value'', s 272; ''oil exploration'', s 164N(1); ''qualifying company'', s 164G.
Cross references—See TCGA 1992 s 164A(13) (disapplication of this section in deciding whether an acquisition made after 28 November 1994 is a qualifying investment).
TCGA 1992 s 164F(2A) (disapplication of this section after 28 November 1994 for the purpose of deciding whether a company is a qualifying company within sub-s (2)(*b*)).
Amendments—¹ This Chapter inserted by FA 1993 s 87 and Sch 7 para 3 in relation to disposals made after 15 March 1993, and repealed by FA 1998 s 165, Sch 27 Part III(32) with effect for acquisitions made after 5 April 1998.
² Words in sub-s (1) repealed by FA 1994 Sch 11 paras 1, 5 and Sch 26 Pt V(7).

[3] Words in sub-s (1) added by FA 1994 s 91(3), (4) and apply to determine whether a company is a qualifying company on or after 30 November 1993.
[4] Word in sub-s (1) substituted by FA 1994 s 91(3), (4).

[164I Qualifying trades

(1) For the purposes of this Chapter—

    (a) a trade is a qualifying trade if it complies with the requirements of this section [and is carried on wholly or mainly in the United Kingdom][3]; and

    (b) the carrying on[, wholly or mainly in the United Kingdom,][3] of any activities of research and development from which it is intended that a trade complying with those requirements[, and to be carried on wholly or mainly in the United Kingdom,][3] will be derived shall be treated as the carrying on of a qualifying trade.

(2) Subject to the following provisions of this section, a trade complies with this section if neither that trade nor a substantial part of it consists in one or more of the following activities, that is to say—

    (a) dealing in land, in commodities or futures or in shares, securities or other financial instruments;

    (b) dealing in goods otherwise than in the course of an ordinary trade of wholesale or retail distribution;

    (c) banking, insurance, money-lending, debt-factoring, hire-purchase financing or other financial activities;

    (d) leasing (including letting ships on charter or other assets on hire) or receiving royalties or licence fees;

    (e) providing legal or accountancy services;

    (f) providing services or facilities for any such trade carried on by another person as—

        (i) consists, to a substantial extent, in activities within any of paragraphs (a) to (e) above; and

        (ii) is a trade in which a controlling interest is held by a person who also has a controlling interest in the trade carried on by the company providing the services or facilities;

    (g) property development;

    (h) farming;

but this subsection shall have effect in relation to a qualifying trade carried on by a member of a group of companies, as if the reference in paragraph (f) above to another person did not include a reference to the principal company of the group.

(3) For the purposes of subsection (2)(b) above—

    (a) a trade of wholesale distribution is one in which the goods are offered for sale and sold to persons for resale by them, or for processing and resale by them, to members of the general public for their use or consumption;

    (b) a trade of retail distribution is one in which the goods are offered for sale and sold to members of the general public for their use or consumption; and

    (c) a trade is not an ordinary trade of wholesale or retail distribution if—

        (i) it consists, to a substantial extent, in dealing in goods of a kind which are collected or held as an investment, or of that activity and any other activity of a kind falling within subsection (2) above, taken together; and

        (ii) a substantial proportion of those goods are held by the company for a period which is significantly longer than the period for which a vendor would reasonably be expected to hold them while endeavouring to dispose of them at their market value.

(4) In determining for the purposes of this Chapter whether a trade carried on by any person is an ordinary trade of wholesale or retail distribution, regard shall be had to the extent to which it has the following features, that is to say—

    (a) the goods are bought by that person in quantities larger than those in which he sells them;

    (b) the goods are bought and sold by that person in different markets;

    (c) that person employs staff and incurs expenses in the trade in addition to the cost of the goods and, in the case of a trade carried on by a company, to any remuneration paid to any person connected with it;

    (d) there are purchases or sales from or to persons who are connected with that person;

    (e) purchases are matched with forward sales or vice versa;

    (f) the goods are held by that person for longer than is normal for goods of the kind in question;

    (g) the trade is carried on otherwise than at a place or places commonly used for wholesale or retail trade;

    (h) that person does not take physical possession of the goods;

and for the purposes of this subsection the features specified in paragraphs (a) to (c) above shall be regarded as indications that the trade is such an ordinary trade and those in paragraphs (d) to (h) above shall be regarded as indications of the contrary.

[(4A) In deciding whether a trade complies with this section at a time falling on or after 29th November 1994 paragraphs (g) and (h) of subsection (2) above shall be ignored.][2]

(5) A trade shall not be treated as failing to comply with this section by reason only of its consisting, to a substantial extent, in receiving royalties or licence fees if—

(a) the company carrying on the trade is engaged in—

(i) the production of films; or
(ii) the production of films and the distribution of films produced by it within the period of 3 years before their distribution;

and

(b) all royalties and licence fees received by it are in respect of films produced by it within the preceding 3 years or sound recordings in relation to such films or other products arising from such films.

(6) A trade shall not be treated as failing to comply with this section by reason only of its consisting, to a substantial extent, in receiving royalties or licence fees if—

(a) the company carrying on the trade is engaged in research and development; and
(b) all royalties and licence fees received by it are attributable to research and development which it has carried out.

(7) A trade shall not be treated as failing to comply with this section by reason only of its consisting in letting ships, other than oil rigs or pleasure craft, on charter if—

(a) every ship let on charter by the company carrying on the trade is beneficially owned by the company;
(b) every ship beneficially owned by the company is registered in the United Kingdom;
(c) the company is solely responsible for arranging the marketing of the services of its ships; and
(d) the conditions mentioned in subsection (8) below are satisfied in relation to every letting of a ship on charter by the company;

but where any of the requirements mentioned in paragraphs (a) to (d) above are not satisfied in relation to any lettings, the trade shall not thereby be treated as failing to comply with this section if those lettings and any other activity of a kind falling within subsection (2) above do not, when taken together, amount to a substantial part of the trade.

(8) The conditions are that—

(a) the letting is for a period not exceeding 12 months and no provision is made at any time (whether in the charterparty or otherwise) for extending it beyond that period otherwise than at the option of the charterer;
(b) during the period of the letting there is no provision in force (whether by virtue of being contained in the charterparty or otherwise) for the grant of a new letting to end, otherwise than at the option of the charterer, more than 12 months after that provision is made;
(c) the letting is by way of a bargain made at arm's length between the company and a person who is not connected with it;
(d) under the terms of the charter the company is responsible as principal—

(i) for taking, throughout the period of the charter, management decisions in relation to the ship, other than those of a kind generally regarded by persons engaged in trade of the kind in question as matters of husbandry; and
(ii) for defraying all expenses in connection with the ship throughout that period, or substantially all such expenses, other than those directly incidental to a particular voyage or to the employment of the ship during that period;

and

(e) no arrangements exist by virtue of which a person other than the company may be appointed to be responsible for the matters mentioned in paragraph (d) above on behalf of the company;

but this subsection shall have effect, in relation to any letting between a company and another company which is a member of the same group of companies as that company, as if paragraph (c) were omitted.

(9) A trade shall not comply with this section unless it is conducted on a commercial basis and with a view to the realisation of profits.][1]

Commentary—*Simon's Direct Tax Service* **C3.921–925.**
Revenue Interpretation RI 120—Consideration of the kinds of "non-qualifying" activities under sub-s (2)(d)—leasing, receiving royalties and receiving licence fees.
Definitions—"Connected person", s 286; "farming", s 164N(1); "film", s 164N(1); "group of companies", Sch 6 para 1(2); "land", s 288(1); "market value", s 272; "oil rig", s 164N(1); "pleasure craft", s 164N(1); "property development", s 164N(1); "research and development", s 164N(1); "shares", s 288(1); "sound recording", s 164N(1); "trade", ss 164J(3), 288(1).
Cross references—See TCGA 1992 s 164J (supplementary provisions).
TCGA 1992 s 164N(2) (interpretation of this section).
Amendments—[1] This Chapter inserted by FA 1993 s 87 and Sch 7 para 3 in relation to disposals made after 15 March 1993, and repealed by FA 1998 s 165, Sch 27 Part III(32) with effect for acquisitions made after 5 April 1998.
[2] Sub-s (4A) inserted by FA 1995 s 46(4).
[3] Words in sub-s (1)(a), (b) inserted by FA 1997 Sch 17 paras 1, 5, 7(1) with effect in relation to shares acquired after 26 November 1996 and, subject to FA 1997 Sch 17 para 7(3), with effect after that date in relation to shares acquired on or before that date and falling within FA 1997 Sch 17 para 7(2).

[164J Provisions supplementary to section 164I

(1) For the purposes of section 164I, in the case of a trade carried on by a company, a person has a controlling interest in that trade if—

(a) he controls the company;

(b) the company is a close company and he or an associate of his is a director of the company and either—

(i) the beneficial owner of, or

(ii) able, directly or through the medium of other companies or by any other indirect means, to control,

more than 30 per cent of the ordinary share capital of the company; or

(c) not less than half of the trade could in accordance with section 344(2) of the Taxes Act be regarded as belonging to him;

and, in any other case, a person has a controlling interest in a trade if he is entitled to not less than half of the assets used for, or of the income arising from, the trade.

(2) For the purposes of subsection (1) above, there shall be attributed to any person any rights or powers of any other person who is an associate of his.

(3) References in section 164I(2)(f) or subsection (1) above to a trade carried on by a person other than the company in question shall be construed as including references to any business, profession or vocation.

(4) In this section "director" shall be construed in accordance with section 417(5) of the Taxes Act.][1]

Commentary—*Simon's Direct Tax Service* **C3.921, 925.**
Definitions—"Asset", s 21(1); "associate", s 164N(1); "close company", s 288(1); "company", s 288(1); "control", s 288(1); "ordinary share capital", s 164N(1).
Amendments—[1] This Chapter inserted by FA 1993 s 87 and Sch 7 para 3 in relation to disposals made after 15 March 1993, and repealed by FA 1998 s 165, Sch 27 Part III(32) with effect for acquisitions made after 5 April 1998.

[164K Foreign residents

(1) This Chapter shall not apply in relation to any person in respect of his acquisition of any eligible shares in a qualifying company if at the time when he acquires them he is neither resident nor ordinarily resident in the United Kingdom.

(2) This Chapter shall not apply in relation to any person in respect of his acquisition of any eligible shares in a qualifying company if—

(a) though resident or ordinarily resident in the United Kingdom at the time when he acquires them, he is regarded for the purposes of any double taxation relief arrangements as resident in a territory outside the United Kingdom; and

(b) by virtue of the arrangements, he would not be liable in the United Kingdom to tax on a gain arising on a disposal of those shares immediately after their acquisition.][1]

Commentary—*Simon's Direct Tax Service* **C3.904.**
Definitions—"Double taxation relief arrangements", s 288(1); "eligible shares", s 164N(1); "ordinarily resident", s 9(1); "qualifying company", s 164G; "resident", s 9(1); "shares", s 288(1).
Amendments—[1] This Chapter inserted by FA 1993 s 87 and Sch 7 para 3 in relation to disposals made after 15 March 1993, and repealed by FA 1998 s 165, Sch 27 Part III(32) with effect for acquisitions made after 5 April 1998.

[164L Anti-avoidance provisions

(1) For the purposes of this Chapter an acquisition of shares in a qualifying company shall not be treated as an acquisition of eligible shares if the arrangements for the acquisition of those shares, or any arrangements made before their acquisition in relation to or in connection with the acquisition, include—

(a) arrangements with a view to the subsequent re-acquisition, exchange or other disposal of the shares;

(b) arrangements for or with a view to the cessation of the company's trade or the disposal of, or of a substantial amount of, its chargeable business assets; or

(c) arrangements for the return of the whole or any part of the value of his investment to the individual acquiring the shares.

(2) If, after any eligible shares in a qualifying company have been acquired by any individual, the whole or any part of the value of that individual's investment is returned to him, those shares shall be treated for the purposes of this Chapter as ceasing to be eligible shares.

(3) For the purposes of this section there shall be treated as being a return of the whole or a part of the value of the investment of an individual who is to acquire or has acquired any shares in a company if the company—

(a) repays, redeems or repurchases any of its share capital or other securities which belong to that individual or makes any payment to him for giving up his right to any of the company's share capital or any security on its cancellation or extinguishment;

(b) repays any debt owed to that individual, other than a debt which was incurred by the company—

(i) on or after the acquisition of the shares; and

(ii) otherwise than in consideration of the extinguishment of a debt incurred before the acquisition of the shares;

(c) makes to that individual any payment for giving up his right to any debt on its extinguishment;

(d) releases or waives any liability of that individual to the company or discharges, or undertakes to discharge, any liability of his to a third person;

(e) provides a benefit or facility for that individual;

(f) disposes of an asset to that individual for no consideration or for a consideration which is or the value of which is less than the market value of the asset;

(g) acquires an asset from that individual for a consideration which is or the value of which is more than the market value of the asset; or

(h) makes any payment to that individual other than a qualifying payment.

(4) For the purposes of this section there shall also be treated as being a return of the whole or a part of the value of the investment of an individual who is to acquire or has acquired any shares in a company if—

(a) there is a loan made by any person to that individual; and

(b) the loan is one which would not have been made, or would not have been made on the same terms, if that individual had not acquired those shares or had not been proposing to do so.

(5) For the purposes of this section a company shall be treated as having released or waived a liability if the liability is not discharged within 12 months of the time when it ought to have been discharged.

(6) References in this section to a debt or liability do not, in relation to a company, include references to any debt or liability which would be discharged by the making by that company of a qualifying payment, and references to a benefit or facility do not include references to any benefit or facility provided in circumstances such that, if a payment had been made of an amount equal to its value, that payment would be a qualifying payment.

(7) References in this section to the making by any person of a loan to an individual include references—

(a) to the giving by that person of any credit to that individual; and

(b) to the assignment or assignation to that person of any debt due from that individual.

(8) In this section ''qualifying payment'' means—

(a) the payment by any company of such remuneration for service as an officer or employee of that company as may be reasonable in relation to the duties of that office or employment;

(b) any payment or reimbursement by any company of travelling or other expenses wholly, exclusively and necessarily incurred by the individual to whom the payment is made in the performance of duties as an officer or employee of that company;

(c) the payment by any company of any interest which represents no more than a reasonable commercial return on money lent to that company;

(d) the payment by any company of any dividend or other distribution which does not exceed a normal return on any investment in shares in or other securities of that company;

(e) any payment for the supply of goods which does not exceed their market value;

(f) the payment by any company, as rent for any property occupied by the company, of an amount not exceeding a reasonable and commercial rent for the property;

(g) any reasonable and necessary remuneration which—

(i) is paid by any company for services rendered to that company in the course of a trade or profession; and

(ii) is taken into account in computing the profits or gains of the trade or profession under Case I or II of Schedule D or would be so taken into account if it fell in a period on the basis of which those profits or gains are assessed under that Schedule;

(h) a payment in discharge of an ordinary trade debt.

(9) In this section—

(a) any reference to a payment or disposal to an individual includes a reference to a payment or disposal made to him indirectly or to his order or for his benefit; and

(b) any reference to an individual includes a reference to an associate of his and any reference to a company includes a reference to a person connected with the company.

(10) This section shall have effect in relation to the acquisition of shares by the trustees of a settlement as if references to the individual acquiring the shares were references to those trustees or [any individual or charity by virtue of whose interest, at the time of the acquisition, section 164B applies to the settled property]².

[(10A) For the purposes of this Chapter, where—

(a) a person has acquired any eligible shares in a qualifying company (''the acquired holding'') for a consideration which is treated as reduced under this Chapter by any amount (''the held-over gain''), and

(b) after that acquisition, he acquires eligible shares in a relevant company, *he shall not be regarded in relation to his acquisition of those shares in the relevant company as acquiring a qualifying investment for the purposes of section 164A.]³*

[(10B) For the purposes of subsection (10A) above a company is a relevant company if—

(a) where that person has disposed of any of the acquired holding, it is the company in which the acquired holding has subsisted or a company which was a member of the same group of companies as that company at any time since the acquisition of the acquired holding,

(b) it is a company in relation to the disposal of any shares in which there has been a claim under this Chapter such that, without that or an equivalent claim, there would have been no held-over gain in relation to the acquired holding, or

(c) it is a company which, at the time of the disposal or acquisition to which the claim relates, was a member of the same group of companies as a company falling within paragraph (b) above.]³

(11) In this section—

"arrangements" includes any scheme, agreement or understanding, whether or not legally enforceable;

["chargeable business asset", in relation to any company, means a chargeable asset (including goodwill but not including shares or securities or other assets held as investments) which is, or is an interest in, an asset used for the purposes of a trade, profession, vocation, office or employment carried on by—

(a) the individual acquiring the shares,

(b) any personal company of that individual,

(c) a member of a trading group of which the holding company is a personal company of that individual, or

(d) a partnership of which that individual is a member.]⁴

"ordinary trade debt" means any debt for goods or services supplied in the ordinary course of a trade or business where any credit given does not exceed six months and is not longer than that normally given to customers of the person carrying on the trade or business.]¹

Commentary—*Simon's Direct Tax Service* **C3.941–944.**
Statement of Practice SP 3/94—As regards holdings of shares issued before 6 April 1998, loans made to acquire shares and available to other borrowers on the same terms do not necessarily preclude relief, but "eligible shares" or associated rights specified as security for the loan would.
SP 6/98—As regards holdings of shares issued after 5 April 1998, loans made to acquire shares do not necessarily preclude relief; the test is whether the lender makes the loan on terms which are influenced by the fact that the borrower, or an associate of the borrower, has acquired, or is proposing to acquire, the shares.
Revenue Interpretation RI 133—Application of SP 3/94 rules relating to loan limited investments to reinvestment relief.
Definitions—"Associate", s 164N(1); "company", s 288(1); "connected", s 286; "eligible shares", s 164N(1); "market value", s 272; "personal company", Sch 6 para 1(2); "qualifying company", s 164G; "shares", s 288(1); "trade", ss 164J(3), 288(1); "trading group", Sch 6 para 1(2).
Amendments—¹ This Chapter inserted by FA 1993 s 87 and Sch 7 para 3 in relation to disposals made after 15 March 1993, and repealed by FA 1998 s 165, Sch 27 Part III(32) with effect for acquisitions made after 5 April 1998.
² Words in sub-s (10) substituted by FA 1994 s 91 and Sch 11 paras 1, 6 in relation to disposals after 29 November 1993.
³ Sub-ss (10A), (10B) inserted by FA 1994 s 91 and Sch 11 paras 1, 10 in relation to disposals after 29 November 1993.
⁴ Definition of "chargeable business asset" in sub-s (11) substituted by FA 1994 s 91 and Sch 11 paras 1, 10.

[164M Exclusion of double relief

Where a person acquires any shares in a company those shares shall not be eligible shares or, as the case may be, shall cease to be eligible shares if that person or any person connected with him has made or makes a claim for relief in relation to those shares under Chapter III of Part VII of the Taxes Act (business expansion scheme) [but the reference in this section to that Chapter is to that Chapter as it applies in relation to shares issued before 1st January 1994]².]¹

Commentary—*Simon's Direct Tax Service* **C3.935.**
Note—For Pt VII Ch III as it applies in relation to shares issued before 1 January 1994, see *Yellow Tax Handbook*, 1993–94, 32nd edition.
Definitions—"Company", s 288(1); "connected", s 286; "eligible shares", s 164N(1); "shares", s 288(1).
Amendments—¹ This Chapter inserted by FA 1993 s 87 and Sch 7 para 3 in relation to disposals made after 15 March 1993, and repealed by FA 1998 s 165, Sch 27 Part III(32) with effect for acquisitions made after 5 April 1998.
² Words inserted by FA 1994 Sch 15 para 31.

[164MA Exclusion of double relief

If a person makes a claim for relief under Chapter III of Part VII of the Taxes Act (enterprise investment scheme) in respect of any shares, those shares shall not be, or be treated as ever having been, eligible shares.]¹

Commentary—*Simon's Direct Tax Service* **C3.935.**
Definitions—"Eligible shares", s 164N(1); "relief", TA 1988 s 312(1); "shares", s 288(1).
Amendments—¹ This section inserted by FA 1994 Sch 15 para 32 in relation to shares issued after 31 December 1993, and repealed by FA 1998 s 165, Sch 27 Part III(32) with effect for acquisitions made after 5 April 1998.

[164N Interpretation of Chapter IA

(1) In this Chapter—

"associate" has the meaning given in subsections (3) and (4) of section 417 of the Taxes Act, except that in those subsections, as applied for the purposes of this Chapter, "relative" shall not include a brother or sister;

"*eligible shares*" *means (subject to sections 164L [164M and 164MA]3) any ordinary shares in a company which do not carry—*

> (a) *any present or future preferential rights to dividends or to that* company's *assets on its winding up; or*
> (b) *any present or future preferential right to be redeemed;*

"*farming*" *has the same meaning as in the Taxes Act;*

"*film*" *means an original master negative of a film, an original master film disc or an original master film tape;*

"*oil exploration*" *means searching for oil (within the meaning of Chapter V of Part XII of the Taxes Act);*

"*oil rig*" *means any ship which is an offshore installation for the purposes of the Mineral Workings (Offshore Installations) Act 1971;*

"*ordinary share capital*" *has the meaning given by section 832(1) of the Taxes Act;*

"*ordinary shares*" *means shares forming part of a company's ordinary share capital;*

"*pleasure craft*" *means any ship of a kind primarily used for sport or recreation;*

"*property development*" *means the development of land, by a company which has, or at any time has had, an interest in the land (within the meaning of section 164H), with the sole or main object of realising a gain from disposing of the land when developed;*

"*research and development*" *means any activity which is intended to result in a patentable invention (within the meaning of the Patents Act 1977) or in a computer program;*

"*sound recording*" *in relation to a film, means its sound track, original master audio disc or original master audio tape; and*

"*unquoted company*" *means a company none of the shares in or other securities of which are [listed]4 on any recognised stock exchange or are dealt in on the Unlisted Securities Market.*

[(1A) Every asset of a company is for the purposes of this Chapter a chargeable asset of that company at any time, except one on the disposal of which by the company at that time no gain accruing to the company would be a chargeable gain.]²

[(2) Section 170 shall apply for the interpretation of sections 164G and 164I as it would apply for the interpretation of sections 171 to 181 if section 170(2)(a) together with the words "(although resident in the United Kingdom)" in section 170(9)(b) were omitted.]⁵

(3) Subject to subsection (2) above, paragraph 1 of Schedule 6 shall have effect for the purposes of this Chapter as it has effect for the purposes of sections 163 and 164 and that Schedule.

(4) References in this Chapter to the reduction of an amount include references to its reduction to nil.

[(5) For the purposes of this Chapter, any allotment of shares before their issue shall be disregarded in determining whether and when a person acquires shares by their issue to him.]⁵]¹

Commentary—*Simon's Direct Tax Service* **C3.911.**
Revenue Interpretation RI 69—Reinvestment relief; investment in non-resident company.
Definitions—"Asset", s 21(1); "chargeable gain", s 15(2); "company, s 288(1).
Amendments—¹ This Chapter inserted by FA 1993 s 87 and Sch 7 para 3 in relation to disposals made after 15 March 1993.
² Sub-s (1A) inserted by FA 1994 s 91 and Sch 11 paras 1, 11 in relation to disposals after 29 November 1993.
³ Words in the definition of "eligible shares" in sub-s (1) substituted by FA 1994 Sch 15 para 33.
⁴ Word in the definition of "unquoted company" in sub-s (1) substituted by FA 1996 Sch 38 para 10(1), (2)(b), (4) with effect in relation to acquisitions of qualifying investments (within the meaning of s 164A) after 31 March 1996.
⁵ Sub-s (2) substituted and sub-s (5) inserted by FA 1997 Sch 17 paras 1, 6, 7(1) with effect in relation to shares acquired after 26 November 1996 and, subject to FA 1997 Sch 17 para 7(3), with effect after that date in relation to shares acquired on or before that date and falling within FA 1997 Sch 17 para 7(2).

CHAPTER II
GIFTS OF BUSINESS ASSETS

165 Relief for gifts of business assets

(1) If—

> (a) an individual ("the transferor") makes a disposal otherwise than under a bargain at arm's length of an asset within subsection (2) below, and
> (b) a claim for relief under this section is made by the transferor and the person who acquires the asset ("the transferee") or, where the trustees of a settlement are the transferee, by the transferor alone,

then, subject to subsection (3) and [sections 166, 167 and 169]², subsection (4) below shall apply in relation to the disposal.

(2) An asset is within this subsection if—

> (a) it is, or is an interest in, an asset used for the purposes of a trade, profession or vocation carried on by—
>> (i) the transferor,
>> (ii) his [personal company]¹, or
>> (iii) a member of a trading group of which the holding company is his [personal company]¹, or
> (b) it consists of shares or securities of a trading company, or of the holding company of a trading group, where—

(i) the shares or securities are [not listed on a recognised stock exchange]², or
(ii) the trading company or holding company is the transferor's [personal company]¹.

(3) Subsection (4) below does not apply in relation to a disposal if—

(*a*) in the case of a disposal of an asset, any gain accruing to the transferor on the disposal is (apart from this section) wholly relieved under Schedule 6, or
(*b*) in the case of a disposal of shares or securities, [the transferee is a company or]² the appropriate proportion determined under paragraph 7(2) or 8(2) of Schedule 6 of any gain accruing to the transferor on the disposal is (apart from this section) wholly relieved under that Schedule, or
(*c*) in the case of a disposal of qualifying corporate bonds, a gain is deemed to accrue by virtue of section 116(10)(*b*), or
(*d*) subsection (3) of section 260 applies in relation to the disposal (or would apply if a claim for relief were duly made under that section).

(4) Where a claim for relief is made under this section in respect of a disposal—

(*a*) the amount of any chargeable gain which, apart from this section, would accrue to the transferor on the disposal, and
(*b*) the amount of the consideration for which, apart from this section, the transferee would be regarded for the purposes of capital gains tax as having acquired the asset or, as the case may be, the shares or securities,

shall each be reduced by an amount equal to the held-over gain on the disposal.

(5) Part I of Schedule 7 shall have effect for extending the relief provided for by virtue of subsections (1) to (4) above in the case of agricultural property and for applying it in relation to settled property.

(6) Subject to Part II of Schedule 7 and subsection (7) below, the reference in subsection (4) above to the held-over gain on a disposal is a reference to the chargeable gain which would have accrued on that disposal apart from subsection (4) above and (in appropriate cases) Schedule 6, and in subsection (7) below that chargeable gain is referred to as the unrelieved gain on the disposal.

(7) In any case where—

(*a*) there is actual consideration (as opposed to the consideration equal to the market value which is deemed to be given by virtue of section 17(1)) for a disposal in respect of which a claim for relief is made under this section, and
(*b*) that actual consideration exceeds the sums allowable as a deduction under section 38,

the held-over gain on the disposal shall be the amount by which the unrelieved gain on the disposal exceeds the excess referred to in paragraph (*b*) above.

(8) Subject to subsection (9) below, in this section and Schedule 7—

(*a*) "[personal company]¹", "holding company", "trading company" and "trading group" have the meanings given by paragraph 1 of Schedule 6, and
(*b*) "trade", "profession" and "vocation" have the same meaning as in the Income Tax Acts.

(9) In this section and Schedule 7 and in determining whether a company is a trading company for the purposes of this section and that Schedule, the expression "trade" shall be taken to include the occupation of woodlands where the woodlands are managed by the occupier on a commercial basis and with a view to the realisation of profits.

(10) Where a disposal after 13th March 1989, in respect of which a claim is made under this section, is (or proves to be) a chargeable transfer for inheritance tax purposes, there shall be allowed as a deduction in computing (for capital gains tax purposes) the chargeable gain accruing to the transferee on the disposal of the asset in question an amount equal to whichever is the lesser of—

(*a*) the inheritance tax attributable to the value of the asset, and
(*b*) the amount of the chargeable gain as computed apart from this subsection,

and, in the case of a disposal which, being a potentially exempt transfer, proves to be a chargeable transfer, all necessary adjustments shall be made, whether by the discharge or repayment of capital gains tax or otherwise.

(11) Where an amount of inheritance tax—

(*a*) falls to be redetermined in consequence of the transferor's death within 7 years of making the chargeable transfer in question, or
(*b*) is otherwise varied,

after it has been taken into account under subsection (10) above, all necessary adjustments shall be made, whether by the making of an assessment to capital gains tax or by the discharge or repayment of such tax.

Commentary—*Simon's Direct Tax Service* C3.501–503.
Statement of Practice SP 8/92—Valuation of gifts in respect of which CGT holdover relief is available.
Revenue Interpretation RI 8—Holdover relief for gifts by reference to the nature of the gifts rather than their value.
RI 222—The withdrawal of business assets gift relief on the transfer of shares or securities to companies does not apply to disposals to a trust with a corporate trustee.
Revenue & other press releases—IR 10-11-81 (as regards an asset used by a family company, payment of rent by the company to an individual does not preclude a claim. Revenue view "a company" does not include the plural "companies").
Hansard 15-2-84 (farmers bringing their land into partnership: roll-over relief is not available to the extent that consideration is received by the transferor of the land).

ICAEW Tax 7/95 20-2-95 (Section C: incorporation of partnership business: company assuming liability for annuities payable to retired persons: relief not restricted under s 162(4) due to Concession D32, but relief is restricted under this section).

IR Tax Bulletin April 1997 p 417 (confirms that Statement of Practice SP 8/92 continues under self-assessment much as before, and explains the introduction of a new claim form).

Definitions—"Asset", s 21(1); "chargeable gain", s 15(2); "company", ss 99, 288(1); "market value", ss 272–274, Sch 11; "personal company", Sch 6 para 1(2); "qualifying corporate bond", s 117; "recognised stock exchange", s 288(1), TA 1988 s 841; "settled property", s 68; "shares", s 288(1); "trade", s 288(1), TA 1988 s 832(1).

Cross references—See TA 1988 s 503 (treatment of the commercial letting of furnished holiday accommodation for the purposes of this section);

TA 1988 Sch 28 para 3(3) (claims under this section in respect of gains from a disposal of an offshore fund).

TCGA 1992 s 74(1) (effect on a claim for relief under this section when trust assets are deemed to be disposed of on termination of life interest).

TCGA 1992 s 81(7) (application of this section where non-resident trustees become resident as a result of a trustee's death).

TCGA 1992 s 168 (claw-back of relief under this section where the donee of the asset migrates before disposing it).

TCGA 1992 s 169 (relief under this section not available for gifts of business assets to dual resident trusts).

TCGA 1992 s 241(3) (commercial letting of furnished holiday accommodation to be treated as a trade for the purposes of this section).

TCGA 1992 s 281(1) (payments by instalments of tax on gifts).

TCGA 1992 Sch 4 para 2 (deferred charges on gains accruing before 31 March 1982).

TCGA 1992 Sch 7 para 2 (application of this section to gifts of settled property).

Amendments—[1] Words in sub-ss (2), (8) substituted by FA 1993 s 87 and Sch 7 para 1(1) in relation to disposals made after 15 March 1993.

[2] Words in sub-ss (1), (2)(b)(i) substituted and words in sub-s (3)(b) inserted by FA 2000 s 90(1), (3), (4), (5) with effect for disposals made after 8 November 1999.

Prospective amendments—Sub-ss (3)(a), (b) and words in sub-s (6) will be repealed by FA 1998 Schedule 27 Part III(31) with effect for disposals in the year 2003–04 and subsequent years of assessment.

Sub-s (8)(a) will be substituted by FA 1998 s 140(4) with effect from the year 2003–04.

166 Gifts to non-residents

(1) Section 165(4) shall not apply where the transferee is neither resident nor ordinarily resident in the United Kingdom.

(2) Section 165(4) shall not apply where the transferee is an individual ...[1] if that individual ...[1]—

   (a) though resident or ordinarily resident in the United Kingdom, is regarded for the purposes of any double taxation relief arrangements as resident in a territory outside the United Kingdom, and

   (b) by virtue of the arrangements would not be liable in the United Kingdom to tax on a gain arising on a disposal of the asset occurring immediately after its acquisition.

Commentary—*Simon's Direct Tax Service* C3.510.

Definitions—"Asset", s 21(1); "company", ss 99, 288(1); "double taxation relief arrangements", s 288(1); "ordinarily resident", s 9(1); "resident", s 9(1).

Amendments—[1] Words in sub-s (2) repealed by FA 1994 s 251(1), (7)(a) and Sch 26 Pt VIII(1) in relation to disposals after 29 November 1993.

167 Gifts to foreign-controlled companies

(1) Section 165(4) shall not apply where the transferee is a company which is within subsection (2) below.

(2) A company is within this subsection if it is controlled by a person who, or by persons each of whom—

   (a) is neither resident nor ordinarily resident in the United Kingdom, and

   (b) is connected with the person making the disposal.

(3) For the purposes of subsection (2) above, a person who (either alone or with others) controls a company by virtue of holding assets relating to that or any other company and who is resident or ordinarily resident in the United Kingdom shall be regarded as neither resident nor ordinarily resident there if—

   (a) he is regarded for the purposes of any double taxation relief arrangements as resident in a territory outside the United Kingdom, and

   (b) by virtue of the arrangements he would not be liable in the United Kingdom to tax on a gain arising on a disposal of the assets.

Commentary—*Simon's Direct Tax Service* C3.511.

Definitions—"Asset", s 21(1); "company", ss 99, 288(1); "connected", s 286; "control", s 288(1), TA 1988 s 416; "double taxation relief arrangements", s 288(1); "ordinarily resident", s 9(1); "resident", s 9(1).

168 Emigration of donee

(1) If—

   (a) relief is given under section 165 in respect of a disposal to an individual or under section 260 in respect of a disposal to an individual ("the relevant disposal"); and

   (b) at a time when he has not disposed of the asset in question, the transferee becomes neither resident nor ordinarily resident in the United Kingdom,

then, subject to the following provisions of this section, a chargeable gain shall be deemed to have accrued to the transferee immediately before that time, and its amount shall be equal to the held-over gain (within the meaning of section 165 or 260) on the relevant disposal.

(2) For the purposes of subsection (1) above the transferee shall be taken to have disposed of an asset before the time there referred to only if he has made a disposal or disposals in connection with

which the whole of the held-over gain on the relevant disposal was represented by reductions made in accordance with section 165(4)(*b*) or 260(3)(*b*) and where he has made a disposal in connection with which part of that gain was so represented, the amount of the chargeable gain deemed by virtue of this section to accrue to him shall be correspondingly reduced.

(3) The disposals by the transferee that are to be taken into account under subsection (2) above shall not include any disposal to which section 58 applies; but where any such disposal is made by the transferee, disposals by his spouse shall be taken into account under subsection (2) above as if they had been made by him.

(4) Subsection (1) above shall not apply by reason of a person becoming neither resident nor ordinarily resident more than 6 years after the end of the year of assessment in which the relevant disposal was made.

(5) Subsection (1) above shall not apply in relation to a disposal made to an individual if—

(*a*) the reason for his becoming neither resident nor ordinarily resident in the United Kingdom is that he works in an employment or office all the duties of which are performed outside the United Kingdom, and

(*b*) he again becomes resident or ordinarily resident in the United Kingdom within the period of 3 years from the time when he ceases to be so, without having meanwhile disposed of the asset in question;

and accordingly no assessment shall be made by virtue of subsection (1) above before the end of that period in any case where the condition in paragraph (*a*) above is, and the condition in paragraph (*b*) above may be, satisfied.

(6) For the purposes of subsection (5) above a person shall be taken to have disposed of an asset if he has made a disposal in connection with which the whole or part of the held-over gain on the relevant disposal would, had he been resident in the United Kingdom, have been represented by a reduction made in accordance with section 165(4)(*b*) or 260(3)(*b*) and subsection (3) above shall have effect for the purposes of this subsection as it has effect for the purposes of subsection (2) above.

(7) Where an amount of tax assessed on a transferee by virtue of subsection (1) above is not paid within the period of 12 months beginning with the date when the tax becomes payable then, subject to subsection (8) below, the transferor may be assessed and charged (in the name of the transferee) to all or any part of that tax.

(8) No assessment shall be made under subsection (7) above more than 6 years after the end of the year of assessment in which the relevant disposal was made.

(9) Where the transferor pays an amount of tax in pursuance of subsection (7) above, he shall be entitled to recover a corresponding sum from the transferee.

(10) Gains on disposals made after a chargeable gain has under this section been deemed to accrue by reference to a held-over gain shall be computed without any reduction under section 165(4)(*b*) or 260(3)(*b*) in respect of that held-over gain.

Commentary—*Simon's Direct Tax Service* **C1.427.**
Definitions—"Asset", s 21(1); "chargeable gain", s 15(2); "ordinarily resident", s 9(1); "resident", s 9(1); "year of assessment", s 288(1).
Cross references—See TCGA 1992 s 67(6) (modification of this section where FA 1980 s 79 (general relief for gifts) has applied).
TCGA 1992 Sch 4 para 4 (deferred charges on gains accruing before 31 March 1982).

169 Gifts into dual resident trusts

(1) This section applies where there is or has been a disposal of an asset to the trustees of a settlement in such circumstances that, on a claim for relief, section 165 or 260 applies, or would but for this section apply, so as to reduce the amounts of the chargeable gain and the consideration referred to in section 165(4) or 260(3).

(2) In this section "a relevant disposal" means such a disposal as is referred to in subsection (1) above.

(3) Relief under section 165 or 260 shall not be available on a relevant disposal if—

(*a*) at the material time the trustees to whom the disposal is made fall to be treated, under section 69, as resident and ordinarily resident in the United Kingdom, although the general administration of the trust is ordinarily carried on outside the United Kingdom; and

(*b*) on a notional disposal of the asset concerned occurring immediately after the material time, the trustees would be regarded for the purposes of any double taxation relief arrangements—

(i) as resident in a territory outside the United Kingdom; and

(ii) as not liable in the United Kingdom to tax on a gain arising on that disposal.

(4) In subsection (3) above—

(*a*) "the material time" means the time of the relevant disposal; and

(*b*) a "notional disposal" means a disposal by the trustees of the asset which was the subject of the relevant disposal.

Commentary—*Simon's Direct Tax Service* **C3.510.**
Definitions—"Asset", s 21(1); "chargeable gain", s 15(2); "double taxation relief arrangements", s 288(1); "ordinarily resident", s 9(1); "resident", s 9(1).

[169A Cessation of trade by limited liability partnership

(1) This section applies where section 59A(1) ceases to apply to a limited liability partnership.

(2) A member of the partnership who immediately before the time at which section 59A(1) ceases to apply holds an asset, or an interest in an asset, acquired by him—

(a) on a disposal to members of a partnership, and

(b) for a consideration which is treated as reduced under section 165(4)(b) or 260(3)(b),

shall be treated as if a chargeable gain equal to the amount of the reduction accrued to him immediately before that time.]¹

Amendments—¹ This section inserted by FA 2001 s 75(3), (5) and deemed to have come into force on 3rd May 2001 and applies where TCGA 1992 s 59A(1) ceased or ceases to apply as mentioned in the above section on or after that date.

PART VI
COMPANIES, OIL, INSURANCE ETC

CHAPTER I
COMPANIES

Groups of companies

170 Interpretation of sections 171 to 181

(1) This section has effect for the interpretation of sections 171 to 181 except in so far as the context otherwise requires, and in those sections—

(a) "profits" means income and chargeable gains, and

(b) "trade" includes "vocation", and includes also an office or employment.

Until 6th April 1993 paragraph (b) shall have effect with the addition at the end of the words "or the occupation of woodlands in any context in which the expression is applied to that in the Income Tax Acts".

(2) Except as otherwise provided—

(a) ...³

(b) subsections (3) to (6) below apply to determine whether companies form a group and, where they do, which is the principal company of the group;

(c) in applying the definition of "75 per cent subsidiary" in section 838 of the Taxes Act any share capital of a registered industrial and provident society shall be treated as ordinary share capital; and

(d) "group" and "subsidiary" shall be construed with any necessary modifications where applied to a company incorporated under the law of a country outside the United Kingdom.

(3) Subject to subsections (4) to (6) below—

(a) a company (referred to below and in sections 171 to 181 as the "principal company of the group") and all its 75 per cent subsidiaries form a group and, if any of those subsidiaries have 75 per cent subsidiaries, the group includes them and their 75 per cent subsidiaries, and so on, but

(b) a group does not include any company (other than the principal company of the group) that is not an effective 51 per cent subsidiary of the principal company of the group.

(4) A company cannot be the principal company of a group if it is itself a 75 per cent subsidiary of another company.

(5) Where a company ("the subsidiary") is a 75 per cent subsidiary of another company but those companies are prevented from being members of the same group by subsection (3)(b) above, the subsidiary may, where the requirements of subsection (3) above are satisfied, itself be the principal company of another group notwithstanding subsection (4) above unless this subsection enables a further company to be the principal company of a group of which the subsidiary would be a member.

(6) A company cannot be a member of more than one group; but where, apart from this subsection, a company would be a member of 2 or more groups (the principal company of each group being referred to below as the "head of a group"), it is a member only of that group, if any, of which it would be a member under one of the following tests (applying earlier tests in preference to later tests)—

(a) it is a member of the group it would be a member of if, in applying subsection (3)(b) above, there were left out of account any amount to which a head of a group is or would be beneficially entitled of any profits available for distribution to equity holders of a head of another group or of any assets of a head of another group available for distribution to its equity holders on a winding-up,

(b) it is a member of the group the head of which is beneficially entitled to a percentage of profits available for distribution to equity holders of the company that is greater than the percentage of those profits to which any other head of a group is so entitled, (*c*) it is a member of the group the head of which would be beneficially entitled to a percentage of any assets of the company available for distribution to its equity holders on a winding-up that is greater than the percentage of those assets to which any other head of a group would be so entitled,

(*d*) it is a member of the group the head of which owns directly or indirectly a percentage of the company's ordinary share capital that is greater than the percentage of that capital owned directly or indirectly by any other head of a group (interpreting this paragraph as if it were included in section 838(1)(*a*) of the Taxes Act).

(7) For the purposes of this section and sections 171 to 181, a company ("the subsidiary") is an effective 51 per cent subsidiary of another company ("the parent") at any time if and only if—

(*a*) the parent is beneficially entitled to more than 50 per cent of any profits available for distribution to equity holders of the subsidiary; and

(*b*) the parent would be beneficially entitled to more than 50 per cent of any assets of the subsidiary available for distribution to its equity holders on a winding-up.

(8) Schedule 18 to the Taxes Act (group relief: equity holders and profits or assets available for distribution) shall apply for the purposes of subsections (6) and (7) above as if the references to subsection (7) ...[4] of section 413 of that Act were references to subsections (6) and (7) above and as if, in paragraph 1(4), the words from "but" to the end and paragraphs 5(3) [and 5B to 5E][1] and 7(1)(*b*) were omitted.

(9) For the purposes of this section and sections 171 to 181, references to a company apply only to—

(*a*) a company within the meaning of the Companies Act 1985 or the corresponding enactment in Northern Ireland, and

(*b*) a company [(other than a limited liability partnership)][5] which is constituted under any other Act or a Royal Charter or letters patent or ...[3] is formed under the law of a country or territory outside the United Kingdom, and

(*c*) a registered industrial and provident society within the meaning of section 486 of the Taxes Act; and

[(cc) an incorporated friendly society within the meaning of the Friendly Societies Act 1992; and][2]

(*d*) a building society.

(10) For the purposes of this section and sections 171 to 181, a group remains the same group so long as the same company remains the principal company of the group, and if at any time the principal company of a group becomes a member of another group, the first group and the other group shall be regarded as the same, and the question whether or not a company has ceased to be a member of a group shall be determined accordingly.

(11) For the purposes of this section and sections 171 to 181, the passing of a resolution or the making of an order, or any other act, for the winding-up of a member of a group of companies shall not be regarded as the occasion of that or any other company ceasing to be a member of the group.

(12) Sections 171 to 181, except in so far as they relate to recovery of tax, shall also have effect in relation to bodies from time to time established by or under any enactment for the carrying on of any industry or part of an industry, or of any undertaking, under national ownership or control as if they were companies within the meaning of those sections, and as if any such bodies charged with related functions (and in particular the Boards and Holding Company established under the Transport Act 1962 and the new authorities within the meaning of the Transport Act 1968 established under that Act of 1968) and subsidiaries of any of them formed a group, and as if also any 2 or more such bodies charged at different times with the same or related functions were members of a group.

(13) Subsection (12) shall have effect subject to any enactment by virtue of which property, rights, liabilities or activities of one such body fall to be treated for corporation tax as those of another, including in particular any such enactment in Chapter VI of Part XII of the Taxes Act.

(14) Sections 171 to 181, except in so far as they relate to recovery of tax, shall also have effect in relation to the Executive for a designated area within the meaning of section 9(1) of the Transport Act 1968 as if that Executive were a company within the meaning of those sections.

Commentary—*Simon's Direct Tax Service* **D2.651.**
Revenue Interpretation RI 224—Circumstances in which Delaware Limited Liability Companies (DLLCs) can be regarded as issuing "ordinary share capital" for the purposes of TCGA 1992 ss 170–181.
Revenue & other press releases—CCAB June 1967 (a company is not treated as leaving a group if it is transferred by its immediate parent to the principal company or to another subsidiary of the principal company).
CCAB June 1968 (the passing of a resolution or an order for winding up of a company will not be regarded as an occasion on which the parent company leaves the group).
ICAEW TR 799 June 1990 (the making of an administration order does not, by itself, break the group relationship, but the approval of the administrator's proposals under IA 1986 s 24 might do so).
Revenue Internal Guidance—Capital Gains Manual CG 45130, CG 45140, CG 45141, CG 45162 (outline the effects of the removal of the residence condition for group membership with effect from 1 April 2000).
Simon's Tax Cases—*Burman v Hedges Butler Ltd* [1979] STC 136*; *Dunlop International A G v Pardoe* [1998] STC 459*.
s 170(3)(*a*), *Dunlop International A G v Pardoe* [1999] STC 909*.
Definitions—"Asset", s 21(1); "the Board", s 288(1); "chargeable gain", s 15(2); "company", ss 99, 288(1); "control", s 288(1), TA 1988 s 416; "resident", s 9(1); "the Taxes Act", s 288(1); "trade", s 288(1), TA 1988 s 832(1).
Cross references—See TCGA 1992 s 140(6) (postponement of charge on transfer of assets to non-resident company).
TCGA 1992 s 181(5) (exception to sub-s (2)(*a*) above).
TCGA 1992 s 190(5) (extension of the application of this section).

TCGA 1992 s 276(8) (modification of this section in its application to disposals of continental shelf exploration and exploitation rights and assets by a non-resident company to a company resident in the same territory, by a resident company to another resident company, or by a non-resident company to a resident company).

FA 2000 Sch 29 para 46 (Sub-s (3)(b) above not to apply in relation to the company for so long as it remains an effective 51 per cent subsidiary of the company which was the principal company of the old group for the purposes of the provisions amended by FA 2000 Sch 29).

TCGA 1992 Sch 3 para 9(3) (rebasing elections by groups of companies).

FA 1999 s 81(7) (application of this section in relation to acquisitions disregarded under insurance companies concession).

Amendments—[1] Words in sub-s (8) inserted by F(No 2)A 1992 Sch 6 paras 5, 10 and deemed always to have had effect.

[2] Sub-s (9)(cc) inserted by FA 1998 s 136(1) with effect for the purpose of determining, in relation to times on and after 17 March 1998, whether a friendly society is a company within the meaning of the provisions of TCGA 1992 ss 170–181.

[3] Sub-s (2)(a) and words in sub-s (9)(b) repealed by FA 2000 ss 102, 156, Sch 29 para 1(1), Sch 40 Pt II(12) with effect—

– broadly (ie for the purposes of TCGA 1992 ss 14, 31A, 106, 138A, 171, 173, 174, 175, 176, 177, 179, 181, 190, 216, 228, 253, Sch A1 para 11, Sch 2 para 5, Sch 3 paras 8, 9, IHTA 1984 s 97, FA 1988 s 132, FA 1993 ss 136, 136A and FA 1996 Sch 9 paras 11, 12) as from 1 April 2000;

– in relation to changes to Schs 7A, 7AA, as for accounting periods ending after 20 March 2000; and

– for the purposes of Sch 7C as from 28 July 2000.

For transitional provisions in respect of this section, see FA 2000 Sch 29 para 46.

[4] Words in sub-s (8) repealed by FA 2000 s 156, Sch 40 Pt II(11) and deemed always to have had effect.

[5] Words in sub-s (9)(b) inserted by FA 2001 s 75(4), (6) with effect from 6 April 2001.

Transactions within groups

171 Transfers within a group: general provisions

[(1) Where—

(a) a company ("company A") disposes of an asset to another company ("company B") at a time when both companies are members of the same group, and

(b) the conditions in subsection (1A) below are met,

company A and company B are treated for the purposes of corporation tax on chargeable gains as if the asset were acquired by company B for a consideration of such amount as would secure that neither a gain nor a loss would accrue to company A on the disposal.

(1A) The conditions referred to in subsection (1)(b) above are—

(a) that company A is resident in the United Kingdom at the time of the disposal, or the asset is a chargeable asset in relation to that company immediately before that time, and

(b) that company B is resident in the United Kingdom at the time of the disposal, or the asset is a chargeable asset in relation to that company immediately after that time.

For this purpose an asset is a "chargeable asset" in relation to a company at any time if, were the asset to be disposed of by the company at that time, any gain accruing to the company would be a chargeable gain and would by virtue of section 10(3) form part of its chargeable profits for corporation tax purposes.][4]

(2) Subsection (1) above shall not apply where the disposal is—

(a) a disposal of a debt due from [company B][4] effected by satisfying the debt or part of it; or

(b) a disposal of redeemable shares in a company on the occasion of their redemption; or

(c) a disposal by or to an investment trust; or

[(cc) a disposal by or to a venture capital trust; or][2]

[(cd) a disposal by or to a qualifying friendly society; or][3]

(d) a disposal to a dual resident investing company; ...[1]

(e) ...[1]

and the reference in subsection (1) above to [company A][4] disposing of an asset shall not apply to anything which under section 122 is to be treated as a disposal of an interest in shares in a company in consideration for a capital distribution (as defined in that section) from that company, whether or not involving a reduction of capital.

(3) Subsection (1) above shall not apply to a transaction treated [by section 127 as it applies by virtue of section 135][5] as not involving a disposal by [company A][4].

(4) For the purposes of subsection (1) above, so far as the consideration for the disposal consists of money or money's worth by way of compensation for any kind of damage or injury to assets, or for the destruction or dissipation of assets or for anything which depreciates or might depreciate an asset, the disposal shall be treated as being to the person who, whether as an insurer or otherwise, ultimately bears the burden of furnishing that consideration.

[(5) In subsection (2)(cd) above "qualifying friendly society" means a company which is a qualifying society for the purposes of section 461B of the Taxes Act (incorporated friendly societies entitled to exemption from income tax and corporation tax on certain profits).][3]

[(6) Subsection (1) above applies notwithstanding any provision in this Act fixing the amount of the consideration deemed to be received on a disposal or given on an acquisition.

But where it is assumed for any purpose that a member of a group of companies has sold or acquired an asset, it shall be assumed also that it was not a sale or acquisition to which this section applies.][4]

Commentary—*Simon's Direct Tax Service* D2.652.

Concession D44—

CGT: rebasing and indexation: shares derived from larger holdings held at 31 March 1982.

Statement of Practice SP 6/88, para 4(ii)—Double tax relief: overseas tax payable on intra-group disposal.

Revenue Interpretation RI 43—Application of no gain/no loss rule in relation to intra-group transfers by members of non-resident group of companies: scope of words "so far as relates to corporation tax on chargeable gains" in sub-s (1) above.

RI 159—Where shares transferred between group companies in exchange for qualifying corporate bonds, such that TCGA 1992 s 116 applies, no gain/no loss rule in sub-s (1) above does not apply to transferee company's acquisition.

RI 224—Circumstances in which Delaware Limited Liability Companies (DLLCs) can be regarded as issuing "ordinary share capital" for the purposes of TCGA 1992 ss 170–181.

Revenue & other press releases—CCAB June 1975 (relief is generally available where an asset is distributed *in specie* by the liquidator of a subsidiary company).

ICAEW TR 588 25-9-85 (application of Furniss v Dawson principle where benefit of capital losses transferred. Revenue will consider amount of loss, period for which loss company has been in the group and circumstances in which losses arose). See now TCGA 1992 Sch 7A.

Revenue Internal Guidance—Capital gains manual CG 45551–45560 (examples showing the operation of sub-s (3)).
Life assurance manual LAM 2.63–2.66 (application to life assurance companies in groups).

Simon's Tax Cases—*Burman v Hedges Butler Ltd* [1979] STC 136*.
s 171(1), *Westcott v Woolcombers Ltd* [1987] STC 600*; *NAP Holdings UK Ltd v Whittles* [1994] STC 979*.
s 171(2), *Innocent v Whaddon Estates Ltd* [1982] STC 115*.

Definitions—"Asset", s 21(1); "chargeable gain", s 15(2); "company", s 170; "double taxation relief arrangements", s 288(1); "dual resident investing company", s 288(1), TA 1988 s 404; "group", s 170; "investment trust", s 288(1), TA 1988 s 842; "resident", s 9(1); "shares", s 288(1).

Cross references—See TA 1988 s 245B(1)(*c*) (restriction on set-off of ACT where asset transferred after change in ownership of company);
TCGA 1992 s 14(2) (application of this section (except sub-ss (1)(*b*), (1A)) to non-resident groups of companies which are members of a non-resident group as it applies to companies which are members of a group of companies).
TCGA 1992 s 19(5) (disposals between members of a group of companies forming part of a series of linked transactions).
TCGA 1992 ss 31(6)(*a*), 32(1) (intra-group transfer of assets under this section may constitute chargeable profits for the purposes of s 31 (value shifting)).
TCGA 1992 s 35(3)(*d*) (application of rebasing provisions).
TCGA 1992 s 42(2) (apportionment of expenditure on part disposals to be made without prejudice to sub-s (1) above).
TCGA 1992 s 55(5) (indexation allowance on a non-no gain/no loss disposal after 31 March 1982 of assets acquired on a no gain/no loss acquisition under this section).
TCGA 1992 s 116(11) (treatment of gain or loss on intra-group disposals on reorganisations, etc involving qualifying corporate bonds).
TCGA 1992 s 117A(7), (8) (to the extent that this section treats disposals as made on a no gain/no loss basis, it does not apply to disposals of certain foreign currency debts involving companies).
TCGA 1992 s 117B(5), (6) (to the extent that this section treats disposals as made on a no gain/no loss basis, it does not apply to disposals of certain foreign currency denominated holdings in unit trusts and offshore funds treated as a right under a creditor relationship of a company).
TCGA 1992 s 134(4) (treatment of gain or loss on intra-group transfer of gilt-edged securities issued on nationalisation in exchange for other securities).
TCGA 1992 s 140(6) (postponement of charge on transfer of assets to non-resident company).
TCGA 1992 s 170(1) (interpretation).
TCGA 1992 s 174 (restriction of capital allowances on assets disposed of outside a group of companies).
TCGA 1992 s 177(2) (restriction of loss relief where transfer to which this section applies is of securities with reduced value as a result of dividend stripping).
TCGA 1992 s 276(8) (modification of this section (except sub-ss (1)(*b*), (1A)) in its application to disposals of continental shelf exploration and exploitation rights and assets by a non-resident company to a company resident in the same territory, by a resident company to another resident company, or by a non-resident company to a resident company).
TCGA 1992 Sch 2 para 4(9) (election for pooling of quoted securities held on 6 April 1965 and disposed of after 19 March 1968 by a disposal to which sub-s (1) above applies).
TCGA 1992 Sch 3 para 2 (inter-group disposal after 5 April 1988 followed by disposal by transferee company to third party: effect on an election under s 35(5) for 31 March 1982 valuation by the group members).
TCGA 1992 Sch 4 para 7 (reduction of deferred charges on gains accruing on disposal of assets not held by the vendor on 31 March 1982 but acquired by him from a person who acquired them before that date on a no gain/no loss disposal in accordance with this section).
FA 1993 s 165 and Sch 17 para 7 (transfers within a group of foreign currency, foreign debts and foreign securities: disapplication of this section in certain circumstances where the currency etc are assets of long term or mutual insurance businesses).
Corporation Tax (Treatment of Unrelieved Surplus Advance Corporation Tax) Regulations, SI 1999/358 reg 18 (application of sub-s (1); restriction on set-off of unrelieved surplus ACT where asset transferred after a change of ownership of a company).
FA 2000 Sch 29 para 2 (the main amendments made to TCGA 1992 s 170 by FA 2000 Sch 29 para 1 have effect for the purposes of this section for disposals after 31 March 2000).

Amendments—[1] Sub-s (2)(*e*) and the preceding word "or" repealed by FA 1994 s 251(1), (7)(*b*) and Sch 26 Pt VIII(1) in relation to disposals after 29 November 1993.
[2] Sub-s (2)(*cc*) inserted by FA 1998 s 135(1) with effect in relation to disposals made on or after 17 March 1998.
[3] Sub-ss (2)(*cd*), (5) inserted by FA 1998 s 136(2), (3) with effect in relation to disposals made on or after 17 March 1998.
[4] Sub-ss (1), (1A) substituted for original sub-s (1) and words in sub-ss (2), (3) substituted, and sub-s (6) inserted, by FA 2000 s 102, Sch 29 para 2 with effect for disposals after 31 March 2000.
[5] Words substituted for the words "by virtue of sections 127 and 135" by FA 2002 s 45, Sch 9 paras 5(1), (10), 7 with effect for shares or debentures issued after 16 April 2002. The reference to shares or debentures includes any interests falling to be treated as shares or debentures for the purposes of TCGA 1992 s 135 or 136 as substituted by FA 2002 Sch 9.

[171A Notional transfers within a group

(1) This section applies where—

(*a*) two companies ("A" and "B") are members of a group of companies; and
(*b*) A disposes of an asset to a person who is not a member of the group ("C").

(2) Subject to subsections (3) and (4) below, A and B may, by notice in writing to an officer of the Board, jointly elect that, for the purposes of corporation tax on chargeable gains—

(*a*) the asset, or any part of it, shall be deemed to have been transferred by A to B immediately before the disposal to C;
(*b*) section 171(1) shall be deemed to have applied to that transfer; . . .[2]
(*c*) the disposal of the asset or part to C shall be deemed to have been made by B[; and
(*d*) any incidental costs to A of making the actual disposal to C shall be deemed to be incidental costs to B of making the deemed disposal to C.][2]

TCGA 1992

(3) No election may be made under subsection (2) above unless section 171(1) would have applied to an actual transfer of the asset or part from A to B.

(4) An election under that subsection must be made [on or before]² the second anniversary of the end of the accounting period of A in which the disposal to C was made.

(5) Any payment by A to B, or by B to A, in pursuance of an agreement between them in connection with the election—

(a) shall not be taken into account in computing profits or losses of either company for corporation tax purposes, and

(b) shall not for any purposes of the Corporation Tax Acts be regarded as a distribution or a charge on income,

provided it does not exceed the amount of the chargeable gain or allowable loss that is treated, as a result of the disposal, as accruing to B.]¹

Revenue Interpretation RI 224—Circumstances in which Delaware Limited Liability Companies (DLLCs) can be regarded as issuing "ordinary share capital" for the purposes of TCGA 1992 ss 170–181.
Revenue Internal Guidance—Capital Gains Manual CG 45351–45359 (operation of this section).
Amendments—¹ This section inserted by FA 2000 s 101 with effect for disposals made after 31 March 2000.
² Sub-s (2)(d) and preceding word "; and" inserted, and words in sub-s (4) substituted for word "before", by FA 2001 s 77 and deemed to have had effect from the time this section was enacted (ie with effect for disposals made after 31 March 2000).

172 Transfer of United Kingdom branch or agency

Commentary—*Simon's Direct Tax Service* D2.315.
Revenue Interpretation RI 224—Circumstances in which Delaware Limited Liability Companies (DLLCs) can be regarded as issuing "ordinary share capital" for the purposes of TCGA 1992 ss 170–181.
Amendments—This section repealed by FA 2000 ss 102, 156, Sch 29 para 3, Sch 40 Pt II(12) with effect for disposals after 31 March 2000.

[173 Transfers within a group: trading stock

(1) Where—

(a) a company ("company A") acquires an asset as trading stock of a trade to which this section applies,

(b) the acquisition is from a company ("company B") that at the time of the acquisition is a member of the same group of companies, and

(c) the asset did not form part of the trading stock of any such trade carried on by company B,

company A is treated for the purposes of section 161 as having acquired the asset otherwise than as trading stock and immediately appropriated it for the purposes of the trade as trading stock.

(2) Where—

(a) a company ("company C") disposes of an asset forming part of the trading stock of a trade to which this section applies carried on by that company,

(b) the disposal is to another company ("company D") that at the time of the disposal is a member of the same group of companies, and

(c) the asset is acquired by company D otherwise than as trading stock of any such trade carried on by it,

company C is treated for the purposes of section 161 as having appropriated the asset immediately before the disposal for some purpose other than the purpose of use as trading stock.

(3) The trades to which this section applies are—

(a) any trade carried on by a company resident in the United Kingdom, and

(b) any trade carried on in the United Kingdom through a branch or agency by a company not so resident.]¹

Commentary—*Simon's Direct Tax Service* D2.656.
Revenue Interpretation RI 224—Circumstances in which Delaware Limited Liability Companies (DLLCs) can be regarded as issuing "ordinary share capital" for the purposes of TCGA 1992 ss 170–181.
Simon's Tax Cases—s 173(1), *Coates v Arndale Properties Ltd* [1984] STC 637*; *Reed v Nova Securities Ltd* [1985] STC 124*.
Revenue Internal Guidance—Capital Gains Manual CG 45905 (outlines the position where acquisitions to trading stock are made on or after 1 April 2000).
Definitions—"Asset", s 21(1); "group", s 170; "trade", ss 170(1), 288(1), TA 1988 s 832(1); "trading stock", s 288(1), TA 1988 s 100(2).
Cross references—See TA 1988 s 440(3) (this section not to apply to certain disposals or acquisitions).
TCGA 1992 s 14(2) (application of this section to non-resident groups of companies which are members of a non-resident group as it applies to companies which are members of a group of companies).
TCGA 1992 s 170(1) (interpretation).
TCGA 1992 s 276(8) (modification of this section in its application to disposals of continental shelf exploration and exploitation rights and assets by a non-resident company to a company resident in the same territory, by a resident company to another resident company, or by a non-resident company to a resident company).
FA 2000 Sch 29 para 11(2) (the main amendments made to TCGA 1992 s 170 by FA 2000 Sch 29 para 1 have effect for the purposes of this section for acquisitions and disposals after 31 March 2000).
Amendments—¹ This section substituted by FA 2000 s 102, Sch 29 para 11 with effect for acquisitions and disposals after 31 March 2000.

174 Disposal or acquisition outside a group

(1)–(3) ...[3]

(4) Schedule 2 shall apply in relation to a disposal of an asset by a company which is or has been a member of a group of companies, and which acquired the asset from another member of the group [in a transfer to which section 171(1) applied][2], as if all members of the group for the time being were the same person, and as if the acquisition or provision of the asset by the group, so taken as a single person, had been the acquisition or provision of it by the member disposing of it.

(5) ...[2].

Commentary—*Simon's Direct Tax Service* **D2.657.**
Revenue Interpretation RI 224—Circumstances in which Delaware Limited Liability Companies (DLLCs) can be regarded as issuing "ordinary share capital" for the purposes of TCGA 1992 ss 170–181.
Definitions—"Asset", s 21(1); "company", s 170; "group", s 170.
Cross references—See TCGA 1992 s 14(2) (application of sub-s (4) to non-resident groups of companies which are members of a non-resident group as it applies to companies which are members of a group of companies).TCGA 1992 s 170(1) (interpretation).
TCGA 1992 s 276(8) (modification of sub-s (4) in its application to disposals of continental shelf exploration and exploitation rights and assets by a non-resident company to a company resident in the same territory, by a resident company to another resident company, or by a non-resident company to a resident company).
F(No 2)A 1992 Sch 17 para 6(1), (3), (6) (privatisation of Northern Ireland Electricity: restriction of losses by reference to capital allowances).
FA 2000 Sch 29 para 13(4) (the main amendments made to TCGA 1992 s 170 by FA 2000 Sch 29 para 1 have effect for the purposes of this section for acquisitions after 31 March 2000).
FA 2000 Sch 29 para 13(5) (any question as to whether a company was a member of a group before 1 April 2000 is determined in accordance with s 170 before it was amended by FA 2000 Sch 29, para 1).
Amendments—[1] Number in sub-ss (2), (3) inserted by F(No 2)A 1992 s 46(1), (5) and deemed always to have had effect.
[2] Words in sub-s (4) substituted and sub-s (5) repealed by FA 2000 ss 102, 156, Sch 29 para 13, Sch 40 Pt II(12) with effect for acquisitions after 31 March 2000.
[3] Sub-ss (1)–(3) repealed by FA 2000 s 156, Sch 40 Pt II(12) with effect for cases where the disposal first referred to in s 41(8) is after 31 March 2000.

175 Replacement of business assets by members of a group

(1) Subject to subsection (2) below, for the purposes of sections 152 to 158 all the trades [to which this section applies][7] carried on by members of a group of companies shall, for the purposes of corporation tax on chargeable gains, be treated as a single trade ...[5]

[(1A) The trades to which this section applies are—

    (*a*) any trade carried on by a company that is resident in the United Kingdom, and
    (*b*) any trade carried on in the United Kingdom through a branch or agency by a company not so resident.][7]

(2) Subsection (1) above does not apply where so much of the consideration for the disposal of the old assets as is applied in acquiring the new assets or the interest in them is so applied by a member of the group which is a dual resident investing company ...[1]

and in this subsection "the old assets" and "the new assets" have the same meanings as in section 152.

[(2A) Section 152 [or 153][6] shall apply where—

    (*a*) the disposal is by a company which, at the time of the disposal, is a member of a group of companies,
    (*b*) the acquisition is by another company which, at the time of the acquisition, is a member of the same group, and
    [(*ba*) the conditions in subsection (2AA) below are met, and][7]
    (*c*) the claim is made by both companies,

as if both companies were the same person.][2]

[(2AA) The conditions referred to in subsection (2A)(*ba*) above are—

    (*a*) that the company making the disposal is resident in the United Kingdom at the time of the disposal, or the assets are chargeable assets in relation to that company immediately before that time, and
    (*b*) that the acquiring company is resident in the United Kingdom at the time of the acquisition, or the assets are chargeable assets in relation to that company immediately after that time.

For this purpose an asset is a "chargeable asset" in relation to a company at any time if, were the asset to be disposed of by the company at that time, any gain accruing to the company would be a chargeable gain and would by virtue of section 10(3) form part of its chargeable profits for corporation tax purposes.][7]

[(2B) Section 152 [or 153][6] shall apply where a company which is a member of a group of companies but is not carrying on a trade—

    (*a*) disposes of assets (or an interest in assets) used, and used only, for the purposes of the trade which (in accordance with subsection (1) above) is treated as carried on by the members of the group which carry on a trade, or
    (*b*) acquires assets (or an interest in assets) taken into use, and used only, for those purposes,

as if the first company were carrying on that trade.][3]

[(2C) [Neither section 152 nor section 153 shall][6] apply if the acquisition of, or of the interest in, the new assets—

(*a*) is made by a company which is a member of a group of companies, and
(*b*) is one to which any of the enactments specified in section 35(3)(*d*) applies.][4]

[(3) Section 154(2) applies where the company making the claim is a member of a group of companies—

(*a*) as if all members of the group for the time being carrying on a trade to which this section applies were the same person, and
(*b*) in accordance with subsection (1) above, as if all those trades were the same trade;

so that the gain accrues to the member of the group holding the asset concerned on the occurrence of the event mentioned in section 154(2).][7]

(4) Subsection (2) above shall apply where the acquisition took place before 20th March 1990 and the disposal takes place within the period of 12 months beginning with the date of the acquisition or such longer period as the Board may by notice allow with the omission of the words from "or a company" to "the acquisition".

Commentary—*Simon's Direct Tax Service* **C3.317; D2.658.**
Statement of Practice D19—Replacement of business assets in groups of companies.
SP 8/81—CGT rollover relief may be claimed where one group member makes a disposal and another makes an acquisition provided relevant conditions are satisfied.
Revenue Interpretation RI 224—Circumstances in which Delaware Limited Liability Companies (DLLCs) can be regarded as issuing "ordinary share capital" for the purposes of TCGA 1992 ss 170–181.
Revenue & other press releases—IR 30-11-78 (payment for group roll-over relief is not included in computing profits of either company for CT purposes).
IR 15-9-92 (a trading company may obtain rollover relief if the replacement asset is acquired by another trading member of the same group).
Revenue Internal Guidance—Capital Gains Manual CG 45945 (sub-s (3): operation of this section).
CG 45949 (sub-s (2A): worked example).
Definitions—"Asset", s 21(1); "the Board", s 288(1); "chargeable gain", s 15(2); "company", s 170; "double taxation relief arrangements", s 288(1); "dual resident investing company", s 288(1), TA 1988 s 404; "group", s 170; "notice", s 288(1); "resident", s 9(1); "trade", ss 170(1), 288(1), TA 1988 s 832(1).
Cross references—See TCGA 1992 s 14(2) (application of sub-s (1) to non-resident groups of companies which are members of a non-resident group as it applies to companies which are members of a group of companies).
TCGA 1992 s 170(1) (interpretation).
TCGA 1992 s 198(4) (modification of this section in its application to oil industry ring fence trades).
FA 2000 Sch 29 para 10(7) (the main amendments made to TCGA 1992 s 170 by FA 2000 Sch 29 para 1 have effect for the purposes of this section for cases in which either the disposal or acquisition is after 31 March 2000, or both the disposal and acquisition are after that date).
FA 2000 Sch 29 para 10(8) (any question as to whether a company was a member of a group where either disposal or acquisition is after 31 March 2000 is determined in accordance with s 170 as amended by FA 2000 Sch 29, para 1).
Modifications—TCGA 1992 Sch 7AB paras 1, 7 (modification of this section for the purposes of TCGA 1992 s 179B (as inserted by FA 2002 s 43) which relates to roll-over of degrouping charge on business assets).
Amendments—[1] Words in sub-s (2) repealed by FA 1994 s 251(1), (8) and Sch 26 Pt VIII(1) and the repeal has effect where disposal of old assets or acquisition of new assets is made after 29 November 1993.
[2] Sub-s (2A) inserted by FA 1995 s 48(1), (3), (4), and is deemed always to have had effect (earlier enactments corresponding to this section are deemed to have contained provision to the same effect), excepting that para (*c*) does not apply unless the claim is made after 28 November 1994.
[3] Sub-s (2B) inserted by FA 1995 s 48(1), (5), with effect for disposals or acquisitions after 28 November 1994.
[4] Sub-s (2C) inserted by FA 1995 s 48(1), (5), with effect for acquisitions after 28 November 1994.
[5] Words omitted from sub-s (1) repealed by FA 1995 Sch 29, Pt VIII(4), with effect for acquisitions of or interests in, new assets after 28 November 1994.
[6] Words in sub-ss (2A), (2B) inserted and words in sub-s (2C) substituted by FA 1996 ss 121(8), 141(3) with effect from the year 1996–97 and, so far as relating to corporation tax, as respects accounting periods ending after 30 June 1999 (by virtue of Finance Act 1994, Section 199, (Appointed Day) Order, SI 1998/3173 art 2).
[7] Words in sub-s (1), and whole of sub-ss (1A), (2A)(*ba*), (2AA) inserted, and sub-s (3) substituted, by FA 2000 s 102, Sch 29 para 10 with effect for cases in which either the disposal or acquisition is after 31 March 2000, or both the disposal and acquisition are after that date.

Losses attributable to depreciatory transactions

176 Depreciatory transactions within a group

(1) This section has effect as respects a disposal of shares in, or securities of, a company ("the ultimate disposal") if the value of the shares or securities has been materially reduced by a depreciatory transaction effected on or after 31st March 1982; and for this purpose "depreciatory transaction" means—

(*a*) any disposal of assets at other than market value by one member of a group of companies to another, or
(*b*) any other transaction satisfying the conditions of subsection (2) below,

except that a transaction shall not be treated as a depreciatory transaction to the extent that it consists of a payment which is required to be or has been brought into account, for the purposes of corporation tax on chargeable gains, in computing a chargeable gain or allowable loss accruing to the person making the ultimate disposal.

(2) The conditions referred to in subsection (1)(*b*) above are—

(*a*) that the company, the shares in which, or securities of which, are the subject of the ultimate disposal, or any 75 per cent subsidiary of that company, was a party to the transaction, and
(*b*) that the parties to the transaction were or included 2 or more companies which at the time of the transaction were members of the same group of companies.

(3) Without prejudice to the generality of subsection (1) above, the cancellation of any shares in or securities of one member of a group of companies under section 135 of the Companies Act 1985 shall, to the extent that immediately before the cancellation those shares or securities were the property of another member of the group, be taken to be a transaction fulfilling the conditions in subsection (2) above.

(4) If the person making the ultimate disposal is, or has at any time been, a member of the group of companies referred to in subsection (1) or (2) above, any allowable loss accruing on the disposal shall be reduced to such extent as [is][1] just and reasonable having regard to the depreciatory transaction, but if the person making the ultimate disposal is not a member of that group when he disposes of the shares or securities, no reduction of the loss shall be made by reference to a depreciatory transaction which took place when that person was not a member of that group.

(5) [A reduction under subsection (4) above shall be made][1] on the footing that the allowable loss ought not to reflect any diminution in the value of the company's assets which was attributable to a depreciatory transaction, but allowance may be made for any other transaction on or after 31st March 1982 which has enhanced the value of the company's assets and depreciated the value of the assets of any other member of the group.

(6) If, under subsection (4) above, a reduction is made in an allowable loss, any chargeable gain accruing on a disposal of the shares or securities of any other company which was a party to the depreciatory transaction by reference to which the reduction was made, being a disposal not later than 6 years after the depreciatory transaction, shall be reduced to such extent as [is][1] just and reasonable having regard to the effect of the depreciatory transaction on the value of those shares or securities at the time of their disposal, but the total amount of any one or more reductions in chargeable gains made by reference to a depreciatory transaction shall not exceed the amount of the reductions in allowable losses made by reference to that depreciatory transaction.

All such adjustments, whether by way of discharge or repayment of tax, or otherwise, as are required to give effect to the provisions of this subsection may be made at any time.

(7) For the purposes of this section—

    (*a*) "securities" includes any loan stock or similar security whether secured or unsecured,

    (*b*) references to the disposal of assets include references to any method by which one company which is a member of a group appropriates the goodwill of another member of the group ...[2]

    (*c*) ...[2].

(8) References in this section to the disposal of shares or securities include references to the occasion of the making of a claim under section 24(2) that the value of shares or securities has become negligible, and references to a person making a disposal shall be construed accordingly.

(9) In any case where the ultimate disposal is not one to which section 35(2) applies, the references above to 31st March 1982 shall be read as references to 6th April 1965.

Commentary—*Simon's Direct Tax Service* D2.665–667.
Revenue Interpretation RI 224—Circumstances in which Delaware Limited Liability Companies (DLLCs) can be regarded as issuing "ordinary share capital" for the purposes of TCGA 1992 ss 170–181.
Revenue & other press releases—IR 3-2-81 (surrender of losses by way of group relief without payment, or where payment is less than value of group relief is not a depreciatory transaction. Revenue will not seek adjustment under s 176(4)).
Revenue Internal Guidance—Capital gains manual CG 46500–46661 (full explanation of the legislation with examples).
CG 46566 (application to group relief surrenders).
CG 46580–46586 (distributions out of pre-acquisition profits are caught).
CG 46640 46641 (effect of rebasing).
CG 46660 (examples of compensating adjustments).
Simon's Tax Cases—*X plc v Roe* [1996] STC (SCD) 139*; *Tesco plc v Crimmin* [1997] STC 981*.
Definitions—"Allowable loss", ss 8(2), 16, 288(1); "asset", s 21(1); "chargeable gain", s 15(2); "company", s 170; "group", s 170; "inspector", s 288(1); "market value", ss 272-274, Sch 11; "resident", s 9(1); "75 per cent subsidiary", s 170(2)(*c*); "shares", s 288(1); "subsidiary", s 170.
Cross references—See TCGA 1992 s 170(1) (interpretation).
TCGA 1992 s 177 (application of this section to dividend stripping transactions).
FA 2000 Sch 29 para 24(2) (the main amendments made to TCGA 1992 s 170 by FA 2000 Sch 29 para 1 have effect for the purposes of this section with effect after 31 March 2000).
Amendments—[1] Words in sub-ss (4)–(6) substituted by FA 1996 s 134(1), (2), Sch 20 para 57 with effect from the year 1996–97 and, for purposes of corporation tax, as respects accounting periods ending after 30 June 1999 (by virtue of Finance Act 1994, Section 199, (Appointed Day) Order, SI 1998/3173 art 2).
[2] Sub-s (7)(*c*) and word "and" preceding it, repealed by FA 2000 ss 102, 156, Sch 29 para 24, Sch 40 Pt II(12) with effect for cases in which the depreciatory transaction (within the meaning of this section) is after 31 March 2000.

177 Dividend stripping

(1) The provisions of this section apply where one company ("the first company") has a holding in another company ("the second company") and the following conditions are fulfilled—

    (*a*) that the holding amounts to, or is an ingredient in a holding amounting to, 10 per cent of all holdings of the same class in the second company,

    (*b*) that the first company is not a dealing company in relation to the holding,

    (*c*) that a distribution is or has been made to the first company in respect of the holding, and

    (*d*) that the effect of the distribution is that the value of the holding is or has been materially reduced.

(2) Where this section applies in relation to a holding, section 176 shall apply, subject to subsection (3) below, in relation to any disposal of any shares or securities comprised in the holding, whether

the disposal is by the first company or by any other company to which the holding is transferred by a transfer to which section [140A,][1] [or 171][2] applies, as if the distribution were a depreciatory transaction and, if the companies concerned are not members of a group of companies, as if they were.

(3) The distribution shall not be treated as a depreciatory transaction to the extent that it consists of a payment which is required to be or has been brought into account, for the purposes of corporation tax on chargeable gains, in computing a chargeable gain or allowable loss accruing to the person making the ultimate disposal.

(4) This section shall be construed as one with section 176, and in any case where the ultimate disposal is not one to which section 35(2) applies, the reference in subsection (1)(*c*) above to a distribution does not include a distribution made before 30th April 1969.

(5) For the purposes of this section a company is "a dealing company" in relation to a holding if a profit on the sale of the holding would be taken into account in computing the company's trading profits.

(6) References in this section to a holding in a company refer to a holding of shares or securities by virtue of which the holder may receive distributions made by the company, but so that—

(*a*) a company's holdings of different classes in another company shall be treated as separate holdings, and

(*b*) holdings of securities which differ in the entitlements or obligations they confer or impose shall be regarded as holdings of different classes.

(7) For the purposes of subsection (1) above—

(*a*) all a company's holdings of the same class in another company are to be treated as ingredients constituting a single holding, and

(*b*) a company's holding of a particular class shall be treated as an ingredient in a holding amounting to 10 per cent of all holdings of that class if the aggregate of that holding and other holdings of that class held by connected persons amounts to 10 per cent of all holdings of that class,

and section 286 shall have effect in relation to paragraph (*b*) above as if, in subsection (7) of that section, after the words "or exercise control of" in each place where they occur there were inserted the words "or to acquire a holding in".

Commentary—*Simon's Direct Tax Service* **D2.667.**
Revenue Interpretation RI 224—Circumstances in which Delaware Limited Liability Companies (DLLCs) can be regarded as issuing "ordinary share capital" for the purposes of TCGA 1992 ss 170–181.
Revenue Internal Guidance—Capital gains manual CG 46680–46683 (operation of this section).
Definitions—"Allowable loss", ss 8(2), 16, 288(1); "chargeable gain", s 15(2); "class", s 288(1); "company", s 170; "connected", s 286; "control", s 288(1), TA 1988 s 416; "group", s 170; "profits", s 170(1); "shares", s 288(1).
Cross references—See TCGA 1992 s 170(1) (interpretation).
FA 2000 Sch 29 para 25(2) (the main amendments made to TCGA 1992 s 170 by FA 2000 Sch 29 para 1 have effect for the purposes of this section with effect for disposals after 31 March 2000).
Amendments—[1] Number in sub-s (2) inserted by F(No 2)A 1992 s 46(1), (6) and deemed always to have had effect.
[2] Words in sub-s (2) substituted by FA 2000 s 102, Sch 29 para 25 with effect for disposals after 31 March 2000.

[177A Restriction on set-off of pre-entry losses

Schedule 7A to this Act (which makes provision in relation to losses accruing to a company before the time when it becomes a member of a group of companies and losses accruing on assets held by any company at such a time) shall have effect.][1]

Commentary—*Simon's Direct Tax Service* **D2.670.**
Revenue Interpretation RI 224—Circumstances in which Delaware Limited Liability Companies (DLLCs) can be regarded as issuing "ordinary share capital" for the purposes of TCGA 1992 ss 170–181.
Amendments—[1] This section inserted by FA 1993 s 88(1).

[Pre-entry gains

177B Restrictions on setting losses against pre-entry gains

Schedule 7AA to this Act (which makes provision restricting the losses that may be set against the chargeable gains accruing to a company in the accounting period in which it joins a group of companies) shall have effect.][1]

Commentary—*Simon's Direct Tax Service* **D2.685.**
Revenue Interpretation RI 224—Circumstances in which Delaware Limited Liability Companies (DLLCs) can be regarded as issuing "ordinary share capital" for the purposes of TCGA 1992 ss 170–181.
Amendments—[1] This section inserted by FA 1998 s 137(1) with effect in relation to any accounting period ending on or after 17 March 1998.

Companies leaving groups

178 Company ceasing to be member of group: pre-appointed day cases

Commentary—*Simon's Direct Tax Service* **D2.661, 662.**
Revenue Interpretation RI 224—
Circumstances in which Delaware Limited Liability Companies (DLLCs) can be regarded as issuing "ordinary share capital" for the purposes of TCGA 1992 ss 170–181.

Amendments—This section (which is spent) repealed by FA 2000 ss 102, 156, Sch 29 para 26, Sch 40 Pt II(12) with effect from 28 July 2000

179 Company ceasing to be member of group: post-appointed day cases

[(1) This section applies where—

(a) a company (''company A'') acquires an asset from another company (''company B'') at a time when company B is a member of a group,

(b) the conditions in subsection (1A) below are met, and

(c) company A ceases to be a member of that group within the period of six years after the time of the acquisition.

References in this section to a company ceasing to be a member of a group of companies do not apply to cases where a company ceases to be a member of a group in consequence of another member of the group ceasing to exist.

(1A) The conditions referred to in subsection (1)(b) above are—

(a) that company A is resident in the United Kingdom at the time it acquires the asset, or the asset is a chargeable asset in relation to that company immediately after that time, and

(b) that company B is resident in the United Kingdom at the time of that acquisition, or the asset is a chargeable asset in relation to that company immediately before that time.

For this purpose an asset is a ''chargeable asset'' in relation to a company at any time if, were the asset to be disposed of by the company at that time, any gain accruing to the company would be a chargeable gain and would by virtue of section 10(3) form part of its chargeable profits for corporation tax purposes.][6]

(2) Where 2 or more associated companies cease to be members of the group at the same time, subsection (1) above shall not have effect as respects an acquisition by one from another of those associated companies.

[(2A) Where—

(a) a company [(''company A'')][6] that has ceased to be a member of a group of companies (''the first group'') acquired an asset from another company [(''company B'')][6] which was a member of that group at the time of the acquisition,

(b) subsection (2) above applies in the case of [company A's][6] ceasing to be a member of the first group so that subsection (1) above does not have effect as respects the acquisition of that asset,

(c) [company A][6] subsequently ceases to be a member of another group of companies (''the second group''), and

(d) there is a connection between the two groups,

subsection (1) above shall have effect in relation to [company A's][6] ceasing to be a member of the second group as if it had been the second group of which both companies had been members at the time of the acquisition.][1]

[(2B) For the purposes of subsection (2A) above there is a connection between the first group and the second group if, at the time when [company A][6] ceases to be a member of the second group, the company which is the principal company of that group is under the control of—

(a) the company which is the principal company of the first group or, if that group no longer exists, which was the principal company of that group when [company A][6] ceased to be a member of it;

(b) any [person or persons who control the company mentioned in paragraph (a) above or who have had it under their][5] control at any time in the period since [company A][6] ceased to be a member of the first group; or

(c) any [person or persons who have, at any time in that period, had under their][3] control either—

   (i) a company which would have [been a person falling][3] within paragraph (b) above if it had continued to exist, or

   (ii) a company which would have [been a person falling][3] within this paragraph (whether by reference to a company which would have [been a person falling][3] within that paragraph or to a company or series of companies falling within this subparagraph).][1]

[(2C) This section shall not have effect as respects any asset if, before the time when [company A][6] ceases to be a member of the group or, as the case may be, the second group, an event has already occurred by virtue of which the company falls by virtue of section 101A(3) to be treated as having sold and immediately reacquired the asset at the time specified in subsection (3) below.][4]

[(2D) This section shall not have effect as respects any asset if, before the time when [company A][6] ceases to be a member of the group or, as the case may be, the second group, an event has already occurred by virtue of which the company falls by virtue of section 101C(3) to be treated as having sold and immediately reacquired the asset at the time specified in subsection (3) below.][5]

(3) If, when [company A][6] ceases to be a member of the group, [company A][6], or an associated company also leaving the group, owns, otherwise than as trading stock—

(a) the asset, or

(b) property to which a chargeable gain has been carried forward from the asset on a replacement of business assets, then, subject to subsection (4) below, [company A][6] shall be treated for all the purposes of this Act as if immediately after its acquisition of the asset it had sold, and immediately reacquired, the asset at market value at that time.

(4) Any chargeable gain or allowable loss [accruing][8] to [company A][6] on the sale referred to in subsection (3) above shall be treated as accruing to [company A][6] [at whichever is the later of the following, that is to say—

    (*a*) the time immediately after the beginning of the accounting period of that company in which or, as the case may be, at the end of which the company ceases to be a member of the group; and

    (*b*) the time when under subsection (3) above it is treated as having reacquired the asset;

[and sections 403A and 403B of the Taxes Act (limits on group relief) shall have effect accordingly as if the actual circumstances were as they were treated as having been.][2]

(5) Where, apart from subsection (6) below, a company ceasing to be a member of a group by reason only of the fact that the principal company of the group becomes a member of another group would be treated by virtue of subsection (3) above as selling an asset at any time, subsections (6) to (8) below shall apply.

(6) The company in question shall not be treated as selling the asset at that time; but if—

    (*a*) within 6 years of that time the company in question ceases at any time (''the relevant time'') to satisfy the following conditions, and

    (*b*) at the relevant time, the company in question, or a company in the same group as that company, owns otherwise than as trading stock the asset or property to which a chargeable gain has been carried forward from the asset on a replacement of business assets,

the company in question shall be treated for all the purposes of this Act as if, immediately after its acquisition of the asset, it had sold and immediately reacquired the asset at the value that, at the time of acquisition, was its market value.

(7) Those conditions are—

    (*a*) that the company is a 75 per cent subsidiary of one or more members of the other group referred to in subsection (5) above, and

    (*b*) that the company is an effective 51 per cent subsidiary of one or more of those members.

(8) Any chargeable gain or allowable loss accruing to the company on that sale shall be treated as accruing at the relevant time.

(9) Where—

    (*a*) by virtue of this section a company is treated as having sold an asset at any time, and

    (*b*) if at that time the company had in fact sold the asset at market value at that time, then, by virtue of section 30, any allowable loss or chargeable gain accruing on the disposal would have been calculated as if the consideration for the disposal were increased by an amount,

subsections (3) and (6) above shall have effect as if the market value at that time had been that amount greater.

[(9A) Section 416(2) to (6) of the Taxes Act (meaning of control) shall have effect for the purposes of subsection (2B) above as it has effect for the purposes of Part XI of that Act; but a person carrying on a business of banking shall not for the purposes of that subsection be regarded as having control of any company by reason only of having, or of the consequences of having exercised, any rights of that person in respect of loan capital or debt issued or incurred by the company for money lent by that person to the company in the ordinary course of that business.][1]

(10) For the purposes of this section—

    (*a*) 2 or more companies are associated companies if, by themselves, they would form a group of companies,

    (*b*) a chargeable gain is carried forward from an asset to other property on a replacement of business assets if, by one or more claims under sections 152 to 158, the chargeable gain accruing on a disposal of the asset is reduced, and as a result an amount falls to be deducted from the expenditure allowable in computing a gain accruing on the disposal of the other property,

    (*c*) an asset acquired by [company A][6] shall be treated as the same as an asset owned at a later time by that company or an associated company if the value of the second asset is derived in whole or in part from the first asset, and in particular where the second asset is a freehold, and the first asset was a leasehold and the lessee has acquired the reversion.

(11), (12) ...[7]

(13) Where under this section [company A][6] is to be treated as having disposed of, and reacquired, an asset, all such recomputations of liability in respect of other disposals, and all such adjustments of tax, whether by way of assessment or by way of discharge or repayment of tax, as may be required in consequence of the provisions of this section shall be carried out.

Commentary—*Simon's Direct Tax Service* D2.661.
Statement of Practice D21—Time limit for an election for valuation on 6 April 1965 under TCGA 1992 Sch 2 para 17: company leaving a group.
Revenue Interpretation RI 64—This section applies only for companies leaving groups on or after 1 October 1993; s 178 above applies for companies leaving groups before 1 October 1993.
RI 224—Circumstances in which Delaware Limited Liability Companies (DLLCs) can be regarded as issuing ''ordinary share capital'' for the purposes of TCGA 1992 ss 170–181.

Revenue & other press releases—IR 19-8-98 (Company purchase schemes: collection of outstanding tax—outcome of consultation).

Definitions—"Allowable loss", ss 8(2), 16, 288(1); "asset", s 21(1); "chargeable gain", s 15(2); "company", s 170; "effective 51 per cent subsidiary", s 170(7); "group", s 170; "lessee", Sch 8 para 10(1); "the Management Act", s 288(1); "market value", ss 272–274, Sch 11; "principal company", s 170(3)–(6); "75 per cent subsidiary", s 170(2)(c); "subsidiary", s 170; "the Taxes Act", s 288(1); "trading stock", s 288(1), TA 1988 s 100(2).

Cross references—See TMA 1970 s 87A(3) (interest on overdue corporation tax assessed under sub-s (11) above);

TCGA 1992 s 14 (this section applies in relation to non-resident "close" company which is a member of non-resident group of companies).

TCGA 1992 s 170(1) (interpretation).

TCGA 1992 s 181 (exemption from charge under this section for certain mergers).

TCGA 1992 s 192(3), (4) (disapplication of this section in certain cases where a company ceases to be a member of a group by reason of a demerger).

TCGA 1992 s 216(2), (4) (transfer of a building society's business to a company with the result that any company ceases to be a member of the same group as the building society).

TCGA 1992 s 276(8) (modification of this section in its application to disposals of continental shelf exploration and exploitation rights and assets by a non-resident company to a company resident in the same territory, by a resident company to another resident company, or by a non-resident company to a resident company).

TCGA 1992 Sch 4 paras 4, 9 (deferred charges on gains accruing before 31 March 1982).

FA 1994 s 250(2) (deemed disposal and reacquisition at market value rule in this section not to apply in the case of a resident company treated as ceasing to be resident on 30 November 1993 solely by virtue of the coming into force of FA 1994 s 249).

FA 2000 Sch 29 para 3 (the main amendments made to TCGA 1992 s 170 by FA 2000 Sch 29 para 1 have effect for the purposes of this section for assets acquired after 31 March 2000).

FA 2000 Sch 29 para 47 (de-grouping charge: deferral until company leaves new group).

Amendments—[1] Sub-ss (2A), (2B), (9A) inserted by FA 1995 s 49, with effect for a company in any case in which the time of the company's ceasing to be a member of the second group is after 28 November 1994.
[2] Words following para (b) in sub-para (4) substituted by F(No 2)A 1997 s 41, Sch 7 paras 8, 9, with effect in relation to any claim for group relief if the accounting period of either the claimant company or the surrendering company ends on or after 2 July 1997 and the overlapping period (see TA 1988 s 403A(8)) would not fall entirely before that date (but see F(No 2)A 1997 Sch 7 para 9(3)–(5) for transitional provisions where the overlapping period straddles 2 July 1997).
[3] Words in sub-s (2B) substituted by FA 1998 s 139(1) with effect in relation to a company in any case in which the time of the company's ceasing to be a member of the second group is on or after 17 March 1998.
[4] Sub-s (2C) inserted by FA 1998 s 133(2) with effect in relation to any company which becomes an investment trust for an accounting period beginning on or after 17 March 1998.
[5] Sub-s (2D) inserted by FA 1998 s 135(3) with effect in relation to a company in respect of which an approval for the purposes of TA 1988 s 842AA (venture capital trusts) has effect as from a time falling on or after 17 March 1998.
[6] Sub-ss (1), (1A) substituted for original sub-s (1), and sub-ss (2A)–(2D), (3), (4), (10)(c), (13) substituted, and words in sub-s (2A) inserted, by FA 2000 s 102, Sch 29 para 4(1)–(4), (5) with effect for assets acquired after 31 March 2000.
[7] Sub-ss (11), (12) repealed by FA 2000 ss 102, 156, Sch 29 para 4(1), (5), (7), Sch 40 Pt II(12) with effect for gains accruing after 31 March 2000.
[8] Word in sub-s (4) substituted by FA 2002 s 44(2), (3), Sch 8 para 2 with effect for disposals after 31 March 2002. This amendment has effect where the company in question ceases to be a member of the group in question after that date: FA 2002 s 44(5).

[179A Reallocation within group of gain or loss accruing under section 179

(1) This section applies where—

(a) a company ("company A") is treated by virtue of section 179(3) or (6) as having sold and immediately reacquired an asset at market value, and

(b) a chargeable gain or an allowable loss accrues to the company on the deemed sale.

(2) In this section "time of accrual" means—

(a) in a case where section 179(3) applies, the time at which, by virtue of section 179(4), the gain or loss referred to in subsection (1) above is treated as accruing to company A;

(b) in a case where section 179(6) applies, the latest time at which the company satisfies the conditions in section 179(7).

(3) If—

(a) a joint election under this section is made by company A and a company ("company C") that was a member of the relevant group at the time of accrual, and

(b) the conditions in subsections (6) to (8) below are all met,

the chargeable gain or allowable loss accruing on the deemed sale, or such part of it as may be specified in the election, shall be treated as accruing not to company A but to company C.

(4) In subsection (3) above "the relevant group" means—

(a) in a case where section 179(3) applies, the group of which company A was a member at the time of accrual;

(b) in a case where section 179(6) applies, the second group referred to in section 179(5).

(5) Where two or more elections are made each specifying a part of the same gain or loss, the total amount specified may not exceed the whole of that gain or loss.

(6) The first condition is that, at the time of accrual, company C—

(a) was resident in the United Kingdom, or

(b) owned assets that were chargeable assets in relation to it.

(7) The second condition is that neither company A nor company C was at that time a qualifying friendly society within the meaning given by section 171(5)).

(8) The third condition is that company C was not at that time an investment trust, a venture capital trust or a dual resident investing company.

(9) A gain or loss treated by virtue of this section as accruing to a company that is not resident in the United Kingdom shall be treated as accruing in respect of a chargeable asset held by that company.

(10) An election under this section must be made—

(*a*) by notice to an officer of the Board;

(*b*) no later than two years after the end of the accounting period of company A in which the time of accrual fell.

(11) Any payment by company A to company C, or by company C to company A, in pursuance of an agreement between them in connection with the election—

(*a*) shall not be taken into account in computing profits or losses of either company for corporation tax purposes, and

(*b*) shall not for any purposes of the Corporation Tax Acts be regarded as a distribution or a charge on income,

provided it does not exceed the amount of the chargeable gain or allowable loss that is treated, as a result of the election, as accruing to company C.

(12) For the purposes of this section an asset is a "chargeable asset" in relation to a company at a particular time if any gain accruing to the company on a disposal of the asset by the company at that time would be a chargeable gain and would by virtue of section 10(3) form part of its chargeable profits for corporation tax purposes.][1]

Amendments—[1] This section inserted by FA 2002 s 42(1), (4) with effect—

(*a*) in relation to a case where a company is treated by virtue of TCGA 1992 s 179(3) as having sold and then reacquired an asset, where the company's ceasing to be a member of the group in question happens after 31 March 2002;
(*b*) in relation to a case where a company is so treated by virtue of TCGA 1992 s 179(6), where the relevant time (within the meaning of that subsection) is after that date.

[179B Roll-over of degrouping charge on business assets

(1) Where a company is treated by virtue of section 179(3) or (6) as having sold and immediately reacquired an asset at market value, relief under section 152 or 153 (roll-over relief on replacement of business assets) is available in accordance with this section in relation to any gain accruing to the company on the deemed sale.

(2) For this purpose, sections 152 and 153 and the other enactments specified in Schedule 7AB apply with the modifications set out in that Schedule.

(3) Where there has been an election under section 179A, any claim for relief available in accordance with this section must be made by company C rather than company A.

(4) For this purpose, the enactments modified by Schedule 7AB have effect as if—

(*a*) references to company A, except those in sections 152(1)(*a*) and (1B), 153(1B), 153A(5), 159(1), 175 and 198(1), were to company C;

(*b*) the references to "that company" in section 159(1) and "the company" in section 185(3)(*b*) were to company C;

(*c*) the reference to "that trade" in section 198(1) were to a ring fence trade carried on by company C.

(5) Where there has been an election under section 179A in respect of part only of the chargeable gain accruing on the deemed sale of an asset, the enactments modified by Schedule 7AB and subsections (3) and (4) above apply as if the deemed sale had been of a separate asset representing a corresponding part of the asset; and any necessary apportionments shall be made accordingly.

(6) A reference in this section to company A or to company C is to the company referred to as such in section 179A.][1]

Amendments—[1] This section inserted by FA 2002 s 43(1), (4) with effect—

(*a*) in relation to a case where a company is treated by virtue of TCGA 1992 s 179(3) as having sold and immediately reacquired an asset, where the company's ceasing to be a member of the group in question happens after 31 March 2002;
(*b*) in relation to a case where a company is so treated by virtue of TCGA 1992 s 179(6), where the relevant time (within the meaning of that subsection) is after that date.

180 Transitional provisions

Commentary—*Simon's Direct Tax Service* D2.661.
Amendment—This section (which is spent) repealed by FA 2000 ss 102, 156, Sch 29 para 27, Sch 40 Pt II(12) with effect from 28 July 2000.

181 Exemption from charge under s 178 or s 179 in the case of certain mergers

(1) Subject to the following provisions of this section, [section 179 shall not][2] shall apply in a case where—

(*a*) as part of a merger, a company ("company A") ceases to be a member of a group of companies ("the A group"); and

(*b*) ...[1] the merger was carried out for bona fide commercial reasons and ...[1] the avoidance of liability to tax was not the main or one of the main purposes of the merger.

(2) In this section "merger" means an arrangement (which in this section includes a series of arrangements)—

(*a*) whereby one or more companies ("the acquiring company" or, as the case may be, "the acquiring companies") none of which is a member of the A group acquires or acquire, otherwise than with a view to their disposal, one or more interests in the whole or part of the business which, before the arrangement took effect, was carried on by company A; and

(*b*) whereby one or more members of the A group acquires or acquire, otherwise than with a view to their disposal, one or more interests in the whole or part of the business or each of the businesses which, before the arrangement took effect, was carried on either by the acquiring company or acquiring companies or by a company at least 90 per cent of the ordinary share capital of which was then beneficially owned by 2 or more of the acquiring companies; and

(*c*) in respect of which the conditions in subsection (4) below are fulfilled.

(3) For the purposes of subsection (2) above, a member of a group of companies shall be treated as carrying on as one business the activities of that group.

(4) The conditions referred to in subsection (2)(*c*) above are—

(*a*) that not less than 25 per cent by value of each of the interests acquired as mentioned in paragraphs (*a*) and (*b*) of subsection (2) above consists of a holding of ordinary share capital, and the remainder of the interest, or as the case may be of each of the interests, acquired as mentioned in subsection (2)(*b*), consists of a holding of share capital (of any description) or debentures or both; and

(*b*) that the value or, as the case may be, the aggregate value of the interest or interests acquired as mentioned in subsection (2)(*a*) above is substantially the same as the value or, as the case may be, the aggregate value of the interest or interests acquired as mentioned in subsection (2)(*b*) above; and

(*c*) that the consideration for the acquisition of the interest or interests acquired by the acquiring company or acquiring companies as mentioned in subsection (2)(*a*) above, disregarding any part of that consideration which is small by comparison with the total, either consists of, or is applied in the acquisition of, or consists partly of and as to the balance is applied in the acquisition of, the interest or interests acquired by members of the A group as mentioned in subsection (2)(*b*) above;

and for the purposes of this subsection the value of an interest shall be determined as at the date of its acquisition.

(5) ...[2]

Commentary—*Simon's Direct Tax Service* D2.664.
Revenue Interpretation RI 224—Circumstances in which Delaware Limited Liability Companies (DLLCs) can be regarded as issuing "ordinary share capital" for the purposes of TCGA 1992 ss 170–181.
Revenue Internal Guidance—Capital Gains Manual CG 45605 (worked examples illustrating the main conditions for relief under the merger provisions).
Definitions—"Company", s 170; "group", s 170; "resident", s 9(1).
Cross references—See TCGA 1992 s 170(1) (interpretation).
TCGA 1992 s 276(8) (modification of this section in its application to disposals of continental shelf exploration and exploitation rights and assets by a non-resident company to a company resident in the same territory, by a resident company to another resident company, or by a non-resident company to a resident company).
FA 2000 Sch 29 para 28(2) (the main amendments made to TCGA 1992 s 170 by FA 2000 Sch 29 para 1 have effect for the purposes of this section with effect for cases in which the company ceases to be a member of a group after 31 March 2000).
Amendments—[1] Words in sub-s (1)(*b*) repealed by FA 1996 s 134(1), (2), Sch 20 para 58, Sch 41 Pt V(10) with effect as respects accounting periods ending after 30 June 1999 (by virtue of Finance Act 1994, Section 199, (Appointed Day) Order, SI 1998/3173 art 2).
[2] Words in sub-s (1) substituted, and sub-s (5) repealed, by FA 2000 ss 102, 156, Sch 29 para 28, Sch 40 Pt II(12) with effect for cases in which the company ceases to be a member of a group after 31 March 2000.

Restriction on indexation allowance for groups and associated companies

182 Disposals of debts

Commentary—*Simon's Direct Tax Service* D2.668.
Amendment—This section repealed by FA 1994 s 93(7), (11) and Sch 26 Pt V(8) in relation to disposals after 29 November 1993.

183 Disposals of shares

Commentary—*Simon's Direct Tax Service* D2.668.
Amendment—This section repealed by FA 1994 s 93(7), (11) and Sch 26 Pt V(8) in relation to disposals after 29 November 1993.

184 Definitions and other provisions supplemental to sections 182 and 183

Commentary—*Simon's Direct Tax Service* D2.668.
Amendment—This section repealed by FA 1994 s 93(7), (11) and Sch 26 Pt V(8) in relation to disposals after 29 November 1993.

Non-resident and dual resident companies

185 Deemed disposal of assets on company ceasing to be resident in UK

(1) This section and section 187 apply to a company if, at any time ("the relevant time"), the company ceases to be resident in the United Kingdom.

(2) The company shall be deemed for all purposes of this Act—

(*a*) to have disposed of all its assets, other than assets excepted from this subsection by subsection (4) below, immediately before the relevant time; and

(*b*) immediately to have reacquired them,

at their market value at that time.

(3) Section 152 shall not apply where the company—

(*a*) has disposed of the old assets, or of its interest in those assets, before the relevant time; and

(*b*) acquires the new assets, or its interest in those assets, after that time,

unless the new assets are excepted from this subsection by subsection (4) below.

(4) If at any time after the relevant time the company carries on a trade in the United Kingdom through a branch or agency—

(*a*) any assets which, immediately after the relevant time, are situated in the United Kingdom and are used in or for the purposes of the trade, or are used or held for the purposes of the branch or agency, shall be excepted from subsection (2) above; and

(*b*) any new assets which, after that time, are so situated and are so used or so held shall be excepted from subsection (3) above;

and references in this subsection to assets situated in the United Kingdom include references to exploration or exploitation assets and to exploration or exploitation rights.

(5) In this section—

(*a*) "designated area", "exploration or exploitation activities" and "exploration or exploitation rights" have the same meanings as in section 276;

(*b*) "exploration or exploitation assets" means assets used or intended for use in connection with exploration or exploitation activities carried on in the United Kingdom or a designated area;

(*c*) "the old assets" and "the new assets" have the same meanings as in section 152;

and a company shall not be regarded for the purposes of this section as ceasing to be resident in the United Kingdom by reason only that it ceases to exist.

Commentary—*Simon's Direct Tax Service* D4.131.
Revenue Internal Guidance—International tax handbook ITH 407–409 (background to the exit charge).
Definitions—"Asset", s 21(1); "branch or agency", s 10(6); "company", ss 99, 288(1); "market value", ss 272–274, Sch 11; "resident", s 9(1).
Cross references—See TCGA 1992 Sch 7B paras 1, 8 (modification of this section in its application to an overseas life insurance company in accounting periods beginning after 31 December 1992).
FA 1994 s 250(3)–(6) (date on which corporation tax is payable by a company on a deemed disposal by virtue of sub-s (2) above where the company is resident but is treated as non-resident under a double taxation relief arrangement and ceases to be resident for tax purposes on 30 November 1993 by virtue of the coming into force of FA 1994 s 249).
Modifications—TCGA 1992 Sch 7AB paras 1, 8 (modification of this section for the purposes of TCGA 1992 s 179B (as inserted by FA 2002 s 43) which relates to roll-over of degrouping charge on business assets).

186 Deemed disposal of assets on company ceasing to be liable to UK taxation

Commentary—*Simon's Direct Tax Service* D4.131.
Definitions—"Asset", s 21(1); "company", ss 99, 288(1); "double taxation relief arrangements", s 288(1); "resident", s 9(1).
Amendments—This section repealed by FA 1994 s 251(9) and Sch 26 Pt VIII(1) where sub-s (1) applies to a company after 29 November 1993.

187 Postponement of charge on deemed disposal under section 185 ...[2]

(1) If—

(*a*) immediately after the relevant time, a company to which this section applies by virtue of section 185 ...[1] ("the company") is a 75 per cent subsidiary of another company ("the principal company") which is resident in the United Kingdom; and

(*b*) the principal company and the company so elect, by notice given to the inspector within 2 years after that time,

this Act shall have effect in accordance with the following provisions.

(2) Any allowable losses accruing to the company on a deemed disposal of foreign assets shall be set off against the chargeable gains so accruing and—

(*a*) that disposal shall be treated as giving rise to a single chargeable gain equal to the aggregate of those gains after deducting the aggregate of those losses; and

(*b*) the whole of that gain shall be treated as not accruing to the company on that disposal but an equivalent amount ("the postponed gain") shall be brought into account in accordance with subsections (3) and (4) below.

(3) If at any time within 6 years after the relevant time the company disposes of any assets ("relevant assets") the chargeable gains on which were taken into account in arriving at the postponed gain, there shall be deemed to accrue to the principal company as a chargeable gain on that occasion the

whole or the appropriate proportion of the postponed gain so far as not already taken into account under this subsection or subsection (4) below.

In this subsection "the appropriate proportion" means the proportion which the chargeable gain taken into account in arriving at the postponed gain in respect of the part of the relevant assets disposed of bears to the aggregate of the chargeable gains so taken into account in respect of the relevant assets held immediately before the time of the disposal.

(4) If at any time after the relevant time—

   (*a*) the company ceases to be a 75 per cent subsidiary of the principal company on the disposal by the principal company of ordinary shares of the company;

   (*b*) after the company has ceased to be such a subsidiary otherwise than on such a disposal, the principal company disposes of such shares; or

   (*c*) the principal company ceases to be resident in the United Kingdom,

there shall be deemed to accrue to the principal company as a chargeable gain on that occasion the whole of the postponed gain so far as not already taken into account under this subsection or subsection (3) above.

(5) If at any time—

   (*a*) the company has allowable losses which have not been allowed as a deduction from chargeable gains; and

   (*b*) a chargeable gain accrues to the principal company under subsection (3) or (4) above,

then, if and to the extent that the principal company and the company so elect by notice given to the inspector within 2 years after that time, those losses shall be allowed as a deduction from that gain.

(6) In this section—

   "deemed disposal" means a disposal which, by virtue of section 185(2) ...[1], is deemed to have been made;

   "foreign assets" means any assets of the company which, immediately after the relevant time, are situated outside the United Kingdom and are used in or for the purposes of a trade carried on outside the United Kingdom;

   "ordinary share" means a share in the ordinary share capital of the company;

   "the relevant time" has the meaning given by section 185(1) ...[1].

(7) For the purposes of this section a company is a 75 per cent subsidiary of another company if and so long as not less than 75 per cent of its ordinary share capital is owned directly by that other company.

Commentary—*Simon's Direct Tax Service* **D4.131, 132.**
Definitions—"Allowable loss", ss 8(2), 16, 288(1); "asset", s 21(1); "chargeable gain", s 15(2); "company", ss 99, 288(1); "inspector", s 288(1); "notice", s 288(1); "resident", s 9(1); "shares", s 288(1); "trade", s 288(1), TA 1988 s 832(1).
Amendments—[1] Words in sub-s (1)(*a*) and in the definitions of "deemed disposal" and "the relevant time" repealed by FA 1994 s 251(9) and Sch 26 Pt VIII(1) where s 186(1) of this Act applies to a company after 29 November 1993.
[2] "or 186" in the heading deleted in view of the amendment[1] above.

188 Dual resident companies: deemed disposal of certain assets

Commentary—*Simon's Direct Tax Service* **D4.132.**
Amendment—This section repealed by FA 1994 s 251(10) and Sch 26 Pt VIII(1) with effect from 30 November 1993.

Recovery of tax otherwise than from tax-payer company

189 Capital distribution of chargeable gains: recovery of tax from shareholder

(1) This section applies where a person who is connected with a company resident in the United Kingdom receives or becomes entitled to receive in respect of shares in the company any capital distribution from the company, other than a capital distribution representing a reduction of capital, and—

   (*a*) the capital so distributed derives from the disposal of assets in respect of which a chargeable gain accrued to the company; or

   (*b*) the distribution constitutes such a disposal of assets;

and that person is referred to below as "the shareholder".

(2) If the corporation tax assessed on the company for the accounting period in which the chargeable gain accrues included any amount in respect of chargeable gains, and any of the tax assessed on the company for that period is not paid within 6 months from the date determined under subsection (3) below, the shareholder may by an assessment made within 2 years from that date be assessed and charged (in the name of the company) to an amount of that corporation tax—

   (*a*) not exceeding the amount or value of the capital distribution which the shareholder has received or become entitled to receive; and

   (*b*) not exceeding a proportion equal to the shareholder's share of the capital distribution made by the company of corporation tax on the amount of that gain at the rate in force when the gain accrued.

(3) The date referred to in subsection (2) above is whichever is the later of—

(a) the date when the tax becomes due and payable by the company; and

(b) the date when the assessment was made on the company.

(4) Where the shareholder pays any amount of tax under this section, he shall be entitled to recover from the company a sum equal to that amount together with any interest paid by him under section 87A of the Management Act on that amount.

(5) The provisions of this section are without prejudice to any liability of the shareholder in respect of a chargeable gain accruing to him by reference to the capital distribution as constituting a disposal of an interest in shares in the company.

(6) With respect to chargeable gains accruing in accounting periods ending on or before such day as the Treasury may by order appoint this section shall have effect—

(a) with the substitution for the words in subsection (3) after "above" of the words "is the date when the tax becomes payable by the company"; and

(b) with the omission of the words in subsection (4) from "together" to the end of the subsection.

(7) In this section "capital distribution" has the same meaning as in section 122.

Commentary—*Simon's Direct Tax Service* D2.302, 313.
Note—The appointed day for the purposes of sub-s (6) above is 30 September 1993 by virtue of Corporation Tax Acts (Provisions for Payment of Tax and Returns) (Appointed Days) Order, SI 1992/3066 art 2(1), (2)(*d*).
Definitions—"Asset", s 21(1); "chargeable gain", s 15(2); "company", ss 99, 288(1); "connected", s 286; "the Management Act", s 288(1); "resident", s 9(1); "shares", s 288(1).

[190 Tax recoverable from another group company or controlling director

(1) This section applies where—

(a) a chargeable gain has accrued to a company ("the taxpayer company"),

(b) the condition in subsection (2) below is met, and

(c) the whole or part of the corporation tax assessed on the company for the accounting period in which the gain accrued ("the relevant accounting period") is unpaid at the end of the period of six months after it became payable.

(2) The condition referred to in subsection (1)(*b*) above is—

(a) that the taxpayer company is resident in the United Kingdom at the time when the gain accrued, or

(b) that the gain forms part of the taxpayer company's chargeable profits for corporation tax purposes by virtue of section 10(3).

(3) The following persons may, by notice under this section, be required to pay the unpaid tax—

(a) if the taxpayer company was a member of a group at the time when the gain accrued—

(i) a company which was at that time the principal company of the group, and

(ii) any other company which in any part of the period of twelve months ending with that time was a member of that group and owned the asset disposed of, or any part of it, or where that asset is an interest or right in or over another asset, owned either asset or any part of either asset; and

(b) if the gain forms part of the chargeable profits of the taxpayer company for corporation tax purposes by virtue of section 10(3), any person who is, or during the period of twelve months ending with the time when the gain accrued was, a controlling director of the taxpayer company or of a company which has, or within that period had, control over the taxpayer company.

(4) The Board may serve a notice on a person within subsection (3) above requiring him, within 30 days of the service of the notice, to pay—

(a) the amount which remains unpaid of the corporation tax assessed on the taxpayer company for the relevant accounting period, or

(b) if less, an amount equal to corporation tax on the amount of the chargeable gain at the rate in force when the gain accrued.

(5) The notice must state—

(a) the amount of corporation tax assessed on the taxpayer company for the relevant accounting period that remains unpaid,

(b) the date when it first became payable, and

(c) the amount required to be paid by the person on whom the notice is served.

(6) The notice has effect—

(a) for the purposes of the recovery from that person of the amount required to be paid and of interest on that amount, and

(b) for the purposes of appeals,

as if it were a notice of assessment and that amount were an amount of tax due from that person.

(7) Any notice under this section must be served before the end of the period of three years beginning with the date on which the liability of the taxpayer company to corporation tax for the relevant accounting period is finally determined.

(8) Where the unpaid tax is charged in consequence of a determination under paragraph 36 or 37 of Schedule 18 to the Finance Act 1998 (determination where no return delivered or return incomplete),

the date mentioned in subsection (7) above shall be taken to be the date on which the determination was made.

(9) Where the unpaid tax is charged in a self-assessment, including a self-assessment that supersedes a determination (see paragraph 40 of Schedule 18 to the Finance Act 1998), the date mentioned in subsection (7) above shall be taken to be the latest of—

(*a*) the last date on which notice of enquiry may be given into the return containing the self-assessment;

(*b*) if notice of enquiry is given, 30 days after the enquiry is completed;

(*c*) if more than one notice of enquiry is given, 30 days after the last notice of completion;

(*d*) if after such an enquiry the Inland Revenue amend the return, 30 days after notice of the amendment is issued;

(*e*) if an appeal is brought against such an amendment, 30 days after the appeal is finally determined.

(10) If the unpaid tax is charged in a discovery assessment, the date mentioned in subsection (7) above shall be taken to be—

(*a*) where there is no appeal against the assessment, the date when the tax becomes due and payable;

(*b*) where there is such an appeal, the date on which the appeal is finally determined.

(11) A person who has paid an amount in pursuance of a notice under this section may recover that amount from the taxpayer company.

(12) A payment in pursuance of a notice under this section is not allowed as a deduction in computing any income, profits or losses for any tax purposes.

(13) In this section—

"director", in relation to a company, has the meaning given by section 168(8) of the Taxes Act (read with subsection (9) of that section) and includes any person falling within section 417(5) of that Act (read with subsection (6) of that section);

"controlling director", in relation to a company, means a director of the company who has control of it (construing control in accordance with section 416 of the Taxes Act);

"group" and "principal company" have the meaning which would be given by section 170 if in that section for references to 75 per cent subsidiaries there were substituted references to 51 per cent subsidiaries.][1]

Commentary—*Simon's Direct Tax Service* **D2.659.**
Definitions—"chargeable gain", s 15(2); "company", ss 99, 288(1).
Cross references—See FA 2000 Sch 29 para 9(3) (the main amendments made to TCGA 1992 s 170 by FA 2000 Sch 29 para 1 have effect for the purposes of this section for gains accruing after 31 March 2000).
FA 2000 Sch 29 para 9(4) (any question as to whether a company was a member of a group during the 12 months ending when a gain accrued after 31 March 2000 is determined in accordance with s 170 as amended by FA 2000 Sch 29, para 1).
Amendment—[1] This section substituted by FA 2000 s 102, Sch 29 para 9 with effect for gains accruing after 31 March 2000.

191 Tax on non-resident company recoverable from another member of group or from controlling director

Amendments—Section 190 above substituted for this section by FA 2000 s 102, Sch 29 para 9 with effect for gains accruing after 31 March 2000.

Demergers

192 Tax exempt distributions

(1) This section has effect for facilitating certain transactions whereby trading activities carried on by a single company or group are divided so as to be carried on by 2 or more companies not belonging to the same group or by 2 or more independent groups.

(2) Where a company makes an exempt distribution which falls within section 213(3)(*a*) of the Taxes Act—

(*a*) the distribution shall not be a capital distribution for the purposes of section 122; and

(*b*) sections 126 to 130 shall, with the necessary modifications, apply as if that company and the subsidiary whose shares are transferred were the same company and the distribution were a reorganisation of its share capital.

(3) Subject to subsection (4) below, [section 179 shall not][1] apply in a case where a company ceases to be a member of a group by reason only of an exempt distribution.

(4) Subsection (3) does not apply if within 5 years after the making of the exempt distribution there is chargeable payment; and the time for making an assessment under section ...[1] 179 by virtue of this subsection shall not expire before the end of 3 years after the making of the chargeable payment.

(5) In this section—

"chargeable payment" has the meaning given in section 214(2) of the Taxes Act;

"exempt distribution" means a distribution which is exempt by virtue of section 213(2) of that Act; and ''group'' means a company which has one or more 75 per cent subsidiaries together with that or those subsidiaries.

(6) In determining for the purposes of this section whether one company is a 75 per cent subsidiary of another, the other company shall be treated as not being the owner of—

(a) any share capital which it owns directly in a body corporate if a profit on a sale of the shares would be treated as a trading receipt of its trade; or

(b) any share capital which it owns indirectly and which is owned directly by a body corporate for which a profit on the sale of the shares would be a trading receipt.

Commentary—*Simon's Direct Tax Service* C2.729; D2.304.
Revenue Internal Guidance—Capital gains manual CG 33900–33920A (implications of this section). CG 33921–33936 (application to trusts).
Simon's Tax Cases—s 192(1), *Combined Technologies Corporation plc v IRC* [1985] STC 348*.
Definitions—''Company'', ss 99, 288(1); ''shares'', s 288(1); ''the Taxes Act'', s 288(1); ''trade'', s 288(1), TA 1988 s 832(1).
Amendments—¹ Words in sub-s (3) substituted for words and words in sub-s (4) repealed by FA 2000 ss 102, 156, Sch 29 para 29, Sch 40 Pt II(12) with effect from 28 July 2000.

[Disposals by companies with substantial shareholding

192A Exemptions for gains or losses on disposal of shares etc

Schedule 7AC (exemptions for disposal of shares etc by companies with substantial shareholding) has effect.]¹

Amendments—¹ This section inserted by FA 2002 s 44(1), (3) with effect for disposals after 31 March 2002.

CHAPTER II
OIL AND MINING INDUSTRIES
Oil exploration and exploitation

193 Roll-over relief not available for gains on oil licences

Commentary—*Simon's Direct Tax Service* C3.303; D4.1024, 1025.
Definition—''Asset'', s 21(1).
Amendments—¹ This section repealed by FA 1999 ss 103, 139, Sch 20 Pt IV(2) with effect for disposals or acquisitions of a licence, or an interest in a licence, after 30 June 1999.

194 Disposals of oil licences relating to undeveloped areas

(1) In this section any reference to a disposal (including a part disposal) is a reference to a disposal made by way of a bargain at arm's length.

(2) If, at the time of the disposal, the licence relates to an undeveloped area, then, to the extent that the consideration for the disposal consists of—

(a) another licence which at that time relates to an undeveloped area or an interest in another such licence, or

(b) an obligation to undertake exploration work or appraisal work in an area which is or forms part of the licensed area in relation to the licence disposed of,

the value of that consideration shall be treated as nil for the purposes of this Act.

(3) If the disposal of a licence which, at the time of the disposal, relates to an undeveloped area is part of a larger transaction under which one party makes to another disposals of 2 or more licences, each of which at the time of the disposal relates to an undeveloped area, the reference in subsection (2)(b) above to the licensed area in relation to the licence disposed of shall be construed as a reference to the totality of the licensed areas in relation to those 2 or more licences.

(4) In relation to a disposal of a licence which, at the time of the disposal, relates to an undeveloped area, being a disposal—

(a) which is a part disposal of the licence in question, and

(b) part but not the whole of the consideration for which falls within paragraph (a) or paragraph (b) of subsection (2) above,

section 42 shall not apply unless the amount or value of the part of the consideration which does not fall within one of those paragraphs is less than the aggregate of the amounts which, if the disposal were a disposal of the whole of the licence rather than a part disposal, would be—

(i) the relevant allowable expenditure, as defined in section 53; and

(ii) the indexation allowance on the disposal.

(5) Where section 42 has effect in relation to such a disposal as is referred to in subsection (4) above, it shall have effect as if, for subsection (2) thereof, there were substituted the following subsection—

''(2) The apportionment shall be made by reference to—

(a) the amount or value of the consideration for the disposal on the one hand (call that amount or value A), and

(b) the aggregate referred to in section 194(4) on the other hand (call that aggregate C), and the fraction of the said sums allowable as a deduction in computing the amount of the gain (if any) accruing on the disposal shall be—

$$\frac{A}{C}$$

and the remainder shall be attributed to the part of the property which remains undisposed of.''

Commentary—*Simon's Direct Tax Service* **D4.1025.**
Definitions—''Appraisal work'', s 196(6); ''exploration work'', s 196(6); ''indexation allowance'', s 53; ''licence'', s 196(5); ''licensed area'', s 196(5); ''oil'', s 196(5); ''part disposal'', s 21(2).
Cross references—See TCGA 1992 s 196 (interpretation).

195 Allowance of certain drilling expenditure etc

(1) On the disposal of a licence, relevant qualifying expenditure incurred by the person making the disposal—

(*a*) in searching for oil anywhere in the licensed area, or
(*b*) in ascertaining the extent or characteristics of any oil-bearing area the whole or part of which lies in the licensed area or what the reserves of oil of any such oil-bearing area are,

shall be treated as expenditure falling within section 38(1)(*b*).

(2) Expenditure incurred as mentioned in subsection (1) above is relevant expenditure if, and only if—

(*a*) it is expenditure of a capital nature on [research and development][1]; and
[(*b*) either it is expenditure in respect of which the person was entitled to an allowance under section 441 of the Capital Allowances Act (research and development allowances) for a relevant chargeable period which began before the date of the disposal or it would have been such expenditure if the trading condition had been fulfilled, and][2]
[(*c*) on the disposal, section 443 of that Act (disposal values) applies in relation to the expenditure or would apply if the trading condition had been fulfilled (and the expenditure had accordingly been qualifying expenditure under Part 6 of that Act).][2]

(3) In subsection (2) above and subsection (4) below, the expression ''if the trading condition had been fulfilled'' means, in relation to expenditure of a capital nature on [research and development][1], if, after the expenditure was incurred but before the disposal concerned was made, the person incurring the expenditure had set up and commenced a trade connected with that research [and development][1]; and in subsection (2)(*b*) above—

''relevant chargeable period'' has the same meaning as in [section 441 of the Capital Allowances Act][2]; ...[2]
...[2]

(4) Relevant expenditure is qualifying expenditure only to the extent that it does not exceed the [disposal value][2] which, by reason of the disposal—

[(*a*) is required to be brought into account under section 443 of the Capital Allowances Act; or][2]
[(*b*) would be required to be so brought into account if the trading condition had been fulfilled (and the expenditure had accordingly been qualifying expenditure under Part 6 of that Act).][2]

(5) ...[2]

(6) Where, on the disposal of a licence, subsection (1) above has effect in relation to any relevant qualifying expenditure [in respect of which the person had not in fact been entitled to an allowance][2] as mentioned in subsection (2)(*b*) above—

(*a*) no allowance shall be made in respect of that expenditure under [section 441 of the Capital Allowances Act]; ...[2]
(*b*) ...[2]

(7) Where, on the disposal of a licence which is a part disposal, subsection (1) above has effect in relation to any relevant qualifying expenditure, then, for the purposes of section 42, that expenditure shall be treated as wholly attributable to what is disposed of (and, accordingly, shall not be apportioned as mentioned in that section).

[(8) In this section ''research and development'' has the same meaning as in [Part 6 of the Capital Allowances Act (research and development allowances)][2].][3]

Commentary—*Simon's Direct Tax Service* **D4.1025.**
Definitions—''The 1990 Act'', s 288(1); ''asset'', s 21(1); ''chargeable period'', s 288(1); ''connected'', s 286; ''licence'', s 196(5); ''licensed area'', s 196(5); ''oil'', s 196(5); ''part disposal'', s 21(2); ''trade'', s 288(1), TA 1988 s 832(1).
Cross references—See TCGA 1992 s 196 (interpretation).
Amendments—[1] Words in sub-ss (2), (3) substituted, and words ''and development'' in sub-s (3) and whole of sub-s (8) inserted, by FA 2000 s 68, Sch 19 para 12 with effect for the purposes of income tax and capital gains tax from the year 2000–01 and for the purposes of corporation tax, for accounting periods ending after 31 March 2000.
[2] Sub-ss (2)(*b*), (c), (3)(*a*), (*b*), and words in sub-ss (3), (4), (6), (8) substituted, words in sub-s (3) and definition of ''basis year'', word in sub-s (6), sub-s (5), (6)(*b*) repealed by CAA 2001 ss 578, 580, Sch 2 para 79, Sch 4 with effect for income tax purposes, as respects allowances and charges falling to be made for chargeable periods ending after 5 April 2001, and for corporation tax purposes, as respects allowances and charges falling to be made for chargeable periods ending after 31 March 2001.

196 Interpretation of sections 194 and 195

(1) For the purposes of section 194, a [UK licence][1] relates to an undeveloped area at any time if—

(*a*) for no part of the licensed area has consent for development been granted to the licensee by the Secretary of State on or before that time; and

(*b*) for no part of the licensed area has a programme of development been served on the licensee or approved by the Secretary of State on or before that time.

[(1A) For the purposes of section 194 a licence other than a UK licence relates to an undeveloped area at any time if, at that time—

(*a*) no development has actually taken place in any part of the licensed area; and

(*b*) no condition for the carrying out of development anywhere in that area has been satisfied—

(i) by the grant of any consent by the authorities of a country or territory exercising jurisdiction in relation to the area; or

(ii) by the approval or service on the licensee, by any such authorities, of any programme of development.][1]

(2) Subsections (4) and (5) of section 36 of the Finance Act 1983 (meaning of "development") shall have effect in relation to [subsections (1) and (1A) above][1] as they have effect in relation to subsection (2) of that section.

(3) In relation to a licence under the Petroleum (Production) Act (Northern Ireland) 1964 any reference in subsection (1) above to the Secretary of State shall be construed as a reference to the Department of Economic Development.

(4) In relation to a disposal to which section 194 applies of a licence under which the buyer acquires an interest in the licence only so far as it relates to part of the licensed area, any reference in subsection (1) or subsection (3) of that section or subsection (1) above to the licensed area shall be construed as a reference only to that part of the licensed area to which the buyer's acquisition relates.

[(5) In sections 194 and 195 and this section—

"foreign oil concession" means any right to search for or win overseas petroleum, being a right conferred or exercisable (whether or not by virtue of a licence) in relation to a particular area;

"interest" in relation to a licence, includes, where there is an agreement which—

(*a*) relates to oil from the whole or any part of the licensed area, and

(*b*) was made before the extraction of the oil to which it relates,

any entitlement under that agreement to, or to a share of, either that oil or the proceeds of its sale;

"licence" means any UK licence or foreign oil concession;

"licensed area" (subject to subsection (4) above)—

(*a*) in relation to a UK licence, has the same meaning as in Part I of the Oil Taxation Act 1975; and

(*b*) in relation to a foreign oil concession, means the area to which the concession applies;

"licensee"—

(*a*) in relation to a UK licence, has the same meaning as in Part I of the Oil Taxation Act 1975; and

(*b*) in relation to a foreign oil concession, means the person with the concession or any person having an interest in it;

"oil"—

(*a*) except in relation to a UK licence, means any petroleum (within the meaning of [Part I of the Petroleum Act 1998][2]); and

(*b*) in relation to such a licence, has the same meaning as in Part I of the Oil Taxation Act 1975;

"overseas petroleum" means any oil that exists in its natural condition at a place to which neither [Part I of the Petroleum Act 1998][2] nor the Petroleum (Production) Act (Northern Ireland) 1964 applies; and

"UK licence" means a licence within the meaning of Part I of the Oil Taxation Act 1975.][1]

[(5A) References in sections 194 and 195 to a part disposal of a licence shall include references to the disposal of any interest in a licence.][1]

(6) In section 194—

(*a*) "exploration work", in relation to any area, means work carried out for the purpose of searching for oil anywhere in that area;

(*b*) "appraisal work", in relation to any area, means work carried out for the purpose of ascertaining the extent or characteristics of any oil-bearing area the whole or part of which lies in the area concerned or what the reserves of oil of any such oil-bearing area are.

Commentary—*Simon's Direct Tax Service* **D4.1025.**
Amendments—[1] Words in sub-ss (1), (2) substituted, sub-s (1A) inserted, sub-ss (5), (5A) substituted for sub-s (5) by FA 1996 s 181(1)–(4) with effect in relation to disposals after 12 September 1995 and sub-ss (5), (5A) as so inserted have effect, and are deemed always to have had effect, for the construction of s 195 *ante* in its application to disposals before that date (see also FA 1996 s 181(5) for transitional provision regarding former enactments).
[2] Words in sub-s (5) substituted by the Petroleum Act 1998 s 50, Sch 4 para 32 with effect from 15 February 1999 (by virtue of SI 1999/161).

197 Disposals of interests in oil fields etc: ring fence provisions

(1) This section applies where in pursuance of a transfer by a participator in an oil field of the whole or part of his interest in the field, there is—

    (*a*) a disposal of an interest in oil to be won from the oil field; or

    (*b*) a disposal of an asset used in connection with the field;

and section 12 of the Oil Taxation Act 1975 (interpretation of Part I of that Act) applies for the interpretation of this subsection and the reference to the transfer by a participator in an oil field of the whole or part of his interest in the field shall be construed in accordance with paragraph 1 of Schedule 17 to the Finance Act 1980.

(2) In this section ''material disposal'' means—

    (*a*) a disposal falling within paragraph (*a*) or paragraph (*b*) of subsection (1) above; or

    (*b*) the sale of an asset referred to in section ...[1] 179(3) where the asset was acquired by the chargeable company (within the meaning of that section) on a disposal falling within one of those paragraphs.

(3) For any chargeable period in which a chargeable gain or allowable loss accrues to any person (''the chargeable person'') on a material disposal (whether taking place in that period or not), subject to subsection (6) below there shall be aggregated—

    (*a*) the chargeable gains accruing to him in that period on such disposals, and

    (*b*) the allowable losses accruing to him in that period on such disposals,

and the lesser of the 2 aggregates shall be deducted from the other to give an aggregate gain or, as the case may be, an aggregate loss for that chargeable period.

(4) For the purposes of tax in respect of chargeable gains—

    (*a*) the several chargeable gains and allowable losses falling within paragraphs (*a*) and (*b*) of subsection (3) above shall be left out of account; and

    (*b*) the aggregate gain or aggregate loss referred to in that subsection shall be treated as a single chargeable gain or allowable loss accruing to the chargeable person in the chargeable period concerned on the notional disposal of an asset; and

    (*c*) if in any chargeable period there is an aggregate loss, then, except as provided by subsection (5) below, it shall not be allowable as a deduction against any chargeable gain arising in that or any later period, other than an aggregate gain treated as accruing in a later period by virtue of paragraph (*b*) above (so that the aggregate gain of that later period shall be reduced or extinguished accordingly); and

    (*d*) if in any chargeable period there is an aggregate gain, no loss shall be deducted from it except in accordance with paragraph (*c*) above; and

    (*e*) without prejudice to any indexation allowance which was taken into account in determining an aggregate gain or aggregate loss under subsection (3) above, no further indexation allowance shall be allowed on a notional disposal referred to in paragraph (*b*) above.

(5) In any case where—

    (*a*) by virtue of subsection (4)(*b*) above, an aggregate loss is treated as accruing to the chargeable person in any chargeable period, and

    (*b*) before the expiry of the period of 2 years beginning at the end of the chargeable period concerned, the chargeable person makes a claim under this subsection,

the whole, or such portion as is specified in the claim, of the aggregate loss shall be treated for the purposes of this Act as an allowable loss arising in that chargeable period otherwise than on a material disposal.

(6) In any case where a loss accrues to the chargeable person on a material disposal made to a person who is connected with him—

    (*a*) the loss shall be excluded from those referred to in paragraph (*b*) of subsection (3) above and, accordingly, shall not be aggregated under that subsection; and

    (*b*) except as provided by subsection (7) below, section 18 shall apply in relation to the loss as if, in subsection (3) of that section, any reference to a disposal were a reference to a disposal which is a material disposal; and

    (*c*) to the extent that the loss is set against a chargeable gain by virtue of paragraph (*b*) above, the gain shall be excluded from those referred to in paragraph (*a*) of subsection (3) above and, accordingly, shall not be aggregated under that subsection.

(7) In any case where—

    (*a*) the losses accruing to the chargeable person in any chargeable period on material disposals to a connected person exceed the gains accruing to him in that chargeable period on material disposals made to that person at a time when they are connected persons, and

    (*b*) before the expiry of the period of 2 years beginning at the end of the chargeable period concerned, the chargeable person makes a claim under this subsection,

the whole, or such part as is specified in the claim, of the excess referred to in paragraph (*a*) above shall be treated for the purposes of section 18 as if it were a loss accruing on a disposal in that chargeable period, being a disposal which is not a material disposal and which is made by the chargeable person to the connected person referred to in paragraph (*a*) above.

(8) Where a claim is made under subsection (5) or subsection (7) above, all such adjustments shall be made whether by way of discharge or repayment of tax or otherwise, as may be required in consequence of the operation of that subsection.

Commentary—*Simon's Direct Tax Service* **D4.1024.**
Definitions—"Allowable loss", ss 8(2), 16, 288(1); "asset", s 21(1); "chargeable gain", s 15(2); "chargeable period", s 288(1); "company", ss 99, 288(1); "connected", s 286; "indexation allowance", s 53.
Amendments—¹ Words in sub-s (2)(*b*) repealed by FA 2000 s 156, Sch 40 Pt II(12) with effect from 28 July 2000.

198 Replacement of business assets used in connection with oil fields

(1) If the consideration which a person obtains on a material disposal is applied, in whole or in part, as mentioned in subsection (1) of section 152 or 153, that section shall not apply unless the new assets are taken into use, and used only, for the purposes of the ring fence trade.

(2) Subsection (1) above has effect notwithstanding subsection (8) of section 152.

(3) Where section 152 or 153 applies in relation to any of the consideration on a material disposal, the asset which constitutes the new assets for the purposes of that section shall be conclusively presumed to be a depreciating asset, and section 154 shall have effect accordingly, except that—

(*a*) the reference in subsection (2)(*b*) of that section to a trade carried on by the claimant shall be construed as a reference solely to his ring fence trade; and
(*b*) subsections (4) to (7) of that section shall be omitted.

(4) In any case where sections 152 to 154 have effect in accordance with subsections (1) to (3) above, the operation of section 175 shall be modified as follows—

(*a*) only those members of a group which actually carry on a ring fence trade shall be treated for the purposes of those sections as carrying on a single trade which is a ring fence trade; and
(*b*) only those activities which, in relation to each individual member of the group, constitute its ring fence trade shall be treated as forming part of that single trade.

(5) In this section—

(*a*) "material disposal" has the meaning assigned to it by section 197; and
(*b*) "ring fence trade" means a trade consisting of either or both of the activities mentioned in paragraphs (*a*) and (*b*) of subsection (1) of section 492 of the Taxes Act.

Commentary—*Simon's Direct Tax Service* **D4.1024.**
Definitions—"Asset", s 21(1); "the Taxes Act", s 288(1).
Modifications—TCGA 1992 Sch 7AB paras 1, 9 (modification of this section for the purposes of TCGA 1992 s 179B (as inserted by FA 2002 s 43) which relates to the roll-over of degrouping charge on business assets).

199 Exploration or exploitation assets: deemed disposals

(1) Where an exploration or exploitation asset which is a mobile asset ceases to be chargeable in relation to a person by virtue of ceasing to be dedicated to an oil field in which he, or a person connected with him, is or has been a participator, he shall be deemed for all purposes of this Act—

(*a*) to have disposed of the asset immediately before the time when it ceased to be so dedicated, and
(*b*) immediately to have reacquired it,

at its market value at that time.

(2) Where a person who is not resident and not ordinarily resident in the United Kingdom ceases to carry on a trade in the United Kingdom through a branch or agency, he shall be deemed for all purposes of this Act—

(*a*) to have disposed immediately before the time when he ceased to carry on the trade in the United Kingdom through a branch or agency of every asset to which subsection (3) below applies, and
(*b*) immediately to have reacquired every such asset,

at its market value at that time.

(3) This subsection applies to any exploration or exploitation asset, other than a mobile asset, used in or for the purposes of the trade at or before the time of the deemed disposal.

(4) A person shall not be deemed by subsection (2) above to have disposed of an asset if, immediately after the time when he ceases to carry on the trade in the United Kingdom through a branch or agency, the asset is used in or for the purposes of exploration or exploitation activities carried on by him in the United Kingdom or a designated area.

(5) Where in a case to which subsection (4) above applies the person ceases to use the asset in or for the purposes of exploration or exploitation activities carried on by him in the United Kingdom or a designated area, he shall be deemed for all purposes of this Act—

(*a*) to have disposed of the asset immediately before the time when he ceased to use it in or for the purposes of such activities, and
(*b*) immediately to have reacquired it,

at its market value at that time.

(6) For the purposes of this section an asset is at any time a chargeable asset in relation to a person if, were it to be disposed of at that time, any chargeable gains accruing to him on the disposal—

(*a*) would be gains in respect of which he would be chargeable to capital gains tax under section 10(1), or

(*b*) would form part of his chargeable profits for corporation tax purposes by virtue of section 10(3).

(7) In this section—

(*a*) "exploration or exploitation asset" means an asset used in connection with exploration or exploitation activities carried on in the United Kingdom or a designated area;

(*b*) "designated area" and "exploration or exploitation activities" have the same meanings as in section 276; and

(*c*) the expressions "dedicated to an oil field" and "participator" shall be construed as if this section were included in Part I of the Oil Taxation Act 1975.

Commentary—*Simon's Direct Tax Service* **D4.1024.**
Definitions—"Asset", s 21(1); "branch or agency", s 10(6); "connected", s 286; "market value", ss 272–274, Sch 11; "ordinarily resident", s 9(1); "resident", s 9(1); "trade", s 288(1), TA 1988 s 832(1).

200 Limitation of losses on disposal of oil industry assets held on 31st March 1982

Commentary—*Simon's Direct Tax Service* **D4.1024.**
Amendment—[1] This section repealed by FA 1994 s 93(7), (11) and Sch 26 Pt V(8) in relation to disposals after 29 November 1993.

Mineral leases

201 Royalties

(1) A person resident or ordinarily resident in the United Kingdom who in any chargeable period is entitled to receive any mineral royalties under a mineral lease or agreement shall be treated for the purposes of this Act as if there accrued to him in that period a chargeable gain equal to one-half of the total of the mineral royalties receivable by him under that lease or agreement in that period.

(2) This section shall have effect notwithstanding any provision of section 119(1) of the Taxes Act making the whole of certain kinds of mineral royalties chargeable to tax under Schedule D, ...[1]

(3) The amount of the chargeable gain treated as accruing to any person by virtue of subsection (1) above shall, notwithstanding any other provision of this Act, be the whole amount calculated in accordance with that subsection, and, accordingly, no reduction shall be made on account of expenditure incurred by that person or of any other matter whatsoever.

(4) In any case where, before the commencement of section 122 of the Taxes Act, for the purposes of the 1979 Act or corporation tax on chargeable gains a person was treated as if there had accrued to him in any chargeable period ending before 6th April 1988 a chargeable gain equal to the relevant fraction, determined in accordance with section 29(3)(*b*) of the Finance Act 1970 of the total of the mineral royalties receivable by him under that lease or agreement in that period, subsection (1) above shall have effect in relation to any mineral royalties receivable by him under that lease or agreement in any later chargeable period with the substitution for the reference to one-half of a reference to the relevant fraction as so determined.

Commentary—*Simon's Direct Tax Service* **C2.1111.**
Definitions—"The 1979 Act", s 288(1); "chargeable gain", s 15(2); "chargeable period", s 288(1); "lease", Sch 8 para 10(1); "ordinarily resident", s 9(1); "resident", s 9(1); "the Taxes Act", s 288(1).
Cross references—See TCGA 1992 s 202(10) (equation of terminal loss with gain treated as accruing under sub-s (1) above). TCGA 1992 s 203 (supplementary provisions).
Amendment—[1] Words in sub-s (2) repealed by FA 1995 s 162, Sch 29 Pt VIII (22) with effect for payments made after 1 May 1995.

202 Capital losses

(1) This section has effect in relation to capital losses which accrue during the currency of a mineral lease or agreement, and applies in any case where, at the time of the occurrence of a relevant event in relation to a mineral lease or agreement, the person who immediately before that event occurred was entitled to receive mineral royalties under the lease or agreement ("the taxpayer") has an interest in the land to which the mineral lease or agreement relates ("the relevant interest").

(2) For the purposes of this section, a relevant event occurs in relation to a mineral lease or agreement—

(*a*) on the expiry or termination of the mineral lease or agreement;

(*b*) if the relevant interest is disposed of, or is treated as having been disposed of by virtue of any provision of this Act.

(3) On the expiry or termination of a mineral lease or agreement the taxpayer shall, if he makes a claim in that behalf, be treated for purposes of tax in respect of chargeable gains as if he had disposed of and immediately reacquired the relevant interest for a consideration equal to its market value, but a claim may not be made under this subsection—

(*a*) if the expiry or termination of the mineral lease or agreement is also a relevant event falling within subsection (2)(*b*) above; nor

(b) unless, on the notional disposal referred to above, an allowable loss would accrue to the taxpayer.

(4) In this section "the terminal loss", in relation to a relevant event in respect of which a claim is made under subsection (3) above, means the allowable loss which accrues to the taxpayer by virtue of the notional disposal occurring on that relevant event by virtue of that subsection.

(5) On making a claim under subsection (3) above, the taxpayer shall specify whether he requires the terminal loss to be dealt with in accordance with subsection (6) or subsections (9) to (11) below.

(6) Where the taxpayer requires the loss to be dealt with in accordance with this subsection it shall be treated as an allowable loss accruing to him in the chargeable period in which the mineral lease or agreement expires.

(7) If on the occurrence of a relevant event falling within subsection (2)(b) above, an allowable loss accrues to the taxpayer on the disposal or notional disposal which constitutes that relevant event, the taxpayer may make a claim under this subsection requiring the loss to be dealt with in accordance with subsections (9) to (11) below and not in any other way.

(8) In subsections (9) to (11) below "the terminal loss" in relation to a relevant event in respect of which a claim is made under subsection (7) above means the allowable loss which accrues to the taxpayer as mentioned in that subsection.

(9) Where, as a result of a claim under subsection (3) or (7) above, the terminal loss is to be dealt with in accordance with this subsection, then, subject to subsection (10) below, it shall be deducted from or set off against the amount on which the taxpayer was chargeable to capital gains tax, or as the case may be corporation tax, for chargeable periods preceding that in which the relevant event giving rise to the terminal loss occurred and falling wholly or partly within the period of 15 years ending with the date of that event.

(10) The amount of the terminal loss which, by virtue of subsection (9) above, is to be deducted from or set off against the amount on which the taxpayer was chargeable to capital gains tax, or as the case may be corporation tax, for any chargeable period shall not exceed the amount of the gain which in that period was treated, by virtue of section 201(1), as accruing to the taxpayer in respect of mineral royalties under the mineral lease or agreement in question; and subject to this limit any relief given to the taxpayer by virtue of subsection (9) above shall be given as far as possible for a later rather than an earlier chargeable period.

(11) If in any case where relief has been given to the taxpayer in accordance with subsections (9) and (10) above there remains an unexpended balance of the terminal loss which cannot be applied in accordance with those subsections, there shall be treated as accruing to the taxpayer in the chargeable period in which the relevant event occurs an allowable loss equal to that unexpended balance.

Commentary—*Simon's Direct Tax Service* **B3.416, C2.1111.**
Definitions—"Allowable loss", ss 8(2), 16, 288(1); "chargeable gain", s 15(2); "chargeable period", s 288(1); "land", s 288(1); "lease", Sch 8 para 10(1); "market value", ss 272–274, Sch 11.
Cross references—See TCGA 1992 s 203 (supplementary provisions).

203 Provisions supplementary to sections 201 and 202

(1) Subsections (5) to (7) of section 122 of the Taxes Act (meaning of "minerals" etc) shall apply for the interpretation of this section and sections 201 and 202 as they apply for the interpretation of that section.

(2) No claim under section 202(3) or (7) shall be allowed unless it is made within 6 years from the date of the relevant event by virtue of which the taxpayer is entitled to make the claim.

(3) All such repayments of tax shall be made as may be necessary to give effect to any such claim.

Commentary—*Simon's Direct Tax Service* **B3.416.**
Definition—"The Taxes Act", s 288(1).

CHAPTER III
INSURANCE

204 Policies of insurance

(1) The rights of the insurer under any policy of insurance shall not constitute an asset on the disposal of which a gain may accrue, whether the risks insured relate to property or not; and the rights of the insured under any policy of insurance of the risk of any kind of damage to, or the loss or depreciation of, assets shall constitute an asset on the disposal of which a gain may accrue only to the extent that those rights relate to assets on the disposal of which a gain may accrue or might have accrued.

(2) Notwithstanding subsection (1) above, sums received under a policy of insurance of the risk of any kind of damage to, or the loss or depreciation of, assets are for the purposes of this Act, and in particular for the purposes of section 22, sums derived from the assets.

(3) Where any investments or other assets are or have been, in accordance with a policy issued in the course of life assurance business carried on by an insurance company, transferred to the policy holder on or after 6th April 1967, the policy holder's acquisition of the assets and the disposal of

them to him shall be deemed to be, for the purposes of this Act, for a consideration equal to the market value of the assets.

(4) In subsections (1) and (2) above "policy of insurance" does not include a policy of assurance on human life and in subsection (3) "life assurance business" and "insurance company" have the same meaning as in Chapter I of Part XII of the Taxes Act.

Commentary—*Simon's Direct Tax Service* **C1.409.**
Simon's Tax Cases—s 204(1), (2), *IRC v Montgomery* [1975] STC 182*.
Definitions—"Asset", s 21(1); "company", ss 99, 288(1); "market value", ss 272–274, Sch 11; "the Taxes Act", s 288(1).

205 Disallowance of insurance premiums as expenses

Without prejudice to the provisions of section 39, there shall be excluded from the sums allowable as a deduction in the computation of the gain accruing on the disposal of an asset any premiums or other payments made under a policy of insurance of the risk of any kind of damage or injury to, or loss or depreciation of, the asset.

Commentary—*Simon's Direct Tax Service* **C2.220.**
Definition—"Asset", s 21(1).

206 Underwriters

Amendments—This section repealed by FA 1993 Sch 23 Pt III (12) with effect from the year 1992–93, as respects sub-s (1) and with effect from the year 1994–95 as respects sub-ss (2)–(5).

207 Disposal of assets in premiums trust fund etc

Amendments—This section repealed by FA 1993 Sch 23 Pt III (12) with effect from the underwriting year 1994.

208 Premiums trust funds: indexation

Amendments—This section repealed by FA 1993 Sch 23 Pt III (12) with effect from the underwriting year 1994.

209 Interpretation, regulations about underwriters etc

Amendments—This section repealed by FA 1993 Sch 23 Pt III (12) with effect from the year 1992–93 as respects sub-ss (3)–(5) and with effect from the year 1994–95 as respects sub-ss (1), (2), (6).

210 Life assurance and deferred annuities

(1) This section has effect as respects any policy of assurance or contract for a deferred annuity on the life of any person.

(2) No chargeable gain shall accrue on the disposal of, or of an interest in, the rights under any such policy of assurance or contract except where the person making the disposal is not the original beneficial owner and acquired the rights or interest for a consideration in money or money's worth.

(3) Subject to subsection (2) above, the occasion of—

    (*a*) the payment of the sum or sums assured by a policy of assurance, or
    (*b*) the transfer of investments or other assets to the owner of a policy of assurance in accordance with the policy,

and the occasion of the surrender of a policy of assurance, shall be the occasion of a disposal of the rights under the policy of assurance.

(4) Subject to subsection (2) above, the occasion of the payment of the first instalment of a deferred annuity, and the occasion of the surrender of the rights under a contract for a deferred annuity, shall be the occasion of a disposal of the rights under the contract for a deferred annuity and the amount of the consideration for the disposal of a contract for a deferred annuity shall be the market value at that time of the right to that and further instalments of the annuity.

Commentary—*Simon's Direct Tax Service* **C1.409.**
Statement of Practice SP 4/92—Capital gains rebasing elections.
Revenue Internal Guidance—Capital Gains Manual CG 69040–69047 (general explanation of this section).
CG 69060–69063 (partnerships; circumstances in which exemption applies).
CG 69080, 69081 (policies linked to unit trusts).
CG 69100–69143 (insurance agents; acquisition and disposals of "books"—financial interests held by agents in their agencies).
Definitions—"Asset", s 21(1); "chargeable gain", s 15(2); "market value", ss 272–274, Sch 11.

211 Transfers of business

[(1) This section applies where an insurance business transfer scheme has effect to transfer business which consists of the effecting or carrying out of contracts of long-term insurance from one person ("the transferor") to another ("the transferee").][4]

[(1A) In subsection (1)—

    "insurance business transfer scheme" means a scheme falling within section 105 of the Financial Services and Markets Act 2000, including an excluded scheme falling within Case 2, 3 or 4 of subsection (3) of that section;

"contracts of long-term insurance" means contracts which fall within Part II of Schedule 1 to the Financial Services and Markets Act 2000 (Regulated Activities) Order 2001.][4]

(2) ...[3] Where this section applies section 139 shall not be prevented from having effect in relation to any asset included in the transfer by reason that—

    (a) the transfer is not part of a scheme of reconstruction [within the meaning of that section][5] ...[6], [or][3]

    (b) ...[3]

    (c) the asset is within subsection (2) of that section;

and where section 139 applies by virtue of paragraph (a) above the references in subsection (5) of that section to the reconstruction ...[6] shall be construed as references to the transfer.

[(2A) Where section 139 has effect in relation to an asset by virtue of subsection (2) above, the reference in subsection (1A) of that section to section 10(3) shall be construed as a reference to section 11(2)(b), (c), (d) or (e) of the Taxes Act.][3]

(3) ...[3]

Commentary—*Simon's Direct Tax Service* **D4.528.**
Statement of Practice SP 7/93—Revenue's interpretation of provisions allowing deferral of corporation tax when a life insurance company transfers the whole or part of its long term business to another company.
Revenue & other press releases—IR 27-7-90 (clearance applications details).
Revenue Internal Guidance—Life assurance manual Chapter 16, para 16.11 (this section does not affect entitlement to relief under s 139 (reconstructions)).
Definitions—"Asset", s 21(1); "chargeable gain", s 15(2); "company", ss 99, 288(1); "double taxation relief arrangements", s 288(1).
Cross references—See TCGA 1992 Sch 7B para 9A (modification of this section in the case of its application to an overseas life insurance company; reference in sub-s (1) above to a transfer of the whole or part of a company's long term business to be treated as including any qualifying overseas trade within TA 1988 Sch 19AC para 4A).
Modification—Sub-para (1) is modified in relation to specified transactions by the Friendly Societies (Modification of the Corporation Tax Acts) Regulations, SI 1997/473 reg 44.
Amendments—[1] "(b)" substituted for "(c)" in sub-s (2)(b) by FA 1993 s 90 in relation to transfers made after 16 July 1992.
[2] Words in sub-s (3) repealed by FA 1994 s 251(1), (11) and Sch 26 Pt VIII(1) where the transfer is made after 29 November 1993.
[3] Words in sub-s (2) and whole of sub-s (3) repealed, word in sub-s (2) and whole of sub-s (2A) inserted, by FA 2000 ss 102, 156, Sch 29 para 30, Sch 40 Pt II(12) with effect for disposals made after 31 March 2000.
[4] Sub-ss (1), (1A) substituted for sub-s (1) by the Financial Services and Markets Act 2000 (Consequential Amendments) (Taxes) Order, SI 2001/3629 arts 61, 66 with effect from 1 December 2001 immediately after the coming into force of the Financial Services and Markets Act 2000 ss 411, 432(1), Sch 20. SI 2001/3629 art 66 has effect in relation to any transfer under a scheme falling within the Financial Services and Markets Act 2000 s 105, including an excluded scheme falling within Case 2, 3 or 4 of the Financial Services and Markets Act 2000 s 105(3).
[5] Words inserted by FA 2002 s 45, Sch 9 paras 5(1), (11), 7 with effect for shares or debentures issued after 16 April 2002. The reference to shares or debentures includes any interests falling to be treated as shares or debentures for the purposes of TCGA 1992 s 135 or 136 as substituted by FA 2002 Sch 9.
[6] Words "or amalgamation" repealed by FA 2002 s 141, Sch 40 Pt 3(2) with effect in accordance with FA 2002 Sch 9 paras 7, 8.

[211A Gains of insurance company from venture capital investment partnership

Schedule 7AD to this Act has effect with respect to the gains of an insurance company from a venture capital investment partnership.][1]

Amendments—[1] This section inserted by FA 2002 s 85 with effect from 24 July 2002.

212 Annual deemed disposal of holdings of unit trusts etc

(1) Where at the end of an accounting period the assets of an insurance company's [long-term insurance][10] fund include—

    (a) rights under an authorised unit trust, or

    (b) relevant interests in an offshore fund,

then, subject to the following provisions of this section and to section 213, the company shall be deemed for the purposes of corporation tax on capital gains to have disposed of and immediately reacquired each of the assets concerned at its market value at that time.

(2) Subsection (1) above shall not apply to assets linked solely to pension business [or life reinsurance business][7] or to assets of the overseas life assurance fund, ...[1]

[(2A) Subsection (1) above shall not apply to assets falling by virtue of paragraph 4 of Schedule 10 to the Finance Act 1996 (company holdings in unit trusts) to be treated for the accounting period in question as representing rights under a creditor relationship of the company.][9]

(3), (4) ...[2]

(5) For the purposes of this section an interest is a "relevant interest in an offshore fund" if—

    (a) it is a material interest in an offshore fund for the purposes of Chapter V of Part XVII of the Taxes Act, or

    [(b) it would be such an interest if either or both of the assumptions mentioned in subsection (6A) below were made.][5]

(6) ...[2]

[(6A) The assumptions referred to in subsection (5)(b) above are—

(a) that the companies, unit trust schemes and arrangements referred to in paragraphs (a) to (c) of subsection (1) of section 759 of the Taxes Act are not limited to those which are also collective investment schemes;

(b) that the shares and interests excluded by subsections (6) and (8) of that section are limited to shares or interests in trading companies.][6]

(7) In this section "trading company" means a company—

(a) whose business consists of the carrying on of insurance business, or the carrying on of any other trade which does not consist to any extent of dealing in commodities, currency, securities, debts or other assets of a financial nature, or

(b) whose business consists wholly or mainly of the holding of shares or securities of trading companies which are its 90 per cent subsidiaries;

and in this section and sections 213 [to 214A][3] other expressions have the same meanings as in Chapter I of Part XII of the Taxes Act.

[(7A) In a case where the profits of a company's life assurance business are charged to tax in accordance with Case I of Schedule D subsection (1) above has effect subject to section 440B(5) of the Taxes Act.][8]

(8) ...[4]

Commentary—*Simon's Direct Tax Service* **D4.527.**
Note—By virtue of FA 1990 s 46 (Appointed Day) Order, SI 1991/2860, the appointed day for the purposes of sub-s (8) above is 1 January 1992. FA 1990 s 46 is re-enacted by this section.
Definitions—"Accounting period", TA 1988 s 834(1); "asset", s 21(1); "authorised unit trust", s 99; "company", ss 99, 288(1); "insurance company", TA 1988 s 431(2); "life reinsurance business", TA 1988 s 431(2); "long term business fund", TA 1988 s 431(2); "market value", ss 272–274, Sch 11; "overseas life assurance fund", TA 1988 s 431(2); "pension business", s 431(2); "shares", s 288(1); "the Taxes Act", s 288(1), TA 1988 s 832(1); "trade", s 288(1), TA 1988 s 832(1); "unit trust scheme", s 99.
Cross references—See TCGA 1992 s 214 (transitional provisions).
TCGA 1992 Sch 7A para 1(8) (restriction on set-off of a loss on a disposal under this section suffered by a company before it becomes a member of a group).
TCGA 1992 Sch 7B paras 1, 10 (modification of this section in the case of its application to an overseas life insurance company in relation to accounting periods beginning after 31 December 1992).
FA 1993 s 91(1) (this section has effect in relation to accounting periods beginning after 31 December 1992 and does not have effect in relation to any earlier accounting period).
Modification—This section is modified so far as it applies to the life or endowment business carried on by friendly societies and non-directive societies by the Friendly Societies (Modification of the Corporation Tax Acts) Regulations, SI 1997/473 reg 45.
Sub-s (2) modified by SI 1998/1871 reg 23 in relation to individual savings account business of insurance companies, with effect from 6 April 1999.
Amendments—[1] Words in sub-s (2) repealed by FA 1993 s 91(2)(b) and Sch 23 Pt III (8) in relation to accounting periods beginning after 31 December 1992.
[2] Sub-ss (3), (4), (6) repealed by FA 1993 s 91(2)(b) and Sch 23 Pt III (8).
[3] Words in sub-s (7) substituted by FA 1993 s 91(3).
[4] Sub-s (8) repealed by FA 1993 Sch 23 Pt III (8) in relation to accounting periods beginning after 31 December 1992.
[5] Sub-s (5)(b) substituted by FA 1995 s 134(6), (10), with effect where it falls to be decided whether an interest is, at any time after 28 November 1994, a relevant interest in an offshore fund.
[6] Sub-s (6A) inserted by FA 1995 s 134(6), (10), s 134(7), (10).
[7] Words in sub-s (2) inserted by FA 1995 s 134(6), (10), s 134(7), (10), Sch 8 paras 9(2), 57, with effect for accounting periods beginning after 31 December 1994.
[8] Sub-s (7A) inserted by FA 1995 s 134(6), (10), s 134(7), (10), Sch 8 para 28(5).
[9] Sub-s (2A) inserted by FA 1996 ss 104, 105(1), Sch 14 para 63 with effect in relation to accounting periods ending after 31 March 1996, subject to transitional provisions in FA 1996 Sch 15.
[10] Words in sub-s (1) substituted by the Financial Services and Markets Act 2000 (Consequential Amendments) (Taxes) Order, SI 2001/3629 arts 61, 73(1)(a) with effect from 1 December 2001 immediately after the coming into force of the Financial Services and Markets Act 2000 ss 411, 432(1), Sch 20.

213 Spreading of gains and losses under section 212

(1) Any chargeable gains or allowable losses which would otherwise accrue on disposals deemed by virtue of section 212 to have been made at the end of a company's accounting period shall be treated as not accruing to it, but instead—

(a) there shall be ascertained the difference ("the net amount") between the aggregate of those gains and the aggregate of those losses, and

(b) one-seventh of the net amount shall be treated as a chargeable gain or, where it represents an excess of losses over gains, as an allowable loss accruing to the company at the end of the accounting period, and

(c) a further one-seventh shall be treated as a chargeable gain or, as the case may be, as an allowable loss accruing at the end of each succeeding accounting period until the whole amount has been accounted for.

[(1A) Subsection (1) above shall not apply to chargeable gains or allowable losses except so far as they are gains or losses which—

(a) are referable to basic life assurance and general annuity business; or

(b) would (apart from that subsection) be taken into account in computing the profits of any business treated as a separate business under section 458 of the Taxes Act;

and that subsection shall apply separately in relation to the gains and losses falling within paragraph (a) above and those falling within paragraph (b) above for the purpose of determining what chargeable gains or allowable losses so referable are to be treated as accruing under that subsection and what chargeable gains or allowable losses to be so taken into account are to be treated as so accruing.][1]

(2) For any accounting period of less than one year, the fraction of one-seventh referred to in subsection (1)(c) above shall be proportionately reduced; and where this subsection has had effect in relation to any accounting period before the last for which subsection (1)(c) above applies, the fraction treated as accruing at the end of that last accounting period shall also be adjusted appropriately.

(3) [Subject to subsection (3A) below,][5] where—

(a) the net amount for an accounting period of an insurance company represents an excess of gains over losses,

(b) the net amount for one of the next 6 accounting periods (after taking account of any reductions made by virtue of this subsection) represents an excess of losses over gains,

(c) there is (after taking account of any such reductions) no net amount for any intervening accounting period,

[(ca) none of the intervening accounting periods is an accounting period in which the company joined a group of companies, and][5]

(d) within 2 years after the end of the later accounting period the company makes a claim for the purpose in respect of the whole or part of the net amount for that period,

the net amounts for both the earlier and the later period shall be reduced by the amount in respect of which the claim is made.

[(3A) Subsection (3) above shall have effect where the company in question joins a group of companies in the later period, as if a claim could not be made in respect of the net amount for that period except to the extent (if any) that the net amount is an amount which, assuming there to be gains accruing to the company immediately after the beginning of that period, would fall to be treated under paragraph 4 of Schedule 7AA as a qualifying loss in relation to those gains.

(3B) References in subsections (3) and (3A) above to a company joining a group of companies shall be construed in accordance with paragraph 1 of Schedule 7AA as if those references were contained in that Schedule.][6]

(4) Subject to subsection (5) below, where a company ceases to carry on [long-term][8] business before the end of the last of the accounting periods for which subsection (1)(c) above would apply in relation to a net amount, the fraction of that amount that is treated as accruing at the end of the accounting period ending with the cessation shall be such as to secure that the whole of the net amount has been accounted for.

(5) [Subject to subsections (5A) to (7) below][4] where [an insurance business transfer scheme has effect to transfer business which consists of the effecting or carrying out of contracts of long-term insurance from one person ("the transferor") to another ("the transferee")][7], any chargeable gain or allowable loss which (assuming that the transferor had continued to carry on the business transferred) would have accrued to the transferor by virtue of subsection (1) above after the transfer shall instead be deemed to accrue to the transferee.

[(5A) Subsection (5) above shall not apply where the transferee is resident outside the United Kingdom unless the business to which the transfer relates is carried on by the transferee, for a period beginning with the time when the transfer takes effect, through a branch or agency in the United Kingdom.][4]

(6) Where subsection (5) above has effect, the amount of the gain or loss accruing at the end of the first accounting period of the transferee ending after the day when the transfer takes place shall be calculated as if that accounting period began with the day after the transfer.

(7) Where the transfer is of part only of the transferor's [long-term][8] business, subsection (5) above shall apply only to such part of any amount to which it would otherwise apply as is appropriate.

(8) Any question arising as to the operation of subsection (7) above shall be determined by the Special Commissioners who shall determine the question in the same manner as they determine appeals; but both the transferor and transferee shall be entitled to appear and be heard or to make representations in writing.

(9) ...[2]

Commentary—*Simon's Direct Tax Service* D4.527.
Definitions—"Allowable loss", ss 8(2), 16, 288(1); "branch or agency", s 10(6); "basic life assurance and general annuity business", TA 1988 s 431(2); "chargeable gain", s 15(2); "company", ss 99, 288(1); "insurance company", TA 1988 s 431(2); "long term business", TA 1988 s 431(2); "resident", s 9(1).
Cross references—See TCGA 1992 s 214A(2) (claim by an insurance company under s 214A for the reduction of certain chargeable gains).
TCGA 1992 Sch 7B paras 1, 11 (modification of sub-s (4) above in the application of this section to an overseas life insurance company in relation to events occurring in accounting periods beginning after 31 December 1992).
Modification—Sub-s (1A) is modified so far as it applies to the life or endowment business carried on by friendly societies, and sub-s (5) is modified in relation to specified transactions by the Friendly Societies (Modification of the Corporation Tax Acts) Regulations, SI 1997/473 regs 46, 47.
Sub-s (1A) is modified in applying life assurance provisions of the Corporation Tax Acts to insurance companies carrying on capital redemption business with effect for accounting periods ending after 30 June 1999: see Insurance Companies (Capital Redemption Business) (Modification of the Corporation Tax Acts) Regulations, SI 1999/498 reg 11.
Amendments—[1] Sub-s (1A) inserted by FA 1993 s 91(4).
[2] Sub-s (9) repealed by FA 1993 Sch 23 Pt III (8) in relation to accounting periods beginning after 31 December 1992.

³ ...
⁴ Words in sub-s (5) inserted, and whole of sub-s (5A) inserted, by FA 1995 s 53, Sch 9 para 4.
⁵ Words in sub-s (3) inserted, and sub-s (3)(ca) substituted by FA 1998 s 137(3) with effect in relation to any intervening period ending on or after 17 March 1998.
⁶ Sub-ss (3A), (3B) inserted by FA 1998 s 137(4) with effect in any case where the earlier accounting period is one ending on or after 17 March 1998.
⁷ Words in sub-s (5) substituted by the Financial Services and Markets Act 2000 (Consequential Amendments) (Taxes) Order, SI 2001/3629 arts 61, 67 with effect from 1 December 2001 immediately after the coming into force of the Financial Services and Markets Act 2000 ss 411, 432(1), Sch 20. SI 2001/3629 art 67 has effect in relation to any transfer under a scheme falling within the Financial Services and Markets Act 2000 s 105, including an excluded scheme falling within Case 2, 3 or 4 of the Financial Services and Markets Act 2000 s 105(3).
⁸ Word in sub-ss (4), (7) substituted by SI 2001/3629 arts 61, 73(2)(*a*) with effect from 1 December 2001 immediately after the coming into force of the Financial Services and Markets Act 2000 ss 411, 432(1), Sch 20.

214 Transitional provisions

(1) In this section—

    (*a*) "section 212 assets" means rights under authorised unit trusts and relevant interests in offshore funds which are assets of a company's long term business fund;

    (*b*) "linked section 212 assets" means section 212 assets which are linked assets;

    (*c*) "relevant linked liabilities", in relation to a company, means such of the liabilities of its basic life assurance and general annuity business as are liabilities in respect of benefits under pre-commencement policies or contracts, being benefits to be determined by reference to the value of linked assets;

    (*d*) "pre-commencement policies or contracts" means—

        (i) policies issued in respect of insurances made before 1st April 1990, and

        (ii) annuity contracts made before that date,

but excluding policies or annuity contracts varied on or after that date so as to increase the benefits secured or to extend the term of the insurance or annuity (any exercise of rights conferred by a policy or annuity contract being regarded for this purpose as a variation);

    (*e*) "basic life assurance and general annuity business" means life assurance business, other than pension business and overseas life assurance business.

(2) The assets which are to be regarded for the purposes of this section as linked solely to an insurance company's basic life assurance and general annuity business at any time before the first accounting period of the company which begins on or after 1st January 1992 are all the assets which at that time—

    (*a*) are or were linked solely to the company's basic life assurance business or general annuity business, or

    (*b*) although not falling within paragraph (*a*) above, would be, or would have been, regarded as linked solely to the company's basic life assurance business, were its general annuity business treated as forming, or having at all times formed, part of its basic life assurance business and as not being a separate category of business.

(3)–(5) ...¹

(6) Subject to subsection (7) below, subsection (9) below applies where—

    (*a*) after the end of 1989 [and before the time when it is first deemed under section 212 to have made a disposal of any assets]² an insurance company exchanges section 212 assets ("the old assets") for other assets ("the new assets") to be held as assets of the long term business fund,

    (*b*) the new assets are not section 212 assets but are assets on the disposal of which any gains accruing would be chargeable gains,

    (*c*) both the old assets and the new assets are linked solely to basic life assurance and general annuity business, or both are neither linked solely to basic life assurance and general annuity business or pension business nor assets of the overseas life assurance fund, and

    (*d*) the company makes a claim for the purpose within 2 years after the end of the accounting period in which the exchange occurs.

(7) Subsection (6) above shall have effect in relation to old assets only to the extent that their amount, when added to the amount of any assets to which subsection (9) below has already applied and which are assets of the same class, does not exceed the aggregate of—

    (*a*) the amount of the assets of the same class included in the long term business fund at the beginning of 1990, other than assets linked solely to pension business and assets of the overseas life assurance fund, and

    (*b*) 110 per cent of the amount of the assets of that class which represents any subsequent increases in the company's relevant linked liabilities in respect of benefits to be determined by reference to the value of assets of that class.

(8) The reference in subsection (7)(*b*) above to a subsequent increase in liabilities is a reference to any amount by which the liabilities at the end of an accounting period ending after 31st December 1989 exceed those at the beginning of the period (or at the end of 1989 if that is later); and for the purposes of that provision the amount of assets which represents an increase in liabilities is the excess of—

(*a*) the amount of assets whose value at the later time is equivalent to the liabilities at that time, over

(*b*) the amount of assets whose value at the earlier time is equivalent to the liabilities at that time.

(9) Where this subsection applies, the insurance company (but not any other party to the exchange) shall be treated for the purposes of corporation tax on capital gains as if the exchange had not involved a disposal of the old assets or an acquisition of the new, but as if the old and the new assets were the same assets acquired as the old assets were acquired.

(10) References in subsections (6) to (9) above to the exchange of assets include references to the case where the consideration obtained for the disposal of assets (otherwise than by way of an exchange within subsection (6)) is applied in acquiring other assets within 6 months after the disposal; and for the purposes of those subsections the time when an exchange occurs shall be taken to be the time when the old assets are disposed of.

(11) Where at any time after the end of 1989 there is a transfer of long term business of an insurance company (''the transferor'') to another company (''the transferee'') in accordance with a scheme sanctioned by a court under [Part I of Schedule 2C to the Insurance Companies Act 1982][3]—

(*a*) if the transfer is of the whole of the long term business of the transferor, subsections (1) to (10) above shall have effect in relation to the assets of the transferee as if that business had at all material times been carried on by him;

(*b*) if the transfer is of part of the long term business of the transferor, those subsections shall have effect in relation to assets of the transferor and the transferee to such extent as is appropriate;

and any question arising as to the operation of paragraph (*b*) above shall be determined by the Special Commissioners who shall determine the question in the same manner as they determine appeals; but both the transferor and the transferee shall be entitled to appear and be heard or to make representations in writing.

Commentary—*Simon's Direct Tax Service* **D4.527.**
Definitions—''Asset'', s 21(1); ''authorised unit trust'', s 99; ''chargeable gain'', s 15(2); ''company'', ss 99, 288(1).
Cross references—See TCGA 1992 s 214A(11) (sub-s (11) of this section to apply for the purposes of s 214A in relation to transfers before 1 January 1993).
TCGA 1992 Sch 7B paras 1, 12 (modification of this section in its application to an overseas life insurance company where the accounting period mentioned in sub-s (6)(*d*) begins after 31 December 1992).
Modifications—Sub-s (1) is modified in its application to the life or endowment business carried on by friendly societies by the Friendly Societies (Modification of the Corporation Tax Acts) Regulations, SI 1997/473 reg 48.
Modification of sub-s (1)(c) in applying life assurance provisions of the Corporation Tax Acts to insurance companies carrying on capital redemption business with effect for accounting periods ending after 30 June 1999: see Insurance Companies (Capital Redemption Business) (Modification of the Corporation Tax Acts) Regulations, SI 1999/498 reg 12.
Amendments—[1] Sub-ss (3)–(5) repealed by FA 1993 s 91(5), Sch 23 Pt III (8) in relation to accounting periods beginning after 31 December 1992.
[2] Words in sub-s (6)(*a*) inserted by FA 1993 s 91(6).
[3] Words in sub-s (11) substituted by FA 1995 s 53, Sch 9 para 1(1), (2)(*d*), with effect for any transfers sanctioned or authorised after 30 June 1994.

[214A Further transitional provisions

(1) This section applies where within two years after the end of an accounting period beginning on or after 1st January 1993 (''the relevant period'')—

(*a*) an insurance company makes a claim for the purposes of this section in relation to that period; and

(*b*) that period is one of the company's first eight accounting periods after the end of 1992.

(2) Where this section applies, section 213 shall have effect as if—

(*a*) the amount of the chargeable gains which—

(i) apart from that section and this section, would be treated as accruing on disposals deemed by virtue of section 212 to have been made at the end of the relevant period, and

(ii) satisfy the condition specified in paragraph (*a*) of section 213(1A),

were reduced by the protected proportion of that amount; and

(*b*) an amount equal to the appropriate part of that reduction were (subject to section 213) a chargeable gain satisfying that condition and accruing at the end of each of the accounting periods in which the reduction is to be taken into account.

(3) For the purposes of subsection (2) above the protected proportion, in relation to the relevant period, of the amount mentioned in paragraph (*a*) of that subsection shall be an amount equal to the amount calculated in accordance with the following formula—

$$\left(A + \frac{B \times C}{D} \right) \times \frac{E}{F} \times \frac{G}{8}$$

(4) In subsection (3) above—

A is so much of the amount mentioned in subsection (2)(*a*) above as represents chargeable gains on section 212 assets which at the end of the relevant period were linked solely to the basic life assurance and general annuity business of the company in question;

B is so much of the amount so mentioned as represents chargeable gains on linked section 212 assets which at the end of that period were partially linked to that business;

C is the amount of such of the closing liabilities at the end of that period of the company's basic life assurance and general annuity business as were liabilities in respect of benefits to be determined by reference to the value of linked section 212 assets which were then partially linked to that business;

D is the amount of all the closing liabilities of the company at the end of that period which were long term business liabilities in respect of benefits to be so determined;

E is the amount of such of the closing liabilities of the company on the relevant date as were relevant linked liabilities in respect of benefits determined by reference to linked section 212 assets;

F is the amount of all the closing liabilities on the relevant date of the company's basic life assurance and general annuity business which were liabilities in respect of such benefits; and;

G is the number of accounting periods in the first nine accounting periods of the company after the end of 1992 which remain after the end of the relevant period or, as the case may be, which would so remain apart from any cessation of the carrying on of any business of the company;

and for the purposes of this subsection the relevant date is, subject to subsection (7) below, the time of the first disposal which is deemed to have been made by the company in question under section 212.

(5) For the purposes of this section and subject to subsection (6) below—

(a) a reduction made under subsection (2) above in relation to the accounting period of any company shall be taken into account in every succeeding accounting period of that company which is included in the first nine accounting periods of that company after the end of 1992; and
(b) in relation to any accounting period in which a reduction is to be taken into account, the appropriate part of the reduction is—

(i) if that is the only accounting period in which it falls to be taken into account, the whole of the reduction; and
(ii) in any other case, the amount of the reduction divided by the number of the accounting periods after the period in which the reduction is made in which the reduction falls to be taken into account or, as the case may be, would so fall apart from any cessation of the carrying on of any business of the company.

(6) Subject to subsection (7) below, where a company ceases to carry on long term business before the end of the first nine accounting periods after the end of 1992, the appropriate part of any reduction in relation to the accounting period ending with the cessation shall be such as to secure that the whole of the reduction has been taken into account under subsection (2)(b) above.

(7) [Subject to subsections (7A) and (8) below][4] where at any time on or after 1st January 1993 there is a transfer of the whole or part of the long term business of an insurance company (''the transferor'') to another company (''the transferee'') in accordance with a scheme sanctioned by a court under [Part I of Schedule 2C to the Insurance Companies Act 1982][3], this section shall have effect so that—

(a) the relevant date for the purposes of subsection (4) above shall be determined in relation to any disposal deemed to have been made after the transfer—

(i) by the transferee, or
(ii) in a case where the transfer is of part of the transferer's long term business, by the transferee or the transferor,

as if there had been no deemed disposals under section 212 before the transfer; and
(b) any reduction which (on the assumption that the transferor had continued to carry on the transferred business) would have fallen to be taken into account under subsection (2)(b) above shall be taken into account instead in relation to the transferee.

[(7A) Paragraph (b) of subsection (7) above shall not apply where the transferee is resident outside the United Kingdom unless the business to which the transfer relates is carried on by the transferee, for a period beginning with the time when the transfer takes effect, through a branch or agency in the United Kingdom.][4]

(8) Where the transfer is of part only of the transferor's long term business, subsection (7)(b) above shall apply only to such part of any reduction to which it would otherwise apply as is appropriate.

(9) Any question arising as to the operation of subsection (8) above shall be determined by the Special Commissioners who shall determine the question in the same manner as they determine appeals; but both the transferor and transferee shall be entitled to appear and be heard or to make representations in writing.

(10) This section shall have effect in relation to any cases in which there is such a transfer as is mentioned in subsection (7) above as if the accounting periods to be taken into account in any calculation for the purposes of this section of the number of accounting periods of the transferee after the end of 1992, and the only accounting periods in relation to which any reduction is to be taken into account under paragraph (b) of that subsection were—

(a) the accounting periods of the transferor which began on or after 1st January 1993 and ended on or before the day of the transfer (including any which, by reference to a transfer in relation to which the transferor is a transferee, are taken into account in accordance with this subsection as accounting periods of the transferor); and
(b) the accounting periods of the transferee ending after the day of the transfer,

and this section shall have effect in relation to such a reduction as if the first accounting period of the transferee to end after the day of the transfer began with the day after the transfer.

(11) For the purposes of this section assets shall be taken to be partially linked to a company's basic life assurance and general annuity business if they are not linked solely to that business and are neither—

    (*a*) linked solely to [any pension business or life reinsurance business of that company or to][2] or long term business of that company other than life assurance business; nor

    (*b*) assets of the company's overseas life assurance fund;

and subsection (1) of section 214 shall apply for the purposes of this section as it applies for the purposes of that section.

(12) Subject to subsection (10) above, the references in this section, in relation to any company, to the first eight accounting periods of a company after the end of 1992 are references to the first accounting period of that company to begin on or after 1st January 1993 and to the succeeding seven accounting periods of that company, and references to the first nine accounting periods of a company after the end of 1992 shall be construed accordingly.][1]

Commentary—*Simon's Direct Tax Service* **D4.527.**
Definitions—''Accounting period'', TA 1988 s 834(1); ''asset'', s 21(1); ''branch or agency'', s 10(6); ''chargeable gain'', s 15(2); ''life reinsurance business'', TA 1988 s 431(2); ''pension business'', s 431(2); ''resident'', s 9(1).
Cross references—See TCGA 1992 Sch 7B paras 1, 13 (modification of this section in its application to an overseas life insurance company).
Modification— Sub-ss (4), (11) modified so far as this section applies to the life or endowment business carried on by friendly societies, and sub-s (7) is modified in relation to specified transactions by the Friendly Societies (Modification of the Corporation Tax Acts) Regulations, SI 1997/473 regs 49, 50.
Sub-s (11)(*a*) modified by SI 1998/1871 reg 23 in relation to individual savings account business of insurance companies, with effect from 6 April 1999.
Amendments—[1] This section inserted by FA 1993 s 91(5).
[2] Words in sub-s (11)(*a*) substituted by FA 1995 Sch 8 paras 9(3), 57, with effect for accounting periods beginning after 31 December 1994.
[3] Words in sub-s (7) substituted by FA 1995 s 53, Sch 9 para 1(1), (2)(*d*), with effect for any transfer sanctioned or authorised after 30 June 1994.
[4] Sub-s (7A), and words in sub-s (7), inserted by FA 1995 s 53, Sch 9 para 5.

[214B Modification of Act in relation to overseas life insurance companies

Schedule 7B (which makes modifications of this Act in relation to overseas life insurance companies) shall have effect.][1]

Commentary—*Simon's Direct Tax Service* **D4.537.**
Amendments—[1] This section inserted by FA 1993 s 102.

CHAPTER IV
MISCELLANEOUS CASES

[Re-organisations of mutual businesses

214C Gains not eligible for taper relief

(1) A gain shall not be eligible for taper relief if—

    (*a*) it is a gain accruing on a disposal in connection with any relevant re-organisation; or

    (*b*) it is a gain accruing on anything which, in a case in which capital sums are received under or in connection with a relevant re-organisation, falls under section 22 to be treated as a disposal.

(2) In this section ''a relevant re-organisation'' means—

    (*a*) any scheme of reconstruction ...[3] applying to a mutual company;

    (*b*) the transfer of the whole of a building society's business to a company in accordance with section 97 and the other applicable provisions of the Building Societies Act 1986; or

    (*c*) the incorporation of a registered friendly society under the Friendly Societies Act 1992.

(3) In this section—

[''insurance company'' means an undertaking carrying on the business of effecting or carrying out contracts of insurance and, for the purposes of this definition, ''contract of insurance'' has the meaning given by Article 3(1) of the Financial Services and Markets Act 2000 (Regulated Activities) Order 2001;][2]

''mutual company'' means—

    (*a*) a mutual insurance company; or

    (*b*) a company of another description carrying on a business on a mutual basis;

''mutual insurance company'' means an insurance company carrying on a business without having a share capital; and

''scheme of reconstruction ...''[3] has the same meaning as in section 136.][1]

Commentary—*Simon's Direct Tax Service* **D4.739.**
Amendments—[1] This section inserted by FA 1998 Sch 21 para 7 with effect from the year 1998–99.
[2] In sub-s (3), definition of ''insurance company'' substituted by the Financial Services and Markets Act 2000 (Consequential Amendments) (Taxes) Order, SI 2001/3629 arts 61, 68 with effect for the purposes of determining whether, at any time after

30 November 2001, a company is a mutual company within the meaning of the Taxation of Chargeable Gains Act 1992 s 214C(3).
[3] Words "or amalgamation" repealed by FA 2002 s 141, Sch 40 Pt 3(2) with effect in accordance with FA 2002 Sch 9 paras 7, 8.

Building societies etc

215 Disposal of assets on amalgamation of building societies etc

If, in the course of or as part of an amalgamation of 2 or more building societies or a transfer of engagements from one building society to another, there is a disposal of an asset by one society to another, both shall be treated for the purposes of corporation tax on chargeable gains as if the asset were acquired from the one making the disposal for a consideration of such amount as would secure that on the disposal neither a gain nor a loss would accrue to the one making the disposal.

Commentary—*Simon's Direct Tax Service* **D4.739.**
Definitions—"Asset", s 21(1); "building society", s 288(1); "chargeable gain", s 15(2).
Cross references—See TCGA 1992 s 35(3)(*d*) (application of rebasing provisions).
TCGA 1992 s 55(5) (indexation allowance by reference to market value on 31 March 1982).
TCGA 1992 Sch 3 para 1 (assets treated as held on 31 March 1982).
TCGA 1992 Sch 4 para 7 (reduction of deferred charges on gains accruing on disposal of assets not held by the vendor on 31 March 1982 but acquired by him from a person who acquired them before that date on a no gain/no loss disposal in accordance with this section).

216 Assets transferred from society to company

(1) This section and section 217 apply where there is a transfer of the whole of a building society's business to a company ("the successor company") in accordance with section 97 and the other applicable provisions of the Building Societies Act 1986.

(2) Where the society and the successor company are not members of the same group at the time of the transfer—

(*a*) they shall be treated for the purposes of corporation tax on capital gains as if any asset disposed of as part of the transfer were acquired by the successor company for a consideration of such amount as would secure that on the disposal neither a gain nor a loss would accrue to the society, and

(*b*) if because of the transfer any company ceases to be a member of the same group as the society, that event shall not cause section ...[1] 179 to have effect as respects any asset acquired by the company from the society or any other member of the same group.

(3) Where the society and the successor company are members of the same group at the time of the transfer but later cease to be so, that later event shall not cause section ...[1] 179 to have effect as respects—

(*a*) any asset acquired by the successor company on or before the transfer from the society or any other member of the same group, or

(*b*) any asset acquired from the society or any other member of the same group by any company other than the successor company which is a member of the same group at the time of the transfer.

(4) Subject to subsection (6) below, where a company which is a member of the same group as the society at the time of the transfer—

(*a*) ceases to be a member of that group and becomes a member of the same group as the successor company, and

(*b*) subsequently ceases to be a member of that group,

section ...[1] 179 shall have effect on that later event as respects any relevant asset acquired by the company otherwise than from the successor company as if it had been acquired from the successor company.

(5) In subsection (4) above "relevant asset" means any asset acquired by the company—

(*a*) from the society, or

(*b*) from any other company which is a member of the same group at the time of the transfer,

when the company and the society, or the company, the society and the other company, were members of the same group.

(6) Subsection (4) above shall not apply if the company which acquired the asset and the company from which it was acquired (one being a 75 per cent subsidiary of the other) cease simultaneously to be members of the same group as the successor company but continue to be members of the same group as one another.

(7) For the purposes of this section "group" shall be construed in accordance with section 170.

Commentary—*Simon's Direct Tax Service* **D4.771–773.**
Definitions—"Asset", s 21(1); "building society", s 288(1); "company", ss 99, 288(1).
Cross references—See TCGA 1992 s 35(3)(*d*) (application of rebasing provisions).
TCGA 1992 s 55(5) (indexation allowance on a non-no gain/no loss disposal after 31 March 1982 of assets acquired on a no gain/no loss acquisition under this section).
TCGA 1992 s 271(4) (exemption from capital gains tax in respect of contractual savings schemes and TESSA).
TCGA 1992 Sch 4 para 7 (reduction of deferred charges on gains accruing on disposal of assets not held by the vendor on 31 March 1982 but acquired by him from a person who acquired them before that date on a no gain/no loss disposal in accordance with this section).

TCGA 1992

FA 2000 Sch 29 para 31 (the main amendments made to TCGA 1992 s 170 by FA 2000 Sch 29 para 1 have effect for the purposes of this section for transfers after 31 March 2000).
Amendments—¹ Words in sub-s (2)(*b*), (3), (4) repealed by FA 2000 s 156, Sch 40 Pt II(12) with effect from 28 July 2000.

217 Shares, and rights to shares, in successor company

(1) Where, in connection with the transfer, there are conferred on members of the society—

(*a*) any rights to acquire shares in the successor company in priority to other persons, or
(*b*) any rights to acquire shares in that company for consideration of an amount or value lower than the market value of the shares, or
(*c*) any rights to free shares in that company,

any such right so conferred on a member shall be regarded for the purposes of tax on chargeable gains as an option (within the meaning of section 144) granted to, and acquired by, him for no consideration and having no value at the time of that grant and acquisition.

(2) Where, in connection with the transfer, shares in the successor company are issued by that company, or disposed of by the society, to a member of the society, those shares shall be regarded for the purposes of tax on chargeable gains—

(*a*) as acquired by the member for a consideration of an amount or value equal to the amount or value of any new consideration given by him for the shares (or, if no new consideration is given, as acquired for no consideration); and
(*b*) as having, at the time of their acquisition by the member, a value equal to the amount or value of the new consideration so given (or, if no new consideration is given, as having no value);

but this subsection is without prejudice to the operation of subsection (1) above, where applicable.

(3) Subsection (4) below applies in any case where—

(*a*) in connection with the transfer, shares in the successor company are issued by that company, or disposed of by the society, to trustees on terms which provide for the transfer of those shares to members of the society for no new consideration; and
(*b*) the circumstances are such that in the hands of the trustees the shares constitute settled property.

(4) Where this subsection applies, then, for the purposes of tax on chargeable gains—

(*a*) the shares shall be regarded as acquired by the trustees for no consideration;
(*b*) the interest of any member in the settled property constituted by the shares shall be regarded as acquired by him for no consideration and as having no value at the time of its acquisition;
(*c*) where a member becomes absolutely entitled as against the trustees to any of the settled property, both the trustees and the member shall be treated as if, on his becoming so entitled, the shares in question had been disposed of and immediately reacquired by the trustees, in their capacity as trustees within section 60(1), for a consideration of such an amount as would secure that on the disposal neither a gain nor a loss would accrue to the trustees (and accordingly section 71 shall not apply in relation to that occasion); and
(*d*) on the disposal by a member of an interest in the settled property, other than the disposal treated as occurring for the purposes of paragraph (*c*) above, any gain accruing shall be a chargeable gain (and accordingly section 76(1) shall not apply in relation to the disposal).

(5) Where, in connection with the transfer, the society disposes of any shares in the successor company, then, for the purposes of this Act, any gains arising on the disposal shall not be chargeable gains.

(6) In this section—

"free shares", in relation to a member of the society, means any shares issued by the successor company, or disposed of by the society, to that member in connection with the transfer but for no new consideration;
"member", in relation to the society, means a person who is or has been a member of it, in that capacity, and any reference to a member includes a reference to a member of any particular class or description;
"new consideration" means consideration other than—

(*a*) consideration provided directly or indirectly out of the assets of the society; or
(*b*) consideration derived from a member's shares or other rights in the society.

(7) References in this section to the case where a member becomes absolutely entitled to settled property as against the trustees shall be taken to include references to the case where he would become so entitled but for being an infant or otherwise under disability.

Commentary—*Simon's Direct Tax Service* **D4.773.**
Revenue & other press releases—IR 21-3-96 and IR 27-3-97 (Revenue views on treatment of cash/shares received by investors on building society conversions, takeovers, mergers).
Definitions—"Absolutely entitled as against trustee", s 60(2); "asset", s 21(1); "chargeable gain", s 15(2); "company", ss 99, 288(1); "issued", s 288(5); "market value", ss 272–274, Sch 11; "settled property", s 68; "shares", s 288(1).
Cross references—See TCGA 1992 s 216(1) (application of this section on transfer of a building society's business to a company).

[Friendly societies][1]

[217A Transfer of assets on incorporation of registered friendly society

(1) This section and section 217B apply where a registered friendly society is incorporated under the Friendly Societies Act 1992 (''the 1992 Act'').

(2) In this section and section 217B—

    (*a*) ''the registered society'' means the society before the incorporation, and

    (*b*) ''the incorporated society'' means the society after the incorporation.

(3) For the purposes of corporation tax on chargeable gains—

    (*a*) any asset of the registered society that by virtue of section 6(2) or (3) of the 1992 Act is transferred to the incorporated society,

    (*b*) any asset of a branch of the registered society that by virtue of section 6(4) of the 1992 Act is transferred to the incorporated society, and

    (*c*) any asset of a branch of the registered society that is identified in a scheme under section 6(5) of the 1992 Act,

shall be taken to be disposed of by the registered society or branch and acquired by the incorporated society on the incorporation for a consideration of such amount as to secure that on the disposal neither a gain nor a loss accrues to the registered society or branch.]*[1]

Commentary—*Simon's Direct Tax Service* **C1.217.**
Definition—''Chargeable gain'', s 15(2).
Amendments—[1] This section inserted by F(No 2)A 1992 Sch 9 paras 21(1), (3), 22 with effect from 19 February 1993 by virtue of F(No 2)A 1992 Sch 9 (Appointed Day) Order, SI 1993/236.

[217B Rights of members in registered society equated with rights in incorporated society

(1) In this section, ''change of membership'' means a change effected by Schedule 4 to the 1992 Act whereby a member of the registered society or of a branch of the registered society becomes a member of the incorporated society or of a branch of the incorporated society.

(2) For the purposes of this Act, a change of membership shall not be taken to involve any disposal or acquisition of an asset by the member concerned, but all the interests and rights in the incorporated society or a branch of the incorporated society that he has immediately after the change, taken together, shall be treated as a single asset which—

    (*a*) was acquired by the first relevant acquisition, and

    (*b*) was added to by any subsequent relevant acquisitions.

(3) In subsection (2) above, ''relevant acquisition'' means an acquisition by which the member acquired any interest or right in the registered society or a branch of the registered society that he had immediately before the change of membership.]*[1]

Commentary—*Simon's Direct Tax Service* **C1.217.**
Definitions—''The incorporated society'', s 217A(2); ''the 1992 Act'', s 217A(1); ''the registered society'', s 217A(2).
Cross references—See TCGA 1992 s 217A (transfer of assets on incorporation).
Amendments—[1] This section inserted by F(No 2)A 1992 Sch 9 paras 21(1), (3), 22 with effect from 19 February 1993 by virtue of F(No 2)A 1992 Sch 9 (Appointed Day) Order, SI 1993/236.

[217C Subsequent disposal of assets by incorporated society etc

(1) Where any asset acquired on a disposal to which section 217A(3) applies is subsequently disposed of by the incorporated society, section 41 shall apply as if any capital allowance made to the registered society in respect of the asset had been made to the incorporated society.

[(2) If the disposal by the incorporated society is in the circumstances mentioned in subsection (8) of section 41, the disposal to which section 217A(3) applies shall for the purposes of that subsection be taken to have been a previous transfer of the asset in such circumstances.]*[2]

Commentary—*Simon's Direct Tax Service* **C1.217.**
Definitions—''The incorporated society'', s 217A(2); ''the registered society'', s 217A(2).
Amendments—[1] This section inserted by F(No 2)A 1992 Sch 9 paras 21(1), (3), 22 with effect from 19 February 1993 by virtue of F(No 2)A 1992 Sch 9 (Appointed Day) Order, SI 1993/236.
[2] Sub-s (2) substituted by FA 2000 s 102, Sch 29 para 32 with effect for cases in which the disposal by the incorporated society is after 31 March 2000.

The Housing Corporation, [the Secretary of State][1]*, Scottish Homes and housing associations*

218 Disposals of land between the Housing Corporation, [the Secretary of State]¹or Scottish Homes and housing associations

(1) Where—

    (*a*) in accordance with a scheme approved under section 5 of the Housing Act 1964 or paragraph 5 of Schedule 7 to the Housing Associations Act 1985 the Housing Corporation acquires from a housing association the association's interest in all the land held by the association for carrying out its objects, or

    (*b*) after the Housing Corporation has so acquired from a housing association all the land so held by it the Corporation disposes to a single housing association of the whole of that land (except any part previously disposed of or agreed to be disposed of otherwise than to a housing association), together with all related assets,

then both parties to the disposal of the land to or, as the case may be, by the Housing Corporation shall be treated for the purposes of corporation tax in respect of chargeable gains as if the land and any related assets disposed of therewith (and each part of that land and those assets) were acquired from the party making the disposal for a consideration of such an amount as would secure that on the disposal neither a gain nor a loss accrued to that party.

(2) In subsection (1) above, "housing association" has the same meaning as in the Housing Associations Act 1985 and "related assets" means, in relation to an acquisition of land by the Housing Corporation, assets acquired by the Corporation in accordance with the same scheme as that land, and in relation to a disposal of land by the Housing Corporation, assets held by the Corporation for the purposes of the same scheme as that land.

(3) This section shall also have effect with the substitution of the words ["the Secretary of State"][1] for the words "the Housing Corporation" and "the Corporation" in each place where they occur.

(4) This section shall also have effect with the substitution of the words "Scottish Homes" for the words "the Housing Corporation" and "the Corporation" in each place where they occur.

Commentary—*Simon's Direct Tax Service* **D4.641.**
Definitions—"Asset", s 21(1); "chargeable gain", s 15(2); "land", s 288(1).
Cross references—See TCGA 1992 s 35(3)(d) (application of rebasing provisions).
TCGA 1992 s 55(5) (indexation allowance on a non-no gain/no loss disposal after 31 March 1982 of assets acquired on a no gain/no loss acquisition under this section).
TCGA 1992 Sch 4 para 7 (reduction of deferred charges on gains accruing on disposal of assets not held by the vendor on 31 March 1982 but acquired by him from a person who acquired them before that date on a no gain/no loss disposal in accordance with this section).
Amendment—[1] Words in the heading, the sidenote and sub-s (3) substituted by the Government of Wales Act 1998 Sch 16 paras 78 and 80 with effect from 1 November 1998, by virtue of the Government of Wales Act 1998 (Commencement No 1) Order 1998, SI 1998/2244.
Prospective amendments—Sub-s (4) to be repealed by the Housing (Scotland) Act 2001 ss 112, 113(1), Sch 10 para 18(1) with effect from such day as the Scottish Ministers may by order appoint.

[219 Disposals by Housing Corporation, [the Secretary of State][2], Scottish Homes and certain housing associations

(1) In any case where—

(a) the Corporation disposes of any land to a relevant housing association, or

(b) a relevant housing association disposes of any land to another relevant housing association, or

(c) in pursuance of a direction of the Corporation given under Part I of the Housing Act 1996 or Part I of the Housing Associations Act 1985 (as the case may be) requiring it to do so, a relevant housing association disposes of any of its property, other than land, to another relevant housing association, or

(d) a relevant housing association or an unregistered self-build society disposes of any land to the Corporation,

both parties to the disposal shall be treated for the purposes of tax on chargeable gains as if the land or property disposed of were acquired from the Corporation, relevant housing association or unregistered self-build society making the disposal for a consideration of such an amount as would secure that on the disposal neither a gain nor a loss accrued to the Corporation or, as the case may be, that association or society.

(2) In this section—"the Corporation" means the Housing Corporation, [the Secretary of State][2] or Scottish Homes; "relevant housing association" means a registered social landlord within the meaning of Part I of the Housing Act 1996 or a registered housing association within the meaning of the Housing Associations Act 1985; "unregistered self-build society" has the same meaning as in the Housing Associations Act 1985.][1]

Commentary—*Simon's Direct Tax Service* **D4.642.**
Definitions—"Chargeable gain", s 15(2); "land", s 288(1).
Cross references—See TCGA 1992 s 35(3)(d) (application of rebasing provisions).
TCGA 1992 s 55(5) (indexation allowance on a non-no gain/no loss disposal after 31 March 1982 of assets acquired on a no gain/no loss acquisition under this section).
TCGA 1992 Sch 4 para 7 (reduction of deferred charges on gains accruing on disposal of assets not held by the vendor on 31 March 1982 but acquired by him from a person who acquired them before that date on a no gain/no loss disposal in accordance with this section).
Amendments—[1] This section substituted by the Housing Act 1996 (Consequential Provisions) Order SI 1996/2325 Sch 2 para 20(1), (2), with effect from 1 October 1996.
[2] Words in the provision heading and sub-s (2) substituted by the Government of Wales Act 1998 Sch 16 paras 79–80 with effect from 1 November 1998, by virtue of the Government of Wales Act 1998 (Commencement No 1) Order 1998, SI 1998/2244.
Prospective amendments—Sub-s (2) to be amended by the Housing (Scotland) Act 2001 ss 112, 113(1), Sch 10 para 18(2) with effect from such day as the Scottish Ministers may by order appoint.

220 Disposals by Northern Ireland housing associations

(1) In any case where—

(a) a registered Northern Ireland housing association disposes of any land to another such association, or (*b*) in pursuance of a direction of the Department of the Environment for Northern Ireland given under Chapter II of Part VII of the Housing (Northern Ireland) Order 1981 requiring it to do so, a registered Northern Ireland housing association disposes of any of its property, other than land, to another such association,

both parties to the disposal shall be treated for the purposes of tax on chargeable gains as if the land or property disposed of were acquired from the association making the disposal for a consideration of such an amount as would secure that on the disposal neither a gain nor a loss accrued to that association.

(2) In subsection (1) above "registered Northern Ireland housing association" means a registered housing association within the meaning of Part VII of the Order referred to in paragraph (*b*) of that subsection.

Commentary—*Simon's Direct Tax Service* **D4.642.**
Definitions—"Chargeable gain", s 15(2); "land", s 288(1).
Cross references—See TCGA 1992 s 35(3)(*d*) (application of rebasing provisions).
TCGA 1992 s 55(5) (indexation allowance on a non-no gain/no loss disposal after 31 March 1982 of assets acquired on a no gain/no loss acquisition under this section).
TCGA 1992 Sch 4 para 7 (reduction of deferred charges on gains accruing on disposal of assets not held by the vendor on 31 March 1982 but acquired by him from a person who acquired them before that date on a no gain/no loss disposal in accordance with this section).

Other bodies

221 Harbour authorities

(1) For the purposes of this Act any asset transferred on the transfer of the trade shall be deemed to be for a consideration such that no gain or loss accrues to the transferor on its transfer; and for the purposes of Schedule 2 the transferee shall be treated as if the acquisition by the transferor of any asset so transferred had been the transferee's acquisition thereof.

(2) This section applies only where the trade transferred is transferred from any body corporate other than a limited liability company to a harbour authority by or under a certified harbour reorganisation scheme (within the meaning of section 518 of the Taxes Act) which provides also for the dissolution of the transferor.

Commentary—*Simon's Direct Tax Service* **D2.503.**
Definitions—"Asset", s 21(1); "company", ss 99, 288(1); "the Taxes Act", s 288(1); "trade", s 288(1), TA 1988 s 832(1).
Cross references—See TCGA 1992 s 35(3)(*d*) (application of rebasing provisions).
TCGA 1992 s 55(5) (indexation allowance by reference to market value on 31 March 1982).
TCGA 1992 Sch 4 para 7 (reduction of deferred charges on gains accruing on disposal of assets not held by the vendor on 31 March 1982 but acquired by him from a person who acquired them before that date on a no gain/no loss disposal in accordance with this section).

PART VII

OTHER PROPERTY, BUSINESSES, INVESTMENTS ETC

Private residences

222 Relief on disposal of private residence

(1) This section applies to a gain accruing to an individual so far as attributable to the disposal of, or of an interest in—

(*a*) a dwelling-house or part of a dwelling-house which is, or has at any time in his period of ownership been, his only or main residence, or
(*b*) land which he has for his own occupation and enjoyment with that residence as its garden or grounds up to the permitted area.

(2) In this section "the permitted area" means, subject to subsections (3) and (4) below, an area (inclusive of the site of the dwelling-house) of 0.5 of a hectare.

[(3) Where the area required for the reasonable enjoyment of the dwelling-house (or of the part in question) as a residence, having regard to the size and character of the dwelling-house, is larger than 0.5 of a hectare, that larger area shall be the permitted area.][1]

(4) Where part of the land occupied with a residence is and part is not within subsection (1) above, then (up to the permitted area) that part shall be taken to be within subsection (1) above which, if the remainder were separately occupied, would be the most suitable for occupation and enjoyment with the residence.

(5) So far as it is necessary for the purposes of this section to determine which of 2 or more residences is an individual's main residence for any period—

(*a*) the individual may conclude that question by notice to the inspector given within 2 years from the beginning of that period but subject to a right to vary that notice by a further notice to the inspector as respects any period beginning not earlier than 2 years before the giving of the further notice,
(*b*) ...[1]
...[1]

(6) In the case of a man and his wife living with him—

(a) there can only be one residence or main residence for both, so long as living together and, where a notice under subsection (5)(a) above affects both the husband and the wife, it must be given by both, ...[1]

(b) ...[1]

(7) In this section and sections 223 to 226, "the period of ownership" where the individual has had different interests at different times shall be taken to begin from the first acquisition taken into account in arriving at the expenditure which under Chapter III of Part II is allowable as a deduction in the computation of the gain to which this section applies, and in the case of a man and his wife living with him—

(a) if the one disposes of, or of his or her interest in, the dwelling-house or part of a dwelling-house which is their only or main residence to the other, and in particular if it passes on death to the other as legatee, the other's period of ownership shall begin with the beginning of the period of ownership of the one making the disposal, and

(b) if paragraph (a) above applies, but the dwelling-house or part of a dwelling-house was not the only or main residence of both throughout the period of ownership of the one making the disposal, account shall be taken of any part of that period during which it was his only or main residence as if it was also that of the other.

(8) If at any time during an individual's period of ownership of a dwelling-house or part of a dwelling-house he—

(a) resides in living accommodation which is for him job-related . . .[2], and

(b) intends in due course to occupy the dwelling-house or part of a dwelling-house as his only or main residence,

this section and sections 223 to 226 shall apply as if the dwelling-house or part of a dwelling-house were at that time occupied by him as a residence.

[(8A) Subject to subsections (8B), (8C) and (9) below, for the purposes of subsection (8) above living accommodation is job-related for a person if—

(a) it is provided for him by reason of his employment, or for his spouse by reason of her employment, in any of the following cases—

(i) where it is necessary for the proper performance of the duties of the employment that the employee should reside in that accommodation;

(ii) where the accommodation is provided for the better performance of the duties of the employment, and it is one of the kinds of employment in the case of which it is customary for employers to provide living accommodation for employees;

(iii) where, there being a special threat to the employee's security, special security arrangements are in force and the employee resides in the accommodation as part of those arrangements;

or

(b) under a contract entered into at arm's length and requiring him or his spouse to carry on a particular trade, profession or vocation, he or his spouse is bound—

(i) to carry on that trade, profession or vocation on premises or other land provided by another person (whether under a tenancy or otherwise); and

(ii) to live either on those premises or on other premises provided by that other person.

(8B) If the living accommodation is provided by a company and the employee is a director of that or an associated company, subsection (8A)(a)(i) or (ii) above shall not apply unless—

(a) the company of which the employee is a director is one in which he or she has no material interest; and

(b) either—

(i) the employment is as a full-time working director, or

(ii) the company is non-profit making, that is to say, it does not carry on a trade nor do its functions consist wholly or mainly in the holding of investments or other property, or

(iii) the company is established for charitable purposes only.

(8C) Subsection (8A)(b) above does not apply if the living accommodation concerned is in whole or in part provided by—

(a) a company in which the borrower or his spouse has a material interest; or

(b) any person or persons together with whom the borrower or his spouse carries on a trade or business in partnership.

(8D) For the purposes of this section—

(a) a company is an associated company of another if one of them has control of the other or both are under the control of the same person; and

(b) "employment", "director", "full-time working director", "material interest" and "control", in relation to a body corporate, have the same meanings as they have for the purposes of Chapter II of Part V of the Taxes Act.][2]

(9) [Subsections (8A)(*b*) and (8C) above][2] shall apply for the purposes of subsection (8) above only in relation to residence on or after 6th April 1983 in living accommodation which is job-related [for the purposes of that section][2].

(10) Apportionments of consideration shall be made wherever required by this section or sections 223 to 226 and, in particular, where a person disposes of a dwelling-house only part of which is his only or main residence.

Commentary—*Simon's Direct Tax Service* C2.1301–1305.
Concession D6—Private residence relief: separated couples.
ESC D21—Private residence relief: late claims in dual residence cases.
ESC D26—Relief for exchange of joint interests.
ESC D33—CGT on compensation and damages. This Concession has been revised.
ESC D37—Private residence relief: relocation arrangements.
ESC D49—Private residence relief: short delay by owner-occupier in taking up residence.
Revenue Interpretation RI 22—Private residence relief: joint but unrelated owner occupiers.
RI 75—Revenue interpretation of scope of the dwellinghouse; sale of a house and garden after it has ceased to be used as a residence; periods of absence; the apportionment rules; elections by married couples; successive interests; deceased person's estates; and disposals by beneficiaries.
RI 89—Revenue interpretation of the application of sub-s (5) to residences occupied under licence.
RI 119—Revenue interpretation of the circumstances in which land is to be regarded as occupied and enjoyed with a residence as its garden or grounds; conditions to be met.
Revenue & other press releases—CCAB June 1976 (private residence exemption will not be lost on a garden where taxpayer ceased to occupy the house before sale, unless the garden had development value).
Hansard 21-3-85 (houseboats may exceptionally qualify as private residences, but are normally exempt assets under s 45).
IR Tax Bulletin February 1992 p 10 (advice on determining the size and location of the "permitted area" of land associated with a dwelling).
Revenue Internal Guidance—Capital gains manual CG 64230–64330 (meaning and definition of "dwelling-house" in sub-s (1)(*a*))
CG 64240–64373 (identification of garden and grounds).
CG 64377–64394 (the test of occupation and enjoyment is to be applied at the date of disposal; period between contract and disposal is dealt with at CG 64381–64384; separate interests in the land and dwelling house are dealt with at CG 64390–64394).
CG 64427–64456 (meaning of "residence" in sub-s (1)).
CG 64470–64473, 64536–64537 (only residences in which the taxpayer has an interest are considered: residence occupied under a licence is not considered).
CG 64486–64489 (a dwelling house which is not one of the taxpayer's residences cannot be nominated under sub-s (5)).
CG 64495–64503 (time limit for a notice under sub-s (5)(*a*): a new period begins when there is a change in the combination of residences).
CG 64523 (notice under sub-s (5)(*a*) must be signed by the taxpayer, not by his agent).
CG 64555–64572 (application of sub-s (8)).
CG 64603 (the gain eligible for relief may arise on the grant, assignment or surrender of a lease, the grant of an easement, surrender of rights of occupation, receipt of a capital sum, as well as on a simple disposal).
CG 64800–64834 (meaning of "permitted area" in sub-s (1)).
CG 64860–64870 (procedures involving the District Valuer).
CG 64882–64888 (appeals procedure).
CG 64895–64901 (valuations and apportionments).
CG 64932, 64944–64945 (worked examples illustrating sub-s (7)).
CG 64955 (transfer between spouses: worked example).
CG 65300–65378 (transfer of interest in a residence following separation or divorce).
Simon's Tax Cases—*Moore v Thompson* [1986] STC 170*; *Owen v Elliott* [1990] STC 469*; *Griffin v Craig-Harvey* [1994] STC 54*; *Wakeling v Pearce* [1995] STC (SCD) 96*.
s 222(1), *Green v IRC* [1982] STC 485*; *Goodwin v Curtis* [1998] STC 475*.
s 222(1)(*a*), *Batey v Wakefield* [1981] STC 521; *Westcott v Woolcombers Ltd* [1987] STC 600*; *Lewis v Lady Rook* [1992] STC 171*; *Honour v Norris* [1992] STC 304*.
s 222(1)(*b*), *Varty v Lynes* [1976] STC 508*.
s 222(2), *Green v IRC* [1982] STC 485*.
s 222(3), *Longson vBaker (Inspector of Taxes)* [2001] STC 6.
Definitions—"Land", s 288(1); "legatee", s 64(2), (3); "notice", s 288(1); "the Taxes Act", s 288(1).
Cross references—See TCGA 1992 s 223(1) (private residence exemption).
TCGA 1992 s 223(4) (treatment of gain under this section in relation to dwelling-house let as residential accommodation during ownership).
TCGA 1992 s 225 (private residence occupied under terms of settlement).
TCGA 1992 s 226 (relief under this section in respect of private residence occupied by dependent relative before 6 April 1988).
TCGA 1992 s 230 (roll-over relief for private residence not available where it qualifies for relief under this section).
TCGA 1992 s 241(6) (restriction of relief under this section where private residence is let as furnished holiday letting).
TCGA 1992 Sch 11 para 19 (transitional provisions: notice period in sub-s (5) above to include notice given before the end of the year 1966–67, if later).
Amendments—[1] Sub-s (3) substituted, and words omitted from sub-ss (5), (6) repealed, by FA 1996 s 134(1), (2), Sch 20 para 59, Sch 41 Pt V(10) with effect from the year 1996–97.
[2] Words in sub-s (8)(*a*) repealed, words in sub-s (9) substituted and sub-ss (8A)–(8D) inserted, by FA 1999 s 38(8), Sch 4 paras 17, 18(4), Sch 20 Pt III para 7 with effect from the year 2000–01.

223 Amount of relief

(1) No part of a gain to which section 222 applies shall be a chargeable gain if the dwelling-house or part of a dwelling-house has been the individual's only or main residence throughout the period of ownership, or throughout the period of ownership except for all or any part of the last 36 months of that period.

(2) Where subsection (1) above does not apply, a fraction of the gain shall not be a chargeable gain, and that fraction shall be—

    (*a*) the length of the part or parts of the period of ownership during which the dwelling-house or the part of the dwelling-house was the individual's only or main residence, but inclusive of the last 36 months of the period of ownership in any event, divided by (*b*) the length of the period of ownership.

(3) For the purposes of subsections (1) and (2) above—

    (*a*) a period of absence not exceeding 3 years (or periods of absence which together did not exceed 3 years), and in addition

    (*b*) any period of absence throughout which the individual worked in an employment or office all the duties of which were performed outside the United Kingdom, and in addition

    (*c*) any period of absence not exceeding 4 years (or periods of absence which together did not exceed 4 years) throughout which the individual was prevented from residing in the dwelling-house or part of the dwelling-house in consequence of the situation of his place of work or in consequence of any condition imposed by his employer requiring him to reside elsewhere, being a condition reasonably imposed to secure the effective performance by the employee of his duties,

shall be treated as if in that period of absence the dwelling-house or the part of the dwelling-house was the individual's only or main residence if both before and after the period there was a time when the dwelling-house was the individual's only or main residence.

(4) Where a gain to which section 222 applies accrues to any individual and the dwellinghouse in question or any part of it is or has at any time in his period of ownership been wholly or partly let by him as residential accommodation, the part of the gain, if any, which (apart from this subsection) would be a chargeable gain by reason of the letting, shall be such a gain only to the extent, if any, to which it exceeds whichever is the lesser of—

    (*a*) the part of the gain which is not a chargeable gain by virtue of the provisions of subsections (1) to (3) above or those provisions as applied by section 225; and

    (*b*) £40,000.

(5) Where at any time the number of months specified in subsections (1) and (2)(*a*) above is 36, the Treasury may by order amend those subsections by substituting references to 24 for the references to 36 in relation to disposals on or after such date as is specified in the order.

(6) Subsection (5) above shall also have effect as if 36 (in both places) read 24 and as if 24 read 36.

(7) In this section—

    ''period of absence'' means a period during which the dwelling-house or the part of the dwelling-house was not the individual's only or main residence and throughout which he had no residence or main residence eligible for relief under this section; and

    ''period of ownership'' does not include any period before 31st March 1982.

Commentary—*Simon's Direct Tax Service* **C2.1307.**
Concession D3—Private residence exemption: periods of absence (*a*).
D4—Private residence exemption: periods of absence (*b*).
Statement of Practice SP 4/92—Capital gains rebasing elections.
Revenue & other press releases—CCAB TR500 10-3-83 (where absence exceeds three years or four years under s 223(3) only the excess does not qualify for exemption, provided other conditions are satisfied).
Hansard 27–1–93 (receipt of ''rent a room relief'' F(No 2)A 1992 s 59, Sch 10 does not normally cause a CGT liability to arise on disposal of main residence).
Simon's Tax Cases—*Owen v Elliott* [1990] STC 469*; *Lewis v Lady Rook* [1992] STC 171*; *Honour v Norris* [1992] STC 304*, *Griffin v Craig-Harvey* [1994] STC 54*.
s 223(1), *Makins v Elson* [1977] STC 46*; *Green v IRC* [1982] STC 485*.
s 223(4), *Owen v Elliott* [1990] STC 469*.
Definitions—''Chargeable gain'', s 15(2); ''period of ownership'', s 222(7).
Cross references—See TCGA 1992 s 222(8) (job-related living accommodation intended to be used in due course as private residence).
TCGA 1992 s 222(10) (apportionment of consideration required by this section).
TCGA 1992 s 224 (amount of relief: further provisions).
TCGA 1992 s 225 (private residence occupied under the terms of a settlement).
TCGA 1992 s 226 (relief under this section in respect of private residence occupied by dependent relative before 6 April 1988).
TCGA 1992 s 241(6) (furnished holiday lettings).
TCGA 1992 Sch 2 para 16(10) (time apportionment of gain or loss on disposal of private residence owned on 6 April 1965).

224 Amount of relief: further provisions

(1) If the gain accrues from the disposal of a dwelling-house or part of a dwelling-house part of which is used exclusively for the purpose of a trade or business, or of a profession or vocation, the gain shall be apportioned and section 223 shall apply in relation to the part of the gain apportioned to the part which is not exclusively used for those purposes.

(2) If at any time in the period of ownership there is a change in what is occupied as the individual's residence, whether on account of a reconstruction or conversion of a building or for any other reason, or there have been changes as regards the use of part of the dwelling-house for the purpose of a trade or business, or of a profession or vocation, or for any other purpose, the relief given by section 223 [may be adjusted in a manner which is just and reasonable][1].

(3) Section 223 shall not apply in relation to a gain if the acquisition of, or of the interest in, the dwelling-house or the part of a dwelling-house was made wholly or partly for the purpose of realising a gain from the disposal of it, and shall not apply in relation to a gain so far as attributable to any expenditure which was incurred after the beginning of the period of ownership and was incurred wholly or partly for the purpose of realising a gain from the disposal.

Commentary—*Simon's Direct Tax Service* **C2.1309.**
Revenue Interpretation RI 75—Revenue interpretation of application of sub-s (3).

Revenue Internal Guidance—Capital gains manual CG 64670–64674 (in small cases, any reasonable apportionment under sub-s (1) is accepted: otherwise the District Valuer will apportion the consideration by reference to the value of the respective parts of the property; worked example at CG 64674).
CG 64771 (worked example illustrating sub-s (2)).
CG 65200–65231 (sub-s (3) applies *inter alia* to trading transactions and to transactions caught by TA 1988 s 776).
CG 65240–65271 (explanation of sub-s (3) with worked examples).
Simon's Tax Cases—s 224(2), *Green v IRC* [1982] STC 485*.
s 224(3), *Jones v Wilcock* [1996] STC (SCD) 389.
Definitions—''Period of ownership'', s 222(7); ''trade'', s 288(1), TA 1988 s 832(1).
Cross references—See TCGA 1992 s 222(8) (job-related living accommodation intended to be used in due course as private residence).
TCGA 1992 s 222(10) (apportionment of consideration required by this section).
TCGA 1992 s 225 (private residence occupied under the terms of a settlement).
TCGA 1992 s 226 (relief under this section in respect of private residence occupied by dependent relative before 6 April 1988).
Amendments—¹ Words in sub-s (2) substituted by FA 1996 s 134(1), (2), Sch 20 para 60 with effect from the year 1996–97.

225 Private residence occupied under terms of settlement

Sections 222 to 224 shall also apply in relation to a gain accruing to a trustee on a disposal of settled property being an asset within section 222(1) where, during the period of ownership of the trustee, the dwelling-house or part of the dwelling-house mentioned in that subsection has been the only or main residence of a person entitled to occupy it under the terms of the settlement, and in those sections as so applied—

(a) references to the individual shall be taken as references to the trustee except in relation to the occupation of the dwelling-house or part of the dwelling-house, and
(b) the notice which may be given to the inspector under section 222(5)(a) shall be a joint notice by the trustee and the person entitled to occupy the dwelling-house or part of the dwelling-house.

Commentary—*Simon's Direct Tax Service* C2.1306.
Concession D5—Private residence exemption: property held by personal representatives.
Revenue Internal Guidance—Capital gains manual CG 65400–65491 (Revenue interpretation of this section).
Simon's Tax Cases—*Sansom v Peay* [1976] STC 494*.
Definitions—''Asset'', s 21(1); ''inspector'', s 288(1); ''notice'', s 288(1); ''period of ownership'', s 222(7); ''settled property'', s 68.
Cross references—See TCGA 1992 s 222(8) (job-related living accommodation intended to be used in due course as private residence).
TCGA 1992 s 222(10) (apportionment of consideration required by this section).
TCGA 1992 s 223(4) (treatment of gain under this section in relation to dwelling-house let as residential accommodation during ownership).

226 Private residence occupied by dependent relative before 6th April 1988

(1) Subject to subsection (3) below, this section applies to a gain accruing to an individual so far as attributable to the disposal of, or of an interest in, a dwelling-house or part of a dwelling-house which, on 5th April 1988 or at any earlier time in his period of ownership, was the sole residence of a dependent relative of the individual, provided rent-free and without any other consideration.

(2) If the individual so claims, such relief shall be given in respect of it and its garden or grounds as would be given under sections 222 to 224 if the dwelling-house (or part of the dwelling-house) had been the individual's only or main residence in the period of residence by the dependent relative, and shall be so given in addition to any relief available under those sections apart from this section.

(3) If in a case within subsection (1) above the dwelling-house or part ceases, whether before 6th April 1988 or later, to be the sole residence (provided as mentioned above) of the dependent relative, any subsequent period of residence beginning on or after that date by that or any other dependent relative shall be disregarded for the purposes of subsection (2) above.

(4) Not more than one dwelling-house (or part of a dwelling-house) may qualify for relief as being the residence of a dependent relative of the claimant at any one time nor, in the case of a man and his wife living with him, as being the residence of a dependent relative of the claimant or of the claimant's husband or wife at any one time.

(5) ...¹

(6) In this section ''dependent relative'' means, in relation to an individual—

(a) any relative of his or of his wife who is incapacitated by old age or infirmity from maintaining himself, or
(b) his or his wife's mother who, whether or not incapacitated, is either widowed, or living apart from her husband, or a single woman in consequence of dissolution or annulment of marriage.

(7) If the individual mentioned in subsection (6) above is a woman the references in that subsection to the individual's wife shall be construed as references to the individual's husband.

Commentary—*Simon's Direct Tax Service* C2.1311.
Concession D20—The condition that the house be provided rent-free without consideration regarded as satisfied where the dependent relative pays all or part of the council tax and cost of repairs attributable to normal wear and tear, certain other payments also permitted provided no set income is received.
Revenue & other press releases—ICAEW TR739 13-2-89 (if a dependent relative is obliged to move temporarily from home to a nursing home or to nurse another individual, absence is not treated as a cessation of occupation).
Revenue Internal Guidance—Capital gains manual CG 65550–65681 (Revenue interpretation of this section).
Definitions—''Period of ownership'', s 222(7); ''rent'', Sch 8 para 10(1).
Cross references—See TCGA 1992 s 222(8) (job-related living accommodation intended to be used in due course as private residence).

TCGA 1992

TCGA 1992 s 222(10) (apportionment of consideration required by this section).

Amendments—¹ Sub-s (5) repealed by FA 1996 s 134(1), (2), Sch 20 para 61, Sch 41 Pt V(10) with effect from the year 1996–97.

Employee share ownership trusts

227 Conditions for roll-over relief

(1) Relief is available under section 229(1) where each of the 6 conditions set out in subsections (2) to (7) below is fulfilled.

(2) The first condition is that a person ("the claimant") makes a disposal of shares, or his interest in shares, to the trustees of a trust which—

    (a) is a qualifying employee share ownership trust at the time of the disposal, and

    (b) was established by a company ("the founding company") which immediately after the disposal is a trading company or the holding company of a trading group.

(3) The second condition is that the shares—

    (a) are shares in the founding company,

    (b) form part of the ordinary share capital of the company,

    (c) are fully paid up,

    (d) are not redeemable, and

    (e) are not subject to any restrictions other than restrictions which attach to all shares of the same class or a restriction authorised by paragraph 7(2) of Schedule 5 to the Finance Act 1989.

(4) The third condition is that, at any time in the entitlement period, the trustees—

    (a) are beneficially entitled to not less than 10 per cent of the ordinary share capital of the founding company,

    (b) are beneficially entitled to not less than 10 per cent of any profits available for distribution to equity holders of the founding company, and

    (c) would be beneficially entitled to not less than 10 per cent of any assets of the founding company available for distribution to its equity holders on a winding-up.

(5) The fourth condition is that the claimant obtains consideration for the disposal and, at any time in the acquisition period, all the amount or value of the consideration is applied by him in making an acquisition of assets or an interest in assets ("replacement assets") which—

    (a) are, immediately after the time of the acquisition, chargeable assets in relation to the claimant, and

    (b) are not shares in, or debentures issued by, the founding company or a company which is (at the time of the acquisition) in the same group as the founding company;

but the preceding provisions of this subsection shall have effect without the words ", at any time in the acquisition period," if the acquisition is made pursuant to an unconditional contract entered into in the acquisition period.

(6) The fifth condition is that, at all times in the proscribed period, there are no unauthorised arrangements under which the claimant or a person connected with him may be entitled to acquire any of the shares, or an interest in or right deriving from any of the shares, which are the subject of the disposal by the claimant.

(7) The sixth condition is that no chargeable event occurs in relation to the trustees in—

    (a) the chargeable period in which the claimant makes the disposal,

    (b) the chargeable period in which the claimant makes the acquisition, or

    (c) any chargeable period falling after that mentioned in paragraph (a) above and before that mentioned in paragraph (b) above.

Commentary—*Simon's Direct Tax Service* **C1.431.**

Definitions—"Acquisition period", s 228(3); "asset", s 21(1); "chargeable asset", s 228(6); "chargeable event", s 228(7), FA 1989 s 69; "chargeable period", s 288(1); "class" (shares), s 288(1); "company", ss 99, 288(1); "connected", s 286; "entitlement period", s 228(2); "group", ss 170, 228(8); "holding company", s 228(8), Sch 6 para 1; "issued", s 288(5); "ordinary share capital", s 228(9); "proscribed period", s 228(4); "qualifying employee share ownership trust", s 228(7), FA 1989 Sch 5; "shares", s 288(1); "trading company", s 228(8), Sch 6 para 1; "trading group", s 228(8), Sch 6 para 1; "unauthorised arrangements", s 228(5).

Cross references—See TCGA 1992 s 228 (supplementary provisions).

TCGA 1992 s 229(2) (relief where part only of the amount or value mentioned in sub-s (5) above is applied).

TCGA 1992 s 230 (dwelling-houses: special provisions).

TCGA 1992 s 231 (roll-over relief for shares not available where business expansion scheme relief is claimed).

228 Conditions for relief: supplementary

(1) This section applies for the purposes of section 227.

(2) The entitlement period is the period beginning with the disposal and ending on the expiry of 12 months beginning with the date of the disposal.

(3) The acquisition period is the period beginning with the disposal and ending on the expiry of 6 months beginning with—

    (a) the date of the disposal, or

    (b) if later, the date on which the third condition (set out in section 227(4)) first becomes fulfilled.

(4) The proscribed period is the period beginning with the disposal, and ending on—

(a) the date of the acquisition, or

(b) if later, the date on which the third condition (set out in section 227(4)) first becomes fulfilled.

(5) All arrangements are unauthorised unless—

(a) they arise wholly from a restriction authorised by paragraph 7(2) of Schedule 5 to the Finance Act 1989 or

(b) they only allow one or both of the following as regards shares, interests or rights, namely, acquisition by a beneficiary under the trust and appropriation under an approved profit sharing scheme.

(6) An asset is a chargeable asset in relation to the claimant at a particular time if, were the asset to be disposed of at that time, any gain accruing to him on the disposal would be a chargeable gain, and either—

(a) at that time he is resident or ordinarily resident in the United Kingdom, or

(b) he would be chargeable to capital gains tax under section 10(1) in respect of the gain, or it would form part of his chargeable profits for corporation tax purposes by virtue of section 10(3),

unless (were he to dispose of the asset at that time) the claimant would fall to be regarded for the purposes of any double taxation relief arrangements as not liable in the United Kingdom to tax on any gains accruing to him on the disposal.

(7) The question whether a trust is at a particular time a qualifying employee share ownership trust shall be determined in accordance with Schedule 5 to the Finance Act 1989; and "chargeable event" in relation to trustees has the meaning given by section 69 of that Act.

(8) The expressions "holding company", "trading company" and "trading group" have the meanings given by paragraph 1 of Schedule 6; and "group" (except in the expression "trading group") shall be construed in accordance with section 170.

(9) "Ordinary share capital" in relation to the founding company means all the issued share capital (by whatever name called) of the company, other than capital the holders of which have a right to a dividend at a fixed rate but have no other right to share in the profits of the company.

(10) Schedule 18 to the Taxes Act (group relief: equity holders and profits or assets available for distribution) shall apply for the purposes of section 227(4) as if—

(a) the trustees were a company,

(b) the references to section 413(7) ...¹ of that Act were references to section 227(4),

(c) the reference in paragraph 7(1)(a) to section 413(7) of that Act were a reference to section 227(4), and

(d) paragraph 7(1)(b) were omitted.

Commentary—*Simon's Direct Tax Service* **C1.431.**
Definitions—"Asset", s 21(1); "chargeable gain", s 15(2); "company", ss 99, 288(1); "double taxation relief arrangements", s 288(1); "issued", s 288(5); "ordinarily resident", s 9(1); "resident", s 9(1); "shares", s 288(1); "the Taxes Act", s 288(1).
Cross references—See TCGA 1992 Sch 7B paras 1, 14 (modification of sub-s (6)(b) above in the case of application of this section to an overseas life insurance company in relation to acquisitions made in chargeable periods beginning after 31 December 1992).
FA 2000 Sch 29 para 33 (the main amendments made to TCGA 1992 s 170 by FA 2000 Sch 29 para 1 have effect for the purposes of this section for disposals after 31 March 2000).
Amendments—¹ Words in sub-s (10)(b) repealed by FA 2000 s 156, Sch 40 Pt II(11) and deemed always to have had effect.
Prospective amendment—Words in sub-s (8) will be substituted by FA 1998 s 140(5) with effect from the year 2003–04.

229 The relief

(1) In a case where relief is available under this subsection the claimant shall, on making a claim in the period of 2 years beginning with the acquisition, be treated for the purposes of this Act—

(a) as if the consideration for the disposal were (if otherwise of a greater amount or value) of such amount as would secure that on the disposal neither a gain nor a loss accrues to him, and

(b) as if the amount or value of the consideration for the acquisition were reduced by the excess of the amount or value of the actual consideration for the disposal over the amount of the consideration which the claimant is treated as receiving under paragraph (a) above.

(2) Relief is available under subsection (3) below where—

(a) relief would be available under subsection (1) above but for the fact that part only of the amount or value mentioned in section 227(5) is applied as there mentioned, and

(b) all the amount or value so mentioned except for a part which is less than the amount of the gain (whether all chargeable gain or not) accruing on the disposal is so applied.

(3) In a case where relief is available under this subsection the claimant shall, on making a claim in the period of 2 years beginning with the acquisition, be treated for the purposes of this Act—

(a) as if the amount of the gain accruing on the disposal were reduced to the amount of the part mentioned in subsection (2)(b) above, and

(b) as if the amount or value of the consideration for the acquisition were reduced by the amount by which the gain is reduced under paragraph (a) above.

(4) Nothing in subsection (1) or (3) above shall affect the treatment for the purposes of this Act of the other party to the disposal or of the other party to the acquisition.

(5) The provisions of this Act fixing the amount of the consideration deemed to be given for a disposal or acquisition shall be applied before the preceding provisions of this section are applied.

Commentary—*Simon's Direct Tax Service* **C1.431.**
Revenue Internal Guidance—Capital Gains Manual CG 62070–62150 (operation of this section including worked examples).
Definition—''Chargeable gain'', s 15(2).
Cross references—See TCGA 1992 s 154 (modification of this section in its application to new assets which are depreciating assets).
TCGA 1992 s 227(1) (conditions for relief under sub-s (1) above).
TCGA 1992 s 230 (dwelling-houses: special provisions where a claim is made under this section).
TCGA 1992 s 231 (shares: special provisions where a claim is made under this section).
TCGA 1992 s 232 (effect on relief under sub-s (1) or (3) above if claimant or a connected person owns replacement assets and there is a chargeable event as defined).
TCGA 1992 s 233 (effect on relief under sub-s (1) or (3) above if claimant or a connected person owns new assets and there is a chargeable event as defined).
TCGA 1992 s 234 (effect on relief under this section where new shares replacing old assets are exchanged for qualifying corporate bonds and there is a chargeable event as defined).
TCGA 1992 s 235(1) (inspector may require the trustees to make a return where a claim is made under sub-s (1) or (3) above).
TCGA 1992 s 235(7) (inspector's duty to send a certificate to trustees where sub-s (1) or (3) above has been applied).
TCGA 1992 s 236(1) (prevention of double charge in respect of gain carried forward by virtue of sub-s (1) or (3) above).
FA 2000 s 54 (no claim for relief under sub-s (1) or (3) may be made for a disposal of shares, or an interest in shares, made after 5 April 2001).

230 Dwelling-houses: special provision

(1) Subsection (2) below applies where—

(*a*) a claim is made under section 229,

(*b*) immediately after the time of the acquisition mentioned in section 227(5) and apart from this section, any replacement asset was a chargeable asset in relation to the claimant,

(*c*) the asset is a dwelling-house or part of a dwelling-house or land, and

(*d*) there was a time in the period beginning with the acquisition and ending with the time when section 229(1) or (3) falls to be applied such that, if the asset (or an interest in it) were disposed of at that time, it would be within section 222(1) and the individual there mentioned would be the claimant or the claimant's spouse.

(2) In such a case the asset shall be treated as if, immediately after the time of the acquisition mentioned in section 227(5), it was not a chargeable asset in relation to the claimant.

(3) Subsection (4) below applies where—

(*a*) the provisions of section 229(1) or (3) have been applied,

(*b*) any replacement asset which, immediately after the time of the acquisition mentioned in section 227(5) and apart from this section, was a chargeable asset in relation to the claimant consists of a dwelling-house or part of a dwelling-house or land, and

(*c*) there is a time after section 229(1) or (3) has been applied such that, if the asset (or an interest in it) were disposed of at that time, it would be within section 222(1) and the individual there mentioned would be the claimant or the claimant's spouse.

(4) In such a case—

(*a*) the asset shall be treated as if, immediately after the time of the acquisition mentioned in section 227(5), it was not a chargeable asset in relation to the claimant and adjustments shall be made accordingly, but

(*b*) any gain treated as accruing in consequence of the application of paragraph (*a*) above shall be treated as accruing at the time mentioned in subsection (3)(*c*) above or, if there is more than one such time, at the earliest of them.

(5) Subsection (6) below applies where—

(*a*) a claim is made under section 229,

(*b*) immediately after the time of the acquisition mentioned in section 227(5) and apart from this section, any replacement asset was a chargeable asset in relation to the claimant,

(*c*) the asset was an option to acquire (or to acquire an interest in) a dwelling-house or part of a dwelling-house or land,

(*d*) the option has been exercised, and

(*e*) there was a time in the period beginning with the exercise of the option and ending with the time when section 229(1) or (3) falls to be applied such that, if the asset acquired on exercise of the option were disposed of at that time, it would be within section 222(1) and the individual there mentioned would be the claimant or the claimant's spouse.

(6) In such a case the option shall be treated as if, immediately after the time of the acquisition mentioned in section 227(5), it was not a chargeable asset in relation to the claimant.

(7) Subsection (8) below applies where—

(*a*) the provisions of section 229(1) or (3) have been applied,

(*b*) any replacement asset which, immediately after the time of the acquisition mentioned in section 227(5) and apart from this section, was a chargeable asset in relation to the claimant consisted of an option to acquire (or to acquire an interest in) a dwelling-house or part of a dwelling-house or land,

(*c*) the option has been exercised, and

(*d*) there is a time after section 229(1) or (3) has been applied such that, if the asset acquired on exercise of the option were disposed of at that time, it would be within section 222(1) and the individual there mentioned would be the claimant or the claimant's spouse.

(8) In such a case—

(*a*) the option shall be treated as if, immediately after the time of the acquisition mentioned in section 227(5), it was not a chargeable asset in relation to the claimant and adjustments shall be made accordingly, but

(*b*) any gain treated as accruing in consequence of the application of paragraph (*a*) above shall be treated as accruing at the time mentioned in subsection (7)(*d*) above or, if there is more than one such time, at the earliest of them.

(9) References in this section to an individual include references to a person entitled to occupy under the terms of a settlement.

Commentary—*Simon's Direct Tax Service* **C1.432.**
Definitions—"Asset", s 21(1); "land", s 288(1).

231 Shares: special provision

(1) Subsection (2) below applies where—

(*a*) a claim is made under section 229,

(*b*) immediately after the time of the acquisition mentioned in section 227(5) and apart from this section, any replacement asset was a chargeable asset in relation to the claimant,

(*c*) the asset consists of shares, and

(*d*) in the period beginning with the acquisition and ending when section 229(1) or (3) falls to be applied relief is claimed under Chapter III of Part VII of the Taxes Act ...[1] in respect of the asset.

(2) In such a case the asset shall be treated as if, immediately after the time of the acquisition mentioned in section 227(5), it was not a chargeable asset in relation to the claimant.

(3) Subsection (4) below applies where—

(*a*) the provisions of section 229(1) or (3) have been applied,

(*b*) any replacement asset which, immediately after the time of the acquisition mentioned in section 227(5) and apart from this section, was a chargeable asset in relation to the claimant consists of shares, and

(*c*) after section 229(1) or (3) has been applied relief is claimed under Chapter III of Part VII of the Taxes Act in respect of the asset.

(4) In such a case the asset shall be treated as if, immediately after the time of the acquisition mentioned in section 227(5), it was not a chargeable asset in relation to the claimant and adjustments shall be made accordingly.

(5) Subsection (4) above shall also apply where section 33(1) or (3) of the Finance Act 1990 has applied and the claimant acquired the replacement asset in a chargeable period beginning before 6th April 1992.

Commentary—*Simon's Direct Tax Service* **C1.432.**
Definitions—"Asset", s 21(1); "chargeable period", s 288(1); "shares", s 288(1); "the Taxes Act", s 288(1).
Amendments—[1] Words in sub-s (1)(*d*) repealed by FA 1994 Sch 15 para 34 and Sch 26 Pt V(17).

232 Chargeable event when replacement assets owned

(1) Subsection (3) below applies where—

(*a*) the provisions of section 229(1) or (3) are applied,

(*b*) a chargeable event occurs in relation to the trustees on or after the date on which the disposal is made (and whether the event occurs before or after the provisions are applied),

(*c*) the claimant was neither an individual who died before the chargeable event occurs nor trustees of a settlement which ceased to exist before the chargeable event occurs, and

(*d*) the condition set out below is fulfilled.

(2) The condition is that, at the time the chargeable event occurs, the claimant or a person then connected with him is beneficially entitled to all the replacement assets.

(3) In a case where this subsection applies, the claimant or connected person (as the case may be) shall be deemed for all purposes of this Act—

(*a*) to have disposed of all the replacement assets immediately before the time when the chargeable event occurs, and

(*b*) immediately to have reacquired them,

at the relevant value.

(4) The relevant value is such value as secures on the deemed disposal a chargeable gain equal to—

(*a*) the amount by which the amount or value of the consideration mentioned in section 229(1)(*b*) was treated as reduced by virtue of that provision (where it applied), or

(*b*) the amount by which the amount or value of the consideration mentioned in section 229(3)(*b*) was treated as reduced by virtue of that provision (where it applied).

(5) In a case where subsection (3) above would apply if "all" read "any of" in subsection (2) above, subsection (3) shall nevertheless apply, but as if—

  (a) in subsection (3)(a) "all the replacement assets" read "the replacement assets concerned", and

  (b) the relevant value were reduced to whatever value is just and reasonable.

(6) Subsection (7) below applies where—

  (a) subsection (3) above applies (whether or not by virtue of subsection 5 above), and

  (b) before the time when the chargeable event occurs anything has happened as regards any of the replacement assets such that it can be said that a charge has accrued in respect of any of the gain carried forward by virtue of section 229(1) or (3).

(7) If in such a case it is just and reasonable for subsection (3) above to apply as follows, it shall apply as if—

  (a) the relevant value were reduced (or further reduced) to whatever value is just and reasonable, or

  (b) the relevant value were such value as secures that on the deemed disposal neither a gain nor a loss accrues (if that is just and reasonable);

but paragraph (a) above shall not apply so as to reduce the relevant value below that mentioned in paragraph (b) above.

(8) For the purposes of subsection (6)(b) above the gain carried forward by virtue of section 229(1) or (3) is the gain represented by the amount which by virtue of either of those provisions falls to be deducted from the expenditure allowable in computing a gain accruing on the disposal of replacement assets (that is, the amount found under subsection (4)(a) or (b) above, as the case may be).

(9) In this section "chargeable event" in relation to trustees has the meaning given by section 69 of the Finance Act 1989.

Commentary—*Simon's Direct Tax Service* C1.433.
Definitions—"Asset", s 21(1); "chargeable gain", s 15(2); "connected", s 286.
Cross references—See TCGA 1992 s 233 (chargeable event when replacement property owned).
TCGA 1992 s 234 (chargeable event when qualifying corporate bonds owned).
TCGA 1992 s 235 (Board's power to obtain information for the purposes of this section).
TCGA 1992 s 236 (prevention of double charge under this section and ss 152–158).

233 Chargeable event when replacement property owned

(1) Subsection (3) below applies where—

  (a) paragraphs (a) to (c) of section 232(1) are fulfilled, and

  (b) the condition set out below is fulfilled.

(2) The condition is that—

  (a) before the time when the chargeable event occurs, all the gain carried forward by virtue of section 229(1) or (3) was in turn carried forward from all the replacement assets to other property on a replacement of business assets, and

  (b) at the time the chargeable event occurs, the claimant or a person then connected with him is beneficially entitled to all the property.

(3) In a case where this subsection applies, the claimant or connected person (as the case may be) shall be deemed for all purposes of this Act—

  (a) to have disposed of all the property immediately before the time when the chargeable event occurs, and

  (b) immediately to have reacquired it,

at the relevant value.

(4) The relevant value is such value as secures on the deemed disposal a chargeable gain equal to—

  (a) the amount by which the amount or value of the consideration mentioned in section 229(1)(b) was treated as reduced by virtue of that provision (where it applied), or

  (b) the amount by which the amount or value of the consideration mentioned in section 229(3)(b) was treated as reduced by virtue of that provision (where it applied).

(5) In a case where subsection (3) above would apply if "all the" in subsection (2) above (in one or more places) read "any of the", subsection (3) shall nevertheless apply, but as if—

  (a) in subsection (3)(a) "all the property" read "the property concerned", and

  (b) the relevant value were reduced to whatever value is just and reasonable.

(6) Subsection (7) below applies where—

  (a) subsection (3) above applies (whether or not by virtue of subsection (5) above), and

  (b) before the time when the chargeable event occurs anything has happened as regards any of the replacement assets, or any other property, such that it can be said that a charge has accrued in respect of any of the gain carried forward by virtue of section 229(1) or (3).

(7) If in such a case it is just and reasonable for subsection (3) above to apply as follows, it shall apply as if—

(*a*) the relevant value were reduced (or further reduced) to whatever value is just and reasonable, or

(*b*) the relevant value were such value as secures that on the deemed disposal neither a gain nor a loss accrues (if that is just and reasonable);

but paragraph (*a*) above shall not apply so as to reduce the relevant value below that mentioned in paragraph (*b*) above.

(8) For the purposes of subsections (2) and (6)(*b*) above the gain carried forward by virtue of section 229(1) or (3) is the gain represented by the amount which by virtue of either of those provisions falls to be deducted from the expenditure allowable in computing a gain accruing on the disposal of replacement assets (that is, the amount found under subsection (4)(*a*) or (*b*) above, as the case may be).

(9) For the purposes of subsection (2) above a gain is carried forward from assets to other property on a replacement of business assets if, by one or more claims under sections 152 to 158, the chargeable gain accruing on a disposal of the assets is reduced, and as a result an amount falls to be deducted from the expenditure allowable in computing a gain accruing on the disposal of the other property.

Commentary—*Simon's Direct Tax Service* **C1.433.**
Definitions—''Asset'', s 21(1); ''chargeable gain'', s 15(2); ''connected'', s 286.
Cross references—See TCGA 1992 s 235 (Board's power to obtain information for the purposes of this section).
TCGA 1992 s 236 (prevention of double charge under this section and ss 152–158).

234 Chargeable events when bonds owned

(1) Subsection (3) below applies where—

  (*a*) paragraphs (*a*) to (*c*) of section 232(1) are fulfilled, and
  (*b*) the condition set out below is fulfilled.

(2) The condition is that—

  (*a*) all the replacement assets were shares (new shares) in a company or companies,
  (*b*) there has been a transaction to which section 116(10) applies and as regards which all the new shares constitute the old asset and qualifying corporate bonds constitute the new asset, and
  (*c*) at the time the chargeable event occurs, the claimant or a person then connected with him is beneficially entitled to all the bonds.

(3) In a case where this subsection applies, a chargeable gain shall be deemed to have accrued to the claimant or connected person (as the case may be); and the gain shall be deemed to have accrued immediately before the time when the chargeable event occurs and to be of an amount equal to the relevant amount.

(4) The relevant amount is an amount equal to the lesser of—

  (*a*) the first amount, and
  (*b*) the second amount.

(5) The first amount is—

  (*a*) the amount of the chargeable gain that would be deemed to accrue under section 116(10)(*b*) if there were a disposal of all the bonds at the time the chargeable event occurs, or
  (*b*) nil, if an allowable loss would be so deemed to accrue if there were such a disposal.

(6) The second amount is an amount equal to—

  (*a*) the amount by which the amount or value of the consideration mentioned in section 229(1)(*b*) was treated as reduced by virtue of that provision (where it applied), or
  (*b*) the amount by which the amount or value of the consideration mentioned in section 229(3)(*b*) was treated as reduced by virtue of that provision (where it applied).

(7) In a case where subsection (3) above would apply if ''all the'' in subsection (2) above (in one or more places) read ''any of the'', subsection (3) shall nevertheless apply, but as if—

  (*a*) in subsection (5) above ''all the bonds'' read ''the bonds concerned'',
  (*b*) the second amount were reduced to whatever amount is just and reasonable, and
  (*c*) the relevant amount were reduced accordingly.

(8) Subsection (9) below applies where—

  (*a*) subsection (3) above applies (whether or not by virtue of subsection (7) above), and
  (*b*) before the time when the chargeable event occurs anything has happened as regards any of the new shares, or any of the bonds, such that it can be said that a charge has accrued in respect of any of the gain carried forward by virtue of section 229(1) or (3).

(9) If in such a case it is just and reasonable for subsection (3) above to apply as follows, it shall apply as if—

  (*a*) the second amount were reduced (or further reduced) to whatever amount is just and reasonable, and
  (*b*) the relevant amount were reduced (or further reduced) accordingly (if the second amount is less than the first amount),

but nothing in this subsection shall have the effect of reducing the second amount below nil.

(10) For the purposes of subsection (8)(*b*) above the gain carried forward by virtue of section 229(1) or (3) is the gain represented by the amount which by virtue of either of those provisions falls to be deducted from the expenditure allowable in computing a gain accruing on the disposal of replacement assets (that is, the amount found under subsection (6)(*a*) or (*b*) above, as the case may be).

Commentary—*Simon's Direct Tax Service* **C1.433.**
Definitions—''Allowable loss'', ss 8(2), 16, 288(1); ''asset'', s 21(1); ''chargeable gain'', s 15(2); ''company'', ss 99, 288(1); ''connected'', s 286; ''qualifying corporate bond'', s 117; ''shares'', s 288(1).
Cross references—See TCGA 1992 s 235 (Board's power to obtain information for the purposes of this section).
TCGA 1992 s 236(3) (reduction or cancellation of a charge under this section where on a disposal of the bonds a chargeable gain is deemed to accrue under s 116(10)(*b*)).

235 Information

(1) An inspector may by notice require a return to be made by the trustees of an employee share ownership trust in a case where—

  (*a*) a disposal of shares, or an interest in shares, has at any time been made to them, and
  (*b*) a claim is made under section 229(1) or (3).

(2) Where he requires such a return to be made the inspector shall specify the information to be contained in it.

(3) The information which may be specified is information the inspector needs for the purposes of sections 232 to 234 and may include information about—

  (*a*) expenditure incurred by the trustees;
  (*b*) assets acquired by them;
  (*c*) transfers of assets made by them.

(4) The information which may be required under subsection (3)(*a*) above may include the purpose of the expenditure and the persons receiving any sums.

(5) The information which may be required under subsection (3)(*b*) above may include the persons from whom the assets were acquired and the consideration furnished by the trustees.

(6) The information which may be required under subsection (3)(*c*) above may include the persons to whom assets were transferred and the consideration furnished by them.

(7) In a case where section 229(1) or (3) has been applied, the inspector shall send to the trustees of the employee share ownership trust concerned a certificate stating—

  (*a*) that the provision concerned has been applied, and
  (*b*) the effect of the provision on the consideration for the disposal or on the amount of the gain accruing on the disposal (as the case may be).

(8) For the purposes of this section, the question whether a trust is an employee share ownership trust shall be determined in accordance with Schedule 5 to the Finance Act 1989.

Commentary—*Simon's Direct Tax Service* **C1.431.**
Definitions—''Asset'', s 21(1); ''inspector'', s 288(1); ''notice'', s 288(1); ''shares'', s 288(1).

236 Prevention of double charge

(1) Where a charge can be said to accrue by virtue of section 232 or 233 in respect of any of the gain carried forward by virtue of section 229(1) or (3), so much of the gain charged shall not be capable of being carried forward (from assets to other property or from property to other property) under sections 152 to 158 on a replacement of business assets.

(2) For the purpose of construing subsection (1) above—

  (*a*) what of the gain has been charged shall be found in accordance with what is just and reasonable;
  (*b*) section 233(8) and (9) shall apply.

(3) In a case where—

  (*a*) section 234 applies in the case of bonds,
  (*b*) subsequently a disposal of the bonds occurs as mentioned in section 116(10)(*b*), and
  (*c*) a chargeable gain is deemed to accrue under section 116(10)(*b*),

the chargeable gain shall be reduced by the relevant amount found under section 234 or (if the amount exceeds the gain) shall be reduced to nil.

(4) The relevant amount shall be apportioned where the subsequent disposal is of some of the bonds mentioned in subsection (3)(*a*) above; and subsection (3) shall apply accordingly.

Commentary—*Simon's Direct Tax Service* **C1.433.**
Definitions—''Asset'', s 21(1); ''chargeable gain'', s 15(2).

[Employee share ownership plans

236A Relief for transfers to employee share ownership plans

Schedule 7C (which makes provision for roll-over relief where shares are transferred to an approved employee share ownership plan) shall have effect.]¹

Amendment—¹ This section inserted by FA 2000 s 48(1) with effect from 28 July 2000.

239 Employee trusts

(1) Where—

  (*a*) a close company disposes of an asset to trustees in circumstances such that the disposal is a disposition which by virtue of section 13 of the Inheritance Tax Act 1984 (employee trusts) is not a transfer of value for the purposes of inheritance tax, or

  (*b*) an individual disposes of an asset to trustees in circumstances such that the disposal is an exempt transfer by virtue of section 28 of that Act (employee trusts: inheritance tax),

this Act shall have effect in relation to the disposal in accordance with subsections (2) and (3) below.

(2) Section 17(1) shall not apply to the disposal; and if the disposal is by way of gift or is for a consideration not exceeding the sums allowable as a deduction under section 38—

  (*a*) the disposal, and the acquisition by the trustees, shall be treated for the purposes of this Act as being made for such consideration as to secure that neither a gain nor a loss accrues on the disposal, and

  (*b*) where the trustees dispose of the asset, its acquisition by the company or individual shall be treated as its acquisition by the trustees.

Paragraph (*b*) above also applies where section 149(1) of the 1979 Act applied on the disposal of an asset to trustees who have not disposed of it before the coming into force of this section.

(3) Where the disposal is by a close company, section 125(1) shall apply to the disposal as if for the reference to market value there were substituted a reference to market value or the sums allowable as a deduction under section 38, whichever is the less.

(4) Subject to subsection (5) below, this Act shall also have effect in accordance with subsection (2) above in relation to any disposal made by a company other than a close company if—

  (*a*) the disposal is made to trustees otherwise than under a bargain made at arm's length, and

  (*b*) the property disposed of is to be held by them on trusts of the description specified in section 86(1) of the Inheritance Tax Act 1984 (that is to say, those in relation to which the said section 13 of that Act has effect) and the persons for whose benefit the trusts permit the property to be applied include all or most of either—

    (i) the persons employed by or holding office with the company, or

    (ii) the persons employed by or holding office with the company or any one or more subsidiaries of the company.

(5) Subsection (4) above does not apply if the trusts permit any of the property to be applied at any time (whether during any such period as is referred to in the said section 86(1) or later) for the benefit of—

  (*a*) a person who is a participator in the company ("the donor company"), or

  (*b*) any other person who is a participator in any other company that has made a disposal of property to be held on the same trusts as the property disposed of by the donor company, being a disposal in relation to which this Act has had effect in accordance with subsection (2) above, or

  (*c*) any other person who has been a participator in the donor company or any such company as is mentioned in paragraph (*b*) above at any time after, or during the 10 years before, the disposal made by that company, or

  (*d*) any person who is connected with a person within paragraph (*a*), (*b*) or (*c*) above.

(6) The participators in a company who are referred to in subsection (5) above do not include any participator who—

  (*a*) is not beneficially entitled to, or to rights entitling him to acquire, 5 per cent or more of, or of any class of the shares comprised in, its issued share capital, and

  (*b*) on a winding-up of the company would not be entitled to 5 per cent or more of its assets;

and in determining whether the trusts permit property to be applied as mentioned in that subsection, no account shall be taken—

  (i) of any power to make a payment which is the income of any person for any of the purposes of income tax, or would be the income for any of those purposes of a person not resident in the United Kingdom if he were so resident, or

  (ii) if the trusts are those of a profit sharing scheme approved under Schedule 9 to the Taxes Act of any power to appropriate shares in pursuance of the scheme.

(7) In subsection (4) above "subsidiary" has the meaning given by section 736 of the Companies Act 1985 and in subsections (5) and (6) above "participator" has the meaning given in section 417(1) of the Taxes Act, except that it does not include a loan creditor.

(8) In this section "close company" includes a company which, if resident in the United Kingdom, would be a close company as defined in section 288.

Commentary—*Simon's Direct Tax Service* **C1.430.**
Concession D35—Employee trusts: transfers of assets to beneficiaries.
Definitions—"The 1979 Act", s 288(1); "asset", s 21(1); "class", s 288(1); "close company", s 288(1), TA 1988 ss 414, 415; "connected", s 286; "issued", s 288(5); "market value", ss 272–274, Sch 11; "resident", s 9(1); "shares", s 288(1); "the Taxes Act", s 288(1).

Superannuation funds, profit sharing schemes, employee trusts etc

237 Superannuation funds, annuities and annual payments

No chargeable gain shall accrue to any person on the disposal of a right to, or to any part of—

(a) any allowance, annuity or capital sum payable out of any superannuation fund, or under any superannuation scheme, established solely or mainly for persons employed in a profession, trade, undertaking or employment, and their dependants,

(b) an annuity granted otherwise than under a contract for a deferred annuity by a company as part of its business of granting annuities on human life, whether or not including instalments of capital, or an annuity granted or deemed to be granted under the Government Annuities Act 1929 or

(c) annual payments which are due under a covenant made by any person and which are not secured on any property.

Commentary—*Simon's Direct Tax Service* C1.410.
Statement of Practice SP 4/92—Capital gains rebasing elections.
Revenue Internal Guidance—Capital gains manual CG 67692 (interpretation of para (a))
Simon's Tax Cases—s 237(c), *Rank Xerox Ltd v Lane* [1979] STC 740*.
Definitions—"Asset", s 21(1); "chargeable gain", s 15(2); "company", ss 99, 288(1); "trade", s 288(1), TA 1988 s 832(1).

[237A Share option schemes: release and replacement of options

(1) This section applies in any case where a right to acquire shares in a body corporate ("the old right") which was obtained by an individual by reason of his office or employment as a director or employee of that or any other body corporate is released in whole or in part for a consideration which consists of or includes the grant to that individual of another right ("the new right") to acquire shares in that or any other body corporate.

(2) As respects the person to whom the new right is granted—

(a) without prejudice to subsection (1) above, the new right shall not be regarded for the purposes of capital gains tax as consideration for the release of the old right;

(b) the amount or value of the consideration given by him or on his behalf for the acquisition of the new right shall be taken for the purposes of section 38(1) to be the amount or value of the consideration given by him or on his behalf for the old right; and

(c) any consideration paid for the acquisition of the new right shall be taken to be expenditure falling within section 38(1)(b).

(3) As respects the grantor of the new right, in determining for the purposes of this Act the amount or value of the consideration received for the new right, the release of the old right shall be disregarded.][1]

Commentary—*Simon's Direct Tax Service* C2.1005, E4.579.
Definitions—"Shares", s 288(1).
Amendments—[1] This section inserted by FA 1996 s 112(1), (3) with effect in relation to transactions effected after 27 November 1995.

238 Approved profit sharing and share option schemes

(1) Notwithstanding anything in a profit sharing scheme approved under Schedule 9 of the Taxes Act or in paragraph 2(2) of that Schedule or in the trust instrument relating to that scheme, for the purposes of capital gains tax a person who is a participant in relation to that scheme shall be treated as absolutely entitled to his shares as against the trustees of the scheme.

(2) For the purposes of capital gains tax—

(a) no deduction shall be made from the consideration for the disposal of any shares by reason only that an amount determined under section 186 or 187 of or Schedule 9 or 10 to the Taxes Act is chargeable to income tax under section 186(3) or (4) of that Act;

(b) any charge to income tax by virtue of section 186(3) of that Act shall be disregarded in determining whether a distribution is a capital distribution within the meaning of section 122(5)(b);

(c) nothing in any provision of section 186 or 187 of or Schedule 9 or 10 to that Act with respect to—

    (i) the order in which any of a participant's shares are to be treated as disposed of for the purposes of those provisions as they have effect in relation to profit sharing schemes, or

    (ii) the shares in relation to which an event is to be treated as occurring for any such purpose,

shall affect the rules applicable to the computation of a gain accruing on a part disposal of a holding of shares or other securities which were acquired at different times; and

(d) a gain accruing on an appropriation of shares to which section 186(11) of that Act applies shall not be a chargeable gain.

(3) In this section "participant" and "the trust instrument" have the meanings given by section 187 of the Taxes Act.

(4) ...[1]

Commentary—*Simon's Direct Tax Service* C2.732, E4.568, 579.
Definitions—"Absolutely entitled as against trustees", s 60(2); "chargeable gain", s 15(2); "part disposal", s 21(2); "shares", s 288(1); "the Taxes Act", s 288(1).
Amendments—[1] Sub-s (4) repealed by FA 1996 s 112(2), (3), Sch 41 Pt V(5) with effect in relation to transactions effected after 27 November 1995.

[Retirement benefits schemes][1]

[239A Cessation of approval of certain schemes

(1) This section applies where tax is charged in accordance with section 591C of the Taxes Act (tax on certain retirement benefits schemes whose approval ceases to have effect).

(2) For the purposes of this Act the assets which at the relevant time are held for the purposes of the scheme—

(*a*) shall be deemed to be acquired at that time for a consideration equal to the amount on which tax is charged by virtue of section 591C(2) of the Taxes Act by the person who would be chargeable in respect of a chargeable gain accruing on a disposal of the assets at that time; but
(*b*) shall not be deemed to be disposed of by any person at that time;

and in this subsection "the relevant time" means the time immediately before the date of the cessation of the approval of the scheme.

(3) Expressions used in subsection (2) above and in section 591C of the Taxes Act have the same meanings in that subsection as in that section.]¹

Commentary—*Simon's Direct Tax Service* E7.271.
Definitions—"The Taxes Act", s 288(1); "tax", TA 1988 s 832(1).
Cross references—See TA 1988 s 591D (supplementary provisions).
Amendments—¹ This section, and the preceding cross-heading, inserted by FA 1995 s 61(2), (3), with effect in relation to any approval of a retirement benefits scheme which ceases to have effect after 1 November 1994 other than an approval ceasing to have effect by virtue of a notice given before that day under TA 1988 s 591B(1).

[Personal pension schemes]

239B Withdrawal of approval of approved arrangements

(1) This section applies where tax is charged in accordance with section 650A of the Taxes Act (tax charged on the withdrawal of the Board's approval in relation to approved personal pension arrangements).

(2) For the purposes of this Act the appropriate part of the assets which at the relevant time are held for the purposes of the relevant scheme—

(*a*) shall be deemed to be acquired at that time for a consideration equal to the amount on which tax is charged by virtue of section 650A(2) of the Taxes Act; but
(*b*) shall not be deemed to be disposed of by any person at that time.

(3) The person who shall be deemed in accordance with subsection (2)(*a*) above to have acquired the appropriate part of the assets shall be the person who would be chargeable in respect of a chargeable gain accruing on a disposal of the assets at the relevant time.

(4) In this section—

"the appropriate part" and "the relevant time" have the meanings given by subsection (3) of section 650A of the Taxes Act for the purposes of subsection (2) of that section; and
"the relevant scheme" has the same meaning as in that section.]¹

Amendments—¹ This section inserted by FA 1998 s 95(3) with effect in relation to any case in which the date from which the Board's approval is withdrawn is a date on or after 17 March 1998, except a case where the notice under TA 1988 s 650(2) was given before that date.

Leases

240 Leases of land and other assets

Schedule 8 shall have effect as respects leases of land and, to the extent specified in paragraph 9 of that Schedule, as respects leases of property other than land.

Commentary—*Simon's Direct Tax Service* C2.1210.
Concession D39—Extension of leases.
Simon's Tax Cases—*Lewis v Walters* [1992] STC 97*.
Definitions—"Asset", s 21(1); "company", ss 99, 288(1); "land", s 288(1); "lease", Sch 8 para 10(1).

241 Furnished holiday lettings

(1) The following provisions of this section shall have effect with respect to the treatment for the purposes of tax on chargeable gains of the commercial letting of furnished holiday accommodation in the United Kingdom.

(2) Section 504 of the Taxes Act (definitions relating to furnished holiday lettings) shall have effect for the purposes of this section as it has effect for the purposes of section 503 of that Act.

(3) [Subject to subsections (4) to (8) below, for the purposes of the provisions mentioned in subsection (3A) below—]³

[(*a*) any Schedule A business (within the meaning of the Taxes Act) which consists in the commercial letting of furnished holiday accommodation in the United Kingdom shall be treated as a trade, and]²
(*b*) all such lettings made by a particular person or partnership or body of persons shall be treated as one trade.

[(3A) The provisions referred to in subsection (3) above are—

sections 152 to 157 (roll-over relief on replacement of business asset),
section 165 (gifts relief),
section 253 (relief for loans to traders),
Schedule A1 (taper relief),
Schedule 6 (retirement relief etc), and
Schedule 7AC (exemptions for disposals by companies with substantial shareholding).][3]

(4) Subject to subsection (5) below, for the purposes of the [provisions mentioned in subsection (3A)][3] above as they apply by virtue of this section, where in any chargeable period a person makes a commercial letting of furnished holiday accommodation—

(a) the accommodation shall be taken to be used in that period only for the purposes of the trade of making such lettings; and
(b) that trade shall be taken to be carried on throughout that period.

(5) Subsection (4) above does not apply to any part of a chargeable period during which the accommodation is neither let commercially nor available to be so let unless it is prevented from being so let or available by any works of construction or repair.

(6) Where—

(a) a gain to which section 222 applies accrues to any individual on the disposal of an asset; and
(b) by virtue of subsection (3) above the amount or value of the consideration for the acquisition of the asset is treated as reduced under section 152 or 153,

the gain to which section 222 applies shall be reduced by the amount of the reduction mentioned in paragraph (b) above.

(7) Where there is a letting of accommodation only part of which is holiday accommodation such apportionments shall be made for the purposes of this section as [are][1] just and reasonable.

(8) Where a person has been charged to tax in respect of chargeable gains otherwise than in accordance with the provisions of this section, such assessment, reduction or discharge of an assessment or, where a claim for repayment is made, such repayment, shall be made as may be necessary to give effect to those provisions.

Commentary—*Simon's Direct Tax Service* **B7.206; C3.319.**
Definitions—''Asset'', s 21(1); ''chargeable gain'', s 15(2); ''chargeable period'', s 288(1); ''inspector'', s 288(1); ''Schedule A business'', TA 1988 s 832(1); ''the Taxes Act'', s 288(1); ''trade'', s 288(1), TA 1988 s 832(1).
Amendments—[1] Word in sub-s (7) substituted by FA 1996 s 134(1), (2), Sch 20 para 62 with effect from the year 1996–97 and, for the purposes of corporation tax, as respects accounting periods ending after 30 June 1999 (by virtue of Finance Act 1994, Section 199, (Appointed Day) Order, SI 1998/3173 art 2).
[2] Sub-s (3)(a) substituted by FA 1998 Sch 5 para 62 with effect from the year 1998–99 for income tax purposes, and from 1 April 1998 for corporation tax, subject to the transitional provisions in FA 1998 Sch 5 Part IV.
[3] Sub-s (3A) inserted, and words in sub-ss (3), (4) substituted, by FA 2002 s 44(2), (3), Sch 8 para 3 with effect for disposals after 31 March 2002.
Prospective amendment—Words in sub-s (3) repealed by FA 1998 s 165, Sch 27 Part III(31) with effect for disposals in the year 2003–04 and subsequent years of assessment.

Part disposals

242 Small part disposals

(1) This section applies to a transfer of land forming part only of a holding of land, where—

(a) the amount or value of the consideration for the transfer does not exceed one-fifth of the market value of the holding as it subsisted immediately before the transfer, and
(b) the transfer is not one which, by virtue of section 58 or 171(1), is treated as giving rise to neither a gain nor a loss.

(2) Subject to subsection (3) below, if the transferor so claims, the transfer shall not be treated for the purposes of this Act as a disposal, but all sums which, if it had been so treated, would have been brought into account as consideration for that disposal in the computation of the gain shall be deducted from any expenditure allowable under Chapter III of Part II as a deduction in computing a gain on any subsequent disposal of the holding.

[(2A) A claim under subsection (2) above shall be made—

(a) for the purposes of capital gains tax, on or before the first anniversary of the 31st January next following the year of assessment in which the transfer is made;
(b) for the purposes of corporation tax, within 2 years after the end of the accounting period in which the transfer is made.][1]

(3) This section shall not apply—

(a) if the amount or value of the consideration for the transfer exceeds £20,000, or
(b) where in the year of assessment in which the transfer is made, the transferor made any other disposal of land, if the total amount or value of the consideration for all disposals of land made by the transferor in that year exceeds £20,000.

(4) No account shall be taken under subsection (3) above of any transfer of land to which section 243 applies.

(5) In relation to a transfer which is not for full consideration in money or money's worth "the amount or value of the consideration" in this section shall mean the market value of the land transferred.

(6) For the purposes of this section the holding of land shall comprise only the land in respect of which the expenditure allowable under paragraphs (*a*) and (*b*) of section 38(1) would be apportioned under section 42 if the transfer had been treated as a disposal (that is, as a part disposal of the holding).

(7) In this section references to a holding of land include references to any estate or interest in a holding of land, not being an estate or interest which is a wasting asset, and references to part of a holding shall be construed accordingly.

Commentary—*Simon's Direct Tax Service* **C2.1103.**
Statement of Practice D1—Part disposals of land.
Definitions—"Accounting period", TA 1988 s 834(1); "asset", s 21(1); "land", s 288(1); "market value", ss 272–274, Sch 11; "part disposal", s 21(2); "wasting asset", ss 44, 288(1), Sch 8 para 1; "year of assessment", s 288(1).
Cross references—See TCGA 1992 s 244 (allowable expenditure under sub-s (2) of this section less than the consideration for the part disposal).
Amendments—[1] Sub-s (2A) inserted by FA 1996 s 135(1), (2), Sch 21 para 37 with effect from the year 1996–97 and, for purposes of corporation tax, as respects accounting periods ending after 30 June 1999 (by virtue of Finance Act 1994, Section 199, (Appointed Day) Order, SI 1998/3173 art 2).

243 Part disposal to authority with compulsory powers

(1) This section applies to a transfer of land forming part only of a holding of land to an authority exercising or having compulsory powers where—

    (*a*) the amount or value of the consideration for the transfer, or if the transfer is not for full consideration in money or money's worth, the market value of the land transferred, is small, as compared with the market value of the holding as it subsisted immediately before the transfer, and
    (*b*) the transferor had not taken any steps by advertising or otherwise to dispose of any part of the holding or to make his willingness to dispose of it known to the authority or others.

(2) If the transferor so claims, the transfer shall not be treated for the purposes of this Act as a disposal, but all sums which, if it had been so treated, would have been brought into account as consideration for that disposal in the computation of the gain shall be deducted from any expenditure allowable under Chapter III of Part II as a deduction in computing a gain on any subsequent disposal of the holding.

[(2A) A claim under subsection (2) above shall be made—

    (*a*) for the purposes of capital gains tax, on or before the first anniversary of the 31st January next following the year of assessment in which the transfer is made;
    (*b*) for the purposes of corporation tax, within 2 years after the end of the accounting period in which the transfer is made.][1]

(3) For the purposes of this section the holding of land shall comprise only the land in respect of which the expenditure allowable under paragraphs (*a*) and (*b*) of section 38(1) would be apportioned under section 42 if the transfer had been treated as a disposal (that is, as a part disposal of the holding).

(4) In this section references to a holding of land include references to an estate or interest in a holding of land, not being an estate or interest which is a wasting asset, and references to part of a holding shall be construed accordingly.

(5) In this section "authority exercising or having compulsory powers" means, in relation to the land transferred, a person or body of persons acquiring it compulsorily or who has or have been, or could be, authorised to acquire it compulsorily for the purposes for which it is acquired, or for whom another person or body of persons has or have been, or could be, authorised so to acquire it.

Commentary—*Simon's Direct Tax Service* **C2.1117.**
Revenue Interpretation RI 164—From 24 February 1997, the Revenue regard a receipt as "small" wherever its amount or value is £3,000 or less, whether or not it would also meet the 5% test (see Revenue and other press releases below).
Revenue & other press releases—CCAB June 1965 ("small" is regarded by Revenue as not exceeding 5 per cent of the relevant amount) See now also Revenue Interpretation RI 164 above.
Definitions—"Accounting period", TA 1988 s 834(1); "asset", s 21(1); "land", s 288(1); "market value", ss 272–274, Sch 11; "part disposal", s 21(2); "wasting asset", ss 44, 288(1), Sch 8 para 1; "year of assessment", s 288(1).
Cross references—See TCGA 1992 s 242(4) (part disposals under this section to be disregarded for small part disposals relief).
TCGA 1992 s 244 (allowable expenditure under sub-s (2) of this section less than the consideration for the part disposal).
TCGA 1992 s 248(4) (no claim may be made under this section where relief is claimed under s 247).
Amendments—[1] Sub-s (2A) inserted by FA 1996 s 135(1), (2), Sch 21 para 38 with effect from the year 1996–97 and, for purposes of corporation tax, as respects accounting periods ending after 30 June 1999 (by virtue of Finance Act 1994, Section 199, (Appointed Day) Order, SI 1998/3173 art 2).

244 Part disposal: consideration exceeding allowable expenditure

(1) The provisions of sections 242(2) and 243(2) shall have effect subject to this section.

(2) Where the allowable expenditure is less than the consideration for the part disposal (or is nil)—

    (*a*) the said provisions shall not apply, and
    (*b*) if the recipient so elects (and there is any allowable expenditure)—

(i) the consideration for the part disposal shall be reduced by the amount of the allowable expenditure, and

(ii) none of that expenditure shall be allowable as a deduction in computing a gain accruing on the occasion of the part disposal or on any subsequent occasion.

In this subsection "allowable expenditure" means expenditure which, immediately before the part disposal, was attributable to the holding of land under paragraphs (*a*) and (*b*) of section 38(1).

[(3) An election under subsection (2)(*b*) above shall be made—

(*a*) for the purposes of capital gains tax, on or before the first anniversary of the 31st January next following the year of assessment in which the part disposal is made;

(*b*) for the purposes of corporation tax, within 2 years after the end of the accounting period in which the part disposal is made.]¹

Commentary—*Simon's Direct Tax Service* **C2.1117.**
Definitions—"Accounting period", TA 1988 s 834(1); "land", s 288(1); "part disposal", s 21(2); "year of assessment", s 288(1).
Cross references—See TCGA 1992 Sch 3 para 4(2) (application of this section where TCGA 1992 s 35(2) (rebasing) applies in relation to the disposal of an asset).
Amendments—¹ Sub-s (3) inserted by FA 1996 s 135(1), (2), Sch 21 para 39 with effect from the year 1996–97 and, for purposes of corporation tax, as respects accounting periods ending after 30 June 1999 (by virtue of Finance Act 1994, Section 199, (Appointed Day) Order, SI 1998/3173 art 2).

Compulsory acquisition

245 Compensation paid on compulsory acquisition

(1) Where land or an interest in or right over land is acquired and the acquisition is, or could have been, made under compulsory powers, then in considering whether, under section 52(4), the purchase price or compensation or other consideration for the acquisition should be apportioned and treated in part as a capital sum within section 22(1)(*a*), whether as compensation for loss of goodwill or for disturbance or otherwise, or should be apportioned in any other way, the fact that the acquisition is or could have been made compulsorily, and any statutory provision treating the purchase price or compensation or other consideration as exclusively paid in respect of the land itself, shall be disregarded.

(2) In any case where land or an interest in land is acquired as mentioned in subsection (1) above from any person and the compensation or purchase price includes an amount in respect of severance of the land comprised in the acquisition or sale from other land in which that person is entitled in the same capacity to an interest, or in respect of that other land as being injuriously affected, there shall be deemed for the purposes of this Act to be a part disposal of that other land.

Commentary—*Simon's Direct Tax Service* **C2.1115.**
Revenue & other press releases—IR 22-5-96 (compulsory acquisition of property: scale fees for valuation services, new Ryde's scale of charges effective from 1–7–96).
Definitions—"Land", s 288(1); "part disposal", s 21(2).
Cross references—See TCGA 1992 s 247(6) (disapplication of certain provisions of this section where roll-over relief is claimed under s 247).

246 Time of disposal and acquisition

Where an interest in land is acquired, otherwise than under a contract, by an authority possessing compulsory purchase powers, the time at which the disposal and acquisition is made is the time at which the compensation for the acquisition is agreed or otherwise determined (variations on appeal being disregarded for this purpose) ...¹

Commentary—*Simon's Direct Tax Service* **C1.322.**
Definition—"Land", s 288(1).
Amendments—¹ Words repealed by FA 1996 ss 121(8), 141(4), Sch 41 Pt V(6) with effect from the year 1996–97 and, so far as relating to corporation tax, as respects accounting periods ending after 30 June 1999 (by virtue of Finance Act 1994, Section 199, (Appointed Day) Order, SI 1998/3173 art 2).

247 Roll-over relief on compulsory acquisition

(1) This section applies where—

(*a*) land ("the old land") is disposed of by any person ("the landowner") to an authority exercising or having compulsory powers; and

(*b*) the landowner did not take any steps, by advertising or otherwise, to dispose of the old land or to make his willingness to dispose of it known to the authority or others; and

(*c*) the consideration for the disposal is applied by the landowner in acquiring other land ("the new land") not being land excluded from this paragraph by section 248.

(2) Subject to section 248, in a case where the whole of the consideration for the disposal was applied as mentioned in subsection (1)(*c*) above, the landowner, on making a claim as respects the consideration so applied, shall be treated for the purposes of this Act—

(*a*) as if the consideration for the disposal of the old land were (if otherwise of a greater amount or value) of such amount as would secure that on the disposal neither a gain nor a loss accrues to him; and (*b*) as if the amount or value of the consideration for the acquisition of the new land were reduced by the excess of the amount or value of the actual consideration for the disposal of the old land over the amount of the consideration which he is treated as receiving under paragraph (*a*) above.

(3) If part only of the consideration for the disposal of the old land was applied as mentioned in subsection (1)(*c*) above, then, subject to section 248, if the part of the consideration which was not so applied ("the unexpended consideration") is less than the amount of the gain (whether all chargeable gain or not) accruing on the disposal of the old land, the landowner, on making a claim as respects the consideration which was so applied, shall be treated for the purposes of this Act—

(*a*) as if the amount of the gain so accruing were reduced to the amount of the unexpended consideration (and, if not all chargeable gain, with a proportionate reduction in the amount of the chargeable gain); and

(*b*) as if the amount or value of the consideration for the acquisition of the new land were reduced by the amount by which the gain is reduced (or, as the case may be, the amount by which the chargeable gain is proportionately reduced) under paragraph (*a*) above.

(4) Nothing in subsection (2) or subsection (3) above affects the treatment for the purposes of this Act of the authority by whom the old land was acquired or of the other party to the transaction involving the acquisition of the new land.

(5) For the purposes of this section—

(*a*) subsection (2) of section 152 shall apply in relation to subsection (2)(*a*) and subsection (2)(*b*) above as it applies in relation to subsection (1)(*a*) and subsection (1)(*b*) of that section; and

(*b*) [subsections (3) and (4)][2] of that section shall apply as if any reference to the new assets were a reference to the new land, any reference to the old assets were a reference to the old land and any reference to that section were a reference to this.

[(5A) Subsections (2A) and (2C) of section 175 shall apply in relation to this section as they apply in relation to section 152 (but as if the reference in subsection (2C) to the new assets were a reference to the new land).][1]

(6) Where this section applies, any such amount as is referred to in subsection (2) of section 245 shall be treated as forming part of the consideration for the disposal of the old land and, accordingly, so much of that subsection as provides for a deemed disposal of other land shall not apply.

(7) The provisions of this Act fixing the amount of the consideration deemed to be given for the acquisition or disposal of assets shall be applied before this section is applied.

(8) In this section—

"land" includes any interest in or right over land; and
"authority exercising or having compulsory powers" shall be construed in accordance with section 243(5).

Commentary—*Simon's Direct Tax Service* C2.1116.
Concession D26—Relief for exchange of joint interests.
Statement of Practice SP 13/93—Compulsory acquisition of freehold reversion by tenant.
Revenue Interpretation RI 205—Compulsory acquisition of freehold reversion or extension of lease by tenant: extension of SP 13/93 where a tenant's right to buy under the Housing Acts 1985–1996 is preserved following a transfer of housing stock into the private sector.
Definitions—"Asset", s 21(1); "chargeable gain", s 15(2); "land", s 288(1).
Cross references—See TCGA 1992 s 247A (provisional application of this section upon declaration of intention to acquire other land).
TCGA 1992 s 248 (supplementary provisions).
TCGA 1992 Sch 4 para 2 (deferred charges on gains accruing before 31 March 1982).
Amendments—[1] Sub-s (5A) inserted by FA 1995 s 48(2), (6), with effect, so far as it relates to s 175(2A), where the disposal or the acquisition occurs after 28 November 1994, and so far as relating to s 175(2C), where the acquisition occurs after that date.
[2] Words in sub-s (5)(*b*) substituted by FA 1996 ss 121(8), 141(5) with effect from the year 1996–97 and, so far as relating to corporation tax, as respects accounting periods ending after 30 June 1999 (by virtue of Finance Act 1994, Section 199, (Appointed Day) Order, SI 1998/3173 art 2).

[247A Provisional application of section 247

(1) This section applies where a person who disposes of land ("the old land") to an authority exercising or having compulsory powers declares, in his return for the chargeable period in which the disposal takes place—

(*a*) that the whole or any specified part of the consideration for the disposal will be applied in the acquisition of other land ("the new land");

(*b*) that the acquisition will take place as mentioned in subsection (3) of section 152; and

(*c*) that the new land will not be land excluded from section 247(1)(*c*) by section 248.

(2) Until the declaration ceases to have effect, section 247 shall apply as if the acquisition had taken place and the person had made a claim under that section.

(3) For the purposes of this section, subsections (3) to (5) of section 153A shall apply as if the reference to section 152 or 153 were a reference to section 247 and the reference to the old assets were a reference to the old land.

(4) In this section "land" and "authority exercising or having compulsory powers" have the same meaning as in section 247.][1]

Commentary—*Simon's Direct Tax Service* **C2.1116.**
Definitions—"Chargeable period", s 288(1); "land", s 288(1).
Amendments—¹ This section inserted by FA 1996 ss 121(8), 141(6) with effect from the year 1996–97 and, so far as relating to corporation tax, as respects accounting periods ending after 30 June 1999 (by virtue of Finance Act 1994, Section 199, (Appointed Day) Order, SI 1998/3173 art 2).

248 Provisions supplementary to section 247

(1) Land is excluded from paragraph (c) of subsection (1) of section 247 if—

(a) it is a dwelling-house or part of a dwelling-house (or an interest in or right over a dwelling-house), and

(b) by virtue of, or of any claim under, any provision of sections 222 to 226 the whole or any part of a gain accruing on a disposal of it by the landowner at a material time would not be a chargeable gain;

and for the purposes of this subsection "a material time" means any time during the period of 6 years beginning on the date of the acquisition referred to in the said paragraph (c).

(2) If, at any time during the period of 6 years referred to in subsection (1) above, land which at the beginning of that period was not excluded from section 247(1)(c) by virtue of that subsection becomes so excluded, the amount of any chargeable gain accruing on the disposal of the old land shall be redetermined without regard to any relief previously given under section 247 by reference to the amount or value of the consideration for the acquisition of that land; and all such adjustments of capital gains tax, whether by way of assessment or otherwise, may be made at any time, notwithstanding anything in section 34 of the Management Act (time limit for assessments).

This subsection also applies where the period of 6 years referred to above began before the commencement of this section (and accordingly the references to section 247 include references to section 111A of the 1979 Act).

(3) Where the new land is a depreciating asset, within the meaning of section 154, that section has effect as if—

(a) any reference in subsection (1) or subsection (4) to section 152 or 153 were a reference to subsection (2) or subsection (3) respectively of section 247; and

(b) paragraph (b) of subsection (2) were omitted; and

(c) the reference in subsection (5) to section 152(3) were a reference to that provision as applied by section 247(5).

(4) No claim may be made under section 243 in relation to a transfer which constitutes a disposal in respect of which a claim is made under section 247.

(5) Expressions used in this section have the same meaning as in section 247.

Commentary—*Simon's Direct Tax Service* **C2.1116.**
Definitions—"The 1979 Act", s 288(1); "asset", s 21(1); "chargeable gain", s 15(2); "land", s 288(1); "the Management Act", s 288(1).
Cross references—See TCGA 1992 Sch 4 para 4(2), (5) (deferred charges on gains accruing before 31 March 1982).

Agricultural land and woodlands

249 Grants for giving up agricultural land

For the purposes of capital gains tax, a sum payable to an individual by virtue of a scheme under section 27 of the Agriculture Act 1967 (grants for relinquishing occupation of uncommercial agricultural units) shall not be treated as part of the consideration obtained by him for, or otherwise as accruing to him on, the disposal of any asset.

Commentary—*Simon's Direct Tax Service* **C1.329; C2.1105.**
Definitions—"Asset", s 21(1); "land", s 288(1).

250 Woodlands

(1) Consideration for the disposal of trees standing or felled or cut on woodlands managed by the occupier on a commercial basis and with a view to the realisation of profits shall be excluded from the computation of the gain if the person making the disposal is the occupier.

(2) Capital sums received under a policy of insurance in respect of the destruction of or damage or injury to trees by fire or other hazard on such woodlands shall be excluded from the computation of the gain if the person making the disposal is the occupier.

(3) Subsection (2) above has effect notwithstanding section 22(1).

(4) In the computation of the gain so much of the cost of woodland in the United Kingdom shall be disregarded as is attributable to trees growing on the land.

(5) In the computation of the gain accruing on a disposal of woodland in the United Kingdom so much of the consideration for the disposal as is attributable to trees growing on the land shall be excluded.

(6) References in this section to trees include references to saleable underwood.

Commentary—*Simon's Direct Tax Service* **C2.1112.**
Definition—"Land", s 288(1).

Debts

251 General provisions

(1) Where a person incurs a debt to another, whether in sterling or in some other currency, no chargeable gain shall accrue to that (that is the original) creditor or his personal representative or legatee on a disposal of the debt, except in the case of the debt on a security (as defined in section 132).

(2) Subject to the provisions of sections [132, 135 and 136][4] and subject to subsection (1) above, the satisfaction of a debt or part of it (including a debt on a security as defined in section 132) shall be treated as a disposal of the debt or of that part by the creditor made at the time when the debt or that part is satisfied.

(3) Where property is acquired by a creditor in satisfaction of his debt or part of it, then subject to the provisions of sections [132, 135 and 136][4] the property shall not be treated as disposed of by the debtor or acquired by the creditor for a consideration greater than its market value at the time of the creditor's acquisition of it; but if under subsection (1) above (and in a case not falling within [section 132, 135 or 136][4]) no chargeable gain is to accrue on a disposal of the debt by the creditor (that is the original creditor), and a chargeable gain accrues to him on a disposal by him of the property, the amount of the chargeable gain shall (where necessary) be reduced so as not to exceed the chargeable gain which would have accrued if he had acquired the property for a consideration equal to the amount of the debt or that part of it.

(4) A loss accruing on the disposal of a debt acquired by the person making the disposal from the original creditor or his personal representative or legatee at a time when the creditor or his personal representative or legatee is a person connected with the person making the disposal, and so acquired either directly or by one or more purchases through persons all of whom are connected with the person making the disposal, shall not be an allowable loss.

(5) Where the original creditor is a trustee and the debt, when created, is settled property, subsections (1) and (4) above shall apply as if for the references to the original creditor's personal representative or legatee there were substituted references to any person becoming absolutely entitled, as against the trustee, to the debt on its ceasing to be settled property, and to that person's personal representative or legatee.

[(6) For the purposes of this section a debenture issued by any company on or after 16th March 1993 shall be deemed to be a security (as defined in section 132) if—

   (a) it is issued on a reorganisation (as defined in section 126(1)) or in pursuance of its allotment on any such reorganisation;

   (b) it is issued in exchange for shares in or debentures of another company and in a case [to which section 135 applies and which is unaffected by section 137(1)][4];

   (c) it is issued under any such arrangements as are mentioned in subsection (1)(a) of section 136 and in a case unaffected by section 137 where section 136 requires shares or debentures in another company to be treated as exchanged for, or for anything that includes, that debenture; or

   (d) it is issued in pursuance of rights attached to any debenture issued on or after 16th March 1993 and falling within paragraph (a), (b) or (c) above.][1]

[and any debenture which results from a conversion of securities within the meaning of section 132, or is issued in pursuance of rights attached to such a debenture, shall be deemed for the purposes of this section to be a security (as defined in that section).][3]

[(7) Where any instrument specified in subsection (8) below is not a security (as defined in section 132), that instrument shall be deemed to be such a security for the purposes of this section, other than the purposes of determining what is or is not an allowable loss in any case.][2]

[(8) The instruments mentioned in subsection (7) above are—

   (a) any instrument that would fall to be treated for the purposes of this Act as an asset representing a loan relationship of a company if the provisions of sections 92(4) and 93(4) of the Finance Act 1996 (convertible securities and assets linked to the value of chargeable assets) were disregarded; or

   (b) any instrument which (even apart from those provisions) is not a loan relationship of a company but which would be a relevant discounted security for the purposes of Schedule 13 to that Act if paragraph 3(2)(c) of that Schedule (excluded indexed securities) were omitted.][2]

Commentary—*Simon's Direct Tax Service* **C1.408.**
Regulations—European Single Currency (Taxes) Regulations, SI 1998/3177 reg 37.
Statement of Practice SP 4/92—
Capital gains rebasing elections.
Revenue & other press releases—CCAB June 1969 (definition of "security" is regarded as exhaustive).
Law Society's Gazette 26-4-95 (Revenue consider that sub-s (4) above does not apply to a debt on a security).
Inland Revenue 15-11-01 (legislation to be introduced so that debentures deemed to be securities for certain purposes by sub-s (6) above will also be treated as securities for taper relief).
Revenue Internal Guidance—Capital gains manual CG 53400–53530 (treatment of debts).
CG 53400, 53495–53496 (whether a debt exists).
CG 53450–53455 (treatment of debts on a security).
CG 53470–53485 (treatment of other debts).
CG 53501–53502 (subsequent disposal of debt by guarantor).
CG 53514–53515 (example of adjustment under sub-s (3)).

Simon's Tax Cases—*Tarmac Roadstone Holdings Ltd v Williams* [1996] STC (SCD) 409*, *Whittles v Uniholdings Ltd* [1996] STC 914*; *Taylor Clark International Ltd v Lewis* [1998] STC 1259*.
s 251(1), *Marson v Marriage* [1980] STC 177*; *Marren v Ingles* [1980] STC 500*; *W T Ramsay Ltd v IRC* [1981] STC 174*.
Definitions—"Absolutely entitled as against trustees", s 60(2); "allowable loss", ss 8(2), 16, 288(1); "chargeable gain", s 15(2); "company", ss 99, 288(1); "connected", s 286; "legatee", s 64(2), (3); "loan relationship", TA 1988 s 834(1), FA 1996 s 81; "market value", ss 272–274, Sch 11; "settled property", s 68.
Cross references—See FA 1990 Sch 12 para 2(3) (transfer of debts owed to Independent Broadcasting Authority).
TCGA 1992 s 252(1) (sub-s (1) of this section not to apply to a foreign currency bank account unless it is used for personal expenses).
FA 1996 Sch 13 paras 3(1), (1A), 10(4), 13(9) (application of these sub-paras (as inserted by FA 1999 s 65) concerning the meaning of "relevant discounted securities" for the purposes of sub-s (8) above with effect for any disposal, in whole or in part of an asset after 14 February 1999: FA 1999 s 65(11)).
Amendments—[1] Sub-s (6) inserted by FA 1993 s 84(2), (3) in relation to any chargeable period ending after 15 March 1993.
[2] Sub-ss (7), (8) inserted by FA 1996 ss 104, 105(1), Sch 14 para 64 with effect for accounting periods ending after 31 March 1996 subject to transitional provisions in FA 1996 Sch 15.
[3] Words after sub-s (6)(*d*) inserted by FA 1997 s 88(5), (6) with effect for the purposes of the application of this Act in relation to any disposal after 25 November 1996 and so as to have effect, where a conversion took place at a time before 26 November 1996, as if they had come into force before that time.
[4] Words in sub-s (2) substituted for the words "132 and 135", words in sub-s (3) substituted for the words "132 and 135" and words "either section 132 or 135" respectively, and words in sub-s (6) substituted for words shown below, by FA 2002 s 45, Sch 9 paras 5(1), (12), 7 with effect for shares or debentures issued after 16 April 2002. The reference to shares or debentures includes any interests falling to be treated as shares or debentures for the purposes of TCGA 1992 s 135 or 136 as substituted by FA 2002 Sch 9. Words in sub-s (6) substituted for the following words—

"unaffected by section 137 where one or more of the conditions mentioned in paragraphs (*a*) to (*c*) of section 135(1) is satisfied in relation to the exchange;".

252 Foreign currency bank accounts

(1) Subject to subsection (2) below, section 251(1) shall not apply to a debt owed by a bank which is not in sterling and which is represented by a sum standing to the credit of a person in an account in the bank.

(2) Subsection (1) above shall not apply to a sum in an individual's bank account representing currency acquired by the holder for the personal expenditure outside the United Kingdom of himself or his family or dependants (including expenditure on the provision or maintenance of any residence outside the United Kingdom).

Commentary—*Simon's Direct Tax Service* C1.608.
Statement of Practice SP 10/84—CGT: foreign bank accounts.
Revenue Internal Guidance—Capital gains manual CG 78330–78333 (operation of this section).
Cross references—See TCGA 1992 s 13(5) (chargeable gains accruing to a non-resident close company on disposal of currency or debt within sub-s (1) above).

253 Relief for loans to traders

(1) In this section "a qualifying loan" means a loan in the case of which—

(*a*) the money lent is used by the borrower wholly for the purposes of a trade carried on by him, not being a trade which consists of or includes the lending of money, and
(*b*) the borrower is resident in the United Kingdom, and
(*c*) the borrower's debt is not a debt on a security as defined in section 132;

and for the purposes of paragraph (*a*) above money used by the borrower for setting up a trade which is subsequently carried on by him shall be treated as used for the purposes of that trade.

(2) In subsection (1) above references to a trade include references to a profession or vocation; and where money lent to a company is lent by it to another company in the same group, being a trading company, that subsection shall apply to the money lent to the first-mentioned company as if it had used it for any purpose for which it is used by the other company while a member of the group.

(3) [Where a person who has made a qualifying loan makes a claim and at that time][2]—

(*a*) any outstanding amount of the principal of the loan has become irrecoverable, and
(*b*) the claimant has not assigned his right to recover that amount, and
(*c*) the claimant and the borrower were not each other's spouses, or companies in the same group, when the loan was made or at any subsequent time,

[then, to the extent that that amount is not an amount which, in the case of the claimant, falls to be brought into account as a debit given for the purposes of Chapter II of Part IV of the Finance Act 1996 (loan relationships),][1] this Act shall have effect as if an allowable loss equal to that amount had accrued to the claimant [at the time of the claim or (subject to subsection (3A) below) any earlier time specified in the claim.][3]

[(3A) For the purposes of subsection (3) above, an earlier time may be specified in the claim if:

(*a*) the amount to which that subsection applies was also irrecoverable at the earlier time; and either
(*b*) for capital gains tax purposes the earlier time falls not more than two years before the beginning of the year of assessment in which the claim is made; or
(*c*) for corporation tax purposes the earlier time falls on or after the first day of the earliest accounting period ending not more than two years before the time of the claim.][3]

(4) [Where a person who has guaranteed the repayment of a loan which is, or but for subsection (1)(*c*) above would be, a qualifying loan makes a claim and at that time][3]—

(*a*) any outstanding amount of, or of interest in respect of, the principal of the loan has become irrecoverable from the borrower, and

(*b*) the claimant has made a payment under the guarantee (whether to the lender or a co-guarantor) in respect of that amount, and

(*c*) the claimant has not assigned any right to recover that amount which has accrued to him (whether by operation of law or otherwise) in consequence of his having made the payment, and

(*d*) the lender and the borrower were not each other's spouses, or companies in the same group, when the loan was made or at any subsequent time and the claimant and the borrower were not each other's spouses, and the claimant and the lender were not companies in the same group, when the guarantee was given or at any subsequent time,

this Act shall have effect as if an allowable loss had accrued to the claimant when the payment was made; and the loss shall be equal to the payment made by him in respect of the amount mentioned in paragraph (*a*) above less any contribution payable to him by any co-guarantor in respect of the payment so made.

[(4A) A claim under subsection (4) above shall be made—

(*a*) for the purposes of capital gains tax, on or before the fifth anniversary of the 31st January next following the year of assessment in which the payment was made;

(*b*) for the purposes of corporation tax, within 6 years after the end of the accounting period in which the payment was made.][2]

(5) Where an allowable loss has been treated under subsection (3) or (4) above as accruing to any person and the whole or any part of the outstanding amount mentioned in subsection (3)(*a*) or, as the case may be, subsection (4)(*a*) is at any time recovered by him, this Act shall have effect as if there had accrued to him at that time a chargeable gain equal to so much of the allowable loss as corresponds to the amount recovered.

(6) Where—

(*a*) an allowable loss has been treated under subsection (4) above as accruing to any person, and

(*b*) the whole or any part of the amount of the payment mentioned in subsection (4)(*b*) is at any time recovered by him,

this Act shall have effect as if there had accrued to him at that time a chargeable gain equal to so much of the allowable loss as corresponds to the amount recovered.

(7) Where—

(*a*) an allowable loss has been treated under subsection (3) above as accruing to a company ("the first company"), and

(*b*) the whole or any part of the outstanding amount mentioned in subsection (3)(*a*) is at any time recovered by a company ("the second company") in the same group as the first company,

this Act shall have effect as if there had accrued to the second company at that time a chargeable gain equal to so much of the allowable loss as corresponds to the amount recovered.

(8) Where—

(*a*) an allowable loss has been treated under subsection (4) above as accruing to a company ("the first company"), and

(*b*) the whole or any part of the outstanding amount mentioned in subsection (4)(*a*), or the whole or any part of the amount of the payment mentioned in subsection (4)(*b*), is at any time recovered by a company ("the second company") in the same group as the first company,

this Act shall have effect as if there had accrued to the second company at that time a chargeable gain equal to so much of the allowable loss as corresponds to the amount recovered.

(9) For the purposes of subsections (5) to (8) above, a person shall be treated as recovering an amount if he (or any other person by his direction) receives any money or money's worth in satisfaction of his right to recover that amount or in consideration of his assignment of the right to recover it; and where a person assigns such a right otherwise than by way of a bargain made at arm's length he shall be treated as receiving money or money's worth equal to the market value of the right at the time of the assignment.

(10) No amount shall be treated under this section as giving rise to an allowable loss or chargeable gain in the case of any person if it falls to be taken into account in computing his income for the purposes of income tax or corporation tax.

(11) Where an allowable loss has been treated as accruing to a person under subsection (4) above by virtue of a payment made by him at any time under a guarantee—

(*a*) no chargeable gain shall accrue to him otherwise than under subsection (5) above, and

(*b*) no allowable loss shall accrue to him under this Act,

on his disposal of any rights that have accrued to him (whether by operation of law or otherwise) in consequence of his having made any payment under the guarantee at or after that time.

(12) References in this section to an amount having become irrecoverable do not include references to cases where the amount has become irrecoverable in consequence of the terms of the loan, of any arrangements of which the loan forms part, or of any act or omission by the lender or, in a case within subsection (4) above, the guarantor.

(13) For the purposes of subsections (7) and (8) above, 2 companies are in the same group if they were in the same group when the loan was made or have been in the same group at any subsequent time.

(14) In this section—

(a) "spouses" means spouses who are living together (construed in accordance with section 288(3)),

(b) "trading company" has the meaning given by paragraph 1 of Schedule 6, and

(c) "group" shall be construed in accordance with section 170.

(15) Subsection (3) above does not apply where the loan was made before 12th April 1978 and subsection (4) above does not apply where the guarantee was given before that date.

Commentary—*Simon's Direct Tax Service* C3.701–705.
Revenue Internal Guidance—Capital gains tax manual, CG 65933 (loan used partly for trade; relief available for trade use portion).
CG 65950–65958 (sub-s (3)(a) meaning of "irrecoverable").
CG 66000 (sub-s (4) loan must be irrecoverable from borrower).
CG 66010–66013 (sub-s (4)(b): co-guarantors, relief available worked examples CG 66033).
CG 66071–66081 (sub-s (6) examples of recoveries).
CG 66132–66134 (novation of debts: new lender making loan for the purpose of this section; not true for assignment of debt).
Revenue & other press releases—CCAB June 1978 (guarantee s 253(4) includes where an individual's property is charged as security for a qualifying loan. An indemnity is not a qualifying guarantee. S.253(4) applies to overdrafts but not to HP agreements).
Simon's Tax Cases—s 253(3), (12), *Cann v Woods* [1999] STC (SCD) 77.
s 253(4), *Leisureking Ltd v Cushing* [1993] STC 46*.
s 253(15), *Rigby v Jayatilaka* [1999] STC (SCD) 243.
Definitions—"Accounting period", TA 1988 s 834(1); "allowable loss", ss 8(2), 16, 288(1); "chargeable gain", s 15(2); "company", ss 99, 288(1); "market value", ss 272–274, Sch 11; "resident", s 9(1); "trade", s 288(1), TA 1988 s 832(1); "year of assessment", s 288(1).
Cross references—See TA 1988 s 503 (treatment of the commercial letting of furnished holiday accommodation for the purposes of this section).
TCGA 1992 s 241(3) (commercial letting of furnished holiday accommodation to be treated as a trade for the purposes of this section).
TCGA 1992 s 254 (relief for debts on qualifying corporate bonds).
TCGA 1992 s 255(5) (provisions of this section to apply for the purposes of s 254 above (relief for qualifying corporate bonds).
FA 2000 Sch 29 para 34 (the main amendments made to TCGA 1992 s 170 by FA 2000 Sch 29 para 1 have effect for the purposes of this section for loans made, or guarantees given, after 31 March 2000).
Amendments—[1] Words in sub-s (3) inserted by FA 1996 ss 104, 105(1), Sch 14 para 65 with effect for accounting periods ending after 31 March 1996, subject to transitional provisions in FA 1994 Sch 15.
[2] Sub-s (4A) inserted by FA 1996 s 135(1), (2), Sch 21 para 40 with effect from the year 1996–97 and, for the purposes of corporation tax, as respects accounting periods ending after 30 June 1999 (by virtue of Finance Act 1994, Section 199, (Appointed Day) Order, SI 1998/3173 art 2).
[3] Words in sub-ss (3), (4) substituted, and sub-s (3A) inserted, by FA 1996 Sch 39 para 8 with effect in relation to claims made after 5 April 1996.
Prospective amendment—Words in sub-s (14)(b) will be substituted by FA 1998 s 140(5) with effect in relation to the year 2003–04 and subsequent years of assessment.

[254 Relief for debts on qualifying corporate bonds

(1) In this section "a qualifying loan" means a loan in the case of which—

(a) the borrower's debt is a debt on a security as defined in section 132,

(b) but for that fact, the loan would be a qualifying loan within the meaning of section 253, and

(c) the security is a qualifying corporate bond [but is not a relevant discounted security for the purposes of Schedule 13 to the Finance Act 1996][2].

(2) [Where a person who has made a qualifying loan makes a claim and at that time]1 one of the following 3 conditions is fulfilled, this Act shall have effect as if an allowable loss equal to the allowable amount had accrued to the claimant [at the time of the claim or (subject to subsection (8A) below) any earlier time specified in the claim][1].

(3) The first condition is that—

(a) the value of the security has become negligible,

(b) the claimant has not assigned his right to recover any outstanding amount of the principal of the loan, and

(c) the claimant and the borrower are not companies which have been in the same group at any time after the loan was made.

(4) The second condition is that—

(a) the security's redemption date has passed,

(b) all the outstanding amount of the principal of the loan was irrecoverable (taking the facts existing on that date) or proved to be irrecoverable (taking the facts existing on a later date), and

(c) subsection (3)(b) and (c) above are fulfilled.

(5) The third condition is that—

(a) the security's redemption date has passed,

(b) part of the outstanding amount of the principal of the loan was irrecoverable (taking the facts existing on that date) or proved to be irrecoverable (taking the facts existing on a later date), and

(c) subsection (3)(b) and (c) above are fulfilled.

(6) In a case where ...[1] the first or second condition is fulfilled, the allowable amount is the lesser of—

(a) *the outstanding amount of the principal of the loan;*
(b) *the amount of the security's acquisition cost;*

and if any amount of the principal of the loan has been recovered the amount of the security's acquisition cost shall for this purpose be treated as reduced (but not beyond nil) by the amount recovered.

(7) In a case where ...¹ the third condition is fulfilled, then—

(a) *if the security's acquisition cost exceeds the relevant amount, the allowable amount is an amount equal to the excess;*
(b) *if the security's acquisition cost is equal to or less than the relevant amount, the allowable amount is nil.*

(8) For the purposes of subsection (7) above the relevant amount is the aggregate of—

(a) *the amount (if any) of the principal of the loan which has been recovered, and*
(b) *the amount (if any) of the principal of the loan which has not been recovered but which ...¹ is recoverable.*

[(8A) For the purposes of subsection (2) above, an earlier time may be specified in the claim if—

(a) *the condition which was fulfilled at the time of the claim was also fulfilled at the earlier time; and either*
(b) *for capital gains tax purposes the earlier time falls not more than two years before the beginning of the year of assessment in which the claim is made; or*
(c) *for corporation tax purposes the earlier time falls on or after the first day of the earliest accounting period ending not more than two years before the time of the claim.]¹*

(9) Where an allowable loss has been treated under subsection (2) above as accruing to any person and the whole or any part of the relevant outstanding amount is at any time recovered by him, this Act shall have effect as if there had accrued to him at that time a chargeable gain equal to so much of the allowable loss as corresponds to the amount recovered.

(10) Where—

(a) *an allowable loss has been treated under subsection (2) above as accruing to a company ("the first company"), and*
(b) *the whole or any part of the relevant outstanding amount is at any time recovered by a company ("the second company") in the same group as the first company,*

this Act shall have effect as if there had accrued to the second company at that time a chargeable gain equal to so much of the allowable loss as corresponds to the amount recovered.

(11) In subsections (9) and (10) above "the relevant outstanding amount" means—

(a) *the amount of the principal of the loan outstanding when the claim was allowed, in a case where ...¹ the first or second condition was fulfilled;*
(b) *the amount of the part (or the greater or greatest part) arrived at ...¹ under subsection (5)(b) above, in a case where ...¹ the third condition was fulfilled.*

(12) This section does not apply if the security was issued before 15th March 1989 and was not held on 15th March 1989 by the person who made the loan.

[(13) This section does not apply for the purposes of corporation tax.]²]³

Commentary—*Simon's Direct Tax Service* C3.712, 713.
Concession D38—Qualifying corporate bonds.
Statement of Practice SP 8/90—Losses on irrecoverable loans in the form of qualifying corporate bonds: loss on early redemption.
Revenue Internal Guidance—Capital Gains Manual CG 66115–66116 (novation of debts: new lender has made loan for the purpose of this section, not true assignment of debt).
CG 66132–66134 (worked examples).
Definitions—"Accounting period", TA 1988 s 834(1); "acquisition cost", s 255(2); "allowable loss", ss 8(2), 16, 288(1); "chargeable gain", s 15(2); "company", ss 99, 288(1); "group", s 255(3); "issued", s 288(5); "qualifying corporate bond", s 117; "redemption date", s 255(1); "year of assessment", s 288(1).
Cross references—See s 255 (supplementary provisions).
FA 1993 s 165 and Sch 17 para 6 (relief under this section for non-sterling debts on securities).
FA 1996 Sch 13 paras 3(1), (1A), 10(4), 13(9) (application of these sub-paras (as inserted by FA 1999 s 65) concerning the meaning of "relevant discounted securities" for the purposes of sub-s (1)(c) above with effect for any claim made after 14 February 1999: FA 1999 s 65(12)).
Amendments—¹ Words in sub-s (2) substituted, words omitted from sub-ss (6), (7), (8), (11) repealed and sub-s (8A) inserted by FA 1996 Sch 39 para 9, Sch 41 Pt VIII(4) with effect in relation to claims made after 5 April 1996.
² Words in sub-s (1)(c) and sub-s (13) inserted by FA 1996 ss 104, 105(1), Sch 14 para 66 with effect from the year 1996–97.
³ This section repealed by FA 1998 ss 141, 165, Sch 27 Part III(32) with effect in relation to loans made after 16 March 1998.

[255 Provisions supplementary to section 254

(1) For the purposes of section 254 a security's redemption date is the latest date on which, under the terms on which the security was issued, the company or body which issued it can be required to redeem it.

(2) For the purposes of section 254 a security's acquisition cost is the amount or value of the consideration in money or money's worth given, by or on behalf of the person who made the loan, wholly and exclusively for the acquisition of the security, together with the incidental costs to him of the acquisition.

(3) For the purposes of section 254(10) 2 companies are in the same group if they have been in the same group at any time after the loan was made.

(4) Section 253(9) shall apply for the purposes of section 254(6) and (8) to (10) as it applies for the purposes of section 253(5).

(5) Section 253(10), (12) and (14)(c) shall apply for the purposes of section 254 and of this section as they apply for the purposes of section 253, ignoring for this purpose the words following ''lender'' in section 253(12).][1]

Commentary—*Simon's Direct Tax Service* **C3.712, 713.**
Definitions—''Company'', ss 99, 288(1); ''issued'', s 288(5).
Amendments—[1] This section repealed by FA 1998 ss 141, 165, Sch 27 Part III(32) with effect in relation to loans made after 16 March 1998.

Charities and gifts of non-business assets etc

256 Charities

(1) Subject to section 505(3) of the Taxes Act and subsection (2) below, a gain shall not be a chargeable gain if it accrues to a charity and is applicable and applied for charitable purposes.

(2) If property held on charitable trusts ceases to be subject to charitable trusts—

(*a*) the trustees shall be treated as if they had disposed of, and immediately reacquired, the property for a consideration equal to its market value, any gain on the disposal being treated as not accruing to a charity, and
(*b*) if and so far as any of that property represents, directly or indirectly, the consideration for the disposal of assets by the trustees, any gain accruing on that disposal shall be treated as not having accrued to a charity,

and an assessment to capital gains tax chargeable by virtue of paragraph (*b*) above may be made at any time not more than 3 years after the end of the year of assessment in which the property ceases to be subject to charitable trusts.

Commentary—*Simon's Direct Tax Service* **C1.220.**
Concession D47—Temporary loss of charitable status due to reverter of school and other sites; no adverse effect on CGT and income tax exemption.
Revenue Interpretation RI 189—This section applies to exempt gains otherwise chargeable on UK charities under TCGA 1992 s 87.
Revenue Internal Guidance—Capital gains tax manual, CG 67516 (sub-s (2) Reverter of Situs Act 1987, closure of schools held by trustees).
Revenue & other press releases—IR & HM C & E 23-11-89 (tax treatment of disaster funds: guidelines for organisers).
IR leaflet CB(1) ''Setting up a charity in Scotland'' (available from Inland Revenue, Claims (Scotland)).
Simon's Tax Cases—s 256(1), *Prest v Bettinson* [1980] STC 607*; *IRC v Helen Slater Charitable Trust Ltd* [1981] STC 471*.
Definitions—''Asset'', s 21(1); ''chargeable gain'', s 15(2); ''market value'', ss 272–274, Sch 11; ''the Taxes Act'', s 288(1); ''year of assessment'', s 288(1).
Cross references—See TA 1988 s 505(5), (6) (certain gains not relieved under this section; charity's discretion to specify); TA 1988 s 761(6) (offshore income gains).

257 Gifts to charities etc

(1) Subsection (2) below shall apply where a disposal of an asset is made otherwise than under a bargain at arm's length—

(*a*) to a charity, or
(*b*) to any bodies mentioned in Schedule 3 to the Inheritance Tax Act 1984 (gifts for national purposes, etc)

[and the disposal is not one in relation to which section 151A(1) has effect.][1]

(2) Sections 17(1) and 258(3) shall not apply; but if the disposal is by way of gift (including a gift in settlement) or for a consideration not exceeding the sums allowable as a deduction under section 38, then—

(*a*) the disposal and acquisition shall be treated for the purposes of this Act as being made for such consideration as to secure that neither a gain nor a loss accrues on the disposal, and
(*b*) where, after the disposal, the asset is disposed of by the person who acquired it under the disposal, its acquisition by the person making the earlier disposal shall be treated for the purposes of this Act as the acquisition of the person making the later disposal.

(3) Where—

(*a*) otherwise than on the termination of a life interest (within the meaning of section 72) by the death of the person entitled thereto, any assets or parts of any assets forming part of settled property are, under section 71, deemed to be disposed of and reacquired by the trustee, and
(*b*) the person becoming entitled as mentioned in section 71(1) is a charity, or a body mentioned in Schedule 3 to the Inheritance Tax Act 1984 (gifts for national purposes, etc),

then, if no consideration is received by any person for or in connection with any transaction by virtue of which the charity or other body becomes so entitled, the disposal and reacquisition of the assets to which the charity or other body becomes so entitled shall, notwithstanding section 71, be treated for the purposes of this Act as made for such consideration as to secure that neither a gain nor a loss accrues on the disposal.

(4) In subsection (2)(*b*) above the first reference to a disposal includes a disposal to which section 146(2) of the 1979 Act applied where the person who acquired the asset on that disposal disposes of the asset after the coming into force of this section.

Commentary—*Simon's Direct Tax Service* **C1.415.**
Concession D47—Temporary loss of charitable status due to reverter of school and other sites; no adverse effect on CGT and income tax exemption.
Revenue Interpretation RI 23—Gift of qualifying corporate bonds to a charity.
Definitions—"The 1979 Act", s 288(1); "asset", s 21(1); "company", ss 99, 288(1); "settled property", s 68.
Cross references—See TCGA 1992 s 35(3)(*d*) (application of rebasing provisions).
TCGA 1992 s 55(5) (indexation allowance by reference to market value on 31 March 1982).
TCGA 1992 Sch 3 para 1 (assets treated as held on 31 March 1982).
TCGA 1992 Sch 4 para 7 (reduction of deferred gain attributable to a disposal by a person of an asset not held by him on 31 March 1982 but acquired by him on a no gain/no loss disposal in accordance with sub-s (3) above from a person who had held the asset on 31 March 1982).
IHTA 1984 is reproduced in Part II of the *Yellow Tax Handbook*.
FA 2002 Sch 18 para 9(3) (relief for donors in relation to community amateur sports clubs; this section has effect as if a registered club were a charity).
Amendments—¹ Words in sub-s (1) inserted by FA 1995 s 72(5), (8), with effect from the year 1995–96.

258 Works of art etc

(1) ...¹

(2) A gain shall not be a chargeable gain if it accrues on the disposal of an asset with respect to which an inheritance tax undertaking or an undertaking under the following provisions of this section has been given and—

    (*a*) the disposal is by way of sale by private treaty to a body mentioned in Schedule 3 to the [Inheritance Tax Act 1984 ("the 1984 Act")]² (museums, etc), or is to such a body otherwise than by sale, or

    (*b*) the disposal is to the Board in pursuance of section 230 of the 1984 Act or in accordance with directions given by the Treasury under section 50 or 51 of the Finance Act 1946 (acceptance of property in satisfaction of tax).

(3) Subsection (4) below shall have effect in respect of the disposal of any asset which is property which has been or could be designated under section 31 of the 1984 Act, being—

    (*a*) a disposal by way of gift, including a gift in settlement, or

    (*b*) a disposal of settled property by the trustee on an occasion when, under section 71(1), the trustee is deemed to dispose of and immediately reacquire settled property (other than any disposal on which by virtue of section 73 no chargeable gain or allowable loss accrues to the trustee),

if the requisite undertaking described in section 31 of the 1984 Act (maintenance, preservation and access) is given by such person as the Board think appropriate in the circumstances of the case.

(4) The person making a disposal to which subsection (3) above applies and the person acquiring the asset on the disposal shall be treated for all the purposes of this Act as if the asset was acquired from the one making the disposal for a consideration of such an amount as would secure that on the disposal neither a gain nor a loss would accrue to the one making the disposal.

(5) If—

    (*a*) there is a sale of the asset and inheritance tax is chargeable under section 32 of the 1984 Act (or would be chargeable if an inheritance tax undertaking as well as an undertaking under this section had been given), or

    (*b*) the Board are satisfied that at any time during the period for which any such undertaking was given it has not been observed in a material respect,

the person selling that asset or, as the case may be, the owner of the asset shall be treated for the purposes of this Act as having sold the asset for a consideration equal to its market value, and, in the case of a failure to comply with the undertaking, having immediately reacquired it for a consideration equal to its market value.

(6) The period for which an undertaking under this section is given shall be until the person beneficially entitled to the asset dies or it is disposed of, whether by sale or gift or otherwise; and if the asset subject to the undertaking is disposed of—

    (*a*) otherwise than on sale, and

    (*b*) without a further undertaking being given under this section,

subsection (5) above shall apply as if the asset had been sold to an individual.

References in this subsection to a disposal shall be construed without regard to any provision of this Act under which an asset is deemed to be disposed of.

(7) Where under subsection (5) above a person is treated as having sold for a consideration equal to its market value any asset within section 31(1)(*c*), (*d*) or (*e*) of the 1984 Act, he shall also be treated as having sold and immediately reacquired for a consideration equal to its market value any asset associated with it; but the Board may direct that the preceding provisions of this subsection shall not have effect in any case in which it appears to them that the entity consisting of the asset and any assets associated with it has not been materially affected.

For the purposes of this subsection 2 or more assets are associated with each other if one of them is a building falling within section 31(1)(*c*) of the 1984 Act and the other or others such land or objects as, in relation to that building, fall within section 31(1)(*d*) or (*e*) of the 1984 Act.

(8) If in pursuance of subsection (5) above a person is treated as having on any occasion sold an asset and inheritance tax becomes chargeable on the same occasion, then, in determining the value of the asset for the purposes of that tax, an allowance shall be made for the capital gains tax chargeable on any chargeable gain accruing on that occasion.

[(8A) Section 35A of the 1984 Act (variation of undertakings) shall have effect in relation to an undertaking given under this section as it has effect in relation to an undertaking given under section 30 of that Act.][3]

(9) In this section "inheritance tax undertaking" means an undertaking under Chapter II of Part II or section 78 of, or Schedule 5 to, the 1984 Act.

Commentary—*Simon's Direct Tax Service* C1.418.
Statement of Practice SP 4/92—Capital gains rebasing elections.
Revenue Internal Guidance—Capital Gains Manual CG 10281 (works of art etc, historic houses and associated assets and preservation of land for public benefit may qualify for relief from charge).
Definitions—"Allowable loss", ss 8(2), 16, 288(1); "asset", s 21(1); "the Board", s 288(1); "chargeable gain", s 15(2); "land", s 288(1); "market value", ss 272–274, Sch 11; "settled property", s 68.
Cross references—See the CGT Regulations, SI 1967/149 reg 13(4) (where this section applies, a determination or agreement relating to market value of an asset is conclusive for both the person disposing of and the person acquiring the asset).
TCGA 1992 s 35(3)(*d*) (application of rebasing provisions).
TCGA 1992 s 55(5) (indexation allowance by reference to market value on 31 March 1982).
TCGA 1992 s 257 (gifts to charities).
TCGA 1992 Sch 3 para 1 (assets treated as held on 31 March 1982).
TCGA 1992 Sch 4 para 7 (reduction of deferred gain attributable to a disposal by a person of an asset not held by him on 31 March 1982 but acquired by him on a no gain/no loss disposal in accordance with sub-s (4) above from a person who had held the asset on 31 March 1982).
Amendments—[1] Sub-s (1) repealed by FA 1998 s 165, Sch 27 Part IV with effect in relation to any disposal after 16 March 1998.
[2] Words in sub-s (2)(a) substituted by FA 1998 s 143(7) with effect in relation to any disposal after 16 March 1998.
[3] Sub-s (8A) inserted by FA 1998 Sch 25 para 9 with effect in relation to undertakings given after 30 July 1998, subject to FA 1998 Sch 25 para 10.

259 Gifts to housing associations

(1) Subsection (2) below shall apply where—

(*a*) a disposal of an estate or interest in land in the United Kingdom is made to a [relevant][1] housing association otherwise than under a bargain at arm's length, and
(*b*) a claim for relief under this section is made by the transferor and the association.

(2) Section 17(1) shall not apply; but if the disposal is by way of gift or for a consideration not exceeding the sums allowable as a deduction under section 38, then—

(*a*) the disposal and acquisition shall be treated for the purposes of this Act as being made for such consideration as to secure that neither a gain nor a loss accrues on the disposal, and
(*b*) where, after the disposal, the estate or interest is disposed of by the association, its acquisition by the person making the earlier disposal shall be treated for the purposes of this Act as the acquisition of the association.

[(3) In this section "relevant housing association" means—

(*a*) a registered social landlord within the meaning of Part I of the Housing Act 1996
(*b*) a registered housing association within the meaning of the Housing Associations Act 1985 (Scottish registered housing associations), or
(*c*) a registered housing association within the meaning of Part II of the Housing (Northern Ireland) Order 1992.][1]

(4) In subsection (2)(*b*) above the first reference to a disposal includes a disposal to which section 146A(2) of the 1979 Act applied where the association which acquired the estate or interest in land on that disposal disposes of it after the coming into force of this section.

Commentary—*Simon's Direct Tax Service* C1.420.
Definitions—"The 1979 Act", s 288(1); "land", s 288(1).
Cross references—See TCGA 1992 s 55(5) (indexation allowance on a non-no gain/no loss disposal after 31 March 1982 of assets acquired on a no gain/no loss acquisition under sub-s (2) above).
Amendments—[1] Word in sub-s (1)(*a*), and sub-s (3), substituted by the Housing Act 1996 (Consequential Provisions) Order , SI 1996 /2325 Sch 2 para 20(1), (3) with effect from 1 October 1996.

260 Gifts on which inheritance tax is chargeable etc

(1) If—

(*a*) an individual or the trustees of a settlement ("the transferor") make a disposal within subsection (2) below of an asset,
(*b*) the asset is acquired by an individual or the trustees of a settlement ("the transferee"), and
(*c*) a claim for relief under this section is made by the transferor and the transferee or, where the trustees of a settlement are the transferee, by the transferor alone,

then, subject to subsection (6) below and [sections 169 and 261][4], subsection (3) below shall apply in relation to the disposal.

(2) A disposal is within this subsection if it is made otherwise than under a bargain at arm's length and—

   (a) is a chargeable transfer within the meaning of the Inheritance Tax Act 1984 (or would be but for section 19 of that Act) and is not a potentially exempt transfer (within the meaning of that Act),

   (b) is an exempt transfer by virtue of—

      (i) section 24 of that Act (transfers to political parties),

      (ii) ...[3]

      (iii) section 27 of that Act (transfers to maintenance funds for historic buildings etc), or

      (iv) section 30 of that Act (transfers of designated property),

   (c) is a disposition to which section 57A of that Act applies and by which the property disposed of becomes held on trusts of the kind referred to in subsection (1)(b) of that section (maintenance funds for historic buildings etc),

   (d) by virtue of subsection (4) of section 71 of that Act (accumulation and maintenance trusts) does not constitute an occasion on which inheritance tax is chargeable under that section,

   (e) by virtue of section 78(1) of that Act (transfers of works of art etc) does not constitute an occasion on which tax is chargeable under Chapter III of Part III of that Act, or

   (f) is a disposal of an asset comprised in a settlement where, as a result of the asset or part of it becoming comprised in another settlement, there is no charge, or a reduced charge, to inheritance tax by virtue of paragraph 9, 16 or 17 of Schedule 4 to that Act (transfers to maintenance funds for historic buildings etc).

(3) Where this subsection applies in relation to a disposal—

   (a) the amount of any chargeable gain which, apart from this section, would accrue to the transferor on the disposal, and

   (b) the amount of the consideration for which, apart from this section, the transferee would be regarded for the purposes of capital gains tax as having acquired the asset in question,

shall each be reduced by an amount equal to the held-over gain on the disposal.

(4) Subject to subsection (5) below, the reference in subsection (3) above to the held-over gain on a disposal is a reference to the chargeable gain which would have accrued on that disposal apart from this section.

(5) In any case where—

   (a) there is actual consideration (as opposed to the consideration equal to the market value which is deemed to be given by virtue of any provision of this Act) for a disposal in respect of which a claim for relief is made under this section, and

   (b) that actual consideration exceeds the sums allowable as a deduction under section 38,

the held-over gain on the disposal shall be reduced by the excess referred to in paragraph (b) above or, if part of the gain on the disposal is relieved under Schedule 6, by so much, if any, of that excess as exceeds the part so relieved.

(6) Subsection (3) above does not apply in relation to a disposal of assets within section 115(1) on which a gain is deemed to accrue by virtue of section 116(10)(b).

[(6A) Subsection (3) above does not apply, so far as any gain accruing in accordance with paragraphs 4 and 5 of Schedule 5B is concerned, in relation to the disposal which constitutes the chargeable event by virtue of which that gain accrues.][1]

[(6B) Subsection (3) above does not apply, so far as any gain accruing in accordance with paragraphs 4 and 5 of Schedule 5C is concerned, in relation to the disposal which constitutes the chargeable event by virtue of which that gain accrues.][2]

(7) In the case of a disposal within subsection (2)(a) above there shall be allowed as a deduction in computing the chargeable gain accruing to the transferee on the disposal of the asset in question an amount equal to whichever is the lesser of—

   (a) the inheritance tax attributable to the value of the asset; and

   (b) the amount of the chargeable gain as computed apart from this subsection.

(8) Where an amount of inheritance tax is varied after it has been taken into account under subsection (7) above, all necessary adjustments shall be made, whether by the making of an assessment to capital gains tax or by the discharge or repayment of such tax.

(9) Where subsection (3) above applies in relation to a disposal which is deemed to occur by virtue of section 71(1) or 72(1), subsection (5) above shall not apply.

(10) Where a disposal is partly within subsection (2) above, or is a disposal within paragraph (f) of that subsection on which there is a reduced charge such as is mentioned in that paragraph, the preceding provisions of this section shall have effect in relation to an appropriate part of the disposal.

Commentary—*Simon's Direct Tax Service* C1.425.
Statement of Practice SP 8/92—Valuation of gifts in respect of which CGT holdover relief is available.
Revenue & other press releases—IR Tax Bulletin April 1997 p 417 (confirms that Statement of Practice SP 8/92 continues under self-assessment much as before, and explains the introduction of a new claim form).
Revenue Internal Guidance—Capital Gains Manual CG 10283 (effect of a claim for gift hold-over relief).
CG 67101–67103 (worked examples of the application of this section).
Definitions—"Asset", s 21(1); "chargeable gain", s 15(2); "market value", ss 272–274, Sch 11.

Cross references—See TA 1988 Sch 28 para 3(3) (claim under this section in respect of gains from a disposal of an offshore-trust).
TCGA 1992 s 74(1) (effect on a claim for relief under this section where assets are deemed to be disposed of on termination of life interest).
TCGA 1992 s 81(7) (application of this section where non-resident trustees become resident as a result of a trustee's death).
TCGA 1992 s 168 (claw back of relief under this section on migration of donee before disposing of the asset).
TCGA 1992 s 169 (relief under this section not available for gifts of business assets to dual resident trustees).
TCGA 1992 s 281(1) (payments by instalments of tax on gifts).
Amendments—[1] Sub-s (6A) inserted by FA 1995 Sch 13 para 4(2), (4) with effect for gains accruing and events occurring after 28 November 1994.
[2] Sub-s (6B) inserted by FA 1995 s 72(6), (8) with effect from the year 1995–96.
[3] Sub-s (2)(b)(ii) repealed by FA 1998 s 165, Sch 27 Part IV with effect in relation to any disposal after 16 March 1998.
[4] Words in sub-s (1) substituted by FA 2000 s 90(2), (5) with effect for disposals made after 8 November 1999.
Prospective amendment—Words in sub-s (5) repealed by FA 1998 s 165, Sch 27 Part III(31) with effect for disposals in the year 2003–04 and subsequent years of assessment.

261 Section 260 relief: gifts to non-residents

(1) Section 260(3) shall not apply where the transferee is neither resident nor ordinarily resident in the United Kingdom.

(2) Section 260(3) shall not apply where the transferee is an individual who—

(a) though resident or ordinarily resident in the United Kingdom, is regarded for the purposes of any double taxation relief arrangements as resident in a territory outside the United Kingdom, and

(b) by virtue of the arrangements would not be liable in the United Kingdom to tax on a gain arising on a disposal of the asset occurring immediately after its acquisition.

Commentary—*Simon's Direct Tax Service* C1.425, 428.
Definitions—"Asset", s 21(1); "double taxation relief arrangements", s 288(1); "ordinarily resident", s 9(1); "resident", s 9(1).

Miscellaneous reliefs and exemptions

262 Chattel exemption

(1) Subject to this section a gain accruing on a disposal of an asset which is tangible movable property shall not be a chargeable gain if the amount or value of the consideration for the disposal does not exceed £6,000.

(2) Where the amount or value of the consideration for the disposal of an asset which is tangible movable property exceeds £6,000, there shall be excluded from any chargeable gain accruing on the disposal so much of it as exceeds five-thirds of the difference between—

(a) the amount or value of the consideration, and
(b) £6,000.

(3) Subsections (1) and (2) above shall not affect the amount of an allowable loss accruing on the disposal of an asset, but for the purposes of computing under this Act the amount of a loss accruing on the disposal of tangible movable property the consideration for the disposal shall, if less than £6,000, be deemed to be £6,000 and the losses which are allowable losses shall be restricted accordingly.

(4) If 2 or more assets which have formed part of a set of articles of any description all owned at one time by one person are disposed of by that person, and—

(a) to the same person, or
(b) to persons who are acting in concert or who are connected persons,

whether on the same or different occasions, the 2 or more transactions shall be treated as a single transaction disposing of a single asset, but with any necessary apportionments of the reductions in chargeable gains, and in allowable losses, under subsections (2) and (3) above.

(5) If the disposal is of a right or interest in or over tangible movable property—

(a) in the first instance subsections (1), (2) and (3) above shall be applied in relation to the asset as a whole, taking the consideration as including the market value of what remains undisposed of, in addition to the actual consideration,

(b) where the sum of the actual consideration and that market value exceeds £6,000, the part of any chargeable gain that is excluded from it under subsection (2) above shall be so much of the gain as exceeds five-thirds of the difference between that sum and £6,000 multiplied by the fraction equal to the actual consideration divided by the said sum, and

(c) where that sum is less than £6,000 any loss shall be restricted under subsection (3) above by deeming the consideration to be the actual consideration plus the said fraction of the difference between the said sum and £6,000.

(6) This section shall not apply—

(a) in relation to a disposal of commodities of any description by a person dealing on a terminal market or dealing with or through a person ordinarily engaged in dealing on a terminal market, or
(b) in relation to a disposal of currency of any description.

Commentary—*Simon's Direct Tax Service* C1.406.
Statement of Practice SP 4/92—Capital gains rebasing elections.

Revenue Interpretation RI 208—Bottles of wine may constitute a set within sub-s (4) if they are from the same vineyard and vintage year and are worth more collectively than individually.
Revenue Internal Guidance—Capital gains tax manual, CG 76552–76554 (meaning of "tangible moveable property").
CG 76610–76613 (worked examples).
CG 76632 (sub-s (4) assets form a set if they are essentially similar and complementary and their value together exceeds total of individual values).
CG 76635 (sub-s (4) purchase of articles in one lot at auction does not imply that the articles form a set).
CG 76636 (sub-s (4) a collection may include one or more sets of assets).
CG 76870–76884 (assets which are chattels).
CG 76920–76928 (personalised car number plates).
Simon's Tax Cases—*Neely v Ward* [1993] STC 196*.
s 262(3), *Neely v Ward* [1991] STC 656*.
Definitions—"Allowable loss", ss 8(2), 16, 288(1); "asset", s 21(1); "chargeable gain", s 15(2); "connected", s 286; "market value", ss 272–274, Sch 11.
Cross reference—See TMA 1970 s 12(2)(*b*) (information about chargeable gains).

263 Passenger vehicles

A mechanically propelled road vehicle constructed or adapted for the carriage of passengers, except for a vehicle of a type not commonly used as a private vehicle and unsuitable to be so used, shall not be a chargeable asset; and accordingly no chargeable gain or allowable loss shall accrue on its disposal.

Commentary—*Simon's Direct Tax Service* C1.405.
Statement of Practice SP 4/92—Capital gains rebasing elections.
Revenue Internal Guidance—Capital gains tax manuals, CG 76907 (exemption does not apply to taxi cabs, racing cars, single seater sports cars, motor cycles, scooters and motor cycle/side car combinations).
CG 76920–76928 (personalised car number plates not covered by this exemption).
Definitions—"Allowable loss", ss 8(2), 16, 288(1); "asset", s 21(1); "chargeable gain", s 15(2).
Cross reference—See TMA 1970 s 12(2) (information about chargeable gains).

[263A Agreements for sale and repurchase of securities

(1) Subject to subsections (2) to (4) below, in any case falling within subsection (1) of section 730A of the Taxes Act (treatment of price differential on sale and repurchase of securities) and in any case which would fall within that subsection if the sale price and the repurchase price were different—

(*a*) the acquisition of the securities in question by the interim holder and the disposal of those securities by him to the repurchaser; and
(*b*) except where the repurchaser is or may be different from the original owner, the disposal of those securities by the original owner and any acquisition of those securities by the original owner as the repurchaser,

shall be disregarded for the purposes of capital gains tax.

(2) Subsection (1) above does not apply in any case where the repurchase price of the securities in question falls to be calculated for the purposes of section 730A of the Taxes Act by reference to provisions of section 737C of that Act that are not in force in relation to those securities when the repurchase price becomes due.

(3) Subsection (1) above does not apply if—

(*a*) the agreement or agreements under which provision is made for the sale and repurchase are not such as would be entered into by persons dealing with each other at arm's length; or
(*b*) any of the benefits or risks arising from fluctuations, before the repurchase takes place, in the market value of the securities sold accrues to, or falls on, the interim holder.

(4) Subsection (1) above does not apply in relation to any disposal or acquisition of qualifying corporate bonds in a case where the securities disposed of by the original owner or those acquired by him, or by any other person, as the repurchaser are not such bonds.

(5) Expressions used in this section and in section 730A of the Taxes Act have the same meanings in this section as in that section.]

Commentary—*Simon's Direct Tax Service* B3.727.
Definitions—"Securities", TA 1988 s 737B; "the Taxes Act", TA 1988 s 831(2).
Cross reference—See the European Single Currency (Taxes) Regulations, SI 1998/3177 reg 18 (treatment of payment made or deemed to be made by interim holder where there is an arrangement for the sale and repurchase of securities to which sub-s (1) applies as a result of a euroconversion of those securities).
Modifications—Sale and Repurchase of Securities (Modification of Enactments) Regulations, SI 1995/3220 regs 4, 5 (modification of this section in relation to arrangements for the sale and redemption of securities and for the substitution of different securities for the original securities to be repurchased, involving the return of the original securities to the original owner).
Amendment—This section was inserted by FA 1995 s 80(4), (5) with effect where the agreement to sell the securities was entered into on or after 1 May 1995.

[263B Stock lending arrangements

(1) In this section "stock lending arrangement" means so much of any arrangements between two persons ("the borrower" and "the lender") as are arrangements under which—

(*a*) the lender transfers securities to the borrower otherwise than by way of sale; and
(*b*) a requirement is imposed on the borrower to transfer those securities back to the lender otherwise than by way of sale.

(2) Subject to the following provisions of this section and section 263C(2), the disposals and acquisitions made in pursuance of any stock lending arrangement shall be disregarded for the purposes of capital gains tax.

(3) Where—

(a) the borrower under any stock lending arrangement disposes of any securities transferred to him under the arrangement,

(b) that disposal is made otherwise than in the discharge of the requirement for the transfer of securities back to the lender, and

(c) that requirement, so far as it relates to the securities disposed of, has been or will be discharged by the transfer of securities other than those transferred to the borrower,

any question relating to the acquisition of the securities disposed of shall be determined (without prejudice to the provisions of Chapter I of Part IV) as if the securities disposed of were the securities with which that requirement (so far as relating to the securities disposed of) has been or will be discharged.

(4) Where, in the case of any stock lending arrangement, it becomes apparent, at any time after the making of the transfer by the lender, that the requirement for the borrower to make a transfer back to the lender will not be complied with—

(a) the lender shall be deemed for the purposes of this Act to have made a disposal at that time of the securities transferred to the borrower;

(b) the borrower shall be deemed to have acquired them at that time; and

(c) subsection (3) above shall have effect in relation to any disposal before that time by the borrower of securities transferred to him by the lender as if the securities deemed to have been acquired by the borrower in accordance with paragraph (b) above were to be used for discharging a requirement to transfer securities back to the lender.

(5) References in this section, in relation to a person to whom securities are transferred, to the transfer of those securities back to another person shall be construed as if the cases where those securities are taken to be transferred back to that other person included any case where securities of the same description as those securities are transferred to that other person either—

(a) in accordance with a requirement to transfer securities of the same description; or

(b) in exercise of a power to substitute securities of the same description for the securities that are required to be transferred back.

(6) For the purposes of this section securities shall not be taken to be of the same description as other securities unless they are in the same quantities, give the same rights against the same persons and are of the same type and nominal value as the other securities.

(7) In this section—

''interest'' includes dividends; and

''securities'' means United Kingdom equities, United Kingdom securities or overseas securities (within the meaning, in each case, of Schedule 23A to the Taxes Act).][1]

Commentary—*Simon's Direct Tax Service* **B3.1007.**
Cross references—See TCGA 1992 s 263C (stock lending involving redemption).
European Single Currency (Taxes) Regulations, SI 1998/3177 regs 20–23 (stock lending arrangements in relation to the introduction of the euro).
Amendment—[1] This section inserted by FA 1997 Sch 10 paras 5(1), 7(1) with effect in relation to, and to transfers under, any arrangement made on or after 1 July 1997 by virtue of the Finance Act 1997, Schedule 10, (Appointed Day) Order, SI 1997/991.

[263C Stock lending involving redemption

(1) In section 263B references to the transfer back to a person of securities transferred by him shall be taken to include references to the payment to him, in pursuance of an obligation arising on any person's becoming entitled to receive an amount in respect of the redemption of those securities, of an amount equal to the amount of the entitlement.

(2) Where, in pursuance of any such obligation, the lender under any stock lending arrangement is paid any amount in respect of the redemption of any securities to which the arrangement relates—

(a) that lender shall be deemed for the purposes of this Act to have disposed, for that amount, of the securities in respect of whose redemption it is paid (''the relevant lent securities'');

(b) the borrower shall not, in respect of the redemption, be taken for the purposes of this Act to have made any disposal of the relevant lent securities; and

(c) section 263B(3) shall have effect in relation to disposals of any of the relevant lent securities made by the borrower before the redemption as if—

(i) the amount paid to the lender were an amount paid for the acquisition of securities, and

(ii) the securities acquired were to be used by the borrower for discharging a requirement under the arrangement to transfer the relevant lent securities back to the lender.

(3) Expressions used in this section and section 263B have the same meanings in this section as in that section.][1]

Commentary—*Simon's Direct Tax Service* **B3.1007.**
Definitions—''Securities'', s 263B; ''stock lending arrangement'', s 263B.
Amendment—[1] This section inserted by FA 1997 Sch 10 paras 5(1), 7(1) with effect in relation to, and to transfers under, any arrangement made on or after 1 July 1997 by virtue of the Finance Act 1997, Schedule 10, (Appointed Day) Order, SI 1997/991.

264 Relief for local constituency associations of political parties on reorganisation of constituencies

(1) In this section "relevant date" means the date of coming into operation of an Order in Council under the Parliamentary Constituencies Act 1986 (orders specifying new parliamentary constituencies) and, in relation to any relevant date—

    (a) "former parliamentary constituency" means an area which, for the purposes of parliamentary elections, was a constituency immediately before that date but is no longer such a constituency after that date; and

    (b) "new parliamentary constituency" means an area which, for the purposes of parliamentary elections, is a constituency immediately after that date but was not such a constituency before that date.

(2) In this section "local constituency association" means an unincorporated association (whether described as an association, a branch or otherwise) whose primary purpose is to further the aims of a political party in an area which at any time is or was the same or substantially the same as the area of a parliamentary constituency or 2 or more parliamentary constituencies and, in relation to any relevant date—

    (a) "existing association" means a local constituency association whose area was the same, or substantially the same, as the area of a former parliamentary constituency or 2 or more such constituencies; and

    (b) "new association" means a local constituency association whose area is the same, or substantially the same, as the area of a new parliamentary constituency or 2 or more such constituencies.

(3) For the purposes of this section, a new association is a successor to an existing association if any part of the existing association's area is comprised in the new association's area.

(4) In any case where, before, on or after a relevant date—

    (a) an existing association disposes of land to a new association which is a successor to the existing association, or

    (b) an existing association disposes of land to a body (whether corporate or unincorporated) which is an organ of the political party concerned and, as soon as practicable thereafter, that body disposes of the land to a new association which is a successor to the existing association,

the parties to the disposal or, where paragraph (b) above applies, to each of the disposals, shall be treated for the purposes of tax on chargeable gains as if the land disposed of were acquired from the existing association or the body making the disposal for a consideration of such an amount as would secure that on the disposal neither a gain nor a loss accrued to that association or body.

(5) In a case falling within subsection (4) above, the new association shall be treated for the purposes of Schedule 2 as if the acquisition by the existing association of the land disposed of as mentioned in that subsection had been the new association's acquisition of it.

(6) In any case where—

    (a) before, on or after a relevant date, an existing association disposes of any land which was used and occupied by it for the purposes of its functions, and

    (b) the existing association transfers the whole or part of the proceeds of the disposal to a new association which is a successor to the existing association,

then, subject to subsection (7) below, this Act (and, in particular, the provisions of sections 152 to 158) shall have effect as if, since the time it was acquired by the existing association, the land disposed of had been the property of the new association and, accordingly, as if the disposal of it had been by the new association.

(7) If, in a case falling within subsection (6) above, only part of the proceeds of the disposal is transferred to the new association, that subsection shall apply—

    (a) as if there existed in the land disposed of as mentioned in paragraph (a) of that subsection a separate asset in the form of a corresponding undivided share in that land, and subject to any necessary apportionments of consideration for an acquisition or disposal of, or of an interest in, that land; and

    (b) as if the references in that subsection (other than paragraph (a) thereof) to the land disposed of and the disposal of it were references respectively to the corresponding undivided share referred to in paragraph (a) above and the disposal of that share;

and for this purpose a corresponding undivided share in the land disposed of is a share which bears to the whole of that land the same proportion as the part of the proceeds transferred bears to the whole of those proceeds.

(8) In this section "political party" means a political party which qualifies for exemption under section 24 of the Inheritance Tax Act 1984 (gifts to political parties).

Commentary—*Simon's Direct Tax Service* **D4.316.**
Definitions—"Asset", s 21(1); "chargeable gain", s 15(2); "land", s 288(1).

Cross references—See TCGA 1992 s 35(3)(*d*) (application of rebasing provisions).

TCGA 1992 s 55(5) (indexation allowance on a non-no gain/no loss disposal after 31 March 1982 of assets acquired on a no gain/no loss acquisition under this section).

TCGA 1992 Sch 4 para 7 (reduction of deferred gain attributable to a disposal by a person of an asset not held by him on 31 March 1982 but acquired by him on a no gain/no loss disposal in accordance with this section from a person who had held the asset on 31 March 1982).

265 Designated international organisations

(1) Where—

(*a*) the United Kingdom or any of the Communities is a member of an international organisation; and

(*b*) the agreement under which it became a member provides for exemption from tax, in relation to the organisation, of the kind for which provision is made by this section;

the Treasury may by order designate that organisation for the purposes of this section.

(2) The Treasury may by order designate any of the Communities or the European Investment Bank for the purposes of this section.

(3) Where an organisation has been designated for the purposes of this section, then any security issued by the organisation shall be taken, for the purposes of capital gains tax, to be situated outside the United Kingdom.

Commentary—*Simon's Direct Tax Service* **D4.338.**

Definition—''Issued'', s 288(5).

Cross references—See TCGA 1992 s 287(4) (exception for the purposes of this section to the general rule of orders being subject to annulment by Parliament).

266 Inter-American Development Bank

A security issued by the Inter-American Development Bank shall be taken for the purposes of this Act to be situated outside the United Kingdom.

Commentary—*Simon's Direct Tax Service* **D4.921.**

Definition—''Issued'', s 288(5).

267 Sharing of transmission facilities

(1) This section applies to any agreement relating to the sharing of transmission facilities—

(*a*) to which the parties are national broadcasting companies,

(*b*) which is entered into on or after 25th July 1991 (the day on which the Finance Act 1991 was passed) and before 1st January 1992 or such later date as may be specified for the purposes of this paragraph by the Secretary of State, and

(*c*) in relation to which the Secretary of State has certified that it is expedient that this section should apply.

(2) Where under an agreement to which this section applies one party to the agreement disposes of an asset to another party to the agreement, both parties shall be treated for the purposes of corporation tax on chargeable gains as if the asset acquired by the party to whom the disposal is made were acquired for a consideration of such amount as would secure that on the other's disposal neither a gain nor a loss would accrue to that other.

(3) Where under an agreement to which this section applies one party to the agreement disposes of an asset to another party to the agreement and the asset is one which the party making the disposal acquired on a part disposal by the party to whom the disposal under the agreement is made, then in applying subsection (2) above—

(*a*) section 42 shall be deemed to have had effect in relation to the part disposal with the omission of subsection (4),

(*b*) the amount or value of the consideration for the part disposal shall be taken to have been nil, and

(*c*) if the disposal under the agreement is one to which section 35(2) applies, the market value of the asset on 31st March 1982 shall be taken to have been nil.

(4) In this section ''national broadcasting company'' means a body corporate engaged in the broadcasting for general reception by means of wireless telegraphy of radio or television services or both on a national basis.

Commentary—*Simon's Direct Tax Service* **C1.421.**

Definitions—''Asset'', s 21(1); ''chargeable gain'', s 15(2); ''market value'', ss 272–274, Sch 11; ''part disposal'', s 21(2).

Cross references—See TCGA 1992 s 35(3)(*d*) (application of rebasing provisions).

TCGA 1992 s 55(5) (indexation allowance on a non-no gain/no loss disposal after 31 March 1982 of assets acquired on a no gain/no loss acquisition under sub-s (2) above).

TCGA 1992 Sch 4 para 7 (reduction of deferred gain attributable to a disposal by a person of an asset not held by him on 31 March 1982 but acquired by him on a no gain/no loss disposal in accordance with sub-s (2) above from a person who had held the asset on 31 March 1982).

268 Decorations for valour or gallant conduct

A gain shall not be a chargeable gain if accruing on the disposal by any person of a decoration awarded for valour or gallant conduct which he acquired otherwise than for consideration in money or money's worth.

Commentary—*Simon's Direct Tax Service* **C1.405.**
Statement of Practice SP 4/92—Capital gains rebasing elections.

269 Foreign currency for personal expenditure

A gain shall not be a chargeable gain if accruing on the disposal by an individual of currency of any description acquired by him for the personal expenditure outside the United Kingdom of himself or his family or dependants (including expenditure on the provision or maintenance of any residence outside the United Kingdom).

Commentary—*Simon's Direct Tax Service* **C1.608.**
Statement of Practice SP 4/92—Capital gains rebasing elections.
Revenue Internal Guidance—Capital gains manual CG 78315 (scope of this section).
Definition—''Chargeable gain'', s 15(2).
Cross reference—See TMA 1970 s 12(2) (information about chargeable gains).

270 Chevening Estate

The enactments relating to capital gains tax (apart from this section) shall not apply in respect of property held on the trusts of the trust instrument set out in the Schedule to the Chevening Estate Act 1959.

Statement of Practice SP 4/92—Capital gains rebasing elections.
Definition—''Chargeable gain'', s 15(2).

271 Other miscellaneous exemptions

(1) The following gains shall not be chargeable gains—

(a) gains accruing on the disposal of stock—

(i) transferred to accounts in the books of the Bank of England in the name of the Treasury or the National Debt Commissioners in pursuance of any Act of Parliament; or

(ii) belonging to the Crown, in whatever name it may stand in the books of the Bank of England;

(b) any gain accruing to a person from his acquisition and disposal of assets held by him as part of a fund mentioned in section 613(4) of the Taxes Act (Parliamentary pension funds) or of which income is exempt from income tax under section 614(1) of that Act (social security supplementary schemes);

(c) any gain accruing to a person from his acquisition and disposal of assets held by him as part of a fund mentioned in section 614(2) or paragraph (b), (c), (d), (f) or (g) of section 615(2) of the Taxes Act (India etc pension funds) or as part of a fund to which subsection (3) of that section applies (pension funds for overseas employees);

(d) any gain accruing to a person from his acquisition and disposal of assets held by him as part of any fund maintained for the purpose mentioned in subsection (5)(b) of section 620 or subsection (5) of section 621 of the Taxes Act under a scheme for the time being approved under that subsection;

(e) any gain accruing on the disposal by the trustees of any settled property held on trusts in accordance with directions which are valid and effective under section 9 of the Superannuation and Trust Funds (Validation) Act 1927 (trust funds for the reduction of the National Debt);

(f) any gain accruing to a consular officer or employee, within the meaning of section 322 of the Taxes Act, of any foreign state to which that section applies on the disposal of assets which at the time of the disposal were situated outside the United Kingdom;

(g) any gain accruing to a person from his disposal of investments if, or to [the extent][3] that, those investments were held by him or on his behalf for the purposes of a scheme which at the time of the disposal is an exempt approved scheme;

(h) any gain accruing to a person on his disposal of investments held by him for the purposes of an approved personal pension scheme;

(j) any gain accruing to a unit holder on his disposal of units in an authorised unit trust which is also an approved personal pension scheme or is one to which section 592(10) of the Taxes Act applies.

In this subsection ''exempt approved scheme'' and ''approved personal pension scheme'' have the same meanings as in Part XIV of the Taxes Act.

(2) Where a claim is made in that behalf, a gain which accrues to a person on the disposal of investments shall not be a chargeable gain for the purposes of capital gains tax if, or to [the extent][3] that, those investments were held by him or on his behalf for the purposes of a fund to which section 608 of the Taxes Act applies.

A claim under this subsection shall not be allowed unless ...[3] the terms on which benefits are payable from the fund have not been altered since 5th April 1980.

(3) A local authority, a local authority association and a health service body shall be exempt from capital gains tax.

In this subsection "local authority association" and "health service body" have the meanings given by sections 519 and 519A of the Taxes Act respectively.

(4) Any bonus to which section 326 or 326A of the Taxes Act (certified contractual savings schemes and tax-exempt special savings accounts) applies shall be disregarded for all purposes of the enactments relating to capital gains tax.

In any case where there is a transfer to which section 216 applies, this subsection shall have effect in relation to any bonus payable after the transfer under a savings scheme which immediately before the transfer was a certified contractual savings scheme notwithstanding that it ceased to be such a scheme by reason of the transfer.

(5) A signatory to the Operating Agreement made pursuant to the Convention on the International Maritime Satellite Organisation which came into force on 16th July 1979, other than a signatory designated for the purposes of the Agreement by the United Kingdom in accordance with the Convention, shall be exempt from capital gains tax in respect of any payment received by that signatory from the Organisation in accordance with the Agreement.

(6) The following shall, on a claim made in that behalf to the Board, be exempt from tax in respect of all chargeable gains—

  (*a*) the Trustees of the British Museum and the Trustees of the [Natural History Museum][1]; and
  (*b*) an Association within the meaning of section 508 of the Taxes Act (scientific research organisations).

(7) The Historic Buildings and Monuments Commission for England, the Trustees of the National Heritage Memorial Fund, the United Kingdom Atomic Energy Authority and the National Radiological Protection Board shall be exempt from tax in respect of chargeable gains; and for the purposes of this subsection gains accruing from investments or deposits held for the purposes of any pension scheme provided and maintained by the United Kingdom Atomic Energy Authority shall be treated as if those gains and investments and deposits belonged to the Authority.

(8) There shall be exempt from tax any chargeable gains accruing to the issue department of the Reserve Bank of India constituted under an Act of the Indian legislature called the Reserve Bank of India Act 1934 or to the issue department of the State Bank of Pakistan constituted under certain orders made under section 9 of the Indian Independence Act 1947.

[(9) Subject to any regulations under subsection (4) of section 129 of the Taxes Act, any disposal and acquisition made in pursuance of an arrangement mentioned in subsection (1), (2) or (2A) of that section shall be disregarded for the purposes of capital gains tax unless it is one in the case of which subsection (2B) of that section has the effect of preventing that section from applying.][2]

(10) In subsections (1)(*g*) and (*h*) and (2) above "investments" includes futures contracts and options contracts; and paragraph 7(3)(*d*) of Schedule 22 to the Taxes Act shall be construed accordingly.

(11) For the purposes of subsection (10) above a contract is not prevented from being a futures contract or an options contract by the fact that any party is or may be entitled to receive or liable to make, or entitled to receive and liable to make, only a payment of a sum (as opposed to a transfer of assets other than money) in full settlement of all obligations.

[(12) Subsection (1)(*b*), (*c*), (*d*), (*g*) and (*h*) and subsection (2) above do not apply to gains accruing to a person from the acquisition and disposal by him of assets held as a member of a property investment LLP.][4]

Commentary—*Simon's Direct Tax Service* C1.222.
Concession C31—Guidance on the criteria applied in determining whether a body is a scientific research association eligible for relief under sub-s (6) above.
Revenue Internal Guidance—Capital gains manual CG 67650–67664 (examples of funds covered by sub-s (1)).
Definitions—"Asset", s 21(1); "authorised unit trust", s 99; "the Board", s 288(1); "chargeable gain", s 15(2); "land", s 288(1); "local authority", s 288(1), TA 1988 s 842A; "settled property", s 68; "the Taxes Act", s 288(1).
Cross references—See TA 1988 s 438(8) (nothing in this section to be construed as affording relief in respect of any sums to be brought into account under TA 1988 s 438 (pension business: exemption from tax));
TCGA 1992 Sch 22 para 7(3)(*d*) (curtailment under certain circumstances of tax exemption under sub-s (1)(*g*) above);
IT (Stock Lending) Regulations, SI 1989/1299 reg 4 (requirements to be fulfilled for sub-s (9) above to apply);
IT (Stock Lending) Regulations, SI 1989/1299 reg 9(3) (disapplication of sub-s (9) above to a disposal and acquisition involving an arrangement to transfer and redeem securities where the borrower pays the lender an amount equal to the proceeds of redemption unless it is part of an ongoing chain of arrangements).
FA 1990 s 81(8) (repeal of TA 1988 s 659 in relation to disposals after 25 July 1990).
Amendments—[1] Words in sub-s (6)(*a*) substituted by the Museums and Galleries Act 1992 Sch 8 para 1(9) with effect from 1 September 1992 by virtue of Museums and Galleries Act 1992 (Commencement) Order, SI 1992/1874.
[2] Sub-s (9) substituted by FA 1995 s 84(5) and repealed by FA 1997 Sch 10 paras 5(2), 7(1), Sch 18 Pt VI (10) with effect in relation to, transfers under, any arrangement made on or after 1 July 1997 by virtue of the Finance Act 1997, Schedule 10, (Appointed Day) Order, SI 1997/991.
[3] Words in sub-ss (1)(*g*), (2) substituted and words in sub-s (2) repealed by FA 1996 s 134(1), (2), Sch 20 para 63, Sch 41 Pt V(10) with effect for the purposes of capital gains tax from the year 1996–97 and, for the purposes of corporation tax, as respects accounting periods ending after 30 June 1999 (by virtue of Finance Act 1994, Section 199, (Appointed Day) Order, SI 1998/3173 art 2).
[4] Sub-s (12) inserted by FA 2001 s 76, Sch 25 para 4 with effect from 6 April 2001.

PART VIII
SUPPLEMENTAL

272 Valuation: general

(1) In this Act "market value" in relation to any assets means the price which those assets might reasonably be expected to fetch on a sale in the open market.

(2) In estimating the market value of any assets no reduction shall be made in the estimate on account of the estimate being made on the assumption that the whole of the assets is to be placed on the market at one and the same time.

(3) Subject to subsection (4) below, the market value of shares or securities [quoted]¹ in The Stock Exchange Daily Official List shall, except where in consequence of special circumstances prices quoted in that List are by themselves not a proper measure of market value, be as follows—

(a) the lower of the 2 prices shown in the quotations for the shares or securities in The Stock Exchange Daily Official List on the relevant date plus one-quarter of the difference between those 2 figures, or

(b) halfway between the highest and lowest prices at which bargains, other than bargains done at special prices, were recorded in the shares or securities for the relevant date,

choosing the amount under paragraph (a), if less than that under paragraph (b), or if no such bargains were recorded for the relevant date, and choosing the amount under paragraph (b) if less than that under paragraph (a).

(4) Subsection (3) shall not apply to shares or securities for which The Stock Exchange provides a more active market elsewhere than on the London trading floor; and, if the London trading floor is closed on the relevant date, the market value shall be ascertained by reference to the latest previous date or earliest subsequent date on which it is open, whichever affords the lower market value.

(5) In this Act "market value" in relation to any rights of unit holders in any unit trust scheme the buying and selling prices of which are published regularly by the managers of the scheme shall mean an amount equal to the buying price (that is the lower price) so published on the relevant date, or if none were published on that date, on the latest date before.

(6) The provisions of this section, with sections 273 and 274, have effect subject to Part I of Schedule 11.

Commentary—*Simon's Direct Tax Service* **C2.122.**
Statement of Practice D3—Company liquidations: tax on shareholders' capital gains.
D7—Treatment of VAT.
Revenue Interpretation RI 63—Valuation costs for ascertaining gains allowable; subsequent valuation costs not allowable.
RI 110—Valuation of assets at date of death; application of this section where value of asset not ascertained for inheritance tax.
Revenue & other press releases—IR 4-2-97 (individuals may submit post-transaction valuations to their tax office for checking before they submit their returns).
Revenue Internal Guidance—Capital gains manual CG 16375–16377 (Principles governing collective valuation).
CG 59500–59632 (valuation of shares and securities).
Simon's Tax Cases—*Administrators of the Estate of Caton, (decd) v Couch* [1995] STC (SCD) 34*; *Clark (executor of Clark, decd) v Green,* [1995] STC (SCD) 99*; *Hawkings-Byass v Sassen* [1996] STC (SCD) 319*.
Definitions—"Asset", s 21(1); "market value", ss 272–274, Sch 11; "shares", s 288(1); "unit trust scheme", s 99.
Cross references—See CGT Regulations, SI 1967/149 reg 10 (referral of questions of valuation to tribunals);
CGT Regulations, SI 1967/149 reg 11(4) (conclusive effect of a determination on appeal of valuation);
TA 1988 s 83B(11) (modification of sub-s (4) above to determine the market value of an interest in an offshore fund for which there are separate published buying and selling prices).
TA 1988 s 251(5) (sub-s (3) of this section to apply for the purposes of stock dividends).
TCGA 1992 Sch 11 para 1 (transitional provisions for market valuation of assets for periods prior to commencement of this Act).
TCGA 1992 Sch 11 Part I (transitional provisions for valuation of assets for periods before commencement of this Act).
TCGA 1992 Sch 11 para 4(3) (market value determination in accordance with this section of unquoted shares and securities acquired on a death occurring after 30 March 1971 and before 6 July 1973).
TCGA 1992 Sch 11 para 6(1) (transitional provisions for market valuation on 6 April 1965 of quoted securities for periods prior to commencement of this Act).
TCGA 1992 Sch 11 para 7 (modifications of sub-ss (3), (4) above and insertion of sub-s (5A) in relation to their application in ascertaining market value before 25 March 1973 and before 13 December 1979).
Modification—This section is modified, in relation to open-ended investment companies, by the Open-ended Investment Companies (Tax) Regulations, SI 1997/1154, regs 3, 22.
Amendment—¹ Word in sub-s (3) substituted by FA 1996 Sch 38 para 12(1), (3) with effect where the relevant date falls after 31 March 1996.

273 Unquoted shares and securities

(1) The provisions of subsection (3) below shall have effect in any case where, in relation to an asset to which this section applies, there falls to be determined by virtue of section 272(1) the price which the asset might reasonably be expected to fetch on a sale in the open market.

(2) The assets to which this section applies are shares and securities which are not quoted on a recognised stock exchange at the time as at which their market value for the purposes of tax on chargeable gains falls to be determined.

(3) For the purposes of a determination falling within subsection (1) above, it shall be assumed that, in the open market which is postulated for the purposes of that determination, there is available to any prospective purchaser of the asset in question all the information which a prudent prospective purchaser of the asset might reasonably require if he were proposing to purchase it from a willing vendor by private treaty and at arm's length.

Commentary—*Simon's Direct Tax Service* **C2.124.**
Statements of Practice D3—Company liquidations: tax on shareholders' capital gains.
D7—Treatment of VAT.
Simon's Tax Cases—*Administrators of the Estate of Caton, (decd) v Couch* [1995] STC (SCD) 34*; *Clark (executor of Clark, decd) v Green,* [1995] STC (SCD) 99*; *Hawkings-Byass v Sassen* [1996] STC (SCD) 319*.
Definitions—"Asset", s 21(1); "chargeable gain", s 15(2); "market value", ss 272–274, Sch 11; "recognised stock exchange", s 288(1), TA 1988 s 841; "shares", s 288(1).
Cross references—See CGT Regulations, SI 1967/149 reg 10 (referral of questions of valuation to tribunals);
CGT Regulations, SI 1967/149 reg 11(4) (conclusive effect of a determination on appeal of valuation);
TA 1988 s 251(6) (application of this section to determine market value of securities, not quoted on stock exchange, issued in lieu of cash dividends).
TCGA 1992 s 272(6) (provisions of Sch 6 Pt I (valuation of assets before commencement of this Act) to apply as necessary for the purposes of this section).
TCGA 1992 Sch 11 para 1 (transitional provisions for market valuation of assets for periods prior to commencement of this Act).
TCGA 1992 Sch 11 para 3 (application of this section for determining market value of any asset at any time before 6 July 1973).
TCGA 1992 Sch 11 para 4 (market value determination in accordance with this section of unquoted shares and securities acquired on a death occurring after 30 March 1971 and before 6 July 1973).
TCGA 1992 Sch 11 para 5 (computation of chargeable gain on a disposal on or after 6 July 1973 of unquoted shares and securities of which there was part disposal prior to that date).

274 Value determined for inheritance tax

Where on the death of any person inheritance tax is chargeable on the value of his estate immediately before his death and the value of an asset forming part of that estate has been ascertained (whether in any proceedings or otherwise) for the purposes of that tax, the value so ascertained shall be taken for the purposes of this Act to be the market value of that asset at the date of the death.

Commentary—*Simon's Direct Tax Service* **C2.121.**
Revenue Interpretation RI 210—Where a bookmaker's pitch is acquired by a member of a family then where its value has been "ascertained" for inheritance tax purposes, this will also be the acquisition cost.
Definitions—"Asset"; "market value", ss 272–274, Sch 11.
Cross references—See IHTA 1984 s 187 (determination of the market value of "specific investment" for the purposes of capital gains tax under this section).
TCGA 1992 s 272(6) (provisions of Sch 6 Pt I (valuation of assets before commencement of this Act) to apply as necessary for the purposes of this section).
TCGA 1992 Sch 11 para 1 (transitional provisions for market valuation of assets for periods prior to commencement of this Act).

275 Location of assets

For the purposes of this Act—

(a) the situation of rights or interests (otherwise than by way of security) in or over immovable property is that of the immovable property,

(b) subject to the following provisions of this subsection, the situation of rights or interests (otherwise than by way of security) in or over tangible movable property is that of the tangible movable property,

(c) subject to the following provisions of this subsection, a debt secured or unsecured, is situated in the United Kingdom if and only if the creditor is resident in the United Kingdom,

(d) shares or securities issued by any municipal or governmental authority, or by any body created by such an authority, are situated in the country of that authority,

(e) subject to paragraph (d) above, registered shares or securities are situated where they are registered and, if registered in more than one register, where the principal register is situated,

(f) a ship or aircraft is situated in the United Kingdom if and only if the owner is then resident in the United Kingdom, and an interest or right in or over a ship or aircraft is situated in the United Kingdom if and only if the person entitled to the interest or right is resident in the United Kingdom,

(g) the situation of good-will as a trade, business or professional asset is at the place where the trade, business or profession is carried on,

(h) patents, trade marks, ...[1] and registered designs are situated where they are registered, and if registered in more than one register, where each register is situated, and rights or licences to use a patent, trade mark, ...[1] or registered design are situated in the United Kingdom if they or any right derived from them are exercisable in the United Kingdom,

(j) copyright, design right and franchises, and rights or licences to use any copyright work or design in which design rights subsists, are situated in the United Kingdom if they or any right derived from them are exercisable in the United Kingdom,

(k) a judgment debt is situated where the judgment is recorded,

(l) a debt which—

(i) is owed by a bank, and

(ii) is not in sterling, and

(iii) is represented by a sum standing to the credit of an account in the bank of an individual who is not domiciled in the United Kingdom,

is situated in the United Kingdom if and only if that individual is resident in the United Kingdom and the branch or other place of business of the bank at which the account is maintained is itself situated in the United Kingdom.

Commentary—*Simon's Direct Tax Service* **C1.604.**
Concession A11—Residence in the UK: year of commencement or cessation of residence.
D2—Residence in the UK: year of commencement or cessation of residence.
Statement of Practice SP 3/81—Individuals coming to the UK: ordinary residence.

Definitions—"Asset", s 21(1); "branch or agency", s 10(6); "issued", s 288(5); "resident", s 9(1); "shares", s 288(1); "trade", s 288(1).

Amendments—¹ Words omitted from para (h) repealed by the Trade Marks Act 1994 s 106(2) Sch 5, as from 31 October 1994, by virtue of the Trade Marks Act 1994 (Commencement) Order 1994, SI 1994/2550.

276 The territorial sea and the continental shelf

(1) The territorial sea of the United Kingdom shall for all purposes of the taxation of chargeable gains (including the following provisions of this section) be deemed to be part of the United Kingdom.

(2) In this section—

(a) "exploration or exploitation activities" means activities carried on in connection with the exploration or exploitation of so much of the seabed and subsoil and their natural resources as is situated in the United Kingdom or a designated area; and

(b) "exploration or exploitation rights" means rights to assets to be produced by exploration or exploitation activities or to interests in or to the benefit of such assets; and

(c) references to the disposal of exploration or exploitation rights include references to the disposal of shares deriving their value or the greater part of their value directly or indirectly from such rights, other than shares [listed]¹ on a recognised stock exchange; and

(d) "shares" includes stock and any security as defined in section 254(1) of the Taxes Act; and

(e) "designated area" means an area designated by Order in Council under section 1(7) of the Continental Shelf Act 1964.

(3) Any gains accruing on the disposal of exploration or exploitation rights shall be treated for the purposes of this Act as gains accruing on the disposal of assets situated in the United Kingdom.

(4) Gains accruing on the disposal of—

(a) exploration or exploitation assets which are situated in a designated area, or

(b) unquoted shares deriving their value or the greater part of their value directly or indirectly from exploration or exploitation assets situated in the United Kingdom or a designated area or from such assets and exploration or exploitation rights taken together,

shall be treated for the purposes of this Act as gains accruing on the disposal of assets situated in the United Kingdom.

(5) For the purposes of this section, an asset disposed of is an exploration or exploitation asset if either—

(a) it is not a mobile asset and it is being or has at some time been used in connection with exploration or exploitation activities carried on in the United Kingdom or a designated area; or

(b) it is a mobile asset which has at some time been used in connection with exploration or exploitation activities so carried on and is dedicated to an oil field in which the person making the disposal, or a person connected with him, is or has been a participator;

and expressions used in paragraphs (a) and (b) above have the same meaning as if those paragraphs were included in Part I of the Oil Taxation Act 1975.

(6) In subsection (4)(b) above "unquoted shares" means shares other than those which are [listed]¹ on a recognised stock exchange; and references in subsections (7) and (8) below to exploration or exploitation assets include references to unquoted shares falling within subsection (4)(b).

(7) Gains accruing to a person not resident in the United Kingdom on the disposal of exploration or exploitation rights or of exploration or exploitation assets shall, for the purposes of capital gains tax or corporation tax on chargeable gains, be treated as gains accruing on the disposal of assets used for the purposes of a trade carried on by that person in the United Kingdom through a branch or agency.

[(8) The provisions specified in subsection (9) below shall apply in relation to a disposal of exploration or exploitation rights or exploration or exploitation assets if (and only if) the disposal is—

(a) by a company resident in a territory outside the United Kingdom to a company resident in the same territory,

(b) by a company resident in the United Kingdom to another company which is so resident, or

(c) by a company which is not resident in the United Kingdom to another company which is resident there.

(9) Those provisions are—

(a) section 41(8),

(b) section 171 (except subsections (1)(b) and (1A)),

(c) section 173 (with the omission of the words "to which this section applies" in subsections (1)(a) and (2)(a) and "such" in subsections (1)(c) and (2)(c) and with the omission of subsection (3)),

(d) section 174(4) (with the substitution of "at a time when both were members of the group" for "in a transfer to which section 171(1) applied"),

(e) section 179 (except subsections (1)(b) and (1A)), and

(f) section 181.

(10) The provisions specified in subsection (9) above shall apply in accordance with subsection (8) above with the following modifications—

(*a*) for the purposes of paragraph (*a*) of subsection (9) above, section 41(8) applies as if section 170 applied, for the purposes of section 171, with the omission of subsection (9), and

(*b*) for the purposes of paragraphs (*b*) to (*f*) of subsection (9) above, the provisions specified in those paragraphs apply as if in section 170 subsection (9) were omitted.][2]

Commentary—*Simon's Direct Tax Service* C1.604; D4.911.
Statement of Practice SP 6/84—Non-resident lessors.
Cross references—See TMA 1970 s 46B(5)(*b*) (any question as to the application of this section to be determined by the Special Commissioners).
Simon's Tax Cases—*Clark v Oceanic Contractors Inc* [1980] STC 656*.
Definitions—"Asset", s 21(1); "branch or agency", s 10(6); "chargeable gain" s 15(2); "company", ss 99, 288(1); "connected", s 286; "recognised stock exchange", s 288(1), TA 1988 s 841; "resident", s 9(1); "shares", s 288(1); "the Taxes Act", s 288(1); "trade", s 288(1).
Amendments—[1] Words in sub-ss (2)(*c*), (6) substituted by FA 1996 Sch 38 para 10(1), (2)(*d*), (3) with effect in relation to disposals after 31 March 1996.
[2] Sub-ss (8)–(10) substituted for original sub-s (8) by FA 2000 s 102, Sch 29 para 35 with effect in cases in which s 41, 171, 173, 174(4), 179 or 181, as the case may be, have effect as amended by this Schedule.

277 Double taxation relief

(1) For the purpose of giving relief from double taxation in relation to capital gains tax and tax on chargeable gains charged under the law of any [territory][1] outside the United Kingdom, in Chapters I and II of Parts XVIII of the Taxes Act, as they apply for the purposes of income tax, for references to income there shall be substituted references to capital gains and for references to income tax there shall be substituted references to capital gains tax meaning, as the context may require, tax charged under the law of the United Kingdom or tax charged under the law of a [territory][1] outside the United Kingdom.

(2) Any arrangements set out in an order made under section 347 of the Income Tax Act 1952 before 5th August 1965 (the date of the passing of the Finance Act 1965) shall so far as they provide (in whatever terms) for relief from tax chargeable in the United Kingdom on capital gains have effect in relation to capital gains tax.

(3) So far as by virtue of this section capital gains tax charged under the law of a [territory][1] outside the United Kingdom may be brought into account under the said Chapters I and II as applied by this section, that tax, whether relief is given by virtue of this section in respect of it or not, shall not be taken into account for the purposes of those Chapters as they apply apart from this section.

(4) Section 816 of the Taxes Act (disclosure of information for purposes of double taxation) shall apply in relation to capital gains tax as it applies in relation to income tax.

Commentary—*Simon's Direct Tax Service* C1.615, 616.
Definitions—"Chargeable gain", s 15(2); "the Taxes Act", s 288(1).
Cross references—See TCGA 1992 s 278 (allowance for foreign tax).
Amendments—[1] Word substituted for the word "country" by FA 2002 s 88(2)(*f*), (3) with effect on and after the date of the passing of FA 2002 (24 July 2002) in relation to arrangements made before that date (as well as in relation to arrangements made on or after that date).

278 Allowance for foreign tax

[(1)][1] Subject to section 277, the tax chargeable under the law of any [territory][2] outside the United Kingdom on the disposal of an asset which is borne by the person making the disposal shall be allowable as a deduction in the computation of the gain.

[(2) Where the amount of any deduction allowed under subsection (1) above is rendered excessive or insufficient by reason of any adjustment of the amount of any tax payable either—

(*a*) in the United Kingdom, or

(*b*) under the law of any other territory,

nothing in this Act, the Management Act or the Taxes Act limiting the time for the making of assessments or claims for relief shall apply to any assessment or claim to which the adjustment gives rise, being an assessment or claim made not later than six years from the time when all such assessments, adjustments and other determinations have been made, whether in the United Kingdom or elsewhere, as are material in determining whether any and if so what deduction falls to be made under subsection (1) above.

(3) Where—

(*a*) a deduction has been allowed under subsection (1) above in the case of the person making the disposal, and

(*b*) the amount of that deduction is subsequently rendered excessive by reason of an adjustment of the amount of any tax payable under the law of a territory outside the United Kingdom,

that person shall give notice in writing to an officer of the Board that an adjustment has been made that has rendered the amount of the deduction excessive.

(4) A notice under subsection (3) above must be given within one year from the time of the making of the adjustment.

(5) A person who fails to comply with the requirements imposed on him by subsections (3) and (4) above in relation to any adjustment shall be liable to a penalty of an amount not exceeding the amount of the difference specified in subsection (6) below.

(6) The difference is that between—

(a) the amount of tax payable by the person in question for the relevant chargeable period, after giving effect to the deduction that ought to be made under subsection (1) above; and
(b) the amount that would have been the tax so payable after giving effect instead to a deduction under that subsection of the amount rendered excessive as mentioned in subsection (3)(b) above.

(7) For the purposes of subsection (6) above "the relevant chargeable period" means the chargeable period as respects which the deduction was treated as made.][1]

Commentary—_Simon's Direct Tax Service_ C1.617; C2.227.
Definition—"Asset", s 21(1).
Amendments—[1] Sub-s (1) numbered as such and ss (2)–(7) inserted by FA 2000 s 103, Sch 30 para 30 with effect for adjustments made after 20 March 2000.
[2] Word substituted for the word "country" by FA 2002 s 88(2)(f), (3) with effect on and after the date of the passing of FA 2002 (24 July 2002) in relation to arrangements made before that date (as well as in relation to arrangements made on or after that date).

279 Foreign assets: delayed remittances

(1) Subsection (2) below applies where—

(a) chargeable gains accrue from the disposal of assets situated outside the United Kingdom, and
[(b) the person charged or chargeable makes a claim, and][1]
[(c) the conditions set out in subsection (3) below are, so far as applicable, satisfied as respects those gains ("the qualifying gains");][1]

and subsection (2)(b) also applies where a claim has been made under section 13 of the 1979 Act.

(2) For the purposes of capital gains tax—

(a) the amount of the qualifying gains shall be deducted [(before the application of any taper relief)][3] from the amounts on which the claimant is assessed to capital gains tax for the year in which the qualifying gains accrued to the claimant, but
(b) the amount so deducted shall be assessed to capital gains tax on the claimant (or his personal representatives) as if it were an amount of chargeable gains accruing in the year of assessment in which the conditions set out in subsection (3) below cease to be satisfied.

(3) The conditions are—

(a) that the claimant was unable to transfer the qualifying gains to the United Kingdom, and
(b) that that inability was due to the laws of the territory where the assets were situated at the time of the disposal, or to the executive action of its government, or to the impossibility of obtaining foreign currency in that territory, and
(c) that the inability was not due to any want of reasonable endeavours on the part of the claimant.

(4) Where under an agreement entered into under arrangements made by the Secretary of State in pursuance of section 1 of the Overseas Investment and Export Guarantees Act 1972 or section 11 of the Export Guarantees and Overseas Investment Act 1978 any payment is made by the Exports Credits Guarantee Department in respect of any gains which cannot be transferred to the United Kingdom, then, to the extent of the payment, the gains shall be treated as gains with respect to which the conditions mentioned in subsection (3) above are not satisfied (and accordingly cannot cease to be satisfied).

[(5) No claim under this section in respect of a chargeable gain shall be made—

(a) in the case of a claim for the purposes of capital gains tax, at any time after the fifth anniversary of the 31st January next following the year of assessment in which the gain accrues; or
(b) in the case of a claim for the purposes of corporation tax, more than 6 years after the end of the accounting period in which the gain accrues.][2]

(6) The personal representatives of a deceased person may make any claim which he might have made under this section if he had not died.

(7) Where—

(a) a claim under this section is made (or has been made under section 13 of the 1979 Act) by a man in respect of chargeable gains accruing to his wife before 6th April 1990, and
(b) by virtue of this section the amount of the gains falls to be assessed to capital gains tax as if it were an amount of gains accruing in the year 1992–93 or a subsequent year of assessment,

it shall be assessed not on the claimant (or his personal representatives) but on the person to whom the gains accrued (or her personal representatives).

(8) In relation to disposals before 19th March 1991 subsection (3)(b) above shall have effect with the substitution of the words "income arose" for the words "assets were situated at the time of the disposal".

Commentary—_Simon's Direct Tax Service_ C1.605.
Revenue Internal Guidance—Capital gains manual CG 78401–78406 (explanation with worked example).
Simon's Tax Cases—s 279(1), (3), _Furniss v Dawson_ [1983] STC 54*.
Definitions—"The 1979 Act", s 288(1); "accounting period", TA 1988 s 834(1); "asset", s 21(1); "chargeable gain", s 15(2); "personal representatives", s 288(1), TA 1988 s 701(4); "year of assessment", s 288(1).
Amendments—[1] Sub-s (1)(b), (c) substituted for sub-s (1)(b) by FA 1996 s 134(1), (2), Sch 20 para 64 with effect from the year 1996–97, and for the purposes of corporation tax as respects accounting periods ending on or after the appointed day, being not earlier than 1 April 1996.

Sub-s (1)(*b*) formerly read: "(*b*) the person charged or chargeable makes a claim and shows that the conditions set out in subsection (3) below are, so far as applicable, satisfied as respects those gains ("the qualifying gains");".

[2] Sub-s (5) substituted by FA 1996 s 135(1), (2), Sch 21 para 41 with effect from the year 1996–97 and, for the purposes of corporation tax, as respects accounting periods ending after 30 June 1999 (by virtue of Finance Act 1994, Section 199, (Appointed Day) Order, SI 1998/3173 art 2).

[3] Words in sub-s (2)(*a*) inserted by FA 1998 Sch 21 para 9 with effect from the year 1998–99.

280 Consideration payable by instalments

If the consideration, or part of the consideration, taken into account in the computation of the gain is payable by instalments over a period beginning not earlier than the time when the disposal is made, being a period exceeding 18 months, then, [at the option of the person making the disposal, the tax on a chargeable gain accruing on the disposal may][1] be paid by such instalments as the Board may allow over a period not exceeding 8 years and ending not later than the time at which the last of the first-mentioned instalments is payable.

Commentary—*Simon's Direct Tax Service* **C1.108; C2.106.**
Revenue & other press releases—Hansard 22-6-72 ("undue hardship": Revenue considers the resources made available by the transaction in permitting an instalment arrangement if there would otherwise be a bona fide commercial transaction).
Revenue Internal Guidance—Assessed taxes manual AT 6.611 (Revenue procedure for dealing with an instalment application).
Definitions—"The Board", s 288(1); "chargeable gain", s 15(2).
Amendments—[1] Words substituted by FA 1996 s 134(1), (2), Sch 20 para 65 with effect from the year 1996–97, and for the purposes of corporation tax as respects accounting periods ending after 30 June 1999 (by virtue of Finance Act 1994, Section 199, (Appointed Day) Order, SI 1998/3173 art 2).

281 Payment by instalments of tax on gifts

(1) Subsection (2) below applies where—

(*a*) the whole or any part of any assets to which this section applies is disposed of by way of gift or is deemed to be disposed of under section 71(1) or 72(1), and

(*b*) the disposal is one—

(i) to which neither section 165(4) nor section 260(3) applies (or would apply if a claim were duly made), or

(ii) to which either of those sections does apply but on which the held-over gain (within the meaning of the section applying) is less than the chargeable gain which would have accrued on that disposal apart from that section.

(2) Where this subsection applies, the capital gains tax chargeable on a gain accruing on the disposal may, if the person paying it by notice to the inspector so elects, be paid by 10 equal yearly instalments.

(3) The assets to which this section applies are—

(*a*) land or an estate or interest in land,

(*b*) any shares or securities of a company which, immediately before the disposal, gave control of the company to the person by whom the disposal was made or deemed to be made, and

(*c*) any shares or securities of a company not falling under paragraph (*b*) above and not [listed][1] on a recognised stock exchange nor dealt in on the Unlisted Securities Market.

(4) Where tax is payable by instalments by virtue of this section, the first instalment shall be due on the day on which the tax would be payable apart from this section.

(5) Subject to the following provisions of this section—

[(*a*) tax payable by instalments by virtue of this section carries interest in accordance with Part IX of the Management Act as that Part applies where no election is made under subsection (2) above, and][2]

(*b*) the interest on the unpaid portion of the tax shall be added to each instalment and paid accordingly.

(6) Tax payable by instalments by virtue of this section which is for the time being unpaid, with interest [(determined in accordance with subsection (5)(*a*) above)][2] to the date of payment, may be paid at any time.

(7) Tax which apart from this subsection would be payable by instalments by virtue of this section and which is for the time being unpaid, with interest [(determined in accordance with subsection (5)(*a*) above as if the tax were payable by instalments by virtue of this section)][2] to the date of payment, shall become due and payable immediately if—

(*a*) the disposal was by way of gift to a person connected with the donor or was deemed to be made under section 71(1) or 72(1), and

(*b*) the assets are disposed of for valuable consideration under a subsequent disposal (whether or not the subsequent disposal is made by the person who acquired them under the first disposal).

Commentary—*Simon's Direct Tax Service* **C1.108.**
Revenue Internal Guidance—Assessed taxes manual AT 6.611 (Revenue procedure for dealing with an instalment application).
Definitions—"Asset", s 21(1); "chargeable gain", s 15(2); "company", ss 99, 288(1); "connected", s 286; "inspector", s 288(1); "land", s 288(1); "the Management Act", s 288(1); "notice", s 288(1); "recognised stock exchange", s 288(1), TA 1988 s 841; "shares", s 288(1).
Amendments—[1] Word in sub-s (3)(*c*) substituted by FA 1996 Sch 38 para 10(1), (2)(*e*), (3) with effect in relation to disposals after 31 March 1996.

² Sub-s (5)(*a*) substituted and words in sub-ss (6), (7) inserted, by FA 1996 Sch 18 paras 15, 17(3) with effect from the year 1996–97 and in relation to any capital gains tax which is charged by an assessment made after 5 April 1998 which is for the year 1995–96 or any earlier year of assessment. Sub-s (5)(*a*) formerly read: "(*a*) tax payable by instalments by virtue of this section shall carry interest in accordance with Part IX (except section 88) of the Management Act, and."

282 Recovery of tax from donee

(1) If in any year of assessment a chargeable gain accrues to any person on the disposal of an asset by way of gift and any amount of capital gains tax assessed on that person for that year of assessment is not paid within 12 months from the date when the tax becomes payable, the donee may, by an assessment made not later than 2 years from the date when the tax became payable, be assessed and charged (in the name of the donor) to capital gains tax on an amount not exceeding the amount of the chargeable gain so accruing, and not exceeding the grossed up amount of that capital gains tax unpaid at the time when he is so assessed, grossing up at the marginal rate of tax, that is to say, taking capital gains tax on a chargeable gain at the amount which would not have been chargeable but for that chargeable gain.

(2) A person paying any amount of tax in pursuance of this section shall be entitled to recover a sum of that amount from the donor.

(3) References in this section to a donor include, in the case of an individual who has died, references to his personal representatives.

(4) In this section references to a gift include references to any transaction otherwise than by way of a bargain made at arm's length so far as money or money's worth passes under the transaction without full consideration in money or money's worth, and "donor" and "donee" shall be construed accordingly; and this section shall apply in relation to a gift made by 2 or more donors with the necessary modifications and subject to any necessary apportionments.

Commentary—*Simon's Direct Tax Service* **C1.204.**
Definitions—"Asset", s 21(1); "chargeable gain", s 15(2); "personal representatives", s 288(1), TA 1988 s 701(4); "year of assessment", s 288(1).

283 Repayment supplements

(1) Subject to the provisions of this section, where in the case of capital gains tax paid by or on behalf of an individual for a year of assessment [a repayment of that tax is made by the Board or an officer of the Board]¹, the repayment shall be increased under this section by an amount ("a repayment supplement") equal to interest on the amount repaid at the rate applicable under section 178 of the Finance Act 1989 for the period (if any) between the relevant time and [the date on which]¹ the order for the repayment is issued.

[(2) For the purposes of subsection (1) above, [the relevant time is the date on which the tax was paid.]².]¹

(3) A repayment supplement shall not be payable under this section in respect of a repayment or payment made in consequence of an order or judgment of a court having power to allow interest on the repayment or payment.

(4) Subsections (1) to (3) above shall apply in relation to a [trust or]¹, the personal representatives of a deceased person as such (within the meaning of section 701(4) of that Act) as they apply in relation to an individual.

(5) ...¹

Commentary—*Simon's Direct Tax Service* **A3.604.**
Notes—For the purposes of sub-s (1) above, the rate of interest is subject to frequent changes by virtue of the Income Tax (Interest on Unpaid Tax and Repayment Supplement) Orders. For the rates applicable at various periods, see *Simon's Direct Tax Service* , Binder 1.
The reference in sub-s (4) to "that Act" is to TA 1988, an earlier reference in that subsection having been substituted by FA 1994 Sch 19 para 46.
Revenue & other press releases—IR 1-4-96 (details of when payments made to the Revenue are treated as received for the purpose of calculating interest).
Definitions—"The Board", s 288(1); "issued", s 288(5); "personal representatives", s 288(1), TA 1988 s 701(4); "the Taxes Act", s 288(1); "year of assessment", s 288(1).
Cross references—See TMA 1970 s 30(2)(*a*) (recovery of overpayment of tax and any increase of it under this section);
TMA 1970, s 70A (where payment is made to the Board by cheque which is paid on first presentation, payment is treated as having been made on the day on which the cheque was received by the Board).
TA 1988 s 824(8) (repayment supplement paid under this section is not income of the payee for any tax purposes).
Amendments—¹ Words in sub-ss (1), (4), and whole of sub-s (2), substituted, and sub-s (5) repealed by FA 1994 ss 196, 199(2)(*a*), Sch 19 para 46 and Sch 26 Pt V(23) with effect from the year 1996–97.
² Words in sub-s (2) substituted by FA 1997 s 92(5), (6) with effect from the year 1996–97.

284 Income tax decisions

Any assessment to income tax or decision on a claim under the Income Tax Acts, and any decision on an appeal under the Income Tax Acts against such an assessment or decision, shall be conclusive so far as, under any provision of this Act, liability to tax depends on the provisions of the Income Tax Acts.

Simon's Tax Cases—*Bye v Coren* [1985] STC 113*.

[284A Concessions that defer a charge

(1) This section applies where—

(a) a person ("the original taxpayer") has at any time obtained for any chargeable period ("the first chargeable period") the benefit of any capital gains relief to which he had no statutory entitlement;

(b) the benefit of the relief was obtained in reliance on any concession;

(c) the concession was first published by the Board before 9th March 1999 or (having been published on or after that date) replaced a concession satisfying the requirements of this paragraph with a concession to the same or substantially the same effect; and

(d) the concession involved the application (with or without modifications), to a case to which they would not otherwise have applied, of the provisions of any enactment ("the relevant statutory provisions").

(2) This section applies only if, at the time when the original taxpayer obtained the benefit of the relief, the concession was one available generally to any person falling within its terms.

(3) If the benefit obtained for the first chargeable period by the original taxpayer is repudiated for any later chargeable period (whether by the original taxpayer or by another person), the enactments relating to the taxation of chargeable gains shall have effect as if a chargeable gain equal to the amount of that benefit accrued in the later chargeable period to the person repudiating the benefit.

(4) For the purposes of this section—

(a) a capital gains relief for any chargeable period is a relief (of whatever description) the effect of which is that the amount of the chargeable gains taken to have accrued to that person in that period is less than it otherwise would have been; and

(b) the amount of the benefit of any such relief is the amount by which, as a consequence of that relief, those gains are less than they otherwise would have been.

(5) Where, without applying a specific enactment, any concession has the effect that—

(a) any asset is treated as the same as another asset and as acquired as the other asset was acquired,

(b) any two or more assets are treated as a single asset, or

(c) any disposal is treated as having been a disposal on which neither a gain nor a loss accrued,

that concession shall be assumed for the purposes of this section to have involved the application, to a case to which it would not otherwise have applied, of the provisions of an enactment to the corresponding effect.

(6) For the purposes of this section the benefit of any relief obtained by the original taxpayer for the first chargeable period is repudiated by a person for a later chargeable period if—

(a) circumstances arise such that, had the equivalent circumstances arisen in the case of the corresponding relief under the relevant statutory provisions, the whole or a part of the benefit of that relief would have fallen to be recouped from that person in the later chargeable period;

(b) apart from this section, the recoupment in the actual circumstances of the whole or a part of the benefit obtained by the original taxpayer is prevented by the fact that the original taxpayer relied on a concession (rather than on the relevant statutory provisions) to obtain that benefit; and

(c) the person from whom, in the equivalent circumstances, the amount of the benefit or any part of it would have fallen to be recouped is not precluded by subsection (8) below from relying on that fact in relation to that amount or part.

(7) For the purposes of this section an amount of the benefit of a capital gains relief is recouped from any person in a chargeable period to the extent that an amount is so brought into account in his case for that period as to secure that—

(a) the amount of his chargeable gains for that period is taken to be more than it otherwise would have been by an amount directly or indirectly representing the whole or a part of the amount of the benefit; or

(b) the amount of his allowable losses for that period is taken to be less than it otherwise would have been by an amount directly or indirectly representing the whole or a part of the amount of the benefit.

(8) Where—

(a) any such circumstances as are mentioned in subsection (6)(a) above have arisen in relation to the relief the benefit of which has been obtained by the original taxpayer,

(b) the person from whom, in the equivalent circumstances, the whole or any part of the amount of the benefit would have fallen to be recouped has accepted that, in the actual circumstances, the whole or a part of the benefit obtained by the original taxpayer may be recouped from him, and

(c) that acceptance is indicated in writing to the Board (whether by the making or amendment of a self-assessment or otherwise),

that person's rights subsequently to amend, appeal against or otherwise challenge any assessment shall not be exercised in any manner inconsistent with his acceptance of that matter (which shall be irrevocable).

(9) In this section "concession" includes any practice, interpretation or other statement in the nature of a concession.][1]

Commentary—*Simon's Direct Tax Service* **C1.424.**
Revenue Interpretation RI 211—Guidance on concessions that defer a capital gains charge.

Revenue Internal Guidance—Capital gains manual CG 13650–13662 (concessions that defer a capital gains charge).
Amendment—[1] This section inserted by FA 1999 s 76 with effect for deferred gains which would have become chargeable under the corresponding statutory provisions by reason of an event occurring after 8 March 1999, whenever the concessionary relief was obtained.

[284B Provisions supplementary to section 284A

(1) Chargeable gains that are treated as accruing to any person under section 284A(3) shall not be eligible for taper relief.

(2) The total amount of chargeable gains that are treated as accruing to any person under subsection (3) of section 284A in respect of any such benefit as is referred to in that subsection shall not exceed the amount of that benefit.

(3) Where, after any assessment to tax has been made on the basis that any chargeable gain is treated as having accrued to any person under section 284A(3)—

    (*a*) the person assessed, within any of the periods allowed by subsection (4) below, gives an indication for the purposes of section 284A(8), or
    (*b*) a final determination of the original taxpayer's liability to tax for the first chargeable period is made on the basis that the original taxpayer did not, or was not entitled to, rely on the concession in question,

all such adjustments shall be made (whether by way of assessment, amendment of an assessment, repayment of tax or otherwise) as are necessary to secure that no person is subjected to any greater liability by virtue of section 284A(3) than he would have been had the indication been given, or the final determination made, before the making of the assessment.

(4) The periods allowed by this subsection are—

    (*a*) the period of twelve months beginning with the making of the assessment;
    (*b*) the period within which the person is entitled to amend his self-assessment or company tax return for the chargeable period in which the chargeable gain under section 284A(3) is treated as having accrued to him;
    (*c*) where the person makes a claim for any further relief against the amount that may be recouped from him by virtue of his indication under section 284A(8), the period allowed for making that claim.

(5) Subsection (3) above has effect notwithstanding any time limits relating to the making or amendment of an assessment for any chargeable period.][1]

Commentary—*Simon's Direct Tax Service* C1.424.
Revenue Interpretation RI 211—Guidance on concessions that defer a capital gains charge.
Revenue Internal Guidance—Capital gains manual, CG 13650–13662 (concessions that defer a capital gains charge).
Amendment—[1] This section inserted by FA 1999 s 76 with effect for deferred gains which would have become chargeable under the corresponding statutory provisions by reason of an event occurring after 8 March 1999, whenever the concessionary relief was obtained.

285 Recognised investment exchanges

The Board may by regulations make provision securing that enactments relating to tax on chargeable gains and referring to The Stock Exchange have effect, for such purposes and subject to such modifications as may be prescribed by the regulations, in relation to all other recognised investment exchanges (within the meaning [given by section 285(1)(*a*) of the Financial Services and Markets Act 2000][1]), or in relation to such of those exchanges as may be so prescribed.

Commentary—*Simon's Direct Tax Service* A1.160.
Definitions—''The Board'', s 288(1); ''chargeable gain'', s 15(2).
Amendments—[1] Words substituted by the Financial Services and Markets Act 2000 (Consequential Amendments) (Taxes) Order, SI 2001/3629 arts 61, 69 with effect from 1 December 2001 immediately after the coming into force of the Financial Services and Markets Act 2000 ss 411, 432(1), Sch 20.

286 Connected persons: interpretation

(1) Any question whether a person is connected with another shall for the purposes of this Act be determined in accordance with the following subsections of this section (any provision that one person is connected with another being taken to mean that they are connected with one another).

(2) A person is connected with an individual if that person is the individual's husband or wife, or is a relative, or the husband or wife of a relative, of the individual or of the individual's husband or wife.

[(3) A person, in his capacity as trustee of a settlement, is connected with—

    (*a*) any individual who in relation to the settlement is a settlor,
    (*b*) any person who is connected with such an individual, and
    (*c*) any body corporate which is connected with that settlement.

In this subsection ''settlement'' and ''settlor'' have the same meaning as in Chapter IA of Part XV of the Taxes Act (see section 660G(1) and (2) of that Act).][1]

(3A) For the purpose of subsection (3) above a body corporate is connected with a settlement if—

(*a*) it is a close company (or only not a close company because it is not resident in the United Kingdom) and the participators include the trustees of the settlement; or

(*b*) it is controlled (within the meaning of section 840 of the Taxes Act) by a company falling within paragraph (*a*) above.][1]

(4) Except in relation to acquisitions or disposals of partnership assets pursuant to bona fide commercial arrangements, a person is connected with any person with whom he is in partnership, and with the husband or wife or a relative of any individual with whom he is in partnership.

(5) A company is connected with another company—

(*a*) if the same person has control of both, or a person has control of one and persons connected with him, or he and persons connected with him, have control of the other, or

(*b*) if a group of 2 or more persons has control of each company, and the groups either consist of the same persons or could be regarded as consisting of the same persons by treating (in one or more cases) a member of either group as replaced by a person with whom he is connected.

(6) A company is connected with another person, if that person has control of it or if that person and persons connected with him together have control of it.

(7) Any 2 or more persons acting together to secure or exercise control of a company shall be treated in relation to that company as connected with one another and with any person acting on the directions of any of them to secure or exercise control of the company.

(8) In this section "relative" means brother, sister, ancestor or lineal descendant.

Commentary—*Simon's Direct Tax Service* **C2.110.**
Revenue Interpretation RI 38—For the purposes of this section, are settlor and trustees connected at the time of settlement and are trustees and beneficiaries connected after settlor's death and are trustees and beneficiaries connected when beneficiaries become absolutely entitled.
Simon's Tax Cases—s 286(3), *Berry v Warnett* [1978] STC 504*.
Definitions—"Asset", s 21(1); "close company", s 288(1); "company", ss 99, 288(1); "resident", s 9(1); "the Taxes Act", s 288(1).
Cross references—See TCGA 1992 s 177(7) (modification of sub-s (7) of this section in its application to dividend stripping provisions).
Amendments—[1] Sub-ss (3), (3A) substituted for sub-s (3) by FA 1995 s 74, Sch 17 para 31 with effect from the year 1995–96 and apply to every settlement, wherever and whenever it was made or entered into.

287 Orders and regulations made by the Treasury or the Board

(1) Subject to subsection (2) below, any power of the Treasury or the Board to make any order or regulations under this Act or any other enactment relating to the taxation of chargeable gains passed after this Act shall be exercisable by statutory instrument.

(2) Subsection (1) above shall not apply in relation to any power conferred by section 288(6).

(3) Subject to subsection (4) below and to any other provision to the contrary, any statutory instrument to which subsection (1) above applies shall be subject to annulment in pursuance of a resolution of the House of Commons.

(4) Subsection (3) above shall not apply in relation to an order or regulations made under section 3(4) or 265 or paragraph 1 of Schedule 9, or—

(*a*) if any other Parliamentary procedure is expressly provided; or

(*b*) if the order in question is an order appointing a day for the purposes of any provision, being a day as from which the provision will have effect, with or without amendments, or will cease to have effect.

Definitions—"Asset", s 21(1); "the Board", s 288(1); "chargeable gain", s 15(2).

288 Interpretation

(1) In this Act, unless the context otherwise requires—

"the 1979 Act" means the Capital Gains Tax Act 1979; ...[3]

"allowable loss" shall be construed in accordance with sections 8(2) and 16;

"the Board" means the Commissioners of Inland Revenue;

"building society" has the same meaning as in the Building Societies Act 1986;

["the Capital Allowances Act" means the Capital Allowances Act 2001;][3]

"chargeable period" means a year of assessment or an accounting period of a company for purposes of corporation tax;

"class", in relation to shares or securities, means a class of shares or securities of any one company;

"close company" has the meaning given by sections 414 and 415 of the Taxes Act;

"collective investment scheme" has the [meaning given by section 235 of the Financial Services and Markets Act 2000][5];

"company" includes any body corporate or unincorporated association but does not include a partnership, and shall be construed in accordance with section 99;

"control" shall be construed in accordance with section 416 of the Taxes Act;

"double taxation relief arrangements" means, in relation to a company, arrangements having effect by virtue of section 788 of the Taxes Act and, in relation to any other person, means arrangements having effect by virtue of that section as extended to capital gains tax by section 277;

"dual resident investing company" has the meaning given by section 404 of the Taxes Act;

"inspector" means any inspector of taxes;

"investment trust" has the meaning given by section 842 of the Taxes Act;

"land" includes messuages, tenements, and hereditaments, houses and buildings of any tenure;

"local authority" has the meaning given by section 842A of the Taxes Act;

"the Management Act" means the Taxes Management Act 1970;

"notice" means notice in writing;

["period of account" has the meaning given by section 832(1) of the Taxes Act;]⁶

"personal representatives" has the meaning given by section 701(4) of the Taxes Act;

["property investment LLP" has the meaning given by section 842B of the Taxes Act;]⁴

"recognised stock exchange" has the meaning given by section 841 of the Taxes Act;

"shares" includes stock;

"the Taxes Act" means the Income and Corporation Taxes Act 1988;

"trade" has the same meaning as in the Income Tax Acts;

"trading stock" has the meaning given by section 100(2) of the Taxes Act;

["venture capital trust" has the meaning given by section 842AA of the Taxes Act;]¹

"wasting asset" has the meaning given by section 44 and paragraph 1 of Schedule 8;

"year of assessment" means, in relation to capital gains tax, a year beginning on 6th April and ending on 5th April in the following calendar year, and "1992–93" and so on indicate years of assessment as in the Income Tax Acts;

and any reference to a particular section, Part or Schedule is a reference to that section or Part of, or that Schedule to, this Act.

(2) In this Act "retail prices index" has the same meaning as in the Income Tax Acts and, accordingly, any reference in this Act to the retail prices index shall be construed in accordance with section 833(2) of the Taxes Act.

(3) References in this Act to a married woman living with her husband shall be construed in accordance with section 282 of the Taxes Act.

(4) ...²

(5) For the purposes of this Act, shares or debentures comprised in any letter of allotment or similar instrument shall be treated as issued unless the right to the shares or debentures thereby conferred remains provisional until accepted and there has been no acceptance.

(6) In this Act "recognised futures exchange" means the London International Financial Futures Exchange and any other futures exchange which is for the time being designated for the purposes of this Act by order made by the Board.

(7) An order made by the Board under subsection (6) above—

(a) may designate a futures exchange by name or by reference to any class or description of futures exchanges, including, in the case of futures exchanges in a country outside the United Kingdom, a class or description framed by reference to any authority or approval given in that country; and

(b) may contain such transitional and other supplemental provisions as appear to the Board to be necessary or expedient.

(8) The Table below indexes other general definitions in this Act.

Expression defined	Reference
"Absolutely entitled as against the trustee"	s 60(2)
"Authorised unit trust"	s 99
"Branch or agency"	s 10(6)
"Chargeable gain"	s 15(2)
"Connected", in references to persons being connected with one another	s 286
"Court investment fund"	s 100
"Gilt-edged securities"	Sch 9
"Indexation allowance"	s 53
"Lease" and cognate expressions	Sch 8 para 10(1)
"Legatee"	s 64(2), (3)
"Market value"	ss 272 to 274 and Sch 11
"Part disposal"	s 21(2)
"Qualifying corporate bond"	s 117
"Relevant allowable expenditure"	s 53
"Resident" and "ordinarily resident"	s 9(1)
"Settled property"	s 68
"Unit trust scheme"	s 99

Note—For a list of exchanges which have been designated as recognised futures exchanges under s 288(6), see the Miscellaneous section in Part II of this publication (Misc IX).

Simon's Tax Cases—s 288(2), *Gubay v Kington* [1984] STC 99*.

Cross references—See TCGA 1992 s 287(2) (exception for the purposes of sub-s (6) above to the general rule of orders by statutory instruments).
Modification—This section is modified, in relation to open-ended investment companies, by the Open-ended Investment Companies (Tax) Regulations, SI 1997/1154, regs 3, 23.
Amendments—¹ Definition "venture capital trust" in sub-s (1) inserted by FA 1995 s 72(7) with effect from the year 1995–96.
² Sub-s (4) repealed by FA 1996 Sch 41 Pt VIII(3) with effect in relation to times falling after 31 March 1996.
³ Definition of "the 1990 Act" repealed, and definition of "the Capital Allowances Act 2001" inserted by CAA 2001 ss 578, 580, Sch 2 para 80, Sch 4 with effect for income tax purposes, as respects allowances and charges falling to be made for chargeable periods ending after 5 April 2001, and for corporation tax purposes, as respects allowances and charges falling to be made for chargeable periods ending after 31 March 2001.
⁴ Definition of "property investment LLP" in sub-s (1) inserted by FA 2001 s 76, Sch 25 para 1(3) with effect from 6 April 2001.
⁵ In sub-s (1), words in the definition of "collective investment scheme" substituted by the Financial Services and Markets Act 2000 (Consequential Amendments) (Taxes) Order, SI 2001/3629 arts 61, 70 with effect from 1 December 2001 immediately after the coming into force of the Financial Services and Markets Act 2000 ss 411, 432(1), Sch 20.
⁶ In sub-s (1), definition of "period of account" inserted by FA 2002 s 103(3), (6) with effect for the purposes of provisions of FA 2002 using these definitions (including provisions inserted by amendment in other enactments) whenever those provisions are expressed to have effect or to come, or to have come, into force. This is without prejudice to the general effect of those amendments.

289 Commencement

(1) Except where the context otherwise requires, this Act has effect in relation to tax for the year 1992–93 and subsequent years of assessment, and tax for other chargeable periods beginning on or after 6th April 1992, and references to the coming into force of this Act or any provision in this Act shall be construed accordingly.

(2) The following provisions of this Act, that is—

(*a*) so much of any provision of this Act as authorises the making of any order or other instrument, and

(*b*) except where the tax concerned is all tax for chargeable periods to which this Act does not apply, so much of any provision of this Act as confers any power or imposes any duty the exercise or performance of which operates or may operate in relation to tax for more than one chargeable period,

shall come into force for all purposes on 6th April 1992 to the exclusion of the corresponding enactments repealed by this Act.

Definition—"Chargeable period, s 288(1).
Cross references—See TCGA 1992 Sch 11 para 18 (without prejudice to this section, tax postponed under CGTA 1979 s 17(4)(*b*) and FA 1984 s 70 and Sch 14 (provisions repealed by this Act) continue to be postponed in accordance with the repealed provisions).

290 Savings, transitionals, consequential amendments and repeals

(1) Schedules 10 (consequential amendments) and 11 (transitory provisions and savings) shall have effect.

(2) No letters patent granted or to be granted by the Crown to any person, city, borough or town corporate of any liberty, privilege, or exemption from subsidies, tolls, taxes, assessments or aids, and no statute which grants any salary, annuity or pension to any person free of any taxes, deductions or assessments, shall be construed or taken to exempt any person, city, borough or town corporate, or any inhabitant of the same, from tax chargeable in pursuance of this Act.

(3) Subject to Schedule 11, the enactments and instruments mentioned in Schedule 12 to this Act are hereby repealed to the extent specified in the third column of that Schedule (but Schedule 12 shall not have effect in relation to any enactment in so far as it has previously been repealed subject to a saving which still has effect on the coming into force of this section).

(4) The provisions of this Part of this Act are without prejudice to the provisions of the Interpretation Act 1978 as respects the effect of repeals.

291 Short title

This Act may be cited as the Taxation of Chargeable Gains Act 1992.

SCHEDULES

[SCHEDULE A1

APPLICATION OF TAPER RELIEF]¹

Section 2A(7)

Commentary—*Simon's Direct Tax Service* C1.403.
Cross references—See TCGA 1992 Sch 5BA (application of taper relief on the disposal of shares to which EIS deferral relief or income tax relief is attributable).
Amendments—¹ This Schedule inserted by FA 1998 s 121(2), Sch 20 with effect from the year 1998–99.

[Introductory

1—(1) Section 2A shall be construed subject to and in accordance with this Schedule.

(2) The different provisions of this Schedule have effect for construing the other provisions of this Schedule, as well as for construing section 2A.]¹

Amendments—¹ This Schedule inserted by FA 1998 s 121(2), Sch 20 with effect from the year 1998–99.

[Period for which an asset is held and relevant period of ownership

2—(1) In relation to any gain on the disposal of a business or non-business asset, the period after 5th April 1998 for which the asset had been held at the time of its disposal is the period which—

(*a*) begins with whichever is the later of 6th April 1998 and the time when the asset disposed of was acquired by the person making the disposal; and

(*b*) ends with the time of the disposal on which the gain accrued.

(2) Where an asset is disposed of, its relevant period of ownership is whichever is the shorter of—

(*a*) the period after 5th April 1998 for which the asset had been held at the time of its disposal; and

(*b*) the period of ten years ending with that time.

(3) The following shall be disregarded for determining when a person is to be treated for the purposes of this paragraph as having acquired an asset, that is to say—

(*a*) so much of section 73(1)(*b*) as treats the asset as acquired at a date before 6th April 1965; and

(*b*) sections 239(2)(*b*), 257(2)(*b*) and 259(2)(*b*).

(4) Where the period after 5th April 1998 for which an asset had been held at the time of its disposal includes any period which, in accordance with any of paragraphs 10 to 12 below [or paragraph 4 of Schedule 5BA]², is a period that does not count for the purposes of taper relief—

(*a*) the qualifying holding period of the asset shall be treated for the purposes of section 2A as reduced by the length of the period that does not count or, as the case may be, of the aggregate of the periods that do not count; and

(*b*) the period that does not count or, as the case may be, every such period—

(i) shall be left out of account in computing for the purposes of sub-paragraph (2) above the period of ten years ending with the time of the asset's disposal; and

(ii) shall be assumed not to be comprised in the asset's relevant period of ownership.

(5) Sub-paragraphs (1) to (3) above have effect subject to the provisions of paragraphs 13 to 19 below.]¹

Commentary—*Simon's Direct Tax Service* **C2.1410, 1421.**
Revenue Internal Guidance—Capital gains manual CG 17907 (sub-s (3): example illustrating this para).
CG 17928 (examples illustrating relevant period of ownership).
CG 17963 (example covering the situation where shares qualify as business assets for part of the relevant period of ownership following changes in FA 2000 and FA 2001).
CG 17964 (voluntary use of apportionment table for assets owned before 17 March 1998, that were wholly owned non-business assets up to 5 April 2000 and that were wholly business assets from 6 April 2000 to the date of disposal).
Amendments—¹ This Schedule inserted by FA 1998 s 121(2), Sch 20 with effect from the year 1998–99.
² Words in sub-s (4) inserted by FA 1999 s 72(3).

[Rules for determining whether a gain is a gain on the disposal of a business asset or non-business asset

3—(1) Subject to the following provisions of this Schedule, a chargeable gain accruing to any person on the disposal of any asset is a gain on the disposal of a business asset if that asset was a business asset throughout its relevant period of ownership.

(2) Where—

(*a*) a chargeable gain accrues to any person on the disposal of any asset,

(*b*) that gain does not accrue on the disposal of an asset that was a business asset throughout its relevant period of ownership, and

(*c*) that asset has been a business asset throughout one or more periods comprising part of its relevant period of ownership,

a part of that gain shall be taken to be a gain on the disposal of a business asset and, in accordance with sub-paragraph (4) below, the remainder shall be taken to be a gain on the disposal of a non-business asset.

(3) Subject to the following provisions of this Schedule, where sub-paragraph (2) above applies, the part of the chargeable gain accruing on the disposal of the asset that shall be taken to be a gain on the disposal of a business asset is the part of it that bears the same proportion to the whole of the gain as is borne to the whole of its relevant period of ownership by the aggregate of the periods which—

(*a*) are comprised in its relevant period of ownership, and

(*b*) are periods throughout which the asset is to be taken (after applying paragraphs 8 and 9 below) to have been a business asset.

(4) So much of any chargeable gain accruing to any person on the disposal of any asset as is not a gain on the disposal of a business asset shall be taken to be a gain on the disposal of a non-business asset.

(5) Where, by virtue of sub-paragraphs (2) to (4) above, a gain on the disposal of a business asset accrues on the same disposal as a gain on the disposal of a non-business asset—

(*a*) the two gains shall be treated for the purposes of taper relief as separate gains accruing on separate disposals of separate assets; but

(*b*) the periods after 5th April 1998 for which each of the assets shall be taken to have been held at the time of their disposal shall be the same and shall be determined without reference to the length of the periods mentioned in sub-paragraph (3)(*a*) and (*b*) above.]¹

Commentary—*Simon's Direct Tax Service* **C2.1420, 1429.**
Revenue Internal Guidance—Capital gains manual CG 17955 (examples illustrating apportionment of chargeable gain where there have been periods of non-business use of the asset disposed of).
Amendments—¹ This Schedule inserted by FA 1998 s 121(2), Sch 20 with effect from the year 1998–99.

[*Conditions for shares to qualify as business assets*

4—(1) This paragraph applies, in the case of the disposal of any asset, for determining (subject to the following provisions of this Schedule) whether the asset was a business asset at a time before its disposal when it consisted of, or of an interest in, any shares in a company (''the relevant company'').

(2) Where the disposal is made by an individual, the asset was a business asset at that time if at that time the relevant company was a qualifying company by reference to that individual.

(3) Where the disposal is made by the trustees of a settlement, the asset was a business asset at that time if at that time the relevant company was a qualifying company by reference to the trustees of that settlement.

(4) Where the disposal is made by an individual's personal representatives, the asset was a business asset at that time if at that time [the relevant company was a qualifying company by reference to the personal representatives]².

(5) Where the disposal is made by an individual who acquired the asset as legatee (as defined in section 64) and that time is not a time when the asset was a business asset by virtue of sub-paragraph (2) above, the asset shall be taken to have been a business asset at that time if at that time—

(*a*) it was held by the personal representatives of the deceased; and

[(*b*) the relevant company was a qualifying company by reference to the personal representatives.]²]¹

Commentary—*Simon's Direct Tax Service* **C2.1424.**
Amendments—¹ This Schedule inserted by FA 1998 s 121(2), Sch 20 with effect from the year 1998–99.
² Words in sub-paras (4), (5) substituted by FA 2000 s 67(1), (2), (7) with effect for determining whether an asset is a business asset at any time after 5 April 2000. These amendments do not affect the determination after that date whether an asset was a business asset at a time before 6 April 2000; for this purpose, the sub-paras (4), (5) previously read—

    ''(4) Where the disposal is made by an individual's personal representatives, the asset was a business asset at that time if at that time—

        (a) the relevant company was a trading company or the holding company of a trading group; and
        (b) the voting rights in that company were exercisable, as to not less than 25 per cent, by the deceased's personal representatives.

    (5) Where the disposal is made by an individual who acquired the asset as legatee (as defined in section 64) and that time is not a time when the asset was a business asset by virtue of sub-paragraph (2) above, the asset shall be taken to have been a business asset at that time if at that time—

        (a) it was held by the personal representatives of the deceased; and
        (b) the conditions in sub-paragraph (4)(a) and (b) above were satisfied.''

[*Conditions for other assets to qualify as business assets*

5—(1) This paragraph applies, in the case of the disposal of any asset, for determining (subject to the following provisions of this Schedule) whether the asset was a business asset at a time before its disposal when it was neither shares in a company nor an interest in shares in a company.

(2) Where the disposal is made by an individual, the asset was a business asset at that time if at that time it was being used, wholly or partly, for purposes falling within one or more of the following paragraphs—

(*a*) the purposes of a trade carried on at that time by that individual or by a partnership of which that individual was at that time a member;

(*b*) the purposes of any trade carried on by a company which at that time was a qualifying company by reference to that individual;

(*c*) the purposes of any trade carried on by a company which at that time was a member of a trading group the holding company of which was at that time a qualifying company by reference to that individual;

[(*d*) the purposes of any office or employment held by that individual with a person carrying on a trade.]²

(3) Where the disposal is made by the trustees of a settlement, the asset was a business asset at that time if at that time it was being used, wholly or partly, for purposes falling within one or more of the following paragraphs—

(a) the purposes of a trade carried on by the trustees of the settlement [or by a partnership whose members at that time included—

(i) the trustees of the settlement; or

(ii) any one or more of the persons who at that time were the trustees of the settlement (so far as acting in their capacity as such trustees)]⁴;

(b) the purposes of a trade carried on at that time by an eligible beneficiary or by a partnership of which an eligible beneficiary was at that time a member;

(c) the purposes of any trade carried on by a company which at that time was a qualifying company by reference to the trustees of the settlement or an eligible beneficiary;

(d) the purposes of any trade carried on by a company which at that time was a member of a trading group the holding company of which was at that time a qualifying company by reference to the trustees of the settlement or an eligible beneficiary;

[(e) the purposes of any office or employment held by an eligible beneficiary with a person carrying on a trade.]²

(4) Where the disposal is made by an individual's personal representatives, the asset was a business asset at that time if at that time it was being used, wholly or partly, for purposes falling within one or more of the following paragraphs—

(a) the purposes of a trade carried on by the deceased's personal representatives;

(b) the purposes of any trade carried on by a company which at that time was a qualifying company by reference to the deceased's personal representatives;

(c) the purposes of any trade carried on by a company which at that time was a member of a trading group the holding company of which was at that time a qualifying company by reference to the deceased's personal representatives.

(5) Where the disposal is made by an individual who acquired the asset as legatee (as defined in section 64) and that time is not a time when the asset was a business asset by virtue of sub-paragraph (2) above, the asset shall be taken to have been a business asset at that time if at that time it was—

(a) being held by the personal representatives of the deceased, and

(b) being used, wholly or partly, for purposes falling within one or more of paragraphs (a) to (c) of sub-paragraph (4) above.]¹

Commentary—*Simon's Direct Tax Service* C2.1425, 1426, 1427.
Revenue Interpretation RI 210—Bookmakers' pitches comprise business assets within para 5(2)(a).
Revenue Internal Guidance—Capital gains manual CG 17940a (asset rented by its owner to his/her partnership or company by whom is it used for the purpose of a trade, profession or vocation is not prevented from being a business asset).
Cross references—See FA 2002 Sch 10 para 8(3) (the amendment made to TCGA 1992 Sch A1 para 22(1) by FA 2002 Sch 10 para 8(1) does not apply to the reference to shares in this paragraph).
Amendments—¹ This Schedule inserted by FA 1998 s 121(2), Sch 20 with effect from the year 1998–99.
² Sub-para (2)(d) substituted for original sub-para (2)(d), (e) by FA 2000 s 67(1), (3), (7) with effect for determining whether an asset is a business asset at any time after 5 April 2000.This amendment does not affect the determination after that date whether an asset was a business asset at a time before 6 April 2000; for this purpose, the sub-para (2)(d), (e) previously read—

"(d) the purposes of any qualifying office or employment to which that individual was at that time required to devote substantially the whole of his time;

(e) the purposes of any office or employment that does not fall within paragraph (d) above but was an office or employment with a trading company in relation to which that individual falls to be treated as having, at that time, been a full-time working officer or employee."
³ Sub-para (3)(e) substituted for original sub-para (3)(e), (f) by FA 2000 s 67(1), (3), (7) with effect for determining whether an asset is a business asset at any time after 5 April 2000.This amendment does not affect the determination after that date whether an asset was a business asset at a time before 6 April 2000; for this purpose, the sub-para (3)(e), (f) previously read—

"(e) the purposes of any qualifying office or employment to which an eligible beneficiary was at that time required to devote substantially the whole of his time;

(f) the purposes of any office or employment that does not fall within paragraph (e) above but was an office or employment with a trading company in relation to which an eligible beneficiary falls to be treated as having, at that time, been a full-time working officer or employee."
⁴ Words in sub-para (3)(a) inserted by FA 2001 s 78, Sch 26 para 2 with effect (in accordance with the changes made by FA 2000 s 67) for determining whether an asset is a business asset at any time after 5 April 2000. This amendment does not affect the determination after that date whether an asset was a business asset at a time before 6 April 2000.

[Companies which are qualifying companies

[**6**—(1) A company shall be taken to have been a qualifying company by reference to an individual at any time when—

(a) the company was a trading company or the holding company of a trading group, and

(b) one or more of the following conditions was met—

(i) the company was unlisted,

(ii) the individual was an officer or employee of the company, or of a company having a relevant connection with it, or

(iii) the voting rights in the company were exercisable, as to not less than 5%, by the individual.

[(1A) A company shall also be taken to have been a qualifying company by reference to an individual at any time when—

TCGA 1992

(a) the company was a non-trading company or the holding company of a non-trading group,

(b) the individual was an officer or employee of the company, or of a company having a relevant connection with it, and

(c) the individual did not have a material interest in the company or in any company which at that time had control of the company.]³

(2) A company shall be taken to have been a qualifying company by reference to the trustees of a settlement at any time when—

(a) the company was a trading company or the holding company of a trading group, and

(b) one or more of the following conditions was met—

(i) the company was unlisted,

(ii) an eligible beneficiary was an officer or employee of the company, or of a company having a relevant connection with it, or

(iii) the voting rights in the company were exercisable, as to not less than 5%, by the trustees.

[(2A) A company shall also be taken to have been a qualifying company by reference to the trustees of a settlement at any time when—

(a) the company was a non-trading company or the holding company of a non-trading group,

(b) an eligible beneficiary was an officer or employee of the company, or of a company having a relevant connection with it, and

(c) the trustees of the settlement did not have a material interest in the company or in any company which at that time had control of the company.]³

(3) A company shall be taken to have been a qualifying company by reference to an individual's personal representatives at any time when—

(a) the company was a trading company or the holding company of a trading group, and

(b) one or more of the following conditions was met—

(i) the company was unlisted, or

(ii) the voting rights in the company were exercisable, as to not less than 5%, by the personal representatives.]²]¹

[(4) For the purposes of this paragraph an individual shall be regarded as having a material interest in a company if—

(a) the individual,

(b) the individual together with one or more persons connected with him, or

(c) any person connected with the individual, with or without any other such persons,

has a material interest in the company.

(5) For the purposes of this paragraph the trustees of a settlement shall be regarded as having a material interest in a company if—

(a) the trustees of the settlement,

(b) the trustees of the settlement together with one or more persons connected with them, or

(c) any person connected with the trustees of the settlement, with or without any other such persons,

has a material interest in the company.

(6) In this paragraph "company" does not include a unit trust scheme, notwithstanding anything in section 99.

(7) This paragraph is supplemented by paragraph 6A below (meaning of "material interest").]³

Commentary—*Simon's Direct Tax Service* C2.1423.
Revenue Internal Guidance—Capital gains manual CG 17951 (the requirement to be able to exercise 25 per cent, or 5 per cent, or the voting rights does not have to be satisfied by virtue of the particular class of shares disposed of).
CG 17954a (sub-s (6) definition of "material interest" and worked example).
Amendments—¹ This Schedule inserted by FA 1998 s 121(2), Sch 20 with effect from the year 1998–99.
² This paragraph substituted by FA 2000 s 67(1), (4), (7) with effect for determining whether an asset is a business asset at any time after 5 April 2000. This amendment does not affect the determination after that date whether an asset was a business asset at a time before 6 April 2000; for this purpose, para 6 previously read—

"**6**—(1) The times when a company shall be taken to have been a qualifying company by reference to an individual, the trustees of a settlement or an individual's personal representatives are—

(a) in the case of an individual, those set out in sub-paragraphs (2) and (3) below; and

(b) in the case of the trustees of a settlement, those set out in sub-paragraphs (2) and (4) below; and

(c) in the case of personal representatives, those set out in sub-paragraph (2) below.

(2) A company was a qualifying company by reference to an individual, the trustees of a settlement or personal representatives at any time when both the following conditions were satisfied, that is to say—

(a) the company was a trading company or the holding company of a trading group; and

(b) the voting rights in that company were exercisable, as to not less than 25 per cent, by that individual or, as the case may be, the trustees of the settlement or the personal representatives.

(3) A company was also a qualifying company by reference to an individual at any time when all of the following conditions were satisfied, that is to say—

(a) the company was a trading company or the holding company of a trading group;

(b) the voting rights in that company were exercisable, as to not less than 5 per cent, by that individual; and

(c) that individual was a full-time working officer or employee of that company or of a company which at the time had a relevant connection with that company.

(4) A company was also a qualifying company by reference to the trustees of a settlement at any time when all the following conditions were satisfied, that is to say—

(a) the company was a trading company or the holding company of a trading group;

(b) the voting rights in that company were exercisable, as to not less than 5 per cent, by the trustees of that settlement; and

(c) an eligible beneficiary was a full-time working officer or employee of that company or of a company which at the time had a relevant connection with that company.".

³ Sub-paras (1A), (2A), (4)–(7) inserted by FA 2001 s 78, Sch 26 para 3 with effect (in accordance with the changes made by FA 2000 s 67) for determining whether an asset is a business asset at any time after 5 April 2000. These amendments do not affect the determination after that date whether an asset was a business asset at a time before 6 April 2000.

[Meaning of "material interest"

6A—(1) For the purposes of paragraph 6 above, a material interest in a company means possession of, or the ability to control (directly or through the medium of other companies or by any other indirect means),—

(a) more than 10% of the issued shares in the company of any particular class,

(b) more than 10% of the voting rights in the company,

(c) such rights as would, if the whole of the income of the company were distributed among the participators (without regard to any rights of any person as a loan creditor) give an entitlement to receive more than 10% of the amount distributed, or

(d) such rights as would, in the event of the winding up of the company or in any other circumstances, give an entitlement to receive more than 10% of the assets of the company which would then be available for distribution among the participators.

(2) For the purposes of sub-paragraph (1) above a right to acquire shares or rights (however arising) shall be treated as a right to control them.

(3) A person shall be treated for the purposes of this paragraph as having a right to acquire any shares or rights—

(a) which he is entitled to acquire at a future date, or

(b) which he will at a future date be entitled to acquire.

(4) Where—

(a) in the case of any shares or rights, an entitlement falling within sub-paragraph (3)(a) or (b) above is conferred on a person by a contract, but

(b) the contract is conditional,

the person shall be treated for the purposes of this paragraph as having a right to acquire the shares or rights as from the time at which the contract is made.

(5) In any case where—

(a) the shares of any particular class attributed to a person consist of or include shares which he or another person has a right to acquire, and

(b) the circumstances are such that if that right were to be exercised the shares acquired would be shares which were previously unissued and which the company is contractually bound to issue in the event of the exercise of the right,

then in determining at any time prior to the exercise of the right whether the number of shares of that class attributed to the person exceeds a particular percentage of the issued shares of that class, the number of issued shares of that class shall be taken to be increased by the number of unissued shares referred to in paragraph (b) above.

(6) The references in sub-paragraph (5) above to the shares of any particular class attributed to a person are to the shares which in accordance with sub-paragraph (1)(a) above fall to be brought into account in his case to determine whether their number exceeds a particular percentage of the issued shares of the company of that class.

(7) Sub-paragraphs (5) and (6) above shall apply, with the necessary modifications, in relation to—

(a) voting rights in the company (and attribution of such rights to a person in accordance with sub-paragraph (1)(b) above),

(b) rights which would, if the whole of the income of the company were distributed among the participators (without regard to any rights of any person as a loan creditor) give an entitlement to receive any of the amount distributed (and attribution of such rights to a person in accordance with sub-paragraph (1)(c) above), and

(c) rights which would, in the event of the winding up of the company or in any other circumstances, give an entitlement to receive any of the assets of the company which would then be available for distribution among the participators (and attribution of such rights to a person in accordance with sub-paragraph (1)(d) above),

as they apply in relation to shares of any particular class (and their attribution to a person in accordance with sub-paragraph (1)(a) above).

(8) For the purposes of this paragraph "participator" and "loan creditor" have the meaning given by section 417 of the Taxes Act.]¹

Commentary—*Simon's Direct Tax Service* **C2.1422.**

Cross references—See FA 2002 Sch 10 para 8(3) (the amendment made to TCGA 1992 Sch A1 para 22(1) by FA 2002 Sch 10 para 8(1) does not apply to the reference to shares in this paragraph).

Amendments—¹ This paragraph inserted by FA 2001 s 78, Sch 26 para 4 with effect (in accordance with the changes made by FA 2000 s 67) for determining whether an asset is a business asset at any time after 5 April 2000. This amendment does not affect the determination after that date whether an asset was a business asset at a time before 6 April 2000.

[Persons who are eligible beneficiaries

7—(1) An eligible beneficiary, in relation to an asset comprised in a settlement and a time, is any individual having at that time a relevant interest in possession under the settlement in either—

    (*a*) the whole of the settled property; or

    (*b*) a part of the settled property that is or includes that asset.

(2) In this paragraph "relevant interest in possession", in relation to property comprised in a settlement, means any interest in possession under that settlement other than—

    (*a*) a right under that settlement to receive an annuity; or

    (*b*) a fixed-term entitlement.

(3) In sub-paragraph (2) above "fixed-term entitlement", in relation to property comprised in a settlement, means any interest under that settlement which is limited to a term that is fixed and is not a term at the end of which the person with that interest will become entitled to the property.]¹

Revenue Internal Guidance—Capital gains manual CG 17965 (definition of eligible beneficiaries and example).
Amendments—¹ This Schedule inserted by FA 1998 s 121(2), Sch 20 with effect from the year 1998–99.

[Cases where there are non-qualifying beneficiaries

8—(1) This paragraph applies in the case of a disposal of an asset by the trustees of a settlement where the asset's relevant period of ownership is or includes a period ("a sharing period") throughout which—

    (*a*) the asset was a business asset by reference to one or more eligible beneficiaries;

    (*b*) the asset would not otherwise have been a business asset; and

    (*c*) there is a non-qualifying part of the relevant income, or there would be if there were any relevant income for that period.

(2) The period throughout which the asset disposed of is to be taken to have been a business asset shall be determined as if the relevant fraction of every sharing period were a period throughout which the asset was not a business asset.

(3) In sub-paragraph (2) above "the relevant fraction", in relation to any sharing period, means the fraction which represents the proportion of relevant income for that period which is, or (if there were such income) would be, a non-qualifying part of that income.

(4) Where a sharing period is a period in which the proportion mentioned in sub-paragraph (3) above has been different at different times, this paragraph shall require a separate relevant fraction to be determined for, and applied to, each part of that period for which there is a different proportion.

(5) For the purposes of this paragraph the non-qualifying part of any relevant income for any period is so much of that income for that period as is or, as the case may be, would be—

    (*a*) income to which no eligible beneficiary has any entitlement; or

    (*b*) income to which a non-qualifying eligible beneficiary has an entitlement.

(6) In sub-paragraph (5) above "non-qualifying eligible beneficiary", in relation to a period, means an eligible beneficiary who is not a beneficiary by reference to whom (if he were the only beneficiary) the asset disposed of would be a business asset throughout that period.

(7) In this paragraph "relevant income" means income from the part of the settled property comprising the asset disposed of.]¹

Commentary—*Simon's Direct Tax Service* C2.1442.
Revenue Internal Guidance—Capital gains manual CG 17968 (example illustrating this para).
Amendments—¹ This Schedule inserted by FA 1998 s 121(2), Sch 20 with effect from the year 1998–99.

[Cases where an asset is used at the same time for different purposes

9—(1) This paragraph applies in the case of a disposal by any person of an asset where the asset's relevant period of ownership is or includes a period ("a mixed-use period") throughout which the asset—

    (*a*) was a business asset by reference to its use for purposes mentioned in paragraph 5(2) to (5) above; but

    (*b*) was, at the same time, being put to a non-qualifying use.

(2) The period throughout which the asset disposed of is to be taken to have been a business asset shall be determined as if the relevant fraction of every mixed-use period were a period throughout which the asset was not a business asset.

(3) In sub-paragraph (2) above "the relevant fraction", in relation to any mixed-use period, means the fraction which represents the proportion of the use of the asset during that period that was a non-qualifying use.

(4) Where both this paragraph and paragraph 8 above apply in relation to the whole or any part of a period—

    (*a*) effect shall be given to that paragraph first; and

Application of Taper Relief

TCGA 1992 Sch A1

(*b*) further reductions by virtue of this paragraph in the period for which the asset disposed of is taken to have been a business asset shall be made in respect of only the relevant part of any non-qualifying use.

(5) In sub-paragraph (4) above the reference to the relevant part of any non-qualifying use is a reference to the proportion of that use which is not a use to which a non-qualifying part of any relevant income is attributable.

(6) Where a mixed-use period is a period in which—

(*a*) the proportion mentioned in sub-paragraph (3) above has been different at different times, or
(*b*) different attributions have to be made for the purposes of sub-paragraphs (4) and (5) above for different parts of the period,

this paragraph shall require a separate relevant fraction to be determined for, and applied to, each part of the period for which there is a different proportion or attribution.

(7) In this paragraph—

"non-qualifying use", in relation to an asset, means any use of the asset for purposes which are not purposes in respect of which the asset would fall to be treated as a business asset at the time of its use; and "non-qualifying part" and

"relevant income" have the same meanings as in paragraph 8 above.]¹

Commentary—*Simon's Direct Tax Service* **C2.1430.**
Revenue Internal Guidance—Capital gains manual CG 17958 (example illustrating this para).
CG 17970 (where apportionments are required both in relation to para 8 above and this para, the apportionment(s) in relation to para 8 should be made first; accompanied by worked example).
Amendments—¹ This Schedule inserted by FA 1998 s 121(2), Sch 20 with effect from the year 1998–99.

[Periods of limited exposure to fluctuations in value not to count

10—(1) Where, in the case of any asset disposed of ("the relevant asset"), the period after 5th April 1998 for which that asset had been held at the time of its disposal is or includes a period during which—

(*a*) the person making the disposal, or
(*b*) a relevant predecessor of his,

had limited exposure to fluctuations in the value of the asset, the period during which that person or predecessor had that limited exposure shall not count for the purposes of taper relief.

(2) The times when a person shall be taken for the purposes of this paragraph to have had such limited exposure in the case of the relevant asset shall be all the times while he held that asset when a transaction entered into at any time by him, or by a relevant predecessor of his, had the effect that he—

(*a*) was not exposed, or not exposed to any substantial extent, to the risk of loss from fluctuations in the value of the relevant asset; and
(*b*) was not able to enjoy, or to enjoy to any substantial extent, any opportunities to benefit from such fluctuations.

(3) The transactions referred to in sub-paragraph (2) above do not include—

(*a*) any insurance policy which the person in question might reasonably have been expected to enter into and which is insurance against the loss of the relevant asset or against damage to it, or against both; or
(*b*) any transaction having effect in relation to fluctuations in the value of the relevant asset so far only as they are fluctuations resulting from fluctuations in the value of foreign currencies.

(4) In this paragraph "relevant predecessor"—

(*a*) in relation to a person disposing of an asset, means any person other than the person disposing of it who held that asset at a time falling in the period which is taken to be the whole period for which it had been held at the time of its disposal; and
(*b*) in relation to a relevant predecessor of a person disposing of an asset, means any other relevant predecessor of that person.

(5) In sub-paragraph (4) above, the reference, in relation to an asset, to the whole period for which it had been held at the time of its disposal is a reference to the period that would be given for that asset by paragraph 2(1) above if, in paragraph (*a*), the words "whichever is the later of 6th April 1998 and" were omitted.]¹

Commentary—*Simon's Direct Tax Service* **C2.1413.**
Revenue Internal Guidance—Capital gains manual CG 17916–17917 (explanation of this para with example).
CG 17928 (worked example).
Amendments—¹ This Schedule inserted by FA 1998 s 121(2), Sch 20 with effect from the year 1998–99.

[[Periods of share ownership not to count where there is a change of activity by the company

11—*(1) This paragraph applies where—*

(*a*) *there is a disposal of an asset consisting of shares in a close company; and*
(*b*) *the period beginning with the relevant time and ending with the time of the disposal includes at least one relevant change of activity involving that company.*

(2) So much of the period after 5th April 1998 for which the asset had been held at the time of its disposal as falls before the time, or latest time, in that period when there was a relevant change of activity involving the close company shall not count for the purposes of taper relief.

(3) Where—

(a) a close company or any of its 51 per cent subsidiaries has at any time begun to carry on a trade, and

(b) immediately before that time, neither that company nor any of its 51 per cent subsidiaries was carrying on a trade,

a relevant change of activity involving the close company shall be taken to have occurred at that time.

(4) For the purposes of this paragraph where—

(a) at the time of the disposal of the shares, the close company was carrying on a business of holding investments, and

(b) there has been any occasion falling within—

(i) the period of twelve months ending with that time, or

(ii) the period of twelve months ending with any earlier time after the relevant time,

when the close company was not carrying on that business or when the size of that business was small by comparison with its size at the end of that period,

a relevant change of activity involving the close company shall be taken to have occurred immediately after the latest such occasion before the time of the disposal.

(5) For the purposes of sub-paragraph (4) above the size of any business at any time shall be determined by assuming it to correspond to the aggregate of the amounts and values given by way of consideration for the assets held at that time for the purposes of the business.

(6) In determining for the purposes of this paragraph whether a close company is at any time carrying on a business of holding investments, and in determining for those purposes the size at any time of such a business—

(a) all the activities of a close company and of all its 51 per cent subsidiaries shall be taken together as if they were all being carried on by the close company; and

(b) the activities that are included in a business of holding investments shall be taken not to include—

(i) holding shares in a 51 per cent subsidiary of the company holding the shares;

(ii) making loans to an associated company or to a participator in the company making the loan or in an associated company; or

(iii) placing money on deposit.

(7) In this paragraph—

(a) references to a company's carrying on a trade, or to beginning to carry one on, do not include references to its carrying on or beginning to carry on a trade that is merely incidental to any non-trading activities carried on by that company or another company in the same group of companies; and

(b) references to a business of holding investments includes a reference to a business of making investments.

(8) For the purposes of this paragraph a company is to be treated as another's associated company at any time if at that time, or at another time within one year previously—

(a) one of them has had control of the other; or

(b) both have been under the control of the same person or persons.

(9) In this paragraph—

"51 per cent subsidiary", in relation to another company, means a company which, in accordance with section 170(7), is an effective 51 per cent subsidiary of the other company for the purposes of sections 170 to 181; and

"participator", in relation to a company, has the meaning given by section 417(1) of the Taxes Act.

(10) In this paragraph "the relevant time", in relation to the disposal of an asset consisting of shares in a company, means the beginning of the period after 5th April 1998 for which that asset had been held at the time of its disposal.][1][2]

Commentary—*Simon's Direct Tax Service* **C2.1411, 1414.**
Revenue Interpretation 229—Meaning of "carrying on a business of holding investments".
Revenue Internal Guidance—Capital gains manual CG 17919–17920 (explanation of this para with example).
Cross references—See FA 2000 Sch 29 para 36 (the main amendments made to TCGA 1992 s 170 by FA 2000 Sch 29 para I have effect for the purposes of this section for any determination as to whether a company is a 51% subsidiary of another company after 31 March 2000).
FA 2002 Sch 10 para 8(3) (the amendment made to TCGA 1992 Sch A1 para 22(1) by FA 2002 Sch 10 para 8(1) does not apply to the references to shares in this paragraph, save to those in sub-para (6) above).
Amendments—[1] This Schedule inserted by FA 1998 s 121(2), Sch 20 with effect from the year 1998–99.
[2] This paragraph repealed by FA 2002 ss 47, 141, Sch 10 paras 1, 2, Sch 40 Pt 3(3) with effect for disposals after 16 April 2002 This amendment has effect for periods of ownership after that date: FA 2002 Sch 10 paras 2, 4, 7.

[Periods of share ownership not to count if company is not active

11A—(1) Where there is a disposal of an asset consisting of shares in a company, any period after 5th April 1998 during which the asset consisted of shares in a company that—

    (*a*) was a close company, and

    (*b*) was not active,

shall not count for the purposes of taper relief.

(2) Subject to the following provisions of this paragraph, a company is regarded as active at any time when—

    (*a*) it is carrying on a business of any description,

    (*b*) it is preparing to carry on a business of any description, or

    (*c*) it or another person is winding up the affairs of a business of any description that it has ceased to carry on.

(3) In sub-paragraph (2) above—

    (*a*) references to a business include a business that is not conducted on a commercial basis or with a view to the realisation of a profit, and

    (*b*) references to carrying on a business include holding assets and managing them.

(4) For the purposes of this paragraph a company is not regarded as active by reason only of its doing all or any of the following—

    (*a*) holding money (in any currency) in cash or on deposit;

    (*b*) holding other assets whose total value is insignificant;

    (*c*) holding shares in or debentures of a company that is not active;

    (*d*) making loans to an associated company or to a participator or an associate of a participator;

    (*e*) carrying out administrative functions in order to comply with requirements of the Companies Act 1985 (c 6) or the Companies (Northern Ireland) Order 1986 (SI 1986/1032 (NI 6)) or other regulatory requirements.

(5) Notwithstanding anything in sub-paragraphs (2) to (4) above a company shall be treated as active for the purposes of this paragraph if—

    (*a*) it is the holding company of a group of companies that contains at least one active company, or

    (*b*) it has a qualifying shareholding in a joint venture company or is the holding company of a group of companies any member of which has a qualifying shareholding in a joint venture company.

(6) In this paragraph "associated company" has the meaning given by section 416 of the Taxes Act and "participator" and "associate" have the meaning given by section 417 of that Act.

(7) Any reference in this paragraph to shares in or debentures of a company includes an interest in, or option in respect of, shares in or debentures of a company.]¹

Cross references—See FA 2002 Sch 10 para 8(3) (the amendment made to TCGA 1992 Sch A1 para 22(1) by FA 2002 Sch 10 para 8(1) does not apply to the references to shares in this paragraph).

Amendments—¹ This paragraph inserted by FA 2002 s 47, Sch 10 paras 1, 3 with effect for disposals after 16 April 2002.

[Periods of share ownership not to count in a case of value shifting

12—(1) This paragraph applies (subject to sub-paragraph (4) below) where—

    (*a*) there is a disposal of an asset consisting of shares in a close company, and

    (*b*) at least one relevant shift of value involving that asset has occurred between the relevant time and the time of the disposal.

(2) So much of the period after 5th April 1998 for which the asset had been held at the time of its disposal as falls before the time, or latest time, in that period at which there was a relevant shift of value involving that asset shall not count for the purposes of taper relief.

(3) For the purposes of this paragraph a relevant shift of value involving any asset shall be taken to have occurred whenever—

    (*a*) a person having control of a close company exercised his control of that company so that value passed into that asset out of a relevant holding; or

    (*b*) effect was given to any other transaction by virtue of which value passed into that asset out of a relevant holding.

(4) A relevant shift of value involving an asset shall be disregarded for the purposes of this paragraph if—

    (*a*) that shift of value is one in which the value passing into that asset out of the relevant holding is insignificant; or

    (*b*) that shift of value took place at a time when the qualifying holding period for the relevant holding was at least as long as the qualifying holding period for that asset.

(5) In sub-paragraphs (3) and (4) above the references to a relevant holding shall be construed, in relation to any case in which value has passed out of one asset into another asset consisting of shares in a company, as a reference to any holding by—

(*a*) the person who, following the exercise of control or other transaction by virtue of which the value has passed, held the other asset, or

(*b*) a person connected with him,

of any shares in that company or in a company under the control of the same person or persons as that company.

(6) For the purposes of sub-paragraph (4)(*b*) above the reference to the qualifying holding period of a holding or other asset at the time when a shift of value takes place shall be taken to be what, in relation to a disposal at that time of that holding or other asset by the person then entitled to dispose of it, would be taken to have been its qualifying holding period for the purposes of section 2A.

(7) In this paragraph references to shares in a company include references to rights over a company.

(8) In this paragraph ''the relevant time'', in relation to the disposal of an asset consisting of shares in a company, means the beginning of the period after 5th April 1998 for which that asset had been held at the time of its disposal.]¹

Commentary—*Simon's Direct Tax Service* **C2.1411, 1415.**
Revenue Internal Guidance—Capital gains manual CG 17922–17923 (explanation of this para with example).
Cross references—See FA 2002 Sch 10 para 8(3) (the amendment made to TCGA 1992 Sch A1 para 22(1) by FA 2002 Sch 10 para 8(1) does not apply to the references to shares in this paragraph).
Amendments—¹ This Schedule inserted by FA 1998 s 121(2), Sch 20 with effect from the year 1998–99.

[Rules for options

13—(1) This paragraph applies where by virtue of section 144—

(*a*) the grant of an option and the transaction entered into by the grantor in fulfilment of his obligations under the option, or

(*b*) the acquisition of an option and the transaction entered into by the person exercising the option,

fall to be treated as one transaction.

(2) The time of the disposal of any asset disposed of in pursuance of the transaction shall be the time of the following disposal—

(*a*) if the option binds the grantor to sell, the disposal made in fulfilment of the grantor's obligations under the option;

(*b*) if the option binds the grantor to buy, the disposal made to the grantor in consequence of the exercise of the option.

(3) The time of the acquisition of any asset acquired in pursuance of the option, or in consequence of its exercise, shall be the time of the exercise of the option.

(4) Any question whether the asset disposed of or acquired was a business asset at any time shall be determined by reference to the asset to which the option related, and not the option.]¹

Commentary—*Simon's Direct Tax Service* **C2.1450.**
Revenue Internal Guidance—Capital gains manual CG 17908 (example illustrating this para).
Amendments—¹ This Schedule inserted by FA 1998 s 121(2), Sch 20 with effect from the year 1998–99.

[Further rules for assets derived from other assets

14—(1) This paragraph applies if, in a case where—

(*a*) assets have merged,

(*b*) an asset has divided or otherwise changed its nature, or

(*c*) different rights or interests in or over any asset have been created or extinguished at different times,

the value of any asset disposed of is derived (through one or more successive events falling within paragraphs (*a*) to (*c*) above but not otherwise) from one or more other assets acquired into the same ownership at a time before the acquisition of the asset disposed of.

(2) The asset disposed of shall be deemed for the purposes of this Schedule to have been acquired at the earliest time at which any asset from which its value is derived was acquired into the same ownership.

(3) Any determination of whether the asset disposed of was a business asset at a time when another asset from which its value is derived was in the ownership of the person making the disposal shall be made as if that other asset were the asset disposed of or, as the case may be, were comprised in it.]¹

Commentary—*Simon's Direct Tax Service* **C2.1451.**
Revenue Internal Guidance—Capital Gains Manual CG 17909, CG 17942 (examples illustrating this para).
Amendments—¹ This Schedule inserted by FA 1998 s 121(2), Sch 20 with effect from the year 1998–99.

[Special rules for assets transferred between spouses

15—(1) This paragraph applies where a person (''the transferring spouse'') has disposed of any asset to another (''the transferee spouse'') by a disposal falling within section 58(1).

(2) Paragraph 2 above shall have effect in relation to any subsequent disposal of the asset as if the time when the transferee spouse acquired the asset were the time when the transferring spouse acquired it.

(3) Where for the purposes of paragraph 2 above the transferring spouse would be treated—

    (*a*) in a case where there has been one or more previous disposals falling within section 58(1), by virtue of sub-paragraph (2) above, or by virtue of that sub-paragraph together with any other provision of this Schedule, or

    (*b*) in a case where there has not been such a previous disposal, by virtue of such another provision,

as having acquired the asset at a time other than the time when the transferring spouse did acquire it, the reference in that sub-paragraph to the time when the transferring spouse acquired it shall be read as a reference to the time when for the purposes of that paragraph the transferring spouse is treated as having acquired it.

(4) Where there is a disposal by the transferee spouse, any question whether the asset was a business asset at a time before that disposal shall be determined as if—

    (*a*) in relation to times when the asset was held by the transferring spouse, references in paragraph 5(2) above to the individual by whom the disposal is made included references to the transferring spouse; and

    (*b*) the reference in paragraph 5(5) above to the acquisition of the asset as a legatee by the individual by whom the disposal is made included a reference to its acquisition as a legatee by the transferring spouse.

(5) Where, in the case of any asset, there has been more than one transfer falling within section 58(1) during the period after 5th April 1998 for which the transferee spouse has held it at the time of that spouse's disposal of that asset, sub-paragraph (4) above shall have effect as if a reference, in relation to any time, to the transferring spouse were a reference to the individual who was the transferring spouse in relation to the next disposal falling within section 58(1) to have been made after that time.]¹

Commentary—*Simon's Direct Tax Service* **C2.1452.**
Revenue Internal Guidance—Capital gains manual CG 17906 (explanation of this para with example).
CG 17943, CG 17945 (illustrations of transfers of business assets between spouses at no gain/no loss).
Amendments—¹ This Schedule inserted by FA 1998 s 121(2), Sch 20 with effect from the year 1998–99.

[Special rules for postponed gains

16—(1) Sub-paragraph (3) below applies where the whole or any part of any gain which—

    (*a*) would (but for any provision of this Act) have accrued on the disposal of any asset, or

    (*b*) would have accrued on any disposal assumed under any enactment to have been made at any time,

falls by virtue of an enactment mentioned in sub-paragraph (2) below to be treated as accruing on or after 6th April 1998 at a time (whether or not the time of a subsequent disposal) which falls after the time of the actual or assumed disposal mentioned in paragraph (*a*) or (*b*) above ("the charged disposal").

(2) Those enactments are—

    (*a*) section 10A,

    (*b*) section 116(10),

    (*c*) section 134,

    (*d*) section 154(2) or (4),

    (*e*) Schedule 5B or 5C, or

    (*f*) paragraph 27 of Schedule 15 to the Finance Act 1996 (qualifying indexed securities).

(3) In relation to the gain or part of a gain that is treated as accruing after the time of the charged disposal—

    (*a*) references in this Schedule (except this sub-paragraph) to the disposal on which the gain or part accrues are references to the charged disposal; and

    (*b*) references in this Schedule to the asset disposed of by that disposal are references to the asset that was or would have been disposed of by the charged disposal;

and, accordingly, the end of the period after 5th April 1998 for which that asset had been held at the time of the disposal on which that gain or part accrues shall be deemed to have been the time of the charged disposal.

(4) In relation to any gain that is treated by virtue of—

    (*a*) subsection (1) of section 12, or

    (*b*) subsection (2) of section 279,

as accruing after the time of the disposal from which it accrues, references in this Schedule to the disposal on which the gain accrues, to the asset disposed of on that disposal and to the time of that disposal shall be construed disregarding that subsection.

(5) It shall be immaterial for the purposes of this paragraph—

(*a*) that the time of the charged disposal or, as the case may be, the time of the actual disposal from which the gain accrues was before 6th April 1998; and

(*b*) that the time at which the charged disposal is treated as accruing is postponed on more than one occasion under an enactment specified in sub-paragraph (2) above.]¹

Commentary—*Simon's Direct Tax Service* C2.1412.
Revenue Internal Guidance—Capital gains manual CG 17911 (example illustrating this para).
CG 17913 (example illustrating this sub-para (4)).
Amendments—¹ This Schedule inserted by FA 1998 s 121(2), Sch 20 with effect from the year 1998–99.

[Special rule for property settled by a company

17—(1) No part of any chargeable gain accruing to the trustees of a settlement on the disposal of any asset shall be treated as a gain on the disposal of a business asset if—

(*a*) the settlor is a company, and

(*b*) that company has an interest in the settlement at the time of the disposal.

(2) Subject to the following provisions of this paragraph, a company which is a settlor in relation to any settlement shall be regarded as having an interest in a settlement if—

(*a*) any property which may at any time be comprised in the settlement, or any derived property is, or will or may become, payable to or applicable for the benefit of that company or an associated company; or

(*b*) that company or an associated company enjoys a benefit deriving directly or indirectly from any property which is comprised in the settlement or any derived property.

(3) This paragraph does not apply unless the settlor or an associated company is within the charge to corporation tax in respect of chargeable gains for the accounting period in which the chargeable gain accrues.

(4) In this paragraph "derived property", in relation to any property, means income from that property or any other property directly or indirectly representing proceeds of, or of income from, that property or income therefrom.

(5) For the purposes of this section a company is to be treated as another's associated company at any time if at that time, or at another time within one year previously—

(*a*) one of them has had control of the other; or

(*b*) both have been under the control of the same person or persons.

(6) In this section "settlor" has the meaning given by section 660G(1) and (2) of the Taxes Act.

(7) This paragraph has effect subject to paragraph 20 below.]¹

Commentary—*Simon's Direct Tax Service* C2.1441.
Revenue Internal Guidance—Capital gains manual CG 17946–47 (explanation of this para and example).
Amendments—¹ This Schedule inserted by FA 1998 s 121(2), Sch 20 with effect from the year 1998–99.

[Special rules for assets acquired in the reconstruction of mutual businesses etc

18—(1) Where—

(*a*) shares in a company have been issued under any arrangements for the issue of shares in that company in respect of the interests of the members of a mutual company; and

(*b*) a person to whom shares were issued under those arrangements falls by virtue of [subsection (2)(*a*)]³ of section 136 to be treated as having exchanged interests of his as a member of the mutual company for shares issued under those arrangements,

paragraph 2 above shall have effect (notwithstanding that section) as if the time of that person's acquisition of the shares were the time when they were issued to him.

(2) Where—

(*a*) a registered friendly society has been incorporated under the Friendly Societies Act 1992, and

(*b*) there has been a change under Schedule 4 to that Act as a result of which a member of the registered society, or of a branch of the registered society, has become a member of the incorporated society or of a branch of the incorporated society,

paragraph 2 above shall have effect (notwithstanding anything in section 217B) in relation to the interests and rights in the incorporated society, or the branch of the incorporated society, which that person had immediately after the change, as if the time of their acquisition by him were the time of the change.

(3) In this paragraph—

"the incorporated society", in relation to the incorporation of a registered friendly society, means the society after incorporation;

["insurance company" means an undertaking carrying on the business of effecting or carrying out contracts of insurance and, for the purposes of this definition, "contract of insurance" has the meaning given by Article 3(1) of the Financial Services and Markets Act 2000 (Regulated Activities) Order 2001;]²

"mutual company" means—

(*a*) a mutual insurance company; or

(*b*) a company of another description carrying on a business on a mutual basis;

"mutual insurance company" means any insurance company carrying on a business without having a share capital;

"the registered society", in relation to the incorporation of a registered friendly society, means the society before incorporation.]¹

Commentary—*Simon's Direct Tax Service* **C2.1453.**
Revenue Internal Guidance—Capital gains manual CG 17914 (explanation of this para).
Cross references—See FA 2002 Sch 10 para 8(3) (the amendment made to TCGA 1992 Sch A1 para 22(1) by FA 2002 Sch 10 para 8(1) does not apply to the references to shares in sub-para (1) above, except insofar as they relate to shares issued before 17 April 2002).
Amendments—¹ This Schedule inserted by FA 1998 s 121(2), Sch 20 with effect from the year 1998–99.
² In sub-para (3), definition of "insurance company" substituted by the Financial Services and Markets Act 2000 (Consequential Amendments) (Taxes) Order, SI 2001/3629 arts 61, 71 with effect for the purposes of determining whether, at any time after 30 November 2001, a company is a mutual company within the meaning of the Taxation of Chargeable Gains Act 1992 Sch A1 para 18.
³ Words in sub-para (1)(b) substituted for the words "subsection (3)" by FA 2002 s 45, Sch 9 paras 5(1), (13), 7 with effect for shares or debentures issued after 16 April 2002. The reference to shares or debentures includes any interests falling to be treated as shares or debentures for the purposes of TCGA 1992 s 135 or 136 as substituted by FA 2002 Sch 9.

[Special rule for ancillary trust funds

19—(1) Use of an asset as part of an ancillary trust fund of a member of Lloyd's—

(*a*) shall not be regarded as a use in respect of which the asset is to be treated as a business asset at any time; but

(*b*) shall be disregarded in any determination for the purposes of paragraph 9 above of whether it was being put to a non-qualifying use at the same time as it was being used for purposes mentioned in paragraph 5(2) to (5) above.

(2) In this section "ancillary trust fund" has the same meaning as in Chapter III of Part II of the Finance Act 1993.]¹

Commentary—*Simon's Direct Tax Service* **C2.1454.**
Amendments—¹ This Schedule inserted by FA 1998 s 121(2), Sch 20 with effect from the year 1998–99.

[General rules for settlements

20—(1) Where, in the case of any settlement, the settled property originates from more than one settlor, this Schedule shall have effect as if there were a separate and distinct settlement for the property originating from each settlor, and references in this Schedule to an eligible beneficiary shall be construed accordingly.

(2) Subsections (1) to (5) of section 79 apply for the purposes of this paragraph as they apply for the purposes of that section.]¹

Commentary—*Simon's Direct Tax Service* **C2.1440.**
Revenue Internal Guidance—Capital gains manual CG 17966 (example illustrating this para).
Amendments—¹ This Schedule inserted by FA 1998 s 121(2), Sch 20 with effect from the year 1998–99.

[General rule for apportionments under this Schedule

21 Where any apportionment falls to be made for the purposes of this Schedule it shall be made—

(*a*) on a just and reasonable basis; and

(*b*) on the assumption that an amount falling to be apportioned by reference to any period arose or accrued at the same rate throughout the period over which it falls to be treated as having arisen or accrued.]¹

Amendments—¹ This Schedule inserted by FA 1998 s 121(2), Sch 20 with effect from the year 1998–99.

[Interpretation of Schedule

22—(1) In this Schedule—

"51 per cent subsidiary" ...¹¹has the meaning given by section 838 of the Taxes Act;

"commercial association of companies" means a company together with such of its associated companies (within the meaning of section 416 of the Taxes Act) as carry on businesses which are of such a nature that the businesses of the company and the associated companies, taken together, may be reasonably considered to make up a single composite undertaking;

"eligible beneficiary" shall be construed in accordance with paragraphs 7 and 20 above;

"full-time working officer or employee", in relation to any company, means an individual who—

(*a*) *is an officer or employee of that company or of that company and one or more other companies with which that company has a relevant connection; and*

(*b*) *is required in that capacity to devote substantially the whole of his time to the service of that company, or to the service of those companies taken together;*²

"group of companies" means a company which has one or more 51 per cent subsidiaries, together with those subsidiaries;

["holding company" means a company that has one or more 51% subsidiaries;]⁴

["interest in shares" means an interest as a co-owner (whether the shares are owned jointly or in common, and whether or not the interests of the co-owners are equal), and "interest in debentures", in relation to any debentures, has a corresponding meaning;][5]

["joint venture company" has the meaning given by paragraph 23(2) below;][6]

["non-trading company" means a company which is not a trading company;

"non-trading group" means a group of companies which is not a trading group;][3]

"office" and "employment" have the same meanings as in the Income Tax Acts;

["ordinary share capital" has the meaning given by section 832(1) of the Taxes Act;][7]

"qualifying office or employment", in relation to any time, means an office or employment with a person who was at that time carrying on a trade; [2]

"qualifying company" shall be construed in accordance with paragraph 6 above;

["qualifying shareholding", in relation to a joint venture company, has the meaning given by paragraph 23(3) below;][6]

"relevant period of ownership" shall be construed in accordance with paragraph 2 above;

"shares", in relation to a company, [includes—

   (*a*) any securities of that company, and

   (*b*) any debentures of that company that are deemed, by virtue of section 251(6), to be securities for the purposes of that section]8;

"trade" means (subject to section 241(3)) anything which—

   (*a*) is a trade, profession or vocation, within the meaning of the Income Tax Acts; and

   (*b*) is conducted on a commercial basis and with a view to the realisation of profits;

["trading company" has the meaning given by paragraph 22A below;]9

["trading group" has the meaning given by paragraph 22B below;]10

"transaction" includes any agreement, arrangement or understanding, whether or not legally enforceable, and a series of transactions.

["unlisted company" means a company—

   (*a*) none of whose shares is listed on a recognised stock exchange, and

   (*b*) which is not a 51 per cent subsidiary of a company whose shares, or any class of whose shares, is so listed;]2

(2) For the purposes of this Schedule one company has a relevant connection with another company at any time when they are both members of the same group of companies or of the same commercial association of companies.

(3) References in this Schedule to the acquisition of an asset that was provided, rather than acquired, by the person disposing of it are references to its provision.

(4) References in this Schedule, in relation to a part disposal, to the asset disposed of are references to the asset of which there is a part disposal.]1

Commentary—*Simon's Direct Tax Service* C2.1422.
Revenue Interpretation RI 228—Meaning of "trading company" and related issues.
RI 230—Meaning of "security".
Revenue Internal Guidance—Capital gains manual CG 17930 (sub-s (1): meaning of security).
CG 17952b (a detailed examination of the elements making up the definition of "trading company").
CG 17954 (the phrase "devote substantially the whole of his time" as applied to a "full-time working officer or employee" in practice is taken to mean at least three quarters of normal working hours).
Cross references—See FA 2002 Sch 10 para 8(3) (the amendment made to TCGA 1992 Sch A1 para 22(1) by FA 2002 Sch 10 para 8(1) does not apply to the references to shares in the definition of "unlisted company" above).
Amendments—1 This Schedule inserted by FA 1998 s 121(2), Sch 20 with effect from the year 1998–99.
2 In sub-para (1) definition of "unlisted company" inserted and definitions of "full-time working officer or employee" and "qualifying office or employment" repealed by FA 2000 ss 67(1), (5), (7), 156, Sch 40 Pt II(6) with effect for determining whether an asset is a business asset at any time after 5 April 2000. These amendments do not affect the determination after that date whether an asset was a business asset at a time before 6 April 2000.
3 In sub-para (1) definitions of "non-trading company" and "non-trading group" inserted by FA 2001 s 78, Sch 26 para 5 with effect (in accordance with the changes made by FA 2000 s 67) for determining whether an asset is a business asset at any time after 5 April 2000. These amendments do not affect the determination after that date whether an asset was a business asset at a time before 6 April 2000.
4 In sub-para (1), definition of "holding company" substituted by FA 2002 s 47, Sch 10 paras 1, 4(1), (3) with effect for disposals after 16 April 2002. This amendment as applied has effect for periods of ownership after 16 April 2002. The definition of "holding company" previously read as follows—

   "holding company" means a company whose business (disregarding any trade carried on by it) consists wholly or mainly of the holding of shares in one or more companies which are its 51 per cent subsidiaries;"
5 In sub-para (1), definition of "interest in shares" inserted by FA 2002 s 47, Sch 10 paras 1, 5 with effect for disposals after 16 April 2002. This amendment as applied has effect for periods of ownership after 16 April 2002.
6 In para (1), definitions of "joint venture company" and "qualifying shareholding" inserted by FA 2002 s 47, Sch 10 paras 1, 6(1), (3) with effect for disposals after 16 April 2002.
7 In para (1), definition of "ordinary share capital" inserted by FA 2002 s 47, Sch 10 paras 1, 7(1), (3) with effect for disposals after 16 April 2002.
8 In para (1), definition of "shares", words substituted for the words "includes any securities of that company" by FA 2002 s 47, Sch 10 paras 1, 8(1) with effect in accordance with FA 2002 Sch 10 para 8(2)–(4).
9 Definition of "trading company" substituted by FA 2002 s 47, Sch 10 para 9(1), (3) with effect for disposals after 16 April 2002. This amendment as applied has effect for periods of ownership after 16 April 2002. The definition previously read as follows—

   " 'trading company' means a company which is either—

   (*a*) a company existing wholly for the purpose of carrying on one or more trades; or

   (*b*) a company that would fall within paragraph (*a*) above apart from any purposes capable of having no substantial effect on the extent of the company's activities;"

[10] In sub-para (1), definition of "trading group" substituted by FA 2002 s 47, Sch 10 paras 1, 10(1), (3) with effect for disposals after 16 April 2002. This amendment as applied has effect for periods of ownership after 16 April 2002. The definition previously read as follows—

> " 'trading group' means a group of companies the activities of which (if all the activities of the companies in the group are taken together) do not, or not to any substantial extent, include activities carried on otherwise than in the course of, or for the purposes of, a trade; and".

[11] In definition of "51 per cent subsidiary", words "(except in paragraph 11 above)" repealed by FA 2002 s 141, Sch 40 Pt 3(3) with effect for disposals after 17 April 2002. This amendment has effect for periods of ownership after that date: FA 2002 Sch 10 paras 2, 4, 7

[Meaning of "trading company"]

22A—(1) In this Schedule "trading company" means a company carrying on trading activities whose activities do not include to a substantial extent activities other than trading activities.

(2) For the purposes of sub-paragraph (1) above "trading activities" means activities carried on by the company—

    (*a*) in the course of, or for the purposes of, a trade being carried on by it,

    (*b*) for the purposes of a trade that it is preparing to carry on,

    (*c*) with a view to its acquiring or starting to carry on a trade, or

    (*d*) with a view to its acquiring a significant interest in the share capital of another company that—

        (i) is a trading company or the holding company of a trading group, and

        (ii) if the acquiring company is a member of a group of companies, is not a member of that group.

(3) Activities do not qualify as trading activities under sub-paragraph (2)(*c*) or (*d*) above unless the acquisition is made, or (as the case may be) the company starts to carry on the trade, as soon as is reasonably practicable in the circumstances.

(4) The reference in sub-paragraph (2)(*d*) above to the acquisition of a significant interest in the share capital of another company is to an acquisition of ordinary share capital in the other company—

    (*a*) such as would make that company a 51% subsidiary of the acquiring company, or

    (*b*) such as would give the acquiring company a qualifying shareholding in a joint venture company without making the two companies members of the same group of companies.][1]

Amendments—[1] This paragraph inserted by FA 2002 s 47, Sch 10 paras 1, 9(2), (3) with effect for disposals after 16 April 2002. This amendment as applied has effect for periods of ownership after 16 April 2002.

[Meaning of "trading group"]

22B—(1) In this Schedule "trading group" means a group of companies—

    (*a*) one or more of whose members carry on trading activities, and

    (*b*) the activities of whose members, taken together, do not include to a substantial extent activities other than trading activities.

(2) For the purposes of sub-paragraph (1) above "trading activities" means activities carried on by a member of the group—

    (*a*) in the course of, or for the purposes of, a trade being carried on by any member of the group,

    (*b*) for the purposes of a trade that any member of the group is preparing to carry on,

    (*c*) with a view to any member of the group acquiring or starting to carry on a trade, or

    (*d*) with a view to any member of the group acquiring a significant interest in the share capital of another company that—

        (i) is a trading company or the holding company of a trading group, and

        (ii) is not a member of the same group of companies as the acquiring company.

(3) Activities do not qualify as trading activities under sub-paragraph (2)(*c*) or (*d*) above unless the acquisition is made, or (as the case may be) the group member in question starts to carry on the trade, as soon as is reasonably practicable in the circumstances.

(4) The reference in sub-paragraph (2)(*d*) above to the acquisition of a significant interest in the share capital of another company is to an acquisition of ordinary share capital in the other company—

    (*a*) such as would make that company a member of the same group of companies as the acquiring company, or

    (*b*) such as would give the acquiring company a qualifying shareholding in a joint venture company without making the joint venture companies a member of the same group of companies as the acquiring company.

(5) For the purposes of this paragraph the activities of the members of the group shall be treated as one business (with the result that activities are disregarded to the extent that they are intra-group activities).][1]

Amendments—[1] This paragraph inserted by FA 2002 s 47, Sch 10 paras 1, 10(2), (3) with effect for disposals after 16 April 2002. This amendment as applied has effect for periods of ownership after 16 April 2002.

[Qualifying shareholdings in joint venture companies

23—(1) This Schedule has effect subject to the following provisions where a company ("the investing company") has a qualifying shareholding in a joint venture company.

(2) For the purposes of [this Schedule]⁴ a company is a "joint venture company" if, and only if—

    (*a*) it is a trading company or the holding company of a trading group, and
    (*b*) 75% or more of its ordinary share capital (in aggregate) is held by not more than five [persons]⁶.

For the purposes of paragraph (*b*) above the shareholdings of members of a group of companies shall be treated as held by a single company.

(3) For the purposes of [this Schedule]⁴ a company has a "qualifying shareholding" in a joint venture company if—

    (*a*) it holds [10% or more]⁶ of the ordinary share capital of the joint venture company, or
    (*b*) it is a member of a group of companies, it holds ordinary share capital of the joint venture company and the members of the group between them hold [10% or more]⁶ of that share capital.

(4) For the purpose of determining whether the investing company is a trading company—

    (*a*) any holding by it of shares in the joint venture company shall be disregarded, and
    (*b*) it shall be treated as carrying on an appropriate proportion—

        (i) of the activities of the joint venture company, or
        (ii) where the joint venture company is the holding company of a trading group, of the activities of that group.

...³

(5) ...³

(6) For the purpose of determining whether a group of companies is a trading group—

    (*a*) every holding of shares in the joint venture company by a member of the group having a qualifying shareholding in that company shall be disregarded, and
    (*b*) each member of the group having such a qualifying shareholding shall be treated as carrying on an appropriate proportion of the activities—

        (i) of the joint venture company, or
        (ii) where the joint venture company is the holding company of a trading group, of that group.

This sub-paragraph does not apply if the joint venture company is a member of the group.

(7) In sub-paragraphs (4)(*b*)...³ and (6)(*b*) above "an appropriate proportion" means a proportion corresponding to the percentage of the ordinary share capital of the joint venture company held by the investing company or, as the case may be, by the group member concerned.

[(7A) For the purposes of this paragraph the activities of a joint venture company that is a holding company and its 51% subsidiaries shall be treated as a single business (so that activities are disregarded to the extent that they are intra-group activities).]⁶

(8) ...²

(9) ...⁵

(10) ...⁵]¹

Commentary—*Simon's Direct Tax Service* **C2.1428.**
Amendments—¹ This paragraph inserted by FA 2000 ss 67(1), (6), (7) with effect for determining whether an asset is a business asset at any time after 5 April 2000. It does not affect the determination after that date whether an asset was a business asset at a time before 6 April 2000.
² Sub-para (8) repealed by FA 2001 ss 78, 110, Sch 26 para 6, Sch 33 Pt II(7) with effect (in accordance with the changes made by FA 2000 s 67) for determining whether an asset is a business asset at any time after 5 April 2000. This amendment does not affect the determination after that date whether an asset was a business asset at a time before 6 April 2000.
³ In sub-para (4), words "This sub-paragraph does not apply if the investing company is a holding company". repealed; sub-para (5), and ", (5)(*b*)" in sub-para (7) repealed, by FA 2002 ss 47, 141, Sch 10 paras 1, 4(2), (3), Sch 40 Pt 3(3) with effect for disposals after 16 April 2002. This amendment as applied has effect for periods of ownership after 16 April 2002. Sub-para (5) previously read as follows—

"For the purpose of determining whether the investing company is a holding company—

(*a*) any holding by it of shares in the joint venture company shall be disregarded, and
(*b*) it shall be treated as carrying on an appropriate proportion of the activities—

    (i) of the joint venture company, or
    (ii) where the joint venture company is the holding company of a trading group, of that group.

This sub-paragraph does not apply if the joint venture company is a 51 per cent subsidiary of the investing company.".
⁴ In sub-paras (2), (3) words substituted for the words "in this paragraph" by FA 2002 s 47, Sch 10 paras 1, 6(2), (3) with effect for disposals after 16 April 2002.
⁵ Sub-paras (9), (10) repealed by FA 2002 ss 47, 141, Sch 10 paras 1, 7(2), (3), Sch 40 Pt 3(3) with effect for disposals after 16 April 2002. The repeal of sub-para (9) has effect for periods of ownership after 16 April 2002. Sub-paras (9), (10) previously read as follows—

"(9) The acquisition by the investing company of the qualifying shareholding shall not be treated as a relevant change of activity for the purposes of paragraph 11 above."

"(10) For the purposes of this paragraph "ordinary share capital" has the meaning given by section 832(1) of the Taxes Act.".
⁶ In sub-para (2)(*b*), word substituted for the word "companies"; in sub-paras (3)(*a*), (*b*), words substituted for the words "more than 30%"; and sub-para (7A) added; by FA 2002 s 47, Sch 10 paras 1, 11 with effect for disposals after 16 April 2002. The amendments as applied have effect for periods of ownership after 16 April 2002.

[Joint enterprise companies: relevant connection

24—(1) This Schedule has effect subject to sub-paragraph (5) below in any case where a company ("the investing company") has a qualifying shareholding in a joint enterprise company.

(2) For the purposes of this paragraph, a company is a "joint enterprise company" if, and only if, 75% or more of its ordinary share capital (in aggregate) is held by not more than five [persons][3].

(3) For the purposes of sub-paragraph (2) above the shareholdings of members of a group of companies shall be treated as held by a single company.

(4) For the purposes of this paragraph a company has a "qualifying shareholding" in a joint enterprise company if—

(a) it holds [10% or more][3] of the ordinary share capital of the joint enterprise company, or
(b) it is a member of a group of companies, it holds ordinary share capital of the joint enterprise company and the members of the group between them hold [10% or more][3] of that share capital.

(5) The following shall be treated as having a relevant connection with each other—

(a) the investing company;
(b) the joint enterprise company;
(c) any company having a relevant connection with the investing company;
(d) any company having a relevant connection with the joint enterprise company by virtue of being—

(i) a 51 per cent subsidiary of that company, or
(ii) a member of the same commercial association of companies.

(6) ...[2]][1]

Commentary—*Simon's Direct Tax Service* **C2.1428.**
Amendments—[1] This paragraph inserted by FA 2001 s 78, Sch 26 para 7 with effect (in accordance with the changes made by FA 2000 s 67) for determining whether an asset is a business asset at any time after 5 April 2000. This amendment does not affect the determination after that date whether an asset was a business asset at a time before 6 April 2000.
[2] Sub-para (6) repealed by FA 2002 ss 47, 141, Sch 10 paras 1, 7(2), (3), Sch 40 Pt 3(3) with effect for disposals after 16 April 2002. The amendments as applied have effect for periods of ownership after 16 April 2002. Sub-para (6) previously read as follows—

"(6) For the purposes of this paragraph "ordinary share capital" has the meaning given by section 832(1) of the Taxes Act.".
[3] In sub-para (2), word substituted for the word "companies"; and in sub-paras (4)(a), (b), words substituted for the words "more than 30%" by FA 2002 s 47, Sch 10 paras 1, 12 with effect for disposals after 16 April 2002. The amendments as applied have effect for periods of ownership after 16 April 2002.

SCHEDULE 1

APPLICATION OF EXEMPT AMOUNT IN CASES INVOLVING SETTLED PROPERTY

Section 3

1—(1) For any year of assessment during the whole or part of which settled property is held on trusts which secure that, during the lifetime of a mentally disabled person or a person in receipt of attendance allowance or of a disability living allowance by virtue of entitlement to the care component at the highest or middle rate—

(a) not less than half of the property which is applied is applied for the benefit of that person, and
(b) that person is entitled to not less than half of the income arising from the property, or no such income may be applied for the benefit of any other person,

section 3(1) to (6) shall apply to the trustees of the settlement as they apply to an individual.

(2) The trusts on which settled property is held shall not be treated as falling outside sub-paragraph (1) above by reason only of the powers conferred on the trustees by section 32 of the Trustee Act 1925 or section 33 of the Trustee Act (Northern Ireland) 1958 (powers of advancement); and the reference in that sub-paragraph to the lifetime of a person shall, where the income from the settled property is held for his benefit on trusts of the kind described in section 33 of the Trustee Act 1925 (protective trusts), be construed as a reference to the period during which the income is held on trust for him.

(3) In relation to a settlement which is one of 2 or more qualifying settlements comprised in a group, this paragraph shall have effect as if for the references in section 3 to the exempt amount for the year there were substituted references to one-tenth of that exempt amount or, if it is more, to such amount as results from dividing the exempt amount for the year by the number of settlements in the group.

(4) For the purposes of sub-paragraph (3) above—

(a) a qualifying settlement is any settlement (other than an excluded settlement) which is made on or after 10th March 1981 and to the trustees of which this paragraph applies for the year of assessment; and
(b) all qualifying settlements in relation to which the same person is the settlor constitute a group.

(5) If, in consequence of 2 or more persons being settlors in relation to it, a settlement is comprised in 2 or more groups comprising different numbers of settlements, sub-paragraph (3) above shall

apply to it as if the number by which the exempt amount for the year is to be divided were the number of settlements in the largest group.

(6) In this paragraph—

"mentally disabled person" means a person who by reason of mental disorder within the meaning of the Mental Health Act 1983 is incapable of administering his property or managing his affairs;

"attendance allowance" means an allowance under section 64 of the Social Security Contributions and Benefits Act 1992 or section 64 of the Social Security Contributions and Benefits (Northern Ireland) Act 1992;

"disability living allowance" means a disability living allowance under section 71 of the Social Security Contributions and Benefits Act 1992 or section 71 of the Social Security Contributions and Benefits (Northern Ireland) Act 1992; and

"settlor" and "excluded settlement" have the same meanings as in paragraph 2 below.

(7) An inspector may by notice require any person, being a party to a settlement, to furnish him within such time as he may direct (not being less than 28 days) with such particulars as he thinks necessary for the purposes of this paragraph.

Commentary—*Simon's Direct Tax Service* C1.402.
Definitions—"Inspector", s 288(1); "land", s 288(1); "notice", s 288(1); "settled property", s 68.
Cross reference—See TA 1988 s 715(8) (exemption from tax in relation to trusts falling under sub-para (1) above in respect of deemed income on disposal of certain securities).

2—(1) For any year of assessment during the whole or part of which any property is settled property, not being a year of assessment for which paragraph 1(1) above applies, section 3(1) to (6) shall apply to the trustees of a settlement as they apply to an individual but with the following modifications.

(2) In subsections (1) and (5) for "the exempt amount for the year" there shall be substituted "one-half of the exempt amount for the year".

(3) Section 3(6) shall apply only to the trustees of a settlement made before 7th June 1978 and, in relation to such trustees, shall have effect with the substitution for "the exempt amount for the year" and "twice the exempt amount for the year" of "one-half of the exempt amount for the year" and "the exempt amount for the year" respectively.

(4) In relation to a settlement which is one of 2 or more qualifying settlements comprised in a group, sub-paragraph (2) above shall have effect as if for the reference to one-half of the exempt amount for the year there were substituted a reference to one-tenth of that exempt amount or, if it is more, to such amount as results from dividing one-half of the exempt amount for the year by the number of settlements in the group.

(5) For the purposes of sub-paragraph (4) above—

(a) a qualifying settlement is any settlement (other than an excluded settlement) which is made after 6th June 1978 and to the trustees of which this paragraph applies for the year of assessment; and

(b) all qualifying settlements in relation to which the same person is the settlor constitute a group.

(6) If, in consequence of 2 or more persons being settlors in relation to it, a settlement is comprised in 2 or more groups comprising different numbers of settlements, sub-paragraph (4) above shall apply to it as if the number by which one-half of the exempt amount for the year is to be divided were the number of settlements in the largest group.

(7) In this paragraph "settlor" has the meaning given by [section 660G(1) and (2)][1] of the Taxes Act and includes, in the case of a settlement arising under a will or intestacy, the testator or intestate and "excluded settlement" means—

(a) any settlement the trustees of which are not for the whole or any part of the year of assessment treated under section 69(1) as resident and ordinarily resident in the United Kingdom; and

(b) any settlement the property comprised in which—

(i) is held for charitable purposes only and cannot become applicable for other purposes; or

(ii) is held for the purposes of any such scheme or fund as is mentioned in sub-paragraph (8) below.

(8) The schemes and funds referred to in sub-paragraph (7)(b)(ii) above are funds to which section 615(3) of the Taxes Act applies, schemes and funds approved under section 620 or 621 of that Act, sponsored superannuation schemes as defined in section 624 of that Act and exempt approved schemes and statutory schemes as defined in Chapter I of Part XIV of that Act.

(9) An inspector may by notice require any person, being a party to a settlement, to furnish him within such time as he may direct (not being less than 28 days) with such particulars as he thinks necessary for the purposes of this paragraph.

Commentary—*Simon's Direct Tax Service* C1.402.
Definitions—"Inspector", s 288(1); "notice", s 288(1); "ordinarily resident", s 9(1); "resident", s 9(1); "settled property", s 68; "the Taxes Act", s 288(1).
Amendments—[1] Words in sub-para (7) substituted by FA 1995 s 74, Sch 17 para 32 with effect from the year 1995–96 and apply to every settlement, wherever and whenever it was made or entered into.

SCHEDULE 2

ASSETS HELD ON 6TH APRIL 1965

Section 35

PART I
QUOTED SECURITIES

Cross references—See FA 1990 Sch 12 para 2(1) (application of this Schedule in relation to transfer of undertakings of Independent Broadcasting Authority).
TCGA 1992 s 139(1) (transfer of business from one company to another: transferee company treated for the purposes of this Schedule as acquiring assets of business at time when transferor company acquired them).
TCGA 1992 s 174(4), (5) (application of this Schedule to assets acquired by a group company from a member of the same group).
TCGA 1992 s 221 (Harbour authorities as transferees to be in the same position as transferors for the purposes of this Schedule).
TCGA 1992 s 264(5) (new parliamentary associations as transferees to be in the same position as existing associations for the purposes of this Schedule).
TCGA 1992 Sch 11 para 27 (circumstances in which the acquisition or provision of an asset by one person is treated as the acquisition or provision of it by another person).

Deemed acquisition at 6th April 1965 value

1—(1) This paragraph applies—

> (a) to shares and securities which on 6th April 1965 had quoted market values on a recognised stock exchange, or which had such quoted market values at any time in the period of 6 years ending on 6th April 1965, and
> (b) to rights of unit holders in any unit trust scheme the prices of which are published regularly by the managers of the scheme.

(2) For the purposes of this Act it shall be assumed, wherever relevant, that any assets to which this paragraph applies were sold by the owner, and immediately reacquired by him, at their market value on 6th April 1965.

(3) This paragraph shall not apply in relation to a disposal of shares or securities of a company by a person to whom those shares or securities were issued as an employee either of the company or of some other person on terms which restrict his rights to dispose of them.

Commentary—*Simon's Direct Tax Service* **C2.705.**
Statement of Practice SP 18/80—Securities dealt in on the Stock Exchange Unlisted Securities Market: status and valuation for tax purposes.
Definitions—"Asset", s 21(1); "company", ss 99, 288(1); "issued", s 288(5); "market value", ss 272–274, Sch 11; "shares", s 288(1); "unit trust scheme", s 99; "year of assessment", s 288(1).
Cross references—See TCGA 1992 Sch 2 para 2(1) (circumstances in which sub-para (2) of this para does not apply).
TCGA 1992 Sch 11 para 6(1) (transitional provisions for market valuation on 6 April 1965 of quoted securities for periods prior to commencement of this Act).

Restriction of gain or loss by reference to actual cost

2—(1) Subject to paragraph 4 below and section 109(4), paragraph 1(2) above shall not apply in relation to a disposal of assets—

> (a) if on the assumption in paragraph 1(2) a gain would accrue on that disposal to the person making the disposal and either a smaller gain or a loss would so accrue if paragraph 1(2) did not apply, or
> (b) if on the assumption in paragraph 1(2) a loss would so accrue and either a smaller loss or a gain would accrue if paragraph 1(2) did not apply,

and accordingly the amount of the gain or loss accruing on the disposal shall be computed without regard to the preceding provisions of this Schedule except that in a case where this sub-paragraph would otherwise substitute a loss for a gain or a gain for a loss it shall be assumed, in relation to the disposal, that the relevant assets were sold by the owner, and immediately reacquired by him, for a consideration such that, on the disposal, neither a gain nor a loss accrued to the person making the disposal.

(2) For the purpose of—

> (a) identifying shares or securities held on 6th April 1965 with shares or securities previously acquired, and
> (b) identifying the shares or securities held on that date with shares or securities subsequently disposed of, and distinguishing them from shares or securities acquired subsequently,

so far as that identification is needed for the purposes of sub-paragraph (1) above, and so far as the shares or securities are of the same class, shares or securities acquired at a later time shall be deemed to be disposed of before shares or securities acquired at an earlier time.

(3) Sub-paragraph (2) above has effect subject to section 105.

Commentary—*Simon's Direct Tax Service* **C2.705, 706.**
Definitions—"Asset", s 21(1); "class", s 288(1); "shares", s 288(1); "year of assessment", s 288(1).
Cross references—See TCGA 1992 s 109(4) (election to exclude certain securities from this para).
TCGA 1992 Sch 2 para 3(2) (identification rules in sub-para (2) above to apply for the purpose of exclusion of pooling of quoted securities held on 6 April 1965).

3—(1) Where—

(*a*) a disposal was made out of quoted securities before 20th March 1968, and
(*b*) by virtue of paragraph 2 of Schedule 7 to the Finance Act 1965 some of the quoted securities out of which the disposal was made were acquired before 6th April 1965 and some later,

then in computing the gain accruing on any disposal of quoted securities the question of what remained undisposed of on the earlier disposal shall be decided on the footing that paragraph 2 of that Schedule did not apply as respects that earlier disposal.

(2) The rules of identification in paragraph 2(2) above shall apply for the purposes of this paragraph as they apply for the purposes of that paragraph.

Commentary—*Simon's Direct Tax Service* C2.706, 707.
Definition—"Quoted securities", Sch 2 para 8.
Cross references—See TCGA 1992 Sch 2 para 6 (exchange of securities: pooling at 6 April 1965 value).

Election for pooling

4—(1) This paragraph applies in relation to quoted securities as respects which an election under paragraphs 4 to 7 of Schedule 5 to the 1979 Act had not been made before the operative date, within the meaning of Part II of Schedule 13 to the Finance Act 1982 (so that they do not constitute a 1982 holding within the meaning of section 109), but does not apply in relation to relevant securities within the meaning of section 108.

(2) If a person so elects, quoted securities covered by the election shall be excluded from paragraph 2 above, so that paragraph 1(2) above is not excluded by that paragraph as respects those securities, and sub-paragraphs (3) to (7) (which re-enact section 65 of the 1979 Act) apply.

(3) Subject to section 105, any number of quoted securities of the same class held by one person in one capacity shall for the purposes of this Act be regarded as indistinguishable parts of a single asset (in this paragraph referred to as a holding) growing or diminishing on the occasions on which additional securities of the class in question are acquired, or some of the securities of the class in question are disposed of.

(4) Without prejudice to the generality of sub-paragraph (3) above, a disposal of quoted securities in a holding, other than the disposal outright of the entire holding, is a disposal of part of an asset and the provisions of this Act relating to the computation of a gain accruing on a disposal of part of an asset shall apply accordingly.

(5) Securities shall not be treated for the purposes of this paragraph as being of the same class unless they are so treated by the practice of a recognised stock exchange or would be so treated if dealt with on such a stock exchange, but shall be treated in accordance with this paragraph notwithstanding that they are identified in some other way by the disposal or by the transfer or delivery giving effect to it.

(6) This paragraph shall apply separately in relation to any securities held by a person to whom they were issued as an employee of the company or of any other person on terms which restrict his rights to dispose of them, so long as those terms are in force, and, while applying separately to any such securities, shall have effect as if the owner held them in a capacity other than that in which he holds any other securities of the same class.

(7) Nothing in this paragraph shall be taken as affecting the manner in which the market value of any asset is to be ascertained.

(8) An election made by any person under this paragraph shall be as respects all disposals made by him at any time, including disposals made before the election but after 19th March 1968—

(*a*) of quoted securities of kinds other than fixed-interest securities and preference shares, or
(*b*) of fixed-interest securities and preference shares,

and references to the quoted securities covered by an election shall be construed accordingly.

Any person may make both of the elections.

(9) An election under this paragraph shall not cover quoted securities which the holder acquired on a disposal after 19th March 1968 in relation to which either section 58 or 171(1) applies, but this paragraph shall apply to the quoted securities so held if the person who made the original disposal (that is to say the wife or husband of the holder, or the other member of the group of companies) makes an election covering quoted securities of the kind in question.

For the purpose of identifying quoted securities disposed of by the holder with quoted securities acquired by him on a disposal in relation to which either section 58 or 171(1) applies, so far as they are of the same class, quoted securities acquired at an earlier time shall be deemed to be disposed of before quoted securities acquired at a later time.

(10) For the avoidance of doubt it is hereby declared—

(*a*) that where a person makes an election under this paragraph as respects quoted securities which he holds in one capacity, that election does not cover quoted securities which he holds in another capacity, and
(*b*) that an election under this paragraph is irrevocable.

(11) An election under this paragraph shall be made by notice to [an officer of the Board given—

    (a) in the case of an election for the purposes of capital gains tax, on or before the first anniversary of the 31st January next following the year of assessment in which the first relevant disposal is made;

    (b) in the case of an election for the purposes of corporation tax, not later than the expiration of 2 years from the end of the accounting period in which the first relevant disposal is made; or

    (c) in either case, within such further time as the Board may allow.]¹

(12) Subject to paragraph 5 below, in this paragraph the "first relevant disposal", in relation to each of the elections referred to in sub-paragraph (8) of this paragraph, means the first disposal after 19th March 1968 by the person making the election of quoted securities of the kind covered by that election.

(13) All such adjustments shall be made, whether by way of discharge or repayment of tax, or the making of assessments or otherwise, as are required to give effect to an election under this paragraph.

Commentary—*Simon's Direct Tax Service* **C2.707, 708.**
Revenue & other press releases—CCAB June 1967 (an election under this paragraph can be made by the taxpayer's legal personal representatives).
Revenue Internal Guidance—Capital Gains Manual CG 51026–51027 (sub-s (11), outlines the background to the acceptance of a late election).
Definitions—"The 1979 Act", s 288(1); "accounting period", TA 1988 s 834(1); "asset", s 21(1); "the Board", s 288(1); "class", s 288(1); "company", ss 99, 288(1); "fixed interest security", Sch 2 para 8; "issued", s 288(5); "market value", ss 272–274, Sch 11; "preference share", Sch 2 para 8; "quoted securities", Sch 2 para 8; "notice", s 288(1); "shares", s 288(1); "year of assessment", s 288(1).
Cross references—See TCGA 1992 s 108(8) (identification of relevant securities where an election is made with respect to them under this paragraph).
TCGA 1992 s 109(5) (modification of this para in its application to an election under s 109(4));
TCGA 1992 Sch 2 para 6 (exchange of securities: pooling at 6 April 1965 value).
TCGA 1992 Sch 2 para 7 (securities excluded from an election under this para).
Amendments—¹ Words in sub-para (11) substituted by FA 1996 s 135(1), (2), Sch 21 para 42(1), (2) with effect from the year 1996–97 and, for the purposes of corporation tax, as respects accounting periods ending after 30 June 1999 (by virtue of Finance Act 1994, Section 199, (Appointed Day) Order, SI 1998/3173 art 2).

Election by principal company of group

5—(1) In the case of companies which at the relevant time are members of a group of companies—

    (a) an election under paragraph 4 above by the company which at that time is the principal company of the group shall have effect also as an election by any other company which at that time is a member of the group, and

    (b) no election under that paragraph may be made by any other company which at that time is a member of the group.

(2) In this paragraph "the relevant time", in relation to a group of companies, and in relation to each of the elections referred to in paragraph 4(8) above, is the first occasion after 19th March 1968 when any company which is then a member of a group disposes of quoted securities of a kind covered by that election, and for the purposes of paragraph 4(11) above that occasion is, in relation to the group, "the first relevant disposal".

(3) This paragraph shall not apply in relation to quoted securities of either kind referred to in paragraph 4(8) above which are owned by a company which, in some period after 19th March 1968 and before the relevant time, was not a member of the group if in that period it had made an election under paragraph 4 above in relation to securities of that kind (or was treated by virtue of this paragraph, in relation to another group, as having done so), or had made a disposal of quoted securities of that kind and did not make an election within the time limited by paragraph 4(11) above.

(4) This paragraph shall apply notwithstanding that a company ceases to be a member of the group at any time after the relevant time.

(5) In this paragraph "company" and "group" shall be construed in accordance with section 170(2) to (9).

Commentary—*Simon's Direct Tax Service* **C2.708.**
Revenue Internal Guidance—Capital Gains Manual CG 51030–51031 (operation of this para).
Definitions—"Company", ss 99, 288(1); "quoted securities", Sch 2 para 8.
Cross references—See TCGA 1992 s 109(5) (modification of this para in its application to an election under s 109(4)).
FA 2000 Sch 29 para 37 (the main amendments made to TCGA 1992 s 170 by FA 2000 Sch 29 para 1 have effect for the purposes of this section for any determination as to whether a company is a member, or the principal company, of a group of companies after 31 March 2000).

Pooling at value on 6th April 1965: exchange of securities etc

6—(1) Where a person who has made only one of the elections under paragraph 4 above disposes of quoted securities which, in accordance with Chapter II of Part IV, are to be regarded as being or forming part of a new holding, the election shall apply according to the nature of the quoted securities disposed of, notwithstanding that under that Chapter the new holding is to be regarded as the same asset as the original holding and that the election would apply differently to the original holding.

(2) Where the election does not cover the disposal out of the new holding but does cover quoted securities of the kind comprised in the original holding, then in computing the gain accruing on the disposal out of the new holding (in accordance with paragraph 3 above) the question of what

remained undisposed of on any disposal out of the original holding shall be decided on the footing that paragraph 3 above applied to that earlier disposal.

(3) In the converse case (that is to say, where the election covers the disposal out of the new holding, but does not cover quoted securities of the kind comprised in the original holding) the question of how much of the new holding derives from quoted securities held on 6th April 1965 and how much derives from other quoted securities, shall be decided as it is decided for the purposes of paragraph 3 above.

Commentary—*Simon's Direct Tax Service* **C2.708.**
Definitions—"Allowable loss", ss 8(2), 16, 288(1); "asset", s 21(1); "quoted securities", Sch 2 para 8.
Cross references—See TCGA 1992 s 109(5) (modification of this para in its application to an election under s 109(4)).

Underwriters

7 No election under paragraph 4 above shall cover quoted securities comprised in any underwriter's premiums trust fund, or premiums trust fund deposits, or personal reserves, being securities comprised in funds to which section 206 applies.

Commentary—*Simon's Direct Tax Service* **C2.708.**
Definition—"Quoted securities", Sch 2 para 8.
Cross references—See TCGA 1992 s 109(5) (modification of this para in its application to an election under s 109(4)).

Interpretation of paragraphs 3 to 7

8—(1) In paragraphs 3 to 7 above—

"quoted securities" means assets to which paragraph 1 above applies,
"fixed interest security" means any security as defined by section 132,
"preference share" means any share the holder whereof has a right to a dividend at a fixed rate,
   but has no other right to share in the profits of the company.

(2) If and so far as the question whether at any particular time a share was a preference share depends on the rate of dividends payable on or before 5th April 1973, the reference in the definition of "preference share" in sub-paragraph (1) above to a dividend at a fixed rate includes a dividend at a rate fluctuating in accordance with the standard rate of income tax.

Commentary—*Simon's Direct Tax Service* **C2.707.**
Definitions—"Asset", s 21(1); "company", ss 99, 288(1).
Cross references—See TCGA 1992 s 109(5) (modification of this para in its application to an election under s 109(4)).

PART II
LAND REFLECTING DEVELOPMENT VALUE

9—(1) Subject to paragraph 17(2) of Schedule 11, this Part of this Schedule shall apply in relation to a disposal of an asset which is an interest in land situated in the United Kingdom—

(a) if, but for this paragraph, the expenditure allowable as a deduction in computing the gain accruing on the disposal would include any expenditure incurred before 6th April 1965, and

(b) if the consideration for the asset acquired on the disposal exceeds the current use value of the asset at the time of the disposal, or if any material development of the land has been carried out after 17th December 1973 since the person making the disposal acquired the asset.

(2) For the purposes of this Act, it shall be assumed that, in relation to the disposal and, if it is a part disposal, in relation to any subsequent disposal of the asset which is an interest in land situated in the United Kingdom, that asset was sold by the person making the disposal, and immediately reacquired by him, at its market value on 6th April 1965.

(3) Sub-paragraph (2) above shall apply also in relation to any prior part disposal of the asset and, if tax has been charged, or relief allowed, by reference to that part disposal on a different footing, all such adjustments shall be made, whether by way of assessment or discharge or repayment of tax, as are required to give effect to the provisions of this sub-paragraph.

(4) Sub-paragraph (2) above shall not apply in relation to a disposal of assets—

(a) on the assumption in that sub-paragraph a gain would accrue on that disposal to the person making the disposal and either a smaller gain or a loss would so accrue (computed in accordance with the provisions of this Act) if it did not apply, or

(b) if on the assumption in sub-paragraph (2) a loss would so accrue and either a smaller loss or a gain would accrue if that sub-paragraph did not apply,

and accordingly the amount of the gain or loss accruing on the disposal shall be computed without regard to the provisions of this Schedule except that in a case where this sub-paragraph would otherwise substitute a loss for a gain or a gain for a loss it shall be assumed, in relation to the disposal, that the relevant assets were sold by the owner, and immediately reacquired by him, for a consideration such that, on the disposal, neither a gain nor a loss accrued to the person making the disposal.

(5) For the purposes of this Part of this Schedule—

(*a*) "interest in land" means any estate or interest in land, any right in or over land or affecting the use or disposition of land, and any right to obtain such an estate, interest or right from another which is conditional on that other's ability to grant the estate, interest or right in question, except that it does not include the interest of a creditor (other than a creditor in respect of a rent charge) whose debt is secured by way of a mortgage, an agreement for a mortgage or a charge of any kind over land, or, in Scotland, the interest of a creditor in a charge or security of any kind over land; and

(*b*) "land" includes buildings.

Commentary—*Simon's Direct Tax Service* **C2.1121.**
Simon's Tax Cases—*Mashiter v Pearmain* [1983] STC 658*; *Morgan v Gibson* [1989] STC 568; *Richart v J Lyons & Co Ltd* [1989] STC 665*.
Sub-para (1), *Mashiter v Pearmain* [1985] STC 165*.
Sub-para (1)(*b*), *Watkins v Kidson* [1979] STC 464*.
Definitions—"Asset", s 21(1); "land", s 288(1); "market value", ss 272–274, Sch 11; "material development", Sch 2 para 13(1); "part disposal", s 21(2).
Cross references—See TCGA 1992 Sch 11 para 17 (allowance for betterment levy).

10—(1) For the purposes of this Part of this Schedule, the current use value of an interest in land shall be ascertained in accordance with the following provisions of this Part, and in this Part the time as at which current use value is to be ascertained is referred to as "the relevant time".

(2) Subject to the following provisions of this Part of this Schedule, the current use value of an interest in land at the relevant time is the market value of that interest at that time calculated on the assumption that it was at that time, and would continue to be, unlawful to carry out any material development of the land other than any material development thereof which, being authorised by planning permission in force at that time, was begun before that time.

In relation to any material development which was begun before 18th December 1973 this sub-paragraph shall have effect with the omission of the words from "other than" to "before that time".

(3) In this paragraph "planning permission" has the same meaning as in the Town and Country Planning Act 1990 or, in Scotland, the Town and Country Planning (Scotland) Act 1972 or, in Northern Ireland, the Planning (Northern Ireland) Order 1991, and in determining for the purposes of this paragraph what material development of any land was authorised by planning permission at a time when there was in force in respect of the land planning permission granted on an outline application (that is to say, an application for planning permission subject to subsequent approval on any matters), any such development of the land which at that time—

(*a*) was authorised by that permission without any requirement as to subsequent approval; or
(*b*) not being so authorised, had been approved in the manner applicable to that planning permission,

but no other material development, shall for those purposes be taken to have been authorised by that permission at that time.

(4) Where the value to be ascertained is the current use value of an interest in land which has been disposed of by way of a part disposal of an asset ("the relevant asset") consisting of an interest in land, the current use value at the relevant time of the interest disposed of shall be the relevant fraction of the current use value of the relevant asset at that time, calculated on the same assumptions as to the lawfulness or otherwise of any material development as fall to be made under this Part in calculating the current use value at that time of the interest disposed of.

(5) For the purposes of sub-paragraph (4) above "the relevant fraction" means that fraction of the sums mentioned in paragraph (6) below which under subsection (2) of section 42 is, or would but for subsection (4) of that section be, allowable as a deduction in computing the amount of the gain accruing on the part disposal.

(6) The sums referred to in sub-paragraph (5) above are the sums which, if the entire relevant asset had been disposed of at the time of the part disposal, would be allowable by virtue of section 38(1)(*a*) and (*b*) as a deduction in computing the gain accruing on that disposal of the relevant asset.

(7) Sub-paragraphs (4) to (6) above shall not apply—

(*a*) in the case of a disposal of an interest in land by way of a part disposal if, on making the disposal, the person doing so no longer has any interest in the land which is subject to that interest; or
(*b*) in a case to which the following provisions of this paragraph apply.

(8) In computing any gain accruing to a person on a part disposal of an interest in land resulting under subsection (1) of section 22 from the receipt as mentioned in paragraph (*a*), (*c*) or (*d*) of that subsection of a capital sum, the current use value at the relevant time of the interest out of which the part disposal was made shall be taken to be what it would have been at that time if the circumstances which caused the capital sum to be received had not arisen.

Commentary—*Simon's Direct Tax Service* **C2.1121.**
Definitions—"Asset", s 21(1); "interest in land", Sch 2 para 9(5); "land", Sch 2 para 9(5); "market value", ss 272–274, Sch 11; "material development", Sch 2 para 13(1); "part disposal", s 21(2).

11—(1) The current use value of an interest in land which is either—

(*a*) a freehold interest which is subject to a lease or an agreement for a lease, or (*b*) an interest under a lease or agreement for a lease,

shall be ascertained without regard to any premium required under the lease or agreement for a lease or any sublease, or otherwise under the terms subject to which the lease or sublease was or is to be granted, but with regard to all other rights under the lease or prospective lease (and, for the current use value of an interest under a lease subject to a sublease, under the sublease).

(2) If under sub-paragraph (1) above an interest under a lease or agreement for a lease would have a negative value, the current use value of the interest shall be nil.

(3) If a lease is granted out of any interest in land after 17th December 1973, then, in computing any gain accruing on any disposal of the reversion on the lease made while the lease subsists, the current use value of the reversion at any time after the grant of the lease shall not exceed what would have been at that time the current use value of the interest in the land of the person then owning the reversion if that interest had not been subject to the lease.

(4) In the application of this paragraph to Scotland, "freehold" means the estate or interest of the proprietor of the dominium utile or, in the case of property other than feudal property, of the owner, and "reversion" means the interest of the landlord in property subject to a lease.

Commentary—*Simon's Direct Tax Service* **C2.1121, 1210.**
Simon's Tax Cases—*Smith v Schofield* [1993] STC 268*.
Sub-para (2), *Bayley v Rogers* [1980] STC 544*.
Definitions—"Interest in land", Sch 2 para 9(5); "land", Sch 2 para 9(5); "lease", Sch 8 para 10(1).

12 In computing any gain accruing to a person on a disposal of a lease which is a wasting asset, the current use value of the lease at the time of its acquisition by the person making the disposal shall be the fraction—

$$\frac{A}{B}$$

of what its current use value at that time would be apart from this paragraph, where—

A is equal to so much of the expenditure attributable to the lease under section 38(1)(*a*) and (*b*) as is not under paragraph 1 of Schedule 8 excluded therefrom for the purposes of the computation of the gain accruing on the disposal, and
B is equal to the whole of the expenditure which would be so attributable to the lease for those purposes apart from the said paragraph 1.

Commentary—*Simon's Direct Tax Service* **C2.1210.**
Statement of Practice D21—Time limit for an election for valuation on 6 April 1965 under TCGA 1992 Sch 2 para 17: company leaving a group.
Simon's Tax Cases—*Henderson v Karmel's Executors* [1984] STC 572*; *Richart v J Lyons & Co Ltd* [1989] STC 665*.
Sub-para (1), *Butler v Evans* [1980] STC 613*.
Sub-para (2), *Butler v Evans* [1980] STC 613*; *Whitaker v Cameron* [1982] STC 665*.
Sub-paras (4), (5), *Whitaker v Cameron* [1982] STC 665*.
Definitions—"Asset", s 21(1); "lease", Sch 8 para 10(1); "wasting asset", ss 44, 288(1), Sch 8 para 1.

13—(1) In this Part of this Schedule, "material development", in relation to any land, means the making of any change in the state, nature or use of the land, but the doing of any of the following things in the case of any land shall not be taken to involve material development of the land, that is to say—

(*a*) the carrying out of works for the maintenance, improvement, enlargement or other alteration of any building, so long as the cubic content of the original building is not exceeded by more than one-tenth;
(*b*) the carrying out of works for the rebuilding, as often as occasion may require, of any building which was in existence at the relevant time, or of any building which was in existence in the period of 10 years immediately preceding the day on which that time falls but was destroyed or demolished before the relevant time, so long as (in either case) the cubic content of the original building is not exceeded by more than one-tenth;
(*c*) the use of any land for the purposes of agriculture or forestry, the use for any of those purposes of any building occupied together with land so used, and the carrying out on any land so used of any building or other operations required for the purposes of that use;
(*d*) the carrying out of operations on land for, or the use of land for, the display of an advertisement announcement or direction of any kind;
(*e*) the carrying out of operations for, or the use of the land for, car parking, provided that such use shall not exceed 3 years;
(*f*) in the case of a building or other land which at the relevant time was used for a purpose falling within any class specified in sub-paragraph (4) below or which, being unoccupied at that time, was last used for any such purpose, the use of that building or land for any other purpose falling within the same class;
(*g*) in the case of a building or other land which at the relevant time was in the occupation of a person by whom it was used as to part only for a particular purpose, the use for that purpose of any additional part of the building or land not exceeding one-tenth of the cubic content of the part of the building used for that purpose at the relevant time or, as the case may be, one-tenth of the area of the land so used at that time;

(*h*) in the case of land which at the relevant time was being temporarily used for a purpose other than the purpose for which it was normally used, the resumption of the use of the land for the last-mentioned purpose;

(i) in the case of land which was unoccupied at the relevant time, the use of the land for the purpose for which it was last used before that time.

References in this paragraph to the cubic content of a building are references to that content as ascertained by external measurement.

(2) For the purposes of sub-paragraph (1)(*a*) and (*b*)—

(*a*) where 2 or more buildings are included in a single development the whole of that development may be regarded as a single building, and where 2 or more buildings result from the redevelopment of a single building the new buildings may together be regarded as a single building, but 2 or more buildings shall not be treated as included in a single development unless they are or were comprised in the same curtilage; and

(*b*) in determining whether or not the cubic content of the original building has been exceeded by more than one-tenth, the cubic content of the building after the carrying out of the works in question shall be treated as reduced by the amount (if any) by which so much of that cubic content as is attributable to one or more of the matters mentioned in sub-paragraph (3) below exceeds so much of the cubic content of the original building as was attributable to one or more of the matters so mentioned.

(3) The matters referred to in sub-paragraph (2)(*b*) are the following, that is to say—

(*a*) means of escape in case of fire;
(*b*) car-parking or garage space;
(*c*) accommodation for plant providing heating, air-conditioning or similar facilities.

(4) The classes of purposes mentioned in sub-paragraph (1)(*f*) are the following—

Class A—Use as a dwelling-house or for the purpose of any activities which are wholly or mainly carried on otherwise than for profit, except use for a purpose falling within Class B, C or E.

Class B—Use as an office or retail shop.

Class C—Use as a hotel, boarding-house or guest-house, or as premises licensed for the sale of intoxicating liquors for consumption on the premises.

Class D—Use for the purpose of any activities wholly or mainly carried on for profit, except—

(*a*) use as a dwelling-house or for the purposes of agriculture or forestry; and
(*b*) use for a purpose falling within Class B, C or E.

Class E—Use for any of the following purposes, namely—

(*a*) the carrying on of any process for or incidental to any of the following purposes, namely—

(i) the making of any article or of any part of any article, or the production of any substance;
(ii) the altering, repairing, ornamenting, finishing, cleaning, washing, packing or canning, or adapting for sale, or breaking up or demolishing of any article; or
(iii) without prejudice to (i) or (ii) above, the getting, dressing or treatment of minerals, being a process carried on in the course of a trade or business other than agriculture or forestry, but excluding any process carried on at a dwelling-house or retail shop;

(*b*) storage purposes (whether or not involving use as a warehouse or repository) other than storage purposes ancillary to a purpose falling within Class B or C.

Commentary—*Simon's Direct Tax Service* C2.706.
Statement of Practice D12—Partnerships.
Definitions—"Agriculture", Sch 2 para 15; "article", Sch 2 para 15; "building", Sch 2 para 15; "class", s 288(1); "forestry", Sch 2 para 15; "land", Sch 2 para 9(5); "minerals", Sch 2 para 15; "retail shop", Sch 2 para 15; "substance", Sch 2 para 15; "trade", s 288(1).

14—(1) For the purposes of this Part, material development shall be taken to be begun on the earliest date on which any specified operation comprised in the material development is begun.

(2) In this paragraph "specified operation" means any of the following, that is to say—

(*a*) any work of construction in the course of the erection of a building;
(*b*) the digging of a trench which is to contain the foundations, or part of the foundations, of a building;
(*c*) the laying of any underground main or pipe to the foundations, or part of the foundations, of a building or to any such trench as is mentioned in (*b*) above;
(*d*) any operation in the course of laying out or constructing a road or part of a road;
(*e*) any change in the use of any land.

(3) Subject to sub-paragraph (4) below, material development shall for the purposes of this Part of this Schedule not be treated as carried out after a particular date if it was begun on or before that date.

(4) If, in the case of any land—

(*a*) material development thereof was begun on or before 17th December 1973 but was not completed on or before that date, and (*b*) the development was on that date to any extent not authorised by planning permission (within the meaning of paragraph 10(3) above) then in force,

then, for the purposes of this Part of this Schedule, so much of the development carried out after that date as was not so authorised on that date shall be treated as begun on the earliest date after 17th December 1973 on which any specified operation comprised therein is begun, and shall accordingly be treated as material development of the land carried out after 17th December 1973.

Commentary—*Simon's Direct Tax Service* C2.706.
Statement of Practice SP 14/79—CGT: unquoted shares or securities held at 6 April 1965.
Simon's Tax Cases—*IRC v Beveridge* [1979] STC 592*.
Definitions—"Building", Sch 2 para 15; "land", Sch 2 para 9(5); "material development", Sch 2 para 13(1); "recognised stock exchange", s 288(1), TA 1988 s 841.

15 In this Part of this Schedule, unless the context otherwise requires—

"agriculture" includes horticulture, fruit growing, seed growing, dairy farming, the keeping and breeding of livestock (including any creature kept for the production of food, wool, skins or fur, or for the purpose of its use in the farming of land), the use of land as grazing land, meadow land, osier land, market gardens and nursery grounds, and the use of land for woodlands where that use is ancillary to the farming of land for other agricultural purposes, and "agricultural" shall be construed accordingly;

"article" means an article of any description;

"building" includes part of a building and references to a building may include references to land occupied therewith and used for the same purposes;

"forestry" includes afforestation;

"minerals" includes all minerals and substances in or under land of a kind ordinarily worked for removal by underground or surface working;

"retail shop" includes any premises of a similar character where retail trade or business (including repair work) is carried on;

"substance" means any natural or artificial substance or material, whether in solid or liquid form or in the form of a gas or vapour.

Definitions—"Land", s 288(1); "trade", s 288(1).

PART III

OTHER ASSETS

Apportionment by reference to straightline growth of gain or loss over period of ownership

16—(1) This paragraph applies subject to Parts I and II of this Schedule.

(2) On the disposal of assets by a person whose period of ownership began before 6th April 1965 only so much of any gain accruing on the disposal as is under this paragraph to be apportioned to the period beginning with 6th April 1965 shall be a chargeable gain.

(3) Subject to the following provisions of this Schedule, the gain shall be assumed to have grown at a uniform rate from nothing at the beginning of the period of ownership to its full amount at the time of the disposal so that, calling the part of that period before 6th April 1965, P, and the time beginning with 6th April 1965 and ending with the time of the disposal T, the fraction of the gain which is a chargeable gain is—

$$\frac{T}{P + T}$$

(4) If any of the expenditure which is allowable as a deduction in the computation of the gain is within section 38(1)(*b*)—

(*a*) the gain shall be attributed to the expenditure, if any, allowable under section 38(1)(*a*) as one item of expenditure, and to the respective items of expenditure under section 38(1)(*b*) in proportion to the respective amounts of those items of expenditure,

(*b*) sub-paragraph (3) of this paragraph shall apply to the part of the gain attributed to the expenditure under section 38(1)(*a*),

(*c*) each part of the gain attributed to the items of expenditure under section 38(1)(*b*) shall be assumed to have grown at a uniform rate from nothing at the time when the relevant item of expenditure was first reflected in the value of the asset to the full amount of that part of the gain at the time of the disposal,

so that, calling the respective proportions of the gain E(O), E(1), E(2) and so on (so that they add up to unity) and calling the respective periods from the times when the items under section 38(1)(*b*) were reflected in the value of the asset to 5th April 1965 P(1), P(2) and so on, and employing also the abbreviations in sub-paragraph (3) above, the fraction of the gain which is a chargeable gain is—

$$E(0)\ \frac{T}{(P + T)}\ + E(1)\ \frac{T}{(P(1) + T)}\ + E(2)\ \frac{T}{(P(2) + T)}\ \text{and so on.}$$

(5) In a case within sub-paragraph (4) above where there is no initial expenditure (that is no expenditure under section 38(1)(*a*)) or that initial expenditure is, compared with any item of

expenditure under section 38(1)(*b*), disproportionately small having regard to the value of the asset immediately before the subsequent item of expenditure was incurred, the part of the gain which is not attributable to the enhancement of the value of the asset due to any item of expenditure under section 38(1)(*b*) shall be deemed to be attributed to expenditure incurred at the beginning of the period of ownership and allowable under section 38(1)(*a*), and the part or parts of the gain attributable to expenditure under section 38(1)(*b*) shall be reduced accordingly.

(6) The beginning of the period over which a gain, or part of a gain, is under sub-paragraphs (3) and (4) above to be treated as growing shall not be earlier than 6th April 1945, and this sub-paragraph shall have effect notwithstanding any provision in this Schedule or elsewhere in this Act.

(7) If in pursuance of section 42 an asset's market value at a date before 6th April 1965 is to be ascertained, sub-paragraphs (3) to (5) above shall have effect as if that asset had been on that date sold by the owner, and immediately reacquired by him, at that market value.

(8) If in pursuance of section 42 an asset's market value at a date on or after 6th April 1965 is to be ascertained sub-paragraphs (3) to (5) above shall have effect as if—

(*a*) the asset on that date had been sold by the owner, and immediately reacquired by him, at that market value, and

(*b*) accordingly, the computation of any gain on a subsequent disposal of that asset shall be computed—

(i) by apportioning in accordance with this paragraph the gain or loss over a period ending on that date (the date of the part disposal), and

(ii) by bringing into account the entire gain or loss over the period from the date of the part disposal to the date of subsequent disposal.

(9) For the purposes of this paragraph the period of ownership of an asset shall, where under section 43 account is to be taken of expenditure in respect of an asset from which the asset disposed of was derived, or where it would so apply if there were any relevant expenditure in respect of that other asset, include the period of ownership of that other asset.

(10) If under this paragraph part only of a gain is a chargeable gain, the fraction in section 223(2) shall be applied to that part instead of to the whole of the gain.

Commentary—*Simon's Direct Tax Service* **C2.611.**
Revenue & other press releases—CCAB TR500 10-3-83 (a period of tenancy prior to the period of ownership can be included as part of the time-apportionment denominator).
Revenue Internal Guidance—Capital gains manual CG 17350 (it is the gain net of indexation relief which is time apportioned; worked examples at CG 17480–17481).
Definitions—''Asset'', s 21(1); ''chargeable gain'', s 15(2); ''market value'', ss 272–274, Sch 11; ''part disposal'', s 21(2).
Cross references—See TCGA 1992 Sch 2 para 17(1), (2) (election for valuation at 6 April 1965);
TCGA 1992 Sch 2 para 19(2) (adaptation of sub-paras (3)–(5) above where a person acquires a new holding after 5 April 1965 in accordance with Pt IV, Ch II of this Act).
TCGA 1992 Sch 2 para 21 (assets transferred to close companies).
TCGA 1992 Sch 3 para 6 (assets held on 31 March 1982: apportionment of pre-1965 gains and losses).

Election for valuation at 6th April 1965

17—(1) If the person making a disposal so elects, paragraph 16 above shall not apply in relation to that disposal and it shall be assumed, both for the purposes of computing the gain accruing to that person on the disposal, and for all other purposes both in relation to that person and other persons, that the assets disposed of, and any assets of which account is to be taken in relation to the disposal under section 43, being assets which were in the ownership of that person on 6th April 1965, were on that date sold, and immediately reacquired, by him at their market value on 6th April 1965.

(2) Sub-paragraph (1) above shall not apply in relation to a disposal of assets if on the assumption in that sub-paragraph a loss would accrue on that disposal to the person making the disposal and either a smaller loss or a gain would accrue if sub-paragraph (1) did not apply, but in a case where this sub-paragraph would otherwise substitute a gain for a loss it shall be assumed, in relation to the disposal, that the relevant assets were sold by the owner, and immediately reacquired by him, for a consideration such that, on the disposal neither a gain nor a loss accrued to the person making the disposal.

The displacement of sub-paragraph (1) above by this sub-paragraph shall not be taken as bringing paragraph 16 above into operation.

(3) An election under this paragraph shall be made by notice to [an officer of the Board given—

(*a*) in the case of an election for the purposes of capital gains tax, on or before the first anniversary of the 31st January next following the year of assessment in which the disposal is made;

(*b*) in the case of an election for the purposes of corporation tax, within 2 years from the end of the accounting period in which the disposal is made; or

(*c*) in either case, within such further time as the Board may by notice allow]¹.

(4) For the avoidance of doubt it is hereby declared that an election under this paragraph is irrevocable.

(5) An election may not be made under this paragraph as respects, or in relation to, an asset the market value of which at a date on or after 6th April 1965, and before the date of the disposal to which the election relates, is to be ascertained in pursuance of section 42.

Commentary—*Simon's Direct Tax Service* C2.611–614, 728.
Revenue & other press releases—Lands Tribunal 31-12-79 (valuation: cost of drainage and acquiring incidental easements must be taken into account in valuing development land).
Statement of Practice D21—Time limit for election: extension.
Revenue Internal Guidance—Capital Gains Manual CG 15530 (Circumstances under which a late election may be made where a charge under s 178 arises).
Definitions—"Accounting period", TA 1988 s 834(1); "asset", s 21(1); "the Board", s 288(1); "company", ss 99, 288(1); "market value", ss 272–274, Sch 11; "notice", s 288(1); "year of assessment", s 288(1).
Amendments—¹ Words in sub-para (3) substituted by FA 1996 s 135(1), (2), Sch 21 para 42(1), (3) with effect from the year 1996–97 and, for the purposes of corporation tax, as respects accounting periods ending after 30 June 1999 (by virtue of Finance Act 1994, Section 199, (Appointed Day) Order, SI 1998/3173 art 2).

Unquoted shares, commodities etc

18—(1) This paragraph has effect as respects shares held by any person on 6th April 1965 other than quoted securities within the meaning of paragraph 8 above and shares as respects which an election is made under paragraph 17 above.

(2) For the purpose of—

(a) identifying the shares so held on 6th April 1965 with shares previously acquired, and

(b) identifying the shares so held on that date with shares subsequently disposed of, and distinguishing them from shares acquired subsequently,

so far as the shares are of the same class, shares bought at a later time shall be deemed to have been disposed of before shares bought at an earlier time.

(3) Sub-paragraph (2) above has effect subject to section 105.

(4) Shares shall not be treated for the purposes of this paragraph as being of the same class unless if dealt with on a recognised stock exchange they would be so treated, but shall be treated in accordance with this paragraph notwithstanding that they are identified in a different way by a disposal or by the transfer or delivery giving effect to it.

(5) This paragraph, without sub-paragraph (4), shall apply in relation to any assets, other than shares, which are of a nature to be dealt with without identifying the particular assets disposed of or acquired.

Commentary—*Simon's Direct Tax Service* C2.709.
Concession D33—CGT on compensation and damages. This Concession has been revised.
Definitions—"Asset", s 21(1).

Reorganisation of share capital, conversion of securities etc

19—(1) For the purposes of this Act, it shall be assumed that any shares or securities held by a person on 6th April 1965 (identified in accordance with paragraph 18 above) which, in accordance with Chapter II of Part IV, are to be regarded as being or forming part of a new holding were sold and immediately reacquired by him on 6th April 1965 at their market value on that date.

(2) If, at any time after 5th April 1965, a person comes to have, in accordance with Chapter II of Part IV, a new holding, paragraph 16(3) to (5) above shall have effect as if—

(a) the new holding had at that time been sold by the owner, and immediately reacquired by him, at its market value at that time, and

(b) accordingly, the amount of any gain on a disposal of the new holding or any part of it shall be computed—

(i) by apportioning in accordance with paragraph 16 above the gain or loss over a period ending at that time, and

(ii) by bringing into account the entire gain or loss over the period from that time to the date of the disposal.

(3) This paragraph shall not apply in relation to a reorganisation of a company's share capital if the new holding differs only from the original shares in being a different number, whether greater or less, of shares of the same class as the original shares.

Commentary—*Simon's Direct Tax Service* C2.728.
Concession D10—Unquoted shares acquired before 6 April 1965: disposal following reorganisation of share capital.
Statement of Practice SP 14/79—CGT: unquoted shares or securities held at 6 April 1965.
Simon's Tax Cases—Para 19(2), (3), *Unilever (UK) Holdings Ltd v Smith (Inspector of Taxes)* [2002] STC 113.
Definitions—"Class", s 288(1); "company", ss 99, 288(1); "market value", ss 272–274, Sch 11; "shares", s 288(1).

PART IV

MISCELLANEOUS

Capital allowances

20 If under any provision in this Schedule it is to be assumed that any asset was on 6th April 1965 sold by the owner, and immediately reacquired by him, sections 41 and 47 shall apply in relation to any capital allowance or renewals allowance made in respect of the expenditure actually incurred by the owner in providing the asset, and so made for the year 1965–66 or for any subsequent year of assessment, as if it were made in respect of the expenditure which, on that assumption, was incurred by him in reacquiring the asset on 7th April 1965.

Commentary—*Simon's Direct Tax Service* C2.612.
Definitions—"Asset", s 21(1); "year of assessment", s 288(1).

Assets transferred to close companies

21—(1) This paragraph has effect where—

(*a*) at any time, including a time before 7th April 1965, any of the persons having control of a close company, or any person who is connected with a person having control of a close company, has transferred assets to the company, and

(*b*) paragraph 16 above applies in relation to a disposal by one of the persons having control of the company of shares or securities in the company, or in relation to a disposal by a person having, up to the time of disposal, a substantial holding of shares or securities in the company, being in either case a disposal after the transfer of the assets.

(2) So far as the gain accruing to the said person on the disposal of the shares is attributable to a profit on the assets so transferred, the period over which the gain is to be treated under paragraph 16 above as growing at a uniform rate shall begin with the time when the assets were transferred to the company, and accordingly a part of a gain attributable to a profit on assets transferred on or after 6th April 1965 shall all be a chargeable gain.

(3) This paragraph shall not apply where a loss, and not a gain, accrues on the disposal.

Commentary—*Simon's Direct Tax Service* **C2.710.**
Definitions—"Asset", s 21(1); "chargeable gain", s 15(2); "close company", s 288(1), TA 1988 ss 414, 415; "company", ss 99, 288(1); "connected", s 286; "shares", s 288(1).

Husbands and wives

22 Where section 58 is applied in relation to a disposal of an asset by a man to his wife, or by a man's wife to him, then in relation to a subsequent disposal of the asset (not within that section) the one making the disposal shall be treated for the purposes of this Schedule as if the other's acquisition or provision of the asset had been his or her acquisition or provision of it.

Commentary—*Simon's Direct Tax Service* **C1.202.**
Definition—"Asset", s 21(1).

Compensation and insurance money

23 Where section 23(4)(*a*) applies to exclude a gain which, in consequence of this Schedule, is not all chargeable gain, the amount of the reduction to be made under section 23(4)(*b*) shall be the amount of the chargeable gain and not the whole amount of the gain; and in section 23(5)(*b*) for the reference to the amount by which the gain is reduced under section 23(5)(*a*) there shall be substituted a reference to the amount by which the chargeable gain is proportionately reduced under section 23(5)(*a*).

Definition—"Chargeable gain", s 15(2).

SCHEDULE 3

ASSETS HELD ON 31ST MARCH 1982

Section 35

Previous no gain/no loss disposals

1—(1) Where—

(*a*) a person makes a disposal, not being a no gain/no loss disposal, of an asset which he acquired after 31st March 1982, and

(*b*) the disposal by which he acquired the asset and any previous disposal of the asset after 31st March 1982 was a no gain/no loss disposal,

he shall be treated for the purposes of section 35 as having held the asset on 31st March 1982.

(2) For the purposes of this paragraph a no gain/no loss disposal is one on which by virtue of any of the enactments specified in section 35(3)(*d*) neither a gain nor a loss accrues to the person making the disposal.

Commentary—*Simon's Direct Tax Service* **C1.202; C2.604, 607.**
Revenue Interpretation RI 26—Rebasing: treatment of enhancement expenditure incurred after 31 March 1982 by a previous owner of an asset deemed to be held on that date by the person making the disposal.
Definition—"Asset", s 21(1).

2—(1) Sub-paragraph (2) below applies where a person makes a disposal of an asset acquired by him on or after 6th April 1988 in circumstances in which section 58 or 171 applied.

(2) Where this sub-paragraph applies—

(*a*) an election under section 35(5) by the person making the disposal shall not cover the disposal, but

(b) the making of such an election by the person from whom the asset was acquired shall cause the disposal to fall outside subsection (3) of that section (so that subsection (2) of that section is not excluded by it) whether or not the person making the disposal makes such an election.

(3) Where the person from whom the asset was acquired by the person making the disposal himself acquired it on or after 6th April 1988 in circumstances in which section 58 or 171 applied, an election made by him shall not have the effect described in sub-paragraph (2)(b) above but an election made by—

   (a) the last person by whom the asset was acquired after 5th April 1988 otherwise than in such circumstances, or

   (b) if there is no such person, the person who held the asset on 5th April 1988,

shall have that effect.

Commentary—*Simon's Direct Tax Service* C1.202; C2.604, 607.
Definition—"Asset", s 21(1).

Capital allowances

3 If under section 35 it is to be assumed that any asset was on 31st March 1982 sold by the person making the disposal and immediately reacquired by him, sections 41 and 47 shall apply in relation to any capital allowance or renewals allowance made in respect of the expenditure actually incurred by him in providing the asset as if it were made in respect of expenditure which, on that assumption, was incurred by him in reacquiring the asset on 31st March 1982.

Commentary—*Simon's Direct Tax Service* C2.602.
Definition—"Asset", s 21(1).

Part disposals etc

4—(1) Where, in relation to a disposal to which section 35(2) applies, section 42 has effect by reason of an earlier disposal made after 31st March 1982 and before 6th April 1988, the sums to be apportioned under section 42 shall for the purposes of the later disposal be ascertained on the assumption stated in section 35(2).

(2) In any case where—

   (a) subsection (2) of section 35 applies in relation to the disposal of an asset,

   (b) if that subsection did not apply, section 23(2), 122(4), 133(4) or 244 would operate to disallow expenditure as a deduction in computing a gain accruing on the disposal, and

   (c) the disallowance would be attributable to the reduction of the amount of the consideration for a disposal made after 31st March 1982 but before 6th April 1988,

the amount allowable as a deduction on the disposal shall be reduced by the amount which would be disallowed if section 35(2) did not apply.

Commentary—*Simon's Direct Tax Service* C2.606.
Definition—"Asset", s 21(1).

Assets derived from other assets

5 Section 35 shall have effect with the necessary modifications in relation to a disposal of an asset which on 31st March 1982 was not itself held by the person making the disposal, if its value is derived from another asset of which account is to be taken in relation to the disposal under section 43.

Commentary—*Simon's Direct Tax Service* C2.602.
Definition—"Asset", s 21(1).

Apportionment of pre-1965 gains and losses

6 In a case where because of paragraph 16 of Schedule 2 only part of a gain or loss is a chargeable gain or allowable loss, section 35(3)(a) and (b) shall have effect as if the amount of the gain or loss that would accrue if subsection (2) did not apply were equal to that part.

Commentary—*Simon's Direct Tax Service* C2.611.
Definition—"Chargeable gain", s 15(2).

Elections under section 35(5): excluded disposals

7—(1) An election under section 35(5) shall not cover disposals such as are specified in sub-paragraph (2) below.

(2) The disposals mentioned in sub-paragraph (1) above are disposals of, or of an interest in—

   (a) plant or machinery,

   (b) an asset which the person making the disposal has at any time held for the purposes of or in connection with—

      (i) a trade consisting of the working of a source of mineral deposits, or

    (ii) where a trade involves (but does not consist of) such working, the part of the trade which involves such working, or

    (c) a licence under [Part I of the Petroleum Act 1998][1] or the Petroleum (Production) Act (Northern Ireland) 1964; or

    (d) shares which, on 31st March 1982, were unquoted and derived their value, or the greater part of their value, directly or indirectly from oil exploration or exploitation assets situated in the United Kingdom or a designated area or from such assets and oil exploration or exploitation rights taken together;

but a disposal does not fall within paragraph (a) or (b) above unless a capital allowance in respect of any expenditure attributable to the asset has been made to the person making the disposal or would have been made to him had he made a claim.

(3) For the purposes of sub-paragraph (2)(d) above,—

    (a) "shares" includes stock and any security, as defined in section 254(1) of the Taxes Act; and
    (b) shares (as so defined) were unquoted on 31st March 1982 if, on that date, they were neither quoted on a recognised stock exchange nor dealt in on the Unlisted Securities Market;

but nothing in this paragraph affects the operation, in relation to such unquoted shares, of sections 126 to 130.

(4) In sub-paragraph (2)(d) above—

    "designated area" means an area designated by Order in Council under section 1(7) of the Continental Shelf Act 1964;
    "oil exploration or exploitation assets" shall be construed in accordance with sub-paragraphs (5) and (6) below; and
    "oil exploration or exploitation rights" means rights to assets to be produced by oil exploration or exploitation activities (as defined in sub-paragraph (6) below) or to interests in or to the benefit of such assets.

(5) For the purposes of sub-paragraph (2)(d) above an asset is an oil exploration or exploitation asset if either—

    (a) it is not a mobile asset and is being or has at some time been used in connection with oil exploration or exploitation activities carried on in the United Kingdom or a designated area; or
    (b) it is a mobile asset which has at some time been used in connection with oil exploration or exploitation activities so carried on and is dedicated to an oil field in which the company whose shares are disposed of by the disposal, or a person connected with that company, is or has been a participator;

and, subject to sub-paragraph (6) below, expressions used in paragraphs (a) and (b) above have the same meaning as if those paragraphs were included in Part I of the Oil Taxation Act 1975.

(6) In the preceding provisions of this paragraph "oil exploration or exploitation activities" means activities carried on in connection with—

    (a) the exploration of land (including the seabed and subsoil) in the United Kingdom or a designated area, as defined in sub-paragraph (4) above, with a view to searching for or winning oil; or
    (b) the exploitation of oil found in any such land;

and in this sub-paragraph "oil" has the same meaning as in Part I of the Oil Taxation Act 1975.

(7) Where the person making the disposal acquired the asset on a no gain/no loss disposal, the references in sub-paragraph (2) above to that person are references to the person making the disposal, the person who last acquired the asset otherwise than on a no gain/no loss disposal or any person who subsequently acquired the asset on such a disposal.

(8) In this paragraph—

    (a) "source of mineral deposits" shall be construed in accordance with [section 394 of the Capital Allowances Act][2], and
    (b) references to a no gain/no loss disposal shall be construed in accordance with paragraph 1 above.

Commentary—*Simon's Direct Tax Service* **C2.604.**
Definitions—"The 1990 Act", s 288(1); "asset", s 21(1); "company", ss 99, 288(1); "connected", s 286; "land", s 288(1); "recognised stock exchange", s 288(1), TA 1988 s 841; "shares", s 288(1); "the Taxes Act", s 288(1); "trade", s 288(1).
Amendments—[1] Words in para (7)(2)(c) substituted by the Petroleum Act 1998 s 50, Sch 4 para 32 with effect from 15 February 1999 (by virtue of the Petroleum Act 1998 (Commencement No 1) Order, SI 1999/161).
[2] Words in sub-para (8) substituted by CAA 2001 s 578, Sch 2 para 81 with effect for income tax purposes, as respects allowances and charges falling to be made for chargeable periods ending after 5 April 2001, and for corporation tax purposes, as respects allowances and charges falling to be made for chargeable periods ending after 31 March 2001.

Elections under section 35(5): groups of companies

8—(1) A company may not make an election under section 35(5) at a time when it is a member but not the principal company of a group unless the company did not become a member of the group until after the relevant time.

(2) Subject to sub-paragraph (3) below, an election under section 35(5) by a company which is the principal company of a group shall have effect also as an election by any other company which at the relevant time is a member of the group.

(3) Sub-paragraph (2) above shall not apply in relation to a company which, in some period after 5th April 1988 and before the relevant time, is not a member of the group if—

(*a*) during that period the company makes a disposal to which section 35 applies, and

(*b*) the period during which an election under subsection (5) of that section could be made expires without such an election having been made.

(4) Sub-paragraph (2) above shall apply in relation to a company notwithstanding that the company ceases to be a member of the group at any time after the relevant time except where—

(*a*) the company is an outgoing company in relation to the group, and

(*b*) the election relating to the group is made after the company ceases to be a member of the group.

(5) In relation to a company which is the principal company of a group the reference in section 35(6) to the first relevant disposal is a reference to the first disposal to which that section applies by a company which is—

(*a*) a member of the group but not an outgoing company in relation to the group, or

(*b*) an incoming company in relation to the group.

Commentary—*Simon's Direct Tax Service* **D2.625.**
Definitions—"Company", ss 99, 288(1); "incoming company", Sch 3 para 9(2); "outgoing company", Sch 3 para 9(2); "relevant time", Sch 3 para 9(1).
Cross references—See FA 2000 Sch 29 para 38 (the main amendments made to TCGA 1992 s 170 by FA 2000 Sch 29 para 1 have effect for the purposes of this section for any determination as to whether a company is a member, or the principal company, of a group of companies after 31 March 2000).

9—(1) In paragraph 8 above "the relevant time", in relation to a group of companies, is—

(*a*) the first time when any company which is then a member of the group, and is not an outgoing company in relation to the group, makes a disposal to which section 35 applies,

(*b*) the time immediately following the first occasion when a company which is an incoming company in relation to the group becomes a member of the group,

(*c*) the time when an election is made by the principal company,

whichever is earliest.

(2) In paragraph 8 above and this paragraph—

"incoming company", in relation to a group of companies, means a company which—

(*a*) makes its first disposal to which section 35 applies at a time when it is not a member of the group, and

(*b*) becomes a member of the group before the end of the period during which an election under section 35(5) could be made in relation to it and at a time when no such election has been made, and

"outgoing company", in relation to a group of companies, means a company which ceases to be a member of the group before the end of the period during which an election under section 35(5) could be made in relation to it and at a time when no such election has been made.

(3) Section 170 shall have effect for the purposes of paragraph 8 above and this paragraph as for those of sections 170 to 181.

Revenue Internal Guidance—Capital Gains Manual CG 46369 (a company joining a group after the group's relevant time has the right to make its own election, subject to the statutory time limit).
Definition—"Company", ss 99, 288(1).
Cross references—See FA 2000 Sch 29 para 38 (the main amendments made to TCGA 1992 s 170 by FA 2000 Sch 29 para 1 have effect for the purposes of this section for any determination as to whether a company is a member, or the principal company, of a group of companies after 31 March 2000).

SCHEDULE 4

DEFERRED CHARGES ON GAINS BEFORE 31ST MARCH 1982

Section 36

Reduction of deduction or gain

1 Where this Schedule applies—

(*a*) in a case within paragraph 2 below, the amount of the deduction referred to in that paragraph, and

(*b*) in a case within paragraph 3 or 4 below, the amount of the gain referred to in that paragraph,

shall be one half of what it would be apart from this Schedule.

Commentary—*Simon's Direct Tax Service* **C2.605.**
Cross references—See TCGA 1992 Sch 4 para 7 (meaning of a no gain/no loss disposal for the purposes of this paragraph).

Charges rolled-over or held-over

2—(1) Subject to sub-paragraphs (2) to (4) below, this Schedule applies on a disposal, not being a no gain/no loss disposal, of an asset if—

 (*a*) the person making the disposal acquired the asset after 31st March 1982,

 (*b*) a deduction falls to be made by virtue of any of the enactments specified in sub-paragraph (5) below from the expenditure which is allowable in computing the amount of any gain accruing on the disposal, and

 (*c*) the deduction is attributable (whether directly or indirectly and whether in whole or in part) to a chargeable gain accruing on the disposal before 6th April 1988 of an asset acquired before 31st March 1982 by the person making that disposal.

(2) This Schedule does not apply where, by reason of the previous operation of this Schedule, the amount of the deduction is less than it otherwise would be.

(3) This Schedule does not apply if the amount of the deduction would have been less had relief by virtue of a previous application of this Schedule been duly claimed.

(4) Where—

 (*a*) the asset was acquired on or after 19th March 1991,

 (*b*) the deduction is partly attributable to a claim by virtue of section 154(4), and

 (*c*) the claim applies to the asset,

this Schedule does not apply by virtue of this paragraph.

(5) The enactments referred to in sub-paragraph (1) above are sections 23(4) and (5), 152, 162, 165 and 247 of this Act and section 79 of the Finance Act 1980.

Commentary—*Simon's Direct Tax Service* **C2.605.**
Definitions—"Asset", s 21(1); "chargeable gain", s 15(2); "no gain/no loss disposal", Sch 4 para 7.
Cross references—See TCGA 1992 Sch 4 para 1 (reduction of amount of deduction referred to in this paragraph to one half in a case within this paragraph).
TCGA 1992 Sch 4 para 3(1) (circumstances in which relief under this Schedule otherwise excluded by sub-para (4) above is available).
TCGA 1992 Sch 4 para 5 (for the purposes of sub-para (1)(*c*) above a person is treated as having acquired an asset before 31 March 1982 in certain circumstances).
TCGA 1992 Sch 4 para 6 (deduction in sub-para (1)(*b*) above to be treated in certain circumstances as falling to be made on a disposal of an asset acquired on or after 31 March 1982).
TCGA 1992 Sch 4 para 7 (meaning of a no gain/no loss disposal for the purposes of this paragraph).
TCGA 1992 Sch 4 para 8 (meaning of "disposal of an asset acquired by a person before 31 March 1982" in sub-para (1)(*c*) above).

3—(1) This paragraph applies where this Schedule would have applied on a disposal but for paragraph 2(4) above.

(2) This Schedule applies on the disposal if paragraph 4 below would have applied had—

 (*a*) section 154(2) continued to apply to the gain carried forward as a result of the claim by virtue of section 154(4), and

 (*b*) the time of the disposal been the time when that gain was treated as accruing by virtue of section 154(2).

Commentary—*Simon's Direct Tax Service* **C2.605.**
Cross references—See TCGA 1992 Sch 4 para 1 (reduction of amount of gain referred to in this paragraph to one half in a case within this paragraph).
TCGA 1992 Sch 4 para 7 (meaning of a no gain/no loss disposal for the purposes of this paragraph).

Postponed charges

4—(1) Subject to sub-paragraphs (3) to (5) below, this Schedule applies where—

 (*a*) a gain is treated as accruing by virtue of any of the enactments specified in sub-paragraph (2) below, and

 (*b*) that gain is attributable (whether directly or indirectly and whether in whole or in part) to the disposal before 6th April 1988 of an asset acquired before 31st March 1982 by the person making that disposal.

(2) The enactments referred to in sub-paragraph (1) above are sections 116(10) and (11), 134, 140, 154(2), 168 (as modified by section 67(6)), ...[1] and 248(3).

(3) ...[1]

(4) Where a gain is treated as accruing in consequence of an event, this Schedule does not apply if—

 (*a*) the gain is attributable (whether directly or indirectly and whether in whole or in part) to the disposal of an asset on or after 6th April 1988, or

 (*b*) the amount of the gain would have been less had relief by virtue of a previous application of this Schedule been duly claimed.

(5) None of sections 134, 140(4), 154(2) and 248(3) shall apply in consequence of an event occurring on or after 6th April 1988 if its application would be directly attributable to the disposal of an asset on or before 31st March 1982.

Commentary—*Simon's Direct Tax Service* **C2.605.**
Definitions—"Asset", s 21(1); "company", ss 99, 288(1).

Cross references—See TCGA 1992 Sch 4 para 1 (reduction of amount of gain referred to in this paragraph to one half in a case within this paragraph).

TCGA 1992 Sch 4 para 5 (for the purposes of sub-para (1)(*b*) above a person is treated as having acquired an asset before 31 March 1982 in certain circumstances).

TCGA 1992 Sch 4 para 7 (meaning of a no gain/no loss disposal for the purposes of this paragraph).

TCGA 1992 Sch 4 para 8 (meaning of "disposal of an asset acquired by a person before 31 March 1982" in sub-para (1)(*b*) above).

Amendments—[1] Words in para (2) and whole of para (3) repealed by FA 2000 s 156, Sch 40 Pt II(12) with effect from 28 July 2000.

Previous no gain/no loss disposals

5 Where—

(*a*) a person makes a disposal of an asset which he acquired on or after 31st March 1982, and

(*b*) the disposal by which he acquired the asset and any previous disposal of the asset on or after 31st March 1982 was a no gain/no loss disposal,

he shall be treated for the purposes of paragraphs 2(1)(*c*) and 4(1)(*b*) above as having acquired the asset before 31st March 1982.

Commentary—*Simon's Direct Tax Service* **C2.605.**
Definitions—"Asset", s 21(1); "no gain/no loss disposal", Sch 4 para 7.
Cross references—See TCGA 1992 Sch 4 para 7 (meaning of a no gain/no loss disposal for the purposes of this paragraph).

6—(1) Sub-paragraph (2) below applies where—

(*a*) a person makes a disposal of an asset which he acquired on or after 31st March 1982,

(*b*) the disposal by which he acquired the asset was a no gain/no loss disposal, and

(*c*) a deduction falling to be made as mentioned in paragraph (*b*) of sub-paragraph (1) of paragraph 2 above which was attributable as mentioned in paragraph (*c*) of that sub-paragraph was made—

(i) on that disposal, or

(ii) where one or more earlier no gain/no loss disposals of the asset have been made on or after 31st March 1982 and since the last disposal of the asset which was not a no gain/no loss disposal, on any such earlier disposal.

(2) Where this sub-paragraph applies the deduction shall be treated for the purposes of paragraph 2 above as falling to be made on the disposal mentioned in sub-paragraph (1)(*a*) above and not on the no gain/no loss disposal.

Commentary—*Simon's Direct Tax Service* **C2.605.**
Definitions—"Asset", s 21(1); "no gain/no loss disposal", Sch 4 para 7.
Cross references—See TCGA 1992 Sch 4 para 7 (meaning of a no gain/no loss disposal for the purposes of this paragraph).

7 For the purposes of this Schedule a no gain/no loss disposal is one on which by virtue of any of the enactments specified in section 35(3)(*d*) neither a gain nor a loss accrues to the person making the disposal.

Commentary—*Simon's Direct Tax Service* **C2.605.**

Assets derived from other assets

8 The references in paragraphs 2(1)(*c*) and 4(1)(*b*) above to the disposal of an asset acquired by a person before 31st March 1982 include references to the disposal of an asset which was not acquired by the person before that date if its value is derived from another asset which was so acquired and of which account is to be taken in relation to the disposal under section 43.

Commentary—*Simon's Direct Tax Service* **C2.605.**
Definitions—"Asset", s 21(1); "no gain/no loss disposal", Sch 4 para 7.

Claims

9—(1) No relief shall be given under this Schedule unless a claim is made—

(*a*) ...[1]

(*b*) in [the case of a disposal made by, or a gain treated as accruing to, a person chargeable to corporation tax][1], within the period of 2 years beginning at the end of the ...[1] accounting period in which the disposal in question is made, or the gain in question is treated as accruing,

[(*c*) in the case of a disposal made by, or a gain treated as accruing to, a person who is chargeable to capital gains tax, on or before the first anniversary of the 31st January next following the year of assessment in which the disposal in question is made or the gain in question is treated as accruing,][1]

or within such longer period [or (as the case may be) on or before such later date][1] as the Board may by notice allow.

(2) A claim under sub-paragraph (1) above shall be supported by such particulars as the inspector may require for the purpose of establishing entitlement to relief under this Schedule and the amount of relief due.

Commentary—*Simon's Direct Tax Service* **C2.605.**
Definitions—"Accounting period", TA 1988 s 834(1); "the Board", s 288(1); "company", ss 99, 288(1); "inspector", s 288(1); "notice", s 288(1); "year of assessment", s 288(1).

Amendments—¹ Words in sub-para (1)(*b*) substituted and repealed; sub-para (1)(*c*) inserted; and words in final paragraph of sub-para (1) inserted, by FA 1996 s 135(1), (2), Sch 21 para 43, Sch 41 Pt V(11) with effect from the year 1996–97 and, for purposes of corporation tax, as respects accounting periods ending after 30 June 1999 (by virtue of Finance Act 1994, Section 199, (Appointed Day) Order, SI 1998/3173 art 2).
Amendments—¹ Sub-para (1)(*a*) repealed by FA 2000 s 156, Sch 40 Pt II(12) with effect from 28 July 2000.

[SCHEDULE 4A

DISPOSAL OF INTEREST IN SETTLED PROPERTY: DEEMED DISPOSAL OF UNDERLYING ASSETS]¹

Section 76A

Amendments—¹ This Schedule inserted by FA 2000 s 91(2), (3), Sch 24 with effect for any disposal of an interest in settled property made, or the effective completion of which falls, after 20 March 2000.

[*Circumstances in which this Schedule applies*

1 This Schedule applies where there is a disposal of an interest in settled property for consideration.]¹

Revenue Internal Guidance—Capital Gains Manual CG 35103 (disposal includes part disposals and the extinction or surrender of an interest).
Amendments—¹ This Schedule inserted by FA 2000 s 91(2), (3), Sch 24 with effect for any disposal of an interest in settled property made, or the effective completion of which falls, after 20 March 2000.

[*Meaning of "interest in settled property"*

2—(1) For the purposes of this Schedule an "interest in settled property" means any interest created by or arising under a settlement.

(2) This includes any right to, or in connection with, the enjoyment of a benefit—

   (*a*) created by or arising directly under a settlement, or

   (*b*) arising as a result of the exercise of a discretion or power—

      (i) by the trustees of a settlement, or

      (ii) by any person in relation to settled property.]¹

Amendments—¹ This Schedule inserted by FA 2000 s 91(2), (3), Sch 24 with effect for any disposal of an interest in settled property made, or the effective completion of which falls, after 20 March 2000.

[*Meaning of "for consideration"*

3—(1) For the purposes of this Schedule a disposal is "for consideration" if consideration is given or received by any person for, or otherwise in connection with, any transaction by virtue of which the disposal is effected.

(2) In determining for the purposes of this Schedule whether a disposal is for consideration there shall be disregarded any consideration consisting of another interest under the same settlement that has not previously been disposed of by any person for consideration.

(3) In this Schedule "consideration" means actual consideration, as opposed to consideration deemed to be given by any provision of this Act.]¹

Amendments—¹ This Schedule inserted by FA 2000 s 91(2), (3), Sch 24 with effect for any disposal of an interest in settled property made, or the effective completion of which falls, after 20 March 2000.

[*Deemed disposal of underlying assets*

4—(1) Where this Schedule applies and the following conditions are met—

   (*a*) the condition as to UK residence of the trustees (see paragraph 5),

   (*b*) the condition as to UK residence of the settlor (see paragraph 6), and

   (*c*) the condition as to settlor interest in the settlement (see paragraph 7),

the trustees of the settlement are treated for all purposes of this Act as disposing of and immediately reacquiring the relevant underlying assets.

This is referred to below in this Schedule as the "deemed disposal".

(2) In paragraphs 5, 6 and 7 "the relevant year of assessment" means the year of assessment in which the disposal of the interest in settled property is made.

(3) The deemed disposal is treated as taking place when the disposal of the interest in settled property is made.

This is subject to paragraph 13(3)(*a*) where the beginning of the disposal and its effective completion fall in different years of assessment.]¹

Amendments—¹ This Schedule inserted by FA 2000 s 91(2), (3), Sch 24 with effect for any disposal of an interest in settled property made, or the effective completion of which falls, after 20 March 2000.

[Condition as to UK residence of trustees

5—(1) The condition as to UK residence of the trustees is that the trustees of the settlement were either—

(a) resident in the United Kingdom during the whole or part of the relevant year of assessment, or

(b) ordinarily resident in the United Kingdom during that year.

(2) For this purpose the trustees shall not be regarded as resident or ordinarily resident in the United Kingdom at any time when they fall to be regarded for the purposes of any double taxation relief arrangements as resident in a territory outside the United Kingdom.

(3) This paragraph has effect subject to paragraph 13(3)(*b*) where the beginning of the disposal and its effective completion fall in different years of assessment.]¹

Amendments—¹ This Schedule inserted by FA 2000 s 91(2), (3), Sch 24 with effect for any disposal of an interest in settled property made, or the effective completion of which falls, after 20 March 2000.

[Condition as to UK residence of settlor

6—(1) The condition as to UK residence of the settlor is that in the relevant year of assessment, or any of the previous five years of assessment, a person who is a settlor in relation to the settlement either—

(a) was resident in the United Kingdom during the whole or part of the year, or

(b) was ordinarily resident in the United Kingdom during the year.

(2) Sub-paragraph (1) has effect subject to paragraph 13(3)(*c*) where the beginning of the disposal and its effective completion fall in different years of assessment.

(3) No account shall be taken for the purposes of this paragraph of any year of assessment before the year 1999–00.]¹

Amendments—¹ This Schedule inserted by FA 2000 s 91(2), (3), Sch 24 with effect for any disposal of an interest in settled property made, or the effective completion of which falls, after 20 March 2000.

[Condition as to settlor interest in the settlement

7—(1) The condition as to settlor interest in the settlement is that at any time in the relevant period the settlement—

(a) was a settlor-interested settlement, or

(b) comprised property derived, directly or indirectly, from a settlement that at any time in that period was a settlor-interested settlement.

(2) The relevant period for this purpose is the period—

(a) beginning two years before the beginning of the relevant year of assessment, and

(b) ending with the date of the disposal of the interest in settled property.

This is subject to paragraph 13(3)(*d*) where the beginning of the disposal and its effective completion fall in different years of assessment.

(3) The relevant period shall not be treated as beginning before 6th April 1999.

If the rule in sub-paragraph (2) (or, where relevant, that in paragraph 13(3)(*d*)) would produce that result, the relevant period shall be treated as beginning on that date.

(4) For the purposes of this paragraph a ''settlor-interested settlement'' means a settlement in which a person who is a settlor in relation to the settlement has an interest or had an interest at any time in the relevant period.

The provisions of section 77(2) to (5) and (8) apply to determine for the purposes of this paragraph whether a settlor has (or had) an interest in the settlement.

(5) The condition as to settlor interest in the settlement is treated as not met in a year of assessment—

(a) where the settlor dies during the year, or

(b) in a case where the settlor is regarded as having an interest in the settlement by reason only of—

(i) the fact that property is, or will or may become, payable to or applicable for the benefit of his spouse, or

(ii) the fact that a benefit is enjoyed by his spouse,

where the spouse dies, or the settlor and the spouse cease to be married, during the year.]¹

Amendments—¹ This Schedule inserted by FA 2000 s 91(2), (3), Sch 24 with effect for any disposal of an interest in settled property made, or the effective completion of which falls, after 20 March 2000.

[The relevant underlying assets

8—(1) Where the interest disposed of is a right in relation to a specific fund or other defined part of the settled property, the deemed disposal is of the whole or part of each of the assets comprised in that fund or part.

In any other case the deemed disposal is of the whole or part of each of the assets comprised in the settled property.

(2) Where the interest disposed of is an interest in a specific fraction or amount of the income or capital of—

(a) the settled property, or

(b) a specific fund or other defined part of the settled property,

the deemed disposal is of a corresponding part of each of the assets comprised in the settled property or, as the case may be, each of the assets comprised in that fund or part.

In any other case the deemed disposal is of the whole of each of the assets so comprised.

(3) Sub-paragraphs (1) and (2) have effect subject to paragraph 13(4)(a) where the identity of the underlying assets changes during the period between the beginning of the disposal and its effective completion.

(4) Where part only of an asset is comprised in a specific fund or other defined part of the settled property, that part of the asset shall be treated for the purposes of this Schedule as if it were a separate asset.]¹

Revenue Internal Guidance—Capital Gains Manual CG 35102 (the type of interest in, or the value of, the settled property is immaterial in deciding what part of it is disposed of).
Amendments—¹ This Schedule inserted by FA 2000 s 91(2), (3), Sch 24 with effect for any disposal of an interest in settled property made, or the effective completion of which falls, after 20 March 2000.

[Character of deemed disposal

9—(1) The deemed disposal shall be taken—

(a) to be for a consideration equal to the whole or, as the case may be, a corresponding part of the market value of each of the assets concerned, and

(b) to be a disposal under a bargain at arm's length.

(2) Sub-paragraph (1)(a) shall be read with paragraph 13(4)(b) where the value of the assets changes during the period between the beginning of the disposal and its effective completion.]¹

Amendments—¹ This Schedule inserted by FA 2000 s 91(2), (3), Sch 24 with effect for any disposal of an interest in settled property made, or the effective completion of which falls, after 20 March 2000.

[Avoidance of double-counting

10—(1) The provisions of this paragraph have effect to prevent there being both a deemed disposal under this Schedule in relation to the disposal of an interest in settled property and a chargeable disposal of the interest itself.

A "chargeable disposal" means one in relation to which section 76(1) does not apply.

(2) If there would be a chargeable gain on the disposal of the interest in the settlement, then—

(a) if—

(i) the chargeable gain on the disposal of the interest would be greater than the net chargeable gain on the deemed disposal, or

(ii) there would be no net chargeable gain on the deemed disposal,

the provisions of this Schedule as to a deemed disposal do not apply; and

(b) in any other case, the provisions of this Schedule as to a deemed disposal apply and no chargeable gain is treated as accruing on the disposal of the interest in the settlement.

(3) If there would be an allowable loss on the disposal of the interest in the settlement, then—

(a) if there would be a greater net allowable loss on the deemed disposal, the provisions of this Schedule as to a deemed disposal do not apply; and

(b) in any other case, the provisions of this Schedule as to a deemed disposal apply and no allowable loss is treated as accruing on the disposal of the interest in the settlement.

(4) If there would be neither a chargeable gain nor an allowable loss on the disposal of the interest in the settlement, then—

(a) if there would be a net allowable loss on the deemed disposal, the provisions of this Schedule as to a deemed disposal do not apply; and

(b) in any other case, the provisions of this Schedule as to a deemed disposal apply.

(5) For the purposes of this paragraph—

(a) there is a net chargeable gain on a deemed disposal if the aggregate of the chargeable gains accruing to the trustees in respect of the assets involved exceeds the aggregate of the allowable losses so accruing; and

(b) there is a net allowable loss on a deemed disposal if the aggregate of the allowable losses accruing to the trustees in respect of the assets involved exceeds the aggregate of the chargeable gains so accruing.]¹

Amendments—¹ This Schedule inserted by FA 2000 s 91(2), (3), Sch 24 with effect for any disposal of an interest in settled property made, or the effective completion of which falls, after 20 March 2000.

TCGA 1992

[Recovery of tax from person disposing of interest

11—(1) This paragraph applies where chargeable gains accrue to the trustees on the deemed disposal and—

(a) tax becomes chargeable on and is paid by the trustees in respect of those gains, or

(b) a person who is a settlor in relation to the settlement recovers from the trustees under section 78 an amount of tax in respect of those gains.

(2) The trustees are entitled to recover the amount of the tax referred to in sub-paragraph (1)(a) or (b) from the person who disposed of the interest in the settlement.

(3) For this purpose the trustees may require an inspector to give that person a certificate specifying—

(a) the amount of the gains in question, and

(b) the amount of tax that has been paid.

Any such certificate shall be conclusive evidence of the facts stated in it.]¹

Amendments—¹ This Schedule inserted by FA 2000 s 91(2), (3), Sch 24 with effect for any disposal of an interest in settled property made, or the effective completion of which falls, after 20 March 2000.

[Meaning of "settlor"

12 The provisions of section 79(1) and (3) to (5) (meaning of "settlor") apply for the purposes of this Schedule as they apply for the purposes of sections 77 and 78.]¹

Amendments—¹ This Schedule inserted by FA 2000 s 91(2), (3), Sch 24 with effect for any disposal of an interest in settled property made, or the effective completion of which falls, after 20 March 2000.

[Cases where there is a period between the beginning of the disposal and its effective completion

13—(1) This paragraph applies in a case where there is a period between the beginning of the disposal of an interest in settled property and the effective completion of the disposal.

(2) For the purposes of this Schedule—

(a) the beginning of the disposal is—

(i) in the case of a disposal involving the exercise of an option, when the option is granted, and

(ii) in any other case of a disposal under a contract, when the contract is entered into; and

(b) the effective completion of the disposal means the point at which the person acquiring the interest becomes for practical purposes unconditionally entitled to the whole of the intended subject matter of the disposal.

(3) Where this paragraph applies and the beginning of the disposal and its effective completion fall in different years of assessment—

(a) the deemed disposal is treated as taking place in the year of assessment in which the disposal is effectively completed;

(b) the condition in paragraph 5 (condition as to residence of trustees) is treated as met if it is met in relation to either of those years of assessment or any intervening year;

(c) the condition in paragraph 6 (condition as to residence of settlor) is treated as met if it is met in relation to either or both of those years of assessment or any intervening year; and

(d) the relevant period for the purposes of paragraph 7 (condition as to settlor interest) is the period—

(i) beginning two years before the beginning of the first of those years of assessment, and

(ii) ending with the effective completion of the disposal.

(4) If the identity or value of the underlying assets changes during the period between the beginning of the disposal and its effective completion, the following provisions apply—

(a) an asset is treated as comprised in the settled property and, where relevant, in any specific fund or other defined part of the settled property to which the deemed disposal relates if it is so comprised at any time in that period;

(b) the market value of any asset for the purposes of the deemed disposal is taken to be its highest market value at any time during that period.

(5) The provisions in sub-paragraph (4) do not apply to an asset if during that period it is disposed of by the trustees under a bargain at arm's length and is not reacquired.]¹

Amendments—¹ This Schedule inserted by FA 2000 s 91(2), (3), Sch 24 with effect for any disposal of an interest in settled property made, or the effective completion of which falls, after 20 March 2000.

[Exception: maintenance funds for historic buildings

14 If the trustees of a settlement have elected that section 691(2) of the Taxes Act (certain income of maintenance funds for historic buildings not to be income of settlor etc) shall have effect in the case of a settlement or part of a settlement in relation to a year of assessment, this Schedule does not apply in relation to the settlement or part for that year.]¹

Amendments—¹ This Schedule inserted by FA 2000 s 91(2), (3), Sch 24 with effect for any disposal of an interest in settled property made, or the effective completion of which falls, after 20 March 2000.

[SCHEDULE 4B

TRANSFERS OF VALUE BY TRUSTEES LINKED WITH TRUSTEE BORROWING][1]

Section 76B

Commentary—*Simon's Direct Tax Service* C4.452.
Amendments—[1] This Schedule inserted by FA 2000 s 92(2), (5), Sch 25 with effect for any transfer of value in relation to which the material time is after 20 March 2000.

[General scheme of this Schedule

1—(1) This Schedule applies where trustees of a settlement—

(a) make a transfer of value (see paragraph 2) in a year of assessment in which the settlement is within section 77, 86 or 87 (see paragraph 3), and

(b) in accordance with this Schedule the transfer of value is treated as linked with trustee borrowing (see paragraphs 4 to 9).

(2) Where this Schedule applies the trustees are treated as disposing of and immediately reacquiring the whole or a proportion of each of the chargeable assets that continue to form part of the settled property (see paragraphs 10 to 13).][1]

Amendments—[1] This Schedule inserted by FA 2000 s 92(2), (5), Sch 25 with effect for any transfer of value in relation to which the material time is after 20 March 2000.

[Transfers of value

2—(1) For the purposes of this Schedule trustees of a settlement make a transfer of value if they—

(a) lend money or any other asset to any person,

(b) transfer an asset to any person and receive either no consideration or a consideration whose amount or value is less than the market value of the asset transferred, or

(c) issue a security of any description to any person and receiver either no consideration or a consideration whose amount or value is less than the value of the security.

(2) References in this Schedule to "the material time", in relation to a transfer of value, are to the time when the loan is made, the transfer is effectively completed or the security is issued.

The effective completion of a transfer means the point at which the person acquiring the asset becomes for practical purposes unconditionally entitled to the whole of the intended subject matter of the transfer.

(3) In the case of a loan, the amount of value transferred is taken to be the market value of the asset.

(4) In the case of a transfer, the amount of value transferred is taken to be—

(a) if any part of the value of the asset is attributable to trustee borrowing, the market value of the asset;

(b) if no part of the value of the asset is attributable to trustee borrowing, the market value of the asset reduced by the amount or value of any consideration received for it.

Paragraph 12 below explains what is meant by the value of an asset being attributable to trustee borrowing.

(5) In the case of the issue of a security, the amount of value transferred shall be taken to be the value of the security reduced by the amount or value of any consideration received by the trustees for it.

(6) References in this paragraph to the value of an asset are to its value immediately before the material time, unless the asset does not exist before that time in which case its value immediately after that time shall be taken.][1]

Amendments—[1] This Schedule inserted by FA 2000 s 92(2), (5), Sch 25 with effect for any transfer of value in relation to which the material time is after 20 March 2000.

[Settlements within section 77, 86 or 87

3—(1) This paragraph explains what is meant in this Schedule by a settlement being "within section 77, 86 or 87" in a year of assessment.

(2) A settlement is "within section 77" in a year of assessment if, assuming—

(a) that there were chargeable gains accruing to the trustees from the disposal of any or all of the settled property, and

(b) that the condition in subsection (1)(b) of that section was met,

chargeable gains would, under that section, be treated as accruing to the settlor in that year.

Expressions used in this sub-paragraph have the same meaning as in section 77.

(3) A settlement is "within section 86" in a year of assessment if, assuming—

(a) that there were chargeable gains accruing to the trustees by virtue of disposals of any of the settled property originating from the settlor, and (*b*) that the other elements of the condition in subsection (1)(*e*) of that section were met,

chargeable gains would, under that section, be treated as accruing to the settlor in that year.

Expressions used in this sub-paragraph have the same meaning as in section 86.

(4) A settlement is "within section 87" in a year of assessment if, assuming—

(*a*) there were trust gains for the year within the meaning of subsection (2) of that section, and
(*b*) that beneficiaries of the settlement received capital payments from the trustees in that year or had received such payments in an earlier year,

chargeable gains would, under that section or section 89(2), be treated as accruing to the beneficiaries in that year.

Expressions used in this sub-paragraph have the same meaning as in section 87.]¹

Amendments—¹ This Schedule inserted by FA 2000 s 92(2), (5), Sch 25 with effect for any transfer of value in relation to which the material time is after 20 March 2000.

[*Trustee borrowing*

4—(1) For the purposes of this Schedule trustees of a settlement are treated as borrowing if—

(*a*) money or any other asset is lent to them, or
(*b*) an asset is transferred to them and in connection with the transfer the trustees assume a contractual obligation (whether absolute or conditional) to restore or transfer to any person that or any other asset.

In the following provisions of this Schedule "loan obligation" includes any such obligation as is mentioned in paragraph (*b*).

(2) The amount borrowed (the "proceeds" of the borrowing) is taken to be—

(*a*) in the case of a loan, the market value of the asset;
(*b*) in the case of a transfer, the market value of the asset reduced by the amount or value of any consideration received for it.

(3) References in this paragraph to the market value of an asset are to its market value immediately before the loan is made, or the transfer is effectively completed, unless the asset does not exist before that time in which case its market value immediately after that time shall be taken.

The effective completion of a transfer means the point at which the person acquiring the asset becomes for practical purposes unconditionally entitled to the whole of the intended subject matter of the transfer.]¹

Amendments—¹ This Schedule inserted by FA 2000 s 92(2), (5), Sch 25 with effect for any transfer of value in relation to which the material time is after 20 March 2000.

[*Transfer of value linked with trustee borrowing*

5—(1) For the purposes of this Schedule a transfer of value by trustees is treated as linked with trustee borrowing if at the material time there is outstanding trustee borrowing.

(2) For the purposes of this Schedule there is outstanding trustee borrowing at any time to the extent that—

(*a*) any loan obligation is outstanding, and
(*b*) there are proceeds of trustee borrowing that have not been either—

(i) applied for normal trust purposes, or
(ii) taken into account under this Schedule in relation to an earlier transfer of value.

(3) An amount of trustee borrowing is "taken into account" under this Schedule in relation to a transfer of value if the transfer of value is in accordance with this Schedule treated as linked with trustee borrowing.

The amount so taken into account is—

(*a*) the amount of the value transferred by that transfer of value, or
(*b*) if less, the amount of outstanding trustee borrowing at the material time in relation to that transfer of value.]¹

Amendments—¹ This Schedule inserted by FA 2000 s 92(2), (5), Sch 25 with effect for any transfer of value in relation to which the material time is after 20 March 2000.

[*Application of proceeds of borrowing for normal trust purposes*

6—(1) For the purposes of this Schedule the proceeds of trustee borrowing are applied for normal trust purposes in the following circumstances, and not otherwise.

(2) They are applied for normal trust purposes if they are applied by the trustees in making a payment in respect of an ordinary trust asset and the following conditions are met—

(*a*) the payment is made under a transaction at arm's length or is not more than the payment that would be made if the transaction were at arm's length;
(*b*) the asset forms part of the settled property immediately after the material time or, if it does not do so, the alternative condition in paragraph 8 below is met; and

(*c*) the sum paid is (or but for section 17 or 39 would be) allowable under section 38 as a deduction in computing a gain accruing to the trustees on a disposal of the asset.

(3) They are applied for normal trust purposes if—

(*a*) they are applied by the trustees in wholly or partly discharging a loan obligation of the trustees, and

(*b*) the whole of the proceeds of the borrowing connected with that obligation (or all but an insignificant amount) have been applied by the trustees for normal trust purposes.

(4) They are applied for normal trust purposes if they are applied by the trustees in making payments to meet bona fide current expenses incurred by them in administering the settlement or any of the settled property.]¹

Amendments—¹ This Schedule inserted by FA 2000 s 92(2), (5), Sch 25 with effect for any transfer of value in relation to which the material time is after 20 March 2000.

[*Ordinary trust assets*

7—(1) The following are "ordinary trust assets" for the purposes of this Schedule—

(*a*) shares or securities;

(*b*) tangible property, whether movable or immovable, or a lease of such property;

(*c*) property not within paragraph (*a*) or (*b*) which is used for the purposes of a trade, profession or vocation carried on—

(i) by the trustees, or

(ii) by a beneficiary who has an interest in possession in the settled property;

(*d*) any right in or over, or any interest in, property of a description within paragraph (*b*) or (*c*).

(2) In sub-paragraph (1)(*a*) "securities" has the same meaning as in section 132.]¹

Amendments—¹ This Schedule inserted by FA 2000 s 92(2), (5), Sch 25 with effect for any transfer of value in relation to which the material time is after 20 March 2000.

[*The alternative condition for assets no longer part of the settled property*

8—(1) The alternative condition referred to in paragraph 6(2)(*b*) in relation to an asset which no longer forms part of the settled property is that—

(*a*) the asset is treated as having been disposed of by virtue of section 24(1), or

(*b*) one or more ordinary trust assets which taken together directly or indirectly represent the asset—

(i) form part of the settled property immediately after the material time, or

(ii) are treated as having been disposed of by virtue of section 24(1).

(2) Where there has been a part disposal of the asset, the condition in paragraph 6(2)(*b*) and the provisions of sub-paragraph (1) above may be applied in any combination in relation to the subject matter of the part disposal and what remains.

(3) References in this paragraph to an asset include part of an asset.]¹

Amendments—¹ This Schedule inserted by FA 2000 s 92(2), (5), Sch 25 with effect for any transfer of value in relation to which the material time is after 20 March 2000.

[*Normal trust purposes: power to make provision by regulations*

9—(1) The Treasury may make provision by regulations as to the circumstances in which the proceeds of trustee borrowing are to be treated for the purposes of this Schedule as applied for normal trust purposes.

(2) The regulations may—

(*a*) add to, amend or repeal any of the provisions of paragraphs 6 to 8 above,

(*b*) make different provision for different cases, and

(*c*) contain such supplementary, incidental, consequential and transitional provision as the Treasury may think fit.]¹

Amendments—¹ This Schedule inserted by FA 2000 s 92(2), (5), Sch 25 with effect for any transfer of value in relation to which the material time is after 20 March 2000.

[*Deemed disposal of remaining chargeable assets*

10—(1) Where in accordance with this Schedule a transfer of value by trustees is treated as linked with trustee borrowing, the trustees are treated for all purposes of this Act—

(*a*) as having at the material time disposed of, and

(*b*) as having immediately reacquired,

the whole or a proportion (see paragraph 11) of each of the chargeable assets that form part of the settled property immediately after the material time ("the remaining chargeable assets").

(2) The deemed disposal and reacquisition shall be taken—

(a) to be for a consideration equal to the whole or, as the case may be, a proportion of the market value of each of those assets, and

(b) to be under a bargain at arm's length.

(3) For the purposes of sub-paragraph (1) an asset is a chargeable asset if a gain on a disposal of the asset by the trustees at the material time would be a chargeable gain.][1]

Amendments—[1] This Schedule inserted by FA 2000 s 92(2), (5), Sch 25 with effect for any transfer of value in relation to which the material time is after 20 March 2000.

[Whether deemed disposal is of whole or a proportion of the assets

11—(1) This paragraph provides for determining whether the deemed disposal and reacquisition is of the whole or a proportion of each of the remaining chargeable assets.

(2) If the amount of value transferred—

(a) is less than the amount of outstanding trustee borrowing, and

(b) is also less than the effective value of the remaining chargeable assets,

the deemed disposal and reacquisition is of the proportion of each of the remaining chargeable assets given by:

$$\frac{VT}{EV}$$

where—

VT is the amount of value transferred, and

EV is the effective value of the remaining chargeable assets.

(3) If the amount of value transferred—

(a) is not less than the amount of outstanding trustee borrowing, but

(b) is less than the effective value of the remaining chargeable assets,

the deemed disposal and reacquisition is of the proportion of each of the remaining chargeable assets given by:

$$\frac{TB}{EV}$$

where—

TB is the amount of outstanding trustee borrowing, and

EV is the effective value of the remaining chargeable assets.

(4) In any other case the deemed disposal and reacquisition is of the whole of each of the remaining chargeable assets.

(5) For the purposes of this paragraph the effective value of the remaining chargeable assets means the aggregate market value of those assets reduced by so much of that value as is attributable to trustee borrowing.

(6) References in this paragraph to amounts or values, except in relation to the amount of value transferred, are to amounts or values immediately after the material time.][1]

Amendments—[1] This Schedule inserted by FA 2000 s 92(2), (5), Sch 25 with effect for any transfer of value in relation to which the material time is after 20 March 2000.

[Value attributable to trustee borrowing

12—(1) For the purposes of this Schedule the value of an asset is attributable to trustee borrowing to the extent determined in accordance with the following rules.

(2) Where the asset itself has been borrowed by trustees, the value of the asset is attributable to trustee borrowing to the extent that the proceeds of that borrowing have not been applied for normal trust purposes.

This is in addition to any extent to which the value of the asset may be attributable to trustee borrowing by virtue of sub-paragraph (3).

(3) The value of any asset is attributable to trustee borrowing to the extent that—

(a) the trustees have applied the proceeds of trustee borrowing in acquiring or enhancing the value of the asset, or

(b) the asset represents directly or indirectly an asset whose value was attributable to the trustees having so applied the proceeds of trustee borrowing.

(4) For the purposes of this paragraph an amount is applied by the trustees in acquiring or enhancing the value of an asset if it is applied wholly and exclusively by them—

(a) as consideration in money or money's worth for the acquisition of the asset,

(b) for the purpose of enhancing the value of the asset in a way that is reflected in the state or nature of the asset,

(c) in establishing, preserving or defending their title to, or to a right over, the asset, or (*d*) where the asset is a holding of shares or securities that is treated as a single asset, by way of consideration in money or money's worth for additional shares or securities forming part of the same holding.

(5) Trustees are treated as applying the proceeds of borrowing as mentioned in sub-paragraph (4) if and to the extent that at the time the expenditure is incurred there is outstanding trustee borrowing.

(6) In sub-paragraph (4)(*d*) "securities" has the same meaning as in section 132.]¹

Amendments—¹ This Schedule inserted by FA 2000 s 92(2), (5), Sch 25 with effect for any transfer of value in relation to which the material time is after 20 March 2000.

[*Assets and transfers*

[**13**—(1) In this Schedule any reference to an asset includes money expressed in sterling. References to the value or market value of such an asset are to its amount.

(2) Subject to sub-paragraph (3), references in this Schedule to the transfer of an asset include anything that is or is treated as a disposal of the asset for the purposes of this Act, or would be if sub-paragraph (1) above applied generally for the purposes of this Act.

(3) References in this Schedule to a transfer of an asset do not include a transfer of an asset that is created by the part disposal of another asset.]¹

Amendments—¹ This Schedule inserted by FA 2000 s 92(2), (5), Sch 25 with effect for any transfer of value in relation to which the material time is after 20 March 2000.

[SCHEDULE 4C

TRANSFERS OF VALUE: ATTRIBUTION OF GAINS TO BENEFICIARIES]¹

Section 85A

Amendments—¹ This Schedule inserted by FA 2000 s 92(4), (5), Sch 26 Pt I with effect for any transfer of value in relation to which the material time is after 20 March 2000.

[*Introduction*

1—(1) This Schedule applies where in any year of assessment a chargeable gain or allowable loss accrues by virtue of Schedule 4B to trustees of a settlement within section 87.

For this purpose a settlement is "within section 87" for a year of assessment if in that year the conditions specified in section 87(1) or section 88(1) are met in relation to the trustees of the settlement.

(2) The provisions of this Schedule have effect in relation to any such chargeable gain or allowable loss as is mentioned in sub-paragraph (1) above in place of the provisions of sections 86A to 95.

(3) No account shall be taken—

    (*a*) of any such chargeable gain or allowable loss in computing the trust gains for a year of assessment in accordance with sections 87 to 89; or

    (*b*) of any chargeable gain or allowable loss to which those sections apply in computing the Schedule 4B trust gains in accordance with this Schedule.]¹

Revenue Internal Guidance—Capital Gains Manual CG 35122 (applicable also to non-resident settlements).
Amendments—¹ This Schedule inserted by FA 2000 s 92(4), (5), Sch 26 Pt I with effect for any transfer of value in relation to which the material time is after 20 March 2000.

[*General scheme of this Schedule*

2 The general scheme of this Schedule is that—

    (*a*) Schedule 4B trust gains are attributed to beneficiaries—

        (i) of the transferor settlement, or

        (ii) of any transferee settlement,

    who have received capital payments from the trustees; and

    (*b*) any allowable loss accruing by virtue of Schedule 4B may only be set against a chargeable gain so accruing.]¹

Revenue Internal Guidance—Capital Gains Manual CG 35125 (sub-s (1) includes the disposals of assets such as government stock and a dwelling house occupied as a beneficiary's principal private residence).
CG 35128 (sub-s (2) illustration of how the term "effectively completed" is applied in practice).
Amendments—¹ This Schedule inserted by FA 2000 s 92(4), (5), Sch 26 Pt I with effect for any transfer of value in relation to which the material time is after 20 March 2000.

[*Computation of Schedule 4B trust gains*

3—(1) This paragraph explains what is meant for the purposes of this Schedule by "Schedule 4B trust gains".

(2) The Schedule 4B trust gains are computed in relation to each transfer of value to which that Schedule applies.

(3) In relation to a transfer of value the amount of the Schedule 4B trust gains for the purposes of this Schedule is given by—

$$CA - SG - AL$$

where—

CA is the chargeable amount computed under paragraph 4 or 5 below,
SG is the amount of any gains attributed to the settlor that fall to be deducted under paragraph 6 below, and
AL is the amount of any allowable losses that may be deducted under paragraph 7 below.]¹

Amendments—¹ This Schedule inserted by FA 2000 s 92(4), (5), Sch 26 Pt I with effect for any transfer of value in relation to which the material time is after 20 March 2000.

[Chargeable amount: non-resident settlement

4—(1) If the transfer of value is made in a year of assessment during which the trustees of the transferor settlement are at no time resident or ordinarily resident in the United Kingdom the chargeable amount is computed under this paragraph.

(2) Where this paragraph applies the chargeable amount is the amount on which the trustees would have been chargeable to tax under section 2(2) by virtue of Schedule 4B if they had been resident or ordinarily resident in the United Kingdom in the year.]¹

Amendments—¹ This Schedule inserted by FA 2000 s 92(4), (5), Sch 26 Pt I with effect for any transfer of value in relation to which the material time is after 20 March 2000.

[Chargeable amount: dual resident settlement

5—(1) If the transfer of value is made in a year of assessment where—

(*a*) the trustees of the transferor settlement are resident in the United Kingdom during any part of the year or ordinarily resident in the United Kingdom during the year, and
(*b*) at any time of such residence or ordinary residence they fall to be regarded for the purposes of any double taxation relief arrangements as resident in a territory outside the United Kingdom,

the chargeable amount is computed under this paragraph.

(2) Where this paragraph applies the chargeable amount is the lesser of—

(*a*) the amount on which the trustees would be chargeable to tax under section 2(2) by virtue of Schedule 4B on the assumption that the double taxation relief arrangements did not apply, and
(*b*) the amount on which the trustees would be so chargeable to tax by virtue of disposals of protected assets.

(3) For this purpose "protected assets" has the meaning given by section 88(4).]¹

Amendments—¹ This Schedule inserted by FA 2000 s 92(4), (5), Sch 26 Pt I with effect for any transfer of value in relation to which the material time is after 20 March 2000.

[Gains attributed to settlor

6—(1) For the purposes of this Schedule the chargeable amount in relation to a transfer of value shall be reduced by the amount of any chargeable gains arising by virtue of that transfer of value that—

(*a*) are by virtue of section 86(4) treated as accruing to the settlor, or
(*b*) where section 10A applies, are treated by virtue of that section (as it has effect subject to paragraph 12 below) as accruing to the settlor in the year of return.

(2) In determining for the purposes of sub-paragraph (1)(*a*) the amount of chargeable gains arising by virtue of a transfer of value that are treated as accruing to the settlor, there shall be disregarded any losses which arise otherwise than by virtue of Schedule 4B.

(3) In computing the chargeable amount in relation to a transfer of value the effect of sections 77 to 79 shall be ignored.]¹

Amendments—¹ This Schedule inserted by FA 2000 s 92(4), (5), Sch 26 Pt I with effect for any transfer of value in relation to which the material time is after 20 March 2000.

[Reduction for allowable losses

7—(1) An allowable loss arising under Schedule 4B in relation to a transfer of value by the trustees of a settlement may be taken into account in accordance with this paragraph to reduce for the purposes of this Schedule the chargeable amount in relation to another transfer of value by those trustees.

(2) Any such allowable loss goes first to reduce chargeable amounts arising from other transfers of value made in the same year of assessment.

If there is more than one chargeable amount and the aggregate amount of the allowable losses is less than the aggregate of the chargeable amounts, each of the chargeable amounts is reduced proportionately.

(3) If in any year of assessment the aggregate amount of the allowable losses exceeds the aggregate of the chargeable amounts, the excess shall be carried forward to the next year of assessment and treated for the purposes of this paragraph as if it were an allowable loss arising in relation to a transfer of value made in that year.

(4) Any reduction of a chargeable amount under this paragraph is made after any deduction under paragraph 6.

Amendments—[1] This Schedule inserted by FA 2000 s 92(4), (5), Sch 26 Pt I with effect for any transfer of value in relation to which the material time is after 20 March 2000.

[Attribution of gains to beneficiaries]

8—(1) The Schedule 4B trust gains relating to a transfer of value shall be treated as chargeable gains accruing to beneficiaries—

    (*a*) of the transferor settlement, and
    (*b*) of any transferee settlement,

in accordance with the following rules.

(2) The Schedule 4B trust gains shall be treated as chargeable gains accruing to beneficiaries who—

    (*a*) receive capital payments from the trustees in the year of assessment in which the transfer of value is made, or
    (*b*) have received such payments in any earlier year,

to the extent that such payments exceed the amount of any gains attributed to the beneficiaries under section 87(4) or 89(2).

(3) Any Schedule 4B trust gains remaining after the application of sub-paragraph (2) in relation to the year of assessment in which the transfer of value was made shall be carried forward to the following year of assessment and treated for the purposes of this paragraph as if they were gains from a transfer of value made in that year.

(4) The attribution of chargeable gains to beneficiaries under this paragraph shall be made in proportion to, but shall not exceed, the amounts of the capital payments received by them.

Amendments—[1] This Schedule inserted by FA 2000 s 92(4), (5), Sch 26 Pt I with effect for any transfer of value in relation to which the material time is after 20 March 2000.

[Attribution of gains to beneficiaries: supplementary]

9—(1) A capital payment shall be left out of account—

    (*a*) for the purposes of paragraph 8, to the extent that chargeable gains have, by reason of it, been treated as accruing to the recipient in an earlier year of assessment; and
    (*b*) for the purposes of sections 87(4) and (5) and 89(2), to the extent that chargeable gains have, by reason of it, been treated as accruing to the recipient under paragraph 8.

(2) A beneficiary shall not be charged to tax on chargeable gains treated by virtue of paragraph 8 as accruing to him in any year unless he is domiciled in the United Kingdom at some time in that year.

(3) For the purposes of paragraph 8 capital payments received—

    (*a*) before 21st March 2000, or
    (*b*) before the year of assessment preceding the year of assessment in which the transfer of value is made,

shall be disregarded.

Amendments—[1] This Schedule inserted by FA 2000 s 92(4), (5), Sch 26 Pt I with effect for any transfer of value in relation to which the material time is after 20 March 2000.

[Residence of trustees from whom capital payment received]

10—(1) Subject to sub-paragraph (2) below, it is immaterial for the purposes of paragraph 8 that the trustees of the transferor settlement, or any transferee settlement, are or have at any time been resident or ordinarily resident in the United Kingdom.

(2) A capital payment received by a beneficiary of a settlement from the trustees in a year of assessment—

    (*a*) during the whole of which the trustees are resident in the United Kingdom, or
    (*b*) in which the trustees are ordinarily resident in the United Kingdom,

shall be disregarded for the purposes of paragraph 8 if it was made before, but was not made in anticipation of, chargeable gains accruing under Schedule 4B or of a transfer of value being made to which that Schedule applies.

(3) For the purposes of sub-paragraph (2) the trustees of a settlement shall not be regarded as resident or ordinarily resident in the United Kingdom at any time when they fall to be regarded for the purposes of any double taxation relief arrangements as resident in a territory outside the United Kingdom.

Amendments—[1] This Schedule inserted by FA 2000 s 92(4), (5), Sch 26 Pt I with effect for any transfer of value in relation to which the material time is after 20 March 2000.

[Taper relief

11 Without prejudice to so much of this Schedule as requires section 2A to be applied in the computation of the amount of Schedule 4B trust gains, chargeable gains that are treated as accruing to beneficiaries under this Schedule shall not be eligible for taper relief.

Amendments—¹ This Schedule inserted by FA 2000 s 92(4), (5), Sch 26 Pt I with effect for any transfer of value in relation to which the material time is after 20 March 2000.

[Attribution of gains to settlor in section 10A cases

12—(1) This paragraph applies where by virtue of section 10A an amount of gains—

  (*a*) arising under Schedule 4B in an intervening year, and
  (*b*) falling within section 86(1)(*e*),

would (apart from this Schedule) be treated as accruing to a person (''the settlor'') in the year of return.

(2) Where this paragraph applies, only so much (if any) of the Schedule 4B trust gains falling within section 86(1)(*e*) as exceeds the amount charged to beneficiaries shall fall in accordance with section 10A to be attributed to the settlor for the year of return.

(3) The ''amount charged to beneficiaries'' means, subject to sub-paragraph (4) below, the total of the amounts on which beneficiaries of the transferor or transferee settlements are charged to tax under this Schedule by reference to those gains for all the intervening years.

(4) Where the property comprised in the transferor settlement has at any time included property not originating from the settlor, only so much (if any) of any capital payment taken into account for the purposes of paragraph 8 above as, on a just and reasonable apportionment, is properly referable to property originating from the settlor shall be taken into account in computing the amount charged to beneficiaries.

(5) Expressions used in this paragraph and section 10A have the same meanings in this paragraph as in that section; and paragraph 8 of Schedule 5 shall apply for the construction of the references in sub-paragraph (4) above to property originating from the settlor as it applies for the purposes of that Schedule.

Amendments—¹ This Schedule inserted by FA 2000 s 92(4), (5), Sch 26 Pt I with effect for any transfer of value in relation to which the material time is after 20 March 2000.

[Increase in tax payable under this Schedule

13—(1) This paragraph applies where—

  (*a*) a capital payment is made by the trustees of a settlement,
  (*b*) the payment is made in circumstances where paragraph 8 above treats chargeable gains as accruing in respect of the payment, and
  (*c*) a beneficiary is charged to tax in respect of the payment by virtue of that paragraph.

(2) The tax payable by the beneficiary in respect of the payment shall be increased by the amount found under sub-paragraph (3) below, except that it shall not be increased beyond the amount of the payment; and an assessment may charge tax accordingly.

(3) The amount is one equal to the interest that would be yielded if an amount equal to the tax which would be payable by the beneficiary in respect of the payment (apart from this paragraph) carried interest for the chargeable period at the specified rate.

The ''specified rate'' means the rate for the time being specified in section 91(3).

(4) The chargeable period is the period which—

  (*a*) begins with the later of the 2 days specified in sub-paragraph (5) below, and
  (*b*) ends with 30th November in the year of assessment following that in which the capital payment is made.

(5) The 2 days are—

  (*a*) 1st December in the year of assessment following that in which the transfer of value was made, and
  (*b*) 1st December falling 6 years before 1st December in the year of assessment following that in which the capital payment is made.

Amendments—¹ This Schedule inserted by FA 2000 s 92(4), (5), Sch 26 Pt I with effect for any transfer of value in relation to which the material time is after 20 March 2000.

[Interpretation

14—(1) In this Schedule—

  (*a*) ''transfer of value'' has the same meaning as in Schedule 4B; and
  (*b*) references to the time at which a transfer of value was made are to the time which is the material time for the purposes of that Schedule.

(2) In this Schedule, in relation to a transfer of value—

(a) references to the transferor settlement are to the settlement the trustees of which made the transfer of value; and

(b) references to a transferee settlement are to any settlement of which the settled property includes property representing, directly or indirectly, the proceeds of the transfer of value.

(3) References in this Schedule to beneficiaries of a settlement include—

(a) persons who have ceased to be beneficiaries by the time the chargeable gains accrue, and

(b) persons who were beneficiaries of the settlement before it ceased to exist,

but who were beneficiaries of the settlement at a time in a previous year of assessment when a capital payment was made to them.]

Amendments—¹ This Schedule inserted by FA 2000 s 92(4), (5), Sch 26 Pt I with effect for any transfer of value in relation to which the material time is after 20 March 2000.

SCHEDULE 5

ATTRIBUTION OF GAINS TO SETTLORS WITH INTEREST IN NON-RESIDENT OR DUAL RESIDENT SETTLEMENT

Section 86

Concession D40—Non-resident trusts: definition of "participator".
Statement of Practice SP 5/92—Revenue's practice in applying the rules (contained in ss 80–98 of this Act and this Schedule) for capital gains of certain offshore trusts.
Revenue & other press releases—IR Tax Bulletin August 1993 p 82 (guidance issued on certain points arising in SP 5/92 relating to rights of reimbursement and administrative expenses).

Construction of section 86(1)(e)

1—(1) In construing section 86(1)(e) as regards a particular year of assessment, the effect of sections 3 and 77 to 79 shall be ignored.

(2) In construing section 86(1)(e) as regards a particular year of assessment—

(a) any deductions provided for by section 2(2) shall be made in respect of disposals of any of the settled property originating from the settlor, and

(b) section 16(3) shall be assumed not to prevent losses accruing to trustees in one year of assessment from being allowed as a deduction from chargeable gains accruing in a later year of assessment (so far as not previously set against gains).

(3) In a case where—

(a) the trustees [are participators in a company in respect of property which originates]¹ from the settlor, and

(b) under section 13 gains or losses would be treated as accruing to the trustees in a particular year of assessment by virtue of [so much of their interest as participators as arises from that property]¹ if the assumption as to residence specified in section 86(3) were made,

the gains or losses shall be taken into account in construing section 86(1)(e) as regards that year as if they had accrued by virtue of disposals of settled property originating from the settlor. [Subsections (12) and (13) of section 13 shall apply for the purposes of this sub-paragraph as they apply for the purposes of that section.]¹

(4) Where, as regards a particular year of assessment, there would be an amount under section 86(1)(e) (apart from this sub-paragraph) and the trustees fall within section 86(2)(b), the following rules shall apply—

(a) assume that the references in section 86(1)(e) and sub-paragraphs (2)(a) and (3) above to settled property originating from the settlor were to such of it as constitutes protected assets;

(b) assume that the reference in sub-paragraph (3)(a) above to shares originating from the settlor were to such of them as constitute protected assets;

(c) find the amount (if any) which would be arrived at under section 86(1)(e) on those assumptions;

(d) if no amount is so found there shall be deemed to be no amount for the purposes of section 86(1)(e);

(e) if an amount is found under paragraph (c) above it must be compared with the amount arrived at under section 86(1)(e) apart from this sub-paragraph and the smaller of the 2 shall be taken to be the amount arrived at under section 86(1)(e).

(5) Sub-paragraphs (2) to (4) above shall have effect subject to sub-paragraphs (6) and (7) below.

(6) The following rules shall apply in construing section 86(1)(e) as regards a particular year of assessment ("the year concerned") in a case where the trustees fall within section 86(2)(a)—

(a) if the conditions mentioned in section 86(1) are not fulfilled as regards the settlement in any year of assessment falling before the year concerned, no deductions shall be made in respect of losses accruing before the year concerned;

(b) if the conditions mentioned in section 86(1) are fulfilled as regards the settlement in any year or years of assessment falling before the year concerned, no deductions shall be made in respect of losses accruing before that year (or the first of those years) so falling, but nothing in the preceding provisions of this sub-paragraph shall prevent deductions being made in respect of losses accruing in a year of assessment in which the conditions mentioned in section 86(1)(*a*) to (*d*) and (*f*) are fulfilled as regards the settlement.

(7) In construing section 86(1)(*e*) as regards a particular year of assessment and in relation to a settlement created before 19th March 1991, no account shall be taken of disposals made before 19th March 1991 (whether for the purpose of arriving at gains or for the purpose of arriving at losses).

(8) For the purposes of sub-paragraph (4) above assets are protected assets if—

(*a*) they are of a description specified in the arrangements mentioned in section 86(2)(*b*), and
(*b*) were the trustees to dispose of them at any relevant time, the trustees would fall to be regarded for the purposes of the arrangements as not liable in the United Kingdom to tax on gains accruing to them on the disposal.

(9) For the purposes of sub-paragraph (8) above—

(*a*) the assumption as to residence specified in section 86(3) shall be ignored;
(*b*) a relevant time is any time, in the year of assessment concerned, when the trustees fall to be regarded for the purposes of the arrangements as resident in a territory outside the United Kingdom;
(*c*) if different assets are identified by reference to different relevant times, all of them are protected assets.

Commentary—*Simon's Direct Tax Service* **C4.440, 447.**
Definitions—"Asset", s 21(1); "chargeable gain", s 15(2); "company", ss 99, 288(1); "participator", s 13(13), TA 1988 s 417(1); "property originating from a person", Sch 5 para 8(1); "resident", s 9(1); "settled property", s 68; "settlor", Sch 5 para 7; "shares", s 288(1); "year of assessment", s 288(1).
Cross references—See TCGA 1992 Sch 5 para 8 (meaning of words "property originating from a person" appearing in s 86 and this Schedule).
TCGA 1992 Sch 5 para 10 (inspector's powers to obtain information for the purposes of this Schedule and s 86).
Amendments—[1] Words in sub-s (3)(*a*), (*b*) substituted, and words at end of sub-s (3) inserted, by FA 1996 s 174(10), (11) with effect in relation to gains accruing after 27 November 1995.

Test whether settlor has interest

2—(1) For the purposes of section 86(1)(*d*) a settlor has an interest in a settlement if—

(*a*) any relevant property which is or may at any time be comprised in the settlement is, or will or may become, applicable for the benefit of or payable to a defined person in any circumstances whatever,
(*b*) any relevant income which arises or may arise under the settlement is, or will or may become, applicable for the benefit of or payable to a defined person in any circumstances whatever, or
(*c*) any defined person enjoys a benefit directly or indirectly from any relevant property which is comprised in the settlement or any relevant income arising under the settlement;

but this sub-paragraph is subject to sub-paragraphs (4) to (6) [and paragraph 2A][1] below.

(2) For the purposes of sub-paragraph (1) above—

(*a*) relevant property is property originating from the settlor,
(*b*) relevant income is income originating from the settlor.

(3) For the purposes of sub-paragraph (1) above each of the following is a defined person—

(*a*) the settlor,
(*b*) the settlor's spouse;
(*c*) any child of the settlor or of the settlor's spouse;
(*d*) the spouse of any such child;
[(*da*) any grandchild of the settlor or of the settlor's spouse;
(*db*) the spouse of any such grandchild;][2]
(*e*) a company controlled by a person or persons falling within paragraphs (*a*) to [(*db*)][2] above;
(*f*) a company associated with a company falling within paragraph (*e*) above.

(4) A settlor does not have an interest in a settlement by virtue of paragraph (*a*) of sub-paragraph (1) above at any time when none of the property concerned can become applicable or payable as mentioned in that paragraph except in the event of—

(*a*) the bankruptcy of some person who is or may become beneficially entitled to the property,
(*b*) any assignment of or charge on the property being made or given by some such person,
(*c*) in the case of a marriage settlement, the death of both parties to the marriage and of all or any of the children of the marriage, or
(*d*) the death under the age of 25 or some lower age of some person who would be beneficially entitled to the property on attaining that age.

(5) A settlor does not have an interest in a settlement by virtue of paragraph (*a*) of sub-paragraph (1) above at any time when some person is alive and under the age of 25 if during that person's life none of the property concerned can become applicable or payable as mentioned in that paragraph except in the event of that person becoming bankrupt or assigning or charging his interest in the property concerned.

(6) Sub-paragraphs (4) and (5) above apply for the purposes of paragraph (*b*) of sub-paragraph (1) above as they apply for the purposes of paragraph (*a*), reading "income" for "property".

[(7) In this paragraph—

"child" includes a stepchild; and

"grandchild" means a child of a child.][3]

(8) For the purposes of sub-paragraph (3) above the question whether a company is controlled by a person or persons shall be construed in accordance with section 416 of the Taxes Act; but in deciding that question for those purposes no rights or powers of (or attributed to) an associate or associates of a person shall be attributed to him under section 416(6) if he is not a participator in the company.

(9) For the purposes of sub-paragraph (3) above the question whether a company is associated with another shall be construed in accordance with section 416 of the Taxes Act; but where in deciding that question for those purposes it falls to be decided whether a company is controlled by a person or persons, no rights or powers of (or attributed to) an associate or associates of a person shall be attributed to him under section 416(6) if he is not a participator in the company.

(10) In sub-paragraphs (8) and (9) "participator" has the meaning given by section 417(1) of the Taxes Act.

Commentary—*Simon's Direct Tax Service* **C4.439.**
Revenue & other press releases—ICAEW TAX 20/92 14-12-92 (1. the settlor has an interest if any defined person can be added to the class of beneficiaries, but where there is no prima facie possibility of a defined person benefiting, the Revenue will not treat the settlor as having an interest unless the terms of the settlement and the circumstances of the case indicate an intention to benefit a person who is likely to become an defined person. 2. a separated spouse is a spouse unless the separation is permanent).
Definitions—"Company", ss 99, 288(1); "control", s 288(1), TA 1988 s 416; "income originating from a person", Sch 5 para 8(2); "property originating from a person", Sch 5 para 8(1); "recognised stock exchange", s 288(1), TA 1988 s 841; "settlor", Sch 5 para 7; "the Taxes Act", s 288(1).
Cross references—See TCGA 1992 Sch 5 paras 4, 5, (s 86 does not apply if certain conditions in respect of any person falling within sub-para (3)(b)–(d) above are satisfied).
Amendments—[1] Words in sub-para (1) inserted by FA 1998 Sch 22 para 2 with effect from the year 1998–99, and shall be deemed to have applied for the year 1997–98.
[2] Sub-paras (3)(da), (db) inserted, and word in sub-para (3)(e) substituted by FA 1998 s 131(1) with effect from the year 1998–99, and shall be deemed to have applied for the year 1997–98.
[3] Sub-para (7) substituted by FA 1998 s 131(2) with effect from the year 1998–99, and shall be deemed to have applied for the year 1997–98.

[Settlements created before 17th March 1998

2A—(1) In determining for the purposes of section 86(1)(d) whether the settlor has an interest at any time during any year of assessment in a settlement created before 17th March 1998, paragraphs (da) and (db) of paragraph 2(3) above, and the reference to those paragraphs in paragraph 2(3)(e), shall be disregarded unless—

    (a) that year is a year in which one of the four conditions set out in the following provisions of this paragraph becomes fulfilled as regards the settlement; or

    (b) one of those conditions became fulfilled as regards that settlement in any previous year of assessment ending on or after 5th April 1998.

(2) The first condition is (subject to sub-paragraph (3) below) that on or after 17th March 1998 property or income is provided directly or indirectly for the purposes of the settlement—

    (a) otherwise than under a transaction entered into at arm's length, and

    (b) otherwise than in pursuance of a liability incurred by any person before that date.

(3) For the purposes of the first condition, where the settlement's expenses relating to administration and taxation for a year of assessment exceed its income for the year, property or income provided towards meeting those expenses shall be ignored if the value of the property or income so provided does not exceed the difference between the amount of those expenses and the amount of the settlement's income for the year.

(4) The second condition is that—

    (a) the trustees become on or after 17th March 1998 neither resident nor ordinarily resident in the United Kingdom, or

    (b) the trustees, while continuing to be resident and ordinarily resident in the United Kingdom, become on or after 17th March 1998 trustees who fall to be regarded for the purposes of any double taxation relief arrangements as resident in a territory outside the United Kingdom.

(5) The third condition is that on or after 17th March 1998 the terms of the settlement are varied so that any person falling within sub-paragraph (7) below becomes for the first time a person who will or might benefit from the settlement.

(6) The fourth condition is that—

    (a) on or after 17th March 1998 a person falling within sub-paragraph (7) below enjoys a benefit from the settlement for the first time, and

    (b) the person concerned is not one who (looking only at the terms of the settlement immediately before 17th March 1998) would be capable of enjoying a benefit from the settlement on or after that date.

(7) Each of the following persons falls within this sub-paragraph—

    (a) any grandchild of the settlor or of the settlor's spouse;

    (b) the spouse of any such grandchild;

(c) a company controlled by a person or persons falling within paragraph (a) or (b) above;

(d) a company controlled by any such person or persons together with any person or persons (not so falling) each of whom is for the purposes of paragraph 2(1) above a defined person in relation to the settlement;

(e) a company associated with a company falling within paragraph (c) or (d) above.

(8) For the purposes of sub-paragraph (7) above the question whether a company is controlled by a person or persons shall be construed in accordance with section 416 of the Taxes Act; but in deciding that question for those purposes no rights or powers of (or attributed to) an associate or associates of a person shall be attributed to him under section 416(6) if he is not a participator in the company.

(9) For the purposes of sub-paragraph (7) above the question whether one company is associated with another shall be construed in accordance with section 416 of the Taxes Act; but where in deciding that question for those purposes it falls to be decided whether a company is controlled by a person or persons, no rights or powers of (or attributed to) an associate or associates of a person shall be attributed to him under section 416(6) if he is not a participator in the company.

(10) In this paragraph—

"child" includes a step-child;

"grandchild" means a child of a child;

"participator" has the meaning given by section 417(1) of the Taxes Act.]¹

Commentary—*Simon's Direct Tax Service* **C4.439.**
Amendments—¹ This paragraph inserted by FA 1998 Sch 22 para 2 with effect from the year 1998–99, and shall be deemed to have applied for the year 1997–98.

Exceptions from section 86

3 Section 86 does not apply if the settlor dies in the year.

Commentary—*Simon's Direct Tax Service* **C4.439.**
Definition—"Settlor", Sch 5 para 7.

4—(1)This paragraph applies where for the purposes of section 86(1)(d) the settlor has no interest in the settlement at any time in the year except for one of the following reasons, namely, that—

(a) property is, or will or may become, applicable for the benefit of or payable to one of the persons falling within paragraph 2(3)(b) to [(db)]¹ above,

(b) income is, or will or may become, applicable for the benefit of or payable to one of those persons, or

(c) one of those persons enjoys a benefit from property or income.

(2) This paragraph also applies where sub-paragraph (1) above is fulfilled by virtue of 2 or all of paragraphs (a) to (c) being satisfied by reference to the same person.

(3) Where this paragraph applies, section 86 does not apply if the person concerned dies in the year.

(4) In a case where—

(a) this paragraph applies, and

(b) the person concerned falls within paragraph 2(3)(b)[, (d) or (db)]¹ above,

section 86 does not apply if during the year the person concerned ceases to be married to the settlor[, child or grandchild]¹ concerned (as the case may be).

Commentary—*Simon's Direct Tax Service* **C4.439.**
Definition—"Settlor", Sch 5 para 7.
Amendments—¹ Words in sub-paras (1) and (4) substituted by FA 1998 Sch 22 para 3 with effect from the year 1998–99, and shall be deemed to have applied for the year 1997–98.

5—(1) This paragraph applies where for the purposes of section 86(1)(d) the settlor has no interest in the settlement at any time in the year except for the reason that there are 2 or more persons, each of whom—

(a) falls within paragraph 2(3)(b) to [(db)]¹ above, and

(b) stands to gain for the reason stated in sub-paragraph (2) below.

(2) The reason is that—

(a) property is, or will or may become, applicable for his benefit or payable to him,

(b) income is, or will or may become, applicable for his benefit or payable to him,

(c) he enjoys a benefit from property or income, or

(d) 2 or all of paragraphs (a) to (c) above apply in his case.

(3) Where this paragraph applies, section 86 does not apply if each of the persons concerned dies in the year.

Commentary—*Simon's Direct Tax Service* **C4.439.**
Definition—"Settlor", Sch 5 para 7.
Amendments—¹ Word in sub-para (1) substituted by FA 1998 Sch 22 para 3 with effect from the year 1998–99, and shall be deemed to have applied for the year 1997–98.

Right of recovery

6—(1) This paragraph applies where any tax becomes chargeable on, and is paid by, a person in respect of gains treated as accruing to him in a year under section 86(4).

(2) The person shall be entitled to recover the amount of the tax from any person who is a trustee of the settlement.

(3) For the purposes of recovering that amount, the person shall also be entitled to require an inspector to give him a certificate specifying—

    (*a*) the amount of the gains concerned, and
    (*b*) the amount of tax paid,

and any such certificate shall be conclusive evidence of the facts stated in it.

Commentary—*Simon's Direct Tax Service* **C4.440, 447.**
Statement of Practice SP 5/92—Revenue's practice in applying the rules (contained in ss 80–98 of this Act and this Schedule) for capital gains of certain offshore trusts.
Definition—''Notice'', s 288(1).

Meaning of ''settlor''

7 For the purposes of section 86 and this Schedule, a person is a settlor in relation to a settlement if the settled property consists of or includes property originating from him.

Commentary—*Simon's Direct Tax Service* **C4.439.**
Definitions—''Property originating from a person'', Sch 5 para 8(1); ''settled property'', s 68.

Meaning of ''originating''

8—(1) References in section 86 and this Schedule to property originating from a person are references to—

    (*a*) property provided by that person;
    (*b*) property representing property falling within paragraph (*a*) above;
    (*c*) so much of any property representing both property falling within paragraph (*a*) above and other property as, on a just apportionment, can be taken to represent property so falling.

(2) References in this Schedule to income originating from a person are references to—

    (*a*) income from property originating from that person;
    (*b*) income provided by that person.

(3) Where a person who is a settlor in relation to a settlement makes reciprocal arrangements with another person for the provision of property or income, for the purposes of this paragraph—

    (*a*) property or income provided by the other person in pursuance of the arrangements shall be treated as provided by the settlor, but
    (*b*) property or income provided by the settlor in pursuance of the arrangements shall be treated as provided by the other person (and not by the settlor).

(4) For the purposes of this paragraph—

    (*a*) where property is provided by a qualifying company controlled by one person alone at the time it is provided, that person shall be taken to provide it;
    (*b*) where property is provided by a qualifying company controlled by 2 or more persons (taking each one separately) at the time it is provided, those persons shall be taken to provide the property and each one shall be taken to provide an equal share of it;
    (*c*) where property is provided by a qualifying company controlled by 2 or more persons (taking them together) at the time it is provided, the persons who are participators in the company at the time it is provided shall be taken to provide it and each one shall be taken to provide so much of it as is attributed to him on the basis of a just apportionment;

but where a person would be taken to provide less than one-twentieth of any property by virtue of paragraph (*c*) above and apart from this provision, he shall not be taken to provide any of it by virtue of that paragraph.

(5) For the purposes of sub-paragraph (4) above a qualifying company is a close company or a company which would be a close company if it were resident in the United Kingdom.

(6) For the purposes of this paragraph references to property representing other property include references to property representing accumulated income from that other property.

(7) For the purposes of this paragraph property or income is provided by a person if it is provided directly or indirectly by the person.

(8) For the purposes of this paragraph the question whether a company is controlled by a person or persons shall be construed in accordance with section 416 of the Taxes Act; but in deciding that question for those purposes no rights or powers of (or attributed to) an associate or associates of a person shall be attributed to him under section 416(6) if he is not a participator in the company.

(9) In this paragraph ''participator'' has the meaning given by section 417(1) of the Taxes Act.

(10) ...[1]

Commentary—*Simon's Direct Tax Service* **C4.439.**
Concession D40—Non-resident trusts: definition of ''participator''.

Definitions—"Close company", s 288(1), TA 1988 ss 414, 415; "company", ss 99, 288(1); "control", s 288(1), TA 1988 s 416; "resident", s 9(1); "settlor", Sch 5 para 7; "shares", s 288(1); "the Taxes Act", s 288(1).
Amendments—¹ Sub-para (10) repealed by FA 1996 Sch 41 Pt V(30) with effect in relation to gains accruing after 27 November 1995.

Qualifying settlements, and commencement

9—(1) A settlement created on or after 19th March 1991 is a qualifying settlement for the purposes of section 86 and this Schedule in—

(a) the year of assessment in which it is created, and

(b) subsequent years of assessment.

[(1A) Subject to sub-paragraph (1B) below, a settlement created before 19th March 1991 is a qualifying settlement for the purposes of section 86 and this Schedule in—

(a) the year 1999-00, and

(b) subsequent years of assessment.]¹

[(1B) Where a settlement created before 19th March 1991 is a protected settlement immediately after the beginning of 6th April 1999, that settlement shall be treated as a qualifying settlement for the purposes of section 86 and this Schedule in a year of assessment mentioned in sub-paragraph (1A)(a) or (b) above only if—

(a) any of the five conditions set out in subsections (3) to (6A) below becomes fulfilled as regards the settlement in that year; or

(b) any of those five conditions became so fulfilled in any previous year of assessment ending after 19th March 1991.]¹

(2) ...³

(3) The first condition is that on or after 19th March 1991 property or income is provided directly or indirectly for the purposes of the settlement—

(a) otherwise than under a transaction entered into at arm's length, and

(b) otherwise than in pursuance of a liability incurred by any person before that date;

but if the settlement's expenses relating to administration and taxation for a year of assessment exceed its income for the year, property or income provided towards meeting those expenses shall be ignored for the purposes of this condition if the value of the property or income so provided does not exceed the difference between the amount of those expenses and the amount of the settlement's income for the year.

(4) The second condition is that—

(a) the trustees become on or after 19th March 1991 neither resident nor ordinarily resident in the United Kingdom, or

(b) the trustees, while continuing to be resident and ordinarily resident in the United Kingdom, become on or after 19th March 1991 trustees who fall to be regarded for the purposes of any double taxation relief arrangements as resident in a territory outside the United Kingdom.

(5) The third condition is that on or after 19th March 1991 the terms of the settlement are varied so that any person falling within sub-paragraph (7) below becomes for the first time a person who will or might benefit from the settlement.

(6) The fourth condition is that—

(a) on or after 19th March 1991 a person falling within sub-paragraph (7) below enjoys a benefit from the settlement for the first time, and

(b) the person concerned is not one who (looking only at the terms of the settlement immediately before 19th March 1991) would be capable of enjoying a benefit from the settlement on or after that date.

[(6A) The fifth condition is that the settlement ceases to be a protected settlement at any time on or after 6th April 1999.]¹

(7) Each of the following persons falls within this sub-paragraph—

(a) a settlor;

(b) the spouse of a settlor;

(c) any child of a settlor or of a settlor's spouse;

(d) the spouse of any such child;

[(da) any grandchild of a settlor or of a settlor's spouse;

(db) the spouse of any such grandchild;]²

(e) a company controlled by a person or persons falling within paragraphs (a) to [(db)]² above;

(f) a company associated with a company falling within paragraph (e) above.

(8) ...⁴

(9) For the purposes of sub-paragraph (7) above the question whether a company is controlled by a person or persons shall be construed in accordance with section 416 of the Taxes Act; but in deciding that question for those purposes no rights or powers of (or attributed to) an associate or associates of a person shall be attributed to him under section 416(6) if he is not a participator in the company.

(10) For the purposes of sub-paragraph (7) above the question whether one company is associated with another shall be construed in accordance with section 416 of the Taxes Act; but where in deciding that question for those purposes it falls to be decided whether a company is controlled by a person or persons, no rights or powers of (or attributed to) an associate or associates of a person shall be attributed to him under section 416(6) if he is not a participator in the company.

[(10A) Subject to sub-paragraph (10B) below, a settlement is a protected settlement at any time in a year of assessment if at that time the beneficiaries of that settlement are confined to persons falling within some or all of the following descriptions, that is to say—

    (*a*) children of a settlor or of a spouse of a settlor who are under the age of eighteen at that time or who were under that age at the end of the immediately preceding year of assessment;

    (*b*) unborn children of a settlor, of a spouse of a settlor, or of a future spouse of a settlor;

    (*c*) future spouses of any children or future children of a settlor, a spouse of a settlor or any future spouse of a settlor;

    (*d*) a future spouse of a settlor;

    (*e*) persons outside the defined categories.

(10B) For the purposes of sub-paragraph (10A) above a person is outside the defined categories at any time if, and only if, there is no settlor by reference to whom he is at that time a defined person in relation to the settlement for the purposes of paragraph 2(1) above.

(10C) For the purposes of sub-paragraph (10A) above a person is a beneficiary of a settlement if—

    (*a*) there are any circumstances whatever in which relevant property which is or may become comprised in the settlement is or will or may become applicable for his benefit or payable to him;

    (*b*) there are any circumstances whatever in which relevant income which arises or may arise under the settlement is or will or may become applicable for his benefit or payable to him;

    (*c*) he enjoys a benefit directly or indirectly from any relevant property comprised in the settlement or any relevant income arising under the settlement.

(10D) In sub-paragraph (10C) above—

"relevant property" means property originating from a settlor; and

"relevant income" means income originating from a settlor.][1]

[(11) In this paragraph—

"child" includes a step-child;

"grandchild" means a child of a child;

"participator" has the meaning given by section 417(1) of the Taxes Act.][2]

Commentary—*Simon's Direct Tax Service* **C4.438.**
Concession D40—Non-resident trusts: definition of "participator".
Statement of Practice SP 5/92—Revenue's practice in applying the rules (contained in ss 80–89 of this Act and this Schedule) for capital gains of certain offshore trusts.
Revenue Interpretation RI 198—As regards a trust which is set up before 19 March 1991 where the beneficiaries, at 6 April 1999, include both children under 18 and grandchildren as the only members of the settlor's immediate family who can benefit from the trust, the Revenue will not regard the existence of the grandchildren as causing the relevant settlement to fall outside the definition of "protected settlement" for the purposes of sub-paras (10A)–(10D).
Definitions—"Company", ss 99, 288(1); "control", s 288(1), TA 1988 s 416; "double taxation relief arrangements", s 288(1); "ordinarily resident", s 9(1); "resident", s 9(1); "settlor", Sch 5 para 7; "the Taxes Act", s 288(1); "year of assessment", s 288(1).
Amendments—[1] Sub-paras (1A)–(1B), (6A), (10A)–(10D) inserted by FA 1998 s 132 with effect from 31 July 1998, and subject to detailed commencement provisions in FA 1998 Sch 23.
[2] Sub-paras (7)(*da*), (*db*), (11), and word in sub-para (7)(*e*) substituted by FA 1998 Sch 22 para 4 with effect from the year 1998–99, and shall be deemed to have applied for the year 1997–98.
[3] Sub-para (2) repealed prospectively by FA 1998 s 132(2), Sch 27 Pt III(30) for the purpose of determining whether any settlement is a qualifying settlement in the year 1999–00 or any subsequent year of assessment.
[4] Sub-para (8) repealed by FA 1998 s 165, Sch 27 Pt III(30) with effect for the year 1998–99 onwards, and shall be deemed to apply for the year 1997–98.

Information

10 An inspector may by notice require any person who is or has been a trustee of, a beneficiary under, or a settlor in relation to, a settlement to give him within such time as he may direct (which must not be less than 28 days beginning with the day the notice is given) such particulars as he thinks necessary for the purposes of section 86 and this Schedule and specifies in the notice.

Commentary—*Simon's Direct Tax Service* **C4.441.**
Definitions—"Inspector", s 288(1); "notice", s 288(1); "settlor", Sch 5 para 7.

11–14 ...

Commentary—*Simon's Direct Tax Service* **C4.441.**
Amendment—Paras 11–14 repealed by FA 1994 s 97(4), (5) and Sch 26 Pt V(10) where the relevant day falls on or after the day on which FA 1994 is passed (ie 3 May 1994).

[SCHEDULE 5A

SETTLEMENTS WITH FOREIGN ELEMENT: INFORMATION][1]

Section 98A

Amendments—[1] This Schedule inserted by FA 1994 s 97(1), (3).

[1 In this Schedule "the commencement day" means the day on which the Finance Act 1994 was passed.]¹

Note—FA 1994 was passed on 3 May 1994.
Amendments—¹ This Schedule inserted by FA 1994 s 97(1), (3).

[2—(1) This paragraph applies if—

  (a) a settlement was created before [17th March 1998]²,
  (b) on or after the commencement day a person transfers property to the trustees otherwise than under a transaction entered into at arm's length and otherwise than in pursuance of a liability incurred by any person before that day,
  (c) the trustees are not resident or ordinarily resident in the United Kingdom at the time the property is transferred, and
  (d) the transferor knows, or has reason to believe, that the trustees are not so resident or ordinarily resident.

(2) Before the expiry of the period of twelve months beginning with the relevant day, the transferor shall deliver to the Board a return which—

  (a) identifies the settlement, and
  (b) specifies the property transferred, the day on which the transfer was made, and the consideration (if any) for the transfer.

(3) For the purposes of sub-paragraph (2) above the relevant day is the day on which the transfer is made.]¹

Commentary—*Simon's Direct Tax Service* **C4.441.**
Definitions—"the Board", s 832(1); "United Kingdom", s 830.
Cross references—See TCGA 1992 Sch 5A para 6 (exceptions as regards returns and information in returns).
Amendments—¹ This Schedule inserted by FA 1994 s 97(1), (3).
² Words "19 March 1991" in sub-para (1)(a) substituted by FA 1998 Sch 22 para 5 with effect in relation to transfers after 16 March 1998.

[3—(1) This paragraph applies if a settlement is created on or after the commencement day, and at the time it is created—

  (a) the trustees are not resident or ordinarily resident in the United Kingdom, or
  (b) the trustees are resident or ordinarily resident in the United Kingdom but fall to be regarded for the purposes of any double taxation relief arrangements as resident in a territory outside the United Kingdom.

(2) Any person who—

  (a) is a settlor in relation to the settlement at the time it is created, and
  (b) at that time fulfils the condition mentioned in sub-paragraph (3) below,

shall, before the expiry of the period of three months beginning with the relevant day, deliver to the Board a return specifying the particulars mentioned in sub-paragraph (4) below.

(3) The condition is that the person concerned is domiciled in the United Kingdom and is either resident or ordinarily resident in the United Kingdom.

(4) The particulars are—

  (a) the day on which the settlement was created;
  (b) the name and address of the person delivering the return;
  (c) the names and addresses of the persons who are the trustees immediately before the delivery of the return.

(5) For the purposes of sub-paragraph (2) above the relevant day is the day on which the settlement is created.]¹

Commentary—*Simon's Direct Tax Service* **C4.441.**
Definitions—"the Board", s 832(1); "commencement day", Sch 5A para 1; "United Kingdom", s 830.
Cross references—See TCGA 1992 Sch 5A para 6 (exceptions as regards returns and information in returns).
Amendments—¹ This Schedule inserted by FA 1994 s 97(1), (3).

[4—(1)This paragraph applies if a settlement is created on or after 19th March 1991, and at the time it is created—

  (a) the trustees are not resident or ordinarily resident in the United Kingdom, or
  (b) the trustees are resident or ordinarily resident in the United Kingdom but fall to be regarded for the purposes of any double taxation relief arrangements as resident in a territory outside the United Kingdom.

(2) Any person who—

  (a) is a settlor in relation to the settlement at the time it is created,
  (b) at that time does not fulfil the condition mentioned in sub-paragraph (3) below, and
  (c) first fulfils that condition at a time falling on or after the commencement day,

shall, before the expiry of the period of twelve months beginning with the relevant day, deliver to the Board a return specifying the particulars mentioned in sub-paragraph (4) below.

(3) The condition is that the person concerned is domiciled in the United Kingdom and is either resident or ordinarily resident in the United Kingdom.

(4) The particulars are—

(*a*) the day on which the settlement was created;

(*b*) the name and address of the person delivering the return;

(*c*) the names and addresses of the persons who are the trustees immediately before the delivery of the return.

(5) For the purposes of sub-paragraph (2) above the relevant day is the day on which the person first fulfils the condition as mentioned in paragraph (*c*) of that sub-paragraph.][1]

Commentary—*Simon's Direct Tax Service* **C4.441.**
Definitions—"the Board", s 832(1); "commencement day", Sch 5A para 1; "United Kingdom", s 830.
Cross references—See TCGA 1992 Sch 5A para 6 (exceptions as regards returns and information in returns).
Amendments—[1] This Schedule inserted by FA 1994 s 97(1), (3).

[5—(1) This paragraph applies if—

(*a*) the trustees of a settlement become at any time (the relevant time) on or after the commencement day neither resident nor ordinarily resident in the United Kingdom, or

(*b*) the trustees of a settlement, while continuing to be resident and ordinarily resident in the United Kingdom, become at any time (the relevant time) on or after the commencement day trustees who fall to be regarded for the purposes of any double taxation relief arrangements as resident in a territory outside the United Kingdom.

(2) Any person who was a trustee of the settlement immediately before the relevant time shall, before the expiry of the period of twelve months beginning with the relevant day, deliver to the Board a return specifying—

(*a*) the day on which the settlement was created,

(*b*) the name and address of each person who is a settlor in relation to the settlement immediately before the delivery of the return, and

(*c*) the names and addresses of the persons who are the trustees immediately before the delivery of the return.

(3) For the purposes of sub-paragraph (2) above the relevant day is the day when the relevant time falls.][1]

Commentary—*Simon's Direct Tax Service* **C4.441.**
Definitions—"the Board", s 832(1); "commencement day", Sch 5A para 1; "United Kingdom", s 830.
Cross references—See TCGA 1992 Sch 5A para 6 (exceptions as regards returns and information in returns).
Amendments—[1] This Schedule inserted by FA 1994 s 97(1), (3).

[6—(1) Nothing in paragraph 2, 3, 4 or 5 above shall require information to be contained in the return concerned to the extent that—

(*a*) before the expiry of the period concerned the information has been provided to the Board by any person in pursuance of the paragraph concerned or of any other provision, or

(*b*) after the expiry of the period concerned the information falls to be provided to the Board by any person in pursuance of any provision other than the paragraph concerned.

(2) Nothing in paragraph 2, 3, 4 or 5 above shall require a return to be delivered if—

(*a*) before the expiry of the period concerned all the information concerned has been provided to the Board by any person in pursuance of the paragraph concerned or of any other provision, or

(*b*) after the expiry of the period concerned all the information concerned falls to be provided to the Board by any person in pursuance of any provision other than the paragraph concerned.][1]

Commentary—*Simon's Direct Tax Service* **C4.441.**
Definitions—"Board", s 832(1).
Amendments—[1] This Schedule inserted by FA 1994 s 97(1), (3).

[SCHEDULE 5AA

MEANING OF "SCHEME OF RECONSTRUCTION"][1]

Amendments—[1] Schedule inserted by FA 2002 s 45, Sch 9 paras 3, 7 with effect for shares or debentures issued after 16 April 2002. The reference to shares or debentures includes any interests falling to be treated as shares or debentures for the purposes of TCGA 1992 s 135 or 136 as substituted by FA 2002 Sch 9 paras 1, 2.

[Introductory

1 In section 136 "scheme of reconstruction" means a scheme of merger, division or other restructuring that meets the first and second, and either the third or the fourth, of the following conditions.][1]

Amendments—[1] Schedule inserted by FA 2002 s 45, Sch 9 paras 3, 7 with effect for shares or debentures issued after 16 April 2002. The reference to shares or debentures includes any interests falling to be treated as shares or debentures for the purposes of TCGA 1992 s 135 or 136 as substituted by FA 2002 Sch 9 paras 1, 2.

[First condition: issue of ordinary share capital

2 The first condition is that the scheme involves the issue of ordinary share capital of a company ("the successor company") or of more than one company ("the successor companies")—

(*a*) to holders of ordinary share capital of another company ("the original company") or, where there are different classes of ordinary share capital of that company, to holders of one or more classes of ordinary share capital of that company (the classes "involved in the scheme of reconstruction"), or

(*b*) to holders of ordinary share capital of more than one other company ("the original companies") or, where there are different classes of ordinary share capital of one or more of the original company or companies, to holders of ordinary share capital of any of those companies or of one or more classes of ordinary share capital of any of those companies (the classes "involved in the scheme of reconstruction"),

and does not involve the issue of ordinary share capital of the successor company, or (as the case may be) any of the successor companies, to anyone else.]¹

Amendments—¹ Schedule inserted by FA 2002 s 45, Sch 9 paras 3, 7 with effect for shares or debentures issued after 16 April 2002. The reference to shares or debentures includes any interests falling to be treated as shares or debentures for the purposes of TCGA 1992 s 135 or 136 as substituted by FA 2002 Sch 9 paras 1, 2.

[Second condition: equal entitlement to new shares

3—(1) The second condition is that under the scheme the entitlement of any person to acquire ordinary share capital of the successor company or companies by virtue of holding relevant shares, or relevant shares of any class, is the same as that of any other person holding such shares or shares of that class.

(2) For this purpose "relevant shares" means shares comprised—

(*a*) where there is one original company, in the ordinary share capital of that company or, as the case may be, in the ordinary share capital of that company of a class involved in the scheme of reconstruction;

(*b*) where there is more than one original company, in the ordinary share capital of any of those companies or, as the case may be, in the ordinary share capital of any of those companies of a class involved in the scheme of reconstruction.]¹

Amendments—¹ Schedule inserted by FA 2002 s 45, Sch 9 paras 3, 7 with effect for shares or debentures issued after 16 April 2002. The reference to shares or debentures includes any interests falling to be treated as shares or debentures for the purposes of TCGA 1992 s 135 or 136 as substituted by FA 2002 Sch 9 paras 1, 2.

[Third condition: continuity of business

4—(1) The third condition is that the effect of the restructuring is—

(*a*) where there is one original company, that the business or substantially the whole of the business carried on by the company is carried on—

(i) by a successor company which is not the original company, or

(ii) by two or more successor companies (which may include the original company);

(*b*) where there is more than one original company, that all or part of the business or businesses carried on by one or more of the original companies is carried on by a different company, and the whole or substantially the whole of the businesses carried on by the original companies are carried on—

(i) where there is one successor company, by that company (which may be one of the original companies), or

(ii) where there are two or more successor companies, by those companies (which may be the same as the original companies or include any of those companies).

(2) The reference in sub-paragraph (1)(*a*)(ii) or (*b*)(ii) to the whole or substantially the whole of a business, or businesses, being carried on by two or more companies includes the case where the activities of those companies taken together embrace the whole or substantially the whole of the business, or businesses, in question.

(3) For the purposes of this paragraph a business carried on by a company that is under the control of another company is treated as carried on by the controlling company as well as by the controlled company.

Section 840 of the Taxes Act (meaning of "control") applies for the purposes of this sub-paragraph.

(4) For the purposes of this paragraph the holding and management of assets that are retained by the original company, or any of the original companies, for the purpose of making a capital distribution in respect of shares in the company shall be disregarded.

In this sub-paragraph "capital distribution" has the same meaning as in section 122.]¹

Amendments—¹ Schedule inserted by FA 2002 s 45, Sch 9 paras 3, 7 with effect for shares or debentures issued after 16 April 2002. The reference to shares or debentures includes any interests falling to be treated as shares or debentures for the purposes of TCGA 1992 s 135 or 136 as substituted by FA 2002 Sch 9 paras 1, 2.

[Fourth condition: compromise or arrangement with members

5 The fourth condition is that—

    (*a*) the scheme is carried out in pursuance of a compromise or arrangement—

        (i) under section 425 of the Companies Act 1985 or Article 418 of the Companies (Northern Ireland) Order 1966), or

        (ii) under any corresponding provision of the law of a country or territory outside the United Kingdom, and

    (*b*) no part of the business of the original company, or of any of the original companies, is transferred under the scheme to any other person.]¹

Amendments—¹ Schedule inserted by FA 2002 s 45, Sch 9 paras 3, 7 with effect for shares or debentures issued after 16 April 2002. The reference to shares or debentures includes any interests falling to be treated as shares or debentures for the purposes of TCGA 1992 s 135 or 136 as substituted by FA 2002 Sch 9 paras 1, 2.

[Preliminary reorganisation of share capital to be disregarded

6 Where a reorganisation of the share capital of the original company, or of any of the original companies, is carried out for the purposes of the scheme of reconstruction, the provisions of the first and second conditions apply in relation to the position after the reorganisation.]¹

Amendments—¹ Schedule inserted by FA 2002 s 45, Sch 9 paras 3, 7 with effect for shares or debentures issued after 16 April 2002. The reference to shares or debentures includes any interests falling to be treated as shares or debentures for the purposes of TCGA 1992 s 135 or 136 as substituted by FA 2002 Sch 9 paras 1, 2.

[Subsequent issue of shares or debentures to be disregarded

7 An issue of shares in or debentures of the successor company, or any of the successor companies, after the latest date on which any ordinary share capital of the successor company, or any of them, is issued—

    (*a*) in consideration of the transfer of any business, or part of a business, under the scheme, or

    (*b*) in pursuance of the compromise or arrangement mentioned in paragraph 5(*a*),

shall be disregarded for the purposes of the first and second conditions.]¹

Amendments—¹ Schedule inserted by FA 2002 s 45, Sch 9 paras 3, 7 with effect for shares or debentures issued after 16 April 2002. The reference to shares or debentures includes any interests falling to be treated as shares or debentures for the purposes of TCGA 1992 s 135 or 136 as substituted by FA 2002 Sch 9 paras 1, 2.

[Interpretation

8—(1) In this Schedule "ordinary share capital" has the meaning given by section 832(1) of the Taxes Act and also includes—

    (*a*) in relation to a unit trust scheme, any rights that are treated by section 99(1)(*b*) of this Act (application of Act to unit trust schemes) as shares in a company, and

    (*b*) in relation to a company that has no share capital, any interests in the company possessed by members of the company.

(2) Any reference in this Schedule to a reorganisation of a company's share capital is to a reorganisation within the meaning of section 126.]¹

Amendments—¹ Schedule inserted by FA 2002 s 45, Sch 9 paras 3, 7 with effect for shares or debentures issued after 16 April 2002. The reference to shares or debentures includes any interests falling to be treated as shares or debentures for the purposes of TCGA 1992 s 135 or 136 as substituted by FA 2002 Sch 9 paras 1, 2.

[SCHEDULE 5B

ENTERPRISE INVESTMENT SCHEME: RE-INVESTMENT]¹

Section 150C

Cross references—See TCGA 1992 Sch 5BA (application of taper relief on the disposal of shares to which EIS deferral relief under this Schedule is attributable).
Amendments—¹ This Schedule inserted by FA 1995 Sch 13 para 4(3), (4) with effect for gains accruing and events occurring after 28 November 1994.

Application of Schedule

[1—(1) This Schedule applies where—

    (*a*) there would (apart from paragraph 2(2)(*a*) below) be a chargeable gain ("the original gain") accruing to an individual ("the investor") at any time ("the accrual time") on or after 29th November 1994;

    (*b*) the gain is one accruing either on the disposal by the investor of any asset or in accordance with [section 164F or 164FA,]² paragraphs 4 and 5 below or paragraphs 4 and 5 of Schedule 5C;

    (*c*) the investor makes a qualifying investment; and

(*d*) the investor is resident or ordinarily resident in the United Kingdom at the accrual time and the time when he makes the qualifying investment and is not, in relation to the qualifying investment, a person to whom sub-paragraph (4) below applies.

[(2) The investor makes a qualifying investment for the purposes of this Schedule if—

(*a*) eligible shares in a company for which he has subscribed wholly in cash are issued to him at a qualifying time and, where that time is before the accrual time, the shares are still held by the investor at the accrual time,

(*b*) the company is a qualifying company in relation to the shares,

(*c*) at the time when they are issued the shares are fully paid up (disregarding for this purpose any undertaking to pay cash to the company at a future date),

(*d*) the shares are subscribed for, and issued, for bona fide commercial purposes and not as part of arrangements the main purpose or one of the main purposes of which is the avoidance of tax,

(*e*) the requirements of section 289(1A) of the Taxes Act are satisfied in relation to the company,

(*f*) all the shares comprised in the issue are issued in order to raise money for the purpose of a qualifying business activity, ...[4]

[(*g*) at least 80% of the money raised by the issue is employed wholly for the purpose of that activity not later than the time mentioned in section 289(3) of the Taxes Act, and][3]

[(*h*) all of the money so raised is employed wholly for that purpose not later than 12 months after that time,][3]

and for the purposes of this Schedule, [conditions in paragraphs (*g*) and (*h*) above do][3] not fail to be satisfied by reason only of the fact that an amount of money which is not significant is employed for another purpose.

(3) In sub-paragraph (2) above "a qualifying time", in relation to any shares subscribed for by the investor, means—

(*a*) any time in the period beginning one year before and ending three years after the accrual time, or

(*b*) any such time before the beginning of that period or after it ends as the Board may by notice allow.][2]

(4) This sub-paragraph applies to the investor in relation to a qualifying investment if—

(*a*) though resident or ordinarily resident in the United Kingdom at the time when he makes the investment, he is regarded for the purposes of any double taxation relief arrangements as resident in a territory outside the United Kingdom, and

(*b*) were section 150A to be disregarded, the arrangements would have the effect that he would not be liable in the United Kingdom, to tax on a gain arising on a disposal, immediately after their acquisition, of the shares acquired in making that investment.][1]

Commentary—*Simon's Direct Tax Service* E3.145.
Revenue Internal Guidance—Capital gains manual 62843 (The Board of Inland Revenue have not delegated to District Inspectors the power to extend the time limits for EIS deferral relief purposes).
CG 62900–62904 (summary of changes to existing rules where shares acquired on or after 6 April 1998).
Definitions—"The Board", s 288(1); "double taxation arrangements", s 288(1); "ordinarily resident", s 9(1); "relevant shares", Sch 5B para 1(2); "resident", s 9(1); "shares", s 288(1); "the Taxes Act", s 288(1).
Amendments—[1] This Schedule inserted by FA 1995 Sch 13 para 4(3), (4) with effect for gains accruing and events occurring after 28 November 1994.
[2] Words in sub-para (1) inserted and sub-paras (2), (3) substituted by FA 1998 Sch 13 para 27 with effect for shares issued after 5 April 1998.
[3] Sub-paras 2(*g*), (*h*) substituted for sub-para 2(*g*), and words in sub-para 2 substituted for the words "the condition in paragraph (*g*) above does" by FA 2001 s 63, Sch 15 paras 25, 26, 40 with effect—

(*a*) in relation to shares issued after 6 March 2001, and
(*b*) in respect of the application of TA 1988 Pt VII Chapter III and TCGA 1992 Sch 5B after 6 March 2001 in relation to shares—
    (i) that were issued after 31 December 1993 but before 7 March 2001, and
    (ii) to which income tax relief or deferral relief was attributable immediately before 7 March 2001.
Previously sub-para 2(*g*) read—

    "(*g*) the money raised by the issue is employed not later than the time mentioned in section 289(3) of the Taxes Act wholly for the purpose of that activity,".
[4] In sub-para (2)(*f*), the word "and" repealed by FA 2001 s 110, Sch 33 Pt II(3) with effect—

(*a*) in relation to shares issued after 6 March 2001, and
(*b*) in respect of the application of TA 1988 Pt VII Chapter III and TCGA 1992 Sch 5B after 6 March 2001 in relation to shares—
    (i) that were issued after 31 December 1993 but before 7 March 2001, and
    (ii) to which income tax relief or deferral relief was attributable immediately before 7 March 2001.

[*Failure of conditions of application*

1A—(1) If the condition in sub-paragraph (2)(*b*) of paragraph 1 above is not satisfied in consequence of an event occurring after the issue of eligible shares, the shares shall be treated for the purposes of this Schedule as ceasing to be eligible shares on the date of the event.

(2) If the condition in sub-paragraph (2)(*e*) of that paragraph is not satisfied in consequence of an event occurring after the issue of eligible shares, the shares shall be treated for the purposes of this Schedule as ceasing to be eligible shares on the date of the event.

(3) If the condition in sub-paragraph (2)(*f*) of that paragraph is not satisfied in relation to an issue of eligible shares, the shares shall be treated for the purposes of this Schedule as never having been eligible shares.

(4) If the condition in sub-paragraph (2)(*g*) [or (*h*)]² of that paragraph is not satisfied in relation to an issue of eligible shares, the shares shall be treated for the purposes of this Schedule—

    (*a*) if the claim under this Schedule is made after the time mentioned in [sub-paragraph (4A) below]², as never having been eligible shares; and

    (*b*) if that claim is made before that time, as ceasing to be eligible shares at that time.

[(4A) The time referred to in sub-paragraph (4) above is—

    (*a*) in a case relating to the condition in sub-paragraph (2)(*g*) of paragraph 1 above, the time mentioned in section 289(3) of the Taxes Act, and

    (*b*) in a case relating to the condition in sub-paragraph (2)(*h*) of that paragraph, the time 12 months after that time.]²

(5) None of the preceding sub-paragraphs applies unless—

    (*a*) the company has given notice under paragraph 16(2) or (4) below or section 310(2) of the Taxes Act; or

    (*b*) an inspector has given notice to the company stating that, by reason of the matter mentioned in that sub-paragraph, the shares should, in his opinion, be treated for the purposes of this Schedule as never having been or, as the case may be, as ceasing to be eligible shares.

(6) The giving of notice by an inspector under sub-paragraph (5) above shall be taken, for the purposes of the provisions of the Management Act relating to appeals against decisions on claims, to be a decision refusing a claim made by the company.

(7) Where any issue has been determined on an appeal brought by virtue of section 307(1B) of the Taxes Act (appeal against notice that relief was not due), the determination shall be conclusive for the purposes of any appeal brought by virtue of sub-paragraph (6) above on which that issue arises.]¹

Commentary—*Simon's Direct Tax Service* **E3.145.**
Revenue Internal Guidance—Capital gains manual CG 62910 (Revenue procedures in relation to this para).
Amendments—¹ This paragraph inserted by FA 1998 Sch 13 para 28 with effect for shares issued after 5 April 1998.
² In sub-para 4, words inserted, and words substituted for the words "section 289(3) of the Taxes Act"; and the whole of sub-para 4A inserted, by FA 2001 s 63, Sch 15 paras 25, 27, 40 with effect—

    (*a*) in relation to shares issued after 6 March 2001, and
    (*b*) in respect of the application of TA 1988 Pt VII Chapter III and TCGA 1992 Sch 5B after 6 March 2001 in relation to shares—
       (i) that were issued after 31 December 1993 but before 7 March 2001, and
       (ii) to which income tax relief or deferral relief was attributable immediately before 7 March 2001.

Postponement of original gain

[2—(1) On the making of a claim by the investor for the purposes of this Schedule, so much of the investor's unused qualifying expenditure on [the relevant shares]³ as—

    (*a*) is specified in the claim, and
    (*b*) does not exceed so much of the original gain as is unmatched,

shall be set against a corresponding amount of the original gain.

(2) Where an amount of qualifying expenditure on [the relevant shares]³ is set under this Schedule against the whole or part of the original gain—

    (*a*) so much of that gain as is equal to that amount shall be treated as not having accrued at the accrual time; but
    (*b*) paragraphs 4 and 5 below shall apply for determining the gain that is to be treated as accruing on the occurrence of any chargeable event in relation to any of [the relevant shares]³.

(3) For the purposes of this Schedule—

    [(*a*) the investor's qualifying expenditure on [the relevant shares]³ is the amount subscribed by him for the shares; and]²
    (*b*) that expenditure is unused to the extent that it has not already been set under this Schedule against the whole or any part of a chargeable gain.

(4) For the purposes of this paragraph the original gain is unmatched, in relation to any qualifying expenditure on [the relevant shares]³, to the extent that it has not had any other expenditure set against it under this Schedule or Schedule 5C.]¹

Commentary—*Simon's Direct Tax Service* **E3.146.**
Revenue Internal Guidance—Capital Gains Manual CG 62911 (operation of this para).
Definitions—"Relevant shares", Sch 5B para 19(1A).
Amendments—¹ This Schedule inserted by FA 1995 Sch 13 para 4(3), (4) with effect for gains accruing and events occurring after 28 November 1994.
² Sub-para (3)(*a*) substituted by FA 1998 Sch 13 para 29 with effect for shares issued after 5 April 1998.
³ Words in sub-paras (2), (3), (4) substituted by FA 1999 s 73, Sch 8 para 4 with effect for shares issued after 5 April 1999.

Chargeable events

[**3**—(1) Subject to the following provisions of this paragraph, there is for the purposes of this Schedule a chargeable event in relation to [any of the relevant shares]³ if, after the making of the qualifying investment—

(*a*) the investor disposes of those shares otherwise than by way of a disposal within marriage;

(*b*) those shares are disposed of, otherwise than by way of a disposal to the investor, by a person who acquired them on a disposal made by the investor within marriage;

(*c*) the investor becomes a non-resident while holding those shares and [before the termination date relating to those shares]⁴;

(*d*) a person who acquired those shares on a disposal within marriage becomes a non-resident while holding those shares and [before the termination date relating to those shares]⁴; [or

(*e*) those shares cease (or are treated for the purposes of this Schedule as ceasing) to be eligible shares.]²

(2) ...²

(3) For the purposes of this Schedule there shall not be a chargeable event by virtue of sub-paragraph (1)(*c*) or (*d*) above in relation to any shares if—

(*a*) the reason why the person in question becomes a non-resident is that he works in an employment or office all the duties of which are performed outside the United Kingdom, and

(*b*) he again becomes resident or ordinarily resident in the United Kingdom within the period of three years from the time when he became a non-resident, without having meanwhile disposed of any of those shares;

and accordingly no assessment shall be made by virtue of sub-paragraph (1)(*c*) or (*d*) above before the end of that period in a case where the condition in paragraph (*a*) above is satisfied and the condition in paragraph (*b*) above may be satisfied.

(4) For the purposes of sub-paragraph (3) above a person shall be taken to have disposed of any shares if and only if there has been such a disposal as would have been a chargeable event in relation to those shares if the person making the disposal had been resident in the United Kingdom.

(5) Where in any case—

(*a*) the investor or a person who has acquired [any of the relevant shares]³ on a disposal within marriage dies, and

(*b*) an event occurs at or after the time of the death which (apart from this sub-paragraph) would be a chargeable event in relation to [any of the relevant shares]³ held by the deceased immediately before his death,

that event shall not be chargeable event in relation to the shares so held.]¹

[(6) Any reference in the following provisions of this Schedule to a chargeable event falling within a particular paragraph of sub-paragraph (1) above is a reference to a chargeable event arising for the purposes of this Schedule by virtue of that paragraph.]²

Commentary—*Simon's Direct Tax Service* **E3.147.**
Revenue Internal Guidance—Capital Gains Manual CG 62914–62916 (operation of this para where shares acquired on or after 6 April 1998).
Definitions—"Company", s 288(1); "disposal within marriage", Sch 5B para 6(2); "non-resident", Sch 5B para 6(2); "ordinarily resident", s 9(1); "qualifying investment", Sch 5B para 1(2); "relevant shares", Sch 5B para 19(1A).
Amendments—¹ This Schedule inserted by FA 1995 Sch 13 para 4(3), (4) with effect for gains accruing and events occurring after 28 November 1994.
² Words in sub-para (1)(*e*) substituted, sub-para (2) repealed and sub-para (6) inserted by FA 1998 Sch 13 para 30 with effect for shares issued after 5 April 1998.
³ Words in sub-paras (1), (5)(*a*), (*b*) substituted by FA 1999 s 73, Sch 8 para 4 with effect for shares issued after 5 April 1999.
⁴ Words in sub-para 1(*c*), (*d*) substituted for the words "within the designated period" by FA 2001 s 63, Sch 15 paras 25, 29, 40 with effect—

(*a*) in relation to shares issued after 6 March 2001, and

(*b*) in respect of the application of TA 1988 Pt VII Chapter III and TCGA 1992 Sch 5B after 6 March 2001 in relation to shares—

(i) that were issued after 31 December 1993 but before 7 March 2001, and

(ii) to which income tax relief or deferral relief was attributable immediately before 7 March 2001.

Gain accruing on chargeable event

[**4**—(1) On the occurrence of a chargeable event in relation to [any of the relevant shares]³ in relation to which there has not been a previous chargeable event—

(*a*) a chargeable gain shall be treated as accruing at the time of the event; and

[(*b*) the amount of the gain shall be equal to so much of the deferred gain as is attributable to the shares in relation to which the chargeable event occurs.]³

[(2) Any question for the purposes of capital gains tax as to whether any shares to which a disposal (including a disposal within marriage) relates are shares to which deferral relief is attributable shall be determined in accordance with sub-paragraphs (3) and (4) below.

(3) Where shares of any class in a company have been acquired by an individual on different days, any disposal by him of shares of that class shall be treated as relating to those acquired on an earlier day rather than to those acquired on a later day.

(4) Where shares of any class in a company have been acquired by an individual on the same day, any of those shares disposed of by him shall be treated as disposed of in the following order, namely—

(a) first any to which neither deferral relief nor relief under Chapter III of Part VII of the Taxes Act is attributable;

(b) next any to which deferral relief, but not relief under that Chapter, is attributable;

(c) next any to which relief under that Chapter, but not deferral relief, is attributable; and

(d) finally any to which both deferral relief and relief under that Chapter are attributable.

(4A) The following, namely—

(a) any shares to which deferral relief, but not relief under Chapter III of Part VII of the Taxes Act, is attributable and which were disposed of to an individual by a disposal within marriage; and

(b) any shares to which relief under that Chapter is attributable and which were transferred to an individual as mentioned in section 304 of that Act,

shall be treated for the purposes of sub-paragraphs (3) and (4) above as acquired by him on the day on which they were issued.

(4B) Chapter I of Part IV of this Act has effect subject to sub-paragraphs (2) to (4A) above.

(4C) Sections 104, 105 and 106A shall not apply to shares to which deferral relief, but not relief under Chapter III of Part VII of the Taxes Act, is attributable.][2]

(5) Where at the time of a chargeable event [any of the relevant shares][3] are treated for the purposes of this Act as represented by assets which consist of or include assets other than those shares—

[(a) so much of the deferred gain as is attributable to those shares shall be treated, in determining for the purposes of this paragraph the amount of the deferred gain to be treated as attributable to each of those assets, as apportioned in such manner as may be just and reasonable between those assets; and][3]

(b) as between different assets treated as representing [the same shares][3], [sub-paragraphs (3) to (4A) above][2] shall apply with the necessary modifications in relation to those assets as they would apply in relation to the shares.][1]

[(6) In order to determine, for the purposes of this paragraph, the amount of the deferred gain attributable to any shares, a proportionate part of the amount of the gain shall be attributed to each of the relevant shares held, immediately before the occurrence of the chargeable event in question, by the investor or a person who has acquired any of the relevant shares from the investor on a disposal within marriage.

(7) In this paragraph ''the deferred gain'' means—

(a) the amount of the original gain against which expenditure has been set under this Schedule, less

(b) the amount of any gain treated as accruing under this paragraph previously as a result of a disposal of any of the relevant shares.][3]

Commentary—*Simon's Direct Tax Service* **E3.148.**
Revenue Internal Guidance—CG 62852–62854 (worked examples—same day acquisitions: deferral relief claimed on some but not all shares).
CG 62917–62918 (operation of this para where shares acquired on or after 6 April 1998).
Capital gains manual CG 62919–62921 (examples illustrating identification of disposals).
Definitions—''Chargeable gain'', s 15(2); ''disposal within marriage'', Sch 5B para 6(2); ''relevant shares'', Sch 5B para 19(1A).
Cross references—See TCGA 1992 s 260(6A) (disapplication of sub-s (3) in relation to a disposal which constitutes a chargeable event by virtue of which a gain accrues under this para).
Amendments—[1] This Schedule inserted by FA 1995 Sch 13 para 4(3), (4) with effect for gains accruing and events occurring after 28 November 1994.
[2] Sub-paras (2)–(4C), and words in sub-para (5)(b) substituted by FA 1998 Sch 13 para 31 with effect for disposals made after 5 April 1998.
[3] Sub-paras (1)(b), (5)(a), (6), (7) and words in sub-paras (1), (5) substituted by FA 1999 s 73, Sch 8 paras 2, 4 with effect for shares issued after 5 April 1999.

Person to whom gain accrues

[5—(1) The chargeable gain which accrues, in accordance with paragraph 4 above, on the occurrence in relation to [any of the relevant shares][3] of a chargeable event shall be treated as accruing, as the case may be—

(a) to the person who makes the disposal,

(b) to the person who becomes a non-resident,

[or

(c) to the person who holds the shares in question when they cease (or are treated for the purposes of this Schedule as ceasing) to be eligible shares.][2]

(2) Where—

(a) sub-paragraph (1) above provides for the holding of shares at a particular time to be what identifies the person to whom any chargeable gain accrues, and

(b) at that time, some of those shares are held by the investor and others are held by a person to whom the investor has transferred them by a disposal within marriage, the amount of the chargeable gain accruing by virtue of paragraph 4 above shall be computed separately in relation to the investor and that person without reference to the shares held by the other.]¹

Commentary—*Simon's Direct Tax Service* **E3.148.**
Definitions—"Disposal within marriage", Sch 5B para 6(2); "non-resident", Sch 5B para 6(2); "relevant shares", Sch 5B para 19(1A); "shares", s 288(1).
Cross references—See TCGA 1992 s 260(6A) (disapplication of sub-s (3) in relation to a disposal which constitutes the chargeable event by virtue of which a gain accrues under this para).
Amendments—¹ This Schedule inserted by FA 1995 Sch 13 para 4(3), (4) with effect for gains accruing and events occurring after 28 November 1994.
² Sub-para (1)(c) substituted for sub-paras (1)(c), (d) by FA 1998 Sch 13 para 32 with effect in relation to shares issued on or after 6 April 1998.
³ Words in sub-para (1) substituted by FA 1999 s 73, Sch 8 para 4 with effect for shares issued after 5 April 1999.

[Claims

6—(1) Subject to sub-paragraph (2) below, section 306 of the Taxes Act shall apply in relation to a claim under this Schedule in respect of [the relevant shares]² as it applies in relation to a claim for relief under Chapter III of Part VII of that Act in respect of eligible shares.

(2) That section, as it so applies, shall have effect as if—

(*a*) any reference to the conditions for the relief were a reference to the conditions for the application of this Schedule;
(*b*) in subsection (1), the words "(or treated by section 289B(5) as so issued)" were omitted; and
(*c*) subsections (7) to (9) were omitted.]¹

Commentary—*Simon's Direct Tax Service* **E3.148.**
Revenue Internal Guidance—Capital gains manual CG 62930 (deferral relief must not be claimed until the investor has received form EIS3 from the company in which the investment is made).
Definitions—"Relevant shares", Sch 5B para 19(1A).
Amendments—¹ This paragraph substituted by FA 1998 Sch 13 para 33 with effect in relation to shares issued on or after 6 April 1998.
² Words in sub-para (1) substituted by FA 1999 s 73, Sch 8 para 4 with effect for shares issued after 5 April 1999.

[Reorganisations

7—(1) Where an individual holds shares which form part of the ordinary share capital of a company and include shares of more than one of the following kinds, namely—

(*a*) shares to which deferral relief and relief under Chapter III of Part VII of the Taxes Act are attributable;
(*b*) shares to which deferral relief but not relief under that Chapter is attributable; and
(*c*) shares to which deferral relief is not attributable,

then, if there is within the meaning of section 126 a reorganisation affecting those shares, section 127 shall apply (subject to the following provisions of this paragraph) separately to shares falling within paragraph (*a*), (*b*) or (*c*) above (so that shares of each kind are treated as a separate holding of original shares and identified with a separate new holding).

(2) Where—

(*a*) an individual holds shares ("the existing holding") which form part of the ordinary share capital of a company,
(*b*) there is, by virtue of any such allotment for payment as is mentioned in section 126(2)(*a*), a reorganisation affecting the existing holding, and
(*c*) immediately following the reorganisation, the existing holding or the allotted shares are shares to which deferral relief is attributable,

sections 127 to 130 shall not apply in relation to the existing holding.]¹

Commentary—*Simon's Direct Tax Service* **E3.148.**
Revenue Internal Guidance—Capital Gains Manual CG 62935–62938 (matters arising from share reorganisations following which shares acquired are categorised between those attracting income tax relief and those which attract only deferral relief).
Amendments—¹ This paragraph inserted by FA 1998 Sch 13 para 34 with effect in relation to shares issued on or after 6 April 1998.

[Acquisition of share capital by new company

8—(1) This paragraph applies where—

(*a*) a company ("the new company") in which the only issued shares are subscriber shares acquires all the shares ("old shares") in another company ("the old company");
(*b*) the consideration for the old shares consists wholly of the issue of shares ("new shares") in the new company;
(*c*) the consideration for new shares of each description consists wholly of old shares of the corresponding description;
(*d*) new shares of each description are issued to the holders of old shares of the corresponding description in respect of and in proportion to their holdings;
(*e*) at some time before the issue of the new shares—
(i) the old company issued eligible shares; and

(ii) a certificate in relation to those eligible shares was issued by that company for the purposes of subsection (2) of section 306 of the Taxes Act (as applied by paragraph 6 above) and in accordance with that section (as so applied); and

(f) by virtue of section 127 as applied by section 135(3), the exchange of shares is not treated as involving a disposal of the old shares or an acquisition of the new shares.

(2) For the purposes of this Schedule, deferral relief attributable to any old shares shall be attributable instead to the new shares for which they are exchanged.

(3) Where, in the case of any new shares held by an individual to which deferral relief becomes so attributable, the old shares for which they were exchanged were subscribed for by and issued to the individual, this Schedule shall have effect as if—

(a) the new shares had been subscribed for by him at the time when, and for the amount for which, the old shares were subscribed for by him;

(b) the new shares had been issued to him by the new company at the time when the old shares were issued to him by the old company; and

(c) the claim under this Schedule made in respect of the old shares had been made in respect of the new shares.

(4) Where, in the case of any new shares held by an individual to which deferral relief becomes so attributable, the old shares for which they are exchanged were acquired by the individual on a disposal within marriage, this Schedule shall have effect as if—

(a) the new shares had been subscribed for at the time when, and for the amount for which, the old shares were subscribed for;

(b) the new shares had been issued by the new company at the time when the old shares were issued by the old company; and

(c) the claim under this Schedule made in respect of the old shares had been made in respect of the new shares.

(5) Where deferral relief becomes so attributable to any new shares—

(a) this Schedule shall have effect as if anything which, under paragraph 1A(5) above, paragraph 16 below or section 306(2) of the Taxes Act as applied by paragraph 6 above has been done, or is required to be done, by or in relation to the old company had been done, or were required to be done, by or in relation to the new company; and

(b) any appeal brought by the old company against a notice under paragraph 1A(5)(b) may be prosecuted by the new company as if it had been brought by that company.

(6) For the purposes of this paragraph old shares and new shares are of a corresponding description if, on the assumption that they were shares in the same company, they would be of the same class and carry the same rights; and in sub-paragraph (1) above references to shares, except in the expressions "eligible shares" and "subscriber shares", include references to securities.

(7) Nothing in section 293(8) of the Taxes Act, as applied by the definition of "qualifying company" in paragraph 18(1) below, shall apply in relation to such an exchange of shares, or shares and securities, as is mentioned in sub-paragraph (1) above or arrangements with a view to such an exchange.]¹

Commentary—*Simon's Direct Tax Service* **E3.148.**
Amendments—¹ This paragraph inserted by FA 1998 Sch 13 para 34 with effect in relation to shares issued on or after 6 April 1998.

[Other reconstructions and amalgamations

9—(1) Subject to sub-paragraphs (2) and (3) below, sections 135 and 136 shall not apply in respect of shares to which deferral relief, but not relief under Chapter III of Part VII of the Taxes Act, is attributable.

(2) Sub-paragraph (1) above shall not have effect to disapply section 135 or 136 where—

(a) the new holding consists of new ordinary shares ("the new shares") carrying no present or future preferential right to dividends or to a company's assets on its winding up and no present or future right to be redeemed,

(b) the new shares are issued after the end of the relevant period, and

(c) the condition in sub-paragraph (4) below is satisfied.

(3) Sub-paragraph (1) above shall not have effect to disapply section 135 where shares to which deferral relief, but not relief under Chapter III of Part VII of the Taxes Act, is attributable are exchanged for other shares in such circumstances as are mentioned in paragraph 8(1) above.

(4) The condition is that at some time before the issue of the new shares—

(a) the company issuing them issued eligible shares, and

(b) a certificate in relation to those eligible shares was issued by the company for the purposes of subsection (2) of section 306 of the Taxes Act (as applied by paragraph 6 above) and in accordance with that section (as so applied).

(5) In sub-paragraph (2) above "new holding" shall be construed in accordance with sections 126, 127, 135 and 136.]¹

Commentary—*Simon's Direct Tax Service* **E3.148.**
Amendments—¹ This paragraph inserted by FA 1998 Sch 13 para 34 with effect in relation to shares issued on or after 6 April 1998.

[Re-investment in same company etc

10—(1) An individual to whom any eligible shares in a qualifying company are issued shall not be regarded for the purposes of this Schedule as making a qualifying investment if, where the asset disposed of consisted of shares in or other securities of any company ("the initial holding"), the qualifying company—

    (*a*) is the company in which the initial holding subsisted; or

    (*b*) is a company that was, at the time of the disposal of the initial holding, or is, at the time of the issue of the eligible shares, a member of the same group of companies as the company in which the initial holding subsisted.

(2) Where—

    (*a*) any eligible shares in a qualifying company ("the acquired holding") are issued to an individual;

    (*b*) an amount of qualifying expenditure on those shares has been set under this Schedule against the whole or part of any chargeable gain (the "postponed gain"); and

    (*c*) after the issue of those shares, eligible shares in a relevant company are issued to him,

he shall not be regarded in relation to the issue to him of the shares in the relevant company as making a qualifying investment for the purposes of this Schedule.

(3) For the purposes of sub-paragraph (2) above a company is a relevant company if—

    (*a*) where that individual has disposed of any of the acquired holding, it is the company in which the acquired holding has subsisted or a company which was a member of the same group of companies as that company at any time since the acquisition of the acquired holding;

    (*b*) it is a company in relation to the disposal of any shares in which there has been a claim under this Schedule such that, without that claim, there would have been no postponed gain in relation to the acquired holding; or

    (*c*) it is a company which, at the time of the disposal or acquisition to which the claim relates, was a member of the same group of companies as a company falling within paragraph (*b*) above.]¹

Commentary—*Simon's Direct Tax Service* **E3.148.**
Amendments—¹ This paragraph inserted by FA 1998 Sch 13 para 35 with effect in relation to shares issued on or after 6 April 1998.

[Pre-arranged exits

11—(1) Where an individual subscribes for eligible shares ("the shares") in a company, the shares shall be treated as not being eligible shares for the purposes of this Schedule if the relevant arrangements include—

    (*a*) arrangements with a view to the subsequent repurchase, exchange or other disposal of the shares or of other shares in or securities of the same company;

    (*b*) arrangements for or with a view to the cessation of any trade which is being or is to be or may be carried on by the company or a person connected with the company;

    (*c*) arrangements for the disposal of, or of a substantial amount of, the assets of the company or of a person connected with the company;

    (*d*) arrangements the main purpose of which, or one of the main purposes of which, is (by means of any insurance, indemnity or guarantee or otherwise) to provide partial or complete protection for persons investing in shares in that company against what would otherwise be the risks attached to making the investment.

(2) The arrangements referred to in sub-paragraph (1)(*a*) above do not include any arrangements with a view to such an exchange of shares, or shares and securities, as is mentioned in paragraph 8(1) above.

(3) The arrangements referred to in sub-paragraph (1)(*b*) and (*c*) above do not include any arrangements applicable only on the winding up of a company except in a case where—

    (*a*) the relevant arrangements include arrangements for the company to be wound up; or

    (*b*) the company is wound up otherwise than for bona fide commercial reasons.

(4) The arrangements referred to in sub-paragraph (1)(*d*) above do not include any arrangements which are confined to the provision—

    (*a*) for the company itself, or

    (*b*) in the case of a company which is a parent company of a trading group, for the company itself, for the company itself and one or more of its subsidiaries or for one or more of its subsidiaries,

of any such protection against the risks arising in the course of carrying on its business as it might reasonably be expected so to provide in normal commercial circumstances.

(5) The reference in sub-paragraph (4) above to the parent company of a trading group shall be construed in accordance with the provision contained for the purposes of section 293 of the Taxes Act in that section.

(6) In this paragraph ''the relevant arrangements'' means—

(*a*) the arrangements under which the shares are issued to the individual; and
(*b*) any arrangements made before the issue of the shares to him in relation to or in connection with that issue.]¹

Commentary—*Simon's Direct Tax Service* **E3.148.**
Amendments—¹ This paragraph inserted by FA 1998 Sch 13 para 35 with effect in relation to shares issued on or after 6 April 1998.

[Put options and call options

12—(1) Sub-paragraph (2) below applies where an individual subscribes for eligible shares (''the shares'') in a company and—

(*a*) an option, the exercise of which would bind the grantor to purchase such shares, is granted to the individual during the relevant period; or
(*b*) an option, the exercise of which would bind the individual to sell such shares, is granted by the individual during the relevant period.

(2) The shares to which the option relates shall be treated for the purposes of this Schedule—

(*a*) if the option is granted on or before the date of the issue of the shares, as never having been eligible shares; and
(*b*) if the option is granted after that date, as ceasing to be eligible shares on the date when the option is granted.

(3) The shares to which the option relates shall be taken to be those which, if—

(*a*) the option were exercised immediately after the grant; and
(*b*) any shares in the company acquired by the individual after the grant were disposed of immediately after being acquired,

would be treated for the purposes of this Schedule as disposed of in pursuance of the option.

(4) Nothing in this paragraph shall prejudice the operation of paragraph 11 above.

(5) An individual who acquires any eligible shares on a disposal within marriage shall be treated for the purposes of this paragraph and paragraphs 13 to 15 below as if he subscribed for those shares.]¹

Commentary—*Simon's Direct Tax Service* **E3.148.**
Revenue Internal Guidance—Capital Gains Manual CG 63016 (explains the meaning of relevant period).
Amendments—¹ This paragraph inserted by FA 1998 Sch 13 para 35 with effect in relation to shares issued on or after 6 April 1998.

[Value received by investor

13—(1) Where an individual who subscribes for eligible shares (''the shares'') in a company receives any value [(other than insignificant value)]² from the company at any time in the [period of restriction]², the shares shall be treated as follows for the purposes of this Schedule—

(*a*) if the individual receives the value on or before the date of the issue of the shares, as never having been eligible shares; and
(*b*) if the individual receives the value after that date, as ceasing to be eligible shares on the date when the value is received.

[(1A) This paragraph is subject to paragraph 13B below.]²

[(1B) Where—

(*a*) the individual who subscribes for the shares receives value (''the relevant receipt'') from the company during the period of restriction,
(*b*) the individual has received from the company one or more receipts of insignificant value at a time or times—

(i) during that period, but
(ii) not later than the time of the relevant receipt, and

(*c*) the aggregate amount of the value of the receipts within paragraphs (*a*) and (*b*) above is not an amount of insignificant value,

the individual shall be treated for the purposes of this Schedule as if the relevant receipt had been a receipt of an amount of value equal to the aggregate amount.

For this purpose a receipt does not fall within paragraph (*b*) above if it has previously been aggregated under this sub-paragraph.]²

(2) For the purposes of this paragraph an individual receives value from the company if the company—

(*a*) repays, redeems or repurchases any of its share capital or securities which belong to the individual or makes any payment to him for giving up his right to any of the company's share capital or any security on its cancellation or extinguishment;
(*b*) repays, in pursuance of any arrangements for or in connection with the acquisition of the shares, any debt owed to the individual other than a debt which was incurred by the company—

(i) on or after the date on which he subscribed for the shares; and

(ii) otherwise than in consideration of the extinguishment of a debt incurred before that date;

(c) makes to the individual any payment for giving up his right to any debt on its extinguishment;

(d) releases or waives any liability of the individual to the company or discharges, or undertakes to discharge, any liability of his to a third person;

(e) makes a loan or advance to the individual which has not been repaid in full before the issue of the shares;

(f) provides a benefit or facility for the individual;

(g) disposes of an asset to the individual for no consideration or for a consideration which is or the value of which is less than the market value of the asset;

(h) acquires an asset from the individual for a consideration which is or the value of which is more than the market value of the asset; or

(i) makes any payment to the individual other than a qualifying payment.

(3) For the purposes of sub-paragraph (2)(e) above there shall be treated as if it were a loan made by the company to the individual—

(a) the amount of any debt (other than an ordinary trade debt) incurred by the individual to the company; and

(b) the amount of any debt due from the individual to a third person which has been assigned to the company.

(4) ...[2]

(5) For the purposes of this paragraph an individual also receives value from the company if any person who would, for the purposes of section 291 of the Taxes Act, be treated as connected with the company—

(a) purchases any of its share capital or securities which belong to the individual; or

(b) makes any payment to him for giving up any right in relation to any of the company's share capital or securities.

(6) Where an individual's disposal of shares in a company gives rise to a chargeable event falling within paragraph 3(1)(a) or (b) above, the individual shall not be treated for the purposes of this paragraph as receiving value from the company in respect of the disposal.

(7) In this paragraph "qualifying payment" means—

(a) the payment by any company of such remuneration for service as an officer or employee of that company as may be reasonable in relation to the duties of that office or employment;

(b) any payment or reimbursement by any company of travelling or other expenses wholly, exclusively and necessarily incurred by the individual to whom the payment is made in the performance of duties as an officer or employee of that company;

(c) the payment by any company of any interest which represents no more than a reasonable commercial return on money lent to that company;

(d) the payment by any company of any dividend or other distribution which does not exceed a normal return on any investment in shares in or other securities of that company;

(e) any payment for the supply of goods which does not exceed their market value;

(f) any payment for the acquisition of an asset which does not exceed its market value;

(g) the payment by any company, as rent for any property occupied by the company, of an amount not exceeding a reasonable and commercial rent for the property;

(h) any reasonable and necessary remuneration which—

(i) is paid by any company for services rendered to that company in the course of a trade or profession; and

(ii) is taken into account in computing the profits of the trade or profession under Case I or II of Schedule D or would be so taken into account if it fell in a period on the basis of which those profits are assessed under that Schedule;

(i) a payment in discharge of an ordinary trade debt.

(8) For the purposes of this paragraph a company shall be treated as having released or waived a liability if the liability is not discharged within 12 months of the time when it ought to have been discharged.

(9) In this paragraph—

(a) references to a debt or liability do not, in relation to a company, include references to any debt or liability which would be discharged by the making by that company of a qualifying payment; and

(b) references to a benefit or facility do not include references to any benefit or facility provided in circumstances such that, if a payment had been made of an amount equal to its value, that payment would be a qualifying payment.

(10) In this paragraph [and paragraph 13A(1) below][2]—

(a) any reference to a payment or disposal to an individual includes a reference to a payment or disposal made to him indirectly or to his order or for his benefit;

(b) any reference to an individual includes a reference to an associate of his; and

(c) any reference to a company includes a reference to a person who at any time in the relevant period is connected with the company, whether or not he is so connected at the material time.

(11) In this paragraph ''ordinary trade debt'' means any debt for goods or services supplied in the ordinary course of a trade or business where any credit given—

    (*a*) does not exceed six months; and

    (*b*) is not longer than that normally given to customers of the person carrying on the trade or business.][1]

[(12) In paragraphs 13A to 13C below (except paragraph 13C(4))—

    (*a*) references to ''the shares'' shall be construed in accordance with sub-paragraph (1) above, and

    (*b*) references to ''the period of restriction'' shall be construed as references to the period of restriction relating to the shares.][2]

Commentary—*Simon's Direct Tax Service* **E3.148.**
Revenue Internal Guidance—Capital Gains Manual CG 63020–63037 (operation of this para).
Amendments—[1] This paragraph inserted by FA 1998 Sch 13 para 35 with effect in relation to shares issued on or after 6 April 1998.
[2] In sub-para 1, words inserted, and words substituted for the words ''designated period'', sub-paras 1A, 1B inserted, sub-para 4 repealed, words in sub-para 10 inserted, and sub-para 12 inserted by FA 2001 ss 63, 110, Sch 15 paras 25, 30, 40, Sch 33 Pt II(3) with effect—
    (*a*) in relation to shares issued on or after 7 March 2001, and
    (*b*) in relation to shares issued before that date, in respect of the application of TA 1988 Pt VII Chapter III and TCGA 1992 Sch 5B in relation to—
      (i) value received (within the meaning of TA 1988 s 300 or TCGA 1992 Sch 5B para 13 of Schedule 5B), and
      (ii) repayments made,
on or after that date.
Previously sub-para 4 read—
''(4) For the purposes of this paragraph an individual also receives value from the company if he receives in respect of ordinary shares held by him any payment or asset in a winding up or in connection with a dissolution of the company, being a winding up or dissolution falling within section 293(6) of the Taxes Act.''

[Provision supplemental to paragraph 13

13A—(1) For the purposes of paragraph 13 above, the value received by the individual in question is—

    (*a*) in a case within sub-paragraph (2)(*a*), (*b*) or (*c*) of that paragraph, the amount received by the individual or, if greater, the market value of the share capital, securities or debt in question;
    (*b*) in a case within sub-paragraph (2)(*d*) of that paragraph, the amount of the liability;
    (*c*) in a case within sub-paragraph (2)(*e*) of that paragraph, the amount of the loan or advance reduced by the amount of any repayment made before the issue of the shares;
    (*d*) in a case within sub-paragraph (2)(*f*) of that paragraph, the cost to the company of providing the benefit or facility less any consideration given for it by the individual;
    (*e*) in a case within sub-paragraph (2)(*g*) or (*h*) of that paragraph, the difference between the market value of the asset and the consideration (if any) given for it;
    (*f*) in a case within sub-paragraph (2)(*i*) of that paragraph, the amount of the payment;
    (*g*) in a case within sub-paragraph (5) of that paragraph, the amount received by the individual or, if greater, the market value of the share capital or securities in question.

(2) In this paragraph and paragraph 13 above references to a receipt of insignificant value (however expressed) are references to a receipt of an amount of insignificant value.
This is subject to sub-paragraph (4) below.

(3) For the purposes of this paragraph and paragraph 13 above ''an amount of insignificant value'' means an amount of value which—

    (*a*) does not exceed £1,000, or
    (*b*) if it exceeds that amount, is insignificant in relation to the total amount of expenditure on the shares which is set under this Schedule against a corresponding total amount of the whole or any part of any chargeable gains.

(4) For the purposes of paragraph 13 above, if, at any time in the period—

    (*a*) beginning one year before the shares are issued, and
    (*b*) expiring at the end of the issue date,

arrangements are in existence which provide for the individual who subscribes for the shares to receive or to be entitled to receive, at any time in the period of restriction, any value from the company that issued the shares, no amount of value received by the individual shall be treated as a receipt of insignificant value.

(5) In sub-paragraph (4) above—

    (*a*) any reference to the individual includes a reference to any person who, at any time in the period of restriction, is an associate of his (whether or not he is such an associate at the material time), and
    (*b*) the reference to the company includes a reference to any person who, at any time in the period of restriction, is connected with the company (whether or not that person is so connected at the material time).][1]

Commentary—*Simon's Direct Tax Service* **C3.1030.**
Revenue Internal Guidance—Capital Gains Manual CG 63038 (operation of this para including worked examples).

Amendments—[1] Paras 13A–13C inserted by FA 2001 s 63, Sch 15 paras 25, 31, 40 with effect—

(*a*) in relation to shares issued on or after 7 March 2001, and

(*b*) in relation to shares issued before that date, in respect of the application of TA 1988 Pt VII Chapter III and TCGA 1992 Sch 5B in relation to—

(i) value received (within the meaning of TA 1988 s 300 or TCGA 1992 Sch 5B para 13 of Schedule 5B), and

(ii) repayments made,

on or after that date.

[*Receipt of replacement value*

13B—(1) Where—

(*a*) by reason of a receipt of value within sub-paragraph (2) (other than paragraph (*b*)) or sub-paragraph (5) of paragraph 13 above ("the original value"), the shares would, in the absence of this paragraph, be treated as never having been eligible shares or as ceasing to be eligible shares on the date when the value is received,

(*b*) the original supplier receives value ("the replacement value") from the original recipient by reason of a qualifying receipt, and

(*c*) the amount of the replacement value is not less than the amount of the original value,

the receipt of the original value shall be disregarded for the purposes of paragraph 13 above.

(2) This paragraph is subject to paragraph 13C below.

(3) For the purposes of this paragraph and paragraph 13C below—

"the original recipient" means the person who receives the original value, and

"the original supplier" means the person from whom that value was received.

(4) A receipt of the replacement value is a qualifying receipt for the purposes of sub-paragraph (1) above if it arises—

(*a*) by reason of the original recipient doing one or more of the following—

(i) making a payment to the original supplier, other than a payment which falls within paragraph (*c*) below or to which sub-paragraph (5) below applies;

(ii) acquiring any asset from the original supplier for a consideration the amount or value of which is more than the market value of the asset;

(iii) disposing of any asset to the original supplier for no consideration or for a consideration the amount or value of which is less than the market value of the asset;

(*b*) where the receipt of the original value was within paragraph 13(2)(*d*) above, by reason of an event the effect of which is to reverse the event which constituted the receipt of the original value; or

(*c*) where the receipt of the original value was within paragraph 13(5) above, by reason of the original recipient repurchasing the share capital or securities in question, or (as the case may be) reacquiring the right in question, for a consideration the amount or value of which is not less than the amount of the original value.

(5) This sub-paragraph applies to—

(*a*) any payment for any goods, services or facilities, provided (whether in the course of a trade or otherwise) by—

(i) the original supplier, or

(ii) any other person who, at any time in the period of restriction, is an associate of, or connected with, that supplier (whether or not that person is such an associate, or so connected, at the material time),

which is reasonable in relation to the market value of those goods, services or facilities;

(*b*) any payment of any interest which represents no more than a reasonable commercial return on money lent to—

(i) the original recipient, or

(ii) any person who, at any time in the period of restriction, is an associate of his (whether or not he is such an associate at the material time);

(*c*) any payment for the acquisition of an asset which does not exceed its market value;

(*d*) any payment, as rent for any property occupied by—

(i) the original recipient, or

(ii) any person who, at any time in the period of restriction, is an associate of his (whether or not he is such an associate at the material time),

of an amount not exceeding a reasonable and commercial rent for the property;

(*e*) any payment in discharge of an ordinary trade debt (within the meaning of paragraph 13(11) above); and

(*f*) any payment for shares in or securities of any company in circumstances that do not fall within sub-paragraph (4)(*a*)(ii) above.

(6) For the purposes of this paragraph, the amount of the replacement value is—

(*a*) in a case within paragraph (*a*) of sub-paragraph (4) above, the aggregate of—

(i) the amount of any payment within sub-paragraph (i) of that paragraph, and

(ii) the difference between the market value of any asset within sub-paragraph (ii) or (iii) of that paragraph and the amount or value of the consideration (if any) received for it,

(b) in a case within sub-paragraph (4)(b) above, the same as the amount of the original value, and
(c) in a case within sub-paragraph (4)(c) above, the amount or value of the consideration received by the original supplier,

and paragraph 13A(1) above applies for the purposes of determining the amount of the original value.

(7) In this paragraph any reference to a payment to a person (however expressed) includes a reference to a payment made to him indirectly or to his order or for his benefit.]¹

Commentary—*Simon's Direct Tax Service* **C3.1030A**.
Revenue Internal Guidance—Capital Gains Manual CG 63039–63039C (operation of this para).
Amendments—¹ Paras 13A–13C inserted by FA 2001 s 63, Sch 15 paras 25, 31 with effect—
(a) in relation to shares issued on or after 7 March 2001, and
(b) in relation to shares issued before that date, in respect of the application of TA 1988 Pt VII Chapter III and TCGA 1992 Sch 5B in relation to—
(i) value received (within the meaning of TA 1988 s 300 or TCGA 1992 Sch 5B para 13 of Schedule 5B), and
(ii) repayments made,
on or after that date.

[Provision supplemental to paragraph 13B

13C—(1) The receipt of the replacement value by the original supplier shall be disregarded for the purposes of paragraph 13B above, as it applies in relation to the shares, to the extent to which that receipt has previously been set (under that paragraph) against any receipts of value which are, in consequence, disregarded for the purposes of paragraph 13 above as that paragraph applies in relation to those shares or any other shares subscribed for by the individual in question ("the individual").

(2) The receipt of the replacement value by the original supplier ("the event") shall also be disregarded for the purposes of paragraph 13B above if—
(a) the event occurs before the start of the period of restriction, or
(b) in a case where the event occurs after the time the original recipient receives the original value, it does not occur as soon after that time as is reasonably practicable in the circumstances, or
(c) where an appeal has been brought by the individual against an assessment made by virtue of paragraph 3(1)(e) above by reason of that receipt, the event occurs more than 60 days after the appeal has been finally determined.

But nothing in paragraph 13B above or this paragraph requires the replacement value to be received after the original value.

(3) Sub-paragraph (4) below applies where—
(a) the receipt of the replacement value by the original supplier is a qualifying receipt for the purposes of paragraph 13B(1) above, and
(b) the event which gives rise to the receipt is (or includes) a subscription for shares by—
(i) the individual, or
(ii) any person who, at any time in the period of restriction, is an associate of the individual, whether or not he is such an associate at the material time.

(4) Where this sub-paragraph applies, the person who subscribes for the shares shall not—
(a) be eligible for any relief under Chapter III of Part VII of the Taxes Act (enterprise investment scheme: income tax relief) in relation to those shares or any other shares in the same issue, or
(b) by virtue of his subscription for those shares or any other shares in the same issue, be treated as making a qualifying investment for the purposes of this Schedule.

(5) In this paragraph "the original value" and "the replacement value" shall be construed in accordance with paragraph 13B above.]¹

Commentary—*Simon's Direct Tax Service* **C3.1030A**.
Amendments—¹ Paras 13A–13C inserted by FA 2001 s 63, Sch 15 paras 25, 31 with effect—
(a) in relation to shares issued on or after 7 March 2001, and
(b) in relation to shares issued before that date, in respect of the application of TA 1988 Pt VII Chapter III and TCGA 1992 Sch 5B in relation to—
(i) value received (within the meaning of TA 1988 s 300 or TCGA 1992 Sch 5B para 13 of Schedule 5B), and
(ii) repayments made,
on or after that date.

[Value received by other persons

14—(1) Sub-paragraph (2) below applies where an individual subscribes for eligible shares ("the shares") in a company and at any time in the [period of restriction]³ the company or any subsidiary—
(a) repays, redeems or repurchases any of its share capital which belongs to any member other than the individual or [a person]² falling within sub-paragraph (3) below, or
(b) makes any payment (directly or indirectly) to any such member, or to his order or for his benefit, for the giving up of his right to any of the share capital of the company or subsidiary on its cancellation or extinguishment.

[This is subject to [paragraphs 14AA and 14A][3] below.][2]

(2) The shares shall be treated for the purposes of this Schedule—

(*a*) if the repayment, redemption, repurchase or payment in question is made or effected on or before the date of the issue of the shares, as never having been eligible shares; and

(*b*) if it is made or effected after that date, as ceasing to be eligible shares on the date when it is made or effected.

(3) [A person][2] falls within this sub-paragraph if the repayment, redemption, repurchase or payment in question—

(*a*) gives rise to a qualifying chargeable event in respect of him, or

(*b*) causes any relief under Chapter III of Part VII of the Taxes Act attributable to his shares in the company to be withdrawn or reduced by virtue of section 299 or 300(2)(*a*) of that Act[, or

(*c*) causes any investment relief [attributable to shares held by that person][3] (within the meaning of Schedule 15 to the Finance Act 2000) to be withdrawn or reduced by virtue of paragraph 46 (disposal of shares) or 49(1)(*a*) (repayment etc of share capital or securities) of that Schedule][2] [,

or it would have the effect mentioned in paragraph (*a*), (*b*) or (*c*) above were it not a receipt of insignificant value for the purposes of paragraph 13 above, section 300 of the Taxes Act or paragraph 47 of Schedule 15 to the Finance Act 2000, as the case may be.][3]

(4) In sub-paragraph (3) above "qualifying chargeable event" means—

(*a*) a chargeable event falling within paragraph 3(1)(*a*) or (*b*) above; or

(*b*) a chargeable event falling within paragraph 3(1)(*e*) above by virtue of sub-paragraph (1)(*b*) of paragraph 13 above (as it applies by virtue of sub-paragraph (2)(*a*) of that paragraph).

(5) Where—

(*a*) a company issues share capital ("the original shares") of nominal value equal to the authorised minimum (within the meaning of the Companies Act 1985) for the purposes of complying with the requirements of section 117 of that Act (public company not to do business unless requirements as to share capital complied with); and

(*b*) after the registrar of companies has issued the company with a certificate under section 117, it issues eligible shares,

the preceding provisions of this paragraph shall not apply in relation to any redemption of any of the original shares within 12 months of the date on which those shares were issued.

(6) In relation to companies incorporated under the law of Northern Ireland references in sub-paragraph (5) above to the Companies Act 1985 and to section 117 of that Act shall have effect as references to the Companies (Northern Ireland) Order 1986 and to Article 127 of that Order.

(7) References in this paragraph [and paragraph 14AA below][3] to a subsidiary of a company are references to a company which at any time in the relevant period is a 51 per cent subsidiary of the first mentioned company, whether or not it is such a subsidiary at the time of the repayment, redemption, repurchase or payment in question.][1]

Commentary—*Simon's Direct Tax Service* E3.148.
Amendments—[1] This paragraph inserted by FA 1998 Sch 13 para 35 with effect for shares issued after 5 April 1998.
[2] Words in sub-paras (1) substituted for words "an individual", words in sub-para (3) substituted for "An individual", words at end of sub-para (1) inserted and sub-para (3)(*c*), and word "or" preceding it, inserted by FA 2000 s 63(2), (4), Sch 16 para 4(1), (2) with effect for shares issued after 31 March 2000 but before 1 April 2010.
[3] In sub-para 1, words substituted for the words "designated period", "paragraphs 14AA and 14A" substituted for "paragraph 14A"; and words in sub-paras 3, 7 inserted, by FA 2001 s 63, Sch 15 paras 25, 32, 40 with effect—

(*a*) in relation to shares issued on or after 7 March 2001, and
(*b*) in relation to shares issued before that date, in respect of the application of TA 1988 Pt VII Chapter III and TCGA 1992 Sch 5B in relation to—
(i) value received (within the meaning of TA 1988 s 300 or TCGA 1992 Sch 5B para 13 of Schedule 5B), and
(ii) repayments made,

on or after that date.

[Insignificant repayments disregarded for purposes of paragraph 14

14AA—(1) Any repayment shall be disregarded for the purposes of paragraph 14 above if whichever is the greater of—

(*a*) the market value of the shares to which it relates ("the target shares") immediately before the event occurs, and

(*b*) the amount received by the member in question,

is insignificant in relation to the market value of the remaining issued share capital of the company in question (or, as the case may be, subsidiary in question) immediately after the event occurs.

This is subject to sub-paragraph (4) below.

(2) For the purposes of this paragraph "repayment" means a repayment, redemption, repurchase or payment mentioned in paragraph 14(1) above.

(3) For the purposes of sub-paragraph (1) above it shall be assumed that the target shares are cancelled at the time the repayment is made.

(4) Where an individual subscribes for eligible shares in a company, sub-paragraph (1) above does not apply to prevent paragraph 14(2) above having effect in relation to the shares if, at a relevant time, arrangements are in existence that provide—

  (a) for a repayment by the company or any subsidiary of the company (whether or not it is such a subsidiary at the time the arrangements are made), or

  (b) for anyone to be entitled to such a repayment,

at any time in the period of restriction.

(5) For the purposes of sub-paragraph (4) above "a relevant time" means any time in the period—

  (a) beginning one year before the eligible shares were issued, and

  (b) expiring at the end of the issue date.]¹

Commentary—*Simon's Direct Tax Service* **C3.1031.**
Revenue Internal Guidance—Capital Gains Manual CG 63042 ("insignificant" should be given its dictionary meaning—"trifling, or completely unimportant").
Amendments—¹ This paragraph inserted by FA 2001s 63, Sch 15 paras 25, 33, 40 with effect—
  (a) in relation to shares issued on or after 7 March 2001, and
  (b) in relation to shares issued before that date, in respect of the application of TA 1988 Pt VII Chapter III and TCGA 1992 Sch 5B in relation to—
    (i) value received (within the meaning of TA 1988 s 300 or TCGA 1992 Sch 5B para 13 of Schedule 5B), and
    (ii) repayments made,
  on or after that date.

[Certain receipts to be disregarded for purposes of paragraph 14

14A—(1) Sub-paragraph (4) below applies where, by reason of a repayment, any investment relief which is attributable under Schedule 15 to the Finance Act 2000 to any shares is withdrawn under paragraph 56(2) of that Schedule.

[(2) For the purposes of this paragraph "repayment" has the meaning given in paragraph 14AA(2) above.]²

(3) For the purposes of sub-paragraph (4) below "the relevant amount" is the amount determined by the formula—

$$X - 5Y$$

Where—

  X is the amount of the repayment, and
  Y is the aggregate amount of the investment relief withdrawn by reason of the repayment.

(4) Where the relevant amount does not exceed £1,000, the repayment shall be disregarded for the purposes of paragraph 14 above, unless repayment arrangements are in existence at any time in the period—

  (a) beginning one year before the shares mentioned in sub-paragraph (1) above are issued, and
  (b) expiring at the end of the issue date of those shares.

(5) For this purpose "repayment arrangements" means arrangements which provide—

  (a) for a repayment by the company that issued the shares ("the issuing company") or any subsidiary of that company, or
  (b) for anyone to be entitled to such a repayment,

at any time.

(6) Sub-paragraph (5)(a) above applies in relation to a subsidiary of the issuing company whether or not it was such a subsidiary—

  (a) at the time of the repayment mentioned in sub-paragraph (1) above, or
  (b) when the arrangements were made.

(7) ...²

(8) In this paragraph—

  (a) "investment relief" has the same meaning as in [Schedule 15 to the Finance Act 2000 (corporate venturing scheme)]²; and
  (b) references to the withdrawal of investment relief include its reduction.]¹

Commentary—*Simon's Direct Tax Service* **C3.1031.**
Amendment—¹ This paragraph inserted by FA 2000 s 63(2), (4), Sch 16 para 4(1), (3) with effect for shares issued after 31 March 2000 but before 1 April 2010.
² Sub-para 2 substituted, sub-para 7 repealed, and words in sub-para 8(a) substituted for the words "that Schedule" by FA 2001 ss 63, 110, Sch 15 paras 25, 34, 40, Sch 33 Pt II(3) with effect—
  (a) in relation to shares issued on or after 7 March 2001, and
  (b) in relation to shares issued before that date, in respect of the application of TA 1988 Pt VII Chapter III and TCGA 1992 Sch 5B in relation to—
    (i) value received (within the meaning of TA 1988 s 300 or TCGA 1992 Sch 5B para 13 of Schedule 5B), and
    (ii) repayments made,
  on or after that date.
Previously, sub-para 2 read—
  "(2) For the purposes of this paragraph "repayment" means a repayment, redemption, repurchase or payment mentioned in paragraph 56(1) of that Schedule (repayments etc which cause withdrawal of investment relief)."
Previously, sub-para 7 read—
  "(7) Where, but for the existence of paragraph 57(1) of Schedule 15 to the Finance Act 2000 (receipts causing insignificant changes to share capital to be disregarded), any investment relief would be withdrawn by reason of a repayment, the repayment shall be disregarded for the purposes of paragraph 14 above."

[Investment-linked loans

15—(1) Where at any time in the relevant period an investment-linked loan is made by any person to an individual who subscribes for eligible shares ("the shares") in a company, the shares shall be treated for the purposes of this Schedule—

(a) if the loan is made on or before the date of the issue of the shares, as never having been eligible shares; and

(b) if the loan is made after that date, as ceasing to be eligible shares on the date when the loan is made.

(2) A loan made by any person to an individual is an investment-linked loan for the purposes of this paragraph if the loan is one which would not have been made, or would not have been made on the same terms, if the individual had not subscribed for the shares or had not been proposing to do so.

(3) References in this paragraph to the making by any person of a loan to an individual include references—

(a) to the giving by that person of any credit to that individual; and

(b) to the assignment or assignation to that person of any debt due from that individual.

(4) In this paragraph any reference to an individual includes a reference to an associate of his.]¹

Commentary—*Simon's Direct Tax Service* **E3.148.**
Amendments—¹ This paragraph inserted by FA 1998 Sch 13 para 35 with effect in relation to shares issued on or after 6 April 1998.

[Information

16—(1) Where, in relation to [any of the relevant shares]² held by an individual—

(a) a chargeable event falling within paragraph 3(1)(a) or (b) above occurs at any time [before the termination date relating to those shares]⁴,

(b) a chargeable event falling within paragraph 3(1)(c) or (d) above occurs, or

(c) a chargeable event falling within paragraph 3(1)(e) above occurs by virtue of paragraph 12(2)(b), 13(1)(b) or 15(1)(b) above,

the individual shall within 60 days of his coming to know of the event give a notice to the inspector containing particulars of the circumstances giving rise to the event.

(2) Where, in relation to [any of the relevant shares]² in a company, a chargeable event falling within paragraph 3(1)(e) above occurs by virtue of paragraph 1A(1) or (2), 13(1)(b) or 14(2)(b) above—

(a) the company, and

(b) any person connected with the company who has knowledge of that matter,

shall within 60 days of the event or, in the case of a person within paragraph (b) above, of his coming to know of it, give a notice to the inspector containing particulars of the circumstances giving rise to the event.

[(2A) In determining, for the purposes of sub-paragraph (1) or (2) above, whether a chargeable event falling within paragraph 3(1)(e) above has occurred by virtue of paragraph 13(1)(b) above, the effect of paragraph 13B above shall be disregarded.]⁴

(3) A chargeable event falling within paragraph 3(1)(e) above which, but for paragraph 1A(5) above, would occur at any time by virtue of paragraph 1A(1) or (2) above shall be treated for the purposes of sub-paragraph (2) above as occurring at that time.

[(3A) Where—

(a) a person is required to give a notice under sub-paragraph (1) or (2) above in respect of a chargeable event which occurs by virtue of paragraph 13(1)(b) above or would occur by virtue of that paragraph but for the operation of paragraph 13B above, and

(b) that person has knowledge of the replacement value received (or expected to be received) from the original recipient by the original supplier by reason of a qualifying receipt,

the notice shall include particulars of that receipt of the replacement value (or expected receipt).

In this sub-paragraph "the replacement value", "the original recipient", "the original supplier" and "qualifying receipt" shall be construed in accordance with paragraph 13B above.]⁴

(4) Where a company has issued a certificate under section 306(2) of the Taxes Act (as applied by paragraph 6 above) in respect of any eligible shares in the company, and the condition in paragraph 1(2)(g) above is not satisfied in relation to the shares—

(a) the company, and

(b) any person connected with the company who has knowledge of that matter,

shall within 60 days of the time mentioned in section 289(3) of the Taxes Act or, in the case of a person within paragraph (b) above, of his coming to know that the condition is not satisfied, give notice to the inspector setting out the particulars of the case.

[(4A) Sub-paragraph (4) above shall apply in relation to the condition in paragraph 1(2)(h) above as it applies in relation to the condition in paragraph 1(2)(g) above, except that the reference to the time mentioned in section 289(3) of the Taxes Act shall be read as a reference to the time 12 months after that time.][3]

[(5) If the inspector has reason to believe—

    (*a*) that a person has not given a notice which he is required to give—

        (i) under sub-paragraph (1) or (2) above in respect of any chargeable event, or

        (ii) under sub-paragraph (4) above in respect of any particular case, or

    (*b*) that a person has given or received value (within the meaning of paragraph 13(2) or (5) above) which, but for the fact that the amount given or received was an amount of insignificant value (within the meaning of paragraph 13A(3) above), would have triggered a requirement to give a notice under sub-paragraph (1) or (2) above, or

    (*c*) that a person has made or received any repayment (within the meaning of paragraph 14AA(2) above) which, but for the fact that it falls to be disregarded for the purposes of paragraph 14 above by virtue of paragraph 14AA(1) above, would have triggered a requirement to give a notice under sub-paragraph (2) above,][4]

the inspector may by notice require that person to furnish him within such time (not being less than 60 days) as may be specified in the notice with such information relating to the event or case as the inspector may reasonably require for the purposes of this Schedule.

(6) Where a claim is made under this Schedule in respect of shares in a company and the inspector has reason to believe that it may not be well founded by reason of any such arrangements as are mentioned in paragraphs 1(2)(*d*) or 11(1) above, or section 293(8) or 308(2)(*e*) of the Taxes Act, he may by notice require any person concerned to furnish him within such time (not being less than 60 days) as may be specified in the notice with—

    (*a*) a declaration in writing stating whether or not, according to the information which that person has or can reasonably obtain, any such arrangements exist or have existed;

    (*b*) such other information as the inspector may reasonably require for the purposes of the provision in question and as that person has or can reasonably obtain.

(7) For the purposes of sub-paragraph (6) above, the persons who are persons concerned are—

    (*a*) in relation to paragraph 1(2)(*d*) above, the claimant, the company and any person controlling the company;

    (*b*) in relation to paragraph 11(1) above, the claimant, the company and any person connected with the company; and

    (*c*) in relation to section 293(8) or 308(2)(*e*) of the Taxes Act, the company and any person controlling the company;

and for those purposes the references in paragraphs (*a*) and (*b*) above to the claimant include references to any person to whom the claimant appears to have made a disposal within marriage of any of the shares in question.

(8) Where deferral relief is attributable to shares in a company—

    (*a*) any person who receives from the company any payment or asset which may constitute value received (by him or another) for the purposes of paragraph 13 above; and

    (*b*) any person on whose behalf such a payment or asset is received,

shall, if so required by the inspector, state whether the payment or asset received by him or on his behalf is received on behalf of any person other than himself and, if so, the name and address of that person.

(9) Where a claim has been made under this Schedule in relation to shares in a company, any person who holds or has held shares in the company and any person on whose behalf any such shares are or were held shall, if so required by the inspector, state—

    (*a*) whether the shares which are or were held by him or on his behalf are or were held on behalf of any person other than himself; and

    (*b*) if so, the name and address of that person.

(10) No obligation as to secrecy imposed by statute or otherwise shall preclude the inspector from disclosing to a company that relief has been given or claimed in respect of a particular number or proportion of its shares.][1]

Commentary—*Simon's Direct Tax Service* E3.148.
Revenue Internal Guidance—Capital Gains Manual CG 63050–63053 (operation of this para).
Definitions—"Relevant shares", Sch 5B para 19(1A).
Amendments—[1] This paragraph inserted by FA 1998 Sch 13 para 36 with effect in relation to shares issued on or after 6 April 1998.
[2] Words in sub-paras (1), (2) substituted by FA 1999 s 73, Sch 8 para 4 with effect for shares issued after 5 April 1999.
[3] Sub-para (4A) inserted by FA 2001 s 63, Sch 15 paras 25, 28, 40 with effect—

    (*a*) in relation to shares issued after 6 March 2001, and
    (*b*) in respect of the application of TA 1988 Pt VII Chapter III and TCGA 1992 Sch 5B after 6 March 2001 in relation to shares—
        (i) that were issued after 31 December 1993 but before 7 March 2001, and
        (ii) to which income tax relief or deferral relief was attributable immediately before 7 March 2001.
[4] Words in sub-para (1)(*a*) substituted for the words "in the designated period", sub-paras (2A), (3A) inserted, words in sub-para 5 substituted for the words "If the inspector has reason to believe that a person has not given a notice which he is required to give—(*a*) under sub-paragraph (1) or (2) above in respect of any chargeable event; or (*b*) under sub-paragraph (4) above in respect of any particular case,", by FA 2001 s 63, Sch 15 paras 25, 35 in relation to events occurring after 6 March 2001.

[Trustees

17—(1) Subject to the following provisions of this paragraph, this Schedule shall apply as if—

(a) any reference to an individual included a reference to the trustees of a settlement, and

(b) in relation to any such trustees, the reference in paragraph 1(1) above to any asset were a reference to any asset comprised in any settled property to which this paragraph applies (a "trust asset").

(2) This paragraph applies—

(a) to any settled property in which the interests of the beneficiaries are not interests in possession, if all the beneficiaries are individuals, and

(b) to any settled property in which the interests of the beneficiaries are interests in possession, if any of the beneficiaries are individuals.

(3) If, at the time of the disposal of the trust asset in a case where this Schedule applies by virtue of this paragraph—

(a) the settled property comprising that asset is property to which this paragraph applies by virtue of sub-paragraph (2)(b) above, but

(b) not all the beneficiaries are individuals,

only the relevant proportion of the gain which would accrue to the trustees on the disposal shall be taken into account for the purposes of this Schedule as it so applies.

(4) This Schedule shall not apply by virtue of this paragraph in a case where, at the time of the disposal of the trust asset, the settled property which comprises that asset is property to which this paragraph applies by virtue of sub-paragraph (2)(a) above unless, immediately after the acquisition of the relevant shares, the settled property comprising the shares is also property to which this paragraph applies by virtue of sub-paragraph (2)(a) above.

(5) This Schedule shall not apply by virtue of this paragraph in a case where, at the time of the disposal of the trust asset, the settled property which comprises that asset is property to which this paragraph applies by virtue of sub-paragraph (2)(b) above unless, immediately after the acquisition of the relevant shares—

(a) the settled property comprising the shares is also property to which this paragraph applies by virtue of sub-paragraph (2)(b) above, and

(b) if not all the beneficiaries are individuals, the relevant proportion is not less than the proportion which was the relevant proportion at the time of the disposal of the trust asset.

(6) If, at any time, in the case of settled property to which this paragraph applies by virtue of sub-paragraph (2)(b) above, both individuals and others have interests in possession, "the relevant proportion" at that time is the proportion which the amount specified in paragraph (a) below bears to the amount specified in paragraph (b) below, that is—

(a) the total amount of the income of the settled property, being income the interests in which are held by beneficiaries who are individuals, and

(b) the total amount of all the income of the settled property.

(7) Where, in the case of any settled property in which any beneficiary holds an interest in possession, one or more beneficiaries ("the relevant beneficiaries") hold interests not in possession, this paragraph shall apply as if—

(a) the interests of the relevant beneficiaries were a single interest in possession, and

(b) that interest were held, where all the relevant beneficiaries are individuals, by an individual and, in any other case, by a person who is not an individual.

(8) In this paragraph references to interests in possession do not include interests for a fixed term and, except in sub-paragraph (1), references to individuals include any charity.]¹

Commentary—*Simon's Direct Tax Service* E3.148.
Revenue Internal Guidance—Capital gains manual CG 63055–63065 (Revenue procedures with illustrative examples, relating to the calculation of the proportion of the chargeable gain arising to trustees which is eligible for deferral relief).
Amendments—¹ This paragraph inserted by FA 1998 Sch 13 para 36 with effect in relation to shares issued on or after 6 April 1998.

[Trustees: anti-avoidance

18—(1) Paragraphs 13 [to 13C]² and 15 above shall have effect in relation to the subscription for shares by the trustees of a settlement as if references to the individual subscribing for the shares were references to

(a) those trustees;

(b) any individual or charity by virtue of whose interest, at a relevant time, paragraph 17 above applies to the settled property; or

(c) any associate of such an individual, or any person connected with such a charity.

(2) The relevant times for the purposes of sub-paragraph (1)(b) above are the time when the shares are issued and

(*a*) in a case where [sub-paragraph (1) of paragraph 13 above applies, or that sub-paragraph would apply were it not for the fact that the amount of value is an amount of insignificant value for the purposes of that sub-paragraph][2], the time when the value is received;

[(*ab*) in a case where paragraph 13(1) above would apply were it not for the operation of paragraph 13B above, the time when the original value (within the meaning of paragraph 13B above) in question is received;][2]

(*b*) in a case where paragraph 15 above applies, the time when the loan is made.][1]

Commentary—*Simon's Direct Tax Service* **E3.148.**
Amendments—[1] This paragraph inserted by FA 1998 Sch 13 para 36 with effect in relation to shares issued on or after 6 April 1998.
[2] Words in sub-para 1 inserted, words in sub-para 2 substituted for the words "paragraph 13 above applies", and sub-para 2(*ab*) inserted, by FA 2001 s 63, Sch 15 paras 25, 36, 40 with effect—

    (*a*) in relation to shares issued on or after 7 March 2001, and
    (*b*) in relation to shares issued before that date, in respect of the application of TA 1988 Pt VII Chapter III and TCGA 1992 Sch 5B in relation to—
        (i) value received (within the meaning of TA 1988 s 300 or TCGA 1992 Sch 5B para 13 of Schedule 5B), and
        (ii) repayments made,

on or after that date.

[Interpretation

19—(1) For the purposes of this Schedule—

"arrangements" includes any scheme, agreement or understanding, whether or not legally enforceable;

"associate" has the meaning that would be given by subsections (3) and (4) of section 417 of the Taxes Act if in those subsections "relative" did not include a brother or sister;

...[5]

"eligible shares" has the meaning given by section 289(7) of that Act;

"the five year period", in the case of [any of the relevant shares][2], means the period of five years beginning with the issue of the shares;[3]

"non-resident" means a person who is neither resident nor ordinarily resident in the United Kingdom;

"ordinary share capital" has the same meaning as in the Taxes Act;

"ordinary shares", in relation to a company, means shares forming part of its ordinary share capital;

["the period of restriction", in relation to any shares, means the period—

    (*a*) beginning one year before the shares are issued, and
    (*b*) ending immediately before the termination date relating to the shares;][4]

"qualifying business activity" has the meaning given by section 289(2) of the Taxes Act;

"qualifying company", in relation to any eligible shares, means a company which, in relation to those shares, is a qualifying company for the purposes of Chapter III of Part VII of that Act [(except that for the purposes of this Schedule the reference in section 293(1B)(*b*)(i) of that Act to section 304A of that Act shall be read as a reference to paragraph 8 above)][4];

"the relevant period", in the case of any shares, means the period found by applying section 312(1A)(*a*) of that Act by reference to the company that issued the shares and by reference to the shares;

...[2]

"the seven year period" has the meaning given by section 291(6) of the Taxes Act.[3]

["termination date", in relation to any shares, means the date found by applying the definition of "termination date" in section 312(1) of the Taxes Act by reference to the company that issued the shares and by reference to the shares.][4]

[(1A) For the purposes of this Schedule, "the relevant shares", in relation to a case to which this Schedule applies, means the shares which—

    (*a*) are acquired by the investor in making the qualifying investment, and
    (*b*) where the qualifying investment is made before the time at which the original gain accrues, are still held by the investor at that time.

This is subject to sub-paragraphs (1B) and (1D) below.

(1B) If any corresponding bonus shares in the same company are issued to the investor or any person who has acquired any of the relevant shares from the investor on a disposal within marriage, this Schedule shall apply as if references to the relevant shares were to all the shares comprising the relevant shares and the bonus shares so issued.

(1C) In sub-paragraph (1B) above "corresponding bonus shares" means bonus shares which—

    (*a*) are issued in respect of the relevant shares; and
    (*b*) are of the same class, and carry the same rights, as those shares.

(1D) If, in circumstances in which paragraph 8 above applies, new shares are issued in exchange for old shares, references in this Schedule to the relevant shares, so far as they relate to the old shares, shall be construed as references to the new shares and not to the old shares.

(1E) In sub-paragraph (1D) above "new shares" and "old shares" have the same meaning as in paragraph 8 above.]²

(2) For the purposes of this Schedule, "deferral relief" is attributable to any shares if—

(a) expenditure on the shares has been set under this Schedule against the whole or part of any gain; and

(b) in relation to the shares there has been no chargeable event for the purposes of this Schedule.

(3) In this Schedule—

(a) references (however expressed) to an issue of eligible shares in any company are to any eligible shares in the company that are of the same class and are issued on the same day;

(b) references to a disposal within marriage are references to any disposal to which section 58 applies; and

(c) references to Chapter III of Part VII of the Taxes Act or any provision of that Chapter are to that Chapter or provision as it applies in relation to shares issued on or after 1st January 1994.

(4) For the purposes of this Schedule shares in a company shall not be treated as being of the same class unless they would be so treated if dealt with on the Stock Exchange.

(5) Notwithstanding anything in section 288(5), shares shall not for the purposes of this Schedule be treated as issued by reason only of being comprised in a letter of allotment or similar instrument.]¹

Commentary—*Simon's Direct Tax Service* E3.148.
Amendments—¹ This paragraph inserted by FA 1998 Sch 13 para 36 with effect in relation to shares issued on or after 6 April 1998.
² Words in sub-para (1) substituted, definition of "relevant shares" in sub-para (1) repealed and sub-paras (1A)–(1E) inserted by FA 1999 s 73, Sch 8 paras 3, 4, Sch 20 Pt III(18) with effect for shares issued after 5 April 1999.
³ In sub-para (1), definitions of "the five year period" and "the seven year period" repealed by FA 2000 ss 64, 156, Sch 17 para 7(1), (2), 8, Sch 40 Pt II(5) with effect for shares issued after 5 April 2000.
⁴ Definition of "the period of restriction", and "termination date" inserted, and words inserted in the definition of "qualifying company", by FA 2001 s 63, Sch 15 paras 25, 37, 40 with effect—

(a) in relation to shares issued after 6 March 2001, and
(b) in respect of the application of TA 1988 Pt VII Chapter III and TCGA 1992 Sch 5B after 6 March 2001 in relation to shares—
    (i) that were issued after 31 December 1993 but before 7 March 2001, and
    (ii) to which income tax relief or deferral relief was attributable immediately before 7 March 2001.
⁵ Definition of "the designated period" repealed by FA 2001 s 110, Sch 33 Pt II(3) with effect—

(a) in relation to shares issued after 6 March 2001, and
(b) in respect of the application of TA 1988 Pt VII Chapter III and TCGA 1992 Sch 5B after 6 March 2001 in relation to shares—
    (i) that were issued after 31 December 1993 but before 7 March 2001, and
    (ii) to which income tax relief or deferral relief was attributable immediately before 7 March 2001.
Previously, the text read—
    " 'the designated period', in the case of any shares, means the period found by applying section 291(6) of that Act by reference to the company that issued the shares and by reference to the shares;".

[SCHEDULE 5BA

ENTERPRISE INVESTMENT SCHEME: APPLICATION OF TAPER RELIEF]¹

Section 150D

Commentary—*Simon's Direct Tax Service* C1.403, E3.145.
Revenue Internal Guidance—Capital Gains Manual CG 63160–63170 (the application of taper relief for serial EIS investments including worked examples).
Amendments—¹ Schedule 5BA inserted by FA 1999 s 72(2), Sch 7.

Application of Schedule

1—(1) This Schedule applies where—

(a) a chargeable gain ("the original gain") accrues on the disposal of shares ("the original shares") to which deferral relief or relief under Chapter III of Part VII of the Taxes Act (EIS income tax relief), or both, is attributable;

(b) the whole or part of the original gain is treated as not having accrued at the time of that disposal because of expenditure on shares being set against it under paragraph 2 of Schedule 5B; and

(c) a chargeable gain ("the revived gain") is subsequently treated as accruing in accordance with paragraph 4 of Schedule 5B as a result of the disposal ("the relevant disposal") of shares expenditure on which has been set under paragraph 2 of Schedule 5B against the whole or part of the original gain or the whole or part of a gain derived from the original gain.

(2) This Schedule applies only if the original shares were issued on or after 6th April 1998 and disposed of on or after 6th April 1999.

Taper relief on revived gains

2—(1) Where this Schedule applies, the provisions of paragraphs 3 to 5 below have effect for applying taper relief under section 2A in relation to the revived gain.

(2) Those provisions do not apply to the extent that the revived gain is treated as not having accrued at the time of the relevant disposal because of expenditure being set against it under paragraph 2 of Schedule 5B.

Qualifying holding period

3—(1) The qualifying holding period of the original shares for the purposes of taper relief is the period beginning with the date of issue of the original shares and ending with the date of the relevant disposal.

(2) Sub-paragraph (1) is subject to paragraph 2(4) of Schedule A1 (periods that do not count for taper relief purposes).

Periods that do not count

4 A period—

(a) which falls within the period beginning with the date of issue of the original shares and ending with the date of the relevant disposal, and

(b) during which neither the original shares nor any relevant re-investment shares were held, does not count for the purposes of taper relief.

Gains on disposal of business or non-business assets

5—(1) The following rules apply to determine whether, or to what extent, the revived gain is for taper relief purposes a gain on the disposal of a business asset or a gain on the disposal of a non-business asset.

(2) The revived gain is treated as a gain on the disposal of an asset which was acquired on the issue of the original shares and disposed of on the date of the relevant disposal.

(3) That asset is treated as being the original shares during the period for which they were held.

(4) That asset is treated as being any relevant re-investment shares during the period for which those shares were held, or so much of that period as is not an overlap period in relation to those shares.

(5) For the purposes of sub-paragraph (4) an "overlap period", in relation to any relevant re-investment shares, means a period during which those shares and also—

(a) any of the original shares, or

(b) any relevant re-investment shares issued before the relevant re-investment shares in question, are held.

Savings

6 The application of paragraphs 3 to 5 above in relation to the revived gain does not affect the treatment for the purposes of taper relief under section 2A of—

(a) any gain which is treated as accruing in accordance with paragraph 4 of Schedule 5B at the same time as the revived gain, or

(b) any part of a gain where no expenditure was set under paragraph 2 of Schedule 5B against that part of the gain.

Relevant re-investment shares

7 For the purposes of this Schedule—

(a) shares are "re-investment shares" if expenditure on them is set under paragraph 2 of Schedule 5B against all or part of a gain; and

(b) re-investment shares are "relevant re-investment shares", in relation to a revived gain, if—

(i) their disposal results in a gain being treated as accruing under paragraph 4 of Schedule 5B, and

(ii) that gain is the revived gain or a gain from which the revived gain is derived.

Derivation of gains

8 For the purposes of this Schedule a gain ("the later gain") is derived from another gain ("the earlier gain") if—

(a) the later gain is treated as accruing in accordance with paragraph 4 of Schedule 5B on the disposal of any shares, and

(b) expenditure on those shares has been set under paragraph 2 of Schedule 5B against all or part of the earlier gain or a gain which, by virtue of this paragraph, is derived from the earlier gain.

Interpretation

9 Expressions defined for the purposes of Schedule 5B (apart from "the original gain") have the same meaning for the purposes of this Schedule as they have for the purposes of that Schedule.

[SCHEDULE 5C

VENTURE CAPITAL TRUSTS: DEFERRED CHARGE ON RE-INVESTMENT][1]

Section 151A

Amendments—[1] This Schedule inserted by FA 1995 s 72(4), Sch 16 with effect from the year 1995–96.

Application of Schedule

[1—(1) This Schedule applies where—

(a) there would (apart from paragraph 2(2)(a)below) be a chargeable gain ("the original gain") accruing to an individual ("the investor") at any time ("the accrual time") on or after 6th April 1995;

(b) that gain is one accruing on the disposal by the investor of any asset or in accordance with paragraphs 4 and 5 of Schedule 5B or paragraphs 4 and 5 below;

(c) the investor makes a qualifying investment; and

(d) the investor is resident or ordinarily resident in the United Kingdom at the accrual time and the time when he makes the qualifying investment and is not, in relation to the qualifying investment, a person to whom sub-paragraph (4) below applies.

(2) The investor makes a qualifying investment for the purposes of this Schedule if—

(a) he subscribes for any shares by reference to which he is given relief under Part I of Schedule 15B to the Taxes Act on any amount;

(b) those shares are issued at a qualifying time; and

(c) where that time is before the accrual time, those shares are still held by the investor at the accrual time;

and in this Schedule "relevant shares", in relation to a case to which this Schedule applies, means any of the shares in a venture capital trust which are acquired by the investor in making the qualifying investment.

(3) In this Schedule "a qualifying time", in relation to any shares subscribed for by the investor, means—

(a) any time in the period beginning twelve months before the accrual time and ending twelve months after the accrual time, or

(b) any such time before the beginning of that period or after it ends as the Board may by notice allow.

(4) This sub-paragraph applies to an individual in relation to a qualifying investment if—

(a) though resident or ordinarily resident in the United Kingdom at the time when he makes the investment, he is regarded for the purposes of any double taxation relief arrangements as resident in a territory outside the United Kingdom; and

(b) were section 151A(1) to be disregarded, the arrangements would have the effect that he would not be liable in the United Kingdom to tax on a gain arising on a disposal, immediately after their acquisition, of the shares acquired in making that investment.][1]

Commentary—*Simon's Direct Tax Service* **C3.1111.**
Amendments—[1] This Schedule inserted by FA 1995 s 72(4), Sch 16 with effect from the year 1995–96.

The postponement of the original gain

[2—(1) On the making of a claim by the investor for the purposes of this Schedule, so much of the investor's unused qualifying expenditure on relevant shares as—

(a) is specified in the claim, and

(b) does not exceed so much of the original gain as is unmatched,

shall be set against a corresponding amount of the original gain.

(2) Where the amount of any qualifying expenditure on any relevant shares is set under this Schedule against the whole or any part of the original gain—

(a) so much of that gain as is equal to that amount shall be treated as not having accrued at the accrual time; but

(b) paragraphs 4 and 5 below shall apply for determining the gain that is to be treated as accruing on the occurrence of any chargeable event in relation to any of those relevant shares.

(3) For the purposes of this Schedule, but subject to the following provisions of this paragraph—

(a) the investor's qualifying expenditure on any relevant shares is the sum equal to the amount on which he is given relief under Part I of Schedule 15B to the Taxes Act by reference to those shares; and

(b) that expenditure is unused to the extent that it has not already been set under this Schedule against the whole or any part of a chargeable gain.

(4) For the purposes of this paragraph the original gain is unmatched, in relation to any qualifying expenditure on relevant shares, to the extent that it has not had any other amount set against it under this Schedule or Schedule 5B.][1]

Commentary—*Simon's Direct Tax Service* **C3.1111.**
Amendments—[1] This Schedule inserted by FA 1995 s 72(4), Sch 16 with effect from the year 1995–96.

Chargeable events

[3—(1) Subject to the following provisions of this paragraph, there is for the purposes of this Schedule a chargeable event in relation to any relevant shares if, after the making of the qualifying investment—

    (*a*) the investor disposes of those shares otherwise than by way of a disposal within marriage;
    (*b*) those shares are disposed of, otherwise than by way of a disposal to the investor, by a person who acquired them on a disposal made by the investor within marriage;
    (*c*) there is, in a case where those shares fall within section 151B(3)(*c*), such an actual or deemed exchange of those shares for any non-qualifying holdings as, under section 135 or 136, requires, or but for section 116 would require, those holdings to be treated for the purposes of this Act as the same assets as those shares;
    (*d*) the investor becomes a non-resident while holding those shares and within the relevant period;
    (*e*) a person who acquired those shares on a disposal within marriage becomes a non-resident while holding those shares and within the relevant period;
    (*f*) the company in which those shares are shares has its approval as a venture capital trust withdrawn in a case to which section 842AA(8) of the Taxes Act does not apply; or
    (*g*) the relief given under Part I of Schedule 15B to the Taxes Act by reference to those shares is withdrawn or reduced in circumstances not falling within any of paragraphs (*a*) to (*f*) above.

(2) In sub-paragraph (1) above—

    "non-qualifying holdings" means any shares or securities other than any ordinary shares (within the meaning of section 151A) in a venture capital trust; and
    "the relevant period", in relation to any relevant shares, means the period of [three]² years beginning with the time when the investor made the qualifying investment by virtue of which he acquired those shares.

(3) For the purposes of sub-paragraph (1) above there shall not be a chargeable event by virtue of sub-paragraph (1)(*d*) or (*e*) above in relation to any shares if—

    (*a*) the reason why the person in question becomes a non-resident is that he works in an employment or office all the duties of which are performed outside the United Kingdom, and
    (*b*) he again becomes resident or ordinarily resident in the United Kingdom within the period of three years from the time when he became a non-resident, without having meanwhile disposed of any of those shares;

and, accordingly, no assessment shall be made by virtue of sub-paragraph (1)(*d*)or (*e*) above before the end of that period in any case where the condition in paragraph (*a*) above is satisfied and the condition in paragraph (*b*) above may be satisfied.

(4) For the purposes of sub-paragraph (3) above a person shall be taken to have disposed of any shares if and only if there has been such a disposal as would, if the person making the disposal had been resident in the United Kingdom, have been a chargeable event in relation to those shares.

(5) Where in any case—

    (*a*) the investor or a person who has acquired any relevant shares on a disposal within marriage dies, and
    (*b*) an event occurs at or after the time of the death which (apart from this sub-paragraph) would be a chargeable event in relation to any relevant shares held by the deceased immediately before his death,

that event shall not be chargeable event in relation to the shares so held.

(6) Without prejudice to the operation of paragraphs 4 and 5 below in a case falling within sub-paragraph (1)(*f*) above, the references in this paragraph to a disposal shall not include references to the disposal which by virtue of section 151B(6) is deemed to take place in such a case.]¹

Commentary—*Simon's Direct Tax Service* C3.1112.
Amendments—¹ This Schedule inserted by FA 1995 s 72(4), Sch 16 with effect from the year 1995–96.
² Word in sub-para (2) substituted for word "five" by FA 2000 s 65, Sch 18 paras 2, 3 with effect for shares issued after 5 April 2000.

Gain accruing on chargeable event

[4—(1) On the occurrence of a chargeable event in relation to any relevant shares in relation to which there has not been a previous chargeable event—

    (*a*) a chargeable gain shall be treated as accruing at the time of the event; and
    (*b*) the amount of the gain shall be equal to so much of the original gain as is an amount against which there has under this Schedule been set any expenditure on those shares.

(2) In determining for the purposes of this Schedule any question whether any shares to which a chargeable event relates are shares the expenditure on which has under this Schedule been set against the whole or any part of any gain, the assumptions in sub-paragraph (3) below shall apply and, in a

case where the shares are not (within the meaning of section 151B) eligible for relief under section 151A(1), shall apply notwithstanding anything in any of sections 104, 105 and [106A][2].

(3) Those assumptions are that—

(a) as between shares acquired by the same person on different days, those acquired on an earlier day are disposed of by that person before those acquired on a later day; and

(b) as between shares in a company that were acquired on the same day, those the expenditure on which has been set under this Schedule against the whole or any part of any gain are disposed of by that person only after he has disposed of any other shares in that company that were acquired by him on that day.

(4) Where at the time of a chargeable event any relevant shares are treated for the purposes of this Act as represented by assets which consist of or include assets other than the relevant shares—

(a) the expenditure on those shares which was set against the gain in question shall be treated, in determining for the purposes of this paragraph the amount of expenditure on each of those assets which is to be treated as having been set against that gain, as apportioned in such manner as may be just and reasonable between those assets; and

(b) as between different assets treated as representing the same relevant shares, the assumptions mentioned in sub-paragraph (3) above shall apply with the necessary modifications in relation to those assets as they would apply in relation to the shares.][1]

Commentary—*Simon's Direct Tax Service* **C3.1113.**
Amendments—[1] This Schedule inserted by FA 1995 s 72(4), Sch 16 with effect from the year 1995–96.
[2] Section number in sub-para (2) substituted by FA 1998 s 124(6) with effect in relation to any disposal on or after 6 April 1998, subject to FA 1998, s 124(8).

Persons to whom gain accrues

[5—(1) The chargeable gain which accrues in accordance with paragraph 4 above on the occurrence in relation to any relevant shares of a chargeable event shall be treated as accruing, as the case may be—

(a) to the person who makes the disposal,

(b) to the person who holds the shares in question at the time of the exchange or deemed exchange,

(c) to the person who becomes a non-resident,

(d) to the person who holds the shares in question when the withdrawal of the approval takes effect, or

(e) to the person who holds the shares in question when the circumstances arise in respect of which the relief is withdrawn or reduced.

(2) Where—

(a) sub-paragraph (1) above provides for the holding of shares at a particular time to be what identifies the person to whom any chargeable gain accrues, and

(b) at that time, some of those shares are held by the investor and others are held by a person to whom the investor has transferred them by a disposal within marriage,

the amount of the chargeable gain accruing by virtue of paragraph 4 above shall be computed separately in relation to the investor and that person without reference to the shares held by the other.

Commentary—*Simon's Direct Tax Service* **C3.1112.**
Amendments—[1] This Schedule inserted by FA 1995 s 72(4), Sch 16 with effect from the year 1995–96.

Interpretation

6—(1) In this Schedule "non-resident" means a person who is neither resident nor ordinarily resident in the United Kingdom.

(2) In this Schedule references to a disposal within marriage are references to any disposal to which section 58 applies.

(3) Notwithstanding anything in section 288(5), shares shall not for the purposes of this Schedule be treated as issued by reason only of being comprised in a letter of allotment or similar instrument.][1]

Commentary—*Simon's Direct Tax Service* **E3.650–655.**
Amendments—[1] This Schedule inserted by FA 1995 s 72(4), Sch 16 with effect from the year 1995–96.

SCHEDULE 6

RETIREMENT RELIEF ETC

Sections 163, 164

Concession D31—Retirement relief: date of disposal.
D33—CGT on compensation and damages. This Concession has been revised.
Revenue Interpretation RI 202—Disallowance of retirement relief for disposals after 5 April 2003.
Cross references—See TCGA 1992 s 165 (relief for gifts of business assets).
TCGA 1992 s 241(3) (commercial letting of furnished holiday accommodation to be treated as a trade for the purposes of this Schedule).
TCGA 1992 Sch 6 para 4(3) (in relation to a qualifying disposal, reference in this Schedule to amount available for relief means amount determined under paras 13–16 below).

TCGA 1992 Sch 7 para 8 (reduction of held-over gain partly relieved by retirement relief under this Schedule).
Prospective amendment—This Schedule will be repealed by FA 1998 s 165, Sch 27 Part III(31) with effect for disposals in the year 2003–04 and subsequent years of assessment.

PART I
INTERPRETATION

1—(1) This paragraph and paragraphs 2 and 3 below have effect for the purposes of this Schedule and sections 163 and 164.

(2) In the provisions referred to above—

"commercial association of companies" means a company together with such of its associated companies, within the meaning of section 416 of the Taxes Act, as carry on businesses which are of such a nature that the businesses of the company and the associated companies taken together may be reasonably considered to make up a single composite undertaking;
...[3]

["full-time working officer or employee", in relation to one or more companies, means any officer or employee who is required to devote substantially the whole of his time to the service of that company, or those companies taken together, in a managerial or technical capacity;][1]

"group of companies" means a company which has one or more 51 per cent subsidiaries, together with those subsidiaries;

"holding company" means a company whose business (disregarding any trade carried on by it) consists wholly or mainly of the holding of shares or securities of one or more companies which are its 51 per cent subsidiaries;

"permitted period" means a period of one year or such longer period as the Board may, in any particular case, by notice allow;

["personal company", in relation to an individual, means any company the voting rights in which are exercisable, as to not less than 5 per cent, by that individual;][2]

"trade", "profession", "vocation", "office" and "employment" have the same meaning as in the Income Tax Acts;

"trading company" means a company whose business consists wholly or mainly of the carrying on of a trade or trades;

"trading group" means a group of companies the business of whose members, taken together, consists wholly or mainly of the carrying on of a trade or trades.

(3)–(4) ...[3]

Commentary—*Simon's Direct Tax Service* C3.602.
Revenue Interpretation RI 134—Definition of "personal company"—Voting rights attached to shares held by trustees cannot be regarded as exercisable by the first named trustee, as an individual.
RI 202—Definition of "full-time working officer or employee"—the Revenue continue to interpret "substantially the whole of his time" as meaning at least three quarters of the normal working hours in a week, pending the final outcome in *Palmer v Maloney and Shipleys*.
Revenue Internal Guidance—Capital gains manual CG 63582–63583 (extension of "permitted period").
Simon's Tax Cases—Sub-para (2), *Palmer v Moloney* [1999] STC 890; *Hatt v Newman* [2000] STC 113.
Definitions—"The Board", s 288(1); "company", ss 99, 288(1); "notice", s 288(1); "settled property", s 68; "shares", s 288(1); "the Taxes Act", s 288(1); "trade", s 288(1), TA 1988 s 832(1).
Amendments—[1] Definition of "full-time working officer or employee" in sub-para (2) substituted for the definition of "full-time working director" by FA 1993 s 87 and Sch 7 para 2(4) in relation to disposals made after 15 March 1993.
[2] Definition of "personal company" in sub-para (2) inserted by FA 1993 s 87 and Sch 7 para 1(2) in relation to disposals made after 15 March 1993.
[3] Sub-paras (3), (4) and definitions of "family company", "family" and "relative" in sub-para (2) repealed by FA 1993 Sch 23 Pt III (7) in relation to disposals made after 15 March 1993.

2—(1) For the purposes of the provisions referred to in paragraph 1(1) above, where, as part of a reorganisation, within the meaning of section 126, there is a disposal of shares or securities of a company and, apart from this sub-paragraph, the shares disposed of and the new holding (as defined in that section) would fall to be treated, by virtue of section 127, as the same asset, section 127 shall not apply if the individual concerned so elects or, in the case of a trustees' disposal, if the trustees and the individual concerned jointly so elect; and an election under this sub-paragraph shall be made by notice given to the Board [on or before the first anniversary of the 31st January next following][1] the year of assessment in which the disposal occurred.

(2) In sub-paragraph (1) above, the reference to a reorganisation, within the meaning of section 126, includes a reference to an exchange of shares or securities which is treated as such a reorganisation by virtue of [section 135 or 136][2].

Commentary—*Simon's Direct Tax Service* C3.608.
Definitions—"Asset", s 21(1); "the Board", s 288(1); "company", ss 99, 288(1); "notice", s 288(1); "shares", s 288(1); "trade", s 288(1), TA 1988 s 832(1); "year of assessment", s 288(1).
Amendments—[1] Words in sub-para (1) substituted by FA 1996 s 135(1), (2), Sch 21 para 44(1), (2) with effect from the year 1996–97.
[2] Words in sub-para (2) substituted for words "section 135(3)" by FA 2002 s 45, Sch 9 paras 5(1), (14), 7 with effect for shares or debentures issued after 16 April 2002. The reference to shares or debentures includes any interests falling to be treated as shares or debentures for the purposes of TCGA 1992 s 135 or 136 as substituted by FA 2002 Sch 9.

3—(1) A person who has been concerned in the carrying on of a business shall be treated as having retired on ill-health grounds if, ...[2]—

(a) [he][2] has ceased to be engaged in and, by reason of ill-health, is incapable of engaging in work of the kind which he previously undertook in connection with that business; and

(b) [he][2] is likely to remain permanently so incapable.

(2) In sub-paragraph (1) above, the reference to a person being concerned in the carrying on of a business is a reference to his being so concerned personally or as a member of a partnership carrying on the business; and the business which is relevant for the purposes of the provisions referred to in paragraph 1(1) above is that referred to—

(a) in subsection (3) or subsection (4) of section 163 in relation to a material disposal of business assets;

(b) in subsection (5) of section 164 in relation to a trustees' disposal; and

(c) in subsection (7) of section 164 in relation to an associated disposal.

(3) A person who has been a [full-time working officer or employee][1] of a company or of two or more companies shall be treated as having retired on ill-health grounds if, ...[2]—

(a) [he][2] has ceased to serve and, by reason of ill-health, is incapable of serving that company or, as the case may be, those companies in a managerial or technical capacity; and

(b) [he][2] is likely to remain permanently incapable of serving in such a capacity that company or those companies (as the case may be) or any other company engaged in business of a kind carried on by that company or those companies.

(4) In relation to an employee's disposal, a person who has been exercising any office or employment shall be treated as having retired on ill-health grounds if, ...[2]—

(a) [he][2] has ceased to exercise and, by reason of ill-health, is incapable of exercising that office or employment; and

(b) [he][2] is likely to remain permanently so incapable.

[(5) In any case where—

(a) an officer of the Board gives notice to any person under section 9A(1) of, or paragraph 5(1) of Schedule 1A to, the Management Act (notice of intention to enquire into a return or claim or an amendment of a return or claim), and

(b) the enquiry to any extent relates to the question whether or not a person falls to be treated as having retired on ill-health grounds by virtue of the foregoing provisions of this paragraph,

then, without prejudice to any other powers of such an officer in relation to such an enquiry, an officer of the Board may at the same or any subsequent time by notice in writing require that person, within such time (which shall not be less than 30 days) as may be specified in the notice, to produce such evidence relating to the question mentioned in paragraph (b) above as may reasonably be specified in the notice.][2]

Commentary—*Simon's Direct Tax Service* **C3.603.**
Revenue Interpretation RI 6—Disallowance of retirement relief on account of ill-health where it is claimed by a person affected by the ill-health of another person.
Simon's Tax Cases—*Mayes v Woods* [1997] STC (SCD) 206*.
Definitions—''Asset'', s 21(1); ''associated disposal'', s 164(7), Sch 6 para 4(1); ''the Board'', s 288(1); ''company'', ss 99, 288(1); ''employment'', Sch 6 para 1(2); ''full-time working officer or employee'', Sch 6 para 1(2); ''the Management Act'', s 288(1); ''material disposal of business assets'', s 163, Sch 6 para 4(1); ''office'', Sch 6 para 1(2).
Amendments—[1] Words in sub-para (3) substituted by FA 1993 s 87 and Sch 7 para 2(1) in relation to disposals made after 15 March 1993.
[2] Words omitted from sub-paras (1), (3), (4) repealed, words in sub-paras (1)(a), (b), (3)(a), (b), (4)(a), (b) substituted, and sub-para (5) inserted, by FA 1996 s 134(1), (2), Sch 20 para 66, Sch 41 Pt V(10), with effect from the year 1996–97.

4—(1) In this Schedule—

(a) ''material disposal of business assets'' has the same meaning as in section 163;

(b) ''employee's disposal'' means a disposal falling within subsection (1) of section 164;

(c) ''trustee's disposal'' means a disposal falling within subsection (3) of section 164 and, in relation to such a disposal, ''the qualifying beneficiary'' has the meaning assigned to it by paragraph (b) of that subsection;

(d) ''associated disposal'' has the meaning assigned to it by section 164(7);

and ''qualifying disposal'' means any of the disposals referred to in paragraphs (a) to (d) above.

(2) Any reference in this Schedule to the qualifying period is a reference to the period of at least one year which—

(a) in relation to a material disposal of business assets, is referred to in subsection (3), subsection (4)(a) or subsection (5) (as the case may require) of section 163;

(b) in relation to an employee's disposal, is referred to in section 164(2)(a);

(c) in relation to a trustees' disposal, is referred to in subsection (4) or subsection (5) (as the case may require) of section 164;

and, in relation to an associated disposal, any reference in this Schedule to the qualifying period is a reference to that period which is the qualifying period in relation to the material disposal of business assets with which the associated disposal is associated in accordance with section 164(7).

(3) In relation to a qualifying disposal, any reference in this Schedule to the amount available for relief is a reference to the amount determined in accordance with paragraphs 13 to 16 below.

Commentary—*Simon's Direct Tax Service* **C3.608, 609.**
Definition—"Asset", s 21(1).

PART II
THE OPERATION OF THE RELIEF
Disposals on which relief may be given

5—(1) Relief in accordance with this Schedule shall not be given in respect of any disposal unless the qualifying period relating to that disposal ends on or after 6th April 1985.

(2) Except in the case of a disposal which is made by an individual who has attained [the age of 50]¹, relief in accordance with this Schedule shall be given only on the making of a claim [on or before the first anniversary of the 31st January next following]² the year of assessment in which the disposal occurred.

(3) In the case of a trustees' disposal, relief in accordance with this Schedule shall be given only on a claim made jointly by the trustees and the beneficiary concerned.

(4) Where a claim for relief in accordance with this Schedule is dependent upon an individual having retired on ill-health grounds below [the age of 50]¹, the claim shall be made to the Board.

Commentary—*Simon's Direct Tax Service* **C3.603, 605.**
Definitions—"The Board", s 288(1); "qualifying period", Sch 6 para 4(2); "year of assessment", s 288(1).
Amendments—¹ Words in sub-paras (2), (4) substituted by FA 1996 s 176 with effect in relation to disposals after 27 November 1995.
² Words in sub-para (2) substituted by FA 1996 s 135(1), (2), Sch 21 para 44(3) with effect from the year 1996–97.

Gains qualifying for relief

6 Subject to paragraphs 9 and 10 below, in the case of any qualifying disposal other than one of shares or securities of a company, the gains accruing to the individual or, in the case of a trustees' disposal, the trustees on the disposal of chargeable business assets comprised in the qualifying disposal shall be aggregated, and only so much of that aggregate as exceeds the amount available for relief shall be chargeable gains (but not so as to affect liability in respect of gains accruing on the disposal of assets other than chargeable business assets).

Commentary—*Simon's Direct Tax Service* **C3.603.**
Simon's Tax Cases—*Durrant v IRC* [1995] STC (SCD) 145*.
Definitions—"Amount available for relief", Sch 6 para 4(3); "asset", s 21(1); "chargeable business assets", Sch 6 para 12(2); "chargeable gain", s 15(2); "company", ss 99, 288(1); "qualifying disposal", Sch 6 para 4(1); "shares", s 288(1).
Cross references—See TCGA 1992 Sch 6 para 12 (computation of aggregate gains under this para).

7—(1) Subject to paragraphs 9 to 11 below, in the case of a qualifying disposal of shares or securities of a trading company which is not a holding company,—

   (*a*) the gains which on the disposal accrue to the individual or, as the case may be, the trustees shall be aggregated, and

   (*b*) of the appropriate proportion of the aggregated gains, only so much as exceeds the amount available for relief shall constitute chargeable gains (but not so as to affect liability in respect of gains representing the balance of the aggregated gains).

(2) For the purposes of sub-paragraph (1)(*b*) above, "the appropriate proportion" is that which that part of the value of the company's chargeable assets immediately before the end of the qualifying period which is attributable to the value of the company's chargeable business assets bears to the whole of that value, but, in the case of a company which has no chargeable assets, "the appropriate proportion" is the whole.

(3) For the purposes of this paragraph, every asset is a chargeable asset except one, on the disposal of which by the company immediately before the end of the qualifying period, no gain accruing to the company would be a chargeable gain.

Commentary—*Simon's Direct Tax Service* **C3.608.**
Revenue & other press releases—IR 17-10-78 (a "chargeable asset" is an asset on disposal of which, the gain or loss arising would be a chargeable gain or allowable loss).
IR 23-11-78 ("chargeable asset" includes plant and machinery with a CGT cost of more than £6,000 and a market value less than cost, whether the market value is more or less than £6,000).
Revenue Internal Guidance—Capital gains manual CG 63783–63784 (explanation with worked examples).
Definitions—"Amount available for relief", Sch 6 para 4(3); "asset", s 21(1); "chargeable business assets", Sch 6 para 12(2); "chargeable gain", s 15(2); "company", ss 99, 288(1); "holding company", Sch 6 para 1(2); "qualifying disposal", Sch 6 para 4(1); "qualifying period", Sch 6 para 4(2); "shares", s 288(1); "trading company", Sch 6 para 1(2).
Cross references—See TCGA 1992 s 165(3)(*b*) (relief for gifts of business assets not applicable where relief under this Schedule is available on proportion of gains determined under this paragraph).
TCGA 1992 Sch 6 para 12 (computation of aggregate gains under this para).

8—(1) Subject to paragraphs 9 to 11 below, in the case of a qualifying disposal of shares or securities of a holding company—

TCGA 1992

(*a*) the gains which on the disposal accrue to the individual or, as the case may be, the trustees shall be aggregated, and

(*b*) of the appropriate proportion of the aggregated gains, only so much as exceeds the amount available for relief shall constitute chargeable gains (but not so as to affect liability in respect of gains representing the balance of the aggregated gains).

(2) For the purposes of sub-paragraph (1)(*b*) above, "the appropriate proportion" is that which that part of the value of the trading group's chargeable assets immediately before the end of the qualifying period which is attributable to the value of the trading group's chargeable business assets bears to the whole of that value; but, in the case of a trading group which has no chargeable assets, "the appropriate proportion" is the whole.

(3) For the purposes of sub-paragraph (2) above—

(*a*) any reference to the trading group's chargeable assets or chargeable business assets is a reference to the chargeable assets or, as the case may be, chargeable business assets of every member of the trading group; and

(*b*) subject to paragraph (*c*) below, every asset is a chargeable asset except one, on the disposal of which by the member of the group concerned immediately before the end of the qualifying period no gain accruing to that member would be a chargeable gain; and

(*c*) a holding by one member of the trading group of the ordinary share capital of another member of the group is not a chargeable asset.

(4) Where the whole of the ordinary share capital of a 51 per cent subsidiary of the holding company is not owned directly or indirectly by that company, then, for the purposes of sub-paragraph (2) above, the value of the chargeable assets and chargeable business assets of that subsidiary shall be taken to be reduced by multiplying it by a fraction of which the denominator is the whole of the ordinary share capital of the subsidiary and the numerator is the amount of that share capital owned, directly or indirectly, by the holding company.

(5) Expressions used in sub-paragraph (4) above have the same meaning as in section 838 of the Taxes Act (subsidiaries).

Commentary—*Simon's Direct Tax Service* **C3.608.**
Revenue Internal Guidance—Capital gains manual CG 63785–63787 (explanation with worked example).
Definitions—"Amount available for relief", Sch 6 para 4(3); "asset", s 21(1); "chargeable business assets", Sch 6 para 12(2); "chargeable gain", s 15(2); "holding company", Sch 6 para 1(2); "qualifying disposal", Sch 6 para 4(1); "qualifying period", Sch 6 para 4(2); "shares", s 288(1); "the Taxes Act", s 288(1); "trading group", Sch 6 para 1(2).
Cross references—See TCGA 1992 s 165(3)(*b*) (relief for gifts of business assets not applicable where relief under this Schedule is available on proportion of gains determined under this paragraph).
TCGA 1992 Sch 6 para 12 (computation of aggregate gains under this para).

9—(1) If, in the case of a trustees' disposal, there is, in addition to the qualifying beneficiary, at least one other beneficiary who, at the end of the qualifying period, has an interest in possession in the whole of the settled property or, as the case may be, in a part of it which consists of or includes the shares, securities or asset which is the subject matter of the disposal, only the relevant proportion of the gain which accrues to the trustees on the disposal shall be brought into account under paragraph 6, paragraph 7 or paragraph 8 above (as the case may require) and the balance of the gain shall, accordingly, be a chargeable gain.

(2) For the purposes of sub-paragraph (1) above, the relevant proportion is that which, at the end of the qualifying period, the qualifying beneficiary's interest in the income of the part of the settled property comprising the shares, securities or asset in question bears to the interests in that income of all the beneficiaries (including the qualifying beneficiary) who then have interests in possession in that part.

(3) The reference in sub-paragraph (2) above to the qualifying beneficiary's interest is a reference to the interest by virtue of which he is the qualifying beneficiary and not to any other interest he may hold.

Commentary—*Simon's Direct Tax Service* **C3.605.**
Definitions—"Asset", s 21(1); "chargeable gain", s 15(2); "qualifying beneficiary", s 164(3), Sch 6 para 4(1); "qualifying period", Sch 6 para 4(2); "settled property", s 68; "shares", s 288(1).
Cross references—See TCGA 1992 Sch 6 para 12 (computation of aggregate gains).

10—(1) If, in the case of an associated disposal—

(*a*) the asset in question was in use for the purposes of a business as mentioned in section 164(7)(*c*) for only part of the period in which it was in the ownership of the individual making the disposal, or

(*b*) for any part of the period in which the asset in question was in use for the purposes of a business as mentioned in section 164(7)(*c*), the individual making the disposal was not concerned in the carrying on of that business (whether personally, as a member of a partnership or as a [full-time working officer or employee]¹ of any such company as is referred to in section 163(3)(*b*)), or

(*c*) for the whole or any part of the period in which the asset in question was in use for the purposes of a business as mentioned in section 164(7)(*c*), its availability for that use was dependent upon the payment of rent, only such part of the gain which accrues on the disposal as [is]² just and reasonable shall be brought into account under paragraph 6, paragraph 7 or paragraph 8 above (as the case may require) and the balance of the gain shall, accordingly, be a chargeable gain.

(2) In determining how much of a gain it is just and reasonable to bring into account as mentioned in sub-paragraph (1) above, [regard shall be had]² to the length of the period the asset was in use as mentioned in that sub-paragraph and the extent to which any rent paid was less than the amount which would have been payable in the open market for the use of the asset.

(3) In sub-paragraphs (1) and (2) above "rent" includes any form of consideration given for the use of the asset.

Commentary—*Simon's Direct Tax Service* **C3.609.**
Revenue Internal Guidance—Capital gains manual CG 63830–63843 (explanation with worked examples).
Definitions—"Asset", s 21(1); "associated disposal", s 164(7), Sch 6 para 4(1); "chargeable gain", s 15(2); "company", ss 99, 288(1); "full-time working officer or employee", Sch 6 para 1(2); "rent", Sch 8 para 10(1).
Cross references—See TCGA 1992 Sch 6 para 12 (computation of aggregate gains).
Amendments—¹ Words in sub-para (1)(b) substituted by FA 1993 s 87 and Sch 7 para 2(1) in relation to disposals made after 15 March 1993.
² Words in sub-paras (1), (2) substituted by FA 1996 s 134(1), (2), Sch 20 para 66(4) with effect from the year 1996–97.

11—(1) This paragraph applies where—

(a) there is a material disposal of business assets or a trustees' disposal which (in either case) consists of a disposal which the individual or trustees is or are treated as making by virtue of section 122 in consideration of a capital distribution; and
(b) the capital distribution consists wholly of chargeable business assets of the company or partly of such assets and partly of money or money's worth.

(2) Where the capital distribution consists wholly of chargeable business assets, no relief shall be given under this Schedule in respect of the gains accruing on the disposal.

(3) Where the capital distribution consists only partly of chargeable business assets, the gains accruing on the disposal (aggregated as mentioned in paragraph 7(1)(a) or paragraph 8(1)(a) above) shall be reduced for the purposes of this Schedule by multiplying them by the fraction—

$$\frac{A}{B}$$

where—

A is the part of the capital distribution which does not consist of chargeable business assets; and

B is the entire capital distribution;

and it shall be to that reduced amount of aggregated gains that, in accordance with sub-paragraph (1)(b) of paragraph 7 or, as the case may be, paragraph 8 above, the appropriate proportion determined under sub-paragraph (2) of that paragraph shall be applied.

(4) Any question whether or to what extent a capital distribution consists of chargeable business assets shall be determined by reference to the status of the assets immediately before the end of the qualifying period.

Commentary—*Simon's Direct Tax Service* **C3.608.**
Definitions—"Asset", s 21(1); "chargeable business assets", Sch 6 para 12(2); "company", ss 99, 288(1); "material disposal of business assets", s 163, Sch 6 para 4(1); "qualifying period", Sch 6 para 4(2).
Cross references—See TCGA 1992 Sch 6 para 12 (computation of aggregate gains).

12—(1) Subject to paragraphs 9 to 11 above, in arriving at the aggregate gains under any of paragraphs 6, 7(1) and 8(1) above—

(a) the respective amounts of the gains shall be computed in accordance with the provisions of this Act fixing the amount of chargeable gains, and
(b) any allowable loss which accrues on the qualifying disposal concerned shall be deducted,

and the provisions of this Schedule shall not affect the computation of the amount of any allowable loss.

(2) Subject to the following provisions of this paragraph, in paragraphs 6 to 11 above, "chargeable business asset" means an asset (including goodwill but not including shares or securities or other assets held as investments) which is, or is an interest in, an asset used for the purposes of a trade, profession, vocation, office or employment carried on by—

(a) the individual concerned; or
(b) that individual's [personal company]¹; or
(c) a member of a trading group of which the holding company is that individual's [personal company]¹; or
(d) a partnership of which the individual concerned is a member.

(3) An asset is not a chargeable business asset if, on the disposal of it, no gain which might accrue would be a chargeable gain.

(4) In relation to a trustees' disposal, references in sub-paragraph (2) above to the individual shall be construed as references to the beneficiary concerned.

(5) Sub-paragraph (6) below applies if—

(*a*) a qualifying disposal falling within paragraph 7 or paragraph 8 above is a disposal which the individual or trustees concerned is or are treated as making by virtue of section 122 in consideration of a capital distribution; and

(*b*) [on or before the first anniversary of the 31st January next following][2] the year of assessment in which the individual or the trustees received the capital distribution, the individual or trustees by notice to [an officer of the Board][2] elects or elect that that sub-paragraph should apply.

(6) If, in a case where this sub-paragraph applies in relation to a qualifying disposal, any part of the assets of the company concerned consists, as at the end of the qualifying period, of the proceeds of the sale of an asset sold not more than 6 months before the end of that period, then, sub-paragraph (2) above and paragraph 7 or, as the case may be, paragraph 8 above shall have effect as if, at that time—

(*a*) the asset remained the property of the company and was in use for the purposes for which it was used before its sale; and

(*b*) the proceeds of sale of the asset did not form part of the assets of the company.

Commentary—*Simon's Direct Tax Service* **C3.602, 608.**
Simon's Tax Cases—Sub-para (2), *Durrant v IRC* [1995] STC (SCD) 145*.
Definitions—''Allowable loss'', ss 8(2), 16, 288(1); ''asset'', s 21(1); ''the Board'', s 288(1); ''chargeable gain'', s 15(2); ''company'', ss 99, 288(1); ''employment'', Sch 6 para 1(2); ''holding company'', Sch 6 para 1(2); ''notice'', s 288(1); ''office'', Sch 6 para 1(2); ''personal company'', Sch 6 para 1(2); ''profession'', Sch 6 para 1(2); ''qualifying disposal'', Sch 6 para 4(1); ''qualifying period'', Sch 6 para 4(2); ''shares'', s 288(1); ''trade'', Sch 6 para 1(2); ''trading group'', Sch 6 para 1(2); ''vocation'', Sch 6 para 1(2); ''year of assessment'', s 288(1).
Amendments—[1] Words in sub-para (2)(*b*), (*c*) substituted by FA 1993 s 87 and Sch 7 para 1(1) in relation to disposals made after 15 March 1993.
[2] Words in sub-para (5)(*b*) substituted by FA 1996 s 135(1), (2), Sch 21 para 44(4) with effect from the year 1996–97.

The amount available for relief: the basic rule

13—(1) Subject to the following provisions of this Part of this Schedule, on a qualifying disposal by an individual the amount available for relief by virtue of sections 163 and 164 is an amount equal to the aggregate of—

(*a*) so much of the gains qualifying for relief as do not exceed the appropriate percentage of [£100,000][1]; and

(*b*) one half of so much of those gains as exceed the appropriate percentage of [£100,000][1] but do not exceed that percentage of [£400,000][1];

and for the purposes of this sub-paragraph ''the appropriate percentage'' is a percentage determined according to the length of the qualifying period which is appropriate to the disposal on a scale rising arithmetically from 10 per cent where that period is precisely one year to 100 per cent where it is 10 years.

(2) In sub-paragraph (1) above ''the gains qualifying for relief'' means, in relation to any qualifying disposal, so much of the gains accruing on that disposal (aggregated under paragraph 6, 7(1)(*a*) or 8(1)(*a*) above) as would, by virtue of this Schedule, not be chargeable gains if—

(*a*) sub-paragraph (1) above had specified as the amount available for relief a fixed sum in excess of those aggregate gains; and

(*b*) paragraphs 14 to 16 below were disregarded.

(3) The amount available for relief by virtue of section 164 on a trustees' disposal shall be determined, subject to sub-paragraph (4) below, in accordance with sub-paragraph (1) above on the assumption that the trustees' disposal is a qualifying disposal by the qualifying beneficiary.

(4) If, on the same day, there is both a trustees' disposal and a material disposal of business assets by the qualifying beneficiary, the amount available for relief shall be applied to the beneficiary's disposal in priority to the trustees' disposal.

Commentary—*Simon's Direct Tax Service* **C3.605, 610.**
Revenue Internal Guidance—Capital gains manual CG 63861 (history of the limits in sub-para (1)).
CG 63871–63873 (worked examples).
CG 63920, 63921 (worked example on sub-paras (2), (3)).
Definitions—''Amount available for relief'', Sch 6 para 4(3); ''asset'', s 21(1); ''chargeable gain'', s 15(2); ''material disposal of business assets'', s 163, Sch 6 para 4(1); ''qualifying beneficiary'', s 164(3), Sch 6 para 4(1); ''qualifying disposal'', Sch 6 para 4(1); ''qualifying period'', Sch 6 para 4(2).
Amendments—[1] Amounts in sub-para (1)(*a*), (*b*) substituted by the table in FA 1998 s 140(1) with effect for the year 2001–02.
Prospective amendments—Amounts in sub-para (1)(*a*), (*b*) will be substituted by the table in FA 1998 s 140(1) with effect for the year 2002–03.

Aggregation of earlier business periods

14—(1) If, apart from this paragraph, the qualifying period appropriate to a qualifying disposal (''the original qualifying period'') would be less than 10 years but throughout some period (''the earlier business period'') which—

(*a*) ends not earlier than 2 years before the beginning of the original qualifying period, and

(*b*) falls, in whole or in part, within the period of 10 years ending at the end of the original qualifying period,

the individual making the disposal or, as the case may be, the relevant beneficiary was concerned in the carrying on of another business (''the previous business'') then, for the purpose of determining the amount available for relief on the qualifying disposal, the length of the qualifying period appropriate to that disposal shall be redetermined on the assumptions and subject to the provisions set out below.

(2) For the purposes of the redetermination referred to in sub-paragraph (1) above, it shall be assumed that the previous business is the same business as the business at retirement and, in the first instance, any time between the end of the earlier business period and the beginning of the [original][2] qualifying period shall be disregarded (so that those 2 periods shall be assumed to be one continuous period).

(3) The reference in sub-paragraph (1) above to a person being concerned in the carrying on of a business is a reference to his being so concerned personally or as a member of a partnership or, if the business was owned by a company, then as a [full-time working officer or employee][1] of that company or, as the case may be, of any member of the group or commercial association of which it is a member; and the reference in sub-paragraph (2) above to the business at retirement is a reference to that business which, in relation to the qualifying disposal, is referred to—

   (*a*) in subsection (3), subsection (4) or subsection (5) of section 163 where the qualifying disposal is a material disposal of business assets;

   (*b*) in subsection (5) of section 164 where that disposal is a trustees' disposal; and

   (*c*) in subsection (7) of section 164 where that disposal is an associated disposal.

(4) Any extended qualifying period resulting from the operation of sub-paragraph (2) above shall not begin earlier than the beginning of the period of 10 years referred to in sub-paragraph (1)(*b*) above.

(5) If the earlier business period ended before the beginning of the original qualifying period, any extended qualifying period which would otherwise result from the operation of the preceding provisions of this paragraph shall be reduced by deducting therefrom a period equal to that between the ending of the earlier business period and the beginning of the original qualifying period.

(6) Where there is more than one business which qualifies as the previous business and, accordingly, more than one period which qualifies as the earlier business period, this paragraph shall apply first in relation to that one of those businesses in which the individual in question was last concerned and shall then again apply (as if any extended qualifying period resulting from the first application were the original qualifying period) in relation to the next of those businesses and so on.

[(7) In relation to the expression "the original qualifying period", the questions whether a disposal is a qualifying disposal and whether the period relating to that disposal is a qualifying period shall be determined without regard to the requirement that the length of the period be at least one year.][2]

[(8) This paragraph shall not apply if the extended qualifying period resulting from the operation of subparagraphs (1) to (7) would be a period of less than one year.][2]

Commentary—*Simon's Direct Tax Service* **C3.611.**
Revenue Interpretation RI 165—If the relevant business is owned for some period by a company which is not the individual's personal company, the qualifying conditions will not all be met and the qualifying period cannot be extended.
Revenue Internal Guidance—Capital gains manual CG 63890–63895 (explanation with worked examples).
Definitions—"Amount available for relief", Sch 6 para 4(3); "asset", s 21(1); "associated disposal", s 164(7), Sch 6 para 4(1); "company", ss 99, 288(1); "full-time working officer or employee", Sch 6 para 1(2); "material disposal of business assets", s 163, Sch 6 para 4(1); "qualifying disposal", Sch 6 para 4(1); "qualifying period", Sch 6 para 4(2).
Cross references—See TCGA 1992 Sch 6 para 13 (amount available for retirement relief).
Amendments—[1] Words in sub-para (3) substituted by FA 1993 s 87 and Sch 7 para 2(1) in relation to disposals made after 15 March 1993.
[2] Word in sub-para (2) and whole of sub-paras (7), (8) inserted by FA 1996 Sch 39 para 7 with effect in relation to disposals made after 5 April 1996.

Relief given on earlier disposal

5—(1) In any case where—

   (*a*) an individual makes a qualifying disposal or is the qualifying beneficiary in relation to a trustees' disposal, and

   (*b*) relief has been (or falls to be) given under this Schedule in respect of an earlier disposal which was either a qualifying disposal made by the individual or a trustees' disposal in respect of which he was the qualifying beneficiary,

the amount which, apart from this paragraph, would be the amount available for relief on the disposal mentioned in paragraph (*a*) above shall not exceed the limit in sub-paragraph (3) below.

(2) In the following provisions of this paragraph—

   (*a*) the disposal falling within sub-paragraph (1)(*a*) above is referred to as "the later disposal"; and

   (*b*) the disposal falling within sub-paragraph (1)(*b*) above or, if there is more than one such disposal, each of them is referred to as "the earlier disposal".

(3) The limit referred to in sub-paragraph (1) above is the difference between—

   (*a*) the amount which would be available for relief on the later disposal—

      (i) if the gains qualifying for relief on that disposal were increased by the amount of the underlying gains relieved on the earlier disposal (or the aggregate amount of the underlying gains relieved on all the earlier disposals, as the case may be); and

(ii) if the qualifying period appropriate to the later disposal (as redetermined where appropriate under paragraph 14 above) were extended by the addition of a period equal to so much (if any) of the qualifying period appropriate to the earlier disposal (or, as the case may be, to each of the earlier disposals) as does not already fall within the qualifying period appropriate to the later disposal; and

(b) the amount of relief given under this Schedule on the earlier disposal or, as the case may be, the aggregate of the relief so given on all the earlier disposals.

(4) Where there is only one earlier disposal, or where there are 2 or more such disposals but none of them took place on or after 6th April 1988, then, for the purposes of sub-paragraph (3)(a)(i) above—

(a) if the earlier disposal took place on or after 6th April 1988, the amount of the underlying gains relieved on that disposal is the aggregate of—

(i) so much of the gains qualifying for relief on that disposal as were, by virtue of paragraph 13(1)(a) above, not chargeable gains; and

(ii) twice the amount of so much of those gains as were, by virtue of paragraph 13(1)(b) above, not chargeable gains; and

(b) if the earlier disposal took place before 6th April 1988, the amount of the underlying gains retrieved on that disposal (or on each such disposal) is so much of the gains qualifying for relief on that disposal as were, by virtue of paragraph 13 of Schedule 20 to the Finance Act 1985 not chargeable gains.

(5) Where there are 2 or more earlier disposals and at least one of them took place on or after 6th April 1988, then, for the purposes of sub-paragraph (3)(a)(i) above, the aggregate amount of the underlying gains relieved on all those disposals shall be determined as follows—

(a) it shall be assumed for the purposes of paragraph (b) below—

(i) that the amount which resulted from the calculation under sub-paragraph (3)(a) above on the last of those disposals ("the last disposal") was the amount of the gains qualifying for relief on that disposal which were, by virtue of this Schedule, not chargeable gains ("the gains actually relieved");

(ii) that the qualifying period appropriate to that disposal (as redetermined where appropriate under paragraph 14 above) was that period as extended in accordance with sub-paragraph (3)(a)(ii) above; and

(iii) that the last disposal was the only earlier disposal;

(b) there shall then be ascertained in accordance with paragraph 13(1) above (but on the assumptions in paragraph (a) above)—

(i) how much of the gains actually relieved would, by virtue of paragraph 13(1)(a) above, not have been chargeable gains; and

(ii) how much of those gains would, by virtue of paragraph 13(1)(b) above, not have been chargeable gains; and

(c) the aggregate amount of the underlying gains relieved on all the earlier disposals is the sum of—

(i) the amount ascertained under paragraph (b)(i) above; and

(ii) twice the amount ascertained under paragraph (b)(ii) above.

(6) In this paragraph "the gains qualifying for relief" has the meaning given by paragraph 13(2) above.

(7) References in this paragraph to relief given under this Schedule include references to relief given under section 34 of the Finance Act 1965 or section 124 of the 1979 Act; and—

(a) in relation to relief given under either of those sections, paragraph (b) of sub-paragraph (1) above shall have effect as if, for the words from "which was" onwards, there were substituted "made by the individual"; and

(b) for the purpose of determining the limit in sub-paragraph (3) above where the earlier disposal (or any of the earlier disposals) was a disposal in respect of which relief was given under either of those sections—

(i) the underlying gains relieved on that disposal shall (subject to sub-paragraph (5) above) be taken to be gains of an amount equal to the relief given under the section in question in respect of that disposal; and

(ii) the reference in sub-paragraph (3)(a)(ii) above to the qualifying period appropriate to the earlier disposal shall be taken to be a reference to the qualifying period within the meaning of the section in question.

Commentary—*Simon's Direct Tax Service* **C3.612.**
Revenue Internal Guidance—Capital Gains Manual CG 63880–63881 (cases are to be submitted to Head Office).
Definitions—"The 1979 Act", s 288(1); "amount available for relief", Sch 6 para 4(3); "chargeable gain", s 15(2); "qualifying beneficiary", s 164(3), Sch 6 para 4(1); "qualifying disposal", Sch 6 para 4(1); "qualifying period", Sch 6 para 4(2).
Cross references—See TCGA 1992 Sch 6 para 13 (amount available for retirement relief).

Aggregation of spouse's interest in the business

16—(1) In any case where—

(a) an individual makes a material disposal of business assets, and (*b*) the subject matter of that disposal (whether business, assets or shares or securities) was acquired, in whole or in part, from that individual's spouse, and

(*c*) that acquisition was either under the will or intestacy of the spouse or by way of lifetime gift and in the year of assessment in which occurred the spouse's death or, as the case may be, the lifetime gift, the individual and his spouse were living together, and

(*d*) as a result of the acquisition the individual acquired the whole of the interest in the business, assets, shares or securities concerned which, immediately before the acquisition or, as the case may be, the spouse's death, was held by the spouse, and

(*e*) [on or before the first anniversary of the 31st January next following]¹ the year of assessment in which the material disposal occurred, the individual elects that this paragraph should apply,

the period which, apart from this paragraph, would be the qualifying period appropriate to that disposal shall be extended by assuming that, in the conditions which under section 163 are the relevant conditions applicable to the disposal, any reference to the individual were a reference either to the individual or his spouse.

(2) An election under sub-paragraph (1)(*e*) above shall be made by notice to [an officer of the Board]¹.

(3) Where the acquisition referred to in sub-paragraph (1)(*c*) above was by way of lifetime gift, the amount available for relief on the material disposal concerned, having regard to the extension of the qualifying period under sub-paragraph (1) above, shall not exceed the limit specified in sub-paragraph (4) below.

(4) The limit referred to in sub-paragraph (3) above is the amount which would have been available for relief on the material disposal if—

(*a*) the lifetime gift had not occurred; and

(*b*) the material disposal had been made by the spouse; and

(*c*) anything done by the individual in relation to the business concerned after the lifetime gift was in fact made had been done by the spouse.

Commentary—*Simon's Direct Tax Service* **C3.613.**
Revenue Internal Guidance—Capital Gains Manual CG 63900–63908 (explanation with examples).
Definitions—''Amount available for relief'', Sch 6 para 4(3); ''asset'', s 21(1); ''the Board'', s 288(1); ''material disposal of business assets'', s 163, Sch 6 para 4(1); ''notice'', s 288(1); ''qualifying period'', Sch 6 para 4(2); ''shares'', s 288(1); ''year of assessment'', s 288(1).
Cross references—See TCGA 1992 Sch 6 para 13 (amount available for retirement relief).
Amendments—¹ Words in sub-paras (1)(*e*), (2) substituted by FA 1996 s 135(1), (2), Sch 21 para 44(5) with effect from the year 1996–97.

SCHEDULE 7

RELIEF FOR GIFTS OF BUSINESS ASSETS

Section 165

PART I

AGRICULTURAL PROPERTY AND SETTLED PROPERTY

Agricultural property

1—(1) This paragraph applies where—

(*a*) there is a disposal of an asset which is, or is an interest in, agricultural property within the meaning of Chapter II of Part V of the Inheritance Tax Act 1984 (inheritance tax relief for agricultural property), and

(*b*) apart from this paragraph, the disposal would not fall within section 165(1) by reason only that the agricultural property is not used for the purposes of a trade carried on as mentioned in section 165(2)(*a*).

(2) Where this paragraph applies, section 165(1) shall apply in relation to the disposal if the circumstances are such that a reduction in respect of the asset—

(*a*) is made under Chapter II of Part V of the Inheritance Tax Act 1984 in relation to a chargeable transfer taking place on the occasion of the disposal, or

(*b*) would be so made if there were a chargeable transfer on that occasion, or

(*c*) would be so made but for section 124A of that Act (assuming, where there is no chargeable transfer on that occasion, that there were).

Commentary—*Simon's Direct Tax Service* **C3.505.**
Statement of Practice SP 8/92—Valuation of gifts in respect of which CGT holdover relief is available.
Revenue Interpretation RI 8—(Holdover relief for gifts by reference to the nature of the gifted assets rather than their value).
Revenue & other press releases—Law Society 18-3-92 (valuation of agricultural tenancies: principles to be applied).
Definitions—''Asset'', s 21(1); ''trade'', s 165(8), TA 1988 s 832(1).

Settled property

2—(1) If—

(*a*) the trustees of a settlement make a disposal otherwise than under a bargain at arm's length of an asset within sub-paragraph (2) below, and

(*b*) a claim for relief under section 165 is made by the trustees and the person who acquires the asset ("the transferee") or, where the trustees of a settlement are also the transferee, by the trustees making the disposal alone,

then, subject to sections 165(3), 166, 167 and 169, section 165(4) shall apply in relation to the disposal.

(2) An asset is within this sub-paragraph if—

(*a*) it is, or is an interest in, an asset used for the purposes of a trade, profession or vocation carried on by—

(i) the trustees making the disposal, or

(ii) a beneficiary who had an interest in possession in the settled property immediately before the disposal, or

(*b*) it consists of shares or securities of a trading company, or of the holding company of a trading group, where—

(i) the shares or securities are [not listed on a recognised stock exchange]², or

(ii) not less than 25 per cent of the voting rights exercisable by shareholders of the company in general meeting are exercisable by the trustees at the time of the disposal.

(3) Where section 165(4) applies by virtue of this paragraph, references to the trustees shall be substituted for the references in section 165(4)(*a*) to the transferor; and where it applies in relation to a disposal which is deemed to occur by virtue of section 71(1) or 72(1) section 165(7) shall not apply.

Commentary—*Simon's Direct Tax Service* C3.506.
Statement of Practice SP 8/92—Valuation of gifts in respect of which CGT holdover relief is available.
Definitions—"Asset", s 21(1); "company", ss 99, 288(1); "holding company", s 165(8), Sch 6 para 1; "profession", s 165(8); "settled property", s 68; "shares", s 288(1); "trade", s 165(8), TA 1988 s 832(1); "trading company", s 165(8), Sch 6 para 1; "trading group", s 165(8), Sch 6 para 1; "vocation", s 165(8).
Cross references—See TCGA 1992 Sch 7 para 3 (disposal of agricultural property not used for purposes of trade).
Amendments—¹ Word in sub-para (2)(*b*)(i) substituted by FA 1996 Sch 38 para 10(1), (2)(*f*), (3) with effect in relation to disposals after 31 March 1996.
² Words in sub-para (2)(*b*)(i) substituted by FA 2000 s 90(3), (5) with effect for disposals after 8 November 1999.

3—(1) This paragraph applies where—

(*a*) there is a disposal of an asset which is, or is an interest in, agricultural property within the meaning of Chapter II of Part V of the Inheritance Tax Act 1984 and

(*b*) apart from this paragraph, the disposal would not fall within paragraph 2(1)(*a*) above by reason only that the agricultural property is not used for the purposes of a trade as mentioned in paragraph 2(2)(*a*) above.

(2) Where this paragraph applies paragraph 2(1) above shall apply in relation to the disposal if the circumstances are such that a reduction in respect of the asset—

(*a*) is made under Chapter II of Part V of the Inheritance Tax Act 1984 in relation to a chargeable transfer taking place on the occasion of the disposal, or

(*b*) would be so made if there were a chargeable transfer on that occasion, or

(*c*) would be so made but for section 124A of that Act (assuming, where there is no chargeable transfer on that occasion, that there were).

Statement of Practice SP 8/92—Valuation of gifts in respect of which CGT holdover relief is available.
Definitions—"Asset", s 21(1); "trade", s 165(8), TA 1988 s 832(1).

PART II

REDUCTIONS IN HELD-OVER GAIN

Application and interpretation

4—(1) The provisions of this Part of this Schedule apply in cases where a claim for relief is made under section 165.

(2) In this Part of this Schedule—

(*a*) "the principal provision" means section 165(2), or, as the case may require, sub-paragraph (2) of paragraph 2 above,

(*b*) "shares" includes securities,

(*c*) "the transferor" has the same meaning as in section 165 except that, in a case where paragraph 2 above applies, it refers to the trustees mentioned in that paragraph, and

(*d*) "unrelieved gain", in relation to a disposal, has the same meaning as in section 165(7).

(3) In this Part of this Schedule—

(*a*) any reference to a disposal of an asset is a reference to a disposal which falls within subsection (1) of section 165 by virtue of subsection (2)(*a*) of that section or, as the case may be, falls within sub-paragraph (1) of paragraph 2 above by virtue of sub-paragraph (2)(*a*) of that paragraph, and

(*b*) any reference to a disposal of shares is a reference to a disposal which falls within subsection (1) of section 165 by virtue of subsection (2)(*b*) of that section or, as the case may be, falls within sub-paragraph (1) of paragraph 2 above by virtue of sub-paragraph (2)(*b*) of that paragraph.

(4) In relation to a disposal of an asset or of shares, any reference in the following provisions of this Part of this Schedule to the held-over gain is a reference to the held-over gain on that disposal as determined under subsection (6) or, where it applies, subsection (7) of section 165.

Definitions—"Asset", s 21(1); "shares", s 288(1).

Reductions peculiar to disposals of assets

5—(1) If, in the case of a disposal of an asset, the asset was not used for the purposes of the trade, profession or vocation referred to in paragraph (*a*) of the principal provision throughout the period of its ownership by the transferor, the amount of the held-over gain shall be reduced by multiplying it by the fraction—

$$\frac{A}{B}$$

where—

A is the number of days in that period of ownership during which the asset was so used, and

B is the number of days in that period.

(2) This paragraph shall not apply where the circumstances are such that a reduction in respect of the asset—

(*a*) is made under Chapter II of Part V of the Inheritance Tax Act 1984 in relation to a chargeable transfer taking place on the occasion of the disposal, or

(*b*) would be so made if there were a chargeable transfer on that occasion, or

(*c*) would be so made but for section 124A of that Act (assuming, where there is no chargeable transfer on that occasion, that there were).

Commentary—*Simon's Direct Tax Service* **C3.504.**
Definitions—"Asset", s 21(1); "disposal of an asset", Sch 7 para 4(3); "held-over gain", Sch 7 para 4(4); "principal provision", Sch 7 para 4(2); "profession", s 165(8); "trade", s 165(8), TA 1988 s 832(1); "transferor", Sch 7 para 4(2); "vocation", s 165(8).

6—(1) If, in the case of a disposal of an asset, the asset is a building or structure and, over the period of its ownership by the transferor or any substantial part of that period, part of the building or structure was, and part was not, used for the purposes of the trade, profession or vocation referred to in paragraph (*a*) of the principal provision, there shall be determined the fraction of the unrelieved gain on the disposal which it is just and reasonable to apportion to the part of the asset which was so used, and the amount of the held-over gain (as reduced, if appropriate, under paragraph 5 above) shall be reduced by multiplying it by that fraction.

(2) This paragraph shall not apply where the circumstances are such that a reduction in respect of the asset—

(*a*) is made under Chapter II of Part V of the Inheritance Tax Act 1984 in relation to a chargeable transfer taking place on the occasion of the disposal, or

(*b*) would be so made if there were a chargeable transfer on that occasion, or

(*c*) would be so made but for section 124A of that Act (assuming, where there is no chargeable transfer on that occasion, that there were).

Commentary—*Simon's Direct Tax Service* **C3.504.**
Definitions—"Asset", s 21(1); "disposal of an asset", Sch 7 para 4(3); "held-over gain", Sch 7 para 4(4); "principal provision", Sch 7 para 4(2); "profession", s 165(8); "trade", s 165(8), TA 1988 s 832(1); "transferor", Sch 7 para 4(2); "unrelieved gain", Sch 7 para 4(2); "vocation", s 165(8).

Reduction peculiar to disposal of shares

7—(1) If in the case of a disposal of shares assets which are not business assets are included in the chargeable assets of the company whose shares are disposed of, or, where that company is the holding company of a trading group, in the group's chargeable assets, and either—

(*a*) at any time within the period of 12 months before the disposal not less than 25 per cent of the voting rights exercisable by shareholders of the company in general meeting are exercisable by the transferor, or

(*b*) the transferor is an individual and, at any time within that period, the company is his [personal company]¹, the amount of the held-over gain shall be reduced by multiplying it by the fraction—

$$\frac{A}{B}$$

where—

A is the market value on the date of the disposal of those chargeable assets of the company or of the group which are business assets, and

B is the market value on that date of all the chargeable assets of the company, or as the case may be of the group.

(2) For the purposes of this paragraph—

(*a*) an asset is a business asset in relation to a company or a group if it is or is an interest in an asset used for the purposes of a trade, profession or vocation carried on by the company, or as the case may be by a member of the group; and

(*b*) an asset is a chargeable asset in relation to a company or a group at any time if, on a disposal at that time, a gain accruing to the company, or as the case may be to a member of the group, would be a chargeable gain.

(3) Where the shares disposed of are shares of the holding company of a trading group, then for the purposes of this paragraph—

(*a*) the holding by one member of the group of the ordinary share capital of another member shall not count as a chargeable asset, and

(*b*) if the whole of the ordinary share capital of a 51 per cent subsidiary of the holding company is not owned directly or indirectly by that company, the value of the chargeable assets of the subsidiary shall be taken to be reduced by multiplying it by the fraction—

$$\frac{A}{B}$$

where—

A is the amount of the ordinary share capital of the subsidiary owned directly or indirectly by the holding company, and

B is the whole of that share capital.

(4) Expressions used in sub-paragraph (3) above have the same meanings as in section 838 of the Taxes Act.

Commentary—*Simon's Direct Tax Service* **C3.504.**
Definitions—"Asset", s 21(1); "chargeable gain", s 15(2); "company", ss 99, 288(1); "disposal of an asset", Sch 7 para 4(3); "disposal of shares", Sch 7 para 4(3); "held-over gain", Sch 7 para 4(4); "holding company", s 165(8), Sch 6 para 1; "market value", Sch 7 para 7; "personal company", s 165(8) Sch 6 para 1; "profession", s 165(8); "shares", s 288(1), Sch 7 para 4(2); "the Taxes Act", s 288(1); "trade", s 165(8), TA 1988 s 832(1); "trading group", s 165(8), Sch 6 para 1; "transferor", Sch 7 para 4(2); "vocation", s 165(8).
Amendments—[1] Words in sub-para (1)(*b*) substituted by FA 1993 s 87 Sch 7 para 1(1) in relation to disposals made after 15 March 1993.

Reduction where gain partly relieved by retirement relief

8—(1) If, in the case of a disposal of an asset—

(*a*) the disposal is of a chargeable business asset and is comprised in a disposal of the whole or part of a business in respect of gains accruing on which the transferor is entitled to relief under Schedule 6, and

(*b*) apart from this paragraph, the held-over gain on the disposal (as reduced, where appropriate, under the preceding provisions of this Part of this Schedule) would exceed the amount of the chargeable gain which, apart from section 165 would accrue on the disposal,

the amount of that held-over gain shall be reduced by the amount of the excess.

(2) In sub-paragraph (1) above "chargeable business asset" has the same meaning as in Schedule 6

(3) If, in the case of a disposal of shares—

(*a*) the disposal is or forms part of a disposal of shares in respect of the gains accruing on which the transferor is entitled to relief under Schedule 6, and

(*b*) apart from this paragraph, the held-over gain on the disposal (as reduced, where appropriate under paragraph 7 above) would exceed an amount equal to the relevant proportion of the chargeable gain which, apart from section 165, would accrue on the disposal,

the amount of that held-over gain shall be reduced by the amount of the excess.

(4) In sub-paragraph (3) above "the relevant proportion", in relation to a disposal falling within paragraph (*a*) of that sub-paragraph, means the appropriate proportion determined under Schedule 6 in relation to the aggregate sum of the gains which accrue on that disposal.

Commentary—*Simon's Direct Tax Service* **C3.503, 630.**
Definitions—"Asset", s 21(1); "chargeable gain", s 15(2); "disposal of an asset", Sch 7 para 4(3); "disposal of shares", Sch 7 para 4(3); "held-over gain", Sch 7 para 4(4); "shares", s 288(1), Sch 7 para 4(2); "transferor", Sch 7 para 4(2).
Prospective amendment—This paragraph will be repealed by FA 1998 s 165, Sch 27 Part III(31) with effect for disposals in the year 2003–04 and subsequent years of assessment.

[SCHEDULE 7A

RESTRICTION ON SET-OFF OF PRE-ENTRY LOSSES][1]

Section 177A

Commentary—*Simon's Direct Tax Service* D2.670–675.
Revenue Internal Guidance—Capital gains manual CG 47989 (outlines the effects of FA 2000 changes to group definition on the operation of Schedule 7A).
CG 47944 (Revenue interpretation of para 9(6) and example).
Amendments—[1] This Schedule inserted by FA 1993 s 88 and Sch 8. It has effect for any accounting period ending after 15 March 1993 in relation to losses of a company joining the group after 30 March 1987; but see FA 1993 s 88(3) for detailed commencement provisions.

Application and construction of Schedule

[1—(1) This Schedule shall have effect, in the case of a company which is or has been a member of a group of companies ("the relevant group"), in relation to any pre-entry losses of that company.

(2) In this Schedule "pre-entry loss", in relation to any company, means—

(*a*) any allowable loss that accrued to that company at a time before it became a member of the relevant group; or

(*b*) the pre-entry proportion of any allowable loss accruing to that company on the disposal of any pre-entry asset;

and for the purposes of this Schedule the pre-entry proportion of any loss shall be calculated in accordance with paragraphs 2 to 5 below.

(3) In this Schedule "pre-entry asset", in relation to any disposal, means (subject to sub-paragraph (4) below) any asset which was held, at the time immediately before [the relevant event occurred in relation to it][2], by any company (whether or not the one which makes the disposal) which is or has at any time been a member of [the relevant group][2].

(3A) In this paragraph references to the relevant event occurring in relation to a company—

(*a*) in a case in which—

(i) the company was resident in the United Kingdom at the time when it became a member of the relevant group, or

(ii) the asset was a chargeable asset in relation to the company at that time,

are references to the company becoming a member of that group;

(*b*) in any other case, are references to whichever is the first of—

(i) the company becoming resident in the United Kingdom, or

(ii) the asset becoming a chargeable asset in relation to the company.

For this purpose an asset is a "chargeable asset" in relation to a company at any time if, were the asset to be disposed of by the company at that time, any gain accruing to the company would be a chargeable gain and would by virtue of section 10(3) form part of its chargeable profits for corporation tax purposes.][2]

(4) Subject to paragraph 3 below, an asset is not a pre-entry asset if—

(*a*) the company which held the asset at the time [the relevant event occurred in relation to it][2] is not the company which makes the disposal; and

(*b*) since that time that asset has been disposed of otherwise than by a disposal to which section 171 applies;

but (without prejudice to sub-paragraph (8) below) where, on a disposal to which section 171 does not apply, any asset would cease to be a pre-entry asset by virtue of this sub-paragraph but the company making the disposal retains any interest in or over the asset in question, that interest shall be a pre-entry asset for the purposes of this Schedule.

(5) References in this Schedule, in relation to a pre-entry asset, to the relevant time are references to the time when [the relevant event occurred in relation to the company by reference to which that asset is a pre-entry asset][2]; and for the purposes of this Schedule—

(*a*) where [a relevant event has occurred in relation to a company][2] on more than one occasion, an asset is a pre-entry asset by reference to that company if it would be a pre-entry asset by reference to that company in respect of any one of those occasions; but

(*b*) references in the following provisions of this Schedule to the time when [a relevant event occurred in relation to a company][2], in relation to assets held on more than one such occasion as is mentioned in paragraph (*a*) above, are references to the later or latest of those occasions.

(6) Subject to so much of sub-paragraph (6) of paragraph 9 below as requires groups of companies to be treated as separate groups for the purposes of that paragraph, if—

(*a*) the principal company of a group of companies ("the first group") has at any time become a member of another group ("the second group") so that the two groups are treated as the same by virtue of subsection (10) of section 170, and

(*b*) the second group, together in pursuance of that subsection with the first group, is the relevant group, then, except where sub-paragraph (7) below applies, the members of the first group shall be treated for the purposes of this Schedule as having become members of the relevant group at that time, and not by virtue of that subsection at the times when they became members of the first group.

(7) This sub-paragraph applies where—

(*a*) the persons who immediately before the time when the principal company of the first group became a member of the second group owned the shares comprised in the issued share capital of the principal company of the first group are the same as the persons who, immediately after that time, owned the shares comprised in the issued share capital of the principal company of the relevant group; and

(*b*) the company which is the principal company of the relevant group immediately after that time—

(i) was not the principal company of any group immediately before that time; and

(ii) immediately after that time had assets consisting entirely, or almost entirely, of shares comprised in the issued share capital of the principal company of the first group.

(8) For the purposes of this Schedule, but subject to paragraph 3 below—

(*a*) an asset acquired or held by a company at any time and an asset held at a later time by that company, or by any company which is or has been a member of the same group of companies as that company, shall be treated as the same asset if the value of the second asset is derived in whole or in part from the first asset; and

(*b*) if—

(i) any asset is treated (whether by virtue of paragraph (*a*) above or otherwise) as the same as an asset held by a company at a later time, and

(ii) the first asset would have been a pre-entry asset in relation to that company,

the second asset shall also be treated as a pre-entry asset in relation to that company;

and paragraph (*a*) above shall apply, in particular, where the second asset is a freehold and the first asset is a leasehold the lessee of which acquires the reversion.

(9) In determining for the purposes of this Schedule whether any allowable loss accruing to a company under section 116(10)(*b*) is a loss that accrued before the company became a member of the relevant group, any loss so accruing shall be deemed to have accrued at the time of the relevant transaction within the meaning of section 116(2).

(10) In determining for the purposes of this Schedule whether any allowable loss accruing to a company on a disposal under section 212 is a loss that accrued before the company became a member of the relevant group, the provisions of section 213 shall be disregarded.][1]

Commentary—*Simon's Direct Tax Service* **D2.671**.
Revenue Internal Guidance—Capital Gains Manual CG 47569 (sub-s (6), operation of this section).
Definitions—"Allowable loss", s 288(1); "asset", s 21(1); "company", ss 170, 288(1); "group of companies", s 170; "leasehold", Sch 8 para 10(1); "lessee", Sch 8 para 10(1).
Cross references—See TCGA 1992 Sch 7A para 9 (connected groups of companies: identification of relevant group and application of this Schedule to every connected group).
Exchange Gains and Losses (Transitional Provisions) Regulations, SI 1994/3226 reg 16(12) (no deduction under this Schedule for allowable losses within an election to set-off pre-commencement losses against exchange gains).
FA 2000 Sch 29 para 7(6)–(8) (any question as to whether a company was a member of a group before 20 March 2000 is construed in accordance with the position under TCGA 1992 s 170 before the amendments made by Sch 29, para 1, and as to whether a company was a member of a group before 6 April 1992 see the Capital Gains Tax Act 1979).
FA 2000 Sch 29 para 7(9) (the main amendments made to TCGA 1992 s 170 by FA 2000 Sch 29 para 1 have effect for the purposes of this paragraph for any accounting period ending after 20 March 2000).
Amendments—[1] This Schedule inserted by FA 1993 s 88(2) and Sch 8. It has effect for any accounting period ending after 15 March 1993 in relation to losses of a company joining the group after 30 March 1987; but see FA 1993 s 88(3) for detailed commencement provisions.
[2] Words in sub-paras (3)–(5) substituted, and sub-para (3A) inserted, by FA 2000 s 102, Sch 29 para 7 with effect in relation to the amount to be included in respect of chargeable gains in a company's total profits for any accounting period ending after 20 March 2000.

Pre-entry proportion of losses on pre-entry assets

[2—(1) Subject to paragraphs 3 to 5 below, the pre-entry proportion of an allowable loss accruing on the disposal of a pre-entry asset shall be whatever would be the allowable loss accruing on that disposal if that loss were the sum of the amounts determined, for every item of relevant allowable expenditure, according to the following formula—

$$A \times \frac{B}{C} \times \frac{D}{E}$$

(2) In sub-paragraph (1) above, in relation to any disposal of a pre-entry asset—

A is the total amount of the allowable loss;

[B is the amount of the item of relevant allowable expenditure for which an amount falls to be determined under this paragraph;][2]

[C is the total amount of all the relevant allowable expenditure;][2]

D is the length of the period beginning with the relevant pre-entry date and ending with the relevant time or, if that date is after that time, nil; and

E is the length of the period beginning with the relevant pre-entry date and ending with the day of the disposal.

(3) In sub-paragraph (2) above "the relevant pre-entry date", in relation to any item of relevant allowable expenditure, means whichever is the later of—

(a) the date on which that item of expenditure is, or (on the [assumptions applying by virtue of sub-paragraphs (4) to (6B)][7] below) would be, treated for the purposes of section 54 as having been incurred; and

(b) 1st April 1982.

(4) Where any asset ("the second asset") is treated by virtue of section 127 as the same as another asset ("the first asset") previously held by any company, this paragraph and (so far as applicable) paragraph 3 below shall have effect, ...[4]—

(a) as if any item of relevant allowable expenditure consisting in consideration given for the acquisition of the second asset had been incurred at the same time as the expenditure consisting in the consideration for the acquisition of the first asset; and

(b) where there is more than one such time as if that item were incurred at those different times in the same proportions as the consideration for the acquisition of the first asset.

(5) Without prejudice to sub-paragraph (4) above, this paragraph shall have effect in relation to any asset which—

(a) was held by a company at the time when it became a member of the relevant group, and

(b) is treated as having been acquired by that company for such a consideration as secured that on the disposal in pursuance of which it was acquired neither a gain nor a loss accrued,

as if that company and every person who acquired that asset or the equivalent asset at a material time had been the same person and, accordingly, as if the asset had been acquired by that company when it or the equivalent asset was acquired by the first of those persons to have acquired it at a material time and the time at which any expenditure had been incurred were to be determined accordingly.

(6) In sub-paragraph (5) above, the reference, in relation to any asset, to a material time is a reference to any time which—

(a) is before the occasion on which the company in question is treated as having acquired the asset for such a consideration as is mentioned in that sub-paragraph; and

(b) is or is after the last occasion before that occasion on which any person acquired that asset or the equivalent asset otherwise than by virtue of an acquisition which—

(i) is treated as an acquisition for such a consideration; or

(ii) is the acquisition by virtue of which any asset is treated as the equivalent asset;

and this paragraph shall have effect in relation to any asset to which that sub-paragraph applies without regard to the provisions of section 56(2).

[(6A) Notwithstanding anything in section 56(2), where in the case of the disposal of any pre-entry asset—

(a) any company has at any time between the relevant time and the time of the disposal acquired that asset or the equivalent asset, and

(b) the acquisition was either an acquisition in pursuance of a disposal on which there is treated by virtue of section 171 as having been neither a gain nor a loss accruing or an acquisition by virtue of which an asset is treated as the equivalent asset,

the items of relevant allowable expenditure and the times when those items shall be treated as having been incurred shall be determined for the purposes of this paragraph on the assumptions specified in sub-paragraph (6B) below.][6]

[(6B) Those assumptions are that—

(a) the company by reference to which the asset in question is a pre-entry asset, and

(b) the company mentioned in sub-paragraph (6A) above and every other company which has made an acquisition which, in relation to the disposal of that asset, falls within that sub-paragraph,

were the same person and, accordingly, that the pre-entry asset had been acquired by the company disposing of it at the time when it or the equivalent asset would have been treated for the purposes of this paragraph as acquired by the company mentioned in paragraph (a) above.][6]

[(7) In sub-paragraphs (5) to (6B) above the references to the equivalent asset, in relation to another asset acquired or disposed of by any company, are references to any asset which falls in relation to that company to be treated (whether by virtue of paragraph 1(8) above or otherwise) as the same as the other asset or which would fall to be so treated after applying, as respects other assets, the assumptions for which those sub-paragraphs provide.][6]

(8) The preceding provisions of this paragraph and (so far as applicable) paragraph 3 below shall have effect where—

(a) a loss accrues to any company under section 116(10)(b), and

(b) the old asset consists in or is treated for the purposes of that paragraph as including pre-entry assets,

as if the disposal on which the loss accrues were that disposal of the old asset which is assumed to have been made for the purposes of the calculation required by section 116(10)(a).

[(8A) Where by virtue of section 55(8) the allowable loss accruing on the disposal of a pre-entry asset, or any part of the loss, is attributable to an amount ("the rolled-up amount") of rolled-up indexation (as defined in section 55(9) to (11)), then, for the purposes of this paragraph—

    (a) the total amount of all the relevant allowable expenditure shall be treated as increased by the rolled-up amount, and

    (b) the amount of each item of relevant allowable expenditure shall be treated as increased by so much (if any) of the rolled-up amount as is attributable to that item.][3]

[(8B) Where—

    (a) section 56(3) applies on the disposal of a pre-entry asset on which an allowable loss accrues, and

    (b) in accordance with that subsection, the total amount of all the relevant allowable expenditure is reduced by any amount ("the global reduction"),

the amount of each item of relevant allowable expenditure shall be treated for the purposes of this paragraph as reduced by so much (if any) of the global reduction as is attributable to that item.][3]

(9) In this paragraph—

    ...[5]

    "relevant allowable expenditure", in relation to any allowable loss, means the expenditure which falls by virtue of section 38(1)(a) or (b) to be taken into account in the computation of that loss.][1]

Commentary—*Simon's Direct Tax Service* D2.672.
Definitions—"Allowable loss", s 288(1); "asset", s 21(1); "pre-entry asset", Sch 7A para 1(3).
Amendments—[1] This Schedule inserted by FA 1993 s 88(2) and Sch 8. It has effect for any accounting period ending after 15 March 1993 in relation to losses of a company joining the group after 30 March 1987; but see FA 1993 s 88(3) for detailed commencement provisions.
[2] Definitions of "B" and "C" in sub-para (2) substituted by FA 1994 s 93(8), (11) in relation to disposals after 29 November 1993.
[3] Sub-paras (8A), (8B) inserted by FA 1994 s 93(8), (11).
[4] Words in sub-para (4) repealed by FA 1994 s 93(8), (11) and Sch 26 Pt V(8).
[5] Definition of "indexed rise" in sub-para (9) repealed by FA 1994 s 93(8), (11).
[6] Sub-paras (6A), (6B), (7) substituted for sub-para (7) by FA 1994 s 94(1), (2), (4) and apply in relation to the making in respect of any loss of any deduction from a chargeable gain where either the gain or the loss is one accruing after 10 March 1994.
[7] Words in sub-para (3)(a) substituted by FA 1994 s 94(1), (2), (4).

Disposals of pooled assets

[3—(1) This paragraph shall apply (subject to paragraphs 4 and 5 below) where any assets acquired by any company fall to be treated with other assets as indistinguishable parts of the same asset ("a pooled asset") and the whole or any part of that asset is referable to pre-entry assets.

(2) For the purposes of this Schedule, where a pooled asset has at any time contained a pre-entry asset—

    (a) the pooled asset shall be treated, until all the pre-entry assets included in that asset have (on the assumptions for which this paragraph provides) been disposed of, as incorporating a part which is referable to pre-entry assets; and

    (b) the size of that part shall be determined in accordance with the following provisions of this paragraph.

(3) Where there is a disposal of any part of a pooled asset and the proportion of the asset which is disposed of does not exceed the proportion of that asset which is represented by any part of it which is not, at the time of the disposal, referable to pre-entry assets, that disposal shall be deemed for the purposes of this Schedule to be confined to assets which are not pre-entry assets so that—

    (a) except where paragraph 4(2) below applies, no part of any loss accruing on that disposal shall be deemed to be a pre-entry loss, and

    (b) the part of the pooled asset which after the disposal is to be treated as referable to pre-entry assets shall be correspondingly increased.

(4) Where there is a disposal of any part of a pooled asset and the proportion of the asset which is disposed of does exceed the proportion of that asset mentioned in sub-paragraph (3) above, that disposal shall be deemed for the purposes of this Schedule to relate to pre-entry assets only so far as required for the purposes of the excess, so that—

    (a) any loss accruing on that disposal shall be deemed for the purposes of this Schedule to be an allowable loss on the disposal of a pre-entry asset;

    (b) the pre-entry proportion of that loss shall be deemed (except where paragraph 4(3) below applies) to be the amount (so far as it does not exceed the amount of the loss actually accruing) which would have been the pre-entry proportion under paragraph 2 above of any loss accruing on the disposal of the excess if the excess were a separate asset; and

    (c) the pooled asset shall be treated after the disposal as referable entirely to pre-entry assets.

(5) Where there is a disposal of the whole of a pooled asset or of any part of a pooled asset which, at the time of the disposal, is referable entirely to pre-entry assets, paragraphs (a) and (b) of sub-paragraph (4) above shall apply to the disposal of the asset or the part as they apply in relation to the assumed disposal of the excess mentioned in that sub-paragraph but, in the case of the disposal of

the whole of a pooled asset only a part of which is referable to pre-entry assets, as if the reference in paragraph (*b*) of that sub-paragraph to the excess were a reference to that part.

(6) For the purpose of determining, under sub-paragraph (4) or (5) above, what would have been the pre-entry proportion of any loss accruing on the disposal of any assets as a separate asset it shall be assumed that none of the assets treated as comprised in that asset has ever been comprised in a pooled asset with any assets other than those which are taken to constitute that separate asset for the purposes of the determination.

(7) The assets which are comprised in any asset which is treated for any of the purposes of this paragraph as a separate asset shall be identified on the following assumptions, that is to say—

    (*a*) that assets are disposed of in the order of the dates which for the purposes of paragraph 2 above are the relevant pre-entry dates in relation to the consideration for their acquisition;
    (*b*) subject to that, that assets with earlier relevant times are disposed of before those with later relevant times;
    (*c*) that disposals made when a company was not a member of the relevant group are made in accordance with the preceding provisions of this paragraph, as they have effect in relation to the group of companies of which the company was a member at the time of the disposal or, as the case may be, of which it had most recently been a member before that time; and
    (*d*) subject to paragraphs (*a*) to (*c*) above, that a company disposes of assets in the order in which it acquired them.

(8) Where in the case of any asset there is more than one date which is the relevant pre-entry date in relation to the consideration for its acquisition, the date taken into account for the purposes of sub-paragraph (7)(*a*) above shall be the date which is the earlier or earliest of those dates if any date which is the relevant pre-entry date in relation to the acquisition of an option to acquire that asset is disregarded.

(9) In applying the formula set out in paragraph 2(1) above in relation to the disposal of an asset which is treated for any of the purposes of this paragraph as comprised in a separate asset—

    (*a*) the amount or value of any consideration for the acquisition or disposal of that asset; and
    (*b*) the incidental costs of the acquisition or disposal of that asset,

shall be determined (to the exclusion of any apportionment under section 129 or 130) by apportioning any consideration or costs relating to both that asset and other assets acquired or disposed of at the same time according to the proportion that is borne by that asset to all the assets to which the consideration or costs related.

(10) Where—

    (*a*) any asset ("the latest asset") falls (whether by virtue of paragraph 1(8) above or otherwise) to be treated as acquired at the same time as another asset ("the original asset") which was acquired before the latest asset, and
    (*b*) the latest asset is either comprised in a pooled asset a part of which is referable to pre-entry assets or is or includes an asset which is to be treated as so comprised,

sub-paragraph (7) above shall apply not only in relation to the latest asset as if it were the original asset but also, in the first place, for identifying the asset which is to be treated as the original asset for the purposes of this paragraph.

(11) Sub-paragraphs (3)(*b*) and (4)(*c*) above shall have effect in relation to any disposal without prejudice to the effect of any subsequent acquisition of assets falling to be treated as part of a pooled asset on the determination of whether, and to what extent, any part of that pooled asset is to be treated as referable to pre-entry assets.]¹

Commentary—*Simon's Direct Tax Service* D2.672, 680–682.
Definitions—"Allowable loss", s 288(1); "asset", s 21(1); "company", s 288(1); "group of companies", s 170; "pre-entry asset", Sch 7A para 1(3); "pre-entry loss", Sch 7A para 1(2); "relevant group", Sch 7A para 1(1).
Amendments—¹ This Schedule inserted by FA 1993 s 88(2) and Sch 8. It has effect for any accounting period ending after 15 March 1993 in relation to losses of a company joining the group after 30 March 1987; but see FA 1993 s 88(3) for detailed commencement provisions.

Rule to prevent pre-entry losses on pooled assets being treated as post-entry losses

[4—(1) This paragraph shall apply if—

    (*a*) there is a disposal of any part of a pooled asset which for the purposes of paragraph 3 above is treated as incorporating a part which is referable to pre-entry assets;
    (*b*) the assets disposed of are or include assets ("the post-entry element of the disposal") which for the purposes of that paragraph are treated as having been incorporated in the part of the pooled asset which is not referable to pre-entry assets;
    (*c*) an allowable loss ("the actual loss") accrues on the disposal; and
    (*d*) the amount which in computing the allowable loss is allowed as a deduction of relevant allowable expenditure ("the expenditure actually allowed") exceeds the relevant allowable expenditure attributable to the post-entry element of the disposal.

(2) Subject to sub-paragraph (6) below, where the post-entry element of the disposal comprises all of the assets disposed of—

(a) the actual loss shall be treated for the purposes of this Schedule as a loss accruing on the disposal of a pre-entry asset; and

(b) the pre-entry proportion of that loss shall be treated as being the amount (so far as it does not exceed the amount of the actual loss) by which the expenditure actually allowed exceeds the relevant allowable expenditure attributable to the post-entry element of the disposal.

(3) Subject to sub-paragraph (6) below, where—

(a) the actual loss is treated by virtue of paragraph 3 above as a loss accruing on the disposal of a pre-entry asset, and

(b) the expenditure actually allowed exceeds the actual cost of the assets to which the disposal is treated as relating,

the pre-entry proportion of the loss shall be treated as being the amount which (so far as it does not exceed the amount of the actual loss) is equal to the sum of that excess and what would, apart from this paragraph and paragraph 5 below, be the pre-entry proportion of the loss accruing on the disposal.

(4) For the purposes of sub-paragraph (3) above the actual cost of the assets to which the disposal is treated as relating shall be taken to be the sum of—

(a) the relevant allowable expenditure attributable to the post-entry element of the disposal; and

(b) the amount which, in computing the pre-entry proportion of the loss in accordance with paragraph 3(4)(b) and (6) above, would be treated for the purposes of C in the formula in paragraph 2(1) above as the total amount allowable as a deduction of relevant allowable expenditure in respect of such of the assets disposed of as are treated as having been incorporated in the part of the pooled asset which is referable to pre-entry assets.

(5) Without prejudice to sub-paragraph (6) below, where sub-paragraph (2) or (3) above applies for the purpose of determining the pre-entry proportion of any loss, no election shall be capable of being made under paragraph 5 below for the purpose of enabling a different amount to be taken as the pre-entry proportion of that loss.

(6) Where—

(a) the pre-entry proportion of the loss accruing to any company on the disposal of any part of a pooled asset falls to be determined under sub-paragraph (2) or (3) above,

(b) the amount determined under that sub-paragraph exceeds the amount determined under sub-paragraph (7) below ("the alternative pre-entry loss"), and

(c) the company makes an election for the purposes of this sub-paragraph,

the pre-entry proportion of the loss determined under sub-paragraph (2) or (3) above shall be reduced to the amount of the alternative pre-entry loss.

(7) For the purposes of sub-paragraph (6) above the alternative pre-entry loss is whatever apart from this paragraph would have been the pre-entry proportion of the loss on the disposal in question, if for the purposes of this Schedule the identification of the assets disposed of were to be made disregarding the part of the pooled asset which was not referable to pre-entry assets, except to the extent (if any) by which the part referable to pre-entry assets fell short of what was disposed of.

(8) An election for the purposes of sub-paragraph (6) above with respect to any loss shall be made by the company to which the loss accrued by notice to the inspector given within—

(a) the period of two years beginning with the end of the accounting period of that company in which the disposal is made on which the loss accrues; or

(b) such longer period as the Board may by notice allow;

and paragraph 5 below may be taken into account under sub-paragraph (7) above in determining the amount of the alternative pre-entry loss as if an election had been made under that paragraph but shall be so taken into account only if the election for the purposes of sub-paragraph (6) above contains an election corresponding to the election that, apart from this paragraph, might have been made under that paragraph.

(9) For the purposes of this paragraph the relevant allowable expenditure attributable to the post-entry element of the disposal shall be the amount which, in computing any allowable loss accruing on a disposal of that element as a separate asset, would have been allowed as a deduction of relevant allowable expenditure if none of the assets comprised in that element had ever been comprised in a pooled asset with any assets other than those which are taken to constitute that separate asset for the purposes of this sub-paragraph.

(10) For the purpose of identifying the assets which are to be treated for the purposes of sub-paragraph (9) above as comprised in the post-entry element of the disposal, a company shall be taken to dispose of assets in the order in which it acquired them.

(11) Paragraph 3(9) above shall apply for the purposes of sub-paragraph (9) above as it applies for the purposes of the application as mentioned in paragraph 3(9) above of the formula so mentioned; and paragraph 3(10) above shall apply for the purposes of this paragraph in relation to sub-paragraph (10) above as it applies for the purposes of paragraph 3 above in relation to sub-paragraph (7) of that paragraph.

(12) In this paragraph references to an amount allowed as a deduction of relevant allowable expenditure are references to the amount falling to be so allowed in accordance with section 38(1)(*a*) and (*b*) and (so far as applicable) section 42, ...².

(13) ...²

(14) Nothing in this paragraph shall affect the operation of the rules contained in paragraph 3 above for determining, for any purposes other than those of sub-paragraph (7) above, how much of any pooled asset at any time consists of a part which is referable to pre-entry assets.]¹

Commentary—*Simon's Direct Tax Service* D2.672, 680, 682, 683.
Revenue Internal Guidance—Capital Gains Manual CG 47691 (sub-s (4), worked examples—actual costs). CG 47694 (sub-s (6), worked example—election for alternative pre-entry loss).
Definitions—''Accounting period'', TA 1988 s 834(1); ''allowable loss'', s 288(1); ''asset'', s 21(1); ''the Board'', s 288(1); ''company'', s 288(1); ''inspector'', s 288(1); ''notice'', s 288(1); ''pre-entry asset'', Sch 7A para 1(3).
Amendments—¹ This Schedule inserted by FA 1993 s 88(2) and Sch 8. It has effect for any accounting period ending after 15 March 1993 in relation to losses of a company joining the group after 30 March 1987; but see FA 1993 s 88(3) for detailed commencement provisions.
² Sub-para (13) and words in sub-para (12) repealed by FA 1994 s 93(9), (11) and Sch 26 Pt V(8) in relation to disposals after 29 November 1993.

Alternative calculation by reference to market value

[5—(1) Subject to paragraph 4(5) above and the following provisions of this paragraph, if—

(*a*) an allowable loss accrues on the disposal by any company of any pre-entry asset; and
(*b*) that company makes an election for the purposes of this paragraph in relation to that loss,

the pre-entry proportion of that loss (instead of being the amount determined under the preceding provisions of this Schedule) shall be whichever is the smaller of the amounts mentioned in sub-paragraph (2) below.

(2) Those amounts are—

(*a*) the amount of any loss which would have accrued if that asset had been disposed of at the relevant time at its market value at that time; and
(*b*) the amount of the loss accruing on the disposal mentioned in sub-paragraph (1)(*a*) above.

[(2A) In determining for the purposes of sub-paragraph (2)(*a*) above the amount of any loss which would have accrued if the asset had been disposed of at the relevant time at its market value at that time—

(*a*) it shall be assumed that the amendments of this Act made by section 93(1) to (5) of the Finance Act 1994 (indexation losses) had effect in relation to that disposal and, accordingly,
(*b*) references in those amendments and in subsection (11) of that section to 30th November 1993 shall be read as references to the day on which the relevant time falls.]²

(3) Where no loss would have accrued on the disposal assumed for the purposes of sub-paragraph (2)(*a*) above, the loss accruing on the disposal mentioned in sub-paragraph (1)(*a*) above shall be deemed not to have a pre-entry proportion.

(4) Sub-paragraph (5) below shall apply where—

(*a*) an election is made for the purposes of this paragraph in relation to any loss accruing on the disposal (''the real disposal'') of the whole or any part of a pooled asset; and
(*b*) the case is one in which (but for the election) paragraph 3 above would apply for determining the pre-entry proportion of a loss accruing on the real disposal.

(5) In a case falling within sub-paragraph (4) above, this paragraph shall have effect as if the amount specified in sub-paragraph (2)(*a*) above were to be calculated—

(*a*) on the basis that the disposal which is assumed to have taken place was a disposal of all the assets falling within sub-paragraph (6) below; and
(*b*) by apportioning any loss that would have accrued on that disposal between—

(i) such of the assets falling within paragraph (6) below as are assets to which the real disposal is treated as relating, and
(ii) the remainder of the assets so falling,

according to the proportions of any pooled asset whose disposal is assumed which would have been, respectively, represented by assets mentioned in sub-paragraph (i) above and by assets mentioned in sub-paragraph (ii) above,

and where assets falling within sub-paragraph (6) below have different relevant times there shall be assumed to have been a different disposal at each of those times.

(6) Assets fall within this sub-paragraph if—

(*a*) immediately before the time which is the relevant time in relation to those assets, they were comprised in a pooled asset which consisted of or included assets which fall to be treated for the purposes of paragraph 3 above as—

(i) comprised in the part of the pooled asset referable to pre-entry assets; and
(ii) disposed of on the real disposal;

(*b*) they were also comprised in such a pooled asset immediately after that time; and (*c*) the pooled asset in which they were so comprised immediately after that time was held by a member of the relevant group.

(7) Where—

(*a*) an election is made under paragraph 4(6) above requiring the determination by reference to this paragraph of the alternative pre-entry loss accruing on the disposal of any assets comprised in a pooled asset, and

(*b*) in pursuance of that election any amount of the loss that would have accrued on an assumed disposal is apportioned in accordance with sub-paragraph (5) above to assets ("the relevant assets") which—

(i) are treated for the purposes of that determination as assets to which the disposal related, but

(ii) otherwise continue after the disposal to be treated as incorporated in the part of that pooled asset which is referable to pre-entry assets,

then, on any further application of this paragraph for the purpose of determining the pre-entry proportion of the loss accruing on a subsequent disposal of assets comprised in that pooled asset, that amount (without being apportioned elsewhere) shall be deducted from so much of the loss accruing on the same assumed disposal as, apart from the deduction, would be apportioned to the relevant assets on that further application of this paragraph.

(8) An election under this paragraph with respect to any loss shall be made by the company in question by notice to the inspector given within—

(*a*) the period of two years beginning with the end of the accounting period of that company in which the disposal is made on which the loss accrues; or

(*b*) such longer period as the Board may by notice allow.]¹

Commentary—*Simon's Direct Tax Service* D2.672, 680, 682, 683.
Revenue Internal Guidance—Capital Gains Manual CG 47720 (worked example—alternative market value calculation).
Definitions—"Accounting period", TA 1988 s 834(1); "allowable loss", s 288(1); "the Board", s 288(1); "company", s 288(1); "inspector", s 288(1); "market value", ss 272–274; "notice", s 288(1); "pre-entry assets", Sch 7A para 1(3); "pre-entry loss", Sch 7A para 1(2); "relevant group", Sch 7A para 1(1).
Amendments—¹ This Schedule inserted by FA 1993 s 88(2) and Sch 8. It has effect for any accounting period ending after 15 March 1993 in relation to losses of a company joining the group after 30 March 1987; but see FA 1993 s 88(3) for detailed commencement provisions.
² Sub-para (2A) inserted by FA 1994 s 93(10), (11) in relation to disposals after 29 November 1993.

Restrictions on the deduction of pre-entry losses

[**6**—(1) In the calculation of the amount to be included in respect of chargeable gains in any company's total profits for any accounting period—

(*a*) if in that period there is any chargeable gain from which the whole or any part of any pre-entry loss accruing in that period is deductible in accordance with paragraph 7 below, the loss or, as the case may be, that part of it shall be deducted from that gain;

(*b*) if, after all such deductions as may be made under paragraph (*a*) above have been made, there is in that period any chargeable gain from which the whole or any part of any pre-entry loss carried forward from a previous accounting period is deductible in accordance with paragraph 7 below, the loss or, as the case may be, that part of it shall be deducted from that gain;

(*c*) the total chargeable gains (if any) remaining after the making of all such deductions as may be made under paragraph (*a*) or (*b*) above shall be subject to deductions in accordance with section 8(1) in respect of any allowable losses that are not pre-entry losses; and

(*d*) any pre-entry loss which has not been the subject of a deduction under paragraph (*a*) or (*b*) above (as well as any other losses falling to be carried forward under section 8(1)) shall be carried forward to the following accounting period of that company.

(2) Subject to sub-paragraph (1) above, any question as to which or what part of any pre-entry loss has been deducted from any particular chargeable gain shall be decided—

(*a*) where it falls to be decided in respect of the setting of losses against gains in any accounting period ending before 16th March 1993 as if—

(i) pre-entry losses accruing in any such period had been set against chargeable gains before any other allowable losses accruing in that period were set against those gains;

(ii) pre-entry losses carried forward to any such period had been set against chargeable gains before any other allowable losses carried forward to that period were set against those gains; and

(iii) subject to sub-paragraphs (i) and (ii) above, the pre-entry losses carried forward to any accounting period ending on or after 16th March 1993 were identified with such losses as may be determined in accordance with such elections as may be made by the company to which they accrued;

and

(*b*) in any other case, in accordance with such elections as may be made by the company to which the loss accrued;

and any question as to which or what part of any pre-entry loss has been carried forward from one accounting period to another shall be decided accordingly.

(3) An election by any company under this paragraph shall be made by notice to the inspector given—

    (*a*) in the case of an election under sub-paragraph (2)(*a*)(iii) above, before the end of the period of two years beginning with the end of the accounting period of that company which was current on 16th March 1993; and

    (*b*) in the case of an election under sub-paragraph (2)(*b*) above, before the end of the period of two years beginning with the end of the accounting period of that company in which the gain in question accrued.

(4) For the purposes of this Schedule where any matter falls to be determined under this paragraph by reference to an election but no election is made, it shall be assumed, so far as consistent with any elections that have been made—

    (*a*) that losses are set against gains in the order in which the losses accrued; and

    (*b*) that the gains against which they are set are also determined according to the order in which they accrued with losses being set against earlier gains before they are set against later ones.]¹

Commentary—*Simon's Direct Tax Service* **D2.673, 678.**
Definitions—''Accounting period'', TA 1988 s 834(1); ''allowable loss'', s 288(1); ''chargeable gain'', s 15(2); ''company'', s 288(1); ''inspector'', s 288(1); ''notice'', s 288(1); ''pre-entry loss'', Sch 7A para 1(2); ''profits'', s 170(1).
Cross references—See TCGA 1992 Sch 7A para 9(4) (connected groups of companies: identification of relevant group and application of this Schedule to every connected group).
Amendments—¹ This Schedule inserted by FA 1993 s 88(2) and Sch 8. It has effect for any accounting period ending after 15 March 1993 in relation to losses of a company joining the group after 30 March 1987; but see FA 1993 s 88(3) for detailed commencement provisions.

Gains from which pre-entry losses are to be deductible

[**7**—(1) A pre-entry loss that accrued to a company before it became a member of the relevant group shall be deductible from a chargeable gain accruing to that company if the gain is one accruing—

    (*a*) on a disposal made by that company before the date on which it became a member of the relevant group (''the entry date'');

    (*b*) on the disposal of an asset which was held by that company immediately before the entry date; or

    (*c*) on the disposal of any asset which—

        (i) was acquired by that company on or after the entry date from a person who was not a member of the relevant group at the time of the acquisition; and

        (ii) since its acquisition from that person has not been used or held for any purposes other than those of a trade which was being carried on by that company at the time immediately before the entry date and which continued to be carried on by that company until the disposal.

(2) The pre-entry proportion of an allowable loss accruing to any company on the disposal of a pre-entry asset shall be deductible from a chargeable gain accruing to that company if—

    (*a*) the gain is one accruing on a disposal made, before the date on which it became a member of the relevant group, by that company and that company is the one (''the initial company'') by reference to which the asset on the disposal of which the loss accrues is a pre-entry asset;

    (*b*) the pre-entry asset and the asset on the disposal of which the gain accrues were each held by the same company at a time immediately before it became a member of the relevant group; or

    (*c*) the gain is one accruing on the disposal of an asset which—

        (i) was acquired by the initial company (whether before or after it became a member of the relevant group) from a person who, at the time of the acquisition, was not a member of that group; and

        (ii) since its acquisition from that person has not been used or held for any purposes other than those of a trade which was being carried on, immediately before it became a member of the relevant group, by the initial company and which continued to be carried on by the initial company until the disposal.

(3) Where two or more companies become members of the relevant group at the same time and those companies were all members of the same group of companies immediately before they became members of the relevant group, then, without prejudice to paragraph 9 below—

    (*a*) an asset shall be treated for the purposes of sub-paragraph (1)(*b*) above as held, immediately before it became a member of the relevant group, by the company to which the pre-entry loss in question accrued if that company is one of those companies and the asset was in fact so held by another of those companies;

    (*b*) two or more assets shall be treated for the purposes of sub-paragraph (2)(*b*) above as assets held by the same company immediately before it became a member of the relevant group wherever they would be so treated if all those companies were treated as a single company; and

    (*c*) the acquisition of an asset shall be treated for the purposes of sub-paragraphs (1)(*c*) and (2)(*c*) above as an acquisition by the company to which the pre-entry loss in question accrued if that company is one of those companies and the asset was in fact acquired (whether before or after they became members of the relevant group) by another of those companies.

(4) Paragraph 1(4) above shall apply for determining for the purposes of this paragraph whether an asset on the disposal of which a chargeable gain accrues was held at the time when a company

became a member of the relevant group as it applies for determining whether that asset is a pre-entry asset in relation to that group by reference to that company.

(5) Subject to sub-paragraph (6) below, where a gain accrues on the disposal of the whole or any part of—

(*a*) any asset treated as a single asset but comprising assets only some of which were held at the time mentioned in paragraph (*b*) of sub-paragraph (1) or (2) above, or

(*b*) an asset which is treated as held at that time by virtue of a provision requiring an asset which was not held at that time to be treated as the same as an asset which was so held,

a pre-entry loss shall be deductible by virtue of paragraph (*b*) of sub-paragraph (1) or (2) above from the amount of that gain to the extent only of such proportion of that gain as is attributable to assets held at that time or, as the case may be, represents the gain that would have accrued on the asset so held.

(6) Where—

(*a*) a chargeable gain accrues by virtue of subsection (10) of section 116 on the disposal of a qualifying corporate bond,

(*b*) that bond was not held as required by paragraph (*b*) of sub-paragraph (1) or (2) above at the time mentioned in that paragraph, and

(*c*) the whole or any part of the asset which is the old asset for the purposes of that section was so held,

the question whether that gain is one accruing on the disposal of an asset the whole or any part of which was held by a particular company at that time shall be determined for the purposes of this paragraph as if the bond were deemed to have been so held to the same extent as the old asset.]¹

Commentary—*Simon's Direct Tax Service* **D2.673, 674, 677, 679.**
Revenue Internal Guidance—Capital Gains Manual CG 47802–47803 (sub-s (5), operation of this section).
CG 47821 (sub-s (6), operation of this section).
Definitions—"Allowable loss", s 288(1); "chargeable gain", s 15(2); "company", s 288(1); "group of companies", s 170; "pre-entry asset", Sch 7A para 1(3); "pre-entry loss", Sch 7A para 1(2); "relevant group", Sch 7A para 1(1); "trade", s 170(1).
Cross references—See TCGA 1992 Sch 7A para 6 (restrictions on the deduction of pre-entry losses),
TCGA 1992 Sch 7A para 8 (trade undergoing major change in its nature or conduct or becoming negligible within a certain period of a company becoming a member of a group to be disregarded for the purposes of sub-paras (1)(c), (2)(c) above).
Amendments—¹ This Schedule inserted by FA 1993 s 88(2) and Sch 8. It has effect for any accounting period ending after 15 March 1993 in relation to losses of a company joining the group after 30 March 1987; but see FA 1993 s 88(3) for detailed commencement provisions.

Change of a company's nature

[**8**—(1) If—

(*a*) within any period of three years, a company becomes a member of a group of companies and there is (either earlier or later in that period, or at the same time) a major change in the nature or conduct of a trade carried on by that company, or

(*b*) at any time after the scale of the activities in a trade carried on by a company has become small or negligible, and before any considerable revival of the trade, that company becomes a member of a group of companies,

the trade carried on before that change, or which has become small or negligible, shall be disregarded for the purposes of paragraph 7(1)(*c*) and (2)(*c*) above in relation to any time before the company became a member of the group in question.

(2) In sub-paragraph (1) above the reference to a major change in the nature or conduct of a trade includes a reference to—

(*a*) a major change in the type of property dealt in, or services or facilities provided, in the trade; or

(*b*) a major change in customers, markets or outlets of the trade;

and this paragraph shall apply even if the change is the result of a gradual process which began outside the period of three years mentioned in sub-paragraph (1)(*a*) above.

(3) Where the operation of this paragraph depends on circumstances or events at a time after the company becomes a member of any group of companies (but not more than three years after), an assessment to give effect to this paragraph shall not be out of time if made within six years from that time or the latest such time.]¹

Commentary—*Simon's Direct Tax Service* **D2.674.**
Definitions—"Company", s 288(1); "group of companies", s 170; "trade", s 170(1).
Amendments—¹ This Schedule inserted by FA 1993 s 88(2) and Sch 8. It has effect for any accounting period ending after 15 March 1993 in relation to losses of a company joining the group after 30 March 1987; but see FA 1993 s 88(3) for detailed commencement provisions.

Identification of "the relevant group" and application of Schedule to every connected group

[**9**—(1) This paragraph shall apply where there is more than one group of companies which would be the relevant group in relation to any company.

(2) Where any loss has accrued on the disposal by any company of any asset, this Schedule shall not apply by reference to any group of companies in relation to any loss accruing on that disposal unless—

(a) that group is a group in relation to which that loss is a pre-entry loss by virtue of paragraph 1(2)(a) above or, if there is more than one such group, the one of which that company most recently became a member;

(b) that group, in a case where there is no group falling within paragraph (a) above, is either—

    (i) the group of which that company is a member at the time of the disposal, or

    (ii) if it is not a member of a group of companies at that time, the group of which that company was last a member before that time;

(c) that group, in a case where there is a group falling within paragraph (a) [or (b)]² above, is a group of which that company was a member at any time in the accounting period of that company in which it became a member of the group falling within that paragraph;

(d) that group is a group the principal company of which is or has been, or has been under the control of—

    (i) the company by which the disposal is made, or

    (ii) another company which is or has been a member of a group by reference to which this Schedule applies in relation to the loss in question by virtue of paragraph (a), (b) or (c) above; or

(e) that group is a group of which either—

    (i) the principal company of a group by reference to which this Schedule so applies, or

    (ii) a company which has had that principal company under its control,

is or has been a member;

and sub-paragraphs (3) to (5) below shall apply in the case of any loss accruing on the disposal of any asset where, by virtue of this sub-paragraph, there are two or more groups ("connected groups") by reference to which this Schedule applies.

(3) This Schedule shall apply separately in relation to each of the connected groups (so far as they are not groups in relation to which the loss is a pre-entry loss by virtue of paragraph 1(2)(a) above) for the purpose of—

(a) determining whether the loss on the disposal of any asset is a loss on the disposal of a pre-entry asset; and

(b) calculating the pre-entry proportion of that loss.

(4) Subject to sub-paragraph (5) below, paragraph 6 above shall have effect—

(a) as if the pre-entry proportion of any loss accruing on the disposal of an asset which is a pre-entry asset in the case of more than one of the connected groups were the largest pre-entry proportion of that loss calculated in accordance with sub-paragraph (3) above; and

(b) so that, where the loss accruing on the disposal of any asset is a pre-entry loss by virtue of paragraph 1(2)(a) above in the case of any of the connected groups, that loss shall be the pre-entry loss for the purposes of paragraph 6 above, and not any amount which is the pre-entry proportion of that loss in relation to any of the other groups.

(5) Where, on the separate application of this Schedule in the case of each of the groups by reference to which this Schedule applies, there is, in the case of the disposal of any asset, a pre-entry loss by reference to each of two or more of the connected groups, no amount in respect of the loss accruing on the disposal shall be deductible under paragraph 7 above from any chargeable gain if any of the connected groups is a group in the case of which, on separate applications of that paragraph in relation to each group, the amount deductible from that gain in respect of that loss is nil.

(6) Notwithstanding that the principal company of one group ("the first group") has become a member of another ("the second group"), those two groups shall not by virtue of section 170(10) be treated [in relation to any company that is or has become a member of the second group ("the relevant company") as the same group for the purposes of this paragraph if—

(a) the time at which the relevant company became a member of the first group is a time in the same accounting period as that in which the principal company of the first group became a member of the second group; or

(b)]³ the principal company of the first group was under the control, immediately before it became a member of the second group, of a company which at that time was already a member of the second group.

(7) Where, in the case of the disposal of any asset—

(a) two or more groups which but for sub-paragraph (6) above would be treated as the same group are treated as separate groups by virtue of that sub-paragraph; and

(b) one of those groups is a group of which either—

    (i) the principal company of a group by reference to which this Schedule applies by virtue of sub-paragraph (2)(a), (b) or (c) above in relation to any loss accruing on the disposal, or

    (ii) a company which has had that principal company under its control,

is or has been a member,

this paragraph shall have effect as if that principal company had been a member of each of the groups mentioned in paragraph (*a*) above.]¹

Commentary—*Simon's Direct Tax Service* D2.675.
Definitions—''Accounting period'', TA 1988 s 834(1);''asset'', s 21(1);''chargeable gain'', s 15(2);''company'', s 288(1);''control'', s 288(1);''group of companies'', s 170;''pre-entry asset'', Sch 7A para 1(3);''pre-entry loss'', Sch 7A para 1(2);''relevant group'', Sch 7A para 1(1).
Amendments—¹ This Schedule inserted by FA 1993 s 88(2) and Sch 8. It has effect for any accounting period ending after 15 March 1993 in relation to losses of a company joining the group after 30 March 1987; but see FA 1993 s 88(3) for detailed commencement provisions.
² ''or (*b*)'' in sub-para (2)(*c*) inserted by FA 1994 s 94(1), (3), (4) in relation to the making in respect of any loss of any deduction from a chargeable gain where either the gain or the loss is one accruing after 10 March 1994.
³ Words in sub-para (6) substituted by FA 1998 s 138(1) with effect in relation to any accounting period ending on or after 17 March 1998.

Appropriations to stock in trade

[**10** Where, but for an election under subsection (3) of section 161, there would be deemed to have been a disposal at any time by any company of any asset—

(*a*) the amount by which the market value of the asset may be treated as increased in pursuance of that election shall not include the amount of any pre-entry loss that would have accrued on that disposal; and
(*b*) this Schedule shall have effect as if the pre-entry loss of the last mentioned amount had accrued to that company at that time.]¹

Commentary—*Simon's Direct Tax Service* D2.679.
Definitions—''Asset'', s 21(1); ''company'', s 288(1); ''market value'', ss 272–274; ''pre-entry loss'', Sch 7A para 1(2).
Amendments—¹ This Schedule inserted by FA 1993 s 88(2) and Sch 8. It has effect for any accounting period ending after 15 March 1993 in relation to losses of a company joining the group after 30 March 1987; but see FA 1993 s 88(3) for detailed commencement provisions.

Continuity provisions

[**11**—(1) This paragraph applies where provision has been made by or under any enactment (''the transfer legislation'') for the transfer of property, rights and liabilities to any person from—

(*a*) a body established by or under any enactment for the purpose, in the exercise of statutory functions, of carrying on any undertaking or industrial or other activity in the public sector or of exercising any other statutory functions;
(*b*) a subsidiary of such a body; or
(*c*) a company wholly owned by the Crown.

(2) A loss shall not be a pre-entry loss for the purposes of this Schedule in relation to any company to whom a transfer has been made by or under the transfer legislation if that loss—

(*a*) accrued to the person from whom the transfer has been made; and
(*b*) falls to be treated, in accordance with any enactment made in relation to transfers by or under that legislation, as a loss accruing to that company.

(3) For the purposes of this Schedule where a company became a member of the relevant group by virtue of the transfer by or under the transfer legislation of any shares in or other securities of that company or any other company—

(*a*) a loss that accrued to that company before it so became a member of that group shall not be a pre-entry loss in relation to that group; and
(*b*) no asset held by that company when it so became a member of that group shall by virtue of that fact be a pre-entry asset.

(4) For the purposes of this paragraph a company shall be regarded as wholly owned by the Crown if it is—

(*a*) a company limited by shares in which there are no issued shares held otherwise than by, or by a nominee of, the Treasury, a Minister of the Crown, a Northern Ireland department or another company wholly owned by the Crown; or
(*b*) a company limited by guarantee of which no person other than the Treasury, a Minister of the Crown or a Northern Ireland department, or a nominee of the Treasury, a Minister of the Crown or a Northern Ireland department, is a member.

(5) In this paragraph—

''enactment'' includes any provision of any Northern Ireland legislation, within the meaning of section 24 of the Interpretation Act 1978; and
''statutory functions'' means functions under any enactment, under any subordinate legislation, within the meaning of the Interpretation Act 1978 or under any statutory rules, within the meaning of the Statutory Rules (Northern Ireland) Order 1979.]¹

Commentary—*Simon's Direct Tax Service* D2.679.
Definitions—''Asset'', s 21(1); ''company'', s 288(1); ''pre-entry assets'', Sch 7A para 1(3); ''pre-entry loss'', Sch 7A para 1(2); ''relevant group'', Sch 7A para 1(1); ''shares'', s 288(1).
Amendments—¹ This Schedule inserted by FA 1993 s 88(2) and Sch 8. It has effect for any accounting period ending after 15 March 1993 in relation to losses of a company joining the group after 30 March 1987; but see FA 1993 s 88(3) for detailed commencement provisions.

Companies changing groups on certain transfers of shares etc

[12 For the purposes of this Schedule, and without prejudice to paragraph 11 above, where—

(*a*) a company which is a member of a group of companies becomes at any time a member of another group of companies as the result of a disposal of shares in or other securities of that company or any other company; and

(*b*) that disposal is one on which, by virtue of any enactment specified in section 35(3)(*d*), neither a gain nor a loss would accrue,

this Schedule shall have effect in relation to the losses that accrued to that company before that time and the assets held by that company at that time as if any time when it was a member of the first group were included in the period during which it is treated as having been a member of the second group.]¹

Commentary—*Simon's Direct Tax Service* **D2.679.**
Definitions—"Assets", s 21(1); "company", s 288(1); "group of companies", s 170; "shares", s 288(1).
Amendments—¹ This Schedule inserted by FA 1993 s 88(2) and Sch 8. It has effect for any accounting period ending after 15 March 1993 in relation to losses of a company joining the group after 30 March 1987; but see FA 1993 s 88(3) for detailed commencement provisions.

[SCHEDULE 7AA

RESTRICTIONS ON SETTING LOSSES AGAINST PRE-ENTRY GAINS]¹

Section 177B

Commentary—*Simon's Direct Tax Service* **D2.685.**
Revenue Internal Guidance—*Capital gains manual CG 48200–48224 (Revenue interpretation and examples).*
Cross references—See FA 2000 Sch 29 para 8(1) (the main amendments made to TCGA 1992 s 170 by FA 2000 Sch 29 para 1 have effect for the purposes of this Schedule for any accounting period ending after 20 March 2000).
FA 2000 Sch 29 para 8(2) (any question as to whether a company was a member of a group before 20 March 2000 is construed in accordance with the position under TCGA 1992 s 170 before the amendments made by Sch 29, para 1).
Amendments—¹ This Schedule inserted by FA 1998 s 137(2) and Sch 24. It has effect for any accounting period ending on or after 17 March 1998.

Introductory

[1—(1) This Schedule applies in the case of any company ("the relevant company") in relation to any accounting period ("the gain period") in which a pre-entry gain has accrued to that company.

(2) Subject to sub-paragraph (3) below, references in this Schedule to a pre-entry gain are references to any chargeable gain accruing to a company in an accounting period in which that company joins a group of companies after the gain has accrued to it.

(3) References in this Schedule to a company joining a group of companies—

(*a*) are references to its becoming a member of any group of companies of which it was not a member immediately before becoming a member; but

(*b*) do not include references to a company becoming a member of a group of companies at any time before 17th March 1998.

(4) Nothing in section 170(10) shall prevent all the companies of one group from being treated for the purposes of this Schedule as joining another group of companies when the principal company of the first group becomes a member of the other group.]¹

Commentary—*Simon's Direct Tax Service* **D2.685.**
Amendments—¹ This Schedule inserted by FA 1998 s 137(2) and Sch 24. It has effect for any accounting period ending on or after 17 March 1998.

Restriction on setting off losses

[2—(1) Notwithstanding anything in section 8 or Schedule 7A, the amount to be included in respect of chargeable gains in the relevant company's total profits for the gain period shall be computed by adding together—

(*a*) the adjusted amounts of the pre-entry gains accruing to the relevant company in the gain period; and

(*b*) the amount which, in accordance with that section and (where applicable) that Schedule, would fall to be included in respect of chargeable gains in those profits if the amounts specified in sub-paragraph (2) below were disregarded.

(2) The amounts to be disregarded as mentioned in sub-paragraph (1)(*b*) above are—

(*a*) all the pre-entry gains accruing to the relevant company in the gain period; and

(*b*) so much of any amount falling within subsection (1)(*a*) or (*b*) of section 8 as is applied in accordance with paragraph 3 below in reducing the amount of any such pre-entry gain;

and, accordingly, amounts which are applied in accordance with paragraph 3 below in reducing the amount of any pre-entry gain accruing in the gain period shall not be available to be carried forward for the purposes of section 8(1)(*b*) or paragraph 6 of Schedule 7A to any subsequent accounting period.]¹

Commentary—*Simon's Direct Tax Service* **D2.688.**
Amendments—¹ This Schedule inserted by FA 1998 s 137(2) and Sch 24. It has effect for any accounting period ending on or after 17 March 1998.

Adjustment of pre-entry gains

[**3**—(1) For the purposes of paragraph 2 above the adjusted amount of any pre-entry gain accruing to the relevant company in the gain period is the amount of that gain after any amount that may be set against it under this paragraph has been applied in reducing it.

(2) Subject to sub-paragraphs (3) and (4) below, the whole or any part of any amount which under paragraph 4 below is a qualifying loss in relation to a pre-entry gain may be set against that gain, except so far as it has been set against another pre-entry gain.

(3) Nothing in this Schedule shall authorise the reduction of a pre-entry gain by the deduction of the whole or any part of any amount to which paragraph 7 of Schedule 7A applies (pre-entry losses) unless that gain is a gain from which that amount is deductible in accordance with that paragraph.

(4) Nothing in this Schedule shall authorise the reduction of a pre-entry gain by the deduction of any amount which section 18(3) prevents from being deductible from that gain.][1]

Commentary—*Simon's Direct Tax Service* **D2.686, 687.**
Amendments—[1] This Schedule inserted by FA 1998 s 137(2) and Sch 24. It has effect for any accounting period ending on or after 17 March 1998.

Meaning of "qualifying losses"

[**4**—(1) Any amount which, in the case of the relevant company, would fall within section 8(1)(*b*) for the gain period is a qualifying loss in relation to any pre-entry gain accruing to the relevant company in that period.

(2) Any allowable loss accruing to the relevant company in the gain period is a qualifying loss in relation to a pre-entry gain accruing to that company in that period if—

(*a*) the time when the loss accrued is the same as or before the time when the gain accrued; or
(*b*) the loss having accrued after the time when the gain accrued, there is no time falling within sub-paragraph (3) below between—

(i) the time when the gain accrued; and
(ii) the time immediately after the time when the loss accrued.

(3) A time falls within this sub-paragraph, in relation to any allowable loss, if—

(*a*) it is a time at which the relevant company joined a group of companies; and
(*b*) the relevant asset was not in relevant ownership immediately before that time.

(4) For the purposes of sub-paragraph (3) above the relevant asset was in relevant ownership at the time immediately before the relevant company joined a group of companies if, and only if, it was at that time held by the relevant company or by another company which—

(*a*) joined that group of companies ("the new group") at the same time as the relevant company; and
(*b*) had been a member of the same group of companies as the relevant company immediately before joining the new group.

(5) In this paragraph "relevant asset", in relation to an allowable loss, means the asset on the disposal of which that loss accrued.][1]

Commentary—*Simon's Direct Tax Service* **D2.686.**
Amendments—[1] This Schedule inserted by FA 1998 s 137(2) and Sch 24. It has effect for any accounting period ending on or after 17 March 1998.

Special rule for disposal of pooled assets

[**5**—(1) This paragraph applies where—

(*a*) any holding of securities falls by virtue of any provision of Chapter I of Part IV to be treated as a single asset;
(*b*) one or more disposals of securities comprised in that holding is made by the relevant company in the gain period at or after the relevant entry time for that company; and
(*c*) an allowable loss accrues to the relevant company on that disposal or, as the case may be, on one or more of them.

(2) The extent to which any allowable loss falling within sub-paragraph (1)(*c*) above is to be treated for the purposes of paragraph 4(4) above as a loss accruing on the disposal of an asset held at any entry time for the relevant company shall be determined—

(*a*) by computing the notional net pre-entry loss accruing to the relevant company in the gain period;
(*b*) by setting allowable losses falling within sub-paragraph (1)(*c*) above against that notional net pre-entry loss in the order in which those losses accrued; and
(*c*) by treating the allowable loss as accruing on the disposal of an asset held at the entry time to the extent only that there is or remains an amount against which it can be set under paragraph (*b*) above.

(3) For the purposes of this paragraph the notional net pre-entry loss accruing to the relevant company in the gain period shall be determined—

    (a) by computing all the chargeable gains and allowable losses that, on the relevant assumptions, would have accrued to the relevant company on the disposals falling within sub-paragraph (4) below;

    (b) in a case where the aggregate amount of those gains is equal to or exceeds the aggregate amount of those losses, taking nil as the amount of the notional net pre-entry loss; and

    (c) in any other case, taking the amount by which the aggregate of those losses exceeds the aggregate of those gains as the amount of the notional net pre-entry loss.

(4) A disposal falls within this sub-paragraph to the extent that—

    (a) it is made by the relevant company in the gain period at or after the relevant entry time for that company; and

    (b) on the relevant assumptions, it would be taken to be a disposal of securities that are pre-entry securities in relation to the relevant entry time for that company.

(5) For the purposes of this paragraph the relevant assumptions, in relation to any company, are—

    (a) that securities which are pre-entry securities in relation to the relevant entry time for that company are not to be regarded as part of a single asset with any securities which are post-entry securities in relation to that time;

    (b) that securities disposed of in the gain period at or after that time are identified with securities that are pre-entry securities in relation to that time, rather than with securities which are post-entry securities in relation to that time; and

    (c) subject to paragraphs (a) and (b) above, that securities disposed of in the gain period are identified in accordance with the provisions applicable apart from paragraphs (a) and (b) above.

(6) For the purpose of applying the relevant assumptions in relation to any disposal of securities by the relevant company, it shall be further assumed—

    (a) that the relevant assumptions applied to every previous disposal in the gain period of securities by one company to another company in the same group of companies;

    (b) that (subject to paragraph (c) below) securities disposed of by one member of a group of companies to another member of that group retain the same status (as pre-entry securities or as post-entry securities) in relation to a particular time as they had before the disposal; and

    (c) that securities acquired by the relevant company at or after the relevant entry time for that company are to be taken to be pre-entry securities in relation to that time only if they fall within sub-paragraph (7) below.

(7) Securities fall within this sub-paragraph if, on the relevant assumptions and the assumptions set out in sub-paragraph (6)(a) and (b) above, they fall to be identified with securities which—

    (a) were held by the relevant company or any associated company of the relevant company at the time which is the relevant entry time for the relevant company; and

    (b) have not, between that time and the time when they are disposed of by the relevant company, been disposed of otherwise than by a disposal made by one company in a group of companies to another company in the same group.

(8) Where anything is treated by virtue of section 127 as the same asset as any securities comprised in any holding of securities falling to be regarded as a single asset by virtue of any provision of Chapter I of Part IV, so much of that section as determines the time at which anything comprised in the asset is taken to have been acquired shall be disregarded in determining for the purposes of this paragraph whether securities comprised in the asset are pre-entry securities or post-entry securities.

(9) Subject to sub-paragraphs (6) to (8) above, in this paragraph—

    "associated company" means a company which—

        (a) at the time which is the relevant entry time in the case of the relevant company joined the group of companies that was also joined at that time by the relevant company; and

        (b) had been a member of the same group of companies as the relevant company immediately before that time;

    "entry time", in relation to a company, means any time in the gain period at which the company joins a group of companies;

    "pre-entry securities", in relation to an entry time, means such securities acquired by the company in question before that time as have not already been disposed of before that time;

    "post-entry securities", in relation to an entry time, means securities acquired by the company in question at or after that time;

    "the relevant entry time" in relation to any company means—

        (a) if there is only one entry time for that company, that time; and

        (b) if there is more than one such time, the earlier or earliest such time.

    "securities" has the meaning given for the purposes of section 104 by subsection (3) of that section.]¹

Commentary—*Simon's Direct Tax Service* **D2.689.**
Amendments—¹ This Schedule inserted by FA 1998 s 137(2) and Sch 24. It has effect for any accounting period ending on or after 17 March 1998.

Special rule for losses on disposal of certain assets acquired at different times

[**6**—(1) This paragraph applies in relation to any allowable loss accruing to the relevant company in the gain period on the disposal of the whole or any part of an asset if—

(*a*)   the asset is one falling within sub-paragraph (2) below;

(*b*)   the disposal is one made at or at any time after an entry time; and

(*c*)   the loss is not one in relation to which paragraph 5(2) above applies.

(2)   An asset falls within this sub-paragraph if it is—

(*a*)   an asset treated as a single asset but comprising assets only some of which were held immediately before the entry time by the relevant company or by an associated company; or

(*b*)   an asset which is treated as held immediately before the entry time by the relevant company or by an associated company by virtue of a provision requiring an asset which was not held immediately before that time to be treated as the same as an asset which was so held.

(3)   Only such proportions of the loss as fall within sub-paragraph (4) below shall be taken for the purposes of paragraph 4(4) above to have accrued on the disposal of an asset held at the entry time.

(4)   Those proportions are—

(*a*)   the proportion of the loss which, on a just and reasonable apportionment, is properly attributable to assets in fact held at the entry time; and

(*b*)   such proportion of the loss not falling within paragraph (*a*) above as represents the loss that would have accrued if the asset disposed of had been the asset in fact held at that time.

(5)   In this paragraph—

"associated company", in relation to any entry time, means a company which—

(*a*)   at that time joined the group of companies that was also joined at that time by the relevant company; and

(*b*)   had been a member of the same group of companies as the relevant company immediately before that time;

"entry time" means any time in the gain period at which the relevant company joins a group of companies.]¹

Commentary—*Simon's Direct Tax Service* **D2.690.**
Amendments—¹ This Schedule inserted by FA 1998 s 137(2) and Sch 24. It has effect for any accounting period ending on or after 17 March 1998.

Special rule for gains and losses on deemed annual disposal

[**7** Where—

(*a*)   a chargeable gain or allowable loss is treated as accruing at the end of a company's accounting period by virtue of section 213(1)(*c*) or 214A(2)(*b*), and

(*b*)   that accounting period is one in which that company has joined a group of companies,

this Schedule shall have effect as if the gain or loss had accrued before the time or, as the case may be, the earliest time at which the company joined a group of companies in that period.]¹

Commentary—*Simon's Direct Tax Service* **D2.691.**
Amendments—¹ This Schedule inserted by FA 1998 s 137(2) and Sch 24. It has effect for any accounting period ending on or after 17 March 1998.

[SCHEDULE 7AB

ROLL-OVER OF DEGROUPING CHARGE: MODIFICATION OF ENACTMENTS]¹

Amendments—¹ This Schedule inserted by FA 2002 s 43(2), (4), Sch 7 with effect—

(*a*) in relation to a case where a company is treated by virtue of TCGA 1992 s 179(3) as having sold and immediately reacquired an asset, where the company's ceasing to be a member of the group in question happens after 31 March 2002;

(*b*) in relation to a case where a company is so treated by virtue of TCGA 1992 s 179(6), where the relevant time (within the meaning of that subsection) is after that date.

Introductory

[**1**—(1)This Schedule sets out how sections 152 and 153 and other related enactments are modified for the purposes of section 179B (roll-over of degrouping charge on business assets).

(2)   In the enactments as so modified—

"company A" and "company B" have the same meanings as in section 179;

"relevant asset" means the asset mentioned in section 179B(1);

"deemed sale" means the sale of the relevant asset that is treated as taking place by virtue of section 179(3) or (6);

"deemed sale consideration" means the amount for which company A is treated as having sold the relevant asset; "time of accrual" means—

> (*a*) in a case where section 179(3) applies, the time at which, by virtue of section 179(4), the gain or loss accruing on the deemed sale is treated as accruing to company A;
> (*b*) in a case where section 179(6) applies, the latest time at which the company satisfies the conditions in section 179(7).]¹

Amendments—¹ This Schedule inserted by FA 2002 s 43(2), (4) Sch 7 with effect—

(*a*) in relation to a case where a company is treated by virtue of TCGA 1992 s 179(3) as having sold and immediately reacquired an asset, where the company's ceasing to be a member of the group in question happens after 31 March 2002;
(*b*) in relation to a case where a company is so treated by virtue of TCGA 1992 s 179(6), where the relevant time (within the meaning of that subsection) is after that date.

[Section 152

2—(1) For subsection (1) of section 152 (roll-over relief) substitute—

"(1) If—

> (*a*) company B was carrying on a trade at the time when it disposed of the relevant asset to company A.
> (*b*) the relevant asset was used, and used only, for the purposes of that trade throughout the period when it was owned by company B,
> (*c*) an amount that is not less than the deemed sale consideration is applied by company A in acquiring other assets, or an interest in other assets ("the new assets"),
> (*d*) on acquisition the new assets are taken into use, and used only, for the purposes of a trade carried on by company A,
> (*e*) both the relevant asset and the new assets are within the classes of assets listed in section 155, and
> (*f*) company A makes a claim as respects the amount applied as mentioned in paragraph (*c*),

company A shall be treated for the purposes of this Act as if the deemed sale consideration were (if otherwise of a greater amount) reduced to such amount as would secure that neither a gain nor a loss accrues to the company in respect of the deemed sale.

(1A) Where subsection (1) applies, company A shall be treated for the purposes of this Act as if the amount or value of the consideration for the acquisition of, or of the interest in, the new assets were reduced by the same amount as the amount of the reduction under that subsection.

(1B) Subsection (1) does not affect the value at which company A is treated by virtue of section 179 as having reacquired the relevant asset.

(1C) Subsection (1A) does not affect the treatment for the purposes of this Act of the other party to the transaction involving the new assets.".

(2) In subsection (2) of that section (application of subsection (1) where old assets held on 6th April 1965)—

> (*a*) for "subsection (1)(*a*)" substitute "subsection (1)";
> (*b*) for "subsection (1)(*b*)" substitute "subsection (1A)".

(3) In subsection (3) of that section (reinvestment period), for "after the disposal of, or of the interest in, the old assets" substitute "after the time of accrual".

(4) In subsection (5) of that section (new assets must be acquired for purposes of trade), for "the trade" substitute "the trade carried on by company A".

(5) In subsection (6) of that section (apportionment where part of building etc not used for purposes of trade), omit "or disposal" and insert at the end "or of the deemed sale consideration".

(6) After that subsection insert—

"(6A) In subsection (6) "period of ownership", in relation to the relevant asset, means the period during which the asset was owned by company B.".

(7) In subsection (7) of that section (apportionment where old assets not used for purposes of trade throughout period of ownership)—

> (*a*) for the words from the beginning to "period of ownership" substitute "If the relevant asset was not used for the purposes of the trade carried on by company B throughout the period during which it was owned by that company";
> (*b*) for the words from "or disposal" to the end substitute "of the asset or of the deemed sale consideration".

(8) In subsection (9) of that section ("period of ownership" does not include period before 31st March 1982), for ""period of ownership" does not" substitute "the references to the period during which the relevant asset was owned by company B do not".

(9) In subsection (11) of that section (apportionment of consideration for assets not all of which are subject of claim), omit "or disposal" and insert at the end "; and similarly in relation to the deemed sale consideration".]¹

Amendments—¹ This Schedule inserted by FA 2002 s 43(2), (4) Sch 7 with effect—

(*a*) in relation to a case where a company is treated by virtue of TCGA 1992 s 179(3) as having sold and immediately reacquired an asset, where the company's ceasing to be a member of the group in question happens after 31 March 2002;

(*b*) in relation to a case where a company is so treated by virtue of TCGA 1992 s 179(6), where the relevant time (within the meaning of that subsection) is after that date.

[Section 153

3 For subsection (1) of section 153 (assets only partly replaced) substitute—

"(1) If—

(*a*) an amount that is less than the deemed sale consideration is applied by company A in acquiring other assets, or an interest in other assets ("the new assets"),

(*b*) the difference between the deemed sale consideration and the amount so applied ("the shortfall") is less than the amount of the gain (whether all chargeable gain or not) accruing on the deemed sale,

(*c*) the conditions in paragraphs (*a*), (*b*), (*d*) and (*e*) of section 152(1) are satisfied, and

(*d*) company A makes a claim as respects the amount applied as mentioned in paragraph (*a*) above,

company A shall be treated for the purposes of this Act as if the amount of the gain accruing as mentioned in paragraph (*b*) above were reduced to the same amount as the shortfall (with a proportionate reduction, if not all of that gain is chargeable gain, in the amount of the chargeable gain).

(1A) Where subsection (1) applies, company A shall be treated for the purposes of this Act as if the amount or value of the consideration for the acquisition of, or of the interest in, the new assets were reduced by the amount by which the gain is reduced (or as the case may be the amount by which the chargeable gain is proportionately reduced) under that subsection.

(1B) Subsection (1) does not affect the value at which company A is treated by virtue of section 179 as having reacquired the relevant asset.

(1C) Subsection (1A) does not affect the treatment for the purposes of this Act of the other party to the transaction involving the new assets.".]¹

Amendments—¹ This Schedule inserted by FA 2002 s 43(2), (4) Sch 7 with effect—

(*a*) in relation to a case where a company is treated by virtue of TCGA 1992 s 179(3) as having sold and immediately reacquired an asset, where the company's ceasing to be a member of the group in question happens after 31 March 2002;

(*b*) in relation to a case where a company is so treated by virtue of TCGA 1992 s 179(6), where the relevant time (within the meaning of that subsection) is after that date.

[Section 153A

4—(1) In subsection (1) of section 153A (provisional application of sections 152 and 153)—

(*a*) for the words from "a person" to "takes place" substitute "company A declares, in its return for the chargeable period in which the time of accrual falls";

(*b*) for "the trade" substitute "a trade carried on by company A";

(*c*) for "the whole or any specified part of the consideration" substitute "an amount equal to the deemed sale consideration or any specified part of that amount".

In subsection (5) of that section (meaning of "relevant day"), for paragraphs (*a*) and (*b*) substitute "the fourth anniversary of the last day of the accounting period of company A in which the time of accrual falls".]¹

Amendments—¹ This Schedule inserted by FA 2002 s 43(2), (4) Sch 7 with effect—

(*a*) in relation to a case where a company is treated by virtue of TCGA 1992 s 179(3) as having sold and immediately reacquired an asset, where the company's ceasing to be a member of the group in question happens after 31 March 2002;

(*b*) in relation to a case where a company is so treated by virtue of TCGA 1992 s 179(6), where the relevant time (within the meaning of that subsection) is after that date.

[Section 155

5 In section 155 (relevant classes of assets), in Head A of Class 1, after paragraph 2 insert—

"In Head A "the trade" means—

(*a*) for the purposes of determining whether the relevant asset is within this head, the trade carried on by company B;

(*b*) for the purposes of determining whether the new assets are within this head, the trade carried on by company A.".]¹

Amendments—¹ This Schedule inserted by FA 2002 s 43(2), (4) Sch 7 with effect—

(*a*) in relation to a case where a company is treated by virtue of TCGA 1992 s 179(3) as having sold and immediately reacquired an asset, where the company's ceasing to be a member of the group in question happens after 31 March 2002;

(*b*) in relation to a case where a company is so treated by virtue of TCGA 1992 s 179(6), where the relevant time (within the meaning of that subsection) is after that date.

[Section 159

6—(1) In subsection (1) of section 159 (new assets must be chargeable assets), for the words from "in the case of a person" to the second "in relation to him" substitute "if the relevant asset (or, as the case may be, the property mentioned in section 179(3)(*b*)) is a chargeable asset in relation to company A at the time of accrual, unless the new assets are chargeable assets in relation to that company''.

(2) In subsection (2) of that section (subsection (1) not to apply where new assets acquired by UK resident after disposal of old ones)—

    (*a*) for paragraph (*a*) substitute—

        ''(*a*) company A acquires the new assets after the time of accrual, and'';

    (*b*) in paragraph (*b*) for ''the person'' substitute ''that company''.

(3) In subsection (3) of that section (subsection (2) not to apply in certain cases where new assets acquired by dual resident), for ''the person'' substitute ''company A''.

(4) In subsection (6) of that section (definitions)—

    (*a*) in paragraph (*a*) for ''''the old assets'' and ''the new assets'' have the same meanings'' substitute ''''the new assets'' has the same meaning'';

    (*b*) omit paragraph (*b*).

(5) Omit subsection (7) of that section (acquisitions before 14th March 1989).][1]

Amendments—[1] This Schedule inserted by FA 2002 s 43(2), (4) Sch 7 with effect—

  (*a*) in relation to a case where a company is treated by virtue of TCGA 1992 s 179(3) as having sold and immediately reacquired an asset, where the company's ceasing to be a member of the group in question happens after 31 March 2002;

  (*b*) in relation to a case where a company is so treated by virtue of TCGA 1992 s 179(6), where the relevant time (within the meaning of that subsection) is after that date.

[Section 175

7—(1) In subsection (2) of section 175 (single-trade rule for group members not to apply in case of dual resident investing company)—

    (*a*) for ''the consideration for the disposal of the old assets'' substitute ''the amount of the deemed sale consideration'';

    (*b*) for ''''the old assets'' and ''the new assets'' have the same meanings'' substitute ''''the new assets'' has the same meaning''.

(2) In subsection (2A) of that section (claim by two group members to be treated as same person for roll-over purposes), for paragraph (*a*) substitute—

        ''(*a*) company A is a member of a group of companies at the time of accrual,''.

(3) In subsection (2AA) of that section (conditions for claim under subsection (2A))—

    (*a*) in paragraph (*a*) for the words from the beginning to ''chargeable assets'' substitute ''that company A is resident in the United Kingdom at the time of accrual, or the relevant asset (or, as the case may be, the property mentioned in section 179(3)(*b*)) is a chargeable asset'';

    (*b*) in paragraph (*b*) for ''the assets'' substitute ''the new assets (within the meaning of section 152)''.

(4) Immediately before subsection (2B) of that section (roll-over relief for group member not itself carrying on trade) insert—

    ''(2AB) Section 152 or 153 shall apply where—

        (*a*) company B was not carrying on a trade at the time when it disposed of the relevant asset to company A, but was a member of a group of companies at that time, and

        (*b*) immediately before that time the relevant asset was used, and used only, for the purposes of the trade which (in accordance with subsection (1) above) is treated as carried on by the members of the group which carried on a trade,

    as if company B had been carrying on that trade.''.

(5) In subsection (2B) of that section—

    (*a*) omit paragraph (*a*);

    (*b*) in paragraph (*b*), for ''those purposes'' substitute ''the purposes of the trade which (in accordance with subsection (1) above) is treated as carried on by the members of the group which carry on a trade''.

(6) Omit subsection (4) of that section (acquisitions before 20th March 1990).][1]

Amendments—[1] This Schedule inserted by FA 2002 s 43(2), (4) Sch 7 with effect—

  (*a*) in relation to a case where a company is treated by virtue of TCGA 1992 s 179(3) as having sold and immediately reacquired an asset, where the company's ceasing to be a member of the group in question happens after 31 March 2002;

  (*b*) in relation to a case where a company is so treated by virtue of TCGA 1992 s 179(6), where the relevant time (within the meaning of that subsection) is after that date.

[Section 185

8—(1) In subsection (3) of section 185 (no roll-over relief in certain cases where company acquires new assets after becoming non-resident)—

    (*a*) omit it ''the company''

    (*b*) for paragraph (*a*) substitute—

        ''(*a*) the time of accrual falls before the relevant time; and'';

(*c*) insert ''the company'' at the beginning of paragraph (*b*).

(2) In subsection (5) of that section (definitions), in paragraph (*c*) for ''''the old assets'' and ''the new assets'' have the same meanings'' substitute ''''the new assets'' has the same meaning''.][1]

Amendments—[1] This Schedule inserted by FA 2002 s 43(2), (4) Sch 7 with effect—

(*a*) in relation to a case where a company is treated by virtue of TCGA 1992 s 179(3) as having sold and immediately reacquired an asset, where the company's ceasing to be a member of the group in question happens after 31 March 2002;
(*b*) in relation to a case where a company is so treated by virtue of TCGA 1992 s 179(6), where the relevant time (within the meaning of that subsection) is after that date.

[Section 198

9—(1) For subsection (1) of section 198 (replacement of business assets used in connection with oil fields) substitute—

''(1) If at the time of accrual the relevant asset (or, as the case may be, the property mentioned in section 179(3)(*b*)) was used by company A for the purposes of a ring fence trade carried on by it, section 152 or 153 shall not apply unless the new assets are on acquisition taken into use, and used only, for the purposes of that trade.''.

(2) In subsection (3) of that section (new asset conclusively presumed to be depreciating asset), for ''in relation to any of the consideration on a material disposal'' substitute ''in a case falling within subsection (1) above''.

(3) In subsection (5) of that section (definitions), omit paragraph (*a*).][1]

Amendments—[1] This Schedule inserted by FA 2002 s 43(2), (4) Sch 7 with effect—

(*a*) in relation to a case where a company is treated by virtue of TCGA 1992 s 179(3) as having sold and immediately reacquired an asset, where the company's ceasing to be a member of the group in question happens after 31 March 2002;
(*b*) in relation to a case where a company is so treated by virtue of TCGA 1992 s 179(6), where the relevant time (within the meaning of that subsection) is after that date.

[Schedule 22 to the Finance Act 2000

10 In sub-paragraph (2) of paragraph 67 of Schedule 22 to the Finance Act 2000 (c 17) (no roll-over relief for tonnage tax assets)—

(*a*) after ''the disposal'', in the first and third places, insert ''or deemed sale'';
(*b*) in paragraph (*a*) after ''Asset No 1'' insert ''or, as the case may be, the deemed sale consideration''.][1]

Amendments—[1] This Schedule inserted by FA 2002 s 43(2), (4) Sch 7 with effect—

(*a*) in relation to a case where a company is treated by virtue of TCGA 1992 s 179(3) as having sold and immediately reacquired an asset, where the company's ceasing to be a member of the group in question happens after 31 March 2002;
(*b*) in relation to a case where a company is so treated by virtue of TCGA 1992 s 179(6), where the relevant time (within the meaning of that subsection) is after that date.

[SCHEDULE 7AC[1]

EXEMPTIONS FOR DISPOSALS BY COMPANIES WITH SUBSTANTIAL SHAREHOLDING][1]

Amendments—[1] This Schedule inserted by FA 2002 s 44(2), (3), Sch 8 para 1 with effect for disposals after 31 March 2002.

[PART 1

THE EXEMPTIONS

The main exemption

1—(1) A gain accruing to a company (''the investing company'') on a disposal of shares or an interest in shares in another company (''the company invested in'') is not a chargeable gain if the requirements of this Schedule are met.

(2) The requirements are set out in—

Part 2 (the substantial shareholding requirement), and
Part 3 (requirements to be met in relation to the investing company and the company invested in).

(3) The exemption conferred by this paragraph does not apply in the circumstances specified in paragraph 5 or the cases specified in paragraph 6.][1]

Amendments—[1] This Schedule inserted by FA 2002 s 44(2), (3), Sch 8 para 1 with effect for disposals after 31 March 2002.

[Subsidiary exemption: disposal of asset related to shares where main exemption conditions met

2—(1) A gain accruing to a company (''company A'') on a disposal of an asset related to shares in another company (''company B'') is not a chargeable gain if either of the following conditions is met.

(2) The first condition is that—

(*a*) immediately before the disposal company A holds shares or an interest in shares in company B, and

(*b*) any gain accruing to company A on a disposal at that time of the shares or interest would, by virtue of paragraph 1, not be a chargeable gain.

(3) The second condition is that—

(*a*) immediately before the disposal company A does not hold shares or an interest in shares in company B but is a member of a group and another member of that group does hold shares or an interest in shares in company B, and

(*b*) if company A, rather than that other company, held the shares or interest, any gain accruing to company A on a disposal at that time of the shares or interest would, by virtue of paragraph 1, not be a chargeable gain.

(4) Where assets of a company are vested in a liquidator under section 145 of the Insolvency Act 1986 (c 45) or Article 123 of the Insolvency (Northern Ireland) Order 1989 or otherwise, this paragraph applies as if the assets were vested in, and the acts of the liquidator in relation to the assets were the acts of, the company (acquisitions from or disposals to him by the company being disregarded accordingly).

(5) The exemption conferred by this paragraph does not apply in the circumstances specified in paragraph 5 or the cases specified in paragraph 6.]¹

Amendments—¹ This Schedule inserted by FA 2002 s 44(2), (3), Sch 8 para 1 with effect for disposals after 31 March 2002.

[Subsidiary exemption: disposal of shares or related asset where main exemption conditions previously met

3—(1) A gain accruing to a company (''company A'') on a disposal of shares, or an interest in shares or an asset related to shares, in another company (''company B'') is not a chargeable gain if the following conditions are met.

(2) The conditions are—

(*a*) that at the time of the disposal company A meets the requirement in paragraph 7 (the substantial shareholding requirement) in relation to company B;

(*b*) that a chargeable gain or allowable loss would, apart from this paragraph, accrue to company A on the disposal (but see sub-paragraph (3) below);

(*c*) that at the time of the disposal—

(i) company A is resident in the United Kingdom, or

(ii) any chargeable gain accruing to company A on the disposal would, by virtue of section 10(3), form part of that company's chargeable profits for corporation tax purposes;

(*d*) that there was a time within the period of two years ending with the disposal (''the relevant period'') when, if—

(i) company A, or

(ii) a company that at any time in the relevant period was a member of the same group as company A,

had disposed of shares or an interest in shares in company B that it then held, a gain accruing would, by virtue of paragraph 1, not have been a chargeable gain; and

(*e*) that, if at the time of the disposal the requirements of paragraph 19 (requirements relating to company invested in) are not met in relation to company B, there was a time within the relevant period when company B was controlled by—

(i) company A, or

(ii) company A together with any persons connected with it, or

(iii) a company that at any time in the relevant period was a member of the same group as company A, or

(iv) any such company together with any persons connected with it.

(3) Sub-paragraph (1) does not apply if—

(*a*) the condition in sub-paragraph (2)(*b*) is met but would not be met but for a failure to meet the requirement in paragraph 18(1)(*b*) (requirement as to investing company to be met immediately after the disposal), and

(*b*) the failure to meet that requirement is not due to—

(i) the fact that company A has been wound up or dissolved, or

(ii) where the winding up or dissolution takes place as soon as is reasonably practicable in the circumstances, the fact that company A is about to be wound up or dissolved.

(4) In determining for the purpose of sub-paragraph (2)(*d*) whether a gain accruing on the hypothetical disposal referred to would have been a chargeable gain, the requirements of paragraph 18(1)(*b*) and of paragraph 19(1)(*b*) (requirement as to company invested in to be met immediately after the disposal) shall be assumed to be met.

(5) Where—

(*a*) immediately before the disposal company B holds an asset, (*b*) the expenditure allowable in computing any gain or loss on that asset, were it to be disposed of by company B immediately before that disposal, would fall to be reduced because of a claim to relief under section 165 (gifts relief) in relation to an earlier disposal, and

(*c*) that earlier disposal took place within the relevant period,

sub-paragraph (1) does not prevent a gain accruing to company A on the disposal from being a chargeable gain but any loss so accruing is not an allowable loss.

(6) Where assets of company B are vested in a liquidator under section 145 of the Insolvency Act 1986 or Article 123 of the Insolvency (Northern Ireland) Order 1989 or otherwise, sub-paragraph (5)(*a*) applies as if the assets were vested in the company.

(7) In determining "the relevant period" for the purposes of sub-paragraph (2)(*d*) or (*e*) or sub-paragraph (5)(*c*), section 28 (time of disposal under contract) applies with the omission of subsection (2) (postponement of time of disposal in case of conditional contract).

(8) The exemption conferred by this paragraph does not apply in the circumstances specified in paragraph 5 or the cases specified in paragraph 6.]¹

Amendments—¹ This Schedule inserted by FA 2002 s 44(2), (3), Sch 8 para 1 with effect for disposals after 31 March 2002.

[Application of exemptions in priority to provisions deeming there to be no disposal etc

4—(1) For the purposes of determining whether an exemption conferred by this Schedule applies, the question whether there is a disposal shall be determined without regard to—

(*a*) section 116(10) (reorganisation, conversion of securities, etc treated as not involving disposal),

(*b*) section 127 (share reorganisations etc treated as not involving disposal), or

(*c*) section 192(2)(*a*) (distribution not treated as capital distribution).

(2) Sub-paragraph (1) does not apply to a disposal of shares if the effect of its applying would be that relief attributable to the shares under Schedule 15 to the Finance Act 2000 (corporate venturing scheme) would be withdrawn or reduced under paragraph 46 of that Schedule (withdrawal or reduction of investment relief on disposal of shares).

(3) Where or to the extent that an exemption conferred by this Schedule does apply—

(*a*) the provisions mentioned in sub-paragraph (1)(*a*) and (*b*) do not apply in relation to the disposal, and

(*b*) the provision mentioned in sub-paragraph (1)(*c*) does not apply in relation to the subject matter of the disposal.

(4) Where section 127 is disapplied by sub-paragraph (3)(*a*) in a case in which that section would otherwise have applied in relation to the disposal by virtue of paragraph 84 of Schedule 15 to the Finance Act 2000 (corporate venturing scheme: share exchanges), paragraph 85 of that Schedule (attribution of relief to new shares) does not apply.

(5) In this paragraph any reference to section 127 includes a reference to that provision as applied by any enactment relating to corporation tax.]¹

Amendments—¹ This Schedule inserted by FA 2002 s 44(2), (3), Sch 8 para 1 with effect for disposals after 31 March 2002.

[Circumstances in which exemptions do not apply

5—(1) Where in pursuance of arrangements to which this paragraph applies—

(*a*) an untaxed gain accrues to a company ("company A") on a disposal of shares, or an interest in shares or an asset related to shares, in another company ("company B"), and

(*b*) before the accrual of that gain—

(i) company A acquired control of company B, or the same person or persons acquired control of both companies, or

(ii) there was a significant change of trading activities affecting company B at a time when it was controlled by company A, or when both companies were controlled by the same person or persons,

none of the exemptions in this Schedule applies to the disposal.

(2) This paragraph applies to arrangements from which the sole or main benefit that (but for this paragraph) could be expected to arise is that the gain on the disposal would, by virtue of this Schedule, not be a chargeable gain.

(3) For the purposes of sub-paragraph (1)(*a*) a gain is "untaxed" if the gain, or all of it but a part that is not substantial, represents profits that have not been brought into account (in the United Kingdom or elsewhere) for the purposes of tax on profits for a period ending on or before the date of the disposal.

(4) The reference in sub-paragraph (3) to profits being brought into account for the purposes of tax on profits includes a reference to the case where—

(*a*) an amount in respect of those profits is apportioned to a company resident in the United Kingdom by virtue of subsection (3) of section 747 of the Taxes Act 1988 (imputation of chargeable profits etc of controlled foreign companies), and

(b) a sum is chargeable on that company in respect of that amount by virtue of subsection (4) of that section for an accounting period of that company ending on or before the date of disposal.

(5) For the purposes of sub-paragraph (1)(b)(ii) there is a "significant change of trading activities affecting company B" if—

(a) there is a major change in the nature or conduct of a trade carried on by company B or a 51% subsidiary of company B, or

(b) there is a major change in the scale of the activities of a trade carried on by company B or a 51% subsidiary of company B, or

(c) company B or a 51% subsidiary of company B begins to carry on a trade.

(6) In this paragraph—

"arrangements" includes any scheme, agreement or understanding, whether or not legally enforceable;

"major change in the nature or conduct of a trade" has the same meaning as in section 768 of the Taxes Act (change of ownership of company: disallowance of trading losses);

"profits" means income or gains (including unrealised income or gains).]¹

Amendments—¹ This Schedule inserted by FA 2002 s 44(2), (3), Sch 8 para 1 with effect for disposals after 31 March 2002.

[Other cases excluded from exemptions

6—(1) The exemptions conferred by this Schedule do not apply—

(a) to a disposal that by virtue of any enactment relating to chargeable gains is deemed to be for a consideration such that no gain or loss accrues to the person making the disposal,

(b) to a disposal a gain on which would, by virtue of any enactment not contained in this Schedule, not be a chargeable gain, or

(c) to a deemed disposal under section 440(1) or (2) of the Taxes Act (deemed disposal on transfer of asset of insurance company from one category to another).

(2) The hypothetical disposal referred to in paragraph 2(2)(b) or (3)(b) or paragraph 3(2)(d) shall be assumed not to be a disposal within sub-paragraph (1)(a), (b) or (c) above.]¹

Amendments—¹ This Schedule inserted by FA 2002 s 44(2), (3), Sch 8 para 1 with effect for disposals after 31 March 2002.

[PART 2
THE SUBSTANTIAL SHAREHOLDING REQUIREMENT
The requirement

7 The investing company must have held a substantial shareholding in the company invested in throughout a twelve-month period beginning not more than two years before the day on which the disposal takes place.]¹

Amendments—¹ This Schedule inserted by FA 2002 s 44(2), (3), Sch 8 para 1 with effect for disposals after 31 March 2002.

[Meaning of "substantial shareholding"

8—(1) For the purposes of this Schedule a company holds a "substantial shareholding" in another company if it holds shares or interests in shares in that company by virtue of which—

(a) it holds not less than 10% of the company's ordinary share capital,

(b) it is beneficially entitled to not less than 10% of the profits available for distribution to equity holders of the company, and

(c) it would be beneficially entitled on a winding up to not less than 10% of the assets of the company available for distribution to equity holders.

This is without prejudice to what is meant by "substantial" where the word appears in other contexts.

(2) Schedule 18 to the Taxes Act 1988 (meaning of equity holder and determination of profits or assets available for distribution) applies for the purposes of sub-paragraph (1).

(3) In that Schedule as it applies for those purposes—

(a) for any reference to sections 403C and 413(7) of that Act, or either of those provisions, substitute a reference to sub-paragraph (1) above;

(b) omit the words in paragraph 1(4) from "but" to the end;

(c) omit paragraph 5(3) and paragraphs 5B to 5F; and

(d) omit paragraph 7(1)(b).]¹

Amendments—¹ This Schedule inserted by FA 2002 s 44(2), (3), Sch 8 para 1 with effect for disposals after 31 March 2002.

[Aggregation of holdings of group companies

9—(1) For the purposes of paragraph 7 (the substantial shareholding requirement) a company that is a member of a group is treated—

(a) as holding any shares or interest in shares held by any other company in the group, and (*b*) as having the same entitlement as any such company to any rights enjoyed by virtue of holding shares or an interest in shares.

(2) Sub-paragraph (1) is subject to paragraph 17(4) (exclusion of aggregation in case of assets of long-term insurance fund of insurance company).][1]

Amendments—[1] This Schedule inserted by FA 2002 s 44(2), (3), Sch 8 para 1 with effect for disposals after 31 March 2002.

[Effect of earlier no-gain/no-loss transfer

10—(1) For the purposes of this Part the period for which a company has held shares is treated as extended by any earlier period during which the shares concerned, or shares from which they are derived, were held—

(*a*) by a company from which the shares concerned were transferred to the first-mentioned company on a no-gain/no-loss transfer, or

(*b*) by a company from which the shares concerned, or shares from which they are derived, were transferred on a previous no-gain/no-loss transfer—

    (i) to a company within paragraph (*a*), or

    (ii) to another company within this paragraph.

(2) For the purposes of sub-paragraph (1)—

(*a*) a "no-gain/no-loss transfer" means a disposal and corresponding acquisition that by virtue of any enactment relating to chargeable gains are deemed to be for a consideration such that no gain or loss accrues to the person making the disposal;

(*b*) a transfer shall be treated as if it had been a no-gain/no-loss transfer if it is a transfer to which subsection (1) of section 171 (transfers within a group) would apply but for subsection (3) of that section.

(3) Where sub-paragraph (1) applies to extend the period for which a company ("company A") is treated as having held any shares, that company shall be treated for the purposes of this Part as having had at any time the same entitlement—

(*a*) to shares, and

(*b*) to any rights enjoyed by virtue of holding shares,

as the company ("company B") that at that time held the shares concerned or, as the case may be, the shares from which they are derived.

(4) The shares and rights to be so attributed to company A include any holding or entitlement attributed at that time to company B under paragraph 9 (aggregation of holdings of group companies).

(5) In this paragraph, except in paragraphs (*a*) to (*c*) of sub-paragraph (6), "shares" includes an interest in shares.

(6) For the purposes of this paragraph shares are "derived" from other shares only where—

(*a*) a company becomes a co-owner of shares previously owned by it alone, or vice versa,

(*b*) a company's interest in shares as co-owner changes (without the company ceasing to be a co-owner),

(*c*) one holding of shares is treated by virtue of section 127 as the same asset as another, or

(*d*) there is a sequence of two or more of the occurrences mentioned in paragraphs (*a*) to (*c*).

The reference in paragraph (*c*) to section 127 includes a reference to that provision as applied by any enactment relating to corporation tax.][1]

Amendments—[1] This Schedule inserted by FA 2002 s 44(2), (3), Sch 8 para 1 with effect for disposals after 31 March 2002.

[Effect of deemed disposal and reacquisition

11—(1) For the purposes of this Part a company is not regarded as having held shares throughout a period if, at any time during that period, there is a deemed disposal and reacquisition of—

(*a*) the shares concerned, or

(*b*) shares, or an interest in shares, from which those shares are derived.

(2) For the purposes of this Part a company is not regarded as having held an interest in shares throughout a period if, at any time during that period, there is a deemed disposal and reacquisition of—

(*a*) the interest concerned, or

(*b*) shares, or an interest in shares, from which that interest is derived.

(3) In this paragraph—

    "deemed disposal and reacquisition" means a disposal and immediate reacquisition treated as
      taking place under any enactment relating to corporation tax;

    "derived" has the same meaning as in paragraph 10.][1]

Amendments—[1] This Schedule inserted by FA 2002 s 44(2), (3), Sch 8 para 1 with effect for disposals after 31 March 2002.

[Effect of repurchase agreement

...where—

...shares in another company transfers the shares under a repurchase

...A(1) (agreements for sale and repurchase of securities) the disposal is ...s of the enactments relating to chargeable gains.

...repurchase agreement—

...be treated for the purposes of this Part as continuing to hold the shares ...as retaining his entitlement to any rights attached to them, and ...be treated for those purposes as not holding the shares transferred and ...any such rights.

This is subject to the following qualification.

(3) If at any time before the end of the period of the repurchase agreement the original owner, or another member of the same group as the original owner, becomes the holder—

    (*a*) of any of the shares transferred, or
    (*b*) of any shares directly or indirectly representing any of the shares transferred,

sub-paragraph (2) does not apply after that time in relation to those shares or, as the case may be, in relation to the shares represented by those shares.

(4) In this paragraph a "repurchase agreement" means an agreement under which—

    (*a*) a person ("the original owner") transfers shares to another person ("the interim holder") under an agreement to sell them, and
    (*b*) the original owner or a person connected with him is required to buy them back either—

        (i) in pursuance of an obligation to do so imposed by that agreement or by any related agreement, or
        (ii) in consequence of the exercise of an option acquired under that agreement or any related agreement.

For the purposes of paragraph (*b*) agreements are related if they are entered into in pursuance of the same arrangements (regardless of the date on which either agreement is entered into).

(5) Any reference in this paragraph to the period of a repurchase agreement is to the period beginning with the transfer of the shares by the original owner to the interim holder and ending with the repurchase of the shares in pursuance of the agreement.]¹

Amendments—¹ This Schedule inserted by FA 2002 s 44(2), (3), Sch 8 para 1 with effect for disposals after 31 March 2002.

[Effect of stock lending arrangements

13—(1) This paragraph applies where—

    (*a*) a company that holds shares in another company transfers the shares under a stock lending arrangement, and
    (*b*) by virtue of section 263B(2) (stock lending arrangements) the disposal is disregarded for the purposes of the enactments relating to chargeable gains.

(2) During the period of the stock lending arrangement—

    (*a*) the lender shall be treated for the purposes of this Part as continuing to hold the shares transferred and accordingly as retaining his entitlement to any rights attached to them, and
    (*b*) the borrower shall be treated for those purposes as not holding the shares transferred and as not becoming entitled to any such rights.

This is subject to the following qualification.

(3) If at any time before the end of the period of the stock lending arrangement the lender, or another member of the same group as the lender, becomes the holder—

    (*a*) of any of the shares transferred, or
    (*b*) of any shares directly or indirectly representing any of the shares transferred,

sub-paragraph (2) does not apply after that time in relation to those shares or, as the case may be, in relation to the shares represented by those shares.

(4) In this paragraph a "stock lending arrangement" means arrangements between two persons ("the borrower" and "the lender") under which—

    (*a*) the lender transfers shares to the borrower otherwise than by way of sale, and
    (*b*) a requirement is imposed on the borrower to transfer those shares back to the lender otherwise than by way of sale.

(5) Any reference in this paragraph to the period of a stock lending arrangement is to the period beginning with the transfer of the shares by the lender to the borrower and ending—

    (*a*) with the transfer of the shares back to the lender in pursuance of the arrangement, or
    (*b*) when it becomes apparent that the requirement for the borrower to make a transfer back to the lender will not be complied with.

(6) The following provisions apply for the purposes of this paragra[...] of section 263B—

(a) subsections (5) and (6) of that section (references to transf[...] transfer of other securities of the same description);

(b) section 263C (references to transfer back of securities to redemption).]¹

Amendments—¹ This Schedule inserted by FA 2002 s 44(2), (3), Sch 8 para 1 with effec[...]

[Effect in relation to company invested in of earlier compar[...]

14—(1) This paragraph applies where shares in one company (''comp[...]

(a) are exchanged (or deemed to be exchanged) for shares in anoth[...] or

(b) are deemed to be exchanged by virtue of section 136 for share[...] another company (''company Y''),

in circumstances such that, under section 127 as that section applies b[...] the original shares and the new holding are treated as the same asset.

(2) Where company Y—

(a) is the company invested in, and is accordingly the comp[...] requirement of paragraph 7 (the substantial shareholding requirem[...]

(b) is a company by reference to which, by virtue of this paragra[...] or

(c) is a company by reference to which, by virtue of paragraph [...] requirement may be met,

that requirement may instead be met, in relation to times before the ex[...] by reference to company X.

(3) If in any case that requirement can be met by virtue of this paragraph (or by virtue of this paragraph together with paragraph 15), it shall be treated as met.

(4) In sub-paragraph (1) ''original shares'' and ''new holding'' shall be construed in accordance with sections 126, 127, 135 and 136.]¹

Amendments—¹ This Schedule inserted by FA 2002 s 44(2), (3), Sch 8 para 1 with effect for disposals after 31 March 2002.

[Effect in relation to company invested in of earlier demerger

15—(1) This paragraph applies where shares in one company (''the subsidiary'') are transferred by another company (''the parent company'') on a demerger.

(2) Where the subsidiary—

(a) is the company invested in, and is accordingly the company by reference to which the requirement of paragraph 7 (the substantial shareholding requirement) falls to be met, or

(b) is a company by reference to which, by virtue of this paragraph, that requirement may be met, or

(c) is a company by reference to which, by virtue of paragraph 14 (effect of earlier company reconstruction etc), that requirement may be met,

that requirement may instead be met, in relation to times before the transfer, by reference to the parent company.

(3) If in any case that requirement can be met by virtue of this paragraph (or by virtue of this paragraph together with paragraph 14), it shall be treated as met.

(4) In this paragraph a ''transfer of shares on a demerger'' means a transfer such that, by virtue of section 192(2)(b), sections 126 to 130 apply as if the parent company and the subsidiary were the same company and the transfer were a reorganisation of that company's share capital not involving a disposal or acquisition.]¹

Amendments—¹ This Schedule inserted by FA 2002 s 44(2), (3), Sch 8 para 1 with effect for disposals after 31 March 2002.

[Effect of investing company's liquidation

16 Where assets of the investing company, or of a company that is a member of the same group as the investing company, are vested in a liquidator under section 145 of the Insolvency Act 1986 (c 45) or Article 123 of the Insolvency (Northern Ireland) Order 1989 (SI 1989/2405 (NI 19)) or otherwise, this Part applies as if the assets were vested in, and the acts of the liquidator in relation to the assets were the acts of, the company (acquisitions from or disposals to him by the company being disregarded accordingly).]¹

Amendments—¹ This Schedule inserted by FA 2002 s 44(2), (3), Sch 8 para 1 with effect for disposals after 31 March 2002.

[Special rules for assets of insurance company's long-term insurance fund

17—(1) In the following two cases paragraph 8(1) (meaning of substantial shareholding) has effect as if, in paragraphs (*a*), (*b*) and (*c*), "30%" were substituted for "10%".

(2) The first case is where the investing company is an insurance company and the disposal is of an asset of its long-term insurance fund.

(3) The second case is where—

    (*a*) the investing company is a 51% subsidiary of an insurance company, and
    (*b*) the insurance company holds as an asset of its long-term insurance fund shares or an interest in shares—

       (i) in the investing company, or
       (ii) in another company through which it owns shares in the investing company.

The reference in paragraph (*b*)(ii) to owning shares through another company has the same meaning as in section 838 of the Taxes Act (subsidiaries).

(4) Where the investing company is a member of a group that includes an insurance company, paragraph 9 (aggregation of holdings of group companies) does not apply in relation to shares or an interest in shares held by the insurance company as assets of its long-term insurance fund.

(5) In this paragraph "insurance company" and "long-term insurance fund" have the meanings given by section 431(2) of the Taxes Act.]¹

Amendments—¹ This Schedule inserted by FA 2002 s 44(2), (3), Sch 8 para 1 with effect for disposals after 31 March 2002.

[PART 3
REQUIREMENTS TO BE MET IN RELATION TO INVESTING COMPANY AND COMPANY INVESTED IN
Requirements relating to the investing company

18—(1) The investing company must—

    (*a*) have been a sole trading company or a member of a qualifying group throughout the period ("the qualifying period")—

       (i) beginning with the start of the latest twelve-month period by reference to which the requirement of paragraph 7 (the substantial shareholding requirement) is met, and
       (ii) ending with the time of the disposal, and

    (*b*) be a sole trading company or a member of a qualifying group immediately after the time of the disposal.

(2) For this purpose a "qualifying group" means—

    (*a*) a trading group, or
    (*b*) a group that would be a trading group if the activities of any group member that is not established for profit were disregarded to the extent that they are carried on otherwise than for profit.

In determining whether a company is established for profit, no account shall be taken of any object or power of the company that is only incidental to its main objects.

(3) The requirement in sub-paragraph (1)(*a*) is met if the investing company was a sole trading company for some of the qualifying period and a member of a qualifying group for the remainder of that period.

(4) The requirement in sub-paragraph (1)(*a*) is treated as met if at the time of the disposal—

    (*a*) the investing company is a member of a group, and
    (*b*) there is another member of the group in relation to which that requirement would have been met if—

       (i) the subject matter of the disposal had been transferred to it immediately before the disposal in circumstances in which section 171(1) (transfers within a group) applied, and
       (ii) it had made the disposal.

(5) If the disposal is by virtue of section 28(1) or (2) (asset disposed of under contract) treated as made at a time before the asset is conveyed or transferred, the requirements in sub-paragraph (1)(*a*) and (*b*) must also be complied with as they would have effect if the references in those provisions and sub-paragraph (4) to the time of the disposal were to the time of the conveyance or transfer.

(6) In this paragraph a "sole trading company" means a trading company that is not a member of a group.]¹

Amendments—¹ This Schedule inserted by FA 2002 s 44(2), (3), Sch 8 para 1 with effect for disposals after 31 March 2002.

[Requirements relating to the company invested in

19—(1) The company invested in must—

    (*a*) have been a qualifying company throughout the period—

TCGA 1992

(i) beginning with the start of the latest twelve-month period by reference to which the requirement of paragraph 7 (the substantial shareholding requirement) is met, and

(ii) ending with the time of the disposal, and

(b) be a qualifying company immediately after the time of the disposal.

(2) For this purpose a ''qualifying company'' means a trading company or the holding company of a trading group or a trading subgroup.

(3) If the disposal is by virtue of section 28(1) or (2) (asset disposed of under contract) treated as made at a time before the asset is conveyed or transferred, the requirements in sub-paragraph (1)(a) and (b) must also be complied with as they would have effect if the references there to the time of the disposal were to the time of the conveyance or transfer.][1]

Amendments—[1] This Schedule inserted by FA 2002 s 44(2), (3), Sch 8 para 1 with effect for disposals after 31 March 2002.

[Meaning of ''trading company'']

20—(1) In this Schedule ''trading company'' means a company carrying on trading activities whose activities do not include to a substantial extent activities other than trading activities.

(2) For the purposes of sub-paragraph (1) ''trading activities'' means activities carried on by the company—

(a) in the course of, or for the purposes of, a trade being carried on by it,

(b) for the purposes of a trade that it is preparing to carry on,

(c) with a view to its acquiring or starting to carry on a trade, or

(d) with a view to its acquiring a significant interest in the share capital of another company that—

(i) is a trading company or the holding company of a trading group or trading subgroup, and

(ii) if the acquiring company is a member of a group, is not a member of that group.

(3) Activities do not qualify as trading activities under sub-paragraph (2)(c) or (d) unless the acquisition is made, or (as the case may be) the company starts to carry on the trade, as soon as is reasonably practicable in the circumstances.

(4) The reference in sub-paragraph (2)(d) to the acquisition of a significant interest in the share capital of another company is to an acquisition of ordinary share capital in the other company—

(a) such as would make that company a 51% subsidiary of the acquiring company, or

(b) such as would give the acquiring company a qualifying shareholding in a joint venture company without making the two companies members of the same group.][1]

Amendments—[1] This Schedule inserted by FA 2002 s 44(2), (3), Sch 8 para 1 with effect for disposals after 31 March 2002.

[Meaning of ''trading group'']

21—(1) In this Schedule ''trading group'' means a group—

(a) one or more of whose members carry on trading activities, and

(b) the activities of whose members, taken together, do not include to a substantial extent activities other than trading activities.

(2) For the purposes of sub-paragraph (1) ''trading activities'' means activities carried on by a member of the group—

(a) in the course of, or for the purposes of, a trade being carried on by any member of the group,

(b) for the purposes of a trade that any member of the group is preparing to carry on,

(c) with a view to any member of the group acquiring or starting to carry on a trade, or

(d) with a view to any member of the group acquiring a significant interest in the share capital of another company that—

(i) is a trading company or the holding company of a trading group or trading subgroup, and

(ii) is not a member of the same group as the acquiring company.

(3) Activities do not qualify as trading activities under sub-paragraph (2)(c) or (d) unless the acquisition is made, or (as the case may be) the group member in question starts to carry on the trade, as soon as is reasonably practicable in the circumstances.

(4) The reference in sub-paragraph (2)(d) to the acquisition of a significant interest in the share capital of another company is to an acquisition of ordinary share capital in the other company—

(a) such as would make that company a member of the same group as the acquiring company, or

(b) such as would give the acquiring company a qualifying shareholding in a joint venture company without making the joint venture company a member of the same group as the acquiring company.

(5) For the purposes of this paragraph the activities of the members of the group shall be treated as one business (with the result that activities are disregarded to the extent that they are intra-group activities).][1]

Amendments—[1] This Schedule inserted by FA 2002 s 44(2), (3), Sch 8 para 1 with effect for disposals after 31 March 2002.

[Meaning of "trading subgroup"

22—(1) In this Schedule "trading subgroup" means a subgroup—

 (*a*) one or more of whose members carry on trading activities, and
 (*b*) the activities of whose members, taken together, do not include to a substantial extent activities other than trading activities.

(2) For the purposes of sub-paragraph (1) "trading activities" means activities carried on by a member of the subgroup—

 (*a*) in the course of, or for the purposes of, a trade being carried on by any member of the subgroup,
 (*b*) for the purposes of a trade that any member of the subgroup is preparing to carry on,
 (*c*) with a view to any member of the subgroup acquiring or starting to carry on a trade, or
 (*d*) with a view to any member of the subgroup acquiring a significant interest in the share capital of another company that—

  (i) is a trading company or the holding company of a trading group or trading subgroup, and
  (ii) is not a member of the same group as the acquiring company.

(3) Activities do not qualify as trading activities under sub-paragraph (2)(*c*) or (*d*) unless the acquisition is made, or (as the case may be) the subgroup member in question starts to carry on the trade, as soon as is reasonably practicable in the circumstances.

(4) The reference in sub-paragraph (2)(*d*) to the acquisition of a significant interest in the share capital of another company is to an acquisition of ordinary share capital in the other company—

 (*a*) such as would make that company a member of the same subgroup as the acquiring company, or
 (*b*) such as would give the acquiring company a qualifying shareholding in a joint venture company without making the two companies members of the same group.

(5) For the purposes of this paragraph the activities of the members of the subgroup shall be treated as one business (with the result that activities are disregarded to the extent that they are intra-subgroup activities).][1]

Amendments—[1] This Schedule inserted by FA 2002 s 44(2), (3), Sch 8 para 1 with effect for disposals after 31 March 2002.

[Treatment of holdings in joint venture companies

23—(1) This paragraph applies where a company ("the company") has a qualifying shareholding in a joint venture company.

(2) In determining whether the company is a trading company—

 (*a*) its holding of shares in the joint venture company shall be disregarded, and
 (*b*) it shall be treated as carrying on an appropriate proportion—

  (i) of the activities of the joint venture company, or
  (ii) where the joint venture company is a holding company, of the activities of that company and its 51% subsidiaries.

This sub-paragraph does not apply if the company is a member of a group and the joint venture company is a member of the same group.

(3) In determining whether the company is a member of a trading group or the holding company of a trading group—

 (*a*) every holding of shares in the joint venture company by a member of the group having a qualifying shareholding in that company shall be disregarded, and
 (*b*) each member of the group having a qualifying shareholding in the joint venture company shall be treated as carrying on an appropriate proportion—

  (i) of the activities of the joint venture company, or
  (ii) where the joint venture company is a holding company, of the activities of that company and its 51% subsidiaries.

This sub-paragraph does not apply if the joint venture company is a member of the group.

(4) In determining whether the company is the holding company of a trading subgroup—

 (*a*) every holding of shares in the joint venture company by the company and any of its 51% subsidiaries having a qualifying shareholding in the joint venture company shall be disregarded, and
 (*b*) the company and each of its 51% subsidiaries having a qualifying shareholding in the joint venture company shall be treated as carrying on an appropriate proportion—

  (i) of the activities of the joint venture company, or
  (ii) where the joint venture company is a holding company, of the activities of that company and its 51% subsidiaries.

This sub-paragraph does not apply if the joint venture company is a member of the same group as the company.

(5) In sub-paragraphs (2)(*b*), (3)(*b*) and (4)(*b*) "an appropriate proportion" means a proportion corresponding to the percentage of the ordinary share capital of the joint venture company held by the company concerned.

(6) In this paragraph "shares", in relation to a joint venture company, includes securities of that company or an interest in shares in or securities of that company.

(7) For the purposes of this paragraph the activities of a joint venture company that is a holding company and its 51% subsidiaries shall be treated as a single business (so that activities are disregarded to the extent that they are intra-group activities or, as the case may be, intra-subgroup, activities).]¹

Amendments—¹ This Schedule inserted by FA 2002 s 44(2), (3), Sch 8 para 1 with effect for disposals after 31 March 2002.

[Meaning of "joint venture company" and "qualifying shareholding"

24—(1) For the purposes of this Schedule a company is a "joint venture company" if, and only if—

(*a*) it is a trading company or the holding company of a trading group or trading subgroup, and
(*b*) there are five or fewer persons who between them hold 75% or more of its ordinary share capital.

In determining whether there are five or fewer such persons as are mentioned in paragraph (*b*), the members of a group are treated as if they were a single company.

(2) For the purposes of this Schedule—

(*a*) a company that is not a member of a group has a "qualifying shareholding" in a joint venture company if, and only if, it holds shares or an interest in shares in the joint venture company by virtue of which it holds 10% or more of that company's ordinary share capital;
(*b*) a company that is a member of a group has a "qualifying shareholding" in a joint venture company if, and only if—

(i) it holds ordinary share capital of the joint venture company, and
(ii) the members of the group between them hold 10% or more of the ordinary share capital of that company.]¹

Amendments—¹ This Schedule inserted by FA 2002 s 44(2), (3), Sch 8 para 1 with effect for disposals after 31 March 2002.

[Effect in relation to company invested in of earlier company reconstruction, demerger etc

25 The provisions of—

(*a*) paragraph 14 (effect of earlier company reconstruction etc), and
(*b*) paragraph 15 (effect of earlier demerger),

have effect in relation to the requirements of paragraph 19 (requirements in relation to company invested in) as they have effect in relation to the requirement of paragraph 7 (the substantial shareholding requirement).]¹

Amendments—¹ This Schedule inserted by FA 2002 s 44(2), (3), Sch 8 para 1 with effect for disposals after 31 March 2002.

[PART 4

INTERPRETATION

Meaning of "company", "group" and related expressions

26—(1) In this Schedule—

(*a*) "company" has the meaning given by section 170(9); and
(*b*) references to a group, or to membership of a group, shall be construed in accordance with the provisions of section 170 read as if "51 per cent" were substituted for "75 per cent".

(2) References in this Schedule to a "subgroup" are to companies that would form a group but for the fact that one of them is a 51% subsidiary of another company.

(3) In this Schedule "holding company"—

(*a*) in relation to a group, means the company described in section 170 as the principal company of the group;
(*b*) in relation to a subgroup, means a company that would be the holding company of a group but for being a 51% subsidiary of another company.

(4) In this Schedule "51% subsidiary" has the meaning given by section 838 of the Taxes Act.

In applying that section for the purposes of this Schedule, any share capital of a registered industrial and provident society shall be treated as ordinary share capital.

(5) References in this Schedule to a "group" or "subsidiary" shall be construed with any necessary modifications where applied to a company incorporated under the law of a country or territory outside the United Kingdom.]¹

Amendments—¹ This Schedule inserted by FA 2002 s 44(2), (3), Sch 8 para 1 with effect for disposals after 31 March 2002.

[Meaning of "trade"

27 In this Schedule "trade" means anything that—

   (*a*) is a trade, profession or vocation, within the meaning of the Income Tax Acts, and

   (*b*) is conducted on a commercial basis with a view to the realisation of profits.]¹

Amendments—¹ This Schedule inserted by FA 2002 s 44(2), (3), Sch 8 para 1 with effect for disposals after 31 March 2002.

[Meaning of "twelve-month period"

28 For the purposes of this Schedule a "twelve-month period" means a period ending with the day before the first anniversary of the day with which, or in the course of which, the period began.]¹

Amendments—¹ This Schedule inserted by FA 2002 s 44(2), (3), Sch 8 para 1 with effect for disposals after 31 March 2002.

[Meaning of "interest in shares"

29—(1) References in this Schedule to an interest in shares are to an interest as a co-owner of shares.

(2) It does not matter whether the shares are owned jointly or in common, or whether the interests of the co-owners are equal.]¹

Amendments—¹ This Schedule inserted by FA 2002 s 44(2), (3), Sch 8 para 1 with effect for disposals after 31 March 2002.

[Meaning of "asset related to shares"

30—(1) This paragraph explains what is meant by an asset related to shares in a company.

(2) An asset is related to shares in a company if it is—

   (*a*) an option to acquire or dispose of shares or an interest in shares in that company, or

   (*b*) a security to which are attached rights by virtue of which the holder is or may become entitled to acquire or dispose of (whether by conversion or exchange or otherwise)—

      (i) shares or an interest in shares in that company, or

      (ii) an option to acquire or dispose of shares or an interest in shares in that company, or

      (iii) another security falling within this paragraph, or

   (*c*) an option to acquire or dispose of any security within paragraph (*b*)or an interest in any such security, or

   (*d*) an interest in, or option over, any such option or security as is mentioned in paragraph (*a*), (*b*) or (*c*), or

   (*e*) any interest in, or option over, any such interest or option as is mentioned in paragraph (*d*) or this paragraph.

(3) In determining whether a security is within sub-paragraph (2)(*b*), no account shall be taken—

   (*a*) of any rights attached to the security other than rights relating, directly or indirectly, to shares of the company in question, or

   (*b*) of rights as regards which, at the time the security came into existence, there was no more than a negligible likelihood that they would in due course be exercised to a significant extent.

(4) The references in this paragraph to an interest in a security or option have a meaning corresponding to that given by paragraph 29 in relation to an interest in shares.]¹

Amendments—¹ This Schedule inserted by FA 2002 s 44(2), (3), Sch 8 para 1 with effect for disposals after 31 March 2002.

[Index of defined expressions

31 In this Schedule the expressions listed below are defined or otherwise explained by the provisions indicated:

asset related to shares	paragraph 30
company	paragraph 26(i)(*a*)
company invested in	paragraph 1
51% subsidiary	paragraph 26(4) and (5)
group (and member of group)	paragraph 26(i)(*b*) and (5)
holding company	paragraph 26(3)
interest in shares	paragraph 29
investing company	paragraph 1
joint venture company	paragraph 24(1)
qualifying shareholding (in joint venture company)	paragraph 24(2)
subgroup	paragraph 26(2)
trade	paragraph 27
trading company	paragraph 20
trading group	paragraph 21
trading subgroup	paragraph 22
twelve-month period	paragraph 28]¹

Amendments—¹ This Schedule inserted by FA 2002 s 44(2), (3), Sch 8 para 1 with effect for disposals after 31 March 2002.

[PART 5

CONSEQUENTIAL PROVISIONS

Meaning of "chargeable shares" or "chargeable asset"

32 Any exemption conferred by this Schedule shall be disregarded in determining whether shares are "chargeable shares", or an asset is a "chargeable asset", for the purposes of any enactment relating to corporation tax or capital gains tax.]¹

Amendments—¹ This Schedule inserted by FA 2002 s 44(2), (3), Sch 8 para 1 with effect for disposals after 31 March 2002.

[Negligible value claims

33—(1) This paragraph applies where—

(*a*) a company makes a claim under section 24(2) (assets of negligible value) in relation to shares held by it, and

(*b*) by virtue of this Schedule any loss accruing to the company on a disposal of the shares at the time of the claim would not be an allowable loss.

(2) Where this paragraph applies the company may not exercise the option under section 24(2) to specify a time earlier than the time of the claim as the time when the shares are treated as sold and reacquired by virtue of that subsection.

(3) This paragraph applies to—

(*a*) an interest in shares in a company, or

(*b*) an asset related to shares in a company,

as it applies to shares in that company.]¹

Amendments—¹ This Schedule inserted by FA 2002 s 44(2), (3), Sch 8 para 1 with effect for disposals after 31 March 2002.

[Reorganisations etc: deemed accrual of chargeable gain or allowable loss held over on earlier transaction

34—(1) The exemptions conferred by this Schedule do not apply to or affect a chargeable gain or allowable loss deemed to accrue on a disposal by virtue of section 116(10)(*b*) (reorganisations, conversions and reconstructions: deemed accrual of gain or loss held over on earlier transaction).

(2) Sub-paragraph (1) does not apply where the relevant earlier transaction was a deemed disposal and reacquisition under section 92(7) of the Finance Act 1996 (c 8) (convertible securities etc).]¹

Amendments—¹ This Schedule inserted by FA 2002 s 44(2), (3), Sch 8 para 1 with effect for disposals after 31 March 2002.

[Recovery of charge postponed on transfer of assets to non-resident company

35—(1) This paragraph applies where—

(*a*) a company disposes of an asset in circumstances falling within section 140(4) (recovery of charge postponed on transfer of assets to non-resident company), and

(*b*) by virtue of this Schedule any gain accruing to the company on the disposal would not be a chargeable gain.

(2) Where this paragraph applies the amount by which the consideration received on the disposal would be treated as increased by virtue of section 140(4) shall instead be treated as accruing to the company, at the time of the disposal, as a chargeable gain to which this Schedule does not apply.

(3) Any reference in section 140 to an amount being brought or taken into account under or in accordance with subsection (4) of that section includes a reference to an amount being treated, by virtue of sub-paragraph (2) above, as accruing as a chargeable gain.]¹

Amendments—¹ This Schedule inserted by FA 2002 s 44(2), (3), Sch 8 para 1 with effect for disposals after 31 March 2002.

[Appropriation of asset to trading stock

36—(1) Where—

(*a*) an asset acquired by a company otherwise than as trading stock of a trade carried on by it is appropriated by the company for the purposes of the trade as trading stock (whether on the commencement of the trade or otherwise), and

(*b*) if the company had then sold the asset for its market value, a chargeable gain or allowable loss would have accrued to the company but for an exemption conferred by this Schedule,

the company is treated for the purposes of the enactments relating to chargeable gains as if it had thereby disposed of the asset for its market value.

(2) Section 173 (transfers within a group: trading stock) applies in relation to this paragraph as it applies in relation to section 161 (appropriations to and from stock).]¹

Amendments—¹ This Schedule inserted by FA 2002 s 44(2), (3), Sch 8 para 1 with effect for disposals after 31 March 2002.

(5) The reduction is made by applying to that amount the fraction:

$$\frac{A - B}{A}$$

where—

A is the book value of all shares and securities held by the partnership at the end of the period of account of the partnership in which the amount of capital in question is fully invested by the partnership, and

B is the book value of all qualifying corporate bonds held by the partnership at the end of that period of account,

(6) For the purposes of sub-paragraph (5) the "book value" means the value shown in the partnership's accounts at the end of the period of account.]¹

Amendments—¹ This Schedule inserted by FA 2002 s 85(2), Sch 31 with effect from 24 July 2002.

[Deemed disposal of single asset in case of distribution

5—(1) There is a disposal of the single asset on each occasion on which the company receives a distribution from the partnership that does not consist entirely of income or the proceeds of sale or redemption of assets that are not relevant assets.

(2) The disposal is taken to be for a consideration equal to the amount of the distribution or of so much of it as does not consist of income or the proceeds of sale or redemption of assets that are not relevant assets.

(3) Where—

(a) the partnership disposes of relevant assets on which a chargeable gain or allowable loss would accrue if they were held by the company alone, and

(b) no distribution of the proceeds of the disposal is made within twelve months of the disposal,

the company is treated as having received its share of the proceeds as a distribution at the end of the period of account of the partnership following that in which the disposal took place, or at the end of the period of six months after the date of the disposal, whichever is the later.

(4) The operation of sub-paragraph (3) is not affected by the partnership having ceased to be a venture capital investment partnership before the time at which the distribution is treated as received by the company.

(5) Where sub-paragraph (3) applies, any subsequent actual distribution of the proceeds is disregarded.]¹

Amendments—¹ This Schedule inserted by FA 2002 s 85(2), Sch 31 with effect from 24 July 2002.

[Apportionment in case of part disposal

6—(1) For the purposes of section 42 (apportionment of cost etc in case of part disposal) the market value of the property remaining undisposed of on a part disposal of the single asset shall be determined as follows.

(2) If there is no further disposal of that asset in the period of account in which the part disposal in question takes place, the market value of the property remaining undisposed of shall be taken to be equal to the company's share of the book value of the relevant assets of the partnership as shown in the partnership's accounts at the end of that period of account.

(3) If there is a further disposal of that asset in the period of account in which the part disposal in question takes place, or more than one, the market value of the property remaining undisposed of shall be taken to be equal to the sum of—

(a) the amount or value of the consideration on the further disposal or, as the case may be, the total amount or value of the consideration on the further disposals, and

(b) the amount (if any) of the company's share of the book value of the relevant assets of the partnership as shown in the partnership's accounts at the end of that period of account.]¹

Amendments—¹ This Schedule inserted by FA 2002 s 85(2), Sch 31 with effect from 24 July 2002.

[Disposal of partnership asset giving rise to offshore income gain

7—(1) Nothing in this Schedule shall be read as affecting the operation of Chapter 5 of Part 17 of the Taxes Act (offshore funds).

(2) Where an offshore income gain accrues to the company under that Chapter from the disposal of any relevant asset of the partnership, the amount of any distribution received or treated as received by the company from the partnership that represents the whole or part of the proceeds of disposal of that asset is treated for the purposes of this Schedule as reduced by the amount of the whole or a corresponding part of the offshore income gain.]¹

Amendments—¹ This Schedule inserted by FA 2002 s 85(2), Sch 31 with effect from 24 July 2002.

[Exclusion of negligible value claim

8 No claim may be made in respect of the single asset under section 24(2) (assets that have become of negligible value).]¹

Amendments—¹ This Schedule inserted by FA 2002 s 85(2), Sch 31 with effect from 24 July 2002.

[Investment in other venture capital investment partnerships

9—(1) For the purposes of paragraph 2 (meaning of ''venture capital investment partnership'') an investment by way of capital contribution to another venture capital investment partnership shall be treated as an investment in unquoted shares or securities.

(2) The Treasury may by regulations make provision, in place of but corresponding to that made by paragraphs 3 to 8, in relation to gains accruing on a disposal of relevant assets by such a partnership.

(3) The regulations may make provision for any period of account to which, in accordance with paragraphs 11 to 13, this Schedule applies.]¹

Amendments—¹ This Schedule inserted by FA 2002 s 85(2), Sch 31 with effect from 24 July 2002.

[Interpretation

10—(1) In this Schedule—

''insurance company'', ''long-term business'' and ''long-term insurance fund'' have the same meaning as in Chapter 1 of Part 12 of the Taxes Act (see section 431(2) of that Act); ''limited partner'' means—

(a) a person carrying on a business as a limited partner in a partnership registered under the Limited Partnership Act 1907, or

(b) a person carrying on a business jointly with others who, under the law of a country or territory outside the United Kingdom, is not entitled to take part in the management of the business and is not liable beyond a certain limit for debts or obligations incurred for the purposes of the business;

''relevant assets'' has the meaning given by paragraph 3(3);

''securities'' has the same meaning as in section 132 and also includes any debentures;

''unquoted'' and quoted'', in relation to shares or securities, refer to listing on a recognised stock exchange.

(2) References in this Schedule to the partnership's accounts are to accounts drawn up in accordance with generally accepted accounting practice.

If no such accounts are drawn up, the references to the treatment of any matter, or the amount shown, in the accounts of the partnership are to what would have appeared if accounts had been drawn up in accordance with generally accepted accounting practice.

(3) References in this Schedule to capital contributed to a limited partnership include amount purporting to be provided by way of loan if—

(a) the loan carries no interest,

(b) all the limited partners are required to make such loans, and

(c) the loans are accounted for as partners' capital, or partners' equity, in the accounts of the partnership.

(4) For the purposes of this Schedule the assets of—

(a) a Scottish partnership, or

(b) a partnership under the law of any other country or territory under which assets of a partnership are regarded as held by or on behalf of the partnership as such,

shall be treated as held by the members of the partnership in the proportions in which they are entitled to share in the profits of the partnership.

References in this Schedule to the company's interest in, or share of, the partnership's assets shall be construed accordingly.]¹

Amendments—¹ This Schedule inserted by FA 2002 s 85(2), Sch 31 with effect from 24 July 2002.

[General commencement and transitional provisions

11—(1) Subject to paragraph 12 (election to remain outside Schedule), this Schedule applies—

(a) to periods of account of the partnership beginning on or after 1st January 2002, and

(b) to a period of account of the partnership beginning before that date and ending on or after it unless the company elects that it shall not do so.

(2) Where the company became a member of the partnership before the beginning of the first period of account of the partnership to which this Schedule applies, the cost of the single asset at the beginning of that period of account shall be taken to be equal to the total of the relevant indexed base costs.

(3) For the purposes of sub-paragraph (2)—

(a) the ''indexed base cost'' means—

(i) in relation to a holding that by virtue of section 104 is to be treated as a single asset, what would be the indexed pool of expenditure within the meaning of section 110 if the holding were disposed of, and

(ii) in relation to any other asset, the amount of expenditure together with the indexation allowance that would be fall to be deducted if the asset were disposed of; and

(*b*) the "relevant indexed base costs" means the indexed base costs that would be taken into account in computing in accordance with section 59 the gain or loss of the company if all the shares and securities (other than qualifying corporate bonds) held by the partnership were disposed of on the last day of the company's accounting period immediately preceding its first accounting period beginning on or after 1st January 2002.

(4) No account shall be taken under this Schedule of a distribution by the partnership in a period of account to which this Schedule applies to the extent that it represents a chargeable gain accruing in an earlier period to which this Schedule does not apply.]¹

Amendments—¹ This Schedule inserted by FA 2002 s 85(2), Sch 31 with effect from 24 July 2002.

[*Election to remain outside Schedule*

12—(1) If the company—

(*a*) became a member of the partnership before the beginning of the first period of account of the partnership to which this Schedule would otherwise apply, or

(*b*) made its first contribution of capital to the partnership before 17th April 2002,

it may elect that the provisions of this Schedule shall not apply to it in relation to that partnership.]¹

Amendments—¹ This Schedule inserted by FA 2002 s 85(2), Sch 31 with effect from 24 July 2002.

[*How and when election to be made*

13 Any election under paragraph 10 or 11 must be made—

(*a*) by notice to an officer of the Board,

(*b*) not later than the end of the period of two years after the end of the company's first accounting period beginning on or after 1st January 2002.]¹

Amendments—¹ This Schedule inserted by FA 2002 s 85(2), Sch 31 with effect from 24 July 2002.

[SCHEDULE 7B

MODIFICATION OF ACT IN RELATION TO OVERSEAS LIFE INSURANCE COMPANIES]¹

Section 214B

Amendments—¹ This Schedule inserted by FA 1993 s 102(2), Sch 11.

[1 In its application to an overseas life insurance company (as defined in section 431(2) of the Taxes Act) this Act shall have effect with the following modifications; and in those modifications any reference to the Taxes Act is a reference to that Act as it has effect in relation to such a company by virtue of Schedule 19AC to that Act.]¹

Amendments—¹ This Schedule inserted by FA 1993 s 102(2), Sch 11.

[2—(1) In section 13(5)(*d*), the words "section 11(2)(*b*), (*c*), (*d*) or (*e*) of the Taxes Act" shall be treated as substituted for the words "section 10(3)".

(2) This paragraph shall apply in relation to chargeable gains accruing to companies in accounting periods beginning after 31st December 1992.]¹

Definitions—"Accounting period", TA 1988 s 834(1); "chargeable gain", s 15(2); "company", Sch 7B para 1.
Amendments—¹ This Schedule inserted by FA 1993 s 102(2), Sch 11.

[3—(1) In section 16(3), the words "under section 11(2)(*b*), (*c*), (*d*) or (*e*) of the Taxes Act" shall be treated as substituted for the words "under section 10".

(2) This paragraph shall apply in relation to accounting periods beginning after 31st December 1992.]¹

Definitions—"Accounting period", TA 1988 s 834(1).
Amendments—¹ This Schedule inserted by FA 1993 s 102(2), Sch 11.

[4—(1) In section 25, the following subsection shall be treated as substituted for sub-section (7)—

"(7) For the purposes of this section an asset is at any time a chargeable asset in relation to an overseas life insurance company if, were it to be disposed of at that time, any chargeable gains accruing to the company on the disposal would form part of its chargeable profits for corporation tax purposes by virtue of section 11(2)(*b*), (*c*), (*d*) or (*e*) of the Taxes Act."

(2) This paragraph shall apply in relation to accounting periods beginning after 31st December 1992.][1]

Definitions—"Accounting period", TA 1988 s 834(1); "asset", s 21(1); "chargeable gain", s 15(2); "overseas life insurance company", Sch 7B para 1.
Amendments—[1] This Schedule inserted by FA 1993 s 102(2), Sch 11.

[5—(1) In section 140A(2), the words "section 11(2)(*b*), (*c*) or (*d*) of the Taxes Act" shall be treated as substituted for the words "section 10(3)".

(2) This paragraph shall apply in relation to transfers taking place in accounting periods of company B beginning after 31st December 1992.][1]

Definitions—"Accounting period", TA 1988 s 834(1).
Amendments—[1] This Schedule inserted by FA 1993 s 102(2), Sch 11.

[6—(1) In section 159(4)(*b*), the words "section 11(2)(*b*), (*c*) or (*d*) of the Taxes Act" shall be treated as substituted for the words "section 10(3)".

(2) This paragraph shall apply in relation to disposals or acquisitions made in accounting periods beginning after 31st December 1992.][1]

Definitions—"Accounting period", TA 1988 s 834(1).
Amendments—[1] This Schedule inserted by FA 1993 s 102(2), Sch 11.

[6A In section 171(1A), the words "section 11(2)(*b*), (*c*), (*d*) or (*e*) of the Taxes Act" shall be treated as substituted for the words "section 10(3)"][1].

Amendment—[1] This paragraph inserted by FA 2000 s 102, Sch 29 para 39(1), (2), (5) with effect for cases where s 171, or as the case may be, s 175 has effect as amended by FA 2000 Sch 29.

[6B In section 175(2AA), the words "section 11(2)(*b*), (*c*), (*d*) or (*e*) of the Taxes Act" shall be treated as substituted for the words "section 10(3)".][1]

Amendment—[1] This paragraph inserted by FA 2000 s 102, Sch 29 para 391), (2), (5) with effect for cases where s 171, or as the case may be, s 175 has effect as amended by FA 2000 Sch 29.

[7...][1]

Definitions—"Accounting period", TA 1988 s 834(1).
Amendments—[1] This paragraph repealed by FA 2000 s 156, Sch 40 Pt II(12) with effect in relation to disposals after 31 March 2000.

[7A In section 179A(12), the words "section 11(2)(*b*), (*c*) or (*d*) of the Taxes Act" shall be treated as substituted for "section 10(3)"][1]

Amendments—[1] This paragraph inserted by FA 2002 s 42(2), (4) with effect—
(*a*) in relation to a case where a company is treated by virtue of TCGA 1992 s 179(3) as having sold and then reacquired an asset, where the company's ceasing to be a member of the group in question happens after 31 March 2002;
(*b*) in relation to a case where a company is so treated by virtue of TCGA 1992 s 179(6), where the relevant time (within the meaning of that subsection) is after that date.

[8—(1) In subsections (2)(*a*) and (3) of section 185, the words "or (4A)" shall be treated as inserted after the words "subsection (4)".

(2) The following subsections shall be treated as inserted after subsection (4) of that section—

"(4A) Subject to subsection (4B) below, if at any time after the relevant time the company is an overseas life insurance company—

(*a*) any assets of its [long-term insurance][2] fund which, immediately after the relevant time—

(i) are situated outside the United Kingdom and are used or held for the purposes of the branch or agency in the United Kingdom through which the company carries on life assurance business; or

(ii) are attributed to the branch or agency by virtue of section 11B of the Taxes Act,

shall be excepted from subsection (2) above; and

(*b*) any new assets of its [long-term insurance][2] fund which, after that time—

(i) are so situated and are so used or held; or

(ii) are so attributed,

shall be excepted from subsection (3) above.

(4B) Subsection (4A) above shall not apply if the relevant time falls before the relevant day; and for the purposes of this subsection the relevant day is the first day of the company's first accounting period to begin after 31st December 1992."

(3) In subsection (5) of that section, the following paragraph shall be treated as inserted after paragraph (*b*)—

"(*ba*) "life assurance business" and "[long-term insurance][2] fund" have the meanings given by section 431(2) of the Taxes Act;".][1]

Definitions—"Accounting period", TA 1988 s 834(1); "asset", s 21(1); "branch or agency", s 10(6); "overseas life insurance company", Sch 7B para 1; "relevant time", s 185(1).
Amendments—[1] This Schedule inserted by FA 1993 s 102(2), Sch 11.

[2] Words in sub-paras (2), (3) substituted by the Financial Services and Markets Act 2000 (Consequential Amendments) (Taxes) Order, SI 2001/3629 arts 61, 73(1)(*b*) with effect from 1 December 2001 immediately after the coming into force of the Financial Services and Markets Act 2000 ss 411, 432(1), Sch 20.

[9 In [section 190(2)(*b*)][2], the words "section 11(2)(*b*), (*c*), (*d*) or (*e*) of the Taxes Act" shall be treated as substituted for the words "section 10(3)".

(2) This paragraph shall apply in relation to accounting periods beginning after 31st December 1992.]¹

Definitions—"Accounting period", TA 1988 s 834(1).
Amendments—¹ This Schedule inserted by FA 1993 s 102(2), Sch 11.
² Words substituted by FA 2000 s 102, Sch 29 para 39(3), (6) with effect for cases where s 190 has effect as amended by FA 2000 Sch 29.

[9A In section 211(1), the reference to [an insurance business transfer scheme][2] shall be treated as including a reference to any qualifying overseas transfer (within the meaning of paragraph 4A of Schedule 19AC to the Taxes Act).]¹

Amendments—¹ Para 9A inserted by FA 1995 s 53, Sch 9 para 6(2) with effect for any transfers sanctioned or authorised after 30 June 1994.
² Words substituted by the Financial Services and Markets Act 2000 (Consequential Amendments) (Taxes) Order, SI 2001/3629 arts 61, 72 with effect from 1 December 2001 immediately after the coming into force of the Financial Services and Markets Act 2000 ss 411, 432(1), Sch 20. SI 2001/3629 art 72 has effect in relation to any transfer under a scheme falling within the Financial Services and Markets Act 2000 s 105, including an excluded scheme falling within Case 2, 3 or 4 of the Financial Services and Markets Act 2000 s 105(3).

[10—(1) In section 212, the following subsection shall be treated as inserted after sub-section (5)—

"(5A) In its application to an overseas life insurance company this section shall have effect as if the references in subsections (1) and (2) to assets were to such of the assets concerned as are—

    (*a*) section 11(2)(*b*) assets;

    (*b*) section 11(2)(*c*) assets; or

    (*c*) assets which by virtue of section 11B of the Taxes Act are attributed to the branch or agency in the United Kingdom through which the company carries on life assurance business; and any expression used in this subsection to which a meaning is given by section 11A of the Taxes Act has that meaning."

(2) This paragraph shall apply in relation to accounting periods beginning after 31st December 1992.]¹

Definitions—"Asset", s 21(1); "branch or agency", s 10(6); "overseas life insurance company", Sch 7B para 1.
Amendments—¹ This Schedule inserted by FA 1993 s 102(2), Sch 11.

[11—(1) In section 213(4), the words "in the United Kingdom through a branch or agency" shall be treated as inserted after the words "[long-term][4] business".

[(1A) In section 213(5), the reference to [an insurance business transfer scheme][3] shall be treated as including a reference to any qualifying overseas transfer (within the meaning of paragraph 4A of Schedule 19AC to the Taxes Act).]²

(2) This paragraph shall apply in relation to events occurring in accounting periods beginning after 31st December 1992.]¹

Definitions—"Accounting period", TA 1988 s 834(1); "branch or agency", s 10(6).
Amendments—¹ This Schedule inserted by FA 1993 s 102(2), Sch 11.
² Sub-para (1A) inserted by FA 1995 s 53, Sch 9 para 6(3), with effect for any transfers sanctioned or authorised after 30 June 1994.
³ Words in sub-para (1A) substituted by the Financial Services and Markets Act 2000 (Consequential Amendments) (Taxes) Order, SI 2001/3629 arts 61, 72 with effect from 1 December 2001 immediately after the coming into force of the Financial Services and Markets Act 2000 ss 411, 432(1), Sch 20. SI 2001/3629 art 72 has effect in relation to any transfer under a scheme falling within the Financial Services and Markets Act 2000 s 105, including an excluded scheme falling within Case 2, 3 or 4 of the Financial Services and Markets Act 2000 s 105(3).
⁴ Word in sub-para (1) substituted by SI 2001/3629 arts 61, 73(2)(*b*) with effect from 1 December 2001 immediately after the coming into force of the Financial Services and Markets Act 2000 ss 411, 432(1), Sch 20.

[12—(1) In section 214, the following subsection shall be treated as inserted after subsection (11)—

"(12) In its application to an overseas life insurance company this section shall have effect as if—

    (*a*) the references in subsections (1), (2) and (6) to (10) to assets were to such of the assets concerned as are—

        (i) section 11(2)(*b*) assets; or

        (ii) section 11(2)(*c*) assets;

    (*b*) the references in subsections (1), (7) and (8) to liabilities were to such of the liabilities concerned as are attributable to the branch or agency in the United Kingdom through which the company carries on life assurance business;

    [(*c*) the reference in subsection (11) to a transfer of the whole or part of a company's long term business in accordance with a scheme sanctioned by a court under Part I of Schedule 2C to the Insurance Companies Act 1982 were to be treated as including a reference to any qualifying overseas transfer (within the meaning of paragraph 4A of Schedule 19AC to the

Taxes Act), and the references in that subsection to the business to which the transfer relates were to be construed accordingly;].[2]

and any expression used in this subsection to which a meaning is given by section 11A of the Taxes Act has that meaning."

(2) This paragraph shall apply where the accounting period mentioned in section 214(6)(*d*) begins after 31st December 1992.][1]

Definitions—"Asset", s 21(1); "branch or agency", s 10(6); "overseas life insurance company", Sch 7B para 1.
Amendments—[1] This Schedule inserted by FA 1993 s 102(2), Sch 11.
[2] Para (*c*) of s 214(12) as set out in this paragraph, inserted by FA 1995 s 53, Sch 9 para 6(4), with effect for any transfers sanctioned or authorised after 30 June 1994.

[13—(1) In subsection (4) of section 214A, in item G the words "in the United Kingdom through a branch or agency" shall be treated as inserted after the words "cessation of the carrying on".

(2) In subsection (6) of that section, the words "in the United Kingdom through a branch or agency" shall be treated as inserted after the words "long term business".

[(2A) In subsection (7) of that section, the reference to a transfer of the whole or part of a company's long term business in accordance with a scheme sanctioned by a court under Part I of Schedule 2C to the Insurance Companies Act 1982 shall be treated as including a reference to any qualifying overseas transfer (within the meaning of paragraph 4A of Schedule 19AC to the Taxes Act); and the references in that subsection and in subsection (8) of that section to the business to which the transfer relates shall be construed accordingly.][2]

(3) In subsection (11) of that section, the following words shall be treated as inserted at the end "; and, as it applies for the purposes of this section, the words "(with the modifications set out in subsection (12) of that section)" shall be treated as inserted after the words "section 214".][1]

Definitions—"Branch or agency", s 10(6); "overseas life insurance company", Sch 7B para 1.
Amendments—[1] This Schedule inserted by FA 1993 s 102(2), Sch 11.
[2] Para (2A) inserted by FA 1995 s 53, Sch 9 para 6(5), with effect in relation to any transfers sanctioned or authorised after 30 June 1994.

[14—(1) In section 228(6)(*b*), the words "section 11(2)(*b*), (*c*) or (*d*) of the Taxes Act" shall be treated as substituted for the words "section 10(3)".

(2) This paragraph shall apply in relation to acquisitions made in chargeable periods beginning after 31st December 1992.][1]

Commentary—*Simon's Direct Tax Service* D4.527, 537.
Definitions—"Chargeable period", s 288(1).
Amendments—[1] This Schedule inserted by FA 1993 s 102(2), Sch 11.

[15—(1) In Schedule 7A, in sub-paragraph (3A) of paragraph 1, the words "section 11(2)(*b*), (*c*), (*d*) or (*e*) of the Taxes Act" shall be treated as substituted for the words "section 10(3)".

(2) In that paragraph, the following sub-paragraph shall be treated as inserted after sub-paragraph (4)—

"(4A) Where—

    (*a*) an asset is held by an overseas life insurance company, and
    (*b*) section 440 of the Taxes Act applies at any time in relation to the asset,

the asset shall not be treated for the purposes of sub-paragraph (3A)(*b*) above as having become a chargeable asset at that time."][1]

Amendment—[1] This paragraph inserted by FA 2000 s 102, Sch 29 para 39(4), (7) with effect for cases where Schedule 7A has effect as amended by FA 2000 Sch 29.

[16 In Schedule 7AC, in paragraph 3(2)(*c*)(ii), the words "section 11(2)(*b*), (*c*) or (*d*) of the Taxes Act" shall be treated as substituted for the words "section 10(3)]][1]

Amendment—[1] This paragraph added by FA 2002 s 44(2), (3), Sch 8 para 4 with effect for disposals after 31 March 2002.

[SCHEDULE 7C

RELIEF FOR TRANSFERS TO APPROVED SHARE PLANS][1]

Section 236A

Commentary—*Simon's Direct Tax Service* E4.536.
Revenue Internal Guidance—Capital Gains Manual CG 61970–61981 (operation of this Schedule including worked examples).
Cross references—See FA 2000 Sch 29 para 40 (the main amendments made to TCGA 1992 s 170 by FA 2000 Sch 29 para 1 have effect for the purposes of this Schedule).
Amendments—[1] This Schedule inserted by FA 2000 s 48(2), Sch 9 with effect from 28 July 2000.

Introductory

[**1**—(1) A person ("the claimant") who makes a disposal of shares ("the disposal") to the trustees of the plan trust of an employee share ownership plan ("the plan") is entitled to claim relief under paragraph 5 if—

(*a*) the conditions in paragraph 2 are fulfilled, and

(*b*) paragraph 3(1) or (2) applies.

(2) Sub-paragraph (1) does not apply to a company that makes a disposal of shares.

(3) In this paragraph the references to a disposal of shares include a disposal of an interest in shares.]¹

Commentary—*Simon's Direct Tax Service* **C1.440**.
Amendments—¹ This Schedule inserted by FA 2000 s 48(2), Sch 9 with effect from 28 July 2000.

Conditions relating to the disposal

[**2**—(1) The first condition is that, at the time of the disposal, the plan is approved under Schedule 8 to the Finance Act 2000.

(2) The second condition is that the relevant shares meet the requirements in Part VIII of that Schedule (types of shares that may be used in plan) in relation to the plan.

For this purpose that Part applies as if paragraph 61(*a*) and (*c*) (listed shares and shares in a company under the control of a company whose shares are listed) were omitted.

(3) The third condition is that, at any time in the entitlement period, the trustees hold, for the beneficiaries of the plan trust, shares in the relevant company that—

(*a*) constitute not less than 10% of the ordinary share capital of the company, and

(*b*) carry rights to not less than 10% of—

(i) any profits available for distribution to shareholders of the company, and

(ii) any assets of that company available for distribution to its shareholders in the event of a winding up.

(4) For the purposes of sub-paragraph (3), shares that have been appropriated to, or acquired on behalf of, an individual under the plan shall continue to be treated as held by the trustees of the plan trust for the beneficiaries of that trust until such time as they cease to be subject to the plan (within the meaning of Schedule 8 to the Finance Act 2000).

(5) The fourth condition is that, at all times in the proscribed period, there are no unauthorised arrangements under which the claimant or a person connected with him may be entitled to acquire (directly or indirectly) from the trustees of the plan trust any shares, or an interest in or right deriving from any shares.

(6) For the purposes of this paragraph—

"ordinary share capital" has the meaning given in section 832(1) of the Taxes Act;

"the relevant company" means the company of whose share capital the relevant shares form part; and

"the relevant shares" means the shares that are, or an interest in which is, the subject of the disposal.]¹

Commentary—*Simon's Direct Tax Service* **C1.440**.
Amendments—¹ This Schedule inserted by FA 2000 s 48(2), Sch 9 with effect from 28 July 2000.

Reinvestment of disposal proceeds

3—(1) This sub-paragraph applies if the claimant obtains consideration for the disposal and, at any time in the acquisition period, all of the amount or value of the consideration is applied by him in making an acquisition of assets or an interest in assets ("replacement assets") which—

(*a*) are, immediately after the time of the acquisition, chargeable assets in relation to the claimant, and

(*b*) are not shares in, or debentures issued by, the relevant company or a company which is (at the time of the acquisition) in the same group as the relevant company;

but the preceding provisions of this sub-paragraph shall have effect without the words ", at any time in the acquisition period," if the acquisition is made pursuant to an unconditional contract entered into in the acquisition period.

(2) This sub-paragraph applies if—

(*a*) sub-paragraph (1) would have applied but for the fact that part only of the amount or value mentioned in that sub-paragraph is applied as there mentioned, and

(*b*) all the amount or value so mentioned except for a part which is less than the amount of the gain (whether all chargeable gain or not) accruing on the disposal is so applied.

(3) In sub-paragraph (1)(*b*)—

"relevant company" has the meaning given in paragraph 2(6); and

"group" shall be construed in accordance with section 170.]¹

Commentary—*Simon's Direct Tax Service* **C1.440**.
Amendments—¹ This Schedule inserted by FA 2000 s 48(2), Sch 9 with effect from 28 July 2000.

Provision supplementary to paragraphs 2 and 3

[**4**—(1) This paragraph applies for the purposes of paragraphs 2 and 3.

(2) The entitlement period is the period beginning with the disposal and ending on the expiry of 1: months beginning with the date of the disposal.

(3) The acquisition period is the period beginning with the disposal and ending on the expiry of six months beginning with—

(*a*) the date of the disposal, or
(*b*) if later, the date on which the third condition (set out in paragraph 2(3)) is first fulfilled.

(4) The proscribed period is the period beginning with the disposal and ending on—

(*a*) the date of the acquisition, or
(*b*) if later, the date on which the third condition (set out in paragraph 2(3)) is first fulfilled.

(5) All arrangements are unauthorised unless they only allow shares to be appropriated to or acquired on behalf of an individual under the plan.][1]

Commentary—*Simon's Direct Tax Service* **C1.440.**
Amendments—[1] This Schedule inserted by FA 2000 s 48(2), Sch 9 with effect from 28 July 2000.

The relief

[**5**—(1) Where the claimant is entitled to claim relief under this paragraph and paragraph 3(1) applies he shall, on making a claim in the period of 2 years beginning with the acquisition, be treated for the purposes of this Act—

(*a*) as if the consideration for the disposal were (if otherwise of a greater amount or value) of such amount as would secure that on the disposal neither a gain nor a loss accrues to him, and
(*b*) as if the amount or value of the consideration for the acquisition were reduced by the exces of the amount or value of the actual consideration for the disposal over the amount of the consideration which the claimant is treated as receiving under paragraph (*a*).

(2) Where the claimant is entitled to claim relief under this paragraph and paragraph 3(2) applies, he shall, on making a claim in the period of 2 years beginning with the acquisition, be treated for th purposes of this Act—

(*a*) as if the amount of the gain accruing on the disposal were reduced to the amount of the pa mentioned in paragraph 3(2)(*b*), and
(*b*) as if the amount or value of the consideration for the acquisition were reduced by the amoun by which the gain is reduced under paragraph (*a*) above.

(3) Nothing in sub-paragraph (1) or (2) shall affect the treatment for the purposes of this Act of th other party to the disposal or of the other party to the acquisition.

(4) The provisions of this Act fixing the amount of the consideration deemed to be given for disposal or acquisition shall be applied before the preceding provisions of this paragraph ar applied.][1]

Commentary—*Simon's Direct Tax Service* **C1.440.**
Amendments—[1] This Schedule inserted by FA 2000 s 48(2), Sch 9 with effect from 28 July 2000.

Dwelling-houses: special provision

[**6**—(1) Sub-paragraph (2) applies where—

(*a*) a claim is made under paragraph 5,
(*b*) immediately after the time of the acquisition mentioned in paragraph 3 and apart from thi paragraph, any replacement asset was a chargeable asset in relation to the claimant,
(*c*) the asset is a dwelling-house or part of a dwelling-house or land, and
(*d*) there was a time in the period beginning with the acquisition and ending with the time whe paragraph 5(1) or (2) falls to be applied such that, if the asset (or an interest in it) were dispose of at that time, it would be within section 222(1) and the individual there mentioned would be th claimant or the claimant's spouse.

(2) In such a case the asset shall be treated as if, immediately after the time of the acquisitio mentioned in paragraph 3, it was not a chargeable asset in relation to the claimant.

(3) Sub-paragraph (4) applies where—

(*a*) the provisions of paragraph 5(1) or (2) have been applied,
(*b*) any replacement asset which, immediately after the time of the acquisition mentioned i paragraph 3 and apart from this paragraph, was a chargeable asset in relation to the claima consists of a dwelling-house or part of a dwelling-house or land, and
(*c*) there is a time after paragraph 5(1) or (2) has been applied such that, if the asset (or an intere in it) were disposed of at that time, it would be within section 222(1) and the individual ther mentioned would be the claimant or the claimant's spouse.

(4) In such a case—

(*a*) the asset shall be treated as if, immediately after the time of the acquisition mentioned in paragraph 3, it was not a chargeable asset in relation to the claimant and adjustments shall be made accordingly, but

(*b*) any gain treated as accruing in consequence of the application of paragraph (*a*) shall be treated as accruing at the time mentioned in sub-paragraph (3)(*c*) or, if there is more than one such time, at the earliest of them.

(5) Sub-paragraph (6) applies where—

(*a*) a claim is made under paragraph 5,

(*b*) immediately after the time of the acquisition mentioned in paragraph 3 and apart from this paragraph, any replacement asset was a chargeable asset in relation to the claimant,

(*c*) the asset was an option to acquire (or to acquire an interest in) a dwelling-house or part of a dwelling-house or land,

(*d*) the option has been exercised, and

(*e*) there was a time in the period beginning with the exercise of the option and ending with the time when paragraph 5(1) or (2) falls to be applied such that, if the asset acquired on exercise of the option were disposed of at that time, it would be within section 222(1) and the individual there mentioned would be the claimant or the claimant's spouse.

(6) In such a case the option shall be treated as if, immediately after the time of the acquisition mentioned in paragraph 3, it was not a chargeable asset in relation to the claimant.

(7) Sub-paragraph (8) applies where—

(*a*) the provisions of paragraph 5(1) or (2) have been applied,

(*b*) any replacement asset which, immediately after the time of the acquisition mentioned in paragraph 3 and apart from this paragraph, was a chargeable asset in relation to the claimant consisted of an option to acquire (or to acquire an interest in) a dwelling-house or part of a dwelling-house or land,

(*c*) the option has been exercised, and

(*d*) there is a time after paragraph 5(1) or (2) has been applied such that, if the asset acquired on exercise of the option were disposed of at that time, it would be within section 222(1) and the individual there mentioned would be the claimant or the claimant's spouse.

(8) In such a case—

(*a*) the option shall be treated as if, immediately after the time of the acquisition mentioned in paragraph 3, it was not a chargeable asset in relation to the claimant and adjustments shall be made accordingly, but

(*b*) any gain treated as accruing in consequence of the application of paragraph (*a*) shall be treated as accruing at the time mentioned in sub-paragraph (7)(*d*) or, if there is more than one such time, at the earliest of them.

(9) References in this paragraph to an individual include a person entitled to occupy under the terms of a settlement.][1]

Commentary—*Simon's Direct Tax Service* **C1.441**.
Amendments—[1] This Schedule inserted by FA 2000 s 48(2), Sch 9 with effect from 28 July 2000.

Shares: special provision

[7—(1) Sub-paragraph (2) applies where—

(*a*) a claim is made under paragraph 5,

(*b*) immediately after the time of the acquisition mentioned in paragraph 3 and apart from this paragraph, any replacement asset was a chargeable asset in relation to the claimant,

(*c*) the asset consists of shares, and

(*d*) relief is claimed under Chapter III of Part VII of the Taxes Act (enterprise investment scheme) at any time in the period beginning with the acquisition and ending when paragraph 5(1) or (2) falls to be applied.

(2) In such a case the asset shall be treated as if, immediately after the time of the acquisition mentioned in paragraph 3, it was not a chargeable asset in relation to the claimant.

(3) Sub-paragraph (4) applies where—

(*a*) the provisions of paragraph 5(1) or (2) have been applied,

(*b*) any replacement asset which, immediately after the time of the acquisition mentioned in paragraph 3 and apart from this paragraph, was a chargeable asset in relation to the claimant consists of shares, and

(*c*) at any time after paragraph 5(1) or (2) has been applied relief is claimed in respect of the asset under Chapter III of Part VII of the Taxes Act (enterprise investment scheme).

(4) In such a case the asset shall be treated as if, immediately after the time of the acquisition mentioned in paragraph 3, it was not a chargeable asset in relation to the claimant and adjustments shall be made accordingly.][1]

Commentary—*Simon's Direct Tax Service* **C1.441**.
Amendments—[1] This Schedule inserted by FA 2000 s 48(2), Sch 9 with effect from 28 July 2000.

Meaning of "chargeable asset"

[8 For the purposes of this Schedule an asset is a chargeable asset in relation to the claimant at a particular time if, were the asset to be disposed of at that time, any gain accruing to him on the disposal would be a chargeable gain, and either—

(*a*) at that time he is resident or ordinarily resident in the United Kingdom, or

(*b*) he would be chargeable to capital gains tax under section 10(1) (non-resident with United Kingdom branch or agency) in respect of the gain,

unless (were he to dispose of the asset at that time) the claimant would fall to be regarded for the purposes of any double taxation relief arrangements as not liable in the United Kingdom to tax on any gains accruing to him on the disposal.][1]

Commentary—*Simon's Direct Tax Service* **C1.440**.
Amendments—[1] This Schedule inserted by FA 2000 s 48(2), Sch 9 with effect from 28 July 2000.

SCHEDULE 8

LEASES

Section 240

Concession D39—Extension of leases.
D42—Mergers of leases: rules for calculating indexation allowance when a lease is merged with a superior lease or the freehold reversion.
Simon's Tax Cases—*Lewis v Walters* [1992] STC 97*.

Leases of land as wasting assets: curved line restriction of allowable expenditure

1—(1) A lease of land shall not be a wasting asset until the time when its duration does not exceed 50 years.

(2) If at the beginning of the period of ownership of a lease of land it is subject to a sublease not at a rackrent and the value of the lease at the end of the duration of the sublease, estimated as at the beginning of the period of ownership, exceeds the expenditure allowable under section 38(1)(*a*) in computing the gain accruing on a disposal of the lease, the lease shall not be a wasting asset until the end of the duration of the sublease.

(3) In the case of a wasting asset which is a lease of land the rate at which expenditure is assumed to be written off shall, instead of being a uniform rate as provided by section 46, be a rate fixed in accordance with the Table below.

(4) Accordingly, for the purposes of the computation of the gain accruing on a disposal of a lease, and given that—

(*a*) the percentage derived from the Table for the duration of the lease at the beginning of the period of ownership is P(1),

(*b*) the percentage so derived for the duration of the lease at the time when any item of expenditure attributable to the lease under section 38(1)(*b*) is first reflected in the nature of the lease is P(2), and

(*c*) the percentage so derived for the duration of the lease at the time of the disposal is P(3), then—

(i) there shall be excluded from the expenditure attributable to the lease under section 38(1)(*a*) a fraction equal to—

$$\frac{P(1) - P(3)}{P(1)}$$

and—

(ii) there shall be excluded from any item of expenditure attributable to the lease under section 38(1)(*b*) a fraction equal to—

$$\frac{P(2) - P(3)}{P(2)}$$

(5) This paragraph applies notwithstanding that the period of ownership of the lease is a period exceeding 50 years and, accordingly, no expenditure shall be written off under this paragraph in respect of any period earlier than the time when the lease becomes a wasting asset.

(6) Section 47 shall apply in relation to this paragraph as it applies in relation to section 46.

TABLE

Years	Percentage	Years	Percentage
50 (or more)	100	25	81·100
49	99·657	24	79·622
48	99·289	23	78·055
47	98·902	22	76·399
46	98·490	21	74·635

TABLE—*continued*

Years	Percentage	Years	Percentage
45	98·059	20	72·770
44	97·595	19	70·791
43	97·107	18	68·697
42	96·593	17	66·470
41	96·041	16	64·116
40	95·457	15	61·617
39	94·842	14	58·971
38	94·189	13	56·167
37	93·497	12	53·191
36	92·761	11	50·038
35	91·981	10	46·695
34	91·156	9	43·154
33	90·280	8	39·399
32	89·354	7	35·414
31	88·371	6	31·195
30	87·330	5	26·722
29	86·226	4	21·983
28	85·053	3	16·959
27	83·816	2	11·629
26	82·496	1	5·983
		0	0

If the duration of the lease is not an exact number of years the percentage to be derived from the Table above shall be the percentage for the whole number of years plus one-twelfth of the difference between that and the percentage for the next higher number of years for each odd month counting an odd 14 days or more as one month.

Commentary—*Simon's Direct Tax Service* C2.1201, 1204, 1210, 1211.
Revenue Internal Guidance—Capital Gains Manual CG 71146, 71148 (worked examples illustrating the operation of this para).
Definitions—"Asset", s 21(1); "land", s 288(1); "lease", Sch 8 para 10(1); "rent", Sch 8 para 10(1); "wasting asset", ss 44, 288(1), Sch 8 para 1.
Cross references—See TCGA 1992 Sch 8 para 9(1) (application of this para to leases of property other than land).

Premiums for leases

2—(1) Subject to this Schedule where the payment of a premium is required under a lease of land, or otherwise under the terms subject to which a lease of land is granted, there is a part disposal of the freehold or other asset out of which the lease is granted.

(2) In applying section 42 to such a part disposal, the property which remains undisposed of includes a right to any rent or other payments, other than a premium, payable under the lease, and that right shall be valued as at the time of the part disposal.

Commentary—*Simon's Direct Tax Service* **C2.1215, 1216.**
Revenue Internal Guidance—Capital gains manual CG 70833–70838, 70850–70852 (reverse premiums are generally not taxable on the recipient, but may be if an existing lease is surrendered or if the premium derives from the tenant's goodwill; the payer normally gets a deduction under s 38(1)(*b*)).
Simon's Tax Cases—Sub-para (1), *Clarke v United Real (Moorgate) Ltd* [1988] STC 273*.
Definitions—"Asset", s 21(1); "land", s 288(1); "lease", Sch 8 para 10(1); "part disposal", s 21(2); "premium", Sch 8 para 10(2); "rent", Sch 8 para 10(1).
Cross references—See TCGA 1992 Sch 8 para 9(1) (application of this para to leases of property other than land).

3—(1) This paragraph applies in relation to a lease of land.

(2) Where under the terms subject to which a lease is granted, a sum becomes payable by the tenant in lieu of the whole or part of the rent for any period, or as consideration for the surrender of the lease, the lease shall be deemed for the purposes of this Schedule to have required the payment of a premium to the landlord (in addition to any other premium) of the amount of that sum[, being a premium which—

(*a*) is due when the sum is payable by the tenant; and
(*b*) where the sum is payable in lieu of rent, is in respect of the period in relation to which the sum is payable.]¹

(3) Where, as consideration for the variation or waiver of any of the terms of a lease, a sum becomes payable by the tenant otherwise than by way of rent, the lease shall be deemed for the purposes of this Schedule to have required the payment of a premium to the landlord (in addition to any other premium) of the amount of that sum[, being a premium which—

(*a*) is due when the sum is payable by the tenant; and
(*b*) is in respect of the period from the time when the variation or waiver takes effect to the time when it ceases to have effect.]¹

[(4) Where under sub-paragraph (2) or (3) above a premium is deemed to have been received by the landlord, that shall not be the occasion of any recomputation of the gain accruing on the receipt of any other premium, and the premium shall be regarded—

(*a*) in the case of a premium deemed to have been received for the surrender of a lease, as consideration for a separate transaction which is effected when the premium is deemed to be due and consists of the disposal by the landlord of his interest in the lease; and

(*b*) in any other case, as consideration for a separate transaction which is effected when the premium is deemed to be due and consists of a further part disposal of the freehold or other asset out of which the lease is granted.][1]

[(5) If under sub-paragraph (2) or (3) above a premium is deemed to have been received by the landlord, otherwise than as consideration for the surrender of the lease, and the landlord is a tenant under a lease the duration of which does not exceed 50 years, this Schedule shall apply—

(*a*) as if an amount equal to the amount of that premium deemed to have been received had been given by way of consideration for the grant of the part of the sublease covered by the period in respect of which the premium is deemed to have been paid; and

(*b*) as if that consideration were expenditure incurred by the sublessee and attributable to that part of the sublease under section 38(1)(*b*).][1]

(7) Sub-paragraph (3) above shall apply in relation to a transaction not at arm's length, and in particular in relation to a transaction entered into gratuitously, as if such sum had become payable by the tenant otherwise than by way of rent as might have been required of him if the transaction had been at arm's length.

Commentary—*Simon's Direct Tax Service* C2.904, 1231–1233.
Definitions—"Land", s 288(1); "lease", Sch 8 para 10(1); "lessee", Sch 8 para 10(1); "premium", Sch 8 para 10(2); "rent", Sch 8 para 10(1).
Cross references—See TCGA 1994 Sch 8 para 9(1) (application of this para to leases of property other than land).
Amendments—[1] Words in sub-paras (2), (3) substituted and sub-paras (4), (5) substituted for sub-paras (4)–(6) by FA 1996 s 142 with effect as respects sums payable after 5 April 1996.

Subleases out of short leases

4—(1) In the computation of the gain accruing on the part disposal of a lease which is a wasting asset by way of the grant of a sublease for a premium the expenditure attributable to the lease under paragraphs (*a*) and (*b*) of section 38(1) shall be apportioned in accordance with this paragraph, and section 42 shall not apply.

(2) Out of each item of the expenditure attributable to the lease under paragraphs (*a*) and (*b*) of section 38(1) there shall be apportioned to what is disposed of—

(*a*) if the amount of the premium is not less than what would be obtainable by way of premium for the said sublease if the rent payable under that sublease were the same as the rent payable under the lease, the fraction which, under paragraph 1(3) of this Schedule, is to be written off over the period which is the duration of the sublease, and

(*b*) if the amount of the premium is less than the said amount so obtainable, the said fraction multiplied by a fraction equal to the amount of the said premium divided by the said amount so obtainable.

(3) If the sublease is a sublease of part only of the land comprised in the lease this paragraph shall apply only in relation to a proportion of the expenditure attributable to the lease under paragraphs (*a*) and (*b*) of section 38(1) which is the same as the proportion which the value of the land comprised in the sublease bears to the value of that and the other land comprised in the lease; and the remainder of that expenditure shall be apportioned to what remains undisposed of.

Commentary—*Simon's Direct Tax Service* C2.904, 1216, 1217.
Definitions—"Asset", s 21(1); "land", s 288(1); "lease", Sch 8 para 10(1); "part disposal;", s 21(2); "premium", Sch 8 para 10(2); "rent", Sch 8 para 10(1); "wasting asset", ss 44, 288(1), Sch 8 para 1.
Cross references—See TCGA 1992 Sch 8 para 9(1) (application of this para to leases of property other than land).

Exclusion of premiums taxed under Schedule A etc

5—(1)Where by reference to any premium [any amount is brought into account by virtue of section 34 of the Taxes Act as a receipt of a Schedule A business (within the meaning of that Act)][1], that amount out of the premium shall be excluded from the consideration brought into account in the computation of the gain accruing on the disposal for which the premium is consideration except where the consideration is taken into account in the denominator of the fraction by reference to which an apportionment is made under section 42.

(2) Where by reference to any premium in respect of a sublease granted out of a lease the duration of which (that is of the lease) does not, at the time of granting the lease, exceed 50 years, [any amount is brought into account by virtue of section 34 of the Taxes Act as a receipt of a Schedule A business (within the meaning of that Act)][1] that amount shall be deducted from any gain accruing on the disposal for which the premium is consideration as computed in accordance with the provisions of this Act apart from this sub-paragraph, but not so as to convert the gain into a loss, or to increase any loss.

(3) Subject to subsection (4) below, where [any amount is brought into account by virtue of section 36 of the Taxes Act (sale of land with right of re-conveyance) as a receipt of a Schedule A business (within the meaning of that Act)][1] a sum of that amount shall be excluded from the consideration brought into account in the computation of the gain accruing on the disposal of the estate or interest in respect of which income tax becomes so chargeable, except where the consideration is taken into account in the denominator of the fraction by reference to which an apportionment is made under section 42.

(4) If what is disposed of is the remainder of a lease or a sublease out of a lease the duration of which does not exceed 50 years, sub-paragraph (3) shall not apply but the amount there referred to shall be deducted from any gain accruing on the disposal as computed in accordance with the provisions of this Act apart from this sub-paragraph and sub-paragraph (3), but not so as to convert the gain into a loss, or to increase any loss.

(5) References in sub-paragraphs (1) and (2) above to a premium include references to a premium deemed to have been received under subsection (4) or (5) of section 34 of the Taxes Act (which correspond to paragraph 3(2) and (3) of this Schedule).

(6) Section 37 shall not be taken as authorising the exclusion of any amount from the consideration for a disposal of assets taken into account in the computation of the gain by reference to any amount chargeable to tax under section 348 or 349 of the Taxes Act.

Commentary—*Simon's Direct Tax Service* C2.1108, 1218.
Definitions—"Asset", s 21(1); "land", s 288(1); "lease", Sch 8 para 10(1); "premium", Sch 8 para 10(2); "the Taxes Act", s 288(1).
Cross references—See TCGA 1992 Sch 8 para 9(1) (application of this para to leases of property other than land).
Amendments—[1] Words in sub-paras (1)–(3) substituted by FA 1998 Sch 5 para 63 with effect from the year 1998–99 for income tax purposes, and from 1 April 1998 for corporation tax, subject to the transitional provisions in FA 1998 Sch 5 Part IV.

6—(1) If under section 37(4) of the Taxes Act (allowance where, by the grant of a sublease, a lessee has converted a capital amount into a right to income) a person is to be treated as paying additional rent in consequence of having granted a sublease, the amount of any loss accruing to him on the disposal by way of the grant of the sublease shall be reduced by the total amount of rent which he is thereby treated as paying over the term of the sublease (and without regard to whether relief is thereby effectively given over the term of the sublease), but not so as to convert the loss into a gain, or to increase any gain.

(2) Nothing in section 37 of this Act shall be taken as applying in relation to any amount [brought into account by virtue of section 35 of the Taxes Act (charge on assignment of a lease granted at an undervalue) as a receipt of a Schedule A business (within the meaning of that Act)][2].

(3) If any adjustment is made under section 36(2)(b) of the Taxes Act on a claim under that paragraph, any necessary adjustment shall be made to give effect to the consequences of the claim on the operation of this paragraph or paragraph 5 above.

Commentary—*Simon's Direct Tax Service* C2.1219.
Definitions—"Lease", Sch 8 para 10(1); "lessee", Sch 8 para 10(1); "rent", Sch 8 para 10(1); "the Taxes Act", s 288(1).
Modification—[1] Except in so far as it applies for the purposes of corporation tax, sub-para (2) applies from the year 1995–96 as if the words "brought into account by virtue of section 35 of the Taxes Act (charge on assignment of a lease granted at an undervalue) as a receipt of a Schedule A business (within the meaning of that Act)" were substituted for the words in square brackets. However, this modification does not apply in respect of certain sources of income which ceased during the year 1995–96: FA 1995 s 39(4), (5), Sch 6 para 37.
Amendments—[2] Words in sub-para (2) substituted by FA 1998 Sch 5 para 63 with effect from the year 1998–99 for income tax purposes, and from 1 April 1998 for corporation tax, subject to the transitional provisions in FA 1998 Sch 5 Part IV.

7 If under section 34(2) and (3) of the Taxes Act [any amount is brought into account by virtue of section 34(2) and (3) of the Taxes Act as a receipt of a Schedule A business (within the meaning of that Act) which is or is treated as carried on by any person, that person][2] shall be treated for the purposes of the computation of any gain accruing to him as having incurred at the time the lease was granted expenditure of that amount (in addition to any other expenditure) attributable to the asset under section 38(1)(b).

Commentary—*Simon's Direct Tax Service* C2.1201.
Definitions—"Asset", s 21(1); "lease", Sch 8 para 10(1); "premium", Sch 8 para 10(2); "the Taxes Act", s 288(1).
Modification—[1] Except in so far as it applies for the purposes of corporation tax, this para applies from the year 1995–96 as if the words "any amount is brought into account by virtue of section 34(2) and (3) of the Taxes Act as a receipt of a Schedule A business (within the meaning of that Act) which is or is treated as carried on by any person, that person" were substituted for the words in square brackets. However, this modification does not apply in respect of certain sources of income which ceased during the year 1995–96: FA 1995 s 39(4), (5), Sch 6 para 37.
Amendments—[2] Words substituted by FA 1998 Sch 5 para 63 with effect from the year 1998–99 for income tax purposes, and from 1 April 1998 for corporation tax, subject to the transitional provisions in FA 1998 Sch 5 Part IV.

[**7A** References in paragraphs 5 to 7 above to an amount brought into account as a receipt of a Schedule A business include references to an amount brought into account as a receipt of an overseas property business.][1]

Amendments—[1] This paragraph substituted by FA 1998 Sch 5 para 63 with effect from the year 1998–99 for income tax purposes, and from 1 April 1998 for corporation tax, subject to the transitional provisions in FA 1998 Sch 5 Part IV.

Duration of leases

8—(1) In ascertaining for the purposes of this Act the duration of a lease of land the following provisions shall have effect.

(2) Where the terms of the lease include provision for the determination of the lease by notice given by the landlord, the lease shall not be treated as granted for a term longer than one ending at the earliest date on which it could be determined by notice given by the landlord.

(3) Where any of the terms of the lease (whether relating to forfeiture or to any other matter) or any other circumstances render it unlikely that the lease will continue beyond a date falling before the expiration of the term of the lease, the lease shall not be treated as having been granted for a term longer than one ending on that date.

(4) Sub-paragraph (3) applies in particular where the lease provides for the rent to go up after a given date, or for the tenant's obligations to become in any respect more onerous after a given date, but includes provision for the determination of the lease on that date, by notice given by the tenant, and those provisions render it unlikely that the lease will continue beyond that date.

(5) Where the terms of the lease include provision for the extension of the lease beyond a given date by notice given by the tenant this paragraph shall apply as if the term of the lease extended for as long as it could be extended by the tenant, but subject to any right of the landlord by notice to determine the lease.

(6) It is hereby declared that the question what is the duration of a lease is to be decided, in relation to the grant or any disposal of the lease, by reference to the facts which were known or ascertainable at the time when the lease was acquired or created.

Commentary—*Simon's Direct Tax Service* **C2.904, 1202.**
Revenue Internal Guidance—Capital gains manual CG 72422 (except in Scotland, an agricultural tenancy is a wasting asset if the tenant's life expectancy is less than 50 years).
Definitions—''Land'', s 288(1); ''lease'', Sch 8 para 10(1); ''notice'', s 288(1); ''rent'', Sch 8 para 10(1).
Cross references—See TCGA 1992 Sch 8 para 9(1) (application of this para to leases of property other than land).

Leases of property other than land

9—(1) Paragraphs 2, 3, 4 and 8 of this Schedule shall apply in relation to leases of property other than land as they apply to leases of land, but subject to any necessary modifications.

(2) Where by reference to any capital sum within the meaning of section 785 of the Taxes Act (leases of assets other than land) any person has been charged to income tax on any amount, that amount out of the capital sum shall be deducted from any gain accruing on the disposal for which that capital sum is consideration, as computed in accordance with the provisions of this Act apart from this sub-paragraph, but not so as to convert the gain into a loss, or increase any loss.

(3) In the case of a lease of a wasting asset which is movable property the lease shall be assumed to terminate not later than the end of the life of the wasting asset.

Commentary—*Simon's Direct Tax Service* **C2.904, 1202.**
Definitions—''Asset'', s 21(1); ''land'', s 288(1); ''lease'', Sch 8 para 10(1); ''wasting asset'', ss 44, 288(1), Sch 8 para 1.

Interpretation

10—(1) In this Act, unless the context otherwise requires ''lease''—

(*a*) in relation to land, includes an underlease, sublease or any tenancy or licence, and any agreement for a lease, underlease, sublease or tenancy or licence and, in the case of land outside the United Kingdom, any interest corresponding to a lease as so defined,
(*b*) in relation to any description of property other than land, means any kind of agreement or arrangement under which payments are made for the use of, or otherwise in respect of, property,

and ''lessor'', ''lessee'' and ''rent'' shall be construed accordingly.

(2) In this Schedule ''premium'' includes any like sum, whether payable to the intermediate or a superior landlord, and for the purposes of this Schedule any sum (other than rent) paid on or in connection with the granting of a tenancy shall be presumed to have been paid by way of premium except in so far as [other sufficient consideration for the payment can be shown to have been given][1].

(3) In the application of this Schedule to Scotland ''premium'' includes in particular a grassum payable to any landlord or intermediate landlord on the creation of a sublease.

Commentary—*Simon's Direct Tax Service* C2.904, 1201, 1215.
Simon's Tax Cases—Sub-para (2), *Clarke v United Real (Moorgate) Ltd* [1988] STC 273*.
Amendments—[1] Words in sub-para (2) substituted by FA 1996 s 134(1), (2), Sch 20 para 67 with effect from the year 1996-97, and for the purposes of corporation tax, as respects accounting periods ending after 30 June 1999 (by virtue of Finance Act 1994, Section 199, (Appointed Day) Order, SI 1998/3173 art 2).

SCHEDULE 9
GILT-EDGED SECURITIES
Section 288

PART I
GENERAL

Cross references—See TCGA 1992 Sch 11 para 15 (for the purposes of this and other Acts "gilt-edged securities" include previous gilt-edged securities listed in CGTA 1979 Sch 2 Pt II.

1 For the purposes of this Act "gilt-edged securities" means the securities specified in Part II of this Schedule, and such stocks and bonds issued under section 12 of the National Loans Act 1968 denominated in sterling and issued after 15th April 1969, as may be specified by order made by the Treasury.

Commentary—*Simon's Direct Tax Service* **C2.806.**
Orders—CGT (Gilt-edged Securities) Orders, SI 1993/950, SI 1994/2656, SI 1996/1031, SI 2001/1122.
Definition—"Issued", s 288(5).
Cross references—See TCGA 1992 s 287(4) (exception for the purposes of this paragraph to the general rule of orders being subject to annulment by Parliament).

[1A—(1) Any security which is a strip of a security which is a gilt-edged security for the purposes of this Act is also itself a gilt-edged security for those purposes.

(2) In this paragraph "strip" has the same meaning as in section 47 of the Finance Act 1942.]¹

Commentary—*Simon's Direct Tax Service* **C2.806.**
Amendment—¹ Para 1A inserted by FA 1996 Sch 40 para 8.

2 The Treasury shall cause particulars of any order made under paragraph 1 above to be published in the London and Edinburgh Gazettes as soon as may be after the order is made.

Commentary—*Simon's Direct Tax Service* **C2.806.**

3 Section 14(*b*) of the Interpretation Act 1978 (implied power to amend orders made by statutory instrument) shall not apply to the power of making orders under paragraph 1 above.

Commentary—*Simon's Direct Tax Service* **C2.806.**

PART II
EXISTING GILT-EDGED SECURITIES
Stocks and bonds charged on the National Loans Fund

12¾%	Treasury Loan 1992
8%	Treasury Loan 1992
10%	Treasury Stock 1992
3%	Treasury Stock 1992
12¼%	Exchequer Stock 1992
13½%	Exchequer Stock 1992
10½%	Treasury Convertible Stock 1992
2%	Index-linked Treasury Stock 1992
12½%	Treasury Loan 1993
6%	Funding Loan 1993
13¾%	Treasury Loan 1993
10%	Treasury Loan 1993
8¼%	Treasury Stock 1993
14½%	Treasury Loan 1994
12½%	Exchequer Stock 1994
9%	Treasury Loan 1994
10%	Treasury Loan 1994
13½%	Exchequer Stock 1994
8½%	Treasury Stock 1994
8½%	Treasury Stock 1994 "A"
2%	Index-linked Treasury Stock 1994
3%	Exchequer Gas Stock 1990–95
12%	Treasury Stock 1995
10¼%	Exchequer Stock 1995
12¾%	Treasury Loan 1995
9%	Treasury Loan 1992–96
15¼%	Treasury Loan 1996
13¼%	Exchequer Loan 1996

14%	Treasury Stock 1996
2%	Index-linked Treasury Stock 1996
10%	Conversion Stock 1996
13¼%	Treasury Loan 1997
10½%	Exchequer Stock 1997
8¾%	Treasury Loan 1997
8¾%	Treasury Loan 1997 ''B''
8¾%	Treasury Loan 1997 ''C''
15%	Exchequer Stock 1997
6¾%	Treasury Loan 1995–98
15½%	Treasury Loan 1998
12%	Exchequer Stock 1998
12%	Exchequer Stock 1998 ''A''
9¾%	Exchequer Stock 1998
9¾%	Exchequer Stock 1998 ''A''
9½%	Treasury Loan 1999
10½%	Treasury Stock 1999
12¼%	Exchequer Stock 1999
12¼%	Exchequer Stock 1999 ''A''
12¼%	Exchequer Stock 1999 ''B''
2½%	Index-linked Treasury Convertible Stock 1999
10¼%	Conversion Stock 1999
9%	Conversion Stock 2000
9%	Conversion Stock 2000 ''A''
13%	Treasury Stock 2000
8½%	Treasury Loan 2000
14%	Treasury Stock 1998–2001
2½%	Index-linked Treasury Stock 2001
9¾%	Conversion Stock 2001
10%	Treasury Stock 2001
9½%	Conversion Loan 2001
12%	Exchequer Stock 1999–2002
12%	Exchequer Stock 1999–2002 ''A''
9½%	Conversion Stock 2002
10%	Conversion Stock 2002
9%	Exchequer Stock 2002
9¾%	Treasury Stock 2002
13¾%	Treasury Stock 2000–2003
13¾%	Treasury Stock 2000–2003 ''A''
2½%	Indexed-linked Treasury Stock 2003
9¾%	Conversion Loan 2003
10%	Treasury Stock 2003
3½%	Funding Stock 1999–2004
11½%	Treasury Stock 2001–2004
9½%	Conversion Stock 2004
10%	Treasury Stock 2004
12½%	Treasury Stock 2003–2005
12½%	Treasury Stock 2003–2005 ''A''
10½%	Exchequer Stock 2005
9½%	Conversion Stock 2005
9½%	Conversion Stock 2005 ''A''
8%	Treasury Loan 2002–2006
8%	Treasury Loan 2002–2006 ''A''
2%	Indexed-linked Treasury Stock 2006
9¾%	Conversion Stock 2006
11¾%	Treasury Stock 2003–2007
11¾%	Treasury Stock 2003–2007 ''A''
8½%	Treasury Loan 2007
13½%	Treasury Stock 2004–2008
9%	Treasury Loan 2008
9%	Treasury Loan 2008 ''A''
2½%	Indexed-linked Treasury Stock 2009
8%	Treasury Stock 2009
2½%	Indexed-linked Treasury Stock 2011
9%	Conversion Loan 2011
5½%	Treasury Stock 2008–2012
2½%	Indexed-linked Treasury Stock 2013
7¾%	Treasury Loan 2012–2015
2½%	Treasury Stock 1986–2016

2½%	Indexed-linked Treasury Stock 2016
2½%	Indexed-linked Treasury Stock 2016 "A"
12%	Exchequer Stock 2013–2017
2½%	Indexed-linked Treasury Stock 2020
2½%	Indexed-linked Treasury Stock 2024
2½%	Annuities 1905 or after
2¾%	Annuities 1905 or after
2½%	Consolidated Stock 1923 or after
4%	Consolidated Loan 1957 or after
3½%	Conversion Loan 1961 or after
2½%	Treasury Stock 1975 or after
3%	Treasury Stock 1966 or after
3½%	War Loan 1952 or after
10%	Conversion Stock 1996 "A"
10%	Conversion Stock 1996 "B"
12%	Exchequer Stock 1998 "B"
9%	Conversion Stock 2000 "B"
13%	Treasury Stock 2000 "A"
10%	Treasury Stock 2001 "A"
10%	Treasury Stock 2001 "B"
9¾%	Treasury Stock 2002 "A"
9¾%	Treasury Stock 2002 "B"
10%	Treasury Stock 2003 "A"
9½%	Conversion Stock 2004 "A"
9%	Treasury Loan 2008 "B"
9%	Treasury Loan 2008 "C"
9%	Conversion Loan 2011 "A"

Cross references—See CGT (Gilt-edged Securities) Orders, SI 1993/950, SI 1994/2656 and SI 1996/1031 (further gilt-edged Securities specified under para 1 above).

Securities issued by certain public corporations and guaranteed by the Treasury

3%   North of Scotland Electricity Stock 1989–92

Commentary—*Simon's Direct Tax Service* C2.806.

SCHEDULE 10

CONSEQUENTIAL AMENDMENTS

Section 290

Post Office Act 1969 c 48

1 (*amended* s 74, *repealed by* the Postal Services Act 2000 (Consequential Modifications No 1) Order, SI 2001/1149 art 3, Sch 2 with effect from 26 March 2001).

Taxes Management Act 1970 c 9

2—(1), (2) (*amend* TMA 1970 ss 11, 27, 47, 57, 78, 111, 119; *repealed in part* by FA 1995 Sch 29 Pt VIII(16) from the year 1996–97).

(3)–(9) (*amend* ss 12, 25, 30, 31, 86, 87A and *substitute* s 28).

This sub-paragraph shall come into force on the day appointed under section 95 of the Finance (No 2) Act 1987 for the purposes of section 85 of that Act.

(10), (11) (*amend* ss 98, 118).

Note—The appointed day mentioned under sub-para (9) above is 30 September 1993 by virtue of Corporation Tax Acts (Provisions for Payment of Tax and Returns) (Appointed Days) Order, SI 1992/3066 art 2(1), (2)(a).

Finance Act 1973 c 51

3—(1), (2) (*amend* s 38, Sch 15, paras 2, 4).

British Aerospace Act 1980 c 26

4 (*amends* s 12).

British Telecommunications Act 1981 c 38

5 (*amends* s 82).

Value Added Tax Act 1983 c 55

6 (*amended* Sch 6 Group 11; *repealed* by the Value Added Tax Act 1994 s 100(2) Sch 15).

Telecommunications Act 1984 c 12

7 (*amends* s 72).

Inheritance Tax Act 1984 c 51

8—(1)–(13) (*amend* IHTA 1984 ss 31, 79, 97, 107, 113A, 124A, 135, 138, 165, 183, 187, 194, 270, 272).

Finance Act 1985 c 54

9 (*amends* s 81).

Trustee Savings Bank Act 1985 c 58

10 (*amend* Sch 2, paras 2, 3, 4, 9).

Transport Act 1985 c 67

11 (*amends* s 130).

Airports Act 1986 c 31

12 (*amends* s 77).

Gas Act 1986 c 44

13 (*amends* s 60).

Income and Corporation Taxes Act 1988 c 1

14—(1) The Income and Corporation Taxes Act 1988 shall have effect subject to the following amendments.

(2)–(5) (*amend* ss 11, 56, 119, 122).

(6) (*inserted* s 126A; *repealed* by FA 1996 Sch 41 Pt V(3) with effect for accounting periods ending after 31 March 1996, subject to transitional provisions in FA 1996 Sch 15).

(7) (*amends* s 128).

(8) (*amended* s 129; *repealed* by FA 1997 Sch 18 Pt VI(10) with effect in relation to, and to transfers under, any arrangement made on or after 1 July 1997 by virtue of the Finance Act 1997, Schedule 10, (Appointed Day) Order, SI 1997/991).

(9)–(14) (*amend* ss 137, 139, 140, 162, 185, 187, 220).

(15) (*amended* s 245B; *repealed* by FA 1998 s 165, Sch 27 Part III(2) with effect for disposals made after 5 April 1999).

(16)–(26) (*amend* ss 251, 299, 305, 312, 399, 400, 438, 440, 440A, 442, 444A, 450).

(27) (*amended* s 473; *repealed in part* by FA 1996 Sch 41 Pt V(24) with effect for accounting periods beginning after 31 December 1995).

(28) (*amends* s 477B).

(29) (*amended* s 484; *repealed* by FA 1996 Sch 41 Pt V(3) with effect for accounting periods ending after 31 March 1996, subject to transitional provisions in FA 1996 Sch 15).

(30)–(38) (*amend* ss 502, 505, 513, 574, 575, 576, 710, 715, 723).

(39) (*amended* s 727; *repealed* by FA 1997 Sch 18 Pt VI(10) with effect in relation to, and to transfers under, any arrangement made on or after 1 July 1997 by virtue of the Finance Act 1997 Schedule 10, (Appointed Day) Order, SI 1997/991).

(40), (41) (*amend* ss 731, 734).

(42) (*amended* s 740; *repealed* by FA 2000 s 156, Sch 40 Pt II(10) with effect for any transfer of value for which the material time is after 21 March 2000).

(43)–(56) (*amend* ss 757–763, 776, 777, 824, 831, 832, 842, 843).

(57) (*amended* Sch 4 paras 1, 2, 7, 12, 19, 20; *repealed* by FA 1996 Sch 41 Pt V(3) with effect for accounting periods ending after 31 March 1996, subject to transitional provisions in FA 1996 Sch 15).

(58)–(60) (*amend* Sch 10, para 5, Sch 20, para 12, Sch 22, para 7).

(61) (*amended* Sch 23A; *repealed* by FA 1997 Sch 18 Pt VI(10) with effect in relation to, and to transfers under, any arrangement made on or after 1 July 1997 by virtue of the Finance Act 1997 Schedule 10, (Appointed Day) Order, SI 1997/991).

(62) (*amends* Sch 26, para 3).

(63) In Schedule 28—

    (a) (*amends* para 2);

    (b) (*amends* para 3; *and repealed in part* by FA 1995 Sch 29 Pt VIII(5) in relation to accounting periods beginning after 31 October 1994);

    (c) (*amends* paras 4, 8).

British Steel Act 1988 c 35

15 (*amends* s 11).

Finance Act 1988 c 39

16 (*amend FA 1988* ss 50, 68, 82, 84, 132, Sch 12, para 6).

Health and Medicines Act 1988 c 49

17 (*amends* s 6).

Water Act 1989 c 15

18 (*amends* s 95).

Finance Act 1989 c 26

19—(1)–(5) (*amend* ss 69, 70, 158, 178, Sch 5, paras 8, 11).

(6) (*amended* Sch 11, paras 1, 19; *repealed* by FA 1996 Sch 41 Pt V(3) with effect for accounting periods ending after 31 March 1996, subject to transitional provisions in FA 1996 Sch 15).

Electricity Act 1989 c 29

20 (*amend* Sch 11, paras 2–5).

Capital Allowances Act 1990 c 1

21 (*inserted* ss 118A, 138(8); *repealed* by CAA 2001 s 580, Sch 4 with effect in accordance with CAA 2001 s 579).

Finance Act 1990 c 29

22—(1) The Finance Act 1990 shall have effect subject to the following amendments.

(2), (3) (*amend* ss 116, 120).

(4) (*amended* Sch 10, para 24; *repealed* by FA 1996 Sch 41 Pt V(3) with effect for accounting periods ending after 31 March 1996, subject to transitional provisions in FA 1996 Sch 15).

(5) (*amend* Sch 12 paras 2, 4–7, 10).

Finance Act 1991 c 31

23 (*amends* s 72).

Ports Act 1991 c 52

24 (*amend* ss 16–18, 20, 35, 40).

British Technology Group Act 1991 c 66

25 (*amends* s 12).

SCHEDULE 11

TRANSITIONAL PROVISIONS AND SAVINGS

Section 290

PART I

VALUATION

Preliminary

—(1) This Part of this Schedule has effect in cases where the market value of an asset at a time before the commencement of this Act is material to the computation of a gain under this Act; and in this Part any reference to an asset includes a reference to any part of an asset.

(2) Where sub-paragraph (1) above applies, the market value of an asset (or part of an asset) at any time before the commencement of this Act shall be determined in accordance with sections 272 to 274 but subject to the following provisions of this Part.

(3) In any case where section 274 applies in accordance with sub-paragraph (2) above the reference in that section to inheritance tax shall be construed as a reference to capital transfer tax.

Revenue Interpretation RI 63—Valuation costs for ascertaining gains allowable; subsequent valuation costs not allowable.
Definition—"Asset", s 21(1).
Cross references—See TCGA 1992 Sch 11 para 2 (gifts and series of transactions between connected persons before 20 March 1985).

Gifts and transactions between connected persons before 20th March 1985

2—(1) Where sub-paragraph (1) above applies for the purpose of determining the market value of any asset at any time before 20th March 1985 (the date when section 71 of the Finance Act 1985, now section 19, replaced section 151 of the 1979 Act, which is reproduced below) sub-paragraphs(2) to(4) below shall apply.

(2) Except as provided by sub-paragraph (4) below section 19 shall not apply in relation to transactions occurring before 20th March 1985.

(3) If a person is given, or acquires from one or more persons with whom he is connected, by way of 2 or more gifts or other transactions, assets of which the aggregate market value, when considered separately, in relation to the separate gifts or other transactions, is less than their aggregate market value when considered together, then for the purposes of this Act their market value shall be taken to be the larger market value, to be apportioned rateably to the respective disposals.

(4) Where—

(*a*) one or more transactions occurred on or before 19th March 1985 and one or more after that date, and

(*b*) had all the transactions occurred before that date sub-paragraph (3) above would apply, and had all the transactions occurred after that date section 19 would have applied,

then those transactions which occurred on or before that date and not more than 2 years before the first of those which occurred after that date shall be treated as material transactions for the purposes of section 19.

Definitions—"Asset", s 21(1);
"connected", s 286.

Valuation of assets before 6th July 1973

3 Section 273 shall apply for the purposes of determining the market value of any asset at any time before 6th July 1973 (the date when the provisions of section 51(1) to (3) of the Finance Act 1973 which are now contained in section 273, came into force) notwithstanding that the asset was acquired before that date or that the market value of the asset may have been fixed for the purposes of a contemporaneous disposal, and in paragraphs 4 and 5 below a "section 273 asset" is an asset to which section 273 applies.

Commentary—*Simon's Direct Tax Service* **C2.124.**
Definition—"Asset", s 21(1).

4—(1) This paragraph applies if, in a case where the market value of a section 273 asset at the time of its acquisition is material to the computation of any chargeable gain under this Act—

(*a*) the acquisition took place on the occasion of a death occurring after 30th March 1971 and before 6th July 1973, and

(*b*) by virtue of paragraph 9 below, the principal value of the asset for the purposes of estate duty on that death would, apart from this paragraph, be taken to be the market value of the asset at the date of the death for the purposes of this Act.

(2) If the principal value referred to in sub-paragraph (1)(*b*) above falls to be determined as mentioned in section 55 of the Finance Act 1940 or section 15 of the Finance (No 2) Act (Northern Ireland) 1946 (certain controlling shareholdings to be valued on an assets basis), nothing in section 273 shall affect the operation of paragraph 9 below for the purpose of determining the market value of the asset at the date of the death.

(3) If sub-paragraph (2) above does not apply, paragraph 9 below shall not apply as mentioned in sub-paragraph (1)(*b*) above and the market value of the asset on its acquisition at the date of the death shall be determined in accordance with sections 272 (but with the same modifications as are made by paragraphs 7 and 8 below) and 273.

Commentary—*Simon's Direct Tax Service* **C2.124.**
Definitions—"Asset", s 21(1); "chargeable gain", s 15(2).
Cross references—See TCGA 1992 Sch 11 para 3 (meaning of "section 273 asset" in this paragraph).

5—(1) In any case where—

(*a*) before 6th July 1973 there has been a part disposal of a section 273 asset ("the earlier disposal"), and (*b*) by virtue of any enactment, the acquisition of the asset or any part of it was deemed to be for a consideration equal to its market value, and

(*c*) on or after 6th July 1973 there is a disposal (including a part disposal) of the property which remained undisposed of immediately before that date (''the later disposal''),

sub-paragraph (2) below shall apply in computing any chargeable gain accruing on the later disposal.

(2) Where this sub-paragraph applies, the apportionment made by virtue of paragraph 7 of Schedule 6 to the Finance Act 1965 (corresponding to section 42 of this Act) on the occasion of the earlier disposal shall be recalculated on the basis that section 273(3) of this Act was in force at the time, and applied for the purposes, of the determination of—

(*a*) the market value referred to in sub-paragraph (1)(*b*) above, and

(*b*) the market value of the property which remained undisposed of after the earlier disposal, and

(*c*) if the consideration for the earlier disposal was, by virtue of any enactment, deemed to be equal to the market value of the property disposed of, that market value.

Commentary—*Simon's Direct Tax Service* **C2.741.**
Definitions—''Asset'', s 21(1); ''chargeable gain'', s 15(2); ''part disposal'', s 21(2).
Cross references—See TCGA 1992 Sch 11 para 3 (meaning of ''section 273 asset'' in this paragraph).

Valuation of assets on 6th April 1965

6—(1) For the purpose of ascertaining the market value of any shares or securities in accordance with paragraph 1(2) of Schedule 2, section 272 shall have effect subject to the provisions of this paragraph.

(2) Subsection (3)(*a*) shall have effect as if for the words, ''one-quarter'' there were substituted the words ''one-half'', and as between the amount under paragraph (*a*) and the amount under paragraph (*b*) of that subsection the higher, and not the lower, amount shall be chosen.

(3) Subsection (5) shall have effect as if for the reference to an amount equal to the buying price there were substituted a reference to an amount halfway between the buying and selling prices.

(4) Where the market value of any shares or securities not within section 272(3) falls to be ascertained by reference to a pair of prices quoted on a stock exchange, an adjustment shall be made so as to increase the market value by an amount corresponding to that by which any market value is increased under sub-paragraph (2) above.

Commentary—*Simon's Direct Tax Service* **C2.122, 123.**
Definition—''Shares'', s 288(1).

References to the London Stock Exchange before 25th March 1973 and Exchange Control restrictions before 13th December 1979

7—(1) For the purposes of ascertaining the market value of an asset before 25th March 1973 section 272(3) and (4) shall have effect subject to the following modifications—

(*a*) for ''[quoted]¹ in The Stock Exchange Daily Official List'' and ''quoted in that List'' there shall be substituted respectively ''quoted on the London Stock Exchange'' and ''so quoted'';

(*b*) for ''The Stock Exchange Daily Official List'' there shall be substituted ''the Stock Exchange Official Daily List'';

(*c*) for ''The Stock Exchange provides a more active market elsewhere than on the London trading floor'' there shall be substituted ''some other stock exchange in the United Kingdom affords a more active market''; and

(*d*) for ''if the London trading floor is closed'' there shall be substituted ''if the London Stock Exchange is closed''.

(2) For the purposes of ascertaining the market value of an asset before 13th December 1979 section 272 shall have effect as if the following subsection were inserted after subsection (5)—

(5A) In any case where the market value of an asset is to be determined at a time before 13th December 1979 and the asset is of a kind the sale of which was (at the time the market value is to be determined) subject to restrictions imposed under the Exchange Control Act 1947 such that part of what was paid by the purchaser was not retainable by the seller, the market value, as arrived at under subsection (1), (3), (4) or (5) above, shall be subject to such adjustment as is appropriate having regard to the difference between the amount payable by a purchaser and the amount receivable by a seller.

Commentary—*Simon's Direct Tax Service* **C2.122.**
Definition—''Asset'', s 21(1).
Amendment—¹ Word in sub-para (1)(*a*) substituted by FA 1996 Sch 38 para 12(2), (3) with effect where the relevant date falls after 31 March 1996.

Depreciated valuations referable to deaths before 31st March 1973

In any case where this Part applies, section 272(2) shall have effect as if the following proviso were inserted at the end—

Provided that where capital gains tax is chargeable, or an allowable loss accrues, in consequence of a death before 31st March 1973 and the market value of any property on the date of death taken into account for the purposes of that tax or loss has been depreciated by reason of the death the estimate of the market value shall take that depreciation into account.

Definition—"Allowable loss", ss 8(2), 16, 288(1).

Estate duty

9—(1) Where estate duty (including estate duty leviable under the law of Northern Ireland) i chargeable in respect of any property passing on a death after 30th March 1971 and the principa value of an asset forming part of that property has been ascertained (whether in any proceedings o otherwise) for the purposes of that duty, the principal value so ascertained shall, subject to paragrap 4(3) above, be taken for the purposes of this Act to be the market value of that asset at the date of th death.

(2) Where the principal value has been reduced under section 35 of the Finance Act 1968 or sectio 1 of the Finance Act (Northern Ireland) 1968 (tapering relief for gifts inter vivos etc), the referenc in sub-paragraph (1) above to the principal value as ascertained for the purposes of estate duty is reference to that value as so ascertained before the reduction.

Definition—"Asset", s 21(1).

PART II
OTHER TRANSITORY PROVISIONS
Value-shifting

10—(1) Section 30 applies only where the reduction in value mentioned in subsection (1) of tha section (or, in a case within subsection (9) of that section, the reduction or increase in value) is afte 29th March 1977.

(2) No account shall be taken by virtue of section 31 of any reduction in the value of an asse attributable to the payment of a dividend before 14th March 1989.

(3) No account shall be taken by virtue of section 32 of any reduction in the value of an asse attributable to the disposal of another asset before 14th March 1989.

(4) Section 34 shall not apply where the reduction in value, by reason of which the amount referre to in subsection (1)(b) of that section falls to be calculated, occurred before 14th March 1989.

Commentary—*Simon's Direct Tax Service* **C2.116; D2.669.**
Definition—"Asset", s 21(1).

Assets acquired on disposal chargeable under Case VII of Schedule D

11—(1) In this paragraph references to a disposal chargeable under Case VII are references to case where the acquisition and disposal was in circumstances that the gain accruing on it was chargeabl under Case VII of Schedule D, or where it would have been so chargeable if there were a gain s accruing.

(2) The amount or value of the consideration for the acquisition of an asset by the person acquirin it on a disposal chargeable under Case VII shall not under any provision of this Act be deemed to b an amount greater than the amount taken into account as consideration on that disposal for th purposes of Case VII.

(3) Any apportionment of consideration or expenditure falling to be made in relation to a disposa chargeable under Case VII in accordance with section 164(4) of the Income and Corporation Taxe Act 1970 and in particular in a case where section 164(6) of that Act (enhancement of value of lan by acquisition of adjoining land) applied, shall be followed for the purposes of this Act both i relation to a disposal of the assets acquired on the disposal chargeable under Case VII and, where th disposal chargeable under Case VII was a part disposal, in relation to a disposal of what remain undisposed of.

(4) Sub-paragraph (3) above has effect notwithstanding section 52(4).

Commentary—*Simon's Direct Tax Service* **C2.101.**
Definitions—"Asset", s 21(1); "land", s 288(1); "part disposal", s 21(2).

Unrelieved Case VII losses

12 Where no relief from income tax (for a year earlier than 1971–72) has been given in respect of loss or part of a loss allowable under Case VII of Schedule D, the loss or part shall, notwithstandin that the loss accrued before that year, be an allowable loss for the purposes of capital gains tax, bu subject to any restrictions imposed by section 18.

Definition—"Allowable loss", ss 8(2), 16, 288(1).

Devaluation of sterling: securities acquired with borrowed foreign currency

13—(1) This paragraph applies where, in pursuance of permission granted under the Exchange Control Act 1947 currency other than sterling was borrowed before 19th November 1967 for the purpose of investing in foreign securities (and had not been repaid before that date), and it was a condition of the permission—

> (a) that repayment of the borrowed currency should be made from the proceeds of the sale in foreign currency of the foreign securities so acquired or out of investment currency, and
>
> (b) that the foreign securities so acquired should be kept in separate accounts to distinguish them from others in the same ownership,

and securities held in such a separate account on 19th November 1967 are in this paragraph referred to as "designated securities".

(2) In computing the gain accruing to the borrower on the disposal of any designated securities or on the disposal of any currency or amount standing in a bank account on 19th November 1967 and representing the loan, the sums allowable as a deduction under section 38(1)(a) shall, subject to sub-paragraph (3) below, be increased by multiplying them by seven-sixths.

(3) The total amount of the increases so made in computing all gains (and losses) which are referable to any one loan (made before 19th November 1967) shall not exceed one-sixth of the sterling parity value of that loan at the time it was made.

(4) Designated securities which on the commencement of this paragraph constitute a separate 1982 holding (within the meaning of section 109), shall continue to constitute a separate 1982 holding until such time as a disposal takes place on the occurrence of which sub-paragraph (3) above operates to limit the increases which would otherwise be made under sub-paragraph (2) in allowable deductions.

(5) In this paragraph and paragraph 14 below, "foreign securities" means securities expressed in a currency other than sterling, or shares having a nominal value expressed in a currency other than sterling, or the dividends on which are payable in a currency other than sterling.

Commentary—*Simon's Direct Tax Service* **C2.737.**
Definition—"Shares", s 288(1).

Devaluation of sterling: foreign insurance funds

14—(1) The sums allowable as a deduction under section 38(1)(a) in computing any gains to which this paragraph applies shall be increased by multiplying by seven-sixths.

(2) This paragraph applies to gains accruing—

> (a) to any underwriting member of Lloyd's, or
>
> (b) to any company engaged in the business of marine protection and indemnity insurance on a mutual basis,

on the disposal by that person after 18th November 1967 of any foreign securities which on that date formed part of a trust fund—

> (i) established by that person in any country or territory outside the United Kingdom, and
>
> (ii) representing premiums received in the course of that person's business, and
>
> (iii) wholly or mainly used for the purpose of meeting liabilities arising in that country or territory in respect of that business.

Commentary—*Simon's Direct Tax Service* **C1.212.**
Definitions—"Company", ss 99, 288(1); "foreign securities", Sch 11 para 13(5).

Gilt-edged securities past redemption date

15 So far as material for the purposes of this or any other Act, the definition of "gilt-edged securities" in Schedule 9 to this Act shall include any securities which were gilt-edged securities for the purposes of the 1979 Act, and the redemption date of which fell before 1st January 1992.

Definition—"The 1979 Act", s 288(1).

Qualifying corporate bonds, company reorganisations, share conversions etc

16—(1) Part IV of this Act has effect subject to the provisions of this paragraph.

(2) The substitution of Chapter II of that Part for the enactments repealed by this Act shall not alter the law applicable to any reorganisation or reduction of share capital, conversion of securities or company amalgamation taking place before the coming into force of this Act.

(3) Sub-paragraph (2) above applies in particular to the law determining whether or not any assets arising on an event mentioned in that sub-paragraph are to be treated as the same asset as the original holding of shares, securities or other assets.

(4) In relation to a disposal or exchange on or after 6th April 1992, the following amendments shall be regarded as always having had effect, that is to say, the amendments to section 64 of, or Schedule 3 to, the Finance Act 1984 made by section 139 of, or paragraph 6 of Schedule 14 to, the Finance Act 1989 paragraph 28 of Schedule 10 to the Finance Act 1990 or section 98 of, or paragraph 1 of

Schedule 10 to, the Finance Act 1991 or by virtue of the amendments to paragraph 1 of Schedule 18 to the Taxes Act made by section 77 of the Finance Act 1991.

Commentary—*Simon's Direct Tax Service* C2.730.
Definitions—"Asset", s 21(1); "company", ss 99, 288(1); "shares", s 288(1); "the Taxes Act", s 288(1).

Land: allowance for betterment levy

17—(1) Where betterment levy charged in the case of any land in respect of an act or event which fell within Case B or Case C or, if it was the renewal, extension or variation of a tenancy, Case F—

(a) has been paid, and

(b) has not been allowed as a deduction in computing the profits or gains or losses of a trade for the purposes of Case I of Schedule D;

then, if the person by whom the levy was paid disposes of the land or any part of it and so claims, the following provisions of this paragraph shall have effect.

(2) Paragraph 9 of Schedule 2 shall apply where the condition stated in sub-paragraph (1)(a) of that paragraph is satisfied, notwithstanding that the condition in sub-paragraph (1)(b) of that paragraph is not satisfied.

(3) Subject to the following provisions of this paragraph, there shall be ascertained the excess, if any, of—

(a) the net development value ascertained for the purposes of the levy, over

(b) the increment specified in sub-paragraph (6) below;

and the amount of the excess shall be treated as an amount allowable under section 38(1)(b).

(4) Where the act or event in respect of which the levy was charged was a part disposal of the land, section 38 shall apply as if the part disposal had not taken place and sub-paragraph (5) below shall apply in lieu of sub-paragraph (3) above.

(5) The amount or value of the consideration for the disposal shall be treated as increased by the amount of any premium or like sum paid in respect of the part disposal, and there shall be ascertained the excess, if any, of—

(a) the aggregate specified in sub-paragraph (7) below, over

(b) the increment specified in sub-paragraph (6) below;

and the amount of the excess shall be treated as an amount allowable under section 38(1)(b).

(6) The increment referred to in sub-paragraphs (3)(b) and (5)(b) above is the excess, if any, of—

(a) the amount or value of the consideration brought into account under section 38(1)(a), over

(b) the base value ascertained for the purposes of the levy.

(7) The aggregate referred to in sub-paragraph (5)(a) above is the aggregate of—

(a) the net development value ascertained for the purposes of the levy, and

(b) the amount of any premium or like sum paid in respect of the part disposal, in so far as charged to tax under Schedule A (or, as the case may be, Case VIII of Schedule D), and

(c) the chargeable gain accruing on the part disposal.

(8) Where betterment levy in respect of more than one act or event has been charged and paid as mentioned in sub-paragraph (1) above, sub-paragraphs (2) to (7) above shall apply without modifications in relation to the betterment levy in respect of the first of them; but in relation to the other or others sub-paragraph (3) or, as the case may be, (5) above shall have effect as if the amount to be treated thereunder as allowable under section 38(1)(b) were the net development value specified in sub-paragraph (3)(a) or, as the case may be, the aggregate referred to in sub-paragraph (5)(a) of this paragraph.

(9) Where the disposal is of part only of the land sub-paragraphs (2) to (8) above shall have effect subject to the appropriate apportionments.

(10) References in this paragraph to a premium include any sum payable as mentioned in section 34(4) or (5) of the Taxes Act (sums payable in lieu of rent or as consideration for the surrender of lease or for variation or waiver of term) and, in relation to Scotland, a grassum.

Commentary—*Simon's Direct Tax Service* C2.1122.
Definitions—"Chargeable gain", s 15(2); "land", s 288(1); "lease", Sch 8 para 10(1); "part disposal", s 21(2); "rent", Sch para 10(1); "the Taxes Act", s 288(1); "trade", s 288(1), TA 1988 s 832(1).

Non-resident trusts

18 Without prejudice to section 289 or Part III of this Schedule—

(a) any tax chargeable on a person which is postponed under subsection (4)(b) of section 17 of the 1979 Act, shall continue to be postponed until that person becomes absolutely entitled to the part of the settled property concerned or disposes of the whole or part of his interest, as mentioned in that subsection; and

(b) section 70 of and Schedule 14 to the Finance Act 1984 shall continue to have effect in relation to amounts of tax which are postponed under that Schedule, and accordingly in paragraph 12 of that Schedule the references to section 80 of the Finance Act 1981 and to subsections (3) and (4) of that section include references to section 87 of this Act and subsections (4) and(5) of that section respectively.

Definitions—"The 1979 Act", s 288(1); "absolutely entitled as against trustees", s 60(2); "settled property", s 68.

Private residences

19 The reference in section 222(5)(*a*) to a notice given by any person within 2 years from the beginning of the period mentioned in section 222(5) includes a notice given before the end of the year 1966–67, if that was later.

Definition—"Notice", s 288(1).

Works of art etc

20 The repeals made by this Act do not affect the continued operation of sections 31 and 32 of the Finance Act 1965 in the form in which they were before 13th March 1975, in relation to estate duty in respect of deaths occurring before that date.

Disposal before acquisition

21 The substitution of this Act for the corresponding enactments repealed by this Act shall not alter the effect of any provision enacted before this Act (whether or not there is a corresponding provision in this Act) so far as it relates to an asset which—

    (*a*) was disposed of before being acquired, and

    (*b*) was disposed of before the commencement of this Act.

Definition—"Asset", s 21(1).

Estate duty

22 Nothing in the repeals made by this Act shall affect any enactment as it applies to the determination of any principal value for the purposes of estate duty.

Validity of subordinate legislation

23 So far as this Act re-enacts any provision contained in a statutory instrument made in exercise of powers conferred by any Act, it shall be without prejudice to the validity of that provision, and any question as to its validity shall be determined as if the re-enacted provision were contained in a statutory instrument made under those powers.

Amendments in other Acts

24—(1) The repeal by this Act of the Income and Corporation Taxes Act 1970 does not affect—

    (*a*) the amendment made by paragraph 3 of Schedule 15 of that Act to section 26 of the Finance Act 1956 or

    (*b*) paragraph 10 of that Schedule so far as it applies in relation to the Management Act.

(2) The repeal by this Act of Schedule 7 to the 1979 Act does not affect the amendments made by that Schedule to any enactment not repealed by this Act.

Definition—"The 1979 Act", s 288(1).

Savings for Part III of this Schedule

25 The provisions of this Part of this Schedule are without prejudice to the generality of Part III of this Schedule.

PART III
ASSETS ACQUIRED BEFORE COMMENCEMENT

Cross references—See TCGA 1992 Sch 11 para 18 (non-resident trusts: continuation of postponement of tax). TCGA 1992 Sch 11 para 25 (savings for this Part of this Schedule).

26—(1) The substitution of this Act for the enactments repealed by this Act shall not alter the effect of any provision enacted before this Act (whether or not there is a corresponding provision in this Act) so far as it determines—

    (*a*) what amount the consideration is to be taken to be for the purpose of the computation under this Act of any chargeable gain; or

    (*b*) whether and to what extent events in, or expenditure incurred in, or other amounts referable to, a period earlier than the chargeable periods to which this Act applies may be taken into account for any tax purposes in a chargeable period to which this Act applies.

(2) Without prejudice to sub-paragraph (1) above, the repeals made by this Act shall not affect—

TCGA 1992

(*a*) the enactments specified in Part V of Schedule 14 to the Finance Act 1971 (charge on death) so far as their operation before repeal falls to be taken into account in chargeable periods to which this Act applies,

(*b*) the application of the enactments repealed by the 1979 Act to events before 6th April 1965 in accordance with paragraph 31 of Schedule 6 to the Finance Act 1965.

(3) This paragraph has no application to the law relating to the determination of the market value of assets.

Simon's Tax Cases—Sub-para (2)(*b*), *Mashiter v Pearmain* [1985] STC 165*.
Definitions—"The 1979 Act", s 288(1); "asset", s 21(1); "chargeable gain", s 15(2); "chargeable period", s 288(1); "the Management Act", s 288(1); "market value", ss 272–274, Sch 11 Part I.

27 Where the acquisition or provision of any asset by one person was, immediately before the commencement of this paragraph and by virtue of any enactment, to be taken for the purposes of Schedule 5 to the 1979 Act to be the acquisition or disposal of it by another person, then, notwithstanding the repeal by this Act of that enactment, Schedule 2 to this Act shall also have effect as if the acquisition or provision of the asset by the first-mentioned person had been the acquisition or provision of it by that other person.

Definitions—"The 1979 Act", s 288(1); "asset", s 21(1).

PART IV

OTHER GENERAL SAVINGS

28 Where under any Act passed before this Act and relating to a country or territory outside the United Kingdom there is a power to affect Acts passed or in force before a particular time, or instruments made or having effect under such Acts, and the power would, but for the passing of this Act, have included power to change the law which is reproduced in, or is made or has effect under, this Act, then that power shall include power to make such provision as will secure the like change in the law reproduced in, or made or having effect under, this Act notwithstanding that this Act is not an Act passed or in force before that time.

29—(1) The continuity of the law relating to the taxation of chargeable gains shall not be affected by the substitution of this Act for the enactments repealed by this Act and earlier enactments repealed by and corresponding to any of those enactments ("the repealed enactments").

(2) Any reference, whether express or implied, in any enactment, instrument or document (including this Act or any Act amended by this Act) to, or to things done or falling to be done under or for the purposes of, any provision of this Act shall, if and so far as the nature of the reference permits, be construed as including, in relation to the times, years or periods, circumstances or purposes in relation to which the corresponding provision in the repealed enactments has or had effect, a reference to, or as the case may be, to things done or falling to be done under or for the purposes of, that corresponding provision.

(3) Any reference, whether express or implied, in any enactment, instrument or document (including the repealed enactments and enactments, instruments and documents passed or made after the passing of this Act) to, or to things done or falling to be done under or for the purposes of, any of the repealed enactments shall, if and so far as the nature of the reference permits, be construed as including, in relation to the times, years or periods, circumstances or purposes in relation to which the corresponding provision of this Act has effect, a reference to, or as the case may be to things done or falling to be done under or for the purposes of, that corresponding provision.

Definition—"Chargeable gain", s 15(2).

FINANCE (NO 2) ACT 1992

(1992 Chapter 48)

ARRANGEMENT OF SECTIONS

PART II
INCOME TAX, CORPORATION TAX AND CAPITAL GAINS TAX

CHAPTER I
GENERAL

CHAPTER II

CAPITAL ALLOWANCES

PART III

MISCELLANEOUS AND GENERAL

Inheritance tax

Petroleum revenue tax

General and Special Commissioners

Miscellaneous

General

SCHEDULES:

Schedule 4—*Car tax: abolition of fiscal frontiers.* (repealed)
Schedule 5—Married couple's allowance etc.
Schedule 6—Group relief etc: amendments.
Schedule 7—*Deep gain securities.* (repealed)
Schedule 8—Rights in pursuance of deposits.
Schedule 9—Friendly societies.
Schedule 10—Furnished accommodation.
Schedule 11—Paying and collecting agents etc.
Schedule 12—Banks etc in compulsory liquidation.
Schedule 13—Capital allowances: enterprise zones.
Schedule 14—*Inheritance tax.* (see *Yellow Tax Handbook, Part II, IHT*)
Schedule 15—*Amendments relating to oil exported directly from off-shore fields.* (see *Yellow Tax Handbook, Part II, PRT*)
Schedule 16—General and Special Commissioners.
Schedule 17—Northern Ireland Electricity.
Schedule 18—*Repeals.* (not printed)

An Act to grant certain duties, to alter other duties, and to amend the law relating to the National Debt and the Public Revenue, and to make further provision in connection with Finance.

[16th July 1992]

PART II
INCOME TAX, CORPORATION TAX AND CAPITAL GAINS TAX

CHAPTER I
GENERAL
Lower rate

19 Lower rate: further provisions

(1) (*amends* TMA 1970 s 7).

(2) (*amends* TMA 1970 s 91 and TA 1988 ss 550, 599A).

(3) (*amends* TA 1988 ss 167, 233, 353, 369, 549, 683, 684, 689, 699, 819 and Sch 7 para 19 *and is repealed in part by* FA 1994 s 258, Sch 26 Pt V(2) and FA 1995 Sch 29 Pt VIII(8)).

(4) (*repealed* by FA 1996 Sch 41 Pt V(1) with effect from the year 1996–97).

(5) (*amended* TA 1988 s 369 and is repealed by FA 1994 s 258, Sch 26 Pt V(2), in relation to interest payments made after 5 April 1994).

(6) (*amends* TA 1988 s 421).

(7) This section shall apply for the year 1992–93 and subsequent years of assessment.

Married couple's allowance etc

20 Married couple's allowance etc

Schedule 5 to this Act (which makes provision in relation to the married couple's allowance) shall have effect.

Corporation tax charge and rate

21 Charge and rate of corporation tax for 1992

(*spent*).

Commentary—*Simon's Direct Tax Service* **D2.108.**

22 Small companies

(*spent*).

Commentary—*Simon's Direct Tax Service* **D2.109.**

Capital gains tax

23 Capital gains tax: rates

Amendment—This section repealed by FA 1999 s 139, Sch 20 Pt III(1) with effect from the year 1999–00.

Groups etc

24 Amendments relating to group relief etc

Schedule 6 to this Act (which contains amendments relating to group relief etc) shall have effect.

25 Companies ceasing to be members of groups

(1) (*amended* TCGA 1992 ss 178, 179; *repealed by* FA 2000 s 156, Sch 40 Pt II(12) with effect for assets acquired after 31 March 2000).

(2) Subject to the repeals made by the Taxation of Chargeable Gains Act 1992 in relation to a company which ceases to be a member of a group of companies on or after 15th November 1991 section 278 of the Income and Corporation Taxes Act 1970 (deemed sale etc where company ceases to be member of a group) shall have effect, and be deemed to have had effect, with the substitution in subsection (1) of the words "in consequence of another member of the group ceasing to exist" for the words from "by being wound up" to the end of the subsection.

Charities etc

26 Donations to charity: minimum limits

(*amended* TA 1988 s 339, FA 1990 s 25; *repealed by* FA 1993 s 213, Sch 23 Pt III(2) *with effect from 16 March 1993*).

27 Covenanted payments to charity

(*amended* TA 1988 s 67; *repealed by* FA 1995 Sch 29 Pt VIII(8), *with effect from the year 1995–96*).

28 Powers of inspection

(1) Subsection (2) below applies if—

(*a*) an exempt body has made a claim for exemption from tax under section 505(1), 507 or 508 of the Taxes Act 1988 and

(*b*) the exemption results in, or (where it has yet to be granted or allowed) would if granted or allowed result in, the repayment of income tax or the payment of a tax credit.

(2) The Board may require the body to produce for inspection by an officer of the Board all such books, documents and other records in the possession, or under the control, of the body as contain information relating to the claim.

(3) For the purposes of subsection (1) above each of the following is an exempt body—

(*a*) any body of persons or trust established for charitable purposes only;

(*b*) each of the bodies mentioned in section 507 of the Taxes Act 1988 (heritage bodies);

(*c*) any Association of a description specified in section 508 of that Act (scientific research organisations).

(4) (*amends* TMA 1970 s 98 Table).

(5) (*repeals* FA 1990 s 94).

(6) This section shall apply in relation to claims made after the day on which this Act is passed.

Commentary—*Simon's Direct Tax Service* **C4.540.**

Interest, dividends and distributions

29 Returns of interest

(1) (*amends* TMA 1970 s 17).

(2) This section shall apply to interest paid or credited after the day on which this Act is passed.

Commentary—*Simon's Direct Tax Service* **C4.540.**

30 Foreign dividends

Amendment—This section repealed by FA 1996 Sch 41 Pt V(2).

31 Equity notes

(1), (2) (*insert* TA 1988 s 209(2)(*e*)(vii), (9), (10), (11)).

(3) (*amends* TA 1988 s 212).

(4) This section shall apply where the interest or other distribution is paid after 14th May 1992.

32 Information relating to distributions

(1)–(3) (*insert* TA 1988 s 234A and *amend* TA 1988 s 234 and 468).

(4) This section shall apply in relation to distributions begun after the day on which this Act is passed.

Securities and deposits

33 Deep gain securities

Amendments—This section repealed by FA 1996 Sch 41 Pt V(3) with effect so far as relating to income tax from the year 1996–97 and so far as relating to corporation tax for accounting periods ending after 31 March 1996, subject to transitional provisions in FA 1996 Sch 15.

34 Rights in pursuance of deposits

Schedule 8 to this Act (which contains provisions about arrangements relating to rights in pursuance of deposits) shall have effect.

35 Exchange of securities

(1) (*amends* TCGA 1992 s 135, and *repealed by* FA 2002 s 141, Sch 40 Pt 3(2) with effect in accordance with FA 2002 Sch 9 paras 7, 8.).

(2) Subject to the repeals made by the Taxation of Chargeable Gains Act 1992 in relation to exchanges made on or after 1st January 1992 section 85 of the Capital Gains Tax Act 1979 (exchange of securities for those in another company) shall have effect, and be deemed to have had effect, with the insertion after subsection (1)(*b*) of

"or

(*c*) company A holds, or in consequence of the exchange will hold, the greater part of the voting power in company B".

Employee shares

36 Employee share ownership trusts

(1) (*inserts* FA 1989 s 69(3A)).

(2) This section applies in relation to exchanges made on or after 1st January 1992.

37 Employee share schemes: special benefits

(1)–(5) (*amend* FA 1988 s 80).

(6) This section shall apply in relation to benefits received on or after 12th November 1991.

Business expansion scheme

38 No relief for shares issued after 1993

Amendment—This section repealed by FA 1994 Sch 26 Pt V(17) (amended TA 1988 s 289).

39 Extension of relief for private rented housing: property managing companies

Amendment—This section repealed by FA 1994 Sch 26 Pt V(17) (amended FA 1988 Sch 4 para 11).

40 Extension of relief for private rented housing: lettings to former owner-occupiers

Amendment—This section repealed by FA 1994 Sch 26 Pt V(17) (amended FA 1988 Sch 4 para 15).

Films

40A Revenue nature of expenditure on master versions of films

(1) Expenditure incurred on the production or acquisition of a master version of a film is to be regarded for the purposes of the Tax Acts as expenditure of a revenue nature unless an election under section 40D below has effect with respect to it.

(2) If expenditure on the master version of a film is regarded as expenditure of a revenue nature under subsection (1) above, sums received from the disposal of the master version are to be regarded for the purposes of the Tax Acts as receipts of a revenue nature (if they would not be so regarded apart from this subsection).

(3) For the purposes of subsection (2) above sums received from the disposal of a master version of a film include—

(*a*) sums received from the disposal of any interest or right in or over the master version, including an interest or right created by the disposal, and

(*b*) insurance, compensation or similar money derived from the master version.

(4) In this section—

(*a*) "expenditure of a revenue nature" means expenditure which, if it were incurred in the course of a trade the profits of which are chargeable to tax under Case I of Schedule D, would be taken into account for the purpose of computing the profits or losses of the trade, and

(*b*) "receipts of a revenue nature" means receipts which, if they were receipts of such a trade, would be taken into account for that purpose.

(5) For the purposes of this section and sections 40B to 40D below, a "master version" of a film means a master negative, master tape or master audio disc of the film and includes any rights in the film (or its soundtrack) that are held or acquired with the master negative, master tape or master audio disc.][1]

Commentary—*Simon's Direct Tax Service* **B3.1307, 1307A.**
Modifications—CAA 2001 Sch 3 para 116(1) (F(No 2)A 1992 ss 40A–40D apply with the necessary modifications in relation to—
   (*a*) expenditure on the production of a film—
      (i) completed before 21st March 2000, or
      (ii) completed on or after that date, if the first day of principal photography is before that date, unless the person incurring
      the expenditure elects that those modifications should not apply;
   (*b*) expenditure on the acquisition of a film, tape or disc incurred before 6 April 2000.
For the necessary modifications see CAA 2001 Sch 3 para 116(2)).
Amendments—[1] This section inserted by CAA 2001 s 578, Sch 2 para 82 with effect for income tax purposes, as respects allowances and charges falling to be made for chargeable periods ending after 5 April 2001, and for corporation tax purposes, as respects allowances and charges falling to be made for chargeable periods ending after 31 March 2001.

[40B Allocation of expenditure to periods

(1) In computing the profits or gains accruing to any person from a trade or business which consists of or includes the exploitation of master versions of films, expenditure which is—

   (*a*) incurred on the production or acquisition of a master version of a film, and
   (*b*) expenditure of a revenue nature (whether as a result of section 40A above or otherwise),

must be allocated to relevant periods in accordance with this section.

(2) Subsection (1) above does not apply if an election under section 40D below has effect with respect to the expenditure.

(3) In this section "relevant period" means—

   (*a*) a period for which the accounts of the trade or business concerned are made up, or
   (*b*) if no accounts of the trade or business concerned are made up for a period—

      (i) if the profits or gains accrue to a company within the charge to corporation tax, the accounting period of the company;
      (ii) in any other case, the period the profits or gains of which are taken into account in assessing the income of the trade or business for a year of assessment.

(4) The amount of expenditure falling within subsection (1) above which falls to be allocated to any relevant period is so much as is just and reasonable, having regard to—

   (*a*) the amount of that expenditure which remains unallocated at the beginning of that period,
   (*b*) the proportion which the estimated value of the master version of the film which is realised in that period (whether by way of income or otherwise) bears to the aggregate of the value so realised and the estimated remaining value of the master version at the end of that period, and
   (*c*) the need to bring the whole of the expenditure falling within subsection (1) above into account over the time during which the value of the master version is expected to be realised.

(5) In addition to any expenditure which is allocated to a relevant period in accordance with subsection (4) above, if a claim is made, there must also be allocated to that period so much of the unallocated expenditure as is specified in the claim and does not exceed the difference between—

   (*a*) the amount allocated to that period in accordance with subsection (4) above, and
   (*b*) the value of the master version of the film which is realised in that period (whether by way of income or otherwise).

(6) A claim under subsection (5) above must be made—

   (*a*) for the purposes of income tax, on or before the first anniversary of the 31st January next following the year of assessment in which ends the relevant period mentioned in that subsection;
   (*b*) for the purposes of corporation tax, not later than two years after the end of the relevant period to which the claim relates.

(7) In subsection (5) above "the unallocated expenditure", in relation to a relevant period, is any expenditure falling within subsection (1) above—

   (*a*) which does not fall to be allocated to that period in accordance with subsection (4) above, and
   (*b*) which has not been allocated to any earlier relevant period in accordance with subsection (4) or (5) above.][1]

Commentary—*Simon's Direct Tax Service* **B3.1307A.**
Modifications—CAA 2001 Sch 3 para 116(1) (F(No 2)A 1992 ss 40A–40D apply with the necessary modifications in relation to—
   (*a*) expenditure on the production of a film—
      (i) completed before 21st March 2000, or
      (ii) completed on or after that date, if the first day of principal photography is before that date, unless the person incurring
      the expenditure elects that those modifications should not apply;
   (*b*) expenditure on the acquisition of a film, tape or disc incurred before 6 April 2000.
For the necessary modifications see CAA 2001 Sch 3 para 116(2)).
Amendments—[1] This section inserted by CAA 2001 s 578, Sch 2 para 82 with effect for income tax purposes, as respect allowances and charges falling to be made for chargeable periods ending after 5 April 2001, and for corporation tax purposes as respects allowances and charges falling to be made for chargeable periods ending after 31 March 2001.

[40C Cases where section 40B does not apply

(1) To the extent that a deduction has been made in respect of any expenditure for a relevant period under section 42 below—

(a) that expenditure must not be allocated under section 40B above, and

(b) no other expenditure incurred on the production or acquisition of the master version of the film is to be allocated under section 40B above to the relevant period.

(2) Section 40B above does not apply to the profits of a trade in which the master version of the film constitutes trading stock, as defined by section 100(2) of the Taxes Act 1988.]¹

Commentary—*Simon's Direct Tax Service* B3.1307A.
Modifications—CAA 2001 Sch 3 para 116(1) (F(No 2)A 1992 ss 40A–40D) apply with the necessary modifications in relation to—
(a) expenditure on the production of a film—
    (i) completed before 21st March 2000, or
    (ii) completed on or after that date, if the first day of principal photography is before that date, unless the person incurring the expenditure elects that those modifications should not apply;
(b) expenditure on the acquisition of a film, tape or disc incurred before 6 April 2000.
For the necessary modifications see CAA 2001 Sch 3 para 116(2)).
Amendments—¹ This section inserted by CAA 2001 s 578, Sch 2 para 82 with effect for income tax purposes, as respects allowances and charges falling to be made for chargeable periods ending after 5 April 2001, and for corporation tax purposes, as respects allowances and charges falling to be made for chargeable periods ending after 31 March 2001.

[40D Election for sections 40A and 40B not to apply

(1) Sections 40A and 40B above do not apply to expenditure—

(a) in relation to which an election is made under this section, and

(b) which meets the conditions in subsection (2) below.

(2) The conditions are that—

(a) the expenditure is incurred—

(i) by a person who carries on a trade or business which consists of or includes the exploitation of master versions of films, and

(ii) on the production or acquisition of a master version of a film,

(b) the master version is certified by the Secretary of State under paragraph 3 of Schedule 1 to the Films Act 1985 as a qualifying film, tape or disc for the purposes of this section, and

(c) the value of the master version is expected to be realisable over a period of not less than two years.

(3) An election under this section—

(a) must relate to all expenditure incurred (or to be incurred) on the production or acquisition of the master version in question,

(b) must be made by giving notice to the Inland Revenue, in such form as the Board of Inland Revenue may determine, and

(c) is irrevocable.

(4) Notice under subsection (3)(b) above must be given—

(a) for the purposes of income tax, on or before the first anniversary of the 31st January next following the year of assessment in which ends the relevant period in which the master version of the film is completed;

(b) for the purposes of corporation tax, not later than two years after the end of the relevant period in which the master version of the film is completed.

(5) In subsection (4) above ''relevant period'' has the same meaning as in section 40B above.

(6) For the purposes of subsection (4) above, the master version of a film is completed—

(a) at the time when it is first in a form in which it can reasonably be regarded as ready for copies of it to be made and distributed for presentation to the public, or

(b) if the expenditure in question was incurred on the acquisition of the master version and it was acquired after the time mentioned in paragraph (a) above, at the time it was acquired.

(7) An election may not be made under this section in relation to expenditure on a master version of a film if a claim has been made in respect of any of that expenditure under section 41 or 42 below.]¹

Commentary—*Simon's Direct Tax Service* B3.1307B.
Cross references—See FA 2002 s 99 (relief under this section restricted to films genuinely intended for theatrical release).
Modifications—CAA 2001 Sch 3 para 116(1) (F(No 2)A 1992 ss 40A–40D) apply with the necessary modifications in relation to—
(a) expenditure on the production of a film—
    (i) completed before 21st March 2000, or
    (ii) completed on or after that date, if the first day of principal photography is before that date, unless the person incurring the expenditure elects that those modifications should not apply;
(b) expenditure on the acquisition of a film, tape or disc incurred before 6 April 2000.
For the necessary modifications see CAA 2001 Sch 3 para 116(2)).
CAA 2001 Sch 3 para 117 (the above section applies with the omission of—
(a) paragraph (a) of subsection (1); and
(b) subsections (3) to (7),
if the film, tape or disc of the film was completed before 10 March 1992)

Amendments—[1] This section inserted by CAA 2001 s 578, Sch 2 para 82 with effect for income tax purposes, as respects allowances and charges falling to be made for chargeable periods ending after 5 April 2001, and for corporation tax purposes, as respects allowances and charges falling to be made for chargeable periods ending after 31 March 2001.

41 Relief for preliminary expenditure

(1) Subject to the following provisions of this section and any other provisions of the Tax Acts, in computing for tax purposes the profits or gains accruing to a person in a relevant period from a trade or business which consists of or includes the exploitation of films, that person shall (on making a claim) be entitled to deduct the amount of any expenditure of a revenue nature payable by him in that or an earlier relevant period—

(*a*) which is expenditure to which this section applies,

(*b*) in respect of which no deduction has previously been made (whether under this section or otherwise) in computing for tax purposes the profits or gains accruing from the trade or business, and

(*c*) in respect of which no election has been made under [section 40D above][2].

(2) This section applies to any expenditure that—

(*a*) can reasonably be said to have been incurred with a view to enabling a decision to be taken as to whether or not to make a film,

(*b*) is payable before the first day of principal photography (where the decision that is taken is to make the film), and

(*c*) is not payable under any contract or other arrangement whereby it may fall to be repaid if the film is not made.

(3) A deduction shall not be made in respect of a film that has been completed unless the master negative of the film or any master tape or master disc of the film is a qualifying film, tape or disc.

(4) A deduction shall not be made in respect of a film that has not been completed unless it is reasonably likely that if the film were completed the master negative of the film or any master tape or master disc of the film would be a qualifying film, tape or disc.

(5) The total amount deducted under this section in respect of a film shall not exceed 20 per cent of the budgeted total expenditure on the film, as calculated at the first day of principal photography.

[(6) A claim under this section shall be made—

(*a*) for the purposes of income tax, on or before the first anniversary of the 31st January next following the year of assessment in which ends the relevant period in which the expenditure to which it relates becomes payable;

(*b*) for the purposes of corporation tax, not later than two years after the end of the relevant period in which the expenditure to which it relates becomes payable.][1]

(7) To the extent that a deduction has been made in respect of any expenditure under this section, no further deduction shall be made in respect of it in computing for tax purposes the profits or gains of the trade or business concerned.

(8) This section shall have effect in relation to expenditure payable on or after 10th March 1992.

Commentary—*Simon's Direct Tax Service* **B3.1307B.**
Statement of Practice SP1/93—Tax treatment of expenditure on films and certain similar assets.
Cross references—See FA 2002 s 99 (relief under this section restricted to films genuinely intended for theatrical release).
Amendments—[1] Sub-s (6) substituted by FA 1996 s 135(1), (2), Sch 21 para 45 with effect for the purposes of income tax from the year 1996–97 and, for purposes of corporation tax, as respects accounting periods ending after 30 June 1999 (by virtue of Finance Act 1994, Section 199, (Appointed Day) Order, SI 1998/3173 art 2).
[2] Words in sub-s (1)(*c*) substituted by CAA 2001 s 578, Sch 2 para 83 with effect for income tax purposes, as respects allowances and charges falling to be made for chargeable periods ending after 5 April 2001, and for corporation tax purposes, as respects allowances and charges falling to be made for chargeable periods ending after 31 March 2001.

42 Relief for production or acquisition expenditure

(1) Subject to the following provisions of this section and any other provisions of the Tax Acts, in computing for tax purposes the profits or gains accruing to a person in a relevant period from a trade or business which consists of or includes the exploitation of films, that person shall (on making a claim) be entitled to deduct an amount in respect of any expenditure—

(*a*) which is expenditure to which subsection (2) or (3) below applies, and

(*b*) in respect of which no deduction has been made by virtue of [section 40B above][4] and no election has been made under [section 40D above][4].

(2) This subsection applies to any expenditure of a revenue nature incurred by the claimant on the production of a film—

(*a*) which was completed in the relevant period to which the claim relates or an earlier relevant period, and

(*b*) the master negative of which or any master tape or master disc of which is a qualifying film, tape or disc.

(3) This subsection applies to any expenditure of a revenue nature incurred by the claimant on the acquisition of the master negative of a film or any master tape or master disc of a film where;—

(a) the film was completed in the relevant period to which the claim relates or an earlier relevant period, and

(b) the master negative, tape or disc is a qualifying film, tape or disc.

(4) Any amount deducted for a relevant period under subsection (1) above shall not exceed—

(a) one third of the total expenditure incurred by the claimant on the production of the film concerned or the acquisition of the master negative or any master tape or master disc of it,

(b) one third of the sum obtained by deducting from the amount of that total expenditure the amount of so much of that total expenditure as has already been deducted by virtue of section 41 above, or

(c) so much of that total expenditure as has not already been deducted by virtue of [section 40B or]⁴ 41 above or this section,

whichever is less.

(5) In relation to a relevant period of less than twelve months, the references to one third in subsection (4) above shall be read as references to a proportionately smaller fraction.

[(6) A claim under this section shall be made—

(a) for the purposes of income tax, on or before the first anniversary of the 31st January next following the year of assessment in which ends the relevant period to which the claim relates,

(b) for the purposes of corporation tax, not later than two years after the end of the relevant period to which the claim relates,

and shall be irrevocable.]¹

(7) Where any expenditure is deducted by virtue of [section 40B above]⁴ in computing the profits or gains of a trade or business for a relevant period, no deduction shall be made under this section for that relevant period in respect of expenditure incurred on the production or acquisition of the film concerned.

(8) This section does not apply to the [profits]² of a trade in which the film concerned constitutes trading stock, as defined in section 100(2) of the Taxes Act 1988.

[(9) This section has effect in relation to expenditure incurred—

(a) on the production of a film completed on or after 10th March 1992, or

(b) on the acquisition of the master negative, master tape or master disc of a film completed on or after that date.]³

Commentary—*Simon's Direct Tax Service* **B3.1307B.**
Statement of Practice SP1/93—Tax treatment of expenditure on films and certain similar assets.
Cross references—See FA 1997 Sch 12 para 11(9), (10) (clawback of allowances in any case where an occasion occurs after 25 November 1996 on which a "major lump sum"—see FA 1997 Sch 12 para 3(2)—falls to be paid in the case of the lease of an asset).
FA 2002 s 99 (relief under this section restricted to films genuinely intended for theatrical release).
Amendments—¹ Sub-s (6) substituted by FA 1996 s 135(1), (2), Sch 21 para 46 with effect for the purposes of income tax from the year 1996–97 and, for purposes of corporation tax, as respects accounting periods ending after 30 June 1999 (by virtue of Finance Act 1994, Section 199, (Appointed Day) Order, SI 1998/3173 art 2).
² Word "profits" in sub-s (8) substituted for "profits or gains" by FA 1998 Sch 7 para 8 with effect from 31 July 1998.
³ Sub-s (9) substituted by FA 2000 s 113(3), (5), (6). This amendment has effect for expenditure on the production of a film—

(a) if the first day of principal photography is after 20 March 2000, or

(b) if the first day of principal photography is before that date but—

(i) the film is completed on or after that date, and

(ii) the person incurring the expenditure elects that the provisions of this section should apply.

For this purpose a film is completed at the time when it is first in a form in which it can reasonably be regarded as ready for copies of it to be made and distributed for presentation to the general public.
This section also has effect for expenditure incurred on the acquisition of a master negative, master tape or master audio disc of a film (as defined in F(No 2)A 1992 s 43) after 5 April 2000.
⁴ Words in sub-ss (1)(b), (4)(c) and (7) substituted by CAA 2001 s 578, Sch 2 para 84 with effect for income tax purposes, as respects allowances and charges falling to be made for chargeable periods ending after 5 April 2001, and for corporation tax purposes, as respects allowances and charges falling to be made for chargeable periods ending after 31 March 2001.
Modification—This section has effect in relation to expenditure to which F(No 2)A 1997 s 48 applies (see below) as if the following subsection were substituted for sub-ss (4), (5) above:

"(4) The amount deducted for a relevant period under subsection (1) above shall not exceed so much of the total expenditure incurred by the claimant on—

(a) the production of the film concerned, or

(b) the acquisition of the master negative or any master tape or master disc of it, as has not already been deducted by virtue of section 68(3)–(6) of the 1990 Act, section 41 above or this section.".

F(No 2)A 1997 s 48 applies to so much of any expenditure falling within sub-s (1)(a) and (b) above as is incurred after 1 July 1997 and before 2 July 2000 where the film concerned has a "total production expenditure" of £15 million or less and is completed after 1 July 1997. It does not apply to so much of any expenditure falling within sub-s (3) above as exceeds the "total production expenditure" on the film concerned. See F(No 2)A 1997 s 48 for the detailed provisions, including definitions and relief available where only part of the expenditure is expenditure to which that section applies.

43 Interpretation of sections 41 and 42

(1) In sections [40A to 42]² above and this section—

"expenditure of a revenue nature" has the meaning given in [section 40A(4) above]²,

"master disc", in relation to a film, means the original master film disc or the original master audio disc of the film,

"master negative", in relation to a film, means the original master negative of the film and its soundtrack (if any), "master tape", in relation to a film, means the original master film tape or the original master audio tape of the film,

"qualifying disc" means a master disc of a film certified by the Secretary of State under Schedule 1 to the Films Act 1985 as a qualifying disc for the purposes of [section 40D above][2],

"qualifying film" means a master negative of a film certified by the Secretary of State under Schedule 1 to the Films Act 1985 as a qualifying film for the purposes of [section 40D above][2],

"qualifying tape" means a master tape of a film certified by the Secretary of State under Schedule 1 to the Films Act 1985 as a qualifying tape for the purposes of [section 40D above][2],

"relevant period" has the meaning given in [section 40B(3) above][2], and

...[2]

(2) In sections 41 and 42 and this section—

(a) any reference to a film shall be construed in accordance with paragraph 1 of Schedule 1 to the Films Act 1985 and

(b) any reference to the acquisition of a master negative, master tape or master disc of a film includes a reference to the acquisition of [any rights in the film (or its soundtrack) that are held or acquired with the master negative, master tape or master audio disc][1].

(3) For the purposes of sections 41 and 42 above a film is completed—

(a) at the time when it is first in a form in which it can reasonably be regarded as ready for copies of it to be made and distributed for presentation to the general public, ...[1]

(b) ...[1]

Commentary—*Simon's Direct Tax Service* B3.1307.

Amendments—[1] Words in sub-s (2)(b) substituted, and sub-s (3)(b) and the word "or" preceding it repealed, by FA 2000 ss 113(4), (5), (6), 156, Sch 40 Pt II(18) This amendment has effect for expenditure on the production of a film—

(a) if the first day of principal photography is after 20 March 2000, or

(b) if the first day of principal photography is before 21 March 2000 but—

(i) the film is completed on or after that date, and

(ii) the person incurring the expenditure elects that the provisions of FA 2000 s 113 should apply,

and for this purpose a film is completed at the time when it is first in a form in which it can reasonably be regarded as ready for copies of it to be made and distributed for presentation to the general public.

This amendment also has effect for expenditure incurred on the acquisition of a master negative, master tape or master audio disc of a film (as defined in F(No 2)A 1992 s 43) after 5 April 2000.

[2] In sub-s (1), words substituted, and definition of "the 1990 Act" repealed by CAA 2001 ss 578, 580, Sch 2 para 85, Sch 4 with effect for income tax purposes, as respects allowances and charges falling to be made for chargeable periods ending after 5 April 2001, and for corporation tax purposes, as respects allowances and charges falling to be made for chargeable periods ending after 31 March 2001.

Transfers of trade

44 Transfer of a UK trade: amendment of 1992 Act

(*inserts* TCGA 1992 ss 140A, 140B).

45 Transfer of a non-UK trade: amendment of 1992 Act

(*inserts* TCGA 1992 ss 140C, 140D).

46 Transfer of a trade: supplementary (1)

(*amend* TCGA 1992 ss 35, 116, 174, 177, 184 and *insert* s 140(6A)).

47 Transfer of a UK trade: amendment of 1970 Act

(*inserted* TA 1970 ss 269A, 269B which have now been repealed).

48 Transfer of a non-UK trade: amendment of 1970 Act

(*inserted* TA 1970 ss 269C, 269D which have now been repealed).

49 Transfer of a trade: supplementary (2)

(*amends* TA 1988 s 268A, 275, 281, FA 1984 Sch 13 para 10(2), FA 1985 s 68(7A)(b), FA 1988 Sch 8 para 1(3)(b), Sch 11 para 5).

Double taxation relief

50 Transfer of a non-UK trade

(*inserts* TA 1988 s 815A).

51 The Arbitration Convention

(*insert* TA 1988 ss 815B, 816(2A), 182A).

52 Interest

(1) (*inserts* TA 1988 s 808A).

(2) This section shall apply in relation to interest (as defined in the arrangements) paid after 14th May 1992.

Miscellaneous

53 Car fuel: cash equivalents

(*amends* TA 1988 s 158).

54 Foreign earnings

(1) (*inserts* TA 1988 Sch 12 para 1A).

(2) This section shall have effect for the year 1992–93 and subsequent years of assessment.

55 Oil extraction activities: extended transportation

(1) (*amends* TA 1988 s 502).

(2) Subsection (1) above has effect with respect to chargeable periods ending after 27th November 1991.

(3) In so far as the amendments made by paragraph 3 of Schedule 15 to this Act amend the definitions of "initial storage" and "initial treatment" as they have effect, by virtue of section 502(2) of the Taxes Act 1988 for the purposes of Chapter V of Part XII of that Act, those amendments have effect with respect to chargeable periods ending after 27th November 1991.

56 Friendly societies

Schedule 9 to this Act (which makes provision in relation to friendly societies) shall have effect.

57 Rents or receipts between connected persons

Amendments—This section repealed by FA 1998 s 165, Sch 27 Part III(4) with effect from 1998-99 for income tax purposes, and from 1 April 1998 for corporation tax, subject to the transitional provisions in FA 1998 Sch 5 Part IV.

58 Rents etc chargeable under Case VI

Amendments—This section repealed by FA 1998 s 165, Sch 27 Part III(4) with effect from 1998-99 for income tax purposes, and from 1 April 1998 for corporation tax, subject to the transitional provisions in FA 1998 Sch 5 Part IV.

59 Furnished accommodation

Schedule 10 to this Act (which makes provision about furnished accommodation) shall have effect.

60 Deduction on account of certain payments

(1) (*amends* TA 1988 s 347A and FA 1988 s 38).

(2) This section shall have effect for the year 1992–93 and subsequent years of assessment.

61 Qualifying maintenance payments: extension to member States

(1) (*amends* TA 1988 s 347B).

(2) This section shall have effect for the year 1992–93 and subsequent years of assessment.

62 Qualifying maintenance payments: maintenance assessments etc

(1) (*inserts* TA 1988 s 347B(8)–(12)).

(2), (3) (*insert* FA 1988 ss 36(5A), 38(8A)).

(4) This section shall come into force on such date as the Secretary of State may by order provide.

(5) The power conferred by subsection (4) above shall be exercisable by statutory instrument.

(6) The provision made by this section shall have effect, so far as it concerns orders under section 106 of the Social Security Administration Act 1992 or section 101 of the Social Security Administration (Northern Ireland) Act 1992 only in relation to payments which fall due after the coming into force of this section.

63 Paying and collecting agents etc

Schedule 11 to this Act (which makes provision in relation to the payment of income tax on foreign dividends etc) shall have effect.

64 Reduced and composite rate

(1) For the purposes of this section each of the following is a relevant order—

(*a*) the Income Tax (Reduced and Composite Rate) Order 1985 (which sets out 25·25 per cent as the reduced rate for building societies and the composite rate for deposit-takers for the year 1986–87);

(*b*) the Income Tax (Reduced and Composite Rate) Order 1986 (which sets out 24·75 per cent as the rate for the year 1987–88);

(*c*) the Income Tax (Reduced and Composite Rate) Order 1987 (which sets out 23·25 per cent as the rate for the year 1988–89);

(*d*) the Income Tax (Reduced and Composite Rate) Order 1988 (which sets out 21·75 per cent as the rate for the year 1989–90).

(2) If apart from this section a relevant order would not be so taken, it shall be taken to be and always to have been effective to determine the rate set out in the order as the reduced rate and the composite rate for the year of assessment for which the order was made.

Commentary—*Simon's Direct Tax Service* **D4.704, 1112.**
Simon's Tax Cases—*National & Provincial Building Society v United Kingdom* [1997] STC 1466.

65 Life assurance business: I minus E basis

(1) For the purposes of this section a claim is a relevant claim if it is made under or by virtue of any of the following provisions—

(*a*) section 393(1) of the Taxes Act 1988 (claim for carry forward of trading losses);

(*b*) section 393A(1) of the Taxes Act 1988 (claim for carry sideways and backwards of trading losses);

(*c*) section 402(2) of the Taxes Act 1988 (surrender of relief between members of groups and consortia: group claim);

(*d*) section 402(3) of the Taxes Act 1988 (surrender of relief between members of groups and consortia: consortium claim);

(*e*) any provision reproduced in any of the provisions mentioned in paragraphs (*a*) to (*d*) above (whether directly or indirectly and whether with or without modification).

(2) For the purposes of this section the following are relevant provisions—

[(*aa*) section 434(1) and (1A) of the Taxes Act 1988 (section 208 not to apply in relation to life assurance profits computed in accordance with Case I of Schedule D etc);

(*ab*) section 434(1C) and (1D) of the Taxes Act 1988 (which makes corresponding provision in relation to overseas life insurance companies and is notionally inserted by paragraph 9(1) of Schedule 19AC to that Act);][5]

[(*a*) section 434A(1) of the Taxes Act 1988 (profits derived from investments held for purposes of life assurance business treated as profits of that business in ascertaining loss);][2]

(*b*), (*c*) ...[4]

[(*d*) section 83(2) of the Finance Act 1989 (amounts to be taken into account as receipts or expenses);][3]

(*e*) section 37(1) of the Taxation of Chargeable Gains Act 1992 (exclusion from consideration for disposal of asset of any money or moneys worth taken into account in computing profits or losses etc);

(*f*) any provision reproduced in any of the provisions mentioned in paragraphs (*a*) to (*c*)[4] and (*e*) above (whether directly or indirectly and whether with or without modification).

(3) For the purposes of this section—

(*a*) the I minus E basis is the basis commonly so called (under which a company carrying on life assurance business is charged to tax in respect of that business otherwise than under Case I of Schedule D);

(*b*) life assurance business includes annuity business.

(4) Neither the making of a relevant claim in respect of a trading loss incurred by a company in an accounting period nor the application of any commercial or accounting principle or practice in computing that loss—

(*a*) shall prevent the I minus E basis being applied for that or any other accounting period in respect of the company's life assurance business;

(*b*) shall affect the calculation of the income or gains of that business for that or any other accounting period in applying that basis.

(5) The application of a relevant provision as regards a company for an accounting period shall not—

(*a*) prevent the I minus E basis being applied for that or any other accounting period in respect of its life assurance business;

(*b*) affect the calculation of the income or gains of that business for that or any other accounting period in applying that basis.

(6) This section—

(*a*) shall apply in relation to accounting periods beginning on or after the day on which this Act is passed;

(*b*) shall apply and be deemed always to have applied in relation to accounting periods beginning before that day;

[but, in relation to any case in which by virtue of section 99 of the Finance Act 1990 losses may be set off under subsection (1) of section 393 of the Taxes Act 1988 without the making of a claim, this section shall have effect as if references to the making of a claim under that subsection were references to the setting off of any loss under that subsection.][1]

Commentary—*Simon's Direct Tax Service* **D4.503, 513.**
Simon's Tax Cases—*Johnson v The Prudential Assurance Co Ltd* [1998] STC 439.
Modifications—Insertion of words "and capital redemption business" at the end of sub-s (3)(*b*) in applying life assurance provisions of the Corporation Tax Acts to insurance companies carrying on capital redemption business with effect for accounting periods ending after 30 June 1999: see Insurance Companies (Capital Redemption Business) (Modification of the Corporation Tax Acts) Regulations, SI 1999/498 reg 13.
Amendments—[1] Words in sub-s (6) inserted by FA 1993 Sch 14 para 9.
[2] Sub-s (2)(*a*) substituted by FA 1995 s 51, Sch 8 para 20(2), with effect for accounting periods beginning after 31 December 1994.
[3] Sub-s (2)(*d*) substituted by FA 1995 s 51, Sch 8 para 16(6), with effect for accounting periods beginning after 31 December 1994.
[4] Sub-s (2)(*b*), (*c*) and words in italics in sub-s (2)(*f*) repealed by FA 1996 Sch 41 Pt V(3) with effect for accounting periods ending after 31 March 1996, subject to transitional provisions in FA 1996 Sch 15.
[5] Sub-s (2)(*aa*), (*ab*) inserted by F(No 2)A 1997 s 23, Sch 3 para 15.

66 Banks etc in compulsory liquidation

Schedule 12 to this Act (which makes provision in relation to companies that are or have been carrying on a deposit-taking business and are in compulsory liquidation) shall have effect.

CHAPTER II
CAPITAL ALLOWANCES

67 Transfer of a UK trade

(*inserted CAA* 1990 s 152B, *repealed by* CAA 2001 s 580, Sch 4 with effect in accordance with CAA 2001 s 579).

68 Computer software

Amendment—This section repealed by the Capital Allowances Act 2001 s 580, Sch 4 with effect for income tax purposes, as respects allowances and charges falling to be made for chargeable periods ending after 5 April 2001, and for corporation tax purposes, as respects allowances and charges falling to be made for chargeable periods ending after 31 March 2001.

69 Films etc

Amendment—This section repealed by the Capital Allowances Act 2001 s 580, Sch 4 with effect for income tax purposes, as respects allowances and charges falling to be made for chargeable periods ending after 5 April 2001, and for corporation tax purposes, as respects allowances and charges falling to be made for chargeable periods ending after 31 March 2001.

70 Enterprise zones

Amendment—This section repealed by the Capital Allowances Act 2001 s 580, Sch 4 with effect for income tax purposes, as respects allowances and charges falling to be made for chargeable periods ending after 5 April 2001, and for corporation tax purposes, as respects allowances and charges falling to be made for chargeable periods ending after 31 March 2001.

71 Expensive motor cars

Amendment—This section repealed by the Capital Allowances Act 2001 s 580, Sch 4 with effect for income tax purposes, as respects allowances and charges falling to be made for chargeable periods ending after 5 April 2001, and for corporation tax purposes, as respects allowances and charges falling to be made for chargeable periods ending after 31 March 2001.

PART III
MISCELLANEOUS AND GENERAL
General and Special Commissioners

75 Change of name

(1) The Lord Chancellor may, with the consent of the [Secretary of State][1], make regulations providing for—

(*a*) Commissioners for the general purposes of the income tax to hold office by a different name (and to be referred to otherwise than as "General Commissioners"), and

(*b*) Commissioners for the special purposes of the Income Tax Acts to hold office by a different name (and to be referred to otherwise than as "Special Commissioners").

(2) The regulations may make such consequential amendments of any Act or instrument made under any Act as the Lord Chancellor thinks appropriate.

(3) Regulations under this section shall be made by statutory instrument subject to annulment in pursuance of a resolution of either House of Parliament.

Commentary—*Simon's Direct Tax Service* A2.501.
Amendments—¹ Words in sub-s (1) substituted by virtue of the Transfer of Functions (Lord Advocate and Secretary of State) Order, SI 1999/678 art 2(1), Sch with effect from 19 May 1999.

76 Miscellaneous

Schedule 16 to this Act (which makes provision in relation to the remuneration, jurisdiction, practice and procedure of the General and Special Commissioners etc) shall have effect.

Miscellaneous

77 Northern Ireland Electricity

Schedule 17 to this Act (which makes provision in relation to the transfer of the undertaking of Northern Ireland Electricity) shall have effect.

General

81 Interpretation

In this Act "the Taxes Act 1988" means the Income and Corporation Taxes Act 1988.

83 Short title

This Act may be cited as the Finance (No 2) Act 1992.

SCHEDULE 5

MARRIED COUPLE'S ALLOWANCE

Section 20

1 The Taxes Act 1988 shall be amended in accordance with paragraphs 2 to 8 below.

2 (*substitutes* ss 257BA, 257BB for s 257B).

3–7 (*amended* ss 257D, 257F, 259, 261A, 262; *repealed* by FA 1999 s 139, Sch 20 Pt III(3) with effect from the year 2000–01).

8 (*amends* s 265; *repealed in part* by FA 1994 s 258, Sch 26 Pt V(1)).

9—(1) The Taxes Management Act 1970 shall be amended as follows.

(2)–(4) (*insert* ss 36(3A), 43A(2A) and *amend* s 37A).

10 This Schedule shall apply in relation to tax for the year 1993–94 and subsequent years of assessment.

SCHEDULE 6

GROUP RELIEF ETC: AMENDMENTS

Section 24

Main amendments

1 (*substitutes* TA 1988 Sch 18 para 5A for Sch 18, para 5(5)).

2 (*inserts* TA 1988 Sch 18 paras 5B–5E).

Other amendments

3 (*Repealed* by FA 2000 s 156, Sch 40 Pt II(11) in accordance with FA 2000 Sch 27 para 6)).

4 In section 272 of the Income and Corporation Taxes Act 1970 (groups of companies: definitions) in subsection (1F) (application of Schedule 18 but without paragraph 5(3) etc) after "5(3)" there shall be inserted "and 5B to 5E".

5 (*amends* TCGA 1992 s 170).

Application of amendments

6—(1) Sub-paragraph (2) below shall apply where either of the following events occurs on or after 15th November 1991—

(*a*) any shares or securities of the relevant company are issued in circumstances where they carry both rights referred to in paragraph 4(1) of Schedule 18 and rights referred to in paragraph 5(1) of Schedule 18;

(*b*) any shares or securities of the relevant company issued before 15th November 1991 begin to carry both rights referred to in paragraph 4(1) of Schedule 18 and rights referred to in paragraph 5(1) of Schedule 18 (whether or not they previously carried rights referred to in one of those paragraphs).

(2) In such a case paragraph 1 above shall apply in relation to the accounting period in which the event occurs and subsequent accounting periods.

(3) In this paragraph—

    (*a*) references to the relevant company are to the second company referred to in paragraphs 2(1) and 3(1) of Schedule 18;

    (*b*) references to accounting periods are to accounting periods of that company.

7 Paragraph 2 above shall apply where the option arrangements are made on or after 15th November 1991.

8 Paragraph 3 above shall apply in accordance with paragraphs 6 and 7 above.

9 Subject to the repeals made by the Taxation of Chargeable Gains Act 1992 paragraph 4 above shall apply in accordance with paragraph 7 above.

10 The Taxation of Chargeable Gains Act 1992 shall have effect, and be deemed always to have had effect, with the amendment made by paragraph 5 above.

SCHEDULE 7

DEEP GAIN SECURITIES

Section 33

Amendments—This Schedule repealed by FA 1996 Sch 41 Pt V(3) with effect so far as relating to income tax from the year 1996–97 and so far as relating to corporation tax for accounting periods ending after 31 March 1996, subject to transitional provisions in FA 1996 Sch 15.

SCHEDULE 8

RIGHTS IN PURSUANCE OF DEPOSITS

Section 34

Disposal or exercise of rights

1 (*inserts* TA 1988 s 56A).

Building societies

2, 3 (*amend* TA 1988 ss 349, 477A).

Deposit-takers

4 (*inserts* TA 1988 s 481(5A)).

Accrued income scheme

5 (*inserts* TA 1988 s 710(3)(*da*)).

General

6 This Schedule shall apply in relation to arrangements made after the day on which this Act is passed.

SCHEDULE 9

FRIENDLY SOCIETIES

Section 56

Amendments of the Taxes Act 1988

1 The Taxes Act 1988 shall be amended in accordance with paragraphs 2 to 19 below.

2–13 (*amend* ss 266, 376, 459–461, 462, 463, 464 and *insert* ss 461A–461C. 462A(9), 465(6), 465A; (paras 3, 5(5)(*c*) and 6(*b*) *repealed by the* Financial Services and Markets Act 2000 (Consequential Amendments) (Taxes) Order, SI 2001/3629 art 109, Schedule *with effect from 1 December 2001*)).

14 (*amends* s 466 (sub-para (2) *repealed by* FA 1996 Sch 41 Pt V(28))).

15–17 (*amend* ss 539, 599, 630).

18—(1) Schedule 14 (provisions ancillary to section 266) shall be amended as follows.

(2), (3) (*amend* paras 2, 3).

19—(1) Schedule 15 (qualifying policies) shall be amended as follows.

(2)–(5) (*amends* para 3 (sub-para (3) *repealed* by FA 1995 Sch 29 Pt VIII(6))).

(6), (7) (*amend* paras 4, 6).

Amendments of enactments relating to chargeable gains

20—(1) (*inserts* CGTA 1979 ss 143A, 143B).

(2) (*amends* FA 1985 s 68 and FA 1988 Sch 8 para 1(3)).

21—(1) The Taxation of Chargeable Gains Act 1992 shall be amended as follows.

(2) (*amends* s 35).

(3) (*inserts* ss 217A–217C).

Commencement

22—(1) This Schedule shall come into force on such day as the Treasury may by order made by statutory instrument appoint, and different days may be appointed for different provisions or different purposes.

(2) An order under this paragraph may contain such transitional provisions and savings (whether or not involving the modification of any statutory provision) as appear to the Treasury necessary or expedient in connection with the provisions brought into force.

SCHEDULE 10

FURNISHED ACCOMMODATION

Section 59

Commentary—*Simon's Direct Tax Service* **B7.206A.**

Introduction

1 Paragraphs 2 to 8 below apply for the purposes of this Schedule.

2—(1) An individual is a qualifying individual for a year of assessment if apart from this Schedule he would be chargeable for the year to income tax [under Schedule A or Case I of Schedule D (or under both together)][1] in respect of all relevant sums accruing to him in respect of a qualifying residence or qualifying residences; and it is immaterial whether the sums are treated for income tax purposes as derived from one source or from two or more separate sources.

(2) Relevant sums are sums accruing in respect of the use of furnished accommodation in the residence or any of the residences or in respect of relevant goods or services supplied in connection with that use.

(3) In a case where—

   (*a*) the individual is chargeable for the year to income tax in respect of sums falling within sub-paragraph (4) below, and

   (*b*) any of those sums are treated for income tax purposes as derived from a source mentioned in sub-paragraph (1) above,

the individual is not a qualifying individual for the year (if he would be apart from this sub-paragraph).

(4) Sums fall within this sub-paragraph if they are not relevant sums accruing to the individual in respect of the residence or residences.

Revenue Internal Guidance—Property Income Manual PIM4002 (letting of room as office accommodation does not qualify for exemption).
Amendments—[1] Words in para 2(1) substituted by FA 1995 Sch 6 para 38, with effect from the year 1995–96. However, this amendment does not apply in relation to certain sources of income which ceased during the year 1995–96: see FA 1995 s 39(5).

3 As regards a year of assessment a period is a basis period for a source mentioned in paragraph 2(1) above if it is a period on whose profits or gains income tax for the year falls to be finally computed in respect of the source.

4 A residence is a qualifying residence if it is the individual's only or main residence at any time in any period which as regards the year of assessment concerned is a basis period for a source mentioned in paragraph 2(1) above.

Revenue Internal Guidance—Property Income Manual PIM4015 (taxpayer going abroad or occupying job-related accommodation unlikely to qualify: worked examples).

5—(1) This paragraph applies to determine an individual's limit for a year of assessment.

(2) Subject to the following provisions of this paragraph, the limit is the basic amount for the year.

(3) For the purposes of sub-paragraph (4) below a relevant period is—

(*a*) any period which as regards the year is a basis period for a source mentioned in paragraph 2(1) above;

(*b*) any period of one year which begins at the same time as any period which is less than one year and falls within paragraph (*a*) above;

(*c*) any period of one year which ends at the same time as any period which is less than one year and falls within paragraph (*a*) above.

(4) In a case where—

(*a*) at any time in a relevant period sums accrue to a person or persons other than the individual in respect of the use of residential accommodation in the residence or any of the residences, or in respect of relevant goods or services supplied in connection with that use, and

(*b*) at that time the residence concerned is the individual's only or main residence,

the limit is the amount equal to half the basic amount for the year.

Revenue Internal Guidance—Property Income Manual PIM4010 (joint ownership: each qualifying owner gets exemption equal to half the basic amount).
PIM4010, 4012 (where an individual has more than one qualifying source, rental income is aggregated and the basic amount is applied to the aggregate).

6 The basic amount for a year of assessment is—

(*a*) such sum as may be specified for the year by order made by the Treasury;

(*b*) £3,250 if no sum is so specified.

Note—The sum specified pursuant to sub-para (*a*) with effect from the year 1997/98 is £4,250 (IT (Furnished Accommodation) (Basic Amount) Order 1996, SI 1996/2953). For previous years, no sum was so specified.

7 "Residence" means a building, or part of a building, occupied or intended to be occupied as a separate residence, or a caravan or house-boat; but a building, or part of a building, which is designed for permanent use as a single residence shall be treated as a single residence notwithstanding that it is temporarily divided into two or more parts which are occupied or intended to be occupied as separate residences.

Revenue Internal Guidance—Property Income Manual PIM4002 (words following semi-colon do not, in the Revenue's view, allow the letting of a room as office accommodation to qualify for relief).
PIM4004 (meaning of "temporary division").

8 Relevant goods and services are meals, cleaning, laundry and goods and services of a similar nature.

Exemption etc

9—(1) This paragraph applies if—

(*a*) an individual is a qualifying individual for a year of assessment,

(*b*) the amount of the sums mentioned in paragraph 2(1) above does not exceed the individual's limit for the year, and

(*c*) no election that this paragraph shall not apply to the individual for the year has effect under paragraph 10 below.

(2) Where this paragraph applies the following shall be treated as nil for the purposes of the Tax Acts—

(*a*) the profits or gains of any period which as regards the year is a basis period for a source mentioned in paragraph 2(1) above;

(*b*) the losses of any such period.

(3) Where this paragraph applies no allowance or balancing charge shall be made for the year to or on the individual under [section 55 of the Capital Allowances Act][1] in respect of any [plant or machinery][1] provided for the purposes of any trade from which any of the sums mentioned in paragraph 2(1) above are derived.

(4) In a case where—

(*a*) apart from this sub-paragraph the preceding provisions of this paragraph would apply, and

(*b*) the amount of the sums mentioned in paragraph 2(1) above together with the amount of any relevant balancing charges would exceed the individual's limit for the year,

the preceding provisions of this paragraph shall not apply.

(5) For the purposes of sub-paragraph (4) above a relevant balancing charge is a balancing charge which (apart from this paragraph) would be made for the year on the individual under [section 55 of the Capital Allowances Act][1] in respect of any [plant or machinery][1] provided for the purposes of any trade from which any of the sums mentioned in paragraph 2(1) above are derived.

(6) In ascertaining the amount of sums for the purposes of this paragraph no deduction shall be made in respect of expenses or any other matter.

Revenue Internal Guidance—Property Income Manual PIM4020 (limit applies to the amount of "all relevant sums" including sums from the provision of meals, goods and services provided in connection with the accommodation, such as cleaning and laundry services).
PIM4040 (use of exemption cannot create a loss; if there is a loss then election under para 10 in point).

Amendments—[1] Words in sub-paras (3), (5) substituted by CAA 2001 s 578, Sch 2 paras 86(1), (2) with effect for income tax purposes, as respects allowances and charges falling to be made for chargeable periods ending after 5 April 2001, and for corporation tax purposes, as respects allowances and charges falling to be made for chargeable periods ending after 31 March 2001.

10—(1) An individual may elect that paragraph 9 above shall not apply to him for a year of assessment, and (unless withdrawn) the election shall have effect accordingly.

(2) An election under this paragraph shall have effect only for the year of assessment for which it is made.

(3) An individual who has made an election under this paragraph for a year of assessment may give a notice to withdraw the election, and if he does so the election shall not have effect for that year.

(4) An election, or notice of withdrawal, under this paragraph—

    (a) must be made or given [on or before—

        (i) the first anniversary of the 31st January next following the year of assessment concerned, or

        (ii) such later date as the Board may in any particular case allow, and][1]

    (b) must be made or given in writing to [an officer of the Board][1].

(5) In a case where—

    (a) an election is made, or a notice to withdraw an election is given, under this paragraph, and

    (b) in order to give effect to the election or its withdrawal it is necessary to make an adjustment by way of an assessment.

the assessment shall not be out of time if it is made [on or before the first anniversary of the 31st January next following the year of assessment in which][1] the election was made or (as the case may be) the notice to withdraw was given.

Revenue Internal Guidance—Property Income Manual PIM4020 (election appropriate where loss arises or potential capital allowances exceed income).
PIM4050 (circumstances in which late election accepted; Revenue procedure).
Amendments—[1] Words in para 10(4)(a), (b), (5) substituted by FA 1996 s 135(1), (2) Sch 21 para 47(1)–(3) with effect from the year 1996–97.

Adjusted profits etc

11—(1) This paragraph applies if—

    (a) an individual is a qualifying individual for a year of assessment.

    (b) the amount of the sums mentioned in paragraph 2(1) above exceeds the individual's limit for the year, and

    (c) an election that this paragraph shall apply to the individual for the year has effect under paragraph 12 below.

(2) In a case where—

    (a) this paragraph applies, and

    (b) the sums mentioned in paragraph 2(1) above are treated for income tax purposes as derived from a single source,

the profits or gains of any period which as regards the year is a basis period for the source shall be treated for the purposes of Tax Acts as equal to the amount found by deducting amount B from amount A.

(3) For the purposes of sub-paragraph (2) above—

    (a) amount A is the amount of the sums mentioned in paragraph 2(1) above;

    (b) amount B is the amount of the individual's limit for year.

(4) In a case where—

    (a) this paragraph applies, and

    (b) the sums mentioned in paragraph 2(1) above are treated for income tax purposes as derived from two or more separate sources,

the profits or gains of any period which as regards the year is a basis period for a separate source shall be treated for the purposes of the Tax Acts as equal to the amount found by deducting amount D from amount C.

(5) For the purposes of sub-paragraph (4) above—

    (a) amount C is the amount of such of the sums mentioned in paragraph 2(1) above as are treated for income tax purposes as derived from the separated source, and

    (b) amount D is the amount found by multiplying the amount of the individual's limit for the year by the appropriate fraction;

and the appropriate fraction is the fraction whose numerator is equal to the number of pounds in amount C and whose denominator is equal to the number of pounds in the sums mentioned in paragraph 2(1) above.

(6) Where this paragraph applies no allowance shall be made for the year to the individual under [section 55 of the Capital Allowances Act][1] in respect of any [plant or machinery][1] provided for the purposes of any trade from which any of the sums mentioned in paragraph 2(1) above are derived.

(7) In ascertaining the amount of sums for the purposes of this paragraph no deduction shall be made in respect of expenses or any other matter.

Amendments—¹ Words in sub-para (6) substituted by CAA 2001 s 578, Sch 2 para 86(3) with effect for income tax purposes, as respects allowances and charges falling to be made for chargeable periods ending after 5 April 2001, and for corporation tax purposes, as respects allowances and charges falling to be made for chargeable periods ending after 31 March 2001.

12—(1) An individual may elect that paragraph 11 above shall apply to him for a year of assessment.

(2) An election under this paragraph—

  (a) shall (unless withdrawn) have effect for the year of assessment for which it is made and for subsequent years of assessment,

  (b) must be made [on or before—

    (i) the first anniversary of the 31st January next following the year of assessment for which it is made, or

    (ii) such later date as the Board may in any particular case allow, and]¹

  (c) must be made in writing to [an officer of the Board]¹.

(3) An individual who has made an election under this paragraph may give a notice to withdraw the election, and if he does so, the election shall not have effect for the year of assessment for which the notice is given or any subsequent year.

(4) A notice of withdrawal under this paragraph—

  (a) must be given [on or before—

    (i) the first anniversary of the 31st January next following the year of assessment for which it is given, or

    (ii) such later date as the Board may in any particular case allow,]¹

  (b) must be given in writing to [an officer of the Board]¹, and

  (c) shall not prejudice the making of a fresh election for any subsequent year of assessment.

(5) Sub-paragraph (6) below applies where—

  (a) an individual is a qualifying individual for a year of assessment,

  (b) the amount of the sums mentioned in paragraph 2(1) above does not exceed the individual's limit for the year, and

  (c) an election under this paragraph has effect (apart from sub-paragraph (6) below) for the year.

(6) In such a case—

  (a) the individual shall be deemed to have given notice to withdraw the election for the year of assessment concerned,

  (b) the notice shall be deemed to have been given on the [first anniversary of the 31st January next following]¹ the year of assessment concerned, and

  (c) sub-paragraphs (3) and (4)(c) above and (7) below shall apply accordingly.

(7) In a case where—

  (a) an election is made, or a notice to withdraw an election is given, under this paragraph, and

  (b) in order to give effect to the election or its withdrawal it is necessary to make an adjustment by way of an assessment,

the assessment shall not be out of time if it is made [on or before the first anniversary of the 31st January next following the year of assessment in which]¹ the election was made or (as the case may be) the notice to withdraw was given.

Revenue Internal Guidance—Property Income Manual PIM4050 (circumstances in which late election accepted; Revenue procedure).
Amendments—¹ Words in para 12(2)(b), (c), (4)(a), (b), (6)(b), (7) substituted by FA 1996 s 135(1), (2) Sch 21 para 47(1), (4)–(7) with effect from the year 1996–97.

Application of Schedule

13 This Schedule shall apply in relation to the year 1992–93 and subsequent years of assessment (whatever the basis period or periods for the source or sources mentioned in paragraph 2(1) above may be as regards the year of assessment concerned).

SCHEDULE 11

PAYING AND COLLECTING AGENTS ETC
Section 63

1–2 (*Repealed* by FA 1996 Sch 41 Pt V(2) with effect from the year 1996–97).

3 (*amends* TMA 1970 s 86).

4–5 (*Repealed* by FA 1996 Sch 41 Pt V(2) with effect from the year 1996–97).

6 This Schedule shall have effect in relation to transactions effected on or after 1st October 1992.

SCHEDULE 12

BANKS ETC IN COMPULSORY LIQUIDATION

Section 66

Commentary—*Simon's Direct Tax Service* **D4.1121.**

Introductory

1—(1) This Schedule applies where—

(*a*) a company is being, or has been, wound up by the court in the United Kingdom,

(*b*) the company was, at any time in the period mentioned in sub-paragraph (2) below, lawfully carrying on a [business of accepting deposits as—

(i) a person falling within section 840A(1)(*b*) of the Taxes Act 1988, or

(ii) an EEA firm of the kind mentioned in paragraph 5(*b*) of Schedule 3 to the Financial Services and Markets Act 2000 with permission under paragraph 15 of that Schedule (as a result of qualifying for authorisation by virtue of paragraph 12 of that Schedule) to accept deposits,][1]

(*c*) the trade of the company that included the [business of accepting deposits][1] (referred to in this Schedule as "the relevant trade") has been permanently discontinued, and

(*d*) the company is insolvent and either was so when the winding-up proceedings were commenced or became so at any time in the period of twelve months following the day on which they were commenced.

(2) The period mentioned in sub-paragraph (1)(*b*) above is the period of twelve months ending with—

(*a*) the day on which the winding-up proceedings were commenced, or

(*b*) the day on which the relevant trade was discontinued,

whichever was the earlier.

Amendments—[1] Words in sub-para (1) substituted by the Financial Services and Markets Act 2000 (Consequential Amendments) (Taxes) Order, SI 2001/3629 art 74 effect for—

(*a*) any period mentioned in sub-para (2) above ("a relevant period") which begins after 30 November 2001; or
(*b*) any part of a relevant period which falls after that date.

2—(1) Sub-paragraphs (2) to (5) below apply for the purposes of this Schedule.

(2) "Company" means—

(*a*) any company as defined in section 735 of the Companies Act 1985 or Article 3 of the Companies (Northern Ireland) Order 1986, or

(*b*) any unregistered company as defined in section 220 of the Insolvency Act 1986 or Article 184 of the Insolvency (Northern Ireland) Order 1989.

(3) Winding-up proceedings shall be taken to have been commenced against a company at the time of the presentation of the petition for its winding up by the court.

(4) A company's ceasing to carry on a trade, or to be within the charge to corporation tax in respect of a trade, shall be treated as the permanent discontinuance of the trade, whether or not the trade is in fact discontinued.

(5) A company shall be taken to be insolvent, or to have been insolvent at any time, if—

(*a*) it is unable to pay its debts as they fall due, or was at that time unable to pay its debts as they fell due, or

(*b*) the value of its assets is, or was at that time, less than the amount of its liabilities (taking into account its contingent and prospective liabilities).

Taxation of certain receipts under Case VI of Schedule D

3—(1) Tax shall be charged under Case VI of Schedule D in respect of any sums within sub-paragraph (2) below that are received by the company or its liquidator after—

(*a*) the commencement of the winding-up proceedings, or

(*b*) the discontinuance of the relevant trade,

whichever was the later.

(2) Subject to sub-paragraph (3) below, any sum arising from the carrying on of the relevant trade is within this sub-paragraph, insofar as its value was not brought into account in computing the profits or gains of the trade for any period before the discontinuance.

(3) The following are not within sub-paragraph (2) above—

(*a*) any sum received on behalf of a person who is entitled to it to the exclusion of the company and its liquidator;

(*b*) any sum realised by the transfer of an asset required to be valued under section 100 of the Taxes Act 1988 (valuation of trading stock at discontinuance);

(*c*) ...[2]

(4) Where tax is chargeable in respect of any sum by virtue of this paragraph, any other provision charging that sum to tax shall not apply.

[(5) This paragraph and paragraph 4 below have effect for the purposes of corporation tax notwithstanding anything in section 80(5) of the Finance Act 1996 (matters to be brought into account in the case of loan relationships only under Chapter 2 of Part 4 of that Act).]²

Amendment—¹ Word "profits" in sub-para (3)(c) substituted for "profits or gains" by FA 1998 Sch 7 para 8 with effect from 31 July 1998.
² Sub-para (3)(c) repealed, and sub-para (5) inserted, by FA 2002 ss 107(1)–(3), 5), 141, Sch 40 Pt 3(18) with effect for accounting periods beginning after 30 September 2002. Sub-para (3)(c) previously read as follows—

"(c) any interest or dividend that, by reason of its having been subjected to tax under other provisions, would not have been taken into account under Case I of Schedule D in computing the [profits]¹ of the relevant trade, had it continued.".

Relief from tax

4—(1) In computing the tax that is chargeable by virtue of paragraph 3 above for any chargeable period, there shall be deducted from the amount that would otherwise be chargeable to tax the aggregate amount of all losses, expenses and debits within sub-paragraph (2) below incurred in that chargeable period or before it, in so far as relief (whether under this sub-paragraph, sub-paragraph (3) below or any other provision of the Tax Acts) has not been given in respect of them already.

(2) Any loss, expense or debit (other than a loss, expense or debit arising directly or indirectly from the discontinuance itself) incurred—

   (*a*) after the later of the two events mentioned in paragraph 3(1) above, or
   (*b*) in the case of a loss, at or before the discontinuance of the relevant trade,

is within this sub-paragraph if it would have been deducted in computing for tax purposes the [profits]¹ of the trade for any period, or deducted from or set off against those [profits]¹ as so computed, had the trade continued.

(3) ...²

Amendment—¹ Word in sub-para (2) substituted by FA 1998 Sch 7 para 8 with effect from 31 July 1998.
² Sub-para (3) repealed by FA 2002 ss 107(1), (4), (5), 141, Sch 40 Pt 3(18) with effect for accounting periods beginning after 30 September 2002. Sub-para (3) previously read as follows—

"(3) If the aggregate amount exceeds the amount from which it is to be deducted under sub-paragraph (1) above, the company or its liquidator may make a claim requiring the excess to be deducted from or set off against the amount assessed to tax for the chargeable period in respect of any sums—

(*a*) received after the later of the two events mentioned in paragraph 3(1) above, and
(*b*) excluded from paragraph 3(2) above by paragraph 3(3)(c) above,
and relief, by repayment or otherwise, shall be given in respect of the excess accordingly.".

Application of charge etc where rights to payments transferred

5 Where the right of the company or its liquidator to receive any sum which is within paragraph 3(2) above (or which would be, if the right to receive it were not transferred) is transferred for value, any tax chargeable by virtue of paragraph 3 above shall be charged in respect of the amount or value of the consideration (or, in the case of a transfer otherwise than at arm's length, in respect of the value of the right transferred as between parties at arm's length); and references in this Schedule to sums received shall be construed accordingly.

Election for carry-back

6—(1) Where any sum is—

   (*a*) chargeable to tax by virtue of paragraph 3 above, and
   (*b*) received in any chargeable period beginning in the period of six years following the day on which the relevant trade was discontinued,

the company or its liquidator may, by notice sent to the inspector within two years after that chargeable period, elect that the tax so chargeable shall be charged as if the sum in question were received on the day on which the trade was discontinued.

(2) Where such an election has been made, an assessment shall (notwithstanding anything in the Tax Acts) be made accordingly.

Commencement

7 This Schedule shall have effect in relation to chargeable periods ending after 10th March 1992.

SCHEDULE 13

CAPITAL ALLOWANCES: ENTERPRISE ZONES

Section 70

Commentary—*Simon's Direct Tax Service* **B2.263.**
Amendment—This Schedule repealed by the Capital Allowances Act 2001 s 580, Sch 4 with effect for income tax purposes, as respects allowances and charges falling to be made for chargeable periods ending after 5 April 2001, and for corporation tax purposes, as respects allowances and charges falling to be made for chargeable periods ending after 31 March 2001.

SCHEDULE 16

GENERAL AND SPECIAL COMMISSIONERS

Section 76

1 The Taxes Management Act 1970 shall be amended in accordance with paragraphs 2 to 5 below.

Remuneration of General Commissioners etc

2 (*substitutes* ss 2(5), 3(2) and *amends* s 3(3)).

Jurisdiction

3 (*inserts* s 46A).

Practice and procedure

4, 5 (*insert* ss 56B–56D and *repeal* s 57B).

Oil taxation appeals

6–7 (see PRT section of *Yellow Tax Handbook, Part II*)

Inheritance tax appeals

8 (see IHT section of *Yellow Tax Handbook, Part II*).

SCHEDULE 17

NORTHERN IRELAND ELECTRICITY

Section 77

Commentary—*Simon's Direct Tax Service* **B3.246; D2.411.**

Interpretation

1—(1) In this Schedule—

"the final accounting period" means the last complete accounting period of NIE ending before the transfer date;

"NIE" means Northern Ireland Electricity;

"the Order" means the Electricity (Northern Ireland) Order 1992;

"successor company" means a company nominated under Article 69(2) of the Order for the purposes of Article 69(1) of the Order;

"transfer date" means the day appointed under Article 69(3) of the Order for the purposes of Article 69(4) of the Order;

"transfer scheme" means a scheme under Article 69(1) of the Order.

(2) This Schedule, so far as it relates to corporation tax on chargeable gains, shall be construed as one with the Capital Gains Tax Act 1979 or, where appropriate, the Taxation of Chargeable Gains Act 1992.

(3) For the purposes of this Schedule a transfer or agreement shall be regarded as made in pursuance of Schedule 10 to the Order if the making of that transfer or agreement is required or authorised by or under paragraph 3 or 5 of that Schedule (allocation of assets and liabilities and variation of transfers by agreement).

Transfer to successor companies: general

2—(1) Subject to sub-paragraph (2) below, the following provisions shall apply for the purposes of the Corporation Tax Acts, namely—

(*a*) any part of the trade carried on by NIE which is transferred by the Order to a successor company shall be treated as having been, at the time when it began to be carried on by NIE or any predecessor and at all times since that time, a separate trade carried on by the successor company;

(*b*) the trade carried on by a successor company after the transfer date shall be treated as the same trade as that which, by virtue of paragraph (*a*) above, it is treated as having carried on before that date;

(*c*) all property, rights and liabilities of NIE which are transferred by the Order to a successor company shall be treated as having been, at the time when they became vested in NIE or any predecessor and at all times since that time, property, rights and liabilities of the successor company; and (*d*) anything done by NIE or any predecessor in relation to any property, rights and liabilities which are transferred by the Order to a successor company shall be deemed to have been done by the successor company.

(2) There shall be made such apportionments of unallowed tax losses, and of expenditure by reference to which capital allowances may be made, as may be specified in the transfer scheme.

(3) In sub-paragraph (2) above "unallowed tax losses" means any losses, allowances or amounts which, as at the end of the final accounting period, are tax losses within the meaning given by section 400(2)(*a*), (*c*) or (*d*) of the Taxes Act 1988.

(4) This paragraph shall have effect in relation to accounting periods beginning after the final accounting period.

Roll-over relief

3 Where NIE has before the transfer date disposed of (or of its interest in) any assets used, throughout the period of ownership, wholly or partly for the purposes of the part of its trade transferred by the Order to a successor company, sections 115 to 119 of the Capital Gains Tax Act 1979 or, where appropriate, sections 152 to 156 of the Taxation of Chargeable Gains Act 1992 (roll-over relief on replacement of business assets) shall have effect in relation to that disposal as if NIE and the successor company were the same person.

Unallowed capital losses

4—(1) Any unallowed capital losses of NIE shall be apportioned between the successor companies in accordance with the transfer scheme; and any such losses which are so apportioned to a successor company shall be treated as allowable capital losses accruing to the successor company on the disposal of an asset on the transfer date.

(2) In sub-paragraph (1) above—

    "allowable capital losses" means losses which are allowable losses for the purposes of corporation tax on chargeable gains;

    "unallowed capital losses" means any allowable capital losses which have accrued to NIE before the transfer date, in so far as they have not been allowed as deductions from chargeable gains.

Arrangements in favour of other successor companies

5—(1) Sub-paragraph (3) below applies to any disposal of an asset which is effected, and sub-paragraphs (4) to (6) below apply to any lease which is granted, in pursuance of a provision included in the transfer scheme by virtue of Article 70(1)(*c*) of the Order (scheme may require successor company to enter into arrangements in favour of any other successor company).

(2) Sub-paragraph (3) below also applies to any disposal of an asset which is effected in pursuance of an agreement under paragraph 3(2) of Schedule 10 to the Order and which is either the grant of a lease of land or the creation of other liabilities and rights over land.

(3) A disposal to which this sub-paragraph applies shall be taken for the purposes of corporation tax on chargeable gains to be effected for a consideration of such amount as would secure that on the disposal neither a gain nor a loss would accrue to the successor company making the disposal.

(4) Section 38(1)(*a*) and (4) of the Taxes Act 1988 (rules for ascertaining duration of leases) shall be disregarded in determining for the purposes of [section 290 of the Capital Allowances Act 2001 (election to treat grant of lease exceeding 50 years as sale)][1] whether a lease to which this sub-paragraph applies is a [lease which satisfies the condition in subsection (1)(*c*)][1] of that section; in relation to any such lease which is, on that basis, such a long lease—

    (*a*) the lessee shall be deemed for the purposes of that section to have paid in consideration for the grant of the lease a capital sum of an amount equal to the residue of expenditure immediately before the lease takes effect, computed in accordance with [Chapter 8 of Part 3][1] of that Act, and

    (*b*) [section 291(1)][1] of that Act shall be disregarded;

and [sections 567 to 570][1] of that Act shall not apply in relation to the grant of a lease in respect of which, by virtue of this sub-paragraph, an election is made under [section 290] of that Act.

(5) Where the conditions in [section 183(1)(*a*) and (*b*) of the Capital Allowances Act (incoming lessee where lessor entitled to allowances)][1] are fulfilled in relation to a lease to which this sub-paragraph applies—

    (*a*) the lessee shall be deemed to have given as consideration for the lease a capital sum which falls to be treated for the purposes of [Part 2 of that Act][1] as expenditure on the provision of the fixture concerned; [and][1]

    (*b*) the amount of that capital sum shall be equal to the amount of expenditure which is attributed to the fixture concerned for the purposes of apportioning, in accordance with the transfer scheme, expenditure by reference to which capital allowances may be made; ...[1]

    (*c*) ...[1]

(6) Section 38(1)(*a*) and (4) of the Taxes Act 1988 shall be disregarded in ascertaining for the purposes of section 35 of that Act (Schedule D charge on assignment of lease granted at an undervalue) the duration of a lease to which this sub-paragraph applies.

(7) Subject to the repeals made by the Taxation of Chargeable Gains Act 1992 in section 68(7A) of the Finance Act 1985 (modification of indexation allowance: list of no gain/no loss provisions) there shall be added after paragraph (i) the words

"and
(*j*) paragraph 5(3) of Schedule 17 to the Finance (No 2) Act 1992."

(8) Subject to the repeals made by the Taxation of Chargeable Gains Act 1992 in paragraph 1(3) of Schedule 8 to the Finance Act 1988 (rebasing to 1982: list of no gain/no loss provisions) there shall be added after paragraph (i) the words

"and
(*j*) paragraph 5(3) of Schedule 17 to the Finance (No 2) Act 1992."

(9) Section 35(3)(*d*) of the Taxation of Chargeable Gains Act 1992 (assets held on 31st March 1982: list of no gain/no loss provisions) shall have effect, and be deemed always to have had effect, with the omission of the word "and" at the end of sub-paragraph (vi) and the addition after sub-paragraph (vii) of the words

"and
(viii) paragraph 5(3) of Schedule 17 to the Finance (No 2) Act 1992."

Amendments—[1] Words in sub-paras (4), (5) substituted, word "and" in sub-para (5)(*a*) added, word "and" and sub-para (5)(*c*) repealed, by CAA 2001 ss 578, 580, Sch 2 paras 87(1), (2), Sch 4 with effect for corporation tax purposes, as respects allowances and charges falling to be made for chargeable periods ending after 31 March 2001.

Restriction of losses by reference to capital allowances

6—(1) Where by virtue of sub-paragraph (4) of paragraph 5 above an election is made under [section 290 of the Capital Allowances Act 2001][1] in respect of a lease to which that sub-paragraph applies, sub-paragraph (2) and, if the relevant condition is met, sub-paragraph (3) below shall apply; and for the purposes of this sub-paragraph the relevant condition is that, as a result of a disposal by the lessee in relevant circumstances, section 275(1) of the Income and Corporation Taxes Act 1970 or section 174(1) of the Taxation of Chargeable Gains Act 1992 applies in relation to a subsequent disposal.

(2) Where this sub-paragraph applies, section 34 of the Capital Gains Tax Act 1979 or, as the case may be, section 41 of the Taxation of Chargeable Gains Act 1992 (restriction of losses by reference to capital allowances etc) shall apply in relation to any disposal by the lessee as if any capital allowance made to—

(*a*) NIE or any predecessor, or
(*b*) the lessor,

in respect of expenditure incurred on the construction of the building or structure comprised in the lease had been made to the lessee.

(3) Where this sub-paragraph applies, section 275(1) of the Income and Corporation Taxes Act 1970 or, as the case may be, section 174(1) of the Taxation of Chargeable Gains Act 1992 shall apply as if the reference to capital allowances made to the person from which the asset was acquired included capital allowances made to—

(*a*) NIE or any predecessor, or
(*b*) the lessor,

in respect of expenditure incurred on the construction of the building or structure comprised in the lease but only so far as not taken into account in relation to any previous disposal.

(4) Where by virtue of sub-paragraph (5) of paragraph 5 above an election is made under [section 183 of the Capital Allowances Act 2001][1] in respect of a lease to which that sub-paragraph applies, sub-paragraph (5) and, if the relevant condition is met, sub-paragraph (6) below shall apply; and the relevant condition for the purposes of this sub-paragraph is the same as the relevant condition for the purposes of sub-paragraph (1) above.

(5) Where this sub-paragraph applies, section 34 of the Capital Gains Tax Act 1979 or, as the case may be, section 41 of the Taxation of Chargeable Gains Act 1992 shall apply in relation to any disposal by the lessee as if any capital allowance made to—

(*a*) NIE or any predecessor, or
(*b*) the lessor,

in respect of expenditure incurred on the provision of the fixture comprised in the lease had been made to the lessee.

(6) Where this sub-paragraph applies, section 275(1) of the Income and Corporation Taxes Act 1970 or, as the case may be, section 174(1) of the Taxation of Chargeable Gains Act 1992 shall apply as if the reference to capital allowances made to the person from which the asset was acquired included capital allowances made to—

(*a*) NIE or any predecessor, or
(*b*) the lessor,

in respect of expenditure incurred on the provision of the fixture comprised in the lease but only so far as not taken into account in relation to any previous disposal.

Amendments—¹ Words in sub-paras (1), (4) substituted by CAA 2001 s 578, Sch 2 paras 87(3), (4) with effect for income tax purposes, as respects allowances and charges falling to be made for chargeable periods ending after 5 April 2001, and for corporation tax purposes, as respects allowances and charges falling to be made for chargeable periods ending after 31 March 2001.

Transfers between successor companies

7 Where any property, rights and liabilities transferred by the Order to a successor company (the first company) are, in pursuance of Schedule 10 to the Order, transferred to another successor company (the second company)—

(*a*) the preceding provisions of this Schedule shall have effect as if the transfer effected by the Order had been a transfer to the second company; and

(*b*) anything which, in relation to the property, rights and liabilities transferred in pursuance of that Schedule, was done by the first company for the purposes of its trade shall be deemed to have been done by the second company for the purposes of its trade.

Apportionments etc

8—(1) This paragraph applies where any apportionment or other matter arising under the preceding provisions of this Schedule appears to be material as respects the liability to tax (for whatever period) of two or more successor companies.

(2) Any question which arises as to the manner in which the apportionment is to be made or the matter is to be dealt with shall be determined, or the purposes of the tax of the successor companies concerned—

(*a*) in a case where the same body of General Commissioners have jurisdiction with respect to the companies concerned, by those Commissioners, unless the companies agree that it shall be determined by the Special Commissioners;

(*b*) in a case where different bodies of General Commissioners have jurisdiction with respect to the companies concerned, by such of those bodies as the Board may direct, unless the companies agree that it shall be determined by the Special Commissioners; and

(*c*) in any other case, by the Special Commissioners.

(3) The Commissioners by whom the question falls to be determined shall make the determination in like manner as if it were an appeal except that the successor companies concerned shall be entitled to appear and be heard by the Commissioners or to make representations to them in writing.

Securities of successor companies

9—(1) Any share issued by a successor company in pursuance of Article 73 of the Order (initial government holding in successor companies) shall be treated for the purposes of the Corporation Tax Acts as if it had been issued wholly in consideration of a subscription paid to the company of an amount equal to the nominal value of the share.

(2) Any debenture issued by a successor company in pursuance of Article 73 of the Order shall be treated for the purposes of the Corporation Tax Acts as if it had been issued—

(*a*) wholly in consideration of a loan made to the company of an amount equal to the principal sum payable under the debenture; and

(*b*) wholly and exclusively for the purposes of the trade carried on by the company.

(3) If any such debenture includes provision for the payment of a sum expressed as interest in respect of a period which falls wholly or partly before the issue of the debenture, any payment made in pursuance of that provision in respect of that period shall be treated for the purposes of the Corporation Tax Acts as if the debenture had been issued at the commencement of that period and, accordingly, as interest on the principal sum payable under the debenture.

Stamp duty reserve tax

10 (see *Orange Tax Handbook*).

FINANCE ACT 1993

(1993 Chapter 34)

ARRANGEMENT OF SECTIONS

PART II
INCOME TAX, CORPORATION TAX AND CAPITAL GAINS TAX

CHAPTER I
GENERAL

CHAPTER II

EXCHANGE GAINS AND LOSSES

Accrual of gains and losses

An Act to grant certain duties, to alter other duties, and to amend the law relating to the National Debt and the Public Revenue, and to make further provision in connection with Finance.
[27th July 1993]

PART II
INCOME TAX, CORPORATION TAX AND CAPITAL GAINS TAX

CHAPTER I
GENERAL

Income tax: charge, rates and allowances

51 Charge and rates of income tax for 1993–94
(Spent).

Commentary—*Simon's Direct Tax Service* **E1.102.**

52 Personal and married couple's allowances
(Spent).

Commentary—*Simon's Direct Tax Service* **E2.201, 202, 302, 303.**

Corporation tax charge and rate

53 Charge and rate of corporation tax for 1993
(Spent).

Commentary—*Simon's Direct Tax Service* **D2.108.**

54 Small companies

(*Spent*).

Commentary—*Simon's Direct Tax Service* **D2.109.**

Interest: general

55 Relief for interest

(*Spent*).

Commentary—*Simon's Direct Tax Service* **E1.539.**

56 Interest relief: substitution of security

(*Inserts* TA 1988 ss 357A, 357B, 357C).

Amendment—This section repealed by FA 1999 s 139, Sch 20 Pt III (7) with effect for payments of interest within FA 1999 s 38(3), (4).

57 Temporary relief for interest payments

(1), (2) ...²

(3) (*inserts* TA 1988 s 365(1A), (1B)).

(4) ...²

(5) This section shall have effect in relation to payments of interest made on or after 16th March 1993 (whenever falling due).

(6) ...²

(7) ...¹

Commentary—*Simon's Direct Tax Service* **A3.431; E1.539, 553.**
Amendments—¹ Sub-s (7) repealed by FA 1994 s 81(5), (6), Sch 9 para 12 and Sch 26, Pt V(2) for payments of interest made after 5 April 1994, whenever falling due (and for relevant loan interest due after 5 April 1994 but paid between 30 November 1993 and 5 April 1994).
² Sub-ss (1), (2), (4), (6) repealed by FA 1999 s 139, Sch 20 Pt III(7) with effect for payments of interest within FA 1999 s 38(3), (4).

58 Overclaims in respect of deductions of mortgage interest

(1) (*inserts* TA 1988 s 369(7)).

(2) This section shall not apply in relation to any payment if the payment, or the claim on which it is made, was made before the day on which this Act is passed.

Commentary—*Simon's Direct Tax Service* **A3.433.**

59 Interest payments to persons not ordinarily resident in UK

(*Inserts* TA 1988 s 349(3)(*h*)).

60 Certain interest not allowed as a deduction

(1) This section applies where—

(a) a qualifying company becomes subject to a qualifying debt, and

(b) the interest payable exceeds a commercial return on the capital repayable, expressing that capital in the settlement currency of the debt.

(2) In computing the corporation tax chargeable for an accounting period of the company, so much of the excess interest as is paid in the accounting period shall not be allowed as a deduction against the total profits for the period (if it would be allowed apart from this section).

(3) In this section—

"qualifying company" has the meaning given by section 152 below;

"qualifying debt" has the meaning given by section 153(10) below;

"settlement currency", in relation to a debt, shall be construed in accordance with section 161 below.

(4) This section applies where the company becomes subject to the debt (whether as the original debtor or otherwise) on or after the day which is its commencement day for the purposes of section 165 below.

Revenue Internal Guidance—Company Taxation Manual COT13902 (worked example).
Amendment—This section repealed by FA 2002 s 141, Sch 40 Pt 3 (10) with effect for accounting periods beginning after 30 September 2002.

Interest etc on debts between associated companies

61 Qualifying debts for purposes of sections 63 to 66

Commentary—*Simon's Direct Tax Service* **D2.225.**
Amendments—This section repealed by FA 1996 Sch 41 Pt V(3) with effect for accounting periods ending after 31 March 1996, subject to transitional provisions in FA 1996 Sch 15.

62 Exempted debts for those purposes

Commentary—*Simon's Direct Tax Service* **D2.225.**
Amendments—This section repealed by FA 1996 Sch 41 Pt V(3) with effect for accounting periods ending after 31 March 1996, subject to transitional provisions in FA 1996 Sch 15.

[62A Application of sections 63 to 66: supplementary]

Commentary—*Simon's Direct Tax Service* **D2.225.**
Amendments—This section (inserted by FA 1995 s 88(2)) repealed by FA 1996 Sch 41 Pt V(3) with effect for accounting periods ending after 31 March 1996, subject to transitional provisions in FA 1996 Sch 15.

63 Accrued income securities

Commentary—*Simon's Direct Tax Service* **D2.225.**
Amendments—This section repealed by FA 1996 Sch 41 Pt V(3) with effect for accounting periods ending after 31 March 1996, subject to transitional provisions in FA 1996 Sch 15.

64 Deep discount securities

Commentary—*Simon's Direct Tax Service* **D2.225.**
Amendments—This section repealed by FA 1996 Sch 41 Pt V(3) with effect for accounting periods ending after 31 March 1996, subject to transitional provisions in FA 1996 Sch 15.

65 Deep gain securities

Commentary—*Simon's Direct Tax Service* **D2.225.**
Amendments—This section repealed by FA 1996 Sch 41 Pt V(3) with effect for accounting periods ending after 31 March 1996, subject to transitional provisions in FA 1996 Sch 15.

66 Avoidance of double charging

Commentary—*Simon's Direct Tax Service* **D2.225.**
Amendments—This section repealed by FA 1996 Sch 41 Pt V(3) with effect for accounting periods ending after 31 March 1996, subject to transitional provisions in FA 1996 Sch 15.

Charitable donations

67 Donations from companies and individuals

(1) (*amends* TA 1988 s 339(3A)).

(2) (*amends* FA 1990 s 25(2)(*g*)).

(3) Subsection (1) above shall apply in relation to payments made on or after 16th March 1993.

(4) Subsection (2) above shall apply in relation to gifts made on or after 16th March 1993.

68 Payroll deduction schemes

(1) (*amends* TA 1988 s 202(7)).

(2) This section shall have effect for the year 1993–94 and subsequent years of assessment.

69 Contributions to agent's expenses

(*Inserts* TA 1988 s 86A).

Benefits in kind

70 Car benefits: 1993–94

(*Spent*).

71 Car fuel: 1993–94

(*Spent*).

72 Car and car fuel benefits: 1994–95 onwards

Schedule 3 to this Act (which contains provisions, having effect for the year 1994–95 and subsequent years of assessment, about cars available for private use and car fuel) shall have effect.

Commentary—*Simon's Direct Tax Service* **E4.614B, 615.**

73 Vans

Schedule 4 to this Act (which contains provisions about vans available for private use) shall have effect.

Commentary—*Simon's Direct Tax Service* **E4.615A.**

74 Heavier commercial vehicles

(1) (*inserts* TA 1988 s 159AC).

(2) ...[1]

(3) This section shall have effect for the year 1993–94 and subsequent years of assessment.

Amendment—[1] Sub-s (2) repealed by FA 1999 s 139, Sch 20 Pt III(9) with effect from the year 1999–00.

75 Sporting and recreational facilities

(1) (*inserts* TA 1988 s 197G).

(2) This section shall apply for the year 1993–94 and subsequent years of assessment.

76 Removal expenses and benefits

Schedule 5 to this Act (which relates to the payment of expenses, and the provision of benefits, in respect of removals) shall have effect.

Taxation of distributions etc

77 Application of lower rate

(1), (2) ...[1]

(3) (*amends* TA 1988 s 249).

(4) (*amends* TA 1988 s 421(1)).

(5) This section shall apply in relation to the year 1993–94 and subsequent years of assessment.

Commentary—*Simon's Direct Tax Service* E4.641–646.
Amendments—[1] Sub-ss (1), (2) repealed by FA 1996 Sch 41 Pt V(1) with effect from the year 1996–97.

78 Rate of advance corporation tax and tax credits

Commentary—*Simon's Direct Tax Service* D1.303, 402.
Amendments—This section repealed by FA 1998 s 165, Sch 27 Part III(2) with effect for distributions made after 5 April 1999.

79 Provisions supplemental to sections 77 and 78

(1) Schedule 6 to this Act (which makes further provision for the purposes of and in connection with the provisions of sections 77 and 78 above) shall have effect.

(2) Subject to that Schedule, subsection (3) of section 687 of the Taxes Act 1988 (definition of pool for the purposes of payments under discretionary trusts) shall have effect, and be deemed always to have had effect, as if—

    (*a*) the repeal of paragraph (*b*) which was made by Part V of Schedule 17 to the Finance Act 1989 in relation to accounting periods beginning after 31st March 1989 had been confined to the following words in that paragraph, that is to say, "under section 426(2) as applied by section 686(4) or"; and

    (*b*) (*inserts* TA 1988 s 687(3)(*j*)).

(3) ...[1]

Commentary—*Simon's Direct Tax Service* C4.225.
Amendments—[1] Sub-s (3) repealed by FA 1996 Sch 41 Pt V(1) with effect from the year 1996–97.

80 Transitional relief for charities etc

(1) In any case where—

    (*a*) a qualifying distribution is made on or after 6th April 1993 and before 6th April 1997 by a company resident in the United Kingdom;

    (*b*) the recipient of the distribution is a section 505 body; and

    (*c*) the section 505 body is entitled to the payment of a tax credit in respect of the distribution,

the section 505 body, on a claim made under this section to the Board, shall (in addition to its entitlement to payment of the tax credit) be entitled to be paid by the Board out of money provided by Parliament an amount determined in accordance with subsection (2) below.

(2) The amount referred to in subsection (1) above is an amount equal to—

    (*a*) one-fifteenth of the amount or value of the distribution if the distribution is made on or after 6th April 1993 and before 6th April 1994;

    (*b*) one-twentieth of that amount or value if the distribution is made on or after 6th April 1994 and before 6th April 1995;

    (*c*) one-thirtieth of that amount or value if the distribution is made on or after 6th April 1995 and before 6th April 1996;

    (*d*) one-sixtieth of that amount or value if the distribution is made on or after 6th April 1996 and before 6th April 1997.

(3) For the purposes of this section each of the following is a section 505 body—

    (*a*) any charity (as defined in section 506(1) of the Taxes Act 1988);

(*b*)　each of the bodies mentioned in section 507 of that Act (heritage bodies);

(*c*)　any Association of a description specified in section 508 of that Act (scientific research organisations).

(4)　Any entitlement of a section 505 body to a payment under the preceding provisions of this section shall be subject to a power of the Board to determine (whether before or after any payment is made) that, having regard to the operation in relation to the qualifying distribution in question of section 235, 237 or 703 of the Taxes Act 1988 (distributions of exempt funds, bonus issues and tax avoidance provisions), that body is to be treated as if it had had no entitlement to that payment or to so much of it as they may determine.

(5)　No claim may be made under this section later than two years after the end of the chargeable period of the section 505 body in which the distribution is made.

(6)　An appeal may be brought against any decision of the Board under this section by giving written notice to the Board within thirty days of receipt of written notice of the decision.

(7)　An appeal under this section shall lie to the Special Commissioners, and the provisions of the Taxes Management Act 1970 relating to appeals under the Tax Acts shall apply to an appeal under this section as they apply to those appeals.

(8)　Any payment of an amount under this section shall be treated for the purposes of section 252 of the Taxes Act 1988 (rectification of excessive set-off etc of ACT or tax credit) as a payment of tax credit.

Commentary—*Simon's Direct Tax Service* **C4.520.**

81 Restriction of set-off of ACT

Amendments—This section repealed by FA 1998 s 165, Sch 27 Part III(2) with effect for changes of ownership occurring after 5 April 1999 (previously inserted TA 1988 s 245(3A), (3B)).

Chargeable gains

82 Annual exempt amount for 1993–94

(*Spent*).

Commentary—*Simon's Direct Tax Service* **C1.401.**

83 Annual exempt amount: indexation for 1994–95 onwards

(1)　(*amends* TCGA 1992 s 3(3)).

(2)　This section shall have effect for the year 1994–95 and subsequent years of assessment.

84 Re-organisations etc involving debentures

(1), (2)　(*insert* TCGA 1992 ss 117(6A), 251(6)).

(3)　This section shall have effect in relation to any chargeable period ending on or after 16th March 1993 but, in relation to any accounting period of a company which began before 6th April 1992, this section shall have effect as if the references in this section, and in the amendments made by this section, to provisions of the Taxation of Chargeable Gains Act 1992 were references to such of the provisions of the Capital Gains Tax Act 1979 and the Finance Act 1984 as correspond to those provisions and have effect in relation to that accounting period.

85 Personal equity plans

(*Inserts TCGA* 1992 s 151(4)).

86 Roll-over relief

(1)　(*inserts* TCGA 1992 s 155 Class 6).

(2)　The Treasury may by order made by statutory instrument amend that section so as to add one or more further classes of assets to the classes specified in that section. [Any such order may make such consequential amendments of Schedule 7AB as appear to the Treasury to be appropriate.][1]

(3)　A statutory instrument containing an order under subsection (2) above shall be subject to annulment in pursuance of a resolution of the House of Commons.

(4)　Subsection (1) above shall apply where the disposal of the old assets (or an interest in them) or the acquisition of the new assets (or an interest in them) is on or after 1st January 1993; but, in relation to any accounting period of a company which began before 6th April 1992, subsection (1) above shall have effect as if the inserted class were numbered 5 and were inserted after Class 4 in section 118 of the Capital Gains Tax Act 1979.

Commentary—*Simon's Direct Tax Service* **C3.303.**
Regulations—Finance Act 1993, Section 86(2), (Fish Quota) Order, SI 1999/564.
Amendments—[1] Words in sub-s (2) inserted by FA 2002 s 43(3), (4) with effect—

(*a*) in relation to a case where a company is treated by virtue of TCGA 1992 s 179(3) as having sold and immediately reacquired an asset, where the company's ceasing to be a member of the group in question happens after 31 March 2002;

(*b*) in relation to a case where a company is so treated by virtue of TCGA 1992 s 179(6), where the relevant time (within the meaning of that subsection) is after that date.

87 Relief on retirement or re-investment

(1) Schedule 7 to this Act (which amends the provisions of the Taxation of Chargeable Gains Act 1992 with respect to retirement relief and makes new provision in relation to relief on the re-investment of certain gains) shall have effect.

(2) This section and that Schedule shall have effect in relation to any disposal made on or after 16th March 1993.

Commentary—*Simon's Direct Tax Service* C3.602, Division C3.9.

88 Restriction on set-off of pre-entry losses

(1) (*inserts* TCGA 1992 s 177A).

(2) The Schedule set out in Schedule 8 to this Act shall be inserted after Schedule 7 to that Act.

(3) This section and that Schedule—

> (*a*) shall apply for the calculation of the amount to be included in respect of chargeable gains in a company's total profits for any accounting period ending on or after 16th March 1993; but
> (*b*) shall so apply only in relation to the deduction from chargeable gains accruing on or after 16th March 1993 of amounts in respect of, or of amounts carried forward in respect of—

>> (i) pre-entry losses accruing before it became a member of the relevant group to a company whose membership of that group began or begins at a time on or after 1st April 1987; and
>> (ii) losses accruing on the disposal of any assets so far as it is by reference to such a company that the assets fall to be treated as being or having been pre-entry assets or assets incorporating a part referable to pre-entry assets.

(4) In relation to accounting periods beginning before 6th April 1992 this section and that Schedule shall have effect as if—

> (*a*) the section and Schedule inserted by subsections (1) and (2) above were inserted in the Capital Gains Tax Act 1979; and
> (*b*) references in the Schedule so inserted to provisions of the Taxation of Chargeable Gains Act 1992 were references to such of the provisions of that Act of 1979 or of any other enactment as correspond to the provisions referred to and have effect in relation to that accounting period.

Commentary—*Simon's Direct Tax Service* D2.670, 671, 675, 678, 679.

89 De-grouping charges

(1) (*amends* TCGA 1992 s 179(4)).

(2) This section shall have effect in relation to accounting periods ending after the day appointed for the purposes of section 180(1)(*b*) of that Act.

Notes—The appointed day referred to in sub-s (2) is 30 September 1993.

90 Insurance: transfers of business

Amendments—This section repealed by FA 2000 s 156, Sch 40 Pt II(12) with effect for disposals made after 31 March 2000.

91 Deemed disposals of unit trusts by insurance companies

(1) Section 212 of the Taxation of Chargeable Gains Act 1992 (annual deemed disposal by insurance companies of unit trusts) shall have effect in relation to accounting periods beginning on or after 1st January 1993; and neither that section nor section 46 of the Finance Act 1990 (which is consolidated in that section) shall have effect in relation to any earlier accounting period in relation to which either of them would have applied apart from this subsection.

(2) In relation to any accounting period beginning on or after 1st January 1993—

> (*a*) section 432A of the Taxes Act 1988 shall have effect with the omission of subsection (10) (which disapplies the apportionment rules in that section in the case of a deemed disposal under section 212 of that Act of 1992); and
> (*b*) that section 212 shall have effect with the omission, in subsection (2), of the words from "and in relation to" onwards and of subsections (3), (4) and (6) (which provide for a different apportionment rule in the case of the deemed disposal).

(3) (*amends* TCGA 1992 s 212(7)).

(4) (*inserts* TCGA 1992 s 213(1A)).

(5) (*repeals* TCGA 1992 s 214(3)–(5) and inserts s 214A).

(6) (*amends* TCGA 1992 s 214(6)(*a*)).

Commentary—*Simon's Direct Tax Service* D4.527.

Corporation tax: currency

[92 The basic rule: sterling to be used

(1) Where a company carries on a business, the profits or losses of the business for an accounting period shall for the purposes of corporation tax be computed and expressed in sterling; but this is subject to [sections 93 and 93A][3] below.

(2) In this section—

"losses" includes management expenses and any allowances falling to be made under [section 19 or 253 of the Capital Allowances Act][2];

"profits" includes gains, income and any charges falling to be made under [section 19 or 253 of that Act][2].][1]

Commentary—*Simon's Direct Tax Service* **D2.910, 912.**
Cross references—See FA 1994 s 226(1) (this section not to apply for computing for corporation tax profits or losses of Lloyd's corporate member's underwriting business).
Amendments—[1] This section substituted, together with ss 93, 94 (for ss 92–94, 94A, 95) by FA 2000 s 105 with effect for accounting periods beginning after 31 December 1999 and ending after 20 March 2000. Any company which did not, for the accounting period immediately preceding the first accounting period falling within these commencement dates, make an election in respect of a trade or part of a trade under the Local Currency Elections Regulations 1994 may, by notice given to an officer of the Board before 1 September 2000, elect that this amendment shall not have effect in relation to it until the first accounting period beginning after 30 June 2000. This section previously read—
"**92 The basic rule: sterling to be used**
Where a company carries on a trade, the profits or losses of the trade for an accounting period shall for the purposes of corporation tax be computed and expressed in sterling; but this is subject to any regulations under section 93 or 94 below.".
[2] Words substituted by CAA 2001 s 578, Sch 2 para 88 with effect for corporation tax purposes as respects allowances and charges falling to be made for chargeable periods ending after 31 March 2001.
[3] In sub-s (1), words substituted for the words "section 93" by FA 2002 s 80, Sch 24 paras 1, 2 with effect for accounting periods beginning after 30 September 2002.

[93 [Use of currency other than sterling: accounts as a whole etc in foreign currency.][3]

(1) This section applies where in an accounting period a company carries on a business and [the condition in subsection (2) below][3] is fulfilled.

(2) [The condition is][3] that—

(a) the accounts of the company as a whole are prepared in a currency other than sterling in accordance with [generally accepted accounting practice][4]; and
(b) in the case of a company which is not resident in the United Kingdom, the company makes a return of accounts for its branch in the United Kingdom prepared in such a currency in accordance with such practice.

(3) The second condition is that—

(a) the accounts of the company as a whole are prepared in sterling but, so far as relating to the businesss, they are prepared, using the closing rate/net investment method, from financial statements prepared in a currency other than sterling; or
(b) in the case of a company which is not resident in the United Kingdom, the company makes a return of accounts for its branch in the United Kingdom prepared in sterling but, so far as relating to the business, it is prepared, using that method, from financial statements prepared in such a currency. [3]

(4) The profits or losses of the business for an accounting period shall for the purposes of corporation tax be found by—

(a) taking the amount of all the profits and losses of the business for the period computed and expressed in the relevant foreign currency;
(b) taking account of any of the following which are so computed and expressed—
(i) any management expenses brought forward under section 75(3) of the Taxes Act 1988 from an earlier accounting period;
(ii) any losses of the business brought forward under section 392B or 393 of that Act from such a period; and
(iii) any non-trading deficits on loan relationships brought forward under section 83 of the Finance Act 1996 from the previous accounting period; and
(c) taking the sterling equivalent of the amount found by applying paragraphs (a) and (b) above.

(5) In the application of [section 578A(2) or (3) of the Taxes Act 1988 or section 43(3), 74(2), 75(1), 76(2), (3) or (4), 99(1), (2) or (3) or 208(1) of the Capital Allowances Act][2] for the purposes of subsection (4)(a) or (b) above, it shall be assumed that any sterling amount mentioned in any of those sections is its equivalent expressed in the relevant foreign currency.

(6) Where in an accounting period—

(a) a company carries on different parts of a business through different branches (whether within or outside the United Kingdom); and
(b) this section would apply differently in relation to different parts if they were separate businesses,
those parts shall be treated for the purposes of this section as if they were separate businesses for that period. [3]

(7) In this section, unless the context otherwise requires—

"accounts", in relation to a company, means—

    (a) the annual accounts of the company prepared in accordance with Part VII of the Companies Act 1985 or Part VIII of the Companies (Northern Ireland) Order 1986; or

    (b) if the company is not required to prepare such accounts, the accounts which it is required to keep under the law of its home State; or

    (c) if the company is not so required to keep accounts, such of its accounts as most closely correspond to accounts which it would have been required to prepare if the provisions of that Part applied to it;

"*branch*" *includes any collection of assets and liabilities;* [3]

"*the closing rate/net investment method*" *means the method so called as described under the title* "*Foreign currency translation*" *in the Statement of Standard Accounting Practice issued in April 1983 by the Institute of Chartered Accountants in England and Wales;* [3]

"home State", in relation to a company, means the country or territory under whose laws the company is incorporated;

"losses" has the same meaning as in section 92 above except that it does not include allowable losses within the meaning of the Taxation of Chargeable Gains Act 1992;

"profits" has the same meaning as in section 92 above except that it does not include chargeable gains within the meaning of that Act;

"the relevant foreign currency" means the currency other than sterling or, where [the condition in sub-s (2) above][3] is fulfilled and two different such currencies are involved, the currency in which the return of accounts is prepared;

"return of accounts", in relation to a branch in the United Kingdom, means a return of such accounts of the branch as may be required by the Inland Revenue under paragraph 3 of Schedule 18 to the Finance Act 1998 (company tax returns, assessments and related matters).][1]

Commentary—*Simon's Direct Tax Service* **D2.910, 912, 934.**
Statement of Practice SP 2/01—Tax treatment for businesses that draw up their accounts in a foreign currency, specifically for businesses carried out by partnerships that include companies.
Revenue Internal Guidance—Company Taxation Manual COT13620 (worked example showing effect of using local currency).
Regulations—Local Currency Elections Regulations, SI 1994/3230.
European Single Currency (Taxes) Regulations, SI 1998/3177.
Cross references—See FA 1994 s 226(1) (this section not to apply for computing for corporation tax profits or losses of Lloyd's corporate member's underwriting business).
FA 2000 s 105(2) (treatment of items referred to in sub-s (4)(*b*) where they fall to be taken into account in the first accounting period in relation to which FA 2000 s 105 has effect).
Amendments—[1] This section substituted, together with ss 92, 94 (for ss 92–94, 94A, 95) by FA 2000 s 105 with effect for accounting periods beginning after 31 December 1999 and ending after 20 March 2000. Any company which did not, for the accounting period immediately preceding the first accounting period falling within these commencement dates, make an election in respect of a trade or part of a trade under the Local Currency Elections Regulations 1994 may, by notice given to an officer of the Board before 1 September 2000, elect that this amendment shall not have effect in relation to it until the first accounting period beginning after 30 June 2000.
[2] Words in sub-s (5) substituted by CAA 2001 s 578, Sch 2 para 89 with effect for corporation tax purposes as respects allowances and charges falling to be made for chargeable periods ending after 31 March 2001.
[3] In sub-s (1), words substituted for the words "either the first condition or the second condition"; in sub-s (2), words substituted for the words "The first condition is"; sub-ss (3), (6) repealed; in sub-s (7), definitions of "branch" and "the closing rate/net investment method" repealed, in the definition of "the relevant foreign currency", words substituted for the words "the first condition"; and Heading which previously read: "Use of currency other than sterling" substituted; by FA 2002 ss 80, 141, Sch 24 paras 1, 3, Sch 40 Pt 3(11) with effect for accounting periods beginning after 30 September 2002.
[4] In sub-s (2), words substituted for the words "normal accountancy practice" by FA 2002 s 103(4)(*b*) with effect from the 24 July 2002.

[93A Use of other currency: accounts partly from statements in foreign currency

(1) This section applies where in an accounting period a company carries on a business and either the first condition or the second condition is fulfilled.

(2) The first condition is that—

    (a) the accounts of the company as a whole are prepared in sterling but, so far as relating to part of the business, they are prepared, using the closing rate/net investment method, from financial statements and records prepared in a currency other than sterling; or

    (b) in the case of a company which is not resident in the United Kingdom, the company makes a return of accounts for its branch in the United Kingdom prepared in sterling but, so far as relating to part of the business, it is prepared, using that method, from financial statements and records prepared in a currency other than sterling.

(3) The second condition is that—

    (a) the accounts of the company as a whole are prepared in a currency other than sterling ("the first currency") in accordance with generally accepted accounting practice but, so far as relating to part of the business, they are prepared, using the closing rate/net investment method, from financial statements and records prepared in a currency ("the second currency") which is neither sterling nor the first currency; or

    (b) in the case of a company which is not resident in the United Kingdom, the company makes a return of accounts for its branch in the United Kingdom prepared in a currency other than sterling ("the first currency") in accordance with generally accepted accounting practice, but, so far as relating to part of the business, it is prepared, using the closing rate/net investment method, from

financial statements and records prepared in a currency ("the second currency") which is neither sterling nor the first currency.

(4) The profits or losses of the part of the business for an accounting period shall for the purposes of corporation tax be found by—

(a) taking the amount of all the profits and losses of the part of the business for the period computed and expressed in the relevant foreign currency; and

(b) taking—

(i) in a case where the first condition is fulfilled, the sterling equivalent, or

(ii) in a case where the second condition is fulfilled, the equivalent in the first currency,

of the amount found by applying paragraph (a) above.

(5) In a case where the second condition is fulfilled, effect shall be given to subsection (4) above before effect is given to section 93(4) above.

(6) In the application for the purposes of subsection (4)(a) above of—

(a) section 578A(2) or (3) of the Taxes Act 1988, or

(b) section 43(3), 74(2), 75(1), 76(2), (3) or (4), 99(1), (2) or (3) or 208(1) of the Capital Allowances Act,

it shall be assumed that any sterling amount mentioned in any of those sections is its equivalent expressed in the relevant foreign currency.

(7) Where for any accounting period—

(a) the accounts of the company, so far as relating to a part of its business, are prepared, using the closing rate/net investment method, from financial statements and records prepared in a currency which is not sterling and, where the second condition is fulfilled, is not the first currency, or

(b) in the case of a company which is not resident in the United Kingdom, its return of accounts for its branch in the United Kingdom, so far as relating to a part of the company's business, is prepared, using that method, from such financial statements and records,

then, if different such financial statements and records are prepared in different currencies, the company shall be treated for the purposes of this section as having a separate part of a separate business for each such different currency (and this section shall accordingly apply separately in relation to each such part).

(8) In this section, "part of a business" includes any collection of assets and liabilities.

(9) In this section, unless the context otherwise requires—

"accounts" has the same meaning as in section 93 above;

"the closing rate/net investment method" means the method so called as described under the title "Foreign currency translation" in the Statement of Standard Accounting Practice issued in April 1983 by the Institute of Chartered Accountants in England and Wales;

"losses" has the same meaning as in section 92 above, except that it does not include allowable losses within the meaning of the Taxation of Chargeable Gains Act 1992;

"profits" has the same meaning as in section 92 above, except that it does not include chargeable gains within the meaning of that Act;

"the relevant foreign currency" means the currency in which the financial statements and records mentioned in subsection (2) or, as the case may be, (3) above are prepared;

"return of accounts" has the same meaning as in section 93 above.]¹

Amendments—¹ This section inserted by FA 2002 s 80, Sch 24 paras 1, 4 with effect for accounting periods beginning after 30 September 2002.

[94AA Rules for ascertaining currency equivalents: general

(1) Where any receipt or expense, or the value of any asset, liability or derivative contract, of a company—

(a) is to be taken into account in making a computation under subsection (1) of section 92 above for an accounting period, and

(b) is denominated in a currency other than sterling,

it shall be translated into its sterling equivalent by reference to a rate determined in accordance with subsection (4) below.

(2) Where the amount of any receipt or expense, or the value of any asset, liability or derivative contract, of a company—

(a) falls to be brought into account for the purposes of the accounts mentioned in paragraph (a), or the return of accounts mentioned in paragraph (b), of subsection (2) of section 93 above,

(b) is denominated in a currency other than the relevant foreign currency, within the meaning of that section, and

(c) accordingly falls to be translated into the relevant foreign currency,

the amount or value shall for the purposes of that section be translated from the currency mentioned in paragraph (b) above into the relevant foreign currency by reference to a rate determined in accordance with subsection (4) below.

(3) Where, for any purpose of any provision of section 93A(4) or (6) above, any profit or loss denominated in one currency falls to be translated into its equivalent expressed in another currency, the translation shall be made by reference to a rate determined in accordance with subsection (4) below.

(4) The rate is—

    (*a*) the rate used in the preparation of the accounts of the company for the accounting period in question, if that rate is an arm's length exchange rate for the relevant day, or

    (*b*) in any other case, the London closing exchange rate for the relevant day.

(5) The reference in subsection (4)(*a*) above to the exchange rate used in the preparation of the accounts of the company includes a reference to any exchange rate implied by a derivative contract whose underlying subject matter is currency.

(6) Nothing in this section affects the operation of Chapter 4 of Part 17 of the Taxes Act 1988 (controlled foreign companies).

(7) Nothing in paragraph 88 of Schedule 18 to the Finance Act 1998 (company tax returns, assessments and related matters) shall be taken to prevent an amount being translated under this section for an accounting period by reference to an exchange rate which was not the exchange rate used to translate that amount for the purposes of the Corporation Tax Acts for another accounting period (whether of the same or a different company).

(8) In this section—

    ''accounts'' has the same meaning as in section 93 above;

    ''arm's length exchange rate'' means such exchange rate as might reasonably be expected to be agreed between persons dealing at arm's length;

    ''derivative contract'' shall be construed in accordance with Schedule 26 to the Finance Act 2002;

    ''the relevant day''—

        (*a*) where the rate used in the preparation of the accounts is an exchange rate for a particular day, means that day; and

        (*b*) where the rate used in the preparation of the accounts is an average rate for a number of days, means each of those days;

''underlying subject matter'', in relation to a derivative contract, shall be construed in accordance with Schedule 26 to the Finance Act 2002.]¹

Commentary—*Simon's Direct Tax Service* **D2.910, 912.**
Statement of Practice SP 2/01—Tax treatment for businesses that draw up their accounts in a foreign currency, specifically for businesses carried out by partnerships that include companies.
Regulations—Local Currency Elections Regulations, SI 1994/3230.
European Single Currency (Taxes) Regulations, SI 1998/3177.
Cross references—See FA 1994 s 226(1) (this section not to apply for computing for corporation tax profits or losses of Lloyd's corporate member's underwriting business).
Amendments—¹ Section 94AA substituted for section 94 by FA 2002 s 80, Sch 24 paras 1, 5 with effect for accounting periods beginning after 30 September 2002. Section 94A previously read as follows—

''94 Rules for ascertaining currency equivalents

(1) Any receipt or expense which is to be taken into account in making a computation under subsection (1) of section 92 above for an accounting period, and is denominated in a currency other than sterling, shall be translated into its sterling equivalent—
(*a*) if either of the conditions mentioned in subsection (2) below is fulfilled, by reference to the rate used in the preparation of the accounts of the company as a whole for that period;
(*b*) if neither of those conditions is fulfilled, by reference to the London closing exchange rate for the relevant day.
(2) The conditions are—
(*a*) that the rate is an arm's length exchange rate for the relevant day;
(*b*) that the rate is an average arm's length exchange rate for a period ending with that day, or for a period not exceeding three months which includes that day, and the arm's length exchange rate for any day in that period (except the first) is not significantly different from that for the preceding day.
(3) Subject to subsections (5) and (7) below, any amount found by applying paragraphs (*a*) and (*b*) of subsection (4) of section 93 above shall be translated into its sterling equivalent by reference to the London closing exchange rate for the relevant day.
(4) The following—
(*a*) any receipt or expense which is to be taken into account in making a calculation for the purposes of subsection (4)(*a*) or (*b*) of section 93 above, and is denominated in a currency other than the relevant foreign currency; and
(*b*) any such sterling amount as is referred to in subsection (5) of that section,
shall be translated into its equivalent expressed in the relevant foreign currency by reference to the London closing exchange rate for the relevant day.
(5) Where section 93 above applies by virtue of the first condition mentioned in that section, then, as regards the business or part of the business, the company—
(*a*) may elect, by a notice given to an officer of the Board, that as from the first day of the accounting period in which the notice is given, an average arm's length exchange rate shall be used for the purposes of subsection (3) above instead of the rate there mentioned; and
(*b*) may withdraw such an election, by a notice so given, as from the first day of the first accounting period beginning on or after the date of the notice.
(6) Where an election under subsection (5) above is withdrawn, no further election may be made under that subsection so as to take effect before the third anniversary of the day on which the withdrawal takes effect.
(7) Where—
(*a*) section 93 above applies by virtue of the second condition mentioned in that section; and
(*b*) the accounts of the company, so far as relating to the business or part of the business, are prepared by reference to an average arm's length exchange rate,
that exchange rate shall be used for the purposes of subsection (3) above instead of the rate there mentioned.
(8) In this section—

"accounts" has the same meaning as in section 93 above;

"arm's length exchange rate" means such exchange rate as might reasonably be expected to be agreed between persons dealing at arm's length;

"average arm's length exchange rate", in relation to a period, means the rate which represents an appropriate average of arm's length exchange rates for the period;

"the relevant day" means—

(a) for the purposes of subsections (1), (2) and (4)(a) above, the day on which the company becomes entitled to the receipt or incurs (or is treated as incurring) the expense;

(b) for the purposes of subsection (3) above, the last day of the accounting period in question;

(c) for the purposes of subsection (4)(b) above, the day on which the company incurs the capital expenditure.

(9) Nothing in this section affects the operation of Chapter IV of Part VII of the Taxes Act 1988 (controlled foreign companies) or Chapter II of this Part.

(10) Nothing in paragraph 88 of Schedule 18 to the Finance Act 1998 (company tax returns, assessments and related matters) shall be taken to prevent any amount which is taken to be conclusively determined for the purposes of the Corporation Tax Acts from being translated under this section by reference to an exchange rate which was not used to determine the amount which can no longer be altered.".

[94AB Rules for ascertaining sterling equivalent for section 93(4) or (5)

(1) Where the amount of any receipt or expense, or the value of any asset, liability or derivative contract, of a company falls to be translated into its sterling equivalent for the purposes of section 93(4) or (5) above, the translation shall be made by reference to a rate which is an arm's length exchange rate for the appropriate day.

(2) For the purposes of subsection (1) above, the "appropriate day" is the day the rate for which would have been used if the accounts, or return of accounts, of the company were translated into sterling in accordance with generally accepted accounting practice in relation to foreign currency translation.

(3) Nothing in this section affects the operation of Chapter 4 of Part 17 of the Taxes Act 1988 (controlled foreign companies).

(4) Nothing in paragraph 88 of Schedule 18 to the Finance Act 1998 (company tax returns, assessments and related matters) shall be taken to prevent an amount being translated under this section for an accounting period by reference to an exchange rate which was not the exchange rate used to translate that amount for the purposes of the Corporation Tax Acts for another accounting period (whether of the same or a different company).

(5) In this section—

"accounts" has the same meaning as in section 93 above;

"arm's length exchange rate" has the same meaning as in section 94AA;

"derivative contract" shall be construed in accordance with Schedule 26 to the Finance Act 2002.][1]

Amendments—[1] This section inserted by FA 2002 s 80, Sch 24 paras 1, 6 with effect for accounting periods beginning after 30 September 2002.

[94A Parts of trades: petroleum extraction companies]

Commentary—*Simon's Direct Tax Service* D2.910, 911.

Amendments—[1] This section substituted by ss 92–94 by FA 2000 s 105 with effect for accounting periods beginning after 31 December 1999 and ending after 20 March 2000. Any company which did not, for the accounting period immediately preceding the first accounting period falling within these commencement dates, make an election in respect of a trade or part of a trade under the Local Currency Elections Regulations 1994 may, by notice given to an officer of the Board before 1 September 2000, elect that this amendment shall not have effect in relation to it until the first accounting period beginning after 30 June 2000. This section (originally inserted by FA 1994 s 136(1)) previously read—

"**94A Parts of trades: petroleum extraction companies**

(1) If a trade carried on by a petroleum extraction company is a ring fence trade—

(a) subsection (1) of section 94 above shall not apply as regards the trade, but

(b) regulations may make provision under that section as regards a case where in an accounting period the company carries on the trade and the condition mentioned in subsection (2) below is fulfilled.

(2) The condition is that—

(a) part of the trade consists of activities which relate to oil and are carried on under the authority of a petroleum licence in the United Kingdom or a designated area, and

(b) part of the trade consists of activities which relate to gas and are carried on under the authority of a petroleum licence in the United Kingdom or a designated area.

(3) For the purposes of this section—

(a) a petroleum licence is a licence granted under Part I of the Petroleum Act 1998 or the Petroleum (Production) Act (Northern Ireland) 1964;

(b) a petroleum extraction company is a company which carries on activities under the authority of such a licence;

(c) a designated area is an area designated by Order in Council under section 1(7) of the Continental Shelf Act 1964.

(4) For the purposes of this section "ring fence trade" means activities which—

(a) fall within any of paragraphs (a) to (c) of subsection (1) of section 492 of the Taxes Act 1988 (oil extraction etc), and

(b) constitute a separate trade (whether by virtue of that subsection or otherwise).

(5) For the purposes of this section—

(a) "oil" means such substance as falls within the meaning of oil contained in section 502(1) of the Taxes Act 1988 and is not gas;

(b) "gas" means such substance as falls within the meaning of oil contained in section 502(1) of the Taxes Act 1988 and is gas of which the largest component by volume, measured at a temperature of 15 degrees centigrade and a pressure of one atmosphere, is methane or ethane or a combination of those gases."

95 Currency to be used: supplementary

Commentary—*Simon's Direct Tax Service* D2.910, 911.

Amendments—[1] This section substituted by ss 92–94 by FA 2000 s 105 with effect for accounting periods beginning after 31 December 1999 and ending after 20 March 2000. Any company which did not, for the accounting period immediately preceding the first accounting period falling within these commencement dates, make an election in respect of a trade or part of a trade under the Local Currency Elections Regulations 1994 may, by notice given to an officer of the Board before 1 September 2000, elect that this amendment shall not have effect in relation to it until the first accounting period beginning after 30 June 2000. This section previously read—

"**95 Currency to be used: supplementary**

(1) Regulations under section 93 or 94 above may include—

    (a) provision that an election may in prescribed circumstances have effect from a time before it is made;
    (b) provision that prescribed conditions shall be treated as fulfilled in prescribed circumstances (subject to any provision under paragraph (c) below);
    (c) provision that prescribed conditions shall be treated as not having been fulfilled if the inspector notifies the company that he is not satisfied that they are fulfilled;
    (d) provision for an appeal from the inspector's notification;

and any provision under paragraph (c) above may allow a notification to be made after the accounting period ends.

(2) The power to make regulations under section 93 or 94 above shall be exercisable by the Treasury by statutory instrument subject to annulment in pursuance of a resolution of the House of Commons.

(3) In sections 93 and 94 above ''prescribed'' means prescribed by regulations made under the section concerned.

(4) Where as regards a trade and for an accounting period—

    (a) an election is made under regulations made under section 93 above, or
    (b) an election is made under regulations made under section 94 above,

no election may be made as regards the trade for the period under regulations made under the other section.

(5) For the purposes of sections 93 and 94 above the ecu shall be regarded as a currency other than sterling; and the reference here to the ecu is to the European currency unit as defined for the time being in Council Regulation No 3180/78/EEC or in any Community instrument replacing it.

(6) Sections 92 to 94A above apply in relation to any accounting period beginning on or after the day appointed under section 165(7)(b) below.''

96 Foreign companies: trading currency

Amendments—This section repealed by FA 1995 Sch 29 Pt VIII(17) and is deemed never to have been enacted.

Overseas life insurance companies

97 Modification of Taxes Act 1988

(1) (*inserts* TA 1988 s 444B).

(2) Schedule 9 to this Act (which inserts Schedule 19AC into that Act and makes further provision) shall have effect.

98 Modification of section 440 of Taxes Act 1988

(1) (*inserts* TA 1988 s 444C).

(2) This section shall apply—

    (a) so far as section 440(1) is concerned, as regards events falling on or after the first day of the relevant accounting period of the company concerned;
    (b) so far as section 440(2) is concerned, as regards events falling on or after the first day of the relevant accounting period of the transferor company or on or after the first day of the relevant accounting period of the acquiring company (whichever of those days falls later).

(3) For the purposes of subsection (2) above a company's relevant accounting period is its first accounting period to begin after 31st December 1992.

99 Qualifying distributions, tax credits, etc

Amendment—This section repealed by FA 1995 Sch 29 Pt VIII(5), with effect for accounting periods beginning after 31 December 1994.

100 Income from investments attributable to BLAGAB, etc

(1) (*inserted* TA 1988 s 444E; repealed by FA 1995 Sch 29 Pt VIII(5), with effect for accounting periods beginning after 31 December 1994).

(2) (*amends* TA 1988 s 475(6); repealed in part by FA 1995 Sch 29 Pt VIII(5), with effect for accounting periods beginning after 31 December 1994).

(3) This section shall apply in relation to accounting periods beginning after 31st December 1992.

101 Modification of Finance Act 1989

(1) (*inserts* FA 1989 s 89A).

(2) Schedule 10 to this Act (which inserts Schedule 8A into that Act) shall have effect.

Commentary—*Simon's Direct Tax Service* D4.537.

102 Modification of Taxation of Chargeable Gains Act 1992

(1) (*inserts* TCGA 1992 s 214B).

(2) Schedule 11 to this Act (which inserts Schedule 7B into that Act) shall have effect.

Commentary—*Simon's Direct Tax Service* **D4.537.**

103 Amendment of definition and repeals

(1) (*amends* TA 1988 s 431(2)).

(2) (*repeals* provisions in TA 1988 ss 445–449, 724, 811, Sch 19AB para 1).

(3) Subject to subsection (4) below, this section shall apply in relation to accounting periods beginning after 31st December 1992.

(4) ...[1]

Commentary—*Simon's Direct Tax Service* **D4.537.**
Amendments—[1] Sub-s (4) repealed by FA 1996 Sch 41 Pt V(3) with effect for accounting periods ending after 31 March 1996, subject to transitional provisions in FA 1996 Sch 15.

Approved share option schemes

104 Calculation of consideration

(*Inserts TCGA* 1992 s 149A).

105 Expenditure on shares

(1) (*amends* TCGA 1992 s 120(6)).

(2) The amendments made by subsection (1) above shall be deemed always to have had effect.

(3) (*amends* CGTA 1979 s 32A(5)).

(4) The amendments made by subsection (3) above shall be deemed to have come into force on 1st January 1992 (but shall have effect subject to the repeals made by the Taxation of Chargeable Gains Act 1992).

Indexation: miscellaneous

106 Earnings cap etc: no indexation in 1993–94

(*Spent*).

107 Indexation of allowances etc for 1994–95 onwards

(1) The Taxes Act 1988 shall be amended as mentioned in subsections (2) to (6) below.

(2)–(6) (*amend* ss 1, 257C, 590C(4), (5), 590B, 592, 594, 599, 640A and *insert* s 590C(5A)).

(7) (*amends* FA 1989 Sch 6 paras 20, 22).

(8) This section shall have effect for the year 1994–95 and subsequent years of assessment.

Miscellaneous provisions about reliefs

108 Counselling services for employees

(*Inserts TA* 1988 ss 589A, 589B).

109 Pre-trading expenditure

(1)–(3) (*amend* TA 1988 s 401(1), 338(5)(*b*) and *insert* s 401(1A)).

(4) Subsections (1) and (2) above shall have effect where the time when the person begins to carry on the trade, profession or vocation falls after 31st March 1993, and subsection (3) above shall have effect in relation to payments made after that date.

Revenue Interpretation RI 117—For income tax, where a business commences after 5 April 1995, relief for pre-trading expenditure is given as a deduction in computing taxable profits. A separate income tax loss relief claim is not necessary.

110 Waste disposal expenditure

(1), (2) (*insert* TA 1988 ss 91A(6)(*c*), 91B(10A)).

(3) This section shall have effect in relation to any case where the trade in question is begun after 31st March 1993.

111 Business expansion scheme: loan linked investments

(1)–(3) (*inserts* TA 1988 ss 299A, 307(6)(*ca*) and *amend* ss 289, 310).

(4) This section shall apply in relation to any case in which the claim for relief is made on or after 16th March 1993.

112 Employers' pension contributions

(1) (*amends* TA 1988 s 592(4)).

(2) Subsection (1) above shall have effect in the case of any employer in relation to, as the case may be—

> (*a*) any accounting period of that employer ending with a day after 5th April 1993; or
>
> (*b*) any year of assessment the employer's basis period for which ends with a day after that date.

(3) Where—

> (*a*) there is after 5th April 1993 an actual payment by an employer of a contribution under an exempt approved scheme,
>
> (*b*) that payment would, apart from this subsection, be allowed to be deducted as an expense, or expense of management, of the employer in relation to any chargeable period in relation to which subsection (1) above has effect, and
>
> (*c*) the total of previously allowed deductions exceeds the relevant maximum,

the amount allowed to be so deducted in respect of the payment mentioned in paragraph (*a*) above and of any other actual payments of contributions under the scheme which, having been made after 5th April 1993, fall within paragraph (*b*) above in relation to the same chargeable period shall be reduced by whichever is the smaller of the excess and the amount which reduces the deduction to nil.

(4) In relation to any such actual payment by an employer of a contribution under an exempt approved scheme as would be allowed to be deducted as mentioned in subsection (3) above in relation to any chargeable period—

> (*a*) the reference in that subsection to the total of previously allowed deductions is a reference to the aggregate of every amount in respect of the making, or any provision for the making, of that or any other contributions under the scheme, which has been allowed to be deducted as an expense, or expense of management, of that person in relation to a previous chargeable period; and
>
> (*b*) the reference to the relevant maximum is a reference to the amount which would have been that aggregate if the restriction on deductions imposed by virtue of subsection (1) above had been applied in relation to every previous chargeable period;

and for the purposes of this subsection an amount the deduction of the whole or any part of which falls to be taken into account as allowed in relation to more than one chargeable period shall be treated as if the amount allowed were a different amount in the case of each of those periods.

(5) For the purposes of this section any payment which is treated under subsection (6) of section 592 of the Taxes Act 1988 as spread over a period of years shall be treated as actually paid at the time when it is treated as paid in accordance with that subsection.

(6) (*inserts* TA 1988 s 592(6A)).

> and this subsection shall have effect in relation to any payment made on or after the day on which this Act is passed.

(7) In this section—

> "basis period", in relation to any person, means a period on the profits or gains of which income tax for any year of assessment falls to be finally computed under Case I or II of Schedule D in respect of the trade, profession or vocation of that person (being the later period in any case where the profits and gains of an earlier period are taken to be the profits and gains of a later period); and
>
> "exempt approved scheme" has the meaning given by section 592(1) of the Taxes Act 1988.

Capital allowances

113 Initial allowances: industrial buildings and structures

Commentary—*Simon's Direct Tax Service* B.233A, 233B.
Amendment—This section repealed by the Capital Allowances Act 2001 s 580, Sch 4 with effect for income tax purposes, as respects allowances and charges falling to be made for chargeable periods ending after 5 April 2001, and for corporation tax purposes, as respects allowances and charges falling to be made for chargeable periods ending after 31 March 2001.

114 Initial allowances: agricultural buildings etc

Commentary—*Simon's Direct Tax Service* B2.507A.
Amendment—This section repealed by the Capital Allowances Act 2001 s 580, Sch 4 with effect for income tax purposes, as respects allowances and charges falling to be made for chargeable periods ending after 5 April 2001, and for corporation tax purposes, as respects allowances and charges falling to be made for chargeable periods ending after 31 March 2001.

115 First year allowances: machinery and plant

Commentary—*Simon's Direct Tax Service* B2.324A.
Amendment—This section repealed by the Capital Allowances Act 2001 s 580, Sch 4 with effect for income tax purposes, as respects allowances and charges falling to be made for chargeable periods ending after 5 April 2001, and for corporation tax purposes, as respects allowances and charges falling to be made for chargeable periods ending after 31 March 2001.

116 Leasing

Amendment—This section repealed by the Capital Allowances Act 2001 s 580, Sch 4 with effect for income tax purposes, as respects allowances and charges falling to be made for chargeable periods ending after 5 April 2001, and for corporation tax purposes, as respects allowances and charges falling to be made for chargeable periods ending after 31 March 2001.

117 Transactions between connected persons etc

Amendment—This section repealed by the Capital Allowances Act 2001 s 580, Sch 4 with effect for income tax purposes, as respects allowances and charges falling to be made for chargeable periods ending after 5 April 2001, and for corporation tax purposes, as respects allowances and charges falling to be made for chargeable periods ending after 31 March 2001.

Miscellaneous

118 Scottish trusts

(1) Where—

    (a) any of the income of a trust having effect under the law of Scotland is income to which a beneficiary of the trust would have an equitable right in possession if that trust had effect under the law of England and Wales, and

    (b) the trustees of that trust are resident in the United Kingdom,

the rights of that beneficiary shall be deemed for the purposes of the Income Tax Acts to include such a right to that income notwithstanding that no such right is conferred according to the law of Scotland.

(2) This section shall have effect in relation to the income of any trust for the year 1993–94 or any subsequent year of assessment.

Commentary—*Simon's Direct Tax Service* **C4.220.**
Revenue & other press releases—Hansard 13-2-96 (the lower rate of tax applies to income from life rent trusts under s 1(a)).

119 Controlled foreign companies

(1) (*amends* TA 1988 s 750(1)).

(2) Subsection (1) above shall apply in relation to accounting periods beginning on or after 16th March 1993.

(3) Where a company is by virtue of section 749(1) or (2) of the Taxes Act 1988 regarded as resident in a territory outside the United Kingdom and (apart from this section)—

    (a) an accounting period of the company would begin before 16th March 1993 and end on or after that date, and

    (b) the company would not be considered to be subject, by virtue of section 750(1) of that Act, to a lower level of taxation in that accounting period in the territory in which it is regarded as resident,

for the purposes of Chapter IV of Part XVII of that Act that accounting period shall be treated as ending on 15th March 1993.

Commentary—*Simon's Direct Tax Service* **D4.1205.**

120 Pay and file: miscellaneous amendments

Schedule 14 to this Act (which makes various amendments of the Taxes Management Act 1970 the Taxes Act 1988 and the Finance Act 1989 with a view to, or in connection with, the introduction of "pay and file") shall have effect.

[121 Repayments and payments to friendly societies

(1) The Treasury may by regulations provide, in relation to accounting periods beginning on or after 1st January 1994, for Schedule 19AB of the Taxes Act 1988 (payments on account of exempt pension business) to have effect, with such modifications and exceptions as may be specified in the regulations, in relation to any business to which this section applies as it has effect in relation to the pension business of an insurance company.

(2) This section applies to any business of a friendly society the profits arising from which are exempt from income tax and corporation tax under section 460(1), 461(1) or 461B(1) of the Taxes Act 1988 (life or endowment and other business), not being a business carried on by a friendly society all of whose profits are so exempt.

(3) Regulations under this section may make different provision for different cases.

(4) This section shall be without prejudice to section 463(1) of the Taxes Act 1988 (application of the Corporation Tax Acts to life or endowment business carried on by friendly societies).][1]

Commentary—*Simon's Direct Tax Service* **D4.606, 611.**
Regulations—Friendly Societies (Provisional Repayments for Exempt Business) Regulations, SI 1993/3112 (revoked for accounting periods ending after 30 June 1999).
Friendly Societies (Provisional Repayments for Exempt Business) Regulations, SI 1999/622.
Friendly Societies (Gilt-edged Securities) (Periodic Accounting for Tax on Interest) Regulations, SI 1999/624.

Cross references—See F(No 2)A 1997 Sch 3 para 12 (for the purposes of this section, TA 1988 Sch 19AB to have effect for pre-6 April 1999 distributions without the amendments otherwise made to it by F(No 2)A 1997 Sch 3 paras 10, 11).
Amendments—¹ This section repealed by FA 2001 s 110, Sch 33 Pt 2(12) with effect in accordance with FA 2001 s 87.

122 Application of Income Tax Acts etc to public departments

(1) (*amends TA 1988 s 829(2)*).

(2) The provisions of Parts IX and X of the Taxes Management Act 1970 (interest and penalties) shall apply in relation to public offices and departments of the Crown for the purposes, so far as they so apply, of the other provisions of that Act and of the provisions of the Income Tax Acts mentioned in section 829(1) of the Taxes Act 1988.

(3) This section shall have effect in relation to the year 1993–94 and subsequent years of assessment.

Commentary—*Simon's Direct Tax Service* **A3.1101; E4.955.**

123 Expenditure involving crime

(1) (*inserts TA 1988 s 577A*).

(2) This section shall apply in relation to expenditure incurred on or after 11th June 1993.

Commentary—*Simon's Direct Tax Service* **A4.301; B3.1202; D4.408.**

124 Expenses of Members of Parliament

(1) (*inserts TA 1988 s 200(2)*).

(2) This section shall apply in relation to sums paid on or after 1st January 1992.

(3) Any such adjustment (whether by way of discharge or repayment of tax, the making of an assessment or otherwise) as is appropriate in consequence of this section may be made.

Commentary—*Simon's Direct Tax Service* **E4.334.**

CHAPTER II
EXCHANGE GAINS AND LOSSES

Regulations—European Single Currency (Taxes) Regulations, SI 1998/3177 (Application of this chapter on the introduction of the European single currency).
Statement of Practice SP 4/98—Application of foreign exchange and financial instruments legislation to partnerships which include companies.
Revenue & other press releases—IR Booklet ''Exchange gains and losses and financial instruments—explanatory statement''.
Revenue Internal Guidance—Company Taxation Manual Volume VI gives a detailed description of the exchange gains and losses legislation.
COT13339 (Hansard extract confirming that where exchange differences are already included in a company's accounts on the translation basis, no adjustment is needed in the tax computation).
COT13340 (worked example).
COT13620–13651 (local currency).
Cross references—See FA 1994 s 177(6)(*b*) (Treasury's powers to amend provisions of this Chapter which relate to currency contracts),
FA 1994 s 226(2) (provisions of this Chapter not applicable to corporate members of Lloyd's).

Accrual of gains and losses

125 Accrual on qualifying assets and liabilities

(1) Subsection (2) below applies where a qualifying company holds a qualifying asset and there is a difference between—

    (a) the local currency equivalent, at the translation time with which an accrual period as regards the asset begins, of the basic valuation of the asset, and
    (b) the local currency equivalent, at the translation time with which the accrual period ends, of the basic valuation of the asset.

(2) There is as regards the asset an exchange difference for the accrual period, and—

    (a) if the difference represents an increase over the period, an initial exchange gain of an amount equal to the difference accrues to the company as regards the asset for the period;
    (b) if the difference represents a decrease over the period, an initial exchange loss of an amount equal to the difference accrues to the company as regards the asset for the period.

(3) Subsection (4) below applies where a qualifying company owes a qualifying liability and there is a difference between—

    (a) the local currency equivalent, at the translation time with which an accrual period as regards the liability begins, of the basic valuation of the liability, and
    (b) the local currency equivalent, at the translation time with which the accrual period ends, of the basic valuation of the liability.

(4) There is as regards the liability an exchange difference for the accrual period, and—

    (a) if the difference represents a decrease over the period, an initial exchange gain of an amount equal to the difference accrues to the company as regards the liability for the period;

(b) if the difference represents an increase over the period, an initial exchange loss of an amount equal to the difference accrues to the company as regards the liability for the period.

Note—This section repealed by FA 2002 ss 79(1)(*b*), (3), 141, Sch 40 Pt 3(10) with effect for accounting periods beginning after 30 September 2002.
Commentary—*Simon's Direct Tax Service* **D2.910, 913, 918.**
Revenue Internal Guidance—Company Taxation Manual COT13339 (separate computation for each contract not required; legislation mirrors accounting practice).
Cross references—See FA 1993 s 152 (meaning of ''qualifying companies'').
FA 1993 s 153 (meaning of ''qualifying assets'' and ''qualifying liabilities'').

126 Accrual on currency contracts

(1) This section applies where a qualifying company enters into a contract (a currency contract) under which—

(a) it becomes entitled to a right and subject to a duty to receive payment at a specified time of a specified amount of one currency (the first currency), and
(b) it becomes entitled to a right and subject to a duty to pay in exchange and at the same time a specified amount of another currency (the second currency).

[(1A) In deciding whether a contract falls within subsection (1) above it is immaterial that the rights and duties there mentioned may be exercised and discharged by a payment made to or, as the case may require, by the qualifying company of an amount (in whatever currency) designed to represent any difference in value at the specified time between the two payments referred to in that subsection.][1]

(2) Subsection (3) below applies if there is a difference between—

(a) the local currency equivalent, at the translation time with which an accrual period as regards the contract begins, of the amount of the first currency, and
(b) the local currency equivalent, at the translation time with which the accrual period ends, of the amount of the first currency.

(3) There is as regards the contract an exchange difference for the accrual period, and—

(a) if the difference represents an increase over the period, an initial exchange gain of an amount equal to the difference accrues to the company as regards the contract for the period;
(b) if the difference represents a decrease over the period, an initial exchange loss of an amount equal to the difference accrues to the company as regards the contract for the period.

(4) Subsection (5) below applies if there is a difference between—

(a) the local currency equivalent, at the translation time with which an accrual period as regards the contract begins, of the amount of the second currency, and
(b) the local currency equivalent, at the translation time with which the accrual period ends, of the amount of the second currency.

(5) There is as regards the contract an exchange difference for the accrual period, and—

(a) if the difference represents a decrease over the period, an initial exchange gain of an amount equal to the difference accrues to the company as regards the contract for the period;
(b) if the difference represents an increase over the period, an initial exchange loss of an amount equal to the difference accrues to the company as regards the contract for the period.

[(6) Subsection (7) below applies where—

(a) under a contract a qualifying company becomes entitled to a right and subject to a duty to receive or make a payment at a specified time, and
(b) the amount of the payment (in whatever currency) is computed in such a way as to be equal to the amount of the payment referred to in subsection (1A) above which would have fallen to be computed if—

(i) the qualifying company had been entitled and subject as mentioned in subsection (1) above, and
(ii) a payment such as is referred to in subsection (1A) above were to be made to or by the qualifying company.][2]

[(7) For the purposes of this Chapter—

(a) the qualifying company shall be deemed to have become entitled and subject as mentioned in subsection (1) above under the contract referred to in subsection (6) above;
(b) the payment made under the contract shall be treated as if it were a payment falling within subsection (1A) above in the exercise and discharge of the rights and duties to which the qualifying company is deemed to have become entitled and subject by virtue of paragraph (a) above.][2][3]

Note—This section repealed by FA 2002 ss 79(1)(*b*), (3), 141, Sch 40 Pt 3(10) with effect for accounting periods beginning after 30 September 2002.
Commentary—*Simon's Direct Tax Service* **D2.908, 910, 913, 925.**
Revenue Internal Guidance—Company Taxation Manual COT13546, 13547 (examples of currency contracts).
Cross references—See FA 1994 s 177(6)(*a*) (Treasury's powers to make amendments to this section).
Amendments—[1] Sub-s (1A) inserted by FA 1994 s 115(1).
[2] Sub-ss (6), (7) added by the Currency Contracts and Options (Amendment of Enactments) Order 1994, SI 1994/3233 art 3, with effect from 23 March 1995.

127 Accrual on debts whose amounts vary

(1) In a case where—

(a) a qualifying company holds an asset consisting of a right to settlement under a qualifying debt or owes a liability consisting of a duty to settle under such a debt, and

(b) the nominal amount of the debt outstanding varies during an accrual period (whether because of an increase or a decrease or both),

the following provisions of this section shall apply for the period and section 125 above shall not.

[(1A) For the purposes of this section if, in the case of any debt—

(a) an amount in respect of any discount or premium relating to that debt is treated, on an accruals basis of accounting, as accruing at any time for the purposes of Chapter II of Part IV of the Finance Act 1996 (loan relationships), or

(b) any such amount would be treated as so accruing if the authorised method of accounting used for those purposes as respects the loan relationship relating to that debt were an accruals basis of accounting, instead of a mark to market basis,

then, for the purposes of this section, there shall be deemed to be such a variation at that time of the nominal amount of the debt outstanding as is specified in subsection (1B) below.]¹

[(1B) That variation is—

(a) if the amount mentioned in paragraph (a) or (b) of subsection (1A) above relates to a discount, a variation that increases the nominal amount of the debt outstanding by the amount so mentioned; and

(b) if the amount so mentioned relates to a premium, a variation that decreases the nominal amount of the debt outstanding by the amount so mentioned.]¹

(2) In such a case—

(a) take the local currency equivalent, at the translation time with which the accrual period begins, of the nominal amount of the debt then outstanding;

(b) take the local currency equivalent, at each time (if any) immediately after the nominal amount of the debt outstanding increases in the accrual period, of the amount by which it then increases;

(c) take the local currency equivalent, at each time (if any) immediately after the nominal amount of the debt outstanding decreases in the accrual period, of the amount by which it then decreases;

(d) take the figure found under paragraph (a) above, add each figure found under paragraph (b) above, subtract each figure found under paragraph (c) above, and call the resulting figure the first amount;

(e) take the local currency equivalent, at the translation time with which the accrual period ends, of the nominal amount of the debt then outstanding, and call the figure so found the second amount.

(3) Where the qualifying company has a right to settlement under the debt the following provisions apply in relation to the asset consisting of the right—

(a) if the second amount exceeds the first an initial exchange gain of an amount equal to the difference between them accrues to the company as regards the asset for the accrual period;

(b) if the second amount is less than the first an initial exchange loss of an amount equal to the difference between them accrues to the company as regards the asset for the accrual period.

(4) Where the qualifying company has a duty to settle under the debt the following provisions apply in relation to the liability consisting of the duty—

(a) if the second amount is less than the first an initial exchange gain of an amount equal to the difference between them accrues to the company as regards the liability for the accrual period;

(b) if the second amount exceeds the first an initial exchange loss of an amount equal to the difference between them accrues to the company as regards the liability for the accrual period.

(5) If the first amount has a negative value, for the purposes of this section the second amount (however small its value) shall be taken to exceed the first amount (however large its value).

(6) Subsection (7) below modifies the preceding provisions of this section in their application to an asset or liability where there is a difference between—

(a) the basic valuation of the asset or liability, and

(b) the nominal amount of the debt outstanding at the translation time with which the accrual period begins.

(7) In such a case—

(a) the reference in subsection (2)(a) above to the nominal amount of the debt outstanding shall be taken to be a reference to the basic valuation of the asset or liability;

(b) the reference in subsection (2)(c) above to the amount by which the nominal amount of the debt outstanding decreases shall be taken to be a reference to the amount found under subsection (8) below;

(c) the reference in subsection (2)(e) above to the nominal amount of the debt outstanding shall be taken to be a reference to the amount found under subsection (10) below.

(8) The amount referred to in subsection (7)(b) above is the amount given by the formula—

$$A \times \frac{B}{C}$$

(9) For the purposes of subsection (8) above—

   A is the basic valuation of the asset or liability;
   B is the amount by which, at the time of the decrease mentioned in subsection (2)(c) above, the nominal amount of the debt outstanding then decreases;
   C is the nominal amount of the debt outstanding at the translation time with which the accrual period begins.

(10) The amount referred to in subsection (7)(c) above is the amount given by the formula—

$$D + E - F$$

(11) For the purposes of subsection (10) above—

   D is the basic valuation of the asset or liability;
   E is the amount (if any) by which the nominal amount of the debt outstanding has at any time increased in the accrual period or, if it has increased more than once, the aggregate of such amounts;
   F is the amount (if any) found under subsection (8) above or, if the nominal amount of the debt outstanding has decreased more than once in the accrual period, the aggregate of the amounts so found.

Note—This section repealed by FA 2002 ss 79(1)(b), (3), 141, Sch 40 Pt 3(10) with effect for accounting periods beginning after 30 September 2002.
Commentary—*Simon's Direct Tax Service* **D2.910, 913, 919.**
Revenue Internal Guidance—Company Taxation Manual COT13344 (worked examples). COT13339 (separate computation for each contract not required; legislation mirrors accounting practice).
Cross references—See FA 1996 Sch 15 para 22(1)–(3) (transitional provisions in respect of loan relationships existing immediately before and on 1 April 1996: continuing debts treated as entered into on 1 April 1996 for the purposes of sub-s (1A) above).
Amendments—¹ Sub-ss (1A), (1B) inserted by FA 1996 ss 104, 105(1), Sch 14 para 67 with effect for accounting periods ending after 31 March 1996, subject to transitional provisions in FA 1996 Sch 15.

Trading gains and losses

128 Trading gains and losses

(1) Subsections (2) to (4) below apply where—

   (a) as regards an asset, liability or contract an initial exchange gain accrues to a qualifying company for an accrual period, and
   (b) at any time in the period the asset or contract was held, or the liability was owed, by the company for the purposes of a trade or part of a trade carried on by it.

(2) If throughout the accrual period the asset or contract was held, or the liability was owed, by the company solely for the purposes of the trade or part the whole of the gain is an exchange gain of the trade or part for the period.

(3) In any other case the gain shall be apportioned on a just and reasonable basis and so much as is attributable to the trade or part is an exchange gain of the trade or part for the period.

(4) The company shall be treated for the purposes of the Tax Acts as—

   (a) receiving in respect of the trade or part an amount equal to the exchange gain of the trade or part for the accrual period, and
   (b) receiving the amount in respect of the accounting period which constitutes the accrual period or in which the accrual period falls.

(5) Subsections (6) to (8) below apply where—

   (a) as regards an asset, liability or contract an initial exchange loss accrues to a qualifying company for an accrual period, and
   (b) at any time in the period the asset or contract was held, or the liability was owed, by the company for the purposes of a trade or part of a trade carried on by it.

(6) If throughout the accrual period the asset or contract was held, or the liability was owed, by the company solely for the purposes of the trade or part the whole of the loss is an exchange loss of the trade or part for the period.

(7) In any other case the loss shall be apportioned on a just and reasonable basis and so much as is attributable to the trade or part is an exchange loss of the trade or part for the period.

(8) The company shall be treated for the purposes of the Tax Acts as—

   (a) incurring in the trade or part a loss of an amount equal to the exchange loss of the trade or part for the accrual period, and
   (b) incurring the loss in respect of the accounting period which constitutes the accrual period or in which the accrual period falls.

[(9) For the purposes of this section a part of a trade is any part of a trade which is treated for the purposes of section 93 above as if it were a separate business for the relevant accounting period;

and the relevant accounting period is the accounting period which constitutes the accrual period concerned or in which that accrual period falls.]²

(10) The preceding provisions of this section apply—

(a) whether the asset or contract is at any time held, or the liability is at any time owed, on revenue account or capital account, and

(b) notwithstanding anything in section 74 of the Taxes Act 1988 (general rules as to deductions not allowable).

[(10A) In a case where—

(a) an exchange gain of a trade or part of a trade or an exchange loss of a trade or part of a trade would (apart from this subsection) accrue to a company as regards a liability consisting of a duty to settle under a qualifying debt, and

(b) a charge is allowed to the company in respect of the debt under section 338 of the Taxes Act 1988 (allowance of charges on income and capital),

the exchange gain or loss shall be treated as not accruing.]¹

[(10B) A charge shall be treated as allowed as mentioned in subsection (10A) above if—

(a) it would be so allowed if the company's total profits were sufficient,

(b) it would be so allowed if the duty mentioned in that subsection were settled, and if in settling it payment were made out of the company's profits brought into charge to corporation tax, or

(c) it would be so allowed if the facts were as mentioned in both paragraph (a) and paragraph (b) above.]¹

(11) In a case where—

(a) an accounting period of a qualifying company begins on or after its commencement day, and

(b) but for this subsection, a gain or loss falling within subsection (12) below would be taken into account in calculating for the purposes of corporation tax the profits or losses for the period of a trade carried on by the company,

the gain or loss shall be left out of account in calculating the profits or losses.

(12) A gain or loss falls within this subsection if it—

(a) accrues to the company, otherwise than by virtue of this Chapter, as regards a qualifying asset or liability or a currency contract, and

(b) is attributable to fluctuations in currency exchange rates;

and it is immaterial whether the gain or loss is realised.

Note—This section repealed by FA 2002 ss 79(1)(b), (3), 141, Sch 40 Pt 3(10) with effect for accounting periods beginning after 30 September 2002.
Commentary—*Simon's Direct Tax Service* **D2.940.**
Revenue Internal Guidance—Company Taxation Manual COT13347 (this section over-rides TA 1988 s 74).
Amendments—¹ Sub-ss (10A), (10B) inserted by FA 1995 Sch 24 para 2, and are deemed always to have had effect.
² Sub-s (9) substituted by FA 2000 s 106(6), (17) with effect for accounting periods beginning after 31 December 1999 and ending after 20 March 2000.

Non-trading gains and losses

129 Non-trading gains and losses: general

(1) In a case where—

(a) as regards an asset, liability or contract an initial exchange gain accrues to a qualifying company for an accrual period, and

(b) the whole or part of the gain is not an exchange gain of a trade or part of a trade for the period,

the whole or part (as the case may be) is a non-trading exchange gain for the period.

(2) The company shall be treated as—

(a) receiving in respect of the asset, liability or contract an amount equal to the non-trading exchange gain for the accrual period, and

(b) receiving the amount in the accounting period which constitutes the accrual period or in which the accrual period falls;

[and the rule in section 130(1) below shall apply.]³

(3) In a case where—

(a) as regards an asset, liability or contract an initial exchange loss accrues to a qualifying company for an accrual period, and

(b) the whole or part of the loss is not an exchange loss of a trade or part of a trade for the period,

the whole or part (as the case may be) is a non-trading exchange loss for the period.

(4) The company shall be treated as—

(a) incurring in respect of the asset, liability or contract a loss of an amount equal to the non-trading exchange loss for the accrual period, and

(b) incurring the loss in the accounting period which constitutes the accrual period or in which the accrual period falls;

[and the rule in section 130(2) below shall apply.]³

(5), (6)...³

(7) In a case where—

> *(a) a non-trading exchange gain or loss would (apart from this subsection) accrue as regards an asset consisting of a right to settlement under a qualifying debt, and*
> *(b) the right is a right to receive income [that is not interest falling to be brought into account for the purposes of Chapter II of Part IV of the Finance Act 1996 (loan relationships) as interest accruing, or (according to the authorised method of accounting used) becoming due and payable, in an accounting period ending after 31st March 1996]³,*

the non-trading exchange gain or loss shall be treated as not accruing.

(8) In a case where—

> *(a) a non-trading exchange gain or loss would (apart from this subsection) accrue to a company as regards a liability consisting of a duty to settle under a qualifying debt, and*
> *(b) a charge is allowed to the company in respect of the debt under section 338 of the Taxes Act 1988 (allowance of charges on income and capital) ...,¹*

the non-trading exchange gain or loss shall be treated as not accruing.

[(8A) A charge shall be treated as allowed as mentioned in subsection (8) above if—

> *(a) it would be so allowed if the company's total profits were sufficient,*
> *(b) it would be so allowed if the duty mentioned in that subsection were settled, and if in settling it payment were made out of the company's profits brought into charge to corporation tax, or*
> *(c) it would be so allowed if the facts were as mentioned in both paragraph (a) and paragraph (b) above.]²*

(9) Section 396 of the Taxes Act 1988 (Case VI losses) shall not be taken to apply to a loss which a company is treated as incurring by virtue of this section; and an amount which a company is treated as receiving by virtue of this section shall not be regarded, for the purposes of subsection (1) of section 396, as income arising as mentioned in that subsection.

Note—This section repealed by FA 2002 ss 79(1)(b), (3), 141, Sch 40 Pt 3(10) with effect for accounting periods beginning after 30 September 2002.
Commentary—*Simon's Direct Tax Service* D2.941, 942.
Amendments—¹ Words omitted from sub-s (8) repealed by FA 1995 Sch 24 para 3(2), Sch 29 Pt VIII(17), and are deemed always to have been omitted.
² Sub-s (8A) inserted by FA 1995 Sch 24 para 3(3), and is deemed always to have had effect.
³ Words in sub-ss (2), (4), (7)(b) substituted and sub-ss (5), (6) repealed by FA 1996 ss 104, 105(1), Sch 14 para 68, Sch 41 Pt V(3) with effect for accounting periods ending after 31 March 1996, but subject to transitional provisions in FA 1996 Sch 15.

[130 Non-trading gains and losses

(1) Where a company is treated by virtue of section 129 above as receiving any amount in an accounting period, that amount shall be brought into account for that accounting period as if it were a non-trading credit falling for the purposes of Chapter II of Part IV of the Finance Act 1996 (loan relationships) to be brought into account in respect of a loan relationship of the company.

(2) Where a company is treated by virtue of section 129 above as incurring any loss in an accounting period, the amount of the loss shall be brought into account for that accounting period as if it were a non-trading debit falling for the purposes of Chapter II of Part IV of the Finance Act 1996 to be brought into account in respect of a loan relationship of the company.]¹

Note—This section repealed by FA 2002 ss 79(1)(b), (3), 141, Sch 40 Pt 3(10) with effect for accounting periods beginning after 30 September 2002.
Commentary—*Simon's Direct Tax Service* D2.942, 943.
Amendments—¹ This section substituted for ss 130–133 by FA 1996 ss 104, 105(1), Sch 14 para 69 with effect for accounting periods ending after 31 March 1996, but subject to transitional provisions in FA 1996 Sch 15.

Alternative calculation

134 Alternative calculation

Schedule 15 to this Act (which provides for the amount of an initial exchange gain or loss to be found in accordance with an alternative method of calculation in certain cases) shall have effect.

Note—This section repealed by FA 2002 ss 79(1)(b), (3), 141, Sch 40 Pt 3(10) with effect for accounting periods beginning after 30 September 2002.
Commentary—*Simon's Direct Tax Service* D2.930.

Main benefit test

135 Loss disregarded if the main benefit

(1) In a case where—

> *(a) an exchange loss would (apart from this section) accrue to a company for an accrual period,*
> *(b) the loss would accrue as regards an asset or liability falling within section 153(1)(a) or (2)(a) below, [and]¹*

(c) the nominal currency of the asset or liability is such that the main benefit or one of the main benefits that might be expected to arise from the company's holding the asset or owing the liability is the accrual of the loss, ...[2]

(d) ...[2]

the loss shall be treated as not accruing.

(2) *References in subsection (1) above to an exchange loss are to an exchange loss of a trade or an exchange loss of part of a trade or a non-trading exchange loss.*

Note—This section repealed by FA 2002 ss 79(1)(*b*), (3), 141, Sch 40 Pt 3(10) with effect for accounting periods beginning after 30 September 2002.
Commentary—*Simon's Direct Tax Service* **D2.955.**
Revenue and other press releases—IR 21-1-98 (the introduction of the Euro will not, of itself, trigger the anti-avoidance provisions provided no abuse takes place).
Revenue Internal Guidance—Company Taxation Manual COT13886 (examples on main benefit test).
Amendments—[1] Inserted by FA 1998 s 109 with effect for transactions entered into at any time as respects accounting periods ending on or after the day appointed by FA 1994 s 199 for the purposes of Chapter III of Part IV of that Act (1 July 1999).
[2] Repealed by FA 1998 s 109, Sch 27 Part III(26) with effect for transactions entered into at any time as respects accounting periods ending after 30 June 1999 (by virtue of Finance Act 1994, Section 199, (Appointed Day) Order, SI 1998/3173 art 2)..
Where a direction given after 16 March 1998 under FA 1993 s 135(1)(*d*) relates to any accounting period ending before the appointed day (1 July 1999), all such adjustments shall be made, whether by assessment, repayment of tax or otherwise, as are necessary to give effect to that direction.

[135A Sterling used if avoidance of gain is the main benefit

(1) *This section applies where, as regards qualifying assets and liabilities of a company—*

(a) *a currency other than sterling would (apart from this section) be the local currency for the purposes of sections 125 to 129 above; and*

(b) *the main benefit that might be expected to accrue from that currency being the local currency is that no net exchange gain would accrue to the company for those purposes.*

(2) *If a net exchange gain would accrue to the company if sterling were the local currency for the purposes of sections 125 to 129 above, then, as regards the assets and liabilities concerned, sterling shall be the local currency for those purposes.*

(3) *For the purposes of this section a net exchange gain accrues to a company if its initial exchange gains (as determined in accordance with this Chapter) exceed its initial exchange losses (as so determined).*][1]

Note—This section repealed by FA 2002 ss 79(1)(*b*), (3), 141, Sch 40 Pt 3(10) with effect for accounting periods beginning after 30 September 2002.
Commentary—*Simon's Direct Tax Service* **D2.959.**
Amendment—[1] This section inserted by FA 2000 s 106(7), (17) with effect for accounting periods beginning after 31 December 1999 and ending after 20 March 2000.

Arm's length test

136 Arm's length test: assets and liabilities

(1) *Subject to the following provisions of this section, subsection (2) below applies where—*

(a) *a qualifying company becomes entitled to a qualifying asset falling within section 153(1)(a) below or subject to a qualifying liability falling within section 153(2)(a) below,*

(b) *the transaction as a result of which the company becomes entitled or subject to the asset or liability would not have been entered into at all if the parties to the transaction had been dealing at arm's length, or the transaction's terms would have been different if they had been so dealing, [and]*[1]

(c) *as regards the asset or liability an exchange loss accrues to the company for an accrual period (or would so accrue apart from this section), ...*[2]

(d) *...*[2]

and any reference in this section to an exchange loss is to an exchange loss of a trade or an exchange loss of part of a trade or a non-trading exchange loss.

(2) *The exchange loss shall be treated as not accruing to the company for the accrual period.*

(3) *Where subsection (2) above applies and the accrual period is not the last to occur as regards the asset or liability while it is held or owed by the company—*

(a) *an amount equal to the amount of the loss shall be set off against appropriate exchange gains accruing to the company as regards the asset or liability for subsequent accrual periods, and*

(b) *any such gain shall then be treated as reduced by that amount or by so much of it as cannot be set off under this subsection against any such gain accruing for an earlier accrual period;*

and an appropriate exchange gain is an exchange gain of the trade concerned (if the exchange loss is an exchange loss of a trade) or an exchange gain of the part of the trade concerned (if the exchange loss is an exchange loss of part of a trade) or a non-trading exchange gain (if the exchange loss is a non-trading exchange loss).

(4) *Subsection (5) below applies where the circumstances are such that, had the parties to the transaction been dealing at arm's length, its terms would have been the same except that the amount*

of the debt would have been an amount (the adjusted amount) greater than nil but less than its actual amount.

(5) In such a case—

    (a) subsection (2) above shall not apply, and

    (b) the exchange loss accruing to the company for the accrual period shall be treated as reduced to the amount it would have been if the amount of the debt had been the adjusted amount;
...²

(6) Where subsection (5)(b) above applies and the accrual period is not the last to occur as regards the asset or liability while it is held or owed by the company—

    (a) an amount equal to the amount by which the loss is treated as reduced shall be set off against appropriate exchange gains accruing to the company as regards the asset or liability for subsequent accrual periods, and

    (b) any such gain shall then be treated as reduced by that amount or by so much of it as cannot be set off under this subsection against any such gain accruing for an earlier accrual period;

and an appropriate exchange gain is an exchange gain of the trade concerned (if the exchange loss is an exchange loss of a trade) or an exchange gain of the part of the trade concerned (if the exchange loss is an exchange loss of part of a trade) or a non-trading exchange gain (if the exchange loss is a non-trading exchange loss).

(7) Subsection (2) above shall not apply in a case where—

    (a) the right constituting the asset mentioned in subsection (1) above arises under a loan made by the company,

    (b) the circumstances are such that, had the parties to the transaction been dealing at arm's length, its terms would have been the same except that interest would have been charged on the loan or, as the case may be, charged at a higher rate, and

    (c) in computing for tax purposes the profits or losses of the company for the accounting period which constitutes the accrual period or in which the accrual period falls the whole of the loan [falls to be treated in accordance with Schedule 28AA to]³ the Taxes Act 1988 (undervalue or overvalue) as if interest had been charged on it or, as the case may be, charged at a higher rate.

(8) Subsection (9) below applies where—

    (a) paragraphs (a) and (b) of subsection (7) above apply, and

    (b) in computing for tax purposes the profits or losses of the company for the accounting period which constitutes the accrual period or in which the accrual period falls part of the loan [falls to be treated in accordance with Schedule 28AA to]³ the Taxes Act 1988 as if interest had been charged on it or, as the case may be, charged at a higher rate;

and in subsection (9) below the reference to the adjusted amount is to an amount equal to the part of the loan that has been so treated.

(9) In such a case—

    (a) subsection (2) above shall not apply, and

    (b) the exchange loss accruing to the company for the accrual period shall be treated as reduced to the amount it would have been if the amount of the loan had been the adjusted amount;
...²

(10) Where subsection (9)(b) above applies and the accrual period is not the last to occur as regards the asset while it is held by the company—

    (a) an amount equal to the amount by which the loss is treated as reduced shall be set off against appropriate exchange gains accruing to the company as regards the asset for subsequent accrual periods, and

    (b) any such gain shall then be treated as reduced by that amount or by so much of it as cannot be set off under this subsection against any such gain accruing for an earlier accrual period;

and an appropriate exchange gain is an exchange gain of the trade concerned (if the exchange loss is an exchange loss of a trade) or an exchange gain of the part of the trade concerned (if the exchange loss is an exchange loss of part of a trade) or a non-trading exchange gain (if the exchange loss is a non-trading exchange loss).

(11) Subsections (2) to (10) above shall not apply where—

    (a) the transaction is entered into by the company mentioned in subsection (1) above (company A) and another company (company B),

    (b) the companies are members of the same group when the transaction is entered into and throughout the accounting period which constitutes the accrual period mentioned in subsection (1) above or in which the accrual period falls,

    (c) as a result of the transaction, not only does company A become entitled or subject to the asset or liability falling within section 153(1)(a) or (2)(a) below but company B also becomes subject or entitled to the corresponding liability or asset (as the case may be) falling within section 153(2)(a) or (1)(a) below,

    (d) as regards that liability or asset an appropriate exchange gain accrues to company B for an accrual period coterminous with that mentioned in subsection (1) above,

(e) throughout the accrual period concerned company A holds or owes the asset or liability either for the purposes of one trade or for non-trading purposes,

(f) throughout the accrual period concerned company B owes or holds the liability or asset either for the purposes of one trade or for non-trading purposes, and

(g) amount X is the same as amount Y.

(12) For the purposes of subsection (11) above—

(a) an appropriate exchange gain is an exchange gain of a trade or a non-trading exchange gain found (in either case) in the currency in which the exchange loss mentioned in subsection (1) above is found;

(b) amount X is the amount of the exchange loss mentioned in subsection (1) above;

(c) amount Y is the amount of the exchange gain mentioned in subsection (11)(d) above, found without regard to section 139 below;

[(d) any question whether companies are members of the same group shall be determined in accordance with section 170 of the Taxation of Chargeable Gains Act 1992.][4]

(13) Where the exchange loss mentioned in subsection (1) above represents the whole or part of an initial exchange loss accruing under section 127 above, this section shall have effect as if subsections (4) to (12) were omitted.

(14) Regulations may make provision designed to supplement this section in its application to a case where the exchange loss mentioned in subsection (1) above represents the whole or part of an initial exchange loss accruing under section 127 above; and the regulations may in particular contain provision based on subsections (4) to (12) above but differing from those subsections to such extent as the Treasury think fit.

(15) In applying subsections (1)(b), (4) and (7)(b) above all factors shall be taken into account including any interest or other sums that would have been payable, any currency that would have been involved, and the amount that any loan would have been.

Note—This section repealed by FA 2002 ss 79(1)(b), (3), 141, Sch 40 Pt 3(10) with effect for accounting periods beginning after 30 September 2002.

Commentary—*Simon's Direct Tax Service* **D2.956.**

Revenue and other press releases—IR 21-1-98 (the introduction of the Euro will not, of itself, trigger the anti-avoidance provisions provided no abuse takes place).

Revenue Internal Guidance—Company Taxation Manual COT 13898, 13899 (worked examples).

Cross references—See FA 1993 s 136A (arm's length test: debts of varying amounts, disapplication of sub-s (2) above in certain circumstances).

Exchange Gains and Losses (Transitional Provisions) Regulations, SI 1994/3226 reg 2 (order of calculation under s 136 above and under the Regulations for existing assets, liabilities or contracts).

Exchange Gains and Losses (Alternative Method of Calculation of Gain or Loss) Regulations, SI 1994/3227 reg 12 (in applying sub-s (11) above exempt circumstances and matching elections to be ignored).

FA 2000 Sch 29 para 41(2) (the main amendments made to TCGA 1992 s 170 by FA 2000 Sch 29 para 1 have effect for the purposes of this section with effect for accruals periods beginning after 31 March 2000).

Amendments—[1] Inserted by FA 1998 s 109 with effect for transactions entered into at any time as respects accounting periods ending on or after the day appointed by FA 1994 s 199 for the purposes of Chapter III of Part IV of that Act (1 July 1999 by virtue of Finance Act 1994, Section 199, (Appointed Day) Order, SI 1998/3173 art 2).

[2] Words repealed by FA 1998 s 109, Sch 27 Part III(26) with effect for transactions entered into at any time as respects accounting periods ending on or after the day appointed by FA 1994 s 199 for the purposes of Chapter III of Part IV of that Act (1 July 1999 by virtue of SI 1998/3173 art 2). Where a direction given after 16 March 1998 under FA 1993 s 136(1)(d), (5) or (9) relates to any accounting period ending before the appointed day (1 July 1999), all such adjustments shall be made, whether by assessment, repayment of tax or otherwise, as are necessary to give effect to that direction.

[3] Words substituted in sub-ss (7) and (8) by FA 1998 s 108 with effect for corporation tax as respects accounting periods ending after 30 June 1999 (by virtue of SI 1998/3173 art 2), and for the purposes of income tax as respects any year of assessment ending after that date.

[4] Sub-s (12)(d) substituted by FA 2000 s 102, Sch 29 para 41 with effect for accrual periods beginning after 31 March 2000.

[136A *Arm's length test: debts of varying amounts*]

(1) The provisions of this section shall have effect in relation to any exchange loss mentioned in section 136(1) above which represents the whole or part of an initial exchange loss accruing under section 127 above.

(2) Subsection (3) below applies where the circumstances are such that, had the parties to the transaction referred to in section 136(1)(b) above been dealing at arms' length, the terms of the transaction would have been the same except that the amount of the debt at any time during the accrual period referred to in section 136(1)(c) would have been an amount (in subsection (3) below referred to as "the adjusted amount") less than its actual amount at that time.

(3) Where this subsection applies in relation to a debt—

(a) section 136(2) above shall not apply, and

(b) the exchange loss accruing to the company for the accrual period shall be treated as reduced to the amount it would have been if the amount of the debt had, at any time in the accrual period when the actual amount of the debt exceeded the adjusted amount, been equal to the adjusted amount;

...[2]

(4) Where subsection (3)(b) above applies and the accrual period is not the last to occur as regards the asset or liability while it is held or owed by the company—

(a) an amount equal to the amount by which the loss is treated as reduced shall be set off against appropriate exchange gains accruing to the company as regards the asset or liability for subsequent accrual periods, and

(b) any such gain shall then be treated as reduced by that amount or by so much of it as cannot be set off under this subsection against any such gain accruing for an earlier accrual period;

and an appropriate exchange gain is an exchange gain of the trade concerned (if the exchange loss is an exchange loss of a trade) or an exchange gain of the part of the trade concerned (if the exchange loss is an exchange loss of part of a trade) or a non-trading exchange gain (if the exchange loss is a non-trading exchange loss).

(5) Section 136(2) above shall not apply in a case where—

(a) the right constituting the asset mentioned in section 136(1)(a) above arises under a loan made by the company,

(b) the circumstances are such that, had the parties to the transaction been dealing at arm's length, its terms would have been the same except that interest would have been charged on the loan or, as the case may be, charged at a higher rate, and

(c) in computing for tax purposes the profits or losses of the company for the accounting period which constitutes the accrual period or in which the accrual period falls the whole of the loan [falls to be treated in accordance with Schedule 28AA to]³ the Taxes Act 1988 (transactions at an undervalue or overvalue) as if interest had been charged on it or, as the case may be, charged at a higher rate.

(6) Subsection (7) below applies where—

(a) paragraphs (a) and (b) of subsection (5) above apply, and

(b) in computing for tax purposes the profits or losses of the company for the accounting period which constitutes the accrual period or in which the accrual period falls, part of the loan [falls in relation to any time in that accrual period to be treated in accordance with Schedule 28AA to]³ the Taxes Act 1988 as if interest had been charged on it or, as the case may be, charged at a higher rate;

and in subsection (7) any reference to the adjusted amount is to an amount equal to the part of the loan that has been so treated.

(7) In any case where subsection (6) applies—

(a) section 136(2) above shall not apply, and

(b) the exchange loss accruing to the company for the accrual period shall be treated as reduced to the amount it would have been if the amount of the debt had, at any time in the accrual period when the actual amount of the debt exceeded the adjusted amount at that time, been equal to that adjusted amount (and if there is no adjusted amount at any time, the actual amount of the debt at that time shall be taken to be zero);

...²

(8) Where subsection (7)(b) above applies and the accrual period is not the last to occur as regards the asset while it is held by the company—

(a) an amount equal to the amount by which the loss is treated as reduced shall be set off against appropriate exchange gains accruing to the company as regards the asset for subsequent accrual periods, and

(b) any such gain shall then be treated as reduced by that amount or by so much of it as cannot be set off under this subsection against any such gain accruing for an earlier accrual period;

and an appropriate exchange gain is an exchange gain of the trade concerned (if the exchange loss is an exchange loss of a trade) or an exchange gain of the part of the trade concerned (if the exchange loss is an exchange loss of part of a trade) or a non-trading exchange gain (if the exchange loss is a non-trading exchange loss).

(9) Section 136(2) and subsections (2) to (8) above shall not apply where—

(a) the transaction is entered into by the company mentioned in section 136(1) above (company A) and another company (company B),

(b) the companies are members of the same group when the transaction is entered into and throughout the accounting period which constitutes the accrual period mentioned in section 136(1) above or in which the accrual period falls,

(c) as a result of the transaction, not only does company A become entitled or subject to the asset or liability falling within section 153(1)(a) or (2)(a) below but company B also becomes subject or entitled to the corresponding liability or asset (as the case may be) falling within section 153(2)(a) or (1)(a) below,

(d) as regards that liability or asset an appropriate exchange gain accrues to company B for an accrual period coterminous with that mentioned in section 136(1) above,

(e) throughout the accrual period concerned company A holds or owes the asset or liability either for the purposes of one trade or for non-trading purposes,

(f) throughout the accrual period concerned company B owes or holds the liability or asset either for the purposes of one trade or for non-trading purposes, and

(g) amount X is the same as amount Y.

(10) For the purposes of subsection (9) above—

    (a) an appropriate exchange gain is an exchange gain of a trade or a non-trading exchange gain found (in either case) in the currency in which the exchange loss mentioned in section 136(1) above is found;

    (b) amount X is the amount of the exchange loss mentioned in section 136(1) above;

    (c) amount Y is the amount of the exchange gain mentioned in subsection (9)(d) above, found without regard to section 139 below; and

    [(d) any question whether companies are members of the same group shall be determined in accordance with section 170 of the Taxation of Chargeable Gains Act 1992.][4].

(11) In applying subsections (2) and (5)(b) above all factors shall be taken into account including any interest or other sums that would have been payable, any currency that would have been involved, and the amount that any loan would have been.][1]

Note—This section repealed by FA 2002 ss 79(1)(b), (3), 141, Sch 40 Pt 3(10) with effect for accounting periods beginning after 30 September 2002.

Commentary—*Simon's Direct Tax Service* **D2.956.**

Cross references—See Exchange Gains and Losses (Alternative Method of Calculation of Gain or Loss) Regulations, SI 1994/3227 reg 12 (in applying sub-s (9) above, exempt circumstances and matching elections to be ignored).

FA 2000 Sch 29 para 42(2) (the main amendments made to TCGA 1992 s 170 by FA 2000 Sch 29 para 1 have effect for the purposes of this section with effect for accruals periods beginning after 31 March 2000).

Amendment—[1] Section inserted by the Exchange Gains and Losses (Debts of Varying Amounts) Regulations, SI 1994/3232 reg 2, with effect from 23 March 1995.

[2] Repealed by FA 1998 s 109, Sch 27 with effect for transactions entered into at any time as respects accounting periods ending after 30 June 1999 (by virtue of Finance Act 1994, Section 199, (Appointed Day) Order, SI 1998/3173 art 2). Where a direction given on or after 17 March 1998 under FA 1993 s 136A(3) or (7) relates to any accounting period ending before 1 July 1999, all such adjustments shall be made, whether by assessment, repayment of tax or otherwise, as are necessary to give effect to that direction.

[3] Words substituted in sub-ss (5) and (6) by FA 1998 s 108 with effect for corporation tax as respects accounting periods ending after 30 June 1999 (by virtue of SI 1998/3173 art 2), and for the purposes of income tax as respects any year of assessment ending after that date.

[4] Sub-s (10)(d) substituted by FA 2000 s 102, Sch 29 para 42 with effect for accruals periods beginning after 31 March 2000.

137 Arm's length test: currency contracts

(1) Subsection (2) below applies where—

    (a) a qualifying company enters into a currency contract,

    (b) the contract would not have been entered into at all if the parties to it had been dealing at arm's length, or the contract's terms would have been different if they had been so dealing, [and][1]

    (c) as regards the contract an exchange loss accrues to the company for an accrual period (or would so accrue apart from this section), ...[2]

...[2]

and any reference in this section to an exchange loss is to an exchange loss of a trade or an exchange loss of part of a trade or a non-trading exchange loss.

(2) The exchange loss shall be treated as not accruing to the company for the accrual period.

(3) Where subsection (2) above applies and the accrual period is not the last to occur as regards the contract while it is held by the company—

    (a) an amount equal to the amount of the loss shall be set off against appropriate exchange gains accruing to the company as regards the contract for subsequent accrual periods, and

    (b) any such gain shall then be treated as reduced by that amount or by so much of it as cannot be set off under this subsection against any such gain accruing for an earlier accrual period;

and an appropriate exchange gain is an exchange gain of the trade concerned (if the exchange loss is an exchange loss of a trade) or an exchange gain of the part of the trade concerned (if the exchange loss is an exchange loss of part of a trade) or a non-trading exchange gain (if the exchange loss is a non-trading exchange loss).

(4) In applying subsection (1)(b) above all factors shall be taken into account including any currency that would have been involved and any amounts that would have been involved.

Note—This section repealed by FA 2002 ss 79(1)(b), (3), 141, Sch 40 Pt 3(10) with effect for accounting periods beginning after 30 September 2002.

Commentary—*Simon's Direct Tax Service* **D2.957.**

Cross reference—See Exchange Gains and Losses (Transitional Provisions) Regulations, SI 1994/3226 reg 2 (order of calculations under this section and Regulations for existing assets, liabilities or contracts).

Amendments—[1] Inserted by FA 1998 s 109 with effect for transactions entered into at any time as respects accounting periods ending after 30 June 1999 (by virtue of Finance Act 1994, Section 199, (Appointed Day) Order, SI 1998/3173 art 2)

[2] Repealed by FA 1998 s 109, Sch 27 with effect for transactions entered into at any time as respects accounting periods ending after 30 June 1999 (by virtue of SI 1998/3173 art 2). Where a direction given after 16 March 1998 under FA 1993 s 137(1)(d) relates to any accounting period ending before 1 July 1999, all such adjustments shall be made, whether by assessment, repayment of tax or otherwise, as are necessary to give effect to that direction.

138 Arm's length test: non-sterling trades

(1) Subsection (2) below applies where—

    (a) an exchange gain of a trade, or of part of a trade, accruing to a company for an accrual period falls to be reduced by virtue of section 136(3), (6) or (10) or 137(3) above, and

(b) the amount falling to be set off is expressed in a currency (the first currency) different from the currency in which the gain is expressed (the second currency).

(2) For the purposes of section 136(3), (6) or (10) or 137(3) the amount falling to be set off shall be treated as the equivalent, expressed in the second currency, of the amount expressed in the first currency.

(3) The translation required by subsection (2) above shall be made by reference to the London closing exchange rate for the two currencies concerned for the first day of the accounting period which constitutes the relevant accrual period or in which that accrual period falls; and the relevant accrual period is the accrual period mentioned in subsection (1)(a) above.

(4) Subsection (2) above shall have effect subject to the application for succeeding accrual periods of this section as regards an amount falling to be set off.

(5) References in subsections (1) and (2) above to the amount falling to be set off include references to so much of that amount as remains after any application of section 136(3), (6) or (10) or 137(3) for earlier accrual periods.

Note—This section repealed by FA 2002 ss 79(1)(*b*), (3), 141, Sch 40 Pt 3(10) with effect for accounting periods beginning after 30 September 2002.
Commentary—*Simon's Direct Tax Service* **D2.956, 957.**

Deferral of unrealised gains

Cross reference—See European Single Currency (Taxes) Regulations, SI 1998/3177 reg 7 (deferral of unrealised gains in relation to the introduction of the euro).

139 Claim to defer unrealised gains

(1) This section applies where (apart from a claim under this section as regards an accounting period) an unrealised exchange gain would accrue to a company—

    (a) for an accrual period constituting or falling within the accounting period, and
    (b) as regards a long-term capital asset or a long-term capital liability;

and the reference here to an exchange gain is to an exchange gain of a trade or an exchange gain of part of a trade or a non-trading exchange gain.

(2) This section does not apply unless an amount is available for relief under this section for the accounting period.

(3) The company may claim that—

    (a) the gain, or part of it, shall be treated in accordance with section 140(3) below, and
    (b) an amount shall be treated in accordance with section 140(4) to (10) below as regards the asset or liability.

(4) The claim must—

    (a) stipulate the amount of the gain or part to be treated as mentioned in subsection (3)(a) above,
    (b) stipulate the amount to be treated as mentioned in subsection (3)(b) above;
    (c) identify the asset or liability concerned.

(5) The following rules apply to a claim—

    (a) only one claim may be made as regards an accounting period, but where this section applies in relation to two or more gains which would accrue to a company for an accrual period or accrual periods constituting or falling within the accounting period the claim may be made in relation to more than one of the gains;
    (b) the amount stipulated under subsection (4)(b) above as regards an asset or liability must be the same as, and must be expressed in the same currency as, the amount of the gain or part stipulated under subsection (4)(a) above as regards the asset or liability;
    (c) the amount (or total of the amounts) stipulated under subsection (4)(a) above as regards an accounting period must not exceed the amount available for relief under this section for the accounting period.

(6) A claim may not be made or withdrawn as regards an accounting period if—

    (a) the company has been assessed to corporation tax for the period, and
    (b) the assessment has become final and conclusive;

but the preceding provisions of this subsection do not apply if the claim or withdrawal is made before the expiry of the period of two years beginning with the end of the accounting period.

(7) In a case where—

    (a) the period of six years beginning with the end of an accounting period expires, and
    (b) no assessment of the company to corporation tax for the accounting period has become final and conclusive,

a claim may not be made or withdrawn as regards that accounting period.

(8) In a case where—

    (a) subsection (6) or (7) above would otherwise prevent a claim being made in a particular case, and

(b) the Board make a determination under this subsection,

a claim may be made on or before such day as the Board allow.

Note—This section repealed by FA 2002 ss 79(1)(b), (3), 141, Sch 40 Pt 3(10) with effect for accounting periods beginning after 30 September 2002.
Commentary—*Simon's Direct Tax Service* **D2.945, 949.**
Revenue Internal Guidance—Inspector's manual IM 2380a–2380g (whether foreign exchange profits are of a capital nature for sub-s (1)(b)).
Cross references—See Exchange Gains and Losses (Transitional Provisions) Regulations, SI 1994/3226 reg 2 (order of calculation under this section and Regulations for existing assets, liabilities or contracts).
Exchange Gains and Losses (Deferral of Gains and Losses) Regulations, SI 1994/3228 reg 4(2) (modification of sub-s (5) where claim made by a member of a group).
FA 2002 Sch 23 para 26 (the repeal of FA 1993 ss 139–143 does not prevent the making of a claim under FA 1993 s 139 in certain prescribed conditions).

140 Deferral of unrealised gains

1) This section applies where a claim is made under section 139 above as regards an asset or liability.

2) For the purposes of this section—

(a) the first accrual period is the accrual period mentioned in section 139(1) above, and
(b) the second accrual period is the accrual period next occurring as regards the asset or liability while it is held or owed by the company.

3) Any gain or part whose amount is stipulated under section 139(4)(a) above as regards the asset or liability shall be treated as not accruing as regards the asset or liability for the first accrual period.

4) If throughout the second accrual period the asset is held, or the liability is owed, by the company solely for the purposes of a trade or part of a trade—

(a) an exchange gain of the trade or part for the accrual period shall be treated as accruing to the company as regards the asset or liability,
(b) the amount of the gain shall be the amount stipulated under section 139(4)(b) above as regards the asset or liability, and
(c) section 128(4) above shall apply.

5) If throughout the second accrual period the asset is held, or the liability is owed, by the company solely for purposes other than trading purposes—

(a) a non-trading exchange gain for the accrual period shall be treated as accruing to the company as regards the asset or liability,
(b) the amount of the gain shall be the amount stipulated under section 139(4)(b) above as regards the asset or liability, and
(c) section 129(2) above shall apply.

6) Where as regards the second accrual period neither subsection (4) nor subsection (5) above applies—

(a) the amount stipulated under section 139(4)(b) above as regards the asset or liability shall be apportioned for the period on a just and reasonable basis, and
(b) subsections (7) and (8) below shall apply.

7) Where for the second accrual period part of an amount is attributed to a trade or part of a trade under subsection (6) above—

(a) an exchange gain of the trade or part for the accrual period shall be treated as accruing to the company as regards the asset or liability,
(b) the amount of the gain shall be the amount of the part so attributed, and
(c) section 128(4) above shall apply.

8) Where for the second accrual period part of an amount is attributed to purposes other than trading purposes under subsection (6) above—

(a) a non-trading exchange gain for the accrual period shall be treated as accruing to the company as regards the asset or liability,
(b) the amount of the gain shall be the amount of the part so attributed, and
(c) section 129(2) above shall apply.

9) In a case where—

(a) an exchange gain of a trade or of part of a trade for the second accrual period is treated as accruing to a company by virtue of the preceding provisions of this section (or would be so treated apart from this subsection), and
(b) in that period the asset or liability is to any extent held or owed by the company in exempt circumstances,

to that extent the gain shall be treated as a non-trading exchange gain (and not as a gain of the trade or part) and section 129(2) above shall apply.

10) Any apportionment required by subsection (9) above shall be made on a just and reasonable basis.

(11) Subsections (4) to (10) above shall have effect subject to any further application of section 13: above as regards the asset or liability.

[(12) For the purposes of this section a part of a trade is any part of a trade which is treated for th purposes of section 93 above as if it were a separate business for the relevant accounting period and the relevant accounting period is the accounting period which constitutes the second accrua period or in which that accrual period falls.][1]

Note—This section repealed by FA 2002 ss 79(1)(*b*), (3), 141, Sch 40 Pt 3(10) with effect for accounting periods beginning afte 30 September 2002.

Commentary—*Simon's Direct Tax Service* **D2.945, 949.**

Cross reference—See Exchange Gains and Losses (Transitional Provisions) Regulations, SI 1994/3226 reg 2 (order of calculatio under this section and Regulations for existing assets, liabilities or contracts). FA 2002 Sch 23 para 26 (the repeal of FA 199 ss 139–143 does not prevent the making of a claim under FA 1993 s 139 in certain prescribed conditions).

Amendment—[1] Sub-s (12) substituted by FA 2000 s 106(8) (17) with effect for accounting periods beginning after 31 Decembe 1999 and ending after 20 March 2000.

141 Deferral: amount available for relief

(1) An amount is available for relief under section 139 above for an accounting period if amount is exceeded by amount B or (if amount C is lower than amount B) amount A is exceeded by amour C; and the amount available for relief for the period is the amount of the difference between amour A and amount B or (as the case may be) between amount A and amount C.

(2) Amount A is one tenth of the amount falling within subsection (3) below.

(3) The amount falling within this subsection is an amount equal to the amount of the company' profits for the accounting period on which corporation tax would fall finally to be borne apart from–

    (a) a claim under section 139 above as regards the accounting period, and

    (b) section 402 of the Taxes Act 1988 (group relief);

and section 238(4) of the Taxes Act 1988 (amount of profits on which corporation tax falls finally t be borne) shall apply for the purposes of this subsection.

(4) Amount B is the amount found by deducting amount B(2) from amount B(1) where—

    (a) amount B(1) is the total amount of unrealised exchange gains which accrue or would (apar from a claim under section 139 above as regards the accounting period) accrue to the compan in an accrual period or accrual periods constituting or falling within the accounting period, a regards long-term capital assets or long-term capital liabilities or both;

    (b) amount B(2) is the total amount of unrealised exchange losses accruing to the company i such an accrual period or accrual periods as regards such assets or liabilities or both.

(5) Amount C is the amount found by deducting amount C(2) from amount C(1) where—

    (a) amount C(1) is the total amount of exchange gains which accrue or would (apart from a clair under section 139 above as regards the accounting period) accrue to the company, in an accru period or accrual periods falling within the accounting period, as regards relevant items;

    (b) amount C(2) is the total amount of exchange losses accruing to the company in such a accrual period or periods as regards relevant items.

(6) In subsections (4) and (5) above the references to exchange gains and losses are to exchang gains and losses of a trade and exchange gains and losses of part of a trade and non-tradin exchange gains and losses.

(7) For the purposes of subsection (5) above relevant items are—

    (a) assets falling within section 153(1)(a) below;

    (b) liabilities falling within section 153(2)(a) below;

    (c) currency contracts.

Note—This section repealed by FA 2002 ss 79(1)(*b*), (3), 141, Sch 40 Pt 3(10) with effect for accounting periods beginning af 30 September 2002.

Commentary—*Simon's Direct Tax Service* **D2.945, 947.**

Cross references—See Exchange Gains and Losses (Transitional Provisions) Regulations, SI 1994/3226 reg 2 (order calculation under this section and Regulations for existing assets, liabilities or contracts).

Exchange Gains and Losses (Deferral of Gains and Losses) Regulations, SI 1994/3228 reg 4 (modification of this section whe claim made by member of a group).

FA 2002 Sch 23 para 26 (the repeal of FA 1993 ss 139–143 does not prevent the making of a claim under FA 1993 s 139 certain prescribed conditions).

142 Deferral: non-sterling trades

(1) Where apart from this subsection—

    (a) a gain falling within section 139(1) above would be expressed in a currency other tha sterling, or

    (b) a gain or loss falling within section 141(4) or (5) above would be expressed in a curren other than sterling,

the amount of the gain or loss shall be treated for the purposes of sections 139 to 141 above as t sterling equivalent of its amount expressed in the other currency.

[(2) For the purposes of subsection (1) above the sterling equivalent of an amount is the sterlin equivalent calculated by reference to such rate of exchange as applies by virtue of section 94 abov

n the case of the profits or losses for the accounting period concerned of the business or part of
vhich the gain or loss is a gain or loss (or would be apart from section 139 above).]¹

3) Subsection (4) below applies where—

(a) part of an exchange gain of a [business]¹, or part of an exchange gain of part of a [business]¹,
is treated as not accruing to a company for an accrual period by virtue of section 140(3) above,
and

(b) the local currency of the [business]¹ or part for the accounting period which constitutes the
accrual period or in which it falls is a currency other than sterling.

(4) The amount the company is treated as receiving under section 128(4) or 129(2) above in respect
f the accounting period and by virtue of the gain (as reduced) shall be the amount computed and
xpressed in that currency.]¹

5) In a case where—

(a) an exchange gain of a [business]¹, or of part of a [business]¹, for an accrual period is treated
as accruing to a company under section 140 above, and

(b) the local currency of the [business]¹ or part for the accounting period which constitutes the
accrual period or in which it falls is a currency other than sterling,

he amount of the gain shall be treated as the local currency equivalent of its amount expressed in
terling.

5) The translation required by subsection (5) above shall be made by reference to the London
losing exchange rate for the two currencies concerned—

(a) for the last day of the accrual period mentioned in subsection (5) above, or

(b) if that accrual period does not end with the end of a day, for the day on which that accrual
period ends.

ote—This section repealed by FA 2002 ss 79(1)(b), (3), 141, Sch 40 Pt 3(10) with effect for accounting periods beginning after
30 September 2002.
ommentary—*Simon's Direct Tax Service* **D2.945, 948.**
ross references—FA 2002 Sch 23 para 26 (the repeal of FA 1993 ss 139–143 does not prevent the making of a claim under
FA 1993 s 139 in certain prescribed conditions).
mendments—¹ Sub-ss (2), (4) and words in sub-ss (3), (5) substituted by FA 2000 s 106(9)–(11), (17) with effect for accounting
periods beginning after 31 December 1999 and ending after 20 March 2000.

43 Deferral: supplementary

1) For the purposes of sections 139 and 141 above and this section an exchange gain or loss is
nrealised if the accrual period concerned is one which ends solely by virtue of an accounting period
f the company coming to an end.

2) In a case where—

(a) an unrealised exchange gain would accrue as mentioned in section 139(1) above,

(b) the gain represents the whole or part of an initial exchange gain accruing under section 127
above, and

(c) the whole or part of the unrealised exchange gain is attributable to any part by which the
nominal amount of the debt has decreased,

te company may not claim under section 139 above as regards so much of the unrealised exchange
ain as is so attributable.

3) In applying subsection (2)(c) above the gain shall be apportioned on a just and reasonable
asis.

4) For the purposes of sections 139 and 141 above an asset or liability is a long-term capital asset
r liability if the following conditions are fulfilled—

(a) the asset or liability falls within section 153(1)(a) or (2)(a) below,

(b) the debt under which it subsists is such that, under the terms as originally entered into, the
time for settlement is not less than one year from the time when the debt was created, and

(c) the asset or liability represents capital throughout the accounting period mentioned in section
139(1) above;

1d the time for settlement is the earliest time at which the creditor can require settlement if he
cercises all available options and rights.

') For the purposes of section 140 above an asset is held, or a liability is owed, in exempt
rcumstances at a given time if it is then held or owed—

(a) for the purposes of [long-term]¹ insurance business;

(b) for the purposes of mutual insurance business;

(c) for the purposes of the occupation of commercial woodlands;

(d) by a housing association approved at that time for the purposes of section 488 of the Taxes
Act 1988;

(e) by a self-build society approved at that time for the purposes of section 489 of that Act.

) In subsection (5) above—

["long-term insurance business" means business which consists of the effecting or carrying out of contracts which fall within Part II of Schedule 1 to the Financial Services and Markets Act 2000 (Regulated Activities) Order 2001;][1]
"commercial woodlands" means woodlands in the United Kingdom which are managed on a commercial basis and with a view to the realisation of profits.

(7) Regulations may—

(a) make provision modifying the effect of sections 139 to 142 above and the preceding provisions of this section in a case where the debt under which a long-term capital asset or liability subsists is settled and replaced to any extent by another debt under which (or other debts under each of which) such an asset or liability subsists;
(b) make provision modifying the effect of sections 139 to 142 above and the preceding provisions of this section in a case where a group of companies is involved;
(c) provide that the amount falling within section 141(3) above shall be treated as reduced in accordance with prescribed rules;

and any provision under paragraph (a) above may include provision that realised gains or losses are to be treated as wholly or partly unrealised.

Note—This section repealed by FA 2002 ss 79(1)(*b*), (3), 141, Sch 40 Pt 3(10) with effect for accounting periods beginning after 30 September 2002.
Commentary—*Simon's Direct Tax Service* **D2.945.**
Regulations—Exchange Gains and Losses (Deferral of Gains and Losses) Regulations, SI 1994/3228.
Cross references—FA 2002 Sch 23 para 26 (the repeal of FA 1993 ss 139–143 does not prevent the making of a claim under FA 1993 s 139 in certain prescribed conditions).
Amendments—[1] Word in sub-s (5)(*a*) substituted, and in sub-s (6), definition of "long-term insurance business" substituted, by the Financial Services and Markets Act 2000 (Consequential Amendments) (Taxes) Order, SI 2001/3629 arts 75, 76 with effect from 1 December 2001 immediately after the coming into force of the Financial Services and Markets Act 2000 ss 411, 432(1), Sch 20.

Irrecoverable debts

144 Irrecoverable debts

(1) In a case where—

(a) a qualifying company holds an asset consisting of a right to settlement under a qualifying debt or owes a liability consisting of a duty to settle under such a debt, and
(b) ...[1] as regards any accounting period of the company, ...[1] all of the debt outstanding immediately before the end of the period could at that time reasonably have been regarded as irrecoverable,
the company shall be treated for the purposes of this Chapter as if immediately before the end of that accounting period it ceased to be entitled to the asset or subject to the liability.

(2) Subsection (3) below applies in a case where—

(a) paragraph (a) of subsection (1) above applies, and
(b) ...1 as regards any accounting period of the company, ...1 part of the debt outstanding immediately before the end of the period could at that time reasonably have been regarded as irrecoverable.

(3) The company shall be treated for the purposes of this Chapter as if—

(a) immediately after the beginning of the accounting period next following the accounting period mentioned in subsection (2) above there were a decrease in the nominal amount of the debt outstanding, and
(b) the decrease were of an amount equal to so much of the debt, expressed in its settlement currency, as was outstanding immediately before the end of the accounting period mentioned in subsection (2) above and ...[1] could at that time reasonably have been regarded as irrecoverable.

(4) ..[1]

Note—This section repealed by FA 2002 ss 79(1)(*b*), (3), 141, Sch 40 Pt 3(10) with effect for accounting periods beginning after 30 September 2002.
Commentary—*Simon's Direct Tax Service* **D2.918.**
Revenue Internal Guidance—Company Taxation Manual COT13383 (Inspectors will adopt the same approach as for the purposes of TA 1988 s 74(1)(j)).
Cross reference—See Exchange Gains and Losses (Transitional Provisions) Regulations, SI 1994/3226 reg 4 (bad debts in respect of existing assets or liabilities).
Amendments—[1] Words in sub-ss (1)–(3) and whole of sub-s (4) repealed by FA 1996 s 134(1), (2), Sch 20 para 68, Sch 41 Pt V(10) with effect for accounting periods ending after 30 June 1999 (by virtue of Finance Act 1994, Section 199, (Appointed Day) Order, SI 1998/3173 art 2).

145 Irrecoverable debts that become recoverable

(1) Subsection (2) below applies where—

(a) a company has been treated as mentioned in section 144(1) above as regards a debt,
(b) at a time (the later time) falling after the end of the accounting period mentioned in section 144(1)(b) above all or part of the debt is actually outstanding, and
(c) ...[1] all or part of the amount actually outstanding at the later time could at that time reasonably have been regarded as recoverable.

(2) *The company shall be treated for the purposes of this Chapter as if—*

(a) *immediately after the later time it had become entitled to an asset consisting of a right to settlement under the debt or (as the case may be) subject to a liability consisting of a duty to settle under the debt, and*

(b) *the nominal amount of the debt outstanding, at the time the company became entitled or subject to the asset or liability, were an amount equal to so much of the debt, expressed in its settlement currency, as was actually outstanding at the later time and ...[1] could at that time reasonably have been regarded as recoverable.*

(3) *Subsections (4) and (5) below apply where—*

(a) *a company has been treated as mentioned in section 144(3) above as regards a debt, or*

(b) *a company has been treated as mentioned in subsection (2) above as regards a debt by virtue of the fact that ...[1] part of the debt could, at the later time, reasonably have been regarded as recoverable.*

(4) *In a case where—*

(a) *at a time (the relevant time) falling after the end of the accounting period mentioned in section 144(2)(b) above or (as the case may be) falling after the later time all or part of the debt is actually outstanding,*

(b) *...[1] all or part of the amount actually outstanding at the relevant time could at that time reasonably have been regarded as recoverable, and*

(c) *the recoverable amount exceeds the amount which (taking into account section 144(3) above, subsection (2) above and any previous application of this subsection) is the nominal amount of the debt outstanding at the relevant time,*

the company shall be treated for the purposes of this Chapter as if, immediately after the relevant time, there were an increase in the nominal amount of the debt outstanding and the increase were of an amount equal to the excess mentioned in paragraph (c) above.

(5) *For the purposes of subsection (4) above the recoverable amount is an amount equal to so much of the debt, expressed in its settlement currency, as was actually outstanding at the relevant time and ...[1] could at that time reasonably have been regarded as recoverable.*

(6) *...[1].*

Note—This section repealed by FA 2002 ss 79(1)(*b*), (3), 141, Sch 40 Pt 3(10) with effect for accounting periods beginning after 30 September 2002.
Commentary—*Simon's Direct Tax Service* **D2.918.**
Amendments—[1] Words in sub-ss (1)–(5) and whole of sub-s (6) repealed by FA 1996 s 134(1), (2), Sch 20 para 69, Sch 41 Pt V(10) with effect for accounting periods ending after 30 June 1999 (by virtue of Finance Act 1994, Section 199, (Appointed Day) Order, SI 1998/3173 art 2).

Currency contracts: special cases

146 Early termination of currency contract

(1) *This section applies where—*

(a) *a qualifying company ceases to be entitled to rights and subject to duties under a currency contract, and*

(b) *at the time it so ceases it has neither received nor made payment of any currency in pursuance of the contract.*

[(1A) *This section also applies where—*

(a) *a qualifying company ceases to be entitled to rights and subject to duties under a currency contract, and*

(b) *it so ceases by virtue of the making of a payment to or by the company of an amount (in whatever currency) designed to represent any difference in value at the specified time between the two payments referred to in section 126(1) above.]*[1]

(2) *If the company has a net contractual gain of a trade it shall be treated for the purposes of the Tax Acts as—*

(a) *incurring in the trade a loss of an amount equal to that gain, and*

(b) *incurring the loss in respect of the last relevant accounting period.*

(3) *If the company has a net contractual loss of a trade it shall be treated for the purposes of the Tax Acts as—*

(a) *receiving in respect of the trade an amount equal to that loss, and*

(b) *receiving the amount in respect of the last relevant accounting period.*

(4) *If the company has a net contractual non-trading gain—*

(a) *it shall be treated as incurring by virtue of section 129 above a loss of an amount equal to the amount of that gain,*

(b) *it shall be treated as incurring the loss in the last relevant accounting period, and*

(c) *in relation to that accounting period references to amount B shall be construed accordingly.*

(5) *If the company has a net contractual non-trading loss—*

(a) it shall be treated as receiving by virtue of section 129 above an amount equal to the amount of that loss,

(b) it shall be treated as receiving the amount in the last relevant accounting period, and

(c) in relation to that accounting period references to amount A shall be construed accordingly.

(6) For the purposes of this section—

(a) the termination time is the time mentioned in subsection (1)(b) above;

(b) the last relevant accounting period is the company's accounting period in which the termination time falls;

(c) the relevant accounting periods are that accounting period and the company's accounting periods preceding it.

(7) This is how to find out whether the company has a net contractual gain or loss of a trade and (if it has) its amount—

(a) take the aggregate of the amounts (if any) the company is treated as receiving under section 128(4) above in respect of the trade and the contract and the relevant accounting periods;

(b) take the aggregate of the amounts (if any) of the losses the company is treated as incurring under section 128(8) above in the trade and in respect of the contract and the relevant accounting periods;

(c) if the amount found under paragraph (a) above exceeds that found under paragraph (b) above the company has a net contractual gain of the trade of an amount equal to the excess;

(d) if the amount found under paragraph (b) above exceeds that found under paragraph (a) above the company has a net contractual loss of the trade of an amount equal to the excess;

and in applying paragraphs (a) and (b) above ignore the effect of subsections (2) and (3) above.

(8) This is how to find out whether the company has a net contractual non-trading gain or loss and (if it has) its amount—

(a) take the aggregate of the amounts (if any) the company is treated as receiving under section 129(2) above in respect of the contract in the relevant accounting periods;

(b) take the aggregate of the amounts (if any) of the losses the company is treated as incurring under section 129(4) above in respect of the contract in the relevant accounting periods;

(c) if the amount found under paragraph (a) above exceeds that found under paragraph (b) above the company has a net contractual non-trading gain of an amount equal to the excess;

(d) if the amount found under paragraph (b) above exceeds that found under paragraph (a) above the company has a net contractual non-trading loss of an amount equal to the excess;

and in applying paragraphs (a) and (b) above ignore the effect of subsections (4) and (5) above.

(9) For the purposes of subsection (7) above—

(a) an amount the company is treated as receiving under section 128(4) above in respect of part of the trade concerned shall be treated as received in respect of the trade;

(b) a loss the company is treated as incurring under section 128(8) above in part of the trade shall be treated as incurred in the trade.

(10) Where any amount or loss the company is treated as receiving or incurring as mentioned in subsection (7)(a) or (b) above would (apart from this subsection) be expressed in a currency other than the local currency of the trade for the last relevant accounting period, it shall be treated for the purposes of this section as being the local currency equivalent of the amount or loss expressed in that other currency.

(11) For the purposes of subsection (10) above the local currency equivalent of an amount is the equivalent—

(a) expressed in the local currency of the trade for the last relevant accounting period, and

(b) calculated by reference to the London closing exchange rate for the day in which the termination time falls.

(12) Subsection (13) below applies where the company has (apart from that subsection) a net contractual gain or loss of a trade and—

(a) the trade concerned has ceased before the termination time, or

(b) the company carries on exempt activities immediately before the termination time.

(13) In such a case the company shall be treated for the purposes of this section as if—

(a) it did not have the net contractual gain or loss of the trade, and

(b) it had a net contractual non-trading gain or loss (as the case may be) equal to the amount which would have been the amount of the net contractual gain or loss of the trade apart from paragraph (a) above.

(14) Where any amount found under subsection (13)(b) above would (apart from this subsection) be expressed in a currency other than sterling, it shall be treated for the purposes of this section as being the sterling equivalent of the amount expressed in that other currency; and any translation required by this subsection shall be made by reference to the London closing exchange rate for the currencies concerned for the day in which the termination time falls.

(15) For the purposes of this section a company carries on exempt activities at a given time if—

(a) the activities it then carries on are or include any of the activities mentioned in subsection (16) below,

(b) it is a housing association approved at that time for the purposes of section 488 of the Taxes Act 1988 or

(c) it is a self-build society approved at that time for the purposes of section 489 of that Act.

(16) The activities referred to in subsection (15)(a) above are—

(a) the activity of [long-term]² insurance business;

(b) the activity of mutual insurance business;

(c) the activity of the occupation of commercial woodlands;

and section 143(6) above applies for the purposes of this subsection.

Note—This section repealed by FA 2002 ss 79(1)(b), (3), 141, Sch 40 Pt 3(10) with effect for accounting periods beginning after 30 September 2002.

Commentary—*Simon's Direct Tax Service* **D2.926.**

Cross references—See FA 1994 s 150(9), 151(2)(c) (treatment of net payments and receipts where contract does not go to delivery).

Modifications—The effect of this section is modified by the Exchange Gains and Losses (Miscellaneous Modifications) Regulations, SI 2000/3315 reg 11 so that where—

(a) the Exchange Gains and Losses (Alternative Method of Calculation of Gain or Loss) Regulations, SI 1994/3227 reg 5(2)(b) applies so as to reduce the amount of an initial exchange gain or initial exchange loss which, apart from that regulation, would accrue to a company as respects a liability, and

(b) this section applies.

this section has effect as if the reduction referred to in (a) above had not been made.

Amendments—¹ Sub-s (1A) inserted by FA 1994 s 115(2).

Word in sub-s (16) substituted by the Financial Services and Markets Act 2000 (Consequential Amendments) (Taxes) Order, SI 2001/3629 arts 75, 77 with effect from 1 December 2001 immediately after the coming into force of the Financial Services and Markets Act 2000 ss 411, 432(1), Sch 20.

147 Reciprocal currency contracts

1) This section applies where—

(a) a qualifying company enters into a currency contract (the first contract), and

(b) the company closes out that contract by entering into another currency contract (the second contract) with rights and duties which are reciprocal to those under the first contract.

2) For the purposes of this Chapter the company shall be treated as ceasing, at the time it enters into the second contract, to be entitled to rights and subject to duties under the first contract without having received or made payment of any currency in pursuance of the first contract.

3) For the purposes of this Chapter the second contract shall be ignored (except in applying the preceding provisions of this section).

Note—This section repealed by FA 2002 ss 79(1)(b), (3), 141, Sch 40 Pt 3(10) with effect for accounting periods beginning after 30 September 2002.

Commentary—*Simon's Direct Tax Service* **D2.926.**

Cross references—See FA 1994 s 153(3) (treatment of payment or receipt where contract closed by reciprocal contract).

Excess gains or losses

148 Excess gains or losses

1) Regulations may provide that where prescribed conditions are fulfilled as regards an asset or liability relief from tax shall be afforded in respect of it; and subsections (2) to (4) below shall apply for the purposes of the regulations.

2) The prescribed conditions must be or include ones that are met where it can reasonably be said that—

(a) a loss other than an exchange loss has accrued to a qualifying company as regards the asset or liability and no relief from tax is available under the Tax Acts in respect of the loss, and

(b) exchange gains have accrued to the company as regards the asset or liability without being matched (or fully matched) by exchange losses accruing to the company as regards the asset or liability.

3) The relief shall take such form as is prescribed and shall be such that the amount relieved does not exceed the amount of the unmatched gains.

4) The regulations may provide that if the loss mentioned in subsection (2)(a) above is made good to any extent the relief afforded by the regulations shall be cancelled (to the extent prescribed) by an assessment to tax.

5) Regulations may provide that where prescribed conditions are fulfilled as regards an asset or liability a charge to tax shall be imposed in respect of it; and subsections (6) and (7) below shall apply for the purposes of the regulations.

6) The prescribed conditions must be or include ones that are met where it can reasonably be said that—

(a) a gain other than an exchange gain has accrued to a qualifying company as regards the asset or liability and no charge to tax is imposed under the Tax Acts in respect of the gain, and

(b) exchange losses have accrued to the company as regards the asset or liability without being matched (or fully matched) by exchange gains accruing to the company as regards the asset or liability.

(7) The charge shall take such form as is prescribed and shall be such that the amount charged does not exceed the amount of the unmatched losses.

(8) Regulations under this section may include provision that the relief—

(a) is subject to a claim being made;
(b) is not available in prescribed circumstances.

(9) Where (apart from this subsection) an exchange gain or loss would be expressed in a currency other than sterling, the amount of the gain or loss shall be treated for the purposes of this section as the sterling equivalent of its amount expressed in the other currency.

(10) The translation required by subsection (9) above shall be made by reference to the London closing exchange rate for the two currencies concerned—

(a) for the last day of the accrual period for which the gain or loss accrues, or
(b) if that accrual period does not end with the end of a day, for the day on which that accrual period ends.

(11) In this section—

(a) references to an exchange gain are to an exchange gain of a trade or an exchange gain of part of a trade or a non-trading exchange gain;
(b) references to an exchange loss are to an exchange loss of a trade or an exchange loss of part of a trade or a non-trading exchange loss.

Note—This section repealed by FA 2002 ss 79(1)(b), (3), 141, Sch 40 Pt 3(10) with effect for accounting periods beginning after 30 September 2002.
Commentary—*Simon's Direct Tax Service* **D2.965.**
Regulations—Exchange Gains and Losses (Excess Gains and Losses) Regulations, SI 1994/3229.

Local currency to be used

149 Local currency to be used

(1) Subject to the following provisions of this section, the local currency for the purposes of sections 125 to 127 above is sterling.

(2) Subsections (4) to (6) below apply where—

(a) at any time in an accrual period an asset or contract was held, or a liability was owed, by a qualifying company for the purposes of a [business or businesses]¹ carried on by it or of part or parts of a [business or businesses]¹ carried on by it, and
(b) the local currency of [any such business]¹ or part for the relevant accounting period is a currency other than sterling.

(3) References in this section to the relevant accounting period are to the accounting period which constitutes the accrual period or in which the accrual period falls.

(4) If throughout the accrual period ...² only one local currency is involved, [sections 125 to 129]² above shall be applied by reference to that currency.

(5) If throughout the accrual period ...² more than one local currency is involved, [sections 125 to 129]² above shall be applied separately by reference to each local currency involved and any exchange gain or loss of a [business]² or part shall be ignored unless found in the currency which is the local currency of the [business]² or part for the relevant accounting period.

[(6) In any other case—

(a) sections 125 to 129 above shall be applied by reference to sterling;
(b) those sections shall then be applied separately by reference to each local currency involved (other than sterling); and
(c) any exchange gain or loss of a business or part shall be ignored unless found in the currency which is the local currency of the business or part for the relevant accounting period (whether sterling or otherwise).]²

[(7) For the purposes of this section a part of a business is any part of a business which is treated for the purposes of section 93 above as if it were a separate business for the relevant accounting period.]²

Note—This section repealed by FA 2002 ss 79(1)(b), (3), 141, Sch 40 Pt 3(10) with effect for accounting periods beginning after 30 September 2002.
Commentary—*Simon's Direct Tax Service* **D2.910, 911, 913.**
Amendments—¹ Words in sub-s (2)(a) substituted for words "trade or trades" in both places, and words in sub-s (2)(b) substituted for words "any such trade" by FA 2000 ss 106(1)–(5), (17), 156, Sch 40 Pt II(15) with effect for accounting periods beginning after 31 December 1999 and ending after 20 March 2000.
² Words in sub-ss (4), (5) and whole of sub-ss (6), (7) substituted, and words in sub-ss (4), (5) repealed, by FA 2000 ss 106(1)–(5), (17), 156, Sch 40 Pt II(15) with effect for accounting periods beginning after 31 December 1999 and ending after 20 March 2000.

Exchange rate to be used

150 Exchange rate at translation times

(1) This section has effect to determine the exchange rate to be used in finding for the purposes of this Chapter the local currency equivalent at a translation time of—

    (a) the basic valuation of an asset or liability,

    (b) the nominal amount of a debt outstanding, or

    (c) an amount of currency.

(2) References in this section to the two currencies are to—

    (a) the local currency and the nominal currency of the asset or liability concerned (where this section applies by virtue of subsection (1)(a) or (1)(b) above), or

    (b) the local currency and the currency mentioned in subsection (1)(c) above (where this section applies by virtue of subsection (1)(c) above).

(3) References in this section to an arm's length rate are to such exchange rate for the two currencies as might reasonably be expected to be agreed between persons dealing at arm's length.

(4) Subsections (5) to (7) below apply where the translation time is a translation time solely by virtue of an accounting period of the company coming to an end.

(5) In a case where—

    (a) an exchange rate for the two currencies is used (as regards the asset, liability or currency contract concerned) in the accounts of the company for the last day of the accounting period, and

    (b) the rate is an arm's length rate,

that is the exchange rate to be used as regards the asset, liability or contract.

(6) In a case where—

    (a) the provision for whose purposes the local currency equivalent falls to be found is section 126 above,

    (b) an exchange rate for the two currencies is not used (as regards the currency contract concerned) in the accounts of the company for the last day of the accounting period,

    (c) the fact that such an exchange rate is not so used conforms with [generally accepted accounting practice][1], and,

    (d) the exchange rate for the two currencies that is implied by the currency contract concerned is an arm's length rate,

the exchange rate mentioned in paragraph (d) above is the exchange rate to be used as regards the contract.

(7) In a case where neither subsection (5) nor subsection (6) above applies, the London closing exchange rate for the two currencies for the last day of the accounting period is the exchange rate to be used.

(8) Subsections (9) to (14) below apply where the translation time is a translation time otherwise than solely by virtue of an accounting period of the company coming to an end.

(9) In a case where—

    (a) an exchange rate for the two currencies is used (as regards the asset, liability or currency contract concerned) in the accounts of the company at the translation time,

    (b) the rate represents the average of arm's length rates for all the days falling within a period, and

    (c) the arm's length rate for any given day (other than the first) falling within the period is not significantly different from the arm's length rate for the day preceding the given day,

that is the exchange rate to be used as regards the asset, liability or contract.

(10) In a case where—

    (a) subsection (9) above does not apply,

    (b) an exchange rate for the two currencies is used (as regards the asset, liability or currency contract concerned) in the accounts of the company at the translation time, and

    (c) the rate is an arm's length rate,

that is the exchange rate to be used as regards the asset, liability or contract.

(11) In a case where—

    (a) the provision for whose purposes the local currency equivalent falls to be found is section 126 above,

    (b) an exchange rate for the two currencies is not used (as regards the currency contract concerned) in the accounts of the company at the translation time,

    (c) the fact that such an exchange rate is not so used conforms with [generally accepted accounting practice][1], and

    (d) the exchange rate for the two currencies that is implied by the currency contract concerned is an arm's length rate,

the exchange rate mentioned in paragraph (d) above is the exchange rate to be used as regards the contract.

(12) In a case where—

(a) none of subsections (9) to (11) above applies,

(b) it is the company's normal practice, when using an exchange rate in its accounts, to use a rate which represents an average of exchange rates obtaining for a period, and

(c) the London closing exchange rate for the two currencies for any given day (other than the first) falling within the relevant period is not significantly different from the London closing exchange rate for the two currencies for the day preceding the given day,

the rate which represents the average of the London closing exchange rates for the currencies for all the days falling within the relevant period is the exchange rate to be used.

(13) In a case where none of subsections (9) to (12) above applies, the London closing exchange rate for the day in which the translation time falls is the exchange rate to be used.

(14) References in subsection (12) above to the relevant period are to the period which—

(a) begins when the relevant accounting period begins, and

(b) ends at the end of the day in which the translation time falls;

and the relevant accounting period is the accounting period in which the translation time falls.

Note—This section repealed by FA 2002 ss 79(1)(b), (3), 141, Sch 40 Pt 3(10) with effect for accounting periods beginning after 30 September 2002.
Commentary—*Simon's Direct Tax Service* D2.914, 975.
Revenue Internal Guidance—Company Taxation Manual COT13563 (exchange rates on currency contracts).
COT13334 (period of averaging not specified: monthly average used in accounts may be accepted; weighted average may be appropriate in some circumstances).
Cross reference—See Exchange Gains and Losses (Transitional Provisions) Regulations, SI 1994/3226 reg 5 (application of this section to an existing asset liability or contract).
Amendments—¹ In sub-ss (6)(c), (11)(c), words substituted for the words "normal accountancy practice" by FA 2002 s 103(4)(b) with effect from the 24 July 2002.

151 Exchange rate for debts whose amounts vary

(1) Subsection (2) below has effect to determine the exchange rate to be used in finding for the purposes of this Chapter the local currency equivalent, at a time immediately after the nominal amount of a debt outstanding increases or decreases, of any amount.

(2) Subsections (9) to (14) of section 150 above (ignoring subsection (11)) shall apply for that purpose, but in so applying them—

(a) references to the translation time shall be construed as references to the time mentioned in subsection (1) above;

(b) references to the two currencies shall be construed as references to the local currency and the settlement currency of the debt.

Note—This section repealed by FA 2002 ss 79(1)(b), (3), 141, Sch 40 Pt 3(10) with effect for accounting periods beginning after 30 September 2002.
Commentary—*Simon's Direct Tax Service* D2.914.

Interpretation: companies

152 Qualifying companies

(1) Subject to the following provisions of this section, any company is a qualifying company.

(2) ...¹

(3) Where a unit trust scheme is an authorised unit trust as respects an accounting period the trustees (who are deemed to be a company for certain purposes by section 468(1) of the Taxes Act 1988) are not a qualifying company as regards that period.

(4) A company which is approved for the purposes of section 842 of the Taxes Act 1988 (investment trusts) for an accounting period is not a qualifying company as regards that period.

(5) In this section—

"unit trust scheme" has the same meaning as in section 469 of the Taxes Act 1988;

"authorised unit trust" has the same meaning as in section 468 of that Act.

Note—This section repealed by FA 2002 ss 79(1)(b), (3), 141, Sch 40 Pt 3(10) with effect for accounting periods beginning after 30 September 2002.
Commentary—*Simon's Direct Tax Service* D2.901, 905, 971.
Modification—This section is modified, for open-ended investment companies, by the Open-ended Investment Companies (Tax) Regulation, SI 1997/1154, regs 3, 5, 17.
Amendments—¹ Sub-s (2) repealed by FA 1996 Sch 41 Pt V(3) with effect for accounting periods ending after 31 March 1996, but subject to transitional provisions in FA 1996 Sch 15.

Interpretation: assets, liabilities and contracts

153 Qualifying assets and liabilities

(1) As regards a qualifying company, each of the following is a qualifying asset—

(a) a right to settlement under a qualifying debt (whether or not the debt is a debt on a security);

(b) a unit of currency;

(c) a share held in qualifying circumstances;

but paragraph (a) above shall have effect subject to subsections (3) and (4) below.

(2) As regards a qualifying company, each of the following is a qualifying liability—

    (a) a duty to settle under a qualifying debt (whether or not the debt is a debt on a security);

    (b) a liability that takes the form of a provision made by the company in respect of a duty to which it may become subject and which (if it were to become subject to it) would be a duty to settle under a qualifying debt;

    (c) a duty to transfer a right to settlement under a qualifying debt on a security, where the duty subsists under a contract and the company is not entitled to the right;

    (d) a duty to transfer a share or shares, where the duty subsists under a contract and the company is not entitled to the share or shares;

but paragraphs (a) to (d) above shall have effect subject to subsections (5) to (9) below.

(3) A right to settlement under a qualifying debt is not a qualifying asset if it is a right under a currency contract.

[(4) A right to settlement under a qualifying debt is not a qualifying asset where the company having the right holds an asset representing the debt and that asset is—

    (a) an asset to which section 92 of the Finance Act 1996 applies (convertible securities); or

    (b) an asset representing a loan relationship to which section 93 of that Act (relationships linked to the value of chargeable assets) applies.][1]

(5) A duty to settle under a qualifying debt is not a qualifying liability if it is a duty under a currency contract.

(6) ...[1]

(7) A liability falling within subsection (2)(b) above is not a qualifying liability unless—

    (a) the duty to settle would (if the company were to become subject to it) be owed for the purposes of a trade, and

    (b) the provision falls to be taken into account (apart from this Chapter) in computing the profits or losses of the trade for corporation tax purposes.

(8) A duty falling within subsection (2)(c) above is not a qualifying liability unless the right would be a qualifying asset if the company were entitled to it.

(9) A duty falling within subsection (2)(d) above is not a qualifying liability unless the share (or each of the shares) would be a qualifying asset if the company were entitled to it.

(10) For the purposes of this section each of the following is a qualifying debt—

    (a) a debt falling to be settled by the payment of money;

    (b) a debt falling to be settled by the transfer of a right to settlement under another debt, itself falling to be settled by the payment of money;

and for the purposes of this subsection an ecu shall be regarded as money.

(11) For the purposes of subsections (1)(c) and (4) above qualifying circumstances, in relation to an asset consisting of a share or a right to settlement, are circumstances where the qualifying company carries on a trade and—

    (a) if the company were to transfer the asset, the transfer would fall to be taken into account (apart from this Chapter) in computing the profits or losses of the trade for corporation tax purposes, and

    (b) if the asset were held by the company at the end of an accounting period, the valuation of the asset to be shown in the company's accounts for that time would fall to be found by taking the local currency equivalent at that time of the valuation put on the asset by the company (whether at that time or earlier) expressed in the nominal currency of the asset;

and the reference here to the local currency is to the local currency of the trade for the accounting period.

[(11A) ...][2]

(12) Interest accrued in respect of a debt shall not be treated as part of the debt.

Note—This section repealed by FA 2002 ss 79(1)(*b*), (3), 141, Sch 40 Pt 3(10) with effect for accounting periods beginning after 30 September 2002.

Commentary—*Simon's Direct Tax Service* **D2.906, 907.**

Revenue Internal Guidance—Company Taxation Manual COT13308 (examples of qualifying assets and liabilities).

Cross reference—See FA 1996 Sch 15 para 22(4) (transitional provisions in respect of loan relationships existing immediately before and on 1 April 1996: asset or liability treated as a qualifying asset or liability by virtue of the amendment of sub-s (4) or repeal of sub-s (6) held both immediately before and on 1 April 1996 treated as acquired on 1 April 1996).

Amendments—[1] Sub-s (4) substituted and sub-s (6) repealed by FA 1996 ss 104, 105(1), Sch 14 para 70, Sch 41 Pt V(3) with effect for accounting periods ending after 31 March 1996, but not applying as respects times before 1 April 1996: FA 1996 Sch 15 para 22(4), (5).

[2] Sub-s (11A) inserted by FA 1995 Sch 24 para 4(4) and providing a definition for the purposes of sub-ss (4), (6).

154 Definitions connected with assets

(1) Subject to the following provisions of this section, a company becomes entitled to an asset when it becomes unconditionally entitled to it.

(2) In determining whether or not a company is unconditionally entitled to an asset, any transfer by way of security of the asset or of any interest or right in or over the asset shall be ignored.

(3) Where a company agrees to acquire an asset by transfer it becomes entitled to it when the contract is made and not on a later transfer made pursuant to the contract; but the preceding provisions of this subsection do not apply where the agreement is by way of a currency contract.

(4) Where a company agrees to dispose of an asset by transfer it ceases to be entitled to it when the contract is made and not on a later transfer made pursuant to the contract.

(5) If a contract is conditional (whether on the exercise of an option or otherwise) for the purposes of subsections (3) and (4) above it is made when the condition is satisfied.

[(5A) The question whether a company becomes unconditionally entitled at a particular time to an asset falling within section 153(1)(a) above shall be determined without reference to the fact that there is or is not a later time when, or before which, the whole or any part of the debt is required to be paid.]¹

[(5B) Where an asset falling within section 153(1)(a) above consists of a right to interest—

    (a) a company becomes unconditionally entitled to the asset at the time when or (as the case may be) before which the interest is required to be paid to the company, and

    (b) subsection (5A) above shall not apply.]¹

(6) Where a company ceases to be entitled to an asset and at a later time becomes entitled to the same asset, with effect from the later time the asset shall be treated as if it were a different asset.

(7) In a case where—

    (a) at different times a company becomes entitled to rights to settlement under debts on securities, and

    (b) the rights are of the same kind,

the rights shall be treated as different assets and not part of the same asset.

(8) Whether a transaction involves a company becoming entitled to—

    (a) one asset consisting of a right to settlement under a debt on a security, or

    (b) a number of such assets,

shall be determined according to the facts of the case concerned.

(9) For the purpose of deciding whether rights to settlement under debts on securities of a particular kind are held by a company, rights of that kind acquired earlier shall be treated as disposed of before rights of that kind acquired later; and references here to acquisition and disposal are references to becoming entitled and ceasing to be entitled.

(10) For the purpose of deciding whether shares of a particular kind are held by a company, shares of that kind acquired earlier shall be treated as disposed of before shares of that kind acquired later; and references here to acquisition and disposal are references to becoming entitled and ceasing to be entitled.

(11) In a case where—

    (a) a rule is used for the purpose mentioned in subsection (9) or (10) above when the company's accounts are prepared,

    (b) the rule differs from that contained in the subsection, and

    (c) the accounts are prepared in accordance [generally accepted accounting practice]³,

the rule used when the accounts are prepared (and not the rule in the subsection) shall be used for the purpose.

(12) In a case where—

    (a) a company would (apart from this subsection) become entitled to an asset at a particular time (the later time) by virtue of the preceding provisions of this section,

    (b) the asset falls within section 153(1)(a) above,

    (c) the time at which the company, in drawing up its accounts, regards itself as becoming entitled to the asset is a time (the earlier time) earlier than the later time, and

    (d) the accounts are drawn up in accordance with [generally accepted accounting practice]³,

the company shall be taken to have become entitled to the asset at the earlier time and not at the later time.

[(12A) So much of any asset as consists in a right to receive interest as respects which any sums fall to be brought into account for the purposes of Chapter II of Part IV of the Finance Act 1996 (loan relationships) shall be taken to be an asset to which the company became entitled at the following time (instead of the time for which subsection (12) above provides), that is to say—

    (a) where the sums fall to be brought into account for the purposes of that Chapter in accordance with an authorised accruals basis of accounting, the time when the interest is taken for those purposes to have accrued, and

    (b) where the sums fall to be brought into account for the purposes of that Chapter in accordance with an authorised mark to market basis of accounting, the time when the interest is taken for those purposes to have become due and payable.]²

(13) Where subsection (12) above applies, as regards any time beginning with the earlier time and ending immediately before the later time the nominal amount of the debt shall be taken to be—

    (a) such amount as the company treats as the nominal amount in its accounts, or

(b) such amount as it would so treat in accordance with [generally accepted accounting practice]³ (if that amount is different from the amount found under paragraph (a) above).

[(13A) In a case where—

(a) a company would (apart from this subsection) become entitled to an asset at a particular time (the earlier time) by virtue of subsections (1) to (11) above,

(b) the asset falls within section 153(1)(a) above and the debt concerned is a debt on a security, or the asset is a share,

(c) the time at which the company, in drawing up its accounts, regards itself as becoming entitled to the asset is a time (the later time) later than the earlier time, and

(d) the accounts are drawn up in accordance with [generally accepted accounting practice]³,

the company shall be taken to become entitled to the asset at the later time and not at the earlier time.]¹

[(13B) In a case where—

(a) a company would (apart from this subsection) cease to be entitled to an asset at a particular time (the earlier time) by virtue of subsections (1) to (11) above,

(b) the asset falls within section 153(1)(a) above and the debt concerned is a debt on a security, or the asset is a share,

(c) the time at which the company, in drawing up its accounts, regards itself as ceasing to be entitled to the asset is a time (the later time) later than the earlier time, and

(d) the accounts are drawn up in accordance with [generally accepted accounting practice]³, the company shall be taken to cease to be entitled to the asset at the later time and not at the earlier time.]¹

(14) A company holds an asset at a particular time if it is entitled to it at that time.

Note—This section repealed by FA 2002 ss 79(1)(*b*), (3), 141, Sch 40 Pt 3(10) with effect for accounting periods beginning after 30 September 2002.
Commentary—*Simon's Direct Tax Service* D2.915.
Amendments—¹ Sub-ss (5A), (5B), (13A), (13B) inserted by FA 1994 s 114(1), (2).
² Sub-s (12A) inserted by FA 1996 ss 104, 105(1), Sch 14 para 71 with effect for accounting periods ending after 31 March 1996, subject to transitional provisions in FA 1996 Sch 15.
³ Words substituted for the words ''normal accountancy practice'' by FA 2002 s 103(4)(*b*) with effect from 24 July 2002.

155 Definitions connected with liabilities

(1) Subject to the following provisions of this section, a company becomes subject to a liability falling within section 153(2)(a) above when it becomes unconditionally subject to it.

(2) Where a company agrees to acquire a liability falling within section 153(2)(a) above by transfer it becomes subject to it when the contract is made and not on a later transfer made pursuant to the contract.

(3) Where a company agrees to dispose of a liability falling within section 153(2)(a) above by transfer it ceases to be subject to it when the contract is made and not on a later transfer made pursuant to the contract.

(4) If a contract is conditional (whether on the exercise of an option or otherwise) for the purposes of subsections (2) and (3) above it is made when the condition is satisfied.

[(4A) The question whether a company becomes unconditionally subject at a particular time to a liability falling within section 153(2)(a) above shall be determined without reference to the fact that there is or is not a later time when, or before which, the whole or any part of the debt is required to be paid.]¹

[(4B) Where a liability falling within section 153(2)(a) above consists of a duty to pay interest—

(a) a company becomes unconditionally subject to the liability at the time when or (as the case may be) before which the company is required to pay the interest, and

(b) subsection (4A) above shall not apply.]¹

(5) Where a company ceases to be subject to a liability falling within section 153(2)(a) above and at a later time becomes subject to the same liability, with effect from the later time the liability shall be treated as if it were a different liability.

(6) A company becomes subject to a liability falling within section 153(2)(b) above at the time with effect from which it makes the provision.

(7) A company ceases to be subject to a liability falling within section 153(2)(b) above at the time with effect from which it deletes the provision or (if different) the time with effect from which it would delete the provision under [generally accepted accounting practice]³.

(8) Where a company makes a provision falling within section 153(2)(b) above and later changes the amount, the company shall be treated as—

(a) deleting (with effect from the time when the change becomes effective) the provision representing the amount before the change, and

(b) making (with effect from that time) a new provision representing the amount as changed; and so on for further changes.

(9) A company ceases to be subject to a liability falling within section 153(2)(c) above when it becomes entitled to the right concerned, unless it ceases to be subject to the liability earlier apart from this subsection.

(10) A company ceases to be subject to a liability falling within section 153(2)(d) above when it becomes entitled to the share or shares, unless it ceases to be subject to the liability earlier apart from this subsection.

(11) In a case where—

(a) *a company would (apart from this subsection) become subject to a liability at a particular time (the later time) by virtue of the preceding provisions of this section,*
(b) *the liability falls within section 153(2)(a) above,*
(c) *the time at which the company, in drawing up its accounts, regards itself as becoming subject to the liability is a time (the earlier time) earlier than the later time, and*
(d) *the accounts are drawn up in accordance with [generally accepted accounting practice]³,*

the company shall be taken to have become subject to the liability at the earlier time and not at the later time.

[(11A) So much of any liability consisting in a liability to pay interest as respects which debits fall to be brought into account for the purposes of Chapter II of Part IV of the Finance Act 1996 (loan relationships) shall be taken to be a liability to which the company became subject at the following time (instead of at the time for which subsection (11) above provides), that is to say—

(a) *where the debits fall to be brought into account for the purposes of that Chapter in accordance with an authorised accruals basis of accounting, the time when the interest is taken for those purposes to have accrued, and*
(b) *where the debits fall to be brought into account for the purposes of that Chapter in accordance with an authorised mark to market basis of accounting, the time when the interest is taken for those purposes to have become due and payable.]²*

(12) Where subsection (11) above applies, as regards any time beginning with the earlier time and ending immediately before the later time the nominal amount of the debt shall be taken to be—

(a) *such amount as the company treats as the nominal amount in its accounts, or*
(b) *such amount as it would so treat in accordance with[generally accepted accounting practice]³ (if that amount is different from the amount found under paragraph (a) above).*

(13) A company owes a liability at a particular time if it is subject to it at that time.

Note—This section repealed by FA 2002 ss 79(1)(b), (3), 141, Sch 40 Pt 3(10) with effect for accounting periods beginning after 30 September 2002.
Commentary—*Simon's Direct Tax Service* **D2.915, 916.**
Amendments—¹ Sub-ss (4A), (4B) inserted by FA 1994 s 114(3).
² Sub-s (11A) inserted by FA 1996 ss 104, 105(1), Sch 14 para 72 with effect for accounting periods ending after 31 March 1996, subject to transitional provisions in FA 1996 Sch 15.
³ Words substituted for the words "normal accountancy practice" by FA 2002 s 103(4)(b) with effect from 24 July 2002.

156 Assets and liabilities: other matters

(1) Each of the following questions shall be determined according to the facts of the case concerned—

(a) *whether a transaction (or series of transactions) involves the creation of one asset consisting of a right to settlement under a debt or a number of assets consisting of a number of such rights;*
(b) *whether a transaction (or series of transactions) involves the creation of one liability consisting of a duty to settle under a debt or a number of liabilities consisting of a number of such duties;*
(c) *whether a transaction (or series of transactions) involves the creation of both an asset (or assets) held and a liability (or liabilities) owed by the same company.*

(2) Subsection (3) below applies where—

(a) *a company, in drawing up its accounts, regards itself as becoming entitled or subject to an asset or liability at a particular time,*
(b) *the company, in drawing up its accounts, regards itself as ceasing to be entitled or subject to the asset or liability at a later time,*
(c) *at the time mentioned in paragraph (a) above it could reasonably be expected that the company would become entitled or subject to such an asset or liability,*
(d) *the asset or liability does not in fact come into existence before the later time but (if it did) it would fall within section 153(1)(a) or (2)(a) above, and*
(e) *the accounts are drawn up in accordance with [generally accepted accounting practice]¹.*

(3) The company shall be taken to—

(a) *become entitled or subject to such an asset or liability at the time it regards itself as becoming so entitled or subject, and*
(b) *cease to be entitled or subject to such an asset or liability at the time it regards itself as ceasing to be so entitled or subject.*

(4) Where subsection (3) above applies, as regards any time beginning with the time mentioned in subsection (3)(a) and ending with the time mentioned in subsection (3)(b) the nominal amount of the debt shall be taken to be—

    (a) such amount as the company treats as the nominal amount in its accounts, or
    (b) such amount as it would so treat in accordance with [generally accepted accounting practice]¹ (if that amount is different from the amount found under paragraph (a) above).

Note—This section repealed by FA 2002 ss 79(1)(*b*), (3), 141, Sch 40 Pt 3(10) with effect for accounting periods beginning after 30 September 2002.
Commentary—*Simon's Direct Tax Service* **D2.915.**
Amendments—¹ Words substituted for the words "normal accountancy practice" by FA 2002 s 103(4)(*b*) with effect from 24 July 2002.

157 Definitions connected with currency contracts

(1) A company becomes entitled to rights and subject to duties under a currency contract when it enters into the contract.

(2) A company holds a currency contract at a particular time if it is then entitled to rights and subject to duties under the contract; and it is immaterial when the rights and duties fall to be exercised and performed.

Note—This section repealed by FA 2002 ss 79(1)(*b*), (3), 141, Sch 40 Pt 3(10) with effect for accounting periods beginning after 30 September 2002.
Commentary—*Simon's Direct Tax Service* **D2.908.**

Interpretation: other provisions

158 Translation times and accrual periods

(1) Where a qualifying company holds a qualifying asset the following are translation times as regards the asset—

    (a) the time immediately after the company becomes entitled to the asset;
    (b) the time immediately before the company ceases to be entitled to the asset;
    (c) any time which is a time when an accounting period of the company ends and which falls after the time mentioned in paragraph (a) above and before the time mentioned in paragraph (b) above.

(2) Where a qualifying company owes a qualifying liability the following are translation times as regards the liability—

    (a) the time immediately after the company becomes subject to the liability;
    (b) the time immediately before the company ceases to be subject to the liability;
    (c) any time which is a time when an accounting period of the company ends and which falls after the time mentioned in paragraph (a) above and before the time mentioned in paragraph (b) above.

(3) Where a qualifying company enters into a currency contract the following are translation times as regards the contract—

    (a) the time immediately after the company becomes entitled to rights and subject to duties under the contract;
    (b) the time immediately before the company ceases to be entitled to those rights and subject to those duties;
    (c) any time which is a time when an accounting period of the company ends and which falls after the time mentioned in paragraph (a) above and before the time mentioned in paragraph (b) above.

(4) As regards a qualifying asset, a qualifying liability or a currency contract an accrual period is a period which—

    (a) begins with a time which is a translation time (other than the last to fall) as regards the asset, liability or contract, and
    (b) ends with the time which is the next translation time to fall as regards the asset, liability or contract.

Note—This section repealed by FA 2002 ss 79(1)(*b*), (3), 141, Sch 40 Pt 3(10) with effect for accounting periods beginning after 30 September 2002.
Commentary—*Simon's Direct Tax Service* **D2.909.**

159 Basic valuation

(1) Subject to the following provisions of this section, the basic valuation of an asset or liability is—

    (a) such valuation as the company puts on it with regard to the time immediately after the company becomes entitled or subject to it, or
    (b) such valuation as the company would put on it with regard to that time under [generally accepted accounting practice]², if that valuation is different from that found under paragraph (a) above.

(2) Where (apart from this subsection) the valuation under subsection (1) above would be in a currency (the actual currency) other than the nominal currency, it shall be taken to be the equivalent, expressed in terms of the nominal currency, of the valuation in the actual currency; and the translation required by this subsection shall be made by reference to the London closing exchange

rate for the two currencies concerned for the day in which the time mentioned in subsection (1) above falls.

(3) The basic valuation of a liability falling within section 153(2)(c) or (d) above is the consideration for the company becoming subject to the liability; and any consideration or part that is not pecuniary shall be taken to be equal to its open market value—

    (a) found at the time when the company becomes subject to the liability, and
    (b) if part of the consideration is pecuniary, expressed in the same currency as that part.

(4) Where (apart from this subsection) the valuation under subsection (3) above would be in a currency (the actual currency) other than the nominal currency, it shall be taken to be the equivalent, expressed in terms of the nominal currency, of the valuation in the actual currency; and the translation required by this subsection shall be made by reference to the London closing exchange rate for the two currencies concerned for the day on which the company becomes subject to the liability.

[(5) Where—

    (a) a company becomes entitled, on any transfer by virtue of which it becomes a party to a loan relationship, to a right of settlement under a qualifying debt on a security, and
    (b) that transfer is a transfer with accrued interest,
    the basic valuation of that right shall be found by taking the consideration for the company's becoming entitled to the right and then deducting the amount of the accrued interest the right to which is transferred.][1]

(10) Subsections (11) and (12) below apply where—

    (a) section 127 above applies as regards an asset or liability for an accrual period (the earlier period), and
    (b) section 125 or 127 above applies as regards the asset or liability for the next accrual period (the later period).

(11) As regards the later period the basic valuation of the asset or liability shall be taken to be—

    (a) the nominal amount of the debt outstanding immediately before the beginning of the later period, or
    (b) if section 127(7) above also applies as regards the earlier period, the amount found under section 127(10) for that period.

(12) As regards an accrual period which falls after the later period the basic valuation of the asset or liability shall be the amount found under subsection (11) above, subject to any subsequent application of that subsection.

Note—This section repealed by FA 2002 ss 79(1)(b), (3), 141, Sch 40 Pt 3(10) with effect for accounting periods beginning after 30 September 2002.
Commentary—*Simon's Direct Tax Service* **D2.917.**
Cross reference—See Exchange Gains and Losses (Transitional Provisions) Regulations, SI 1994/3226 reg 6 (basic valuation of an existing asset or liability).
Amendments—[1] Sub-s (5) substituted for sub-ss (5)–(9) by FA 1996 ss 104, 105(1), Sch 14 para 73 with effect for accounting periods ending after 31 March 1996 except for transfers before 1 April 1996 and subject to transitional provisions in FA 1996 Sch 15.
[2] Words substituted for the words "normal accountancy practice" by FA 2002 s 103(4)(b) with effect from 24 July 2002.

160 Nominal currency of assets and liabilities

(1) As regards an asset mentioned in section 153(1)(a) above, or a liability mentioned in section 153(2)(a) or (b) or (c) above, the nominal currency is the settlement currency of the debt mentioned in the paragraph concerned.

(2) As regards an asset mentioned in section 153(1)(b) above, the nominal currency is the currency concerned.

(3) As regards an asset mentioned in section 153(1)(c) above, the nominal currency is the currency in which the share is denominated.

(4) As regards a liability mentioned in section 153(2)(d) above, the nominal currency is the currency in which the share is (or shares are) denominated.

Note—This section repealed by FA 2002 ss 79(1)(b), (3), 141, Sch 40 Pt 3(10) with effect for accounting periods beginning after 30 September 2002.
Commentary—*Simon's Direct Tax Service* **D2.913.**
Revenue Internal Guidance—Company Taxation Manual COT13313 (meaning of "nominal currency").

161 Settlement currency of a debt

(1) Subject to the following provisions of this section, the settlement currency of a debt is the currency in which ultimate settlement of the debt falls to be made.

(2) In a case where—

    (a) ultimate settlement of a debt falls to be made in a particular currency, but
    (b) the amount of the currency falls to be determined by reference to the value at any time of an asset consisting of or denominated in another currency,

the settlement currency of the debt is the other currency.

(3) As regards a debt mentioned in section 153(2)(b) above, and as regards a case where section 156(3) above applies, in subsections (1) and (2) above "falls" (in each place) shall be read as "would fall".

(4) Where the settlement currency of a debt cannot be determined under subsections (1) to (3) above, the settlement currency of the debt is the currency that can reasonably be regarded as the most appropriate—

(a) deeming the state of affairs at settlement to be the same as the state of affairs at the material time, and

(b) having regard to subsections (1) to (3) above;

and the material time is the time immediately after the company becomes entitled to the asset mentioned in section 153(1)(a) above or subject to the liability mentioned in section 153(2)(a) or (b) or (c) above.

(5) For the purposes of this section the ecu shall be regarded as a currency.

Note—This section repealed by FA 2002 ss 79(1)(b), (3), 141, Sch 40 Pt 3(10) with effect for accounting periods beginning after 30 September 2002.
Commentary—*Simon's Direct Tax Service* **D2.913.**

162 Nominal amount of a debt

(1) The nominal amount of a debt outstanding at any time is the amount of the debt outstanding at that time, expressed in terms of the settlement currency of the debt.

(2) In a case where—

(a) a payment or repayment is made at any time in a currency other than the settlement currency of a debt, and

(b) it falls to be decided whether there is in consequence an increase or decrease in the nominal amount of the debt outstanding,

the amount of the payment or repayment shall be taken to be its equivalent expressed in terms of the settlement currency of the debt.

(3) Any translation required by this section shall be made by reference to the London closing exchange rate for the currencies concerned for the day in which the time concerned falls.

Note—This section repealed by FA 2002 ss 79(1)(b), (3), 141, Sch 40 Pt 3(10) with effect for accounting periods beginning after 30 September 2002.
Commentary—*Simon's Direct Tax Service* **D2.919.**
Revenue Internal Guidance—Company Taxation Manual COT13316 (meaning of "translation time").

163 Local currency of a trade

(1) Subject to subsection (2) below, the local currency of a [business]¹ for an accounting period is sterling.

[(2) Where by virtue of section 93 above the profits or losses of a business or part of a business for an accounting period are to be computed and expressed in a currency other than sterling for the purposes of corporation tax, that other currency is the local currency of the business or part for that period.]¹

(4) For the purposes of this section the ecu shall be regarded as a currency other than sterling; and references in this Chapter to a currency other than sterling shall be construed accordingly.

Note—This section repealed by FA 2002 ss 79(1)(b), (3), 141, Sch 40 Pt 3(10) with effect for accounting periods beginning after 30 September 2002.
Commentary—*Simon's Direct Tax Service* **D2.911.**
Amendments—¹ Words in sub-s (1) substituted for word "trade" and whole of sub-s (2) substituted (for original sub-ss (2), (3)) by FA 2000 s 106(12), (13), (17) with effect for accounting periods beginning after 31 December 1999 and ending after 20 March 2000.

164 Interpretation: miscellaneous

(1) References to—

(a) initial exchange gains and losses,

(b) exchange gains and losses of a trade or of part of a trade,

(c) non-trading exchange gains and losses, and

(d) the accrual of gains and losses mentioned in paragraphs (a) to (c) above,

shall be construed in accordance with sections 125 to 129 above and Schedule 15 to this Act.

(2) References to a currency contract shall be construed in accordance with section 126(1) [and (1A)]¹ above.

(3) References to a qualifying debt shall be construed in accordance with section 153(10) above.

(4) References to a company's commencement day shall be construed in accordance with section 165(7) below.

(5) The local currency equivalent of a valuation of an asset or liability, or of an amount, is that valuation or amount expressed in terms of the local currency (a process sometimes known as translation).

(6), (7) ...[3]

(8) References to a share are to a share in a company (whether or not the qualifying company).

(9) Shares are of the same kind if they are treated as being of the same kind by the practice of a recognised stock exchange or would be so treated if dealt with on such a stock exchange.

(10) Rights to settlement under debts on securities are of the same kind if the securities are treated as being of the same kind by the practice of a recognised stock exchange or would be so treated if dealt with on such a stock exchange.

(11) "Security", in the expression "debt on a security", has the meaning given by section 132 of the Taxation of Chargeable Gains Act 1992.

(12) ...[2]

(13) References to the ecu are to the European currency unit as defined for the time being in Council Regulation No 3180/78/EEC or in any Community instrument replacing it.

(14) "Prescribed" means prescribed by regulations made under this Chapter.

(15) A reference to this Chapter includes a reference to regulations made under it and a reference to a provision of this Chapter includes a reference to regulations made under the provision, unless otherwise required by the context or regulations.

(16) Sections 152 to 163 above, and the preceding provisions of this section, apply for the purposes of this Chapter.

Note—This section repealed by FA 2002 ss 79(1)(*b*), (3), 141, Sch 40 Pt 3(10) with effect for accounting periods beginning after 30 September 2002.
Commentary—*Simon's Direct Tax Service* **D2.914.**
Amendments—[1] Words in sub-s (2) inserted by FA 1994 s 115(3).
[2] Sub-s (12) repealed by FA 1996 Sch 41 Pt V(3) with effect for accounting periods ending after 31 March 1996, but subject to transitional provisions in FA 1996 Sch 15.
[3] Sub-ss (6), (7) repealed by FA 2000 ss 106(14), (17), 156, Sch 40 Pt II(15) with effect for accounting periods beginning after 31 December 1999 and ending after 20 March 2000.

Miscellaneous

165 Commencement and transitionals

(1) This Chapter applies where—

   (a) a qualifying asset is one to which the company becomes entitled on or after the company's commencement day;
   (b) a qualifying liability is one to which the company becomes subject on or after that day;
   (c) the rights and duties under a currency contract are ones to which the company becomes entitled and subject on or after that day.

(2) Where a qualifying asset or liability is held or owed by a qualifying company both immediately before and at the beginning of its commencement day, for the purposes of this Chapter the company shall be treated as becoming entitled or subject to the asset or liability at the beginning of its commencement day.

(3) Where both immediately before and at the beginning of its commencement day a qualifying company is entitled to rights and subject to duties under a currency contract, for the purposes of this Chapter the company shall be treated as becoming entitled and subject to them at the beginning of its commencement day.

(4) Regulations may provide that where—

   (a) a qualifying asset or liability is held or owed by a qualifying company both immediately before and at the beginning of its commencement day, and
   (b) the asset or liability is of a prescribed description,

subsection (2) above shall not apply and for the purposes of this Chapter the company shall be treated as becoming entitled or subject to the asset or liability at such time (falling after its commencement day) as is found in accordance with prescribed rules.

(5) Regulations may provide that any rule made under subsection (4) above shall not apply, and that subsection (2) above shall accordingly apply, in a case where the company so elects in accordance with prescribed rules.

(6) Schedule 16 to this Act (which contains transitional provisions) shall have effect.

(7) For the purposes of this section—

   (a) a company's commencement day is the first day of its first accounting period to begin after the day preceding the appointed day;
   (b) the appointed day is such day as may be appointed by order.

(8) Subsections (1) to (6) above do not apply for the purposes of construing Schedule 17 to this Act (which contains its own commencement provisions).

Note—This section repealed by FA 2002 ss 79(1)(*b*), (3), 141, Sch 40 Pt 3(10) with effect for accounting periods beginning after 30 September 2002.
Commentary—*Simon's Direct Tax Service* **D2.975.**
Regulations—Exchange Gains and Losses (Transitional Provisions) Regulations, SI 1994/3226.
Note—The day appointed under sub-s (7) is 23 March 1995, by Finance Act 1993 section 165 (Appointed Day) Order, SI 1995/3224.

166 Anti-avoidance: change of accounting period

(1) This section applies where—

(a) a company changes the date on which any accounting period is to begin,
(b) if the change had not been made an exchange gain or gains not accruing to the company would have accrued or an exchange loss or losses accruing to the company would not have accrued or an exchange gain or gains accruing would have been bigger or an exchange loss or losses accruing would have been smaller, and
(c) the change mentioned in paragraph (a) above was made for the purpose, or for purposes which include the purpose, of securing the non-accrual or reduction of the gain or gains or the accrual or increase of the loss or losses.

(2) In such a case the inspector or on appeal the Commissioners concerned—

(a) may in arriving at the exchange gains and losses accruing to the company assume that there had been no such change as is mentioned in subsection (1)(a) above, and
(b) may accordingly make, with regard to the accounting period mentioned in subsection (1)(a) above, such adjustment to the company's corporation tax liability as is just and reasonable.

(3) For the purposes of this section—

(a) an exchange gain is an exchange gain of a trade or an exchange gain of part of a trade or a non-trading exchange gain;
(b) an exchange loss is an exchange loss of a trade or an exchange loss of part of a trade or a non-trading exchange loss.

Note—This section repealed by FA 2002 ss 79(1)(*b*), (3), 141, Sch 40 Pt 3(10) with effect for accounting periods beginning after 30 September 2002.
Commentary—*Simon's Direct Tax Service* **D2.958.**
Revenue Internal Guidance—Company Taxation Manual COT13905 (worked example).

167 Orders and regulations

(1) Any power to make an order or regulations under this Chapter shall be exercisable by the Treasury.

(2) Any power to make an order under this Chapter shall be exercisable by statutory instrument.

(3) Any power to make regulations under this Chapter shall be exercisable by statutory instrument subject to annulment in pursuance of a resolution of the House of Commons.

(4) Any power to make regulations under this Chapter—

(a) may be exercised as regards prescribed cases or descriptions of case;
(b) may be exercised differently in relation to different cases or descriptions of case.

(5) Regulations under this Chapter may make provision in such way as the Treasury think fit, and in particular may amend or modify the effect of any enactment (whether or not contained in this Chapter).

[(5A) Without prejudice to the generality of any power of the Treasury to amend regulations made under this Chapter, every such power shall include power to make such modifications of any regulations so made as the Treasury consider appropriate in consequence of—

[(a) the provisions of Chapter II of Part IV of the Finance Act 1996 (loan relationships); or
(b) the provisions of sections 105 and 106 of the Finance Act 2000 (use of local currency)]².]¹

[(5B) The power to make any such modifications as are mentioned in [subsection (5A)(a)]² above shall be exercisable so as to apply those modifications in relation to any accounting period of a company ending on or after 1st April 1996.]¹

[(5C) The power to make any such modifications as are mentioned in subsection (5A)(b) above shall be exercisable so as to apply those modifications in relation to any accounting period of a company beginning on or after 1st January 2000.]²

(6) Regulations under this Chapter may include such supplementary, incidental, consequential or transitional provisions as appear to the Treasury to be necessary or expedient.

(7) No specific provision of this Chapter about regulations shall prejudice the generality of subsections (4) to (6) above.

Note—This section repealed by FA 2002 ss 79(1)(*b*), (3), 141, Sch 40 Pt 3(10) with effect for accounting periods beginning after 30 September 2002.
Regulations—Exchange Gains and Losses (Alternative Method of Calculation of Gain or Loss) Regulations, SI 1994/3227.
Amendments—¹ Sub-ss (5A), (5B) inserted by FA 1996 ss 104, 105(1), Sch 14 para 74 with effect for accounting periods ending after 31 March 1996.
² Words in sub-ss (5A), (5B) substituted and words in sub-s (5C) inserted by FA 2000 s 106(15), (17) with effect for accounting periods beginning after 31 December 1999 and ending after 20 March 2000.

168 Insurance companies

(1) Subject to the following provisions of this section, this Chapter shall apply in relation to insurance companies as it applies in relation to other qualifying companies.

(2) Regulations may make provision about the treatment for corporation tax purposes of exchange differences arising as regards assets and liabilities held or owed by insurance companies.

(3) Any such provision may be made—

  (a) about exchange differences arising as regards assets or liabilities (or both) generally or about a proportion of such differences;
  (b) about exchange differences arising as regards prescribed descriptions of assets or liabilities (or both) or about a proportion of such differences;
  (c) about exchange differences arising as regards individual assets or liabilities.

(4) Any such provision may be made about assets or liabilities that are qualifying assets or liabilities, or about those that are not, or about both.

(5) Regulations under this section may—

  (a) contain exceptions (whether by reference to categories of insurance business or otherwise);
  (b) contain provision about the circumstances in which a charge or relief is to arise, its amount, and other matters relating to it;
  (c) provide for consequential adjustments in a company's corporation tax liability;
  (d) exclude or modify the effect of any of the provisions of this Chapter.

(6) References in this section to exchange differences are to gains and losses attributable to fluctuations in currency exchange rates.

(7) For the purposes of this section an insurance company is [any company which carries on [the business of effecting or carrying out contracts of insurance and, for the purposes of this subsection, "contract of insurance" has the meaning given by Article 3(1) of the Financial Services and Markets Act 2000 (Regulated Activities) Order 2001.]²]¹

Note—This section repealed by FA 2002 ss 79(1)(*b*), (3), 141, Sch 40 Pt 3(10) with effect for accounting periods beginning after 30 September 2002.
Commentary—*Simon's Direct Tax Service* **D2.966.**
Regulations—Exchange Gains and Losses (Insurance Companies) Regulations, SI 1994/3231.
Amendments—¹ Words in sub-s (7) substituted by FA 1995 s 52(2), with effect for any accounting period ending after 30 June 1994.
² Words in sub-s (7) substituted by the Financial Services and Markets Act 2000 (Consequential Amendments) (Taxes) Order, SI 2001/3629 arts 75, 78 with effect from 1 December 2001 immediately after the coming into force of the Financial Services and Markets Act 2000 ss 411, 432(1), Sch 20.

[168A Application of Chapter to certain companies becoming resident in the United Kingdom

(1) In a case where—

  (a) by virtue of section 751 of the Taxes Act 1988 an exchange gain or an exchange loss accrues to a company for an accrual period constituting or falling within an accounting period during which the company is resident outside the United Kingdom, and
  (b) the company subsequently becomes resident in the United Kingdom,

the company shall be treated, for the purposes of applying this Chapter to accounting periods beginning on or after the date when the company becomes resident in the United Kingdom, as if the exchange gain or loss mentioned in paragraph (a) above never existed.

(2) In this section—

  (a) references to an exchange gain are to an exchange gain of a trade or an exchange gain of part of a trade or a non-trading exchange gain;
  (b) references to an exchange loss are to an exchange loss of a trade or an exchange loss of part of a trade or a non-trading exchange loss;
  (c) the reference in paragraph (a) of subsection (1) above to an exchange gain or an exchange loss accruing is to the gain or loss accruing before the application of any of sections 131, 136, 137 and 140 above in relation to the accounting period mentioned in that paragraph.]¹

Note—This section repealed by FA 2002 ss 79(1)(*b*), (3), 141, Sch 40 Pt 3(10) with effect for accounting periods beginning after 30 September 2002.
Commentary—*Simon's Direct Tax Service* **D2.967.**
Amendment—¹ Section inserted by FA 1995 Sch 25 para 7.

169 Chargeable gains

Schedule 17 to this Act (provisions which relate to the taxation of chargeable gains and are connected with other provisions of this Chapter) shall have effect.

Note—This section repealed by FA 2002 ss 79(1)(*b*), (3), 141, Sch 40 Pt 3(10) with effect for accounting periods beginning after 30 September 2002.
Commentary—*Simon's Direct Tax Service* **D2.969.**

170 Amendments

Schedule 18 to this Act (which contains amendments) shall have effect.

CHAPTER III
LLOYD'S UNDERWRITERS ETC

Cross reference—See FA 1993 s 182(*ca*) (the Board may make regulations modifying the application of this Chapter where assets forming part of a premiums trust fund are the subject of certain arrangements under TA 1988 ss 129(1), (2), (2A), 737E(2)–(8)).
TCGA 1992 s 155 (rights of a member of Lloyd's under a syndicate within the meaning of this Chapter are qualifying assets for roll-over relief).

Main provisions

171 Taxation of profits and allowance of losses

(1) Income tax for any year of assessment on the profits arising from a member's underwriting business shall be computed on the profits of that year of assessment.

(2) As respects the profits arising to a member from his underwriting business for any year of assessment—

  (*a*) the aggregate of those profits shall be chargeable to tax under Case I of Schedule D; and
  (*b*) accordingly, no part of those profits shall be chargeable to tax under any other Schedule or any other Case of Schedule D;

but nothing in this subsection shall affect the manner in which the amount of any profits arising from assets forming part of an ancillary trust fund is to be computed.

[(2A) ...]¹

[(2B) Section 231(1) of the Taxes Act 1988 (entitlement to tax credit) shall not apply where the distribution there mentioned is a distribution in respect of any asset of a member's [premium]⁴ trust fund.]³

(3) ...²

(4) Subsection (2) above does not apply in relation to any profits arising before 6th April 1993 from assets forming part of an ancillary trust fund.

Commentary—*Simon's Direct Tax Service* E5.611.
Simon's Tax Cases—s 171(2), *Deeny v Gooda Walker Ltd (in voluntary liquidation) (IRC third party)* [1996] STC 299.
Cross references—See Lloyd's Underwriters (Tax) Regulations, SI 1995/351 reg 4 (application to tax charged under this section of provisions in TMA and TA 1988 relating to assessment and collection of tax).
Lloyd's Underwriters (Tax) (1992–93 to 1996–97) Regulations, SI 1995/352 reg 13 (running-off syndicates—allocation of profits or losses).
Amendments—¹ Sub-s (2A) repealed by F(No 2)A 1997 s 36(4), Sch 6 para 20, Sch 8 Pt II(11) with effect for distributions made after 5 April 1999 (originally inserted by FA 1994 Sch 21 para 1(1), (3)(*a*)).
² Sub-s (3) repealed by FA 1994 Sch 21 para 1(2), (3)(*b*) and Sch 26 Pt V(25) with effect from the year 1996–97.
³ Sub-s (2B) inserted by F(No 2)A 1997 s 22(1), (7) with effect for distributions made after 1 July 1997.
⁴ Word in sub-s (2B) substituted by the Financial Services and Markets Act 2000 (Consequential Amendments) (Taxes) Order, SI 2001/3629 arts 75, 82(*a*) with effect from 1 December 2001 immediately after the coming into force of the Financial Services and Markets Act 2000 ss 411, 432(1), Sch 20.

172 Year of assessment in which profits or losses arise

(1) Subject to the provisions of this Chapter, for the purposes of section 171 above and all other purposes of the Income Tax Acts the profits or losses in any year of assessment of a member's underwriting business shall be taken to be—

  [(*a*) in the case of profits or losses arising directly from his membership of one or more syndicates, those of any previous year or years which are declared in the corresponding underwriting year;
  (*b*) in the case of profits or losses arising from assets forming part of a [premium]² trust fund, those allocated under the rules or practice of Lloyd's to any previous year or years the profits or losses of which are declared in the corresponding underwriting year; and]¹
  (*c*) in the case of other profits or losses, those derived from payments received or made in the corresponding underwriting year.

(2) Subsection (1)(*c*) above does not apply in relation to payments received or made before 6th April 1993.

Commentary—*Simon's Direct Tax Service* E5.613.
Amendments—¹ Sub-s (1)(*a*), (*b*) substituted by FA 1994 Sch 21 para 2 with effect from the year 1997–98. As originally enacted, they did not apply for the years 1994–95 to 1996–97.
² Word in sub-s (1)(*b*) substituted by the Financial Services and Markets Act 2000 (Consequential Amendments) (Taxes) Order, SI 2001/3629 arts 75, 82(*b*) with effect from 1 December 2001 immediately after the coming into force of the Financial Services and Markets Act 2000 ss 411, 432(1), Sch 20.

173 Assessment and collection of tax

(1) Schedule 19 to this Act (assessment and collection of tax) shall have effect.

(2) (*amended* TA 1988 Sch 19A para 1(3) and is now superseded).

(3) Subsection (2) above applies in relation to regulations made after the passing of this Act.

Commentary—*Simon's Direct Tax Service* E5.619.

Members' trust funds

174 [Premium][4] trust funds

[(1) For the purposes of the Income Tax Acts and the Gains Tax Acts—

(a) a member shall be treated as absolutely entitled as against the trustees to the assets forming part of a [premium][4] trust fund of his; and

(b) where a deposit required by a regulatory authority in a country or territory outside the United Kingdom is paid out of such a fund, the money so paid shall be treated as still forming part of that fund.][1]

(2) Where an asset forms part of a [premium][4] trust fund at the beginning of any underwriting year, for the purposes of the Income Tax Acts—

(a) the trustees of the fund shall be treated as acquiring it on that day, and

(b) they shall be treated as paying in respect of the acquisition an amount equal to the value of the asset at the time of the acquisition.

(3) Where an asset forms part of a [premium][4] trust fund at the end of any underwriting year, for the purposes of the Income Tax Acts—

(a) the trustees of the fund shall be treated as disposing of it on that day, and

(b) they shall be treated as obtaining in respect of the disposal an amount equal to the value of the asset at the time of the disposal.

(4), (5) ...[3]

(6) ...[2]

(7) In this section—

...[2]

"underwriting year" does not include the year 1993 or any earlier underwriting year.

Commentary—*Simon's Direct Tax Service* **E5.631.**
Amendments—[1] Sub-s (1) substituted by FA 1994 Sch 21 para 3 with effect from the year 1994–95.
[2] Sub-s (6) and definitions omitted from sub-s (7) repealed by FA 1996 Sch 41 Pt V(18) with effect for the purposes of income tax from the year 1996–97.
[3] Sub-ss (4), (5) repealed by FA 1997 Sch 10 paras 6(a), 7(1) Sch 18 Pt VI(10) with effect in relation to, and to transfers under, any arrangement made on or after 1 July 1997 by virtue of the Finance Act 1997, Schedule 10, (Appointed Day) Order, SI 1997/991.
[4] Word in Heading and sub-ss (1)(a), (2), (3) substituted by the Financial Services and Markets Act 2000 (Consequential Amendments) (Taxes) Order, SI 2001/3629 arts 75, 82(c) with effect from 1 December 2001 immediately after the coming into force of the Financial Services and Markets Act 2000 ss 411, 432(1), Sch 20.

175 Special reserve funds

(1) If arrangements are made by the Council of Lloyd's which—

(a) enable such a special reserve fund as is referred to in Part I of Schedule 20 to this Act to be set up in relation to each member; and

(b) comply with the requirements of that Part and are approved by the Board,

the provisions of that Part relating to taxation shall have effect in relation to any special reserve fund of a member set up under the arrangements.

(2) The arrangements may from time to time be varied with the consent of the Board.

(3) If, after giving notice of their intention to do so to the Council of Lloyd's, the Board cancel the approval which they have given with respect to the arrangements, paragraph 3 of Schedule 20 to this Act shall not apply, in the case of any member, to any year of assessment after the year of assessment in which the approval is cancelled.

(4) The provisions of Part II of Schedule 20 to this Act shall have effect as respects the winding up of any special reserve fund which—

(a) was set up under the arrangements mentioned in section 452(1) of the Taxes Act 1988; and

(b) belongs to a member for whom a special reserve fund may be set up under the arrangements mentioned in subsection (1) above.

Commentary—*Simon's Direct Tax Service* **E5.641.**
Cross reference—See Lloyd's Underwriters (Tax) Regulations, SI 1995/351 reg 15 (cessation on death or winding up of old-style fund).

176 Ancillary trust funds

(1) A member shall be treated for the purposes of the Income Tax Acts and the Gains Tax Acts as absolutely entitled as against the trustees to the assets forming part of an ancillary trust fund of his.

(2) The cost of acquisition and the consideration for the disposal of assets forming part of an ancillary trust fund—

(a) shall be left out of account in computing for the purposes of income tax the profits or losses of the member's underwriting business; and

(b) accordingly, shall not be excluded for the purposes of capital gains tax under section 37 or 39 of the Gains Tax Act.

(3) None of the following provisions (which apply where an individual entitled to securities dies), namely—

(a) subsections (1) to (4) of section 721 of the Taxes Act 1988 (accrued income scheme);

(b)–(d) ...[1]

shall apply where the individual concerned is a member and the security concerned forms part of an ancillary trust fund of his.

(4) In a case where subsection (3)(a) above applies, the deceased's personal representatives shall be treated for the purposes of sections 710 to 728 of the Taxes Act 1988 as the transferor or transferee in relation to transfers of securities as to which the deceased was the transferor or transferee (as the case may be) in the interest period in which he died.

Commentary—*Simon's Direct Tax Service* **E5.632.**
Amendment—[1] Sub-s (3)(b)–(d) repealed by FA 1996 Sch 41 Pt V(3) with effect from the year 1996–97 subject to transitional provisions in FA 1996 Sch 15.

Other special cases

177 Reinsurance to close

Commentary—*Simon's Direct Tax Service* **E5.605.**
Amendments—This section repealed by FA 2000 ss 107(11), (12)(c), 156, Sch 40 Pt II(16) with effect for profits of underwriting members' trades which are declared in periods of account beginning after 31 December 1999. FA 2000 s 107 supersedes this section.

178 Stop-loss and quota share insurance

(1) In computing for the purposes of income tax the profits of a member's underwriting business, each of the following shall be deductible as an expense, namely—

(a) any premium payable by him under a stop-loss insurance, and any repayment of insurance money paid to him under such an insurance;

(b) any amount payable by him into the High Level Stop Loss Fund, and any repayment of an amount paid to him out of that Fund; and

[(c) where an amount is payable by him under a quota share contract—

(i) so much of that amount as exceeds the amount of transferred losses that are declared on or before the date the contract takes effect ("the declared amount"), or

(ii) if the contract does not take effect, the amount so payable under the contract.][2]

(2) Subject to subsection (3) below, each of the following, namely—

(a) any insurance money payable to [a member][1] under a stop-loss insurance in respect of a loss in his underwriting business; and

(b) any amount payable to a member out of the High Level Stop Loss Fund in respect of such a loss,

shall be treated as a trading receipt in computing the profits arising from that business for the year of assessment which corresponds to the underwriting year in which the loss [was declared][1].

(3) Where, as respects the payment of any such insurance money or amount as is mentioned in subsection (2) above—

(a) the inspector is not notified of the payment at least 30 days before the time after which any assessment or further assessment of profits for the year of assessment is precluded by section 34 of the Management Act (ordinary time limit of six years), and

(b) the inspector is not entitled, after that time, to make any such assessment or further assessment by virtue of section 36 (fraudulent or negligent conduct) or 40(2) (assessment on personal representatives) of that Act,

that subsection shall have effect in relation to that insurance money or amount as if it referred instead to the year of assessment which corresponds to the underwriting year in which the payment is made.

[(3A) Where the amount payable by a member under a quota share contract is less than the declared amount, the difference between the two amounts shall be treated as a trading receipt in computing the profits arising from the member's underwriting business in the year of assessment which corresponds to the underwriting year in which the contract takes effect.][2]

[(3B) Where a member has entered a quota share contract, any amount paid by him to cover a cash call in respect of transferred losses that are not declared at the time the contract takes effect shall be treated—

(a) for the purposes of subsection (1)(c)(i) and (3A) above, as an amount payable under the contract, and

(b) for the purposes of section 172, as a payment made at the time the contract takes effect.][2]

[(4) For the purposes of this section—

"cash call" has the same meaning as in Part 1 of Schedule 20 to this Act;

"quota share contract" means any contract between a member and another person which—

(a) is made in accordance with the rules or practice of Lloyd's, and

(b) provides for that other person to take over any rights and liabilities of the member under any of the syndicates of which he is a member;

and where the taking over of a member's rights and liabilities is conditional upon the occurrence of any event, the contract does not take effect until that event occurs; and

''transferred loss'', in relation to such a contract, means a loss for which that other person takes over liability under the contract (disregarding, in the case of a loss that has been declared at the time it is taken over, any part of it in respect of which the member has paid a cash call before that time).][2]

Commentary—*Simon's Direct Tax Service* **E5.614.**
Amendments—[1] Words in sub-s (2) substituted by FA 1994 Sch 21 para 5 as respects insurance money and other amounts payable in respect of losses declared in the underwriting year 1997 and subsequent underwriting years.
[2] Sub-ss (1)(c), (4), substituted, and sub-ss (3A), (3B) inserted, by FA 2002 s 86, Sch 32 paras 1–4 with effect for quota share contracts (within the meaning of FA 1993 s 178 or FA 1994 s 225) entered into after 16 April 2002.
Sub-s (1)(c) previously read as follows—

''(c) any amount payable by him under a quota share contract, irrespective of the purpose for which the contract was entered into.''
Sub-s (4) previously read as follows—

''(4) In this section ''quota share contract'' means any contract between a member and another person which—

(a) is made in accordance with the rules or practice of Lloyd's; and
(b) provides for that other person to take over any rights and liabilities of the member under any of the syndicates of which he is a member.''

Miscellaneous

179 Cessation: final year of assessment

(1) Subject to subsection (5) below, this section applies where a member ceases to carry on his underwriting business, whether by reason of death or otherwise.

(2) Subject ...[1] to the provisions of any regulations made by the Board, the member's final year of assessment shall be that which corresponds to the underwriting year in which his deposit at Lloyd's is paid over to him or his personal representatives or assigns.

(3) ...[1]

(4) For the purposes of section 171 above and all other purposes of the Income Tax Acts, any profits or losses arising to the member from his underwriting business which are not taken (by virtue of the provisions of this Chapter) to be profits or losses of an earlier year of assessment shall be taken to be profits or losses of his final year of assessment.

(5) This section does not apply in any case where the member's deposit at Lloyd's is paid over to him or his personal representatives or assigns before 1st January 1993.

Commentary—*Simon's Direct Tax Service* **E5.613.**
Amendments—[1] Sub-s (3) and words omitted from sub-s (2) repealed by FA 1994 Sch 21 para 6(1), (3) and Sch 26 Pt V(25) in any case where the member dies after the end of the year 1993–94.

[179A Death of member

(1) This section applies where a member ceases to carry on his underwriting business by reason of death.

(2) For the purposes of assessing the profits of the member's underwriting business, the member shall be treated as having died at the end of the year of assessment which corresponds to the underwriting year immediately preceding that in which he actually died.

(3) For the purposes of the Income Tax Acts—

(a) the carrying on of the member's underwriting business by his personal representatives shall not be treated as a change in the persons engaged in the carrying on of that business; and
(b) subject to the provisions of any regulations made by the Board, the business shall be treated as continuing until the member's deposit at Lloyd's is paid over to his personal representatives.][1]

Commentary—*Simon's Direct Tax Service* **E5.613.**
Amendments—[1] This section inserted by FA 1994 Sch 21 para 6(2), (3) and has effect in any case where the member dies after the end of the year 1993–94.

180 Underwriting profits to be earned income

(1) In relation to any member, all profits arising to him from his underwriting business—

(a) shall be treated for the purposes of the Income Tax Acts as immediately derived from the carrying on by him of that business, and
(b) accordingly, shall constitute earned income for those purposes.

(2) This section does not apply in relation to profits of the year 1992–93 or earlier years of assessment.

Commentary—*Simon's Direct Tax Service* **E5.653.**

181 Lloyd's underwriting agents

In section 43 of the Finance Act 1989 (Schedule D: computation), subsections (6) and (7) (which extend certain time limits for persons permitted by the Council of Lloyd's to act as underwriting agents at Lloyd's) shall cease to have effect in relation to periods of account ending on or after 30th June 1993.

Supplemental

182 Regulations

(1) The Board may by regulations provide—

(a) for the assessment and collection of tax charged in accordance with section 171 above (so far as not provided for by Schedule 19 to this Act);

(b) for making, in the event of any changes in the rules or practice of Lloyd's, such amendments of this Chapter as appear to the Board to be expedient having regard to those changes;

(c) for modifying the application of this Chapter in cases where a syndicate continues after the end of its closing year or a member dies or otherwise ceases to carry on his underwriting business;

[(ca) for modifying the application of this Chapter in relation to cases where assets forming part of a [premium]⁴ trust fund are the subject of—

(i) ...³

(ii) any such arrangements or agreements as are mentioned in section 737E(2) and (8) of the Taxes Act 1988 (sale and repurchase of securities etc);]¹

(d) for giving credit for foreign tax.

(2)–(4) ...²

(5) Regulations made, or deemed to have been made, under any of the following enactments (regulations about Lloyd's underwriters), namely—

(a) section 451(1) or (1A) of the Taxes Act 1988

(b) section 92(5) of the Finance Act 1989 or

(c) section 209(4) of the Gains Tax Act,

which were in force immediately before 6th April 1992 shall continue in force for the year 1992–93 and subsequent years of assessment notwithstanding the repeal of that enactment by this Act, and shall be deemed to have been made under this section.

Commentary—*Simon's Direct Tax Service* E5.613.
Regulations—Lloyd's Underwriters (Tax) Regulations, SI 1995/351.
Lloyd's Underwriters (Tax) (1992–93 to 1996–97) Regulations, SI 1995/352.
Lloyd's Underwriters (Special Reserve Funds) Regulations, SI 1995/353.
Lloyd's Underwriters (Double Taxation Relief) Regulations, SI 1997/405.
Amendments—¹ Sub-s (1)(ca) inserted by FA 1995 s 83(2).
² Sub-ss (2)–(4) repealed by FA 1994 Sch 21 para 7 and Sch 26 Pt V(25) with effect from the year 1997–98.
³ Sub-s (1)(ca)(i) repealed by FA 1997 Sch 10 paras 6(a), 7(1), Sch 18 Pt VI(10) with effect in relation to, and to transfers under, any arrangement made on or after 1 July 1997 by virtue of the Finance Act 1997, Schedule 10, (Appointed Day) Order, SI 1997/991.
⁴ Word in sub-s (1)(ca) substituted by the Financial Services and Markets Act 2000 (Consequential Amendments) (Taxes) Order, SI 2001/3629 arts 75, 82(d) with effect from 1 December 2001 immediately after the coming into force of the Financial Services and Markets Act 2000 ss 411, 432(1), Sch 20.

183 Consequential amendments

(1) (*amends* TA 1988 s 20(2) Schedule F).

(2) (*amends* TA 1988 s 481(5)(f)).

(3) (*amended* TA 1988 ss 627(5), 641(2)).

(4) (*amended* TA 1988 s 710(14)).

(5) (*amended* TA 1988 s 720(3), Sch 4 para 18(1), FA 1989 Sch 11 para 10(1) and FA 1990 Sch 10 para 18(1)).

(6) (*amended* TA 1988 s 721(5), Sch 4 para 18(8), FA 1989 Sch 11 para 10(6) and FA 1990 Sch 10 para 18(6)).

(7) (*amended* TCGA 1992 s 206(2)).

(8) (*amended* TCGA 1992 s 209).

Amendments—Sub-s (3) repealed by FA 1994 ss 228(2)(c), (4), 258 and Sch 26 Pt VI(25) with effect from the year 1997–98.
Sub-ss (4)–(6) repealed by s 213 of, and Sch 23 Pt III(12) to this Act as respects the year 1994 and subsequent underwriting years and sub-ss (7), (8) repealed by those provisions as respects the year 1994–95 and subsequent years of assessment.

184 Interpretation and commencement

(1) In this Chapter, unless the context otherwise requires—

"ancillary trust fund", in relation to a member, does not include a [premium]⁵ trust fund of his or his special reserve fund (if any) but, subject to that, means any trust fund required or authorised by the rules of Lloyd's, or required by a members' agent of his ...¹;

"closing year"—

(*a*) in relation to a year of assessment, means the year of assessment next but one following that year;

(*b*) in relation to an underwriting year, means the underwriting year next but one following that year; and

(*c*) in relation to a syndicate, means the closing year of the underwriting year for which it was formed;

"the Gains Tax Act" means the Taxation of Chargeable Gains Act 1992 and "the Gains Tax Acts" means that Act and any other enactments relating to capital gains tax;

"the High Level Stop Loss Fund" means the fund of that name which, under the rules of Lloyd's, has been established for the year 1993 and subsequent underwriting years;

"inspector" includes any officer of the Board;

"the Management Act" means the Taxes Management Act 1970;

"managing agent", in relation to a syndicate and a year of assessment, means—

(*a*) the person registered as a managing agent at Lloyd's who was acting as such an agent for the syndicate at the end of the corresponding underwriting year, or

(*b*) such other person as may be determined in accordance with regulations made by the Board;

"member" means [an individual who is a member of Lloyd's and][2] is or has been an underwriting member;

"members' agent", in relation to a member of a syndicate and a year of assessment, means—

(*a*) the person registered as a members' agent at Lloyd's who was acting as such an agent for the member at the end of the corresponding underwriting year, or

(*b*) if two or more such persons were so acting and one of them was appointed by the member to be responsible for complying with the requirements of Part II of Schedule 19 to this Act in relation to all of the syndicates of which he is a member, that person, or

(*c*) if two or more such persons were so acting and none of them was so appointed, the person who was so acting for the member in his capacity as a member of the syndicate, or

(*d*) such other person as may be determined in accordance with regulations made by the Board;

["premium trust fund" means a trust fund into which premiums receivable by members are paid in compliance with a trust deed under section 10.3 of the Lloyd's Sourcebook made by the Financial Services Authority under the Financial Services and Markets Act 2000;][4]

"prescribed" means prescribed by regulations made by the Board;

"profits" includes gains;

"special reserve fund", unless the contrary intention appears, means a special reserve fund set up under the arrangements mentioned in section 175(1) above;

"stop-loss insurance" means any insurance taken out by a member against losses in his underwriting business[, except insurance taken out by entering a quota share contract (within the meaning of section 178 above)][6];

"syndicate" means a syndicate of underwriting members of Lloyd's formed for an underwriting year;

"underwriting business", in relation to a member, means his underwriting business as a member of Lloyd's, whether carried on personally or through an underwriting agent, and does not include any other business carried on by him, and in particular, where he is himself an underwriting agent, does not include his business as such an agent;

"underwriting year" means the calendar year.

(2) For the purposes of this Chapter—

(*a*) an underwriting year and a year of assessment shall be deemed to correspond to each other if the underwriting year ends in the year of assessment;

(*b*) the profits or losses of a member's underwriting business include profits or losses arising to him from assets forming part of a [premium][5] trust fund or an ancillary trust fund; and

(*c*) any charge made on a member by the [managing agent][3] of a syndicate of which he is a member, and any expense incurred on his behalf by the [managing agent][3] of such a syndicate, shall be treated as expenses arising directly from his membership of that syndicate.

(3) Subject to any provision to the contrary, the provisions of this Chapter have effect for the year 1992–93 and subsequent years of assessment.

Simon's Tax Cases—s 184(1), *Deeny v Gooda Walker Ltd (in voluntary liquidation) (IRC third party)* [1996] STC 299.
Amendments—[1] Words in the definition of "ancillary trust fund" repealed by FA 1994 Sch 21 para 8 and Sch 26 Pt V(25) with effect from the year 1994–95..
[2] Words in the definition of "member" in sub-s (1) substituted by FA 1994 Sch 21 para 8 with effect from the year 1994–95.
[3] Words in sub-s (2)(*c*) substituted by FA 1994 Sch 21 para 8.
[4] In sub-s (1), definition of "premium trust fund" substituted for definition of "premiums trust fund" by the Financial Services and Markets Act 2000 (Consequential Amendments) (Taxes) Order, SI 2001/3629 arts 75, 79 with effect from 1 December 2001 immediately after the coming into force of the Financial Services and Markets Act 2000 ss 411, 432(1), Sch 20.
[5] Word in sub-s (1) (in the definition of "ancillary trust fund"), and sub-s (2)(*b*) substituted by SI 2001/3629 arts 75, 82(*e*) with effect from 1 December 2001 immediately after the coming into force of the Financial Services and Markets Act 2000 ss 411, 432(1), Sch 20.
[6] In sub-s (1), words in definition of "stop-loss insurance" added by FA 2002 s 86, Sch 32 paras 1, 5 with effect for quota share contracts (within the meaning of FA 1993 s 178 or FA 1994 s 225) entered into after 16 April 2002.

PART VI
MISCELLANEOUS AND GENERAL
Statutory effect of resolutions etc

205 The 1968 Act

(1) The Provisional Collection of Taxes Act 1968 shall be amended as follows.

(2)–(5) (*amend* PCTA 1968 s 1).

(6) (*amends* PCTA 1968 s 5).

(7) This section shall apply in relation to resolutions passed after the day on which this Act is passed.

206 Corporation tax

(1) (*repeals* TA 1988 s 8(4)–(6)).

(2) (*inserted* TA 1988 s 8A, and is repealed by FA 1996 Sch 41 Pt V(13)).

(3) (*amends* TA 1988 s 246(2)(*b*) and is repealed by F(No 2)A 1997 Sch 8 Pt III).

Miscellaneous

208 Residence: available accommodation

(1) (*inserts* TA 1988 s 336(3)).

(2) (*inserts* TCGA 1992 s 9(4)).

(3) (*amends* IHTA 1984 s 267(4)).

(4) Subsections (1) and (2) above shall have effect for the year 1993–94 and subsequent years of assessment.

(5) Subsection (3) above shall have effect where the year of assessment concerned is 1993–94 or a subsequent year of assessment.

General

212 Interpretation

In this Act "the Taxes Act 1988" means the Income and Corporation Taxes Act 1988.

214 Short title

This Act may be cited as the Finance Act 1993.

SCHEDULES

SCHEDULE 3

CAR AND CAR FUEL BENEFITS: 1994–95 ONWARDS
Section 72

Introductory

1 The Taxes Act 1988 shall be amended as follows.

Car benefits

2 (*amends* s 157).

3 (*amends* s 168).

4 (*inserts* ss 168A–168G).

5 (*substitutes* Sch 6).

Car fuel benefits

6 (*substitutes* s 158(2) Tables *and amends* s 158(5)).

General

7 This Schedule shall have effect for the year 1994–95 and subsequent years of assessment.

SCHEDULE 4

Vans

Section 73

1 The Taxes Act 1988 shall be amended as follows.

2–4 (*amend* ss 154(2), 155(1) and *insert* ss 159AA, 159AB).

5 (*amended* s 159A(8)(*a*); *repealed* by FA 1999 s 139, Sch 20 Pt III(9) with effect from the year 1999–00).

6 (*inserts* s 168(5A), (6)(*c*), (*d*)).

7 (*inserts* Sch 6A).

SCHEDULE 5

REMOVAL EXPENSES AND BENEFITS

Section 76

1, 2 (*insert* TA 1988 ss 191A, 191B, Sch 11A).

SCHEDULE 6

TAXATION OF DISTRIBUTIONS: SUPPLEMENTAL PROVISIONS

Section 79

The Taxes Act 1988

1 (*amends* ss 167(2A), 819(2), Sch 7 para 19(1) and remainder *repealed in part* by FA 1994 s 258, Sch 26 Pt V(2) in relation to interest payments made after 5 April 1994, and by FA 1995 Sch 29 Pt VIII(8) with effect from the year 1995–96).

2 (*amends* s 233(1), (2) and inserts s 233(1A), (1B)).

3 (*repealed* by F(No 2)A 1997 Sch 8 Pt II(9) with effect in relation to distributions made after 5 April 1999).

4 (*amended* s 468E(2) and *repealed* by FA 1994 Sch 26 Pt V(13)).

5 (*amended* s 468F(2) and *inserted* s 468F(2A), (2B) and *repealed* by FA 1994 Sch 26 Pt V(13)).

6 (*amends* ss 549(2), 699(2); and remainder *repealed in part* by FA 1995 Sch 29 Pt VIII(8) with effect from the year 1995–96).

7–11 (*amend* ss 677(2), (6), (7), 686(1), (6), 687(2), (3), 694(2A), 695(4), 696(3)–(5), 698(2) and *insert* s 686(1A), (2A), 698A, 701(3A)).

12 (*amends* s 703(5); *repealed by* FA 1998 Sch 27 Part III(2) *with effect for the year 1999–00 and subsequent years of assessment*).

13 (*amends* ss 720(5), 764).

14 (*repealed* by FA 1996 Sch 41 Pt V(1) with effect from the year 1996–97).

15 (*amends* s 832(1)).

16 (*repealed* by FA 1998 Sch 27 Part III (2) *with effect in relation to distributions made after 5 April 1999*).

17, 18 (*repealed* by FA 1996 Sch 41 Pt V(2) with effect from the year 1996–97).

19 (*inserted* Sch 23A para 2(5); *repealed* by FA 1997 Sch 18 Pt VI(10) with effect in relation to payments made on or after 1 July 1997 by virtue of the Finance Act 1997, Schedule 10, (Appointed Day) Order, SI 1997/991).

The Finance Act 1989 (c 26)

20 (*amends* ss 68(2), 71(4); and *repealed in part* by FA 1996 Sch 41 Pt V(3) with effect from the year 1996–97).

The Finance Act 1990 (c 29)

21 (*repealed* by FA 1996 Sch 41 Pt V(3) with effect from the year 1996–97).

The Taxation of Chargeable Gains Act 1992 (c 12)

22 (*inserted* s 4(3A), (3B) and *amended* s 4(4); *repealed* by FA 1999 s 139, Sch 20 Pt III(1)).

23 (*repealed* by FA 1998 Sch 27 Pt III(29) with effect from the year 1998–99).

24 (*amended* s 6(1); *repealed* by FA 1995 Sch 29 Pt VIII(8) with effect from the year 1995–96).

Commencement

25—(1) This Schedule, except the provisions to which sub-paragraphs (2) to (5) below apply, shall have effect for the year 1993–94 and subsequent years of assessment.

(2) (*repealed* by FA 1994 Sch 26 Pt V(13)).

(3), (4) ...[1]

(5) (*repealed* by FA 1996 Sch 41 Pt V(2) with effect from the year 1996–97).

Amendments—[1] Sub-paras (3), (4) repealed by FA 1997 Sch 18 Pt VI(10) with effect for payment made on or after 1 July 1997 by virtue of the Finance Act 1997, Schedule 10, (Appointed Day) Order, SI 1997/991.

SCHEDULE 7

RELIEF ON RETIREMENT OR RE-INVESTMENT

Section 87

PART I

RETIREMENT RELIEF ETC

Extension of references to "family company"

1 (*amends* TCGA 1992 ss 157, 163–165, Sch 6 paras 1(2), 12(2), Sch 7 para 7(1)).

Prospective amendments—Para 1(2) will be repealed by FA 1998 Sch 27 Pt III(31) with effect for disposals from the year 2003–04.

Extension of references to full-time working directors etc

2 (*amends* TCGA 1992 ss 163, 164, Sch 6).

Prospective amendments—This paragraph will be repealed by FA 1998 Sch 27 Pt III(31) with effect for disposals in the year 2003–04 and subsequent years of assessment.

PART II

ROLL-OVER RELIEF ON RE-INVESTMENT

3 (*inserts* TCGA 1992 ss 164A–164N).

SCHEDULE 8

RESTRICTION ON SET-OFF OF PRE-ENTRY LOSSES

Section 88

(*Inserts TCGA* 1992 Sch 7A).

SCHEDULE 9

OVERSEAS LIFE INSURANCE COMPANIES: AMENDMENT OF TAXES ACT 1988 ETC

Section 97

1 (*inserts* TA 1988 Sch 19AC).

Deemed disposal and reacquisition

2—(1) Where immediately before the relevant day the company referred to in section 11(2) of the Taxes Act 1988 is an overseas life insurance company, then, subject to sub-paragraph (4) below, it shall be deemed for the purposes of corporation tax on chargeable gains—

    (*a*) to have disposed immediately before the relevant day of every asset to which sub-paragraph (2) below applies, and

    (*b*) immediately to have reacquired every such asset,

at its market value at the time of the deemed disposal.

(2) This sub-paragraph applies to any asset which—

    (*a*) was held by the company immediately before the relevant day, and

    (*b*) at the beginning of that day is a chargeable asset in relation to the company.

(3) For the purposes of sub-paragraph (2) above an asset is at the beginning of the relevant day a chargeable asset in relation to the company if, were it to be disposed of at that time, any chargeable gains accruing to the company on the disposal would form part of its chargeable profits by virtue of

paragraph (*c*), (*d*) or (*e*) of section 11(2) of the Taxes Act 1988 (as that paragraph has effect by virtue of Schedule 19AC to that Act).

(4) Sub-paragraph (1) above shall not have effect in applying paragraph 2(2) of Schedule 28 to that Act in the case of a disposal by the company.

(5) For the purposes of this paragraph the relevant day is the first day of the company's first accounting period to begin after 31st December 1992.

Commentary—*Simon's Direct Tax Service* **D4.537.**
Revenue Internal Guidance—Life Assurance manual (17.141–17.143: para 2 above applies only to a company which is an overseas life insurance company before the "relevant day", that is it must have a UK branch before the relevant day (TA 1988 s 431(2)).

SCHEDULE 10

OVERSEAS LIFE INSURANCE COMPANIES: AMENDMENT OF FINANCE ACT 1989

Section 101

(*Inserts FA 1989 Sch 8A*).

SCHEDULE 11

OVERSEAS LIFE INSURANCE COMPANIES: AMENDMENT OF TAXATION OF CHARGEABLE GAINS ACT 1992

Section 102

(*Inserts TCGA 1992 Sch 7B*).

SCHEDULE 12

INITIAL ALLOWANCES FOR AGRICULTURAL BUILDINGS

Section 114

Amendment—This Schedule repealed by the Capital Allowances Act 2001 s 580, Sch 4 with effect for income tax purposes, as respects allowances and charges falling to be made for chargeable periods ending after 5 April 2001, and for corporation tax purposes, as respects allowances and charges falling to be made for chargeable periods ending after 31 March 2001.

SCHEDULE 13

FIRST-YEAR ALLOWANCES FOR MACHINERY AND PLANT

Section 115

Amendment—This Schedule repealed by the Capital Allowances Act 2001 s 580, Sch 4 with effect for income tax purposes, as respects allowances and charges falling to be made for chargeable periods ending after 5 April 2001, and for corporation tax purposes, as respects allowances and charges falling to be made for chargeable periods ending after 31 March 2001.

SCHEDULE 14

PAY AND FILE: MISCELLANEOUS AMENDMENTS

Section 120

Failure to give notice of liability for corporation tax

1 (*amends* TMA 1970 s 10(3)).

Amendments—This paragraph repealed by FA 1998 s 165, Sch 27 Part III(28) with effect for accounting periods ending after 30 June 1999 (by virtue of Finance Act 1994, Section 199, (Appointed Day) Order, SI 1998/3173 art 2).

Further claims etc where assessment made

2 (*amends* TMA 1970 s 43A(1)).

Amendments—This paragraph repealed by FA 1998 s 165, Sch 27 Part III(28) with effect for accounting periods ending after 30 June 1999 (by virtue of Finance Act 1994, Section 199, (Appointed Day) Order, SI 1998/3173 art 2).

Interest on overdue corporation tax: transitional cases

3 (*amends* TMA 1970 s 86(3) and *inserts* s 86(4A), (4B)).

Interest on overdue corporation tax: pay and file cases

4 (*amends* TMA 1970 s 87A(4) and *substitutes* s 87A(6), (7) for sub-s (6)).

Amendments—Para 4(1) repealed by FA 1998 Sch 27 Part III with effect where the later period mentioned in TMA 1970 s 87A begins after 5 April 1999.

Effect on interest of reliefs

5 (*amends* TMA 1970 s 91(1B)).

Failure to make return for corporation tax

6 (*amends* TMA 1970 s 94(6), (7)).

Amendments—This paragraph repealed by FA 1998 s 165, Sch 27 Part III(28) with effect for accounting periods ending after 30 June 1999 (by virtue of Finance Act 1994, Section 199, (Appointed Day) Order, SI 1998/3173 art 2).

Things to be done by companies

7 (*amends* TMA 1970 s 108(1)).

Relief under section 393 of the Taxes Act 1988

8—(1) In relation to any case in which by virtue of section 99 of the Finance Act 1990 losses may be set off under subsection (1) of section 393 or of section 396 of the Taxes Act 1988 without the making of a claim, the Taxes Act 1988 shall have effect with the following amendments.

(2)–(5) (*amend* TA 1988 ss 343(3), 395(1), (4), 398, 400(2)).

9 (*amends* F(No 2)A 1992 s 65(6)).

Interest on tax overpaid

10—(1) ...¹

(2) (*amends* TA 1988 ss 826(7A)).

(3) ...¹

(4) (*amends* TA 1988 ss 826(7B)).

(5), (6) ...¹

Amendments—Sub-paras (1), (3), (5) and (6) repealed by FA 1998 Sch 27 Part III(2) with effect where the later period mentioned in TA 1988 s 826(7) begins after 5 April 1999, and where the earlier period mentioned in TA 1988 s 826(7AA)(7CA) begins after 5 April 1999.

Surrender of refunds

11 (*inserts* FA 1989 s 102(4A)).

SCHEDULE 15

EXCHANGE GAINS AND LOSSES: ALTERNATIVE CALCULATION

Section 134

Note—This Schedule repealed by FA 2002 s 141, Sch 40 Pt 3(10) with effect for accounting periods beginning after 30 September 2002.

Regulations—Exchange Gains and Losses (Alternative Method of Calculation of Gain or Loss) Regulations, SI 1994/3227.

Introduction

1—(1) This paragraph applies where regulations under this Schedule provide that the amount of an initial exchange gain or initial exchange loss accruing to a company as regards an asset, liability or contract for an accrual period shall be found in accordance with the alternative method of calculation.

(2) In such a case the amount shall not be found in accordance with section 125(2) or (4) of this Act or section 126(3) or (5) or section 127(3) or (4) (as the case may be) but shall be found by—

(a) taking the accrued amount for each day in the accrual period, and

(b) adding the amounts found under paragraph (a) above.

(3) Subject to regulations under this Schedule, the accrued amount for a day in the accrual period shall be found by—

(a) taking the amount of the initial exchange gain or initial exchange loss found in accordance with section 125(2) or (4) of this Act or section 126(3) or (5) or section 127(3) or (4) (as the case may be), and

(b) dividing it by the number of days in the period.

(4) Where an accrual period does not begin at the beginning of a day, the part of the day that falls within the accrual period shall be treated for the purposes of this Schedule as a complete day.

(5) Where an accrual period does not end at the end of a day, the part of the day that falls within the accrual period shall be treated for the purposes of this Schedule as a complete day.

Commentary—*Simon's Direct Tax Service* **D2.930.**

Exempt circumstances

2—(1) Regulations may provide that where—

> *(a) as regards an asset, liability or contract an initial exchange gain or initial exchange loss accrues to a company for an accrual period under section 125, 126 or 127 of this Act or would so accrue apart from regulations under this Schedule,*
>
> *(b) at any time on a day in the period the asset or contract was held, or the liability was owed, by the company in exempt circumstances, and*
>
> *(c) such other conditions as may be prescribed are fulfilled,*

the amount of the gain or loss shall be found in accordance with the alternative method of calculation.

(2) Regulations may also provide that as regards any such day as is mentioned in sub-paragraph (1) above the accrued amount shall be ascertained in accordance with prescribed rules.

(3) Regulations may be so framed that the accrued amount as regards a day depends on the extent to which an asset or contract is held, or a liability is owed, in exempt circumstances.

(4) For the purposes of this paragraph an asset or contract is held, or a liability is owed, in exempt circumstances at a given time if it is then held or owed—

> *(a) for the purposes of [long-term][1] insurance business;*
>
> *(b) for the purposes of mutual insurance business;*
>
> *(c) for the purposes of the occupation of commercial woodlands;*
>
> *(d) by a housing association approved at that time for the purposes of section 488 of the Taxes Act 1988;*
>
> *(e) by a self-build society approved at that time for the purposes of section 489 of that Act.*

(5) In this paragraph—

> *["long-term insurance business" means business which consists of the effecting or carrying out of contracts which fall within Part II of Schedule 1 to the Financial Services and Markets Act 2000 (Regulated Activities) Order 2001;][1]*
>
> *"commercial woodlands" means woodlands in the United Kingdom which are managed on a commercial basis and with a view to the realisation of profits.*

Commentary—*Simon's Direct Tax Service* **D2.931.**
Amendments—[1] Word in sub-para (4)(a) substituted, and in sub-para (5), definition of "long-term insurance business" substituted by the Financial Services and Markets Act 2000 (Consequential Amendments) (Taxes) Order, SI 2001/3629 arts 75 80 with effect from 1 December 2001 immediately after the coming into force of the Financial Services and Markets Act 2000 ss 411, 432(1), Sch 20.

Unremittable income

3—(1) Regulations may provide that where—

> *(a) as regards an asset falling within section 153(1)(a) or (b) of this Act an initial exchange gain or initial exchange loss accrues to a company for an accrual period under section 125 or 127 of this Act or would so accrue apart from regulations under this Schedule,*
>
> *(b) at any time on a day in the period income represented by the asset was unremittable, and*
>
> *(c) such other conditions as may be prescribed are fulfilled,*

the amount of the gain or loss shall be found in accordance with the alternative method of calculation

(2) Regulations may also provide that as regards any such day as is mentioned in sub-paragraph (1) above the accrued amount shall be ascertained in accordance with prescribed rules.

(3) Regulations may be so framed that the accrued amount as regards a day depends on the extent to which the income represented by an asset is unremittable.

(4) For the purposes of this paragraph income is unremittable if—

> *[(a) a claim under subsection (2) of section 584 of the Taxes Act 1988 (relief for unremittable income) has been made in relation to the income,][1]*
>
> *[(b) paragraphs (a) and (b) of that subsection apply to it, and][1]*
>
> *[(c) those paragraphs have not ceased to apply to it.][1]*

Commentary—*Simon's Direct Tax Service* **D2.932.**
Amendments—[1] Sub-para 3(4)(a)–(c) substituted by FA 1996 s 134(2), Sch 20 para 70 with effect as respects accounting period ending after 30 June 1999 (by virtue of Finance Act 1994, Section 199, (Appointed Day) Order, SI 1998/3173 art 2).

Matched liabilities

4—(1) Regulations may provide that where—

> *(a) as regards a liability an initial exchange gain or initial exchange loss accrues to a company for an accrual period under section 125 or 127 of this Act or would so accrue apart from regulations under this Schedule,*
>
> *(b) the liability falls within section 153(2)(a) of this Act,*

(c) the liability is eligible to be matched on any day in the accrual period with an asset held by the company, and such other conditions as may be prescribed are fulfilled, and

(d) an election is made in accordance with the regulations to match the liability with the asset on any such day and the election has effect by virtue of the regulations,

the amount of the gain or loss shall be found in accordance with the alternative method of calculation.

(2) Regulations may also provide that as regards any day in respect of which an election has effect the accrued amount shall be ascertained in accordance with prescribed rules.

(3) The question whether a liability is eligible to be matched with an asset shall be determined in accordance with prescribed rules, and in particular regulations may include provision that—

(a) only liabilities of a prescribed description are eligible to be matched with assets;

(b) only assets of a prescribed description are eligible to be matched with liabilities;

(c) liabilities of a prescribed description are eligible to be matched only with assets of a prescribed description.

(4) Regulations may include provision that on any day—

(a) a liability may be partially matched;

(b) an asset may be partially matched;

(c) one asset may be matched with two or more liabilities (wholly or partially);

(d) one liability may be matched with two or more assets (wholly or partially).

(5) Regulations may include provision that an election relating to an asset or assets shall be treated as made in relation to another asset or other assets (as where assets are replaced by others).

(6) Regulations may include provision—

(a) that an election may in prescribed circumstances have effect from a time before it is made;

(b) that an election may be varied;

(c) that an election may not be revoked;

(d) that an election must be made by the company (subject to any provision under sub-paragraph (7) below).

(7) Regulations may provide that where the company is a relevant controlled foreign company an election may be made by a United Kingdom resident company which has (or may be made jointly by United Kingdom resident companies which together have) a majority interest in the company; and—

(a) a company is a relevant controlled foreign company if Chapter IV of Part XVII of the Taxes Act 1988 applies in relation to the accounting period of the company which constitutes the accrual period or in which the accrual period falls;

(b) paragraph 4(3) of Schedule 24 to that Act (majority interest) applies for the purposes of this sub-paragraph.

(8) Regulations may include provision—

(a) that prescribed conditions shall be treated as fulfilled in prescribed circumstances (subject to any provision under paragraph (b) below);

(b) that prescribed conditions shall be treated as not having been fulfilled if the inspector gives notification that he is not satisfied that they are fulfilled;

(c) for an appeal from the inspector's notification;

(d) for a notification to be given to the company or companies making the election.

(9) Regulations may be so framed that the accrued amount as regards a day depends on the extent to which a liability is matched.

(10) Regulations may also provide as mentioned in one or more of the following paragraphs—

(a) that a chargeable gain (or chargeable gains) shall be treated as accruing to a relevant person for the purposes of the Taxation of Chargeable Gains Act 1992;

(b) that an allowable loss (or allowable losses) shall be treated as accruing to a relevant person for the purposes of that Act;

(c) that the operation of that Act as regards a relevant person shall be otherwise adjusted in accordance with prescribed rules (whether the adjustment results in the incidence of tax on the person being greater or smaller).

(11) For the purposes of sub-paragraph (10) above each of the following is a relevant person—

(a) the company mentioned in sub-paragraph (1) above;

(b) any person who has at any time acquired a matched asset (or part of a matched asset) since the company acquired it;

and a matched asset is an asset which has at any time been to any extent matched with a liability in pursuance of an election.

(12) Regulations may make provision—

(a) as to the occasion on which a chargeable gain or allowable loss mentioned in sub-paragraph (10) above is to be treated as accruing, as to the amount to be treated as the amount of the gain or loss, and as to other matters relating to the gain or loss;

(b) as to the timing and extent of any adjustment mentioned in sub-paragraph (10)(c) above and as to other matters relating to the adjustment.

[Currency contracts: matching]¹

[4A—(1) Regulations may provide that where—

(a) as regards a contract an initial exchange gain or initial exchange loss accrues to a company for an accrual period under section 126(5) of this Act or would so accrue apart from regulations under this Schedule,

(b) the relevant duty is eligible to be matched on any day in the accrual period with an asset held by the company, and such other conditions as may be prescribed are fulfilled, and

(c) an election is made in accordance with the regulations to match the duty with the asset on any such day and the election has effect by virtue of the regulations,

the amount of the gain or loss shall be found in accordance with the alternative method of calculation.

(2) Regulations may also provide that as regards any day in respect of which an election has effect the accrued amount shall be ascertained in accordance with prescribed rules.

(3) The reference in sub-paragraph (1) above to the relevant duty is to the duty to which, under the contract, the company becomes subject as regards the second currency (within the meaning given by section 126 of this Act).

(4) Where regulations are made under this paragraph, sub-paragraphs (3) to (12) of paragraph 4 above shall apply as they apply where regulations are made under that paragraph; but in the application of those sub-paragraphs by virtue of this sub-paragraph—

(a) the references to a liability in sub-paragraphs (3), (4), (9) and (11) shall be construed as references to a duty,

(b) the references to liabilities in sub-paragraphs (3) and (4) shall be construed as references to duties, and

(c) the reference in sub-paragraph (11)(a) to sub-paragraph (1) of paragraph 4 shall be construed as a reference to sub-paragraph (1) above.]¹

Amendment—¹ This paragraph inserted by FA 1994 s 116(1), (2).

Combination of circumstances

5—(1) This paragraph applies where regulations under more than one of paragraphs 2 to 4 above apply—

(a) as regards the same asset or liability, and

(b) for the same accrual period.

(2) Regulations may provide that, as regards any day falling within the period and identified in accordance with prescribed rules, the accrued amount shall be ascertained in accordance with rules prescribed under this paragraph (rather than provisions made under any of those paragraphs).

Commentary—*Simon's Direct Tax Service* **D2.930.**

[5A—(1) This paragraph applies where regulations under both paragraph 2 and paragraph 4A above apply—

(a) as regards the same contract, and

(b) for the same accrual period.

(2) Regulations may provide that, as regards any day falling within the period and identified in accordance with prescribed rules, the accrued amount shall be ascertained in accordance with rules prescribed under this paragraph (rather than provisions made under either of those paragraphs).]¹

Commentary—*Simon's Direct Tax Service* **D2.930.**
Amendment—¹ This paragraph inserted by FA 1994 s 116(1), (3).

Arm's length test

6 Where regulations make provision under any of [the relevant paragraphs]¹, they may provide that for the purposes of section 136(11) of this Act amounts X and Y shall be found without regard to matters which are prescribed and would otherwise have had to be taken into account under the regulations [; and the relevant paragraphs are paragraphs 2, 3, 4 and 5 above]².

Amendments—¹ Words substituted by FA 1994 s 116(1), (4).
² Words inserted by FA 1994 s 116(1), (4).

Local currency

7 Where regulations make provision under any of paragraphs 2 to [5A]¹ above, section 149 of this Act shall have effect as if the references to sections 125 to 127 included references to this Schedule and the provisions of the regulations.

Commentary—*Simon's Direct Tax Service* **D2.930.**
Amendment—¹ "5A" substituted by FA 1994 s 116(1), (5).

General

8 *Regulations may be so framed that the accrued amount as regards a day is nil (so that, depending on the circumstances, an initial exchange gain or initial exchange loss may be extinguished).*

9 *Regulations may make different provision about exchange gains (on the one hand) and exchange losses (on the other).*

Commentary—*Simon's Direct Tax Service* **D2.930**.

SCHEDULE 16

EXCHANGE GAINS AND LOSSES: TRANSITIONALS

Section 165

Note—This Schedule repealed by FA 2002 s 141, Sch 40 Pt 3(10) with effect for accounting periods beginning after 30 September 2002.

Regulations—Exchange Gains and Losses (Transitional Provisions) Regulations, SI 1994/3226.

Introduction

1 *For the purposes of this Schedule an existing asset, liability or contract is an asset, liability or contract to which this Chapter applies by virtue of section 165(2) or (3) of this Act or by virtue of regulations under section 165(4) of this Act.*

General provision

2—*(1) Regulations may make such provision as the Treasury think fit with regard to the application of this Chapter to an existing asset, liability or contract (such as provision for finding the basic valuation of an asset or liability).*

(2) Nothing in the following provisions of this Schedule shall prejudice the generality of sub-paragraph (1) above.

Attributed gain or loss

3—*(1) Regulations may provide that—*

(a) an amount found in accordance with prescribed rules shall be attributed to an existing asset or liability, and

(b) the amount shall be characterised as a gain or loss in accordance with prescribed rules.

(2) The regulations may provide that an attributed gain or loss shall be set off against exchange losses or exchange gains accruing as regards the asset or liability; and for this purpose—

(a) an exchange gain is an exchange gain of a trade or an exchange gain of part of a trade or a non-trading exchange gain;

(b) an exchange loss is an exchange loss of a trade or an exchange loss of part of a trade or a non-trading exchange loss.

(3) The regulations may provide that if an event of a prescribed description occurs as regards the asset or liability at a time falling on or after the commencement day of the company concerned and at a time when all or part of an attributed gain or loss is outstanding—

(a) an initial exchange gain or initial exchange loss of an amount found in accordance with prescribed rules shall be treated as accruing to the company as regards the asset or liability, or

(b) a chargeable gain or allowable loss of an amount found in accordance with prescribed rules shall be treated as accruing to the company as regards the asset or liability for the purposes of the Taxation of Chargeable Gains Act 1992.

(4) The regulations may provide that where—

(a) apart from provision under this sub-paragraph, an allowable loss would be treated as accruing by virtue of provision made under sub-paragraph (3)(b) above, and

(b) the company concerned makes an election in accordance with prescribed rules,

the loss shall not be treated as accruing and relief of an amount equal to it shall be given to the company in such form and manner as may be prescribed.

(5) The regulations may provide that where provision under this paragraph has effect the outstanding attributed gain or loss shall be treated as reduced or extinguished.

(6) The regulations may make provision—

(a) as to the time when an initial exchange gain or initial exchange loss is to be treated as accruing and as to the extent to which it is to be treated as an exchange gain or loss of a trade or of part of a trade or as a non-trading exchange gain or loss;

(b) as to the occasion on which a chargeable gain or allowable loss is to be treated as accruing;

(c) as to other matters relating to setting off against, or the accrual of, gains or losses as mentioned in this paragraph.

Adjustment of exchange gain or loss

4—(1) Regulations may provide that where an exchange gain or exchange loss accrues to a company as regards an existing asset or liability (or would so accrue apart from the regulations)—

(a) the amount of the gain or loss shall be deemed to be increased in accordance with prescribed rules,

(b) the amount of the gain or loss shall be deemed to be reduced in accordance with prescribed rules, or

(c) the gain or loss shall be deemed not to accrue.

(2) For the purposes of this paragraph—

(a) an exchange gain is an exchange gain of a trade or an exchange gain of part of a trade or a non-trading exchange gain;

(b) an exchange loss is an exchange loss of a trade or an exchange loss of part of a trade or a non-trading exchange loss.

(3) The regulations may be framed by reference to—

(a) exchange differences arising as regards the asset or liability at any time while the company actually holds or owes it (whether any such time falls before, on or after the company's commencement day);

(b) such other factors as the Treasury think fit;

and for this purpose exchange differences are gains and losses attributable to fluctuations in currency exchange rates.

(4) The regulations may include provision designed to prevent provision under them being avoided by the replacement (or partial replacement) of assets or liabilities by other assets or liabilities.

Allowable losses

5—(1) Regulations may provide that where—

(a) an allowable loss of a prescribed description has accrued to a qualifying company for the purposes of the Taxation of Chargeable Gains Act 1992

(b) the loss has accrued before the company's commencement day,

(c) all or part of the loss has not been allowed as a deduction under that Act, and

(d) prescribed conditions (whether relating to the making of a claim or otherwise) are fulfilled,

the loss shall be set off against exchange gains accruing to the company.

(2) For the purposes of this paragraph an exchange gain is an exchange gain of a trade or an exchange gain of part of a trade or a non-trading exchange gain.

(3) The regulations may provide that the loss may only be set off—

(a) to the extent that it has not been allowed as a deduction under the Taxation of Chargeable Gains Act 1992;

(b) against exchange gains accruing as regards assets or liabilities of a prescribed description.

(4) The regulations may include rules for ascertaining whether an allowable loss of a prescribed description has or has not been allowed as a deduction under the Taxation of Chargeable Gains Act 1992.

Miscellaneous

6—(1) Regulations may provide—

(a) that provision under paragraph 3 above or provision under paragraph 4 above or provision under neither of them shall apply in the case of an asset or liability according to the circumstances of the case;

(b) that provision under paragraph 3(3)(a) above or provision under paragraph 3(3)(b) above shall apply in the case of an asset or liability according to the circumstances of the case.

(2) The circumstances may be framed by reference to—

(a) whether, and how, exchange differences arising as regards the asset or liability would be taken into account for tax purposes apart from this Chapter;

(b) such other factors as the Treasury think fit;

and for this purpose exchange differences are gains and losses attributable to fluctuations in currency exchange rates.

SCHEDULE 17

EXCHANGE GAINS AND LOSSES: CHARGEABLE GAINS

Section 169

Note—This Schedule repealed by FA 2002 s 141, Sch 40 Pt 3(10) with effect for accounting periods beginning after 30 September 2002.

Introduction

1 In this Schedule "the 1992 Act" means the Taxation of Chargeable Gains Act 1992.

Currency

2—(1) In a case where—

(a) there is for the purposes of the 1992 Act a disposal of currency other than sterling by a qualifying company, and

(b) immediately before the disposal the company did not hold the currency in exempt circumstances (within the meaning given by paragraph 3 below),

for the purposes of that Act no chargeable gain or allowable loss shall accrue on the disposal.

(2) This paragraph applies to disposals on or after the company's commencement day.

Commentary—*Simon's Direct Tax Service* **D2.969.**

3—(1) For the purposes of paragraph 2 above a company holds currency in exempt circumstances at a given time if—

(a) the purposes for which it then holds the currency are or include any of the purposes mentioned in sub-paragraph (2) below,

(b) it is a housing association approved at that time for the purposes of section 488 of the Taxes Act 1988 or

(c) it is a self-build society approved at that time for the purposes of section 489 of that Act.

(2) The purposes referred to in sub-paragraph (1)(a) above are—

(a) the purposes of [long-term]¹ insurance business;

(b) the purposes of mutual insurance business;

(c) the purposes of the occupation of commercial woodlands.

(3) In this paragraph—

["long-term insurance business" means business which consists of the effecting or carrying out of contracts which fall within Part II of Schedule 1 to the Financial Services and Markets Act 2000 (Regulated Activities) Order 2001;]¹

"commercial woodlands" means woodlands in the United Kingdom which are managed on a commercial basis and with a view to the realisation of profits.

Commentary—*Simon's Direct Tax Service* **D2.969.**
Amendments—¹ Word in sub-para (2)(a) and definition of "long-term insurance business" in sub-para (3) substituted by the Financial Services and Markets Act 2000 (Consequential Amendments) (Taxes) Order, SI 2001/3629 arts 75, 81(1), (2) with effect from 1 December 2001 immediately after the coming into force of the Financial Services and Markets Act 2000 ss 411, 432(1), Sch 20.

[Debts other than securities]¹

4 ...

Commentary—*Simon's Direct Tax Service* **D2.969.**
Amendments—This paragraph repealed by FA 1996 Sch 41 Pt V(3) with effect for accounting periods ending after 31 March 1996, but not for any disposal before 1 April 1996: FA 1996 Sch 15 para 22(6).

[Debts on securities: disposals

5 ...

Commentary—*Simon's Direct Tax Service* **D2.969.**
Amendments—This paragraph repealed by FA 1996 Sch 41 Pt V(3) with effect for accounting periods ending after 31 March 1996, but not for any disposal before 1 April 1996: FA 1996 Sch 15 para 22(6) (previously substituted by FA 1995 Sch 24 para 6).

Debts on securities: relief

6 ...

Commentary—*Simon's Direct Tax Service* **D2.969.**
Amendments—This paragraph repealed by FA 1996 Sch 41 Pt V(3) with effect for accounting periods ending after 31 March 1996, but not for any disposal before 1 April 1996: FA 1996 Sch 15 para 22(6).

Reconstructions, groups etc

7—(1) This paragraph applies where there is for the purposes of the 1992 Act a disposal or acquisition of an asset which is—

(a) currency,

(b) a debt which is not a debt on a security and the right to settlement under which is a qualifying asset,

(c) a security (as defined in section 132 of the 1992 Act) where the right to settlement under the debt on the security is a qualifying asset, or

(d) an obligation which by virtue of section 143 of the 1992 Act (futures and options) is regarded as an asset to the disposal of which that Act applies and which is a duty under a currency contract.

(2) In a case where—

(a) the condition mentioned in sub-paragraph (3) below is fulfilled, and

(b) section 139, [or 171][1] of the 1992 Act (reconstructions, groups etc) would, apart from this paragraph, apply as regards the disposal or acquisition,

the section concerned shall not apply as regards the disposal and the corresponding acquisition or (as the case may be) shall not apply as regards the acquisition and the corresponding disposal.

(3) The condition is that stated in paragraph (a) or (b) below (as the case may be)—

(a) the disposal is by a qualifying company and immediately before the disposal the asset is held wholly for qualifying purposes;

(b) the acquisition is by a qualifying company and immediately after the acquisition the asset is held wholly for qualifying purposes.

(4) For the purposes of this paragraph qualifying purposes are purposes which constitute one or both of the following—

(a) purposes of [long-term][2] insurance business;

(b) purposes of mutual insurance business;

[and "long-term insurance business" means business which consists of the effecting or carrying out of contracts which fall within Part II of Schedule 1 to the Financial Services and Markets Act 2000 (Regulated Activities) Order 2001.][2]

(5) This paragraph applies where the disposal or acquisition (as the case may be) is made on or after the commencement day of the company mentioned in sub-paragraph (3)(a) or (b) above (as the case may be).

Commentary—*Simon's Direct Tax Service* **D2.966.**
Amendments—[1] Words in sub-para (2)(b) substituted by FA 2000 s 102, Sch 29 para 43 with effect for disposals after 31 March 2000.
[2] Words in sub-para (4) substituted by the Financial Services and Markets Act 2000 (Consequential Amendments) (Taxes) Order, SI 2001/3629 arts 75, 82(1), (3) with effect from 1 December 2001 immediately after the coming into force of the Financial Services and Markets Act 2000 ss 411, 432(1), Sch 20.

Indexation allowance

8 ...

Amendment—This paragraph repealed by FA 1994 s 258, Sch 26 Pt V(8) for disposals made after 29 November 1993. For transitional relief for the years 1993–94, 1994–95, see Sch 12 to that Act.

SCHEDULE 18

EXCHANGE GAINS AND LOSSES: AMENDMENTS

Section 170

Taxes Management Act 1970 (c 9)

1 (inserts s 87A(4A)).

Income and Corporation Taxes Act 1988 (c 1)

2 (inserts s 56(3A)–(3D); repealed by FA 2002 s 141, Sch 40 Pt 3 (10) with effect for accounting periods beginning after 30 September 2002).

3 (inserted s 242(2)(f), (8)(e) and repealed by FA 1996 Sch 41 Pt V(3) with effect for accounting periods ending after 31 March 1996, subject to transitional provisions in FA 1996 Sch 15).

4 (inserts s 407(2)(c)).

5 (inserts s 826(7C)).

6 (inserts Sch 27 para 5(2A)).

Finance Act 1989 (c 26)

7 (inserted Sch 11 para 5A and repealed by FA 1996 Sch 41 Pt V(3) with effect for accounting periods ending after 31 March 1996, subject to transitional provisions in FA 1996 Sch 15).

SCHEDULE 19

LLOYD'S UNDERWRITERS: ASSESSMENT AND COLLECTION OF TAX

Section 173

Cross reference—See FA 1994 s 221 (extension of the application of this Schedule to corporate members of Lloyd's).

PART I
DETERMINATION OF A SYNDICATE'S PROFIT OR LOSS
Preliminary

1 In this Part of this Schedule "profit or loss", in relation to a syndicate, means the aggregate amount of such of the profits or losses of all the members of the syndicate (taken together) as arise—

(a) directly from their membership of the syndicate, or

(b) from assets forming part of [premium][1] trust funds,

and "profits" and "losses" shall be construed accordingly.

Cross reference—See FA 1994 s 221 (extension of the application of this Schedule to corporate members of Lloyd's).
Amendments—[1] Word in sub-para (1)(b) substituted by the Financial Services and Markets Act 2000 (Consequential Amendments) (Taxes) Order, SI 2001/3629 arts 75, 82(f) with effect from 1 December 2001 immediately after the coming into force of the Financial Services and Markets Act 2000 ss 411, 432(1), Sch 20.

Returns by managing agent

2—(1) An inspector may, at any time [after the beginning of a year of assessment][1] by notice in writing to a syndicate's managing agent require him to deliver to the inspector, on or before the final day determined under sub-paragraph (2) below, a return of the syndicate's profit or loss for the year of assessment—

(a) containing such information as may be required in pursuance of the notice; and

(b) accompanied by such accounts, statements and reports as may be so required.

(2) The final day for the delivery of any return required by a notice under sub-paragraph (1) above is whichever is the later of—

(a) [1st September in the year of assessment][1]; and

(b) the end of the period of three months beginning on the day following that on which the notice was served.

(3) If a syndicate's managing agent, having been required by a notice under sub-paragraph (1) above to deliver a return, fails to deliver the return on or before the final date for its delivery, he shall be liable to a penalty equal to the prescribed amount multiplied by the number of days on which the failure continues.

(4) In sub-paragraph (3) above "the prescribed amount" means £60 for each fifty members of the syndicate (counting any number of members less than fifty, and any number left over, as fifty).

(5) If a syndicate's managing agent fraudulently or negligently delivers an incorrect return under sub-paragraph (1) above, he shall be liable to a penalty not exceeding £3,000 multiplied by the number of members of the syndicate.

(6) In relation to a return required by a notice under sub-paragraph (1) above—

(a) any reference in sub-paragraph (2) or (3) above to the delivery of the return is a reference to its delivery together with the accompanying documents referred to in sub-paragraph (1) above; and

(b) the reference in sub-paragraph (5) above to the return being incorrect includes a reference to any of those documents being incorrect.

Commentary—*Simon's Direct Tax Service* E5.619.
Cross references—See FA 1994 s 221 (extension of the application of this Schedule to corporate members of Lloyd's).
Lloyd's Underwriters (Tax) Regulations, SI 1995/351 reg 7 (non-delivery of return—reasonable excuse).
Amendment—[1] Words in sub-ss (1), (2) substituted by FA 1994 Sch 21 para 9 with effect from the year 1997–98.

Determinations by inspector

3—(1) If the inspector is satisfied that a return under paragraph 2(1) above affords correct and complete information concerning the syndicate's profit or loss for a year of assessment, he shall determine that profit or loss accordingly.

(2) If for a year of assessment the inspector is dissatisfied with a return under paragraph 2(1) above, or there is no such return, the inspector shall determine the syndicate's profit or loss for that year to the best of his judgment.

(3) If the inspector discovers that a determination under sub-paragraph (1) or (2) above—

(a) understates the syndicate's profits for the year of assessment; or

(b) overstates the syndicate's losses for that year,

he may, by a determination under this sub-paragraph, vary the first-mentioned determination accordingly.

(4) Notice of a determination under this paragraph shall be served on the syndicate's managing agent and shall state the time within which any appeal against the determination may be made under paragraph 4 below.

(5) After notice of a determination under this paragraph has been served on the syndicate's managing agent, the determination shall not be altered except in accordance with the express provisions of the Taxes Acts.

Commentary—*Simon's Direct Tax Service* **E5.619.**
Cross reference—See FA 1994 s 221 (extension of the application of this Schedule to corporate members of Lloyd's).

Appeals

4—(1) A syndicate's managing agent may appeal against a determination under paragraph 3 above by a notice of appeal in writing given to the inspector within thirty days after the date of the notice of determination.

(2) An appeal under this paragraph shall be to the General Commissioners, except that the agent may elect (in accordance with section 46(1) of the Management Act) to bring the appeal before the Special Commissioners instead of the General Commissioners.

(3) Subsections [(5) and (6) of section 31A and subsections (2) to (7) of section 31D][1] of the Management Act shall apply for the purposes of an election under sub-paragraph (2) above as they apply for the purposes of an election under subsection [(1) of section 31D of that Act][1].

Commentary—*Simon's Direct Tax Service* **E5.619.**
Cross reference—See FA 1994 s 221 (extension of the application of this Schedule to corporate members of Lloyd's).
Amendments—[1] In sub-para (3), words substituted for the words "(5) to (5E) of section 31", and the words "(1) of section 31D of that Act" substituted for the words "(4) of that section", by FA 2001 s 88, Sch 29 para 36(1), (2) with effect from the passing of FA 2001 in relation to returns whether made before or after the passing of FA 2001, and whether relating to periods before or after the passing of FA 2001.

Modification of determinations pending appeal

5—(1) Where a syndicate's managing agent appeals against a determination under paragraph 3 above, then, for the purpose of establishing, in the event of a member of the syndicate appealing against an assessment made on him, the amount of tax the payment of which should, pending the determination of that appeal, be postponed under section 55 of the Management Act, that section shall apply to the first-mentioned appeal with the modifications specified in sub-paragraph (2) below.

(2) The modifications are as follows—

(a) any reference to the notice of assessment shall be construed as a reference to the notice of determination;

(b) any reference to the appellant believing that he is overcharged to tax by the assessment shall be construed as a reference to him believing that the determination overstates the syndicate's profits, or understates the syndicate's losses, for the year of assessment;

(c) any reference to the appellant having grounds for so believing, or there being reasonable grounds for so believing, shall be construed in accordance with paragraph (b) above;

(d) any reference to a determination of the amount of tax the payment of which should be postponed pending the determination of the appeal shall be construed as a reference to a direction that the determination shall, pending the determination of the appeal, have effect for the purpose stated in sub-paragraph (1) above as if the syndicate's profits there stated were reduced, or the syndicate's losses there stated were increased, by such amount as may be specified in the direction;

(e) any reference to an amount of tax so determined, or to the amount of tax which should be so postponed, shall be construed in accordance with paragraph (d) above; and

(f) subsections (2) and (9) and, in subsection (6), paragraphs (a) and (b) and the word "and" immediately preceding paragraph (a) shall be omitted.

Commentary—*Simon's Direct Tax Service* **E5.619.**
Cross reference—See FA 1994 s 221 (extension of the application of this Schedule to corporate members of Lloyd's).

Apportionments of syndicate's profit or loss

6—(1) Where a determination of a syndicate's profit or loss for a year of assessment is made, varied or modified (whether under the foregoing provisions of this Schedule or on appeal), the inspector may, by notice in writing to the syndicate's managing agent, require him to make to the inspector, within the specified period, a return apportioning, between the members of the syndicate, the syndicate's profit or loss as stated in the determination as so made, varied or modified.

(2) If a syndicate's managing agent, having been required by a notice under sub-paragraph (1) above to deliver a return within the specified period, fails to deliver the return within that period, he shall be liable to a penalty equal to the prescribed amount multiplied by the number of days on which the failure continues.

(3) In sub-paragraph (2) above "the prescribed amount" means £5 for each fifty members of the syndicate (counting any number of members less than fifty, and any number left over, as fifty).

(4) In this paragraph "the specified period" means such period, not being less than thirty days and beginning with the day following the date of the notice under sub-paragraph (1) above, as may be specified in that notice.

Commentary—*Simon's Direct Tax Service* **E5.619.**
Cross references—See FA 1994 s 221 (extension of the application of this Schedule to corporate members of Lloyd's).
Lloyd's Underwriters (Tax) Regulations, SI 1995/351 reg 7 (non-delivery of return—reasonable excuse).

Individual members: effect of determinations

7—(1) A determination of a syndicate's profit or loss for a year of assessment (whether as originally made or as varied or modified) shall, for the purpose of determining the liability to tax of each member of the syndicate, be conclusive against that member that the syndicate's profit or loss for that year is as there stated.

(2) Where a determination of a syndicate's profit or loss for a year of assessment is varied or modified at any time after the issue of a notice of assessment assessing any member of the syndicate to tax—

(*a*) [section 31A][1] of the Management Act (right of appeal) and section 55 of that Act (postponement of tax) shall have effect, in relation to that member, as if any reference to the date of the notice of assessment, or the date of the issue of the notice of assessment, were a reference to the date of the variation or modification; and

(*b*) in the case of a variation, an assessment which gives effect to the determination as varied shall not be out of time if it is made within one year of the date of the variation.

(3) Sub-paragraph (2)(*b*) above shall not apply in the case of a variation under paragraph 3(3) above which is made later than six years after the end of the closing year.

Commentary—*Simon's Direct Tax Service* E5.619.
Cross reference—See FA 1994 s 221 (extension of the application of this Schedule to corporate members of Lloyd's).
FA 2000 s 107(11) (nothing in this para affects the operation of FA 2000 s 107(2)–(4) concerning general insurance reserves).
Amendments—[1] In sub-para (2)(*a*), "section 31A" substituted for "section 31" by FA 2001 s 88, Sch 29 para 36(1), (3) with effect from the passing of FA 2001 in relation to returns whether made before or after the passing of FA 2001, and whether relating to periods before or after the passing of FA 2001.

Assessment of individual members: time limits

8 For the purposes of sections 36 and 40 of the Management Act (extension of time in cases of fraudulent or negligent conduct) anything done or omitted to be done by a syndicate's managing agent shall be deemed to have been done or omitted to be done by each member of the syndicate.

Commentary—*Simon's Direct Tax Service* E5.619.
Cross references—See FA 1994 s 221 (extension of the application of this Schedule to corporate members of Lloyd's).

PART II
PAYMENTS ON ACCOUNT OF TAX

Amendment—This Part of this Schedule repealed by FA 1994 s 228(3), Sch 21 para 10 and Sch 26 Pt V(25) with effect from the year 1994–95.

PART III
REPAYMENT OF TAX DEDUCTED ETC FROM INVESTMENT INCOME

13—(1) In relation to an underwriting year, a syndicate's managing agent may, by notice in writing at any time during the period of six years beginning with the 1st March next following the end of the closing year for that year, make a claim to the inspector—

(*a*) for the repayment of tax suffered by way of deduction on such of the syndicate's investment income as is allocated to that year in accordance with the rules or practice of Lloyd's; *or*
(*b*) ...[1]

(2) The syndicate's managing agent shall provide such information in support of the claim as the inspector may reasonably require.

(3) Where an amount is repaid ...[1] to a syndicate's managing agent under this paragraph, he shall—

(*a*) apportion that amount between the members of the syndicate in proportion to their interests in that part of the syndicate's investment income which has suffered tax by way of deduction ...[1]; and
(*b*) except in so far as it is required to meet a share of a loss of the syndicate, pay the amount so apportioned to each member, within 90 days of the repayment, to the members' agent of that member.

[(3A) ...][1]

(4) The provisions of section 824 of the Taxes Act 1988 (repayment supplements: individuals and others) shall not apply to any repayment of tax made under this paragraph.

[(4A) ...][1]

(5) In this paragraph "investment income", in relation to a syndicate, means the aggregate amount of the profits arising to all the members of the syndicate (taken together) from assets forming part of premiums trust funds.

Commentary—*Simon's Direct Tax Service* E5.613.
Cross reference—See FA 1994 s 221 (extension of the application of this Schedule with modification of this paragraph to corporate members of Lloyd's).
Amendments—[1] Sub-para (1)(*b*), words in sub-para (3), and sub-paras (3A), (4A) (inserted by FA 1994 Sch 21 para 11 with effect as respects under writing years from 1992 onwards), repealed by F(No 2)A 1997 Sch 8 Pt II(5) with effect for distributions made on or after 2 July 1997.

SCHEDULE 20

LLOYD'S UNDERWRITERS: SPECIAL RESERVE FUNDS

Section 175

Cross reference—See Lloyd's Underwriters (Special Reserve Funds) Regulations, SI 1995/353 (additional matters relating to special reserve funds).

PART I

REQUIREMENTS FOR AND TAX CONSEQUENCES OF NEW-STYLE FUNDS

Preliminary

1—(1) In this Part of this Schedule—

''the arrangements'' means the arrangements mentioned in section 175(1) of this Act;

''cash call'' means a request for funds which, in pursuance of a contract made in accordance with the rules and practices of Lloyd's, is made to a member by the agent of a syndicate of which he is a member;

''overall premium limit'', in relation to a member and an underwriting year, means the maximum amount which, under the rules of Lloyd's, the member may accept by way of premiums in that year;

[''payment'', unless the contrary intention appears, means a payment in money;][1]

''stop-loss payment'' means a payment of insurance money under a stop-loss insurance or a payment out of the High Level Stop Loss Fund;

''syndicate profit'', in relation to a member and an underwriting year, means the amount by which the aggregate of his profits exceeds the aggregate of his losses for the year, and ''syndicate loss'' shall be construed accordingly.

(2) For the purposes of the definitions of ''syndicate profit'' and ''syndicate loss'' in sub-paragraph (1) above—

(a) any reference to profits or losses of a member is a reference to profits or losses which, in the accounts of the syndicates of which he is a member, are shown as arising to him, ...[2]

(b) any payments under paragraph 3(1), 4(1), (2), (3) or (6), 5(1), (4) or (7) or 6(2) below shall be disregarded.

[(c) where the accounts of a syndicate remain open beyond the end of the underwriting year which is the closing year for that syndicate, profits or losses shown in the accounts of the syndicate as arising to a member in any subsequent underwriting year shall be profits or losses of the member for the last underwriting year but one preceding that subsequent underwriting year.][2]

Commentary—*Simon's Direct Tax Service* **E5.645.**
Modifications—See Lloyd's Underwriters (Special Reserve Funds) Regulations, SI 1995/353 reg 7 (modification of this paragraph where a member dies and his underwriting business is carried on by his personal representatives).
Amendments—[1] Definition of ''payment'' in sub-para (1) inserted by FA 1994 Sch 21 para 12(1), (3), with effect from the year 1992–93.
[2] Word omitted from sub-para (2)(a) repealed, and sub-para (2)(c) added, by the Lloyd's Underwriters (Special Reserve Funds) Regulations 1995, SI 1995/353, reg 3, with effect from the year 1992–93.

General requirements

2—(1) The arrangements must provide—

(a) for the setting up, in relation to any member, of a special reserve fund vested in one or more trustees who have control over it, and

(b) for the appointment of an authorised fund manager (who may be the trustees or one of the trustees) to invest the capital of the fund and to vary the investments;

and in this sub-paragraph ''authorised'' means authorised under the rules of Lloyd's.

[(2) The arrangements must be such as to secure that—

(a) any income arising to the trustee or trustees of the special reserve fund shall be added to the capital of the fund and held on the same trusts as the fund; and

(b) except as required or permitted by this Schedule, no payments shall be made into or out of the special reserve fund.][1]

Commentary—*Simon's Direct Tax Service* **E5.645.**
Amendment—[1] Sub-para (2) substituted (for original sub-paras (2), (3)) by FA 1995 s 143(2), and is deemed always to have had effect.

Payments into fund out of syndicate profits

3—(1) The arrangements must be such as to secure that, if the member has made a syndicate profit for an underwriting year, he has the right to make, into his special reserve fund, payments the amount of which is not in the aggregate greater than whichever of the following is the less, namely—

(a) 50 per cent of that profit; and

(b) the amount (if any) by which 50 per cent of the member's overall premium limit for the closing year exceeds the value of the fund as at the end of that year.

(2) Any payments which a member is entitled to make by virtue of sub-paragraph (1) above must be made before the end of such period as may be prescribed.

(3) Where the member did not accept premiums in the closing year, the reference in sub-paragraph (1)(b) above to the member's overall premium limit for that year shall be construed as a reference to that limit for the latest underwriting year in which he did so.

Commentary—*Simon's Direct Tax Service* E5.645.
Cross reference—See Lloyd's Underwriters (Special Reserve Funds) Regulations, SI 1995/353 reg 5(1) (prescribed period for the purposes of para 3(2) above).
Modifications—Lloyd's Underwriters (Special Reserve Funds) Regulations, SI 1995/353 reg 7 (modification of this paragraph where a member dies and his underwriting business is carried on by his personal representatives).

Payments out of fund to cover cash calls

4—(1) The arrangements must be such as to secure that, if a cash call is made on the member in respect of an underwriting year, there shall be made into a [premium]² trust fund of his, out of his special reserve fund, payments the amount of which is equal in the aggregate to the amount of the call, or the amount of his special reserve fund, whichever is the less.

[(1A) References in sub-paragraph (1) above to a cash call include references to a cash call made in respect of an underwriting year determined by paragraph 1(2)(c) above ("the relevant call") if and to the extent that the aggregate amount of the relevant cash call and any previous cash calls made on the member in respect of the syndicate concerned exceeds the net amount of losses arising to the member from that syndicate which have been declared before the date of the relevant cash call after deducting the amount of profits arising to him from that syndicate which have been so declared.]¹

(2) Where the aggregate amount of any payments made under sub-paragraph (1) above in respect of any year is found to exceed the amount of the member's syndicate loss for the year, there shall be made into his special reserve fund, out of a [premium]² trust fund or ancillary trust fund of his, payments the amount of which is equal in the aggregate to the amount of the excess.

(3) Where a stop-loss payment is made to the member in respect of his syndicate loss for any year, so much of the stop-loss payment as does not exceed the requisite amount shall be paid into his special reserve fund.

(4) In sub-paragraph (3) above "the requisite amount" means so much of the amount (if any) given by sub-paragraph (5) below as does not exceed the aggregate amount mentioned in paragraph (b) of that sub-paragraph.

(5) The amount given by this sub-paragraph is the amount by which—

    (a) the amount of the stop-loss payment, and
    (b) the aggregate amount of the payments under sub-paragraph (1) above as reduced by the aggregate amount of any payments under sub-paragraph (2) above,

exceeds in the aggregate the amount of the member's syndicate loss.

(6) Where the whole or any part of a stop-loss payment made to a member is repaid, there shall be made to the member or his personal representatives or assigns, out of his special reserve fund, payments the amount of which is equal in the aggregate to the amount (if any) to which sub-paragraph (7) below applies or the amount of his special reserve fund, whichever is the less.

(7) This sub-paragraph applies to any amount which—

    (a) has been paid into the member's special reserve fund under sub-paragraph (2) or (3) above, but
    (b) would not have been so paid but for the stop-loss payment or (as the case may be) the part repaid.

(8) Any payments required by sub-paragraph (1), (2), (3) or (6) above shall be made before the end of such period as may be prescribed.

Commentary—*Simon's Direct Tax Service* E5.645.
Cross reference—See Lloyd's Underwriters (Special Reserve Funds) Regulations, SI 1995/353 reg 5(2)–(5) (prescribed period for the purposes of para 4(1), (2), (3), (6) above).
Modifications—Lloyd's Underwriters (Special Reserve Funds) Regulations, SI 1995/353 reg 7 (modification of this paragraph where a member dies and his underwriting business is carried on by his personal representatives).
Amendment—¹ Sub-para (1A) inserted by the Lloyd's Underwriters (Special Reserve Funds) Regulations, SI 1995/353 reg 4, with effect from the year 1992–93.
² Word in sub-paras (1), (2) substituted by the Financial Services and Markets Act 2000 (Consequential Amendments) (Taxes) Order, SI 2001/3629 arts 75, 82(g)(i) with effect from 1 December 2001 immediately after the coming into force of the Financial Services and Markets Act 2000 ss 411, 432(1), Sch 20.

Payments out of fund to cover syndicate losses

5—(1) The arrangements must be such as to secure that, if the member has sustained a syndicate loss for an underwriting year, there shall be made into a [premium]¹ trust fund of his, out of his special reserve fund, payments the amount of which is equal in the aggregate to the net amount of the loss or the amount of his special reserve fund, whichever is the less.

(2) Sub-paragraphs (3) and (4) below apply where a stop-loss payment is made to the member in respect of his syndicate loss for any year.

(3) If any payments are subsequently made for the year under sub-paragraph (1) above, the aggregate amount of those payments shall be determined as if the net amount of the syndicate loss were reduced by the amount of the stop-loss payment.

(4) If any payments have previously been made for the year under sub-paragraph (1) above, so much of the stop-loss payment as does not exceed the requisite amount shall be paid into his special reserve fund.

(5) In sub-paragraph (4) above "the requisite amount" means so much of the amount (if any) given by sub-paragraph (6) below as does not exceed the amount mentioned in paragraph (b) of that sub-paragraph.

(6) The amount given by this sub-paragraph is the amount by which—

    (a) the amount of the stop-loss payment, and

    (b) the aggregate amount of the payments made under sub-paragraph (1) above,

exceeds in the aggregate the net amount of the member's syndicate loss.

(7) Where the whole or any part of a stop-loss payment made to a member is repaid, there shall be made to the member or his personal representatives or assigns, out of his special reserve fund, payments the amount of which is equal in the aggregate to the aggregate of the amounts (if any) to which sub-paragraphs (8) and (9) below apply or the amount of his special reserve fund, whichever is the less.

(8) This sub-paragraph applies to any amount which—

    (a) has not been paid out of the member's special reserve fund under sub-paragraph (1) above, but

    (b) would have been so paid but for the stop-loss payment or (as the case may be) the part repaid.

(9) This sub-paragraph applies to any amount which—

    (a) has been paid into the member's special reserve fund under sub-paragraph (4) above, but

    (b) would not have been so paid but for the stop-loss payment or (as the case may be) the part repaid.

(10) Any payments required by sub-paragraph (1), (4) or (7) above shall be made before the end of such period as may be prescribed.

(11) In this paragraph "net amount", in relation to a member's syndicate loss for any year, means the amount of the loss as reduced by the amount of any payments made under paragraph 4(1) above for the year.

Commentary—*Simon's Direct Tax Service* **E5.645.**
Cross references—See Lloyd's Underwriters (Special Reserve Funds) Regulations, SI 1995/353 reg 5(6)–(8) (prescribed periods for para 5(1), (4) and (7) above).
Lloyd's Underwriters (Special Reserve Funds) Regulations, SI 1995/353 reg 6 (valuation of fund and other matters to be reported to the member).
Modifications—Lloyd's Underwriters (Special Reserve Funds) Regulations, SI 1995/353 reg 7 (modification of this paragraph where a member dies and his underwriting business is carried on by his personal representatives).
Amendments—[1] Word in sub-para (3) substituted by the Financial Services and Markets Act 2000 (Consequential Amendments) (Taxes) Order, SI 2001/3629 arts 75, 82(g)(ii) with effect from 1 December 2001 immediately after the coming into force of the Financial Services and Markets Act 2000 ss 411, 432(1), Sch 20.

Valuation and payments out of fund of excess amounts

6—(1) The arrangements must be such as to secure that the fund manager of a member's special reserve fund—

    (a) shall determine in the prescribed manner the value of the fund as at the end of the year 1994 and each subsequent underwriting year; and

    (b) shall report the value so determined to the member;

and the report shall also state such other matters as may be prescribed.

(2) If the value [(determined under sub-paragraph (1) above) of the fund as at the end][1] of any underwriting year exceeds 50 per cent of—

    [(a) the higher of—

        (i) the member's overall premium limit for that year, and

        (ii) his overall premium limit for the immediately preceding year; or][1]

    (b) where he did not accept premiums in [either of those years][1], his overall premium limit for the last underwriting year in which he did so,

there shall be made to the member or his personal representatives or assigns, out of his special reserve fund, payments the amount of which is equal in the aggregate to the excess.

(3) The payments required by sub-paragraph (2) above shall be made before the end of such period as may be prescribed.

Commentary—*Simon's Direct Tax Service* **E5.645.**
Cross reference—See Lloyd's Underwriters (Special Reserve Funds) Regulations, SI 1995/353 reg 5(9) (prescribed period for the purposes of para 6(2) above).

Modifications—See Lloyd's Underwriters (Special Reserve Funds) Regulations, SI 1995/353 reg 7 (modification of this paragraph where a member dies and his underwriting business is carried on by his personal representatives).
Amendments—[1] Words substituted by the Lloyd's Underwriters (Special Reserve Funds) Regulations, SI 1999/3308, reg 3, with effect from 31 December 1999.

Payments out of fund on cessation

7—(1) The arrangements must provide that, on the member ceasing to carry on his underwriting business, whether by reason of death or otherwise, the amount of his special reserve fund, so far as not required for giving effect to the requirements of paragraph 4 or 5 above, shall be paid over to the member or his personal representatives or assigns.

(2) For the purposes of sub-paragraph (1) above, a payment of an amount shall be in money or [in assets forming part of the fund][1] or both, as the member or his personal representatives or assigns may direct.

Commentary—*Simon's Direct Tax Service* E5.645.
Amendment—[1] Words in sub-para (2) substituted by FA 1994 Sch 21 para 12(2), (3) with effect from the year 1992–93.

Entitlement of member for tax purposes

[8—(1) Subject to sub-paragraph (2) [and paragraph 11(2) to (4)][2] below, a member shall be treated for the purposes of the Income Tax Acts and the Gains Tax Acts as absolutely entitled as against the trustees to the assets forming part of his special reserve fund.

(2) Where an asset is disposed of by a member to the trustees of his special reserve fund, nothing in sub-paragraph (1) above shall affect the operation of the Gains Tax Acts in relation to that disposal.][1]

Commentary—*Simon's Direct Tax Service* E5.645.
Modifications—See Lloyd's Underwriters (Special Reserve Funds) Regulations, SI 1995/353 reg 7 (modification of this paragraph where a member dies and his underwriting business is carried on by his personal representatives).
Amendment—[1] This paragraph substituted by FA 1994 Sch 21 para 13 with effect from the year 1994–95.
[2] Words inserted by the Lloyd's Underwriters (Special Reserve Funds) Regulations, SI 1999/3308, reg 4, with effect from the year 2000–2001, and for payments made after 31 December 1999.

Tax exemption for profits arising from assets of fund

9—(1) Profits or losses arising from assets forming part of a special reserve fund shall be excluded for the purposes of income tax under the Income Tax Acts, and for the purposes of capital gains tax under the Gains Tax Acts.

(2) Where for any underwriting year income tax has been deducted from any profits arising from assets forming part of a special reserve fund, the fund manager may, at any time after the end of that year, claim repayment of that tax.

(3) ...[1]

Commentary—*Simon's Direct Tax Service* E5.645.
Modifications—Sub-paras (1)–(3) modified for profits or losses arising after the death of the member from the investment of income retained by the trustees by the Lloyd's Underwriters (Special Reserve Funds) Regulations, SI 1995/353 reg 7A, as inserted by SI 1995/1185 reg 4, with effect for the year 1994–95 and subsequent years of assessment.
Amendment—[1] Sub-para (3) repealed by F(No 2)A 1997 s 34, Sch 4 para 30, Sch 8 Pt II(10) with effect for distributions made after 5 April 1999.

Tax consequences of payments into and out of fund

10—(1) In computing for the purposes of income tax the profits of a member's underwriting business for any year of assessment, the aggregate amount of any payments which, in respect of the [relevant][1] underwriting year, are made into his special reserve fund under paragraph 3(1) above shall be deducted as an expense.

(2) In computing for the purposes of income tax the profits of a member's underwriting business for any year of assessment—

   (*a*) the aggregate amount of any payments which, in respect of the [relevant][1] underwriting year, are made out of his special reserve fund under paragraph 4(1) or 5(1) above shall be treated as a trading receipt; and
   (*b*) the aggregate amount of any payments which, in respect of that year, are made into that fund under paragraph 4(2) or (3) or 5(4) above shall be deducted as an expense.

(3) In computing for the purposes of income tax the profits of a member's underwriting business for any year of assessment, the aggregate amount of any payments which, as a result of the repayment of stop-loss payments in the [relevant][1] underwriting year, are made out of his special reserve fund under paragraph 4(6) or 5(7) above shall be treated as a trading receipt.

(4) In computing for the purposes of income tax the profits of a member's underwriting business for any year of assessment, the aggregate amount of any payments which, in respect of the [relevant][1] underwriting year's closing year, are made out of his special reserve fund under paragraph 6(2) above [(including where they are also made under paragraph 7(1) above)][2] shall be treated as a trading receipt.

[(5) In this paragraph "the relevant underwriting year", in relation to a year of assessment, means the underwriting year next but two before its corresponding underwriting year.]¹

Commentary—*Simon's Direct Tax Service* **E5.645.**
Modifications—See Lloyd's Underwriters (Special Reserve Funds) Regulations, SI 1995/353 reg 7 (modification of this paragraph where a member dies and his underwriting business is carried on by his personal representatives).
Amendments—¹ Words in square brackets in sub-paras (1)–(4) substituted and sub-para (5) inserted by FA 1994 Sch 21 para 14 with effect from the year 1997–98. For the years 1994–95 to 1996–97 this paragraph did not apply; see FA 1994 Sch 21 para 14(3).
² Words inserted by the Lloyd's Underwriters (Special Reserve Funds) Regulations, SI 1999/3308, reg 5, with effect from the year 2000–2001, and for payments made after 31 December 1999.

Tax consequences of cessation

11—(1) This paragraph applies where a member ceases to carry on his underwriting business, whether by reason of death or otherwise.

(2) In computing for the purposes of income tax the profits of the member's underwriting business for [the relevant year of assessment]¹, any payment [which is made by the trustees to him or his personal representatives or assigns out of his special reserve fund under paragraph 7(1) above, or otherwise than]⁵ out of his special reserve fund shall be treated—

   (a) as made immediately after the end of [the relevant underwriting year]²; and
   (b) as being a trading receipt of an amount equal to that mentioned in sub-paragraph (3) below.

(3) The amount referred to in sub-paragraph (2) above is the value of the fund, as determined under paragraph 6(1) above for [the penultimate underwriting year]³ and—

   (a) as reduced by the aggregate amount of any payments under paragraph 4(1) or (6) or 5(1) or (7) above made after the end of that year;
   (b) as increased by the aggregate amount of any payments under paragraph 4(2) or (3) or 5(4) above so made; and
   (c) as increased by the amount of any tax repayment ...⁸ under paragraph 9(2) ...⁸ above after the end of that year.

(4) Where an asset is transferred to the member or his personal representatives or assigns under paragraph 7(1) above, the transfer shall be treated, for the purposes of the Gains Tax Acts, to be an acquisition of the asset by the member or his personal representatives or assigns for a consideration equal to its market value as at the end of [the penultimate underwriting year]³.

[(5) In this paragraph, subject to the provisions of any regulations made by the Board—

   "the penultimate underwriting year" means the underwriting year [corresponding to the year of assessment immediately preceding the member's final year of assessment;]⁶
   ["the relevant underwriting year" means—
      (a) where a member dies before the occurrence of any of the events specified in sub-paragraph (6) below, the underwriting year immediately preceding that corresponding to the relevant year of assessment; and
      (b) in any other case, the underwriting year corresponding to the year of assessment immediately preceding the member's final year of assessment.]⁶
   "the relevant year of assessment" means—
      [(a) where a member dies before the occurrence of any of the events specified in sub-paragraph (6) below, the year of assessment at the end of which he is treated, by virtue of section 179A(2) of this Act, as having died;]⁶
      (b) in any other case, his final year of assessment.]⁴

[(6) For the purposes of the definitions of "the relevant underwriting year" and "the relevant year of assessment" in sub-paragraph (5) above the events specified before the occurrence of which a member dies are the following—

   (a) the member's deposit at Lloyd's is paid over to him or his assigns, or to a person other than the member or his assigns;
   (b) the member or another person is released from any arrangement entered into by the member or that person in order to satisfy the requirement on the part of the member to provide a deposit at Lloyd's;
   (c) the last open year of account of any syndicate of which he was a member is closed.]⁷

[(7) For the purposes of sub-paragraph (6)(c) above, the last open year of account of any syndicate of which a person was a member shall be regarded as having closed either—

   (a) when the member is treated under the rules or practice of Lloyd's as having been discharged of all his liabilities in relation to that syndicate, whether by the syndicate closing its accounts or by the member or his personal representatives or assigns entering into a quota share contract, or
   (b) in a case where the member entered, or his personal representatives or assigns have entered, into a quota share contract before the end of the closing year of the syndicate, at the end of the underwriting year in which the contract was made.]⁷

Commentary—*Simon's Direct Tax Service* **E5.645.**
Amendments—¹ Words in sub-para (2) substituted by FA 1994 s 228(3) and Sch 21 para 15 with effect from the year 1994–95.
² Words in sub-para (2)(a) substituted by FA 1994 s 228(3) and Sch 21 para 15.
³ Words in sub-paras (3), (4) substituted by FA 1994 s 228(3) and Sch 21 para 15.

PART II

WINDING UP OF OLD-STYLE FUNDS

Preliminary

12—(1) In this Part of this Schedule—

"new-style fund" means a special reserve fund set up under the arrangements mentioned in section 175(1) of this Act;

"old-style fund" means a special reserve fund set up under the arrangements mentioned in section 452(1) of the Taxes Act 1988;

"the relevant period", in relation to an old-style fund, means the period of three months beginning with the closing date.

(2) For the purposes of sub-paragraph (1) above, the closing date for an old-style fund shall be the earliest date on which each of the following has occurred as respects the year 1991–92 and earlier years of assessments, namely—

(a) the time for making any payments into the fund under section 452(5) of the Taxes Act 1988 has expired, or the member has given notice to the inspector that he will not be making any (or any further) such payments; and

(b) any payments required by section 453(1) of that Act to be made out of the fund have been so made.

Commentary—*Simon's Direct Tax Service* E5.644.

Winding up of old-style funds

13—(1) A member may, at any time before the end of the relevant period, direct that so much of the capital of any old-style fund of his as represents sums paid into it under section 452(5) of the Taxes Act 1988 shall be transferred, at the end of that period, into his new-style fund; ...[1].

(2) Where an amount of capital is transferred into a member's new-style fund under sub-paragraph (1) above, there shall be paid into that fund by the Board an amount equal to the amount of tax which, if the amount transferred were a net amount corresponding to a gross amount from which income tax had been duly deducted at the basic rate for the year 1992–93, would have been so deducted.

(3) If a member does not give a direction under sub-paragraph (1) above in relation to any old-style fund of his, so much of the capital of that fund as represents sums paid into it under section 452(5) of the Taxes Act 1988 shall be paid over, at the end of the relevant period, to the member or his personal representatives or assigns.

(4) In either event, the remaining capital of any old-style fund of a member shall be paid over, at the end of the relevant period, to the member or his personal representatives or assigns.

(5) For the purposes of sub-paragraphs (1) and (3) above, any payments made out of an old-style fund under section 453(1) of the Taxes Act 1988 shall be treated as having been met, so far as possible, out of payments made into the fund under section 452(5) of that Act.

[(6) A transfer or payment under this paragraph of an amount of capital shall be in money or in assets forming part of the fund or both, as the member may direct.][2]

Commentary—*Simon's Direct Tax Service* E5.644.
Amendments—[1] Words omitted from sub-para (1) repealed by FA 1994 Sch 21 para 16(1), (3) and Sch 26 Pt V(25) with effect from the year 1992–93.
[2] Sub-para (6) inserted by FA 1994 Sch 21 para 16(2), (3) with effect from the year 1992–93.

Tax consequences of winding up

14—(1) Where an asset is transferred into a member's new-style fund under paragraph 13(1) above, the transfer shall be treated, for the purposes of the Gains Tax Acts, to be a disposal of the asset by the member for a consideration equal to its market value.

(2) Sub-paragraph (3) below applies where an amount is paid over to the member or his personal representatives or assigns under paragraph 13(3) above.

(3) In computing for the purposes of income tax the profits of the member's underwriting business for the year 1992–93, it shall be assumed—

(*a*) that the amount paid were a net amount corresponding to a gross amount from which income tax had been duly deducted at the basic rate for that year; and

(*b*) that the corresponding gross amount were a trading receipt for that year.

Commentary—*Simon's Direct Tax Service* **E5.644.**

FINANCE ACT 1994

(1994 Chapter 9)

ARRANGEMENT OF SECTIONS

PART IV

INCOME TAX, CORPORATION TAX AND CAPITAL GAINS TAX

CHAPTER I
GENERAL

CHAPTER II
INTEREST RATE AND CURRENCY CONTRACTS
Qualifying contracts

Interest rate and currency contracts and options

Other basic definitions

Accrual of profits and losses

Treatment of profits and losses

Special cases

Anti-avoidance and related provisions

Miscellaneous

Supplemental

CHAPTER III
MANAGEMENT: SELF-ASSESSMENT ETC
Income tax and capital gains tax

CHAPTER IV

CHANGES FOR FACILITATING SELF-ASSESSMENT

CHAPTER V

LLOYD'S UNDERWRITERS: CORPORATIONS ETC

Main provisions

Trust funds

Other special cases

Miscellaneous

Supplemental

PART V

OIL TAXATION

CHAPTER I

ELECTION BY REFERENCE TO PIPE-LINE USAGE

CHAPTER II

MISCELLANEOUS

PART VII

INHERITANCE TAX

PART VIII

MISCELLANEOUS AND GENERAL

Companies treated as non-resident

Privatisations

Management

Assigned matters

General

257   Interpretation and construction.
258   Repeals.
259   Short title.

SCHEDULES:

*An Act to grant certain duties, to alter other duties, and to amend the law relating to the National
Debt and the Public Revenue, and to make further provision in connection with Finance.*

[3rd May 1994]

PART IV
INCOME TAX, CORPORATION TAX AND CAPITAL GAINS TAX

CHAPTER I
GENERAL

Income tax: charge, rates and reliefs

75 Charge and rates of income tax for 1994–95

(*Spent*).

Commentary—*Simon's Direct Tax Service* E1.102.

76 Personal allowance

(*Spent*).

Commentary—*Simon's Direct Tax Service* E1.201.

77 Rate of relief to married couples etc

(1)–(5) (*amend* TA 1988 ss 256, 257A, 259, 261A, 262).

(6) The Taxes Act 1988 and the Taxes Management Act 1970 shall have effect with the amendments
specified in Schedule 8 to this Act (which supplements the provisions of this section).

(7) This section and Schedule 8 to this Act shall have effect for the year 1994–95 and, subject to the
following provisions of this section, for subsequent years of assessment.

(8) (*amends* TA 1988 s 256 from the year 1995–96).

(9) (*amended* TA 1988 s 257A for the year 1995–96 and is now superseded).

(10) Section 257C(1) of the Taxes Act 1988 (indexation), so far as relating to section 257A(1) to (3) of that Act, shall not apply for the year 1994–95 or for the year 1995–96 but shall not be prevented by anything in this section from applying for the year 1996–97 or any subsequent year of assessment.

Commentary—*Simon's Direct Tax Service* E2.201, 202, 303; E2.501, 502.
Amendments—Sub-s (2)(*a*) repealed by FA 1999 s 139, Sch 20 Pt III(3) with effect from the year 2000–01.
Sub-ss (3), (4) repealed by FA 1999 s 139, Sch 20 Pt III(4) with effect from the year 2000–01.
Prospective amendments—Sub-s (5) repealed by FA 1999 s 139, Sch 20 Pt III(5) with effect from the year 2001–02.

78 Amount by reference to which MCA is reduced

(*Spent*).

Commentary—*Simon's Direct Tax Service* E2.304.

79 Relief for maintenance payments

(1) Sections 347A and 347B of the Taxes Act 1988 and section 38 of the Finance Act 1988 (which contain provision with respect to the deductions from income allowed on account of maintenance payments) shall have effect in relation to payments becoming due on or after 6th April 1994 with the following modifications.

(2) Section 347A (which restricts the making of deductions) shall apply to any payment made—

(*a*) in pursuance of any obligation which falls within paragraphs (*a*) to (*c*) of subsection (4) of section 36 of the Finance Act 1988 (existing obligations) and is an obligation under an order made by a court, a written or oral agreement or a deed executed for giving effect to an agreement, and

(*b*) for the benefit, maintenance or education of a person (whether or not the person to whom the payment is made) who attained the age of 21 on or before the day on which the payment became due but after 5th April 1994,

as if that obligation were not an existing obligation within the definition contained in that subsection.

(3)–(6) (*amend* TA 1988 s 347B).

(7), (8) (*amend* FA 1988 s 38).

Prospective amendments— Sub-ss (2), (5), (7), (8), and words in sub-s (1), repealed by FA 1999 s 139, Sch 20 Pt III(6) with effect for any payment falling due after 5 April 2000.

80 Limit on relief for interest

(*Spent*).

Commentary—*Simon's Direct Tax Service* A3.431.

81 Mortgage interest relief etc

(1), (2) (*amend* TA 1988 s 353).

(3) ...[1]

(4) (*amends* TA 1988 s 369).

(5) Schedule 9 to this Act (which for the purposes of or in connection with the provisions of this section makes further modifications of certain enactments in relation to tax relief on interest payments) shall have effect.

(6) The preceding provisions of this section and that Schedule—

(*a*) shall have effect in relation to payments of interest made on or after 6th April 1994 (whenever falling due); and

(*b*) shall also have effect, so far as they relate to relevant loan interest, in relation to any payments of interest becoming due on or after 6th April 1994 which have been made at any time before that date but on or after 30th November 1993.

(7) Any provision made before the passing of this Act by reference to the basic rate of income tax and contained in any instrument or agreement under or in accordance with which payments of relevant loan interest have been or are to be made shall be taken, in relation to any such payment as is mentioned in subsection (6)(*a*) or (*b*) above, to have been made, instead, by reference to a rate which, in the case of that payment, is the applicable percentage for the purposes of subsection (1) of section 369 of the Taxes Act 1988.

(8) ...[1]

(9) In this section ''relevant loan interest'' has the same meaning as in Part IX of the Taxes Act 1988.

Amendment—[1] Sub-ss (3), (8) repealed by FA 1999 s 139, Sch 20 Pt III(7) with effect for payments of interest made—
– after 5 April 2000;
– after 8 March 1999 and before 6 April 2000 in respect of interest falling due after 5 April 2000; or
– after 8 March 1999 and before 6 April 2000 under a scheme made for a tax avoidance purpose after 8 March 1999.

82 Relief for blind persons

(*amended TA* 1988 s 265(1) and is now superseded).

Commentary—*Simon's Direct Tax Service* E2.802.

83 Medical insurance

Commentary—*Simon's Direct Tax Service* E2.902.
Amendments—This section repealed by F(No 2)A 1997 Sch 8 Pt II(2) with effect for 1997–98 and subsequent years of assessment except in relation to cases in which relief due under FA 1989 s 54 in respect of any payment is unaffected by the provisions of F(No 2)A 1997 s 17(1) (see the Amendments note to FA 1989 s 54).

84 Relief for vocational training

(1)–(3) (*amend* FA 1991 s 32).

(4) This section has effect in relation to payments made on or after 1st January 1994.

Prospective amendment—This section repealed by FA 1999 s 139, Sch 20 Pt III(15) with effect for payments made after such date after 5 April 2000 as the Treasury may by order appoint.

Corporation tax charge and rate

85 Charge and rate of corporation tax for 1994

(*Spent*).

Commentary—*Simon's Direct Tax Service* D2.108.

86 Small companies

(1) (*spent*).

(2) (*amends* TA 1988 s 13(3)).

(3) Subsection (2) above shall have effect for the financial year 1994 and subsequent financial years; and where by virtue of that subsection section 13 of the Taxes Act 1988 has effect with different relevant maximum amounts in relation to different parts of a company's accounting period, then for the purposes of that section those parts shall be treated as if they were separate accounting periods and the profits and basic profits of the company for that period shall be apportioned between those parts.

Commentary—*Simon's Direct Tax Service* D2.109.

Benefits in kind

87 Car fuel

(1) (*amended* TA 1988 s 158(2) and is now superseded).

(2) This section shall have effect for the year 1994–95 and subsequent years of assessment.

Commentary—*Simon's Direct Tax Service* E4.631, 632.

88 Beneficial loan arrangements

(1)–(4) (*amend* TA 1988 ss 160, 161, Sch 7).

(5) ...[1]

(6) This section shall have effect for the year 1994–95 and subsequent years of assessment.

Commentary—*Simon's Direct Tax Service* E4.631, 632.
Amendments—[1] Sub-s (5) repealed by FA 2000 s 156, Sch 40 Pt II(2) with effect from the year 2000–01.

89 Vouchers and credit-tokens

(*amend* TA 1988 ss 141–144).

Chargeable gains

90 Annual exempt amount for 1994–95

(*Spent*).

Commentary—*Simon's Direct Tax Service* C1.401, 402.

91 Relief on re-investment

(1) Schedule 11 to this Act (which extends the relief on re-investment for individuals and trustees provided by Chapter IA of Part V of the Taxation of Chargeable Gains Act 1992) shall have effect.

(2) That Schedule shall have effect in relation to disposals made on or after 30th November 1993.

(3) (*amends* TCGA 1992 s 164H(1)).

(4) Subsection (3) above shall apply to determine whether a company is a qualifying company on or after 30th November 1993.

Commentary—*Simon's Direct Tax Service* **C3.901, 941, 952, 966, 967.**

92 Relief on retirement

(1) (*amends* TCGA 1992 Sch 6 para 13(1)).

(2) This section shall have effect in relation to disposals made on or after 30th November 1993.

Prospective amendments—This section will be repealed by FA 1998 s 165, Sch 27 Pt III(32) with effect for disposals made from the year 2003–04.

93 Indexation losses

(1)–(10) (*amend* TCGA 1992 ss 53, 56, Sch 7A, paras 2, 4, *insert* ss 55(7)–(11), 110(6A), Sch 7A, para 5(2A) and *repeal* ss 103, 111, 182–184, 200).

(11) This section shall have effect in relation to disposals made on or after 30th November 1993 and Schedule 12 to this Act (which gives transitional relief) shall have effect for the years 1993–94 and 1994–95.

Cross-references—See TCGA 1992 s 24(2)(*c*) (this section and Sch 12 have effect in relation to an asset which becomes of negligible value as if the sale and reacquisition occurred at the time the claim for relief is made).

94 Set-off of pre-entry losses

(1) Schedule 7A to the Taxation of Chargeable Gains Act 1992 (set off of pre-entry losses) shall be amended as follows.

(2), (3) (*amends* TCGA 1992 Sch 7A paras 2, 9(2)).

(4) This section shall apply in relation to the making in respect of any loss of any deduction from a chargeable gain where either the gain or the loss is one accruing on or after 11th March 1994.

95 Commodity and financial futures

(1) (*amends* TCGA 1992 s 143).

(2) This section shall apply in relation to contracts entered into on or after 30th November 1993.

96 Cash-settled options

(1) (*inserts* TCGA 1992 s 144A).

(2) This section shall apply in relation to options granted on or after 30th November 1993.

Note—Sub-s (1) inserts TCGA 1992 s 144A.

97 Settlements with foreign element: information

(1) The Taxation of Chargeable Gains Act 1992 shall be amended as mentioned in subsections (2) to (4) below.

(2)–(4) (*insert* TCGA 1992 s 98A, Sch 5A and *repeal* Sch 5 paras 11–14).

(5) Subsection (4) above shall have effect where the relevant day falls on or after the day on which this Act is passed.

(6) (*amends* TMA 1970 s 98 Table).

Profit-related pay

98 The distributable pool

(1) *Schedule 8 to the Taxes Act 1988 (profit-related pay schemes: conditions for registration) shall be amended as follows.*

(2), (3) (*inserted* TA 1988 Sch 8 paras 13A, 14A).

(4) *This section shall have effect in relation to any scheme not registered before 1st December 1993.*[1]

Amendments—[1] This section repealed by FA 1997 Sch 18 Pt VI(3) with effect for any payment made by reference to a profit period beginning after 31 December 1999 in accordance with FA 1997 s 61(2), (3), but subject to FA 1997 Sch 18 Pt VI(3) notes 2, 3.

99 Parts of undertakings

(1) (*inserted* TA 1988 Sch 8 paras 23, 24).

(2) *This section shall have effect in relation to any scheme not registered before 1st December 1993.*[1]

Amendments—[1] This section repealed by FA 1997 Sch 18 Pt VI(3) with effect for any payment made by reference to a profit period beginning after 31 December 1999 in accordance with FA 1997 s 61(2), (3), but subject to FA 1997 Sch 18 Pt VI(3) notes 2, 3.

Profit sharing schemes

100 Relevant age for purpose of appropriate percentage

(1) Schedule 10 to the Taxes Act 1988 (profit sharing schemes) shall be amended as follows.

(2), (3) (*amend* TA 1988 Sch 10 para 3 and *insert* Sch 10, para 3A).

101 Acceptance of qualifying corporate bonds for shares

(1) Schedule 10 to the Taxes Act 1988 (profit sharing schemes) shall be amended as mentioned in subsections (2) to (4) below.

(2)–(5) (*amend* TA 1988 Sch 9 para 32(1), Sch 10 para 1 and *insert* Sch 10 para 5A).

(6) In paragraph 33(*a*) of Schedule 9 to the Taxes Act 1988 (which provides that the trust instrument must contain certain provision by reference to new shares within the meaning of paragraph 5 of Schedule 10) the reference to paragraph 5 of Schedule 10 shall be construed as including a reference to that paragraph as applied by paragraph 5A.

(7) Subsections (2) and (3) above shall have effect where a direction is made on or after the day on which this Act is passed.

(8) Subsection (4) above shall have effect where what would be the new holding comes into being on or after the day on which this Act is passed; but this is subject to subsection (13) below.

(9) Subsection (5) above shall have effect in relation to any scheme not approved before the day on which this Act is passed.

(10) In a case where—

(*a*) a scheme is approved before the day on which this Act is passed, and
(*b*) on or after that day the trust instrument is altered in such a way that paragraph 32(1) of Schedule 9 to the Taxes Act 1988 would be fulfilled if subsection (5) above applied in relation to the scheme,

subsection (5) above shall apply in relation to the scheme with effect from the time the alteration is made.

(11) Subsection (6) above shall have effect in relation to any scheme not approved before the day on which this Act is passed.

(12) In a case where—

(*a*) a scheme is approved before the day on which this Act is passed, and
(*b*) on or after that day the trust instrument is altered in such a way that paragraph 33(*a*) of Schedule 9 to the Taxes Act 1988 would be fulfilled if subsection (6) above applied in relation to the scheme,

subsection (6) above shall apply in relation to the scheme with effect from the time the alteration is made.

(13) In a case where—

(*a*) a scheme is approved before the day on which this Act is passed,
(*b*) subsection (4) above would apply in relation to the scheme by virtue of subsection (8) above and apart from this subsection, and
(*c*) the trust instrument is not altered as mentioned in subsection (12)(*b*) above before what would be the new holding comes into being,

subsection (4) above shall not apply in relation to the scheme.

(14) Subsection (6) above shall not imply a contrary intention for the purposes of section 20(2) of the Interpretation Act 1978 in its application to other references to paragraph 5 of Schedule 10 to the Taxes Act 1988.

Employee share ownership trusts

102 Employee share ownership trusts

Schedule 13 to this Act (which contains provisions about employee share ownership trusts) shall have effect.

Commentary—*Simon's Direct Tax Service* **E4.591–599.**

Retirement benefits schemes

103 The administrator

(1), (2) (*insert* TA 1988 s 611AA and *amend* s 612(1)).

(3) This section—

(*a*) so far as it relates to section 591B(1) of the Taxes Act 1988 shall apply in relation to notices given on or after the day on which this Act is passed;
(*b*) so far as it relates to section 593(3) of that Act, shall apply in relation to contributions paid on or after that day;

(*c*) so far as it relates to section 596A(3) of that Act, shall apply in relation to benefits received on or after that day;

(*d*) so far as it relates to sections 598(2) and (4), 599(3) and 599A(2) of that Act, shall apply in relation to payments made on or after that day;

(*e*) so far as it relates to section 602(1) and (2) of that Act and regulations made under section 602, shall apply in relation to amounts becoming recoverable on or after that day;

(*f*) so far as it relates to section 604(1) of that Act, shall apply in relation to applications made on or after that day;

(*g*) so far as it relates to section 605(1) and (4) of that Act, shall apply in relation to notices given on or after that day.

104 Default of administrator etc

(1), (2) (*substitute* TA 1988 s 606 and *amend* s 607(3)).

(3) This section shall apply where the time in question falls on or after the day on which this Act is passed.

105 Information

(1) The Taxes Act 1988 shall be amended in accordance with subsections (2) and (3) below.

(2)–(3) (*amend* TA 1988 s 605).

(4) (*amends* TMA 1970 s 98 Table).

(5) Subsections (3) and (4)(*b*) above shall come into force on such day as the Treasury may by order appoint.

Commentary—*Simon's Direct Tax Service* **E7.217.**
Notes—The appointed day referred to in sub-s (5) is 1 January 1996.

106 False statements etc

(1) (*inserts* TA 1988 s 605A).

(2) This section shall apply in relation to things done or omitted after the day on which this Act is passed.

107 Discretionary approval

(1)–(3) (*amend* TA 1988 s 591).

(4) This section shall apply in relation to a scheme not approved by virtue of section 591 of the Taxes Act 1988 before 1st July 1994.

108 Taxation of benefits of non–approved schemes

(1)–(5) (*amend* TA 1988 s 596A).

(6) The amendments of section 596A made by this section shall have effect in relation to retirement benefit schemes—

(*a*) entered into on or after 1st December 1993, or

(*b*) entered into before that day if the scheme is varied on or after that day with a view to the provision of the benefit.

(7) Subject to subsection (8) below, in the Taxes Act 1988—

(*a*) in section 188(1), paragraph (*c*), and

(*b*) in section 189, paragraph (*b*),

(exemption from tax where recipient of benefit or lump sum chargeable to tax in respect of sums paid or treated as paid with a view to the provision of the benefit or lump sum) shall cease to have effect in relation to any benefit provided or lump sum paid on or after 1st December 1993.

(8) The repeals made by subsection (7) above shall not have effect in relation to any benefit provided or lump sum paid on or after 1st December 1993 in pursuance of a scheme or arrangement entered into before that day unless the scheme or arrangement is varied on or after that day with a view to the provision of the benefit or lump sum.

Annuities

109 Annuities derived from personal pension schemes

(1) (*inserts* TA 1988 s 648A).

(2) This section shall apply in relation to payments which are made under annuities on or after 6th April 1995.

110 Annuities derived from retirement benefits schemes

(1) (*inserts* TA 1988 s 597(3)).

(2) This section shall apply in relation to payments which are made under annuities on or after the day on which this Act is passed.

Authorised unit trusts

111 Rate of corporation tax

Amendments—¹ Section repealed by FA 1996 Sch 41 Pt V(1) with effect from the year 1996–97.

112 Distributions of authorised unit trusts

Schedule 14 to this Act (distributions of authorised unit trusts) shall have effect.

Commentary—*Simon's Direct Tax Service* **D4.414.**

113 Umbrella schemes

(1)–(3) (*amend* TA 1988 ss 468, 469).

(4) Subject to what follows, the amendments made by subsections (1) to (3) above shall have effect on and after 1st April 1994 in relation to unit trust schemes and their participants.

(5) Nothing in those amendments shall have effect before the relevant date in relation to a unit trust scheme which immediately before 1st April 1994 falls within the definition of an umbrella scheme contained in those amendments.

(6) In this section "the relevant date", means, in relation to a unit trust scheme, the day after the end of the last distribution period of the scheme which commences before 1st April 1994.

(7) On and after the relevant date, the amendments made by subsections (1) to (3) above shall have effect in relation to a scheme—

    (*a*) to which subsection (5) above applies, and
    (*b*) which immediately before the relevant date falls within the definition of an umbrella scheme contained in those amendments,

subject to subsections (8) to (10) below.

(8) The amendments made by subsections (1) to (3) above shall not prevent the trustees of the scheme on and after the relevant date—

    (*a*) making a claim under section 239(3) of the Taxes Act 1988 (carry back of surplus advance corporation tax) in respect of accounting periods of the scheme ending before the relevant date; or
    (*b*) continuing anything which immediately before that date was in the process of being done for the purposes of tax in relation to such accounting periods.

(9) Where immediately before the relevant date the trustees of the scheme are entitled to carry forward an excess under—

    (*a*) section 75(3) of the Taxes Act 1988 (carry forward of management expenses and sums treated as management expenses), or
    (*b*) section 241 of that Act (carry forward of franked investment income),

then, on the relevant date, that right shall be translated into a right in each successor company to carry forward a proportionate part of that excess.

(10) Where immediately before the relevant date the trustees of the scheme have an amount of surplus advance corporation tax which—

    (*a*) has not been dealt with under subsection (3) of section 239 of the Taxes Act 1988 and
    (*b*) is due to be treated under subsection (4) of that section as if it were advance corporation tax paid by them in their next accounting period,

then, on and after the relevant date, a proportionate part of that amount shall be treated as paid under subsection (4) of that section by each successor company in its first accounting period.

(11) In subsections (9) and (10) above "successor company" means, in relation to a scheme, each part of the scheme which on the relevant date becomes an authorised unit trust.

Exchange gains and losses

114 Assets and liabilities

(1)–(3) (*inserted* FA 1993 ss 154(5A), (5B), (13A), (13B), 155(4A), (4B); *repealed by* FA 2002 s 141, Sch 40 Pt 3(10)).

115 Currency contracts: net payments

(1)–(3) (*inserted* FA 1993 ss 126(1A), 146(1A), 164(2); *repealed by* FA 2002 s 141, Sch 40 Pt 3(10)).

116 Currency contracts: matching

(1) Schedule 15 to the Finance Act 1993 (alternative calculation) shall be amended as follows.

(2)–(5) (*inserted* FA 1993 Sch 15 paras 4A, 5A and *amended* Sch 15 paras 6, 7).

Amendment—This section repealed by FA 2002 s 141, Sch 40 Pt 3(10) with effect for accounting periods beginning after 30 September 2002.

Capital allowances

117 Expenditure on machinery or plant

Amendment—This section repealed by the Capital Allowances Act 2001 s 580, Sch 4 with effect for income tax purposes, as respects allowances and charges falling to be made for chargeable periods ending after 5 April 2001, and for corporation tax purposes, as respects allowances and charges falling to be made for chargeable periods ending after 31 March 2001.

118 Expenditure on machinery or plant: notification

(1)–(5) ...[2]

(6) For the purposes of—

    (a) ...[3]

    (b) section 44(4) of the Finance Act 1971 (provision corresponding to section 25(1) applicable to earlier chargeable periods),][2]

expenditure which has not formed part of a person's qualifying expenditure for a previous chargeable period may not form part of his qualifying expenditure for a subsequent chargeable period unless the machinery or plant on which the expenditure was incurred belongs to that person at some time in that subsequent period ...[1].

(7)–(9) ...[2]

Commentary—*Simon's Direct Tax Service* B2.325A.

Statement of Practice SP 6/94—This Statement explains how the Board will exercise their power under sub-s (5) above.

Revenue & other press releases—IR letter August 1994 (where time limit not met, allowance can be claimed in next chargeable period if asset still held; where expenditure claimed as revenue is subsequently reclassified as capital, the original computation is treated as a notification under these provisions).

Revenue Internal Guidance—Inspector's Manual IM 3753b (failure to give notice of expenditure on machinery and plant under this section cannot be rectified by means of an error or mistake claim).

Amendments—[1] Words in sub-s (6) repealed by Sch 26 Pt V(24) of this Act with effect from the year 1997–98 as respects trades etc commenced before 6 April 1994 and with effect from the year 1994–95 as respects trades etc commenced after 5 April 1994.

[2] Sub-ss (1)–(5), (7)–(9) repealed, and words in sub-s (6) substituted, by FA 2000 ss 73, 156, Sch 40 Pt II(8) with effect for chargeable periods as respects which the period specified in sub-s (3A) ends after 31 March 2000. Sub-ss (1)–(9) previously read as follows—

"(1) A first year allowance shall not be made under—

    (a) section 22 of the Capital Allowances Act 1990 (first-year allowances in respect of expenditure on machinery or plant), or

    (b) section 41 of the Finance Act 1971 (provision corresponding to section 22 applicable to earlier chargeable periods),

for any chargeable period (whenever ending) unless the relevant condition is fulfilled with respect to that period.

(2) For the purposes of—

    (a) section 25(1) of the 1990 Act (meaning of qualifying expenditure for the purposes of writing-down allowances for expenditure on machinery or plant), and

    (b) section 44(4) of the 1971 Act (provision corresponding to section 25(1) applicable to earlier chargeable periods),

no expenditure may form part of a person's qualifying expenditure for any chargeable period (whenever ending) unless the relevant condition is fulfilled with respect to that period.

(3) The relevant condition is fulfilled with respect to a chargeable period ending on or after 30th November 1993 if notice of the expenditure is given to an officer of the Board, in such form as the Board may require, within the period specified in subsection (3A) below.

(3A) A notice under subsection (3) above—

    (a) for the purposes of income tax, shall be given on or before the first anniversary of the 31st January next following the year of assessment in which ends the chargeable period mentioned in that subsection;

    (b) for the purposes of corporation tax, shall be given no later than two years after the end of the chargeable period mentioned in that subsection.

(4) The relevant condition is fulfilled with respect to a chargeable period ending before 30th November 1993 if—

    (a) the expenditure was included in a computation which—

        (i) was required to be made for any tax purpose,

        (ii) was given before that date to an inspector, and

        (iii) was not contained in a document prepared primarily for a purpose which was not a tax purpose; or

    (b) notice of the expenditure is given to the inspector, in such form as the Board may require, not later than three years after the end of that period; or

    (c) if the chargeable period ends on or after 1st December 1990, notice of the expenditure is so given before the passing of this Act.

(5) If in a particular case it appears to the Board appropriate to do so, having regard to all the circumstances of the case (including in particular any unforeseeable circumstances which have delayed the giving of any notice or computation), they may extend the period within which for the purposes of subsection (3) or (4) above any notice or computation is to be given to the inspector.

(6) For the purposes of the provisions mentioned in subsection (2) above expenditure which has not formed part of a person's qualifying expenditure for a previous chargeable period may not form part of his qualifying expenditure for a subsequent chargeable period unless the machinery or plant on which the expenditure was incurred belongs to that person at some time in that subsequent period.

(7) No relief shall be given under—

    (a) section 33, 33A or 42 of the Taxes Management Act 1970, or (*b*) paragraph 51 or 56 of Schedule 18 to the Finance Act 1998,

in respect of a claim of error or mistake to the extent that the error or mistake consists of or arises from a failure to fulfil the relevant condition in relation to a chargeable period.

(8) In this section "the 1990 Act" means the Capital Allowances Act 1990 and "the 1971 Act" means the Finance Act 1971; and expressions used in subsections (1) to (6) above have the same meaning as in the 1990 Act or (as the case may be) the 1971 Act.

(9) Any such adjustment as is appropriate in consequence of this section may be made (whether by way of discharge or repayment of tax, the making of an assessment or otherwise).".

³ Sub-s (6)(*a*) repealed by the Capital Allowances Act 2001 s 580, Sch 4 with effect for income tax purposes, as respects allowances and charges falling to be made for chargeable periods ending after 5 April 2001, and for corporation tax purposes, as respects allowances and charges falling to be made for chargeable periods ending after 31 March 2001.

119 Transactions between connected persons

(1) ...¹

(2) Paragraph 4(2) of Schedule 7 to the Capital Allowances Act 1968 (provision corresponding to section 158(2)) shall be assumed always to have had effect subject to amendments corresponding to those made to section 158(2) of the 1990 Act by section 117(2) and (3) of the Finance Act 1993.

Commentary—*Simon's Direct Tax Service* **B2.108.**
Amendments—¹ Sub-s (1) repealed by the Capital Allowances Act 2001 s 580, Sch 4 with effect for income tax purposes, as respects allowances and charges falling to be made for chargeable periods ending after 5 April 2001, and for corporation tax purposes, as respects allowances and charges falling to be made for chargeable periods ending after 31 March 2001.

120 Balancing charge on realisation of capital value

Amendment—This section repealed by the Capital Allowances Act 2001 s 580, Sch 4 with effect for income tax purposes, as respects allowances and charges falling to be made for chargeable periods ending after 5 April 2001, and for corporation tax purposes, as respects allowances and charges falling to be made for chargeable periods ending after 31 March 2001.

121 Used buildings etc in enterprise zones

Commentary—*Simon's Direct Tax Service* **B2.263.**
Amendment—This section repealed by the Capital Allowances Act 2001 s 580, Sch 4 with effect for income tax purposes, as respects allowances and charges falling to be made for chargeable periods ending after 5 April 2001, and for corporation tax purposes, as respects allowances and charges falling to be made for chargeable periods ending after 31 March 2001.

Securities

122 Sale and repurchase of securities: deemed manufactured payments

(*Inserts TA* 1988 ss 737A–737C).

123 Manufactured payments

(1) (*amends TA* 1988 s 715(6)).

(2)–(5) ...¹

(6) Subsection (1) above shall apply where any of the contracts mentioned in section 715(6) of the Taxes Act 1988 is made on or after 30th November 1993.

(7) ...*1*

Amendments—¹ Sub-ss (2)–(5) (which amended TA 1988 Sch 23A para 5), (7) repealed by FA 1997 Sch 18 Pt VI (10) with effect in relation to payments made on or after 1 July 1997 by virtue of the Finance Act 1997, Schedule 10, (Appointed Day) Order, SI 1997/991.

124 Overseas dividend manufacturers: limitation of double taxation relief

(*Inserted TA* 1988 Sch 23A para 4(7A), and is repealed by FA 1996 Sch 41 Pt V(21) with effect from 29 April 1996).

PAYE

125 Payment by intermediary

(*Inserts TA* 1988 s 203B).

126 Employees working for persons other than their employers, etc

(*Inserts TA* 1988 ss 203C–203E).

127 Tradeable assets

(*Inserts TA* 1988 s 203F).

128 Non-cash vouchers

(*Inserts TA* 1988 s 203G).

129 Credit-tokens

(*Inserts* TA 1988 s 203H).

130 Cash vouchers

(*Inserts* TA 1988 s 203I).

131 Supplementary

(*Inserts* TA 1988 ss 203J–203L).

132 Payments etc received free of tax

(*Inserts* TA 1988 s 144A).

133 PAYE regulations: past cases

(1) Regulation 4 of the 1993 Regulations (intermediate employers) is hereby revoked; but in relation to any time before its revocation it shall be deemed to have been validly made.

(2) Regulation 3 of the 1973 Regulations (intermediate employers) shall, in relation to any time before its revocation, be deemed to have been validly made.

(3) Where, at any time before the passing of this Act—

(*a*) a payment has been made of, or on account of, any income of an employee not resident or, if resident, not ordinarily resident in the United Kingdom,

(*b*) at the time when the payment was made it appeared that some of the income would be assessable to income tax under Case II of Schedule E, but that some of the income might prove not to be assessable to income tax under that Schedule, and

(*c*) the payment or any proportion of it was treated for the purposes of the 1993 Regulations or the 1973 Regulations as a payment to which the regulations applied,

then the treatment of that payment or that proportion of the payment as being a payment to which the regulations applied shall be deemed to have been lawful.

(4) In this section—

(*a*) "employee" means a person holding an office or employment under or with any other person;

(*b*) "the 1993 Regulations" means the Income Tax (Employments) Regulations 1993; and

(*c*) "the 1973 Regulations" means the Income Tax (Employments) Regulations 1973.

Commentary—*Simon's Direct Tax Service* **E4.989.**
Note—This Act was passed on 3 May 1994.

Miscellaneous provisions about companies

134 Controlled foreign companies

(1) In Schedule 25 to the Taxes Act 1988 Part I (acceptable distribution policy) shall be amended as follows.

(2)–(4) (*amend* TA 1988 Sch 25 paras 2, 3 and *insert* Sch 25, para 2A).

(5) This section shall apply to determine whether a controlled foreign company pursues an acceptable distribution policy in respect of accounting periods ending on or after 30th November 1993.

135 Prevention of avoidance of corporation tax

(1)–(5) (*insert* TA 1988 ss 767A, 767B and *amend* s 769).

(6) The amendments made by this section shall have effect in relation to any change in ownership occurring on or after 30th November 1993 other than a change occurring in pursuance of a contract entered into before that day.

136 Parts of trades: computations in different currencies

(*insert* FA 1993 s 94A and *amend* FA 1993, s 95(6)).

Miscellaneous

137 Enterprise investment scheme

(1) Schedule 15 to this Act shall have effect to revive Chapter III of Part VII of the Taxes Act 1988 (relief for investment in corporate trades) in relation to shares issued on or after 1st January 1994.

(2) That Chapter shall have effect in relation to such shares with the amendments made by that Schedule; and, in relation to such shares, that Chapter as so amended shall apply for the year 1993–94 and subsequent years of assessment.

(3) The Taxation of Chargeable Gains Act 1992 shall have effect with the amendments made by that Schedule.

Commentary—*Simon's Direct Tax Service* **C3.952; E1.812.**

138 Foreign income dividends

Schedule 16 to this Act (which contains provisions about foreign income dividends) shall have effect.

Commentary—*Simon's Direct Tax Service* **Division D1.7.**

139 Taxation of incapacity benefit

(1) For the year 1995–96 and subsequent years of assessment incapacity benefit, except—

(a) benefit payable for an initial period of incapacity, and
(b) so much of any benefit as is attributable in any case to an increase in respect of a child,

shall be treated as income for the purposes of the Income Tax Acts and charged to income tax under Schedule E.

(2) Subsection (1) above shall not apply to incapacity benefit to which a person is entitled for any day of incapacity for work falling in a period of incapacity for work which is treated for the purposes of that benefit as having begun before 13th April 1995 if the part of that period which is treated as having fallen before that date includes a day for which that person was entitled to invalidity benefit.

(3) Incapacity benefit shall for the purposes of this section be a benefit in relation to which section 41 of the Finance Act 1989 (year of assessment in which benefit to be charged) applies.

(4) Enactments relating to the payment of incapacity benefit shall have effect subject to such provision as may be contained for the purposes of this section in regulations under section 203 of the Taxes Act 1988 (PAYE regulations).

(5) In this section—

"incapacity benefit" means any benefit which by virtue of provisions contained in the Social Security (Incapacity for Work) Act 1994 or any corresponding provisions made for Northern Ireland is to be known as incapacity benefit;
["initial period of incapacity", in relation to incapacity benefit, means any period for which short-term incapacity benefit is payable otherwise than at the higher rate; and][1]
"invalidity benefit" means invalidity benefit under Part II of the Social Security Contributions and Benefits Act 1992 or under Part II of the Social Security Contributions and Benefits (Northern Ireland) Act 1992.

[(6) The reference in subsection (5) above to short-term incapacity benefit payable at the higher rate shall be construed in accordance with sections 30B(5), 40(8) and 41(7) of the Social Security Contributions and Benefits Act 1992 and the corresponding provisions of the Social Security Contributions and Benefits (Northern Ireland) Act 1992.][2]

Commentary—*Simon's Direct Tax Service* **E4.328.**
Concession A24—Extension of the exemption under this section to payments made by foreign governments which correspond to those categories of incapacity benefit which are exempt from income tax.
Amendments—[1] Definition "initial period of incapacity" in sub-s (5) substituted by FA 1995 s 141(2), and is deemed always to have had effect.
[2] Sub-s (6) inserted by FA 1995 s 141(3).

140 Restriction on deduction from income

(1) (*amends* TA 1988 s 808).

(2) This section shall apply where it is sought to exclude receipts from income or profits of an accounting period beginning on or after 30th November 1993.

141 Expenditure involving crime

(1)–(3) (*amend* TA 1988 s 577A).

(4) This section shall apply in relation to expenditure incurred on or after 30th November 1993.

142 Mortgage interest payable under deduction of tax: qualifying lenders

(1), (2) (*amended* TA 1988 s 376 and *inserted* s 376A, (sub-s (1) *repealed by the* Financial Services and Markets Act 2000 (Consequential Amendments) (Taxes) Order, SI 2001/3629 art 109, Schedule *with effect from 1 December 2001*)).

(3) Any body which is, immediately before the date on which this Act is passed, a prescribed body for the purposes of section 376 of the Taxes Act 1988 (by virtue of an order made under subsection (5) of that section) shall be entitled to be entered in the register maintained under section 376A of that Act as a qualifying lender except that if it was, immediately before that date, a qualifying lender only in relation to such description of loan as was specified in the order, it shall be entitled to be entered in the register as a qualifying lender only in relation to that description of loan.

(4) Until such time as the Board enter any such body in the register, that body shall be deemed to have been registered in accordance with its entitlement.

143 Premiums referred to pension business

Amendment—This section (which amended TA 1988 s 431(4), 431AA) repealed by FA 1995 Sch 29 Pt VIII(5) with effect for accounting periods beginning after 31 December 1994.

144 Debts released in voluntary arrangement: relief from tax

(1)–(5) (*amend* TA 1988 ss74, 94, 103(4), (4A)).

(6) Subsection (1) above shall have effect, for the purposes of determining (in computing the amount of profits or gains to be charged under Case I or Case II of Schedule D) whether any sum should be deducted in respect of any debt, in relation to debts—

  (*a*) proved to be bad,

  (*b*) released as part of—

    (i) a voluntary arrangement which has taken effect under or by virtue of the Insolvency Act 1986 or the Insolvency (Northern Ireland) Order 1989, or,

    (ii) a compromise or arrangement which has taken effect under section 425 of the Companies Act 1985 or Article 418 of the Companies (Northern Ireland) Order 1986, and

  (*c*) estimated to be bad,

if the proof, release or estimation occurs on or after 30th November 1993.

(7) Subsection (3) above shall have effect in relation to the release on or after 30th November 1993 of the whole or any part of any debt.

145 Relief for business donations

(1) (*repealed* by FA 2000 s 156, Sch 40 Pt II(9) with effect from 28 July 2000).

(2)–(5) (*amend* TA 1988 s 79A).

146 Minor corrections

Schedule 17 to this Act (which corrects various mistakes made in or introduced into the Taxes Act 1988) shall have effect.

CHAPTER II

INTEREST RATE AND CURRENCY CONTRACTS

Regulations—European Single Currency (Taxes) Regulations, SI 1998/3177 (Treatment of currency contracts etc on the introduction of the European single currency).
Statement of Practice SP 4/98—Application of foreign exchange and financial instruments legislation to partnerships which include companies.
Revenue & other press releases—Inland Revenue Tax Bulletin February 1995 (summary of time limits for election under the legislation and SIs).
Revenue Internal Guidance—Banking manual BM 11.11–11.3.4.1 (background to the legislation and application of the previous law to banks).
Company Taxation Manual COT13451–13533 (detailed explanation of the legislation relating to foreign exchange gains and losses).
COT13540–13606 (currency contracts and options).
COT13880–13930 (anti-avoidance provisions).
Cross-references—
FA 1996 s 101(1) (this Chapter does not apply to any profit or loss accruing to a company for an accounting period where that profit or loss is brought into account for that period for the purposes of FA 1996 Pt IV Ch II (loan relationships)).

Qualifying contracts

147 Qualifying contracts

(1) For the purposes of this Chapter—

  (a) an interest rate contract or option, or

  (b) a currency contract or option,

is a qualifying contract as regards a qualifying company if the company becomes entitled to rights or subject to duties under the contract or option on or after its commencement day.

(2) Where both immediately before and at the beginning of its commencement day—

  (a) a company to which this paragraph applies is entitled to rights or subject to duties under an interest rate contract or option, or

  (b) a qualifying company is entitled to rights or subject to duties under a currency contract or option,

for the purposes of this Chapter the company shall be treated as becoming entitled or subject to them at the beginning of that day.

(3) A qualifying company is a company to which paragraph (a) of subsection (2) above applies if its commencement day falls outside the period of twelve months beginning with the appointed day.

(4) For the purposes of this Chapter—

(a) a company's commencement day is the first day of its first accounting period to begin after the day preceding the appointed day; and

(b) the appointed day is such day as the Treasury may by order appoint.

Commentary—*Simon's Direct Tax Service* **D2.1010, 1106.**
Note—The Finance Act 1994 Chapter II of Part IV, (Appointed Day) Order 1994, SI 1994/3225, appoints 23 March 1995 for the purposes of Pt IV, Ch II to this Act.
This section repealed by FA 2002 ss 83(2), (3), 141, Sch 40 Pt 3(13) with effect for accounting periods beginning after 30 September 2002.

[147A Debt contracts and options to be qualifying contracts

(1) For the purposes of this Chapter a debt contract or option is a qualifying contract as regards a qualifying company if the company becomes entitled to rights, or subject to duties, under the contract or option at any time on or after 1st April 1996.

(2) For the purposes of this Chapter a qualifying company which is entitled to rights, or subject to duties, under a debt contract or option both immediately before and on 1st April 1996 shall be deemed to have become entitled or subject to those rights or duties on that date.

(3) This section has effect subject to paragraph 25 of Schedule 15 to the Finance Act 1996 (transitional provisions).]¹

Note—This section repealed by FA 2002 ss 83(2), (3), 141, Sch 40 Pt 3(13) with effect for accounting periods beginning after 30 September 2002.
Commentary—*Simon's Direct Tax Service* **D2.1010, 1106; D4.540.**
Amendment—¹ This section inserted by FA 1996 ss 101(2), 105(1) with effect for the purposes of corporation tax for accounting periods ending after 31 March 1996, but subject to transitional provisions in FA 1996 Sch 15.

148 Contracts which may become qualifying contracts

(1) A qualifying company is a company to which this section applies if its commencement day falls within the period of twelve months beginning with the appointed day.

(2) Subject to subsection (3) below, all quasi-qualifying contracts which, at the end of the period of six years beginning with its commencement day, are held by a company to which this section applies shall be treated for the purposes of this Chapter as if the company became entitled to rights or subject to duties under them on the first day of its first accounting period beginning after the end of the period of six years.

(3) Subject to subsection (5) below, if a company to which this section applies so elects, all quasi-qualifying contracts held by the company on its commencement day shall be treated for the purposes of this Chapter as if the company became entitled to rights or subject to duties under them on that day.

(4) An election by a company under subsection (3) above shall be irrevocable and shall be made by notice served on the inspector before the end of the period of three months beginning with its commencement day.

(5) A company may not make an election under subsection (3) above at a time when it is a member but not the principal company of a group unless the company did not become a member of the group until after the relevant day.

(6) An election under subsection (3) above by a company which is the principal company of a group shall have effect also as an election by any other company to which this section applies and which on the relevant day is a member of the group.

(7) Subsection (6) above shall apply in relation to a company notwithstanding that the company ceases to be a member of the group at any time after the relevant day except where—

(a) the company is an outgoing company in relation to the group, and

(b) the election relating to the group is made after the company ceases to be a member of the group.

(8) In this section—

"outgoing company", in relation to a group of companies, means a company which ceases to be a member of the group before the end of the period during which an election under subsection (3) above could be made in relation to it and at a time when no such election has been made;

"quasi-qualifying contract", in relation to a qualifying company, means an interest rate contract or option which would be a qualifying contract if the company became entitled to rights or subject to duties under it on or after the company's commencement day;

"the relevant day" means the principal company's commencement day.

(9) Section 170 of the Taxation of Chargeable Gains Act 1992 (groups of companies) shall have effect for the purposes of this section as for those of sections 171 to 181 of that Act.

Note—This section repealed by FA 2002 ss 83(2), (3), 141, Sch 40 Pt 3(13) with effect for accounting periods beginning after 30 September 2002.
Revenue Interpretation RI 114—Foreign exchange and financial instruments "grandfathering" and other elections.
Revenue Internal Guidance—Company Taxation Manual COT13455–13460 (effect of election under sub-s(3) for companies joining and leaving a group).

Interest rate and currency contracts and options

149 Interest rate contracts and options

(1) A contract is an interest rate contract for the purposes of this Chapter if—

(a) *the condition mentioned below is fulfilled, and*
(b) *the only transfers of money or money's worth for which the contract provides are payments falling within subsection (2), (3) or (4) or section 151 below.*

(2) The condition is that under the contract, whether unconditionally or subject to conditions being fulfilled, a qualifying company becomes entitled to a right to receive, or becomes subject to a duty to make, at a time specified in the contract a variable rate payment.

(3) An interest rate contract may include provision under which, as the consideration or part of the consideration for a payment falling within subsection (2) above, the qualifying company becomes subject to a duty to make, or (as the case may be) becomes entitled to a right to receive, at a time specified in the contract a fixed or fixed rate payment.

(4) In so far as the rights and duties mentioned in subsections (2) and (3) above relate to two payments—

(a) *which fall to be made at the same time, and*
(b) *of which one falls to be made to and the other by the qualifying company,*

it is immaterial for the purposes of this section that those rights and duties may be exercised and discharged by a payment made to or, as the case may require, by the company of an amount equal to the difference between the amounts of those payments.

(5) Each of the following, namely—

(a) *an option to enter into an interest rate contract, and*
(b) *an option to enter into such an option,*

is an interest rate option for the purposes of this Chapter if the only transfers of money or money's worth for which it provides are payments falling within section 151 below.

(6) In this section—

"fixed payment" means a payment of a fixed amount specified in the contract;
"fixed rate payment" means a payment the amount of which falls to be determined (wholly or mainly) by applying to a notional principal amount specified in the contract, for a period so specified, a rate the value of which at all times is the same as that of a fixed rate of interest so specified;
"variable rate payment" means a payment the amount of which falls to be determined (wholly or mainly) by applying to a notional principal amount specified in the contract, for a period so specified, a rate the value of which at any time is the same as that of a variable rate of interest so specified.

Note—This section repealed by FA 2002 ss 83(2), (3), 141, Sch 40 Pt 3(13) with effect for accounting periods beginning after 30 September 2002.
Commentary—*Simon's Direct Tax Service* **D2.1011, 1012.**
Revenue Internal Guidance—Company Taxation Manual COT13472 (meaning of "rate of interest").
COT13473 (netting off of amounts payable against amounts receivable does not prevent contract from being a qualifying contract).
Cross reference—European Single Currency (Taxes) Regulations, SI 1998/3177 regs 7–12 (treatment of interest rate contracts, including options, in relation to the introduction of the euro).

150 Currency contracts and options

(1) A contract is a currency contract for the purposes of this Chapter if—

(a) *the condition mentioned below is fulfilled, and*
(b) *the only transfers of money or money's worth for which the contract provides are payments falling within subsection (2), (3), (4) or (9) or section 151 below.*

(2) The condition is that under the contract a qualifying company—

(a) *becomes entitled to a right and subject to a duty to receive payment at a specified time of a specified amount of one currency (the first currency), and*
(b) *becomes entitled to a right and subject to a duty to pay in exchange and at the same time a specified amount of another currency (the second currency).*

(3) A currency contract may include provision under which the qualifying company—

(a) *becomes entitled to a right to receive at a time specified in the contract a payment the amount of which falls to be determined (wholly or mainly) by applying a specified rate of interest to a specified amount of the first currency, and*
(b) *becomes subject to a duty to make at a time so specified a payment the amount of which falls to be determined (wholly or mainly) by applying a specified rate of interest to a specified amount of the second currency.*

(4) A currency contract may also include provision under which the qualifying company—

(a) *becomes entitled to a right and subject to a duty to receive payment at a specified time of a specified amount of the second currency, and*

(b) becomes entitled to a right and subject to a duty to pay in exchange and at the same time a specified amount of the first currency.

(5) In subsections (3) and (4) above—

(a) any reference to a time is a reference to a time earlier than that specified in the contract for the purposes of subsection (2) above, and

(b) any reference to a specified rate of interest is a reference to a rate the value of which at any time is the same as that of the specified rate of interest.

(6) Each of the following, namely—

(a) an option to enter into a currency contract, and

(b) an option to enter into such an option,

is a currency option for the purposes of this Chapter if the only transfers of money or money's worth for which it provides are payments falling within section 151 below.

(7) An option the exercise of which at any time would result in a qualifying company—

(a) becoming entitled to a right and subject to a duty to receive payment at that time of a specified amount of one currency, and

(b) becoming entitled to a right and subject to a duty to pay in exchange and at that time a specified amount of another currency,

is a currency option for the purposes of this Chapter if the only transfers of money or money's worth for which it provides are payments falling within this subsection and section 151 below.

(8) Where, in the case of a contract which is subject to a condition precedent, the fulfilment of the condition at any time would result in a qualifying company becoming entitled and subject as mentioned in paragraphs (a) and (b) of subsection (7) above, that subsection and the following provisions of this Chapter shall have effect as if—

(a) the contract before the fulfilment of the condition were such an option as is mentioned in that subsection,

(b) the fulfilment of the condition were the exercise of the option, and

(c) the contract after the fulfilment of the condition were the contract resulting from the exercise of the option.

(9) It is immaterial for the purposes of this section that the rights and duties mentioned in subsection (2), (4) or (7) above may be exercised and discharged by a payment made to or, as the case may require, by the qualifying company of an amount (in whatever currency) which, at the specified time or the time when the option is exercised, is equivalent in value to the difference between—

(a) the local currency equivalent at that time of one of the payments there mentioned, and

(b) the local currency equivalent at that time of the other of those payments.

(10) Subsection (9) above shall be read as applying equally to such of the rights and duties mentioned in subsection (3) above as fall to be exercised and discharged at the same time, and for that purpose shall have effect with such modifications as may be requisite.

[(11) Subsection (12) below applies where—

(a) under a contract or as a result of the exercise of an option, a qualifying company becomes entitled to a right and subject to a duty to receive or make a payment at a specified time or at the time when the option is exercised, and

(b) the amount of the payment (in whatever currency) is computed in such a way as to be equal to the amount of the payment referred to in subsection (9) above which would have fallen to be computed if—

(i) the qualifying company had been entitled and subject as mentioned in subsection (2) or (7) above, and

(ii) a payment such as is referred to in subsection (9) were to be made to or by the qualifying company.][1]

[(12) For the purposes of this Chapter—

(a) the qualifying company shall be deemed to have become entitled and subject as mentioned in subsection (2) above under the contract referred to in subsection (11) above or, as the case may be, shall be deemed to have become entitled and subject as mentioned in subsection (7) above as a result of the exercise of the option referred to in subsection (11);

(b) the payment made under the contract or as a result of the exercise of the option shall be treated as if it were a payment falling within subsection (9) above in the exercise and discharge of the rights and duties to which the qualifying company is deemed to have become entitled and subject by virtue of paragraph (a) above.][1]

Note—This section repealed by FA 2002 ss 83(2), (3), 141, Sch 40 Pt 3(13) with effect for accounting periods beginning after 30 September 2002.

Commentary—*Simon's Direct Tax Service* **D2.1013, 1014.**

Revenue Internal Guidance—Company Taxation Manual COT13548, 13549 (examples of currency options).

Cross reference—European Single Currency (Taxes) Regulations, SI 1998/3177 regs 7–12 (treatment of currency contracts, including options, in relation to the introduction of the euro).

Amendments—[1] Sub-ss (11), (12) added by the Currency Contracts and Options (Amendment of Enactments) Order 1994, SI 1994/3233 art 2 with effect from 23 March 1995.

[150A Debt contracts and options

(1) A contract is a debt contract for the purposes of this Chapter if, not being an interest rate contract or option or a currency contract or option—

    (a) it is a contract under which, whether unconditionally or subject to conditions being fulfilled, a qualifying company has any entitlement, or is subject to any duty, to become a party to a loan relationship; and

    (b) the only transfers of money or money's worth for which the contract provides (apart from those that will be made under the loan relationship) are payments falling within subsection (5) below and payments falling within section 151 below.

(2) A contract is also a debt contract for the purposes of this Chapter if, not being a debt contract by virtue of subsection (1) above or an interest rate contract or option or a currency contract or option—

    (a) it is a contract under which, whether unconditionally or subject to conditions being fulfilled, a qualifying company has any entitlement, or is subject to any duty, to become treated as a person with rights and liabilities corresponding to those of a party to a loan relationship; and

    (b) the only transfers of money or money's worth for which the contract provides are payments falling within subsection (6) below and payments falling within section 151 below.

(3) In this section references to an entitlement to become a party to a loan relationship, or to a duty to become such a party, shall be taken to include references, in relation to a specified loan relationship, to either of the following, namely—

    (a) an entitlement or, as the case may be, a duty to become a party to an equivalent relationship; and

    (b) an entitlement or, as the case may be, a duty relating to the making of any one or more such payments as fall within subsection (5) below.

(4) Subsection (3) above shall apply in relation to references in this section to an entitlement or a duty to become treated as a person with rights and liabilities corresponding to those of a party to a loan relationship as it applies to references to an entitlement or, as the case may be, a duty to become such a party.

(5) The payments falling within this subsection are—

    (a) a payment of an amount representing the price for becoming a party to the relationship;

    (b) a payment of an amount determined by reference to the value at any time of the money debt by reference to which the relationship subsists;

    (c) a settlement payment of an amount determined by reference to the difference at specified times between—

        (i) the price for becoming a party to the relationship; and

        (ii) the value of the money debt by reference to which the relationship subsists, or (if the relationship were in existence) would subsist.

(6) A payment falls within this subsection if it is a settlement payment of an amount determined by reference to the difference at specified times between—

    (a) the price for becoming treated as a person with rights and liabilities corresponding to those of a party to a relationship; and

    (b) the value of the money debt by reference to which the relationship subsists or (if the relationship existed) would subsist.

(7) Each of the following, namely—

    (a) an option to enter into a contract which would be a debt contract, and

    (b) an option to enter into such an option,

is a debt option for the purposes of this Chapter if the only transfers of money or money's worth for which the option provides are payments falling within section 151 below.

(8) For the purposes of this Chapter where any contract contains both—

    (a) provisions under which, whether unconditionally or subject to conditions being fulfilled, a qualifying company has any entitlement, or is subject to any duty, to become a party to a loan relationship, and

    (b) any provisions that have effect otherwise than for the purposes of or in relation to the provisions conferring that entitlement or imposing that duty,

the provisions mentioned in paragraph (a) above, together with the other contents of that contract so far as they are attributable on a just and reasonable basis to the provisions mentioned in that paragraph, shall be treated as a separate contract.

(9) For the purposes of this Chapter where—

    (a) any attribution of the contents of a contract falls to be made between provisions falling within paragraph (a) of subsection (8) above and provisions falling within paragraph (b) of that subsection, and

    (b) that contract provides for the making of any payment constituting a transfer of money or money's worth which cannot be attributed to the provisions falling within only one of those paragraphs,

that payment shall be treated as apportioned between the provisions falling within each of those paragraphs in such manner as may be just and reasonable.

(10) Expressions used in this section and in Chapter II of Part IV of the Finance Act 1996 have the same meanings in this section as in that Chapter; but references in this section to a loan relationship do not include—

    (a) any loan relationship represented by an asset to which section 92 of that Act (convertible securities) applies; or

    (b) any loan relationship to which section 93 of that Act (securities indexed to chargeable assets) applies.

(11) For the purposes of this section and, so far as it relates to a debt contract or option, of section 151 below the transfer of money's worth having a value of any amount shall be treated as the payment of that amount.][1]

Note—This section repealed by FA 2002 ss 83(2), (3), 141, Sch 40 Pt 3(13) with effect for accounting periods beginning after 30 September 2002.
Commentary—*Simon's Direct Tax Service* **D2.1015, 1106; D4.540.**
Revenue Internal Guidance—Company Taxation Manual COT13479 (the legislation covers instruments where the underlying asset is a loan relationship, instruments such as futures and options and instruments based on synthetic debt).
COT13482 (treatment of warrants).
Cross reference—European Single Currency (Taxes) Regulations, SI 1998/3177 regs 7–12 (treatment of debt contracts, including options, in relation to the introduction of the euro).
Modifications—Words ''but references'' onwards in sub-s (10) above treated as omitted for the purposes of Pt IV Ch II in relation to contracts and options held for the purposes of a life assurance or capital redemption business of an insurance company for any accounting period where the I minus E basis is applied: FA 1994 Sch 18 para 1A.
Amendments—[1] This section inserted by FA 1996 ss 101(3), 105(1), Sch 12 with effect for accounting periods ending after 31 March 1996, but subject to transitional provisions in FA 1996 Sch 15.

151 Provisions which may be included

(1) An interest rate contract or option, [a currency contract or option or a debt contract or option][1] *may include provision under which the qualifying company—*

    (a) becomes entitled to a right to receive a payment in consideration of its entering into the contract or option, or

    (b) becomes subject to a duty to make a payment in consideration of another person's entering into the contract or option.

(2) An interest rate contract or option, [a currency contract or option or a debt contract or option][1] *may also include provision for all or any of the following—*

    (a) a payment of a reasonable fee for arranging the contract or option;

    (b) a payment of reasonable costs incurred in respect of the contract or option;

    (c) a payment for securing, or made in consequence of, the variation or termination of the contract or option; and

    (d) a payment by way of compensation for, or made in consequence of, a failure to comply with the contract or option.

Note—This section repealed by FA 2002 ss 83(2), (3), 141, Sch 40 Pt 3(13) with effect for accounting periods beginning after 30 September 2002.
Commentary—*Simon's Direct Tax Service* **D2.1017.**
Revenue Internal Guidance—Company Taxation Manual COT13487 (treatment of arrangement fees: meaning of ''reasonable'' in relation thereto).
Amendments—[1] Words in sub-ss (1), (2) substituted by FA 1996 ss 101(4), 105(1) with effect for accounting periods ending after 31 March 1996, but subject to transitional provisions in FA 1996 Sch 15.

152 Provisions which may be disregarded

(1) Where—

    (a) but for the inclusion in a contract or option of provisions for one or more transfers of money or money's worth, the contract or option would be a qualifying contract; and

    (b) as regards the qualifying company and the relevant time, the present value of the transfer, or the aggregate of the present values of the transfers, is small when compared with the aggregate of the present values of all relevant payments,

the contract or option shall be treated for the purposes of section 149 or, as the case may be, section 150 [or 150A][1] *above as if those provisions were not included in it.*

(2) For the purposes of subsection (1) above—

    (a) any present value of a relevant payment which is a negative value shall be treated as if it were the equivalent positive value; and

    (b) any relevant payment the amount of which represents the difference between two other amounts shall be treated as if it were a payment of an amount equal to the aggregate of those amounts.

(3) In this section—

    ''relevant payments'' means—

       (a) in relation to a contract, qualifying payments under the contract;

(b) in relation to an option, qualifying payments under the option and payments which, if it were exercised, would be qualifying payments under the contract arising by virtue of its exercise;

"the relevant time" means the time when the contract or option was entered into or, if later, the time when the provisions were included in the contract or option.

Note—This section repealed by FA 2002 ss 83(2), (3), 141, Sch 40 Pt 3(13) with effect for accounting periods beginning after 30 September 2002.
Commentary—*Simon's Direct Tax Service* D2.1017.
Revenue and other press releases—
IR 21-1-98 (conversion of a currency into the Euro will not constitute a relevant time under sub-s (3)).
Revenue Internal Guidance—Company Taxation Manual COT13493 (worked example on present values).
Amendments—¹ Words in sub-s (1) inserted by FA 1996 s 101(5) with effect for accounting periods ending after 31 March 1996, subject to transitional provisions in FA 1996 Sch 15.

Other basic definitions

153 Qualifying payments

(1) Subject to subsections (2) to (5) below, in this Chapter "qualifying payment" means—

(a) in relation to a qualifying contract which is an interest rate contract, a payment falling within section 149(2), (3) or (4) above;
(b) in relation to a qualifying contract which is a currency contract a payment falling within subsection (3) or (9) of section 150 above;
(c) in relation to a qualifying contract which is a currency option, a payment falling within subsection (9) of that section;
[(ca) in relation to a qualifying contract which is a debt contract, a payment falling within section 150A(5) or (6) above; and]¹
(d) in relation to any qualifying contract, a payment falling within section 151 above.

(2) In this Chapter "qualifying payment" includes, in relation to a qualifying contract—

(a) a payment which, if it were a payment under the contract, would be a payment falling within section 151 above; and
(b) a payment for securing the acquisition or disposal of the contract.

(3) Where a qualifying company closes out a qualifying contract which is an interest rate or currency contract by entering into another contract with obligations which are reciprocal to those of the qualifying contract—

(a) any payment received by the company in consideration of its entering into the reciprocal contract, or paid by the company in consideration of another person's entering into that contract, is for the purposes of this Chapter a qualifying payment in relation to the qualifying contract; and
(b) all other payments under the reciprocal contract, and all subsequent payments under the qualifying contract, shall be ignored for all purposes of the Tax Acts.

[(5) For the purposes of this Chapter, in the case of any qualifying contract which is a currency contract,—

(a) the amount of any forward discount arising under the contract to a qualifying company shall be treated as a qualifying payment received by the company; and
(b) the amount of any forward premium arising under the contract from a qualifying company shall be treated as a qualifying payment made by the company.]²

[(6) The amounts of any forward discounts and premiums arising under a contract to a qualifying company shall be determined for the purposes of subsection (5) above—

(a) in accordance with subsections (7) to (9) below in the case of a currency contract which provides for a rate of exchange between the reporting currency and another currency, and
(b) in accordance with subsection (10) below in the case of a currency contract which provides for a rate of exchange between two currencies, neither of which is the reporting currency.]²

[(7) For the purposes of subsection (5)(a) above, the cases where a forward discount arises under a currency contract to a company are those cases where—

(a) the acquisition spot price exceeds the acquisition contract price, or
(b) the sale contract price exceeds the sale spot price;

and the amount of the forward discount is the amount of the excess mentioned in paragraph (a) or (b) above, as the case may be.]²

[(8) For the purposes of subsection (5)(b) above, the cases where a forward premium arises under a currency contract from a company are those cases where—

(a) the acquisition contract price exceeds the acquisition spot price, or
(b) the sale spot price exceeds the sale contract price;

and the amount of the forward premium is the amount of the excess mentioned in paragraph (a) or (b) above, as the case may be.]²

[(9) In subsections (7) and (8) above—

"*the acquisition contract price*" *means the amount of any currency (other than the reporting currency) to be acquired under the contract by the company, expressed in the reporting currency, using the rate of exchange determined by the terms of the contract;*

"*the acquisition spot price*" *means the amount of any currency (other than the reporting currency) to be acquired under the contract by the company, expressed in the reporting currency, using such rate of exchange for the date on which the company becomes entitled to rights and subject to duties under the contract as is used for the purposes of the company's accounts (as defined in section 156(6) below);*

"*the sale contract price*" *means the amount of any currency (other than the reporting currency) to be disposed of under the contract by the company, expressed in the reporting currency, using the rate of exchange determined by the terms of the contract;*

"*the sale spot price*" *means the amount of any currency (other than the reporting currency) to be disposed of under the contract by the company, expressed in the reporting currency, using such rate of exchange for the date on which the company becomes entitled to rights and subject to duties under the contract as is used for the purposes of the company's accounts (as defined in section 156(6) below).]²*

[(10) Where this subsection has effect in accordance with subsection (6)(b) above, the amounts of any forward premiums and discounts arising under the contract are the amounts which, in accordance with generally accepted accounting practice, are brought into account in the same way as any forward premiums and discounts which fall to be determined in accordance with subsections (7) and (8) above.]²

[(11) Subsection (5) above is subject to subsection (12) below.]²

[(12) Where a qualifying company is using, as respects a qualifying contract which is a currency contract, a basis of accounting which conforms to generally accepted accounting practice and—

(a) an amount which would, but for this subsection, fall to be treated as a qualifying payment by virtue of subsection (5) above is brought into account by the company, in accordance with that basis of accounting, as a qualifying payment made or received by the company but otherwise than by virtue of being a forward premium or discount, or

(b) that basis of accounting is such that no forward premiums or discounts are treated as arising under a qualifying contract,

subsection (5) above shall not have effect in relation to that amount or, as the case may be, in relation to that contract.]²

[(13) In this section "the reporting currency" means sterling, unless the case is one where section 93 of the Finance Act 1993 (c 34) (use of foreign currency) applies, in which case it means the currency which is the relevant foreign currency for the purposes of that section.]²

Note—This section repealed by FA 2002 ss 83(2), (3), 141, Sch 40 Pt 3(13) with effect for accounting periods beginning after 30 September 2002.

Commentary—*Simon's Direct Tax Service* **D2.1021.**

Revenue Internal Guidance—Company Taxation Manual COT13497 (description of payments falling within this section). COT13498 (reciprocal contracts). COT13605, 13606 (worked examples).

Amendments—¹ Sub-s (1)(*ca*) substituted for word "and" formerly appearing at end of sub-s (1)(*c*) by FA 1996 ss 101(6), 105(1) with effect for accounting periods ending after 31 March 1996, but subject to transitional provisions in FA 1996 Sch 15.
² Sub-ss (5)–(13) substituted for original sub-ss (4), (5) by FA 2002 s 70 with effect for accounting periods ending after 25 July 2001 in relation to any currency contract to which a company is party, unless the company has ceased to be a party to the contract before that date. Sub-ss (4)–(5) previously read as follows—

"(4) Subsection (5) below applies where, in the case of a qualifying contract which is a currency contract, there is a difference between—

(a) the local currency equivalent, at the time immediately after the qualifying company becomes entitled to rights and subject to duties under the contract, of the amount of the first currency (the first currency equivalent), and
(b) the local currency equivalent, at that time, of the amount of the second currency (the second currency equivalent).
(5) The amount of the difference shall be treated for the purposes of this Chapter—

(a) where the first currency equivalent exceeds the second currency equivalent, as a qualifying payment received by the qualifying company at the time specified in the contract for the purposes of section 150(2) above, and
(b) where the first currency equivalent is less than the second currency equivalent, as a qualifying payment made by the qualifying company at that time."

154 Qualifying companies

(1) Subject to subsections (2) and (3) below, any company is a qualifying company for the purposes of this Chapter.

(2) Where a unit trust scheme is an authorised unit trust as respects an accounting period the trustees (who are deemed to be a company for certain purposes by section 468(1) of the Taxes Act 1988) are not, as regards that period, a qualifying company for the purposes of this Chapter.

(3) A company which is approved for the purposes of section 842 of the Taxes Act 1988 (investment trusts) for an accounting period is not, as regards that period, a qualifying company for the purposes of this Chapter so far as it relates to currency contracts and options.

(4) In this section—

"authorised unit trust" has the same meaning as in section 468 of the Taxes Act 1988;
"unit trust scheme" has the same meaning as in section 469 of that Act.

Note—This section repealed by FA 2002 ss 83(2), (3), 141, Sch 40 Pt 3(13) with effect for accounting periods beginning after 30 September 2002.
Commentary—*Simon's Direct Tax Service* **D2.1004.**
Modification—This section is modified, in relation to open-ended investment companies, by the Open-ended Investment Companies (Tax) Regulations 1997, SI 1997/1154, regs 3, 5, 18.

Accrual of profits and losses

155 Accrual of profits and losses

(1) Where, as regards a qualifying contract held by a qualifying company and an accounting period, amount A exceeds amount B, a profit on the contract of an amount equal to the excess accrues to the company for the period.

(2) Where, as regards a qualifying contract held by a qualifying company and an accounting period, amount B exceeds amount A, a loss on the contract of an amount equal to the excess accrues to the company for the period.

(3) Subsections (4) and (5) below have effect for the purposes of this section, sections 158 and 161 to 167 below and paragraph 2 of Schedule 18 to this Act; and any reference in any of those sections or that paragraph to amount A or amount B is a reference to that amount after the making of any adjustments under such of those sections as precede that section or paragraph.

(4) Where as regards a qualifying contract a qualifying company's profit or loss for an accounting period falls to be computed on a mark to market basis incorporating a particular method of valuation—

(a) amount A is the aggregate of—

(i) the amount or aggregate amount of the qualifying payment or payments becoming due and payable to the company in the period, and
(ii) any increase for the period, or the part of the period for which the contract is held by the company, in the value of the contract as determined by that method, and

(b) amount B is the aggregate of—

(i) the amount or aggregate amount of the qualifying payment or payments becoming due and payable by the company in the period, and
(ii) any reduction for the period, or the part of the period for which the contract is held by the company, in the value of the contract as so determined.

(5) Where as regards a qualifying contract a qualifying company's profit or loss for an accounting period falls to be computed on a particular accruals basis—

(a) amount A is so much of the qualifying payment or payments received or falling to be received by the company as is allocated to the period on that basis, and
(b) amount B is so much of the qualifying payment or payments made or falling to be made by the company as is so allocated.

(6) Where a qualifying contract is such a contract by reason of being treated, by virtue of section 152 above, as if any provisions for one or more transfers of money or money's worth were not included in it—

(a) so much of any qualifying payment as relates to the transfer or transfers shall be ignored for the purposes of subsections (4) and (5) above, and
(b) so much of any such increase or reduction as is mentioned in paragraph (a) or (b) of subsection (4) above as so relates shall be ignored for the purposes of that subsection.

(7) Subject to subsection (8) below, where a qualifying contract—

(a) becomes held by a qualifying company at any time in an accounting period, or
(b) ceases to be so held at any such time,
it shall be assumed for the purposes of subsection (4) above that its value is nil immediately after it becomes so held or, as the case may be, immediately before it ceases to be so held.

(8) Subsection (7)(b) above does not apply where a qualifying contract is discharged by the making of payments none of which is a qualifying payment for the purposes of this Chapter.

Note—This section repealed by FA 2002 ss 83(2), (3), 141, Sch 40 Pt 3(13) with effect for accounting periods beginning after 30 September 2002.
Revenue Internal Guidance—Company Taxation Manual COT13513 (worked example).

156 Basis of accounting: general

(1) Where, for the purposes of a qualifying company's accounts, profits and losses for an accounting period on a qualifying contract held by the company are computed on—

(a) a mark to market basis of accounting which satisfies the requirements of this section, or
(b) an accruals basis of accounting which satisfies those requirements,
profits and losses for the period on the contract shall be computed on that basis for the purposes of this Chapter.

(2) Where subsection (1) above does not apply in the case of a qualifying contract held by a qualifying company and an accounting period, profits and losses for the period on the contract shall

be computed for the purposes of this Chapter on a mark to market or accruals basis of accounting which—

(a) satisfies the requirements of this section, and

(b) is specified in an agreement between the company and the inspector or, in default of such an agreement, in a notice served on the company by the inspector.

(3) A mark to market basis of accounting satisfies the requirements of this section as regards a qualifying contract if—

(a) computing the profits or losses on the contract on that basis is in accordance with [generally accepted accounting practice]¹;

(b) all relevant payments under the contract are allocated to the accounting periods in which they become due and payable; and

(c) the method of valuation adopted is such as to secure the contract is brought into account at a fair value.

(4) An accruals basis of accounting satisfies the requirements of this section as regards a qualifying contract if—

(a) computing the profits or losses on the contract on that basis is in accordance with [generally accepted accounting practice]¹;

(b) all relevant payments under the contract are allocated to the accounting periods to which they relate, without regard to the accounting periods in which they are made or received, or become due and payable; and

(c) where such payments relate to two or more such periods, they are apportioned between those periods on a just and reasonable basis.

(5) In determining whether, as regards a qualifying contract, a relevant payment is dealt with as mentioned in subsection (4) above—

(a) regard shall be had to the accounting period or periods to which any reciprocal payment or payments are allocated, and to the basis on which any such payment or payments are apportioned between two or more such periods, but

(b) no regard shall be had to the accounting period or periods to which any other payment or payments are allocated, or to the basis on which any such payment or payments are so apportioned.

(6) References in this section to a qualifying company's accounts shall be construed as follows—

(a) in the case of a company formed and registered under the Companies Act 1985 as references to its accounts drawn up in accordance with the requirements of that Act;

(b) in the case of a company formed and registered under the Companies (Northern Ireland) Order 1986, as references to its accounts drawn up in accordance with the requirements of that Order;

(c) in any other case, as references to the accounts which it is required to keep under the law of its home State or, if it is not so required to keep accounts, such of its accounts as most closely correspond to the accounts mentioned in paragraph (a) above;

and for the purposes of paragraph (c) above the home State of a company is the country or territory under whose law the company is incorporated.

(7) In this section—

"fair value", in relation to a qualifying contract, means the amount which, if the qualifying company disposed of the contract to a knowledgeable and willing party dealing at arm's length, it would be able to obtain or, as the case may be, would have to pay;

"reciprocal payment", in relation to a relevant payment, means another such payment which is the consideration or part of the consideration for that payment;

"relevant payment" means a qualifying payment made or received, or falling to be made or received, by the company.

(8) In the above definition of "reciprocal payment", the second reference to a relevant payment includes a reference to any payment which—

(a) is subject to a condition precedent, and

(b) would be a relevant payment if the condition were fulfilled.

Note—This section repealed by FA 2002 s 83(2), (3) with effect for accounting periods beginning after 30 September 2002.
Commentary—*Simon's Direct Tax Service* **D2.1022, 1023.**
Revenue Internal Guidance—Company Taxation Manual COT13513–13515, 13575 (worked examples).
Amendments—¹ Words substituted for the words "normal accountancy practice" by FA 2002 s 103(4)(c) with effect from 24 July 2002.

157 Basis of accounting for linked currency options

(1) As regards a qualifying contract which is a linked currency option, a qualifying company's profit or loss for an accounting period shall be computed on a mark to market basis of accounting.

(2) Accordingly if, as regards such an option, a qualifying company's profit or loss for an accounting period would, apart from subsection (1) above, fall to be computed on an accruals basis of accounting, that profit or loss shall be computed for the purposes of this Chapter on a mark to market basis of accounting which—

(a) satisfies the requirements of section 156 above, or would satisfy those requirements if paragraph (a) of subsection (3) of that section were omitted, and

(b) is specified in an agreement between the company and the inspector or, in default of such an agreement, in a notice served on the company by the inspector.

(3) A currency option is a linked currency option for the purposes of this section if each of the conditions mentioned below is fulfilled.

(4) The first condition is that—

(a) in the case of an option exercisable by the qualifying company against the other party, another currency option is exercisable by that party against the company; or

(b) in the case of an option exercisable by the other party against the qualifying company, another currency option is exercisable by the company against that party.

(5) For the purposes of subsection (4) above, another currency option which is exercisable by or against an associated company of the qualifying company, or by or against an associated company of the other party to the currency option in question, shall be treated as exercisable by or against the qualifying company or that party.

(6) The second condition is that the terms of the two options are such that—

(a) they must be exercised (if at all) at the same, or substantially the same, time, and

(b) the rights and duties under the contract which would arise if the one option were exercised are the same, or substantially the same, as those under the contract which would arise if the other option were exercised.

(7) Where the currency option in question is such an option by virtue of section 150(8) above, subsections (4) and (5) above shall be construed as if—

(a) any reference to an option being exercisable by any person were a reference to a contract subject to a condition precedent the fulfilment of which would result in a transfer of value to that person, and

(b) any reference to an option being exercisable against any person were a reference to a contract subject to a condition precedent the fulfilment of which would result in a transfer of value by that person.

(8) For the purposes of subsection (7) above there is a transfer of value to or by any person if, immediately after the fulfilment of the condition, the value of that person's net assets is more or, as the case may be, less than it would have been but for the fulfilment of the condition.

(9) Any reference in subsection (8) above to the value of a person's net assets being more or less than it would have been but for the fulfilment of the condition includes a reference to the value of that person's net liabilities being less or, as the case may be, more than it would have been but for the fulfilment of the condition.

(10) In this section "associated company" shall be construed in accordance with section 416 of the Taxes Act 1988 and any reference to a currency option is a reference to one which is a qualifying contract.

Note—This section repealed by FA 2002 ss 83(2), (3), 141, Sch 40 Pt 3(13) with effect for accounting periods beginning after 30 September 2002.

Commentary—*Simon's Direct Tax Service* **D2.1038.**

Revenue Internal Guidance—Company Taxation Manual COT13581 (worked example on cross options).

158 Adjustments for changes in basis of accounting

(1) Subsections (2) to (5) below apply where, as regards a qualifying contract and an accounting period, a qualifying company's profit or loss is computed on a basis of accounting (the new basis) other than that adopted for the immediately preceding accounting period.

(2) There shall be added to amount A an amount equal to any amount, or the aggregate of any amounts—

(a) which have not been included in amount A for a preceding accounting period, and

(b) which would have been so included if the new basis had been adopted for that period.

(3) There shall be deducted from amount A or, as the case may require, added to amount B an amount equal to any amount, or the aggregate of any amounts—

(a) which have been included in amount A for a preceding accounting period, and

(b) which would not have been so included if the new basis had been adopted for that period.

(4) There shall be added to amount B an amount equal to any amount, or the aggregate of any amounts—

(a) which have not been included in amount B for a preceding accounting period, and

(b) which would have been so included if the new basis had been adopted for that period.

(5) There shall be deducted from amount B or, as the case may require, added to amount A an amount equal to any amount, or the aggregate of any amounts—

(a) which have been included in amount B for a preceding accounting period, and

(b) which would not have been so included if the new basis had been adopted for that period.

(6) Subject to subsection (7) below, subsections (2) to (5) above also apply where a contract or option becomes a qualifying contract by virtue of section 147(2) or 148(2) or (3) above at the beginning of the first day of an accounting period of a qualifying company.

(7) Where subsections (2) to (5) above apply by virtue of subsection (6) above, they shall have effect as if—

(a) any reference to the new basis were a reference to the basis of accounting on which, as regards the qualifying contract, the company's profit or loss for the accounting period is calculated,

(b) any reference to being or not being included in amount A for a preceding accounting period were a reference to being or not being taken into account as receipts or increases in value in computing the company's profits or losses for such a period, and

(c) any reference to being or not being included in amount B for a preceding accounting period were a reference to being or not being taken into account as deductions or reductions in value in computing the company's profits or losses for such a period.

Note—This section repealed by FA 2002 ss 83(2), (3), 141, Sch 40 Pt 3(13) with effect for accounting periods beginning after 30 September 2002.
Commentary—*Simon's Direct Tax Service* **D2.1024, 1050.**
Revenue Internal Guidance—Company Taxation Manual COT13530 (worked example).

Treatment of profits and losses

159 Trading profits and losses

(1) Subsections (2) and (3) below apply where—

(a) as regards a qualifying contract a profit or loss accrues to a qualifying company for an accounting period, and

(b) the qualifying contract was at any time in the period held by the company for the purposes of a trade or part of a trade carried on by it.

(2) If throughout the accounting period the qualifying contract was held by the company solely for the purposes of the trade or part, the whole of the profit or loss shall be treated for the purposes of the Tax Acts as a profit or loss of the trade or part for the period.

(3) In any other case the profit or loss shall be apportioned on a just and reasonable basis and so much as is attributable to the trade or part shall be treated for the purposes of the Tax Acts as a profit or loss of the trade or part for the period.

(4) The preceding provisions of this section apply notwithstanding anything in section 74 of the Taxes Act 1988 (general rules as to deductions not allowable).

Note—This section repealed by FA 2002 ss 83(2), (3), 141, Sch 40 Pt 3(13) with effect for accounting periods beginning after 30 September 2002.
Commentary—*Simon's Direct Tax Service* **D2.1030.**

160 Non-trading profits and losses

(1) In a case where—

(a) as regards a qualifying contract a profit or loss accrues to a qualifying company for an accounting period, and

(b) the whole or part of the profit or loss does not fall to be treated for the purposes of the Tax Acts as a profit or loss of a trade or part of a trade for the period,

the whole or part (as the case may be) shall be treated for the purposes of this section as a non-trading profit or loss of the company for the period.

[(2) Any amount which for the purposes of this section is treated as a non-trading profit of a company for any accounting period shall be brought into account for that accounting period as if it were a non-trading credit falling to be brought into account for the purposes of Chapter II of Part IV of the Finance Act 1996 in respect of a loan relationship of the company.]¹

[(2A) Any amount which for the purposes of this section is treated as a non-trading loss of a company for any accounting period shall be brought into account for that accounting period as if it were a non-trading debit falling to be brought into account for the purposes of Chapter II of Part IV of the Finance Act 1996 in respect of a loan relationship of the company.]¹

Note—This section repealed by FA 2002 ss 83(2), (3), 141, Sch 40 Pt 3(13) with effect for accounting periods beginning after 30 September 2002.
Commentary—*Simon's Direct Tax Service* **D2.1031.**
Cross reference—TA 1988 s 434A(3)(*b*) (companies carrying on life assurance business: limitations on relief: exchange gains and losses).
Amendments—¹ Sub-ss (2), (2A) substituted for sub-ss (2)–(4) by FA 1996 ss 104, 105(1), Sch 14 para 75 with effect for accounting periods ending after 31 March 1996, subject to transitional provisions in FA 1996 Sch 15.

Special cases

161 Termination etc of qualifying contracts

(1) This section applies where at any time (the relevant time) in an accounting period of a qualifying company—

(a) a qualifying contract held by the company is terminated,

(b) such a contract is disposed of by the company, or

(c) a contract held by the company is so varied as to cease to be such a contract.

(2) If, as regards the contract and the period, amounts A and B fall to be determined under section 155(5) above—

(a) there shall be deducted from amount A or, as the case may require, added to amount B so much of any qualifying payment as has not become due and payable to the company before the relevant time but has been included in amount A for the period or any previous accounting period, and

(b) there shall be deducted from amount B or, as the case may require, added to amount A so much of any qualifying payment as has not become due and payable by the company before the relevant time but has been included in amount B for the period or any previous accounting period.

Note—This section repealed by FA 2002 ss 83(2), (3), 141, Sch 40 Pt 3(13) with effect for accounting periods beginning after 30 September 2002.

Revenue Internal Guidance—Company Taxation Manual COT13514 (worked example).

162 Exchange gains and losses on currency contracts

Where, as regards a currency contract held by a qualifying company and an accounting period, amounts A and B fall to be determined under section 155(4) above—

(a) the amount of any exchange gain which as regards the contract accrues to the company for the period shall be deducted from amount A or, as the case may require, added to amount B; and

(b) the amount of any exchange loss which as regards the contract accrues to the company for the period shall be deducted from amount B or, as the case may require, added to amount A.

Note—This section repealed by FA 2002 ss 83(2), (3), 141, Sch 40 Pt 3(13) with effect for accounting periods beginning after 30 September 2002.

Commentary—*Simon's Direct Tax Service* **D2.1025.**

163 Irrecoverable payments

(1) Subsections (2) and (3) below apply in any case [where a qualifying company—

(a) is entitled to a right to receive a qualifying payment, and

(b) makes a claim][1] within two years after the end of an accounting period of the company, that the whole or any part of the payment outstanding immediately before the end of that period could at that time reasonably have been regarded as having become irrecoverable in that period.

(2) If, as regards the contract and the period, amounts A and B fall to be determined under section 155(4) above, an amount equal to so much of the payment as—

(a) [may reasonably be regarded as having][1] become irrecoverable in the period, and

(b) became due and payable in the period or any previous accounting period,

shall be deducted from amount A, or as the case may require, added to amount B.

(3) If, as regards the contract and the period, amounts A and B fall to be determined under section 155(5) above, an amount equal to so much of the payment as—

(a) [may reasonably be regarded as having][1] become irrecoverable in the period, and

(b) was allocated to the period or any previous accounting period,

shall be deducted from amount A, or as the case may require, added to amount B.

(4) In any case where—

(a) as regards a qualifying contract and an accounting period of a qualifying company, an amount has been deducted or added as mentioned in subsection (2) or (3) above, and

(b) the whole or any part of so much of the qualifying payment as [fell within paragraphs (a) and (b) of that subsection][1] is recovered in a later accounting period of the company,

an amount equal to so much of the payment as is so recovered shall, as regards the qualifying contract and the later accounting period, be deducted from amount B, or as the case may require, added to amount A.

Note—This section repealed by FA 2002 ss 83(2), (3), 141, Sch 40 Pt 3(13) with effect for accounting periods beginning after 30 September 2002.

Commentary—*Simon's Direct Tax Service* **D2.1026.**

Amendments—[1] Words in sub-ss (1)–(4) substituted by FA 1996 s 134(1), (2), Sch 20 para 71 with effect as respects accounting periods ending after 30 June 1999 (by virtue of Finance Act 1994, Section 199, (Appointed Day) Order, SI 1998/3173 art 2).

164 Released payments

(1) Subsections (2) and (3) below apply in any case where—

(a) a qualifying company is subject to a duty to make a qualifying payment, and

(b) at any time in an accounting period of the company, the whole or any part of the payment then outstanding is released by the person to whom the duty is owed.

(2) If, as regards the contract and the period, amounts A and B fall to be determined under section 155(4) above, an amount equal to so much of the payment as—

(a) is released in the period, and
(b) became due and payable in the period or any previous accounting period,

shall be deducted from amount B, or as the case may require, added to amount A.

(3) If, as regards the contract and the period, amounts A and B fall to be determined under section 155(5) above, an amount equal to so much of the payment as—

(a) is released in the period, and
(b) was allocated to the period or any previous accounting period,

shall be deducted from amount B, or as the case may require, added to amount A.

Note—This section repealed by FA 2002 ss 83(2), (3), 141, Sch 40 Pt 3(13) with effect for accounting periods beginning after 30 September 2002.

Commentary—*Simon's Direct Tax Service* **D2.1026.**

Anti-avoidance and related provisions

165 Transfers of value by qualifying companies

(1) Subsection (2) below applies where, as a result of—

(a) a qualifying company entering into a relevant transaction on or after its commencement day, or
(b) the expiry on or after a qualifying company's commencement day of an option held by the company which, until its expiry, was a qualifying contract,

there is a transfer of value by the qualifying company to an associated company or an associated third party.

(2) For the accounting period of the qualifying company in which the transaction was entered into or the option expired, there shall be deducted from amount B or, as the case may require, added to amount A an amount equal to the value transferred by that company.

(3) For the purposes of subsection (1) above there is a transfer of value by the qualifying company to an associated company or an associated third party if, immediately after the transaction or expiry—

(a) the value of the qualifying company's net assets is less, and
(b) the value of the associated company's or associated third party's net assets is more,

than it would have been but for the transaction or expiry; and the amount by which the value mentioned in paragraph (a) above is less is the value transferred by the qualifying company for the purposes of subsection (2) above.

(4) Any reference in subsection (3) above to the value of a person's net assets being less or more than it would have been but for the transaction or expiry includes a reference to the value of that person's net liabilities being more or, as the case may be, less than it would have been but for the transaction or expiry.

(5) In applying subsection (3) above, no account shall be taken of any such payment as is mentioned in section 151(2)(a) or (b) above.

(6) A third party, that is to say, a person who is not an associated company, is an associated third party for the purposes of this section at the time when the relevant transaction is entered or the option expires if, at that time, each of the two conditions mentioned below is fulfilled.

(7) The first condition is that the relevant transaction is entered into or the option is allowed to expire in pursuance of arrangements made with the third party.

(8) The second condition is that, in pursuance of those arrangements, a transfer of value has been or will be made to an associated company (directly or indirectly) by the third party or by a company which was at the time when the arrangements were made an associated company of that party.

(9) Where it appears to the inspector that there is a transfer of value by the qualifying company to a third party, he may by notice in writing require the company, within such time (which shall not be less than 30 days) as may be specified in the notice, to furnish to the inspector such information—

(a) as is in its possession or power, and
(b) as the inspector reasonably requires for the purpose of determining whether the third party is an associated third party for the purposes of this section.

(10) Subsection (3) above shall (with the necessary modifications) apply for the purposes of subsections (7) to (9) above as it applies for the purposes of subsection (1) above.

(11) In this section—

''associated company'' shall be construed in accordance with section 416 of the Taxes Act 1988;
''relevant transaction'' means a transaction as a result of which—

(a) a qualifying company becomes party to a qualifying contract, or
(b) the terms of a qualifying contract to which a qualifying company is party are varied;

and any reference to an associated company is, unless the contrary intention appears, a reference to an associated company of the qualifying company.

Note—This section repealed by FA 2002 ss 83(2), (3), 141, Sch 40 Pt 3(13) with effect for accounting periods beginning after 30 September 2002.

Commentary—*Simon's Direct Tax Service* **D2.1035.**
Revenue Internal Guidance—Company Taxation Manual COT13915 (worked example).
Cross references—See SI 1994/3226 reg 5 (FA 1993 s 150 applies for the purposes of sub-s(3)).

166 Transfers of value to associated companies

(1) Subsection (2) below applies where subsection (2) of section 165 above applies and either—

(a) the transfer of value by the qualifying company is to an associated company which is itself a qualifying company; or

(b) the transfer of value by the qualifying company is to an associated third party, and the transfer of value mentioned in subsection (8) of that section—

(i) is to an associated company which is itself a qualifying company, and

(ii) results from that company entering into a relevant transaction.

(2) For the corresponding accounting period or periods of the associated company, there shall be deducted from amount A or, as the case may require, added to amount B an amount equal to the value transferred to the associated company.

(3) Subsection (3) of section 165 above shall (with the necessary modifications) apply for the purposes of subsection (2) above as it applies for the purposes of subsection (2) of that section.

(4) In subsection (2) above "corresponding accounting period or periods", in relation to the associated company, means the accounting period or periods of that company comprising or together comprising the accounting period of the qualifying company in which the transaction was entered into or the option expired, and any necessary apportionment shall be made between corresponding accounting periods if more than one.

(5) In this section any expressions which are also used in section 165 above shall be construed in accordance with the provisions of that section.

Note—This section repealed by FA 2002 ss 83(2), (3), 141, Sch 40 Pt 3(13) with effect for accounting periods beginning after 30 September 2002.
Commentary—*Simon's Direct Tax Service* **D2.1035.**

167 Transactions not at arm's length

(1) A transaction entered into on or after a qualifying company's commencement day is a relevant transaction for the purposes of this section if as a result of the transaction—

(a) the qualifying company becomes party to a qualifying contract, or

(b) the terms of a qualifying contract to which the qualifying company is party are varied.

(2) Subsections (3) to (5) below apply where—

(a) if the parties to a relevant transaction had been dealing at arm's length, the transaction—

(i) would not have been entered into at all, or

(ii) would have been entered into on different terms, ...[2]

(b) ...[2]

but subject, in a case falling within paragraph (a)(ii) above, to the modifications made by subsection (7) below.

(3) For each relevant accounting period for the whole of which the other party is a qualifying company, the following deductions shall be made—

(a) from amount B, a deduction of such amount as may be necessary to reduce amount B to nil, and

(b) from amount A, a deduction of such amount as may be necessary to reduce amount A to nil.

(4) For each relevant accounting period for any part of which the other party is not a qualifying company, the following deductions shall be made—

(a) from amount B, a deduction of such amount as may be necessary to reduce amount B to nil, and

(b) from amount A, a deduction of the same amount or (where that amount exceeds amount A) a deduction of so much of that amount as may be necessary to reduce amount A to nil.

(5) For each relevant accounting period (except the first) for any part of which the other party is not a qualifying company, there shall also be deducted from amount A or, as the case may require, added to amount B such amount as may be necessary to secure that amount C does not exceed amount D where—

(a) amount C is any amount by which the aggregate of adjusted amounts A exceeds the aggregate of adjusted amounts B, and

(b) amount D is any amount by which the aggregate of unadjusted amounts A exceeds the aggregate of unadjusted amounts B.

(6) In subsection (5) above—

"adjusted" means adjusted under subsections (4) and (5) above and "unadjusted" shall be construed accordingly;

"the aggregate of adjusted amounts A", in relation to a relevant accounting period, means the aggregate of—

(a) adjusted amount A for that period, and

(b) adjusted amount A for each preceding relevant accounting period,

and similar expressions shall be construed accordingly.

(7) In a case falling within subsection (2)(a)(ii) above—

(a) subsections (3) to (5) above shall have effect as if any reference to amount A or amount B were a reference to the relevant proportion of that amount; and

(b) the definitions in subsection (6) above of "the aggregate of adjusted amounts A" and similar expressions shall have effect as if any reference to adjusted amount A were a reference to the adjusted relevant proportion of amount A;

and in this subsection "the relevant proportion" means such proportion as may be just and reasonable having regard to the differences between the terms mentioned in subsection (2)(a)(ii) above and the terms on which the relevant transaction was actually entered into.

(8) In applying subsections (2) and (7) above—

(a) no account shall be taken of any transfer of value in respect of which an adjustment is made under section 165 or 166 above, but

(b) subject to that, all factors shall be taken into account.

(9) The factors which may be so taken into account include—

(a) in a case where the qualifying contract is an interest rate contract or option, any notional principal amounts and rates of interest that would have been involved;

(b) in a case where the qualifying contract is a currency contract or option, any currencies and amounts that would have been involved;

[(ba) in a case where the qualifying contract is a debt contract or option, the amount of the debt by reference to which any loan relationship that would have been involved would have subsisted, and any terms as to repayment, redemption or interest that, in the case of that debt or any asset representing it, would have been involved;]¹ and

(c) in [any such]¹ case, any transactions which are related to the relevant transaction.

(10) In this section "relevant accounting period", in relation to a relevant transaction, means—

(a) the accounting period of the qualifying company in which the transaction was entered into, and

(b) each subsequent accounting period of that company for the whole or part of which it is party to the contract.

Note—This section repealed by FA 2002 ss 83(2), (3), 141, Sch 40 Pt 3(13) with effect for accounting periods beginning after 30 September 2002.
Commentary—*Simon's Direct Tax Service* **D2.1036.**
Revenue Internal Guidance—Company Taxation Manual COT13929 (worked example on sub-s(4)).
Amendments—¹ Sub-s (9)(ba) inserted and words in sub-s (9)(c) substituted by FA 1996 Sch 14 para 76 with effect for accounting periods ending after 31 March 1996, subject to transitional provisions in FA 1996 Sch 15.
² Words in sub-s (2) repealed by FA 1998 s 109, Sch 27 Part III(27) with effect in relation to transactions entered into at any time as respects accounting periods ending after 30 June 1999 (by virtue of Finance Act 1994, Section 199, (Appointed Day) Order, SI 1998/3173 art 2).

168 Qualifying contracts with non-residents

(1) Subject to subsections (3) to (5) below, subsections (4) and (5) of section 167 above ("the relevant subsections") also apply where, as a result of any transaction entered into on or after a qualifying company's commencement day—

(a) the qualifying company and a non-resident, that is, a person who is not resident in the United Kingdom, both become party to a qualifying contract;

(b) the qualifying company becomes party to a qualifying contract to which a non-resident is party; or

(c) a non-resident becomes party to a qualifying contract to which the qualifying company is party.

(2) For the purposes of the relevant subsections as so applied, the definition of "relevant accounting period" in subsection (10) of that section shall have effect as if—

(a) any reference to a relevant transaction were a reference to the transaction mentioned in subsection (1) above; and

(b) in paragraph (b), for the words "it is" there were substituted the words "both it and the non-resident are".

(3) The relevant subsections shall not apply where the qualifying company is a bank, building society or financial trader and—

(a) it holds the qualifying contract solely for the purposes of a trade or part of a trade carried on by it in the United Kingdom, and

(b) it is party to the contract otherwise than as agent or nominee of another person.

(4) The relevant subsections shall not apply where—

(a) the non-resident holds the qualifying contract solely for the purposes of a trade or part of a trade carried on by him in the United Kingdom through a branch or agency, and

(b) he is party to the contract otherwise than as agent or nominee of another person.

(5) The relevant subsections shall not apply where arrangements made with the government of the territory in which the non-resident is resident—

(a) have effect by virtue of section 788 of the Taxes Act 1988 and

(b) make provision, whether for relief or otherwise, in relation to interest (as defined in the arrangements).

(6) Where the non-resident is party to the contract as agent or nominee of another person, subsection (5) above shall have effect as if the reference to the territory in which the non-resident is resident were a reference to the territory in which that other person is resident.

Note—This section repealed by FA 2002 ss 83(2), (3), 141, Sch 40 Pt 3(13) with effect for accounting periods beginning after 30 September 2002.

Commentary—*Simon's Direct Tax Service* **D2.1037.**

[168A Qualifying contracts for unallowable purposes

(1) Where in any accounting period a qualifying contract to which a company is party has an unallowable purpose, any amounts which for that period fall, in the case of the company, to be brought into account for the purposes of section 155 above as part of amount B shall (subject to subsection (2) below) not include so much of the amounts given by the accounting method used as respects the contract as, on a just and reasonable apportionment, is referable to the unallowable purpose.

(2) The total of any amounts which by virtue of subsection (1) above are not to be brought into account in the accounting period as part of amount B may not exceed the maximum amount.

(3) For the purposes of subsection (2) above, the maximum amount, in relation to the accounting period, is—

(a) if in the accounting period amount B exceeds amount A, the amount by which amount B exceeds amount A; and

(b) if in the accounting period amount A exceeds or equals amount B, nil.

(4) For the purposes of subsection (3) above, amount A and amount B shall be determined in relation to the qualifying contract in accordance with section 155 above and, in so determining amount B, so much of any amount as is referable to the unallowable purpose of the contract shall (notwithstanding subsection (1) above) be brought into account.

(5) For the purposes of this section a qualifying contract to which a company is party shall be taken to have an unallowable purpose in an accounting period where the purposes for which, at times during that period, the company is party to the contract include a purpose ("the unallowable purpose") which is not amongst the business or other commercial purposes of the company.

(6) For the purposes of this section the business and other commercial purposes of a company do not include the purposes of any part of its activities in respect of which it is not within the charge to corporation tax.

(7) For the purposes of this section, where one of the purposes for which a company is party to a qualifying contract at any time is a tax avoidance purpose, that purpose shall be taken to be a business or other commercial purpose of the company only where it is not the main purpose, or one of the main purposes, for which the company is party to the contract at that time.

(8) The reference in subsection (7) above to a tax avoidance purpose is a reference to any purpose that consists in securing a tax advantage (whether for the company or any other person).

(9) In this section "tax advantage" has the same meaning as in Chapter 1 of Part 17 of the Taxes Act 1988 (tax avoidance).][1]

Note—This section repealed by FA 2002 ss 83(2), (3), 141, Sch 40 Pt 3(13) with effect for accounting periods beginning after 30 September 2002.

Cross references—FA 2002 s 69(3) (apportionment of amounts where an accounting period begins before 26 July 2001).

FA 2002 s 69(4) (modification of sub-s (3) above where an accounting period begins before 26 July 2001).

Amendments—[1] This section inserted by FA 2002 s 69 with effect for accounting periods ending after 25 July 2001 in relation to any qualifying contract to which a company is party, unless the company has ceased to be a party to the contract before that date. This is, however, subject to FA 2002 s 69(3).

Miscellaneous

169 Insurance and mutual trading companies

(1) Subject to the provisions of Schedule 18 to this Act and subsection (2) below, this Chapter shall apply in relation to insurance companies and mutual trading companies as it applies in relation to other qualifying companies.

(2) The Treasury may by regulations provide that this Chapter shall have effect in relation to currency contracts held by insurance companies with such modifications as may be specified in the regulations.

(3) Regulations under subsection (2) above may make different provision as respects contracts held for different purposes or in different circumstances.

Note—This section repealed by FA 2002 ss 83(2), (3), 141, Sch 40 Pt 3(13) with effect for accounting periods beginning after 30 September 2002.

Commentary—*Simon's Direct Tax Service* **D2.1040.**

170 Investment trusts

(1) For the purpose of determining whether a qualifying company may be approved for the purposes of section 842 of the Taxes Act 1988 (investment trusts) for any accounting period, any non-trading profits which the company is treated for the purposes of section 160 above as having for that period shall be treated as income derived from shares or securities.

(2) In this section "shares" has the same meaning as in section 842 of the Taxes Act 1988.

Note—This section repealed by FA 2002 ss 83(2), (3), 141, Sch 40 Pt 3(13) with effect for accounting periods beginning after 30 September 2002.
Commentary—*Simon's Direct Tax Service* **D2.1043.**

171 Charities

Commentary—*Simon's Direct Tax Service* **.D2.1041**
Amendments—This section repealed by FA 1996 Sch 41 Pt V(3) with effect for accounting periods ending after 31 March 1996, subject to transitional provisions in FA 1996 Sch 15.

172 Partnerships involving qualifying companies

(1) Subject to the provisions of this section, this Chapter shall have effect as if qualifying partnerships were qualifying companies.

(2) A partnership is a qualifying partnership for the purposes of this section if one or more of the partners are qualifying companies.

(3) Subsections (4) to (6) below apply where—

(a) one or more of the members of a qualifying partnership are not qualifying companies, and
(b) as regards one or more qualifying contracts, one or more profits or losses accrue to the partnership for an accounting period.

(4) Two computations of the profits and losses for the period shall be made under subsection (1) of section 114 of the Taxes Act 1988 (partnerships involving companies: special rules for computing profits and losses)—

(a) one (the first computation) on the basis that the partnership is a qualifying partnership, and
(b) the other (the second computation) on the basis that the partnership is not such a partnership.

(5) The first computation shall be used for the purpose of determining, under subsection (2) of that section, the share or shares of such of the partners as are qualifying companies.

(6) The second computation shall be used for the purpose of determining, under that subsection, the share or shares of such of the partners as are not qualifying companies.

Note—This section repealed by FA 2002 ss 83(2), (3), 141, Sch 40 Pt 3(13) with effect for accounting periods beginning after 30 September 2002.
Commentary—*Simon's Direct Tax Service* **D2.1042.**

Supplemental

173 Prevention of double charging etc

(1) Subsection (2) below applies to any amount—

(a) which under or by virtue of this Chapter is chargeable to corporation tax as profits of a qualifying company, or
(b) which falls to be taken into account as a receipt in computing for the purposes of this Chapter the profits or losses of such a company.

(2) An amount to which this subsection applies—

(a) shall not otherwise than under or by virtue of this Chapter be chargeable to corporation tax as profits of the company,
(b) shall not be taken into account as a receipt in computing for other purposes of the Tax Acts the profits or losses of the company, and
(c) for the purposes of the Taxation of Chargeable Gains Act 1992 shall be excluded from the consideration for a disposal of assets taken into account in the computation of the gain.

(3) Subsection (4) below applies to any amount—

(a) which is allowable as a deduction in computing for the purposes of this Chapter the profits or losses of a qualifying company, or
(b) which under or by virtue of this Chapter is allowable as a deduction in computing any other income or profits or gains or losses of such a company for the purposes of the Tax Acts, or
(c) which, although not so allowable as a deduction in computing any losses, would be so allowable but for an insufficiency of income or profits or gains;

and that subsection applies to any such amount irrespective of whether effect is or would be given to the deduction in computing the amount of tax chargeable or by discharge or repayment of tax or in any other way.

(4) An amount to which this subsection applies—

(a) shall not be allowable as a deduction in computing for other purposes of the Tax Acts the profits or losses of the company,

(b) shall not otherwise than under or by virtue of this Chapter be allowable as a deduction in computing any other income or profits or gains or losses of the company for the purposes of the Tax Acts,

(c) shall not be treated as a charge on income for the purposes of corporation tax, and

(d) shall be excluded from the sums allowable under section 38 of the Taxation of Chargeable Gains Act 1992 as a deduction in the computation of the gain.

(5) In this section—

(a) references to the purposes of this Chapter include references to the purposes of [Chapter II of Part IV of the Finance Act 1996 (loan relationships), so far as that Chapter is applied by virtue of section 160(2) or (2A) above,][1] and

(b) references to other purposes of the Tax Acts are references to the purposes of those Acts other than those of this Chapter.

Note—This section repealed by FA 2002 ss 83(2), (3), 141, Sch 40 Pt 3(13) with effect for accounting periods beginning after 30 September 2002.

Revenue Internal Guidance—Company Taxation Manual COT13591 (the amount of any capital gain is reduced under TCGA 1992 ss 37, 39 to the extent that exchange differences, or any deemed forward premium, or discount are taken into account on the contract under this legislation).

COT13592 (treatment of residual capital gain or loss).

COT13598, 13599 (worked examples).

Amendments—[1] Words in sub-s (5)(a) substituted by FA 1996 ss 104, 105(1), Sch 14 para 77 with effect for accounting periods ending after 31 March 1996, subject to transitional provisions in FA 1996 Sch 15.

174 Prevention of deduction of tax

Notwithstanding anything in section 349 of the Taxes Act 1988 or any other provision of the Tax Acts, a qualifying company shall not be required, on making a qualifying payment, to deduct out of it any sum representing an amount of income tax on it.

Note—This section repealed by FA 2002 ss 83(2), (3), 141, Sch 40 Pt 3(13) with effect for accounting periods beginning after 30 September 2002.

Revenue and other press releases—IR 21-1-98 (fixed rate swaps of two currencies which convert into the Euro will continue within the financial instruments legislation).

175 Transitional provisions

(1) In a case where—

(a) at any time, a currency contract held by a qualifying company becomes a qualifying contract by virtue of section 147(2) above, and

(b) at that time, it is held for the purposes of a trade or part of a trade carried on by the company, [and][1]

[(c) the circumstances are such that if any profit or loss accrues (or were to accrue) to the company as regards the contract for an accounting period beginning before that time it falls (or would fall) to be taken into account as a profit or loss of the trade or part,][1]

subsection (4) of section 153 above shall have effect in relation to the contract and the company as if section 147(2) above applied for the purposes of this Chapter except those of that subsection.

[(2) In a case where—

(a) at any time, a currency contract held by a qualifying company becomes a qualifying contract by virtue of section 147(2) above, and

(b) the circumstances are such that if any profit or loss accrues (or were to accrue) to the company as regards the contract for the accounting period beginning with that time it does not fall (or would not fall) to be taken into account as a profit or loss of a trade or part of a trade carried on by the company,

in applying section 158(2) and (4) above in relation to the contract and the period section 153(4) and (5) above shall be treated as omitted.][2]

Note—This section repealed by FA 2002 ss 83(2), (3), 141, Sch 40 Pt 3(13) with effect for accounting periods beginning after 30 September 2002.

Revenue Interpretation RI 113—Operation of transitional rules in relation to foreign exchange gains and losses on currency contracts where company has been, or may be, subject to a direction under TA 1988 s 747, the controlled foreign company provisions.

Amendments—[1] In sub-s (1) word at end of sub-para (b) added, and sub-para (c) inserted, by FA 1995 s 132(2), and is deemed to have been enacted with the amendments made.

[2] Sub-s (2) substituted by FA 1995 s 132(3).

176 Minor and consequential amendments

(1) (amended TA 1988 s 434A(1); repealed by FA 1995 Sch 29 Pt VIII(5), with effect for accounting periods beginning on or after 31 December 1994).

(2) (substitutes TA 1988 Sch 27 para 5(2A)).

177 Interpretation of Chapter II

(1) In this Chapter—

    "appointed day" has the meaning given by section 147(4) above;

    "bank" means any of the following—

        (a) the Bank of England;

        [(b) any person falling within section 840A(1)(b) of the Taxes Act 1988; and]³

        [(c) any firm falling within section 840A(1)(c) of that Act;]³

    "commencement day" [—

        (a) for the purposes of this Chapter as it has effect in relation to any debt contract or option, means (subject to paragraph 25 of Schedule 15 to the Finance Act 1996) 1st April 1996; and

        (b) for all other purposes]² has the meaning given by section 147(4) above;

    "currency contract" and "currency option" shall be construed in accordance with section 150 above;

    ["debt contract" and "debt option" shall be construed in accordance with section 150A above;]²

    ...³

    ...³

    ["financial trader" means—

        (a) any person who—

            (i) falls within section 31(1)(a), (b) or (c) of the Financial Services and Markets Act 2000, and

            (ii) has permission under that Act to carry on one or more of the activities specified in Article 14 and, in so far as it applies to that Article, Article 64 of the Financial Services and Markets Act 2000 (Regulated Activities) Order 2001; or

        (b) any person not falling within paragraph (a) above who is approved by the Board for the purposes of this paragraph;]³

    "inspector" includes any officer of the Board;

    "insurance company" means a company [which [effects or carries out contracts of insurance and, for the purposes of this definition, "contract of insurance" has the meaning given by Article 3(1) of the Financial Services and Markets Act 2000 (Regulated Activities) Order 2001;]³]¹;

    "interest rate contract" and "interest rate option" shall be construed in accordance with section 149 above;

    ...³

    "mutual trading company" means a company carrying on any business of mutual trading or mutual insurance or other mutual business;

    "qualifying company" has the meaning given by section 154 above;

    "qualifying contract" has the meaning given by section 147(1) above;

    "qualifying payment" shall be construed in accordance with section 153 above.

(2) For the purposes of this Chapter—

    (a) a company becomes entitled to rights or subject to duties under an interest rate contract or option, [a currency contract or option or a debt contract or option]² when it becomes party to the contract or option; and

    (b) a company holds such a contract or option at a particular time if it is then entitled to rights or subject to duties under it;

and it is immaterial for the purposes of paragraph (b) above when the rights or duties fall to be exercised or performed.

(3) Any provision of this Chapter other than section 167 above which requires any amount (the relevant amount) to be deducted from amount A or, as the case may require, added to amount B shall be construed as requiring the following deductions or additions to be made—

    (a) where amount A is not less than the relevant amount, a deduction from amount A of an amount equal to the relevant amount;

    (b) where amount A is less than the relevant amount but is more than nil—

        (i) a deduction from amount A of an amount equal to so much of the relevant amount as may be necessary to reduce amount A to nil, and

        (ii) an addition to amount B of an amount equal to the remainder of the relevant amount;

    (c) where amount A is nil, an addition to amount B of an amount equal to the relevant amount.

(4) Subsection (3) above shall be read as applying equally to any such provision which requires any amount to be deducted from amount B or, as the case may be, added to amount A, and for that purpose shall have effect with such modifications as may be requisite.

(5) In this Chapter expressions which are not defined or otherwise explained but are used in Chapter II of Part II of the Finance Act 1993 (exchange gains and losses) have the same meanings as in that Chapter.

(6) The Treasury may by order amend any of sections 149 to 153 above; and any such order may—

    (a) make corresponding amendments to section 126 of the Finance Act 1993;

(b) make consequential amendments to such of the provisions of this Chapter or Chapter II of Part II of that Act as relate to currency contracts; and

(c) contain such other consequential provisions, and such supplementary, incidental or transitional provisions, as appear to the Treasury to be necessary or expedient.

Note—This section repealed by FA 2002 ss 83(2), (3), 141, Sch 40 Pt 3(13) with effect for accounting periods beginning after 30 September 2002.

Statement of Practice SP 3/95—Definition of financial trader for the purposes of FA 1994 s 177(1).

Amendments—¹ Words in definition of "insurance company" in sub-s (1) substituted by FA 1995 s 52(3) with effect for any accounting period ending after 30 June 1994.

² Words in definition of "commencement day" and whole of definition of "debt contract" and "debt option" in sub-s (1) inserted, and words in sub-s (2)(*a*) substituted by FA 1996 ss 104, 105(1), Sch 14 para 78 with effect for accounting periods ending after 31 March 1996, subject to transitional provisions in FA 1996 Sch 15.

³ In sub-s (1), words in the definition of "bank" and "insurance company" substituted, definitions of "deposit", "European authorised institution" and "investment business" revoked, and definition of "financial trader" substituted, by the Financial Services and Markets Act 2000 (Consequential Amendments) (Taxes) Order, SI 2001/3629 arts 83, 84 with effect from 1 December 2001 immediately after the coming into force of the Financial Services and Markets Act 2000 ss 411, 432(1), Sch 20.

CHAPTER III
MANAGEMENT: SELF-ASSESSMENT ETC

Revenue & other press releases—IR Booklet SAT 2 (self-assessment—the legal framework—a guide for practitioners, available from the Inland Revenue Library at Somerset House).

IR Leaflet IR 142 (explanation for taxpayers).

Income tax and capital gains tax

178 Personal and trustee's returns

(1) (*substitutes* TMA 1970 s 8(1), (1A)–(1C) for s 8(1)).

(2) (*substitutes* TMA 1970 s 8A(1), (1A) for s 8A(1)).

Commentary—*Simon's Direct Tax Service* A3.101; E1.101.

179 Returns to include self-assessment

(*Substitutes* TMA 1970 s 9).

180 Power to enquire into returns

(*Inserted* TMA 1970 s 9A, *repealed* by FA 2001 s 110, Sch 33 Pt II(13) with effect in accordance with FA 2001 s 88, Sch 29).

Corporation tax

181 Return of profits

Commentary—*Simon's Direct Tax Service* A3.101.

Amendment—This section repealed by FA 1998 s 165, Sch 27 Part III(28) with effect in relation to accounting periods ending after 30 June 1999 (by virtue of Finance Act 1994, Section 199, (Appointed Day) Order, SI 1998/3173 art 2).

182 Return of profits to include self-assessment

Amendment—This section repealed by FA 1998 s 165, Sch 27 Part III(28) with effect in relation to accounting periods ending after 30 June 1999 (by virtue of Finance Act 1994, Section 199, (Appointed Day) Order, SI 1998/3173 art 2).

183 Power to enquire into return of profits

Amendment—This section repealed by FA 1998 s 165, Sch 27 Part III(28) with effect in relation to accounting periods ending after 30 June 1999 (by virtue of Finance Act 1994, Section 199, (Appointed Day) Order, SI 1998/3173 art 2).

Partnerships

184 Partnership return

(*Inserts* TMA 1970 s 12AA).

185 Partnership return to include partnership statement

(*Inserts* TMA 1970 s 12AB).

186 Power to enquire into partnership return

(*Inserted* TMA 1970 s 12AC; *repealed by* FA 2001 s 110, Sch 33 Pt II(13) with effect in accordance with FA 2001 s 88, Sch 29).

187 Power to call for documents

(*Inserts TMA* 1970 s 19A).

188 Amendment of self-assessment

(*Inserted TMA* 1970 s 28A; *repealed by* FA 2001 s 110, Sch 33 Pt II(13) with effect in accordance with FA 2001 s 88, Sch 29).

189 Amendment of partnership statement

(*Inserted TMA* 1970 s 28B; *repealed by* FA 2001 s 110, Sch 33 Pt II(13) with effect in accordance with FA 2001 s 88, Sch 29).

Determinations and assessments to protect revenue

190 Determination of tax where no return delivered

(*Inserts TMA* 1970 s 28C).

191 Assessment where loss of tax discovered

(1) (*substitutes* TMA 1970 s 29).

(2) This section, so far as it relates to partnerships whose trades, professions or businesses are set up and commenced before 6th April 1994, has effect as respects the year 1997–98 and subsequent years of assessment.

Commentary—*Simon's Direct Tax Service* **A3.101, 201.**

Payment of tax

192 Payments on account of income tax

(*Inserts TMA* 1970 s 59A and the Part heading preceding it).

193 Payment of income tax and capital gains tax

(*Inserts TMA* 1970 s 59B).

194 Surcharges on unpaid income tax and capital gains tax

(*Inserts TMA* 1970 s 59C).

195 Payment of corporation tax

Amendment—This section repealed by FA 1998 s 165, Sch 27 Part III(28) with effect in relation to accounting periods ending after 30 June 1999 (by virtue of Finance Act 1994, Section 199, (Appointed Day) Order, SI 1998/3173 art 2).

Miscellaneous and supplemental

196 Management: other amendments

Schedule 19 to this Act (which makes other amendments relating to the management of tax) shall have effect.

Commentary—*Simon's Direct Tax Service* **A3.101, 150, 201, 601, 801, 1301.**

197 Construction of certain references

Commentary—*Simon's Direct Tax Service* **A3.101, 1301.**
Amendments—This section repealed by FA 1998 s 165, Sch 27 Part III(28) with effect in relation to accounting periods ending after 30 June 1999 (by virtue of Finance Act 1994, Section 199, (Appointed Day) Order, SI 1998/3173 art 2).

198 Transitional provisions

Commentary—*Simon's Direct Tax Service* **A3.101, 1301.**
Amendments—This section repealed by FA 1995 s 116(2), Sch 29 Pt VIII(14).

199 Interpretation and commencement of Chapter III

(1) In this Chapter "the Management Act" means the Taxes Management Act 1970.

(2) Unless the contrary intention appears, this Chapter—

(a) so far as it relates to income tax and capital gains tax, has effect as respects the year 1996–97 and subsequent years of assessment, and

(b) so far as it relates to corporation tax, has effect as respects accounting periods ending on or after the appointed day.

(3) For the purposes of this Chapter the appointed day is such day, not earlier than 1st April 1996, as the Treasury may by order appoint.

Commentary—*Simon's Direct Tax Service* A3.101, 1301.

Note—The 'appointed day' in sub-s (3) is 1 July 1999 by virtue of Finance Act 1994, Section 199, (Appointed Day) Order SI 1998/3173.

CHAPTER IV
CHANGES FOR FACILITATING SELF-ASSESSMENT

Revenue & other press releases. IR Booklet SAT 1 (guide for Inland Revenue Officers and tax practitioners, available from the Inland Revenue Library at Somerset House).

Assessment under Cases I and II of Schedule D

200 Assessment on current year basis
(*Substitutes* TA 1988 s 60).

Commentary—*Simon's Direct Tax Service* E1.201.

201 Basis of assessment at commencement
(*Substitutes* TA 1988 s 61).

Commentary—*Simon's Direct Tax Service* E1.201.

202 Change of basis period
(*Substitutes* TA 1988 s 62).

203 Conditions for such a change
(*Substitutes* TA 1988 s 62A).

204 Basis of assessment on discontinuance
(*Substitutes* TA 1988 s 63).

205 Overlap profits and overlap losses
(*Substitutes* TA 1988 s 63A).

Assessment under Cases III to VI of Schedule D

206 Basis of assessment under Case III
(*Substitutes* TA 1988 s 64).

207 Basis of assessment under Cases IV and V
(1)–(3) (*modify* TA 1988 s 65; for details, see TA 1988 s 65 *ante*).

(4) (*repeals* TA 1988 ss 66, 67; for details of when the repeals are in force, see TA 1988 ss 66, 67 *ante*).

(5) (*modifies* TA 1988 s 68; for details, see TA 1988 s 68 *ante*).

(6) In its application to trades, professions or vocations set up and commenced before 6th April 1994, subsection (2) above has effect as respects the year 1997–98 and subsequent years of assessment.

Commentary—*Simon's Direct Tax Service* E1.201, 301.

208 Basis of assessment under Case VI
(*Substitutes* TA 1988 s 69).

Loss relief

209 Loss relief: general
(1) (*modifies* TA 1988 s 380).

(2) (*modifies* TA 1988 s 381).

(3) (*modifies* TA 1988 s 382).

(4)–(5) (*modify* TA 1988 s 385).

(6) (*modifies* TA 1988 s 388).

[(7) Subsections (1), (2) and (6) above—

(a) except in their application to a trade set up and commenced on or after 6th April 1994, have effect in relation to losses sustained in the year 1996–97 and subsequent years of assessment; and (*b*) in their application to a trade so set up and commenced, have effect in relation to losses sustained in the year 1994–95 and subsequent years of assessment.

(8) Subsections (3) to (5) above—

(*a*) except in their application to a trade set up and commenced on or after 6th April 1994, have effect in relation to losses sustained in the year 1997–98 and subsequent years of assessment; and

(*b*) in their application to a trade so set up and commenced, have effect in relation to losses sustained in the year 1994–95 and subsequent years of assessment.

(9) Any reference in subsection (7) or (8) above to a trade includes a reference to a profession, vocation or employment.]¹

Commentary—*Simon's Direct Tax Service* **E1.201.**
Amendments—¹ Sub-ss (7), (8), (9) substituted for sub-s (7) by FA 1995 s 118, and are deemed always to have had effect.

210 Relief for losses on unquoted shares

(1) (*substitutes* TA 1988 s 574(1), (2)).

(2) This section has effect [in relation to losses incurred in]¹ the year 1994–95 and subsequent years of assessment.

Commentary—*Simon's Direct Tax Service* **E1.201, 627.**
Amendment—¹ Words in sub-s (2) substituted by FA 1995 s 119, and are deemed always to have had effect.

Capital allowances

211 Income tax allowances and charges in taxing a trade etc

(1) (*modified* CAA 1990 s 140; *repealed by* CAA 2001 s 580, Sch 4 with effect in accordance with CAA 2001 s 579).

(2) Subject to section 214(7) below, this section and sections 212 to 214 below, in their application to trades, professions or vocations set up and commenced before 6th April 1994 or employments or offices entered into before that date, have effect as respects the year 1997–98 and subsequent years of assessment.

Commentary—*Simon's Direct Tax Service* **E1.201.**

212 Chargeable periods for income tax purposes

Commentary—*Simon's Direct Tax Service* **E1.201.**
Amendment—This section repealed by the Capital Allowances Act 2001 s 580, Sch 4 with effect for income tax purposes, as respects allowances and charges falling to be made for chargeable periods ending after 5 April 2001, and for corporation tax purposes, as respects allowances and charges falling to be made for chargeable periods ending after 31 March 2001.

213 Other amendments of Capital Allowances Act 1990

Commentary—*Simon's Direct Tax Service* **E1.201.**
Amendment—This section repealed by the Capital Allowances Act 2001 s 580, Sch 4 with effect for income tax purposes, as respects allowances and charges falling to be made for chargeable periods ending after 5 April 2001, and for corporation tax purposes, as respects allowances and charges falling to be made for chargeable periods ending after 31 March 2001.

214 Amendments of other enactments

(1) (*modifies* TA 1988 ss 96, 383, 384, 388, 389).

(2) (*modifies* TA 1988 s 384(6)).

(3) (*modifies* TA 1988 s 397(1)).

(4)–(5) ...¹

(7) Subsection (1)(*a*) above—

(*a*) except in its application to a trade set up and commenced on or after 6th April 1994, has effect where the first of the two years of assessment to which the claim relates is the year 1996–97 or any subsequent year, and

(*b*) in its application to a trade so set up and commenced, has effect where the first of those two years of assessment is the year 1995–96 or any subsequent year.

Commentary—*Simon's Direct Tax Service* **E1.201.**
Amendments—¹ Sub-ss (4)–(6) repealed by the Capital Allowances Act 2001 s 580, Sch 4 with effect for income tax purposes, as respects allowances and charges falling to be made for chargeable periods ending after 5 April 2001, and for corporation tax purposes, as respects allowances and charges falling to be made for chargeable periods ending after 31 March 2001.

Miscellaneous and supplemental

215 Treatment of partnerships

(1) (*enacts* TA 1988 s 111 (new version) as amended by FA 1995 s 117(1)(*a*), (2)).

[(1A) (*amends* TA 1988 s 110(2) as inserted by FA 1995 s 117(1)(*b*), (3) (and deemed always to have had effect).]

(2) (*modifies* TA 1988 s 114 *as* amended by FA 1995 s 117(1)(*c*)).

(3) *(modifies* TA 1988 ss 114, 115, 277, as amended by FA 1995 s 117(1)(*d*)).

(4) This section and section 216 below—

(*a*) except in their application to partnerships mentioned in subsection (5) below, have effect as respects the year 1997–98 and subsequent years of assessment, and

(*b*) in its application to partnerships so mentioned, have effect as respects the year 1994–95 and subsequent years of assessment.

(5) The partnerships referred to in subsection (4) above are partnerships—

(*a*) whose trades, professions or businesses are set up and commenced on or after 6th April 1994; ...¹

(*b*) ...¹

Commentary—*Simon's Direct Tax Service* **E1.201, E5.301.**
Amendments—¹ In sub-s (5) word omitted from para (*a*), and whole of para (*b*), repealed by FA 1995 Sch 29 Pt VIII(16), with effect from the year 1995–96.

216 Effect of change in ownership of trade, profession or vocation

(1), (2) *(modify* TA 1988 s 113*)*.

(3) *(modifies* TA 1988 ss 96, 380, 381, 384–386, 389).

(4) *(modifies* TA 1988 s 389(4)).

(5) Subsection (3)(*a*) above—

(*a*) except in its application to a trade set up and commenced on or after 6th April 1994, has effect where the first of the two years of assessment to which the claim relates is the year 1996–97 or any subsequent year, and

(*b*) in its application to a trade so set up and commenced, has effect where the first of those two years of assessment is the year 1995–96 or any subsequent year.

Commentary—*Simon's Direct Tax Service* **E1.201, E5.301.**

217 Double taxation relief in respect of overlap profits

(modifies TA 1988 s 804*)*.

Commentary—*Simon's Direct Tax Service* **E1.201.**

218 Commencement, transitional provisions and savings

(1) Unless the contrary intention appears, this Chapter—

(*a*) except in its application to a trade set up and commenced on or after 6th April 1994 or income from a source arising to a person on or after that date, has effect as respects the year 1996–97 and subsequent years of assessment, and

(*b*) in its application to a trade so set up and commenced or income from a source so arising, has effect as respects the year 1994–95 and subsequent years of assessment.

[(1A) In a case where—

(*a*) a trade is set up and commenced by a company, and

(*b*) it is not set up and commenced before 6th April 1994,

sections 213(4) and (8) and 214(4) and (6) have effect only if it is set up and commenced on or after 6th April 1995.]¹

(2) Any reference in subsection (1) above to a trade includes a reference to a profession, vocation, employment or office.

(3) Where the first underwriting year of the underwriting business of a member of Lloyd's is the year 1994, subsection (1) above shall have effect in relation to that business as if it had been set up and commenced on 6th April 1994.

(4) Where, as respects income from any source, income tax is to be charged under Case IV or V of Schedule D by reference to the amounts of income received in the United Kingdom, the source shall be treated for the purposes of subsection (1) above as arising on the date on which the first amount of income is so received.

(5) This Chapter shall have effect subject to the transitional provisions and savings contained in Schedule 20 to this Act.

Commentary—*Simon's Direct Tax Service* **E1.201, 301.**
Amendments—¹ Sub-s (1A) inserted by FA 1995 s 102(2), and is deemed always to have had effect.

CHAPTER V
LLOYD'S UNDERWRITERS: CORPORATIONS ETC
Main provisions

219 Taxation of profits

(1) Corporation tax for any accounting period on the profits arising from a corporate member's underwriting business shall be computed on the profits of that accounting period.

(2) As respects the profits arising to a corporate member for any accounting period directly from its membership of one or more syndicates, or from assets forming part of a [premium][2] trust fund—

    (a) the aggregate of those profits shall be computed for tax purposes under Case I of Schedule D; and

    (b) accordingly, no part of those profits shall be computed for those purposes under any other Schedule or any other Case of Schedule D.

(3) [Subject to subsection (4A) below,][1] the profits arising to a corporate member for any accounting period—

    (a) from assets forming part of an ancillary trust fund; or

    (b) from assets employed by it in, or in connection with, its underwriting business,

shall be computed for tax purposes under Case I of Schedule D if, and to the extent that, they do not fall to be computed for those purposes under any other Schedule or any other Case of Schedule D.

(4) Where the profits arising for any accounting period from the assets of a corporate member's [premium][2] trust fund include [UK distributions][1], subsection (2) above shall apply in relation to those distributions ...[1] notwithstanding anything in section 11(2)(a) or 208 of the Taxes Act 1988.

[(4A) Notwithstanding anything in section 11(2)(a) or 208 of the Taxes Act 1988, UK distributions in respect of any assets of a corporate member which are mentioned in paragraph (a) or (b) of subsection (3) above—

    (a) shall be taken into account in computing profits of the corporate members for tax purposes; and

    (b) shall be so taken into account under Case I of Schedule D (and not under any other Schedule or any other Case of Schedule D).

(4B) Section 231(1) of the Taxes Act 1988 (entitlement to tax credit) shall not apply where the distribution there mentioned is a distribution in respect of any asset of a corporate member's [premium][2] trust fund.

(4C) In this section "UK distributions" means dividends or other distributions of a company resident in the United Kingdom.][1]

(5) (amends TA 1988 s 20(2)).

Commentary—*Simon's Direct Tax Service* E5.607, 611, 613, 620.
Cross reference—See Lloyd's Underwriters (Tax) Regulations, SI 1995/351 reg 4 (application to tax charged under this section of provisions in TMA 1970 and TA 1988 relating to assessment and collection of tax).
Revenue Internal Guidance—Inspector's manual IM 14264–14264c (treatment of income arising under accrued income scheme).
Amendments—[1] Words in sub-s (3), and sub-ss (4A), (4B), (4C), inserted, words in sub-s (4) substituted and repealed by F(No 2)A 1997 s 22(2), (3), (4), (7), Sch 8 Pt II(5) with effect in relation to distributions made after 1 July 1997.
[2] Word in sub-ss (2), (4) and (4B) substituted by the Financial Services and Markets Act 2000 (Consequential Amendments) (Taxes) Order, SI 2001/3629 arts 83, 87(a) with effect from 1 December 2001 immediately after the coming into force of the Financial Services and Markets Act 2000 ss 411, 432(1), Sch 20.

220 Accounting period in which certain profits or losses arise

(1) For the purposes of section 219 above and all other purposes of the Corporation Tax Acts, the profits or losses arising to a corporate member in any accounting period directly from its membership of one or more syndicates, or from assets forming part of a [premium][1] trust fund, shall be taken to be—

    (a) if two underwriting years each fall partly within that period, the aggregate of the apportioned parts of those profits or losses in those years; and

    (b) if a single underwriting year falls wholly or partly within that period, those profits or losses or (as the case may be) the apportioned part of those profits or losses in that year.

(2) Subject to the provisions of this Chapter, for the purposes of subsection (1) above and all other purposes of the Corporation Tax Acts—

    (a) the profits or losses arising to a corporate member in any underwriting year directly from its membership of one or more syndicates shall be taken to be those of any previous year or years which are declared in that year; and

    (b) the profits or losses arising to a corporate member in any underwriting year from assets forming part of a [premium][1] trust fund shall be taken to be those allocated under the rules or practice of Lloyd's to any previous year or years the profits or losses of which are declared in that year.

(3) In this section "apportioned part", in relation to the profits or losses of an underwriting year, means a part apportioned under section 72 of the Taxes Act 1988.

Commentary—*Simon's Direct Tax Service* **E5.607, 620.**
Amendments—¹ Word in sub-ss (1), (2)(*b*) substituted by the Financial Services and Markets Act 2000 (Consequential Amendments) (Taxes) Order, SI 2001/3629 with effect from 1 December 2001 immediately after the coming into force of the Financial Services and Markets Act 2000 ss 411, 432(1), Sch 20.

221 Assessment and collection of tax

(1) Subject to subsection (2) below, Schedule 19 (Lloyd's underwriters: assessment and collection of tax) to the Finance Act 1993 (''the 1993 Act'') shall apply in relation to corporate members as it applies in relation to other members.

(2) In its application to a corporate member, paragraph 13 of that Schedule shall have effect as if—

　(*a*) in sub-paragraph (3)(*b*), the reference to the members' agent of each member were a reference to each corporate member itself;

　(*b*) ...¹

　(*c*) in sub-paragraph (4), the reference to section 824 of the Taxes Act 1988 were a reference to section 826 of that Act (interest on tax overpaid); ...¹

　(*d*) ...¹

Commentary—*Simon's Direct Tax Service* **E5.607, 620.**
Amendments—¹ Sub-s (2)(*b*), (*d*) repealed by F(No 2)A 1997 Sch 8 Pt II(5) with effect in relation to distributions made after 1 July 1997.

Trust funds

222 Premiums trust funds

(1) For the purposes of the Corporation Tax Acts—

　(*a*) a corporate member shall be treated as absolutely entitled as against the trustees to the assets forming part of a premiums trust fund belonging to it; and

　(*b*) where a deposit required by a regulatory authority in a country or territory outside the United Kingdom is paid out of such a fund, the money so paid shall be treated as still forming part of that fund.

(2) Where an asset forms part of a corporate member's premiums trust fund at the beginning of any underwriting year, for the purposes of the Corporation Tax Acts—

　(*a*) the trustees of the fund shall be treated as acquiring it on that day, and

　(*b*) they shall be treated as paying in respect of the acquisition an amount equal to the value of the asset at the time of the acquisition.

(3) Where an asset forms part of a corporate member's premiums trust fund at the end of any underwriting year, for the purposes of the Corporation Tax Acts—

　(*a*) the trustees of the fund shall be treated as disposing of it on that day, and

　(*b*) they shall be treated as obtaining in respect of the disposal an amount equal to the value of the asset at the time of the disposal.

(4), (5) ...²

(6), (7) ...¹

Commentary—*Simon's Direct Tax Service* **E5.607, 620.**
Amendments—¹ Sub-ss (6), (7) repealed by FA 1996 Sch 41 Pt V(18) with effect for accounting periods ending after 31 March 1996.
² Sub-ss (4), (5) repealed by FA 1997 Sch 10 paras 6(*b*), 7(1), Sch 18 Pt VI (10) with effect in relation to, and to transfers under, any arrangement made on or after 1 July 1997 by virtue of the Finance Act 1997, Schedule 10, (Appointed Day) Order, SI 1997/991.

223 Ancillary trust funds

A corporate member shall be treated for the purposes of the Corporation Tax Acts as absolutely entitled as against the trustees to the assets forming part of an ancillary trust fund belonging to it.

Commentary—*Simon's Direct Tax Service* **E5.607, 620.**

Other special cases

224 Reinsurance to close

Commentary—*Simon's Direct Tax Service* **E5.607, 620.**
Amendments—This section repealed by FA 2000 ss 107(11), (12)(*c*), 156, Sch 40 Pt II(16) with effect for profits of underwriting members' trades which are declared in periods of account beginning after 31 December 1999. FA 2000 s 107 supersedes this section.

225 Stop-loss and quota share insurance

(1) In computing for the purposes of corporation tax the profits of a corporate member's underwriting business, each of the following shall be deductible as an expense, namely—

　(*a*) any premium payable by it under a stop-loss insurance, and any repayment of insurance money paid to it under such an insurance; and

　[(*b*) where an amount is payable by it under a quota share contract—

(i) so much of that amount as exceeds the amount of transferred losses that are declared on or before the date the contract takes effect (''the declared amount''), or

(ii) if the contract does not take effect, the amount so payable under the contract.]¹

(2) Subject to subsection (3) below, the following provisions apply where any insurance money is payable to a corporate member under a stop-loss insurance in respect of a loss in its underwriting business—

(a) if the underwriting year in which the loss is declared falls within two or more accounting periods, the apportioned part of the insurance money shall be treated as a trading receipt in computing the profits arising from the business for each of those periods; and

(b) if the underwriting year in which the loss is declared falls within a single accounting period, the insurance money shall be treated as a trading receipt in computing the profits arising from the business for that period.

(3) Where, as respects the payment of any such insurance money as is mentioned in subsection (2) above—

(a) the inspector is not notified of the payment at least 30 days before the time after which any assessment or further assessment of profits for any of the accounting periods or (as the case may be) the accounting period is precluded by section 34 of the Management Act (ordinary time limit), and

(b) the inspector is not entitled, after that time, to make any such assessment or further assessment by virtue of section 36 (fraudulent or negligent conduct) of that Act,

that subsection shall have effect in relation to the apportioned part of that insurance money or (as the case may be) that insurance money as if, instead of that accounting period, it referred to the accounting period in which the payment is made.

[(3A) Where the amount payable by a corporate member under a quota share contract is less than the declared amount—

(a) if the underwriting year in which the contract takes effect falls within a single accounting period, the difference between the two amounts (''the surplus'') shall be treated as a trading receipt in computing the profits arising from the member's underwriting business for that period, and

(b) if that underwriting year falls within two or more accounting periods, the apportioned part of the surplus shall be treated as a trading receipt in computing the profits arising from the member's underwriting business for each of those periods.]¹

[(3B) Where a corporate member has entered a quota share contract, any amount paid by it to cover a cash call in respect of transferred losses that are not declared at the time the contract takes effect shall be treated for the purposes of subsections (1)(b)(i) and (3A) above, as an amount payable under the contract at that time.]¹

[(4) In this section—

''apportioned part'', in relation to any insurance money or other amount, means a part apportioned under section 72 of the Taxes Act 1988;

''cash call'' means a request for funds which, in pursuance of a contract made in accordance with the rules and practices of Lloyd's, is made to a corporate member by the agent of a syndicate of which it is a member;

''quota share contract'' means any contract between a corporate member and another person which—

(a) is made in accordance with the rules or practice of Lloyd's; and

(b) provides for that other person to take over any rights and liabilities of the member under any of the syndicates of which it is a member;

and where the taking over of a member's rights and liabilities is conditional upon the occurrence of any event, the contract does not take effect until that event occurs; and

''transferred loss'', in relation to such a contract, means a loss for which that other person takes over liability under the contract (disregarding, in the case of a loss that has been declared at the time it is taken over, any part of it in respect of which the member has paid a cash call before that time).]¹

Commentary—*Simon's Direct Tax Service* E5.607, 620.
Amendments—¹ Sub-ss (1)(b), (4) substituted, sub-ss (3A), (3B) inserted, by FA 2002 s 86, Sch 32 paras 6–9 with effect for quota share contracts (within the meaning of FA 1993 s 178 or FA 1994 s 225) entered into after 16 April 2002.
Sub-s (1)(b) previously read as follows—

''(b) any amount payable by it under a quota share contract, irrespective of the purpose for which the contract was entered into.''.

Sub-s (4) previously read as follows—

''(4) In this section—

''apportioned part'', in relation to any insurance money, means a part apportioned under section 72 of the Taxes Act 1988;
''quota share contract'' means any contract between a corporate member and another person which—

(a) is made in accordance with the rules or practice of Lloyd's; and
(b) provides for that other person to take over any rights and liabilities of the member under any of the syndicates of which it is a member.''.

Miscellaneous

226 Provisions which are not to apply

(1) ...[1]

(2) ...[3]

[(3) No relevant contract (within the meaning of Schedule 26 to the Finance Act 2002) forming part of a premium trust fund of a corporate member shall be a derivative contract.][2]

Commentary—*Simon's Direct Tax Service* E5.607, 620.
Cross references—FA 2002 Sch 24 para 7 (on the repeal of sub-s (1) above, FA 1993 s 92–92AB shall apply for the purposes of computing for corporation tax the profits or losses of a corporate member's underwriting business).
Amendments—[1] Sub-s (1) repealed by FA 2002 ss 80, 141, Sch 24 paras 1, 7, Sch 40 Pt 3(11) with effect for accounting periods beginning after 30 September 2002. Sub-s (1) previously read as follows—

"(1) Sections 92 to 95 of the 1993 Act (corporation tax: currency to be used) shall not apply for the purposes of computing for the purposes of corporation tax the profits or losses of a corporate member's underwriting business.".
[2] Sub-s (3) substituted by FA 2002 s 83(1)(*b*), (3) Sch 27 para 16 with effect for accounting periods beginning after 30 September 2002. Sub-s (3) previously read as follows—

"(3) No contract or option forming part of a premiums trust fund of a corporate member shall be a qualifying contract for the purposes of Chapter II of this Part of this Act (interest rate and currency contracts and options).".
[3] Sub-s (2) repealed by FA 2002 s 141, Sch 40 Pt 3(10) with effect for accounting periods beginning after 30 September 2002. Sub-s (2) previously read as follows—

"No asset forming part of or liability attaching to a premiums trust fund of a corporate member shall be a qualifying asset or liability for the purposes of Chapter II of Part II of the 1993 Act (exchange gains and losses); and no contract forming part of such a fund shall be a currency contract for those purposes.".

227 Cessation: final underwriting year

(1) This section applies where a corporate member ceases to carry on its underwriting business, whether by reason of being wound up or otherwise.

(2) Subject to the provisions of any regulations made by the Board—

(*a*) the member's final underwriting year shall be that in which its deposit at Lloyd's is paid over to it or its liquidator, and

(*b*) the member's underwriting business shall be treated as continuing until the end of that year.

Commentary—*Simon's Direct Tax Service* E5.607, 620.
Regulations—Lloyd's Underwriters (Tax) Regulations, SI 1995/351 reg 16.

228 Lloyd's underwriters: individuals

(1) Chapter III of Part II of the 1993 Act (Lloyd's underwriters: individuals) shall have effect subject to the amendments specified in Schedule 21 to this Act.

(2) The following provisions shall cease to have effect, namely—

(*a*) section 627 of the Taxes Act 1988 (elections by Lloyd's underwriters with respect to retirement annuities);

(*b*) in section 641 of that Act, subsection (2) (elections by Lloyd's underwriters with respect to carry-back of contributions); and

(*c*) in section 183 of the 1993 Act, subsection (3) (amendments of sections 627(5) and 641(2) of the Taxes Act 1988).

(3) Subject to any provision to the contrary, the provisions of Schedule 21 to this Act have effect for the year 1994–95 and subsequent years of assessment.

(4) Subsection (2) above has effect for the year 1997–98 and subsequent years of assessment.

Commentary—*Simon's Direct Tax Service* E5.604, 607, 620.

Supplemental

229 Regulations

The Board may by regulations provide—

(*a*) for the assessment and collection of tax charged in accordance with section 219 above (so far as not provided for by Schedule 19 to the 1993 Act as applied by section 221 above);

(*b*) for making, in the event of any changes in the rules or practice of Lloyd's, such amendments of this Chapter as appear to the Board to be expedient having regard to those changes;

(*c*) for modifying the application of this Chapter in cases where a syndicate continues after the end of its closing year or a corporate member becomes insolvent or otherwise ceases to carry on its underwriting business;

[(*ca*) for modifying the application of this Chapter in relation to cases where assets forming part of a premiums trust fund are the subject of—

(i) ...[2]

(ii) any such arrangements or agreements as are mentioned in section 737E(2) and (8) of the Taxes Act 1988 (sale and repurchase of securities etc);][1]

(*d*) for giving credit for foreign tax.

4549 Income Tax, Corporation Tax and Capital Gains Tax FA 1994 s 230

Commentary—*Simon's Direct Tax Service* **E5.607, 620.**
Amendments—[1] Para (*ca*) inserted by FA 1995 s 83(2).
[2] Para (*ca*)(i) repealed by FA 1997 Sch 10 paras (6)(*b*), 7(1), Sch 18 Pt VI (10) with effect in relation to, and to transfers under, any arrangement made on or after 1 July 1997 by virtue of the Finance Act 1997, Schedule 10, (Appointed Day) Order, SI 1997/991.

230 Interpretation and commencement

(1) In this Chapter, unless the context otherwise requires—

"the 1993 Act" means the Finance Act 1993;
"ancillary trust fund", in relation to a corporate member, does not include a premiums trust fund but, subject to that, means any trust fund required or authorised by the rules of Lloyd's, or required by a members' agent or regulating trustee of the corporate member;
"closing year"—

(*a*) in relation to an underwriting year, means the underwriting year next but one following that year; and
(*b*) in relation to a syndicate, means the closing year of the underwriting year for which it was formed;

"corporate member" means a body corporate which is a member of Lloyd's and is or has been an underwriting member;
"inspector" includes any officer of the Board;
"the Management Act" means the Taxes Management Act 1970;
"managing agent", in relation to a syndicate and an underwriting year, means—

(*a*) the person registered as a managing agent at Lloyd's who was acting as such an agent for the syndicate at the end of that year, or
(*b*) such other person as may be determined in accordance with regulations made by the Board;

"member" means a member of Lloyd's who is or has been an underwriting member;
"members' agent", in relation to a corporate member, means a person registered as a members' agent at Lloyd's who has been appointed by the corporate member to act as its members' agent in respect of all or any part of its underwriting business;
["premium trust fund" means a trust fund into which premiums receivable by members are paid in compliance with a trust deed under section 10.3 of the Lloyd's Sourcebook made by the Financial Services Authority under the Financial Services and Markets Act 2000;][1]
"prescribed" means prescribed by regulations made by the Board;
"profits" includes gains;
"regulating trustee", in relation to a corporate member, means a person designated as such by the terms of any trust deed by which a premiums trust fund of the corporate member is constituted;
"stop-loss insurance" means any insurance taken out by a corporate member against losses in its underwriting business [except insurance taken out by entering a quota share contract (within the meaning of section 225 above)][2];
"syndicate" means a syndicate of underwriting members of Lloyd's formed for an underwriting year;
"underwriting business", in relation to a corporate member, means its underwriting business as a member of Lloyd's;
"underwriting year" means the calendar year.

(2) For the purposes of this Chapter, unless the contrary intention appears—

(*a*) the profits or losses of a corporate member's underwriting business include profits or losses arising to it—

(i) from assets forming part of a premiums trust fund or an ancillary trust fund; or
(ii) from assets employed by it in, or in connection with, its underwriting business; and

(*b*) any charge made on a corporate member by the managing agent of a syndicate of which it is a member, and any expense incurred on its behalf by the managing agent of such a syndicate, shall be treated as expenses arising directly from its membership of that syndicate.

(3) Subject to any provision to the contrary, the provisions of this Chapter have effect for accounting periods ending on or after 1st January 1994 or, as the case may require, for the underwriting year 1994 and subsequent underwriting years.

Commentary—*Simon's Direct Tax Service* **E5.607, 620.**
Amendments—[1] In sub-s (1), definition of "premium trust fund" substituted by the Financial Services and Markets Act 2000 (Consequential Amendments) (Taxes) Order, SI 2001/3629 arts 83, 85 with effect from 1 December 2001 immediately after the coming into force of the Financial Services and Markets Act 2000 ss 411, 432(1), Sch 20.
[2] In sub-s (1), words in definition of "stop-loss insurance" inserted by FA 2002 s 86, Sch 32 paras 6, 10 with effect for quota share contracts (within the meaning of FA 1993 s 178 or FA 1994 s 225) entered into after 16 April 2002.

PART VIII

MISCELLANEOUS AND GENERAL

Companies treated as non-resident

249 Certain companies treated as non-resident

(1) A company which—

(a) would (apart from this section) be regarded as resident in the United Kingdom for the purposes of the Taxes Acts, and

(b) is regarded for the purposes of any double taxation relief arrangements as resident in a territory outside the United Kingdom and not resident in the United Kingdom,

shall be treated for the purposes of the Taxes Acts as resident outside the United Kingdom and not resident in the United Kingdom.

(2) For the purpose of deciding whether the company is regarded as mentioned in subsection (1)(b) above it shall be assumed that—

(a) the company has made a claim for relief under the arrangements, and

(b) in consequence of the claim it falls to be decided whether the company is to be regarded as mentioned in subsection (1)(b) above.

(3) This section shall apply whether the company would otherwise be regarded as resident in the United Kingdom for the purposes of the Taxes Acts by virtue of section 66(1) of the Finance Act 1988 (company incorporated in UK to be regarded as resident there) or by virtue of some other rule of law.

(4) In this section—

(a) "double taxation relief arrangements" means arrangements having effect by virtue of section 788 of the Taxes Act 1988;

(b) "the Taxes Acts" has the same meaning as in the Taxes Management Act 1970.

(5) This section shall be deemed to have come into force on 30th November 1993.

Commentary—*Simon's Direct Tax Service* **D4.108.**

250 Companies treated as non-resident: supplementary

(1) Sections 130(1) to (6) and 131(1) to (5) of the Finance Act 1988 (securing payment of outstanding tax) shall not apply where the company concerned ceases to be resident in the United Kingdom on 30th November 1993 solely by virtue of the coming into force of section 249 above.

(2) References in section 179 of the Taxation of Chargeable Gains Act 1992 to a company ceasing to be a member of a group of companies do not apply to cases where a company ceases to be a member of a group by virtue of that company, or another company, ceasing to be resident in the United Kingdom on 30th November 1993 solely by virtue of the coming into force of section 249 above.

(3) Subsection (4) below applies where—

(a) a company ceases to be resident in the United Kingdom on 30th November 1993 solely by virtue of the coming into force of section 249 above, and

(b) by virtue of section 185(2) of the Taxation of Chargeable Gains Act 1992 it is deemed to have disposed of assets immediately before the time it so ceases.

(4) In such a case—

(a) if the company makes an actual disposal of the assets on or before the day when (apart from this subsection) corporation tax is due and payable in respect of the deemed disposal, the tax shall be due and payable on that day;

(b) in any other case the tax shall be due and payable on the day the company makes an actual disposal of the assets or on 30th November 1999 (whichever falls first).

(5) Where subsection (4) above applies, for the purposes of section 87A of the Taxes Management Act 1970 (interest on overdue corporation tax) the tax shall be treated as becoming due and payable on the relevant day in accordance with section 10 of the Taxes Act 1988; and the relevant day is the day on which the tax is due and payable by virtue of subsection (4) above.

(6) If the company makes an actual disposal of part of the assets subsections (4) and (5) above shall be applied separately as regards the different parts and the tax shall be apportioned (and carry interest) accordingly.

Commentary—*Simon's Direct Tax Service* **D4.108.**
Revenue Internal Guidance—Capital Gains Tax Manual CG 42456 (sub-s (4) expanded explanation of the due and payable date provisions).

251 Companies treated as non-resident: repeals

(1) For the purposes of this section—

(a) the relevant date is 30th November 1993;

(b) the 1992 Act is the Taxation of Chargeable Gains Act 1992.

4551 Supplemental Provisions Relating to Personal Reliefs FA 1994 Sch 8

(2) (*amended* TA 1988 s 468F which has itself been repealed).

(3), (4) (*amend* TA 1988 ss 742(8), 745(4), 749, 751).

(5)–(11) (*repeal* TCGA 1992 ss 139(3), 160, 186, 188 and *amend* ss 166(2), 171(2), 172(3), 175(2), 187, 211(3)).

(12) (*repealed* FA 1993 s 61(3) and is itself repealed by FA 1996 Sch 41 Pt V(3) with effect for accounting periods ending after 31 March 1996).

Commentary—*Simon's Direct Tax Service.*

Privatisations

252 Railways

(1) Schedule 24 to this Act (which makes provision in connection with transfers and other disposals under or by virtue of the Railways Act 1993) shall have effect.

(2) Paragraphs 4(1) and 17 of that Schedule, and this section so far as relating to those provisions, shall be taken to have come into force on 5th November 1993 (the date on which the Railways Act 1993 was passed).

(3) Subject to subsection (2) above, this section and that Schedule shall be taken to have come into force on 11th January 1994.

Commentary—*Simon's Direct Tax Service* **B3.246.**

253 Northern Ireland Airports Limited

Schedule 25 to this Act (which makes provision in connection with the transfer of the undertaking of Northern Ireland Airports Limited) shall have effect.

Commentary—*Simon's Direct Tax Service* **B3.246.**

Management

254 Practice and procedure in connection with appeals

(*Amends* TMA 1970 s 56B).

255 Calling for documents of taxpayers and others

(*Amends* TMA 1970 s 20).

General

257 Interpretation and construction

(1) In this Act "the Taxes Act 1988" means the Income and Corporation Taxes Act 1988.

(2) Part V of this Act shall be construed as one with Part I of the Oil Taxation Act 1975 and in Part V that Act is referred to as "the principal Act".

(3) Part VI of this Act shall be construed as one with the Stamp Act 1891.

258 Repeals

The enactments specified in Schedule 26 to this Act (which include provisions which are already spent) are hereby repealed to the extent specified in the third column of that Schedule, but subject to any provision of that Schedule.

259 Short title

This Act may be cited as the Finance Act 1994.

SCHEDULE 8

SUPPLEMENTAL PROVISIONS RELATING TO PERSONAL RELIEFS

Section 77

The Taxes Act 1988

1 (*amends* s 257A(6)).

2—(1), (2) (*amend* s 257BA(1), (2), (3)).

(3) Any election made for the purposes of section 257BA of the Taxes Act 1988 which—

    (a) has been made before the coming into force of this paragraph, and

    (b) apart from this paragraph, would have effect in accordance with that section for the year 1994–95 or any subsequent year, shall so have effect as if it were an election for the purposes of that section as amended by this paragraph.

3 (*amends* s 257BB).

4–9 (*repealed* by FA 1999 s 139, Sch 20 Pt III(3) with effect from the year 2000–01).

10–12 (*amend* ss 265(3), 796(1) and *insert* 276(1A)).

The Taxes Management Act 1970 (c 9)

13 (*amends* s 37A).

SCHEDULE 9
MORTGAGE INTEREST RELIEF ETC
Section 81

The Taxes Act 1988

1 (*amends* s 74(*o*)).

2 (*amended* s 237(5); and *repealed* in relation to distributions made after 5 April 1999 by F(No 2)A 1997 Sch 8 Pt II (9)).

3 (*repeals* s 353(4), (5)).

4–6 (*amended* TA 1988 ss 355(4), 356(1), 356A(3); *repealed* in relation to any payment of interest made after 5 April 1995 by FA 1995 Sch 29 Pt VIII(2).)

7—(1) (*amends* ss 356D(1), 357(1))[1].

(2)–(4) (*amended* ss 357A(7), 357B(1), (6), 357C(1), (2); *repealed* in relation to any payment of interest made after 5 April 1995 by FA 1995 Sch 29 Pt VIII(2).)

Amendment—[1] Sub-para (1) repealed by FA 1999 s 139, Sch 20 Pt III(7) with effect for payments of interest within FA 1999 s 38(3), (4).

8 (*inserted* s 358(4A); *repealed* in relation to any payment of interest made after 5 April 1995 by FA 1995 Sch 29 Pt VIII(2).)

9 (*amends* s 368(1)).

10—(1) (*amends* s 370(2)).

(2) (*inserts* s 370(6A))[1].

Amendment—[1] Sub-para (2) repealed by FA 1999 s 139, Sch 20 Pt III(7) with effect for payments of interest within FA 1999 s 38(3), (4).

11 (*amends* s 375(3)).

The Finance Act 1993 (c 34)

12 (*repeals* s 57(7)).

[SCHEDULE 10
MEDICAL INSURANCE][1]
Section 83

Amendments—[1] This Schedule repealed by F(No 2)A 1997 Sch 8 Pt II(2) with effect for 1997–98 and subsequent years of assessment except in relation to cases in which relief due under FA 1989 s 54 in respect of any payment is unaffected by the provisions of F(No 2)A 1997 s 17(1) (see the Amendments note to FA 1989 s 54).

Introductory

1 *In this Schedule "the 1989 Act" means the Finance Act 1989.*

Reduction of relief

2—(1)–(3) (*amend* FA 1989 s 54).

(4) *This paragraph shall apply in relation to payments made on or after 6th April 1994.*

3—(1) (*repeals* TA 1988 ss 257D(8)(d), 265(3)(d)).

(2) *This paragraph shall apply in relation to payments made on or after 6th April 1994.*

Surviving spouse

4—*(1) (inserts FA 1989 s 54(2A)).*

(2) This paragraph shall apply where the first or only payment to be made in respect of a premium under the contract after the death occurs is made on or after 6th April 1994.

Small benefits and abolition of certification

5—*(1)–(7) (amend FA 1989 s 55).*

(8) This paragraph shall apply where the time which is the relevant time for the purposes of section 55 falls on or after 1st July 1994.

6 *The Board shall not certify a contract under section 56 of the 1989 Act in such a way that the certification is expressed to take effect on or after 1st July 1994.*

SCHEDULE 11

EXTENSION OF ROLL-OVER RELIEF ON RE-INVESTMENT

Section 91

1 Chapter IA of Part V of the Taxation of Chargeable Gains Act 1992 shall be amended as follows.

Disposals on which relief available

2–6 *(amend ss 164A, 164H(1), 164L(10), substitute s 164B and repeal ss 164C–164E).*

Acquisitions on which relief available

7 *(substitutes s 164A(8)).*

Retirement relief

8 *(repeals s 164A(11) and inserts s 164BA).*

Clawback

9—*(1) (amends s 164F).*

(2) Section 164F as amended by sub-paragraph (1) above shall have effect as follows—

    (a) the reference in subsection (1) to consideration treated as reduced under section 164A includes consideration treated as reduced under section 164D,
    (b) the reference in subsection (3) to a gain having been charged on any disposal includes any gain having been carried forward from any disposal of shares, and
    (c) the amounts referred to in subsection (4A)(a) and (b)(i) shall be treated as reduced by any amounts carried forward from any disposal of shares.

(3) References in sub-paragraph (2) above to an amount being carried forward from a disposal of shares are references to the reduction by that amount, in accordance with section 164D(3)(a), of the amount of the consideration for the disposal of those shares.

Anti-avoidance

10 *(inserts s 164L(10A), (10B) and amends s 164L(11)).*

Miscellaneous

11 *(inserts s 164N(1A)).*

SCHEDULE 12

INDEXATION LOSSES: TRANSITIONAL RELIEF

Section 93

(Spent; see FA 1994 s 93(11)).

Commentary—*Simon's Direct Tax Service* **C2.301, D2.630.**

SCHEDULE 13

EMPLOYEE SHARE OWNERSHIP TRUSTS

Section 102

Introduction

1 The Finance Act 1989 shall be amended as provided in this Schedule.

Trustees

2–5 (*insert* Sch 5 para 3(5), 3A–3C, 12A and *amend* Sch 5, para 12).

Securities

6, 7 (*amend* s 69, Sch 5, para 9).

Interpretation

8 (*inserts* Sch 5 para 17).

SCHEDULE 14

DISTRIBUTIONS OF AUTHORISED UNIT TRUSTS

Section 112

1 Chapter III of Part XII of the Taxes Act 1988 shall be amended in accordance with paragraphs 2 to 5 of this Schedule.

The new sections

2 (*inserts* ss 468H–468R).

Other amendments

3–6 (*amend* TA 1988 ss 468, 469, 834(3) and *repeal* ss 468F, 468G).

Commencement

7—(1) Subject to sub-paragraph (2) below, this Schedule shall have effect in relation to distribution periods beginning on or after 1st April 1994.

(2) Nothing in the amendments made by this Schedule shall be taken to permit—

    (*a*) the total amount shown in the distribution accounts for a distribution period of an authorised unit trust, or

    (*b*) a part of that total amount,

to be shown as available for distribution as foreign income dividends unless the distribution date for that distribution period is 1st July 1994 or a subsequent date.

SCHEDULE 15

ENTERPRISE INVESTMENT SCHEME

Section 137

Amendments of the Taxes Act 1988

1 Chapter III of Part VII of the Taxes Act 1988 shall be amended as follows:

2 (*substitutes* ss 289, 289A, 289B for s 289 and also substitutes the heading preceding it).

3—(1) (*substitutes* s 290(2)).

(2) Sub-paragraph (1) above shall have effect for the year 1994–95 and subsequent years of assessment.

(3) An individual shall not be eligible for relief in respect of the year 1993–94 in respect of any amount subscribed for eligible shares (whether the shares are issued in that or a subsequent year) which, when aggregated with the amounts (if any) on which relief is claimed under the old scheme in respect of that year, exceeds £40,000.

(4) In this paragraph the "old scheme" means Chapter III of Part VII of the Taxes Act 1988 as it had effect before the amendments made by this Schedule.

4—(1) (*amends* s 290A).

(2) References in that section to amounts raised through the issue of eligible shares include amounts raised through the issue before 1st January 1994 of shares which were eligible shares under the old scheme; and the ''old scheme'' has the same meaning as in paragraph 3 above.

5 (*substitutes* ss 291, 291A, 291B for s 291).

6–9 (*amend* ss 292, 293, 294 and *repeal* s 296(6)).

10 (*amends* TA 1988 s 297).

Amendments—Para 10(*c*) repealed by FA 2000 s 156, Sch 40 Pt II(5) with effect for shares issued after 5 April 2000.
Para 10(*d*) repealed by FA 2001 s 110, Sch 33 Pt II(3) with effect—

(*a*) in relation to shares issued after 6 March 2001, and
(*b*) in respect of the application of TA 1988 Pt VII Chapter III and TCGA 1992 Sch 5B after 6 March 2001 in relation to shares—
    (i) that were issued after 31 December 1993 but before 7 March 2001, and
    (ii) to which income tax relief or deferral relief was attributable immediately before 7 March 2001.

11–20 (*amend* ss 298–305A).

Amendments—Para 17(*b*), (*c*) repealed by FA 2001 s 110, Sch 33 Pt II(3) with effect—

(*a*) in relation to shares issued on or after 7 March 2001, and
(*b*) in relation to shares issued before that date, in respect of the application of TA 1988 Pt VII Chapter III and TCGA 1992 Sch 5B in relation to—
    (i) value received (within the meaning of TA 1988 s 300 or TCGA 1992 Sch 5B para 13) and
    (ii) repayments made,

on or after that date.

21 (*amends* s 306; *repealed in part* by FA 1996 Sch 41 Pt V(11) with effect for purposes of income tax from the year 1996–97 and for purposes of corporation tax as respects accounting periods ending on or after the appointed day (1 July 1999 by virtue of Finance Act 1994, Section 199, (Appointed Day) Order, SI 1998/3173; *repealed in part* by FA 2001 s 110, Sch 33 Pt II(3) with effect for shares issued after 5 April 2001.)).

22–24 (*amend* ss 307, 308 and *repeal* s 309).

25 (*amended* s 310).[1]

Amendments—[1] Para 25(*d*) repealed by FA 1998 Sch 27 Part III(13) with effect in relation to shares issued after 1 July 1997.

26, 27 (*amend* ss 311, 312).

Amendments of the Taxation of Chargeable Gains Act 1992

28 The Taxation of Chargeable Gains Act 1992 shall be amended as follows:

29–31 (*amend* ss 150, 164M and *insert* s 150A).

32—(1) (*inserts* s 164MA).

(2) This paragraph has effect in relation to shares issued on or after 1st January 1994.

33, 34 (*amend* ss 164N(1), 231(1)).

SCHEDULE 16

FOREIGN INCOME DIVIDENDS

Section 138

PART I

THE NEW CHAPTER

1 (*repealed* by F(No 2)A 1997 Sch 8 Pt II (11)).

PART II

LIABILITY FOR AND COLLECTION OF ADVANCE CORPORATION TAX

2 (*repealed by* FA 1998 Sch 27 Part III(2) with effect in relation to distributions made after 5 April 1999).

3 ...[1, 2]

Amendments—[1] Sub-paras (5)–(10), (12) repealed by F(No 2)A 1997 Sch 8 Pt II(11) with effect in relation to distributions made after 5 April 1999.
[2] Sub-paras (1)–(4), (11), (13) repealed by FA 1998 Sch 27 Pt III(2) with effect in relation to return periods and accounting periods beginning after 5 April 1999.

PART III
INSURANCE COMPANIES ETC

4 (*repealed* by F(No 2)A 1997 Sch 8 Pt II (11)).

5 (*repealed in part* by FA 1995 Sch 29 Pt VIII(5) with effect for accounting periods beginning after 31 December 1994; and *in part* by F(No 2)A 1997 Sch 8 Pt II (11) with effect for accounting periods beginning after 5 April 1999).

6–9 (*repealed* by F(No 2)A 1997 Sch 8 Pt II(6), (11)).

PART IV
OTHER PROVISIONS
Penalties

10 (*amends* TMA 1970 s 98 Table).

Small companies' relief

11 (*repealed* by F(No 2)A 1997 Sch 8 Pt II).

Expenses of management

12 (*repealed* by F(No 2)A 1997 Sch 8 Pt II).

Group income

13 (*repealed* by F(No 2)A 1997 Sch 8 Pt II (11)).

Mutual business etc

14 (*repealed* by F(No 2)A 1997 Sch 8 Pt II (11)).

Discretionary trusts

15 (*repealed* by F(No 2)A 1997 Sch 8 Pt II (11)).

Personal representatives

16 (*repealed by* F(No 2)A 1997 Sch 8 Pt II (11)).

Purchase and sale of securities

17 (*amends* TA 1988 s 731).

Manufactured dividends

18, 19 (*repealed* by FA 1997 Sch 18 Pt IV(10) with effect in relation to payments made on or after 1 July 1997 by virtue of the Finance Act 1997, Schedule 10, (Appointed Day) Order, SI 1997/991).

Interest on tax overpaid

20 (*repealed by* FA 1998 Sch 27 Part III(2) with effect in relation to return periods and accounting periods beginning after 5 April 1999).

SCHEDULE 17
MINOR CORRECTIONS
Section 146

1–3 (*amend* TA 1988 ss 43(1), 271(1), (2), 356D(6)).

Amendment—This paragraph repealed by FA 1999 s 139, Sch 20 Pt III(7) with effect for payments of interest within FA 1999 s 38(3), (4).

4 (*amended* TA 1988 s 431(5); *repealed* by FA 1995 Sch 29 Pt VIII(5), with effect for accounting periods beginning after 31 December 1994).

5–9 (*amend* TA 1988 ss 561(2), 576(5), 768(6), 842(4), 843(2), Sch 11, para 8(*b*)).

SCHEDULE 18

INTEREST RATE AND CURRENCY CONTRACTS: INSURANCE AND MUTUAL TRADING COMPANIES

Section 169

Note—This Schedule repealed by FA 2002 ss 83(2), (3), 141, Sch 40 Pt 3(13) with effect for accounting periods beginning after 30 September 2002.
Commentary—*Simon's Direct Tax Service* **Division D2.10.**

[Application of insurance companies provisions relating to loan relationships][1]

*[**1**—(1) Part I of Schedule 11 to the Finance Act 1996 (special provision with respect to loan relationships for insurance companies) shall have effect (subject to sub-paragraph (2) below) in relation to qualifying contracts as it has effect in relation to loan relationships which are creditor relationships within the meaning of Chapter II of Part IV of that Act.*

(2) That Part of that Schedule shall have effect in its application in relation to qualifying contracts, as if—

    (a) references to section 82(2) of the Finance Act 1996 were references to section 159 of this Act, and

    (b) references to credits and debits given by Chapter II of Part IV of that Act in respect of a loan relationship were references, respectively, to the profits and losses deriving from the contract.][1]

*[**1A**—(1) Where the I minus E basis is applied for any accounting period in respect of the life assurance business or capital redemption business of any insurance company, this Chapter shall have effect for that period in relation to contracts and options held for the purposes of that business as if the words in subsection (10) of section 150A from ''but references'' onwards were omitted.*

(2) Expressions used in sub-paragraph (1) above and in Part I of Schedule 11 to the Finance Act 1996 have the same meanings in this paragraph as in that Part of that Schedule.][1]

Modifications—Words ''or capital redemption business'' in para 1A(1) omitted in applying life assurance provisions of the Corporation Tax Acts to insurance companies carrying on capital redemption business with effect for accounting periods ending after 30 June 1999: see Insurance Companies (Capital Redemption Business) (Modification of the Corporation Tax Acts) Regulations, SI 1999/498 reg 13.
Amendments—[1] Paras 1, 1A and preceding heading substituted for paras 1, 2 by FA 1996 ss 104, 105(1), Sch 14 para 79 with effect for accounting periods ending after 31 March 1996, subject to transitional provisions in FA 1996 Sch 15.

Non-life mutual business

*3**—(1) Subject to sub-paragraph (2) below, sub-paragraph (3) below applies where a qualifying contract was at any time in an accounting period of a mutual trading company held by the company for the purposes of any non-life mutual business carried on by it.*

(2) Where the qualifying contract was held partly for the purposes of the non-life mutual business and partly for other purposes—

    (a) the profit or loss on the contract for the period shall be apportioned on a just and reasonable basis, and

    (b) any reference in sub-paragraph (3) below to that profit or loss shall be construed as a reference to so much of it as is referable to the non-life mutual business.

(3) Notwithstanding anything in section 159 of this Act—

    (a) no part of the profit or loss on the contract for the period shall be treated for the purposes of the Tax Acts as a profit or loss of a trade or part of a trade, and

    (b) accordingly, the whole of that profit or loss shall be treated for the purposes of section 160 of this Act as a non-trading profit or loss.

Commentary—*Simon's Direct Tax Service* **D2.1040.**

Interpretation

4 In this Schedule—

    ...[2]

    ...[1]

    ''non-life mutual business'' means any mutual trading, or any mutual insurance or other mutual business, which (in either case) is not life assurance business.

...[2]

Commentary—*Simon's Direct Tax Service* **D2.1040.**
Amendments—[1] Definition ''life assurance business'' repealed by FA 1995 Sch 8 para 10(4), with effect for accounting periods beginning on or after 1 January 1995.
[2] Definition ''the I minus E basis'' and final words (which were added by FA 1995 Sch 8 para 10(4)) repealed by FA 1996 Sch 41 Pt V(3) with effect for accounting periods ending after 31 March 1996, subject to transitional provisions in FA 1996 Sch 15.

SCHEDULE 19

MANAGEMENT: OTHER AMENDMENTS

Section 196

PART I

AMENDMENTS OF MANAGEMENT ACT

Notice of liability to income tax and capital gains tax

1—(1) (*substitutes* TMA 1970 s 7).

(2) This paragraph has effect as respects the year 1995–96 and subsequent years of assessment.

European Economic Interest Groupings

2 (*amends* TMA 1970 s 12A(2)).

Records for purposes of returns

3 (*inserts* TMA 1970 s 12B).

Recovery of overpayment of tax etc

4 (*inserts* TMA 1970 s 30(1B) and *substitutes* s 30(5)).

Assessing procedure

5—(1) (*inserts* TMA 1970 s 30A).

(2) This paragraph, so far as it relates to partnerships whose trades, professions or businesses are set up and commenced before 6th April 1994, has effect as respects the year 1997–98 and subsequent years of assessment.

Amendment of partnership statement where loss of tax discovered

6 (*inserts* TMA 1970 s 30B).

Right of appeal

7 (*substituted* TMA 1970 s 31(1)–(3); *repealed by* FA 2001 s 110, Sch 33 Pt II(13) with effect in accordance with FA 2001 s 88, Sch 29).

Error or mistake

8—(1) ...[1]

(2) (*repeals* TMA 1970 s 33(2) proviso and *inserts* TMA 1970 s 33(2A)).

Amendments—[1] Sub-para (1) repealed by FA 1998 s 165, Sch 27 Part III(28) with effect in relation to accounting periods ending after 30 June 1999 (by virtue of Finance Act 1994, Section 199, (Appointed Day) Order, SI 1998/3173 art 2).

9 (*inserts* TMA 1970 s 33A).

Time limits for assessments

10 ...

Amendments—This paragraph repealed by FA 1998 s 165, Sch 27 Part III(28) with effect in relation to accounting periods ending after 30 June 1999 (by virtue of Finance Act 1994, Section 199, (Appointed Day) Order, SI 1998/3173 art 2).

11, 12 (*amend* TMA 1970 ss 36(1), 40(1), (2) and *substitute* s 36(2)).

Claims etc

13 (*substitutes* TMA 1970 s 42).

14, 15 ...

Amendments—These paragraphs repealed by FA 1998 s 165, Sch 27 Part III(28) with effect in relation to accounting periods ending after 30 June 1999 (by virtue of Finance Act 1994, Section 199, (Appointed Day) Order, SI 1998/3173 art 2).

Determination of Commissioners

16 ...

Amendments—This paragraph repealed by FA 1998 s 165, Sch 27 Part III(28) with effect in relation to accounting periods ending after 30 June 1999 (by virtue of Finance Act 1994, Section 199, (Appointed Day) Order, SI 1998/3173 art 2).

Procedure on appeal

17—(1) (*substitutes* TMA 1970 s 50(6), (7); *amended by* the General and Special Commissioners (Amendment of Enactments) Regulations, SI 1994/1813, Sch 1 para 25(*b*) and Sch 2 Pt I).

(2) (*amends* TMA 1970 s 50(8)).

(3) ...[1]

Amendments—[1] Sub-para (3) repealed by FA 1998 s 165, Sch 27 Part III(28) with effect in relation to accounting periods ending after 30 June 1999 (by virtue of Finance Act 1994, Section 199, (Appointed Day) Order, SI 1998/3173 art 2).

Postponement of tax pending appeal

18 (*substitutes* TMA 1970 s 55(1) and *amends* s 55(2), (10)).

Collection and recovery

19 ...

Amendments—This paragraph repealed by FA 1998 s 165, Sch 27 Part III(28) with effect in relation to accounting periods ending after 30 June 1999 (by virtue of Finance Act 1994, Section 199, (Appointed Day) Order, SI 1998/3173 art 2).

20 (*amends* TMA 1970 ss 69, 70(2) and *repeals* s 70(3); *repealed* by FA 2001 s 110, Sch 33 Pt II(14) with effect for proceedings begun, or a counterclaim made, and a set-off first claimed after the passing of FA 2001).

21 (*amends* TMA 1970 ss 69, 70(2) and *repeals* s 70(3)).

22—(1) (*inserts* TMA 1970 s 70A).

(2) This paragraph has effect as respects cheques received on or after 6th April 1996.

Interest on overdue tax or tax recovered

23 (*repealed* by FA 1996 s 131(3), Sch 41 Pt V(6)).

24 (*amends* TMA 1970 s 87A).

Penalties

25–33 (*substitute* TMA 1970 ss 93, 98(2), (2A), (2B) (for s 98(2)), *insert* ss 93A, 95A, 97AA, 103AA and *amend* ss 95(1), (3), 98B(3), (4), 100B(1), (2), 103(2)).

Interpretation

34—(1) (*amends* TMA 1970 s 118(1); *amended by* the General and Special Commissioners (Amendment of Enactments) Regulations, SI 1994/1813, reg 2(1), Sch 1 para 25(*c*)).

(2) (*repeals* TMA 1970 s 118(3)).

(3) Sub-paragraph (2) above, so far as it relates to partnerships whose trades, professions or businesses are set up and commenced before 6th April 1994, has effect as respects the year 1997–98 and subsequent years of assessment.

Claims etc not included in returns

35 (*inserts* TMA 1970 Sch 1A).

36—(1) (*amended* TMA 1970 Sch 2 para 1; *repealed* by FA 1996 Sch 41 Pt V(12) with effect in relation to any proceedings relating to the year 1996–97 or any subsequent year of assessment, and any proceedings relating to an accounting period ending on or after the appointed day (1 July 1999 by virtue of Finance Act 1994, Section 199, (Appointed Day) Order, SI 1998/3173)).

(2) (*amended* TMA 1970 Sch 2 para 2; *repealed* by FA 1996 Sch 41 Pt V(12) with effect in relation to any proceedings relating to the year 1996–97 or any subsequent year of assessment, and any proceedings relating to an accounting period ending on or after the appointed day (1 July 1999 by virtue of SI 1998/3173)).

(3) (*substitutes* TMA 1970 Sch 2 para 3; *repealed* by FA 1996 Sch 41 Pt V(12) with effect in relation to any proceedings relating to the year 1996–97 or any subsequent year of assessment, and any proceedings relating to an accounting period ending on or after the appointed day (1 July 1999 by virtue of SI 1998/3173)).

PART II
AMENDMENTS OF TAXES ACT 1988

Time limits for claims under section 96

37—(1) (*amends* TA 1988 s 96(8)).

(2) This paragraph has effect where the first of the two years of assessment to which the claim relates is the year 1996–97 or any subsequent year.

Interest on Schedule E tax

38 (*amends* TA 1988 s 203(2)(*dd*)).

Time limits for claims under sections 534 and 537A

39, 40 (*amend* TA 1988 ss 534(5), 537A(5)).

Repayment supplements: income tax

41—(1)–(3) (*substitute* TA 1988 ss 824(1), (3) and *repeal* s 824(5), (9) (in part), (10)).

(4) This paragraph, so far as it relates to partnerships whose trades, professions or businesses are set up and commenced before 6th April 1994, has effect as respects the year 1997–98 and subsequent years of assessment.

Interest on tax overpaid

42 (*amends* TA 1988 s 826(2)).

Time limits for elections under Schedule 5

43 (*amends* TA 1988 Sch 5 para 2(3), *substitutes* Sch 5 paras 2(4)(*a*), (*b*), 6(2)–(4) and *inserts* Sch 5 para 2(5), (6)).

PART III
AMENDMENTS OF OTHER ENACTMENTS

Setting of rates of interest

44 (*amends* FA 1989 s 178(2)(*f*)).

Class 4 contributions

45 (*amends* Social Security Contributions and Benefits Act 1992 s 16(1)—see Orange Book).

Repayment supplements: capital gains tax

46 (*amends* TCGA 1992 s 283(1), (4), *substitutes* s 283(2) and *repeals* TCGA 1992 s 283(5)).

SCHEDULE 20

CHANGES FOR FACILITATING SELF-ASSESSMENT: TRANSITIONAL PROVISIONS AND SAVINGS

Section 218

Commentary—*Simon's Direct Tax Service* E1.201, 301.
Revenue Interpretation RI 123—Changes of accounting date in advance of transition to current year basis of assessment.
RI 129—Timing of refunds of VAT to opticians.
Cross Reference—See FA 1995 s 123, Sch 22 (prevention of exploitation of provisions of this Schedule).

Assessment under Cases I and II of Schedule D

1—(1) Subject to paragraph 3(2) below, this paragraph applies in the case of a trade, profession or vocation set up and commenced before 6th April 1994 and continuing after 5th April 1997.

(2) The basis period for the year 1996–97 shall be as follows—

 (*a*) where an accounting date falls within the year, the period of twelve months ending with that accounting date; and

 (*b*) in any other case, the period of twelve months ending with 5th April 1997.

(3) Where the basis period for the year 1996–97 is given by paragraph (*b*) of sub-paragraph (2) above, section 62 of the Taxes Act 1988 shall have effect in relation to the accounting change by virtue of which that paragraph applies as if that change were made in the first year of assessment in which accounts are made up to the new date.

(4) In this paragraph "accounting date" and "the new date" have the same meanings as in section 62 of the Taxes Act 1988.

2—(1) Subject to paragraph 3(2) and (4) below, this paragraph applies in the case of a trade, profession or vocation set up and commenced before 6th April 1994 and continuing after 5th April 1997.

(2) Subject to sub-paragraph (3) below, sections 60 to 63A of the Taxes Act 1988 shall have effect in relation to the year 1996–97 as if they required income tax under Case I or II of Schedule D to be charged on the appropriate percentage of the aggregate of—

   (*a*) the full amount of the profits or gains of the basis period for that year, and
   (*b*) the full amount of the profits or gains of the relevant period.

(3) Where, in the case of the year 1995–96, the period on the profits or gains of which income tax is chargeable under Case I or II of Schedule D is that year, sub-paragraph (2) above shall have effect as if for the words from "the appropriate percentage" to the end there were substituted the words "the full amount of the profits or gains of that year".

(4) Section 63A of the Taxes Act 1988 shall have effect as if the amount of profits or gains of the basis period for the year 1997–98 which arise [after the end of—

   (*a*) the basis period for the year 1996–97; or
   (*b*) in the case of a trade or profession carried on by a person in partnership with other persons, the basis period of the partnership for that year,

and (in either case)][1] before 6th April 1997 were an overlap profit for the purposes of that section.

[(4A) In calculating the amount of the profits or gains of the basis period for the year 1997–98 which arise as mentioned in sub-paragraph (4) above, any deduction of a capital allowance and any addition of a balancing charge shall be ignored.][2]

[(4B) Sub-paragraph (4A) above does not apply in the case of a trade or profession carried on by persons who include both an individual and a company.][2]

(5) In this paragraph—

   "the appropriate percentage" means the following expressed as a percentage, that is, 365 divided by the number of days in the basis period for the year 1996–97 and the relevant period taken together;
   "the relevant period" means the period which—

      (*a*) begins immediately after the end of the period on the profits or gains of which tax is chargeable for the year 1995–96, and
      (*b*) ends immediately before the beginning of the basis period for the year 1996–97.

Revenue Interpretation RI 190—Application of sub-para (4) above to cases involving farmers' averaging under TA 1988 s 96.
RI 193—Use of apportionment in the calculation of transitional overlap profit.
Cross reference—See FA 1995 s 123 Sch 22 (prevention of exploitation of provisions of sub-paras (2), (4) above).
Amendments—[1] Words in sub-para (4) inserted by FA 1995 s 122(2).
[2] Sub-paras (4A), (4B) inserted by FA 1995 s 122(3).

3—(1) In the case of a trade, profession or vocation set up and commenced before 6th April 1994 and ceasing before 6th April 1997, sections 60 to 63 of the Taxes Act 1988 shall have effect as if sections 200 to 205 of this Act had not been enacted.

(2) If, in the case of a trade, profession or vocation set up and commenced before 6th April 1994 and ceasing on or after 6th April 1997 but before 6th April 1998, an officer of the Board so directs—

   (*a*) paragraphs 1 and 2 above shall not apply, and
   (*b*) sections 60 to 63 of the Taxes Act 1988 shall have effect as if sections 200 to 205 of this Act had not been enacted.

(3) Sub-paragraph (4) below applies where, in the case of a trade, profession or vocation set up and commenced before 6th April 1994 and ceasing on or after 6th April 1998 but before 6th April 1999, the profits or gains arising in the year 1996–97 exceed—

   (*a*) the amount on which income tax has been charged for that year; or
   (*b*) the amount on which income tax would have been charged for that year if no deduction or set-off under section 385 of the Taxes Act 1988 had been allowed.

(4) Notwithstanding anything in sections 60 to 63A of the Taxes Act 1988 if an officer of the Board so directs, income tax for the year 1996–97 shall be charged instead, but subject to any deduction or set-off under section 385 of that Act, on the amount of the profits or gains arising in that year.

(5) All such adjustments shall be made, whether by way of an assessment to tax or a reduction or discharge of such an assessment or otherwise, as may be necessary to give effect to a direction under sub-paragraph (2) or (4) above.

Cross reference—See FA 1998 s 56(5) (officer of the Board prevented from giving a direction under this section in the case of a person whose trade is deemed to cease on 5 April 1998 under FA 1998 s 56(2)).

Assessment under Case III of Schedule D

4—(1) Subject to sub-paragraph (3) below, this paragraph applies in the case of income which—

(a) is from a source arising before 6th April 1994 and continuing after 5th April 1998, and

(b) is chargeable to tax under Case III of Schedule D.

(2) Section 64 of the Taxes Act 1988 shall have effect in relation to the year 1996–97 as if it required income tax under Case III of Schedule D to be computed on 50 per cent of the aggregate of—

(a) the full amount of the income arising within that year; and

(b) the full amount of the income arising within the year 1995–96.

(3) This paragraph does not apply if section 66(1)(c) of that Act applied in relation to the year 1995–96.

Cross reference—See FA 1995 s 123, Sch 22 (prevention of exploitation of provisions of sub-para (2), above).

5 In the case of income which—

(a) is from a source arising before 6th April 1994 and ceasing before 6th April 1998, and

(b) is chargeable to tax under Case III of Schedule D,

sections 64, 66 and 67 of the Taxes Act 1988 shall have effect as if section 206 of this Act had not been enacted.

Assessment under Cases IV and V of Schedule D

6—(1) This paragraph applies in the case of income which—

(a) is from a source arising before 6th April 1994 and continuing after 5th April 1998, and

(b) is chargeable to tax under Case IV or V of Schedule D.

(2) Subject to sub-paragraph (3) below, section 65 of the Taxes Act 1988 shall have effect in relation to the year 1996–97 as if—

(a) subsection (1) required income tax chargeable under Case IV or V of Schedule D to be computed on 50 per cent of the aggregate of—

(i) the full amount of the income arising within that year; and

(ii) the full amount of the income arising within the year 1995–96,

subject (in either case) to the deductions and allowances there mentioned in the case of income not received in the United Kingdom;

(b) paragraph (a) of subsection (5) required income tax chargeable under Case IV of Schedule D to be computed on 50 per cent of the aggregate of—

(i) the full amount, so far as it can be computed, of the sums received in the United Kingdom in that year; and

(ii) the full amount, so far as it can be computed, of the sums received in the United Kingdom in the year 1995–96,

without (in either case) any deduction or abatement; and

(c) paragraph (b) of that subsection required income tax chargeable under Case V of Schedule D to be computed on 50 per cent of the aggregate of—

(i) the full amount of the actual sums received in the United Kingdom in that year; and

(ii) the full amount of the actual sums received in the United Kingdom in the year 1995–96,

without (in either case) any deduction or abatement other than as there mentioned.

(3) Sub-paragraph (2) above does not apply if section 66(1)(c) of that Act applied in relation to the year 1995–96.

(4) Section 63A of the Taxes Act 1988 (as applied by section 65(3) of that Act) shall have effect as if the amount of profits or gains of the basis period for the year 1997–98 which arise before 6th April 1997 were an overlap profit for the purposes of that section.

Cross reference—See FA 1995 s 123, Sch 22 (prevention of exploitation provisions of sub-paras (2)(a), (4) above).

7 In the case of income which—

(a) is from a source arising before 6th April 1994 and ceasing before 6th April 1998, and

(b) is chargeable to tax under Case IV or V of Schedule D,

sections 65 to 68 of that Act shall have effect as if section 207 of this Act and its associated repeals had not been enacted.

Loss relief

8 (*Spent.*)

Capital allowances

9—(1) This paragraph applies in the case of a trade, profession or vocation set up and commenced before 6th April 1994 and continuing after 5th April 1997.

(2) Section 140 of the Capital Allowances Act 1990 shall have effect as if the allowances which fall to be made in taxing the trade, profession or vocation for the first period of account ending after 5th April 1997 under the provisions of that Act as they apply for the purposes of income tax included any allowance or part of any allowance—

(*a*) which falls to be made in taxing the trade, profession or vocation for the year 1996–97, or is carried forward to that year from a previous year of assessment, and

(*b*) to which full effect cannot be given in the year 1996–97.

Double taxation relief

10—(1) Subject to paragraph 12(2) below, this paragraph applies in the case of—

(*a*) a trade, profession or vocation set up and commenced before 6th April 1994 and continuing after 5th April 1998; or

(*b*) income from a source arising before the former date and continuing after the latter date.

(2) Subject to sub-paragraph (3) below, the amount of foreign tax to be taken into account in determining whether and, if so, what credit is allowable under Part XVIII of the Taxes Act 1988 against income tax which, in respect of income from any source, is chargeable under Case I or II of Schedule D for the year 1996–97 shall be the appropriate percentage of the aggregate of—

(*a*) the amount of foreign tax paid on income from that source arising in the basis period for that year, and

(*b*) the amount of foreign tax paid on income from that source arising in the relevant period.

(3) Where the period on the profits or gains of which income tax is chargeable under Case I or II of Schedule D for the year 1995–96 is that year, sub-paragraph (2) above shall have effect as if for the words from ''the appropriate percentage'' to the end there were substituted the words ''the amount of foreign tax paid on income arising in that year''.

(4) Where—

(*a*) the amount of the profits or gains on which income tax is chargeable under Case I or II of Schedule D for the year 1996–97 is given by paragraph 2(2) above, and

(*b*) that amount includes income from any source in respect of which credit is allowable under Part XVIII of the Taxes Act 1988,

the amount of income from that source to be taken into account in determining what credit is so allowable shall be the appropriate percentage of the aggregate of the full amount of the income of the basis period for that year and the full amount of the income of the relevant period.

(5) [Subject to sub-paragraph (5A) below,][1] the amount of foreign tax to be taken into account in determining whether and, if so, what credit is allowable under Part XVIII of the Taxes Act 1988 against income tax which, in respect of income from any source, is chargeable for the year 1996–97 under Case IV or V of Schedule D shall be 50 per cent of the aggregate of—

(*a*) the amount of foreign tax paid on income from that source arising, or (as the case may require) received in the United Kingdom, in that year; and

(*b*) the amount of foreign tax paid on income from that source arising, or (as the case may require) received in the United Kingdom, in the year 1995–96.

[(5A) Where the period on the profits or gains of which income tax is chargeable under Case IV or V of Schedule D for the year 1995–96 is that year, sub-paragraph (5) above shall have effect as if for the words from ''50 per cent'' to the end there were substituted the words ''the amount of foreign tax paid on income arising, or (as the case may require) received in the United Kingdom, in that year.][2]

(6) In this paragraph—

''the appropriate percentage'' and ''the relevant period'' have the same meanings as in paragraph 2 above;

''double taxation arrangements'' means arrangements having effect by virtue of section 788 of the Taxes Act 1988;

''foreign tax'' means tax chargeable under the law of a territory outside the United Kingdom for which credit may be allowed under double taxation arrangements or section 790(1) of that Act.

Amendments—[1] Words in sub-para (5) inserted by FA 1995 s 122(4).
[2] Sub-para (5A) inserted by FA 1995 s 122(5).

11—(1) Subject to paragraph 12(2) below, this paragraph applies in the case of—

(*a*) a trade, profession or vocation set up and commenced before 6th April 1994 and continuing after 5th April 1998; or

(*b*) income from a source arising before the former date and continuing after the latter date.

(2) Sub-paragraph (3) below applies where—

(*a*) credit against income tax for the year 1995–96 or any earlier year of assessment is or has been allowed by virtue of subsection (1) of section 804 of the Taxes Act 1988 in respect of any income (''the original income''), and

(*b*) the source of that income ceases in a subsequent year of assessment (''the subsequent year'').

(3) The following shall be set off one against the other, namely—

(a) the amount of the credit which, under Part XVIII of the Taxes Act 1988 (including section 804), has been allowed against income tax in respect of the original income, and
(b) the aggregate of—

(i) the amount of the credit which, apart from that section, would have been so allowed, and
(ii) the difference between the amount of the credit which, on the assumptions mentioned in sub-paragraph (4) below, would have been allowable under Part XVIII of that Act for the year 1996–97 and the amount of credit which has been so allowed;

and if the amount given by paragraph (a) exceeds that given by paragraph (b) above, the person chargeable in respect of income (if any) arising in the subsequent year from the same source as the original income shall be treated as having received in that year a payment chargeable under Case VI of Schedule D of an amount such that income tax on it at the basic rate is equal to the excess.

(4) The assumptions are—

(a) that the words "the appropriate percentage of" were omitted from paragraph 2(2) above;
(b) that the words "50 per cent of" were omitted from paragraphs (a), (b) and (c) of paragraph 6(2) above; and
(c) that paragraph 10 above had not been enacted.

(5) Where the period on the income of which income tax is chargeable for the year 1996–97 is that year, sub-paragraph (3) above shall have effect as if for paragraph (b) there were substituted the following paragraph—

"(b) the amount of the credit which, apart from that section, would have been so allowed;".

(6) Any reference in sub-paragraph (2) or (3) above to section 804 or Part XVIII of the Taxes Act 1988 includes a reference to the corresponding provisions of any earlier enactments.

(7) Any payment which a person is treated by virtue of sub-paragraph (3) above as having received shall not on that account constitute income of his for any of the purposes of the Income Tax Acts other than that sub-paragraph and in particular no part of it shall constitute profits or gains brought into charge to income tax for the purposes of section 348 of the Taxes Act 1988.

12—(1) In the case of—

(a) a trade, profession or vocation set up and commenced before 6th April 1994 and ceasing before 6th April 1998, being a trade, profession or vocation in respect of which a direction has been given under paragraph 3(2) above, or
(b) income from a source arising before the former date and ceasing before the latter date, being income to which paragraph 7 above applies,

section 804 of the Taxes Act 1988 shall have effect as if section 217 of this Act and its associated repeals had not been enacted.

(2) In the case of a trade, profession or vocation set up and commenced before 6th April 1994 and ceasing on or after 6th April 1998 but before 6th April 1999, being a trade, profession or vocation in respect of which a direction has been given under paragraph 3(4) above—

(a) paragraphs 10 and 11 above shall not apply, and
(b) section 804 of the Taxes Act 1988 shall have effect as if section 217 of this Act and its associated repeals had not been enacted.

13 Paragraphs 2(2) and 6(2) above shall have effect as if any reference to the full amount of any profits or gains, or the full amount of any income, were a reference to that amount after any reduction which is treated as made by section 811 of the Taxes Act (deduction for foreign tax where no credit allowable).

Supplemental

14—(1) In this Schedule—

(a) any reference to a source of income arising before any date ("the earlier date") and continuing after or ceasing before some other date ("the later date") is a reference to a source of income arising to any person before the earlier date and continuing to be possessed by that person after, or (as the case may be) ceasing to be possessed by that person before, the later date; and
(b) any reference to a source of income includes a reference to a part of such a source.

(2) Where, as respects income from any source, income tax is to be charged under Case IV or V of Schedule D by reference to the amounts of income received in the United Kingdom, the source shall be treated for the purposes of this Schedule as arising on the date on which the first amount of income is so received.

SCHEDULE 21

LLOYD'S UNDERWRITERS: INDIVIDUALS

Section 228

Year of assessment in which profits or losses arise

1—(1) ...[1]

(2) Subsection (3) of that section shall cease to have effect.

(3) In this paragraph—

    (*a*) ...[1]

    (*b*) sub-paragraph (2) has effect for the year 1996–97 and subsequent years of assessment.

Amendments—[1] Sub-para (1) and (3)(*a*) repealed by F(No 2)A 1997 Sch 8 Pt II(11) with effect in relation to distributions made after 5 April 1999.

2—(1) (*substitutes* FA 1993 s 172(1)(*a*), (*b*)).

(2) Sub-paragraph (1) above does not have effect for the years 1994–95, 1995–96 and 1996–97, but in relation to those years that section shall have effect as if paragraphs (*a*) and (*b*) of subsection (1) were omitted.

Premiums trust funds

3 (*substitutes* FA 1993 s 174(1)).

Reinsurance to close

4—(1) (*inserts* FA 1993 s 177(5)).

(2) This paragraph has effect for the underwriting year 1993 and subsequent underwriting years.

Stop-loss and quota share insurance

5—(1) (*amends* FA 1993 s 178(2)).

(2) This paragraph has effect as respects insurance money and other amounts payable in respect of losses declared in the underwriting year 1997 or subsequent underwriting years.

Cessation etc

6—(1) (*amends* FA 1993 s 179(2) and *repeals* sub-s (3)).

(2) (*inserts* FA 1993 s 179A).

(3) This paragraph has effect in any case where the member dies after the end of the year 1993–94.

Regulations

7—(1) (*repeals* FA 1993 s 182 (2)–(4)).

(2) This paragraph has effect for the year 1997–98 and subsequent years of assessment.

Interpretation

8 (*amends* FA 1993 s 184(1), (2)).

Assessment and collection of tax

9—(1), (2) (*amend* FA 1993 Sch 19 para 2(1), (2)).

(3) This paragraph has effect for the year 1997–98 and subsequent years of assessment.

10 (*repeals* FA 1993 Sch 19 Pt II (paras 9–12)).

11 ...

Amendments—Paragraph 11 repealed by F(No 2)A 1997 Sch 8 Pt II(5) with effect in relation to distributions made after 1 July 1997.

Special reserve funds

12—(1) (*inserts* definition of "payment" in FA 1993 Sch 20 para 1(1)).

(2) (*amends* FA 1993 Sch 20 para 7(2)).

(3) This paragraph has effect for the year 1992–93 and subsequent years of assessment.

13—(1) (*substitutes* FA 1993 Sch 20 para 8).

(2) This paragraph has effect for the year 1994–95 and subsequent years of assessment.

14—(1) (*amends* FA 1993 Sch 20 para 10(1)–(4)).

(2) (*inserts* FA 1993 Sch 20 para 10(5)).

(3) Sub-paragraphs (1) and (2) above do not have effect for the years 1994–95, 1995–96 and 1996–97, but in relation to those years that Schedule shall have effect as if paragraph 10 were omitted.

15 (*amends* FA 1993 Sch 20 para 11).

16—(1), (2) (*amend* FA 1993 Sch 20 para 13(1) and *insert* Sch 20 para 13(6)).

(3) This paragraph has effect for the year 1992–93 and subsequent years of assessment.

SCHEDULE 24

PROVISIONS RELATING TO THE RAILWAYS ACT 1993

Section 252

Commentary—*Simon's Direct Tax Service* **B3.246.**

Interpretation

1—(1) In this Schedule—

...[1]

"the Board" means the British Railways Board;

["the Capital Allowances Act" means the Capital Allowances Act 2001 and includes, where the context admits, enactments which under the Taxes Act 1988 are to be treated as contained in the Capital Allowances Act 2001;][1]

"fixture" has the same meaning as it has in [Chapter 14 of Part 2 of the Capital Allowances Act][1];

"franchise company" has the meaning given by section 85(8) of the Railways Act 1993;

"the Franchising Director" means the Director of Passenger Rail Franchising;

"the Gains Act" means the Taxation of Chargeable Gains Act 1992;

"predecessor", in relation to any relevant transfer, means the body from which the property, rights or liabilities in question are transferred by virtue of the restructuring scheme in question;

"property", "rights" and "liabilities" have the same meaning as they have in Part II of the Railways Act 1993;

"publicly owned railway company" has the same meaning as it has in the Railways Act 1993;

"relevant transfer" means a transfer of any property, rights or liabilities by virtue of a restructuring scheme;

"restructuring scheme" means a section 85 transfer scheme made by, or pursuant to a direction of, the Secretary of State, if and to the extent that the transfer scheme provides for the transfer of property, rights or liabilities from—

   (*a*) the Board,
   (*b*) a wholly owned subsidiary of the Board,
   (*c*) a publicly owned railway company, or
   (*d*) a company which is wholly owned by the Franchising Director,

to any other body falling within paragraphs (*a*) to (*d*) above;

"section 85 transfer scheme" means a scheme made under or by virtue of section 85 of the Railways Act 1993;

"subsidiary" has the meaning given by section 736 of the Companies Act 1985;

"successor company" has the same meaning as it has in Part II of the Railways Act 1993;

"transfer date" shall be construed in accordance with section 85(6) of the Railways Act 1993;

"transfer scheme" means a scheme made under or by virtue of section 85 or 86 of the Railways Act 1993;

"transferee", in relation to a relevant transfer, means the body to which the property, rights or liabilities in question are transferred by virtue of the restructuring scheme in question;

"wholly owned subsidiary" has the meaning given by section 736 of the Companies Act 1985.

(2) Section 151(2) and (3) of the Railways Act 1993 (companies wholly owned by the Crown or the Franchising Director) shall have effect for the purposes of this Schedule as it has effect for the purposes of that Act.

(3) Any reference in this Schedule to "assignment" shall be construed in Scotland as a reference to "assignation".

(4) This Schedule—

   (*a*) so far as it relates to income tax, shall be construed as one with the Income Tax Acts,
   (*b*) so far as it relates to corporation tax, shall be construed as one with the Corporation Tax Acts, and
   (*c*) so far as it relates to capital allowances, shall be construed as one with [the Capital Allowances Act][1].

Amendments—[1] In sub-para (1), definition of "the Allowances Act" repealed, definition of "the Capital Allowances Act" inserted, words in definition of "fixture" substituted, and in sub-para (4)(*c*), words substituted by CAA 2001 ss 578, 580, Sch 2 paras 91(1), (2), Sch 4 with effect for income tax purposes, as respects allowances and charges falling to be made for chargeable periods ending after 5 April 2001, and for corporation tax purposes, as respects allowances and charges falling to be made for chargeable periods ending after 31 March 2001.

Chargeable gains: transfer to be without gain or loss

2—(1) For the purposes of the Gains Act, where there is a relevant transfer, the disposal of property, rights and liabilities which is constituted by that transfer shall, subject to the following provisions of this Schedule, be taken, in relation to the transferee as well as the predecessor, to be for a consideration such that no gain or loss accrues to the predecessor.

(2) Section 35(3)(*d*) of the Gains Act (list of provisions for transfers without gain or loss for purposes of provisions applying to assets held on 31st March 1982) shall have effect with the omission of the word "and" at the end of sub-paragraph (vii) and with the insertion, after sub-paragraph (viii), of the following sub-paragraph—

    "(ix) paragraphs 2(1), 7(2), 11(3) and (4) and 25(2) of Schedule 24 to the Finance Act 1994;".

(3) Section 171(1) of the Gains Act (which makes provision in relation to the disposal of assets from one member of a group of companies to another member of the group) shall not apply where the disposal in question is a relevant transfer.

Chargeable gains: receipt of compensation or insurance policies

3—(1) Subsection (4) of section 23 of the Gains Act (adjustments where compensation or insurance money used for purchase of replacement asset) shall have effect in accordance with sub-paragraph (3) below in any case where—

    (*a*) there is a relevant transfer such that—

        (i) any capital sum received by the predecessor by way of compensation for the loss or destruction of any asset, or under a policy of insurance of the risk of the loss or destruction of any asset, becomes available to the transferee; or
        (ii) any right of the predecessor to receive such a sum is transferred to the transferee, and the transferee receives that sum; and

    (*b*) the transferee acquires an asset in circumstances where—

        (i) had there been no such relevant transfer, and
        (ii) had the predecessor acquired the asset by the application of that sum,

the predecessor would be treated for the purposes of that subsection as having so acquired the asset in replacement for the asset lost or destroyed.

(2) Subsection (5) of that section (adjustments where a part of any compensation or insurance money is used for the purchase of a replacement asset) shall have effect in accordance with sub-paragraph (3) below in any case where—

    (*a*) there is a relevant transfer such that—

        (i) any capital sum received by the predecessor by way of compensation for the loss or destruction of any asset, or under a policy of insurance of the risk of the loss or destruction of any asset, becomes available to the transferee; or
        (ii) any right of the predecessor to receive such a sum is transferred to the transferee, and the transferee receives that sum; and

    (*b*) the transferee acquires an asset in circumstances where—

        (i) had there been no such relevant transfer, and
        (ii) had the predecessor acquired the asset by the application of all of that sum except for a part which was less than the amount of the gain (whether all chargeable gain or not) accruing on the disposal of the asset lost or destroyed,

the predecessor would be treated for the purposes of that subsection as having so acquired the asset in replacement for the asset lost or destroyed.

(3) In a case falling within sub-paragraph (1) or (2) above, subsection (4) or, as the case may be, subsection (5) of section 23 of the Gains Act shall have effect as if the transferee and the predecessor were the same person, except that—

    (*a*) in a case falling within sub-paragraph (1)(*a*)(i) or (2)(*a*)(i) above—

        (i) any claim under the subsection in question must be made by the predecessor and the transferee; and
        (ii) any adjustment to be made in consequence of paragraph (*a*) of that subsection shall be made for the purposes only of the taxation of the predecessor; and

    (*b*) in a case falling within sub-paragraph (1)(*a*)(ii) or (2)(*a*)(ii) above—

        (i) any claim under the subsection in question must be made by the transferee; and
        (ii) any adjustment to be made in consequence of paragraph (*a*) of that subsection shall be made for the purposes only of the taxation of the transferee.

Chargeable gains: section 30 of the Gains Act

4—(1) Nothing in Part II or III of the Railways Act 1993 and no instrument or agreement made, or other thing done, under or by virtue of either of those Parts, shall be regarded as a scheme or arrangement for the purposes of section 30 of the Gains Act (value-shifting).

(2) In any case where—

(*a*) an asset which is the subject of a relevant transfer or qualifying disposal has previously been the subject of a scheme or arrangements falling within subsection (1) of that section,

(*b*) in consequence, subsection (5) of that section (consideration on disposal to be treated as increased for certain purposes) would, apart from sub-paragraph (3) below, have had effect in relation to the consideration for the relevant transfer or qualifying disposal, and

(*c*) the consideration for the relevant transfer or qualifying disposal falls to be determined under paragraph 2 above or paragraph 7(2), 11(3) or 25(2) below,

sub-paragraph (3) below shall apply.

(3) Where this sub-paragraph applies—

(*a*) the said subsection (5) shall not have effect in relation to the consideration for the relevant transfer or qualifying disposal; but

(*b*) on the first subsequent disposal of the asset which is neither a relevant transfer or qualifying disposal nor a group disposal—

(i) that subsection shall have effect in relation to the consideration for that disposal (whether or not it would otherwise have done so); and

(ii) the increase that falls to be made under that subsection shall be so calculated as to include any increase which would, but for paragraph (*a*) above, have fallen to be made in relation to the relevant transfer or qualifying disposal.

(4) In this paragraph—

"group disposal" means a disposal which falls to be treated by virtue of section 171(1) of the Gains Act as made for a consideration such that no gain or loss accrues to the person making the disposal;

"qualifying disposal" means—

(*a*) a disposal to which paragraph 7(2) below applies; or

(*b*) a disposal falling within paragraph 11(3) or 25(2) below.

Chargeable gains: section 41 of the Gains Act

5 Subsection (1) of section 174 of the Gains Act (which applies section 41 of that Act to cases where assets have been acquired without gain or loss) shall have effect, without prejudice to paragraph 2 above or paragraph 7(2), 11(3) or (4) or 25(2) below, where there has been—

(*a*) a relevant transfer,

(*b*) a disposal to which paragraph 7(2) below applies, or

(*c*) a disposal falling within paragraph 11(3) or (4) or 25(2) below,

as if the asset to which the transfer or disposal relates had thereby been transferred and acquired in relevant circumstances, within the meaning of that subsection.

Chargeable gains: roll-over relief

6—(1) Subject to the following provisions of this paragraph, where any asset, or any interest in an asset, is the subject of a relevant transfer, sections 152 to 160 of the Gains Act (roll-over relief on replacement of business assets) shall have effect as if—

(*a*) the asset or interest had been acquired by the transferee—

(i) at the time at which, and for the consideration for which, the predecessor acquired it; and

(ii) for the purpose of the asset's use in a trade carried on by the transferee (and not wholly or partly for the purpose of realising a gain from the disposal of the asset or interest), but only to the extent that the predecessor's acquisition was for the purpose of the asset's use in a trade carried on by him (and not wholly or partly for the purpose of realising a gain from the disposal of the asset or interest);

(*b*) throughout the period during which the asset or interest was owned by the predecessor, it had been owned by the transferee; and

(*c*) to the extent that the predecessor—

(i) used the asset, or

(ii) in the case of an asset falling within head A of Class 1 in section 155 of that Act, used and occupied the asset,

during that period for the purposes of a trade carried on by him, the transferee had used or, as the case may be, used and occupied the asset for the purposes of a trade carried on by him.

(2) In any case where—

(*a*) a held-over gain would, but for the provisions of section 154 of the Gains Act (depreciating assets), have been carried forward to a depreciating asset, and

(*b*) that asset is the subject of a relevant transfer,

that section shall have effect as if the gain had accrued to, and the claim for it to be held over had been made by, the transferee and as if the predecessor's acquisition of the depreciating asset had been the transferee's acquisition of that asset.

(3) Where an asset, or an interest in an asset, is the subject of a relevant transfer, the predecessor shall not be entitled at any time after the coming into force of the relevant transfer to make any claim under section 152 or 153 of the Gains Act in respect of his acquisition of the asset or interest.

(4) Where an asset, or an interest in an asset, is the subject of a relevant transfer, the transferee shall not, by virtue of any provision of this Schedule, be treated for the purposes of sections 152 to 154 of the Gains Act as having applied the whole or any part of the consideration for any disposal—

    (*a*)   in acquiring the asset or interest by virtue of the relevant transfer; or

    (*b*)   in acquiring the asset or interest as postulated in sub-paragraph (1)(*a*) above, if the predecessor has made a claim under section 152 or 153 of that Act in respect of his acquisition of the asset or interest.

(5) Without prejudice to paragraph 1(4)(*b*) above, expressions used in sub-paragraph (2) above and in section 154 of the Gains Act have the same meaning in that sub-paragraph as they have in that section.

Chargeable gains: agreements and instruments by virtue of section 91(1)(c) of the Railways Act 1993

7—(1) Sub-paragraph (2) below applies to any disposal effected pursuant to an obligation imposed by a section 85 transfer scheme by virtue of section 91(1)(*c*) of the Railways Act 1993 (obligations to enter into agreements or execute instruments) if the person making the disposal is—

    (*a*)   the Board,

    (*b*)   a wholly owned subsidiary of the Board,

    (*c*)   a publicly owned railway company, or

    (*d*)   a company which is wholly owned by the Franchising Director,

and the person to whom the disposal is made is either a person falling within paragraphs (*a*) to (*d*) above or the Franchising Director.

(2) A disposal to which this sub-paragraph applies shall be taken for the purposes of corporation tax on chargeable gains, in relation to the person to whom the disposal is made as well as the person making the disposal, to be effected for a consideration such that no gain or loss accrues to the person making the disposal.

(3) Section 171(1) of the Gains Act (transfers within a group) shall not apply where the disposal in question is one to which sub-paragraph (2) above applies.

(4) Section 17 of that Act (disposals and acquisitions treated as made at market value) shall not have effect in relation to a disposal or the corresponding acquisition if—

    (*a*)   the disposal is effected pursuant to an obligation imposed by a section 85 transfer scheme by virtue of section 91(1)(*c*) of the Railways Act 1993

    (*b*)   the person making the disposal is either a person falling within paragraphs (*a*) to (*d*) of sub-paragraph (1) above or the Franchising Director, and

    (*c*)   the person making the corresponding acquisition is neither a person falling within those paragraphs nor the Franchising Director,

unless the person making the disposal is connected with the person to whom the disposal is made.

(5) In this paragraph, "the corresponding acquisition", in the case of any disposal, means the acquisition made by the person to whom the disposal is made.

Chargeable gains: group transactions

8—(1) For the purposes of section 179 of the Gains Act (company ceasing to be a member of a group), where any company ("the degrouped company") ceases, by virtue of a qualifying transaction, to be a member of a group of companies, the degrouped company shall not, by virtue of that qualifying transaction, be treated under that section as having sold, and immediately reacquired, any asset acquired from a company which was at the time of acquisition a member of that group.

(2) Where sub-paragraph (1) above applies in relation to any asset, section 179 of the Gains Act shall have effect on the first subsequent occasion on which the degrouped company ceases to be a member of a group of companies (the "subsequent group"), otherwise than by virtue of a qualifying transaction, as if both the degrouped company and the company from which the asset was acquired had been members of the subsequent group at the time of acquisition.

(3) Where, disregarding any preparatory transactions, a company would be regarded for the purposes of section 179 of the Gains Act (and, accordingly, of this paragraph) as ceasing to be, or becoming, a member of a group of companies by virtue of a qualifying transaction, it shall be regarded for those purposes as so doing by virtue of the qualifying transaction and not by virtue of any preparatory transactions.

(4) In this paragraph—

    "preparatory transaction" means anything done under or by virtue of Part II of the Railways Act 1993 for the purpose of initiating, advancing or facilitating the qualifying transaction in question;

    "qualifying transaction" means—

(*a*) a relevant transfer;

(*b*) any other transfer or disposal under or by virtue of section 85, 88(6) or (7) or 89 of the Railways Act 1993.

(5) Expressions used in this paragraph and in section 179 of the Gains Act have the same meaning in this paragraph as they have in that section.

Chargeable gains: disposal of debts

9—(1) Where by virtue of any relevant transfer—

(*a*) any debt owed to the predecessor is transferred to the transferee, and

(*b*) the predecessor would, apart from this sub-paragraph, be the original creditor in relation to that debt for the purposes of section 251 of the Gains Act (disposal of debts),

that Act shall have effect as if the transferee and not the predecessor were the original creditor for those purposes.

(2) Where, by virtue of any relevant transfer, any obligations of the predecessor under a guarantee of the repayment of a loan are transferred to the transferee, the transferee shall be treated for the purposes of section 253(4) of the Gains Act (relief for guarantors) as a person who gave the guarantee.

(3) In any case where—

(*a*) by virtue of any relevant transfer, a debt owed to the predecessor is transferred to the transferee,

(*b*) that debt is either—

(i) a right to the repayment of any amount outstanding as principal on a loan which is a qualifying loan for the purposes of either of sections 253 *and 254*¹ of the Gains Act (relief for irrecoverable debts owed by traders and payments under guarantees), or

(ii) a right to recover any amount paid under a guarantee of the repayment of such a loan or of a loan which would be such a loan but for section 253(1)(*c*) of that Act (exclusion of debts not on security), and

(*c*) no allowable loss in respect of the amount mentioned in paragraph (*b*)(i) or (ii) above has been claimed by the predecessor under either of sections 253 *and 254*¹ of that Act before the coming into force of the relevant transfer,

those sections shall have effect with the modifications set out in sub-paragraph (4) below.

(4) Those modifications are—

(*a*) that the loan or, as the case may be, the guarantee shall be treated as if it had been made or given by the transferee, and

(*b*) that any payment made under the guarantee by the predecessor shall be treated as if it had been made by the transferee,

and those sections shall accordingly have effect as if there had been no assignment of the right to recover the principal of the loan or of any right to recover an amount paid under the guarantee.

(5) In any case where—

(*a*) a debt falling within sub-paragraph (3)(*b*) above is transferred by virtue of a relevant transfer, and

(*b*) before the coming into force of the relevant transfer, the predecessor has claimed a loss in respect of the amount mentioned in sub-paragraph (3)(*b*)(i) or (ii) above under section 253 *or 254*¹ of the Gains Act,

the relevant transfer shall not be treated as an assignment of the debt for the purposes of those sections and sub-paragraph (2) above shall not have effect in relation to the transferee, so far as relating to the amount mentioned in paragraph (*b*) above.

(6) In any case where—

(*a*) any right to the recovery of an amount falling within subsection (3) of section 253 of the Gains Act (relief in respect of certain irrecoverable loans) is transferred by virtue of a relevant transfer,

(*b*) an allowable loss determined by reference to that amount has been treated under that subsection as accruing to the predecessor, and

(*c*) the whole or any part of that amount is at any time recovered by the transferee or by a company in the same group of companies as the transferee,

that Act shall have effect as if a chargeable gain equal to so much of the allowable loss as corresponds to the amount recovered had accrued to the transferee or, as the case may be, to the company in the same group as the transferee.

(7) In any case where—

(*a*) any right to the recovery of an amount falling within subsection (4) of section 253 of the Gains Act is transferred by virtue of a relevant transfer,

(*b*) an allowable loss determined by reference to that amount has been treated under that subsection as accruing to the predecessor, and

(c) the whole or any part of the amount mentioned in subsection (4)(*a*), or the whole or any part of the amount of the payment mentioned in subsection (4)(*b*), of that section is at any time recovered by the transferee or by a company in the same group of companies as the transferee,

that Act shall have effect as if a chargeable gain equal to so much of the allowable loss as corresponds to the amount recovered had accrued to the transferee or, as the case may be, to the company in the same group as the transferee.

(8) In any case where—

(*a*) any right to recovery of the relevant outstanding amount, as defined in subsection (11) of section 254 of the Gains Act, is transferred by virtue of a relevant transfer,

(*b*) an allowable loss determined by reference to that amount has been treated under subsection (2) of that section (relief for debts on qualifying corporate bonds) as accruing to the predecessor, and

(*c*) the whole or any part of that amount is at any time recovered by the transferee or by a company in the same group of companies as the transferee,

that Act shall have effect as if a chargeable gain equal to so much of the allowable loss as corresponds to the amount recovered had accrued to the transferee or, as the case may be, to the company in the same group as the transferee.

(9) In any case where sub-paragraph (6), (7) or (8) above applies in relation to an allowable loss, subsections (7) and (8) of section 253 of the Gains Act ...[1] (which deem a chargeable gain to arise where an amount treated as an allowable loss is recovered by another company in same group) shall not apply in relation to that allowable loss.

(10) Expressions used in this paragraph and in section 253 *or* 254[1] of the Gains Act have the same meaning in this paragraph as they have in that section.

Amendments—[1] Words in sub-para (9) repealed by FA 1996 Sch 41 Pt V(3) with effect for accounting periods ending after 31 March 1996, subject to transitional provisions in FA 1996 Sch 15.

Chargeable gains: assets held before 6th April 1965

10 Schedule 2 to the Gains Act (assets held on 6th April 1965) shall have effect in relation to any assets which vest in the transferee by virtue of a relevant transfer as if—

(*a*) the predecessor and the transferee were the same person; and

(*b*) those assets, to the extent that they were in fact acquired or provided by the predecessor, were acquired or, as the case may be, provided by the transferee.

Chargeable gains: miscellaneous disposals and acquisitions

11—(1) In this paragraph, "relevant disposal" means—

(*a*) a disposal by virtue of a section 85 transfer scheme, other than a restructuring scheme, to the extent that the scheme provides for the transfer of property, rights and liabilities of—

   (i) the Board,
   (ii) a wholly owned subsidiary of the Board,
   (iii) a publicly owned railway company, or
   (iv) a company which is wholly owned by the Franchising Director,

to a franchise company or to the Franchising Director;

(*b*) a disposal pursuant to a direction under section 88(6) or (7) or 89 of the Railways Act 1993;

(*c*) a disposal by or pursuant to an agreement or instrument made or executed, transaction effected or direction given under or by virtue of paragraph 2, 3 or 14(2) of Schedule 8 to that Act, in a case where the transfer scheme in question is a section 85 transfer scheme, other than a restructuring scheme; or

(*d*) a disposal pursuant to a requirement imposed under paragraph 7(2)(*b*) of that Schedule, in a case where the transfer to which that Schedule applies is a transfer by virtue of a section 85 transfer scheme.

(2) Subject to sub-paragraph (3) below, section 17 of the Gains Act (disposals and acquisitions treated as made at market value) shall not have effect—

(*a*) in relation to a relevant disposal or the corresponding acquisition,

(*b*) in relation to an acquisition by a franchise company, in a case where the corresponding disposal is a disposal by the Franchising Director by virtue of a section 85 transfer scheme, or

(*c*) in relation to a disposal of a historical record or artefact in accordance with directions under section 125 of the Railways Act 1993 (railway heritage),

unless, in a case falling within paragraph (*a*) or (*b*) above, the person making the disposal is connected with the person making the acquisition.

(3) Where there is a relevant disposal of an asset of—

(*a*) the Board,
(*b*) a subsidiary of the Board,
(*c*) a publicly owned railway company, or
(*d*) a company wholly owned by the Franchising Director,

to the Franchising Director or a company wholly owned by the Crown, the disposal shall be taken for the purposes of the Gains Act, in relation to the person making the disposal and, if the disposal is made to a company wholly owned by the Crown, the person to whom the disposal is made, to be for a consideration such that no gain or loss accrues on the disposal.

(4) Where there is a disposal of a historical record or artefact in accordance with directions under section 125 of the Railways Act 1993 and the disposal is either—

(a) for a consideration not exceeding the sums which are allowable as a deduction under section 38 of the Gains Act (consideration for, and incidental costs of, original acquisition etc), or

(b) for no consideration,

the disposal shall be taken for the purposes of the Gains Act, in relation to the person to whom the disposal is made as well as the person making the disposal, to be for a consideration such that no gain or loss accrues on the disposal.

(5) In this paragraph—

"the corresponding acquisition", in the case of any disposal, means the acquisition made by the person to whom the disposal is made;

"the corresponding disposal" in the case of any acquisition, means the disposal to the person by whom the acquisition is made.

Transfers of trading stock

12—(1) This paragraph applies in any case where—

(a) by virtue of a relevant transfer, any trading stock belonging to a trade carried on by the predecessor ("the predecessor's trade") vests in the transferee, and

(b) the trading stock is acquired by the transferee as trading stock for the purposes of a trade which he carries on or which he begins to carry on after the relevant transfer ("the transferee's trade").

(2) Where this paragraph applies, the trading stock in question shall, for the purposes (whether in relation to the predecessor or the transferee) of computing for the purposes of the Corporation Tax Acts the [profits]¹ of the predecessor's trade and the transferee's trade,—

(a) be taken to have been both disposed of by the predecessor and acquired by the transferee in the course of those trades and (subject to that) at the time when the transfer comes into force; and

(b) be valued in each case as if that disposal and acquisition had been for a consideration which in relation to the predecessor would have resulted in neither a profit nor a loss being brought into account in respect of the disposal in the accounting period of the predecessor which is current at that time.

(3) In this paragraph "trading stock" has the same meaning as in section 100 of the Taxes Act 1988.

Amendments—¹ Words substituted by FA 1998 Sch 7 para 9 with effect from 31 July 1998.

Transfer of rights to receipts

13 Where, by virtue of any relevant transfer, there is transferred any right of the predecessor to receive any amount which is for the purposes of corporation tax—

(a) an amount brought into account as a trading receipt of the predecessor for any accounting period ending before the time when the transfer comes into force, or

(b) an amount falling to be so brought into account if it is assumed, where it is not the case, that the accounting period of the predecessor current on the day before the transfer comes into force ends immediately before that time,

the transfer shall not require any modification of the way in which that amount has been and is to be treated in relation to the predecessor for those purposes or entitle any amount due or paid in respect of that right to be treated as a trading receipt of the transferee for any accounting period.

Transfer of liabilities

14—(1) If the whole or any part of the amount of a liability transferred by virtue of a relevant transfer falls, for the purposes of corporation tax,—

(a) to be brought into account as deductible in computing the predecessor's profits, or any description of the predecessor's profits, for any accounting period ending before the time when the transfer comes into force, or

(b) to be so brought into account if it is assumed, where it is not the case, that the accounting period of the predecessor current on the day before the transfer comes into force ends immediately before that time,

then the transfer shall not require any modification of the way in which that amount or, as the case may be, that part of that amount has been or is to be treated in relation to the predecessor for those purposes or entitle any amount due or paid in respect of that liability or, as the case may be, the corresponding part of that liability to be deductible in computing the transferee's profits, or any description of the transferee's profits, for any accounting period.

(2) If and to the extent that the amount of any liability which, in consequence of any relevant transfer, falls to be discharged by the transferee is an amount which would (but for that and any other transfer) have fallen to be deductible in computing the predecessor's profits, or any description of the predecessor's profits, for any accounting period beginning with the coming into force of the transfer or at any subsequent time, that amount shall, to that extent,—

(*a*) not be so deductible; but

(*b*) subject to sub-paragraph (3) below, be deductible in computing the transferee's profits to the same extent as if the transferee had become subject to the obligation in pursuance of which the liability arises or has arisen at the same time and for the same consideration, and otherwise on the same terms and in the same circumstances, as the predecessor;

and for the purposes of this sub-paragraph it shall be assumed, where it is not the case, that the accounting period of the predecessor current on the day before the transfer comes into force ends immediately before the coming into force of that transfer.

(3) For the purposes of corporation tax, where any relevant transfer has the effect that any liability falls to any extent to be discharged by the transferee instead of by the predecessor, the amounts deductible in computing the transferee's profits, or any description of the transferee's profits, for any accounting period shall not include any amount in respect of so much of that liability as falls to be so discharged unless it is an amount which (but for that and any other transfer) would have fallen to be deductible in computing the predecessor's profits, or any description of the predecessor's profits, for any accounting period beginning or ending after the coming into force of that transfer.

(4) The preceding provisions of this paragraph shall apply in relation to the deduction of charges on income against the total profits of the predecessor or transferee for any period as they apply in relation to the deduction of any amount in the computation for that period of the profits of the predecessor or, as the case may be, of the transferee.

(5) For the purposes of Chapter II of Part VI of the Taxes Act 1988 (definition of distributions), where in the case of any relevant transfer any consideration given or treated as given in respect of a security relating to—

(*a*) any liability, or

(*b*) the use of the principal to which any liability, being a liability to interest or an equivalent liability, relates,

would fall (apart from this sub-paragraph) to be regarded for those purposes as new consideration received by the predecessor, that consideration shall be treated instead, to the extent that it relates to so much of the liability as falls in consequence of the transfer to be discharged by the transferee, as if it were new consideration received by the transferee.

Trading losses

15—(1) Subject to the following provisions of this paragraph, where as a result of a relevant transfer, the predecessor falls to be regarded for the purposes of section 343 of the Taxes Act 1988 (company reconstructions without change of ownership) as ceasing to carry on a trade and the transferee falls to be regarded for the purposes of that section as beginning to carry on that trade—

(*a*) the transferee shall not, by virtue of those matters, be entitled to any relief under section 393(1) (trading losses) of that Act to which it would, apart from this paragraph, have been entitled by virtue of section 343(3) of that Act; and

(*b*) after the coming into force of the relevant transfer, the loss in question shall continue to be regarded for the purposes of the Corporation Tax Acts as a loss incurred in the trade for the time being carried on by the predecessor to the same extent as it would have been so regarded apart from the relevant transfer (and shall be eligible for relief accordingly).

(2) The following provisions of this paragraph apply in any case where—

(*a*) a restructuring scheme makes express provision for the transfer from the predecessor to the transferee of the right to obtain tax relief in respect of such an amount of the predecessor's unrelieved trading losses or unrelieved transferred losses as may be specified in, or determined in accordance with, the scheme; and

(*b*) after the relevant date the transferee carries on, or begins to carry on, any trade (whether or not the trade, or a part of the trade, carried on by the predecessor);

and any reference in this paragraph to a transferred loss is a reference to the amount mentioned in paragraph (*a*) above.

(3) The transferee shall be entitled to relief under section 393(1) of the Taxes Act 1988 for the transferred loss, as for a loss sustained by the transferee in carrying on its trade, but the transferred loss may only be set off against trading income of the transferee which arises in an accounting period throughout which the transferee is a public sector railway company.

(4) Where the transferee ceases to be a public sector railway company, it shall be assumed for the purposes of giving relief by virtue of sub-paragraph (3) above that—

(*a*) on the occasion of the cessation (unless a true accounting period of the transferee ends then) an accounting period of the transferee ends and a new one begins, the new accounting period to end with the end of the true accounting period; and (*b*) the amount of the trading income for the true accounting period of the transferee against which the relief may be allowed is apportioned to the component accounting periods;

and any apportionment under this sub-paragraph shall be on a time basis according to the respective lengths of the component accounting periods except that, if it appears that that method would work unreasonably or unjustly, such other method shall be used as appears just and reasonable.

(5) Relief by virtue of sub-paragraph (3) above in respect of a transferred loss shall be given against the trading income of any accounting period of the transferee before relief is given against that income in respect of losses incurred by the transferee after the relevant date.

(6) As from the relevant date—

(*a*) the amount of the predecessor's unrelieved losses (if any) shall be regarded for the purposes of this paragraph as reduced by an amount equal to the transferred loss; and

(*b*) if the transferred loss exceeds the amount of the predecessor's unrelieved transferred losses before the reduction under paragraph (*a*) above, or if there are no such losses, the predecessor's unrelieved trading losses shall be regarded for the purposes of the Corporation Tax Acts as reduced by the amount of that excess or, as the case may be, by an amount equal to the transferred loss.

(7) Without prejudice to the generality of sub-paragraphs (1) and (3) above, if the conditions in subsection (1) of section 343 of the Taxes Act 1988 become satisfied at any time on or after the relevant date in relation to any trade (or, where subsection (8) of that section applies, any part of a trade which falls to be treated for the purposes of that section as a separate trade), the company which is the successor, within the meaning of that section, shall not become entitled to relief by virtue of subsection (3) of that section in respect of any amount for which the company which is the predecessor, within the meaning of that section, would have been entitled to relief by virtue of sub-paragraph (3) above had it continued to carry on the trade (or the part of the trade which falls to be treated as a separate trade).

(8) Subject to sub-paragraph (9) below, the provisions of a restructuring scheme providing for the determination of the amount which is to be that of any transferred loss may include provision—

(*a*) for such a determination to be made by the Secretary of State in such manner as may be described in the scheme;

(*b*) for any amount determined to be calculated by reference to such factors, or to the opinion of such person, as may be so described; and

(*c*) for a determination under those provisions to be capable of being modified, on one or more occasions, in such manner and in such circumstances as may be so described.

(9) The consent of the Treasury shall be required for the making or modification of a determination of any such amount as is mentioned in sub-paragraph (8) above; and the consent of the transferee shall also be required for any such modification after the coming into force of the relevant transfer.

(10) Where there is a determination, or a modification of a determination, for any purposes of this paragraph, all necessary adjustments shall be made by making assessments or by repayment or discharge of tax, and shall be so made notwithstanding any limitation on the time within which assessments may be made.

(11) For the purposes of this paragraph, a transferee is at any time a "public sector railway company" if, and only if, it is at that time—

(*a*) the Board;

(*b*) a wholly owned subsidiary of the Board;

[(*ba*) a wholly owned subsidiary of the Strategic Rail Authority;]¹

(*c*) a publicly owned railway company; or

(*d*) a company wholly owned by the Crown.

(12) In this paragraph—

"the relevant date" means the date on which the transfer mentioned in sub-paragraph (2)(*a*) above takes effect;

"trading income" has the same meaning as it has in section 393 of the Taxes Act 1988;

"unrelieved trading losses" means any losses—

(*a*) which were incurred by the predecessor in carrying on a trade in accounting periods ending before the relevant date, or

(*b*) for which the predecessor has, by virtue of section 343(3) of the Taxes Act 1988 become entitled to relief under section 393(1) of that Act,

and which would, apart from the restructuring scheme mentioned in sub-paragraph (2)(*a*) above, have fallen to be set off under the said section 393(1) against trading income of the predecessor arising in the accounting period in which the relevant date falls;

"unrelieved transferred losses" means so much of a transferred loss as would, apart from the restructuring scheme mentioned in sub-paragraph (2)(*a*) above, have fallen to be set off under section 393(1) of the Taxes Act 1988 as it applies by virtue of sub-paragraph (3) above, against trading income of the predecessor arising in the accounting period in which the relevant date falls.

(13) It shall be assumed for the purposes of the definitions of "unrelieved trading losses" and "unrelieved transferred losses" in sub-paragraph (12) above (if it is not in fact the case) that the

trading income mentioned in those definitions is at least equal to the aggregate amount of the losses in question of each of those descriptions.

Amendments—¹ Sub-s (11)(*ba*) inserted by the Transport Act 2000 s 252, Sch 27 para 50 with effect from 15 January 2001.

No reduction in allowable losses on extinguishment of certain liabilities

16 Where any of the liabilities of a successor company are extinguished by virtue of section 106(1) of the Railways Act 1993 section 400 of the Taxes Act 1988 (reduction of allowable losses on write-off of government investment) shall not have effect in relation to any amount of government investment in a body corporate which, apart from this paragraph, would thereby fall to be regarded as written-off for the purposes of that section.

Group relief

17—(1) The existence of the powers of the Secretary of State or the Franchising Director under Part II of the Railways Act 1993 shall not be regarded as constituting arrangements falling within subsection (1) or (2) of section 410 of the Taxes Act 1988 (arrangements for the transfer of a company to another group or consortium).

(2) Nothing in Part II of the Railways Act 1993 and no direction given by the Secretary of State under or by virtue of any provision of that Part, shall be regarded as constituting option arrangements for the purposes of paragraph 5B of Schedule 18 to the Taxes Act 1988.

(3) Arrangements relating to the transfer, pursuant to any provision of Part II of the Railways Act 1993 of shares of a subsidiary of the Board to—

    (*a*) the Secretary of State,
    (*b*) the Franchising Director,
    (*c*) a publicly owned railway company,
    (*d*) a company which is wholly owned by the Crown, or
    (*e*) a person acting on behalf of a person falling within any of paragraphs (*a*) to (*d*) above,

shall not, so far as so relating, be regarded as constituting arrangements falling within subsection (1)(*b*)(i) or (ii) of section 410 of the Taxes Act 1988.

(4) Arrangements relating to the transfer, by virtue of a section 85 transfer scheme, of the whole or any part of a trade carried on by the Board or a wholly owned subsidiary of the Board to—

    (*a*) a publicly owned railway company, or
    (*b*) a company wholly owned by the Franchising Director,

shall not, so far as so relating, be regarded as constituting arrangements falling within section 410(1)(*b*)(iii) of the Taxes Act 1988.

(5) Arrangements relating to the transfer, pursuant to any provision of Part II of the Railways Act 1993 of shares of a subsidiary of the Board, or shares of a company owned by a consortium, to—

    (*a*) the Secretary of State,
    (*b*) the Franchising Director,
    (*c*) a publicly owned railway company,
    (*d*) a company which is wholly owned by the Crown, or
    (*e*) person acting on behalf of a person falling within any of paragraphs (*a*) to (*d*) above,

shall not, so far as so relating, be regarded as constituting arrangements falling within section 410(2)(*b*)(ii) of the Taxes Act 1988.

(6) None of sub-paragraphs (3) to (5) above shall have effect in relation to any arrangements if—

    (*a*) notwithstanding the provisions of those sub-paragraphs, the arrangements to any extent fall within section 410(1) or (2) of the Taxes Act 1988; or
    (*b*) the arrangements form part of a series of subsisting arrangements which to any extent—
        (i) relate to the transfer of any shares or assets of, or the whole or any part of the trade carried on by, a company to which the first-mentioned arrangements relate, and
        (ii) notwithstanding the provisions of sub-paragraphs (3) to (5) above, fall within section 410(1) or (2) of the Taxes Act 1988.

(7) Section 413(6)(*a*) of the Taxes Act 1988 (company owned by a consortium) shall have effect for the purposes of sub-paragraph (5) above as it has effect for the purposes of Chapter IV of Part X of that Act.

(8) In this paragraph—

    "arrangements" has the same meaning as in section 410 of the Taxes Act 1988;
    "shares" includes stock.

Securities issued under section 98 or 106 of the Railways Act 1993

18—(1) Subject to sub-paragraph (2) below, any shares issued by a relevant company in pursuance of section 98 or 106 of the Railways Act 1993 (initial share holding in, and extinguishment of certain liabilities of, successor companies) shall be treated for the purposes of the Corporation Tax Acts as if they had been issued wholly in consideration of a subscription paid to that company (and attributable equally between those shares) of an amount equal—

  (a) in the case of shares issued under section 98 of that Act, to the value, as at the transfer date, of the property, rights and liabilities vested in that company in accordance with the transfer scheme mentioned in subsection (1) of that section, or

  (b) in the case of shares issued under section 106 of that Act, to the amount of the liabilities extinguished by the order under subsection (1) of that section,

reduced, in either case, by the principal sum payable under any debentures issued by the company in pursuance of the section in question.

(2) Where two or more classes of share are issued by a relevant company in pursuance of section 98 or, as the case may be, section 106 of the Railways Act 1993—

  (a) the issued shares of each of those classes shall be valued, as at the day on which, in consequence of section 98(4) or, as the case may be, section 106(5) of that Act, no more shares can be directed to be issued by the company under the section in question;

  (b) the amount of the consideration mentioned in sub-paragraph (1) above shall be apportioned between those classes of share in proportion to the aggregate value of the issued shares of each of those classes, as determined pursuant to paragraph (a) above; and

  (c) the portion attributed to any class of share pursuant to paragraph (b) above shall be divided by the number of issued shares of that class, the resulting amount being referred to in the following provisions of this sub-paragraph as the "appropriate price" for a share of that class;

and each of the issued shares of any of those classes shall be treated for the purposes of the Corporation Tax Acts as if it had been issued wholly in consideration of a subscription paid to the relevant company of an amount equal to the appropriate price for a share of that class.

(3) Any debenture issued by a relevant company in pursuance of section 98 or 106 of the Railways Act 1993 shall be treated for the purposes of the Corporation Tax Acts as if it had been issued—

  (a) wholly in consideration of a loan made to that company of an amount equal to the principal sum payable under the debenture; and

  (b) wholly and exclusively for the purposes of the trade or business carried on by that company.

(4) If any debenture issued as mentioned in sub-paragraph (3) above includes provisions for the payment of a sum expressed as interest in respect of a period which falls wholly or partly before the issue of the debenture, any payment made in pursuance of that provision in respect of that period shall be treated for the purposes of the Corporation Tax Acts as if the debenture had been issued at the commencement of that period and, accordingly, as interest on the principal sum payable under the debenture.

(5) The value required to be determined for the purposes of sub-paragraph (1)(a) or (2)(a) above is market value, as defined in section 272 of the Gains Act.

(6) In this paragraph—

  "company" means a body corporate;

  "relevant company" means a company which is—

    (a) a successor company; or

    (b) in the application of this paragraph in relation to shares or debentures issued pursuant to section 106 of the Railways Act 1993 the company, or one of the companies, wholly owning (within the meaning of that section) the successor company whose liabilities are extinguished by the order under subsection (1) of that section.

Leased assets

19—(1) For the purposes of section 781 of the Taxes Act 1988 (assets leased to traders and others), where the interest of the lessor or the lessee under a lease, or any other interest in an asset, vests in any person by virtue of a relevant transfer—

  (a) the transfer shall (notwithstanding anything in section 783(4) of that Act) be treated as made without any capital sum having been obtained in respect of that interest by the predecessor or the transferee; and

  (b) in a case where the interest is an interest under a lease, payments made by the predecessor under the lease before the coming into force of the transfer shall be treated as if they had been made under that lease by the transferee.

(2) No charge shall arise under section 781(1) of the Taxes Act 1988 by virtue of section 783(2) of that Act in a case where the capital sum mentioned in section 781(1)(b)(i) or (ii) of that Act is the consideration obtained (or treated by section 783(4) of that Act as obtained) by the Board on a disposal pursuant to a direction under Part II of the Railways Act 1993 of securities of a subsidiary of the Board.

(3) The grant of a lease of an asset—

  (a) by a person to an associate of his, pursuant to an obligation imposed by a restructuring scheme by virtue of section 91(1)(c) of the Railways Act 1993

  (b) by a person to an associate of his, pursuant to paragraph 2 of Schedule 8 to that Act in connection with a restructuring scheme, or

(c) by the Board, any of the Board's wholly owned subsidiaries, a publicly owned railway company or a company wholly owned by the Franchising Director to an associate of the grantor, pursuant to a direction under that Act,

shall be treated for the purposes of section 781 of the Taxes Act 1988 (notwithstanding anything in section 783(4) of that Act) as made without any capital sum having been obtained by the grantor.

(4) No charge shall arise under section 781(1) of the Taxes Act 1988 in a case where the capital sum mentioned in section 781(1)(b)(i) or (ii) of that Act is the consideration obtained (or treated by section 783(4) of that Act as obtained) on a disposal of, or of an interest in, rolling stock by—

(a) the Board,
(b) a wholly owned subsidiary of the Board,
(c) a publicly owned railway company,
(d) a company wholly owned by the Franchising Director, or
(e) a body which, at the time when it acquired the rolling stock, fell within paragraph (b), (c) or (d) above,

in any case where before, at or after the time when the disposal is made the lessee's interest in a lease of the rolling stock has belonged to an associate of the person making the disposal.

(5) Section 782 of the Taxes Act 1988 (leased assets: special cases) shall not apply to payments made by—

(a) the Board,
(b) a wholly owned subsidiary of the Board,
[(ba) the Strategic Rail Authority,
(bb) a wholly owned subsidiary of the Strategic Rail Authority,][1]
(c) a publicly owned railway company,
(d) a company wholly owned by the Franchising Director,
(e) a successor company, or
(f) a franchise company,

under a lease of an asset which at any time before the creation of the lease was used by a body falling within paragraphs (a) to (d) above for the purposes of a trade carried on by that body and which was, when so used, owned by that body.

(6) Section 781 of the Taxes Act 1988 shall not, by virtue of sub-paragraph (5) above, apply to any payments to which, by virtue of section 782 of that Act, it would not have applied apart from that sub-paragraph.

(7) In this paragraph—

"asset" has the meaning given by section 785 of the Taxes Act 1988;
"associate" shall be construed in accordance with section 783(10) of that Act;
"capital sum" has the meaning given by section 785 of that Act;
"lease" has the meaning given by section 785 of that Act;
"rolling stock" has the meaning given by section 83(1) of the Railways Act 1993;
"securities" has the meaning given by section [74(5) of the Financial Services and Markets Act 2000][2].

Amendments—[1] Sub-para (5)(ba), (bb) inserted by the Transport Act 2000 s 252, Sch 27 para 50 with effect from 15 January 2001.
[2] Words in sub-para (7) in the definition of "securities" substituted by the Financial Services and Markets Act 2000 (Consequential Amendments) (Taxes) Order, SI 2001/3629 arts 83, 86 with effect for disposals of securities made after 30 November 2001.

Continuity in relation to capital allowances etc where trade transferred

20—(1) Subject to the following provisions of this Schedule, where, apart from this paragraph—

(a) the predecessor would be treated for the purposes of the Corporation Tax Acts as having ceased, by virtue of the coming into force of a relevant transfer, to carry on any trade, and
(b) the transferee would be treated as having begun, on the coming into force of that transfer, to carry it on,

then the trade shall not be treated as permanently discontinued, nor a new trade as set up, for the purposes of the allowances and charges provided for by [the Capital Allowances Act][1], but sub-paragraphs (2) to (4) below shall apply.

(2) Subject to sub-paragraphs (3) and (4) below, in a case falling within sub-paragraph (1) above—

(a) there shall be made to or on the transferee in accordance with [the Capital Allowances Act][1] all such allowances and charges as would, if the predecessor had continued to carry on the trade, have fallen to be made to or on the predecessor; and
(b) the amount of any such allowance or charge shall be computed as if—

(i) the transferee had been carrying on the trade since the predecessor began to do so; and
(ii) everything done to or by the predecessor had been done to or by the transferee (but so that the relevant transfer itself, so far as it relates to any assets in use for the purpose of the trade, shall not be treated as giving rise to any such allowance or charge).

(3) For the purposes of the Corporation Tax Acts, only such amounts (if any) as may be specified in or determined in accordance with the restructuring scheme providing for a relevant transfer shall be

allocated to the transferee in respect of expenditure by reference to which capital allowances may be made by virtue of sub-paragraph (2) above in relation to anything to which the transfer relates.

(4) Sub-paragraph (2) above shall affect the amounts falling to be taken into account in relation to the predecessor as expenditure by reference to which capital allowances may be made only so far as necessary to give effect to a reduction of any such amount by a sum equal to so much of that amount as is allocated to the transferee as mentioned in sub-paragraph (3) above.

(5) Subject to sub-paragraph (6) below, the provisions of a restructuring scheme providing for the determination of any amount which for the purposes of sub-paragraph (3) above is to be allocated, in the case of any relevant transfer, to the transferee may include provision—

(a) for such a determination to be made by the Secretary of State in such manner as may be described in the scheme;

(b) for any amount determined to be calculated by reference to such factors or to the opinion of such person as may be so described; and

(c) for a determination under those provisions to be capable of being modified, on one or more occasions, in such manner and in such circumstances as may be so described.

(6) The consent of the Treasury shall be required for the making or modification of a determination of any such amount as is mentioned in sub-paragraph (5) above; and the consent of the transferee shall also be required for any such modification after the coming into force of the relevant transfer.

(7) This sub-paragraph applies in any case where assets which are the subject of a relevant transfer became vested in the predecessor by virtue of a transfer made by a company; and in any such case—

(a) if the predecessor held a direct or indirect interest in the company at the time of the transfer by the company, that interest shall be treated for the purposes of sub-paragraph (2)(b)(ii) above as if it had instead been held by the transferee;

(b) if the company held a direct or indirect interest in the predecessor at the time of the transfer by the company, the interest which the company held in the predecessor shall be treated for the purposes of sub-paragraph (2)(b)(ii) above as if it had instead been the corresponding interest in the transferee; and

(c) if there was a person who, at the time of the transfer by the company, held—

(i) a direct or indirect interest in the predecessor, and

(ii) a direct or indirect interest in the company,

the interest which that person held at that time in the predecessor shall be treated for the purposes of sub-paragraph (2)(b)(ii) above as if it had instead been the corresponding interest in the transferee.

(8) Neither section 343 of the Taxes Act 1988 (company reconstructions without change of ownership) nor [sections 266 and 267 of the Capital Allowances Act (election where predecessor and successor are connected persons)][1] shall have effect in a case falling within sub-paragraph (1) above.

(9) In determining whether sub-paragraph (1) above has effect in relation to a relevant transfer in a case where—

(a) the predecessor continues to carry on any trade or part of a trade after the coming into force of the transfer, or

(b) the transferee was carrying on any trade before the coming into force of the transfer,

the trade or part of a trade which is continued or, as the case may be, was being carried on shall for the purposes of that sub-paragraph be treated in relation to any trade or part of a trade which is transferred by virtue of the transfer as a separate trade and shall accordingly be disregarded.

(10) Where there is a determination, or a modification of a determination, for any purposes of this paragraph, all necessary adjustments shall be made by making assessments or by repayment or discharge of tax, and shall be so made notwithstanding any limitation on the time within which assessments may be made.

Amendments—[1] Words in sub-paras (1), (2)(a), and (8) substituted by CAA 2001 s 578, Sch 2 paras 91(3), (4) with effect for corporation tax purposes as respects allowances and charges falling to be made for chargeable periods ending after 31 March 2001.

Capital allowances in certain cases where paragraph 20 does not apply

21—(1) [The Capital Allowances Act][1] shall have effect in accordance with this paragraph in relation to any property if—

(a) it is property to which a relevant transfer relates; and

(b) paragraph 20 above does not apply in relation to its transfer to the transferee;

and in this paragraph "the relevant scheme", in relation to property to which a relevant transfer relates, means the restructuring scheme that provides for that transfer.

(2) In any case where—

(a) [section 573 of the Capital Allowances Act (transfers treated as sales) as it applies for the purposes of Part 3 of that Act][1] applies on the relevant transfer in relation to the property, and (*b*) the relevant scheme contains provision for the sale of that property which is deemed to occur by virtue of [that section][1] to be deemed for the purposes of [that Act] to be at a price specified in or determined in accordance with the scheme,

that deemed sale shall be treated as a sale at the price so specified or determined (instead of at the price determined [under that section or any other provision of the Capital Allowances Act), sections 567 to 570 of that Act][1] shall not apply and that provision of the scheme shall have an equivalent effect in relation to the expenditure which the transferee is to be treated as having incurred in making the corresponding purchase.

(3) Where the property is plant or machinery which would, for the purposes of [the Capital Allowances Act][1], be treated on the coming into force of the relevant transfer as disposed of by the predecessor to the transferee and the relevant scheme contains provision for the disposal value of that property to be deemed for the purposes of [that Act][1] to be of such amount as may be specified in or determined in accordance with the scheme—

(*a*) that provision shall have effect, instead of [section 61(2) to (4), 72(3) to (5), 171, 196 or 423 of the Capital Allowances Act][1], for determining an amount as the disposal value of the property or, as the case may be, as the price at which any fixture is to be treated as sold;

(*b*) the transferee shall be deemed to have incurred expenditure of that amount on the provision of that property; and

(*c*) in the case of a fixture, the expenditure which falls to be treated as incurred by the transferee shall be deemed for the purposes of [sections 181(1) and 182(1)][1] of that Act to be incurred by the giving of a consideration consisting in a capital sum of that amount.

(4) Sub-paragraphs (5) and (6) of paragraph 20 above shall apply in relation to any determination of any amount in accordance with any provision made by a restructuring scheme for the purposes of this paragraph as they apply for the purposes of a determination such as is mentioned in those sub-paragraphs.

(5) Where there is a determination, or a modification of a determination, for any purposes of this paragraph, all necessary adjustments shall be made by making assessments or by repayment or discharge of tax, and shall be so made notwithstanding any limitation on the time within which assessments may be made.

Amendments—[1] Words in sub-paras (1), (2) and (3) substituted by CAA 2001 s 578, Sch 2 paras 91(5)–(7) with effect for income tax purposes, as respects allowances and charges falling to be made for chargeable periods ending after 5 April 2001, and for corporation tax purposes, as respects allowances and charges falling to be made for chargeable periods ending after 31 March 2001.

Capital allowances: actual consideration to be the disposal value in certain other cases

22—(1) In this paragraph, "relevant disposal" means—

(*a*) a disposal by virtue of a section 85 transfer scheme, other than a restructuring scheme, to the extent that the scheme provides for the transfer of property, rights and liabilities of—

(i) the Board,
(ii) a wholly owned subsidiary of the Board,
(iii) a publicly owned railway company, or
(iv) a company which is wholly owned by the Franchising Director,

to a franchise company or to the Franchising Director;

(*b*) a disposal pursuant to a direction under section 89 of the Railways Act 1993;

(*c*) a disposal in accordance with directions under section 125 of that Act;

(*d*) a disposal by or pursuant to an agreement or instrument made or executed, transaction effected or direction given under or by virtue of paragraph 2, 3 or 14(2) of Schedule 8 to that Act, in a case where the transfer scheme in question is a section 85 transfer scheme, other than a restructuring scheme; or

(*e*) a disposal pursuant to a requirement imposed under paragraph 7(2)(*b*) of that Schedule, in a case where the transfer to which that Schedule applies is a transfer by virtue of a section 85 transfer scheme.

(2) A relevant disposal of the relevant interest in—

(*a*) an industrial [building][1], or

(*b*) a qualifying hotel or a commercial [building][1],

shall be treated for the purposes of [Part 3 of the Capital Allowances Act][1], and the other provisions of that Act which are relevant to that Part, as a sale of that relevant interest; and [sections 567 to 570][1] of that Act (sales between connected persons or without change of control) shall not have effect in relation to that sale.

(3) Where there is a relevant disposal of [plant or machinery][1], the amount which, in consequence of that disposal, is to be brought into account as the disposal value of that [plant or machinery][1] for the purposes of [section 55 of the Capital Allowances Act (determination of entitlement or liability) shall, subject to section 62 of that Act (general limit on amount of disposal value)][1] be taken—

(*a*) if consideration is given in respect of the relevant disposal, to be an amount equal to the amount or value of that consideration, or

(b) if no such consideration is given, to be nil,

notwithstanding any other provision of [the Capital Allowances Act]¹.

(4) Where, in consequence of a relevant disposal, a fixture is treated by [section 188 of the Capital Allowances Act]¹ as ceasing to belong to a person at any time, the amount which, in consequence of that disposal, is to be brought into account as the disposal value of the fixture for the purposes of [section 55 of that Act shall, subject to section 62]¹ of that Act, be taken—

(a) if consideration is given in respect of the relevant disposal, to be an amount equal to that portion of the amount or value of that consideration which falls (or, if the person to whom the relevant disposal is made were entitled to an allowance, would fall) to be treated for the purposes of [Part 2]¹ of that Act as expenditure incurred by that person on the provision of the fixture, or

(b) if no such consideration is given, to be nil,

notwithstanding any other provision of [the Capital Allowances Act]¹.

Amendments—¹ Words in sub-paras (2), (3), and (4) substituted by CAA 2001 s 578, Sch 2 paras 91(8)–(10) with effect for income tax purposes, as respects allowances and charges falling to be made for chargeable periods ending after 5 April 2001, and for corporation tax purposes, as respects allowances and charges falling to be made for chargeable periods ending after 31 March 2001.

Sale and lease-back: limitation on tax reliefs

23—(1) Section 779 of the Taxes Act 1988 (sale and lease-back) shall not apply by virtue of subsection (1) or (2) of that section in any case where the liability of the transferor, or of the person associated with the transferor, is—

(a) a liability under an access agreement, within the meaning of Part I of the Railways Act 1993;
(b) a liability under an agreement or instrument made or executed—

(i) pursuant to an obligation imposed by a restructuring scheme by virtue of section 91(1)(c) of that Act; or
(ii) pursuant to paragraph 2 of Schedule 8 to that Act;

(c) a liability under an exempt lease; or
(d) a liability to pay exempt rent or to make other exempt payments.

(2) A lease is "exempt" for the purposes of sub-paragraph (1)(c) above if—

(a) the transfer mentioned in subsection (1) of section 779 of the Taxes Act 1988 is—

(i) a transfer by virtue of a restructuring scheme;
(ii) a transfer pursuant to an obligation imposed by a restructuring scheme by virtue of section 91(1)(c) of the Railways Act 1993; or
(iii) a transfer pursuant to paragraph 2 of Schedule 8 to that Act; and

(b) the lease is granted after that transfer and otherwise than pursuant to—

(i) an obligation imposed by a restructuring scheme by virtue of section 91(1)(c) of the Railways Act 1993; or
(ii) paragraph 2 of Schedule 8 to that Act.

(3) Rent or other payments are "exempt" for the purposes of paragraph (d) of sub-paragraph (1) above if—

(a) the rent or other payments would, apart from that paragraph, be rent or other payments to which section 779 of the Taxes Act 1988 applies by virtue of subsection (1) or (2) of that section;
(b) the transfer mentioned in subsection (1) or, as the case may be, subsection (2)(a) of that section is—

(i) a transfer by virtue of a restructuring scheme;
(ii) a transfer pursuant to an obligation imposed by a restructuring scheme by virtue of section 91(1)(c) of the Railways Act 1993; or
(iii) a transfer pursuant to paragraph 2 of Schedule 8 to that Act; and

(c) the transaction or series of transactions mentioned in subsection (1)(b) or, as the case may be, subsection (2)(b) of the said section 779 is effected after that transfer.

(4) In this paragraph "transferor", "lease" and "rent" have the same meaning as they have in section 779 of the Taxes Act 1988 and "associated" shall be construed in accordance with subsection (11) of that section.

Sales of land with right to reconveyance

24 No charge to tax shall arise by virtue of section 36 of the Taxes Act 1988 (charge on sale of land with right to reconveyance) where the sale in question is constituted by a disposition to a franchise company—

(a) by virtue of a transfer scheme;
(b) pursuant to an obligation imposed by a transfer scheme by virtue of section 91(1)(c) of the Railways Act 1993; or
(c) pursuant to paragraph 2 of Schedule 8 to that Act.

Modifications of restructuring scheme

25—(1) Subject to sub-paragraph (2) below, where the effect of a restructuring scheme is modified in pursuance of an agreement or direction under paragraph 2 or 3 of Schedule 8 to the Railways Act 1993 the Corporation Tax Acts and this Schedule shall have effect as if—

(a) the scheme originally made had been the scheme as modified; and

(b) anything done by or in relation to the preceding holder had, so far as relating to the property, rights or liabilities affected by the modification, been done by or in relation to the subsequent holder.

(2) A disposal of an asset—

(a) which is effected in pursuance of an agreement or direction under paragraph 2 of Schedule 8 to the Railways Act 1993 and

(b) which is either the grant of a lease of land or the creation of other liabilities and rights over land,

shall be taken for the purposes of corporation tax on chargeable gains, in relation to the person to whom the disposal is made as well as the person making the disposal, to be effected for a consideration such that no gain or loss accrues to the person making the disposal.

(3) Section 171(1) of the Gains Act (transfers within a group) shall not apply where the disposal in question falls within sub-paragraph (2) above.

(4) Any reference in sub-paragraph (1) or (2) above to an agreement or direction under paragraph 2 or 3 of Schedule 8 to the Railways Act 1993 includes a reference to such an agreement or direction as varied in accordance with a direction given by the Secretary of State under paragraph 14(2) of that Schedule.

(5) For the purposes of sub-paragraph (1)(b) above—

"the preceding holder" means the person who without the modification in question—

(a) became, by virtue of the restructuring scheme in question, entitled or subject to the property, rights or liabilities affected by the modification, or

(b) remained, notwithstanding the restructuring scheme in question, entitled or subject to the property, rights or liabilities affected by the modification,

as the case may be;

"the subsequent holder" means the person who, in consequence of the modification in question, becomes, or resumes being, entitled or subject to the property, rights or liabilities affected by the modification.

Income tax exemption for certain interest

26 Where liability for a loan made to the Board is vested in a successor company by virtue of a section 85 transfer scheme, the vesting shall not affect any direction given, or having effect as if given, by the Treasury under section 581 of the Taxes Act 1988 (income tax exemption for interest on foreign currency securities) in respect of the loan.

Employee benefits: transport vouchers

27—(1) This paragraph applies to any person (an "eligible person")—

(a) who on 11th January 1994 was in the employment of—

(i) the Board,

(ii) a wholly owned subsidiary of the Board, or

(iii) any other subsidiary of the Board which, at that date, was a passenger transport undertaking; and

(b) who at that date was provided, or was eligible to be provided, by reason of that employment, with a transport voucher falling within subsection (6) of section 141 of the Taxes Act 1988 (exclusion of subsection (1) of that section in relation to certain transport vouchers);

but this sub-paragraph is subject to sub-paragraph (2) below.

(2) This paragraph shall not apply, or shall cease to apply, to a person if, on or after 11th January 1994, any of the following conditions became or becomes satisfied in his case, that is to say—

(a) he ceases, otherwise than—

(i) by virtue of anything done under or by virtue of, or pursuant to, the Railways Act 1993 or

(ii) by virtue of any other enactment or statutory instrument, in consequence of anything so done,

to be in the employment of a person falling within sub-paragraph (i) or, as the case may be, sub-paragraph (ii) or (iii) of sub-paragraph (1)(a) above;

(b) he is not in the employment of any person engaged in the railway industry; or

(c) the continuity of the period of his employment is broken.

(3) Subsection (6) of section 141 of the Taxes Act 1988 shall, if and so long as the conditions in sub-paragraph (4) below are satisfied, have effect in relation to a transport voucher provided for an eligible person, notwithstanding—

(*a*) that the employer of the eligible person does not fall to be regarded as a passenger transport undertaking;

(*b*) that the arrangements under which the transport voucher is provided were not in operation on 25th March 1982; or

(*c*) that the passenger transport services which may be obtained by means of the transport voucher are provided, in whole or in part, otherwise than as mentioned in paragraphs (*a*) to (*d*) of that subsection;

but this sub-paragraph is subject to sub-paragraph (2) above.

(4) The conditions mentioned in sub-paragraph (3) above are—

(*a*) that the eligible person is in the employment of an employer engaged in the railway industry;

(*b*) that the transport voucher is provided by reason of the eligible person's being in the employment of such an employer;

(*c*) that the transport voucher is intended to enable the eligible person or a relation of his to obtain passenger transport services; and

(*d*) that the current transport voucher benefits in the case of the eligible person are not significantly better than the former transport voucher benefits for comparable employees.

(5) The Secretary of State may, with the consent of the Treasury, by order prescribe for any purposes of this paragraph circumstances—

(*a*) in which a person who ceases, or ceased, as mentioned in sub-paragraph (2)(*a*) above to be in the employment there mentioned shall be treated—

(i) as if he had not ceased to be in that employment, or

(ii) as if he had not so ceased to be in that employment;

(*b*) in which a person shall be treated for a period during which he is not or was not in the employment of any person engaged in the railway industry as if he were or had been in the employment of such a person;

(*c*) in which a break in the continuity of a person's period of employment shall be disregarded; or

(*d*) in which a transport voucher shall be treated as if it were, or had been, provided for a person by reason of his being in the employment of an employer engaged in the railway industry.

(6) The employers who are to be regarded for the purposes of this paragraph as "engaged in the railway industry" are those who carry on activities of a class or description specified for the purposes of this sub-paragraph in an order made by the Secretary of State with the consent of the Treasury; and the Secretary of State may so specify any class or description of activity which, in his opinion, falls within, or is related to or connected with, the railway industry.

(7) Any power to make an order under this paragraph shall be exercisable by statutory instrument; and a statutory instrument containing such an order shall be subject to annulment pursuant to a resolution of the House of Commons.

(8) In determining for the purposes of sub-paragraph (4)(*d*) above whether the current transport voucher benefits in the case of an eligible person are not significantly better than the former transport voucher benefits for comparable employees, regard shall be had, in particular, to—

(*a*) the passenger transport services which may be, or (as the case may be) might have been, obtained by means of transport vouchers under the arrangements in question,

(*b*) whether, and (if so) the extent to which, free or concessionary travel is or (as the case may be) was available under those arrangements,

(*c*) the rate of any discount to the standard fare which is or (as the case may be) was available in the case of concessionary travel under those arrangements, and

(*d*) any limitations on the availability or use of transport vouchers under the arrangements in question.

[(9) Chapter I of Part XIV of the Employment Rights Act 1996, except section 218(6), shall apply for the purposes of this paragraph as it applies for the purposes of that Act.]¹

(12) In this paragraph—

"the current transport voucher benefits", in the case of an eligible person, means the totality of the benefits which, by reason of his employment by an employer engaged in the railway industry, are available in the year in question—

(*a*) to the eligible person, and

(*b*) to relations of his,

by way of transport voucher under the arrangements under which the transport voucher in question is provided;

"the former transport voucher benefits for comparable employees", in the case of an eligible person, means the totality of the benefits which would, by reason of the employment by the Board of a person of similar status to the eligible person ("the comparable person"), have been available in the year 1993–94—

(*a*) to the comparable person, and

(*b*) to relations of his,

by way of transport voucher under arrangements in operation on 25th March 1982.

(13) Subject to paragraph 1(1) and [sub-paragraph]¹ (12) above, expressions used in this paragraph and in section 141 of the Taxes Act 1988 have the same meaning in this paragraph as they have in that section.

(14) This paragraph has effect—

    (*a*) in relation to transport vouchers received by an employee on or after 11th January 1994; and

    (*b*) in relation to expense incurred on or after that date in, or in connection with, the provision of—

        (i) any transport voucher, or

        (ii) the money, goods or services for which it is capable of being exchanged,

irrespective of when the transport voucher falls to be regarded as received by the employee in question.

Amendments—¹ Para 27(9) substituted for para 27(9)–(11) and words in para 27(13) substituted by the Employment Rights Act 1996 Sch 1 para 62 with effect from 22 August 1996.

SCHEDULE 25

NORTHERN IRELAND AIRPORTS LIMITED

Section 253

Commentary—*Simon's Direct Tax Service* **B3.246.**

Interpretation

1—(1) In this Schedule—

    "the final accounting period" means the last complete accounting period of NIAL ending before the transfer date;

    "the Holding Company" means the Northern Ireland Transport Holding Company established under section 47 of the Transport Act (Northern Ireland) 1967;

    "NIAL" means the subsidiary of the Holding Company incorporated under the name of Northern Ireland Airports Limited;

    "the Order" means the Airports (Northern Ireland) Order 1994 and any reference to an Article is to an Article of the Order;

    "the successor company" means the company nominated under Article 51(1) as the successor company for the purposes of the Order;

    "the transfer date" means the day appointed under Article 54(2);

    "the transferred trade" means the trade carried on by NIAL and transferred under Article 54(2) to the successor company.

(2) This Schedule, so far as it relates to corporation tax on chargeable gains, shall be construed as one with the Taxation of Chargeable Gains Act 1992.

Transfers from NIAL to successor company: general

2—(1) The following shall apply for the purposes of the Corporation Tax Acts—

    (*a*) the transferred trade shall be treated as having been, at the time when it began to be carried on by NIAL and at all times since that time, a separate trade carried on by the successor company;

    (*b*) the trade carried on by the successor company on and after the transfer date shall be treated as the same trade as that which, by virtue of paragraph (*a*) above, it is treated as having carried on before that date;

    (*c*) all property, rights and liabilities of NIAL which are transferred under Article 54(2) to the successor company shall be treated as having been, at the time when they became vested in NIAL and at all times since that time, property, rights and liabilities of the successor company; and

    (*d*) anything done by NIAL in relation to any property, rights and liabilities which are transferred under Article 54(2) to the successor company shall be deemed to have been done by the successor company.

(2) This paragraph shall have effect in relation to accounting periods beginning after the final accounting period.

Roll-over relief

3—(1) This paragraph applies where NIAL has, before the transfer date, disposed of (or of its interest in) any assets used, throughout the period of ownership, wholly or partly for the purposes of the transferred trade.

(2) Sections 152 to 156 of the Taxation of Chargeable Gains Act 1992 (roll-over relief on replacement of business assets) shall have effect in relation to that disposal as if NIAL and the successor company were the same person.

Transfers from Holding Company to successor company

4—(1) This paragraph applies where under Article 54(2) an asset of the Holding Company is transferred to the successor company.

(2) The disposal of the asset by the Holding Company shall be taken for the purposes of corporation tax on chargeable gains to be effected for a consideration of such amount as would secure that on the disposal neither a gain nor a loss would accrue to the Holding Company.

(3) (*inserts* TCGA 1992 s 35(3)(*d*)(x)).

Leasehold interests in industrial buildings or structures

5—(1) This paragraph applies where—

  (*a*) NIAL is entitled, under a lease granted by the Holding Company, to a leasehold interest in a building or structure,
  (*b*) by virtue of Article 52(2)(*b*) that interest is deemed to have been surrendered by NIAL,
  (*c*) under Article 52(3) the Holding Company and NIAL enter into a lease under which NIAL is entitled to a leasehold interest (''the new interest'') in the property, and
  (*d*) under Article 54(2) that interest is transferred to the successor company.

(2) For the purposes of [the Capital Allowances Act 2001]¹—

  (*a*) the surrender shall be deemed to be for such an amount (by way of sale, insurance, salvage or compensation moneys) as would secure that no balancing allowance or balancing charge would be made to or on NIAL by reason of the surrender (''the surrender value'');
  (*b*) the successor company shall be treated for the purposes of [the Capital Allowances Act 2001]¹—
    (i) as if the new interest were the relevant interest in relation to the capital expenditure incurred on the construction of the property; and
    (ii) as if the amount of the residue of that expenditure immediately after the transfer of the new interest were equal to the surrender value.

(3) In this paragraph—

  ...¹
  ''balancing allowance'' and ''balancing charge'' have the same meanings as in [Chapter 7 of Part 3 of the Capital Allowances Act 2001]¹;
  ''the property'' means the building or structure referred to in sub-paragraph (1); and
  ''relevant interest'' has the same meaning as in [Chapter 3 of Part 3 of the Capital Allowances Act 2001]¹.

Amendments—¹ Words in sub-paras (2), (3) substituted, and in sub-para (3), definition of ''the 1990 Act'' repealed by CAA 2001 ss 578, 580, Sch 2 para 92, Sch 4 with effect for corporation tax purposes as respects allowances and charges falling to be made for chargeable periods ending after 31 March 2001.

Securities of successor company

6—(1) Any share issued by the successor company under Article 57 shall be treated for the purposes of the Corporation Tax Acts as if it had been issued wholly in consideration of a subscription paid to the company of an amount equal to the nominal value of the share.

(2) Any debenture issued by the successor company under Article 57 shall be treated for the purposes of the Corporation Tax Acts as if it had been issued—

  (*a*) wholly in consideration of a loan made to the company of an amount equal to the principal sum payable under the debenture, and
  (*b*) wholly and exclusively for the purposes of the trade carried on by the company.

(3) If any such debenture includes provision for the payment of a sum expressed as interest in respect of a period which falls wholly or partly before the issue of the debenture, any payment made in pursuance of that provision in respect of that period shall be treated for the purposes of the Corporation Tax Acts as if the debenture had been issued at the commencement of that period and, accordingly, as interest on the principal sum payable under the debenture.

FINANCE ACT 1995

(1995 Chapter 4)

ARRANGEMENT OF SECTIONS

PART III

INCOME TAX, CORPORATION TAX AND CAPITAL GAINS TAX

Income tax: charge, rates and reliefs

Part I—The new provisions.
Part II—Minor and consequential amendments of the Taxes Act 1988.
Part III—Consequential amendments of other enactments.
Schedule 18—Deceased persons' estates.
Schedule 19—*Stock lending: interest on cash collateral.* (repealed)
Schedule 20—Claims etc not included in returns.
Schedule 21—Self-assessment etc: transitional provisions.
Schedule 22—Prevention of exploitation of Schedule 20 to Finance Act 1994.
Part I—Cases I and II of Schedule D.
Part II—Cases III, IV and V of Schedule D.
Part III—Procedural and other provisions.
Part IV—Interpretation.
Schedule 23—Obligations etc imposed on UK representatives.
Schedule 24—Exchange gains and losses.
Part I—Amendments of Finance Act 1993.
Part II—Amendments of other provisions.
Schedule 25—Controlled foreign companies.
Schedule 26—Change in ownership of investment company: deductions.
Schedule 27—Sub-contractors in the construction industry.
Schedule 28—Electronic lodgement of tax returns, etc.
Schedule 29—Repeals.
Part VIII—Income tax, corporation tax and capital gains tax.

An Act to grant certain duties, to alter other duties, and to amend the law relating to the National Debt and the Public Revenue, and to make further provision in connection with Finance.

[1st May 1995]

PART III
INCOME TAX, CORPORATION TAX AND CAPITAL GAINS TAX
Income tax: charge, rates and reliefs

35 Charge and rates of income tax for 1995–96
(*Spent*).

Commentary—*Simon's Direct Tax Service* **E1.102.**

36 Personal allowance
(*Spent*).

Commentary—*Simon's Direct Tax Service* **E2.302.**

Corporation tax: charge and rate

37 Charge and rate of corporation tax for 1995
(*Spent*).

Commentary—*Simon's Direct Tax Service* **D2.108.**

38 Small companies
(*Spent*).

Commentary—*Simon's Direct Tax Service* **D2.109.**

Taxation of income from land

39 Income chargeable under Schedule A

Amendments—This section repealed by FA 1998 s 165, Sch 27 Part III(4) with effect for income tax for the year 1998–99 and subsequent years of assessment, and for corporation tax from 1 April 1998 subject to transitional provisions in FA 1998 Sch 5 Part IV.

40 Non-residents and their representatives

(1) (*inserts* TA 1988 s 42A).

(2) (*amends* TMA 1970 s 98, Table).

(3) Section 43 of the Taxes Act 1988 (payments to non-residents of amounts chargeable under Schedule A) shall not have effect in relation to any payment made on or after 6th April 1996.

Commentary—*Simon's Direct Tax Service* **A3.141.**

41 Income from overseas property

Commentary—*Simon's Direct Tax Service* **A4.101.**
Amendments—This section repealed by FA 1998 s 165, Sch 27 Part III(4) with effect for income tax for the year 1998–99 and subsequent years of assessment, and for corporation tax from 1 April 1998 subject to transitional provisions in FA 1998 Sch 5 Part IV.

42 Abolition of interest relief for commercially let property

(1) ...².

(2) (*amends* TA 1988 ss 353(1B), 355, 356(1), 356B(5), 357A(7), 357B(1)(*c*), (6), 357C(1)(*e*), (2))².

(3) Subject to subsections (4) to (6) below, this section shall have effect in relation to any payment of interest made on or after 6th April 1995.

(4) Where—

(*a*) the profits or gains of any source of income that ceases in the course of the year 1995-96 are taxed, by virtue of section 39(5) or 41(9) above without reference to the Schedule A that has effect by virtue of section 39(1) above, and
(*b*) that source of income includes any land, caravan or house-boat with respect to which the condition specified in section 355(1)(*b*) of the Taxes Act 1988 would be satisfied in the case of any loan,

this section shall not apply to any payment of interest on that loan which is made before the time in the year 1995-96 when that source of income ceases.

(5) Subject to paragraph 19(3) of Schedule 6 to this Act, no relief in respect of any payment of interest before 6th April 1995 shall be given under section 355(4) of the Taxes Act 1988 (income against which relief available) against any income for the year 1995-96 or any subsequent year of assessment except in a case where the income falls within subsection (4)(*a*) above.

(6) ...¹

Commentary—*Simon's Direct Tax Service* **A4.101.**
Amendments—¹ Sub-s (6) repealed by FA 1996 Sch 41 Pt V(3) with effect for accounting periods ending after 31 March 1996, subject to transitional provisions in FA 1996 Sch 15.
² Sub-s (1), and sub-s (2)(*b*)–(*e*) repealed by FA 1999 s 139, Sch 20 Pt III(7) with effect for payments of interest within FA 1999 s 38(3), (4).

Benefits in kind

43 Cars available for private use

(1)–(3) (*insert* TA 1988 ss 157A, 167(2B)–(2D) and *amend* ss 158, 167(2)).

(4) This section shall have effect for the year 1995-96 and subsequent years of assessment.

44 Cars: accessories for the disabled

(1), (2) (*amend* TA 1988 s 168A(11) and *insert* s 168AA).

(3) This section shall have effect for the year 1995-96 and subsequent years of assessment.

45 Beneficial loan arrangements: replacement loans

(1) In Chapter II of Part V of the Taxes Act 1988 (benefits in kind, &c), section 160 (beneficial loan arrangements) is amended as follows.

(2)–(4) (*repeal* TA 1988 s 160(5)(*b*), *insert* s 160(3A) and *renumber* Sch 7 para 4 as para 4(1) and *insert* para 4(2)).

(5) The above amendments have effect for the year 1995-96 and subsequent years of assessment and apply to loans whether made before or after the passing of this Act.

Chargeable gains

46 Relief on re-investment: property companies etc

(1) Chapter IA of Part V of the Taxation of Chargeable Gains Act 1992 (roll-over relief on re-investment) shall be amended as follows.

(2)–(4) (*insert* TCGA 1992 ss 164A(13), 164F(2A), 164I(4A)).

47 Relief on re-investment: amount of relief, etc

(1) Chapter IA of Part V of the Taxation of Chargeable Gains Act 1992 (roll-over relief on re-investment) shall be amended as follows.

(2)–(5) (*insert* TCGA 1992 ss 164A(14), 164F(10C), 164FF, 164FG).

(6) Subsection (4) above (and subsections (1) to (3) above so far as relating to subsection (4) above) shall apply to a claim as respects a qualifying investment if—

(*a*) the qualifying investment is acquired on or after 20th June 1994; or
(*b*) the claim is under section 164A(2) and relates to a disposal on or after that day; or

(*c*) the claim is under subsection (10A) of section 164F and relates to a gain which (apart from that subsection) would accrue on or after that day.

(7) Subsection (5) above (and subsections (1) to (3) above so far as relating to subsection (5) above) shall apply to a claim as respects a qualifying investment if—

(*a*) the qualifying investment is acquired on or after 20th June 1994; or
(*b*) the claim is under section 164A(2) and relates to a disposal on or after that day; or
(*c*) the claim is under subsection (10A) of section 164F and relates to a gain which (apart from that subsection) would accrue on or after that day; or
(*d*) there is another claim as respects that qualifying investment which is under section 164A(2) and which relates to a disposal on or after that day; or
(*e*) there is another claim as respects that qualifying investment which is under subsection (10A) of section 164F and which relates to a gain which (apart from that subsection) would accrue on or after that day.

(8) Any such adjustment as is appropriate in consequence of this section may be made (whether by discharge or repayment of tax, the making of an assessment or otherwise).

Commentary—*Simon's Direct Tax Service* **C3.901.**

48 Roll-over relief and groups of companies

(1), (2) (*insert* TCGA 1992 ss 175(2A)–(2C), 247(5A)).

(3) Subject to subsection (4) below—

(*a*) the subsection inserted into section 175 of the Taxation of Chargeable Gains Act 1992 by subsection (1) above as subsection (2A) shall be deemed always to have had effect; and
(*b*) the earlier enactments corresponding to that section shall be deemed to have contained provision to the same effect as that subsection (2A).

(4) Paragraph (*c*) of that subsection (2A) shall not apply unless the claim is made on or after 29th November 1994.

(5) The subsection inserted into section 175 of the Taxation of Chargeable Gains Act 1992 by subsection (1) above as subsection (2B) shall apply where the disposal or the acquisition is on or after 29th November 1994; and the subsection so inserted as subsection (2C) shall apply where the acquisition is on or after that date.

(6) The subsection inserted into section 247 of the Taxation of Chargeable Gains Act 1992 by subsection (2) above shall apply—

(*a*) so far as it relates to section 175(2A), where the disposal or the acquisition is on or after 29th November 1994; and
(*b*) so far as it relates to section 175(2C), where the acquisition is on or after that date.

Commentary—*Simon's Direct Tax Service* **C3.317.**

49 De-grouping charges

(1), (2) (*insert* TCGA 1992 s 179(2A), (2B), (9A)).

(3) This section has effect in relation to a company in any case in which the time of the company's ceasing to be a member of the second group is on or after 29th November 1994.

50 Corporate bonds

(*inserted* TCGA 1992 s 117(2A); repealed by FA 1996 Sch 41 Pt V(3) with effect for accounting periods ending after 31 March 1996, subject to transitional provisions in FA 1996 Sch 15).

Insurance companies and friendly societies

51 Companies carrying on life assurance business

Schedule 8 to this Act has effect in relation to companies carrying on life assurance business, as follows—

Part I contains general amendments,
Part II contains amendments of provisions relating to overseas life insurance companies, and
Part III contains supplementary provisions.

Commentary—*Simon's Direct Tax Service* **B2.360; D4.501, 503, 509.**

52 Meaning of "insurance company"

(1) (*amended* TA 1988 s 431(2), *repealed by the* Financial Services and Markets Act 2000 (Consequential Amendments) (Taxes) Order, SI 2001/3629 art 109, Schedule *with effect from 1 December 2001*)).

(2) (*amends* FA 1993 s 168(7); *repealed by* FA 2002 s 141, Sch 40 Pt 3(10) *with effect for accounting periods beginning after 30 September 2002*).

(3) (*amended* FA 1994 s 177(1); *repealed by* FA 2002 s 141, Sch 40 Pt 3(13) *with effect for accounting periods beginning after 30 September 2002.*).

(4) (*amends* Inheritance Tax Act 1984 s 59(3)(*b*) (see Orange Book)).

(5) Subsections (1) to (3) above shall have effect in relation to any accounting period ending after 30th June 1994; and subsection (4) above shall have effect for the purposes of the making, on an anniversary or other occasion after that date, of any charge to tax under section 64 or 65 of the Inheritance Tax Act 1984.

53 Transfer of life insurance business

(1) The amendments specified in Schedule 9 to this Act (which relate to enactments referring to the transfer of the whole or part of the long term business of an insurance company) shall have effect.

(2) This section and that Schedule shall have effect in relation to any transfers sanctioned or authorised after 30th June 1994.

Commentary—*Simon's Direct Tax Service* **D4.501.**

54 Friendly societies

Schedule 10 to this Act (which makes provision about friendly societies) shall have effect.

Commentary—*Simon's Direct Tax Service* **D4.603.**

Insurance policies

55 Qualifying life insurance policies

(1) Subject to subsections (2) and (3) below—

   (*a*) paragraph 21 of Schedule 15 to the Taxes Act 1988 (certification of policies and of standard forms etc) shall not apply, in relation to any time on or after [the appointed date][1], for determining whether a policy is or would be a qualifying policy at that time; and

   (*b*) no certificate may be issued under that paragraph at any time on or after that date except, in the case of a certificate under sub-paragraph (1)(*a*) of that paragraph, in relation to a time before that date.

(2) Subsection (1) above shall not affect the right of any person to bring or continue with an appeal under paragraph 21(3) of that Schedule against either a refusal before [the appointed date][1] to certify any policy or a refusal on or after that date to certify any policy in relation to times before that date.

(3) A certificate issued—

   (*a*) before [the appointed date][1] in pursuance of paragraph 21(1)(*a*) of that Schedule, or

   (*b*) in pursuance of a determination on an appeal determined after that date by virtue of subsection (2) above,

shall, in relation to any time on or after that date or, as the case may be, the date on which it is issued, be conclusive evidence that the policy to which it relates is (subject to any variation of the policy) a qualifying policy.

(4) Paragraph 22 of that Schedule (certificates from body issuing policy) shall cease to have effect in relation to any time on or after [the appointed date][1].

(5) Paragraph 24 of that Schedule (policies issued by non-resident companies) shall have effect in relation to times on or after [the appointed date][1]—

   (*a*), (*b*) (*amend* TA 1988 Sch 15 para 24(3)).

(6) (*substitutes* TA 1988 Sch 15 para 25(2)).

(7) In paragraph 27(1) of that Schedule, except so far as it has effect for the purposes of any case to which paragraph 21 of that Schedule applies by virtue of the preceding provisions of this section, for "paragraphs 21 and" there shall be substituted "paragraph".

(8) In section 553 of the Taxes Act 1988 (which contains provisions referring to paragraph 24(3) or (4) of Schedule 15 to that Act)—

   (*a*) in subsection (2), for the words from "neither" to "fulfilled" there shall be substituted "the conditions in paragraph 24(3) of Schedule 15 to this Act are not fulfilled"; and

   (*b*) in subsection (7), for "either sub-paragraph (3) or sub-paragraph (4)" there shall be substituted "sub-paragraph (3)";

but this subsection shall not affect the operation of Chapter II of Part XIII of that Act in relation to any policy in relation to which the conditions in paragraph 24(4) of Schedule 15 to that Act, as it then had effect, were fulfilled at times in accounting periods before those in relation to which section 103 of the Finance Act 1993 (which repealed section 445 of the Taxes Act 1988) had effect.

[(9) In this section "the appointed date" means such date as may be specified for the purpose in an order made by the Board.][1]

Commentary—*Simon's Direct Tax Service* **E3.502.**
Amendments—[1] Words in sub-ss (1)–(5) substituted and sub-s (9) inserted by FA 1996 s 162(1).

56 Foreign life policies etc

(1) (*amends* TA 1988 s 547(5A) and inserts TA 1988 s 547(6A)).

(2) (*amends* TA 1988 s 553(6) and inserts TA 1988 s 553(6A)).

(3) For the purpose of securing that section 547(5) of the Taxes Act 1988 has effect in other cases (in addition to those specified in sections 547(6A) and 553(6A)) where it appears to the Board appropriate for section 547(6) or 553(6) to be disapplied by reference to tax chargeable under the laws of a territory outside the United Kingdom, the Board may by regulations provide that the cases described in subsection (6A) of each of sections 547 and 553 of that Act are to be treated as including cases, being cases which would not otherwise fall within the subsection, where the conditions specified in the regulations are fulfilled in relation to any time (including one before the making of the regulations).

(4) This section shall apply in relation to any gain arising on or after 29th November 1994 and in relation to any gain arising before that date the income tax on which has not been the subject of an assessment that became final and conclusive before that date.

Commentary—*Simon's Direct Tax Service* E3.502.

57 Duties of insurers in relation to life policies etc

(1), (2) (*insert* TA 1988 s 552(2A), (4A)–(4C)).

(3) (*amends* TMA 1970 s 98, Table).

Pensions

58 Personal pensions: income withdrawals

Schedule 11 to this Act has effect for the purpose of enabling income withdrawals to be made under a personal pension scheme where the purchase of an annuity is deferred.

Commentary—*Simon's Direct Tax Service* E7.311, 406.

59 Pensions: meaning of insurance company etc

(1) Part XIV of the Taxes Act 1988 (pension schemes etc) shall be amended as follows.

(2)–(5) (*substitute* TA 1988 ss 591(3), 599(8), *amend* s 630 and *insert* ss 659B, 659C).

60 Application of section 59

(1) Section 59(2) above and the new section 659B, so far as relating to section 591(2)(*g*), shall apply in relation to a scheme not approved by virtue of section 591 before the day on which this Act is passed.

(2) Section 59(3) above and the new section 659B, so far as relating to section 599(7), shall apply where tax is charged under section 599 on or after the day on which this Act is passed.

(3) Section 59(4) above and the new section 659B, so far as relating to Chapter IV of Part XIV, shall apply in relation to a scheme not approved under that Chapter before the day on which this Act is passed.

(4) Subsection (5) below applies where—

(*a*) a scheme is approved under Chapter IV of Part XIV before the day on which this Act is passed,

(*b*) on or after that day the person who established the scheme proposes to amend it, and

(*c*) the scheme as proposed to be amended would make provision such that, if the scheme had not been approved before that day, section 59(4) above and the new section 659B (so far as relating to that Chapter) would allow the Board to approve it.

(5) The Board may at their discretion approve the amendment notwithstanding anything in Chapter IV of Part XIV, and if the amendment is made—

(*a*) section 59(4) above and the new section 659B, so far as relating to that Chapter, shall apply in relation to the scheme, and

(*b*) any question as to the validity of the Board's approval of the scheme shall be determined accordingly.

Commentary—*Simon's Direct Tax Service* E7.215, 406A.

61 Cessation of approval of certain retirement benefits schemes

(1) (*inserts* TA 1988 ss 591C, 591D).

(2) (*inserts* TCGA 1992 s 239A).

(3) This section shall apply in relation to any approval of a retirement benefits scheme which ceases to have effect on or after 2nd November 1994 other than an approval ceasing to have effect by virtue of a notice given before that day under section 591B(1) of the Taxes Act 1988.

Saving and investment: general

62 Follow-up TESSAs

(*Inserts* TA 1988 ss 326BB, 326C(1)(*cc*), (*cd*), 326C(1A), (1B) and *amends* s 326C(1)(*e*), (2)).

63 TESSAs: European institutions

(1)–(4) (*amend* TA 1988 s 326A(4) and *insert* ss 326A(10), 326D; sub-s (3) *repealed by the Financial Services and Markets Act 2000 (Consequential Amendments) (Taxes) Order*, SI 2001/3629 art 109, Schedule *with effect from 1 December 2001*)).

(5) Subsection (2) above shall apply in relation to accounts opened after such day as the Board may by order made by statutory instrument appoint.

Notes—The appointed day referred to in sub-s (5) is 1 January 1996.

64 Personal equity plans: tax representatives

(1) (*inserts* TA 1988 s 333A).

(2) (*inserts* TCGA 1992 s 151(2A)).

65 Contractual savings schemes

Schedule 12 to this Act (which contains provisions about contractual savings schemes) shall have effect.

Commentary—*Simon's Direct Tax Service* B5.210; D4.733; E4.588.

66 Enterprise investment scheme: ICTA amendments

(1) Chapter III of Part VII of the Taxes Act 1988 as it has effect in relation to shares issued on or after 1st January 1994 (the enterprise investment scheme) shall be amended as follows.

(2)–(4) (*insert* TA 1988 ss 292(5), 293(8B), 305(5), (6)).

67 Enterprise investment scheme: TCGA amendments

Schedule 13 to this Act (which contains amendments relating to chargeable gains as regards the enterprise investment scheme) shall have effect.

68 Business expansion scheme: ICTA amendments

(1) Chapter III of Part VII of the Taxes Act 1988 as it has effect in relation to shares issued before 1st January 1994 (the business expansion scheme) shall be amended as follows.

(2) In section 289 (the relief) the following subsection shall be inserted after subsection (12) (which defines "the relevant period" for the purposes of the Chapter)—

"(12A) In arriving at the relevant period for the purposes of sections 294 to 296 any time falling on or after 29 November 1994 shall be ignored; and subsection (12) above shall have effect subject to the preceding provisions of this subsection."

(3) In section 305 (reorganisation of share capital) the following subsections shall be inserted after subsection (4)—

"(5) Subsection (2) above shall not apply where the reorganisation occurs on or after 29 November 1994.

(6) Subsection (2) above shall not apply by virtue of subsection (3) above where the rights are disposed of on or after 29 November 1994."

Commentary—*Simon's Direct Tax Service* E3.145–148.

69 Business expansion scheme: TCGA amendments

(*Inserts* TCGA 1992 s 150(8A)–(8C)).

Venture capital trusts

70 Approval of companies as trusts

(1) (*inserts* TA 1988 s 842AA).

(2) Schedule 14 to this Act (meaning of "qualifying holdings") shall be inserted, before Schedule 29 to the Taxes Act 1988 as Schedule 28B to that Act, and shall be construed accordingly.

71 Income tax relief

(1) (*inserts* TA 1988 s 332A).

(2) Schedule 15 to this Act (relief in respect of holdings in a venture capital trust) shall be inserted, before Schedule 16 to the Taxes Act 1988 as Schedule 15B to that Act, and shall be construed accordingly.

(3) (*amends* TMA 1970 s 98, Table).

(4) This section has effect for the year 1995-96 and subsequent years of assessment.

72 Capital gains

(1) The Taxation of Chargeable Gains Act 1992 shall be amended as follows.

(2), (3) (*amend* TCGA 1992 s 100(1) and *insert* ss 151A, 151B).

(4) Schedule 16 to this Act (relief on re-investment in venture capital trusts) shall be inserted before Schedule 6, as Schedule 5C, and shall be construed accordingly.

(5)–(7) (*amends* TCGA 1992 s 257(1), 288(1) and *insert* s 260(6B)).

(8) Subsection (2) above shall have effect in relation to gains accruing on or after 6th April 1995 and the other provisions of this section have effect for the year 1995-96 and subsequent years of assessment.

73 Regulations

(1) The Treasury may by regulations make such provision as they may consider appropriate for—

(*a*) giving effect to any relief for which provision is made by Schedule 15B to the Taxes Act 1988 or section 151A of, and Schedule 5C to, the Taxation of Chargeable Gains Act 1992; and

(*b*) preventing such relief from being given except where a claim is made in accordance with the regulations and where such other requirements as may be imposed by the regulations have been complied with.

(2) Without prejudice to the generality of subsection (1) above, regulations under this section may make provision—

(*a*) as to the making of applications for approvals under section 842AA of the Taxes Act 1988 and otherwise as to the procedure in relation to any such applications and the giving of such approvals;

(*b*) as to the procedure to be followed in connection with the withdrawal of any such approval;

(*c*) as to the manner in which, and the persons by whom, relief is to be claimed;

(*d*) as to the obligations of a company which is a venture capital trust if it should appear to the company that the conditions for it to continue to be approved as such a trust are not satisfied;

(*e*) as to the accounts, records, returns and other information to be kept, and furnished or otherwise made available to the Board, by companies which are or have been venture capital trusts and by persons who hold or have held shares in such companies; and

(*f*) as to the persons liable to account for any tax becoming due where the approval of a company as a venture capital trust is withdrawn.

(3) Regulations under this section may make provision, in relation to tax credits to which any persons are entitled in respect of distributions of venture capital trusts—

(*a*) for the credits not to be set against income tax but to be claimed by and paid to the trusts; and

(*b*) for amounts equal to the credits to be paid by the trusts to the persons who receive or are entitled to receive the distributions;

and any such regulations may provide for sections 234 and 252 of the Taxes Act 1988 (information relating to distributions and rectification of excessive tax credit) to have effect, in relation to the distributions of venture capital trusts or, as the case may be, any provision made by virtue of paragraph (*a*) or (*b*) above, with such modifications as may be specified in the regulations.

(4) Regulations under this section may apply the following provisions of the Management Act, as they have effect in the case of repayments in respect of income tax, in relation to cases where amounts are paid to any person in pursuance of regulations made by virtue of subsection (3) above, that is to say—

(*a*) [section 29(1)(*c*)][1] (excessive relief);

(*b*) section 30 (tax repaid in error);

(*c*) [section 86][2] (interest); and

(*d*) section 95 (incorrect return or accounts);

[and section 86 of that Act may be so applied with such modifications as respects the relevant date as may be specified in the regulations].[2]

(5) (*amends* TMA 1970 s 98, Table).

(6) In this section "venture capital trust" has the meaning given by section 842AA of the Taxes Act 1988.

Commentary—*Simon's Direct Tax Service* **E3.601.**
Regulations—Venture Capital Trust Regulations, SI 1995/1979.
Cross-references—See FA 2002 Sch 33 para 14 (extension of this section to give effect to VCT reliefs).
Amendments—[1] Words in sub-ss (4)(*a*) substituted by FA 1996 Sch 18 paras 16, 17(1) with effect for purposes of income tax and capital gains tax from the year 1996–97 and, for purposes of corporation tax, as respects accounting periods ending after 30 June 1999 (by virtue of Finance Act 1994, Section 199, (Appointed Day) Order, SI 1998/3173 art 2).
[2] Words in sub-s (4)(*c*) substituted for "section 88", and words after sub-s (4)(*d*) inserted, by FA 1996 Sch 18 paras 16, 17(3) with effect from the year 1996–97, and in relation to any income and capital gains tax which is charged by an assessment made on or after 6 April 1998 and is for the year 1995–96 or any earlier year of assessment.

Settlements and estates

74 Settlements: liability of settlor

(1) Schedule 17 to this Act has effect with respect to settlements and the liability of the settlor, as follows—

 Part I inserts new provisions in place of sections 660 to 676 and 683 to 685 of the Taxes Act 1988
 Part II makes minor and consequential amendments of that Act, and
 Part III contains consequential amendments of other enactments.

(2) The amendments made by Schedule 17 have effect for the year 1995–96 and subsequent years of assessment and apply to every settlement, wherever and whenever it was made or entered into.

Commentary—*Simon's Direct Tax Service* **Division C3.4.**

75 Deceased persons' estates: taxation of beneficiaries

Part XVI of the Taxes Act 1988 (deceased persons' estates) shall have effect with the amendments specified in Schedule 18 to this Act.

Commentary—*Simon's Direct Tax Service* **C4.110.**

76 Untaxed income of a deceased person's estate

(1) (*inserts* TA 1988 s 246D(3A), and is repealed prospectively by F(No 2)A 1997 Sch 8 Pt II (11)).

(2)–(5) (*amend* TA 1988 s 547(1)(*c*) and *insert* ss 547(7A), 553(7A), 699A, 701(10A)).

(6) This section has effect for the year 1995-96 and subsequent years of assessment.

Securities

77 Interest on gilt-edged securities payable without deduction of tax

(*Inserted* TA 1988 s 51A, and repealed prospectively by F(No 2)A 1997 Sch 8 Pt II (13)).

78 Periodic accounting for tax on interest on gilt-edged securities

Amendment—This section repealed by FA 1998 s 165, Sch 27 Pt II(3) with effect in relation only to payments of interest falling
 due after 31 March 1999 by virtue of Finance Act 1998, Section 37, (Appointed Day) Order, SI 1999/619.

79 Sale and repurchase of securities: exclusion from accrued income scheme

(1), (2) (*insert* TA 1988 s 727A and *amend* s 728(1), (5)).

(3) The above amendments have effect where the agreement to sell the securities is entered into on or after the date on which this Act is passed.

(4) If the appointed day for the purposes of section 737A of the Taxes Act 1988 in relation to any description of securities falls after the date on which this Act is passed, the reference in subsection (3) above to the date on which this Act is passed shall be construed in relation to an agreement relating to securities of that description and to which section 737A would apply if it were in force as a reference to that appointed day.

80 Treatment of price differential on sale and repurchase of securities

(1) (*inserts* TA 1988 ss 730A, 730B).

(2) ...¹

(3) (*amends* TA 1988 s 737C(3)(*b*), (9), (11)(*c*) and *inserts* s 737C(11A) thereof).

(4) (*inserts* TCGA 1992 s 263A).

(5) This section shall have effect where the agreement to sell the securities is entered into on or after the date on which this Act is passed.

Amendments—¹ Sub-s (2) (which amended TA 1988 s 729(5A)) repealed by FA 1996 Sch 41 Pt V(21) with effect except in
 relation to cases where the initial agreement to sell or transfer securities or other property was made before a date to be
 appointed under FA 1996 s 159(1), (10).

81 Manufactured interest payments: exclusion from bond-washing provisions

(1) Section 731 of the Taxes Act 1988 (application of sections 732 to 734) is amended as follows.

(2), (3) (*insert* TA 1988 s 731(2A) and *amend* s 731(2), (3)).

(4) The above amendments have effect where the date on which the payment referred to in the inserted subsection (2A) is required to be made, or treated as required to be made, is after the passing of this Act.

82 Manufactured interest on gilt-edged securities

Amendments—This section repealed by FA 1997 Sch 17 Pt VI (9) with effect in relation to payments made on or after 1 July by
 virtue of the Finance Act 1997, Schedule 10, (Appointed Day) Order, SI 1997/991.

83 Power to make special provision for special cases

(1) (*inserts* TA 1988 ss 737D, 737E).

(2) (*inserts* FA 1993 s 182(1)(*ca*) and FA 1994 s 229(*ca*)).

84 Stock lending: power to modify rules

Amendments—This section repealed by FA 1997 Sch 17 Pt VI (9) with effect in relation to, and to transfers under, any arrangement made on or after 1 July 1997 by virtue of the Finance Act 1997, Schedule 10, (Appointed Day) Order, SI 1997/991.

85 Stock lending: interest on cash collateral

Amendments—This section repealed by FA 1997 Sch 17 Pt VI(9) with effect in relation to, and to transfers under, any arrangement made on or after 1 July 1997 by virtue of the Finance Act 1997, Schedule 10, (Appointed Day) Order, SI 1997/991.

Interest

86 Deduction of tax from interest on deposits

(1)–(9) (*insert* TA 1988 ss 481(4)(*d*), (4A), (5B), 482(5A), (11)(*ab*), *amend* ss 481(5)(*k*), (5B), 482(6), 482A(1) and *substitute* s 482(2)(*a*)).

(10) The preceding provisions of this section apply in relation to any payments made on or after 6th April 1996.

(11) Notwithstanding the repeal of section 67 of the Taxes Act 1988 by the Finance Act 1994 or anything contained in the transitional provisions relating to that repeal, where—

(*a*) this section has effect so as to require any deposit made before 6th April 1996 to be treated in relation to payments made after a time falling before 6th April 1998 as a relevant deposit for the purposes of section 480A(1) of the Taxes Act 1988 and

(*b*) section 67(2) of that Act does not otherwise apply in relation to the liability to deduction of tax that begins at that time,

section 67(1) of the Taxes Act 1988 shall apply in respect of payments made before that time as if the deposit were a source of income that the trustees in question ceased to possess at that time.

(12) An officer of the Board may, by notice to any of the trustees of a trust, require the trustees to provide the Board with the following, that is to say—

(*a*) information about any notification given by any of the trustees for the purposes of subsection (5B) of section 481 of the Taxes Act 1988; and

(*b*) such information as the Board may reasonably require for the purposes of themselves giving a notification under that subsection with respect to any income arising to the trustees;

and section 98 of the Management Act (penalties in respect of special returns) shall have effect with a reference to this subsection inserted at the end of the first column of the Table.

(13) Where a notice given by the Board before the passing of this Act requires any such information as is mentioned in subsection (12) above to be provided to the Board, and the period within which that information was required to be so provided does not expire until at least one month after the passing of this Act, that notice shall have effect as if given after the passing of this Act in accordance with that subsection.

(14) Without prejudice to section 20(2) of the Interpretation Act 1978 (references to other enactments) and subject to any provision to the contrary made in exercise of any power to make, revoke or amend any subordinate legislation, the enactments and subordinate legislation having effect, apart from this section, in relation to any provisions of the Taxes Act 1988 amended by this section shall be assumed, in cases where this section applies, to have the corresponding effect in relation to those provisions as so amended.

(15) In this section "subordinate legislation" has the same meaning as in the Interpretation Act 1978.

Commentary—*Simon's Direct Tax Service* **D4.1115**.

87 Interest payments deemed to be distributions

(1)–(5) (*insert* TA 1988 ss 209(2)(*da*), (8A)–(8F), 212(4) and *amend* ss 209(2)(*e*), (3), 212(1), (3), 710(3)(*a*)).

(6) ...[1]

(7) This section has effect, subject to subsection (8) below, in relation to any interest or other distribution paid on or after 29th November 1994.

(8) This section shall not have effect in relation to any interest or other distribution paid before 1st April 1995 in respect of any security if the security is one in the case of which a notice given before 29th November 1994 under Regulation 2(2) of the Double Taxation Relief (Taxes on Income) (General) Regulations 1970 was in force immediately before 29th November 1994 as regards payments of interest or other distributions made in respect of that security.

Commentary—*Simon's Direct Tax Service* **D1.106.**
Amendments—[1] Sub-s (6) (which amends TA 1988 Sch 4 para 5(5)) repealed by FA 1996 Sch 41 Pt V(3) with effect for purposes of income tax from the year 1996–97 and, for purposes of corporation tax, for accounting periods ending after 31 March 1996, subject to transitional provisions in FA 1996 Sch 15.

Debts

88 Generalisation of ss 63 to 66 of Finance Act 1993

Commentary—*Simon's Direct Tax Service* **D2.240.**
Amendments—This section (which amends FA 1993 ss 63–66 and inserts s 62A) repealed by FA 1996 Sch 41 Pt V(3) with effect in relation to accounting periods ending after 31 March 1996, subject to transitional provisions in FA 1996 Sch 15.

89 Application of ss 63 to 66 to debts held by associates of banks

Commentary—*Simon's Direct Tax Service* **D2.240.**
Amendments—This section repealed by FA 1996 Sch 41 Pt V(3) with effect for accounting periods ending after 31 March 1996, subject to transitional provisions in FA 1996 Sch 15.

Reliefs

90 Relief for post-cessation expenditure

(1) (*inserts* TA 1988 s 109A).

(2) (*modified* TA 1988 s 109A(1) as respects the years 1994–95 and 1995–96).

(3) (*amends* TA 1988 s 110(1)).

(4) Where under section 109A of the Taxes Act 1988 (inserted by subsection (1) above) a person makes a claim for relief for a year of assessment in respect of an amount which is available for relief under that section, he may in the notice by which the claim is made make a claim to have so much of that amount as cannot be set off against his income for the year (the ''excess relief'') treated for the purposes of capital gains tax as an allowable loss accruing to him in that year.

(5) No relief shall be available by virtue of subsection (4) above in respect of so much of the excess relief as exceeds the amount on which the claimant would be chargeable to capital gains tax for that year if the following (and the effect of that subsection) were disregarded—

(*a*) any allowable losses falling to be carried forward to that year from a previous year for the purposes of section 2(2) of the Taxation of Chargeable Gains Act 1992;
(*b*) section 3(1) of that Act (the annual exempt amount); and
(*c*) any relief against capital gains tax under section 72 of the Finance Act 1991 (deduction of trading losses).

(6) (*amends* TA 1988 s 105(2)).

(7) This section has effect in relation to payments made or treated as made (see subsection (4) of section 109A of the Taxes Act 1988 inserted by subsection (1) above) on or after 29th November 1994.

Commentary—*Simon's Direct Tax Service* **B3.921; B4.111A.**

91 Employee liabilities and indemnity insurance

(1), (2) (*insert* TA 1988 s 201AA and *amend* ss 141(3), 142(2), 153(2), 156(8)).

(3) This section has effect for the year 1995-96 and subsequent years of assessment.

92 Post-employment deductions

(1) Subject to the following provisions of this section, where any individual who has held any office or employment (''the former employee'') defrays any amount to which this section applies, he shall be entitled, on making a claim for the purpose, to a deduction of that amount in computing, for income tax purposes, his total income for the year of assessment in which that amount is defrayed.

(2) This section applies to any amount defrayed by the former employee where that amount—

(*a*) is defrayed by him in the period beginning when he ceased to hold the relevant office or employment and ending with the sixth year of assessment after that in which he ceased to hold it; and
(*b*) is not deductible in pursuance of section 201AA of the Taxes Act 1988 from the emoluments of that office or employment to be assessed for tax but would be so deductible if—

(i) the former employee had continued to hold that office or employment, and
(ii) that amount had been defrayed out of the emoluments of that office or employment for the year of assessment in which it is in fact defrayed.

(3) In determining for the purposes of subsection (2) above whether any amount would be deductible as mentioned in paragraph (*b*) of that subsection, the assumption in sub-paragraph (i) of that paragraph shall be disregarded when identifying the liabilities which are to be regarded as qualifying liabilities within the meaning of section 201AA of the Taxes Act 1988.

(4) This section shall not apply to any amount defrayed by the former employee in so far as the cost of defraying that amount, without being met out of his relevant retirement benefits or post-employment emoluments, is borne—

   (a) by the person under whom he held the relevant office or employment;
   (b) by a person for the time being carrying on the whole or any part of the business or other undertaking for the purposes of which the former employee held that office or employment;
   (c) by a person who is for the time being subject to any of the liabilities with respect to that business or other undertaking of the person mentioned in paragraph (a) above;
   (d) by a person who within the terms of section 839 of the Taxes Act 1988 is connected with a person falling within any of paragraphs (a) to (c) above; or
   (e) out of the proceeds of any contract of insurance relating to the matters in respect of which the amount is defrayed.

(5) In so far as the amount of any expenditure which is either—

   (a) defrayed by any person mentioned in subsection (4)(a) to (d) above, or
   (b) borne as mentioned in subsection (4)(a) to (e) above,

is an amount which falls to be treated as a relevant retirement benefit or post-employment emolument of the former employee, that amount shall be deemed for the purposes of this section to be an amount defrayed by the former employee out of that benefit or emolument.

(6) Subject to subsection (7) below, if an amount to which this section applies exceeds by any amount ("the excess relief") the amount from which it is deductible in accordance with subsection (1) above, the former employee shall be entitled, on making a claim for the purpose, to have the amount of the excess relief treated for the purposes of capital gains tax as an allowable loss accruing to that person for that year of assessment.

(7) No relief shall be available by virtue of this section in respect of so much of the excess relief for any year of assessment as exceeds the maximum amount.

(8) For the purposes of subsection (7) above the maximum amount, in relation to the excess relief for any year of assessment, is the amount on which the claimant would be chargeable to capital gains tax for that year if the following (together with any relief available under this section) were disregarded, that is to say—

   (a) any allowable losses falling to be carried forward to that year from a previous year for the purposes of section 2(2) of the Taxation of Chargeable Gains Act 1992;
   (b) section 3(1) of that Act (the annual exempt amount); and
   (c) any relief against capital gains tax under section 72 of the Finance Act 1991 (deduction of trading losses) or under section 90(4) of this Act.

(9) In this section—

   "post-employment emolument", in relation to the former employee, means so much of any amount as, having been received when the relevant office or employment is no longer held by the former employee, is treated for the purposes of the Income Tax Acts as an emolument of that office or employment;
   "the relevant office or employment", in relation to the former employee, means the office or employment in respect of which he is the former employee; and
   "relevant retirement benefit", in relation to the former employee, means so much of any amount as, in accordance with section 596A of the Taxes Act 1988 is chargeable to tax as a benefit received by him under a retirement benefits scheme of which he is a member in respect of the relevant office or employment.

[(10) Tax shall not be charged under section 148 of the Taxes Act 1988 (payments and other benefits in connection with termination of employment etc) in respect of a payment or other benefit received by an individual, or an individual's executors or administrators, in so far as—

   (a) in the case of a cash benefit, it is provided for meeting the cost of an amount to which this subsection applies, or
   (b) in the case of a non-cash benefit, it is or represents a benefit equivalent to the cost of defraying such an amount.

This subsection applies to an amount which, without being an amount to which this section applies, would fall to be treated as such an amount if subsection (4) of this section were omitted and, where the individual has died, he had not died but had himself defrayed any amounts defrayed by his executors or administrators.]¹

(11) This section applies for the year 1995-96 and subsequent years of assessment.

Commentary—*Simon's Direct Tax Service* **E4.718B.**
Amendments—¹ Sub-s (10) substituted by FA 1998 Sch 9 para 5 with effect from 31 July 1998.

93 Incidental overnight expenses etc

(1)–(4) (*insert* TA 1988 ss 141(6C), (6D), 142(3C), (3D), 155(1B), (1C), 200A).

(5) This section shall have effect for determining what emoluments are received by any person on or after 6th April 1995.

Capital allowances: ships

94 Deferment of balancing charges in respect of ships

(*Inserted* CAA 1990 s 33A, 33B, *repealed by* CAA 2001 s 580, Sch 4 with effect in accordance with CAA 2001 s 579).

95 Reimposition of deferred charge

(*Inserted* CAA 1990 s 33C, *repealed by* CAA 2001 s 580, Sch 4 with effect in accordance with CAA 2001 s 579).

96 Ships in respect of which charge may be deferred

(*Inserted* CAA 1990 ss 33D, 33E, *repealed by* CAA 2001 s 580, Sch 4 with effect in accordance with CAA 2001 s 579).

97 Procedural provisions relating to deferred charges

...

Amendments—This section repealed by the Capital Allowances Act 2001 s 580, Sch 4 with effect for income tax purposes, as respects allowances and charges falling to be made for chargeable periods ending after 5 April 2001, and for corporation tax purposes, as respects allowances and charges falling to be made for chargeable periods ending after 31 March 2001.

98 Deferred charges: commencement and transitional provisions

...

Commentary—*Simon's Direct Tax Service* **B2.335A.**
Amendment—This section repealed by the Capital Allowances Act 2001 s 580, Sch 4 with effect for income tax purposes, as respects allowances and charges falling to be made for chargeable periods ending after 5 April 2001, and for corporation tax purposes, as respects allowances and charges falling to be made for chargeable periods ending after 31 March 2001.

Capital allowances: other provisions

99 Highway concessions

...

Amendment—This section repealed by the Capital Allowances Act 2001 s 580, Sch 4 with effect for income tax purposes, as respects allowances and charges falling to be made for chargeable periods ending after 5 April 2001, and for corporation tax purposes, as respects allowances and charges falling to be made for chargeable periods ending after 31 March 2001.

100 Arrangements affecting the value of a relevant interest

...

Commentary—*Simon's Direct Tax Service* **B2.110, 222, 263.**
Amendment—This section repealed by the Capital Allowances Act 2001 s 580, Sch 4 with effect for income tax purposes, as respects allowances and charges falling to be made for chargeable periods ending after 5 April 2001, and for corporation tax purposes, as respects allowances and charges falling to be made for chargeable periods ending after 31 March 2001.

101 Import warehouses etc

...

Commentary—*Simon's Direct Tax Service* **B2.208.**
Amendment—This section repealed by the Capital Allowances Act 2001 s 580, Sch 4 with effect for income tax purposes, as respects allowances and charges falling to be made for chargeable periods ending after 5 April 2001, and for corporation tax purposes, as respects allowances and charges falling to be made for chargeable periods ending after 31 March 2001.

102 Commencement of certain provisions

(1) Chapter IV of Part IV of the Finance Act 1994 (changes for facilitating self-assessment) shall be deemed to have been enacted with the following modification.

(2) (*Inserts* FA 1994 s 218(1A)).

Management: self-assessment etc

103 Liability of trustees

(1)–(6) (*amends* TMA 1970 s 7(2), 8A(1), 118 and *insert* ss 7(9), 8A(5), 107A).

(7) Unless the contrary intention appears, this section, sections 104 to 115 below and Schedule 20 to this Act—

    (*a*) so far as they relate to income tax and capital gains tax, have effect as respects the year 1996-97 and subsequent years of assessment, and

    (*b*) so far as they relate to corporation tax, have effect as respects accounting periods ending on or after the appointed day for the purposes of Chapter III of Part IV of the Finance Act 1994.

Commentary—*Simon's Direct Tax Service* **E1.802.**

104 Returns and self-assessments

(*Amends* TMA 1970 ss 8(1A), (1B), 9(1), 11AA(1), 12AB(5), 8A(1A), *inserts* s 8(5) and *substitutes* s 12AA(1), (1A) (for s 12AA(1)), 12AB(1)).

Commentary—*Simon's Direct Tax Service* E1.806.
Amendment—Sub-s (5) repealed by FA 1998 s 165, Sch 27 Part III(28) with effect in relation to accounting periods ending after 30 June 1999 (by virtue of Finance Act 1994, Section 199, (Appointed Day) Order, SI 1998/3173 art 2).

105 Records for purposes of returns

(*Substitutes* TMA 1970 s 12B(1)(*b*), *amend* s 12B(2), (3), (4), (5) and *inserts* s 12B(2A), (5A)).

Commentary—*Simon's Direct Tax Service* E1.809.

106 Return of employees' emoluments etc

(1) (*substitutes* TMA 1970 s 15).

(2) This section has effect as respects payments made or benefits provided on or after 6th April 1996.

107 Procedure for making claims etc

(1)–(4) (*insert* TMA 1970 s 42(1A), (3A), (3B) and *amend* TMA 1970 s 42(2), (3)).

(5), (6) (*repealed* by F(No 2)A 1997 s 52, Sch 8 Pt II(9) and FA 1998 s 165, Sch 27 Part III(28)).

(7)–(10) (*amend* TMA 1970 s 42(5), (7)(*a*), (10), (11)).

(11) Schedule 1A to that Act (claims etc not included in returns) shall have effect subject to the amendments specified in Schedule 20 to this Act.

Commentary—*Simon's Direct Tax Service* E1.831.

108 Payments on account of income tax

(*Amends* TMA 1970 s 59A(1), (2), (5), *inserts* s 59A(4A) and *substitutes* s 59A(8), (9) (for s 59A(8))).

Commentary—*Simon's Direct Tax Service* E1.821.

109 Surcharges on unpaid tax

(1) (*amends* TMA 1970 s 59C(4)).

(2) That section of that Act shall apply in relation to any income tax or capital gains tax which—

   (*a*) is charged by an assessment made on or after 6th April 1998; and
   (*b*) is for the year 1995-96 or an earlier year of assessment,

as it applies in relation to any income tax or capital gains tax which becomes payable in accordance with section 55 or 59B of that Act and is for the year 1996-97 or a subsequent year of assessment.

Commentary—*Simon's Direct Tax Service* E1.823.

110 Interest on overdue tax

(1) (*substitutes* TMA 1970 s 86).

(2) That section of that Act shall apply in relation to any income tax or capital gains tax which—

   (*a*) is charged by an assessment made on or after 6th April 1998; and
   (*b*) is for the year 1995-96 or an earlier year of assessment,

as it applies in relation to any income tax or capital gains tax which becomes due and payable in accordance with section 55 or 59B of that Act and is for the year 1996-97 or a subsequent year of assessment.

(3) In that section of that Act as it so applies, "the relevant date" means the 31st January next following the year of assessment.

[(4) So far as it relates to partnerships whose trades, professions or businesses were set up and commenced before 6th April 1994, subsection (1) above has effect as respects the year 1997–98 and subsequent years of assessment.]¹

Commentary—*Simon's Direct Tax Service* E1.825.
Amendments—¹ Sub-s (4) inserted by FA 1996 s 131(1) and is deemed to have always had effect.

111 Assessments in respect of income taken into account under PAYE

(*substitutes* TA 1988 s 205 and *amends* s 206).

Commentary—*Simon's Direct Tax Service* E1.802.

112 Recovery of certain amounts deducted or paid under MIRAS

(1)–(4) (*insert* TA 1988 ss 374A, 375(2)(*aa*), (8A) and *substitute* s 375(4), (4A) (for s 375(4))).

(5) This section applies in relation to deductions made by borrowers, and payments made by the Board, after the passing of this Act.

Commentary—*Simon's Direct Tax Service* E1.802.

113 Allowable losses: capital gains tax

(1) (*inserts* TCGA 1992 s 16(2A)).

(2) Deductions under that Act in respect of allowable losses shall be given preference as follows—

(*a*) a deduction in respect of a loss accruing to a person in the year 1996-97 or a subsequent year of assessment shall be preferred to a deduction in respect of a loss accruing to him in an earlier year of assessment; and

(*b*) a deduction in respect of a loss accruing to a company in an accounting period ending on or after the appointed day for the purposes of Chapter III of Part IV of the Finance Act 1994 shall be preferred to a deduction in respect of a loss accruing to the company in an accounting period ending before that day.

Commentary—*Simon's Direct Tax Service* E1.802.

114 Liability of trustees and personal representatives: capital gains tax

(*Substitutes* TCGA 1992 s 65(1) and *inserts* s 65(3), (4)).

Commentary—*Simon's Direct Tax Service* E1.802.

115 Minor amendments and repeals

(1)–(8) (*amend* TMA 1970 ss 7(7), 9(3), 12AA(2), 30B(1)(*c*), 59B(6), 100B(1), 103A and *repeal* s 11A).

(9)–(11) (*repeal* TA 1988 s 73, Sch 3 para 6E(1), (3) and *amend* ss 536(2), (4), 537B(2), (4)).

(12) (*repeals* TCGA 1992 s 7).

(13) Subsection (3) above has effect as respects the year 1995-96 and subsequent years of assessment.

Commentary—*Simon's Direct Tax Service* E1.802.

116 Transitional provisions

(1) The provisions of the Management Act specified in Schedule 21 to this Act shall have effect subject to the transitional provisions contained in that Schedule.

(2) Section 198 of the Finance Act 1994 (which is superseded by this section) shall cease to have effect.

Commentary—*Simon's Direct Tax Service* E1.802.

Changes for facilitating self-assessment

117 Treatment of partnerships

(1)–(3) (*amend* FA 1994 s 215(1), (2), (3) and insert s 215(1A), which amendments are deemed always to have had effect.)

(4) (*modified* TA 1988 s 111 as set out in sub-s (2) of this section, as respects the year 1994–95).

Commentary—*Simon's Direct Tax Service* E5.311–315.

118 Loss relief: general

(*Substitutes* FA 1994 s 209(7)–(9) for s 209(7), which amendment is deemed always to have had effect).

119 Relief for losses on unquoted shares

(*Amends* FA 1994 s 210(2), which amendment is deemed always to have had effect).

120 Relief for pre-trading expenditure

(1) (*amends* TA 1988 s 401(1) and repeals s 401(2)).

(2) This section has effect as respects trades, professions and vocations which are set up and commenced on or after 6th April 1995.

121 Basis of apportionment for Cases I, II and VI of Schedule D

(*Amends* TA 1988 s 72(2)).

122 Amendments of transitional provisions

(1) Schedule 20 to the Finance Act 1994 (changes for facilitating self-assessment: transitional provisions and savings) shall be amended as follows.

(2)–(5) (*amend* FA 1994 Sch 20 paras 2(4), 10(5) and *insert* Sch 20 paras 2(4A), (4B), 10(5A)).

123 Prevention of exploitation of transitional provisions

Schedule 22 to this Act shall have effect for preventing the exploitation of, and (in certain cases) penalising attempts to exploit, the transitional provisions set out in paragraphs 2(2) and (4), 4(2) and 6(2)(*a*) and (4) of Schedule 20 to the Finance Act 1994 (changes for facilitating self-assessment: transitional provisions and savings).

Commentary—*Simon's Direct Tax Service* E1.216, 301, 304, 531.

Change of residence and non-residents

124 Change of residence

(1) (*inserts* TA 1988 s 110A).

(2) This section shall have effect as respects the year 1997-98 and subsequent years of assessment and also, in relation only to a trade, profession or vocation set up and commenced on or after 6th April 1994, as respects the years 1995-96 and 1996-97.

Commentary—*Simon's Direct Tax Service* B3.101.

125 Non-resident partners

(1) The provisions of the Taxes Act 1988 to which sections 215 and 216 of the Finance Act 1994 (partnerships and change of ownership of trade etc) relate shall have effect as respects the year 1995-96 and subsequent years of assessment as if subsection (5)(*b*) of section 215 (amendments not to apply until the year 1997-98 to partnerships controlled abroad) were omitted; and the Taxes Act 1988 shall have effect—

    (*a*) as respects the year 1997-98 and subsequent years of assessment, and

    (*b*) in its application with the amendments made by those sections to partnerships whose trades, professions or businesses were set up and commenced on or after 6th April 1994, as respects the years 1995-96 and 1996-97,

with the further amendments specified in the following provisions of this section.

(2)–(5) (*substitute* TA 1988 s 112(1), (1A), (1B) (for s 112(1)–(3)), 115(4), (5) and *amend* ss 112(4)(*a*), (6), 114(1)).

Commentary—*Simon's Direct Tax Service* E5.301.

126 UK representatives of non-residents

(1) Schedule 23 to this Act shall have effect for imposing obligations and liabilities in relation to income tax, corporation tax and capital gains tax on a branch or agency which, under this section, is the UK representative of a person who is not resident in the United Kingdom ("the non-resident").

(2) Subject to the following provisions of this section and to section 127 below, a branch or agency in the United Kingdom through which the non-resident carries on (whether solely or in partnership) any trade, profession or vocation shall, for the purposes of this section and Schedule 23 to this Act, be the non-resident's UK representative in relation to the following amounts, that is to say—

    (*a*) the amount of any such income from the trade, profession or vocation as arises, directly or indirectly, through or from that branch or agency;

    (*b*) the amount of any income from property or rights which are used by, or held by or for, that branch or agency;

    (*c*) amounts which, by reference to that branch or agency, are chargeable to capital gains tax under section 10 of the Taxation of Chargeable Gains Act 1992 (non-residents) or fall under that section to be included in the chargeable profits of the non-resident; and

    (*d*) in a case where the non-resident is an overseas life insurance company, any other amounts which by virtue of paragraph 3 of Schedule 19AC to the Taxes Act 1988 fall by reference to that branch or agency to be included in the company's chargeable profits for the purposes of corporation tax.

(3) For the purposes of this section and Schedule 23 to this Act, the non-resident's UK representative in relation to any amount shall continue to be the non-resident's UK representative in relation to that amount even after ceasing to be a branch or agency through which the non-resident carries on the trade, profession or vocation in question.

(4) For the purposes of this section and Schedule 23 to this Act, the non-resident's UK representative in relation to any amount shall be treated, where he would not otherwise be so treated, as if he were a separate and distinct person from the non-resident.

(5) Where the branch or agency through which the non-resident carries on the trade, profession or vocation is one carried on by persons in partnership, the partnership, as such, shall be deemed for the

purposes of this section and Schedule 23 to this Act to be the non-resident's UK representative in relation to the amounts mentioned in subsection (2) above.

(6) Where a trade or profession carried on by the non-resident through a branch or agency in the United Kingdom is one carried on by him in partnership, the trade or profession carried on through that branch or agency shall be deemed, for the purposes of this section and Schedule 23 to this Act, to include the deemed trade or profession from which the non-resident's share in the partnership's [profits][1] or losses is treated for the purposes of section 111 or 114 of the Taxes Act 1988 as deriving.

(7) For the purposes of this section and Schedule 23 to this Act where—

    (*a*) a trade or profession carried on by the non-resident in the United Kingdom is one carried on by him in partnership, and
    (*b*) any member of that partnership is resident in the United Kingdom,

the deemed trade or profession from which the non-resident's share in the partnership's [profits][1] or losses is treated for the purposes of section 111 or 114 of the Taxes Act 1988 as deriving shall be treated (in addition, where subsection (6) above also applies, to being treated as included in a trade or profession carried on through any such branch or agency as is mentioned in that subsection) as a trade carried on in the United Kingdom through the partnership as such.

(8) In this section "branch or agency" has the same meaning as in the Management Act.

(9) This section and Schedule 23 to this Act apply—

    (*a*) for the purposes of income tax and capital gains tax, in relation to the year 1996-97 and subsequent years of assessment; and
    (*b*) for the purposes of corporation tax, in relation to accounting periods beginning after 31st March 1996.

Commentary—*Simon's Direct Tax Service* B3.125.
Statement of Practice SP 1/01—Treatment of investment managers and their overseas clients
Amendments—[1] Words substituted by FA 1998 Sch 7 para 10 with effect from 31 July 1998.

127 Persons not treated as UK representatives

(1) For the purposes of section 126 above and Schedule 23 to this Act, none of the following persons shall be capable of being the non-resident's UK representative in relation to income or other amounts falling within paragraphs (*a*) to (*d*) of section 126(2) above, that is to say—

    (*a*) where the income arises from, or the other amounts are chargeable by reference to, so much of any business as relates to transactions carried out through a person who (though an agent of the non-resident) does not act in relation to the transactions in the course of carrying on a regular agency for the non-resident, that agent;
    (*b*) where the income arises from, or the other amounts are chargeable by reference to, so much of any business as relates to transactions carried out through a broker and falling within subsection (2) below, that broker;
    (*c*) where the income arises from, or the other amounts are chargeable by reference to, so much of any business as relates to investment transactions carried out through an investment manager and falling within subsection (3) below, that manager; and
    (*d*) where the non-resident is a member of Lloyd's and the income arises from, or the other amounts are chargeable by reference to, his underwriting business, any person who, in relation to or to matters connected with that income or those amounts, has been the non-resident's members' agent or the managing agent of the syndicate in question.

(2) For the purposes of subsection (1)(*b*) above where any income arises from, or other amounts are chargeable by reference to, so much of any business as relates to any transaction carried out through a broker, that transaction shall be taken, in relation to the income or other amounts ("the taxable sums"), to fall within this subsection if—

    (*a*) at the time of the transaction, the broker was carrying on the business of a broker;
    (*b*) the transaction was carried out by the broker on behalf of the non-resident in the ordinary course of that business;
    (*c*) the remuneration which the broker received for the provision of the services of a broker to the non-resident in respect of that transaction was at a rate not less than that which would have been customary for that class of business; and
    (*d*) the non-resident does not fall (apart from this paragraph) to be treated as having the broker as his UK representative in relation to any income or other amounts not included in the taxable sums but chargeable to tax for the same chargeable period.

(3) For the purposes of subsection (1)(*c*) above where any income arises from, or other amounts are chargeable by reference to, so much of any business as relates to any investment transaction, that transaction shall be taken, in relation to that income or those amounts ("the taxable sums"), to have been carried out through an investment manager and to fall within this subsection if—

    (*a*) the transaction was carried out on behalf of the non-resident by a person ("the manager") who at the time was carrying on a business of providing investment management services;
    (*b*) the transaction was carried out in the ordinary course of that business;
    (*c*) the manager, when he acted on behalf of the non-resident in relation to the transaction, did so in an independent capacity;

(*d*) the requirements of subsection (4) below are satisfied in relation to the transaction;

(*e*) the remuneration which the manager received for the provision to the non-resident of the investment management services in question was at a rate which was not less than that which would have been customary for that class of business; and

(*f*) the non-resident does not fall (apart from this paragraph) to be treated as having the manager as his UK representative in relation to any income or other amounts not included in the taxable sums but chargeable to tax for the same chargeable period.

(4) Subject to subsections (9) to (11) below, the requirements of this subsection are satisfied in relation to any transaction if—

(*a*) there is a qualifying period in relation to which it has been or is the intention of the manager and the persons connected with him that the non-resident's relevant excluded income should, as to at least 80 per cent, consist of amounts to which neither the manager nor any such person has a beneficial entitlement; and

(*b*) to the extent that there is a failure to fulfil that intention, that failure—

(i) is attributable (directly or indirectly) to matters outside the control of the manager and persons connected with him; and

(ii) does not result from a failure by the manager or any of those persons to take such steps as may be reasonable for mitigating the effect of those matters in relation to the fulfilment of that intention.

(5) For the purposes of this section any reference to the relevant excluded income of the non-resident for a qualifying period is a reference to the aggregate of such of the profits and gains of the non-resident for the chargeable periods comprised in the qualifying period as—

(*a*) derive from transactions carried out by the manager while acting on the non-resident's behalf; and

(*b*) for the purposes of section 128 or 129 below would fall (apart from the requirements of subsection (4) above) to be treated as excluded income for any of those chargeable periods.

(6) For the purposes of this section any reference to an amount of relevant excluded income to which a person has a beneficial entitlement is a reference to so much of any amount to which he has or may acquire a beneficial entitlement by virtue of—

(*a*) any interest of his (whether or not an interest giving a right to an immediate payment of a share in the profits or gains) in property in which the whole or any part of that income is represented, or

(*b*) any interest of his in or other rights in relation to the non-resident,

as is or would be attributable to that income.

(7) For the purposes of subsections (4) to (6) above references to a qualifying period, in relation to any transaction, are references to any period consisting in or including the chargeable period for which the taxable sums are chargeable to tax, being, in a case where it is not that chargeable period, a period of not more than five years comprising two or more complete chargeable periods.

(8) Where there is a transaction which would fall within subsection (3) above but for its being a transaction in relation to which the requirements of subsection (4) above are not satisfied, this section shall have effect as if the transaction did fall within subsection (3) above but only in relation to so much of the amount of the taxable sums as does not represent any amount of the non-resident's relevant excluded income to which the manager or a person connected with him has or has had any beneficial entitlement.

(9) Subsections (10) and (11) below shall apply, where amounts arise or accrue to the non-resident as a participant in a collective investment scheme, for the purpose of determining whether a transaction carried out for the purposes of that scheme, in so far as it is a transaction in respect of which any such amounts arise or accrue to him, is one in relation to which the requirements of subsection (4) above are satisfied.

(10) Those requirements shall be deemed to be satisfied in relation to the transaction wherever the collective investment scheme is such that, if the following assumptions applied, namely—

(*a*) that all transactions carried out for the purposes of the scheme were carried out on behalf of a company constituted for the purposes of the scheme and resident outside the United Kingdom, and

(*b*) that the participants did not have any rights in respect of the amounts arising or accruing in respect of those transactions other than the rights which, if they held shares in the company on whose behalf the transactions are assumed to be carried out, would be their rights as shareholders,

the assumed company would not, in relation to the chargeable period in which the taxable sums are chargeable to tax, be regarded for tax purposes as a company carrying on a trade in the United Kingdom.

(11) Where, on those assumptions, the assumed company would be so regarded for tax purposes, subsections (4) to (8) above shall have effect in relation to the transaction as if, applying those assumptions—

(*a*) references to the non-resident were references to the assumed company; and

(*b*) the following subsection were substituted for subsection (5) above, namely—

''(5) In subsection (4) above the reference to the assumed company's relevant excluded income for a qualifying period is a reference to the aggregate of the amounts which would, for the chargeable periods comprised in the qualifying period, be chargeable to tax on that company as profits deriving from the transactions carried out by the manager and assumed to be carried out on the company's behalf.''.

(12) In this section ''investment transaction'' means—

(*a*) transactions in shares, stock, futures contracts, options contracts or securities of any description not mentioned in this paragraph, but excluding futures contracts or options contracts relating to land,

(*b*) transactions consisting in the buying or selling of any foreign currency or in the placing of money at interest, and

(*c*) such other transactions as the Treasury may by regulations designate for the purposes of this section;

and the power to make regulations for the purposes of paragraph (*c*) above shall be exercisable by statutory instrument subject to annulment in pursuance of a resolution of the House of Commons.

(13) For the purposes of subsection (12) above a contract is not prevented from being a futures contract or an options contract by the fact that any party is or may be entitled to receive or liable to make, or entitled to receive and liable to make, only a payment of a sum (as opposed to a transfer of assets other than money) in full settlement of all obligations.

(14) The preceding provisions of this section shall have effect in the case of a person who acts as a broker or provides investment management services as part only of a business as if that part were a separate business.

(15) For the purposes of this section—

(*a*) a person shall be taken to carry out a transaction on behalf of another where he undertakes the transaction himself, whether on behalf of or to the account of that other, and also where he gives instructions for it to be so carried out by another; and

(*b*) the references to the income arising from so much of a business as relates to transactions carried out through a branch or agency on behalf of the non-resident shall include references to income from property or rights which, as a result of the transactions, are used by, or held by or for, that branch or agency.

(16) In paragraph (*d*) of subsection (1) above—

(*a*) the reference to a member of Lloyd's is a reference to any person who is a member within the meaning of Chapter III of Part II of the Finance Act 1993 or a corporate member within the meaning of Chapter V of Part IV of the Finance Act 1994 and

(*b*) the references to a members' agent and to a managing agent shall also be construed in accordance with section 184 of that Act of 1993 or, as the case may be, section 230 of that Act of 1994.

(17) In this section—

''branch or agency'' has the same meaning as in the Management Act;

[''collective investment scheme'' has the meaning given by section 235 of the Financial Services and Markets Act 2000 and ''participant'', in relation to such a scheme, shall be construed in accordance with that section;][1]

and section 839 of the Taxes Act 1988 (connected persons) shall apply for the purposes of this section.

(18) For the purposes of this section a person shall not be regarded as acting in an independent capacity when acting on behalf of the non-resident unless, having regard to its legal, financial and commercial characteristics, the relationship between them is a relationship between persons carrying on independent businesses that deal with each other at arm's length.

(19) This section applies—

(*a*) for the purposes of income tax and capital gains tax, in relation to the year 1996-97 and subsequent years of assessment; and

(*b*) for the purposes of corporation tax, in relation to accounting periods beginning after 31st March 1996.

Commentary—*Simon's Direct Tax Service* B3.125.
Statement of Practice SP 1/01—Treatment of investment managers and their overseas clients.
Amendments—[1] In sub-s (17), definition of ''collective investment scheme'' substituted for definitions of ''collective investment scheme'' and ''participant'' by the Financial Services and Markets Act 2000 (Consequential Amendments) (Taxes) Order, SI 2001/3629 arts 88, 89 with effect from 1 December 2001, immediately after the coming into force of the Financial Services and Markets Act 2000 ss 411, 432(1), Sch 20.

128 Limit on income chargeable on non-residents: income tax

(1) Subject to subsection (5) below, the income tax chargeable for any year of assessment on the total income of any person who is not resident in the United Kingdom shall not exceed the sum of the following amounts, that is to say—

(*a*) the amount of tax which, apart from this section, would be chargeable on that total income if—

(i) the amount of that income were reduced by the amount of any excluded income; and

(ii) there were disregarded any relief under Chapter I of Part VII of the Taxes Act 1988 to which that person is entitled for that year by virtue of section 278(2) of that Act or of any arrangements having effect by virtue of section 788 of that Act;

and

(*b*) the amount of tax deducted from so much of any excluded income as is income the tax on which is deducted at source.

(2) For the purposes of this section income arising for any year to a person who is not resident in the United Kingdom is excluded income in so far as it—

(*a*) falls within subsection (3) below; and

(*b*) is not income in relation to which that person has a UK representative for the purposes of section 126 above and Schedule 23 to this Act.

(3) Income falls within this subsection if—

(*a*) it is chargeable to tax under ...¹ Case III of Schedule D or Schedule F;

(*b*) it is chargeable to tax under Case VI of Schedule D by virtue of section 56 of the Taxes Act 1988 (transactions in deposits);

(*c*) it is chargeable to tax under Schedule E by virtue of section 150 or 617(1) of the Taxes Act 1988 or section 139(1) of the Finance Act 1994 (social security benefits etc);

(*d*) without being chargeable as mentioned in paragraphs (*a*) to (*c*) above or chargeable in accordance with section 171(2) of the Finance Act 1993 (profits of the underwriting business of a member of Lloyd's), it is income arising as mentioned in subsection (1)(*b*) or (*c*) of section 127 above; or

(*e*) it is income of such other description as the Treasury may by regulations designate for the purposes of this subsection;

and the power to make regulations for the purposes of paragraph (*e*) above shall be exercisable by statutory instrument subject to annulment in pursuance of a resolution of the House of Commons.

(4) In subsection (1)(*b*) above—

(*a*) the reference to excluded income the tax on which is deducted at source is a reference to excluded income from which an amount in respect of income tax is or is treated as deducted, on which any such amount is treated as paid or in respect of which there is a tax credit, and

(*b*) the reference, in relation to any such income, to the amount of income tax deducted shall be construed, accordingly, as a reference to the amount which is or is treated as deducted or which is treated as paid or, as the case may be, to the amount of that credit.

(5) This section shall not apply to the income tax chargeable for any year of assessment on the income of trustees not resident in the United Kingdom if there is a relevant beneficiary of the trust who is either—

(*a*) an individual ordinarily resident in the United Kingdom, or

(*b*) a company resident in the United Kingdom.

(6) In subsection (5) above, the reference to a relevant beneficiary, in relation to a trust, is a reference to any person who, as a person falling wholly or partly within any description of actual or potential beneficiaries, is either—

(*a*) a person who is, or will or may become, entitled under the trust to receive the whole or any part of any income under the trust; or

(*b*) a person to or for the benefit of whom the whole or any part of any such income may be paid or applied in exercise of any discretion conferred by the trust;

and for the purposes of this subsection references, in relation to a trust, to income under the trust shall include references to so much (if any) of any property falling to be treated as capital under the trust as represents amounts originally received by the trustees as income.

(7) This section shall apply, subject to subsections (8) and (9) below, in relation to the year 1995-96 and subsequent years of assessment.

(8) This section shall have effect in relation to the year 1995-96 as if the following paragraphs were substituted for paragraph (*b*) of subsection (2) above, that is to say—

"(*aa*) arises on or after 6th April 1995; and

(*b*) is not income in relation to which that person would have a UK representative for the purposes of section 126 above and Schedule 23 to this Act if sections 126 and 127 above and that Schedule applied for the year 1995-96.''

(9) This section shall have effect in relation to the year 1995-96 as if—

(*a*) the income falling within paragraphs (*a*) and (*b*) of subsection (3) above did not include any income arising otherwise than from a transaction falling within subsection (10) below; and

(*b*) the reference in paragraph (*d*) of subsection (3) above to income arising as mentioned in subsection (1)(*b*) or (*c*) of section 127 above were a reference to any income which would be such income if that section applied in relation to the year 1995-96.

(10) A transaction falls within this subsection if—

(*a*) it is either—

(i) a transaction carried out on behalf of the non-resident by a person who, at the time of the transaction, was carrying on the business of a broker; or

(ii) an investment transaction carried out on behalf of the non-resident by a person (''the manager'') who at the time was carrying on a business of providing investment management services;

(*b*) it was carried out by the broker or manager on behalf of the non-resident in the ordinary course of the business referred to in paragraph (*a*) above; and

(*c*) the remuneration which the broker or manager received in respect of that transaction for the provision to the non-resident of the services of a broker or, as the case may be, for the provision of the investment management services in question was at a rate not less than that which would have been customary for that class of business.

(11) In this section ''investment transaction'' has the same meaning as in section 127 above.

Commentary—*Simon's Direct Tax Service* **B3.126.**
Amendments—¹ Words omitted from sub-s (3)(*a*) repealed by FA 1996 Sch 7 paras 31, 32, Sch 41 Pt V(2) with effect from the year 1996–97.
Statement of Practice SP 1/01—Treatment of investment managers and their overseas clients

129 Limit on income chargeable on non-residents: corporation tax

(1) Subject to subsection (4) below, the corporation tax chargeable on the chargeable profits arising in any accounting period to a company which is not resident in the United Kingdom shall not exceed the sum of the following amounts, that is to say—

(*a*) the amount of tax deducted from so much of any excluded income as is income the tax on which is deducted at source; and

(*b*) the amount (if any) of corporation tax which would be chargeable on the chargeable profits arising to that company for that period if the excluded income of the company for that period were not included in those profits.

(2) For the purposes of this section income arising for any accounting period to any company is excluded income in so far as it—

(*a*) is income arising as mentioned in subsection (1)(*b*) or (*c*) of section 127 above; and

(*b*) is not income in relation to which that person has a UK representative for the purposes of section 126 above and Schedule 23 to this Act.

(3) In subsection (1)(*a*) above—

(*a*) the reference to excluded income the tax on which is deducted at source is a reference to excluded income from which an amount in respect of tax is or is treated as deducted, on which any such amount is treated as paid or in respect of which there is a tax credit, and

(*b*) the reference, in relation to any such income, to the amount of tax deducted shall be construed, accordingly, as a reference to the amount which is or is treated as deducted or which is treated as paid or, as the case may be, to the amount of that credit.

(4) This section does not apply in relation to the chargeable profits arising to a company which is a corporate member within the meaning of Chapter V of Part IV of the Finance Act 1994 (corporate Lloyd's underwriters etc).

(5) This section applies, subject to subsection (6) below, in relation to any accounting period ending after 5th April 1995.

(6) This section shall have effect in relation to any accounting period beginning before 1st April 1996 as if the following paragraphs were substituted for paragraphs (*a*) and (*b*) of subsection (2) above, that is to say—

''(*a*) is income arising after 5th April 1995 which would be income arising as mentioned in subsection (1)(*b*) or (*c*) of section 127 above if that section applied in relation to accounting periods beginning before 1st April 1996; and

(*b*) is not income in relation to which that person would have a UK representative for the purposes of section 126 above and Schedule 23 to this Act if sections 126 and 127 above and that Schedule so applied.''

Commentary—*Simon's Direct Tax Service* **D4.123.**
Statement of Practice SP 1/01—Treatment of investment managers and their overseas clients

Exchange gains and losses and currency contracts

130 Exchange gains and losses: general

Schedule 24 to this Act (which amends the provisions of the Finance Act 1993 relating to exchange gains and losses and other provisions connected with exchange gains and losses) shall have effect.

Commentary—*Simon's Direct Tax Service* **B3.1711, 1726, 1768.**

131 Exchange gains and losses: transitional provision

(1) The provisions specified in subsection (2) below, so far as they require a disposal to be treated, for the purposes of the Taxation of Chargeable Gains Act 1992 as a disposal on which neither a

gain nor a loss accrues, shall not apply in relation to any disposal of a qualifying asset which is made—

    (a) by one qualifying company to another such company; and

    (b) at a time before the commencement day of the company making the disposal and on or after the commencement day of the company to which the disposal is made.

(2) The provisions referred to in subsection (1) above are—

    (a) sections 139, 140A, 171, 172, 215, 216 and 217A of the Taxation of Chargeable Gains Act 1992; and

    (b) section 486(8) of the Taxes Act 1988.

(3) In this section—

    "commencement day", in relation to a qualifying company, means that company's commencement day for the purposes of section 165 of the Finance Act 1993;

    "qualifying asset", in relation to a disposal, means anything which, after the disposal, is by virtue of section 153 of that Act a qualifying asset in relation to the company to which the disposal was made; and

    "qualifying company" means any company which is a qualifying company within the meaning of section 152 of that Act.

(4) This section has effect in relation to any disposal of an asset taking place on or after 1st January 1995.

Commentary—*Simon's Direct Tax Service* **B3.1711.**
Revenue Internal Guidance—Company Taxation Manual COT13906 (worked example).
Amendment—This section repealed by FA 2002 ss 79, 141, Sch 23 para 22(1), (2), Sch 40 Pt 3(10) with effect for accounting periods beginning after 30 September 2002.

132 Currency contracts: transitional provisions

(1) Section 175 of the Finance Act 1994 (currency contracts: transitional provisions) shall be deemed to have been enacted with the modifications set out below.

(2), (3) (insert FA 1994 s 175(1)(c) and substitute s 175(2)).

Amendment—This section repealed by FA 2002 s 141, Sch 40 Pt 3(13) with effect for accounting periods beginning after 30 September 2002.

Provisions with a foreign element

133 Controlled foreign companies

Schedule 25 to this Act (which contains amendments of Chapter IV of Part XVII of the Taxes Act 1988 and connected amendments) shall have effect.

Commentary—*Simon's Direct Tax Service* **B3.1716; D4.133.**

134 Offshore funds

(1) Section 759 of the Taxes Act 1988 (material interests in offshore funds) shall be amended as mentioned in subsections (2) and (3) below.

(2)–(4) (*amend* TA 1988 s 759(1), *insert* s 759(1A) and *substitute* Sch 27, Pt I, para 1(2)(*a*), (*b*)).

(5) Section 212 of the Taxation of Chargeable Gains Act 1992 (annual deemed disposal of certain holdings, including holdings consisting of a relevant interest in an offshore fund) shall be amended as mentioned in subsections (6) and (7) below.

(6), (7) (*substitute* TCGA 1992 s 212(5)(*b*) and *insert* s 212(6A)).

(8) Subsections (1) to (3) above shall apply where it falls to be decided—

    (*a*) whether a material interest is, at any time on or after 29th November 1994, a material interest in an offshore fund;

    (*b*) whether a company, unit trust scheme or arrangements in which any person has an interest which is a material interest is, at any time on or after that day, an offshore fund.

(9) Subsection (4) above shall apply in relation to account periods ending on or after 29th November 1994.

(10) Subsections (5) to (7) above shall apply where it falls to be decided whether an interest is, at any time on or after 29th November 1994, a relevant interest in an offshore fund.

Miscellaneous

135 Change in ownership of investment company: deductions

Schedule 26 to this Act (which makes provision for the purposes of corporation tax about deductions following a change in the ownership of an investment company) shall have effect.

Commentary—*Simon's Direct Tax Service* **D4.404.**

[136 Profit-related pay

(1) In Schedule 8 to the Taxes Act 1988 (profit-related pay schemes) paragraph 19 (ascertainment of profits) shall be amended in accordance with subsections (2) to (4) below.

(2) (repealed TA 1988 Sch 8 para 19(6)(g)–(k)).

(3) (inserted TA 1988 Sch 8 para 19(6)(l)).

(4) (inserted TA 1988 Sch 8 para 19(6A)).

(5) Subject to subsections (6) to (10) below, subsections (2) to (4) above shall have effect in relation to the preparation, for the purposes of a scheme, of a profit and loss account in respect of a period beginning on or after the day on which this Act is passed.

(6) Subsections (2) to (4) above shall not have effect in relation to an existing scheme unless, before the end of the period of 6 months beginning with the day on which this Act is passed, the scheme is altered to take account of the amendments made by those subsections.

(7) Subsections (8) to (10) below apply where, before the end of the period mentioned in subsection (6) above, an existing scheme is altered as mentioned in that subsection.

(8) The provision made by the scheme in compliance with paragraph 20(1) of Schedule 8 to the Taxes Act 1988 shall not prevent a profit and loss account being prepared in accordance with the alteration.

(9) Where the distributable pool would but for this subsection be determined by reference—

(a) to an amount shown in a profit and loss account prepared in accordance with the altered scheme, and
(b) to an amount shown in a profit and loss account ("an earlier account") prepared in accordance with the scheme in a form in which it stood before the alteration,

then, for the purposes of the determination of the pool, the amount shown in the earlier account shall be recalculated using the same method as that used to calculate the amount mentioned in paragraph (a) above.

(10) The alteration of the existing scheme shall be treated as being within subsection (8) of section 177B of the Taxes Act 1988 (alterations which are registrable and which once registered cannot give rise to Board's power of cancellation).

(11) In subsections (6) to (10) above "an existing scheme" means a scheme which, immediately before the day on which this Act is passed, is registered under Chapter III of Part V of the Taxes Act 1988.

(12) (inserted TA 1988 Sch 8 para 19A).][1]

Commentary—*Simon's Direct Tax Service* E4.305.
Amendments—[1] Section repealed by FA 1997 Sch 18 Pt VI(3) with effect for any payment made by reference to a profit period beginning after 31 December 1999 in accordance with FA 1997 s 61(2), (3), but subject to FA 1997 Sch 18 Pt VI(3) notes 2, 3.

137 Part-time workers: miscellaneous provisions

[(1) (repealed TA 1988 Sch 8 para 8(a)).][1]

(2)–(4) (amend TA 1988 Sch 9 Pt III para 26(1)(a), Pt IV para 27(4), Pt V para 36(1)(a)).

(5) (amends FA 1989 Sch 5 para 4(2)(c)).

[(6) Subsection (1) above shall apply in relation to any scheme not registered before the day on which this Act is passed.][1]

(7) Subsections (2) to (4) above shall apply in relation to any scheme not approved before the day on which this Act is passed.

(8) In a case where—

(a) a scheme is approved before the day on which this Act is passed, and
(b) on or after that day the scheme is altered in such a way that paragraph 27 of Schedule 9 to the Taxes Act 1988 would be fulfilled if subsection (3) above applied in relation to the scheme,

subsection (3) above shall apply in relation to the scheme with effect from the time the alteration is made.

(9) Subsection (5) above shall apply in relation to trusts established on or after the day on which this Act is passed; and for this purpose a trust is established when the deed under which it is established is executed.

Commentary—*Simon's Direct Tax Service* E4.501.
Amendments—[1] Sub-ss (1), (6) repealed by FA 1997 Sch 18 Pt VI(3) with effect for any payment made by reference to a profit period beginning after 31 December 1999 in accordance with FA 1997 s 61(2), (3), but subject to FA 1997 Sch 18 Pt VI(3) notes 2, 3.

138 Charities, etc: lotteries

(1) (*inserts* TA 1988 s 505(1)(f)).

(2) Subsection (1) above shall apply to chargeable periods beginning—

(*a*) in the case of a company, after 31st March 1995; and

(*b*) in any other case, after 5th April 1995.

139 Sub-contractors in the construction industry

(1) (*amends* TA 1988 s 559(4) *and inserts* TA 1988 s 559(4A)).

(2) Chapter IV of Part XIII of the Taxes Act 1988 (sub-contractors in the construction industry) shall be further amended in accordance with Schedule 27 to this Act.

(3) In this section and that Schedule "the appointed day" means such day, not being a day before 1st August 1998, as the Treasury may by order made by statutory instrument appoint; and different days may be appointed under this subsection for different purposes.

Commentary—*Simon's Direct Tax Service* **E5.501.**
Note—By virtue of the Finance Act 1995, Section 139(3), (Appointed Day) Order 1998, SI 1998/2620 arts 2, 3, the appointed day as regards FA 1995 Sch 27 para 3(2), (3)(*b*) is 23 November 1998 and as regards FA 1995 Sch 27 para 1, 2, 3(1), 4, 5, 6, 7 is 1 August 1999. By virtue of the Finance Act 1995, Section 139(3), (Appointed Day) Order, SI 1999/2156 art 2 the appointed day as regards the repeals effected by FA 1995 Sch 29 Pt VIII(21) in or of TA 1988 s 561(1), (3)–(6) and of FA 1988 s 28 is 6 August 1999. By virtue of the Finance Act 1995, Section 139(3), (Appointed Day) Order, SI 2000/922 art 2 the appointed day as regards FA 1995 s 139(1) is 6 April 2000.

140 Valuation of trading stock on discontinuance of trade

(1) (*amends* TA 1988 s 100(1)(*a*) and inserts s 100(1A)–(1G) thereof).

(2) This section applies in relation to any case in which a trade is discontinued at a time on or after 29th November 1994.

141 Incapacity benefit

(1) Section 139 of the Finance Act 1994 (taxation of incapacity benefit) shall have effect, and be deemed always to have had effect, with the following amendments.

(2), (3) (*amend* FA 1994 s 139(5) and *insert* s 139(6)).

142 Annuities purchased where certain claims or actions are settled

(*Inserted TA* 1988 ss 329A, 329B; repealed by FA 1996 Sch' 41 Pt V(16)).

143 Lloyd's underwriters; new-style special reserve funds

(1) In Schedule 20 to the Finance Act 1993 (Lloyd's underwriters: special reserve funds) paragraph 2 (general requirements about special reserve funds) shall be deemed to have been enacted with the modification in subsection (2) below.

(2) (*substitutes* FA 1993 Sch 20 para 2(2) for para 2(2), (3) thereof).

144 Local government residuary body

(1) (*inserts* TA 1988 s 842A(2)(*h*)).

(2) This section shall be deemed to have come into force on 29th November 1994.

145 Payment of rent &c, under deduction of tax

(1), (2) (*amend* TA 1988 s 119(1) and *substitute* s 121(1) for s 121(1), (2) thereof).

(3) The provisions of this section have effect in relation to payments made after the passing of this Act.

PART VI

MISCELLANEOUS AND GENERAL

Miscellaneous

152 Open-ended investment companies

(1) The Treasury may, by regulations, make such provision as they consider appropriate for securing that the enactments specified in subsection (2) below have effect in relation to—

(*a*) open-ended investment companies of any such description as may be specified in the regulations,

(*b*) holdings in, and the assets of, such co mpanies, and

(*c*) transactions involving such companies,

in a manner corresponding, subject to such modifications as the Treasury consider appropriate, to the manner in which they have effect in relation to unit trusts, to rights under, and the assets subject to, such trusts and to transactions for purposes connected with such trusts.

(2) The enactments referred to in subsection (1) above are—

(*a*) the Tax Acts and the Taxation of Chargeable Gains Act 1992; and

(*b*) the enactments relating to stamp duty and [stamp duty reserve tax][1].

(3) The power of the Treasury to make regulations under this section in relation to any such enactments shall include power to make provision which does any one or more of the following, that is to say—

(a) identifies the payments which are or are not to be treated, for the purposes of any prescribed enactment, as the distributions of open-ended investment companies;

(b) modifies the operation of Chapters II, III and VA of Part VI of the Taxes Act 1988 in relation to open-ended investment companies or in relation to payments falling to be treated as the distributions of such companies;

(c) applies and adapts any of the provisions of [the enactments relating to stamp duty or stamp duty reserve tax][2] for the purpose of making in relation to transactions involving open-ended investment companies any provision corresponding (with or without modifications) to that which applies under [those enactments][2] in the case of equivalent transactions involving unit trusts;

(d) provides for any or all of the provisions of sections 75 to 77 of the Finance Act 1986 to have effect or not to have effect in relation to open-ended investment companies or the undertakings of, or any shares in, such companies;

(e) so modifies the operation of any prescribed enactment in relation to any such companies as to secure that arrangements for treating the assets of an open-ended investment company as assets comprised in separate pools are given an effect corresponding, in prescribed respects, to that of equivalent arrangements constituting the separate parts of an umbrella scheme;

(f) requires prescribed enactments to have effect in relation to an open-ended investment company as if it were, or were not, a member of the same group of companies as one or more other companies;

(g) identifies the holdings in open-ended investment companies which are, or are not, to be treated for the purposes of any prescribed enactment as comprised in the same class of holdings;

(h) preserves a continuity of tax treatment where, in connection with any scheme of re-organisation, assets of one or more unit trusts become assets of one or more open-ended investment companies, or vice versa;

(i) treats the separate parts of the undertaking of an open-ended investment company in relation to which provision is made by virtue of paragraph (e) above as distinct companies for the purposes of any regulations under this section;

(j) amends, adapts or applies the provisions of any subordinate legislation made under or by reference to any enactment modified by the regulations.

(4) The power to make regulations under this section shall be exercisable by statutory instrument and shall include power—

(a) to make different provision for different cases; and

(b) to make such incidental, supplemental, consequential and transitional provision as the Treasury may think fit.

(5) A statutory instrument containing regulations under this section shall be subject to annulment in pursuance of a resolution of the House of Commons.

(6) In this section—

"the enactments relating to stamp duty" means the Stamp Act 1891, and any enactment (including any Northern Ireland legislation) which amends or is required to be construed together with that Act;

["the enactments relating to stamp duty reserve tax" means Part IV of the Finance Act 1986 and any enactment which amends or is required to be construed as one with that Part;][3]

"Northern Ireland legislation" shall have the meaning given by section 24(5) of the Interpretation Act 1978;

["open-ended investment company" shall have the meaning given by section 236 of the Financial Services and Markets Act 2000;][4]

"prescribed" means prescribed by regulations under this section;

"subordinate legislation" means any subordinate legislation within the meaning of the Interpretation Act 1978 or any order or regulations made by statutory instrument under Northern Ireland legislation; and

"umbrella scheme" shall have the meaning given by section 468 of the Taxes Act 1988;

and references in this section to the enactments relating to stamp duty, or to any of them, or to Part IV of the Finance Act 1986 shall have effect as including references to enactments repealed by sections 107 to 110 of the Finance Act 1990.

(7) Any reference in this section to unit trusts has effect—

(a) for the purposes of so much of this section as confers power in relation to the enactments specified in paragraph (a) of subsection (2) above, as a reference to authorised unit trusts (within the meaning of section 468 of the Taxes Act 1988), and

(b) for the purposes of so much of this section as confers power in relation to the enactments specified in paragraph (b) of that subsection, as a reference to any unit trust scheme (within the meaning given by section 57 of the Finance Act 1946).

(8) For the purposes of this section the enactments which shall be taken to make provision in relation to companies that are members of the same group of companies shall include any enactments which make provision in relation to a case—

(*a*) where one company has, or in relation to another company is, a subsidiary, or a subsidiary of a particular description, or

(*b*) where one company controls another or two or more companies are under the same control.

Commentary—*Simon's Direct Tax Service* D4.1336.
Regulations—Open-ended Investment Companies (Tax) Regulations 1997, SI 1997/1154.
Concession C30—Subject to conditions, an open-ended investment company will not be treated for tax purposes as making distributions of the total amount shown in its "distribution accounts" as available for distribution to investors in respect of a distribution period for which it waives a distribution (or accumulation) in accordance with *de minimis* provisions in Financial Services Regulations.
Statements of Practice SP 3/97—Investment trusts investing in authorised unit trusts or open-ended investment companies: tax implications.
SP 2/99—Explains where the Revenue will accept simplified capital gains computations from individuals who have disposed of shares in open-ended investment companies incorporated in the UK acquired through monthly savings schemes before 6 April 1999.
Amendments—¹ Words in sub-s (2)(*b*) substituted for words "Part IV of the Finance Act 1986 (stamp duty reserve tax)" by FA 1999 s 122(4), Sch 19 para 13 with effect from 6 February 2000.
² Words in sub-s (3)(*c*) substituted for words "Part IV of the Finance Act 1986" and words "the enactments relating to stamp duty" respectively by FA 1999 s 122(4), Sch 19 para 13 with effect from 6 February 2000.
³ Definition of "the enactments relating to stamp duty reserve tax" inserted by FA 1999 s 122(4), Sch 19 para 13 with effect from 6 February 2000.
⁴ In sub-s (6), definition of "open-ended investment company" substituted **by the** Financial Services and Markets Act 2000 (Consequential Amendments) (Taxes) Order, SI 2001/3629 art 90 with effect from 1 December 2001, immediately after the coming into force of the Financial Services and Markets Act 2000 ss 411, 432(1), Sch 20.

153 Electronic lodgement of tax returns, etc

Schedule 28 to this Act (which makes provision with respect to the electronic lodgement of certain tax returns and documents required in connection with tax returns) shall have effect.

Commentary—*Simon's Direct Tax Service* A3.166.
Prospective amendment—This section will be repealed by FA 1999 s 139, Sch 20 Pt VII with effect on such day as the Treasury may by order appoint.

154 Short rotation coppice

(1) The cultivation of short rotation coppice shall be regarded for the purposes of the Tax Acts and the Taxation of Chargeable Gains Act 1992 as farming (and, where relevant, as husbandry or agriculture) and not as forestry; and land in the United Kingdom on which the activity is carried on shall accordingly be regarded for those purposes as farm land or agricultural land, as the case may be, and not as woodlands.

(2) For the purposes of the Inheritance Tax Act 1984 the cultivation of short rotation coppice shall be regarded as agriculture; and accordingly for those purposes—

(*a*) land on which short rotation coppice is cultivated shall be regarded as agricultural land, and

(*b*) buildings used in connection with the cultivation of short rotation coppice shall be regarded as farm buildings.

(3) In subsections (1) and (2) "short rotation coppice" means a perennial crop of tree species planted at high density, the stems of which are harvested above ground level at intervals of less than ten years.

(4) Subsection (1) and subsection (3) so far as relating to subsection (1) shall be deemed to have come into force on 29th November 1994.

(5) Subsection (2) and subsection (3) so far as relating to subsection (2) shall have effect in relation to transfers of value or other events occurring on or after 6th April 1995.

Commentary—*Simon's Direct Tax Service* B3.505.
Revenue & other press releases—IR Tax Bulletin October 1995 p 252 (general guidance is given on the tax treatment of short rotation coppice).

156 Proceedings for tax in sheriff court

(1) Section 67 of the Taxes Management Act 1970 (proceedings for tax in sheriff court) shall be amended as follows.

(2), (3) (*amend* TMA 1970 s 67(1) and *insert* s 67(1A)).

(4) This section shall apply in relation to proceedings commenced after the day on which this Act is passed.

157 Certificates of tax deposit

(1) If, whether before or after the passing of this Act—

(*a*) any person ("the depositor") has received any sum on the making, on or after 6th April 1990, of a withdrawal for cash of a tax deposit made before that date,

(*b*) the whole or any part of any qualifying tax liability has been discharged by any payment made otherwise than by the application of a tax deposit, and

(*c*) that payment was made in the period beginning one month before the withdrawal and ending one month afterwards,

the depositor shall be entitled to receive compensation under this section from the Board.

(2) In this section "qualifying tax liability", in relation to a tax deposit, means so much of any liability as is—

(a) a liability of any person for any tax for the year 1990-91 or any subsequent year of assessment, or for interest on such tax;

(b) a liability that relates to tax for a year of assessment during the whole or any part of which that person was married to the depositor; and

(c) a liability of such a description that, if it had been a liability of the depositor (and the withdrawal were to be disregarded), the whole or any part of it could have been discharged, immediately before the time of the payment mentioned in subsection (1)(b) above, by the application of that deposit and of accrued interest thereon.

(3) Subject to the following provisions of this section, the amount of the compensation to which the depositor is entitled under this section in the case of any deposit withdrawn for cash shall be equal to the difference between—

(a) the sum received as mentioned in subsection (1)(a) above on the withdrawal; and

(b) the sum that would have been received if interest had accrued on the relevant part of the sum received at the rate applicable under the relevant terms to sums applied in the payment of tax, instead of at the rate applicable to a withdrawal for cash.

(4) In subsection (3) above, the reference to the relevant part of the sum received on the withdrawal of a deposit is a reference to the following amount, that is to say—

(a) in a case where the sum received on the withdrawal is equal to or smaller than the amount of the liability discharged by the payment mentioned in subsection (1)(b) above, the amount equal to such part of the sum actually received as does not represent interest that has accrued under the relevant terms; and

(b) in any other case, to the amount which would have been the amount specified in paragraph (a) above if the sum actually received on the withdrawal had been equal to the amount of qualifying tax liability so discharged.

(5) The amount of compensation to which any person is entitled under this section shall also include an amount equal to interest, for the period from the withdrawal mentioned in subsection (1)(a) above until the payment of the compensation, on the amount determined in accordance with subsection (3) above; and a liability to compensation under this section shall not bear interest apart from in accordance with this subsection.

(6) Section 178 of the Finance Act 1989 (interest rates) shall apply to subsection (5) above for determining the rate of the interest treated, by virtue of that subsection, as included in any compensation under this section; and any regulations under that section which are in force at the passing of this Act shall be deemed, subject to the powers of the Treasury under that section, to have effect in relation to this section as they have effect in relation to the enactments specified in subsection (2)(f) of that section (interest on overdue tax).

(7) The part of any compensation under this section that represents interest under subsection (5) above shall not be treated as included in the income of the depositor for the purposes of income tax; but the remainder shall be chargeable to income tax under Case III of Schedule D.

(8) No compensation shall be paid under this section unless a claim for it has been made to the Board.

(9) Where any claim is made under this section with respect to any withdrawal for cash of a tax deposit—

(a) this section shall have effect if there is, in the period mentioned in subsection (1)(c) above, more than one such payment as is mentioned in subsection (1)(b) above as if (subject to paragraph (b) below) all the payments in that period were, for the purposes of that claim, to be aggregated and treated as one such payment; and

(b) the amount of compensation payable under this section on that claim shall be computed without regard to so much of any payment discharging a qualifying tax liability as, in pursuance of any claim under this section, has been or is to be so taken into account as to affect the amount of compensation payable in the case of any other withdrawal.

(10) Sums required by the Board for paying compensation under this section shall be issued to the Board by the Treasury out of the National Loans Fund.

(11) A withdrawal for cash of a tax deposit shall be taken for the purposes of this section to occur at the same time as, under the relevant terms, it is deemed to occur for the purposes of the calculation of interest on the amount withdrawn.

(12) This section shall be construed as one with the Tax Acts, and in this section—

(a) references to a tax deposit are references to the whole or any part of any deposit in respect of which a certificate of tax deposit has been issued by the Treasury under section 12 of the National Loans Act 1968; and

(b) references to the relevant terms, in relation to a tax deposit, are references to the terms applicable to that deposit and to the certificate issued in respect of it.

158 Amendment of the Exchequer and Audit Departments Act 1866

Section 10 of the Exchequer and Audit Departments Act 1866 (Commissioners of Customs and Excise and of Inland Revenue to deduct repayments from gross revenues) shall have effect, and be deemed always to have had effect, as if the reference in that section to repayments included references to—

(a) payments in respect of any actual or deemed credits relating to any tax or duty; and

(b) payments of any interest on sums which are or are deemed to be repayments for the purposes of that section.

Commentary—*Simon's Direct Tax Service* A3.1327.

160 Tax simplification

Amendment—This section repealed by Statute Law (Repeals) Act 1998 Sch 1 Pt IV with effect from 19 November 1998.

General

161 Interpretation

(1) In this Act "the Taxes Act 1988" means the Income and Corporation Taxes Act 1988.

(2) In Part III of this Act "the Management Act" means the Taxes Management Act 1970.

(3) (*see* Orange Book).

162 Repeals

The provisions specified in Schedule 29 to this Act (which include provisions which are already spent) are hereby repealed to the extent specified in the third column of that Schedule, but subject to any provision of that Schedule.

163 Short title

This Act may be cited as the Finance Act 1995.

SCHEDULE 6

AMENDMENTS IN CONNECTION WITH CHARGE UNDER SCHEDULE A

Section 39

Commentary—*Simon's Direct Tax Service* Part A4.

The Taxes Act 1988

1 ...

Amendments—This paragraph repealed by FA 1998 s 165, Sch 27 Part III(4) with effect for income tax for the year 1998–99 and subsequent years of assessment, and for corporation tax from 1 April 1998 subject to transitional provisions in FA 1998 Sch 5 Part IV.

2, 3 (*amend* TA 1988 s 18(3) and *repeal* ss 22, 23).

4–7 ...

Amendments—Paras 4–7 repealed by FA 1998 s 165, Sch 27 Part III(4) with effect for income tax for the year 1998–99 and subsequent years of assessment, and for corporation tax from 1 April 1998 subject to transitional provisions in FA 1998 Sch 5 Part IV.

8 (*modified* TA 1988 s 32 except where it is applied for the purposes of corporation tax; *repealed* by FA 1997 Sch 17 Pt VI(11) with effect from the year 1997-98).

9–16 ...

Amendments—Paras 9–16 repealed by FA 1998 s 165, Sch 27 Part III(4) with effect for income tax for the year 1998–99 and subsequent years of assessment, and for corporation tax from 1 April 1998 subject to transitional provisions in FA 1998 Sch 5 Part IV.

17, 18 (*amend* TA 1988 s 368(3), (4) and *insert* s 375A).

Amendment—Paras 17, 18 repealed by FA 1999 s 139, Sch 20 Pt III(7) with effect for payments of interest within FA 1999 s 38(3), (4).

19—(1) (*inserts* TA 1988 s 379A).

(2) Where apart from this Act any person who carries on a Schedule A business in the year 1995-96 would have been entitled—

(a) by virtue of Part II of the Taxes Act 1988 to deduct any amount that became due before the beginning of that year from rent received in that year, being rent which is in fact brought into account in computing the profits or gains of that business, or (*b*) by virtue of section 392 of that Act, to carry forward to that year the amount of any portion of a loss sustained in any transaction, being a transaction of such a nature that if it occurred in that year it would be treated as a transaction in the course of that Schedule A business,

that amount shall be treated for the purposes of income tax as if it were a loss falling, in accordance with section 379A(1) of that Act, to be carried forward from the previous year to the year 1995-96 and (in so far as not used in giving relief for that year) to subsequent years.

(3) Where—

(*a*) any person carrying on a Schedule A business in the year 1995-96 would, by virtue of section 355(4) of the Taxes Act 1988 (power to carry forward excess interest), have been entitled, in respect of an amount of interest representing an excess of interest over the income against which relief was available for any previous year, to be given relief against an equivalent amount of income for the year 1995-96 from the letting of any land, caravan or house-boat, and

(*b*) that business relates to any land, caravan or house-boat in relation to which the condition specified in section 355(1)(*b*) of that Act would have been fulfilled for the year 1995-96,

that amount shall be treated for the purposes of income tax as if it were a loss falling, in accordance with section 379A(1) of that Act, to be carried forward from the previous year to the year 1995-96 and (in so far as not used in giving relief for that year) to subsequent years.

(4) Section 379A(3) of that Act shall have effect for the purposes of the making of a claim in a case where the year to which the claim relates is the year 1995-96 as if the period for making such a claim ended two years after the end of that year.

20–25 ...

Amendments—Paras 20–25 repealed by FA 1998 s 165, Sch 27 Part III(4) with effect for income tax for the year 1998–99 and subsequent years of assessment, and for corporation tax from 1 April 1998 subject to transitional provisions in FA 1998 Sch 5 Part IV.

26–28 (*amend* TA 1988 ss 692(1), 779(13)(*a*), 832(1)).

The Capital Allowances Act 1990 (c 1)

29, 30 ...

Amendments— Paras 29, 30 repealed by FA 1998 s 165, Sch 27 Part III(4) with effect for income tax for the year 1998–99 and subsequent years of assessment, and for corporation tax from 1 April 1998 subject to transitional provisions in FA 1998 Sch 5 Part IV.

31 (*modified* CAA 1990 s 29(1) except so far as it applies for the purposes of corporation tax; *repealed* by FA 1997 Sch 17 Pt VI (11) with effect from the year 1997-98).

32 ...

Amendments—This paragraph repealed by FA 1998 s 165, Sch 27 Part III(4) with effect for income tax for the year 1998–99 and subsequent years of assessment, and for corporation tax from 1 April 1998 subject to transitional provisions in FA 1998 Sch 5 Part IV.

33 (*inserted* CAA 1990 s 73(4); *repealed* by FA 1997 Sch 17 Pt VI(11) with effect for the purposes of income tax from the year 1997-98 and for the purposes of corporation tax in relation to accounting periods ending after 31 March 1997).

34–37 ...

Amendments— Paras 34–37 repealed by FA 1998 s 165, Sch 27 Part III(4) with effect for income tax for the year 1998–99 and subsequent years of assessment, and for corporation tax from 1 April 1998 subject to transitional provisions in FA 1998 Sch 5 Part IV.

The Finance (No 2) Act 1992 (c 48)

38 (*amends* F(No 2)A 1992 Sch 10 para 2(1).

SCHEDULE 7

COMMERCIALLY LET PROPERTY: CORPORATION TAX

Section 42

Amendments—Schedule repealed by FA 1996 Sch 41 Pt V(3) with effect for accounting periods ending after 31 March 1996, subject to transitional provisions in FA 1996 Sch 15.

1 (*amends* TA 1988 s 338(6); *repealed* by FA 1996 Sch 41 Pt V(3) with effect for accounting periods ending after 31 March 1996, subject to transitional provisions in FA 1996 Sch 15).

2 (*inserts* TA 1988 s 338A; *repealed* by FA 1996 Sch 41 Pt V(3) with effect for accounting periods ending after 31 March 1996, subject to transitional provisions in FA 1996 Sch 15).

SCHEDULE 8

LIFE ASSURANCE BUSINESS

Section 51

PART I

GENERAL AMENDMENTS

Classes of life assurance business

1–8 (*amend* TA 1988 ss 76(1)(*d*), 431(2), 432C(2), 438(1), (8), 440(3), Sch 19AA para 5(5), *insert* ss 431B–431F and *substitute* ss 440(4) and 440A(2)(*a*) for s 440(2)(*a*), (*b*)).

9 (*amends* TCGA 1992 ss 212(2), 214A(11)(*a*)).

10 (*amended* FA 1994 Sch 18 paras 1(5), (6), 4; *repealed* by FA 1996 Sch 41 Pt V(3) with effect for accounting periods ending after 31 March 1996, subject to transitional provisions in FA 1996 Sch 15).

Linked assets

11 (*amends* TA 1988 s 431(2) and *inserts* s 432ZA).

12—(1) (*amends* TA 1988 ss 432C(1), 432D(1), 432E(3)(*a*), (*b*), (6)(*a*), Sch 19AB para 1(5)(*b*)(i) and, so far as amending FA 1994 Sch 18 para 1(4)(*b*) *repealed* by FA 1996 Sch 41 Pt V(3) with effect for accounting periods ending after 31 March 1996, subject to transitional provisions in FA 1996 Sch 15; *part repealed by* FA 2001 s 110, Sch 33 Pt II(12) with effect in accordance with FA 2001 s 87.

(2) The amendments made by paragraph 11 above do not affect the meaning of "linked assets", and related expressions, in sections 214 and 214A of the Taxation of Chargeable Gains Act 1992 (transitional provisions relating to changes made in 1990 and 1991).

(3) (*amends* TA 1988 s 432).

13 (*substitutes* TA 1988 s 432A(1)–(3), (7), (9) and *amends* s 432A(5), (6)(*b*)(i)).

14, 15 (*amend* TA 1988 ss 432C(1), (3), (4)(*b*), 432D(1), (2), *repeal* s 432C(5)(*a*) and *substitute* ss 432C(6) and 432D(3), (4) (for s 432D(3))).

Receipts to be brought into account

16 (*substitutes* FA 1989 ss 83, 83A (for s 83) and F(No 2)A 1992 s 65(2)(*d*), *amends* TA 1988 s 432B(1) and *substitutes* s 432B(2) and *amends* TA 1988 s 432E(1) and so far as amending TA 1988 ss 436, 441 *repealed* by FA 1996 Sch 41 Pt V(23) with effect in accordance with FA 1996 Sch 31 para 10(2).).

Supplementary provisions as to apportionment

17 (*amends* TA 1988 ss 432B(1), (2), (3), 432E(1), (5), 444A(5) and *inserts* ss 432F, 444A(3A)).

Franked investment income: supplementary provisions

18 (*amends* TA 1988 ss 238(1), 241(3), (5), 242(1)(*b*), (9), *inserts* s 238(1A) and *substitutes* s 238(3); *sub-paras (7)–(8) repealed*, i.e. in relation to TA 1988 s 242, *by* F(No 2)A 1997 Sch 8 Pt II(4)) with effect for accounting periods ending after 1 July 1997; *remaining paragraph repealed by* FA 1998 Sch 27 Part III(2) with effect in relation to accounting periods beginning after 5 April 1999).

19 (*substitutes* TA 1988 s 434(1), (3);*sub-para (2) repealed by* F(No 2)A 1997 Sch 8 Pt II(6) with effect in relation to distributions made after 1 July 1997; *sub-para (3) repealed by* FA 1998 Sch 27 Pt III(2) with effect in relation to franked investment income which is attributable to distributions made after 5 April 1999).

Computation of losses

20 (*substitutes* TA 1988 s 434A and F(No 2)A 1992 s 65(2)(*a*)).

Treatment of interest and annuities

21 (*inserted* TA 1988 s 434B and *substituted* FA 1989 s 88(3); *repealed* by FA 1997 Sch 18 Pt VI(6) with effect in relation to accounting periods beginning after 5 March 1997).

Interest on repayment of advance corporation tax

22 (*inserts* TA 1988 s 434C; *repealed by* FA 1998 Sch 27 Part III(2) with effect in relation to distributions made after 5 April 1999).

Capital allowances

23 (*inserts* TA 1988 ss 434D, 434E and FA 1989 s 86(5A) and *amends* TA 1988 s 75(4), part *repealed* by CAA 2001 s 580, Sch 4 with effect in accordance with CAA 2001 s 579).

24 (*substituted* CAA 1990 s 28, *repealed by* CAA 2001 s 580, Sch 4 with effect in accordance with CAA 2001 s 579).

Treatment of tax-free income

25 (*amends* TA 1988 ss 474(1)(*b*), 475(2)(*a*) and *inserts* s 474(3)).

Taxation of pure reinsurance business

26 (*inserts* TA 1988 s 439A).

Life reinsurance business: separate charge on profits

27 (*inserts* TA 1988 s 439B and *amends* ss 444A(3)(*a*), 724(3), (4)).

Provisions applicable to charge under Case I of Schedule D

28 (*inserts* TA 1988 ss 440B, 438(9), 440(6), 440A(7) and TCGA 1992 s 212(7A); *part repealed by* F(No 2)A 1997 Sch 8 Pt II(6)).

29 (*amends* TA 1988 ss 438(3), (3AA); *repealed by* F(No 2)A 1997 Sch 8 Pt II(6)).

Overseas life assurance business

30 (*amends* TA 1988 s 444(1)).

31 (*substitutes* TA 1988 s 441A(3)–(5) for s 441A(3)–(6); *repealed by* F(No 2)A 1997 Sch 8 Pt II(10) with effect in relation to distributions made after 5 April 1999).

32, 33 (*insert* TA 1988 s 441B and *amend* Sch 19A, para 1(2)).

Taxation of investment return where risk reinsured

34 (*inserts* TA 1988 s 442A).

PART II
APPLICATION OF PROVISIONS TO OVERSEAS LIFE INSURANCE COMPANIES

35 (*inserts* TA 1988 Sch 19AC paras 5A–5C, 6(4A) and *amends* TA 1988 Sch 19AC para 2(1) and s 475(6) and FA 1989 Sch 8A para 2(2); *part repealed by* F(No 2)A 1997 Sch 8 Pt II(6)).

36 (*amends* TA 1988 Sch 19AC para 5(1); *repealed by* F(No 2)A 1997 Sch 8 Pt II(6)).

37 (*repeals* TA 1988 Sch 19AC para 6(3), (4).

38 (*inserts* TA 1988 Sch 19AC para 6A).

39 (*substitutes* TA 1988 Sch 19AC para 7).

40 (*amends* TA 1988 Sch 19AC para 8(1), (2) and *substitutes* para 8(3)).

41 (*amends* TA 1988 Sch 19AC para 9(1); *repealed by* F(No 2)A 1997 Sch 8 Pt II(6)).

42 (*inserts* TA 1988 Sch 19AC paras 9A–9C).

43 (*amends* TA 1988 Sch 19AC para 10(1), (2); *repealed by* F(No 2)A 1997 Sch 8 Pt II(6)).

44 (*inserts* TA 1988 Sch 19AC paras 10A–10C).

45 (*substitutes* TA 1988 Sch 19AC para 11(1), *repeals* para 11(2) and *amends* para 11(5)).

46 (*inserts* TA 1988 Sch 19AC paras 11A, 11B).

47 (*amends* TA 1988 Sch 19AC para 12(1); *repealed by* F(No 2)A 1997 Sch 8 Pt II(6)).

48 (*inserts* TA 1988 Sch 19AC para 14A).

49 (*substitutes* FA 1989 Sch 8A paras 1, 1A–1C (for para 1), *amends* para 2(7) and *inserts* para 2(7A)).

PART III
SUPPLEMENTARY PROVISIONS
Penalties

50 (*amends* TMA 1970 s 98, Table).

Miscellaneous

51 (*amends* TA 1988 ss 432, 434, 436).

Commencement

52 The amendment made by paragraph 43(2) above shall be deemed always to have had effect.

53—(1) The amendments made by paragraph 17 above have effect in relation to accounting periods ending on or after 1st January 1994.

(2) In the first accounting period of a company ending on or after 1st January 1994 in which the subsection (3) figure for any category of business exceeds the subsection (2) figure, the subsection (2) figure shall be treated as increased by an amount not exceeding the amount or aggregate amount of any subsection (2) excesses in relation to that category of business for accounting periods beginning on or after 1st January 1990 and ending before 1st January 1994, but not so as to produce a subsection (2) excess for that period.

For this purpose the subsection (2) excess for an accounting period beginning on or after 1st January 1990 and ending before 1st January 1994 shall be determined without regard to the fact that in any other such accounting period the subsection (3) figure exceeded the subsection (2) figure.

Expressions used in this sub-paragraph have the same meaning as in section 432F of the Taxes Act 1988.

(3) Where a transfer mentioned in section 444A of the Taxes Act 1988 took place at the end of an accounting period of the transferor beginning on or after 1st January 1990 and ending before 1st January 1994, section 444A(3A) shall have effect in relation to the transfer as if it read—

"(3A) Any subsection (2) excess (within the meaning of section 432F(2)) of the transferor for an accounting period beginning on or after 1st January 1990 and ending before 1st January 1994 which (assuming the transferor had continued to carry on the business transferred after the transfer) would have been available to increase the subsection (2) figure (within the meaning of section 432F(1)) of the transferor in the first accounting period ending on or after 1st January 1994 in which the subsection (3) figure exceeded the subsection (2) figure—

(*a*) shall, instead, be treated as a subsection (2) excess of the transferee, and

(*b*) shall be taken into account to increase the subsection (2) figure of the transferee in its first accounting period ending on or after 1st January 1994 in which the subsection (3) figure exceeds the subsection (2) figure, but not so as to produce a subsection (2) excess for that period,

in relation to the revenue account of the transferee dealing with or including the business transferred.

For this purpose the subsection (2) excess for an accounting period beginning on or after 1st January 1990 and ending before 1st January 1994 shall be determined without regard to the fact that in any other such accounting period the subsection (3) figure exceeded the subsection (2) figure.".

54 The amendment made by paragraph 22 above applies in relation to distributions made by an insurance company in any accounting period ending after 30th September 1993.

55—(1) Subject to sub-paragraphs (2) and (3) below, the amendments made by the following provisions of this Schedule have effect in relation to accounting periods beginning on or after 1st November 1994—

paragraph 1 so far as relating to the definition of "overseas life assurance business",
paragraph 2 so far as relating to sections 431D and 431E of the Taxes Act 1988
paragraphs 3, 25, 30 to 33, 37, 38 and 45(1) and (3),
paragraph 46 so far as relating to paragraph 11A of Schedule 19AC to the Taxes Act 1988 and
paragraphs 48 and 50.

(2) Where the policy or contract for any life assurance business was made before 1st November 1994, the amendments made by this Schedule (and the repeals consequential on those amendments) shall not have effect for determining whether the business is overseas life assurance business.

(3) Where the policy or contract for any life assurance business effected by a company resident in the United Kingdom at or through a branch or agency outside the United Kingdom was made before 29th November 1994, subsections (2) to (8) of section 431D of the Taxes Act 1988 shall not have effect for determining whether the business is overseas life assurance business.

Simon's Tax Cases—*Royal London Mutual Assurance Society Ltd v Barrett (Insp of Taxes)* [2002] STC (SCD) 61.

56 The amendments made by paragraphs 41(*a*) and 43(1) above have effect in relation to foreign income dividends paid after 29th November 1994.

57—(1) Except as provided by paragraphs 52 to 56 above, and subject to sub-paragraph (2) below, the amendments made by provisions of this Schedule have effect in relation to accounting periods beginning on or after 1st January 1995.

(2) Section 442A of the Taxes Act 1988 does not apply in relation to the reinsurance of a policy or contract where the policy or contract was made, and the reinsurance arrangement effected, before 29th November 1994.

58 Any power to make regulations exercisable by virtue of an amendment made by any provision of this Schedule may be exercised so as to make provision having effect in relation to any accounting period in relation to which that provision has effect in accordance with paragraph 55 or 57 above.

SCHEDULE 9

TRANSFER OF LIFE INSURANCE BUSINESS

Section 53

Consequential amendment of references to sanctioned transfers

1 (*amends* TA 1988 ss 12(7A), 440(2)(*a*), 444A(1), (3)(*b*), 460(10A) and TCGA 1992 ss 211(1), 213(5), 214(11), 214A(7); *partly repealed by the* Financial Services and Markets Act 2000 (Consequential Amendments) (Taxes) Order, SI 2001/3629 art 109, Schedule)).

Modification of the Taxes Act 1988 in relation to overseas life insurance companies

2 (*inserts* TA 1988 Sch 19AC paras 4A, 10AA, 11C).

Modification of the Capital Allowances Act 1990

3 (*substituted* CAA 1990 s 152A(1), (1A), (1B) for s 152A(1), *repealed by* CAA 2001 s 580, Sch 4 with effect in accordance with CAA 2001 s 579).

Modification of the Taxation of Chargeable Gains Act 1992

4 (*amends* TCGA 1992 s 213(5) and *inserts* s 213(5A)).

5 (*amends* TCGA 1992 s 214A(7) and *inserts* s 214A(7A)).

6 (*inserts* TCGA 1992 Sch 7B paras 9A, 11(1A), 13(2A) and *amends* para 12(1)).

SCHEDULE 10

FRIENDLY SOCIETIES

Section 54

Tax exempt life or endowment business

1 (*inserts* TA 1988 s 460(2)(*c*)(zai) and *amends* s 460(2)(*c*)(ai), (3), (4A), (4B)).

Maximum benefits payable to members

2 (*inserts* TA 1988 s 464(3)(zza) and *amends* s 464(za), (4A), (4B)).

Qualifying policies

3 (*repeals* TA 1988 Sch 15 para 3(2)(*c*)).

4—(1) This paragraph applies to any policy which—

(*a*) was issued by a friendly society, or a branch of a friendly society, in the course of tax exempt life or endowment business (as defined in section 466 of the Taxes Act 1988); and

(*b*) was effected by a contract made after 31st August 1987 and before the day on which this Act is passed.

(2) Where—

(*a*) the amount payable by way of premium under a policy to which this paragraph applies is increased by virtue of a variation made in the period beginning with the day on which this Act is passed and ending with 31st March 1996, and

(*b*) the variation is not such as to cause a person to become in breach of the limits in section 464 of the Taxes Act 1988

Schedule 15 to that Act, in its application to the policy, shall have effect, in relation to that variation, with the omission of paragraph 4(3)(*a*) and the insertion at the end of paragraph 18(2) of the words set out in sub-paragraph (3) below.

(3) Those words are as follows, that is to say, ''and as if for paragraph 3(2)(*b*) above there were substituted—

'(*b*) subject to sub-paragraph (4) below, the premiums payable under the policy shall be premiums of equal or rateable amounts payable at yearly or shorter intervals—

(i) over the whole of the term of the policy as from the variation, or

(ii) where premiums are not payable for any period after the person liable to pay them or whose life is insured has attained a specified age, being an age attained at a time not less than ten years after the beginning of the term of the policy, over the whole of the remainder of the period for which premiums are payable.''.

SCHEDULE 11

PERSONAL PENSIONS: INCOME WITHDRAWALS

Section 58

Introductory

1—(1) Chapter IV of Part XIV of the Taxes Act 1988 (personal pension schemes) is amended as follows.

(2) The amendments have effect in relation to approvals, of schemes or amendments, given under that Chapter after the passing of this Act.

(3) They do not affect any approval previously given.

Interpretation

2 (*renumbers* TA 1988 s 630 as s 630(1), *amends* the resulting s 630(1) and *inserts* s 630(2)–(4)).

Conditions of approval: benefits that may be provided

3 (*amends* TA 1988 s 633(1)).

Income withdrawals

4 (*inserts* TA 1988 s 634A).

Lump sum to member

5 (*amends* TA 1988 s 635(1), (2), (3)).

Annuity after death of member

6 (*amends* TA 1988 s 636(3)).
7 (*inserts* TA 1988 s 636A).

Lump sum on death of member

8 (*substitutes* TA 1988 ss 637, 637A for s 637).

Other restrictions on approval

9 (*inserts* TA 1988 s 638(7A)).

Maximum amount of deductions

10 (*amends* TA 1988 s 640(3)).

Treatment of personal pension income

11 (*inserts* TA 1988 s 643(5)).

Tax charge on return of contributions after pension date

12 (*repeals* heading before TA 1988 s 648A and *inserts* s 648B).

SCHEDULE 12

CONTRACTUAL SAVINGS SCHEMES

Section 65

Introduction

1 In this Schedule references to section 326 are to section 326 of the Taxes Act 1988 (contractual savings schemes).

Curtailment of schemes

2—(1), (2) (*amend* TA 1988 s 326(2), (3), (4)).

(3) This paragraph shall apply in relation to schemes not certified as mentioned in section 326(2)(*c*), (3)(*b*) or (4)(*b*) before 1st December 1994.

European institutions

3—(1) Section 326 shall be further amended as follows.

(2)–(4) (*insert* TA 1988 s 326(1)(*d*), (5) and *amend* s 326(2)).

(5) Sub-paragraph (2) above shall apply in relation to schemes established after the day on which this Act is passed.

Certification: Treasury specifications

4—(1) Section 326 shall be further amended as follows.

(2) (*amends* TA 1988 s 326(3)(*b*), (4)(*b*), (5)(*b*)).

(3) This paragraph shall apply in relation to schemes not certified as mentioned in section 326(3)(*b*), (4)(*b*) or (5)(*b*) before such day as the Treasury may by order made by statutory instrument appoint.

Treasury authorisation

5—(1) (*inserts* TA 1988 s 326(6)–(8)).

(2) This paragraph shall apply in relation to schemes not certified as mentioned in section 326(3)(*b*), (4)(*b*) or (5)(*b*) before the day appointed under paragraph 4(3) above.

Section 326: supplementary

6—(1) (*inserts* TA 1988 s 326(9)).

(2) (*inserts* TA 1988 Sch 15A).

Payments under certain contracts

7—(1) Any terminal bonus, interest or other sum payable under a scheme shall not be treated as payable under a certified contractual savings scheme for the purposes of section 326 if—

    (*a*) the scheme is not a share option linked scheme, and

    (*b*) the contract under which the sum is payable is not entered into before 1st December 1994.

(2) Any terminal bonus, interest or other sum payable under a scheme shall not be treated as payable under a certified contractual savings scheme for the purposes of section 326 if—

    (*a*) the contract under which the sum is payable provides for contributions to be made by way of investment in a building society or to be made to [a person falling within section 840A(1)(*b*) of the Taxes Act 1988][1] or to a relevant European institution,

    (*b*) the scheme is certified as mentioned in section 326(3)(*b*), (4)(*b*) or (5)(*b*) before the day appointed under paragraph 4(3) above, and

    (*c*) the contract is not entered into before that day.

(3) In this paragraph ''share option linked scheme'' and ''relevant European institution'' have the same meanings as in section 326.

Amendments—[1] Words in sub-para (2)(*a*) substituted by the Financial Services and Markets Act 2000 (Consequential Amendments) (Taxes) Order, SI 2001/3629 art 91 with effect from 1 December 2001, immediately after the coming into force of the Financial Services and Markets Act 2000 ss 411, 432(1), Sch 20.

Transitional

8—(1) The Treasury may by regulations provide that at the beginning of the day appointed under paragraph 4(3) above Treasury authorisation shall be treated as given under section 326(7) to any specified relevant body without any conditions being imposed.

(2) The Treasury may by regulations provide that—

    (*a*) at the beginning of the day appointed under paragraph 4(3) above Treasury authorisation shall be treated as given under section 326(8) to any specified relevant body subject to conditions being met;

    (*b*) the conditions as regards a body shall be such as are specified in, or identified by provision contained in, the regulations as regards that body.

(3) Any authorisation treated as given as mentioned in sub-paragraph (1) or (2) above shall be treated as given as regards schemes generally; but this is subject to any provision to the contrary in the regulations.

(4) For the purposes of this paragraph the following are relevant bodies—

    (*a*) any building society;

    [(*b*) any person falling within section 840A(1)(*b*) of the Taxes Act 1988][1];

    (*c*) any relevant European institution.

(5) In this paragraph—

    (*a*) ''relevant European institution'' has the same meaning as in section 326;

    (*b*) ''specified'' means specified in the regulations.

(6) Regulations under this paragraph shall be made by statutory instrument subject to annulment in pursuance of a resolution of the House of Commons.

Amendments—[1] Sub-para (4)(*b*) substituted by the Financial Services and Markets Act 2000 (Consequential Amendments) (Taxes) Order, SI 2001/3629 art 91 with effect from 1 December 2001, immediately after the coming into force of the Financial Services and Markets Act 2000 ss 411, 432(1), Sch 20.

SCHEDULE 13

ENTERPRISE INVESTMENT SCHEME

Section 67

Introduction

1 The Taxation of Chargeable Gains Act 1992 shall be amended as mentioned in this Schedule.

Amendments of section 150A

2—(1) Section 150A (enterprise investment scheme) shall be amended as mentioned in sub-paragraphs (2) to (4) below; and the amendments made by sub-paragraphs (2) and (3) below shall apply in relation to shares issued on or after 1st January 1994.

(2)–(4) (*insert* s 150A(2A), (3)(*aa*), (8A)–(8C)).

Reduction of relief

3 (*inserts* s 150B).

Re-investment

4—(1)–(3) (*insert* ss 150C, 260(6A), Sch 5B)).

(4) This paragraph has effect in relation to gains accruing and events occurring on or after 29th November 1994.

SCHEDULE 14

VENTURE CAPITAL TRUSTS: MEANING OF

"QUALIFYING HOLDINGS"

Section 70

Commentary—*Simon's Direct Tax Service* **Division E3.6.**
Note—This Schedule sets out TA 1988 Sch 28B.

SCHEDULE 15

VENTURE CAPITAL TRUSTS: RELIEF FROM INCOME TAX

Section 71

Commentary—*Simon's Direct Tax Service* **Division E3.6.**
Note—This Schedule sets out TA 1988 Sch 15B.

SCHEDULE 16

VENTURE CAPITAL TRUSTS: DEFERRED CHARGE ON

RE-INVESTMENT

Section 72

Commentary—*Simon's Direct Tax Service* **Division E3.6.**
Note—This Schedule sets out TCGA 1992 Sch 5C.

SCHEDULE 17

SETTLEMENTS: LIABILITY OF SETTLOR

Section 74

PART I

THE NEW PROVISIONS

1 (*inserts* TA 1988 ss 660A–660G).

PART II
MINOR AND CONSEQUENTIAL AMENDMENTS OF THE TAXES ACT 1988

2, 3 (*amends* TA 1988 ss 125(3)(*a*), 339(1)(*a*)).

4—(1) . . .[1]

(2) (*adds* TA 1988 s 347A(7), (8)).

Amendments—[1] Sub-para (1) repealed by FA 1999 s 139, Sch 20 Pt III(6) with effect for any payment falling due after 5 April 2000.

5–20 (*amend* TA 1988 ss 360A(2)(*b*), 417(3)(*b*), 505(6), 677(2), (9), 687(2)(*a*), 694(3), 720(6), (7), (8)(*a*), 745(6), 783(10)(*b*), *insert* heading before TA 1988 s 677, *repeal* ss 678(7), 689, *insert* s 682A, *substitute* heading before TA 1988 s 686, *substitute* s 686(2)(*b*), 687(1) and s 839(3), (3A) (for s 839(3)) and *add* s 687(5)).

PART III
CONSEQUENTIAL AMENDMENTS OF OTHER ENACTMENTS
Taxes Management Act 1970 (c 9)

21 (*amends* s 27(2)).

22 (*amends* s 31(3); rubric to this paragraph *repealed in part* by FA 1996 Sch 41 Pt V(12) with effect in relation to proceedings relating to the year 1996–97 or any subsequent year of assessment and any proceedings relating to an accounting period ending after 30 June 1999 (by virtue of Finance Act 1994, Section 199, (Appointed Day) Order, SI 1998/3173 art 2).

23 (*amends* s 98, Table).

Finance Act 1989 (c 26)

24, 25 (*amend* ss 59(1)(*c*), 60(4) and *repeal* s 60(3)).

Finance Act 1990 (c 29)

26 (*amends* s 25(12)(*b*)).

Taxation of Chargeable Gains Act 1992 (c 12)

27–32 (*substitute* ss 77, s 286(3), (3A) (for s 286(3)), *amend* ss 78(1), (2), (3), 79(5), 97(7), Sch 1 para 2(7) and *repeal* s 79(2)(*b*), (4)).

SCHEDULE 18
DECEASED PERSONS' ESTATES
Section 75

Commentary—*Simon's Direct Tax Service* **C4.108–119.**

Introductory

1 Part XVI of the Taxes Act 1988 shall be amended as follows.

Limited interests in residue

2—(1) (*amends* s 695(2) and *substitutes* s 695(3)).

(2) This paragraph has effect in relation to any estate the administration of which is completed on or after 6th April 1995.

Absolute interests in residue

3—(1) (*substitutes* s 696(3), (3A), (3B) for s 696(3)).

(2) (*substitutes* s 696(5)).

(3) Sub-paragraph (1) above has effect, subject to sub-paragraph (4) below, in relation to any payment made on or after 6th April 1995; and sub-paragraph (2) above shall have effect in relation to any estate the administration of which is completed on or after 6th April 1995.

(4) Where any sum is deemed by virtue of subsection (3) of section 696 of the Taxes Act 1988 (as it has effect apart from this Schedule) to have been paid to any person as income for the year 1994–95 or any previous year of assessment, that sum shall be treated for the purposes of subsections (3A) and (5) of that section (as they have effect by virtue of this Schedule) as a sum actually paid in respect of that person's absolute interest in that year of assessment.

Supplemental provisions relating to section 696

4—(1), (2) (*insert* s 697(1A) and *amend* s 697(2)).

(3) Sub-paragraph (1) above has effect for ascertaining the residuary income of an estate for the year 1995-96 or any subsequent year of assessment; and sub-paragraph (2) above has effect in relation to any estate the administration of which is completed on or after 6th April 1995.

Special provisions as to successive interests in residue

5—(1) (*substitutes* s 698(1A), (1B), (2) for s 698(2)).

(2) This paragraph has effect in relation to any payment made on or after 6th April 1995 and, so far as it relates to the operation of section 695(3) or 696(5) of the Taxes Act 1988 in relation to any estate the administration of which is completed on or after that date.

Adjustments and information

6 (*inserts* s 700(5), (6)).

Interpretation

7 (*repeals* s 701(14)).

SCHEDULE 19

STOCK LENDING: INTEREST ON CASH COLLATERAL

Section 85

Commentary—*Simon's Direct Tax Service* **B3.1007**.
Note—This Schedule which set out TA 1988 Sch 5A is repealed by FA 1997 Sch 17 Pt VI (9) with effect in relation to, and to transfers under, any arrangement made on or after 1 July 1997 by virtue of the Finance Act 1997, Schedule 10, (Appointed Day) Order, SI 1997/991.

SCHEDULE 20

CLAIMS ETC NOT INCLUDED IN RETURNS

Section 107(11)

Making of claims

1 (*substitutes* TMA 1970 Sch 1A para 2(5)(*b*), (*bb*) for para 2(5)(*b*)).

Keeping and preserving of records

2 (*inserts* TMA 1970 Sch 1A para 2A).

Amendments of claims

3 (*amends* TMA 1970 Sch 1A para 3(1)(*a*)).

Giving effect to claims and amendments

4 (*amends* TMA 1970 Sch 1A para 4(1), (2) and *inserts* para 4(1A), (3)).

Power to enquire into claims

5 (*substitutes* TMA 1970 Sch 1A para 5(2), (3)).

SCHEDULE 21

SELF-ASSESSMENT ETC: TRANSITIONAL PROVISIONS

Section 116(1)

Commentary—*Simon's Direct Tax Service* **E1.821**.

Notice of liability

1 Section 7 of the Management Act (notice of liability) shall have effect as respects the year 1995–96 as if the reference in subsection (7) to a self-assessment made under section 9 of that Act in respect of that year were a reference to assessments made more than six months after the end of that year.

Payments on account of income tax

2—(1) Section 59A of that Act (payments on account of income tax) shall have effect as respects the year 1996-97 with the modifications made by sub-paragraphs (2) to (7) below.

(2) The references in subsections (1)(*a*) and (4A) to a person being assessed to income tax under section 9 of that Act shall be construed as references to his being assessed to income tax under section 29 of that Act.

(3) The reference in subsection (1)(*b*) to the assessed amount shall be construed as a reference to the difference between that amount and the aggregate of the following, namely—

 (*a*) so much of any income tax charged at a higher rate on any income—

  (i) from which tax has been deducted otherwise than under section 203 of the Taxes Act 1988 or

  (ii) from or on which income tax is treated as having been deducted or paid,

 as is attributable to the difference between that rate and the basic rate; and

 (*b*) so much of any income tax charged at a higher rate on any income chargeable under Schedule F as is attributable to the difference between that rate and the lower rate.

(4) The reference in subsection (1)(*c*) to the relevant amount shall be construed as a reference to the difference between that amount and the amount of any income tax charged under Schedule E which—

 (*a*) has not been deducted under section 203 of the Taxes Act 1988; and

 (*b*) is not charged by an assessment made under regulation 103 of the Income Tax (Employments) Regulations 1993.

(5) Subsection (2) shall have effect as if it required—

 (*a*) the first payment on account to be of an amount equal to the aggregate of—

  (i) such part of the relevant amount as represents tax charged under Schedule A or any of Cases III to VI of Schedule D; and

  (ii) 50 per cent of the remaining part of the relevant amount, and

 (*b*) the second payment on account to be of an amount equal to 50 per cent of that remaining part.

(6) Subsection (4) shall have effect as if it provided that, in the circumstances there mentioned—

 (*a*) the amount of the first payment on account should be, and should be deemed always to have been, equal to the aggregate of—

  (i) such part of the stated amount as represents tax charged under Schedule A or any of Cases III to VI of Schedule D; and

  (ii) 50 per cent of the remaining part of the stated amount, and

 (*b*) the amount of the second payment on account should be, and should be deemed always to have been, equal to 50 per cent of that remaining part.

(7) Subsection (4A) shall have effect as if it provided that, in the circumstances and subject as there mentioned—

 (*a*) the amount of the first payment on account should be, and should be deemed always to have been, equal to the aggregate of—

  (i) such part of the relevant amount (as determined on the basis of the assessment or, as the case may be, the assessment as amended) as represents tax charged under Schedule A or any of Cases III to VI of Schedule D; and

  (ii) 50 per cent of the remaining part of the relevant amount, as so determined, and

 (*b*) the amount of the second payment on account should be, and should be deemed always to have been, equal to 50 per cent of that remaining part.

(8) In this paragraph ''higher rate'' means a rate other than the basic rate or the lower rate.

Partnerships

3—(1) This paragraph applies in the case of a partnership whose trade, profession or business is set up and commenced before 6th April 1994.

(2) Section 32 of the Management Act (relief for double assessments to tax) shall have effect, as respects each partner and the year 1996-97, as if the partnership had not been assessed to income tax for that year.

(3) Section 59B of that Act (payment of income tax and capital gains tax) shall have effect, as respects each partner and that year, as if his share of any income tax to which the partnership is assessed for that year were income tax which in respect of that year had been deducted at source.

SCHEDULE 22

PREVENTION OF EXPLOITATION OF SCHEDULE 20 TO FINANCE ACT 1994

Section 123

Commentary—*Simon's Direct Tax Service* **E1.216.**
Regulations—Income Tax (Schedule 22 to the Finance Act 1995) (Prescribed Amounts) Regulations 1997, SI 1997/1158.
Revenue & other press releases—IR Tax Bulletin June 1997 p 434 (article explains, with illustrative examples, the operation of the *de minimis* exemptions from the anti-avoidance provisions in this Schedule).

PART I

CASES I AND II OF SCHEDULE D

Increase of profits or gains of transitional period

1—(1) This paragraph applies where, in the case of a trade, profession or vocation carried on by any person—

(*a*) paragraph 2(2) of Schedule 20 to the Finance Act 1994 applies without the modification made by paragraph 2(3) of that Schedule; and

(*b*) any amount which is included in the profits or gains of the transitional period would not have been so included if—

(i) any relevant change made by that person had not been made; or

(ii) any relevant transaction entered into by that person had not been entered into.

(2) Subject to sub-paragraph (3) below, the said paragraph 2(2) shall have effect as if the reference to the appropriate percentage of the aggregate of the amounts there mentioned were a reference to the aggregate of—

(*a*) that percentage of each of those amounts; and

(*b*) 1·25 times the complementary percentage of each of the amounts falling within sub-paragraph (1)(*b*) above.

(3) Sub-paragraph (2) above does not apply where—

(*a*) the aggregate of the amounts falling within sub-paragraph (1)(*b*) above is less than such amount as may be prescribed by regulations made by the Board;

(*b*) the proportion which the aggregate of those amounts bears to the aggregate of the amounts mentioned in the said paragraph 2(2) is less than such proportion as may be so prescribed; or

(*c*) the appropriate percentage of the turnover for the transitional period is less than such amount as may be so prescribed;

and regulations under this sub-paragraph may make as respects trades or professions carried on by persons in partnership provision different from that made as respects trades, professions or vocations carried on by individuals.

(4) In this paragraph—

"the appropriate percentage" means the following expressed as a percentage, that is, 365 divided by the number of days in the transitional period;

"the complementary percentage" means the difference between 100 per cent. and the appropriate percentage;

"the transitional period" means the basis period for the year 1996-97 and the relevant period (within the meaning of paragraph 2 of Schedule 20 to the Finance Act 1994) taken together.

Cross references—See the Income Tax (Schedule 22 to the Finance Act 1995) (Prescribed Amounts) Regulations 1997, SI 1997/1158, reg 3 (the amounts prescribed for the purposes of paras (*a*) and (*c*) of sub-para (3) for persons other than partners are, respectively, £10,000 and £50,000).

SI 1997/1158, regs 4, 5 (amounts prescribed for purposes of paras (*a*) and (*c*) of sub-para (3) for persons in partnership).

2—(1) This paragraph applies where, in the case of a trade or profession carried on by persons in partnership—

(*a*) paragraph 2(2) of Schedule 20 to the Finance Act 1994 applies without the modification made by paragraph 2(3) of that Schedule;

(*b*) a claim is made under section 353 of the Taxes Act 1988 (relief for interest: general provision) in respect of interest on a loan to defray money contributed or advanced by a partner to the partnership; and

(*c*) sub-paragraph (2) below applies to any of the money so contributed or advanced.

(2) This sub-paragraph applies to money so contributed or advanced unless it was contributed or advanced wholly or mainly—

(*a*) for bona fide commercial reasons; or

(*b*) for a purpose other than the reduction of the partnership's borrowings for a relevant period.

(3) Subject to sub-paragraph (4) below, the amount eligible for relief under the said section 353 in respect of interest paid by the partner in respect of the transitional period on money to which sub-paragraph (2) above applies shall not exceed the appropriate percentage of that interest.

(4) Sub-paragraph (3) above does not apply where—

(*a*) the loan was made before 1st April 1994; or

(*b*) the aggregate amount of interest paid as mentioned in that sub-paragraph is less than such amount as may be prescribed by regulations made by the Board.

(5) Where relief under the said section 353 in respect of interest on any loan ("the original loan") is restricted by sub-paragraph (3) above, relief under that section in respect of interest on any other loan used to defray money applied in paying off the original loan shall be restricted to the same extent as if that other loan were the original loan.

(6) In this paragraph—

(5) In this paragraph—

"relevant period" means a period the whole or part of which falls within the transitional overlap period;

"the transitional overlap period" has the same meaning as in paragraph 3 above;

"the transitional overlap profit" means the amount mentioned in the said paragraph 2(4) (whether having effect with or without the modification made by paragraph 3(2) above).

Cross reference—See the Income Tax (Schedule 22 to the Finance Act 1995) (Prescribed Amounts) Regulations 1997, SI 1997/1158, reg 7 (the amount prescribed for the purposes of sub-para (4)(b) is £7,500).

PART II
CASES III, IV AND V OF SCHEDULE D
Increase of trade etc profits or gains arising in 1995-96 and 1996-97

6—(1) This paragraph applies where, in the case of any income derived by any person from the carrying on by him of a trade, profession or vocation—

(a) paragraph 6(2)(a) of Schedule 20 to the Finance Act 1994 applies; and

(b) any amount which is included in the income arising within the years 1995-96 and 1996-97 would not have been so included if—

(i) any relevant change made by that person had not been made; or

(ii) any relevant transaction entered into by that person had not been entered into.

(2) Subject to sub-paragraph (3) below, the said paragraph 6(2)(a) shall have effect as if the reference to 50 per cent of the aggregate of the amounts there mentioned were a reference to the aggregate of—

(a) 50 per cent of each of those amounts; and

(b) 62.5 per cent of each of the amounts falling within sub-paragraph (1)(b) above.

(3) Sub-paragraph (3) of paragraph 1 above shall apply for the purposes of this paragraph as it applies for the purposes of that paragraph but subject to the following modifications, namely—

(a) the reference to the said paragraph 2(2) shall have effect as a reference to the said paragraph 6(2)(a); and

(b) the reference to the appropriate percentage of the turnover of the transitional period shall have effect as a reference to 50 per cent of the turnover of the years 1995-96 and 1996-97.

Increase of trade etc profits or gains arising in transitional overlap period

7—(1) This paragraph applies where, in the case of any income derived by any person from the carrying on by him of a trade, profession or vocation—

(a) paragraph 6(4) of Schedule 20 to the Finance Act 1994 applies; and

(b) any amount which is included in the transitional overlap profit would not have been so included if—

(i) any relevant change made by that person had not been made; or

(ii) any relevant transaction entered into by that person had not been entered into.

(2) Subject to sub-paragraph (3) below, the said paragraph 6(4) shall have effect as if the reference to the transitional overlap profit were a reference to the amount (if any) by which that profit exceeds 1·25 times the aggregate of the amounts falling within sub-paragraph (1)(b) above.

(3) Sub-paragraph (3) of paragraph 1 above shall apply for the purposes of this paragraph as it applies for the purposes of that paragraph but subject to the following modifications, namely—

(a) the reference to the aggregate of the amounts mentioned in the said paragraph 2(2) shall have effect as a reference to the transitional overlap profit; and

(b) the reference to the appropriate percentage of the turnover for the transitional period shall have effect as a reference to the appropriate percentage of the turnover for the transitional overlap period.

(4) In this paragraph—

"the appropriate percentage" means the following expressed as a percentage, that is, 365 divided by the number of days in the transitional overlap period;

"the transitional overlap period" means the period beginning immediately after the end of—

(a) the basis period for the year 1996-97; or

(b) in the case of any income derived by any person from the carrying on by him of a trade or profession in partnership with other persons, the basis period of the partnership for that year,

and (in either case) ending with 5th April 1997;

"the transitional overlap profit" means the amount mentioned in the said paragraph 6(4).

8—(1) This paragraph applies where, in the case of any income derived by any person from the carrying on by him of a trade or profession in partnership with other persons—

(a) that person ("the retiring partner") ceases to carry on the trade or profession at any time in the transitional overlap period; and

(b) if he had not so ceased, paragraph 7(2) above would have applied in relation to him.

"the appropriate percentage" and "the transitional period" have the same meanings as in paragraph 1 above;

"relevant period" means a period the whole or part of which falls within the transitional period.

Cross reference—See the Income Tax (Schedule 22 to the Finance Act 1995) (Prescribed Amounts) Regulations 1997, SI 1997/1158, reg 6 (the amount prescribed for the purposes of sub-para (4)(*b*) is £15,000).

Increase of profits or gains of transitional overlap period

3—(1) This paragraph applies where, in the case of a trade, profession or vocation carried on by any person—

(*a*) paragraph 2(4) of Schedule 20 to the Finance Act 1994 applies; and

(*b*) any amount which is included in the transitional overlap profit would not have been so included if—

    (i) any relevant change made by that person had not been made; or

    (ii) any relevant transaction entered into by that person had not been entered into.

(2) Subject to sub-paragraph (3) below, the said paragraph 2(4) shall have effect as if the reference to the transitional overlap profit were a reference to the amount (if any) by which that profit exceeds 1·25 times the aggregate of the amounts falling within sub-paragraph (1)(*b*) above.

(3) Sub-paragraph (3) of paragraph 1 above shall apply for the purposes of this paragraph as it applies for the purposes of that paragraph but subject to the following modifications, namely—

(*a*) the reference to the aggregate of the amounts mentioned in the said paragraph 2(2) shall have effect as a reference to the transitional overlap profit; and

(*b*) the reference to the appropriate percentage of the turnover for the transitional period shall have effect as a reference to the appropriate percentage of the turnover for the transitional overlap period.

(4) In this paragraph—

"the appropriate percentage" means the following expressed as a percentage, that is, 365 divided by the number of days in the transitional overlap period;

"the transitional overlap period" means the period beginning immediately after the end of—

    (*a*) the basis period for the year 1996-97; or

    (*b*) in the case of a trade or profession carried on by any person in partnership with other persons, the basis period of the partnership for that year,

and (in either case) ending with 5th April 1997;

"the transitional overlap profit" means the amount mentioned in the said paragraph 2(4).

4—(1) This paragraph applies where, in the case of a trade or profession carried on by any person in partnership with other persons—

(*a*) that person ("the retiring partner") ceases to carry on the trade or profession at any time in the transitional overlap period; and

(*b*) if he had not so ceased, paragraph 3(2) above would have applied in relation to him.

(2) The retiring partner shall for the year 1996-97 be chargeable to income tax under Case I or II of Schedule D on 1·25 times the aggregate of the amounts which would have fallen within paragraph 3(1)(*b*) above.

(3) In this paragraph "the transitional overlap period" has the same meaning as in paragraph 3 above.

5—(1) This paragraph applies where, in the case of a trade or profession carried on by any person in partnership with other persons—

(*a*) paragraph 2(4) of Schedule 20 to the Finance Act 1994 applies with or without the modification made by paragraph 3(2) above;

(*b*) a claim is made under section 353 of the Taxes Act 1988 (relief for interest: general provision) in respect of interest on a loan to defray money contributed or advanced by him ("the partner") to the partnership; and

(*c*) sub-paragraph (2) below applies to any of the money so contributed or advanced.

(2) This sub-paragraph applies to money so contributed or advanced unless it was contributed or advanced wholly or mainly—

(*a*) for bona fide commercial reasons; or

(*b*) for a purpose other than the reduction of the partnership's borrowings for the relevant period.

(3) Subject to sub-paragraph (4) below, the said paragraph 2(4) shall have effect as if the reference to the transitional overlap profit were a reference to the difference between that profit and the amount of interest paid by the partner in respect of the transitional overlap period on money to which sub-paragraph (2) above applies.

(4) Sub-paragraph (3) above does not apply where—

(*a*) the loan was made before 1st April 1994; or

(*b*) the aggregate amount of interest paid as mentioned in that sub-paragraph is less than such amount as may be prescribed by regulations made by the Board.

(2) The retiring partner shall for the year 1996-97 be chargeable to income tax under Case IV or V of Schedule D on 1·25 times the aggregate of the amounts which would have fallen within paragraph 7(1)(*b*) above.

(3) In this paragraph "the transitional overlap period" has the same meaning as in paragraph 7 above.

Increase of interest arising in 1995-96 and 1996-97

9—(1) This paragraph applies where, in the case of any interest arising to any person from any source—

    (*a*) paragraph 4(2) or 6(2)(*a*) of Schedule 20 to the Finance Act 1994 applies; and

    (*b*) any amount which is included in the interest arising within the years 1995-96 and 1996-97 would not have been so included if any relevant arrangements made between that person and another had not been made.

(2) Subject to sub-paragraph (3) below, the said paragraph 4(2) or 6(2)(*a*) shall have effect as if the reference to 50 per cent of the aggregate of the amounts there mentioned were a reference to the aggregate of—

    (*a*) 50 per cent of each of those amounts; and

    (*b*) 62·5 per cent of each of the amounts falling within sub-paragraph (1)(*b*) above.

(3) Sub-paragraph (2) above does not apply where—

    (*a*) the aggregate of the amounts falling within sub-paragraph (1)(*b*) above is less than such amount as may be prescribed by regulations made by the Board; or

    (*b*) the proportion which the aggregate of those amounts bears to the aggregate of the amounts mentioned in the said paragraph 4(2) or 6(2)(*a*) is less than such proportion as may be so prescribed.

Cross reference—See the Income Tax (Schedule 22 to the Finance Act 1995) (Prescribed Amounts) Regulations 1997, SI 1997/1158, reg 8 (the amount prescribed for the purposes of sub-para (3)(*a*) is £7,500).

Increase of other income arising in 1995-96 and 1996-97

10—(1) This paragraph applies where, in the case of any income (other than income falling within paragraph 6 or 9 above) arising to any person from any source—

    (*a*) paragraph 4(2) or 6(2)(*a*) of Schedule 20 to the Finance Act 1994 applies; and

    (*b*) any amount which is included in the income arising within the years 1995-96 and 1996-97 would not have been so included if—

        (i) any relevant arrangements made between that person and another had not been made; or

        (ii) any relevant transaction entered into by that person had not been entered into.

(2) Subject to sub-paragraph (3) below, the said paragraph 4(2) or 6(2)(*a*) shall have effect as if the reference to 50 per cent of the aggregate of the amounts there mentioned were a reference to the aggregate of—

    (*a*) 50 per cent of each of those amounts; and

    (*b*) 62·5 per cent of each of the amounts falling within sub-paragraph (1)(*b*) above.

(3) Sub-paragraph (3) of paragraph 9 above shall apply for the purposes of this paragraph as it applies for the purposes of that paragraph.

PART III
PROCEDURAL AND OTHER PROVISIONS
Time limits for purposes of paragraphs 1, 2, 4, 6 and 8 to 10

11—(1) Nothing in subsection (2) or (3) of section 29 of the Management Act (as substituted by section 191 of the Finance Act 1994) shall prevent an assessment being made under subsection (1) of that section in any case where—

    (*a*) the loss of tax there mentioned is attributable to any failure to give effect to any of paragraphs 1, 2, 4, 6 and 8 to 10 above; and

    (*b*) at the time when the assessment is made, the condition mentioned in sub-paragraph (3) below is fulfilled.

(2) Nothing in subsection (3) or (4) of section 30B of the Management Act (amendment of [partnership return]¹ where loss of tax discovered) shall prevent an amendment being made under subsection (1) of that section in any case where—

    (*a*) the omission, deficiency or excess there mentioned is attributable to any failure to give effect to any of paragraphs 1, 2, 4, 6 and 8 to 10 above; and

    (*b*) at the time when the amendment is made, the condition mentioned in sub-paragraph (3) below is fulfilled.

(3) The condition referred to in sub-paragraphs (1) and (2) above is that either—

(*a*) [a return under section 8 or 8A of the Management Act (personal or trustee return)]¹or, as the case may require, a [partnership return]¹ has been made for the year 1997–98 and that [return]¹ is still capable of being amended; or

[(*b*) no such return has been so made.]¹

Amendments—¹ Words in sub-para (2) substituted for the words "partnership statement"; in sub-para 3(*a*), words substituted for the words "an assessment under section 9 of the Management Act", the words "partnership return" substituted for "partnership statement under section 12AB of that Act", the word "return" substituted for the words "assessment or statement"; and sub-para 3(*b*) substituted by FA 2001 s 88, Sch 29 para 37(1)–(3) with effect from the passing of FA 2001 in relation to returns whether made before or after the passing of FA 2001, and whether relating to periods before or after the passing of FA 2001. Sub-para 3(*b*) previously read—

"(*b*) no such assessment or, as the case may require, statement has been so made."

Advance notice for purposes of paragraphs 3, 5 and 7

12—(1) An officer of the Board shall not so amend [a return under section 8 or 8A of the Management Act (personal or trustee return)]¹ as to give effect to paragraph 3, 5 or 7 above unless a notice stating—

(*a*) in the case of paragraph 3 or 7 above, the aggregate of the amounts falling within sub-paragraph (1)(*b*) of that paragraph; and

(*b*) in the case of paragraph 5 above, the aggregate amount of interest paid as mentioned in sub-paragraph (3) of that paragraph,

is given by such an officer at a time when the condition mentioned in sub-paragraph (2) below is fulfilled.

(2) The condition referred to in sub-paragraph (1) above is that either—

(*a*) [a return under section 8 or 8A of the Management Act (personal or trustee return)]¹ has been made for the year 1998–99 and [that return]¹ is still capable of being amended; or

[(*b*) no such return has been so made.]¹

(3) Subject to sub-paragraph (4) below, a notice under sub-paragraph (1) above shall be conclusive of the matters stated in it.

(4) An appeal may be brought against a notice under sub-paragraph (1) above at any time within the period of 30 days beginning with the date on which the notice is given.

(5) Subject to sub-paragraph (6) below, the provisions of the Management Act relating to appeals shall have effect in relation to an appeal under sub-paragraph (4) above as they have effect in relation to an appeal against an assessment to tax.

(6) On an appeal under sub-paragraph (4) above, section 50(6) to (8) of the Management Act (procedure on appeals) shall not apply but the Commissioners may—

(*a*) if it appears to them that the matters stated in the notice under sub-paragraph (1) above are correct, confirm the notice; or

(*b*) if it does not so appear to them, set aside or modify the notice accordingly.

Amendments—¹ Words in sub-para (1) substituted for words "an assessment made under section 9 of the Management Act (returns to include self-assessment)", words in (2)(*a*) substituted for the words "an assessment under section 9 of the Management Act", the words "that return" substituted for "that assessment"; and sub-para 2(*b*) substituted by FA 2001 s 88, Sch 29 para 37(1), (4) with effect from the passing of FA 2001 in relation to returns whether made before or after the passing of FA 2001, and whether relating to periods before or after the passing of FA 2001. Sub-para 2(*b*) previously read—

"(*b*) no such assessment has been so made."

Penalties not to apply in certain cases

13—(1) Where a relevant return (as originally made) states—

(*a*) that paragraph 1, 3 or 4 above applies in the case of a trade, profession or vocation carried on by any person; or

(*b*) that paragraph 7 or 8 above applies in the case of any income derived by any person from the carrying on by him of a trade, profession or vocation,

sub-paragraph (2) of that paragraph shall have effect, in its application to any amounts stated in the return (as so made) to fall within sub-paragraph (1)(*b*) of that paragraph or, in the case of paragraph 4 or 8 above, to be amounts which would have fallen within sub-paragraph (1)(*b*) of the preceding paragraph, as if the words "1·25 times" were omitted.

(2) Where a relevant return (as originally made) states—

(*a*) that paragraph 6 above applies in the case of any income derived by any person from the carrying on by him of a trade, profession or vocation; or

(*b*) that paragraph 9 or 10 above applies in the case of any income arising to any person from any source,

sub-paragraph (2) of that paragraph shall have effect, in its application to any amounts stated in the return (as so made) to fall within sub-paragraph (1)(*b*) of that paragraph, as if for the words "62·5 per cent." there were substituted the words "50 per cent.".

(3) In this paragraph—

"relevant return" means a return which, for the relevant year, is made under section 8, 8A or 12AA of the Management Act in respect of the trade, profession or vocation or, as the case may be, the source of the income;

"the relevant year" means—

(a) in relation to paragraph 1, 6, 9 or 10 above, the year 1996–97;

(b) in relation to paragraph 3, 4, 7 or 8 above, the year 1997–98.

PART IV

INTERPRETATION

Relevant changes for purposes of paragraphs 1, 3, 6 and 7

14—(1) Any accounting change or change of business practice is a relevant change for the purposes of paragraphs 1, 3, 6 and 7 above unless—

(a) the change is made exclusively for bona fide commercial reasons; or

(b) the obtaining of a tax advantage is not the main benefit that could reasonably be expected to arise from the making of the change.

(2) In this paragraph "accounting change"—

(a) does not include any change of accounting date which brings the end of the basis period for the year 1996-97 closer to 5th April 1997; but

(b) subject to that, means any change of accounting date or other modification of an accounting policy or any substitution of one such policy for another.

(3) In this paragraph "change of business practice" means any change in an established practice of trade, profession or vocation carried on by any person—

(a) as to the timing of any of the following, namely—

(i) the supply of goods or services, the invoicing of customers or clients and the collection of outstanding debts; and

(ii) the obtaining of goods or services, the incurring of business expenses and the settlement of outstanding debts; or

(b) as to the obtaining or making of payments in advance or payments on account.

Relevant transactions for purposes of paragraphs 1, 3, 6 and 7

15 Any self-cancelling transaction or transaction with a connected person is a relevant transaction for the purposes of paragraphs 1, 3, 6 and 7 above unless—

(a) the transaction is entered into exclusively for bona fide commercial reasons; or

(b) the obtaining of a tax advantage is not the main benefit that could reasonably be expected to arise from the entering into of the transaction.

16—(1) An agreement by which the person by whom a trade, profession or vocation is carried on agrees to sell or transfer trading stock or work in progress is a self-cancelling transaction for the purposes of paragraph 15 above if by the same or any collateral agreement that person—

(a) agrees to buy back or re-acquire the trading stock or work in progress; or

(b) acquires or grants an option, which is subsequently exercised, for him to buy back or re-acquire the trading stock or work in progress.

(2) In sub-paragraph (1) above—

"trading stock" has the same meaning as in section 100 of the Taxes Act 1988;

"work in progress", in relation to a profession or vocation, means—

(a) any services performed in the ordinary course of the profession or vocation, the performance of which is wholly or partly completed at the time of the sale or transfer and for which it would be reasonable to expect that a charge would have been made on their completion if the sale or transfer had not been effected; and

(b) any article produced, and any such material as is used, in the performance of any such services,

and references in that sub-paragraph to the sale or transfer of work in progress shall include references to the sale or transfer of any benefits and rights which accrue, or might reasonably be expected to accrue, from the carrying out of the work.

17—(1) For the purposes of paragraph 15 above, any question whether the person by whom a trade, profession or vocation is carried on is connected with another person shall be determined in accordance with sub-paragraphs (2) to (5) below.

(2) An individual carrying on a trade, profession or vocation is connected with another person if they are connected with each other within the meaning of section 839 of the Taxes Act 1988 (disregarding for this purpose the exception in subsection (4) of that section).

(3) Persons carrying on a trade or profession in partnership are connected with an individual if he controls the partnership.

(4) Persons carrying on a trade or profession in partnership are connected with a company if the company controls the partnership or the same person controls both the company and the partnership.

(5) Persons carrying on a trade or profession in partnership are connected with persons carrying on another trade or profession in partnership if the same person controls both partnerships.

(6) In this paragraph—

(*a*) "control" shall be construed—

(*a*) in relation to a company, in accordance with section 416 of the Taxes Act 1988;

(*b*) in relation to a partnership, in accordance with section 840 of that Act; and

(*b*) any reference to a person controlling a company or partnership is a reference to his doing so either alone or with one or more persons connected with him.

Relevant arrangements for purposes of paragraph 9

18—(1) Any arrangements under which—

(*a*) interest arises at irregular intervals during the years 1994-95 to 1997-98, or

(*b*) there are artificial variations in the rate of interest applicable during those years,

are relevant arrangements for the purposes of paragraph 9 above unless the obtaining of a tax advantage is not the main benefit that could reasonably be expected to arise from the making of the arrangements.

(2) Any variations in the rate of interest applicable during the years 1994–95 to 1997–98 are artificial variations for the purposes of this paragraph unless they are based on variations in a variable rate of interest the values of which from time to time are regularly published.

Relevant arrangements for purposes of paragraph 10

19 Any arrangements under which income arises at irregular intervals during the years 1994-95 to 1997-98 are relevant arrangements for the purposes of paragraph 10 above unless—

(*a*) the arrangements are made exclusively for bona fide commercial reasons; or

(*b*) the obtaining of a tax advantage is not the main benefit that could reasonably be expected to arise from the making of the arrangements.

Relevant transactions for purposes of paragraph 10

20—(1) Any transaction with a connected person is a relevant transaction for the purposes of paragraph 10 above unless—

(*a*) the transaction is entered into exclusively for bona fide commercial reasons; or

(*b*) the obtaining of a tax advantage is not the main benefit that could reasonably be expected to arise from the entering into of the transaction.

(2) A person is connected with another person for the purposes of this paragraph if they are connected with each other within the meaning of section 839 of the Taxes Act 1988.

General

21—(1) In this Schedule "turnover", in relation to a trade, profession or vocation, means the amounts derived from the provision of goods or services falling within its ordinary activities, after deduction of trade discounts and value added tax.

(2) Obtaining a tax advantage shall not be regarded as a bona fide commercial reason for the purposes of this Schedule.

SCHEDULE 23

OBLIGATIONS ETC IMPOSED ON UK REPRESENTATIVES

Section 126

Commentary—*Simon's Direct Tax Service* **B3.125.**
Statement of Practice SP 1/01—Treatment of investment managers and their overseas clients

General imposition of obligations etc

1—(1) Subject to the following provisions of this Schedule, the provisions of the Tax Acts, of the Taxation of Chargeable Gains Act 1992 and of any subordinate legislation made under the Tax Acts or that Act of 1992, so far as they—

(*a*) make provision for or in connection with the assessment, collection and recovery of tax, or of interest on any tax, and

(*b*) apply in any case for purposes connected with the taxation of any amounts in relation to which the non-resident has a UK representative, shall have effect in that case with respect to tax chargeable on, and interest payable by, the non-resident as if the obligations and liabilities of the non-resident by virtue of those provisions were also obligations and liabilities of the UK representative.

(2) In this paragraph "subordinate legislation" has the same meaning as in the Interpretation Act 1978.

Discharge of obligations and liabilities

2 Subject to the following provisions of this Schedule—

(*a*) the discharge by the non-resident's UK representative or by the non-resident himself of an obligation or liability which is or corresponds to one to which that representative is subject under this Schedule shall be treated as discharging the corresponding obligation or liability to which the other is subject; and

(*b*) the non-resident shall be bound, as if they were his own, by any acts or omissions of his UK representative in the discharge of the obligations and liabilities imposed on that representative by this Schedule.

Obligations and liabilities requiring notice

3 Where any obligation or liability such as is mentioned in paragraph 2 above arises only if the person on whom it is imposed has been given or served with a notice or other document or has received a request or demand, that obligation or liability shall not by virtue of this Schedule be treated as having been imposed on the non-resident's UK representative unless the notice or document, or a copy of it, was given to or served on that representative, or he was notified of the request or demand.

Information requirements

4—(1) The obligations relating to the furnishing of information which are imposed by this Schedule on the non-resident's UK representative in a case where that representative is his independent agent shall not require that representative to do anything except so far as it is practicable for the representative to do so by acting to the best of his knowledge and belief after having taken all reasonable steps to obtain the necessary information.

(2) Paragraph 2 above shall not have the effect—

(*a*) of discharging the non-resident from any obligation to furnish information in a case where that obligation has been discharged by his UK representative by virtue only of sub-paragraph (1) above; or

(*b*) of requiring the non-resident to be bound by any error or mistake contained, otherwise than as a result of—

    (i) any act or omission of the non-resident himself, or

    (ii) any act or omission to which he consented or in which he connived,

in information furnished by his UK representative in compliance, so far as required by sub-paragraph (1) above, with any obligation imposed by virtue of this Schedule on that representative.

(3) In this paragraph "information" includes anything contained in any return, self-assessment, account, statement or report that is required to be provided to the Board or any officer of the Board, and references to furnishing information shall be construed accordingly.

Criminal offences and penalties etc

5—(1) A person shall not by virtue of this Schedule be guilty of a criminal offence except where he committed the offence himself or consented to, or connived in, its commission.

(2) An independent agent of the non-resident shall not by virtue of this Schedule be liable, in respect of any act or omission, to any civil penalty or surcharge if—

(*a*) the act or omission is neither an act or omission of the agent himself nor an act or omission to which he consented or in which he connived, and

(*b*) he is able to show that he will not, after being indemnified for his other liabilities by virtue of this Schedule, be able to recover the amount of the penalty or surcharge out of any such sums as are mentioned in paragraph 6 below.

Indemnities

6 An independent agent of the non-resident shall be entitled—

(*a*) to be indemnified in respect of the amount of any liability of the non-resident which is discharged by that agent by virtue of paragraph 2 above; and

(*b*) to retain, out of any sums otherwise due from that agent to the non-resident, or received by that agent on behalf of the non-resident, amounts sufficient for meeting any liabilities by virtue of that paragraph which have been discharged by the agent, or to which he is subject.

Meaning of "independent agent"

7—(1) In this Schedule "independent agent", in relation to the non-resident, means any person who is the non-resident's UK representative in respect of any agency from the non-resident in which he was acting on the non-resident's behalf in an independent capacity.

(2) For the purposes of this paragraph a person shall not be regarded as acting in an independent capacity on behalf of the non-resident unless, having regard to its legal, financial and commercial characteristics, the relationship between them is a relationship between persons carrying on independent businesses that deal with each other at arm's length.

SCHEDULE 24

EXCHANGE GAINS AND LOSSES

Section 130

PART I

AMENDMENTS OF FINANCE ACT 1993

Introduction

1 ...

Amendment—Repealed by FA 2002 s 141, Sch 40 Pt 3(10) with effect for accounting periods beginning after 30 September 2002.

Trading gains and losses

2 (*inserted* s 128(10A), (10B), *repealed by* FA 2002 s 141, Sch 40 Pt 3(10) *with effect for accounting periods beginning after 30 September 2002*).

Non-trading gains and losses

3 (*amended* s 129(8)(*b*) and *inserted* s 129(8A), *repealed by* FA 2002 s 141, Sch 40 Pt 3(10)).

Assets and liabilities

4 (*amended* s 153(4), (6) and *inserted* s 153(11A); *repealed by* FA 1996 Sch 41 Pt V(3) with effect for accounting periods ending after 31 March 1996, subject to transitional provisions in FA 1996 Sch 15).

Chargeable gains

5 (*inserted* Sch 17 para 4(2A); *repealed* by FA 1996 Sch 41 Pt V(3) with effect for accounting periods ending after 31 March 1996, subject to transitional provisions in FA 1996 Sch 15).

6 (*substituted* Sch 17 para 5; *repealed by* FA 1996 Sch 41 Pt V(3) with effect for accounting periods ending after 31 March 1996, subject to transitional provisions in FA 1996 Sch 15).

PART II

AMENDMENTS OF OTHER PROVISIONS

Introduction

7 Paragraphs 8 to 12 below shall be deemed to have come into force on [23rd March 1995][1].

Amendments—[1] Words substituted for the words "on the day appointed under section 165(7)(*b*) of the Finance Act 1993 (which relates to exchange gains and losses)" by FA 2002 s 79, Sch 23 para 22(1), (3) with effect for accounting periods beginning after 30 September 2002.

Interest on overdue tax

8 (*amends* TMA 1970 s 87A(4A)).

9 (*amends* TMA 1970 s 87A(4A) and *inserts* s 87A(4B);*repealed by* FA 1998 Sch 27 Part III(2) with effect for relevant periods beginning after 5 April 1999).

10 (*amends* TMA 1970 s 91(1B)).

Interest on tax overpaid

11 (*amends* TA 1988 s 826(7C)).

12—(1), (2) ...[1]

(3) (*amends* FA 1989 s 102(4A)).

(4), (5) ...[1]

Amendments—¹ Sub-paras (1), (2), (4), (5) repealed by FA 1998 Sch 27 Pt III(2) with effect for relevant periods beginning after 5 April 1999.

SCHEDULE 25

CONTROLLED FOREIGN COMPANIES

Section 133

Introduction

1 In this Schedule—

(*a*) paragraph 2 contains an amendment designed to secure that in certain cases the chargeable profits of a company resident outside the United Kingdom are to be computed and expressed in the currency used in its accounts;

(*b*) the other paragraphs contain amendments connected with that amendment.

The principal amendment

2 (*inserts* TA 1988 s 747A).

Connected amendments

3–5 (*insert* TA 1988 s 747(4A), (4B), 748(4), (5), 750(5)–(8)).

6—(1) Schedule 24 to the Taxes Act 1988 (assumptions for calculating chargeable profits etc) shall be amended as mentioned in sub-paragraphs (2) to (5) below; and—

(*a*) the amendment made by sub-paragraph (2) below shall be deemed always to have had effect, and

(*b*) paragraph 1(4) of Schedule 16 to the Finance Act 1984 shall be deemed always to have had effect subject to the same amendment.

(2) (*amends* para 1(4)).

(3) Paragraph 4A (computation of basic profits or losses of a trade) shall be deemed never to have been inserted.

(4), (5) (*insert* paras 11A, 13–19, sub-para (5) *repealed by* FA 2002 s 141, Sch 40 Pt 3(10) *with effect for accounting periods beginning after 30 September 2002*).

7 (*inserted* FA 1993 s 168A; *repealed by* FA 2002 s 141, Sch 40 Pt 3(10) *with effect for accounting periods beginning after 30 September 2002*).

SCHEDULE 26

CHANGE IN OWNERSHIP OF INVESTMENT COMPANY: DEDUCTIONS

Section 135

Introductory

1 The Taxes Act 1988 shall have effect subject to the amendments in paragraphs 2 to 4 below.

Main provisions

2 (*inserts* ss 768B, 768C).

Supplementary provisions

3 (*inserts* Sch 28A).

Consequential amendments

4 (*amends* s 769(1), (2)(*d*), (4), (5) and *inserts* s 769(3A)).

Application of Schedule

5 This Schedule shall apply in relation to a change in ownership occurring on or after 29th November 1994 other than a change occurring in pursuance of a contract entered into before that date.

SCHEDULE 27

SUB-CONTRACTORS IN THE CONSTRUCTION INDUSTRY

Section 139

Commentary—*Simon's Direct Tax Service* **E5.501.**

Cross reference—See FA 1995 s 139 and Finance Act 1995, Section 139(3), (Appointed Day) Order 1998, SI 1998/2620 as to the appointed day for paras 1 to 7.

Payments to which provision for deductions applies

1—(1) ...[1]

(2), (3) (*repeal* TA 1988 s 559(3) and *insert* s 559(3A)).

(4) Sub-paragraphs (1) and (3) above shall have effect in relation to payments made on or after the appointed day.

Amendment—[1] Sub-s (1) (which amended TA 1988 s 559(1)) repealed by FA 1998 s 165, Sch 27 Pt III(7) with effect in relation to any payments made after 5 April 1998 other than any made in respect of services rendered before 6 April 1998, and any payments made before 6 April 1998 in respect of services to be rendered on or after that date.

Persons who are contractors and sub-contractors

2—(1), (2) (*insert* TA 1988 s 560(2)(*aa*), (*ea*) and *amend* s 560(2)(*f*)).

(3) This paragraph applies in relation to any payments made on or after the appointed day.

Individual partners and liabilities for certain contraventions

3 (*amends* TA 1988 s 561(2)(*b*)), (10), (11).

Turnover test etc

4—(1) Section 562 of that Act (conditions for grant of exemption certificate to be satisfied by individuals) shall be amended as follows.

(2)–(7) (*amend* TA 1988 s 562(1), 562(9), (11), *insert* s 562(2A), (2B), *repeal* TA 1988 s 562(3)–(7) and *substitute* TA 1988 s 562(13A), (14)).

5 (*repeals* TA 1988 s 563).

6—(1) (*substitutes* TA 1988 s 564(2A)–(7)).

7 (*inserts* TA 1988 s 565(2A)–(2C), (8A)).

Commencement of paragraphs 3 to 7

8—(1) Except in the case of paragraph 3(2) and (3) above, paragraphs 3 to 7 above shall have effect in relation to any application for the issue or renewal of a certificate under section 561 of the Taxes Act 1988 which is made with respect to any period beginning on or after the appointed day.

(2) Paragraph 3(2) and (3)(*b*) above shall have effect in relation to contraventions of section 561(10) or (11) occurring on or after the appointed day; and paragraph 3(3)(*a*) above shall have effect in relation to forms and other documents in a person's possession at any time after the passing of this Act.

Powers to make regulations

9 (*inserts* TA 1988 s 566(3)).

SCHEDULE 28

ELECTRONIC LODGEMENT OF TAX RETURNS, ETC

Section 153

Commentary—*Simon's Direct Tax Service* **A3.111.**
Prospective amendment—This Schedule will be repealed by FA 1999 s 139, Sch 20 Pt VII with effect on such day as the Treasury may by order appoint.

1, 2 (*insert* TMA 1970 s 115A, Sch 3A).

SCHEDULE 29

REPEALS

Section 162

PART VIII

INCOME TAX, CORPORATION TAX AND CAPITAL GAINS TAX

Note—Details of repeals already in effect have been omitted from this Schedule.

(7) QUALIFYING LIFE INSURANCE POLICIES

Chapter	Short title	Extent of repeal
1988 c 1.	The Income and Corporation Taxes Act 1988.	In Schedule 14, in paragraph 7(1), the words "and paragraphs 9 and 10 of Schedule 15". In Schedule 15, paragraphs 21, 22 and, in paragraph 24, in sub-paragraph (3), the word "first" and sub-paragraph (4).

These repeals come into force, in accordance with section 55(1) to (5) of this Act, on 5th May 1996.

Note—Reference to 5th May 1996 in s 55(1)–(5) now reference to the appointed date under s 55(9).

FINANCE ACT 1996

(1996 Chapter 8)

ARRANGEMENT OF SECTIONS

PART IV
INCOME TAX, CORPORATION TAX AND CAPITAL GAINS TAX

CHAPTER I
PRINCIPAL PROVISIONS

Income tax charge, rates and reliefs

Corporation tax charge and rate

Abolition of Schedule C charge etc

CHAPTER II
LOAN RELATIONSHIPS

Introductory provisions

Taxation of profits and gains and relief for deficits

Computational provisions etc

CHAPTER III

PROVISIONS RELATING TO THE SCHEDULE E CHARGE

CHAPTER IV

SHARE OPTIONS, PROFIT SHARING AND EMPLOYEE SHARE OWNERSHIP

Share options

Savings-related share option schemes

Other share option schemes

Profit sharing schemes

Employee share ownership trusts

CHAPTER V

SELF-ASSESSMENT, GENERAL MANAGEMENT ETC

General

CHAPTER VI

MISCELLANEOUS PROVISIONS

An Act to grant certain duties, to alter other duties, and to amend the law relating to the National Debt and the Public Revenue, and to make further provision in connection with Finance.

[29th April 1996]

PART IV

INCOME TAX, CORPORATION TAX AND CAPITAL GAINS TAX

CHAPTER I

PRINCIPAL PROVISIONS

Income tax charge, rates and reliefs

72 Charge and rates of income tax for 1996–97

(1)–(2) ...

(3) Section 559(4) of the Taxes Act 1988 (deductions from payments to sub-contractors in the construction industry) shall have effect—

(a) ...

(b) (*amends* FA 1995 s 139(1)).

Commentary—*Simon's Direct Tax Service* E1.102.
Cross reference—See FA 1995 s 139 for the meaning of "appointed day" in sub-s (3)(*b*).
Notes—Sub-ss (1), (2) are spent.
Sub-s (3)(*a*) amends TA 1988 s 559(4).

73 Application of lower rate to income from savings

(1)–(2) ...

(3) Subsection (1) above has effect in relation to the year 1996–97 and subsequent years of assessment and subsection (2) above has effect in relation to payments on or after 6th April 1996.

(4) Schedule 6 to this Act (which makes further amendments in connection with the charge at the lower rate on income from savings etc) shall have effect.

(5) Where any subordinate legislation (within the meaning of the Interpretation Act 1978) falls to be construed in accordance with section 4 of the Taxes Act 1988, that legislation (whenever it was made) shall be construed, in relation to payments on or after 6th April 1996, subject to subsection (1A) of that section.

Commentary—*Simon's Direct Tax Service* E1.102.
Note—Sub-s (1) inserts TA 1988 s 1A.
Sub-s (2) inserts TA 1988 s 4(1A).

74 Personal allowances for 1996–97

Commentary—*Simon's Direct Tax Service* E2.201, 302.
Note—This section is spent.

75 Blind person's allowance

(1) ...

(2) This section shall apply for the year 1996–97 and subsequent years of assessment.

Commentary—*Simon's Direct Tax Service* A3.431.
Note—Sub-s (1) amends TA 1988 s 265(1).

76 Limit on relief for interest

Commentary—*Simon's Direct Tax Service* D2.108.
Note—This section is spent.

Corporation tax charge and rate

77 Charge and rate of corporation tax for 1996

Commentary—*Simon's Direct Tax Service* D2.109.
Note—This section is spent.

78 Small companies

Commentary—*Simon's Direct Tax Service* A6.101; B5.101.
Note—This section is spent.

Abolition of Schedule C charge etc

79 Abolition of Schedule C charge etc

(1) The charge to tax under Schedule C is abolished—

   (*a*) for the purposes of income tax, for the year 1996–97 and subsequent years of assessment;

   (*b*) for the purposes of corporation tax, for accounting periods ending after 31st March 1996.

(2) Schedule 7 to this Act (which, together with Chapter II of this Part of this Act, makes provision for imposing a charge under Schedule D on descriptions of income previously charged under Schedule C, and makes connected amendments) shall have effect.

CHAPTER II
LOAN RELATIONSHIPS

Statement of Practice SP 4/98—Application of loan relationships legislation to partnerships which include companies for accounting periods ending after 31 March 1996.
Revenue Internal Guidance—Company taxation manual (Volume V) (detailed coverage of the provisions of this Chapter).
Cross references—See TA 1988 s 337A (no deduction to be made in respect of interest in computing a company's income from any source except in accordance with this Chapter).
TA 1988 s 338(3)(*a*) (annual payments payable in respect of any of a company's loan relationships are *not* charges on income).
TA 1988 s 401(1AA)–(1AC) (interaction between pre-trading expenditure relief provisions and loan relationship debits).
TA 1988 s 440(2A) (transfers of assets between categories of business of insurance companies).
TA 1988 s 487 (no credits or debits to be brought into account in respect of any loan relationship of a credit union as respects which a member of the union stands in the position of debtor or creditor).
TA 1988 s 494(2), (2A) (ring fence profits of oil companies).
TA 1988 s 730A(6), (6A) (treatment of price differential on repos).
TA 1988 ss 768B(10), 768C(9), Sch 28 Pt IV (restriction of debits to be brought into account for purposes of this Chapter on certain changes in ownership of an investment company).
TA 1988 s 797A (provisions concerning relief under double tax agreement for foreign tax in respect of a non-trading credit relating to an amount of interest).
TA 1988 s 807A (double tax relief: disposals and acquisitions of company loan relationships with or without interest).

TCGA 1992 s 117(A1) (for corporation tax purposes, any asset representing a loan relationship of a company is a qualifying corporate bond; but see ss 117A, 117B for exceptions to this rule).
TCGA 1992 s 251(7), (8) (asset representing a loan relationship is generally deemed to be a security, other than for purposes of determining allowable losses).
FA 1993 s 130 (non-trading exchange gains and losses to be brought into account as if they were non-trading credits and debits falling for the purposes of this Chapter to be brought into account in respect of a loan relationship of the company).
FA 1994 s 160(2), (2A) (non-trading profits and losses on "qualifying contracts" under the "interest rate and currency contract" provisions in FA 1994 to be brought into account as if they were non-trading credits and debits falling for the purposes of this Chapter to be brought into account in respect of a loan relationship of the company).

Introductory provisions

80 Taxation of loan relationships

(1) For the purposes of corporation tax all profits and gains arising to a company from its loan relationships shall be chargeable to tax as income in accordance with this Chapter.

(2) To the extent that a company is a party to a loan relationship for the purposes of a trade carried on by the company, profits and gains arising from the relationship shall be brought into account in computing the [profits][1] of the trade.

(3) Profits and gains arising from a loan relationship of a company that are not brought into account under subsection (2) above shall be brought into account as profits and gains chargeable to tax under Case III of Schedule D.

(4) This Chapter shall also have effect for the purposes of corporation tax for determining how any deficit on a company's loan relationships is to be brought into account in any case, including a case where none of the company's loan relationships falls by virtue of this Chapter to be regarded as a source of income.

(5) Subject to any express provision to the contrary, the amounts which in the case of any company are brought into account in accordance with this Chapter as respects any matter shall be the only amounts brought into account for the purposes of corporation tax as respects that matter.

Commentary—*Simon's Direct Tax Service* D2.1102; D4.731A.
Revenue Interpretation RI 207—Taxation of interest received as part of a company's Case I profit does not affect the payer's obligation to deduct income tax from yearly interest under TA 1988 s 349(2).
Note—Provisions contrary to the rule in sub-s (5) include: TA 1988 ss 400(9A) (write-off of government investment), 795(4) (double tax relief), s 798(3A) (double tax relief re interest on certain overseas loans), 811(3) (double tax relief: deduction of foreign tax where no credit available), TCGA 1992 s 116(16) (reorganisation of share capital etc involving qualifying corporate bond).
Amendments—[1] Words substituted by FA 1998 Sch 7 para 11 with effect from 31 July 1998.

81 Meaning of "loan relationship" etc

(1) Subject to the following provisions of this section, a company has a loan relationship for the purposes of the Corporation Tax Acts wherever—

(a) the company stands (whether by reference to a security or otherwise) in the position of a creditor or debtor as respects any money debt; and
(b) that debt is one arising from a transaction for the lending of money;

and references to a loan relationship and to a company's being a party to a loan relationship shall be construed accordingly.

(2) For the purposes of this Chapter a money debt is a debt [which is, or has at any time been, one that falls, or that may at the option of the debtor or of the creditor fall,][1] to be settled—

(a) by the payment of money; or
(b) by the transfer of a right to settlement under a debt which is itself a money debt

[disregarding any other option exercisable by either party][1].

(3) Subject to subsection (4) below, where an instrument is issued by any person for the purpose of representing security for, or the rights of a creditor in respect of, any money debt, then (whatever the circumstances of the issue of the instrument) that debt shall be taken for the purposes of this Chapter to be a debt arising from a transaction for the lending of money.

(4) For the purposes of this Chapter a debt shall not be taken to arise from a transaction for the lending of money to the extent that it is a debt arising from rights conferred by shares in a company.

(5) For the purposes of this Chapter—

(a) references to payments or interest under a loan relationship are references to payments or interest made or payable in pursuance of any of the rights or liabilities under that relationship; and
(b) references to rights or liabilities under a loan relationship are references to any of the rights or liabilities under the agreement or arrangements by virtue of which that relationship subsists;

and those rights or liabilities shall be taken to include the rights or liabilities attached to any security which, being a security issued in relation to the money debt in question, is a security representing that relationship.

(6) In this Chapter "money" includes money expressed in a currency other than sterling.

Commentary—*Simon's Direct Tax Service* D2.1103; D4.731A.
Revenue Internal Guidance—Company Taxation Manual COT12110 (sub-s(3) catches securities issued in consideration for a transfer of assets, for example; an instrument is any legal document, eg a stock certificate).

COT12160 (''related transactions'' include part-disposals, transfers by way of sale, gift and exchange and transactions where rights are extinguished by surrender, redemption or release).
COT12165–12167 (related transactions: repos and stock loans).
Simon's Tax Cases—*HSBC Life (UK) Ltd v Stubbs (Insp of Taxes), Nationwide Life Ltd v Crisp (Insp of Taxes), Abbey Life Assurance Co Ltd v Colclough (Insp of Taxes), TSB Life Ltd v Colclough (Insp of Taxes), Lloyds TSB Life Assurance Co Ltd v Colclough (Insp of Taxes)* [2002] STC (SCD) 9.
Amendments—[1] In sub-s (2) words substituted for the words ''which falls''; and final words inserted, by FA 2002 s 82, Sch 25 paras 1, 2 with effect for accounting periods beginning after 30 September 2002.

Taxation of profits and gains and relief for deficits

82 Method of bringing amounts into account

(1) For the purposes of corporation tax—

(*a*) the profits and gains arising from the loan relationships of a company, and

(*b*) any deficit on a company's loan relationships,

shall be computed in accordance with this section using the credits and debits given for the accounting period in question by the following provisions of this Chapter.

(2) To the extent that, in any accounting period, a loan relationship of a company is one to which it is a party for the purposes of a trade carried on by it, the credits and debits given in respect of that relationship for that period shall be treated (according to whether they are credits or debits) either—

(*a*) as receipts of that trade falling to be brought into account in computing the [profits][1] of that trade for that period; or

(*b*) as expenses of that trade which are deductible in computing those [profits][1].

(3) Where for any accounting period there are, in respect of the loan relationships of a company, both—

(*a*) credits that are not brought into account under subsection (2) above (''non-trading credits''), and

(*b*) debits that are not so brought into account (''non-trading debits''),

the aggregate of the non-trading debits shall be subtracted from the aggregate of the non-trading credits to give the amount to be brought into account under subsection (4) below.

(4) That amount is the amount which for any accounting period is to be taken (according to whether the aggregate of the non-trading credits or the aggregate of the non-trading debits is the greater) to be either—

(*a*) the amount of the company's profits and gains for that period that are chargeable under Case III of Schedule D as profits and gains arising from the company's loan relationships; or

(*b*) the amount of the company's non-trading deficit for that period on its loan relationships.

(5) Where for any accounting period a company has non-trading credits but no non-trading debits in respect of its loan relationships, the aggregate amount of the credits shall be the amount of the company's profits and gains for that period that are chargeable under Case III of Schedule D as profits and gains arising from those relationships.

(6) Where for any accounting period a company has non-trading debits but no non-trading credits in respect of its loan relationships, that company shall have a non-trading deficit on its loan relationships for that period equal to the aggregate of the debits.

(7) Subsection (2) above, so far as it provides for any amount to be deductible as mentioned in paragraph (*b*) of that subsection, shall have effect notwithstanding anything in section 74 of the Taxes Act 1988 (allowable deductions).

Commentary—*Simon's Direct Tax Service* D2.1135; D4.731A.
Cross reference—See TA 1988 s 730A(6A) (treatment of price differential on repos).
Amendments—[1] Words substituted by FA 1998 Sch 7 para 11 with effect from 31 July 1998.

83 Non-trading deficit on loan relationships

(1) This section applies for the purposes of corporation tax where for any accounting period (''the deficit period'') there is a non-trading deficit on a company's loan relationships.

(2) The company may make a claim for the whole or any part of the deficit [(to the extent that it is not surrendered as group relief by virtue of section 403 of the Taxes Act 1988)][2] to be treated in any of the following ways, that is to say—

(*a*) to be set off against any profits of the company (of whatever description) for the deficit period; [or][2]

(*b*)...[2]

(*c*) to be carried back to be set off against profits for earlier accounting periods; ...[2]

(*d*) ...[2]

[(3A) So much of the deficit for the deficit period as is not—

(*a*) surrendered as group relief by virtue of section 403 of the Taxes Act 1988, or

(*b*) treated in any of the ways specified in subsection (2) above,

shall be carried forward and set against non-trading profits of the company for succeeding accounting periods.][2]

(4)...[2]

(5) No part of any non-trading deficit of a company established for charitable purposes only shall be set off against the profits of that or any other company in pursuance of a claim under subsection (2) above.

(6) A claim under subsection (2) above must be made within the period of two years immediately following the end of the relevant period, or within such further period as the Board may allow.

(7) In subsection (6) above "the relevant period"—

(a) in relation to a claim under subsection (2)(a), ...[3] or (c) above, means the deficit period; ...[3]
(b) ...[3]

(8) Different claims may be made under subsection (2) above as respects different parts of a non-trading deficit for any period, but no claim may be made as respects any part of a deficit to which another claim made under that subsection relates.

(9) Schedule 8 to this Act (which makes provision about what happens where a claim is made under [subsection (2)(a) or (c) above or where subsection (3A) above has effect)][3] shall have effect.

Commentary—*Simon's Direct Tax Service* D2.1136, 1145; D4.731A.
Revenue Internal Guidance—Company Taxation Manual COT12816, 12827 (worked examples).
COT12836 (the rules allow partial claims so that foreign income can remain in charge; any part of a deficit not set off under sub-s(2)(a)–(c) is carried forward under sub-s(3) and may be the subject of a further claim under sub-s(2)(d) for the following period etc).
COT12841 (the carry forward under sub-s(3) is automatic: no claim is required).
Cross reference—See TMA 1970 s 87A(4A), (4B) (effect of claim under sub-s (2)(c) on interest on overdue corporation tax for earlier periods).
TA 1988 s 242(2)(f) (deficit may be set against surplus franked investment income).
TA 1988 s 407(1)(b), (2)(c) (relationship between group relief and relief under this section).
TA 1988 s 797(3A), (3B) (allocation, for purposes of computing double tax relief, of deduction in pursuance of claim under sub-s (2)(a) or (2)(d) or in accordance with sub-s (3); see also s 797A).
TA 1988 s 826(7C), (7CA) (interest on tax overpaid as a result of a claim under sub-s (2)(c)).
Amendments—[1] Substituted by FA 1998 s 82 and deemed always to have had effect.
[2] Words inserted in sub-s (2), word "or" in sub-s (2) repealed, sub-ss (2)(b), (d), (4) repealed, sub-s (3A) substituted for sub-s (3), and in sub-s (9) words substituted for the words "subsection (2) above)", by FA 2002 ss 82, 141,Sch 25 paras 1, 3, Sch 40 Pt 3(12) with effect accounting periods beginning after 30 September 2002.
Sub-ss (2)(b), (d), previously read as follows—

"(b) to be eligible for group relief"

"(d) to be carried forward and set against non-trading profits for the next accounting period."
Sub-ss (3), (4) previously read as follows—

"(3) So much of the deficit for the deficit period as is not the subject of a claim under subsection (2) above shall be carried forward and treated as a deficit for the next accounting period.".

"(4) An amount carried forward to an accounting period under subsection (3) above—

(a) may be the subject of a claim under paragraph (d) of subsection (2) above, but not under any other paragraph of that subsection, and
(b) shall be disregarded for the purposes of any claim under that subsection relating to a deficit arising in that period.".
[3] In sub-s (7), "(b)" and "and" and para (b) repealed by FA 2002 s 141, Sch 40 Pt 3(12) with effect for accounting periods beginning after 30 September 2002. Para (b) previously read as follows—

"(b) in relation to a claim under subsection (2)(d) above, means the accounting period immediately following the deficit period.".

Computational provisions etc

84 Debits and credits brought into account

(1) The credits and debits to be brought into account in the case of any company in respect of its loan relationships shall be the sums which, in accordance with an authorised accounting method and when taken together, fairly represent, for the accounting period in question—

(a) all profits, gains and losses of the company, including those of a capital nature, which (disregarding interest and any charges or expenses) arise to the company from its loan relationships and related transactions; and
(b) all interest under the company's loan relationships and all charges and expenses incurred by the company under or for the purposes of its loan relationships and related transactions.

(2) The reference in subsection (1) above to the profits, gains and losses arising to a company—

(a) does not include a reference to any amounts required to be transferred to the company's share premium account; but
(b) does include a reference to any profits, gains or losses which, in accordance with [generally accepted accounting practice][2], are carried to or sustained by any other reserve maintained by the company.

(3) The reference in subsection (1)(b) above to charges and expenses incurred for the purposes of a company's loan relationships and related transactions does not include a reference to any charges or expenses other than those incurred directly—

(a) in bringing any of those relationships into existence;
(b) in entering into or giving effect to any of those transactions;
(c) in making payments under any of those relationships or in pursuance of any of those transactions; or

(*d*) in taking steps for ensuring the receipt of payments under any of those relationships or in accordance with any of those transactions.

(4) Where—

(*a*) any charges or expenses are incurred by a company for purposes connected—

(i) with entering into a loan relationship or related transaction, or

(ii) with giving effect to any obligation that might arise under a loan relationship or related transaction,

(*b*) at the time when the charges or expenses are incurred, the relationship or transaction is one into which the company may enter but has not entered, and

(*c*) if that relationship or transaction had been entered into by that company, the charges or expenses would be charges or expenses incurred as mentioned in subsection (3) above,

those charges or expenses shall be treated for the purposes of this Chapter as charges or expenses in relation to which debits may be brought into account in accordance with subsection (1)(*b*) above to the same extent as if the relationship or transaction had been entered into.

[(4A) Where—

(*a*) different authorised accounting methods are used for the purposes of this Chapter as respects the same loan relationship for different parts of the same accounting period or for successive accounting periods, and

(*b*) no debit or credit falls to be brought into account under subsection (2)(*c*) or (3)(*b*) of section 90 below in consequence of the change of method, but

(*c*) an amount is brought into account for the purposes of the company's statutory accounts in respect of the change of method,

that amount shall be taken for the purposes of this Chapter to be included among the sums in respect of which debits and credits fall to be brought into account for the purposes of this Chapter in accordance with subsection (1)(*a*) above.][2]

(5) [In this Chapter][1] "related transaction", in relation to a loan relationship, means any disposal or acquisition (in whole or in part) of rights or liabilities under that relationship.

(6) The cases where there shall be taken [for the purposes of subsection (5) above][1] to be a disposal and acquisition of rights or liabilities under a loan relationship shall include those where such rights or liabilities are transferred or extinguished by any sale, gift, exchange, surrender, redemption or release.

(7) This section has effect subject to Schedule 9 to this Act (which contains provision disallowing certain debits and credits for the purposes of this Chapter and making assumptions about how an authorised accounting method is to be applied in certain cases).

Commentary—*Simon's Direct Tax Service* D2.1110, 1115, 1117; D4.731A.
Revenue Interpretation RI 156—Explains application of this section in relation to incidental costs of corporate borrowing.
RI 161—Relief is available under sub-s (3)(*a*) for guarantee fees paid by debtor where loan would not be advanced without provision of guarantee.
Revenue Internal Guidance—Company Taxation Manual COT12180, 12181 (meaning of "interest").
Regulations—See the Exchange Gains and Losses (Bringing into Account Gains or Losses) Regulations, SI 2002/1970.
Amendments—[1] In sub-s (5), words substituted for the words "In this section", and in sub-s (6), words substituted for the words "for the purposes of this section", by FA 2002 s 79, Sch 23 paras 1, 2 with effect for accounting periods beginning after 30 September 2002.
[2] In sub-s (2)(*b*), words "generally accepted accounting practice" substituted for the words "normal accountancy practice" by FA 2002 s 82, Sch 25 paras 1, 4 with effect for accounting periods beginning after 30 September 2002. This substitution is also made by FA 2002 s 103(4)(*d*) with effect from 24 July 2002. Sub-s (4A) inserted by FA 2002 s 82, Sch 25 paras 1, 4 with effect for accounting periods beginning after 30 September 2002.

[84A Exchange gains and losses from loan relationships]

(1) The reference in section 84(1)(*a*) above to the profits, gains and losses arising to a company from its loan relationships and related transactions includes a reference to exchange gains and losses arising to the company from its loan relationships.

(2) Subsection (1) above is subject to the following provisions of this section.

(3) Subsection (1) above does not have effect in relation to—

(*a*) so much of an exchange gain or loss arising to a company in relation to an asset representing a loan relationship of the company as falls within subsection (4) below; or

(*b*) so much of an exchange gain or loss arising to a company in relation to a liability representing a loan relationship of the company as falls within subsection (5) below; or

(*c*) so much of any exchange gain or loss arising to a company as results from any translation from one currency to another pursuant to section 93A(4) of the Finance Act 1993 of the profit or loss of part of the company's business and falls within subsection (4) below; or

(*d*) so much of an exchange gain or loss arising to a company in relation to an asset or liability representing a loan relationship of the company as falls within a description prescribed for the purpose in regulations made by the Treasury.

(4) For the purposes of subsection (3)(*a*) or (*c*) above, an exchange gain or loss falls within this subsection to the extent that, in accordance with generally accepted accounting practice, an amount representing the whole or part of it is carried to or sustained by a reserve maintained by the company.

(5) For the purposes of subsection (3)(*b*) above, an exchange gain or loss falls within this subsection to the extent that, in accordance with generally accepted accounting practice, an amount representing the whole or part of it—

(*a*) is carried to or sustained by a reserve maintained by the company; and

(b) is set off by or against an amount falling within subsection (6) below.

(6) An amount falls within this subsection if—

(a) it represents the whole or part of an exchange gain or loss arising to the company in relation to any asset of the company; and

(b) in accordance with generally accepted accounting practice it is carried to or sustained by the reserve mentioned in subsection (5)(a) above.

(7) Where by virtue of subsection (3) above subsection (1) above does not have effect in relation to an amount representing the whole or part of an exchange gain or loss, section 84(2)(b) above shall not have effect in relation to that amount (but this subsection is subject to regulations under subsection (8) below).

(8) The Treasury may by regulations make provision for or in connection with bringing into account in prescribed circumstances amounts in relation to which subsection (1) above does not, by virtue of subsection (3) above, have effect.

(9) The reference in subsection (8) above to bringing amounts into account is a reference to bringing amounts into account—

(a) for the purposes of this Chapter, as credits or debits in respect of the loan relationships of the company concerned; or

(b) for the purposes of the Taxation of Chargeable Gains Act 1992.

(10) Any power to make regulations under this section includes power to make different provision for different cases.]¹

Amendments—¹ This section inserted by FA 2002 s 79, Sch 23 paras 1, 3 with effect for accounting periods beginning after 30 September 2002.

85 Authorised accounting methods

(1) Subject to the following provisions of this Chapter, the alternative accounting methods that are authorised for the purposes of this Chapter are—

(a) an accruals basis of accounting; and

(b) a mark to market basis of accounting under which any loan relationship to which that basis is applied is brought into account in each accounting period at a fair value.

(2) An accounting method applied in any case shall be treated as authorised for the purposes of this Chapter only if—

[(a) subject to paragraphs (b) to (c) below, it is in conformity with generally accepted accounting practice to use that method in that case;]².

(b) it contains proper provision for allocating payments under a loan relationship[, or arising as a result of a related transaction,]² to accounting periods; ...³

[(bb) it contains proper provision for determining exchange gains and losses from loan relationships for accounting periods; and]¹

(c) where it is an accruals basis of accounting, it does not contain any provision (other than [provision in respect of exchange losses or]¹ provision comprised in authorised arrangements for bad debt) that gives debits by reference to the valuation at different times of any asset representing a loan relationship.

(3) In the case of an accruals basis of accounting, proper provision for allocating payments under a loan relationship to accounting periods is provision which—

(a) allocates payments to the period to which they relate, without regard to the periods in which they are made or received or in which they become due and payable;

(b) includes provision which, where payments relate to two or more periods, apportions them on a just and reasonable basis between the different periods;

(c) assumes, subject to authorised arrangements for bad debt, that, so far as any company in the position of a creditor is concerned, every amount payable under the relationship will be paid in full as it becomes due;

(d) secures the making of the adjustments required in the case of the relationship by authorised arrangements for bad debt; and

(e) provides, subject to authorised arrangements for bad debt and for writing off government investments, that, where there is a release of any liability under the relationship, the appropriate amount in respect of the release is credited to the debtor in the accounting period in which the release takes place.

(4) In the case of a mark to market basis of accounting, proper provision for allocating payments under a loan relationship to accounting periods is provision which allocates payments to the accounting period in which they become due and payable.

(5) In this section

(a) the references to authorised arrangements for bad debt are references to accounting arrangements under which debits and credits are brought into account in conformity with the provisions of paragraph 5 of Schedule 9 to this Act; and

(b) the reference to authorised arrangements for writing off government investments is a reference to accounting arrangements that give effect to paragraph 7 of that Schedule.

(6) In this section "fair value", in relation to any loan relationship of a company, means the amount which, at the time as at which the value falls to be determined, is the amount that the company would obtain from or, as the case may be, would have to pay to an independent person for—

(a) the transfer of all the company's rights under the relationship in respect of amounts which at that time are not yet due and payable; and

(b) the release of all the company's liabilities under the relationship in respect of amounts which at that time are not yet due and payable.

Commentary—*Simon's Direct Tax Service* D2.1110–1112; D4.731A.
Revenue Internal Guidance—Company Taxation Manual COT12312 (three methods of apportioning payments relating to more than one accounting period: straight line method, economic accrual or actuarial method, and the rule of 78 method; worked examples).
COT12314 (interest accrues on a day to day basis).
Amendments—¹ Sub-s (2)(bb) inserted, and words inserted in sub-s (2)(c) by FA 2002 s 79, Sch 23 paras 1, 4 with effect for accounting periods beginning after 30 September 2002.
² Sub-s (2)(a) substituted, and in words in sub-s (2)(b) inserted by FA 2002 s 82, Sch 25 paras 1, 5 with effect for accounting periods beginning after 30 September 2002. Sub-s (2)(a) previously read as follows—
"(a) it conforms (subject to paragraphs (b) and (c) below) to generally accepted accounting practice, as followed in cases where such practice allows the use of that method;".
³ Word "and" repealed by FA 2002 s 141, Sch 40 Pt 3(10) with effect for accounting periods beginning after 30 September 2002.

86 Application of accounting methods

(1) This section has effect, subject to the following provisions of this Chapter, for the determination of which of the alternative authorised accounting methods that are available by virtue of section 85 above is to be used as respects the loan relationships of a company.

(2) Different methods may be used as respects different relationships or, as respects the same relationship, for different accounting periods or for different parts of the same accounting period.

(3) If a basis of accounting which is or equates with an authorised accounting method is used as respects any loan relationship of a company in a company's statutory accounts, then the method which is to be used for the purposes of this Chapter as respects that relationship for the accounting period, or part of a period, for which that basis is used in those accounts shall be—

(a) where the basis used in those accounts is an authorised accounting method, that method; and

(b) where it is not, the authorised accounting method with which it equates

[but this subsection is subject to subsections (3A) and (3D) below.]¹

[(3A) If, in the case of a company falling within subsection (8)(c) or (d) below, an authorised mark to market basis of accounting—

(a) would be used as respects some or all of the company's loan relationships, were the company a UK company following generally accepted accounting practice, but

(b) is not the basis of accounting used as respects those loan relationships in the company's statutory accounts,

the company may elect to use an authorised mark to market basis of accounting as its authorised accounting method for the purposes of this Chapter in relation to every loan relationship as respects which that basis would be used if the company were a UK company following generally accepted accounting practice.]¹

[(3B) Any election under subsection (3A) above—

(a) must be made before the expiration of the period of two years following the end of the company's first accounting period beginning on or after 1st October 2002 in which it is party to a loan relationship in relation to which such an election may be made;

(b) has effect for that accounting period and all subsequent accounting periods of the company; and

(c) is irrevocable.]¹

[(3C) A company which makes an election under sub-paragraph (3A) above as respects its loan relationships shall be taken for the purposes of Schedule 26 to the Finance Act 2002 (derivative contracts) to have at the same time made an election under sub-paragraph (2) of paragraph 19 of that Schedule having effect—

(a) for the accounting periods mentioned in subsection (3B)(b) above, and

(b) as respects any derivative contracts to which the company is or may become party in any of those accounting periods,

and that election shall so have effect notwithstanding anything in paragraph (a) or (b) of sub-paragraph (3) of that paragraph.]¹

[(3D) If, in the case of a company falling within subsection (8)(c) or (d) below which has not made an election under subsection (3A) above,—

(a) an authorised mark to market basis of accounting would be used for an accounting period—

(i) as respects some or all of the company's loan relationships, and

(ii) as respects some or all of the company's derivative contracts,

were the company a UK company following generally accepted accounting practice, and

(b) that basis of accounting—

(i) is used in the company's statutory accounts as respects those derivative contracts for that accounting period, but

(ii) is not the basis of accounting used in those accounts as respects those loan relationships for that accounting period,

the company must for that accounting period use an authorised mark to market basis of accounting as its authorised accounting method for the purposes of this Chapter in relation to every loan relationship as respects which that basis would be used if the company were a UK company following generally accepted accounting practice.][1]

(4) For any period or part of a period for which the authorised accounting method to be used as respects a loan relationship of a company is not—

[(*a*) a method determined under subsection (3) above,

(*b*) an authorised mark to market method in accordance with an election under subsection (3A) above, or

(*c*) an authorised mark to market method in accordance with subsection (3D) above,][1],

an authorised accruals basis of accounting shall be used for the purposes of this Chapter as respects that loan relationship.

(5) For the purposes of this section (but subject to subsection (6) below)—

(*a*) a basis of accounting equates with an authorised accruals basis of accounting if it purports to allocate payments under a loan relationship to accounting periods according to when they are taken to accrue; and

(*b*) a basis of accounting equates with an authorised mark to market basis of accounting if (without equating with an authorised accruals basis of accounting) it purports in respect of a loan relationship—

(i) to produce credits or debits computed by reference to the determination, as at different times in an accounting period, of a fair value; and

(ii) to produce credits or debits relating to payments under that relationship according to when they become due and payable.

(6) An accounting method which purports to make any such allocation of payments under a loan relationship as is mentioned in subsection (5)(*a*) above shall be taken for the purposes of this section to equate with an authorised mark to market basis of accounting (rather than with an authorised accruals basis of accounting) if—

(*a*) it purports to bring that relationship into account in each accounting period at a value which would be fair value if the valuation were made on the basis that interest under the relationship were to be disregarded to the extent that it has already accrued; and

(*b*) the credits and debits produced in the case of that relationship by that method (when it is properly applied) correspond, for all practical purposes, to the credits and debits produced in the case of that relationship, and for the same accounting period, by an authorised mark to market basis of accounting.

(7) In this section—

["fair value" has the same meaning as in section 85 above][1].

["UK company" means a company incorporated or formed under the law of a part of the United Kingdom.][1]

(8) [In this Chapter][1] "statutory accounts", in relation to a company, means—

(*a*) any accounts relating to that company that are drawn up in accordance with any requirements of the Companies Act 1985 or the Companies (Northern Ireland) Order 1986 that apply in relation to that company;

(*b*) any accounts relating to that company that are drawn up in accordance with any requirements of regulations under section 70 of the Friendly Societies Act 1992 that apply in relation to that company;

(*c*) any accounts relating to that company which are accounts to which Part I of Schedule 21C to the Companies Act 1985 or Part I of Schedule 21D to that Act (companies with UK branches) applies;

(*d*) in the case of a company which—

(i) is not subject to any such requirements as are mentioned in paragraphs (*a*) or (*b*) above, and

(ii) is a company in whose case there are no accounts for the period in question that fall within paragraph (*c*) above,

any accounts relating to the company drawn up in accordance with requirements imposed in relation to that company under the law of its home State; and

(*e*) in the case of a company which—

(i) is not subject to any such requirements as are mentioned in paragraphs (*a*), (*b*) or (*d*) above, and

(ii) is a company in whose case there are no accounts for the period in question that fall within paragraph (*c*) above, the accounts relating to the company that most closely correspond to the accounts which, in the case of a company formed and registered under the Companies Act 1985, are required under that Act.

(9) For the purposes of subsection (8) above the home State of a company is the country or territory under whose law the company is incorporated.

Commentary—*Simon's Direct Tax Service* **D2.1110; D4.731A.**
Revenue Internal Guidance—Company Taxation Manual COT12340–12345 ("dirty" and "clean" mark to market bases: treatment of accrued interest).
COT12358–12361 (examples of allowable expenses).
COT12361 (deferred consideration on a sale of a loan relationship is brought into account in the period to which it relates (accruals basis), or the period in which due and payable (mark to market basis).
Amendments—[1] Words inserted after sub-s (3)(*b*), sub-ss (3A)–(3D) inserted, sub-s (4)(*a*)–(*c*) substituted for the words "determined under subsection (3) above,"; sub-s (7) amended in order for definition of "UK company" to be inserted; and in sub-s (8), words substituted for the words "In this section"; by FA 2002 s 82, Sch 25 paras 1, 7 with effect for accounting periods beginning after 30 September 2002.

87 Accounting method where parties have a connection

(1) This section applies in the case of a loan relationship of a company where for any accounting period there is a connection between the company and—

(*a*) in the case of a debtor relationship of the company, a person standing in the position of a creditor as respects the debt in question; or

(*b*) in the case of a creditor relationship of the company, a person standing in the position of a debtor as respects that debt.

(2) The only accounting method authorised for the purposes of this Chapter for use by the company as respects the loan relationship shall be an authorised accruals basis of accounting.

(3) For the purposes of this section there is a connection between a company and another person for an accounting period if (subject to subsection (4) and section 88 below)—

(*a*) the other person is a company and there is a time in that period...[1] when one of the companies has had control of the other;

(*b*) the other person is a company and there is a time in that period...[1] when both the companies have been under the control of the same person; ...[1]

(*c*) ...[1]

(4) Two companies which have at any time been under the control of the same person shall not, by virtue of that fact, be taken for the purposes of this section to be companies between whom there is a connection if the person was the Crown, a Minister of the Crown, a government department, a Northern Ireland department, a foreign sovereign power or an international organisation.

(5) The references in subsection (1) above to a person who stands in the position of a creditor or debtor as respects a loan relationship include references to a person who indirectly stands in that position by reference to a series of loan relationships [or money debts which would be loan relationships if a company directly stood in the position of creditor or debtor][1].

[(5A) Where a trade, profession or business is carried on by two or more persons in partnership ("the firm") and the firm stands in the position of a creditor or debtor as respects a money debt, any question—

(*a*) whether there is for the purposes of this Chapter a connection, within the meaning of this section, between any two companies for an accounting period in the case of a loan relationship, or

(*b*) to what extent any amount is to be treated under this Chapter in any particular way as a result of there being, or not being, such a connection,

shall be determined as if to the extent of his appropriate share each of the partners separately, instead of the firm, stood in the position of a creditor or, as the case may be, debtor as respects the money debt.

The reference in the words following paragraph (*b*) above to partners does not include a reference to the general partner of a limited partnership which is a collective investment scheme within the meaning of section 235 of the Financial Services and Markets Act 2000.][1]

[(5B) For the purposes of subsection (5A) above, a partner's "appropriate share" is the share that would be apportioned to him if an apportionment were made in the shares in which any profit or loss computed in accordance with subsection (1) of section 114 of the Taxes Act 1988 for the accounting period in question would be apportioned between the partners under subsection (2) of that section.][1]

(6) ...[1]

(7) ...[1]

(8) ...[1]

Commentary—*Simon's Direct Tax Service* **D2.1118, 1119; D4.731A.**
Concession C28—Bad debt relief allowed in limited circumstances even where lender and borrower connected with one another under this section (see also FA 1996 Sch 9 para 6).
Revenue Interpretation RI 172—Considers the period over which purchase discount should be recognised for tax purposes where purchased loan is repayable on demand and parties are connected persons.
Cross references—See FA 1996 Sch 9 paras 5(3), 6 (treatment of bad debts).
Amendments—[1] In sub-s (3)(*a*), words "", or in the two years before the beginning of that period," repealed, and word inserted; in sub-s (3)(*b*), words "", or in those two years," and "or" repealed; sub-ss (3)(*c*), (6)–(8) repealed, in sub-s (5) words inserted;

and sub-ss (5A), (5B) inserted; by FA 2002 ss 82, 141, Sch 25 paras 1, 7, Sch 40 Pt 3(12) with effect for accounting periods beginning after 30 September 2002.
Sub-s (3)(*c*) previously read as follows—

"(*c*) there is a time in that accounting period, or in those two years, when the company was a close company and the other person was a participator in that company or the associate of a person who was such a participator at that time.";
Sub-ss (6)–(8) previously read as follows—

"(6) Subsections (2) to (6) of section 416 of the Taxes Act 1988 (meaning of control) shall apply for the purposes of this section as they apply for the purposes of Part XI of that Act."

"(7) Subject to subsection (8) below, in this section "participator" and "associate" have the meanings given for the purposes of Part XI of the Taxes Act 1988 by section 417 of that Act.

(8) A person shall not for the purposes of this section be regarded as a participator in relation to a company by reason only that he is a loan creditor of the company.".

[87A Meaning of "control" in section 87

(1) For the purposes of section 87 above, "control", in relation to a company, means the power of a person to secure—

(*a*) by means of the holding of shares or the possession of voting power in or in relation to the company or any other company, or
(*b*) by virtue of any powers conferred by the articles of association or other document regulating the company or any other company,

that the affairs of the company are conducted in accordance with his wishes.

(2) There shall be left out of account for the purposes of this section—

(*a*) any shares held by a company, and
(*b*) any voting power or other powers arising from shares held by a company,

if a profit on a sale of the shares would be treated as a trading receipt of a trade carried on by the company and the shares are not, within the meaning of Chapter 1 of Part 12 of the Taxes Act 1988, assets of an insurance company's long-term insurance fund (see section 431(2) of that Act).

(3) Where section 114 of the Taxes Act 1988 (partnerships involving companies: special rules for computing profits and losses) applies in relation to a partnership, any property, rights or powers held or exercisable for the purposes of the partnership shall be treated for the purposes of this section, as respects any time in an accounting period of the partnership, as if—

(*a*) the property, rights or powers had been apportioned between, and were held or exercisable by, the partners severally, and
(*b*) the apportionment had been in the shares in which the profit or loss of the accounting period of the partnership would be apportioned between the partners under subsection (2) of that section,

but taking the references in paragraphs (*a*) and (*b*) above to partners as not including a reference to the general partner of a limited partnership which is a collective investment scheme within the meaning of section 235 of the Financial Services and Markets Act 2000.]¹

Amendments—This section to be inserted by FA 2002 s 82, Sch 25 paras 1, 8 with effect for accounting periods beginning after 30 September 2002.

88 Exemption from section 87 in certain cases

(1) Subject to subsection (5) below, where a creditor relationship of a company is one to which that company is a party in any accounting period in exempt circumstances, any connection for that accounting period between the company and a person who stands in the position of a debtor as respects the debt shall be disregarded for the purposes of section 87 above.

(2) A company having a credit relationship in any accounting period shall, for that period, be taken for the purposes of this section to be a party to that relationship in exempt circumstances if—

(*a*) the company, in the course of carrying on any activities forming an integral part of a trade carried on by that company in that period, disposes of or acquires assets representing creditor relationships;
(*b*) that period is one for which the company uses an authorised mark to market basis of accounting as respects all the creditor relationships represented by assets acquired in the course of those activities;
(*c*) the asset representing the creditor relationship in question was acquired in the course of those activities;
(*d*) that asset is either—

    (i) listed on a recognised stock exchange at the end of that period; or
    (ii) a security the redemption of which must occur within twelve months of its issue;

(*e*) there is a time in that period when assets of the same kind as the asset representing the loan relationship in question are in the beneficial ownership of persons other than the company; and
(*f*) there is not more than three months, in aggregate, in that accounting period during which the equivalent of 30 per cent or more of the assets of that kind is in the beneficial ownership of connected persons.

(3) An insurance company carrying on basic life assurance and general annuity business and having a creditor relationship in any accounting period shall, for that period, be taken for the purposes of this section to be a party to that relationship in exempt circumstances if—

(*a*) assets of the company representing any of its creditor relationships are linked for that period to its basic life assurance and general annuity business;

(*b*) that period is one for which the company uses an authorised mark to market basis of accounting as respects all the creditor relationships of the company represented by assets that are so linked;

(*c*) the asset representing the creditor relationship in question is so linked;

(*d*) that asset is either—

(i) listed on a recognised stock exchange at the end of that period; or

(ii) a security the redemption of which must occur within twelve months of its issue;

(*e*) there is a time in that period when assets of the same kind as the asset representing the creditor relationship in question are in the beneficial ownership of persons other than the company; and

(*f*) there is not more than three months, in aggregate, in that period during which the equivalent of 30 per cent or more of the assets of that kind is in the beneficial ownership of connected persons.

(4) For the purposes of subsections (2) and (3) above—

(*a*) assets shall be taken to be of the same kind where they are treated as being of the same kind by the practice of any recognised stock exchange, or would be so treated if dealt with on such a stock exchange; and

(*b*) a connected person has the beneficial ownership of an asset wherever there is, or (apart from this section) would be, a connection (within the meaning of section 87 above) between—

(i) the person who has the beneficial ownership of the assets, and

(ii) a person who stands in the position of a debtor as respects the money debt by reference to which any loan relationship represented by that asset subsists.

(5) Where for any accounting period—

(*a*) subsection (1) above has effect in the case of a creditor relationship of a company, and

(*b*) the person who stands in the position of a debtor as respects the debt in question is also a company,

that subsection shall not apply for determining, for the purposes of so much of section 87 above as relates to the corresponding debtor relationship, whether there is a connection between the two companies.

(6) Subsection (5) of section 87 above shall apply for the purposes of this section as it applies for the purposes of that section.

(7) In this section "basic life assurance and general annuity business" and "insurance company" has the same meanings as in Chapter I of Part XII of the Taxes Act 1988, and section 432ZA of that Act (linked assets) shall apply for the purposes of this section as it applies for the purposes of that Chapter.

[88A Accounting method where rate of interest is reset

(1) This section applies where—

(*a*) the conditions in subsections (2) and (3) below are satisfied in relation to an asset representing a creditor relationship of a company; and

(*b*) the object, or one of the main objects, of the company entering into or becoming a party to the creditor relationship was the securing, whether for itself or any other person, of a tax advantage (within the meaning of Chapter 1 of Part 17 of the Taxes Act 1988).

(2) The first condition is that there is or has at any time been a change in—

(*a*) the rate of interest payable in the case of the asset;

(*b*) the amount payable to discharge the debt; or

(*c*) the time at which any payments under the asset (whether of interest or otherwise) fall due.

(3) The second condition is that the difference between—

(*a*) the fair value of the asset immediately after the change, and

(*b*) the issue price of the asset, is equal to at least 5 per cent of the issue price of the asset.

(4) On and after the day on which the conditions in subsections (2) and (3) above become satisfied in the case of an asset, the only accounting method authorised for the purposes of this Chapter for use by any company as respects a creditor relationship represented by the asset shall be an authorised mark to market basis of accounting.

(5) Where section 90 below applies in consequence of subsection (4) above, no debit shall be brought into account under subsection (2)(*c*) or (3)(*b*) of that section.

(6) In determining the fair value of an asset for any purpose of this section it shall be assumed that all amounts payable by the debtor will be paid in full as they fall due.]¹

Amendments—¹ Section inserted by FA 2002 s 71 with effect from the relevant day. The relevant day is—

(*a*) 19 December 2001, in a case where this section applies by reason of a change in the rate of interest payable in the case of the asset in question; or

(*b*) 24 April 2002, in any other case.

89 Inconsistent application of accounting methods

(1) Where there is any inconsistency or other material difference between the way in which any authorised accounting method is applied as respects the same loan relationship in successive accounting periods, a balancing credit or balancing debit shall be brought into account in the second of those periods (''the second period'').

(2) The amount of the balancing credit or debit shall be computed as respects the relationship in question by—

    (a) taking the amount given by subsection (3) below and the amount given by subsection (4) below; and

    (b) then aggregating those amounts (treating any debit as a negative amount) to produce a net credit or net debit.

(3) The amount given by this subsection is whichever of the following is applicable—

    (a) a debit equal to the amount (if any) by which the first of the following amounts exceeds the second, that is to say—

       (i) the aggregate of the credits actually brought into account for all previous periods in which the accounting method was used; and

       (ii) the aggregate of the credits that would have been brought into account if that method had been applied in those periods in the same way as it was applied in the second period;

    (b) a credit equal to the amount (if any) by which the second aggregate mentioned in paragraph (a) above exceeds the first; or

    (c) if both those aggregates are the same, nil.

(4) The amount given by this subsection is whichever of the following is applicable—

    (a) a credit equal to the amount (if any) by which the first of the following amounts exceeds the second, that is to say—

       (i) the aggregate of the debits actually brought into account for all previous periods in which the accounting method was used; and

       (ii) the aggregate of the debits that would have been brought into account if that method had been applied in those periods in the same way as it was applied in the second period;

    (b) a debit equal to the amount (if any) by which the second aggregate mentioned in paragraph (a) above exceeds the first; or

    (c) if both those aggregates are the same, nil.

(5) In this section ''previous period'' means any accounting period before the second period.

Commentary—*Simon's Direct Tax Service* D2.1113.
Revenue Internal Guidance—Company Taxation Manual COT12405, 12406 (worked examples).
Amendment—This section repealed by FA 2002 ss 82, 141, Sch 25 paras 1, 9, Sch 40 Pt 3(12) with effect for accounting periods beginning after 30 September 2002.

90 Changes of accounting method

(1) This section applies where—

    [(a)]² different authorised accounting methods are used for the purposes of this Chapter as respects the same loan relationship for different parts of the same accounting period or for successive accounting periods.

    [(b) the change or method is in pursuance of a requirement of this Chapter as to the basis of accounting to be used for the purposes of this Chapter in the case of the loan relationship; and]²

    [(c) the case does not fall within subsection (1A) below]²

[(1A) The case falls within this subsection if, for the purposes of the company's statutory accounts, the different authorised accounting methods mentioned in subsection (1) above are also used as respects the loan relationship for the same parts of the same accounting period or, as the case may be, for the same successive accounting periods as are mentioned in subsection (1) above.]1

(2) Where, in the case of any loan relationship, the use of any authorised accounting method is superseded in the course of any accounting period by the use of another—

    (a) the assumptions specified in subsection (4) below shall be made;

    (b) each method shall be applied on those assumptions as respects the part of the period for which it is used; and

    (c) the credits and debits given by the application of those methods on those assumptions shall be brought into account in the accounting period in which the change of method takes effect.

(3) Where, in the case of any loan relationship, the use of any authorised accounting method is superseded as from the beginning of an accounting period by the use of another—

    (a) a net credit or debit shall be computed (treating any debit used in the computation as a negative amount) by—

       (i) aggregating the credits and debits which, on the assumptions specified in subsection (4) below, would have been given in respect of that relationship for the successive accounting periods by the use for each period of the accounting method actually used for that period;

       (ii) aggregating the credits and debits so given without the making of those assumptions; and

(iii) subtracting the second aggregate from the first;
and

(b) the net credit or debit shall be brought into account for the purposes of this Chapter in the accounting period as from the beginning of which the change of method takes effect.

(4) The assumptions mentioned in subsections (2) and (3) above are—

(a) that the company ceased to be a party to the relationship immediately before the end of the period, or part of a period, for which the superseded method is used;

(b) that the company again became a party to that relationship as from the beginning of the period or, as the case may be, part of a period for which the other authorised accounting method is used;

(c) that the relationship to which the company is deemed to have become a party is separate and distinct from the one to which it is deemed to have ceased to be a party;

(d) that the amount payable under the transaction comprised in each of the assumptions specified in paragraphs (a) and (b) above was equal to the fair value of the relationship; and

(e) so far as relevant, that that amount became due at the time when the company is deemed to have ceased to be a party to the relationship or, as the case may be, to have again become a party to it.

(5) Where—

(a) a mark-to-market basis of accounting is superseded by an accruals basis of accounting in the case of any loan relationship,

[(aa) the relationship is one to which the company in question is still a party at the end of the period or part of a period for which the accruals basis of accounting is used,] and

(b) the amount which would have accrued in respect of that relationship in the period or part of a period for which the accruals basis of accounting is used falls to be determined for the purposes of this section in accordance with the assumptions mentioned in subsection (4) above,

[that amount shall be computed using for the closing value as at the end of that period or part of a period the amount specified in subsection (6) below.]

[(6) That amount is—

(a) in a case to which subsection (3) above applies, the amount taken for the purposes of subsection (3)(a)(ii) above to be the closing value as at the end of the period for which the accruals basis of accounting is used; and

(b) in a case to which subsection (2) above applies, the amount which, without the making of the assumptions mentioned in subsection (4) above, would be taken to be the closing value as at the end of the part of the period for which that basis is used.]

(7) In this section "fair value" has the same meaning as in section 85 above.

Commentary—*Simon's Direct Tax Service* D2.1113.
Revenue Internal Guidance—Company Taxation Manual COT12402, 12403 (worked examples).
Amendments—¹ Sub-s (5)(aa) inserted and words after sub-s (5)(b), and sub-s (6), substituted by FA 1997 s 81(1)–(5) with effect where the period or part of a period for which the superseded accounting method is or was used is a period ending after 13 November 1996.
² In sub-s (1), "(a)" inserted after "where", paras (b), (c), inserted; and sub-s (1A) inserted, by FA 2002 s 82, Sch 25 paras 1, 10 with effect for accounting periods beginning after 30 September 2002.

91 Payments subject to deduction of tax

(1) This section applies where—

(a) any company receives a payment of interest on which it bears income tax by deduction; and

(b) in the case of that company, a credit relating to that interest has been brought into account for the purposes of this Chapter for an accounting period ending more than two years before the receipt of the payment.

(2) On a claim made by the company to an officer of the Board, section 7(2) or, as the case may be, 11(3) of the Taxes Act 1988 (deducted income tax to be set against liability to corporation tax) shall have effect in relation to the income tax on the payment as if the interest had fallen to be taken into account for the purposes of corporation tax in the accounting period in which the payment of that interest is received.

(3) In determining for the purposes of this section which accounting period is the accounting period for which a credit relating to interest paid subsequently was brought into account, every payment of interest to a company under a loan relationship of that company shall be assumed to be a payment in discharge of the earliest outstanding liability to that company in respect of interest payable under the relationship.

(4) For the purposes of this section, the earliest outstanding liability to interest payable under a loan relationship of a company shall be identified, in relation to any payment of such interest, according to the authorised accounting method most recently used as respects that relationship, so that—

(a) if that method is an authorised accruals basis of accounting, it shall be determined by reference to the time when the interest accrued; and

(b) if that method is an authorised mark to market basis of accounting, it shall be determined by reference to the time when the interest became due and payable.

(5) In subsection (4) above the reference, in relation to a payment of interest made to a company in any accounting period, to the authorised accounting method most recently used as respects that relationship is a reference to the authorised accounting method which, in the case of that company, has been used as respects that relationship for the accounting period which, when the payment is made, is the most recent for which amounts in respect of that relationship have been brought into account for the purposes of this Chapter.

(6) A claim under this section shall not be made in respect of any payment of interest at any time after the later of the following, that is to say—

(a) the time two years after the end of the accounting period in which the payment is received; and

(b) the time six years after the end of the accounting period for which the credit in respect of the interest was brought into account for the purposes of this Chapter.

(7) Where—

(a) there is a payment of interest to a company under a loan relationship of that company, and

(b) the company is prevented by virtue of subsection (6) above from making any claim under this section in respect of that payment,

the company shall not be entitled to make any claim under paragraph 5 of Schedule 16 to the Taxes Act 1988 (set off of income tax borne against income tax payable) in respect of that payment.

Commentary—*Simon's Direct Tax Service* D2.1138.
Amendment—This section repealed by FA 2002 ss 82, 141, Sch 25 paras 1, 11, Sch 40 Pt 3(12) with effect for accounting periods beginning after 30 September 2002.

Special cases

92 [Convertible securities etc: creditor relationships][2]

(1) This section applies to an asset if—

(a) the asset represents a creditor relationship of a company;

(b) the rights attached to the asset include provision by virtue of which the company is or may become entitled to acquire (whether by conversion or exchange or otherwise) [shares in a company][2];

[(bb) the only shares that may be so acquired under any such provision are shares which, at the time when the asset comes or came into existence are or were, and at all times since have been,—

(i) qualifying ordinary shares in one or more companies, or

(ii) mandatorily convertible preference shares in one or more companies;][2]

(c) the extent to which shares may be acquired under that provision is not determined using a cash value which is specified in [any such provision][2] or which is or will be ascertainable by reference to the terms of that provision;

(d) the asset is not a relevant discounted security within the meaning of Schedule 13 to this Act [or an excluded indexed security within the meaning of that Schedule][2];

[(dd) the rights attached to the asset do not include provision by virtue of which the company may require a person other than the issuing company to acquire the asset for an amount which would, if payable on redemption, be an amount involving a deep gain for the purposes of paragraph 3 of that Schedule;][2]

(e) at the time when the asset came into existence there was a more than negligible likelihood that [the rights][2] to acquire shares in a company would in due course be exercised to a significant extent; ...[2]

[(ee) the rights to acquire shares in a company (whether by conversion or exchange or otherwise) are such that exercising them to their full extent would result in the replacement of the asset—

(i) wholly by shares, or

(ii) in a case where exercising the rights to acquire shares to their full extent would not confer an entitlement to a whole number of shares, wholly by shares and a cash adjustment in respect of the fraction of a share so arising,

and the ending of the creditor relationship; and][2]

(f) the asset is not one the disposal of which by the company would fall to be treated as a disposal in the course of activities forming an integral part of a trade carried on by the company.

[(1A) In subsection (1) above—

"the issuing company" means the company that brought into existence the asset mentioned in subsection (1) above;

"mandatorily convertible preference shares" means shares (other than qualifying ordinary shares) which are issued upon terms that stipulate that, by a time no more than 24 hours after their acquisition by a person who immediately before that acquisition had the creditor relationship represented by those shares, they must be converted into or exchanged for qualifying ordinary shares;

"qualifying ordinary shares" means shares in a company which satisfy the conditions in subsections (1B) and (1C) below.][2]

[(1B) The first condition is that the shares are shares representing some or all of the issued share capital (by whatever name called) of the company, other than—

(a) capital the holders of which have a right to a dividend at a fixed rate but have no other right to share in the profits of the company, or

(b) capital the holders of which have no right to a dividend of any description nor any other right to share in the profits of the company.][2]

[(1C) The second condition is that the shares are—

(a) shares which are listed on a recognised stock exchange, or

(b) shares in a company which is a trading company or a holding company;

and for this purpose "trading company" and "holding company" have the meanings given by paragraph 22(1) of Schedule A1 to the Taxation of Chargeable Gains Act 1992 (c 12).][2]

[(1D) For the purposes of subsection (1)(ee)(ii) above, the amount which may be paid by way of a cash adjustment may not exceed five per cent of the value of the relevant shares at the relevant time; and for these purposes—

(a) "the relevant shares" means the shares which would be acquired by exercising the rights attached to the asset to their full extent, and

(b) "the relevant time" means the time at which the rights to acquire those shares are exercised.][2]

[(1E) This section does not apply to an asset representing a creditor relationship of a company if, for the accounting period in which the asset comes into existence, there is a connection between the company and the company which is the issuing company in relation to that asset.][3]

[(1F) If, in the case of an asset representing a creditor relationship of a company, the company and the company which is the issuing company in relation to that asset become companies between which, for any accounting period, there is a connection—

(a) the asset shall cease to be an asset to which this section applies, and

(b) it shall be treated, for the purposes of subsection (7)(a) below, as having ceased to be such an asset at the time when the circumstances giving rise to that connection arose.][3]

[(1G) Section 87(3) above (connection between a company and another person for an accounting period) applies for the purposes of subsections (1E) and (1F) above.][3]

(2) The amounts falling for any accounting period to be brought into account for the purposes of this Chapter in respect of a creditor relationship represented by an asset to which this section applies shall be confined to—

[(a)][4] amounts relating to interest[; and

(b) amounts relating to exchange gains or losses.][4]

(3) Only an authorised accruals basis of accounting shall be used for ascertaining those amounts.

(4) Amounts shall be brought into account in computing the profits of the company for the purposes of corporation tax as if the Taxation of Chargeable Gains Act 1992 had effect in relation to any asset to which this section applies as it has effect in relation to an asset that does not represent a loan relationship.

(5) For the purposes of that Act the amount or value of the consideration for any disposal or acquisition of the asset shall be treated as adjusted so as to exclude so much of it as, on a just and reasonable apportionment, relates to any interest which—

(a) falls to be brought into account under subsections (2) and (3) above as accruing to any company at any time; and

(b) in consequence of, or of the terms of, the disposal or acquisition, is not paid or payable to the company to which it is treated for the purposes of this Chapter as accruing.

[(5A) For the purposes of that Act the amount or value of the consideration for any disposal of the asset—

(a) shall be increased by the addition of any relevant exchange losses, determined in accordance with subsection (5C) below; and

(b) shall (after giving effect to any such increase) be reduced (but not below nil) by the deduction of any relevant exchange gains, determined in accordance with that subsection.][4]

[(5B) In subsection (5C) below—

"relevant accounting period" means any accounting period beginning on or after 1st October 2002; and

"the relevant condition" is that the asset in question is an asset to which this section applies and is held by the company making the disposal.][4]

[(5C) For the purposes of subsection (5A) above, relevant exchange gains or, as the case may be, losses in the case of any asset are—

(a) the amount of any exchange gains or, as the case may be, losses brought into account under subsections (2) and (3) above in respect of the asset, by the company making the disposal, for a relevant accounting period throughout which the relevant condition is satisfied; and

(b) for any relevant accounting period not falling within paragraph (a) above in which the relevant condition is at some time satisfied, an amount which, on a just and reasonable apportionment, represents so much of the amount of any exchange gains or, as the case may be, losses brought into account under subsections (2) and (3) above in respect of the asset, by the company making the disposal, for that period as is referable to the part of the period for which the relevant condition is satisfied.][4]

[(5D) Where—

(a) the amount of the relevant exchange gains falling to be deducted under subsection (5A)(b) above, exceeds

(b) the amount required to reduce the amount or value of the consideration to nil,

the excess shall be treated for the purposes of section 38(1)(c) of the Taxation of Chargeable Gains Act 1992 as incidental costs of making the disposal of the asset.][4]

(6) In [subsections (5) and (5A)][4] above the references to a disposal, in relation to an asset, are references to anything which—

(a) is a disposal of that asset (within the meaning of the Taxation of Chargeable Gains Act 1992); or

(b) would be such a disposal but for section *127 or*[4] 116(10) of that Act (reorganisations etc);

and the references to the acquisition of an asset shall be construed accordingly.

[(7) Where an asset representing a creditor relationship of a company—

(a) ceases at any time to be an asset to which this section applies, but

(b) does not cease at that time to represent a creditor relationship of that company,

the company shall be deemed for the purposes of the Taxation of Chargeable Gains Act 1992 and this Chapter to have disposed of the asset immediately before that time for the relevant consideration, and to have re-acquired it immediately after that time for the relevant consideration.][1]

[(8) Any deemed disposal and re-acquisition under subsection (7) above shall be treated for the purposes of that Act of 1992 as a transaction in the case of which—

(a) sections 127 to 130 of that Act would apply, apart from the provisions of section 116 of that Act, by virtue of any provision of Chapter II of Part IV of that Act;

(b) the asset in question represents both the original shares and the new holding for the purposes of those sections;

(c) the market value of the asset at the time of the transaction is an amount equal to the relevant consideration.][1]

[(9) Subject to [subsections (10) and (10A)][4] below, in subsections (7) and (8) above "the relevant consideration", in relation to an asset, means the amount that would have been taken, in accordance with the relevant accounting method, to be the value of the asset at the time of its deemed disposal if that method had been applied to the asset for tax purposes at all times until then.][1]

[(10) Subsection (5) above shall not apply in the case of a deemed disposal and re-acquisition under subsection (7) above; but the amount of the relevant consideration in such a case shall be treated for the purposes of the Taxation of Chargeable Gains Act 1992 as reduced by so much (if any) of the amount mentioned in subsection (9) above as is referable to interest which—

(a) is not paid or payable to the company before the time of the deemed disposal; but

(b) is interest falling to be brought into account under subsections (2) and (3) above as having accrued before that time.][1]

[(10A) Subsection (5A) above shall not apply in the case of a deemed disposal and re-acquisition under subsection (7) above; but in any such case the amount of the relevant consideration, after any reduction under subsection (10) above, shall be treated for the purposes of the Taxation of Chargeable Gains Act 1992 as further adjusted by making the same additions and deductions (and for the purposes of both the disposal and the re-acquisition) as would fall to be made under subsection (5A) above if it were the consideration for an actual disposal and that subsection also applied in relation to the corresponding acquisition.][4]

[(11) In subsection (9) above "the relevant accounting method", in relation to an asset representing a creditor relationship of a company, means the accounting method which, for the accounting period of that company in which the deemed re-acquisition takes place, is used as respects that asset and the part of that accounting period beginning with the deemed re-acquisition.][1]

Commentary—*Simon's Direct Tax Service* **D2.1126.**
Cross reference—See FA 1993 s 153(4) (debt represented by an asset to which this section applies is not a qualifying asset under FA 1993 "exchange gains and losses" provisions).
FA 1996 Sch 13 paras 3(1)–(1F), 10(4), 13(9) (application of these sub-paras (as inserted by FA 1999 s 65) concerning the meaning of "relevant discounted securities" for the purposes of this section with effect for accounting periods ending on or after 15 February 1999, but not in respect of any disposal if it was completed before that day, by virtue of FA 1999 s 65(9)).
Amendments—[1] Sub-ss (7)–(11) inserted by FA 1999 ss 65(7), (8) with effect for—

– any transfer of a security after 14 February 1999; or
– any occasion after that date on which a person holding a security becomes entitled to any payment on its redemption,

subject to FA 1999 s 68(9)–(12) (concerning effective dates of these amendments for the purposes of FA 1996 s 92, Sch 9 paras 17, 18 and TCGA 1992 ss 117(2AA), 251(8), 254(1)(c)).
[2] In sub-s (1), paras (b), (c), (e) substituted, paras (bb), (dd), (ee) inserted, words in para (d) inserted, and word "and" in para (e) repealed; sub-ss (1A)–(1D) inserted, and Heading substituted; by FA 2002 ss 72, 141, Sch 40 Pt 3(8) with effect in accordance with FA 2002 s 72(13)–(16).
[3] Sub-ss (1E)–(1G) inserted by FA 2002 s 73(1) with effect in accordance with FA 2002 s 73(2)–(7).
[4] In sub-s (2), "(a)" inserted, and para (b) inserted; sub-ss (5A)–(5D), (10A) inserted; in sub-s (6), words substituted for the words "subsection (5)"; in sub-s (6)(b) words "127 or" repealed; and in sub-s (9), words substituted for the words "subsection

(10)''; by FA 2002 ss 79, 82, 141, Sch 23 paras 1, 5, Sch 40 Pt 3(10) with effect for accounting periods beginning after 30 September 2002.

[92A Convertible securities etc: debtor relationships

(1) This section applies to a liability if—

(*a*) the liability represents a debtor relationship of a company (''the debtor company''); and

(*b*) the rights attached to the asset that represents the corresponding creditor relationship include provision by virtue of which a person is or may become entitled to acquire (whether by conversion or exchange or otherwise)—

    (i) any shares in the debtor company, or

    (ii) any shares in another company.

(2) The debits falling for any accounting period to be brought into account for the purposes of this Chapter in respect of a debtor relationship represented by a liability to which this section applies shall not include debits in relation to any of the amounts falling within subsection (3) below.

(3) The amounts are—

(*a*) any amounts payable by the debtor company in respect of, or in connection with, any such acquisition of shares as is described in subsection (1)(*b*)(ii) above, but not any amounts to which subsection (4) below applies; and

(*b*) any charges or expenses incurred by the debtor company as described in paragraph (*b*), (*c*) or (*d*) of section 84(3) above, where the related transaction in question relates to, or is connected with, the acquisition of shares by another person (whether by conversion or exchange or otherwise) as described in subsection (1)(*b*) above.

(4) This subsection applies to amounts payable by the debtor company, as described in subsection (3)(*a*) above, in respect of the debtor relationship in a case where—

(*a*) the debtor company is carrying on a banking business or a business consisting wholly or partly in dealing in securities, and

(*b*) it entered into the debtor relationship in the ordinary course of that business.

(5) For the purposes of subsection (4) above ''securities'' has the same meaning as in section 473 of the Taxes Act.

(6) Subject to subsection (7) below, only an authorised accruals basis of accounting shall be used for ascertaining the amounts which fall to be taken into account as described in subsection (2) above.

(7) The requirement in subsection (6) above to use an authorised accruals basis of accounting does not apply in the case of a debtor relationship where—

(*a*) the debtor company is carrying on a banking business or a business consisting wholly or partly in dealing in securities, and

(*b*) it entered into the debtor relationship in the ordinary course of that business.]¹

Amendments—¹ This section inserted by FA 2002 s 74 with effect for—

    (*a*) any amounts falling within sub-s (3)(*a*) above, where those amounts fall to be paid after 25 July 2001, and

    (*b*) any charges or expenses falling within sub-s (3)(*b*) above, where those charges or expenses accrue after 25th July 2001.

93 Relationships linked to the value of chargeable assets

(1) This section applies in the case of any loan relationship of a company that is linked to the value of chargeable assets [unless

(*a*) in a case where the loan relationship is a creditor relationship, the asset representing the loan relationship is one]¹ the disposal of which by the company would fall to be treated as a disposal in the course of activities forming an integral part of a trade carried on by the company

[(*b*) in a case where the loan relationship is a debtor relationship, the liability representing the loan relationship is a liability entered into by the company in the course of activities forming an integral part of a trade carried on by the company; or]¹

[(*c*) the loan relationship is one to which section 93A below applies.]¹

(2) The amounts falling for any accounting period to be brought into account for the purposes of this Chapter in respect of the relationship shall be confined to amounts relating to interest.

(3) Only an authorised accruals basis of accounting shall be used for ascertaining those amounts.

(4) Amounts shall be brought into account in computing the profits of the company for the purposes of corporation tax as if the Taxation of Chargeable Gains Act 1992 had effect in relation to the asset representing the relationship as it has effect in relation to an asset that does not represent a loan relationship.

(5) For the purposes of that Act the amount or value of the consideration for any disposal or acquisition of the asset shall be treated as adjusted so as to exclude so much of it as, on a just and reasonable apportionment, relates to any interest which—

(*a*) falls to be brought into account under subsections (2) and (3) above as accruing to any company at any time; and

(*b*) in consequence of, or of the terms of, the disposal or acquisition, is not paid or payable to the company to which it is treated for the purposes of this Chapter as accruing.

(6) For the purposes of this section a loan relationship is linked to the value of chargeable assets if, in pursuance of any provision having effect for the purposes of that relationship, the amount that must be paid to discharge the money debt (whether on redemption of a security issued in relation to that debt or otherwise) is equal to the amount determined by applying a relevant percentage change in the value of chargeable assets to the amount falling for the purposes of this Chapter to be regarded as the amount of the original loan from which the money debt arises.

(7) In subsection (6) above the reference to a relevant percentage change in the value of chargeable assets is a reference to the amount of the percentage change (if any) over the relevant period in the value of chargeable assets of any particular description or in any index of the value of any such assets.

(8) In subsection (7) above ''the relevant period'' means—

    (*a*) the period between the time of the original loan and the discharge of the money debt; or

    (*b*) any other period in which almost all of that period is comprised and which differs from that period exclusively for purposes connected with giving effect to a valuation in relation to rights or liabilities under the loan relationship.

(9) If—

    (*a*) there is a provision which, in the case of any loan relationship, falls within subsection (6) above,

    (*b*) that provision is made subject to any other provision applying to the determination of the amount payable to discharge the money debt,

    (*c*) that other provision is to the effect only that the amount so payable must not be less than a specified percentage of the amount falling for the purposes of this Chapter to be regarded as the amount of the original loan, and

    (*d*) the specified percentage is not more than 10 per cent,

that other provision shall be disregarded in determining for the purposes of this section whether the relationship is linked to the value of chargeable assets.

(10) For the purposes of this section an asset is a chargeable asset, in relation to a loan relationship of a company, if [the asset is—

    (*a*) an estate or interest in land (wherever situated), or

    (*b*) qualifying ordinary shares which are listed on a recognised stock exchange.][1]

(11) ...[1]

(12) In subsection (5) above references to a disposal, in relation to an asset, are references to anything which—

    (*a*) is a disposal of that asset (within the meaning of the Taxation of Chargeable Gains Act 1992); or

    (*b*) would be such a disposal but for section 127 or 116(10) of that Act (reorganisations etc);

and the references to the acquisition of an asset shall be construed accordingly.

[(12A) In subsection (10)(*b*) above ''qualifying ordinary shares'', in relation to a company, means shares representing some or all of the issued share capital (by whatever name called) of the company, other than—

    (*a*) capital the holders of which have a right to a dividend at a fixed rate but have no other right to share in the profits of the company, or

    (*b*) capital the holders of which have no right to a dividend of any description nor any other right to share in the profits of the company.][1]

(13) ...[1]

[(14) This section is supplemented by section 93B below.][1]

Commentary—*Simon's Direct Tax Service* **D2.1127.**
Revenue Internal Guidance—Company Taxation Manual COT12143 (worked example on identification rules under sub-ss(6)–(8)).
COT12148 (miscellaneous points on index linked bonds).
Cross reference—See FA 1993 s 153(4) (debt represented by an asset representing a loan relationship to which this section applies is not a qualifying asset under FA 1993 ''exchange gains and losses'' provisions).
Amendments—[1] In sub-s (1), words substituted, and paras (*b*), (*c*) inserted; words in sub-s (10) substituted; sub-ss (11), (13) repealed; sub-s (12A) inserted; and sub-s (14) inserted; by FA 2002 ss 75, 141, Sch 40 Pt 3(8) with effect for accounting periods ending after 25 July 2001 in relation to any loan relationship of a company, unless the loan relationship in question is one to which the company ceased to be a party before 26 July 2001. However, these amendments do not have effect for the purpose of determining, in relation to such part of an accounting period as falls before 26 July 2001, whether a loan relationship is, or has ceased to be, a loan relationship to which this section applies.

[93A Relationships linked to the value of chargeable assets: guaranteed returns]

(1) This section applies to a loan relationship which is a creditor relationship of a company if—

    (*a*) that loan relationship and one or more other transactions are associated transactions designed to produce a guaranteed return;

    (*b*) any such other transaction is [a derivative contract falling within paragraph 6 of Schedule 26 to the Finance Act 2002 (''an associated derivative contract'');][2] and (*c*) the guaranteed return comprises the return consisting of the amount that must be paid to discharge the money debt arising in connection with that loan relationship taken together with the return from any one or more of [the associated derivative contracts][2].

(2) For the purposes of this section a loan relationship of a company and one or more [associated derivative contracts][2] are transactions designed to produce a guaranteed return if, taking the transactions together, it would be reasonable to assume, from considering—

(*a*) the likely effect of the transactions,

(*b*) the circumstances in which the transactions are entered into, or in which any of them is entered into, or

(*c*) the matters in both of paragraphs (*a*) and (*b*),

that the main purpose of the transactions, or one of their main purposes, is or was the production of a guaranteed return from the loan relationship and [any one or more of the associated derivative contracts][2].

(3) For the purposes of this section a guaranteed return is produced from the loan relationship and [any one or more of the associated derivative contracts][2] wherever (taking all the transactions together) risks from fluctuations in the underlying subject matter are so eliminated or reduced as to produce a return from the transactions—

(*a*) ...[2]

(*b*) which equates, in substance, to the return on an investment of money at interest.

(4) For the purposes of subsection (3) above the cases where risks from fluctuations in the underlying subject matter are eliminated or reduced shall be deemed to include any case where the main reason, or one of the main reasons, for the choice of that subject matter is—

(*a*) that there appears to be no risk that that subject matter will fluctuate; or

(*b*) that the risk that it will fluctuate appears to be insignificant.

(5) In this section—

(*a*) the references, in relation to a loan relationship, to the underlying subject matter are references to the value of chargeable assets of a particular description to which that relationship is linked;

[(*b*) the references, in relation to an associated derivative contract, to the underlying subject matter are to be construed in accordance with paragraphs 6(2)(*a*) and 11 of Schedule 26 to the Finance Act 2002.][2]

(6) Subsection (5)(*a*) above is to be construed in accordance with section 93 above.

(7) ...[2].][1]

Amendments—[1] This section inserted by FA 2002 s 76 with effect for accounting periods ending after 25 July 2001 in relation to any loan relationship of a company, unless the loan relationship in question is one to which the company ceased to be a party before 26 July 2001.
[2] In sub-s (1), words substituted for the words "a disposal of futures or options" and the words "the disposals of futures or options"; in sub-s (2), words substituted for the words "disposals of futures or options" and the words "any one or more of the disposals"; in sub-(3), words substituted for the words "any one or more of the disposals of futures or options", and para (*a*) repealed; sub-s (5)(*b*) substituted; and sub-s (7) repealed; by FA 2002 ss 83(1)(*b*), (3), 141, Sch 27 paras 17, 18, Sch 40 Pt 3(13) with effect for accounting periods beginning after 30 September 2002.
Sub-s (3)(*a*) previously read as follows—
"(*a*) the amount of which is not, to any significant extent, attributable (otherwise than incidentally) to any such fluctuations; and".
Sub-s (5)(*b*) previously read as follows—
"(*b*) the references, in relation to a disposal of futures or options, to the underlying subject matter are references to or to the value of the commodities, currencies, shares, stock or securities, interest rates, indices or other matters to which, or to the value of which, those futures or options are referable.".
Sub-s (7) previously read as follows—
"(7) For the purposes of this section—
(*a*) references to the disposal of futures or options are to be construed in accordance with paragraphs 4 and 4A of Schedule 5AA to the Taxes Act 1988;
(*b*) references to the return from one or more disposals of futures or options are to be construed in accordance with paragraph 5 of that Schedule; and
(*c*) references to associated transactions are to be construed in accordance with paragraph 6 of that Schedule.".

[93B Loan relationships ceasing to be within section 93

(1) Where a loan relationship of a company—

(*a*) ceases at any time to be a loan relationship to which section 93 above applies, but

(*b*) does not cease at that time to be a loan relationship of that company,

subsection (2) below shall have effect in relation to the asset representing that relationship.

(2) Where this subsection has effect in relation to an asset representing a loan relationship of a company, the company shall be deemed for the purposes of the Taxation of Chargeable Gains Act 1992 (c 12) and this Chapter—

(*a*) to have disposed of the asset for the relevant consideration immediately before the time when the loan relationship ceases to be one to which section 93 above applies, and

(*b*) to have re-acquired it for the relevant consideration immediately after that time.

(3) Any deemed disposal and re-acquisition of an asset under subsection (2) above shall be treated for the purposes of the Taxation of Chargeable Gains Act 1992 as a transaction in the case of which—

(*a*) sections 127 to 130 of that Act would apply, apart from the provisions of section 116 of that Act, by virtue of any provision of Chapter 2 of Part 4 of that Act;
(*b*) the asset in question represents both the original shares and the new holding for the purposes of those sections;
(*c*) the market value of the asset at the time of the transaction is an amount equal to the relevant consideration.

(4) Subject to subsection (5) below, in subsections (2) and (3) above "the relevant consideration", in relation to an asset, means the amount that would have been taken, in accordance with the relevant accounting method, to be the value of the asset at the time of its deemed disposal if that method had been applied to the asset for tax purposes at all times until then.

(5) Section 93(5) above shall not apply in the case of a deemed disposal and reacquisition under subsection (2) above; but the amount of the relevant consideration in such a case shall be treated for the purposes of the Taxation of Chargeable Gains Act 1992 (c 12) as reduced by so much (if any) of the amount mentioned in subsection (4) above as is referable to interest which—

(*a*) is not paid or payable to the company before the time of the deemed disposal; but
(*b*) is interest falling to be brought into account under section 93(2) and (3) above as having accrued before that time.

(6) In subsection (4) above "the relevant accounting method", in relation to an asset representing a loan relationship of a company, means the accounting method which, for the accounting period of that company in which the deemed reacquisition takes place, is used as respects that asset and the part of that accounting period beginning with the deemed reacquisition.

(7) This section shall be construed as one with section 93 above.]¹

Amendments—¹ This section inserted by FA 2002 s 77 with effect for accounting periods ending after 25 July 2001 in relation to any loan relationship of a company, unless the loan relationship in question is one to which the company ceased to be a party before 26 July 2001. However, this amendment does not have effect for a loan relationship which, before 26 July 2001, ceased to be a loan relationship to which FA 1996 s 93 (as it has effect by virtue of FA 2002 s 75(8)) applies.

94 Indexed gilt-edged securities

(1) In the case of any loan relationship represented by an index-linked gilt-edged security, the adjustment for which this section provides shall be made in computing the credits and debits which fall, for any accounting period, to be brought into account for the purposes of this Chapter in respect of that relationship as non-trading credits or non-trading debits.

(2) The adjustment shall be made wherever—

(*a*) the authorised accounting method applied as respects the index-linked gilt-edged security gives credits or debits by reference to the value of the security at two different times, and
(*b*) there is any change in the retail prices index between those times.

(3) Subject to subsection (4) below the adjustment is such an adjustment of the amount which would otherwise be taken for the purposes of that accounting method to be the value of the security at the earlier time ("the opening value") as results in the amount in fact so taken being equal to the opening value increased or, as the case may be, reduced by the same percentage as the percentage increase or reduction in the retail prices index between the earlier and the later time.

[(3A) Where the authorised accounting method applied is an accruals basis of accounting, the amount which is the opening value shall be taken to be the amount of the value which (disregarding interest) accrued to the company under the loan relationship before the earlier time.]¹

(4) The Treasury may, in relation to any description of index-linked gilt-edged securities, by order provide that—

(*a*) there are to be no adjustments under this section; or
(*b*) that an adjustment specified in the order (instead of the adjustment specified in subsection (3) above) is to be the adjustment for which this section provides.

(5) An order under subsection (4) above—

(*a*) shall not have effect in relation to any gilt-edged security issued before the making of the order; but
(*b*) may make different provision for different descriptions of securities.

(6) For the purposes of this section the percentage increase or reduction in the retail prices index between any two times shall be determined by reference to the difference between—

(*a*) that index for the month in which the earlier time falls; and
(*b*) that index for the month in which the later time falls

[except that where the earlier time falls at the beginning of an accounting period which begins with the first day of a month, the index for the previous month shall be used for the purposes of paragraph (*a*) above.]¹

(7) In this section "index-linked gilt-edged securities" means any gilt-edged securities the amounts of the payments under which are determined wholly or partly by reference to the retail prices index.

Commentary—*Simon's Direct Tax Service* D2.1129.
Revenue Internal Guidance—Company Taxation Manual COT12786 (worked example).

Amendments—¹ Sub-s (3A) inserted,and in sub-s (6), words inserted, by FA 2002 s 82, Sch 25 paras 1, 12 with effect for accounting periods beginning after 30 September 2002.

95 Gilt strips

(1) This section has effect for the purposes of the application of an authorised accruals basis of accounting as respects a loan relationship represented by a gilt-edged security or a strip of a gilt-edged security.

(2) Where a gilt-edged security is exchanged by any person for strips of that security—

(a) the security shall be deemed to have been redeemed at the time of the exchange by the payment to that person of its market value; and

(b) that person shall be deemed to have acquired each strip for the amount which bears the same proportion to that market value as is borne by the market value of the strip to the aggregate of the market values of all the strips received in exchange for the security.

(3) Where strips of a gilt-edged security are consolidated into a single gilt-edged security by being exchanged by any person for that security—

(a) each of the strips shall be deemed to have been redeemed at the time of the exchange by the payment to that person of the amount equal to its market value; and

(b) that person shall be deemed to have acquired the security received in the exchange for the amount equal to the aggregate of the market values of the strips given in exchange for the security.

(4) References in this section to the market value of a security given or received in exchange for another are references to its market value at the time of the exchange.

(5) Without prejudice to the generality of any power conferred by section 202 below, the Treasury may by regulations make provision for the purposes of this section as to the manner of determining the market value at any time of any gilt-edged security (including any strip).

(6) Regulations under subsection (5) above may—

(a) make different provision for different cases; and

(b) contain such incidental, supplemental, consequential and transitional provision as the Treasury may think fit.

(7) In this section "strip" means anything which, within the meaning of section 47 of the Finance Act 1942, is a strip of a gilt-edged security.

Commentary—*Simon's Direct Tax Service* D2.1129.

96 Special rules for certain other gilts

(1) This section applies as respects any loan relationship of a company if—

(a) it is represented by a security of any of the following descriptions—

(i) 3½ % Funding Stock 1999–2004; or

(ii) 5½ % Treasury Stock 2008–2012;

and

(b) it is one to which the company is a party otherwise than in the course of activities that form an integral part of a trade carried on by the company.

(2) The amounts falling for any accounting period to be brought into account for the purposes of this Chapter in respect of a loan relationship to which this section applies shall be confined to amounts relating to interest.

(3) Only an authorised accruals basis of accounting shall be used for ascertaining those amounts.

Commentary—*Simon's Direct Tax Service* D2.1129.

97 Manufactured interest

(1) [For the purposes of the Corporation Tax Acts, a company has a relationship to which this section applies in any case where—]²

(a) any amount ("manufactured interest") is payable by or on behalf of, or to, [the company]² under any contract or arrangements relating to the transfer of an asset representing a loan relationship; and

(b) that amount is, or (when paid) will fall to be treated as, representative of interest under [that loan relationship]² ("the real interest")

[and references to a relationship to which this section applies, and to a company's being party to such a relationship, shall be construed accordingly]²

[(2) Where a company has a relationship to which this section applies—

(a) this Chapter shall have effect in relation to the company and the manufactured interest under the relationship—

(i) as it would have effect if the manufactured interest were interest payable on a loan by, or (as the case may be) to, the company and were accordingly interest under a loan relationship to which the company is a party, and

(ii) where that company is the company to which the manufactured interest is payable, as if that relationship were the one under which the real interest is payable, but

(b) the only credits or (subject to subsection (4A) below) debits to be brought into account for the purposes of this Chapter by virtue of this section in respect of a relationship are those relating to that interest,

and, subject to paragraphs (a)(ii) and (b) above, references in the Corporation Tax Acts to a loan relationship accordingly include a reference to a relationship to which this section applies.][2]

(3) Any question whether debits or credits falling to be brought into account in the case of any company by virtue of this section—

(a) are to be brought into account under section 82(2) above, or

(b) are to be treated as non-trading debits or non-trading credits,

shall be determined according to the extent (if any) to which the manufactured interest is paid for the purposes of a trade carried on by the company or is received in the course of activities forming an integral part of such a trade.

[(3A) To the extent that debits or credits fall to be brought into account by a company under section 82(2) above in the case of a relationship to which this section applies, the company shall be regarded for the purposes of this Chapter as being party to the relationship for the purposes of a trade carried on by the company.][2]

(4) Where section [736B(2) or][2] 737A(5) of the Taxes Act 1988 (deemed manufactured payments) has effect in relation to a transaction relating to an asset representing a loan relationship so as, for the purposes of ...[1] Schedule 23A to, that Act, to deem there to have been a payment representative of interest under that relationship, this section shall apply as it would have applied if such a representative payment had in fact been made.

[(4A) Where, for the purposes of section 736B of the Taxes Act 1988, a company is the borrower under a stock lending arrangement, then (pursuant to subsection (2A) of that section (which precludes deductions or group relief for the borrower)) no debits are to be brought into account for the purposes of this Chapter by that company in respect of the deemed representative payment under that section which is treated under subsection (4) above as if it had in fact been made.][2]

(5) ...[1]

Commentary—*Simon's Direct Tax Service* D2.1128.
Revenue Internal Guidance—Company Taxation Manual COT12730–12732 (explanation of manufactured interest).
Amendments—[1] Words in sub-s (4), and whole of sub-s (5), repealed by FA 1997 Sch 17 Pt VI (9) with effect in relation to payments made on or after 1 July 1997 by virtue of the Finance Act 1997, Schedule 10, (Appointed Day) Order, SI 1997/991.
[2] In sub-s (1), words substituted for the words "This section applies where—", in para (a), words substituted for the words "any company", in para (b), words substituted for the words "that relationship", and words inserted; sub-s (2) substituted; and sub-ss (3A), (4A) inserted; by FA 2002 s 82, Sch 25 paras 1, 13 with effect for accounting periods beginning after 30 September 2002.
Sub-s (2) previously read as follows—

"(2) In relation to that company the manufactured interest shall be treated for the purposes of this Chapter—

(a) as if it were interest under a loan relationship to which the company is a party; and
(b) where that company is the company to which the manufactured interest is payable, as if that relationship were the one under which the real interest is payable.".

98 Collective investment schemes

The provisions of this Chapter have effect subject to the provisions of Schedule 10 to this Act (which makes special provision in relation to certain collective investment schemes).

99 Insurance companies

The preceding provisions of this Chapter have effect subject to Schedule 11 to this Act (which makes special provision in relation to certain insurance companies and in relation to corporate members of Lloyd's).

Miscellaneous other provisions

[100 Interest, and exchange gains and losses, on debts etc not arising from the lending of money

(1) For the purposes of the Corporation Tax Acts, a company has a relationship to which this section applies in any case where—

(a) the company stands, or has stood, in the position of a creditor or debtor as respects a money debt;

(b) the money debt is not one which arose from a transaction for the lending of money (so that, in consequence of section 81(1)(b) above, there is no loan relationship); and

(c) the money debt is one—

(i) on which interest is payable to or by the company; or

(ii) in relation to which exchange gains or losses arise to the company;

and references to a relationship to which this section applies, and to a company's being party to such a relationship, shall be construed accordingly.

(2) Where a company has a relationship to which this section applies—

(a) this Chapter shall have effect in relation to the interest payable under, or the exchange gains or losses arising to the company from, the relationship as it has effect in relation to interest payable under, or (as the case may be) exchange gains or losses arising to the company from, a loan relationship to which the company is a party; but

(b) the only credits or debits to be brought into account for the purposes of this Chapter in respect of the relationship are those relating to the interest or (as the case may be) to the exchange gains or losses;

and, subject to paragraph (b) above, references in the Corporation Tax Acts to a loan relationship accordingly include a reference to a relationship to which this section applies.

(3) References in this section to interest payable on a money debt include a reference to any amount which, in pursuance of Schedule 28AA to the Taxes Act 1988 (provision not at arm's length), falls to be treated as—

(a) interest on a money debt; or

(b) interest on an amount which is treated as a money debt;

and references in the other provisions of this section to a money debt accordingly include a reference to the amount on which that amount so falls to be treated as interest.

(4) Except as provided by subsection (7) below, any question whether debits or credits falling to be brought into account by virtue of this section in relation to a company—

(a) are to be brought into account under section 82(2) above, or

(b) are to be treated as non-trading debits or non-trading credits,

shall be determined in accordance with subsection (5) below (in the case of interest) or subsection (6) below (in the case of an exchange gain or loss).

(5) In the case of interest, any such question shall be determined according to the extent (if any) to which the interest—

(a) is paid for the purposes of a trade carried on by the company;

(b) is received in the course of activities forming an integral part of such a trade; or

(c) in the case of deemed interest, would be deemed to be so paid or received.

(6) In the case of an exchange gain or loss, any such question shall be determined according to the extent (if any) to which the money debt—

(a) is owed by the company for the purposes of a trade carried on by the company; or

(b) is held in the course of activities forming an integral part of such a trade.

(7) Any debits or credits which—

(a) relate to interest payable under the Tax Acts, and

(b) fall to be brought into account by virtue of this section in relation to any company,

are to be treated as non-trading debits or credits.

(8) To the extent that debits or credits fall to be brought into account by a company under section 82(2) above in the case of a relationship to which this section applies, the company shall be regarded for the purposes of the Corporation Tax Acts as being party to the relationship for the purposes of a trade carried on by the company.

(9) No exchange gains or losses shall be taken to arise for the purposes of this section if the money debt in question—

(a) is an amount of tax,

(b) is an amount of tax payable under the law of a territory outside the United Kingdom, or

(c) is an amount which would, but for any statutory provision or rule of law to the contrary other than section 74(1)(f) or (g) of the Taxes Act 1988, be deductible as an expense in computing profits in accordance with Case I of Schedule D or as an expense of management within section 75 of the Taxes Act 1988,

except to the extent that, in the case of a money debt falling within paragraph (b) above, a reduction in respect of the tax there mentioned falls to be made under section 811 of the Taxes Act 1988 (double taxation relief: deduction for foreign tax where no credit allowable).

(10) For the purposes of this section so far as relating to exchange gains and losses, each of the following shall be treated as a money debt owed to a company—

(a) any currency held by the company;

(b) in the case of a company carrying on insurance business, any deferred acquisition costs, within the meaning of Assets item G.II in the Balance Sheet Format set out after paragraph 9 of Schedule 9A to Companies Act 1985 (form and content of accounts of insurance companies and groups) as read with note (17) of the Notes on the Balance Sheet Format (which follow immediately after that format).

(11) For the purposes of this section so far as relating to exchange gains and losses, each of the following shall be treated as a money debt owed by a company—

(a) any provision made by the company for the purposes of its statutory accounts in respect of a liability to which the company may become subject;

(b) in the case of a company carrying on insurance business—

    (i) any provision made by the company for unearned premiums, within the meaning of Liabilities item C.1 in the Balance Sheet Format set out after paragraph 9 of Schedule 9A to Companies Act 1985, as read with note (20) of the Notes on the Balance Sheet Format (which follow immediately after that format);

    (ii) any provision for unexpired risks, as defined in paragraph 81(1) of that Schedule.

(12) A provision does not fall within paragraph (*a*) of subsection (11) above unless—

    (*a*) the duty to settle the liability in question would (if the company were to become subject to it) be owed for the purposes of a trade, a Schedule A business or an overseas property business (within the meaning of section 70A of the Taxes Act 1988); and

    (*b*) the provision falls to be taken into account (apart from this Chapter) in computing the profits or losses of the trade, Schedule A business or overseas property business for corporation tax purposes.

(13) This section has effect subject to the provisions of Schedules 9 and 11 to this Act.]¹

Commentary—*Simon's Direct Tax Service* D2.1104.
Revenue Interpretation RI 209—This section applies to interest payable under the Late Payment of Commercial Debts (Interest) Act 1998.
Amendments—¹ This section substituted by FA 2002 s 79, Sch 23 paras 1, 6 with effect for accounting periods beginning after 30 September 2002. This section previously read as follows—

"**100 Interest on judgments, imputed interest, etc**

(1) This Chapter shall have effect in accordance with subsection (2) below where—

(*a*) interest on a money debt is payable to or by any company;
(*b*) that debt is one as respects which it stands, or has stood, in the position of a creditor or debtor; and
(*c*) that debt did not arise from a loan relationship.
(2) It shall be assumed for the purposes of this Chapter—

(*a*) that the interest is interest payable under a loan relationship to which the company is a party; but
(*b*) that the only credits or debits to be brought into account for those purposes in respect of that relationship are those relating to the interest.
(3) References in this section to interest payable on a money debt include references to any amount [which, in pursuance of Schedule 28AA to the Taxes Act 1988 (provision not at arm's length), falls to be treated] as—

(*a*) interest on a money debt; or
(*b*) interest on an amount which is treated as a money debt.
(4) [Except as provided by subsection (4A) below]¹ any question whether debits or credits falling to be brought into account in accordance with this section in relation to any company—

(*a*) are to be brought into account under section 82(2) above, or
(*b*) are to be treated as non-trading debits or non-trading credits,
shall be determined according to the extent (if any) to which the interest in question is paid for the purposes of a trade carried on by the company or is received in the course of activities forming an integral part of such a trade, or (in the case of deemed interest) would be deemed to be so paid or received.

[(4A) Any debits or credits which—

(*a*) relate to interest payable under the Tax Acts, and
(*b*) fall to be brought into account in accordance with this section in relation to any company,
are to be treated as non-trading debits or non-trading credits.]¹

(5) This section has effect subject to the provisions of Schedules 9 and 11 to this Act.".

101 Financial instruments

(1) [Schedule 26 to the Finance Act 2002 (provisions relating to derivative contracts)]¹ shall not apply to any profit or loss which, [in accordance with that Schedule]¹, accrues to a company for any accounting period on [a derivative contract]¹ by virtue of which the company is a party to any loan relationship if—

    (*a*) an amount representing that profit or loss, or
    (*b*) an amount representing the profit or loss accruing to the company on that contract,

is brought into account for that period for the purposes of this Chapter.

(2)–(6) (*inserted* FA 1994 ss 147A, 150A, 153(1)(*ca*) and *amended* ss 151, 152(1); *repealed by* FA 2002 ss 83(1)(*b*), (3), 141, Sch 27 paras 17, 19, Sch 40 Pt 3(13) with effect for accounting periods beginning after 30 September 2002).

Commentary—*Simon's Direct Tax Service* D2.1106.
Amendments—¹ In sub-s (1), words substituted for the words "Chapter II of Part IV of the Finance Act 1994 (provisions relating to certain financial instruments)", "in accordance with that Chapter", and "a qualifying contract"; and sub-ss (2)–(6) (which amended FA 1994) repealed; by FA 2002 s 83(1)(*b*), (3) Sch 27 paras 17, 19 with effect for accounting periods beginning after 30 September 2002.

102 Discounted securities: income tax provisions

Schedule 13 to this Act (which, in connection with the provisions of this Chapter relating to corporation tax, makes provision for income tax purposes about discounted securities) shall have effect.

Supplemental

103 Interpretation of Chapter

(1) In this Chapter—

"authorised accounting method", "authorised accruals basis of accounting" and "authorised mark to market basis of accounting" shall be construed in accordance with section 85 above;

"creditor relationship", in relation to a company, means any loan relationship of that company in the case of which it stands in the position of a creditor as respects the debt in question;

"debt" includes a debt the amount of which falls to be ascertained by reference to matters which vary from time to time;

"debtor relationship", in relation to a company, means any loan relationship of that company in the case of which it stands in the position of a debtor as respects the debt in question;

["derivative contract" has the same meaning as in Schedule 26 to the Finance Act 2002;][3]

["exchange gain" and "exchange loss" shall be construed in accordance with subsections (1A) and (1B) below;][1]

"gilt-edged securities" means any securities which—

(a) are gilt-edged securities for the purposes of the Taxation of Chargeable Gains Act 1992; or

(b) will be such securities on the making of any order under paragraph 1 of Schedule 9 to that Act the making of which is anticipated in the prospectus under which they are issued;

"an independent person" means a knowledgeable and willing party dealing at arm's length;

"international organisation" means an organisation of which two or more sovereign powers, or the governments of two or more sovereign powers, are members;

"loan" includes any advance of money, and cognate expressions shall be construed accordingly;

"money" shall be construed in accordance with section 81(6) above and subsection (5) below;

"money debt" shall be construed in accordance with section 81(2) above;

"non-trading credit" and "non-trading debit" shall be construed in accordance with section 82(3) above;

["related transaction" shall be construed in accordance with section 84 above (see subsections (5) and (6) of that section);][1]

"retail prices index" has the same meaning as it has, by virtue of section 833(2) of the Taxes Act 1988, in the Income Tax Acts;

"share", in relation to a company, means any share in the company under which an entitlement to receive distributions may arise [but does not include a share in a building society][2].

["statutory accounts" has the meaning given by section 86(8) above.][3]

[(1A) References in this Chapter to exchange gains or exchange losses, in the case of any company, are references respectively to—

(a) profits or gains, or

(b) losses,

which arise as a result of comparing at different times the expression in one currency of the whole or some part of the valuation put by the company in another currency on an asset or liability of the company.

If the result of such a comparison is that neither an exchange gain nor an exchange loss arises, then for the purposes of this Chapter an exchange gain of nil shall be taken to arise in the case of that comparison.][1]

[(1B) Any reference in this Chapter to an exchange gain or loss from a loan relationship of a company is a reference to an exchange gain or loss arising to a company in relation to an asset or liability representing a loan relationship of the company.][1]

(2) For the purposes of this Chapter a company shall be taken to be a party to a creditor relationship for the purposes of a trade carried on by that company only if it is a party to that relationship in the course of activities forming an integral part of that trade.

(3) For the purposes of this Chapter, and of so much of any other enactment as contains provision by reference to which amounts fall to be brought into account for the purposes of this Chapter, activities carried on by a company in the course of—

(a) any mutual trading, or

(b) any mutual insurance or other mutual business which is not life assurance business (within the meaning of Chapter I of Part XII of the Taxes Act 1988),

shall be deemed not to constitute the whole or any part of a trade.

(4) If, in any proceedings, any question arises whether a person is an international organisation for the purposes of any provision of this Chapter, a certificate issued by or under the authority of the Secretary of State stating any fact relevant to that question shall be conclusive evidence of that fact.

(5) For the purposes of this Chapter the European currency unit (as for the time being defined in Council Regulation No 3180/78/EEC or in any Community instrument replacing it) shall be taken to be a currency other than sterling.

[(6) Where—

(*a*) a company ceases to be a party to a loan relationship in an accounting period (the "cessation period"),

(*b*) profits, gains or losses arise to the company from the loan relationship or a related transaction in that accounting period, and

(*c*) the credits or debits brought into account for the purposes of this Chapter for that accounting period do not include credits or debits which represent the whole of those profits, gains or losses,

credits or debits in respect of so much of those profits, gains or losses as are not represented by credits or debits brought into account for the cessation period shall continue to be brought into account under this Chapter over one or more subsequent accounting periods ("post-cessation periods") as in the case of a loan relationship to which the company is a party in those periods and subsections (7) and (8) below shall apply.][4]

[(7) In any case falling within subsection (6) above, any question—

(*a*) whether, in a post-cessation period, the company is to any extent a party to the loan relationship—

(i) for the purposes of a trade carried on by it, or

(ii) for any other particular purpose or purposes, or

(*b*) whether, in a post-cessation period, the loan relationship is to any extent referable to a particular business, or a particular class, category or description of business, carried on by the company,

shall be determined by reference to the circumstances immediately before the company ceased to be a party to the loan relationship instead of the circumstances in the post-cessation period.][4]

[(8) In any case falling within subsection (6) above, any question—

(*a*) whether the loan relationship has to any extent a particular purpose in a post-cessation period, or

(*b*) whether there is a connection between the company and any other person for a post-cessation period,

shall be determined by reference to the circumstances in the cessation period instead of the circumstances in the post-cessation period.][4]

Commentary—*Simon's Direct Tax Service* **Division D2.11.**
Revenue Internal Guidance—Company Taxation Manual COT12114, 12118 (ordinary trade debts are not loan relationships). COT12117 (an inter-company account or a director's loan account may be a loan relationship, depending on the circumstances). COT12122 (whether late or deferred consideration is a loan relationship).
Inspectors' Manual IM500 (meaning of "integral part of trade" in sub-s (2)).
Simon's Tax Cases—*HSBC Life (UK) Ltd v Stubbs (Insp of Taxes), Nationwide Life Ltd v Crisp (Insp of Taxes), Abbey Life Assurance Co Ltd v Colclough (Insp of Taxes), TSB Life Ltd v Colclough (Insp of Taxes), Lloyds TSB Life Assurance Co Ltd v Colclough (Insp of Taxes)* [2002] STC (SCD) 9.
Amendments—[1] In sub-s (1), definitions of "exchange gain" and exchange loss" and "related transaction" inserted, and sub-ss (1A), 1B) inserted, by FA 2002 s 79, Sch 23 paras 1, 7 with effect for accounting periods beginning after 30 September 2002.
[2] In sub-s (1), words inserted at the end of the definition of "share" by FA 2002 s 82, Sch 25 paras 1, 14 with effect for accounting periods beginning after 30 September 2002.
[3] Definitions of "derivative contract" and "statutory accounts" inserted in sub-s (1) by FA 2002 s 82, Sch 25 paras 1, 15 with effect for accounting periods beginning after 30 September 2002.
[4] Sub-ss (6)–(8) inserted by FA 2002 s 82, Sch 25 paras 1, 16 with effect for accounting periods beginning after 30 September 2002.

104 Minor and consequential amendments

Schedule 14 to this Act (which, for the purposes of both corporation tax and income tax, makes certain minor and consequential amendments in connection with the provisions of this Chapter) shall have effect.

105 Commencement and transitional provisions

(1) Subject to Schedule 15 to this Act, this Chapter has effect—

(*a*) for the purposes of corporation tax, in relation to accounting periods ending after 31st March 1996; and

(*b*) so far as it makes provision for the purposes of income tax, in relation to the year 1996–97 and subsequent years of assessment.

(2) Schedule 15 to this Act (which contains transitional provisions and savings in connection with the coming into force of this Chapter) shall have effect.

Commentary—*Simon's Direct Tax Service* **D2.1101.**

CHAPTER III

PROVISIONS RELATING TO THE SCHEDULE E CHARGE

106 Living accommodation provided for employees

(1), (2) (*amend* TA 1988 s 145(1) and *insert* s 146A).

(3) This section applies for the year 1996–97 and subsequent years of assessment.

107 Beneficial loans

(1)–(3) (*substitute* TA 1988 s 160(1B), (1BA) (for s 160(1B)), Sch 7 para 5(2) and *amend* TA 1988 Sch 7 para 5(1)).

(4) This section has effect for the year 1996–97 and subsequent years of assessment and applies to loans whenever made.

108 Incidental benefits for holders of certain offices etc

(1) (*inserts* TA 1988 s 200AA).

(2) This section has effect for the year 1996–97 and subsequent years of assessment.

109 Charitable donations: payroll deduction schemes

(1) (*amends* TA 1988 s 202(7)).

(2) This section has effect for the year 1996–97 and subsequent years of assessment.

110 PAYE settlement agreements

(*inserts* TA 1988 s 206A).

CHAPTER IV
SHARE OPTIONS, PROFIT SHARING AND EMPLOYEE SHARE OWNERSHIP

Share options

111 Amount or value of consideration for option

(1) Section 149A of the Taxation of Chargeable Gains Act 1992 (consideration for grant of option under approved share option schemes not to be deemed to be equal to market value of option) shall be amended as follows.

(2)–(4) (*amend* TCGA 1992 s 149A(1), (2), (4)).

(5) (*substitutes* TCGA 1992 s 149A section heading).

(6) This section has effect in relation to any right to acquire shares in a body corporate obtained on or after 28th November 1995 by an individual by reason of his office or employment as a director or employee of a body corporate.

112 Release and replacement

(1), (2) (*insert* TCGA 1992 s 237A and *repeal* s 238(4)).

(3) This section has effect in relation to transactions effected on or after 28th November 1995.

Savings-related share option schemes

113 Exercise of rights by employees of non-participating companies

(1)–(3) (*insert* TA 1988 Sch 9 paras 21(1)(*f*), (4) and *amend* Sch 9 para 26(3)).

Other share option schemes

114 Requirements to be satisfied by approved schemes

(1) Part IV of Schedule 9 to the Taxes Act 1988 (requirements applicable to approved share option schemes which are not savings-related) shall be amended in accordance with subsections (2) and (3) below.

(2) (*amends* TA 1988 Sch 9 para 28(1) and repeals sub-paras (2) and (4) thereof).

(3) (*substituted* TA 1988 Sch 9 para 29(1) for para 29(1)–(6)).

(4) Section 185 of the Taxes Act 1988 (approved share option schemes) shall be amended in accordance with subsections (5) to (7) below.

(5)–(7) (*amends* TA 1988 s 185(2), (7), (8) and *substitutes* TA 1988 s 185(6) (for s 185(6)–(6B))).

(8) (*amends* TCGA 1992 s 120(6)).

(9) Schedule 16 to this Act, which makes provision with respect to share option schemes approved before the day on which this Act is passed, shall have effect.

(10) Subsections (3) to (7) above have effect in relation to rights obtained on or after the day on which this Act is passed.

115 Transitional provisions

Commentary—*Simon's Direct Tax Service* **E4.595.**
Note—This section contains provisions concerning rights acquired under an approved share option scheme between 17 July 1995 and 28 April 1996 inclusive, and is spent.

Profit sharing schemes

116 The release date

(1) (*amends* TA 1988 s 187(2)).

(2) The amendment made by subsection (1) above shall have effect in relation to shares of a participant in a profit sharing scheme if the third anniversary of the appropriation of the shares to the participant occurs on or after the day on which this Act is passed.

(3) If the third anniversary of the appropriation of any shares to a participant in a profit sharing scheme has occurred, but the fifth anniversary of their appropriation to him has not occurred, before the passing of this Act, then, in the application of sections 186 and 187 of, and Schedules 9 and 10 to, the Taxes Act 1988 in relation to those shares, the release date shall be the day on which this Act is passed.

Commentary—*Simon's Direct Tax Service* **E4.569.**

117 The appropriate percentage

(1) (*substitute* TA 1988 Sch 10 para 3 and *repeal* s 187(8)(*b*)).

(3) Subsections (1) and (2) above have effect in relation to the occurrence, on or after the day on which this Act is passed, of events by reason of whose occurrence any provision of section 186 or 187 of, or Schedule 9 or 10 to, the Taxes Act 1988 charges an individual to income tax under Schedule E.

118 The appropriate allowance

(1) (*amends* TA 1988 s 186(12)).

(2) Subsection (1) above has effect for the year 1997–98 and subsequent years of assessment.

Employee share ownership trusts

119 Removal of requirement for at least one year's service

(1) (*amends* FA 1989 Sch 5 para 4(5)(*a*)).

(2) This section applies to trusts established on or after the day on which this Act is passed.

120 Grant and exercise of share options

(1) (*inserts* FA 1989 Sch 5 para 4(2A), (2B)).

(2) In consequence of the amendment made by subsection (1) above, section 69 of, and Schedule 5 to, the Finance Act 1989 (which respectively make provision about chargeable events in relation to the trustees of qualifying employee share ownership trusts and the requirements to be satisfied by such trusts) shall be amended in accordance with the following provisions of this section.

(3)–(11) (*amend* F 1989 s 69(4), Sch 5 paras 4(4), (7), (8), 9(2), 10 and *insert* s 69(4ZA), Sch 5, paras 5(2)(*cc*), 9(2ZA)).

(12) This section has effect in relation to trusts established on or after the day on which this Act is passed.

CHAPTER V
SELF-ASSESSMENT, GENERAL MANAGEMENT ETC
General

121 Returns and self-assessment

(1)–(4) (*amend* TMA 1970 ss 8(1), (1A), 8A(1), (1A), *insert* ss 8(1AA), 8A(1AA) and *substitute* s 9(1)).

(5) ...[1]

(6), (7) (*amend* TMA 1970 s 12AA(1)(*a*) and *substitute* s 12AA(1A)).

(8) This section and sections 122, 123, 125 to 127 and 141 below—

 (*a*) so far as they relate to income tax and capital gains tax, have effect as respects the year 1996–97 and subsequent years of assessment, and

 (*b*) so far as they relate to corporation tax, have effect as respects accounting periods ending on or after the appointed day for the purposes of Chapter III of Part IV of the Finance Act 1994.

Commentary—*Simon's Direct Tax Service* **E1.806.**
Amendments—[1] Sub-s (5) repealed by FA 1998 s 165, Sch 27 Part III(28) with effect in relation to accounting periods ending after 30 June 1999 (by virtue of Finance Act 1994, Section 199, (Appointed Day) Order, SI 1998/3173 art 2).

122 Notional tax deductions and payments

(1)–(4) (*amend* TMA 1970 ss 9(1), 59B(1), 233(1A) and *substitute* s 233(1)(*a*), (*b*)).

(5) (*amends* TA 1988 ss 246D(2)(*a*), 249(4)(*a*) and is part repealed (prospectively) by F(No 2)A 1997 Sch 8 Pt II(11)).

(6), (7) (*amend* TA 1988 ss 421(1)(*b*), 547(5)(*a*), 599A(6) and *repeal* s 599A(7)).

Commentary—*Simon's Direct Tax Service* E1.821.

123 Liability of partners

(1)–(14) (*amend* TMA 1970 ss 12AA(2), (3), (7)(*a*), 12AB(1), (2), 12AC(1)(*b*), 93A(1)(*b*), (3), (4), (6), (7), 95A(1)(*a*), (3), 118(1), insert* s 12AA(11)–(13) and *repeal* s 12AC(6); *part repealed by* FA 2001 s 110, Sch 33 Pt II(13) with effect in accordance with FA 2001 s 88, Sch 29).

124 Retention of original records

(1) The Taxes Management Act 1970, as it has effect—

(*a*) for the purposes of income tax and capital gains tax, as respects the year 1996–97 and subsequent years of assessment, and

(*b*) for the purposes of corporation tax, as respects accounting periods ending on or after the day appointed under section 199 of the Finance Act 1994 for the purposes of Chapter III of Part IV of that Act (self-assessment management provisions),

shall be amended in accordance with the following provisions of this section.

(2)–(8) (*amend* TMA 1970 s 12B(4), (5), Sch 1A, para 2A(3), (4), (5) and *insert* ss 12B(4A), (5B)).

(9) The amendments made by this section shall not have effect in relation to—

(*a*) any time before this Act is passed, or

(*b*) any records which a person fails to preserve before this Act is passed.

125 Determination of tax where no return delivered

(*substitutes* TMA 1970 s 28C(1), (1A) (for s 28C(1)), *amends* s 28C(3), (6) and *inserts* s 59B(5A)).

126 PAYE regulations

(*inserts* TMA 1970 ss 59A(10), 59B(8)).

127 Repayment postponed pending completion of enquiries

(*Inserts* TMA 1970 s 59B (4A)).

128 Claims for reliefs involving two or more years

(1), (2) (*repeal* TMA 1970 s 42(3A), (3B), *amend* s 42(7)(*a*) and *insert* s 42(11A), Sch 1B).

(3)–(10) (*substitute* TA 1988 ss 96(9), 534 (5)–(5B) (for s 534(5)), 537A(5)–(5B) (for s 537A(5)), *amend* ss 108, 534(5), (6), *insert* TA 1988 s 534(6A), 535(8A), 538(4) and *repeal* s 535(5), (7); *part repealed* by FA 2001 s 110, Sch 33 Pt II(6) with effect for payments actually receivable after 5 April 2001).

(11) This section (except subsections (1)(*b*) and (6) above) and Schedule 17 to this Act have effect as respects claims made (or deemed to be made) in relation to the year 1996–97 or later years of assessment.

(12) Subsection (1)(*b*) above has effect as respects claims made in relation to the year 1997–98 or later years of assessment.

129 Claims for medical insurance and vocational training relief

(1) Nothing in section 42 of the Taxes Management Act 1970 (procedure for making claims etc), or Schedule 1A to that Act (claims etc not included in returns), shall apply in relation to—

(*a*) any claim under subsection (6)(*b*) of section 54 (medical insurance relief) of the Finance Act 1989 (''the 1989 Act''); or[1]

(*b*) ...[2]

(2) (*amends* FA 1989 s 54(6)(*b*) and FA 1991 s 32(5)(*b*) and is repealed to the former extent by F(No 2)A 1997 Sch 8 Pt II (2)).

(3) (*inserts* FA 1989 s 57(1)(*aa*) and is repealed by F(No 2)A 1997 Sch 8 Pt II (2)).

(4) (*inserts* FA 1991 s 33(1)(*aa*) and is repealed by FA 1999 s 139, Sch 20 Pt III(15) with effect for payments made after 31 August 2000 (by virtue of SI 2000/2004)).

(5) *Subsection (1)(a) above shall not apply in relation to claims made before the coming into force of regulations made by virtue of section 57(1)(aa) of the 1989 Act.*[1]

(6) ...[2]

Commentary—*Simon's Direct Tax Service* **E2.902, 1303.**
Amendments—¹ Sub-ss (1)(*a*), (5) repealed by F(No 2)A 1997 Sch 8 Pt II(2) with effect for 1997–98 and subsequent years
except in relation to cases in which relief due under FA 1989 s 54 in respect of any payment is unaffected by the provisions of
F(No 2)A 1997 s 17(1) (see the Amendments note to FA 1989 s 54).
² Sub-s (1)(*b*), (6) repealed by by FA 1999 s 139, Sch 20 Pt III(15) with effect for payments made after 31 August 2000 (by virtue
of SI 2000/2004).

130 Procedure for giving notices

(1) Section 42 of, and Schedule 1A to, the Taxes Management Act 1970, as they have effect—

(*a*) for the purposes of income tax and capital gains tax, as respects the year 1996–97 and
subsequent years of assessment, and

(*b*) for the purposes of corporation tax, as respects accounting periods ending on or after the day
appointed under section 199 of the Finance Act 1994 for the purposes of Chapter III of Part IV of
that Act (self-assessment management provisions),

shall be amended in accordance with the following provisions of this section.

(2)–(5) (*amend* TMA 1970 ss 42(7)(*a*), (*c*), (10), (11), Sch 1A para 1).

131 Interest on overdue tax

(1) (*inserts* FA 1995 s 110(4) which is deemed to have always had effect).

(2) (*amends* TMA 1970 s 86(3)).

(3) (*repeals* FA 1994 Sch 19 para 23).

132 Overdue tax and excessive payments by the Board

Schedule 18 to this Act (which amends enactments relating to overdue tax or excessive payments by
the Board) shall have effect.

Commentary—*Simon's Direct Tax Service* **E1.825, 827.**

133 Claims and enquiries

Schedule 19 to this Act (which, for purposes connected with self-assessment, further amends
provisions relating to claims and enquiries) shall have effect.

Commentary—*Simon's Direct Tax Service* **E1.830–832.**

134 Discretions exercisable by the Board etc

(1) Schedule 20 to this Act (which in connection with self-assessment modifies enactments by virtue
of which a decision or other action affecting an assessment may be or is required to be taken by the
Board, or one of their officers, before the making of the assessment) shall have effect.

(2) Subject to subsection (3) below, the amendments made by that Schedule shall have effect—

(*a*) for the purposes of income tax and capital gains tax, as respects the year 1996–97 and
subsequent years of assessment; and

(*b*) for the purposes of corporation tax, as respects accounting periods ending on or after the day
appointed under section 199 of the Finance Act 1994 for the purposes of Chapter III of Part IV of
that Act (self-assessment management provisions).

(3) Paragraphs 22 and 23 of that Schedule shall have effect in relation to shares issued on or after
6th April 1996.

Commentary—*Simon's Direct Tax Service* **E1.807.**
Notes—The appointed day is 1 July 1999 by virtue of Finance Act 1994, Section 199, (Appointed Day) Order, SI 1998/3173
art 2.

135 Time limits for claims etc

(1) Schedule 21 to this Act (which in connection with self-assessment modifies enactments which
impose time limits on the making of claims, elections, adjustments and assessments and the giving
of notices, and enactments which provide for the giving of notice to the inspector) shall have effect.

(2) Subject to subsections (3) to (5) below, the amendments made by that Schedule shall have
effect—

(*a*) for the purposes of income tax and capital gains tax, as respects the year 1996–97 and
subsequent years of assessment; and

(*b*) for the purposes of corporation tax, as respects accounting periods ending on or after the day
appointed under section 199 of the Finance Act 1994 for the purposes of Chapter III of Part IV of
that Act (self-assessment management provisions).

(3) ...¹

(4) ...¹

(5) ...¹

Commentary—*Simon's Direct Tax Service* E1.835.
Amendments—Sub-ss (3)–(5) repealed by the Capital Allowances Act 2001 s 580, Sch 4 with effect for income tax purposes, as respects allowances and charges falling to be made for chargeable periods ending after 5 April 2001, and for corporation tax purposes, as respects allowances and charges falling to be made for chargeable periods ending after 31 March 2001.

136 Appeals

Schedule 22 to this Act (which makes provision, in connection with self-assessment, about appeals) shall have effect.

Commentary—*Simon's Direct Tax Service* E1.839.

Companies

137 Schedules 13 and 16 to the Taxes Act 1988

(1) Schedule 23 to this Act shall have effect.

(2) The amendments made by that Schedule shall have effect as respects return periods ending on or after the appointed day for the purposes of Chapter III of Part IV of the Finance Act 1994.

(3) In subsection (2) above "return period" means—

(*a*) so far as relating to Schedule 13 to the Taxes Act 1988, a period for which a return is required to be made under paragraph 1 of that Schedule; and
(*b*) so far as relating to Schedule 16 to that Act, a period for which a return is required to be made under paragraph 2 of that Schedule.

Commentary—*Simon's Direct Tax Service* D1.605, 615.
Notes—The appointed day is 1 July 1999 by virtue of Finance Act 1994, Section 199, (Appointed Day) Order, SI 1998/3173 art 2.

138 Accounting periods

Schedule 24 to this Act (which makes provision, in connection with self-assessment, in relation to accounting periods) shall have effect.

Commentary—*Simon's Direct Tax Service* D2.107, 731.

139. Surrenders of advance corporation tax

Commentary—*Simon's Direct Tax Service* D2.655, 731.
Amendments—This section repealed by FA 1998 s 165, Sch 27 Pt III(2) with effect in relation to distributions made after 5 April 1999.

Chargeable gains

140 Transfer of company's assets to investment trust

(1) (*inserts* TCGA 1992 s 101(1A)).

(2) This section shall have effect as respects accounting periods ending on or after the day appointed under section 199 of the Finance Act 1994 for the purposes of Chapter III of Part IV of that Act (self-assessment management provisions).

Commentary—*Simon's Direct Tax Service* D2.303.
Notes—The appointed day is 1 July 1999 by virtue of Finance Act 1994, Section 199, (Appointed Day) Order, SI 1998/3173.

141 Roll-over relief

(1)–(6) (*amend* TCGA 1992 ss 152(4), 175(2A), (2B), (2C), 246, 247(5)(*b*) and *insert* ss 153A, 247A).

142 Premiums for leases

(1) Paragraph 3 of Schedule 8 to the Taxation of Chargeable Gains Act 1992 (premiums for leases) shall be amended as follows.

(2), (3) (*amend* TCGA 1992 Sch 8 para 3(2), (3) and *substitute* Sch 8 para 3(4), (5) (for para 3(4)–(6))).

(4) (*substitutes* TCGA 1992 Sch 8 para 3(4), (5) for para 3(4)–(6)).

(5) This section has effect as respects sums payable on or after 6th April 1996.

CHAPTER VI
MISCELLANEOUS PROVISIONS
Reliefs

143 Annual payments under certain insurance policies

(1) (*inserts* TA 1988 ss 580A, 580B).

(2) This section has effect for the year 1996–97 and subsequent years of assessment in relation to—

(*a*) any payment which under the policy in question falls to be paid at any time on or after 6th April 1996; and

(*b*) any payment not falling within paragraph (*a*) above in relation to which the conditions mentioned in subsection (3)(*a*) and (*b*) below are satisfied.

(3) This section shall also be deemed to have had effect for earlier years of assessment in relation to any payment in relation to which the following conditions are satisfied, that is to say—

(*a*) the payment was made under a policy in relation to which the requirements of subsection (4) below were fulfilled; and

(*b*) the policy in question provided for the right to annual payments under the policy to cease when all the liabilities in question were discharged.

(4) The requirements of this subsection are fulfilled in relation to any policy if—

(*a*) the only or main purpose of the insurance under the policy was to secure that the insured would be able to meet (in whole or in part) liabilities that would or might arise from any transaction;

(*b*) the policy expressly identified the transaction or, as the case may be, all the transactions (whether actual or proposed) by reference to which the insurance was taken out; and

(*c*) none of the transactions which would or might give rise to the liabilities mentioned in paragraph (*a*) above could be one entered into after any of the circumstances insured against arose.

(5) In subsection (4) above "transaction" includes any arrangements for the provision of credit or for the supply of services to residential premises.

Commentary—*Simon's Direct Tax Service* **B5.301.**

144 Vocational training

...

Amendment—This section repealed by FA 1999 s 139, Sch 20 Pt III(15) with effect for payments made after made after 31 August 2000 (by virtue of SI 2000/2004).

145 Personal reliefs for non-resident EEA nationals

(1), (2) (*amend* TA 1988 s 278(2)(*a*) and *insert* s 278(9)).

(3) This section has effect for the year 1996–97 and subsequent years of assessment.

146 Exemptions for charities

(1) Section 505(1) of the Taxes Act 1988 (exemptions for charities) shall be amended as follows.

(2)–(4) (*substitutes* TA 1988 s 505(1)(*a*) and *amend* s 505(1)(*c*), (*e*)).

(5) This section has effect—

(*a*) for the purposes of income tax, for the year 1996–97 and subsequent years of assessment; and

(*b*) for the purposes of corporation tax, in relation to accounting periods ending after 31st March 1996.

147 Withdrawal of relief for Class 4 contributions

(1) (*repeals* TA 1988 s 617(5)).

(2) (*amends* SSC & BA 1992 Sch 2 para 3(2) and SSC & B (NI)A 1992 Sch 2 para 3(2)).

(3) This section shall have effect in relation to the year 1996–97 and subsequent years of assessment.

Commentary—*Simon's Direct Tax Service* **E1.447.**

148 Mis-sold personal pensions etc

(1) Income tax shall not be chargeable on any payment falling within subsection (3) or (5) below.

(2) Receipt of a payment falling within subsection (3) below shall not be regarded for the purposes of capital gains tax as the disposal of an asset.

(3) A payment falls within this subsection if it is a capital sum by way of compensation for loss suffered, or reasonably likely to be suffered, by a person in a case where that person, or some other person, acting in reliance on bad investment advice at least some of which was given during the period beginning with 29th April 1988 and ending with 30th June 1994,—

(*a*) has, while eligible, or reasonably likely to become eligible, to be a member of an occupational pension scheme, instead become a member of a personal pension scheme or entered into a retirement annuity contract;

(*b*) has ceased to be a member of, or to pay contributions to, an occupational pension scheme and has instead become a member of a personal pension scheme or entered into a retirement annuity contract;

(*c*) has transferred to a personal pension scheme accrued rights of his under an occupational pension scheme; or (*d*) has ceased to be a member of an occupational pension scheme and has instead (by virtue of such a provision as is mentioned in section 591(2)(*g*) of the Taxes Act 1988) entered into arrangements for securing relevant benefits by means of an annuity contract.

(4) A payment chargeable to income tax apart from subsection (1) above may nevertheless be regarded as a capital sum for the purpose of determining whether it falls within subsection (3) above.

(5) A payment falls within this subsection if and to the extent that it is a payment of interest, on the whole or any part of a capital sum such as is mentioned in subsection (3) above, for a period ending on or before the earliest date on which a determination (whether or not subsequently varied on an appeal or in any other proceedings) of the amount of the particular capital sum in question is made, whether by agreement or by a decision of—

    (*a*) a court, tribunal or commissioner,
    (*b*) an arbitrator or (in Scotland) arbiter, or
    (*c*) any other person appointed for the purpose.

(6) In this section—

"bad investment advice" means investment advice in respect of which an action against the person who gave it has been, or may be, brought—

    (*a*) in or for negligence;
    (*b*) for breach of contract;
    (*c*) by reason of a breach of a fiduciary obligation; or
    [(*d*) by reason of a contravention which is actionable—

        (i) under section 62 of the Financial Services Act 1986; or
        (ii) under section 150 of the Financial Services and Markets Act 2000;][1]

["investment advice"—

    (*a*) in relation to a time before 1st December 2001, means advice such as is mentioned in paragraph 15 of Schedule 1 to the Financial Services Act 1986; and
    (*b*) in relation to a time on or after that date, means advice such as is mentioned in Article 53 of the Financial Services and Markets Act 2000 (Regulated Activities) Order 2001;][1]

"occupational pension scheme" means—

    (*a*) a scheme approved, or being considered for approval, under Chapter I of Part XIV of the Taxes Act 1988 (retirement benefit schemes);
    (*b*) a relevant statutory scheme, as defined in section 611A(1) of that Act; or
    (*c*) a fund to which section 608 of that Act applies (superannuation funds approved before 6th April 1980 etc);

"personal pension scheme" has the meaning given by section 630(1) of the Taxes Act 1988;
"relevant benefits" has the meaning given by section 612(1) of the Taxes Act 1988;
"retirement annuity contract" means a contract made before 1st July 1988 and approved by the Board under or by virtue of any provision of Chapter III of Part XIV of the Taxes Act 1988.

(7) This section shall have effect, and be taken always to have had effect, in relation to any payment falling within subsection (3) or (5) above, whether made before or after the passing of this Act.

Commentary—*Simon's Direct Tax Service* **E7.401.**
Amendments—[1] In sub-s (6), definition of "investment advice" and words in definition of "bad investment advice" substituted by the Financial Services and Markets Act 2000 (Consequential Amendments) (Taxes) Order, SI 2001/3629 arts 92, 93 with effect from 1 December 2001 immediately after the coming into force of the Financial Services and Markets Act 2000 ss 411, 432(1), Sch 20.

149 Annual payments in residuary cases

Commentary—*Simon's Direct Tax Service* **B5.301.**
This section repealed by FA 1999 s 139, Sch 20 Pt III(6) with effect for any payment falling due after 5 April 2000.

150 Income tax exemption for periodical payments of damages and compensation for personal injury

(1) The sections set out in Schedule 26 to this Act shall be inserted after section 329 of the Taxes Act 1988.

(2) The first of those sections supersedes sections 329A and 329B inserted by the Finance Act 1995 and applies to payments received after the passing of this Act irrespective of when the agreement or order referred to in that section was made or took effect.

(3) Subsections (1) and (2) of the second of those sections supersede section 329C inserted by the Criminal Injuries Compensation Act 1995 and apply to payments received after the passing of that Act.

(4) The repeal of sections 329A and 329B does not affect the operation of those sections in relation to payments received before the passing of this Act.

Commentary—*Simon's Direct Tax Service* **B5.310.**

Taxation of benefits

151 Benefits under pilot schemes

(1) The Treasury may by order make provision for the Income Tax Acts to have effect in relation to any amount of benefit payable by virtue of a Government pilot scheme as if it was, as they think fit, either—

    (*a*) wholly or partly exempt from income tax and, accordingly, to be disregarded in computing the amount of any receipts brought into account for income tax purposes; or

    (*b*) to the extent specified in the order, to be brought into account for the purposes of income tax as income of a description so specified or as a receipt of a description so specified.

(2) The Treasury may by order provide for any amount of benefit payable by virtue of a Government pilot scheme to be left out of account, to the extent specified in the order, in the determination for the purposes of [section 532 of the Capital Allowances Act (exclusion of expenditure met by contributions)][1] of how far any expenditure has been or is to be met directly or indirectly by the Crown or by an authority or person other than the person actually incurring it.

(3) In this section ''Government pilot scheme'' means any arrangements (whether or not contained in a scheme) which—

    (*a*) are made, under any enactment or otherwise, by the Secretary of State or any Northern Ireland department;

    (*b*) make provision for or about the payment of amounts of benefit either—

        (i) for purposes that are similar to those for which any social security or comparable benefit is payable; or

        (ii) for purposes connected with the carrying out of any functions of the Secretary of State or any such department in relation to employment or training for employment;

    (*c*) are arrangements relating to a temporary experimental period; and

    (*d*) are made wholly or partly for the purpose of facilitating a decision as to whether, or to what extent, it is desirable for provision to be made on a permanent basis for or in relation to any benefit.

(4) In subsection (3)(*b*) above the reference to making provision for or about the payment of amounts of benefit for purposes that are similar to those for which any social security or comparable benefit is payable shall include a reference to making provision by virtue of which there is a modification of the conditions of entitlement to, or the conditions for the payment of, an existing social security or comparable benefit.

(5) An order under this section may—

    (*a*) make different provision for different cases, and

    (*b*) contain such incidental, supplemental, consequential and transitional provision (including provision modifying provision made by or under the Income Tax Acts) as the Treasury may think fit.

(6) In this section ''benefit'' includes any allowance, grant or other amount the whole or any part of which is payable directly or indirectly out of public funds.

(7) The power to make an order under this section—

    (*a*) shall be exercisable for the year 1996–97 and subsequent years of assessment; and

    (*b*) so far as exercisable for the year 1996–97, shall be exercisable in relation to benefits, allowances and other amounts paid at times on or after 6th April 1996 but before the making of the order.

(8) The Treasury shall not make an order under this section containing any such provision as is mentioned in subsection (1)(*b*) above unless a draft of the order has been laid before, and approved by a resolution of, the House of Commons.

Commentary—*Simon's Direct Tax Service* **E4.328.**
Order—Taxation of Benefits under Pilot Schemes (Earnings Top-up) Order 1996, SI 1996/2396.
Amendments—[1] Words in sub-s (2) substituted by CAA 2001 s 578, Sch 2 para 95 with effect for income tax purposes as respects allowances and charges falling to be made for chargeable periods ending after 5 April 2001.

152 Jobfinder's grant

(1) The Income Tax Acts shall have effect, and be deemed always to have had effect, as if jobfinder's grant were exempt from income tax and, accordingly, were to be disregarded in computing the amount of any receipts brought into account for income tax purposes.

(2) In this section ''jobfinder's grant'' means grant paid under that name by virtue of arrangements made in pursuance of section 2 of the Employment and Training Act 1973 or section 1 of the Employment and Training Act (Northern Ireland) 1950 (arrangements for assisting persons to select, train for, obtain or retain employment).

Commentary—*Simon's Direct Tax Service* **E4.328.**

Investments

153 Foreign income dividends

Schedule 27 to this Act (which makes provision relating to foreign income dividends) shall have effect.

Commentary—*Simon's Direct Tax Service* **D1.701.**

154 FOTRA securities

(1) The modifications which, under section 60 of the Finance Act 1940, may be made for the purposes of any issue of securities to the conditions about tax exemption specified in section 22 of the Finance (No 2) Act 1931 shall include a modification by virtue of which the tax exemption contained in any condition of the issue applies, as respects capital, irrespective of where the person with the beneficial ownership of the securities is domiciled.

(2) Subject to subsections (3) to (5) below, nothing in the Tax Acts shall impose any charge to tax on any person in respect of so much of any profits or gains arising from a FOTRA security, or from any loan relationship represented by a FOTRA security, as is expressed to be exempt from tax in the tax exemption condition applying to that security.

(3) Exemption from tax shall not be conferred by virtue of subsection (2) above in relation to any security unless the requirements imposed as respects that exemption by the conditions with which the security is issued (including any requirement as to the making of a claim) are complied with.

(4) The tax exemption condition of a FOTRA security shall not be taken to confer any exemption from any charge to tax imposed by virtue of the provisions of Chapter IA of Part XV or Chapter III of Part XVII of the Taxes Act 1988 (anti-avoidance provisions for residents etc).

(5) Nothing in this section shall entitle any person to any repayment of tax which he has not claimed within the time limit which would be applicable under the Tax Acts (apart from this section) to a claim for the repayment of that tax.

(6) A person with the beneficial ownership of a FOTRA security who would, by virtue of this section, be exempt from tax in respect of some or all of the profits and gains arising from that security, or from any loan relationship represented by it, shall not be entitled for the purposes of income tax or corporation tax to bring into account any amount—

(*a*) in respect of changes in the value of that security;

(*b*) as expenses or disbursements incurred in, or in connection with, the holding of the security or any transaction relating to the security; or

(*c*) as a debit given, in respect of any loan relationship represented by that security, by any provision of Chapter II of this Part of this Act in respect of such a relationship.

(7) Schedule 28 to this Act (which contains amendments consequential on the provisions of this section) shall have effect.

(8) References in this section to a FOTRA security are references to—

(*a*) any security issued with such a condition about exemption from taxation as is authorised in relation to its issue by virtue of section 22 of the Finance (No 2) Act 1931; or

(*b*) any $3\frac{1}{2}$ % War Loan 1952 Or After which was issued with a condition authorised by virtue of section 47 of the Finance (No 2) Act 1915;

and references, in relation to such a security, to the tax exemption condition shall be construed accordingly.

(9) This section and Schedule 28 to this Act shall have effect—

(*a*) for the purposes of income tax, for the year 1996–97 and subsequent years of assessment; and

(*b*) for the purposes of corporation tax, for accounting periods ending after 31st March 1996.

Commentary—*Simon's Direct Tax Service* **B5.215.**
Concession **A14**—Exemption in respect of residuary income which is deemed to be received during the administration period of a deceased person's estate by a non-resident beneficiary.
B18—Payments out of a discretionary trust: entitlement to relief from UK tax where the beneficiary would otherwise have been entitled to exemption in respect of FOTRA securities issued in accordance with this section.

155 Directions for payment without deduction of tax

(*Inserts TA* 1988 s 51AA).

156 Paying and collecting agents etc

Schedule 29 to this Act (which amends the rules relating to paying and collecting agents) shall have effect.

Commentary—*Simon's Direct Tax Service* **Division A7.9.**

157 Stock lending fees

(1) (*inserts* TA 1988 s 129B).

(2) This section has effect in relation to any arrangements entered into on or after 2nd January 1996.

158 Transfers on death under the accrued income scheme

(1)–(4) (*amend* TA 1988 s 710(5), *repeal* s 721(1), (4) and *substitute* s 721(2)).

(5) This section has effect as respects deaths on or after 6th April 1996.

159 Manufactured payments, repos, etc

(1) (*repeals* TA 1988 ss 729, 737A(2)(*b*), 786(4)).

(2), (3) ...¹

(4)–(6) (*amend* TA 1988 Sch 23A paras 4(3), (7) and *insert* TA 1988 Sch 23A para 4(3A), (3B), (7AA)).

(7) ...¹

(8) (*inserts* TA 1988 Sch 23A para 8(1A)).

(9) Subsections (2), (4) and (5) above have effect—

(*a*) for the purposes of corporation tax, in relation to accounting periods ending after 31st March 1996; and

(*b*) for the purposes of income tax, in relation to the year 1996–97 and subsequent years of assessment.

(10) In this section ''the appointed day'' means such day as the Treasury may by order appoint, and different days may be appointed under this subsection for different purposes.

Notes—The day appointed under sub-s (10) for the purposes of sub-ss (1), (3) is 6 November 1996, SI 1996/2646.
Amendments—¹ Sub-ss (2), (3), and sub-s (7) insofar as it amends the words after TA 1988 Sch 23A para 8(1)(*b*), repealed by FA 1997 Sch 17 Pt VI(9) with effect in relation to payments made on or after 1 July 1997 by virtue of the Finance Act 1997, Schedule 10, (Appointed Day) Order, SI 1997/991.

160 Investments in housing

Schedule 30 to this Act (which makes provision conferring relief from corporation tax on companies that invest in housing) shall have effect.

Commentary—*Simon's Direct Tax Service* **D4.422.**

161 Venture capital trusts: control of companies etc

(1) Schedule 28B to the Taxes Act 1988 (venture capital trusts: meaning of qualifying holdings) shall have effect, and be deemed always to have had effect, subject to the amendments in subsections (2) and (3) below.

(2) (*amends* TA 1988 Sch 28B para 9(1) and repeals sub-para (2) thereof).

(3) (*substitutes* TA 1988 Sch 28B para 13(2)–(5) for para 13(2), (3)).

Insurance policies

162 Qualifying life insurance policies: certification

(1) (*amends* FA 1995 s 55).

(2) (*amends* TA 1988 Sch 15 paras 24(2A), 25(2)).

Insurance companies

163 Life assurance business losses

Schedule 31 to this Act, which makes provision about losses arising to insurance companies in the carrying on of life assurance business, shall have effect.

Commentary—*Simon's Direct Tax Service* **D4.503.**

164 Limits on relief for expenses

(1) (*substitutes* TA 1988 s 76(2), (2A), (2B), (2C), (2D), (5) for s 76(2)–(5)).

(2) (*amends* TA 1988 s 76(8) and is part repealed by F(No 2)A 1997 Sch 8 Pt II(6)).

(3) (*amends* TA 1988 Sch 19AC para 5(1) and inserts sub-para (1A) thereof and is part repealed by F(No 2)A 1997 Sch 8 Pt II(6)).

(4) (*amends* TA 1988 s 56(4)).

(5) Subject to subsection (6) below, this section has effect in relation to accounting periods beginning on or after 1st January 1996.

(6) Notwithstanding anything in the previous provisions of this section, section 76 of the Taxes Act 1988 has effect in relation to accounting periods beginning on or after 1st January 1996—

(*a*) as if the reference in subsection (2D) of that section to a previous accounting period included a reference to an accounting period beginning before that date, and

(*b*) in relation to such a previous accounting period, as if the references—

(i) to the amount deductible by virtue of this section, and

(ii) to the basic deduction,

were to be construed by reference to whatever provisions had effect in relation to that previous period for purposes corresponding to those of that section as amended by this section.

Commentary—*Simon's Direct Tax Service* **D4.504.**

165 Annual payments under insurance policies: deductions

(1), (2) (*insert* TA 1988 s 337(2A), (2B) and *amend* s 338(2)).

(3) (*repeals* TA 1988 s 434B(1) and amends sub-s (2) thereof, and is itself repealed by FA 1997 Sch 18 Pt VI(6)).

(4) Subject to subsection (5) below, this section has effect in relation to accounting periods beginning on or after 1st January 1996.

(5) In relation to any accounting period beginning on or after 1st January 1996 but ending before 1st April 1996, this section shall have effect as if any reference in provisions inserted by this section to an annuity payable or paid by an insurance company included a reference to any such interest as was mentioned in section 434B(1) of the Taxes Act 1988 before its repeal by virtue of this section.

166 Equalisation reserves

Schedule 32 to this Act (which makes provision about the tax treatment of equalisation reserves maintained by insurance companies) shall have effect.

Commentary—*Simon's Direct Tax Service* **D4.538.**

167 Industrial assurance business

(1) (*repeals* TA 1988 s 432(2)).

(2) (*substitutes* TA 1988 s 432A(2)(*d*) for s 432A(*d*), (*e*)).

(3) (*amends* FA 1989 s 86(1)(*a*), (2)).

(4) In section 832 of the Taxes Act 1988 (interpretation), in the definition of "industrial assurance business" for "has" there shall be substituted "means any such business carried on before the day appointed for the coming into force of section 167(4) of the Finance Act 1996 as was industrial assurance business within".

(5), (6) (*amend* TA 1988 Sch 14 para 8(4) and *insert* Sch 14 para 8(8)).

(7) In Schedule 15 to the Taxes Act 1988 (qualifying policies)—

    (*a*) in paragraph 1(6) (calculation of amount included in premiums of whole life and term insurances in respect of their payment otherwise than annually), for "and if the policy is issued in the course of an industrial assurance business," there shall be substituted "and if the policy provides for payment otherwise than annually without providing for the amount of the premiums if they are paid annually,"; and
    (*b*) in paragraph 2(2) (the equivalent calculation for endowment assurances), for "issued in the course of an industrial assurance business," there shall be substituted "that provides for the payment of premiums otherwise than annually without providing for the amount of the premiums if they are paid annually,".

(8), (9) (*insert* TA 1988 Sch 15 paras 8A, 18(3)(*c*)).

(10) Subsections (1) to (3) above have effect in relation to accounting periods beginning on or after 1st January 1996.

(11) Subsection (4) above shall come into force on such day as the Board may by order appoint.

(12) Subsection (7) above shall have effect in relation to policies issued on or after such day as the Board may by order appoint.

Commentary—*Simon's Direct Tax Service* **D4.526.**

168 Capital redemption business

(1) (*substitutes* TA 1988 s 458(3)).

(2) Schedule 33 to this Act (which makes provision for the application of the I minus E basis of charging tax to companies carrying on capital redemption business) shall have effect.

(3) (*inserts* TA 1988 s 458A).

(4) (*amends* TA 1988 s 539(3)).

(5) (*amends* TA 1988 s 553(10)).

(6) Subsection (1) above shall have effect as respects accounting periods ending on or after the day appointed under section 199 of the Finance Act 1994 for the purposes of Chapter III of Part IV of that Act (self-assessment management provisions), and subsections (4) and (5) above shall have effect as respects contracts effected on or after that day.

Commentary—*Simon's Direct Tax Service* **D4.530.**
Notes—The appointed day is 1 July 1999 by virtue of Finance Act 1994, Section 199, (Appointed Day) Order, SI 1998/3173 art 2.

[169 Provisional repayments in connection with pension business

(1) Schedule 19AB to the Taxes Act 1988 (pension business: payments on account of tax credits and deducted tax) shall be amended in accordance with the provisions of Part I of Schedule 34 to this Act.

(2) Schedule 19AC to the Taxes Act 1988 (modification of that Act in relation to overseas life insurance companies) shall be amended in accordance with the provisions of Part II of Schedule 34 to this Act.

(3) The amendments made by Schedule 34 to this Act shall have effect in relation to provisional repayment periods, within the meaning of Schedule 19AB to the Taxes Act 1988, falling in accounting periods ending on or after the day appointed under section 199 of the Finance Act 1994 for the purposes of Chapter III of Part IV of that Act (self-assessment management provisions).][1]

Commentary—*Simon's Direct Tax Service* **D4.534.**
Notes—The appointed day is 1 July 1999 by virtue of Finance Act 1994, Section 199, (Appointed Day) Order, SI 1998/3173 art 2.
Amendments—[1] This section repealed by FA 2001 s 110, Sch 33 Pt II(12) with effect in accordance with FA 2001 s 87.

170 Time for amending and enquiring into returns

Commentary—*Simon's Direct Tax Service* **A3.110.**
Amendments—This section repealed by FA 1998 s 165, Sch 27 Part III(28) with effect in relation to accounting periods ending after 30 June 1999 (by virtue of Finance Act 1994, Section 199, (Appointed Day) Order, SI 1998/3173 art 2).

Friendly societies

171 Life or endowment business

(1)–(4) (*substitute* TA 1988 s 466(1)–(1B) for s 466(1), *amend* s 466(2) and *insert* s 266(6)(*c*), (6A)).

(5) (*amends* TA 1988 s 463(1)).

(6) The amendment made by subsection (5) above shall have effect in relation to accounting periods ending on or after 1st September 1996.

Personal pension schemes

172 Return of contributions on or after death of member

(1) (*amends* TA 1988 s 633(1)).

(2) (*substitutes* TA 1988 s 637A).

(3) This section—

    (*a*) has effect in relation to approvals, of schemes or amendments, given under Chapter IV of Part XIV of the Taxes Act 1988 (personal pension schemes) after the passing of this Act; and
    (*b*) does not affect any approval previously given.

Participators in close companies

173 Loans to participators etc

(1) Section 419 of the Taxes Act 1988 (loans to participators etc) shall be amended in accordance with subsections (2) to (4) below.

(2)–(4) (*substitute* TA 1988 s 419(3), *insert* s 419(4A) and *amend* s 419(6)).

(5) (*substitutes* TA 1988 s 826(4)(*a*)).

(6) This section has effect in relation to any loan or advance made in an accounting period ending on or after 31st March 1996.

174 Attribution of gains to participators in non-resident companies

(1) Section 13 of the Taxation of Chargeable Gains Act 1992 (attribution of gains to members of non-resident companies) shall be amended in accordance with subsections (2) to (9) below.

(2)–(9) (*amend* TCGA 1992 ss 13(2), 13(7), (9), (10), *substitute* s 13(3), (4), *repeal* s 13(5)(*a*) and *insert* s 13(5A), (7A), (12)–(15)).

(10) (*amends* TCGA 1992 Sch 5 para 1(3)).

(11) This section applies to gains accruing on or after 28th November 1995.

Cancellation of tax advantages

175 Transactions in certain securities

(1) (*amends* TA 1988 s 704 para D(2)(*b*)).

(2), (3) ...[1]

(4) ...[1] this section—

(*a*) so far as relating to sub-paragraph (2) of paragraph D of section 704 of the Taxes Act 1988 as it applies for the purposes of sub-paragraph (1) of that paragraph or paragraph E of that section, shall have effect where the relevant transaction takes place after the passing of this Act; and

(*b*) so far as relating to paragraph D of that section as it applies for the purposes of section 210(3) or 211(2) of that Act, shall have effect—

(i) in the case of section 210(3), in relation to share capital issued after the passing of this Act; or

(ii) in the case of section 211(2), in relation to distributions made after the passing of this Act.

(5) In this section "the relevant transaction" means—

(*a*) the transaction in securities mentioned in paragraph (*b*) of section 703(1) of the Taxes Act 1988, or

(*b*) the first of the two or more such transactions mentioned in that paragraph,

as the case may be.

Amendments—¹ Sub-ss (2),(3) and words "Except as provided by subsection (3) above," in sub-s (4) repealed by FA 1996 Sch 41 Pt V(31) with effect from the date on which the Unlisted Securities Market closed (31 December 1996).

Chargeable gains: reliefs

176 Retirement relief: age limits

(1) (*amends* TCGA 1992 ss 163, 164, Sch 6 para 5).

(2) The amendments made by this section shall apply in relation to disposals on or after 28th November 1995.

Prospective amendments—This section will be repealed by FA 1998 s 165, Sch 27 Pt III(31) with effect in relation to disposals in the year 2003–04 and subsequent years of assessment.

177 Reinvestment relief on disposal of qualifying corporate bond

(*Inserts* TCGA 1992 s 164A(2A), (2B)).

Special cases

178 Sub-contractors in the construction industry

(1) (*inserts* TA 1988 s 566(2A)–(2F)).

(2) (*amends* TMA 1970 s 98, Table).

179 Roll-over relief in respect of ships

...

Commentary—*Simon's Direct Tax Service* B2.335A.

Amendment—This section repealed by the Capital Allowances Act 2001 s 580, Sch 4 with effect for income tax purposes, as respects allowances and charges falling to be made for chargeable periods ending after 5 April 2001, and for corporation tax purposes, as respects allowances and charges falling to be made for chargeable periods ending after 31 March 2001.

180 Scientific research expenditure: oil licences

...

Amendment—This section repealed by the Capital Allowances Act 2001 s 580, Sch 4 with effect for income tax purposes, as respects allowances and charges falling to be made for chargeable periods ending after 5 April 2001, and for corporation tax purposes, as respects allowances and charges falling to be made for chargeable periods ending after 31 March 2001.

181 Overseas petroleum

(1) (*amends* TCGA 1992 s 196(1)).

(2) (*inserts* TCGA 1992 s 196(1A) and amends sub-s (2) thereof).

(3) (*substitutes* TCGA 1992 s 196(5), (5A) for s 196(5)).

(4) Subsections (1) to (3) above shall have effect in relation to any disposal on or after 13th September 1995 and subsection (3) shall also have effect, and be deemed always to have had effect, for the construction of section 195 of the Taxation of Chargeable Gains Act 1992 in its application to disposals before that date.

(5) Where enactments re-enacted in the Taxation of Chargeable Gains Act 1992 apply, instead of that Act, in the case of any disposal before 13th September 1995, this section shall have effect as if it required amendments equivalent to those made by subsection (3) above to have effect, and be deemed always to have had effect, for the construction of any enactment corresponding to section 195 of that Act.

Commentary—*Simon's Direct Tax Service* D4.1025.

182 Controlled foreign companies

Schedule 36 to this Act (which contains amendments of Chapter IV of Part XVII of the Taxes Act 1988) shall have effect in relation to accounting periods of a controlled foreign company, within the meaning of that Chapter, beginning on or after 28th November 1995.

Commentary—*Simon's Direct Tax Service* **D4.138.**

PART VII

MISCELLANEOUS AND SUPPLEMENTAL

Miscellaneous: direct taxation

198 Banks

Schedule 37 to this Act (which re-defines "bank" for certain purposes, and makes related amendments) shall have effect.

Commentary—*Simon's Direct Tax Service* **A3.405.**

199 Quotation or listing of securities

Schedule 38 to this Act (which contains amendments of enactments referring to the quotation or listing of securities) shall have effect.

200 Domicile for tax purposes of overseas electors

(1) In determining—

(a) for the purposes of inheritance tax, income tax or capital gains tax where a person is domiciled at any time on or after 6th April 1996, or

(b) for the purposes of section 267(1)(a) of the Inheritance Tax Act 1984 (deemed UK domicile for three years after ceasing to be so domiciled) where a person was domiciled at any time on or after 6th April 1993,

there shall be disregarded any relevant action taken by that person (whether before, on or after that date) in connection with electoral rights.

(2) Relevant action is taken by a person in connection with electoral rights where—

(a) he does anything with a view to, or in connection with, being registered as an overseas elector; or

(b) when registered as an overseas elector, he votes in any election at which he is entitled to vote by virtue of being so registered.

(3) For the purposes of this section, a person is registered as an overseas elector if he is—

(a) registered in any register [of parliamentary electors in pursuance of such a declaration as is mentioned in section 1(1)(a)][1] of the Representation of the People Act 1985 (extension of parliamentary franchise to certain non-resident British citizens); or

(b) registered under section 3 of that Act 1985 (certain non-resident peers entitled to vote at European Parliamentary elections).

(4) Nothing in subsection (1) above prevents regard being had, in determining the domicile of a person at any time, to any relevant action taken by him in connection with electoral rights if—

(a) his domicile at that time falls to be determined for the purpose of ascertaining his or any other person's liability to any of the taxes mentioned in subsection (1)(a) above; and

(b) the person whose liability is being ascertained wishes regard to be had to that action;

and a person's domicile determined in accordance with any such wishes shall be taken to have been so determined for the purpose only of ascertaining the liability in question.

Commentary—*Simon's Direct Tax Service* **E6.301.**
Amendments—[1] Words in sub-s (3)(a) substituted by the Representation of the People Act 2000 s 16, Sch 6 para 19 with effect from 29 Jan 2001 for the purpose only of making regulations and 16 Feb 2001 for all other purposes (by virtue of SI 2001/116).

201 Enactment of Inland Revenue concessions

Schedule 39 to this Act has effect for the purpose of enacting certain extra-statutory concessions relating to income tax, corporation tax, capital gains tax, and stamp duty.

Miscellaneous: other matters

202 Gilt stripping

(1)–(4) ...

(5) The Treasury may by regulations make provision for securing that enactments and subordinate legislation which—

(a) apply in relation to government securities or to any description of such securities, or (*b*) for any other purpose refer (in whatever terms) to such securities or to any description of them,

have effect with such modifications as the Treasury may think appropriate in consequence of the making of any provision or arrangements for, or in connection with, the issue or transfer of strips of government securities or the consolidation of such strips into other securities.

(6) Regulations under subsection (5) above may—

(*a*) impose a charge to income tax, corporation tax, capital gains tax, inheritance tax, stamp duty or stamp duty reserve tax;

(*b*) include provision applying generally to, or to any description of, enactments or subordinate legislation;

(*c*) make different provision for different cases; and

(*d*) contain such incidental, supplemental, consequential and transitional provision as the Treasury think appropriate.

(7) The power to make regulations under subsection (5) above shall be exercisable by statutory instrument subject to annulment in pursuance of a resolution of the House of Commons.

(8) Schedule 40 to this Act (which makes provision in relation to strips for taxation purposes) shall have effect.

(9) The enactments that may be modified by regulations under this section shall include section 95 above and the enactments contained in Schedule 40 to this Act.

(10) In this section—

"government securities" means any securities included in Part I of Schedule 11 to the Finance Act 1942;

"modifications" includes amendments, additions and omissions; and

"subordinate legislation" has the same meaning as in the Interpretation Act 1978;

and expressions used in this section and in section 47 of the Finance Act 1942 have the same meanings in this section as in that section.

Commentary—*Simon's Direct Tax Service* **B5.101; C2.806.**
Note—Sub-ss (1)–(4) outside the scope of this handbook.

203 Modification of the Agriculture Act 1993

(1) Part I of Schedule 2 to the Agriculture Act 1993 (taxation provisions applying to the reorganisation of the milk marketing boards) shall have effect, and be deemed always to have had effect, in accordance with subsections (2) to (4) below where—

(*a*) any approved scheme has made provision as to the functions of a milk marketing board in the period after the transfers taking effect on the vesting day under section 11 of that Act;

(*b*) regulations have been made by virtue of section 14(2) of that Act (provision following re-organisation) for giving effect to that provision; and

(*c*) a transaction is or has been entered into by that board in pursuance of any obligation under those regulations to carry out those functions so far as they relate to a subsidiary of the board.

(2) For the purposes of that Part of that Schedule—

(*a*) anything done by way of entering into the transaction, or for the purpose of carrying it out, shall be deemed to have been done under and in accordance with the scheme; and

(*b*) the terms and other provisions having effect in relation to that transaction by virtue of anything contained in, or anything done in exercise of powers conferred by, any regulations under section 14(2) of the Agriculture Act 1993 shall be deemed to be terms for which the scheme provided or, as the case may be, to be provisions of the scheme.

(3) Sub-paragraph (1) of paragraph 16 of Schedule 2 to the Agriculture Act 1993 (distributions) shall have effect, and be deemed always to have had effect, in a case where the terms and provisions mentioned in subsection (2)(*b*) above involved or involve—

(*a*) the issue or transfer of any shares in, or securities of, any body,

(*b*) the conferring of any right to a distribution out of the assets of any body,

(*c*) the conferring of any right to, or to acquire, shares in any body, or

(*d*) the transfer to any person of any property or rights of a milk marketing board, or of the subsidiary of such a board,

as if the references to the vesting day in paragraphs (*a*), (*c*), (*d*) and (*e*) of that sub-paragraph were references to the day on which the winding up of the board is completed.

(4) Sub-paragraph (4) of paragraph 31 of Schedule 2 to the Agriculture Act 1993 (condition to be satisfied if body to be qualifying body by virtue of sub-paragraph (1)(*c*)) shall have effect, and be deemed always to have had effect, as if—

(*a*) the reference, in relation to a company, to 90 per cent. of its ordinary share capital were a reference to 70 per cent. of its ordinary share capital; and

(*b*) the references to shares having been issued to any person included references to their having been allotted to that person.

(5) Paragraph 1 of Schedule 2 to the Agriculture Act 1993 (tax continuity with successor bodies) shall have effect, and be deemed to have had effect, in relation to any relevant transfer after 31st December 1995 to a society registered under the Industrial and Provident Societies Act 1965 of—

    (*a*) a trade, or part of a trade, of a milk marketing board, or

    (*b*) any property, rights or liabilities of such a board,

as it has effect in relation to any transfer under section 11 of that Act to a qualifying body.

(6) Paragraphs 16, 20, 25, 26, 28 and 29 of Schedule 2 to the Agriculture Act 1993 shall have effect, and be deemed to have had effect, in relation to any relevant transfer after 31st December 1995 of assets of a milk marketing board to a society registered under the Industrial and Provident Societies Act 1965 as if—

    (*a*) the terms and other provisions of the transaction for effecting the transfer were contained in an approved scheme;

    (*b*) the society were a relevant successor of that board; and

    (*c*) references in those paragraphs to the vesting day were references to the day on which the winding up of the board is completed.

(7) For the purposes of subsections (5) and (6) above, a transfer of anything to a society registered under the Industrial and Provident Societies Act 1965 is a relevant transfer if—

    (*a*) it is a transfer in pursuance of regulations made by virtue of section 14(2) of the Agriculture Act 1993;

    (*b*) it is not a transfer of shares in a subsidiary of a milk marketing board; and

    (*c*) the condition mentioned in sub-paragraph (5) of paragraph 31 of Schedule 2 to that Act would have been met in relation to that society if the provision made as to the persons to whom the membership of the society is open were contained in an approved scheme providing for the transfer.

(8) Paragraph 20 of Schedule 2 to the Agriculture Act 1993 (treatment of acquisition of certain shares and securities) shall not apply, and shall be deemed never to have applied, in relation to the acquisition of any security after 31st December 1995 if the indebtedness acknowledged by that security does not fall, for the purposes of the Taxation of Chargeable Gains Act 1992, to be treated as a debt on a security (as defined in section 132 of that Act of 1992).

(9) For the purposes of Chapter II of Part IV of this Act, so far as it has effect for any accounting period ending after 31st March 1996 in relation to any creditor relationship represented by a debenture issued on or after 31st December 1995, paragraph 25 of Schedule 2 to the Agriculture Act 1993 shall have effect as if sub-paragraph (2)(*a*) of that paragraph (deemed consideration for issue of debenture issued under approved scheme) were omitted.

(10) For the purposes of the Taxation of Chargeable Gains Act 1992, where any debenture to which paragraph 25 of Schedule 2 to the Agriculture Act 1993 applies has been or is issued at any time after 31st December 1995, the indebtedness acknowledged by that debenture shall be deemed (where that would not otherwise be the case) to be, and always to have been, a debt on a security (as defined in section 132 of that Act of 1992).

(11) Expressions used in this section and in Part I of the Agriculture Act 1993 have the same meanings in this section as in that Part.

Commentary—*Simon's Direct Tax Service* **C2.715.**

Supplemental

204 Interpretation

In this Act "the Taxes Act 1988" means the Income and Corporation Taxes Act 1988.

205 Repeals

(1) The enactments mentioned in Schedule 41 to this Act (which include spent provisions) are hereby repealed to the extent specified in the third column of that Schedule.

(2) The repeals specified in that Schedule have effect subject to the commencement provisions and savings contained in, or referred to, in the notes set out in that Schedule.

206 Short title

This Act may be cited as the Finance Act 1996.

SCHEDULE 6

TAXATION OF SAVINGS AT THE LOWER RATE

Section 73

Commentary—*Simon's Direct Tax Service* **B5.222.**

The Taxes Management Act 1970 (c 9)

1 (*amends* TMA 1970 s 86(2)(*b*) (old version)).

The Taxes Act 1988

2 (*amends* TA 1988 s 4(2)).

3 (*amends* TA 1988 s 5(4)).

4 ...

Amendments—This paragraph repealed by FA 1998 Sch 27 Pt III(3) with effect in relation only to payments of interest falling due after 31 March 1999 by virtue of Finance Act 1998, Section 37, (Appointed Day) Order, SI 1999/619).

5 ...

Amendments—This paragraph *repealed* by F(No 2)A 1997 Sch 8 Pt II (11)).

6 (*amends* TA 1988 s 249(4)(*c*)).

7—(1) (*amends* TA 1988 s 326B(2)(*b*)).

(2) (*inserts* TA 1988 s 326B(2A)).

(3) This paragraph has effect as respects withdrawals on or after 6th April 1996.

8 (*amends* TA 1988 s 350(1) and *inserts* s 350(1A)).

9 (*amends* TA 1988 s 421(1)(*c*)).

10—(1) (*inserts* TA 1988 s 468(1A)).

(2) Sub-paragraph (1) above has effect in relation to any accounting period ending after 31st March 1996.

(3) (*repeals* TA 1988 ss 468E, 468EE for accounting periods ending after 31 March 1996 except so far as relating to the financial year 1995).

11—(1), (2) (*insert* TA 1988 s 468L(1A), (8)–(14)).

(3) This paragraph has effect in relation to distribution periods ending on or after 1st April 1996.

12 (*amends* TA 1988 s 469(2)).

13 (*amends* TA 1988 ss 549(2), 686(1), 699(2), 819(2)).

14 (*amends* TA 1988 s 582(2)(*a*) and *inserts* s 582(2A)).

15 (*inserts* TA 1988 s 686(2B)).

16 (*inserts* TA 1988 Pt XV Chapter ID (ss 689A, 689B).

17 (*amends* TA 1988 s 698A(1),(2)).

18, 19 (*repealed* by FA 1997 Sch 17 Pt VI(9) with effect in relation to payments made on or after 1 July 1997 by virtue of the Finance Act 1997, Schedule 10, (Appointed Day) Order, SI 1997/991.

20 (*amends* TA 1988 s 743(1)).

21 (*amends* TA 1988 s 789(2)).

22 (*amends* TA 1988 s 821(1)).

23 (*amends* TA 1988 s 822(1)).

24 (*amends* TA 1988 s 835(6)(*a*)).

25—(1) (*amends* TA 1988 Sch 3 paras 1(*c*), 6A(1) and *repeals* para 6A(4)).

(2) This paragraph has effect in relation to payments made on or after 6th April 1996 and before the day on which this Act is passed.

The Finance Act 1989 (c 26)

26—(1)–(3) (*amend* FA 1989 s 88(1), 89(1), (2) and *insert* s 88A).

(4) This paragraph shall have effect for the financial year 1996 and subsequent financial years.

The Taxation of Chargeable Gains Act 1992 (c 12)

27 (*amended* TCGA 1992 s 4(3A); *repealed* by FA 1999 s 139, Sch 20 Pt III(1) with effect from the year 1999–00).

Commencement of Schedule

28 Subject to any express provisions as to commencement that are contained in the preceding provisions of this Schedule, this Schedule has effect for the year 1996–97 and subsequent years of assessment.

SCHEDULE 7

TRANSFER OF CHARGE UNDER SCHEDULE C TO SCHEDULE D

Section 7

Amendments of the Taxes Act 1988

1 The Taxes Act 1988 shall be amended in accordance with paragraphs 2 to 28 below.

2 (*amends* TA 1988 s 1(1)).

3 (*repeals* TA 1988 s 17).

4 (*amends* TA 1988 s 18(1), (3), (5) and *inserts* s 18(3B)–(3E)).

5 (*amends* TA 1988 s 19(1) (Schedule E para 2).

6 (*substitutes* heading to TA 1988 Pt III).

7 (*repeals* TA 1988 s 44).

8 (*repeals* TA 1988 s 45).

9 (*repeals* TA 1988 s 48).

10 (*inserts* TA 1988 s 49(3)).

11 (*amends* TA 1988 ss 50(1), 51A(1)).

12 (*repeals* TA 1988 s 52).

13 (*repeals* TA 1988 s 123).

14 (*amends* TA 1988 s 124(6) and *repeals* s 124(7)).

15 (*amends* TA 1988 s 322(1)).

16 (*amends* TA 1988 s 398(*b*)).

17 (*substitutes* TA 1988 s 468M(4)(*cc*) for s 468M(4)(*c*) – (*e*)).

18 (*repeals* TA 1988 s 474(1), (3)).

19 (*repeals* TA 1988 s 505(1)(*c*)(i), *substitutes* s 505(1)(*d*) and *inserts* s 505(1A)).

20 (*amends* TA 1988 s 512(1)(*a*),(*b*) and *inserts* s 512(3)).

21 (*amends* TA 1988 s 516(1), (2)).

22 (*repeals* TA 1988 s 582A(3)).

23 (*amends* TA 1988 s 730(2), (4), (6), (8)).

24 (*amends* TA 1988 s 828(2)).

25 (*amends* TA 1988 s 832(1)).

26 (*inserts* TA 1988 s 841A).

27 (*repeals* TA 1988 Sch 3).

28 (*amends* TA 1988 Sch 23A para 1(1) and *substitutes* Sch 23A para 4(8)(*b*), (*c*) for para 4(8)(*a*)–(*d*); *repealed* by FA 2000 s 156, Sch 40 Pt II(17) with effect in relation to payments of interest made after 31 March 2001).

Other amendments

29 (*amends* TMA 1970 s 98, Table).

30 (*amends* FA 1989 s 178(2)(*m*)).

31 (*amends* FA 1995 s 128(3)(*a*)).

Commencement, etc

32 Subject to paragraphs 33 and 34 below, this Schedule has effect—

(*a*) for the purposes of income tax, for the year 1996–97 and subsequent years of assessment;

(*b*) for the purposes of corporation tax, for accounting periods ending after 31st March 1996.

Position of paying and collecting agents

33 (*spent*).

Position of taxpayers

34 (*spent*).

Times to which paragraphs 33 and 34 apply

35 Paragraphs 33 and 34 above apply in relation to times falling—

(*a*) within a year of assessment or an accounting period mentioned in paragraph 32 above, but

(*b*) before the day on which this Act was passed.

SCHEDULE 8

LOAN RELATIONSHIPS: [CLAIMS ETC][1] RELATING TO DEFICITS

Section 83

Commentary—*Simon's Direct Tax Service* **Division D2.11.**
Amendments—Words substituted for the word "claims" by FA 2002 s 82, Sch 25 paras 1, 19(5) with effect for accounting periods beginning after 30 September 2002.

Claim to set off deficit against other profits for the deficit period

1—(1) This paragraph applies where a claim is made under section 83(2)(*a*) of this Act for the whole or any part of the deficit to be set off against profits of any description for the deficit period.

(2) Subject to the following provisions of this paragraph—

(*a*) the amount to which the claim relates shall be set off against the profits of the company for the deficit period that are identified in the claim; and

(*b*) those profits shall be treated as reduced accordingly.

(3) Any reduction by virtue of sub-paragraph (2) above shall be made—

(*a*) after relief has been given for any loss incurred in a trade in an earlier accounting period; and

(*b*) before any relief is given against profits for that period either—

[(i) under section 392A(1) or 393A(1) of the Taxes Act 1988 (losses set against profits for the same or preceding accounting periods); or][1]

(ii) by virtue of any claim made, in respect of a deficit for a subsequent period, under section 83(2)(*c*) of this Act.

(4) Relief shall not be given by virtue of a claim under section 83(2) (*a*) of this Act against any ring fence profits of the company within the meaning of Chapter V of Part XII of the Taxes Act 1988 (petroleum extraction activities).

Commentary—*Simon's Direct Tax Service* **D2.1136.**
Amendments—[1] Substituted by FA 1998 Sch 5 para 64 with effect for 1998–99 and subsequent years of assessment for income tax, and from 1 April 1998 for corporation tax.

Claim to treat deficit as eligible for group relief

2—*(1) This paragraph applies where the company makes a claim under section 83(2)(b) of this Act for the whole or any part of the deficit to be treated as eligible for group relief.*

[(2) Section 403 of the Taxes Act 1988 (amounts which may be surrendered by way of group relief) applies in accordance with section 403ZC(2) of that Act.]

Commentary—*Simon's Direct Tax Service* **D2.1136.**
Amendments—This paragraph repealed by FA 2002 ss 82, 141, Sch 25 paras 1, 17, Sch 40 Pt 3(12) with effect for accounting periods beginning after 30 September 2002.

Claim to carry back deficit to previous accounting periods

3—(1) This paragraph applies where a claim is made under section 83(2)(*c*) of this Act for the whole or any part of the deficit to be carried back to be set off against profits for earlier accounting periods.

(2) The claim shall have effect only if it relates to an amount that is equal to whichever is smaller of the following amounts, that is to say—

(*a*) so much of that deficit as is neither—

(i) an amount in relation to which a claim is made [under subsection (2)(*a*)][3] of section 83 of this Act, nor

(ii) an amount excluded by virtue of subsection (4) of that section from the amounts in relation to which claims may be made under subsection (2) of that section;

and

(*b*) the total amount of the profits available for relief under this paragraph.

(3) Where the claim has effect, the amount to which the claim relates shall be set off against the profits available for relief under this paragraph—

(*a*) by treating those profits as reduced accordingly; and

(*b*) to the extent that those profits are profits for more than one accounting period, by applying the relief to profits for a later period before setting off any remainder of the amount to which the claim relates against profits for an earlier period.

(4) Subject to sub-paragraph (5) below, the profits available for relief under this paragraph are the amounts which, for accounting periods ending within the permitted period, would be taken—

(*a*) apart from any relief under this paragraph, and

(*b*) after the giving of every relief which under sub-paragraph (6) below falls to be given in priority to relief under this paragraph,

to be chargeable under Case III of Schedule D as profits and gains arising from the company's loan relationships.

(5) Where any accounting period begins before the beginning of the permitted period but ends in the course of it—

    (*a*) any amount chargeable in respect of that accounting period under Case III of Schedule D as profits and gains of the company's loan relationships shall be apportioned according to the proportions of the accounting period falling before and after the beginning of the permitted period; and

    (*b*) the amount attributable, on that apportionment, to before the beginning of the permitted period shall not be available for relief under this paragraph.

(6) The reliefs which fall to be given in priority to relief under this paragraph in respect of any loss are—

    (*a*) any relief in respect of a loss or deficit incurred or treated as incurred in an accounting period before the deficit period;

    (*b*) any relief under section 338 of the Taxes Act 1988 (charges on income) in respect of payments made wholly and exclusively for the purposes of a trade;

    (*c*) where the company is an investment company for the purposes of Part IV of that Act—

        (i) any allowance under [Part 2 of the Capital Allowances Act (plant and machinery allowances)]²;

        (ii) any deduction in respect of management expenses under section 75 of the Taxes Act 1988; and

        (iii) any relief under section 338 of the Taxes Act 1988 in respect of payments made wholly and exclusively for the purposes of its business;

    (*d*) any relief under section 393A of the Taxes Act 1988 (trading losses set against profits of the same or any preceding accounting periods); and

    (*e*) any relief in pursuance of a claim [under section 83(2)(*a*)]³ of this Act.

(7) In this paragraph ''the permitted period'' means the period of [twelve months]¹ immediately preceding the beginning of the deficit period so far as that [twelve months]¹ period falls after 31st March 1996.

Commentary—*Simon's Direct Tax Service* **D2.1136.**
Amendments—¹ Words in sub-para (7) substituted by F(No 2)A 1997 s 40(1), (2), (7) with effect in relation to any deficit for a deficit period (see para 5 below) ending on or after 2 July 1997, but see F(No 2)A 1997 s 40(8), (10)—(12) for transitional provisions where the deficit period begins before but ends on or after that date.
² Words in sub-para (6)(*c*)(i) substituted by CAA 2001 s 578, Sch 2 para 96 with effect for income tax purposes, as respects allowances and charges falling to be made for chargeable periods ending after 5 April 2001, and for corporation tax purposes, as respects allowances and charges falling to be made for chargeable periods ending after 31 March 2001.
³ In sub-para (2)(*a*)(i), words substituted for the words ''under subsection (2)(*a*) or (*b*)''; and in sub-para (6)(*e*), words substituted for the words ''under section 83(2)(*a*) or (*b*)''; by FA 2002 s 82, Sch 25 paras 1, 18 with effect for accounting periods beginning after 30 September 2002.

*[Carry forward of deficit to succeeding accounting periods]*¹

4—[(1) This paragraph applies where, pursuant to section 83(3A) of this Act, any of the deficit for a deficit period is to be carried forward and set against non-trading profits for succeeding accounting periods.]¹

(2) [The amount carried forward from the deficit period, reduced by any amount claimed under sub-paragraph (3) below,]¹ shall be set off against the non-trading profits of the company for the accounting period immediately following the deficit period, and those profits shall be treated as reduced accordingly.

[(3) The company may make a claim for so much of the amount carried forward from the deficit period as may be specified in the claim to be excepted from being set against non-trading profits of the accounting period immediately following the deficit period.]¹

[(4) Any claim under sub-paragraph (3) above must be made before the expiration of the period of 2 years following the end of that accounting period.]¹

[(5) So much of the amount carried forward from the deficit period as—

    (*a*) cannot be relieved under sub-paragraph (2) above against non-trading profits of the accounting period immediately following the deficit period, or

    (*b*) is the subject of a claim under sub-paragraph (3) above in respect of that accounting period,

shall be treated for the purposes of this Chapter as if it were an amount of non-trading deficit on the company's loan relationships for that accounting period which, pursuant to section 83(3A) of this Act, falls to be carried forward and set against non-trading profits of succeeding accounting periods (and this paragraph shall apply accordingly).]¹

[(6)]¹ In this paragraph ''non-trading profits'', in relation to a company, means so much of any profits of the company (of whatever description) as do not consist in trading income for the purposes of section 393A of the Taxes Act 1988 (setting-off of trading losses against profits of the same or an earlier period).

Commentary—*Simon's Direct Tax Service* **D2.1136.**
Amendments—¹ Sub-para (1) substituted, in sub-para (2), words substituted for the words ''The amount to which the claim relates'', former sub-para (3) renumbered as para (6) and sub-paras (3)–(5) inserted, and Heading amended; by FA 2002 s 82, Sch 25 paras 1, 19(1)–(4), (5)(a), with effect for accounting periods beginning after 30 September 2002.

Sub-para (1) previously read as follows—

"(1) This paragraph applies where a claim is made under section 83(2)(d) of this Act for the whole or any part of the deficit to be carried forward and set against non-trading profits for the next accounting period.".

Construction of Schedule

5 In this Schedule "the deficit" and "the deficit period" shall be construed by reference to section 83(1) of this Act.

SCHEDULE 9

LOAN RELATIONSHIPS: SPECIAL COMPUTATIONAL PROVISIONS

Section 84

Commentary—*Simon's Direct Tax Service* **Division D2.11.**

Distributions

1—[(1)][1] The credits and debits to be brought into account for the purposes of this Chapter shall not include any credits or debits relating to any amount falling, when paid, to be treated as a distribution.

[(2) Nothing in section 80(5) of this Act prevents an amount which, by virtue of sub-paragraph (1) above, is not brought into account for the purposes of this Chapter from being brought into account for the purposes of corporation tax apart from this Chapter.][1]

Commentary—*Simon's Direct Tax Service* **D2.1115.**
Amendments—[1] Figure inserted, and sub-para (2) added, by FA 2002 s 82, Sch 25 paras 1, 20 with effect for accounting periods beginning after 30 September 2002.

[Life assurance policies and capital redemption policies

1A—(1) The credits and debits to be brought into account for the purposes of this Chapter shall not include any credits or debits relating to—

(a) a policy of life assurance; or
(b) a capital redemption policy, within the meaning of Chapter 2 of Part 13 of the Taxes Act 1988.

(2) Nothing in section 80(5) of this Act prevents an amount which, by virtue of sub-paragraph (1) above, is not brought into account for the purposes of this Chapter from being brought into account for the purposes of corporation tax apart from this Chapter.][1]

Amendments—[1] This paragraph to be inserted by FA 2002 s 82, Sch 25 paras 1, 21 with effect for accounting periods beginning after 30 September 2002.

Late interest

2—(1) This paragraph applies for the purpose of bringing debits into account for the purposes of this Chapter in respect of a debtor relationship of a company [("the debtor company") in a case falling within any of sub-paragraphs (1A) to (1D) below.][1]

[(1A) The first case is where there is, for the relevant accounting period, a connection (within the meaning of section 87 of this Act) between the debtor company and a person standing in the position of creditor as respects the loan relationship.][1]

[(1B) The second case is where there is a time in the relevant accounting period when the debtor company is a close company and a person standing in the position of a creditor as respects the loan relationship is—

(a) a participator in the debtor company,
(b) the associate of a person who is such a participator at that time, or
(c) a company of which such a participator has control or in which such a participator has a major interest,

and the debt is not one that is owed to, or to persons acting for, a limited partnership which is a collective investment scheme within the meaning of section 235 of the Financial Services and Markets Act 2000.][1]

[(1C) The third case is where—

(a) a person standing in the position of a creditor as respects the loan relationship is a company ("the creditor company"); and
(b) there is a time in the relevant accounting period when the debtor company has a major interest in the creditor company or the creditor company has a major interest in the debtor company.][1]

[(1D) The fourth case is where the loan is one made by trustees of a retirement benefits scheme (as defined in section 611 of the Taxes Act 1988) and—

(a) there is a time in the relevant accounting period when the debtor company is the employer of employees to whom the scheme relates; or (*b*) there is for the relevant accounting period a connection, within the meaning of section 87 of this Act, between the debtor company and such an employer; or

(*c*) a company is such an employer and there is a time in the relevant accounting period when the debtor company has a major interest in that company or that company has a major interest in the debtor company.]¹

(2) If—

(*a*) interest payable under that relationship is not paid within the period of twelve months following the end of the accounting period in which it would (apart from this paragraph) be treated as accruing, and

(*b*) credits representing the full amount of the interest are not for any accounting period brought into account for the purposes of this Chapter in respect of the corresponding creditor relationship,

then debits relating to that interest shall be brought into account on the assumption that the interest does not accrue until it is paid.

[(3) References in this paragraph to a person who stands in the position of a creditor as respects a loan relationship include references to a person who indirectly stands in that position by reference to a series of loan relationships or money debts which would be loan relationships if a company directly stood in the position of creditor or debtor.]¹

[(4) Where this paragraph applies in relation to a debtor relationship by virtue of sub-paragraph (3) above, the reference to the corresponding creditor relationship in sub-paragraph (2)(*b*) above is a reference to the creditor relationship of the person who indirectly stands in the position of a creditor as respects the debtor relationship.]¹

[(5) For the purposes of this section, section 414 of the Taxes Act 1988 (meaning of "close company" in the Tax Acts) shall have effect with the omission of subsection (1)(*a*) (exclusion of companies not resident in the United Kingdom).]¹

[(6) In this paragraph—

"associate" has the meaning given by section 417(3) and (4) of the Taxes Act 1988;

"control" has the same meaning as in section 87 of this Act (see section 87A);

"participator", in relation to a close company, means a person who, by virtue of section 417 of the Taxes Act 1988, is a participator in the company for the purposes of Part 11 of that Act, other than a person who is a participator for those purposes by virtue only of being a loan creditor of the company;

"the relevant accounting period" means the accounting period mentioned in sub-paragraph (2)(*a*) above.]¹

[(7) Paragraph 20 below (major interests) applies for the purposes of this paragraph.]¹

Revenue Internal Guidance—Company Taxation Manual COT12200 (meaning of "paid" in relation to interest). COT12426 (meaning of "brought into account"). COT12426 (examples of interest allowed when paid). **Amendments**—¹ In sub-para (1), words substituted for the words "where an authorised accruals basis of accounting is used as respects that relationship in pursuance of section 87 of this Act", and sub-paras (1A)–(1D), (3)–(7) inserted by FA 2002 s 82, Sch 25 paras 1, 22 with effect for accounting periods beginning after 30 September 2002.

Options etc

3—(1) This paragraph applies for determining the credits and debits to be brought into account for any accounting period in accordance with an authorised accruals basis of accounting, where—

(*a*) the answer to the question whether any amount will become due under a loan relationship after the end of that period,

(*b*) the amount which will become due under a loan relationship after the end of that period, or

(*c*) the time after the end of that period when an amount will become due under a loan relationship,

depends on the exercise of an option by a party to the relationship or an associate of his, or is otherwise under the control of such a party or an associate of his.

(2) It shall be assumed that the party or his associate will exercise his power to determine whether and on what date any amount will become due in the manner which (apart from taxation) appears, as at the end of the accounting period in question, to be the most advantageous to that party.

(3) In this paragraph "associate" has the meaning given for the purposes of Part XI of the Taxes Act 1988 by section 417(3) and (4) of that Act.

Foreign exchange gains and losses

4—(1) *The credits and debits to be brought into account for the purposes of this Chapter shall be computed disregarding so much of any authorised accounting method as, by requiring the translation or conversion of amounts from one currency into another, has the effect that credits and debits produced by that method include sums in which profits, gains or losses arising from fluctuations in the value of a currency are to any extent represented.*

(2) *This paragraph is without prejudice to the provisions of Chapter II of Part II of the Finance Act 1993 (exchange gains and losses).*

Cross reference—See Exchange Gains and Losses (Insurance Companies) Regulations, SI 1994/3231 reg 8A (insurance company may elect to disregard this paragraph where the assets representing a loan relationship fall within SI 1994/3231 reg 7).
Amendment—This paragraph repealed by FA 2002 ss 79(1)(a), (3), 141, Sch 40 Pt 3(10) with effect for accounting periods beginning after 30 September 2002.

Bad debt etc

5—(1) In determining the credits and debits to be brought into account in accordance with an accruals basis of accounting, a departure from the assumption in the case of the creditor relationships of a company that every amount payable under those relationships will be paid in full as it becomes due shall be allowed (subject to paragraph 6 below) to the extent only that—

   (a) a debt is a bad debt;
   (b) a doubtful debt is estimated to be bad; or
   (c) a liability to pay any amount is released.

[(1A) Such a departure shall be made only where the first and second conditions (set out in sub-paragraphs (2) and (2A) below) are satisfied.]¹

(2) [The first condition is that]¹ the accounting arrangements allowing the departure also require appropriate adjustments, in the form of credits, to be made if the whole or any part of an amount taken or estimated to represent an amount of bad debt is paid or otherwise ceases to be an amount in respect of which such a departure is allowed.

[(2A) The second condition is that, in determining the credits and debits to be brought into account in respect of exchange gains and losses, the accounting arrangements allowing the departure require a debt—

   (a) to be left out of account, to the extent that such a departure is allowed; and
   (b) to be taken into account again, to the extent that it is represented by credits brought into account under subparagraph (2) above.]¹

(3) Where—

   (a) a liability to pay any amount under a debtor relationship of a company is released, and
   (b) the release takes place in an accounting period for which an authorised accruals basis of accounting is used as respects that relationship,

no credit in respect of the release shall be required to be brought into account in the case of that company if the release is part of a relevant arrangement or compromise (within the meaning given by section 74(2) of the Taxes Act 1988) or the relationship is one as respects which section 87 of this Act requires the use of an authorised accruals basis of accounting.

Commentary—*Simon's Direct Tax Service* **D2.1120.**
Revenue Internal Guidance—Company Taxation Manual COT12471 (if debt written off in accounts, rather than merely provided against, this suggests it is bad rather than just doubtful; general provision for doubtful debts not allowed; debt is released only when creditor has formally waived debtor's obligation to pay).
COT12557, 12558 (worked examples on purchase of debt).
Amendments—¹ Sub-paras (1A), (2A) inserted, and in sub-para (2), words substituted for the words "Such a departure shall be made only where"; by FA 2002 s 79, Sch 23 paras 1, 8 with effect for accounting periods beginning after 30 September 2002.

Bad debt etc where parties have a connection

6—(1) This paragraph applies where for any accounting period section 87 of this Act requires an authorised accruals basis of accounting to be used as respects a creditor relationship of a company.

(2) The credits and debits which for that period are to be brought into account for the purposes of this Chapter in accordance with that accounting method shall be computed subject to sub-paragraphs (3) to (6) [and paragraphs 6A and 6B]² below.

(3) The assumption that every amount payable under the relationship will be paid in full shall be applied as if no departure from that assumption were authorised by virtue of [paragraph 5(1)]¹ above except where it is allowed by sub-paragraph (4) [or paragraph 6A or 6B]²below.

(4) A departure from that assumption shall be allowed in relation to a liability to pay any amount to the company ("the creditor company") under the creditor relationship where—

   (a) in consideration of, or of any entitlement to, any shares forming part of the ordinary share capital of the company on whom the liability would otherwise have fallen, the creditor company treats the liability as discharged; and
   (b) the condition specified in sub-paragraph (5) below is satisfied.

(5) That condition is that there would be no connection between the two companies for the accounting period in which that consideration is given if the question whether there is such a connection for that period fell to be determined, in accordance with section 87 of this Act, by reference only to times before the creditor company acquired possession of, or any entitlement to, the shares in question.

(6) Where the company ceases in the accounting period in question to be a party to the relationship—

   (a) the debits brought into account for that period in respect of that relationship shall not (subject to sub-paragraph (7) below) be more than they would have been had the company not ceased to be a party to the relationship; and (*b*) the credits brought into account for that period in respect of the relationship shall not (subject to that sub-paragraph) be less than they would have been in those circumstances.

(7) In determining for the purposes of sub-paragraph (6) above the debits and credits that would have been brought into account if a company had not ceased to be a party to a loan relationship, no account shall be taken of any amounts that would have accrued at times after it ceased to be a party to the relationship.

[(8) Nothing in this paragraph affects the debits or credits to be brought into account for the purposes of this Chapter in respect of exchange gains or losses arising from a debt.][1]

Commentary—*Simon's Direct Tax Service* **D2.1121, 1122, 1161.**
Concession C28—Bad debt relief allowed in limited circumstances even where lender and borrower connected with one another under FA 1996 s 87.
Revenue Internal Guidance—Company Taxation Manual COT12520–12531 (worked examples on change from connected to unconnected and vice versa).
COT12551 (worked example on sale of debt after connection ceased).
COT12557, 12558 (worked examples on purchase of debt).
COT12570–12581 (application of sub-ss (4)–(6): debt for equity swaps: worked examples).
Amendments—[1] In sub-para (3), words substituted for the words "paragraph 5"; and sub-para (8) inserted, by FA 2002 s 79, Sch 23 paras 1, 9 with effect for accounting periods beginning after 30 September 2002.
[2] Words inserted in sub-paras (2), (3) by FA 2002 s 82, Sch 25 paras 1, 24 with effect for accounting periods beginning after 30 September 2002.

[Bad debt etc parties having connection and creditor in insolvent liquidation etc

6A—(1) This paragraph applies in any case falling within paragraph 6(1) above where—

(*a*) the company which has the creditor relationship ("the creditor company") has gone into insolvent liquidation;
(*b*) an administration order is in force in relation to that company under Part 2 of the Insolvency Act 1986 or Part 3 of the Insolvency (Northern Ireland) Order 1989;
(*c*) an appointment of a provisional liquidator is in force in relation to that company under section 135 of that Act or Article 115 of that Order; or
(*d*) under the law of a country or territory outside the United Kingdom, an event has occurred, or circumstances exist, corresponding to any of those described in paragraphs (*a*) to (*c*) above.

(2) Where this paragraph applies, a departure from the assumption that every amount payable under the relationship will be paid in full shall be allowed in relation to any amount accruing to the creditor company under the relationship—

(*a*) in a case falling within paragraph (*a*) of sub-paragraph (1) above, at a time after the commencement of the winding up;
(*b*) in a case falling within paragraph (*b*) of that sub-paragraph, at a time when the administration order is in force;
(*c*) in a case falling within paragraph (*c*) of that sub-paragraph, at a time when the appointment of the provisional liquidator is in force; or
(*d*) in a case falling within paragraph (*d*) of that sub-paragraph, at a time corresponding to that described in paragraph (*a*), (*b*) or (*c*) above (as the case may be).

(3) For the purposes of this paragraph, a company goes into insolvent liquidation if it goes into liquidation, as defined in section 247(2) of the Insolvency Act 1986 or Article 6(2) of the Insolvency (Northern Ireland) Order 1989, at a time when its assets are insufficient for the payment of its debts and other liabilities and the expenses of the winding up.][1]

Amendments—[1] This paragraph inserted by by FA 2002 s 82, Sch 25 paras 1, 25 with effect for accounting periods beginning after 30 September 2002.

[Bad debt etc: companies becoming connected

6B—(1) Where—

(*a*) paragraph 6 above applies in relation to a creditor relationship of a company (the "creditor company") in the case of an accounting period, and
(*b*) another company (the "debtor company") stands in the position of a debtor as respects the money debt,

a departure from the assumption mentioned in paragraph 6(3) above shall be allowed in accordance with sub-paragraphs (2) to (4) or (5) to (7) below.

(2) A departure from the assumption mentioned in paragraph 6(3) above shall be allowed in the case of the creditor relationship if—

(*a*) a departure has been allowed under paragraph 5(1) above in respect of the creditor relationship for a previous accounting period for which there was no connection between the creditor company and the debtor company; and
(*b*) the first accounting period of the creditor company for which there is or was such a connection is an accounting period beginning on or after 1st October 2002.

(3) A departure shall be allowed under sub-paragraph (2) above to the extent only that the debits brought into account by the creditor company for the accounting period in respect of the relationship are not more than they would have been if it were assumed that the aggregate of the amounts payable

in respect of the creditor relationship were equal to the pre-connection value of the asset representing the creditor relationship.

(4) The "pre-connection value" of the asset representing the creditor relationship is the value of that asset as shown in the accounts of the creditor company at the end of the accounting period immediately preceding the accounting period mentioned in sub-paragraph (2)(b) above.

(5) A departure from the assumption mentioned in paragraph 6(3) above shall be allowed for the accounting period in respect of the creditor relationship, if the conditions in sub-paragraph (6) below are satisfied.

(6) The conditions are that—

(a) the creditor company acquired its rights under the relationship by virtue of an arm's length transaction;

(b) for the accounting period in which it acquired those rights, there was no connection between the creditor company and the person from whom it acquired the asset; and

(c) there had been no such connection between the creditor company and the debtor company at any time in the period which—

(i) begins 4 years before the date on which the company acquired those rights; and

(ii) ends twelve months before that date.

(7) A departure shall be allowed under sub-paragraph (5) above to the extent only that the debits brought into account by the creditor company for the accounting period in respect of the relationship are not more than they would have been if—

(a) it were assumed that the aggregate of the amounts payable in respect of the relationship were equal to the price paid by the company to acquire its rights; and

(b) no departure were allowed from the assumption in paragraph (a) above.

(8) For the purposes of this paragraph, there is a connection between a company and another person at any time if at that time—

(a) the other person is a company and one of the companies has control of the other, or

(b) the other person is a company and both companies are under the control of the same person,

and there is a connection between a company and another person for an accounting period if there is a connection (within paragraph (a) or (b) above) between the company and the person at any time in that accounting period.

(9) For the purposes of sub-paragraph (8) above "control" has the meaning given for the purposes of section 87 by section 87A of this Act.]¹

Amendments—¹ This paragraph inserted by by FA 2002 s 82, Sch 25 paras 1, 26 with effect for accounting periods beginning after 30 September 2002.

[Bad debt etc: departure not permitted by paragraph 6: cessation of connection

6C—(1) Where, in the case of a creditor relationship of a company,—

(a) a departure that would otherwise have been allowed under paragraph 5(1) above in respect of an amount is or was, by virtue of paragraph 6 above, not allowed in the case of an accounting period; and

(b) there is a subsequent accounting period for which there is, within the meaning of section 87 of this Act, no connection between the company and any person standing in the position of a debtor as respects that debt,

sub-paragraphs (2) and (3) below shall apply.

(2) Where this sub-paragraph applies, no credit shall be required to be brought into account by virtue of paragraph 5(2) above in respect of an amount—

(a) for the first accounting period falling within sub-paragraph (1)(b) above, or

(b) for any subsequent such accounting period,

to the extent that the amount in question corresponds to the amount mentioned in sub-paragraph (1)(a) above.

(3) Where this sub-paragraph applies, no debit shall be brought into account in respect of an amount—

(a) for the first accounting period falling within sub-paragraph (1)(b) above, or

(b) for any subsequent such accounting period,

to the extent that the amount in question represents the amount mentioned in sub-paragraph (1)(a) above.]¹

Amendments—¹ This paragraph inserted by by FA 2002 s 82, Sch 25 paras 1, 27 with effect for accounting periods beginning after 30 September 2002.

Writing-off of government investments

7—(1) Where any government investment in a company is written off by the release of a liability to pay any amount under a debtor relationship of the company, no credit shall be required, in the case of that company, to be brought into account for the purposes of this Chapter in respect of that release.

(2) Subsections (7) and (8) of section 400 of the Taxes Act 1988 shall apply, as they apply for the purposes of that section, for construing the reference in sub-paragraph (1) above to the writing-off of a government investment.

Restriction on writing off overseas sovereign debt etc

8—(1) This paragraph applies for the purposes of the use, as respects any loan relationship of a company and in conformity with paragraph 5 above, of an authorised accruals basis of accounting.

(2) Where the company is one to which a relevant overseas debt is owed, the debits and credits to be brought into account on that basis for the purposes of this Chapter shall be determined, for any accounting period of the company, on the assumption that it is not permissible for more than the relevant percentage of the debt to be estimated to be bad.

(3) For the purposes of this paragraph the relevant percentage of a debt for any accounting period of a company is (subject to sub-paragraph (4) below) such percentage (which may be zero) as may be determined, by reference to the position at the end of the relevant period of account, in accordance with regulations made by the Treasury.

(4) Where, apart from this sub-paragraph, the relevant percentage of a debt for any accounting period is more than the adjusted base percentage of that debt for that period, the relevant percentage of the debt for that period shall be taken to be equal to its adjusted base percentage for that period.

(5) For the purposes of this paragraph the adjusted base percentage of a debt for any accounting period shall be calculated by—

(a) taking the percentage which, in accordance with section 88B of the Taxes Act 1988 and any regulations made under that section, was or (assuming the debt to have been a debt of the company at the end of the base period) would have been the base percentage for that debt; and

(b) increasing that base percentage by five percentage points for every complete year (except the first) between—

(i) the time by reference to which the base percentage was, or would have been, determined, and

(ii) the end of the relevant period of account.

(6) In this paragraph "the relevant period of account", in relation to any accounting period of a company, means the period of account ending with that accounting period or, if a period of account does not end with that accounting period, the last period of account of the company to end before the end of that accounting period.

(7) In this paragraph "relevant overseas debt" means any debt which—

(a) satisfies one of the conditions specified in sub-paragraph (8) below; but

(b) is neither interest on a debt nor a debt which represents the consideration for the provision of goods or services.

(8) Those conditions are—

(a) that the debt is owed by an overseas State authority; or

(b) that payment of the debt is guaranteed by an overseas State authority; or

(c) that the debt is estimated to be bad for the purposes of this Chapter wholly or mainly because due payment is or may be prevented, restricted or subjected to conditions—

(i) by virtue of any law of a State or other territory outside the United Kingdom or any act of an overseas State authority; or

(ii) under any agreement entered into in consequence or anticipation of such a law or act.

(9) In this paragraph "overseas State authority" means—

(a) a State or other territory outside the United Kingdom;

(b) the government of such a State or territory;

(c) the central bank or other monetary authority of such a State or territory;

(d) a public or local authority in such a State or territory; or

(e) a body controlled by such a State, territory, government, bank or authority;

and for this purpose "controlled" shall be construed in accordance with section 840 of the Taxes Act 1988.

(10) The Treasury shall not make any regulations under this paragraph unless a draft of them has been laid before and approved by a resolution of the House of Commons.

Further restriction on bringing into account losses on overseas sovereign debt etc

9—(1) This paragraph applies where—

(a) for an accounting period in which a company ceases to be a party to a loan relationship ("the loss period") any amount falls for the purposes of this Chapter to be brought into account in respect of that relationship in accordance with an authorised accruals basis of accounting;

(b) by the bringing into account of that amount in that period a loss incurred in connection with a relevant overseas debt falling within sub-paragraph (2) below is treated for the purposes of this Chapter as arising in that period;

(c) the amount of the loss is greater than 5 per cent. of the debt; and (*d*) the loss is not one incurred on a disposal of the debt to an overseas State authority in a case in which the State or territory by reference to which it is an overseas State authority is the same as that by reference to which the debt is a relevant overseas debt.

(2) A relevant overseas debt falls within this sub-paragraph if—

(*a*) a deduction has been made in respect of the debt in accordance with section 74(1)(*j*) of the Taxes Act 1988 for any period of account of the company ending before 1st April 1996;

(*b*) any debit relating to the debt has been brought into account for the purposes of this Chapter in accordance with so much of any authorised accruals basis of accounting as relates to the matters mentioned in paragraph 5(1)(*a*) to (*c*) above; or

(*c*) the debt is one acquired by the company on or after 20th March 1990 for a consideration greater than the price which it might reasonably have been expected to fetch on a sale in the open market at the time of acquisition.

(3) Where this paragraph applies, the amounts brought into account for the purposes of this Chapter in the loss period shall be such as to secure that only so much of the loss as does not exceed 5 per cent. of the debt is treated for the purposes of this Chapter as arising in the loss period; but sub-paragraph (4) below applies as respects further parts of that loss until the loss is exhausted.

(4) A part of the loss may, in accordance with sub-paragraph (5) below, be brought into account for the purposes of this Chapter in the form of a debit for any accounting period after the loss period ("a subsequent period").

(5) The amount of the debit brought into account under sub-paragraph (4) above for any subsequent period shall not exceed such amount as, together with any parts of the loss which for earlier periods have been represented by—

(*a*) the amount of the loss treated as arising in the loss period in accordance with sub-paragraph (3) above, or

(*b*) debits brought into account in accordance with this sub-paragraph,

is equal to 5 per cent. of the debt for each complete year that has elapsed between the beginning of the loss period and the end of the subsequent period.

(6) In this paragraph "overseas State authority" and "relevant overseas debt" have the same meanings as in paragraph 8 above.

(7) References in this paragraph to a loss do not include so much of any loss as falls to be disregarded for the purposes of this Chapter by virtue of paragraph 10 below or to any loss incurred before 1st April 1996.

Imported losses etc

10—(1) This paragraph applies in the case of a company ("the chargeable company") for an accounting period ("the loss period") where—

(*a*) an authorised accruals basis of accounting is used as respects a loan relationship of that company for the loss period;

(*b*) in accordance with that basis of accounting there is an amount which would fall (apart from this paragraph) to be brought into account for the purposes of this Chapter in respect of that relationship;

(*c*) by the bringing into account of that amount in that period a loss incurred in connection with that loan relationship would be treated for the purposes of this Chapter as arising in that period; and

(*d*) that loss is referable in whole or in part to a time when the relationship was not subject to United Kingdom taxation.

(2) The amounts brought into account for the purposes of this Chapter in the loss period shall be such as to secure that no part of the loss that is referable to a time when the relationship was not subject to United Kingdom taxation shall be treated for the purposes of this Chapter as arising in the loss period or any other accounting period of the chargeable company.

(3) For the purposes of this paragraph a loss is referable to a time when a relationship is not subject to United Kingdom taxation to the extent that, at the time to which the loss is referable, the chargeable company would not have been chargeable to tax in the United Kingdom on any profits or gains arising from the relationship.

(4) Sub-paragraph (3) above shall have effect where the chargeable company was not a party to the relationship at the time to which the loss is referable as if the reference to that company were a reference to the person who at that time was in the same position as respects the relationship as is subsequently held by the chargeable company.

[(5) Amounts which, by virtue of this paragraph, are not brought into account for the purposes of this Chapter as respects any matter are in consequence also amounts which, in accordance with section 80(5) of this Act, are not to be brought into account for the purposes of corporation tax as respects that matter apart from this Chapter.][1]

Commentary—*Simon's Direct Tax Service* D2.1123.
Revenue Internal Guidance—Company Taxation Manual COT12633, 12640 (worked examples).
Amendments—[1] Sub-para (5) inserted by FA 2002 s 82, Sch 25 paras 1, 28 with effect for accounting periods beginning after 30 September 2002.

Transactions not at arm's length

11—(1) [Subject to sub-paragraphs (2) to (3A) below][2], where—

(*a*) debits or credits in respect of a loan relationship of a company fall to be brought into account for the purposes of this Chapter in accordance with an authorised accounting method,

(*b*) those debits or credits relate to amounts arising from, or incurred for the purposes of, a related transaction, and

(*c*) that transaction is not a transaction at arm's length,

the debits or credits given by that method shall be determined on the assumption that the transaction was entered into on the terms on which it would have been entered into between independent persons.

(2) Sub-paragraph (1) above shall not apply to debits arising from the acquisition of rights under a loan relationship where those rights are acquired for less than market value.

(3) Sub-paragraph (1) above does not apply—

[(*a*) in the case of any related transaction between two companies that are—

(i) members of the same group, and

(ii) within the charge to corporation tax in respect of that transaction; or

(*b*) in relation to a member of a group of companies, in the case of any transaction which is part of a series of transactions having the same effect as a transaction falling within paragraph (*a*) above.][1]

[(3A) Sub-paragraph (1) above shall not apply to any exchange gains or losses.][2]

(4) ...[3]

[(5) In this paragraph references to a company which is a member of a group of companies shall be construed in accordance with section 170 of the Taxation of Chargeable Gains Act 1992.][1]

Commentary—*Simon's Direct Tax Service* **D2.1150.**
Cross references—See FA 2000 Sch 29 para 44(5) (the main amendments made to TCGA 1992 s 170 by FA 2000 Sch 29 para 1 have effect for the purposes of this section with effect for transactions after 31 March 2000).
Amendments—[1] Sub-paras (3)(*a*), (*b*), (5) substituted by FA 2000 s 102, Sch 29 para 44(1)–(3), (5) with effect for transactions entered into, or series of transactions begun, after 31 March 2000.
[2] In sub-para (1), words substituted for the words ''Subject to sub-paragraphs (2) and (3) below,''; and sub-para (3A) inserted, by FA 2002 s 79, Sch 23 para 1, 10 with effect for accounting periods beginning after 30 September 2002.
[3] Sub-para (4) repealed by FA 2002 s 141, Sch 40 Pt 3(10) with effect for accounting periods beginning after 30 September 2002. Sub-para (4) previously read—

''(4) In this paragraph ''related transaction'' has the same meaning as in section 84 of this Act.''.

[Exchange gains and losses where loan not on arm's length terms

11A—(1) Where a company has a debtor relationship in an accounting period and in the case of that accounting period—

(*a*) the whole of any interest or other distribution out of the assets of the company in respect of securities of the company that represent the relationship falls by virtue of section 209(2)(*da*) or (*e*)(vii) of the Taxes Act 1988 to be regarded as a distribution for the purposes of the Corporation Tax Acts, or

(*b*) the profits and losses of the company fall by virtue of Schedule 28AA to that Act (provision not at arm's length) to be computed for tax purposes as if the loan had not been made,

any exchange gains or losses which arise in that accounting period in respect of a liability representing the debtor relationship shall be left out of account in determining the debits or credits to be brought into account for the purposes of this Chapter.

(2) Where a company has a debtor relationship in an accounting period and in the case of that accounting period—

(*a*) part of any interest or other distribution out of the assets of the company in respect of securities of the company that represent the relationship falls by virtue of section 209(2)(*da*) or (*e*)(vii) of the Taxes Act 1988 to be regarded as a distribution for the purposes of the Corporation Tax Acts, or

(*b*) the profits and losses of the company fall by virtue of Schedule 28AA to that Act to be computed for tax purposes as if the loan had in part not been made,

the proportionate part of any exchange gains or losses which arise in that accounting period in respect of a liability representing the debtor relationship shall be left out of account in determining the debits or credits to be brought into account for the purposes of this Chapter.

(3) In sub-paragraph (2) above, the ''proportionate part'' of an exchange gain or loss is that part which bears to the whole the proportion which—

(*a*) in a case falling within paragraph (*a*) of that sub-paragraph, the part of the interest or other distribution out of assets that falls to be regarded as a distribution for the purposes of the Corporation Tax Acts bears to the whole of that interest or other distribution out of assets; or (*b*) in a case falling within paragraph (*b*) of that sub-paragraph, the part of the loan that falls to be treated as if it had not been made bears to the whole of the loan.

(4) Where—

(*a*) a company has a creditor relationship in an accounting period,

(*b*) the transaction giving rise to the loan is such that it would not have been entered into at all if the parties had been dealing at arm's length, and

(*c*) there is no corresponding debtor relationship such that there would, or would apart from section 84A(2) to (10) of this Act, fall to be brought into account for the purposes of this Chapter, in respect of exchange gains or losses from that debtor relationship, debits or (as the case may be) credits corresponding to, and of the same amount as, the credits or debits that would (apart from this paragraph) fall to be brought into account for the purposes of this Chapter in respect of exchange gains or losses from the creditor relationship,

any exchange gains or losses which arise in that accounting period in respect of an asset representing the creditor relationship shall be left out of account in determining the debits or credits to be brought into account for the purposes of this Chapter.

(5) Where—

(*a*) a company has a creditor relationship in an accounting period,

(*b*) the circumstances are such that, had the parties to the transaction giving rise to the loan been dealing at arm's length, the terms would have been the same, except that the amount of the loan would have been an amount (referred to in sub-paragraph (6) below as "the adjusted amount") greater than nil but less than its actual amount, and

(*c*) there is no such corresponding debtor relationship as satisfies, in relation to that creditor relationship, the condition set out in sub-paragraph (4)(*c*) above,

sub-paragraph (4) above shall not apply, but the excess portion of any exchange gain or loss which arises in the accounting period in respect of an asset representing the creditor relationship shall be left out of account in determining the debits or credits to be brought into account for the purposes of this Chapter.

(6) In sub-paragraph (5) above, the "excess portion" of an exchange gain or loss is so much of the gain or loss as remains after subtracting that part which bears to the whole the proportion which the adjusted amount bears to the amount of the loan.]¹

Amendments—¹ This paragraph inserted by FA 2002 s 79, Sch 23 paras 1, 11 with effect for accounting periods beginning after 30 September 2002.

Continuity of treatment: groups etc

12—(1) Subject to paragraph 15 below, this paragraph applies where, as a result of—

[(*a*) a related transaction between two companies that are—

(i) members of the same group, and

(ii) within the charge to corporation tax in respect of that transaction,

(*b*) a series of transactions having the same effect as a related transaction between two companies each of which—

(i) has been a member of the same group at any time in the course of that series of transactions, and

(ii) is within the charge to corporation tax in respect of the related transaction,]¹

[(*c*) a transfer between two companies of business consisting of the effecting or carrying out of contracts of long-term insurance which has effect under an insurance business transfer scheme;]²

(*d*) any transfer between two companies which is a qualifying overseas transfer within the meaning of paragraph 4A of Schedule 19AC to the Taxes Act 1988 (transfer of business of overseas life insurance company),

one of those companies ("the transferee company") directly or indirectly replaces the other ("the transferor company") as a party to a loan relationship.

(2) The credits and debits to be brought into account for the purposes of this Chapter in the case of the two companies shall be determined as follows—

(*a*) the transaction, or series of transactions, by virtue of which the replacement takes place shall be disregarded except for the purpose of identifying the company in whose case any debit or credit not relating to that transaction, or those transactions, is to be brought into account; and

(*b*) the transferor company and the transferee company shall be deemed (except for that purpose) to be the same company.

[(2A) This paragraph does not apply where the transferor company uses an authorised mark to market basis of accounting as respects the loan relationship, but in any such case—

(*a*) the amount to be brought into account by the transferee company in respect of the transaction, the result of the series of transactions, or the transfer must be the fair value of the asset, or of the rights under or interest in the asset, as at the date on which the transferee company becomes party to the loan relationship; and (*b*) paragraph (*b*) of sub-paragraph (2) above shall have effect for the purposes of section 90 of this Act (changes of accounting method).][5]

(3) This paragraph does not apply by virtue of sub-paragraph (1)(*a*) or (*b*) above in relation to any transfer of an asset, or of any rights under or interest in an asset, where the asset was within one of the categories set out in section 440(4)(*a*) to (*e*) of the Taxes Act 1988 (assets held for certain categories of [long-term][3] business) either immediately before the transfer or immediately afterwards.

(4) This paragraph does not apply by virtue of sub-paragraph (1)(*c*) or (*d*) above in relation to any transfer of an asset, or of any rights under or interest in an asset, where—

(*a*) the asset was within one of the categories set out in section 440(4) of the Taxes Act 1988 immediately before the transfer; and

(*b*) is not within that category immediately afterwards.

(5) For the purposes of sub-paragraph (4) above, where one of the companies is an overseas life insurance company an asset shall be taken to be within the same category both immediately before the transfer and immediately afterwards if it—

(*a*) was within one category immediately before the transfer; and

(*b*) is within the corresponding category immediately afterwards.

(6) References in this paragraph to one company replacing another as a party to a loan relationship shall include references to a company becoming a party to any loan relationship under which its rights are equivalent to those of the other company under a loan relationship of which that other company has previously ceased to be a party.

(7) For the purposes of sub-paragraph (6) above a person's rights under a loan relationship are equivalent to rights under another such relationship if they entitle the holder of an asset representing the relationship—

(*a*) to the same rights against the same persons as to capital, interest and dividends, and

(*b*) to the same remedies for the enforcement of those rights,

notwithstanding any difference in the total nominal amounts of the assets, in the form in which they are held or in the manner in which they can be transferred.

[(8) Sub-paragraph (5) of paragraph 11 above has effect for the purposes of this paragraph as it has effect for the purposes of that paragraph.][4]

[(9) In this paragraph—

"contracts of long-term insurance" means contracts which fall within Part II of Schedule 1 to the Financial Services and Markets Act 2000 (Regulated Activities) Order 2001;

"insurance business transfer scheme" means a scheme falling within section 105 of the Financial Services and Markets Act 2000, including an excluded scheme falling within Case 2, 3 or 4 of subsection (3) of that section;

"overseas life insurance company" has the same meaning as in Chapter 1 of Part 12 of the Taxes Act 1988.][2]

Commentary—*Simon's Direct Tax Service* **D2.1125.**
Revenue Internal Guidance—Company Taxation Manual COT12621 (worked examples).
COT12624 (series of transactions can include a novation of the loan relationship; the word "indirectly" in sub-para (1) does not extend the scope of the provision further than the reference to a series of transactions).
This paragraph modified in relation to specified transactions by the Friendly Societies (Modification of the Corporation Tax Acts) Regulations, SI 1997/473 reg 52.
Cross references—See FA 1999 s 81(9) (application of this sub-para (2) above in relation to acquisitions disregarded under insurance companies concession).
FA 2000 Sch 29 para 44(5) (the main amendments made to TCGA 1992 s 170 by FA 2000 Sch 29 para 1 have effect for the purposes of this section with effect for transactions after 31 March 2000).
Amendments—[1] Sub-para (1)(*a*), (*b*) substituted by FA 2000 s 102, Sch 29 para 44(1), (4), (5) with effect for transactions entered into, or series of transactions begun, after 31 March 2000.
[2] Sub-paras (1)(*c*), (9) substituted by the Financial Services and Markets Act 2000 (Consequential Amendments) (Taxes) Order, SI 2001/3629 arts 92, 94 with effect from 1 December 2001 immediately after the coming into force of the Financial Services and Markets Act 2000 ss 411, 432(1), and Schedule 20. This amendment has effect for any transfer under a scheme falling within the Financial Services and Markets Act 2000 s 105, including an excluded scheme falling within Case 2, 3 or 4 of the Financial Services and Markets Act 2000 s 105(3).
[3] Word in sub-para (3) substituted by SI 2001/3629 arts 92, 96 with effect from 1 December 2001 immediately after the coming into force of the Financial Services and Markets Act 2000 ss 411, 432(1), and Schedule 20.
[4] Sub-para (8) substituted by FA 2002 s 79, Sch 23 paras 1, 12 with effect for accounting periods beginning after 30 September 2002. Sub-para (8) previously read as follows—
"(8) Sub-paragraphs (4) and (5) of paragraph 11 above have effect for the purposes of this paragraph as they have effect for the purposes of that paragraph."
[5] Sub-para (2A) inserted by FA 2002 s 82, Sch 25 paras 1, 29 with effect for accounting periods beginning after 30 September 2002.

Loan relationships for unallowable purposes

13—(1) Where in any accounting period a loan relationship of a company has an unallowable purpose,—

[(*a*) the debits, and

(*b*) the credits in respect of exchange gains,][1]

which, for that period fall, in the case of that company, to be brought into account for purposes of this Chapter shall not include so much of the debits [or credits (as the case may be)][1] given by the authorised accounting method used as respects that relationship as, on a just and reasonable apportionment, is attributable to the unallowable purpose.

[(1A) Amounts which, by virtue of this paragraph, are not brought into account for the purposes of this Chapter as respects any matter are in consequence also amounts which, in accordance with section 80(5) of this Act, are not to be brought into account for the purposes of corporation tax as respects that matter apart from this Chapter.][2]

(2) For the purposes of this paragraph a loan relationship of a company shall be taken to have an unallowable purpose in an accounting period where the purposes for which, at times during that period, the company—

  (a) is a party to the relationship, or
  (b) enters into transactions which are related transactions by reference to that relationship,

include a purpose ("the unallowable purpose") which is not amongst the business or other commercial purposes of the company.

(3) For the purposes of this paragraph the business and other commercial purposes of a company do not include the purposes of any part of its activities in respect of which it is not within the charge to corporation tax.

(4) For the purposes of this paragraph, where one of the purposes for which a company—

  (a) is a party to a loan relationship at any time, or
  (b) enters into a transaction which is a related transaction by reference to any loan relationship of the company,

is a tax avoidance purpose, that purpose shall be taken to be a business or other commercial purpose of the company only where it is not the main purpose, or one of the main purposes, for which the company is a party to the relationship at that time or, as the case may be, for which the company enters into that transaction.

(5) The reference in sub-paragraph (4) above to a tax avoidance purpose is a reference to any purpose that consists in securing a tax advantage (whether for the company or any other person).

(6) In this paragraph—

  ...[3]

  "tax advantage" has the same meaning as in Chapter I of Part XVII of the Taxes Act 1988 (tax avoidance).

Commentary—*Simon's Direct Tax Service* D2.1151.
Amendments—[1] Sub-paras (1)(a), (b) substituted for the words "the debits" where first occurring", words inserted by FA 2002 s 79, Sch 23 paras 1, 13 with effect for accounting periods beginning after 30 September 2002.
[2] Sub-para (1A) inserted by FA 2002 s 82, Sch 25 paras 1, 30 with effect for accounting periods beginning after 30 September 2002.
[3] The following definition of "related transaction" repealed by FA 2002 s 141, Sch 40 Pt 3(10) with effect for accounting periods beginning after 30 September 2002.

  " 'related transaction'has the same meaning as in section 84 of this Act; and".

Debits and credits treated as relating to capital expenditure

14—(1) This paragraph applies where any debit or credit given by an authorised accounting method for any accounting period in respect of a loan relationship of a company is allowed by [generally accepted accounting practice][1] to be treated, in the accounts of the company, as an amount brought into account in determining the value of a fixed capital asset or project.

(2) Notwithstanding the application to it of the treatment allowed by [generally accepted accounting practice][1]the debit or credit shall be brought into account for the purposes of corporation tax, for the accounting period for which it is given, in the same way as a debit or credit which, in accordance with normal accountancy practice, is brought into account in determining the company's profit or loss for that period.

[(3) No debit may be brought into account by virtue of this paragraph if it is taken into account in arriving at the amount of expenditure in relation to which a debit may be given by Schedule 29 to the Finance Act 2002 (gains and losses of a company from intangible fixed assets).][1]

Commentary—*Simon's Direct Tax Service* D2.1124.
Revenue Internal Guidance—Company Taxation Manual COT12440 (interest debited to work in progress is allowed as and when written off in the accounts: WIP is not regarded as relating to capital expenditure).
Amendments—[1] In sub-paras (1), (2) words "generally accepted accounting practice" substituted for the words "normal accountancy practice", and sub-para (3) inserted by FA 2002 s 82, Sch 25 paras 1, 31 with effect for accounting periods beginning after 30 September 2002. This substitution is also made by FA 2002 s 103(4)(d) with effect from 24 July 2002.

Repo transactions and stock-lending

15—(1) In determining the debits and credits to be brought into account for the purposes of this Chapter in respect of any loan relationship, it shall be assumed that a disposal or acquisition to which this paragraph applies is not a related transaction...[2].

(2) This paragraph applies to any such disposal or acquisition of rights or liabilities under the relationship as is made in pursuance of any repo or stock-lending arrangements.

(3) In this paragraph "repo or stock-lending arrangements" means any arrangements consisting in or involving an agreement or series of agreements under which provision is made—

    (*a*) for the transfer from one person to another of any rights under that relationship; and

    (*b*) for the transferor, or a person connected with him, subsequently to be or become entitled, or required—

        (i) to have the same or equivalent rights transferred to him; or

        (ii) to have rights in respect of benefits accruing in respect of that relationship on redemption.

(4) For the purposes of sub-paragraph (3) above rights under a loan relationship are equivalent to rights under another such relationship if they entitle the holder of an asset representing the relationship—

    (*a*) to the same rights against the same persons as to capital, interest and dividends, and

    (*b*) to the same remedies for the enforcement of those rights,

notwithstanding any difference in the total nominal amounts of the assets, in the form in which they are held or in the manner in which they can be transferred.

[(4A) In consequence of sub-paragraph (1) above—

    (*a*) the person transferring the rights mentioned in sub-paragraph (3)(*a*) above does not, as a result of the transfer, fall to be regarded for the purposes of this Chapter as ceasing to be party to the loan relationship; and

    (*b*) the person to whom those rights are transferred does not, as a result of the transfer, fall to be regarded for the purposes of this Chapter as being party to the loan relationship;

but nothing in sub-paragraph (1) or paragraph (*b*) above shall prevent any credit in respect of interest from being brought into account for the purposes of this Chapter by the person described in that paragraph.][1]

(5) Nothing in this paragraph shall prevent any redemption or discharge of rights or liabilities under a loan relationship to which any repo or stock-lending arrangements relate from being treated for the purposes of this Chapter as a related transaction (within the meaning of section 84 of this Act).

(6) This paragraph is without prejudice to section 730A(2) and (6) of the Taxes Act 1988 (deemed payments of loan interest in the case of the sale and repurchase of securities).

[(6A) Nothing in this paragraph affects section 807A(2A) of the Taxes Act 1988 (double taxation relief in the case of repo or stock lending agreement).][1]

(7) Section 839 of the Taxes Act 1988 (connected persons) applies for the purposes of this paragraph.

Commentary—*Simon's Direct Tax Service* **D2.1117.**
Modification—This paragraph shall have effect as if the definition of "repo or stock lending arrangements" in sub-para (3) also
    included provision under an agreement for the original owner, or a person connected with him, to become entitled to either the
    rights accruing on a euroconversion of the loan relationship, or, where the rights include payment or payments on the
    euroconversion other than interest of an amount which results in an aggregate that does not exceed 500 euros, either the whole
    of those rights or the whole of those rights apart from that payment: see European Single Currency (Taxes) Regulations,
    SI 1998/3177 reg 19.
Amendments—[1] Sub-paras (4A), (6A) inserted by FA 2002 s 82, Sch 25 paras 1, 32 with effect for accounting periods beginning
    after 30 September 2002.
[2] Words "for the purposes of section 84 of this Act" repealed by FA 2002 s 141, Sch 40 Pt 3(10) with effect for accounting
    periods beginning after 30 September 2002.

Imputed interest

16—(1) This paragraph applies where, in pursuance of [Schedule 28AA to the Taxes Act 1988 (provision not at arm's length)][1], any amount falls to be treated as interest payable under a loan relationship of a company.

(2) [That Schedule][1] shall have effect, notwithstanding the provisions of any authorised accounting method, so as to require credits or debits relating to the deemed interest to be brought into account for the purposes of this Chapter to the same extent as they would be in the case of an actual amount of interest accruing or becoming due and payable under the loan relationship in question.

Amendments—[1] Words substituted in sub-ss (1) and (2) by FA 1998 s 108 with effect for corporation tax in relation to accounting
    periods ending after 30 June 1999 (by virtue of Finance Act 1994, Section 199, (Appointed Day) Order, SI 1998/3173 art 2).

Discounted securities where companies have a connection

17—(1) This paragraph applies as respects any accounting period ("the relevant period") where—

    (*a*) a debtor relationship of a company ("the issuing company") is represented by a relevant discounted security issued by that company;

    [(*b*) at any time in that period another company stands in the position of a creditor as respects that security;][1]

    (*c*) for that period there is a connection between the issuing company and the other company; and

    (*d*) credits representing the full amount of the discount that is referable to that period are not for any accounting period brought into account for the purposes of this Chapter in respect of the corresponding creditor relationship.

(2) The debits falling in the case of the issuing company to be brought into account for the purposes of this Chapter in respect of the loan relationship shall be adjusted so that every debit relating to the

amount of the discount that is referable to the relevant period is brought into account for the accounting period in which the security is redeemed, instead of for the relevant period.

(3) References in this paragraph to the amount of the discount that is referable to the relevant period are references to the amount relating to the difference between—

 (a) the issue price of the security, and

 (b) the amount payable on redemption,

which (apart from this paragraph) would for the relevant period be brought into account for the purposes of this Chapter in the case of the issuing company.

(4) In this paragraph "relevant discounted security" has the same meaning as in Schedule 13 to this Act; and the provisions of that Schedule shall apply for the purposes of this paragraph for determining the difference between the issue price of a security and the amount payable on redemption as they apply for the purposes of paragraph 3(3) of that Schedule.

(5) For the purposes of this paragraph there is a connection between one company and another for the relevant period if (subject to the following provisions of this paragraph)—

 (a) there is a time in that period ...¹, when one of the companies has had control of[, or a major interest in,]¹ the other; or

 (b) there is a time in that period ...¹ when both the companies have been under the control of the same person.

(6) ...²

(7) ...²

[(8) Any reference in this paragraph to a person who stands in the position of a creditor as respects a relevant discounted security includes a reference to a person who indirectly stands in that position by reference to a series of relevant discounted securities.]¹

[(8A) Where this paragraph applies by virtue of sub-paragraph (8) above, the reference to the corresponding creditor relationship in sub-paragraph (1)(d) above is a reference to the creditor relationship of the company which indirectly stands in the position of a creditor as respects the relevant discounted security.]¹

[(9) For the purposes of this paragraph "control", in relation to a company, has the same meaning as in section 87 of this Act (see section 87A).]¹

[(10) Paragraph 20 below (major interests) applies for the purposes of this paragraph.]¹

Commentary—*Simon's Direct Tax Service* D2.1119.
Cross reference—See FA 1996 Sch 13 paras 3(1), (1A), 10(4), 13(9) (application of these sub-paras (as inserted by FA 1999 s 61) concerning the meaning of "relevant discounted securities" for the purposes of this paragraph with effect for accounting periods ending on or after 15 February 1999, but not in respect of any amount brought into account where the debtor company was no longer subject to any liability under it on that day, by virtue of FA 1999 s 65(10))).
Amendments—¹ Sub-para (1)(b) substituted, in sub-para (5), words ", or in the period of two years before the beginning of that period" repealed, and words inserted; in sub-para (5)(b), words ", or in those two years" repealed; sub-paras (8), (8A) substituted for sub-para (8), and sub-paras (9), 10) substituted for sub-para (9), by FA 2002 ss 82, 141, Sch 25 paras 1, 33, Sch 40 Pt 3(12) with effect for accounting periods beginning after 30 September 2002.
Sub-para (1)(b) previously read as follows—
 "(b) the benefit of that security is available to another company at any time in that period;"
Sub-para (8) previously read as follows—
 "(8) For the purposes of this paragraph the benefit of a security is available to a company if—
 (a) that security, or any entitlement to rights attached to it, is beneficially owned by that company; or
 (b) that company is indirectly entitled, by reference to a series of loan transactions, to the benefit of any rights attached to the security."
Sub-para (9) previously read as follows—
 "(9) Subsections (2) to (6) of section 416 of the Taxes Act 1988 (meaning of "control") shall apply for the purposes of this paragraph as they apply for the purposes of Part XI of that Act.".
² Sub-paras (6), (7) repealed by FA 2002 s 141, Sch 40 Pt 3(12) with effect for accounting periods beginning after 30 September 2002. Sub-paras (6), (7) previously read thus—
 ("6) Two companies which have at any time been under the control of the same person shall not, by virtue of that fact, be taken for the purposes of this paragraph to be companies between whom there is a connection if the person was the Crown, a Minister of the Crown, a government department, a Northern Ireland department, a foreign sovereign power or an international organisation.
 (7) Section 88 of this Act shall apply for the purposes of this paragraph in the case of a debtor relationship of a company represented by a relevant discounted security as it would apply for the purposes of section 87 of this Act in the case of the corresponding creditor relationship of the company holding that security and, accordingly, as if—
 (a) the reference to section 87 of this Act in section 88(4)(b) were a reference to this paragraph; and
 (b) section 88(5) were omitted.".

Discounted securities of close companies

18—(1) This paragraph applies for any accounting period [("the relevant period")]¹ where—

 (a) a debtor relationship of a close company [("the issuing company")]¹is represented by a relevant discounted security issued by the company; ...¹

 [(b) at any time in that period there is a person who stands in the position of a creditor as respects that security and who at that time is—]¹

  (i) a participator in the company;

  (ii) an associate of such a participator; or

(iii) a company of which such a participator has control[; and

(c) the debt is not one that is owed to, or to persons acting for, a limited partnership which is a collective investment scheme within the meaning of section 235 of the Financial Services and Markets Act 2000.][1]

[(1A) But for any such accounting period this paragraph shall not apply in relation to that debtor relationship if—

(a) at all times in the period when there is such a person as is described in sub-paragraph (1)(b) above, that person is a company; and

(b) credits representing the full amount of the discount that is referable to the period are brought into account for the purposes of this Chapter in respect of the corresponding creditor relationship.][1]

[(2) The debits falling in the case of the issuing company to be brought into account for the purposes of this Chapter in respect of the loan relationship shall be adjusted so that every debit relating to the amount of the discount that is referable to the relevant period ("the relevant debits") is brought into account for the accounting period in which the security is redeemed, instead of for the relevant period.

This sub-paragraph does not apply where the relevant period is the accounting period in which the security is redeemed.][1]

[(2A) Where at some (but not all) times in the relevant period there is such a person as is described in sub-paragraph (1)(b) above—

(a) part only of the relevant debits shall be brought into account in accordance with sub-paragraph (2) above; and

(b) that part is the part which bears to the whole of the relevant debits the proportion which the part of the relevant period for which there is such a person bears to the whole of that period.][1]

[(2B) References in this paragraph to the amount of the discount that is referable to an accounting period are references to the amount relating to the difference between—

(a) the issue price of the security, and

(b) the amount payable on redemption,

which (apart from sub-paragraphs (2) and (2A) above) would for that accounting period be brought into account for the purposes of this Chapter in the case of the issuing company.][1]

[(2C) Any reference in this paragraph to a person who stands in the position of a creditor as respects a relevant discounted security includes a reference to a person who indirectly stands in that position by reference to a series of relevant discounted securities.][1]

[(2D) Where this paragraph applies by virtue of sub-paragraph (2C) above, the reference to the corresponding creditor relationship in sub-paragraph (1A)(c) above is a reference to the creditor relationship of the person who indirectly stands in the position of a creditor as respects the relevant discounted security.][1]

(3) In this paragraph "relevant discounted security" has the same meaning as in Schedule 13 to this Act; and the provisions of that Schedule shall apply for the purposes of this paragraph for determining the difference between the issue price of a security and the amount payable on redemption as they apply for the purposes of paragraph 3(3) of that Schedule.

[(3A) For the purposes of this paragraph there is a connection between one company and another for an accounting period if—

(a) there is a time in that period when one of the companies has had control of the other, or

(b) there is a time in that period when both the companies have been under the control of the same person.][1]

[(3B) In this paragraph "control", in relation to a company, has the same meaning as in section 87 of this Act (see section 87A).][1]

(4) In this paragraph—

"associate" has the meaning given in section 417(3) and (4) of the Taxes Act 1988;
...[1]

"participator" [, in relation to a company,][1] means a person who, by virtue of section 417 of that Act, is a participator in the company for the purposes of Part XI of that Act, other than a person who is a participator for those purposes [by reason only that he is a loan creditor of the company.][1]

(5) In determining whether a person who carries on a business of banking is a participator in a company for the purposes of this paragraph, there shall be disregarded any securities of the company acquired by him in the ordinary course of his business.

Commentary—*Simon's Direct Tax Service* D2.1119.
Cross reference—See FA 1996 Sch 13 paras 3(1), (1A), 10(4), 13(9) (application of these sub-paras (as inserted by FA 1999 s 61) concerning the meaning of "relevant discounted securities" for the purposes of this paragraph with effect for accounting periods ending on or after 15 February 1999, but not in respect of any amount brought into account where the debtor company was no longer subject to any liability under it on that day, by virtue of FA 1999 s 65(10)).
Amendments—In sub-para (1), words inserted; and word "and" repealed; in sub-para (1)(b), words substituted for the words "at any time in or before that period that security has been beneficially owned by a person who at the time was—;" sub-paras (1)(c), (1A), (2B)–(2D), (3A), (3B) inserted; sub-paras (2), (2A) substituted for sub-para (2); in sub-para (4), definiton of

"control" repealed, and definition of "participator" amended; by FA 2002 ss 82, 141, Sch 25 paras 1, 34, Sch 40 Pt 3(12) with effect for accounting periods beginning after 30 September 2002.
Sub-para (2) previously read as follows—

"(2) The debits falling in the case of the company to be brought into account for the purposes of this Chapter in respect of the loan relationship shall be adjusted so that no amount is brought into account in respect of the difference between—

(a) the issue price of the security, and
(b) the amount payable on redemption,

for any accounting period before that in which the security is redeemed.".
Definition of "control" in sub-para (4) previously read as follows—

" 'control' shall be construed in accordance with section 416(2) to (6) of that Act; ...".
Definition of "participator" previously read as follows—

" 'participator' means a person who, by virtue of section 417 of that Act, is a participator in the company for the purposes of Part XI of that Act, other than a person who is a participator for those purposes by virtue only of his holding a relevant discounted security issued by the company.".

[Partnerships involving companies

19—(1) This paragraph applies where—

(a) a trade, profession or business is carried on by persons in partnership ("the firm");
(b) any of those persons is a company (a "company partner"); and
(c) a money debt is owed by or to the firm.

(2) In any such case—

(a) in computing the profits and losses of the trade, profession or business for the purposes of corporation tax in accordance with section 114(1) of the Taxes Act 1988 (computation as if the partnership were a company) no debits or credits shall be brought into account under this Chapter in relation to the money debt or any loan relationship that would fall to be treated for the purposes of the computation as arising from the money debt; but
(b) debits and credits shall be brought into account under this Chapter in relation to the money debt (and any loan relationship treated as arising from it) in accordance with the following provisions of this paragraph by each company partner for each of its accounting periods in which the conditions in sub-paragraph (1) above are satisfied.

(3) The debits and credits to be brought into account as mentioned in sub-paragraph (2)(b) above shall be determined separately in the case of each company partner.

(4) For the purpose of determining those debits and credits in the case of any particular company partner—

(a) the money debt owed by or to the firm shall be treated as if it were instead owed by or, as the case may be, to that company partner, for the purposes of the trade, profession or business which that company partner carries on,
(b) the money debt shall continue to be regarded as arising from a transaction for the lending of money if that is in fact the case (so that the company partner is treated as having a loan relationship), and
(c) anything done by or in relation to the firm in connection with the money debt shall be treated as done by or in relation to the company partner,

and debits and credits (the "gross debits and credits") shall be determined accordingly.

(5) The debits and credits to be brought into account under this Chapter pursuant to sub-paragraph (2)(b) above in the case of any particular company partner shall be that company partner's appropriate share of the gross debits and credits determined in accordance with sub-paragraph (4) above in the case of that company partner.

(6) For the purposes of sub-paragraph (5) above, the "appropriate share", in the case of a company partner, is the share that would be apportioned to that company partner if—

(a) the gross debits and credits determined in accordance with sub-paragraph (4) above in the case of that company partner fell to be apportioned between the partners; and
(b) the apportionment fell to be made in the shares in which any profit or loss computed in accordance with subsection (1) of section 114 of the Taxes Act 1988 would be apportioned between them under subsection (2) of that section.

(7) If, in a case where the money debt owed by or to the firm arises from a transaction for the lending of money, there is a time in an accounting period of any company at which—

(a) a person who is a company partner stands in relation to the debt in the position of a creditor (if it is owed by the firm) or a debtor (if it is owed to the firm) and accordingly has a creditor relationship or debtor relationship (as the case may be),
(b) that company partner, whether alone or taken together with one or more other company partners connected with it, controls the partnership, and
(c) that or any other company partner falls to be treated in accordance with sub-paragraph (4) above as if it had the debtor relationship or creditor relationship that corresponds to the creditor relationship or debtor relationship mentioned in paragraph (a) above,

sub-paragraph (8) below shall apply with respect to that accounting period, if it is an accounting period of a company partner mentioned in paragraph (a) or (c) above.

(8) Where this sub-paragraph applies, there shall be taken for the purposes of this Chapter to be a connection by virtue of section 87(3)(*a*) of this Act for the accounting period of the company partner mentioned in paragraph (*a*) of sub-paragraph (7) above, between that company partner and each company partner (including that company partner) that falls within paragraph (*c*) of that sub-paragraph.

(9) For the purposes of sub-paragraph (7) above, one company partner is connected with another at any time in an accounting period if at that or any other time in the accounting period one controls the other or both are under the control of the same person.

(10) The only accounting method authorised for use by a company partner in determining the debits and credits to be brought into account under this paragraph is an authorised accruals basis of accounting, but this sub-paragraph is subject to sub-paragraph (11) below.

(11) Where the company partner uses an authorised mark to market basis of accounting in relation to its interest in the partnership, the only accounting method authorised for use in determining the debits and credits to be brought into account under this paragraph by that company partner is an authorised mark to market basis of accounting, unless a provision of this Chapter requires the use of an authorised accruals basis of accounting.

(12) Subsection (3) of section 84A of this Act does not apply in relation to a company partner as respects the debits and credits to be brought into account by virtue of this paragraph except to the extent that, in the accounts of the firm, exchange gains and losses are carried to or sustained by a reserve in a manner corresponding to that described in that section in relation to a company.

(13) Where the firm holds a relevant discounted security, within the meaning of paragraph 17 above, each of the partners shall be treated for the purposes of this paragraph as beneficially entitled to that share of the security to which he would be entitled if all the partners were companies and such an apportionment as is described in sub-paragraph (6)(*b*) above were made.

(14) In this paragraph ''control''—

    (*a*) in relation to a company, has the same meaning as in section 87 of this Act (see section 87A); and

    (*b*) in relation to a partnership, has the meaning given by section 840 of the Taxes Act 1988.]¹

Amendments—¹ This paragraph inserted by FA 2002 s 82, Sch 25 paras 1, 35 with effect for accounting periods beginning after 30 September 2002.

[Interpretation of references to major interests

20—(1) For the purposes of any provision which applies this paragraph, the cases where a company (''company A'') has a major interest in another company (''company B'') at any time are those cases where at that time—

    (*a*) company A and one other person, taken together, have control of company B; and

    (*b*) company A and the other person each have interests, rights and powers representing at least 40 per cent of the holdings, rights and powers in respect of which company A and the other person fall to be taken as having control of company B; and

    (*c*) company A, or a company connected with it, and the other person, or, if that person is a company, a company connected with it, both satisfy the first condition, or both satisfy the second condition, in sub-paragraph (2) below.

(2) A person—

    (*a*) satisfies the first condition if he stands in the position of a creditor in relation to a loan relationship as respects which company B stands in the position of a debtor; and

    (*b*) satisfies the second condition if he stands in the position of a debtor in relation to a loan relationship as respects which company B stands in the position of a creditor.

(3) The reference in sub-paragraph (1)(*b*) above to interests, rights and powers does not include interests, rights or powers arising from shares held by a company if—

    (*a*) a profit on a sale of the shares would be treated as a trading receipt of a trade carried on by the company; and

    (*b*) the shares are not, within the meaning of Chapter 1 of Part 12 of the Taxes Act 1988, assets of an insurance company's long-term insurance fund (see section 431(2) of that Act).

(4) For the purposes of sub-paragraph (1) above, any question—

    (*a*) whether two persons taken together have control of a company at any time, or

    (*b*) whether a person has at any time interests, rights and powers representing at least 40 per cent of the holdings, rights and powers in respect of a company,

shall be determined after attributing to any person which is a company all the interests, rights and powers of any company connected with it.

(5) Where section 114 of the Taxes Act 1988 (partnerships involving companies: special rules for computing profits and losses) applies in relation to a partnership, any property, rights or powers held or exercisable for the purposes of the partnership shall be treated for the purposes of this paragraph, as respects any time in an accounting period of the partnership, as if—

(*a*) the property, rights or powers had been apportioned between, and were held or exercisable by, the partners severally, and

(*b*) the apportionment had been in the shares in which the profit or loss of the accounting period of the partnership would be apportioned between the partners under subsection (2) of that section,

but taking the references in paragraphs (*a*) and (*b*) above to partners as not including a reference to the general partner of a limited partnership which is a collective investment scheme within the meaning of section 235 of the Financial Services and Markets Act 2000.

(6) Where a trade, profession or business is carried on by two or more persons in partnership (''the firm'') and the firm stands in the position of a creditor or debtor as respects a money debt, any question—

(*a*) whether a company has a major interest (within the meaning of this paragraph) in another company for an accounting period in the case of a loan relationship, or

(*b*) to what extent any amount is to be treated under this Chapter in any particular way as a result of a company having, or (as the case may be) not having, such a major interest in another company,

shall be determined as if to the extent of his appropriate share each of the partners separately, instead of the firm, stood in the position of a creditor or, as the case may be, debtor as respects the money debt.

The reference in the words following paragraph (*b*) above to partners does not include a reference to the general partner of a limited partnership which is a collective investment scheme within the meaning of section 235 of the Financial Services and Markets Act 2000.

(7) For the purposes of sub-paragraph (6) above, a partner's ''appropriate share'' is the share that would be apportioned to him if an apportionment were made in the shares in which any profit or loss computed in accordance with subsection (1) of section 114 of the Taxes Act 1988 for the accounting period in question would be apportioned between the partners under subsection (2) of that section.

(8) For the purposes of this paragraph, a company is connected with another company if one controls the other or both are controlled by the same company.

(9) For the purposes of this paragraph, ''control'', in relation to a company, has the same meaning as in section 87 of this Act (see section 87A).

(10) Where two or more persons taken together have the power mentioned in subsection (1) of section 87A of this Act (as read with the other provisions of that section) they shall be taken for the purposes of sub-paragraph (1)(*a*) above to have control of the company in question.]¹

Amendments—¹ This paragraph inserted by FA 2002 s 82, Sch 25 paras 1, 36 with effect for accounting periods beginning after 30 September 2002.

SCHEDULE 10

LOAN RELATIONSHIPS: COLLECTIVE INVESTMENT SCHEMES

Section 98

Commentary—*Simon's Direct Tax Service* **Division D2.11.**
Modification—See the Open-ended Investment Companies (Tax) Regulations, SI 1997/1154 regs 3, 5,19 (modifications of this Schedule as it has effect in relation to open-ended investment companies).

[Investment trusts and venture capital trusts: capital reserves

1A—(1) Where any profits, gains or losses arising to an investment trust from a creditor relationship for an accounting period are carried to or sustained by a capital reserve in accordance with the Statement of Recommended Practice used for that accounting period, those profits, gains or losses must not be brought into account as credits or debits for the purposes of this Chapter, notwithstanding section 84(2)(*b*) of this Act.

(2) Where any profits, gains or losses arising to a venture capital trust from a creditor relationship for an accounting period—

(*a*) are carried to or sustained by a capital reserve in accordance with the Statement of Recommended Practice used for the accounting period as if the venture capital trust were an investment trust, or

(*b*) would be carried to or sustained by a capital reserve if the venture capital trust were an investment trust and were using that Statement of Recommended Practice,

those profits, gains or losses must not be brought into account as credits or debits for the purposes of this Chapter, notwithstanding section 84(2)(*b*) of this Act.

(3) For the purposes of this paragraph, the Statement of Recommended Practice used for an accounting period is—

(*a*) in relation to an accounting period for which it is permitted to be used, the Statement of Recommended Practice relating to Investment Trust Companies, issued by the Association of Investment Trust Companies in December 1995, as from time to time modified, amended or revised, or (*b*) in relation to any accounting period for which it is permitted to be used, any subsequent Statement of Recommended Practice relating to investment trusts, as from time to time modified, amended or revised.]¹

Commentary—*Simon's Direct Tax Service* **D2.1142.**
Orders—Investment Trusts (Approval of Accounting Methods for Creditor Relationships) Order, SI 2001/391.
Cross references—See Investment Trusts (Approval of Accounting Methods for Creditor Relationships) Order, SI 2001/391 (approves the use of two accounting methods for the creditor relationships of investment trusts).
Amendments—¹ Paragraph 1A substituted for paragraph 1 by FA 2002 s 82, Sch 25 paras 1, 37 with effect for accounting periods beginning after 30 September 2002. Paragraph 1 previously read as follows—

"Investment trusts

1—(1) This paragraph applies for the purposes of the application of this Chapter in relation to investment trusts and venture capital trusts.

(2) If the Treasury by order approve the use of an accounting method for the creditor relationships of investment trusts or venture capital trusts—

(*a*) that method, instead of any method for which section 85 of this Act provides, shall be used as respects the creditor relationships of the trusts for which it is approved; and
(*b*) this Chapter shall have effect (subject to the provisions of the order) as if the accounting method were, for the purposes for which it is approved, an authorised accruals basis of accounting.
(3) Where an approval is given under this paragraph, it must be an approval of one of the following—

(*a*) the use of an accruals basis of accounting appearing to the Treasury to be recognised by [generally accepted accounting practice] for use in the case of investment trusts;
(*b*) the use, with such modifications as may be provided for in the order, of an accruals basis of accounting appearing to them to be so recognised; or
(*c*) the use, with such modifications as may be so provided for, of an accounting method which, apart from the order, would be an authorised accruals basis of accounting.
(4) An order under this paragraph may provide for any approval of the use (with or without modifications) of a basis of accounting recognised by [generally accepted accounting practice] to have effect in relation to accounting periods beginning before the time as from which the use of that method is recognised and before the making of the order.".

[Authorised unit trusts

2A—(1) Where any profits, gains or losses arising to an authorised unit trust from a creditor relationship in an accounting period are capital profits, gains or losses, those profits, gains or losses must not be brought into account as credits or debits for the purposes of this Chapter, notwithstanding section 84(2)(*b*) of this Act.

(2) For the purposes of this paragraph, capital profits, gains or losses arising from a creditor relationship in an accounting period are such profits, gains or losses arising from a creditor relationship as fall to be dealt with under—

(*a*) the heading "net gains/losses on investments during the period", or
(*b*) the heading "other gains/losses",

in the statement of total return for the accounting period.

(3) For the purposes of sub-paragraph (2) above, the statement of total return for an accounting period is the statement of total return which, in accordance with the Statement of Recommended Practice used for the accounting period, must be included in the accounts contained in the annual report of the authorised unit trust which deals with the accounting period.

(4) For the purposes of sub-paragraph (3) above, "Statement of Recommended Practice" means—

(*a*) in relation to any accounting period for which it is required or permitted to be used, the Statement of Recommended Practice relating to Authorised Unit Trust Schemes issued by the Investment Management Regulatory Organisation Limited in January 1997, as from time to time modified, amended or revised; or
(*b*) in relation to any accounting period for which it is required or permitted to be used, any subsequent Statement of Recommended Practice relating to authorised unit trust schemes, as from time to time modified, amended or revised.

(5) The Treasury may by order amend this paragraph so as to alter the definition of capital profits, gains or losses in consequence of the modification, amendment, revision or replacement of a Statement of Recommended Practice.

(6) The power to make an order under this paragraph includes power—

(*a*) to make different provision for different cases; and

(*b*) to make such consequential, supplementary, incidental or transitional provision, or savings, as appear to the Treasury to be necessary or expedient (including provision amending any enactment or any instrument made under any enactment).]¹

Commentary—*Simon's Direct Tax Service* **D2.1140.**
Amendments—¹ Paragraphs 2A, 2B substituted for paragraph 2 by FA 2002 s 82, Sch 25 paras 1, 38 with effect for accounting periods beginning after 30 September 2002.
Paragraph 2 previously read as follows—

"Authorised unit trusts

2—(1) The provisions of this Chapter so far as they relate to the creditor relationships of a company shall not apply for the purposes of corporation tax in computing the profits or losses of an authorised unit trust.

(2) For the purposes of corporation tax the profits and gains, and losses, that are to be taken to arise from the creditor relationships of an authorised unit trust shall be computed—

(*a*) in accordance with the provisions applicable, in the case of unauthorised unit trusts, for the purposes of income tax; and

(b) as if the provisions so applicable had effect in relation to an accounting period of an authorised unit trust as they have effect, in the case of unauthorised unit trusts, in relation to a year of assessment.

(3) In relation to the first accounting period of any authorised unit trust to end after 31st March 1996, the reference in sub-paragraph (2)(a) above to the provisions applicable for the purposes of income tax is a reference to the provisions so applicable for the year 1996–97.

(4) In this paragraph "unauthorised unit trust" means the trustees of any unit trust scheme which is not an authorised unit trust but is a unit trust scheme for the purposes of section 469 of the Taxes Act 1988.".

[Open-ended investment companies

2B—(1) Where any profits, gains or losses arising to an open-ended investment company from a creditor relationship in an accounting period are capital profits, gains or losses, those profits, gains or losses must not be brought into account as credits or debits for the purposes of this Chapter, notwithstanding section 84(2)(b) of this Act.

(2) For the purposes of this paragraph, capital profits, gains or losses arising from a creditor relationship in an accounting period are such profits, gains or losses arising from a creditor relationship as fall to be dealt with under—

    (a) the heading "net gains/losses on investments during the period", or

    (b) the heading "other gains/losses",

in the statement of total return for the accounting period.

(3) For the purposes of sub-paragraph (2) above, the statement of total return for an accounting period is the statement of total return which, in accordance with the Statement of Recommended Practice used for the accounting period, must be included in the accounts contained in the annual report of the open-ended investment company which deals with the accounting period.

(4) For the purposes of sub-paragraph (3) above, "Statement of Recommended Practice" means—

    (a) in relation to any accounting period for which it is required or permitted to be used, the Statement of Recommended Practice relating to Open-Ended Investment Companies issued by the Financial Services Authority in November 2000, as from time to time modified, amended or revised; or

    (b) in relation to any accounting period for which it is required or permitted to be used, any subsequent Statement of Recommended Practice relating to open-ended investment companies, as from time to time modified, amended or revised.

(5) The Treasury may by order amend this paragraph so as to alter the definition of capital profits, gains or losses in consequence of the modification, amendment, revision or replacement of a Statement of Recommended Practice.

(6) The power to make an order under this paragraph includes power—

    (a) to make different provision for different cases; and

    (b) to make such consequential, supplementary, incidental or transitional provision, or savings, as appear to the Treasury to be necessary or expedient (including provision amending any enactment or any instrument made under any enactment).]¹

Amendments—¹ Paragraphs 2A, 2B substituted for paragraph 2 by FA 2002 s 82, Sch 25 paras 1, 38 with effect for accounting periods beginning after 30 September 2002.

Distributing offshore funds

[3—(1) For the purposes of paragraph 5(1) of Schedule 27 to the Taxes Act 1988 (computation of UK equivalent profit), the assumptions to be made in determining what, for any period, would be the total profits of an offshore fund are to include the assumptions in sub-paragraphs (2) and (3) below.

(2) The first assumption is that the provisions of this Chapter so far as they relate to the creditor relationships of a company do not apply for the purposes of corporation tax in computing the profits or loss of an offshore fund.

(3) The second assumption is that for the purposes of corporation tax the profits and gains, and losses, that are to be taken to arise from the creditor relationships of an offshore fund are to be computed—

    (a) in accordance with the provisions applicable, in the case of unauthorised unit trusts, for the purposes of income tax; and

    (b) as if the provisions so applicable had effect in relation to an accounting period of an offshore fund as they have effect, in the case of unauthorised unit trusts, in relation to a year of assessment.

(4) In this paragraph "unauthorised unit trust" means the trustees of any unit trust scheme which is not an authorised unit trust but is a unit trust scheme for the purposes of section 469 of the Taxes Act 1988.]¹

Commentary—*Simon's Direct Tax Service* **D2.1141.**
Modification—This section is modified, in relation to open-ended investment companies, by the Open-ended Investment Companies (Tax) Regulations 1997, SI 1997/1154, regs 3, 5.
Amendments—¹ This paragraph substituted by FA 2002 s 82, Sch 25 paras 1, 39 with effect for accounting periods beginning after 30 September 2002. Paragraph 3 previously read as follows—

"**3**—(1) For the purposes of paragraph 5(1) of Schedule 27 to the Taxes Act 1988 (computation of UK equivalent profit), the assumptions to be made in determining what, for any period, would be the total profits of an offshore fund are to include an assumption that paragraph 2 above applies in the case of that offshore fund as it applies in the case of any authorised unit trust.".

Company holdings in unit trusts and offshore funds

4—(1) This paragraph applies for the purposes of corporation tax in relation to any company where—

(a) at any time in an accounting period that company holds any of the following ("a relevant holding"), that is to say, any rights under a unit trust scheme or any relevant interests in an offshore fund; and

(b) there is a time in that period when that scheme or fund fails to satisfy the non-qualifying investments test.

(2) The Corporation Tax Acts shall have effect for that accounting period in accordance with sub-paragraphs (3) and (4) below as if the relevant holding were rights under a creditor relationship of the company.

(3) An accruals basis of accounting shall not be used for the purposes of this Chapter as respects the company's relevant holdings.

(4) The authorised mark to market basis of accounting used for any accounting period as respects a relevant holding shall not be taken, for the purposes of this Chapter, to require the bringing into account of any credit relating to any distributions of an authorised unit trust which become due and payable in that period other than interest distributions within the meaning of section 468L(3) of the Taxes Act 1988.

Commentary—*Simon's Direct Tax Service* **D2.1152.**
Cross references—See TCGA 1992 s 117B ("relevant holdings" within this paragraph not to be treated as qualifying corporate bonds in certain circumstances).
TCGA 1992 s 212(2A) (annual deemed disposal by insurance company of holdings of unit trusts etc.)

Holding becoming or ceasing to be paragraph 4 holding

5—(1) Section 116 of the 1992 Act (reorganisations etc involving qualifying corporate bonds) shall have effect in accordance with the assumptions for which this paragraph provides if—

(a) a relevant holding is held by a company both at the end of one accounting period and at the beginning of the next; and

(b) paragraph 4 above applies to that holding for one of those periods but not for the other.

(2) Where—

(a) the accounting period for which paragraph 4 above applies to the relevant holding is the second of the periods mentioned in sub-paragraph (1) above, and

(b) the first of those periods is not a period ending on 31st March 1996 or a period at the end of which there is deemed under section 212 of the 1992 Act to have been a disposal of the relevant holding,

the holding shall be assumed to have become a holding to which paragraph 4 above applies for the second of those periods in consequence of the occurrence, at the end of the first period, of a transaction such as is mentioned in section 116(1) of that Act.

(3) In relation to the transaction that is deemed to have occurred as mentioned in sub-paragraph (2) above—

(a) the relevant holding immediately before the beginning of the second accounting period shall be assumed to be the old asset for the purposes of section 116 of the 1992 Act; and

(b) the relevant holding immediately after the beginning of that period shall be assumed for those purposes to be the new asset.

(4) Where the accounting period for which paragraph 4 above applies to the relevant holding is the first of the periods mentioned in sub-paragraph (1) above, then, for the purposes of the 1992 Act—

(a) the holding shall be assumed to have become a holding to which paragraph 4 above does not apply for the second of those periods in consequence of the occurrence at the beginning of the second of those periods of a transaction such as is mentioned in section 116(1) of that Act;

(b) the relevant holding immediately before the beginning of that second period shall be assumed, in relation to that transaction, to be the old asset for the purposes of section 116 of the 1992 Act; and

(c) the relevant holding immediately after the beginning of that period shall be assumed, in relation to that transaction, to be the new asset for those purposes.

(5) In this paragraph "the 1992 Act" means the Taxation of Chargeable Gains Act 1992.

Commentary—*Simon's Direct Tax Service* **D2.1152.**

Opening valuation of paragraph 4 holding

6 Where—

(a) paragraph 5(2) above applies in the case of any relevant holding of a company, and

(b) for the purpose of bringing amounts into account for the purposes of this Chapter on the mark to market basis used for that period in pursuance of paragraph 4 above, an opening valuation of the holding falls to be made as at the beginning of that period,

the value of that asset at the beginning of that period shall be taken for the purpose of the opening valuation to be equal to whatever, in relation to a disposal immediately before the end of the previous accounting period, would have been taken to be the market value of the holding for the purposes of the Taxation of Chargeable Gains Act 1992.

Meaning of offshore funds

7—(1) For the purposes of paragraph 4 above an interest is a relevant interest in an offshore fund if—

(*a*) it is a material interest in an offshore fund for the purposes of Chapter V of Part XVII of the Taxes Act 1988; or

(*b*) it would be such an interest if the assumption mentioned in sub-paragraph (2) below were made.

(2) That assumption is that the unit trust schemes and arrangements referred to in paragraphs (*b*) and (*c*) of subsection (1) of section 759 of the Taxes Act 1988 are not limited to those which are also collective investment schemes.

Commentary—*Simon's Direct Tax Service* **D2.1152.**

Non-qualifying investments test

8—(1) For the purposes of paragraph 4 above a unit trust scheme or offshore fund fails to satisfy the non-qualifying investments test at any time when the market value of the qualifying investments exceeds 60 per cent of the market value of all the investments of the scheme or fund.

(2) Subject to sub-paragraph (8) below, in this paragraph ''qualifying investments'', in relation to a unit trust scheme or offshore fund, means investments of the scheme or fund which are of any of the following descriptions—

(*a*) money placed at interest;

(*b*) securities;

(*c*) shares in a building society;

(*d*) qualifying holdings in a unit trust scheme or an offshore fund [or an open-ended investment company][1]

[(*e*) derivative contracts whose underlying subject matter consists wholly of any one or more of the matters referred to in paragraphs (*a*) to (*d*) above;][4]

[(*f*) contracts for differences whose underlying subject matter consists wholly of interest rates or creditworthiness or both of those matters][4].

(3) For the purposes of sub-paragraph (2) above a holding in a unit trust scheme or offshore fund [or an open-ended investment company][1] is a qualifying holding at any time if—

(*a*) at that time, or

(*b*) at any other time in the same accounting period,

that scheme or fund [or company][1] would itself fail (even on the relevant assumption) to satisfy the non-qualifying investments test.

[(3A) For the purposes of sub-paragraph (3) above an open-ended investment company fails to satisfy the non-qualifying investments test at any time when the market value of the investments of the company which are qualifying investments exceeds 60 per cent of the market value of all its investments.][1]

(4) For the purposes of [sub-paragraphs (3) and (3A)][2] above the relevant assumption is that investments of the scheme or fund [or company][1] are qualifying investments in relation to that scheme or fund [or company][2] only if they fall within paragraphs (*a*) to (*c*)[, (*e*) and (*f*)][4] of sub-paragraph (2) above.

(5) References in this paragraph to investments of a unit trust scheme or offshore fund are references, as the case may be—

(*a*) to investments subject to the trusts of the scheme, or

(*b*) to assets of the fund,

but in neither case do they include references to cash awaiting investment.

[(5A) References in this paragraph to investments of an open-ended investment company are references to investments comprised in the scheme property of that company, but do not include references to cash awaiting investment.][1]

(6) References in this paragraph to a holding—

(*a*) in relation to a unit trust scheme, are references to an entitlement to a share in the investments of the scheme; and

(*b*) in relation to an offshore fund, are references to shares in any company by which that fund is constituted or any entitlement to a share in the investments of the fund;

[and

(*c*) in relation to an open-ended investment company, are references to shares in that company.][1]

[(6A) For the purposes of sub-paragraph (6)(*c*) above, where in respect of a given class of shares of an open-ended investment company—

(*a*) shares issued of that class consist of both smaller denomination shares and larger denomination shares, and (*b*) a person owns both smaller denomination shares and larger denomination shares of that class,

those shares owned by him shall be treated as being securities of the same class for the purposes of the provisions of the Tax Acts and the 1992 Act relating to ownership of shares in a company.]¹

[(6B) In sub-paragraph (6A) above, ''smaller denomination shares'' means shares to which are attached rights specified in the open-ended investment company's instrument of incorporation that are expressed in the smaller of two denominations, and ''larger denomination shares'' means shares to which are attached rights so specified that are expressed in the larger of two denominations.]¹

(7) In this paragraph ''security'' does not include shares in a company.

[(7A) In this paragraph—

(*a*) ''collective investment scheme'' has the meaning given by section [235 of the Financial Services and Markets Act 2000];

(*b*) ''open-ended investment company'' means, subject to sub-paragraph (7B) below, an open-ended investment company within the meaning given by section [236 of the Financial Services and Markets Act 2000] which is incorporated in the United Kingdom;

(*c*) ''scheme property'' of an open-ended investment company means, subject to sub-paragraph (7C)(*b*) below, the property subject to the collective investment scheme constituted by the company;

(*d*) references to a person owning shares in an open-ended investment company are references to—

(i) the beneficial owner of the shares,

(ii) where the shares are held on trust (other than a bare trust), the trustees of the trust, or

(iii) where the shares are comprised in the estate of a deceased person, the deceased's personal representatives.]¹

[(7B) Each of the parts of an umbrella company shall be regarded for the purposes of this paragraph as an open-ended investment company and the umbrella company as a whole shall not be so regarded and shall not be regarded as a company.]¹

[(7C) In relation to a part of an umbrella company—

(*a*) references in this paragraph to investments of an open-ended investment company shall have effect as references to such of the investments as under the arrangements referred to in sub-paragraph (7D) below form part of the separate pool to which that part of the umbrella company relates;

(*b*) references in this paragraph to the scheme property of an open-ended investment company shall have effect as if they were references to such property subject to the collective investment scheme constituted by the umbrella company as is comprised in the separate pool to which that part of the umbrella company relates;

(*c*) a person for the time being having rights in that part shall be regarded as the owner of shares in the open-ended investment company which that part is deemed to be by virtue of sub-paragraph (7B) above, and not as the owner of shares in the umbrella company itself.]¹

[(7D) In sub-paragraphs (7B) and (7C) above ''umbrella company'' means a company—

(*a*) which falls within the definition of ''open-ended investment company'' in section [236 of the Financial Services and Markets Act 2000],

(*b*) which is incorporated in the United Kingdom,

(*c*) whose instrument of incorporation provides for arrangements for such pooling as is mentioned in section [235(3)(*a*)]⁴ of that Act in relation to separate parts of the scheme property of the company, and

(*d*) the owners of shares in which are entitled to exchange rights in one part for rights in another;

and any reference to a part of an umbrella company is a reference to such of the arrangements as relate to a separate pool.]¹

[(7E) For the purposes of this paragraph—

''contract for differences'' has the same meaning as in paragraph 12 of Schedule 26 to the Finance Act 2002;

''derivative contract'' means—

(*a*) contract which is a derivative contract within the meaning of that Schedule, or

(*b*) a contract which is, in the accounting period in question, treated as if it were a derivative contract by virtue of paragraph 36 of that Schedule (contracts relating to holdings in unit trust schemes, open-ended investment companies and offshore funds);

''underlying subject matter'' has the same meaning as in paragraph 11 of that Schedule.]⁴

(8) The Treasury may by order amend this paragraph so as to extend or restrict the descriptions of investments of a unit trust scheme or offshore fund that are qualifying investments for the purposes of this paragraph.

Commentary—*Simon's Direct Tax Service* **D2.1152.**
Modification—This section is modified, in relation to open-ended investment companies, by the Open-ended Investment Companies (Tax) Regulations 1997, SI 1997/1154, regs 3, 5, 19(3)–(10).
Amendments—¹ Words in sub-paras (2), (3), (4), and sub-paras (3A), (5A), (6)(*c*), (6A), (6B), (7A) to (7D), inserted by Unit Trust Schemes and Offshore Funds (Non-qualifying Investments Test) Order 1997, SI 1997/213, with effect from 25 February 1997.

² Words in sub-para (4) substituted by Unit Trust Schemes and Offshore Funds (Non-qualifying Investments Test) Order 1997, SI 1997/213 reg 6(*a*) with effect from 25 February 1997.
³ Words in sub-paras (7A), (7D) substituted by the Financial Services and Markets Act 2000 (Consequential Amendments) (Taxes) Order, SI 2001/3629 arts 92, 95 with effect from 1 December 2001 immediately after the coming into force of the Financial Services and Markets Act 2000 ss 411, 432(1), Sch 20.
⁴ Sub-para (2)(*d*), (*e*) inserted, words in sub-para (4) inserted, and sub-para (7E) inserted, by FA 2002 s 83(1)(*b*), (3) Sch 27 para s 17, 20 with effect for accounting periods beginning after 30 September 2002.

Powers to make orders

9—(1) An order made by the Treasury under any provision of this Schedule may—

(*a*) make different provision for different cases; and

(*b*) contain such incidental, supplemental, consequential and transitional provision as the Treasury may think fit.

(2) Without prejudice to the generality of sub-paragraph (1) above, an order under paragraph 8(8) above may make such incidental modifications of paragraph 8(4) above as the Treasury may think fit.

Orders—Investment Trusts (Approval of Accounting Methods for Creditor Relationships) Order, SI 2001/391.

SCHEDULE 11

LOAN RELATIONSHIPS: SPECIAL PROVISIONS FOR INSURERS

Section 99

PART I

INSURANCE COMPANIES

I minus E basis

1—(1) Nothing in this Chapter shall be construed as preventing profits and gains arising from loan relationships of an insurance company from being included, where—

(*a*) the relationship is referable to any life assurance business or capital redemption business carried on by the company, and

(*b*) that business is business in respect of which the I minus E basis is applied,

in profits and gains on which the company is chargeable to tax in accordance with that basis.

[(1A) Where—

(*a*) the I minus E basis is applied for any accounting period in respect of any life assurance business carried on by an insurance company, and

(*b*) in that accounting period the insurance company is a party to a loan relationship which is to any extent referable to that business,

then, in applying the I minus E basis to that business, sections 92(1)(*f*), 93(1)(*a*) and (*b*) and 96(1)(*b*) of this Act shall be disregarded in relation to that loan relationship to that extent.]²

[(1B) In applying the I minus E basis for any accounting period in respect of any life assurance business carried on by an insurance company, no exchange gains or losses shall be taken to arise for the purposes of section 100 of this Act except to the extent that the money debt for the purposes of that section—

(*a*) arises as a result of an amount of income or expenses which falls to be taken into account in applying the I minus E basis not being paid when it is due and payable; or

(*b*) is one that is treated as a money debt for the purposes of that section by virtue of subsection (11)(a) of that section in accordance with subsection (12) of that section by reference to a Schedule A business or an overseas property business.

This sub-paragraph has effect notwithstanding sub-paragraph (1) above.]¹

(2) Where, for any accounting period, the I minus E basis is applied in respect of any life assurance business or capital redemption business carried on by an insurance company, the effect of applying that basis shall be—

(*a*) that none of the credits or debits falling for the purposes of this Chapter to be brought into account in respect of loan relationships of the company that are referable to that business shall be brought into account as mentioned in section 82(2) of this Act; but

(*b*) that (subject to the following provisions of this Schedule) all those credits and debits shall, instead, be brought into account, in applying that basis to that business, as non-trading credits or, as the case may be, non-trading debits;

and the reference in paragraph 2(1) below to non-trading credits and non-trading debits shall be construed accordingly.

Modification—In para 1(1)(*a*), (2), words "or capital redemption business" omitted in applying life assurance provisions of the Corporation Tax Acts to insurance companies carrying on capital redemption business with effect for accounting periods ending after 30 June 1999: see Insurance Companies (Capital Redemption Business) (Modification of the Corporation Tax Acts) Regulations, SI 1999/498 reg 15(2).

Amendments—[1] Sub-para (1B) inserted by FA 2002 s 79, Sch 23 paras 1, 14 with effect for accounting periods beginning after 30 September 2002.
[2] Sub-para (1A) inserted by FA 2002 s 82, Sch 25 paras 1, 40 with effect for accounting periods beginning after 30 September 2002.

Rules for different categories of business

2—(1) Where an insurance company carries on basic life assurance and general annuity business or capital redemption business or both of them, a separate computation, using only the non-trading credits and non-trading debits referable to the business in question, shall be made for the purposes of this Chapter in relation to that business or, as the case may be, in relation to each of them.

(2) References in any enactment to the computation of any profits of an insurance company in accordance with the provisions of the Taxes Act 1988 applicable to Case I of Schedule D shall have effect as if those provisions included the provisions of this Chapter but, in accordance with sub-paragraph (3) below, only to the extent that they relate to the bringing into account in accordance with section 82(2) of this Act of credits and debits in respect of a company's debtor relationships.

(3) Where an insurance company carries on—

    (a) life assurance business or any category of life assurance business, or
    (b) capital redemption business,

the credits and debits referable to that business, or category of business, that are given by this Chapter in respect of creditor relationships of the company shall be disregarded for the purposes of any computations falling to be made, in relation to that business or category of business, in accordance with provisions applicable to Case I of Schedule D.

(4) Accordingly (and notwithstanding section 80(5) of this Act), the amounts which are to be brought into account in any computations such as are mentioned in sub-paragraph (3) above shall be determined under the provisions applicable apart from this Chapter.

(5) To the extent that any profits of an insurance company in respect of any business or category of business fall to be computed in accordance with provisions applicable to Case I of Schedule D the credits and debits referable to that business or category of business that fall to be disregarded under sub-paragraph (3) above shall also be disregarded in any computations falling to be made for the purposes of this Chapter otherwise than in accordance with sub-paragraph (1) above.

Modifications—Sub-para (1) modified so far as this Schedule applies to the life or endowment business carried on by friendly societies (Modification of the Corporation Tax Acts) Regulations, SI 1997/473 regs 53, 53A (as amended by SI 1999/2636).
Substitution of sub-para (1), and substitution of words in sub-para (3), in applying life assurance provisions of the Corporation Tax Acts to insurance companies carrying on capital redemption business with effect for accounting periods ending after 30 June 1999: see the Insurance Companies (Capital Redemption Business) (Modification of the Corporation Tax Acts) Regulations, SI 1999/498 reg 15(3).
Sub-para (1) modified further in relation to companies carrying on capital redemption business by the Insurance Companies (Capital Redemption Business) (Modification of the Corporation Tax Acts) Regulations, SI 1999/498 reg 15, and so far as this Schedule (as so modified) applies to the life or endowment business carried on by friendly societies for accounting periods ending after 30 June 1999, by the Friendly Societies (Modification of the Corporation Tax Acts) Regulations, SI 1997/473 reg 53ZA (as inserted by SI 1999/2636).

Apportionments

3 Where—

    (a) any creditor relationship of an insurance company is represented by an asset which is an asset of a fund of the company or is linked to any category of insurance business, and
    (b) any question arises for the purposes of the Corporation Tax Acts as to the extent to which credits or debits given for the purposes of this Chapter in respect of that relationship are referable to any category of the company's [long-term][1] business,

section 432A of the Taxes Act 1988 (apportionment of insurance companies' income) shall have effect in relation to the credits and debits so given in respect of that relationship as it has effect in relation to the income arising from an asset.

Amendments—[1] Word in sub-para (b) substituted by the Financial Services and Markets Act 2000 (Consequential Amendments) (Taxes) Order, SI 2001/3629 arts 92, 96(b)(i) with effect from 31 December 2001 immediately after the coming into force of the Financial Services and Markets Act 2000 ss 411, 432(1), and Schedule 20.

[3A—(1) This paragraph applies where—

    (a) any [loan relationship][4] of an insurance company is represented by a liability which is a liability of the [long-term insurance][3] fund of the company; and
    (b) any question arises for the purposes of the Corporation Tax Acts as to the extent to which any debits or credits given for the purposes of this Chapter in respect of that *debt or*[4] liability are referable to any category of the company's [long-term][2] business.

(2) If any debits relate to interest payable in respect of the late payment of any benefits, they are referable to the category of [long-term][2] business which comprises the effecting and carrying out of the policies or contracts under which the benefits are payable.

(3) If the liability is a liability of an internal linked fund of the company, any debits or credits are referable—

(a) to the category of [long-term]² business to which the fund relates; or

(b) where the fund relates to two or more categories of such business, to those categories in the same proportion as the linked assets in the fund are apportioned to them under section 432ZA(4) of the Taxes Act 1988 (linked assets).

(4) In any case not falling within sub-paragraph (2) or (3) above, there shall be referable to any category of [long-term]² business the relevant fraction of any debits or credits.

(5) For the purpose of determining that fraction, subsections (6) and (8) of section 432A of the Taxes Act 1988 (apportionment of income and gains) shall have effect as if—

(a) the debits or credits were income not directly referable to any category of business;

(b) the reference in subsection (6)(a) to assets directly referable to a category of business were a reference to assets linked to that category of business; and

(c) subsection (9) of that section were omitted.

(6) In this paragraph ''internal linked fund'' has the same meaning as in section 432ZA of the Taxes Act 1988 (linked assets).]¹

Amendments—¹ This paragraph inserted by FA 2000 s 109(8) with effect for accounting periods beginning after 31 December 1999 and ending after 20 March 2000.
² Words in sub-paras (1)(b), (2), (3)(a), (4) substituted by the Financial Services and Markets Act 2000 (Consequential Amendments) (Taxes) Order, SI 2001/3629 arts 92, 96(b)(i) with effect from 31 December 2001 immediately after the coming into force of the Financial Services and Markets Act 2000 ss 411, 432(1), and Schedule 20.
³ Words in sub-para (1)(a) substituted by SI 2001/3629 arts 92, 96(2) with effect from 31 December 2001 immediately after the coming into force of the Financial Services and Markets Act 2000 ss 411, 432(1), and Schedule 20.
⁴ In sub-para (1)(a), words substituted for the words "money debt", and in sub-para (1)(b), words "debt or" repealed, by FA 2002 ss 79, 141, Sch 23 paras 1, 15, Sch 40 Pt 3(10) with effect for accounting periods beginning after 30 September 2002.

Treatment of deficit

4—(1) Where, in the case of any insurance company, a non-trading deficit on its loan relationships is produced for any accounting period (''the deficit period'') by any separate computation made under paragraph 2 above for—

(a) basic life assurance and general annuity business, or

(b) capital redemption business,

the following provisions of this paragraph shall apply in relation to that deficit, instead of section 83 of, and Schedule 8 to, this Act.

(2) On a claim made by the company in relation to the whole or any part of the deficit—

(a) the amount to which the claim relates shall be set off against any net income and gains of the deficit period referable to the relevant category of business and arising or accruing otherwise than in respect of loan relationships; and

(b) the amount of the net income and gains against which it is set off shall be treated as reduced accordingly;

and any such reductions shall be made before any deduction by virtue of section 76 of the Taxes Act 1988 of any expenses of management.

(3) Subject to the following provisions of this paragraph, on a claim made by the company in relation to the whole or any part of so much (if any) of the deficit as exceeds the amount of the net income and gains for the deficit period that are referred to in sub-paragraph (2)(a) above, the amount to which the claim relates shall be—

[(a) carried back to accounting periods falling wholly or partly within the period of twelve months immediately preceding the deficit period; and]¹

(b) in accordance with sub-paragraph (5) below, set against the eligible profits of the company for [up to three such periods.]¹

(4) If the whole or any amount of the deficit is not set off under sub-paragraph (2) or (3) above, so much of it as is not set off shall be—

(a) carried forward to the accounting period immediately following the deficit period; and

(b) treated for the purposes of the Corporation Tax Acts (including the following provisions of this paragraph) as an amount to be included in the company's expenses of management for the period following the deficit period.

(5) Subject to sub-paragraph (6) below, where, in pursuance of a claim under sub-paragraph (3) above, any amount falls to be carried back to be set off against the eligible profits of the company for [accounting periods falling wholly or partly within the period of twelve months mentioned in sub-paragraph (3)(a) above]¹, that amount shall be set off against those profits as follows, that is to say—

(a) the amount shall be applied, up to the limit for the first set-off period, in reducing the company's eligible profit for that period;

(b) any remainder of that amount after the limit for the first set-off period is reached shall be applied, up to the limit for the second set-off period, in reducing the company's eligible profit for the second set-off period; and (*c*) any remainder of that amount after the limit for the second set-off period has been reached shall be applied, up to the limit for third set-off period, in reducing the company's eligible profit for the third set-off period.

(6) No reduction shall be made in pursuance of any such claim in a company's eligible profit for any accounting period ending before 1st April 1996.

(7) For the purposes of this paragraph the eligible profit of the company for an accounting period is the amount (if any) which, in pursuance of any separate computation made for that period for the relevant category of business, is chargeable to tax for that period under Case III of Schedule D as profits and gains arising from the company's loan relationships.

(8) For the purpose of this paragraph—

(*a*) the first set-off period is the accounting period immediately preceding the deficit period,
(*b*) the second set-off period is the accounting period [(if any) which falls wholly or partly within the period of twelve months mentioned in sub-paragraph (3)(*a*) above and immediately precedes]¹ the first set-off period, and
(*c*) the third set-off period is the accounting period [(if any) which falls wholly or partly within the period of twelve months mentioned in sub-paragraph (3)(*a*) above and immediately precedes]¹ the second set-off period, and
(*d*) the limit for a set-off period is the amount equal to the adjusted amount of the company's eligible profit for that period.

(9) In sub-paragraph (8) above, the reference to the adjusted amount of a company's eligible profit for a set-off period is [(subject to sub-paragraph (9A) below)]¹ a reference to so much (if any) of the company's eligible profit for that period as remains after reducing it by an amount equal to the unused part of the relevant deductions for that period.

[(9A) Where a set-off period falls only partly within the period of twelve months mentioned in sub-paragraph (3)(*a*) above, the adjusted amount of a company's eligible profit for that period shall be taken to be confined to the part of the amount computed under sub-paragraph (9) above which is proportionate to the part of the set-off period that falls within that period of twelve months.]¹

(10) For the purposes of sub-paragraph (9) above the unused part of the relevant deductions for any set-off period is the amount (if any) by which the aggregate of—

(*a*) so much of the amount of any deductions for the set-off period by virtue of section 76 of the Taxes Act 1988 as is referable to the relevant category of business, and
(*b*) so much of the aggregate of the deductions made in the case of the company in respect of charges on income for that period as is so referable,

exceeds the aggregate of the amounts referable to the relevant category of business that could for that period be applied in making deductions by virtue of that section, or in respect of charges on income, if the eligible profit of the company for that period were disregarded.

(11) In sub-paragraph (10) above, the references, in relation to a claim under sub-paragraph (3) above ("the relevant claim"), to deductions by virtue of section 76 of the Taxes Act 1988 for a set-off period are references to the deductions by way of management expenses that would have fallen to be made by virtue of that section for that period if—

(*a*) no account were taken of either—
(i) the relevant claim; or
(ii) any claim under sub-paragraph (3) above relating to a deficit for an accounting period after the deficit period;
but
(*b*) there were made all such adjustments required by virtue of any sum having been carried back to that set-off period—
(i) under the Corporation Tax Acts, but
(ii) otherwise than in pursuance of the relevant claim or of any other such claim as is mentioned in paragraph (*a*) above.

(12) Where—

(*a*) in pursuance of a claim under sub-paragraph (3) above any amount is set-off against the eligible profit of a company for any set-off period, and
(*b*) there is a section 76(5) amount for that period which is attributable to that claim,

that section 76(5) amount shall not be carried forward by virtue of section 75(3) of the Taxes Act 1988 but, if that set-off period is the first or second set-off period, sub-paragraph (13) below shall apply to that amount instead.

(13) Where this sub-paragraph applies to a section 76(5) amount for any set-off period, the amount available in accordance with sub-paragraph (5) above to be carried back from that set-off period to be set off against eligible profits of previous set-off periods (or, as the case may be, against the eligible profit of the previous set-off period) shall be treated as increased by an amount equal to the amount to which this sub-paragraph applies.

(14) In relation to any claim under sub-paragraph (3) above, the amount which for any set-off period is, for the purposes of this paragraph, to be taken to be the section 76(5) amount attributable to that

claim is the amount (if any) by which the amount specified in paragraph (*a*) below is exceeded by the amount specified in paragraph (*b*) below, that is to say—

(*a*) the amount that would have fallen to be carried forward by virtue of section 75(3) of the Taxes Act 1988 if the claim had not been made; and

(*b*) the amount which, after the making of the claim, would have fallen to be carried forward to a subsequent period by virtue of section 75(3) of that Act if sub-paragraphs (12) and (13) above, so far as they relate to that claim, were to be disregarded.

(15) A claim for the purposes of sub-paragraph (2) or (3) above must be made within the period of two years immediately following the end of the deficit period or within such further period as the Board may allow.

(16) In this paragraph—

"net income and gains" has the meaning given by subsection (1) of section 76 of the Taxes Act 1988; and

"the relevant category of business", in relation to a deficit, means the category of business in relation to which the deficit was produced.

Cross references—See TMA 1970 s 87A(4A), (4B) (effect of claim under sub-para (3) on interest on overdue corporation tax for earlier periods).
TA 1988 s 242(2)(*f*) (deficit may be set against surplus franked investment income).
TA 1988 s 407(1)(*b*), (2)(*c*) (relationship between group relief and relief under this paragraph).
TA 1988 s 797(3A) (allocation, for purposes of computing double tax relief, of deduction in pursuance of claim under sub-para (2); see also s 797A).
TA 1988 s 826(7C), (7CA) (interest on tax overpaid as a result of a claim under sub-para (3)).
TA 1988 Sch 19AC para 5B(2)(*e*) (deficit may be set against UK distribution income of an overseas life insurance company).
FA 1989 s 88(3)(*aa*) (effect of non-trading deficits on calculation of policy holders' fraction of profits).
Modifications—Sub-para (1) modified so far as this Schedule applies to the life or endowment business carried on by friendly societies by the Friendly Societies (Modification of the Corporation Tax Acts) Regulations, SI 1997/473 reg 53.
Words in sub-paras (1), (2)(*a*), (7), (10) substituted, and words in sub-para (16) omitted, in applying life assurance provisions of the Corporation Tax Acts to insurance companies carrying on capital redemption business with effect for accounting periods ending after 30 June 1999: see Insurance Companies (Capital Redemption Business) (Modification of the Corporation Tax Acts) Regulations, SI 1999/498 reg 15(4).
Sub-paras (1), (2)(*a*), (7), (10) modified further in relation to companies carrying on capital redemption business by the Insurance Companies (Capital Redemption Business) (Modification of the Corporation Tax Acts) Regulations, SI 1999/498 reg 15, and so far as this Schedule (as so modified) applies to the life or endowment business carried on by friendly societies for accounting periods ending after 30 June 1999, by the Friendly Societies (Modification of the Corporation Tax Acts) Regulations, SI 1997/473 reg 53ZA (as inserted by SI 1999/2636).
Amendments—[1] Sub-para (3)(*a*) and words in sub-paras (3)(*b*), (5), (8)(*b*), (*c*) substituted and words in sub-para (9) and whole of sub-para (9A) inserted by F(No 2)A 1997 s 40 with effect in relation to any deficit for a deficit period ending on or after 2 July 1997.

Election for accruals basis for long term business assets

5—(1) Subject to sub-paragraphs (3) to (6) below, sub-paragraph (2) below applies for any accounting period to so much of any creditor relationship of an insurance company as—

(*a*) for the whole or any part of that period is an asset within one of the categories set out in section 440(4)(*d*) and (*e*) of the Taxes Act 1988 (assets held for certain categories of long term business); and

(*b*) is an asset in relation to which an election under this paragraph is made by the company for that period.

(2) Where—

(*a*) this sub-paragraph applies for any accounting period to any asset, and

(*b*) apart from this paragraph, a mark to market basis of accounting would have had to be used for the purposes of this Chapter as respects that asset for the whole or any part of that period,

this Chapter shall have effect as if an authorised accruals basis of accounting had to be used for the purposes of this Chapter as respects that asset for that period or part.

(3) Sub-paragraph (2) above shall not apply to any holding to which paragraph 4(3) of Schedule 10 to this Act applies.

(4) An election under this paragraph shall not be made except by notice in writing given to an officer of the Board not more than three months after the end of the accounting period to which the election relates.

(5) An election under this paragraph shall be irrevocable, and shall not be varied, once it has been made.

(6) An election shall not be made under this paragraph for any accounting period ending after [31st March 2000][1].

(7) The Treasury may, if they think fit, by order—

(*a*) amend sub-paragraph (6) above to substitute a later date for the date for the time being specified in that sub-paragraph; or

(*b*) repeal that sub-paragraph.

Amendments—[1] Date in sub-para (6) substituted by Insurance Companies (Loan Relationships) (Election for Accruals Basis) Order, SI 1999/1643, with effect from 2 July 1999.

Interpretation of Part I

6 In this Part of this Schedule—

"basic life assurance and general annuity business" and "long term business" have the same meanings as in Chapter I of Part XII of the Taxes Act 1988;

"capital redemption business" means any capital redemption business, within the meaning of section 458 of that Act, which is business to which that section applies;

"the I minus E basis" means the basis commonly so called (under which a company carrying on life assurance business or capital redemption business is charged to tax on that business otherwise than under Case I of Schedule D);

"life assurance business" includes any annuity business within the meaning of Chapter I of Part XII of that Act.

Modifications—This paragraph modified, by the addition of a definition of "taxable basic life and general assurance business", so far as this Schedule applies to the life or endowment business carried on by friendly societies by the Friendly Societies (Modification of the Corporation Tax Acts) Regulations, SI 1997/473 reg 53.
Definition of "capital redemption business" omitted, and definition of "life assurance business" amended, in applying life assurance provisions of the Corporation Tax Acts to insurance companies carrying on capital redemption business with effect for accounting periods ending after 30 June 1999: see Insurance Companies (Capital Redemption Business) (Modification of the Corporation Tax Acts) Regulations, SI 1999/498 reg 15(5).

PART II

CORPORATE MEMBERS OF LLOYD'S

7—(1) This Chapter does not apply as respects any loan relationship of a corporate member of Lloyd's in so far as rights or liabilities making up that relationship, or any securities representing them, are—

(a) assets forming part of that member's premiums trust fund; or
(b) liabilities attached to that fund.

(2) Section 230 of the Finance Act 1994 (interpretation of provisions applying to corporate members of Lloyd's) shall apply for the purposes of this paragraph as it applies for the purposes of Chapter V of Part IV of that Act.

SCHEDULE 12

MEANING OF DEBT CONTRACT OR OPTION

Section 101

Note—This Schedule, which set out FA 1994 s 150A inserted by FA 1996 s 101(3) is repealed by FA 2002 ss 83(1)(b), (3), 141, Sch 27 paras 17, 21, Sch 40 Pt 3(13) with effect for accounting periods beginning after 30 September 2002..

SCHEDULE 13

DISCOUNTED SECURITIES: INCOME TAX PROVISIONS

Section 102

Commentary—*Simon's Direct Tax Service* **Division A7.6.**
Cross references—See TCGA 1992 s 117(2AA), (8A) ("qualifying corporate bond" defined to include any asset which is a relevant discounted security).
TCGA 1992 s 254(1) (relief under that section for debts on qualifying corporate bonds does not apply if the security in question is relevant discounted security).
European Single Currency (Taxes) Regulations, SI 1998/3177 regs 7–12 (exchange or conversion of relevant discounted securities in relation to the introduction of the euro).

Charge to tax on realised profit comprised in discount

1—(1) Where a person realises the profit from the discount on a relevant discounted security, he shall be charged to income tax on that profit under Case III of Schedule D or, where the profit arises from a security out of the United Kingdom, under Case IV of that Schedule.

(2) For the purposes of this Schedule a person realises the profit from the discount on a relevant discounted security where—

(a) he transfers such a security or becomes entitled, as the person holding the security, to any payment on its redemption; and
(b) the amount payable on the transfer or redemption exceeds the amount paid by that person in respect of his acquisition of the security.

(3) For the purposes of this Schedule the profit shall be taken—

(a) to be equal to the amount of the excess reduced by the amount of any relevant costs; and
(b) to arise, for the purposes of income tax, in the year of assessment in which the transfer or redemption takes place.

(4) In this paragraph "relevant costs", in relation to a security that is transferred or redeemed, are all the following costs—

(*a*) the costs incurred in connection with the acquisition of the security by the person making the transfer or, as the case may be, the person entitled to a payment on the redemption; and

(*b*) the costs incurred by that person, in connection with the transfer or redemption of the security;

and for the purposes of this Schedule costs falling within paragraph (*a*) above shall not be regarded as amounts paid in respect of the acquisition of a security.

Realised losses on discounted securities

2—(1) Subject to the following provisions of this Schedule, where—

(*a*) a person sustains a loss in any year of assessment from the discount on a relevant discounted security, and

(*b*) makes a claim for the purposes of this paragraph before the end of twelve months from the 31st January next following that year of assessment,

that person shall be entitled to relief from income tax on an amount of the claimant's income for that year equal to the amount of the loss.

(2) For the purposes of this Schedule a person sustains a loss from the discount on a relevant discounted security where—

(*a*) he transfers such a security or becomes entitled, as the person holding the security, to any payment on its redemption; and

(*b*) the amount paid by that person in respect of his acquisition of the security exceeds the amount payable on the transfer or redemption.

(3) For the purposes of this Schedule the loss shall be taken—

(*a*) to be equal to the amount of the excess increased by the amount of any relevant costs; and

(*b*) to be sustained for the purposes of this Schedule in the year of assessment in which the transfer or redemption takes place.

(4) Sub-paragraph (4) of paragraph 1 above applies for the purposes of this paragraph as it applies for the purposes of that paragraph.

Meaning of "relevant discounted security"

3—[(1) Subject to the following provisions of this paragraph and paragraph 14(1) below, in this Schedule "relevant discounted security" means any security which (whenever issued) is such that, taking the security as at the time of its issue, the amount payable on redemption—

(*a*) on maturity, or

(*b*) in the case of a security of which there may be a redemption before maturity, on at least one of the occasions on which it may be redeemed,

is or would be an amount involving a deep gain, or might be an amount which would involve a deep gain.][1]

[(1A) The occasions that are to be taken into account for the purpose of determining whether a security is a relevant discounted security by virtue of sub-paragraph (1)(*b*) above shall not include any of the following occasions on which it may be redeemed, that is to say—

(*a*) any occasion not falling within sub-paragraph (1C) below on which there may be a redemption otherwise than at the option of the person who holds the security;

(*b*) in a case where a redemption may occur as a result of the exercise of an option that is exercisable—

(i) only on the occurrence of an event adversely affecting the holder, or

(ii) only on the occurrence of a default by any person,

any occasion on which that option is unlikely (judged as at the time of the security's issue) to be exercisable;

but nothing in this sub-paragraph shall require an occasion on which a security may be redeemed to be disregarded by reason only that it is or may be an occasion that coincides with an occasion mentioned in this sub-paragraph.][1]

[(1B) In sub-paragraph (1A) above "event adversely affecting the holder", in relation to a security, means an event which (judged as at the time of the security's issue) is such that, if it occurred and there were no provision for redemption, the interests of the person holding the security at the time of the event would be likely to be adversely affected.][1]

[(1C) An occasion on which there may be a redemption of a security falls within this sub-paragraph if—

(*a*) the security is a security issued to a person connected with the issuer; or

(*b*) the obtaining of a tax advantage by any person is the main benefit, or one of the main benefits, that might have been expected to accrue from the provision in accordance with which it may be redeemed on that occasion.][1]

[(1D) In sub-paragraph (1C) above "tax advantage" has the meaning given by section 709(1) of the Taxes Act 1988.][1]

[(1E) Subject to sub-paragraph (1F) below, where a security which is not a relevant discounted security but which would have been such a security if it had been issued to a person connected with the issuer—

    (*a*) is acquired by a person who is so connected, or

    (*b*) is held by a person who becomes so connected,

this Schedule shall have effect, in relation to times falling at or after the time of the acquisition or, as the case may be, the time when that person became so connected, as if the security were a relevant discounted security.][1]

[(1F) Where a security which—

    (*a*) is a relevant discounted security, but

    (*b*) would not be such a security but for sub-paragraph (1C)(*a*) or (1E) above,

is acquired by a person who is not connected with the issuer, this Schedule shall have effect, in relation to that person, as if the security ceased to be a relevant discounted security at the time of the acquisition.][1]

(2) The following are not relevant discounted securities for the purposes of this Schedule—

    (*a*) shares in a company;

    (*b*) gilt-edged securities that are not strips;

    (*c*) excluded indexed securities;

    (*d*) life assurance policies;

    (*e*) capital redemption policies (within the meaning of Chapter II of Part XIII of the Taxes Act 1988); and

    (*f*) subject to paragraph 10 below, securities issued (at whatever time) under the same prospectus as other securities which have been issued previously but (disregarding that paragraph) are not themselves relevant discounted securities.

[(2A) Nothing in sub-paragraph (2)(*c*) above shall prevent a security that would have been a relevant discounted security if it had been issued to a person connected with the issuer from being treated as a relevant discounted security by virtue of sub-paragraph (1E) above.][1]

[(2B) Nothing in sub-paragraph (2)(*f*) above shall prevent a security from being treated as a relevant discounted security by virtue of sub-paragraph (1C)(*a*) or (1E) above.][1]

(3) For the purposes of this Schedule the amount payable on redemption of a security involves a deep gain if—

    (*a*) the issue price is less than the amount so payable; and

    (*b*) the amount by which it is less represents more than the relevant percentage of the amount so payable.

(4) In this paragraph "the relevant percentage", in relation to the amount payable on redemption of a security, means—

    (*a*) the percentage figure equal, in a case where the period between the date of issue and the date of redemption is less than thirty years, to one half of the number of years between those dates; and

    (*b*) in any other case, 15 per cent.;

and for the purposes of this paragraph the fraction of a year to be used for the purposes of paragraph (*a*) above in a case where the period mentioned in that paragraph is not a number of complete years shall be calculated by treating each complete month, and any remaining part of a month, in that period as one twelfth of a year.

(5) ...[1]

(6) For the purposes of this paragraph the amount payable on redemption shall not be taken to include any amount payable on that occasion by way of interest.

[(7) Section 839 of the Taxes Act 1988 (connected persons) applies for the purposes of this paragraph.][1]

[(8) In determining for the purposes of sub-paragraph (1C), (1E), (1F) or (2A) above whether a person is or becomes connected with the issuer, no account shall be taken of—

    (*a*) the security mentioned in that sub-paragraph; or

    (*b*) any security issued under the same prospectus as that security.][1]

Amendments—[1] Sub-para (1) substituted, sub-paras (1A)–(1F), (2A), (2B), (7), (8) inserted, and sub-para (5) repealed by FA 1999 ss 65(1)–(4), (8), 139, Sch 20 Pt III(16) with effect for—

    – any transfer of a security after 14 February 1999; or

    – any occasion after that date on which a person holding a security becomes entitled to any payment on its redemption,

subject to FA 1999 s 68(9)–(12) (concerning effective dates of these amendments for the purposes of FA 1996 s 92, Sch 9 paras 17, 18 and TCGA 1992 ss 117(2AA), 251(8), 254(1)(*c*)).

[Issue price etc of securities issued in accordance with qualifying earn-out right

3A—(1) This paragraph applies where a security is issued to a person in accordance with the terms of a qualifying earn-out right.

(2) In any such case the issue price of the security shall be taken for the purposes of this Schedule to be the sum of—

(*a*) the market value, immediately before the issue of the security, of the right to be issued with the security in accordance with the terms of the qualifying earn-out right, and

(*b*) any amount payable for the issue of the security in accordance with those terms,

and any reference in this Schedule to the amount paid by the person in respect of his acquisition of the security shall be taken as a reference to that sum.

(3) For the purposes of this paragraph a "qualifying earn-out right" is so much of any right conferred on a person as—

(*a*) constitutes the whole or any part of the consideration for the transfer by him of shares in or debentures of a company or for the transfer of the whole or part of a business or interest in a business carried on by him or by him and others in partnership;

(*b*) consists in either a right to be issued with securities of another company or a right which is capable of being discharged in accordance with its terms by the issue of such securities; and

(*c*) is such that the value of the consideration mentioned in paragraph (*a*) above is unascertainable at the time when the right is conferred.]¹

Amendments—¹ This paragraph inserted by FA 2002 s 104(1), (2), (4) and deemed always to have had effect.

Meaning of "transfer"

4—(1) Subject to sub-paragraph (2) below, in this Schedule references to a transfer, in relation to a security, are references to any transfer of the security by way of sale, exchange, gift or otherwise.

(2) Where an individual who is entitled to a relevant discounted security dies, then for the purposes of this Schedule—

(*a*) he shall be treated as making a transfer of the security immediately before his death;

(*b*) he shall be treated as obtaining in respect of the transfer an amount equal to the market value of the security at the time of the transfer; and

(*c*) his personal representatives shall be treated as acquiring the security for that amount on his death.

(3) For the purposes of this Schedule a transfer or acquisition of a security made in pursuance of an agreement shall be deemed to take place at the time when the agreement is made, if the person to whom the transfer is made, or who makes the acquisition, becomes entitled to the security at that time.

(4) If an agreement is conditional, whether on the exercise of an option or otherwise, it shall be taken for the purposes of this paragraph to be made when the condition is satisfied (whether by the exercise of the option or otherwise).

(5) This paragraph is without prejudice to paragraph 14(2) to (4) below.

Cross reference—See IHTA 1984 s 174(1)(*b*) (see *Yellow Tax Handbook Part II*) (any income tax liability on a transfer within sub-para (2) to be allowed for in determining value of a person's death estate for inheritance tax).
European Single Currency (Taxes) Regulations, SI 1998/3177 reg 12 (a euroconversion of relevant discounted securities that is effected solely by means of an exchange or transfer of those securities does not constitute a "transfer" within this paragraph. Where a euroconversion is effected by an exchange or transfer of such securities, a formula is provided for determining the acquisition cost of the new securities. A formula is also given for calculating the deemed acquisition cost of relevant discounted securities where a cash payment is made as a result of a euroconversion which involves a simple redenomination of those securities, accompanied by renominalisation and/or reconventioning, and is not effected by a transfer or exchange or conversion of those securities).

Redemption to include conversion

5—(1) This paragraph applies where a relevant discounted security is extinguished by being converted, in pursuance of rights conferred by the security, into shares in a company or into any other securities (including other relevant discounted securities).

(2) For the purposes of this Schedule the conversion shall be deemed—

(*a*) to constitute the redemption of the security which is extinguished; and

(*b*) to involve a payment on redemption of an amount equal to whatever, at the time of the conversion, is the market value of the shares or other securities into which the security in question is converted.

(3) This paragraph does not apply to an exchange to which paragraph 14 below applies.

Cross reference—See European Single Currency (Taxes) Regulations, SI 1998/3177 regs 7–12 (a euroconversion of relevant discounted securities does not constitute a "conversion" within this paragraph. Where a euroconversion is effected by a conversion of such securities, a formula is provided for determining the acquisition cost of the new securities. A formula is also given for calculating the deemed acquisition cost of relevant discounted securities where a cash payment is made as a result of a euroconversion which involves a simple redenomination of those securities, accompanied by renominalisation and/or reconventioning, and is not effected by a transfer or exchange or conversion of those securities).

Trustees and personal representatives

6—(1) Where, on a transfer or redemption of a security by trustees, an amount is treated as income chargeable to tax by virtue of this Schedule—

(a) that amount shall be taken for the purposes of Chapters IA and IB of Part XV of the Taxes Act 1988 (settlements: liability of settlor etc) to be income arising—

    (i) under the settlement of which the trustees are trustees; and

    (ii) from that security;

(b) that amount shall be taken for the purposes of Chapter IC of Part XV of that Act (settlements: liability of trustees) to be income arising to the trustees; and

(c) to the extent that tax on that amount is charged on the trustees, the rate at which it is chargeable shall be taken (where it would not otherwise be the case) to be the rate applicable to trusts for the year of assessment in which the transfer or redemption is made.

(2) Where the trustees are trustees of a scheme to which section 469 of the Taxes Act 1988 (unauthorised unit trusts) applies, sub-paragraph (1) above shall not apply if or to the extent that the amount is treated as income in the accounts of the scheme.

(3) Without prejudice to paragraph 12 below, paragraphs 1(1) and 2(1) above do not apply in the case of—

(a) any transfer of a security for the time being held under a settlement the trustees of which are not resident in the United Kingdom; or

(b) any redemption of a security which is so held immediately before its redemption.

(4) Relief shall not be given to trustees under paragraph 2 above except from income tax on income chargeable under paragraph 1 above.

(5) Sub-paragraph (6) below applies where, in the case of any trustees, the amount mentioned in paragraph (a) below exceeds in any year of assessment the amount mentioned in paragraph (b) below, that is to say—

(a) the aggregate amount of the losses in respect of which relief from income tax may be given to the trustees for that year under paragraph 2 above (including any amount treated as such a loss by virtue of that sub-paragraph); and

(b) the income of those trustees chargeable for that year to tax under paragraph 1 above.

(6) Subject to paragraph 7(2) below, the excess shall for the purposes of this Schedule be—

(a) carried forward to the immediately following year of assessment; and

(b) in relation to the year to which it is carried forward, treated as if it were a loss sustained in that year by the trustees from a discount on a relevant discounted security.

(7) Where a relevant discounted security is transferred by personal representatives to a legatee, they shall be treated for the purposes of this Schedule as obtaining in respect of the transfer an amount equal to the market value of the security at the time of the transfer.

(8) In this paragraph "legatee" includes any person taking (whether beneficially or as trustee) under a testamentary disposition or on an intestacy or partial intestacy, including any person taking by virtue of an appropriation by the personal representatives in or towards satisfaction of a legacy or other interest or share in the deceased's property.

Treatment of losses where income exempt

7—(1) Where—

(a) on the transfer or redemption of any relevant discounted security, a loss is sustained from the discount on that security, and

(b) if the person sustaining that loss had realised a profit from that discount on that transfer or redemption, the profit would have been an exempt profit for the year of assessment in which the loss is sustained,

relief shall not be given to that person under paragraph 2 above in respect of that loss except from income tax on income chargeable for that year under paragraph 1 above.

(2) No part of any loss to which sub-paragraph (1) above applies shall be carried forward under paragraph 6(6) above.

(3) The reference in sub-paragraph (1) above to an exempt profit for a year of assessment is a reference to any income for that year which—

(a) is eligible for relief from tax by virtue of section 505(1) of the Taxes Act 1988, or would be so eligible but for section 505(3) of that Act (charities); or

(b) is eligible for relief from tax by virtue of section 592(2), 608(2)(a), 613(4), 614(2), (3), (4) or (5), 620(6) or 643(2) of that Act (pension scheme funds etc).

(4) Where a loss to which sub-paragraph (1) above applies is sustained in a case in which the profit mentioned in paragraph (b) of that sub-paragraph would be eligible for relief under section 592(2) of the Taxes Act 1988—

(a) relief shall be given under paragraph 2 above in accordance with sub-paragraph (1) above before any computation is made under paragraph 7 of Schedule 22 to that Act, and

(b) that paragraph 7 shall have effect, accordingly, so that the amount of income to which the specified percentage is applied by virtue of sub-paragraph (3)(a) of that paragraph is reduced by the amount of the relief.

Transfers between connected persons

8—(1) This paragraph applies where a relevant discounted security is transferred from one person to another and they are connected with each other.

(2) For the purposes of this Schedule—

(a) the person making the transfer shall be treated as obtaining in respect of it an amount equal to the market value of the security at the time of the transfer; and

(b) the person to whom the transfer is made shall be treated as paying in respect of his acquisition of the security an amount equal to that market value.

(3) Section 839 of the Taxes Act 1988 (connected persons) shall apply for the purposes of this paragraph.

Other transactions deemed to be at market value

9—(1) This paragraph applies where a relevant discounted security is transferred from one person to another in a case in which—

(a) the transfer is made for a consideration which consists of or includes consideration not in money or money's worth; or

(b) the transfer is made otherwise than by way of a bargain made at arm's length.

(2) For the purposes of this Schedule—

(a) the person making the transfer shall be treated as obtaining in respect of it an amount equal to the market value of the security at the time of the transfer, and

(b) the person to whom the transfer is made shall be treated as paying in respect of his acquisition of the security an amount equal to that market value.

[Securities issued to connected person etc at price in excess of market value: transfer to connected person

9A—(1) Where a relevant discounted security is transferred by a person ("the relevant person") to a person connected with him and—

(a) the occasion of the relevant person's acquisition of the security was its issue to him,

(b) the relevant person was, at the time of issue, connected with the issuer or the conditions in sub-paragraph (2) below are satisfied, and

(c) the amount paid by the relevant person in respect of his acquisition of the security exceeds the market value of the security at the time of issue,

the relevant person shall be taken for the purposes of this Schedule not to sustain a loss from the discount on the relevant discounted security.

(2) The conditions mentioned in sub-paragraph (1)(b) above are that—

(a) the security is a security issued by a close company;

(b) at the time of issue, the relevant person was not connected with the company;

(c) securities of the same kind as that issued to him were also issued to other persons; and

(d) he and some or all of those other persons, taken together, controlled the company.

(3) In sub-paragraph (2)(d) above, "control" shall be construed in accordance with section 416 of the Taxes Act 1988.

(4) For the purposes of this section, section 414 of the Taxes Act 1988 (meaning of "close company" in the Tax Acts) shall have effect with the omission of subsection (1)(a) (exclusion of companies not resident in the United Kingdom).

(5) Section 839 of the Taxes Act 1988 (connected persons) shall apply for the purposes of this paragraph.]¹

Amendments—¹ This paragraph inserted by FA 2002 s 104(1), (3), (5) with effect for transfers after 25 March 2002.

Issue of securities in separate tranches

10—(1) In a case where—

(a) none of the securities issued on the occasion of the original issue of securities under a particular prospectus would be a relevant discounted security apart from this paragraph,

(b) some of the securities subsequently issued under the prospectus would be relevant discounted securities apart from paragraph 3(2)(f) above, and

(c) there is a time (whether before, at or after the beginning of the year 1996–97) when the aggregate nominal value as at that time of the securities falling within paragraph (b) above exceeds the aggregate nominal value as at that time of the securities which have been issued under the prospectus and do not fall within that paragraph,

sub-paragraph (2) below shall apply in relation to every security which has been or is issued under the prospectus at any time (whether before, at or after the time mentioned in paragraph (c) above).

(2) As regards any event occurring in relation to the security after the time mentioned in sub-paragraph (1)(c) above, this Schedule shall have effect as if the security—

(a) were a relevant discounted security; and

(b) had been acquired as such (whatever the time of its acquisition).

(3) For the purposes of sub-paragraph (2) above events, in relation to a security, include anything constituting a transfer, redemption or acquisition for the purposes of this Schedule.

[(4) For the purpose of determining whether a security held by a person who is not connected with the issuer is a relevant discounted security by virtue of this paragraph, a security which—

(a) is a relevant discounted security, but

(b) would not be such a security but for paragraph 3(1C)(a) or (1E) above,

shall be assumed not to be a security falling within sub-paragraph (1)(b) above.]¹

Amendments—¹ Sub-para (4) inserted by FA 1999 ss 65(5), (8) with effect for—

   – any transfer of a security after 14 February 1999; or

   – any occasion after that date on which a person holding a security becomes entitled to any payment on its redemption,

   subject to FA 1999 s 68(9)–(12) (concerning effective dates of these amendments for the purposes of FA 1996 s 92, Sch 9 paras 17, 18 and TCGA 1992 ss 117(2AA), 251(8), 254(1)(c)).

Accrued income scheme

11 In a case where—

(a) paragraph 1 or 2 above applies on the transfer of any security, and

(b) apart from this paragraph, the transfer would be a transfer for the purposes of sections 710 to 728 of the Taxes Act 1988,

the transfer shall be treated as if it were not a transfer for those purposes.

Assets transferred abroad

12 For the purposes of sections 739 and 740 of the Taxes Act 1988 (prevention of avoidance of tax by transfer of assets abroad), where a person resident or domiciled outside the United Kingdom realises a profit from the discount on a relevant discounted security, that profit shall be taken to be income of that person.

Excluded indexed securities

13—(1) For the purposes of this Schedule a security is an excluded indexed security if the amount payable on redemption is linked to the value of chargeable assets.

(2) For the purposes of this paragraph an amount is linked to the value of chargeable assets if, in pursuance of any provision having effect for the purposes of the security, it is equal to an amount determined by applying a relevant percentage change in the value of chargeable assets to the amount for which the security was issued.

(3) In sub-paragraph (2) above the reference to a relevant percentage change in the value of chargeable assets is a reference to the amount of the percentage change (if any) over the relevant period in the value of chargeable assets of any particular description or in any index of the value of any such assets.

(4) In sub-paragraph (3) above "the relevant period" means—

(a) the period between the time of the issue of the security and its redemption; or

(b) any other period in which almost all of that period is comprised and which differs from that period exclusively for purposes connected with giving effect to a valuation in relation to rights or liabilities under the security.

(5) If—

(a) there is a provision which, in the case of the amount payable on the redemption of any security, falls within sub-paragraph (2) above,

(b) that provision is made subject to any other provision applying to the determination of that amount,

(c) that other provision is to the effect only that that amount must not be less than a specified percentage of the amount for which the security is issued, and

(d) the specified percentage is not more than 10 per cent,

that other provision shall be disregarded in determining for the purposes of this paragraph whether the amount payable on redemption is linked to the value of chargeable assets.

(6) For the purposes of this paragraph an asset is a chargeable asset in relation to any security if any gain accruing to a person on a disposal of that asset would, on the assumptions specified in sub-paragraph (7) below, be a chargeable gain for the purposes of the Taxation of Chargeable Gains Act 1992.

(7) Those assumptions are—

(a) where it is not otherwise the case, that the asset is an asset of the person in question and that that person does not have the benefit of any exemption conferred by section 100 of that Act of 1992 (exemption for authorised unit trusts etc);

(*b*) that the asset is not one the disposal of which by that person would fall to be treated for the purposes of income tax as a disposal in the course of a trade, profession or vocation carried on by that person; and

    (*c*) that chargeable gains that might accrue under section 116(10) of that Act are to be disregarded.

(8) For the purposes of this paragraph neither—

    (*a*) the retail prices index, nor

    (*b*) any similar general index of prices published by the government of any territory or by the agent of any such government,

shall be taken to be an index of the value of chargeable assets.

[(9) In this paragraph references to redemption, in relation to a security, do not include references to redemption of the security on any such occasion as, by reason of sub-paragraph (1A) of paragraph 3 above, is not to be taken into account for the purpose of determining whether the security is a relevant discounted security by virtue of sub-paragraph (1)(*b*) of that paragraph.]¹

Cross reference—See TCGA 1992 s 117(6B) (excluded indexed security issued after 5 April 1996 is not a corporate bond for purposes of that section (meaning of ''qualifying corporate bond''); such a security issued before 6 April 1996 is to be taken to be a corporate bond only in limited circumstances).
Amendments—¹ Sub-para (9) inserted by FA 1999 s 65(6), (8) with effect for—

  – any transfer of a security after 14 February 1999; or
  – any occasion after that date on which a person holding a security becomes entitled to any payment on its redemption,

subject to FA 1999 s 68(9)–(12) (concerning effective dates of these amendments for the purposes of FA 1996 s 92, Sch 9 paras 17, 18 and TCGA 1992 ss 117(2AA), 251(8), 254(1)(*c*)).

Gilt strips

14—(1) Every strip is a relevant discounted security for the purposes of this Schedule.

(2) For the purposes of this Schedule, where a person exchanges a gilt-edged security for strips of that security, the person who receives the strips in the exchange shall be deemed to have paid, in respect of his acquisition of each strip, the amount which bears the same proportion to the market value of the security as is borne by the market value of the strip to the aggregate of the market values of all the strips received in exchange for the security.

(3) For the purposes of this Schedule, where strips are consolidated into a single gilt-edged security by being exchanged by any person for that security, each of the strips shall be deemed to have been redeemed at the time of the exchange by the payment to that person of the amount equal to its market value.

(4) A person who holds a strip on the 5th April in any year of assessment, and who (apart from this sub-paragraph) does not transfer or redeem it on that day, shall be deemed for the purposes of this Schedule—

    (*a*) to have transferred that strip on that day;

    (*b*) to have received in respect of that transfer an amount equal to the strip's market value on that day; and

    (*c*) to have re-acquired the strip on the next day on payment of an amount equal to the amount for which it is deemed to have been disposed of on the previous day;

and the deemed transfer and re-acquisition shall be assumed for the purposes of paragraphs 1 and 2 above to be transactions in connection with which no relevant costs are incurred.

(5) Without prejudice to the generality of any power conferred by section 187 of this Act, the Treasury may by regulations provide that this Schedule is to have effect with such modifications as they may think fit in relation to any relevant discounted security which is a strip.

(6) Regulations made by the Treasury under this paragraph may—

    (*a*) make provision for the purposes of sub-paragraphs (2) to (4) above as to the manner of determining the market value at any time of any security;

    (*b*) make different provision for different cases; and

    (*c*) contain such incidental, supplemental, consequential and transitional provision as the Treasury may think fit.

(7) References in sub-paragraphs (2) and (3) above to the market value of a security given or received in exchange for another are references to its market value at the time of the exchange.

General interpretation

15—(1) In this Schedule—

    ''deep gain'' shall be construed in accordance with paragraph 3(3) above;

    ''excluded indexed security'' has the meaning given by paragraph 13 above;

    ''market value'' (except in paragraph 14 above) has the same meaning as in the Taxation of Chargeable Gains Act 1992;

    ''relevant discounted security'' has the meaning given by paragraphs 3 and 14(1) above;

    ''strip'' means anything which, within the meaning of section 47 of the Finance Act 1942, is a strip of a gilt-edged security.

(2) Where a person, having acquired and transferred any security, subsequently re-acquires it, references in this Schedule to his acquisition of the security shall have effect, in relation to—

   (*a*) the transfer by him of that security, or
   (*b*) the redemption of the security in a case where he becomes entitled to any amount on its redemption,

as references to his most recent acquisition of the security before the transfer or redemption in question.

Application of Schedule for income tax purposes only

16—(1) This Schedule does not apply for the purposes of corporation tax.

(2) Sub-paragraph (1) above is without prejudice to any enactment not contained in this Schedule by virtue of which the definition of a relevant discounted security, or any other provision of this Schedule, is applied for the purposes of corporation tax.

SCHEDULE 14

LOAN RELATIONSHIPS: MINOR AND CONSEQUENTIAL AMENDMENTS

Section 104

The Taxes Management Act 1970 (c 9)

1 (1) (*amends* TMA 1970 s 87A(4A)(*a*), (*b*), (4B)).

(2) ...[1]

Amendments—[1] Para 1(2) repealed by FA 1998 s 165, Sch 27 Pt III(2) with effect for any relevant period beginning after 5 April 1999.

The Inheritance Tax Act 1984 (c 51)

2—(1) (*amends* IHTA 1984 s 174(1)(*b*)—*see Pt II of this Handbook*).

(2) This paragraph applies in relation to deaths on or after 6th April 1996.

The Airports Act 1986 (c 31)

3 (*amends* Airports Act 1986 s 77—not reproduced).

The Gas Act 1986 (c 44)

4 (*amends* Gas Act 1986 s 60—not reproduced).

The Taxes Act 1988

5 (*inserts* TA 1988 s 18(3A)).

6 (*inserts* TA 1988 s 56(4A), (4B)).

7 (*amends* TA 1988 s 70(3)).

8 (*inserts* TA 1988 s 75(1A)).

9 (*inserts* TA 1988 s 77(8)).

10—(1) (*repeals* TA 1988 s 78)).

(2) Where any bill so drawn is paid on or after 1st April 1996—

   (*a*) the amount which subsection (2) of that section provides to be treated as a deduction against total profits and as a charge on income shall (instead of being so treated) be brought into account for the purposes of this Chapter as a non-trading debit; and
   (*b*) that amount shall be the only amount brought into account for the purposes of this Chapter in respect of the discount in question.

11—(1) (*inserts* TA 1988 s 209(3A)).

(2) Sub-paragraph (1) above does not apply to distributions made before 1st April 1996.

12 ...

Amendments—This paragraph *repealed* by F(No 2)A 1997 Sch 8 Pt II(4).

13 (*amended* TA 1988 s 247(4) and *inserted* s 247(4A); *repealed* by FA 2001 s 110, Sch 33 Pt II(10) with effect for payments made after 11 May 2001).

14 (*amends* TA 1988 s 337(2)(*b*) and *repeals* s 337(3)).

15 (*inserts* TA 1988 s 337A).

16 (*amends* TA 1988 ss 338(3), (5)(*a*) and *repeals* s 338(4)(*b*), (*c*), (6)).

17 (*repeals* TA 1988 ss 338A, 340, 341).

18 (*amends* TA 1988 s 349(2)).

19 (*inserts* TA 1988 s 400(9A)).

20 (*inserts* TA 1988 s 401(1AA), (1AB), (1AC) and *repeals* s 401(1A)).

21 (*amends* TA 1988 s 404(6)(*a*), (*c*) and *inserts* s 404(7).

22 (*amends* TA 1988 s 407(1)(*b*), (2)).

23—(1) (spent).

(2), (3) (*insert* TA 1988 s 434A(2A) and *amend* s 434A(3)).

24 (spent)

25 (*inserts* TA 1988 s 440(2A)).

26 (*amends* TA 1988 s 468L(5)).

27 (*substitutes* TA 1988 s 475(2) and *amends* s 475(4)).

28 (*substitutes* TA 1988 s 477A(3)(*a*), (*aa*) for s 477A(3)(*a*) and *repeals* s 477A(3A) – (3C)).

29 (*repeals* TA 1988 ss 484, 485).

30 (*amends* TA 1988 s 486(1),(7)).

31 (*substitutes* TA 1988 s 487(1)(*b*), *amends* s 487(3) and *inserts* s 487(3A)).

32—(1)–(3) (*amend* TA 1988 s 494(1), (2), and *insert* s 494(2A)).

(4) ...¹

Amendments—¹ Repealed by FA 1998 s 165, Sch 27 Part III(4) with effect for income tax from the year 1998–99, and for corporation tax from 1 April 1998 subject to transitional provisions in FA 1998 Sch 5 Part IV.

33 (*amends* TA 1988 s 587A(1)).

34 (*inserts* TA 1988 s 614(2A)).

35 (*inserts* TA 1988 s 687(3)(*k*)).

36 (*inserts* TA 1988 s 710(1A)).

37 (*substitutes* TA 1988 s 730A(6), (6A) for s 730A(6)).

38 ...

Amendments—This paragraph *repealed* by FA 1997 Sch 17 Pt VI(9) with effect in relation to payments made on or after 1 July 1997 by virtue of the Finance Act 1997, Schedule 10, (Appointed Day) Order, SI 1997/991.

39 (*substitutes* TA 1988 s 768B(10) for s 768B(10), (11) and *amends* s 768B(13)).

40 (*substitutes* TA 1988 s 768C(9) for s 768C(9), (10)).

41 (*inserts* TA 1988 s 795(4)).

42 (*inserts* TA 1988 s 797(3A), (3B), (6)).

43 (*inserts* TA 1988 s 797A).

44 (*inserts* TA 1988 s 798(2A), (3A)).

45 (*inserts* TA 1988 s 807(6)).

46 (*inserts* TA 1988 s 807A).

47 (*inserts* TA 1988 s 811(3)).

48—(1) (*amends* TA 1988 s 826(7C)).

(2) ...¹

Amendments—Sub-para (2) repealed by FA 1998 s 165, Sch 27 Pt III(2) with effect for any relevant period beginning after 5 April 1999.

49 (*amends* TA 1988 s 834(1)).

50 (*repeals* TA 1988 Sch 4).

51 ...

Amendments—This paragraph *repealed* by F(No 2)A 1997 Sch 8 Pt II(6).

52—(1) Schedule 23A to that Act (manufactured payments) shall be amended as follows.

(2), (3) ...

(4) (*inserts* TA 1988 Sch 23A para 4(9)).

(5), (6) ...

(7) (*inserts* TA 1988 Sch 23A para 7(1A)).

Amendments—Sub-paras (2), (3), (5), (6) *repealed* by FA 1997 Sch 17 Pt VI(9) with effect in relation to payments made on or after 1 July 1997 by virtue of SI 1997/991.

53 (*amends* TA 1988 Sch 26(1)(3)).

54 (*amends* TA 1988 Sch 28A).

The British Steel Act 1988 (c 35)

55 (*amends* British Steel Act 1988 s 11—not reproduced).

The Finance Act 1989 (c 26)

56, 57 (*insert* FA 1989 s 88(3)(*aa*) and *repeal* FA 1989 Sch 11).

The Finance Act 1990 (c 29)

58 (*repeals* FA 1990 Sch 10).

The Taxation of Chargeable Gains Act 1992 (c 12)

59–66 (*inserts* TCGA 1992 ss 108(1)(*aa*), 116(4A), (8A), (16), 117(A1), (2AA), (6B), (6C), (8A), 117A, 117B, 212(2A), 251(7), (8), 254(13) and *amend* ss 253(3), 254(1)(*c*)).

The Finance Act 1993 (c 34)

67 (*inserted* FA 1993 s 127(1A), (1B); *repealed by* FA 2002 s 141, Sch 40 Pt 3(10) with effect for accounting periods beginning after 30 September 2002).

68 (*amended* FA 1993 s 129(2), (4), (7)(*b*) and *repeals* s 129(5), (6); *repealed by* FA 2002 s 141, Sch 40 Pt 3(10) with effect for accounting periods beginning after 30 September 2002).

69 (*substituted* FA 1993 s 130 for ss 130–133; *repealed by* FA 2002 s 141, Sch 40 Pt 3(10) with effect for accounting periods beginning after 30 September 2002).

70 (*substituted* FA 1993 s 153(4) and *repeals* s 153(6); *repealed by* FA 2002 s 141, Sch 40 Pt 3(10) with effect for accounting periods beginning after 30 September 2002).

71 (*inserted* FA 1993 s 154(12A); *repealed by* FA 2002 s 141, Sch 40 Pt 3(10) with effect for accounting periods beginning after 30 September 2002).

72 (*inserted* FA 1993 s 155(11A); *repealed by* FA 2002 s 141, Sch 40 Pt 3(10) with effect for accounting periods beginning after 30 September 2002).

73—(1) (*substituted* FA 1993 s 159(5) for s 159(5)–(9); *repealed by* FA 2002 s 141, Sch 40 Pt 3(10) with effect for accounting periods beginning after 30 September 2002).

(2) This paragraph does not apply in relation to transfers before 1st April 1996.

Amendment—This paragraph repealed by FA 2002 s 141, Sch 40 Pt 3(10) with effect for accounting periods beginning after 30 September 2002

74 (*inserts* FA 1993 s 167(5A), (5B); *repealed by* FA 2002 s 141, Sch 40 Pt 3(10) with effect for accounting periods beginning after 30 September 2002).

The Finance Act 1994 (c 9)

75 (*substituted* FA 1994 s 160(2), (2A) for s 160(2) – (4); *repealed by* FA 2002 s 141, Sch 40 Pt 3(13) with effect for accounting periods beginning after 30 September 2002).

76 (*inserted* FA 1994 s 167(9)(*ba*) and *amended* s 167(9)(*c*); *repealed by* FA 2002 s 141, Sch 40 Pt 3(13) with effect for accounting periods beginning after 30 September 2002).

77 (*amended* FA 1994 s 173(5)(*a*); *repealed by* FA 2002 s 141, Sch 40 Pt 3(13) with effect for accounting periods beginning after 30 September 2002).

78 (*amended* FA 1994 s 177(1), (2)(*a*); *repealed by* FA 2002 s 141, Sch 40 Pt 3(13) with effect for accounting periods beginning after 30 September 2002).

79 (*substituted* FA 1994 Sch 18 paras 1, 1A for paras 1, 2; *repealed by* FA 2002 s 141, Sch 40 Pt 3(13) with effect for accounting periods beginning after 30 September 2002).

SCHEDULE 15

LOAN RELATIONSHIPS: SAVINGS AND TRANSITIONAL PROVISIONS

Section 105

Commentary—*Simon's Direct Tax Service* **Division D2.11.**

PART I

CORPORATION TAX

Application and interpretation of Part I

1—(1) This Part of this Schedule has effect for the purposes of corporation tax.

(2) In this Part of this Schedule—

    ''the 1992 Act'' means the Taxation of Chargeable Gains Act 1992;

    ''continuing loan relationship'', in relation to any company, means any loan relationship to which the company was a party both immediately before and on 1st April 1996;

    ''first relevant accounting period'', in relation to a company, means the first accounting period of the company to end after 31st March 1996; and "transitional accounting period", in relation to a company, means any accounting period of the company beginning before and ending on or after 1st April 1996.

(3) Any question as to whether, or to what extent, credits or debits falling to be brought into account for the purposes of this Chapter by virtue of this Part of this Schedule are referable to any category of an insurance company's [long-term][1] business shall be determined according to any apportionment in relation to the loan relationship in question which is made for the company's first relevant accounting period.

(4) In this Part of this Schedule references to this Chapter include references to any repeals having effect for the purposes of this Chapter.

Commentary—*Simon's Direct Tax Service* **D2.1155.**
Amendments—[1] Words in sub-para (3) substituted by the Financial Services and Markets Act 2000 (Consequential Amendments) (Taxes) Order, SI 2001/3629 arts 92, 96(1)(c) with effect from 1 December 2001 (immediately after the coming into force of the Financial Services and Markets Act 2000 ss 411, 432(1), Sch 20).

Loan relationships terminated before 1st April 1996

2 Subject to paragraph 13(6) below, the amounts which are to be brought into account for the purposes of corporation tax in any transitional accounting period of a company by reference to any loan relationship to which it was a party only at a time before 1st April 1996—

    (*a*) shall not be computed in accordance with this Chapter; but

    (*b*) shall, instead, be computed as they would be for an accounting period ending on 31st March 1996.

Commentary—*Simon's Direct Tax Service* **D2.1155.**

Basic rules for transitional accounting periods

3—(1) This paragraph applies as respects any continuing loan relationship of a company.

(2) In a transitional accounting period an amount accruing before 1st April 1996 in respect of a continuing loan relationship (whether it accrues as a right or liability) shall be brought into account for the purposes of this Chapter in accordance with an authorised accruals basis of accounting only if it is an amount accruing as interest.

(3) In a transitional accounting period an amount becoming due and payable before 1st April 1996 in respect of a continuing loan relationship shall be brought into account for the purposes of this Chapter in accordance with an authorised mark to market basis of accounting only if it is an amount becoming so due and payable as interest.

(4) Except where sub-paragraph (6) below applies and subject to the following provisions of this Part of this Schedule, any opening valuation that is to be made for the purpose of bringing amounts into account for the purposes of this Chapter in a transitional accounting period on a mark to market basis of accounting shall be made as at 1st April 1996, instead of as at any earlier time.

(5) Where any opening valuation is made in accordance with sub-paragraph (4) above for any transitional accounting period—

    (*a*) that valuation, and

    (*b*) any closing valuation made as at the end of that period for the purposes mentioned in that sub-paragraph,

shall each be made disregarding any amount of interest that has accrued in respect of any part of that period.

[(5A) Where—

    (*a*) sub-paragraph (5) above applies for determining the closing value of a continuing loan relationship of a company for a transitional accounting period ending on or after 14th November 1996, and

    (*b*) an opening valuation of that relationship falls to be made, as at the beginning of the immediately following accounting period, for the purpose of bringing amounts into account in that company's case on a mark to market basis of accounting,

the opening value given by that opening valuation shall be taken to be the same as the closing value given in accordance with that sub-paragraph.][1]

(6) This sub-paragraph applies in the case of a continuing loan relationship if, apart from this Chapter—

    (*a*) a mark to market basis of accounting would have been used, in the case of the relationship, for the purpose of bringing amounts into account in the transitional accounting period; and

    (*b*) on that basis, an opening valuation as respects the relationship would have fallen to be made for that purpose as at a time before 1st April 1996.

(7) Notwithstanding anything in sub-paragraph (2) or (3) above, where—

    (*a*) there is an amount that accrued or became due and payable before 1st April 1996 in respect of a continuing loan relationship of a company,

    (*b*) that amount is not interest, and

(*c*) that amount would, apart from this Chapter, have been brought into account for the purposes of corporation tax in the accounting period in which it accrued or, as the case may be, became due and payable,

that amount shall be brought into account in that period for the purposes of corporation tax to the same extent as it would have been so brought into account apart from this Chapter and shall not otherwise be brought into account by virtue of the application in relation to times on or after 1st April 1996 of any authorised accounting method.

Commentary—*Simon's Direct Tax Service* **D2.1155, 1158.**
Amendments—[1] Sub-para (5A) inserted by FA 1997 Sch 13 paras 1, 2, 7(1) with effect for the purpose of determining the credits and debits to be brought into account in any accounting period ending after 13 November 1996.

[Adjustment of opening value where new accounting basis adopted as from an accounting period beginning on 1st April 1996

3A—(1) This paragraph applies in the case of a continuing loan relationship of a company where—

(*a*) the company's first relevant accounting period begins on 1st April 1996;
(*b*) in that period amounts are brought into account for the purposes of this Chapter in respect of the relationship on a mark to market basis of accounting;
(*c*) amounts falling to be brought into account in respect of the relationship for the purposes of corporation tax in the accounting period ending with 31st March 1996 were or (if there had been any) would have been so brought into account otherwise than on a mark to market basis of accounting; and
(*d*) an opening valuation of the relationship falls to be made, as at the beginning of the accounting period immediately following the first relevant accounting period, for the purpose of bringing amounts into account on a mark to market basis of accounting.

(2) Where this paragraph applies in the case of a continuing loan relationship of a company, the opening valuation mentioned in sub-paragraph (1)(*d*) above shall be made disregarding any amount of interest that has accrued in the company's first relevant accounting period or in any of its accounting periods preceding that period.][1]

Commentary—*Simon's Direct Tax Service* **D2.1158.**
Amendments—[1] This paragraph inserted by FA 1997 Sch 13 paras 1, 3, 7(1) with effect for the purpose of determining the credits and debits to be brought into account in any accounting period ending after 13 November 1996.

Application of accruals basis to pre-commencement relationships

4 Subject to the following provisions of this Schedule, any question for the purposes of this Chapter as to the amounts which are to be treated (in accordance with an authorised accruals basis of accounting) as accruing to a company on or after 1st April 1996 shall be determined by applying that basis of accounting for determining, first, what amounts had accrued before that date.

Adjustments in respect of pre-commencement trading relationships

5—(1) This paragraph applies in the case of any continuing loan relationship of a company as respects which any amounts would have been brought into account for the purposes of corporation tax in computing the profits or losses of the company from any trade carried on by it if—

(*a*) the company had ceased to be a party to the relationship on 31st March 1996; and
(*b*) where it is not otherwise the case, an accounting period of the company had ended on that date.

(2) Where there is a difference between—

(*a*) the notional closing value of the relationship as at 31st March 1996, and
(*b*) the adjusted closing value of that relationship as at that date,

that difference shall be brought into account as provided for in paragraph 6 below.

(3) Except where sub-paragraph (4) or (6) below applies, the notional closing value as at 31st March 1996 of a loan relationship of a company shall be taken for the purposes of this paragraph to be the amount which, for the purposes of computing the profits or losses of the company from any trade carried on by it—

(*a*) was as at that date, or
(*b*) had an accounting period of the company ended on that date, would have been,

the amount falling to be brought into account as representing the value of the company's rights or liabilities under the relationship.

(4) Except where sub-paragraph (6) below applies, if no amount is given by sub-paragraph (3) above, the notional closing value as at 31st March 1996 of a loan relationship of a company shall be taken for the purposes of this paragraph to be the amount which, for the purposes of computing the profits or losses of the company from any trade carried on by it, would have been deductible as representing the cost of becoming a party to the relationship if the company had ceased to be a party to the relationship on 31st March 1996.

[(4A) In sub-paragraph (4) above the reference, in relation to a creditor relationship, to the amount deductible as representing the cost of a company's becoming a party to the relationship shall not, except where sub-paragraph (4B) or (4C) below applies, include a reference to so much of that amount as would represent the cost of acquiring any right to accrued interest under the loan relationship.][1]

[(4B) This sub-paragraph applies where—

(a) the company became a party to the relationship before the beginning of its first relevant accounting period,

(b) interest accruing under the relationship before the company became a party to it was paid to the company after it became a party to it but before the beginning of the company's first relevant accounting period, and

(c) the interest under the relationship which, in the case of that company, has been brought into account for the purposes of corporation tax has included interest accruing under the relationship before the company became a party to it but paid afterwards.][1]

[(4C) This sub-paragraph applies where—

(a) the company became a party to the loan relationship in a transitional accounting period, and

(b) in the case of that company, interest under the relationship which—

(i) accrued before the company became a party to the relationship, but

(ii) became due and payable afterwards,

is brought into account for the purposes of this Chapter in accordance with an authorised mark to market basis of accounting.][1]

(5) Except where sub-paragraph (6) below applies, the adjusted closing value of that relationship as at that date shall be taken for the purposes of this paragraph to be the amount which for the purposes of this Chapter is the opening value as at 1st April 1996 of the company's rights and liabilities under the relationship.

(6) For the purposes of this paragraph where the asset representing a loan relationship of a company is a relevant qualifying asset of the company, or the liabilities of the company under the relationship are relevant liabilities—

(a) the notional closing value of the relationship as at 31st March 1996 shall be taken for the purposes of this paragraph to be the value given by paragraph 12 below as the notional closing value as at 31st March 1996 of that asset or, as the case may be, of those liabilities; and

(b) the adjusted closing value of the relationship as at 31st March 1996 shall be taken for those purposes to be the amount which is as at 1st April 1996 the opening value of the asset or liabilities for the purposes of this Chapter.

(7) For the purposes of this paragraph, where an accruals basis of accounting is used as respects a loan relationship for the first relevant accounting period of the company, the opening value as at 1st April 1996 of the company's rights and liabilities under the relationship shall be taken to be the value which (disregarding interest) is treated in accordance with paragraph 4 above as having accrued to the company before that date.

(8) In this paragraph—

"attributed amount" means any attributed gain or loss falling to be calculated in accordance with any regulations made under Schedule 16 to the Finance Act 1993 (transitional provisions for exchange gains and losses) which contain any such provision as is mentioned in paragraph 3(1) of that Schedule;

"commencement day", in relation to a company, means its commencement day for the purposes of Chapter II of Part II of the Finance Act 1993;

"market value" has the same meaning as in the 1992 Act;

"relevant liability", in relation to a company, means any liability under a loan relationship the value of which has been determined as at the company's commencement day for the purpose of calculating any attributed amount;

"relevant qualifying asset", in relation to a company, means any qualifying asset for the purposes of Chapter II of Part II of the Finance Act 1993 the value of which has been determined as at the company's commencement day for the purpose of calculating any attributed amount.

Commentary—*Simon's Direct Tax Service* D2.1159.
Amendments—[1] Sub-paras (4A)–(4C) inserted by FA 1997 Sch 13 paras 1, 4, 7(1), subject to FA 1997 Sch 13 para 7(2), with effect for the purpose of determining the credits and debits to be brought into account in any accounting period ending after 13 November 1996.

Method of giving effect to paragraph 5 adjustments

6—(1) Subject to sub-paragraph (4) below, the difference mentioned in paragraph 5(2) above shall be brought into account in accordance with sub-paragraph (2) or (3) below in the accounting period in which the company ceases to be a party to the relationship.

(2) If—

(a) the relationship is a creditor relationship and the difference consists in an excess of the amount mentioned in paragraph 5(2)(b) above over the amount mentioned in paragraph 5(2)(a) above, or (*b*) the relationship is a debtor relationship and the difference consists in an excess of the amount mentioned in paragraph 5(2)(*a*) above over the amount mentioned in paragraph 5(2)(*b*) above,

the difference shall be brought into account as a credit given for the purposes of this Chapter for the period mentioned in sub-paragraph (1) above.

(3) In any other case, the difference shall be brought into account as a debit given for the purposes of this Chapter for the period so mentioned.

(4) Where the company, by notice in writing given on or before 30th September 1996 to an officer of the Board, makes an election for the purposes of this sub-paragraph—

(*a*) sub-paragraphs (1) to (3) above shall not apply; and

(*b*) instead, one sixth of every credit and debit which would have fallen, in accordance with those sub-paragraphs, to be brought into account on the relevant assumption shall be brought into account for each year in the period of six years beginning with the company's first relevant accounting period;

and for this purpose "the relevant assumption" is that the company had ceased on 1st April 1996 to be a party to every one of its continuing loan relationships to which paragraph 5 above applies.

(5) Where any amount representing a fraction of a credit or debit falls to be brought into account for any year under sub-paragraph (4) above, that amount shall be—

(*a*) apportioned between the accounting periods beginning or ending in that year; and

(*b*) brought into account in the periods to which it is allocated in accordance with that apportionment.

(6) An apportionment between accounting periods of an amount to be brought into account under sub-paragraph (4) above for any year shall be made according to how much of the year is included in each period; and, if that year and the accounting period are the same, the apportionment shall be effected by the allocation of the whole amount to that accounting period.

(7) If the company ceases to be within the charge to corporation tax before the end of the six years mentioned in sub-paragraph (4)(*b*) above, the whole amount of the excess, so far as it has not fallen to be brought into account for an earlier accounting period, shall be brought into account as a debit or credit for the accounting period ending when the company ceases to be within that charge.

(8) Where any credit or debit falls to be brought into account under this paragraph for any accounting period for the whole or any part of which the company carries on the trade in question, the credit or debit shall be brought into account under section 82(2) of this Act in relation to that trade; and, in any other case, it shall be brought into account as a non-trading credit or non-trading debit.

Commentary—*Simon's Direct Tax Service* **D2.1159.**
Cross reference—See FA 1997 Sch 13 para 7(3) (commencement of that Schedule, which amends *this* Schedule, as it affects determination of credits and debits within sub-para (4) above).
FA 1999 s 81 (acquisitions disregarded under insurance companies concession).

General savings for the taxation of chargeable gains

7 The amendments of the 1992 Act contained in Schedule 14 to this Act and the related repeals made by this Act—

(*a*) so far as they relate to section 253 of the 1992 Act, do not apply to any loan the outstanding amount of principal on which became irrecoverable before 1st April 1996;

(*b*) so far as they relate to section 254 of the 1992 Act, do not apply to any security whose value became negligible before 1st April 1996;

(*c*) so far as they relate to anything else, do not apply in relation to any disposal made, or deemed to be made, before 1st April 1996.

Transitional provision for chargeable assets held after commencement

8—(1) This paragraph applies where—

(*a*) on 31st March 1996 any company ("the relevant company") held any asset representing, in whole or in part, any loan relationship to which it was a party on that date;

(*b*) the company did not dispose of that asset on that date and does not fall (apart from by virtue of this paragraph) to be treated for the purposes of the 1992 Act as having made a disposal of it on that date;

(*c*) the asset is not one to which section 92 of this Act or paragraph 15 below applies;

(*d*) that asset is not an asset representing a loan relationship to which section 93 of this Act applies;

(*e*) that asset is not a relevant qualifying asset; and

(*f*) a relevant event occurs.

(2) For the purposes of this paragraph a relevant event occurs on the first occasion after 31st March 1996 when the relevant company or any other company falls to be treated for the purposes of the 1992 Act as making a disposal, other than one to which section 139, 140A, [or 171(1)][2] of that Act (disposals on which neither a gain nor a loss accrues) applies, of—

(*a*) the asset in question, so far as it has not come to be represented by an asset falling within paragraph (*b*) below, or

(b) any such asset as falls to be treated for the purposes of that Act as the same as that asset.

(3) The amount of any chargeable gain or allowable loss which would have been treated as accruing to the relevant company on the assumption—

    (a) that it had made a disposal of the asset on 31st March 1996, and

    (b) (so far as relevant for the purpose of computing the amount of that gain or loss) that the disposal had been for a consideration equal to the market value of the asset,

shall be brought into account (subject to the following provisions of this paragraph and to paragraph 9 below) as one accruing to the company ("the chargeable company") which makes the disposal constituting the relevant event, and shall be so brought into account in the accounting period in which that event occurs.

(4) The amount of the deemed chargeable gain or deemed allowable loss falling to be brought into account in accordance with sub-paragraph (3) above shall be treated as reduced by the extent (if any) to which it is, in relation to the company, an amount that already has been, or falls to be, taken into account for the purposes of corporation tax by virtue of the use of any accruals or mark to market basis of accounting—

    (a) for those purposes;

    (b) as respects times before 1st April 1996; and

    (c) in relation to the asset in question.

(5) To the extent that any deemed chargeable gain or deemed allowable loss falling to be brought into account under sub-paragraph (3) above includes any gain or loss deemed to accrue under section 116(10)(b) of the 1992 Act (qualifying corporate bonds acquired in a reorganisation etc), that gain or loss shall be deemed to have accrued for the purposes of that sub-paragraph and (without prejudice to its being brought into account in accordance with that sub-paragraph) shall not be taken to accrue again on the occurrence of the relevant event or any subsequent disposal of any asset.

[(5A) In any case where the relevant event has not occurred before 14th November 1996, the deemed chargeable gain or deemed allowable loss falling to be brought into account in accordance with sub-paragraph (3) above shall be computed without any account being taken of the provisions of section 119(6) and (7) of the 1992 Act (transfer of securities with or without accrued interest).]¹

(6) In any case where—

    (a) the relevant company is one which at any time before 1st April 1996 was not resident in the United Kingdom,

    (b) the asset was held by the relevant company at such a time, and

    (c) if the asset had been disposed of at that time and a gain had accrued to the relevant company on that disposal, it would not have been included in the company's chargeable profits by virtue of section 10(3) of the 1992 Act (gain on a disposal by a branch or agency of a non-resident company),

the relevant company shall be deemed for the purposes of sub-paragraph (3) above to have acquired the asset, at market value, on the first day on which any relevant gain would have been included in the company's chargeable profits for the purposes of corporation tax (whether because it is a day on which the company became resident, or the asset became situated, in the United Kingdom or for any other reason).

(7) In sub-paragraph (6) above the reference, in relation to a company, to a relevant gain is a reference to any gain which would have accrued to the company on the following assumptions, that is to say—

    (a) that the relevant company disposed of the asset on the day in question;

    (b) that that disposal gave rise to a gain; and

    (c) that any allowable losses which might have been available for deduction under section 8(1) of, or Schedule 7A to, the 1992 Act were to be disregarded.

(8) In any case where the company acquired the asset on a disposal on which, by virtue of any enactment specified in section 35(3)(d) of the 1992 Act, neither a gain nor a loss accrued to the person making the disposal, the reference in sub-paragraph (6) or (7) above to the relevant company includes—

    (a) a reference to the company from which it acquired the asset; and

    (b) if that company also acquired the asset on such a disposal, a reference to the company from which the asset was acquired by that company, and so on through any number of such disposals.

(9) In any case where section 176 of the 1992 Act (depreciatory transactions within a group) would have applied in relation to the disposal referred to in sub-paragraph (3) above if that disposal had actually taken place, that section shall apply for the calculation of any deemed allowable loss to be brought into account by virtue of that sub-paragraph.

(10) For the purposes of this paragraph a company that ceases to be within the charge to corporation tax shall be deemed to make a disposal of all its assets at their market value immediately before ceasing to be within that charge.

(11) In this paragraph—

"market value" has the same meaning as in the 1992 Act; and

"relevant qualifying asset" has the same meaning as in paragraph 5 above.

Commentary—*Simon's Direct Tax Service* **D2.1162.**
Amendments—¹ Sub-para (5A) inserted by FA 1997 Sch 13 paras 1, 5, 7(1) with effect for the purpose of determining the credits and debits to be brought into account in any accounting period ending after 13 November 1996.
² Words in sub-para (2) substituted by FA 2000 s 102, Sch 29 para 45 with effect for disposals after 31 March 2000.

Election for alternative treatment of amounts specified in paragraph 8

9—(1) Subject to the following provisions of this paragraph, where (apart from this paragraph) any amount representing a deemed allowable loss would fall in the case of any company to be brought into account for any accounting period in accordance with sub-paragraph (3) of paragraph 8 above, the chargeable company may elect for that amount to be brought into account for that period for the purposes of this Chapter, instead of in accordance with that sub-paragraph.

(2) An amount brought into account for the purposes of this Chapter by virtue of an election under this paragraph shall be so brought into account as a debit given for that period for the purposes of this Chapter.

(3) The question whether or not any debit brought into account for any accounting period in accordance with sub-paragraph (2) above is to be brought into account for that period as a non-trading debit shall be determined according to how other credits or debits relating to the loan relationship in question are, or (if there were any) would be, brought into account for that period.

(4) No election shall be made under this paragraph in respect of any deemed allowable loss in any case where the asset in respect of which that loss is deemed to have accrued was one which, as at 1st April 1996, either—

    (*a*) fell in accordance with section 127 or 214(9) of the 1992 Act (equation of new holding with previous holding) to be treated as the same as an asset which was not an asset representing a loan relationship; or

    (*b*) would have so fallen but for section 116(5) of that Act.

(5) An election shall not be made under this paragraph at any time more than two years after the occurrence of the relevant event by virtue of which the amount to which the election relates would fall to be brought into account in accordance with paragraph 8(3) above.

Commentary—*Simon's Direct Tax Service* **D2.1162.**

Adjustments of opening value for mark to market accounting in the case of chargeable assets

10—(1) Where—

    (*a*) a mark to market basis of accounting is used as respects any loan relationship of a company for the company's first relevant accounting period,

    (*b*) for the purpose of bringing amounts into account for the purposes of this Chapter on that basis, an opening valuation of an asset representing that relationship falls to be made as at 1st April 1996, and

    (*c*) that asset is a chargeable asset held by that company on 31st March 1996,

the value of that asset on 1st April 1996 shall be taken for the purpose of the opening valuation to be equal to whatever, in relation to a disposal on 31st March 1996, would have been taken to be its market value for the purposes of the 1992 Act.

(2) In this paragraph "chargeable asset", in relation to a company, means (subject to sub-paragraph (3) below) any asset in the case of which one of the following conditions is satisfied, that is to say—

    (*a*) a gain accruing to the company on a disposal of that asset on 31st March 1996 would have fallen to be treated in relation to the company as a chargeable gain; or

    (*b*) a chargeable gain or allowable loss would be deemed to have accrued to the company on any disposal of that asset on that date.

(3) An asset is not a chargeable asset for the purposes of this paragraph if (disregarding the provisions of this Chapter) it is an asset any disposal of which on 31st March 1996 would have fallen to be regarded for the purposes of the 1992 Act as a disposal of a qualifying corporate bond.

Commentary—*Simon's Direct Tax Service* **D2.1162.**

Other adjustments in the case of chargeable assets etc

11—(1) Where—

    (*a*) an authorised accruals basis of accounting is applied as respects any continuing loan relationship of a company for the company's first relevant accounting period,

    (*b*) an asset representing that relationship is a relevant asset or any liability under it is a relevant liability, and

    (*c*) the relationship is not one as respects which, if the company had ceased to be a party to the relationship on 31st March 1996, any amounts would have been brought into account in computing, for an accounting period ending on or after that date, the profits or losses of the company from any trade carried on by it,

that accounting method shall be taken for the purposes of this Chapter to require the asset or liability to be given a notional closing value as at 31st March 1996 in accordance with paragraph 12 below and the following provisions of this paragraph shall apply if there is any difference in the case of that relationship between the amounts mentioned in sub-paragraph (2) below.

[(2) Those amounts are—

    (a) the notional closing value of the relationship as at 31st March 1996; and

    (b) the amount which would be taken on a computation made—

        (i) in accordance with an authorised accruals basis of accounting, and

        (ii) on the assumption that such a basis of accounting had always been used as respects that relationship,

to represent the accrued value of the loan relationship in question on 1st April 1996.][1]

[(2A) If, in a case where the continuing loan relationship is a creditor relationship,—

    (a) the company acquired its rights under the relationship on or before 31st March 1996 by virtue of an arm's length transaction,

    (b) for the accounting period in which it acquired those rights—

        (i) there was no connection (as defined in sub-paragraph (2C) below) between the company and the person from whom the company acquired the asset, but

        (ii) there was such a connection between the company and a company standing in the position of a debtor as respects the money debt, and

    (c) there had been no such connection between the companies mentioned in paragraph (b)(ii) above at any time in the period which—

        (i) begins 4 years before the date on which the company acquired those rights, and

        (ii) ends twelve months before that date,

this paragraph shall have effect as if the amount mentioned in sub-paragraph (2)(b) above were an amount equal to the greater of the amounts mentioned in sub-paragraph (2B) below.][2]

[(2B) Those amounts are—

    (a) the fair value of the rights at the time when the company ceases to be a party to the loan relationship; and

    (b) the fair value of the rights on 1st April 1996.][2]

[(2C) For the purposes of sub-paragraph (2A) above there is a connection between a company and another person at any time if at that time—

    (a) the other person is a company and one of the companies has control of the other,

    (b) the other person is a company and both companies are under the control of the same person, or

    (c) the company is a close company and the other person is a participator in that company or the associate of a person who is such a participator,

and there is a connection between a company and another person for an accounting period if there is a connection (within paragraphs (a) to (c) above) between the company and the person at any time in that accounting period.][2]

[(2D) For the purposes of sub-paragraph (2C) above—

    (a) subsections (2) to (6) of section 416 of the Taxes Act 1988 (meaning of control) shall apply as they apply for the purposes of Part 11 of that Act;

    (b) subject to paragraph (c) below, "participator" and "associate" have the meaning given for the purposes of that Part by section 417 of that Act;

    (c) a person shall not be regarded as a participator in relation to a company by reason only that he is a loan creditor of the company.][2]

[(3) Where there is a difference between the amounts mentioned in sub-paragraph (2) above, that difference shall be brought into account—

    (a) where the amount mentioned in paragraph (a) of that sub-paragraph is the smaller, as a credit given for the purposes of this Chapter for the accounting period in which the company ceases to be a party to the relationship; and

    (b) in any other case, as a debit so given.][1]

(5) Where the company ceases to be within the charge to corporation tax, it shall be deemed for the purposes of this paragraph to have ceased to be a party to the relationship in question immediately before ceasing to be within that charge.

(6) A credit or debit brought into account under this paragraph shall be brought into account as a non-trading credit or non-trading debit.

(7) In this paragraph—

    "chargeable asset", in relation to a company, means (subject to sub-paragraph (8) below) any asset held by the company on 31st March 1996 in the case of which one of the following conditions is satisfied, that is to say—

        (a) a gain accruing to the company on a disposal of that asset on that date would have fallen to be treated in relation to the company as a chargeable gain; or

        (b) a chargeable gain or allowable loss would be deemed to have accrued to the company on any disposal of that asset on that date;

and

"relevant asset" means a chargeable asset or a relevant qualifying asset.

(8) An asset is not a chargeable asset for the purposes of this paragraph if (disregarding the provisions of this Chapter) it is an asset any disposal of which on 31st March 1996 would have fallen to be regarded for the purposes of the 1992 Act as a disposal of a qualifying corporate bond.

(9) Expressions used in this paragraph and paragraph 5 above have the same meanings in this paragraph as in that paragraph.

Commentary—*Simon's Direct Tax Service* **D2.1163.**
Amendments—¹ Sub-paras (2), (3) substituted for sub-paras (2)–(4) by FA 1997 Sch 13 paras 1, 6, 7(1), subject to FA 1997 Sch 13 para 7(2), with effect for the purpose of determining the credits and debits to be brought into account in any accounting period ending after 13 November 1996.
² Sub-paras (2A)–(2D) inserted by FA 2002 s 82, Sch 25 paras 1, 41 with effect for accounting periods beginning after 30 September 2002.

[*Reduction of para. 11 credit where s.251(4) of 1992 Act prevents para. 8 loss*

11A—(1) This paragraph applies where, in the case of any asset representing in whole or in part a loan relationship of a company, an amount representing a deemed allowable loss would (apart from this paragraph) fall or have fallen to be brought into account in accordance with paragraph 8(3) above for an accounting period (whenever beginning or ending), but for section 251(4) of the 1992 Act (no allowable loss on disposal of debt acquired from connected person).

(2) Where this paragraph applies, the amount of any credit falling within sub-paragraph (3) below shall be treated for the purposes of this Chapter as reduced (but not below nil) by the amount described in sub-paragraph (1) above.

(3) A credit falls within this sub-paragraph if (apart from this paragraph)—

(a) the credit falls to be given by virtue of paragraph 11(3)(a) above for an accounting period beginning on or after 1st October 2002; and
(b) the loan relationship mentioned in paragraph 11(1)(a) above in the case of the credit is the same loan relationship as the one mentioned in sub-paragraph (1) above.]¹

Amendments—¹ This paragraph inserted by FA 2002 s 82, Sch 25 paras 1, 42 with effect for accounting periods beginning after 30 September 2002.

Notional closing values of relevant assets

12—(1) Subject to sub-paragraph (2) below, the notional closing value as at 31st March 1996 of any relevant asset representing a loan relationship of a company, or of any relevant liability, shall be taken for the purposes of paragraphs 5 and 11 above, to be an amount equal to the following amount, that is to say—

(a) in the case of a chargeable asset, its market value on that date;
(b) in the case of a relevant qualifying asset or relevant liability, the value given to it as at the company's commencement day for the purpose of computing any attributed amount.

(2) Sub-paragraph (3) below applies where a company, by notice in writing given on or before 30th September 1996 to an officer of the Board, makes an election for the purposes of that sub-paragraph in relation to all of its relevant qualifying assets which—

(a) apart from the election, would be given a notional closing value as at 31st March 1996 by sub-paragraph (1) above; and
(b) but for Chapter II of Part II of the Finance Act 1993 (exchange gains and losses), would be chargeable assets.

(3) Where such an election is made as respects those assets—

(a) sub-paragraph (1) above shall not apply as respects those assets; but
(b) the value of each of those assets as at 1st April 1996 shall be taken for the purposes of this Chapter to be its market value on that date.

(4) In this paragraph "chargeable asset" and "relevant asset" have the same meanings as in paragraph 11 above; and expressions used in this paragraph and paragraph 5 above have the same meanings in this paragraph as in that paragraph.

Commentary—*Simon's Direct Tax Service* **D2.1163.**

Further transitional rules for interest under loan relationships

13—(1) Where—

(a) an amount of interest under a loan relationship of a company accrues or becomes due and payable in an accounting period ending on or after 1st April 1996, but
(b) the amount accruing or becoming due and payable has already, in the case of that company, been brought into account for the purposes of corporation tax for an old accounting period,

no credit or, as the case may be, debit relating to that amount shall be brought into account in the case of that company for the purposes of this Chapter.

(2) This Chapter shall have effect in accordance with sub-paragraphs (3) and (4) below in relation to any pre-commencement late interest, that is to say, interest which—

    (*a*) has accrued or become due and payable in an old accounting period, but
    (*b*) is paid in an accounting period ending on or after 1st April 1996.

(3) Where—

    (*a*) an amount of pre-commencement late interest under a debtor relationship of a company is paid by that company,
    (*b*) the amount paid is not interest which, in the case of that company, was brought into account for the purposes of corporation tax for any old accounting period,
    (*c*) relief would have been allowable in respect of the amount paid if the provisions of this Chapter had not been enacted, and
    (*d*) the amount paid is not interest in relation to which any debit falls (apart from under this sub-paragraph) to be brought into account for the purposes of this Chapter in case of that company,

debits shall be brought into account for the purposes of this Chapter in the case of that company as if the amount paid were interest accruing, and becoming due and payable, at the time when it is paid.

(4) Where—

    (*a*) an amount of pre-commencement late interest under a creditor relationship of a company is paid to that company,
    (*b*) the amount paid is not interest which, in the case of that company, was brought into account for the purposes of corporation tax for any old accounting period,
    (*c*) the amount paid is not interest in relation to which any credit falls (apart from under this sub-paragraph) to be brought into account for the purposes of this Chapter in the case of that company,
    (*d*) the amount paid is not an amount of interest which in relation to a transfer before 1st April 1996 was unrealised interest within the meaning of section 716 of the Taxes Act 1988,

credits shall be brought into account for the purposes of this Chapter in the case of that company as if the amount paid were interest accruing, and becoming due and payable, at the time when it is paid.

(5) Where—

    (*a*) any interest under a debtor relationship of a company was paid by that company at a time on or after 20th December 1995 but during an old accounting period,
    (*b*) the company was not required to make the payment at or before that time by virtue of any contractual obligation entered into by that company before 20th December 1995, and
    (*c*) the interest paid is not interest which, if brought into account for the purposes of corporation tax in accordance with an authorised accruals basis of accounting, would fall to be so brought into account in an old accounting period,

the interest paid shall not, in the case of that company, be brought into account for the purposes of corporation tax in any old accounting period.

(6) Where on 1st April 1996 any interest under a loan relationship remains to be paid to or by a company that ceased to be a party to that relationship before that date, this Chapter (including the preceding provisions of this paragraph) shall have effect, so far as relating to interest under a loan relationship, as if the relationship were a continuing loan relationship.

(7) Sub-paragraphs (8) and (9) below apply where the accounting period for which any credits or debits relating to interest under a loan relationship are brought into account for the purposes of this Chapter is determined either—

    (*a*) in accordance with an accruals basis of accounting, by reference to the time when by virtue of this paragraph that interest is deemed to accrue; or
    (*b*) in accordance with a mark to market basis of accounting, by reference to the time when by virtue of this paragraph the interest is deemed to become due and payable.

(8) If—

    (*a*) at the time when the interest in fact accrued or (as the case may be) when the interest in fact became due and payable, the company was a party to the relationship in question for the purposes of a trade carried on by it, and
    (*b*) the credits or debits relating to that interest fall to be brought into account for an accounting period determined as mentioned in sub-paragraph (7) above which is a period for the whole or any part of which that company carries on that trade,

those credits or debits shall be so brought into account under section 82(2) of this Act.

(9) In a case not falling within sub-paragraph (8) above, credits or debits relating to any interest that fall to be brought into account for the purposes of this Chapter for an accounting period determined as mentioned in sub-paragraph (7) above shall be so brought into account as non-trading credits or, as the case may be, non-trading debits.

(10) References in this paragraph to interest under a loan relationship include references to any amounts brought into account for the purposes of corporation tax in accordance with the provisions of section 477A(3) of the Taxes Act 1988 (whether under those provisions as they had effect apart from the amendments made by this Act or under those provisions as amended by this Act).

(11) In this paragraph "old accounting period", in relation to a company, means any accounting period of that company ending before 1st April 1996.

Commentary—*Simon's Direct Tax Service* **D2.1156, 1157.**

Transitional in respect of incidental expenses already allowed

14 To the extent that any deduction in respect of any charges or expenses incurred as mentioned in section 84(3) of this Act has been made for the purposes of corporation tax in any accounting period ending before 1st April 1996, those charges or expenses shall not be included in the charges or expenses in relation to which debits may be brought into account for the purposes of this Chapter.

Commentary—*Simon's Direct Tax Service* **D2.1160.**

Holdings of unit trusts etc

15—(1) This paragraph applies to any asset which—

(a) is an asset of an insurance company's long term business fund (within the meaning of Chapter I of Part XII of the Taxes Act 1988) both on and immediately after 31st March 1996; and

(b) falls by virtue of paragraph 4 of Schedule 10 to this Act to be treated for a transitional accounting period of the company as representing rights under a creditor relationship of the company.

(2) Sections 212 and 213 of the 1992 Act (annual disposal of holdings of unit trusts etc) shall have effect (without the amendment made by this Chapter) in relation to the assets to which this paragraph applies as if (where it would not otherwise be the case) 31st March 1996 were the last day of an accounting period of the company holding the asset.

(3) Nothing in this Chapter shall prejudice the effect of section 213 of the 1992 Act in relation to any disposal which (whether by virtue of sub-paragraph (2) above or otherwise) is deemed under section 212 of that Act to be made on or before 31st March 1996.

Bad debt relieved before commencement

16—(1) This paragraph applies where—

(a) an amount becomes, or is to become, due and payable under a creditor relationship of a company in an accounting period ending on or after 1st April 1996, but

(b) by virtue of any of sub-paragraphs (i) to (iii) of section 74(1)(j) of the Taxes Act 1988 (or any enactment re-enacted in those sub-paragraphs), a deduction of an amount representing the whole or any part of the amount payable was authorised to be made, and was made, in computing for the purposes of corporation tax the profits of the company for any accounting period ending before that date.

(2) Subject to sub-paragraph (3) below, nothing in this Chapter shall require it to be assumed for the purposes of this Chapter that any part of the amount to which the deduction relates will be paid in full as it becomes due.

(3) Subject to sub-paragraph (4) below, where—

(a) the deduction relates to an amount payable under a creditor relationship of a company which has been proved or estimated to be a bad debt, but

(b) in an accounting period ending on or after 1st April 1996 the whole or any part of the liability under that relationship to pay that amount is discharged by payment,

this Chapter shall have effect, in the case of that company, as if there were a credit equal to the amount of the payment to be brought into account for the purposes of this Chapter for that period.

(4) Sub-paragraph (3) above does not apply to so much of any payment as is an amount in relation to which a credit falls to be brought into account for the purposes of this Chapter in accordance with paragraph 13(4) above.

Commentary—*Simon's Direct Tax Service* **D2.1161.**

Transitional for overseas sovereign debt etc

17—(1) Subject to any regulations under sub-paragraph (4) below and notwithstanding anything in the preceding provisions of this Schedule, the value which for the purposes of this Chapter is to be taken to be the value as at 1st April 1996 of a company's rights under any creditor relationship relating to a relevant overseas debt any part of which falls to be estimated as bad, is the following amount—

(a) where the company was not entitled to the debt before the end of its last period of account to end before 1st April 1996, the amount for which the company acquired those rights; and

(b) in any other case, the amount of so much of that debt as did not fall, in accordance with section 88B of the Taxes Act 1988, to be estimated as at the end of that period to be bad.

(2) Subject to any regulations under sub-paragraph (4) below, sub-paragraph (3) below shall apply where there is a loss incurred before 1st April 1996 to which section 88C of the Taxes Act 1988 has applied or applies by virtue of paragraph 2 above.

(3) Where, apart from this Chapter, any amount would have been allowed in respect of the loss as a deduction for any accounting period ending after 31st March 1996, that amount shall not be so allowed but shall, instead, be brought into account for the purposes of this Chapter as if it were a debit given for that accounting period by paragraph 9 of Schedule 9 to this Act in respect of a loss incurred on or after 1st April 1996.

(4) The Treasury may by regulations—

(a) make such transitional provision as they consider appropriate for purposes connected with the coming into force of paragraphs 8 and 9 of Schedule 9 to this Act and the repeal of sections 88A to 88C of the Taxes Act 1988 (which contained corresponding provisions); and

(b) in connection with any such provision, make such modifications of this Schedule (including sub-paragraphs (1) to (3) above) as they consider appropriate;

and regulations made by virtue of this sub-paragraph may have retrospective effect in relation to any accounting periods ending on or after 1st April 1996.

(5) The Treasury shall not make any regulations under sub-paragraph (4) above unless a draft of them has been laid before and approved by a resolution of the House of Commons.

(6) In this paragraph "relevant overseas debt" has the same meaning as in paragraphs 8 and 9 of Schedule 9 to this Act.

Transitional for accrued income scheme

18—(1) Subject to sub-paragraph (2) below, where, apart from this Chapter, any company would be treated under subsection (2) or (4) of section 714 of the Taxes Act 1988 (treatment of deemed sums and reliefs under accrued income scheme)—

(a) as receiving any amount at the end of a period beginning before and ending on or after 1st April 1996, or

(b) as entitled to any allowance of any amount in such a period,

that amount shall be brought into account as a non-trading credit or, as the case may be, non-trading debit given for the purposes of this Chapter for the company's first relevant accounting period, instead of in accordance with that subsection.

(2) A debit in respect of an allowance relating to a security shall not, in the case of any company, be brought into account for the purposes of this Chapter in accordance with sub-paragraph (1) above if—

(a) the security was transferred to that company with accrued interest in a transitional accounting period; and

(b) for the purposes of this Chapter an authorised accruals basis of accounting is used for that period as respects the creditor relationship of the company represented by that security.

(3) Where any excess would, apart from this Chapter, be available by virtue of section 103(4) of the Finance Act 1993 (transitional provision in connection with the repeal of section 724(7) of the Taxes Act 1988) to be applied in reducing the annual profits or gains of a company (if any) for its first relevant accounting period, that excess shall be brought into account for the purposes of this Chapter in the case of that company as a non-trading debit for that period.

(4) Subsection (6) of section 807 of the Taxes Act 1988 shall not prevent that section from having effect for an accounting period ending on or after 1st April 1996 in relation to amounts brought into account under this paragraph.

(5) The repeal by this Act of section 63 of the Finance Act 1993 (deemed transfers for the purposes of the accrued income scheme) and of enactments relating to that section shall not apply in relation to relevant days falling before 1st April 1996; but for the purposes of that section and this sub-paragraph 31st March 1996 shall be deemed (where it would not otherwise be so) to be the last day of an accounting period.

Commentary—*Simon's Direct Tax Service* **D2.1164.**

Deep discount securities

19—(1) This Chapter shall not affect—

(a) the application of paragraph 3 of Schedule 4 to the Taxes Act 1988 (charge to tax after acquisition of deep discount securities) in relation to occasions before 1st April 1996;

(b) the application of paragraph 4 of that Schedule (charge to tax on disposal of such securities) in relation to any disposal before that date; or

(c) the application of paragraph 5 of that Schedule (relief in respect of the income element), in accordance (where applicable) with paragraphs 9 and 10 of that Schedule, in relation to income periods ending before that date.

(2) For the purposes of paragraph 5 of Schedule 4 to the Taxes Act 1988 and sub-paragraph (1)(c) above every income period current on 31st March 1996 shall be deemed to end on that date.

(3) The repeal by this Act of section 64 of the Finance Act 1993 (deemed transfers in the case of deep discount securities) and of enactments relating to that section shall not apply in relation to relevant times falling before 1st April 1996; but for the purposes of that section and this sub-

paragraph 31st March 1996 shall be deemed (where it would not otherwise be so) to be the last day of an accounting period.

[(3A) Any income that is treated as arising at the time mentioned in subsection (5) of that section, as it applies by virtue of sub-paragraph (3) above, shall be brought into account as a non-trading credit given for the purposes of this Chapter for the accounting period in which that time falls.][1]

(4) Where—

 (a) a company issued a deep discount security before 1st April 1996 which was not redeemed before that date, and

 (b) there is a difference between the adjusted issue price of the security as at 31st March 1996 and the adjusted closing value of that security as at that date,

the amount of that difference shall, in the case of that company, be brought into account for the purposes of this Chapter in accordance with sub-paragraph (5) below.

(5) An amount falling to be brought into account for the purposes of this Chapter in accordance with this sub-paragraph shall be brought into account for those purposes for the accounting period in which the security is redeemed—

 (a) if the adjusted issue price of the security as at 31st March 1996 is greater than the adjusted closing value of the security as at that date, as a non-trading credit; and

 (b) if the adjusted closing value of the security as at that date is the greater, as a non-trading debit.

(6) Where—

 (a) a company held a deep discount security on 31st March 1996,

 (b) the company did not make any disposal of that security on that date,

 (c) the security is not one in relation to which there is, or is deemed to be, a relevant time on that date for the purposes of section 64 of the Finance Act 1993, and

 (d) there is an amount which, if the company had made a disposal of that security on that date, would have been treated under paragraph 4 of Schedule 4 to the Taxes Act 1988 as income chargeable to tax under Case III or IV of Schedule D,

that amount shall be brought into account as a non-trading credit given for the purposes of this Chapter for the accounting period mentioned in sub-paragraph (9) below.

(7) Where—

 (a) a company held a deep discount security on 31st March 1996,

 [(b) the company did not make any disposal of that security on that date,][2]

 (c) the security is not an asset falling to be treated as a relevant asset of the company for the purposes of paragraph 11 above, and

 (d) there is a difference between the adjusted issue price of the security as at 31st March 1996 and the adjusted closing value of that security as at that date,

the amount of that difference (in addition to any amount given by sub-paragraph (6) above) shall, in the case of that company, be brought into account for the purposes of this Chapter in accordance with sub-paragraph (8) below.

(8) An amount falling to be brought into account for the purposes of this Chapter in accordance with this sub-paragraph shall be brought into account for those purposes for the accounting period mentioned in sub-paragraph (9) below—

 (a) if the adjusted issue price of the security as at 31st March 1996 is greater than the adjusted closing value of the security as at that date, as a non-trading debit; and

 (b) if the adjusted closing value of the security as at that date is the greater, as a non-trading credit.

(9) That period is the accounting period in which falls whichever is the earliest of the following, that is to say—

 (a) the earliest day after 31st March 1996 on which, under the terms on which the security was issued, the company holding the security is entitled to require it to be redeemed;

 (b) the day on which the security is redeemed; and

 (c) the day on which the company makes a disposal of that security.

(10) The repeal by this Act of the reference in any enactment to, or to any provision of, paragraph 5 of Schedule 4 to the Taxes Act 1988 shall not have effect in relation to amounts treated as paid before 1st April 1996.

(11) For the purposes of this paragraph, in relation to any company—

 (a) the adjusted issue price of a deep discount security as at 31st March 1996 is whatever for the purposes of Schedule 4 to the Taxes Act 1988 would have been the adjusted issue price for that security for an income period beginning with 1st April 1996; and

 (b) the adjusted closing value of a security as at 31st March 1996 is the amount which for the purposes of this Chapter is the opening value as at 1st April 1996 if the company's rights and liabilities under the loan relationship of the company that is represented by that security;

and sub-paragraph (7) of paragraph 5 above shall apply for the purposes of this sub-paragraph as it applies for the purposes of that paragraph.

(12) In this paragraph "deep discount security", "disposal" and "income period" have the same meanings as in Schedule 4 to the Taxes Act 1988.

Commentary—*Simon's Direct Tax Service* **D2.1165.**
Amendments—¹ Sub-para (3A) inserted by FA 1999 s 67(1), (6) with effect for income treated as arising after 14 February 1999.
² Sub-para (7)(*b*) substituted by FA 1999 s 67(3), (7) where the day mentioned in sub-para (9) above falls after 14 February 1999.

Deep gain securities

20—(1) This Chapter shall not affect the application of paragraph 5 of Schedule 11 to the Finance Act 1989 (charge on deep gain securities) in relation to any transfer or redemption occurring before 1st April 1996.

(2) The repeal by this Act of section 65 of the Finance Act 1993 (deemed transfers in the case of deep gain securities) and of enactments relating to that section shall not apply in relation to relevant days falling before 1st April 1996; but for the purposes of that section and this sub-paragraph 31st March 1996 shall be deemed (where it would not otherwise be so) to be the last day of an accounting period.

[(2A) Any income that is treated as arising on the day mentioned in subsection (5) of that section, as it applies by virtue of sub-paragraph (2) above, shall be brought into account as a non-trading credit given for the purposes of this Chapter for the accounting period in which that day falls.]¹

(3) Where—

    (*a*) a company held a deep gain security on 31st March 1996,
    (*b*) the security was not transferred or redeemed by that company on that date,
    (*c*) the security is not one in relation to which that date is, or is deemed to be, a relevant day for the purposes of section 65 of the Finance Act 1993, and
    (*d*) there is an amount which, if the company had made a transfer of that security on that date, by selling it for its adjusted closing value, would have been treated under paragraph 5 of Schedule 11 to the Finance Act 1989 as income chargeable to tax under Case III or IV of Schedule D,

that amount shall be brought into account as a non-trading credit given for the purposes of this Chapter for the accounting period mentioned in sub-paragraph (4) below.

(4) That period is the accounting period in which falls whichever is the earliest of the following, that is to say—

    (*a*) the earliest day after 31st March 1996 on which, under the terms on which the security was issued, the company holding the security is entitled to require it to be redeemed;
    (*b*) the day on which the security is redeemed; and
    (*c*) the day on which the company makes a disposal of that security.

(5) For the purposes of this paragraph the adjusted closing value of a deep gain security held by a company on 31st March 1996 shall be the amount which for the purposes of this Chapter is the opening value as at 1st April 1996 of the company's rights and liabilities under the relationship represented by that security; and sub-paragraph (7) of paragraph 5 above shall apply for the purposes of this sub-paragraph as it applies for the purposes of that paragraph.

(6) In this paragraph "deep gain security" and "transfer" have the same meanings as in Schedule 11 to the Finance Act 1989.

Commentary—*Simon's Direct Tax Service* **D2.1166.**
Amendments—¹ Sub-para (2A) inserted by FA 1999 s 67(2), (6) with effect for income treated as arising after 14 February 1999.

Convertible securities

21—(1) This Chapter shall not affect—

    (*a*) the application of paragraph 12 of Schedule 10 to the Finance Act 1990 (charge in the case of convertible securities) in relation to any chargeable event occurring before 1st April 1996; or
    (*b*) the application of paragraph 25 of that Schedule (relief in the case of convertible securities) in relation to any redemption occurring before that date.

(2) Where—

    (*a*) a company held a qualifying convertible security on 31st March 1996,
    (*b*) that date was not a date on which any chargeable event occurred in relation to that security, and
    (*c*) there is an amount which, if there had been a chargeable event on that date, would have been treated under paragraph 12 of Schedule 10 to the Finance Act 1990 as income chargeable to tax under Case III or IV of Schedule D,

that amount shall be brought into account, in the case of that company, as a non-trading credit given for the purposes of this Chapter for the accounting period mentioned in sub-paragraph (3) below.

(3) That period is the accounting period in which falls whichever is the earliest of the following, that is to say—

    (*a*) the earliest day after 31st March 1996 on which, under the terms on which the security was issued, the company holding the security is entitled to require it to be redeemed;

(*b*) the day on which the security is redeemed; and

(*c*) the day on which the company makes a disposal of that security.

(4) Where—

(*a*) any qualifying convertible security is redeemed, and

(*b*) that security is one in the case of which any amount falls to be brought into account under sub-paragraph (2) above,

an amount equal to that amount shall be brought into account, in the case of the company that issued the security, as a non-trading debit given for the purposes of this Chapter for the accounting period in which the redemption occurs.

(5) In this paragraph "chargeable event" and "qualifying convertible security" have the same meanings as in Schedule 10 to the Finance Act 1990.

Commentary—*Simon's Direct Tax Service* D2.1167.

Transitional and savings for Chapter II of Part II of the Finance Act 1993

22—(*1*) *Chapter II of Part II of the Finance Act 1993 (exchange gains and losses) shall have effect in the case of any continuing loan relationship as follows.*

(*2*) *Subsection (1A) of section 127 of that Act (deemed variation of debt in respect of amounts accruing in respect of discounts and premiums) shall have effect in relation to the debt by reference to which the continuing loan relationship at any time subsists as if that debt is one to which the company became subject or entitled on 1st April 1996; and, accordingly, that subsection shall require the nominal amount of the debt outstanding to be treated as varied only where the time of the deemed variation is on or after 1st April 1996.*

(*3*) *Where section 127 of that Act has effect in relation to any debt by reference to which a continuing loan relationship at any time subsists, it shall so have effect, so far as the debt is one to which the company is deemed by virtue of sub-paragraph (2) above to have become subject or entitled on 1st April 1996, as if the nominal amount of the debt outstanding on that date were an amount equal to what it would have been if—*

(*a*) *sub-paragraph (2) above did not apply; and*

(*b*) *section 127(1A) of the Finance Act 1993 and the provisions to which it refers had always had effect.*

(*4*) *The amendment by this Act of section 153(4) of the Finance Act 1993 (assets excluded from being qualifying assets) shall not apply as respects times before 1st April 1996; and, where a company holds an asset immediately before and on 1st April 1996 and that asset is one which falls to be treated as a qualifying asset by virtue of that amendment—*

(*a*) *the company shall be treated as having become entitled to that asset on that date; and*

(*b*) *the basic valuation of the asset shall be taken to be its market value on 31st March 1996 (instead of any amount given by section 159 of that Act of 1993);*

and in this sub-paragraph "market value" has the same meaning as in the 1992 Act.

(*5*) *The repeal by this Act of section 153(6) of the Finance Act 1993 (liabilities excluded from being qualifying liabilities) shall not have effect as respects times before 1st April 1996; and, where a company is subject to a liability immediately before and on 1st April 1996 and that liability is one which falls to be treated as a qualifying liability by virtue of that repeal, the company shall be treated as having become subject to that liability on that date.*

(*6*) *The repeal by this Act of paragraphs 4 to 6 of Schedule 17 to the Finance Act 1993 (exchange gains and losses) shall not have effect in relation to any disposal before 1st April 1996.*

Amendment—This paragraph repealed by FA 2002 ss 79, 141, Sch 23 paras 1, 16, Sch 40 Pt 3(10) with effect for accounting periods beginning after 30 September 2002.

Carrying back non-trading losses against exchange profits etc

23—(*1*) *Subject to sub-paragraph (2) below, for the purpose of setting any amount against exchange profits for an accounting period beginning before 1st April 1996—*

(*a*) *a claim may be made under section 131(5) or (6) of the Finance Act 1993 (treatment of exchange gains and losses) in relation to any relievable amount for an accounting period ending on or after 1st April 1996; and*

(*b*) *the provisions of sections 129 to 133 of that Act shall be deemed to have effect for the purposes of that claim without the amendments made by Schedule 14 to this Act.*

(*2*) *If any claim is made by virtue of sub-paragraph (1) above in respect of the relievable amount for an accounting period beginning on or after 1st April 1996, then an amount equal to the amount to which the claim relates shall be deemed, for the purposes of the computation falling to be made for that accounting period under section 82 of this Act, to be brought into account for that period as a non-trading credit.*

(*3*) *The references in this paragraph and paragraph 24 below to provisions of the Finance Act 1993 shall have effect as including references to those sections as applied by the provisions of Chapter II of Part IV of the Finance Act 1994.*

(4) Sub-paragraph (3) above is without prejudice to the generality of section 20(2) of the Interpretation Act 1978 (references to other enactments).

Cross reference—See F(No 2)A 1997 s 40(9) (modification of FA 1993 s 131(10)(*b*) (as it is applied by this para) in relation to a relievable amount for an accounting period ending on or after 2 July 1997).
Amendment—This paragraph repealed by FA 2002 ss 79, 141, Sch 23 paras 1, 16, Sch 40 Pt 3(10) with effect for accounting periods beginning after 30 September 2002.

Exchange losses etc carried forward from before 1st April 1996

24 *Where there is any amount which apart from this Chapter would fall under section 131(12) of the Finance Act 1993 (carrying forward of exchange gains and losses) to be carried forward to an accounting period ending on or after 1st April 1996, that amount shall be treated in relation to that period as an amount carried forward to that period in pursuance of section 83(3) of this Act.*

Amendment—This paragraph repealed by FA 2002 ss 79, 141, Sch 23 paras 1, 16, Sch 40 Pt 3(10) with effect for accounting periods beginning after 30 September 2002.

Transitional for debt contracts and options to which Chapter II of Part IV of the Finance Act 1994 is applied

25—*(1) This paragraph applies in the case of any debt contract or option held by a company both immediately before and on 1st April 1996 if (apart from this Chapter)—*

> *(a) the contract or option is an asset in the case of which the following condition is satisfied, that is to say, a gain accruing to the company on a disposal of that asset on 31st March 1996 would have fallen to be treated as a chargeable gain in relation to the company; or*
> *(b) had there been a disposal of that asset on 31st March 1996, amounts with respect to it would have fallen to be brought into account for any accounting period beginning before 1st April 1996 in computing any profits or gains of the company from a trade carried on by it.*

(2) Chapter II of Part IV of the Finance Act 1994 (provisions relating to certain financial instruments) shall have effect in relation to the debt contract or option as if references in that Chapter to 1st April 1996 were references to the beginning of the company's first relevant accounting period.

(3) For the accounting period mentioned in sub-paragraph (2) above, section 158(2) to (5) of that Act (adjustments for changes of basis of accounting) shall have effect in relation to the debt contract or option as if—

> *(a) any reference to the new basis were a reference to the basis of accounting on which, as regards the contract or option, the company's profit or loss for the accounting period so mentioned is calculated;*
> *(b) any reference to being or not being included in amount A for a preceding accounting period were a reference to being or not being taken into account as receipts or increases in value in computing the company's profits or losses for such a period; and*
> *(c) any reference to being or not being included in amount B for a preceding accounting period were a reference to being or not being taken into account as deductions or reductions in value in computing the company's profits or losses for such a period.*

(4) Expressions used in this paragraph and in Chapter II of Part IV of the Finance Act 1994 have the same meanings in this paragraph as in that Chapter.

Amendment—This paragraph repealed by FA 2002 s 141, Sch 40 Pt 3(13) with effect for accounting periods beginning after 30 September 2002.

PART II
INCOME TAX AND CAPITAL GAINS TAX
Application and interpretation of Part II

26—(1) This Part of this Schedule (except paragraph 29) has effect for the purposes of income tax and capital gains tax but not for the purposes of corporation tax.

(2) In this Part of this Schedule—

> ''the 1992 Act'' means the Taxation of Chargeable Gains Act 1992;
> ''market value'' has the same meaning as in the 1992 Act;
> ''qualifying indexed security'' has the meaning given by paragraph 2 of Schedule 11 to the Finance Act 1989; and
> ''relevant discounted security'' has the meaning given for the purposes of Schedule 13 to this Act.

(3) References in this Part of this Schedule to a disposal within marriage are references to any disposal to which section 58 of the 1992 Act applies.

Qualifying indexed securities

27—(1) This paragraph applies where—

> (a) on 5th April 1996 any person (''the relevant person'') held a qualifying indexed security;

(*b*) that person did not dispose of that security on that date and does not fall (apart from by virtue of this paragraph) to be treated for the purposes of the 1992 Act as having made a disposal of it on that date; and

(*c*) a relevant event occurs.

(2) For the purposes of this paragraph a relevant event occurs on the first occasion after 5th April 1996 when the relevant person, or a person to whom that person has made a disposal of the security within marriage, falls to be treated for the purposes of the 1992 Act as making a disposal (otherwise than within marriage) which is—

(*a*) a disposal of the security in question; or

(*b*) a disposal of any such asset as falls to be treated for the purposes of that Act as the same as that security.

(3) The amount of any chargeable gain or allowable loss which would have been treated as accruing to the relevant person if—

(*a*) he had made a disposal of the asset on 5th April 1996, and

(*b*) that disposal had been for a consideration equal to the market value of the asset,

shall be brought into account as one accruing to the person who makes the disposal constituting the relevant event in the year of assessment in which that event occurs.

28 For the purposes of Schedule 13 to this Act where—

(*a*) a person held a qualifying indexed security both on and immediately after 5th April 1996, and

(*b*) that security is a relevant discounted security,

the amount which that person shall be taken to have paid in respect of his acquisition of that security on or before 5th April 1996 shall be an amount equal to its market value on that date.

29 For the purposes of paragraph 2 of Schedule 10 to this Act paragraphs 27 and 28 above shall have effect in relation to an authorised unit trust for the first of its accounting periods to end after 31st March 1996 as if references in those paragraphs to 5th April 1996 were references to 31st March 1996.

Transitional in relation to qualifying corporate bonds

30—(1) This paragraph applies where—

(*a*) any person holds any asset on and immediately after 5th April 1996;

(*b*) that asset is one which came to be held by that person as a result of a transaction to which section 127 of the 1992 Act applies; and

(*c*) that asset falls from 5th April 1996 to be treated as a relevant discounted security but is neither a qualifying indexed security nor such that it would have fallen to be treated as a qualifying corporate bond in relation to any disposal of it on that date.

(2) Section 116 of the 1992 Act (reorganisations etc involving qualifying corporate bonds) shall have effect as if—

(*a*) there had been a transaction on 5th April 1996 by which the person holding the asset had disposed of it and immediately re-acquired it;

(*b*) the asset re-acquired had been a qualifying corporate bond; and

(*c*) the transaction had been a transaction to which section 127 of the 1992 Act would have applied but for section 116(5) of that Act.

Revenue Internal Guidance—Company Taxation Manual COT12900–13085 (explanation of the transitional rules with worked examples).

SCHEDULE 16

SHARE OPTION SCHEMES APPROVED BEFORE PASSING OF THIS ACT
Section 114

Commentary—*Simon's Direct Tax Service* E4.595.

Preliminary

1—(1) Subject to sub-paragraphs (2) and (3) below, this Schedule applies to any share option scheme approved by the Board before the day on which this Act is passed in consequence of their being satisfied that the scheme fulfils the requirements of Part IV of Schedule 9 to the Taxes Act 1988 (as well as such requirements of Parts I and II of that Schedule as apply in relation to the scheme).

(2) This Schedule shall not apply to a share option scheme if, before the end of 1996, the grantor gives notice to the Board that it is not to apply.

(3) Where a notice is given to the Board under sub-paragraph (2) above, the scheme shall, with effect from the day on which the notice is given, cease to be approved.

Limit on aggregate value of options

2—(1) A scheme to which this Schedule applies shall have effect, notwithstanding anything included in it to the contrary, as if it provided that no person shall, on or after the day on which this Act is passed, obtain rights under it which would, at the time they are obtained, cause the aggregate market value of the shares which that person may acquire in pursuance of rights obtained under the scheme or under any other share option scheme, not being a savings related share option scheme, approved under Schedule 9 to the Taxes Act 1988 and established by the grantor or an associated company of the grantor (and not exercised) to exceed or further exceed £30,000.

(2) Sub-paragraph (3) of paragraph 28 of Schedule 9 to the Taxes Act 1988 (market value of shares to be calculated as at time when rights obtained etc) shall have effect for the purposes of sub-paragraph (1) above as it has effect for the purposes of sub-paragraph (1) of that paragraph.

Price at which scheme shares may be obtained

3 A scheme to which this Schedule applies shall have effect, notwithstanding anything included in it to the contrary, as if it provided that the price at which scheme shares may be acquired by the exercise of a right obtained, on or after the day on which this Act is passed, under the scheme must not be manifestly less than the market value of shares of the same class at that time or, if the Board and the grantor agree in writing, at such earlier time or times as may be provided in the agreement.

Approval of the Board to alterations

4 For the purposes of paragraph 4 of Schedule 9 to the Taxes Act 1988 (approval not to have effect from the date of any alteration in the scheme unless the Board have approved the alteration) the alterations made by paragraphs 2 and 3 above in any scheme to which this Schedule applies shall be taken to have been approved by the Board before the day on which this Act is passed.

Interpretation

5—(1) Section 187 of the Taxes Act 1988 (interpretation of sections 185 and 186 and Schedules 9 and 10) applies for the purposes of this Schedule as it applies for the purposes of sections 185 and 186 of, and Schedules 9 and 10 to, that Act.

(2) In this Schedule "scheme shares" has the same meaning as in Part IV of Schedule 9 to the Taxes Act 1988.

SCHEDULE 17

CLAIMS FOR RELIEF INVOLVING TWO OR MORE YEARS

Section 128

Note—This Schedule inserted as TMA 1970 Sch 1B.

SCHEDULE 18

OVERDUE TAX AND EXCESSIVE PAYMENTS BY THE BOARD

Section 132

The Taxes Management Act 1970

1 (*substitutes* TMA 1970 s 55(1)(*b*)).

2 (*amends* TMA 1970 s 59A(2), (4A), (5) and *inserts* s 59A(4B)).

3 (*amends* TMA 1970 s 86(4), (6)).

4 (*repeals* TMA 1970 ss 88, 88A, 113(1C) and *amends* s 91(1)).

The Taxes Act 1988

5 (*amends* TA 1988 s 307(6)).

6 (*amends* TA 1988 s 369).

7 (*amends* TA 1988 s 374A(4)).

8 (*amends* TA 1988 s 375(4)).

9 (*amends* TA 1988 s 412(4)).

10 (*amends* TA 1988 s 588(5)).

11 (*amends* TA 1988 Sch 14).

The Finance Act 1989

12 ...

Amendments—This paragraph repealed by F(No 2)A 1997 Sch 8 Pt II(2) with effect for 1997–98 and subsequent years of assessment except in relation to cases in which relief due under FA 1989 s 54 in respect of any payment is unaffected by the provisions of F(No 2)A 1997 s 17(1) (see the Amendments note to FA 1989 s 54).

13 (*amends* FA 1989 s 178)

The Finance Act 1991

14 (*amends* FA 1991 s 33).

Amendment—This paragraph repealed by FA 1999 s 139, Sch 20 Pt III(15) with effect for payments made after 31 August 2000 (by virtue of SI 2000/2004).

The Taxation of Chargeable Gains Act 1992

15 (*substitutes* TCGA 1992 s 281(5)(*a*) and *amends* s 281(6), (7)).

The Finance Act 1995

16 (*amends* FA 1995 s 73(4)).

Commencement

17—(1) Paragraphs 1 to 3, 6(2)(*a*) and (*b*), 8, 10, 11(3)(*a*) and (*b*), *12(2)(a) and (b)*[1], 14(2)(*a*) and (*b*) and 16(*a*) above have effect, subject to sub-paragraph (2) below—

    (*a*) for the purposes of income tax and capital gains tax, as respects the year 1996–97 and subsequent years of assessment; and

    (*b*) for the purposes of corporation tax, as respects accounting periods ending on or after the day appointed under section 199 of the Finance Act 1994 for the purposes of Chapter III of Part IV of that Act (self-assessment management provisions).

(2) Paragraphs 1, 3, 6(2)(*a*) and (*b*), 10, 11(3)(*a*) and (*b*), *12(2)(a) and (b)*[1] and 14(2)(*a*) and (*b*) above, so far as relating to partnerships whose trades, professions or businesses are set up and commenced before 6th April 1994, has effect as respects the year 1997–98 and subsequent years of assessment.

(3) Paragraphs 4, 5, 6(2)(*c*) and (3), 11(3)(*c*) and (4), *12(2)(c) and (3)*[1], 13, 14(2)(*c*) and (3), 15 and 16(*b*) and (*c*) above have effect, subject to sub-paragraph (4) below—

    (*a*) as respects the year 1996–97 and subsequent years of assessment; and

    (*b*) in relation to any income tax or capital gains tax which—

        (i) is charged by an assessment made on or after 6th April 1998; and

        (ii) is for the year 1995–96 or any earlier year of assessment;

and where sub-paragraph (4) of paragraph 11, sub-paragraph (3) of paragraph 12, or sub-paragraph (3) of paragraph 14 has effect by virtue of paragraph (*b*) of this sub-paragraph it shall have effect with the substitution, in the provision inserted by that sub-paragraph, for "section 29(1)(*c*)" of "section 29(3)(*c*)".

(4) Paragraphs 4, 6(2)(*c*) and (3), 11(3)(*c*) and (4), *12(2)(c) and (3)*[1], 13 and 14(2)(*c*) and (3) above, so far as relating to partnerships whose trades, professions or businesses were set up and commenced before 6th April 1994 have effect—

    (*a*) as respects the year 1997–98 and subsequent years of assessment; and

    (*b*) in relation to any income tax which—

        (i) is charged by an assessment made on or after 6th April 1998; and

        (ii) is for the year 1995–96 or any earlier year of assessment.

(5) Paragraphs 7 and 11(2) above have effect—

    (*a*) as respects the year 1996–97 and subsequent years of assessment; and

    (*b*) subject to sub-paragraphs (6) and (7) below, in relation to any income tax or capital gains tax which—

        (i) is charged by an assessment made on or after 6th April 1998; and

        (ii) is for the year 1995–96 or any earlier year of assessment.

(6) Sub-paragraph (5)(*b*) above does not apply to paragraph 7 above so far as paragraph 7 provides for the omission of—

    (*a*) paragraph (*a*) of subsection (4) of section 374A of the Taxes Act 1988, and

    (*b*) the words "and as if" so far as they relate to paragraph (*a*) of that subsection.

(7) Sub-paragraph (5)(*b*) above does not apply to paragraph 11(2) above so far as paragraph 11(2) provides for the omission of—

    (*a*) the words "sections 55(1) (recovery of tax not postponed) and", and

    (*b*) the words "and as if—

(*a*) the assessment were among those specified in''

so far as those words relate to the words mentioned in paragraph (*a*) of this sub-paragraph.

(8) Paragraphs 6(2)(*d*), 11(3)(*d*), *12(2)(d)* [1] and 14(2)(*d*) above shall not apply in relation to any payment if the payment, or the claim on which it is made, was made before the day on which this Act is passed.

(9) Paragraph 9 above has effect as respects accounting periods ending on or after the day appointed under section 199 of the Finance Act 1994 for the purposes of Chapter III of Part IV of that Act (self-assessment management provisions).

(10) Any power to make regulations exercisable by virtue of an amendment made by any of the preceding provisions of this Schedule may be exercised so as to make provision having effect in relation to any year of assessment in relation to which that provision has effect in accordance with sub-paragraphs (1) to (9) above.

Amendments—[1] References to para 12 repealed by F(No 2)A 1997 Sch 8 Pt II(2) with effect for 1997–98 and subsequent years of assessment except in relation to cases in which relief due under FA 1989 s 54 in respect of any payment is unaffected by the provisions of F(No 2)A 1997 s 17(1) (see the Amendments note to FA 1989 s 54).

SCHEDULE 19

SELF-ASSESSMENT: CLAIMS AND ENQUIRIES

Section 133

Commentary—*Simon's Direct Tax Service* **E1.831.**

Introductory

1 The Taxes Management Act 1970, as it has effect—

(*a*) for the purposes of income tax and capital gains tax, as respects the year 1996–97 and subsequent years of assessment, and

(*b*) for the purposes of corporation tax, as respects accounting periods ending on or after the day appointed under section 199 of the Finance Act 1994 for the purposes of Chapter III of Part IV of that Act (self-assessment management provisions),

shall be amended in accordance with the following provisions of this Schedule.

Notes—The appointed day is 1 July 1999 by virtue of Finance Act 1994, Section 199, (Appointed Day) Order, SI 1998/3173 art 2.

Matters subject to enquiry

2 (*inserts* TMA 1970 ss 9A(1)(*c*), 12AC(1)(*c*), 19A(1)(*c*), 28A(1)(*c*), 28B(1)(*c*); *part repealed by* FA 1998 s 165, Sch 27 Part III(28) with effect in relation to accounting periods ending after 30 June 1999 (by virtue of Finance Act 1994, Section 199, (Appointed Day) Order, SI 1998/3173 art 2); *part repealed by* FA 2001 s 110, Sch 33 Pt II(13) with effect in accordance with FA 2001 s 88, Sch 29).).

Power to call for documents

3 (*inserts* TMA 1970 s 19A(2A), *amends* s 19A(3), (4), (5), (7), (9)(*a*), (10) and *amends* TMA 1970 s 97AA(1)).

Further amendments of section 28A

4 (*amended* TMA 1970 s 28A(2), (4), (5) and *inserted* s 28A(4A), (4B), (7A), (7B), (7C); *repealed by* FA 2001 s 110, Sch 33 Pt II(13) with effect in accordance with FA 2001 s 88, Sch 29).

Further amendments of section 28B

5 (*amended* TMA 1970 s 28B(3)(*b*), (5)(*b*) and *inserted* s 28B(6A), (6B); *repealed by* FA 2001 s 110, Sch 33 Pt II(13) with effect in accordance with FA 2001 s 88, Sch 29).

Right of appeal against notice disallowing claim in return

6 (*amended* TMA 1970 s 31(1)(*c*), (5) and *inserted* s 31(1)(*aa*), (1AA); *repealed by* FA 2001 s 110, Sch 33 Pt II(13) with effect in accordance with FA 2001 s 88, Sch 29).

7 (*inserts* TMA 1970 s 50(7A)).

Claims not included in returns

8 (*amends* TMA 1970 Sch 1A para 4(1),(2) and *inserts* para 4(4)).

9 (*inserted* TMA 1970 Sch 1A para 7(3A), (3B) and *amended* para 7(4)(*b*); *repealed by* FA 2001 s 110, Sch 33 Pt II(13) with effect in accordance with FA 2001 s 88, Sch 29).

Right of appeal against notice disallowing claim not in return

10 (*substitutes* TMA 1970 Sch 1A para 9(1), *amends* para 9(2), (3) and *inserts* para 9(5); *part repealed by* FA 2001 s 110, Sch 33 Pt II(13) with effect in accordance with FA 2001 s 88, Sch 29).

SCHEDULE 20

SELF-ASSESSMENT: DISCRETIONS EXERCISABLE BY THE BOARD ETC

Section 134

Revenue Internal Guidance—Capital Gains Manual CG 10305 ("Taxpayer control" charges: examples of Revenue "satisfaction", "judgement" and "direction").

The Taxes Act 1988

1–14 (*amend* TA 1988 s 24(2), 38(4), 65(4), 74(1)(*j*), 109A(4), 132(1), 145(7), 159(1), 161(3), (4), 168(3), (6)(*b*), (*d*), 186(10)(*c*), 231(3A), 257(1), (2), (3), 257A(2), (3), *insert* s 109(4A), *repeal* s 159(4)–(6) and *substitute* s 186(10)(*b*)).

Amendments—Sub-para 14(2) repealed by FA 1999 s 139, Sch 20 Pt III(3) with effect from the year 2000–01.

15–18 ...

Amendments—Paras 15–18 repealed by FA 1999 s 139, Sch 20 Pt III(3), (4) with effect from the year 2000–01.

19–27 (*amend* TA 1988 ss 265(1), 274(4), 278(2), 306(2), 311(4), 381(4), 384(1), 393A(3)(*b*), 397(3) and *substitute* ss 384(9), 393A(4)(*a*)).

28 (1)–(4) (*amend* TA 1988 s 488).

(5) ...¹

Amendments—¹ Sub-para (5) repealed by FA 1998 s 165, Sch 27 Part III(28) with effect for accounting periods ending after 30 June 1999 (by virtue of Finance Act 1994, Section 199, (Appointed Day) Order, SI 1998/3173 art 2). It is also repealed by FA 1999 s 139, Sch 20 Pt III(7) with effect for interest payments within FA 1999 s 38(3), (4).

29 (*amend* TA 1988 s 489).

30 ...¹

Amendments—¹ Repealed by FA 1998 s 165, Sch 27 Part III(4) with effect for income tax for the year 1998–99 and subsequent years of assessment, and for corporation tax from 1 April 1998 subject to transitional provisions in FA 1998 Sch 5 Part IV.

31 (*amends* TA 1988 s 570(2)).

32 (*amends* TA 1988 s 582(2), (*b*)).

33 (*amend* TA 1988 s 584).

34 (*amends* TA 1988 s 585(1)).

35 (*amends* TA 1988 s 717(9)).

36 (*amends* TA 1988 s 731(3)).

37 (*amends* TA 1988 s 769(2)(*d*)).

38 (*repeals* TA 1988 s 812(4)(*a*) and *amends* s 812(7)).

39 (*substitutes* TA 1988 s 815A(2) for s 815A(2) – (4)).

40 (*amends* TA 1988 Sch 6 para 2(1), (2)).

Prospective amendments—This paragraph to be repealed by FA 2000 s 156, Sch 40 Pt II(3) with effect from the year 2002–03.

41 (*amends* TA 1988 Sch 7 para 1(5)).

42 (*amends* TA 1988 Sch 12 para 2(2)).

43 (*repeals* TA 1988 Sch 21 para 3).

The Capital Allowances Act 1990

44 (*amended* CAA 1990 s 29(3), *repealed by* CAA 2001 s 580, Sch 4 with effect in accordance with CAA 2001 s 579).

The Taxation of Chargeable Gains Act 1992

45 In the following provisions of this Schedule "the Gains Act" means the Taxation of Chargeable Gains Act 1992.

46 (*amends* TCGA 1992 s 30(4)).

47 (*amends* TCGA 1992 ss 30(5), (6), 32(4)(*b*), 33(7), (8)).

48 (*amends* TCGA 1992 s 48).

49 (*substitutes* TCGA 1992 s 49(2)).

50 (*amends* TCGA 1992 s 52(4)).

51 (*amends* TCGA 1992 s 116(13)).

52 (*amends* TCGA 1992 s 122(2), (4)(*a*) and *repeals* s 122(3)).

53 (*amends* TCGA 1992 s 133(2), (4)(*a*) and *repeals* s 133(3)).

54 (*amends* TCGA 1992 ss 150(10)(*a*), 150A(9)(*a*)).

55 (*amends* TCGA 1992 s 164F(8)(*a*)).

56 (*amends* TCGA 1992 s 164FG(2)).

57 (*amends* TCGA 1992 s 176(4), (5), (6)).

58 (*amends* TCGA 1992 s 181(1)(*b*)).

59 (*substitutes* TCGA 1992 s 222(3), *amends* s 222(5) and *repeals* s 222(6)(*b*)).

60 (*amends* TCGA 1992 s 224(2)).

61 (*repeals* TCGA 1992 s 226(5)).

62 (*amends* TCGA 1992 s 241(7)).

63 (*amends* TCGA 1992 s 271(1), (2)).

64 (*substitutes* TCGA 1992 s 279(1)(*b*), (*c*) for s 279(1)(*b*)).

65 (*amends* TCGA 1992 s 280).

66 (*amend* TCGA 1992 Sch 6).

Prospective amendments—Para 66 will be repealed by FA 1998 s 165, Sch 27 Pt III(31) with effect for disposals from the year 2003–04.

67 (*amends* TCGA 1992 Sch 8 para 10(2)).

The Finance Act 1993

68 (*amends* FA 1993 s 144; *repealed by* FA 2002 s 141, Sch 40 Pt 3(10) with effect for accounting periods beginning after 30 September 2002).

69 (*amends* FA 1993 s 145; *repealed by* FA 2002 s 141, Sch 40 Pt 3(10) with effect for accounting periods beginning after 30 September 2002).

70 (*substitutes* FA 1993 Sch 15 para 3(4)(*a*)–(*c*); *repealed by* FA 2002 s 141, Sch 40 Pt 3(10) with effect for accounting periods beginning after 30 September 2002).

The Finance Act 1994

71 (*amended* FA 1994 s 163(1), (2)(*a*), (3)(*a*), (4)(*b*); *repealed by* FA 2002 s 141, Sch 40 Pt 3(13) with effect for accounting periods beginning after 30 September 2002).

SCHEDULE 21

SELF-ASSESSMENT: TIME LIMITS

Section 135

The Taxes Act 1988

1 (*amends* TA 1988 s 62A(3)).

2 (*amends* TA 1988 s 84 (3) and *inserts* s 84(3A), (3B)).

3 (*amends* TA 1988 s 101(2) and *inserts* s 101(2A)).

4 (*amends* TA 1988 s 257BB(5)(*a*)).

5 (*amended* TA 1988 s 257D(9)(*a*); *repealed by* FA 1999 s 139, Sch 20 Pt III(3) with effect from the year 2000–01).

6 (*amends* TA 1988 s 265(5)(*a*)).

7 (*substitutes* TA 1988 s 306(1)(*b*)).

8 (*amends* TA 1988 s 356B(2)(*a*), (4)(*b*)).

Amendments—This paragraph repealed by FA 1999 s 139, Sch 20 Pt III(7) with effect for payments of interest within FA 1999 s 38(3), (4).

9 (*substitutes* TA 1988 s 356C(6)(*a*)).

Amendments—This paragraph repealed by FA 1999 s 129, Sch 20 Pt III(7) with effect for payments of interest within FA 1999 s 38(3), (4).

10 (*amends* TA 1988 s 381(1)).

11 (*amends* TA 1988 s 392(5)).

12, 13 ...

Amendments—Paras 12, 13 repealed by FA 1998 s 165, Sch 27 Part III(23) with effect in relation to exchanges made after 31 July 1998.

14 (*amends* TA 1988 s 504(6) and *inserts* s 504(6A)).

15 (*amends* TA 1988 s 524(2), (4) and *inserts* s 524(2A)).

16 (*amends* TA 1988 s 585(6)).

17 (*amends* TA 1988 s 619(4)).

18 (*amends* TA 1988 s 641(4)).

Amendments—Para 18 repealed by FA 2000 s 156, Sch 40 Pt II(4) with effect in accordance with FA 2000 Sch 13 para 17 (no election made under TA 1988 s 641 for contributions paid after 5 April 2001).

19 (*amends* TA 1988 s 691(4)).

20 (*amends* TA 1988 s 700(3)).

21 (*amends* TA 1988 s 781(8) and *inserts* s 781(8A)).

22 (*amends* TA 1988 s 804(7)).

23 (*amends* TA 1988 s 806(1)).

24 ...

Amendments—This paragraph repealed by FA 1998 s 165, Sch 27 Pt III(9) with effect in relation to payments or other benefits received after 5 April 1998, except where the payment or other benefit or the right to receive it has been brought into charge to tax before 6 April 1998 (FA 1998 s 58(4)).

The Finance Act 1988 (c 39)

25 (*amended* FA 1988 s 39(2)(*b*); *repealed* by FA 1999 s 139, Sch 20 Pt III(6) with effect for any payment falling due after 5 April 2000.).

The Capital Allowances Act 1990 (c 1)

26–34 (*amended* CAA 1990 s 25, 30, 31 33, 37, 53, 68, 129, 141; *repealed by* CAA 2001 s 580, Sch 4 with effect in accordance with CAA 2001 s 579).

The Taxation of Chargeable Gains Act 1992 (c 12)

35 (*amends* TCGA 1992 s 35(6)).

36 (*inserts* TCGA 1992 s 161(3A)).

37 (*inserts* TCGA 1992 s 242(2A)).

38 (*inserts* TCGA 1992 s 243(2A)).

39 (*inserts* TCGA 1992 s 244(3)).

40 (*inserts* TCGA 1992 s 253(4A)).

41 (*substitutes* TCGA 1992 s 279(5)).

42 (*amends* TCGA 1992 Sch 2 paras 4(11), 17(3)).

43 (*amends* TCGA 1992 Sch 4 para 9(1)).

44 (*amends* TCGA 1992 Sch 6 paras 2(1), 5(2), 12(5)(*b*), 16(1)(*e*), (2)).

Prospective amendments—Para 44 will be repealed by FA 1998 s 165, Sch 27 Pt III(31) with effect in relation to disposals from the year 2003–04.

The Finance (No 2) Act 1992 (c 48)

45 (*substitutes* F(No 2)A 1992 s 41(6)).

46 (*substitutes* F(No 2)A 1992 s 42(6)).

47 (*amends* F(No 2)A 1992 Sch 10 paras 10(4), (5), 12(2), (4), (6)(*b*), (7)).

The Finance Act 1994 (c 9)

48 (*amends* FA 1994 s 118(3) and *inserts* s 118(3A)).

SCHEDULE 22

SELF-ASSESSMENT: APPEALS

Section 136

Commentary—*Simon's Direct Tax Service* **E1.838, 839.**

The Taxes Management Act 1970

1 The Taxes Management Act 1970 shall be amended in accordance with paragraphs 2 to 10 below.

2 (*substitutes* TMA 1970 s 19A(11)).

3 (*substituted* TMA 1970 s 28A(6), (6A), (7) for s 28A(6), (7); *repealed by* FA 2001 s 110, Sch 33 Pt II(13) with effect in accordance with FA 2001 s 88, Sch 29).

4 (*substituted* TMA 1970 s 31(3); *repealed by* FA 2001 s 110, Sch 33 Pt II(13) with effect in accordance with FA 2001 s 88, Sch 29).

5 (*substitutes* TMA 1970 s 33A(8), (8A) for s 33A(8)).

6 (*repeals* TMA 1970 s 42(12), Sch 2).

7 (*substitutes* TMA 1970 ss 46B, 46C, 46D, for s 47).

8 (*amends* TMA 1970 s 57(3)(*c*)).

9 (*inserts* TMA 1970 Sch 1A paras 10,11).

10 (*substitutes* TMA 1970 Sch 3).

Section 102 of the Taxes Act 1988

11 (*amends* TA 1988 s 102(1)(*a*)).

Commencement of Schedule

12 This Schedule has effect in relation to—

(*a*) any proceedings relating to the year 1996–97 or any subsequent year of assessment, and

(*b*) any proceedings relating to an accounting period ending on or after the day appointed under section 199 of the Finance Act 1994 for the purposes of Chapter III of Part IV of that Act (self-assessment).

Notes—The appointed day is 1 July 1999 by virtue of Finance Act 1994, Section 199, (Appointed Day) Order, SI 1998/3173 art 2.

SCHEDULE 23

SELF-ASSESSMENT: SCHEDULES 13 AND 16 TO THE TAXES ACT 1988

Section 137

PART I

SCHEDULE 13 TO THE TAXES ACT 1988

1–3 ...

Amendments—Paras 1–3 repealed by FA 1998 Sch 27 Part III(2) with effect for return periods and accounting periods beginning after 5 April 1999.

4 (*amends* TA 1988 Sch 13 para 3B(1), (3); *repealed* by F(No 2)A 1997 Sch 8 Pt II(11) for return periods beginning after 5 April 1999).

5 (*amends* TA 1988 Sch 13 para 5; *repealed* by FA 1998 Sch 27 Part III with effect in relation for return periods and accounting periods beginning after 5 April 1999).

6 (*amends* TA 1988 Sch 13 para 6A(1); *repealed* prospectively by F(No 2)A 1997 Sch 8 Pt II(11)).

7–9 ...

Amendments—Paras 7–9 repealed by FA 1998 Sch 27 Part III with effect for return periods and accounting periods beginning after 5 April 1999.

PART II

SCHEDULE 16 TO THE TAXES ACT 1988

10 Schedule 16 to the Taxes Act 1988 (collection of income tax on company payments which are not distributions) shall be amended in accordance with the following provisions of this Part of this Schedule.

11 (*amends* TA 1988 Sch 16 para 4(2)).

12 (*inserts* TA 1988 Sch 16 para 7A).

13 (*amends* TA 1988 Sch 16 para 8).

SCHEDULE 24

SELF-ASSESSMENT: ACCOUNTING PERIODS ETC

Section 138

Commentary—*Simon's Direct Tax Service* **D2.732, 733.**

PART I
AMENDMENTS OF THE TAXES MANAGEMENT ACT 1970
Introductory

1 The Taxes Management Act 1970 shall be amended in accordance with this Part of this Schedule.

2 ...

Amendments—This paragraph repealed by FA 1998 s 165, Sch 27 Part III(28) with effect in relation to accounting periods ending after 30 June 1999 (by virtue of Finance Act 1994, Section 199, (Appointed Day) Order, SI 1998/3173 art 2).

Power to enquire into return for wrong period, etc

3 ...

Amendments— This paragraph repealed by FA 1998 s 165, Sch 27 Part III(28) with effect in relation to accounting periods ending after 30 June 1999 (by virtue of Finance Act 1994, Section 199, (Appointed Day) Order, SI 1998/3173 art 2).

4 ...

Amendments— This paragraph repealed by FA 1998 s 165, Sch 27 Part III(28) with effect in relation to accounting periods ending after 30 June 1999 (by virtue of Finance Act 1994, Section 199, (Appointed Day) Order, SI 1998/3173 art 2).

5 (*inserted* TMA 1970 s 19A(1)(*d*); *repealed by* FA 2001 s 110, Sch 33 Pt II(13) with effect in accordance with FA 2001 s 88, Sch 29).

Amendment of return for wrong period

6 ...

Amendments— This paragraph repealed by FA 1998 s 165, Sch 27 Part III(28) with effect in relation to accounting periods ending after 30 June 1999 (by virtue of Finance Act 1994, Section 199, (Appointed Day) Order, SI 1998/3173 art 2).

Failure to deliver return: determinations

7 ...

Amendments— This paragraph repealed by FA 1998 s 165, Sch 27 Part III(28) with effect in relation to accounting periods ending after 30 June 1999 (by virtue of Finance Act 1994, Section 199, (Appointed Day) Order, SI 1998/3173 art 2).

Commencement

8—(1) Paragraphs 3 to 6 above have effect in relation to returns made for periods ending on or after the day appointed under section 199 of the Finance Act 1994 for the purposes of Chapter III of Part IV of that Act (self-assessment).

(2) ...[1]

Amendments—[1] Sub-para (2) repealed by FA 1998 s 165, Sch 27 Part III(28) with effect in relation to accounting periods ending after 30 June 1999 (by virtue of Finance Act 1994, Section 199, (Appointed Day) Order, SI 1998/3173 art 2).

PART II
OTHER AMENDMENTS
General

9 In this Part of this Schedule "the appointed day" means the day appointed as mentioned in paragraph 8(1) above.

Repeal of section 8A of the Taxes Act 1988

10 (*repeals* TA 1988 s 8A).

Determination of accounting date

11—(1)–(3) (*amend* TA 1988 s 12).

(4) This paragraph has effect where each of the different dates referred to in section 12(5) of the Taxes Act 1988 occurs on or after the appointed day.

Companies in liquidation

12—(1)–(3) (*amend* TA 1988 s 342).

(4) This paragraph has effect in relation to the winding up of a company if the date on which the affairs of the company are completely wound up does not occur before the appointed day.

Construction of references to assessments

13 ...

Amendments—This paragraph repealed by FA 1998 s 165, Sch 27 Part III(28) with effect in relation to accounting periods ending after 30 June 1999 (by virtue of Finance Act 1994, Section 199, (Appointed Day) Order, SI 1998/3173 art 2).

SCHEDULE 25

SELF-ASSESSMENT: SURRENDERS OF ADVANCE CORPORATION TAX

Section 139

Commentary—*Simon's Direct Tax Service* **D2.739.**
Amendments—This Schedule repealed by FA 1998 Sch 27 Part III(2) with effect in relation to accounting periods of the surrendering company beginning after 5 April 1999.

SCHEDULE 26

DAMAGES AND COMPENSATION FOR PERSONAL INJURY

Section 150

Note—This Schedule sets out TA 1988 ss 329AA, 329AB inserted by FA 1996 s 150.

SCHEDULE 27

FOREIGN INCOME DIVIDENDS

Section 153

Companies that pay FIDs

1 ...
Amendments—This paragraph repealed F(No 2)A 1997 Sch 8 Pt II(11).

Recipients of FIDs

2 ...
Amendments—This paragraph repealed F(No 2)A 1997 Sch 8 Pt II(11).

Calculation of the distributable foreign profit and the notional foreign source ACT

3 ...
Amendments—This paragraph repealed by F(No 2)A 1997 Sch 8 Pt II(11) with effect for accounting periods beginning after 5 April 1999.

International headquarters company

4 ...
Amendments—This paragraph repealed by F(No 2)A 1997 Sch 8 Pt II(11) with effect in relation to accounting periods beginning after 5 April 1999.

Life assurance business charged under Case I of Schedule D

5 ...
Amendments—This paragraph repealed by F(No 2)A 1997 Sch 8 Pt II(6) with effect in relation to distributions after 1 July 1997.

Foreign income distributions to corporate unit holders

6 ...
Amendments—This paragraph repealed by F(No 2)A 1997 Sch 8 Pt II(11) with effect in relation to distributions after 5 April 1999.

SCHEDULE 28

FOTRA SECURITIES: CONSEQUENTIAL AMENDMENTS

Section 154

The Taxes Act 1988

1–6 (*repeal* TA 1988 s 47, 474(2), 475(6), (7), *substitute* s 475(1), Sch 19AC para 5C(2)–(4) and *amend* s 475(3), (8), Sch 24 paras 1(3), Sch 27 para 5(5)).

Amendments—Para 4 (which substituted Sch 19AA para 5(7)) repealed by the Overseas Life Assurance Fund (Amendment) Order, SI 2000/2188 art 6(2) with effect for accounting periods beginning after 31 December 1999 and ending after 31 August 2000.

The Inheritance Tax Act 1984 (c 51)

7, 8 (*amends* IHTA 1984 ss 6, 48(4)).

SCHEDULE 29

PAYING AND COLLECTING AGENTS ETC
Section 156

Amendments—This Schedule to be repealed by FA 2000 s 156, Sch 40 Pt II(17) with effect for relevant payments or receipts in relation to which the chargeable date for the purposes of Pt IV, Ch VIIA is after 31 March 2001.

PART I
THE NEW CHAPTER

1 (*inserts* TA 1988 ss 118A – 118K).

PART II
OTHER PROVISIONS
Penalties

2 (*amends* TMA 1970 s 98, Table).

Amendments of the Taxes Act 1988

3 The Taxes Act 1988 shall be amended in accordance with paragraphs 4 to 7 below.

4 (*substitutes* TA 1988 s 124(2) – (5) for s 124(2) – (4)).

5 (*amends* TA 1988 ss 348(3), 349(1) and *inserts* s 349(3)(*e*)).

6 (*amends* TA 1988 s 582A(1)).

7 (*amends* TA 1988 Sch 23A para 4(8)).

Amendment of the Finance Act 1989

8 (*amends* FA 1987 s 178(2)(*m*)).

SCHEDULE 30

INVESTMENTS IN HOUSING
Section 160

Reduced rate of corporation tax

1 (*inserts* TA 1988 ss 508A, 508B).

Investments in housing by investment trusts

2 (*amends* TA 1988 s 842(1)(*a*), (*e*) and *inserts* s 842(1AA)).

Commencement

3 This Schedule has effect in relation to accounting periods beginning on or after the day on which this Act is passed.

SCHEDULE 31

LIFE ASSURANCE BUSINESS LOSSES
Section 163

Expenses of management

1 (*inserts* TA 1988 s 76(1)(*aa*), (*ab*)).

Computation of losses and limitation on relief

2—(1) (*amends* TA 1988 s 434A(2A) and *introduces* sub-para (2) below, in relation to accounting periods beginning on or after 1 January 1996 and ending after 31 March 1996).

(2) (*substitutes* TA 1988 s 434A(2)).

(3) (spent).

Spreading of relief for acquisition expenses

3 (*amends* FA 1989 s 86(1) and *inserts* s 86(1A), (1B)).

Ascertainment of losses

4 (*substituted* FA 1989 s 83(3) – (8) for s 83(3)).

Application of surplus in reduction of certain losses

5 (*inserts* FA 1989 ss 83AA, 83AB).

Meaning of "brought into account" in sections 83AA and 83AB

6 (*amends* FA 1989 s 83A(1), (2)).

Enactments disapplying section 83(3) of the Finance Act 1989

7 (*repeals* TA 1988 ss 436(3)(*aa*), 439B(3)(*b*), 441(4)(*aa*)).

Overseas life insurance companies

8—(1) Schedule 8A to the Finance Act 1989 (modifications of sections 83 and 89 in relation to overseas life insurance companies) shall be amended in accordance with the following provisions of this paragraph.

(2)–(6) (*amend* FA 1989 Sch 8A heading, paras 1(1), 1A(4), 1C(4) and *insert* Sch 8A para 1A(5)).

Transitional provisions

9—(1) In the application of section 83AA or 83AB of the Finance Act 1989 in a case where one or more relevant amounts added to a company's long term business fund on or before 25th March 1996 are brought into account for a period of account beginning on or after 1st January 1996—

(*a*) the amount of any loss which, before any application of section 83(3) of that Act in relation to that period, would have arisen to the company in that period shall be treated as reduced (but not below nil) by the aggregate of those relevant amounts; and

(*b*) except as provided by paragraph (*a*) above, those relevant amounts shall be disregarded.

(2) In the application of sub-paragraph (1) above in relation to an overseas life insurance company, any reference to an amount added to a company's long term business fund shall be taken as a reference to any assets which became assets of the long term business fund of an overseas life insurance company used or held for the purposes of the company's United Kingdom branch or agency, having immediately previously been—

(*a*) held by the company otherwise than as assets of that fund, or

(*b*) used or held otherwise than for those purposes.

(3) If the relevant accounting period mentioned in subsection (3) of section 83AA of the Finance Act 1989 is a period beginning before 1st January 1996, only the appropriate portion of the eligible loss shall be reduced pursuant to that subsection; and for the purposes of this sub-paragraph—

(*a*) "the eligible loss" means so much of the loss arising to the transferor company in the relevant accounting period as, on a just and reasonable apportionment of the loss for the purposes of that subsection, is referable to the business which is the subject of the particular transfer of business in question; and

(*b*) "the appropriate portion" of the eligible loss is the amount which bears to the eligible loss the proportion which A bears to B where—

A is the number of days in the relevant accounting period which fall on or after 1st January 1996; and

B is the total number of days in the relevant accounting period.

(4) Paragraph 10(2) below shall not prevent—

(*a*) an amount of surplus for a period of account of a company beginning on or after 1st January 1996, or

(*b*) an amount of surplus for any period of account of a company which, by virtue of the operation of this sub-paragraph, derives from an amount of surplus falling within paragraph (*a*) above,

from being treated by virtue of section 83AB of the Finance Act 1989 as an amount of surplus for the period of account of another company last preceding its earliest period of account ending on or after 1st January 1996 (whenever beginning) or from being applied accordingly under section 83AA(6) or 83AB of that Act.

(5) In this paragraph—

"add" has the same meaning as in section 83 of the Finance Act 1989;

"brought into account" has the same meaning as it has in sections 83 to 83AB of that Act by virtue of section 83A of that Act;

"relevant amount" has the same meaning as in section 83AA of that Act;

"surplus" has the same meaning as in sections 83AA and 83AB of that Act.

Commencement

10—(1) Subject to paragraph 2(1) and (3) above, paragraphs 1 to 3 above have effect in relation to accounting periods beginning on or after 1st January 1996.

(2) Subject to paragraph 9 above, paragraphs 4 to 8 above have effect in relation to periods of account beginning on or after 1st January 1996.

SCHEDULE 32

EQUALISATION RESERVES

Section 166

1 (*inserts* TA 1988 ss 444BA, 444BB, 444BC, 444BD).

2 (*amends* TMA 1970 s 98, Table)

SCHEDULE 33

MANAGEMENT EXPENSES OF CAPITAL REDEMPTION BUSINESS

Section 168

Commentary—*Simon's Direct Tax Service* **D4.530.**

Amendment of section 76 of Taxes Act

1 (*inserts* TA 1988 s 76(5A) and *amends* s 76(6), (8)).

Treatment of capital redemption business

2 (*amends* TA 1988 s 458(1)).

Overseas life insurance companies

3 (*amends* TA 1988 Sch 19AC para 5(1)).

Commencement

4 This Schedule has effect as respects accounting periods ending on or after the day appointed under section 199 of the Finance Act 1994 for the purposes of Chapter III of Part IV of that Act (self-assessment management provisions).

Notes—The appointed day is 1 July 1999 by virtue of Finance Act 1994, Section 199, (Appointed Day) Order, SI 1998/3173 art 2.

SCHEDULE 34

PROVISIONAL REPAYMENTS IN CONNECTION WITH PENSION BUSINESS

Section 169

Commentary—*Simon's Direct Tax Service* **D4.534.**

PART I

AMENDMENTS OF SCHEDULE 19AB TO THE TAXES ACT 1988

Amendments—This Schedule repealed by FA 2001, s 110, Sch 33 Pt II(12) with effect in accordance with FA 2001 s 87

[1—(1)–(6) (*amends* TA 1988 Sch 19AB para 1).

(7) ...1

(8) ...2][3]

Amendments—¹ Sub-para (7) *repealed by* F(No 2)A 1997 Sch 8 Pt II (6).
² Sub-para (8) repealed by FA 1998 Sch 27 Part III with effect in relation to accounting periods ending after 30 June 1999 (by virtue of Finance Act 1994, Section 199, (Appointed Day) Order, SI 1998/3173 art 2).
³ This Schedule repealed by FA 2001, s 110, Sch 33 Pt II(12) with effect in accordance with FA 2001 s 87

2 (*substitutes* TA 1988 Sch 19AB para 2(1), (2) and *amends* para 2(3); *repealed by* FA 2001, s 110, Sch 33 Pt II(12) with effect in accordance with FA 2001 s 87).

3—*(1) Paragraph 3 (repayment, with interest, of excessive provisional repayments) shall be amended in accordance with the following provisions of this paragraph.*

(2)–(6) (substitute TA 1988 Sch 19AB para 3(1)(a), (b), insert para 3(1A), (1B), (1C), (1D), (8), (9) and amend para 3(3), (b), (4)).

(4) (amends para 3(3), (b)).

(5) (amends para 3(4)).

(6) (inserts para 3(8), (9)).

Amendments—This Schedule repealed by FA 2001, s 110, Sch 33 Pt II(12) with effect in accordance with FA 2001 s 87

4 (*amends* TA 1988 Sch 19AB para 6(1), *repeals* para 6(3) and *inserts* para 6(4)–(6); *repealed by* FA 2001, s 110, Sch 33 Pt II(12) with effect in accordance with FA 2001 s 87).

PART II

AMENDMENTS OF SCHEDULE 19AC TO THE TAXES ACT 1988

5 (*repeals* TA 1988 Sch 19AC para 15(1) and *inserts* para 15(3); *part repealed by* F(No 2)A 1997 Sch 8 Pt II (6); *repealed by* FA 2001, s 110, Sch 33 Pt II(12) with effect in accordance with FA 2001 s 87).

SCHEDULE 35

ROLL-OVER RELIEF IN RESPECT OF SHIPS

Section 179

Amendments—This Schedule repealed by the Capital Allowances Act 2001 s 580, Sch 4 with effect for income tax purposes, as respects allowances and charges falling to be made for chargeable periods ending after 5 April 2001, and for corporation tax purposes, as respects allowances and charges falling to be made for chargeable periods ending after 31 March 2001.

SCHEDULE 36

CONTROLLED FOREIGN COMPANIES

Section 182

1 (*repeals* TA 1988 s 747A(7) and *amends* s 747A(8)).

2 (*amends* TA 1988 s 748(3)(*a*)).

3 (*amends* TA 1988 Sch 24 paras 1, 2, 4, 9, 10, 11).

Amendments—Sub-paras 6(*b*), (7) repealed by FA 1998 Sch 27 Part III(27) with effect in relation to accounting periods ending after 30 June 1999 (by virtue of Finance Act 1994, Section 199, (Appointed Day) Order, SI 1998/3173 art 2).

4—(1) (*amends* TA 1988 Sch 25 paras 2, 2A, 3, 6, 16).

SCHEDULE 37

BANKS

Section 198

Commentary—*Simon's Direct Tax Service* **A3.405.**

PART I

"BANK" RE-DEFINED FOR CERTAIN PURPOSES

1 (*inserts* TA 1988 s 840A and *amends* s 828(4)).

PART II

AMENDMENTS OF THE TAXES ACT 1988

Provisions in which new meaning of "bank" applies

2 (*inserts* TA 1988 ss 234A(8A), 349(3AA), 745(5A), 816(3A), Sch 20 paras 7(3), 10(2)).

Related amendments

3 (*amends* TA 1988 s 349(3)(*a*), (*b*)).

4 (*inserts* TA 1988 s 349(3AB)).

5 (*amends* TA 1988 Sch 20 paras 7(1), 10).

Application

6 The amendments of the Taxes Act 1988 made by paragraphs 2 to 5 above apply as mentioned in paragraphs 7 to 10 below.

7 The amendment of section 234A applies in relation to payments made on or after the day on which this Act is passed.

8—(1) The amendment of subsection (3)(*a*) of section 349, and inserted subsection (3AA) of that section so far as it relates to subsection (3)(*a*), apply in accordance with sub-paragraphs (2) to (6) below.

(2) The amendments do not apply in relation to interest payable before the day on which this Act is passed.

(3) In the case of an institution which—

    (*a*) immediately before the day on which this Act is passed, is treated for the purposes of section 349(3)(*a*) as a bank carrying on a bona fide banking business in the United Kingdom, and
    (*b*) on that day, falls within the definition of ''bank'' given by section 840A(1),

the amendments apply in relation to interest payable on an advance made before that day as well as in relation to interest payable on an advance made on or after that day.

(4) In the case of an institution which—

    (*a*) immediately before the day on which this Act is passed, is not treated for the purposes of section 349(3)(*a*) as a bank carrying on a bona fide banking business in the United Kingdom, and
    (*b*) on that day, falls within the definition of ''bank'' given by section 840A(1),

the amendments apply only in relation to interest payable on an advance made on or after that day.

(5) Sub-paragraph (6) below applies in the case of an institution which—

    (*a*) immediately before the day on which this Act is passed, is treated for the purposes of section 349(3)(*a*) as a bank carrying on a bona fide banking business in the United Kingdom; and
    (*b*) on that day does not fall within the definition of ''bank'' given by section 840A(1).

(6) The amendments apply in relation to—

    (*a*) interest payable on an advance made on or after the day on which this Act is passed; and
    (*b*) interest payable on an advance made before that day, if at the time when the interest is paid the person beneficially entitled to the interest is not within the charge to corporation tax as respects the interest.

(7) The amendment of subsection (3)(*b*) of section 349, and inserted subsection (3AA) of that section so far as it relates to subsection (3)(*b*), apply in relation to interest paid on or after the day on which this Act is passed on an advance made on or after that day.

(8) In relation to interest paid on an advance made before the day on which this Act is passed, section 349(3)(*b*) shall have effect as if for the words ''such a bank'' there were substituted ''a bank carrying on a bona fide banking business in the United Kingdom'' (and section 349(3AA) shall be disregarded).

9 The amendments of sections 745 and 816 apply in relation to requirements imposed on or after the day on which this Act is passed.

10 The amendments of paragraphs 7 and 10 of Schedule 20 apply in relation to deposits made or, as the case may be, money placed on or after the day on which this Act is passed.

PART III
OTHER AMENDMENTS
Amendments of the Management Act

11—(1)–(4) (*insert* TMA 1970 ss 17(1A), 18(3AA), 24(3A) and *amend* ss 17(1), 18(3))).

(5) This paragraph applies as follows—

    (*a*) the amendments of section 17 apply in relation to interest paid on or after the day on which this Act is passed; and
    (*b*) the amendments of sections 18 and 24 apply in relation to requirements imposed on or after the day on which this Act is passed.

Amendments of the Inheritance Tax Act 1984

12 ...

Note—Para 12 is reproduced in the Pt II of this Handbook.

SCHEDULE 38

QUOTATION OR LISTING OF SECURITIES

Section 199

The Finance Act 1973

1—(1) (*amends FA 1973 s 38(2)(c)*).

(2) This paragraph has effect in relation to disposals of shares on or after 1st April 1996.

The Inheritance Tax Act 1984

2–5 ...

Note—Paragraphs 2–5 are reproduced in Pt II of this Handbook.

The Taxes Act 1988

6 (*amends TA 1988 ss 124(6)(b), 209(2)(e), 246S(3)(c), (e), 254(11), 349(3A)(b), 415(1)(b),
477A(1A), 576(4), Sch 9 para 11(a), (c), Sch 18 para 1(5C)(c), Sch 20 para 5, Sch 25 para 13(2)(c);
part repealed* (prospectively) by F(No 2)A 1997 Sch 8 Pt II(11) and FA 2000 s 156 Sch 40 Pt II(17)).

7 (*amends TA 1988 ss 210(4), 842(1)(c), 842AA(2)(e)*).

8 (*amends TA 1988 s 251(5)*).

9 (*amends TA 1988 s 735(3), (4), (5)*).

The Taxation of Chargeable Gains Act 1992

10 (*amends TCGA 1992 ss 144(8)(b), 164N(1), 165(2)(b), 276(2)(c), (6), 281(3)(c), Sch 7
para 2(2)(b); part repealed* by FA 2000 s 156, Sch 40 Pt II(10) with effect for disposals made after 8
November 1999).

11 (*amends TCGA 1992 s 146(4)(b)*).

12 (*amends TCGA 1992 s 272(3), Sch 11 para 7(1)(a)*).

SCHEDULE 39

ENACTMENT OF CERTAIN INLAND REVENUE EXTRA-STATUTORY CON-
CESSIONS

Section 201

PART I

INCOME TAX AND CORPORATION TAX

Capital Allowances

1—(1) ...[2]

(2) ...[1]

(3) ...[2]

(4) ...[2]

Amendments—[1] Sub-para (2) and words in sub-para (4) repealed by FA 1998 s 165, Sch 27 Part III(4) with effect for income
tax for the year 1998–99 and subsequent years of assessment, and for corporation tax from 1 April 1998 subject to transitional
provisions in FA 1998 Sch 5 Part IV.
[2] Sub-paras (1), (3) and (4) repealed by the Capital Allowances Act 2001 s 580, Sch 4 with effect for income tax purposes, as
respects allowances and charges falling to be made for chargeable periods ending after 5 April 2001, and for corporation tax
purposes, as respects allowances and charges falling to be made for chargeable periods ending after 31 March 2001.

Contributions to overseas pension schemes

2—(1)–(3) (*amends FA 1989 s 76(2), (3), (5), (6) and inserts s 76(6A)–(6C)*).

(4) The amendments made by this paragraph shall have effect in relation to expenses incurred on or
after the day on which this Act is passed.

PART II
CHARGEABLE GAINS
Treatment of compensation and insurance money

3—(1), (2) (*substitutes* TCGA 1992 s 23(6)–(8) for s 23(6)).

(3) The amendments made by this paragraph shall have effect in relation to capital sums received on or after 6th April 1996.

Assets of negligible value

4—(1) (*substitutes* TCGA 1992 s 24(2)).

(2) The amendment made by this paragraph shall have effect in relation to claims made on or after 6th April 1996.

Settled Property

5—(1)–(3) (*amends* TCGA 1992 s 72(1), (2), (5) and *substitutes* s 72(3), (4)).

(4) The amendments made by this paragraph shall have effect in relation to deaths occurring on or after 6th April 1996.

6—(1)–(4) (*amends* TCGA 1992 s 73(1), (2), (3)).

(5) The amendments made by this paragraph shall have effect in relation to deaths occurring on or after 6th April 1996.

Retirement Relief

7—(1)–(3) (*amends* TCGA 1992 Sch 6 para 14(2) and *inserts* para 14(7), (8)).

(4) The amendments made by this paragraph shall have effect in relation to disposals made on or after 6th April 1996.

Prospective amendments—This paragraph to be repealed by FA 1998 s 165, Sch 27 Pt III(31) with effect for disposals from the year 2003–04.

Relief for loans to traders

8—(1)–(4) (*amends* TCGA 1992 s 253(3), (4) and *inserts* s 253(3A)).

(5) The amendments made by this paragraph shall have effect in relation to claims made on or after 6th April 1996.

Relief for debts on qualifying corporate bonds

9—(1)–(6) (*amends* TCGA 1992 s 254(2), (6), (7), (8), (11) and *inserts* s 254(8A)).

(7) The amendments made by this paragraph shall have effect in relation to claims made on or after 6th April 1996.

SCHEDULE 40
GILT STRIPPING: TAXATION PROVISIONS
Section 202

Commentary—*Simon's Direct Tax Service* **B5.101; C2.806.**

The Stamp Act 1891 (c39)

1, 2 ...

Note—Paras 1, 2 are reproduced in the *Orange Tax Handbook*.

The Taxes Act 1988

3 (*amends* TA 1988 s 710(5) and *inserts* s 710(13A), (13B)).

4 (*inserts* TA 1988 s 711(6A)).

5 (*inserts* TA 1988 s 712(4)).

6 (*inserts* TA 1988 s 722A).

7 (*inserts* TA 1988 s 730C).

The Taxation of Chargeable Gains Act 1992 (c 12)

8 (*inserts* TCGA 1992 Sch 9 para 1A).

FINANCE ACT 1997

(1997 Chapter 16)

ARRANGEMENT OF SECTIONS

PART V

INCOME TAX, CORPORATION TAX AND CAPITAL GAINS TAX

An Act to grant certain duties, to alter other duties, and to amend the law relating to the National Debt and the Public Revenue, and to make further provision in connection with Finance.

[19th March 1997]

PART V

INCOME TAX, CORPORATION TAX AND CAPITAL GAINS TAX

Income tax charge, rates and reliefs

54 Charge and rates of income tax for 1997–98

(1), (2) (*Spent*).

(3), (4) (*amend* TA 1988 s 686 (1A)).

(5) (*amends* TA 1988 s 559(4)).

Commentary—*Simon's Direct Tax Service* **E1.102.**

55 Modification of indexed allowances

(*Spent*).

Commentary—*Simon's Direct Tax Service* **E2.105.**

56 Blind person's allowance.

(1) (*Spent*).

(2) (*inserts* TA 1988 s 265 (1A)).

(3) Subsection (1) above shall apply for the year 1997–98 and, subject to subsection (2) above, for subsequent years of assessment.

Commentary—*Simon's Direct Tax Service* **E2.802.**

57 Limit on relief for interest.

(*Spent*).

Commentary—*Simon's Direct Tax Service* **A3.431; E1.539.**

Corporation tax charge and rate

58 Charge and rate of corporation tax for 1997

Commentary—*Simon's Direct Tax Service* **D2.109.**
Amendments—This section repealed by F(No 2)A 1997 Sch 8 Pt II(3) and deemed never to have had effect. Superseded by F(No 2)A 1997 s 18(1).

59 Small companies

Commentary—*Simon's Direct Tax Service* **D2.109.**
Amendments—Sub-para (*a*) repealed by F(No 2)A 1997 Sch 8 Pt II(3) and deemed never to have had effect. Superseded by F(No 2)A 1997 s 18(2); sub-para (*b*) spent.

Payments for wayleaves

60 Wayleaves for electricity cables, telephone lines, etc

(1), (2) (*amend* TA 1988 s 120(1)).

(3) (*inserts* TA 1988 s 120(1A)).

(4) (*repeals* TA 1988 s 120 (2)–(4) and (5)(*c*)).

(5) This section has effect in relation to payments made on or after 6th April 1997.

Commentary—*Simon's Direct Tax Service* **A3.141.**

Schedule E

61 Phasing out of relief for profit-related pay

(1) Chapter III of Part V of the Taxes Act 1988 (profit-related pay) shall have effect as if, in section 171(4) (£4,000 limit on relief for profit period of twelve months), for "£4,000" there were substituted—

(*a*) in relation to profit-related pay paid by reference to profit periods beginning on or after 1st January 1998 and before 1st January 1999, "£2,000"; and

(*b*) in relation to profit-related pay paid by reference to profit periods beginning on or after 1st January 1999 and before 1st January 2000, "£1,000".

(2) That Chapter shall not have effect in relation to any payment made by reference to a profit period beginning on or after 1st January 2000.

(3) Accordingly—

  (*a*) a scheme shall not be registered under that Chapter if the only payments for which it provides are payments by reference to profit periods beginning on or after 1st January 2000; and

  (*b*) registration under that Chapter shall end on 31st December 2000.

Commentary—*Simon's Direct Tax Service* E4.302.

62 Travelling expenses etc

(1)–(3) ...[1]

(4) (*amends* TA 1988 s 168(5)(c), (5A)(c)).

(5) This section has effect for the year 1998–99 and subsequent years of assessment.

Commentary—*Simon's Direct Tax Service* E4.708.
Amendments—[1] Sub-ss (1)–(3) repealed by FA 1998 s 165, Sch 27 Part III(10) with effect for the year 1998–99 and subsequent years of assessment.

63 Work-related training

(1), (2) (*insert* TA 1988 s 200B, s 200C and s 200D and *amend* s 200A(3)(*b*)).

(3) This section applies for the year 1997–98 and subsequent years of assessment.

Commentary—*Simon's Direct Tax Service* E2.1301.

Relieved expenditure, losses etc

64 Postponed company donations to charity

(1) (*inserts* TA 1988 s 339 (7AA), (7AB) and (7AC)).

(2) This section has effect in relation to donations made in accounting periods beginning on or after 1st April 1997.

Commentary—*Simon's Direct Tax Service* C4.522.

65 National Insurance contributions

(1)–(3) (*amend* TA 1988 s 617(3), (4)).

(4) Subsection (2) above has effect in relation to the year 1996–97 and subsequent years of assessment.

(5) Subsection (3) above has effect in relation to contributions paid on or after 26th November 1996.

Commentary—*Simon's Direct Tax Service* B3.1428.

66 Expenditure on production wells etc

(1) (*inserts* TA 1988 s 91C).

(2) ...[1]

(3) Subsection (1) above applies to expenditure which—

  (*a*) is incurred on or after 26th November 1996; but

  (*b*) is not incurred before 26th November 1997 in pursuance of a contract entered into before 26th November 1996.

(4) The reference in subsection (3) above to expenditure incurred in pursuance of a contract entered into before 26th November 1996 does not, in the case of a contract varied on or after that date, include a reference to so much of any expenditure of the sort described in section 91C of the Taxes Act 1988 as exceeds the amount of expenditure of that sort that would have been incurred if that contract had not been so varied.

(5) ...[1]

Commentary—*Simon's Direct Tax Service* B3.405.
Amendments—[1] Sub-ss (2), (5) repealed by the Capital Allowances Act 2001 s 580, Sch 4 with effect for income tax purposes, as respects allowances and charges falling to be made for chargeable periods ending after 5 April 2001, and for corporation tax purposes, as respects allowances and charges falling to be made for chargeable periods ending after 31 March 2001.

67 Annuity business of insurance companies

(1) (*amends* TA 1988 s 437(1A), (1B)).

(2), (3) (*amend* TA 1988 s 437(1C) and *insert* s 437(1CA)–(1CD), 437A).

(4) (*repeals* TA 1988 s 434B(2), *amends* TA 1988 s 76(2A)(*b*) and s 337(2B)).

(5) (*amends* TA 1988 Sch 19AC para 9B).

(6) (*amends* FA 1991 Sch 7 para 16(1)).

(7) Subsections (1) and (4) to (6) above have effect in relation to accounting periods beginning after 5th March 1997.

(8) Subsections (2) and (3) above have effect in relation to accounting periods ending on or after 5th March 1997 but do not affect the computation of the capital elements contained in any annuity payments made before that date.

Commentary—*Simon's Direct Tax Service* **D4.520A.**

68 Consortium claims for group relief

(*Amends* TA 1988 s 410(5)).

Commentary—*Simon's Direct Tax Service* **D2.642A.**

Distributions etc

69 Special treatment for certain distributions

Schedule 7 to this Act (which makes provision for the treatment of distributions arising on the purchase etc by a company of its own shares and for cases where a distribution has a connection with a transaction in securities) shall have effect.

Commentary—*Simon's Direct Tax Service* **D1.110.**

70 Distributions of exempt funds

Commentary—*Simon's Direct Tax Service* **B3.734.**
Amendment—This section repealed by F(No 2)A 1997 Sch 8 Pt II(9) with effect in relation to distributions made after 5 April 1999.

71 Set-off against franked investment income

Commentary—*Simon's Direct Tax Service* **B5.101.**
Amendments—This section repealed by F(No 2)A 1997 Sch 8 Pt II(4) with effect generally in relation to accounting periods beginning after 1 July 1997 but subject to the detailed provisions of F(No 2)A 1997 s 20(1)–(4).

72 FIDs paid to unauthorised unit trusts

Commentary—*Simon's Direct Tax Service* **D1.707.**
Amendment—This section repealed by F(No 2)A 1997 Sch 8 Pt II(11) with effect in relation to distributions made after 5 April 1999.

73 Tax advantages to include tax credits

(1) (*inserts* TA 1988 s 709(2A)).

(2) This section—

(*a*) has effect for the purposes of the application of provisions of Chapter I of Part XVII of the Taxes Act 1988 in relation to chargeable periods ending at any time, including times before the passing of this Act, but

(*b*) without prejudice to the construction of that Chapter apart from this section, does not apply in the case of a tax credit in respect of a distribution made before 8th October 1996.

Commentary—*Simon's Direct Tax Service* **A7.103**

Investments etc

74 Enterprise investment scheme

Schedule 8 to this Act (which amends the provisions in Chapter III of Part VII of the Taxes Act 1988 about the companies which are qualifying companies for the purposes of the enterprise investment scheme and makes related amendments to that Chapter) shall have effect.

Commentary—*Simon's Direct Tax Service* **E3.117.**

75 Venture capital trusts

(1) (*amends* TA 1988 s 842AA(5A),(5B)).

(2) (*inserts* TA 1988 s 842AA(6)(ca)).

(3) Schedule 9 to this Act (which amends the provisions of Schedule 28B to the Taxes Act 1988 defining "qualifying holdings") shall have effect.

Commentary—*Simon's Direct Tax Service* **E3.602.**

76 Stock lending and manufactured payments

Schedule 10 to this Act (which makes provision for the treatment for the purposes of income tax, corporation tax and capital gains tax of stock lending arrangements and manufactured payments) shall have effect.

Commentary—*Simon's Direct Tax Service* **B3.1007.**

77 Bond washing and repos

(1) (*inserts* TA 1988 s 731(2B)–(2F)).

(2) This section applies in relation to cases in which the interest becomes payable on or after the day on which this Act is passed.

Commentary—*Simon's Direct Tax Service* A7.302.

78 National Savings Bank interest

(1) (*inserts* TA 1988 s 349(3)(*ba*)).

(2) This section applies to interest whenever paid (including interest paid before the day on which this Act is passed).

Commentary—*Simon's Direct Tax Service* B5.103.

79 Payments under certain life insurance policies

(1) In this section "relevant excepted benefit" means so much of any qualifying payment under a relevant life insurance policy as—

> (*a*) is a sum falling, but for this section, to be treated for the purposes of the Tax Acts as an amount of interest or as an annual payment;
> (*b*) is not a sum paid or falling to be paid by virtue of provisions of that policy which, taken alone, would constitute a different sort of policy; and
> (*c*) does not represent interest for late payment on—
>> (i) any other part of that qualifying payment, or
>> (ii) the whole or any part of any other qualifying payment under the policy.

(2) For the purposes of subsection (1)(*c*) above, interest on the whole or any part of a qualifying payment under a policy ("the relevant amount") is interest for late payment if it is interest for a period beginning on or after the date of the occurrence of the event or contingency as a result of the occurrence of which the relevant amount falls to be paid.

(3) The Tax Acts shall have effect, and be deemed always to have had effect, as if—

> (*a*) a relevant excepted benefit were neither an amount of interest nor an annual payment;
> (*b*) the payments which are relevant capital payments for the purposes of section 541 of the Taxes Act 1988 (computation of gain in the case of life policies) included the payment of a relevant excepted benefit;
> (*c*) on the payment of a relevant excepted benefit there were a surrender—
>> (i) except in a case falling within sub-paragraph (ii) below, of a part of the rights conferred by the policy in question; and
>> (ii) in a case where the payment of the benefit (or of that benefit together with any interest falling within subsection (1)(*c*) above) comprises the whole of the last payment to be made under the policy, of all of the remaining rights so conferred;

> and

> (*d*) the value of the part or rights treated as surrendered on the payment of a relevant excepted benefit were equal to the amount of the payment.

(4) For the purposes of this section a qualifying payment under a relevant life insurance policy is any amount which has been or is to be paid under that policy by the insurer.

(5) In this section "relevant life insurance policy" means any contract of insurance (whenever effected) which—

> [(*a*) is a contract which falls within paragraph I or III of Part II of Schedule 1 to the Financial Services and Markets Act 2000 (Regulated Activities) Order 2001;][1]
> (*b*) is neither—
>> (i) an annuity contract, nor
>> (ii) a contract effected in the course of a company's pension business (within the meaning given by section 431B of the Taxes Act 1988 or the corresponding enactment in force when the contract was effected).

(6) In subsection (1)(*b*) above, the reference to a different sort of policy is a reference to any contract [which falls within Part I or II of Schedule 1 to the Financial Services and Markets Act 2000 (Regulated Activities) Order 2001 other than a contract which falls within paragraph I or III of Part II of that Schedule.][1]

(7) This section shall be deemed to have had effect, for the purposes of the cases to which the enactments applied, in relation to enactments directly or indirectly re-enacted in the Tax Acts, as it has effect in relation to those Acts.

(8) For the purposes of subsection (7) above the reference in subsection (3)(*b*) above to section 541 of the Taxes Act 1988 shall be taken to include a reference to any corresponding provision contained in the enactments directly or indirectly re-enacted in the Tax Acts.

Commentary—*Simon's Direct Tax Service* **E3.502.**
Amendments—[1] Sub-s (5)(*a*), and words in sub-s (6), substituted by the Financial Services and Markets Act 2000 (Consequential Amendments) (Taxes) Order, SI 2001/3629 arts 97, 98 with effect from 1 December 2001 (immediately after the coming into force of the Financial Services and Markets Act 2000 ss 411, 432(1), Sch 20)

80 Futures and options: transactions with guaranteed returns

(1) (*inserts* TA 1988 s 127A).

(2) (*inserts* TA 1988 Sch 5AA).

(3) (*amends* TA 1988 s 128).

(4) (*inserts* TA 1988 s 399(1A)).

(5) (*amends* TA 1988 s 469(9)).

(6) Subject to subsection (7) below, this section and Schedule 11 to this Act shall have effect, and be deemed to have had effect, for chargeable periods ending on or after 5th March 1997 in relation to profits and gains realised, and losses sustained, on or after that date.

(7) In relation to profits and gains realised, and losses sustained, on or after 5th March 1997, paragraph 1(6) and (7) of the Schedule 5AA to the Taxes Act 1988 (rule against double counting) inserted by this section shall be deemed to have had effect for chargeable periods beginning before that date (as well as for those beginning on or after that date).

Commentary—*Simon's Direct Tax Service* **B7.204.**

Transfer of assets abroad

81 Transfer of assets abroad

(1) (*inserts* TA 1988 s 739(1A)).

(2) This section applies irrespective of when the transfer or associated operations took place, but applies only to income arising on or after 26th November 1996.

Commentary—*Simon's Direct Tax Service* **E1.721.**

Leasing and loan arrangements

82 Finance leases and loans

Schedule 12 to this Act (which makes provision about arrangements such as are treated for certain accounting purposes as finance leases or loans) shall have effect.

Commentary—*Simon's Direct Tax Service* **B3.1310.**

83 Loan relationships: transitions

(1) Chapter II of Part IV of the Finance Act 1996 (loan relationships) shall be amended as follows.

(2)–(4) (*insert* FA 1996 s 90(5)(*aa*) and *amend* FA 1996 s 90 (5), (6)).

(5) Subsections (2) to (4) above apply where the period or part of a period for which the superseded accounting method is or was used is a period ending on or after 14th November 1996.

(6) Schedule 13 to this Act (which contains amendments of the transitional provisions in Schedule 15 to the Finance Act 1996) shall have effect.

Commentary—*Simon's Direct Tax Service* **B5.101.**

Capital allowances

84 Writing-down allowances on long-life assets

...

Commentary—*Simon's Direct Tax Service* **B2.320.**
Amendment—This section repealed by the Capital Allowances Act 2001 s 580, Sch 4 with effect for income tax purposes, as respects allowances and charges falling to be made for chargeable periods ending after 5 April 2001, and for corporation tax purposes, as respects allowances and charges falling to be made for chargeable periods ending after 31 March 2001.

85 Schedule A cases etc

Schedule 15 to this Act (which makes provision in relation to capital allowances for cases where persons have income chargeable to tax under Schedule A or make lettings of furnished holiday accommodation in the United Kingdom) shall have effect.

Commentary—*Simon's Direct Tax Service* **A4.331.**

86 Capital allowances on fixtures

...

Commentary—*Simon's Direct Tax Service* **B2.351.**
Amendment—This section repealed by the Capital Allowances Act 2001 s 580, Sch 4 with effect for income tax purposes, as respects allowances and charges falling to be made for chargeable periods ending after 5 April 2001, and for corporation tax purposes, as respects allowances and charges falling to be made for chargeable periods ending after 31 March 2001.

Chargeable gains

87 Re-investment relief

Schedule 17 to this Act (which amends Chapter IA of Part V of the Taxation of Chargeable Gains Act 1992) shall have effect.

Commentary—*Simon's Direct Tax Service* C3.917.

88 Conversion of securities: QCBs and debentures

(1) The Taxation of Chargeable Gains Act 1992 shall be amended as follows.

(2), (3) (*amend* TCGA 1992 s 132(3)(*a*) and *insert* s 132(3)(*a*), (ia), (ib) 132(4), (5)).

(4) (*amends* TCGA 1992 s 116(2)).

(5) (*amends* TCGA 1992 s 251(6)(*d*)).

(6) This section has effect for the purposes of the application of the Taxation of Chargeable Gains Act 1992 in relation to any disposal on or after 26th November 1996 and shall so have effect, where a conversion took place at a time before that date, as if it had come into force before that time.

Commentary—*Simon's Direct Tax Service* C2.804.

89 Earn-out rights

(1) (*inserts* TCGA 1992 s 138A).

(2) Subject to subsections (3) to (8) below—

  (*a*) the section 138A inserted by subsection (1) above shall be deemed always to have been a section of the Taxation of Chargeable Gains Act 1992; and
  (*b*) the enactments applying to chargeable periods beginning before 6th April 1992 shall be deemed always to have included a corresponding section.

(3) Subject to subsections (4) to (6) below, an election under section 138A of the Taxation of Chargeable Gains Act 1992 in respect of a right conferred on any person before 26th November 1996 may be made at any time before the end of the period for the making of such an election in respect of a right conferred on that person on that date.

(4) An election in respect of a right conferred on any person shall not be made by virtue of subsection (3) above at any time after the final determination of his liability to corporation tax or capital gains tax for the chargeable period in which the right was in fact conferred on him.

(5) A notice given to an officer of the Board before the day on which this Act is passed shall not have effect as an election under section 138A of the Taxation of Chargeable Gains Act 1992, or the corresponding provision applying to chargeable periods beginning before 6th April 1992, except in accordance with subsection (6) below.

(6) Where—

  (*a*) any person has given a notification to an officer of the Board before the day on which this Act is passed, and
  (*b*) that notification was given either—

    (i) in anticipation of the right to make an election under section 138A of the Taxation of Chargeable Gains Act 1992, or
    (ii) for the purposes of an extra-statutory concession available to be used by that person for purposes similar to those of that section,

that notification shall, unless the Board otherwise direct, be treated as if it were a valid and irrevocable election made by that person for the purposes of that section or, as the case may be, the corresponding provision.

(7) Where any notification given as mentioned in subsection (6)(*b*)(ii) above is treated as an election for the purposes of section 138A of the Taxation of Chargeable Gains Act 1992 or any corresponding provision, that section or, as the case may be, the corresponding provision shall be taken to have no effect by virtue of that election in relation to any disposal before 26th November 1996 of any asset which—

  (*a*) was issued to any person in pursuance of an earn-out right;
  (*b*) was issued to any person in pursuance of any such right as is mentioned in subsection (4) of that section; or
  (*c*) falls for the purposes of that Act to be treated as the same as an asset issued at any time to any person in pursuance of such a right as is mentioned in paragraph (*a*) or (*b*) above but is not an asset first held by that person before that time.

(8) Subsection (7) above shall not prevent section 138A of the Taxation of Chargeable Gains Act 1992 from being taken, for the purposes of applying that Act to any disposal on or after 26th November 1996, to have had effect in relation to—

  (*a*) any disposal before that date on which, by virtue of any of the enactments specified in section 35(3)(*d*) of that Act, neither a gain nor a loss accrued, (*b*) any deemed disposal before that date by reference to which a gain or loss falls to be calculated in accordance with section 116(10)(*a*) of that Act, or

(*c*) any transaction before that date that would have fallen to be treated as a disposal but for section 127 of that Act.

Commentary—*Simon's Direct Tax Service* **C2.727.**

Double taxation relief

90 Restriction of relief for underlying tax

(1) (*inserts* TA 1988 s 801A).

(2) This section has effect in relation to dividends paid to a company resident in the United Kingdom at any time on or after 26th November 1996.

Commentary—*Simon's Direct Tax Service* **F2.106.**

91 Disposals of loan relationships with or without interest

(1) Section 807A of the Taxes Act 1988 (disposals and acquisitions of company loan relationships with or without interest) shall be amended as follows.

(2), (3) (*amend* TA 1988 s 807A(2) and *insert* s 807A(2A)).

(4) (*amends* TA 1988 s 807A(3)(*b*)).

(5) (*inserts* TA 1988 s 807A(6A)).

(6) Subsections (2) and (3) above have effect in relation to interest accruing on or after 1st April 1996.

(7) Subsection (4) above has effect in relation to transactions made on or after 26th November 1996.

Commentary—*Simon's Direct Tax Service* **B3.1007.**

Repayment supplement

92 Time from which entitlement runs

(1) Section 824 of the Taxes Act 1988 (repayment supplements), where it has effect as amended by paragraph 41 of Schedule 19 to the Finance Act 1994, shall be amended in accordance with subsections (2) to (4) below.

(2)–(4) (*amend* TA 1988 s 824(3)(*a*), (*b*), (*c*), (4) and *insert* s 824(4A)).

(5) (*amends* TCGA 1992 s 283(2)).

(6) This section has effect as respects the year 1997–98 and subsequent years of assessment and shall be deemed to have had effect as respects the year 1996–97.

Commentary—*Simon's Direct Tax Service* **E1.827.**

PART VIII
MISCELLANEOUS AND SUPPLEMENTAL
Obtaining information

110 Obtaining information from social security authorities

(1) This section applies to—

(*a*) any information held by the Secretary of State or the Department of Health and Social Services for Northern Ireland for the purposes of any of his or its functions relating to social security; and

(*b*) any information held by a person in connection with the provision by him to the Secretary of State or that Department of any services which that person is providing for purposes connected with any of those functions.

(2) Subject to the following provisions of this section, the person holding any information to which this section applies shall be entitled to supply it to—

(*a*) the Commissioners of Customs and Excise or any person by whom services are being provided to those Commissioners for purposes connected with any of their functions; or

(*b*) the Commissioners of Inland Revenue or any person by whom services are being provided to those Commissioners for purposes connected with any of their functions.

(3) Information shall not be supplied to any person under this section except for one or more of the following uses—

(*a*) use in the prevention, detection, investigation or prosecution of criminal offences which it is a function of the Commissioners of Customs and Excise, or of the Commissioners of Inland Revenue, to prevent, detect, investigate or prosecute;

(*b*) use in the prevention, detection or investigation of conduct in respect of which penalties which are not criminal penalties are provided for by or under any enactment;

(*c*) use in connection with the assessment or determination of penalties which are not criminal penalties;

(*d*) use in checking the accuracy of information relating to, or provided for purposes connected with, any matter under the care and management of the Commissioners of Customs and Excise or the Commissioners of Inland Revenue;

(*e*) use (where appropriate) for amending or supplementing any such information; and

(*f*) use in connection with any legal or other proceedings relating to anything mentioned in paragraphs (*a*) to (*e*) above.

(4) An enactment authorising the disclosure of information by a person mentioned in subsection (2)(*a*) or (*b*) above shall not authorise the disclosure by such a person of information supplied to him under this section except to the extent that the disclosure is also authorised by a general or specific permission granted by the Secretary of State or by the Department of Health and Social Services for Northern Ireland.

(5) In this section references to functions relating to social security include references to—

(*a*) functions in relation to ...[1] social security benefits (whether contributory or not) or national insurance numbers; and

(*b*) functions under the Jobseekers Act 1995 or the Jobseekers (Northern Ireland) Order 1995.

[(5AA) The reference to social security benefits in subsection (5)(*a*) above does not include a reference to working families' tax credit or disabled person's tax credit.][3]

[(5A) Nothing in this section affects any disclosure authorised by section 121F of the Social Security Administration Act 1992 (supply to Inland Revenue of information for purposes of contributions, statutory sick pay or statutory maternity pay of information held by Secretary of State) [or section 115E of the Social Security Administration (Northern Ireland) Act 1992 (supply to Inland Revenue of information for purposes of contributions, statutory sick pay or statutory maternity pay of information held by the Department of Health and Social Services for Northern Ireland)][2] [or paragraph 3 of Schedule 5 to the Tax Credits Act 1999 (supply to Inland Revenue for purposes of tax credit of information so held)][3].][1]

(6) In this section "conduct" includes acts, omissions and statements.

(7) This section shall come into force on such day as the Treasury may by order made by statutory instrument appoint, and different days may be appointed under this subsection for different purposes.

Commentary—*Simon's Direct Tax Service* A2.803.
Note—The day appointed for the purposes of this section is 2 July 1997 (Finance Act 1997, Section 110, (Appointed Day) Order, SI 1997/1603).
Amendments—[1] Words in sub-s (5)(*a*) repealed, and sub-s (5A) inserted, by the Social Security Contributions (Transfer of Functions, etc) Act 1999 s 28(3), Sch 6 para 10 with effect from 1 April 1999 by virtue of the Social Security (Transfer of Functions, etc) Act 1999 (Commencement No 1 and Transitional Provisions) Order, SI 1999/527 art 2, Sch 2.
[2] Words in sub-s (5A) inserted by the Social Security Contributions (Transfer of Functions, etc) (Northern Ireland) Order, SI 1999/671, art 6, Sch 5 para 9 with effect from 1 April 1999 (by virtue of the Social Security Contributions (Transfer of Functions, etc) (1999 Order) (Commencement No 1 and Transitional Provisions) Order (Northern Ireland), SR 1999/149, art 2(*c*), Sch 2).
[3] Sub-s (5AA) and words in sub-s (5A) inserted by Tax Credits Act 1999 s 12(6), Sch 5 para 7 with effect from 5 October 1999.

Supplemental

112 Interpretation

In this Act "the Taxes Act 1988" means the Income and Corporation Taxes Act 1988.

113 Repeals

(1) The enactments mentioned in Schedule 18 to this Act (which include spent provisions) are hereby repealed to the extent specified in the third column of that Schedule.

(2) The repeals specified in that Schedule have effect subject to the commencement provisions and savings contained or referred to in the notes set out in that Schedule.

114 Short title

This Act may be cited as the Finance Act 1997.

SCHEDULES

SCHEDULE 7

SPECIAL TREATMENT FOR CERTAIN DISTRIBUTIONS

Section 69

Commentary—*Simon's Direct Tax Service* D1.110.
Revenue & other press releases—IR Tax Bulletin June 1997 p 429 (article explains scope of this legislation and provides illustrative examples).
Amendments—See the corresponding note to the individual paragraphs in this Schedule, where relevant.

Distributions to which Schedule applies

1 ...

Amendment—This paragraph repealed by F(No 2)A 1997 Sch 8 Pt II(12) with effect in relation to distributions made after 5 April 1999.

Distributions treated as FIDs

2 ...

Amendment—This paragraph repealed by F(No 2)A 1997 s 36(4), Sch 6 para 21(1), (2), (4), Sch 8 Pt II(11) with effect in relation to distributions made after 5 April 1999.

Distributions treated as section 686 income of trustees

3 ...

Amendment—This paragraph repealed by F(No 2)A 1997 Sch 8 Pt II(9) with effect in relation to distributions made after 5 April 1999.

Stock options

4 ...

Amendment—This paragraph repealed by F(No 2)A 1997 s 36(4), Sch 6 para 21(1), (3), (4), Sch 8 Pt II(11) with effect in relation to distributions made after 5 April 1999.

Dividends on fixed rate preference shares

5 ...

Amendments—This paragraph repealed by F(No 2)A 1997 s 36(4), Sch 6 para 21(1), (3), (4), Sch 8 Pt II(11) with effect in relation to distributions made after 5 April 1999.

Pre-sale distributions

6 ...

Amendment—This paragraph repealed by F(No 2)A 1997 s 36(4), Sch 6 para 21(1), (3), (4), Sch 8 Pt II(11) with effect in relation to distributions made after 5 April 1999.

Manufactured payments

7 ...

Amendment—This paragraph repealed by F(No 2)A 1997 Sch 8 Pt II(12) with effect in relation to payments which are representative of distributions made after 5 April 1999.

Amendment of section 95 of the Taxes Act 1988

8—(1) (*amends* TA 1988 s 95(1)–(3) and *inserts* s 95 (1A), (1B)).

(2) (*amends* TA 1988 s 20(1) Sch F para 1 and TA 1988 s 234(1)).

(3) This paragraph has effect in relation to distributions made on or after 26th November 1996.

Information to be provided about deemed FID

9 ...

Amendment—This paragraph repealed by F(No 2)A 1997 Sch 8 Pt II(11) with effect in relation to distributions made after 5 April 1999.

Group income

10 ...

Amendment—This paragraph repealed by F(No 2)A 1997 Sch 8 Pt II(11) with effect in relation to distributions made after 5 April 1999.

Distribution accounts

11 ...

Amendment—This paragraph repealed by F(No 2)A 1997 Sch 8 Pt II(11) with effect for distribution periods (within the meaning of TA 1988 s 468H) the distribution date for which falls after 5 April 1999.

Amendments consequential on paragraph 3 above

12—(1) (*repeals* TA 1988 s 686(2)(d) and *inserts* s 686(2AA)).

(2) (*amends* TA 1988 s 686(2A)).

(3) (*amends* TA 1988 s 233(1A)(a)(ii)).

(4) This paragraph has effect for the year 1997–98 and subsequent years of assessment and shall be deemed to have had effect for the year 1996–97.

SCHEDULE 8

ENTERPRISE INVESTMENT SCHEME: QUALIFYING COMPANIES

Section 74

Commentary—*Simon's Direct Tax Service* **E3.117.**

Introductory

1 Chapter III of Part VII of the Taxes Act 1988 (the enterprise investment scheme)—

    (*a*) in its application in relation to shares issued after 26th November 1996, and

    (*b*) in its application after 26th November 1996 in relation to shares which—

       (i) were issued on or after 1st January 1994 but before 27th November 1996, and

       (ii) immediately before 27th November 1996 were held by an individual and at that time were shares to which, within the meaning of that Chapter, any relief was attributable,

    shall have effect with the following amendments.

Requirements to be satisfied by the company for whose business activity money is raised

2 (*inserts* TA 1988 s 289(1)(*ba*) and s 289(1A)–(1D)).

Limit on relief for trading groups which let or operate ships

3 (*repeals* TA 1988 s 290A(6)(*b*)(*c*) and *inserts* s 290A(6)(*aa*) and s 290A(6A), (6B)).

Meaning of "qualifying company"

4 (*inserts* TA 1988 s 293(2)(*aa*) and s 293(3A)–(3F)).

Consequential amendments of section 297

5 (*amends* TA 1988 s 297(3)(*c*)(i) and s 297(6)(*d*)).

Consequential repeals of provisions about subsidiaries

6 (*repeals* TA 1988 s 308(1)(*b*) and s 308(5)(*a*), (*b*)).

SCHEDULE 9

VENTURE CAPITAL TRUSTS: QUALIFYING HOLDINGS

Section 75

Commentary—*Simon's Direct Tax Service* **E3.602.**

Introductory

1 Schedule 28B to the Taxes Act 1988 (venture capital trusts: meaning of "qualifying holdings") shall be amended as follows.

Requirements as to business of company whose shares etc are qualifying holdings

2 (*amends* TA 1988 Sch 28B para 3(2) and *inserts* paras (6)–(11)).

Consequential amendment of paragraph 4(7)

3 (*amends* TA 1988 Sch 28B para 4(7)).

Application of investment

4 (*inserts* TA 1988 Sch 28B para 6(2A)–(2C)).

Qualifying subsidiaries

5 (*amends* TA 1988 Sch 28B para 10(1), *repeals* para 10(2) and *amends* para 10(4), (5)).

Commencement

6 This Schedule has effect for the purposes of determining whether shares or securities are, as at any time after 26th November 1996, to be regarded as comprised in a company's qualifying holdings.

SCHEDULE 10

STOCK LENDING ARRANGEMENTS AND MANUFACTURED PAYMENTS

Section 76

Commentary—*Simon's Direct Tax Service* **B3.1007.**

PART I

STOCK LENDING

Approved stock lending arrangements: traders

1 (*repeals* TA 1988 s 129, s 129A and Sch 5A)).

Stock lending fees

2 (*amends* TA 1988 s 129B(3) and *substitutes* s 129B(4).

Stock lending agreements under which manufactured payments are not made

3 (*inserts* TA 1988 s 736B)).

Manufactured payments in stock lending cases etc

4 (*repeals* TA 1988 Sch 23A para 6 and *amends* Sch 23A para 7(3)).

Stock lending arrangements: capital gains

5— (1) (*inserts* TCGA 1992 ss 263B, 263C)).

(2) (*repeals* TCGA 1992 s 271(9)).

(3) (*amends* TA 1988 s 727(2)).

Premiums trust funds of Lloyd's members

6 (*repeals* FA 1993 s 174 (4), (5), s 182(1)(*ca*)(i), FA 1994 s 222(4), (5)and s 229(*ca*)(i))

Commencement

7—(1) This Part of this Schedule (except paragraph 4 above) has effect in relation to, and to transfers under, any arrangement made on or after such day as the Treasury may by order made by statutory instrument appoint.

(2) Paragraph 4 above has effect in relation to any manufactured payment made on or after the day appointed under sub-paragraph (1) above.

Note—The day appointed under sub-para (1) is 1 July 1997 (Finance Act 1997, Schedule 10, (Appointed Day) Order, SI 1997/991).

PART II

MANUFACTURED PAYMENTS

Repeal of section 737 of the Taxes Act 1988

8 (*repeals* TA 1988 s 737).

Meaning of "foreign income dividend"

9 ...

Amendment—This paragraph repealed by F(No 2)A 1997 Sch 8 Pt II(11) with effect in relation to manufactured dividends which are representative of dividends paid after 5 April 1999).

Manufactured dividends on UK equities

10—(1) (*amends* TA 1988 Sch 23A para 2 and *inserts* Sch 23A paras 2A and 2B).

(2) (*repealed by* F(No 2)A 1997 Sch 8 Pt II(11) *with effect for accounting periods beginning after 5 April 1999*).

(3) (*repealed by* F(No 2)A 1997 Sch 8 Pt II(11) *with effect in relation to manufactured dividends which are representative of dividends paid after 5 April 1999*).

Manufactured interest on UK securities

11—(1) (*amends* TA 1988 Sch 23A paras 3 and 3A).

(2) (*amends* TA 1988 s 737C(8)(*a*), (*b*)).

Repeal of paragraph 5 of Schedule 23A

12 (*repeals* TA 1988 Sch 23A para 5).

Consequential amendments in Schedule 23A

13 (*amends* TA 1988 Sch 23A para 8(1),(2) and *inserts* Sch 23A para 8(2A)).

Amendments of Taxes Management Act 1970

14 (*amends* TMA 1970 s 21(1)–(5), *inserts* s 21(5A) and *substitutes* s 21(7)).

Repeal of powers to modify information provisions

15 (*repeals* FA 1986 Sch 18 paras 7 and 9).

Commencement

16—(1) Subject to the following provisions of this paragraph, this Part of this Schedule has effect in relation to any payment of a manufactured dividend or manufactured interest which is a payment made on or after such day as the Treasury may by order made by statutory instrument appoint.

(2) Paragraph 14 above has effect (instead of in accordance with sub-paragraph (1) above but subject to sub-paragraph (3) below) for the purpose of conferring powers for obtaining information about—

(*a*) transactions entered into on or after such day as the Treasury may by order made by statutory instrument appoint; and

(*b*) payments made on or after that day (whether under such transactions or under transactions entered into before that day).

(3) Nothing in this Part of this Schedule shall affect the exercise, at any time on or after the day appointed under sub-paragraph (2) above, of the powers conferred apart from this Schedule by—

(*a*) section 21 of the Taxes Management Act 1970, or by any regulations modifying that section, or

(*b*) section 737(8) of the Taxes Act 1988,

for obtaining information about transactions entered into, or payments made, before that day.

Note—The day appointed under each of sub-paras (1) and (2) is 1 July 1997 (Finance Act 1997, Schedule 10, (Appointed Day) Order, SI 1997/991).

SCHEDULE 11

FUTURES AND OPTIONS: TAXATION OF GUARANTEED RETURNS

Section 80

Commentary—*Simon's Direct Tax Service* **B7.204.**
Note—This Schedule inserts TA 1988 Sch 5AA.

SCHEDULE 12

LEASING ARRANGEMENTS: FINANCE LEASES AND LOANS

Section 82

Commentary—*Simon's Direct Tax Service* **B3.1310.**
Revenue & other press releases—IR Tax Bulletin April 1997 p 414 (sets out in some detail the Revenue's view on a number of points of interpretation regarding this Schedule).

PART I

LEASING ARRANGEMENTS WHERE ANY OF THE RETURN ON INVESTMENT IS IN CAPITAL FORM

Purpose of this Part of this Schedule

1—(1) This Part of this Schedule is concerned with arrangements—

(*a*) which involve the lease of an asset;

(*b*) which are or have been entered into by companies or other persons;

(*c*) which are of such a kind as ...² falls ...² to be treated in accordance with [generally accepted accounting practice]¹ as finance leases or loans; and

(*d*) whose effect is that some or all of the return on investment in respect of the finance lease or loan—

(i) is or may be in the form of a sum which is not rent; and

(ii) would not, apart from this Schedule, be wholly brought into account for tax purposes as rent from the lease.

(2) The principal purpose of this Part of this Schedule is, in the case of any such arrangements,—

(*a*) to charge any person entitled to the lessor's interest under the lease of the asset to tax from time to time on amounts of income determined by reference to those which fall for accounting purposes to be treated in accordance with normal [generally accepted accounting practice][1] as the income return, on and after 26th November 1996, on investment in respect of the finance lease or loan (taking into account the substance of the matter as a whole, including in particular the state of affairs as between connected persons, or within a group of companies, as reflected or falling to be reflected in accounts of any of those persons or in consolidated group accounts);

(*b*) where the sum mentioned in sub-paragraph (1)(*d*) above falls due, to recover by reference to that sum the whole or any part of any reliefs, allowances or deductions which are or have been allowed or made in respect of capital expenditure incurred in respect of the leased asset.

Amendments—[1] Words substituted for the words "normal accountancy practice" by FA 2002 s 103(4)(*e*) with effect from 24 July 2002.
[2] In sub-para (1)(*c*), the words "and in paragraph (*a*) above "period of account" means a period for which the accounts of the trade are made up" and the words "for the purposes of accounts of such companies" repealed by FA 2002 s 141, Sch 40 Pt 3(16) with effect from 24 July 2002.

Application of this Part of this Schedule

2—(1) This Part of this Schedule applies in any case where (whether before or after the passing of this Act)—

(*a*) a lease of an asset is or has been granted; and
(*b*) in the case of the lease, the conditions in paragraph 3 below are or have been satisfied at some time in a period of account of the current lessor.

(2) Where the conditions in paragraph 3 below have been satisfied at some time in a period of account of the person who was at that time the lessor, they shall be taken to continue to be satisfied for the purposes of this Part of this Schedule unless and until—

(*a*) the asset ceases to be leased under the lease; or
(*b*) the lessor's interest under the lease is assigned to a person who is not connected with any of the persons described in sub-paragraph (3) below.

(3) Those persons are—

(*a*) the assignor;
(*b*) any person who was the lessor at some time before the assignment; or
(*c*) any person who at some time after the assignment becomes the lessor pursuant to arrangements made by a person who was the lessor, or was connected with the lessor, at some time before the assignment.

(4) Nothing in sub-paragraph (2) above prevents this Part of this Schedule from again applying in the case of the lease if the conditions for its application are satisfied after the assignment.

The conditions

3—(1) The condition in this sub-paragraph is that at the relevant time the leasing arrangements are such as fall for accounting purposes to be treated in accordance with [generally accepted accounting practice][2] as a finance lease or a loan and—

(*a*) the lessor, or a person connected with him, falls for accounting purposes to be treated in accordance with [generally accepted accounting practice][2] as the finance lessor in relation to the finance lease or loan, or
(*b*) the finance lease or loan falls for accounting purposes to be treated, in accordance with [generally accepted accounting practice][2], as subsisting for the purposes of consolidated group accounts of a group of companies of which the lessor is a member.

(2) The condition in this sub-paragraph is that, under the leasing arrangements, there is or may be payable to the lessor, or to a person connected with him, a sum (a "major lump sum") which is not rent but is a sum such as falls for accounting purposes to be treated in accordance with [generally accepted accounting practice][2]—

(*a*) as to part, as repayment of some or all of the investment in respect of a finance lease or loan; and
(*b*) as to part, as a return on investment in respect of a finance lease or loan.

(3) The condition in this sub-paragraph is that not all of that part of a major lump sum which falls within paragraph (*b*) of sub-paragraph (2) above would, apart from this Schedule, fall to be brought into account for tax purposes in chargeable periods of the lessor ending with the relevant chargeable period as the normal rent from the lease for periods of account of the lessor.

(4) The condition in this sub-paragraph is that, as respects the lessor at the relevant time,—

(*a*) the period of account of his in which the relevant time falls, or
(*b*) an earlier period of account of his during which he was the lessor,

is a period of account for which the accountancy rental earnings in respect of the lease exceed the normal rent for the period.

(5) The condition in this sub-paragraph is that at the relevant time—

(*a*) arrangements falling within sub-paragraph (1) of paragraph 4 below exist; or

(*b*) if the condition in paragraph (*a*) above is not satisfied, circumstances falling within sub-paragraph (2) of that paragraph exist.

(6) ...[1]

(7) In determining the normal rent for a period of account for the purpose of determining whether the condition in sub-paragraph (4) above is satisfied, rent which falls to be brought into account for tax purposes as it falls due shall be treated—

(*a*) as accruing evenly throughout the period to which, in accordance with the terms of the lease, each payment falling due relates, and

(*b*) as falling due as it so accrues,

unless any such payment falls due more than 12 months after the time at which any of the rent to which that payment relates is so treated as accruing.

(8) In this paragraph—

"the relevant chargeable period", in the case of any major lump sum, means—

(*a*) the chargeable period of the lessor which is related to his period of account in which that major lump sum is or may be payable in accordance with the leasing arrangements; or

(*b*) if there are two or more such chargeable periods, the latest of them;

"the relevant time" means the time as at which it falls to be determined for the purposes of sub-paragraph (1) or (2) of paragraph 2 above whether the conditions in this paragraph are or, as the case may be, were satisfied.

Amendments—[1] Repealed by FA 1998 Sch 5 para 74, Sch 27 Part III(4) with effect for income tax for the year 1998–99 and subsequent years of assessment, and for corporation tax from 1 April 1998.
[2] Words substituted for the words "normal accountancy practice" by FA 2002 s 103(4)(*e*) with effect from 24 July 2002.

The arrangements and circumstances in paragraph 3(5)

4—(1) The arrangements mentioned in paragraph 3(5)(*a*) above are arrangements under which—

(*a*) the lessee or a person connected with him may acquire, whether directly or indirectly, the leased asset, or an asset representing the leased asset, from the lessor or a person connected with the lessor; and

(*b*) in connection with that acquisition, the lessor or a person connected with him may receive, whether directly or indirectly, a qualifying lump sum from the lessee or a person connected with the lessee.

(2) The circumstances mentioned in paragraph 3(5)(*b*) above are circumstances which make it more likely—

(*a*) that the events described in sub-paragraph (3) below will occur, than

(*b*) that the event described in sub-paragraph (4) below will occur.

(3) The events mentioned in sub-paragraph (2)(*a*) above are—

(*a*) that the lessee or a person connected with him will acquire, whether directly or indirectly, the leased asset or an asset representing the leased asset from the lessor or a person connected with the lessor; and

(*b*) that, in connection with that acquisition, the lessor or a person connected with him will receive, whether directly or indirectly, a qualifying lump sum from the lessee or a person connected with the lessee.

(4) The event mentioned in sub-paragraph (2)(*b*) above is that, before any such acquisition as is mentioned in sub-paragraph (3) above takes place, the leased asset or, as the case may be, the asset representing the leased asset, will have been acquired, in a sale on the open market, by a person who is not the lessor or the lessee and who is not connected with either of them.

(5) In this paragraph, "qualifying lump sum" means any sum which is not rent but at least part of which would ...[2] fall for accounting purposes to be treated in accordance with [generally accepted accounting practice][1] as a return on investment in respect of a finance lease or loan.

Amendments—[1] Words substituted for the words "normal accountancy practice" by FA 2002 s 103(4)(*e*) with effect from 24 July 2002.
[2] Words ", if the recipient were a company incorporated in the United Kingdom," repealed by FA 2002 s 141, Sch 40 Pt 3(16) with effect from 24 July 2002.

Current lessor to be taxed by reference to accountancy rental earnings

5—(1) Where, in the case of any period of account of the current lessor,—

(*a*) this Part of this Schedule applies in the case of the lease, and

(*b*) the accountancy rental earnings in respect of the lease for that period of account exceed the normal rent for that period,

he shall be treated for tax purposes as if in that period of account he had been entitled to, and there had arisen to him, rent from the lease of an amount equal to those accountancy rental earnings (instead of the normal rent referred to in paragraph (*b*) above).

(2) Where a person is treated under sub-paragraph (1) above as if he had in a period of account been entitled to, and there had arisen to him, any rent from a lease of an asset, the rent shall be treated for tax purposes—

    (*a*) as if it had accrued at an even rate throughout so much of the period of account as falls within the period for which the asset is leased; and

    (*b*) as if that person had become entitled to it as it accrued.

Reduction of taxable rent by certain excesses

6—(1) Subject to sub-paragraph (6)(*b*) below, if in the case of the lease—

    (*a*) the normal rent for a period of account of the current lessor throughout which the leasing arrangements are such as fall for accounting purposes to be treated in accordance with [generally accepted accounting practice][2] as a finance lease or loan, exceeds

    (*b*) the accountancy rental earnings for the period,

there is for the purposes of this paragraph a "normal rental excess" for that period of an amount equal to the excess.

(2) In this paragraph the "cumulative normal rental excess" in the case of the lease and a period of account of the current lessor means so much of the aggregate of the normal rental excesses for previous periods of account of his as (after taking account of any increases under paragraph 10 below) has not been—

    (*a*) set off under this paragraph against the taxable rent for any such previous period; or

    (*b*) reduced under paragraph 10 below.

(3) Subject to sub-paragraph (8)(*b*) below, if the taxable rent in the case of the lease for a period of account of the current lessor is, by virtue of paragraph 5 above, an amount equal to the accountancy rental earnings, there is for the purposes of this paragraph an "accountancy rental excess" for that period of an amount equal to the difference between—

    (*a*) the accountancy rental earnings for the period of account; and

    (*b*) the normal rent for the period.

(4) In this paragraph the "cumulative accountancy rental excess", in the case of the lease and a period of account of the current lessor, means so much of the aggregate of the accountancy rental excesses for previous periods of account of his as (after taking account of any increases under paragraph 9 below) has not been—

    (*a*) set off under this paragraph against the taxable rent for any such previous period;

    (*b*) reduced under paragraph 9 below; or

    (*c*) set off under paragraph 12 below against the consideration for a disposal.

(5) If a period of account of the current lessor is one—

    (*a*) for which the normal rent exceeds the accountancy rental earnings, and

    (*b*) for which there is any cumulative accountancy rental excess,

sub-paragraph (6) below shall apply.

(6) Where this sub-paragraph applies—

    (*a*) the taxable rent for the period of account shall be reduced (but not below the accountancy rental earnings) by setting against it the cumulative accountancy rental excess; and

    (*b*) the normal rental excess for the period shall be the amount (if any) by which—

        (i) the normal rent, reduced by an amount equal to the reduction under paragraph (*a*) above, exceeds

        (ii) the accountancy rental earnings,

    and if there is no such excess, there is no normal rental excess for the period.

(7) If a period of account of the current lessor is one—

    (*a*) for which the taxable rent in the case of the lease is, by virtue of paragraph 5 above, an amount equal to the accountancy rental earnings, and

    (*b*) there is any cumulative normal rental excess,

sub-paragraph (8) below shall apply.

(8) Where this sub-paragraph applies—

    (*a*) the taxable rent for the period of account shall be reduced (but not below the normal rent) by setting against it the cumulative normal rental excess, and

    (*b*) the accountancy rental excess for the period shall be the amount (if any) by which—

        (i) the accountancy rental earnings, reduced by an amount equal to the reduction under paragraph (*a*) above, exceeds

        (ii) the normal rent,

and if there is no such excess, there is no accountancy rental excess for the period.

(9) In this paragraph "the taxable rent", in the case of a period of account of the current lessor, means the amount which would, apart from this paragraph and paragraph 8(6) below, be treated for tax purposes as rent from the lease—

    (*a*) which arises to him, and

(b) ...[1]

in that period of account for the purpose of determining his liability to tax for the related chargeable period or periods.

Amendments—[1] Repealed by FA 1998 Sch 5 para 74, Sch 27 Part III(4) with effect for income tax for the year 1998–99 and subsequent years of assessment, and for corporation tax from 1 April 1998.
[2] Words substituted for the words "normal accountancy practice" by FA 2002 s 103(4)(e) with effect from 24 July 2002.

Assignments on which neither a gain nor a loss accrues

7—(1) This paragraph applies in any case where—

(a) the current lessor assigns the lessor's interest under the lease; and
(b) the assignment is a disposal on which, by virtue of any of the enactments specified in section 35(3)(d) of the Taxation of Chargeable Gains Act 1992, neither a gain nor a loss accrues.

(2) Where this paragraph applies, this Schedule shall have effect as if—

(a) a period of account of the assignor ended, and
(b) a period of account of the assignee began,

with the assignment.

(3) Where this paragraph applies—

(a) any unused cumulative accountancy rental excess, or
(b) any unused cumulative normal rental excess,

of the assignor shall become the cumulative accountancy rental excess or the cumulative normal rental excess (as the case may be) for the period of account of the assignee which begins with the assignment.

(4) In sub-paragraph (3) above—

"unused cumulative accountancy rental excess", in relation to the assignor, means the aggregate of—

(a) any cumulative accountancy rental excess, and
(b) any accountancy rental excess,

for the period of account of his which ends with the assignment;

"unused cumulative normal rental excess", in relation to the assignor, means the aggregate of—

(a) any cumulative normal rental excess, and
(b) any normal rental excess,

for the period of account of his which ends with the assignment.

Relief for bad debts etc: corporation tax under Schedule A

8 ...

Amendments—This paragraph repealed by FA 1998 Sch 5 para 74, Sch 27 Part III with effect for income tax for the year 1998–99 and subsequent years of assessment, and for corporation tax from 1 April 1998.

Relief for bad debts etc: cumulative accountancy rental excess

9—(1) If, in the case of the lease, for any period of account—

(a) the accountancy rental earnings exceed the normal rent,
(b) a bad debt deduction falls to be made in respect of rent from the lease,
(c) the amount of the bad debt deduction exceeds the amount of the accountancy rental earnings, and
(d) there is a cumulative accountancy rental excess,

the cumulative accountancy rental excess for the period of account shall be reduced (but not below nil) by the amount by which the bad debt deduction exceeds the accountancy rental earnings.

(2) If, in the case of the lease, for any period of account—

(a) the accountancy rental earnings do not exceed the normal rent,
(b) a bad debt deduction falls to be made in respect of rent from the lease, and
(c) there is a cumulative accountancy rental excess for that period of account, sub-paragraph (3) below shall apply.

(3) Where this sub-paragraph applies, the amount of the cumulative accountancy rental excess which may be set against the taxable rent for the period of account shall not exceed the amount (if any) by which the normal rent exceeds the bad debt deduction (and, if the normal rent does not exceed the bad debt deduction, shall be nil).

(4) If, in a case where sub-paragraph (3) above applies, the bad debt deduction exceeds the normal rent for the period of account, the cumulative accountancy rental excess for the period of account shall be reduced (but not below nil) by the amount by which the bad debt deduction exceeds the normal rent.

(5) Where—

(a) the cumulative accountancy rental excess for any period of account of the current lessor has been reduced under sub-paragraph (1) or (4) above by reason of a bad debt deduction, but

(b) in a subsequent period of account of his, an amount ("the relevant credit") is recovered or credited in respect of the amount which constituted the bad debt deduction,

the cumulative accountancy rental excess (if any) for the period of account mentioned in paragraph (b) above shall, subject to sub-paragraph (6) below, be increased by the relevant credit.

(6) If, in a case falling within sub-paragraph (5) above,—

(a) the relevant credit, exceeds

(b) the aggregate of the reductions falling within paragraph (a) of that sub-paragraph,

the amount of the increase under that sub-paragraph shall not exceed that aggregate.

(7) In this paragraph—

"bad debt deduction", in relation to a period of account, means the aggregate of any sums falling within sub-paragraph (i), (ii) or (iii) of section 74(1)(j) of the Taxes Act 1988 in respect of amounts in respect of rents from the lease of the asset which are deductible as expenses for that period, whether by virtue of paragraph 8(4) above or otherwise;

"taxable rent" has the same meaning as in paragraph 6 above.

Relief for bad debts etc: cumulative normal rental excess

10—(1) If, in the case of the lease, for any period of account—

(a) the accountancy rental earnings do not exceed the normal rent,

(b) a bad debt deduction falls to be made in respect of rent from the lease,

(c) the amount of the bad debt deduction exceeds the amount of the normal rent, and

(d) there is a cumulative normal rental excess,

the cumulative normal rental excess for the period of account shall be reduced (but not below nil) by the amount by which the bad debt deduction exceeds the normal rent.

(2) If, in the case of the lease, for any period of account—

(a) the accountancy rental earnings exceed the normal rent,

(b) a bad debt deduction falls to be made in respect of rent from the lease, and

(c) there is a cumulative normal rental excess for that period of account,

sub-paragraph (3) below shall apply.

(3) Where this sub-paragraph applies, the amount of the cumulative normal rental excess which may be set against the taxable rent for the period of account shall not exceed the amount (if any) by which the accountancy rental earnings exceed the bad debt deduction (and, if the accountancy rental earnings do not exceed the bad debt deduction, shall be nil).

(4) If, in a case where sub-paragraph (3) above applies, the bad debt deduction exceeds the accountancy rental earnings for the period of account, the cumulative normal rental excess for the period of account shall be reduced (but not below nil) by the amount by which the bad debt deduction exceeds the accountancy rental earnings.

(5) Where—

(a) the cumulative normal rental excess for any period of account of the current lessor has been reduced under sub-paragraph (1) or (4) above by reason of a bad debt deduction, but

(b) in a subsequent period of account of his, an amount ("the relevant credit") is recovered or credited in respect of the amount which constituted the bad debt deduction,

the cumulative normal rental excess (if any) for the period of account mentioned in paragraph (b) above shall, subject to sub-paragraph (6) below, be increased by the relevant credit.

(6) If, in a case falling within sub-paragraph (5) above,—

(a) the relevant credit, exceeds

(b) the aggregate of the reductions falling within paragraph (a) of that sub-paragraph,

the amount of the increase under that sub-paragraph shall not exceed that aggregate.

(7) In this paragraph—

"bad debt deduction", in relation to a period of account, means the aggregate of any sums falling within sub-paragraph (i), (ii) or (iii) of section 74(1)(j) of the Taxes Act 1988 in respect of amounts in respect of rents from the lease of the asset which are deductible as expenses for that period, whether by virtue of paragraph 8(4) above or otherwise;

"taxable rent" has the same meaning as in paragraph 6 above.

Capital allowances

11—(1) This paragraph applies in any case where an occasion occurs on or after 26th November 1996 on which a major lump sum falls to be paid in the case of the lease of the asset.

(2) In this paragraph "the relevant occasion" means the occasion mentioned in sub-paragraph (1) above.

(3) If capital expenditure incurred by the current lessor in respect of the leased asset is or has been taken into account for the purposes of any allowance or charge under any of the following groups of provisions, that is to say—

    [(a) Part 2 of the Capital Allowances Act (plant and machinery allowances),
    (b) Part 5 of that Act (mineral extraction allowances), or
    (c) Part 8 of that Act (patent allowances)]¹,

the group of provisions in question ("the relevant provisions") shall have effect as if the relevant occasion were an event by reason of which a disposal value is to be brought into account of an amount equal (subject to any applicable limiting provision) to the amount or value of the major lump sum.

(4) In this paragraph "limiting provision" means a provision to the effect that the disposal value of the asset in question is not to exceed an amount ("the limit") described by reference to capital expenditure incurred in respect of the asset.

(5) Where—

    (a) by virtue of sub-paragraph (3) above, a disposal value ("the relevant disposal value") falls or has fallen to be brought into account by a person in respect of the leased asset for the purposes of the relevant provisions, and
    (b) a limiting provision has effect in the case of those provisions,

sub-paragraph (6) below shall apply.

(6) Where this sub-paragraph applies, the limiting provision shall have effect (if or to the extent that it would not otherwise do so)—

    (a) in the case of the relevant disposal value, and
    (b) in the case of any simultaneous or subsequent disposal value,

as if, instead of any particular disposal value, it were the aggregate amount of all the disposal values brought into account for the purposes of the relevant provisions by the current lessor in respect of the leased asset which is not to exceed the limit.

(7) In sub-paragraph (6) above "simultaneous or subsequent disposal value" means any disposal value which falls to be brought into account by the current lessor in respect of the leased asset by reason of any event occurring subsequent to, or at the same time as, the event by reason of which the relevant disposal value falls to be brought into account.

(8) If any allowance is or has been given in respect of capital expenditure incurred by the current lessor in respect of the leased asset under any provision of [the Capital Allowances Act]¹ other than those specified in sub-paragraph (3) above, an amount equal to the lesser of—

    (a) the aggregate of the allowances so given (so far as not previously recovered or withdrawn),
    (b) the amount or value of the major lump sum,

shall, in relation to the current lessor, be treated as if it were a balancing charge to be made on him for the chargeable period ...¹ in which falls the relevant occasion.

(9) If there is or has been allowed to the current lessor in respect of expenditure incurred in connection with the leased asset any deduction by virtue of [section 40B(1) or 42 of the Finance (No 2) Act 1992 (expenditure in connection with films etc)]¹, sub-paragraph (10) below shall apply.

(10) Where this sub-paragraph applies, the current lessor shall be treated as if receipts of a revenue nature of an amount equal to the amount (if any) by which—

    (a) the amount or value of the major lump sum, exceeds
    (b) the amount or value of so much of the major lump sum as is treated as receipts of a revenue nature [under section 40A(2) of the Finance (No 2) Act 1992]¹,

arose to him from the trade or business in question on the relevant occasion.

(11) If there is or has been allowed to the current lessor in respect of capital expenditure incurred in connection with the leased asset any deduction by virtue of—

    (a) section 91 of the Taxes Act 1988 (cemeteries etc), or
    (b) section 91A or 91B of that Act (restoration and preparation expenditure in relation to a waste disposal site),

sub-paragraph (12) below shall apply.

(12) Where this sub-paragraph applies, the current lessor shall be treated as if trading receipts of an amount equal to the lesser of—

    (a) the amount or value of the major lump sum,
    (b) the deductions previously allowed,

arose to him from the trade in question on the relevant occasion.

(13) If, in a case where this paragraph applies, allowances are or have been made to a person ("the contributor") by virtue of [sections 537 to 542 of the Capital Allowances Act]¹ (allowances in respect of contributions to capital expenditure) in respect of his contribution of a capital sum to expenditure on the provision of the leased asset, the foregoing provisions of this paragraph shall have effect in relation to the contributor and allowances by virtue of that section in respect of the

contribution as they have effect in relation to the current lessor and allowances in respect of capital expenditure incurred by him in respect of the leased asset.

[(14) In sub-paragraph (8) above—

"the Capital Allowances Act" includes enactments which under the Taxes Act 1988 are to be treated as contained in the Capital Allowances Act;

"chargeable period" has the meaning given by section 6 of the Capital Allowances Act.]¹

(15) ...¹

Amendments—¹ Sub-paras (3)(*a*)–(*c*), (14) substituted, words in sub-para (8) repealed and substituted, words in sub-paras (10), and (13) substituted, words substituted for sub-paras (9)(*a*), (*b*), sub-para (15) repealed, by CAA 2001 ss 578, 580, Sch 2 para 98, Sch 4 with effect for income tax purposes, as respects allowances and charges falling to be made for chargeable periods ending after 5 April 2001, and for corporation tax purposes, as respects allowances and charges falling to be made for chargeable periods ending after 31 March 2001.

Chargeable gains

12—(1) If, in the case of the lease,—

(*a*) the current lessor or a person connected with him disposes of—

(i) the lessor's interest under the lease, or

(ii) the leased asset, or

(iii) an asset representing the leased asset, and

(*b*) there is, for the period of account of the current lessor in which the disposal takes place, any cumulative accountancy rental excess,

then, in determining for the purposes of the Taxation of Chargeable Gains Act 1992 the amount of any gain accruing to the person making the disposal, the consideration for the disposal shall be treated as reduced (but not below nil) by setting against it the cumulative accountancy rental excess.

(2) If the disposal mentioned in sub-paragraph (1) above is, for the purposes of the Taxation of Chargeable Gains Act 1992, a part-disposal of an asset—

(*a*) the cumulative accountancy rental excess mentioned in sub-paragraph (1) above shall be apportioned between—

(i) the property disposed of, and

(ii) the property which remains undisposed of,

in the proportions in which the sums which under paragraph (*a*) or (*b*) of section 38(1) of that Act are attributable to the asset fall to be apportioned under section 42 of that Act; and

(*b*) only that portion of the cumulative accountancy rental excess which is so apportioned to the property disposed of shall be set against the consideration for the part-disposal in accordance with sub-paragraph (1) above.

(3) Sub-paragraph (1) above is without prejudice to section 37 of the Taxation of Chargeable Gains Act 1992 (deduction for money or money's worth charged to income tax etc) except as provided in sub-paragraph (4) below.

(4) Section 37 of that Act shall not apply if or to the extent that any money or money's worth which, apart from this sub-paragraph, would be excluded by virtue of that section from the consideration for a disposal is represented by any cumulative accountancy rental excess which in accordance with sub-paragraph (1) above—

(*a*) falls to be set against the consideration for the disposal; or

(*b*) has fallen to be set against the consideration for a previous disposal made by the person making the disposal in question or a person connected with him.

(5) Where the current lessor or a person connected with him disposes of—

(*a*) the lessor's interest under the lease, or

(*b*) the leased asset, or

(*c*) an asset representing the leased asset,

this Schedule shall have effect as if a period of account of the current lessor ended, and another period of account of his began, immediately before the disposal.

(6) If two or more disposals falling within sub-paragraph (1) above are made at the same time—

(*a*) the cumulative accountancy rental excess mentioned in sub-paragraph (1) above shall, subject to sub-paragraph (2) above, be apportioned between them in such proportions as are just and reasonable; and

(*b*) sub-paragraph (5) above shall have effect in relation to those disposals as if they together constituted a single disposal.

(7) In this paragraph "dispose" and "disposal" shall be construed in accordance with the Taxation of Chargeable Gains Act 1992.

Existing schemes where this Part does not at first apply

13—(1) This paragraph applies in any case where—

(*a*) the lease of the asset forms part of an existing scheme, but (*b*) the conditions in paragraph 3 above become satisfied after 26th November 1996.

(2) This Schedule shall have effect as if a period of account of the current lessor ended, and another period of account of his began—

    (*a*) immediately before the time at which the conditions in paragraph 3 above become satisfied as mentioned in sub-paragraph (1)(*b*) above; and

    (*b*) immediately after the time at which those conditions become so satisfied.

(3) If, on the assumption that this Part of this Schedule (other than this paragraph) had applied in the case of the lease at all times on or after 26th November 1996, there would be an amount of cumulative accountancy rental excess for the period of account of the current lessor in which the conditions in paragraph 3 above become satisfied, then—

    (*a*) that amount shall be the cumulative accountancy rental excess for that period of account; and

    (*b*) the current lessor shall be treated for tax purposes as if, in the immediately preceding period of account, he had been entitled to, and there had arisen to him, rent from the lease of an amount equal to that cumulative accountancy rental excess.

(4) If, on the assumption that this Part of this Schedule (other than this paragraph) had applied in the case of the lease at all times on or after 26th November 1996, there would be an amount of cumulative normal rental excess for the period of account of the current lessor in which the conditions in paragraph 3 above become satisfied, that amount shall be the cumulative normal rental excess for that period of account.

(5) The amount of rent mentioned in sub-paragraph (3)(*b*) above—

    (*a*) is in addition to any other rent from the lease for the period of account there mentioned; and

    (*b*) shall be left out of account for the purposes of paragraph 5 above.

(6) Where a person is treated under sub-paragraph (3)(*b*) above as if he had in a period of account been entitled to, and there had arisen to him, any rent, the rent shall be treated for tax purposes as if it had accrued, and he had become entitled to it, immediately before the end of that period of account.

(7) ...[1]

Amendments—[1] Sub-para (7) repealed by FA 1998 s 165, Sch 27 Part III(4) with effect for income tax for the year 1998-99 and subsequent years of assessment, and for corporation tax from 1 April 1998 subject to transitional provisions in FA 1998 Sch 5 Part IV.

New schemes where this Part begins to apply after Part II has applied

14 If—

    (*a*) the conditions in paragraph 3 above become satisfied in the case of the lease of the asset, and

    (*b*) immediately before those conditions became so satisfied, Part II of this Schedule applied in the case of the lease,

then, in determining the cumulative accountancy rental excess or the cumulative normal rental excess for any period of account ending after those conditions become satisfied, this Schedule shall have effect as if this Part of this Schedule had applied in relation to the lease at any time when Part II of this Schedule applied in relation to it.

PART II
OTHER FINANCE LEASES
Purpose of this Part of this Schedule

15—(1) This Part of this Schedule is concerned with arrangements (other than arrangements with which Part I of this Schedule is concerned)—

    (*a*) which involve the lease of an asset;

    (*b*) which are or have been entered into by companies or other persons; and

    (*c*) which are of such a kind as ...[2] falls ...[2] to be treated in accordance with [generally accepted accounting practice][1] as finance leases or loans.

(2) The principal purpose of this Part of this Schedule is, in the case of any such arrangements, to charge any person entitled to the lessor's interest under the lease of the asset to tax from time to time on amounts of income determined by reference to those which fall for accounting purposes to be treated in accordance with [generally accepted accounting practice][1] as the income return, on and after 26th November 1996, on investment in respect of the finance lease or loan (taking into account the substance of the matter as a whole, including in particular the state of affairs as between connected persons, or within a group of companies, as reflected or falling to be reflected in accounts of any of those persons or in consolidated group accounts).

Amendments—[1] Words substituted for the words "normal accountancy practice" by FA 2002 s 103(4)(*e*) with effect from 24 July 2002.
[2] Words ", in the case of companies incorporated in any part of the United Kingdom," and "for the purposes of accounts of such companies" repealed by FA 2002 s 141, Sch 40 Pt 3(16) with effect from 24 July 2002.

Application of this Part of this Schedule

16—(1) This Part of this Schedule applies in any case where—

(*a*) a lease of an asset is or has been granted on or after 26th November 1996;

(*b*) the lease forms part of a new scheme;

(*c*) in the case of the lease, the condition in sub-paragraph (1) of paragraph 3 above is or has been satisfied at some time on or after 26th November 1996 in a period of account of the current lessor; and

(*d*) Part I of this Schedule does not apply in the case of the lease by reason of the conditions in sub-paragraphs (2) to (5) of that paragraph not all being, or having been, satisfied as mentioned in paragraph 2 above.

(2) Where the condition in paragraph 3(1) above has been satisfied at any time on or after 26th November 1996 in a period of account of the person who was at that time the lessor, it shall be taken to continue to be satisfied unless and until—

(*a*) the asset ceases to be leased under the lease; or

(*b*) the lessor's interest under the lease is assigned to a person who is not connected with any of the persons described in sub-paragraph (3) below.

(3) Those persons are—

(*a*) the assignor;

(*b*) any person who was the lessor at some time before the assignment; or

(*c*) any person who at some time after the assignment becomes the lessor pursuant to arrangements made by a person who was the lessor, or was connected with the lessor, at some time before the assignment.

(4) Nothing in sub-paragraph (2) above prevents this Part of this Schedule from again applying in the case of the lease if the conditions for its application are satisfied after the assignment.

Application of provisions of Part I for purposes of Part II

17 Paragraphs 5 to 10 and 12 above shall apply for the purposes of this Part of this Schedule as they apply for the purposes of Part I of this Schedule.

PART III

INSURANCE COMPANIES

Accounting purposes

18[—(1)][1] In the application of this Schedule in relation to companies carrying on insurance business, "accounting purposes" does not include the purposes of accounts which [the rules contained in Chapter 9 of the Prudential Sourcebook (Insurers)][1] requires to be prepared.

[(2) In sub-paragraph (1) above "the Prudential Sourcebook (Insurers)" means the Interim Prudential Sourcebook for Insurers made by the Financial Services Authority under the Financial Services and Markets Act 2000.][1]

Amendments—[1] Words substituted, sub-para (1) renumbered as such, and sub-para (2) added, by the Financial Services and Markets Act 2000 (Consequential Amendments) (Taxes) Order, SI 2001/3629 arts 97, 102(1), (2), (4) with effect for periods of account ending after 30 November 2001.

Companies carrying on life assurance business

19—(1) This paragraph applies if the current lessor is a company carrying on life assurance business.

(2) Where the leased asset is an asset of the company's [long-term insurance][1] fund, no amount shall be brought into account by virtue of this Schedule in any computation of profits of life assurance business, or any class of life assurance business, carried on by the company where the computation is made in accordance with the provisions of the Taxes Act 1988 applicable to Case I of Schedule D.

(3) In determining whether the condition in sub-paragraph (3) or (4) of paragraph 3 above is satisfied in the case of the company, an amount shall not be regarded—

(*a*) as falling to be brought into account for tax purposes as rent which arises to the company from the lease, or to which the company is entitled, in a period of account, or

(*b*) as representing a portion of that part of a major lump sum which falls within paragraph 3(2)(*b*) above,

by reason only that it falls to be taken into account for any purpose by virtue of section 83(2) of the Finance Act 1989 (investment income from, and increases in value of, assets of [long-term insurance][1] fund treated as receipts of period).

(4) Where—

(*a*) under paragraph 5 or 13 above the company is treated for tax purposes as if in a period of account it had been entitled to, and there had arisen to it, any rent from the lease, and

(*b*) the leased asset is an asset of the company's [long-term insurance][1] fund or is linked to any category of insurance business, and

(c) any question arises for the purposes of the Corporation Tax Acts as to the extent to which that rent is referable to any category of the company's [long-term][1] business,

section 432A of the Taxes Act 1988 (apportionment of insurance companies' income) shall have effect in relation to the rent as it has effect in relation to the income arising from an asset.

Modification—Sub-para (5) inserted above in applying life assurance provisions of the Corporation Tax Acts to insurance companies carrying on capital redemption business with effect for accounting periods ending after 30 June 1999: see Insurance Companies (Capital Redemption Business) (Modification of the Corporation Tax Acts) Regulations, SI 1999/498 reg 16.
Amendments—[1] Words in sub-paras (2), (3), (4)(b), (c) substituted by the Financial Services and Markets Act 2000 (Consequential Amendments) (Taxes) Order, SI 2001/3629 arts 97, 102(1), (3) with effect from 1 December 2001 (immediately after the coming into force of the Financial Services and Markets Act 2000 ss 411, 432(1), Sch 20).

PART IV
SUPPLEMENTARY PROVISIONS
Normal rent

20 For the purposes of this Schedule, the "normal rent" in respect of a lease for a period of account of the lessor is the amount which he would, apart from this Schedule, bring into account as rent from the lease—

(a) which arises to him, and
(b) ...[1]

in that period of account for the purpose of determining his liability to tax for the related chargeable period or periods.

Amendments—[1] Sub-para (b) repealed by FA 1998 Sch 5 para 74, Sch 27 Part III(4) with effect for income tax for the year 1998–99 and subsequent years of assessment, and for corporation tax from 1 April 1998.

Accountancy rental earnings

21—(1) For the purposes of this Schedule, the "accountancy rental earnings" in respect of the lease for a period of account of the lessor is the greatest of the amounts specified in sub-paragraph (2) below.

(2) Those amounts are—

(a) the rental earnings for the relevant period in respect of the lease, in the case of the lessor;
(b) the rental earnings for the relevant period in respect of the lease, in the case of a person connected with the lessor;
(c) the rental earnings for the relevant period in respect of the lease, for the purposes of consolidated group accounts of a group of companies of which the lessor is a member.

(3) In sub-paragraph (2) above, "the relevant period" means the period of account of the lessor which is mentioned in sub-paragraph (1) above.

Rental earnings

22 In this Schedule "the rental earnings" for any period in respect of the lease of the asset is, in the case of any person or any consolidated group accounts, the amount which falls for accounting purposes to be treated in accordance with [generally accepted accounting practice][1] as the gross return for that period on investment in respect of a finance lease or loan in respect of the leasing arrangements.

Amendments—[1] Words substituted for the words "normal accountancy practice" by FA 2002 s 103(4)(e) with effect from 24 July 2002.

Periods of account which straddle 26th November 1996

23 This Schedule shall apply in relation to a period of account which begins before 26th November 1996 and ends on or after that date as if—

(a) so much of the period as falls before 26th November 1996, and
(b) so much of the period as falls on or after that date,

were separate periods of account.

Time apportionment where periods do not coincide

24—(1) This paragraph applies in any case where—

(a) a period of account of the lessor does not coincide with a period of account of a person connected with the lessor, or
(b) a period of account of the lessor does not coincide with a period for which consolidated group accounts of a group of companies of which the lessor is a member fall to be prepared.

(2) Where this paragraph applies, any amount which falls for the purposes of this Schedule to be found for the lessor's period of account but by reference to the connected person or, as the case may be, the consolidated group accounts shall be found by making such apportionments as may be necessary—

(*a*) between two or more periods of account of the connected person, or

(*b*) between two or more periods for which consolidated group accounts of the group fall to be prepared,

as the case may be.

(3) Any apportionment under sub-paragraph (2) above shall be made in proportion to the number of days in the respective periods which fall within the lessor's period of account.

Connected persons

25—(1) If a person is connected with another at some time during the period which—

(*a*) begins at the earliest time at which any of the leasing arrangements were made, and

(*b*) ends when the current lessor finally ceases to have an interest in the asset or any arrangements relating to it,

he shall be treated for the purposes of this Schedule, in its application in consequence of those leasing arrangements, as being connected with that other throughout that period.

(2) Section 839 of the Taxes Act 1988 shall apply for the purposes of this Schedule.

Assets which represent the leased asset

26 For the purposes of this Schedule, the following assets shall be treated as representing the leased asset—

(*a*) any asset derived from, or created out of, the leased asset;

(*b*) any asset from or out of which the leased asset was derived or created;

(*c*) any asset derived from or created out of an asset from or out of which the leased asset was derived or created; or

(*d*) any asset which derives the whole or a substantial part of its value from the leased asset or from an asset which itself represents the leased asset.

Existing schemes and new schemes

27—(1) For the purposes of this Schedule, a lease of an asset—

(*a*) forms part of an existing scheme if, and only if, the conditions in sub-paragraph (2) or (3) below are satisfied; and

(*b*) in any other case, forms part of a new scheme.

(2) The conditions in this sub-paragraph are that—

(*a*) a contract in writing for the lease of the asset has been made before 26th November 1996;

(*b*) either—

    (i) the contract is unconditional; or

    (ii) if the contract is conditional, the conditions have been satisfied before that date; and

(*c*) no terms remain to be agreed on or after that date.

(3) The conditions in this sub-paragraph are that—

(*a*) a contract in writing for the lease of the asset has been made before 26th November 1996;

(*b*) the condition in paragraph (*b*) or (*c*) of sub-paragraph (2) above is not satisfied in the case of the contract;

(*c*) either the contract is unconditional or, if it is conditional, the conditions are satisfied before the end of the finalisation period or within such further period as the Commissioners of Inland Revenue may allow in the particular case;

(*d*) no terms remain to be agreed after the end of the finalisation period or such further period as the Commissioners of Inland Revenue may allow in the particular case; and

(*e*) the contract in its final form is not materially different from the contract as it stood when it was made as mentioned in paragraph (*a*) above.

(4) In sub-paragraph (3) above, ''the finalisation period'' means the period which ends with the later of—

(*a*) 31st January 1997;

(*b*) the expiration of the period of six months next following the day on which the contract was made as mentioned in sub-paragraph (3)(*a*) above.

Accounting purposes and normal accountancy practice

28—(1)–(4) ...²

(5) This Schedule shall have effect in relation to a body corporate (wherever incorporated) which is a parent undertaking but which, for accounting purposes, is not required to prepare consolidated group accounts in accordance with [generally accepted accounting practice]¹ as if the body corporate were required to do so.

(6) In sub-paragraph (5) above ''parent undertaking'' shall be construed in accordance with—

(*a*) section 258 of the Companies Act 1985, or

(*b*) in Northern Ireland, Article 266 of the Companies (Northern Ireland) Order 1986.

Amendments—¹ Words substituted for the words "normal accountancy practice" by FA 2002 s 103(4)(e) with effect from 24 July 2002.
² Sub-paras (1)–(4) repealed by FA 2002 s 141, Sch 40 Pt 3(16) with effect from 24 July 2002. Sub-paras (1)–(4) previously read thus—

"(1) In the application of any provisions of this Schedule which relate to accounting purposes or normal accountancy practice, it shall be assumed, if it is not the case, that the person who is at any time entitled to the lessor's interest under the lease of the asset, and any person connected with that person, is a company incorporated in a part of the United Kingdom.

(2) A person who is not in fact a body corporate shall not by virtue of sub-paragraph (1) above be treated as a member of a group of companies for any purpose of this Schedule.

(3) This Schedule shall have effect in relation to a person who, for accounting purposes, is not required to prepare accounts in accordance with normal accountancy practice as if he were required to do so.

(4) Nothing in sub-paragraph (3) above applies in relation to consolidated group accounts."

Assessments and adjustments

29 All such assessments and adjustments shall be made as are necessary to give effect to the provisions of this Schedule.

Interpretation

30—(1) In this Schedule, unless the context otherwise requires—

"accountancy rental earnings" has the meaning given by paragraph 21(1) above;
"accountancy rental excess" shall be construed—

(a) for the purposes of Part I of this Schedule, in accordance with paragraph 6 above; and
(b) for the purposes of Part II of this Schedule, in accordance with paragraph 6 above as it has effect by virtue of paragraph 17 above;

"accounting purposes" means the purposes of—

(a) accounts of companies incorporated in any part of the United Kingdom, or
(b) consolidated group accounts for groups all the members of which are companies incorporated in any part of the United Kingdom;

"asset" means any form of property or rights;
"asset representing the leased asset" shall be construed in accordance with paragraph 26 above;
"assignment", in the application of this Schedule to Scotland, means assignation;
"consolidated group accounts" means group accounts which satisfy the requirements—

(a) of section 227 of the Companies Act 1985, or
(b) in Northern Ireland, of Article 235 of the Companies (Northern Ireland) Order 1986;

"cumulative accountancy rental excess" and "cumulative normal rental excess" shall be construed—

(a) for the purposes of Part I of this Schedule, in accordance with paragraph 6 above; and
(b) for the purposes of Part II of this Schedule, in accordance with paragraph 6 above as it has effect by virtue of paragraph 17 above;

"the current lessor", in the case of a lease of an asset, means the person who is for the time being entitled to the lessor's interest under the lease;
"existing scheme" shall be construed in accordance with paragraph 27(1)(a) above;
"finance lessor" means a person who for accounting purposes is treated in accordance with [generally accepted accounting practice]¹ as the person with—

(i) the grantor's interest in relation to a finance lease; or
(ii) the lender's interest in relation to a loan;

"group of companies" means a group as defined—

(a) in section 262(1) of the Companies Act 1985, or
(b) in Northern Ireland, in Article 270(1) of the Companies (Northern Ireland) Order 1986,

and "member", in relation to a group of companies, means a company comprised in the group;
"lease"—

(a) in relation to land, includes an underlease, sublease or any tenancy or licence, and any agreement for a lease, underlease, sublease or tenancy or licence and, in the case of land outside the United Kingdom, any interest corresponding to a lease as so defined; and
(b) in relation to any form of property or right other than land, means any kind of agreement or arrangement under which payments are made for the use of, or otherwise in respect of, an asset;

and "rent" shall be construed accordingly;
"the leasing arrangements", in the case of a lease of an asset, means—

(a) the lease of the asset,
(b) any arrangements relating to or connected with the lease of the asset, and
(c) any other arrangements of which the lease of the asset forms part,

and includes a reference to any of the leasing arrangements;
"the lessee", in the case of a lease of an asset, means (except in the expression "the lessee's interest under the lease") the person entitled to the lessee's interest under the lease;

"the lessor", in the case of a lease of an asset, means (except in the expression "the lessor's interest under the lease") the person entitled to the lessor's interest under the lease;

"major lump sum" shall be construed in accordance with paragraph 3(2) above;

"new scheme" shall be construed in accordance with paragraph 27(1)(*b*) above;

"normal rent" shall be construed in accordance with paragraph 20 above;

"normal rental excess" shall be construed—

>(*a*) for the purposes of Part I of this Schedule, in accordance with paragraph 6 above; and
>
>(*b*) for the purposes of Part II of this Schedule, in accordance with paragraph 6 above as it has effect by virtue of paragraph 17 above;

"period of account" means a period for which accounts are made up and, except for the purposes of paragraphs 2 to 4 and 23 above, means such a period which begins on or after 26th November 1996;

"related chargeable period" shall be construed in accordance with sub-paragraph (2) below;

"sum" includes any money or money's worth (and "pay" and cognate expressions shall be construed accordingly);

"the rental earnings", in relation to the lease of the asset and any period, has the meaning given by paragraph 22 above.

(2) For the purposes of this Schedule a chargeable period is related to a period of account (and a period of account is related to a chargeable period) if—

>(*a*) the chargeable period is an accounting period which consists of or includes the whole or any part of the period of account; or
>
>(*b*) the chargeable period is a year of assessment whose basis period for the purposes of Case I or Case II of Schedule D consists of or includes the whole or any part of the period of account.

Amendments—¹ Words substituted for the words "normal accountancy practice" by FA 2002 s 103(4)(*e*) with effect from 24 July 2002.

SCHEDULE 13

LOAN RELATIONSHIPS: AMENDMENT OF TRANSITIONAL PROVISIONS

Section 83

Commentary—*Simon's Direct Tax Service* **Division B3.19; B5.101**.

Introductory

1 Schedule 15 to the Finance Act 1996 (transitional provisions and savings for loan relationships) shall be amended as follows.

Transitional rules for transitional accounting periods

2 (*inserts* FA 1996 Sch 15 para 3(5A).

Opening valuations as at 1st April 1996

3 (*inserts* FA 1996 Sch 15 para 3A).

Adjustments in the case of pre-commencement trading relationships

4 (inserts FA 1996 Sch 15 para 5 (4A)–(4C)).

Chargeable assets held after commencement

5 (*inserts* FA 1996 Sch 15 para 8(5A)).

Adjustments in the case of chargeable assets

6 (*amends* FA 1996 Sch 15 para 11(2)).

Commencement of Schedule

7—(1) Subject to sub-paragraph (2) below, this Schedule has effect for the purpose of determining the credits and debits to be brought into account in any accounting period ending on or after 14th November 1996.

(2) Paragraphs 4 and 6 above do not apply in the case of a loan relationship to which the company in question has ceased to be a party before 14th November 1996 unless—

>(*a*) that company ceased to be a party to the relationship as a result of being directly or indirectly replaced as a party to that relationship by another company, and
>
>(*b*) the transaction, or series of transactions, by virtue of which the replacement took place fell within any of paragraphs (*a*) to (*d*) of paragraph 12(1) of Schedule 9 to the Finance Act 1996 (continuity of treatment in the case of groups and certain transfers of insurance business).

(3) A credit or debit a fraction of which falls to be brought into account under paragraph 6(4) of Schedule 15 to the Finance Act 1996 (election as to adjustments) in an accounting period ending on or after 14th November 1996 shall be determined, for the purposes mentioned in sub-paragraph (1) above, without applying sub-paragraph (2) above in relation to the relevant assumption.

SCHEDULE 14

CAPITAL ALLOWANCES ON LONG-LIFE ASSETS

Section 84

Commentary—*Simon's Direct Tax Service* **B2.320.**
Amendment—This Schedule repealed by the Capital Allowances Act 2001 s 580, Sch 4 with effect for income tax purposes, as respects allowances and charges falling to be made for chargeable periods ending after 5 April 2001, and for corporation tax purposes, as respects allowances and charges falling to be made for chargeable periods ending after 31 March 2001.

SCHEDULE 15

CAPITAL ALLOWANCES: SCHEDULE A CASES ETC

Section 85

Commentary—*Simon's Direct Tax Service* **A4.331.**

Repeal of existing rules

1 (*repeals* TA 1988 s 32).

Removal of restriction on set-off of losses

2 (*amends* TA 1988 s 379A(2)(*a*), (*b*) and *inserts* TA 1988 s 503(1A)).

Amendments—Sub-para 2(2) repealed by FA 1998 Sch 27 Part III(4) with effect for income tax for the year 1998–99 and subsequent years of assessment, and for corporation tax from 1 April 1998 subject to transitional arrangements in FA 1998 Sch 5 Part IV.

New general provision

3 (*inserted* CAA 1990 s 28A, *repealed by* CAA 2001 s 580, Sch 4 with effect in accordance with CAA 2001 s 579).

4 (*amended* CAA 1990 s 29(1) and *inserted* 29(1A), *repealed by* CAA 2001 s 580, Sch 4 with effect in accordance with CAA 2001 s 579).

Manner of making allowances and charges

5 (*amended* CAA 1990 s 67(3) and *inserted* s 67(3A),(4A)).

Amendments—Sub-paras (1), (2) repealed by FA 1998 s 165, Sch 27 Part III(4) with effect for income tax for the year 1998–99 and subsequent years of assessment, and for corporation tax from 1 April 1998 subject to transitional provisions in FA 1998 Sch 5 Part IV. Sub-para (3) repealed by the Capital Allowances Act 2001 s 580, Sch 4 with effect for income tax purposes, as respects allowances and charges falling to be made for chargeable periods ending after 5 April 2001, and for corporation tax purposes, as respects allowances and charges falling to be made for chargeable periods ending after 31 March 2001.

6 ...

Amendments—This paragraph repealed by FA 1998 s 165, Sch 27 Part III(4) with effect for income tax for the year 1998-99 and subsequent years of assessment, and for corporation tax from 1 April 1998 subject to transitional provisions in FA 1998 Sch 5 Part IV.

Meaning of capital expenditure

7 (*inserted* CAA 1990 s 159(1A), *repealed by* CAA 2001 s 580, Sch 4 with effect in accordance with CAA 2001 s 579).

Consequential amendment of section 434E of the Taxes Act 1988

8 (*amends* TA 1988 s 424E(2), *repealed by* CAA 2001 s 580, Sch 4 with effect in accordance with CAA 2001 s 579).

Commencement

9—(1) Subject to sub-paragraph (2) below, this Schedule has effect—
(*a*) for the purposes of income tax, in relation to the year 1997–98 and subsequent years of assessment; and
(*b*) for the purposes of corporation tax, in relation to accounting periods ending on or after 1st April 1997.
(2) ...¹

Amendments—[1] Sub-para (2) repealed by the Capital Allowances Act 2001 s 580, Sch 4 with effect for income tax purposes, as respects allowances and charges falling to be made for chargeable periods ending after 5 April 2001, and for corporation tax purposes, as respects allowances and charges falling to be made for chargeable periods ending after 31 March 2001.

SCHEDULE 16

CAPITAL ALLOWANCES ON FIXTURES

PART I

AMENDMENTS OF THE CAPITAL ALLOWANCES ACT 1990

Section 86

Commentary—*Simon's Direct Tax Service* B2.351.
Amendment—This Schedule repealed by the Capital Allowances Act 2001 s 580, Sch 4 with effect for income tax purposes, as respects allowances and charges falling to be made for chargeable periods ending after 5 April 2001, and for corporation tax purposes, as respects allowances and charges falling to be made for chargeable periods ending after 31 March 2001.

SCHEDULE 17

CHARGEABLE GAINS: RE-INVESTMENT RELIEF

Section 87

Commentary—*Simon's Direct Tax Service* C3.917.

Introductory

1 The Taxation of Chargeable Gains Act 1992 shall be amended in accordance with the provisions of this Schedule.

Qualifying investments

2 (*amends* TCGA 1992 s 164A(8) and *inserts* s 164A(8A), (8B))

Loss of relief

3 (*amends* TCGA 1992 s 164F(1) and *inserts* s 164FA).

Meaning of "qualifying company"

4 (*amends* TCGA 1992 s 164G(2)(*b*),(*c*), *inserts* s 164G(4A)–(4F) and *repeals* s 164G(5))

Meaning of "qualifying trade"

5 (*amends* TCGA 1992 s 164I(1)(*a*), (*b*)).

Interpretation of Chapter IA of Part V

6 (*amends* TCGA 1992 s 164N(2) and *inserts* s 164N(5))

Commencement

7—(1) This Schedule—

    (*a*) applies in relation to shares acquired after 26th November 1996; and
    (*b*) subject to sub-paragraph (3) below, applies after 26th November 1996 in relation to shares that fall within sub-paragraph (2) below.

(2) Shares fall within this sub-paragraph if—

    (*a*) they were acquired by a person at any time on or before 26th November 1996;
    (*b*) they were held by him throughout the period beginning with that time and ending with 26th November 1996; and
    (*c*) at all times in that period they were, for the purposes of Chapter IA of Part V of the Taxation of Chargeable Gains Act 1992, eligible shares in a qualifying company.

(3) The application of the preceding provisions of this Schedule in relation to any shares falling within sub-paragraph (2) above shall not prevent those shares from being (or having been) shares in a qualifying company at any relevant time when those shares would have been shares in such a company if this Schedule had not been enacted.

(4) For the purposes of sub-paragraph (3) above a time is a relevant time in relation to any shares falling within sub-paragraph (2) above if it is a time after 26th November 1996 and within the period of 3 years after the acquisition of the shares.

SCHEDULE 18

REPEALS

Section 113

PART VI

INCOME TAX, CORPORATION TAX AND
CAPITAL GAINS TAX

Note—Details of repeals already in effect have been omitted from this Schedule

(3) PROFIT-RELATED PAY

Chapter	Short title	Extent of repeal
1970 c 9	The Taxes Management Act 1970	In section 98, in the Table— (*a*) in the first column, the entry relating to section 181(1) of the Taxes Act 1988; and (*b*) in the second column, the entry relating to section 180(1) of that Act.
1988 c 1	The Income and Corporation Taxes Act 1988	Sections 169 to 184. Schedule 8.
1988 c 39	The Finance Act 1988	In Schedule 13, paragraph 4.
1989 c 26	The Finance Act 1989	Section 42(4). Section 61. Schedule 4. In Schedule 12, paragraph 18.
1989 c 40	The Companies Act 1989	In Schedule 10, paragraph 38(2).
SI 1990/593 (NI 5).	The Companies (Northern Ireland) Order 1990	In Schedule 10, paragraph 30(1).
1991 c 31	The Finance Act 1991	Section 37.
1994 c 9	The Finance Act 1994	Sections 98 and 99.
1995 c 4	The Finance Act 1995	Section 136. Section 137(1) and (6).

1 These repeals have effect (subject to Notes 2 and 3 below) in accordance with section 61(2) and (3) of this Act.

2 These repeals do not affect the operation of any of the repealed provisions, or prevent the exercise of any power under those provisions, in relation to profit periods beginning before 1st January 2000 or for purposes connected with, or with the doing or not doing of anything in or in relation to, any such periods.

3 The repeal of Schedule 8 to the Taxes Act 1988 does not affect the application of any of the provisions of paragraph 7 of that Schedule by any of—

    (*a*) section 360A(5) and (7) of that Act;

    (*b*) paragraph 40(2) and (4) of Schedule 9 to that Act; and

    (*c*) paragraph 16(4) and (6) of Schedule 5 to the Finance Act 1989.

Arrangement of Sections

(1997 Chapter 58)

ARRANGEMENT OF SECTIONS

PART III

INCOME TAX AND CORPORATION TAX

Reliefs for interest and private medical insurance

PART IV

MISCELLANEOUS AND SUPPLEMENTAL

Stamp duty

SCHEDULES:

Schedule 3—Insurance companies and friendly societies.
Schedule 4—Tax credits, taxation of distributions etc.
         Part I—General.
         Part II—Insurance companies and Lloyd's underwriters.
Schedule 5—Limitation of entitlement to relief under section 35.
         Part I—Qualifying distributions other than bonus issues.
         Part II—Bonus issues.
Schedule 6—Foreign income dividends.
Schedule 7—Restrictions on group relief.
Schedule 8—*Repeals.* (not printed)

An Act to grant certain duties, to alter other duties, and to amend the law relating to the National Debt and the Public Revenue, and to make further provision in connection with Finance.

[31st July 1997]

PART III

INCOME TAX AND CORPORATION TAX

Reliefs for interest and private medical insurance

[15 Mortgage interest payments

(1) (*amends* TA 1988 s 353(1G)).

(2) (*amends* TA 1988 s 369(1A)).

(3) *Subsection (1) above has effect in relation to any payment of interest (whenever falling due) made in the year 1998–99 or any subsequent year of assessment; and subsection (2) above has effect in relation to any payment of interest which becomes due in the year 1998–99 or any subsequent year of assessment.*][1]

Commentary—*Simon's Direct Tax Service* **A3.430; E1.102A.**
Amendment—[1] This section repealed by FA 1999 s 139, Sch 20 Pt III(7) with effect for payments of interest within FA 1999 s 38(3), (4).

16 Limit on relief for interest for 1998–99

For the year 1998–99 the qualifying maximum defined in section 367(5) of the Taxes Act 1988 (limit on relief for interest on certain loans) shall be £30,000.

Commentary—*Simon's Direct Tax Service* **A3.430; E1.102A.**

17 Withdrawal of relief on medical insurance premiums

(1) Subject to subsections (2) and (3) below, relief under section 54 of the Finance Act 1989 (medical insurance) shall not be given in respect of any payment where either—

     (*a*) the premium in respect of which the payment is made is a premium under a contract entered into on or after 2nd July 1997; or

     (*b*) the payment is received by the insurer on or after 6th April 1999.

(2) Subsection (1) above shall not affect the giving of relief in respect of a payment received by an insurer before 6th April 1999 where—

     (*a*) the premium in respect of which the payment is made is a premium under a contract entered into on or after 2nd July 1997 but before 1st August 1997;

     (*b*) the contract is one entered into in pursuance of a written proposal received by or on behalf of the insurer before 2nd July 1997;

     (*c*) the contract is not a contract entered into by way of the renewal of an earlier contract; and

     (*d*) if the payment is not itself a payment received before 1st August 1997, the insurer had before 1st August 1997 received an earlier payment in respect of a premium under the contract in question.

(3) Subsection (1) above shall not affect the giving of relief in respect of a payment received by an insurer before 6th April 1999 where—

     (*a*) the premium in respect of which the payment is made is a premium under a contract entered into on or after 2nd July 1997 but before 1st August 1997;

     (*b*) that contract is one entered into by way of the renewal of an earlier contract;

     (*c*) the period of insurance under the earlier contract ended before 2nd July 1997; and

     (*d*) if the payment is not itself a payment received before 1st August 1997, the insurer had before 1st August 1997 received an earlier payment in respect of a premium under the renewal contract.

(4) For the purposes of the preceding provisions of this section a contract shall be taken to have been entered into by way of the renewal of an earlier contract only if—

(*a*) it was entered into by way of the renewal of a contract which was an eligible contract for the purposes of section 54 of the Finance Act 1989 when that earlier contract was entered into;

(*b*) the insurer under the earlier contract and the insurer under the contract by which it has been renewed are the same; and

(*c*) the period of insurance under the earlier contract ended immediately before the beginning of the period of insurance under the contract by which it has been renewed.

(5) This section has effect for the year 1997–98 and subsequent years of assessment.

Commentary—*Simon's Direct Tax Service* **E1.102A; E2.901.**

Corporation tax

18 Rates for financial year 1997

Commentary—*Simon's Direct Tax Service* **D2.108, 109.**
Note—This section is spent.

Distributions, tax credits etc on and after 2nd July 1997

19 Pension funds no longer entitled to payment of tax credits

Commentary—*Simon's Direct Tax Service* **D1.402.**
Amendment—This section repealed by F(No 2)A 1997 Sch 8 Pt II(9) with effect in relation to distributions made after 5 April 1999.

20 Losses etc not to be set against surplus franked investment income

(1) No claim shall be made under section 242 or 243 of the Taxes Act 1988 (set off of losses etc against surplus of franked investment income) for any accounting period beginning on or after 2nd July 1997; and section 244(1) of that Act shall cease to have effect accordingly.

(2) Sections 242(5) and (6) and 243(4) of the Taxes Act 1988 (restoration of loss etc in later accounting period for which there is a surplus of franked payments) shall not have effect where the later accounting period mentioned in section 242(5)(*b*) begins on or after 2nd July 1997.

(3) No amount shall be deducted under paragraph (*a*), or carried forward and deducted under paragraph (*b*), of section 244(2) (deduction of tax credit paid from ACT subsequently available for set off or surrender) for any accounting period beginning on or after 2nd July 1997.

(4) For the purposes of sections 242 and 243 of the Taxes Act 1988, if—

(*a*) a company has a surplus of franked investment income for an accounting period beginning before 2nd July 1997 and ending on or after that date, and

(*b*) that surplus exceeds the surplus of franked investment income which the company would have had for that accounting period had it ended on 1st July 1997,

the surplus shall be treated as reduced by the excess.

(5), (6) (*repeals* TA 1988 ss 242–244 and *amend* TA 1988 s 237(4)).

(7) Subsection (6) above has effect in accordance with subsection (5) above.

Commentary—*Simon's Direct Tax Service* **D2.413; D4.304.**

21 Estates in administration: distributions to which s 233(1) applies

(1) Section 699A of the Taxes Act 1988 (untaxed sums comprised in the income of the estate) shall be amended as follows.

(2) (*amends* TA 1988 s 699A(1))

(3) (*inserts* TA 1988 s 699A(1A), (1B))

(4) (*amends* TA 1988 s 699A(4))

(5) This section has effect in relation to amounts which a person is deemed by virtue of Part XVI of the Taxes Act 1988 (estates in the course of administration) to receive, or to have a right to receive, on or after 2nd July 1997.

Commentary—*Simon's Direct Tax Service* **C4.116; D1.111.**

22 Lloyd's underwriters

(1) (*inserts* FA 1993 s 171(2B))

(2)–(4) (*amend* FA 1994 s 219(3), (4) and *insert* s 219(4A), (4B), (4C)).

(5), (6) (*amend* TA 1988 s 20(1), 231(1))

(7) This section has effect in relation to distributions made on or after 2nd July 1997.

Commentary—*Simon's Direct Tax Service* **E5.611.**

23 Insurance companies and friendly societies

Schedule 3 to this Act (which makes provision in relation to insurance companies and friendly societies) shall have effect.

Commentary—*Simon's Direct Tax Service* **D4.503**.

Distributions, tax credits etc: avoidance

24 Taxation of dealers in respect of distributions etc

(1) Section 95 of the Taxes Act 1988 (taxation of dealers in respect of certain qualifying distributions etc) shall be amended in accordance with subsections (2) to (9) below.

(2) (*substitutes* TA 1988 s 95(1))

(3) (*amends* TA 1988 s 95(1A))

(4) (*repeals* TA 1988 s 95(1B))

(5) (*amends* TA 1988 s 95(2))

(6) (*inserts* TA 1988 s 95(2A))

(7) (*repeals* TA 1988 s 95(4))

(8) (*repeals* TA 1988 s 95(5))

(9) (*substitutes sidenote to* TA 1988 s 95)

(10) (*amends* TA 1988 s 20(1))

(11) (*amends* TA 1988 s 234)

(12) (*amends* TA 1988 s 246D(1))

(13) (*repeals* TA 1988 Sch 23A para 2A(2))

(14) (*amends* FA 1997 Sch 7 para 2(3))

(15) This section has effect in relation to—

    (*a*) any distribution made on or after 2nd July 1997; and

    (*b*) any payment which is representative of such a distribution.

Commentary—*Simon's Direct Tax Service* **D4.411**.

25 Repeal of s 95(5) of the Taxes Act 1988: consequential amendments

(1) (*amends* TA 1988 s 246A(9))

(2), (3) (*amend* TA 1988 Sch 28B para 13)

(4) (*inserts* TA 1988 Sch 28B para 13(6))

(5), (6) (*amend* FA 1997 Sch 7 para 5(2))

(7) (*inserts* FA 1997 Sch 7 para 5(3))

(8) This section has effect on and after 2nd July 1997.

Commentary—*Simon's Direct Tax Service* **D4.411**.

26 Purchase and sale of securities

(1) Section 732 of the Taxes Act 1988 (dealers in securities) shall be amended as follows.(2) (*inserts* TA 1988 s 732(1A))

(3) (*repeals* TA 1988 s 732(2), (2A))

(4), (5) (*amend* TA 1988 s 732(4))

(6) (*repeals* TA 1988 s 732(5), (5A))

(7) (*repeals* TA 1988 s 732(6), (7))

(8) This section has effect where, for the purposes of section 731(2) of the Taxes Act 1988, the interest receivable by the first buyer is paid on or after 2nd July 1997.

Commentary—*Simon's Direct Tax Service* **B3.727A**.

27 Payments to companies under section 687 of the Taxes Act 1988

(1) (*inserts* TA 1988 s 687A)

(2) This section has effect in relation to payments made by trustees to companies on or after 2nd July 1997.

Commentary—*Simon's Direct Tax Service* **C4.226; D1.402**.

28 Arrangements to pass on value of tax credit

(1) (*inserts* TA 1988 s 231B)

(2) This section has effect in relation to distributions made on or after 2nd July 1997.

Commentary—*Simon's Direct Tax Service* **D1.402**.

29 Unauthorised unit trusts

(1) Where a qualifying distribution—

(*a*) is made on or after 2nd July 1997 but before 6th April 1999 by a company resident in the United Kingdom, and

(*b*) falls to be regarded by virtue of subsection (2) of section 469 of the Taxes Act 1988 (unit trusts other than authorised unit trusts) as income of the trustees of a unit trust scheme to which that section applies, and

(*c*) is not a foreign income dividend and does not fall to be regarded by virtue of any provision of the Tax Acts apart from this section as a foreign income dividend arising to the trustees,

the trustees shall be treated for all purposes of the Tax Acts (apart from this section) as if the qualifying distribution were a foreign income dividend.

(2) Subsection (1) above shall not apply—

(*a*) if the unit trust scheme is a common investment fund established under section 42 of the Administration of Justice Act 1982; or

(*b*) if, apart from section 469(2) of the Taxes Act 1988, the whole of the qualifying distribution would fall to be regarded as income of section 505 bodies.

(3) In this section—

"foreign income dividend" shall be construed in accordance with Chapter VA of Part VI of the Taxes Act 1988;

"section 505 body" means—

(*a*) a charity, as defined in section 506(1) of the Taxes Act 1988;

(*b*) a body mentioned in section 507 (heritage bodies) of that Act; or

(*c*) an Association of a description specified in section 508 of that Act (scientific research organisations).

Commentary—*Simon's Direct Tax Service* **D4.1326.**

Distributions, tax credits etc in and after 1999–00

Revenue Interpretation RI 199—The taxation of Schedule F income received by trustees after 6 April 1999.

30 Tax credits

(1) Section 231 of the Taxes Act 1988 (tax credits for certain recipients of qualifying distributions) shall be amended in accordance with subsections (2) to (7) below.

(2) (*amends* TA 1988 s 231(1)).

(3) (*inserts* TA 1988 s 231(1A)).

(4) (*repeals* TA 1988 s 231(2)).[1]

(5) (*amends* TA 1988 s 231(3)).

(6) (*inserts* TA 1988 s 231(3AA)).

(7) (*repeals* TA 1988 s 231(3A)–(3D)).

(8) (*repeals* TA 1988 s 231A).

(9) The amendments made by subsections (5) and (6) above do not affect the entitlement of a person who is not resident in the United Kingdom to payment in respect of a tax credit by virtue of arrangements having effect under section 788 of the Taxes Act 1988 (relief by agreement with other countries).

(10) Where—

(*a*) arrangements having effect by virtue of section 788 of the Taxes Act 1988 confer on a person not resident in the United Kingdom the right to a tax credit under section 231 of the Taxes Act 1988 in respect of a dividend of a company resident in the United Kingdom, and

(*b*) the arrangements contain provision for permitting—

(i) tax to be charged or deducted, or

(ii) a reduction in the amount of the tax credit that is paid to be made,

by reference to the aggregate of the dividend and the tax credit, and

(*c*) the amount of that tax or that reduction exceeds the amount of the tax credit,

that provision shall only have the effect of reducing to nil the amount of the payment to which the person is entitled in respect of the tax credit.

(11) This section has effect in relation to distributions made on or after 6th April 1999.

Commentary—*Simon's Direct Tax Service* **D1.402.**
Modifications—Modified by FA 1998 s 76 with effect from 31 July 1998 where a distribution is made before 6 April 2004, if it is received by an individual in respect of an investment made under a plan for which provision is made by regulations under TA 1988 s 333 (individual savings accounts and personal equity plans) and that investment is one in respect of which that individual is entitled to relief in accordance with such regulations. The section is modified as if—

(*a*) subsection (5) did not make the substitution set out in paragraph (*a*) or the repeal set out in paragraph (*b*);
(*b*) subsections (6), (7) and (9) were to be disregarded.

Amendments—[1] Sub-s (4) does not have effect in relation to certain distributions made to friendly societies before 6 April 2004 (FA 1998 s 90(1)).

Income Tax and Corporation TaxFN 2A 1997 s 35

31 Rates of tax applicable to Schedule F income etc

(1) Section 1A of the Taxes Act 1988 (application of lower rate to income from savings and distributions) shall be amended in accordance with subsections (2) to (4) below.

(2) (*amends* TA 1988 s 1A(1)).

(3) (*inserts* TA 1988 s 1A(1A)).

(4) (*substitutes* TA 1988 s 1A(5)).

(5) (*inserts* TA 1988 s 1B).

(6) This section has effect in relation to distributions made on or after 6th April 1999.

Commentary—*Simon's Direct Tax Service* **D1.402.**

32 Trusts

(1) Section 686 of the Taxes Act 1988 (income arising to trustees which is to be chargeable at the rate applicable to trusts) shall be amended as follows.

(2) (*amends* TA 1988 s 686(1)).

(3) (*inserts* TA 1988 s 686(1AA)).

(4) (5) (*amend* TA 1988 s 686(1A)).

(6) (*amends* TA 1988 s 686(2AA)).

(7) (*inserts* TA 1988 s 686(5A)).

(8) (*substitutes sidenote to* TA 1988 s 686).

(9) (*inserts* TA 1988 s 686A).

(10) The amendment made by subsection (5) above has effect on and after 6th April 1999.

(11) The other amendments made by this section have effect in relation to distributions made on or after 6th April 1999.

Commentary—*Simon's Direct Tax Service* **C4.203.**

33 Estates of deceased persons in administration

(1) (*substitutes* TA 1988 s 698A).

(2) Section 699A of the Taxes Act 1988 (untaxed sums comprised in the income of the estate) shall be amended in accordance with subsections (3) to (6) below.

(3) (*amends* TA 1988 s 699A(1A)).

(4) (*amends* TA 1988 s 699A(2)).

(5) (*amends* TA 1988 s 699A(4)).

(6) (*amends* TA 1988 s 699A(6)).

(7) In section 701 of the Taxes Act 1988 (interpretation of Part XVI) subsection (3A) (which defines the "applicable rate" as basic rate or lower rate, according to the rate at which the income of the residue out of which the payment to the beneficiary is made bears tax) shall be amended in accordance with subsections (8) and (9) below.

(8) (9) (*amend* TA 1988 s 701(3A)).

(10) The amendment made by subsection (3) above has effect in relation to distributions made on or after 6th April 1999.

(11) The amendments made by subsections (1) and (4) to (9) above have effect for the year 1999–00 and subsequent years of assessment.

Commentary—*Simon's Direct Tax Service* **C4.122.**

34 Tax credits and taxation of distributions: miscellaneous provisions

Schedule 4 to this Act (which contains provisions relating to tax credits and the taxation of distributions) shall have effect.

Commentary—*Simon's Direct Tax Service* **D1.402.**

35 Transitional relief for charities etc

(1) In any case where—

(a) a qualifying distribution is made on or after 6th April 1999 and before 6th April 2004 by a company resident in the United Kingdom; and

(b) the recipient of the distribution is a section 505 body; and

(c) if the section 505 body falls within neither paragraph (b) nor paragraph (c) of subsection (3) below, entitlement to exemption from tax by virtue of subsection (1)(c)(iii) of section 505 of the Taxes Act 1988 (charities) in respect of the distribution is not prevented by anything in that section, the section 505 body, on a claim made under this section to the Board, shall be entitled to be paid by the Board out of money provided by Parliament an amount determined in accordance with subsection (2) below.

(2) The amount referred to in subsection (1) above is an amount equal to—

(a) 21 per cent of the amount or value of the distribution if the distribution is made on or after 6th April 1999 and before 6th April 2000;

(b) 17 per cent of that amount or value if the distribution is made on or after 6th April 2000 and before 6th April 2001;

(c) 13 per cent of that amount or value if the distribution is made on or after 6th April 2001 and before 6th April 2002;

(d) 8 per cent of that amount or value if the distribution is made on or after 6th April 2002 and before 6th April 2003;

(e) 4 per cent of that amount or value if the distribution is made on or after 6th April 2003 and before 6th April 2004.

(3) For the purposes of this section each of the following is a section 505 body—

(a) any charity (as defined in section 506(1) of the Taxes Act 1988);

(b) each of the bodies mentioned in section 507 of that Act (heritage bodies);

(c) any Association of a description specified in section 508 of that Act (scientific research organisations).

(4) Schedule 5 to this Act shall have effect to remove or restrict entitlement to payment under this section in certain circumstances.

(5) For the purposes of Chapter I of Part XVII of the Taxes Act 1988 (cancellation of tax advantages) payment of an amount under this section shall be treated as repayment of tax.

(6) Any entitlement of a section 505 body to a payment under subsection (1) above shall be subject to a power of the Board to determine (whether before or after any payment is made) that, having regard to the operation in relation to the distribution in question of section 703 of the Taxes Act 1988 (cancellation of tax advantages) that body is to be treated as if it had had no entitlement to that payment or to so much of it as they may determine.

(7) No claim may be made under this section later than two years after the end of the chargeable period of the section 505 body in which the distribution is made.

(8) An appeal may be brought against any decision of the Board under this section or under Schedule 5 by giving written notice to the Board within thirty days of receipt of written notice of the decision.

(9) An appeal under this section shall lie to the Special Commissioners, and the provisions of the Taxes Management Act 1970 relating to appeals under the Tax Acts shall apply to an appeal under this section as they apply to those appeals.

(10) Any payment of an amount under this section shall be treated for the purposes of section 252 of the Taxes Act 1988 (rectification of excessive set-off etc of ACT or tax credit) as a payment of tax credit.

Commentary—*Simon's Direct Tax Service* **C4.521.**

36 Foreign income dividends

(1) No election shall be made under section 246A of the Taxes Act 1988 (election for dividend to be treated as foreign income dividend) in respect of any distributions made on or after 6th April 1999.

(2) No amount shall be shown as available for distribution as foreign income dividends in the distribution accounts of an authorised unit trust for a distribution period the distribution date for which falls on or after 6th April 1999.

(3) No distribution made on or after 6th April 1999 shall be treated as a foreign income dividend by virtue of paragraph 2(1) of Schedule 7 to the Finance Act 1997 (Tax Acts to have effect as if qualifying distributions to which Schedule 7 applies were foreign income dividends).

(4) Schedule 6 to this Act (which makes provision for and in connection with the repeal of provisions relating to foreign income dividends) shall have effect.

(5) In subsection (2) above, "distribution accounts", "distribution date" and "distribution period" shall be construed in accordance with section 468H of the Taxes Act 1988 (interpretation of sections 468I to 468R of that Act).

Commentary—*Simon's Direct Tax Service* **D1.701.**

Gilt-edged securities

37 Interest to be paid gross

(1) The Taxes Act 1988 shall be amended as follows.

(2)–(5) (*inserts* TA 1988 s 50(A1), amend s 50(1)–(5), (7) and *repeal* s 51A.)

(6) (*substituted* TA 1988 s 51B(5) *and inserted* s 51B(5A)).[1]

(7) (*amends* TA 1988 s 722A(5), s 730C(9) and Sch 23A para 3A(2)(a).)

(8) Subject to subsections (9) to (13) below, this section has effect in relation to payments of interest falling due on or after 6th April 1998.

(9) Subsection (3)(*d*) above has effect in relation to applications made and notices given at any time on or after the day on which this Act is passed.

(10) Where—

(*a*) any person holds any gilt-edged securities in relation to which a direction was given under section 50(1) of the Taxes Act 1988 at any time before 6th April 1998, and

(*b*) that person at any time before that date made an application under section 50(2) of that Act with respect to those securities,

that application (unless withdrawn) shall have effect in relation to any interest on those securities to which section 50(A1) of that Act applies as it previously had effect in relation to any interest on those securities to which that direction applied.

(11) [Section 50][2] of the Taxes Act 1988 shall have effect in relation to any gilt-edged securities issued before 6th April 1998 which—

(*a*) are securities the interest on which, if paid immediately before that date, would have fallen to be paid after deduction of income tax, and

(*b*) are registered within the meaning of section 50 of that Act but are not securities in relation to which any direction under section 50 of that Act was given before that date,

as if the appropriate person had so made an application under section 50(2) of that Act as to enable that application to take effect in relation to payments of interest made on or after that date.

(12) In subsection (11) above "the appropriate person" means—

(*a*) in the case of securities transferred before 6th April 1998 but after the time when the balance was struck for a dividend on them falling due on or after that date, the person who held the securities at the time when the balance was so struck;

(*b*) in any other case, the person holding the securities in question immediately before 6th April 1998.

(13) Section 50(5) of the Taxes Act 1988 shall have effect in relation to an application treated as made by virtue of subsection (11) above as if a notice withdrawing that application was capable of being given at any time on or after the passing of this Act.

Commentary—*Simon's Direct Tax Service* A7.1103..
Amendment—[1] Sub-s (6), repealed by FA 1998 s 165, Sch 27 Part III(3) with effect in relation only to payments of interest falling due after 31 March 1999 by virtue of Finance Act 1998, Section 37, (Appointed Day) Order, SI 1999/619.
[2] Words in sub-s (11) substituted by FA 2000 s 111(5), (6)(*a*) with effect for relevant payments or receipts in relation to which the chargeable date for the purposes of TA 1988 Pt IV Ch VIIA is after 31 March 2001.

38 Paying and collecting agents

(1) ...

(2) (*amended* TA 1988 s 118A).

(3) (*inserted* TA 1988 s 118A(2)).

(4) (*amended* TA 1988 s 118D(4)).

(5) (*repealed* TA 1988 s 118G(3)(*b*), (*d*)–(*f*) *and inserts* s 118G(3)(*ca*)).

(6) (*amended* TA 1988 s 118G(7)).

(7) (*repealed* TA 1988 s 118G(8), (10)).

(8) ...

Commentary—*Simon's Direct Tax Service* A7.910, 915–917.
Amendment—This section repealed by FA 2000 s 156, Sch 40 Pt II(17) with effect for relevant payments or receipts in relation to which the chargeable date for the purposes of TA 1988 Pt IV Ch VIIA is after 31 March 2001.

Relief for losses etc

39 Carry-back of trading losses

(1) Section 393A of the Taxes Act 1988 (set-off of trading losses against profits of previous three years) shall be amended in accordance with subsections (2) to (6) below.

(2) (*amends* TA 1988 s 393A(2).)

(3) (*inserts* TA 1988 s 393A(2A)–(2C).)

(4) (*amends* s 393A(7).)

(5) (*inserts* s 393A(7A).)

(6) (*inserts* s 393A(12).)

(7) (*inserts* TA 1988 s 343(4A).)

(8) Subject to subsection (9) below, this section applies to any loss incurred in an accounting period ending on or after 2nd July 1997.

(9) Where a loss in any trade is incurred by a company in an accounting period ending on or after 2nd July 1997 but beginning before that date, section 393A of the Taxes Act 1988 shall have effect

as if subsection (2A) of that section applied to the pre-commencement part of any amount of that loss to which that subsection would not apply apart from this subsection.

(10) In subsection (9) above "the pre-commencement part", in relation to the amount of the whole or any part of a loss in an accounting period, means the part of that amount which, on an apportionment in accordance with subsection (11) or, as the case may be, (12) below, is attributable to the part of that accounting period falling before 2nd July 1997.

(11) Except in a case where subsection (12) below applies, an apportionment for the purposes of subsection (10) above shall be made on a time basis according to the respective lengths of the part of the accounting period falling before 2nd July 1997 and the remainder of that accounting period.

(12) Where the circumstances of a particular case are such that the making of an apportionment on the time basis mentioned in subsection (11) above would work in a manner that would be unjust or unreasonable in relation to any person, the apportionment shall be made instead (to the extent only that is necessary in order to avoid injustice and unreasonableness) in such other manner as may be just and reasonable.

Commentary—*Simon's Direct Tax Service* D2.405.
Simon's Tax Cases—s 39(9)–(12) *Camcrown Ltd v McDonald* [1999] STC (SCD) 255.

40 Carry-back of loan relationship deficits

(1) Chapter II of Part IV of the Finance Act 1996 (loan relationships) shall be amended as follows.

(2) (*amends* FA 1996 Sch 8 para 3(7).)

(3) (*amends* FA 1996 Sch 11 para 4(3).)

(4) (*amends* FA 1996 Sch 11 para 4(5).)

(5) (*amends* FA 1996 Sch 11 para 4(8).)

(6) (*amends* FA 1996 Sch 11 para 4(9) and *inserts* para 4(9A).)

(7) Subject to subsection (8) below, this section has effect in relation to any deficit for a deficit period ending on or after 2nd July 1997.

(8) Paragraph 3 of Schedule 8 to the Finance Act 1996 shall have effect in relation to any deficit for a deficit period beginning before but ending on or after 2nd July 1997 as if the permitted period in relation to the pre-commencement part of the deficit were the period beginning with 1st April 1996 and ending immediately before the beginning of the deficit period.

(9) Where for the purposes of paragraph 23 of Schedule 15 to the Finance Act 1996 (transitional provision in connection with the carrying back of exchange losses) there is a relievable amount for an accounting period ending on or after 2nd July 1997, that paragraph shall have effect, except in relation to any pre-commencement part of that amount, as if, in section 131(10)(*b*) of the Finance Act 1993 (the permitted period) as applied by that paragraph, the words "twelve months" were substituted for the words "three years".

(10) In this section "pre-commencement part", in relation to the deficit for any deficit period or the relievable amount for any accounting period, means the part (if any) of that deficit or relievable amount which, on an apportionment in accordance with subsection (11) or, as the case may be, (12) below, is attributable to such part (if any) of that period as falls before 2nd July 1997.

(11) Except in a case where subsection (12) below applies, an apportionment for the purposes of subsection (10) above shall be made on a time basis according to the respective lengths of the part of the deficit period or, as the case may be, accounting period falling before 2nd July 1997 and the remainder of that period.

(12) Where the circumstances of a particular case are such that the making of an apportionment on the time basis mentioned in subsection (11) above would work in a manner that would be unjust or unreasonable in relation to any person, the apportionment shall be made instead (to the extent only that is necessary in order to avoid injustice and unreasonableness) in such other manner as may be just and reasonable.

Commentary—*Simon's Direct Tax Service* D2.1136.

41 Restrictions on group relief

Schedule 7 to this Act (which imposes new restrictions on the giving of group relief) shall have effect.

Commentary—*Simon's Direct Tax Service* D2.645.

Capital allowances for small and medium-sized businesses

42 Temporary first-year allowances

...

Commentary—*Simon's Direct Tax Service* B2.321, 324.
Amendment—This section repealed by the Capital Allowances Act 2001 s 580, Sch 4 with effect for income tax purposes, as respects allowances and charges falling to be made for chargeable periods ending after 5 April 2001, and for corporation tax purposes, as respects allowances and charges falling to be made for chargeable periods ending after 31 March 2001.

43 Expenditure of a small company or small business

...

Commentary—*Simon's Direct Tax Service* B2.321, 324.
Amendment—This section repealed by the Capital Allowances Act 2001 s 580, Sch 4 with effect for income tax purposes, as respects allowances and charges falling to be made for chargeable periods ending after 5 April 2001, and for corporation tax purposes, as respects allowances and charges falling to be made for chargeable periods ending after 31 March 2001.

Capital allowances and finance leases

44 Writing-down allowances for finance lessors

...

Commentary—*Simon's Direct Tax Service* B2.340.
Amendment—This section repealed by the Capital Allowances Act 2001 s 580, Sch 4 with effect for income tax purposes, as respects allowances and charges falling to be made for chargeable periods ending after 5 April 2001, and for corporation tax purposes, as respects allowances and charges falling to be made for chargeable periods ending after 31 March 2001.

45 Hire-purchase by finance lessors

...

Commentary—*Simon's Direct Tax Service* B2.331.
Amendment—This section repealed by the Capital Allowances Act 2001 s 580, Sch 4 with effect for income tax purposes, as respects allowances and charges falling to be made for chargeable periods ending after 5 April 2001, and for corporation tax purposes, as respects allowances and charges falling to be made for chargeable periods ending after 31 March 2001.

46 Sale and leaseback etc using finance leases

...

Commentary—*Simon's Direct Tax Service* B2.365.
Amendment—This section repealed by the Capital Allowances Act 2001 s 580, Sch 4 with effect for income tax purposes, as respects allowances and charges falling to be made for chargeable periods ending after 5 April 2001, and for corporation tax purposes, as respects allowances and charges falling to be made for chargeable periods ending after 31 March 2001.

47 Meaning of "finance lease"

...

Commentary—*Simon's Direct Tax Service* B2.365.
Amendment—This section repealed by the Capital Allowances Act 2001 s 580, Sch 4 with effect for income tax purposes, as respects allowances and charges falling to be made for chargeable periods ending after 5 April 2001, and for corporation tax purposes, as respects allowances and charges falling to be made for chargeable periods ending after 31 March 2001.

Films

48 Relief for expenditure or production and acquisition

(1) Subject to subsection (4) below, section 42 of the Finance (No 2) Act 1992 shall have effect in relation to any expenditure to which this section applies as if the following subsection were substituted for subsections (4) and (5) (which for any period limit relief for film production and acquisition expenditure to a third, or a proportionately reduced fraction, of the relievable expenditure)—

"(4) The amount deducted for a relevant period under subsection (1) above shall not exceed so much of the total expenditure incurred by the claimant on—

    (*a*) the production of the film concerned, or
    (*b*) the acquisition of the master negative or any master tape or master disc of it,

as has not already been deducted by virtue of [section 40B or]², section 41 above or this section."

(2) Subject to subsection (3) below, this section applies to so much of any expenditure falling within paragraphs (*a*) and (*b*) of section 42(1) of the Finance (No 2) Act 1992 as is expenditure in relation to which each of the following conditions is satisfied, that is to say—

    (*a*) the expenditure is expenditure incurred on or after 2nd July 1997 and before [2nd July 2005]¹;
    (*b*) the film concerned is a film with a total production expenditure of £15 million or less; and
    (*c*) the film concerned is a film completed on or after 2nd July 1997.

(3) This section does not apply to so much of any expenditure falling within section 42(3) of the Finance (No 2) Act 1992 (acquisition expenditure) as exceeds the amount of the total production expenditure on the film concerned.

(4) Where this section applies to only part of any expenditure to which subsection (2) or (3) of section 42 of the Finance (No 2) Act 1992 applies in the case of any film, the amount deducted by virtue of subsection (1) of that section for a relevant period shall not exceed the sum of the following amounts—

    (*a*) the maximum amount of expenditure to which this section applies that is deductible for that period in accordance with subsection (1) above; and
    (*b*) the maximum amount specified in subsection (5) below.

(5) The amount mentioned in subsection (4) above is the maximum amount which would be deductible for the relevant period in accordance with subsection (4) of section 42 of the Finance (No 2) Act 1992 if—

(*a*) in paragraphs (*a*) and (*b*) of that subsection (but not in paragraph (*c*)) the references to expenditure incurred by the claimant did not include references to any expenditure to which this section applies; and

(*b*) the maximum amount mentioned in subsection (4)(*a*) above had already been deducted by virtue of that section.

(6) In this section "total production expenditure", in relation to any claim for relief under section 42 of the Finance (No 2) Act 1992 in the case of any film, means ([subject to subsections (6A) and (7)][3] below) the total of all expenditure on the production of the film, whenever incurred and whether or not incurred by the claimant.

[(6A) For the purposes of this section the production expenditure on a film shall be taken not to include any amount that at the time the film is completed—

(*a*) has not been paid, and

(*b*) is not the subject of an unconditional obligation to pay within four months after the date of completion.][3]

(7) For the purposes of this section where—

(*a*) any part of the expenditure incurred by any person on the production of a film is incurred under or by virtue of any transaction directly or indirectly between that person and a person connected with him, and

(*b*) that part of that expenditure might have been expected to have been of a greater amount ("the arm's length amount") if the transaction had been between independent persons dealing at arm's length,

that part of that expenditure shall be deemed, for the purpose of determining the amount of the total production expenditure on the film, to have been expenditure of an amount equal to the arm's length amount.

(8) Subsection (3) of section 43 of the Finance (No 2) Act 1992 (time of completion of a film) shall apply for the purposes of this section as it applies for the purposes of sections 41 and 42 of that Act, but with the omission of paragraph (*b*) (completion on incurring acquisition expenditure) and the word "or" immediately preceding it.

[(9) Subsections (1) to (5) of section 5 of the Capital Allowances Act 2001 (when capital expenditure is incurred) apply for determining when for the purposes of this section any expenditure is incurred as they apply for determining when for the purposes of that Act any capital expenditure is incurred, but as if, in subsection (6) of that section, "at an earlier time" were substituted for "in an earlier chargeable period".][2]

(10) Section 839 of the Taxes Act 1988 (meaning of "connected person") applies for the purposes of this section.

(11) This section applies for the making of a deduction for any relevant period ending on or after 2nd July 1997.

Commentary—*Simon's Direct Tax Service* **B3.1307**.
Cross references—See FA 2002 s 99 (relief under this section restricted to films genuinely intended for theatrical release).
FA 2002 s 101 (restriction of relief under this section for successive acquisitions of the same film).
Amendments—[1] Words in sub-s (2)(*a*) substituted by FA 2001 s 72 with effect from 11 May 2001.
[2] Words in sub-s (1) substituted, and sub-s (9) substituted, by CAA 2001 s 578, Sch 2 para 99 with effect for income tax purposes, as respects allowances and charges falling to be made for chargeable periods ending after 5 April 2001, and for corporation tax purposes, as respects allowances and charges falling to be made for chargeable periods ending after 31 March 2001.
[3] In sub-s (6), words substituted for the words "subject to subsection (7)", and sub-s (6A) inserted, by FA 2002 s 100 with effect for films completed after 16 April 2002. For this purpose, a film is completed at the time when it is first in a form in which it can reasonably be regarded as ready for copies of it to be made and distributed for presentation to the general public: FA 2002 s 100(4).

PART IV

MISCELLANEOUS AND SUPPLEMENTAL

Provisional collection of taxes

50 Statutory effect of resolutions etc

(1) (*inserts* PCTA 1968(1), (3)(*aa*).)

(2) (*amends* TA 1988 s 246(2)(*b*); *repealed by* FA 1998 Sch 27 Part III(2) *with effect in relation to distributions made after 5 April 1999*)

(3) Subsection (1) above applies in relation to resolutions passed after the day on which this Act is passed.

Supplemental

51 Interpretation

In this Act "the Taxes Act 1988" means the Income and Corporation Taxes Act 1988.

52 Repeals

(1) The enactments mentioned in Schedule 8 to this Act (which include spent provisions) are hereby repealed to the extent specified in the third column of that Schedule.

(2) The repeals specified in that Schedule have effect subject to the commencement provisions and savings contained or referred to in the notes set out in that Schedule.

53 Short title

This Act may be cited as the Finance (No 2) Act 1997.

SCHEDULES

Schedule 3

Insurance Companies and Friendly Societies

Section 23

Commentary—*Simon's Direct Tax Service* **D4.503.**

Section 76 of the Taxes Act 1988

1—(1) Section 76 of the Taxes Act 1988 (expenses of management: insurance companies) shall be amended as follows.

(2) *(amends* TA 1988 s 76(2B)).

(3) *(repeals* TA 1988 s 76(8)).

(4) This paragraph has effect in relation to distributions made on or after 2nd July 1997.

Section 432E of the Taxes Act 1988

2—(1) *(repeals* TA 1988 s 432E(6)(*b*)).

(2) This paragraph has effect in relation to distributions made on or after 2nd July 1997.

Section 434 of the Taxes Act 1988

3—(1) Section 434 of the Taxes Act 1988 (franked investment income etc) shall be amended as follows.

(2) *(substitutes* TA 1988 s 434(1) *and inserts* s 434(1A), (1B)).

(3), (4) ...[1]

(5) Sub-paragraph (2) above has effect in relation to distributions made on or after 2nd July 1997.

(6), (7) ...[1]

(8) In determining, for the purposes of any claim under section 242 of the Taxes Act 1988 made by virtue of section 434(3) of that Act for an accounting period beginning before 2nd July 1997 and ending on or after that date, the policy holders' share of the franked investment income from investments held in connection with an insurance company's life assurance business, there shall be left out of account any distributions which are made on or after 2nd July 1997.

(9) Any amount which, by virtue of sub-paragraph (8) above, is treated as a surplus of franked investment income for the purposes of any such claim as is mentioned in that sub-paragraph shall be disregarded for the purposes of section 20(4) of this Act.

Amendments—[1] Sub-paras (3), (4), (6) and (7) repealed by FA 1998 Sch 27 Part III(2) with effect in relation to distributions made after 5 April 1999.

Section 434A of the Taxes Act 1988

4—(1) *(repeals* TA 1988 s 434A(1)).

(2) This paragraph has effect for accounting periods beginning on or after 2nd July 1997.

Section 436 of the Taxes Act 1988

5—(1) *(repeals* TA 1988 s 436(3)(*d*), (*e*)).

(2) This paragraph has effect in relation to distributions made on or after 2nd July 1997.

Section 438 of the Taxes Act 1988

6—(1) Section 438 of the Taxes Act 1988 (pension business: exemption from tax) shall be amended as follows.

(2)–(4) (*repeal* TA 1988 s 438(3), (3AA), (5) and *amend* TA 1988 s 438(4)).

(5), (6) (*repeal* TA 1988 s 438(6), (7), (9)).

(7) Sub-paragraphs (2) to (4) above have effect in relation to distributions made on or after 2nd July 1997.

(8) Sub-paragraphs (5) and (6) above have effect for accounting periods beginning on or after 2nd July 1997.

(9) In determining, for the purposes of subsections (6) to (7) of section 438 of the Taxes Act 1988, the franked investment income of, or foreign income dividends arising to, an insurance company for an accounting period beginning before 2nd July 1997 and ending on or after that date, there shall be left out of account any distributions which are made on or after 2nd July 1997.

Section 439B of the Taxes Act 1988

7—(1) (*repeals* TA 1988 s 439B(7)).

(2) This paragraph has effect in relation to distributions made on or after 2nd July 1997.

Section 440B of the Taxes Act 1988

8—(1) Section 440B of the Taxes Act 1988 (modifications where tax charged under Case I of Schedule D) shall be amended as follows.

(2) (*repeals* TA 1988 s 440B(1A)).

(3) (*repeals* TA 1988 s 440B(2)).

(4) Sub-paragraph (2) above has effect in relation to distributions made on or after 2nd July 1997.

(5) Sub-paragraph (3) above has effect for accounting periods beginning on or after 2nd July 1997.

Section 441A of the Taxes Act 1988

9—(1) Section 441A of the Taxes Act 1988 (section 441: distributions) shall be amended as follows.

(2), (3) (*repeal* TA 1988 s 441A(1) and *amend* s 441A(2)).

(4) This paragraph has effect in relation to distributions made on or after 2nd July 1997.

Schedule 19AB to the Taxes Act 1988

10—*(1) Schedule 19AB to the Taxes Act 1988 (payments on account of tax credits and deducted tax) shall be amended as follows.*

(2) (amends TA 1988 Sch 19AB para 1(1)).

(3)–(5) (amends TA 1988 Sch 19AB para 1(7), (10), repeals Sch 19AB para 1(1)(b), para 1((7)(b) and para 1(8)).

(6) Sub-paragraph (2) above has effect in relation to distributions made on or after 2nd July 1997.

(7) Sub-paragraphs (3) to (5) above have effect for accounting periods beginning on or after 2nd July 1997.

Amendments—This paragraph repealed by FA 2001 s 110, Sch 33 Pt II(12) with effect in accordance with FA 2001 s 87.

11—*(1) Schedule 19AB to the Taxes Act 1988, as it has effect in relation to provisional repayment periods falling in accounting periods ending on or after the day appointed under section 199 of the Finance Act 1994 for the purposes of Chapter III of Part IV of that Act, shall be amended as follows.*

(2)–(5) (amend TA 1988 Sch 19AB paras 1(7), 3(1A), 3(1B), (8) and repeal para 3(1B)(b), (8)(b)).[1]

Amendments—[1] This paragraph repealed by FA 2001 s 110, Sch 33 Pt II(12) with effect in accordance with FA 2001 s 87.

12—*(1) For the purposes of section 121 of the Finance Act 1993 (repayments and payments to friendly societies), Schedule 19AB to the Taxes Act 1988 shall be deemed to have effect without the amendments made by this Schedule.*[1]

(2) In relation to distributions made on or after 6th April 1999, sub-paragraph (1) above shall not prevent Schedule 19AB to the Taxes Act 1988 having effect for the purposes of section 121 of the Finance Act 1993 with the amendments made by this Schedule.[2]

Amendments—[1] Sub-para 1 repealed by FA 2001 s 110, Sch 33 Pt II(12) with effect in accordance with FA 2001 s 87.
[2] Sub-para 2 repealed by FA 2001 s 110, Sch 33 Pt II(12) with effect from the passing of FA 2001.

Schedule 19AC to the Taxes Act 1988

13—(1) Schedule 19AC to the Taxes Act 1988 (modification of Taxes Act 1988 in relation to overseas life insurance companies) shall be amended as follows.

(2) (*repeals* TA 1988 Sch 19AC para 2).

(3) (*amends* TA 1988 Sch 19AC para 5(1)).

(4) (*inserts* TA 1988 Sch 19AC para 5A(3)).

(5) (*repeals* TA 1988 Sch 19AC para 5B(1)–(3)).

(6) (*amends* TA 1988 Sch 19AC para 9(1)).

(7) (*repeals* TA 1988 Sch 19AC para 9A).

(8) (*repeals* TA 1988 Sch 19AC para 10(1)).

(9) (*repeals* TA 1988 Sch 19AC para 10(2)).

(10) (*repeals* TA 1988 Sch 19AC para 10A).

(11) (*repeals* TA 1988 Sch 19AC para 11A(1)).

(12) (*repeals* TA 1988 Sch 19AC para 12(1)).

(13) (*repeals* TA 1988 Sch 19AC para 15(1); *repealed by* FA 2001 s 110, Sch 33 Pt II(12) with effect in accordance with FA 2001 s 87).

(14) Sub-paragraphs (2), (3), (5), (7), (9), (12) and (13) above have effect for accounting periods beginning on or after 2nd July 1997.

(15) Sub-paragraphs (4), (6), (8), (10) and (11) above have effect in relation to distributions made on or after 2nd July 1997.

(16) In determining, for the purposes of paragraph 5B(1) to (3) of Schedule 19AC to the Taxes Act 1988, the UK distribution income of an overseas life insurance company for an accounting period beginning before 2nd July 1997 and ending on or after that date, there shall be left out of account any distributions which are made on or after 2nd July 1997.

(17) In determining, for the purposes of subsections (6) to (7) of section 438 of the Taxes Act 1988 (as notionally amended by paragraph 10(2) of Schedule 19AC to that Act), the UK distribution income of, or foreign income dividends arising to, an overseas life insurance company for an accounting period beginning before 2nd July 1997 and ending on or after that date, there shall be left out of account any distributions which are made on or after 2nd July 1997.

Section 89 of the Finance Act 1989

14—(1) Section 89 of the Finance Act 1989 (policy holders' share of profits) shall be amended as follows.

(2) (*repeals* FA 1989 s 89(2)(*a*) and *amends* s 89(2)(*b*), (*c*)).

(3) (*repeals* FA 1989 s 89(8)).

(4) This paragraph has effect in relation to distributions made on or after 2nd July 1997.

Section 65 of the Finance (No 2) Act 1992

15 (*inserts* F(No2)A 1992 s 65(2)(*aa*), (*ab*)).

SCHEDULE 4

TAX CREDITS, TAXATION OF DISTRIBUTIONS ETC

Section 34

Commentary—*Simon's Direct Tax Service* **D1.402.**

PART I

GENERAL

THE TAXES MANAGEMENT ACT 1970

Section 7

1—(1) (*amends* TMA 1970 s 7(6)).

(2) This paragraph has effect for the year 1999–00 and subsequent years of assessment.

Section 42 (pre-corporation tax self-assessment version)

2—(1) (*amended* TMA 1970 s 42(5) *and repealed* s 42(5A), (10A), *before substitution of* s 42 by FA 1994 ss 196, 199, Sch 19 para 13).

(2) This paragraph has effect in relation to tax credits in respect of distributions made on or after 6th April 1999.

Section 42 (corporation tax self-assessment version)

3 ...

Amendment—This paragraph repealed by FA 1998 s 165, Sch 27 Part III(28) with effect for accounting periods ending after 30 June 1999 (by virtue of Finance Act 1994, Section 199, (Appointed Day) Order, SI 1998/3173 art 2).

THE TAXES ACT 1988
Section 231

4—(1) (*amends* TA 1988 s 231(1)).

(2) This paragraph has effect in relation to distributions made on or after 6th April 1999.

Section 232

5—(1) (*repeals* TA 1988 s 232(2), (3)).

(2) This paragraph has effect in relation to distributions made on or after 6th April 1999.

Section 233

6—(1) Section 233 of the Taxes Act 1988 (taxation of certain recipients of distributions and in respect of non-qualifying distributions) shall be amended as follows.

(2)–(4) (*amend* TA 1988 s 233(1)–(1B), (2)).

(5) This paragraph has effect in relation to distributions made on or after 6th April 1999.

Sections 235 to 237

7—(1) (*repeals* TA 1988 ss 235–237).

(2) This paragraph has effect in relation to distributions made on or after 6th April 1999.

Section 238

8 ...

Amendment—This paragraph repealed by FA 1998 ss 31(5), 165, Sch 3 para 45 and Sch 27 Pt III(2) with the effect that the prospective amendment of TA 1988 s 238(1) does not take effect.

Section 241

9 ...

Amendment—This paragraph repealed by FA 1998 ss 31(5), 165, Sch 3 para 46 and Sch 27 Pt III(2) with the effect that the prospective substitution of TA 1988 s 241(2) does not take effect.

Section 249

10—(1) Section 249 of the Taxes Act 1988 (stock dividends treated as income) shall be amended as follows.

(2), (3) (*amend* TA 1988 s 249(4), (6)).

(4) This paragraph has effect in relation to share capital, within the meaning of section 249 of the Taxes Act 1988, issued on or after 6th April 1999.

Section 421

11—(1) (*amends* TA 1988 s 421(1)).

(2) This paragraph has effect in relation to the release or writing off of the whole or part of a debt on or after 6th April 1999.

Section 469

12—(1) Section 469 of the Taxes Act 1988 (unit trusts other than authorised unit trusts) shall be amended as follows.

(2)–(4) (*amend* TA 1988 s 469(2), (9) and *insert* s 469(2A), (2B)).

(5) This paragraph has effect in relation to distributions made on or after 6th April 1999.

Section 549

13—(1) (*amends* TA 1988 s 549(2)).

(2) This paragraph has effect for the year 1999–00 and subsequent years of assessment.

Section 660C

14—(1) Section 660C of the Taxes Act 1988 (settlements where the settlor retains an interest: nature of the charge on settlor) shall be amended as follows.

(2), (3) (*amend* TA 1988 s 660C(1) and *insert* s 660C(1A)).

(4) This paragraph has effect for the year 1999–00 and subsequent years of assessment.

Cross references—See FA 2000 s 46(2) (exemption under FA 2000 s 46(1) for income of a charity is not granted in respect of income chargeable to tax under Schedule D Case VI by virtue of this paragraph).

Section 687

15—(1) In section 687 of the Taxes Act 1988 (payments under discretionary trusts) subsection (3) (amounts which may be set against the amount assessable on trustees) shall be amended as follows.

(2)–(4) (*amend* TA 1988 s 687(3)).

(5) This paragraph has effect for the year 1999–00 and subsequent years of assessment.

Section 689B

16—(1) Section 689B of the Taxes Act 1988 (order in which expenses of trustees are to be set against income) shall be amended as follows.

(2)–(5) (*amend* TA 1988 s 689B(1), (2), (3) and *insert* s 689B(2A)).

(6) This paragraph has effect for the year 1999–00 and subsequent years of assessment.

Section 699

17—(1) (*amends* TA 1988 s 699(2)).

(2) This paragraph has effect for the year 1999–00 and subsequent years of assessment.

Section 703

18 ...

Amendment—This paragraph repealed by FA 1998 ss 31(5), 165, Sch 3 para 47 and Sch 27 Pt III(2) with the effect that the prospective amendment of TA 1988 s 703(5)(*b*) does not take effect.

Section 709

19—(1) (*amends* TA 1988 s 709(2A)).

(2) This paragraph has effect for the year 1999–00 and subsequent years of assessment.

Section 743

20—(1) Section 743 of the Taxes Act 1988 (provisions supplemental to section 739 etc) shall be amended as follows.

(2), (3) (*amend* TA 1988 s 743(1) and *insert* s 743(1A)).

(4) This paragraph has effect for the year 1999–00 and subsequent years of assessment.

Section 819

21—(1) (*amends* TA 1988 s 819(2)).

(2) This paragraph has effect for the year 1999–00 and subsequent years of assessment.

Section 832

22—(1) (*amends* TA 1988 s 832(1)).

(2) This paragraph has effect for the year 1999–00 and subsequent years of assessment.

Schedule 13

23 ...

Amendment—This paragraph repealed by FA 1998 ss 31(5), 165, Sch 3 para 48 and Sch 27 Pt III(2) with the effect that the prospective amendment of TA 1988 Sch 13 paras 2, 4 does not take effect.

THE TAXATION OF CHARGEABLE GAINS ACT 1992

Section 4

24—(1) Section 4 of the Taxation of Chargeable Gains Act 1992 (rates of capital gains tax) shall be amended as follows.

(2), (3) (*amend* TCGA 1992 s 4(2), (3)).

(4), (5) ...¹

(6) This paragraph has effect for the year of assessment 1999–00 and subsequent years of assessment.

Amendment—¹ Sub-paras (4), (5) (which amended TCGA 1992 s 4(3A), (3B)) repealed by FA 1999 s 139, Sch 20 Pt III(1) with effect from the year 1999–00.

Section 6

25—(1) (*amends* TCGA 1992 s 6(3)).

(2) This paragraph has effect for the year of assessment 1999–00 and subsequent years of assessment.

PART II

INSURANCE COMPANIES AND LLOYD'S UNDERWRITERS

THE TAXES ACT 1988
Section 231B

26—(1) (*amends* TA 1988 s 231B(4)).

(2) This paragraph has effect in relation to distributions made on or after 6th April 1999.

Section 434

27—(1) (*amends* TA 1988 s 434(1A)).

(2) This paragraph has effect in relation to distributions made on or after 6th April 1999.

Section 441A

28—(1) (*repeals* TA 1988 s 441A(2)–(8)).

(2) This paragraph has effect in relation to distributions made on or after 6th April 1999.

Schedule 19AC

29—(1) Schedule 19AC to the Taxes Act 1988 (overseas life insurance companies) shall be amended as follows.

(2) (*amends* TA 1988 Sch 19AC para 9(1)).

(3) (*repeals* TA 1988 Sch 19AC para 11A(2)).

(4) This paragraph has effect in relation to distributions made on or after 6th April 1999.

THE FINANCE ACT 1993
Schedule 20

30—(1) (*repeals* FA 1993 Sch 20 para 9(3) *and amends* Sch 20 para 11(3)).

(2) Sub-paragraph (1) above has effect in relation to distributions made on or after 6th April 1999.

SCHEDULE 5

LIMITATION OF ENTITLEMENT TO RELIEF UNDER SECTION 35
Section 35

PART I

QUALIFYING DISTRIBUTIONS OTHER THAN BONUS ISSUES

1 This Part of this Schedule applies where a person ("the claimant")—

(*a*) would, apart from paragraph 2 below, be entitled to a payment under section 35(1) of this Act in respect of a distribution, and

(*b*) his holding (together with any associated holding) of any one class of the shares, securities or rights by virtue of which he is entitled to the distribution amounts to not less than 10 per cent of that class.

2 Where this Part of this Schedule applies, if any part of the distribution is not a part—

(*a*) to which profits arising after the date of acquisition are attributable in accordance with section 236 of the Taxes Act 1988, or

(*b*) in relation to which the date of acquisition is earlier than 6th April 1965,

then no payment under section 35(1) of this Act shall be made to the claimant in respect of the distribution.

3 This Part of this Schedule applies to any qualifying distribution except any amount which is treated as such in accordance with section 209(3) or sections 210 and 211 of the Taxes Act 1988.

4 Notwithstanding the repeal of sections 235 and 236 of the Taxes Act 1988 by this Act, section 236 of the Taxes Act 1988 as it applies in relation to distributions made before 6th April 1999 shall continue to apply for the purposes of this Part of this Schedule as it applies for the purposes of section 235 of the Taxes Act 1988 in relation to such distributions.

5 For the purposes of this Part of this Schedule and section 236 of the Taxes Act 1988 as it applies by virtue of paragraph 4 above, the date of acquisition, in relation to any part of a distribution or profits attributable to it, is the date on which the shares, securities or rights by virtue of which a person is entitled to that part were acquired by him.

PART II
BONUS ISSUES

6 A person (''the claimant'') who receives an amount treated as a distribution by virtue of section 209(3), 210 or 211(1) of the Taxes Act 1988 (''a bonus issue'') shall not be entitled to a payment under section 35(1) of this Act in respect of that distribution, except to the extent that paragraph 7 below otherwise provides.

7 Paragraph 6 above shall not affect a person's entitlement to a payment under section 35 of this Act in respect of that part (if any) of a bonus issue made in respect of any shares or securities which, if it had been declared as a dividend, would represent a normal return to the claimant—

(a) on the consideration provided by him for the relevant shares or securities, that is to say, those in respect of which the bonus issue was made; and

(b) if the relevant shares or securities are derived from shares or securities previously acquired by the claimant, on the shares or securities which were previously acquired.

8 For the purposes of paragraph 7 above—

(a) if the consideration provided by the claimant for any of the relevant shares or securities was in excess of their market value at the time he acquired them, or if no consideration was provided by him for any of the relevant shares or securities, the claimant shall be taken to have provided for those shares or securities consideration equal to their market value at the time he acquired them; and

(b) in determining whether an amount received by way of dividend exceeds a normal return, regard shall be had to the length of time previous to the receipt of that amount since the claimant first acquired any of the relevant shares or securities and to any dividends and other distributions made in respect of them during that time.

SCHEDULE 6

FOREIGN INCOME DIVIDENDS

Section 36

Commentary—*Simon's Direct Tax Service* **D1.701.**

Section 13 of the Taxes Act 1988

1—(1) Section 13 of the Taxes Act 1988 (small companies' relief) shall be amended as follows.

(2) (*amended* TA 1988 s 13(7) *before substitution by* FA 1998 Sch 3 para 7).

(3) (*repeals* TA 1988 s 13(8A)).

(4) This paragraph has effect for accounting periods beginning on or after 6th April 1999.

Section 75 of the Taxes Act 1988

2—(1) Section 75 of the Taxes Act 1988 (expenses of management: investment companies) shall be amended as follows.

(2), (3) (*amend* TA 1988 s 75(2) and *repeal* s 75(6)).

(4) This paragraph has effect in relation to distributions made on or after 6th April 1999.

Chapter VA of Part VI of the Taxes Act 1988

3—(1) (*repeals* TA 1988 ss 246A–246Y).

(2) The repeal of sections 246A to 246E and 246G of the Taxes Act 1988 has effect in relation to distributions made on or after 6th April 1999.

(3) The repeal of sections 246F, 246H to 246J and 246N to 246Y of the Taxes Act 1988 has effect for accounting periods beginning on or after 6th April 1999.

(4) The repeal of sections 246K to 246M of the Taxes Act 1988 has effect for accounting periods of the parent (within the meaning of those sections) beginning on or after 6th April 1999.

Section 247 of the Taxes Act 1988

4—(1) (*repeals* TA 1988 s 247(5A)–(5D)).

(2) This paragraph has effect in relation to distributions made on or after 6th April 1999.

Section 431 of the Taxes Act 1988

5—(1) (*amends* TA 1988 s 431(2)).

(2) This paragraph has effect for accounting periods beginning on or after 6th April 1999.

Section 434 of the Taxes Act 1988

6—(1) Section 434 of the Taxes Act 1988 (franked investment income etc) shall be amended as follows.

(2), (3) (*repeal* TA 1988 s 434(3B)–(3D) and *amend* s 434(6A)).

(4) This paragraph has effect for accounting periods beginning on or after 6th April 1999.

Section 458 of the Taxes Act 1988

7—(1) (*amends* TA 1988 s 458(2)).

(2) This paragraph has effect in relation to distributions made on or after 6th April 1999.

Chapter III of Part XII of the Taxes Act 1988

8—(1) (*repeals* TA 1988 s 468H(5) and *amends* s 468H(6)).

(2) (*amends* TA 1988 s 468I(2) and *repeals* s 468I(3), (5), (5A), (7)).

(3) (*amends* TA 1988 s 468J(1), (2) and *repeals* s 468J(3)).

(4) (*repeals* TA 1988 s 468K).

(5) (*amends* TA 1988 s 468M(5)).

(6) (*amends* TA 1988 s 468Q(2), (3) and *repeals* s 468Q(4)).

(7) (*repeals* TA 1988 s 468R).

(8) Sub-paragraphs (1)(*a*), (5) and (6) above have effect for distribution periods beginning on or after 6th April 1999.

(9) Sub-paragraphs (1)(*b*), (2) to (4) and (7) above have effect for distribution periods the distribution date for which falls on or after 6th April 1999.

Section 490 of the Taxes Act 1988

9—(1) Section 490 of the Taxes Act 1988 (companies carrying on a mutual business or not carrying on a business) shall be amended as follows.

(2)–(4) (*amend* TA 1988 s 490(1), (4) and *repeal* s 490(5)).

(5) This paragraph has effect in relation to distributions made on or after 6th April 1999.

Section 687 of the Taxes Act 1988

10—(1) (*amends* TA 1988 s 687(3)).

(2) This paragraph has effect in relation to distributions made on or after 6th April 1999.

Section 689B of the Taxes Act 1988

11—(1) (*amends* TA 1988 s 689B(2)).

(2) This paragraph has effect in relation to distributions made on or after 6th April 1999.

Section 699A of the Taxes Act 1988

12—(1) (*amends* TA 1988 s 699A(1), (4)).

(2) This paragraph has effect in relation to distributions made on or after 6th April 1999.

Section 701 of the Taxes Act 1988

13—(1) (*amends* TA 1988 s 701(8)).

(2) This paragraph has effect in relation to distributions made on or after 6th April 1999.

Section 731 of the Taxes Act 1988

14—(1) Section 731 of the Taxes Act 1988 (application and interpretation of sections 732 to 734) shall be amended as follows.

(2), (3) (*amend* TA 1988 s 731(9A) and *repeal* s 731(9B)–(9D)).

(4) This paragraph has effect in relation to distributions made on or after 6th April 1999.

Section 802 of the Taxes Act 1988

15—(1) Section 802 of the Taxes Act 1988 (UK insurance companies trading overseas) shall be amended as follows.

(2), (3) (*amend* TA 1988 s 802(2) and *repeal* s 802(4)).

(4) This paragraph has effect in relation to distributions made on or after 6th April 1999.

Schedule 13 to the Taxes Act 1988

16—(1) Schedule 13 to the Taxes Act 1988 shall be amended as follows.

(2) (*amends* TA 1988 Sch 13 para 1(1)).

(3)–(10) (*amend* TA 1988 Sch 13 paras 1(4), 2(1), 3, 4(2), 7(3) and *repeal* Sch 13 paras 2(5), (6), 3A, 3B, 4A, 6A).

(11) (*repeals* TA 1988 Sch 13 para 9A).

(12) Sub-paragraph (2) above has effect for accounting periods beginning on or after 6th April 1999.

(13) Sub-paragraphs (3) to (10) above have effect for return periods beginning on or after 6th April 1999.

(14) Sub-paragraph (11) above has effect in relation to manufactured dividends which are representative of dividends paid on or after 6th April 1999.

Schedule 23A to the Taxes Act 1988

17—(1) Schedule 23A to the Taxes Act 1988 (manufactured dividends and interest) shall be amended as follows.

(2)–(4) (*repeal* TA 1988 Sch 23A para 1(1), 2B and *amend* Sch 23A para 2(6)).

(5) This paragraph has effect in relation to manufactured dividends which are representative of dividends paid on or after 6th April 1999.

Section 88A of the Finance Act 1989

18—(1) (*amends* FA 1989 s 88A(3)).

(2) This paragraph has effect in relation to distributions made on or after 6th April 1999.

Section 89 of the Finance Act 1989

19—(1) Section 89 of the Finance Act 1989 (policy holders' share of profits) shall be amended as follows.

(2), (3) (*amend* FA 1989 s 89(2) and *repeal* s 89(2A)).

(4) This paragraph has effect in relation to distributions made on or after 6th April 1999.

Section 171 of the Finance Act 1993

20—(1) Section 171 of the Finance Act 1993 (taxation of profits and allowance of losses of Lloyd's underwriters) shall be amended as follows.

(2) (*repeals* FA 1993 s 171(2A)).

(3) This paragraph has effect in relation to distributions made on or after 6th April 1999.

Schedule 7 to the Finance Act 1997

21—(1) Schedule 7 to the Finance Act 1997 shall be amended as follows.

(2), (3) (*repeal* FA 1997 Sch 7 paras 2, 4–6).

(4) Sub-paragraphs (2) and (3) above have effect in relation to distributions made on or after 6th April 1999.

Transitional provisions

22—(1) Where, in the case of an accounting period of a company beginning before 6th April 1999 and ending on or after 5th April 1999 (''a transitional period''), there would (apart from this sub-paragraph) be such an excess as is mentioned in section 246F(3) of the Taxes Act 1988, no such excess shall be deemed to have arisen.

(2) In their application in relation to foreign income dividends paid in an accounting period of a company beginning before 6th April 1999, sections 246J(5) and 246K(10) of the Taxes Act 1988 shall have effect as if the reference to any subsequent accounting period—

    (*a*) included an accounting period which immediately follows a transitional period, but
    (*b*) did not include any later accounting period.

23 Where a foreign income dividend paid by a company before 6th April 1999—

    (*a*) is received by a person on or after that date, and
    (*b*) is not one in relation to which section 246D of the Taxes Act 1988 applies,

the recipient shall be treated, for all purposes of the Tax Acts, as receiving instead a qualifying distribution made by a company resident in the United Kingdom of an amount equal to nine tenths of the amount of the foreign income dividend.

SCHEDULE 7

RESTRICTIONS ON GROUP RELIEF

Section 41

Commentary—*Simon's Direct Tax Service* **D2.645.**

Introductory

1 Chapter IV of Part X of the Taxes Act 1988 (group relief) shall be amended in accordance with paragraphs 2 to 7 below.

New limits

2 (*inserts* TA 1988 ss 403A–403C).

Consequential amendments

3 ...

Amendments—This paragraph repealed by FA 1998 s 165, Sch 27 Part III(4) with effect for income tax for the year 1998–99 and subsequent years of assessment, and for corporation tax from 1 April 1998 subject to transitional provisions in FA 1998 Sch 5 Part IV. Originally this paragraph repealed TA 1988 s 403(9).

4 (*amends* TA 1988 s 405(4)).

5 (*amends* TA 1988 s 406(2), (3), (6)–(8)).

6 (*repeals* TA 1988 ss 408–409, and s 411(2)–(9)).

7 (*inserts* TA 1988 s 413(2A)).

8 (*amends* TCGA 1992 s 179(4)).

Commencement

9—(1) This Schedule has effect, subject to sub-paragraphs (2) to (4) below, in relation to any claim for group relief if—

    (*a*) the accounting period of the claimant company for which relief is claimed, or

    (*b*) the accounting period of the surrendering company to which that claim relates,

is an accounting period ending on or after 2nd July 1997.

(2) This Schedule does not apply in relation to any claim for group relief for which the overlapping period for the purposes of section 403A of the Taxes Act 1988 would be a period falling entirely before 2nd July 1997.

(3) Where in the case of any claim for group relief the overlapping period begins before but ends on or after 2nd July 1997, the maximum amount which in the claimant's case is allowable on that claim by way of group relief shall (instead of being determined in accordance with this Schedule) be the amount determined by—

    (*a*) taking the maximum amount that would have been allowable on that claim if this Schedule had not been enacted; and

    (*b*) reducing that amount by the amount (if any) of the relief withdrawn in respect of the part of the claimant company's accounting period beginning with 2nd July 1997.

(4) For the purposes of sub-paragraph (3) above the relief withdrawn in respect of the part of the claimant company's accounting period beginning with 2nd July 1997 is the amount (if any) by which the amount specified in paragraph (*a*) below exceeds the amount specified in paragraph (*b*) below, that is to say—

    (*a*) the maximum amount which would have been allowable by way of group relief on the claimant company's claim if this Schedule had not been enacted but it were assumed that the qualifying conditions were not satisfied in relation to that claim at any time before 2nd July 1997; and

    (*b*) the maximum amount which would be allowable by way of group relief on that claim if that were assumed but relief fell to be given in accordance with Chapter IV of Part X of the Taxes Act 1988 as amended by this Schedule.

(5) For the purposes of sub-paragraph (4) above an assumption in relation to any claim that the qualifying conditions were not satisfied at a particular time is an assumption that, at that time, the claimant company and the surrendering company—

    (*a*) were not both members of the same group; and

    (*b*) did not satisfy in relation to each other the conditions specified in section 402(3) of the Taxes Act 1988 for the making of a consortium claim.

FINANCE ACT 1998

(1998 Chapter 36)

ARRANGEMENT OF SECTIONS

PART III
INCOME TAX, CORPORATION TAX AND CAPITAL GAINS TAX

CHAPTER I
INCOME TAX AND CORPORATION TAX

CHAPTER II

TAXATION OF CHARGEABLE GAINS

An Act to grant certain duties, to alter other duties, and to amend the law relating to the National Debt and the Public Revenue, and to make further provision in connection with Finance.

[31 July 1998]

PART III

INCOME TAX, CORPORATION TAX AND CAPITAL GAINS TAX

CHAPTER I

INCOME TAX AND CORPORATION TAX

Income tax charge, rates and reliefs

25 Charge and rates for 1998–99

(Spent).

Commentary—*Simon's Direct Tax Service* E1.102.

26 Relief for a woman with a child and an incapacitated husband

Commentary—*Simon's Direct Tax Service* E2.105.
Amendments—This section repealed by FA 1999 s 139, Sch 20 Pt III(4) with effect from the year 2000–01.

27 Married couple's allowance etc in and after 1999–00

(1) (*Amends* TA 1988 ss 256(2)(*a*), 347B(5A)(*a*)).

(2) (*spent*).

Commentary—*Simon's Direct Tax Service* E2.105

Corporation tax charge and rates

28 Charge and rates for financial year 1998

(*Spent*).

Commentary—*Simon's Direct Tax Service* D2.108.

29 Charge and rates for financial year 1999

(*Spent*)

Commentary—*Simon's Direct Tax Service* D2 108.

Corporation tax: periodic payments etc

30 Corporation tax: due and payable date

(1) (*inserts* TMA 1970 s 59E).

(2) The Treasury may by regulations make provision for or in connection with the payment to the Board of an amount or amounts determined by or under the regulations in any case where, on or after 25th November 1997 and before 30th June 2002, a company takes any action specified in the regulations which has the effect—

(*a*) of delaying the application, or

(*b*) of delaying or avoiding the full effect,

in relation to the company of any regulations made under section 59E of the Taxes Management Act 1970.

(3) Any amount determined by or under regulations under this section shall be computed as if it were interest on a sum determined by or under the regulations; and any amount so determined shall be treated for the purposes of the Tax Acts as if it were interest due to the Board.

(4) The action which may be specified in regulations under this section includes—

(*a*) a change by a company in the date or dates on which any of its accounting periods begin or end; or

(*b*) a transfer by a company of any property, rights or liabilities to a company which belongs to the same group as that company.

(5) In subsection (4) above "group" means a company which has one or more 51 per cent. subsidiaries together with that or those subsidiaries.

(6) Regulations under this section—

(*a*) may make different provision in relation to different cases or in relation to companies of different descriptions;

(*b*) may make such supplementary, incidental, consequential or transitional provision as appears to the Treasury to be necessary or expedient.

Commentary—*Simon's Direct Tax Service* D2.841, 842.
Regulations—Corporation Tax (Instalment Payments) Regulations, SI 1998/3175.

31 Abolition of advance corporation tax

(1) No company resident in the United Kingdom shall be liable to pay advance corporation tax in respect of any qualifying distribution made on or after 6th April 1999.

(2) For the purposes of the Tax Acts, no distribution made on or after 6th April 1999 shall be treated as giving rise to the making of a franked payment.

(3) No franked investment income which is attributable to a distribution made on or after 6th April 1999 shall be used to frank any distributions of a company.

(4) Section 238(3) of the Taxes Act 1988 shall apply for the purposes of subsection (3) above as it applies for the purposes of Chapter V of Part VI of that Act.

(5) Schedule 3 to this Act (which makes provision for and in connection with the abolition of advance corporation tax) shall have effect.

Commentary—*Simon's Direct Tax Service* D1.302.

32 Unrelieved surplus advance corporation tax

(1) The Treasury may by regulations make provision for or in connection with enabling unrelieved surplus advance corporation tax to be set against liability to corporation tax on profits charged to corporation tax for accounting periods ending on or after 6th April 1999 (and thus to discharge a corresponding amount of any such liability).

(2) Without prejudice to the generality of subsection (1) above, regulations under this section may make provision—

(*a*) for or in connection with imposing a limit or limits on the amount of unrelieved surplus advance corporation tax which may be set against liability to corporation tax on profits charged to corporation tax for an accounting period;

(*b*) for or in connection with the carrying forward of unrelieved surplus advance corporation tax from earlier accounting periods to later accounting periods;

(*c*) for or in connection with the recovery of corporation tax from companies in prescribed circumstances where any such liability as is mentioned in paragraph (*a*) above is or has been discharged by the set-off of unrelieved surplus advance corporation tax;

(*d*) for or in connection with the reduction or extinguishment of unrelieved surplus advance corporation tax;

(*e*) for or in connection with treating notional amounts of advance corporation tax ("shadow ACT") as paid by companies in respect of distributions made on or after 6th April 1999;

(*f*) for or in connection with the determination of amounts of shadow ACT which are treated as paid by companies in respect of distributions made on or after 6th April 1999;

(*g*) in relation to the treatment of shadow ACT;

(*h*) in relation to the treatment of companies which have prescribed relationships or connections with each other;

(*i*) in relation to the treatment of prescribed events, arrangements or transactions involving companies with unrelieved surplus advance corporation tax.

(3) The provision which may be made by regulations under this section includes provision—

(*a*) for or in connection with treating shadow ACT as reducing any limit or limits on the amount of unrelieved surplus advance corporation tax which may be set against any such liability as is mentioned in subsection (2)(*a*) above;

(*b*) for or in connection with the carrying forward of shadow ACT from earlier accounting periods to later accounting periods;

(*c*) for or in connection with the carrying back of shadow ACT from later accounting periods to earlier accounting periods;

(*d*) for or in connection with the transfer of shadow ACT between companies;

(*e*) for or in connection with the reduction or extinguishment of shadow ACT.

(4) The provision which may be made by virtue of subsection (2)(*c*) above includes provision for or in connection with the recovery of corporation tax from a company which has a prescribed relationship or connection with a company whose liability to corporation tax is or has been discharged by the set-off of unrelieved surplus advance corporation tax.

(5) The provision which may be made by regulations under this section includes provision for or in connection with enabling unrelieved surplus advance corporation tax to be set against liability to a sum chargeable under section 747(4)(*a*) of the Taxes Act 1988 (controlled foreign companies) as if it were an amount of corporation tax for an accounting period.

(6) In this section "unrelieved surplus advance corporation tax" means the advance corporation tax (if any) which, apart from sub-paragraph (3) of [paragraph 12][1] of Schedule 3 to this Act but otherwise in accordance with that paragraph, would be treated by virtue of section 239(4) of the Taxes Act 1988 as paid in respect of distributions made by a company in the first accounting period of the company to begin on or after 6th April 1999.

(7) The reference in subsection (6) above to an accounting period beginning on or after 6th April 1999 includes a reference to a separate accounting period mentioned in section 245(2) of the Taxes Act 1988 which begins on 6th April 1999.

(8) Regulations under this section—

(*a*) may make such modifications of any provisions of the Tax Acts, or

(*b*) may apply such provisions of the Tax Acts,

as the Treasury think necessary or expedient for or in connection with giving effect to the provisions of this section.

(9) Regulations under this section which apply any provisions of the Tax Acts may apply those provisions either without modifications or with such modifications as the Treasury think necessary or expedient for or in connection with giving effect to the provisions of this section.

(10) Regulations under this section—

(*a*) may make different provision for different purposes, cases or circumstances;

(*b*) may make different provision in relation to companies or accounting periods of different descriptions;

(*c*) may make such supplementary, incidental, consequential or transitional provision as appears to the Treasury to be necessary or expedient.

(11) Regulations under this section may make provision in relation to accounting periods beginning before (as well as accounting periods beginning on or after) the date on which the regulations are made.

(12) In this section—

"modifications" includes amendments, additions and omissions;

"prescribed" means prescribed by regulations made under this section.

Commentary—*Simon's Direct Tax Service* D1.312.
Regulations—Corporation Tax (Treatment of Unrelieved Surplus Advance Corporation Tax) Regulations, SI 1999/358.
Revenue and other press releases—IR 16-2-99 (operation of "shadow" ACT rules, with worked example).
Amendments—[1] Words in sub-s (6) substituted by FA 1999 s 91(4), (5) and deemed always to have had effect.

33 Relief for interest payable under the Tax Acts

(1) Section 90 of the Taxes Management Act 1970 (interest on overdue tax to be paid without deduction of income tax and not to be allowed as a deduction in computing income, profits or losses) shall be amended as follows.

(2) (*amends* TMA 1970 s 90).

(3) (*amends* TMA 1970 s 90(1)(*b*)).

(4) (*inserts* TMA 1970 s 90(2)).

(5) The amendments made by subsections (3) and (4) above have effect in relation to—

    (*a*) interest on corporation tax for accounting periods ending on or after the day appointed under section 199 of the Finance Act 1994 for the purposes of Chapter III of Part IV of that Act (corporation tax self-assessment); and

    (*b*) interest on tax assessable in accordance with Schedule 13 or 16 to the Taxes Act 1988 for return periods in accounting periods ending on or after that day.

Commentary—*Simon's Direct Tax Service* **D2.844.**
Note—The appointed day for the purposes of sub-s (5) is 1 July 1999, by virtue of the Finance Act 1994, Section 199, (Appointed Day) Order, SI 1998/3173.

34 Charge to tax on interest payable under the Tax Acts

(1) Section 826 of the Taxes Act 1988 (interest on tax overpaid) shall be amended as follows.

(2) (*amends* TA 1988 s 826(5)).

(3) (*amends* TA 1988 s 826(5)(*b*)).

(4) (*inserts* TA 1988 s 826(5A)).

(5) The amendments made by subsections (3) and (4) above have effect in relation to interest payable by virtue of any paragraph of section 826(1) of the Taxes Act 1988 if the accounting period mentioned in that paragraph is one which ends on or after the day appointed under section 199 of the Finance Act 1994 for the purposes of Chapter III of Part IV of that Act (corporation tax self-assessment).

Commentary—*Simon's Direct Tax Service* **D2.845.**
Note—The appointed day for the purposes of sub-s (5) is 1 July 1999, by virtue of the Finance Act 1994, Section 199, (Appointed Day) Order, SI 1998/3173.

35 Further provision about interest payable under the Tax Acts

Schedule 4 to this Act (which makes further amendments relating to interest payable under the Tax Acts by or to companies) shall have effect.

Commentary—*Simon's Direct Tax Service* **D2.844, 845.**

36 Arrangements with respect to payment of corporation tax

(1) The Board may enter into arrangements with some or all of the members of a group of companies for one of those members to discharge any liability of each of those members to pay corporation tax for the accounting periods to which the arrangements relate.

(2) Any such arrangements—

    (*a*) may make provision in relation to cases where companies become or cease to be members of a group of companies;

    (*b*) may make provision in relation to the discharge of liability to pay interest or penalties;

    (*c*) may make provision in relation to the discharge of liability to pay any amount treated as corporation tax;

    (*d*) may make provision for or in connection with the termination of the arrangements;

    (*e*) may make such supplementary, incidental, consequential or transitional provision as is necessary or expedient for the purposes of the arrangements.

(3) Any such arrangements—

    (*a*) shall not affect the liability to corporation tax, or to pay corporation tax, of any company to which the arrangements relate; and

    (*b*) shall not affect any other liability of any such company under the Tax Acts.

(4) For the purposes of this section a company and all its 51 per cent. subsidiaries form a group of companies and, if any of those subsidiaries have 51 per cent. subsidiaries, the group of companies includes them and their 51 per cent. subsidiaries, and so on.

(5) The reference in subsection (2)(*c*) above to any amount treated as corporation tax is a reference—

    (*a*) to any amount due from a company under section 419 of the Taxes Act 1988 (loans to participators etc) as if it were an amount of corporation tax chargeable on the company;

    (*b*) to any sum chargeable on a company under section 747(4)(*a*) of the Taxes Act 1988 (controlled foreign companies) as if it were an amount of corporation tax.

Commentary—*Simon's Direct Tax Service* **D2.843.**

Gilt-edged securities

37 Abolition of periodic accounting

(1) (*repeals* TA 1988 s 51B).

(2) (*amends* TA 1988 Sch 19AB para 3(1C); *repealed by* FA 2001 s 110, Sch 33 Pt II(12) with effect in accordance with FA 2001 s 87).

(3) The preceding provisions of this section have effect in relation only to payments of interest falling due on or after such day as the Treasury may by order appoint.

Commentary—*Simon's Direct Tax Service* **A7.1115.**
Note—The appointed day for the purposes of this section is 1 April 1999, by virtue of the Finance Act 1998, Section 37, (Appointed Day) Order, SI 1999/619.

Rents and other receipts from land

38 Taxation of rents and other receipts from land

(1) The provisions of Schedule 5 to this Act have effect with respect to tax on rents and other receipts from land.

Part I contains amendments relating to the charge to tax under Schedule A or Case V of Schedule D on rents and other receipts from land.
Part II contains amendments about relief for losses incurred in a Schedule A business or overseas property business, and the relationship between such relief and other reliefs.
Part III contains minor and consequential amendments.

(2) So far as relating to income tax, the provisions of Parts I to III of that Schedule have effect for the year 1998-99 and subsequent years of assessment.

(3) So far as relating to corporation tax, the provisions of Parts I to III of that Schedule come into force on 1st April 1998, subject to the transitional provisions in Part IV of the Schedule.

Commentary—*Simon's Direct Tax Service* **A4.102.**

39 Land managed as one estate and maintenance funds for historic buildings

Sections 26 and 27 of the Taxes Act 1988 (deductions from rent: land managed as one estate and maintenance funds for historic buildings) shall cease to have effect—

   (*a*) for income tax purposes, on and after 6th April 2001;
   (*b*) for corporation tax purposes, for accounting periods beginning on or after 1st April 2001.

Commentary—*Simon's Direct Tax Service* **A4.311, 312.**

40 Treatment of premiums as rent

(1)–(4) (*amend* TA 1988 s 34(1), (4), (5)).

(5) The above amendments have effect in relation to amounts treated as received under section 34 of the Taxes Act 1988 on or after 17th March 1998.

Commentary—*Simon's Direct Tax Service* **A4.201, 202.**

41 Tied premises: receipts and expenses treated as those of trade

(1) (*substitutes* TA 1988 s 98).

(2) (*substitutes* TCGA 1992 s 156(4)).

(3) The above amendments have effect on and after 17th March 1998, subject to the following transitional provisions.
In those provisions–
   "before commencement" and "after commencement" mean, respectively, before 17th March 1998 and on or after that date; and
   "the new section 98" means the section as substituted by subsection (1) above.

(4) To the extent that receipts or expenses have been taken into account before commencement, they shall not be taken into account again under the new section 98 after commencement.

(5) To the extent that receipts or expenses would under the new section 98 have been brought into account before commencement, and were not so brought into account, they shall be brought into account immediately after commencement.

(6) If any estate, interest or rights in or over land is or are transferred from one person to another, the references in subsections (4) and (5) above to receipts or expenses being taken into account shall be construed as references to their being taken into account in relation to either of those persons.

(7) For the purposes of those subsections an amount is "taken into account" if—
   (*a*) it is brought into account for tax purposes, or
   (*b*) it would have been so brought into account if the person concerned were chargeable to tax.

42 Computation of profits of trade, profession or vocation

(1) For the purposes of Case I or II of Schedule D the profits of a trade, profession or vocation must be computed [in accordance with generally accepted accounting practice][1], subject to any adjustment required or authorised by law in computing profits for those purposes.

(2) This does not—

(a) require a person to comply with the requirements of the Companies Act 1985 or the Companies (Northern Ireland) Order 1986 except as to the basis of computation, or

(b) impose any requirements as to audit or disclosure.

(3) This section applies to periods of account beginning after 6th April 1999.

A period of account beginning on or before 6th April 1999 which is still current on 7th April 2000 shall be treated for the purposes of this section as having ended on 6th April 1999 and a new period as having begun on 7th April 1999.

(4) This section is subject to the exemption in section 43 below (barristers and advocates in early years of practice).

(5) This section does not affect provisions of the Tax Acts relating to the computation of the profits of Lloyd's underwriters or companies carrying on life insurance, or otherwise laying down special rules for the computation of the profits of a particular description of business.

Commentary—*Simon's Direct Tax Service* B4.203, 212.
Revenue & other press releases—IR Tax Bulletin December 1998 p 606 (interpretation of "true and fair view" in sub-s (1) above).
Cross-references—See FA 2002 s 65(2) (postponement of charge to mark to market basis in certain cases).
Amendments—[1] Words substituted for the words "on an accounting basis which gives a true and fair view" by FA 2002 s 103(5) with effect from 24 July 2002.

43 Barristers and advocates in early years of practice

(1) The profits of a barrister or advocate in actual practice for a period of account ending not more than seven years after the commencement of such practice may be computed in accordance with this section.

(2) For this purpose barristers and advocates are regarded as commencing in actual practice when they first hold themselves out as available for fee-earning work.

(3) The profits of a barrister or advocate for a period of account to which this section applies may be computed—

(a) on a cash basis, or

(b) by reference to fees earned whose amount has been agreed or in respect of which a fee note has been delivered.

Once a particular basis has been adopted it must be applied consistently.

(4) The exemption given by this section ceases if for any period of account an accounting basis is adopted that complies with section 42 above.

In that case, that section applies to all subsequent periods of account.

Commentary—*Simon's Direct Tax Service* B4.212, 216.

44 Change of accounting basis

(1) The provisions of Schedule 6 to this Act apply where there is a change, from one period of account to the next of a trade, profession or vocation, of the accounting basis on which profits are computed for tax purposes.

(2) The Schedule only applies if the old basis accords with the law and practice applicable immediately before the change and the new basis accords with the law and practice applicable immediately after the change.

(3) The provisions of the Schedule replace section 104(4) of the Taxes Act 1988 and any rule of law as to the adjustments necessary for tax purposes in those circumstances.

(4) They apply to any change of accounting basis taking effect on or after 6th April 1999.

Note—The rules set out in FA 2002 s 64, Sch 22 have effect in place of the provisions of FA 1998 s 44, Sch 6: FA 2002 s 64(6).
Commentary—*Simon's Direct Tax Service* B4.202, 212.
Amendment—This section repealed by FA 2002 s 141, Sch 40 Pt 3(8) with effect in accordance with FA 2002 s 64(6), Sch 22 paras 16, 17.

45 Meaning of "period of account"

In sections 42 to 44 above a "period of account" means any period for which accounts of the trade, profession or vocation are drawn up.

Commentary—*Simon's Direct Tax Service* B4.203.
Amendment—This section repealed by FA 2002 s 141, Sch 40 Pt 3(16) with effect from 24 July 2002.

46 Minor and consequential provisions about computations

(1) In provisions of the Tax Acts relating to the computation of the profits of a trade, profession or vocation references to receipts and expenses are (except where otherwise expressly provided) to any items brought into account as credits or debits in computing such profits.

There is no implication that an amount has been actually received or expended.

(2) Except where otherwise expressly provided, the same rules apply in computing losses of a trade, profession or vocation for any purpose of the Tax Acts as apply in computing profits.

(3) (*amends provisions listed in* FA 1998 Sch 7).

Commentary—*Simon's Direct Tax Service* **B4.203.**

Gifts to charities

47 Gifts in kind for relief in poor countries

Commentary—*Simon's Direct Tax Service* **B3.1445A.**
Regulations—Gifts for Relief in Poor Countries (Designation) Order, SI 1998/1868.
Revenue & other press releases—IR 31-7-98 (Eighty countries eligible for Millennium Gift Aid).
Revenue Internal Guidance—Inspectors manual IM1139 (claim must be made within the time specified and must specify the article given and name of charity to whom it is donated).
Cross references—See TA 1988 s 83A (relief for gifts in kind to charities generally).
Amendment—This section repealed by FA 1999 ss 55(2), (3), 139, Sch 20 Pt III(12) with effect for gifts made after 26 July 1999.

48 Gifts of money for relief in poor countries

(1) This section applies to any gift of a sum of money by an individual to a charity that has given the required notification to the Board if that gift is made—

    (*a*) in the period beginning with [31 July 1998][1] and ending with 31st December 2000; and
    (*b*) in circumstances giving rise to a reasonable expectation that the sum given will be applied for, or in connection with, [one or more][1] of the purposes specified in subsection (2) below.

(2) Those purposes are—

    (*a*) the relief of poverty in any one or more [countries or territories designated for the purposes of this paragraph][1], ...[3]
    (*b*) the advancement of education in any one or more [countries or territories designated for the purposes of this paragraph][1][; and,
    (*c*) the relief of poverty in the case of persons from a country or territory designated for the purposes of this paragraph who are refugees or who have suffered displacement as a result of organised intimidation or oppression or of war or other armed conflict.][1]

(3) *Subject to the following provisions of this section, subsection (2)(g) of section 25 of the Finance Act 1990 (minimum payment for which relief given on gift by an individual) shall have effect in relation to any gift to which this section applies as if for "£250" there were substituted "£100".*[4]

(4) Where—

    (*a*) a relevant gift of less than £100 is made [before 6th April 2000][4] by an individual to a charity that has given the required notification to the Board,
    (*b*) the aggregate of that gift and any one or more subsequent relevant gifts made by that individual to that charity is £100 or more,
    [(*bb*) the subsequent gift, or at least one of the subsequent gifts, is made on or after 6th April 2000;][4]
    (*c*) that individual gives an [appropriate declaration][5] in relation to that aggregate to that charity, and
    (*d*) the condition specified in paragraph (*e*) of subsection (2) of section 25 of the Finance Act 1990 (limit on benefit for the donor) would be satisfied if the aggregated gifts constituted a single gift by that individual to that charity made at the time of the making of the last of them to be made,

the aggregated gifts shall be treated for the purposes of that section [(but subject to sub-section (4A) below)][2] as if they together constituted a single qualifying donation made by that individual to that charity at that time.

[(4A) Subsection (10) of section 25 of the Finance Act 1990 (receipts of gifts by a charity to be treated as payments of grossed-up amounts after deduction of basic rate income tax) shall have effect where—

    (*a*) any aggregated gifts are treated under this section as a single qualifying donation made to a charity, and
    (*b*) the aggregated gifts include gifts made in different years of assessment,

as if that single qualifying donation had been received by the charity in the year of assessment in which the first of the aggregated gifts was made and as if that were the relevant year of assessment for the purposes of that subsection.][2]

(5) The gifts aggregated for the purposes of subsection (4) above must not include either—

(*a*) a relevant gift of £250 or more; or

(*b*) more than one relevant gift of £100 or more.

(6) *The reference in paragraph (c) of subsection (4) above to an appropriate certificate is a reference to a certificate which states—*

(*a*) *that each of the gifts being aggregated qualifies as a relevant gift for the purposes of this section;*

(*b*) *that if those gifts are treated in accordance with this section as a single qualifying donation made at the time specified in subsection (4) above, the single donation will satisfy the taxation condition; and*

(*c*) *that the condition in paragraph (d) of that subsection is satisfied in the case of those gifts taken together.*[4]

(7) *For the purposes of subsection (6) above the taxation condition in the case of any relevant gift is that, either directly or by deduction from profits or gains brought into charge to tax in the relevant year of assessment, the individual making the gift has paid or will pay to the Board income tax of an amount equal to income tax at the basic rate for the relevant year of assessment on the grossed up amount of that gift.*[4]

(8) In this section—

...[3]

[''relevant gift'' means a gift to which this section applies—

(*a*) which satisfies the requirements of subsection (2) of section 25 of the Finance Act 1990 (as amended by section 39 of the Finance Act 2000); or

(*b*) which would satisfy those requirements if paragraph (*e*) of that subsection were disregarded.][6]

and

''required notification'', in relation to a charity, means a notification (including one given before the passing of this Act) which–

(i) is in such form, and contains such information, as may have been required by the Board, and

(ii) contains a statement to the effect that the charity proposes to accept gifts to which this section applies.

(9) A country or territory is a designated country or territory for the purposes of [paragraph (*a*), (*b*), or (*c*) of subsection 2 above][1] if—

(*a*) it is designated as such by an order made for those purposes by the Treasury; or

(*b*) it is of a description specified in an order so made;

and a description specified in such an order may be expressed by reference to the opinion of any person so specified or by reference to the contents from time to time of a document prepared by a person so specified.

(10) Expressions used in this section and in section 25 of the Finance Act 1990 have the same meanings in this section as in that section.

Commentary—*Simon's Direct Tax Service* **E1.504B.**
Regulations—Gifts for Relief in Poor Countries (Designation) Order, SI 1998/1868.
Gifts for Relief in Poor Countries (Designation of Kosovo) Order, SI 1999/2118.
Revenue & other press releases—IR 31-7-98 (Eighty countries eligible for Millennium Gift Aid).
Cross references—See FA 1999 s 56(5) (any Order made under sub-s (9) before the date of Royal Assent has effect only for the purposes of sub-s (2)(*a*), (*b*)).
FA 1999 s 56(8) (any Order made for the purposes of sub-s (2)(*c*) under sub-s (9) may have effect retrospectively for such times falling on or after the date specified in the Order).
Note—Kosovo designated as a territory for the purposes of sub-s (2)(*c*) (Gifts for Relief in Poor Countries (Designation of Kosovo) Order, SI 1999/2118).
Amendments—[1] Words in sub-ss (1)(*a*), (*b*), (2), (9) substituted, and sub-s (2)(*c*) and preceding word ''and'' inserted, by FA 1999 ss 56(1)–(4), (7), 139, with effect for gifts made after 5 April 1999.
[2] Words in sub-s (4), and sub-s (4A), inserted by FA 1999 s 57, and are deemed always to have had effect.
[3] Definition of ''the first designation date'' in sub-s (8), and word ''and'' at the end of sub-s (2)(*a*), repealed by FA 1999 s 139, Sch 20 Pt III(13) with effect for gifts made after 5 April 1999.
[4] Sub-ss (3), (6), (7) repealed, words in sub-s (4)(*a*) and whole of sub-s (4)(*bb*) inserted by FA 2000 ss 42, 156, Sch 40 Pt II(1) with effect from 28 July 2000.
[5] Words in sub-s 4(*c*) substituted for words ''appropriate certificate'' by FA 2000 s 42(2) with effect from 28 July 2000.
[6] Definition of ''relevant gift'' in sub-s 8 substituted by FA 2000 s 42(2) with effect from 28 July 2000.

Employee share incentives

49 Employee share options

(1) (*amends* TA 1988 s 135(2), (5)).

(2) Subsection (1) above has effect in relation to rights obtained on or after 6th April 1998.

Commentary—*Simon's Direct Tax Service* **E4.511.**

50 Conditional acquisition of shares

(1) (*inserts* TA 1988 ss 140A, 140B, 140C).

(2), (3) (*amend* FA 1988 s 77(1) and *insert* s 79(6A)).

(4) The preceding provisions of this section apply in relation to interests acquired on or after 17th March 1998.

Commentary—*Simon's Direct Tax Service* **E4.511.**

51 Convertible shares provided to directors and employees

(1) (*inserts* TA 1988 ss 140D, 140E, 140F).

(2) (*inserts* FA 1988 s 79(6B)).

(3) The preceding provisions of this section apply in relation to shares acquired on or after 17th March 1998.

Commentary—*Simon's Direct Tax Service* **E4.511.**

52 Information powers

(1) (*inserts* TA 1988 s 140G).

(2) (*amends column 2 of Table in* TMA 1970 s 98).

Commentary—*Simon's Direct Tax Service* **E4.511.**

53 Provision supplemental to sections 50 to 52

(*inserts* TA 1988 s 140H).

Commentary—*Simon's Direct Tax Service* **E4.511.**

54 Amendments consequential on sections 50 to 53

(1) The Taxation of Chargeable Gains Act 1992 shall be amended as follows.

(2)–(5) (*insert* TCGA 1992 s 120(5A), (5B), (8), 149B and *amend* s 120(7)).

(6) This section has effect in relation to disposals on or after 17th March 1998 of interests and shares acquired on or after that date.

Commentary—*Simon's Direct Tax Service* **E4.511.**

Construction industry workers

55 Construction workers supplied by agencies

(1) (*repeals* TA 1988 s 134(5)(*c*)).

(2) (*amends* TA 1988 s 559(1) *and inserts* TA 1988 s 559(1A)).

(3) Subsections (1) and (2) above have effect in relation to—

(*a*) any payments made on or after 6th April 1998 other than any made in respect of services rendered before that date; and

(*b*) any payments made before 6th April 1998 in respect of services to be rendered on or after that date.

Commentary—*Simon's Direct Tax Service* **E5.501.**

56 Transitional provisions in connection with section 55

(1) Subject to subsection (6) below, subsection (2) below applies if—

(*a*) a construction trade is being carried on by a person ("the sub-contractor") at the end of the year 1997–98; and

(*b*) there are receipts of that trade which, but for section 134(5)(*c*) of the Taxes Act 1988, would have fallen to be treated for the year 1997–98 as the emoluments of an office or employment.

(2) Where this subsection applies, then, subject to subsections (4) and (5) below—

(*a*) the trade shall be deemed to have been permanently discontinued at the end of the year 1997–98; and

(*b*) to the extent (if any) that the trade includes activities in addition to the rendering of services falling by virtue of section 55 to be treated as the duties of an office or employment, a new trade shall be deemed to have been set up and commenced on 6th April 1998.

(3) Subsection (4) below applies if—

(*a*) a construction trade ("the old trade") is deemed by virtue of subsection (2)(*a*) above to have been permanently discontinued; and

(*b*) a construction trade ("the new trade")–

(i) is deemed by virtue of subsection (2)(*b*) above to have been set up and commenced; or

(ii) (where sub-paragraph (i) above does not apply) is actually set up and commenced in the year 1998–99.

(4) Where this subsection applies then, notwithstanding the deemed discontinuance, the old trade and the new trade shall be treated as the same for the purposes of section 385 of the Taxes Act 1988 (carry-forward of losses against subsequent profits).

(5) An officer of the Board shall not become entitled by virtue of anything in this section to give a direction under paragraph 3(2) of Schedule 20 to the Finance Act 1994 (power to revise assessment so that made on the actual basis) in the case of a person whose trade is deemed under subsection (2) above to cease on 5th April 1998.

(6) Subsection (2) above does not apply if the sub-contractor by notice to an officer of the Board otherwise elects.

(7) An election under subsection (6) above—

(a) if it relates to a trade carried on by an individual, must be included in a return under section 8 of the Taxes Management Act 1970 which is made and delivered in that individual's case on or before the day on which it is required to be made and delivered under that section; and

(b) if it relates to a trade carried on by persons in partnership, must be included in a return under section 12AA of that Act which is made and delivered in the partners' case, or in the case of any one or more of them, on or before the day specified in relation to that return under subsection (2) or (3) of that section.

(8) In this section "construction trade" means a trade consisting in or including the rendering of services under contracts relating to construction operations (within the meaning of Chapter IV of Part XIII of the Taxes Act 1988).

(9) Where at any time on or after 17th March 1998 and before the day on which this Act is passed any election corresponding to an election under subsection (6) above has been made under a resolution of the House of Commons having effect in accordance with the provisions of the Provisional Collection of Taxes Act 1968, this section has effect, on and after the day on which this Act is passed, as if that election were an election under subsection (6) above.

Commentary—*Simon's Direct Tax Service* **E5.501.**

57 Sub-contractors in the construction industry

Schedule 8 to this Act (which makes provision in relation to sub-contractors in the construction industry) shall have effect.

Commentary—*Simon's Direct Tax Service* **E5.502.**

Payments and other benefits in connection with termination of employment etc

58 Payments and other benefits in connection with termination of employment etc

(1) (*substitutes* TA 1988 s 148).

(2) In the Taxes Act 1988, for Schedule 11 (relief as respects tax on payments on retirement or removal from office or employment) substitute the Schedule set out in Part I of Schedule 9 to this Act.

(3) The enactments mentioned in Part II of Schedule 9 to this Act have effect with the amendments specified there which are consequential on this section.

(4) This section applies to payments or other benefits received (within the meaning of section 148 of the Taxes Act 1988 as substituted by subsection (1) above) on or after 6th April 1998, except where the payment or other benefit or the right to receive it has been brought into charge to tax before that date.

Commentary—*Simon's Direct Tax Service* **E4.805.**
Cross reference—See IT (Employments) Regulations, SI 1993/744 reg 46ZA (information provided to the Revenue by employers in respect of termination payments and other benefits exceeding £30,000).

Benefits in kind

59 Car fuel

(1) (*amended* TA 1988 s 158(2) *and is now superseded*).

(2) This section shall have effect for the year 1998–99 and subsequent years of assessment.

Commentary—*Simon's Direct Tax Service* **E4.615.**

60 Reductions for road fuel gas cars

(1)–(5) (*amend* TA 1988 s 168A(1)), (11), 168B(2), 168C(2) and *insert* TA 1988 s 168AB).

(6) This section has effect for the year 1998–99 and subsequent years of assessment.

Commentary—*Simon's Direct Tax Service* **E4.627.**

61 Travelling expenses

(1) (*substitutes* TA 1988 s 198(1)–(1B)).

(2) In the Taxes Act 1988 insert as Schedule 12A the Schedule set out in Schedule 10 to this Act.

(3) This section has effect for the year 1998–99 and subsequent years of assessment.

Commentary—*Simon's Direct Tax Service* **E4.708A**.

Profit-related pay

62 Provision preventing manipulation of profit periods

Schedule 11 to this Act (which makes provision to prevent the manipulation of profit periods in relation to the phasing out of relief for profit-related pay) shall have effect.

Commentary—*Simon's Direct Tax Service* **E4.302**.

Foreign earnings deduction

63 Withdrawal except in relation to seafarers

(1) (*repeals* TA 1988 s 193(1)).

(2) (*inserts* TA 1988 s 192A).

(3) The references in the Taxes Act 1988 to section 193(1) are amended as follows—

   (*a*) (*amends* TA 1988 s 19(1)).

   (*b*) (*amended* TA 1988 Sch 11 para 10 *before substitution by* FA 1998 Sch 9 Part I).

   (*c*) (*amends* TA 1988 s 132(3), Sch 12 paras 1, 1A, 2(1), 3(1), (3), 5, 6).

(4) In Schedule 12 to that Act—

   (*a*) (*amends* TA 1988 Sch 12 para 3(2)).

   (*b*) (*amends* TA 1988 Sch 12 para 5).

(5) Subsections (1) to (4) above have effect in relation to—

   (*a*) emoluments attributable to qualifying periods beginning on or after 17th March 1998, and

   (*b*) emoluments attributable to qualifying periods beginning before 17th March 1998 which are received on or after that date.

(6) Nothing in those subsections affects the question what deduction (if any) falls to be made under section 193(1) of the Taxes Act 1988 in the case of emoluments attributable to a qualifying period beginning before 17th March 1998 and received before that date.

(7) For the purposes of subsections (5) and (6) above the question whether emoluments are attributable to a qualifying period beginning before 17th March 1998 shall be determined without reference to any arrangements entered into on or after that date.

Commentary—*Simon's Direct Tax Service* **E4.112**.

PAYE: non-cash benefits etc

64 Transitory provision relating to tradeable assets

(1) In relation to any asset provided on or after 2nd July 1997 and before 6th April 1998, section 203F of the Taxes Act 1988 (application of PAYE where payment is in the form of the provision of a tradeable asset) shall have effect with the following two modifications.

(2) The first modification is the insertion in subsection (2), before the word "and" at the end of paragraph (*b*), of the following paragraph—

"(ba) an asset not falling within paragraph (*a*) or (*b*) above which consists in the rights of an assignee, or any other rights, in respect of a trade debt that is or may become due to the employer;".

(3) The second modification is the insertion in subsection (3), before the word "and" at the end of paragraph (*a*), of the following paragraph—

"(aa) in the case of an asset falling within subsection (2)(*ba*) above, the amount of the debt;".

(4) The preceding provisions of this section shall be deemed, in accordance with subsections (5) and (6) below, to have come into force on 2nd July 1997.

(5) Subject to subsection (6) below, this section shall not be taken to have changed—

   (*a*) the amounts which were deductible by any person under section 203 of the Taxes Act 1988 at any time on or before 17th March 1998; or

   (*b*) the amounts which should have been accounted for to the Board under section 203J(3) of that Act at any time on or before 5th April 1998.

(6) Where, by virtue of this section, any employer would (but for subsection (5) above) be treated as having been under an obligation at any time on or before 17th March 1998 to make deductions from payments made by the employer of, or on account of, an employee's assessable income—

   (*a*) sections 203 and 203J of the Taxes Act 1988, and

   (*b*) the provisions of any regulations under section 203 of that Act,

shall have effect, and be deemed to have had effect, as if the employer had been obliged (subject to section 203J(3) of that Act) to make those deductions from any payments that were so made on or after 24th March 1998 and before 6th April 1998.

(7) Expressions used in subsection (6) above and in section 203J of the Taxes Act 1988 have the same meanings in that subsection as in that section.

65 Payment in the form of a readily convertible asset

(1)–(5) (*amend* TA 1988 s 203F(1), (4), (5), *substitute* s 203F(2)–(3C) and *insert* TA 1988 s 203F(6)).

(6) The preceding provisions of this section have effect in relation to any asset provided on or after 6th April 1998 and shall be deemed, in accordance with subsection (7) below, to have come into force on that date.

(7) This section shall not be taken to have changed—

   (a) the amounts which were deductible by any person under section 203 of the Taxes Act 1988 at any time on or before the day on which this Act is passed; or
   (b) the amounts which should have been accounted for to the Board under section 203J(3) of that Act at any time on or before the fifth of the month following that in which this Act is passed;

but, the amounts which (but for this subsection) would have been deductible, or would have been amounts for which any person should have accounted, shall be deducted or accounted for in accordance with any such provision as may be made by regulations under section 203 of the Taxes Act 1988.

66 Enhancing the value of an asset

(1) (*inserts* TA 1988 s 203FA).

(2) The preceding provisions of this section have effect in relation to any assessable income provided on or after 6th April 1998 and shall be deemed, in accordance with subsection (3) below, to have come into force on that date.

(3) This section shall not be taken to have changed—

   (a) the amounts which were deductible by any person under section 203 of the Taxes Act 1988 at any time on or before the day on which this Act is passed; or
   (b) the amounts which should have been accounted for to the Board under section 203J(3) of that Act at any time on or before the fifth of the month following that in which this Act is passed;

but, the amounts which (but for this subsection) would have been deductible, or would have been amounts for which any person should have accounted, shall be deducted or accounted for in accordance with any such provision as may be made by regulations under section 203 of the Taxes Act 1988.

67 Gains from share options etc

(1) (*inserts* TA 1988 s 203FB).

(2) The preceding provisions of this section have effect in relation to events occurring on or after 6th April 1998 and shall be deemed, in accordance with subsection (3) below, to have come into force on that date.

(3) This section shall not be taken to have changed—

   (a) the amounts which were deductible by any person under section 203 of the Taxes Act 1988 at any time on or before the day on which this Act is passed; or
   (b) the amounts which should have been accounted for to the Board under section 203J(3) of that Act at any time on or before the fifth of the month following that in which this Act is passed;

but, the amounts which (but for this subsection) would have been deductible, or would have been amounts for which any person should have accounted, shall be deducted or accounted for in accordance with any such provision as may be made by regulations under section 203 of the Taxes Act 1988.

68 Vouchers and credit-tokens

(1) (*substitutes* TA 1988 s 203G(3)–(5)).

(2) (*substitutes* TA 1988 s 203H(1)(b) *and repeals* TA 1988 s 203H(2)).

(3) (*inserts* TA 1988 s 203I(3)).

(4) The preceding provisions of this section have effect—

   (a) in relation to non-cash vouchers or cash vouchers received on or after 6th April 1998, and
   (b) in relation to any use of a credit-token on or after that date,

and shall be deemed, in accordance with subsection (5) below, to have come into force on that date.

(5) This section shall not be taken to have changed—

(*a*) the amounts which were deductible by any person under section 203 of the Taxes Act 1988 at any time on or before the day on which this Act is passed; or

(*b*) the amounts which should have been accounted for to the Board under section 203J(3) of that Act at any time on or before the fifth of the month following that in which this Act is passed;

but, the amounts which (but for this subsection) would have been deductible, or would have been amounts for which any person should have accounted, shall be deducted or accounted for in accordance with any such provision as may be made by regulations under section 203 of the Taxes Act 1988.

Commentary—*Simon's Direct Tax Service* **E4.909D.**

69 Intermediaries, non-UK employers, agencies etc

(1) (*amends* TA 1988 s 203C(1)(*b*)–(*d*)).

(2) (*inserts* TA 1988 s 203C(3A), (3B)).

(3) (*substitutes* TA 1988 s 203L(1)–(2)).

(4) (*amends* TA 1988 s 144A(2)).

(5) The preceding provisions of this section have effect in relation to payments made, assets provided and vouchers received at any time on or after 6th April 1998 and in relation to any use of a credit-token on or after that date.

(6) Nothing in this section shall be taken to have changed—

(*a*) the amounts which were deductible by any person under section 203 of the Taxes Act 1988 at any time on or before the day on which this Act is passed; or

(*b*) the amounts which should have been accounted for to the Board under section 203J(3) of that Act at any time on or before the fifth of the month following that in which this Act is passed;

but, the amounts which (but for this subsection) would have been deductible, or would have been amounts for which any person should have accounted, shall be deducted or accounted for in accordance with any such provision as may be made by regulations under section 203 of the Taxes Act 1988.

Commentary—*Simon's Direct Tax Service* **E4.909D.**

The enterprise investment scheme and venture capital trusts

70 Qualifying trades for EIS and VCTs

(1) Schedule 12 to this Act (which amends the definition of qualifying trade for the purposes of the enactments relating to the enterprise investment scheme and venture capital trusts) shall have effect.

(2) (*amends* TA 1988 s 298(4)).

(3) (*amends* TA 1988 Sch 28B para 12(*a*)).

(4) The power conferred by subsection (2) above shall not be exercisable in relation to any shares issued before 17th March 1998.

Commentary—*Simon's Direct Tax Service* **E3.101.**

71 Pre-arranged exits from EIS

(1) (*inserts* TA 1988 s 299B).

(2) (*amends* TA 1988 s 307(6)(*a*)).

(3) (*amends* TA 1988 s 310(5)).

(4) (*substitutes* TA 1988 s 310(6)).

(5) The preceding provisions of this section apply in relation to shares issued on or after 2nd July 1997.

Commentary—*Simon's Direct Tax Service* **E3.101.**

72 Qualifying holdings for VCTs after 2nd July 1997

(1), (2) (*inserts* TA 1988 Sch 28B para 10A, 10B).

(3) Subject to subsections (4) and (5) below, the preceding provisions of this section have effect in relation to accounting periods ending on or after 2nd July 1997.

(4) Subsection (1) above shall not have effect for the purpose of determining whether any shares or securities acquired by a company by means of the investment of—

(*a*) money raised by the issue before 2nd July 1997 of shares in or securities of the trust company, or

(*b*) money derived from the investment by that company of any such money,

constitute qualifying holdings of the trust company at any time.

(5) If at any time the requirement of paragraph 10B of Schedule 28B to the Taxes Act 1988—

(*a*) would be satisfied in relation to a relevant holding and a company if none of the old investments were held by the trust company at that time, but

(*b*) would not otherwise be satisfied,

that paragraph shall apply in relation to that holding as if the old investments were not held by the trust company at that time.

(6) In subsection (5) above, "old investments" means shares in or securities of the relevant company acquired by means of the investment of—

(*a*) money raised by the issue before 2nd July 1997 of shares in or securities of the trust company; or

(*b*) money derived from the investment of such money.

Commentary—*Simon's Direct Tax Service* E3.101.

73 Other changes to requirements for VCTs

(1) (*amends* TA 1988 s 842AA(14), Sch 15B para 6(1)).

(2) (*amends* TA 1988 Sch 28B para 10(3)).

(3) (*amends* TA 1988 Sch 28B para 3(3)).

(4) (*amends* TA 1988 Sch 28B para 6(1)(*b*), (2A)(*c*), (2B) and *inserts* TA 1988 Sch 28B para 6(5)).

(5) (*amends* TA 1988 Sch 28B para 8(1)).

(6) Subsections (1) to (4) above have effect for the purpose of determining whether shares or securities are, as at any time on or after 6th April 1998, to be regarded as comprised in a company's qualifying holdings; and subsection (5) above has effect in relation to relevant holdings issued on or after that date.

Commentary—*Simon's Direct Tax Service* E3.101.

74 Other changes to EIS etc

(1) Schedule 13 to this Act, which amends the provisions mentioned in subsection (2) below, shall have effect.

(2) The provisions are—

(*a*) Chapter III of Part VII of the Taxes Act 1988 (EIS income tax relief);

(*b*) sections 150A and 150B of the Taxation of Chargeable Gains Act 1992 (EIS relief in respect of chargeable gains);

(*c*) Schedule 5B to that Act (EIS deferral of chargeable gains); and

(*d*) that Chapter as it has effect in relation to shares issued before 1st January 1994 (BES income tax relief) and section 150 of that Act (BES relief in respect of chargeable gains).

(3) Unless the contrary intention appears, the amendments made by that Schedule have effect in relation to shares issued on or after 6th April 1998.

Commentary—*Simon's Direct Tax Service* E3.101.

Individual savings accounts etc

75 Use of PEPs powers to provide for accounts

(1)–(5) (*insert* TA 1988 s 333(1A), (4)(*ca*)–(*cd*) and *amend* s 333(3)(*b*), (4)(*b*), (*c*)).

(6) (*amends* TCGA 1992 s 151(2)).

Commentary—*Simon's Direct Tax Service* E3.301.
Regulations—Individual Savings Account Regulations, SI 1998/1870.
Individual Savings Account (Amendment) Regulations, SI 1998/3174.
Revenue & other press releases—IR 31-7-98 (The Individual Savings Account (ISA)—tax regulations).

76 Tax credits for accounts and for PEPs

(1) Section 30 of the Finance (No 2) Act 1997 (which provides, in relation to distributions on or after 6th April 1999, for the excess of tax credit over income tax liability to cease to be payable under section 231(3) of the Taxes Act 1988 to persons who are not companies resident in the United Kingdom) shall have effect in accordance with subsection (2) below in relation to any distribution if—

(*a*) it is a distribution made before 6th April 2004;

(*b*) it is received by an individual in respect of an investment made under a plan for which provision is made by regulations under section 333 of the Taxes Act 1988 (individual savings accounts and personal equity plans); and

(*c*) that investment is one in respect of which that individual is entitled to relief in accordance with such regulations.

(2) That section of that Act of 1997 shall have effect in relation to such a distribution as if—

(*a*) subsection (5) of that section did not make the substitution set out in paragraph (*a*) or the repeal set out in paragraph (*b*);

(*b*) subsections (6), (7) and (9) of that section were to be disregarded; and (*c*) the words "Subject to section 231A," in section 231(3) of the Taxes Act 1988 were omitted.

(3) The Treasury may by regulations make provision for individuals who—

    (*a*) are not resident in the United Kingdom, but

    (*b*) have made investments under plans for which provision is made by regulations under section 333 of the Taxes Act 1988,

to be treated in relation to any such investments as if they were so resident for the purposes of any enactment conferring an entitlement to, or to the payment of, tax credits.

(4) Subsection (4) of section 231 of the Taxes Act 1988 (persons treated as in receipt of a tax credit) applies for the purposes of this section as it applies for the purposes of that section.

(5) Schedule 8 to the Finance (No 2) Act 1997 (repeals), so far as it relates to the repeal made by section 30(5)(*b*) of that Act, shall have effect subject to the preceding provisions of this section.

Commentary—*Simon's Direct Tax Service* **E3.701.**
Regulations—Individual Savings Account Regulations, SI 1998/1870.

77 The insurance element etc

(1) (*inserts* TA 1988 s 333B).

(2) (*amends columns 1 and 2 of* TMA 1970 s 98).

Commentary—*Simon's Direct Tax Service* **E3.301.**

78 Phasing out of TESSAs

(*amends* TA 1988 s 326A(3)).

Commentary—*Simon's Direct Tax Service* **E3.301.**

Relief for interest and losses etc

79 Relief for loan to acquire interest in a close company

(1) (*amends* TA 1988 s 360(3A)).

(2) This section has effect in relation to shares acquired on or after 6th April 1998.

Commentary—*Simon's Direct Tax Service* **E3.101.**

80 Relief for losses on unlisted shares in trading companies

(1)–(4) (*amend* TA 1988 s 576(1), (5), *insert* s 576(1A), (1B) and *substitute* s 576(4)–(4B)).

(5) In this section—

    (*a*) subsections (1) and (2) have effect in relation to disposals made on or after 6th April 1998; and

    (*b*) subsections (3) and (4) have effect in relation to shares issued on or after that date.

Commentary—*Simon's Direct Tax Service* **E3.101.**

81 Group relief: special rules for consortium cases

Commentary—*Simon's Direct Tax Service* **D2.622.**
Amendments—This section repealed by FA 2000 s 156, Sch 40 Pt II(11) and deemed always to have had effect.

82 Carry forward of non-trading deficit on loan relationships

(1) (*substituted* FA 1996 s 83(3), (4); *repealed by* FA 2002 s 141, Sch 40 Pt 3(12) *with effect for accounting periods beginning after 30 September 2002*).

(2) (*amends* TA 1988 ss 797(3B)(*b*), 797A(5)–(7); paras (*c*), (*e*) *repealed by* FA 2002 s 141, Sch 40 Pt 3(12) *with effect for accounting periods beginning after 30 September 2002*).

(3) (*amends* TA 1988 Sch 28A paras 6(*da*), (*db*), (*dc*), 7(1)(*b*), 11(2), 13(1)(*ea*), (*eb*), (*ec*), 16(1)(*b*)).

(4) The amendments made by this section shall be deemed always to have had effect.

Commentary—*Simon's Direct Tax Service* **B3.1931.**

Capital allowances

83 First-year allowances for investment in Northern Ireland

Commentary—
Simon's Direct Tax Service **B2.323. Amendment**—This section repealed by the Capital Allowances Act 2001 s 580, Sch 4 with effect for income tax purposes, as respects allowances and charges falling to be made for chargeable periods ending after 5 April 2001, and for corporation tax purposes, as respects allowances and charges falling to be made for chargeable periods ending after 31 March 2001.

84 First-year allowances for small businesses etc

...

Commentary—*Simon's Direct Tax Service* B2.324.
Amendment—This section repealed by the Capital Allowances Act 2001 s 580, Sch 4 with effect for income tax purposes, as respects allowances and charges falling to be made for chargeable periods ending after 5 April 2001, and for corporation tax purposes, as respects allowances and charges falling to be made for chargeable periods ending after 31 March 2001.

85 First-year allowances: consequential amendments etc

...

Amendment—This section repealed by the Capital Allowances Act 2001 s 580, Sch 4 with effect for income tax purposes, as respects allowances and charges falling to be made for chargeable periods ending after 5 April 2001, and for corporation tax purposes, as respects allowances and charges falling to be made for chargeable periods ending after 31 March 2001.

Insurance, insurance companies and friendly societies

86 Life policies etc

Schedule 14 to this Act (which makes provision in relation to the taxation of life policies etc under Chapter II of Part XIII of the Taxes Act 1988) shall have effect.

Commentary—*Simon's Direct Tax Service* E3.502.

87 Non-resident insurance companies: tax representatives

(*inserts* TA 1988 ss 552A, 552B).

Commentary—*Simon's Direct Tax Service* E3.502.

88 Overseas life assurance business

(*inserts* TA 1988 ss 553A, 553B).

Commentary—*Simon's Direct Tax Service* E3.502.

89 Personal portfolio bonds

(*inserts* TA 1988 s 553C).

Commentary—*Simon's Direct Tax Service* E3.502.

90 Distributions to friendly societies

(1) The repeal by section 30(4) of the Finance (No 2) Act 1997 of section 231(2) of the Taxes Act 1988 (payment of tax credit to a company resident in the UK) shall not have effect in relation to any distribution made to a friendly society before 6th April 2004 which is—

(*a*) a distribution to a friendly society all of whose profits are exempt from corporation tax by virtue of section 460(1) of the Taxes Act 1988 (life or endowment business of friendly society); or

(*b*) a distribution not falling within paragraph (*a*) above in relation to which exemption is given under section 460(1) of that Act.

(2) In relation to any distribution falling within paragraph (*a*) or (*b*) of subsection (1) above—

(*a*) paragraph 3 of Schedule 4 to the Finance (No 2) Act 1997 (which, from 6th April 1999, repeals certain provisions about claims for tax credits for accounting periods to which self-assessment applies) shall have effect as if the reference in sub-paragraph (2) of that paragraph to 6th April 1999 were a reference to 6th April 2004; and

(*b*) paragraph 2 of that Schedule (which repeals certain provisions about claims for tax credits for earlier periods) shall have no effect.

[(*3*) *In the case of any distribution falling within paragraph (b) of subsection (1) above, paragraph 12 of Schedule 3 to the Finance (No 2) Act 1997 (which defers the coming into force of paragraphs 10 and 11 in relation to friendly societies) shall have effect as if the reference in sub-paragraph (2) of that paragraph to 6th April 1999 were a reference to 6th April 2004.*][1]

(4) Schedule 8 to the Finance (No 2) Act 1997 (repeals), so far as it relates to any repeal referred to in the preceding provisions of this section, shall have effect subject to those provisions.

Amendments—[1] Sub-s (3) repealed by FA 2001 s 110, Sch 33 Pt II(12) with effect from the passing of FA 2001.

91 Provisional repayments in connection with pension business

(*1*) (*inserts* TA 1988 Sch 19AB para 3(1ZA)).

(*2*) *The amendment made by subsection (1) above has effect in relation to accounting periods beginning at any time after 1st October 1992 and ending before the day appointed under section 199 of the Finance Act 1994.*

Commentary—*Simon's Direct Tax Service* E7.241.
Amendments—This section repealed by FA 2001 s 110, Sch 33 Pt II(12) with effect in accordance with FA 2001 s 87.

Pensions

92 Approved retirement benefit schemes etc

Schedule 15 to this Act (which makes provision in relation to cases where a scheme has been approved for the purposes of Chapter I of Part XIV of the Taxes Act 1988 or an approval for those purposes has ceased to have effect) shall have effect.

Commentary—*Simon's Direct Tax Service* **E7.241.**

93 Benefits received under non-approved retirement benefits scheme

(1) (*substitutes* TA 1988 s 596A(4)(*b*)).

(2) (*amends* TA 1988 s 596B(9)).

(3) (*inserts* TA 1988 s 596C).

(4) This section applies to benefits received in the year 1998–99 and subsequent years of assessment.

Commentary—*Simon's Direct Tax Service* **E7.241.**

94 Approval of personal pension schemes

(1) (*inserts* TA 1988 s 638A).

(2) (*amends* TA 1988 s 631(2)).

Commentary—*Simon's Direct Tax Service* **E7.241.**

95 Personal pensions: charge on withdrawal of approval

(1) (*inserts* TA 1988 ss 650A).

(2) (*inserts* TA 1988 s 650(6)).

(3) (*inserts* TCGA 1992 s 239B).

(4) This section has effect in relation to any case in which the date from which the Board's approval is withdrawn is a date on or after 17th March 1998, except a case where the notice under section 650(2) of the Taxes Act 1988 was given before that date.

Commentary—*Simon's Direct Tax Service* **E7.241.**

96 Information relating to personal pension schemes etc

(1) (*inserts* TA 1988 s 651A).

(2) Section 652 of the Taxes Act 1988 (information about payments) shall cease to have effect.

(3) In the Table in section 98 of the Taxes Management Act 1970 (penalties for failure to provide information etc)—

    (*a*) (*amends column 1 of Table in* TMA 1970 s 98).

    (*b*) in that column, the entry relating to section 652 of the Taxes Act 1988 shall be omitted; and

    (*c*) (*amends column 2 of Table in* TMA 1970 s 98).

(4) Subsections (2) and (3)(*b*) above shall come into force on such day as the Treasury may by order appoint.

Commentary—*Simon's Direct Tax Service* **E7.241.**
Note—The day appointed for the purposes of sub-s (4) is 1 October 2000 by virtue of the Finance Act 1998, Section 96(4), (Appointed Day) Order, SI 2000/2319.

97 Notices to be given to scheme administrator

(1) (*inserts* TA 1988 s 653A).

(2) This section has effect in relation to the giving of notices at any time on or after the day on which this Act is passed.

Commentary—*Simon's Direct Tax Service* **E7.241.**

98 Assessments on scheme administrators

(1) (*inserts* TA 1988 s 658A).

(2) (*amends* TMA 1970 s 9(1) *and inserts* TMA 1970 s 9(1A)).

(3) Subsection (2) above shall have effect for the year 1998–99 and subsequent years of assessment and shall be deemed to have had effect for the years 1996–97 and 1997–98.

Commentary—*Simon's Direct Tax Service* **E7.241.**

Futures and options

99 Extension of provisions relating to guaranteed returns

(1)–(4) (*insert* TA 1988 Sch 5AA paras 4A, 9(3)–(7), *substitute* Sch 5AA para 9(1), (2) and *amend* Sch 5AA para 4(6); sub-ss (2), (3) *repealed by* FA 2002 s 141, Sch 40 Pt 3(13) *with effect for accounting periods beginning after 30 September 2002*).

(5) This section applies where the transaction consisting in the future running to delivery or the exercise of the option takes place on or after 6th February 1998.

Commentary—*Simon's Direct Tax Service* **B7.204.**

Securities

100 Accrued income scheme

(1), (2) (*amend* TA 1988 s 1A(1) and *insert* s 1A(2)(*aa*)).

(3) Subsections (1) and (2) above apply for the year 1998–99 and subsequent years of assessment.

Commentary—*Simon's Direct Tax Service* **B5.215.**

101 Dealers in securities etc

(1) (*repeals* TA 1988 s 471).

(2) (*repeals* TA 1988 s 472).

(3) Subsection (1) above applies in relation to exchanges made after the day on which this Act is passed.

(4) Subsection (2) above applies in relation to issues of securities occurring after that day.

Commentary—*Simon's Direct Tax Service* **B5.215, D4.410.**

102 Manufactured dividends

(1) (*amends* TA 1988 s 231(1) *and inserts* TA 1988 s 231AA).

(2) (*amends* TA 1988 s 231(1) *and inserts* TA 1988 s 231AB).

(3) (*amends* TA 1988 s 737D(2)).

(4) Schedule 23A to the Taxes Act 1988 (manufactured dividends and interest) shall be amended in accordance with subsections (5) to (8) below.

(5)–(8) (*substitute* TA 1988 Sch 23A para 2, *amend* TA 1988 Sch 23A para 2(3), (6), (6)(*b*), 2A(1), (3) and *repeal* Sch 23A para 2(4), (5)).

(9) Subsection (1) above has effect in relation to qualifying distributions made on or after 8th April 1998 if the manufactured dividend representative of the distribution is paid (or treated for the purposes of Schedule 23A to the Taxes Act 1988 as paid) on or after 6th April 1999.

(10) Subsections (2) to (8) above have effect in relation to manufactured dividends paid (or treated for the purposes of Schedule 23A to the Taxes Act 1988 as paid) on or after 6th April 1999.

Commentary—*Simon's Direct Tax Service* **A7.806, 807.**

Double taxation relief

103 Restriction of relief on certain interest and dividends

(1) (*substitutes* TA 1988 s 798).

(2) This section and sections 104 and 105 do not have effect in relation to foreign interest or foreign dividends paid before 1st January 1999 in pursuance of arrangements which were entered into before, and are not altered on or after, 17th March 1998.

(3) Subject to subsection (2) above, this section and sections 104 and 105 have effect in relation to foreign interest or foreign dividends paid on or after 17th March 1998.

Commentary—*Simon's Direct Tax Service* **F2.114.**

104 Adjustments of interest and dividends for spared tax etc

(*inserts* TA 1988 s 798A).

Commentary—*Simon's Direct Tax Service* **F2.114.**

105 Meaning of "financial expenditure"

(*inserts* TA 1988 s 798B).

Commentary—*Simon's Direct Tax Service* **F2.114.**

106 Underlying tax reflecting interest or dividends

(1)–(10)   (*amends* TA 1988 s 803).

(11) This section does not apply where the overseas dividend is paid before 1st January 1999 in pursuance of arrangements which were entered into before, and are not altered on or after, 17th March 1998.

(12) Subject to subsection (11) above, this section applies where the overseas dividend is paid on or after 17th March 1998.

Commentary—*Simon's Direct Tax Service* **F2.114.**
Revenue Internal Guidance—Double taxation relief manual DT888A (example illustrating the effect of this section).

107 Notification of foreign tax adjustment

(1)   (*inserts* TA 1988 s 806(3)–(6)).

(2) This section shall be deemed to have come into force on 17th March 1998 in relation to adjustments made on or after that date.

Commentary—*Simon's Direct Tax Service* **F3.104, 135.**

Transfer pricing, FOREX and financial instruments

108 New regime for transfer pricing etc

(1)   (*substitutes* TA 1988 s 770A).

(2) After Schedule 28A to that Act there shall be inserted, as Schedule 28AA to that Act, the Schedule set out in Schedule 16 to this Act.

(3)   (*amended* FA 1993 ss 136(7), (8), 136A(5), (6); *repealed by* FA 2002 s 141, Sch 40 Pt 3(10) *with effect for accounting periods beginning after 30 September 2002*).

(4)   (*amends* FA 1996 s 100(3), Sch 9 para 16(1), (2); sub-para (*a*) *repealed by* FA 2002 s 141, Sch 40 Pt 3(10) *with effect for accounting periods beginning after 30 September 2002*).

(5) Subject to subsection (6) below, this section and Schedule 16 to this Act have effect (in relation to provision made or imposed at any time)—

     (*a*) for the purposes of corporation tax, as respects accounting periods ending on or after the day appointed under section 199 of the Finance Act 1994 for the purposes of Chapter III of Part IV of that Act (self-assessment management provisions); and

     (*b*) for the purposes of income tax, as respects any year of assessment ending on or after that day.

(6) The Schedule 28AA to the Taxes Act 1988 that is inserted by subsection (2) above shall not, in the case of any potentially advantaged person, apply as respects the consequences at any time of the difference between the actual provision and the arm's length provision if—

     (*a*) that time falls before 17th March 2001;

     (*b*) the actual provision is a provision made or imposed by means of contractual arrangements entered into by that person before 17th March 1998;

     (*c*) the requirements of paragraph 1(1)(*b*) of Schedule 28AA to that Act (control requirements) are satisfied in the case of the actual provision and that person by reference only to paragraph 4(2)(*b*) of that Schedule (joint ventures etc);

     (*d*) the rights and obligations of that person by virtue of the actual provision are not ones that have been varied or continued in pursuance of any transaction entered into by that person in the period between 17th March 1998 and that time; and

     (*e*) that person is not a party, and has not been a party, to any transaction by virtue of which he could during that period have secured the variation or termination of those rights and obligations.

(7) Expressions used in subsection (6) above and in Schedule 28AA to the Taxes Act 1988 have the same meanings in that subsection as in that Schedule.

Note—The day appointed for the purposes of sub-s (5)(*a*) is 1 July 1999 by virtue of the Finance Act 1994, Section 199, (Appointed Day) Order, SI 1998/3173.

109 Abolition of requirements for direction

(1)   (*amended* FA 1993 ss 135(1), 136(1), (5), (9), 136A(3), (7), 137(1); *repealed by* FA 2002 s 141, Sch 40 Pt 3(10) *with effect for accounting periods beginning after 30 September 2002*).

(2)   (*amended* FA 1993 ss 135(1), 136(1), 137(1); *repealed by* FA 2002 s 141, Sch 40 Pt 3(10) *with effect for accounting periods beginning after 30 September 2002*).

(3)   (*amended* FA 1994 s 167(2); *repealed by* FA 2002 s 141, Sch 40 Pt 3(13) *with effect for accounting periods beginning after 30 September 2002*).

(4) *The preceding provisions of this section shall have effect (in relation to transactions entered into at any time) as respects accounting periods ending on or after the day appointed under section 199 of the Finance Act 1994 for the purposes of Chapter III of Part IV of that Act (self-assessment management provisions).*[1]

(5) Where a direction given on or after 17th March 1998 under—

(a) section 135(1)(d), 136(1)(d), (5) or (9), 136A(3) or (7) or 137(1)(d) of the Finance Act 1993, or

(b) section 167(2)(b) of the Finance Act 1994,

relates to any accounting period ending before the day appointed as mentioned in subsection (4) above, all such adjustments shall be made, whether by assessment, repayment of tax or otherwise, as are necessary to give effect to that direction.[1]

Note—The day appointed for the purposes of sub-s (4) is 1 July 1999 by virtue of the Finance Act 1994, Section 199, (Appointed Day) Order, SI 1998/3173.
Amendments—[1] Sub-s (4), so far as relating to sub-ss (1)–(2) above, and sub-s (5) repealed by FA 2002 s 141, Sch 40 Pt 3(10), (13) with effect for accounting periods beginning after 30 September 2002.

110 Determinations requiring the sanction of the Board

(1) This section has effect where a determination requiring the Board's sanction is made for any of the following purposes, that is to say—

(a) the giving of a closure notice;

(b) the giving of a notice under section 30B(1) of the Taxes Management Act 1970 amending a [partnership return][2]; or

(c) the making of a discovery assessment.

(2) If the closure notice, the notice under section 30B(1) of the Taxes Management Act 1970 or, as the case may be, a notice of the discovery assessment is given to any person—

(a) without the determination, so far as it is taken into account in the notice or assessment, having been approved by the Board, or

(b) without a copy of the Board's approval having been served on that person at or before the time of the giving of the notice,

the closure notice, notice under section 30B(1) of that Act or, as the case may be, the discovery assessment shall be deemed to have been given or made (and in the case of an assessment notified) in the terms (if any) in which it would have been given or made had that determination not been taken into account.

(3) For the purposes of this section the Board's approval of a determination requiring their sanction—

(a) must be given specifically in relation to the case in question and must apply to the amount determined; but

(b) subject to that, may be given by the Board (either before or after the making of the determination) in any such form or manner as they may determine.

(4) In this section references to a determination requiring the Board's sanction are references (subject to subsection (5) below) to any of the following determinations, that is to say—

(a) a determination of an amount falling to be brought into account for tax purposes in respect of any assumption made by virtue of paragraph 1(2) of Schedule 28AA to the Taxes Act 1988 (provision not at arm's length);

(b) ...[3]

(c) a determination of the amount of any adjustment falling to be made for tax purposes in respect of any deduction from, or addition to, any amount in accordance with section 167 of the Finance Act 1994 (arm's length test in relation to financial instruments).

(5) For the purposes of this section a determination shall be taken, in relation to a closure notice, a notice under section 30B(1) of the Taxes Management Act 1970 or a discovery assessment, not to be a determination requiring the Board's sanction if—

(a) an agreement about the matters to which the determination relates has been made between an officer of the Board and the person in whose case it is made;

(b) that agreement is in force at the time of the giving of the notice or, as the case may be, of any notice of the assessment; and

(c) the matters to which the agreement relates include the amount determined.

(6) For the purposes of subsection (5) above an agreement made between an officer of the Board and any person ("the taxpayer") in relation to any matter shall be taken to be in force at any time if, and only if—

(a) the agreement is one which has been made or confirmed in writing;

(b) that time is after the end of the period of thirty days beginning–

(i) in the case of an agreement made in writing, with the day of the making of the agreement, and

(ii) in any other case, with the day of the agreement's confirmation in writing;

and

(c) the taxpayer has not, before the end of that period of thirty days, served a notice on an officer of the Board stating that he is repudiating or resiling from the agreement.

(7) The references in subsection (6) above to the confirmation in writing of an agreement are references to the service on the taxpayer by an officer of the Board of a notice in writing—

(a) stating that the agreement has been made; and

(b) setting out the terms of the agreement.

(8) The matters that may be questioned on so much of any appeal by virtue of any provision of the Taxes Management Act 1970 or Schedule 18 to this Act, as relates to a determination the making of which has been approved by the Board for the purposes of this section shall not include the Board's approval, except to the extent that the grounds for questioning the approval are the same as the grounds for questioning the determination itself.

(9) In this section—

"closure notice" means–

[(a) a closure notice under section 28A(1) or 28B(1) of the Taxes Management Act 1970 in relation to an enquiry into a return under section 8 or 8A of that Act or into a partnership return; or]²

(b) a closure notice under paragraph 32 of Schedule 18 to this Act in relation to an enquiry into a company tax return;

"discovery assessment" means–

(a) an assessment under section 29 of the Taxes Management Act 1970; or

(b) a discovery assessment or discovery determination under paragraph 41 of Schedule 18 to this Act (including an assessment by virtue of paragraph 52 of that Schedule).

(10) This section has effect—

(a) for the purposes of corporation tax, as respects accounting periods ending on or after the day appointed under section 199 of the Finance Act 1994 for the purposes of Chapter III of Part IV of that Act (self-assessment management provisions); and

(b) for the purposes of income tax, as respects any year of assessment ending on or after that day.

Amendments—¹ Words in sub-s (4)(b) inserted by FA 2000 s 106(16), (17) with effect for accounting periods beginning after 31 December 1999 and ending after 20 March 2000.
² The words "partnership return" in sub-s (1)(b) substituted for the words "partnership statement", and in sub-s (9), para (a) of the definition of "closure notice" substituted, by FA 2001 s 88, Sch 29 para 38(1), (2) with effect from the passing of FA 2001 in relation to returns whether made before or after the passing of FA 2001, and whether relating to periods before or after the passing of FA 2001. Previously, para (a) in the definition of "closure notice" read as follows—

"(a) a notice under section 28A(5) or 28B(5) of the Taxes Management Act 1970 stating the conclusions of an officer of the Board in relation to any self-assessment, partnership statement, claim or election; or".
³ Sub-s (4)(b) repealed by FA 2002 s 141, Sch 40 Pt 3(10) with effect for accounting periods beginning after 30 September 2002. Sub-para (4)(b) previously read as follows—

"(b) a determination of the amount of any adjustment falling to be made for tax purposes in respect of the disregarding or reduction, in accordance with section 135, [135A,]¹ 136, 136A or 137 of the Finance Act 1993 (main benefit and arm's length tests in relation to foreign exchange gains and losses), of any exchange loss, or of any exchange gain;".

111 Notice to potential claimants

(1) Where—

(a) a relevant notice is given to any person,

(b) that notice, or anything contained in it, takes account of a determination of an amount falling to be brought into account for tax purposes in respect of any assumption made by virtue of paragraph 1(2) of Schedule 28AA to the Taxes Act 1988 (provision not at arm's length), and

(c) it appears to an officer of the Board that there is a person who is or may be a disadvantaged person by reference to the subject-matter of that determination,

the officer shall give a notice under this section to the person who so appears to him.

(2) A notice under this section is a notice containing particulars of the determination by reference to which the person to whom the notice is given appears to an officer of the Board to be a person who is or may be a disadvantaged person.

(3) Where, in any case, there is a contravention of subsection (1) above or the notice required by that subsection is given after the giving of the relevant notice, the Board—

(a) shall consider whether, as a result of the contravention, any person has been prejudiced with respect to the making or amendment of a claim for the purposes of paragraph 6 of Schedule 28AA to the Taxes Act 1988 (claim for relief by party disadvantaged by transfer pricing adjustment), and

(b) may, if they think fit, treat the period for the making or amendment of such a claim in that case as extended by such further period as appears to them to be appropriate.

(4) Where, in a case in which a relevant notice is given to any person, there is a contravention of this section, that contravention shall not affect the validity of that notice or of any determination to which that notice relates.

(5) For the purposes of this section a person is a disadvantaged person by reference to the subject-matter of a determination such as is mentioned in subsection (1)(b) above if, and only if—

(a) he is entitled, in consequence of the making of the determination, to make a claim for the purposes of paragraph 6 of Schedule 28AA to the Taxes Act 1988;

(b) he is entitled, in consequence of the making of the determination, to amend such a claim; or

(c) he will be entitled, by virtue of paragraph 12(3) of that Schedule, to appear and be heard by the Special Commissioners in any proceedings on an appeal relating to that determination.

(6) In this section "relevant notice" means any of the following, that is to say—

[(a) a closure notice under section 28A(1) or 28B(1) of the Taxes Management Act 1970 in relation to an enquiry into a return under section 8 or 8A of that Act or into a partnership return;][1]

(b) a closure notice under paragraph 32 of Schedule 18 to this Act in relation to an enquiry into a company tax return;

(c) a notice of assessment under section 29 of that Act of 1970;

(d) a notice of any discovery assessment or discovery determination under paragraph 41 of Schedule 18 to this Act (including any notice of an assessment by virtue of paragraph 52 of that Schedule);

(e) a notice under section 30B(1) of that Act of 1970 amending a [partnership return][1].

(7) This section applies to notices given at any time after the day appointed under section 199 of the Finance Act 1994 for the purposes of Chapter III of Part IV of that Act (self-assessment management provisions).

Commentary—*Simon's Direct Tax Service* B3.1817.
Cross references—See FA 1999 s 87(5) (application of this section in determining the effect of advance pricing agreements on non-parties).
Amendments—[1] In sub-s (6), para (a) substituted, and in para (e), "partnership return" substituted for " partnership statement", by FA 2001 s 88, Sch 29 para 38(1), (3), with effect from the passing of FA 2001 in relation to returns whether made before or after the passing of FA 2001, and whether relating to periods before or after the passing of FA 2001.
Previously, sub-s (6)(a) read as follows—

"(a) a notice under section 28A(5) or 28B(5) of the Taxes Management Act 1970 stating the conclusions of an officer of the Board in relation to any self-assessment, partnership statement, claim or election;".

Controlled foreign companies

112 Exempt activities

(1) Part II of Schedule 25 to the Taxes Act 1988 (exempt activities) shall be amended as follows.

(2) (*substitutes* TA 1988 Sch 25 para 9(1A)).

(3) (*amends* TA 1988 Sch 25 para 11(1)).

(4) (*amends* TA 1988 Sch 25 paras 9(3), 11(3)).

(5) This section has effect in relation to accounting periods of a controlled foreign company, within the meaning of Chapter IV of Part XVII of the Taxes Act 1988, beginning on or after 17th March 1998.

Commentary—*Simon's Direct Tax Service* D4.1234.

113 Miscellaneous amendments

Schedule 17 to this Act (which makes provision in relation to controlled foreign companies) shall have effect.

Commentary—*Simon's Direct Tax Service* D4.1201.

Changes in company ownership

114 Postponed corporation tax

(1) (*inserts* TA 1988 s 767AA).

(2) Subsection (1) above has effect in relation to changes in ownership occurring on or after 2nd July 1997 other than any change occurring in pursuance of a contract entered into before 2nd July 1997.

Commentary—*Simon's Direct Tax Service* D2.517.
Revenue & other press releases—IR 19-8-98 (Company purchase schemes: collection of outstanding tax—outcome of consultation).

115 Information powers where ownership changes

(1) (*inserts* TA 1988 s 767C).

(2) (*amends column 1 of Table in* TMA 1970 s 98).

(3) The preceding provisions of this section have effect in relation to changes in ownership occurring on or after 2nd July 1997 other than any change occurring in pursuance of a contract entered into before 2nd July 1997.

Commentary—*Simon's Direct Tax Service* D2.517.
Revenue & other press releases—IR 19-8-98 (Company purchase schemes: collection of outstanding tax—outcome of consultation).

116 Provisions supplemental to sections 114 and 115

(1)–(5) (*insert* TA 1988 ss 767B(1A) and *amend* s 767B(2), (4), (10), 769(1), (2), (2A), (5), (9)).

(6) The preceding provisions of this section have effect in relation to changes in ownership occurring on or after 2nd July 1997 other than any change occurring in pursuance of a contract entered into before 2nd July 1997.

Commentary—*Simon's Direct Tax Service* **D2.517.**
Revenue & other press releases—IR 19-8-98 (Company purchase schemes: collection of outstanding tax—outcome of consultation).

Corporation tax self-assessment

117 Company tax returns, assessments and related matters

(1) The provisions of Schedule 18 to this Act have effect in place of—

   (*a*) the provisions of Parts II and IV of the Taxes Management Act 1970 (returns, assessment and claims), so far as they relate to corporation tax,
   (*b*) certain related provisions of Part X of that Act (penalties), [and]¹
   (*c*) Schedule 17A to the Taxes Act 1988 (group relief: claims), [and also make provision in relation to claims for allowances under the Capital Allowances Act.]¹

(2) Schedule 18 to this Act, the Taxes Management Act 1970 and the Tax Acts shall be construed and have effect as if that Schedule were contained in that Act.

(3) The enactments mentioned in Schedule 19 to this Act have effect with the amendments specified there, which are minor amendments and amendments consequential on Schedule 18.

(4) Except as otherwise provided, the provisions of Schedules 18 and 19 to this Act have effect in relation to accounting periods ending on or after the self-assessment appointed day.

(5) In this section ''the self-assessment appointed day'' means the day appointed by the Treasury under section 199 of the Finance Act 1994 for the purposes of Chapter III of Part IV of that Act (corporation tax self-assessment).

Commentary—*Simon's Direct Tax Service* **D2.801.**
Note—The day appointed for the purposes of sub-s (5)(*a*) is 1 July 1999 by virtue of the Finance Act 1994, Section 199, (Appointed Day) Order, SI 1998/3173.
Amendments—¹ In sub-s (1), word inserted, and words substituted by CAA 2001 s 578, Sch 2 para 100 with effect for corporation tax purposes as respects allowances and charges falling to be made for chargeable periods ending after 31 March 2001.

Telephone claims etc

118 Claims for income tax purposes

(1) Subject to the following provisions of this section, the Board may, by publishing them in such manner as they think fit, give such general directions for the purposes of income tax as they consider appropriate with respect to—

   (*a*) the circumstances in which, and
   (*b*) the conditions subject to which,

claims under the Tax Acts may be made by individuals by the use of a telecommunication system (within the meaning of the Telecommunications Act 1984) or otherwise without producing a claim in writing.

(2) If directions of the Board under this section are for the time being in force with respect to the making to the Board or an officer of the Board of claims of any description, then, notwithstanding any enactment or subordinate legislation requiring claims of that description to be made in writing or by notice, claims of that description may be made to the Board or, as the case may be, an officer of the Board in any manner authorised by the directions.

(3) Where directions of the Board under this section are for the time being in force with respect to the making of claims of any description, claims of that description that are made without producing the claim in writing must be made in accordance with the directions.

(4) The power of the Board to give directions under this section—

   (*a*) shall not be exercisable in relation to the making of any claim by an individual in his capacity as a trustee, partner or personal representative; but
   (*b*) subject to that, shall be exercisable in relation to claims made by an individual through another person acting on his behalf.

(5) The Board shall not give directions under this section with respect to—

   (*a*) the making of any claim to which Schedule 1B to the Taxes Management Act 1970 applies; or
   (*b*) the making of any claim under any provision of [the Capital Allowances Act]¹.

(6) Directions under this section—

   (*a*) shall not be capable of modifying any requirement by or under any enactment as to the period within which any claim is to be made or as to the contents of any claim; but (*b*) may include provision as to how any requirement as to the contents of a claim is to be fulfilled when the claim is not produced in writing.

(7) Different provision may be made by directions under this section with respect to the making of claims of different descriptions; and a direction under this section may revoke or vary any previous direction given under this section.

(8) References in the preceding provisions of this section to the making of a claim include references to any of the following—

(*a*) the making of an election,

(*b*) the giving of a notification or notice,

(*c*) the amendment of any return, claim, election, notification or notice,

(*d*) the withdrawal of any claim, election, notification or notice,

and references in those provisions to a claim shall be construed accordingly.

(9) In this section—

"return" includes any statement or declaration under the Income Tax Acts;

"subordinate legislation" has the same meaning as in the Interpretation Act 1978.

(10) In section 832(1) of the Taxes Act 1988 (interpretation), in the definition of "notice", after "writing" there shall be inserted "or in a form authorised (in relation to the case in question) by directions under section 118 of the Finance Act 1998".

Commentary—*Simon's Direct Tax Service* **A2.301.**
Statements of Practice SP 2/98—Telephone services provided by tax offices generally.
SP 8/98—Telephone services provided by the Revenue's East Kilbride call centre.
Amendments—[1] Words in sub-s (5)(*b*) substituted by CAA 2001 s 578, Sch 2 para 101 with effect for income tax purposes as respects allowances and charges falling to be made for chargeable periods ending after 5 April 2001.

119 Evidential provisions in PAYE regulations

(*inserts* TA 1988 s 203(10)).

Commentary—*Simon's Direct Tax Service* **A2.301.**

CHAPTER II
TAXATION OF CHARGEABLE GAINS
Rate for trustees

120 Rate of CGT for trustees etc

(1) (*inserts* TCGA 1992 s 4(1AA)).

(2) Subsection (1) above applies for the year 1998–99 and subsequent years of assessment.

Commentary—*Simon's Direct Tax Service* **C4.206.**

Taper relief and indexation allowance

121 Taper relief for CGT

(1) (*inserts* TCGA 1992 s 2A).

(2) Before Schedule 1 to the Taxation of Chargeable Gains Act 1992 there shall be inserted, as Schedule A1 to that Act, the Schedule set out in Schedule 20 to this Act.

(3) Schedule 21 to this Act (which makes incidental and consequential provision in connection with the introduction of taper relief) shall have effect.

(4) This section and those two Schedules have effect for the year 1998–99 and subsequent years of assessment.

Commentary—*Simon's Direct Tax Service* **C1.403.**

122 Freezing of indexation allowance for CGT

(1)–(5) (*insert* TCGA 1992 ss 13(11A), 53(1A), 54(1A), 145(1A) and *amend* ss 54(1), 145(1)).

(6) Subject to subsection (7) below, the preceding provisions of this section have effect in relation to disposals on or after 6th April 1998.

(7) This section does not affect the computation of the amount of so much of any gain as—

(*a*) is treated for the purposes of the taxation of chargeable gains as having accrued on a disposal on or after 6th April 1998; but

(*b*) is taken for those purposes to be equal to the whole or any part of a gain that—

(i) would (but for any enactment relating to the taxation of chargeable gains) have accrued on an actual disposal made before that date, or

(ii) would have accrued on a disposal assumed under any such enactment to have been made before that date.

Commentary—*Simon's Direct Tax Service* **C2.301, 302.**

Pooling and identification of shares etc

123 Abolition of pooling for CGT

(1)–(4)   (*amend* TCGA 1992 s 104(2), (3), *insert* TCGA 1992 s 104(2A) and *substitute* s 104(4)).

(5)   (*amends* TA 1988 s 440A, TCGA 1992 ss 104(6), 107, 110).

(6)   The preceding provisions of this section have effect in relation to any disposal on or after 6th April 1998 of any securities (whenever acquired).

(7)   The powers of the Treasury to make provision by regulations under one or both of—

    (*a*)   section 333 of the Taxes Act 1988 (regulations providing for exemptions in respect of investment plans), and

    (*b*)   section 151 of the Taxation of Chargeable Gains Act 1992 (capital gains tax and investment plans),

shall include power to provide, to such extent as appears to them to be appropriate for purposes connected with the enactment of this section and section 124 below, for any provision contained in any such regulations to have effect retrospectively in relation to such times falling on or after 17th March 1998 as may be specified in the regulations.

Commentary—*Simon's Direct Tax Service* **C2.701, 703.**

124 New identification rules for CGT

(1)–(6)   (*insert* TCGA 1992 ss 106A, 108(A1), *amend* ss 105(1), 108(2), (7), 151B(1), (7), Sch 5C para 4(2) and *substitute* TCGA 1992 ss 105(2), 107(1), (2)).

(7)   Subject to subsection (8) below, the preceding provisions of this section have effect in relation to any disposal on or after 6th April 1998.

(8)   For the purposes of capital gains tax for the year 1997–98 (but not for the purposes of corporation tax), the following provisions have effect in relation to any disposal of securities made on or after 17th March 1998 and before 6th April 1998, that is to say—

    (*a*)   the identification rule in subsection (5) of the section 106A of the Taxation of Chargeable Gains Act 1992 set out in subsection (1) above shall apply in accordance with subsections (3) and (4) of that section;

    (*b*)   that rule shall have priority over any other rule, except the one in section 105(1) of that Act; and

    (*c*)   section 104(1) of that Act shall not apply to any securities identified by virtue of this subsection with the securities disposed of.

(9)   In subsection (8) above "securities" means any securities within the meaning of section 104 of the Taxation of Chargeable Gains Act 1992 or any relevant securities within the meaning of section 108 of that Act.

Commentary—*Simon's Direct Tax Service* **C2.701A–703.**
Revenue Internal Guidance—Capital gains manual CG50566 (explanation of sub-s (8) and examples of how the 30 day identification rule works).

125 Indexation and share pooling etc

(1)–(3)   (*amend* TCGA 1992 ss 53(4), 104(3), (5), 110(1), and *insert* s 110A).

(4)   Subject to subsection (5) below, the preceding provisions of this section have effect in relation to disposals on or after 6th April 1998.

(5)   This section does not affect the computation of the amount of so much of any gain as—

    (*a*)   is treated for the purposes of the taxation of chargeable gains as having accrued on a disposal on or after 6th April 1998; but

    (*b*)   is taken for those purposes to be equal to the whole or any part of a gain that–

        (i)   would (but for any enactment relating to the taxation of chargeable gains) have accrued on an actual disposal made before that date, or

        (ii)   would have accrued on a disposal assumed under any such enactment to have been made before that date.

Commentary—*Simon's Direct Tax Service* **C2.703.**

Stock dividends

126 Capital gains on stock dividends

(1)   (*substitutes* TCGA 1992 s 142).

(2)   This section applies to any share capital issued on or after 6th April 1998.

Commentary—*Simon's Direct Tax Service* **C1.101.**

Non-residents etc

127 Charge to CGT on temporary non-residents

(1) (*inserts* TCGA 1992 s 10A).

(2) (*amends* TCGA 1992 s 9(3)).

(3) (*inserts* TCGA 1992 s 96(9A), (9B)).

(4) This section has effect—

(*a*) in any case in which the year of departure is the year 1998–99 or a subsequent year of assessment; and

(*b*) in any case in which the year of departure is the year 1997–98 and the taxpayer was resident or ordinarily resident in the United Kingdom at a time in that year on or after 17th March 1998.

Commentary—*Simon's Direct Tax Service* **C1.601.**

128 Disposal of interests in a settlement

(1)–(3) (*amend* TCGA 1992 s 76 and *insert* s 76(1A), (1B), (3)).

(4) This section has effect in relation to any disposal on or after 6th March 1998.

Commentary—*Simon's Direct Tax Service* **C4.431.**

129 Attribution of gains to settlor in section 10A cases

(1) (*inserts* TCGA 1992 s 86A).

(2) (*amends* TCGA 1992 s 97(1)–(5), (7),(8)).

(3) This section has effect where the year of departure is the year 1997–98 or any subsequent year of assessment.

Commentary—*Simon's Direct Tax Service* **C4.431.**

130 Charge on beneficiaries of settlements with non-resident settlors

(1), (2) (*amend* TCGA 1992 ss 87(1), 88(1)).

(3) Subject to subsection (4) below, the preceding provisions of this section apply for the year 1998–99 and subsequent years of assessment and shall be deemed to have applied for the year 1997–98.

(4) Where section 87 of that Act applies for any year of assessment in relation to any settlement in relation to which it would not have applied for that year but for subsection (1) or (2) above—

(*a*) gains and losses accruing to the trustees of the settlement before 17th March 1998, and

(*b*) capital payments received before that date,

shall be disregarded for the purposes of that section.

Commentary—*Simon's Direct Tax Service* **C4.431.**

131 Charge on settlors of settlements for grandchildren

(1) (*amends* TCGA 1992 Sch 5 para 2(3)).

(2) (*substitutes* TCGA 1992 Sch 5 para 2(7)).

(3) Schedule 22 to this Act (which makes transitional provision and consequential amendments in connection with the provisions of this section) shall have effect.

(4) The preceding provisions of this section and Schedule 22 to this Act apply for the year 1998–99 and subsequent years of assessment and shall be deemed to have applied for the year 1997–98.

Commentary—*Simon's Direct Tax Service* **C4.431.**
Revenue Interpretation RI 198—As regards a trust which is set up before 19 March 1991 where the beneficiaries, at 6 April 1999, include both children under 18 and grandchildren as the only members of the settlor's immediate family who can benefit from the trust, the Revenue will not regard the existence of the grandchildren as causing the relevant settlement to fall outside the definition of ''protected settlement'' for the purposes of TCGA 1992 Sch 5 para 9(10A)–(10D).

132 Charge on settlors of pre-19th March 1991 settlements

(1)–(4) (*insert* TCGA 1992 Sch 5 para 9(1A), (1B), (6A), (10A)–(10D) and *repeal* Sch 5 para 9(2)).

(5) In construing section 86(1)(*e*) of the Taxation of Chargeable Gains Act 1992 (which specifies the amount by reference to which a charge arises under that section) as regards a particular year of assessment and in relation to a settlement created before 19th March 1991 which—

(*a*) is a qualifying settlement in the year 1999–00, but

(*b*) was not a qualifying settlement in any earlier year of assessment,

no account shall be taken of disposals made before 6th April 1999 (whether for the purpose of arriving at gains or for the purpose of arriving at losses).

(6) Schedule 23 (which makes transitional provision in connection with the coming into force of this section) shall have effect.

Commentary—*Simon's Direct Tax Service* **C4.431.**

Revenue Interpretation RI 198—As regards a trust which is set up before 19 March 1991 where the beneficiaries, at 6 April 1999, include both children under 18 and grandchildren as the only members of the settlor's immediate family who can benefit from the trust, the Revenue will not regard the existence of the grandchildren as causing the relevant settlement to fall outside the definition of "protected settlement" for the purposes of TCGA 1992 Sch 5 para 9(10A)–(10D).

RI 232—Change of interpretation: Non-resident trusts—gains and losses accruing in the transitional period to trusts brought within the settlor charge by FA 1988—treatment for tax year 1999/2000.

Groups of companies etc

133 Transfer within group to investment trust

(1), (2) (*insert* TCGA 1992 ss 101A, 179(2C)).

(3) Subsections (1) and (2) above apply to any company which becomes an investment trust for an accounting period beginning on or after 17th March 1998.

Commentary—*Simon's Direct Tax Service* D2.653, 655.

134 Transfer of company's assets to venture capital trust

(1)–(3) (*amend* TCGA 1992 s 139(4) and *insert* ss 101(1B), 101B).

(4) Subsection (1) above applies to transfers made on or after 17th March 1998.

(5) Subsections (2) and (3) above apply to a company in respect of which an approval for the purposes of section 842AA of the Taxes Act 1988 (venture capital trusts) has effect as from a time falling on or after 17th March 1998.

Commentary—*Simon's Direct Tax Service* D2.303.

135 Transfer within group to venture capital trust

(1) (*amends* TCGA 1992 s 171(2)).

(2), (3) (*insert* TCGA 1992 ss 101C, 179(2D)).

(4) Subsection (1) above applies to disposals made on or after 17th March 1998.

(5) Subsections (2) and (3) above apply to a company in respect of which an approval for the purposes of section 842AA of the Taxes Act 1988 (venture capital trusts) has effect as from a time falling on or after 17th March 1998.

Commentary—*Simon's Direct Tax Service* D2.655.

136 Incorporated friendly societies

(1) (*amends* TCGA 1992 s 170(9)).

(2), (3) (*amend* TCGA 1992 s 171(2) and *insert* s 171(5)).

(4) Subsection (1) above applies for the purpose of determining, in relation to times on and after 17th March 1998, whether a friendly society is a company within the meaning of the provisions of sections 170 to 181 of the Taxation of Chargeable Gains Act 1992.

(5) Subsections (2) and (3) above apply in relation to disposals made on or after 17th March 1998.

Commentary—*Simon's Direct Tax Service* C1.217, D2.652.

137 Pre-entry gains

(1) (*inserts* TCGA 1992 s 177B).

(2) After Schedule 7A to that Act there shall be inserted, as Schedule 7AA to that Act, the Schedule set out in Schedule 24 to this Act.

(3), (4) (*amend* TCGA 1992 s 213(3) and *insert* s 213(3A), (3B)).

(5) Subsections (1) and (2) above and Schedule 24 to this Act have effect in relation to any accounting period ending on or after 17th March 1998.

(6) Subsection (3) above has effect in relation to any intervening period ending on or after 17th March 1998.

(7) Subsection (4) above has effect in any case where the earlier accounting period is one ending on or after 17th March 1998.

Commentary—*Simon's Direct Tax Service* C2.685.

138 Pre-entry losses

(1) (*amends* TCGA 1992 Sch 7A para 9(6)).

(2) This section has effect in relation to any accounting period ending on or after 17th March 1998.

Commentary—*Simon's Direct Tax Service* D2.670.

139 De-grouping charges

(1) (*amends* TCGA 1992 s 179(2B)).

(2) Subsection (1) above has effect in relation to a company in any case in which the time of the company's ceasing to be a member of the second group is on or after 17th March 1998.

Commentary—*Simon's Direct Tax Service* **D2.663.**

Abolition of reliefs

140 Phasing out of retirement relief

(1) In Schedule 6 to the Taxation of Chargeable Gains Act 1992 (retirement relief etc), paragraph 13(1) (amount available for relief: basic rule) shall have effect, in relation to qualifying disposals in a year of assessment specified in the first column of the following Table, as if—

    (*a*) for the references to £250,000 there were substituted references to the amount specified in the second column of that Table; and

    (*b*) for the reference to £1 million there were substituted a reference to the amount specified in the third column of that Table.

TABLE

Year	£250,000	£1 million
1999–00	£200,000	£800,000
2000–01	£150,000	£600,000
2001–02	£100,000	£400,000
2002–03	£50,000	£200,000

(2) The following provisions, namely—

    (*a*) section 163 of that Act (relief for disposals by individuals on retirement from family business);

    (*b*) section 164 of that Act (other retirement relief); and

    (*c*) Schedule 6 to that Act,

shall cease to have effect in relation to disposals in the year 2003–04 and subsequent years of assessment.

(3) In section 157 of that Act (trade carried on by family company), for the words "within the meaning of Schedule 6" there shall be substituted the words "that is to say, a company the voting rights in which are exercisable, as to not less than 5 per cent, by him".

(4) In subsection (8) of section 165 of that Act (relief for gifts of business assets), for paragraph (*a*) there shall be substituted the following paragraphs—

    "(*a*) "personal company", in relation to an individual, means a company the voting rights in which are exercisable, as to not less than 5 per cent, by that individual;

    (*aa*) "holding company", "trading company" and "trading group" have the meanings given by paragraph 22 of Schedule A1; and".

(5) In the following provisions, namely—

    (*a*) subsection (8) of section 228 of that Act (conditions for roll-over relief: supplementary); and

    (*b*) subsection (14)(*b*) of section 253 of that Act (relief for loans to traders),

for the words "paragraph 1 of Schedule 6" there shall be substituted the words "paragraph 22 of Schedule A1".

(6) Subsections (3) to (5) above have effect in relation to the year 2003–04 and subsequent years of assessment.

Commentary—*Simon's Direct Tax Service* **C3.601.**

141 Abolition of certain other CGT reliefs

(1) (*repeals* TCGA 1992 Part V Chapter IA *and* TCGA 1992 ss 254, 255).

(2) In subsection (1) above—

    (*a*) paragraph (*a*) has effect in relation to acquisitions made on or after 6th April 1998; and

    (*b*) paragraph (*b*) has effect in relation to loans made on or after 17th March 1998.

Commentary—*Simon's Direct Tax Service* **C3.771, 901.**

PART IV
INHERITANCE TAX ETC

142 Property of historic interest etc

Schedule 25 to this Act (which makes provision about the designation of property of historic interest, etc and about undertakings in relation to such property) shall have effect.

Commentary—*Simon's Direct Tax Service* **C1.418.**

143 Removal of exemption for gifts for public benefit

(7) (*amends* TCGA 1992 s 258(2)).

Commentary—*Simon's Direct Tax Service* **I7.501.**

PART VI
MISCELLANEOUS AND SUPPLEMENTAL
Government borrowing

161 Non-FOTRA securities

(1) Subject to the following provisions of this section, any gilt-edged security issued before 6th April 1998 without FOTRA conditions shall be treated in relation to times on or after that date as if—

(*a*) it were a security issued with the post-1996 Act conditions; and
(*b*) those conditions had been authorised in relation to the issue of that security by virtue of section 22 of the Finance (No 2) Act 1931.

(2) Where a gilt-edged security falls to be treated as mentioned in subsection (1) above that treatment shall have effect—

(*a*) for the purposes of sections 711 to 728 of the Taxes Act 1988 (accrued income scheme), in relation only to amounts which a person is treated under those sections as receiving on or after 6th April 1998;
(*b*) for the other purposes of the Tax Acts, in relation only to payments of interest falling due on or after that date; and
(*c*) for the purposes of the Inheritance Tax Act 1984, in relation only to a determination of whether property is excluded property at a time falling on or after that date.

(3) No charge to tax shall be treated as arising under section 65 of the Inheritance Tax Act 1984 (property becoming excluded property) by reason only of the coming into force of this section.

(4) In this section "FOTRA conditions" means any such conditions about exemption from taxation as are authorised in relation to the issue of a gilt-edged security by virtue of section 22 of the Finance (No 2) Act 1931.

(5) In this section "the post-1996 Act conditions" means the FOTRA conditions with which 7.25% Treasury Stock 2007 was first issued by virtue of section 22 of the Finance (No 2) Act 1931.

(6) In this section "gilt-edged securities" means any securities which are gilt-edged securities for the purposes of the Taxation of Chargeable Gains Act 1992.

(7) This section does not apply to any $3\frac{1}{2}$% War Loan 1952 Or After which was issued with a condition authorised by virtue of section 47 of the Finance (No 2) Act 1915.

The European Single Currency

163 Adoption of single currency by other member states

(1) The Treasury may, to such extent as appears to them appropriate in connection with any of the matters falling within subsection (2) below, by regulations modify the application and effect as respects—

(*a*) transactions in a currency other than sterling,
(*b*) instruments denominated in such a currency, and
(*c*) the bringing into account of amounts expressed in, or by reference to, such a currency,

of any enactment or subordinate legislation relating to any matter under the care and management of the Commissioners of Inland Revenue.

(2) The matters falling within this subsection are—

(*a*) the adoption or proposed adoption by other member States of the single currency; and
(*b*) any transitional measures or other arrangements applying or likely to apply in relation to the adoption of the single currency by other member States.

(3) Without prejudice to the generality of subsection (1) above, the power conferred by that subsection includes power by regulations to provide—

(a) for liabilities to pay amounts to the Commissioners of Inland Revenue under any enactment or subordinate legislation relating to taxation to be capable of being discharged, in accordance with the regulations, by payments in the single currency;

(b), (c) ...¹

(4) The power to make regulations under this section includes—

(a) power to impose charges to taxation;

(b) power to amend or repeal any enactment; and

(c) power to make such incidental, supplemental, consequential and transitional provision as appears to the Treasury to be appropriate.

(5) The power to make regulations under this section shall be exercisable by statutory instrument subject to annulment in pursuance of a resolution of the House of Commons.

(6) In this section—

"enactment" includes any enactment contained in this Act (other than this section) and any enactment passed after this Act;

"other member State" means a member State other than the United Kingdom;

"subordinate legislation" has the same meaning as in the Interpretation Act 1978.

(7) References in this section to the adoption of the single currency are references to the adoption of the single currency in accordance with the Treaty establishing the European Community, and the reference in subsection (3)(a) above to that currency shall be construed accordingly.

Regulations—European Single Currency (Taxes) Regulations, SI 1998/3177.
Amendments—¹ Sub-ss (3)(b), (c) repealed by FA 2002 s 141, Sch 40 Pt 3(11) with effect for accounting periods beginning after 30 September 2002. Sub-ss (3)(b), (c) previously read as follows—

"(b) for elections made for the purposes of section 93(1)(b) or 94(2)(b) of the Finance Act 1993 (computation of a company's profits in a foreign currency) to have effect as modified in accordance with the regulations; and

(c) for such persons as may be described in the regulations to be treated as having made elections for any of those purposes in such terms as may be provided for in the regulations.".

Supplemental

164 Interpretation

In this Act "the Taxes Act 1988" means the Income and Corporation Taxes Act 1988.

165 Repeals

(1) The enactments mentioned in Schedule 27 to this Act (which include spent provisions) are hereby repealed to the extent specified in the third column of that Schedule.

(2) The repeals specified in that Schedule have effect subject to the commencement provisions and savings contained or referred to in the notes set out in that Schedule.

166 Short title

This Act may be cited as the Finance Act 1998.

SCHEDULES

SCHEDULE 3

ADVANCE CORPORATION TAX

Section 31

Section 1 of the Provisional Collection of Taxes Act 1968

1—(1) Section 1 of the Provisional Collection of Taxes Act 1968 (temporary statutory effect of House of Commons resolutions) shall be amended as follows.

(2) (*amends* PCTA 1968 s 1(1)).

(3) This paragraph has effect in relation to distributions made on or after 6th April 1999.

Section 10 of the Taxes Management Act 1970

2—(1) Section 10 of the Taxes Management Act 1970 (notice of liability to corporation tax) shall be amended as follows.

(2) (*repeals* TMA 1970 s 10(4)).

(3) This paragraph has effect in relation to accounting periods beginning on or after 6th April 1999.

Section 87 of the Taxes Management Act 1970

3—(1) Section 87 of the Taxes Management Act 1970 (interest on overdue ACT and income tax on company payments) shall be amended as follows.

(2)–(5) (*amend* TMA 1970 s 87(1), (2), (6), (7)).

(6) This paragraph has effect in relation to accounting periods beginning on or after 6th April 1999.

Section 87A of the Taxes Management Act 1970

4—(1) Section 87A of the Taxes Management Act 1970 (interest on overdue corporation tax etc) shall be amended as follows.

(2) (*repeals* TMA 1970 s 87A(4)).

(3) (*repeals* TMA 1970 s 87A(4B), (7)).

(4) Sub-paragraph (2) above has effect where the later period mentioned in subsection (4) of section 87A begins on or after 6th April 1999.

(5) Sub-paragraph (3) above has effect where the earlier period mentioned in subsections (4B) and (7) of section 87A begins on or after 6th April 1999.

Section 94 of the Taxes Management Act 1970

5 ...

Amendment—This paragraph (which repealed TMA 1970 s 94(8) with effect for accounting periods ending after 5 April 1999) repealed by FA 1998 s 165, Sch 27 Part III(28) with effect for accounting periods ending after 30 June 1999 by virtue of the Finance Act 1994, Section 199, (Appointed Day) Order, SI 1998/3173.

Section 109 of the Taxes Management Act 1970

6—(1) Section 109 of the Taxes Management Act 1970 (corporation tax on close company in connection with loans to participators etc) shall be amended as follows.

(2) (*amends* TMA 1970 s 109(3A)).

(3) This paragraph has effect in relation to the release or writing off of the whole or part of a debt on or after 6th April 1999.

Section 13 of the Taxes Act 1988

7—(1) Section 13 of the Taxes Act 1988 (small companies' relief) shall be amended as follows.

(2), (3) (*amend* TA 1988 s 13(7) and *insert* s 13(8AA), (8AB)).

(4) This paragraph has effect in relation to distributions made on or after 6th April 1999.

Section 14 of the Taxes Act 1988

8—(1) Section 14 of the Taxes Act 1988 (ACT and qualifying distributions) shall be amended as follows.

(2) (*repeals* TA 1988 s 14(1), (3)–(5)).

(3) This paragraph has effect in relation to distributions made on or after 6th April 1999.

Section 75 of the Taxes Act 1988

9—(1) Section 75 of the Taxes Act 1988 (expenses of management: investment companies) shall be amended as follows.

(2) (*amends* TA 1988 s 75(2)).

(3) This paragraph has effect in relation to distributions made on or after 6th April 1999.

Section 116 of the Taxes Act 1988

10—(1) Section 116 of the Taxes Act 1988 (arrangements for transferring relief) shall be amended as follows.

(2) (*amends* TA 1988 s 116(2)).

(3) This paragraph has effect in relation to accounting periods beginning on or after 6th April 1999.

Section 238 of the Taxes Act 1988

11—(1) (*repeals* TA 1988 s 238).

(2) This paragraph has effect in relation to accounting periods beginning on or after 6th April 1999.

Section 239 of the Taxes Act 1988

12—(1) (*repeals* TA 1988 s 239).

(2) Sub-paragraph (1) above has effect in relation to accounting periods beginning on or after 6th April 1999.

(3) No advance corporation tax shall, by virtue of section 239(4) of the Taxes Act 1988, be treated as if it were paid in respect of distributions made in accounting periods beginning on or after 6th April 1999.

(4) The limit under section 239(2) of the Taxes Act 1988 on the set-off of advance corporation tax for an accounting period of a company beginning before, and ending on or after, 6th April 1999 (a "straddling period") shall be determined as if—

(a) the straddling period were an accounting period beginning at the beginning of the straddling period and ending on 5th April 1999 ("the notional period"); and

(b) there were apportioned to the notional period a proportionate amount of the profits of the company which, apart from this sub-paragraph, would be taken into account in determining the limit under section 239(2) of that Act.

(5) The references in sub-paragraphs (2) and (3) above to accounting periods beginning on or after 6th April 1999 include a reference to a separate accounting period mentioned in section 245(2) of the Taxes Act 1988 which begins on 6th April 1999.

(6) The reference in sub-paragraph (4) above to an accounting period beginning before, and ending on or after, 6th April 1999 includes a reference to a separate accounting period mentioned in section 245(2) of the Taxes Act 1988 which begins before, and ends on or after, that date.

Section 240 of the Taxes Act 1988

13—(1) (*repeals* TA 1988 s 240).

(2) This paragraph has effect in relation to accounting periods of the surrendering company (as defined in section 240(1) of the Taxes Act 1988) beginning on or after 6th April 1999.

Commentary—*Simon's Direct Tax Service* **D2.602.**

Section 241 of the Taxes Act 1988

14—(1) (*repeals* TA 1988 s 241).

(2) This paragraph has effect in relation to accounting periods beginning on or after 6th April 1999.

Section 245 of the Taxes Act 1988

15—(1) (*repeals* TA 1988 s 245).

(2) This paragraph has effect in relation to changes in ownership (within the meaning of section 245 of that Act) occurring on or after 6th April 1999.

Section 245A of the Taxes Act 1988

16—(1) (*repeals* TA 1988 s 245A).

(2) This paragraph has effect in relation to changes in ownership (within the meaning of section 245A of that Act) occurring on or after 6th April 1999.

Section 245B of the Taxes Act 1988

17—(1) (*repeals* TA 1988 s 245B).

(2) Sub-paragraph (1) above has effect in relation to disposals on or after 6th April 1999.

(3) In relation to an accounting period beginning before, and ending on or after, 6th April 1999, the reference in section 245B(4)(a) of the Taxes Act 1988 to the end of the relevant period shall be taken to be a reference to the end of a period which ends on 5th April 1999.

Section 246 of the Taxes Act 1988

18—(1) (*repeals* TA 1988 s 246).

(2) This paragraph has effect in relation to distributions made on or after 6th April 1999.

Section 247 of the Taxes Act 1988

19—(1) Section 247 of the Taxes Act 1988 (dividends etc paid by one member of a group to another) shall be amended as follows.

(2)–(7) (*repeal* TA 1988 s 247(1), (2), (3), and *amend* s 247(4)–(7), (10); *part repealed* by FA 2001 s 110, Sch 33 Pt II(10) with effect for payments made after 11 May 2001).

(8) This paragraph has effect in relation to distributions made on or after 6th April 1999.

Commentary—*Simon's Direct Tax Service* **D2.602, 605, 606, 620.**

Section 248 of the Taxes Act 1988

20—(1) Section 248 of the Taxes Act 1988 (provisions supplemental to section 247) shall be amended as follows.

(2) (*amends* TA 1988 s 248(2), (3)).

(3) This paragraph has effect in relation to distributions made on or after 6th April 1999.

Section 252 of the Taxes Act 1988

21—(1) Section 252 of the Taxes Act 1988 (rectification of excessive set-off of ACT or tax credit) shall be amended as follows.

(2) (*amends* TA 1988 s 252(1)).

(3) This paragraph has effect in relation to accounting periods beginning on or after 6th April 1999.

Section 253 of the Taxes Act 1988

22—(1) Section 253 of the Taxes Act 1988 (power to modify or replace section 234(5) to (9) and Schedule 13) shall be amended as follows.

(2)–(4) (*amend* TA 1988 s 253(1), (3) and *repeal* s 253(2)).

(5) This paragraph has effect in relation to accounting periods beginning on or after 6th April 1999.

Section 255 of the Taxes Act 1988

23—(1) (*repeals* TA 1988 s 255).

(2) This paragraph has effect in relation to distributions made on or after 6th April 1999.

Section 419 of the Taxes Act 1988

24—(1) Section 419 of the Taxes Act 1988 (loans to participators etc) shall be amended as follows.

(2) (*amends* TA 1988 s 419(1)).

(3) (*amends* TA 1988 s 419(4)).

(4) (*amends* TA 1988 s 419(4A)).

(5) Sub-paragraph (2) above has effect in relation to loans or advances made on or after 6th April 1999.

(6) Sub-paragraphs (3) and (4) above have effect in relation to the release or writing off of the whole or part of a debt on or after 6th April 1999.

Section 434 of the Taxes Act 1988

25—(1) Section 434 of the Taxes Act 1988 (franked investment income etc) shall be amended as follows.

(2) (*repeals* TA 1988 s 434(3)).

(3) (*repeals* TA 1988 s 434(6)).

(4) (*repeals* TA 1988 s 434(8)).

(5) Sub-paragraph (2) above has effect in relation to franked investment income which is attributable to distributions made on or after 6th April 1999.

(6) Sub-paragraphs (3) and (4) above have effect in relation to accounting periods beginning on or after 6th April 1999.

Section 434C of the Taxes Act 1988

26—(1) (*repeals* TA 1988 s 434C).

(2) This paragraph has effect in relation to distributions made on or after 6th April 1999.

Section 468Q of the Taxes Act 1988

27—(1) Section 468Q of the Taxes Act 1988 (dividend distribution to corporate unit holder) shall be amended as follows.

(2)–(4) (*amend* TA 1988 s 468Q(3), and *insert* s 468Q(3A), (5A), (5B), (5C)).

(5) This paragraph has effect in relation to distribution periods beginning on or after 6th April 1999.

Section 490 of the Taxes Act 1988

28—(1) Section 490 of the Taxes Act 1988 (companies carrying on a mutual business or not carrying on a business) shall be amended as follows.

(2) (*amends* TA 1988 s 490(1)).

(3) This paragraph has effect in relation to distributions made on or after 6th April 1999.

Section 497 of the Taxes Act 1988

29—(1) (*repeals* TA 1988 s 497).

(2) This paragraph has effect in relation to accounting periods beginning on or after 6th April 1999.

Section 498 of the Taxes Act 1988

30—(1) (*repeals* TA 1988 s 498).

(2) Sub-paragraph (1) above has effect in relation to accounting periods of the surrendering company (as defined in section 240(1) of the Taxes Act 1988) beginning on or after 6th April 1999.

(3) The limit under section 498(5) of the Taxes Act 1988 for an accounting period of the surrendering company (as defined in section 240(1) of that Act) beginning before, and ending on or after, 6th April 1999 (a "straddling period") shall be determined as if—

(*a*) the straddling period were an accounting period beginning at the beginning of the straddling period and ending on 5th April 1999 ("the notional period"); and

(*b*) there were apportioned to the notional period a proportionate amount of the limit which, apart from this sub-paragraph, would apply for the purposes of section 498(5) of the Taxes Act 1988.

Section 499 of the Taxes Act 1988

31—(1) (*repeals* TA 1988 s 499).

(2) This paragraph has effect in relation to distributions made on or after 6th April 1999.

Section 703 of the Taxes Act 1988

32—(1) Section 703 of the Taxes Act 1988 (cancellation of tax advantage) shall be amended as follows.

(2) (*inserts* TA 1988 s 703(3A)).

(3) (*repeals* TA 1988 s 703(4)–(6)).

(4) Sub-paragraph (2) above has effect in relation to assessments under section 703(3) of the Taxes Act 1988 made on or after 6th April 1999.

(5) Sub-paragraph (3) above has effect for the year 1999–00 and subsequent years of assessment.

Section 704 of the Taxes Act 1988

33—(1) Section 704 of the Taxes Act 1988 (the prescribed circumstances) shall be amended as follows.

(2) (*amends* TA 1988 s 704).

(3) This paragraph has effect in relation to distributions made on or after 6th April 1999.

Section 705 of the Taxes Act 1988

34—(1) Section 705 of the Taxes Act 1988 (appeals against Board's notices under section 703) shall be amended as follows.

(2) (*repeals* TA 1988 s 705(6)–(8)).

(3) This paragraph has effect for the year 1999–00 and subsequent years of assessment.

Section 797 of the Taxes Act 1988

35—(1) Section 797 of the Taxes Act 1988 (limits on credit: corporation tax) shall be amended as follows.

(2) (*repeals* TA 1988 s 797(4), (5)).

(3) This paragraph has effect in relation to accounting periods beginning on or after 6th April 1999.

Section 802 of the Taxes Act 1988

36—(1) Section 802 of the Taxes Act 1988 (UK insurance companies trading overseas) shall be amended as follows.

(2) (*amends* TA 1988 s 802(2)).

(3) This paragraph has effect in relation to distributions made on or after 6th April 1999.

Section 813 of the Taxes Act 1988

37—(1) Section 813 of the Taxes Act 1988 (recovery of tax credits incorrectly paid) shall be amended as follows.

(2) (*repeals* TA 1988 s 813(6)).

(3) This paragraph has effect in relation to accounting periods beginning on or after 6th April 1999.

Section 826 of the Taxes Act 1988

38—(1) Section 826 of the Taxes Act 1988 (interest on tax overpaid) shall be amended as follows.

(2) (*repeals* TA 1988 s 826(2A)).

(3) (*repeals* TA 1988 s 826(7)).

(4) (*repeals* TA 1988 s 826(7AA), (7AC)).

(5) Sub-paragraph (2) above has effect in relation to accounting periods beginning on or after 6th April 1999.

(6) Sub-paragraph (3) above has effect where the later period mentioned in subsection (7) of section 826 begins on or after 6th April 1999.

(7) Sub-paragraph (4) above has effect where the earlier period mentioned in subsections (7AA) and (7CA) of section 826 begins on or after 6th April 1999.

Section 832 of the Taxes Act 1988

39— (1) Section 832 of the Taxes Act 1988 (interpretation of the Tax Acts) shall be amended as follows.

(2)–(6) (*amends* TA 1988 s 832(1)).

(7) (*inserts* TA 1988 s 832(4)).

(8) Sub-paragraphs (2), (3), (6) and (7) above have effect in relation to accounting periods beginning on or after 6th April 1999.

(9) Sub-paragraphs (4) and (5) above have effect in relation to distributions made on or after 6th April 1999.

Section 835 of the Taxes Act 1988

40—(1) Section 835 of the Taxes Act 1988 ("total income" in the Income Tax Acts) shall be amended as follows.

(2) (*amends* TA 1988 s 835(6)).

(3) This paragraph has effect in relation to distributions made on or after 6th April 1999.

Schedule 13 to the Taxes Act 1988

41—(1) (*repeals* TA 1988 Sch 13).

(2) This paragraph has effect—

  (*a*) in relation to return periods beginning on or after 6th April 1999; and
  (*b*) in relation to accounting periods beginning on or after that date.

Schedule 13A to the Taxes Act 1988

42—(1) (*repeals* TA 1988 Sch 13A).

(2) This paragraph has effect in relation to accounting periods of the surrendering company (as defined in section 240(1) of the Taxes Act 1988) beginning on or after 6th April 1999.

Schedule 24 to the Taxes Act 1988

43—(1) Schedule 24 to the Taxes Act 1988 (assumptions in relation to controlled foreign companies etc) shall be amended as follows.

(2) (*amends* TA 1988 Sch 24 para 6(1), (2)).

(3) (*repeals* TA 1988 Sch 24 para 7).

(4) This paragraph has effect in relation to accounting periods of companies resident outside the United Kingdom which begin on or after 6th April 1999.

Schedule 26 to the Taxes Act 1988

44—(1) Schedule 26 to the Taxes Act 1988 (controlled foreign companies: relief against liability for tax in respect of chargeable profits) shall be amended as follows.

(2) (*repeals* TA 1988 Sch 26 para 2).

(3) Sub-paragraphs (1) and (2) above have effect in relation to accounting periods beginning on or after 6th April 1999.

(4) The relevant maximum (as defined in paragraph 2(3) of Schedule 26 to the Taxes Act 1988) for an accounting period beginning before, and ending on or after, 6th April 1999 (a "straddling period") shall be determined as if—

  (*a*) the straddling period were an accounting period beginning at the beginning of the straddling period and ending on 5th April 1999 ("the notional period"); and
  (*b*) there were apportioned to the notional period a proportionate amount of the amounts mentioned in paragraph 2(3)(*a*) and (*b*) of Schedule 26 to the Taxes Act 1988.

Paragraph 8 of Schedule 4 to the Finance (No 2) Act 1997

45 (*repeals* F(No 2)A 1997 Sch 4 para 8).

Paragraph 9 of Schedule 4 to the Finance (No 2) Act 1997

46 (*repeals* F(No 2)A 1997 Sch 4 para 9).

Paragraph 18 of Schedule 4 to the Finance (No 2) Act 1997

47 (*repeals* F(No 2)A 1997 Sch 4 para 18).

Paragraph 23 of Schedule 4 to the Finance (No 2) Act 1997

48 (*repeals* F(No 2)A 1997 Sch 4 para 23).

SCHEDULE 4

INTEREST PAYABLE UNDER THE TAX ACTS BY OR TO COMPANIES
Section 35

Interest on overpaid or early paid corporation tax

Commentary—*Simon's Direct Tax Service* **D2.845.**

1—(1) (*amends* TA 1988 s 826(2)).

(2) (*inserts* TA 1988 s 826A).

(3) (*amends* FA 1989 s 178(2)).

The "material date" for interest on a repayment of income tax

2—(1) (*amends* TA 1988 s 826(3)).

(2) This paragraph has effect in relation to accounting periods ending on or after the day appointed under section 199 of the Finance Act 1994 for the purposes of Chapter III of Part IV of that Act (corporation tax self-assessment).

Note—The appointed day for the purposes of sub-para (2) is 1 July 1999, by virtue of the Finance Act 1994, Section 199, (Appointed Day) Order, SI 1998/3173.

Recovery of interest overpaid under section 826(1)(a)

3—(1) (*inserts* TA 1988 s 826(8A), (8B), (8C)).

(2) (*amended* TMA 1970 s 69; *repealed* by FA 2001 s 110, Sch 33 Pt II(14) with effect for proceedings begun, or a counterclaim made, and a set-off first claimed after the passing of FA 2001).

(3) The amendments made by this paragraph have effect in relation to interest on repayments of corporation tax paid for accounting periods ending on or after the day appointed under section 199 of the Finance Act 1994 for the purposes of Chapter III of Part IV of that Act (corporation tax self-assessment).

Note—The appointed day for the purposes of sub-para (3) is 1 July 1999, by virtue of the Finance Act 1994, Section 199, (Appointed Day) Order, SI 1998/3173.

Interest on underpaid tax where reliefs are carried back

4—(1) Section 87A of the Taxes Management Act 1970 (interest on overdue corporation tax etc) shall be amended as follows.

(2) (*amends* TMA 1970 s 87A(4), (4A), (6)).

(3) (*inserts* TMA 1970 s 87A(8)).

(4) (*inserts* TMA 1970 s 87A(9)).

(5) The amendments made by this paragraph have effect where the accounting period whose due and payable date falls to be determined is an accounting period ending on or after the day appointed under section 199 of the Finance Act 1994 for the purposes of Chapter III of Part IV of that Act (corporation tax self-assessment).

(6) In sub-paragraph (5) above "due and payable date", in relation to an accounting period, means the date on which corporation tax for that period becomes, or (as the case may be) would become, due and payable.

Note—The appointed day for the purposes of sub-para (5) is 1 July 1999, by virtue of the Finance Act 1994, Section 199, (Appointed Day) Order, SI 1998/3173.

Interest on overpaid tax where reliefs are carried back

5—(1) Section 826 of the Taxes Act 1988 (interest on tax overpaid) shall be amended as follows.

(2)–(4) (*amend* TA 1988 s 826(7), (7A), (7B), (7C) and *insert* s 826(7D), (7E)).

(5) The amendments made by this paragraph have effect where the accounting period whose due and payable date falls to be determined is an accounting period ending on or after the day appointed under section 199 of the Finance Act 1994 for the purposes of Chapter III of Part IV of that Act (corporation tax self-assessment).

(6) In sub-paragraph (5) above "due and payable date", in relation to an accounting period, means the date on which corporation tax for that period becomes, or (as the case may be) would become, due and payable.

Note—The appointed day for the purposes of sub-para (5) is 1 July 1999, by virtue of the Finance Act 1994, Section 199, (Appointed Day) Order, SI 1998/3173.

Company liquidations

6—(1) Section 342 of the Taxes Act 1988 (tax on company in liquidation) shall be amended as follows.

(2), (3) (*amend* TA 1988 s 342(2) and *insert* s 342(3A)).

(4) This paragraph has effect in relation to final accounting periods ending on or after the day appointed under section 199 of the Finance Act 1994 for the purposes of Chapter III of Part IV of that Act (corporation tax self-assessment).

Note—The appointed day for the purposes of sub-para (4) is 1 July 1999, by virtue of the Finance Act 1994, Section 199, (Appointed Day) Order, SI 1998/3173.

Loan relationships

7—*(1) Section 100 of the Finance Act 1996 (loan relationships: interest on judgments, imputed interest etc) shall be amended as follows.*

(2), (3) (amend FA 1996 s 100(4) and insert FA 1996 s 100(4A)).

(4) This paragraph has effect in relation to accounting periods ending on or after the day appointed under section 199 of the Finance Act 1994 for the purposes of Chapter III of Part IV of that Act (corporation tax self-assessment).

Note—The appointed day for the purposes of sub-para (4) is 1 July 1999, by virtue of the Finance Act 1994, Section 199, (Appointed Day) Order, SI 1998/3173.
Amendment—Repealed by FA 2002 s 141, Sch 40 Pt 3(10) with effect for accounting periods beginning after 30 September 2002.

SCHEDULE 5

RENT AND OTHER RECEIPTS FROM LAND

Section 38(1)

PART I

MAIN CHARGING PROVISIONS

Revenue Interpretation RI 197—As from 1 April 1998, residential service charges received by occupier controlled flat management companies will ordinarily be outside the scope of Schedule A.

1 (*amends* TA 1988 s 15(1)).

2 (*inserts* TA 1988 s 15(1A)).

3 (*substitutes heading of* TA 1988 Part II).

4 (*substitutes* TA 1988 ss 21, 21A, 21B).

5 (*inserts* TA 1988 s 21C).

6 (*repeals* TA 1988 s 25).

7 (*amend* TA 1988 s 26).

8 (*substitutes* TA 1988 s 27(3)).

9 (*repeals* TA 1988 s 28).

10 (*repeals* TA 1988 s 29).

11 (*amends* TA 1988 s 30(1)).

12 (*repeals* TA 1988 s 31).

13 (*repeals* TA 1988 s 33).

14 (*repeals* TA 1988 ss 33A, 33B).

15 (*amend* TA 1988 s 34).

16 (*amend* TA 1988 s 35).

17 (*amend* TA 1988 s 36).

18 (*amend* TA 1988 s 37).

19 (*substitutes heading before* TA 1988 s 40).

20 (*amend* TA 1988 s 40).

21 (*repeals* TA 1988 s 41).

22 (*repeals* TA 1988 s 42A(8)).

23 (*repeals* TA 1988 s 65(2A), (2B) *and amends* TA 1988 s 65(4)).

24 (*substitutes* TA 1988 s 65A).

25 (*inserts* TA 1988 s 70A).

PART II
TREATMENT OF LOSSES

26 (*amends heading before* TA 1988 s 379A).

27 (*inserts* TA 1988 s 379B).

28 (*inserts* TA 1988 ss 392A, 392B).

29 (*substitutes* TA 1988 ss 403, *and inserts* TA 1988 ss 403ZA–403ZE).

30 (*inserts* TA 1988 s 494A).

31 (*inserts* TA 1988 s 768D).

32 (*amends* TA 1988 s 769(1), (2), (3), (4), (5)).

PART III
MINOR AND CONSEQUENTIAL AMENDMENTS
Taxes Management Act 1970 (c 9)

33 ...

Amendment—This paragraph (which amended TMA 1970 s 41A(9)) repealed by FA 1998 s 165, Sch 27 Part III(28) with effect
for accounting periods ending after 30 June 1999 by virtue of the Finance Act 1994, Section 199, (Appointed Day) Order,
SI 1998/3173.

Income and Corporation Taxes Act 1988 (c 1)

34 (*amends* TA 1988 s 87(1)).

35 (*amends* TA 1988 s 118(1), (2)).

36 (*amends* TA 1988 s 400(2)).

37 (*amend* TA 1988 s 404).

38 (*amends* TA 1988 s 413(6)).

39 (*inserts* TA 1988 ss 432AA, 432AB).

40 (*amended* TA 1988 s 434E, *repealed by* CAA 2001 s 580, Sch 4 with effect in accordance with
CAA 2001 s 579).

41 (*inserts* TA 1988 s 441B(2A)).

42 (*substitutes* TA 1988 s 503).

43 (*repeals* TA 1988 s 579(4) *and amends* TA 1988 s 579(5)).

44 (*amends* TA 1988 s 787(3)).

45 (*amends* TA 1988 s 832(1)).

46 (*amends* TA 1988 Sch 26 para 1(3)).

Capital Allowances Act 1990 (c 1)

47–61 (*amended* CAA 1990, *repealed by* CAA 2001 s 580, Sch 4 with effect in accordance with
CAA 2001 s 579).

Taxation of Chargeable Gains Act 1992 (c 12)

62 (*amends* TCGA 1992 s 241(3)).

63 (*amends* TCGA 1992 Sch 8 para 5(1), (2), (3)), 6(2), 7 *and substitutes* Sch 8 para 7A).

Finance Act 1996 (c 8)

64 (*amends* FA 1996 Sch 8 para 1(3) *and substitutes* Sch 8 para 2(2)).

PART IV
TRANSITIONAL PROVISIONS FOR CORPORATION TAX
Introduction

65—(1) This Part of this Schedule makes provision with respect to the application of the provisions of Parts I to III of this Schedule for corporation tax purposes.

(2) In this Part of this Schedule—

''before commencement'' and ''after commencement'' mean, respectively, before 1st April 1998 and on or after that date; and

''the new rules'' means the provisions of the Tax Acts relating to Schedule A taxation or, as the case may be, to the taxation under Case V of Schedule D of income from land outside the United Kingdom, as they have effect after commencement.

Receipts and expenses not to be counted twice

66—(1) To the extent that receipts or expenses have been taken into account before commencement, they shall not be taken into account again under the new rules after commencement.

(2) Nothing in section 43 of the Finance Act 1989 (computation of profits: effect of delayed payment of emoluments) shall be construed as affecting the rule in sub-paragraph (1) above.

Receipts and expenses not to be left out of account

67 To the extent that receipts or expenses would under the new rules have been brought into account before commencement, and were not so brought into account, they shall be brought into account immediately after commencement.

Expenses not to be carried back to before commencement

68 Expenses which were incurred before commencement but were not taken into account before commencement shall not, by virtue of section 25(3) or 31(3) of the Taxes Act 1988, be carried back and taken into account before commencement.

Effect of transfer of underlying rights

69 If any estate, interest or rights in or over land is or are transferred from one person to another, the references in paragraphs 66 to 68 to receipts or expenses being taken into account shall be construed as references to their being taken into account in relation to either of those persons

Bad debt relief

70—(1) Where relief under section 41 of the Taxes Act 1988 (relief for rent, etc not paid) has been given in respect of an amount before commencement, any receipt after commencement shall be taken into account under the new rules.

(2) Any writing off of an amount after commencement shall be taken into account under the new rules, even where it relates to a receipt brought into account before commencement.

Meaning of ''taken into account''

71 For the purposes of paragraphs 66 to 70 an amount is ''taken into account'' if—

    (a) it is brought into account for tax purposes, or

    (b) it would have been so brought into account if the person concerned were chargeable to tax.

Unrelieved Case VI losses

72—(1) A loss to which this paragraph applies which a company would, apart from this Schedule, have been entitled to carry forward under section 396 of the Taxes Act 1988 (Case VI losses) shall be treated after commencement as a loss of an earlier period within section 392A or 392B of that Act and accordingly available to be set off under those provisions.

(2) This paragraph applies to a loss sustained in a business or transaction of a kind that after commencement would be treated as carried on or entered into in the course of a Schedule A business or overseas property business carried on by the company.

Source ceasing in transitional accounting period

73—(1) The provisions of Parts I to III of this Schedule do not apply in relation to a source which ceases in the course of a company's transitional accounting period to be a source within the charge to tax under Schedule A or Case V or VI of Schedule D in relation to that company and any other person.

(2) This paragraph does not apply if the company acquired the source in that accounting period or in the preceding twelve months.

Superseded provisions relating to finance leasing

74—(1) In Schedule 12 to the Finance Act 1997 (leasing arrangements: finance leases and loans), the following provisions (which apply concepts from Case I of Schedule D in relation to rent taxed under Schedule A) shall cease to have effect in accordance with this paragraph.

(2) Paragraphs 3(6), 6(9)(*b*), 8(1) to (7) and 20(*b*) do not apply in relation to periods of account beginning on or after 1st April 1998.

"period of account" means a period for which accounts are made up.

(3) Paragraph 8(8) does not apply if the time mentioned in that provision is on or after 1st April 1998.

(4) Paragraph 8(9) does not apply if the time mentioned in paragraph (*a*) of that provision is on or after 1st April 1998.

Computation of amounts available for surrender as group relief

75 In computing under section 403 of the Taxes Act the amounts available for surrender as group relief in a company's transitional accounting period, the amounts referable to the period before commencement shall be computed separately from the amounts referable to the period after commencement.

Commentary—*Simon's Direct Tax Service* **D2.624.**

Meaning of "transitional accounting period"

76 For the purposes of paragraphs 73 and 75 a "transitional accounting period" means an accounting period beginning before, and ending on or after, 1st April 1998.

SCHEDULE 6

ADJUSTMENT ON CHANGE OF ACCOUNTING BASIS
Section 44

Note—The rules set out in FA 2002 s 64, Sch 22 have effect in place of the provisions of FA 1998 s 44, Sch 6.
Revenue & other press releases—IR Tax Bulletin February 1999 p 625 (guidance on "catching-up charge" under this Schedule).
Amendment—This Schedule repealed by FA 2002 s 141, Sch 40 Pt 3(8) with effect in accordance with FA 2002 s 64(6), Sch 22 paras 16, 17.

Introduction

1 The provisions of this Schedule apply in the circumstances specified in section 44(1) and (2).

Adjustment on change of accounting basis

2—*(1) The amount required by way of adjustment must be calculated (in accordance with paragraph 3) and*—

(a) *if the amount is positive, it is chargeable to tax, and*
(b) *if it is negative, it is allowable as a deduction in computing profits.*

(2) An amount chargeable to tax under this paragraph—

(a) *is treated as income arising on the first day of the first period of account for which the new basis is adopted, subject to paragraphs 4 and 5 (spreading of adjustment charge in certain cases and election to accelerate payment);*
(b) *is chargeable to tax under Case VI of Schedule D;*
(c) *in the case of an individual whose income from the trade, profession or vocation in question is*—

(i) *relevant earnings within section 623(2)(c) or 644(2)(c) of the Taxes Act 1988, or*
(ii) *earned income within section 833(4)(c) of that Act,*

is similarly relevant earnings or earned income for the year of assessment in which it is charged to tax; and
(d) *is treated for the purposes of Chapters I and II of Part X of the Taxes Act 1988 (loss relief) as profits of the trade, profession or vocation for the chargeable period for which it is charged to tax.*

(3) An amount allowable under this paragraph as a deduction in computing profits is treated as an expense of the trade, profession or vocation in the first period for which the new basis is adopted.

Commentary—*Simon's Direct Tax Service* **B4.212, 213.**

Calculation of adjustment

3—*(1) The amount of the adjustment is calculated as follows.*
First step

Add together any amounts representing the extent to which, comparing the two bases, profits were understated (or losses overstated) on the old basis:

1. Receipts which on the new basis would have been brought into account in computing the profits of a period before the change of basis, to the extent that they were not so brought into account.

2. Expenses which on the new basis fall to be brought into account in computing the profits of a period after the change, to the extent that they were brought into account in computing the profits of a period of account before the change of basis.

3. Deductions in respect of opening trading stock or opening work in progress in the first period of account on the new basis to the extent to which they are not matched by credits in respect of closing trading stock or closing work in progress in the last period of account before the change.

Second step

Then deduct any amounts representing the extent to which, comparing the two bases, profits were overstated (or losses understated) on the old basis:

1. Receipts which were taken into account in a period before the change, to the extent that they would not have been taken into account for such a period if the profits had been computed on the new basis.

2. Expenses which were not taken into account in computing the profits of a period before the change, to the extent that they would have been taken into account for such a period if the profits had been computed on the new basis.

3. Credits in respect of closing trading stock or closing work in progress in the last period of account before the change of accounting basis to the extent to which they are not matched by deductions in respect of opening trading stock or opening work in progress in the first period of account on the new basis.

An amount so deducted may not be deducted again in computing the profits of a period of account.

Third step

In the case of a profession or vocation adopting a new accounting basis to comply with section 42 (true and fair view), a further deduction may be made by way of adjustment in respect of any change of accounting basis before 6th April 1999.

The amount deductible is calculated as follows—

A Add together the amounts by which profits were overstated (or losses understated) by reason of the previous change of accounting basis:

1. Receipts to the extent that by reason of the change of accounting basis they were brought into account in more than one period of account.

2. Expenses to the extent that by reason of the change of accounting basis they were not deducted in any period of account.

3. Credits in respect of closing trading stock or closing work in progress in the last period of account before the change of accounting basis to the extent that they were not matched by deductions in respect of opening trading stock or opening work in progress in the first period of account following the change.

B Then deduct the amounts by which profits were understated (or losses overstated) by reason of that change:

1. Receipts to the extent that by reason of the change of accounting basis they were not brought into account in any period of account.

2. Expenses to the extent that by reason of the change of accounting basis they were deducted in more than one period of account.

3. Deductions in respect of opening trading stock or opening work in progress in the first period of account following the change of accounting basis to the extent that they were not matched by credits in respect of closing trading stock or closing work in progress in the last period of account before the change.

An amount may not be so deducted if it has previously been brought into account; and it may not be deducted again on a subsequent change of accounting basis.

(2) The references in this paragraph to items being brought into account in a period of account before the change of basis are to their being brought into account—

    (a) in computing the profits of the same trade, profession or vocation, and
    (b) in accordance with the law and practice then applicable.

For the purposes of paragraph (a) a trade, profession or vocation is not regarded as the same if section 113(1) or 337(1) of the Taxes Act 1988 applies (deemed discontinuance on change of persons carrying on trade, profession or vocation).

Commentary—*Simon's Direct Tax Service* **B4.212, 213.**

Spreading of adjustment charge in certain cases

4—(1) This paragraph provides for the spreading of the adjustment charge in certain cases where an individual—

    (a) has been entitled to compute the profits of a profession or vocation on a basis that does not comply with section 42 of this Act (true and fair view), or would not have complied with that section if it had been in force, and

    (b) changes to an accounting basis that does comply with that section.

(2) The cases in which this paragraph applies are where a change of basis is made to comply with that section—

    (a) on that section coming into effect in relation to periods of account beginning after 6th April 1999, or

    (b) on the exemption given by section 43 of this Act (barristers and advocates in early years of practice) coming to an end or ceasing to apply.

(3) Where this paragraph applies the adjustment charge is spread over ten years of assessment, as follows.

(4) In each of the nine years of assessment beginning with that in which the whole amount would otherwise be chargeable to tax, an amount equal to whichever is the less of—

    (a) one-tenth of the amount of the adjustment charge, and

    (b) 10% of the profits of the profession or vocation for that year of assessment,

is treated as arising and chargeable to tax.

For the purposes of paragraph (b) the profits of the profession or vocation means the profits as computed for the purposes of Case II of Schedule D, leaving out of account any allowances or charges under [the Capital Allowances Act][1].

(5) In the tenth year of assessment the balance of the adjustment charge is treated as arising and chargeable to tax.

(6) If before the whole of the adjustment charge has been charged to tax the profession or vocation—

    (a) is permanently discontinued, or

    (b) is treated as permanently discontinued under section 113(1) of the Taxes Act 1988 (change of persons carrying on profession or vocation),

the preceding provisions of this paragraph continue to apply, but with the omission of the alternative limit in paragraph (4)(b) by reference to profits of the profession or vocation.

(7) This paragraph has effect subject to any election under paragraph 5.

Commentary—*Simon's Direct Tax Service* **B4.213.**
Amendments—[1] Words in sub-para (4) substituted by CAA 2001 s 578, Sch 2 para 102 with effect for income tax purposes as respects allowances and charges falling to be made for chargeable periods ending after 5 April 2001.

Election to accelerate payment of adjustment charge

5—(1) A person who under paragraph 4 is chargeable to tax for a year of assessment on an amount representing part of an adjustment charge may elect that the amount treated as income arising in that year of assessment should be increased.

(2) The election must be made—

    (a) by notice in writing,

    (b) to an officer of the Board,

    (c) before the 31st January following the year of assessment in question.

(3) The election must specify the amount to be treated as income arising in the year of assessment, which may be any amount up to the whole of the adjustment charge so far as not previously charged to tax.

(4) Where an election has been made, paragraph 4 applies in relation to any subsequent year of assessment as if the original amount of the adjustment charge were reduced by the additional amount treated as arising in the year for which the election was made.

Commentary—*Simon's Direct Tax Service* **B4.213.**

Application of provisions to partnerships

6—(1) In the case of a trade, profession or vocation carried on in partnership, the amount of any adjustment under this Schedule shall be computed—

    (a) for income tax purposes, as if the partnership were an individual resident in the United Kingdom, and

    (b) for corporation tax purposes, as if the partnership were a company resident in the United Kingdom.

(2) Subject to the following provisions of this paragraph, each partner's share of any amount chargeable to tax under paragraph 2 shall be determined according to the profit-sharing

arrangements for the twelve months ending immediately before the date on which the new accounting basis was adopted.

(3) If paragraph 4 applies (spreading of adjustment charge in certain cases), then, subject to sub-paragraph (4) below—

   (a) each partner's share of the amount chargeable in any year of assessment shall be determined—

      (i) for the first year of assessment, according to the profit-sharing arrangements for the twelve months ending immediately before the date on which the new accounting basis was adopted, and

      (ii) for any subsequent year of assessment, according to the profit-sharing arrangements for the twelve months immediately preceding the anniversary in that year of that date; and

   (b) any election under paragraph 5 (election for accelerated payment) in relation to a year of assessment must be made jointly by all the persons who have been members of the partnership in the relevant twelve month period.

(4) If paragraph 4(6) applies (effect of discontinuance of profession or vocation), then—

   (a) each partner's share of any amount chargeable on or after the discontinuance is determined as follows—

      (i) if the discontinuance occurs on the date on which the new accounting basis was adopted, according to the profit-sharing arrangements for the twelve months ending immediately before that date;

      (ii) if the discontinuance occurs after that date but before the first anniversary of that date, according to the profit-sharing arrangements for the period between that date and the date of discontinuance;

      (iii) if the discontinuance occurs after the first anniversary of the date on which the new accounting basis was adopted, according to the profit-sharing arrangements for the period between the immediately preceding anniversary of that date and the date of discontinuance; and

   (b) any election under paragraph 5 after the discontinuance must be made by each former partner separately.

(5) For the purposes of this paragraph—

   (a) "profit-sharing arrangements" means the rights of the partners to share in the profits of the trade, profession or vocation for the period in question; and

   (b) references to the date on which a new accounting basis was adopted are to the first day of the first period of account for which the new basis was adopted.

(6) The provisions of section 111 of the Taxes Act (general provisions as to taxation of partnerships), except subsection (1) (partnership not to be treated as separate entity), do not apply to the extent that the preceding provisions of this paragraph apply.

Commentary—*Simon's Direct Tax Service* **B4.214.**

Liability of personal representatives in case of death of person chargeable

7 In the case of the death of a person who, if he had not died, would have been chargeable to tax under paragraph 4 on an amount representing part of an adjustment charge—

   (a) the tax which would have been so chargeable shall be assessed and charged on his personal representatives and shall be a debt due from and payable out of his estate, and

   (b) his personal representatives may make any election under paragraph 5 which he might have made.

Commentary—*Simon's Direct Tax Service* **B4.215.**

Interpretation

8—(1) In this Schedule—

"adjustment charge" means a charge under paragraph 2 above; and

"period of account" means any period for which accounts of the trade, profession or vocation are drawn up.

SCHEDULE 7

REMOVAL OF UNNECESSARY REFERENCES TO GAINS

Section 46(3)

Commentary—*Simon's Direct Tax Service* **B4.203.**
Note—Details of amendments already in force have been omitted from the Schedule.

SCHEDULE 8

SUB-CONTRACTORS IN THE CONSTRUCTION INDUSTRY

Section 57

Introductory

1 Chapter IV of Part XIII of the Taxes Act 1988 shall be amended in accordance with paragraphs 2 to 6 below.

Application of deductions to public departments etc

2—(1) (*inserted* TA 1988 s 559(5A), *repealed by* FA 2002 s 141, Sch 40 Pt 3(1) *with effect for deductions made under TA 1988 s 559 after 5 April 2002*).

(2) (*amends* TA 1988 s 560(2) *and inserts* TA 1988 s 560(2A), (2B)).

(3) This paragraph has effect in relation to any payments made on or after the day, or first day, that is appointed under subsection (3) of section 139 of the Finance Act 1995 (commencement of changes to sub-contractors scheme) for the purposes of paragraph 2 of Schedule 27 to that Act (additional public bodies etc that may be contractors).

(4) The reference in subsection (2B) of section 560 of the Taxes Act 1988 to a period of three years in relation to which the condition provided for in subsection (2A) of that section has been satisfied does not include a reference to any such period ending more than a year before the day or, as the case may be, first day mentioned in sub-paragraph (3) above.

Note—The appointed day for the purposes of sub-para (3) is 1 August 1999, by virtue of the Finance Act 1995, Section 139(3), (Appointed Day) Order, SI 1998/2620.

Conditions for exemption of partnerships

3 ...

Amendment—This paragraph (which amended TA 1988 s 564(2A) and inserted s 564(2AA), (2C)) repealed by FA 1999 ss 53(1), 139, Sch 20 Pt III(11) with effect retrospectively for any application for the issue or renewal of a certificate under TA 1988 s 561 made for a period beginning after 31 July 1999.

Conditions of exemption for companies

4 ...

Amendment—This paragraph (which substituted TA 1988 s 565(2A), (2B) and inserted s 565(2BB), (2D)) repealed by FA 1999 ss 53(1), 139, Sch 20 Pt III(11) with effect retrospectively for any application for the issue or renewal of a certificate under TA 1988 s 561 made for a period beginning after 31 July 1999.

Commencement of paragraphs 3 and 4

5 ...

Amendment—This paragraph repealed by FA 1999 ss 53(1), 139, Sch 20 Pt III(11) with effect retrospectively for any application for the issue or renewal of a certificate under TA 1988 s 561 made for a period beginning after 31 July 1999.

Powers to make regulations

6 (*inserts* TA 1988 s 566(4), (5)).

Transitional provision for commencement of 1995 Act amendments

7 An order under subsection (3) of section 139 of the Finance Act 1995 (commencement of changes to sub-contractors scheme) appointing a day for the purposes of a provision of that section or Schedule 27 to that Act may also provide that certificates under section 561 of the Taxes Act 1988 which have been issued or renewed before the making of the order for periods ending on or after the appointed day are to cease to have effect at the end of the day immediately preceding the appointed day.

Cross references—See Finance Act 1995, Section 139(3), (Appointed Day) Order, SI 1998/2620 art 4 (certificates under TA 1988 s 561 for periods ending after 31 July 1999, cease to have effect at the end of 31 July 1999).

SCHEDULE 9

PAYMENTS AND OTHER BENEFITS IN CONNECTION WITH TERMINATION OF EMPLOYMENT ETC

Section 58(2)

PART I

SCHEDULE 11 TO THE TAXES ACT 1988

(*substitutes* TA 1988 Sch 11).

PART II
CONSEQUENTIAL AMENDMENTS
Income and Corporation Taxes Act 1988 (c 1)

1 (*amends* TA 1988 s 189 (exemption from Schedule E charge of lump sum payments under approved retirement benefits schemes, etc)).

2 (*amends* TA 1988 s 190).

3 (*amends* TA 1988 s 202B(8)).

4 (*amends* TA 1988 s 833(3)(*a*)).

Finance Act 1995 (c 4)

5 (*substitutes* FA 1995 s 92(10)).

SCHEDULE 10
ORDINARY COMMUTING AND PRIVATE TRAVEL
Section 61(2)

(*inserts* TA 1988 Sch 12A).

SCHEDULE 11
TRANSITIONAL PROVISIONS FOR PROFIT-RELATED PAY
Section 62

Application of Schedule

1—(1) This Schedule applies for the purposes of Chapter III of Part V of the Taxes Act 1988 (profit-related pay) where—

(*a*) profit-related pay is or has been paid to an employee by reference to any period (''the relevant period'') and in accordance with a registered scheme (''the affected scheme''), and

(*b*) sub-paragraph (2) or (3) below applies in the employee's case to the relevant period.

(2) This sub-paragraph applies in the employee's case to the relevant period if—

(*a*) that period is a period beginning for the employee at a time on or after 17th March 1998 and ending before 31st December 2000;

(*b*) the employee has been eligible in accordance with a related scheme to receive profit-related pay by reference to the whole or a part of any profit period for the related scheme (''the earlier period'');

(*c*) the earlier period is (or, by virtue of sub-paragraph (4) below, is treated as being) a period beginning before the first day of the relevant period; and

(*d*) the relevant anniversary is (or, by virtue of that sub-paragraph, is treated as being) in a later calendar year than the first day of the relevant period.

(3) This sub-paragraph applies in the employee's case to the relevant period if—

(*a*) that period is a period beginning for the employee at a time on or after 17th March 1998 and ending before 31st December 2000;

(*b*) the employee has been eligible in accordance with either the affected scheme or a related scheme to receive profit-related pay by reference to the whole or any part of a profit period (''the earlier period'');

(*c*) the earlier period is a period beginning twelve months or less before the first day of the relevant period;

(*d*) the section 171(4) limit for the earlier period is a limit computed in accordance with this Schedule; and

(*e*) the relevant anniversary is in a later calendar year than the first day of the relevant period.

(4) Where—

(*a*) the conditions in paragraphs (*a*) and (*b*) of sub-paragraph (2) above are satisfied in relation to the relevant period in the case of any employee, and

(*b*) the person who is the scheme employer in relation to the affected scheme, by notice to the employee, elects that this sub-paragraph shall apply in relation to the related scheme,

the earlier period referred to in that sub-paragraph shall be assumed for the purposes of this Schedule to be a period beginning with the 1st January next before the first day of the relevant period.

Rule for determining section 171(4) limit

2—(1) The section 171(4) limit applicable to any profit-related pay paid to the employee in accordance with the affected scheme and by reference to the relevant period shall be—

(*a*) if the relevant period does not begin for the employee before the apportionment date, the limit for the part of the profit period falling on or after that date; and

(*b*) in any other case the sum of–

(i) the limit for the part of the relevant period falling on or after the apportionment date; and

(ii) the limit for the part of the relevant period falling before that date.

(2) For the purposes of sub-paragraph (1) above the limit for a part of the relevant period shall be computed by—

(*a*) taking the amount given by virtue of section 61 of the Finance Act 1997 (phasing out of relief for profit-related pay) as the section 171(4) limit for a profit period beginning with the first day of that part of that period and ending with the last day of that part of that period;

(*b*) making a proportionate reduction for so much of that part of that period (if any) as is not included in any period by reference to which the employee is eligible for profit-related pay in accordance with the affected scheme; and

(*c*) using–

(i) the amount produced by the reduction, or

(ii) (if no reduction has been made) the amount taken in accordance with paragraph (*a*) above,

as the limit for that part of the relevant period.

(3) Subject to sub-paragraph (4) below, the apportionment date in the case of any employee is for the purposes of this paragraph—

(*a*) except where the person who is the scheme employer for the affected scheme otherwise elects by notice to that employee, the 1st January that falls next after the first day of the relevant period; and

(*b*) where that person does so elect, the date which is the relevant anniversary for the purposes of whichever of sub-paragraphs (2) and (3) of paragraph 1 above applies to the relevant period in the employee's case.

(4) Where—

(*a*) both sub-paragraphs (2) and (3) of paragraph 1 above apply to the relevant period in the employee's case, or

(*b*) there is, for any other reason, more than one date which (but for this sub-paragraph) would be taken in accordance with sub-paragraph (3)(*b*) above to be the apportionment date,

the apportionment date shall be the earliest of those dates to fall in the calendar year immediately following that in which the first day of the relevant period falls.

Meaning of related scheme

3—(1) In the case of any employee a scheme is, in relation to the affected scheme, a related scheme for the purposes of this Schedule if—

(*a*) it was a registered scheme at any relevant time and the conditions set out in sub-paragraph (2) below are satisfied with respect to it; or

(*b*) notice that for the purposes of this Schedule it is to be treated as a related scheme in relation to the affected scheme is given to the employee by the scheme employer for the affected scheme.

(2) Those conditions are satisfied with respect to a scheme (''the relevant scheme'') if a person who is the scheme employer for the affected scheme was, at a relevant time—

(*a*) the scheme employer for the relevant scheme; or

(*b*) connected with a person who was, at that or another relevant time, the scheme employer for the relevant scheme.

(3) In this paragraph ''relevant time'' means any time on the day of the beginning for the employee of the relevant period or in the period of twelve months preceding that day.

(4) Section 839 of the Taxes Act 1988 (connected persons) applies for the purposes of this paragraph.

(5) Without prejudice to sub-paragraph (4) above, for the purposes of this paragraph—

(*a*) each of the members of a partnership shall be regarded as connected with the partnership and with any person (including another partnership) with whom the partnership is connected; and

(*b*) a partnership shall be regarded as connected with each of its members and with any person (including another partnership) with whom any of its members is connected.

Meaning of ''relevant anniversary''

4 For the purposes of this Schedule the relevant anniversary is—

(*a*) for the purposes of paragraph 1(2) above, the first anniversary of the first day of the earlier period; and

(*b*) for the purposes of paragraph 1(3) above, the first anniversary of the date that is taken to be the relevant anniversary for the purpose of computing the section 171(4) limit for the earlier period in accordance with this Schedule.

General interpretation

5—(1) Expressions used in this Schedule and in Chapter III of Part V of the Taxes Act 1988 have the same meanings in this Schedule as in that Chapter.

(2) References in this Schedule to the section 171(4) limit are references to the second of the limits mentioned in section 171(2) of the Taxes Act 1988; and this Schedule shall have effect on the basis that that limit is nil for any period (or part of a period) beginning on or after 1st January 2000.

(3) References in this Schedule to the beginning for the employee of any profit period by reference to which he is eligible to receive profit-related pay are references—

(*a*) where sub-paragraph (4) below applies, to the earliest time in that period which is included in a part of that period by reference to which he is so eligible; and

(*b*) in any other case, to the beginning of the first day of the period in question.

(4) This sub-paragraph applies where—

(*a*) the employee is eligible to receive profit-related pay by reference to only a part of the relevant period; and

(*b*) that part of that period begins after the beginning of that period.

SCHEDULE 12

EIS AND VCTS: MEANING OF QUALIFYING TRADE

Section 70

New exclusions for the enterprise investment scheme

1 (*inserts* TA 1988 s 297(2)(*fa*)–(*fe*), (3A) and *amends* TA 1988 s 297(2)(*g*)).

Definition of excluded activities for the enterprise investment scheme

2 (*amend* TA 1988 s 298(5) and *inserts* s 298(5A)–(5C)).

New exclusions for VCTs

3 (*inserts* TA 1988 Sch 28B para 4(2)(*ea*)–(*ee*), (3A) and *amends* Sch 28B para 4(2)(*f*)).

Definition of excluded activities for VCTs

4 (*amend* TA 1988 Sch 28B para 5(1), (5) and *inserts* Sch 28B para 5(6), (7)).

Commencement

5—(1) Paragraphs 1 and 2 above have effect in relation to shares issued on or after 17th March 1998.

(2) Subject to sub-paragraph (3) below, paragraphs 3 and 4 above have effect for the purpose of determining whether any shares or securities are, as at any time on or after 17th March 1998, to be regarded as comprised in the qualifying holdings of any company (''the trust company'').

(3) Paragraphs 3 and 4 above shall not have effect for the purpose of making such a determination in relation to any shares or securities acquired by the trust company by means of the investment of—

(*a*) money raised by the issue before 17th March 1998 of shares in or securities of the trust company, or

(*b*) money derived from the investment by that company of any such money.

SCHEDULE 13

CHANGES TO EIS ETC

Section 74(1)

PART I

EIS INCOME TAX RELIEF

Eligibility for relief

1 (*amends* TA 1988 s 289(1), (1A)(*c*), (6), (7) and *inserts* s 289(9)).

Form of relief

2 (*amends* TA 1988 s 289A(4)).

Attribution of relief to shares

3—(1), (2) (*amend* TA 1988 s 289B(3)(*b*) and *insert* s 289B(3A)).

(3), (4) (*substitute* TA 1988 s 289B(4) and *amend* s 289B(5)).

(5) Sub-paragraphs (1) and (2) above have effect in relation to bonus shares issued on or after 6th April 1998.

Maximum subscriptions etc

4 (*amends* TA 1988 s290(2)).

5 (*repeals* TA 1988 s 290A)

Individuals qualifying for relief

6 (*amends* TA 1988 s 291(1), (2), *substitutes* s 291(3) and *inserts* TA 1988 s 291(6)).

Amendments—Sub-para (1) repealed by FA 2001 s 110, Sch 33 Pt II(3) with effect—

   (*a*) in relation to shares issued after 6 March 2001, and
   (*b*) in respect of the application of TA 1988 Pt VII Chapter III and TCGA 1992 Sch 5B after 6 March 2001 in relation to shares—
      (i) that were issued after 31 December 1993 but before 7 March 2001, and
      (ii) to which income tax relief or deferral relief was attributable immediately before 7 March 2001.

Connected persons: directors

7 (*amends* TA 1988 s 291A(1), (5)).

Amendments—Sub-para (1) repealed by FA 2001 s 110, Sch 33 Pt II(3) with effect—

   (*a*) in relation to shares issued after 6 March 2001, and
   (*b*) in respect of the application of TA 1988 Pt VII Chapter III and TCGA 1992 Sch 5B after 6 March 2001 in relation to shares—
      (i) that were issued after 31 December 1993 but before 7 March 2001, and
      (ii) to which income tax relief or deferral relief was attributable immediately before 7 March 2001.

Connected persons: persons interested in capital etc

8 (*inserts* TA 1988 s 291B(5A) and *substitutes* s 291B(6)).

Qualifying companies and qualifying trades

9—(1) (*amends* TA 1988 s 293(3B)).

(2) (*amends* TA 1988 s 293(6)).

(3)–(5) (*insert* TA 1988 s 293(6A)–(6B), *repeal* s 293(7) and *amends* s 293(8)).

(6) Sub-paragraph (2) above has effect in relation to events occurring on or after 6th April 1998.

10 (*amends* TA 1988 s 297(1)).

11 (*amends* TA 1988 s 298(1)).

Disposal of shares

12—(1), (2) (*amend* TA 1988 s 299(1), (3)).

(3) (*amends* TA 1988 s 299(4)).

(4) (*inserts* TA 1988 s 299(5A)).

(5), (6) (*substitute* TA 1988 s 299(6)–(6D) and *repeal* s 299(7)).

(7) (*amends* TA 1988 s 299(8)).

(8) Sub-paragraphs (1), (3)(*b*), (5) and (6) above have effect in relation to disposals made on or after 6th April 1998.

(9) Sub-paragraph (4) above has effect in relation to options granted on or after that date.

Value received from company

13—(1), (2) (*substitute* TA 1988 s 300(1), (1C)).

(3) (*inserts* TA 1988 s 300(6)).

(4) Sub-paragraph (3) above has effect in relation to disposals made on or after 6th April 1998.

14—(1) (*inserts* TA 1988 s 301(4A)).

(2) (*amends* TA 1988 s 301(5)).

(3) Sub-paragraph (1) above has effect in relation to value received (within the meaning of section 300 of that Act) on or after 6th April 1998.

Value received by persons other than claimants

15 (*substitutes* TA 1988 s 303(1), (1A)–(1D), (2), *amends* s 303(3) and *inserts* s 303(9A)).

Amendments—Sub-para (2) repealed by FA 2001 s 110, Sch 33 Pt II(3) with effect—

(*a*) in relation to shares issued on or after 7 March 2001, and
(*b*) in relation to shares issued before that date, in respect of the application of TA 1988 Pt VII Chapter III and TCGA 1992 Sch 5B in relation to—
(i) value received (within the meaning of TA 1988 s 300 or TCGA 1992 Sch 5B para 13) and
(ii) repayments made,
on or after that date.

Husband and wife

16—(1) (*inserts* TA 1988 s 304(4)).

(2) This paragraph has effect in relation to disposals made on or after 6th April 1998.

Acquisition of share capital by new company

17—(1) (*inserts* TA 1988 s 304A).

(2) This paragraph has effect in relation to new shares (within the meaning of section 304A of the Taxes Act 1988) issued on or after 6th April 1998.

Relief for loss on disposal of shares

18—(1) (*amends* TA 1988 s 305A(2)).

(2) This paragraph has effect in relation to disposals made on or after 6th April 1998.

Claims

19 (*amends* TA 1988 s 306(1), (2), *substitutes* s 306(3), (4), (5) and *amends* s 306(3A)).

Withdrawal of relief

20 (*amends* TA 1988 s 307(1A), (4), (6)(*b*) and *inserts* s 307(1C)).

Amendments—Sub-para (1)(*a*) repealed by FA 2001 s 110, Sch 33 Pt II(3) with effect—

(*a*) in relation to shares issued after 6 March 2001, and
(*b*) in respect of the application of TA 1988 Pt VII Chapter III and TCGA 1992 Sch 5B after 6 March 2001 in relation to shares—
(i) that were issued after 31 December 1993 but before 7 March 2001, and
(ii) to which income tax relief or deferral relief was attributable immediately before 7 March 2001.

Application to subsidiaries

21 (*amends* TA 1988 s 308(2)).

Information

22 (*amend* TA 1988 s 310(1), (2), (7) and *insert* s 310(9A)).

(5) This paragraph has effect in relation to events occurring on or after 6th April 1998.

Interpretation of Chapter III

23—(1) (*amends* TA 1988 s 312(1), (1A), (1B), (2), (7) and *inserts* s 312(4A), (4B)).

PART II
EIS RELIEF AGAINST CHARGEABLE GAINS

24—(1)–(3) (*amend* TCGA 1992 s 150A(1), (2), (4), (5)).

(4) (*substitutes* TCGA 1992 s 150A(6), (6A)).

(5) (*amends* TCGA 1992 s 150A(8A)).

(6) (*inserts* TCGA 1992 s 150A(8D)).

(7) (*inserts* TCGA 1992 s 150A(10A)).

(8) In this paragraph—

(*a*) sub-paragraphs (1) to (3) have effect in relation to disposals made on or after 6th April 1998;
(*b*) sub-paragraph (4) has effect in relation to reorganisations taking effect on or after that date;
(*c*) sub-paragraph (5) has effect in relation to new shares (within the meaning of section 150A(8A) of the Taxation of Chargeable Gains Act 1992) issued on or after that date;
(*d*) sub-paragraph (6) has effect in relation to new shares (within the meaning of section 304A of the Taxes Act 1988) issued on or after that date; and
(*e*) sub-paragraph (7) has effect in relation to events occurring on or after that date.

25—(1) (*amend* TA 1988 s 150B).

(2) This paragraph has effect in relation to disposals made on or after 6th April 1998.

PART III
EIS DEFERRAL OF CHARGEABLE GAINS

Preliminary

26 Schedule 5B to the Taxation of Chargeable Gains Act 1992 (enterprise investment scheme: re-investment) shall be amended in accordance with the following provisions of this Part.

Application of Schedule

27 (*amends* TCGA 1992 Sch 5B para 1(1) and *substitutes* Sch 5B para 1(2), (3)).

Failure of conditions of application

28 (*inserts* TCGA 1992 Sch 5B para 1A).

Postponement of original gain

29 (*amends* TCGA 1992 Sch 5B para 2(3)).

Chargeable events

30 (*amends* Sch 5B para 3(1), *repeals* TCGA 1992 Sch 5B para 3(2) and *inserts* Sch 5B para 3(6)).

Amendments—Sub-para (1)(*a*) repealed by FA 2001 s 110, Sch 33 Pt II(3) with effect—
    (*a*) in relation to shares issued after 6 March 2001, and
    (*b*) in respect of the application of TA 1988 Pt VII Chapter III and TCGA 1992 Sch 5B after 6 March 2001 in relation to shares—
        (i) that were issued after 31 December 1993 but before 7 March 2001, and
        (ii) to which income tax relief or deferral relief was attributable immediately before 7 March 2001.

Gains accruing on chargeable event

31—(1), (2) (*substitute* TCGA 1992 Sch 5B para 4(2)–(4C) and *amend* Sch 5B para 3(5)).
(3) This paragraph has effect in relation to disposals made on or after 6th April 1998.

Persons to whom gain accrues

32 (*amends* TCGA 1992 Sch 5B para 5(1)).

Claims

33 (*substitutes* TCGA 1992 Sch 5B para 6).

Reorganisations and reconstructions

34 (*inserts* TCGA 1992 Sch 5B paras 7–9).

Anti-avoidance provisions

35 (*inserts* TCGA 1992 Sch 5B paras 10–15).

Supplementary provisions

36 (*inserts* TCGA 1992 Sch 5B paras 16–19).

PART IV
BES INCOME TAX RELIEF AND RELIEF AGAINST CHARGEABLE GAINS

37 Any reference in this Part to a provision of Chapter III of Part VII of the Taxes Act 1988 is a reference to that provision as it has effect in relation to shares issued before 1st January 1994.

38—(1) (*amends* TA 1988 s 293(8)).
(2) This paragraph has effect in relation to new shares (within the meaning of section 304A of the Taxes Act 1988) issued on or after 6th April 1998.

39—(1), (2) (*amend* TA 1988 s 299(1) and *substitute* s 299(4)–(4C)).
(3) This paragraph has effect in relation to disposals made on or after 6th April 1998.

40—(1) (*inserts* TA 1988 s 304(7)).
(2) This paragraph has effect in relation to disposals made on or after 6th April 1998.

41—(1) (*inserts* TA 1988 s 304A).
(2) This paragraph has effect in relation to new shares (within the meaning of section 304A of the Taxes Act 1988) issued on or after 6th April 1998.

42—(1) (*amends* TA 1988 s 150(4)(*a*), (5)).

(3) (*amends* TA 1988 s 150(7)).

(4) (*amends* TA 1988 s 150(8)).

(5) (*amends* TA 1988 s 150(8A)(*a*)).

(6) (*inserts* TA 1988 s 150(8D)).

(7) (*inserts* TA 1988 s 150(12)).

(8) In this paragraph—

(*a*) sub-paragraphs (1) and (2) have effect in relation to disposals made on or after 6th April 1998;

(*b*) sub-paragraph (3) has effect in relation to subsequent disposals made on or after that date;

(*c*) sub-paragraph (4) has effect in relation to events occurring on or after that date;

(*d*) sub-paragraph (5) has effect in relation to new shares (within the meaning of section 150(8A) of the Taxation of Chargeable Gains Act 1992) issued on or after that date;

(*e*) sub-paragraph (6) has effect in relation to new shares (within the meaning of section 304A of the Taxes Act 1988) issued on or after that date; and

(*f*) sub-paragraph (7) has effect in relation to events occurring on or after that date.

SCHEDULE 14

LIFE POLICIES, LIFE ANNUITIES AND CAPITAL REDEMPTION POLICIES

Section 86

Section 547

1—(1) Section 547 of the Taxes Act 1988 (method of charging gain to tax) shall be amended as follows.

(2)–(7) (*amends* TA 1988 s 547(1), (4), (5), *repeal* s 547(3) and *insert* s 547(5A)).

(8) (*renumbers* TA 1988 s 547(9) as s 547(13) *and inserts* s 547(9)–(12)).

(9), (10) (*amends* TA 1988 s 547(13) and *insert* s 547(14)).

Multiple interests

2 (*inserts* TA 1988 s 547A).

Right of company to recover tax from trustees

3 (*inserts* TA 1988 s 551A).

Foreign institution policies: no reduction under section 553

4—(1) Section 553 of the Taxes Act 1988 (non-resident policies and capital redemption policies) shall be amended as follows.

(2)–(4) (*amends* TA 1988 s 553(3), (10) and *insert* s 553(5A)).

Consequential amendments

5 (*amends* TMA 1970 s 7(9)).

6 (*substitutes* FA 1989 s 151(2)).

Commencement

7—(1) Paragraph (*d*) of section 547(1) of the Taxes Act 1988 shall not have effect in relation to the amount of a gain if—

(*a*) the gain is treated as arising on the happening of a chargeable event on or after 6th April 1998 in relation to a pre-commencement policy or contract; and

(*b*) the trusts in question were created before 17th March 1998 and the person, or (disregarding section 547A(6) of that Act) at least one of the persons, who created them was an individual who died before that date.

(2) In sub-paragraph (1) above, "pre-commencement policy or contract" means—

(*a*) a policy of life insurance issued in respect of an insurance made before 17th March 1998,

(*b*) a contract for a life annuity made before that date, or

(*c*) a capital redemption policy where the contract was effected before that date,

but does not include a policy or contract varied on or after that date so as to increase the benefits secured or to extend the term of the insurance, annuity or capital redemption policy (any exercise of rights conferred by the policy or contract being regarded for this purpose as a variation).

(3) The amendment made by paragraph 6 above has effect in relation to income arising on or after 6th April 1998.

(4) In that amendment, the express references to gains treated as arising under Chapter II of Part XIII of the Taxes Act 1988 are references to gains treated as so arising on the happening of chargeable events on or after 6th April 1998.

(5) Except as provided by the preceding provisions of this paragraph, this Schedule has effect in relation to chargeable events happening on or after 6th April 1998.

SCHEDULE 15

APPROVED RETIREMENT BENEFITS SCHEMES

Section 92

Amendment of section 591C of the Taxes Act 1988

1—(1) Section 591C of the Taxes Act 1988 (charge to tax arising on cessation of approval) shall be amended as follows.

(2)–(5) (*amend* TA 1988 s 591C(4), (7) and *insert* s 591C(6A), (8), (9)).

(6) This paragraph has effect in relation to any case in which the date of the cessation of the approval is on or after 17th March 1998.

Amendment of section 591D

2—(1) (*amends* TA 1988 s 591D(3)).

(2) This paragraph has effect in relation to any case in which the date of the cessation of the approval of the scheme is on or after 17th March 1998.

Application for scheme approval

3—(1), (2) (*amend* TA 1988 s 604(1) and *insert* s 604(1A)).

(3) This paragraph has effect in relation to any application made on or after the day on which this Act is passed.

Information powers

4 (*amends* TA 1988 s 605(1B)).

Employers responsible for discharging administrator's duties

5—(1) (*inserts* TA 1988 s 606(9A), (11A)).

(2) (*inserts* TA 1988 s 606(11A)).

(3) Sub-paragraph (2) above has effect for determinations made in relation to any time on or after 17th March 1998.

Recourse to scheme members in respect of section 591C charge

6—(1) (*inserts* TA 1988 s 606A).

(2) This paragraph has effect in relation to any case in which the date of the cessation of the approval is on or after 17th March 1998.

Modification of certain existing approved schemes

7—(1) This paragraph applies in relation to any retirement benefits scheme which—

(*a*) was approved by the Board on or before 17th March 1998; and

(*b*) contains provision requiring one of the trustees of the scheme to be an approved independent trustee.

(2) Notwithstanding anything to the contrary in the scheme or its rules, the appointment (whenever made) of any person to be a trustee of the scheme, and any requirement on him or entitlement of his to act as such, shall be (and be treated as having been) incapable of termination at any time on or after 17th March 1998 except—

(*a*) by the death of that person;

(*b*) by an order of the court;

(*c*) by virtue of section 3, 4 or 29 of the Pensions Act 1995 or Article 3, 4 or 29 of the Pensions (Northern Ireland) Order 1995 (prohibition, suspension or disqualification); or

(*d*) in circumstances mentioned in sub-paragraph (3)(*a*), (*b*) or (*c*) below, in accordance with the rules of the scheme.

(3) Those circumstances are—

(*a*) where the trustee is not the trustee by reference to whom the requirement mentioned in sub-paragraph (1)(*b*) above was satisfied immediately before the termination;

(*b*) where immediately after the termination that requirement is satisfied by reference to a trustee whose appointment takes effect at that time;

(*c*) where the trustee whose appointment is terminated has committed a fraudulent breach of trust in relation to the scheme and that is the reason for the termination.

(4) Any provisions of the scheme or of any instrument by which the administration of the scheme is governed which require a successor to an approved independent trustee of the scheme to be appointed in specified circumstances shall have effect, in relation to any case in which those circumstances arise at a time on or after the day on which this Act is passed, as if they required the appointment to be made no more than 30 days after that time.

(5) Subsection (5) of section 591D of the Taxes Act 1988 (meaning of "approved independent trustee") shall apply for the purposes of this paragraph as it applies for the purposes of that section.

(6) In this paragraph "retirement benefits scheme" has the same meaning as in Chapter I of Part XIV of the Taxes Act 1988, and "approved" means approved for the purposes of that Chapter or any enactment re-enacted in that Chapter.

SCHEDULE 16

TRANSFER PRICING ETC: NEW REGIME

Section 108

(*inserts* TA 1988 Sch 28AA).

SCHEDULE 17

CONTROLLED FOREIGN COMPANIES

Section 113

Section 747

1 (*amends* TA 1988 s 747(1), (3), (4), (5)).

Commentary—*Simon's Direct Tax Service* **D4.1250.**

Section 747A

2 (*amends* TA 1988 s 747A(6), (8), (9)).

Commentary—*Simon's Direct Tax Service* **D4.1217.**

Section 748

3 (*amends* TA 1988 s 748(1), (3), *inserts* s 748(1A) and *repeals* s 748(2)).

Commentary—*Simon's Direct Tax Service* **D4.1206.**

Section 749

4 (*substitutes* TA 1988 ss 749, 749A, 749B).

Commentary—*Simon's Direct Tax Service* **D4.1203A, 1204, 1204A.**

Section 750

5 (*amends* TA 1988 s 750(1), (3)).

Commentary—*Simon's Direct Tax Service* **D4.1205.**

Section 751

6 (*amends* TA 1988 s 751(1), (4), (5), (6) and *inserts* s 751(5A)).

Commentary—*Simon's Direct Tax Service* **D4.1203.**

Section 752

7 (*substitutes* TA 1988 ss 752, 752A, 752B, 752C).

Commentary—*Simon's Direct Tax Service* **D4.1203A, 1258.**

Section 753

8 (*repeals* TA 1988 s 753).

Commentary—*Simon's Direct Tax Service* **D4.1250.**

Section 754

9 (*amends* TA 1988 s 754(1), (6)–(8), *inserts* s 754(1A), (2A)–(2E), *substitutes* s 754(2), (3), (3A), (3B) and *repeals* s 754(4)).
Commentary—*Simon's Direct Tax Service* **D4.1255, 1259A, 1259B.**

Returns where it is not established whether acceptable distribution policy applies

10 (*inserts* TA 1988 s 754A).
Commentary—*Simon's Direct Tax Service* **D4.1257.**

Determinations requiring the sanction of the Board

11 (*inserts* TA 1988 s 754B).

Section 755

12 (*repeals* TA 1988 s 755).
Commentary—*Simon's Direct Tax Service* **D4.1270.**

Treatment of chargeable profits and creditable tax apportioned to company carrying on life assurance business

13 (*inserts* TA 1988 s 755A).

Amendment of return where general insurance business of foreign company accounted for on non-annual basis

14 (*inserts* TA 1988 s 755B).

Application of Chapter where general insurance business of foreign company accounted for on non-annual basis.

15 (*inserts* TA 1988 s 755C).

Section 756

16—(1) Section 756 of the Taxes Act 1988 (interpretation and construction of Chapter IV) shall be amended as follows.
(2) (*amends* TA 1988 s 756(1)).

Paragraph 1 of Schedule 24

17 (*amends* TA 1988 Sch 24 para 1(3A), (4)).
Commentary—*Simon's Direct Tax Service* **D4.1211.**

Paragraph 2 of Schedule 24

18 (*amends* TA 1988 Sch 24 para 2(1)).
Commentary—*Simon's Direct Tax Service* **D4.1211.**

Paragraph 4 of Schedule 24

19—(1) Paragraph 4 of Schedule 24 to the Taxes Act 1988 (assumption that claims or elections giving maximum relief have been made, subject to notice to the contrary) shall be amended as follows.
(2)–(6) (*amend* TA 1988 Sch 24 para 4(1A), (2), (3), (3A) and *repeal* Sch 24 para 4(2A)).
Commentary—*Simon's Direct Tax Service* **D4.1213.**

Paragraph 9 of Schedule 24

20—(1) Paragraph 9 of Schedule 24 to the Taxes Act 1988 (losses in pre-direction accounting periods) shall be amended as follows.
(2)–(9) (*amend* TA 1988 Sch 24 para 9(1), (3), *repeal* Sch 24 para 9(2), (5), (6), *substitute* Sch 24 para 9(4) and *insert* Sch 24 para 9(7)).
Commentary—*Simon's Direct Tax Service* **D4.1211.**

Paragraph 10 of Schedule 24

21 (*amends* TA 1988 Sch 24 para 10(1)).
Commentary—*Simon's Direct Tax Service* **D4.1215.**

Paragraph 11 of Schedule 24

22 (*repeals* TA 1988 Sch 24 para 11).

Commentary—*Simon's Direct Tax Service* **D4.1211, 1214.**

Paragraph 11A of Schedule 24

23 (*repeals* TA 1988 Sch 24 para 11A(3), (6)).

Transfer pricing

24 (*inserts* TA 1988 Sch 24 para 20).

Commentary—*Simon's Direct Tax Service* **D4.1216.**

Schedule 25

25 (*substitutes heading to* TA 1988 Sch 25).

Commentary—*Simon's Direct Tax Service* **D4.1220.**

Paragraph 1 of Schedule 25

26 (*amends* TA 1988 Sch 25 para 1).

Commentary—*Simon's Direct Tax Service* **D4.1220.**

Paragraph 2A of Schedule 25

27—(1) Paragraph 2A of Schedule 25 to the Taxes Act 1988 (acceptable distribution policy: modifications of paragraph 2) shall be amended as follows.

(2)–(5) (*amend* TA 1988 Sch 25 para 2A(2), (4), (8)).

Commentary—*Simon's Direct Tax Service* **D4.1220, 1221.**

Paragraph 3 of Schedule 25

28 (*amends* TA 1988 Sch 25 para 3(4A)).

Commentary—*Simon's Direct Tax Service* **D4.1220.**

Paragraph 5 of Schedule 25

29 (*amends* TA 1988 Sch 25 para 5(2)).

Paragraph 6 of Schedule 25

30—(1) Paragraph 6 of Schedule 25 to the Taxes Act 1988 (exemption for controlled foreign companies engaged in exempt activities) shall be amended as follows.

(2)–(9) (*amend* TA 1988 Sch 25 para 6(1)–(4), (5) and *insert* Sch 25 para 6(4A), (4B), (4C), (5A)).

Commentary—*Simon's Direct Tax Service* **D4.1203A, 1233, 1237, 1237A.**

Paragraph 8 of Schedule 25

31—(1) Paragraph 8 of Schedule 25 to the Taxes Act 1988 (which relates to the condition in paragraph 6(1)(*b*) of that Schedule) shall be amended as follows.

(2) (*amends* TA 1988 Sch 25 para 8(3)).

Commentary—*Simon's Direct Tax Service* **D4.1237A.**

Paragraph 12 of Schedule 25

32—(1) Paragraph 12 of Schedule 25 to the Taxes Act 1988 (meaning of "holding company" in paragraphs 6 and 8(3)) shall be amended as follows.

(2), (3) (*amend* TA 1988 Sch 25 para 12(1), (5)).

Superior holding companies: supplementary provisions

33 (*inserts* TA 1988 Sch 25 para 12A).

Commentary—*Simon's Direct Tax Service* **D4.1237A.**

Paragraph 1 of Schedule 26

34—(1) In Schedule 26 to the Taxes Act 1988 (reliefs against liability for tax in respect of chargeable profits apportioned to UK resident company) paragraph 1 (trading losses and group relief etc) shall be amended as follows.

(2)–(5) (*amend* TA 1988 Sch 26 para 1(1), (2) and *repeal* Sch 26 para 1(4), (6)).

Commentary—*Simon's Direct Tax Service* **D4.1254.**

Paragraph 3 of Schedule 26

35—(1) Paragraph 3 of Schedule 26 to the Taxes Act 1988 (gains on disposal of shares in controlled foreign companies) shall be amended as follows.

(2)–(7) (*amend* TA 1988 Sch 26 para 3(1), (3), (4) and *insert* Sch 26 para 3(6A)).

Commentary—*Simon's Direct Tax Service* **D4.1263.**

Paragraph 4 of Schedule 26

36—(1) Paragraph 4 of Schedule 26 to the Taxes Act 1988 (dividends from the controlled foreign company) shall be amended as follows.

(2)–(5) (*amend* TA 1988 Sch 26 para 4(1), (2), (5)).

Commentary—*Simon's Direct Tax Service* **D4.1254.**

Commencement and transitional provision

37—(1) The preceding provisions of this Schedule have effect as respects accounting periods of companies resident in the United Kingdom which end on or after the corporation tax self-assessment appointed day.

(2) Where by virtue of sub-paragraph (1) above any question as to liability (if any) to tax by virtue of Chapter IV of Part XVII of the Taxes Act 1988 as respects any particular accounting period of a non-resident company which ends before the corporation tax self-assessment appointed day falls to be determined—

> (*a*) in the case of at least one company resident in the United Kingdom, for an accounting period of its which ends on or after that day, and
>
> (*b*) in the case of at least one other such company, for an accounting period of its which ends before that day,

such separate determinations and computations shall be made as are necessary for determining the liability of the companies which fall within paragraph (*a*) above and the liability of the companies which fall within paragraph (*b*) above.

(3) For the purposes of sub-paragraph (2) above—

> (*a*) any question as to the liability (if any) of a company falling within paragraph (*a*) shall be determined as if, in the case of every company resident in the United Kingdom, the accounting period of the non-resident company ended in an accounting period of the company ending on or after the corporation tax self-assessment appointed day; and
>
> (*b*) any question as to the liability (if any) of a company falling within paragraph (*b*) shall be determined as if, in the case of every company resident in the United Kingdom, the accounting period of the non-resident company ended in an accounting period of the company ending before the corporation tax self-assessment appointed day.

(4) In this paragraph—

"accounting period", in relation to a non-resident company, has the same meaning as it has in Chapter IV of Part XVII of the Taxes Act 1988;

"the corporation tax self-assessment appointed day" means the day which is the appointed day for the purposes of section 199 of the Finance Act 1994 (corporation tax self-assessment);

"non-resident company" means a company resident outside the United Kingdom.

SCHEDULE 18

COMPANY TAX RETURNS, ASSESSMENTS AND RELATED MATTERS

Section 117(1)

Revenue & other press releases—IR Tax Bulletin October 1998 (Issue 38) p 587 (record keeping requirements under corporation tax self-assessment.

PART I

INTRODUCTION

Meaning of "tax"

1 In this Schedule "tax" means corporation tax including, except as otherwise indicated, any amount assessable or chargeable as if it was corporation tax.

Amounts are assessable or chargeable as if they were corporation tax under—

section 419(1) of the Taxes Act 1988 (tax on loan or advance made by close company to a participator),

[section 501A(1) of that Act (supplementary charge in respect of ring fence trades), and]¹

section 747(4)(*a*) of that Act (tax on profits of controlled foreign company).

Commentary—*Simon's Direct Tax Service* **D2.801.**

Amendments—¹ Words substituted for the word "and" by FA 2002 s 92(3) with effect from 24 July 2002.

Duty to give notice of chargeability

2—(1) A company which—

(*a*) is chargeable to tax for an accounting period, and
(*b*) has not received a notice requiring a company tax return,

must give notice to the Inland Revenue that it is so chargeable.

(2) The notice must be given within twelve months from the end of the accounting period.

(3) A company which fails to comply with this paragraph is liable to a penalty not exceeding the amount of tax payable for the accounting period in question that remains unpaid twelve months after the end of the period.

(4) In computing the amount of unpaid tax for this purpose, no account shall be taken of any relief under section 419(4) of the Taxes Act 1988 (relief in respect of repayment, etc of loan) which is deferred under subsection (4A) of that section.

Commentary—*Simon's Direct Tax Service* **D2.802.**

PART II

COMPANY TAX RETURN

Company tax return

3—(1) The Inland Revenue may by notice require a company to deliver a return (a "company tax return") of such information, accounts, statements and reports—

(*a*) relevant to the tax liability of the company, or
(*b*) otherwise relevant to the application of the Corporation Tax Acts to the company,

as may reasonably be required by the notice.

(2) Different information, accounts, statements and reports may be required from different descriptions of company.

(3) A company tax return must include a declaration by the person making the return that the return is to the best of his knowledge correct and complete.

(4) The return must be delivered to the officer of the Board by whom the notice was issued not later than the filing date.

Commentary—*Simon's Direct Tax Service* **D2.805, 806, 809.**

Meaning of delivery of return

4 References in this Schedule to the delivery of a company tax return are to the delivery of all the information, accounts, statements and reports required to comply with the notice requiring the return.

Commentary—*Simon's Direct Tax Service* **D2.809.**

Period for which return required

5—(1) A notice requiring a company tax return must specify the period to which the notice relates.

(2) If an accounting period of the company ended during (or at the end of) the specified period, a return is required for that accounting period.

If there is more than one, a separate company tax return is required for each of them.

(3) If sub-paragraph (2) does not apply but an accounting period of the company began during the specified period, a company tax return is required for the part of the specified period before the accounting period began.

(4) If the company was outside the charge to corporation tax for the whole of the specified period, a company tax return is required for the whole of the specified period.

(5) If none of the above provisions applies, no company tax return is required in response to the notice.

Commentary—*Simon's Direct Tax Service* **D2.805.**

Notice relating to period beginning before appointed day

6—(1) A notice requiring a company tax return may be given on or after the self-assessment appointed day in relation to a period beginning before that day.

(2) Where the effect of such a notice is to require a return for an accounting period ending before that day, the provisions of the Tax Acts apply as if it were a notice under section 11 of the Taxes Management Act 1970.

(3) The provisions of this Act relating to company tax returns, or amending other provisions of the Tax Acts so as to refer to such returns, do not affect the operation of those Acts in relation to such a notice.

Commentary—*Simon's Direct Tax Service* **D2.805.**

Return to include self-assessment

7—(1) Every company tax return for an accounting period must include an assessment (a "self-assessment") of the amount of tax which is payable by the company for that period—

(*a*) on the basis of the information contained in the return, and

(*b*) taking into account any relief or allowance for which a claim is included in the return or which is required to be given in relation to that accounting period.

(2) For this purpose a company tax return is regarded as a return for an accounting period if the period is treated in the return as an accounting period and is not longer than twelve months, even though it is not, or may not be, an accounting period.

Commentary—*Simon's Direct Tax Service* **D2.805, 808.**

Calculation of tax payable

8—(1) The amount of tax payable for an accounting period is calculated as follows.

First step

Calculate the corporation tax chargeable on the company's profits:

1. Take the amount of the company's profits for that period on which corporation tax is chargeable.

2. Apply the rate or rates of corporation tax applicable to the company.

Second step

Then give effect to any reliefs or set-offs available against corporation tax chargeable on profits:

1. Any reduction under section 13(2) [or 13AA(2)][1] of the Taxes Act 1988 (marginal small companies' relief).

[1A. Any relief under Part V of Schedule 15 to the Finance Act 2000 (corporate venturing scheme: investment relief).][2]

2. Any double taxation relief under section 788 or 790 of that Act.

3. Any set off for advance corporation tax under section 239 of that Act or under regulations made under section 32 of this Act.

Third step

Then add any amounts assessable or chargeable as if they were corporation tax (reduced by any reliefs specific to those amounts):

1. Any amount due under section 419(1) of the Taxes Act 1988 (tax on a loan or advance made by close company to a participator).

[1A Any sum chargeable under section 501A(1) of that Act (supplementary charge in respect of ring fence trades).][3]

2. Any sum chargeable under section 747(4)(*a*) of that Act (tax on profits of a controlled foreign company).

Fourth step

Then deduct any amounts to be set off against the company's overall tax liability for that period:

1. Any amount to be set off under section 7(2) or 11(3) of the Taxes Act 1988 (income tax borne by deduction).

2. Any amount to be set off under section 246N or 246Q of that Act (advance corporation tax paid in respect of foreign income dividend).

(2) Except as otherwise provided, references in this Schedule to the amount of tax payable by a company for an accounting period are to the amount shown in the company's self-assessment as the amount payable.

Commentary—*Simon's Direct Tax Service* **D2.808.**
Amendments—[1] Words in sub-para (1) inserted by FA 1999 s 28(5), (6) with effect for corporation tax from the financial year 2000, subject to FA 1999 s 28(7) (concerning accounting periods straddling 1 April 2000).
[2] In sub-para (1), para (1A) of the Second step inserted by FA 2000 s 63(2), Sch 16 para 5(1), (2) with effect for shares issued after 31 March 2000 but before 1 April 2010.
[3] Sub-para 1A of the Third step inserted by FA 2002 s 92(4) with effect from 24 July 2002.
Prospective amendments—In sub-para (1), para 1B of the Second step inserted by FA 2002 s 57, Sch 17 para 5 with effect from such day as the Treasury may by order appoint. This amendment will have effect for accounting periods ending on or after that day: FA 2002 s 574(*c*). Para 1B as inserted to read as follows—

"1B. Any relief under Part 5 of Schedule 16 to the Finance Act 2002 (community investment tax relief)."

Claims that cannot be made without a return

9—(1) No claim to which this paragraph applies may be made by a company before it delivers a company tax return for the period to which the claim relates.

(2) This paragraph applies to a claim by a company for any repayment of income tax called for by virtue of—

(a) section 6(2) of the Taxes Act 1988 (exclusion of income tax charge in case of UK resident company or income within chargeable profits for corporation tax), or
(b) exemptions from income tax conferred by the Corporation Tax Acts.

(3) This paragraph applies to a claim by a company for payment of a tax credit, unless—

(a) the company is wholly exempt from corporation tax or is only not so exempt in respect of trading income, *and*
(b) *the tax credit is not one in respect of which a payment on account may be claimed by the company under Schedule 19AB to the Taxes Act 1988 (pension business).*[2]

[(4) This paragraph applies to a claim by a company for relief under Part V of Schedule 15 to the Finance Act 2000 (corporate venturing scheme: investment relief).][1]

Commentary—*Simon's Direct Tax Service* **D2.831.**
Amendment—[1] Sub-para (4) inserted by FA 2000 s 63(2), Sch 16 para 5(1), (3) with effect for shares issued after 31 March 2000 but before 1 April 2010.
[2] The word "and" in sub-para (3)(a), and the whole of sub-para (3)(b) repealed by FA 2001 s 110, Sch 33 Pt II(12) with effect in accordance with FA 2001 s 87.

Other claims and elections to be included in return

10—(1) In Part VII of this Schedule (general provisions as to claims and elections) paragraphs 57 to 59 contain provisions as to the circumstances in which a claim or election may or must be made, or is to be treated as having been made, in a company tax return.

[(2) A claim to which Part VIII, IX or IXA of this Schedule applies (claims for group relief, capital allowances or R&D tax credit) can only be made by being included in a company tax return (see paragraphs 67, 79 and 83B).][1]

[(2A) A claim to which Part IXB of this Schedule applies (claims for land remediation tax credit and life assurance company tax credit) can only be made by being included in a company tax return (see paragraph 83H).][2]

Commentary—*Simon's Direct Tax Service* **D2.831, 835, 836; 1416.**
Amendment—[1] Sub-para (2) substituted by FA 2000 s 69(2), Sch 21 para 2 with effect for accounting periods ending after 31 March 2000.
[2] Sub-para (2A) inserted by FA 2001 s 70(3), Sch 23 para 4 with effect for accounting periods ending after 31 March 2001.
Prospective amendments—Sub-para (3) to be inserted by FA 2002 s 54, Sch 14 paras 2, 5 with effect for tax credits payable under FA 2002 Sch 13 in respect of expenditure incurred on or after such day as the Treasury may appoint under FA 2002 Sch 13 para 28. Sub-para (3) as inserted to read as follows—

"(3) A claim to which Part 9C of this Schedule applies (claims for tax credits under Schedule 13 to the Finance Act 2002) can only be made by being included in a company tax return (see paragraph 83N).".

Accounts required in case of Companies Act company

11—(1) In the case of a company which—

(a) is required to deliver a company tax return for a period,
(b) is resident in the United Kingdom throughout that period, and
(c) is required under the Companies Act 1985 to prepare accounts for a period consisting of or including the whole of that period,

the power to require the delivery of accounts as part of the return is limited to such accounts, containing such information and having annexed to them such documents, as are required to be prepared under that Act.

(2) In relation to a company registered in Northern Ireland, for the reference in sub-paragraph (1) to the Companies Act 1985 substitute a reference to the Companies (Northern Ireland) Order 1986.

Commentary—*Simon's Direct Tax Service* **D2.807.**

Information about business carried on in partnership

12—(1) A company tax return of a company which carries on a trade, profession or business in partnership must include any amount which in a relevant partnership statement is stated to be its share of any income, loss, consideration, tax, credit or charge.

(2) A "relevant partnership statement" means a statement under section 12AB of the Taxes Management Act 1970 for the period for which the return is made or a period which includes that period or any part of it.

Commentary—*Simon's Direct Tax Service* **D2.807.**

Information about chargeable gains

13—(1) A notice requiring a company tax return may require details of assets acquired by the company in the period specified in the notice.

The details required may include details of the person from whom the asset was acquired and the consideration for its acquisition.

(2) The power in sub-paragraph (1) does not apply to—

(*a*) assets exempted by–

section 121 of the Taxation of Chargeable Gains Act 1992 (government non-marketable securities), or

section 263 of that Act (passenger vehicles); or

(*b*) tangible movable property, unless–

(i) the amount or value of the consideration for its acquisition exceeded £6,000, or

(ii) it is within the exceptions in section 262(6) of the Taxation of Chargeable Gains Act 1992 (terminal markets and currency); or

(*c*) assets acquired as trading stock, unless they are held for the purposes of [long-term][1] business carried on by an insurance company.

(3) In sub-paragraph (2)(*c*)—

"trading stock" has the meaning given by section 100(2) of the Taxes Act 1988, and

"[long-term][1] business" and "insurance company" have the meaning given by section 431(2) of that Act.

Commentary—*Simon's Direct Tax Service* **D2.807.**
Amendments—[1] Word in sub-paras (2)(*c*) and (3) substituted by the Financial Services and Markets Act 2000 (Consequential Amendments) (Taxes) Order, SI 2001/3629 art 103(1), (2) with effect from 1 December 2001 (immediately after the coming into force of the Financial Services and Markets Act 2000 ss 411, 432(1), Sch 20).

Filing date

14—(1) The filing date for a company tax return is the last day of whichever of the following periods is the last to end—

(*a*) twelve months from the end of the period for which the return is made;

(*b*) if the company's relevant period of account is not longer than 18 months, twelve months from the end of that period;

(*c*) if the company's relevant period of account is longer than 18 months, 30 months from the beginning of that period;

(*d*) three months from the date on which the notice requiring the return was served.

(2) In sub-paragraph (1) "relevant period of account" means, in relation to a return for an accounting period, the period of account of the company in which the last day of that accounting period falls.
...[1]

Commentary—*Simon's Direct Tax Service* **A3.1631, D2.809.**
Amendments—[1] The following sentence repealed by FA 2002 s 141, Sch 40 Pt 3(16) with effect from 24 July 2002—
"For this purpose "period of account" means a period for which the company makes up accounts.".

Amendment of return by company

15—(1) A company may amend its company tax return by notice to the Inland Revenue.

(2) The notice must be in such form as the Inland Revenue may require.

(3) The notice must contain such information and be accompanied by such statements as the Inland Revenue may reasonably require.

(4) Except as otherwise provided, an amendment may not be made more than twelve months after—

(*a*) the filing date, or

(*b*) in the case of a return for the wrong period, what would be the filing date if the period for which the return was made were an accounting period.

Commentary—*Simon's Direct Tax Service* **D2.810.**

Correction of return by Revenue

16—(1) The Inland Revenue may amend a company tax return so as to correct obvious errors or omissions in the return (whether errors of principle, arithmetical mistakes or otherwise).

(2) A correction under this paragraph is made by notice to the company concerned.

(3) No such correction may be made more than nine months after—

(*a*) the day on which the return was delivered, or

(*b*) if the correction is required in consequence of an amendment by the company under paragraph 15, the day on which that amendment was made.

(4) A correction under this paragraph is of no effect if the company—

(*a*) amends its return so as to reject the correction, or

(b) after the end of the period within which it may amend its return, but within three months from the date of issue of the notice of correction, gives notice rejecting the correction.

(5) Notice under sub-paragraph (4)(b) must be given—

(a) in writing,

(b) to the officer of the Board by whom notice of the correction was given.

Commentary—*Simon's Direct Tax Service* **D2.810.**

Failure to deliver return: flat-rate penalty

17—(1) A company which is required to deliver a company tax return and fails to do so by the filing date is liable to a flat-rate penalty under this paragraph.

It may also be liable to a tax-related penalty under paragraph 18.

(2) The penalty is—

(a) £100, if the return is delivered within three months after the filing date, and

(b) £200, in any other case.

(3) The amounts are increased to £500 and £1000 for a third successive failure, that is, where—

(a) the company is within the charge to corporation tax for three consecutive accounting periods (and at no time between the beginning of the first of those periods and the end of the last is it outside the charge to corporation tax),

(b) a company tax return is required for each of those accounting periods,

(c) the company was liable to a penalty under this paragraph in respect of each of the first two of those periods, and

(d) the company is again liable to a penalty under this paragraph in respect of the third period.

(4) The first or second period mentioned in sub-paragraph (3) may be a period ending before the self-assessment appointed day, in relation to which—

(a) the reference in paragraph (b) to a company tax return shall be construed as a reference to a return under section 11 of the Taxes Management Act 1970, and

(b) the references in paragraphs (c) and (d) to a penalty under this paragraph shall be construed as a reference to a penalty under section 94 of that Act.

Commentary—*Simon's Direct Tax Service* **D2.809, 846.**

Failure to deliver return: tax-related penalty

18—(1) A company which is required to deliver a company tax return for an accounting period and fails to do so—

(a) within 18 months after the end of that period, or

(b) if the filing date is later than that, by the filing date,

is liable to a tax-related penalty under this paragraph.

This is in addition to any flat-rate penalty under paragraph 17.

(2) The penalty is—

(a) 10% of the unpaid tax, if the return is delivered within two years after the end of the period for which the return is required, and

(b) 20% of the unpaid tax, in any other case.

(3) The "unpaid tax" means the amount of tax payable by the company for the accounting period for which the return was required which remains unpaid on the date when the liability to the penalty arises under sub-paragraph (1).

(4) In determining that amount no account shall be taken of any relief under section 419(4) of the Taxes Act 1988 (relief in respect of repayment, etc of loan) which is deferred under subsection (4A) of that section.

Commentary—*Simon's Direct Tax Service* **D2.809, 846.**
Cross references—See FA 1989 s 102(6) (ascertainment of the date of payment of corporation tax where there is a penalty liability under this section arising from surrender of company tax refund within group).

Excuse for late delivery of return

19 A company is not liable to a penalty under paragraph 17 (flat rate penalty) if—

(a) the period for which the return is required is one for which the company is required to deliver accounts under the Companies Act 1985, and

(b) the return is delivered no later than the last day for the delivery of those accounts to the registrar of companies.

In relation to a company registered in Northern Ireland, for the reference in paragraph (a) to the Companies Act 1985 substitute a reference to the Companies (Northern Ireland) Order 1986.

Commentary—*Simon's Direct Tax Service* **D2.809.**

Penalty for incorrect or uncorrected return

20—(1) A company which—

(a) fraudulently or negligently delivers a company tax return which is incorrect, or

(b) discovers that a company tax return delivered by it (neither fraudulently nor negligently) is incorrect and does not remedy the error without unreasonable delay,

is liable to a tax-related penalty.

(2) The penalty is an amount not exceeding the amount of tax understated, that is, the difference between—

(a) the amount of tax payable by the company for the period for which the return is made, and

(b) the amount which would have been so payable on the basis of the return delivered.

(3) In computing for this purpose the amount of tax payable, no account shall be taken of any relief under section 419(4) of the Taxes Act 1988 (relief in respect of repayment, etc of loan) which is deferred under subsection (4A) of that section.

Commentary—*Simon's Direct Tax Service* **D2.846.**

PART III

DUTY TO KEEP AND PRESERVE RECORDS

Duty to keep and preserve records

21—(1) A company which may be required to deliver a company tax return for any period must—

(a) keep such records as may be needed to enable it to deliver a correct and complete return for the period, and

(b) preserve those records in accordance with this paragraph.

(2) The records must be preserved for six years from the end of the period for which the company may be required to deliver a company tax return.

(3) If the company is required to deliver a company tax return by notice given before the end of that six year period, the records must be preserved until any later date on which—

(a) any enquiry into the return is completed, or

(b) if there is no enquiry, the Inland Revenue no longer have power to enquire into the return.

(4) If the company is required to deliver a company tax return by notice given after the end of that six year period and has in its possession at that time any records that may be needed to enable it to deliver a correct and complete return, it is under a duty to preserve those records until the date on which—

(a) any enquiry into the return is completed, or

(b) if there is no enquiry, the Inland Revenue no longer have power to enquire into the return.

(5) The records required to be kept and preserved under this paragraph include records of—

(a) all receipts and expenses in the course of the company's activities, and the matters in respect of which the receipts and expenses arise, and

(b) in the case of a trade involving dealing in goods, all sales and purchases made in the course of the trade.

(6) The duty to preserve records under this paragraph includes a duty to preserve all supporting documents relating to the items mentioned in sub-paragraph (5)(a) and (b).

"Supporting documents" includes accounts, books, deeds, contracts, vouchers and receipts.

Commentary—*Simon's Direct Tax Service* **D2.811.**

Preservation of information instead of original records

22—(1) The duty under paragraph 21 to preserve records may be satisfied by the preservation of the information contained in them, except in the case of records of the kinds specified in sub-paragraph (3) below.

(2) Where information is so preserved a copy of any document forming part of the records is admissible in evidence in any proceedings before the Commissioners to the same extent as the records themselves.

(3) The records excluded from sub-paragraph (1) are—

(a) any statement in writing such as is mentioned in–

(i) section 234(1) of the Taxes Act 1988 (amount of qualifying distribution and tax credit), or

(ii) section 352(1) of that Act (gross amount, tax deducted and actual amount paid, in certain cases where payments are made under deduction of tax),

provided by the company or person there mentioned whether after the making of a request or otherwise;

(b) any certificate or other record (however described) required by regulations under section 566(1) of the Taxes Act 1988 to be given to a sub-contractor (within the meaning of Chapter IV of Part XIII of that Act) on the making of a payment to which section 559 of that Act applies (deductions on account of tax);

(c) any record relating to an amount of tax–

(i) paid under the law of a territory outside the United Kingdom, or

(ii) which would have been so payable but for a relief to which section 788(5) of the Taxes Act 1988 applies (relief for promoting development or contemplated by double taxation arrangements).

Commentary—*Simon's Direct Tax Service* **D2.811.**

Penalty for failure to keep and preserve records

23—(1) A company which fails to comply with paragraph 21 in relation to an accounting period is liable to a penalty not exceeding £3,000, subject to the following exceptions.

(2) No penalty is incurred if the records which the company fails to keep or preserve are records which might have been needed only for the purposes of claims, elections or notices not included in the return.

(3) No penalty is incurred if—

(a) the records which the company fails to keep or preserve are statements in writing such as are mentioned in–

(i) section 234(1) of the Taxes Act 1988 (amount of qualifying distribution and tax credit), or

(ii) section 352(1) of that Act (gross amount, tax deducted and actual amount paid, in certain cases where payments are made under deduction of tax),

provided by the company or person there mentioned whether after the making of a request or otherwise, and

(b) the Inland Revenue are satisfied that any facts which they reasonably require to be proved, and which would have been proved by the records, are proved by other documentary evidence furnished to them.

Commentary—*Simon's Direct Tax Service* **D2.811.**

PART IV
ENQUIRY INTO COMPANY TAX RETURN
Notice of enquiry

24—(1) The Inland Revenue may enquire into a company tax return if they give notice to the company of their intention to do so (''notice of enquiry'') within the time allowed.

(2) If the return was delivered on or before the filing date, notice of enquiry may be given at any time up to twelve months from the filing date.

(3) If the return was delivered after the filing date, notice of enquiry may be given at any time up to and including the 31st January, 30th April, 31st July or 31st October next following the first anniversary of the day on which the return was delivered.

(4) If the company amends its return, notice of enquiry may be given at any time up to and including the 31st January, 30th April, 31st July or 31st October next following the first anniversary of the day on which the amendment was made.

(5) A return which has been the subject of one notice of enquiry may not be the subject of another, except one given in consequence of an amendment (or another amendment) by the company of its return.

Commentary—*Simon's Direct Tax Service* **D2.815.**
Statement of Practice SP 1/02—Deals with situation where an enquiry into a company tax return remains open after expiry of the period within which a notice of enquiry may be issued solely because of an unagreed valuation for chargeable gains purposes.
Revenue Internal Guidance—Enquiry Handbook EH 1083–1095 (operation of this para).

Scope of enquiry

25—(1) An enquiry into a company tax return extends to anything contained in the return, or required to be contained in the return, including-

(a) any claim or election included in the return,

(b) any amount that affects or may affect–

(i) the tax payable by that company for another accounting period, or

(ii) the tax liability of another company for any accounting period,

subject to the following limitation.

(2) If the notice of enquiry is given-

(*a*) as a result of an amendment by the company of its return, and

(*b*) at a time when it is no longer possible to give notice of enquiry under paragraph 24(2) or (3),

the enquiry into the return is limited to matters to which the amendment relates or which are affected by the amendment.

Commentary—*Simon's Direct Tax Service* **D2.815.**

Enquiry into return for wrong period

26—(1) In the case of a company tax return which appears to the Inland Revenue-

(*a*) is or may be a return for the wrong period, or

(*b*) has become a return for the wrong period as a result of a direction under section 12(5A) of the Taxes Act 1988 (power of Board to direct which accounting date to be used where company carries on several trades),

the power to enquire into the return includes power to enquire into the period for which the return ought to have been made.

(2) A return is a "return for the wrong period" in the following cases.

(3) The first case is where the return is made for a period which is treated in the return as an accounting period, but which is not an accounting period of the company.

(4) The second case is where the return is made on the basis that there is no accounting period ending in or at the end of the specified period, but there is such an accounting period.

(5) In relation to a return for the wrong period the references to the filing date in paragraph 24(2) and (3) (period within which notice of enquiry may be given) are to the date that would be the filing date if the period for which the return was made were a period of the kind it is treated as in the return.

(6) In this paragraph "the specified period" means the period specified in the notice requiring a company tax return.

Commentary—*Simon's Direct Tax Service* **D2.815.**

Notice to produce documents, etc for purposes of enquiry

27—(1) If the Inland Revenue give a notice of enquiry to a company, they may by notice require the company-

(*a*) to produce to them such documents in the company's possession or power, and

(*b*) to provide them with such information, in such form,

as they may reasonably require for the purposes of the enquiry.

(2) A notice under this paragraph (which may be given at the same time as the notice of enquiry) must specify the time (which must not be less than 30 days) within which the company is to comply with it.

(3) In complying with a notice under this paragraph copies of documents may be produced instead of originals, but-

(*a*) the copies must be photographic or other facsimiles, and

(*b*) the Inland Revenue may by notice require the original to be produced for inspection.

A notice under paragraph (*b*) must specify the time (which must not be less than 30 days) within which the company is to comply with it.

(4) The Inland Revenue may take copies of, or make extracts from, any document produced to them under this paragraph.

(5) A notice under this paragraph does not oblige the company to produce documents or provide information relating to the conduct of [—

(*a*) any pending appeal by the company, or

(*b*) any pending referral to the Special Commissioners under paragraph 31A to which the company is a party.][1].

Commentary—*Simon's Direct Tax Service* **A3.1634; D2.816, 841.**
Revenue Internal Guidance—Enquiry Handbook EH 1113–1136 (operation of this para).
Amendments—[1] Words in sub-para (5) substituted for the words "any pending appeal by the company" by FA 2001 s 88, Sch 29 para 38(4) with effect from the passing of FA 2001 in relation to returns whether made before or after the passing of FA 2001, and whether relating to periods before or after the passing of FA 2001.

Appeal against notice to produce documents, etc

28—(1) An appeal may be brought against a requirement imposed by a notice under paragraph 27 to produce documents or provide information.

(2) Notice of appeal must be given-

(*a*) in writing,

(*b*) within 30 days after the notice was given to the company,

(*c*) to the officer of the Board by whom that notice was given.

(3) An appeal under this paragraph shall be heard and determined in the same way as an appeal against an assessment.

(4) On an appeal under this paragraph the Commissioners-

(*a*) shall set aside the notice so far as it requires the production of documents, or the provision of information, which appears to them not reasonably required for the purposes of the enquiry, and

(*b*) shall confirm the notice so far as it requires the production of documents, or the provision of information, which appears to them reasonably required for the purposes of the enquiry.

(5) A notice which is confirmed by the Commissioners (or so far as it is confirmed) has effect as if the period specified in it for complying was 30 days from the determination of the appeal.

(6) The decision of the Commissioners on an appeal under this paragraph is final and conclusive.

Commentary—*Simon's Direct Tax Service* **D2.816, 841.**

Penalty for failure to produce documents, etc

29—(1) A company which fails to comply with a notice under paragraph 27 (notice to produce documents, etc for purposes of enquiry) is liable-

(*a*) to a penalty of £50, and

(*b*) if the failure continues after a penalty is imposed under paragraph (*a*) above, to a further penalty or penalties not exceeding the amount specified in sub-paragraph (2) below for each day on which the failure continues.

(2) The amount referred to in sub-paragraph (1)(*b*) is-

(*a*) £30 if the penalty is determined by an officer of the Board under section 100 of the Taxes Management Act 1970, and

(*b*) £150 if the penalty is determined by the Commissioners under section 100C of that Act.

(3) An officer of the Board authorised by the Board for the purposes of section 100C of the Taxes Management Act 1970 may commence proceedings under that section for any penalty under sub-paragraph (1)(*b*) above.

(4) No penalty shall be imposed under this paragraph in respect of a failure at any time after the failure has been remedied.

Commentary—*Simon's Direct Tax Service* **D2.816, 841.**

Amendment of self-assessment during enquiry to prevent loss of tax

30—(1) If after notice of enquiry has been given and before the enquiry is completed the Inland Revenue form the opinion—

(*a*) that the amount stated in the company's self-assessment as the amount of tax payable is insufficient, and

(*b*) that unless the assessment is immediately amended there is likely to be a loss of tax to the Crown,

they may by notice to the company amend its self-assessment to make good the deficiency.

(2) In the case of an enquiry which under paragraph 25(2) is limited to matters arising from an amendment of the return, sub-paragraph (1) above only applies so far as the deficiency is attributable to the amendment.

(3) An appeal may be brought against an amendment of a company's self-assessment by the Inland Revenue under this paragraph.

(4) Notice of appeal must be given—

(*a*) in writing,

(*b*) within 30 days after the amendment was notified to the company,

(*c*) to the officer of the Board by whom the notice of amendment was given.

(5) The appeal shall not be heard and determined before the completion of the enquiry.

Commentary—*Simon's Direct Tax Service* **D2.817, 842.**
Revenue Internal Guidance—Enquiry Handbook EH 1140–1145 (conditions under which Revenue may make a jeopardy payment).

Amendment of return by company during enquiry

31—(1) This paragraph applies if a company amends its company tax return at a time when an enquiry is in progress into the return.

(2) The amendment does not restrict the scope of the enquiry but may be taken into account (together with any matters arising) in the enquiry.

(3) So far as the amendment affects—

(*a*) the amount stated in the company's self-assessment as the amount of tax payable, or

(*b*) any amount that affects or may affect—

(i) the tax payable by the company for another accounting period, or

(ii) the tax liability of another company for any accounting period,

it does not take effect until after the enquiry is completed.

This does not affect any claim by the company under section 59DA of the Taxes Management Act 1970 (claim for repayment in advance of liability being established).

(4) An amendment whose effect is deferred under sub-paragraph (3) takes effect as follows—

(*a*) if the conclusions in the closure notice state either—

(i) that the amendment was not taken into account in the enquiry, or

(ii) that no amendment of the return is required arising from the enquiry,

the amendment takes effect on the completion of the enquiry;

(*b*) in any other case, the amendment shall be taken into account by the company in amending its return to accord with the conclusions stated in the closure notice and takes effect accordingly as part of those amendments.

(5) For the purposes of this paragraph the period during which an enquiry is in progress is the whole of the period—

(*a*) beginning with the day on which the Inland Revenue give notice of enquiry into the return, and

(*b*) ending with the day on which the enquiry is completed.

Commentary—*Simon's Direct Tax Service* **D2.817, 842.**

[Referral of questions to Special Commissioners during enquiry

31A—(1) At any time when an enquiry is in progress into a company's tax return any question arising in connection with the subject-matter of the enquiry may be referred to the Special Commissioners for their determination.

(2) Notice of referral must be given—

(*a*) jointly by the company and the Inland Revenue,

(*b*) in writing,

(*c*) to the Special Commissioners.

(3) The notice of referral must specify the question or questions being referred.

(4) More than one notice of referral may be given under this paragraph in relation to an enquiry.

(5) For the purposes of this paragraph the period during which an enquiry is in progress is the whole of the period—

(*a*) beginning with the day on which the Inland Revenue give notice of enquiry into the return, and

(*b*) ending with the day on which the enquiry is completed.]¹

Amendments—¹ Sections 31A–31D inserted by FA 2001 s 88, Sch 29 para 7 with effect for an enquiry under FA 1998 Sch 18 Pt IV in relation to which notice of enquiry is given after the passing of FA 2001, or which is in progress (within the meaning of FA 1998 Sch 18 para 31(5)) immediately before the passing of FA 2001.

[Withdrawal of notice of referral

31B—(1) The Inland Revenue or the company may withdraw a notice of referral under paragraph 31A by notice in accordance with this paragraph.

(2) Notice of withdrawal must be given—

(*a*) in writing,

(*b*) to the other party to the referral and to the Special Commissioners,

(*c*) before the first hearing by the Special Commissioners in relation to the referral.]¹

Amendments—¹ Sections 31A–31D inserted by FA 2001 s 88, Sch 29 para 7 with effect for an enquiry under FA 1998 Sch 18 Pt IV in relation to which notice of enquiry is given after the passing of FA 2001, or which is in progress (within the meaning of FA 1998 Sch 18 para 31(5)) immediately before the passing of FA 2001.

[Effect of referral on enquiry

31C—(1) While proceedings on a referral under paragraph 31A are in progress in relation to an enquiry—

(*a*) no closure notice shall be given in relation to the enquiry, and

(*b*) no application may be made for a direction to give such a notice.

(2) For the purposes of this paragraph proceedings on a referral are in progress where—

(*a*) notice of referral has been given,

(*b*) the notice has not been withdrawn, and

(*c*) the questions referred have not been finally determined.

(3) For the purposes of sub-paragraph (2)(*c*) a question referred is finally determined when—

(*a*) it has been determined by the Special Commissioners, and

(*b*) there is no further possibility of that determination being varied or set aside (disregarding any power to grant permission to appeal out of time).]¹

Amendments—¹ Sections 31A–31D inserted by FA 2001 s 88, Sch 29 para 7 with effect for an enquiry under FA 1998 Sch 18 Pt IV in relation to which notice of enquiry is given after the passing of FA 2001, or which is in progress (within the meaning of FA 1998 Sch 18 para 31(5)) immediately before the passing of FA 2001.

[Effect of determination

31D—(1) The determination of a question referred to the Special Commissioners under paragraph 31A is binding on the parties to the referral in the same way, and to the same extent, as a decision on a preliminary issue in an appeal.

(2) The determination shall be taken into account by the Inland Revenue in reaching their conclusions on the enquiry.

(3) Any right of appeal under paragraph 30 or 34(3) may not be exercised so as to reopen the question determined except to the extent (if any) that it could be reopened if it had been determined as a preliminary issue in that appeal.]¹

Amendments—¹ Sections 31A–31D inserted by FA 2001 s 88, Sch 29 para 7 with effect for an enquiry under FA 1998 Sch 18 Pt IV in relation to which notice of enquiry is given after the passing of FA 2001, or which is in progress (within the meaning of FA 1998 Sch 18 para 31(5)) immediately before the passing of FA 2001.

Completion of enquiry

32—(1) An enquiry is completed when the Inland Revenue by notice (a ''closure notice'') inform the company they have completed their enquiry and state their conclusions.

The notice takes effect when it is issued.

(2) If the Inland Revenue conclude that the return was a return for the wrong period, the closure notice must designate the accounting period for which a return should have been made (specifying the dates on which the period begins and ends).

(3) If there is more than one accounting period ending in or at the end of the period specified in the notice requiring a return, the closure notice shall only designate the first of those accounting periods for which no return has been delivered.

Paragraph 35 provides for a return to be delivered for any other outstanding accounting period.

Commentary—*Simon's Direct Tax Service* D2.818.
Revenue Internal Guidance—Enquiry Handbook EH 1168 (sub-s (2): worked example).

Direction to complete enquiry

33—(1) The company may apply to the Commissioners for a direction that the Inland Revenue give a closure notice within a specified period.

(2) Any such application shall be heard and determined in the same way as an appeal.

(3) The Commissioners hearing the application shall give a direction unless they are satisfied that the Inland Revenue have reasonable grounds for not giving a closure notice within a specified period.

Commentary—*Simon's Direct Tax Service* D2.818.

Amendment of return after enquiry

34—(1) The company has 30 days beginning with the day on which the enquiry is completed in which—

    (*a*) to amend the return that was the subject of the enquiry—
        (i) to accord with the conclusions stated in the closure notice, and
        (ii) in the case of a return for the wrong period, to make it a return appropriate to the designated period, and
    (*b*) to make any amendments of other company tax returns delivered by it which are required to give effect to the conclusions stated in the closure notice.

The time limits otherwise applicable to amendment of a company tax return do not prevent an amendment being made under paragraph (*a*) or (*b*).

(2) If after the end of that period of 30 days the Inland Revenue are not satisfied—

    (*a*) that the return that was the subject of the enquiry—
        (i) is correct and complete, and
        (ii) in the case of a return for the wrong period, is a return appropriate to the designated period, and
    (*b*) that any necessary amendments have been made to any other return delivered by the company that are required to give effect to the conclusions stated in the closure notice,

they may, within the following period of 30 days, by notice to the company make such amendments of that return or those returns as they consider necessary.

(3) An appeal may be brought against any such amendment of a company's return.

(4) Notice of appeal must be given—

    (*a*) in writing,
    (*b*) within 30 days after the amendment was notified to the company,
    (*c*) to the officer of the Board by whom the notice of amendment was given.

(5) In this paragraph ''the designated period'' means the period designated in the closure notice.

Commentary—*Simon's Direct Tax Service* **D2.818.**
Revenue Internal Guidance—Enquiry Handbook EH 1174–1190 (operation of this para).

Further return for outstanding period

35—(1) Where, following an enquiry into a company tax return—

(a) it is finally determined—

(i) that the return is a return for the wrong period, and

(ii) what the period is for which the return should have been made, and

(b) the effect of the determination is that there is a further period ("the outstanding period") for which a company tax return should have been made under the original notice requiring a return,

then, if there is no such return delivered by the company which can be amended so as to become a return for the outstanding period, the original notice shall be taken to require the company to deliver a return in respect of that period.

(2) The filing date for such a return for an outstanding period is whichever is the later of—

(a) the original filing date, and

(b) the last day of the period of 30 days beginning with the day on which the matters mentioned in sub-paragraph (1)(a) are finally determined.

Commentary—*Simon's Direct Tax Service* **D2.818.**

PART V
REVENUE DETERMINATIONS AND ASSESSMENTS
Determination of tax payable if no return delivered in response to notice

36—(1) If no return is delivered in response to a notice requiring a company tax return, the Inland Revenue may determine to the best of their information and belief the amount of tax payable by the company.

(2) The power to make a determination under this paragraph becomes exercisable if no return is delivered on or before the following date—

(a) if the filing date for any return required by the notice can be ascertained, that date;

(b) if no such date can be ascertained, the later of—

(i) 18 months from the end of the period specified in the notice, or

(ii) three months from the day on which the notice was served.

(3) The accounting period or periods for which a determination may be made are—

(a) if there is only one accounting period ending in or at the end of the period specified in the notice, that period;

(b) if there is more than one accounting period ending in or at the end of the period specified in the notice, each of those periods;

(c) if the Inland Revenue have insufficient information to identify the accounting periods of the company, such period or periods ending in or at the end of the period specified in the notice as they may determine.

(4) Notice of a determination under this paragraph must be served on the company, stating the date on which the determination is issued.

(5) No determination under this paragraph may be made more than five years after the day on which the power becomes exercisable.

(6) If the company shows—

(a) that there is no accounting period of the company ending in or at the end of the period specified in the notice, or

(b) that it has delivered a return for the accounting period, or each accounting period, ending in or at the end of the period specified in the notice, or

(c) that no return is yet due for any such period,

any determination under this paragraph is of no effect.

Commentary—*Simon's Direct Tax Service* **D2.821, 843.**
Cross references—See FA 2000 Sch 28 para 4(2) (time limit for giving notice in respect of recovery of tax payable by non-resident company where unpaid tax is charged following a determination under this para).

Determination of tax payable if notice complied with in part

37—(1) If a notice requiring a company tax return is served on a company and—

(a) a return is delivered for an accounting period ending in or at the end of the period specified in the notice, but

(b) there is another period so ending (the "outstanding period") which appears to the Inland Revenue is or may be an accounting period,

the Inland Revenue may determine to the best of their information and belief the amount of corporation tax payable by the company for the outstanding period.

(2) The power to make a determination under this paragraph becomes exercisable—

(a) if the filing date for the outstanding period can be ascertained and no return is delivered on or before that date;

(b) if no such date can be ascertained and no return for that period is delivered by the later of—

(i) 30 months from the end of the period specified in the notice, or

(ii) three months from the day on which the notice was served.

(3) Notice of a determination under this paragraph must be served on the company, stating the date on which the determination is issued.

(4) No determination under this paragraph may be made more than five years after the day on which the power first became exercisable.

(5) If the company shows—

(a) that the outstanding period is not an accounting period, or

(b) that it has delivered a return for that period,

any determination under this paragraph is of no effect.

Commentary—*Simon's Direct Tax Service* **D2.821.**
Cross references—See FA 2000 Sch 28 para 4(2) (time limit for giving notice in respect of recovery of tax payable by non-resident company where unpaid tax is charged following a determination under this para).

Extent of power to make determination

38—(1) The power to make a determination under paragraph 36 or 37 includes power to determine—

(a) any of the amounts mentioned in paragraph 8(1) (calculation of amount of tax payable), and

(b) any amount forming part of the calculation of any of those amounts.

(2) Notice of a determination under either of those paragraphs may be accompanied by notice of any determination by the Inland Revenue relating to the dates on which amounts of tax become due and payable under section 59D or 59E of the Taxes Management Act 1970.

Commentary—*Simon's Direct Tax Service* **D2.821.**

Determination to have effect as self-assessment

39—(1) A determination under paragraph 36 or 37 has effect for enforcement purposes as if it were a self-assessment by the company.

(2) In sub-paragraph (1) "for enforcement purposes" means for the purposes of—

(a) the following Parts of the Taxes Management Act 1970—
Part VA (payment),
Part VI (collection and recovery),
Part IX (interest on overdue tax), and
Part XI (miscellaneous and supplementary provisions);

(b) the provisions of this Schedule imposing tax-related penalties; and

(c) the provisions of the Corporation Tax Acts enabling unpaid tax assessed on a company to be assessed on other persons.

(3) For those purposes the period for which the determination is made shall be treated as an accounting period of the company, even though—

(a) in the case of a determination under paragraph 36, the Inland Revenue have insufficient information to determine the accounting periods of the company and exercise their power under sub-paragraph (3)(c) of that paragraph, or

(b) in the case of a determination under paragraph 37, the Inland Revenue have insufficient information to determine whether the outstanding period is an accounting period.

Commentary—*Simon's Direct Tax Service* **D2.822.**

Determination superseded by actual self-assessment

40—(1) If after a determination has been made under paragraph 36—

(a) the company delivers a company tax return for a period ending in or at the end of the period specified in the notice requiring a company tax return, and

(b) the period is, or is treated in the return as, an accounting period,

the self-assessment included in that return supersedes the determination or, if there is more than one, the determination for the period which is, or most closely approximates to, the period for which the return is made.

(2) If after a determination has been made under paragraph 37—

(a) the company delivers a further company tax return for a period ending in or at the end of the period specified in the notice requiring a company tax return, and

(b) the period is, or is treated in the return as, an accounting period,

the self-assessment included in that return supersedes the determination.

(3) Sub-paragraphs (1) and (2) do not apply to a return made—

(a) more than five years after the day on which the power to make the determination first became exercisable (see paragraph 36(2) or 37(2)), or

(b) more than twelve months after the date of the determination,

whichever is the later.

(4) Where—

(a) [proceedings have been begun][1] for the recovery of any tax charged by a determination under paragraph 36 or 37, and

(b) before the proceedings are concluded the determination is superseded by a self-assessment,

the proceedings may be continued as if they were proceedings for the recovery of so much of the tax charged by the self-assessment as is due and payable and has not been paid.

Commentary—*Simon's Direct Tax Service* **D2.822.**
Cross references—See FA 2000 Sch 28 para 4(3) (time limit for giving notice in respect of recovery of tax payable by non-resident company where unpaid tax is charged in a self-assessment, including one that supersedes a determination (under this para)).
Amendments—[1] Words in sub-para (4)(a) substituted for the words "the Inland Revenue have begun proceedings" by FA 2001 s 88, Sch 29 para 17(2) with effect for proceedings begun after the passing of FA 2001.

Assessment where loss of tax discovered or determination of amount discovered to be incorrect

41—(1) If the Inland Revenue discover as regards an accounting period of a company that—

(a) an amount which ought to have been assessed to tax has not been assessed, or

(b) an assessment to tax is or has become insufficient, or

(c) relief has been given which is or has become excessive,

they may make an assessment (a "discovery assessment") in the amount or further amount which ought in their opinion to be charged in order to make good to the Crown the loss of tax.

(2) If the Inland Revenue discover that a company tax return delivered by a company for an accounting period incorrectly states—

(a) an amount that affects, or may affect, the tax payable by that company for another accounting period, or

(b) an amount that affects, or may affect, the tax liability of another company,

they may make a determination (a "discovery determination") of the amount which in their opinion ought to have been stated in the return.

Commentary—*Simon's Direct Tax Service* **A3.1632; D2.823.**

Restrictions on power to make discovery assessment or determination

42—(1) The power to make—

(a) a discovery assessment for an accounting period for which the company has delivered a company tax return, or

(b) a discovery determination,

is only exercisable in the circumstances specified in paragraph 43 or 44 and subject to paragraph 45 below.

(2) Those restrictions do not apply to an assessment or determination which only gives effect to a discovery determination duly made with respect to an amount stated in another company's company tax return.

(3) Any objection to a discovery assessment or determination on the ground that those paragraphs have not been complied with can only be made on an appeal against the assessment or determination.

Commentary—*Simon's Direct Tax Service* **A3.1632; D2.823.**

Fraudulent or negligent conduct

43 A discovery assessment for an accounting period for which the company has delivered a company tax return, or a discovery determination, may be made if the situation mentioned in paragraph 41(1) or (2) is attributable to fraudulent or negligent conduct on the part of—

(a) the company, or

(b) a person acting on behalf of the company, or

(c) a person who was a partner of the company at the relevant time.

Commentary—*Simon's Direct Tax Service* **A3.1632; D2.823.**

Situation not disclosed by return or related documents etc

44—(1) A discovery assessment for an accounting period for which the company has delivered a company tax return, or a discovery determination, may be made if at the time when the Inland Revenue—

(a) ceased to be entitled to give a notice of enquiry into the return, or

(b) completed their enquiries into the return,

they could not have been reasonably expected, on the basis of the information made available to them before that time, to be aware of the situation mentioned in paragraph 41(1) or (2).

(2) For this purpose information is regarded as made available to the Inland Revenue if—

(*a*) it is contained in a relevant return by the company or in documents accompanying any such return, or

(*b*) it is contained in a relevant claim made by the company or in any accounts, statements or documents accompanying any such claim, or

(*c*) it is contained in any documents, accounts or information produced or provided by the company to the Inland Revenue for the purposes of an enquiry into any such return or claim, or

(*d*) it is information the existence of which, and the relevance of which as regards the situation mentioned in paragraph 41(1) or (2)—

(i) could reasonably be expected to be inferred by the Inland Revenue from information falling within paragraphs (*a*) to (*c*) above, or

(ii) are notified in writing to the Inland Revenue by the company or a person acting on its behalf.

(3) In sub-paragraph (2)—

"relevant return" means the company's company tax return for the period in question or either of the two immediately preceding accounting periods, and

"relevant claim" means a claim made by or on behalf of the company as regards the period in question.

Commentary—*Simon's Direct Tax Service* **A3.1632; D2.823.**

Return made in accordance with prevailing practice

45 No discovery assessment for an accounting period for which the company has delivered a company tax return, or discovery determination, may be made if—

(*a*) the situation mentioned in paragraph 41(1) or (2) is attributable to a mistake in the return as to the basis on which the company's liability ought to have been computed, and

(*b*) the return was in fact made on the basis or in accordance with the practice generally prevailing at the time when it was made.

Commentary—*Simon's Direct Tax Service* **A3.1632; D2.823.**

General time limits for assessments

46—(1) Subject to any provision of the Taxes Acts allowing a longer period in any particular class of case no assessment may be made more than six years after the end of the accounting period to which it relates.

(2) In a case involving fraud or negligence on the part of—

(*a*) the company, or

(*b*) a person acting on behalf of the company, or

(*c*) a person who was a partner of the company at the relevant time,

an assessment may be made up to 21 years after the end of the accounting period to which it relates.

(3) Any objection to the making of an assessment on the ground that the time limit for making it has expired can only be made on an appeal against the assessment.

Commentary—*Simon's Direct Tax Service* **D2.824.**

Assessment procedure

47—(1) Notice of an assessment to tax on a company must be served on the company stating—

(*a*) the date on which the notice is issued, and

(*b*) the time within which any appeal against the assessment may be made.

(2) After that notice has been served on the company, the assessment may not be altered except in accordance with the express provisions of the Taxes Acts.

Commentary—*Simon's Direct Tax Service* **D2.824.**

Appeal against assessment

48—(1) An appeal may be brought against any assessment to tax on a company which is not a self-assessment.

(2) Notice of appeal must be given—

(*a*) in writing,

(*b*) within 30 days after notice of the assessment was issued,

(*c*) to the officer of the Board by whom the notice of the assessment was given.

Commentary—*Simon's Direct Tax Service* **D2.824.**

Application of provisions to discovery determinations

49 The provisions of paragraphs 46 to 48 (assessments: general provisions as to time limits, procedure and appeals) apply to a discovery determination as they apply to an assessment.

Commentary—*Simon's Direct Tax Service* **D2.824.**

PART VI

EXCESSIVE ASSESSMENTS OR REPAYMENTS, ETC

Relief in case of double assessment

50—(1) A company which believes it has been assessed to tax more than once for the same cause and for the same accounting period may make a claim for relief—

(a) by notice in writing,
(b) given to the Board.

(2) If on a claim being made the Board are satisfied that the company has been assessed to tax more than once for the same cause and for the same accounting period, they shall amend the assessment or assessments concerned, or give relief by way of discharge or repayment of tax or otherwise, so as to eliminate the double charge.

(3) An appeal against the Board's decision on a claim for relief under this paragraph may be brought to the Commissioners having jurisdiction to hear an appeal relating to the assessment, or the later of the assessments, to which the claim relates.

Commentary—*Simon's Direct Tax Service* **D2.825.**

Relief in case of mistake in return

51—(1) A company which believes it has paid tax under an assessment which was excessive by reason of some mistake in a return may make a claim for relief—

(a) by notice in writing,
(b) given to the Board,
(c) not more than six years after the end of the accounting period to which the return relates.

(2) On receiving the claim the Board shall enquire into the matter and give by way of repayment such relief in respect of the mistake as is reasonable and just.

(3) No relief shall be given under this paragraph—

(a) in respect of a mistake as to the basis on which the liability of the claimant ought to have been computed when the return was in fact made on the basis or in accordance with the practice generally prevailing at the time when it was made, or
(b) in respect of a mistake in a claim or election which is included in the return.

(4) In determining a claim under this paragraph the Board shall have regard to all the relevant circumstances of the case.

They shall, in particular, consider whether the granting of relief would result in amounts being excluded from charge to tax.

For that purpose they may take into consideration the liability of the claimant company, and assessments made on it, for accounting periods other than that to which the claim relates.

(5) On an appeal against the Board's decision on the claim, the Special Commissioners shall hear and determine the claim in accordance with the same principles as apply to the determination by the Board of claims under this paragraph.

(6) Neither the company nor the Board may appeal under section 56A of the Taxes Management Act 1970 against the determination of the Special Commissioners, except on a point of law arising in connection with the computation of—

(a) the profits of the company for the purposes of corporation tax,
(b) any amount assessable under section 419(1) of the Taxes Act 1988 (tax on loan or advance made by close company to a participator), or
(c) any amount chargeable under section 747(4)(a) of that Act (tax on profits of controlled foreign company).

Commentary—*Simon's Direct Tax Service* **D2.825.**
Cross references—See FA 1994 s 118(7) (no relief in respect of an error or mistake consisting in a failure to satisfy the relevant condition for notification of expenditure on machinery or plant).

Recovery of excessive repayments etc

52—(1) The provisions of paragraphs 41 to 48 relating to discovery assessments apply to an amount to which this paragraph applies as if it were unpaid tax, unless—

(a) it is assessable under those provisions apart from this paragraph, or
(b) it is recoverable under section 826(8A) of the Taxes Act 1988 (interest overpaid which is recoverable in same way as interest charged).

(2) This paragraph applies to an amount paid to a company by way of—

(*a*) repayment of tax (or income tax) or payment of a tax credit,

(*b*) repayment supplement under section 825 of the Taxes Act 1988,

[(*ba*) R&D tax credit under Schedule 20 to the Finance Act 2000,][1]

[(*bb*) land remediation tax credit or life assurance company tax credit under Schedule 22 to the Finance Act 2001][2] or

(*c*) interest paid under section 826 of [the Taxes Act 1988][2],

to the extent that it ought not to have been paid.

(3) For the purposes of this paragraph—

(*a*) an amount is regarded as paid if it is allowed by way of set-off, and

(*b*) an amount is regarded as a repayment if it was intended as repayment but exceeds the amount paid by the company.

(4) An assessment made by virtue of this paragraph shall be made under Case VI of Schedule D.

(5) An assessment to recover—

(*a*) an amount of tax repaid to a company in respect of an accounting period, or interest on any such repayment,

[(*ab*) an amount of R&D tax credit paid to a company for an accounting period,][1]

[(*ac*) an amount of land remediation tax credit or life assurance company tax credit paid to a company for an accounting period,][2]or

(*b*) an amount of income tax repaid to a company in respect of a payment received by the company in an accounting period, or interest on any such repayment,

shall be treated as an assessment to tax for the accounting period referred to in paragraph (*a*)[, (*ab*)][1][, (*ac*)][2] or (*b*).

(6) The sum assessed shall carry interest at the prescribed rate for the purposes of section 87A of the Taxes Management Act 1970 (interest on overdue corporation tax, etc) from the date when the payment being recovered was made until payment.

Commentary—*Simon's Direct Tax Service* **D2.826; 1416.**
Cross references—See FA 2000 s 46(2) (exemption under FA 2000's 46(1) for income of a charity is not granted in respect of income chargeable to tax under Schedule D Case VI by virtue of sub-para (4) above).
Amendment—[1] Words in sub-paras (2), (5) inserted by FA 2000 s.69(2), Sch 21 para 3 with effect for accounting periods ending after 31 March 2000.
[2] Sub-para (2)(*bb*) inserted, words in sub-para 2(*c*) substituted, and sub-para (5)(*ac*) and words in sub-para (5) inserted by FA 2001 s 70(3), Sch 23 para 5 with effect for accounting periods ending after 31 March 2001.
Prospective amendments—Sub-paras (2)(*bc*), (5)(*ad*) to be inserted, and in sub-para (5), "(*ad*)" to be inserted after "(*ac*)", by FA 2002 s 54, Sch 14 paras 3, 5 with effect for tax credits payable under FA 2002 Sch 13 in respect of expenditure incurred on or after such day as the Treasury may appoint under FA 2002 Sch 13 para 28.
Sub-para (2)(*bc*) as inserted to read as follows—
  "(*bc*) tax credit under Schedule 13 to the Finance Act 2002,",
Sub-para (5)(*ad*) as inserted to read as follows—
  "(*ad*) an amount of tax credit under Schedule 13 to the Finance Act 2002 paid to a company for an accounting period,".

Time limit for recovery of excessive repayments, etc

53—(1) An assessment made by virtue of paragraph 52 is not out of time under paragraph 46(1) (general six year time limit for assessments) if it is made—

(*a*) before the end of the accounting period following that in which the amount assessed was paid, or

(*b*) if later, before the end of the period of three months beginning with the day on which the Inland Revenue complete an enquiry into a relevant company tax return by the company concerned.

(2) Sub-paragraph (1) above is without prejudice to paragraph 46(2) (time limit for assessment in case of fraud or negligence).

Commentary—*Simon's Direct Tax Service* **D2.826.**

PART VII
GENERAL PROVISIONS AS TO CLAIMS AND ELECTIONS
Claims must be quantified

54 A claim under any provision of the Corporation Tax Acts for a relief, an allowance or a repayment of tax must be for an amount which is quantified at the time when the claim is made.

Commentary—*Simon's Direct Tax Service* **D2.831.**

General time limit for making claims

55 Subject to any provision prescribing a longer or shorter period, a claim for relief under any provision of the Corporation Tax Acts must be made within six years from the end of the accounting period to which it relates.

Commentary—*Simon's Direct Tax Service* **D2.831.**

Supplementary claim or election

56. A company which has made a claim or election under any provision of the Corporation Tax Acts (by including it in a return or otherwise) and subsequently discovers that a mistake has been made in it may make a supplementary claim or election within the time allowed for making the original claim or election.

Commentary—*Simon's Direct Tax Service* **D2.831.**
Cross references—See FA 1994 s 118(7) (no relief in respect of an error or mistake consisting in a failure to satisfy the relevant condition for notification of expenditure on machinery or plant).

Claims or elections affecting a single accounting period

57—(1) This paragraph applies to a claim or election for tax purposes which affects only one accounting period (''the relevant accounting period'').

(2) If notice has been given under paragraph 3 requiring a company to deliver a company tax return for the relevant accounting period, a claim or election by the company which can be made by being included in the return (as originally made or by amendment) must be so made.

(3) If a company has delivered a company tax return for the relevant accounting period, a claim or election made by the company which could be made by amending the return is treated as an amendment of the return.

The provisions of paragraph 15 (amendment of return by company) apply.

(4) Schedule 1A to the Taxes Management Act 1970 (claims and elections not included in returns) applies to a claim or election made by a company which cannot be included in a company tax return for the relevant accounting period.

This applies in particular to a claim or election made—

   (*a*) before any notice is given under paragraph 3 requiring a company tax return for the relevant accounting period, or
   (*b*) at a time when its return for the relevant accounting period cannot be amended.

Commentary—*Simon's Direct Tax Service* **D2.831.**

Claims or elections involving more than one accounting period

58—(1) This paragraph applies to a claim or election for tax purposes if—

   (*a*) the event or occasion giving rise to it occurs in one accounting period (the period to which it ''relates''), and
   (*b*) it affects one or more other accounting periods (whether or not it also affects the period to which it relates).

(2) If a company makes a claim or election which—

   (*a*) relates to an accounting period for which the company has delivered a company tax return and could be made by amendment of the return, or
   (*b*) affects an accounting period for which the company has delivered a company tax return and could be given effect by amendment of the return,

the claim or election is treated as an amendment of the return.

The provisions of paragraph 15 (amendment of return by company) apply.

(3) Schedule 1A to the Taxes Management Act 1970 (claims and elections not included in returns) applies to a claim or election made by a company if or to the extent that it is not—

   (*a*) made by being included (by amendment or otherwise) in the company tax return for the accounting period to which it relates, and
   (*b*) given effect by being included (by amendment or otherwise) in company tax returns for the accounting periods affected by it.

Commentary—*Simon's Direct Tax Service* **D2.831.**

Other claims and elections

59—(1) Schedule 1A to the Taxes Management Act 1970 applies to a claim or election for tax purposes which is not within paragraph 57 or 58, whether or not it is included (by amendment or otherwise) in a company tax return.

(2) The provisions of this Schedule do not apply where or to the extent that the provisions of Schedule 1A apply.

Commentary—*Simon's Direct Tax Service* **D2.836.**

Provisions supplementary to paragraphs 57 to 59

60—(1) Paragraphs 57 to 59 have effect subject to any express provision to the contrary.

(2) Nothing in those paragraphs affects the time limit or any other conditions for making a claim or election.

(3) Where Schedule 1A to the Taxes Management Act 1970 applies by virtue of any of those paragraphs and the claim or election results in an increase in the amount of tax payable, all such adjustments by way of assessment or otherwise shall be made as are necessary to give effect to it.

Commentary—*Simon's Direct Tax Service* **D2.831, 832.**

Consequential claims, etc arising out of certain Revenue amendments or assessments

61—(1) Paragraphs 62 to 64 have effect to allow certain claims, elections, applications and notices to be made or given, or if previously given to be revoked or varied, where—

(*a*) an amendment of a company tax return is made under paragraph 34(2)(*b*) (amendments of other returns required in consequence of closure notice) which has the effect of increasing the amount of tax payable by a company,

(*b*) a discovery assessment is made, or

(*c*) an assessment is made under paragraph 76 (recovery of excessive group relief).

(2) Paragraphs 62 to 64 do not apply in relation to an assessment made in a case involving fraudulent or negligent conduct on the part of—

(*a*) the company, or

(*b*) a person acting on behalf of the company, or

(*c*) a person who was a partner of the company at the relevant time.

In such a case more limited provision is made by paragraph 65.

(3) In paragraphs 62 to 64 "the relevant accounting period", in relation to the time limit for making a consequential claim, election, application or notice, means—

(*a*) in relation to an amendment of a company tax return under paragraph 34(2)(*b*), the accounting period in which the closure notice was issued;

(*b*) in relation to an assessment, the accounting period in which the assessment was made.

Commentary—*Simon's Direct Tax Service* **D2.834.**

Consequential claims etc that may be made

62—(1) A claim, election, application or notice to which this paragraph applies—

(*a*) may be made or given at any time within one year from the end of the relevant accounting period, or

(*b*) if previously made or given may at any such time be revoked or varied–

(i) in the same manner as it was made or given, and

(ii) by or with the consent of the same person or persons who made, gave or consented to it (or, if a person has died, by or with the consent of his personal representatives),

unless, by virtue of any enactment, it is irrevocable.

(2) This paragraph applies to a claim, election, application or notice—

(*a*) relating to the accounting period in respect of which the amendment or assessment is made, or

(*b*) made or given by reference to an event occurring in that period,

whose making, giving, revocation or variation has or could have the effect of reducing a relevant liability of the company.

(3) The following are relevant liabilities of the company for this purpose—

(*a*) the increased liability to tax resulting from the amendment or assessment;

(*b*) any other liability to tax of the company–

(i) for the accounting period to which the amendment or assessment relates, or

(ii) for any subsequent accounting period ending not later than one year after the end of the relevant accounting period.

(4) Where a claim, election, application or notice is made, given, revoked or varied by virtue of this paragraph, all such adjustments shall be made, whether by way of discharge or repayment of tax or the making of amendments, assessments or otherwise, as are required to take account of the effect of the taking of that action on any person's liability to tax for any chargeable period.

(5) The provisions of the Taxes Management Act 1970 relating to appeals against decisions on claims apply with any necessary modifications to a decision on the revocation or variation of a claim by virtue of this paragraph.

(6) This paragraph has effect subject to—

paragraph 63 (consequential claims etc affecting tax liability of another person), and

paragraph 64 (consequential claims etc not to give rise to reduction in liability).

Commentary—*Simon's Direct Tax Service* **D2.834.**

Consequential claims etc affecting tax liability of another person

63—(1) If the effect of the exercise by any person of a power conferred by paragraph 62 would be to alter the liability to tax of another person, the power may not be exercised except with the consent in writing of that other person or, if he has died, of his personal representatives.

(2) Where such a power is exercised so as to increase the liability to tax of another person, neither paragraph 61 above nor section 43A of the Taxes Management Act 1970 (which makes corresponding provision in relation to income tax or capital gains tax) applies in relation to any amendment or assessment made because of that increased liability.

(3) In this paragraph "tax" includes income tax or capital gains tax.

Commentary—*Simon's Direct Tax Service* **D2.834.**

Consequential claims etc not to give rise to reduction in liability

64—(1) If in any case—

　(*a*) one or more claims, elections, applications or notices are made, given, revoked or varied under paragraph 62 in consequence of an amendment or assessment, and

　(*b*) the total of the reductions in liability to tax resulting from that action would exceed the additional liability to tax resulting from the amendment or assessment,

the excess is not available to reduce any liability to tax.

(2) Where sub-paragraph (1) has the effect of limiting either—

　(*a*) the reduction in a person's liability to tax for more than one period, or

　(*b*) the reduction in the liability to tax of more than one person,

the limited amount shall be apportioned between the periods or persons concerned.

(3) The apportionment shall be made in such manner as the Inland Revenue may specify by notice in writing to the person or persons concerned, unless notice is given under the following provision.

(4) If the person concerned gives (or the persons concerned jointly give) notice in writing to the Inland Revenue within the period of 30 days beginning with—

　(*a*) the day on which notice under sub-paragraph (3) is given to the person concerned, or

　(*b*) where more than one person is concerned, the latest date on which such notice is given to any of them,

the apportionment shall be made in such manner as may be specified in the notice given by the person or persons concerned.

(5) In this paragraph "tax" includes income tax or capital gains tax.

Commentary—*Simon's Direct Tax Service* **D2.834.**

Consequential claims in case of fraud or negligence

65—(1) This paragraph applies where an assessment is made on a company in a case involving fraudulent or negligent conduct on the part of—

　(*a*) the company, or

　(*b*) a person acting on behalf of the company, or

　(*c*) a person who was a partner of the company at the relevant time.

(2) If the company so requires, effect shall be given in determining the amount of the tax charged by the assessment to any relief or allowance to which the company would have been entitled for that accounting period on a claim or application made within the time allowed by the Taxes Acts.

Commentary—*Simon's Direct Tax Service* **D2.834.**

PART VIII
CLAIMS FOR GROUP RELIEF

Cross references—See FA 2000 Sch 22 para 81 (the provisions of this Part, except para 77, apply for relief under FA 2000 Sch 22 para 81 (tonnage tax: surrender of unrelieved qualifying expenditure) as they apply to group relief).

Introduction

66 This Part of this Schedule applies to claims for relief under Chapter IV of Part X of the Taxes Act 1988 (group relief).

Commentary—*Simon's Direct Tax Service* **D2.630, 836.**

Claim to be included in company tax return

67—(1) A claim for group relief must be made by being included in the claimant company's company tax return for the accounting period for which the claim is made.

(2) It may be included in the return originally made or by amendment.

Commentary—*Simon's Direct Tax Service* **D2.630, 836.**

Content of claims

68—(1) A claim for group relief must specify—

  (a) the amount of relief claimed, and

  (b) the name of the surrendering company.

(2) The amount specified must be an amount which is quantified at the time the claim is made.

[(3) A claim for group relief must also state whether or not there is a company mentioned in sub-paragraph (4) that was not resident in the United Kingdom in either or both of the following periods—

  (a) the accounting period of the surrendering company to which the surrender relates,

  (b) the corresponding accounting period of the claimant company.

(4) Those companies are the claimant company, the surrendering company and any other company by reference to which—

  (a) the claimant company and the surrendering company are members of the same group, or

  (b) the conditions specified in section 402(3) of the Taxes Act 1988 for the making of the claim are satisfied in the case of the claimant company and the surrendering company.][1]

Commentary—*Simon's Direct Tax Service* **D2.630.**

Amendment—[1] Sub-paras (3), (4) inserted by FA 2000 s 97, Sch 27 para 11 with effect for accounting periods ending after 31 March 2000.

Claims for more or less than the amount available for surrender

69—(1) A claim for group relief may be made for less than the amount available for surrender at the time the claim is made.

(2) A claim is ineffective if the amount claimed exceeds the amount available for surrender at the time the claim is made.

(3) For these purposes the amount available for surrender at any time is calculated as follows.

First step

Determine the total amount available for surrender under section 403 of the Taxes Act 1988—

  (a) on the basis of the information in the company's company tax return, and

  (b) disregarding any amendments whose effect is deferred under paragraph 31(3).

Second step

Then deduct the total of all amounts for which notices of consent have been given by the company and not withdrawn.

(4) Where one or more claims are withdrawn on the same day as one or more claims are made, the withdrawals are given effect first.

(5) Where more than one claim is made on the same day, and the claims together take the amount claimed over the limit of what is available for surrender, the Inland Revenue may determine which of the claims is to be ineffective.

(6) The power under sub-paragraph (5) shall not be exercised to any greater extent than is necessary to bring the total amount claimed within the amount available for surrender.

Commentary—*Simon's Direct Tax Service* **D2.630.**

Consent to surrender

70—(1) A claim for group relief requires the consent of the surrendering company.

(2) A consortium claim also requires the consent of each member of the consortium.

(3) The necessary consent or consents must be given—

  (a) by notice in writing,

  (b) to the officer of the Board to whom the surrendering company makes its company tax returns,

  (c) at or before the time the claim is made.

Otherwise the claim is ineffective.

(4) A claim for group relief is ineffective unless it is accompanied by a copy of the notice of consent to surrender given by the surrendering company.

(5) A consortium claim is ineffective unless it is also accompanied by a copy of the notice of consent to surrender given by each member of the consortium.

Commentary—*Simon's Direct Tax Service* **D2.630.**

Notice of consent

71—(1) Notice of consent by the surrendering company must contain all the following details—

  (a) the name of the surrendering company;

  (b) the name of the company to which relief is being surrendered;

  (c) the amount of relief being surrendered;

  (d) the accounting period of the surrendering company to which the surrender relates;

(*e*) the tax district references of the surrendering company and the company to which relief is being surrendered.

Otherwise the notice is ineffective.

(2) Notice of consent may not be amended, but it may be withdrawn and replaced by another notice of consent.

(3) Notice of consent may be withdrawn by notice to the officer of the Board to whom the notice of consent was given.

(4) Except where the consent is withdrawn under paragraph 75 (withdrawal in consequence of reduction of amount available for surrender), the notice of withdrawal must be accompanied by a notice signifying the consent of the claimant company to the withdrawal.

Otherwise the notice is ineffective.

(5) The claimant company must, so far as it may do so, amend its company tax return for the accounting period for which the claim was made so as to reflect the withdrawal of consent.

Commentary—*Simon's Direct Tax Service* **D2.630.**

Notice of consent requiring amendment of return

72—(1) Where notice of consent by the surrendering company is given after the company has made a company tax return for the period to which the surrender relates, the surrendering company must at the same time amend its return so as to reflect the notice of consent.

(2) Where notice of consent by the surrendering company relates to a loss in respect of which relief has been given under section 393(1) of the Taxes Act 1988 (carry forward of trading losses), the surrendering company must at the same time amend its company tax return for the period or, if more than one, each of the periods in which relief for that loss has been given under section 393(1) so as to reflect the new notice of consent.

For this purpose relief under section 393(1) is treated as given for losses incurred in earlier accounting periods before losses incurred in later accounting periods.

(3) The time limits otherwise applicable to amendment of a company tax return do not prevent an amendment being made under sub-paragraph (1) or (2).

(4) If the surrendering company fails to comply with sub-paragraph (1) or (2), the notice of consent is ineffective.

Commentary—*Simon's Direct Tax Service* **D2.630.**

Withdrawal or amendment of claim

73—(1) A claim for group relief may be withdrawn by the claimant company only by amending its company tax return.

(2) A claim for group relief may not be amended, but must be withdrawn and replaced by another claim.

Commentary—*Simon's Direct Tax Service* **D2.630.**

Time limit for claims

74—(1) A claim for group relief may be made or withdrawn at any time up to whichever is the last of the following dates—

(*a*) the first anniversary of the filing date for the company tax return of the claimant company for the accounting period for which the claim is made;

(*b*) if notice of enquiry is given into that return, 30 days after the enquiry is completed;

(*c*) if after such an enquiry the Inland Revenue amend the return under paragraph 34(2), 30 days after notice of the amendment is issued;

(*d*) if an appeal is brought against such an amendment, 30 days after the date on which the appeal is finally determined.

(2) A claim for group relief may be made or withdrawn at a later time if the Inland Revenue allow it.

(3) The time limits otherwise applicable to amendment of a company tax return do not apply to an amendment to the extent that it makes or withdraws a claim for group relief within the time allowed by or under this paragraph.

(4) The references in sub-paragraph (1) to an enquiry into a company tax return do not include an enquiry restricted to a previous amendment making or withdrawing a claim for group relief.

An enquiry is so restricted if—

(*a*) the scope of the enquiry is limited as mentioned in paragraph 25(2), and

(*b*) the amendment giving rise to the enquiry consisted of the making or withdrawing of a claim for group relief.

Commentary—*Simon's Direct Tax Service* **D2.631.**

Reduction in amount available for surrender

75—(1) This paragraph applies if, after the surrendering company has given one or more notices of consent to surrender, the [total amount available for surrender][1] is reduced to less than the amount stated in the notice, or the total of the amounts stated in the notices, as being surrendered.

(2) The company must within 30 days withdraw the notice of consent, or as many of the notices as is necessary to bring the total amount surrendered within the new [total][1] amount available for surrender, and may give one or more new notices of consent.

(3) The company must give notice in writing of the withdrawal of consent, and send a copy of any new notice of consent—

   (*a*) to each of the companies affected, and
   (*b*) to the Inland Revenue.

(4) If the surrendering company fails to act in accordance with sub-paragraph (2), the Inland Revenue may by notice to the surrendering company give such directions as they think fit as to which notice or notices are to be ineffective or are to have effect in a lesser amount.

This power shall not be exercised to any greater extent than is necessary to secure that the total amount stated in the notice or notices is consistent with the [total][1] amount available for surrender.

(5) The Inland Revenue must at the same time send a copy of the notice to the claimant company, or each claimant company, affected by their action.

(6) A claimant company which receives—

   (*a*) notice of the withdrawal of consent, or a copy of a new notice of consent, under sub-paragraph (3), or
   (*b*) a copy of a notice containing directions by the Inland Revenue under sub-paragraph (4),

must, so far as it may do so, amend its company tax return for the accounting period for which the claim is made so that it is consistent with the new position with regard to consent to surrender.

(7) An appeal may be brought by the surrendering company against any directions given by the Inland Revenue under sub-paragraph (4).

(8) Notice of appeal must be given—

   (*a*) in writing,
   (*b*) within 30 days after the notice containing the directions was issued,
   (*c*) to the officer of the Board by whom the notice was given.

Commentary—*Simon's Direct Tax Service* D2.630.
Amendment—[1] Words in sub-para (1) substituted, and word in sub-paras (2), (4) inserted, by FA 1999 s 92(2), (7) with effect for accounting periods ending after 30 June 1999.

[Assessment on other claimant companies

75A—(1) This paragraph applies where, after the surrendering company has given notice of consent to surrender, a claimant company (''the chargeable company'') has become liable to tax in consequence of receiving—

   (*a*) notice of the withdrawal of consent, or a copy of a new notice of consent, under paragraph 75(3), or
   (*b*) a copy of a notice containing directions by the Inland Revenue under paragraph 75(4).

(2) If any of the tax is unpaid six months after the chargeable company's time limit for claims, the Inland Revenue may make an assessment to tax in the name of the chargeable company on any other company that has obtained group relief as a result of the surrender.

(3) The assessment may not be made more than two years after that time limit.

(4) The amount of the assessment must not exceed—

   (*a*) the amount of the unpaid tax, or
   (*b*) if less, the amount of tax which the other company saves by virtue of the surrender.

(5) A company assessed to an amount of tax under sub-paragraph (2) is entitled to recover from the chargeable company—

   (*a*) a sum equal to that amount, and
   (*b*) any interest on that amount which it has paid under section 87A of the Taxes Management Act 1970 (interest on unpaid corporation tax).

(6) For the purposes of this paragraph the chargeable company's time limit for claims is the last of the dates mentioned in paragraph 74(1) on which the chargeable company could make or withdraw a claim for group relief for the accounting period for which the claim in question is made.][1]

Commentary—*Simon's Direct Tax Service* D2.630.
Cross references—See TMA 1970 s 87A (interest on overdue corporation tax).
Amendment—[1] This paragraph inserted by FA 1999 s 92(3), (7) with effect for accounting periods ending after 30 June 1999.

Assessment to recover excessive group relief

76—(1) If the Inland Revenue discover that any group relief which has been given is or has become excessive, they may make an assessment to tax in the amount which in their opinion ought to be charged.

(2) This power is without prejudice to—

(*a*) the power to make a discovery assessment under paragraph 41(1);

(*b*) the making of all such adjustments by way of discharge or repayment of tax or otherwise as may be required where a claimant company has obtained too much relief, or a surrendering company has forgone relief in respect of a corresponding amount.

[(3) If an assessment under this paragraph is made because a claimant company fails, or is unable, to amend its company tax return under paragraph 75(6), the assessment is not out of time if it is made within one year from—

(*a*) the date on which the surrendering company gives notice of the withdrawal of consent, or (if later) sends a copy of a new notice of consent, to the claimant company under paragraph 75(3), or

(*b*) the date on which the Inland Revenue send the claimant company a copy of a notice containing their directions under paragraph 75(4).][1]

Commentary—*Simon's Direct Tax Service* **D2.639.**
Amendment—[1] Sub-para (3) inserted by FA 1999 s 92(4), (7) with effect for accounting periods ending after 30 June 1999.

Joint amended returns

77—(1) The Treasury may by regulations make provision for arrangements under which—

(*a*) a claim for group relief may be made without being accompanied by a copy of the notice of consent to surrender given by the surrendering company[, provided authority for the claim being so made is given by a company which is authorised in relation to the claimant company as mentioned in paragraph (*b*)][1], and

(*b*) one company may be authorised to act on behalf of two or more companies in the same group in amending their company tax returns for the purpose of claiming or surrendering group relief or revising the amounts of group relief claimed or surrendered by them.

(2) Regulations under this paragraph may add to, exclude or modify the operation of any provisions of this Part of this Schedule to such extent as the Treasury think necessary or expedient for the purpose of, or in connection with, such arrangements.

(3) Provision may in particular be made—

(*a*) altering the conditions for making and withdrawing claims for group relief, and

(*b*) giving the Inland Revenue power to recover from the authorised company or another company in the group any amount which might be recovered from the claimant company by an assessment under paragraph 76.

Commentary—*Simon's Direct Tax Service* **D2.630.**
Amendment—[1] Words in sub-para (1) inserted by FA 2000 s 99 with effect from 28 July 2000.

PART IX
CLAIMS FOR CAPITAL ALLOWANCES
Introduction

[**78** This Part of this Schedule applies to claims for allowances under the Capital Allowances Act which—

(*a*) are made for corporation tax purposes, and

(*b*) are required under section 3 of that Act to be included in a tax return.][1]

Commentary—*Simon's Direct Tax Service* **D2.835.**
Amendments—[1] Substituted by CAA 2001 s 578, Sch 2 para 103(1) with effect for corporation tax purposes as respects allowances and charges falling to be made for chargeable periods ending after 31 March 2001.

Claim to be included in company tax return

[**79**—(1) A claim for capital allowances must be included in the claimant company's company tax return for the accounting period for which the claim is made.][1]

(2) It may be included in the return originally made or by amendment.

Commentary—*Simon's Direct Tax Service* **D2.835.**
Amendments—[1] Sub-para (1) substituted by CAA 2001 s 578, Sch 2 para 103(2) with effect for income tax purposes, as respects allowances and charges falling to be made for chargeable periods ending after 5 April 2001, and for corporation tax purposes, as respects allowances and charges falling to be made for chargeable periods ending after 31 March 2001.

Content of claims

80 A claim for capital allowances must specify the amount claimed, which must be an amount which is quantified at the time the claim is made.

Commentary—*Simon's Direct Tax Service* **D2.835.**

Amendment or withdrawal of claim

81 A claim for capital allowances may be amended or withdrawn by the claimant company only by amending its company tax return.

Commentary—*Simon's Direct Tax Service* **D2.835.**

Time limit for claims

82—(1) A claim for capital allowances may be made, amended or withdrawn at any time up to whichever is the last of the following dates—

    (*a*) the first anniversary of the filing date for the company tax return of the claimant company for the accounting period for which the claim is made;

    (*b*) if notice of enquiry is given into that return, 30 days after the enquiry is completed;

    (*c*) if after such an enquiry the Inland Revenue amend the return under paragraph 34(2), 30 days after notice of the amendment is issued;

    (*d*) if an appeal is brought against such an amendment, 30 days after the date on which the appeal is finally determined.

(2) A claim for capital allowances may be made, amended or withdrawn at a later time if the Inland Revenue allow it.

(3) The time limits otherwise applicable to amendment of a company tax return do not apply to an amendment to the extent that it makes, amends or withdraws a claim for capital allowances within the time allowed by or under this paragraph.

(4) The references in sub-paragraph (1) to an enquiry into a company tax return do not include an enquiry restricted to a previous amendment making, amending or withdrawing a claim for capital allowances.

An enquiry is so restricted if—

    (*a*) the scope of the enquiry is limited as mentioned in paragraph 25(2), and

    (*b*) the amendment giving rise to the enquiry consisted of the making, amending or withdrawing of a claim for capital allowances.

Commentary—*Simon's Direct Tax Service* **D2.835.**

Consequential amendment of return for another accounting period

83—(1) This paragraph applies if the effect of a claim for capital allowances is to reduce the amount available by way of capital allowances for another accounting period of the company for which a company tax return has been delivered.

(2) The company has 30 days within which to make any necessary amendments of the company tax return for that other period.

(3) If it does not do so, the Inland Revenue may by notice in writing to the company amend the return to make it consistent with the amount available by way of capital allowances.

(4) The time limits otherwise applicable to amendment of a company tax return do not prevent an amendment being made under sub-paragraph (2) or (3).

(5) An appeal may be brought by the company against any such amendment.

(6) Notice of appeal must be given—

    (*a*) in writing,

    (*b*) within 30 days after notice of the amendment was issued,

    (*c*) to the officer of the Board by whom the notice of amendment was issued.

Commentary—*Simon's Direct Tax Service* **D2.835.**

[PART IXA
CLAIMS FOR R&D TAX CREDIT
Introduction

83A This Part of this Schedule applies to claims for R&D tax credits under Schedule 20 to the Finance Act 2000.][1]

Amendments—[1] This Part (paras 83A–83F) inserted by FA 2000 s 69(2), Sch 21 para 4 with effect for accounting periods ending after 31 March 2000.

[Claim to be included in company tax return

83B—(1) A claim for an R&D tax credit must be made by being included in the claimant company's company tax return for the accounting period for which the claim is made.

(2) It may be included in the return originally made or by amendment.][1]

Amendments—[1] This Part (paras 83A–83F) inserted by FA 2000 s 69(2), Sch 21 para 4 with effect for accounting periods ending after 31 March 2000.

[Content of claim

83C A claim for an R&D tax credit must specify the amount of the relief claimed, which must be an amount quantified at the time the claim is made.][1]

Amendments—[1] This Part (paras 83A–83F) inserted by FA 2000 s 69(2), Sch 21 para 4 with effect for accounting periods ending after 31 March 2000.

[Amendment or withdrawal of claim

83D A claim for an R&D tax credit may be amended or withdrawn by the claimant company only by amending its company tax return.][1]

Amendments—[1] This Part (paras 83A–83F) inserted by FA 2000 s 69(2), Sch 21 para 4 with effect for accounting periods ending after 31 March 2000.

[Time limit for claims

83E—(1) A claim for an R&D tax credit may be made, amended or withdrawn at any time up to the first anniversary of the filing date for the company tax return of the claimant company for the accounting period for which the claim is made.

(2) The claim may be made, amended or withdrawn at a later date if the Inland Revenue allow it.][1]

Amendments—[1] This Part (paras 83A–83F) inserted by FA 2000 s 69(2), Sch 21 para 4 with effect for accounting periods ending after 31 March 2000.

[Penalty

83F—(1) The company is liable to a penalty where it—

(a) fraudulently or negligently makes a claim for an R&D tax credit which is incorrect, or

(b) discovers that a claim for an R&D tax credit made by it (neither fraudulently or negligently) is incorrect and does not remedy the error without unreasonable delay.

(2) The penalty is an amount not exceeding the excess R&D tax credit claimed, that is, the difference between—

(a) the amount of the R&D tax credit to which the company is entitled for the accounting period to which the claim relates, and

(b) the amount of the R&D tax credit claimed by the company for that period.][1]

Amendments—[1] This Part (paras 83A–83F) inserted by FA 2000 s 69(2), Sch 21 para 4 with effect for accounting periods ending after 31 March 2000.

[PART IXB

CLAIMS RELATING TO REMEDIATION OF CONTAMINATED LAND

Introduction

83G This Part of this Schedule applies to claims for—

(a) land remediation tax credits under paragraph 14 of Schedule 22 to the Finance Act 2001 (''land remediation tax credits''), and

(b) life assurance company tax credits under paragraph 24 of that Schedule (''life assurance company tax credits'').][1]

Commentary—*Simon's Direct Tax Service* **D2.1416**.
Amendments—[1] This Part (paras 83G–83L) inserted by FA 2001 s 70(3), Sch 23 para 6 with effect for accounting periods ending after 31 March 2001.

[Claim to be included in company tax return

83H—(1) A claim for a land remediation tax credit or a life assurance company tax credit must be made by being included in the claimant company's company tax return for the accounting period for which the claim is made.

(2) It may be included in the return originally made or by amendment.][1]

Commentary—*Simon's Direct Tax Service* **D2.1416**.
Amendments—[1] This Part (paras 83G–83L) inserted by FA 2001 s 70(3), Sch 23 para 6 with effect for accounting periods ending after 31 March 2001.

[Content of claim

83I A claim for a land remediation tax credit or a life assurance company tax credit must specify the amount of the tax credit claimed, which must be an amount quantified at the time the claim is made.]

Commentary—*Simon's Direct Tax Service* **D2.1416**.
Amendments—[1] This Part (paras 83G–83L) inserted by FA 2001 s 70(3), Sch 23 para 6 with effect for accounting periods ending after 31 March 2001.

[Amendment or withdrawal of claim

83J A claim for a land remediation tax credit or a life assurance company tax credit may be amended or withdrawn by the claimant company only by amending its company tax return.][1]

Commentary—*Simon's Direct Tax Service* **D2.1416**.
Amendments—[1] This Part (paras 83G–83L) inserted by FA 2001 s 70(3), Sch 23 para 6 with effect for accounting periods ending after 31 March 2001.

[Time limit for claims

83K—(1) A claim for a land remediation tax credit or a life assurance company tax credit may be made, amended or withdrawn at any time up to the first anniversary of the filing date for the company tax return of the claimant company for the accounting period for which the claim is made.

(2) The claim may be made, amended or withdrawn at a later date if the Inland Revenue allow it.][1]

Commentary—*Simon's Direct Tax Service* **D2.1416**.
Amendments—[1] This Part (paras 83G–83L) inserted by FA 2001 s 70(3), Sch 23 para 6 with effect for accounting periods ending after 31 March 2001.

[Penalty

83L—(1) The company is liable to a penalty where it—

(a) fraudulently or negligently makes a claim for a land remediation tax credit or a life assurance company tax credit and that claim is incorrect, or
(b) discovers that such a claim made by it (neither fraudulently nor negligently) is incorrect and does not remedy the error without unreasonable delay.

(2) The penalty is an amount not exceeding the excess land remediation tax credit or excess life assurance company tax credit claimed, that is, the difference between—

(a) the amount of the land remediation tax credit or the life assurance company tax credit claimed by the company for the accounting period to which the claim relates, and
(b) the amount of the land remediation tax credit or the life assurance company tax credit to which the company is entitled for that period.][1]

Commentary—*Simon's Direct Tax Service* **D2.1416**.
Amendments—[1] This Part (paras 83G–83L) inserted by FA 2001 s 70(3), Sch 23 para 6 with effect for accounting periods ending after 31 March 2001.

PART 9C
CLAIMS FOR TAX CREDIT UNDER SCHEDULE 13 TO THE FINANCE ACT 2002

Prospective amendments—Part 9C inserted by FA 2002 s 54, Sch 14 paras 4, 5 with effect for tax credits payable under FA 2002 Sch 13 in respect of expenditure incurred on or after such day as the Treasury may appoint under FA 2002 Sch 13 para 28. Part 9C as inserted to read as follows—

"Introduction

83M This Part of this Schedule applies to claims for tax credits under Schedule 13 to the Finance Act 2002 (vaccine research etc).

Claim to be included in company tax return

83N—(1) A claim to which this Part of this Schedule applies must be made by being included in the claimant company's company tax return for the accounting period for which the claim is made.

(2) It may be included in the return originally made or by amendment.

Content of claim

83O A claim to which this Part of this Schedule applies must specify the amount of the relief claimed, which must be an amount quantified at the time the claim is made.

Amendment or withdrawal of claim

83P A claim to which this Part of this Schedule applies may be amended or withdrawn by the claimant company only by amending its company tax return.

Time limit for claims

83Q—(1) A claim to which this Part of this Schedule applies may be made, amended or withdrawn at any time up to the first anniversary of the filing date for the company tax return of the claimant company for the accounting period for which the claim is made.

(2) The claim may be made, amended or withdrawn at a later date if the Inland Revenue allow it.

Penalty

83R—(1) The company is liable to a penalty where it—

(a) fraudulently or negligently makes a claim to which this Part of this Schedule applies which is incorrect, or
(b) discovers that such a claim made by it (neither fraudulently nor negligently) is incorrect and does not remedy the error without unreasonable delay.
(2) The penalty is an amount not exceeding the excess credit claimed, that is, the difference between—
(a) the amount of the credit to which the company is entitled under Schedule 13 to the Finance Act 2002 for the accounting period to which the claim relates, and
(b) the amount of such credit claimed by the company for that period.".

PART X
SPECIAL PROVISIONS
Choice between different Cases of Schedule D

84—(1) This paragraph applies in the following cases.

(2) The first case is where amounts may be brought into charge to tax either—

(*a*) in computing profits chargeable to tax under Case I of Schedule D, or

(*b*) as amounts within Case III or V of that Schedule.

(3) The second case is where amounts may be brought into charge to tax either—

(*a*) in computing profits charged to tax under Case I of Schedule D, or

(*b*) for the purpose of applying the basis commonly called the I minus E basis under which a company carrying on life assurance business is charged to tax on that business otherwise than under Case I of Schedule D.

In paragraph (*b*) ''life assurance business'' includes annuity business within the meaning of Chapter I of Part XII of the Taxes Act 1988.

(4) Where this paragraph applies, the Inland Revenue may by notice require a company—

(*a*) to produce to them such documents in the company's power or possession, and

(*b*) to provide them with such information, in such form,

as they may reasonably require for the purpose of determining which basis of charge is to be used for an accounting period.

The provisions of paragraphs 27 to 29 (notice to produce documents, etc for purposes of enquiry: supplementary provisions and penalty) apply in relation to such a notice.

(5) A determination by the Inland Revenue under this paragraph is final and conclusive as to the basis of charge to be used for the accounting period concerned.

Commentary—*Simon's Direct Tax Service* **D2.851.**

Non-annual accounting of general insurance business

85—(1) This paragraph applies where a company carrying on insurance business delivers a company tax return based wholly or partly on accounts drawn up using the method described in paragraph 52 of Schedule 9A to the Companies Act 1985.

That paragraph provides for a technical provision to be made in the accounts which is later replaced by a provision for estimated claims outstanding.

(2) Where this paragraph applies—

(*a*) the company may make any amendments of its return arising from the replacement of the technical provision at any time within twelve months from the date on which the provision was replaced, and

(*b*) the Inland Revenue may give notice of enquiry into the return at any time up to two years from that date.

(3) Nothing in this paragraph prevents notice of enquiry being given at any later time in accordance with the general rule in paragraph 24(3).

Commentary—*Simon's Direct Tax Service* **D2.852.**

Insurance companies with non-annual actuarial investigations

86—(1) This paragraph applies where a company tax return is delivered by an insurance company which is permitted by [a direction under section 148 of the Financial Services and Markets Act 2000][1] to cause investigations to be made into its financial condition less frequently than is required by section 18 of that Act.

(2) Where this paragraph applies—

(*a*) the company may make any amendments of its return arising from the relevant investigation at any time within twelve months from the date as at which that investigation is carried out, and

(*b*) the Inland Revenue may give notice of enquiry into the return at any time up to two years from that date.

(3) ''The relevant investigation'' means—

(*a*) if the return is for a period as at the end of which there is carried out an investigation under section [9.4 of the Prudential Sourcebook (Insurers)][2] into the financial condition of the company, that investigation;

(*b*) if the return is not for such a period, the first such investigation to be made into the financial condition of the company as at the end of a subsequent period.

[(4) In sub-paragraph (1) ''the Prudential Sourcebook (Insurers)'' means the Interim Prudential Sourcebook for Insurers made by the Financial Services Authority under the Financial Services and Markets Act 2000.][2]

Commentary—*Simon's Direct Tax Service* **D2.852.**
Amendments—[1] Words in sub-para (1) substituted by the Financial Services and Markets Act 2000 (Consequential Amendments) (Taxes) Order, SI 2001/3629 art 103(1), (3)(*a*) with effect from 1 December 2001 (immediately after the coming into force of the Financial Services and Markets Act 2000 ss 411, 432(1), Sch 20).
[2] Words in sub-para (3) substituted, and sub-para (4) added, by SI 2001/3629 art 103(1), (3)(*b*), (*c*), (5) with effect for periods of account ending after 30 November 2001.

Friendly societies with non-annual actuarial investigations

87—(1) This paragraph applies where a company tax return is delivered by a friendly society which is required by section [5.2 of the Prudential Sourcebook (Friendly Societies)][1] to cause an investigation to be made into its financial condition at least once in every period of three years.

(2) Where this paragraph applies—

(*a*) the society may make any amendments of its return arising from the relevant investigation at any time within 15 months from the date as at which that investigation is carried out, and
(*b*) the Inland Revenue may give notice of enquiry into the return at any time up to 27 months from that date.

(3) ''The relevant investigation'' means—

(*a*) if the return is for a period as at the end of which there is carried out an investigation under section [5.2 of the Prudential Sourcebook (Friendly Societies)][1] into the financial condition of the society, that investigation;
(*b*) if the return is not for such a period, the first such investigation to be made into the financial condition of the company as at the end of a subsequent period.

[(4) In this paragraph ''the Prudential Sourcebook (Friendly Societies)'' means the Interim Prudential Sourcebook for Friendly Societies made by the Financial Services Authority under the Financial Services and Markets Act 2000.][1]

Commentary—*Simon's Direct Tax Service* **D2.853.**
Amendments—[1] Words in sub-paras (1), (3) substituted, and sub-para (4) added, by the Financial Services and Markets Act 2000 (Consequential Amendments) (Taxes) Order, SI 2001/3629 art 103(1), (4), (5) with effect for periods of account ending after 30 November 2001.

PART XI
SUPPLEMENTARY PROVISIONS
Conclusiveness of amounts stated in return

88—(1) This paragraph applies to an amount stated in a company tax return for an accounting period which is required to be included in the return and which affects or may affect—

(*a*) the tax payable by the company making the return for another accounting period, or
(*b*) the tax liability of another company for any accounting period.

(2) If such an amount can no longer be altered it is taken to be conclusively determined for the purposes of the Corporation Tax Acts in relation to that other period or other company.

Sub-paragraphs (3) to (5) explain what is meant by ''can no longer be altered''.

(3) An amount is regarded as one that can no longer be altered if—

(*a*) the period specified in paragraph 15(4) (general period for amendment by company) has ended,
(*b*) any enquiry into the return has been completed and the period specified in paragraph 34(1) (period for amendment by company after enquiry) has ended,
(*c*) if the Inland Revenue amend the return under paragraph 34(2), the period within which an appeal may be brought against that amendment has ended, and
(*d*) if an appeal is brought, the appeal has been finally determined.

(4) If the return is amended by the company under a provision that allows an amendment after the end of the period specified in paragraph 15(4), an amount affected by the amendment ceases to be regarded as one that can no longer be altered until after whichever is the last of the following—

(*a*) the end of the period within which notice of enquiry into the return may be given in consequence of the amendment;
(*b*) if such a notice is given, the end of the period specified in paragraph 34(1);
(*c*) if the Inland Revenue amend the return under paragraph 34(2), the end of the period within which an appeal against that amendment may be brought;
(*d*) if an appeal is brought, the date on which the appeal is finally determined.

(5) If the return is amended by the Inland Revenue under paragraph 83(3) (consequential amendment of return where amount available by way of capital allowances is reduced), an amount affected by the amendment ceases to be regarded as one that can no longer be altered until after—

(*a*) the end of the period within which an appeal against that amendment may be brought, or
(*b*) if an appeal is brought, the date on which the appeal is finally determined.

(6) For the purposes of this paragraph an amount carried forward from a period for which a return was made under section 11 of the Taxes Management Act 1970 is not regarded as one required to be included in a company tax return for a later period.

(7) Nothing in this paragraph affects any power to make an assessment other than a self-assessment or the power to make a discovery determination.

Commentary—*Simon's Direct Tax Service* **D2.812.**

Penalty for fraud or negligence

89—(1) A company which fraudulently or negligently—

    (*a*) makes any incorrect return, statement or declaration in connection with a claim for any allowance, deduction or relief in respect of tax, or

    (*b*) submits to the Inland Revenue, or to the Special or General Commissioners, any incorrect accounts in connection with ascertainment of the company's tax liability,

is liable to a tax-related penalty.

(2) The penalty is an amount not exceeding the amount of tax understated, that is, the difference between—

    (*a*) the amount of tax payable by the company for the accounting period or periods to which the claim or accounts relate, and

    (*b*) the amount which would have been so payable on the basis of the return, statement or declaration made, or the accounts submitted.

(3) In computing for this purpose the amount of tax payable, no account shall be taken of any relief under section 419(4) of the Taxes Act 1988 (relief in respect of repayment, etc of loan) which is deferred under subsection (4A) of that section.

(4) For the purposes of this paragraph any accounts submitted on behalf of a company shall be taken to be submitted by it unless the company proves that they were submitted without its consent or connivance.

Commentary—*Simon's Direct Tax Service* **D2.846.**

Multiple tax-related penalties in respect of same accounting period

90—(1) This paragraph applies where a company incurs more than one penalty whose amount falls to be determined by reference to the tax payable by it for an accounting period.

(2) Each penalty after the first shall be reduced so that the total amount of the penalties, so far as determined by reference to any particular part of the tax, does not exceed whichever is, or but for this paragraph would be, the greater or greatest of them, so far as so determined.

Commentary—*Simon's Direct Tax Service* **D2.846.**

European Economic Interest Groupings

91 An act or omission such as is mentioned in section 98B of the Taxes Management Act 1970 (European Economic Interest Groupings: acts or omissions attracting penalties) on the part of a grouping, or a member of a grouping, is treated as the act or omission of each member of the grouping for the purposes of—

    paragraphs 43 and 46(2) (assessment in case of fraud or negligence), and

    paragraphs 61(2) and 65(1) (consequential claims in case of such an assessment).

Commentary—*Simon's Direct Tax Service* **D2.854.**

Notices of appeal

92—(1) This paragraph applies in relation to any appeal under this Schedule.

(2) The notice of appeal shall specify the grounds of appeal.

(3) On the hearing of the appeal the Commissioners may allow the appellant to put forward grounds not specified in the notice, and take them into consideration, if satisfied that the omission was not wilful or unreasonable.

Commentary—*Simon's Direct Tax Service* **D2.837.**

General jurisdiction of Special or General Commissioners

93—(1) This paragraph applies in relation to an appeal against—

    (*a*) an amendment of a self-assessment under paragraph 30, or

    (*b*) an amendment of a company tax return under paragraph 34(2), or

    (*c*) an assessment to tax other than a self-assessment, or

    (*d*) a discovery determination.

(2) An appeal against a decision of the Board shall be to the Special Commissioners.

[(2A) Unless the Special Commissioners otherwise direct, an appeal under paragraph 30 or 34(3) shall be to the Special Commissioners if—

(*a*) the appeal relates to a return in relation to which notice of enquiry has been given under paragraph 24, and
(*b*) notice has been given under paragraph 31A referring a question relating to the subject-matter of that enquiry to the Special Commissioners.

This applies even if the notice of referral was subsequently withdrawn.][1]

(3) Any other appeal shall be to the General Commissioners, subject—

(*a*) to any provision made by or under Part V of the Taxes Management Act 1970, and
(*b*) to any election under paragraph 94 below.

Commentary—*Simon's Direct Tax Service* **D2.837.**
Amendments—[1] Sub-para (2A) inserted by FA 2001 s 88, Sch 29 para 13 with effect as from the passing of FA 2001 in relation to returns whether made before or after the passing of FA 2001, and whether relating to periods before or after the passing of FA 2001.

Election to take appeal to Special Commissioners

94—(1) The appellant may elect (in accordance with section 46(1) of the Taxes Management Act 1970) to bring an appeal to which paragraph 93(3) would otherwise apply before the Special Commissioners.

(2) Such an election shall be disregarded if—

(*a*) the appellant and the Inland Revenue agree in writing, at any time before the determination of the appeal, that it is to be disregarded, or
(*b*) the General Commissioners have given a direction under sub-paragraph (4) and have not revoked it.

(3) At any time before the determination of an appeal in respect of which an election has been made, the inspector or other officer of the Board for the time being concerned with the proceedings, after giving notice to the appellant, may refer the election to the General Commissioners.

(4) On any such reference the Commissioners shall, unless they are satisfied that the appellant has arguments to present or evidence to adduce on the [merits of the appeal][1], direct that the election be disregarded.

(5) If, at any time [after the giving][1] of such a direction (but before the determination of the appeal) the General Commissioners are satisfied that the appellant has arguments to present or evidence to adduce on the merits of the appeal, they shall revoke the direction.

(6) Any decision to give or revoke such a direction shall be final.

Commentary—*Simon's Direct Tax Service* **D2.837.**
Amendment—[1] Words in sub-paras 4, 5 substituted by FA 1999 s 93, Sch 11 para 9 with effect for accounting periods ending after 30 June 1999.

Meaning of "the Inland Revenue"

95—(1) References in this Schedule to "the Inland Revenue" are to any officer of the Board, except as otherwise provided.

(2) Functions under these provisions are functions of the Board—

paragraph 50 (relief in case of double assessment),
paragraph 51 (relief in case of mistake in return).

(3) Functions under these provisions are exercisable by the Board or an officer of the Board—

paragraph 41(1) or (2) (power to make discovery assessment or determination),
paragraph 52 (recovery of excessive repayments, etc).

(4) Functions exercisable by the Board under sub-paragraph (2) or (3) are within section 4A of the Inland Revenue Regulation Act 1890 (functions of Board exercisable by officer acting with their authority).

(5) These provisions require things to be done by or in relation to the officer of the Board indicated in the Table—

Provision	Subject-matter	Officer
Paragraph 3(4)	Delivery of return	Officer by whom notice requiring return was issued.
Paragraph 16(5)(*b*)	Notice rejecting correction of return.	Officer by whom notice of correction was given.
Paragraph 28(2)(*c*)	Notice of appeal against requirement to produce documents, etc	Officer by whom notice was given making the requirement.
Paragraph 30(4)(*c*)	Notice of appeal against amendment of self-assessment during enquiry.	Officer by whom notice of amendment was given.

Provision	Subject-matter	Officer
Paragraph 34(4)(*c*)	Notice of appeal against amendment of return after enquiry.	Officer by whom notice of amendment was given.
Paragraph 48(2)(*c*)	Notice of appeal against assessment other than self-assessment.	Officer by whom notice of assessment was given.
Paragraph 70(3)(*b*)	Notice of consent to surrender group relief.	Officer to whom the surrendering company makes its company tax returns.
Paragraph 71(3)	Notice of withdrawal of consent to surrender group relief.	Officer to whom the notice of consent was given.
Paragraph 75(8)(*c*)	Notice of appeal against amendment of consent to surrender group relief.	Officer by whom notice of amendment was given.
Paragraph 83(6)(*c*)	Appeal against amendment of return to reduce claim for capital allowances.	Officer by whom notice of amendment was given.
Paragraph 94(3)	Election to take appeal to Special Commissioners.	Inspector or other officer of the Board for the time being concerned with the proceedings.

(6) In this Schedule "the Board" means the Commissioners of Inland Revenue.

Commentary—*Simon's Direct Tax Service* A2.302.

The self-assessment appointed day

96 In this Schedule "the self-assessment appointed day" means the day appointed by the Treasury under section 199 of the Finance Act 1994 for the purposes of Chapter III of Part IV of that Act (corporation tax self-assessment).

Commentary—*Simon's Direct Tax Service* D2.801.
Note—The appointed day is 1 July 1999 by virtue of the Finance Act 1994, Section 199, (Appointed Day) Order, SI 1998/3173 art 2.

Construction of references to assessment

97 Any reference in the Tax Acts (however expressed) to a person being assessed to tax, or being charged to tax by an assessment, include a reference to his being so assessed, or being so charged—

(*a*) by a self-assessment under this Schedule, or an amendment of such a self-assessment, or
(*b*) by a determination under paragraph 36 or 37 of this Schedule (which, until superseded by a self-assessment, has effect as if it were one).

Index of defined expressions

98 In this Schedule the expressions listed below are defined or otherwise explained by the provisions indicated—

The Board	paragraph 95(6)
Closure notice	paragraph 32(1)
Company tax return	paragraph 3(1)
Delivery (in relation to company tax return)	paragraph 4
Discovery assessment	paragraph 41(1)
Discovery determination	paragraph 41(2)
Filing date	paragraph 14
Inland Revenue	paragraph 95
Notice of enquiry	paragraph 24(1)
Notice requiring company tax return	paragraph 3(1)
Self-assessment	paragraph 7
Self-assessment appointed day	paragraph 96
Tax	paragraph 1 (and see paragraphs 63(3) and 64(5))
Tax payable	paragraph 8
Wrong period (return for)	paragraph 26(2) to (4)

SCHEDULE 19

COMPANY TAX RETURNS, ETC: MINOR AND CONSEQUENTIAL AMENDMENTS

Section 117(3)

Taxes Management Act 1970 (c 9)

1 (*repeals* TMA 1970 ss 10, 11, 11AA–AE).

2 (*amends* TMA 1970 s 12(2)).

3 (*amends* TMA 1970 s 12AA(7)).

4 (*substituted* TMA 1970 s 12AB(4); *repealed by* FA 2001 s 110, Sch 33 Pt II(13) with effect in accordance with FA 2001 s 88, Sch 29).

5 (*substituted* TMA 1970 s 12AC(3); *repealed by* FA 2001 s 110, Sch 33 Pt II(13) with effect in accordance with FA 2001 s 88, Sch 29).

6 (*amends* TMA 1970 s 12B(1)).

7 (*amends* TMA 1970 s 19A(1)).

8 (*amended* TMA 1970 s 28A; *repealed by* FA 2001 s 110, Sch 33 Pt II(13) with effect in accordance with FA 2001 s 88, Sch 29).

9 (*repeals* TMA 1970 ss 28AA, 28AB).

10 (*amended* TMA 1970 s 28B; *repealed by* FA 2001 s 110, Sch 33 Pt II(13) with effect in accordance with FA 2001 s 88, Sch 29).

11 (*repeals* TMA 1970 ss 28D, 28E, 28F).

12 (*amends* TMA 1970 s 29).

13 (*amends* TMA 1970 s 30).

14 (*amends* TMA 1970 s 30B; *part repealed by* FA 2001 s 110, Sch 33 Pt II(13) with effect in accordance with FA 2001 s 88, Sch 29).

15 (*amends* TMA 1970 s 33).

16 (*amends* TMA 1970 s 33A; *part repealed by* FA 2001 s 110, Sch 33 Pt II(13) with effect in accordance with FA 2001 s 88, Sch 29).

17 (*amends* TMA 1970 s 34(1)).

18 (*amends* TMA 1970 s 36(1)).

19 (*repeals* TMA 1970 ss 41A, 41B, 41C).

20 (*amends* TMA 1970 s 42).

21 (*substitutes* TMA 1970 s 43(1)).

22 (*amends* TMA 1970 s 43A).

Commentary—*Simon's Direct Tax Service* **D2.834.**

23 (*amends* TMA 1970 s 46(2)).

24 (*amended* TMA 1970 s 46B(2); *repealed by* FA 2001 s 110, Sch 33 Pt II(13) with effect in accordance with FA 2001 s 88, Sch 29).

25 (*amended* TMA 1970 s 46C(2); *repealed by* FA 2001 s 110, Sch 33 Pt II(13) with effect in accordance with FA 2001 s 88, Sch 29).

26 (*amended* TMA 1970 s 46D(2); *repealed by* FA 2001 s 110, Sch 33 Pt II(13) with effect in accordance with FA 2001 s 88, Sch 29).

27 (*amends* TMA 1970 s 50; *part repealed by* FA 2001 s 110, Sch 33 Pt II(13) with effect in accordance with FA 2001 s 88, Sch 29).

Commentary—*Simon's Direct Tax Service* **D2.837.**

28 (*amends* TMA 1970 s 55(1)).

Commentary—*Simon's Direct Tax Service* **D2.841.**

29—(1) (*inserts heading before* TMA 1970 s 59A).

(2) (*substitutes* TMA 1970 ss 59D, 59DA).

Commentary—*Simon's Direct Tax Service* **D2.841.**

30 (*amends* TMA 1970 s 65).

31 (*amends* TMA 1970 s 69; *repealed* by FA 2001 s 110, Sch 33 Pt II(14) with effect for proceedings begun, or a counterclaim made, and a set-off first claimed after the passing of FA 2001).

32 (*amends* TMA 1970 s 70(2)).

33 (*repeals* TMA 1970 s 94).

34 (*repeals* TMA 1970 s 96).

35 (*amends* TMA 1970 s 97(1), (2)).

36 (*amends* TMA 1970 s 97AA(1)).

37 (*amends* TMA 1970 s 97A).

38 (*amends* TMA 1970 s 100(6)).

39 (*substitutes* TMA 1970 s 101).

40 (*amends* TMA 1970 s 103A).

41 (*amends* TMA 1970 s 113(1B)).

42 (*amends* TMA 1970 Sch 1A).

Commentary—*Simon's Direct Tax Service* **D2.832.**

43 (*amends* TMA 1970 Sch 3A paras 1(4), 8(2)).

Prospective amendment—This paragraph to be repealed by FA 1999 s 139, Sch 20 Pt VII with effect on such day as the Treasury may by order appoint.

Income and Corporation Taxes Act 1988 (c 1)

44 (*amends* TA 1988 s 246Q(6), (7)).

45 (*amends* TA 1988 s 246U(7), (8)).

46 (*substitutes* TA 1988 s 412).

47 (*amends* TA 1988 s 419(3), (4) and *inserts* s 419(4B)).

Commentary—*Simon's Direct Tax Service* **D2.845.**

48 (*amends* TA 1988 s 488(11A) and *substitutes* s 488(12)).

49 (*amends* TA 1988 s 489(9A)).

50 (*amends* TA 1988 Sch 13A para 5(1), 14(1), (6), (8) and *substitutes* Sch 13A para 5(2)).

51 (*amends* TA 1988 Sch 19AB paras 1(4), (7), 2(1), 3(1), 3(1A), (3), (7), (9), 6(4) and *substitutes* Sch 19AB paras 1(6), (10), (11), 3(1D); *repealed by* FA 2001 s 110, Sch 33 Pt II(12) with effect in accordance with FA 2001 s 87).

SCHEDULE 20

APPLICATION OF TAPER RELIEF

Section 121

(*inserts* TCGA 1992 Sch A1).

SCHEDULE 21

AMENDMENTS IN CONNECTION WITH TAPER RELIEF

Section 121

Introductory

1 The Taxation of Chargeable Gains Act 1992 shall be amended in accordance with the following provisions of this Schedule.

Gains of trustees attributed to settlor

2 (*inserts* TCGA 1992 s 2(4), (5)).

Annual exempt amount

3 (*substitutes* TCGA 1992 s 3(5), (5A)–(5C)).

Commentary—*Simon's Direct Tax Service* **C1.401, 403, 502, 503.**

Gains attributed to members of non-resident companies

4 (*inserts* TCGA 1992 s 13(10A)).

Commentary—*Simon's Direct Tax Service* **C1.403.**

Carry back of losses on death

5 (*inserts* TCGA 1992 s 62(2A), (2B)).

Commentary—*Simon's Direct Tax Service* **C1.403.**

Gains attributed to settlors and beneficiaries

6—(1) (*inserts* TCGA 1992 ss 77(6A), 86(4A), 87(6A) and *amends* s 89(3); *repealed by* FA 2002 s 141, Sch 40 Pt 3(4) *with effect for chargeable gains treated as accruing to a person by virtue of* TCGA 1992 s 77 or 86 (*read, where appropriate, with* TCGA 1992 s 10A) *from 2003–04*).

Commentary—*Simon's Direct Tax Service* **C1.403.**
Cross reference—FA 2002 Sch 11 para 8 (election for prospective amendments made by FA 2002 s 141, Sch 40 Pt 3(4) to apply with effect for chargeable gains treated as accruing to a person by virtue of TCGA 1992 s 77 or 86 (read, where appropriate, with TCGA s 10A) in any or all of the tax years 2000–01, 2001–02, and 2002–03).

Gains on assets deriving from reorganisation of body carrying on a mutual business etc

7 (*inserts* TCGA 1992 s 214C).

Commentary—*Simon's Direct Tax Service* **C1.403.**

Commercial letting of furnished holiday dwellings

8 (*amends* TCGA 1992 s 241(3)).

Commentary—*Simon's Direct Tax Service* **C1.403.**

Delayed remittances in respect of foreign assets

9 (*amends* TCGA 1992 s 279(2)).

Commentary—*Simon's Direct Tax Service* **C1.403.**

SCHEDULE 22

TRANSITIONAL PROVISION AND CONSEQUENTIAL AMENDMENTS FOR SECTION 131

Section 131

Introductory

1 The Taxation of Chargeable Gains Act 1992 shall be amended as follows.

Transitional for settlements created before 17th March 1998

2—(1) (*amends* TCGA 1992 Sch 5 para 2(1)).

(2) (*inserts* TCGA 1992 Sch 5 para 2A).

(3) In construing section 86(1)(*e*) as regards any year of assessment and in relation to a settlement which—

    (*a*) was created before 17th March 1998, and
    (*b*) is a settlement in which the settlor has an interest during that year by virtue only of the fulfilment for the purposes of the paragraph inserted by sub-paragraph (2) above of one of the conditions set out in that paragraph,

no account shall be taken of disposals made before the relevant day (whether for the purpose of arriving at gains or for the purpose of arriving at losses).

(4) In sub-paragraph (3) above "the relevant day" means—

    (*a*) for the year 1997-98, 17th March 1998; and
    (*b*) for any other year of assessment, the 6th April which is the first day of that year.

Consequential amendments of paragraphs 4 and 5 of Schedule 5 to the 1992 Act

3 (*amends* TCGA 1992 Sch 5 paras 4(1), (4), 5(1)).

Consequential amendment of paragraph 9 of Schedule 5 to the 1992 Act

4—(1) (*amends* TCGA 1992 Sch 5 para 9(7)).

(2) (*substitutes* TCGA 1992 Sch 5 para 9(11)).

(3) Sub-paragraph (1) above shall be disregarded for the purpose of determining whether either of the conditions set out in sub-paragraphs (5) and (6) of that paragraph became fulfilled at any time before 17th March 1998.

Consequential amendment of Schedule 5A

5—(1) (*amends* TCGA 1992 Sch 5A para 2(1)).

(2) This paragraph has effect in relation to transfers on or after 17th March 1998.

SCHEDULE 23

TRANSITIONAL PROVISION IN CONNECTION WITH SECTION 132

Section 132

Pre-6th April 1999 gains and losses of settlements that become qualifying

1—(1) This paragraph applies to a settlement in the case of any person who is a settlor in relation to that settlement if that settlement—

(*a*) is one created before 19th March 1991;

(*b*) is not a qualifying settlement in the year 1998–99; and

(*c*) is a qualifying settlement in the year 1999–00 without having been a protected settlement in relation to that settlor immediately after the beginning of 6th April 1999.

(2) Subject to sub-paragraph (3) below, section 86 of the 1992 Act (attribution of gains to settlor of non-resident or dual resident trusts) shall have effect in relation to any settlement to which this paragraph applies—

(*a*) as if any relevant gains or relevant losses accruing to the trustees of the settlement on or after 17th March 1998 and before 6th April 1999 were gains or losses accruing to those trustees on 6th April 1999; and

(*b*) where it is not the case, as if the trustees fulfilled the condition as to residence in the year 1999–00.

(3) Where (apart from sub-paragraph (2)(*b*) above) the trustees of a settlement to which this paragraph applies do not fulfil the condition as to residence in the year 1999–00, section 86 of the 1992 Act shall have effect (without prejudice to any charge imposed otherwise than by virtue of that section) as if the only gains and losses accruing to the trustees of that settlement in that year were those which are treated as accruing to those trustees on 6th April 1999 by virtue of sub-paragraph (2)(*a*) above.

(4) The gains and losses that are relevant gains or relevant losses for the purposes of this paragraph are those which (apart from this paragraph) accrue to the trustees of a settlement to which this paragraph applies in any year of assessment in which those trustees fulfil the condition as to residence.

Pre-6th April 1999 gains and losses where there is a transfer to another settlement

2—(1) This paragraph applies, subject to sub-paragraph (5) below, to any chargeable gain or loss accruing on the disposal of any asset by the trustees of a settlement (''the transferor settlement'') if—

(*a*) that settlement was created before 19th March 1991;

(*b*) the disposal on which the gain or loss accrues is one made–

(i) on or after 17th March 1998 and before 6th April 1999; and

(ii) in a year of assessment in which the trustees of the transferor settlement fulfil the condition as to residence but the settlement is not a qualifying settlement;

(*c*) a person who is a settlor in relation to the transferor settlement (''the chargeable settlor'')–

(i) is domiciled in the United Kingdom at some time in the year 1999-00 and in the year of assessment in which the disposal is made;

(ii) is either resident in the United Kingdom during any part of each of those years or ordinarily resident in the United Kingdom during each of those years; and

(iii) is alive at the end of the year 1999–00;

(*d*) the asset disposed of is property originating from the chargeable settlor;

(*e*) the property comprised in another settlement (''the transferee settlement'') at any time after the disposal and before 6th April 1999 is or includes (whether in consequence of the disposal or otherwise) the asset disposed of or any relevant property;

(*f*) the transferor settlement has a relevant connection with the transferee settlement; and

(*g*) the gain or loss in question is not one treated under paragraph 1 above as accruing on 6th April 1999 to the trustees of the transferor settlement.

(2) If, in the case of the chargeable settlor, section 86 of the 1992 Act applies (apart from this paragraph) for the year 1999–00 in relation to the transferee settlement, that section shall apply for that year in relation to that settlement as if any chargeable gain or loss to which this paragraph applies—

(*a*) were a gain or loss accruing on 6th April 1999 to the trustees of the transferee settlement; and

(*b*) so accrued on the disposal by those trustees of any asset that was property originating from the chargeable settlor.

(3) Where sub-paragraph (2) above does not apply, section 86 of the 1992 Act shall have effect in relation to the chargeable settlor as if—

(*a*) in the year 1999-00 the conditions specified in paragraphs (*a*) to (*d*) and (*f*) of subsection (1) of that section were fulfilled in his case in relation to the transferee settlement;

(*b*) any gain or loss to which this paragraph applies–

    (i) were a gain or loss accruing on 6th April 1999 to the trustees of the transferee settlement; and

    (ii) so accrued on the disposal by them of an asset that was property originating from the chargeable settlor;

and

(*c*) any chargeable gains and losses accruing to the trustees of the transferee settlement which are not gains or losses to which this paragraph applies were to be disregarded for the purposes of that section.

(4) Where (but for this sub-paragraph) the same gain or loss would fall to be treated by virtue of sub-paragraph (2) or (3) above as a gain or loss accruing to the trustees of more than one settlement—

    (*a*) that gain or loss shall be apportioned between those settlements in such manner as may be just and reasonable; and

    (*b*) only such part of the gain or loss as on that apportionment is attributable to a particular settlement shall be treated in accordance with that sub-paragraph as accruing to that settlement.

(5) This paragraph does not apply to any chargeable gain or loss accruing on any disposal if, for the year of assessment in which that disposal is made, section 86 of the 1992 Act would, on the relevant assumption, have been prevented by virtue of paragraph 3, 4 or 5 of Schedule 5 to that Act—

    (*a*) from applying in the case of the chargeable settlor in relation to the transferor settlement; or

    (*b*) from applying in his case in relation to the transferee settlement.

(6) The relevant assumption for the purposes of sub-paragraph (5) above is that section 86 of the 1992 Act would have applied in the case of the chargeable settlor apart from paragraphs 3 to 5 of Schedule 5 to that Act.

(7) In this paragraph "relevant property", in relation to any disposal made by the trustees of the transferor settlement, means any property (not being the asset disposed of) which—

    (*a*) is or represents property or income originating from the chargeable settlor;

    (*b*) has been comprised in, or has arisen to, the transferor settlement at any time after the time of that disposal; and

    (*c*) is property or income of the trustees of the transferee settlement acquired or otherwise deriving, directly or indirectly, from the trustees of the transferor settlement.

(8) For the purposes of this paragraph the transferor settlement has, in relation to a disposal by its trustees, a relevant connection with the transferee settlement if—

    (*a*) immediately before the time of the disposal, the beneficiaries of the transferor settlement are or include persons who are defined persons in relation to that settlement at that time;

    (*b*) the transferor settlement is not a protected settlement at that time in relation to the chargeable settlor;

    (*c*) at the beginning of 6th April 1999, the beneficiaries of the transferee settlement are or include persons who–

        (i) have attained the age of eighteen; and

        (ii) have been defined persons in relation to the transferor settlement;

and

    (*d*) the property comprised in the transferee settlement in respect of which some or all of the persons mentioned in paragraph (*c*) above are beneficiaries of that settlement at the beginning of 6th April 1999 is or includes anything which, in relation to either that settlement or the transferor settlement, is property or income originating from the chargeable settlor.

(9) For the purposes of this paragraph a person is a defined person in relation to a settlement at a time if he would fall at that time to be treated, by reference to the chargeable settlor, as a defined person in relation to that settlement for the purposes of paragraph 2 of Schedule 5 to the 1992 Act.

(10) Sub-paragraph (3)(*c*) above is without prejudice to any charge imposed otherwise than by virtue of this paragraph.

Pre-6th April 1999 gains and losses where there is a transfer to a foreign institution

3—(1) This paragraph applies, subject to sub-paragraphs (4) and (6) below, to a chargeable gain or loss accruing on the disposal of any asset by the trustees of a settlement ("the transferor settlement") if—

    (*a*) that settlement was created before 19th March 1991;

    (*b*) the disposal on which the gain or loss accrues is one made—

        (i) on or after 17th March 1998 and before 6th April 1999; and

        (ii) in a year of assessment in which the trustees of the transferor settlement fulfil the condition as to residence but the settlement is not a qualifying settlement;

    (*c*) a person who is a settlor in relation to the transferor settlement ("the chargeable settlor")—

        (i) is domiciled in the United Kingdom at some time in the year 1999–00 and in the year of assessment in which the disposal is made;

(ii) is either resident in the United Kingdom during any part of each of those years or ordinarily resident in the United Kingdom during each of those years; and

(iii) is alive at the end of the year 1999–00;

(*d*) the asset disposed of is property originating from the chargeable settlor;

(*e*) the property comprised in a foreign institution ("the transferee institution") at any time after the disposal and before 6th April 1999 is or includes (whether in consequence of the disposal or otherwise) the asset disposed of or any relevant property;

(*f*) the transferor settlement has a relevant connection with the transferee institution; and

(*g*) the gain or loss in question is neither—

(i) a gain or loss treated under paragraph 1 above as accruing on 6th April 1999 to the trustees of any settlement; nor

(ii) a gain or loss to which paragraph 2 above applies.

(2) If, in the case of the chargeable settlor, section 86 of the 1992 Act applies (apart from this paragraph) for the year 1999–00 in relation to the transferor settlement, that section shall apply for that year in relation to that settlement as if any chargeable gain or loss to which this paragraph applies—

(*a*) were a gain or loss accruing on 6th April 1999 to the trustees of the transferor settlement; and

(*b*) so accrued on the disposal by them of an asset that was property originating from the chargeable settlor.

(3) Where sub-paragraph (2) above does not apply, section 86 of the 1992 Act shall have effect in relation to the chargeable settlor as if—

(*a*) (where it is not the case) the transferor settlement existed in the year 1999–00;

(*b*) that settlement were a settlement in relation to which all the conditions specified in paragraphs (*a*) to (*d*) and (*f*) of subsection (1) of that section were fulfilled in the case of the chargeable settlor in that year;

(*c*) any gain or loss to which this paragraph applies—

(i) were a gain or loss accruing on 6th April 1999 to the trustees of the transferor settlement; and

(ii) so accrued on the disposal by them of an asset that was property originating from the chargeable settlor;

and

(*d*) any chargeable gains and losses which are not gains or losses to which this paragraph applies were to be disregarded for the purposes of that section.

(4) This paragraph does not apply to any chargeable gain or loss accruing on any disposal if, for the year of assessment in which that disposal is made, section 86 of the 1992 Act would, on the relevant assumption, have been prevented by virtue of paragraph 3, 4 of 5 of Schedule 5 to that Act from applying in the case of the chargeable settlor in relation to the transferor settlement.

(5) The relevant assumption for the purposes of sub-paragraph (4) above is that section 86 of the 1992 Act would have applied in the case of the chargeable settlor apart from paragraphs 3 to 5 of Schedule 5 to that Act.

(6) This paragraph does not apply to any chargeable gain or loss accruing on any disposal if the chargeable settlor stands in such a relationship to the foreign institution that if—

(*a*) that institution were a settlement,

(*b*) property of the institution were property comprised in the settlement, and

(*c*) income arising to the institution were income arising under the settlement,

paragraph 4 or 5 of Schedule 5 to the 1992 Act would (assuming that nothing else did) prevent section 86 of that Act from applying in the case of the chargeable settlor in relation to that settlement for the year of assessment in which that disposal is made.

(7) In this paragraph "relevant property", in relation to any disposal made by the trustees of the transferor settlement, means any property which—

(*a*) is or represents property or income originating from the chargeable settlor;

(*b*) has been comprised in, or has arisen to, the transferor settlement at any time after the time of that disposal; and

(*c*) is property or income of the transferee institution acquired or otherwise deriving, directly or indirectly, from the trustees of the transferor settlement.

(8) For the purposes of this paragraph the transferor settlement has, in relation to a disposal by its trustees, a relevant connection with the transferee institution if—

(*a*) immediately before the time of the disposal, the beneficiaries of the transferor settlement are or include persons who are defined persons in relation to that settlement at that time;

(*b*) the transferor settlement is not a protected settlement at that time in relation to the chargeable settlor; and

(*c*) the transferee institution is—

(i) one in which a relevant defined person is a participator at the beginning of 6th April 1999;

(ii) one which is under the control of a company in which, or two or more companies in any of which, a relevant defined person is a participator at that time; or

(iii) one whose relevant property or relevant income includes property or income in which a relevant defined person has an interest at that time.

(9) For the purposes of this paragraph a person is a relevant defined person at any time if he—

(a) has attained the age of eighteen; and

(b) has been, by reference to the chargeable settlor, a defined person in relation to the transferor settlement.

(10) For the purposes of this paragraph a person has an interest in any property or income of a foreign institution at any time if—

(a) there are any circumstances whatever in which that property or income is or will or may become applicable for his benefit or payable to him;

(b) there are any circumstances whatever in which income which is or may arise from that property or income is or will or may become applicable for his benefit or payable to him;

(c) he enjoys a benefit directly or indirectly from that property or income or from any income arising from that property or income.

(11) For the purposes of this paragraph a person is a defined person in relation to a settlement at a time if he would fall at that time to be treated, by reference to the chargeable settlor, as a defined person in relation to that settlement for the purposes of paragraph 2 of Schedule 5 to the 1992 Act.

(12) In this paragraph—

"foreign institution" means any company or other institution resident outside the United Kingdom;

"participator" has the meaning given (for the purposes of Part XI of the Taxes Act 1988 (close companies)) by section 417(1) of that Act;

"relevant income", in relation to a foreign institution, means any income of that institution which, if that institution were a settlement, would be treated for the purposes of Schedule 5 to the 1992 Act as originating from the chargeable settlor;

"relevant property", in relation to a foreign institution, means any property of that institution which, if that institution were a settlement, would be treated for the purposes of Schedule 5 to the 1992 Act as originating from the chargeable settlor.

(13) Sub-paragraph (3)(d) above is without prejudice to any charge imposed otherwise than by virtue of this paragraph.

Rule to prevent a double charge

4—(1) This paragraph applies, in the case of a person who is a settlor in relation to any settlement ("the relevant settlement"), to so much (if any) of the amount falling in his case within section 86(1)(e) of the 1992 Act for the year 1999–00 as (apart from this paragraph) would be treated by virtue only of the preceding provisions of this Schedule, as gains accruing to him in that year.

(2) Where there is an excess of the relevant chargeable amounts for the transitional period over the amount of the section 87 pool on 17th March 1998, only so much (if any) of the amount to which this paragraph applies as exceeds that excess shall fall in accordance with this Schedule to be, or (as the case may be) to be included in, the amount treated as accruing to the settlor in the year 1999–00.

(3) In sub-paragraph (2) above, the reference to the relevant chargeable amounts for the transitional period is (subject to sub-paragraph (5) below) a reference to the aggregate of the amounts on which beneficiaries of the relevant settlement are charged to tax under section 87 or 89(2) of the 1992 Act for any year of assessment ending after 17th March 1998 and before 6th April 1999 in respect of capital payments received by them.

(4) In sub-paragraph (2) above, the reference to the section 87 pool on 17th March 1998 is (subject to sub-paragraph (5) below) a reference to the amount (if any) which, in accordance with subsection (2) of section 87 of the 1992 Act, would have fallen in relation to the relevant settlement to be carried forward from the year 1997–98 to be included in the amount of the trust gains for the year 1998–99 if—

(a) the year 1997–98 had ended with 16th March 1998; and

(b) the year 1998–99 had begun with 17th March 1998.

(5) Where the property comprised in the relevant settlement has at any time included property not originating from the settlor, only so much (if any) of any capital payment or of any amount that would have been carried forward in accordance with section 87(2) of the 1992 Act as, on a just and reasonable apportionment, is properly referable to property originating from the settlor shall be taken into account for the purposes of sub-paragraphs (3) and (4) above.

(6) Where any reduction falls to be made by virtue of sub-paragraph (2) above in the amount to be attributed in accordance with this Schedule to any settlor for the year 1999–00, the reduction to be treated as made for that year in accordance with section 87(3) of the 1992 Act in the case of the settlement in question shall not be made until—

(a) the reduction (if any) falling to be made by virtue of that sub-paragraph has been made in the case of every settlor to whom any amount is so attributed; and (*b*) effect has been given to any reduction required to be made under paragraph 5(1) below.

(7) In this paragraph "the transitional period" means the period beginning with 17th March 1998 and ending with 5th April 1999.

5—(1) Where in the case of any settlement there is (after the making of any reduction or reductions in accordance with paragraph 4(2) above) any amount or amounts falling in accordance with this Schedule to be attributed for the year 1999–00 to settlors of the settlement, the amount or (as the case may be) aggregate amount falling in accordance with this Schedule to be so attributed shall be applied in reducing the amount which (after any reductions in accordance with section 86A(7) of that Act) is carried forward to that year in accordance with section 87(2) of that Act.

(2) Where an amount or aggregate amount has been applied, in accordance with sub-paragraph (1) above, in reducing the amount which in the case of any settlement is carried forward to the year 1999–00 in accordance with section 87(2) of the 1992 Act, that amount (or, as the case may be, so much of it as does not exceed the amount which it is applied in reducing) shall be deducted from the amount used for that year in the case of that settlement for making the reduction under section 87(3) of that Act.

Interpretation of Schedule

6—(1) In this Schedule—

"the 1992 Act" means the Taxation of Chargeable Gains Act 1992;

"qualifying settlement", in relation to any year of assessment, means a settlement that is a qualifying settlement in that year for the purposes of section 86 of and Schedule 5 to the 1992 Act;

"settlor", in relation to a settlement, has the same meaning as in Schedule 5 to the 1992 Act.

(2) In this Schedule "protected settlement", in relation to any time and any settlor, means (subject to sub-paragraph (3) below)—

    (*a*) a settlement that is a protected settlement at that time, within the meaning given by sub-paragraph (10A) of paragraph 9 of Schedule 5 to the 1992 Act, or
    (*b*) a settlement that would be such a settlement at that time if that settlor were the only settlor of the settlement.

(3) For the purposes of construing, in accordance with sub-paragraph (2) above, the references in paragraphs 2(8) and 3(8) above to a protected settlement, paragraph 9(10A)(*a*) of Schedule 5 to the 1992 Act shall be deemed to have effect with the omission of the words "or who were under that age at the end of the immediately preceding year of assessment".

(4) References in this Schedule to the condition as to residence are references to the condition set out in section 86(2) of the 1992 Act.

(5) For the purposes of this Schedule a person is a beneficiary of a settlement if—

    (*a*) there are any circumstances whatever in which property which is or may become comprised in the settlement is or will or may become applicable for his benefit or payable to him;
    (*b*) there are any circumstances whatever in which income which arises or may arise from property comprised in the settlement is or will or may become applicable for his benefit or payable to him;

    (*c*) he enjoys a benefit directly or indirectly from any property comprised in the settlement or any income arising from any such property;

and references in this paragraph to the property comprised in the settlement in respect of which a person is a beneficiary shall be construed accordingly.

(6) For the purposes of this paragraph, paragraph 8 of Schedule 5 to the 1992 Act shall apply for determining if property is property originating from any person as it applies for the purposes of that Schedule.

(7) Expressions used in this Schedule and in the 1992 Act have the same meanings in this Schedule as in that Act.

SCHEDULE 24

RESTRICTIONS ON SETTING LOSSES AGAINST PRE-ENTRY GAINS

Section 137

(*inserts* TCGA 1992 Sch 7AA).

Commentary—*Simon's Direct Tax Service* **D2.670, 685.**

SCHEDULE 25

PROPERTY OF HISTORIC INTEREST ETC

Section 142

Variation of undertakings

9—(1) (*inserts* TCGA 1992 s 258(8A)).

(2) Subject to paragraph 10 below, this paragraph has effect in relation to undertakings given on or after the day on which this Act is passed.

10—(1) Section 35A of the 1984 Act applies in relation to a relevant undertaking given with respect to any property before the day on which this Act is passed except in a case where there has been a chargeable event with respect to that property at any time after the giving of the undertaking but before that day.

(2) In its application to such a relevant undertaking, section 35A of the 1984 Act applies with the modifications set out in sub-paragraphs (3) and (4) below.

(3) The first modification is the substitution, for paragraph (*a*) of subsection (2), of the following paragraph—

"(*a*) the Board have made a proposal to the person bound by such an undertaking for the undertaking to be varied so as to include (where it does not already do so) an extended access requirement or a publication requirement (or both those requirements),".

(4) The second modification is the insertion, after subsection (4), of the following subsections—

"(5) For the purposes of subsection (2)(*a*) above—

(*a*) an extended access requirement is a requirement for the taking of steps ensuring that the access to the public that is secured is not confined to access only where a prior appointment has been made; and

(*b*) a publication requirement is a requirement for the taking of steps involving the publication of any matter mentioned in paragraph (*a*) or (*b*) of section 31(4FB) above.

(6) In determining for the purposes of subsection (2)(*a*) above whether an undertaking already includes an extended access requirement, there shall be disregarded so much of the undertaking as includes provision for the property with respect to which the undertaking was given to be made available temporarily for the purposes of special exhibitions."

(5) In this paragraph "relevant undertaking" means any of the following—

(*a*) an undertaking given under section 30, 32, 32A, 78 or 79 of the 1984 Act;

(*b*) an undertaking given under paragraph 3(3) of Schedule 4 to the 1984 Act or paragraph 5(2) of Schedule 5 to that Act;

(*c*) an undertaking given under section 76, 78, 81 or 82 of the Finance Act 1976;

(*d*) an undertaking given under section 34(2) of the Finance Act 1975;

(*e*) an undertaking given under section 258 of the Taxation of Chargeable Gains Act 1992.

(6) In this paragraph "chargeable event", in relation to any property means—

(*a*) an event which under section 32 or 32A of the 1984 Act is a chargeable event with respect to that property; or

(*b*) an event which under either of those sections would be such an event if (where it is not the case) the undertaking in question had been given under section 30 of that Act.

SCHEDULE 27

REPEALS

Section 165

Note—Details of repeals already in force have been omitted from the Schedule.

PART III

INCOME TAX, CORPORATION TAX AND CAPITAL GAINS TAX

(5) LAND MANAGED AS ONE ESTATE ETC

Chapter	Short title	Extent of repeal
1988 c 1.	The Income and Corporation Taxes Act 1988.	Sections 26 and 27.
1998 c 36	The Finance Act 1998.	In Schedule 5, paragraphs 6 and 7.

These repeals have effect in accordance with section 39 of this Act.

(21) PERSONAL PENSION SCHEMES

Chapter	Short title	Extent of repeal
1970 c 9.	The Taxes Management Act 1970.	In section 98, in the Table, the entry relating to section 652 of the Taxes Act 1988.
1988 c 1.	The Income and Corporation Taxes Act 1988.	Section 652.

Subsection (4) of section 96 of this Act applies in relation to these repeals as it applies in relation to subsections (2) and (3)(*b*) of that section.

(31) RETIREMENT RELIEF

Chapter	Short title	Extent of repeal
1992 c 12.	The Taxation of Chargeable Gains Act 1992.	Sections 163 and 164.
		In section 165, in subsection (3), paragraphs (*a*) and (*b*) and, in subsection (6), the words "and (in appropriate cases) Schedule 6".
		In section 241(3), the words "and Schedule 6".
		In section 260(5), the words from "or, if part of the gain" to the end.
		Schedule 6.
		In Schedule 7, paragraph 8.
1993 c 34.	The Finance Act 1993.	In Schedule 7, paragraphs 1(2) and 2.
1994 c 9.	The Finance Act 1994.	Section 92.
1996 c 8.	The Finance Act 1996.	Section 176.
		In Schedule 20, paragraph 66.
		In Schedule 21, paragraph 44.
		In Schedule 39, paragraph 7.

The above repeals have effect in relation to disposals in the year 2003–04 and subsequent years of assessment.

HUMAN RIGHTS ACT 1998

(1998 Chapter 42)

ARRANGEMENT OF SECTIONS

An Act to give further effect to rights and freedoms guaranteed under the European Convention on Human Rights; to make provision with respect to holders of certain judicial offices who become judges of the European Court of Human Rights; and for connected purposes.

[9th November 1998]

Note—This Act was brought into force as follows—
ss 1–17 on 2 October 2000 (by the Human Rights Act 1998 (Commencement No 2) Order, SI 2000/1851 art 2).
s 19 on 24 November 1998 (by the Human Rights Act 1998 (Commencement) Order, SI 1998/2882 art 2).
s 20 on 9 November 1998 (RA).

s 21(1)–(4) (by the Human Rights Act 1998 (Commencement) Order, SI 1998/2882 art 2).
s 21(5) on 9 November 1998 (RA).
s 22 on 9 November 1998 (RA).
Schs 1, 2 (by the Human Rights Act 1998 (Commencement) Order, SI 1998/2882 art 2).

Introduction

1 The Convention Rights

(1) In this Act "the Convention rights" means the rights and fundamental freedoms set out in—

  (*a*) Articles 2 to 12 and 14 of the Convention,
  (*b*) Articles 1 to 3 of the First Protocol, and
  (*c*) Articles 1 and 2 of the Sixth Protocol,

as read with Articles 16 to 18 of the Convention.

(2) Those Articles are to have effect for the purposes of this Act subject to any designated derogation or reservation (as to which see sections 14 and 15).

(3) The Articles are set out in Schedule 1.

(4) The [Lord Chancellor][1] may by order make such amendments to this Act as he considers appropriate to reflect the effect, in relation to the United Kingdom, of a protocol.

(5) In subsection (4) "protocol" means a protocol to the Convention—

  (*a*) which the United Kingdom has ratified; or
  (*b*) which the United Kingdom has signed with a view to ratification.

(6) No amendment may be made by an order under subsection (4) so as to come into force before the protocol concerned is in force in relation to the United Kingdom.

Amendment—[1] In sub-s (4), words in square brackets substituted by the Transfer of Functions (Miscellaneous) Order, SI 2001/3500 art 8, Sch 2 para 7 with effect from 26 November 2001.

2 Interpretation of Convention rights

(1) A court or tribunal determining a question which has arisen in connection with a Convention right must take into account any—

  (*a*) judgment, decision, declaration or advisory opinion of the European Court of Human Rights,
  (*b*) opinion of the Commission given in a report adopted under Article 31 of the Convention,
  (*c*) decision of the Commission in connection with Article 26 or 27(2) of the Convention, or
  (*d*) decision of the Committee of Ministers taken under Article 46 of the Convention,

whenever made or given, so far as, in the opinion of the court or tribunal, it is relevant to the proceedings in which that question has arisen.

(2) Evidence of any judgment, decision, declaration or opinion of which account may have to be taken under this section is to be given in proceedings before any court or tribunal in such manner as may be provided by rules.

(3) In this section "rules" means rules of court or, in the case of proceedings before a tribunal, rules made for the purposes of this section—

  (*a*) by the Lord Chancellor or the Secretary of State, in relation to any proceedings outside Scotland;
  (*b*) by the Secretary of State, in relation to proceedings in Scotland; or
  (*c*) by a Northern Ireland department, in relation to proceedings before a tribunal in Northern Ireland—
    (i) which deals with transferred matters; and
    (ii) for which no rules made under paragraph (*a*) are in force.

Legislation

3 Interpretation of legislation

(1) So far as it is possible to do so, primary legislation and subordinate legislation must be read and given effect in a way which is compatible with the Convention rights.

(2) This section—

  (*a*) applies to primary legislation and subordinate legislation whenever enacted;
  (*b*) does not affect the validity, continuing operation or enforcement of any incompatible primary legislation; and
  (*c*) does not affect the validity, continuing operation or enforcement of any incompatible subordinate legislation if (disregarding any possibility of revocation) primary legislation prevents removal of the incompatibility.

4 Declaration of incompatibility

(1) Subsection (2) applies in any proceedings in which a court determines whether a provision of primary legislation is compatible with a Convention right.

(2) If the court is satisfied that the provision is incompatible with a Convention right, it may make a declaration of that incompatibility.

(3) Subsection (4) applies in any proceedings in which a court determines whether a provision of subordinate legislation, made in the exercise of a power conferred by primary legislation, is compatible with a Convention right.

(4) If the court is satisfied—

(a) that the provision is incompatible with a Convention right, and
(b) that (disregarding any possibility of revocation) the primary legislation concerned prevents removal of the incompatibility,

it may make a declaration of that incompatibility.

(5) In this section "court" means—

(a) the House of Lords;
(b) the Judicial Committee of the Privy Council;
(c) the Courts-Martial Appeal Court;
(d) in Scotland, the High Court of Justiciary sitting otherwise than as a trial court or the Court of Session;
(e) in England and Wales or Northern Ireland, the High Court or the Court of Appeal.

(6) A declaration under this section ("a declaration of incompatibility")—

(a) does not affect the validity, continuing operation or enforcement of the provision in respect of which it is given; and
(b) is not binding on the parties to the proceedings in which it is made.

5 Right of Crown to intervene

(1) Where a court is considering whether to make a declaration of incompatibility, the Crown is entitled to notice in accordance with rules of court.

(2) In any case to which subsection (1) applies—

(a) a Minister of the Crown (or a person nominated by him),
(b) a member of the Scottish Executive,
(c) a Northern Ireland Minister,
(d) a Northern Ireland department,

is entitled, on giving notice in accordance with rules of court, to be joined as a party to the proceedings.

(3) Notice under subsection (2) may be given at any time during the proceedings.

(4) A person who has been made a party to criminal proceedings (other than in Scotland) as the result of a notice under subsection (2) may, with leave, appeal to the House of Lords against any declaration of incompatibility made in the proceedings.

(5) In subsection (4)—

"criminal proceedings" includes all proceedings before the Courts-Martial Appeal Court; and
"leave" means leave granted by the court making the declaration of incompatibility or by the House of Lords.

Public authorities

6 Acts of public authorities

(1) It is unlawful for a public authority to act in a way which is incompatible with a Convention right.

(2) Subsection (1) does not apply to an act if—

(a) as the result of one or more provisions of primary legislation, the authority could not have acted differently; or
(b) in the case of one or more provisions of, or made under, primary legislation which cannot be read or given effect in a way which is compatible with the Convention rights, the authority was acting so as to give effect to or enforce those provisions.

(3) In this section "public authority" includes—

(a) a court or tribunal, and
(b) any person certain of whose functions are functions of a public nature,

but does not include either House of Parliament or a person exercising functions in connection with proceedings in Parliament.

(4) In subsection (3) "Parliament" does not include the House of Lords in its judicial capacity.

(5) In relation to a particular act, a person is not a public authority by virtue only of subsection (3)(b) if the nature of the act is private.

(6) "An act" includes a failure to act but does not include a failure to—

(a) introduce in, or lay before, Parliament a proposal for legislation; or
(b) make any primary legislation or remedial order.

Simon's Tax Cases—*R (oao Wilkinson) v IRC* [2002] STC 347.

7 Proceedings

(1) A person who claims that a public authority has acted (or proposes to act) in a way which is made unlawful by section 6(1) may—

(a) bring proceedings against the authority under this Act in the appropriate court or tribunal, or

(b) rely on the Convention right or rights concerned in any legal proceedings,

but only if he is (or would be) a victim of the unlawful act.

(2) In subsection (1)(a) "appropriate court or tribunal" means such court or tribunal as may be determined in accordance with rules; and proceedings against an authority include a counterclaim or similar proceeding.

(3) If the proceedings are brought on an application for judicial review, the applicant is to be taken to have a sufficient interest in relation to the unlawful act only if he is, or would be, a victim of that act.

(4) If the proceedings are made by way of a petition for judicial review in Scotland, the applicant shall be taken to have title and interest to sue in relation to the unlawful act only if he is, or would be, a victim of that act.

(5) Proceedings under subsection (1)(a) must be brought before the end of—

(a) the period of one year beginning with the date on which the act complained of took place; or

(b) such longer period as the court or tribunal considers equitable having regard to all the circumstances,

but that is subject to any rule imposing a stricter time limit in relation to the procedure in question.

(6) In subsection (1)(b) "legal proceedings" includes—

(a) proceedings brought by or at the instigation of a public authority; and

(b) an appeal against the decision of a court or tribunal.

(7) For the purposes of this section, a person is a victim of an unlawful act only if he would be a victim for the purposes of Article 34 of the Convention if proceedings were brought in the European Court of Human Rights in respect of that act.

(8) Nothing in this Act creates a criminal offence.

(9) In this section "rules" means—

(a) in relation to proceedings before a court or tribunal outside Scotland, rules made by the Lord Chancellor or the Secretary of State for the purposes of this section or rules of court,

(b) in relation to proceedings before a court or tribunal in Scotland, rules made by the Secretary of State for those purposes,

(c) in relation to proceedings before a tribunal in Northern Ireland—

(i) which deals with transferred matters; and

(ii) for which no rules made under paragraph (a) are in force,

rules made by a Northern Ireland department for those purposes,

and includes provision made by order under section 1 of the Courts and Legal Services Act 1990.

(10) In making rules, regard must be had to section 9.

(11) The Minister who has power to make rules in relation to a particular tribunal may, to the extent he considers it necessary to ensure that the tribunal can provide an appropriate remedy in relation to an act (or proposed act) of a public authority which is (or would be) unlawful as a result of section 6(1), by order add to—

(a) the relief or remedies which the tribunal may grant; or

(b) the grounds on which it may grant any of them.

(12) An order made under subsection (11) may contain such incidental, supplemental, consequential or transitional provision as the Minister making it considers appropriate.

(13) "The Minister" includes the Northern Ireland department concerned.

8 Judicial remedies

(1) In relation to any act (or proposed act) of a public authority which the court finds is (or would be) unlawful, it may grant such relief or remedy, or make such order, within its powers as it considers just and appropriate.

(2) But damages may be awarded only by a court which has power to award damages, or to order the payment of compensation, in civil proceedings.

(3) No award of damages is to be made unless, taking account of all the circumstances of the case, including—

(a) any other relief or remedy granted, or order made, in relation to the act in question (by that or any other court), and

(b) the consequences of any decision (of that or any other court) in respect of that act, the court is satisfied that the award is necessary to afford just satisfaction to the person in whose favour it is made.

(4) In determining—

(a) whether to award damages, or

(b) the amount of an award,

the court must take into account the principles applied by the European Court of Human Rights in relation to the award of compensation under Article 41 of the Convention.

(5) A public authority against which damages are awarded is to be treated—

(a) in Scotland, for the purposes of section 3 of the Law Reform (Miscellaneous Provisions) (Scotland) Act 1940 as if the award were made in an action of damages in which the authority has been found liable in respect of loss or damage to the person to whom the award is made;

(b) for the purposes of the Civil Liability (Contribution) Act 1978 as liable in respect of damage suffered by the person to whom the award is made.

(6) In this section—

"court" includes a tribunal;

"damages" means damages for an unlawful act of a public authority; and

"unlawful" means unlawful under section 6(1).

9 Judicial acts

(1) Proceedings under section 7(1)(a) in respect of a judicial act may be brought only—

(a) by exercising a right of appeal;

(b) on an application (in Scotland a petition) for judicial review; or

(c) in such other forum as may be prescribed by rules.

(2) That does not affect any rule of law which prevents a court from being the subject of judicial review.

(3) In proceedings under this Act in respect of a judicial act done in good faith, damages may not be awarded otherwise than to compensate a person to the extent required by Article 5(5) of the Convention.

(4) An award of damages permitted by subsection (3) is to be made against the Crown; but no award may be made unless the appropriate person, if not a party to the proceedings, is joined.

(5) In this section—

"appropriate person" means the Minister responsible for the court concerned, or a person or government department nominated by him;

"court" includes a tribunal;

"judge" includes a member of a tribunal, a justice of the peace and a clerk or other officer entitled to exercise the jurisdiction of a court;

"judicial act" means a judicial act of a court and includes an act done on the instructions, or on behalf, of a judge; and

"rules" has the same meaning as in section 7(9).

Remedial action

10 Power to take remedial action

(1) This section applies if—

(a) a provision of legislation has been declared under section 4 to be incompatible with a Convention right and, if an appeal lies—

(i) all persons who may appeal have stated in writing that they do not intend to do so;

(ii) the time for bringing an appeal has expired and no appeal has been brought within that time; or

(iii) an appeal brought within that time has been determined or abandoned; or

(b) it appears to a Minister of the Crown or Her Majesty in Council that, having regard to a finding of the European Court of Human Rights made after the coming into force of this section in proceedings against the United Kingdom, a provision of legislation is incompatible with an obligation of the United Kingdom arising from the Convention.

(2) If a Minister of the Crown considers that there are compelling reasons for proceeding under this section, he may by order make such amendments to the legislation as he considers necessary to remove the incompatibility.

(3) If, in the case of subordinate legislation, a Minister of the Crown considers—

(a) that it is necessary to amend the primary legislation under which the subordinate legislation in question was made, in order to enable the incompatibility to be removed, and

(b) that there are compelling reasons for proceeding under this section,

he may by order make such amendments to the primary legislation as he considers necessary.

(4) This section also applies where the provision in question is in subordinate legislation and has been quashed, or declared invalid, by reason of incompatibility with a Convention right and the Minister proposes to proceed under paragraph 2(*b*) of Schedule 2.

(5) If the legislation is an Order in Council, the power conferred by subsection (2) or (3) is exercisable by Her Majesty in Council.

(6) In this section "legislation" does not include a Measure of the Church Assembly or of the General Synod of the Church of England.

(7) Schedule 2 makes further provision about remedial orders.

Other rights and proceedings

11 Safeguard for existing human rights

A person's reliance on a Convention right does not restrict—

(*a*) any other right or freedom conferred on him by or under any law having effect in any part of the United Kingdom; or

(*b*) his right to make any claim or bring any proceedings which he could make or bring apart from sections 7 to 9.

12 Freedom of expression

(1) This section applies if a court is considering whether to grant any relief which, if granted, might affect the exercise of the Convention right to freedom of expression.

(2) If the person against whom the application for relief is made ("the respondent") is neither present nor represented, no such relief is to be granted unless the court is satisfied—

(*a*) that the applicant has taken all practicable steps to notify the respondent; or

(*b*) that there are compelling reasons why the respondent should not be notified.

(3) No such relief is to be granted so as to restrain publication before trial unless the court is satisfied that the applicant is likely to establish that publication should not be allowed.

(4) The court must have particular regard to the importance of the Convention right to freedom of expression and, where the proceedings relate to material which the respondent claims, or which appears to the court, to be journalistic, literary or artistic material (or to conduct connected with such material), to—

(*a*) the extent to which—

(i) the material has, or is about to, become available to the public; or

(ii) it is, or would be, in the public interest for the material to be published;

(*b*) any relevant privacy code.

(5) In this section—

"court" includes a tribunal; and

"relief" includes any remedy or order (other than in criminal proceedings).

13 Freedom of thought, conscience and religion

(1) If a court's determination of any question arising under this Act might affect the exercise by a religious organisation (itself or its members collectively) of the Convention right to freedom of thought, conscience and religion, it must have particular regard to the importance of that right.

(2) In this section "court" includes a tribunal.

Derogations and reservations

14 Derogations

(1) In this Act "designated derogation" means—

...[1] any derogation by the United Kingdom from an Article of the Convention, or of any protocol to the Convention, which is designated for the purposes of this Act in an order made by the [Lord Chancellor][2].

(2) ...[1]

(3) If a designated derogation is amended or replaced it ceases to be a designated derogation.

(4) But subsection (3) does not prevent the [Lord Chancellor][2] from exercising his power under subsection (1)...[1] to make a fresh designation order in respect of the Article concerned.

(5) The [Lord Chancellor][2] must by order make such amendments to Schedule 3 as he considers appropriate to reflect—

(*a*) any designation order; or

(*b*) the effect of subsection (3).

(6) A designation order may be made in anticipation of the making by the United Kingdom of a proposed derogation.

Amendments—[1] In sub-s (1), para (*a*), and letter "(*b*)" revoked; sub-s (2) revoked; and letter "(*b*)" in sub-s (4) revoked; by the Human Rights Act (Amendment) Order, SI 2001/1216 art 2 with effect from 1 April 2001.

[2] In sub-ss (1), (4) and (5), words in square brackets substituted by the Transfer of Functions (Miscellaneous) Order, SI 2001/3500 art 8, Sch 2 para 7 with effect from 26 November 2001.

15 Reservations

(1) In this Act "designated reservation" means—

   (a) the United Kingdom's reservation to Article 2 of the First Protocol to the Convention; and
   (b) any other reservation by the United Kingdom to an Article of the Convention, or of any protocol to the Convention, which is designated for the purposes of this Act in an order made by the [Lord Chancellor][1].

(2) The text of the reservation referred to in subsection (1)(a) is set out in Part II of Schedule 3.

(3) If a designated reservation is withdrawn wholly or in part it ceases to be a designated reservation.

(4) But subsection (3) does not prevent the [Lord Chancellor][1] from exercising his power under subsection (1)(b) to make a fresh designation order in respect of the Article concerned.

(5) The [Lord Chancellor][1] must by order make such amendments to this Act as he considers appropriate to reflect—

   (a) any designation order; or
   (b) the effect of subsection (3).

[1] In sub-ss (1)(b), (4) and (5), words in square brackets substituted by the Transfer of Functions (Miscellaneous) Order, SI 2001/3500 art 8, Sch 2 para 7 with effect from 26 November 2001.

16 Period for which designated derogations have effect

(1) If it has not already been withdrawn by the United Kingdom, a designated derogation ceases to have effect for the purposes of this Act—

   ...[1] at the end of the period of five years beginning with the date on which the order designating it was made.

(2) At any time before the period—

   (a) fixed by subsection (1)...[1], or
   (b) extended by an order under this subsection,

comes to an end, the [Lord Chancellor][2] may by order extend it by a further period of five years.

(3) An order under section 14(1)...[1] ceases to have effect at the end of the period for consideration, unless a resolution has been passed by each House approving the order.

(4) Subsection (3) does not affect—

   (a) anything done in reliance on the order; or
   (b) the power to make a fresh order under section 14(1)...[1].

(5) In subsection (3) "period for consideration" means the period of forty days beginning with the day on which the order was made.

(6) In calculating the period for consideration, no account is to be taken of any time during which—

   (a) Parliament is dissolved or prorogued; or
   (b) both Houses are adjourned for more than four days.

(7) If a designated derogation is withdrawn by the United Kingdom, the [Lord Chancellor][2] must by order make such amendments to this Act as he considers are required to reflect that withdrawal.

Amendments—[1] Words in sub-ss (1), (2)(a) revoked, and the letter "(b)" in sub-ss (3), (4) revoked; and letter "(b)" in sub-s (4) revoked; by the Human Rights Act (Amendment) Order, SI 2001/1216 art 3 with effect from 1 April 2001.
[2] Words in sub-ss (2), (7) in square brackets substituted by the Transfer of Functions (Miscellaneous) Order, SI 2001/3500 art 8, Sch 2 para 7 with effect from 26 November 2001.

17 Periodic review of designated reservations

(1) The appropriate Minister must review the designated reservation referred to in section 15(1)(a)—

   (a) before the end of the period of five years beginning with the date on which section 1(2) came into force; and
   (b) if that designation is still in force, before the end of the period of five years beginning with the date on which the last report relating to it was laid under subsection (3).

(2) The appropriate Minister must review each of the other designated reservations (if any)—

   (a) before the end of the period of five years beginning with the date on which the order designating the reservation first came into force; and
   (b) if the designation is still in force, before the end of the period of five years beginning with the date on which the last report relating to it was laid under subsection (3).

(3) The Minister conducting a review under this section must prepare a report on the result of the review and lay a copy of it before each House of Parliament.

Judges of the European Court of Human Rights

18 Appointment to European Court of Human Rights

[not reproduced: see *Halsbury's Statutes* (4th edn) CIVIL RIGHTS and LIBERTIES].

Parliamentary procedure

19 Statements of compatibility

(1) A Minister of the Crown in charge of a Bill in either House of Parliament must, before Second Reading of the Bill—

(*a*) make a statement to the effect that in his view the provisions of the Bill are compatible with the Convention rights (''a statement of compatibility''); or

(*b*) make a statement to the effect that although he is unable to make a statement of compatibility the government nevertheless wishes the House to proceed with the Bill.

(2) The statement must be in writing and be published in such manner as the Minister making it considers appropriate.

Note—This section was brought into force on 24 November 1998 by the Human Rights Act 1998 (Commencement) Order, SI 1998/2882 art 2.

Supplemental

20 Orders etc under this Act

(1) Any power of a Minister of the Crown to make an order under this Act is exercisable by statutory instrument.

(2) The power of the Lord Chancellor or the Secretary of State to make rules (other than rules of court) under section 2(3) or 7(9) is exercisable by statutory instrument.

(3) Any statutory instrument made under section 14, 15 or 16(7) must be laid before Parliament.

(4) No order may be made by the Lord Chancellor or the Secretary of State under section 1(4), 7(11) or 16(2) unless a draft of the order has been laid before, and approved by, each House of Parliament.

(5) Any statutory instrument made under section 18(7) or Schedule 4, or to which subsection (2) applies, shall be subject to annulment in pursuance of a resolution of either House of Parliament.

(6) The power of a Northern Ireland department to make—

(*a*) rules under section 2(3)(*c*) or 7(9)(*c*), or

(*b*) an order under section 7(11),

is exercisable by statutory rule for the purposes of the Statutory Rules (Northern Ireland) Order 1979.

(7) Any rules made under section 2(3)(*c*) or 7(9)(*c*) shall be subject to negative resolution; and section 41(6) of the Interpretation Act (Northern Ireland) 1954 (meaning of ''subject to negative resolution'') shall apply as if the power to make the rules were conferred by an Act of the Northern Ireland Assembly.

(8) No order may be made by a Northern Ireland department under section 7(11) unless a draft of the order has been laid before, and approved by, the Northern Ireland Assembly.

21 Interpretation, etc

(1) In this Act—

''amend'' includes repeal and apply (with or without modifications);

''the appropriate Minister'' means the Minister of the Crown having charge of the appropriate authorised government department (within the meaning of the Crown Proceedings Act 1947);

''the Commission'' means the European Commission of Human Rights;

''the Convention'' means the Convention for the Protection of Human Rights and Fundamental Freedoms, agreed by the Council of Europe at Rome on 4th November 1950 as it has effect for the time being in relation to the United Kingdom;

''declaration of incompatibility'' means a declaration under section 4;

''Minister of the Crown'' has the same meaning as in the Ministers of the Crown Act 1975;

''Northern Ireland Minister'' includes the First Minister and the deputy First Minister in Northern Ireland;

''primary legislation'' means any—

(*a*) public general Act;

(*b*) local and personal Act;

(*c*) private Act;

(*d*) Measure of the Church Assembly;

(*e*) Measure of the General Synod of the Church of England;

(*f*) Order in Council—

(i) made in exercise of Her Majesty's Royal Prerogative;

(ii) made under section 38(1)(*a*) of the Northern Ireland Constitution Act 1973 or the corresponding provision of the Northern Ireland Act 1998; or

(iii) amending an Act of a kind mentioned in paragraph (*a*), (*b*) or (*c*);

and includes an order or other instrument made under primary legislation (otherwise than by the National Assembly for Wales, a member of the Scottish Executive, a Northern Ireland Minister or a Northern Ireland department) to the extent to which it operates to bring one or more provisions of that legislation into force or amends any primary legislation;

"the First Protocol" means the protocol to the Convention agreed at Paris on 20th March 1952;

"the Sixth Protocol" means the protocol to the Convention agreed at Strasbourg on 28th April 1983;

"the Eleventh Protocol" means the protocol to the Convention (restructuring the control machinery established by the Convention) agreed at Strasbourg on 11th May 1994;

"remedial order" means an order under section 10;

"subordinate legislation" means any—

    (*a*) Order in Council other than one—

        (i) made in exercise of Her Majesty's Royal Prerogative;

        (ii) made under section 38(1)(*a*) of the Northern Ireland Constitution Act 1973 or the corresponding provision of the Northern Ireland Act 1998; or

        (iii) amending an Act of a kind mentioned in the definition of primary legislation;

    (*b*) Act of the Scottish Parliament;

    (*c*) Act of the Parliament of Northern Ireland;

    (*d*) Measure of the Assembly established under section 1 of the Northern Ireland Assembly Act 1973;

    (*e*) Act of the Northern Ireland Assembly;

    (*f*) order, rules, regulations, scheme, warrant, byelaw or other instrument made under primary legislation (except to the extent to which it operates to bring one or more provisions of that legislation into force or amends any primary legislation);

    (*g*) order, rules, regulations, scheme, warrant, byelaw or other instrument made under legislation mentioned in paragraph (*b*), (*c*), (*d*) or (*e*) or made under an Order in Council applying only to Northern Ireland;

    (*h*) order, rules, regulations, scheme, warrant, byelaw or other instrument made by a member of the Scottish Executive, a Northern Ireland Minister or a Northern Ireland department in exercise of prerogative or other executive functions of Her Majesty which are exercisable by such a person on behalf of Her Majesty;

"transferred matters" has the same meaning as in the Northern Ireland Act 1998; and

"tribunal" means any tribunal in which legal proceedings may be brought.

(2) The references in paragraphs (*b*) and (*c*) of section 2(1) to Articles are to Articles of the Convention as they had effect immediately before the coming into force of the Eleventh Protocol.

(3) The reference in paragraph (*d*) of section 2(1) to Article 46 includes a reference to Articles 32 and 54 of the Convention as they had effect immediately before the coming into force of the Eleventh Protocol.

(4) The references in section 2(1) to a report or decision of the Commission or a decision of the Committee of Ministers include references to a report or decision made as provided by paragraphs 3, 4 and 6 of Article 5 of the Eleventh Protocol (transitional provisions).

(5) Any liability under the Army Act 1955, the Air Force Act 1955 or the Naval Discipline Act 1957 to suffer death for an offence is replaced by a liability to imprisonment for life or any less punishment authorised by those Acts; and those Acts shall accordingly have effect with the necessary modifications.

22 Short title, commencement, application and extent

(1) This Act may be cited as the Human Rights Act 1998.

(2) Sections 18, 20 and 21(5) and this section come into force on the passing of this Act.

(3) The other provisions of this Act come into force on such day as the Secretary of State may by order appoint; and different days may be appointed for different purposes.

(4) Paragraph (*b*) of subsection (1) of section 7 applies to proceedings brought by or at the instigation of a public authority whenever the act in question took place; but otherwise that subsection does not apply to an act taking place before the coming into force of that section.

(5) This Act binds the Crown.

(6) This Act extends to Northern Ireland.

(7) Section 21(5), so far as it relates to any provision contained in the Army Act 1955, the Air Force Act 1955 or the Naval Discipline Act 1957, extends to any place to which that provision extends.

SCHEDULE 1
THE ARTICLES
Section 1(3)

PART I
THE CONVENTION

RIGHTS AND FREEDOMS

[Article 2 (Right to life), Article 3 (Prohibition of torture), Article 4 and Article 5 (Right to liberty and security) (Prohibition of slavery and forced labour) are not reproduced here: see *Halsbury's Statutes* (4th edn) CIVIL RIGHTS and LIBERTIES].

Article 6
Right to a fair trial

1 In the determination of his civil rights and obligations or of any criminal charge against him, everyone is entitled to a fair and public hearing within a reasonable time by an independent and impartial tribunal established by law. Judgment shall be pronounced publicly but the press and public may be excluded from all or part of the trial in the interest of morals, public order or national security in a democratic society, where the interests of juveniles or the protection of the private life of the parties so require, or to the extent strictly necessary in the opinion of the court in special circumstances where publicity would prejudice the interests of justice.

2 Everyone charged with a criminal offence shall be presumed innocent until proved guilty according to law.

3 Everyone charged with a criminal offence has the following minimum rights:

(*a*) to be informed promptly, in a language which he understands and in detail, of the nature and cause of the accusation against him;
(*b*) to have adequate time and facilities for the preparation of his defence;
(*c*) to defend himself in person or through legal assistance of his own choosing or, if he has not sufficient means to pay for legal assistance, to be given it free when the interests of justice so require;
(*d*) to examine or have examined witnesses against him and to obtain the attendance and examination of witnesses on his behalf under the same conditions as witnesses against him;
(*e*) to have the free assistance of an interpreter if he cannot understand or speak the language used in court.

Article 7
No punishment without law

[not reproduced: see *Halsbury's Statutes* (4th edn) CIVIL RIGHTS and LIBERTIES].

Article 8
Right to respect for private and family life

1 Everyone has the right to respect for his private and family life, his home and his correspondence.

2 There shall be no interference by a public authority with the exercise of this right except such as is in accordance with the law and is necessary in a democratic society in the interests of national security, public safety or the economic well-being of the country, for the prevention of disorder or crime, for the protection of health or morals, or for the protection of the rights and freedoms of others.

[Article 9 (Freedom of thought, conscience and religion), Article 10 (Freedom of expression), Article 11 (Freedom of assembly and association) and Article 12 (Right to marry) not reproduced here: see *Halsbury's Statutes* (4th edn) CIVIL RIGHTS and LIBERTIES].

Article 14
Prohibition of discrimination

The enjoyment of the rights and freedoms set forth in this Convention shall be secured without discrimination on any ground such as sex, race, colour, language, religion, political or other opinion, national or social origin, association with a national minority, property, birth or other status.

Simon's Tax Cases—*Aston Cantlow and Wilmcote with Billesley Parochial Church Council v Wallbank* [2002] STC 313; *R (oao Wilkinson) v IRC* [2002] STC 347.

[Article 16 (Restrictions on political activity of aliens) not reproduced here: see *Halsbury's Statutes* (4th edn) CIVIL RIGHTS and LIBERTIES].

Article 17
Prohibition of abuse of rights

Nothing in this Convention may be interpreted as implying for any State, group or person any right to engage in any activity or perform any act aimed at the destruction of any of the rights and freedoms set forth herein or at their limitation to a greater extent than is provided for in the Convention.

Article 18
Limitation on use of restrictions on rights

The restrictions permitted under this Convention to the said rights and freedoms shall not be applied for any purpose other than those for which they have been prescribed.

PART II
THE FIRST PROTOCOL
Article 1
Protection of property

Every natural or legal person is entitled to the peaceful enjoyment of his possessions. No one shall be deprived of his possessions except in the public interest and subject to the conditions provided for by law and by the general principles of international law.

The preceding provisions shall not, however, in any way impair the right of a State to enforce such laws as it deems necessary to control the use of property in accordance with the general interest or to secure the payment of taxes or other contributions or penalties.

Simon's Tax Cases—*Aston Cantlow and Wilmcote with Billesley Parochial Church Council v Wallbank* [2002] STC 313; *R (oao Wilkinson) v IRC* [2002] STC 347.

[Article 2 (Right to education) and Article 3 (Right to free elections) not reproduced: see *Halsbury's Statutes* (4th edn) CIVIL RIGHTS and LIBERTIES].

PART III
THE SIXTH PROTOCOL

[Article 1 (Abolition of the death penalty) and Article 2 (Death penalty in time of war) not reproduced: see *Halsbury's Statutes* (4th edn) CIVIL RIGHTS and LIBERTIES].

SCHEDULE 2

REMEDIAL ORDERS
Section 10

Orders

1—(1) A remedial order may—

(*a*) contain such incidental, supplemental, consequential or transitional provision as the person making it considers appropriate;
(*b*) be made so as to have effect from a date earlier than that on which it is made;
(*c*) make provision for the delegation of specific functions;
(*d*) make different provision for different cases.

(2) The power conferred by sub-paragraph (1)(*a*) includes—

(*a*) power to amend primary legislation (including primary legislation other than that which contains the incompatible provision); and
(*b*) power to amend or revoke subordinate legislation (including subordinate legislation other than that which contains the incompatible provision).

(3) A remedial order may be made so as to have the same extent as the legislation which it affects.

(4) No person is to be guilty of an offence solely as a result of the retrospective effect of a remedial order.

Procedure

2 No remedial order may be made unless—

(*a*) a draft of the order has been approved by a resolution of each House of Parliament made after the end of the period of 60 days beginning with the day on which the draft was laid; or
(*b*) it is declared in the order that it appears to the person making it that, because of the urgency of the matter, it is necessary to make the order without a draft being so approved.

Orders laid in draft

3—(1) No draft may be laid under paragraph 2(*a*) unless—

(*a*) the person proposing to make the order has laid before Parliament a document which contains a draft of the proposed order and the required information; and

(*b*) the period of 60 days, beginning with the day on which the document required by this sub-paragraph was laid, has ended.

(2) If representations have been made during that period, the draft laid under paragraph 2(*a*) must be accompanied by a statement containing—

(*a*) a summary of the representations; and

(*b*) if, as a result of the representations, the proposed order has been changed, details of the changes.

Urgent cases

4—(1) If a remedial order ("the original order") is made without being approved in draft, the person making it must lay it before Parliament, accompanied by the required information, after it is made.

(2) If representations have been made during the period of 60 days beginning with the day on which the original order was made, the person making it must (after the end of that period) lay before Parliament a statement containing—

(*a*) a summary of the representations; and

(*b*) if, as a result of the representations, he considers it appropriate to make changes to the original order, details of the changes.

(3) If sub-paragraph (2)(*b*) applies, the person making the statement must—

(*a*) make a further remedial order replacing the original order; and

(*b*) lay the replacement order before Parliament.

(4) If, at the end of the period of 120 days beginning with the day on which the original order was made, a resolution has not been passed by each House approving the original or replacement order, the order ceases to have effect (but without that affecting anything previously done under either order or the power to make a fresh remedial order).

Definitions

5 In this Schedule—

"representations" means representations about a remedial order (or proposed remedial order) made to the person making (or proposing to make) it and includes any relevant Parliamentary report or resolution; and

"required information" means—

(*a*) an explanation of the incompatibility which the order (or proposed order) seeks to remove, including particulars of the relevant declaration, finding or order; and

(*b*) a statement of the reasons for proceeding under section 10 and for making an order in those terms.

Calculating periods

6 In calculating any period for the purposes of this Schedule, no account is to be taken of any time during which—

(*a*) Parliament is dissolved or prorogued; or

(*b*) both Houses are adjourned for more than four days.

[**7**—(1) This paragraph applies in relation to—

(*a*) any remedial order made, and any draft of such an order proposed to be made—

(i) by the Scottish Ministers; or

(ii) within devolved competence (within the meaning of the Scotland Act 1998) by Her Majesty in Council; and

(*b*) any document or statement to be laid in connection with such an order (or proposed order).

(2) This Schedule has effect in relation to any such order (or proposed order), document or statement subject to the following modifications.

(3) Any reference to Parliament, each House of Parliament or both Houses of Parliament shall be construed as a reference to the Scottish Parliament.

(4) Paragraph 6 does not apply and instead, in calculating any period for the purposes of this Schedule, no account is to be taken of any time during which the Scottish Parliament is dissolved or is in recess for more than four days.]

Amendments—Para 7 inserted by the Scotland Act 1998 (Consequential Modifications) Order, SI 2000/2040 art 2, Schedule para 21 with effect from 27 July 2000.

SCHEDULE 3

DEROGATION AND RESERVATION

[not reproduced: see *Halsbury's Statutes* (4th edn) CIVIL RIGHTS and LIBERTIES].

SCHEDULE 4

JUDICIAL PENSIONS

[not reproduced: see *Halsbury's Statutes* (4th edn) CIVIL RIGHTS and LIBERTIES].

SCOTLAND ACT 1998

(1998 Chapter 46)

PART IV

THE TAX-VARYING POWER

73	Power to fix basic rate for Scottish taxpayers
74	Supplemental provision with respect to resolutions
75	Scottish taxpayers
76	Changes to income tax structure
77	Accounting for additional Scottish tax
78	Effect of tax reduction for Scottish taxpayers
79	Supplemental powers to modify enactments
80	Reimbursement of expenses

An Act to provide for the establishment of a Scottish Parliament and Administration and other changes in the government of Scotland; to provide for changes in the constitution and functions of certain public authorities; to provide for the variation of the basic rate of income tax in relation to income of Scottish taxpayers in accordance with a resolution of the Scottish Parliament; to amend the law about parliamentary constituencies in Scotland; and for connected purposes.   [19th November 1998]

PART IV

THE TAX-VARYING POWER

Note—Sections 73–80 came into force on 6 May 1999 by virtue of the Scotland Act 1998 (Commencement) Order, SI 1998/3178.

73 Power to fix basic rate for Scottish taxpayers

(1) Subject to section 74, this section applies for any year of assessment for which income tax is charged if—

(a) the Parliament has passed a resolution providing for the percentage determined to be the basic rate for that year to be increased or reduced for Scottish taxpayers in accordance with the resolution,

(b) the increase or reduction provided for is confined to an increase or reduction by a number not exceeding three which is specified in the resolution and is either a whole number or half of a whole number, and

(c) the resolution has not been cancelled by a subsequent resolution of the Parliament.

(2) Where this section applies for any year of assessment the Income Tax Acts (excluding this Part) shall have effect in relation to the income of Scottish taxpayers as if any rate determined by the Parliament of the United Kingdom to be the basic rate for that year were increased or reduced in accordance with the resolution of the Scottish Parliament.

(3) In subsection (2) the reference to the income of Scottish taxpayers does not include a reference to any income of Scottish taxpayers which, had it been income for the year 1998–99, would have been income to which section 1A of the Income and Corporation Taxes Act 1988 (income from savings and distributions) applied for that year.

(4) In this section—

(a) a reference, in relation to any year of assessment, to income tax being charged for that year includes a reference to the passing of a PCTA resolution that provides for the charging of that tax for that year, and (*b*) a reference, in relation to a year of assessment, to the determination by the Parliament of the United Kingdom of a rate to be the basic rate for that year includes a reference to the passing of a PCTA resolution specifying a percentage to be the basic rate for that year.

(5) In this section "a PCTA resolution" means a resolution of the House of Commons containing such a declaration as is mentioned in section 1(2)(*b*) of the Provisional Collection of Taxes Act 1968.

74 Supplemental provision with respect to resolutions

(1) This section applies to any resolution of the Parliament ("a tax-varying resolution") which—

(*a*) provides, in accordance with section 73, for an increase or reduction for Scottish taxpayers of the basic rate for any year of assessment, or

(*b*) cancels a previous resolution of the Parliament providing for such an increase or reduction.

(2) Subject to subsection (3), a tax-varying resolution—

(*a*) must be expressed so as to relate to no more than a single year of assessment beginning after, but no more than twelve months after, the passing of the resolution, but

(*b*) shall have effect in relation to a determination by the Parliament of the United Kingdom of the rate to be the basic rate for that year irrespective of whether that determination had been made at the time of the passing of the resolution.

(3) Subsection (2) shall not prevent a tax-varying resolution relating to any year of assessment from being passed and having effect where—

(*a*) a determination by the Parliament of the United Kingdom of the rate to be the basic rate for that year is made after, or less than a month before, the beginning of that year,

(*b*) that determination is not confined to the passing of the enactment by which a determination of the same rate by a PCTA resolution is ratified, and

(*c*) the tax-varying resolution is passed within the period of one month beginning with the day of the making by the Parliament of the United Kingdom of its determination.

(4) Where, in a case to which subsection (3) applies, a tax-varying resolution is passed after the beginning of the year of assessment to which it relates—

(*a*) the resolution shall have effect as from the beginning of that year, and

(*b*) all such payments, repayments, deductions and other adjustments shall be made as are required to restore the position to what it would have been if the resolution had been passed before the beginning of that year.

(5) Standing orders shall ensure that only a member of the Scottish Executive may move a motion for a tax-varying resolution.

(6) A tax-varying resolution shall not be passed so as to have effect in relation to any year of assessment before the year 2000–01.

(7) Subsections (4) and (5) of section 73 apply for the purposes of this section as they apply for the purposes of that section.

75 Scottish taxpayers

(1) For the purposes of this Part a person is a Scottish taxpayer in relation to any year of assessment if—

(*a*) he is an individual who, for income tax purposes, is treated as resident in the United Kingdom in that year, and

(*b*) Scotland is the part of the United Kingdom with which he has the closest connection during that year.

(2) For the purposes of this section an individual who is treated for income tax purposes as resident in the United Kingdom in any year of assessment has his closest connection with Scotland during that year if, but only if, one or more of the following paragraphs applies in his case—

(*a*) he is an individual to whom subsection (3) applies for that year,

(*b*) the number of days which he spends in Scotland in that year is equal to or exceeds the number of days in that year which he spends elsewhere in the United Kingdom,

(*c*) he is an individual who, for the whole or any part of that year, is a member of Parliament for a constituency in Scotland, a member of the European Parliament for Scotland or a member of the Scottish Parliament.

(3) This subsection applies to an individual for a year of assessment if—

(*a*) he spends at least a part of that year in Scotland,

(*b*) for at least a part of the time that he spends in Scotland in that year, his principal UK home is located in Scotland and he makes use of it as a place of residence, and

(*c*) the times in that year when Scotland is where his principal UK home is located comprise (in aggregate) at least as much of that year as the times (if any) in that year when the location of his principal UK home is not in Scotland.

(4) For the purposes of this section—

(*a*) an individual spends a day in Scotland if, but only if, he is in Scotland at the end of that day, and (*b*) an individual spends a day elsewhere in the United Kingdom if, but only if, he is in the United Kingdom at the end of that day and it is not a day that he spends in Scotland.

(5) For the purposes of this section an individual's principal UK home at any time is located in Scotland if at that time—

(*a*) he is an individual with a place of residence in Scotland, and

(*b*) in the case of an individual with two or more places of residence in the United Kingdom, Scotland is the location of such one of those places as at that time is his main place of residence in the United Kingdom.

(6) In this section "place" includes a place on board a vessel or other means of transport.

76 Changes to income tax structure

(1) This section applies where—

(*a*) there has been a proposal for the modification of any provision made by or under the Income Tax Acts,

(*b*) that proposal is one made and published by the Treasury or the Board, or (without having been so made and published) appears to the Treasury to be a proposal to which effect is likely to be given by Act of Parliament, and

(*c*) it appears to the Treasury that the proposed modification would have a significant effect on the practical extent for any year of assessment of the Parliament's tax-varying powers.

(2) It shall be the duty of the Treasury, as soon as reasonably practicable after the publication of the proposal, or (as the case may be) as soon as reasonably practicable after it first appears to the Treasury that the proposal is likely to be enacted, to lay before the House of Commons—

(*a*) a statement of whether, in the Treasury's opinion, an amendment of the Parliament's tax-varying powers is required as a consequence of the proposal, and

(*b*) if in their opinion an amendment of those powers is required, the Treasury's proposals for amending those powers.

(3) Any proposals for amending the Parliament's tax-varying powers that are laid before the House of Commons by the Treasury under this section—

(*a*) must be confined to income tax,

(*b*) must appear to the Treasury to satisfy the conditions set out in subsections (4) and (5), and

(*c*) must not contain any proposal for the Parliament's tax-varying powers to be exercisable in relation to the taxation of income from savings or distributions.

(4) The first condition mentioned in subsection (3)(*b*) is that the proposals would secure—

(*a*) so far as possible, and

(*b*) after making due allowance for annual changes in the retail prices index,

that the practical extent of the Parliament's tax-varying powers would remain broadly the same from year to year as it would be if (apart from any resolution of the Parliament) the law relating to income tax were the same from year to year as it was in relation to the year 1997–98.

(5) The second condition so mentioned is that the proposals would not enable the Parliament's tax-varying powers to be exercised for any year of assessment so as to have an effect on the levels of the after-tax income of Scottish taxpayers generally that would be significantly different from the effect their exercise could have had in any previous year of assessment.

(6) References in this section to the practical extent of the Parliament's tax-varying powers are references to the amounts of income tax for any year of assessment which appear to be or (as the case may be) to have been the maximum amounts capable of being raised and foregone in that year in pursuance of a resolution of the Parliament.

(7) In this section "income from savings or distributions" means income which, had it been income for the year 1998–99, would have been income to which section 1A of the Income and Corporation Taxes Act 1988 applied for that year.

77 Accounting for additional Scottish tax

(1) Where the basic rate for any year of assessment is increased for Scottish taxpayers by a resolution of the Parliament, it shall be the duty of the Board to pay amounts into the Scottish Consolidated Fund in accordance with this section.

(2) The amounts of the payments to be made by the Board under this section, and the times at which they are to be made, shall be determined by the Board and notified to the Scottish Ministers as soon as reasonably practicable after the passing of the resolution providing for the increase to which they relate.

(3) Any determination made by the Board under subsection (2) for any year of assessment shall be such as appears to the Board to be necessary for securing that, in the course of that year, amounts are paid into the Scottish Consolidated Fund which are equal in total to the amount estimated by the Board to represent the proportion of the income tax receipts for that year that is properly attributable to a resolution of the Parliament.

(4) For the purposes of this section the Board shall make and maintain arrangements as to—

(a) the manner of estimating the proportion of the income tax receipts for a year of assessment that is properly attributable to a resolution of the Parliament,

(b) the circumstances and manner in which an estimate of that proportion or of those receipts may be revised before or in the course of the year of assessment to which it relates,

(c) the manner of determining the amount of each payment to be made in respect of any such estimate, and

(d) the times at which, and manner in which, those amounts are to be paid by the Board into the Scottish Consolidated Fund.

(5) Arrangements under subsection (4) may include provision for the making of adjustments to the amounts paid by the Board where any estimate made for the purposes of this section in respect of any year of assessment (whether the current year or a previous year) turns out to have been inaccurate.

(6) Before making or modifying any arrangements under subsection (4) or (5), the Board shall consult with the Scottish Ministers.

(7) In this section ''income tax receipts'', in relation to any year of assessment, means so much as is referable to income tax charged for that year of any sums which, disregarding both—

(a) subsection (8), and

(b) any regulations or direction made or given by the Treasury,

are sums that have to be paid into the Consolidated Fund under section 10 of the Exchequer and Audit Departments Act 1866 (gross revenues of Board's department to be paid into that Fund after the making of specified deductions).

(8) Sums required by the Board for making payments under this section shall be paid out of the gross revenues of the Board's department; and, accordingly, those sums shall be treated as included in the amounts to be deducted from those revenues before they are paid into the Consolidated Fund under section 10 of the Exchequer and Audit Departments Act 1866.

78 Effect of tax reduction for Scottish taxpayers

(1) Where the basic rate for any year of assessment is reduced for Scottish taxpayers by a resolution of the Parliament, payments to the Board in accordance with this section shall be charged on the Scottish Consolidated Fund.

(2) The amounts of the payments to be made out of the Scottish Consolidated Fund under this section, and the times at which they are to be made, shall be determined by the Board and notified to the Scottish Ministers as soon as reasonably practicable after the passing of the resolution providing for the reduction to which they relate.

(3) Any determination made by the Board under subsection (2) for any year of assessment shall be such as appears to the Board to be necessary for securing that in the course of that year amounts are paid to the Board which are equal in total to the amount estimated by the Board to represent the shortfall in income tax receipts for that year that is properly attributable to a resolution of the Parliament.

(4) For the purposes of this section the Board shall make and maintain arrangements as to—

(a) the manner of estimating the shortfall in income tax receipts for any year of assessment that is properly attributable to a resolution of the Parliament,

(b) the circumstances and manner in which an estimate of that shortfall may be revised before or in the course of the year of assessment to which it relates,

(c) the manner of determining the amount of each payment to be made in respect of any such estimate, and

(d) the times at which, and manner in which, those amounts are to be paid to the Board.

(5) Arrangements under subsection (4) may include provision for the making of adjustments to the amounts paid to the Board where any estimate made for the purposes of this section in respect of any year of assessment (whether the current year or a previous year) turns out to have been inaccurate.

(6) Before making or modifying any arrangements under subsection (4) or (5), the Board shall consult with the Scottish Ministers.

(7) In this section ''income tax receipts'' has the same meaning as in section 77.

(8) The sums paid to the Board under this section shall be treated for the purposes of section 10 of the Exchequer and Audit Departments Act 1866 (payment, after the making of the specified deductions, of gross revenues into the Consolidated Fund) as comprised in their department's gross revenues.

79 Supplemental powers to modify enactments

(1) The Treasury may by order make such modifications of any enactment as they consider necessary or expedient in consequence of—

(a) the fact that the Parliament has, or is to have, the power to pass a tax-varying resolution, or

(b) the fact (where it is the case) that the Parliament has passed such a resolution.

(2) The Treasury may by order make provision—

(a) excluding the operation of section 73(2) in relation to any enactment, and (*b*) making any such other modifications of any enactment as they consider necessary or expedient in connection with, or for the purposes of, any such exclusion.

(3) Without prejudice to the generality of the powers conferred by the preceding provisions of this section, an order under this section may provide that, where any tax-varying resolution relating to any year of assessment is passed, that resolution does not require any change in the amounts repayable or deductible under section 203 of the Income and Corporation Taxes Act 1988 (PAYE) between—

(*a*) the beginning of that year, and

(*b*) such day falling after the passing of the resolution as may be specified in the order.

(4) An order under this section may, to the extent that the Treasury consider it to be appropriate, take effect retrospectively from the beginning of the year of assessment in which it is made.

(5) In this section "tax-varying resolution" has the same meaning as in section 74.

80 Reimbursement of expenses

The Scottish Ministers may reimburse any Minister of the Crown or government department for administrative expenses incurred by virtue of this Part at any time after the passing of this Act by the Minister or department.

FINANCE ACT 1999

(1999 Chapter 16)

ARRANGEMENT OF SECTIONS

PART III

INCOME TAX, CORPORATION TAX AND CAPITAL GAINS TAX

An Act to grant certain duties, to alter other duties, and to amend the law relating to the National Debt and the Public Revenue, and to make further provision in connection with Finance.

[27 July 1999]

PART III
INCOME TAX, CORPORATION TAX AND CAPITAL GAINS TAX

Income tax rates and charge etc

22 Starting rate

(1), (2) (*substitute* TA 1988 s 1(2)(*aa*), (2A)).

(3) (*Amends* TA 1988 s 1(3)).

(4) (*Amends* TA 1988 s 1(4)).

(5) Section 1(4) of that Act (indexation), so far as it relates to section 1(2)(*aa*), shall not apply for the year 1999–00.

(6) (*Amends* TA 1988 s 1(6A).

(7) (*Inserts* TA 1988 s 1A(1B), (6A)).

(8)–(10) (*Amend* ss 547(5)(*c*), 549(2), 550(3), 699(2), 819(2), 832(1)

(11) (*Amends* TMA 1970, ss 7(6), 91(3)(*c*)).

(12) Subsections (1) to (3) and (6) to (11) above apply for the year 1999–00 and subsequent years of assessment; and subsection (4) above applies for the year 2000–01 and subsequent years of assessment.

Commentary—*Simon's Direct Tax Service* **E1.102.**

23 Charge and rates for 1999–00

(*Spent*).

Commentary—*Simon's Direct Tax Service* **E1.102.**

24 Personal allowances for 1999–00 for those aged 65 or more

(1) (*Spent*).

(2) Accordingly, section 257C(1) of the Taxes Act 1988 (indexation), so far as it relates to the amounts so specified, shall not apply for the year 1999–00.

Commentary—*Simon's Direct Tax Service* **E2.302.**

25 Operative date of indexation for PAYE

(1) The Taxes Act 1988 shall be amended in accordance with subsections (2) and (3) below.

(2), (3) (*Insert* TA 1988, ss 1(5A), 257C(2A)).

(4) This section has effect for the year 1999–00 and subsequent years of assessment.

Commentary—*Simon's Direct Tax Service* **E1.104, E4.901.**

Rates of capital gains tax

26 Rates of capital gains tax

(1) Section 4 of the Taxation of Chargeable Gains Act 1992 (rates of capital gains tax) shall be amended as follows.

(2)–(5) (*Amend* TCGA 1992, s 4(1), (1AA), (4) and *repeal* s 4(1A), (1B), (3A), (3B)).

(6) This section applies for the year 1999–00 and subsequent years of assessment.

Commentary—*Simon's Direct Tax Service* **C1.107.**

Corporation tax charge and rates

27 Charge and main rate for financial year 2000

Corporation tax shall be charged for the financial year 2000 at the rate of 30 per cent.

Commentary—*Simon's Direct Tax Service* **D2.108.**

28 Corporation tax starting rate

(1) (*Insert* TA 1988, s 13AA).

(2), (3) (*Amend* TA 1988 ss 13A(1), 468(1A)).

(4) (*Amends* FA 1989 Sch 12 para 1(a)).

(5) (*Amends* FA 1998 Sch 18 para 8(1)).

(6) Subsections (1) to (5) above have effect, subject to subsection (7) below, in relation to corporation tax for the financial year 2000 or any subsequent financial year.

(7) In the case of an accounting period beginning before 1st April 2000 and ending on or after that date—

(a) section 13AA of the Taxes Act 1988 shall apply as if the different parts of that accounting period falling in the different financial years were separate accounting periods;

(b) where a claim is made under section 13AA in relation to the part of that period beginning with 1st April 2000, section 13 of that Act shall also so apply; and

(c) for the purposes of treating different parts of an accounting period as separate accounting periods in accordance with paragraphs (a) and (b) above, the profits and basic profits of the company for that period shall be attributed to the different parts of it according to the financial year in which, for the purposes of section 8 of that Act, they are taken to arise.

Commentary—*Simon's Direct Tax Service* **D2.109.**

29 Rate and fraction for corporation tax starting rate

For the financial year 2000—

(a) the corporation tax starting rate shall be 10 per cent; and

(b) the fraction mentioned in section 13AA(3) of the Taxes Act 1988 shall be one fortieth.

Commentary—*Simon's Direct Tax Service* **D2.109.**

Income tax reductions

30 Children's tax credit

(1) The following section shall be inserted after section 257 of the Taxes Act 1988—

"257A Children's tax credit

(1) If a qualifying child (or more than one) is resident with the claimant during the whole or part of the year of assessment, the claimant shall be entitled to an income tax reduction, to be known as a children's tax credit.

(2) The reduction shall be calculated by reference to £4,160.

(3) Where any part of the claimant's income for the year of assessment falls within section 1(2)(b), his children's tax credit for the year shall be calculated as if the amount specified in subsection (2) above were reduced by £2 for every £3 of that part of his income.

(4) In this section 'qualifying child' means, in relation to a person—

(a) a child of his who has not attained the age of 16, or

(b) a child who has not attained the age of 16 and who is maintained by, and at the expense of, the person for any part of the year of assessment;

and 'child' includes illegitimate child and stepchild.

(5) Schedule 13B (which modifies this section where a child lives with more than one adult during a year of assessment) shall have effect."

(2) The Schedule set out in Schedule 3 to this Act shall be inserted after Schedule 13A to the Taxes Act 1988.

(3) In section 257C(1) and (3) of the Taxes Act 1988 (indexation), for the words "sections 257 and 257A" there shall be substituted "sections 257, 257AA(2) and 257A".

(4) The Taxes Management Act 1970 shall be amended as follows—

(a) in section 36(3A) (fraudulent or negligent conduct), there shall be inserted at the end "or under Schedule 13B to that Act (elections as to transfer of children's tax credit)",

(b) in section 37A (effect of assessment where allowances transferred)—

(i) after "spouse" there shall be inserted "or partner", and

(ii) after "Act" there shall be inserted "or paragraph 4 of Schedule 13B to that Act",

(c) in section 43A(2A) (further assessments), there shall be inserted at the end "or under Schedule 13B to that Act (elections as to transfer of children's tax credit)", and

(d) in section 58(3)(b) (proceedings in Northern Ireland), after "repealed by that Act)" there shall be inserted ", paragraph 6 of Schedule 13B to that Act".

(5) Subsections (1), (2) and (4) above have effect for the year 2001-02 and subsequent years of assessment.

(6) Subsection (3) above has effect for the purposes of the application of section 257AA of the Taxes Act 1988 for the year 2002-03 and subsequent years of assessment.

Commentary—*Simon's Direct Tax Service* **E2.502.**

31 Restriction of MCA to those reaching 65 before 2000–01

(1) Section 257A of the Taxes Act 1988 (income tax reduction for married couples) shall be amended as follows.

(2)–(5) (*Repeal* TA 1988, s 257A(1)) and *amend* s 257A(2)–(4)).

(6), (7) (*Amend* TA 1988, s 257A(5) and *insert* s 257(5A)).

(8) (*Amends* TA 1988, s 257A(6)).

(9) After subsection (6) there shall be inserted the following subsections—

"(7) A man who is entitled for any year of assessment to an income tax reduction under this section, or to make a claim for such a reduction, shall not be entitled for that year to any income tax reduction under section 257AA.

(8) Where—

(a) a woman is married to and living with a man for the whole or any part of a year of assessment, and

(b) that man is entitled for that year to an income tax reduction under this section, or to make a claim for such a reduction,

no child shall be regarded for any of the purposes of section 257AA or Schedule 13B as resident with that woman at any time in that year when she is married to and living with that man.

(9) A person may, by notice to an officer of the Board, elect to give up his entitlement for any year of assessment to an income tax reduction under this section; and where he does so and the election is not subsequently revoked, that person shall be taken for the purposes of this section to have no entitlement for that year to a reduction under this section, or to make a claim for such a reduction."

(10) Subsections (2) to (5) and (8) above have effect for the year 2000–01 and subsequent years of assessment.

(11) Subject to section 32(5) below, subsections (6) and (7) above have effect for the year 1999–00 and subsequent years of assessment.

(12) Subsection (9) above has effect for the year 2001-02 and subsequent years of assessment.

Commentary—*Simon's Direct Tax Service* E2.202, 303.

32 Further provision about married couple's allowance

(1) In section 257BA of the Taxes Act 1988 (elections as to transfer of relief under section 257A)—

(a) (*Amend* s 257BA(1)(a), (2)(a), (3)(a), (6)).

(b) (*Amend* s 257BA(2)).

(c) (*Amend* s 257BA(9)).

(2) (*Repeals* TA 1988 ss 257D–257F).

(3) Subsection (1)(a) and (c) above has effect for the year 1999–00 and subsequent years of assessment.

(4) Subsections (1)(b) and (2) above have effect for the year 2000–01 and subsequent years of assessment.

(5) Section 257C of the Taxes Act 1988 (indexation) shall apply in relation to subsection (5A) of section 257A of that Act, but only for the year 2000–01 and subsequent years of assessment.

Commentary—*Simon's Direct Tax Service* E2.202, 303.

33 Abolition of existing relief in respect of children

(1) (*Repeals* TA 1988 ss 259 to 261A).

(2) This section has effect for the year 2000–01 and subsequent years of assessment.

Commentary—*Simon's Direct Tax Service* E2.502.

34 Abolition of widow's bereavement allowance

(1) (*Repeals* TA 1988 s 262).

(2) Subsection (1) above has effect in relation to deaths occurring on or after 6th April 2000.

(3) Where a woman is entitled to an income tax reduction for the year 2000–01 by virtue of paragraph (b) of section 262(1) of the Taxes Act 1988, the reference in that paragraph to the amount specified in section 257A(1) for that year shall be read as a reference to the amount specified in section 257A(5A) for that year.

Commentary—*Simon's Direct Tax Service* E2.501.

35 Order of income tax reductions etc

(1) In section 256(3) of the Taxes Act 1988 (order of income tax reductions etc)—

(a) in paragraph (a), for "section 259 or 261A" there shall be substituted "section 257AA";

(b) paragraph (b) shall cease to have effect;

(c) the words after paragraph (c) shall be omitted.

(2) Subsection (1)(a) and (b) above has effect for the year 2001-02 and subsequent years of assessment.

(3) Subsection (1)(*c*) above has effect for the year 2000–01 and subsequent years of assessment.

(4) For the year 2000–01, section 256(3) of the Taxes Act 1988 shall have effect with the omission of paragraph (*a*) and, in paragraph (*b*), of the words "except section 259 or 261A".

Commentary—*Simon's Direct Tax Service* **E1.102A.**

36 Maintenance payments

(1)–(6) (*Amend* TA 1988, s 347B(1), (2), (3), (5A), (8) and *insert* s 347(1A)).

(7) Sections 347A and 347B of the Taxes Act 1988 shall have effect, notwithstanding anything in subsection (3) of section 36 of the Finance Act 1988 (which provides for the application of those sections), in relation to a payment made in pursuance of an existing obligation (within the meaning of that subsection) as they have effect in relation to a payment made otherwise than in pursuance of such an obligation.

(8) This section has effect in relation to any payment falling due on or after 6th April 2000.

Commentary—*Simon's Direct Tax Service* **E5.104.**

Relief for interest payments

37 Limit on relief for interest

(*Spent*).

Commentary—*Simon's Direct Tax Service* **E1.539.**

38 Withdrawal of relief for interest on loans to buy land etc

(1) A payment of interest falling within subsection (3) or (4) below shall not be eligible for relief under section 353 of the Taxes Act 1988 by virtue of section 354 of that Act (interest on loans to buy land etc).

(2) Section 369(1) of that Act (mortgage interest payable under deduction of tax) shall not apply to any payment of interest falling within subsection (3) or (4) below which (apart from section 353(2) of that Act and subsection (1) above) would be eligible for relief under section 353 of that Act by virtue of section 354 of that Act.

(3) A payment of interest falls within this subsection if it is—

    (*a*) a payment made on or after 6th April 2000 (whenever falling due); or
    (*b*) a payment made before that date, but not before 9th March 1999, of any interest that was not due until on or after 6th April 2000.

(4) A payment of interest falls within this subsection if it is—

    (*a*) made before 6th April 2000 but not before 9th March 1999; and
    (*b*) made under or in accordance with any scheme made for a tax-avoidance purpose on or after 9th March 1999 (whether or not before the making of the payment).

(5) For the purposes of subsection (4) above, a scheme is made for a tax-avoidance purpose if its main purpose, or one of its main purposes, is to secure that a payment of one or more of the following descriptions is a relievable payment, that is to say—

    (*a*) a payment discharging an obligation to make a payment which (but for the scheme) might have been expected to be a non-relievable payment;
    (*b*) a payment made in pursuance of any obligation which has effect, directly or indirectly, in place of an obligation under which a payment which might have been expected to be a non-relievable payment would have become due;
    (*c*) a payment made in pursuance of an obligation which (apart from the purpose of securing that it is a relievable payment) might have been expected to take the form of an obligation—

        (i) to make a non-relievable payment, or
        (ii) to make two or more payments at least one of which would have been a non-relievable payment.

(6) In subsection (5) above—

"non-relievable payment" means a payment falling within subsection (3) above; and
"relievable payment" means a payment which—

    (*a*) is eligible for relief under section 353 of the Taxes Act 1988, or
    (*b*) is a payment to which section 369(1) of that Act applies.

(7) The references in this section to a scheme are references to any scheme, arrangements or understanding of any kind whatever, whether or not legally enforceable.

(8) Schedule 4 to this Act (which contains amendments consequential on the preceding provisions of this section) shall have effect.

Commentary—*Simon's Direct Tax Service* **E1.535.**

39 Withdrawal of relief for interest on new annuity loans

(1), (2) (*Insert* TA 1988 s 365(1)(*aa*), (1AA)).

(3) This section has effect for the year 1998–99 and subsequent years of assessment.

Commentary—*Simon's Direct Tax Service* E1.553.

40 Annuity loans: residence requirements and re-mortgages

(1)–(4) (*Amend* TA 1988 s 365(1)(*d*), *insert* s 365(1AB)–(1AD) and *substitute* s 365(1A)).

(5) This section has effect in relation to any payment of interest (whenever falling due) made on or after the day on which this Act is passed.

Commentary—*Simon's Direct Tax Service* E1.553.

41 Repayments attracting repayment supplement

(1) Section 824 of the Taxes Act 1988 (repayment supplements for individuals) shall have effect, and be deemed always to have had effect, with the following amendments.

(2), (3) (*Insert* TA 1988 s 824(2B), (3)(*aa*)).

(4) This section shall be deemed to have had effect in relation to provisions corresponding to section 824 of the Taxes Act 1988 directly or indirectly re-enacted in that section as it has effect in relation to that section, subject to subsections (5) and (6) below.

(5) For the purposes of subsection (4) above the references in the amendments of section 824 of the Taxes Act 1988 made by this section to provisions of that Act shall be taken to include references to any corresponding provision contained in the enactments directly or indirectly re-enacted in those provisions.

(6) Subsection (4) above applies only if the payments corresponding to payments under section 375(8) of the Taxes Act 1988 were made in the year 1984-85 or a subsequent year of assessment.

Commentary—*Simon's Direct Tax Service* A3.436, 616, E4.975.

Employee benefits etc

42 Conditional acquisition of shares

(1) Section 140A of the Taxes Act 1988 (conditional acquisition of shares) is amended as follows.

(2)–(4) (*Repeal* TA 1988 s 140A(2) and *amend* s 140A(3), (4)).

(5) This section applies in relation to shares acquired on or after the day on which this Act is passed.

Commentary—*Simon's Direct Tax Service* E4.531.

43 Meaning of conditional interests in shares

(1) Section 140C of the Taxes Act 1988 (which describes the cases in which an interest in shares is, or is not, to be treated as only conditional) is amended as follows.

(2)–(6) (*Insert* TA 1988 s 140C(1A), (3A), (6) and *amend* s 140C(2)–(4)).

(7) The amendments made by this section shall be deemed always to have had effect.

Commentary—*Simon's Direct Tax Service* E4.531.

44 Exemption for mobile telephones

(1)–(5) (*Insert* TA 1988 s 155AA, *amend* ss 154, 168A and *repeal* ss 159A, 200AA(3)).

(6) This section has effect for the year 1999–00 and subsequent years of assessment.

Commentary—*Simon's Direct Tax Service* E4.612, 617.

45 Limited exemption for computer equipment

(1), (2) (*Insert* TA 1988 s 156A and *amend* s 154(2)).

(3) This section applies for the year 1999–00 and subsequent years of assessment.

Commentary—*Simon's Direct Tax Service* E4.611, 612.

46 PRP and agricultural pay

(1) An application made at any time on or after 28th July 1998 for the registration of a profit-related pay scheme shall not be required to contain, or to have contained, any such undertaking as is mentioned in section 175(1)(*c*) of the Taxes Act 1988 (undertaking to satisfy minimum wage legislation without taking account of profit-related pay).

(2) (*Repeals* TA 1988 s 178(1)(*d*)).

(3) Subsection (2) above has effect in relation only to failures to comply taking place on or after 28th July 1998; but it shall be deemed so to have had effect at all times on or after that date.

Commentary—*Simon's Direct Tax Service* E4.304, 310.

47 Cars available for private use

(1) Schedule 6 to the Taxes Act 1988 (cars available for private use: cash equivalent of car) shall be amended as follows.

(2)–(5) (*Amend* TA 1988 Sch 6 paras 2(1), (2), 5 and *substitute* para 4(*a*)).

(6) This section has effect for the year 1999–00 and subsequent years of assessment.

Commentary—*Simon's Direct Tax Service* **E4.626.**
Prospective amendments—
This section to be repealed by FA 2000 s 156, Sch 40 Pt II(3) with effect from the year 2002–03.

48 Provision and support of bus services

(1) (*Insert* TA 1988 ss 197AA, 197AB).

(2) This section has effect for the year 1999–00 and subsequent years of assessment.

Commentary—*Simon's Direct Tax Service* **E4.612, 708.**

49 Provision of motor cycle or cycle parking facilities

(1) The provisions listed below (which provide for exemption from tax in relation to the provision of car parking spaces) apply in relation to—

    (*a*) motor cycle parking spaces, and
    (*b*) facilities for parking cycles,

as they apply in relation to car parking spaces.

(2) The provisions referred to above are—

    section 141(6A) of the Taxes Act 1988 (use of non-cash voucher to obtain use of parking space);
    section 142(3A) of that Act (use of credit-token to obtain use of parking space);
    section 155(1A) of that Act (taxable benefits: general charge excluded in relation to provision of parking space); and
    section 197A of that Act (charge on emoluments excluded in relation to expenditure in connection with provision of parking space).

(3) In subsection (1) above—

    ''motor cycle'' has the meaning given by section 185(1) of the Road Traffic Act 1988, and
    ''cycle'' has the meaning given by section 192(1) of that Act.

(4) The provisions of this section have effect for the year 1999–00 and subsequent years of assessment.

Commentary—*Simon's Direct Tax Service* **E4.612, 708.**

50 Cycles and cyclist's safety equipment

(1) (*Inserts* TA 1988 s 197AC).

(2) ...[1]

(3) The provisions of this section have effect for the year 1999–00 and subsequent years of assessment.

Commentary—*Simon's Direct Tax Service* **E4.612, 711.**
Amendment—[1] Sub-s (2) repealed by the Capital Allowances Act 2001 s 580, Sch 4 with effect for income tax purposes, as respects allowances and charges falling to be made for chargeable periods ending after 5 April 2001, and for corporation tax purposes, as respects allowances and charges falling to be made for chargeable periods ending after 31 March 2001.

Members of parliaments and assemblies

51 EU travel expenses

(1) (*Amends* TA 1988, s 200 and *insert* s 200(3)).

(2) This section has effect in relation to sums paid on or after 1st April 1999.

Commentary—*Simon's Direct Tax Service* **E4.334.**

52 Scottish Parliament and devolved assemblies

(1) Schedule 5 to this Act, which makes amendments the effect of which is—

    (*a*) to treat members of the Scottish Parliament, the National Assembly for Wales and the Northern Ireland Assembly in the same way, for tax purposes, as members of Parliament, and
    (*b*) to treat certain office holders under the Scotland Act 1998, the Government of Wales Act 1998 and the Northern Ireland Act 1998 in the same way, for tax purposes, as holders of ministerial and other offices,

shall have effect.

(2) The amendments made by that Schedule have effect for the year 1999–00 and subsequent years of assessment.

Commentary—*Simon's Direct Tax Service* **E4.334; E7.262.**

Sub-contractors in the construction industry

53 Exemption certificates

(1) Sections 562 to 565 of the Taxes Act 1988 (exemption certificates for the scheme for sub-contractors in the construction industry) shall have effect in relation to any application to which this section applies, and shall be deemed always to have had effect in relation to such an application—

(*a*) with the substitution of the subsection set out in subsection (2) below for the subsection (2B) inserted in section 562 by paragraph 4(3) of Schedule 27 to the Finance Act 1995 (which defined the payments to be taken into account in assessing turnover for the purposes of exemption); and

(*b*) as if paragraphs 3 to 5 of Schedule 8 to the Finance Act 1998 (which extended the description of payments for certain cases) had not been enacted.

(2) That subsection is as follows—

''(2B) In subsection (2A) above 'relevant payments' means payments under contracts relating to, or to the work of individuals participating in the carrying out of, any operations which—

(*a*) are of a description specified in subsection (2) of section 567; but

(*b*) are not of a description specified in subsection (3) of that section,

other than so much of the payments as represents the direct cost to the person receiving the payments of materials used or to be used in carrying out the operations in question.''

(3) This section applies to any application for the issue or renewal of a certificate under section 561 of the Taxes Act 1988 which is or has been made with respect to any period beginning on or after 1st August 1999.

Commentary—*Simon's Direct Tax Service* E5.511.

Reverse premiums

54 Tax treatment of reverse premiums

(1) Schedule 6 to this Act (tax treatment of receipts by way of reverse premium) has effect.

(2) The provisions of that Schedule apply in relation to a reverse premium (within the meaning of that Schedule) received on or after 9th March 1999, unless it is a payment or other benefit to which the recipient was entitled immediately before that date.

(3) In determining whether a payment or benefit was one to which the recipient was entitled immediately before 9th March 1999, no account shall be taken of any arrangements made on or after that date.

Commentary—*Simon's Direct Tax Service* A4.221; B3.910.
Revenue Interpretation RI 213—the taxation of reverse premiums.

Charities

55 Gifts in kind to charities etc

(1) (*Inserts* TA 1988 s 83A).

(2) (*Repeals* FA 1998 s 47).

(3) Subsections (1) and (2) above have effect in relation to gifts made on or after the day on which this Act is passed.

Commentary—*Simon's Direct Tax Service* B3.1445.

56 Gifts of money to relieve refugee poverty

(1) Section 48 of the Finance Act 1998 (gifts of money made for relief in poor countries) shall be amended in accordance with subsections (2) to (4) below.

(2)–(4) (*Amend* FA 1998 s 48(1)(*a*), (*b*), (2)(*a*), (9) and *insert* s 48(2)(*c*)).

(5) Any order made before the passing of this Act under subsection (9) of that section (designation of countries or territories in respect of which section 48 has effect) shall have effect as if made for the purposes only of subsection (2)(*a*) and (*b*) of that section.

(6) Any notification given for the purposes of that section, in relation to a charity, before the passing of this Act shall be treated as a notification given for the purposes of that section as amended by this section.

(7) This section has effect in relation to gifts made on or after 6th April 1999.

(8) An order made under subsection (9) of that section for the purposes of subsection (2)(*c*) (as inserted by subsection (3)(*b*) above) may have effect retrospectively in relation to such times falling on or after that date as may be specified in the order.

Commentary—*Simon's Direct Tax Service* E1.504.

57 Aggregation of money gifts for relief in poor countries

(1) Section 48 of the Finance Act 1998 (gifts of money made for relief in poor countries) shall have effect, and be deemed always to have had effect, with the following amendments.

(2), (3) (*Amend* FA 1998, s 48(4) and *insert* s 48(4A)).

Commentary—*Simon's Direct Tax Service* **E1.504.**
Regulations—Gifts for Relief in Poor Countries (Designation of Kosovo) Order, SI 1999/2118.

Education and training

58 Employees seconded to educational establishments

(1) Section 86 of the Taxes Act 1988 (employees seconded to charities and educational establishments) shall be amended as follows.

(2) (*Amends* TA 1988, s 86(3)).

(3), (4) (*Substitute* TA 1988, s 86(3)(*a*)–(*c*) and *insert* TA 1988 s 86(4)–(6)).

(5) The amendment made by subsection (2) above shall be deemed always to have had effect.

(6) The amendments made by subsections (3) and (4) above have effect for the year 1999–00 and subsequent years of assessment.

Commentary—*Simon's Direct Tax Service* **B3.1441.**

59 Phasing out of vocational training relief

(1) (*Substitutes* FA 1991, s 32(2)–(2B) for original s 32(2)).

(2) (*Repeals* FA 1991 ss 32, 33).

(3) In this section—

(*a*) subsection (1) has effect in relation to payments made on or after 6th April 1999; and
(*b*) subsection (2) shall have effect in relation to payments made on or after such date after 6th April 2000 as the Treasury may by order appoint.

Commentary—*Simon's Direct Tax Service* **E2.1301.**
Note—The appointed day for the purposes of sub-s (3) is 31 August 2000 by virtue of the Finance Act 1999, Section 59(3)(*b*), (Appointed Day) Order, SI 2000/2004.

60 Student loans: certain interest to be disregarded

(*Insert* TA 1988 s 331A).

Commentary—*Simon's Direct Tax Service* **B5.210.**

Various other reliefs etc

61 Class 1B National Insurance contributions

(1) (*Amends* TA 1988 s 617).

(2) Subsection (1) above has effect in relation to contributions paid on or after 6th April 1999.

Commentary—*Simon's Direct Tax Service* **B3.1428.**

62 Expenditure on film production and acquisition

(*Amends* F(No 2)A 1987 s 48).

Commentary—*Simon's Direct Tax Service* **B3.1307.**

63 Treatment of transfer fees under existing contracts

(1) Subject to subsection (2) below, where—

(*a*) a contract is or has been entered into by a football or other sports club to secure the services of a player; and
(*b*) the contract is or was entered into before the beginning of the first accounting period of the club in relation to which a relevant financial reporting standard has effect (whether by virtue of the adoption of the standard by the club or otherwise),

nothing in the standard shall be taken to affect the manner in which any fee required to be paid by the club under the contract may be taken into account in computing the club's profits to be charged under Case I of Schedule D.

(2) Subsection (1) above shall not apply if the club so elects by a notice given to an officer of the Board within the period of two years beginning immediately after the accounting period described in subsection (1)(*b*) above.

(3) The relevant financial reporting standards are—

(*a*) Financial Reporting Standard 10 issued by the Accounting Standards Board on 4th September 1997; and
(*b*) Financial Reporting Standard for Smaller Entities issued by that Board on 10th December 1998.

(4) All such adjustments shall be made (whether by way of assessment, amendment of an assessment, repayment of tax or otherwise) as may be necessary to give effect to the provisions of this section.

(5) Subsection (4) above has effect notwithstanding any time limits relating to the making or amendment of an assessment for any accounting period.

Commentary—*Simon's Direct Tax Service* **B3.916.**

Settlements

64 Income of unmarried child of settlor

(1) (*Amends* TA 1988, s 660B(1)).

(2), (3) (*Substitute* TA 1988, s 660B(3)(*a*), (*b*), (*bb*) and *insert* s 600B(3A)).

(4) (*Substitutes* TA 1988, s 660B(5)).

(5) The amendment in subsection (1) above has effect in relation to—

    (*a*) income arising under a settlement made or entered into on or after 9th March 1999, and

    (*b*) income arising under a settlement made or entered into before that date so far as it arises directly or indirectly from funds provided on or after that date;

and the amendment in subsection (4) above has effect accordingly.

Any apportionment required for the purposes of paragraph (*b*) shall be made on a just and reasonable basis.

(6) The amendments in subsections (2) and (3) above have effect in relation to any payment within subsection (2) of section 660B of the Taxes Act 1988 made on or after 9th March 1999.

In relation to such a payment those amendments apply whenever the facts mentioned in subsection (3) of that section occurred.

(7) (*Amends* TA 1988 s 660E(3)).

Commentary—*Simon's Direct Tax Service* **C4.351.**

Securities and investments

65 Relevant discounted securities

(1)–(6) (*Substitute* FA 1996 Sch 13 para 3(1)–(1F) (for original para 3(1)), (7), (8), *insert* para 3(2A), (2B), 10(4), 13(9) and *repeal* para 3(5)).

(7) (*Inserts* FA 1996 s 92(7)–(11)).

(8) Subject to subsections (9) to (12) below, subsections (1) to (7) above have effect in relation to—

    (*a*) any transfer of a security on or after 15th February 1999; or

    (*b*) any occasion on or after that date on which a person holding a security becomes entitled to any payment on its redemption.

(9) For the purposes of section 92 of that Act, subsections (1) to (7) above—

    (*a*) have effect in relation to any accounting period of a company ending on or after 15th February 1999; but

    (*b*) do not affect any amount falling to be brought into account in respect of any disposal (in whole or in part) of an asset representing a creditor relationship if the disposal was one completed before that day.

(10) For the purposes of paragraphs 17 and 18 of Schedule 9 to that Act, subsections (1) to (7) above—

    (*a*) have effect in relation to any accounting period of a company ending on or after 15th February 1999; but

    (*b*) do not affect any amount falling to be brought into account in respect of a security representing a debtor relationship of a company if, on that day, the company was no longer subject to any liability under the relationship.

(11) For the purposes of sections 117(2AA) and 251(8) of the Taxation of Chargeable Gains Act 1992, subsections (1) to (7) above have effect in relation to any disposal (in whole or in part) of an asset on or after 15th February 1999.

(12) For the purposes of subsection (1)(*c*) of section 254 of that Act (which, notwithstanding its repeal by the Finance Act 1998, continues to have effect in relation to loans made before 17th March 1998), subsections (1) to (7) above have effect in relation to any claim made on or after 15th February 1999.

Commentary—*Simon's Direct Tax Service* **A7.602.**

66 Qualifying corporate bonds: provision consequential on s 65

(1) This section applies where—

    (*a*) before 15th February 1999 there occurred a transaction (''the relevant transaction'') to which sections 127 to 130 of the Taxation of Chargeable Gains Act 1992 applied; and

    (*b*) the new holding (within the meaning given by section 126 of that Act) consisted of or included something (''the new asset'') that—

(i) did not fall to be treated as a qualifying corporate bond in relation to the relevant transaction, but

(ii) by virtue of section 65 above, does fall to be so treated in relation to a disposal on or after 15th February 1999.

(2) Section 116 of the Taxation of Chargeable Gains Act 1992 (reorganisations etc involving qualifying corporate bonds) shall have effect in relation to any disposal of the whole or part of the new asset on or after 15th February 1999 as if—

(*a*) there had been a transaction (''the subsequent transaction'') by which the person holding the new asset had disposed of it and immediately re-acquired it;

(*b*) the subsequent transaction had occurred at the time mentioned in subsection (3) below;

(*c*) the asset re-acquired had been a qualifying corporate bond; and

(*d*) the subsequent transaction had been a transaction to which section 127 of that Act would have applied but for section 116(5) of that Act.

(3) That time is—

(*a*) where the relevant transaction took place before 5th April 1996, that date;

(*b*) where the relevant transaction took place on or after that date, immediately after the relevant transaction.

Commentary—*Simon's Direct Tax Service* **C2.802.**

67 Deep discount and deep gain securities

(1), (2) (*Insert* FA 1996 Sch 15 paras 19(3A), 20(2A)).

(3) (*Substitutes* FA 1996 Sch 15 para 19(7)(*b*)).

(4), (5) (*Amend* FA 1993 ss 64(5)(*c*), 65(5)(*c*) and *insert* s 65(5A)).

(6) Subsections (1) and (2) above apply in relation to income treated as arising on or after 15th February 1999.

(7) Subsection (3) above applies in any case where the day mentioned in paragraph 19(9) of Schedule 15 to the Finance Act 1996 falls on or after 15th February 1999.

(8) Subsections (4) and (5) above apply for determining whether a time on or after 15th February 1999—

(*a*) is a time falling within section 64(5)(*c*) of the Finance Act 1993; or

(*b*) is on a day falling within section 65(5)(*c*) of that Act.

Commentary—*Simon's Direct Tax Service* **B3.1958, 1959.**

68 Court common investment funds

(1) (*Inserts* TA 1988 s 469A).

(2) (*Repeals* TA 1988 s 328).

(3) Subsections (1) and (2) above have effect in relation to—

(*a*) any income arising to a common investment fund on or after 6th April 1999; and

(*b*) any distribution made by such a fund for a distribution period beginning on or after that date.

(4) For the purposes of the Tax Acts where any common investment fund was in existence on 5th April 1999—

(*a*) the distribution period of that fund which was current on that date for the purposes of section 469 of the Taxes Act 1988 shall be taken to have ended with that date; and

(*b*) the fund's first accounting period for the purposes of corporation tax, and its first distribution period for the purposes of the enactments relating to authorised unit trusts, shall each be taken to have begun with 6th April 1999.

(5) In this section ''common investment fund'' means any common investment fund established under section 42 of the Administration of Justice Act 1982.

Commentary—*Simon's Direct Tax Service* **D4.414, 420.**

Venture capital trusts

69 Company restructuring and convertible securities

(1) The Taxes Act 1988 shall be amended as follows.

(2) (*Inserts* Sch 28B paras 10C, 10D).

(3) (*Amends* Sch 28B para 13(1)).

(4) (*Insert* s 842AA(5AA)–(5AC)).

(5) This section—

(*a*) shall have effect in relation to any arrangements made, and rights of conversion exercised, on or after 16th June 1999; and

(*b*) shall be deemed to have come into force on that date.

Commentary—*Simon's Direct Tax Service* **E3.620.**

70 Relief on distributions

(1) (*Inserts* TA 1988 Sch 15B para 7(3)(*a*)(*ia*)).

(2) This section applies in relation to shares acquired on or after 9th March 1999.

Commentary—*Simon's Direct Tax Service* E3.643.

Enterprise investment scheme

71 Eligibility for EIS relief

(1) (*Substitutes* TA 1988 s 289(1A)(*a*) and *amend* s 289(1A)(*b*)).

(2) This section applies in relation to shares issued on or after 6th April 1999.

Commentary—*Simon's Direct Tax Service* E3.115.

72 Deferred gains: application of taper relief

(1) (*Inserts* TCGA 1992 s 150D).

(2) Schedule 7 to this Act (which inserts Schedule 5BA into that Act) shall have effect.

(3) In consequence of the insertion of Schedule 5BA, in that Act—

(*a*) in section 2A(8) (qualifying holding period for taper relief), after "that Schedule" insert "and paragraph 3 of Schedule 5BA"; and

(*b*) in paragraph 2(4) of Schedule A1 (effect of periods not counting for taper relief purposes), after "paragraphs 10 to 12 below" insert "or paragraph 4 of Schedule 5BA".

Commentary—*Simon's Direct Tax Service* E3.145.

73 Deferred gains: gain accruing on part disposal, etc

(1) Schedule 8 to this Act (which amends Schedule 5B to the Taxation of Chargeable Gains Act 1992 in relation to cases where there is a disposal of some, but not all, of the shares to which relief under that Schedule is attributable) shall have effect.

(2) The amendments made by Schedule 8 to this Act have effect in relation to shares issued on or after 6th April 1999.

Commentary—*Simon's Direct Tax Service* E3.145.

Chargeable gains

74 Value shifting: tax-free benefits

Schedule 9 to this Act (which makes provision about tax-free benefits in relation to value shifting) shall have effect.

Commentary—*Simon's Direct Tax Service* D2.669.

75 Allowable losses where beneficiary absolutely entitled

(1) (*Substitutes* TCGA 1992, s 71(2)–(2D) for original s 71(2)).

(2) This section applies in relation to any occasion on or after 16th June 1999 on which a person becomes absolutely entitled to settled property as against the trustee.

Commentary—*Simon's Direct Tax Service* C4.229.

76 Concessions that defer a capital gains charge

(1) (*Inserts* TCGA 1992 ss 284A, 284B).

(2) Sections 284A and 284B of the Taxation of Chargeable Gains Act 1992 have effect in relation to any case in which the circumstances arising as mentioned in subsection (6)(*a*) of section 284A are circumstances arising on or after 9th March 1999, whether the benefit mentioned in subsection (1) of that section was obtained as so mentioned before or after the passing of this Act.

Commentary—*Simon's Direct Tax Service* C3.306.

Capital allowances

77 Extension of first-year allowances

Commentary—*Simon's Direct Tax Service* B2.324.
Amendment—This section repealed by the Capital Allowances Act 2001 s 580, Sch 4 with effect for income tax purposes, as respects allowances and charges falling to be made for chargeable periods ending after 5 April 2001, and for corporation tax purposes, as respects allowances and charges falling to be made for chargeable periods ending after 31 March 2001.

78 First-year allowances for investment in Northern Ireland

Commentary—*Simon's Direct Tax Service* B2.324.

Amendment—This section repealed by the Capital Allowances Act 2001 s 580, Sch 4 with effect for income tax purposes, as respects allowances and charges falling to be made for chargeable periods ending after 5 April 2001, and for corporation tax purposes, as respects allowances and charges falling to be made for chargeable periods ending after 31 March 2001.

Pensions and insurance, etc

79 Sharing of pensions on divorce, etc

Schedule 10 to this Act (which, for purposes connected with the sharing of pensions between ex-spouses, makes provision with respect to pensions and annuities) shall have effect.

Commentary—*Simon's Direct Tax Service* E7.101, 201.

80 Purchased life annuities

(*Insert* TA 1988 s 657(2)(*da*)).

Commentary—*Simon's Direct Tax Service* E7.221.

81 Acquisitions disregarded under insurance companies concession

(1) This section applies for the purposes of corporation tax in relation to the disposal by a company (''the relevant company'') of any asset where—

    (*a*) the asset is one acquired by the relevant company from an insurance company at a time when the relevant company and that insurance company were both members of the same group of companies;

    (*b*) there was an occasion before the disposal (whether the occasion of the transfer of the asset to the relevant company or the occasion of an earlier transfer of the asset) in relation to which the non-statutory arrangements for groups of insurance companies were applied in the case of the transferring company;

    (*c*) the application of those arrangements in relation to that occasion had the effect of preventing the cost of the asset's acquisition by the transferring company (''the previous acquisition'') from being brought into account for tax purposes; and

    (*d*) there has not, between that occasion and the making of the disposal, been any relevant event by reference to which the cost of the previous acquisition has been brought into account in computing the profits or losses of any company for tax purposes.

(2) Subject to subsection (5) below, where the computation of the relevant company's profits or losses from any trade requires the cost of the acquisition of the asset by that company to be brought into account in the accounting period in which the disposal takes place, that cost shall be brought into account in that period as if it were an amount equal to the cost of the previous acquisition.

(3) Subject to subsections (4) and (5) below, where—

    (*a*) the asset disposed of represents a creditor relationship,

    (*b*) the disposal is such that paragraph 6 of Schedule 15 to the Finance Act 1996 (adjustment for pre-commencement trading relationships) would require an amount to be brought into account in the accounting period in which the disposal takes place in any case in which there is, for that relationship, a difference such as is mentioned in sub-paragraph (1) of that paragraph, and

    (*c*) the cost of the previous acquisition is less than the amount which for the purposes of paragraph 5(2) of that Schedule would (apart from this subsection) be the notional closing value of the relationship on 31st March 1996,

the question whether an amount falls to be brought into account in accordance with paragraph 6(2) or (3) of that Schedule, and the amount (if any) falling to be so brought into account, shall be determined as if the notional closing value of the relationship on 31st March 1996 had been equal to the cost of the previous acquisition.

(4) In any case where the asset represents a creditor relationship in relation to which an election under paragraph 6(4) of Schedule 15 to the Finance Act 1996 has effect—

    (*a*) subsection (3) above and paragraphs (*b*) and (*c*) below shall be disregarded in determining the amounts falling to be brought into account under paragraph 6(4) to (7) of that Schedule;

    (*b*) paragraph 6(1) and (2) of that Schedule shall be treated as applying, notwithstanding paragraph 6(4)(*a*), if, in the case of that relationship, the amount referred to in subsection (3)(*c*) above exceeds the cost of the previous acquisition; and

    (*c*) the amount falling by virtue of paragraph (*b*) above to be brought into account in accordance with paragraph 6(2) of that Schedule shall be determined as if the excess referred to in paragraph 6(2)(*a*) were the excess mentioned in paragraph (*b*) above.

(5) Where—

    (*a*) there are two or more occasions such as are mentioned in paragraph (*b*) of subsection (1) above, and

    (*b*) paragraph (*d*) of that subsection is satisfied in relation to each of them,

subsections (2) to (4) above shall have effect as if the references to the previous acquisition were references to the acquisition which is the previous acquisition in relation to the earliest of those occasions.

(6) In subsection (1)(*d*) above "relevant event", in relation to any asset, means—

   (*a*) a disposal of the asset; or

   (*b*) any event by reference to which the conditions of the non-statutory arrangements for groups of insurance companies has required the cost of the previous acquisition to be brought into account in computing the profits or losses of any company for tax purposes.

(7) Section 170 of the Taxation of Chargeable Gains Act 1992 (meaning of groups etc) shall apply for construing references in the preceding provisions of this section to a group of companies as it applies for the purposes of sections 171 to 181 of that Act.

(8) In the preceding provisions of this section—

"creditor relationship" has the same meaning as in Chapter II of Part IV of the Finance Act 1996; and

"insurance company" means an insurance company within the meaning of Chapter I of Part XII of the Taxes Act 1988.

(9) References in this section to an asset shall be construed as if section 473 of the Taxes Act 1988 (cases where different assets are treated as the same) applied for the purposes of this section as it applies for the purposes of that Act; and paragraph 12(2) of Schedule 9 to the Finance Act 1996 (cases where different companies are treated as the same) shall apply for the purposes of this section as it applies for the purposes of Chapter II of Part IV of that Act of 1996.

(10) In this section any reference to the non-statutory arrangements for groups of insurance companies is a reference to so much of any arrangements made by the Board otherwise than by virtue of an enactment as—

   (*a*) in relation to an accounting period beginning before 1st January 2000—

      (i) provided for a single assessment of the trading profits of a group of insurance companies to be made on the principal company of the group; and

      (ii) excluded trading profits on intra-group transfers of investments from the group assessment; or

   (*b*) contains transitional provision, in connection with the withdrawal of any arrangements falling within paragraph (*a*) above, for allowing trading profits on intra-group transfers to be excluded from assessments of members of groups of insurance companies that relate to accounting periods beginning on or after 1st January 1999 and before 1st January 2000.

(11) This section—

   (*a*) shall not be construed as requiring any amount representing a gain on the disposal of the asset to be brought into account for tax purposes in so far as an amount representing that gain is or has already been brought into account, as an attributed gain, under any regulations made by virtue of Schedule 16 to the Finance Act 1993 (Forex transitional provisions); and

   (*b*) shall be without prejudice to any power of the Board apart from this section to enforce any conditions subject to which any relief in accordance with the non-statutory arrangements for groups of insurance companies has been allowed.

(12) This section applies in relation to disposals by the relevant company made in accounting periods beginning on or after 1st January 1999.

[(13) If the relevant company changes from—

   (*a*) not recognising a profit or loss on an asset until it is realised, to

   (*b*) bringing assets into account in each period of account at a fair value,

then, in calculating the amount of any adjustment required under Schedule 22 to the Finance Act 2002 (calculation of adjustment on change of basis), the amount to be taken into account as the cost of the asset in relation to a period of account before the change is the cost of the previous acquisition.]¹

Commentary—*Simon's Direct Tax Service* **D4.532.**
Cross references—FA 2002 Sch 22 Pt 5 (commencement provisions).
Amendments—¹ Sub-s (13) inserted by FA 2002 s 67(3), (4)(b) with effect wherever an adjustment falls to be made under FA 2002 Sch 22.

82 Lloyd's: members' agent pooling arrangements

(1) This section applies where a member has entered into a members' agent pooling arrangement ("the arrangement").

(2) Subsections (3) to (9) below shall apply for the purpose of determining any liability of the member's to capital gains tax that may arise from transactions effected in pursuance of the arrangement.

(3) The syndicate rights held by the member under the arrangement shall be treated as a single asset acquired by him at the time when he entered into the arrangement; but, subject to subsection (9) below, he shall not be treated as disposing of the asset (in whole or in part) except as mentioned in subsection (6) below.

(4) The member shall be treated as having given, wholly and exclusively for the acquisition of the asset, consideration equal to any amount paid by him on entering into the arrangement.

(5) Any other amount paid by the member under the arrangement shall, on a disposal of the asset, be treated as expenditure incurred wholly and exclusively on the asset for the purpose of enhancing its value and reflected in its state or nature at the time of the disposal.

(6) If an amount is paid to the member at any time under the arrangement, he shall be treated as disposing of the whole asset or, as the case may be, part of the asset at that time for a consideration equal to that amount.

(7) If syndicate rights held by the member otherwise than under the arrangement become at any time rights held by him under the arrangement, he shall be treated as disposing of those rights at that time for a consideration equal to their market value at that time.

(8) If syndicate rights held by the member under the arrangement become at any time rights held by him otherwise than under the arrangement, he shall be treated as acquiring those rights at that time for a consideration equal to their market value at that time.

(9) Nothing in subsection (3) above shall affect the operation of section 24(1) of the Taxation of Chargeable Gains Act 1992 (disposals where assets extinguished etc) in relation to the asset.

(10) Subject to subsection (11) below this section applies to arrangements entered into on or after 6th April 1999 or subsisting on that date.

(11) In the case of arrangements subsisting on 6th April 1999, this section has effect—

(*a*) as if the time mentioned in subsection (3) above were the earliest time (''the notional time of acquisition'') at which the member acquired any of the syndicate rights held by him under the arrangement immediately before 6th April 1999;
(*b*) as if the consideration referred to in subsection (4) above were the consideration, in money or money's worth, given by him wholly and exclusively for the acquisition of such of those rights as he acquired at the notional time of acquisition; and
(*c*) in relation to times before 6th April 1999, as if the amount mentioned in subsection (5) above were the amount of any consideration, in money or money's worth, given by him wholly and exclusively for the acquisition, after the notional time of acquisition, of rights such as are mentioned in paragraph (*a*) above;

and the incidental costs of any acquisition falling within paragraph (*b*) or (*c*) above shall be taken to be incidental costs of the acquisition of the asset.

Commentary—*Simon's Direct Tax Service* **E5.632.**
Definitions—''member'', s 83(1); ''members' agent'', s 83(1); ''members' agent pooling arrangement'', s 83(1); ''syndicate'', s 83(1); ''syndicate rights'', s 83(1).

83 Provisions supplementary to s 82

(1) In section 82 above and this section, except where the context otherwise requires—

''member'' means an individual who is an underwriting member of Lloyd's;
''members' agent'', in relation to a member, means a person registered as a members' agent at Lloyd's who is acting as such an agent for the member;
''members' agent pooling arrangement'', in relation to a member, means an arrangement—

(i) under which a members' agent arranges for the member's participation in syndicates; and
(ii) which satisfies the conditions set out in subsection (2) below;

''syndicate'' has the same meaning as in Chapter III of Part II of the Finance Act 1993; and
''syndicate rights'', in relation to a member, means rights under a syndicate in which the member participates.

(2) The conditions mentioned in paragraph (ii) of the above definition of ''members' agent pooling arrangement'' are that under the arrangement—

(*a*) the member must participate in each of the syndicates to which the arrangement relates; and
(*b*) the extent to which the member participates in each such syndicate is determined—

(i) by the members' agent; or
(ii) according to a formula provided for in the arrangement.

(3) References in section 82 above to the payment of an amount are references to the payment of an amount in money or money's worth; and to the extent that an amount mentioned in subsection (4), (5) or (6) of that section is paid in money's worth, the amount of the consideration or expenditure there referred to shall be calculated by reference to the market value of the money's worth at the time of the payment mentioned in that subsection.

(4) Section 82 above and this section have effect in relation to a Scottish partnership which is an underwriting member of Lloyd's as they have effect in relation to a member, but as if the reference in section 82(2) to any liability of the member's to capital gains tax that may arise from transactions effected in pursuance of the arrangement were a reference to any such liability of members of the partnership that may so arise.

Commentary—*Simon's Direct Tax Service* **E5.632.**

84 Lloyd's: roll-over relief

(1) (*Inserts* TCGA 1992 s 155 Class 8).

(2) This section applies to—

    (*a*) assets (or interests in them) disposed of on or after 6th April 1999;

    (*b*) assets (or interests in them) acquired on or after that date.

Commentary—*Simon's Direct Tax Service* **C3.303.**

Advance pricing agreements and CFCs

85 Advance pricing agreements etc

(1) This section applies in relation to any chargeable period where—

    (*a*) the Board have made a written agreement with any person ("the taxpayer");

    (*b*) the agreement relates to one or more of the matters mentioned in subsection (2) below and to that chargeable period;

    (*c*) the agreement is one made as a consequence of an application by the taxpayer to the Board for the clarification by agreement of the effect in the taxpayer's case of provisions by reference to which questions relating to any one or more of those matters fall, or might fall, to be determined; and

    (*d*) the agreement contains a declaration that it is an agreement made for the purposes of this section.

(2) Those matters are—

    (*a*) the attribution of income to a branch or agency through which the taxpayer has been carrying on a trade in the United Kingdom, or is proposing so to carry on a trade;

    (*b*) the attribution of income to any permanent establishment of the taxpayer (wherever situated) through which he has been carrying on, or is proposing to carry on, any business;

    (*c*) the extent to which income which has arisen or may arise to the taxpayer is to be taken for any purpose to be income arising in a country or territory outside the United Kingdom;

    (*d*) the treatment for tax purposes of any provision made or imposed (whether before or after the date of the agreement) as between the taxpayer and any associate of his;

    (*e*) the treatment for tax purposes of any provision made or imposed (whether before or after the date of the agreement) as between a ring fence trade carried on by the taxpayer and any other activities so carried on.

(3) Subject to the following provisions of this section and to section 86 below, the Tax Acts shall have effect in the taxpayer's case as if questions relating to the matters mentioned in subsection (2) above were, to the extent provided for in the agreement, to be determined in accordance with the agreement, and without reference to the provisions in accordance with which they would otherwise have fallen to be determined.

(4) In the case of so much of any question as—

    (*a*) relates to any matter mentioned in paragraph (*d*) or (*e*) of subsection (2) above, and

    (*b*) is not comprised in a question falling within another paragraph of that subsection,

the provisions reference to which is capable of being excluded under subsection (3) above by an agreement made for the purposes of this section shall be confined to those contained in Schedule 28AA to the Taxes Act 1988 (transfer pricing rules).

(5) Any such application to the Board as is mentioned in subsection (1)(*c*) above must set out—

    (*a*) the taxpayer's understanding of what would, in his case, be the effect, in the absence of any agreement, of the provisions in relation to which clarification is sought;

    (*b*) the respects in which it appears to the taxpayer that clarification is required in relation to those provisions; and

    (*c*) how the taxpayer proposes that matters should be clarified in a manner consistent with the understanding mentioned in paragraph (*a*) above.

(6) For the purposes of this section two persons are associates, in relation to provision made or imposed as between them if, within the meaning of Schedule 28AA to the Taxes Act 1988—

    (*a*) one of them is directly or indirectly participating, at the time of the making or imposition of the provision, in the management, control or capital of the other; or

    (*b*) the same person or persons is or are, at that time, directly or indirectly participating in the management, control or capital of each of the two persons;

and, in the case of provision made or imposed by or in relation to the terms of any sale of oil (within the meaning of paragraph 9 of that Schedule), two persons shall also be treated as associates for the purposes of this section wherever sub-paragraph (2) of that paragraph would require them for the purposes of that Schedule to be treated in relation to that provision as falling within paragraph (*b*) above.

(7) In this section "ring fence trade", in relation to the taxpayer, means any activities which—

    (*a*) are carried on by the taxpayer as, or as part of, a trade; and (*b*) in accordance with section 492(1) of the Taxes Act 1988 (tax treatment of oil extraction activities), either—

     (i) fall to be treated for tax purposes as a separate trade, distinct from all other activities carried on by the taxpayer; or

     (ii) would so fall if the taxpayer did carry on any other activities as part of that trade.

(8) This section applies in relation to any chargeable period ending on or after the day on which this Act is passed but only if the agreement is one made on or after that day and in relation to that period.

Commentary—*Simon's Direct Tax Service* **B3.1851.**
Statement of Practice SP 3/99—Guidance on administration of advance pricing agreements and on how businesses may reach advance agreement with the Revenue about transfer pricing issues in accordance with FA 1999 ss 85–87.

86 Provisions supplementary to s 85

(1) The chargeable periods in relation to which provision may be made by a section 85 agreement include periods ending before the making of the agreement.

(2) An agreement shall not have effect in accordance with section 85(3) above in relation to any determination of a question which—

     (*a*) relates to a time after a time as from which an officer of the Board has revoked the agreement in accordance with its terms;

     (*b*) relates to a time after or in relation to which there has been a failure by a party to the agreement to comply with any provision of the agreement compliance with which is, under the terms of the agreement, to be a condition of its having effect; or

     (*c*) relates to any matter as respects which any other conditions which, by the terms of the agreement, are to be conditions of its having effect have not been, or are no longer, satisfied.

(3) Where—

     (*a*) there is a section 85 agreement between the Board and any person, and

     (*b*) there is a mutual agreement made under and for the purposes of any double taxation arrangements which is not consistent with the terms of the section 85 agreement,

it shall be the duty of the Board to ensure that all such modifications of the section 85 agreement are made (whether in exercise of powers conferred on the Board by that agreement or otherwise) as may be necessary for enabling effect to be given to the mutual agreement in relation to the subject-matter of the section 85 agreement.

(4) It shall be the duty of any person who is a party to a section 85 agreement to provide the Board from time to time with all such reports and other information as he may be required to provide under the agreement or by virtue of any request made by an officer of the Board in accordance with the terms of the agreement.

(5) Where—

     (*a*) the Board and any person have purported to enter into a section 85 agreement at any time,

     (*b*) before that time, that person fraudulently or negligently provided the Board with information which was false or misleading,

     (*c*) that information was so provided for or in connection with the application to the Board for the making of the agreement or otherwise in connection with its preparation, and

     (*d*) the Board have notified that person that the agreement is nullified by reason of the misrepresentation,

the agreement shall be deemed never to have been made.

(6) Any provision of a section 85 agreement that provides for the modification or revocation of that agreement by the Board, or by an officer of the Board, may provide for the modification or revocation to take effect as from such time (including a time before the modification is made or the agreement revoked) as the Board or officer may determine.

(7) Where a section 85 agreement—

     (*a*) relates to a chargeable period beginning or ending before the making of the agreement, and

     (*b*) provides for the manner in which adjustments are to be made for tax purposes in consequence of that agreement,

the adjustments shall be made for those purposes in the manner provided for in the agreement.

(8) A person shall be liable to a penalty not exceeding £10,000 if he fraudulently or negligently makes any false or misleading statement to the Board or an officer of the Board either—

     (*a*) for or in connection with any application to the Board for them to enter into a section 85 agreement; or

     (*b*) otherwise in connection with the preparation of such an agreement.

(9) (*Amends* TMA 1970 s 98).

(10) In this section—

     ''double taxation arrangements'' means any arrangements having effect under or by virtue of section 788 of the Taxes Act 1988 (double taxation agreements); and

     ''section 85 agreement'' means an agreement made for the purposes of section 85 above.

Commentary—*Simon's Direct Tax Service* **B3.1851.**
Statement of Practice SP 3/99—Guidance on administration of advance pricing agreements and on how businesses may reach advance agreement with the Revenue about transfer pricing issues in accordance with FA 1999 ss 85–87.

87 Effect of section 85 agreements on non-parties

(1) This section applies where—

(*a*) any agreement made for the purposes of section 85 above has effect in relation to any provision (''the actual provision'') made or imposed as between any person (''the taxpayer'') and another (''the other party''); and

(*b*) section 85(3) above has the effect in the taxpayer's case of requiring a question relating to the actual provision to be determined in accordance with the agreement rather than by reference to rules which would otherwise be applicable by virtue of Schedule 28AA to the Taxes Act 1988.

(2) Paragraphs 6 and 7 of Schedule 28AA to the Taxes Act 1988 (relief from double counting in the case of disadvantaged persons) shall have effect in the other party's case on the assumption that any question falling within subsection (3) below is to be determined, to the same extent as in the taxpayer's case, by reference to the agreement.

(3) Those questions are—

(*a*) whether the taxpayer is a person on whom a potential advantage in relation to United Kingdom taxation is conferred by the actual provision; and

(*b*) what constitutes the arm's length provision in relation to the actual provision.

(4) Subsection (2) above shall have effect subject to any agreement made for the purposes of section 85 above between the Board and the other party.

(5) Section 111 of the Finance Act 1998 (notice to persons who may be entitled to claim as disadvantaged persons) shall have effect as if the assumptions referred to in subsection (1)(*b*) of that section included any assumptions falling to be made by virtue of the agreement.

Statement of Practice SP 3/99—Guidance on administration of advance pricing agreements and on how businesses may reach advance agreement with the Revenue about transfer pricing issues in accordance with FA 1999 ss 85–87.

88 Controlled foreign companies

(1) (*Inserts* TA 1988 Sch 25 para 2(1B)).

(2) Subsection (1) above applies for the purpose of determining whether dividends paid on or after 9th March 1999 for accounting periods ending on or after that date fall within sub-paragraph (1)(*d*) of paragraph 2 of that Schedule.

Commentary—*Simon's Direct Tax Service* **D4.1220.**

Management and enforcement

89 Corporation tax: due and payable date

(1) (*Amends* TMA 1970 s 98).

(2) (*Amends* FA 1989 s 102(5)(*a*)).

(3) This section has effect in relation to accounting periods ending on or after 1st July 1999.

Commentary—*Simon's Direct Tax Service* **D2.841, 846.**

90 Release or writing off of debt: interest on tax overpaid

(1) (*Amends* TA 1988 s 826(4)).

(2) This section has effect in relation to the release or writing off of the whole or part of a debt on or after 6th April 1999.

Commentary—*Simon's Direct Tax Service* **D2.708, 845.**

91 Advance corporation tax: consequences of abolition

(1) Schedule 16 to the Taxes Act 1988 (collection of income tax on company payments) is amended as follows.

(2), (3) (*Amend* TA 1988 Sch 16 paras 4, 8)).

(4) (*Amends* FA 1998 s 32(6)).

(5) Subsections (1) to (3) above have effect—

(*a*) in relation to periods for which a return is required under paragraph 2 of Schedule 16 to the Taxes Act 1988 beginning on or after 6th April 1999; and

(*b*) in relation to accounting periods beginning on or after that date.

(6) The amendment made by subsection (4) above shall be deemed always to have had effect.

Commentary—*Simon's Direct Tax Service* **D1.615.**

92 Group relief: consequences of reduction in surrenderable amount

(1) Part VIII of Schedule 18 to the Finance Act 1998 (claims for group relief) is amended as follows.

(2)–(4) (*Amend* FA 1998 Sch 18 para 75 and *add* ss 75A, 76(3)).

(5) (*Amends* TMA 1970 s 87A(3)).

(6) (*Repeals* FA 1990 s 96).

(7) This section has effect in relation to accounting periods ending on or after 1st July 1999.

Commentary—*Simon's Direct Tax Service* **D2.630.**

93 Company tax returns, etc

(1) The enactments mentioned in Schedule 11 to this Act have effect with the amendments specified there, which are minor amendments and amendments consequential on Schedule 18 to the Finance Act 1998 (company tax returns, assessments and claims, etc).

(2) The amendments made by Schedule 11 to this Act have effect in relation to accounting periods ending on or after 1st July 1999.

Commentary—*Simon's Direct Tax Service* **D2.801.**

PART VIII
MISCELLANEOUS AND SUPPLEMENTAL
General administration of tax

131 Economic and monetary union: taxes and duties

The Commissioners of Inland Revenue and the Commissioners of Customs and Excise may incur expenditure in order to secure that, if the United Kingdom were to move to the third stage of economic and monetary union, they would be able to exercise their functions relating to taxes and duties (including agricultural levies of the European Community).

132 Power to provide for use of electronic communications

(1) Regulations may be made, in accordance with this section, for facilitating the use of electronic communications for—

(a) the delivery of information the delivery of which is authorised or required by or under any legislation relating to a taxation matter;

(b) the making of payments under any such legislation.

(2) The power to make regulations under this section is conferred—

(a) on the Commissioners of Inland Revenue in relation to matters which are under their care and management; and

(b) on the Commissioners of Customs and Excise in relation to matters which are under their care and management.

(3) For the purposes of this section provision for facilitating the use of electronic communications includes any of the following—

(a) provision authorising persons to use electronic communications for the delivery of information to tax authorities, or for the making of payments to tax authorities;

(b) provision requiring electronic communications to be used for the making to tax authorities of payments due from persons using such communications for the delivery of information to those authorities;

(c) provision authorising tax authorities to use electronic communications for the delivery of information to other persons or for the making of any payments;

(d) provision as to the electronic form to be taken by any information that is delivered to any tax authorities using electronic communications;

(e) provision requiring persons to prepare and keep records of information delivered to tax authorities by means of electronic communications, and of payments made to any such authorities by any such means;

(f) provision for the production of the contents of records kept in accordance with any regulations under this section;

(g) provision imposing conditions that must be complied with in connection with any use of electronic communications for the delivery of information or the making of any payment;

(h) provision, in relation to cases where use is made of electronic communications, for treating information as not having been delivered, or a payment as not having been made, unless conditions imposed by any such regulations are satisfied;

(i) provision, in relation to such cases, for determining the time when information is delivered or a payment is made;

(j) provision, in relation to such cases, for determining the person by whom information is to be taken to have been delivered or by whom a payment is to be taken to have been made;

(*k*) provision, in relation to cases where information is delivered by means of electronic communications, for authenticating whatever is delivered.

(4) The power to make provision under this section for facilitating the use of electronic communications shall also include power to such provision as the persons exercising the power think fit (including provision for the application of conclusive or other presumptions) as to the manner of proving for any purpose—

(*a*) whether any use of electronic communications is to be taken as having resulted in the delivery of information or the making of a payment;

(*b*) the time of delivery of any information for the delivery of which electronic communications have been used;

(*c*) the time of the making of any payment for the making of which electronic communications have been used;

(*d*) the person by whom information delivered by means of electronic communications was delivered;

(*e*) the contents of anything so delivered;

(*f*) the contents of any records;

(*g*) any other matter for which provision may be made by regulations under this section.

(5) Regulations under this section may—

(*a*) allow any authorisation or requirement for which such regulations may provide to be given or imposed by means of a specific or general direction given by the Commissioners of Inland Revenue or the Commissioners of Customs and Excise;

(*b*) provide that the conditions of any such authorisation or requirement are to be taken to be satisfied only where such tax authorities as may be determined under the regulations are satisfied as to specified matters;

(*c*) allow a person to refuse to accept delivery of information in an electronic form or by means of electronic communications except in such circumstances as may be specified in or determined under the regulations;

(*d*) allow or require use to be made of intermediaries in connection with—

(i) the delivery of information, or the making of payments, by means of electronic communications; or

(ii) the authentication or security of anything transmitted by any such means.

(6) Power to make provision by regulations under this section shall include power—

(*a*) to provide for a contravention of, or any failure to comply with, a specified provision of any such regulations to attract a penalty of a specified amount not exceeding £1,000;

(*b*) to provide that specified enactments relating to penalties imposed for the purposes of any taxation matter (including enactments relating to assessments, review and appeal) are to apply, with or without modifications, in relation to penalties under such regulations;

(*c*) to make different provision for different cases;

(*d*) to make such incidental, supplemental, consequential and transitional provision in connection with any provision contained in any such regulations as the persons exercising the power think fit.

(7) The power to make regulations under this section shall be exercisable by statutory instrument subject to annulment in pursuance of a resolution of the House of Commons.

(8) References in this section to the delivery of information include references to any of the following (however referred to)—

(*a*) the production or furnishing to a person of any information, account, record or document;

(*b*) the giving, making, issue or surrender to, or service on, any person of any notice, notification, statement, declaration, certificate or direction;

(*c*) the imposition on any person of any requirement or the issue to any person of any request;

(*d*) the making of any return, claim, election or application;

(*e*) the amendment or withdrawal of anything mentioned in paragraphs (*a*) to (*d*) above.

(9) References in this section to a taxation matter are references to any of the matters which are under the care and management of the Commissioners of Inland Revenue or of the Commissioners of Customs and Excise.

(10) In this section—

"electronic communications" includes any communications by means of a telecommunication system (within the meaning of the Telecommunications Act 1984);

"legislation" means any enactment, Community legislation or subordinate legislation;

"payment" includes a repayment;

"records" includes records in electronic form;

"subordinate legislation" has the same meaning as in the Interpretation Act 1978;

"tax authorities" means—

(*a*) the Commissioners of Inland Revenue or the Commissioners of Customs and Excise,

(*b*) any officer of either body of Commissioners; or

(*c*) any other person who for the purposes of electronic communications is acting under the authority of either body of Commissioners.

Cross references—See Income Tax (Electronic Communications) Regulations, SI 2000/945 (delivery by electronic means of information in respect of income tax assessments).
FA 2000 Sch 38 para 1(1) (regulations may be made in accordance with FA 2000 Sch 38 for providing incentives to use electronic communications the purposes of mention in sub-s (1) above).

133 Use of electronic communications under other provisions

(1) Without prejudice to section 132 above, where any power to make subordinate legislation for or in connection with the delivery of information or the making of payments is conferred in relation to any taxation matter on—

(*a*) the Commissioners of Inland Revenue,
(*b*) the Commissioners of Customs and Excise, or
(*c*) the Treasury,

that power shall be taken (to the extent that it would not otherwise be so taken) to include power to make any such provision in relation to the delivery of that information or the making of those payments as could be made by any person by regulations in exercise of a power conferred by that section.

(2) Provision made in exercise of the powers conferred by section 132 above or subsection (1) above shall have effect notwithstanding so much of any enactment or subordinate legislation as (apart from the provision so made) would require—

(*a*) any information to be delivered, or
(*b*) any amount to be paid,

in a form or manner that would preclude the use of electronic communications for its delivery or payment, or the use in connection with its delivery or payment of an intermediary.

(3) Schedule 3A to the Taxes Management Act 1970 (electronic lodgment of tax returns etc) shall cease to have effect.

(4) Subsection (3) above shall come into force on such day as the Treasury may by order made by statutory instrument appoint; and different days may be appointed under this subsection for different purposes.

(5) Expressions used in this section and section 132 above have the same meanings in this section as in that section.

Cross references—See Income Tax (Electronic Communications) Regulations, SI 2000/945 (delivery by electronic means of information in respect of income tax assessments).

Supplemental

138 Interpretation

In this Act "the Taxes Act 1988" means the Income and Corporation Taxes Act 1988.

139 Repeals

(1) The enactments mentioned in Schedule 20 to this Act (which include provisions that are spent or of no practical utility) are hereby repealed to the extent specified in the third column of that Schedule.

(2) The repeals specified in that Schedule have effect subject to the commencement provisions and savings contained or referred to in the notes set out in that Schedule.

140 Short title

This Act may be cited as the Finance Act 1999.

SCHEDULES

SCHEDULE 3

NEW SCHEDULE 13B TO THE TAXES ACT 1988

Section 30

Commentary—*Simon's Direct Tax Service* E2.502.

The Schedule inserted after Schedule 13A to the Taxes Act 1988 is as follows—

"SCHEDULE 13B

CHILDREN'S TAX CREDIT

Child living with more than one adult: married and unmarried couples

1—(1) Paragraphs 2 to 5 below apply where at any time in a year of assessment—

(*a*) a husband and wife are living together or a man and a woman are living together as husband and wife, and

(*b*) a relevant child is resident with them.

(2) In those paragraphs—

(*a*) the husband and wife, or the man and the woman, are referred to as the partners,

(*b*) 'the higher-earning partner' means the partner who has the higher total income for the year of assessment,

(*c*) 'the lower-earning partner' means the partner who has the lower total income for the year of assessment, and

(*d*) 'relevant child' means a child who is a qualifying child in relation to both partners.

(3) If the partners have the same total income for the year—

(*a*) they may elect that one of them be treated for the purposes of paragraphs 2 to 5 below as the lower-earning partner, and

(*b*) if they do not make an election, neither shall be entitled to a children's tax credit for the year in respect of a relevant child.

2 Subject to paragraph 3 below, the lower-earning partner shall not be entitled to a children's tax credit for the year in respect of a relevant child.

3—(1) This paragraph applies if no part of either partner's income for the year falls within section 1(2)(*b*).

(2) If the lower-earning partner makes a claim for a children's tax credit for the year in respect of a relevant child—

(*a*) paragraph 2 above shall not apply, and

(*b*) in calculating the credit for each partner, the amount mentioned in section 257AA(2) shall be halved.

(3) If the partners make an election under this sub-paragraph—

(*a*) paragraph 2 above shall not apply, and

(*b*) the higher-earning partner shall not be entitled to a children's tax credit for the year in respect of a relevant child.

4—(1) This paragraph applies where—

(*a*) a partner is entitled to a children's tax credit for a year of assessment,

(*b*) the amount by reference to which his credit falls to be calculated (Amount A) exceeds the amount which would be necessary, in accordance with section 256(2), to reduce his liability for the year to income tax on his total income to nil (Amount B), and

(*c*) he gives notice to an officer of the Board under this paragraph.

(2) Where the other partner would not, by virtue of paragraph 2 or 3 above, be entitled to a children's tax credit for the year in respect of a relevant child—

(*a*) he shall be entitled to a children's tax credit in respect of a relevant child notwithstanding that paragraph, and

(*b*) the amount by reference to which his credit shall be calculated shall be the amount of the difference between Amount A and Amount B.

(3) In any other case, the difference between Amount A and Amount B shall be added to the amount by reference to which children's tax credit would otherwise be calculated for the other partner in respect of a relevant child.

(4) A notice under this paragraph—

(*a*) must be given on or before the fifth anniversary of the 31st January next following the end of the year of assessment to which it relates,

(*b*) shall be in such form as the Board may determine, and

(*c*) shall be irrevocable.

5—(1) This paragraph applies to elections under paragraph 3 above.

(2) An election—

(*a*) shall be made by giving notice to an officer of the Board in such form as the Board may determine, and

(*b*) may be made so as to have effect for a single year of assessment or for two or more consecutive years.

(3) Subject to sub-paragraph (4) below, an election must be made before the first year of assessment for which it is to have effect and on the basis of assumptions about the partners' incomes for that year.

(4) An election may be made, on the basis of such assumptions, at a time during the first year for which it is to have effect if—

(*a*) the election is made within the first 30 days of that year and an officer of the Board has been given written notification before that year that the election will be made, or

(*b*) the partners marry in that year, or

(*c*) the partners start to live together as man and wife in that year, or

(*d*) a relevant child becomes resident with the partners in that year and no relevant child has previously in that year been resident with the partners, or

(*e*) it is assumed that the partner who was the higher-earning partner in the previous year will be the lower-earning partner in that year.

(5) An election may be withdrawn—

(*a*) by the making of another election which supersedes the first, or

(*b*) by notice given to an officer of the Board, in such form as the Board may determine, by either partner.

(6) A withdrawal shall have effect for the year of assessment in which it is given and subsequent years.

(7) If the higher-earning partner for one year of assessment (Year 1) is the lower-earning partner for the next year (Year 2), an election having effect for Year 1 shall not have effect for Year 2 or subsequent years.

Child living with more than one adult: other cases

6—(1) This paragraph applies to a child for a year of assessment if—

(*a*) he is resident with two or more persons at the same time or at different times during the year,

(*b*) he is a qualifying child in relation to two or more of those persons, and

(*c*) paragraphs 2 to 5 above do not apply in relation to him in that year.

(2) The persons in relation to whom the child is a qualifying child are referred to in this paragraph as the taxpayers.

(3) None of the taxpayers shall be entitled to a children's tax credit for the year of assessment by virtue of the residence of any child to whom this paragraph applies except in accordance with the following provisions of this paragraph.

(4) If a taxpayer claims a children's tax credit for the year of assessment by virtue of the residence of any child to whom this paragraph applies, for the amount mentioned in section 257AA(2) (before any reduction) there shall be substituted his allotted proportion of that amount.

(5) A taxpayer's allotted proportion is—

(*a*) such proportion as may be agreed between him and the other taxpayers, or

(*b*) in default of agreement, a proportion which is assigned to him by the Commissioners.

(6) For the purposes of sub-paragraph (5) above—

(*a*) a proportion may be 100 per cent,

(*b*) the sum of the proportions shall not exceed 100 per cent, and

(*c*) 'the Commissioners' means such body of General Commissioners, being the General Commissioners for a division in which one of the taxpayers resides, as the Board may direct or, if none of the taxpayers resides in the United Kingdom, the Special Commissioners.

(7) Where a person—

(*a*) is a member of more than one set of taxpayers in relation to whom this paragraph applies for a year of assessment,

(*b*) has more than one allotted proportion under this paragraph for the year, and

(*c*) claims a children's tax credit for the year,

for the amount mentioned in section 257AA(2) (before any reduction) there shall be substituted the aggregate of his allotted proportions of that amount (not exceeding 100 per cent).

(8) Where—

(*a*) a taxpayer makes a claim under section 257AA, and

(*b*) it appears that an allotted proportion will need to be assigned to him under sub-paragraph (5)(*b*) above for that purpose,

the Board may direct that the claim shall be dealt with, and the assignment shall be made, by a specified body of Commissioners which could be directed under sub-paragraph (6)(*c*) above to make the assignment; and where a direction is given no other body of Commissioners shall have jurisdiction to determine the claim.

(9) For the purposes of any assignment to a taxpayer under sub-paragraph (5)(*b*) above—

(*a*) the Commissioners shall hear and determine the case in the same manner as an appeal, and

(*b*) any of the taxpayers shall be entitled to appear and be heard by the Commissioners or to make representations to them in writing.

Combined cases

7—(1) This paragraph applies where a child is a relevant child for the purposes of paragraphs 2 to 5 above in a year of assessment and—

(a) he is a relevant child for the year in relation to more than one pair of partners, or
(b) paragraph 6 above would apply to him for the year but for the fact that he is a relevant child for the purposes of paragraphs 2 to 5 above.

(2) Where this paragraph applies—

(a) paragraph 6 above shall apply, but with each pair of partners for the purposes of paragraphs 2 to 5 above being treated as a single taxpayer, and
(b) paragraphs 2 to 5 above shall apply in relation to each pair of partners, taking for the amount mentioned in section 257AA(2) (before any reduction) the amount substituted by virtue of paragraph 6 above.

Change of circumstances

8—(1) For the purposes of this paragraph a change of circumstances occurs in relation to a child in a year of assessment if a relevant event takes place in that year and—

(a) as a result of the event the child becomes a qualifying child in relation to any person or stops being a qualifying child in relation to any person, or
(b) the child is, immediately before the event, a qualifying child in relation to both parties to the event.

(2) The following are relevant events—

(a) a marriage or a man and a woman starting to live together as husband and wife;
(b) a separation.

(3) A separation occurs when—

(a) a husband and wife cease to live together, or
(b) a man and a woman cease to live together as husband and wife, having been living together as husband and wife without being married.

(4) In a year of assessment in which a change of circumstances (or more than one) occurs in relation to a child, section 257AA and paragraphs 2 to 7 above shall apply in relation to the child's residence as if each of the following were a separate year of assessment—

(a) the period ending with the day before the first (or only) change of circumstances,
(b) the period starting with the day of the last (or only) change of circumstances, and
(c) any period starting with the day of one change of circumstances and ending with the day before the next.

(5) For the purposes of sub-paragraph (4) above the amount specified in section 257AA(2) (before any reduction or substitution) shall be taken to be the result of the following formula—

$$\frac{\text{Days during the period}}{365} \times \text{Amount in s } 257AA(2)$$

(6) In applying sub-paragraph (4) above a reference in section 257AA or this Schedule to a person's income for the year shall be taken as a reference to his income for the year and not his income for the period.''

SCHEDULE 4

WITHDRAWAL OF RELIEF FOR INTEREST ON LOANS TO BUY LAND ETC

Section 38

Commentary—*Simon's Direct Tax Service* **E1.535.**

Amendments of Part IX of the Taxes Act 1988

1—(1) Section 353 of the Taxes Act 1988 (general provision for relief for interest payments) is amended as follows.

(2)–(4) (*Amend* TA 1988 s 353(1), (1A), (1B) and *substitute* s 353(1G)).

2 (*Repeals* TA 1988 ss 354 to 358).

3—(1) Section 367 of the Taxes Act 1988 (supplementary provisions) is amended as follows.

(2)–(4) (*Repeal* s 367(1) and *amend* s 367(3)–(5)).

4 (*Substitutes* TA 1988 s 369(1A)).

5—(1) Section 370 of the Taxes Act 1988 (meaning of ''relevant loan interest'') is amended as follows.

(2)–(5) (*Amend* s 370(1), (2), (5) and *repeal* s 370(3), (4), (6), (7)).

6 (*Repeals* TA 1988 s 372).

7—(1)–(3) (*Amend* s 373(1), (5), (6), (7) and *repeal* s 373(3), (4)).

8 (*Amends* TA 1988 s 374).

9—(1), (2) (*Insert* TA 1988 s 375(8B) and *repeal* s 375(9), (10)).

10 (*Repeals* TA 1988 s 375A).

11 (*Amends* TA 1988 s 376(3) and *repeals* s 376(6)).

12 (*Repeals* TA 1988 s 377).

13 (*Repeals* TA 1988 s 378(1), (2), (4) and *amends* s 378(3)).

14 (*Amends* TA 1988 s 379).

Other amendments

15 (*Amends* TA 1988 s 488(1), (2), (4), (11A) and *repeal* s 488(12)).

16 (*Substitutes* TA 1988 s 548(3)(*a*)).

17 (*Amends* TCGA 1992 s 222(8), (9) and *insert* s 222(8A)–(8D)).

Commencement

18—(1) Paragraph 9(2) above has effect in relation to any loan the only payments under which are payments falling within subsection (3) or (4) of section 38 of this Act.

(2) Paragraph 15 above has effect in relation to any claim for (or for part of) the year 2000–01 or any subsequent year of assessment.

(3) Paragraph 16 above has effect in relation to loans made on or after 6th April 2000.

(4) Paragraph 17 above has effect for the year 2000–01 and subsequent years of assessment.

(5) The other provisions of this Schedule have effect in relation to any payment of interest falling within subsection (3) or (4) of section 38 of this Act.

SCHEDULE 5

SCOTTISH PARLIAMENT AND DEVOLVED ASSEMBLIES: EXEMPTIONS AND RELIEFS

Section 52

Commentary—*Simon's Direct Tax Service* **E4.334; E7.262.**

Payments on dissolution, etc, or loss of office

1 (*Substitute* TA 1988 s 190).

Payments in respect of overnight expenses or EU travel

2—(1), (2) (*Insert* TA 1988 s 200ZA and *substitute* s 198(4)).

(3) (*Substituted* CAA 1990 s 74, *repealed by* CAA 2001 s 580, Sch 4 with effect in accordance with CAA 2001 s 579).

Office-holders' transport and subsistence

3 (*Inserts* TA 1988 s 200AA(2)(*c*)).

Trustees' income from parliamentary pension funds

4 (*Amends* TA 1988 s 613(4)).

Relevant statutory schemes

5 (*Substitutes* TA 1988 s 611A(1) and *adds* s 611A(5)).

Pensions of members of the Scottish Executive

6—(1) Sub-paragraph (2) below applies if provision under the Scotland Act 1998 is made for the salary paid to members of the Scottish Parliament who are also members of the Scottish Executive to be lower than that of other members of the Scottish Parliament.

(2) In that case, sections 629 and 654 of the Taxes Act 1988 (under which part of the salary of the holder of certain offices is treated as remuneration as a member of the House of Commons) apply in relation to the salary of a member of the Scottish Executive who is also a member of the Scottish Parliament as they apply in relation to the salary of the holder of a qualifying office within the meaning of those sections who is also a member of the House of Commons, with such modifications as the Treasury may specify by order.

(3) In this paragraph references to a member of the Scottish Executive include a junior Scottish Minister.

SCHEDULE 6

TAX TREATMENT OF RECEIPTS BY WAY OF REVERSE PREMIUM

Section 54

Commentary—*Simon's Direct Tax Service* **A4.221; B3.910.**
Revenue Interpretation RI 213—the taxation of reverse premiums.

Application of this Schedule

1—(1) This Schedule applies where—

(*a*) a person receives a payment or other benefit by way of inducement in connection with a transaction being entered into by him or a person connected with him;

(*b*) that transaction (the "relevant transaction") is one under which the person receiving the payment or other benefit, or as the case may be the person connected with him, becomes entitled to an estate or interest in, or a right in or over, land; and

(*c*) the payment or other benefit is paid or provided by—

(i) the person ("the grantor") by whom that estate, interest or right is granted or was granted at an earlier time, or

(ii) a person connected with the grantor, or

(iii) a nominee of, or a person acting on the directions of, the grantor or a person connected with the grantor.

(2) The payment or other benefit is referred to in this Schedule as a "reverse premium".

Tax treatment of receipts by way of reverse premium

2—(1) A reverse premium shall be regarded for the purposes of the Tax Acts as a receipt of a revenue nature.

(2) Where the relevant transaction is entered into—

(*a*) by the person receiving the reverse premium, and

(*b*) for the purposes of a trade, profession or vocation carried on or to be carried on by that person,

the reverse premium shall be taken into account in computing the profits of that trade, profession or vocation under Case I or II of Schedule D.

(3) If sub-paragraph (2) does not apply, the person receiving the reverse premium is chargeable to tax as if it were a receipt of a transaction entered into by him for the exploitation, as a source of rents or other receipts, of an estate, interest or right in or over the land in question.

Arrangements not at arm's length

3—(1) Where—

(*a*) two or more of the parties to the relevant arrangements are connected persons, and

(*b*) the terms of those arrangements are not such as would reasonably have been expected if those persons had been dealing at arm's length,

the whole amount or value of the reverse premium shall be brought into account under paragraph 2(2) or (3) in the first relevant period of account.

(2) The "first relevant period of account" means the period of account in which the relevant transaction is entered into, subject to sub-paragraph (3).

(3) If the relevant transaction is entered into—

(*a*) by the person receiving the reverse premium, and

(*b*) for the purposes of a trade, profession or vocation which is not then carried on by him but which he subsequently begins to carry on,

the first relevant period of account is the first period of account in which he carries on the trade, profession or vocation.

(4) The condition in sub-paragraph (1)(*b*) is met if the terms differ to a significant extent from the terms which at the time the arrangements were entered into would be regarded as normal and reasonable in the market conditions then prevailing between persons dealing with each other at arm's length in the open market.

(5) ...¹

Amendments—¹ Sub-para (5) repealed by FA 2002 s 141, Sch 40 Pt 3(16) with effect from 24 July 2002. Sub-para (5) previously read thus—

"(5) In this paragraph "period of account" means a period for which accounts of the trade, profession, vocation or business in question are drawn up.".

Special rules for insurance companies carrying on life assurance business

4—(1) Paragraphs 2 and 3 have effect subject to the provisions of this paragraph.

(2) Nothing in paragraph 2 or 3 shall prevent any amount from being brought into account in accordance with section 83 of the Finance Act 1989 (receipts to be brought into account in Case I computation of profits in respect of life assurance).

(3) Where a reverse premium is received by an insurance company carrying on life assurance business in respect of which it is chargeable to tax otherwise than in accordance with the rules applicable to Case I of Schedule D, there shall be deducted from the amount treated as the company's expenses of management for the accounting period in which the reverse premium is received such part of the reverse premium as is attributable—

    (*a*) to its life assurance business, and
    (*b*) to its basic life assurance and general annuity business.

(4) In this paragraph "insurance company", "life assurance business" and "basic life assurance and general annuity business" have the same meaning as in Chapter I of Part XII of the Taxes Act 1988.

Modification—Sub-paras (3), (4) modified in relation to a reverse premium (within the meaning of this Schedule) received after 8 March 1999 by a friendly society carrying on life or endowment business, not being a payment or other benefit to which the friendly society was entitled immediately before that date, by the Friendly Societies (Modification of the Corporation Tax Acts) Regulations, SI 1997/473 reg 53B (as inserted by SI 1999/2636).

Exclusion of receipts taken into account for capital allowances

5 This Schedule does not apply to a payment or benefit if or to the extent that it is taken into account under [section 532 of the Capital Allowances Act (the general rule excluding contributions)][1] to reduce the recipient's expenditure qualifying for capital allowances.

Amendments—[1] Words substituted by CAA 2001 s 578, Sch 2 para 104 with effect for income tax purposes, as respects allowances and charges falling to be made for chargeable periods ending after 5 April 2001, and for corporation tax purposes, as respects allowances and charges falling to be made for chargeable periods ending after 31 March 2001.

Exclusion of transaction relating to individual's only or main residence

6 This Schedule does not apply to a payment or benefit received in connection with a relevant transaction where the person entering into the transaction is an individual and the transaction relates to premises occupied or to be occupied by him as his only or main residence.

Exclusion of consideration under sale and lease-back arrangement

7 This Schedule does not apply to a payment or benefit to the extent that it is consideration for the transfer of an estate or interest in land which constitutes the sale in a sale and lease-back arrangement.

A "sale and lease-back arrangement" means any such arrangement as is described in section 779(1) or (2) or section 780(1) of the Taxes Act 1988.

Connected persons and relevant arrangements

8—(1) For the purposes of this Schedule persons are connected with each other if they are connected within the meaning of section 839 of the Taxes Act 1988 at any time during the period when the relevant arrangements are entered into.

(2) In this Schedule "the relevant arrangements" means the relevant transaction and any arrangements entered into in connection with it, whether before, at the same time or after it.

SCHEDULE 7

APPLICATION OF TAPER RELIEF TO EIS DEFERRED GAINS

Section 72

(*Inserts* TCGA 1992 Sch 5BA).

Commentary—*Simon's Direct Tax Service* E3.145.

SCHEDULE 8

EIS DEFERRED GAINS: GAINS ACCRUING ON PART DISPOSAL

Section 73

Commentary—*Simon's Direct Tax Service* E3.145.

Introductory

1 Schedule 5B to the Taxation of Chargeable Gains Act 1992 (relief in respect of re-investment under the enterprise investment scheme) is amended as follows.

Paragraph 4

2 (*Amends* TCGA 1992 Sch 5B para 4(1), *substitutes* para 4(5)(*a*) and *inserts* para 4(6), (7)).

Paragraph 19

3 (*Amends* TCGA 1992 Sch 5B para 19(1) and *inserts* para 19(1A)–(1E)).

Consequential amendments

4 In consequence of paragraph 3 above—

   (*a*)–(*j*) (*Amend* TCGA 1992, Sch 5B paras 2, 3, 4, 5, 6, 16, 19).

SCHEDULE 9

CHARGEABLE GAINS: VALUE SHIFTING AND TAX-FREE BENEFITS

Section 74

Commentary—*Simon's Direct Tax Service* **D2.669.**

1 The Taxation of Chargeable Gains Act 1992 shall be amended as follows.

2 (*Inserts* s 31A).

3 (*Amends* TCGA 1992 s 33).

4 (*Amends* TCGA 1992 s 34).

5 This Schedule has effect in relation to any disposal of an asset which occurs on or after 9th March 1999.

SCHEDULE 10

SHARING OF PENSIONS ETC ON DIVORCE OR ANNULMENT

Section 79

Commentary—*Simon's Direct Tax Service* **E7.101, 201.**
Modifications—This Schedule modified by the Retirement Benefits Schemes (Sharing of Pensions on Divorce or Annulment) Regulations, SI 2000/1085.

Definition of "pension business"

1 (*Amends* TA 1988 s 431B).

Approval of retirement benefit schemes

2 (*Amends* TA 1988 s 590).

Discretionary approval of retirement benefit schemes

3 (*Amends* TA 1988 s 591(2)).

Non-approved retirement benefit schemes

4 (*Amends* TA 1988 s 595(5)).
5 (*Inserts* TA 1988 s 596(4)).
6 (*Amends* TA 1988 s 596A(8)(*c*)).

Charge on pensions commuted in special circumstances

7 (*Amends* TA 1988 s 599).

Charge on unauthorised payments

8 (*Amends* TA 1988 s 600).

Definition of "retirement benefits scheme"

9 (*Amends* TA 1988 s 611).

Interpretation of Chapter I

10 (*Amends* TA 1988 s 612).

Overseas pensions

11 (*Amends* TA 1988 s 615).

Rules prohibiting surrender or assignment of annuities etc

12 (*Amends* TA 1988 ss 634, 634A and 635).

Annuity payable on the death of a member

13 (*Amends* TA 1988 s 636).

Rule in section 636A prohibiting assignment or surrender

14 (*Amends* TA 1988 s 636A(7)).

Meaning of ''relevant earnings''

15 (*Inserts* TA 1988 s 644(6EA)).

Purchased life annuities

16 (*Inserts* TA 1988 s 657(2)(*f*)).

Interpretation of Part XIV

17 (*Inserts* TA 1988 s 659D).

Commencement etc

18—(1) In this paragraph—

''the first appointed day'' means such day as the Treasury may by order appoint as the first appointed day for the purposes of this paragraph;

''the second appointed day'' means such day falling after the first appointed day as the Treasury may by order appoint as the second appointed day for the purposes of this paragraph.

(2) The power of the Treasury to appoint a day as the second appointed day for the purposes of this paragraph shall include power so to appoint different days for different purposes.

(3) Subject to sub-paragraph (4) below, paragraphs 2 and 3(*b*) above apply for the purposes of the grant or withdrawal at any time on or after the first appointed day of any approval of a retirement benefits scheme (whenever made or approved).

(4) Section 590(3)(bb) and (da) of the Taxes Act 1988 shall be disregarded for the purposes of determining whether any retirement benefits scheme approved before the first appointed day satisfies the prescribed conditions at any time before the second appointed day.

(5) Every retirement benefits scheme which—

(*a*) has, before the first appointed day, been approved by the Board for the purposes of Chapter I of Part XIV of the Taxes Act 1988, and

(*b*) by virtue of having been approved before that day continues to be so approved on or after the second appointed day,

shall have effect, so long as it continues to be approved on and after the second appointed day and notwithstanding anything in the rules of the scheme, as if (so far as it does not already do so) it contained provision satisfying the conditions set out in section 590(3)(bb) and (da) of the Taxes Act 1988.

(6) Paragraph 6 above applies to any lump sum provided on or after the second appointed day.

(7) Paragraph 8 above applies to any payment on or after the second appointed day.

(8) Subject to sub-paragraph (9) below, paragraphs 12 to 14 above apply for the purposes of—

(*a*) the grant at any time on or after the first appointed day of any approval of a personal pension scheme (whenever made);

(*b*) the withdrawal at any time on or after that day of approval of any personal pension scheme or personal pension arrangements (whenever approved).

(9) Section 636(3A) of the Taxes Act 1988 shall be disregarded for the purposes of determining whether any personal pension scheme approved before the first appointed day, or any of the arrangements made by an individual in accordance with such a scheme, satisfies the prescribed conditions at any time before the second appointed day.

(10) The Board may by regulations provide that, in such circumstances as may be prescribed by the regulations, this Schedule shall apply in the case of retirement benefits schemes approved before the first appointed day with such exceptions, exclusions and modifications as may be so prescribed.

(11) Regulations under sub-paragraph (10) above may include such incidental, supplemental, consequential and transitional provision as the Board think appropriate.

Note—In para (1) ''the first appointed day'' is 10 May 2000 and ''the second appointed day'' is 1 December 2000 by virtue of the Finance Act 1999, Schedule 10, Paragraph 18, (First and Second Appointed Days) Order, SI 1000/1093.

SCHEDULE 11

COMPANY TAX RETURNS, ETC: MINOR AND CONSEQUENTIAL AMENDMENTS

Section 93

Commentary—*Simon's Direct Tax Service* **D2.801.**

Income and Corporation Taxes Act 1988 (c 1)

1 (*Repeals* TA 1988 s 411A).

2 (*Amends* TA 1988 s 588(5)).

Finance Act 1989 (c 26)

3 (*Amends* FA 1989 s 102(6)).

Capital Allowances Act 1990 (c 1)

4–7 (*Amended* CAA 1990, *repealed by* CAA 2001 s 589, Sch 4 with effect in accordance with CAA 2001 s 579).

Finance Act 1994 (c 9)

8 (*Substituted* FA 1994 s 118(7), *repealed by* CAA 2001 s 580, Sch 4 with effect in accordance with CAA 2001 s 579).

Finance Act 1998 (c 36)

9 (*Amends* FA 1998 Sch 18 para 94).

SCHEDULE 20

REPEALS

Section 139

Note—Details of repeals already in force have been omitted from the Schedule.

PART III

INCOME TAX, CORPORATION TAX AND CAPITAL GAINS TAX

(5) WIDOW'S BEREAVEMENT ALLOWANCE

Chapter	Short title	Extent of repeal
1988 c 1.	The Income and Corporation Taxes Act 1988.	Section 256(3)(*b*). Section 262.
1988 c 39.	The Finance Act 1988.	In Schedule 3, paragraph 7(3).
1992 c 48.	The Finance (No 2) Act 1992.	In Schedule 5, paragraph 7.
1994 c 9.	The Finance Act 1994.	Section 77(5). In Schedule 8, paragraph 9.

1. The repeal of section 262 of the Taxes Act 1988 and the repeal in Schedule 3 to the Finance Act 1988 have effect in relation to deaths occurring on or after 6th April 2000.

2. The other repeals have effect for the year 2001–02 and subsequent years of assessment.

(15) VOCATIONAL TRAINING RELIEF

Chapter	Short title	Extent of repeal
1988 c 1.	The Income and Corporation Taxes Act 1988.	In section 265(3), paragraph (*e*) and the word ''or'' immediately preceding it.
1991 c 31.	The Finance Act 1991.	Sections 32 and 33.

1994 c 9.	The Finance Act 1994.	Section 84.
1996 c 8.	The Finance Act 1996.	In section 129—
		(*a*) subsection (1)(*b*);
		(*b*) in subsection (2), the words "section 32(5)(*b*) of the 1991 Act"; and
		(*c*) subsections (4) and (6).
		Section 144.
		In Schedule 18, paragraph 14.
1997 c 44.	The Education Act 1997.	In Schedule 7, paragraph 6.

Section 59(3)(*b*) of this Act shall apply in relation to these repeals as it applies in relation to subsection (2) of that section.

(16) RELEVANT DISCOUNTED SECURITIES

Chapter	Short title	Extent of repeal
1996 c 8.	The Finance Act 1996.	In Schedule 13, paragraph 3(5).

This repeal has effect in accordance with section 65(8) to (12) of this Act.

PART VII
ELECTRONIC COMMUNICATIONS

Chapter	Short title	Extent of repeal
1970 c 9	The Taxes Management Act 1970.	Section 115A.
		Schedule 3A.
1988 c 1.	The Income and Corporation Taxes Act 1988.	In section 203(10), the words from "and, in particular" onwards.
		Section 566(5).
1995 c 4.	The Finance Act 1995.	Section 153.
		Schedule 28.
1998 c 36.	The Finance Act 1998.	In Schedule 19, paragraph 43.

1. Subsection (4) of section 133 of this Act shall apply in relation to these repeals as it applies in relation to subsection (3) of that section.

2. Without prejudice to section 17(2) of the Interpretation Act 1978, any provision made by regulations under an enactment to which any of these repeals relates shall have effect, on and after the coming into force of the repeal and to the extent that it could have been made under section 132 or 133 of this Act, as if it were a provision made under that section of this Act.

FINANCE ACT 2000

(2000 Chapter 17)

ARRANGEMENT OF SECTIONS

PART III
INCOME TAX, CORPORATION TAX AND CAPITAL GAINS TAX

CHAPTER I
CHARGE AND RATES
Income tax

Capital gains tax

CHAPTER II
OTHER PROVISIONS

Giving to charity

Employee share ownership

Other provisions about employment

Pension schemes

Enterprise incentives

Research and development

Capital allowances

PART V

OTHER TAXES

Inheritance Tax

Petroleum revenue tax

PART VI

MISCELLANEOUS AND SUPPLEMENTARY PROVISIONS

Incentives for electronic communications

Compliance

An Act to grant certain duties, to alter other duties, and to amend the law relating to the National Debt and the Public Revenue, and to make further provision in connection with Finance.

[28 July 2000]

PART III
INCOME TAX, CORPORATION TAX AND CAPITAL GAINS TAX

CHAPTER I
CHARGE AND RATES
Income tax

31 Charge and rates for 2000–01
(*Spent*).

Commentary—*Simon's Direct Tax Service* **E1.102**.

32 Extension of starting rate to savings income of individuals

(1) Section 1A of the Taxes Act 1988 (application of lower rate or Schedule F ordinary rate to income from savings and distributions) is amended as follows.

(2) (*Amends* TA 1988 s 1A(1)(*b*)).

(3) (*Inserts* TA 1988 s 1A(1AA)).

(4) This section has effect for the year 2000–01 and subsequent years and shall be deemed to have had effect for the year 1999–00.

Commentary—*Simon's Direct Tax Service* **E1.102**.

33 Deduction of income tax from foreign dividends

(1) (*Inserts* TA 1988 s 4(1B)).

(2) This section has effect for the year 2000–01 and shall be deemed to have had effect for the year 1999–00.

Commentary—*Simon's Direct Tax Service* **B6.203**.

34 Children's tax credit

(1) (*Amends* TA 1988 s 257AA(2)).

(2) This section has effect for the year 2001–02 and subsequent years of assessment.

Commentary—*Simon's Direct Tax Service* **E2.502**.

Corporation tax

35 Charge and main rate for financial year 2001

Corporation tax shall be charged for the financial year 2001 at the rate of 30%.

Commentary—*Simon's Direct Tax Service* **D2.108**.

36 Small companies' rate for financial year 2000

(*Spent*).

Commentary—*Simon's Direct Tax Service* **D2.109**.

Capital gains tax

37 Application of starting rate to capital gains tax

(1) (*Inserts* TCGA 1992 s 4(1AB), (1AC)).

(2) This section has effect for the year 2000–01 and subsequent years of assessment.

Commentary—*Simon's Direct Tax Service* **C1.107, E1.102**.

CHAPTER II
OTHER PROVISIONS
Giving to charity

38 Payroll deduction scheme

(1) Where in accordance with a scheme approved under section 202 of the Taxes Act 1988 (donations to charity: payroll deduction scheme) an agent is to pay to a charity any sum which—

(*a*) is withheld by an employer from a payment which an employee is entitled to receive; and

(*b*) is paid by the employer to the agent,

the agent shall, within a period prescribed by regulations made by the Treasury, pay a supplement equal to 10% of that sum to the charity.

(2) On a claim made by an agent in such form as the Board may prescribe, the Board shall pay to the agent out of money provided by Parliament—

(*a*) such amounts as are required—

(i) to fund the payment of supplements falling to be paid by him; or

(ii) to reimburse him for supplements paid by him the payment of which has not been so funded; and

(*b*) in the case of an agent which is a charity, an amount which is equal to 10% of the aggregate of sums which—

(i) are withheld and paid as mentioned in paragraphs (*a*) and (*b*) of subsection (1) above; and

(ii) are sums to which the agent is itself entitled in its capacity as a charity.

(3) The Treasury may by regulations make provision—

(*a*) requiring agents to notify the Board of any failures of theirs to comply with subsection (1) above, and of the reasons for those failures;

(*b*) requiring agents to keep records of supplements paid by them under that subsection; and

(*c*) for the assessment and recovery under the Taxes Acts of amounts paid to agents under subsection (2) above which ought not to have been so paid.

The regulations may contain such supplementary and incidental provision as appears to the Treasury necessary or expedient.

(4) In this section—

"agent" means any such person or charity as is mentioned in subsection (4) of section 202 of the Taxes Act 1988;

"employee" and "employer" shall be construed in accordance with subsection (1) of that section;

"charity" has the same meaning as in section 506 of that Act and includes each of the bodies mentioned in section 507 of that Act;

"the Taxes Acts" has the same meaning as in the Taxes Management Act 1970.

(5) (*Amends* TA 1988 s 202(6), (11) *and repeals* s 202(7)).

(6) Subsections (1) to (4) above shall have effect in relation to supplements or other amounts payable in respect of sums withheld on or after 6th April 2000 and before 6th April 2003; and no claim under subsection (2) above shall be entertained if made on or after 6th April 2004.

(7) Subsection (5) above shall have effect in relation to sums withheld on or after 6th April 2000.

Commentary—*Simon's Direct Tax Service* **E4.948**.

39 Gift aid payments by individuals

(1) Section 25 of the Finance Act 1990 (donations to charity by individuals) shall be amended in accordance with subsections (2) to (7) below.

(2)–(7) (*Amend* FA 1990 s 25).

(8) (*Amends* TA 1988 s 257BB(1)(*b*), (3)(*b*)).

(9) (*Amends* TA 1988 Sch 13B para 4(1)(*b*)).

(10) This section has effect in relation to—

(*a*) gifts made on or after 6th April 2000 which are not covenanted payments; and

(*b*) covenanted payments falling to be made on or after that date;

and any regulations made under subsection (3) of section 25 of the Finance Act 1990 (as substituted by subsection (4) above) within three months of the passing of this Act may be so made as to apply to any payments in relation to which this section has effect.

Commentary—*Simon's Direct Tax Service* **E1.504**.

40 Gift aid payments by companies

(1) Section 339 of the Taxes Act 1988 (charges on income: donations to charity) shall be amended in accordance with subsections (2) to (8) below.

(2)–(8) (*Amend* TA 1988 s 339).

(9) (*Amends* TA 1988 s 209(1)).

(10) (*Amends* TA 1988 s 338(2)(*a*)).

(11) This section has effect in relation to payments made on or after 1st April 2000; and—

(*a*) so much of an accounting period as falls before that date; and

(*b*) so much of it as falls after 31st March 2000,

shall be treated as separate accounting periods for the purposes of the amendment made by subsection (5) above.

Commentary—*Simon's Direct Tax Service* **D2.212**.
Concession—Temporary (unnumbered) concession allowing charitable companies to continue to be eligible for relief on payments made to another charity under deed of covenant until March 2001.

41 Covenanted payments to charities

(1) (*Amends* TA 1988 s 338(5)(*b*)).

(2) (*Repeals* TA 1988 s 347A(2)(*b*), (7), (8)).

(3) (*Amends* TA 1988 s 348(3)).

(4) (*Amends* TA 1988 s 349(1)).

(5) (*Amends* TA 1988 s 505(6)).

(6) (*Substitutes* TA 1988 s 660A(9)(*b*)).

(7) (*Repeals* FA 1989 s 59).

(8) Where a deed of covenant executed by an individual before 6th April 2000 provides for the payment of specified amounts, any amount payable under the deed on or after that date shall be determined as if the individual were entitled to deduct tax from that amount at the basic rate.

(9) This section shall have effect in relation to covenanted payments—

    (a) falling to be made by individuals on or after 6th April 2000; or

    (b) made by companies on or after 1st April 2000.

Commentary—*Simon's Direct Tax Service* **D2.212A, E1.504**.
Concession—Temporary (unnumbered) concession allowing charitable companies to continue to be eligible for relief on payments made to another charity under deed of covenant until March 2001.

42 Millennium gift aid

(1) *(Repeals* FA 1998 s 48(3), (6), (7)).

(2) *(Amends* FA 1998 s 48(4)).

(3) *(Amends* FA 1998 s 48(8)).

Commentary—*Simon's Direct Tax Service* **D2.212, E1.504**.

43 Gifts of shares and securities to charities etc

(1) *(Inserts* TA 1988 s 587B).

(2) *(Inserts* TA 1988 s 338(2)(*za*)).

(3) This section has effect in relation to—

    (a) disposals made by individuals on or after 6th April 2000; and

    (b) disposals made by companies on or after 1st April 2000.

Commentary—*Simon's Direct Tax Service* **D2.212, E1.504**.

44 Gifts to charity from certain trusts

(1) Chapter IA of Part XV of the Taxes Act 1988 (liability of settlors) shall not apply to any qualifying income which arises under a trust the trustees of which are resident in the United Kingdom (a "UK trust") if—

    (a) it is given by the trustees to a charity in the year of assessment in which it arises; or

    (b) it is income to which a charity is entitled under the terms of the trust.

(2) Subject to subsection (3) below, where in any year of assessment qualifying income arising under a UK trust from different sources exceeds the amount of that income falling within subsection (1) above, that amount shall be rateably apportioned between those sources.

(3) Nothing in subsection (2) above shall affect the operation of any requirement that the whole, or any specified part, of the income from a particular source be given to a charity.

(4) Where in any year of assessment qualifying income arising under a UK trust exceeds the amount of that income falling within subsection (1) above, any management expenses for that year shall be rateably apportioned between—

    (a) so much of that income as is equal to that amount; and

    (b) so much of that income as exceeds that amount.

(5) In this section—

    "charity" has the same meaning as in section 506 of the Taxes Act 1988 and includes each of the bodies mentioned in section 507 of that Act;

    "qualifying income" means—

        (i) income which is to be accumulated;

        (ii) income which is payable at the discretion of the trustees or any other person (whether or not the trustees have power to accumulate it); or

        (iii) income which (before being distributed) is income of any person other than the trustees;

    "resident", in relation to the trustees of a trust, shall be construed in accordance with section 110 of the Finance Act 1989;

and the reference to Chapter IA of Part XV of the Taxes Act 1988 includes a reference to that Chapter as it has effect by virtue of section 660E of that Act (application to settlements by two or more settlors).

(6) This section has effect in relation to qualifying income arising to a UK trust on or after 6th April 2000.

Commentary—*Simon's Direct Tax Service* **C4.310, E1.504**.

45 Loans to charities

(1) In Chapter IA of Part XV of the Taxes Act 1988 "settlement" does not include any arrangement so far as it consists of a loan of money made by an individual to a charity either—

    (a) for no consideration; or

    (b) for a consideration which consists only of interest.

(2) In this section "charity" has the same meaning as in section 44 above.

(3) This section has effect in relation to income arising on or after 6th April 2000 on loans made before, as well as loans made on or after, that date.

Commentary—*Simon's Direct Tax Service* **C4.302**.

46 Exemption for small trades etc

(1) Subject to subsection (2) below, exemption from tax under Case I or VI of Schedule D shall be granted, on a claim made in that behalf to the Board, in respect of any income of a charity if the requirements of subsection (3) below are satisfied with respect to the income.

(2) Exemption shall not be granted under subsection (1) above in respect of income which is chargeable to tax under Case VI of Schedule D by virtue of any of the following—

(*a*) section 30 of the Taxes Management Act 1970;

(*b*) sections 214, 412, 547(1)(*b*) and (6), 553(6), 660C, 677, 703, 776, 788, 790 and 804 of the Taxes Act 1988;

(*c*) paragraph 14 of Schedule 4 to the Finance (No. 2) Act 1997;

(*d*) paragraph 52(4) of Schedule 18, and paragraph 13(7) of Schedule 19, to the Finance Act 1998; and

(*e*) any other enactment specified in an order made by the Treasury.

(3) The requirements of this subsection are satisfied with respect to any income for a chargeable period if it is applied solely for the purposes of the charity and either—

(*a*) the charity's gross income for the chargeable period does not exceed the requisite limit; or

(*b*) the charity had, at the beginning of the period, a reasonable expectation that its gross income for the period would not exceed that limit.

(4) Subject to subsection (5) below, the requisite limit is whichever is the greater of—

(*a*) £5,000; and

(*b*) whichever is the lesser of £50,000 and 25% of all of the charity's incoming resources for the chargeable period.

(5) For a chargeable period of less than twelve months, the amounts of £5,000 and £50,000 specified in subsection (4) above shall be proportionally reduced.

(6) In this section—

"charity" means any body of persons or trust established for charitable purposes only;

"gross income", in relation to a charity, means income before deduction of any expenses;

"income", in relation to a charity, means any profits or gains or other income which is chargeable to tax under Case I or VI of Schedule D and which is not, apart this section, exempted from tax under that Case.

(7) This section applies for the year 2000–01 and subsequent years of assessment or, in the case of charities which are companies, for accounting periods beginning on or after 1st April 2000.

Commentary—*Simon's Direct Tax Service* **C4.523**.

Employee share ownership

47 Employee share ownership plans

Schedule 8 to this Act (employee share ownership plans) shall have effect.

Commentary—*Simon's Direct Tax Service* **E4.528**.

48 Relief for transfers to employee share ownership plans

(1) (*Inserts* TCGA 1992 s 236A).

(2) After Schedule 7B to that Act insert the Schedule 7C set out in Schedule 9 to this Act.

Commentary—*Simon's Direct Tax Service* **E4.536**.

49 Phasing out of approved profit sharing schemes

(1) The Board shall not approve a profit sharing scheme under Schedule 9 to the Taxes Act 1988 (approval of share option schemes and profit sharing schemes) unless the application for approval is received by the Board before 6th April 2001.

(2) For the purposes of subsection (1) an application for approval which is not accompanied by the particulars and evidence referred to in paragraph 1(2) of that Schedule is not regarded as received by the Board until the required particulars and evidence have been received by them.

(3) In section 186 of that Act (approved profit sharing schemes), in subsection (1) (under which the section applies to appropriations of shares made after 5th April 1979) after "5th April 1979" insert "and before 1st January 2003".

Commentary—*Simon's Direct Tax Service* **E4.562**.

50 Phasing out of relief for payments to trustees of profit sharing schemes

(1) This section has effect to phase out deductions under section 85 of the Taxes Act 1988 (corporation tax relief for payments to trustees of approved profit sharing schemes).

(2) In the case of sums paid to the trustees on or after 21st March 2000 and before 6th April 2002 no deduction may be made by virtue of subsection (2)(*a*) of that section (sums applied in acquiring shares for appropriation) unless the trustees appropriate the shares acquired, by the application of the sum, as mentioned in that provision—

(*a*) before the end of the period of nine months beginning on the day following the end of the period of account in which payment to the trustees was made, and
(*b*) before 1st January 2003.

(3) No deduction may be made by virtue of subsection (2)(*a*) of that section in respect of any sum paid to the trustees on or after 6th April 2002.

(4) No deduction may be made by virtue of subsection (2)(*b*) of that section (sums to meet expenses of trustees in administering the scheme) in respect of any sum paid to the trustees more than three years after the date of the last appropriation of shares to individuals which was made—

(*a*) in accordance with the approved profit sharing scheme, and
(*b*) before 1st January 2003.

(5) For the purposes of this section references to a deduction under section 85 are to a deduction under subsection (1)(*a*) or by virtue of subsection (1)(*b*) of that section.

Commentary—*Simon's Direct Tax Service* E4.562, 569.

51 Approved profit sharing scheme: other awards of shares

(1) (*Inserts* TA 1988 Sch 9 para 3(2)(*f*)).
(2) (*Inserts* TA 1988 Sch 9 para 3(4)–(6)).

Commentary—*Simon's Direct Tax Service* E4.562.

52 Approved profit sharing schemes: restriction on type of shares

(1) Schedule 9 to the Taxes Act 1988 (share option schemes and profit sharing schemes) is amended in accordance with subsections (2) to (4).
(2) (*Amends* TA 1988 Sch 9 para 9(1).
(3) (*Inserts* TA 1988 Sch 9 para 11A).
(4) (*Amends* TA 1988 Sch 9 para 12).
(5) Subsections (1) to (4) shall be deemed to have come into force on 21st March 2000.
(6) Subsections (3) and (4) do not have effect in relation to shares acquired before 21st March 2000 by the trustees of a profit sharing scheme approved under Schedule 9 to the Taxes Act 1988.

Commentary—*Simon's Direct Tax Service* E4.562.

53 Approved profit sharing schemes: loan arrangements

(1), (2) (*Inserts* TA 1988 Sch 9 paras 2(2A), (2B), 3(2)(*ca*)).
(3) This section shall be deemed to have come into force on 21st March 2000.

Commentary—*Simon's Direct Tax Service* E4.562.

54 Employee share ownership trusts

No claim for relief under section 229(1) or (3) of the Taxation of Chargeable Gains Act 1992 (roll-over relief where disposal made to employee share ownership trust) may be made in relation to a disposal of shares, or an interest in shares, made on or after 6th April 2001.

Commentary—*Simon's Direct Tax Service* E4.536.

55 Shares transferred from employee share ownership trust

(1) Section 69 of the Finance Act 1989 (chargeable events in relation to employee share ownership trusts) is amended in accordance with subsections (2) to (5).
(2)–(5) (*Amends* FA 1989 s 69).
(6) (*Inserts* FA 1989 s 70(4)).

Commentary—*Simon's Direct Tax Service* E4.531.

56 Further provisions about share options

(1) (*Inserts* TA 1988 s 187A).
Section 187A inserted by this subsection applies to any agreement or election having effect as mentioned in subsection (6) of that section, whether made before or after the passing of this Act.
(2) (*Amends* TA 1988 s 203FB).

These amendments apply where the event giving rise to the charge to tax occurs after the passing of this Act.

(3) *(Amends* TA 1988 s 136(6) *and* FA 1988 s 85(1)).

These amendments apply where the event giving rise to the duty to deliver particulars occurs on or after 6th April 2000.

(4) *(Inserts* TA 1988 s 136(7), (8)).

Section 136(8) inserted by this subsection applies to any amounts recovered or met as mentioned in section 187A(2)(*a*) or (3) of the Taxes Act 1988, whether before or after the passing of this Act.

Other provisions about employment

57 Benefits in kind: deregulatory amendments

(1) Chapter II of Part V of the Taxes Act 1988 (provisions relating to the Schedule E charge: benefits in kind, etc) is amended in accordance with Schedule 10 to this Act.

(2) The amendments have effect for the year 2000-01 and subsequent years of assessment.

Commentary—*Simon's Direct Tax Service* E4.612, 632.

58 Education and training

(1) *(Inserts* TA 1988 ss 200E, 200F, 200G, 200H, 200J).

(2) *(Amends* TA 1988 s 200A(3)(*b*)).

(3) This section applies for the year 2000-01 and subsequent years of assessment.

Commentary—*Simon's Direct Tax Service* E4.422.

59 Cars available for private use

Schedule 11 to this Act (which makes provision in relation to the taxation of cars available for private use) has effect for the year 2002-03 and subsequent years of assessment.

Commentary—*Simon's Direct Tax Service* E4.626.

60 Provision of services through intermediary

Schedule 12 to this Act has effect with respect to the provision of services through an intermediary.

Commentary—*Simon's Direct Tax Service* E4.205–209.

Pension schemes

61 Occupational and personal pension schemes

Schedule 13 to this Act (which makes provision in relation to occupational and personal pension schemes) has effect.

Commentary—*Simon's Direct Tax Service* E7.401.

Enterprise incentives

62 Enterprise management incentives

Schedule 14 to this Act (enterprise management incentives) has effect in relation to any right to acquire shares granted after the passing of this Act.

Commentary—*Simon's Direct Tax Service* E4.543.

63 Corporate venturing scheme

(1) Schedule 15 to this Act (which makes provision for the corporate venturing scheme) has effect.

(2) Schedule 16 to this Act (which makes consequential amendments) has effect.

(3) Paragraph 3(2)(*a*)(i) to (iii) and (3) of Schedule 16 (and paragraph 3(1) so far as it relates to those provisions) have effect—

   (*a*) in relation to claims made under section 573 of the Taxes Act 1988, in respect of disposals on or after 1st April 2000, and

   (*b*) in relation to claims made under section 574 of that Act, in respect of disposals on or after 6th April 2000.

(4) Subject to that, Schedules 15 and 16 apply in relation to shares issued on or after 1st April 2000 but before 1st April 2010.

Commentary—*Simon's Direct Tax Service* Division D2.13.

64 Enterprise investment scheme: amendments

The provisions relating to the enterprise investment scheme are amended in accordance with Schedule 17 to this Act.

In that Schedule—
  Part I makes amendments reducing various periods which apply in relation to the provisions which determine the reliefs under the scheme;
  Part II makes amendments about qualifying companies;
  Part III makes other minor amendments.

Commentary—*Simon's Direct Tax Service* **E3.102**.

65 Venture capital trusts: amendments

The provisions relating to venture capital trusts are amended in accordance with Schedule 18 to this Act.

In that Schedule—
  Part I makes amendments reducing various periods which apply in relation to the provisions which determine the reliefs; and
  Part II makes amendments about qualifying holdings.

Commentary—*Simon's Direct Tax Service* **E3.612, 626**.

66 Taper relief: taper for business assets

(1) Section 2A of the Taxation of Chargeable Gains Act 1992 (taper relief) is amended as follows.

(2) (*Amends* first 2 columns of table in TCGA 1992 s 2A(5)).

(3) (*Substitutes* TCGA 1992 s 2A(8)).

(4) This section applies to disposals on or after 6th April 2000.

Commentary—*Simon's Direct Tax Service* **Division C2.14**.

67 Taper relief: assets qualifying as business assets

(1) Schedule A1 to the Taxation of Chargeable Gains Act 1992 (application of taper relief) is amended as follows.

(2) (*Amends* TCGA 1992 Sch A1 para 4).

(3) (*Amends* TCGA 1992 Sch A1 para 5).

(4) (*Substitutes* TCGA 1992 Sch A1 para 6).

(5) (*Amends* TCGA 1992 Sch A1 para 22(1)).

(6) (*Inserts* TCGA 1992 Sch A1 para 23).

(7) This section has effect for determining whether an asset is a business asset at any time on or after 6th April 2000.

It does not affect the determination on or after that date whether an asset was a business asset at a time before that date.

Commentary—*Simon's Direct Tax Service* **Division C2.14**.

Research and development

68 Meaning of "research and development"

(1) Schedule 19 to this Act (meaning of "research and development") has effect.

In that Schedule—
  Part I contains a new definition of "research and development" for the purposes of the Tax Acts, and
  Part II contains consequential amendments.

(2) The amendments in Part II of that Schedule have effect—
  (*a*) for the purposes of income tax and capital gains tax, in relation to the year 2000–01 and subsequent years of assessment, and
  (*b*) for the purposes of corporation tax, for accounting periods ending on or after 1st April 2000.

Commentary—*Simon's Direct Tax Service* **B2.702**.

69 Tax relief for expenditure on research and development

(1) Schedule 20 to this Act (tax relief for expenditure on research and development) has effect for accounting periods ending on or after 1st April 2000.

In that Schedule—
  Part I provides for entitlement to relief,
  Part II provides for the manner of giving effect to the relief, and
  Part III contains supplementary provisions.

(2) Schedule 21 to this Act (which contains consequential amendments) has effect accordingly.

Commentary—*Simon's Direct Tax Service* **B2.703**.

Capital allowances

70 First year allowances for small or medium-sized enterprises

...

Commentary—*Simon's Direct Tax Service* **B2.321, 324**.
Amendment—This section repealed by the Capital Allowances Act 2001 s 580, Sch 4 with effect for income tax purposes, as respects allowances and charges falling to be made for chargeable periods ending after 5 April 2001, and for corporation tax purposes, as respects allowances and charges falling to be made for chargeable periods ending after 31 March 2001.

71 First year allowances for ICT expenditure by small enterprises

...

Commentary—*Simon's Direct Tax Service* **B2.321, 324**.
Amendment—This section repealed by the Capital Allowances Act 2001 s 580, Sch 4 with effect for income tax purposes, as respects allowances and charges falling to be made for chargeable periods ending after 5 April 2001, and for corporation tax purposes, as respects allowances and charges falling to be made for chargeable periods ending after 31 March 2001.

72 Expenditure of a small enterprise

...

Commentary—*Simon's Direct Tax Service* **B2.321, 324**.
Amendment—This section repealed by the Capital Allowances Act 2001 s 580, Sch 4 with effect for income tax purposes, as respects allowances and charges falling to be made for chargeable periods ending after 5 April 2001, and for corporation tax purposes, as respects allowances and charges falling to be made for chargeable periods ending after 31 March 2001.

73 Repeal of notification requirements

(1) (*Repeals* FA 1994 s 118(1)–(5), (7)–(9) *and amends* s 118(6)).

(2) This section has effect for chargeable periods as respects which the period specified in subsection (3A) of that section ends on or after 1st April 2000.

Commentary—*Simon's Direct Tax Service* **B2.325A**.

74 Pool for certain leased assets and inexpensive cars

(1) (*Amends* CAA 1990 s 41(1), (4)).

(2) Subsection (3) below applies where—

(*a*) immediately before the end of the relevant chargeable period, a person was treated for the purposes of sections 24, 25 and 26 of the Capital Allowances Act 1990 as having incurred expenditure on the provision of machinery or plant wholly and exclusively for the purposes of a separate trade carried on by him;

(*b*) the expenditure fell within subsection (1)(*b*) or (*c*) of section 41 of that Act; and

(*c*) qualifying expenditure in respect of the separate trade for the relevant chargeable period exceeded any disposal value brought into account in respect of that trade for that period.

(3) The balance of the excess (after the deduction of any writing-down allowances made by reference to it) shall be treated for the purposes of sections 24, 25 and 26 of the Capital Allowances Act 1990 as capital expenditure which—

(*a*) was incurred by that person in the relevant chargeable period on the provision of the machinery or plant for the purposes of the trade which is the actual trade for the purposes of section 41 of that Act; and

(*b*) does not form part of his qualifying expenditure for that period.

(4) In this section—

"the relevant chargeable period" means the chargeable period immediately preceding that which begins on or before and ends on or after the relevant date;

"the relevant date" means, subject to subsection (5) below, 6th April 2000 for the purposes of income tax and 1st April 2000 for the purposes of corporation tax.

(5) A person may, by a notice given to an officer of the Board, elect that this section shall have effect in relation to any trade carried on by him as if the relevant date were 6th April 2001 or, as the case may be, 1st April 2001.

Commentary—*Simon's Direct Tax Service* **B2.325**.

75 Machinery and plant allowances for non-residents etc

(1)–(3) ...[1]

(4) (*Inserts* TA 1988 Sch 19AC para 10B(2A).

(5) ...[1]

(6) In this section—

(*a*) subsections (1), (4) and (5) have effect for chargeable periods ending on or after 21st March 2000;

(*b*)–(*c*) ...[1]

Commentary—*Simon's Direct Tax Service* B2.325.
Amendments—¹ Sub-ss (1)–(3), (5), (6)(*b*), (*c*) repealed by the Capital Allowances Act 2001 s 580, Sch 4 with effect for income tax purposes, as respects allowances and charges falling to be made for chargeable periods ending after 5 April 2001, and for corporation tax purposes, as respects allowances and charges falling to be made for chargeable periods ending after 31 March 2001.

76 Production animals

(1) ...¹

(2) (*Amends* TA 1988 Sch 5 para 9(4)).

(3) The enactments amended by subsections (1) and (2) above shall be deemed always to have had effect with the amendments made by those subsections.

Commentary—*Simon's Direct Tax Service* B2.325, B3.503A.
Amendment—¹ Sub-s (1) repealed by the Capital Allowances Act 2001 s 580, Sch 4 with effect for income tax purposes, as respects allowances and charges falling to be made for chargeable periods ending after 5 April 2001, and for corporation tax purposes, as respects allowances and charges falling to be made for chargeable periods ending after 31 March 2001.

77 Sale and leaseback

Commentary—*Simon's Direct Tax Service* B2.343C.
Amendment—This section repealed by the Capital Allowances Act 2001 s 580, Sch 4 with effect for income tax purposes, as respects allowances and charges falling to be made for chargeable periods ending after 5 April 2001, and for corporation tax purposes, as respects allowances and charges falling to be made for chargeable periods ending after 31 March 2001.

78 Meaning of "fixture"

(1) Section 51 of the Capital Allowances Act 1990 (application and interpretation of Chapter VI: plant and machinery: fixtures) is amended as follows.

(2)–(5) (*Amend* CAA 1990 s 51).

(6) The amendments in this section shall be deemed always to have had effect.

Commentary—*Simon's Direct Tax Service* B2.303.

79 Leased assets under the Affordable Warmth Programme

Commentary—*Simon's Direct Tax Service* B2.303.
Amendment—This section repealed by the Capital Allowances Act 2001 s 580, Sch 4 with effect for income tax purposes, as respects allowances and charges falling to be made for chargeable periods ending after 5 April 2001, and for corporation tax purposes, as respects allowances and charges falling to be made for chargeable periods ending after 31 March 2001.

80 Fixtures and machinery and plant on hire-purchase etc

Commentary—*Simon's Direct Tax Service* B2.303.
Amendment—This section repealed by the Capital Allowances Act 2001 s 580, Sch 4 with effect for income tax purposes, as respects allowances and charges falling to be made for chargeable periods ending after 5 April 2001, and for corporation tax purposes, as respects allowances and charges falling to be made for chargeable periods ending after 31 March 2001.

81 Production sharing contracts

Commentary—*Simon's Direct Tax Service* B2.420.
Amendment—This section repealed by the Capital Allowances Act 2001 s 580, Sch 4 with effect for income tax purposes, as respects allowances and charges falling to be made for chargeable periods ending after 5 April 2001, and for corporation tax purposes, as respects allowances and charges falling to be made for chargeable periods ending after 31 March 2001.

Tonnage tax

82 Tonnage tax

Schedule 22 to this Act (tonnage tax) has effect.

Other relieving provisions

83 Relief for interest on loans to buy annuities

(1) (*Amends* TA 1988 s 365(3)).

(2) (*Amends* TA 1988 s 353(1G)).

(3) (*Amends* TA 1988 s 369(1A)).

(4) This section has effect in relation to payments of interest made on or after 6th April 2000.

Commentary—*Simon's Direct Tax Service* E1.553.

84 Exemption of payments under New Deal 50plus

(1) This section applies to—

(*a*) the scheme under section 2(2) of the Employment and Training Act 1973 known as "New Deal 50plus", and (*b*) the corresponding scheme under section 1 of the Employment and Training Act (Northern Ireland) 1950.

(2) A payment to a person as a participant in the scheme by way of an employment credit or training grant under the scheme is exempt from income tax and, accordingly, shall be disregarded in computing the amount of any receipts brought into account for income tax purposes.

(3) This section applies to any such payment made on or after 25th October 1999.

Commentary—*Simon's Direct Tax Service* **E4.328**.

85 Exemption of payments under Employment Zones programme

(1) A payment to a person as a participant in an employment zone programme is exempt from income tax and, accordingly, shall be disregarded in computing the amount of any receipts brought into account for income tax purposes.

(2) An "employment zone programme" means an employment zone programme established for an area or areas designated under section 60 of the Welfare Reform and Pensions Act 1999.

(3) This section applies to any such payment made on or after 6th April 2000.

Commentary—*Simon's Direct Tax Service* **E4.328**.

86 Loan where return bears inverse relationship to results

(1) (*Inserts* TA 1988 s 209(3B)).

This subsection applies to payments made on or after 21st March 2000.

(2) (*Amends* TA 1988 Sch 18 para 1(5E)).

This subsection applies for the purposes of determining whether, at any time on or after 21st March 2000, a loan is a normal commercial loan for the purposes of paragraph 1(1)(*b*) of Schedule 18 to the Taxes Act 1988.

Commentary—*Simon's Direct Tax Service* **D1.106**.

87 Tax treatment of acquisition, disposal or revaluation of certain rights

Schedule 23 to this Act has effect with respect to the treatment of amounts relating to the acquisition, disposal or revaluation of—

(*a*) licences granted under section 1 of the Wireless Telegraphy Act 1949 in accordance with regulations made under section 3 of the Wireless Telegraphy Act 1998 (bidding for licences),
(*b*) indefeasible rights to use a telecommunications cable system, or
(*c*) rights derived, directly or indirectly, from a right within paragraph (*a*) or (*b*).

Commentary—*Simon's Direct Tax Service* **B3.1203**.
Revenue Interpretation RI 223—Guidance on the interpretation of FA 2000 Sch 23 in relation to indefeasible rights to use.

88 Contributions to local enterprise agencies, etc

(*Amends* TA 1988 ss 79(11), 79A(7)).

Commentary—*Simon's Direct Tax Service* **B3.1444**.

89 Waste disposal: entitlement of successor to allowances

(*Inserts* TA 1988 s 91BA).

Commentary—*Simon's Direct Tax Service* **B3.1345**.

Capital gains tax: gifts and trusts

90 Restriction of gifts relief

(1) (*Amends* TCGA 1992 s 165(1)).

(2) (*Amends* TCGA 1992 s 260(1)).

(3) (*Amends* TCGA 1992 s 165(2)(*b*)(i) and Sch 7 para 2(2)(*b*)(i)).

(4) (*Amends* TCGA 1992 s 165(3)(*b*)).

(5) This section has effect in relation to disposals made on or after 9th November 1999.

Commentary—*Simon's Direct Tax Service* **C3.502**.

91 Disposal of interest in settled property: deemed disposal of underlying assets

(1) (*Inserts* TCGA 1992 s 76A).

(2) (*Inserts* TCGA 1992 Sch 4A).

(3) This section applies to any disposal of an interest in settled property made, or the effective completion of which falls, on or after 21st March 2000.

Expressions used in this subsection have the same meaning as in Schedule 4A to the Taxation of Chargeable Gains Act 1992.

Commentary—*Simon's Direct Tax Service* **C4.206, 301**.

92 Transfers of value by trustees linked with trustee borrowing

(1) (*Inserts* TCGA 1992 s 76B).

(2) (*Inserts* TCGA 1992 Sch 4B).

(3) (*Inserts* TCGA 1992 s 85A).

(4) (*Inserts* TCGA 1992 Sch 4C).

The consequential amendments in Part II of Schedule 26 to this Act have effect.

(5) The provisions of this section have effect in relation to any transfer of value in relation to which the material time is on or after 21st March 2000.

The expressions "transfer of value" and "material time" have the same meaning in this subsection as in Schedule 4B to the Taxation of Chargeable Gains Act 1992.

Commentary—*Simon's Direct Tax Service* **C4.206, 301**.

93 Restriction on set-off of trust losses

(1) (*Inserts* TCGA 1992 s 79A).

(2) This section applies to gains accruing on or after 21st March 2000.

Commentary—*Simon's Direct Tax Service* **C4.206, 301**.

94 Attribution to trustees of gains of non-resident companies

(1) (*Inserts* TCGA 1992 s 79B).

(2) This section applies where a chargeable gain accrues on or after 21st March 2000 to a company that is not resident in the United Kingdom.

Commentary—*Simon's Direct Tax Service* **C4.431**.

95 Disposal of interest in non-resident settlement

(1) Section 85 of the Taxation of Chargeable Gains Act 1992 (disposal of interest in non-resident settlements) is amended as follows.

(2)–(4) (*Amend* TCGA 1992 s 85).

(5) This section applies where the material time (within the meaning of section 85(10) of the Taxation of Chargeable Gains Act 1992, inserted by subsection (4) above) falls on or after 21st March 2000.

Commentary—*Simon's Direct Tax Service* **C4.405, 431**.

96 Payments by trustees to non-resident companies

(1) (*Amends* TCGA 1992 s 96(5)).

(2) This section applies to payments received on or after 21st March 2000.

Commentary—*Simon's Direct Tax Service* **C4.431**.

Groups and group relief

97 Group relief for non-resident companies etc

Schedule 27 to this Act has effect.

In that Schedule—

Part I makes amendments of Chapter IV of Part X of the Taxes Act 1988 (group relief), and
Part II contains consequential amendments.

Commentary—*Simon's Direct Tax Service* **D2.623**.

98 Recovery of tax payable by non-resident company

(1) Schedule 28 to this Act has effect with respect to the recovery of unpaid corporation tax payable by a company not resident in the United Kingdom.

(2) The provisions of that Schedule have effect in relation to corporation tax for accounting periods ending on or after 1st April 2000.

Commentary—*Simon's Direct Tax Service* **D2.642**.

99 Joint arrangements for claims

(*Amends* FA 1998 Sch 18 para 77).

Commentary—*Simon's Direct Tax Service* **D2.630**.

100 Limit on amount of group relief in case of consortium claim

(1) (*Substitutes* TA 1988 s 403C).

(2) (*Amends* TA 1988 s 406(6)).

(3) (*Amends* TA 1988 s 402(4) *and repeals* s 413(8), (9)).

(4) (*Amends* TA 1988 Schedule 18 paras 1(1), 2(1), 3(1), 4(3), (4), 5A(3), (4), 5C(3), (4), 5D(3), (4), 5E(3), (4), 6, 7(1)(*b*)).

(5) The amendments in this section shall be deemed always to have had effect.

Commentary—*Simon's Direct Tax Service* **D2.635**.

101 Notional transfers within groups of companies

(1) (*Inserts* TCGA 1992 s 171A).

(2) This section has effect in relation to disposals made on or after 1st April 2000.

Commentary—*Simon's Direct Tax Service* **D2.652**.

102 Chargeable gains: non-resident companies and groups etc

Schedule 29 to this Act has effect.

In that Schedule—

Part I makes provision with respect to the application of the Taxation of Chargeable Gains Act 1992 to companies not resident in the United Kingdom and groups of companies etc,

Part II contains minor and consequential amendments, and

Part III contains transitional provisions.

Commentary—*Simon's Direct Tax Service* **D2.657, 658**.

International matters

103 Double taxation relief

Schedule 30 to this Act (double taxation relief) shall have effect.

Commentary—*Simon's Direct Tax Service* **F1.117**.

104 Controlled foreign companies

Schedule 31 to this Act (which makes provision in relation to controlled foreign companies) shall have effect.

Commentary—*Simon's Direct Tax Service* **D4.1201**.

105 Corporation tax: use of currencies other than sterling

(1) (*Substitutes* FA 1993 ss 92–95).

(2) Where any of the items referred to in section 93(4)(*b*) of the Finance Act 1993 (as substituted by subsection (1) above) fall to be taken into account in the first accounting period in relation to which this section has effect, the amounts of those items shall be computed and expressed in the relevant currency by reference to the London closing exchange rate for the last day of the immediately preceding accounting period.

(3) Where [any amount falls to be taken into account under Chapter 5 of Part 2 of the Capital Allowances Act as available qualifying expenditure][1] for the first accounting period in relation to which this section has effect relate to expenditure which was incurred before the beginning of that period, the amounts of those items shall be computed and expressed in the relevant currency by reference to the London closing exchange rate for the last day of the immediately preceding accounting period.

(4) Subject to subsection (5) below, this section has effect for accounting periods beginning on or after 1st January 2000 and ending on or after 21st March 2000.

(5) Any company which did not, for the accounting period immediately preceding the first accounting period falling within subsection (4) above, make an election in respect of a trade or part of a trade under the Local Currency Elections Regulations 1994 may, by notice given to an officer of the Board on or before 31st August 2000, elect that this section shall not have effect in relation to it until the first accounting period beginning on or after 1st July 2000.

Commentary—*Simon's Direct Tax Service* **D2.910–912**.
Amendments—[1] Words in sub-s (3) substituted by CAA 2001 s 578, Sch 2 para 106 with effect for corporation tax purposes as respects allowances and charges falling to be made for chargeable periods ending after 31 March 2001.

106 Foreign exchange gains and losses: use of local currency

(1)–(5) (*Amend* FA 1993 s 149)

(6) (*Substitutes* FA 1993 s 128(9)).

(7) (*Inserts* FA 1993 s 135A).

(8) (*Substitutes* FA 1993 s 140(12)).

(9)–(11) (*Amend* FA 1993 s 142).

(12)–(13) (*Amend* FA 1993 s 163).

(14) (*Repeals* FA 1993 s 164(6), (7)).

(15) (*Amends* FA 1993 s 167).

(16) (*Amends* FA 1998 s 110(4)(*b*)).

(17) This section has effect for accounting periods beginning on or after 1st January 2000 and ending on or after 21st March 2000.

Amendment—Repealed by FA 2002 s 141, Sch 40 Pt 3(10) with effect for accounting periods beginning after 30 September 2002.
Commentary—*Simon's Direct Tax Service* **D2.913, 914**.

Insurance

107 General insurance reserves

(1) Where an amount representing the whole or any part of the technical provisions which are made by a general insurer for a period of account is taken into account in computing for tax purposes the profits of his trade for that period—

(*a*) subsection (2) below applies if it becomes apparent in a later period of account that the amount taken into account was excessive; and

(*b*) subsection (3) below applies if it becomes apparent in such a period that that amount was insufficient.

(2) For the purpose of making good to the Exchequer the loss occasioned by the excess, an amount calculated by applying, for a prescribed period, a prescribed rate of interest to the amount of the excess shall be treated as a receipt of the general insurer's trade in computing for tax purposes the profits of that trade for the later period of account.

(3) For the purpose of making good to the general insurer the loss occasioned by the deficiency, an amount calculated by applying, for a prescribed period, a prescribed rate of interest to the amount of the deficiency shall be treated as an expense of the general insurer's trade in computing for tax purposes the profits of that trade for the later period of account.

(4) A general insurer may, before the end of a prescribed period, elect that any part of the technical provisions made by him for a period of account shall not be taken into account in computing for tax purposes the profits of his trade for that period; and where he does so, the profits of his trade for the next period of account shall be adjusted accordingly for the purposes of any computation for tax purposes.

(5) The Board may by regulations make provision for giving effect to subsections (1) to (4) above.

(6) The regulations may, in particular—

(*a*) exclude from the operation of subsections (1) to (4) above such descriptions of general insurer as may be prescribed;

(*b*) make such provision as appears to the Board to be appropriate for determining for the purposes of subsections (1) to (3) above whether any amount taken into account was excessive or insufficient and, if so, the amount of the excess or deficiency, including—

(i) provision requiring discounting at a prescribed rate; and

(ii) provision allowing a prescribed margin for error;

(*c*) make provision for applying subsections (1) to (3) above, to such extent and with such modifications as appear to the Board to be appropriate, to cases where it becomes apparent—

(i) that any amount taken into account was or has become insufficient; or

(ii) that any amount treated as a receipt or expense of a trade was excessive;

(*d*) make such provision as appears to the Board to be appropriate for dealing with cases where a general insurer transfers his general business to, or enters into a qualifying contract with, another person; and

(*e*) in the event of any changes in the rules or practice of Lloyd's, make such amendments of this section as appear to the Board to be expedient having regard to those changes.

(7) In this section—

"closing year", in relation to a syndicate, has the same meaning as in Chapter III of Part II of the Finance Act 1993 or Chapter V of Part IV of the Finance Act 1994;

["general business" means business which consists of the effecting or carrying out of contracts that fall within Part I of Schedule 1 to the Financial Services and Markets Act 2000 (Regulated Activities) Order 2001;][1]

"general insurer" means any of the following which carries on general business—

[(*a*) a person (other than a friendly society) who has permission under Part 4 of the Financial Services and Markets Act 2000 to effect or carry out contracts that fall within Part I of Schedule 1 to the Financial Services and Markets Act 2000 (Regulated Activities) Order 2001;][1]

[(*b*) an EEA firm of the kind mentioned in paragraph 5(*d*) of Schedule 3 to that Act which has permission under paragraph 15 of Schedule 3 to that Act (as a result of qualifying for authorisation under paragraph 12(1) of that Schedule) to effect or carry out such contracts;][1]

[(*ba*) a firm which has permission under paragraph 4 of Schedule 4 to that Act (as a result of qualifying for authorisation under paragraph 2 of that Schedule) to effect or carry out such contracts;][1]

(*c*) a controlled foreign company within the meaning of Chapter IV of Part XVII of the Taxes Act 1988; and

(*d*) an underwriting member of Lloyd's ("an underwriting member");

"period of account"—

(*a*) except in relation to an underwriting member, means a period for which an account is made up;

(*b*) in relation to such a member, means an underwriting year in which profits or losses are declared for an earlier underwriting year;

"prescribed" means prescribed by regulations under this section;

"qualifying contract", in relation to a general insurer, means a contract for reinsuring the liabilities to which any technical provisions of his relate;

"reinsurance to close contract" means a contract where, in accordance with the rules or practice of Lloyd's and in consideration of the payment of a premium, one underwriting member agrees with another to meet liabilities arising from the latter's underwriting business for an underwriting year so that the accounts of the business for that year may be closed;

"syndicate" means a syndicate of underwriting members of Lloyd's formed for an underwriting year;

"technical provisions", except in relation to an underwriting member, means any of the following—

(*a*) provisions for claims outstanding;

(*b*) provisions for unearned premiums;

(*c*) provisions for unexpired risks;

and in this definition expressions which are used in Schedule 9A to the Companies Act 1985 have the same meanings as in that Schedule;

"technical provisions", in relation to an underwriting member, means—

(*a*) so much of the premiums paid, or treated (in accordance with the rules or practice of Lloyd's) as paid, by him under reinsurance to close contracts; and

(*b*) so much of any provisions made for the unpaid liabilities of an open syndicate of which he is a member,

as may be determined by or under regulations made by the Board;

"underwriting year" means the calendar year;

and for the purposes of this section a syndicate is an open syndicate at any time after the end of its closing year if, at that time, the accounts of its business for the underwriting year for which it was formed have not been closed.

(8) Regulations under this section may—

(*a*) make different provision for different cases or descriptions of case, including different provision for different entitlements to participate in the general business carried on by syndicates; and

(*b*) make such supplementary, incidental, consequential and transitional provision as appears to the Board to be appropriate.

(9) An amount which under subsection (2) or (3) above is treated as a receipt or expense of an underwriting member's trade—

(*a*) shall not be included in the aggregate amount mentioned in paragraph 1 of Schedule 19 to the Finance Act 1993; but

(*b*) shall be regarded as arising directly from his membership of one or more syndicates for the purposes of section 172(1)(*a*) of the Finance Act 1993 or section 220(2)(*a*) of the Finance Act 1994.

(10) Nothing in paragraph 7 of Schedule 19 to the Finance Act 1993 shall be taken to affect the operation of subsection (2) or (3) above or the exercise of the power conferred by subsection (4) above.

(11) Section 177 of the Finance Act 1993 and section 224 of the Finance Act 1994 (which are superseded by this section) shall cease to have effect.

(12) In this section—

(*a*) subsections (1) to (3), subsections (5) to (8) and (10) so far as relating to those subsections and subsection (9) have effect where—

(i) the first period of account mentioned in subsection (1) begins on or after 1st January 2000; and

(ii) the later period of account mentioned in that subsection begins on or after 1st January 2001;

(*b*) subsection (4), and subsections (5) to (8) and (10) so far as relating to that subsection, have effect in relation to periods of account beginning on or after 1st January 2000;

(*c*) subsection (11) has effect in relation to profits of underwriting members' trades which are declared in periods of account beginning on or after that date.

Commentary—*Simon's Direct Tax Service* D4.538, E5.605.
Regulations—General Insurance Reserves (Tax) Regulations, SI 2001/1757.
Amendments—¹ In sub-s (7), definition of "general business" substituted, and in the definition of "general insurer", sub-paras (*a*), (*b*), (*ba*) substituted for sub-paras (*a*), (*ab*) by the Financial Services and Markets Act 2000 (Consequential Amendments) (Taxes) Order, SI 2001/3629 arts 105, 106 with effect from 1 December 2001, immediately after the coming into force of the Financial Services and Markets Act 2000 ss 411, 432(1), Sch 20.

108 Overseas life assurance business

(1), (2) (*Amend* TA 1988 s 431D).

(3) Where the policy or contract for any life assurance business was made before such day as the Treasury may by order appoint, the amendments made by this section (and any regulations made under them) shall not have effect for determining whether the business is overseas life assurance business.

Commentary—*Simon's Direct Tax Service* D4.524.
Note—The appointed day for the purposes of sub-s (3) is 22 August 2000 by virtue of the Finance Act 2000, Section 108(3), (Appointed Day) Order, SI 2000/2082.

109 Insurance business: apportionment rules

(1), (2) (*Amend* TA 1988 s 432ZA).

(3), (4) (*Amend* TA 1988 ss 432A(6), 432C(4), 432D(3)).

(5), (6) (*Amend* TA 1988 s 432A).

(7) (*Amends* TA 1988 s 432C(5)(*b*)).

(8) (*Inserts* FA 1996 Sch 11 para 3A).

(9) (*Amends* TA 1988 s 431(2), Sch 19AA para 4(2), Sch 19AC para 7(3)).

(10) This section shall have effect in relation to accounting periods beginning on or after 1st January 2000 and ending on or after 21st March 2000.

Commentary—*Simon's Direct Tax Service* D4.526.

Miscellaneous

110 Rent factoring

(1) (*Inserts* TA 1988 ss 43A–43G).

(2) The provisions inserted by subsection (1) have effect in relation to transactions entered into on or after 21st March 2000.

Commentary—*Simon's Direct Tax Service* A4.101.

111 Payments under deduction of tax

(1) Chapter VIIA of Part IV of the Taxes Act 1988 (paying and collecting agents) shall cease to have effect.

(2) (*Amends* TA 1988 s 349(3)(*c*), (3B), (4))

and accordingly section 124 of that Act (interest on quoted Eurobonds) shall cease to have effect.

(3) (*Amends* TA 1988 s 482).

(4) (*Inserts* TA 1988 s 477A(2A)).

(5) (*Amends* F(No 2)A 1997 s 37(11)).

(6) In this section—

(*a*) subsections (1) and (5) apply to relevant payments or receipts in relation to which the chargeable date for the purposes of Chapter VIIA of Part IV is on or after 1st April 2001;

(*b*) subsection (2) applies in relation to payments of interest made on or after that date;

(*c*) subsection (3) applies in relation to declarations under section 481(5)(k)(i) of the Taxes Act 1988 made on or after 6th April 2001.

Commentary—*Simon's Direct Tax Service* A3.405, A7.901, 1001.

112 UK public revenue dividends: deduction of tax

(1) (*Amends* TA 1988 s 50(A1)).

(2), (3) (*Amend* TA 1988 s 349).

(4) (*Inserts* TA 1988 s 350A).

(5) This section applies to payments made on or after 1st April 2001.

Commentary—*Simon's Direct Tax Service* A3.405, A7.1101.

113 Tax treatment of expenditure on production or acquisition of films

Commentary—*Simon's Direct Tax Service* B3.1307.
Amendment—This section repealed by the Capital Allowances Act 2001 s 580, Sch 4 with effect for income tax purposes, as respects allowances and charges falling to be made for chargeable periods ending after 5 April 2001, and for corporation tax purposes, as respects allowances and charges falling to be made for chargeable periods ending after 31 March 2001.

PART VI
MISCELLANEOUS AND SUPPLEMENTARY PROVISIONS
Incentives for electronic communications

143 Power to provide incentives to use electronic communications

(1) Regulations may be made in accordance with Schedule 38 to this Act for providing incentives to use electronic communications.

(2) Anything received by way of incentive under any such regulations shall not be regarded as income for any purposes of the Tax Acts.

Commentary—*Simon's Direct Tax Service* A3.101.

Compliance

144 Offence of fraudulent evasion of income tax

(1) A person commits an offence if he is knowingly concerned in the fraudulent evasion of income tax by him or any other person.

(2) A person guilty of an offence under this section is liable—

(*a*) on summary conviction, to imprisonment for a term not exceeding six months or a fine not exceeding the statutory maximum, or both;
(*b*) on conviction on indictment, to imprisonment for a term not exceeding seven years or a fine, or both.

(3) This section applies to things done or omitted on or after 1st January 2001.

Commentary—*Simon's Direct Tax Service* A3.1502A.
Revenue & other press releases—IR Tax Bulletin October 2000 p 782 (discussion of what conduct amounts to being "knowingly concerned in the fraudulent evasion of income tax").

145 Information about interest etc paid, credited or received

(1)–(3) (*Amend* TMA 1970 s 17).

(4)–(9) (*Amend* TMA 1970 s 18).

(10) Section 482A of Taxes Act 1988 (audit powers in relation to non-residents) shall cease to have effect.

(11) This section has effect in relation to amounts paid, credited or received on or after 6th April 2001.

Commentary—*Simon's Direct Tax Service* A3.152, D4.729.

146 International exchange of information: general

(1) (*Inserts* TA 1988 s 815C).

(2) (*Amends* TA 1988 s 816(2) *and inserts* s 816(2ZA)).

(3) Subsections (1) to (8) and (8C) to (9) of section 20 of the Taxes Management Act 1970 (powers to call for information relevant to liability to income tax, corporation tax or capital gains tax) shall have effect as if the references in those provisions to tax liability included a reference to liability to a tax which—

(*a*) is a tax of a territory outside the United Kingdom; and
(*b*) is covered by arrangements having effect under section 788 or 815C of the Taxes Act 1988 and containing provision with respect to the obtaining (as well as the disclosure) of information.

(4) In their application by virtue of subsection (3) above those provisions shall have effect as if—

(*a*) the reference in section 20(7A) to any provision of the Taxes Acts were a reference to any provision of the law of the territory concerned;
(*b*) the references in subsection (2) of section 20B to an appeal relating to tax were references to an appeal, review or similar proceedings under the law of that territory relating to the tax in question; and
(*c*) the reference in subsection (6) of that section to believing that tax has or may have been lost to the Crown were a reference to believing that the tax in question has or may have been lost to that territory.

Commentary—*Simon's Direct Tax Service* A3.154, F1.264.

148 Use of minimum wage information

(1) Information obtained by an officer acting for the purposes of the National Minimum Wage Act 1998 (''the 1998 Act'') by virtue of section 13(1)(*a*) or (*b*) of that Act (officers) may be supplied by or with the authority of the Secretary of State to the Board for the purpose of any of its functions.

(2) Information obtained by an officer of the Board acting in accordance with section 13(1)(*b*) of the 1998 Act may be used for the purpose of any functions of the Board.

(3) Information supplied to the Secretary of State under section 16(2) of the 1998 Act (information obtained by agricultural wages officers) may be supplied by the Secretary of State to the Board for the purpose of any of its functions.

(4) For section 15(6) of the 1998 Act (restrictions on use of information) there shall be substituted—
   ''(6) This section—
     (*a*) does not limit the circumstances in which information may be supplied or used apart from this section; and
     (*b*) is subject to section 148 of the Finance Act 2000 (use of minimum wage information).''.

Commentary—*Simon's Direct Tax Service* **A3.150**.

149 Orders for the delivery of documents

(1) (*Inserts* TMA 1970 s 20BA).

(2) After Schedule 1 to the Taxes Management Act 1970, insert the Schedule 1AA set out in Schedule 39 to this Act.

(3) (*Amends* TMA 1970 s 20BB).

(4) (*Amends* TMA 1970 s 20D(1)).

Commentary—*Simon's Direct Tax Service* **A3.151**.

150 Search warrants: miscellaneous amendments

(1) Section 20C of the Taxes Management Act 1970 (search warrants) is amended as follows.

(2)–(5) (*Amend* TMA 1970 s 20C).

Commentary—*Simon's Direct Tax Service* **A3.157**.

Supplementary provisions

155 Interpretation

In this Act ''the Taxes Act 1988'' means the Income and Corporation Taxes Act 1988.

156 Repeals

(1) The enactments mentioned in Schedule 40 to this Act (which include provisions that are spent or of no practical utility) are repealed to the extent specified in the third column of that Schedule.

(2) The repeals specified in that Schedule have effect subject to the commencement provisions and savings contained or referred to in the notes set out in that Schedule.

157 Short title

This Act may be cited as the Finance Act 2000.

SCHEDULES

SCHEDULE 8

EMPLOYEE SHARE OWNERSHIP PLANS

Section 47

Revenue Internal Guidance—Capital Gains Manual CG 56490–56497 (operation of this Schedule).

PART I

INTRODUCTORY

Employee share ownership plans

1—(1) In this Schedule an ''employee share ownership plan'' means a plan established by a company providing—

   (*a*) for shares (''free shares'') to be appropriated to employees without payment, or (*b*) for shares (''partnership shares'') to be acquired on behalf of employees out of sums deducted from their salary.

(2) A plan that provides for partnership shares may also provide for shares (''matching shares'') to be appropriated without payment to employees in proportion to the partnership shares acquired by them.

(3) Where a plan contains provision for all, or more than one, of the kinds of shares mentioned in sub-paragraphs (1) and (2), it may leave it for the company to decide when the provisions relating to each kind of share are to have effect.

(4) In this Schedule, in relation to an employee share ownership plan ''the company'' means the company which established the plan.

Commentary—*Simon's Direct Tax Service* **E4.529**.

Group plans

2—(1) An employee share ownership plan established by a company that controls other companies (a ''parent company'') may extend to all or any of those other companies.

In this Schedule a plan established by a parent company which so extends is referred to as a ''group plan''.

(2) In relation to a group plan a ''participating company'' means the parent company or any other company to which for the time being the plan is expressed to extend.

Commentary—*Simon's Direct Tax Service* **E4.529**.

Meaning of ''award of shares'', ''participant'' etc

3—(1) For the purposes of this Schedule an award of shares is made under a plan on each occasion when in accordance with the plan—

  (*a*) matching or free shares are appropriated to employees, or
  (*b*) partnership shares are acquired on behalf of employees.

(2) For the purposes of this Schedule an individual participates in an award of free, matching or partnership shares under the plan if shares (''the individual award'') included in that award are—

  (*a*) in the case of an award of free or matching shares, appropriated to him, or
  (*b*) in the case of an award of partnership shares, acquired on his behalf,

and references to shares awarded to an individual are to free or matching shares appropriated to him, or partnership shares acquired on his behalf, under the plan.

(3) In this Schedule ''participant'', in relation to a plan, means an individual to whom shares have been awarded under the plan.

Application for approval

4—(1) Where an employee share ownership plan has been established, on the application of the company the Inland Revenue shall approve the plan if they are satisfied that it meets the requirements of this Schedule.

(2) An application for approval must contain such particulars and be supported by such evidence as the Inland Revenue may require.

Appeal against refusal of approval

5—(1) If the Inland Revenue refuse to approve the plan, the company may appeal to the Special Commissioners.

(2) Notice of appeal must be given to the Inland Revenue within 30 days after their decision was notified to the company.

(3) If the Special Commissioners allow the appeal they may direct the Inland Revenue to approve the plan with effect from such date (but not earlier than the application for approval) as the Commissioners may specify.

PART II
GENERAL REQUIREMENTS
Introduction

6 The plan must meet the requirements of—

  paragraph 7 (the purpose of plan);
  paragraph 8 (all-employee nature of plan);
  paragraph 9 (participation on same terms);
  paragraph 10 (no preferential treatment for directors, etc);
  paragraph 11 (no further conditions);
  paragraph 12 (no loan arrangements).

Commentary—*Simon's Direct Tax Service* **E4.530**.

The purpose of the plan

7—(1) The purpose of the plan must be to provide benefits to employees in the nature of shares in a company which give them a continuing stake in that company.

(2) The plan must not contain, and the operation of the plan must not involve, features which are neither essential nor reasonably incidental to that purpose.

Commentary—*Simon's Direct Tax Service* **E4.530**.

All-employee nature of plan

8—(1) The plan must provide that every employee who—

(a) meets the requirements mentioned in Part III (eligibility of individuals) in relation to an award of shares under the plan, and

(b) is chargeable to tax under Case I of Schedule E in respect of the employment by reference to which he satisfies the condition in paragraph 14 (the employment requirement),

is eligible to participate in the award, and invited to do so.

(2) The plan must not contain any feature which has or would have the effect of discouraging any description of employees within sub-paragraph (1) from participating in an award of shares under the plan.

This does not apply to any provision required or authorised by this Schedule.

(3) The plan may provide that an employee who—

(a) meets the requirements mentioned in Part III (eligibility of individuals) in relation to an award of shares under the plan, but

(b) is not chargeable to tax as mentioned in sub-paragraph (1)(b),

is eligible to participate in the award, and may be invited to do so.

(4) For the purposes of this Schedule an individual is a "qualifying employee", in relation to an award of shares, if—

(a) he is eligible to participate in the award, and

(b) either—

(i) he must be invited to participate in the award (see sub-paragraph (1)), or

(ii) under the plan he may be invited to participate in the award (see sub-paragraph (3)) and has been so invited.

Commentary—*Simon's Direct Tax Service* **E4.530**.

Participation on same terms

9—(1) The requirement of this paragraph is—

(a) that every employee who is invited to participate in an award must be invited to participate on the same terms, and

(b) that those who do participate must actually do so on the same terms.

(2) The requirement of this paragraph is infringed by the awarding of free shares by reference to factors other than those mentioned in sub-paragraph (3).

(3) The requirement of this paragraph is not infringed by the awarding of free shares by reference to an employee's—

(a) remuneration,

(b) length of service, or

(c) hours worked.

This is subject to sub-paragraph (4).

(4) Where the awarding of free shares is by reference to more than one of the factors mentioned in sub-paragraph (3) the requirement of this paragraph is infringed unless—

(a) each factor gives rise to a separate entitlement related to the level of remuneration, length of service or (as the case may be) hours worked, and

(b) the total entitlement is the sum of those separate entitlements.

(5) In the case of an award of free shares which provides for performance allowances, this paragraph has effect as provided in paragraph 29 (performance allowances: method one) or, as the case may be, paragraph 30 (performance allowances: method two).

For this purpose "performance allowance" has the meaning given in paragraph 25(1).

Commentary—*Simon's Direct Tax Service* **E4.530**.

No preferential treatment for directors etc

10—(1) The first requirement of this paragraph is that no feature of the plan must have or be likely to have the effect of conferring benefits wholly or mainly—

(a) on directors, or

(b) on employees receiving higher levels of remuneration.

(2) The second requirement of this paragraph is that in the case of a plan established by a company that is a member of a group, the identity of the company (or, if it is a group plan, the participating companies) must not be such that the plan has or is likely to have the effect of conferring benefits wholly or mainly—

(a) on employees of companies that are members of the group who receive higher levels of remuneration, or

(b) on directors of such companies.

(3) This paragraph is subject to paragraph 9(3) (award of shares by reference to remuneration etc).

Commentary—*Simon's Direct Tax Service* **E4.530**.

No further conditions

11 No conditions, other than those required or permitted by this Schedule, may be imposed on an employee's participation in an award of shares under the plan.

No loan arrangements

12—(1) The arrangements for the plan must not make any provision, or be in any way associated with any provision made, for loans to some or all of the employees of—

(a) the company, or

(b) in the case of a group plan, any participating company,

and the operation of the plan must not be in any way associated with such loans.

(2) For the purposes of sub-paragraph (1) "arrangements" includes any scheme, agreement, undertaking or understanding, whether or not legally enforceable.

Commentary—*Simon's Direct Tax Service* **E4.530**.

PART III
ELIGIBILITY OF INDIVIDUALS
Introduction

13—(1) The plan must provide that an individual may only participate in an award of shares if—

(a) in the case of free shares, he is eligible to participate in the award at the time it is made, and

(b) in the case of partnership or matching shares—

(i) if there is no accumulation period, he is eligible to participate in the award at the time the partnership share money relating to the award is deducted, and

(ii) if there is an accumulation period, he is eligible to participate in the award at the time of the first deduction of partnership share money relating to the award.

(2) For the purposes of sub-paragraph (1), in the case of an award of matching shares the deduction of partnership share money "relating" to the award is the deduction relating to the award of partnership shares to which the matching shares relate.

(3) An individual is eligible to participate in an award of shares under the plan if and only if—

(a) the requirements of the plan are met as to—

(i) employment (see paragraph 14),

(ii) no material interest (see paragraph 15), and

(iii) not participating in other schemes (see paragraph 16), and

(b) in a case where the individual is not within paragraph 8(1) (employees who must be invited to participate in the award), any further eligibility requirements of the plan are met.

Commentary—*Simon's Direct Tax Service* **E4.531**.

The employment requirement

14—(1) The plan must provide that an individual is not eligible to participate in an award of shares unless—

(a) he is an employee of the company or, in the case of a group plan, of a participating company, and

(b) where the plan provides for a qualifying period, he has at all times during that period been an employee [of a qualifying company.]¹

[(1A) Except in the case of a group plan, a qualifying company means—

(a) the company, or

(b) a company that when the individual was employed by it was an associated company—

(i) of the company, or

(ii) of another company qualifying under this paragraph.

(1B) In the case of a group plan, a qualifying company means—

(a) a company that is a participating company at the end of the qualifying period, or (*b*) a company that when the individual was employed by it was a participating company, or

(*c*) a company that when the individual was employed by it was an associated company of—

    (i) a company qualifying under paragraph (*a*) or (*b*), or

    (ii) another company qualifying under this paragraph.]²

(2) If the plan provides for a qualifying period, that period must be—

(*a*) in the case of free shares, a period of not more than 18 months ending with the date on which the award is made,

(*b*) in the case of partnership or matching shares—

    (i) if the plan does not provide for an accumulation period, a period of not more than 18 months ending with the deduction of partnership share money relating to the award, and

    (ii) if the plan provides for an accumulation period, a period of not more than six months ending with the start of the accumulation period relating to the award.

(3) For the purposes of sub-paragraph (2), in the case of an award of matching shares the deduction of partnership share money or accumulation period "relating" to the award is the deduction or period relating to the award of partnership shares to which the matching shares relate.

(4) In relation to an award, the same qualifying period must apply in relation to all employees of the company or, in the case of a group plan, of the participating companies.

(5) Subject to sub-paragraphs (2) and (4), the plan may authorise the company to specify different qualifying periods in respect of different awards of shares.

Commentary—*Simon's Direct Tax Service* **E4.531**.
Amendment—¹ Words in sub-para (1) substituted by FA 2001 s 61, Sch 13 para 2 with effect for awards of shares (within the meaning of FA 2000 Sch 8) made after the passing of FA 2001. Before amendment, the substituted words were as follows: "—
    (i) of the company, or
    (ii) in the case of a group plan, of a company that is a participating company at the end of that period."
² Sub-paras (1A), (1B) inserted by FA 2001 s 61, Sch 13 para 2 with effect for awards of shares (within the meaning of FA 2000 Sch 8) made after passing of FA 2001.

The "no material interest" requirement

15—(1) The plan must provide that an individual is not eligible to participate in an award of shares if he has, or has within the preceding twelve months had, a material interest in—

(*a*) a close company whose shares may be awarded under the plan, or

(*b*) a company which has control of such a company or is a member of a consortium which owns such a company.

(2) For the purposes of this paragraph an individual is regarded as having a material interest in a company if—

(*a*) the individual,

(*b*) the individual together with one or more associates of his, or

(*c*) any associate of the individual's, with or without any other such associates,

has a material interest in the company.

(3) This paragraph is supplemented—

(*a*) as regards the meaning of "material interest", by paragraphs 17 to 19, and

(*b*) as regards the meaning of "associate", by paragraph 20 (read with paragraphs 21 and 22).

Commentary—*Simon's Direct Tax Service* **E4.531**.

The requirement of non-participation in other relevant share schemes

16—(1) The plan must provide that an individual is not to participate in an award of free shares under the plan in a tax year if in that year—

(*a*) shares have been (or are at the same time to be) appropriated to him in accordance with an approved profit sharing scheme established by the company or a connected company, or

(*b*) he has participated (or is at the same time to participate) in another employee share ownership plan established by the company or a connected company and approved under this Schedule.

(2) The plan must provide that an individual is not eligible to participate in an award of partnership or matching shares under the plan in any tax year if, in that year, he has participated (or at the same time participates) in an award of shares under another employee share ownership plan established by the company or a connected company and approved under this Schedule.

(3) For the purposes of this paragraph an individual is treated as having participated in an award of free shares under an employee share ownership plan if he would have participated in that award but for his failure to obtain a performance allowance (see paragraph 25).

(4) In this paragraph "connected company" means—

(*a*) a company which controls or is controlled by the company or which is controlled by a company which also controls the company, or

(*b*) a company which is a member of a consortium owning the company or which is owned in part by the company as a member of a consortium.

Commentary—*Simon's Direct Tax Service* **E4.531**.

Meaning of "material interest"

17—(1) For the purposes of paragraph 15 (the "no material interest" requirement) a material interest in a company means—

(a) beneficial ownership of, or the ability to control, directly or through the medium of other companies or by any other indirect means, more than 25% of the ordinary share capital of the company; or

(b) where the company is a close company, possession of or entitlement to acquire such rights as would, in the event of the winding up of the company or in any other circumstances, give an entitlement to receive more than 25% of the assets that would then be available for distribution among the participators.

(2) In this paragraph—

"close company" includes a company that would be a close company but for—

(a) section 414(1)(a) of the Taxes Act 1988 (exclusion of companies not resident in the United Kingdom), or

(b) section 415 of that Act (exclusion of certain quoted companies); and

"participator" has the meaning given by section 417(1) of that Act.

(3) This paragraph is supplemented by paragraph 18 (options etc) and paragraph 19 (shares held by trustees of approved profit sharing scheme etc).

Commentary—Simon's Direct Tax Service **E4.531**.

Material interest: options etc

18—(1) For the purposes of paragraph 17(1) (meaning of material interest) a right to acquire shares (however arising) is treated as a right to control them.

(2) In any case where—

(a) the shares attributed to an individual consist of or include shares which he or another person has a right to acquire, and

(b) the circumstances are such that if that right were to be exercised the shares acquired would be shares which were previously unissued and which the company is contractually bound to issue in the event of the exercise of the right,

then in determining at any time prior to the exercise of the right whether the number of shares attributed to the individual exceeds a particular percentage of the ordinary share capital of the company, that ordinary share capital shall be taken to be increased by the number of unissued shares referred to in paragraph (b).

(3) The references in sub-paragraph (2) to the shares attributed to an individual are to the shares which in accordance with paragraph 17(1)(a) fall to be brought into account in his case to determine whether their number exceeds a particular percentage of the company's ordinary share capital.

Commentary—Simon's Direct Tax Service **E4.531**.

Material interest: shares held by trustees of approved profit sharing schemes etc

19 In applying paragraph 17(1) (meaning of material interest) there shall be disregarded—

(a) the interest of the trustees of—

(i) any approved profit sharing scheme, or

(ii) an approved employee share ownership plan,

in any shares held by them in accordance with the scheme or plan but which have not been appropriated to or acquired on behalf of an individual; and

(b) any rights exercisable by those trustees by virtue of any such interest.

Commentary—Simon's Direct Tax Service **E4.531**.

Meaning of "associate"

20—(1) In paragraph 15 (the "no material interest" requirement) "associate", in relation to a person, means—

(a) any relative or partner of that person,

(b) the trustee or trustees of any settlement in relation to which that person, or any relative of his (living or dead), is or was a settlor, and

(c) where that person is interested in any shares or obligations of the company which are subject to any trust, or are part of the estate of a deceased person, the trustee or trustees of the settlement concerned or (as the case may be) the personal representatives of the deceased.

(2) In sub-paragraph (1)(a) and (b) "relative" means husband or wife, parent or remoter forebear, child or remoter issue, or brother or sister.

(3) In sub-paragraph (1)(b) "settlor" and "settlement" have the same meaning as in Chapter IA of Part XV of the Taxes Act 1988 (see section 660G(1) and (2)).

Commentary—Simon's Direct Tax Service **E4.531**.

Meaning of "associate": trustees of employee benefit trust

21—(1) This paragraph applies for the purposes of paragraph 20(1)(c) (meaning of "associate": trustees of settlement) where an individual is interested as a beneficiary of an employee benefit trust in shares or obligations of a company ("the relevant company") in relation to which it falls to be determined whether that individual has an interest.

(2) The trustees of the employee benefit trust are not regarded as associates of the individual by reason only of his being so interested if neither—

    (a) the individual, nor

    (b) the individual together with one or more associates of his, nor

    (c) any associate of the individual's, with or without any other such associates,

has at any time on or after 14th March 1989 been the beneficial owner of, or able (directly or through the medium of other companies or by any other indirect means) to control, more than 25% of the ordinary share capital of the company.

(3) In this paragraph "employee benefit trust" has the same meaning as in paragraph 7 of Schedule 8 to the Taxes Act 1988.

(4) Sub-paragraphs (9) to (12) of that paragraph apply for the purposes of this paragraph in relation to an individual as they apply for the purposes of that paragraph in relation to an employee.

(5) In sub-paragraph (2)(b) and (c) "associate" does not include the trustees of an employee benefit trust by reason only that the individual has an interest in shares or obligations of the trust.

Commentary—*Simon's Direct Tax Service* E4.531.

Meaning of "associate": trustees of discretionary trust

22—(1) This paragraph applies for the purposes of paragraph 20(1)(c) (meaning of "associate": trustees of settlement) where—

    (a) the person in question ("the beneficiary") is one of the objects of a discretionary trust, and

    (b) the property subject to the trust has at any time consisted of, or included, shares or obligations of the company ("the relevant company") in relation to which it falls to be determined whether that person has an interest.

(2) If—

    (a) the beneficiary has ceased to be eligible to benefit under the discretionary trust by reason of—

        (i) an irrevocable disclaimer or release executed by him, or

        (ii) the irrevocable exercise by the trustees of a power to exclude him from the objects of the trust,

    (b) immediately after the beneficiary ceased to be so eligible, no associate of his was interested in the shares or obligations of the relevant company which were subject to the trust, and

    (c) during the period of twelve months ending with the date when the beneficiary ceased to be so eligible, neither he nor any associate of his received any benefit under the trust,

the beneficiary is not regarded by reason only of the matters mentioned in sub-paragraph (1) as having been interested in the shares or obligations of the relevant company at any time during the period of twelve months mentioned in paragraph (c).

(3) In sub-paragraph (2) "associate" has the meaning given by paragraph 20, but with the omission of sub-paragraph (1)(c) of that paragraph (trusts and estates).

PART IV

FREE SHARES

Introduction

23 If the plan provides for free shares it must comply with the requirements of this Part of this Schedule.

Maximum annual award

24—(1) The plan must provide that the initial market value of the free shares awarded to a participant in any tax year cannot exceed £3,000.

(2) For this purpose the "initial market value" of shares means their market value on the date on which they are awarded.

(3) For the purposes of this paragraph the market value of shares subject to restrictions or risk of forfeiture shall be determined as if there were no such restriction or risk.

For this purpose shares are "subject to risk of forfeiture" if the interest that may be acquired is only conditional within the meaning of section 140C of the Taxes Act 1988.

Commentary—*Simon's Direct Tax Service* E4.532.

Performance allowances

25—(1) Sub-paragraph (2) applies if the plan provides for performance allowances, that is for—

    (*a*) whether or not free shares will be awarded to an individual, or

    (*b*) the number or value of free shares awarded,

to be conditional on performance targets being met.

(2) Where this sub-paragraph applies—

    (*a*) the requirements of—

        paragraph 26 (performance allowances: general application),

        paragraph 27 (performance measures and targets), and

        paragraph 28 (performance allowances: information to be given to employees), and

    (*b*) the requirements of either paragraph 29 (method one) or paragraph 30 (method two),

must be complied with.

Performance allowances: general application

26 If the plan provides for performance allowances in relation to an award it must make provision for such allowances for all qualifying employees in relation to that award.

Performance allowances: measures and targets

27—(1) If the plan provides for performance allowances the following requirements must be met with respect to performance measures and performance targets.

(2) The performance measures used must—

    (*a*) be based on business results or other objective criteria, and

    (*b*) be fair and objective measures of the performance of the units to which they are or may be applied.

(3) The performance targets must be set for performance units comprising one or more employees.

(4) For the purposes of an award of free shares under the plan an employee must not be a member of more than one performance unit.

Commentary—*Simon's Direct Tax Service* **E4.532**.

Performance allowances: information to be given to employees

28—(1) If the plan provides for performance allowances in relation to an award of shares, the plan must require the company—

    (*a*) to notify each employee participating in the award of the performance targets and measures which, under the plan, will be used to determine the number or value of free shares awarded to him; and

    (*b*) to notify all qualifying employees of the company or, in the case of a group plan, of any participating company, in general terms, of the performance measures to be used to determine the number or value of free shares to be awarded to each employee participating in the award.

(2) The notices must be given as soon as reasonably practicable.

(3) The company may exclude from the notice mentioned in sub-paragraph (1)(*b*) any information the disclosure of which the company reasonably considers would prejudice commercial confidentiality.

Commentary—*Simon's Direct Tax Service* **E4.532**.

Performance allowances: method one

29—(1) The requirements of this paragraph are that if the plan provides for performance allowances in relation to an award of shares—

    (*a*) at least 20% of the shares in the award must be awarded without reference to performance in accordance with the requirement of paragraph 9 (participation on same terms),

    (*b*) the remaining shares must be awarded by reference to performance, and

    (*c*) the highest number of shares within paragraph (*b*) awarded to an individual must be not more than four times the highest number of shares within paragraph (*a*) awarded to an individual.

(2) In determining for the purposes of sub-paragraph (1)(*a*) whether the requirement of paragraph 9 (participation on same terms) is met the shares to which sub-paragraph (1)(*a*) above applies are treated as a separate award of free shares.

(3) Where the plan meets the requirements of sub-paragraph (1), the requirement of paragraph 9 (participation on same terms) does not apply to any provision of the plan relating to the awarding of shares within sub-paragraph (1)(*b*).

(4) If free shares of different classes are awarded, the requirements of sub-paragraph (1) apply separately in relation to each class.

Commentary—*Simon's Direct Tax Service* **E4.532**.

Performance allowances: method two

30—(1) The requirements of this paragraph are that in relation to an award of free shares under the plan—

    (*a*) some or all of the shares must be awarded by reference to performance; and

    (*b*) the awarding of the shares to qualifying employees who are members of the same performance unit must meet the requirement of paragraph 9 (participation on same terms).

(2) In determining for the purposes of sub-paragraph (1)(*b*) whether the requirement of paragraph 9 (participation on same terms) is met the free shares awarded in respect of each performance unit are treated as a separate award of free shares.

(3) If this method is used nothing in paragraph 9 (participation on same terms) requires the awarding of shares to members of different performance units to be on the same terms.

Commentary—*Simon's Direct Tax Service* E4.532.

The holding period

31—(1) The plan must require the company in respect of each award of free shares to specify a period (''the holding period'') during which a participant is bound by contract with the company—

    (*a*) to permit his free shares to remain in the hands of the trustees, and

    (*b*) not to assign, charge or otherwise dispose of his beneficial interest in the shares.

(2) The holding period—

    (*a*) must be a period of at least three years but not more than five years, beginning with the date on which the shares in question are awarded to the participant, and

    (*b*) must be the same in respect of all shares in the same award.

(3) The plan may authorise the company to specify different holding periods from time to time.

But it must prevent the company from increasing the holding period specified in respect of free shares that have been awarded under the plan.

(4) The participant's obligations with respect to the holding period—

    (*a*) come to an end if during the period he ceases to be in relevant employment, and

    (*b*) are subject to—

        paragraph 32 (power to authorise trustees to accept general offers etc);

        paragraph 73 (meeting PAYE obligations); and

        paragraph 121(5) (termination of plan: early removal of shares with participant's consent).

Commentary—*Simon's Direct Tax Service* E4.532.

Holding period: power to authorise trustees to accept general offers etc

32 A participant may direct the trustees to do any of the following during the holding period—

    (*a*) to accept an offer for any of his free shares (''the original shares'') if the acceptance or agreement will result in a new holding being equated with the original shares for the purposes of capital gains tax; or

    (*b*) to accept an offer of a qualifying corporate bond (whether alone or with other assets or cash or both) for his free shares if the offer forms part of such a general offer as is mentioned in paragraph (*c*); or

    (*c*) to accept an offer of cash, with or without other assets, for his free shares if the offer forms part of a general offer which is made to holders of shares of the same class as his or of shares in the same company and which is made in the first instance on a condition such that if it is satisfied the person making the offer will have control of that company, within the meaning of section 416 of the Taxes Act 1988; or

    (*d*) to agree to a transaction affecting his free shares or such of them as are of a particular class, if the transaction would be entered into pursuant to a compromise, arrangement or scheme applicable to or affecting—

        (i) all the ordinary share capital of the company or, as the case may be, all the shares of the class in question, or

        (ii) all the shares, or all the shares of the class in question, which are held by a class of shareholders identified otherwise than by reference to their employment or their participation in an approved employee share ownership plan.

Commentary—*Simon's Direct Tax Service* E4.532.

PART V

PARTNERSHIP SHARES

Introduction

33 If the plan provides for partnership shares it must comply with the requirements of this Part of this Schedule.

Partnership share agreements

34 The plan must provide for qualifying employees to enter into agreements with the company (''partnership share agreements'') under which—

(*a*) the employee authorises the company to deduct part of his salary for the purchase of partnership shares, and

(*b*) the company undertakes to arrange for partnership shares to be awarded to the employee in accordance with the plan.

Commentary—*Simon's Direct Tax Service* **E4.533**.

Deductions from salary

35—(1) The plan must provide for a partnership share agreement to be given effect by deductions from the employee's salary.

Amounts so deducted are referred to in this Part of this Schedule as ''partnership share money''.

(2) The partnership share agreement must specify—

(*a*) what amounts are to be deducted, and

(*b*) at what intervals.

This does not prevent the employee and the company agreeing to vary those amounts or intervals.

(3) For the purposes of sub-paragraph (2)(*a*) the agreement may specify a percentage of the employee's salary.

(4) The plan must require the employer company to calculate the amounts and intervals having regard to the provisions of paragraph 36 (maximum amount of deductions from salary).

For this purpose ''the employer company'' is the company by reference to which the employee meets the requirement of paragraph 14 (the employment requirement) in relation to the plan.

Commentary—*Simon's Direct Tax Service* **E4.533**.

Maximum amount of deductions

36—(1) The amount of partnership share money deducted from an employee's salary must not exceed—

(*a*) £125 in any month, or

(*b*) where the salary is not paid at monthly intervals, such amount as bears to £125 the same proportion as the pay interval in question bears to one month.

(2) The amount of partnership share money deducted from an employee's salary must not exceed 10% of the employee's salary.

This means—

(*a*) if the plan does not provide for an accumulation period, 10% of the salary payment from which the deduction is made;

(*b*) if the plan provides for an accumulation period, 10% of the total of the employee's salary payments over that period.

(3) The plan may authorise the company to specify lower limits than those specified in sub-paragraphs (1) and (2).

Different limits may be specified in relation to different awards of shares.

(4) Any amount deducted in excess of that allowed by sub-paragraph (1) or (2), or any lower limit in the plan, must be paid over to the employee as soon as practicable.

Commentary—*Simon's Direct Tax Service* **E4.533**.

Minimum amount of deductions

37—(1) The plan may provide that the amount to be deducted in pursuance of a partnership share agreement in any month must not be less than a minimum amount specified in the plan.

(2) The specified minimum amount must not be greater than £10.

(3) Sub-paragraphs (1) and (2) apply whatever the intervals at which the employee is paid.

Commentary—*Simon's Direct Tax Service* **E4.533**.

Notice of possible effect of deductions on benefit entitlement

38—(1) The plan must provide that the company may not enter into a partnership share agreement with an employee unless the agreement contains a notice under this paragraph.

(2) A notice under this paragraph is a notice in a prescribed form containing prescribed information as to the possible effect of deductions on an employee's entitlement to social security benefits, statutory sick pay and statutory maternity pay.

(3) In this paragraph ''prescribed'' means prescribed by regulations made by the Board.

Commentary—*Simon's Direct Tax Service* **E4.533**.

Partnership share money held for employee

39—(1) The plan must provide that partnership share money deducted in accordance with a partnership share agreement is—

(a) paid to the trustees as soon as practicable, and

(b) held by them on behalf of the employee until such time as it is applied by them in acquiring partnership shares on the employee's behalf.

This is subject to paragraphs 40(4)(b) and 42(5)(b) and (6) (obligations to pay money to employee).

(2) References in this Schedule to the trustees acquiring partnership shares on behalf of an employee include their appropriating to an employee shares already held by them.

(3) The plan must provide for the trustees to keep any money required to be held by them under this paragraph in an account (interest bearing or otherwise) with—

[(a) a person falling within section 840A(1)(b) of the Taxes Act 1988,][1]

(b) a building society, or

[(c) a firm falling within section 840A(1)(c) of that Act,][1]

(4) If the partnership share money held on behalf of an employee is held in an interest bearing account the plan must provide for the trustees to account to the employee for the interest.

Commentary—*Simon's Direct Tax Service* **E4.533.**
Amendment—[1] Sub-paras (3)(a), (c) substituted by the Financial Services and Markets Act 2000 (Consequential Amendments) (Taxes) Order, SI 2001/3629 arts 105, 107 with effect from 1 December 2001, immediately after the coming into force of the Financial Services and Markets Act 2000 ss 411, 432(1), Sch 20.

Plan with no accumulation period

40—(1) If the plan does not provide for an accumulation period, it must provide for partnership share money to be applied by the trustees in acquiring partnership shares on behalf of the employee on the acquisition date.

(2) For this purpose "the acquisition date" means the date set by the trustees in relation to the award of partnership shares, being a date within 30 days after the last date on which the partnership share money to be applied in acquiring the shares was deducted.

(3) The number of shares awarded to each employee must be determined in accordance with the market value of the shares on the acquisition date.

(4) Any surplus partnership share money remaining after the acquisition of shares by the trustees—

(a) may with the agreement of the employee be carried forward and added to the amount of the next deduction, and

(b) in any other case must be paid over to the employee as soon as practicable.

(5) This paragraph is subject to paragraph 43 (restriction imposed on number of shares awarded).

Commentary—*Simon's Direct Tax Service* **E4.533.**

Plan with accumulation period

41—(1) The plan may provide for accumulation periods not exceeding twelve months.

(2) Where it does so—

(a) the partnership share agreement must specify when each accumulation period begins and ends (the beginning of the first period being not later than the date on which the first deduction is made), and

(b) the accumulation period which applies in relation to each award of partnership shares must be the same for all individuals who are eligible to participate in the award.

(3) The partnership share agreement may specify that an accumulation period comes to an end on the occurrence of a specified event.

This is subject to sub-paragraph (2)(b).

(4) Where the plan provides for accumulation periods, it may also provide that if—

(a) during an accumulation period, a transaction occurs in relation to any of the shares ("the original holding") to be acquired under a partnership share agreement which results in a new holding of shares being equated with the original holding for the purposes of capital gains tax, and

(b) the employee gives his consent for the purposes of this sub-paragraph,

the partnership share agreement shall have effect after the time of that transaction as if it were an agreement for the purchase of shares comprised in the new holding.

Commentary—*Simon's Direct Tax Service* **E4.533.**

Application of money deducted in accumulation period

42—(1) This paragraph applies if the plan provides for one or more accumulation periods.

(2) The plan must provide for the partnership share money deducted in each period to be applied by the trustees in acquiring partnership shares on behalf of the employee on the acquisition date.

This is subject to sub-paragraphs (6) and (7).

(3) In sub-paragraph (2) "the acquisition date" means the date set by the trustees in relation to the award of partnership shares, being a date within 30 days after the end of the accumulation period which applies in relation to the award.

(4) The number of shares awarded to each employee must be determined in accordance with the lower of—

(a) the market value of the shares at the beginning of the accumulation period, and
(b) the market value of the shares on the acquisition date.

(5) Any surplus partnership share money remaining after the acquisition of shares by the trustees—

(a) may with the agreement of the employee be carried forward to the next accumulation period, and
(b) in any other case must be paid over to the employee as soon as practicable.

(6) The plan must provide that where—

(a) partnership share money has been deducted in an accumulation period, and
(b) the employee ceases to be in relevant employment during that period,

the partnership share money is paid over to the individual as soon as practicable.

(7) The partnership share agreement may provide that, where an accumulation period comes to an end on the occurrence of a specified event, the partnership share money deducted in that period must be paid over to the individual as soon as practicable instead of being applied in acquiring shares.

(8) This paragraph is subject to paragraph 43 (restriction imposed on number of shares awarded).

Commentary—*Simon's Direct Tax Service* **E4.533**.

Restriction imposed on number of shares awarded

43—(1) The plan may authorise the company to specify the maximum number of shares ("the award maximum") to be included in an award of partnership shares.

A different number may be specified in relation to different awards.

(2) If the plan so authorises the company, it must require partnership share agreements to contain an undertaking by the company to notify the employee of any restriction on the number of shares to be included in an award.

(3) The plan must require the notice to be given—

(a) if there is no accumulation period, before the deduction of the partnership share money relating to the award, and
(b) if there is an accumulation period, before the beginning of the accumulation period relating to the award.

(4) The plan must provide that where the award maximum in respect of an award of partnership shares is smaller than the number of shares which would otherwise be included in the award, the number of partnership shares included in each individual award under paragraph 40(1) or 42(2) shall be reduced proportionately.

Stopping and re-starting deductions

44—(1) The plan must provide that an employee may at any time give notice in writing to the company to stop deductions in pursuance of a partnership share agreement.

(2) The plan must also provide that an employee who has stopped deductions may subsequently give notice in writing to the company to re-start deductions in pursuance of the agreement, but may not make up deductions that have been missed.

(3) If the plan makes provision for one or more accumulation periods, it may prevent an employee re-starting deductions more than once in any accumulation period.

(4) The plan must provide that unless a later date is specified in the notice—

(a) the company must within 30 days of receiving a notice within sub-paragraph (1), ensure that no further deductions are made by it under the partnership share agreement;
(b) the company must on receiving a notice within sub-paragraph (2) re-start deductions under the partnership share agreement not later than the re-start date.

(5) For the purposes of sub-paragraph (4)(b) "the re-start date" is the date of the first deduction due under the partnership share agreement more than 30 days after receipt of the notice within sub-paragraph (2).

Commentary—*Simon's Direct Tax Service* **E4.533**.

Withdrawal from partnership share agreement

45—(1) The plan must provide that an employee may withdraw from a partnership share agreement at any time by notice in writing to the company.

(2) The plan must provide that, unless a later date is specified in the notice, a notice of withdrawal takes effect 30 days after it is received by the company.

(3) The plan must provide that where an employee withdraws from a partnership share agreement, any partnership share money held on his behalf is to be paid over to him as soon as practicable.

Commentary—*Simon's Direct Tax Service* **E4.533**.

Repayment of partnership share money on withdrawal of approval or termination

46—(1) The plan must provide that where—

(*a*) the approval of the plan is withdrawn (see paragraph 118), or

(*b*) a plan termination notice is issued in respect of the plan (see paragraph 120),

any partnership share money held on behalf of an employee is paid over to him.

(2) The plan must require the payment to be made—

(*a*) in a case within sub-paragraph (1)(*a*), as soon as practicable after notice of the withdrawal is given to the company, and

(*b*) in a case within sub-paragraph (1)(*b*), as soon as practicable after the plan termination notice is notified to the trustees under paragraph 120(2).

Commentary—*Simon's Direct Tax Service* **E4.533**.

Access to partnership shares

47—(1) The plan must provide that when partnership shares have been awarded to an employee, the employee may at any time withdraw any or all of the partnership shares from the plan.

(2) There may be a charge to tax under paragraph 86 (charge on partnership shares ceasing to be subject to plan).

Commentary—*Simon's Direct Tax Service* **E4.533**.

Meaning of "salary"

48 References in this Part of this Schedule to an employee's "salary" are to such of the emoluments of the employment by reference to which he is eligible to participate in the plan as are liable to be paid under deduction of tax pursuant to section 203 of the Taxes Act 1988 (PAYE) [or which would be if that individual were within the scope of Schedule E][1], after deducting amounts included by virtue of Chapter II of Part V of that Act (expenses and benefits in kind) [or which would have been had the individual been within the scope of Schedule E][1] , or would be so liable apart from this Schedule.

Amendment—[1] Words inserted by FA 2001 s 61, Sch 13 para 3 with effect for any award of partnership shares (within the meaning of FA 2000 Sch 8) in relation to which the eligibility time (ie the time at which an individual, in order to participate in the award, is required, in accordance with FA 2000 Sch 8 para 13(1)(*b*), to be eligible to so participate) falls after the passing of FA 2001.

PART VI
MATCHING SHARES
Introduction

49 If the plan provides for matching shares it must comply with the requirements of this Part of this Schedule.

General requirements for matching shares

50—(1) The plan must provide for the matching shares—

(*a*) to be shares of the same class and carrying the same rights as the partnership shares to which they relate;

(*b*) to be awarded on the same day as the partnership shares to which they relate are awarded; and

(*c*) to be awarded to all employees who participate in the award on exactly the same basis.

(2) Sub-paragraph (1) is subject to paragraph 65 (permitted restrictions: provision for forfeiture).

Commentary—*Simon's Direct Tax Service* **E4.534**.

Ratio of matching shares to partnership shares

51—(1) The partnership share agreement must specify—

(*a*) the ratio of matching shares to partnership shares for the time being offered by the company, and (*b*) the circumstances and manner in which the ratio may be changed by the company.

(2) The ratio must not exceed 2:1 and must be applied by reference to the number of shares.

(3) A partnership share agreement must provide for the employee to be informed by the company if the ratio offered by the company changes before partnership shares are awarded to him under the agreement.

Commentary—*Simon's Direct Tax Service* **E4.534**.

Application of provisions relating to holding period etc

52 The provisions of paragraphs 31 and 32 as to the holding period and related matters apply in relation to matching shares as they apply to free shares.

Commentary—*Simon's Direct Tax Service* **E4.534**.

PART VII
REINVESTMENT OF CASH DIVIDENDS
Reinvestment

53—(1) The plan may provide that where the company so directs—

(*a*) all cash dividends in respect of plan shares held on behalf of participants must be applied in acquiring further shares on their behalf, or

(*b*) all cash dividends in respect of plan shares held on behalf of participants who elect to reinvest their dividends must be applied in acquiring further shares on their behalf.

This is referred to in this Part of this Schedule as "reinvestment" and the further plan shares acquired are referred to in this Schedule as "dividend shares".

(2) The company may revoke a direction.

(3) Where cash dividends in respect of plan shares held on behalf of a participant are not required to be reinvested under the plan, the plan must require the dividends to be paid over to the participant as soon as practicable.

(4) This paragraph is subject to paragraph 54 (limit on amount reinvested).

Commentary—*Simon's Direct Tax Service* **E4.535**.

Limit on amount reinvested

54—(1) The plan must provide that the total dividend reinvestment in respect of any participant cannot exceed £1,500 in any tax year.

(2) For this purpose "the total dividend reinvestment" in respect of a participant is the sum of—

(*a*) the amount applied by the trustees in acquiring dividend shares on behalf of the participant under the plan, and

(*b*) the amount applied by the trustees of other employee share ownership plans that are—

  (i) established by the company or an associated company, and
  (ii) approved under this Schedule,

in acquiring dividend shares on his behalf.

(3) If the amounts received by the trustees exceed the limit in sub-paragraph (1), the plan must provide for the balance to be paid over to the participant as soon as practicable.

Commentary—*Simon's Direct Tax Service* **E4.535**.

General requirements for dividend shares

55 The plan must provide that dividend shares are shares—

(*a*) of the same class and carrying the same rights as the shares in respect of which the dividend is paid, and

(*b*) which are not subject to any provision for forfeiture.

Commentary—*Simon's Direct Tax Service* **E4.535**.

Acquisition of dividend shares

56—(1) The plan must provide that in exercising their powers in relation to the acquisition of dividend shares the trustees must treat participants fairly and equally.

(2) The plan must provide for the trustees to apply a cash dividend in acquiring further shares on behalf of participants on the acquisition date.

This does not affect the carrying forward under paragraph 58 of any such amount as is mentioned in sub-paragraph (1) of that paragraph (amounts remaining after acquisition of shares).

(3) For this purpose "the acquisition date" means the date set by the trustees in relation to the acquisition of dividend shares, being a date within 30 days after the dividend is received by them.

(4) The number of dividend shares acquired on behalf of each participant must be determined in accordance with the market value of the shares on the acquisition date.

(5) References in this Part of this Schedule to the trustees acquiring dividend shares on behalf of a participant include their appropriating to a participant shares already held by them.

Commentary—*Simon's Direct Tax Service* **E4.535**.

Holding period for dividend shares

57 The provisions of paragraphs 31 and 32 (holding period and related matters) apply in relation to dividend shares as they apply to free shares, except that the holding period must be three years.

Commentary—*Simon's Direct Tax Service* **E4.535**.

Certain amounts not reinvested to be carried forward

58—(1) Any amount that is not reinvested—

(*a*) because the amount of the cash dividend to which the participant is entitled is not sufficient to acquire a share, or

(*b*) because there is an amount remaining after acquiring one or more dividend shares on the participant's behalf,

may be retained by the trustees and carried forward to be added to the amount of the next cash dividend to be reinvested, but shall be held by them so as to be separately identifiable for the purposes of sub-paragraphs (2) and (3).

(2) An amount retained under this paragraph shall be paid over to the participant—

(*a*) if or to the extent that it is not reinvested within the period of three years beginning with the date on which the dividend was paid, or

(*b*) if during that period the participant ceases to be in relevant employment, or

(*c*) if during that period a plan termination notice is issued in respect of the plan.

(3) An amount required to be paid over to the participant under sub-paragraph (2) shall be paid over as soon as practicable.

(4) For the purposes of this paragraph an amount carried forward under this paragraph derived from an earlier cash dividend is treated as reinvested before an amount derived from a later cash dividend.

Commentary—*Simon's Direct Tax Service* **E4.535**.

PART VIII
TYPES OF SHARE THAT MAY BE USED
Introduction

59 The requirements of the following paragraphs must be met with respect to any shares that may be awarded under the plan ("eligible shares")—

paragraph 60 (must be ordinary share capital);
paragraph 61 (requirement as to listing etc);
paragraph 62 (shares must be fully paid up and not redeemable);
paragraph 63 (only certain kinds of restriction allowed);
paragraph 67 (prohibited companies).

Commentary—*Simon's Direct Tax Service* **E4.536**.

Must be ordinary share capital

60 Eligible shares must form part of the ordinary share capital of—

(*a*) the company; or

(*b*) a company which has control of the company; or

(*c*) a company which either is, or has control of, a company which is a member of a consortium owning either the company or a company having control of the company.

Commentary—*Simon's Direct Tax Service* **E4.536**.

Requirement as to listing etc

61 Eligible shares must be—

(*a*) shares of a class listed on a recognised stock exchange; or

(*b*) shares in a company which is not under the control of another company; or

(*c*) shares in a company which is under the control of a company (other than a company which is, or would if resident in the United Kingdom be, a close company) whose shares are listed on a recognised stock exchange.

Commentary—*Simon's Direct Tax Service* **E4.536**.

Shares must be fully paid up and not redeemable

62—(1) Eligible shares must be—

    (*a*) fully paid up, and

    (*b*) not redeemable.

(2) Shares are not regarded as fully paid up for the purposes of sub-paragraph (1)(*a*) if there is any undertaking to pay cash to the company at a future date.

(3) For the purposes of sub-paragraph (1)(*b*) "redeemable" shares include shares that may become redeemable at a future date.

(4) Sub-paragraph (1)(*b*) does not apply in relation to shares in a co-operative.

(5) In sub-paragraph (4) "co-operative" means a registered industrial and provident society which is a co-operative society.

For this purpose—

    "registered industrial and provident society" means a society registered or deemed to be registered under the Industrial and Provident Societies Act 1965 or the Industrial and Provident Societies Act (Northern Ireland) 1969; and

    "co-operative society" has the same meaning as in section 1 of the 1965 Act or, as the case may be, the 1969 Act.

Commentary—*Simon's Direct Tax Service* **E4.536.**

Only certain kinds of restriction allowed

63—(1) Eligible shares must not be subject to any restrictions other than—

    (*a*) those involved in there being a holding period (see paragraphs 31, 52 and 57); or

    (*b*) those affecting all ordinary shares in the company; or

    (*c*) those permitted by—

    paragraph 64 (voting rights),

    paragraph 65 (provision for forfeiture), or

    paragraph 66 (pre-emption conditions).

(2) For this purpose there is a restriction if there is any contract, agreement, arrangement or condition—

    (*a*) by which a person's freedom to dispose of the shares or of any interest in them or of the proceeds of their sale or to exercise any right conferred by them is restricted, or

    (*b*) by which such a disposal or exercise may result in any disadvantage to him or to a person connected with him,

subject to sub-paragraphs (3) and (4).

(3) Any discretion of the directors under the articles of association of the company to refuse to accept the transfer of shares shall be disregarded for the purposes of this paragraph if the directors—

    (*a*) have undertaken to the Inland Revenue not to exercise it in such a way as to discriminate against participants, and

    (*b*) have notified all qualifying employees of the existence of the undertaking.

(4) There shall also be disregarded for the purposes of this paragraph so much of any contract, agreement, arrangement or condition as contains provisions similar in purpose and effect to any of the provisions of the Model Code as (for the time being) set out in the listing rules issued by the competent authority for listing in the United Kingdom under section 74(4) of the Financial Services and Markets Act 2000.

Commentary—*Simon's Direct Tax Service* **E4.536.**

Permitted restrictions: voting rights

64 Eligible shares may be shares carrying no voting rights or limited voting rights.

Commentary—*Simon's Direct Tax Service* **E4.536.**

Permitted restrictions: provision for forfeiture

65—(1) Free or matching shares may be subject to provision for forfeiture in the following circumstances.

(2) Provision may be made for forfeiture—

    (*a*) on the participant ceasing to be in relevant employment at any time in the forfeiture period,

    (*b*) on the participant withdrawing the shares from the plan in that period, or

    (*c*) in the case of matching shares, on the participant withdrawing the partnership shares in respect of which those shares were awarded from the plan within that period,

otherwise than by reason of an event within paragraph 87(2) (circumstances in which there is no charge to tax on shares ceasing to be subject to plan).

(3) In sub-paragraph (2) "the forfeiture period" means the forfeiture period specified in the plan being a period of not more than three years beginning with the date on which the shares were awarded to the participant.

(4) Forfeiture may not be linked to the performance of any person or persons.

(5) The same provision for forfeiture must apply in relation to all free or matching shares included in the same award under the plan.

(6) In this Schedule "provision for forfeiture" means any provision to the effect that a participant shall cease to be beneficially entitled to the shares on the occurrence of certain events, and references to forfeiture shall be construed accordingly.

Commentary—*Simon's Direct Tax Service* **E4.536**.

Permitted restrictions: pre-emption conditions

66—(1) If the requirements of this paragraph are met, eligible shares may be subject to provision requiring shares—

    (*a*) that were awarded to an employee under the plan, and

    (*b*) that are held by an employee or a permitted transferee,

to be offered for sale on the employee ceasing to be in relevant employment.

(2) For the purposes of sub-paragraph (1)(*b*) a "permitted transferee" means a person to whom, under the articles of association of the company, the employee is permitted to transfer the shares.

(3) The requirements of this paragraph are that under the articles of association of the company—

    (*a*) the same provision applies to all employees of the company or, in the case of a parent company, to all employees of that company or any company of which that company has control;

    (*b*) the shares are required to be offered for sale at a specified consideration; and

    (*c*) anyone disposing of shares of the same class (whether or not as an employee) is required to offer the shares for sale on no better terms.

Commentary—*Simon's Direct Tax Service* **E4.536**.

Prohibited companies

67—(1) Eligible shares must not be shares—

    (*a*) in an employer company, or

    (*b*) in a company that—

        (i) has control of an employer company, and

        (ii) is under the control of a person or persons within sub-paragraph (2)(*b*)(i) in relation to an employer company.

(2) For the purposes of this paragraph a company is "an employer company" if—

    (*a*) the business carried on by it consists substantially in the provision of the services of persons employed by it, and

    (*b*) the majority of those services are provided to—

        (i) a person who has, or two or more persons who together have, control of the company, or

        (ii) a company associated with the company.

(3) For the purposes of sub-paragraph (2)(*b*)(ii) a company shall be treated as associated with another company if both companies are under the control of the same person or persons.

(4) For the purposes of sub-paragraphs (1) to (3)—

    (*a*) references to a person include a partnership, and

    (*b*) where a partner, alone or together with others, has control of a company, the partnership shall be treated as having like control of that company.

(5) For the purposes of this paragraph the question whether a person controls a company shall be determined in accordance with section 416(2) to (6) of the Taxes Act 1988.

Commentary—*Simon's Direct Tax Service* **E4.536**.

PART IX

THE TRUSTEES

Establishment of trustees

68—(1) The plan must provide for the establishment of a body of persons resident in the United Kingdom ("the trustees") who are required by the plan—

    (*a*) in the case of free or matching shares, to acquire shares and appropriate them to employees in accordance with the plan;

    (*b*) in the case of partnership shares, to apply partnership share money in acquiring shares on behalf of employees in accordance with the plan; and

    (*c*) in the case of dividend shares, to apply cash dividends in acquiring shares on behalf of participants in accordance with the plan.

(2) The functions of the trustees with respect to shares held by them must be regulated by a trust (''the plan trust'')—

(a) which is constituted under the law of a part of the United Kingdom, and
(b) the terms of which are embodied in an instrument which complies with the requirements of this Part of this Schedule.

(3) The instrument must not contain any terms which are neither essential nor reasonably incidental to complying with the requirements of this Part of this Schedule.

Commentary—*Simon's Direct Tax Service* **E4.537**.

Power of trustees to borrow

69 The trust instrument may provide that the trustees have power to borrow—

(a) to acquire shares for the purposes of the plan, and
(b) for such other purposes as may be specified in the trust instrument.

Commentary—*Simon's Direct Tax Service* **E4.537**.

Duty to give notice of award of shares etc

70—(1) The trust instrument must make the following provision regarding notices.

(2) It must provide that, as soon as practicable after any free or matching shares have been awarded to an employee, the trustees shall give him notice of the award—

(a) specifying the number and description of those shares,
(b) stating their market value on the date on which they were awarded to him, and
(c) stating the holding period applicable to them.

(3) It must provide that, as soon as practicable after any partnership shares have been awarded to an employee, the trustees shall give him notice of the award—

(a) specifying the number and description of those shares, and
(b) stating—

(i) the amount of partnership share money applied by the trustees in acquiring the shares on his behalf, and
(ii) their market value on the acquisition date (within the meaning of paragraph 40(2) or, if there is an accumulation period, paragraph 42(3)).

(4) It must provide that, as soon as practicable after any dividend shares have been acquired on behalf of a participant, the trustees shall give him notice of the acquisition—

(a) specifying the number and description of those shares,
(b) stating their market value on the acquisition date (within the meaning of paragraph 56(3)),
(c) stating the holding period applicable to them, and
(d) informing him of any amount carried forward under paragraph 58 (certain amounts not reinvested).

(5) It must provide that, where any foreign cash dividend is received in respect of plan shares held on behalf of a participant, the trustees shall give him notice of the amount of any foreign tax deducted from the dividend before it was paid.

Commentary—*Simon's Direct Tax Service* **E4.537**.

General duties of trustees

71—(1) The trust instrument must require the trustees—

(a) to dispose of a participant's plan shares, and
(b) to deal with any right conferred in respect of any of his plan shares to be allotted other shares, securities or rights of any description,

only pursuant to a direction given by or on behalf of the participant.

This is subject to sub-paragraph (3) and to any provision made in the plan in accordance with paragraph 73 (meeting PAYE obligations).

(2) The plan may provide for participants to give such general directions, to such effect and in such terms, as are specified in the plan.

(3) The trust instrument must, in the case of a participant's plan shares that are free, matching or dividend shares, prohibit the trustees from disposing of any of those shares (whether to the participant or otherwise) at any time during the holding period, unless the participant has at that time ceased to be in relevant employment.

This is subject to—

paragraph 32 (holding period: power to authorise trustees to accept general offers etc);
paragraph 72 (power of trustees to raise funds to subscribe for rights issue);
paragraph 73 (meeting PAYE obligations);
paragraph 121(5) (termination of plan: early removal of shares with participant's consent).

(4) The trust instrument must require the trustees to pay over to the participant as soon as practicable any money or money's worth received by them in respect of or by reference to any of his shares, other than money's worth consisting of new shares within the meaning of paragraph 115 (company reconstructions).

This is subject to—

(*a*) the provisions of Part VII (reinvestment of cash dividends);

(*b*) the trustees' obligations under paragraphs 95 and 96 (PAYE: shares ceasing to be subject to the plan and capital receipts); and

(*c*) the trustees' PAYE obligations.

Commentary—*Simon's Direct Tax Service* **E4.537**.

Power of trustees to raise funds to subscribe for rights issue

72—(1) The trustees may dispose of some of the rights arising under a rights issue in order to be able to obtain sufficient funds to exercise other such rights.

This power is subject to paragraph 71(1) (duty to act in accordance with participant's directions).

(2) In this paragraph references to rights arising under a rights issue are to rights conferred in respect of a participant's plan shares to be allotted, on payment, other shares or securities or rights of any description in the same company.

Commentary—*Simon's Direct Tax Service* **E4.537**.

Meeting PAYE obligations

73—(1) The plan must make provision to ensure that, where a PAYE obligation is imposed on the trustees as a result of any of a participant's plan shares ceasing to be subject to the plan, the trustees are able to meet that obligation—

(*a*) by disposing of—

(i) any of those shares, or

(ii) any of the participant's remaining plan shares (if any), or

(*b*) by virtue of the participant paying to the trustees a sum equal to the amount required to discharge the obligation.

(2) In sub-paragraph (1) the reference to a PAYE obligation includes an obligation under paragraph 95 (PAYE: shares ceasing to be subject to the plan).

(3) In sub-paragraph (1)(*a*) the reference to disposing of shares includes the acquisition of the shares by the trustees for the purposes of the trust.

(4) A disposal of any of the participant's plan shares in accordance with provision made under sub-paragraph (1)(*a*)(ii) may give rise to a charge to tax under—

paragraph 81 (charge on free or matching shares ceasing to be subject to plan);

paragraph 86 (charge on partnership shares ceasing to be subject to plan); or

paragraph 93 (charge on dividend shares ceasing to be subject to plan).

Commentary—*Simon's Direct Tax Service* **E4.537**.

Deemed disposal by trustees on disposal of beneficial interest

74—(1) If at any time the participant's beneficial interest in any of his shares is disposed of, the shares in question shall be treated for the purposes of this Schedule as having been disposed of at that time by the trustees for the like consideration as was obtained for the disposal of the beneficial interest.

(2) For this purpose there is no disposal of the participant's beneficial interest if and at the time when—

(*a*) in England and Wales or Northern Ireland, that interest becomes vested in any person on the insolvency of the participant or otherwise by operation of law, or

(*b*) in Scotland, that interest becomes vested in a judicial factor, in a trustee of the participant's sequestrated estate or in a trustee for the benefit of the participant's creditors.

(3) If a disposal of shares falling within this paragraph is not at arm's length, the proceeds of the disposal shall be taken for the purposes of this Schedule to be equal to the market value of the shares at the time of the disposal.

Commentary—*Simon's Direct Tax Service* **E4.537**.

Duties of trustees in relation to tax liabilities

75—(1) The trust instrument must require the trustees—

(*a*) to maintain such records as may be necessary for the purposes of—

(i) their own PAYE obligations, or

(ii) the PAYE obligations of the employer company so far as they relate to the plan, (*b*) where the participant becomes liable to income tax under Case V of Schedule D, Schedule E or Schedule F by reason of the occurrence of any event, to inform him of any facts relevant to determining that liability.

(2) For the purposes of this paragraph—

"employer company" has the same meaning as in paragraph 95 (PAYE: shares ceasing to be subject to the plan); and

"PAYE obligations" includes obligations conferred on the trustees by paragraphs 95 and 96 (PAYE: shares ceasing to be subject to plan and capital receipts).

Commentary—*Simon's Direct Tax Service* **E4.537**.

Acquisition by trustees of shares from employee share ownership trust

76—(1) The trust instrument must provide that, where there is a qualifying transfer of shares to the trustees, those shares—

(*a*) must not be awarded to participants under the plan as partnership shares, and

(*b*) must be included in any award of free or matching shares made after the date of the transfer in priority to other shares available for inclusion in that award.

(2) For the purposes of this paragraph there is a qualifying transfer of shares to the trustees if relevant shares—

(*a*) are transferred to them by the trustees of an employee share ownership trust, and

(*b*) the transfer is a qualifying transfer within section 69(3AA) of the Finance Act 1989 (transfer of shares in, or shares purchased from money in, an employee share ownership trust immediately before 21st March 2000).

Commentary—*Simon's Direct Tax Service* **E4.537**.

PART X
INCOME TAX
Introduction

77—(1) The provisions of this Part of this Schedule apply for income tax purposes in relation to an approved employee share ownership plan.

This is subject to sub-paragraph (2).

(2) Nothing in this Part applies to an individual if, at the time of the award in question, he is not chargeable to tax under Schedule E in respect of the employment by reference to which he meets the requirement of paragraph 14 (the employment requirement) in relation to the plan.

Commentary—*Simon's Direct Tax Service* **E4.538**.

No charge on award of shares etc

78—(1) Notwithstanding that the beneficial interest in the shares passes to the employee—

(*a*) on the award to him of free, matching or partnership shares under the plan, or

(*b*) on the acquisition on his behalf of dividend shares under the plan,

the value of that interest at the time of the award or acquisition is not treated as income of his chargeable to tax.

(2) An employee is not chargeable to tax under Schedule E by virtue of section 162(1) of the Taxes Act 1988 (deemed loan in case of shares acquired at an under-value) in respect of the award to him of shares under the plan.

This does not affect any charge to tax under section 162(6) of that Act (stop-loss provision).

[(3) Incidental expenditure of the trustees or the employer in operating the plan is not treated as giving rise to any charge to income tax on employees.][1]

Commentary—*Simon's Direct Tax Service* **E4.538**.
Amendment—[1] Sub-para (3) inserted by FA 2001 s 61, Sch 13 para 4 with effect from the year 2001–02.

Capital receipts in respect of participant's shares

79—(1) Where—

(*a*) a capital receipt is received by a participant in respect of or by reference to any of his plan shares, and

(*b*) the plan shares in respect of or by reference to which it is received are—

(i) free, matching or partnership shares that were awarded to the participant fewer than five years before he received the capital receipt, or

(ii) dividend shares that were acquired on his behalf fewer than three years before he received that receipt, the participant is chargeable to income tax under Schedule E for the tax year in which the capital receipt is received by him on the amount or value of the receipt.

(2) For the purposes of this paragraph any money or money's worth is a "capital receipt" subject to the following provisions.

(3) Money or money's worth is not a capital receipt for the purposes of this paragraph to the extent that—

(a) it constitutes income in the hands of the recipient for the purposes of income tax (or would do so but for this Part of this Schedule), or

(b) it consists of the proceeds of disposal of the shares, or

(c) it consists of new shares within the meaning of paragraph 115 (company reconstructions).

(4) If, pursuant to a direction given by or on behalf of the participant for the purposes of paragraph 72(1), the trustees—

(a) dispose of some of the rights under a rights issue, and

(b) use the proceeds of that disposal to exercise other such rights,

the money or money's worth that constitutes the proceeds of that disposal is not a capital receipt for the purposes of this paragraph.

The references in this sub-paragraph to rights under a rights issue are to rights, conferred in respect of a participant's plan shares, to be allotted, on payment, other shares or securities or rights of any description in the same company.

(5) This paragraph does not apply in relation to a capital receipt referable to the shares of a participant if it is received by the participant's personal representative after his death.

Commentary—*Simon's Direct Tax Service* **E4.538**.

Exclusion of certain charges in relation to participant's shares

80—(1) There is no charge to tax on the participant under—

(a) section 140A of the Taxes Act 1988 (charge on conditional acquisition of shares), or

(b) section 78 of the Finance Act 1988 (charge on removal of restriction),

when any provision for forfeiture to which the shares are subject, in accordance with paragraph 65 (permitted restrictions: provision for forfeiture), is varied or removed.

(2) A participant is not chargeable to tax under Schedule E by virtue of section 78 of the Finance Act 1988 (charge on removal of restriction) if the chargeable event (within the meaning of that section) is the ending of the holding period in relation to his free, matching or dividend shares.

(3) A participant is not chargeable to tax under Schedule E by virtue of section 79 of that Act (charge on chargeable increase in value) in respect of any shares of his that are subject to the plan at the end of the period for which the chargeable increase is determined for the purposes of that section.

Commentary—*Simon's Direct Tax Service* **E4.538**.

Charge on free or matching shares ceasing to be subject to plan

81—(1) When free or matching shares cease to be subject to the plan, income tax may be chargeable depending on the period that has elapsed between—

(a) the date on which the shares were awarded to the participant, and

(b) the date on which they cease to be subject to the plan.

(2) If the period is less than three years, the participant is chargeable to tax under Schedule E on the market value of the shares when they cease to be subject to the plan.

(3) If the period is three years or more but less than five years, the participant is chargeable to tax under Schedule E on—

(a) the market value of the shares at the date they were awarded to him, or

(b) the market value of the shares when they cease to be subject to the plan,

whichever is less.

(4) Where the participant is charged to tax under sub-paragraph (3)(a) the tax due shall be reduced by the amount or aggregate amount of any tax paid on any capital receipts within paragraph 79 in respect of those shares.

(5) There is no charge to tax under this paragraph on the forfeiture of free or matching shares.

(6) This paragraph has effect subject to—

paragraph 82 (charge to tax on disposal of beneficial interest in shares during the holding period); and

paragraph 87 (circumstances in which there is no charge to tax on shares ceasing to be subject to plan).

(7) Except as provided by this paragraph and paragraph 82 there is no charge to tax on free or matching shares ceasing to be subject to the plan.

Commentary—*Simon's Direct Tax Service* **E4.538**.

Charge on disposal of beneficial interest during the holding period

82—(1) Where free or matching shares cease to be subject to the plan by virtue of a participant, in breach of his obligations under paragraph 31(1)(*b*), assigning, charging or otherwise disposing of his beneficial interest in those shares—

(*a*) paragraph 81 does not apply, and

(*b*) the participant is chargeable to income tax under Schedule E on the market value of the shares when they cease to be subject to the plan.

(2) . . ..[1]

Commentary—*Simon's Direct Tax Service* **E4.538**.
Amendment—[1] Sub-para (2) repealed by FA 2001 ss 61, 110, Sch 13 para 5, Sch 33 Pt II(3), and deemed always to have had effect.

Partnership share money deducted before tax

83—(1) Partnership share money deducted from an employee's salary in accordance with a partnership share agreement is not regarded as income of the employee chargeable to tax under Schedule E.

(2) The deduction of partnership share money shall be disregarded for the purpose of ascertaining the amount of—

(*a*) the employee's remuneration for the purposes of Chapter I of Part XIV of the Taxes Act 1988 (retirement benefit schemes), or

(*b*) the employee's relevant earnings for the purposes of Chapter III or IV of that Part (retirement annuities or personal pension schemes).

Commentary—*Simon's Direct Tax Service* **E4.538**.

Charge on partnership share money paid over to employee

84—(1) An individual is chargeable to income tax under Schedule E on any amount paid over to him under—

paragraph 36(4) (deductions in excess of permitted maximum amount);

paragraph 40(4)(*b*) or 42(5)(*b*) (surplus partnership share money remaining after acquisition of shares);

paragraph 42(6) (partnership share money paid over on individual leaving relevant employment);

paragraph 42(7) (partnership share money paid over where accumulation period brought to an end by event specified in plan);

paragraph 45(3) (partnership share money paid over on withdrawal from partnership share agreement); or

paragraph 46 (partnership share money paid over on withdrawal of plan approval or termination of plan).

(2) A charge to tax under sub-paragraph (1) arises at the time the amount is paid over.

Commentary—*Simon's Direct Tax Service* **E4.538**.

Charge on cancellation payments in respect of partnership share agreement

85 An individual is chargeable to tax under Schedule E on the amount or value of any money or money's worth received by him in respect of the cancellation of a partnership share agreement entered into by him.

Commentary—*Simon's Direct Tax Service* **E4.538**.

Charge on partnership shares ceasing to be subject to plan

86—(1) When partnership shares cease to be subject to the plan, income tax may be chargeable depending on the period that has elapsed between—

(*a*) the acquisition date in respect of those shares (as defined by paragraph 40(2) or, as the case may be, 42(3)), and

(*b*) the date on which they cease to be subject to the plan.

(2) If the period is less than three years, the employee is chargeable to income tax under Schedule E on an amount equal to the market value of the shares when they cease to be subject to the plan.

(3) If the period is three years or more but less than five years, the employee is chargeable to income tax under Schedule E on—

(*a*) the amount of partnership share money used to acquire the shares, or

(*b*) the market value of the shares when they cease to be subject to the plan,

whichever is less.

(4) Where the participant is charged to tax under sub-paragraph (3)(*a*) the tax due shall be reduced by the amount or aggregate amount of any tax paid on any capital receipts within paragraph 79 in respect of those shares.

(5) This paragraph has effect subject to paragraph 87 (circumstances in which there is no charge on shares ceasing to be subject to plan).

(6) Except as provided by this paragraph, there is no charge to income tax on the employee on partnership shares ceasing to be subject to the plan.

Commentary—*Simon's Direct Tax Service* **E4.538**.

Circumstances in which there is no charge on shares ceasing to be subject to plan

87—(1) There is no charge to tax on shares ceasing to be subject to the plan on the occurrence of any of the following events.

(2) Those events are the participant ceasing to be in relevant employment—

(*a*) because of injury or disability;
(*b*) on being dismissed by reason of redundancy;
(*c*) by reason of a transfer to which the Transfer of Undertakings (Protection of Employment) Regulations 1981 apply;
(*d*) by reason of a change of control or other circumstances ending the associated company status of the company by which he is employed;
(*e*) by reason of his retirement on or after he reaches retirement age; or
(*f*) on his death.

(3) In sub-paragraph (2)(*b*) "redundancy" has the same meaning as in the Employment Rights Act 1996 or the Employment Rights (Northern Ireland) Order 1996.

(4) In sub-paragraph (2)(*e*) "retirement age" means the retirement age specified in the plan, which—

(*a*) must be the same for men and women, and
(*b*) must be not less than 50.

Commentary—*Simon's Direct Tax Service* **E4.538**.

Dividends etc in respect of unappropriated shares

88—(1) This paragraph applies to income of the trustees consisting of dividends or other distributions in respect of shares held by them in relation to which the requirements of Part VIII are met.

(2) Income to which this paragraph applies is income to which section 686 of the Taxes Act 1988 (accumulation and discretionary trusts: special rates of tax) applies only if and when—

(*a*) the period applicable to the shares under the following provisions comes to an end without the shares being awarded to a participant in accordance with the plan, or
(*b*) if earlier, the shares are disposed of by the trustees.

(3) [If any of the shares in the company in question are readily convertible assets at the time the shares are acquired by the trustees,][1] the period applicable to the shares is the period of two years beginning with the date on which the shares were acquired by the trustees.

(4) If at the time of the acquisition of the shares by the trustees none of the shares in the company in question are readily convertible assets, the period within which the shares must be awarded is—

(*a*) five years beginning with the date on which the shares were acquired by the trustees, or
(*b*) if within that period [any of the shares in that company][1] become readily convertible assets, two years beginning with the date on which they did so,

whichever ends first.

(5) For the purposes of determining whether shares are awarded to a participant within the period applicable under the above provisions, shares acquired by the trustees at an earlier time are taken to be awarded to a participant before shares of the same class acquired by the trustees at a later time.

(6) For the purposes of this paragraph shares which are subject to provision for forfeiture are treated as acquired by the trustees if and when the forfeiture occurs.

(7) In this paragraph references to the shares being awarded include references to shares being acquired on behalf of a participant as dividend shares.

Commentary—*Simon's Direct Tax Service* **E4.538**.
Amendment—[1] Words in sub-paras (3), (4) substituted by FA 2001 s 61, Sch 13 para 6 with effect for any shares acquired by the trustees of an employee share ownership plan after the passing of FA 2001. For this purpose, "the trustees of an employee share ownership plan" means the body of persons established in accordance with FA 2000 Sch 8 para 68. Before amendment, sub-paras (3), (4) read as follows—

"(3) Subject to sub-paragraph (4), the period applicable to the shares is the period of two years beginning with the date on which the shares were acquired by the trustees.
(4) If at the time of the acquisition of the shares by the trustees none of the shares in the company in question are readily convertible assets, the period within which the shares must be awarded is—

(*a*) five years beginning with the date on which the shares were acquired by the trustees, or
(*b*) if within that period the shares in question become readily convertible assets, two years beginning with the date on which they did so,

whichever ends first.".

Reinvestment of cash dividend on behalf of participant

89—(1) The amount applied by the trustees in acquiring dividend shares on behalf of a participant is not treated as income of the participant for any tax purposes.

(2) The participant has no entitlement to a tax credit in respect of the amounts of dividends so applied.

(3) Sub-paragraphs (1) and (2) do not affect—

(*a*) any charge under paragraph 93(1) (charge on dividend shares ceasing to be subject to plan), or

(*b*) any entitlement to a tax credit in respect of the amount so charged.

(4) Section 234A(4) of the Taxes Act 1988 (information relating to distributions to be provided by nominee) shall not apply in relation to any amount applied by the trustees in acquiring dividend shares on behalf of a participant.

This is subject to paragraph 93(4).

Commentary—*Simon's Direct Tax Service* **E4.538**.

Repayment of excess cash dividend

90 Section 234A(4) to (11) of the Taxes Act 1988 (information relating to distributions to be provided by nominee) shall apply in relation to the balance of any cash dividend paid over to the participant under paragraph 54(3) as if it were a payment to which subsection (4)(*b*) of that section applies.

Commentary—*Simon's Direct Tax Service* **E4.538**.

Treatment of cash dividend retained for reinvestment

91—(1) An amount retained under paragraph 58(1) (amount of cash dividend not reinvested) shall not be treated as income of the participant for any tax purposes.

(2) The participant has no entitlement to a tax credit in respect of any such amount.

(3) This paragraph does not affect any charge—

(*a*) under paragraph 92 (treatment of cash dividend retained and then later paid out), or

(*b*) paragraph 93 (charge on dividend shares ceasing to be subject to plan),

or any tax credit in respect of an amount so charged.

Commentary—*Simon's Direct Tax Service* **E4.538**.

Treatment of cash dividend retained and then later paid out

92—(1) Where a cash dividend is paid over to a participant under paragraph 58(2) (cash dividend paid over if not reinvested), the participant is chargeable to tax on that amount—

(*a*) under Schedule F, or

(*b*) to the extent that the dividend is a foreign cash dividend, under Case V of Schedule D,

for the tax year in which the dividend is paid over to him.

(2) For the purposes of determining the tax credit (if any) to which the participant is entitled under section 231 of the Taxes Act 1988 (tax credits for certain recipients of qualifying distributions), the reference in subsection (1) of that section to the tax credit fraction in force when the distribution is made shall be read as a reference to the fraction in force when the dividend is paid over to him.

(3) Section 234A(4) to (11) of the Taxes Act 1988 (information relating to distributions to be provided by nominee) shall apply in relation to an amount paid under paragraph 58(2) as if—

(*a*) it were a payment to which subsection (4)(*b*) of that section applies, and

(*b*) the cash dividend had been paid when the payment was paid over to the participant under paragraph 58(2).

Commentary—*Simon's Direct Tax Service* **E4.538**.

Charge on dividend shares ceasing to be subject to plan

93—(1) If dividend shares cease to be subject to the plan before the end of the period of three years beginning with the date on which the shares were acquired on his behalf, the participant is chargeable to tax on the amount of the relevant dividend—

(*a*) under Schedule F, or

(*b*) to the extent that the amount represents a foreign cash dividend, under Case V of Schedule D,

for the tax year in which the shares cease to be subject to the plan.

For this purpose "the relevant dividend" is the cash dividend applied to acquire those shares on the participant's behalf.

(2) For the purposes of determining the tax credit (if any) to which the participant is entitled under section 231 of the Taxes Act 1988 (tax credits for certain recipients of qualifying distributions), the

reference in subsection (1) of that section to the tax credit fraction in force when the distribution is made shall be read as a reference to the fraction in force [when the shares cease to be subject to the plan]¹.

(3) Where the participant is charged to tax under this paragraph the tax due shall be reduced by the amount or aggregate amount of any tax paid on any capital receipts within paragraph 79 in respect of those shares.

For this purpose "the tax due" means the amount of tax due after deduction of the tax credit determined under sub-paragraph (2).

(4) Section 234A(4) to (11) of the Taxes Act 1988 (information relating to distributions to be provided by nominee) shall apply in relation to the relevant dividend as if it were a payment to which subsection (4)(*b*) of that section applies.

(5) This paragraph has effect subject to paragraph 87 (circumstances in which there is no charge on shares ceasing to be subject to plan).

(6) Except as provided by this paragraph there is no charge to tax on dividend shares ceasing to be subject to the plan.

Commentary—*Simon's Direct Tax Service* **E4.538**.
Amendment—¹ Words in sub-para (2) substituted by FA 2001 s 61, Sch 13 para 7 and deemed always to have had effect.

PAYE: shares ceasing to be subject to plan

94 Where as a result of shares ceasing to be subject to the plan a participant is chargeable to tax under this Part of this Schedule,

    [(*a*) section 203F of the Taxes Act 1988 (PAYE: readily convertible assets) shall have effect as if the participant were being provided with assessable income in the form of those shares—

        (i) at the time the shares cease to be subject to the plan, and

        (ii) in respect of the relevant employment in which the participant is employed at that time (or, if he is not employed in relevant employment at that time, the relevant employment in which he was last employed before that time), and

    (*b*) subsection (3) of that section]¹ shall have effect as if the reference in that subsection to the amount of income likely to be chargeable to tax under Schedule E in respect of the provision of the asset were a reference to the amount on which tax is likely to be chargeable under this Part of this Schedule by virtue of the shares ceasing to be subject to the plan.

Commentary—*Simon's Direct Tax Service* **E4.538**.
Amendments—¹ Words substituted by FA 2002 s 39(1), (2), (7) with effect from the year 2002–03.

PAYE: shares ceasing to be subject to the plan

95—(1) Sub-paragraphs (2) to (5) apply where as a result of any shares ("the relevant shares") ceasing to be subject to the plan—

    (*a*) a participant is chargeable to income tax under Schedule E in accordance with this Part of this Schedule, and

    (*b*) an obligation to make a PAYE deduction arises in respect of that charge.

(2) The trustees must pay to the employer company a sum which is sufficient to enable the employer company to discharge that obligation.

This is subject to sub-paragraphs (3) and (7).

(3) Sub-paragraph (2) only applies where, or to the extent that, the plan does not require the participant to pay the employer company a sum that is sufficient to discharge the obligation mentioned in sub-paragraph (1)(*b*).

(4) Section 203J(1) of the Taxes Act 1988 (sections 203B to 203I: accounting for tax) shall have effect as if it required the deduction of income tax to be made from any sum or sums received by the employer—

    (*a*) from the trustees under sub-paragraph (2), or

    (*b*) from the participant in accordance with the plan, as mentioned in sub-paragraph (3).

(5) After making the necessary PAYE deduction from the sum or sums received as mentioned in sub-paragraph (4), the employer company shall pay any remaining amounts to the participant.

(6) For the purposes of this paragraph "the employer company" means [the company which employs the participant in relevant employment at the time when the shares cease to be subject to the plan (or, if the participant is not employed in relevant employment at that time, the company which last employed him in relevant employment before that time), provided that that company is one to whom]¹ the PAYE regulations (within the meaning of section 203L(3) of the Taxes Act 1988) at that time apply.

(7) Where, as a result of any shares ceasing to be subject to the plan, a participant is chargeable to income tax under Schedule E in accordance with this Part and either—

    (*a*) there is no company which falls within sub-paragraph (6), or (*b*) the Inland Revenue are of the opinion that it is impracticable for the company which falls within that sub-paragraph to make a PAYE deduction and accordingly direct that this sub-paragraph shall apply,

then sub-paragraph (2) shall not apply and the trustees shall make a PAYE deduction in respect of an amount equal to that on which income tax is payable as if the participant were a former employee of the trustees.

(8) In a case where sub-paragraph (7) applies, section 203C of the Taxes Act 1988 (PAYE: employee of non-UK employer) does not apply.

(9) Where—

    (*a*) a participant disposes of his beneficial interest in any of his plan shares to the trustees, and

    (*b*) the trustees are deemed by virtue of paragraph 74 to have disposed of the shares in question,

this paragraph shall apply as if the consideration payable by the trustees to the participant on the disposal had been received by the trustees as the proceeds of disposal of plan shares.

(10) For the purposes of this paragraph "PAYE deduction" means a deduction required by regulations under section 203 of the Taxes Act 1988.

Commentary—*Simon's Direct Tax Service* **E4.538**.
Amendments—[1] Words in sub-para (6) substituted by FA 2002 s 39(1), (3), (7) with effect from the year 2002–03.

PAYE: capital receipts

96—(1) Where the trustees receive a sum of money which constitutes (or forms part of) a capital receipt in respect of which a participant is chargeable to income tax under Schedule E, in accordance with this Part of this Schedule, when it is received by him—

    (*a*) the trustees shall pay out of that sum of money to the employer company an amount equal to that on which income tax is so payable, and

    (*b*) the employer company shall then pay over that amount to the participant, but in so doing shall make a PAYE deduction.

This is subject to sub-paragraph (3).

(2) For the purposes of this paragraph "the employer company" means [the company which employs the participant in relevant employment at the time the trustees receive the sum of money referred to in sub-paragraph (1) (or, if the participant is not employed in relevant employment at that time, the company which last employed him in relevant employment before that time), provided that that company is one to whom][1] the PAYE regulations (within the meaning of section 203L(3) of the Taxes Act 1988) at that time apply.

(3) Where the trustees receive a sum of money to which sub-paragraph (1) applies but—

    (*a*) there is no company which falls within sub-paragraph (2), or

    (*b*) the Inland Revenue are of the opinion that it is impracticable for the company which falls within that sub-paragraph to make a PAYE deduction and accordingly direct that this sub-paragraph shall apply,

then, in paying over to the participant the capital receipt, the trustees shall make a PAYE deduction in respect of an amount equal to that on which income tax is payable as mentioned in sub-paragraph (1) as if the participant were a former employee of the trustees.

(4) In a case where sub-paragraph (3) applies, section 203C of the Taxes Act 1988 (PAYE: employee of non-UK employer) does not apply.

(5) For the purposes of this paragraph "PAYE deduction" means a deduction required by regulations under section 203 of the Taxes Act 1988.

Commentary—*Simon's Direct Tax Service* **E4.538**.
Amendments—[1] Words in sub-para (2) substituted by FA 2002 s 39(1), (4), (7) with effect from the year 2002–03.

PART XI

CAPITAL GAINS TAX

Introduction

97 The provisions of this Part apply for capital gains tax purposes in relation to an approved employee share ownership plan.

Gains accruing to trustees

98—(1) Any gain accruing to the trustees is not a chargeable gain if the shares—

    (*a*) are shares in relation to which the requirements of Part VIII are met, and

    (*b*) are awarded to employees, or acquired on their behalf as dividend shares, in accordance with the plan within the relevant period.

(2) [If any of the shares in the company in question are readily convertible assets at the time the shares][1] are acquired by the trustees, the relevant period is the period of two years beginning with the date on which the shares are acquired by the trustees.

(3) [If at the time of the acquisition of the shares by the trustees none of the shares in the company in question are readily convertible assets][1], the relevant period is—

    (*a*) the period of five years beginning with the date on which the shares were acquired, or
    (*b*) if within that period [any of the shares in that company][1] become readily convertible assets, the period of two years beginning with the date on which they did so,

whichever ends first.

(4) For the purposes of determining whether shares are awarded to employees within the relevant period, shares acquired by the trustees at an earlier time are taken to be awarded to employees before shares of the same class acquired by the trustees at a later time.

This is subject to paragraph 76(1) (treatment of shares acquired from an employee share ownership trust).

Commentary—*Simon's Direct Tax Service* **E4.539**.
Amendment—[1] Words in sub-paras (2), (3) substituted by FA 2001 s 61, Sch 13 para 8 with effect for any shares acquired by the trustees of an employee share ownership plan after the passing of FA 2001. For this purpose, "the trustees of an employee share ownership plan" means the body of persons established in accordance with FA 2000 Sch 8 para 68. Before amendment, sub-paras (2), (3) read as follows—

    "(2) If the shares are readily convertible assets at the time they are acquired by the trustees, the relevant period is the period of two years beginning with the date on which the shares are acquired by the trustees.
    (3) If at the time of their acquisition by the trustees the shares are not readily convertible assets, the relevant period is—

        (*a*) the period of five years beginning with the date on which the shares were acquired, or
        (*b*) if within that period the shares in question become readily convertible assets, the period of two years beginning with the date on which they did so,

    whichever ends first.".

Participant absolutely entitled as against trustees

99—(1) A participant is treated for capital gains tax purposes as absolutely entitled as against the trustees to any shares awarded to him under the plan.

(2) This applies notwithstanding anything in the plan or the trust instrument.

Commentary—*Simon's Direct Tax Service* **E4.539**.

Different classes of shares

100—(1) For the purposes of Chapter I of Part IV of the Taxation of Chargeable Gains Act 1992 (identification of shares etc) a participant's plan shares are treated, so long as they are subject to the plan, as of a different class from any shares (which would otherwise be treated as of the same class) that are not plan shares.

(2) For the purposes of that Chapter, any shares transferred to the trustees of the plan trust by a qualifying transfer that have not been awarded to participants under the plan shall (notwithstanding that they would otherwise fall to be treated as of the same class) be treated as of a different class from any shares held by the trustees that were not transferred to them by a qualifying transfer.

(3) In sub-paragraph (2) "qualifying transfer" has the meaning given in paragraph 76 (acquisition by trustees of shares from employee share ownership trust).

Commentary—*Simon's Direct Tax Service* **E4.539**.

No chargeable gain on shares ceasing to be subject to the plan

101—(1) Shares which cease to be subject to the plan are treated as having been disposed of and immediately reacquired by the participant at market value.

(2) Any gain accruing on that disposal is not a chargeable gain.

Commentary—*Simon's Direct Tax Service* **E4.539**.

Treatment of forfeited shares

102—(1) If any of the participant's plan shares are forfeited, they are treated as having been disposed of by the participant and acquired by the trustees at market value at the date of forfeiture.

(2) Any gain accruing on that disposal is not a chargeable gain.

Commentary—*Simon's Direct Tax Service* **E4.539**.

Acquisition by trustees of shares from profit sharing scheme

103—(1) Where the trustees acquire shares from the trustees of an approved profit sharing scheme, the disposal and the acquisition by the trustees are treated as being made for such consideration as to secure that neither a gain nor a loss accrues on the disposal.

(2) In such a case the relevant period for the purposes of paragraph 98 is determined as if the shares had been acquired by the trustees at the time they were acquired by the trustees of the other trust.

This does not affect the date on which the trustees are treated as acquiring the shares for the purposes of taper relief.

Commentary—*Simon's Direct Tax Service* **E4.539**.

Disposal of rights under rights issue

104—(1) Any gain accruing on the disposal of rights under paragraph 72 (power of trustees to raise funds to subscribe for rights issue) is not a chargeable gain.

(2) Sub-paragraph (1) does not apply to a disposal of rights unless similar rights are conferred in respect of all ordinary shares in the company.

Commentary—*Simon's Direct Tax Service* **E4.539**.

PART XII
CORPORATION TAX DEDUCTIONS

Introduction

105 References in this Part of this Schedule to deductions are to deductions by a company in calculating for the purposes of corporation tax the profits of a trade carried on by it.

This is subject to paragraph 114 (application of provisions to expenses of management of investment companies etc).

Deduction for providing free or matching shares

106—(1) Where, under an approved employee share ownership plan, shares are awarded to employees as free or matching shares by reason of their employment with a company, a deduction is allowed under this paragraph to that company.

(2) Any such deduction—

(a) is of an amount equal to the market value of the shares at the time they are acquired by the trustees, and

(b) must be made for the period of account in which the shares are awarded to employees in accordance with the plan.

(3) Except as provided by sub-paragraph (1), no deduction may be made by that company or any associated company in respect of the provision of those shares.

This is subject to paragraphs 111 (deduction for costs of setting up the plan) and 112 (deductions for contributions to running expenses of plan).

(4) Where the shares are awarded under a group plan, the market value of the shares at the time they are acquired by the trustees shall for the purposes of this paragraph be taken to be the relevant proportion of the total market value of the shares included in the award.

For this purpose "the relevant proportion" means the proportion that the number of shares in the award awarded to the employees of the company concerned bears to the total number of shares in the award.

(5) In determining the market value of any shares for the purposes of this paragraph, if shares have been acquired by the trustees on different days it shall be assumed that those acquired on an earlier day are awarded to employees under the plan before those acquired by the trustees on a later day.

(6) If a deduction is made under this paragraph by a company, no deduction may be made by any other company under this paragraph in respect of the provision of the shares.

(7) This paragraph has effect subject to paragraph 108 (cases in which no deduction is allowed).

Commentary—*Simon's Direct Tax Service* **E4.540**.

Deduction for additional expenses in providing partnership shares

107—(1) Where under an approved employee share ownership plan—

(a) partnership shares are awarded to employees by reason of their employment with a company, and

(b) the market value of those shares at the time they are acquired by the trustees exceeds the partnership share money paid by the participants to acquire those shares,

a deduction is allowed under this paragraph to that company.

(2) Any such deduction—

(a) is of an amount equal to the amount of the excess referred to in sub-paragraph (1)(b), and

(b) must be made for the period of account in which the shares are awarded to employees in accordance with the plan.

(3) Except as provided by sub-paragraph (1), no deduction may be made by that company or any associated company in respect of the provision of those shares.

This is subject to paragraphs 111 (deduction for costs of setting up the plan) and 112 (deductions for contributions to running expenses of plan).

(4) If a deduction is made under this paragraph by a company, no deduction may be made by any other company under this paragraph in respect of the provision of the shares.

(5) This paragraph has effect subject to paragraph 108 (cases in which no deduction is allowed).
Commentary—*Simon's Direct Tax Service* **E4.540**.

Cases in which no deduction is allowed

108—(1) No deduction is allowed under paragraph 106 or 107 in the following cases.

(2) No deduction is allowed in respect of shares awarded to an individual who is not a Schedule E taxpayer at the date the shares are awarded to him under the plan.

A "Schedule E taxpayer" means an individual who—

   (*a*) is chargeable to tax under Schedule E in respect of emoluments from the employment by reference to which he is eligible to participate in the award, or
   (*b*) would be so chargeable if any such emoluments were remitted to the United Kingdom.

(3) No deduction is allowed in respect of shares that are liable to depreciate substantially in value for reasons that do not apply generally to shares in the company.

(4) No deduction is allowed if a deduction has been made—

   (*a*) by the company, or
   (*b*) by an associated company of the company,

in respect of the provision of the same shares for this or another trust.

This applies whatever the nature or purpose of the other trust and whatever the basis on which the deduction was made.

(5) For the purposes of determining whether the same shares have been provided to more than one trust, if shares have been acquired by the trustees of the plan trust on different days it shall be assumed that those acquired on an earlier day are awarded under the plan before those acquired by the trustees on a later day.

Commentary—*Simon's Direct Tax Service* **E4.540**.

No deduction for expenses in providing dividend shares

109—(1) No deduction is allowed for expenses in providing shares that are acquired on behalf of individuals under an approved employee share ownership plan as dividend shares.

(2) This is subject to paragraph 112 (deductions for contributions to running expenses of plan).

Commentary—*Simon's Direct Tax Service* **E4.540**.

Treatment of forfeited shares

110 If any of a participant's plan shares are forfeited—

   (*a*) the shares are treated for the purposes of this Part as acquired by the trustees—
      (i) when the forfeiture occurs, and
      (ii) for no consideration, and
   (*b*) no deduction is allowed under paragraph 106 or 107 in respect of any subsequent award of those shares under the plan.

Commentary—*Simon's Direct Tax Service* **E4.540**.

Deduction for costs of setting up the plan

111—(1) A deduction is allowed under this paragraph for expenses incurred by a company in establishing an employee share ownership plan which is approved by the Inland Revenue.

(2) No deduction may be made under this paragraph if—

   (*a*) any employee acquires rights under the plan, or
   (*b*) the trustees acquire any shares for the purposes of the plan,

before the Inland Revenue approve the plan.

(3) If Inland Revenue approval of the plan is given more than nine months after the end of that period of account in which the expenses are incurred, the expenses are treated for the purposes of this paragraph as incurred in the period in which the approval is given.

(4) No other deduction is allowed in respect of expenses for which a deduction is allowed under this paragraph.

Commentary—*Simon's Direct Tax Service* **E4.540**.

Deductions for contributions to running expenses of plan

112—(1) Nothing in this Part of this Schedule affects any deduction for expenses incurred by a company in contributing to the expenses of the trustees in operating an approved employee share ownership plan.

(2) For this purpose the expenses of the trustees in operating the plan—

(*a*) do not include expenses in acquiring shares for the purposes of the trust, other than incidental acquisition costs, but

(*b*) do include the payment of interest on money borrowed by them for that purpose.

(3) In sub-paragraph (2)(*a*) "incidental acquisition costs" means any fees, commission, stamp duty and similar incidental costs attributable to the acquisition of the shares.

Commentary—*Simon's Direct Tax Service* **E4.540**.

Withdrawal of deductions on withdrawal of approval

113—(1) If approval of an employee share ownership plan is withdrawn the Inland Revenue may by notice to a company direct that the benefit of any deductions under paragraph 106 (deduction for providing free or matching shares) or 107 (deduction for contributing to additional expenses in providing partnership shares) in relation to the plan is also withdrawn.

(2) The effect of the direction is that the aggregate amount of the deductions is treated as a trading receipt of that company for the period of account in which the Inland Revenue give notice of the withdrawal of approval.

Commentary—*Simon's Direct Tax Service* **E4.540**.

Application of provisions to expenses of management of investment companies etc

114—(1) The provisions of this Part apply in relation to—

(*a*) investment companies, and

(*b*) companies to which section 75 of the Taxes Act 1988 (management expenses) applies by virtue of section 76 of that Act (insurance companies),

in accordance with the following provisions.

(2) The provisions of this Part which allow a deduction in calculating the profits of a trade apply to treat amounts as disbursed as expenses of management.

(3) Paragraph 113(2) (effect of direction as to withdrawal of deductions) applies as if the reference to a trading receipt for the period of account in which the Inland Revenue give notice of the withdrawal of approval were a reference to profits or gains chargeable to tax under Case VI of Schedule D arising when the Inland Revenue give notice of the withdrawal.

Commentary—*Simon's Direct Tax Service* **E4.540**.

PART XIII
SUPPLEMENTARY PROVISIONS
Company reconstructions

115—(1) This paragraph applies where there occurs in relation to any of the participant's plan shares ("the original holding")—

(*a*) a transaction which results in a new holding being equated with the original holding for the purposes of capital gains tax, or

(*b*) a transaction that would have that result but for the fact that what would be the new holding consists of or includes a qualifying corporate bond,

other than a transaction within sub-paragraph (2).

A transaction in relation to which this paragraph applies is referred to below as a "company reconstruction".

(2) Where an issue of shares of any of the following descriptions (in respect of which a charge to income tax arises) is made as part of a company reconstruction, those shares shall be treated for the purposes of this paragraph as not forming part of the new holding—

(*a*) redeemable shares or securities issued as mentioned in section 209(2)(*c*) of the Taxes Act 1988;

(*b*) share capital issued in circumstances such that section 210(1) of that Act applies;

(*c*) share capital to which section 249 of that Act applies.

(3) In this paragraph—

"corresponding shares", in relation to any new shares, means the shares in respect of which the new shares are issued or which the new shares otherwise represent;

"new shares" means shares comprised in the new holding which were issued in respect of, or otherwise represent, shares comprised in the original holding;

"original holding" has the meaning given by sub-paragraph (1).

(4) Subject to the following provisions of this paragraph, in relation to an employee share ownership plan, references in this Schedule to a participant's plan shares shall be construed, after the time of the company reconstruction, as being or, as the case may be, as including references to any new shares.

(5) For the purposes of this Schedule—

(*a*) a company reconstruction shall be treated as not involving a disposal of shares comprised in the original holding,

(*b*) the date on which any new shares are to be treated as having been awarded to the participant shall be that on which the corresponding shares were awarded,

(*c*) the conditions in Part VIII shall be treated as fulfilled with respect to any new shares if they were (or were treated as) fulfilled with respect to the corresponding shares, and

(*d*) the provisions of Part X (income tax) and Part XI (capital gains tax) shall apply in relation to the new shares as they would have applied to the corresponding shares.

Where the corresponding shares were dividend shares, the reference in paragraph (*b*) to the shares being awarded shall be read as a reference to the shares being acquired on behalf of the participant.

(6) Sub-paragraphs (4) and (5) are subject to paragraph 116 (treatment of shares acquired under rights issue).

(7) For the purposes of this Schedule if, as part of a company reconstruction, trustees become entitled to a capital receipt, their entitlement to the capital receipt shall be taken to arise before the new holding comes into being.

(8) In the context of a new holding, any reference in this Schedule to shares includes securities and rights of any description which form part of the new holding for the purposes of Chapter II of Part IV of the Taxation of Chargeable Gains Act 1992.

Commentary—*Simon's Direct Tax Service* **E4.541**.

Treatment of shares acquired under rights issue

116—(1) Where the trustees exercise rights under a rights issue conferred in respect of a participant's plan shares, any shares or securities or rights allotted as a result shall be treated for the purposes of this Schedule as if they were plan shares—

(*a*) identical to the shares in respect of which the rights were conferred, and

(*b*) appropriated to, or acquired on behalf of, the participant under the plan in the same way and at the same time as those shares.

This is subject to sub-paragraphs (2) to (4).

(2) Where the funds used by the trustees to exercise rights under a rights issue are provided otherwise than by virtue of the exercise by the trustees of their powers under paragraph 72 (power of trustees to raise funds to subscribe for rights issue)—

(*a*) any shares, securities or rights allotted are not plan shares, and

(*b*) sections 127 to 130 of the Taxation of Chargeable Gains Act 1992 shall not apply in relation to them.

(3) Sub-paragraph (1) does not apply in relation to rights arising under a rights issue unless similar rights are conferred in respect of all ordinary shares in the company.

(4) Where sub-paragraph (1) does not apply by virtue of sub-paragraph (3)—

(*a*) any shares, securities or rights allotted are not plan shares, and

(*b*) sections 127 to 130 of the Taxation of Chargeable Gains Act 1992 shall not apply in relation to them.

(5) In this paragraph references to rights arising under a rights issue are to be construed in accordance with paragraph 72(2).

Commentary—*Simon's Direct Tax Service* **E4.541**.

[Exemptions from stamp duty and stamp duty reserve tax

116A Where, under an approved employee share ownership plan, partnership shares or dividend shares are transferred by the trustees to an employee—

(*a*) no *ad valorem* stamp duty is chargeable on any instrument by which the transfer is made, and

(*b*) no stamp duty reserve tax is chargeable on any agreement by the trustees to make the transfer.]¹

Amendment—¹ This paragraph inserted by FA 2001 s 95 with effect for instruments executed (within the meaning of SA 1891) after 11 May 2001, and for agreements to transfer shares made after 11 May 2001.

Power to require information

117—(1) The Inland Revenue may by notice require any person to provide them with such information as they reasonably require for the performance of their functions under this Schedule and as the person to whom the notice is addressed has or can reasonably obtain.

(2) The power conferred by this paragraph extends, in particular, to—

(*a*) information to enable the Inland Revenue—

(i) to decide whether to approve an employee share ownership plan or withdraw an approval already given, or

(ii) to determine the liability to tax, including capital gains tax, of any person who has participated in a plan; and (*b*) information about the administration of a plan and any proposed alteration of the terms of a plan.

(3) The notice must require the information to be provided within a specified time, which must not be less than three months.

(4) In section 98 of the Taxes Management Act 1970 (penalties in connection with returns, etc), in the first column of the table, after the final entry insert—

"paragraph 117 of Schedule 8 to the Finance Act 2000".

Commentary—*Simon's Direct Tax Service* **E4.542**.

Withdrawal of approval

118—(1) If any disqualifying event occurs in relation to an approved employee share ownership plan, the Inland Revenue may by notice to the company withdraw the approval with effect from the time at which the disqualifying event occurred or such later time as the Inland Revenue may specify.

(2) The following are disqualifying events—

(*a*) a contravention in relation to the operation of the plan of any of the requirements of this Schedule, the plan itself or the plan trust;

(*b*) any alteration being made in a key feature of the plan, or in the terms of the plan trust, without the approval of the Inland Revenue;

(*c*) if the plan provides for performance allowances in accordance with paragraph 30 (method two), the setting, in respect of an award of shares, of performance targets that, at the time they are set in accordance with the plan, cannot reasonably be viewed as being comparable;

(*d*) any alteration being made in the share capital of the company whose shares are the subject of the plan, or in the rights attaching to any shares of that company, that materially affects the value of participants' plan shares;

(*e*) shares of a class of which shares have been awarded to participants receiving different treatment in any respect from the other shares of that class;

(*f*) the trustees, the company or, in the case of a group plan, a company which is or has been a participating company failing to furnish any information which they are or it is required to furnish under paragraph 117.

(3) For the purposes of sub-paragraph (2)(*b*)—

(*a*) an alteration is an alteration of a "key feature" of the plan if it relates to a provision that is necessary in order to meet the requirements of this Schedule; and

(*b*) the Inland Revenue shall not withhold their approval unless it appears to them that the plan as proposed to be altered would not now be approved on an application under paragraph 4.

(4) For the purposes of sub-paragraph (2)(*c*) performance targets are comparable if they are comparable in terms of the likelihood of their being met by the performance units to which they apply.

(5) Sub-paragraph (2)(*e*) applies, in particular, to different treatment in respect of—

(*a*) the dividend payable;

(*b*) repayment;

(*c*) the restrictions attaching to the shares; or

(*d*) any offer of substituted or additional shares, securities or rights of any description in respect of the shares.

This is subject to sub-paragraph (6).

(6) Sub-paragraph (2)(*e*) does not apply—

(*a*) where the difference in treatment arises from—

(i) a key feature of the plan, or

(ii) any of the participants' shares being subject to provision for forfeiture, or

(*b*) on the ground only that shares which have been newly issued receive, in respect of dividends payable with respect to a period beginning before the date on which they were issued, treatment less favourable than that accorded to shares issued before that date.

(7) The withdrawal of approval of an employee share ownership plan does not affect the operation of this Schedule in relation to shares awarded to participants in the plan before the time with effect from which approval was withdrawn.

References in this Schedule to an approved employee share ownership plan in relation to such shares are to a plan that was approved at the time the shares were awarded.

Commentary—*Simon's Direct Tax Service* **E4.542**.

Appeal against withdrawal of approval

119—(1) The company may appeal against a decision of the Inland Revenue—

(*a*) to withdraw approval of an employee share ownership plan, or

(*b*) to give a direction under paragraph 113 (withdrawal of corporation tax deductions on withdrawal of approval), or (*c*) to refuse approval under paragraph 118(2)(*b*) (approval of alteration of plan or plan trust).

(2) The appeal lies to the Special Commissioners.

(3) Notice of appeal must be given to the Inland Revenue within 30 days after notice of their decision is given to the company.

Termination of plan

120—(1) The plan may provide for the company to issue a plan termination notice in respect of the plan in such circumstances as are specified in the plan.

(2) The plan must provide that, where a plan termination notice is issued, a copy of the notice is to be given, without delay, to—

    (*a*) the Inland Revenue,
    (*b*) the trustees, and
    (*c*) each individual—

        (i) who has plan shares, or
        (ii) who has entered a partnership share agreement which was in force immediately before the notice was issued.

Commentary—*Simon's Direct Tax Service* **E4.542**.

Effect of plan termination notice

121—(1) This paragraph applies where the company has issued a plan termination notice under paragraph 120.

(2) No further shares may be awarded to individuals under the plan.

(3) The trustees must remove the plan shares from the plan as soon as practicable after—

    (*a*) the end of the notice period, or
    (*b*) if later, the first date on which the shares may be removed from the plan without giving rise to a charge to income tax under Part X of this Schedule on the participant on whose behalf they are held.

Paragraph 46 (repayment of partnership share money) and paragraph 58(2) (cash dividend paid over if not reinvested) provide for the payment to employees of money held on their behalf.

(4) In sub-paragraph (3) "the notice period" means the period of three months beginning with the date on which the requirements imposed by the plan in accordance with paragraph 120(2) (copy of termination notice to Inland Revenue, participants etc) are met in respect of the plan termination notice.

(5) The trustees may remove the participant's shares from the plan at an earlier date with the participant's consent.

(6) Any consent given by the participant before he receives a copy of the plan termination notice shall be disregarded for this purpose.

(7) The trustees must as soon as practicable after the plan termination notice is issued pay to an individual any money held on his behalf.

(8) In this paragraph references to the trustees removing the plan shares from the plan are to their—

    (*a*) transferring the shares to the participant on behalf of whom they are held, or to another person, at his direction, or
    (*b*) disposing of the shares and accounting (or holding themselves ready to account) for the proceeds to the participant or to another person at his direction.

(9) Where the participant has died, the references in sub-paragraph (8) to the participant shall be read as references to his personal representatives.

Commentary—*Simon's Direct Tax Service* **E4.542**.

Meaning of shares being withdrawn from or ceasing to be subject to plan

122—(1) For the purposes of this Schedule shares are withdrawn from the plan when—

    (*a*) they are transferred by the trustees to the participant, or another person, on the direction of the participant,
    (*b*) the participant assigns, charges or otherwise disposes of his beneficial interest in the shares, or
    (*c*) they are disposed of by the trustees, on the direction of the participant, in circumstances where the trustees account (or hold themselves ready to account) for the proceeds to the participant or to another person.

(2) Where the participant has died, the references in sub-paragraph (1) to the participant shall be read as references to his personal representatives.

(3) For the purposes of this Schedule plan shares cease to be subject to the plan when—

    (*a*) they are withdrawn from the plan,

(*b*) the participant to whom the shares were awarded ceases to be in relevant employment at a time when the shares are subject to the plan, or

(*c*) the trustees dispose of the shares under provision made in accordance with paragraph 73 (meeting PAYE obligations).

(4) Where an individual participates in an award of partnership shares, if he ceases to be in relevant employment at any time during the acquisition period relating to that award, he shall be treated for the purposes of sub-paragraphs (3) and (7) as ceasing to be in such employment immediately after the shares are awarded to him.

(5) In sub-paragraph (4) "the acquisition period" in relation to an award means—

(*a*) where there was no accumulation period, the period beginning with the deduction of the partnership share money and ending with the acquisition date (within the meaning of paragraph 40(2)); and

(*b*) where there was an accumulation period, the period beginning with the end of that period and ending immediately before the acquisition date (within the meaning of paragraph 42(3)).

(6) For the purposes of determining the charge to income tax (if any) arising on any of the participant's shares ceasing to be subject to the plan—

(*a*) shares shall be taken to cease to be subject to the plan in the order in which they were awarded to the participant under the plan,

(*b*) where shares are awarded to the participant on the same day, the shares shall be treated as ceasing to be subject to the plan in the order which gives rise to the lowest charge to income tax on the participant.

(7) Where a participant ceases to be in relevant employment his plan shares shall be treated as ceasing to be subject to the plan on the date of leaving.

Commentary—*Simon's Direct Tax Service* **E4.542**.

Meaning of participant ceasing to be in relevant employment

123—(1) This paragraph explains what is meant by a participant ceasing to be in relevant employment.

(2) Relevant employment means employment by the company or any associated company.

(3) A participant does not cease to be in relevant employment if he remains in the employment of the company or any associated company.

Commentary—*Simon's Direct Tax Service* **E4.542**.

Exercise of functions conferred on "the Inland Revenue"

124 References in this Schedule to "the Inland Revenue" are to any officer of the Board.

Determination of market value

125—(1) For the purposes of this Schedule the "market value" of shares has the same meaning as, for the purposes of the Taxation of Chargeable Gains Act 1992, it has by virtue of Part VIII of that Act.

This is subject to paragraph 24(3) (determination of value of shares subject to restriction or risk of forfeiture).

(2) Where for the purposes of this Schedule the market value of shares on any date falls to be determined, the Inland Revenue and the trustees may agree that it shall be determined by reference to such date or dates, or to an average of the values on a number of dates, as may be provided in the agreement.

Meaning of "associated company"

126—(1) For the purposes of this Schedule one company is an "associated company" of another company if—

(*a*) one has control of the other, or

(*b*) both are under the control of the same person or persons.

(2) For the purposes of this paragraph the question of whether a person controls a company shall be determined in accordance with section 416(2) to (6) of the Taxes Act 1988.

(3) This paragraph is subject to paragraph 67(3).

Jointly owned companies

127—(1) For the purposes of the provisions of this Schedule relating to group plans, each joint owner of a jointly owned company is treated as controlling—

(*a*) the jointly owned company, and

(*b*) any company controlled by that company.

This paragraph does not apply for the purposes of paragraph 61(*b*) (requirement that plan shares are in a company not under another company's control).

(2) A "jointly owned company" means a company—

   (*a*) of which 50% of the issued share capital is owned by one person and 50% by another, and
   (*b*) which is not controlled by any one person.

(3) A jointly owned company may not be a participating company in more than one group plan.

[(4) A company controlled by a jointly owned company may not—

   (*a*) be a participating company in more than one group plan, or
   (*b*) if the jointly owned company or any other company controlled by it is a participating company in a group plan, be a participating company in a different group plan.]¹

Cross references—See FA 2002 s 39(8) (nothing in FA 2002 s 39(5) prevents a company continuing to be a participating company in a group plan in which it was a participating company immediately before 24 July 2002).
Amendments—¹ Sub-para (4) added by FA 2002 s 39(1), (5), (7) with effect from the year 2002–03.

Meaning of "readily convertible asset"

128—(1) For the purposes of this Schedule "readily convertible asset" has the same meaning as in section 203F of the Taxes Act 1988 (PAYE: tradeable assets).

This is subject to sub-paragraph (2).

(2) In determining for the purposes of this Schedule [(and that section in its application in relation to shares which cease to be subject to a plan)]¹ whether shares are readily convertible assets any market for the shares that—

   (*a*) is created by virtue of the trustees acquiring shares for the purposes of the plan, and
   (*b*) exists solely for the purposes of the plan,

shall be disregarded.

Amendments—¹ Words inserted by FA 2002 s 39(1), (6), (7) with effect from the year 2002–03.

Minor definitions

129—(1) In this Schedule—

   "approved employee share ownership plan" means an employee share ownership plan approved under this Schedule;
   "approved profit sharing scheme" means a profit sharing scheme approved under Schedule 9 to the Taxes Act 1988;
   "articles of association", in relation to a company, includes any other written agreement between the shareholders of the company;
   "company" means a body corporate;
   "control", unless otherwise indicated, has the same meaning as in section 840 of the Taxes Act 1988;
   "foreign cash dividend" means a cash dividend paid in respect of plan shares in a company not resident in the United Kingdom;
   "group of companies" means a company and any other companies of which it has control, and "group company" has a corresponding meaning;
   "ordinary share capital" has the meaning given in section 832(1) of the Taxes Act 1988;
   "participant's plan shares", in relation to an employee share ownership plan, means plan shares that have been awarded to an individual participant;
   "PAYE obligations" means obligations of any person under—

      (*a*) sections 203 to 203L of the Taxes Act 1988, or
      (*b*) regulations under section 203 of that Act;

   "plan shares", in relation to a plan, means—

      (*a*) free, partnership or matching shares that have been awarded to participants under the plan,
      (*b*) dividend shares that have been acquired on behalf of participants under the plan, and
      (*c*) shares in relation to which paragraph 115(5) applies (company reconstructions: new shares),

   that remain subject to the plan;
   "qualifying corporate bond" has the meaning given by section 117 of the Taxation of Chargeable Gains Act 1992;
   "tax year" means a year of assessment.

(2) Section 839 of the Taxes Act 1988 (connected persons) applies for the purposes of this Schedule.

(3) For the purposes of this Schedule references to "shares" include fractions of shares forming part of the share capital of a company registered in a foreign country the law of which recognises such fractions.

(4) For the purposes of this Schedule a company is a member of a consortium owning another company if it is one of a number of companies—

(*a*) which between them beneficially own not less than three-quarters of the other company's ordinary share capital, and
(*b*) each of which beneficially owns not less than one-twentieth of that capital.

Index of defined expressions

130 In this Schedule the following expressions are defined or otherwise explained by the provisions indicated—

SCHEDULE 9

NEW SCHEDULE 7C TO THE TAXATION OF CHARGEABLE GAINS ACT 1992

Section 48

(*inserts* TCGA 1992 Sch 7B)

Commentary—*Simon's Direct Tax Service* **E4.536**.

SCHEDULE 10

BENEFITS IN KIND: DEREGULATORY AMENDMENTS

Section 57

Commentary—*Simon's Direct Tax Service* **E4.612, 632.**

Introduction

1 Chapter II of Part V of the Taxes Act 1988 (provisions relating to the Schedule E charge: benefits in kind, etc) is amended as follows.

Accommodation, supplies or services used in performing duties of employment

2—(1) (*inserts* TA 1988 s 155ZA).

(2) (*amends* TA 1988 s 154(2), (3)).

Power to provide by regulations for exemption of minor benefits

3—(1) (*inserts* TA 1988 s 155ZB).

(2) (*amends* TA 1988 s 154(2)).

Beneficial loans: exception of loan where whole of interest qualifies for relief

4—(1) (*inserts* TA 1988 s 161A).

(2) In section 160—

    (*a*) subsection (1C) shall cease to have effect, and

    (*b*) in subsection (5) after ''161'' insert '', 161A''.

Beneficial loans: loans on ordinary commercial terms

5—(1) (*inserts* TA 1988 s 161A).

(2) (*inserts* TA 1988 Sch 7A).

(3) In section 160(5)—

    (*a*) after ''161A'' (inserted by paragraph 4(2)) insert '', 161B'', and

    (*b*) for ''Schedule 7'' substitute ''Schedules 7 and 7A''.

(4) In section 161, subsections (1A) and (1B) shall cease to have effect.

Beneficial loans: apportionment of benefit in case of joint loan etc

6 (*inserts* TA 1988 Sch 7 para 5A)

SCHEDULE 11

CARS AVAILABLE FOR PRIVATE USE

Section 59

Commentary—*Simon's Direct Tax Service* **E4.626.**

1—(1) Schedule 6 to the Taxes Act 1988 (taxation of directors and others in respect of cars) is amended as follows.

(2) For paragraphs 1 to 5 (which make provision for determining the cash equivalent of the benefit) substitute—

''*Cash equivalent*

1—(1) The cash equivalent of the benefit is the appropriate percentage for the year of the price of the car as regards the year.

(2) This is subject to paragraphs 6 and 7 below (reductions for periods when car unavailable and payments for use of car).

The appropriate percentage

2 The appropriate percentage for the year is determined in accordance with paragraphs 3 to 5G below.

Car with CO_2 emissions figure

3—(1) This paragraph applies where—

    (*a*) the car—

(i) is first registered on or after 1st January 1998 but before 1st October 1999, and

(ii) when so registered conformed to a vehicle type with an EC type-approval certificate, or had a UK approval certificate, that specifies a CO_2 emissions figure in terms of grams per kilometre driven, or

(b) the car—

(i) is first registered on or after 1st October 1999, and

(ii) is so registered on the basis of an EC certificate of conformity or UK approval certificate that specifies a CO_2 emissions figures in terms of grams per kilometre driven.

(2) In this paragraph references to "the applicable CO_2 emissions figure" are—

(a) if the car is within sub-paragraph (1)(a) above, to the figure mentioned in paragraph (ii) of that sub-paragraph, and

(b) if the car is within sub-paragraph (1)(b) above—

(i) where the EC certificate of conformity or UK approval certificate specifies only one CO_2 emissions figure, that figure, and

(ii) where it specifies more than one, the figure specified as the CO_2 emissions (combined) figure.

This is subject to paragraph 5 (bi-fuel cars) and paragraph 5A (disabled drivers).

(3) Where the applicable CO_2 emissions figure does not exceed the lower threshold for the year the appropriate percentage for the year is 15% ("the basic percentage").

(4) Where the applicable CO_2 emissions figure exceeds the lower threshold for the year, the appropriate percentage for the year is whichever is the smaller of—

(a) the basic percentage increased by 1% for each 5 grams per kilometre by which the applicable CO_2 emissions figure exceeds the lower threshold for the year, and

(b) 35%.

(5) This paragraph is subject to paragraph 5D (diesel car supplement) and any regulations under paragraph 5E (power to provide for discounts).

The lower threshold

4—(1) For the purposes of paragraph 3 above the lower threshold is ascertained from the following Table—

TABLE

Year of assessment	Lower threshold (in g/km)
2002–03	165
2003–04	155
2004–05 and subsequent years of assessment	145

(2) The Treasury may by order provide for a lower threshold different from that provided for in the Table in sub-paragraph (1) above to apply for years of assessment beginning on or after 6th April 2005 or such later date as may be specified in the order.

(3) For the purposes of paragraph 3 above the applicable CO_2 emissions figure (if it is not a multiple of five) is rounded down to the nearest multiple of five.

Bi-fuel cars

5 Where the car—

(a) is first registered on or after 1st January 2000, and

(b) is so registered on the basis of an EC certificate of conformity, or UK approval certificate, that specifies separate CO_2 emissions figures in terms of grams per kilometre driven for different fuels,

then, for the purposes of paragraph 3 above, "the applicable CO_2 emissions figure" is the lowest figure specified or, if there is more than one figure specified in relation to each fuel, the lowest CO_2 emissions (combined) figure specified.

Automatic cars made available to disabled drivers

5A—(1) Sub-paragraph (2) below applies where—

(a) paragraph 3 above (car with CO_2 emissions figure) applies to the car,

(b) the car has automatic transmission,

(c) at any time in the year when the car is available to the employee, he holds a disabled person's badge, and

(d) by reason of his disability he must, if he wants to drive a car, drive a car that has automatic transmission.

For this purpose the car is not at any time available to the employee by reason only of its being made available to a member of his family or household.

(2) If the applicable CO_2 figure for the car ("the relevant car") is more than it would have been if the car had been an equivalent manual car, paragraph 3 above shall have effect as if the applicable CO_2 emissions figure in relation to the relevant car were the same as that in relation to an equivalent manual car.

(3) For this purpose "an equivalent manual car" means a car that—

(*a*) is first registered at or about the same time as the relevant car, and

(*b*) does not have automatic transmission, but otherwise is the closest variant available of the make and model of the relevant car.

(4) For the purposes of this paragraph a car has automatic transmission if—

(*a*) the driver of the car is not provided with any means whereby he may vary the gear ratio between the engine and the road wheels independently of the accelerator and the brakes, or

(*b*) he is provided with such means, but they do not include a clutch pedal or lever that he may operate manually.

(5) In this paragraph—

"the applicable CO_2 emissions figure" has the same meaning as in paragraph 3 above; and

"disabled person's badge" has the meaning given in section 168AA(3).

"EC certificate of conformity", "EC type-approval certificate" and "UK approval certificate"

5B In this Schedule—

"EC certificate of conformity" means a certificate of conformity issued by a manufacturer under any provision of the law of a Member State implementing Article 6 of Council Directive 70/156/EEC, as amended;

"EC type-approval certificate" means a type-approval certificate issued under any provision of the law of a Member State implementing Council Directive 70/156/EEC, as amended; and

"UK approval certificate" means a certificate issued under—

(*a*) section 58(1) or (4) of the Road Traffic Act 1988, or

(*b*) Article 31A(4) or (5) of the Road Traffic (Northern Ireland) Order 1981.

Car with no CO_2 emissions figure

5C—(1) This paragraph applies where—

(*a*) the car is first registered on or after 1st January 1998, and

(*b*) paragraph 3 above does not apply.

(2) If the car has an internal combustion engine with one or more reciprocating pistons, the appropriate percentage for the year is ascertained from the following Table—

TABLE

Cylinder capacity of car in cubic centimetres	Appropriate percentage
1,400 or less	15%
More than 1,400 but not more than 2,000	25%
More than 2,000	35%

For this purpose a car's cylinder capacity is the capacity of its engine calculated as for the purposes of the Vehicle Excise and Registration Act 1994.

(3) If sub-paragraph (2) above does not apply the appropriate percentage for the year is—

(*a*) 15%, if the car is an electrically propelled vehicle, and

(*b*) 35%, in any other case.

(4) This paragraph is subject to paragraph 5D (diesel car supplement) and any regulations under paragraph 5E (power to provide for discounts) below.

Diesel car supplement

5D—(1) This paragraph applies where the car—

(*a*) is propelled solely by diesel, and

(*b*) is first registered on or after 1st January 1998.

(2) The appropriate percentage for the year is whichever is the smaller of—

(*a*) the percentage which is 3% greater than the appropriate percentage for the year ascertained in accordance with paragraphs 2 to 5C above, and

(*b*) 35%.

(3) In sub-paragraph (1) "diesel" means any diesel fuel within the definition in Article 2 of Directive 98/70/EC of the European Parliament and of the Council.

(4) This paragraph is subject to any regulations under paragraph 5E below (power to provide for discounts).

Discounts

5E The Treasury may by regulations provide for the value of the appropriate percentage as determined in accordance with paragraphs 2 to 5D above to be reduced by such amount as may be prescribed in the regulations, in such circumstances and subject to such conditions as may be so prescribed.

Car registered before 1st January 1998

5F—(1) This paragraph applies where the car was first registered before 1st January 1998.

(2) Where the car has an internal combustion engine with one or more reciprocating pistons, the appropriate percentage for the year is ascertained from the following Table—

TABLE

Cylinder capacity of car in cubic centimetres	Appropriate percentage
1,400 or less	15%
More than 1,400 but not more than 2,000	22%
More than 2,000	32%

For this purpose a car's cylinder capacity is the capacity of its engine calculated as for the purposes of the Vehicle Excise and Registration Act 1994.

(3) Where sub-paragraph (2) above does not apply, the appropriate percentage for the year is—

(*a*) 15%, if the car is an electrically propelled vehicle, and

(*b*) 32%, in any other case.

Electrically propelled vehicle

5G For the purposes of this Schedule, a vehicle is not an electrically propelled vehicle unless—

(*a*) it is propelled solely by electrical power, and

(*b*) that power is derived from—

    (i) a source external to the vehicle, or

    (ii) an electrical storage battery which is not connected to any source of power when the vehicle is in motion.''.

(3) In paragraph 6 (reduction for periods when car is unavailable) for the words from ''('the full'' to the end substitute—

''multiplied by the fraction—

$$\frac{A}{B}$$

where—

A is the number of days in the year on which the car is available; and
B is the number of days in the year.''.

(4) At the end of paragraph 10 (general interpretation) add—

''This is subject to paragraph 5A(1) above.''

2. In section 168AB of the Taxes Act 1988 (equipment etc to enable car to run on road fuel gas), after subsection (3) insert—

''(4) This section does not apply in relation to cars to which paragraph 5 of Schedule 6 to this Act applies (bi-fuel cars taxed by reference to CO_2 emissions figure).''.

SCHEDULE 12

PROVISION OF SERVICES THROUGH AN INTERMEDIARY

Section 60

Revenue & other press releases—IR Tax Bulletin October 2001 p 819 (Providing services through an intermediary–IR35–what happens next?).

Concession C32 (concession for personal services companies in the construction industry who are liable to PAYE on deemed payments under IR35, and have had tax deducted under CIS).

PART I

APPLICATION OF THIS SCHEDULE

Engagements to which this Schedule applies

1—(1) This Schedule applies where—

(*a*) an individual (''the worker'') personally performs, or is under an obligation personally to perform, services for the purposes of a business carried on by another person (''the client''), (*b*) the services are provided not under a contract directly between the client and the worker but under arrangements involving a third party ("the intermediary"), and

(*c*) the circumstances are such that, if the services were provided under a contract directly between the client and the worker, the worker would be regarded for income tax purposes as an employee of the client.

(2) In sub-paragraph (1)(*a*) "business" includes any activity carried on—

(*a*) by a government or public or local authority (in the United Kingdom or elsewhere), or

(*b*) by a body corporate, unincorporated body or partnership.

(3) The reference in sub-paragraph (1)(*b*) to a "third party" includes a partnership or unincorporated body of which the worker is a member.

(4) The circumstances referred to in sub-paragraph (1)(*c*) include the terms on which the services are provided, having regard to the terms of the contracts forming part of the arrangements under which the services are provided.

(5) The fact that the worker holds an office with the client does not affect the application of this Schedule.

Commentary—*Simon's Direct Tax Service* **E4.1003–1005**.

Worker treated as receiving Schedule E income

2—(1) If, in the case of an engagement to which this Schedule applies, in any tax year—

(*a*) the conditions specified in paragraph 3, 4 or 5 are met in relation to the intermediary, and

(*b*) the worker, or an associate of the worker—

(i) receives from the intermediary, directly or indirectly, a payment or other benefit that is not chargeable to tax under Schedule E, or

(ii) has rights entitling him, or which in any circumstances would entitle him, to receive from the intermediary, directly or indirectly, any such payment or other benefit,

the intermediary is treated as making to the worker in that year, and the worker is treated as receiving in that year, a payment chargeable to income tax under Schedule E ("the deemed Schedule E payment").

(2) The deemed Schedule E payment is treated as made at the end of the tax year, unless paragraph 12 applies (earlier date of deemed payment in certain cases).

(3) A single payment is treated as made in respect of all engagements in relation to which the intermediary is treated as making a payment to the worker in the tax year.

These are referred to in this Schedule as "the relevant engagements" in relation to a deemed Schedule E payment.

Commentary—*Simon's Direct Tax Service* **E4.1005**.

Conditions of liability where intermediary is a company

3—(1) Where the intermediary is a company the conditions are that the intermediary is not an associated company of the client that falls within sub-paragraph (2) and either—

(*a*) the worker has a material interest in the intermediary, or

(*b*) the payment or benefit mentioned in paragraph 2(1)(*b*)—

(i) is received or receivable by the worker directly from the intermediary, and

(ii) can reasonably be taken to represent remuneration for services provided by the worker to the client.

(2) An associated company of the client falls within this sub-paragraph if it is such a company by reason of the intermediary and the client both being under the control—

(*a*) of the worker, or

(*b*) of the worker and another person.

(3) A worker is treated as having a material interest in a company if—

(*a*) the worker, alone or with one or more associates of his, or

(*b*) an associate of the worker, with or without other such associates,

has a material interest in the company.

(4) For this purpose a material interest means—

(*a*) beneficial ownership of, or the ability to control, directly or through the medium of other companies or by any other indirect means, more than 5% of the ordinary share capital of the company; or

(*b*) possession of, or entitlement to acquire, rights entitling the holder to receive more than 5% of any distributions that may be made by the company; or

(*c*) where the company is a close company, possession of, or entitlement to acquire, rights that would in the event of the winding up of the company, or in any other circumstances, entitle the holder to receive more than 5% of the assets that would then be available for distribution among the participators.

(5) In sub-paragraph (4)(*c*) "participator" has the meaning given by section 417(1) of the Taxes Act 1988.

Commentary—*Simon's Direct Tax Service* **E4.1005**.

Conditions of liability where intermediary is a partnership

4—(1) Where the intermediary is a partnership the conditions are as follows.

(2) In relation to payments or benefits received or receivable by the worker as a member of the partnership the conditions are—

    (*a*) that the worker, alone or with one or more relatives, is entitled to 60% or more of the profits of the partnership; or

    (*b*) that most of the profits of the partnership concerned derive from the provision of services under engagements to which this Schedule applies—

        (i) to a single client, or

        (ii) to a single client together with associates of that client; or

    (*c*) that under the profit sharing arrangements the income of any of the partners is based on the amount of income generated by that partner by the provision of services under engagements to which this Schedule applies.

In paragraph (*a*) "relative" means husband or wife, parent or remoter forebear, child or remoter issue, or brother or sister.

(3) In relation to payments or benefits received or receivable by the worker otherwise than as a member of the partnership, the conditions are that the payment or benefit—

    (*a*) is received or receivable by the worker directly from the intermediary, and

    (*b*) can reasonably be taken to represent remuneration for services provided by the worker to the client.

Commentary—*Simon's Direct Tax Service* **E4.1005**.

Conditions of liability where intermediary is an individual

5 Where the intermediary is an individual the conditions are that the payment or benefit—

    (*a*) is received or receivable by the worker directly from the intermediary, and

    (*b*) can reasonably be taken to represent remuneration for services provided by the worker to the client.

Commentary—*Simon's Direct Tax Service* **E4.1005**.

Exception of certain payments subject to deduction of tax

6 This Schedule does not apply to payments subject to deduction of tax under section 555 of the Taxes Act 1988 (payments to non-resident entertainers and sportsmen).

Commentary—*Simon's Direct Tax Service* **E4.1027**.

PART II

THE DEEMED SCHEDULE E PAYMENT

Calculation of deemed Schedule E payment

7 The amount of the deemed Schedule E payment for a tax year is calculated as follows:

Step One

Find the total amount of all payments and other benefits received by the intermediary in that year in respect of the relevant engagements, and reduce that amount by 5%.

Step Two

Add the amount of any payments and other benefits received by the worker in that year in respect of the relevant engagements, otherwise than from the intermediary, that—

    (*a*) are not chargeable to income tax under Schedule E, and

    (*b*) would be so chargeable if the worker were employed by the client.

Step Three

Deduct the amount of any expenses met in that year by the intermediary that would have been deductible from the emoluments of the employment if the worker had been employed by the client and the expenses had been met by the worker out of those emoluments.

Step Four

Deduct the amount of any capital allowances in respect of expenditure incurred by the intermediary that could have been claimed by the worker under [Part 2 of the Capital Allowances Act][1] if the worker had been employed by the client and had incurred the expenditure.

Step Five

Deduct any contributions made in that year for the benefit of the worker by the intermediary to a scheme approved under Chapter I or Chapter IV of Part XIV of the Taxes Act 1988 that if made by an employer for the benefit of an employee would not be chargeable to income tax as income of the employee.

This does not apply to excess contributions made and later repaid.

Step Six

Deduct the amount of any employer's national insurance contributions paid by the intermediary for that year in respect of the worker.

Step Seven

Deduct the amount of any payments or other benefits received in that year by the worker from the intermediary—

    (*a*) in respect of which the worker is chargeable to income tax under Schedule E, and

    (*b*) which do not represent items in respect of which a deduction was made under Step Three.

If the result at this point is nil or a negative amount, there is no deemed Schedule E payment.

Step Eight

Find the amount that together with employer's national insurance contributions on it is equal to the amount resulting from Step Seven.

Step Nine

The result is the amount of the deemed Schedule E payment.

Commentary—*Simon's Direct Tax Service* **E4.1011–1017**.
Amendments—[1] Words in Step Four substituted by CAA 2001 s 578, Sch 2 para 107 with effect for income tax purposes as respects allowances and charges falling to be made for chargeable periods ending after 5 April 2001.

[Reimbursed expenses

7A—(1) The reference in Step Three of the calculation in paragraph 7 to expenses met by the intermediary includes expenses met by the worker and reimbursed by the intermediary.

(2) Where the intermediary is a partnership and the worker is a member of the partnership, expenses met by the worker for and on behalf of the intermediary shall be treated for the purposes of sub-paragraph (1) as expenses met by the worker and reimbursed by the intermediary.][1]

Amendments—[1] This paragraph inserted, with paragraph 7B, by FA 2002 s 38(1), (2), (5) with effect from the year 2002–03.

[Treatment of mileage allowances

7B—(1) Where—

    (*a*) the intermediary provides a vehicle for the worker, and

    (*b*) the worker would have been entitled to an amount of mileage allowance relief for a tax year in respect of the use of the vehicle if the worker had been employed by the client and the vehicle had not been a company vehicle (within the meaning of paragraph 6 of Schedule 12AA to the Taxes Act 1988),

Step Three of the calculation in paragraph 7 has effect as if that amount were an amount of expenses deductible under that Step.

(2) Where—

    (*a*) the intermediary is a partnership,

    (*b*) the worker is a member of the partnership, and

    (*c*) the worker provides a vehicle for the purposes of the business of the partnership,

then for the purposes of sub-paragraph (1) the vehicle shall be regarded as provided by the intermediary for the worker.

(3) Where the worker receives payments from the intermediary that are exempt from income tax under Schedule E by virtue of section 197AD or 197AE of the Taxes Act 1988 (mileage allowance payments and passenger payments), Step Seven of the calculation in paragraph 7 has effect as if the worker were chargeable to income tax under Schedule E in respect of the payments.][1]

Amendments—[1] This paragraph inserted, with paragraph 7A, by FA 2002 s 38(1), (2), (5) with effect from the year 2002–03.

Treatment of payments made under construction industry scheme

8 Where section 559 of the Taxes Act 1988 applies (sub-contractors in the construction industry: payments to be made under deduction), the intermediary is treated for the purposes of Step One of the calculation in paragraph 7 as receiving the amount that would have been received had no deduction been made under that section.

Commentary—*Simon's Direct Tax Service* **E4.1808**.
Concession C32—Personal service companies in the construction industry who are liable to PAYE on deemed payments under IR35 and have suffered a deduction of tax on the same income under the Construction Industry Scheme may claim to defer payment of IR35 liability and ask that CIS tax be set against it.

Apportionments

9 For the purposes of calculating the deemed Schedule E payment any necessary apportionment shall be made on a just and reasonable basis of amounts received by the intermediary that are referable—

(a) to the services of more than one worker, or

(b) partly to the services of the worker and partly to other matters.

Application of Schedule E rules

10—(1) The following provisions apply in relation to the calculation of the deemed Schedule E payment.

(2) A "payment or other benefit" includes anything that, if received by an employee for performing the duties of an employment within Schedule E—

(a) would be an emolument of the employment, or

(b) would be chargeable to tax as an emolument of the employment.

(3) The amount of a payment or other benefit is taken to be—

(a) in the case of a payment or cash benefit, the amount received, and

(b) in the case of a non-cash benefit, the cash equivalent of the benefit.

(4) The cash equivalent of a non-cash benefit is taken to be whichever is the greater of—

(a) the amount that would be chargeable to tax under section 19(1) of the Taxes Act 1988 if the benefit were an emolument chargeable to tax under Case I of Schedule E, and

(b) the cash equivalent determined in accordance with the rules in section 596B of that Act.

(5) A payment or benefit is treated as received—

(a) in the case of a payment or cash benefit, when payment is made of or on account of the payment or benefit;

(b) in the case of a non-cash benefit, when it is used or enjoyed.

Application of Income Tax Acts in relation to deemed Schedule E payment

11—(1) The Income Tax Acts (in particular, the PAYE provisions) apply in relation to the deemed Schedule E payment as follows.

(2) They apply as if—

(a) the worker were employed by the intermediary, and

(b) the relevant engagements were undertaken by the worker in the course of performing the duties of that employment.

(3) The worker is not chargeable to tax in respect of the deemed Schedule E payment if, or to the extent that, by reason of any combination of the following factors—

(a) the worker being resident, ordinarily resident or domiciled outside the United Kingdom,

(b) the client being resident or ordinarily resident outside the United Kingdom, or

(c) the services in question being provided outside the United Kingdom,

he would not be chargeable to tax under Schedule E if the client employed the worker, the worker performed the services in the course of that employment and the deemed Schedule E payment were a payment by the client of emoluments from that employment.

(4) The deemed Schedule E payment is treated as an emolument of that employment—

(a) for the purpose of determining whether it is employment to which Chapter II of Part V of the Taxes Act 1988 applies (benefits in kind: provisions applicable to higher-paid employment);

[(ab) for the purposes of section 197AG of that Act (mileage allowance relief);][1] and

(b) for the purposes of section 198 of that Act (deductions for necessary expenses defrayed out of emoluments).

(5) Where the intermediary is a partnership or unincorporated association, the deemed Schedule E payment is treated as received by the worker in his personal capacity and not as income of the partnership or association.

(6) Where—

(a) the worker is resident in the United Kingdom,

(b) the services in question are provided in the United Kingdom, and

(c) the client or employer carries on business in the United Kingdom,

the intermediary is treated as having a place of business in the United Kingdom, whether or not it in fact does so.

(7) The deemed Schedule E payment is treated as relevant earnings of the worker for the purposes of section 644 of the Taxes Act 1988 (relevant earnings for purposes of permissible pension contributions).

Commentary—*Simon's Direct Tax Service* E4.1010, 1027.
Amendments—[1] Sub-para (4)(ab) inserted by FA 2001 s 57(3), (4), Sch 12 Pt II para 16 with effect from the year 2002–03.

PART III
SUPPLEMENTARY PROVISIONS
Earlier date of deemed Schedule E payment in certain cases

12—(1) If in any tax year—

(a) a deemed Schedule E payment is treated as made, and

(b) before the date on which the payment would be treated as made under paragraph 2(2) any relevant event (as defined below) occurs in relation to the intermediary,

the deemed Schedule E payment for that year is treated as having been made immediately before that event or, if there is more than one, immediately before the first of them.

(2) Where the intermediary is a company the following are relevant events—

[(za) the company ceasing to trade;]¹

(a) where the worker is a member of the company, his ceasing to be such a member;

(b) where the worker holds an office with the company, his ceasing to hold such an office;

(c) where the worker is employed by the company, his ceasing to be so employed.

(3) Where the intermediary is a partnership the following are relevant events—

(a) the dissolution of the partnership or the partnership ceasing to trade or a partner ceasing to act as such;

(b) where the worker is employed by the partnership, his ceasing to be so employed.

(4) Where the intermediary is an individual and the worker is employed by him, it is a relevant event if the worker ceases to be so employed.

(5) The fact that the deemed Schedule E payment is treated as made before the end of the tax year does not affect what receipts and other matters are taken into account in calculating its amount.

Commentary—*Simon's Direct Tax Service* **E.1019**.
Amendments—¹ Sub-para (2)(za) inserted by FA 2002 s 38(1), (3), (5) with effect from the year 2002–03.

Relief in case of distributions by intermediary

13—(1) A claim for relief may be made under this paragraph where the intermediary—

(a) is a company,

(b) is treated as making a deemed Schedule E payment in any tax year, and

(c) either in that tax year (whether before or after that payment is treated as made), or in a subsequent tax year, makes a distribution.

(2) A claim for relief under this paragraph must be made by the intermediary by notice in writing given to the Inland Revenue.

(3) If on a claim being made the Inland Revenue are satisfied that relief should be given in order to avoid a double charge to tax, they shall give such relief by way of amending any assessment, by discharge or repayment of tax, or otherwise, as appears to them appropriate.

(4) Relief under this paragraph shall be given by treating the amount of the distribution as reduced, not the amount of the deemed Schedule E payment.

(5) The Inland Revenue shall exercise the power conferred by this paragraph so as to secure that so far as practicable relief is given by setting the amount of a deemed Schedule E payment—

(a) against relevant distributions of the same tax year before those of other years,

(b) against relevant distributions received by the worker before those received by another person, and

(c) against relevant distributions of earlier years before those of later years.

(6) Where the amount of a distribution is reduced under this paragraph, the amount of any associated tax credit is reduced accordingly.

Commentary—*Simon's Direct Tax Service* **E4.1025**.

Provisions applicable to multiple intermediaries

14—(1) The following provisions apply where in the case of an engagement to which this Schedule applies the arrangements involve more than one relevant intermediary—

paragraph 15 (avoidance of double-counting);
paragraph 16 (joint and several liability for PAYE deductions)

(2) In this paragraph and paragraphs 15 and 16 "relevant intermediary" means an intermediary in relation to which the conditions specified in paragraph 3, 4 or 5 are met.

(3) Except as provided by paragraphs 15 and 16, the provisions of this Schedule apply separately in relation to each relevant intermediary.

Commentary—*Simon's Direct Tax Service* **E4.1026**.

Multiple intermediaries: avoidance of double-counting

15—(1) This paragraph applies where a payment or other benefit has been made or provided, directly or indirectly, from one relevant intermediary to another in respect of the engagement.

(2) In that case, the amount taken into account in relation to any intermediary in Step One or Step Two of the calculation in paragraph 7 shall be reduced to such extent as is necessary to avoid double-counting having regard to the amount so taken into account in relation to any other intermediary.

Commentary—*Simon's Direct Tax Service* **E4.1026**.

Multiple intermediaries: joint and several liability for PAYE deductions

16—(1) All relevant intermediaries in relation to an engagement to which this Schedule applies are jointly and severally liable, subject to sub-paragraph (2), to account for any amount required under the PAYE provisions to be deducted from a deemed Schedule E payment treated as made by any of them—

(*a*) in respect of that engagement, or
(*b*) in respect of that engagement together with other engagements.

(2) An intermediary is not so liable if it has not received any payment or benefit in respect of that engagement or any such other engagement as is mentioned in sub-paragraph (1)(*b*).

Commentary—*Simon's Direct Tax Service* **E4.1026**.

Calculation of profits of intermediary: deduction for deemed Schedule E payment

17—(1) In calculating for tax purposes the profits of a business carried on by an intermediary that is treated as making in connection with that business a deemed Schedule E payment, a deduction is allowed for—

(*a*) the amount of the payment, and
(*b*) the amount of any employer's national insurance contributions paid by the intermediary in respect of it.

(2) The deduction allowed by this paragraph must be taken into account for the period of account in which the deemed Schedule E payment is treated as made.

(3) No deduction in respect of the matters mentioned in sub-paragraph (1) may be made except in accordance with this paragraph.

Commentary—*Simon's Direct Tax Service* **E4.1021**.

Calculation of profits of intermediary: special rules for partnerships

18—(1) The following provisions apply in calculating for tax purposes the profits of a business carried on by a partnership that is treated as making in connection with that business a deemed Schedule E payment.

(2) The amount of the deduction allowed under paragraph 17 is limited to the amount that reduces the profits of the partnership for the tax year to nil.

(3) To the extent that in any tax year the expenses of the partnership in connection with the relevant engagements exceed the sum of—

[(*a*) the amount that, in calculating the deemed Schedule E payment, is deducted under Step Three of the calculation in paragraph 7, and][1]
(*b*) 5% of the amount taken into account in Step One of the calculation in paragraph 7 as the intermediary's receipts in respect of the relevant engagements,

they shall be left out of account in calculating the profits of the business.

Commentary—*Simon's Direct Tax Service* **E4.1021**.
Amendments—[1] Sub-para (3)(*a*) substituted by FA 2002 s 38(1), (4), (5) with effect from the year 2002–03

Meaning of "associate"

19—(1) In this Schedule "associate"—

(*a*) in relation to an individual, has the meaning given by section 417(3) and (4) of the Taxes Act 1988, subject to the following provisions of this paragraph;
(*b*) in relation to a company, means a person connected with the company within the meaning of section 839 of the Taxes Act 1988; and
(*c*) in relation to a partnership, means any associate of a member of the partnership.

(2) Where an individual has an interest in shares or obligations of the company as a beneficiary of an employee benefit trust, the trustees are not regarded as associates of his by reason only of that interest except in the following circumstances.

(3) The exception is where—

(*a*) the individual, either on his own or with any one or more of his associates, or
(*b*) any associate of his, with or without other such associates,

has at any time on or after 14th March 1989 been the beneficial owner of, or able (directly or through the medium of other companies or by any other indirect means) to control more than 5% of the ordinary share capital of the company.

(4) In this paragraph "employee benefit trust" has the meaning given by paragraph 7 of Schedule 8 to the Taxes Act 1988.

(5) Sub-paragraphs (9) to (12) of that paragraph apply for the purposes of this paragraph in relation to an individual as they apply for the purposes of that paragraph in relation to an employee.

(6) In sub-paragraph (3) "associate" does not include the trustees of an employee benefit trust by reason only that the individual has an interest in shares or obligations of the trust.

Meaning of "the Inland Revenue"

20 References in this Schedule to "the Inland Revenue" are to any officer of the Board.

Interpretation

21—(1) In this Schedule—

"associate" has the meaning given by paragraph 19;

"associated company" has the meaning given by section 416 of the Taxes Act 1988;

"business" means any trade, profession or vocation and includes a Schedule A business;

"company" means a body corporate or unincorporated association, and does not include a partnership;

"employer's national insurance contributions" means secondary Class 1 or Class 1A national insurance contributions;

"engagement to which this Schedule applies" means any such engagement as is mentioned in paragraph 1(1);

"national insurance contributions" means contributions under Part I of the Social Security Contributions and Benefits Act 1992 or Part I of the Social Security Contributions and Benefits (Northern Ireland) Act 1992;

"PAYE provisions" means provisions of—

(a) section 203 of the Taxes Act 1988 or regulations under that section, or
(b) sections 203A to 203L of that Act;

"tax year" means a year of assessment.

(2) References in this Schedule to payments or benefits received or receivable from a partnership or unincorporated association include payments or benefits to which a person is or may be entitled in his capacity as a member of the partnership or association.

(3) For the purposes of this Schedule—

(a) anything done by or in relation to an associate of an intermediary is treated as done by or in relation to the intermediary, and
(b) a payment or other benefit provided to a member of an individual's family or household is treated as provided to the individual.

The reference in paragraph (b) to an individual's family or household has the same meaning as in Chapter II of Part V of the Taxes Act 1988 (provisions relating to the Schedule E charge): see section 168(4) of that Act.

(4) For the purposes of this Schedule a man and a woman living together as husband and wife are treated as if they were married to each other.

Transitional provisions: general

22—(1) This Schedule has effect for the tax year 2000–01 and subsequent years and applies in relation to services performed, or to be performed, on or after 6th April 2000.

(2) Payments or other benefits in respect of such services received before that date shall be treated as if received in the tax year 2000–01.

Commentary—*Simon's Direct Tax Service* **E4.1029**.

Transitional provisions: deemed discontinuance of business

23—(1) This paragraph applies where an individual or partnership—

(a) is carrying on a business at the beginning of the year 2000–01, and
(b) is treated as making one or more deemed Schedule E payments for that year in connection with that business.

(2) Where this paragraph applies the individual or partnership may elect that—

(a) the business shall be deemed to have been permanently discontinued at the end of the year 1999–00, and
(b) a new business shall be deemed to have been set up and commenced on 6th April 2000.

(3) Notwithstanding the deemed discontinuance, the old business and the new business shall be treated as the same for the purposes of section 385 of the Taxes Act 1988 (carry-forward of losses against subsequent profits).

(4) Any such election as is mentioned in sub-paragraph (2) must be made by being included in a return made and delivered on or before the due date.

(5) In the case of an election by an individual—

(*a*) the reference in sub-paragraph (4) to a return is to a return under section 8 of the Taxes Management Act 1970 (personal returns), and

(*b*) the ''due date'' means the day specified in relation to the return under subsection (1A) of that section.

(6) In the case of an election by a partnership—

(*a*) the reference in sub-paragraph (4) to a return is to a return under section 12AA(2) or (3) of that Act (partnership returns), and

(*b*) the ''due date'' means the day specified in relation to the return under subsection (2) or, as the case may be, subsection (3) of that section.

Commentary—*Simon's Direct Tax Service* **E4.1029**.

Saving for provisions relating to agency workers

24 Nothing in this Schedule affects the operation of section 134 of the Taxes Act 1988 (workers supplied by agencies).

Commentary—*Simon's Direct Tax Service* **E4.1028**.

SCHEDULE 13

OCCUPATIONAL AND PERSONAL PENSION SCHEMES

Section 61

Commentary—*Simon's Direct Tax Service* **E7.401**.

PART I

AMENDMENTS OF THE TAXES ACT 1988

Introductory

1 Amend the Taxes Act 1988 as follows.

Exception of certain life policies from chargeable events legislation

2—(1), (2) (*inserts* TA 1988 s 539(2)(*d*)).

(3) This paragraph has effect for the year 2000–01 and subsequent years of assessment.

No charge to tax under section 591C on conversion under Schedule 23ZA

3 (*Amends* TA 1988 s 591C(1)).

Definition of ''retirement benefits scheme''

4 (*amends* TA 1988 s 611(1), (3), (4) and *inserts* TA 1988 s 611(1)(*b*) and TA 1988 s 611(6)(*c*)).

Interpretation of Chapter IV of Part XIV

5—(1), (2) (*amend* TA 1988 s 630(1)(*a*), (*b*), and inserts TA 1988 s 630(1)(*b*)(ii)) Amend section 630 as follows.

(3), (4) (*amend* TA 1988 s 630(1)).

(5)–(7) (*insert* TA 1988 s 630(1A), *amend* TA 1988 s 630(2)(*a*), (*b*) and *repeal* TA 1988 s 630(3)).

(8) Paragraphs (*c*) and (*d*) of sub-paragraph (4) have effect for the year 2001–02 and subsequent years of assessment.

Approval of personal pension schemes

6—(1) Amend section 631 as follows.

(2) (*amends* TA 1988 s 631(2)).

(3), (4) (*insert* TA 1988 s 631(2A), (3)(*a*), (*b*)).

(5) Sub-paragraphs (3) and (4) have effect in relation to applications for approval granted on or after 6th April 2001.

Conversion of certain approved retirement benefits schemes

7 (*inserts* TA 1988 s 631A).

Eligibility to make contributions

8—(1) (*inserts* TA 1988 ss 632A, 632B).

(2) This paragraph has effect on and after 6th April 2001.

Insurance against risks relating to non-payment of contributions

9—(1) Amend section 633 (benefits allowed to be provided by approved schemes) as follows.

(2) Omit subsection (2) (approval of schemes making provision for insurance against certain risks not to be prevented by subsection (1)).

(3) This paragraph has effect in relation to insurance under a contract of insurance made on or after 6th April 2001.

Income withdrawals: the relevant date

10—(1) Amend section 634A as follows.

(2)–(4) (*amend* TA 1988 s 634A(4), *substitute* TA 1988 s 634A(5) and *insert* TA 1988 s 634A(5A)–(5D)).

(5) Sub-paragraphs (2)(*a*) and (3) have effect on and after 1st October 2000.

(6) Sub-paragraphs (2)(*b*) and (4) have effect in relation to personal pension arrangements—

  (*a*) under any personal pension scheme to which approval under Chapter IV of Part XIV of the Taxes Act 1988 is given on or after 1st October 2000; or

  (*b*) under any existing approved scheme amended on or after that date, with the approval of the Board under that Chapter, for the purpose of—

    (i) conforming to the amendment made by sub-paragraph (2)(*b*), or

    (ii) imposing such a requirement as is mentioned in the subsection (5A) inserted by sub-paragraph (4),

  as the case may be.

(7) In this paragraph "existing approved scheme" means a personal pension scheme approved under Chapter IV of Part XIV of the Taxes Act 1988 before 1st October 2000.

Income withdrawals: purchase of two or more annuities

11—(1) Amend section 634A as follows.

(2) (*inserts* TA 1988 s 634A(1A)).

(3)–(5) (*amend* TA 1988 s 634A(4), (5D) and *insert* TA 1988 s 634A(4A)).

(6) This paragraph has effect on and after 6th April 2001.

Income withdrawals after death of member

12—(1) Amend section 636A as follows.

(2), (3) (*insert* TA 1988 s 636A(1A) and *substitute* TA 1988 s 636A(5)(*a*), (*b*)).

(4), (5) (*amend* TA 1988 s 636A(5)(*b*) and *insert* TA 1988 s 636A(5A)).

(6) Sub-paragraph (3), and sub-paragraph (1) so far as relating to that sub-paragraph, have effect on and after 1st October 2000.

(7) The other provisions of this paragraph have effect on and after 6th April 2001.

Other restrictions on approval

13—(1) Amend section 638 as follows.

(2), (3) (*amend* TA 1988 s 638(3), (4)).

(4), (5) (*insert* TA 1988 s 638(7B), (9)–(13)).

(6) Sub-paragraph (2) has effect for the year 2001–02 and subsequent years of assessment.

(7) Sub-paragraph (3) has effect in relation to contributions paid in the year 2001–02 or any subsequent year of assessment.

(8) Sub-paragraph (5) has effect in relation to contributions in the year 2001–02 or any subsequent year of assessment.

Multiple pension dates etc

14—(1) (*inserts* TA 1988 s 638ZA).

(2) This paragraph has effect on and after 6th April 2001.

Tax relief on member's contributions

15—(1) Amend section 639 as follows.

(2)–(5) (*substitutes TA 1988 s 639(1)–(4A)*).

(6) (*amends TA 1988 s 639(5)*).

(7) (*inserts TA 1988 s 639(5A), (5B)*).

(8) (*amends TA 1988 s 639(7)*).

(9) This paragraph has effect in relation to contributions paid in the year 2001–02 or any subsequent year of assessment.

Maximum amount of deductions

16—(1) Amend section 640 as follows.

(2) (*amends TA 1988 s 640(1) and inserts TA 1988 s 640(1)(a), (b)*).

(3)–(5) (*amend TA 1988 s 640(3)*).

(6) (*inserts TA 1988 s 640(3A)*).

(7) (*amends TA 1988 s 640(7)*).

(8) Sub-paragraphs (2), (4) and (7) have effect in relation to contributions paid in the year 2001–02 or any subsequent year of assessment.

(9) Sub-paragraphs (5) and (6) have effect in relation to contributions paid to secure benefits satisfying the conditions in section 637 of the Taxes Act 1988 where the contract of life assurance concerned is made on or after 6th April 2001.

Carry-back of contributions

17 No election shall be made under section 641 in respect of contributions paid on or after 6th April 2001.

Election for contributions to be treated as paid in previous year

18—(1) (*inserts TA 1988 s 641A*).

(2) This paragraph has effect in relation to contributions paid in the year 2001–02 or any subsequent year of assessment.

Abolition of carry-forward of relief

19 No relief shall be given by virtue of section 642 (carry-forward of relief) in the year 2001–02 or any subsequent year of assessment.

Earnings from pensionable employment

20 (*inserts TA 1988 s 645(3)(d)*).

Meaning of "net relevant earnings"

21—(1) Amend section 646 as follows.

(2) In subsection (5) (cases where the whole or part of a deduction under subsection (2)(d) falls to be made from income other than relevant earnings) for "an amount is deducted or set off under section 639(1) against the net relevant earnings" substitute "the basic rate limit is increased in accordance with section 639(5A) in the case".

(3) In subsection (6) (reduction of net relevant earnings in subsequent years) for "under section 639(1)" substitute "in accordance with section 639(5A)".

(4) Omit subsection (7) (net relevant earnings to be computed without regard to any deduction or set off under section 639(1)).

(5) This paragraph has effect for the year 2001–02 and subsequent years of assessment.

Presumption of same level of relevant earnings etc for 5 years

22—(1) (*inserts TA 1988 ss 646B, 646C*).

(2) Sub-paragraph (1) above has effect in relation to presumptions for the year 2001–02 and subsequent years of assessment.

Higher level contributions after cessation of actual relevant earnings: modification of section 646B

23—(1) (*inserts TA 1988 s 646D*).

(2) This paragraph has effect where the break year is the year 2001–02 or any subsequent year of assessment.

Appeals

24—(1) Amend section 651 as follows.

(2) In subsection (1)(*a*) (appeal against refusal of application under section 631) after "section 631" insert "or paragraph 3 of Schedule 23ZA".

Old transitional provisions

25—(1) Amend section 655 as follows.

(2) In subsection (1)(*a*) (reduction of relief under section 639 where relief is given for certain qualifying premiums) for "that may be deducted or set off" substitute "of contributions in respect of which relief may be given".

(3) This paragraph has effect for the year 2001–02 and subsequent years of assessment.

Benefits under approved pension arrangements not to be income of settlor

26—(1)–(4) (*repeal* TA 1988 s 660A(7), *amend* TA 1988 s 660A(9) and *insert* TA 1988 s 660A(10), (11)).

(5) This paragraph has effect for the year 2001–02 and subsequent years of assessment.

Conversion of certain approved retirement benefits schemes

27 (*inserts* TA 1988 Sch 23ZA).

PART II
TRANSITIONAL PROVISIONS

Schemes approved before 6th April 2001 deemed to contain certain provisions

28—(1) This paragraph applies to any personal pension scheme which is or has been approved under Chapter IV of Part XIV of the Taxes Act 1988 before 6th April 2001 (an "existing approved scheme").

(2) An existing approved scheme shall be deemed to include provision prohibiting, in relation to arrangements made by a member in accordance with the scheme, the acceptance of—

    (*a*) contributions by the member, or

    (*b*) contributions by an employer of the member,

at a time when the member is not eligible to make contributions.

(3) An existing approved scheme shall be deemed to include provision, in relation to arrangements made by a member in accordance with the scheme, requiring that contributions accepted at a time when the member is not eligible to make contributions are repaid—

    (*a*) to the member, to the extent of his contributions, and

    (*b*) as to the remainder, to his employer,

except that, in a case falling within subsection (6) of section 632B of the Taxes Act 1988, the contributions required to be repaid shall be determined in accordance with that subsection (and their repayment shall have the like consequence).

(4) An existing approved scheme shall be taken to include provisions prohibiting the scheme from making provision for any benefit so far as consisting of insurance against a risk relating to the non-payment of contributions where—

    (*a*) the benefit, so far as so consisting, does not fall within one or more of the paragraphs of section 633(1) of the Taxes Act 1988; and

    (*b*) the insurance is under a contract of insurance made on or after 6th April 2001.

(5) Sections 646B to 646D of the Taxes Act 1988, and any regulations made under those sections, override any provision of an existing approved scheme to the extent that it conflicts with them.

(6) An existing approved scheme shall be deemed to include provision entitling any member who is eligible to make contributions in a year of assessment under arrangements made by him under the scheme to make contributions in that year up to the earnings threshold for the year.

(7) Nothing in sub-paragraph (6) authorises the making, in the case of any member, of total contributions in a year of assessment which exceed the earnings threshold for the year or, if greater, the permitted maximum for the year.

(8) In this paragraph—

    "approved personal pension arrangements" has the same meaning as in Chapter IV of Part XIV of the Taxes Act 1988 (see section 630(1) of that Act);

    "earnings threshold" has the same meaning as in Chapter IV of Part XIV of the Taxes Act 1988 (see section 630(1) of that Act);

    "eligible to make contributions" shall be construed in accordance with sections 632A and 632B of the Taxes Act 1988;

    "the permitted maximum" has the same meaning as in section 638(3) of the Taxes Act 1988;

"personal pension scheme" has the same meaning as in Chapter IV of Part XIV of the Taxes Act 1988 (see section 630(1) of that Act);

"total contributions", in the case of a member and a year of assessment, means the aggregate amount of the contributions made in the year by the member and any employer of his under the approved personal pension arrangements in question, together with the aggregate amounts of such contributions under other approved personal pension arrangements made by that member.

Deemed requisite evidence for the presumptions

29—(1) This paragraph applies where, in the case of any individual and any arrangements made by him under an approved personal pension scheme,—

(*a*) the conditions in regulations 5 and 6 of the Personal Pension Schemes (Relief at Source) Regulations 1988 ("the 1988 Regulations") are satisfied for one or more of the five years of assessment preceding the year 2001–02;

(*b*) the particulars specified in regulation 5(2)(*e*) of the 1988 Regulations have been furnished for a year of assessment ("the relevant year") for which those conditions are satisfied and which is one of those five years of assessment; and

(*c*) such a certificate as is specified in regulation 6(2)(*a*) of the 1988 Regulations has been furnished at some time during, or not later than 60 days after the end of, such a year of assessment.

(2) Where this paragraph applies, it shall be assumed for the purposes of sections 646B to 646D of the Taxes Act 1988—

(*a*) that the individual has provided the scheme administrator with the requisite evidence of the relevant amounts for the relevant year; and

(*b*) that the relevant amounts for that year are the amounts stated in, or deduced from, the relevant particulars and certificates.

(3) In sub-paragraph (2) above, "the relevant particulars and certificates" means the latest particulars and certificates furnished under regulations 5 and 6 of the 1988 Regulations by reference to which the relevant year is a year for which the conditions prescribed in those regulations are satisfied.

Applications for approval

30—(1) An application to the Board for their approval under Chapter IV of Part XIV of the Taxes Act 1988 of—

(*a*) a personal pension scheme, or

(*b*) an amendment to a personal pension scheme approved under that Chapter,

may not be made before 1st October 2000 if the scheme or amendment makes or includes any provision such that the Board could not give their approval apart from the amendments made to the Taxes Act 1988 by the relevant provisions of this Schedule.

(2) For the purposes of sub-paragraph (1) the relevant provisions of this Schedule are any provisions of this Schedule other than paragraphs 10 and 12(3).

SCHEDULE 14

ENTERPRISE MANAGEMENT INCENTIVES

Section 62

Commentary—*Simon's Direct Tax Service* **E4.543**
Statement of Practice SP 2/00—Enterprise Management Incentives—value of "gross assets".
SP 3/00—Enterprise Management Incentives—location of activity.
Revenue Internal Guidance—Capital Gains Manual CG 56440–56449 (operation of this Schedule).

PART I

INTRODUCTORY

Qualifying options

1—(1) In this Schedule a "qualifying option" means an option—

(*a*) in relation to which the requirements of this Schedule are met at the time the option is granted, and

(*b*) of which notice is given to the Inland Revenue in accordance with paragraph 2.

(2) The requirements of this Schedule are—

(*a*) the general requirements in Part II of this Schedule,

(*b*) that the company whose shares are the subject of the option is a qualifying company (see Part III of this Schedule),

(*c*) that the individual to whom the option is granted is an eligible employee in relation to that company (see Part IV of this Schedule),

(*d*) that the option is granted to the employee by reason of his employment—

    (i) with that company, or

    (ii) if that company is a parent company, with that company or another group company, and

  (*e*) the requirements of Part V of this Schedule as to the terms of the option, the circumstances in which it is granted and other matters.

(3) In this Schedule, in relation to an option—

  (*a*) references to "the relevant company" are to the company whose shares are the subject of the option, and

  (*b*) references to "the employer company" are to the company by reference to which the requirement in sub-paragraph (2)(*d*) is met.

Notice of option to be given to Inland Revenue

2—(1) For an option to be a qualifying option notice of the option must be given to the Inland Revenue within [92 days][1] after the grant of the option.

(2) The notice must—

  (*a*) be given by the employer company, and

  (*b*) be in a form required or authorised by the Inland Revenue.

(3) The notice must contain, or be supported by, such information as the Inland Revenue may require for the purpose of determining whether the requirements of this Schedule are met.

(4) The notice must also contain—

  (*a*) a declaration by a director, or the secretary, of the employer company—

    (i) that in his opinion the requirements of this Schedule are met in relation to the option, and

    (ii) that the information provided is to the best of his knowledge correct and complete, and

  (*b*) a declaration by the individual to whom the option was granted that he meets the requirement of paragraph 29 (commitment of working time) in relation to the option.

Commentary—*Simon's Direct Tax Service* **E4.551.**
Amendment—[1] In sub-para (1), words "92 days" substituted for words "30 days" by FA 2001 s 62, Sch 14 paras 2, 13 with effect for any right to acquire shares granted after the passing of FA 2001.

Correction of notice by Revenue

3—(1) The Inland Revenue may amend a notice given under paragraph 2 so as to correct obvious errors or omissions in the notice.

(2) A correction under this paragraph is made by notice to the employer company.

(3) No such correction may be made more than nine months after the day on which the notice under paragraph 2 was given to the Inland Revenue.

(4) A correction under this paragraph is of no effect if the employer company within three months from the date of issue of the notice of correction gives notice rejecting the correction.

Commentary—*Simon's Direct Tax Service* **E4.551.**

Notice of enquiry

4—(1) The Inland Revenue may enquire into an option of which notice is given under paragraph 2 if they give notice to the employer company of their intention to do so in accordance with this paragraph.

(2) Where notice is given under paragraph 2, the Inland Revenue may enquire into whether paragraph 29 (commitment of working time) is met by the individual to whom the option was granted if they give him notice of their intention to do so in accordance with this paragraph.

(3) The Inland Revenue shall give a copy of any notice under sub-paragraph (2) to the employer company.

(4) Notice of enquiry may be given at any time within the period of 12 months beginning with the end of the period of [92 days][1] mentioned in paragraph 2(1) (the period within which notice under that paragraph must be given).

(5) Notice of enquiry may be given at any time if the Inland Revenue discover that any of the information provided in or in connection with the notice under paragraph 2 was false or misleading in a material particular.

(6) An option that has been the subject of one notice of enquiry under sub-paragraph (1) or (2) may not be the subject of another notice under the same sub-paragraph, unless it is given by virtue of sub-paragraph (5).

Commentary—*Simon's Direct Tax Service* **E4.551.**
Amendment—[1] In sub-para (4), words "92 days" substituted for words "30 days" by FA 2001 s 62, Sch 14 paras 3, 13 with effect for any right to acquire shares granted after the passing of FA 2001.

Completion of enquiry

5—(1) An enquiry under paragraph 4(1) is completed when the Inland Revenue by notice inform the employer company that they have completed their enquiry and state their decision whether the requirements of this Schedule are met in relation to the option.

(2) If the Inland Revenue conclude that the requirements of this Schedule are not met, they must also give notice of that decision to the individual to whom the option was granted.

(3) An enquiry under paragraph 4(2) is completed when the Inland Revenue by notice inform the individual concerned and the employer company that they have completed their enquiry and state their decision whether the requirement of paragraph 29 (commitment of working time) is met by that individual in relation to the option.

(4) References in this Part to a "closure notice" are to a notice under sub-paragraph (1) or (3).

(5) A closure notice takes effect when it is issued.

(6) An application may be made by—

(a) the employer company, or
(b) in a case within paragraph 4(2), the individual concerned,

for a direction that the Inland Revenue give a closure notice within a specified period.

(7) An application under sub-paragraph (6) must be made to the General Commissioners or, if the applicant so elects (in accordance with section 46(1) of the Taxes Management Act 1970), to the Special Commissioners.

(8) Any such application shall be heard and determined in the same way as an appeal.

(9) The Commissioners hearing the application shall give a direction unless they are satisfied that the Inland Revenue have reasonable grounds for not giving a closure notice within a specified period.

Commentary—*Simon's Direct Tax Service* **E4.551**.

Effect of enquiry

6—(1) If the Inland Revenue do not give notice of enquiry, the requirements of this Schedule are taken to be met in relation to the option.

(2) If the Inland Revenue do give notice of enquiry, their decision stated in the closure notice is conclusive as to whether the requirements of this Schedule are met in relation to the option, subject—

(a) if their decision is that the requirements are not met, to the outcome of any appeal against that decision;
(b) if their decision is that the requirements are met, to the outcome of any further enquiry under paragraph 4(5) (enquiry arising from discovery of false or misleading information).

(3) This paragraph does not affect the provisions of paragraphs 47 to 53 (which relate to disqualifying events).

Commentary—*Simon's Direct Tax Service* **E4.551**.

Appeals

7—(1) The employer company may appeal against a decision of the Inland Revenue—

(a) that notice of the grant of the option was not given in accordance with paragraph 2, or
(b) that the requirements of this Schedule are not met in relation to the option.

(2) An individual may appeal against a decision of the Inland Revenue that he does not meet the requirement of paragraph 29 (commitment of working time).

(3) Notice of the appeal must be given to the Inland Revenue within 30 days after the closure notice is given to the employer company or individual.

(4) The appeal lies to the General Commissioners or, if the employer company or individual so elects (in accordance with section 46(1) of the Taxes Management Act 1970), to the Special Commissioners.

Commentary—*Simon's Direct Tax Service* **E4.551**.

PART II
GENERAL REQUIREMENTS
Introduction

8 An option is not a qualifying option unless the requirements of this Part of this Schedule are met as to—

(a) the purpose for which the option is granted (see paragraph 9),
(b) the maximum entitlement of an employee (see paragraph 10), and
[(c) the maximum value of the relevant company's shares in respect of which unexercised options can exist (see paragraph 11).]¹

Commentary—*Simon's Direct Tax Service* **E4.544**.
Amendment—[1] Para (*c*) substituted by FA 2001 s 62, Sch 14 paras 4, 13 with effect for any right to acquire shares granted after the passing of FA 2001. Para (*c*) previously read as follows—
   "(*c*) the maximum number of employees who can hold qualifying options (see paragraph 11)."

Purpose of granting the option

9 An option is a qualifying option only if it is granted for commercial reasons in order to recruit or retain [an][1] employee in a company, and not as part of a scheme or arrangement the main purpose, or one of the main purposes, of which is the avoidance of tax.

Commentary—*Simon's Direct Tax Service* **E4.544**.
Amendment—[1] Word "an" substituted for words "a key" by FA 2001 s 62, Sch 14 paras 5, 13 with effect for any right to acquire shares granted after the passing of FA 2001.

Maximum entitlement of employee

10—(1) An employee may not hold unexercised qualifying options which—

   (*a*) are in respect of shares with a total value of more than £100,000, and

   (*b*) were granted by reason of his employment—

      (i) with one company, or

      (ii) with two or more companies which are members of the same group.

(2) An option is not a qualifying option if the limit in sub-paragraph (1) is already exceeded at the time it is granted.

(3) If the grant of an option causes that limit to be exceeded, the option is not a qualifying option so far as it relates to the excess.

(4) Where by reason of his employment with one company, an employee has been granted qualifying options in respect of shares with a total value of £100,000 (whether or not they have been exercised or released), any further option granted by reason of his employment with—

   (*a*) that company, or

   (*b*) if it is a member of a group, any company that is a member of that group,

within three years of the date of the grant of the last qualifying option is not a qualifying option.

(5) Where, by reason of his employment with two or more companies which are members of the same group, an employee has been granted qualifying options in respect of shares with a total value of £100,000 (whether or not they have been exercised or released), any further option granted, by reason of his employment with any member of that group, within three years of the date of the grant of the last qualifying option is not a qualifying option.

(6) Where, at the time an option is granted to an employee, he holds unexercised CSOP options granted by reason of his employment with—

   (*a*) the employer company, or

   (*b*) if that company is a member of a group, any member of that group,

those options shall be treated for the purposes of this paragraph as if they were unexercised qualifying options.

For this purpose a "CSOP option" is an option to acquire shares under a scheme approved under Schedule 9 to the Taxes Act 1988 by reference to the requirements of Part IV of that Schedule (non-savings-related share option schemes).

(7) For the purposes of this paragraph—

   (*a*) the value of shares means the market value at the time the option is granted of shares of the same class as those that may be acquired by exercise of the option; and

   (*b*) an option is treated as granted in respect of the maximum number of shares that may be acquired under it.

(8) For the purposes of this paragraph the market value of shares subject to restrictions or risk of forfeiture shall be determined as if there were no such restriction or risk.

For this purpose shares are "subject to risk of forfeiture" if the interest that may be acquired is only conditional within the meaning of section 140C of the Taxes Act 1988.

Commentary—*Simon's Direct Tax Service* **E4.544**.

[Maximum value of options in respect of relevant company's shares

11—(1) The total value of shares in the relevant company in respect of which unexercised qualifying options exist must not exceed £3 million.

(2) An option is not a qualifying option if the limit in sub-paragraph (1) is already exceeded at the time it is granted.

(3) If the grant of an option causes that limit to be exceeded the option is not a qualifying option so far as it relates to the excess.

(4) Where the grant of two or more options at the same time causes that limit to be exceeded, then, for the purpose of determining which part of each option relates to that excess, the amount of the

excess shall be divided pro rata among the options according to the value of the shares in respect of which each option was granted.

(5) Sub-paragraphs (7) and (8) of paragraph 10 (determination of value of shares) apply for the purposes of this paragraph as they apply for the purposes of that paragraph.]¹

Commentary—*Simon's Direct Tax Service* **E4.544.**
Amendment—¹ This paragraph substituted by FA 2001 s 62, Sch 14 paras 6, 13 with effect for any right to acquire shares granted after the passing of FA 2001. Previously, the paragraph read as follows—

"*Number of employees who may hold qualifying options*

11 Not more than 15 employees may hold qualifying options in respect of shares in the relevant company at the same time.".

PART III
QUALIFYING COMPANIES
Introduction

12 A qualifying company is a company in relation to which the requirements of this Part of this Schedule are met as to—

(a) independence (see paragraph 13),
(b) having only qualifying subsidiaries (see paragraph 14),
(c) gross assets (see paragraph 16), and
(d) trading activities (see paragraph 17).

Commentary—*Simon's Direct Tax Service* **E4.545.**

The independence requirement

13—(1) The independence requirement is that the company is not—

(a) a 51% subsidiary of another company, or
(b) under the control of another company (or of another company and any other person connected with that other company), without being a 51% subsidiary of that other company,

and that no arrangements are in existence by virtue of which the company could become such a subsidiary or fall under such control.

(2) For the purposes of this requirement arrangements with a view to a qualifying exchange of shares (within the meaning of paragraph 60) shall be disregarded.

(3) In this paragraph "control" has the meaning given by section 840 of the Taxes Act 1988.

Commentary—*Simon's Direct Tax Service* **E4.545.**

The qualifying subsidiaries requirement

14—(1) A company that has one or more subsidiaries is not a qualifying company unless every subsidiary of the company is a qualifying subsidiary.

(2) For this purpose—

(a) "subsidiary" means any company which the company controls, either on its own or together with any person connected with it, and
(b) the question whether a person controls a company shall be determined in accordance with section 416(2) to (6) of the Taxes Act 1988.

Commentary—*Simon's Direct Tax Service* **E4.545.**

Meaning of "qualifying subsidiary"

15—(1) A company ("the subsidiary") is a qualifying subsidiary of another company ("the company") if the following conditions are met.

(2) The conditions are—

(a) that the company or another of its subsidiaries possesses not less than 75% of the issued share capital of, and not less than 75% of the voting power in, the subsidiary;
(b) that the company or another of its subsidiaries would—
    (i) in the event of a winding up of the subsidiary, or
    (ii) in any other circumstances,
be beneficially entitled to receive not less than 75% of the assets of the subsidiary which would then be available for distribution to the shareholders of the subsidiary;
(c) that the company or another of its subsidiaries is beneficially entitled to not less than 75% of any profits of the subsidiary which are available for distribution to the shareholders of the subsidiary;
(d) that no person other than the company or another of its subsidiaries has control of the subsidiary within the meaning of section 840 of the Taxes Act 1988; and
(e) that no arrangements are in existence by virtue of which the conditions in paragraphs (a) to (d) would cease to be met.

(3) The subsidiary shall not be regarded, at a time when it or another company is being wound up, as having ceased on that account to be a company in relation to which the conditions in sub-paragraph (2) are met if—

(*a*) the conditions in that sub-paragraph would be met apart from the winding up, and

(*b*) the winding up is for commercial reasons and is not part of a scheme or arrangement the main purpose of which, or one of the main purposes of which, is the avoidance of tax.

(4) The subsidiary shall not be regarded, at any time when arrangements are in existence for the disposal by the company or (as the case may be) by another subsidiary of the company of all its interest in the subsidiary in question, as having ceased on that account to be a qualifying subsidiary if the disposal is to be for commercial reasons and not part of a scheme or arrangement the main purpose of which, or one of the main purposes of which, is the avoidance of tax.

Commentary—*Simon's Direct Tax Service* **E4.545**.

The gross assets requirement

16—(1) The gross assets requirement in the case of a single company is that the value of the company's gross assets does not exceed [£30 million][1].

(2) The gross assets requirement in the case of a parent company is that the consolidated value of the group assets does not exceed [£30 million][1].

(3) The consolidated value of the group assets means the aggregate value of the gross assets of the group, disregarding any that consist in rights against, or shares in or securities of, another company in the group.

Commentary—*Simon's Direct Tax Service* **E4.545**.
Amendments—[1] In paras (1) and (2), "£30 million" substituted for "£15 million" by the Enterprise Management Incentives (Gross Asset Requirement) Order, SI 2001/3799 with effect for any right to acquire shares granted after 31 December 2001.

The trading activities requirement

17—(1) The trading activities requirement in the case of a single company is that the company—

(*a*) disregarding any incidental purposes, exists wholly for the purpose of carrying on one or more qualifying trades, and

(*b*) is carrying on a qualifying trade or preparing to do so.

(2) The trading activities requirement in the case of a parent company is that—

(*a*) the business of the group does not consist wholly or as to a substantial part in the carrying on of non-qualifying activities, and

(*b*) at least one group company—

(i) disregarding any incidental purposes, exists wholly for the purpose of carrying on one or more qualifying trades, and

(ii) is carrying on a qualifying trade or preparing to do so.

(3) The business of the group means what would be the business of the group if the activities of the group companies taken together were regarded as one business.

(4) For the purposes of determining whether a company falls within sub-paragraph (1)(*a*) or (2)(*b*)(i), the purposes for which it exists shall be disregarded to the extent that they consist in the carrying on of the following activities—

(*a*) in the case of a single company, the holding and managing of property used by the company for one or more qualifying trades carried on by it, and

(*b*) in the case of a group company, any activities within sub-paragraph (5).

(5) For the purposes of determining the business of a group, activities of a group company shall be disregarded to the extent that they consist in—

(*a*) the holding of shares in or securities of, or the making of loans to, another group company; or

(*b*) the holding and managing of property used by a group company for the purposes of one or more qualifying trades carried on by a group company; or

(*c*) incidental activities of a company which meets the trading activities requirement for a single company.

(6) In sub-paragraph (2)(*a*) "non-qualifying activities" means—

(*a*) excluded activities other than—

(i) the letting of ships to which paragraph 21 applies (ships other than oil rigs or pleasure craft) in circumstances where the requirements of sub-paragraph (2) of that paragraph are met; or

(ii) the receiving of royalties or licence fees within paragraph 22 in circumstances where the requirements mentioned in sub-paragraph (2) of that paragraph are met; or

(*b*) activities carried on otherwise than in the course of a trade.

(7) In this paragraph—

(*a*) "incidental purposes" means purposes having no significant effect (other than in relation to incidental matters) on the extent of the company's activities; and

(b) "incidental activities" means activities carried on in pursuance of incidental purposes.

Commentary—*Simon's Direct Tax Service* **E4.545**.

Meaning of "qualifying trade"

18—(1) A trade is a qualifying trade if—

(a) it is carried on wholly or mainly in the United Kingdom,

(b) it is conducted on a commercial basis and with a view to the realisation of profits, and

(c) it does not consist wholly or as to a substantial part in the carrying on of excluded activities.

(2) The carrying on of activities of research and development from which it is intended that a connected qualifying trade will be derived or benefit is treated as the carrying on of a qualifying trade.

But preparing to carry on such activities does not count as preparing to carry on a qualifying trade.

(3) For the purposes of sub-paragraph (2) a "connected qualifying trade" means a qualifying trade carried on—

(a) by the company carrying on the activities of research and development, or

(b) if that company is a member of a group, by any other group company.

Commentary—*Simon's Direct Tax Service* **E4.545**.

Excluded activities

19—(1) The following are excluded activities—

(a) dealing in land, in commodities or futures or in shares, securities or other financial instruments;

(b) dealing in goods otherwise than in the course of an ordinary trade of wholesale or retail distribution;

(c) banking, insurance, money-lending, debt-factoring, hire-purchase financing or other financial activities;

(d) leasing (including letting ships on charter or other assets on hire) or receiving royalties or licence fees;

(e) providing legal or accountancy services;

(f) property development;

(g) farming or market gardening;

(h) holding, managing or occupying woodlands, any other forestry activities or timber production;

(i) operating or managing hotels or comparable establishments, or managing property used as a hotel or comparable establishment; and

(j) operating or managing nursing homes or residential care homes, or managing property used as a nursing home or residential care home.

(2) Sub-paragraph (1) is supplemented by the following provisions—

paragraph 20 (wholesale and retail distribution);

paragraph 21 (leasing of ships);

paragraph 22 (receipt of royalties and licence fees);

paragraph 23 (property development);

paragraph 24 (hotels and comparable establishments);

paragraph 25 (nursing homes and residential care homes); and

paragraph 26 (provision of facilities for another business).

Note—This paragraph was prospectively amended by the Regulation of Care (Scotland) Act 2001 ss 79, 81(2), Sch 3 para 24. However, the Scotland Act 1998 (Regulation of Care (Scotland) Act 2001) Order, SI 2001/2478 repeals the Regulation of Care (Scotland) Act 2001 Sch 3 para 24. The effect of this repeal is that the prospective amendments will not now be brought into force.

Commentary—*Simon's Direct Tax Service* **E4.545**.

Excluded activities: wholesale and retail distribution

20—(1) This paragraph supplements paragraph 19(1)(b).

(2) A trade of wholesale distribution is one in which the goods are offered for sale and sold to persons for resale by them, or for processing and resale by them, to members of the general public for their use or consumption.

(3) A trade of retail distribution is one in which the goods are offered for sale and sold to members of the general public for their use or consumption.

(4) A trade is not an ordinary trade of wholesale or retail distribution if—

(a) it consists, to a substantial extent, in dealing in goods of a kind which are collected or held as an investment, or in that activity and any other excluded activity taken together, and

(b) a substantial proportion of those goods are held by the company for a period which is significantly longer than the period for which a vendor would reasonably be expected to hold them while endeavouring to dispose of them at their market value.

(5) In determining whether a trade carried on by any person is an ordinary trade of wholesale or retail distribution, regard shall be had to the extent to which it has the following features—

(*a*) the goods are bought by that person in quantities larger than those in which he sells them;

(*b*) the goods are bought and sold by that person in different markets;

(*c*) that person employs staff and incurs expenses in the trade in addition to the cost of the goods and, in the case of a trade carried on by a company, to any remuneration paid to any person connected with it;

(*d*) there are purchases or sales from or to persons who are connected with that person;

(*e*) purchases are matched with forward sales or vice versa;

(*f*) the goods are held by that person for longer than is normal for goods of the kind in question;

(*g*) the trade is carried on otherwise than at a place or places commonly used for wholesale or retail trade;

(*h*) that person does not take physical possession of the goods;

(6) The features specified in sub-paragraph (5)(*a*) to (*c*) are indications that the trade is such an ordinary trade.

Those in sub-paragraph (5)(*d*) to (*h*) are indications of the contrary.

Commentary—*Simon's Direct Tax Service* **E4.545**.

Excluded activities: leasing of ships

21—(1) This paragraph supplements paragraph 19(1)(*d*) so far as it relates to the leasing of ships other than oil rigs or pleasure craft.

(2) A trade shall not be treated as not being a qualifying trade by reason only of its consisting in letting such ships on charter if the following requirements are met—

(*a*) every ship let on charter by the company carrying on the trade is beneficially owned by the company;

(*b*) every ship beneficially owned by the company is registered in the United Kingdom;

(*c*) the company is solely responsible for arranging the marketing of the services of its ships; and

(*d*) the conditions mentioned in sub-paragraph (3) are satisfied in relation to every letting of a ship on charter by the company.

(3) The conditions are that—

(*a*) the letting is for a period not exceeding 12 months and no provision is made at any time (whether in the charterparty or otherwise) for extending it beyond that period otherwise than at the option of the charterer;

(*b*) during the period of the letting there is no provision in force (whether by virtue of being contained in the charterparty or otherwise) for the grant of a new letting to end, otherwise than at the option of the charterer, more than 12 months after that provision is made;

(*c*) the letting is by way of a bargain made at arm's length between the company and a person who is not connected with it;

(*d*) under the terms of the charter the company is responsible as principal—

(i) for taking, throughout the period of the charter, management decisions in relation to the ship, other than those of a kind generally regarded by persons engaged in trade of the kind in question as matters of husbandry; and

(ii) for defraying all expenses in connection with the ship throughout that period, or substantially all such expenses, other than those directly incidental to a particular voyage or to the employment of the ship during that period;

and

(*e*) no arrangements exist by virtue of which a person other than the company may be appointed to be responsible for the matters mentioned in paragraph (*d*) on behalf of the company.

(4) In relation to any letting between one company and another where—

(*a*) one of those companies is the company carrying on the trade and the other is a qualifying subsidiary of that company, or

(*b*) both companies are qualifying subsidiaries of the company carrying on the trade,

sub-paragraph (3) has effect with the omission of paragraph (*c*).

(5) Where any of the requirements in sub-paragraph (2) are not met in relation to any lettings, the trade shall not thereby be treated as not a qualifying trade if those lettings and any other excluded activities do not, taken together, amount to a substantial part of the trade.

(6) In this paragraph—

"oil rig" means any ship which is an offshore installation for the purposes of the Mineral Workings (Offshore Installations) Act 1971; and

"pleasure craft" means any ship of a kind primarily used for sport or recreation.

Commentary—*Simon's Direct Tax Service* **E4.545**.

Excluded activities: receipt of royalties and licence fees

22—(1) This paragraph supplements paragraph 19(1)(*d*) so far as it relates to the receipt of royalties and licence fees.

(2) A trade shall not be regarded as not being a qualifying trade by reason only that it consists to a substantial extent in the receiving of royalties or licence fees if the royalties and licence fees (or all but for a part that is not a substantial part in terms of value) are attributable to the exploitation of relevant intangible assets.

(3) For this purpose an intangible asset is a "relevant intangible asset" if the whole or greater part (in terms of value) of it has been created—

(a) by the company carrying on the trade, or

(b) by a company which at all times during which it created the asset was—

    (i) the parent company of the company carrying on the trade, or

    (ii) a qualifying subsidiary of that parent company.

(4) In this paragraph "intangible asset" means any asset which falls to be treated as an intangible asset in accordance with [generally accepted accounting practice][1].

...[2]

(5) In the case of a relevant asset that is intellectual property, references in this paragraph to the creation of the asset by a company are to its creation in circumstances in which the right to exploit it vests in the company (whether alone or jointly with others).

(6) In sub-paragraph (5) "intellectual property" means—

(a) any patent, trade mark, registered design, copyright, design right, performer's right or plant breeder's right; and

(b) any rights under the law of a country or territory outside the United Kingdom which correspond or are similar to those falling within paragraph (a).

Commentary—*Simon's Direct Tax Service* **E4.545**.
Amendments—[1] Words substituted for the words "normal accounting practice" by FA 2002 s 103(4)(f) with effect from 24 July 2002.
[2] The following words repealed by FA 2002 s 141, Sch 40 Pt 3(16) with effect from 24 July 2002—

"For this purpose "normal accounting practice" means normal accounting practice in relation to the accounts of companies incorporated in any part of the United Kingdom.".

Excluded activities: property development

23—(1) This paragraph supplements paragraph 19(1)(f).

(2) "Property development" means the development of land—

(a) by a company which has, or at any time has had, an interest in the land, and

(b) with the sole or main object of realising a gain from the disposal of an interest in the land when it is developed.

(3) For this purpose "interest in land" means, subject to sub-paragraph (4)—

(a) any estate, interest or right in or over land, including any right affecting the use or disposition of land, or

(b) any right to obtain such an estate, interest or right from another which is conditional on the other's ability to grant it.

(4) References in this paragraph to an interest in land do not include—

(a) the interest of a creditor (other than a creditor in respect of a rentcharge) whose debt is secured by way of mortgage, an agreement for a mortgage or a charge of any kind over land, or

(b) in the case of land in Scotland, the interest of a creditor in a charge or security of any kind over land.

Commentary—*Simon's Direct Tax Service* **E4.545**.

Excluded activities: hotels and comparable establishments

24—(1) This paragraph supplements paragraph 19(1)(i).

(2) The reference to a comparable establishment is to a guest house, hostel or other establishment the main purpose of maintaining which is the provision of facilities for overnight accommodation (with or without catering services).

(3) The activities of a person shall not be taken to fall within paragraph 19(1)(i) unless that person has an estate or interest in, or is in occupation of, the hotel or comparable establishment in question.

Commentary—*Simon's Direct Tax Service* **E4.545**.

Excluded activities: nursing homes and residential care homes

25—(1) This paragraph supplements paragraph 19(1)(j).

(2) "Nursing home" means an establishment that exists wholly or mainly for the provision of nursing care—

(a) for persons suffering from sickness, injury or infirmity, or

(b) for women who are pregnant or have given birth to children.

(3) "Residential care home" means an establishment that exists wholly or mainly for the provision of residential accommodation, together with board and personal care, for persons in need of personal care by reason of—

(a) old age,

(b) mental or physical disability,

(c) past or present dependence on alcohol or drugs,

(d) any past illness, or

(e) past or present mental disorder.

(4) The activities of a person shall not be taken to fall within paragraph 19(1)(j) unless that person has an estate or interest in, or is in occupation of, the nursing home or residential care home in question.

Note—This paragraph was prospectively amended by the Regulation of Care (Scotland) Act 2001 ss 79, 81(2), Sch 3 para 24. However, the Scotland Act 1998 (Regulation of Care (Scotland) Act 2001) Order, SI 2001/2478 repeals the Regulation of Care (Scotland) Act 2001 Sch 3 para 24. The effect of this repeal is that the prospective amendments will not now be brought into force.

Commentary—*Simon's Direct Tax Service* E4.545.

Excluded activities: provision of facilities for another business

26—(1) Providing services or facilities for a business carried on by another person is an excluded activity if—

(a) the business consists to a substantial extent in excluded activities within paragraph 19(1), and

(b) a controlling interest in the business is held by a person (other than a company of which the company providing the services or facilities is a subsidiary) who also has a controlling interest in the business carried on by the company providing the services or facilities.

(2) Sub-paragraphs (3) to (5) define what is meant by a controlling interest in a business for the purposes of sub-paragraph (1)(b).

(3) In the case of a business carried on by a company, a person has a controlling interest if—

(a) he controls the company,

(b) the company is a close company and he or an associate of his, being a director of the company, either—

(i) is the beneficial owner of more than 30% of the ordinary share capital of the company, or

(ii) is able, directly or through the medium of other companies or by any other indirect means, to control more than 30% of that share capital,

or

(c) not less than half of the business could, in accordance with section 344(2) of the Taxes Act 1988, be regarded as belonging to him for the purposes of section 343 of that Act.

(4) In any other case, a person has a controlling interest in a business if he is entitled to not less than half of the assets used for, or of the income arising from, the business.

(5) For the purposes of sub-paragraph (3)(a) the question whether a person controls a company shall be determined in accordance with section 416(2) to (6) of the Taxes Act 1988.

(6) For the purposes of this paragraph there shall be attributed to any person any rights or powers of any other person who is an associate of his.

(7) In this paragraph—

"associate" has the meaning given in section 417(3) and (4) of the Taxes Act 1988, except that in those subsections as they apply for the purposes of this paragraph "relative" does not include a brother or sister;

"business" includes any trade, profession or vocation; and

"director" shall be construed in accordance with section 417(5) of the Taxes Act 1988.

Commentary—*Simon's Direct Tax Service* E4.545.

PART IV
ELIGIBLE EMPLOYEES
Introduction

27 An individual is an eligible employee in relation to the relevant company if the requirements of this Part of this Schedule are met as to—

(a) employment (see paragraph 28),

(b) commitment of working time (see paragraph 29), and

(c) no material interest (see paragraph 30).

Commentary—*Simon's Direct Tax Service* E4.546.

The employment requirement

28 An employee is an eligible employee in relation to the relevant company only if he is an employee—

    (*a*) of that company, or

    (*b*) if that company is a parent company, of that company or a qualifying subsidiary of that company.

Commentary—*Simon's Direct Tax Service* **E4.546**.

The requirement as to commitment of working time

29—(1) An employee is an eligible employee in relation to the relevant company only if his committed time amounts to—

    (*a*) at least 25 hours a week, or

    (*b*) if less, 75% of his working time.

(2) An employee's "committed time" means the time that he is required as an employee in relevant employment to spend—

    (*a*) on the business of the relevant company, or

    (*b*) if the relevant company is a parent company, on the business of the group.

(3) It includes any time which the employee would have been required to spend as mentioned in sub-paragraph (2) but for—

    (*a*) injury, ill-health or disability,

    (*b*) pregnancy, childbirth, maternity or paternity leave or parental leave,

    (*c*) reasonable holiday entitlement, or

    (*d*) not being required to work during a period of notice of termination of employment.

(4) For the purposes of this paragraph an employee is in "relevant employment" if he is employed—

    (*a*) by the relevant company, or

    (*b*) where the relevant company is a parent company, by any group company.

References to an employee beginning or ceasing to be in relevant employment are to his becoming or no longer being so employed.

(5) In sub-paragraph (1)(*b*) "working time" means—

    (*a*) time spent on remunerative work as an employee or self-employed person, or

    (*b*) time which would have been so spent but for any of the reasons specified in sub-paragraph (3)(*a*) to (*d*).

(6) In sub-paragraph (5)(*a*) "remunerative work" means—

    (*a*) work the income from which is chargeable to tax under Case I of Schedule E, and

    (*b*) work undertaken with a view to profit the profits (if any) from which are (or would be) chargeable to tax under Case I or II of Schedule D,

or, in either case, which would be so chargeable if the employee were resident and ordinarily resident in the United Kingdom.

Commentary—*Simon's Direct Tax Service* **E4.546**.

The "no material interest" requirement

30—(1) An individual is not an eligible employee in relation to the relevant company if he has a material interest in—

    (*a*) that company, or

    (*b*) if that company is a parent company, any group company.

(2) For the purposes of this paragraph an individual is regarded as having a material interest in a company if—

    (*a*) the individual,

    (*b*) the individual together with one or more associates of his, or

    (*c*) any associate of the individual's, with or without any other such associates,

has a material interest in the company.

(3) No account shall be taken for the purposes of this paragraph of shares that an individual may acquire under a qualifying option, but once such shares have been acquired they are taken into account.

(4) This paragraph is supplemented—

    (*a*) as regards the meaning of "material interest", by paragraphs 31 to 33; and

    (*b*) as regards the meaning of "associate", by paragraph 34 (read with paragraphs 35 and 36).

Commentary—*Simon's Direct Tax Service* **E4.546**.

Meaning of "material interest"

31—(1) For the purposes of paragraph 30 a material interest in a company means—

(a) beneficial ownership of, or the ability to control, directly or through the medium of other companies or by any other indirect means, more than 30% of the ordinary share capital of the company; or

(b) where the company is a close company, possession of or entitlement to acquire such rights as would, in the event of the winding up of the company or in any other circumstances, give an entitlement to receive more than 30% of the assets that would then be available for distribution among the participators.

(2) In this paragraph—

"close company" includes a company that would be a close company but for-

(a) section 414(1)(a) of the Taxes Act 1988 (exclusion of companies not resident in the United Kingdom), or

(b) section 415 of that Act (exclusion of certain quoted companies);

"participator" has the meaning given by section 417(1) of that Act.

(3) This paragraph is supplemented by paragraph 32 (options etc) and paragraph 33 (shares held by trustees of approved profit-sharing schemes).

Commentary—*Simon's Direct Tax Service* **E4.546**.

Material interest: options etc

32—(1) For the purposes of paragraph 31 (meaning of "material interest") a right to acquire shares (however arising) is treated as a right to control them.

(2) In any case where—

(a) the shares attributed to an individual consist of or include shares which he or another person has a right to acquire, and

(b) the circumstances are such that if that right were to be exercised the shares acquired would be shares which were previously unissued and which the company is contractually bound to issue in the event of the exercise of the right,

then in determining at any time prior to the exercise of the right whether the number of shares attributed to the individual exceeds a particular percentage of the ordinary share capital of the company, that ordinary share capital shall be taken to be increased by the number of unissued shares referred to in paragraph (b).

(3) The references in sub-paragraph (2) to the shares attributed to an individual are to the shares which in accordance with paragraph 31(1)(a) fall to be brought into account in his case to determine whether their number exceeds a particular percentage of the company's ordinary share capital.

Commentary—*Simon's Direct Tax Service* **E4.546**.

Material interest: shares held by trustees of approved profit-sharing schemes etc

33 In applying paragraph 31 (meaning of "material interest") there shall be disregarded—

(a) the interest of the trustees of—

(i) any profit-sharing scheme approved under Schedule 9 to the Taxes Act 1988, or

(ii) any employee share ownership plan approved under Schedule 8 to this Act,

in any shares which are held by them in accordance with the scheme or plan but which have not been appropriated to, or acquired on behalf of, an individual; and

(b) any rights exercisable by those trustees by virtue of any such interest.

Commentary—*Simon's Direct Tax Service* **E4.546**.

Meaning of "associate"

34—(1) In paragraph 30 (the "no material interest" requirement) "associate", in relation to an individual, means—

(a) any relative or partner of that individual,

(b) the trustee or trustees of any settlement in relation to which that individual, or any relative of his (living or dead), is or was a settlor, and

(c) where that individual is interested in any shares or obligations of the company which are subject to any trust, or are part of the estate of a deceased person, the trustee or trustees of the settlement concerned or, as the case may be, the personal representatives of the deceased.

(2) In sub-paragraph (1)(a) and (b) "relative" means husband or wife, parent or remoter forebear, or child or remoter issue.

(3) In sub-paragraph (1)(b) "settlor" and "settlement" have the same meaning as in Chapter IA of Part XV of the Taxes Act 1988 (see section 660G(1) and (2)).

Commentary—*Simon's Direct Tax Service* **E4.546**.

Meaning of "associate": trustees of employee benefit trust

35—(1) This paragraph applies for the purposes of paragraph 34(1)(c) (meaning of "associate": trustees of settlement) where an individual is interested as a beneficiary of an employee benefit trust in shares or obligations of a company ("the company") in relation to which it falls to be determined whether that individual has an interest.

(2) The trustees of the employee benefit trust are not regarded as associates of the individual by reason only of his being so interested if neither—

  (a) the individual, nor

  (b) the individual together with one or more associates of his, nor

  (c) any associate of the individual's, with or without any other such associates,

has at any time on or after 14th March 1989 been the beneficial owner of, or able (directly or through the medium of other companies or by any other indirect means) to control, more than 30% of the ordinary share capital of the company.

(3) In this paragraph "employee benefit trust" has the same meaning as in paragraph 7 of Schedule 8 to the Taxes Act 1988.

(4) Sub-paragraphs (9) to (12) of that paragraph apply for the purposes of this paragraph in relation to an individual as they apply for the purposes of that paragraph in relation to an employee.

(5) In sub-paragraph (2)(b) and (c) "associate" does not include the trustees of an employee benefit trust by reason only that the individual has an interest in shares or obligations of the trust.

Commentary—*Simon's Direct Tax Service* **E4.546**.

Meaning of "associate": trustees of discretionary trust

36—(1) This paragraph applies for the purposes of paragraph 34(1)(c) (meaning of "associate": trustees of settlement) where—

  (a) an individual ("the beneficiary") is one of the objects of a discretionary trust, and

  (b) the property subject to the trust has at any time consisted of or included shares or obligations of the company ("the company") in relation to which it falls to be determined whether that individual has an interest.

(2) If—

  (a) the beneficiary has ceased to be eligible to benefit under the discretionary trust by reason of—

    (i) an irrevocable disclaimer or release executed by him, or

    (ii) the irrevocable exercise by the trustees of a power to exclude him from the objects of the trust,

  (b) immediately after the beneficiary ceased to be so eligible, no associate of his was interested in the shares or obligations of the company which were subject to the trust, and

  (c) during the period of twelve months ending with the date when the beneficiary ceases to be so eligible, neither he nor any associate of his received any benefit under the trust,

the beneficiary is not regarded by reason only of the matters mentioned in sub-paragraph (1) as having been interested in the shares or obligations of the company at any time during the period of twelve months mentioned in paragraph (c) above.

(3) In sub-paragraph (2) "associate" has the meaning given by paragraph 34, but with the omission of sub-paragraph (1)(c) of that paragraph (trusts and estates).

Commentary—*Simon's Direct Tax Service* **E4.546**.

PART V
REQUIREMENTS AS TO TERMS OF OPTION ETC
Introduction

37 An option is not a qualifying option unless the requirements of this Part of this Schedule are met as to—

  (a) the type of shares that may be acquired (see paragraph 38);

  (b) when the option is capable of being exercised (see paragraph 39);

  (c) the terms being agreed in writing (see paragraph 40); and

  (d) the non-assignability of rights (see paragraph 41).

Commentary—*Simon's Direct Tax Service* **E4.547**.

Type of shares that may be acquired

38—(1) The option must confer a right to acquire shares that—

  (a) form part of the ordinary share capital of the relevant company,

  (b) are fully paid up, and

  (c) are not redeemable.

(2) Shares are not fully paid up for the purposes of sub-paragraph (1)(*b*) if there is any undertaking to pay cash to the relevant company at a future date.

(3) For the purposes of sub-paragraph (1)(*c*) "redeemable" shares include shares that may become redeemable at a future date.

Commentary—*Simon's Direct Tax Service* **E4.547**.

Option to be capable of exercise within 10 years

39—(1) The option must be capable of being exercised within the period of ten years beginning with the date on which it is granted.

(2) Where the exercise of the option is dependent on the fulfilment of conditions, it is taken to be capable of being exercised within the period mentioned in sub-paragraph (1) if the conditions may be fulfilled within that period.

Commentary—*Simon's Direct Tax Service* **E4.547**.

Terms of option to be agreed in writing

40—(1) The option must take the form of a written agreement between the person granting the option and the employee which meets the following requirements.

(2) The agreement must state—

  (*a*) the date on which the option is granted;
  (*b*) that it is granted under the provisions of this Schedule;
  (*c*) the number, or maximum number, of shares that may be acquired;
  (*d*) the price (if any) payable by the employee to acquire them, or the method by which that price is to be determined; and
  (*e*) when and how the option may be exercised.

(3) The agreement must set out any conditions, such as performance conditions, affecting the terms or extent of the employee's entitlement.

(4) The agreement must contain details of any restrictions attaching to the shares.

(5) Where the shares that may be acquired by the employee are subject to risk of forfeiture, the agreement must contain details of the conditions.

For this purpose shares are "subject to risk of forfeiture" if the interest that may be acquired is only conditional within the meaning of Section 140C of the Taxes Act 1988.

Commentary—*Simon's Direct Tax Service* **E4.547**.

Non-assignability of rights

41 An option is not a qualifying option unless the terms on which it is granted—

  (*a*) prohibit the person to whom it is granted from transferring any of his rights under it, and
  (*b*) if they permit its exercise after that person's death, do not permit such exercise more than one year after the death.

Commentary—*Simon's Direct Tax Service* **E4.547**.

PART VI
INCOME TAX
Introduction

42—(1) The provisions of this Part of this Schedule give relief from income tax in respect of the grant or exercise of a qualifying option.

(2) Relief in respect of the exercise of a qualifying option applies only to exercise within the period of ten years after—

  (*a*) the grant of the option, or
  (*b*) if it is a replacement option, the grant of the original option.

(3) In this Part the references to the "original option", where there has been one or more replacement options, are to the option that the replacement option (or, if there has been more than one, the first of them) replaced.

Exclusion of charge on grant

43 Tax is not chargeable under any provision of the Tax Acts in respect of the grant of the option.

Commentary—*Simon's Direct Tax Service* **E4.548**.

Exercise of option to acquire shares at market value

44—(1) This paragraph applies if the option is to acquire shares at not less than their market value—

　(*a*) at the time the option is granted, or

　(*b*) if it is a replacement option, at the time the original option was granted.

(2) In that case no amount is chargeable to income tax under section 135 of the Taxes Act 1988 (taxation of share options) in respect of the exercise of the option.

(3) This paragraph has effect subject to paragraph 53 (effect of disqualifying event).

Commentary—*Simon's Direct Tax Service* **E4.548**.

Exercise of option to acquire shares at less than market value

45—(1) This paragraph applies if the option is to acquire shares at less than their market value—

　(*a*) at the time the option is granted, or

　(*b*) if it is a replacement option, at the time the original option was granted.

[(2) In that case for the purposes of section 135 of the Taxes Act 1988 (taxation of share options) the amount of the gain realised by the exercise of the option is taken to be the amount by which—

　(*a*) the chargeable market value, exceeds

　(*b*) the aggregate of—

　　(i) the amount or value of the consideration given for the grant of the option, and

　　(ii) the amount for which the shares are acquired.

(3) For the purposes of this paragraph "the chargeable market value" means—

　(*a*) the market value of the shares—

　　(i) at the time the option was granted, or

　　(ii) if it is a replacement value, at the time the original option was granted,

or

　(*b*) if lower, the market value of the shares at the time the option is exercised.

(4) If the chargeable market value does not exceed the aggregate of the amounts mentioned in sub-paragraph (2)(*b*)(i) and (ii), no amount is chargeable to income tax under section 135 of the Taxes Act 1988 (taxation of share options) in respect of the exercise of the option.][1]

(5) This paragraph has effect subject to paragraph 53 (effect of disqualifying event).

Commentary—*Simon's Direct Tax Service* **E4.548**.
Amendment—[1] Sub-paras (2)–(4) substituted by FA 2001 s 62, Sch 14 paras 7, 13 with effect for any right to acquire shares exercised after the passing of FA 2001. Previously, sub-paras (2)–(4) read as follows—

"(2) In that case for the purposes of section 135 of the Taxes Act 1988 (taxation of shares options) the amount of the gain realised by the exercise of the option is taken to be—

　(*a*) the amount of the discount, or
　(*b*) if lower, the amount by which the market value of the shares at the time the option is exercised exceeds the amount for which they are acquired.

(3) The amount of the discount means the amount by which the market value of the shares—

　(*a*) at the time the option was granted, or
　(*b*) if it is a replacement option, at the time the original option was granted,

exceeds the amount for which they are acquired.

(4) If the market value of the shares at the time the option is exercised does not exceed the amount for which they are acquired, no amount is chargeable to income tax under section 135 of the Taxes Act 1988 (taxation of share options) in respect of the exercise of the option.".

Exercise of option to acquire shares at nil cost

46—(1) This paragraph applies if the option is to acquire shares at a nil cost.

[(2) In that case for the purposes of section 135 of the Taxes Act 1988 (taxation of share options) the amount of the gain realised by the exercise of the option is taken to be the amount by which—

　(*a*) the chargeable market value (within the meaning of paragraph 45), exceeds

　(*b*) the amount or value of the consideration given for the grant of the option.

(2A) If the chargeable market value does not exceed the amount or value of the consideration given for the grant of the option, no amount is chargeable to income tax under section 135 of the Taxes Act 1988 (taxation of share options) in respect of the exercise of the option.][1]

(3) This paragraph has effect subject to paragraph 53 (effect of disqualifying event).

Commentary—*Simon's Direct Tax Service* **E4.548**.
Amendment—[1] Sub-paras (2), (2A) substituted for sub-para (2) by FA 2001 s 62, Sch 14 paras 8, 13 with effect for any right to acquire shares exercised after the passing of FA 2001. Previously, sub-para (2) read as follows—

"(2) In that case for the purposes of section 135 of the Taxes Act 1988 (taxation of share options) the amount of the gain realised by the exercise of the option is taken to be—

　(a) the market value of the shares—

　　(i) at the time the option was granted, or
　　(ii) if it is a replacement option, at the time the original option was granted, or

　(b) if lower, the market value of the shares at the time the option is exercised.".

Main disqualifying events

47—(1) The following are "disqualifying events" in relation to a qualifying option—

    (*a*) the relevant company—

        (i) becoming a 51% subsidiary of another company, or

        (ii) coming under the control of another company (or of another company and any other person connected with that other company), without being a 51% subsidiary of that other company;

    (*b*) the relevant company ceasing to meet the trading activities requirement;

    (*c*) the employee ceasing to be an eligible employee in relation to the relevant company by reason of ceasing to meet—

        (i) the requirement in paragraph 28 (the employment requirement), or

        (ii) the requirement in paragraph 29 (the requirement as to commitment of working time);

    (*d*) any variation of the terms of the option the effect of which is—

        (i) to increase the market value of the shares that are the subject of the option, or

        (ii) that the requirements of this Schedule would no longer be met in relation to the option;

    [(*e*) any alteration to the share capital of the relevant company that is within paragraph 49(1)—

        (i) where the effect of the alteration is that the requirements of this Schedule would no longer be met in relation to the option, or

        (ii) where the effect of the alteration is to increase the market value of the shares that are the subject of the qualifying option and paragraph 49(2) applies to the alteration;][1]

    (*f*) a conversion of any of the shares to which the option relates into shares of a different class, except in a case within paragraph 50; and

    (*g*) the grant to the employee of a relevant CSOP option, if immediately after it is granted the employee holds unexercised employee options in respect of shares with a total value of more than £100,000.

(2) A disqualifying event is treated as occurring in relation to a qualifying option if—

    (*a*) the relevant company was a qualifying company at the time the option was granted by reason only of preparations to carry on a qualifying trade, and

    (*b*) either—

        (i) the preparations cease to be carried on, or

        (ii) the period of two years from the grant of the original option comes to an end,

without the relevant company or, if it is the parent company of a group, any group company beginning to carry on that qualifying trade.

(3) A disqualifying event is also treated as occurring in relation to a qualifying option if in any tax year the employee's relevant working time amounts to less than 25 hours a week or, if less, 75% of his working time.

(4) This paragraph is supplemented by the following provisions—

    paragraph 48 (company reorganisation);

    paragraph 49 (alterations of share capital);

    paragraph 50 (conversion of shares);

    paragraph 51 (grant of CSOP option); and

    paragraph 52 (actual relevant working time).

Commentary—*Simon's Direct Tax Service* **E4.548**.

Amendment—[1] Sub-para (1)(*e*) substituted by FA 2001 s 62, Sch 14 paras 9, 13 with effect for any alteration made to the share capital of a company after the passing of FA 2001. Previously, sub-para (1)(*e*) read as follows—

"(*e*) any alteration to the share capital of the relevant company that is within paragraph 49 and is made without the prior approval of the Inland Revenue;".

Disqualifying events: company reorganisation

48 Where a replacement option has been granted (see paragraph 61), if an event within paragraph 47(1)(*a*) (loss of independence) has occurred in relation to the old option at any time during the period—

    (*a*) beginning at the same time as the period within which the replacement option had to be granted (see paragraph 62), and

    (*b*) ending with the release of the rights under the old option,

that event shall not be regarded as a disqualifying event in relation to the old option.

Commentary—*Simon's Direct Tax Service* **E4.548**.

Disqualifying events: alterations of share capital

49—(1) An alteration of the share capital of the relevant company is within [this sub-paragraph][1] if—

    (*a*) it affects (or but for the occurrence of some other event would affect) the value of the shares which are the subject of the qualifying option, and

    (*b*) it consists of or includes—

    (i) the creation, variation or removal of a right relating to any shares in the relevant company,
    (ii) the imposition of a restriction relating to any such shares, or
    (iii) the variation or removal of a restriction to which any such shares are subject.

For this purpose references to restrictions relating to shares or to which shares are subject, or to rights relating to shares, include restrictions imposed or rights conferred by any contract or arrangement or in any other way.

[(2) This sub-paragraph applies to an alteration if—

    (a) it is not made by the relevant company for commercial reasons, or
    (b) the main purpose or one of the main purposes for making the alteration is to increase the market value of the shares which are the subject of the qualifying option.][1]

Commentary—*Simon's Direct Tax Service* **E4.548**.
Amendment—[1] In sub-para (1), the words "this sub-paragraph" substituted for the words "this paragraph", and sub-para (2) substituted for sub-paras (2)–(5), by FA 2001 s 62, Sch 14 paras 10, 13 with effect for any alteration made to the share capital of a company after the passing of FA 2001. Previously, sub-paras (2)–(5) read as follows—

"(2) The Inland Revenue shall not withhold their approval under paragraph 47(1)(e) unless it appears to them that the effect of the alteration would be—

    (a) to increase the market value of the shares that are the subject of the qualifying option, or
    (b) that the requirements of this Schedule would no longer be met in relation to the option.

(3) Where the Inland Revenue withhold their approval the employer company may appeal against that decision.
(4) Notice of appeal must be given to the Inland Revenue within 30 days after their notice of their decision was given to the employer company.
(5) An appeal under this paragraph lies to the General Commissioners or, if the employer company so elects (in accordance with section 46(1) of the Taxes Management Act 1970), to the Special Commissioners.".

Disqualifying events: conversion of shares

50—(1) A conversion of shares is not a disqualifying event if—

    (a) the conversion is a conversion of shares of one class only ("the original class") into shares of one other class only ("the new class");
    (b) all shares of the original class are converted into shares of the new class; and
    (c) one of the conditions in sub-paragraph (2) is fulfilled.

(2) The conditions are—

    (a) that immediately before the conversion the majority of the relevant company's shares of the original class are held otherwise than by or for the benefit of—

        (i) directors or employees of the relevant company,
        (ii) an associated company of the relevant company, or
        (iii) directors or employees of such an associated company; and

    (b) that immediately before the conversion the relevant company is employee-controlled by virtue of holdings of shares of the original class.

(3) For the purposes of this paragraph "director", "employee", "associated company" and "employee-controlled" have the same meaning as in section 140D of the Taxes Act 1988 (convertible shares).

Commentary—*Simon's Direct Tax Service* **E4.548**.

Disqualifying events: grant of CSOP option

51—(1) This paragraph applies where it falls to be determined whether a disqualifying event within sub-paragraph (1)(g) of paragraph 47 has occurred in relation to a qualifying option ("the qualifying option") granted to an employee.

(2) For the purposes of that sub-paragraph and this paragraph "CSOP option" has the meaning given in paragraph 10(6).

(3) A CSOP option is a "relevant" CSOP option if it is granted to the employee by reason of his employment with—

    (a) the employer company, or
    (b) if that company is a member of a group, any member of that group.

(4) An option is an "employee option" if it is—

    (a) the qualifying option,
    (b) another qualifying option granted to the employee by reason of his employment with the employer company or, if that company is a member of a group, any member of that group, or
    (c) a relevant CSOP option.

(5) Paragraph 10(7) and (8) (determination of value of shares) apply for the purposes of paragraph 47(1)(g) as they apply for the purposes of paragraph 10.

Commentary—*Simon's Direct Tax Service* **E4.548**.

52—(1) For the purposes of paragraph 47(3) an employee's relevant working time means the time that he in fact spends as an employee in relevant employment—

(*a*) on the business of the relevant company, or

(*b*) if the relevant company is a parent company, on the business of the group.

(2) The time at which the disqualifying event is taken to have occurred is determined in accordance with the following provisions.

(3) Subject to sub-paragraphs (4) and (5), the time at which the disqualifying event occurred is determined as follows:

Method

1 For each calendar month calculate whether over the tax year to date the employee's relevant working time amounts to less than 25 hours a week or, if less, 75% of his working time.

2 If it does, the disqualifying event is taken to have occurred—

(*a*) at the end of the previous calendar month, or

(*b*) if the calendar month for which the calculation is done is April, at the end of the previous tax year.

(4) In the case of an employee who begins or ceases to be in relevant employment during the tax year, the references in sub-paragraph (3) above and paragraph 47(3) to that tax year shall be construed as references to the part of the tax year in which he is in relevant employment.

(5) If the time determined under sub-paragraph (3) or (4) falls before the grant of the option, the option is treated for the purposes of this Schedule as if it had never been a qualifying option.

(6) Expressions used in paragraph 47(3) or this paragraph that are defined for the purposes of paragraph 29 (requirement as to commitment of working time) have the same meaning as in that paragraph.

Commentary—*Simon's Direct Tax Service* **E4.548**.

Effect of disqualifying event

53—(1) This paragraph applies where—

(*a*) a disqualifying event occurs in relation to a qualifying option before the option is exercised, and

(*b*) the option is not exercised within 40 days of that event.

[(2) Where paragraph 44 applies (option to acquire shares at market value), then for the purposes of section 135 of the Taxes Act 1988 (taxation of share options) the amount of the gain realised on the exercise of the option is taken to be—

(*a*) the post-event gain (if any), less

(*b*) the amount or value of the consideration given for the grant of the option.

(2A) Where paragraph 45 applies (option to acquire shares at less than market value), then for the purposes of section 135 of the Taxes Act 1988 (taxation of share options) the amount of the gain realised on the exercise of the option is taken to be—

(*a*) the aggregate of—

(i) the chargeable market value (within the meaning of that paragraph), and

(ii) the post-event gain, less

(*b*) the aggregate of—

(i) the amount or value of the consideration given for the grant of the option, and

(ii) the amount for which the shares are acquired.

(2B) Where paragraph 46 applies (option to acquire shares at nil cost), then for the purposes of section 135 of the Taxes Act 1988 (taxation of share options) the amount of the gain realised on the exercise of the option is taken to be—

(*a*) the aggregate of—

(i) the chargeable market value (within the meaning of paragraph 45), and

(ii) the post-event gain, less

(*b*) the amount or value of the consideration given for the grant of the option.

(2C) For the purposes of this paragraph "the post-event gain" means the amount (if any) by which—

(*a*) the market value of the shares when the option is exercised, exceeds

(*b*) their market value immediately before the disqualifying event.

(2D) Where—

(*a*) the amount of the gain realised on the exercise of an option falls to be determined under sub-paragraph (2), (2A) or (2B) above, and

(*b*) the amount mentioned in paragraph (*b*) of the sub-paragraph concerned exceeds the amount mentioned in paragraph (*a*) of that sub-paragraph, no amount is chargeable to income tax under section 135 of the Taxes Act 1988 (taxation of share options) in respect of the exercise of the option.]¹

(3) Paragraphs 44 to 46 and [sub-paragraphs (2), (2A), and (2B)]¹ of this paragraph do not apply if the amount chargeable under section 135 of the Taxes Act 1988 on the exercise of the option would, in the absence of those provisions, be less than the amount so chargeable by virtue of those provisions.

Commentary—*Simon's Direct Tax Service* **E4.548**.
Amendment—¹ Sub-paras (2)–(2D) substituted for sub-para (2), and words in sub-para (3) substituted for words "sub-paragraph (2)", by FA 2001 s 62, Sch 14 paras 11, 13 with effect for any right to acquire shares exercised after the passing of FA 2001. Previously, sub-para (2) read as follows—

"(2) For the purposes of section 135 of the Taxes Act 1988 (taxation of share options) the amount of the gain realised on the exercise of the option is taken—

(*a*) where paragraph 44 applies (option to acquire shares at market value), to be, and
(*b*) where paragraph 45 or 46 applies (option to acquires shares at less than market value or for nil cost), to be increased by,

the amount (if any) by which the market value of the shares when the option is exercised exceeds their market value immediately before the disqualifying event.

This is subject to sub-paragraph (3).".

Exclusion of charge on acquisition at under-value

54—(1) Section 162(1) of the Taxes Act 1988 (deemed employment-related loan in case of acquisition of shares at an undervalue), as it applies in relation to an employee chargeable to tax under Case I of Schedule E, does not apply in relation to the acquisition of shares by the exercise of a qualifying option.

(2) This does not affect any charge to tax under section 162(6) of that Act (stop-loss provisions).

Commentary—*Simon's Direct Tax Service* **E4.548**.

Saving for other income tax charges

55—(1) Nothing in this Part of this Schedule affects—

(*a*) any charge to tax under section 135 of the Taxes Act 1988 (taxation of share options) in respect of the release of rights conferred by a qualifying option;
(*b*) any charge to tax under section 78 or 80 of the Finance Act 1988 (charge on removal of restrictions etc or on special benefits) in respect of shares acquired under a qualifying option; or
(*c*) subject to sub-paragraph (2), any charge to tax under—

(i) section 140A of the Taxes Act 1988 (charge on interest in shares ceasing to be only conditional), or
(ii) section 140D of that Act (convertible shares),

in respect of shares acquired under a qualifying option.

(2) The amount of relief under this Schedule shall be treated as a deductible amount for the purposes of any charge to tax under section 140A or 140D of the Taxes Act 1988 in respect of shares acquired under a qualifying option.

The amount of relief means the difference between the amount on which tax would have been chargeable under section 135 of that Act in respect of the exercise of the option apart from this Schedule and the amount (if any) in fact so chargeable.

Commentary—*Simon's Direct Tax Service* **E4.548**.

PART VII
CAPITAL GAINS TAX

Qualifying shares

56—(1) In this Part of this Schedule "qualifying shares"—

(*a*) means shares acquired by the exercise of a qualifying option, subject to sub-paragraphs (2) and (3), and
(*b*) includes shares ("replacement shares") which—

(i) are treated under section 127 of the Taxation of Chargeable Gains Act 1992 (company reorganisations etc) as the same asset as a holding of qualifying shares, and
(ii) meet the requirements of paragraph 38 (type of shares that may be acquired under qualifying option).

(2) If a disqualifying event occurs in relation to a qualifying option (whether the original option or a replacement option), shares acquired by the exercise of the option are qualifying shares only if the option is exercised within 40 days of that event.

(3) References in this Part to "the original option", where there has been one or more replacement options, are to the option that the replacement option (or, if there has been more than one, the first of them) replaced.

Commentary—*Simon's Direct Tax Service* **E4.549**.

Taper relief on disposal of qualifying shares

57 For the purposes of computing taper relief on a disposal of qualifying shares, the shares are treated as if they had been acquired when the original option was granted.

Commentary—*Simon's Direct Tax Service* **E4.549**.

Rights issues in respect of qualifying shares

58 Where—

(*a*) an individual holds qualifying shares, and
(*b*) there is, by virtue of any such allotment for payment as is mentioned in section 126(2)(*a*) of the Taxation of Chargeable Gains Act 1992, a reorganisation affecting that holding,

sections 127 to 130 of that Act shall not apply in relation to that holding.

Commentary—*Simon's Direct Tax Service* **E4.549**.

PART VIII
COMPANY REORGANISATIONS.

Introduction

59—(1) The provisions of this Part of this Schedule apply in relation to company reorganisations.

(2) For the purposes of this Part a "company reorganisation" means where a company ("the acquiring company")—

(*a*) obtains control of a company whose shares are subject to a qualifying option which has yet to be exercised—

(i) as a result of making a general offer to acquire the whole of the issued ordinary share capital of that company which is made on a condition such that if it is satisfied the person making the offer will have control of the company, or
(ii) as a result of making a general offer to acquire all the shares in the company which are of the same class as those to which the option relates; or

(*b*) obtains control of such a company in pursuance of a compromise or arrangement sanctioned by the court under section 425 of the Companies Act 1985 or Article 418 of the Companies (Northern Ireland) Order 1986; or

(*c*) becomes bound or entitled under sections 428 to 430 of that Act or Articles 421 to 423 of that Order to acquire shares of the same class as shares that are subject to a qualifying option that has yet to be exercised; or

(*d*) obtains all the shares of a company whose shares are subject to such a qualifying option as a result of a qualifying exchange of shares (see paragraph 60).

(3) In this Part of this Schedule "control" has the meaning given by section 840 of the Taxes Act 1988.

Commentary—*Simon's Direct Tax Service* **E4.550**.

Meaning of "qualifying exchange of shares"

60—(1) For the purposes of this Part of this Schedule there is a "qualifying exchange of shares" where arrangements are made in accordance with which a company ("the new company") acquires all the shares ("old shares") in another company ("the old company") and the following conditions are met.

(2) The conditions are—

(*a*) that the consideration for the old shares consists wholly of the issue of shares ("new shares") in the new company;
(*b*) that new shares are issued in consideration of old shares only at times when there are no issued shares in the new company other than—

(i) subscriber shares, and
(ii) new shares previously issued in consideration of old shares;

(*c*) that the consideration for new shares of each description consists wholly of old shares of the corresponding description;
(*d*) that new shares of each description are issued to the holders of old shares of the corresponding description in respect of, and in proportion to, their holdings; and

(*e*) that by virtue of section 127 of the Taxation of Chargeable Gains Act 1992 as applied by section 135(3) of that Act, the exchange of shares is not treated as involving a disposal of the old shares or an acquisition of the new shares.

(3) For the purposes of this paragraph old shares and new shares are of a corresponding description if, on the assumption that they were shares in the same company, they would be of the same class and carry the same rights.

(4) In this paragraph references to "shares", except in the expression "subscriber shares", include securities.

Commentary—*Simon's Direct Tax Service* **E4.550**.

Grant of replacement option

61—(1) This paragraph applies where in the case of a company reorganisation—

(*a*) the holder of a qualifying option, by agreement with the acquiring company, releases his rights under that option ("the old option") in consideration of the grant to him of rights ("the new option") which are equivalent but relate to shares in the acquiring company, and

(*b*) the requirements of the following paragraphs are met—

    paragraph 62 (period within which replacement option must be granted), and
    paragraph 63 (qualifying requirements for replacement option).

(2) Where this paragraph applies, the new option shall be treated for the purposes of this Schedule as a "replacement option".

(3) Except as otherwise provided—

(*a*) references in this Schedule to a qualifying option include a replacement option, and

(*b*) a replacement option is treated for the purposes of this Schedule as if it had been granted on the date on which the old option was granted.

(4) In this Schedule references to "the old option" or "the new option" shall be construed in accordance with this paragraph.

Commentary—*Simon's Direct Tax Service* **E4.550**.

Period within which replacement option must be granted

62 The new option does not qualify as a replacement option unless it is granted within—

(*a*) if the company reorganisation falls within paragraph 59(2)(*a*), the period of six months beginning with the time when the person making the offer has obtained control of the company and any condition subject to which the offer is made is satisfied;

(*b*) if the company reorganisation falls within paragraph 59(2)(*b*) or (*d*), the period of six months beginning with the time when the acquiring company obtains control of the company whose shares are subject to the old option;

(*c*) if the company reorganisation falls within paragraph 59(2)(*c*), the period during which the acquiring company remains bound or entitled as mentioned in that paragraph.

Commentary—*Simon's Direct Tax Service* **E4.550**.

Qualifying requirements for replacement option

63 A new option qualifies as a replacement option only if—

(*a*) the option is granted to the holder of the old option by reason of his employment—

    (i) with the acquiring company, or
    (ii) if that company is a parent company, with that company or another group company;

(*b*) at the time of the release of rights under the old option, the requirements of—

    (i) paragraph 9 (purpose of granting the option), and
    (ii) paragraph 11 [(maximum value of options in respect of relevant company's shares)][1],

are met in relation to the new option;

(*c*) at that time, the independence requirement and the trading activities requirement are met in relation to the acquiring company;

(*d*) at that time, the individual to whom the new option is granted is an eligible employee in relation to the acquiring company;

(*e*) at that time, the requirements of Part V are met in relation to the new option;

(*f*) the total market value, immediately before the release, of the shares which were subject to the old option is equal to the total market value, immediately after the grant, of the shares in respect of which the new option is granted; and

(*g*) the total amount payable by the employee for the acquisition of shares in pursuance of the new option is equal to the total amount that would have been payable for the acquisition of shares in pursuance of the old option.

Commentary—*Simon's Direct Tax Service* **E4.550**.
Amendment—[1] Words substituted for words "(number of employees who may hold qualifying options)" by FA 2001 s 62, Sch 14 paras 12, 13 with effect for any right to acquire shares granted after the passing of FA 2001.

PART IX
SUPPLEMENTARY PROVISIONS
Power to require information

64—(1) The Inland Revenue may by notice require any person to furnish them, within such time as the Inland Revenue may direct (not being less than three months), with such information as—

(a) the Inland Revenue think necessary for the performance of their functions under this Schedule, and

(b) the person to whom the notice is addressed has or can reasonably obtain.

(2) The power conferred by this paragraph extends, in particular, to information to enable the Inland Revenue—

(a) to decide whether an option is a qualifying option, or

(b) to determine the liability to tax, including capital gains tax, of any person who has been granted a qualifying option.

(3) (*amends* TMA 1970 s 98, Table).

Commentary—*Simon's Direct Tax Service* **E4.551**.

Annual returns

65—(1) A company whose shares are the subject of a qualifying option at any time during a tax year must deliver a return to the Inland Revenue.

(2) The return must—

(a) contain such information as the Inland Revenue may require, and

(b) be made within three months after the end of the tax year to which it relates.

(3) (*amends* TMA 1970 s 98, Table).

Commentary—*Simon's Direct Tax Service* **E4.551**.

Meaning of "market value" of shares

66—(1) For the purposes of this Schedule the "market value" of shares has the same meaning as, for the purposes of the Taxation of Chargeable Gains Act 1992, it has by virtue of Part VIII of that Act.

This is subject to paragraph 10(8) (determination of value of shares subject to restriction or risk of forfeiture).

(2) Where the market value of shares on any date falls to be determined for the purposes of this Schedule, the Inland Revenue and the employer company may agree that it shall be determined by reference to such date or dates, or to an average of the values on a number of dates, as may be provided in the agreement.

Determination of market value

67—(1) The market value of shares for the purposes of this Schedule, if not agreed between the employer company and the Inland Revenue or referred to the Commissioners under sub-paragraph (4), shall be determined by the Inland Revenue.

(2) The employer company may appeal against any such determination.

(3) Notice of appeal must be given to the Inland Revenue within 30 days after their notice of their determination was given to the employer company.

(4) The employer company may, at any time before notice of determination by the Inland Revenue has been given to it, by notice given to the Inland Revenue require the question of the market value of the shares to be referred to the Commissioners.

Any such reference shall be determined by the Commissioners in the same way as an appeal.

(5) An appeal or reference under this paragraph lies to the General Commissioners or, if the employer company so elects (in accordance with section 46(1) of the Taxes Management Act 1970), to the Special Commissioners.

Commentary—*Simon's Direct Tax Service* **E4.551**.

Exercise of functions conferred on "the Inland Revenue"

68 Functions conferred by this Schedule on "the Inland Revenue" may be exercised by any officer of the Board.

Power to amend by Treasury order

69 The Treasury may by order amend this Schedule—

(a) to make such amendments of paragraphs 17 to 26 (the trading activities requirement and related provisions) as they consider expedient;

(*b*) to substitute different sums of money for those for the time being specified in—

paragraph 10(1), (4) and (5) (maximum entitlement of employee), or
paragraph 16(1) and (2) (the gross assets requirement).

Commentary—*Simon's Direct Tax Service* **E4.545**.

Compliance with time limits

70—(1) For the purposes of this Part and Part I of this Schedule a person is not taken to have failed to do anything required to be done within a limited time if—

(*a*) he had a reasonable excuse for not doing it within that time, and
(*b*) if the excuse ceased, he did it without unreasonable delay after the excuse ceased.

(2) Where sub-paragraph (1)(*b*) applies any further time limit expressed by reference to the time when the thing should have been done shall have effect as if it had been expressed by reference to the time when it was done.

Commentary—*Simon's Direct Tax Service* **E4.551**.

Minor definitions

71—(1) In this Schedule—

"arrangements" includes any scheme, agreement or understanding, whether or not legally enforceable;
"company" means any body corporate;
"group", in relation to a parent company, means that company and its 51% subsidiaries;
"group company", in relation to a parent company, means that company or any of its 51% subsidiaries;
"parent company" means a company that has one or more 51% subsidiaries and "single company" means a company that does not;
"option" means any right to acquire shares;
"ordinary share capital" has the meaning given in section 832(1) of the Taxes Act 1988;
"research and development" has the meaning given by section 837A of the Taxes Act 1988;
"shares" includes stock; and
"tax year" means a year of assessment.

(2) Section 839 of the Taxes Act 1988 (connected persons) applies for the purposes of this Schedule.

Index of defined expressions

72 In this Schedule the following expressions are defined or otherwise explained by the provisions indicated:

research and development	paragraph 71(1)
shares	paragraph 71(1) (and see paragraph 60(4))
single company	paragraph 71(1)
tax year	paragraph 71(1)
trading activities requirement	paragraph 17

SCHEDULE 15

THE CORPORATE VENTURING SCHEME

Section 63(1)

Statement of Practice SP 3/00—Corporate venturing scheme—location of activity.
Commentary—*Simon's Direct Tax Service* **D2.13**.

PART I

INVESTMENT RELIEF: INTRODUCTION

Meaning of "investment relief"

1 This Schedule makes provision for—

(a) relief against corporation tax ("investment relief") on amounts subscribed by companies for shares (see this Part and Parts II to VI of this Schedule);

(b) relief against income of companies for losses on disposals of shares to which investment relief is attributable (see Part VII of this Schedule); and

(c) the postponement of certain chargeable gains of companies where the gains are reinvested in shares to which investment relief is attributable (see Part VIII of this Schedule).

Eligibility for investment relief

2 A company ("the investing company") is eligible for investment relief in respect of an amount subscribed by it for an issue of shares in another company ("the issuing company") if—

(a) the shares ("the relevant shares") are issued to the investing company;

(b) the investing company is a qualifying investing company in relation to the relevant shares (see Part II of this Schedule);

(c) the issuing company is a qualifying issuing company in relation to the relevant shares (see Part III of this Schedule); and

(d) the general requirements of Part IV of this Schedule are met in respect of the relevant shares.

Meaning of "the qualification period"

3—(1) In this Schedule "the qualification period", in relation to the relevant shares, means the period beginning with the issue of the shares and ending—

(a) immediately before the third anniversary of the issue date; or

(b) where the money raised by the issuance of the shares is employed wholly or mainly for the purposes of one or more qualifying trades that, on the issue date, were not being carried on—

    (i) by the issuing company, or

    (ii) if it is a parent company, by that company or any of its qualifying subsidiaries,

immediately before the third anniversary of the trading date.

(2) For this purpose "the trading date" means—

(a) the date on which the issuing company or one of its qualifying subsidiaries begins to carry on the qualifying trade to which sub-paragraph (1)(b) refers, or

(b) if there is more than one such trade, the latest date on which the issuing company or one of its qualifying subsidiaries begins to carry on such a trade.

PART II

THE INVESTING COMPANY

Introduction

4 The investing company is a qualifying investing company in relation to the relevant shares if the requirements of this Part are met as to—

(a) no material interest (see paragraph 5);

(b) no reciprocal arrangements (see paragraph 6);

(c) no control (see paragraph 8);

(d) non-financial activities (see paragraph 10);

(e) the shares being a chargeable asset (see paragraph 13); and

(f) no tax avoidance (see paragraph 14).

The "no material interest" requirement

5 The investing company must not, at any time during the qualification period relating to the shares, have a material interest in the issuing company.

The "no reciprocal arrangements" requirement

6—(1) The investing company must not subscribe for the relevant shares as part of any arrangements which provide for any other person to subscribe for shares in a related company.

(2) For this purpose—

    (a) arrangements shall be disregarded to the extent that they provide for the issuing company to subscribe for shares in any of its qualifying subsidiaries, and

    (b) "a related company" means a company in which the investing company, or any other person who is a party to the arrangements, has a material interest.

(3) In sub-paragraph (2)(a) the reference to qualifying subsidiaries of the issuing company is not restricted to companies that were such subsidiaries at the time the arrangements were made.

Meaning of "material interest"

7—(1) For the purposes of paragraphs 5 and 6 a person has a material interest in a company if he (whether alone or together with any person connected with him) directly or indirectly possesses or is entitled to acquire more than 30% of—

    (a) the ordinary share capital of the company or any subsidiary, or

    (b) the voting power in the company or any subsidiary.

(2) For the purposes of sub-paragraph (1) "ordinary share capital", in relation to a company, means—

    (a) all of the issued share capital (by whatever name called) of the company, other than capital comprising relevant preference shares, and

    (b) all of the loan capital of the company that comprises debt which carries (directly or indirectly) any right to conversion into, or to the acquisition of, shares within paragraph (a) (or that would be within that paragraph if issued).

(3) For the purposes of sub-paragraph (2)(b) the loan capital of a company shall be treated as including any debt incurred by the company—

    (a) for any money borrowed or capital assets acquired by the company,

    (b) for any right to receive income created in favour of the company, or

    (c) for consideration the value of which to the company was (at the time when the debt was incurred) substantially less than the amount of the debt (including any premium on it).

This is subject to sub-paragraph (4).

(4) For the purposes of sub-paragraph (3) a debt which—

    (a) is incurred by a company or any subsidiary by overdrawing an account with a person carrying on the business of banking, and

    (b) arises in the ordinary course of that business,

shall not be treated as loan capital of the company.

(5) For the purposes of sub-paragraph (1)—

    (a) a person is treated as entitled to acquire anything which he is entitled to acquire at a future date or will at a future date be entitled to acquire, and

    (b) there are attributed to a person any rights or powers of any other person who is an associate of his.

(6) For the purposes of this paragraph a company is a subsidiary of another company if it is a 51% subsidiary of that company.

The "no control" requirement

8—(1) The investing company must not, at any time during the qualification period relating to those shares, control the issuing company.

(2) For this purpose the question whether the investing company controls the issuing company shall be determined in accordance with section 416(2) to (6) of the Taxes Act 1988 with the following modifications.

(3) The first modification is that, in determining whether the investing company controls the issuing company, there shall be disregarded—

    (a) its or any other person's possession of, or entitlement to acquire, relevant preference shares of the issuing company; and

    (b) its or any other person's possession of, or entitlement to acquire, rights as a loan creditor of the issuing company.

(4) For the purposes of sub-paragraph (3) a person is a "loan creditor" of a company if the person is a creditor in respect of the loan capital of that company (within the meaning of paragraph 7(3)).

(5) The second modification is that in determining whether the conditions of section 416(2) of that Act are satisfied there shall be attributed to the investing company (to the extent that it would not otherwise be the case) any rights or powers in the issuing company, or any of its subsidiaries, that are held by—

(*a*) any person connected with the investing company; or

(*b*) any person who is—

(i) a director of the investing company, or of any company connected with that company, or

(ii) a relative of such a director.

For this purpose "relative" means husband or wife, parent or remoter forebear or child or remoter issue.

Relevant preference shares

9—(1) In paragraphs 7 (meaning of "material interest") and 8 (the "no control" requirement) "relevant preference shares" means shares which—

(*a*) do not for the time being carry voting rights;

(*b*) are issued wholly for new consideration;

(*c*) do not carry any right either to conversion into shares or securities of any other description or to the acquisition of any additional shares or securities; and

(*d*) do not carry any right to dividends other than dividends which—

(i) fall within sub-paragraph (2) or (3);

(ii) are not to any extent dependent on the results of the company's business or any part of it or on the value of any of the company's assets; and

(iii) together with any sum paid on a redemption, represent no more than a reasonable commercial return on the consideration for which the shares were issued.

In paragraph (*b*) "new consideration" has the meaning given by section 254 of the Taxes Act 1988.

(2) Dividends fall within this sub-paragraph if they are of a fixed amount or at a fixed rate per cent of the nominal value of the shares.

This includes dividends where the amount or rate may be changed to another fixed amount or fixed rate in a manner determined under the terms of issue of the shares.

(3) Dividends fall within this sub-paragraph if they are of a rate per cent of the nominal value of the shares and the rate fluctuates in accordance with—

(*a*) a standard published rate of interest,

(*b*) a rate of tax,

(*c*) the retail prices index, or any similar general index of prices which is published by the government, or by an agent of the government, of the country or territory in whose currency the shares are denominated, or

(*d*) a published index of prices of shares quoted in the official list of a recognised stock exchange.

(4) For the purposes of sub-paragraph (1)(*d*)(ii) dividends shall not be treated as being to any extent dependent on the results of the company's business (or any part of it) or on the value of any of the company's assets by reason only of the fact that the amount or rate of the dividends—

(*a*) reduces in the event of the results of the business (or part) improving or the value of any of the company's assets increasing, or

(*b*) increases in the event of the results of the business (or part) deteriorating or the value of any of the company's assets diminishing.

(5) Dividends are not prevented from falling within sub-paragraph (2) or (3) by the fact that the shares carry no rights at all to dividends for a period or periods determined under the terms of issue of the shares.

The non-financial activities requirement

10—(1) Throughout the qualification period relating to the relevant shares the investing company must fall within sub-paragraph (2) or (3).

(2) The company falls within this sub-paragraph at any time when it—

(*a*) is a single company, and

(*b*) disregarding any incidental purposes, exists wholly for the purpose of carrying on one or more non-financial trades.

(3) The company falls within this sub-paragraph at any time when—

(*a*) it is a group company,

(*b*) the group is a non-financial trading group, and

(*c*) sub-paragraph (4) applies.

(4) This sub-paragraph applies where the company—

(*a*) disregarding any incidental purposes, exists wholly for the purpose of carrying on one or more—

(i) non-financial trades, or

(ii) businesses other than trades; or

(b) is the parent company of the group.

(5) For the purposes of determining whether the company falls within sub-paragraph (2)(b) or (4)(a), the purposes for which the company exists shall be disregarded to the extent that they consist in the carrying on of the following activities—

(a) in the case of a single company, the holding and managing of property used by the company for one or more non-financial trades carried on by it,

(b) in the case of a group company, any activities within paragraph 12(3)(a) or (b), and

(c) in any case, the holding of shares to which investment relief is attributable, unless the holding of such shares amounts to a substantial part of the company's business.

(6) In this paragraph "incidental purposes" means purposes having no significant effect (other than in relation to incidental matters) on the extent of the company's activities.

Meaning of "non-financial trade"

11—(1) A trade is a "non-financial trade" if—

(a) it is conducted on a commercial basis and with a view to the realisation of profits, and

(b) it does not consist wholly or as to a substantial part in the carrying on of financial activities.

(2) For this purpose "financial activities" includes—

(a) banking, or money-lending, carried on by a bank, building society or other person;

(b) debt-factoring, finance-leasing or hire-purchase financing;

(c) insurance;

(d) dealing in shares, securities, currency, debts or other assets of a financial nature; and

(e) dealing in commodity or financial futures or options.

Meaning of "non-financial trading group"

12—(1) A group is a "non-financial trading group" unless the business of the group consists wholly or as to a substantial part in the carrying on of one or more of the following—

(a) trades other than non-financial trades;

(b) businesses which are not trades.

(2) The business of the group means what would be the business of the group if the activities of the group companies taken together were regarded as one business.

(3) For this purpose activities of a group company shall be disregarded to the extent that they consist in—

(a) the holding of shares in or securities of, or the making of loans to, another group company;

(b) the holding and managing of property used by a group company for the purposes of one or more non-financial trades carried on by a group company; or

(c) the holding of shares to which investment relief is attributable, unless the holding of such shares amounts to a substantial part of the company's business.

Requirement as to shares being a chargeable asset

13—(1) The investing company is not a qualifying investing company in relation to the relevant shares unless the shares are a chargeable asset of the company immediately after they are issued to it.

(2) For this purpose an asset is a chargeable asset of that company at any time if, on a disposal at that time, a gain accruing to the company would be a chargeable gain.

(3) In this paragraph "asset" has the same meaning as in the 1992 Act.

Requirement as to no tax avoidance

14 The relevant shares must be subscribed for by the investing company for commercial reasons, and not as part of a scheme or arrangement the main purpose or one of the main purposes of which is the avoidance of tax.

PART III

THE ISSUING COMPANY

Introduction

15 The issuing company is a qualifying issuing company in relation to the relevant shares if the requirements of this Part are met as to—

(a) unquoted status (see paragraph 16);

(b) independence (see paragraph 17);

(c) individual-owners (see paragraph 18);

(d) partnerships and joint ventures (see paragraph 19);

(e) qualifying subsidiaries (see paragraph 20);

(*f*) gross assets (see paragraph 22); and
(*g*) trading activities (see paragraph 23).

The "unquoted status" requirement

16—(1) The unquoted status requirement is that, at the time the relevant shares are issued, none of the issuing company's shares, debentures or other securities is (and there are no arrangements in existence for any of them to be)—

(*a*) listed on a recognised stock exchange,
(*b*) listed on a designated exchange in a country outside the United Kingdom, or
(*c*) dealt in outside the United Kingdom by such means as may be designated.

This is subject to sub-paragraph (3).

(2) The unquoted status requirement applies whether or not the company is resident in the United Kingdom.

(3) The unquoted status requirement is treated as not met if at the time the relevant shares are issued—

(*a*) arrangements are in existence for the issuing company to become a subsidiary of another company ("the new company") by virtue of an exchange of shares, or shares and securities, in relation to which paragraph 83 (certain exchanges resulting in acquisition of share capital by new company) applies, and
(*b*) arrangements have been made with a view to any of the new company's shares, debentures or other securities being listed or dealt in as mentioned in paragraph (*a*), (*b*) or (*c*) of sub-paragraph (1).

(4) For the purposes of sub-paragraph (1) "designated" means designated by an order ("a designation order") made for the purposes of subsection (1B) of section 312 of the Taxes Act 1988 (definition of "unquoted company" for the purposes of EIS).

(5) Where the issuing company meets the unquoted status requirement when the relevant shares are issued, it shall not cease to meet it by virtue of—

(*a*) any designation order, or
(*b*) any order under section 841 of the Taxes Act 1988 (designation of exchange as "recognised stock exchange"),

made after that time.

The independence requirement

17—(1) The independence requirement is that—

(*a*) the issuing company is not, at any time during the qualification period relating to the relevant shares—

(i) a 51% subsidiary of another company, or
(ii) under the control of another company (or of another company and any other person connected with that other company), without being a 51% subsidiary of that other company, and

(*b*) no arrangements are in existence at any time during that period by virtue of which the company could become such a subsidiary or fall under such control (whether during that period or otherwise).

(2) For the purposes of sub-paragraph (1)(*b*) arrangements with a view to such an exchange of shares, or shares and securities, as is mentioned in paragraph 83(1) (certain exchanges resulting in acquisition of share capital by new company) shall be disregarded.

(3) In this paragraph "control" has the meaning given by section 840 of the Taxes Act 1988.

The "individual-owners" requirement

18—(1) The "individual-owners" requirement is that, throughout the qualification period relating to the relevant shares, at least 20% of the ordinary share capital of the issuing company is beneficially owned by one or more independent individuals.

(2) For the purposes of sub-paragraph (1) "independent individual" means an individual who is not, at any time during that period when he holds ordinary shares in the issuing company—

(*a*) a director or employee of—

(i) the investing company, or
(ii) any company connected with that company, or

(*b*) a relative of such a director or employee.

For this purpose "relative" means husband or wife, parent or remoter forebear or child or remoter issue.

(3) Where part of the ordinary share capital of the issuing company forms part of the estate of a deceased person who immediately before his death—

(a) was the beneficial owner of the shares in question, and

(b) was an independent individual for the purposes of sub-paragraph (1),

the shares in question shall, by virtue of this sub-paragraph, continue to be treated as beneficially owned by an independent individual for the purposes of sub-paragraph (1) until such time as they cease to form part of the deceased's estate.

The partnerships and joint ventures requirement

19—(1) The requirement as to partnerships and joint ventures is that neither the issuing company nor any of its qualifying subsidiaries is at any time during the qualification period relating to the relevant shares—

(a) a member of a partnership falling within sub-paragraph (2), or

(b) a party to a joint venture falling within sub-paragraph (3).

(2) A partnership of which the issuing company, or any of its qualifying subsidiaries, is a member falls within this paragraph at any time when—

(a) the relevant trade is being carried on, or to be carried on, by the partners in partnership,

(b) the other partners include at least one other company, and

(c) the same person (or persons) are the beneficial owner (or owners) of more than 75% of the issued share capital or the ordinary share capital of both—

(i) the issuing company, and

(ii) at least one of the other partners.

(3) A joint venture to which the issuing company, or any of its qualifying subsidiaries, is a party falls within this paragraph at any time when—

(a) the relevant trade is being carried on, or to be carried on, by that party in its capacity as a party to the joint venture,

(b) the other parties include at least one other company, and

(c) the same person (or persons) are the beneficial owner (or owners) of more than 75% of the issued share capital or the ordinary share capital of both—

(i) the issuing company, and

(ii) at least one of the other parties.

(4) For the purposes of sub-paragraphs (2) and (3)—

(a) "the relevant trade" means any trade by reference to which the trading activities requirement is met in respect of the issuing company in relation to the relevant shares; and

(b) there shall be attributed to any person any issued share capital or ordinary share capital held by any other person who is an associate of his.

The qualifying subsidiaries requirement

20—(1) The issuing company is not a qualifying issuing company in relation to the relevant shares if, at any time during the qualification period relating to those shares, it has a subsidiary which is not a qualifying subsidiary.

(2) For this purpose—

(a) "subsidiary" means any company which the company controls, either on its own or together with any person connected with it; and

(b) the question whether a person controls a company shall be determined in accordance with section 416(2) to (6) of the Taxes Act 1988.

Meaning of "qualifying subsidiary"

21—(1) A company ("the subsidiary") is a qualifying subsidiary of another company ("the relevant company") if the following conditions are met.

(2) The conditions are that—

(a) the relevant company or another of its subsidiaries possesses not less than 75% of the issued share capital of, and not less than 75% of the voting power in, the subsidiary;

(b) the relevant company or another of its subsidiaries would—

(i) in the event of a winding up of the subsidiary; or

(ii) in any other circumstances,

be beneficially entitled to receive not less than 75% of the assets of the subsidiary which would then be available for distribution to the shareholders of the subsidiary;

(c) the relevant company or another of its subsidiaries is beneficially entitled to not less than 75% of any profits of the subsidiary which are available for distribution to the shareholders of the subsidiary;

(d) no person other than the relevant company or another of its subsidiaries has control of the subsidiary within the meaning of section 840 of the Taxes Act 1988; and

(e) no arrangements are in existence by virtue of which the conditions in paragraphs (a) to (d) would cease to be met.

(3) The subsidiary shall not be regarded as ceasing to be a company in relation to which the conditions in sub-paragraph (2) are met by reason only of—

(a) anything done as a consequence of the subsidiary, or any other company, being in administration or receivership, or

(b) the subsidiary, or any other company, being wound up or dissolved without winding up,

if sub-paragraph (4) applies.

(4) This paragraph applies where—

(a) in a case within sub-paragraph (3)(a)—

(i) the making of the order within paragraph (a) or, as the case may be, (b) of paragraph 102(4) (administration orders and orders for appointment of receiver etc), and

(ii) everything done as a consequence of the company being in administration or receivership, or

(b) in a case within sub-paragraph (3)(b), the winding up or dissolution,

is for commercial reasons and is not part of a scheme or arrangement the main purpose or one of the main purposes of which is the avoidance of tax.

(5) The subsidiary shall not be regarded, at any time when arrangements are in existence for the disposal by the relevant company or (as the case may be) by another subsidiary of that company of all its interest in the subsidiary in question, as having ceased on that account to be a qualifying subsidiary if the disposal is to be for commercial reasons and not part of a scheme or arrangement the main purpose of which, or one of the main purposes of which, is the avoidance of tax.

The gross assets requirement

22—(1) The gross assets requirement in the case of a single company is that the value of the company's gross assets—

(a) does not exceed £15 million immediately before the issue of the relevant shares, and

(b) does not exceed £16 million immediately afterwards.

(2) The gross assets requirement in the case of a parent company is that the consolidated value of the group assets—

(a) does not exceed £15 million immediately before the issue of the relevant shares, and

(b) does not exceed £16 million immediately afterwards.

(3) The consolidated value of the group assets means the aggregate value of the gross assets of the group, disregarding any that consist in rights against, or shares in or securities of, another group company.

Statement of Practice SP 2/00—Corporate venturing scheme—value of "gross assets".

The trading activities requirement

23—(1) The issuing company is not a qualifying issuing company in relation to the relevant shares unless it meets the trading activities requirement throughout the qualification period relating to those shares.

(2) The trading activities requirement in the case of a single company is that the company—

(a) disregarding any incidental purposes, exists wholly for the purpose of carrying on one or more qualifying trades, and

(b) is carrying on a qualifying trade or preparing to do so.

(3) The trading activities requirement in the case of a parent company is that—

(a) the business of the group does not consist wholly or as to a substantial part in the carrying on of non-qualifying activities, and

(b) at least one group company—

(i) disregarding any incidental purposes, exists wholly for the purpose of carrying on one or more qualifying trades, and

(ii) is carrying on a qualifying trade or preparing to do so.

(4) For this purpose the business of the group means what would be the business of the group if the activities of the group companies taken together were regarded as one business.

(5) The requirement of sub-paragraph (2) or (3) is not met at any time by reason of the issuing company or a subsidiary preparing to carry on a qualifying trade if the company or subsidiary does not begin to carry on the trade within two years after the issue of the relevant shares.

(6) For the purposes of determining whether the company falls within sub-paragraph (2)(a) or (3)(b)(i), the purposes for which it exists shall be disregarded to the extent that they consist in the carrying on of the following activities—

(a) in the case of a single company, the holding and managing of property used by the company for one or more qualifying trades carried on by it,

(b) in the case of a group company, any activities within sub-paragraph (7)(a), (b) or (d), and

(c) in any case, the holding of shares to which investment relief is attributable, unless the holding of such shares amounts to a substantial part of the company's business.

(7) For the purposes of determining the business of a group, activities of a group company shall be disregarded to the extent that they consist in—

(a) the holding of shares in or securities of, or the making of loans to, another group company;

(b) the holding and managing of property used by a group company for the purposes of one or more qualifying trades carried on by a group company;

(c) the holding of shares to which investment relief is attributable, unless the holding of such shares amounts to a substantial part of the company's business, or

(d) incidental activities of a company which meets the trading activities requirement for a single company.

(8) In sub-paragraph (3)(a) "non-qualifying activities" means—

(a) excluded activities other than—

(i) the letting of ships to which paragraph 28 applies (ships other than oil rigs or pleasure craft) in circumstances where the requirement of sub-paragraph (2) of that paragraph is met; or

(ii) the receiving of royalties or licence fees within paragraph 29 in circumstances where the requirements mentioned in sub-paragraph (2) of that paragraph are met; and

(b) activities carried on otherwise than in the course of a trade.

(9) In this paragraph—

(a) "incidental purposes" means purposes having no significant effect (other than in relation to incidental matters) on the extent of the activities of the company in question;

(b) "incidental activities" means activities carried on in pursuance of incidental purposes.

Ceasing to meet trading activities requirement by reason of administration, receivership, etc

24—(1) A company which is in administration or receivership shall not be regarded as ceasing to meet the trading activities requirement by reason of anything done as a consequence of the company, or any of its qualifying subsidiaries, being in administration or receivership.

This sub-paragraph has effect subject to sub-paragraphs (2) and (3).

(2) Sub-paragraph (1) applies only if—

(a) the making of the order within paragraph (a) or, as the case may be, (b) of paragraph 102(4) (administration orders and orders for appointment of receiver etc), and

(b) everything done as a consequence of the company being in administration or receivership,

is for commercial reasons and is not part of a scheme or arrangement the main purpose or one of the main purposes of which is the avoidance of tax.

(3) A company ceases to meet the trading activities requirement if—

(a) a resolution is passed, or an order is made, for the winding up of the company or any of its qualifying subsidiaries (or, in the case of a winding up otherwise than under the Insolvency Act 1986 or the Insolvency (Northern Ireland) Order 1989, any other act is done for the like purpose), or

(b) the company, or any of its qualifying subsidiaries, is dissolved without winding up.

This is subject to sub-paragraph (4).

(4) A company shall not be regarded as ceasing to meet the trading activities requirement if—

(a) it does so by reason of the company or any of its subsidiaries being wound up or dissolved without winding up, and

(b) the winding up or dissolution is for commercial reasons and not part of a scheme or arrangement the main purpose or one of the main purposes of which is the avoidance of tax.

Meaning of "qualifying trade"

25—(1) A trade is a qualifying trade if—

(a) it is carried on wholly or mainly in the United Kingdom,

(b) it is conducted on a commercial basis and with a view to the realisation of profits, and

(c) it does not consist wholly or as to a substantial part in the carrying on of excluded activities.

(2) The carrying on of activities of research and development from which it is intended that a connected qualifying trade will be derived or benefit is treated as the carrying on of a qualifying trade.

But preparing to carry on such activities does not count as preparing to carry on a qualifying trade.

(3) For the purposes of sub-paragraph (2) a "connected qualifying trade" means a qualifying trade carried on—

(a) by the company carrying on the activities of research and development, or

(b) if that company is a member of a group, by any other group company.

Excluded activities

26—(1) The following are excluded activities—

    (*a*) dealing in land, in commodities or futures or in shares, securities or other financial instruments;

    (*b*) dealing in goods otherwise than in the course of an ordinary trade of wholesale or retail distribution;

    (*c*) banking, insurance, money-lending, debt-factoring, hire-purchase financing or other financial activities;

    (*d*) leasing (including letting ships on charter or other assets on hire) or receiving royalties or other licence fees;

    (*e*) providing legal or accountancy services;

    (*f*) property development;

    (*g*) farming or market gardening;

    (*h*) holding, managing or occupying woodlands, any other forestry activities or timber production;

    (*i*) operating or managing hotels or comparable establishments or managing property used as a hotel or comparable establishment; and

    (*j*) operating or managing nursing homes or residential care homes, or managing property used as a nursing home or residential care home.

(2) Sub-paragraph (1) is supplemented by the following provisions—

    paragraph 27 (wholesale and retail distribution);

    paragraph 28 (leasing of ships);

    paragraph 29 (receipt of royalties and licence fees);

    paragraph 30 (property development);

    paragraph 31 (hotels and comparable establishments);

    paragraph 32 (nursing homes and residential care homes); and

    paragraph 33 (provision of facilities for another business).

Note—This paragraph was prospectively amended by the Regulation of Care (Scotland) Act 2001 ss 79, 81(2), Sch 3 para 24. However, the Scotland Act 1998 (Regulation of Care (Scotland) Act 2001) Order, SI 2001/2478 repeals the Regulation of Care (Scotland) Act 2001 Sch 3 para 24. The effect of this repeal is that the prospective amendments will not now be brought into force.

Excluded activities: wholesale and retail distribution

27—(1) This paragraph supplements paragraph 26(1)(*b*).

(2) A trade of wholesale distribution is one in which the goods are offered for sale and sold to persons for resale by them, or for processing and resale by them, to members of the general public for their use or consumption.

(3) A trade of retail distribution is one in which the goods are offered for sale and sold to members of the general public for their use or consumption.

(4) A trade is not an ordinary trade of wholesale or retail distribution if—

    (*a*) it consists, to a substantial extent, in dealing in goods of a kind which are collected or held as an investment, or in that activity and any other excluded activity taken together, and

    (*b*) a substantial proportion of those goods are held by the company for a period which is significantly longer than the period for which a vendor would reasonably be expected to hold them while endeavouring to dispose of them at their market value.

(5) In determining whether a trade carried on by any person is an ordinary trade of wholesale or retail distribution, regard shall be had to the extent to which it has the following features—

    (*a*) the goods are bought by that person in quantities larger than those in which he sells them;

    (*b*) the goods are bought and sold by that person in different markets;

    (*c*) that person employs staff and incurs expenses in the trade in addition to the cost of the goods and, in the case of a trade carried on by a company, to any remuneration paid to any person connected with it;

    (*d*) there are purchases or sales from or to persons who are connected with that person;

    (*e*) purchases are matched with forward sales or vice versa;

    (*f*) the goods are held by that person for longer than is normal for goods of the kind in question;

    (*g*) the trade is carried on otherwise than at a place or places commonly used for wholesale or retail trade;

    (*h*) that person does not take physical possession of the goods.

(6) The features specified in sub-paragraph (5)(*a*) to (*c*) are indications that the trade is such an ordinary trade.

Those in sub-paragraph (5)(*d*) to (*h*) are indications of the contrary.

Excluded activities: leasing of ships

28—(1) This paragraph supplements paragraph 26(1)(*d*) so far as it relates to the leasing of ships other than oil rigs or pleasure craft.

(2) A trade shall not be treated as not being a qualifying trade by reason only of its consisting in letting such ships on charter if the following requirements are met—

(*a*) every ship let on charter by the company carrying on the trade is beneficially owned by the company;

(*b*) every ship beneficially owned by the company is registered in the United Kingdom;

(*c*) the company is solely responsible for arranging the marketing of the services of its ships; and

(*d*) the conditions mentioned in sub-paragraph (3) are satisfied in relation to every letting of a ship on charter by the company.

(3) The conditions are that—

(*a*) the letting is for a period not exceeding 12 months and no provision is made at any time (whether in the charterparty or otherwise) for extending it beyond that period otherwise than at the option of the charterer;

(*b*) during the period of the letting there is no provision in force (whether by virtue of being contained in the charterparty or otherwise) for the grant of a new letting to end, otherwise than at the option of the charterer, more than 12 months after that provision is made;

(*c*) the letting is by way of a bargain made at arm's length between the company and a person who is not connected with it;

(*d*) under the terms of the charter the company is responsible as principal—

    (i) for taking, throughout the period of the charter, management decisions in relation to the ship, other than those of a kind generally regarded by persons engaged in trade of the kind in question as matters of husbandry; and

    (ii) for defraying all expenses in connection with the ship throughout that period, or substantially all such expenses, other than those directly incidental to a particular voyage or to the employment of the ship during that period;

and

(*e*) no arrangements exist by virtue of which a person other than the company may be appointed to be responsible for the matters mentioned in paragraph (*d*) on behalf of the company.

(4) In relation to any letting between one company and another where—

(*a*) one of those companies is the company carrying on the trade and the other is a qualifying subsidiary of that company, or

(*b*) both companies are qualifying subsidiaries of the company carrying on the trade,

sub-paragraph (3) has effect with the omission of paragraph (*c*).

(5) Where any of the requirements in sub-paragraph (2) are not met in relation to any lettings, the trade shall not thereby be treated as not a qualifying trade if those lettings and any other excluded activities do not, taken together, amount to a substantial part of the trade.

(6) In this paragraph—

"oil rig" means any ship which is an offshore installation for the purposes of the Mineral Workings (Offshore Installations) Act 1971; and

"pleasure craft" means any ship of a kind primarily used for sport or recreation.

Excluded activities: receipt of royalties and licence fees

29—(1) This paragraph supplements paragraph 26(1)(*d*) so far as it relates to the receipt of royalties and licence fees.

(2) A trade shall not be regarded as not being a qualifying trade by reason only that at some time in the qualification period relating to the relevant shares it consists to a substantial extent in the receiving of royalties or licence fees if the royalties and licence fees (or all but for a part that is not a substantial part in terms of value) are attributable to the exploitation of relevant intangible assets.

(3) For this purpose an intangible asset is a "relevant intangible asset" if the whole or greater part (in terms of value) of it has been created—

(*a*) by the company carrying on the trade, or

(*b*) by a company which at all times during which it created the asset was—

    (i) the parent company of the company carrying on the trade, or

    (ii) a qualifying subsidiary of that parent company.

(4) In this paragraph "intangible asset" means any asset which falls to be treated as an intangible asset in accordance with [generally accepted accounting practice][1].

...[2]

(5) In the case of a relevant asset that is intellectual property, references in this paragraph to the creation of the asset by a company are to its creation in circumstances in which the right to exploit it vests in the company (whether alone or jointly with others).

(6) In sub-paragraph (5) "intellectual property" means—

(*a*) any patent, trade mark, registered design, copyright, design right, performer's right or plant breeder's right; and

(*b*) any rights under the law of a country or territory outside the United Kingdom which correspond or are similar to those falling within paragraph (*a*).

Amendments—[1] Words substituted for the words "normal accounting practice" by FA 2002 s 103(4)(*f*) with effect 24 July 2002.

[2] The following words repealed by FA 2002 s 141, Sch 40 Pt 3(16) with effect from 24 July 2002—

"For this purpose "normal accounting practice" means normal accounting practice in relation to the accounts of companies incorporated in any part of the United Kingdom.".

Excluded activities: property development

30—(1) This paragraph supplements paragraph 26(1)(*f*).

(2) "Property development" means the development of land—

(*a*) by a company which has, or at any time has had, an interest in the land, and

(*b*) with the sole or main object of realising a gain from the disposal of an interest in the land when it is developed.

(3) For this purpose "interest in land" means, subject to sub-paragraph (4)—

(*a*) any estate, interest or right in or over land, including any right affecting the use or disposition of land, or

(*b*) any right to obtain such an estate, interest or right from another which is conditional on the other's ability to grant it.

(4) References in this paragraph to an interest in land do not include—

(*a*) the interest of a creditor (other than a creditor in respect of a rentcharge) whose debt is secured by way of mortgage, an agreement for a mortgage or a charge of any kind over land, or

(*b*) in the case of land in Scotland, the interest of a creditor in a charge or security of any kind over land.

Excluded activities: hotels and comparable establishments

31—(1) This paragraph supplements paragraph 26(1)(*i*).

(2) The reference to a comparable establishment is to a guest house, hostel or other establishment the main purpose of maintaining which is the provision of facilities for overnight accommodation (with or without catering services).

(3) The activities of a person shall not be taken to fall within paragraph 26(1)(*i*) unless that person has an estate or interest in, or is in occupation of, the hotel or comparable establishment in question.

Excluded activities: nursing homes and residential care homes

32—(1) This paragraph supplements paragraph 26(1)(*j*).

(2) "Nursing home" means an establishment that exists wholly or mainly for the provision of nursing care—

(*a*) for persons suffering from sickness, injury or infirmity, or

(*b*) for women who are pregnant or have given birth to children.

(3) "Residential care home" means an establishment that exists wholly or mainly for the provision of residential accommodation, together with board and personal care, for persons in need of personal care by reason of—

(*a*) old age,

(*b*) mental or physical disability,

(*c*) past or present dependence on alcohol or drugs,

(*d*) any past illness, or

(*e*) past or present mental disorder.

(4) The activities of a person shall not be taken to fall within paragraph 26(1)(*j*) unless that person has an estate or interest in, or is in occupation of, the nursing home or residential care home in question.

Note—This paragraph was prospectively amended by the Regulation of Care (Scotland) Act 2001 ss 79, 81(2), Sch 3 para 24. However, the Scotland Act 1998 (Regulation of Care (Scotland) Act 2001) Order, SI 2001/2478 repeals the Regulation of Care (Scotland) Act 2001 Sch 3 para 24. The effect of this repeal is that the prospective amendments will not now be brought into force.

Excluded activities: provision of facilities for another business

33—(1) Providing services or facilities for a business carried on by another person is an excluded activity if—

(*a*) the business consists to a substantial extent of excluded activities within sub-paragraph 26(1), and

(*b*) a controlling interest in the business is held by a person who also has a controlling interest in the business carried on by the company providing the services or facilities.

(2) Sub-paragraphs (3) to (5) define what is meant by a controlling interest in a business for the purposes of sub-paragraph (1)(*b*).

(3) In the case of a business carried on by a company, a person has a controlling interest if—

(*a*) he controls the company,

(*b*) the company is a close company and he or an associate of his, being a director of the company, either—

(i) is the beneficial owner of more than 30% of the ordinary share capital of the company, or

(ii) is able, directly or through the medium of other companies or by any other indirect means, to control more than 30% of that share capital,

or

(c) not less than half of the business could, in accordance with section 344(2) of the Taxes Act 1988, be regarded as belonging to him for the purposes of section 343 of that Act.

(4) In any other case, a person has a controlling interest in a business if he is entitled to not less than half of the assets used for, or of the income arising from, the business.

(5) For the purposes of sub-paragraph (3)(a) the question whether a person controls a company shall be determined in accordance with section 416(2) to (6) of the Taxes Act 1988.

(6) For the purposes of this paragraph—

(a) there shall be attributed to any person any rights or powers of any other person who is an associate of his, and

(b) "business" includes any trade, profession or vocation.

PART IV
GENERAL REQUIREMENTS
Introduction

34 The investing company is not eligible for investment relief in respect of the amount subscribed by it for the relevant shares unless the requirements of this Part are met as to—

(a) the shares (see paragraph 35);

(b) the money raised (see paragraph 36);

(c) no pre-arranged exits (see paragraph 37); and

(d) no tax avoidance (see paragraph 38).

Requirement as to the shares

35—(1) The relevant shares must satisfy sub-paragraphs (2) and (3).

(2) Shares satisfy this sub-paragraph if they are—

(a) ordinary shares,

(b) subscribed for wholly in cash, and

(c) fully paid up at the time they are issued.

Shares are not fully paid up for the purposes of paragraph (c) if there is any undertaking to pay cash to the issuing company at a future date.

(3) Shares satisfy this sub-paragraph if they do not, at any time during the qualification period relating to the relevant shares, carry—

(a) any present or future preferential right to dividends or to a company's assets on its winding up, or

(b) any present or future right to be redeemed.

Requirement as to the money raised

36—[(1) At least 80% of the money raised by the issuance of the relevant issue of shares must have been employed wholly for the purposes of a relevant trade not later than the time determined in accordance with sub-paragraph (1B).]¹

[(1A) All of the money so raised must have been so employed not later than 12 months after that time.]¹

[(1B) The time referred to in sub-paragraph (1) is—

(a) the end of the period of 12 months beginning with the issue of the shares, or

(b) where the relevant trade was not being carried on at the time the shares were issued, the end of the period of 12 months beginning when the issuing company or a subsidiary begins to carry on the relevant trade.]¹

[(1C) Sub-paragraphs (1) and (1A) are subject to sub-paragraph (5).]¹

(2) For the purposes of this paragraph—

"the relevant issue of shares" means the issue of shares in the issuing company which includes the relevant shares;

"relevant trade" means a trade by reference to which the issuing company meets the trading activities requirement.

(3) In this paragraph references to employing money for the purposes of a trade (except where the carrying on of the trade is within paragraph 25(2)) include references to employing it for the purpose of preparing to carry on the trade.

(4) In sub-paragraph (2) the reference to a trade by reference to which the trading activities requirement is met includes, where the carrying on of that trade is within paragraph 25(2), a reference to any qualifying trade—

(*a*) which is derived or benefits from that trade, and

(*b*) which is carried on—

  (i) by the issuing company, or

  (ii) if that company is a parent company, by that company or a qualifying subsidiary of that company.

(5) Where—

(*a*) [any of the money raised by the issuance of the relevant issue of shares][1] is employed for the purposes of a trade that is a relevant trade by virtue of sub-paragraph (4), and

(*b*) that trade was not being carried on by the issuing company, or a qualifying subsidiary of that company, at the time the shares were issued,

[the requirement of sub-paragraph (1) does not apply and the requirement of sub-paragraph (1A)][1] is not met unless that money is so employed before the third anniversary of the issue date.

(6) For the purposes of this paragraph money is not treated as employed otherwise than wholly for the purposes of a trade if the only amount employed for other purposes is an amount which is not a significant amount.

Amendments—[1] Sub-paras (1)–(1C) substituted for sub-para (1); in sub-para 5, words substituted for the words "any of the money mentioned in sub-paragraph (1)", and the words "the requirement of sub-paragraph (1) does not apply and the requirement of sub-paragraph (1A)" substituted for "the requirement of sub-paragraph (1)" by FA 2001 s 64, Sch 16 paras 4, 5 with effect—

(*a*) in relation to shares issued after 6 March 2001, and

(b) in respect of the application of this Schedule (corporate venturing scheme) after 6 March 2001 in relation to shares—

  (i) that were issued after 31 March 2000 but before 7 March 2001, and

  (ii) to which investment relief (within the meaning of this Schedule) was attributable immediately before 7 March 2001.

Previously, sub-para 1 read as follows—

"(1) The money raised by the issuance of the relevant issue of shares must have been employed wholly for the purposes of a relevant trade not later than—

(*a*) the end of the period of 12 months beginning with the issue of the shares, or

(*b*) where the relevant trade was not being carried on at the time the shares were issued the end of the period of 12 months beginning when the issuing company or a subsidiary begins to carry on the relevant trade.

This is subject to sub-paragraph (5).".

Requirement as to no pre-arranged exits

37—(1) The issuing arrangements for the relevant shares must not include—

(*a*) arrangements with a view to the subsequent repurchase, exchange or other disposal of those shares or of other shares in or securities of the issuing company;

(*b*) arrangements for or with a view to the cessation of any trade which is being or is to be or may be carried on by the issuing company or a person connected with that company;

(*c*) arrangements for the disposal of, or of a substantial amount (in terms of value) of, the assets of the issuing company or of a person connected with that company; or

(*d*) arrangements the main purpose of which, or one of the main purposes of which, is (by means of any insurance, indemnity or guarantee or otherwise) to provide partial or complete protection for persons investing in shares in the issuing company against what would otherwise be the risks attached to making the investment.

(2) For the purposes of this paragraph "the issuing arrangements" means—

(*a*) the arrangements under which the relevant shares are issued to the investing company,

(*b*) any arrangements made, before the issue of the relevant shares to that company, in relation to or in connection with that issue, and

(*c*) if before the relevant shares were issued information on pre-arranged exits was made available to any prospective subscribers for shares in the relevant issue, any arrangements made—

  (i) on or after the issue of the shares, but

  (ii) before the end of the qualification period relating to them.

(3) For the purposes of sub-paragraph (2)—

(*a*) "information on pre-arranged exits" means any information indicating the possibility of making, on or after the issue of the relevant shares but before the end of the qualification period relating to them, arrangements of the kind described in paragraph (*a*), (*b*), (*c*) or (*d*) of sub-paragraph (1), and

(*b*) "the relevant issue" means the issue of shares in the issuing company which includes the relevant shares.

(4) The arrangements referred to in sub-paragraph (1)(*a*) do not include any arrangements with a view to such an exchange of shares, or shares and securities, as is mentioned in paragraph 83(1) (certain exchanges resulting in acquisition of share capital by new company).

(5) The arrangements referred to in sub-paragraph (1)(*b*) and (*c*) do not include any arrangements applicable only on the winding up of the issuing company except in a case where—

(*a*) the issuing arrangements include arrangements for the issuing company to be wound up, or

(*b*) the issuing company is wound up otherwise than for commercial reasons.

(6) The arrangements referred to in sub-paragraph (1)(*d*) do not include any arrangements which are confined to the provision—

(a) for the issuing company itself, or

(b) where the issuing company is the parent company of a group, for any group company,

of any such protection against the risks arising in the course of carrying on its business as might reasonably be expected to be provided for normal commercial reasons.

Requirement as to no tax avoidance

38 The relevant shares must be issued for commercial reasons, and not as part of a scheme or arrangement the main purpose or one of the main purposes of which is the avoidance of tax.

PART V

INVESTMENT RELIEF

Form of investment relief

39—(1) Where—

(a) the investing company is eligible for investment relief in respect of an amount subscribed by it for an issue of shares, and

(b) it makes a claim under this Part,

the company's liability for corporation tax for the accounting period in which the shares were issued shall be reduced by the appropriate amount.

(2) In sub-paragraph (1) "the appropriate amount" means whichever is the smaller of—

(a) 20% of the amount or aggregate amount—

(i) which was subscribed by the company for shares issued in that period, and

(ii) in respect of which the company is eligible for and claims investment relief, and

(b) the amount which reduces the liability to nil.

Entitlement to claim

40—(1) The investing company is entitled to make a claim to investment relief in respect of the amount subscribed by it for the relevant shares if it appears to it that the requirements for the relief are for the time being met.

This is subject to sub-paragraph (2).

(2) The investing company is not entitled to make a claim to investment relief in relation to the amount subscribed by it for the relevant shares unless—

(a) the funded trade has been carried on by the issuing company or a subsidiary of the company for four months (disregarding any time spent preparing to carry on that trade), and

(b) the investing company has received from the issuing company a compliance certificate in respect of those shares.

(3) For the purposes of this paragraph, "the funded trade" means the trade or trades by reference to which the requirement of paragraph 36 (use of money raised) is met in respect of the relevant issue of shares (as defined by sub-paragraph (2) of that paragraph).

This is subject to sub-paragraph (4).

(4) To the extent that the funded trade would, by virtue of sub-paragraph (3), be a trade derived or benefiting from a trade within paragraph 25(2), the funded trade shall be deemed, for the purposes of this paragraph, to be the trade within that paragraph.

(5) Where—

(a) the company or subsidiary concerned, by reason of its being wound up, or dissolved without winding up, carries on the funded trade for a period shorter than four months, and

(b) the winding up or dissolution was for commercial reasons and was not part of a scheme or arrangement the main purpose or one of the main purposes of which was the avoidance of tax,

sub-paragraph (2)(a) shall have effect as if it referred to that shorter period.

(6) Where—

(a) the company or subsidiary concerned, by reason of anything done as a consequence of its being in administration or receivership, carries on the funded trade for a period shorter than four months, and

(b) the making of the order within paragraph (a) or, as the case may be, (b) of paragraph 102(4) (administration orders and orders for appointment of receiver etc), and everything done as a consequence of the company being in administration or receivership, is for commercial reasons and is not part of a scheme or arrangement the main purpose or one of the main purposes of which is the avoidance of tax,

sub-paragraph (2)(a) shall have effect as if it referred to that shorter period.

(7) No application shall be made under section 55(3) or (4) of the Taxes Management Act 1970 (application for postponement of payment of tax pending appeal) on the ground that the investing

company is eligible for investment relief unless a claim for the relief has been duly made by that company.

Compliance certificates

41—(1) A "compliance certificate" is a certificate which—

(a) is issued by the issuing company in respect of the relevant shares,

(b) states that, except so far as they fall to be met by or in relation to the investing company, the requirements for investment relief are for the time being met in relation to those shares, and

(c) is in such form as the Inland Revenue may direct.

(2) Before issuing a compliance certificate in respect of the relevant shares, the issuing company must provide the Inland Revenue with a compliance statement in respect of the issue of shares which includes the relevant shares.

(3) The issuing company must not issue a compliance certificate without the authority of the Inland Revenue.

(4) Where the company or a person connected with the company has given notice to the Inland Revenue under paragraph 65 (information to be provided by issuing company etc) the authority of the Inland Revenue must be given or renewed after the receipt of the notice.

Compliance statements

42—(1) A "compliance statement" is a statement, in respect of an issue of shares, to the effect that, except so far as they fall to be satisfied by or in relation to companies to which the shares included in that issue have been issued, the requirements for investment relief—

(a) are for the time being met in relation to the shares to which the statement relates, and

(b) have been so met at all times since the shares were issued.

In determining for the purposes of this sub-paragraph whether those requirements are met at any time in relation to the issue of shares, references in this Schedule to "the relevant shares" shall be read as references to the shares included in the issue.

(2) A compliance statement must be in such form as the Inland Revenue direct and must contain—

(a) such additional information as the Inland Revenue reasonably require,

(b) a declaration that the statement is correct to the best of the issuing company's knowledge and belief, and

(c) such other declarations as the Inland Revenue reasonably require.

(3) Without prejudice to the generality of sub-paragraph (2)(a) the information required by the Inland Revenue may include—

(a) information relating to the companies to which compliance certificates may be issued under paragraph 41 in respect of any shares included in the issue of shares to which the statement relates, and

(b) information to enable the Inland Revenue to determine whether the requirements of paragraph 35(2)(b) and (c) (shares to be subscribed for wholly in cash and fully paid up) are met in relation to shares included in that issue subscribed for by such companies.

(4) The issuing company may not provide the Inland Revenue with a compliance statement in respect of any shares issued by it in any accounting period—

(a) before the condition in paragraph 40(2)(a) (no claim until trade carried on for four months) is satisfied; or

(b) later than two years after the end of that accounting period or, if that condition is first satisfied after the end of that accounting period, later than two years after the condition is first satisfied.

Appeal against refusal to authorise compliance certificate

43 For the purposes of the provisions of the Taxes Management Act 1970 relating to appeals, the refusal of the Inland Revenue to authorise the issue of a compliance certificate shall be taken to be a decision disallowing a claim by the issuing company which is not a claim for discharge or repayment of tax.

Penalties for fraudulent certificate or statement etc

44 The issuing company is liable to a penalty not exceeding £3,000 if—

(a) it issues a compliance certificate, or provides a compliance statement, which is made fraudulently or negligently, or

(b) it issues a compliance certificate in contravention of paragraph 41(3) or (4) (no certificate to be issued without Inland Revenue approval).

Attribution of relief to shares

45—(1) References in this Schedule, in relation to a company, to the investment relief attributable to any shares or issue of shares shall be read as references to any reduction made in the company's liability to corporation tax that is attributed to those shares or that issue in accordance with this paragraph.

This is subject to the provisions of Part VI of this Schedule providing for the reduction or withdrawal of investment relief.

(2) Where a company's liability to corporation tax is reduced for an accounting period under paragraph 39 (form of investment relief), then—

    (*a*) where the reduction is obtained by reason of one issue of shares, the amount of the reduction shall be attributed to that issue, and

    (*b*) where the reduction is obtained by reason of two or more issues of shares, the reduction—

        (i) shall be apportioned between those issues in the same proportions as the amounts subscribed by the company for each issue, and

        (ii) shall be attributed to those issues accordingly.

(3) Where under this paragraph an amount of any reduction of corporation tax is attributed to an issue of shares ("the original issue") to a company a proportionate part of that amount shall be attributed to each share comprised in the original issue.

(4) If corresponding bonus shares are issued to the company in respect of any shares ("the original shares") comprised in the original issue that have been continuously held by the company from the time they were issued until the issue of the bonus shares—

    (*a*) a proportionate part of the total amount attributed to the original shares immediately before the bonus shares are issued shall be attributed to each of the shares in the holding comprising the original shares and the bonus shares, and

    (*b*) after the issue of the bonus shares, this Schedule shall apply as if—

        (i) the original issue had included the bonus shares, and

        (ii) the bonus shares had been held by the company continuously from the time the original shares were issued until the bonus shares were issued.

(5) In sub-paragraph (4) "corresponding bonus shares" means bonus shares which are in the same company, of the same class, and carry the same rights as the original shares.

(6) If investment relief attributable to any shares falls to be withdrawn under Part VI of this Schedule the relief attributable to each of the shares shall be reduced to nil.

(7) If investment relief attributable to any shares falls to be reduced under Part VI of this Schedule by any amount the relief attributable to each of the shares shall be reduced by a proportionate part of that amount.

PART VI
WITHDRAWAL OF INVESTMENT RELIEF

Revenue Internal Guidance—Company Taxation Manual CT 4885 (circumstances in which investment relief can be withdrawn or reduced).

Disposal of shares

46—(1) This paragraph applies where—

    (*a*) the investing company disposes of any of the relevant shares which have been held by it continuously from the time they were issued until the disposal,

    (*b*) the disposal takes place during the qualification period relating to the relevant shares, and

    (*c*) investment relief is attributable to the shares.

(2) If the disposal is not—

    (*a*) by way of a bargain made at arm's length for full consideration,

    (*b*) by way of a distribution in the course of dissolving or winding up the issuing company,

    (*c*) a disposal within section 24(1) of the 1992 Act (entire loss, destruction, dissipation or extinction of asset), or

    (*d*) a deemed disposal under section 24(2) of that Act (claim that value of asset has become negligible),

the investment relief attributable to those shares must be withdrawn.

(3) If the disposal is within paragraph (*a*), (*b*), (*c*) or (*d*) of sub-paragraph (2) the investment relief attributable to those shares must—

    (*a*) if it is greater than an amount equal to 20% of the amount or value of the consideration (if any) which the company receives for the shares, be reduced by that amount, and

    (*b*) in any other case, be withdrawn.

(4) Where—

    (*a*) the amount of the reduction ("A") in the investing company's liability to corporation tax obtained under paragraph 39 (form of investment relief) in respect of the relevant shares, is less than (*b*) the amount (''B'') which is equal to 20% of the amount subscribed by the investing company for those shares,

sub-paragraph (3)(*a*) shall have effect in relation to a disposal of any of those shares as if the amount or value referred to in that sub-paragraph were reduced by multiplying it by the fraction—

$$\frac{A}{B}$$

(5) Where the amount of investment relief attributable to any of the relevant shares has been reduced before the investment relief was obtained, the amount of the corporation tax reduction obtained in respect of those shares shall be deemed for the purposes of sub-paragraph (4) to be the amount of the corporation tax reduction that would have been obtained had no such reduction of relief been made before the relief was obtained.

(6) Sub-paragraph (5) does not apply to a reduction by virtue of paragraph 45(4) (attribution of investment relief where there is a corresponding issue of bonus shares).

Revenue Internal Guidance—Company Taxation Manual CT 4887, 4888 (application of this para).

Value received by investing company

47—(1) Sub-paragraph (2) applies where the investing company receives any value (other than insignificant value) from the issuing company during the period of restriction relating to the relevant shares.

(2) Any investment relief attributable to the shares shall—

(*a*) if it exceeds the amount mentioned in sub-paragraph (3), be reduced by that amount, and
(*b*) in any other case, be withdrawn.

(3) The amount referred to in sub-paragraph (2)(*a*) is an amount equal to 20% of the amount of the value received.

(4) This paragraph is subject to the following paragraphs—

paragraph 51 (value received where there is more than one issue of shares);
paragraph 52 (cases where maximum investment relief not obtained); and
paragraph 54 (receipt of replacement value).

(5) Where—

(*a*) value is received (''the relevant receipt'') by the investing company from the issuing company at any time during the period of restriction relating to the relevant shares,
(*b*) the investing company has received from the issuing company one or more receipts of insignificant value at a time or times—

(i) during that period, but
(ii) not later than the time of the relevant receipt, and

(*c*) the aggregate amount of the value of the receipts within paragraph (*a*) and (*b*) is not an amount of insignificant value,

the investing company shall be treated for the purposes of this Part as if the relevant receipt had been a receipt of an amount of value equal to that aggregate amount.

For this purpose a receipt does not fall within paragraph (*b*) if it has been previously aggregated under this sub-paragraph.

(6) If, at any time in the period—

(*a*) beginning one year before the relevant shares are issued, and
(*b*) expiring at the end of the issue date,

arrangements are in existence which provide for the investing company to receive, or to be entitled to receive, any value from the issuing company at any time in the period of restriction relating to those shares, no amount of value received by the investing company shall be treated as a receipt of insignificant value for the purposes of this paragraph.

(7) For the purposes of this paragraph—

(*a*) references to a receipt of insignificant value (however expressed) are references to a receipt of an amount of insignificant value;
(*b*) ''an amount of insignificant value'' means an amount of value which—

(i) does not exceed £1,000, or
(ii) if it exceeds that amount, is insignificant in relation to the amount subscribed by the investing company for the shares.

This is subject to sub-paragraph (6).

(8) Where by reason of the investing company's disposal of any shares any investment relief attributable to those shares is withdrawn or reduced, the investing company shall not be treated for the purposes of this paragraph as receiving value from the issuing company in respect of the disposal.

(9) Value received shall be disregarded, for the purposes of this paragraph, to the extent to which investment relief attributable to any shares has already been reduced or withdrawn on its account.

Revenue Internal Guidance—Company Taxation Manual CT 4897 (Revenue interpretation of what constitutes insignificant value).

Meaning of "the period of restriction"

48 For the purposes of this Schedule "the period of restriction" relating to the relevant shares means the period—

   (*a*) beginning one year before the shares are issued, and

   (*b*) ending at the end of the qualification period relating to the shares.

When value is received

49—(1) For the purposes of paragraphs 47 (value received by investing company) and 51 (value received where there is more than one issue of shares) the investing company receives value from the issuing company at any time when the issuing company—

   (*a*) repays, redeems or repurchases any of its share capital or securities which belong to the investing company or makes any payment to that company for giving up its right to any of the issuing company's share capital or any security on its cancellation or extinguishment;

   (*b*) repays, in pursuance of any arrangements for or in connection with the acquisition of the relevant shares, any debt owed to the investing company other than a debt which was incurred by the issuing company—

      (i) on or after the date of issue of those shares; and

      (ii) otherwise than in consideration of the extinguishment of a debt incurred before that date;

   (*c*) makes to the investing company any payment for giving up the company's right to any debt on its extinguishment;

   (*d*) releases or waives any liability of the investing company to the issuing company or discharges, or undertakes to discharge, any liability of the investing company to a third person;

   (*e*) makes a loan or advance to the investing company which has not been repaid in full before the issue of the relevant shares;

   (*f*) provides a benefit or facility for the directors or employees of the investing company or any of their associates;

   (*g*) disposes of an asset to the investing company for no consideration or for a consideration which is or the value of which is less than the market value of the asset;

   (*h*) acquires an asset from the investing company for a consideration which is or the value of which is more than the market value of the asset; or

   (*i*) makes a payment to the investing company other than a qualifying payment.

(2) For the purposes of sub-paragraph (1)(*e*) there shall be treated as if it were a loan made by the issuing company to the investing company—

   (*a*) the amount of any debt (other than an ordinary trade debt) incurred by the investing company to the issuing company, and

   (*b*) the amount of any debt due from the investing company to a third person which has been assigned to the issuing company.

(3) For the purposes of sub-paragraph (1)(*d*) the issuing company shall be treated as having released or waived a liability if the liability is not discharged within 12 months of the time when it ought to have been discharged.

(4) For the purposes of this paragraph—

   (*a*) references to a debt or liability do not, in relation to a person, include references to any debt or liability which would be discharged by the making by that person of a qualifying payment;

   (*b*) references to a benefit or facility do not include references to any benefit or facility provided in circumstances such that, if a payment had been made of an amount equal to its value, that payment would be a qualifying payment; and

   (*c*) any reference to a payment or disposal to a person includes a reference to a payment or disposal made to that person indirectly or to his order or for his benefit.

In paragraphs (*a*) to (*c*) references to "a person" include references to any person who, at any time in the period of restriction in question, is connected with that person, whether or not he is so connected at the material time.

(5) In this paragraph—

   "ordinary trade debt" means any debt for goods or services supplied in the ordinary course of a trade or business where any credit given—

      (*a*) does not exceed six months, and

      (*b*) is not longer than that normally given to customers of the person carrying on the trade or business; and

   "qualifying payment" means—

      (*a*) any payment by any person for any goods, services or facilities provided by the investing company (in the course of its trade or otherwise) which is reasonable in relation to the market value of those goods, services or facilities;

(*b*) the payment by any person of any interest which represents no more than a reasonable commercial return on money lent to that person;

(*c*) the payment by any company of any dividend or other distribution which does not exceed a normal return on any investment in shares in or other securities of that company;

(*d*) any payment for the acquisition of an asset which does not exceed its market value;

(*e*) the payment by any person, as rent for any property occupied by the person, of an amount not exceeding a reasonable and commercial rent for the property; and

(*f*) a payment in discharge of an ordinary trade debt.

The amount of value received

Revenue Internal Guidance—Company Taxation Manual CT 4894, 4895 (receipt of value: outline of the circumstances in which value may be received by an investing company from an issuing company and how that value is quantified).

50 For the purposes of paragraph 47 the amount of the value received is—

(*a*) in a case within paragraph 49(1)(*a*), (*b*) or (*c*)—

   (i) the amount received by the investing company, or

   (ii) the market value of the shares, securities or debt in question,

whichever is greater;

(*b*) in a case within paragraph 49(1)(*d*), the amount of the liability;

(*c*) in a case within paragraph 49(1)(*e*)—

   (i) the amount of the loan or advance, less

   (ii) the amount of any repayment made before the issue of the relevant shares;

(*d*) in a case within paragraph 49(1)(*f*)—

   (i) the cost to the issuing company of providing the benefit or facility, less

   (ii) any consideration given for it by the recipient or any associate of his;

(*e*) in a case within paragraph 49(1)(*g*) or (*h*), the difference between the market value of the asset and the consideration (if any) received for it; and

(*f*) in a case within paragraph 49(1)(*i*), the amount of the payment.

Value received where there is more than one issue of shares

Revenue Internal Guidance—Company Taxation Manual CT 4894, 4895 (receipt of value: outline of the circumstances in which value may be received by an investing company from an issuing company and how that value is quantified).

51—(1) This paragraph applies where—

(*a*) two or more issues of shares in the issuing company have been made to the investing company (being issues in relation to which the investing company is eligible for and claims investment relief), and

(*b*) the value received falls within the periods of restriction relating to two or more of those issues.

(2) Where this paragraph applies paragraph 47 has effect in relation to the shares comprised in each of the issues referred to in sub-paragraph (1)(*b*) as if the amount of the value received were reduced by multiplying it by the fraction—

$$\frac{A}{B}$$

Where—

A is the amount subscribed by the investing company for the shares comprised in the issue in question to which investment relief is (or, but for paragraph 47 would be) attributable; and

B is the aggregate of that amount and the corresponding amount or amounts for the other issue or issues.

Cases where maximum investment relief not obtained

52—(1) Where—

(*a*) the amount of the reduction ("C") in the investing company's liability to corporation tax obtained in respect of the relevant shares, is less than

(*b*) the amount ("D") which is equal to 20% of the amount subscribed by the investing company for those shares,

paragraph 47 has effect as if the amount of the value received were reduced by multiplying it by the fraction—

$$\frac{C}{D}$$

(2) Where the amount of investment relief attributable to any of the relevant shares has been reduced before the investment relief was obtained, the amount of the corporation tax reduction obtained in respect of those shares shall be deemed for the purposes of sub-paragraph (1) to be the amount of the

corporation tax reduction that would have been obtained had no such reduction of relief been made before the relief was obtained.

(3) Sub-paragraph (2) does not apply to a reduction of investment relief by virtue of paragraph 45(4) (attribution of investment relief where there is a corresponding issue of bonus shares).

Receipts of value by and from connected persons

53 In paragraphs 47, 49 and 50 references to the investing company or the issuing company include references to any person who at any time in the period of restriction relating to the relevant shares is connected with the company concerned, whether or not he is connected at the material time.

Receipt of replacement value

54—(1) Where—

(a) any investment relief attributable to the relevant shares would, in the absence of this paragraph, be reduced or withdrawn under paragraph 47 by reason of a receipt of value within paragraph 49(1) (''the original value''),
(b) the original supplier receives value (''the replacement value'') from the original recipient by reason of a qualifying receipt, and
(c) [the amount of]¹ the replacement value is not less than the amount of the original value,

paragraph 47 shall not, by reason of the receipt of the original value, have effect to reduce or withdraw the investment relief.

(2) For the purposes of this paragraph and paragraph 55—

''the original recipient'' means the person who receives the original value; and
''the original supplier'' means the person from whom that value was received.

[(2A) Where the amount of the original value is, by virtue of paragraph 51, treated as reduced for the purposes of paragraph 47, the reference in sub-paragraph (1)(c) to the amount of the original value shall be read as a reference to the amount of that value disregarding the reduction.]²

(3) A receipt of the replacement value is a qualifying receipt for the purposes of sub-paragraph (1) if it arises—

[(a) by reason of the original recipient doing one or more of the following—

(i) making a payment to the original supplier other than an excepted payment;
(ii) acquiring any asset from the original supplier for a consideration the amount or value of which is more than the market value of the asset;
(iii) disposing of any asset to the original supplier for no consideration or for a consideration the amount or value of which is less than the market value of the asset; or]²

[(b) where the receipt of the original value was within paragraph 49(1)(d), by reason of an event the effect of which is to reverse the event which constituted the receipt of the original value.]²

[(3A) For the purposes of sub-paragraph (3)(a)(i), the following are excepted payments—

(a) any payment for any goods, services or facilities, provided (whether in the course of a trade or otherwise) by—

(i) the original supplier, or
(ii) any other person who, at any time in the period of restriction relating to the relevant shares, is an associate of, or connected with, that supplier (whether or not he is such an associate, or so connected, at the material time),

which is reasonable in relation to the market value of those goods, services or facilities;
(b) any payment of any interest which represents no more than a reasonable commercial return on money lent to—

(i) the original recipient, or
(ii) any other person who, at any time in the period of restriction relating to the relevant shares, is an associate of, or connected with, that recipient (whether or not he is such an associate, or so connected, at the material time);
(c) any payment, as rent for any property occupied by—

(i) that recipient, or
(ii) any person who, at any time in the period of restriction relating to the relevant shares, is an associate of, or connected with, that recipient (whether or not he is such an associate, or so connected, at the material time),

of an amount not exceeding a reasonable and commercial rent for the property;
(d) any payment within paragraph (c), (d) or (f) of the definition of ''qualifying payment'' in paragraph 49(5); and
(e) any payment for shares in or securities of any company in circumstances that do not fall within sub-paragraph (3)(a)(ii).]²

[(4) For the purposes of this paragraph, the amount of the replacement value is—

(a) in a case within paragraph (a) of sub-paragraph (3), the aggregate of—

(i) the amount of any payment within sub-paragraph (i) of that paragraph, and

(ii) the difference between the market value of any asset to which sub-paragraph (ii) or (iii) of that paragraph applies and the amount or value of the consideration (if any) received for it, and

(b) in a case within sub-paragraph (3)(*b*), the amount of the original value,

and paragraph 50 shall apply for the purposes of determining the amount of the original value.]²

Revenue Internal Guidance—Company Taxation Manual CT 4898 (application of this para).
Amendments—¹ Words in sub-para 1(*c*) inserted by FA 2001 s 64, Sch 16 paras 4, 6(1) and deemed always to have had effect.
² Sub-para 2A inserted, sub-paras 3(*a*), (*b*) substituted for original sub-para 3(*a*)–(*c*), sub-para 3A inserted, and sub-para 4 substituted by FA 2001 s 64, Sch 16 paras 4, 6 with effect—

  (*a*) in relation to shares issued after 6 March 2001, and
  (*b*) in relation to shares issued after 31 March 2000 but before 7 March 2001, in respect of value received (within the meaning of FA 2000 Sch 15 para 49) after 6 March 2001.
Previously, sub-paras 3(*a*)–(*c*) read—

  (a) by reason of the original recipient making a payment to the original supplier other than—
    (i) a qualifying payment (within the meaning of paragraph 49(5)), or
    (ii) a payment for shares in or securities of any company in circumstances that do not fall within paragraph (*c*) below;
  (b) where the receipt of the original value was within paragraph 49(1)(*d*), by reason of an event the effect of which is to reverse the event which constituted the receipt of the original value; or
  (c) where the receipt of the original value was within paragraph 49(1)(g) or (h), by reason of—
    (i) the original recipient acquiring any asset from the original supplier for a consideration which is or the value of which is more than the market value of the asset, or
    (ii) the original recipient disposing of any asset to the original supplier for no consideration or for a consideration which is, or the value of which is, less than the market value of the asset.''.
Previously, sub-para 4 read—

  ''(4) For the purposes of this paragraph—
    (*a*) paragraph 50 shall apply for the purposes of determining the amount of the original value; and
    (*b*) the amount of the replacement value is—
     (i) in a case within sub-paragraph (3)(*a*), the amount of the payment,
     (ii) in a case within sub-paragraph (3)(*b*), the same as the amount of the original value, and
     (iii) in a case within sub-paragraph (3)(*c*), the difference between the market value of the asset and the consideration (if any) received for it.''.

Provision supplementary to paragraph 54

55—(1) The receipt of the replacement value shall be disregarded for the purposes of sub-paragraph (1) of paragraph 54 to the extent to which it has previously been set (under that paragraph) against a receipt of value to prevent any reduction or withdrawal of investment relief under paragraph 47.

(2) The receipt of the replacement value by the original supplier (''the event'') shall be disregarded for the purposes of paragraph 54(1) if—

(a) the event occurs before the start of the period of restriction relating to the relevant shares,

(b) there was an unreasonable delay in the event occurring, or

(c) where an appeal has been brought by the investing company against an assessment to withdraw or reduce any investment relief attributable to the relevant shares by reason of the receipt of the original value, the event occurs more than 60 days after the amount of relief which falls to be withdrawn has been finally determined.

But nothing in paragraph 54 or this paragraph requires the replacement value to be received after the original value.

(3) Sub-paragraph (4) applies where—

(a) the receipt of the replacement value is a qualifying receipt for the purposes of paragraph 54(1) (receipt of replacement value which prevents loss of investment relief), and

(b) the event which gives rise to the receipt is (or includes) a subscription for shares by—

(i) the investing company, or

(ii) any person who at any time in the period of restriction relating to the relevant shares is connected with the investing company, whether or not he is connected at the material time.

(4) Where this sub-paragraph applies the person who subscribes for the shares shall not—

(a) be eligible for—

(i) any investment relief, or

(ii) any relief under Chapter III of Part VII of the Taxes Act 1988 (EIS income tax relief),

in relation to those shares or any other shares in the same issue; or

(b) by virtue of his subscription for those shares or any other shares in the same issue, be treated as making a qualifying investment for the purposes of Schedule 5B to the 1992 Act (EIS: deferral relief).

[(5) In this paragraph ''the original value'' and ''the replacement value'' shall be construed in accordance with paragraph 54.]¹

Amendments—¹ Sub-para 5 inserted by FA 2001 s 64, Sch 16 para 7, and deemed always to have had effect.

Value received by other persons

56—(1) Where any investment relief is attributable to such of the relevant shares as are held by the investing company, sub-paragraph (2) shall apply if at any time in the period of restriction relating to the relevant shares the issuing company or any subsidiary—

    (*a*) repays, redeems or repurchases any of its share capital which belongs to any member other than—

        (i) the investing company, or

        (ii) a person who falls within sub-paragraph (3), or

    (*b*) makes any payment to any such member for giving up his right to any of the share capital of the company or subsidiary on its cancellation or extinguishment.

(2) The investment relief—

    (*a*) if it is greater than the amount mentioned in sub-paragraph (4), shall be reduced by that amount, and

    (*b*) in any other case, must be withdrawn.

(3) A person falls within this sub-paragraph if the repayment, redemption, repurchase or payment in question—

    (*a*) causes any investment relief attributable to that person's shares in the issuing company to be withdrawn or reduced by virtue of—

        (i) paragraph 46 (disposal of shares), or

        (ii) paragraph 49(1)(*a*) (receipt of value by virtue of repayment of share capital etc);

    (*b*) causes any relief under Chapter III of Part VII of the Taxes Act 1988 (EIS income tax relief) attributable to that person's shares in the issuing company to be withdrawn or reduced by virtue of—

        (i) section 299 of that Act (disposal of shares), or

        (ii) section 300(2)(*a*) of that Act (receipt of value by virtue of repayment of share capital etc);

or

    (*c*) gives rise to a qualifying chargeable event (within the meaning of paragraph 14(4) of Schedule 5B to the 1992 Act (EIS: deferral relief)) in respect of that person[,

or it would have the effect mentioned in paragraph (*a*), (*b*) or (*c*) were it not a receipt of insignificant value for the purposes of paragraph 47 (value received by the investing company), section 300 of the Taxes Act 1988 or paragraph 13 of Schedule 5B to the 1992 Act, as the case may be.][1]

(4) The amount referred to in sub-paragraph (2) is an amount equal to 20%—

    (*a*) where sub-paragraph (1) does not apply in the case of any other company holding shares in the issuing company, of the amount received by the member, and

    (*b*) where sub-paragraph (1) also applies in the case of one or more such other companies, of the appropriate fraction of that amount.

(5) For the purposes of sub-paragraph (4) "the appropriate fraction" is—

$$\frac{A}{B}$$

Where—

A is the amount subscribed by the investing company for such of the relevant shares as are shares to which investment relief is or, but for sub-paragraph (2)(*b*), would be attributable, and

B is the aggregate of that amount and the amount or amounts subscribed by the other company or companies for such shares which are comprised in the same issue of shares.

(6) Where—

    (*a*) the amount of the reduction ("C") in the investing company's liability to corporation tax obtained under paragraph 39 (form of investment relief) in respect of the relevant shares, is less than

    (*b*) the amount ("D") which is equal to 20% of the amount subscribed by the investing company for those shares,

sub-paragraph (4) has effect as if the amount received by the member, or (as the case may be) the appropriate fraction of that amount, were reduced by multiplying it by the fraction—

$$\frac{C}{D}$$

(7) Where the amount of investment relief attributable to the relevant shares has been reduced before the relief was obtained, the amount of the corporation tax reduction obtained in respect of those shares shall be deemed for the purposes of sub-paragraph (6) to be the amount of the corporation tax reduction that would have been obtained had no such reduction of investment relief been made before the relief was obtained.

(8) Sub-paragraph (7) does not apply to a reduction by virtue of paragraph 45(4) (attribution of investment relief where there is a corresponding issue of bonus shares).

Amendments—[1] Words in sub-para (3) inserted by FA 2001 s 64, Sch 16 para 8, with effect—

(*a*) in relation to shares issued after 6 March 2001, and
(*b*) in respect of shares issued after 31 March 2000 but before 7 March 2001, in relation to any repayment (within the meaning of FA 2000 Sch 15 para 57(2)) made after 6 March 2001.

Insignificant repayments disregarded

57—(1) Any repayment shall be disregarded for the purposes of paragraph 56(1) (repayments etc which cause withdrawal of investment relief) if whichever is the greater of—

(*a*) the market value of the shares to which it relates ("the target shares") immediately before the event occurs, and

(*b*) the amount received by the member in question,

is insignificant in relation to the market value of the remaining [issued]¹ share capital of the issuing company (or, as the case may be, subsidiary) immediately after the event occurs.

This is subject to sub-paragraph (4).

(2) For the purposes of this paragraph "repayment" means a repayment, redemption, repurchase or payment mentioned in paragraph 56(1) (repayments etc which cause withdrawal of investment relief).

(3) For the purposes of sub-paragraph (1) it shall be assumed that the target shares are cancelled at the time the [repayment]² is made.

(4) Sub-paragraph (1) does not apply if, at a relevant time, arrangements are in existence that provide—

(*a*) for a repayment by the issuing company or any subsidiary of that company (whether or not it is such a subsidiary at the time the arrangements are made), or

(*b*) for anyone to be entitled to such a repayment,

at any time in the period of restriction relating to the shares.

(5) For the purposes of sub-paragraph (4) "a relevant time" means any time in the period—

(*a*) beginning one year before the relevant shares are issued, and

(*b*) expiring at the end of the issue date.

Amendments—¹ Word in sub-para 1 inserted by FA 2001 s 64, Sch 16 para 9(1), (3), with effect—
(*a*) in relation to shares issued after 6 March 2001, and
(*b*) in respect of shares issued after 31 March 2000, but before 7 March 2001, in relation to repayments (within the meaning of FA 2000 Sch 15 para 57(2)) made after 6 March 2001.
² The word "repayment" substituted for the word "payment" by FA 2001 s 64, Sch 16 para 9(2), (4), and deemed always to have had effect.

Provision supplementary to paragraph 56 and 57

58—(1) Any repayment shall be disregarded for the purposes of paragraph 56(1) (repayments etc which cause withdrawal of investment relief) to the extent to which investment relief attributable to any shares has already been reduced or withdrawn on its account.

(2) In any case where—

(*a*) investment relief is attributable to such of the relevant shares as are held by the investing company;

(*b*) the issuing company has made one or more other issues of shares each of which includes shares ("designated shares") to which investment relief is attributable, and

(*c*) the repayment falls—

(i) within the period of restriction relating to the relevant shares, and

(ii) within one or more of the equivalent periods relating to any of the designated shares,

paragraph 56(4) shall have effect in relation to each of the issues of shares as if the amount received by the member, or (as the case may be) the appropriate fraction of that amount, were reduced by multiplying it by the relevant fraction.

(3) For the purposes of sub-paragraph (2) "the equivalent period", in relation to any designated shares, means the period—

(*a*) beginning one year before the shares are issued, and

(*b*) ending at the end of the qualification period relating to the shares.

For the purposes of determining the qualification period relating to any designated shares, the references in paragraph 3 to the relevant shares shall be read as references to those designated shares.

(4) In sub-paragraph (2)—

(*a*) "the appropriate fraction" has the meaning given by paragraph 56(5), and

(*b*) "the relevant fraction" means—

$$\frac{E}{F}$$

Where—

E is the amount subscribed by companies for shares which are included in the issue in question and to which investment relief is or, but for paragraph 56(2)(*b*), would be attributable; and

F is the aggregate of that amount and the corresponding amount or amounts for the other issue or issues.

(5) Where—

> (a) a company issues share capital of nominal value equal to the authorised minimum (within the meaning of the Companies Act 1985) for the purposes of complying with the requirements of section 117 of that Act (public company not to do business unless requirements as to share capital complied with), and
>
> (b) the registrar of companies issues the company with a certificate under section 117,

paragraph 56(1) shall not apply in relation to any redemption of those shares within 12 months of the date on which they were issued.

(6) In relation to companies incorporated under the law of Northern Ireland references in sub-paragraph (5) to the Companies Act 1985 and to section 117 of that Act shall have effect as references to the Companies (Northern Ireland) Order 1986 and to Article 127 of that Order.

(7) References in paragraphs 56 and 57 and this paragraph to a subsidiary of the issuing company are references to any company which at any time in the period of restriction relating to the relevant shares is a 51% subsidiary of the issuing company whether or not it is such a subsidiary at the time of the repayment in question.

(8) For the purposes of this paragraph "repayment" has the meaning given in paragraph 57(2).

Put options and call options

59—(1) Sub-paragraph (2) applies where—

> (a) an option, the exercise of which would bind the grantor to purchase any of the relevant shares, is granted to the investing company during the qualification period relating to those shares; or
>
> (b) an option, the exercise of which would bind the investing company to sell such shares, is granted by the investing company during that period.

(2) Any investment relief attributable to the shares to which the option relates must be withdrawn.

(3) The shares to which the option relates are those which, if—

> (a) the option were exercised immediately after the grant, and
>
> (b) any shares in the issuing company acquired by the investing company after the grant were disposed of immediately after being acquired,

would be treated for the purposes of this Schedule as disposed of in pursuance of the option.

(4) Nothing in this paragraph prejudices the operation of paragraph 37 (pre-arranged exits).

Revenue Internal Guidance—Company Taxation Manual CT 4890 (treatment of shares held by the investing company where some are subject to an option and some are not).

Withdrawal of relief

60—(1) Where any investment relief has been obtained which—

> (a) is subsequently found not to have been due, or
>
> (b) falls to be withdrawn under this Part,

it shall be withdrawn by making an assessment to corporation tax under Case VI of Schedule D for the accounting period for which the relief was obtained.

(2) Investment relief obtained by the investing company in respect of the relevant shares may not be withdrawn on the ground—

> (a) that the issuing company is not a qualifying issuing company in relation to those shares,
>
> (b) that the requirements of Part IV of this Schedule are not met in respect of the shares,
>
> (c) by virtue of paragraph 47 (value received by investing company), or
>
> (d) by virtue of paragraph 56 (value received by other persons),

unless sub-paragraph (3) is satisfied.

(3) This sub-paragraph is satisfied if—

> (a) either—
>
>> (i) the issuing company has given notice under paragraph 65 (information to be provided by issuing company etc) in relation to those shares, or
>>
>> (ii) the Inland Revenue have given notice to that company stating that, by reason of the ground in question, the whole or any part of the investment relief obtained by any company or companies in respect of shares included in the relevant issue of shares was not in their opinion due,
>
> and
>
> (b) in the case of a withdrawal within sub-paragraph (2)(c) or (d), the Inland Revenue have given notice to the investing company stating the matters mentioned in paragraph (a)(ii) above.

(4) In this paragraph—

> (a) references to the withdrawal of investment relief include its reduction; and

(b) ''the relevant issue of shares'' means the issue of shares in the issuing company which includes the relevant shares.

Appeals against withdrawal of relief

61 For the purposes of the provisions of the Taxes Management Act 1970 relating to appeals, the giving of notice by the Inland Revenue under paragraph 60(3)(a)(ii) shall be taken to be a decision disallowing a claim by the issuing company which is not a claim for discharge or repayment of tax.

Time limits

62—(1) The Inland Revenue may not—

(a) make an assessment for withdrawing or reducing the investment relief attributable to any of the relevant shares, or

(b) give a notice under paragraph 60(3)(a)(ii) or (b),

more than six years after the end of the relevant accounting period.

(2) In sub-paragraph (1) ''the relevant accounting period'' means—

(a) the accounting period in which the time mentioned in paragraph 36(1) (time limit for employing money raised) falls, or

(b) the accounting period in which the event which causes the investment relief to be withdrawn or reduced occurs,

whichever is later.

(3) This paragraph is subject to sub-paragraphs (2) and (3) of paragraph 46 of Schedule 18 to the Finance Act 1998 (fraud or negligence).

Those sub-paragraphs shall apply in relation to any notice under paragraph 60(3)(a)(ii) or (b) as if it were an assessment relating to the accounting period to which any assessment made by virtue of the notice would relate.

Interest

63—(1) This paragraph applies where—

(a) investment relief is withdrawn or reduced by virtue of—

(i) a failure to meet any of the requirements of paragraphs 5 to 10 or of Part III of this Schedule (requirements to be met in relation to investing company or issuing company);

(ii) paragraph 46 (disposal of shares);

(iii) paragraph 47 (value received by investing company);

(iv) paragraph 56 (value received by other persons); or

(v) paragraph 59 (put options and call options);

(b) as a result, an assessment to corporation tax is made by virtue of paragraph 60; and

(c) the relevant event occurs after the date when the tax assessed became due and payable or, if there is more than one such date, the latest of them.

(2) Section 87A of the Taxes Management Act 1970 (interest on overdue corporation tax etc) has effect in relation to the tax assessed as if it became due and payable on the date the relevant event occurred.

(3) In this paragraph references to ''the relevant event'' are to the event by virtue of which the relief is withdrawn or reduced as mentioned in sub-paragraph (1)(a).

Information to be provided by the investing company

64—(1) This paragraph applies where—

(a) the investing company has obtained investment relief in respect of the relevant shares, and

(b) an event occurs by reason of which—

(i) the company is not a qualifying investing company in relation to those shares,

(ii) the investment relief falls to be withdrawn or reduced by virtue of paragraph 47 (receipt of value by investing company), or

(iii) the investment relief falls to be withdrawn or reduced by virtue of paragraph 59 (put options and call options).

(2) Where this paragraph applies the investing company must give the Inland Revenue a notice containing particulars of the event.

(3) Where the investing company—

(a) is required under this paragraph to give notice of a receipt of value (within paragraph 49(1)), and

(b) has knowledge of any replacement value received (or expected to be received) from the original recipient by the original supplier by reason of a qualifying receipt,

the notice shall include particulars of that receipt of replacement value (or expected receipt).

In this paragraph "replacement value", "original recipient", "original supplier" and "qualifying receipt" shall be construed in accordance with paragraph 54.

(4) Subject to sub-paragraph (5), any notice required to be given by the company under sub-paragraph (2) must be given—

(*a*) within 60 days after the event, or

(*b*) where the event is the receipt of value by a person connected with the company (see paragraph 53), within 60 days after the company's coming to know of the event.

(5) In a case within sub-paragraph (1)(*b*)(ii), where the event occurred before the issue of the relevant shares, any notice required to be given by the investing company under sub-paragraph (2) must be given—

(*a*) within 60 days after the issue of the shares, or

(*b*) where—

(i) the event is the receipt of value by a person connected with the company (see paragraph 53), and

(ii) the company comes to know of the event on or after the issue of the shares,

within 60 days after the company's coming to know of the event.

Information to be provided by the issuing company etc

65—(1) This paragraph applies where—

(*a*) the issuing company has provided the Inland Revenue with a compliance statement in respect of an issue of shares, and

(*b*) an event occurs by reason of which—

(i) the issuing company is not a qualifying issuing company in relation to any of the shares included in that issue, or would not be such a company if investment relief had been obtained in respect of the shares in question,

(ii) the requirements of Part IV of this Schedule are not met in respect of any of the shares included in that issue, or would not be met if investment relief had been obtained in respect of the shares in question, or

(iii) paragraph 47 (value received by investing company) or 56 (value received by other persons) has effect to cause any investment relief attributable to any of the shares included in that issue to be withdrawn or reduced, or would have such an effect if investment relief had been obtained in respect of the shares in question.

(2) Where this paragraph applies—

(*a*) the company, and

(*b*) any person connected with the company who has knowledge of the matters mentioned in sub-paragraph (1),

must give the Inland Revenue a notice containing particulars of the event.

(3) Sub-paragraph (3) of paragraph 64 shall apply in relation to a person required to give notice under this paragraph of a receipt of value within paragraph 49(1) as it applies to a company required to give such a notice under paragraph 64.

(4) Subject to sub-paragraph (6) any notice required to be given by a company under sub-paragraph (2)(*a*) must be given—

(*a*) within 60 days after the event, or

(*b*) where the event is—

(i) a failure by the company to meet the requirement of paragraph 18 (the "individual-owners requirement") in respect of any of those shares; or

(ii) a receipt of value within paragraph 49(1) from a person connected with the company (see paragraph 53),

within 60 days after the company's coming to know of the event.

(5) Subject to sub-paragraph (6) any notice required to be given by a person within sub-paragraph (2)(*b*) must be given within 60 days after the person's coming to know of the event.

(6) In a case within sub-paragraph (1)(*b*)(iii), any notice required to be given by a person under sub-paragraph (2) must be given within 60 days after the issue of the shares if—

(*a*) the event occurred, and

(*b*) the person came to know of it,

before those shares were issued.

Power of Inland Revenue to obtain information

66—(1) This paragraph applies where the Inland Revenue have reason to believe that a company or other person—

(*a*) has not given a notice which it is required to give under paragraph 64 or 65 in respect of any event, or (*b*) has given or received value (within the meaning of paragraph 49(1)) which, but for the fact that the amount given or received was an amount of insignificant value, would have triggered a requirement to give such a notice.

(2) The Inland Revenue may by notice require the person concerned to furnish them, within such time as the Inland Revenue may direct (not being less than 60 days), with such information relating to the event as the Inland Revenue may reasonably require for the purposes of this Schedule.

(3) In sub-paragraph (1)(*b*) the reference to an amount of insignificant value shall be construed in accordance with paragraph 47(7)(*b*).

PART VII
RELIEF FOR LOSSES ON DISPOSALS OF SHARES

Revenue Internal Guidance—Capital Gains Manual CG 63181–63183 (summary of provisions affecting claims for loss relief).

Eligibility for relief against income

67—(1) The investing company is eligible for relief under this Part (''loss relief'') if—

(*a*) it incurs an allowable loss on the disposal of shares to which investment relief is attributable (and not withdrawn in full as a result of the disposal), and
(*b*) the requirements of sub-paragraphs (2) and (3) are met.

(2) The first requirement is that the shares must have been held continuously by the investing company from the time they were issued until the disposal.

(3) The second requirement is that the disposal on which the loss is incurred must be a disposal of the kind described in paragraph (*a*), (*b*), (*c*) or (*d*) of paragraph 46(2).

Entitlement to claim

68—(1) Where the investing company is eligible for loss relief it may make a claim requiring that the loss be set off for the purposes of corporation tax against income—

(*a*) of the accounting period in which the loss is incurred, and
(*b*) if the claim so requires, of accounting periods ending within the preceding 12 month period.

(2) A claim under sub-paragraph (1) must be made within two years after the end of the accounting period in which the loss is incurred.

(3) In this paragraph ''the preceding 12 month period'' means the 12 months ending immediately before the accounting period in which the loss is incurred.

Form of loss relief

69—(1) Where a claim is made under sub-paragraph (1) of paragraph 68, the income of any of the accounting periods mentioned in that sub-paragraph shall then be treated as reduced by the amount of the loss or by so much of it as cannot be relieved under this sub-paragraph against income of a later accounting period.

This is subject to loss relief first being obtained for any earlier loss.

(2) The amount of the reduction which may be made under this paragraph in the income of an accounting period beginning before the preceding 12 month period (within the meaning of paragraph 68(3)) shall not exceed a part of that income proportionate to the part of the accounting period falling within that period.

Priority of loss relief

70—(1) Where loss relief is claimed by the investing company it must be claimed—

(*a*) in priority to any relief claimed by that company under section 573 of the Taxes Act 1988 (relief for loss on disposal of shares in certain trading companies by investment companies), and
(*b*) before any deduction is made for charges on income or other amounts which can be deducted from or set against or treated as reducing profits of any description.

(2) Where loss relief is obtained for an amount of a loss no deduction shall be made in respect of that amount—

(*a*) by virtue of section 573(2) of the Taxes Act 1988 (relief for loss on disposal of shares in certain trading companies by investment companies), or
(*b*) for the purposes of corporation tax on chargeable gains.

Tax avoidance

71—(1) Sub-paragraph (2) applies where shares would, in the absence of paragraph 82 (which disapplies sections 135 and 136 of the 1992 Act in respect of shares to which investment relief is attributable), be the subject of an exchange or arrangement which—

(*a*) is of the kind mentioned in section 135 or 136 of the 1992 Act (company reconstructions etc), and

(*b*) would involve a disposal of shares, by reason of—

   (i) section 137(1) of that Act (schemes with tax avoidance purpose), or
   (ii) paragraph 96(2)(*b*) (company treated as disposing of shares in the case of certain [schemes of reconstruction]¹ involving tax avoidance).

(2) Where this sub-paragraph applies no loss relief may be obtained in respect of any allowable loss incurred on the disposal.

(3) Where a claim is made under this Part in respect of a loss accruing on the disposal of shares, section 30 of the 1992 Act (value-shifting) shall have effect in relation to the disposal as if for the references in subsections (1)(*b*) and (5) of that section to a tax-free benefit there were substituted references to any benefit whether tax-free or not.

Amendments—¹ Words in sub-para (1)(*b*)(ii) substituted for the words "reconstructions and amalgamations" by FA 2002 s 45, Sch 9 paras 6(1), (2), 8(1) with effect for disposals after 16 April 2002.

Adjustment of corporation tax

72 The Inland Revenue shall make any adjustment of corporation tax required as a result of—

(*a*) loss relief being obtained in respect of an allowable loss, or
(*b*) loss relief not being obtained for the whole or part of a loss in respect of which a claim is made under this Part,

whether by way of assessment, discharge or repayment of tax.

PART VIII
DEFERRAL RELIEF

Revenue Internal Guidance—Capital Gains Manual CG 63185–63189 (summary of provisions affecting deferral relief).

Introduction

73—(1) This Part applies where—

(*a*) a chargeable gain ("the original gain") accrues to the investing company at any time ("the accrual time"),
(*b*) the gain is one accruing either—

   (i) on a disposal of shares to which investment relief was attributable immediately before the disposal, or
   (ii) by virtue of paragraph 79 on the occurrence of a chargeable event in relation to shares to which deferral relief is attributable immediately before the event,

and
(*c*) the investing company makes a qualifying investment.

(2) In determining for the purposes of sub-paragraph (1)(*a*) whether or not a chargeable gain accrues at any time paragraph 76 (postponement of original gain) shall be disregarded.

(3) Sub-paragraph (1)(*b*)(i) does not apply to a disposal of shares unless the shares were held by the investing company continuously from the time they were issued until the disposal.

Meaning of "qualifying investment"

74—(1) For the purposes of this Part the investing company makes a qualifying investment if—

(*a*) it subscribes for any shares to which investment relief is attributable,
(*b*) the shares are not issued by a prohibited company,
(*c*) the shares are issued to the investing company at a qualifying time, and
(*d*) where the shares were issued before the accrual time—

   (i) they have been held continuously by the investment company from the time they were issued until that time, and
   (ii) investment relief is attributable to the shares at that time.

(2) For the purposes of sub-paragraph (1)—

"a prohibited company" means—

   (*a*) the company whose shares comprised the original holding, or
   (*b*) a company that was, at the accrual time or the time of the issue of the qualifying shares (or both), a member of the same group as that company; and

"a qualifying time" means any time in the period of four years beginning one year before the accrual time.

(3) For the purposes of the definition of "a prohibited company" in sub-paragraph (2), "the original holding" means—

(*a*) where the original gain accrued as mentioned in sub-paragraph (i) of paragraph 73(1)(*b*), the shares disposed of, and

(*b*) where the original gain accrued as mentioned in sub-paragraph (ii) of paragraph 73(1)(*b*), the shares in relation to which the chargeable event occurred.

Meaning of "the qualifying shares"

75—(1) For the purposes of this Part "the qualifying shares", in relation to a case where this Part applies, means the shares which are acquired by the investing company in making the qualifying investment.

This is subject to sub-paragraphs (2) and (4).

(2) If any corresponding bonus shares are issued to the investing company, this Part shall apply as if references to the qualifying shares were to all the shares comprising the qualifying shares and the bonus shares so issued.

(3) In sub-paragraph (2) "corresponding bonus shares" means bonus shares which—

(*a*) are issued in respect of the qualifying shares, and

(*b*) are in the same company, of the same class and carry the same rights as those shares.

(4) If in circumstances where paragraph 83 (certain exchanges resulting in acquisition of share capital by new company) applies new shares are issued in exchange for old shares, references in this Part to the qualifying shares, so far as they relate to the old shares, shall be construed as references to the new shares.

For this purpose "old shares" and "new shares" have the same meaning as in that paragraph.

Postponement of original gain

76—(1) On the making of a claim by the investing company for the purposes of this Part, so much of the investing company's unused qualifying expenditure on the qualifying shares as—

(*a*) is specified in the claim, and

(*b*) does not exceed so much of the original gain as is unmatched,

shall be set against a corresponding amount of the original gain.

(2) Where an amount of qualifying expenditure on the qualifying shares is set under this paragraph against the whole or part of the original gain, then for the purposes of corporation tax on chargeable gains—

(*a*) so much of that gain as is equal to that amount shall be treated as not having accrued at the accrual time, but

(*b*) paragraph 79 applies for determining the gain that is to be treated as accruing on the occurrence of any chargeable event in relation to any of the qualifying shares.

(3) For the purposes of this Part—

(*a*) the investing company's qualifying expenditure on the qualifying shares is the amount subscribed by it for the shares, and

(*b*) that expenditure is unused to the extent that it has not already been set under this paragraph against the whole or any part of a chargeable gain.

(4) For the purposes of this paragraph the original gain is unmatched in relation to any qualifying expenditure on the qualifying shares to the extent that it has not had any other expenditure set against it under this paragraph.

Meaning of "deferral relief"

77 For the purposes of this Schedule "deferral relief" is attributable to any shares if—

(*a*) expenditure on the shares has been set under paragraph 76 against the whole or part of any gain, and

(*b*) there has been no chargeable event for the purposes of this Part in relation to the shares.

Chargeable events

78—(1) There is, for the purposes of this Part, a chargeable event in relation to any of the qualifying shares if—

(*a*) the investing company disposes of those shares, or

(*b*) any other event occurs by reason of which the investment relief attributable to those shares is reduced or withdrawn otherwise than by virtue of paragraph 46(2) or (3) (withdrawal of investment relief on disposal of shares).

(2) For the purposes of sub-paragraph (1)(*b*), where the qualifying investment is made before the time at which the original gain accrues, any reduction of the investment relief attributable to the qualifying shares that is made by reason of an event that occurs before the accrual time shall be disregarded.

Gain accruing on chargeable event

79—(1) This paragraph applies where a chargeable event occurs in relation to any of the qualifying shares in relation to which there has not been a previous chargeable event.

(2) Where this paragraph applies, then for the purposes of corporation tax on chargeable gains—

(*a*) a chargeable gain shall be treated as accruing to the investing company at the time of the event, and

(*b*) the amount of the gain shall be equal to so much of the deferred gain as is attributable to the shares in relation to which the chargeable event occurs.

(3) In order to determine, for this purpose, the amount of the deferred gain attributable to any shares, a proportionate part of the amount of the gain shall be attributed to each of the qualifying shares held immediately before the occurrence of the chargeable event in question by the investing company.

(4) In this paragraph "the deferred gain" means—

(*a*) the amount of the original gain against which expenditure has been set under paragraph 76, less

(*b*) the amount of any gain treated as accruing under this paragraph previously in consequence of a chargeable event in relation to any of the qualifying shares.

(5) For the purposes of section 10 of the 1992 Act (taxation of chargeable gains accruing to non-resident with UK branch or agency) a chargeable gain treated as accruing by virtue of this paragraph shall be treated as a chargeable gain accruing on the disposal of an asset to which subsection (3) of that section applies.

PART IX

COMPANY RESTRUCTURING

Revenue Internal Guidance—Capital Gains Manual CG 63192–63193 (summary of provisions created by company restructuring).

Share reorganisations

80—(1) Where a company ("the company") holds shares which—

(*a*) form part of the ordinary share capital of another company,

(*b*) are of the same class and held in the same capacity, and

(*c*) include shares falling within two or more of the categories in sub-paragraph (2),

then, where there is a reorganisation affecting those shares to which section 116 or section 127 of the 1992 Act applies, section 116 or (as the case may be) section 127 shall apply separately to shares falling within each of those categories.

(2) The categories referred to in sub-paragraph (1)(*c*) are—

(*a*) shares to which deferral relief is attributable;

(*b*) shares—

(i) to which investment relief but not deferral relief is attributable, and

(ii) which have been held continuously by the company since the time they were issued until the reorganisation; and

(*c*) shares not within paragraph (*a*) or (*b*) above.

(3) In this paragraph "reorganisation" has the meaning given in section 126 of the 1992 Act.

Rights issues etc

81—(1) Where—

(*a*) a company ("the company") holds shares ("the existing holding") which—

(i) form part of the ordinary share capital of another company, and

(ii) are of the same class and held in the same capacity,

(*b*) there is by virtue of such an allotment as is mentioned in section 126(2)(*a*) of the 1992 Act (an allotment of shares or debentures in respect of and in proportion to an original holding), other than an allotment of corresponding bonus shares, a reorganisation affecting the existing holding,

(*c*) immediately following the reorganisation, investment relief is attributable to the shares comprised in the existing holding or the shares allotted in respect of those shares, and

(*d*) if investment relief is attributable to the shares comprised in the existing holding at that time, those shares have been held by the company continuously from the time they were issued until the reorganisation,

sections 127 to 130 of that Act (treatment of share capital following a reorganisation) shall not apply in relation to the existing holding.

(2) Subsection (10) of section 116 of that Act (reorganisations, conversions and reconstructions) shall not apply in any case where the old asset consists of shares held (in the same capacity) by a company—

(*a*) that have been held by it continuously from the time they were issued until the relevant transaction, and

(*b*) to which investment relief is attributable immediately before that transaction.

In this sub-paragraph "old asset" and "the relevant transaction" have the meanings given in section 116 of that Act.

(3) For the purposes of sub-paragraph (1)—

"corresponding bonus shares" means bonus shares that—

(*a*) are issued in respect of shares comprised in the existing holding, and

(*b*) are of the same class, and carry the same rights, as those shares;

"reorganisation" has the meaning given in section 126 of that Act.

Company reconstructions and amalgamations

82—(1) Where—

(*a*) a company ("the company") holds shares ("the existing holding") in a company ("company A"),

(*b*) there is a reconstruction or amalgamation affecting the existing holding,

(*c*) immediately before the reconstruction or amalgamation, investment relief is attributable to the shares comprised in the existing holding, and

(*d*) the shares comprised in the existing holding have been held by the company continuously from the time they were issued until the reconstruction or amalgamation,

sections 135 and 136 of the 1992 Act ([share exchanges and company reconstructions][1]) shall not apply in respect of the existing holding.

This is subject to paragraph 84 (no disposal on certain exchanges of shares).

(2) Sub-paragraph (1)(*a*) applies only where the shares are held by the company in the same capacity.

(3) For the purposes of sub-paragraph (1) a "reconstruction or amalgamation" means an issue by a company ("company B") of shares in or debentures of that company in exchange for or in respect of shares in or debentures of company A.

Amendments—[1] Words in sub-para (1) substituted for the words "company reconstructions and amalgamations" by FA 2002 s 45, Sch 9 paras 6(1), (3), 7 with effect for shares or debentures issued after 16 April 2002. The reference to shares or debentures includes any interests falling to be treated as shares or debentures for the purposes of TCGA 1992 s 135 or 136 as substituted by FA 2002 Sch 9.

Certain exchanges resulting in acquisition of share capital by new company

83—(1) Paragraphs 84 and 85 apply where—

(*a*) arrangements are made in accordance with which a company ("the new company") acquires all the shares ("old shares") in another company ("the old company");

(*b*) the acquisition provided for by the arrangements falls within sub-paragraph (2); and

(*c*) the Inland Revenue have, before any exchange of shares takes place under the arrangements, given an approval notification.

(2) An acquisition of shares falls within this sub-paragraph if—

(*a*) the consideration for the old shares consists wholly of the issue of shares ("new shares") in the new company;

(*b*) new shares are issued in consideration of old shares only at times when there are no issued shares in the new company other than—

(i) subscriber shares, and

(ii) new shares previously issued in consideration of old shares;

(*c*) the consideration for new shares of each description consists wholly of old shares of the corresponding description; and

(*d*) new shares of each description are issued to the holders of old shares of the corresponding description in respect of, and in proportion to, their holdings.

(3) For the purposes of sub-paragraph (1)(*c*) an approval notification is one which, on an application by either the old company or the new company, is given to the applicant company and states that the Inland Revenue are satisfied that the exchange of shares under the arrangements—

(*a*) will be effected for commercial reasons, and

(*b*) will not form part of any such scheme or arrangements as are mentioned in section 137(1) of the 1992 Act (schemes with tax avoidance purpose).

(4) For the purposes of this paragraph old shares and new shares are of a corresponding description if, on the assumption that they were shares in the same company, they would be of the same class and carry the same rights.

(5) In this paragraph references to "shares", except in the expression "subscriber shares", include securities.

(6) References in paragraphs 84 to 87 to "shares", "old shares", "new shares", "the old company" and "the new company" shall be construed in accordance with this paragraph.

No disposal on certain exchanges of shares

84—(1) Where this paragraph applies (see paragraph 83 [and paragraph 4 of Schedule 7AC to the Taxation of Chargeable Gains Act 1992][1]), nothing in paragraph 82 has effect to disapply section 135 of the 1992 Act (exchange of shares etc for those in another company).

Accordingly, by virtue of section 127 of that Act (as applied by section 135(3)), the exchange of shares is not treated as involving a disposal of the old shares or an acquisition of the new shares.

(2) In its application by virtue of sub-paragraph (1), section 127 of the 1992 Act shall have effect subject to paragraph 80 (shares to which investment relief or investment and deferral relief is attributable treated as separate holdings).

Amendments—[1] Words in sub-para (1) inserted by FA 2002 s 44(2), (3), Sch 8 para 5 with effect for disposals after 31 March 2002.

Attribution of relief to new shares

85—(1) Where this paragraph applies (see paragraph 83 [and paragraph 4 of Schedule 7AC to the Taxation of Chargeable Gains Act 1992][1]), any investment relief or deferral relief which is attributable to any old shares shall be attributable instead to the new shares for which they are exchanged.

(2) Where investment relief becomes so attributable to any new shares—

    (a) this Schedule shall have effect as if anything which under paragraph 41, 42, 60 or 65 has been done, or is required to be done, by or in relation to the old company had been done, or were required to be done, by or in relation to the new company; and

    (b) any appeal brought by the old company against—

        (i) the refusal of the Inland Revenue to authorise the issue of a compliance certificate, or

        (ii) a notice under paragraph 60(3)(b),

may be prosecuted by the new company as if it had been brought by that company.

Amendments—[1] Words in sub-para (1) inserted by FA 2002 s 44(2), (3), Sch 8 para 5 with effect for disposals after 31 March 2002.

Substitution of new shares for old shares

86—(1) This paragraph applies where—

    (a) relief becomes attributable, by virtue of paragraph 85, to any new shares held by a company ("the company"), and

    (b) the old shares for which those shares were exchanged ("the relevant old shares") were—

        (i) subscribed for by and issued to the company, and

        (ii) held by it continuously from the time they were issued until the exchange.

(2) Where this paragraph applies this Schedule shall have effect as if—

    (a) the matching new shares had been subscribed for by the company at the time when, and for the amount for which, the relevant old shares were subscribed for,

    (b) the matching new shares had—

        (i) been issued at the time when the relevant old shares were issued, and

        (ii) been held continuously by the company from that time until the exchange,

    (c) any claim for relief under Part V (investment relief), or Part VIII (deferral relief), of this Schedule made in respect of the relevant old shares had been made in respect of the matching new shares, and

    (d) the company's liability to corporation tax had been reduced under Part V of this Schedule in respect of the matching new shares for the same accounting period as that for which its liability was so reduced in respect of the relevant old shares.

(3) For the purposes of this paragraph old shares and new shares are matching shares in relation to each other if the old shares are the shares for which those new shares are exchanged under the arrangements.

Operation of requirements of Parts II and III in relation to new shares

87—(1) This paragraph applies where paragraph 86 (substitution of new shares for old shares) applies in relation to any new shares held by a company.

(2) If, immediately before the exchange, any of the requirements of paragraphs 5, 8 and 13 (requirements to be met by a qualifying investing company in relation to the relevant shares) was (or was deemed to be) met to any extent by the company in relation to the matching old shares, the requirement shall be deemed to be met by the company to the same extent in relation to the new shares.

(3) If, immediately before the exchange, any of the requirements of paragraphs 16 to 22 (requirements to be met by a qualifying issuing company) was (or was deemed to be) met to any extent by the old company in relation to the matching old shares, it shall be deemed to be met to the same extent by the new company in relation to the new shares.

(4) In determining whether the requirements of paragraphs 17 (the independence requirement) and 20 (the qualifying subsidiaries requirement) are met in relation to the old company or the new company at a time in the period for giving effect to the arrangements, both—

(a) the arrangements themselves, and

(b) any exchange of new shares for old shares that has already taken place under the arrangements,

shall be disregarded.

(5) If, immediately before the period for giving effect to the arrangements, the requirement of paragraph 23(1) (the trading activities requirement) was (or was deemed to be) met to any extent by the old company in relation to the matching old shares—

(a) it shall be deemed to be met to the same extent by the new company in relation to the new shares, and

(b) to the extent that it would not otherwise be the case, it shall also be deemed to be met by that company in relation to those shares at all times which—

(i) fall in the period for giving effect to the arrangements, and

(ii) do not fall after a time when (apart from the arrangements) the requirement would have ceased to have been met by the old company in relation to the matching old shares.

(6) For the purposes of this paragraph—

(a) "the period for giving effect to the arrangements" means the period which—

(i) begins when those arrangements first come into existence; and

(ii) ends when the new company completes its acquisition under the arrangements of all the old shares;

and

(b) references to matching shares shall be construed in accordance with paragraph 86(3).

Relationship between this Part and the 1992 Act

88 The following provisions of the 1992 Act have effect subject to paragraphs 80, 81, 82 and 84 (which make special provision in respect of company reorganisations etc involving shares to which investment relief is attributable)—

section 116 (reorganisations, conversions and reconstructions); and

Chapter II of Part IV (reorganisation of share capital, conversion of securities etc).

PART X
ADVANCE CLEARANCE

Statement of Practice SP 1/00—Corporate venturing scheme—applications for advance clearance under FA 2000 Sch 15 Part X.

Application for advance clearance notice

89—(1) A company ("the applicant") may, before issuing any shares, make an application to the Board for an advance clearance notice in respect of that issue.

(2) An advance clearance notice is a notice issued by the Board in respect of an issue of shares which states that, on the basis of the particulars, declarations and undertakings provided by the applicant, the Board are satisfied that, at the time the shares are issued, the requirements of Parts III and IV of this Schedule will be met (or, in the case of any requirement that cannot be met until a future date, will be met for the time being) in relation to the shares.

(3) For the purposes of determining whether they are satisfied as mentioned in sub-paragraph (2) the Inland Revenue shall assume that the shares included in the issue of shares are "the relevant shares".

(4) An application under this paragraph must—

(a) contain the particulars, declarations and undertakings required by the Board, and

(b) disclose all facts and circumstances material for the decision of the Board.

(5) In this Part references to an "application" are to an application under this paragraph.

Provision of further information

90—(1) On receiving an application for an advance clearance notice, the Board may by notice ("an information notice") require the applicant to provide them, within such time as the Board may direct (not being less than 30 days), with such further particulars as the Board deem necessary to enable them to decide whether or not to issue an advance clearance notice.

(2) An information notice must be given—

(a) within 30 days after the receipt of the application, or

(b) if further particulars have already been provided in response to an earlier information notice, within 30 days after the receipt of those particulars.

(3) If the applicant does not comply with an information notice within the period specified in the notice, the Board need not proceed further on the application.

Decision on application and review procedure

91—(1) The Board must within 30 days after receiving an application or, where an information notice is given in relation to the application, within 30 days after that notice being complied with—

(a) issue an advance clearance notice in respect of the shares to which the application relates, or

(b) notify the applicant that the Board are not satisfied as mentioned in paragraph 89(2) in respect of those shares.

This is subject to sub-paragraph (3) and to paragraph 90(3) (circumstances in which Board need not proceed on application).

(2) In a case where two or more information notices are given in relation to the application, the time limit in sub-paragraph (1) is calculated by reference to the time when the later (or last) of the notices is complied with.

(3) If before the Board issue an advance clearance notice in respect of the issue of shares to which the application relates, or notify the applicant under sub-paragraph (1), the applicant issues the shares in question, the Board need not proceed further on the application.

(4) If the Board—

(a) notify the applicant that they are not satisfied as mentioned in paragraph 89(2), or

(b) in a case to which sub-paragraph (3) does not apply, fail to notify their decision to the applicant in accordance with sub-paragraph (1),

the applicant may, within 30 days after the notification or failure, require the Board to transmit the application, together with any information notices given and further particulars provided under paragraph 90, to the Special Commissioners.

(5) Where sub-paragraph (4) applies any notification by the Special Commissioners that they are satisfied as mentioned in paragraph 89(2) shall have effect as if it were an advance clearance notice issued by the Board in respect of the issue of shares in question.

Effect of advance clearance notice

92—(1) For the purposes of this Schedule, where an advance clearance notice is issued in respect of an issue of shares before the shares are issued, the requirements of Parts III and IV of this Schedule shall be treated as met (or, in the case of any requirement that cannot be met until a future date, as met for the time being) in relation to those shares at the time they are issued.

(2) If—

(a) any particulars provided in the application for the notice, or in response to any information notice relating to the application, do not fully and accurately disclose all facts and circumstances material for the decision of the Board or the Special Commissioners, or

(b) the applicant or any of its subsidiaries fails to act in accordance with any declaration or undertaking which was given in, or in connection with, the application,

any resulting advance clearance notice shall be void.

(3) Sub-paragraph (2)(b) applies in relation to a subsidiary of the applicant whether or not it was such a subsidiary at the time the declaration or undertaking in question was given.

PART XI

SUPPLEMENTARY AND GENERAL

Identification of shares on a disposal

93—(1) In any case where—

(a) a company (''the company'') disposes of part of a holding of shares (''the holding''), and

(b) the holding includes shares to which investment relief is attributable that have been held continuously by the company from the time they were issued until the disposal,

this paragraph applies for the purpose of identifying the shares disposed of.

(2) For the purposes of this paragraph ''holding'' means any number of shares of the same class in another company held by the company in the same capacity, growing or diminishing as shares of that class are acquired or disposed of.

(3) Where shares included in the holding have been acquired by the company on different days, then, for the purposes of corporation tax on chargeable gains and of this Schedule, any disposal by the company of any of those shares shall be treated as relating to those acquired on an earlier day rather than to those acquired on a later day.

(4) Where shares included in the holding have been acquired by the company on the same day, then, for the purposes of corporation tax on chargeable gains and of this Schedule, if there is a disposal by the company of any of those shares, any shares—

(a) to which investment relief is attributable, and

(b) which have been held by the company continuously from the time they were issued until the time of disposal, shall be treated as disposed of after any other shares included in the holding which were acquired by the company on that day.

(5) Chapter I of Part IV of the 1992 Act (share pooling, etc) shall have effect subject to this paragraph.

(6) Sections 104 to 106 and 107 of that Act (which make provision for the purposes of corporation tax on chargeable gains for the identification of shares on a disposal) shall not apply to shares to which investment relief is attributable.

(7) In a case to which section 127 of that Act (equation of original shares and new holding) applies [(including a case where that section applies by virtue of any enactment relating to chargeable gains)]¹, shares comprised in the new holding shall be treated for the purposes of sub-paragraphs (3) and (4) as acquired when the original shares were acquired.

In this sub-paragraph "new holding" and "original shares" [have the same meaning as in section 127 of the 1992 Act (or, as the case may be, that section as applied by virtue of the enactment concerned)]¹.

Amendments—¹ In sub-para (7), words substituted for the words "(whether or not by virtue of section 135(3) of that Act)", and words substituted for the words "shall be construed in accordance with sections 126, 127, 135 and 136 of that Act." by FA 2002 s 45, Sch 9 paras 6(1), (4), 8(1) with effect for disposals after 16 April 2002.

Determination of loss where investment relief is attributable to shares

94—(1) This paragraph applies for the purposes of corporation tax on chargeable gains where—

(a) a company disposes of shares which were held by it continuously from the time they were issued until the disposal,
(b) investment relief is attributable to the shares (and not withdrawn in full as a result of the disposal), and
(c) apart from sub-paragraph (2), there would be a loss on the disposal.

(2) For the purpose of determining the gain or loss on the disposal the consideration given by the company for the shares is treated as reduced by the amount of the investment relief attributable to the shares immediately after the disposal.

(3) Any gain which accrues by virtue of sub-paragraph (2) is not a chargeable gain.

(4) Notwithstanding the definition of "allowable loss" in section 834(1) of the Taxes Act 1988 (interpretation of the Corporation Tax Acts), nothing in sub-paragraph (3) has effect in relation to any loss determined in accordance with sub-paragraph (2) to prevent it being an allowable loss.

Nominees

95 Shares subscribed for by, issued to, acquired or held by or disposed of by a nominee for any person shall be treated for the purposes of this Schedule as subscribed for by, issued to, acquired or held by or disposed of by that person.

Meaning of "disposal"

96—(1) Subject to sub-paragraph (2), in this Schedule "disposal" shall be construed in accordance with the 1992 Act, and cognate expressions shall be construed accordingly.

(2) A company shall be treated for the purposes of this Schedule, and for the purposes of corporation tax on chargeable gains, as disposing of any shares which but for paragraph 82 (company reconstructions and amalgamations) it—

(a) would be treated as exchanging for other shares by virtue of [section 136]¹of the 1992 Act, or
(b) would be so treated but for section 137(1) of the 1992 Act (which restricts [section 136 of that Act to bona fide schemes of reconstruction]¹).

Amendments—¹ Words in sub-para (2)(a) substituted for the words "section 136(1)", and in sub-para (2)(b), words substituted for the words "sections 135 and 136 of that Act to bona fide reconstructions and amalgamations" by FA 2002 s 45, Sch 9 paras 6(1), (5), 8(1) with effect for disposals after 16 April 2002.

Construction of references to shares being "held continuously"

97—(1) This paragraph applies where for the purposes of this Schedule it falls to be determined whether a company has held shares continuously throughout any period.

(2) The company shall not be treated as having held shares continuously throughout a period if—

(a) it is deemed, under any provision of the 1992 Act, to have disposed of and immediately reacquired the shares at any time during the period, or
(b) it is treated as having disposed of the shares at any such time, by virtue of paragraph 96(2) (on reconstruction or amalgamation company treated as disposing of shares continuously held by it to which investment relief is attributable).

Meaning of "issue of shares"

98 In this Schedule—

(a) references (however expressed) to an issue of shares in any company are to such of the shares in the company as are of the same class and issued on the same day; and

(b) references (however expressed) to an issue of shares in a company to a person are references to such of the shares in an issue of shares in that company as are issued to that person in one capacity.

Meaning of "associate"

99—(1) In this Schedule "associate", in relation to a person, means—

(a) any relative or partner of that person,

(b) the trustee or trustees of any settlement in relation to which that person, or any relative of his (living or dead), is or was a settlor, and

(c) where that person is interested in any shares or obligations of a company which are subject to any trust, or are part of the estate of a deceased person—

(i) the trustee or trustees of the settlement concerned or, as the case may be, the personal representatives of the deceased, and

(ii) if that person is a company, any other company interested in those shares or obligations.

(2) In sub-paragraph (1)(a) and (b) "relative" means husband or wife, parent or remoter forebear or child or remoter issue.

(3) In sub-paragraph (1)(b) "settlor" and "settlement" have the same meaning as in Chapter IA of Part XV of the Taxes Act 1988 (see section 660G(1) and (2)).

"The Board" and "the Inland Revenue"

100 In this Schedule—

(a) "the Board" means the Commissioners of Inland Revenue; and

(b) references to "the Inland Revenue" are to any officer of the Board.

Power to amend by Treasury order

101 The Treasury may by order amend this Schedule—

(a) to make such amendments of—

(i) paragraphs 10 to 12 (the non-financial activities requirement), or

(ii) paragraphs 23 to 33 (the trading activities requirement),

as they consider expedient;

(b) to substitute different sums of money for those for the time being specified in paragraph 22 (gross assets requirement).

Minor definitions etc

102—(1) In this Schedule—

"allowable loss" means an allowable loss for the purposes of corporation tax on chargeable gains;

"arrangements" includes any scheme, agreement or understanding, whether or not legally enforceable;

"chargeable gain" means a chargeable gain for the purposes of corporation tax on chargeable gains;

"class", in relation to shares or securities, means a class of shares in or securities of any one company (see sub-paragraph (2));

"director" shall be construed in accordance with section 417(5) of the Taxes Act 1988;

"group" means a parent company and its 51% subsidiaries;

"group company", in relation to a group, means the parent company and any of its 51% subsidiaries;

"ordinary share capital", except in paragraph 7 (meaning of "material interest"), has the meaning given in section 832(1) of the Taxes Act 1988;

"ordinary shares" means shares forming part of a company's ordinary share capital;

"parent company" means a company that—

(a) has one or more 51% subsidiaries, but

(b) is not itself a 51% subsidiary of another company;

"research and development" has the meaning given by section 837A of the Taxes Act 1988;

"single company" means a company that is not a parent company or a 51% subsidiary of a parent company;

"the 1992 Act" means the Taxation of Chargeable Gains Act 1992.

(2) For the purposes of this Schedule shares in or securities of a company shall not be treated as being of the same class unless they would be so treated if dealt with on the Stock Exchange.

(3) Section 839 of the Taxes Act 1988 (connected persons) applies for the purposes of this Schedule.

(4) References in this Schedule to a company being in administration or receivership shall be construed as follows—

    (a) references to a company being "in administration" are to there being in force in relation to it—

        (i) an administration order under Part II of the Insolvency Act 1986 or Part III of the Insolvency (Northern Ireland) Order 1989, or

        (ii) any corresponding order under the law of a country or territory outside the United Kingdom;

    (b) references to a company being "in receivership" are to there being in force in relation to it—

        (i) an order for the appointment of an administrative receiver, a receiver and manager or a receiver under Chapter I or II of Part III of the Insolvency Act 1986 or Part IV of the Insolvency (Northern Ireland) Order 1989, or

        (ii) any corresponding order under the law of a country or territory outside the United Kingdom.

(5) For the purposes of this Schedule the market value at any time of any asset is the price which it might reasonably be expected to fetch on a sale at that time in the open market free from any interest or right which exists by way of security in or over it.

(6) In this Schedule—

    (a) references to investment relief obtained by a company in respect of any shares include references to investment relief obtained by it in respect of those shares at any time after it has disposed of them, and

    (b) references to the withdrawal or reduction of investment relief obtained by a company in respect of any shares include references to the withdrawal or reduction of investment relief obtained in respect of those shares at any such time.

(7) In the case of a requirement that cannot be met until a future date—

    (a) references in this Schedule to a requirement being met for the time being are to nothing having occurred to prevent its being met, and

    (b) references to its continuing to be met are to nothing occurring to prevent its being met.

Index of defined expressions

103 In this Schedule the following expressions are defined or otherwise explained by the provisions indicated:

the period of restriction	paragraph 48
the qualification period	paragraph 3
the qualifying shares (in Part VIII)	paragraph 75
qualifying subsidiary	paragraph 21
qualifying trade	paragraph 25
in receivership	paragraph 102(4)(*b*)
relevant preference shares	paragraph 9
the relevant shares	paragraph 2
relief attributable to shares	
investment relief	paragraph 45
deferral relief	paragraph 77
research and development	paragraph 102(1)
single company	paragraph 102(1)
the 1992 Act	paragraph 102(1)
trading activities requirement	paragraph 23(2) and (3)

SCHEDULE 16

CORPORATE VENTURING SCHEME: CONSEQUENTIAL AMENDMENTS

Section 63(2)

Commentary—*Simon's Direct Tax Service* **D2.13**.

Penalties in connection with returns etc

1—(1) (*amends* TMA 1970 s 98, Table).

Enterprise investment scheme

2—(1) Chapter III of Part VII of the Taxes Act 1988 is amended as follows.

(2) (*inserts* TA 1988 s 303(1AA) and *amends* TA 1988 s 303(1B)).

(3) (*inserts* TA 1988 s 303A).

Loss relief

3—(1) Chapter VI of Part XIII of the Taxes Act 1988 (relief on losses on shares in trading companies etc) is amended as follows.

(2) (*amends* TA 1988 s 573(4) and *inserts* TA 1988 s 573(4A)).

(3) (*amends* TA 1988 s 575(1)).

(4) (*amends* TA 1988 s 576(1) and *inserts* TA 1988 s 576(1C)).

EIS: deferral relief

4 (*amends* TCGA 1992 Sch 5B para 14(1), (3) and *inserts* TCGA 1992 Sch 5B para 14A).

Company tax returns, assessments etc

5 (*amends* FA 1998 Sch 18 para 8 and *inserts* FA 1998 Sch 18 para 9(4)).

SCHEDULE 17

ENTERPRISE INVESTMENT SCHEME: AMENDMENTS

Section 64

Commentary—*Simon's Direct Tax Service* **E3.102**.

PART I

REDUCTION OF APPLICABLE PERIODS

Meaning of "eligible shares"

1 (*amends* TA 1988 s 289(7)).

Conditions relating to individuals

2 (*amended* TA 1988 s 291(1) and *inserted* TA 1988 s 291(6)).

Amendments—This paragraph repealed by FA 2001 s 110, Sch 33 Pt II(3) with effect—

(*a*) in relation to shares issued after 6 March 2001, and

(b) in respect of the application of TA 1988 Pt VII Chapter III and TCGA 1992 Sch 5B after 6 March 2001 in relation to shares—
  (i) that were issued after 31 December 1993 but before 7 March 2001, and
  (ii) to which income tax relief or deferral relief was attributable immediately before 7 March 2001.

Conditions relating to further investment by connected person

3 (*amends* TA 1988 s 291A(1), (5)).

Amendments—Sub-para (2) repealed by FA 2001 s 110, Sch 33 Pt II(3) with effect—

(*a*) in relation to shares issued after 6 March 2001, and
(*b*) in respect of the application of TA 1988 Pt VII Chapter III and TCGA 1992 Sch 5B after 6 March 2001 in relation to shares—
  (i) that were issued after 31 December 1993 but before 7 March 2001, and
  (ii) to which income tax relief or deferral relief was attributable immediately before 7 March 2001.

Value received from company

4 (*amends* TA 1988 s 300(1)).

Amendments—This paragraph repealed by FA 2001 s 110, Sch 33 Pt II(3) with effect—

(*a*) in relation to shares issued on or after 7 March 2001, and
(*b*) in relation to shares issued before that date, in respect of the application of TA 1988 Pt VII Chapter III and TCGA 1992 Sch 5B in relation to—
  (i) value received (within the meaning of TA 1988 s 300 or TCGA 1992 Sch 5B para 13) and
  (ii) repayments made,
on or after that date.

Value received by persons other than claimants

5 (*amends* TA 1988 s 303(1), (2), (5) and *inserts* TA 1988 s 303(2A)).

Amendments—Sub-paras (2), (5) repealed by FA 2001 s 110, Sch 33 Pt II(3) with effect—

(*a*) in relation to shares issued on or after 7 March 2001, and
(*b*) in relation to shares issued before that date, in respect of the application of TA 1988 Pt VII Chapter III and TCGA 1992 Sch 5B in relation to—
  (i) value received (within the meaning of TA 1988 s 300 or TCGA 1992 Sch 5B para 13) and
  (ii) repayments made,
on or after that date.

Meaning of "termination date" and "relevant period"

6 (*amends* TA 1988 s 312(1) and *substitutes* TA 1988 s 312(1A)).

Amendments—Sub-para (2) repealed by FA 2001 s 110, Sch 33 Pt II(3) with effect—

(*a*) in relation to shares issued after 6 March 2001, and
(*b*) in respect of the application of TA 1988 Pt VII Chapter III and TCGA 1992 Sch 5B after 6 March 2001 in relation to shares—
  (i) that were issued after 31 December 1993 but before 7 March 2001, and
  (ii) to which income tax relief or deferral relief was attributable immediately before 7 March 2001.

Postponement of chargeable gains on reinvestment

7—(*amended* TCGA 1992 Sch 5B paras 3(1)(*c*), (*d*), 13(1), 14(1), 16(1)(*a*), 19(1)).

Amendments—This paragraph repealed by FA 2001 s 110, Sch 33 Pt II(3) with effect, so far as it amended TCGA 1992 Sch 5B paras 13(1), 14(1)—

(*a*) in relation to shares issued on or after 7 March 2001, and
(*b*) in relation to shares issued before that date, in respect of the application of TA 1988 Pt VII Chapter III and TCGA 1992 Sch 5B in relation to—
  (i) value received (within the meaning of TA 1988 s 300 or TCGA 1992 Sch 5B para 13) and
  (ii) repayments made,
on or after that date.
So far as it amended TCGA 1992 Sch 5B paras 3(1)(*c*), (*d*), 16(1)(*a*), 19(1), this paragraph repealed with effect—

(*a*) in relation to shares issued after 6 March 2001, and
(*b*) in respect of the application of TA 1988 Pt VII Chapter III and TCGA 1992 Sch 5B after 6 March 2001 in relation to shares—
  (i) that were issued after 31 December 1993 but before 7 March 2001, and
  (ii) to which income tax relief or deferral relief was attributable immediately before 7 March 2001.

Commencement

8 The amendments in this Part of this Schedule have effect in relation to shares issued on or after 6th April 2000.

PART II
QUALIFYING COMPANIES
Company in administration or receivership

9—(1) (*inserts* TA 1988 s 293(4A), (4B)).

(2) (*amends* TA 1988 s 289(1D)).

(3) (*inserts* TA 1988 s 289A(8A)).

(4) (*inserts* TA 1988 s 312(2A)).

Company in liquidation

10 (*repeals* TA 1988 s 293(6)).

Independence of qualifying company

11 (*substitutes* TA 1988 s 293(8), (8AA)).

Commencement

12—(1) The amendments in this Part of this Schedule have effect—

(*a*) in relation to shares issued on or after 21st March 2000, and

(*b*) in respect of the application of section 293 of the Taxes Act 1988 on or after that date in relation to shares—

(i) that were issued after 31st December 1993 but before 21st March 2000, and

(ii) to which income tax relief or deferral relief was attributable immediately before 21st March 2000.

(2) In sub-paragraph (1)—

"income tax relief" means relief under Chapter III of Part VII of the Taxes Act 1988 (enterprise investment scheme); and

"deferral relief" has the same meaning as in Schedule 5B to the Taxation of Chargeable Gains Act 1992.

PART III
OTHER AMENDMENTS
Qualifying trades

13—(1) (*substitutes* TA 1988 s 297(4)–(5C)).

(2) This paragraph has effect in relation to shares issued on or after 6th April 2000.

Meaning of "arrangements"

14—(1) (*amends* TA 1988 s 312(1)).

(2) This paragraph has effect—

(*a*) in relation to shares issued on or after 21st March 2000, and

(*b*) in respect of the application of section 312 of the Taxes Act 1988 on or after that date in relation to shares—

(i) that were issued after 31st December 1993 but before 21st March 2000, and

(ii) to which income tax relief or deferral relief was attributable immediately before 21st March 2000.

(3) In sub-paragraph (2)—

"income tax relief" means relief under Chapter III of Part VII of the Taxes Act 1988 (enterprise investment scheme); and

"deferral relief" has the same meaning as in Schedule 5B to the Taxation of Chargeable Gains Act 1992.

Meaning of "research and development"

15—(1) (*amends* TA 1988 s 312(1)).

(2) This paragraph has effect in relation to shares issued on or after 6th April 2000.

(3) Nothing in this paragraph affects the operation of any of the following provisions in relation to shares issued before 6th April 2000—

(*a*) Chapter III of Part VII of the Taxes Act 1988 (enterprise investment scheme);

(*b*) sections 573 and 574 of that Act (relief for losses on shares in trading companies);

(*c*) Schedule 5B to the Taxation of Chargeable Gains Act 1992.

SCHEDULE 18

VENTURE CAPITAL TRUSTS: AMENDMENTS

Section 65

Commentary—*Simon's Direct Tax Service* **E3.612, 626**.

PART I

REDUCTION OF APPLICABLE PERIODS

Relief from income tax

1 (*amends* TA 1988 Sch 15B paras 2(3), 3(1)(*b*) and 6(1)).

Deferred CGT charge on reinvestment

2 (*amends* TCGA 1992 Sch 5C para 3(2)).

Commencement

3 The amendments made by this Part of this Schedule have effect in relation to shares issued on or after 6th April 2000.

PART II

QUALIFYING HOLDINGS

Introductory

4 Schedule 28B to the Taxes Act 1988 (venture capital trusts: qualifying holdings) is amended as follows.

Qualifying trade: receipt of royalties or licence fees

5—(1) (*substitutes* TA 1988 Sch 28B para 4(5)–(6D)).

(2) This paragraph has effect for the purpose of determining whether shares or securities issued on or after 6th April 2000 are, for the purposes of section 842AA of the Taxes Act 1988, to be regarded as comprised in a company's qualifying holdings.

Meaning of "research and development"

6—(1) (*amends* TA 1988 Sch 28B para 5(1)).

(2) This paragraph has effect for the purpose of determining whether shares or securities issued on or after 6th April 2000 are, for the purposes of section 842AA of the Taxes Act 1988, to be regarded as comprised in a company's qualifying holdings.

(3) Nothing in this paragraph affects the operation of Schedule 28B to the Taxes Act 1988 as it has effect for the purpose of determining whether shares or securities issued before that date are, for the purposes of section 842AA of that Act, to be regarded as comprised in a company's qualifying holdings.

Company in administration or receivership

7—(1) (*inserts* TA 1988 Sch 28B para 11A).

(2) This paragraph has effect for the purposes of determining whether shares or securities are, as at any time on or after 21st March 2000, to be regarded as comprised in a company's qualifying holdings.

Company reorganisations etc involving exchange of shares

8—(1) (*inserts* TA 1988 Sch 28B para 11B).

(2) (*inserts* TA 1988 s 842AA(5AD), (5AE)).

(3) (*amends* TMA 1970 s 98, Table).

(4) This paragraph applies to exchanges of shares or securities (within the meaning of paragraph 11B(1) of Schedule 28B to the Taxes Act 1988) taking effect on or after 21st March 2000.

SCHEDULE 19

MEANING OF "RESEARCH AND DEVELOPMENT"

Section 68

Commentary—*Simon's Direct Tax Service* **B2.702**.

PART I
THE NEW DEFINITION
Research and development

1 (*inserts* TA 1988 s 837A).

Oil and gas exploration and appraisal

2 (*inserts* TA 1988 s 837B).

PART II
CONSEQUENTIAL AMENDMENTS
Income and Corporation Taxes Act 1988 (c.1)

3 The Income and Corporation Taxes Act 1988 is amended as follows.

4 In section 495 (regional development grants), in subsection (1)(*b*) for "scientific research" substitute "research and development".

5—(1) (*inserts* TA 1988 ss 82A, 82B).

(2) Any approval given by the Secretary of State for the purposes of section 136(*b*) or (*c*) of the Capital Allowances Act 1990 and in force immediately before the commencement of this paragraph has effect as if given under section 82B(1)(*a*) or (*b*) of the Taxes Act 1988 as inserted by sub-paragraph (1) above.

(3) So far as is necessary for continuing its effect, any decision made by the Secretary of State under section 139(3) of the Capital Allowances Act 1990 before the commencement of this paragraph has effect as if given under section 82B(4) of the Taxes Act 1988 as inserted by sub-paragraph (1) above.

6 (*amends* TA 1988 Sch 18 para 1(6)(*b*)(iii)).

Capital Allowances Act 1990 (c.1)

7–11 (*amended* CAA 1990 ss 4(5), (9), (10), 8(5), 56D(1)(*a*), 118(2), 137(1), (1A), (3), 138(1), (3A)(*a*), (5)(*b*), 138A(3), 139(1)(*b*), (1)(*c*), (1)(*d*), 158(2)(*d*) and section 161, 161(2); *repealed by* CAA 2001 s 580, Sch 4 with effect in accordance with CAA 2001 s 579).

Taxation of Chargeable Gains Act 1992 (c.12)

12—(1) (*amends* TCGA 1992 s 195(2), (3) and *inserts* TCGA 1992 s 195(8)).

SCHEDULE 20

TAX RELIEF FOR EXPENDITURE ON RESEARCH AND DEVELOPMENT

Section 69(1)

Commentary—*Simon's Direct Tax Service* **B2.703**.

PART I
ENTITLEMENT TO RELIEF
Entitlement to R&D tax relief

1—(1) A company is entitled to R&D tax relief for an accounting period if—

(*a*) the company qualifies as a small or medium-sized enterprise in the period (see paragraph 2), and

(*b*) [the aggregate of its qualifying R&D expenditure (see paragraph 3) and its qualifying sub-contracted R&D expenditure (within the meaning of paragraph 8 of Schedule 12 to the Finance Act 2002)][1] deductible in that period is not less than—

(i) £25,000, if the accounting period is a period of 12 months, or

(ii) such amount as bears to £25,000 the same proportion as the accounting period bears to 12 months.

(2) For the purposes of sub-paragraph (1) a company's qualifying R&D expenditure is deductible in an accounting period if—

(*a*) it is allowable as a deduction in computing for tax purposes the profits for that period of a trade carried on by the company, or

(*b*) it would have been allowable as such a deduction had the company, at the time the expenditure was incurred, been carrying on a trade consisting of the activities in respect of which it was incurred.

(3) For the purposes of sub-paragraph (2)(*a*) no account shall be taken of section 401 of the Taxes Act 1988 (pre-trading expenditure treated as incurred when trading begins).

[(3A) For the purposes of sub-paragraph (1)(*b*) a company's qualifying sub-contracted R&D expenditure (within the meaning of paragraph 8 of Schedule 12 to the Finance Act 2002) is deductible in an accounting period if it is allowable as a deduction in computing for tax purposes the profits for that period of a trade carried on by the company.]¹

(4) In relation to an accounting period beginning before and ending on or after 1st April 2000, the references in sub-paragraph (1)(*b*)(i) and (ii) to the accounting period shall be read as references to so much of it as falls on or after that date.

Amendments—¹ Words in sub-para (1)(*b*) substituted, and sub-para (3A) inserted, by FA 2002 s 56, Sch 15 paras 1, 2 with effect for accounting periods ending after 31 March 2002. These amendments do not apply in relation to a company's qualifying sub-contracted R&D expenditure (within the meaning of FA 2002 Sch 12 para 8) incurred before 1 April 2002; for this purpose no account is taken of TA 1988 s 401.

Meaning of "small or medium-sized enterprise"

2—(1) For the purposes of this Schedule a "small or medium-sized enterprise" means a small or medium-sized enterprise as defined in Commission Recommendation 96/280/EC of 3rd April 1996.

(2) The Treasury may by order amend sub-paragraph (1) so as to substitute another definition of "small or medium-sized enterprise" for the definition that is for the time being effective for the purposes of this Schedule.

Qualifying R&D expenditure

3—(1) For the purposes of this Schedule "qualifying R&D expenditure" of a company means expenditure that meets the following conditions.

(2) The first condition is that the expenditure is not of a capital nature.

(3) The second condition is that the expenditure is attributable to relevant research and development (see paragraph 4) directly undertaken by the company or on its behalf.

(4) The third condition is that the expenditure is incurred—

    (*a*) on staffing costs (see paragraph 5), or
    (*b*) on consumable stores (see paragraph 6),

or is qualifying expenditure on sub-contracted research and development (see paragraphs 9 to 12).

(5) The fourth condition is that any intellectual property (see paragraph 7) created as a result of the research and development to which the expenditure is attributable is, or will be, vested in the company (whether alone or with other persons).

(6) The fifth condition is that the expenditure is not incurred by the company in carrying on activities the carrying on of which is contracted out to the company by any person.

(7) The sixth condition is that the expenditure is not subsidised (see paragraph 8).

Relevant research and development

4—(1) For the purposes of this Schedule "relevant research and development", in relation to a company, means research and development—

    (*a*) related to a trade carried on by the company, or
    (*b*) from which it is intended that a trade to be carried on by the company will be derived.

(2) For the purposes of this Schedule research and development related to a trade carried on by the company includes—

    (*a*) research and development which may lead to or facilitate an extension of that trade, and
    (*b*) research and development of a medical nature which has a special relation to the welfare of workers employed in that trade.

Staffing costs

5—(1) For the purposes of this Schedule the staffing costs of a company are—

    (*a*) the emoluments paid by the company to directors or employees of the company, including all salaries, wages, perquisites and profits whatsoever other than benefits in kind;
    (*b*) the secondary Class 1 national insurance contributions paid by the company; and
    (*c*) the contributions paid by the company to any pension fund ...¹ operated for the benefit of directors or employees of the company.

[(1A) In sub-paragraph (1)(*c*) "pension fund" means any scheme, fund or other arrangements established and maintained (whether in the United Kingdom or elsewhere) for the purpose of providing pensions, retirement annuities, allowances, lump sums, gratuities or other superannuation benefits (with or without subsidiary benefits).

In this sub-paragraph "scheme" includes any deed, agreement or series of agreements.]¹

(2) The staffing costs of a company attributable to relevant research and development are those paid to, or in respect of, directors or employees directly and actively engaged in such research and development.

(3) In the case of a director or employee partly engaged directly and actively in relevant research and development the following rules apply—

(a) if the time he spends so engaged is less than 20% of his total working time, none of the staffing costs relating to him are treated as attributable to relevant research and development;
(b) if the time he spends so engaged is more than 80% of his total working time, the whole of the staffing costs relating to him are treated as attributable to relevant research and development;
(c) in any other case, an appropriate proportion of the staffing costs relating to him are treated as attributable to relevant research and development.

(4) For the purpose of sub-paragraphs (2) and (3) persons who provide services, such as secretarial or administrative services, in support of activities carried on by others, are not, by virtue of providing those services, to be treated as themselves directly and actively engaged in those activities.

Amendments—[1] Words in sub-para (1)(c) repealed, and sub-para (1A) inserted, by FA 2002 ss 56, 141, Sch 15 paras 1, 3, Sch 40 Pt 3(5) with effect for accounting periods ending after 31 March 2002.

Expenditure on consumable stores

6—(1) For the purposes of this Schedule expenditure on consumable stores means expenditure that would be treated as expenditure on consumable stores in accordance with [generally accepted accounting practice][1].

(2) Expenditure on consumable stores is attributable to relevant research and development if the stores are employed directly in such research and development.

Amendments—[1] words substituted for the words "normal accounting practice" by FA 2002 s 103(4)(f) with effect from 24 July 2002.

Meaning of "intellectual property"

7 In this Schedule "intellectual property" means—

(a) any industrial information or techniques likely to assist in—

(i) the manufacture or processing of goods or materials, or
(ii) the working of a mine, oil well or other source of mineral deposits or the winning of access thereto, or
(iii) the carrying out of any agricultural, forestry or fishing operations;

(b) any patent, trade mark, registered design, copyright, design right or plant breeder's right; and
(c) any rights under the law of a country outside the United Kingdom which correspond or are similar to those falling within paragraph (b).

Subsidised expenditure

8—(1) For the purposes of this Schedule a company's expenditure is treated as subsidised—

(a) if a notified State aid is, or has been, obtained in respect of—

(i) the whole or part of the expenditure, or
(ii) any other expenditure (whenever incurred) attributable to the same research and development project;

(b) to the extent that a grant or subsidy (other than a notified State aid) is obtained in respect of the expenditure;
(c) to the extent that it is otherwise met directly or indirectly by any person other than the company.

(2) For the purposes of sub-paragraph (1) "notified State aid" means a State aid notified to and approved by the European Commission.

[For this purpose the following are not State aids—

(a) R&D tax relief and R&D tax credits;
(b) tax relief under Schedule 12 to the Finance Act 2002 (tax relief for expenditure on research and development);
(c) tax relief and tax credits under Schedule 13 to that Act (tax relief for expenditure on vaccine research etc).][1]

(3) For the purposes of this Schedule a notified State aid, grant, subsidy or payment that is not allocated to particular expenditure shall be allocated to expenditure of the recipient in such manner as is just and reasonable.

Amendments—[1] Words in sub-para (2) substituted by FA 2002 s 56, Sch 15 paras 1, 4 with effect for accounting periods ending after 31 March 2002.

Qualifying expenditure on sub-contracted research and development

9—(1) The provisions of paragraphs 10 to 12 have effect for determining the amount of the qualifying expenditure of a company (''the company'') on sub-contracted research and development.

(2) For the purposes of this Schedule the company incurs expenditure on sub-contracted research and development if it makes a payment (a ''sub-contractor payment'') to another person (''the sub-contractor'') in respect of relevant research and development contracted out by the company to that person.

Treatment of expenditure where company and sub-contractor are connected persons

10—(1) Where—

   (*a*) the company and the sub-contractor are connected persons, and
   (*b*) in accordance with [generally accepted accounting practice]¹—

      (i) the whole of the sub-contractor payment has been brought into account in determining the sub-contractor's profit or loss for a relevant period, and
      (ii) all of the sub-contractor's relevant expenditure has been so brought into account,

the whole of the payment (up to the amount of the sub-contractor's relevant expenditure) is qualifying expenditure on sub-contracted research and development.

(2) In sub-paragraph (1)—

   (*a*) references to the ''relevant expenditure'' of the sub-contractor are to expenditure that—

      (i) is incurred by the sub-contractor in carrying on, on behalf of the company, the activities to which the sub-contractor payment relates,
      (ii) is not of a capital nature,
      (iii) is incurred on staffing costs or on consumable stores, and
      (iv) is not subsidised;

   (*b*) a ''relevant period'' means a period

      (i) for which accounts are drawn up for the sub-contractor, and
      (ii) that ends not more than twelve months after the end of the company's period of account in which the sub-contractor payment is, in accordance with [generally accepted accounting practice]¹, brought into account in determining the company's profit or loss.

(3) Paragraph 5 (staffing costs) and paragraph 8 (subsidised expenditure) apply for the purposes of determining whether the sub-contractor's expenditure meets the requirements of sub-paragraph (2)(*a*)(iii) and (iv).

For this purpose the references in those paragraphs to a company shall be read as references to the sub-contractor.

(4) Any apportionment of expenditure of the company or the sub-contractor necessary for the purposes of this paragraph shall be made on a just and reasonable basis.

Amendments—¹ Words substituted for the words ''normal accounting practice'' by FA 2002 s 103(4)(*f*) with effect from 24 July 2002.

Election for connected persons treatment

11—(1) The company and the sub-contractor may in any case jointly elect that paragraph 10 shall apply to sub-contractor payments made by the company to the sub-contractor.

(2) Any such election must be made in relation to all sub-contractor payments paid under the same contract or other arrangement.

(3) The election must be made by notice in writing given to the Inland Revenue.

(4) The notice must be given before the end of the period of two years beginning with the end of the company's accounting period in which the contract or other arrangement is entered into.

(5) An election under this paragraph, once made, is irrevocable.

Treatment of sub-contractor payment in other cases

12 Where—

   (*a*) the company makes a sub-contractor payment, ...²
   [(*b*) the company and the sub-contractor are not connected persons, and
   (*c*) no election is made under paragraph 11,]¹

65% of the amount of the sub-contractor payment is treated as qualifying expenditure on sub-contracted research and development.

Amendments—¹ Sub-paras (*b*), (*c*) substituted for original sub-para (*b*) by FA 2002 s 56, Sch 15 paras 1, 5 with effect for accounting periods ending after 31 March 2002.
² Word in para (*a*) repealed by FA 2002 s 141, Sch Pt 3(5) with effect for accounting periods ending after 31 March 2002.

PART II
MANNER OF GIVING EFFECT TO RELIEF

Deduction in computing profits of trade

13 Where—

    (*a*) a company is entitled to R&D tax relief for an accounting period,

    (*b*) it is carrying on a trade in that period, and

    (*c*) it has qualifying R&D expenditure that is allowable as a deduction in computing for tax purposes the profits of the trade for that period,

it may (on making a claim) treat that qualifying R&D expenditure as if it were an amount equal to 150% of the actual amount.

Alternative treatment of pre-trading expenditure

14—(1) This paragraph applies where a company—

    (*a*) is entitled to R&D tax relief for an accounting period, and

    (*b*) has incurred qualifying R&D expenditure in that accounting period which—

        (i) is not allowable as a deduction in computing, for tax purposes, the profits of a trade that was carried on by it at the time the expenditure was incurred, but

        (ii) would have been so allowable had the company, at that time, been carrying on a trade consisting of the activities in respect of which the expenditure was incurred.

(2) The company may elect to be treated as if it had incurred a trading loss in the accounting period equal to 150% of the amount of that qualifying R&D expenditure.

(3) Where an election is made under this paragraph in respect of the accounting period, section 401 of the Taxes Act 1988 (relief for pre-trading expenditure) does not apply to that qualifying R&D expenditure.

(4) An election under this paragraph must specify the accounting period in respect of which it is made.

(5) The election must be made by notice in writing to the Inland Revenue.

(6) The notice must be given before the end of the period of two years beginning with the end of the company's accounting period to which the election relates.

Entitlement to R&D tax credit

15—(1) A company may claim an R&D tax credit for an accounting period in which it has a surrenderable loss.

(2) A company has a "surrenderable loss" for this purpose if in an accounting period—

    (*a*) paragraph 13 applies and the company incurs a trading loss in that period in the trade mentioned in sub-paragraph (1)(*b*) of that paragraph, or

    (*b*) paragraph 14 applies and the company is treated under that paragraph as incurring a trading loss.

(3) The amount of the surrenderable loss is equal to—

    (*a*) so much of that trading loss as is unrelieved, or

    (*b*) if less, 150% of the related qualifying R&D expenditure.

(4) For this purpose the amount of a trading loss that is "unrelieved" means the amount of that loss reduced by the amount of—

    (*a*) any relief that was or could have been obtained by the company making a claim under section 393A(1)(*a*) of the Taxes Act 1988 to set the loss against profits of whatever description of the same accounting period,

    (*b*) any other relief obtained by the company in respect of the loss, including relief under section 393A(1)(*b*) of that Act (losses set against profits of an earlier accounting period), and

    (*c*) any loss surrendered under section 403(1) (surrender of relief to group or consortium members) of that Act.

(5) No account shall be taken for this purpose of any losses—

    (*a*) brought forward from an earlier accounting period under section 393(1) of the Taxes Act 1988, or

    (*b*) carried back from a later accounting period under section 393A(1)(*b*) of that Act.

Amount of credit

16—(1) The amount of the R&D tax credit to which a company is entitled for an accounting period is an amount equal to—

    (*a*) 16% of the amount of the surrenderable loss for the period, or

    (*b*) if less, the total amount of the company's PAYE and NICs liabilities for payment periods ending in the accounting period.

(2) The Treasury may by order substitute for the percentage for the time being specified in sub-paragraph (1)(*a*) such other percentage as they think fit.

(3) An order under sub-paragraph (2) may make such incidental, supplemental, consequential and transitional provision as the Treasury think fit.

Total amount of company's PAYE and NICs liabilities

17—(1) For the purposes of paragraph 16 the total amount of the company's PAYE and NICs liabilities for a payment period is the total of—

(*a*) the amount of income tax for which the company is required to account to the Inland Revenue for that period under the PAYE regulations, disregarding any deduction the company is authorised to make in respect of the working families' tax credit or disabled person's tax credit, and

(*b*) the Class 1 national insurance contributions for which the company is required to account to the Inland Revenue for that period, disregarding any deduction the company is authorised to make in respect of payments of statutory sick pay, statutory maternity pay, working families' tax credit or disabled person's tax credit.

(2) A "payment period" means a period which ends on the 5th day of a month and for which the company is liable to account for income tax and national insurance contributions to the Inland Revenue.

Payment in respect of R&D tax credit

18—(1) Where—

(*a*) the company is entitled to an R&D tax credit for an accounting period, and

(*b*) makes a claim,

the Inland Revenue shall pay to the company the amount of the credit.

(2) An amount payable in respect of—

(*a*) an R&D tax credit, or

(*b*) interest on an R&D tax credit under section 826 of the Taxes Act 1988,

may be applied in discharging any liability of the company's to pay corporation tax, and to the extent that it is so applied the Inland Revenue's obligation under sub-paragraph (1) is discharged.

(3) Where the company's company tax return for the accounting period is enquired into by the Inland Revenue, no payment in respect of an R&D tax credit for that period need be made before the Inland Revenue's enquiries are completed (see paragraph 32 of Schedule 18 to the Finance Act 1998).

In those circumstances the Inland Revenue may make a payment on a provisional basis of such amount as they think fit.

(4) No payment need be made in respect of an R&D tax credit for an accounting period before the company has paid to the Inland Revenue any amount that it is required to pay for payment periods ending in that accounting period—

(*a*) under the PAYE regulations, or

(*b*) in respect of Class 1 national insurance contributions.

Restriction on losses carried forward

19—(1) For the purposes of section 393 of the Taxes Act 1988 (relief of trading losses against future trading profits), a company's trading loss for a period for which it claims an R&D tax credit is treated as reduced by the amount of the loss surrendered.

(2) The amount of the loss surrendered is—

(*a*) where the maximum amount of R&D tax credit was claimed, the whole of the surrenderable loss for that period;

(*b*) where less than the maximum amount was claimed, a corresponding proportion of the surrenderable loss for that period.

The "maximum amount" here means the amount specified in paragraph 16(1)(*a*).

Payment in respect of R&D tax credit not income

20 A payment in respect of an R&D tax credit is not income of the company for any tax purposes.

PART III
SUPPLEMENTARY PROVISIONS
Artificially inflated claims for deduction or R&D tax credit

21—(1) To the extent that a transaction is attributable to arrangements entered into wholly or mainly for a disqualifying purpose, it shall be disregarded in determining for an accounting period the amount of—

(*a*) any relief to which a company is entitled under paragraph 13 or 14, and

(*b*) any R&D tax credit to which a company is entitled.

(2) Arrangements are entered into wholly or mainly for a "disqualifying purpose" if their main object, or one of their main objects, is to enable a company to obtain—

(*a*) relief under paragraph 13 or 14 to which it would not otherwise be entitled or of a greater amount than that to which it would otherwise be entitled; or

(*b*) an R&D tax credit to which it would not otherwise be entitled or of a greater amount than that to which it would otherwise be entitled.

(3) In this paragraph "arrangements" includes any scheme, agreement or understanding, whether or not legally enforceable.

Restriction on consortium relief

22 Where—

(*a*) the company claims relief under paragraph 13 or 14 in respect of an accounting period, and

(*b*) at any time during that period the company is owned by a consortium at least one of the members of which is a company which is not a small or medium-sized enterprise,

no amount in respect of that period may be surrendered by the company, for the purposes of a claim to group relief under section 402(3) of the Taxes Act 1988 (group relief available where surrendering company owned by consortium), to any other company that is not a small or medium-sized enterprise.

Treatment of deemed trading loss

23—(1) This paragraph applies where under paragraph 14 (alternative treatment of pre-trading expenditure) a company is treated as incurring a trading loss in an accounting period ("the accounting period").

(2) The trading loss may not be set off against profits of a preceding accounting period under section 393A(1)(*b*) of the Taxes Act 1988 unless the company is entitled to R&D tax relief under paragraph 14 above for that earlier period.

(3) If the company begins, in the accounting period or a later period, to carry on a trade which falls within sub-paragraph (4), then—

(*a*) subject to paragraph 19 (restriction on losses carried forward), and

(*b*) to the extent that—

(i) the company has not obtained relief in respect of the trading loss under any other provision, and

(ii) the loss has not been surrendered under section 403(1) of the Taxes Act 1988 (surrender of relief to group or consortium members),

the loss shall be treated as if it were a loss of that trade brought forward under section 393 of the Taxes Act 1988 (relief of trading losses against future trading profits).

(4) A trade falls within this sub-paragraph if it is derived from the research and development in relation to which the R&D tax relief in question was obtained under paragraph 14.

Funding of R&D tax credits

24 Section 10 of the Exchequer and Audit Departments Act 1866 (gross revenues to be paid to Exchequer) shall be construed as allowing the Commissioners of Inland Revenue to deduct payments for or in respect of R&D tax credits before causing the gross revenues of their department to be paid to the accounts mentioned in that section.

Interpretation

25—(1) In this Schedule—

"the Inland Revenue" means any officer of the Board;

"national insurance contributions" means contributions under Part I of the Social Security Contributions and Benefits Act 1992 or Part I of the Social Security Contributions and Benefits (Northern Ireland) Act 1992;

...¹

"PAYE regulations" means regulations under section 203 of the Taxes Act 1988;

"payment period" has the meaning given in paragraph 17(2);

"research and development" has the meaning given by section 837A of the Taxes Act 1988; and

"surrenderable loss" has the meaning given in paragraph 15(2).

(2) Section 839 of the Taxes Act 1988 (connected persons) applies for the purposes of this Schedule.

(3) For the purposes of this Schedule a company not within the charge to corporation tax which incurs qualifying R&D expenditure is treated as having such accounting periods as it would have if—

(*a*) it carried on a trade consisting of the activities in respect of which the expenditure is incurred, and (*b*) it had started to carry on that trade when it started to carry on relevant research and development.

Amendments—¹ Definition of "normal accounting practice" repealed by FA 2002 s 141, Sch 40 Pt 3(16) with effect from 24 July 2002. The definition previously read—

"normal accounting practice" means normal accounting practice in relation to the accounts of companies incorporated in any part of the United Kingdom;".

Transitional provisions

26—(1) This Schedule does not apply to expenditure incurred before 1st April 2000.

(2) For this purpose no account shall be taken of section 401 of the Taxes Act 1988 (pre-trading expenditure treated as incurred when trading begins).

SCHEDULE 21

R&D TAX CREDITS: CONSEQUENTIAL AMENDMENTS

Section 69(2)

Commentary—*Simon's Direct Tax Service* **B2.703**.

Interest

1 (*amends* TA 1988 s 826(1), (8A) and *inserts* TA 1988 s 826(3A), (8BA)).

Claim must be made in tax return

2 (*substitutes* FA 1998 Sch 18 para 10(2)).

Recovery of excessive R&D tax credit

3 (*Inserts* FA 1998 Sch 18 para 52(2)(*ba*), (5)(*ab*) and *amends* FA 1998 Sch 18 para 52(5)).

Claims for R&D tax credits

4 (*Inserts* FA 1998 Part IXA (paras 83A–83F)).

SCHEDULE 22

TONNAGE TAX

Section 82

Cross references—Tonnage Tax (Training Requirement) Regulations, SI 2000/2129 (provision for training requirement referred to in this Schedule).
Tonnage Tax Regulations, SI 2000/2303 (supplementary provisions with respect to tonnage tax).

PART I

INTRODUCTORY

Tonnage tax

1—(1) This Schedule provides an alternative regime ("tonnage tax") for calculating the profits of a shipping company for the purposes of corporation tax.

(2) The regime applies only if an election to that effect (a "tonnage tax election") is made (see Part II of this Schedule).

Companies that are members of a group must join in a group election.

(3) A tonnage tax election may only be made if—

(*a*) the company or group is a qualifying company or group (see Part III of this Schedule), and
(*b*) certain requirements are met as to training (see Part IV of this Schedule) and other matters (see Part V of this Schedule).

Tonnage tax companies and groups

2—(1) In this Schedule a "tonnage tax company" or "tonnage tax group" means a company or group in relation to which a tonnage tax election has effect.

(2) References in this Schedule to a company entering or leaving tonnage tax are to its becoming or ceasing to be a tonnage tax company.

References to a company being subject to tonnage tax have a corresponding meaning.

Commentary—*Simon's Direct Tax Service* **D4.1401**.

Profits of tonnage tax company

3—(1) In the case of a tonnage tax company, its tonnage tax profits are brought into charge to corporation tax in place of its relevant shipping profits (see Part VI of this Schedule).

(2) Where profits would be relevant shipping income, any loss accruing to the company is similarly left out of account for the purposes of corporation tax.

Commentary—*Simon's Direct Tax Service* **D4.1401**.

Tonnage tax profits: method of calculation

4—(1) A company's tonnage tax profits for an accounting period are calculated in accordance with this paragraph by reference to the net tonnage of the qualifying ships operated by the company.

For the purposes of the calculation the net tonnage of a ship is rounded down (if necessary) to the nearest multiple of 100 tons.

(2) The calculation is as follows:

Step One

Determine the daily profit for each qualifying ship operated by the company by reference to the following table and the net tonnage of the ship:

For each 100 tons up to 1,000 tons	£0.60
For each 100 tons between 1,000 and 10,000 tons	£0.45
For each 100 tons between 10,000 and 25,000 tons	£0.30
For each 100 tons above 25,000 tons	£0.15

Step Two

Work out the ship's profit for the accounting period by multiplying the daily profit by—

    (*a*) the number of days in the accounting period, or
    (*b*) if the ship was operated by the company as a qualifying ship for only part of the period, by the number of days in that part.

Step Three

Follow Steps One and Two for each of the qualifying ships operated by the company in the accounting period.

Step Four

Add together the resulting amounts and the total is the amount of the company's tonnage tax profits for that accounting period.

Tonnage tax profits: calculation in case of joint operation etc

5—(1) If two or more companies fall to be regarded as operators of a ship by virtue of a joint interest in the ship, or in an agreement for the use of the ship, the tonnage tax profits of each are calculated as if each were entitled to a share of the profits proportionate to its share of that interest.

(2) If two or more companies fall to be treated as the operator of a ship otherwise than as mentioned in sub-paragraph (1), the tonnage tax profits of each are computed as if each were the only operator.

Commentary—*Simon's Direct Tax Service* **D4.1401**.

Measurement of tonnage of ship

6—(1) References in this Schedule to the gross or net tonnage of a ship are to that tonnage as determined—

    (*a*) in the case of a vessel of 24 metres in length or over, in accordance with the IMO International Convention on Tonnage Measurement of Ships (ITC69);
    (*b*) in the case of a vessel under 24 metres in length, in accordance with tonnage regulations.

(2) A ship shall not be treated as a qualifying ship for the purposes of this Schedule unless there is in force—

    (*a*) a valid International Tonnage Certificate (1969), or
    (*b*) a valid certificate recording its tonnage as measured in accordance with tonnage regulations.

(3) In this paragraph "tonnage regulations" means regulations under section 19 of the Merchant Shipping Act 1995 or provisions of the law of a country or territory outside the United Kingdom corresponding to those regulations.

Commentary—*Simon's Direct Tax Service* **D4.1401**.

PART II
TONNAGE TAX ELECTIONS
Company or group election

7—(1) A tonnage tax election may be made in respect of—

  (*a*) a qualifying single company (a "company election"), or
  (*b*) a qualifying group (a "group election").

(2) A group election has effect in relation to all qualifying companies in the group.

Commentary—*Simon's Direct Tax Service* **D4.1402**.

Method of making election

8—(1) A tonnage tax election is made by notice to the Inland Revenue.

(2) The notice must contain such particulars and be supported by such evidence as the Inland Revenue may require.

Commentary—*Simon's Direct Tax Service* **D4.1402**.

Person by whom election to be made

9—(1) A company election must be made by the company concerned.

(2) A group election must be made jointly by all the qualifying companies in the group.

Commentary—*Simon's Direct Tax Service* **D4.1402**.

When election may be made

10—(1) A tonnage tax election may be made at any time before the end of the period of twelve months beginning with the day on which this Act is passed ("the initial period").

After the end of the initial period a tonnage tax election may only be made—

  (*a*) in the circumstances specified in the following provisions of this paragraph, or
  (*b*) as provided by an order under paragraph 11 (power to provide further opportunities for election).

(2) An election may be made after the end of the initial period in respect of a single company that—

  (*a*) becomes a qualifying company, and
  (*b*) has not previously been a qualifying company at any time after the passing of this Act.

Any such election must be made before the end of the period of twelve months beginning with the day on which the company became a qualifying company.

(3) An election may be made after the end of the initial period in respect of a group that becomes a qualifying group by virtue of a member of the group becoming a qualifying company, not previously having been a qualifying company at any time after the passing of this Act.

This does not apply if the group—

  (*a*) was previously a qualifying group at any time after the passing of this Act, or
  (*b*) is substantially the same as a group that was previously a qualifying group at any such time.

An election under this sub-paragraph must be made before the end of the period of twelve months beginning with the day on which the group became a qualifying group.

(4) This paragraph does not prevent an election being made under the provisions of Part XII of this Schedule relating to mergers and demergers.

Commentary—*Simon's Direct Tax Service* **D4.1402**.

Power to provide further opportunities for election

11—(1) The Treasury may by order provide for further periods during which tonnage tax elections may be made.

(2) Any such order may provide for this Part of this Schedule to apply, with such consequential adaptations as appear to the Treasury to be appropriate, in relation to any such further period as it applies in relation to the initial period.

The consequential adaptations that may be made include adaptations of the references to the passing of this Act or to 1st January 2000.

When election takes effect

12—(1) The general rule is that a tonnage tax election has effect from the beginning of the accounting period in which it is made.

This is subject to the following exceptions.

(2) A tonnage tax election cannot have effect in relation to an accounting period beginning before 1st January 2000.

If the general rule would produce that effect, the election has effect instead from the beginning of the accounting period following that in which it is made.

(3) The Inland Revenue may agree that a tonnage tax election made before the end of the initial period shall have effect from the beginning of an accounting period earlier than that in which it is made (but not one beginning before 1st January 2000).

(4) The Inland Revenue may agree that a tonnage tax election made before the end of the initial period shall have effect from the beginning of the accounting period following that in which it is made.

In exceptional circumstances they may agree that it shall have effect from the beginning of the accounting period following that one.

(5) In the case of a group election in respect of a group where the members have different accounting periods—

(a) sub-paragraph (1), or
(b) any agreement under sub-paragraph (3) or (4),

has effect in relation to each qualifying company by reference to that company's accounting periods.

(6) A tonnage tax election under paragraph 10(2) or (3) (election in consequence of company becoming a qualifying company) has effect from the time at which the company in question became a qualifying company.

This is subject to paragraph 38(2)(a) and (b) (effect in certain cases of exceeding the 75% limit on chartered in tonnage).

Commentary—*Simon's Direct Tax Service* **D4.1402**.

Period for which election is in force

13—(1) The general rule is that a tonnage tax election remains in force until it expires at the end of the period of ten years beginning—

(a) in the case of a company election, with the first day on which the election has effect in relation to the company;
(b) in the case of a group election, with the first day on which the election has effect in relation to any member of the group.

This is subject to the following exceptions.

(2) A tonnage tax election ceases to be in force—

(a) in the case of a company election, if the company ceases to be a qualifying company;
(b) in the case of a group election, if the group ceases to be a qualifying group.

(3) A tonnage tax election may also cease to be in force under—

(a) the provisions of Part V of this Schedule, or
(b) the provisions of Part XII of this Schedule relating to mergers and demergers.

(4) This paragraph has effect subject to paragraph 15(4) (election superseded by renewal election).

Effect of election ceasing to be in force

14 A tonnage tax election that ceases to be in force ceases to have effect in relation to any company.

Commentary—*Simon's Direct Tax Service* **D4.1402**.

Renewal election

15—(1) At any time when a tonnage tax election is in force in respect of a single company or group a further tonnage tax election (a "renewal election") may be made in respect of that company or group.

(2) This is subject to paragraph 32(5) (training requirement: no renewal election if non-compliance notice in force).

(3) The provisions of—

paragraphs 7 to 9 (type of election, method of election and person by whom election to be made), and
paragraphs 13 and 14 (period for which election is in force and when election ceases to have effect),

apply in relation to a renewal election as they apply in relation to an original tonnage tax election.

(4) A renewal election supersedes the existing tonnage tax election.

Commentary—*Simon's Direct Tax Service* **D4.1402**.

PART III

QUALIFYING COMPANIES AND GROUPS

Qualifying companies and groups

16—(1) For the purposes of this Schedule a company is a "qualifying company" if—

(a) it is within the charge to corporation tax,

(b) it operates qualifying ships, and

(c) those ships are strategically and commercially managed in the United Kingdom.

(2) A "qualifying group" means a group of which one or more members are qualifying companies.

Commentary—*Simon's Direct Tax Service* **D4.1403**.

Effect of temporarily ceasing to operate qualifying ships

17—(1) This paragraph applies where a company temporarily ceases to operate any qualifying ships. It does not apply where a company continues to operate a ship that temporarily ceases to be a qualifying ship.

(2) If the company gives notice to the Inland Revenue stating—

(a) its intention to resume operating qualifying ships, and

(b) its wish to remain within tonnage tax,

the company shall be treated for the purposes of this Schedule as if it had continued to operate the qualifying ship or ships it operated immediately before the temporary cessation.

(3) The notice must be given not later than the date which is the filing date for the company's company tax return for the accounting period in which the temporary cessation begins.

"Filing date" and "company tax return" here have the same meaning as in Schedule 18 to the Finance Act 1998.

(4) This paragraph ceases to apply if and when the company—

(a) abandons its intention to resume operating qualifying ships, or

(b) again in fact operates a qualifying ship.

Commentary—*Simon's Direct Tax Service* **D4.1403**.

Meaning of operating a ship

18—(1) A company is regarded for the purposes of this Schedule as operating any ship owned by, or chartered to, the company, subject to the following provisions.

(2) A company is not regarded as the operator of a ship where part only of the ship has been chartered to it.

For this purpose a company is not to be taken as having part only of a ship chartered to it by reason only of the ship being chartered to it jointly with one or more other persons.

(3) A company is not regarded as the operator of a ship that has been chartered out by it on bareboat charter terms, except as provided by the following provisions.

(4) A company is regarded as operating a ship that has been chartered out by it on bareboat charter terms if the person to whom it is chartered is not a third party.

For this purpose a "third party" means—

(a) in the case of a single company, any other person;

(b) in the case of a member of a group—

(i) any member of the group that is not a tonnage tax company (and does not become a tonnage tax company by virtue of the ship being chartered to it), or

(ii) any person who is not a member of the group.

(5) A company is not regarded as ceasing to operate a ship that has been chartered out by it on bareboat charter terms if—

(a) the ship is chartered out because of short-term over-capacity, and

(b) the term of the charter does not exceed three years.

(6) A company is regarded as operating a ship that has been chartered out by it on bareboat charter terms if the ship—

(a) is registered in the United Kingdom, and

(b) is in the service of a government department by reason of a charter by demise to the Crown,

and there is in force under section 308(2) of the Merchant Shipping Act 1995 an Order in Council providing for the registration of government ships in the service of that department.

In this sub-paragraph "government department" includes a Northern Ireland department.

Commentary—*Simon's Direct Tax Service* **D4.1403**.

Qualifying ships

19—(1) For the purposes of this Schedule a "qualifying ship" means, subject to sub-paragraph (2), a seagoing ship of 100 tons or more gross tonnage used for—

   (*a*) the carriage of passengers,

   (*b*) the carriage of cargo,

   (*c*) towage, salvage or other marine assistance, or

   (*d*) transport in connection with other services of a kind necessarily provided at sea.

(2) A vessel is not a qualifying ship for the purposes of this Schedule if the main purpose for which it is used is the provision of goods or services of a kind normally provided on land.

(3) Sub-paragraph (1) is also subject to paragraph 20 (vessels excluded from being qualifying ships).

(4) For the purposes of this paragraph a ship is a seagoing ship if it is certificated for navigation at sea by the competent authority of any country or territory.

Commentary—*Simon's Direct Tax Service* **D4.1404.**

Vessels excluded from being qualifying ships

20—(1) The following kinds of vessel are not qualifying ships for the purposes of this Schedule—

   (*a*) fishing vessels or factory ships;

   (*b*) pleasure craft;

   (*c*) harbour or river ferries;

   (*d*) offshore installations;

   (*e*) tankers dedicated to a particular oil field;

   (*f*) dredgers.

(2) In sub-paragraph (1)(*a*) "factory ship" means a vessel providing processing services for the fishing industry.

(3) In sub-paragraph (1)(*b*) "pleasure craft" means a vessel of a kind whose primary use is for the purposes of sport or recreation.

(4) In sub-paragraph (1)(*c*) "harbour or river ferry" means a vessel used for harbour, estuary or river crossings.

(5) In sub-paragraph (1)(*d*) "offshore installation" means—

   (*a*) an offshore installation within the meaning of the Mineral Workings (Offshore Installations) Act 1971, or

   (*b*) what would be such an installation if the references in that Act to controlled waters were to any waters.

(6) For the purposes of sub-paragraph (1)(*e*) whether a tanker is dedicated to a particular oil field shall be determined in accordance with section 2 of the Oil Taxation Act 1983 (dedicated mobile assets).

Commentary—*Simon's Direct Tax Service* **D4.1404.**

Power to modify exclusions

21 The Treasury may make provision by order amending paragraph 20 so as to add any description of vessel to, or remove any description of vessel from, the kinds of vessel that are excluded from being qualifying ships for the purposes of this Schedule.

Commentary—*Simon's Direct Tax Service* **D4.1404.**

Effect of change of use

22—(1) A qualifying ship that begins to be used as a vessel of an excluded kind ceases to be a qualifying ship when it begins to be so used, subject to the following provisions.

(2) If—

   (*a*) a company operates a ship throughout an accounting period of the company, and

   (*b*) in that period the ship is used as a vessel of an excluded kind on not more than 30 days,

that use shall be disregarded in determining whether the ship is a qualifying ship at any time during that period.

(3) In the case of an accounting period shorter than a year, the figure of 30 days in sub-paragraph (2) shall be proportionately reduced.

(4) If a company operates a ship during part only of an accounting period of the company, sub-paragraph (2) has effect as if for "30 days", or the number of days substituted by sub-paragraph (3), there were substituted the number of days that bear to the length of that part of the accounting period the same proportion that 30 days does to a year.

(5) In this paragraph references to use as a vessel of an excluded kind are to use as a vessel of a kind excluded by paragraph 20 from being a qualifying ship.

Commentary—*Simon's Direct Tax Service* **D4.1404.**

PART IV

THE TRAINING REQUIREMENT

Introduction

23—(1) It is a condition of entering tonnage tax or making a renewal election that—

    (*a*) in the case of a single company, the company, or

    (*b*) in the case of a group, the group,

meets certain minimum obligations in connection with the training of seafarers.

(2) The provisions of this Part of this Schedule have effect for securing that result.

Commentary—*Simon's Direct Tax Service* **D4.1405**.

The minimum training obligation

24—(1) The Secretary of State may make provision by regulations as to the minimum obligation of a tonnage tax company as regards the training of seafarers.

(2) The regulations may—

    (*a*) require the company to provide training for a minimum number of seafarers calculated on such basis as may be prescribed, and

    (*b*) impose different requirements with respect to the training of officers and ratings.

Paragraph (*b*) is without prejudice to the general power to make different provision for different cases (see paragraph 36(2)(*a*)).

(3) The regulations may impose such requirements as to the nationality and ordinary residence of trainees as appear to the Secretary of State to be appropriate.

(4) References in this Part of this Schedule to "the minimum training obligation" are—

    (*a*) in relation to a single company, to the minimum obligation of that company, and

    (*b*) in relation to a group, to the minimum obligations of the qualifying companies in the group taken as a whole.

Meaning of "training commitment"

25—(1) References in this Part of this Schedule to a "training commitment" are to a statement by a company or group setting out how it proposes to meet the minimum training obligation.

(2) A training commitment is not effective for the purposes of this Part of this Schedule unless approved by the Secretary of State.

(3) Sub-paragraphs (1) and (2) are subject to—

    paragraph 27(4) and (5) (power of Secretary of State to set training commitment), and

    paragraph 28(2) (power of Secretary of State to adjust training commitment to take account of changed circumstances).

Commentary—*Simon's Direct Tax Service* **D4.1405**.

Approval of initial training commitment

26—(1) A company or group proposing to make a tonnage tax election must produce, and submit to the Secretary of State for approval, an initial training commitment.

(2) If the Secretary of State is satisfied that the proposals are adequate to meet the minimum training obligation, he shall approve the initial training commitment and issue a certificate to that effect.

(3) A tonnage tax election is ineffective unless such a certificate of approval is in force with respect to the training commitment of the company or group in respect of which the election is made.

Commentary—*Simon's Direct Tax Service* **D4.1405**.

Annual training commitment

27—(1) The Secretary of State may by regulations require a tonnage tax company or tonnage tax group—

    (*a*) to produce a training commitment at such annual or other intervals as may be prescribed in respect of such period as may be prescribed, and

    (*b*) to submit it to the Secretary of State for approval.

(2) If the Secretary of State is satisfied that the proposals are adequate to meet the minimum training obligation, he shall approve the training commitment and issue a certificate to that effect.

(3) It is an offence to fail to comply with any requirement imposed by regulations under sub-paragraph (1).

(4) The Secretary of State may make provision by regulations enabling him—

    (*a*) to set the training commitment for a company or group if, after such period as may be prescribed, no training commitment has been submitted to and approved by him; and (*b*) on the application of the company or group concerned, made after consultation with any prescribed person involved in the training of seafarers, to vary a training commitment set by him.

(5) A training commitment set by the Secretary of State has effect as if submitted by the company or group and approved by him.

Supplementary provisions about training commitments

28—(1) The Secretary of State may make provision by regulations—

(*a*) as to the form and contents of a training commitment;

(*b*) requiring an application for approval of a training commitment to be in such form and contain such information as may be prescribed;

(*c*) authorising the Secretary of State, when considering a training commitment, to consult any prescribed person involved in the training of seafarers;

(*d*) as to the procedure to be followed where the Secretary of State is minded not to approve a training commitment.

(2) The Secretary of State may make provision by regulations—

(*a*) enabling him, on the application of the company or group concerned, to adjust a training commitment (to any extent) to take account of changed circumstances;

(*b*) requiring an application for adjustment to be in such form and contain such information as may be prescribed;

(*c*) authorising the Secretary of State, when considering an application for adjustment, to consult any prescribed person involved in the training of seafarers;

(*d*) as to the procedure to be followed where the Secretary of State is minded not to make the adjustment applied for.

(3) The Secretary of State may by regulations make such provision as he thinks appropriate as to the effect in relation to a training commitment of a merger or other transaction resulting in a change of control of one or more companies.

Payments in lieu of training

29—(1) The Secretary of State may make provision by regulations—

(*a*) allowing a company or group, in such circumstances and to such extent as may be prescribed, to propose in its training commitment to meet the minimum training obligation by making payments in lieu of training; and

(*b*) requiring a company or group to make payments in lieu of training—

    (i) where its training commitment provides for such payments;

    (ii) where training is not provided in accordance with its training commitment.

(2) The regulations shall provide for payments in lieu of training—

(*a*) to be calculated on such basis as may be prescribed,

(*b*) to be made to or for the benefit of any prescribed person involved in the training of seafarers, and

(*c*) to be made at such intervals and in such manner as may be prescribed.

(3) The regulations may provide that if in any case there is a failure in relation to a company or group to comply with the requirements of this Part of this Schedule with respect to—

(*a*) the submission of training commitments, or

(*b*) the making of returns or provision of information,

the Secretary of State may determine to the best of his information and belief the amount of the payments in lieu of training to be made by the company or group.

(4) The regulations may provide that a payment in lieu of training that has become due but is unpaid—

(*a*) is a debt due to the Secretary of State or any prescribed person involved in the training of seafarers, and

(*b*) carries interest at such rate as may be prescribed.

(5) The regulations may provide for the costs or expenses of any legal or other proceedings for recovering the debt or interest to be recoverable, and to carry interest, in the same way as the debt.

Commentary—*Simon's Direct Tax Service* **D4.1405.**

Monitoring of compliance with training commitment

30—(1) The Secretary of State may make provision by regulations—

(*a*) requiring a return to be made to the Secretary of State or any prescribed person involved in the training of seafarers, at such intervals as may be prescribed, of such information as may be prescribed relating to—

    (i) the training provided, and

    (ii) any payments in lieu of training made,

by a tonnage tax company or tonnage tax group;

(*b*) authorising the Secretary of State to direct any person to provide such information as the Secretary of State may reasonably require for the purposes of ascertaining—

    (i) what the minimum training obligation of a company or group should be,

    (ii) whether the proposals in a training commitment are adequate to meet the minimum training obligation of a company or group, or

    (iii) whether a company or group has complied with its training commitment;

(*c*) enabling an audit to be carried on behalf of the Secretary of State of the accounts or other records—

    (i) of a qualifying single company, or

    (ii) of the qualifying companies in a group,

for the purpose of checking that any return or information provided to the Secretary of State is correct.

(2) A person commits an offence if without reasonable excuse—

(*a*) he fails to make a return that he is required to make by regulations under sub-paragraph (1)(*a*),

(*b*) having been directed under regulations under sub-paragraph (1)(*b*) to provide any information, he fails to comply with the direction, or

(*c*) he obstructs a person carrying out an audit under regulations under sub-paragraph (1)(*c*).

Commentary—*Simon's Direct Tax Service* **D4.1405**.

Higher rate of payment in case of failure to meet training commitment

31—(1) The Secretary of State may by regulations provide that—

(*a*) if a company fails to meet its training commitment in any period, the amount of any payments in lieu of training that fall to be made by the company in a subsequent period shall be at a higher rate; and

(*b*) if a group fails to meet its training commitment in any period, the amount of any payments in lieu of training that fall to be made by any member of the group in a subsequent period shall be at a higher rate.

(2) The regulations may contain provision as to—

(*a*) the periods by reference to which it is to be determined whether a company or group has met its training commitment;

(*b*) the circumstances in which a company or group is to be treated as failing to meet its training commitment;

(*c*) the method of calculating the higher rate of payment; and

(*d*) any circumstances in which the higher rate is not to be payable despite the failure of a company or group to meet its training commitment.

(3) The regulations may make provision having the effect that the rate of payments in lieu of training is progressively increased if a company or group fails to meet its training commitment in successive periods.

Commentary—*Simon's Direct Tax Service* **D4.1405**.

Certificate of non-compliance

32—(1) The Secretary of State may by regulations make provision authorising the Secretary of State to issue a certificate of non-compliance in the following cases.

(2) The regulations may authorise the issue of a certificate of non-compliance in respect of a single company if—

(*a*) the company fails to meet its training commitment for successive periods amounting to not less than two years, or

(*b*) the company, or any of its officers, commits an offence under this Schedule.

(3) The regulations may authorise the issue of a certificate of non-compliance in respect of a group if—

(*a*) the group fails to meet its training commitment for successive periods amounting to not less than two years, or

(*b*) a member of the group, or an officer of a member, commits an offence under this Schedule.

(4) If such regulations are made they shall provide that a certificate of non-compliance must be issued unless the Secretary of State is satisfied that there are good reasons why a certificate should not be issued.

(5) No renewal election may be made in respect of a company or group in relation to which a certificate of non-compliance is in force.

Certificates of non-compliance: supplementary provisions

33—(1) The Secretary of State may make provision by regulations—

(*a*) enabling a company or group in respect of which a certificate of non-compliance has been issued to apply to the Secretary of State to cancel the certificate;

(b) requiring any such application to be in such form and contain such information as may be prescribed;

(c) authorising or requiring the Secretary of State, when considering such an application, to consult any prescribed person involved in the training of seafarers;

(d) as to the procedure to be followed where the Secretary of State is minded not to cancel a certificate of non-compliance.

(2) The Secretary of State may by regulations make such provision as he thinks appropriate as to the effect on a certificate of non-compliance of a merger or demerger relating to the company or group in respect of which the certificate is in force.

Commentary—*Simon's Direct Tax Service* **D4.1405**.

Disclosure of information

34—(1) No obligation as to secrecy or other restriction on the disclosure of information imposed by statute or otherwise prevents the disclosure of information—

(a) by the Secretary of State to the Inland Revenue for the purpose of assisting the Inland Revenue to discharge their functions under the Corporation Tax Acts so far as relating to matters arising under this Schedule, or

(b) by the Inland Revenue to the Secretary of State for the purpose of assisting the Secretary of State to discharge his functions under this Part of this Schedule.

(2) No obligation as to secrecy or other restriction on the disclosure of information imposed by statute or otherwise prevents the disclosure of information—

(a) by the Secretary of State to any prescribed person involved in the training of seafarers, or

(b) by any such person to the Secretary of State,

for the purposes of assisting the Secretary of State to discharge his functions under this Part of this Schedule.

(3) Information obtained by such disclosure as is mentioned in sub-paragraph (1) or (2) shall not be further disclosed except for the purposes of legal proceedings arising out of the functions referred to.

Commentary—*Simon's Direct Tax Service* **D4.1405**.
Cross references—Tonnage Tax (Training Requirement) Regulations, SI 2000/2129 reg 25 (the Merchant Navy Training Board and the Maritime Training Trust are prescribed persons for the purposes of sub-para (2)).

Offences

35—(1) It is an offence for a person to provide for any of the purposes of this Part of this Schedule information that he knows or has reasonable cause to believe is false in a material particular.

(2) A person committing any offence under this Part of this Schedule, is liable—

(a) on summary conviction, to a fine not exceeding the statutory maximum, and

(b) on conviction on indictment, to a fine.

Commentary—*Simon's Direct Tax Service* **D4.1405**.

General provisions about regulations

36—(1) Regulations under this Part of this Schedule shall be made by statutory instrument which shall be subject to annulment in pursuance of a resolution of the House of Commons.

(2) Regulations under this Part of this Schedule—

(a) may make different provision for different cases, and

(b) may contain such supplementary, incidental and transitional provisions as appear to the Secretary of State to be necessary or expedient.

(3) In this Part of this Schedule ''prescribed'' means prescribed by regulations made by the Secretary of State.

(4) Regulations under this Part of this Schedule may make provision as to the obligations of a company in respect of any part of the period—

(a) beginning with 1st January 2000, and

(b) ending immediately before the first regulations under this Part come into force,

during which the company is, or is treated as having been, subject to tonnage tax.

This includes power to require payments in lieu of training to be made in respect of any such part of that period.

PART V
OTHER REQUIREMENTS

The requirement that not more than 75% of fleet tonnage is chartered in

37—(1) It is a requirement of entering or remaining within tonnage tax—

(a) in the case of a single company, that not more than 75% of the net tonnage of the qualifying ships operated by it is chartered in;

(*b*) in the case of a group, that not more than 75% of the aggregate net tonnage of the qualifying ships operated by the members of the group that are qualifying companies is chartered in.

(2) For this purpose a ship is ''chartered in''—

(*a*) in relation to a single company, if it is chartered to the company otherwise than on bareboat charter terms, or

(*b*) in relation to a group, if it is chartered otherwise than on bareboat charter terms to a qualifying member of the group by a person who is not a qualifying member of the group.

In paragraph (*b*) ''qualifying member of the group'' means a qualifying company that is a member of the group.

(3) A ship shall not be counted more than once in determining for the purposes of sub-paragraph (1)(*b*) the aggregate net tonnage of the qualifying ships operated by the members of a group that are qualifying companies.

(4) In the following provisions the requirement in this paragraph is referred to as ''the 75% limit''—

paragraph 38 (election not effective if limit exceeded), and

paragraphs 39 and 40 (exclusion of company or group where limit exceeded).

(5) References to the limit being exceeded in an accounting period are to its being exceeded on average over the period in question.

Commentary—*Simon's Direct Tax Service* **D4.1406**.

The 75% limit: election not effective if limit exceeded

38—(1) Where a tonnage tax election is made before the end of the initial period and the 75% limit is exceeded in the first relevant accounting period, the election is treated as never having been of any effect.

(2) Where a tonnage tax election is made after the end of the initial period, then—

(*a*) if the 75% limit is exceeded in the first relevant accounting period, the election does not have effect in relation to that period;

(*b*) if the 75% limit is exceeded in the first and second relevant accounting periods, the election does not have effect in relation to either of those periods; and

(*c*) if the 75% limit is exceeded in the first, second and third relevant accounting periods, the election is treated as never having been of any effect.

(3) For the purposes of sub-paragraphs (1) and (2) the first, second or third relevant accounting period means—

(*a*) in relation to a single company, the accounting period that, if the election had been effective, would have been the first, second or third accounting period of the company after its entry into tonnage tax;

(*b*) in relation to a group, the accounting period that, if the election had been effective, would have been the first, second or third accounting period of a member of the group that would have been a tonnage tax company.

(4) Sub-paragraphs (1) and (2) do not apply to a renewal election.

Commentary—*Simon's Direct Tax Service* **D4.1406**.

The 75% limit: exclusion of company if limit exceeded

39—(1) If the 75% limit is exceeded in two or more consecutive accounting periods of a single company subject to tonnage tax, the Inland Revenue may give notice excluding the company from tonnage tax.

(2) The effect of the notice is that the company's tonnage tax election ceases to be in force from such date as may be specified in the notice.

The specified date must not be earlier than the beginning of the accounting period of the company that follows the second consecutive accounting period of the company in which the limit is exceeded.

Commentary—*Simon's Direct Tax Service* **D4.1406**.

The 75% limit: exclusion of group if limit exceeded

40—(1) If the 75% limit is exceeded in relation to a tonnage tax group in two or more consecutive accounting periods of any tonnage tax company that is a member of the group (''the relevant company''), the Inland Revenue may give notice excluding the group from tonnage tax.

(2) The effect of the notice is that the group's tonnage tax election ceases to be in force from such date as may be specified in the notice.

The specified date must not be earlier than the beginning of the accounting period of the relevant company that follows the second consecutive accounting period of that company in which the limit is exceeded.

(3) Notice under this paragraph need only be given to the relevant company.

This is subject to any arrangements under paragraph 120 (arrangements for dealing with group matters).

Commentary—*Simon's Direct Tax Service* **D4.1406**.

The requirement not to enter into tax avoidance arrangements

41—(1) It is a condition of remaining within tonnage tax that a company is not a party to any transaction or arrangement that is an abuse of the tonnage tax regime.

(2) A transaction or arrangement is such an abuse if in consequence of its being, or having been, entered into the provisions of this Schedule fall to be applied in a way that results (or would but for this paragraph result) in—

(*a*) a tax advantage being obtained for—

(i) a company other than a tonnage tax company, or

(ii) a tonnage tax company in respect of its non-tonnage tax activities,

or

(*b*) the amount of the tonnage tax profits of a tonnage tax company being artificially reduced.

(3) In this paragraph "tax advantage" has the same meaning as in Chapter I of Part XVII of the Taxes Act 1988 (tax avoidance) (see section 709 of that Act).

(4) A finance lease is not to be taken as being an abuse of the tonnage tax regime by reason of the lessor obtaining capital allowances as a result of the lease being, or having been, entered into.

In this sub-paragraph "finance lease", and "lessor" in relation to such a lease, have the meaning given by [section 219 of the Capital Allowances Act 2001][1].

Commentary—*Simon's Direct Tax Service* **D4.1407**.
Amendments—[1] Words in sub-para (4) substituted by CAA 2001 s 578, Sch 2 para 108(1) with effect for corporation tax purposes as respects allowances and charges falling to be made for chargeable periods ending after 31 March 2001.

Tax avoidance: exclusion from tonnage tax

42—(1) If a tonnage tax company is a party to any such transaction or arrangement as is mentioned in paragraph 41(1), the Inland Revenue may—

(*a*) if it is a single company, give notice excluding it from tonnage tax;

(*b*) if it is a member of a group, give notice excluding the group from tonnage tax.

(2) The effect of the notice in the case of a single company is that the company's tonnage tax election ceases to be in force from the beginning of the accounting period in which the transaction or arrangement was entered into.

(3) The effect of such a notice in the case of a group is that the group's tonnage tax election ceases to be in force from such date as may be specified in the notice.

The specified date must not be earlier than the beginning of the earliest accounting period in which any member of the group entered into the transaction or arrangement in question.

(4) The provisions of paragraphs 138 and 139 (exit charge: chargeable gains and balancing charges) apply where a company ceases to be a tonnage tax company by virtue of this paragraph.

(5) Notice under this sub-paragraph (1)(*b*) need only be given to the company mentioned in the opening words of that sub-paragraph.

This is subject to any arrangements under paragraph 120 (arrangements for dealing with group matters).

Commentary—*Simon's Direct Tax Service* **D4.1407**.

Appeals

43—(1) An appeal lies to the Special Commissioners against a notice given by the Inland Revenue under—

paragraph 39 or 40 (exclusion of company or group from tonnage tax if 75% limit exceeded), or

paragraph 42 (exclusion from tonnage tax of company or group where tax avoidance arrangement entered into).

(2) Notice of appeal must be given to the Inland Revenue within 30 days of the date of issue of the notice appealed against.

(3) In the case of a notice under paragraph 40 or 42(1)(*b*) only one appeal may be brought, but it may be brought jointly by two or more members of the group concerned.

Commentary—*Simon's Direct Tax Service* **D4.1407**.

PART VI
RELEVANT SHIPPING PROFITS
Introduction

44—(1) For the purposes of this Schedule the relevant shipping profits of a tonnage tax company are—

(*a*) its relevant shipping income (as defined below), and

(*b*) so much of its chargeable gains as is effectively excluded from the charge to tax by the provisions of Part VIII of this Schedule.

(2) The "relevant shipping income" of a tonnage tax company means—

(*a*) its income from tonnage tax activities (see paragraphs 45 to 48), and

(*b*) any income that is relevant shipping income under—

paragraph 49 (distributions of overseas shipping companies), or

paragraph 50 (certain interest etc),

but subject to paragraph 51 (general exclusion of investment income).

Commentary—*Simon's Direct Tax Service* **D4.1408**.

Tonnage tax activities

45—(1) References in this Schedule to the "tonnage tax activities" of a tonnage tax company are to—

(*a*) its core qualifying activities (see paragraph 46),

(*b*) its qualifying secondary activities to the extent that they do not exceed the permitted level (see paragraph 47), and

(*c*) its qualifying incidental activities (see paragraph 48).

(2) Sub-paragraph (1) has effect subject to paragraph 51(2) (exclusion of activities giving rise to investment income).

Commentary—*Simon's Direct Tax Service* **D4.1408**.

Core qualifying activities

46—(1) A tonnage tax company's "core qualifying activities" are—

(*a*) its activities in operating qualifying ships, and

(*b*) other ship-related activities that are a necessary and integral part of the business of operating its qualifying ships.

(2) A company's activities in operating qualifying ships means the activities mentioned in paragraph 19(1)(*a*) to (*d*) by virtue of which the ship is a qualifying ship.

Commentary—*Simon's Direct Tax Service* **D4.1408**.

Qualifying secondary activities

47—(1) The Inland Revenue may make provision by regulations as to—

(*a*) the descriptions of activity that are to be regarded as qualifying secondary activities, and

(*b*) the permitted level in relation to any such activity or description of activity.

(2) The regulations may set the permitted level or provide for its determination by reference to such factors as may be specified in the regulations.

Qualifying incidental activities

48—(1) A company's incidental activities means its ship-related activities that—

(*a*) are incidental to its core qualifying activities, and

(*b*) are not qualifying secondary activities.

(2) If the turnover in an accounting period of the company from its incidental activities (taken together) does not exceed 0.25% of the company's turnover in that period from—

(*a*) its core qualifying activities, and

(*b*) its qualifying secondary activities to the extent that they do not exceed the permitted level,

the company's incidental activities in that period are qualifying incidental activities.

Commentary—*Simon's Direct Tax Service* **D4.1408**.

Relevant shipping income: distributions of overseas shipping companies

49—(1) Income of a tonnage tax company consisting in a dividend or other distribution of an overseas company is relevant shipping income if the following conditions are met.

(2) The conditions are—

(*a*) that the overseas company operates qualifying ships;

(*b*) that more than 50% of the voting power in the overseas company is held by a company resident in a member State, or that two or more companies each of which is resident in a member State hold in aggregate more than 50% of that voting power;

(*c*) that the 75% limit is not exceeded in relation to the overseas company in any accounting period in respect of which the distribution is paid;

(*d*) that all the income of the overseas company is such that, if it were a tonnage tax company, it would be relevant shipping income;

(*e*) that the distribution is paid entirely out of profits arising at a time when—

    (i) the conditions in paragraphs (*a*) to (*d*) were met, and

    (ii) the tonnage tax company was subject to tonnage tax; and

(*f*) the profits of the overseas company out of which the distribution is paid are subject to a tax on profits (in the country of residence of the company or elsewhere, or partly in that country and partly elsewhere).

(3) For the purposes of sub-paragraph (2)(*c*) the "75% limit" is the requirement set out in paragraph 37 (requirement that not more than 75% of tonnage is chartered in) as it applies to a single company.

(4) In this paragraph an "overseas company" means a company that is not resident in the United Kingdom.

Commentary—*Simon's Direct Tax Service* **D4.1408**.

Relevant shipping income: certain interest etc

50—(1) Income to which this paragraph applies is relevant shipping income only to the extent that it would apart from this Schedule fall to be taken into account as trading income from a trade consisting of the company's tonnage tax activities.

(2) This paragraph applies to—

(*a*) anything giving rise to a credit that would fall to be brought into account for the purposes of Chapter II of Part IV of the Finance Act 1996 (loan relationships); [and][1]

(*b*) ...[3]

[(*c*) any credit falling to be brought into account under Schedule 26 to the Finance Act 2002 (derivative contracts).][2]

Commentary—*Simon's Direct Tax Service* **D4.1408**.
Amendments—[1] Word inserted after sub-para (*a*) by FA 2002 s 79, Sch 23 para 23(1), (2) with effect for accounting periods beginning after 30 September 2002.
[2] Sub-para (2)(*c*) substituted by FA 2002 s 83(1)(*b*), (3) Sch 27 paras 22, 23(1), (3) with effect for accounting periods beginning after 30 September 2002. Sub-para (2)(*c*) previously read as follows—

"(*c*) any profit on a qualifying contract under Chapter II of Part IV of the Finance Act 1994 (interest rate and currency contracts).".

[3] Sub-para (2)(*b*) repealed by FA 2002 s 141, Sch 40 Pt 3(10) with effect for accounting periods beginning after 30 September 2002. Sub-para (2)(*b*) previously read as follows—

"(*b*) any exchange gain under Chapter II of Part II of the Finance Act 1993 (exchange gains and losses); and".

General exclusion of investment income

51—(1) Income from investments is not relevant shipping income.

(2) To the extent that an activity gives rise to income from investments it is not regarded as part of a company's tonnage tax activities.

(3) For the purposes of this paragraph "income from investments" includes—

(*a*) any income chargeable to tax under Schedule A or Case III of Schedule D, and

(*b*) any equivalent foreign income.

(4) "Equivalent foreign income" means income chargeable under Case V of Schedule D that—

(*a*) consists in income of an overseas property business, or

(*b*) is equivalent to a description of income chargeable to tax under Case III of Schedule D but arises from a possession outside the United Kingdom.

(5) Sub-paragraph (1) above does not affect income that is relevant shipping income under—

paragraph 49 (distributions of overseas shipping companies), or

paragraph 50 (certain interest etc).

Commentary—*Simon's Direct Tax Service* **D4.1408**.

PART VII

THE RING FENCE: GENERAL PROVISIONS

Accounting period ends on entry or exit

52 An accounting period ends (if it would not otherwise do so) when a company enters or leaves tonnage tax.

Commentary—*Simon's Direct Tax Service* **D4.1410**.

Tonnage tax trade

53—(1) The tonnage tax activities of a tonnage tax company are treated for corporation tax purposes as a separate trade (the company's "tonnage tax trade") distinct from all other activities carried on by the company.

(2) Sub-paragraph (1) shall not be read as requiring a company to be treated—

(a) as setting up and commencing a new trade on entry into tonnage tax, or

(b) as permanently ceasing to carry on a trade on leaving tonnage tax.

Commentary—*Simon's Direct Tax Service* **D4.1410**.

Profits of controlled foreign companies

54—(1) A tonnage tax company is not subject to any liability under section 747 of the Taxes Act 1988 in any accounting period in respect of profits of a controlled foreign company if in that period distributions of the controlled foreign company made to the tonnage tax company would be relevant shipping income of the latter (see paragraph 49).

(2) Schedule 24 to that Act (assumptions for calculating chargeable profits of controlled foreign companies) has effect subject to the following provisions.

(3) If a company in relation to which that Schedule applies—

(a) is a member of a tonnage tax group, and

(b) is a tonnage tax company by virtue of the group's tonnage tax election, or would be if it were within the charge to corporation tax,

it shall be assumed for the purposes for which that Schedule applies to be a single company that is a tonnage tax company.

(4) Nothing in paragraph 5(1) of that Schedule (controlled foreign company assumed not to be member of a group) affects sub-paragraph (3) above.

For accounting periods ending before 1st April 2000 the reference to paragraph 5(1) has effect as a reference to paragraph 5 of that Schedule.

(5) Paragraph 20 of that Schedule (provisions for avoiding double charge) does not apply where, or to the extent that, the transaction in question is one any profits from which would be, or would be reflected in, relevant shipping profits of a party to the transaction.

Commentary—*Simon's Direct Tax Service* **D4.1410**.

General exclusion of reliefs, deductions and set-offs

55 No relief, deduction or set-off of any description is allowed against the amount of a company's tonnage tax profits.

Commentary—*Simon's Direct Tax Service* **D4.1410**.

Exclusion of loss relief

56—(1) When a company enters tonnage tax, any losses that have accrued to it before entry and are attributable—

(a) to activities that under tonnage tax become part of the company's tonnage tax trade, or

(b) to a source of income that under tonnage tax becomes relevant shipping income,

are not available for loss relief in any accounting period beginning on or after the company's entry into tonnage tax.

(2) Any apportionment necessary to determine the losses so attributable shall be made on a just and reasonable basis.

(3) In sub-paragraph (1) "loss relief" includes any means by which a loss might be used to reduce the amount in respect of which that company, or any other company, is chargeable to tax.

Commentary—*Simon's Direct Tax Service* **D4.1410**.

Exclusion of relief or set-off against tax liability

57—(1) Any relief or set-off against a company's tax liability for an accounting period does not apply in relation to—

(a) so much of that tax liability as is attributable to the company's tonnage tax profits, or

(b) so much of that tax liability as is attributable to tonnage profits of a controlled foreign company apportioned to the company under section 747(3) of the Taxes Act 1988.

(2) Relief to which this paragraph applies includes, but is not limited to, any relief or set-off under—

(a) section 788 or 790 of the Taxes Act 1988 (double taxation relief), or

(b) regulations under section 32 of the Finance Act 1998 (unrelieved surplus advance corporation tax).

(3) Sub-paragraph (1)(b) applies whether or not the company to which the profits are apportioned is subject to tonnage tax.

(4) For the purposes of sub-paragraph (1)(*b*)—

(*a*) ''tonnage profits'' means so much of the chargeable profits of the controlled foreign company as, on the assumptions in Schedule 24 to the Taxes Act 1988, are calculated in accordance with paragraph 4 of this Schedule; and

(*b*) so much of a controlled foreign company's chargeable profits for any accounting period as are tonnage profits shall be treated as apportioned under section 747(3) of that Act in the same proportions as those chargeable profits (taken generally) are apportioned.

(5) For the purposes of any such regulations as are mentioned in sub-paragraph (2)(*b*), a company's tonnage tax profits shall be left out of account in determining the company's profits charged to corporation tax.

This does not affect the computation under those regulations of shadow ACT on distributions made by a tonnage tax company, whether paid out of tonnage tax profits or other profits.

(6) This paragraph does not affect—

(*a*) any reduction under section 13(2) of the Taxes Act 1988 (marginal small companies' relief), or

(*b*) any set off under section 7(2) or 11(3) of the Taxes Act 1988 (set off for income tax borne by deduction).

Commentary—*Simon's Direct Tax Service* **D4.1410**.

Transactions not at arm's length: between tonnage tax company and another person

58—(1) In relation to provision made or imposed as between a tonnage tax company and another person by a transaction or series of transactions that—

(*a*) falls in relation to the tonnage tax company to be regarded as made or imposed in the course of, or with respect to, its tonnage tax trade, and

(*b*) does not fall in relation to the other person to be regarded as made or imposed in the course of, or with respect to, a tonnage tax trade carried on by that person,

Schedule 28AA to the Taxes Act 1988 (transactions not at arm's length) has effect with the omission of paragraphs 5(2) to (6), 6 and 7 (exclusion of intra-UK transactions).

(2) Expressions used in Schedule 28AA have the same meaning in this paragraph.

(3) Nothing in this paragraph affects the computation of a company's tonnage tax profits.

Commentary—*Simon's Direct Tax Service* **D4.1410**.

Transactions not at arm's length: between tonnage tax trade and other activities of same company

59—(1) Schedule 28AA of the Taxes Act 1988 (transactions not at arm's length) applies to provision made or imposed as between a company's tonnage tax trade and other activities carried on by it as if—

(*a*) that trade and those activities were carried on by two different persons,

(*b*) the provision were made or imposed between those persons by means of a transaction, and

(*c*) the two persons were both controlled by the same person at the time of the making or imposition of the provision.

(2) As applied by sub-paragraph (1), Schedule 28AA has effect with the omission of paragraphs 5(2) to (6), 6 and 7 (exclusion of intra-UK transactions).

(3) Expressions used in Schedule 28AA have the same meaning in this paragraph.

(4) Nothing in this paragraph affects the computation of a company's tonnage tax profits.

Commentary—*Simon's Direct Tax Service* **D4.1410**.

Transactions not at arm's length: duty to give notice

60—(1) Not more than 90 days after—

(*a*) the making of an election under this Schedule, or the occurrence of any other event, as a result of which a company enters, or is taken to have entered, tonnage tax, or

(*b*) the making of an election under this Schedule as a result of which a company will become a tonnage tax company at a later date,

the company shall give notice under this paragraph to any person whose tax liability may be affected by paragraph 58 (transactions not at arm's length).

(2) The notice must state—

(*a*) that the company has become a tonnage tax company, or

(*b*) that an election has been made under this Schedule as a result of which the company will become a tonnage tax company,

and inform the person to whom it is given of the possible application of the provisions of Schedule 28AA in relation to transactions between the company and that person.

Commentary—*Simon's Direct Tax Service* **D4.1410**.

Treatment of finance costs: single company

61—(1) This paragraph applies to a tonnage tax company which is a single company carrying on tonnage tax activities and other activities.

(2) An adjustment shall be made if it appears, in relation to an accounting period of the company, that the company's deductible finance costs outside the ring fence exceed a fair proportion of the company's total finance costs.

(3) The company's "deductible finance costs outside the ring fence" means the total of the amounts that may be brought into account in respect of finance costs in calculating for the purposes of corporation tax the company's profits other than relevant shipping profits.

(4) A company's "total finance costs" means so much of the company's finance costs as could, if there were no tonnage tax election, be brought into account in calculating the company's profits for the purposes of corporation tax.

(5) What proportion of the company's total finance costs should be deductible outside the ring fence shall be determined on a just and reasonable basis by reference to the extent to which the funding in relation to which the costs are incurred is applied in such a way that any profits arising, directly or indirectly, would be relevant shipping profits.

(6) Where an adjustment falls to be made under this paragraph, an amount equal to the excess referred to in sub-paragraph (2) shall be brought into account as if it were a non-trading credit falling for the purposes of Chapter II of Part IV of the Finance Act 1996 (loan relationships) to be brought into account in respect of a loan relationship of the company in respect of non-tonnage tax activities.

Commentary—*Simon's Direct Tax Service* **D4.1410**.

Treatment of finance costs: group company

62—(1) This paragraph applies to a tonnage tax company which is a member of a tonnage tax group where the activities carried on by the members of the group include activities other than tonnage tax activities.

(2) An adjustment shall be made if it appears, in relation to an accounting period of the company, that the group's deductible finance costs outside the ring fence exceed a fair proportion of the total finance costs of the group.

(3) A group's "deductible finance costs outside the ring fence" means so much of the group's finance costs as may be brought into account in calculating for the purposes of corporation tax—

   (*a*) in the case of a group member that is a tonnage tax company, the company's profits other than relevant shipping profits, and
   (*b*) in the case of a group member that is not a tonnage tax company, the company's profits.

(4) A group's "total finance costs" means so much of the group's finance costs as could, if there were no tonnage tax election, be brought into account in calculating for the purposes of corporation tax the profits of any member of the group.

(5) What proportion of the group's total finance costs should be deductible outside the ring fence shall be determined on a just and reasonable basis by reference to the extent to which the funding in relation to which the costs are incurred is applied in such a way that any profits arising, directly or indirectly, would be relevant shipping profits.

(6) Where an adjustment falls to be made under this paragraph, an amount equal to the relevant proportion of the excess referred to in sub-paragraph (2) shall be brought into account as if it were a non-trading credit falling for the purposes of Chapter II of Part IV of the Finance Act 1996 (loan relationships) to be brought into account in respect of a loan relationship of the company in respect of non-tonnage tax activities.

For this purpose "the relevant proportion" is the proportion that the company's tonnage tax profits bear to the tonnage tax profits of all the members of the group.

Commentary—*Simon's Direct Tax Service* **D4.1410**.

Meaning of "finance costs"

63—(1) For the purposes of paragraphs 61 and 62 "finance costs" means the costs of debt finance.

(2) In calculating the costs of debt finance, the matters to be taken into account include—

   (*a*) any costs giving rise to a trading or non-trading debit under Chapter II of Part IV of the Finance Act 1996 (loan relationships);
   [(*b*) any credit or debit falling to be brought into account under Schedule 26 to the Finance Act 2002 (derivative contracts), in relation to debt finance;][2]
   (*c*) any exchange gain or loss [within the meaning given by section 103(1A) of the Finance Act 1996][1] in relation to debt finance;
   (*d*) the finance cost—
      (i) implicit in a payment under a finance lease, or
      (ii) payable on debt factoring or any similar transaction; and

(*e*) any other costs arising from what would be considered on normal accounting principles to be a financing transaction.

(3) No adjustment shall be made under paragraph 61 or 62 if, in calculating for a period the company's, or as the case may be, the group's deductible finance costs outside the ring fence, the amount taken into account in respect of costs and losses is exceeded by the amount taken into account in respect of profits and gains.

Commentary—*Simon's Direct Tax Service* **D4.1410**.
Amendments—¹ In sub-para (2)(*c*), words substituted for the words "within the meaning of Chapter II of Part II of the Finance Act 1993" by FA 2002 s 79, Sch 23 paras 22, 23(1), (3) with effect for accounting periods beginning after 30 September 2002.
² Sub-para (2)(*b*) substituted by FA 2002 s 83(1)(*b*), (3) Sch 27 paras 22, 23(1), (3) with effect for accounting periods beginning after 30 September 2002. Sub-para (2)(*b*) previously read as follows—

"(*b*) any trading profit or loss, under Chapter II of Part IV of the Finance Act 1994 (interest rate and currency contracts), in relation to debt finance;".

PART VIII
CHARGEABLE GAINS AND ALLOWABLE LOSSES ON TONNAGE TAX ASSETS

Chargeable gains: tonnage tax assets

64—(1) In this Part of this Schedule a "tonnage tax asset" means an asset that is used wholly and exclusively for the purposes of the tonnage tax activities of a tonnage tax company.

(2) Where for one or more continuous periods of at least a year part of an asset has been used wholly and exclusively for the purposes of the tonnage tax activities of a tonnage tax company and part has not, this Part of this Schedule shall apply as if the part so used were a separate asset.

(3) Where sub-paragraph (2) applies, any necessary apportionment of the gain or loss on the whole asset shall be made on a just and reasonable basis.

Commentary—*Simon's Direct Tax Service* **D4.1411**.

Chargeable gains: disposal of tonnage tax asset

65—(1) When an asset is disposed of that is or has been a tonnage tax asset—

(*a*) any gain or loss on the disposal is a chargeable gain or allowable loss only to the extent (if any) to which it is referable to periods during which the asset was not a tonnage tax asset, and
(*b*) any such chargeable gain or allowable loss on a disposal by a tonnage tax company is treated as arising otherwise than in the course of the company's tonnage tax trade.

(2) For the purposes of sub-paragraph (1) the amount of the gain or loss on a disposal means what would be the amount of the chargeable gain or allowable loss apart from this paragraph.

(3) The proportion of that gain or loss referable to periods during which the asset was not a tonnage tax asset is given by:

$$\frac{P - PTTA}{P}$$

where:
P is the total length of the period since the asset was created or, if later, the last third-party disposal, and
PTTA is the length of the period (or the aggregate length of the periods) since—

(*a*) the asset was created, or
(*b*) if later, the last third-party disposal,

during which the asset was a tonnage tax asset.

(4) In sub-paragraph (3) a "third-party disposal" means a disposal (or deemed disposal) that is not treated as one on which neither a gain nor a loss accrues to the person making the disposal.

Chargeable gains: losses brought forward

66 A tonnage tax election does not affect the deduction under section 8(1) of the Taxation of Chargeable Gains Act 1992 (corporation tax: computation of chargeable gains) of allowable losses that accrued to a company before it became a tonnage tax company.

Commentary—*Simon's Direct Tax Service* **D4.1411**.

Chargeable gains: roll-over relief for business assets

67—(1) Sections 152 and 153 of the Taxation of Chargeable Gains Act 1992 (roll-over relief for business assets) do not apply if or to the extent that the new assets are tonnage tax assets.

(2) Where relief under either of those sections is, or has been, claimed in respect of the disposal of an asset ("Asset No.1") and the acquisition of another asset ("Asset No.2") that subsequently

becomes a tonnage tax asset, the claimant is not (or, as the case may be, shall cease to be) entitled under that section to—

(*a*) a reduction of the consideration for the disposal of Asset No.1, and

(*b*) a corresponding reduction of the expenditure for the acquisition of Asset No.2,

but so much of the chargeable gain arising on the disposal of Asset No.1 as is equal to the amount of the reduction that would have been made is treated as not accruing until Asset No.2 is disposed of.

(3) Any chargeable gain accruing as a result of the rules in sub-paragraph (1) or (2) is treated as arising otherwise than in the course of the company's tonnage tax trade.

Commentary—*Simon's Direct Tax Service* **D4.1411**.
Modifications—TCGA 1992 Sch 7AB paras 1, 10 (modification of this paragraph for the purposes of TCGA 1992 s 17B (as inserted by FA 2002 s 43) which relates to roll-over of degrouping charge on business assets).

PART IX
THE RING FENCE: CAPITAL ALLOWANCES: GENERAL
Introduction

68—(1) This Part of this Schedule makes provision about capital allowances where a company enters, leaves or is subject to tonnage tax.

(2) The general scheme of this Part of this Schedule is that—

(*a*) entry of a company into tonnage tax does not of itself give rise to any balancing charges or balancing allowances,

(*b*) a company subject to tonnage tax is not entitled to capital allowances in respect of expenditure incurred for the purposes of its tonnage tax trade, whether before or after its entry into tonnage tax, and

(*c*) on leaving tonnage tax a company is put broadly in the position it would have been in if it had never been subject to tonnage tax.

(3) A company's tonnage tax trade is not a qualifying activity for the purposes of determining the company's entitlement to capital allowances.

Commentary—*Simon's Direct Tax Service* **D4.1412**.

Entry: plant and machinery: assets to be used wholly for tonnage tax trade

69—(1) On a company's entry into tonnage tax any unrelieved qualifying expenditure attributable to plant or machinery that is to be used wholly for the purposes of the company's tonnage tax trade is taken to a single pool (the company's "tonnage tax pool").

[(2) In this paragraph "unrelieved qualifying expenditure" has the same meaning as in Chapter 5 of Part 2 of the Capital Allowances Act 2001.][1]

(3) The amount of unrelieved qualifying expenditure attributable to plant or machinery in a class pool, or the main pool, is the proportion of the whole given by:

$$\frac{AV}{PV}$$

where:

AV is the aggregate market value of the assets concerned immediately before entry into tonnage tax, and

PV is the aggregate market value at that time of all the assets in the pool.

(4) References in this paragraph to unrelieved qualifying expenditure include qualifying expenditure to the extent to which it is unrelieved by virtue of notice having been given under [section 130 of the Capital Allowances Act 2001 (notice postponing first-year or writing-down allowance).][1]

No allowance may be claimed in respect of any such expenditure taken to the company's tonnage tax pool.

Commentary—*Simon's Direct Tax Service* **D4.1412**.
Amendments—[1] Sub-para (2) substituted, and words in sub-para (4) substituted by CAA 2001 s 578, Sch 2 paras 108(2), (3) with effect for corporation tax purposes as respects allowances and charges falling to be made for chargeable periods ending after 31 March 2001.

Entry: plant and machinery: assets to be used partly for tonnage tax trade

70—(1) This paragraph applies where, on a company's entry into tonnage tax, plant and machinery is to be used partly for the purposes of the company's tonnage tax trade and partly for the purposes of a qualifying activity carried on by the company.

[(2) Sections 61(1)(*e*), 206(3) and 207 of the Capital Allowances Act 2001 (effect of use partly for qualifying activity and partly for other purposes) apply as follows—

(*a*) references to a qualifying activity shall be read as not including references to the tonnage tax trade, and

(*b*) references to purposes other than those of a qualifying activity shall be read as including references to the purposes of the tonnage tax trade.][1]

Commentary—*Simon's Direct Tax Service* **D4.1412**.
Amendments—[1] Sub-para (2) substituted by CAA 2001 s 578, Sch 2 para 108(4) with effect for corporation tax purposes, as respects allowances and charges falling to be made for chargeable periods ending after 31 March 2001.

Entry: ships acquired and disposed of within twelve months

71—(1) This paragraph applies if a company—

(*a*) acquires a qualifying ship within the period of six months before the company enters tonnage tax, and

(*b*) disposes of the ship before the end of the period of twelve months beginning with the day on which the ship was acquired.

(2) The aggregate amount of the capital allowances to which the company is entitled for the period or periods before entry into tonnage tax in respect of its expenditure on acquiring the ship is limited to the amount by which that expenditure exceeds the market value of the ship on the company's entry into tonnage tax.

Commentary—*Simon's Direct Tax Service* **D4.1412**.

Entry: deferred balancing charge on disposal of ship

72—(1) This paragraph applies where deferment of a balancing charge has been claimed under [sections 135 to 156 of the Capital Allowances Act 2001][1] (balancing charge on disposal of ship to be deferred and set against new expenditure incurred within six years) by a company that subsequently enters tonnage tax.

(2) Expenditure on new shipping incurred by a company subject to tonnage tax shall not be taken into account for the purposes of those sections unless the company that incurred the balancing charge—

(*a*) was a qualifying company for the purposes of this Schedule at the time the balancing charge arose, or

(*b*) would have been such a company had this Schedule been in force at that time.

(3) Subject to sub-paragraph (2)—

(*a*) the company's entry into tonnage tax does not affect the operation of those sections, and

(*b*) the expenditure on new shipping that is to be taken into account for the purposes of those sections shall be determined as if the company was not subject to tonnage tax.

Commentary—*Simon's Direct Tax Service* **D4.1412**.
Amendments—[1] Words in sub-para (1) substituted by CAA 2001 s 578, Sch 2 para 108(5) with effect for corporation tax purposes as respects allowances and charges falling to be made for chargeable periods ending after 31 March 2001.

During: plant and machinery: new expenditure partly for tonnage tax purposes

73—(1) This paragraph applies where a company subject to tonnage tax incurs expenditure on the provision of plant or machinery partly for the purposes of its tonnage tax trade and partly for the purposes of a qualifying activity.

[(2) Sections 206(1), (2) and (4) and 207 of the Capital Allowances Act 2001 (operation of single asset pool for mixed use assets) apply as follows—

(*a*) references to a qualifying activity shall be read as not including references to the tonnage tax trade, and

(*b*) references to purposes other than those of a qualifying activity shall be read as including references to the purposes of the tonnage tax trade.][1]

Commentary—*Simon's Direct Tax Service* **D4.1412**.
Amendments—[1] Sub-para (2) substituted by CAA 2001 s 578, Sch 2 para 108(6) with effect for corporation tax purposes as respects allowances and charges falling to be made for chargeable periods ending after 31 March 2001.

During: plant and machinery: asset beginning to be used for tonnage tax trade

74 A company's tonnage tax pool is not increased by reason of an asset beginning to be used for the purposes of the company's tonnage tax trade after the company's entry into tonnage tax.

Commentary—*Simon's Direct Tax Service* **D4.1412**.

During: plant and machinery: change of use of tonnage tax asset

75—(1) This paragraph applies where, at a time when a company is subject to tonnage tax, plant or machinery used for the purposes of the company's tonnage tax trade begins to be used wholly or partly for purposes other than those of that trade.

[(2) If the asset was acquired before entry into tonnage tax, section 61(1)(*e*) of the Capital Allowances Act 2001 applies (disposal event if plant or machinery begins to be used wholly or partly for purposes other than those of the qualifying activity), but reading the reference in that provision to the qualifying activity as a reference to the tonnage tax trade.][1]

[(3) If the asset was acquired after entry into tonnage tax and begins to be used wholly or partly for the purposes of a qualifying activity carried on by the company, section 13 of the Capital Allowances

Act 2001 (use for qualifying activity of plant or machinery provided for other purposes) applies as follows—

(*a*) references to purposes which were not those of any qualifying activity shall be read as including references to the purposes of the tonnage tax trade, and

(*b*) references to the qualifying activity carried on by him shall be read as not including references to the tonnage tax trade.][1]

Commentary—*Simon's Direct Tax Service* **D4.1412**.
Amendments—[1] Sub-paras (2), (3) substituted by CAA 2001 s 578, Sch 2 para 108(7) with effect for corporation tax purposes as respects allowances and charges falling to be made for chargeable periods ending after 31 March 2001.

During: plant and machinery: change of use of non-tonnage tax asset

76—(1) This paragraph applies where, at a time when a company is subject to tonnage tax, plant or machinery used for the purposes of a qualifying activity carried on by the company begins to be used wholly or partly for the purposes of the company's tonnage tax trade.

[(2) Sections 61(1)(*e*), 206(3) and 207 of the Capital Allowances Act 2001 (effect of use partly for qualifying activity and partly for other purposes) apply as follows—

(*a*) references to a qualifying activity shall be read as not including references to the tonnage tax trade, and

(*b*) references to purposes other than those of a qualifying activity shall be read as including references to the purposes of the tonnage tax trade.][1]

Commentary—*Simon's Direct Tax Service* **D4.1412**.
Amendments—[1] Sub-para (2) substituted by CAA 2001 s 578, Sch 2 para 108(8) with effect for corporation tax purposes as respects allowances and charges falling to be made for chargeable periods ending after 31 March 2001.

During: plant and machinery: disposals

77—(1) This paragraph applies if when a company is subject to tonnage tax a disposal event occurs in relation to plant or machinery—

(*a*) in respect of which qualifying expenditure was incurred by the company before its entry into tonnage tax,

(*b*) some or all of the expenditure on which was carried to the tonnage tax pool on the company's entry into tonnage tax, and

(*c*) which is used by the company for the purposes of its tonnage tax trade.

(2) A "disposal event" means an event as a result of which the company is required under [Part 2 of the Capital Allowances Act 2001][1] to bring a disposal value into account.

In determining whether such an event has occurred [references in that Part of that Act to a qualifying activity][1] shall be read as including the company's tonnage tax trade.

(3) Where this paragraph applies—

(*a*) the disposal value to be brought into account in respect of any plant or machinery is limited to its market value when the company entered tonnage tax, and

(*b*) the disposal value is set against the unrelieved qualifying expenditure in the company's tonnage tax pool.

(4) If the amount of the disposal value is less than or equal to the amount of unrelieved qualifying expenditure in the company's tonnage tax pool, the amount of unrelieved qualifying expenditure is reduced or extinguished accordingly.

(5) If—

(*a*) the amount of the disposal value exceeds the amount of unrelieved qualifying expenditure, or

(*b*) there is no unrelieved qualifying expenditure in the pool,

the company is liable to a balancing charge.

(6) The amount of the balancing charge is—

(*a*) where sub-paragraph (5)(*a*) applies, the amount of the excess, or

(*b*) where sub-paragraph (5)(*b*) applies, the amount of the disposal value.

This is subject to any reduction under paragraph 78.

Commentary—*Simon's Direct Tax Service* **D4.1412**.
Amendments—[1] Words in sub-para (2) substituted by CAA 2001 s 578, Sch 2 para 108(9) with effect for corporation tax purposes as respects allowances and charges falling to be made for chargeable periods ending after 31 March 2001.

During: plant and machinery: reduction of balancing charges

78—(1) The amount of any balancing charge under this Part of this Schedule is reduced by reference to the number of whole years the company has been subject to tonnage tax at the time of the disposal event giving rise to the charge.

(2) The following table shows the percentage reduction:

Number of years	Percentage reduction
1	15%
2	30%
3	45%
4	60%
5	75%
6	90%
7 or more	100%

Commentary—*Simon's Direct Tax Service* **D4.1412**.

During: plant and machinery: giving effect to balancing charge

79—(1) A balancing charge under this Part of this Schedule—

(*a*) is treated as arising in connection with a trade (other than its tonnage tax trade) carried on by the company, and

(*b*) is made in taxing that trade.

(2) Subject to paragraph 80 (deferment of balancing charge in case of reinvestment), the charge must be given effect in the accounting period in which it arises.

Commentary—*Simon's Direct Tax Service* **D4.1412**.

During: plant and machinery: deferment of balancing charge

80—(1) If—

(*a*) a balancing charge under this Part of this Schedule arises in connection with the disposal of a qualifying ship, and

(*b*) within the requisite period the company incurs capital expenditure on acquiring one or more other qualifying ships, and

(*c*) the company claims relief under this paragraph,

only the amount (if any) by which the balancing charge exceeds that expenditure must be given effect in the accounting period in which the charge arises and the rest may be held over.

(2) For the purposes of this paragraph—

(*a*) the disposal of a qualifying ship includes any event within [section 61(1)(*a*) to (*d*) of the Capital Allowances Act 2001][1] occurring with respect to a qualifying ship, and

(*b*) the requisite period is the period beginning one year before, and ending two years after, the date of the disposal.

(3) If the new qualifying ship (or any of them) is disposed of before the end of the period of seven years after the company in question entered tonnage tax—

(*a*) there is a balancing charge under this paragraph when the disposal occurs, and

(*b*) the amount of that charge is equal to the amount held over under sub-paragraph (1) by reference to the acquisition of that ship.

This is subject to any reduction under paragraph 78 and to any further deferment under this paragraph.

(4) [Sections 135 to 156 of the Capital Allowances Act 2001][1] (deferment of balancing charges) do not apply in relation to balancing charges arising when the company is subject to tonnage tax.

(5) The fact that there is a balancing charge under this paragraph does not affect the operation of paragraph 77 in a case where that paragraph also applies.

Commentary—*Simon's Direct Tax Service* **D4.1412**.
Amendments—[1] Words in sub-paras (2), (4) substituted by CAA 2001 s 578, Sch 2 paras 108(10), (11) with effect for corporation tax purposes as respects allowances and charges falling to be made for chargeable periods ending after 31 March 2001.

During: plant and machinery: surrender of unrelieved qualifying expenditure

81—(1) This paragraph applies where—

(*a*) a company subject to tonnage tax is liable to a balancing charge under this Part of this Schedule,

(*b*) another tonnage tax company which is a member of the same group has unrelieved qualifying expenditure in its tonnage tax pool, and

(*c*) the two companies have been members of the same group for not less than a year at the date of the disposal giving rise to the balancing charge.

(2) The latter company may surrender to the former all or part of its unrelieved qualifying expenditure, and the amount of the balancing charge shall be reduced or extinguished accordingly.

(3) The provisions of Part VIII of Schedule 18 to the Finance Act 1998 (corporation tax self-assessment: claims for group relief), except paragraph 77 (joint amended returns), apply in relation to relief under this paragraph as they apply in relation to group relief.

Commentary—*Simon's Direct Tax Service* **D4.1412**.

During: industrial buildings: mixed use

[82 If any identifiable part of a building or structure is used for the purposes of a company's tonnage tax trade, that part is treated for the purposes of Part 3 of the Capital Allowances Act 2001 as used otherwise than as an industrial building.][1]

Commentary—*Simon's Direct Tax Service* **D4.1412**.
Amendments—[1] Para 82 substituted by CAA 2001 s 578, Sch 2 para 108(12) with effect for corporation tax purposes as respects allowances and charges falling to be made for chargeable periods ending after 31 March 2001.

During: industrial buildings: balancing charges

83—(1) This paragraph applies where, in an accounting period during which a company is subject to tonnage tax, a [balancing event occurs in relation to an industrial building][1] in respect of which qualifying expenditure was incurred by the company before its entry into tonnage tax.

[(2) A "balancing event" means an event by reason of which the company is required by Part 3 of the Capital Allowances Act 2001 to bring into account any proceeds.][1]

In determining whether such an event has occurred references in that Part of that Act to a trade or undertaking shall be read as including the company's tonnage tax trade.

(3) Where this paragraph applies—

[(a) the proceeds to be brought into account in respect of the industrial building are limited to the market value of the relevant interest when the company entered tonnage tax; and][1]
(b) the amount of any balancing charge under that Part is reduced in accordance with paragraph 78.

Commentary—*Simon's Direct Tax Service* **D4.1412**.
Amendments—[1] Words in sub-paras (1), (2) substituted, and sub-para (3)(a) substituted by CAA 2001 s 578, Sch 2 para 108(13)–(15) with effect for corporation tax purposes as respects allowances and charges falling to be made for chargeable periods ending after 31 March 2001.

During: industrial buildings: residue of qualifying expenditure

84—(1) This paragraph applies where a company subject to tonnage tax disposes of the relevant interest in an industrial building ...[1].

(2) [Section 313 and Chapter 8 of Part 3 of the Capital Allowances Act 2001 (meaning of "residue of qualifying expenditure" and writing off qualifying expenditure)][1] apply to determine the residue of expenditure in the hands of the person who acquires the relevant interest, as if—

(a) the company had not been subject to tonnage tax, and
(b) all writing-down allowances, and balancing allowances and charges, had been made as could have been made if the company had not been subject to tonnage tax.

Commentary—*Simon's Direct Tax Service* **D4.1412**.
Amendments—[1] Words "or structure" in sub-para (1) repealed, and words in sub-para (2) substituted by CAA 2001 ss 578, 580, Sch 2 paras 108(16), (17), Sch 4 with effect for corporation tax purposes as respects allowances and charges falling to be made for chargeable periods ending after 31 March 2001.

Exit: plant and machinery

85—(1) If a company leaves tonnage tax—

(a) the amount of qualifying expenditure under [Part 2 of the Capital Allowances Act 2001 (plant and machinery allowances)][1], and
(b) the pools to which such expenditure is to be allocated for the purposes of that Part,

shall be determined under this paragraph.

(2) For each asset used by the company for the purposes of its tonnage tax activities and held by the company when it leaves tonnage tax there shall be determined—

(a) the amount of expenditure incurred on the provision of the asset that would have been qualifying expenditure if the company had not been subject to tonnage tax, and
(b) the written down value of that amount by reference to the period since the expenditure was incurred.

(3) The Inland Revenue shall make provision by regulations as to the basis on which the writing down is to be done.

The regulations may make different provision for different descriptions of asset.

Commentary—*Simon's Direct Tax Service* **D4.1412**.
Amendments—[1] Words in sub-para (1) substituted by CAA 2001 s 578, Sch 2 para 108(18) with effect for corporation tax purposes as respects allowances and charges falling to be made for chargeable periods ending after 31 March 2001.

Exit: industrial buildings

86 If a company leaves tonnage tax the amount of unrelieved qualifying expenditure under [Part 3 of the Capital Allowances Act 2001 (industrial buildings allowances)][1] is calculated as if—

(a) the company had never been subject to tonnage tax, and
(b) all such allowances and charges under that Part had been made as could have been made.

Commentary—*Simon's Direct Tax Service* **D4.1412.**
Amendments—[1] Words substituted by CAA 2001 s 578, Sch 2 para 108(19) with effect for corporation tax purposes as respects allowances and charges falling to be made for chargeable periods ending after 31 March 2001.

Meaning of ''not entitled to capital allowances''

87—(1) Where any provision of this Part of this Schedule states that a person is not entitled to capital allowances in respect of expenditure on plant or machinery—

(*a*) a first-year allowance shall not be given in respect of that expenditure, and

[(*b*) the expenditure shall be disregarded for the purposes of calculating the person's entitlement to a writing-down allowance or balancing allowance or liability to a balancing charge.][1]

(2) If there is no entitlement to capital allowances in respect of expenditure, there is no entitlement to capital allowances in respect of any additional VAT liability incurred in respect of it.

Commentary—*Simon's Direct Tax Service* **D4.1412.**
Amendments—[1] Sub-para (1)(*b*) substituted by CAA 2001 s 578, Sch 2 para 108(20) with effect for corporation tax purposes as respects allowances and charges falling to be made for chargeable periods ending after 31 March 2001.

Interpretation

88—(1) In this Part of this Schedule—

[''capital allowance'' means any allowance under the Capital Allowances Act 2001;][1]

[''qualifying activity'' means any activity in respect of which a person may be entitled to a capital allowance;][1]

''qualifying expenditure'' means expenditure in respect of which a person is or may be entitled to a capital allowance.

[(2) In this Part of this Schedule any reference to pooling or to single asset pools, class pools or the main pool shall be construed in accordance with sections 53 and 54 of the Capital Allowances Act 2001.][1]

(4) Other expressions relating to capital allowances have the same meaning in this Part of this Schedule as in [the Capital Allowances Act 2001][1].

Amendments—[1] Definitions of ''capital allowances'' and ''qualifying activity'' substituted, sub-para (2) substituted for sub-paras (2), (3), and words in sub-para (4) substituted, by CAA 2001 s 578, Sch 2 para 108(21)–(23) with effect for corporation tax purposes as respects allowances and charges falling to be made for chargeable periods ending after 31 March 2001.

PART X
THE RING FENCE: CAPITAL ALLOWANCES: SHIP LEASING
Introduction

89—(1) In the case of a finance lease of a qualifying ship provided, directly or indirectly, to a company within tonnage tax, the provisions of [Part 2 of the Capital Allowances Act 2001][1] have effect subject to and in accordance with the provisions of—

paragraphs 90 and 91 (defeased leasing),
paragraph 92 (sale and lease back arrangements), and
paragraphs 94 to 102 (quantitative restrictions on allowances).

(2) In this Part of this Schedule ''finance lease'', and ''lessor'' and ''lessee'' in relation to a finance lease, have the same meaning as in that Part (see [section 219 of that Act][1]).

(3) Other expressions used in this Part of this Schedule have the same meaning as in Part IX of this Schedule (the ring fence: capital allowances: general).

Commentary—*Simon's Direct Tax Service* **D4.1413.**
Amendments—[1] Words in sub-paras (1), (2) substituted by CAA 2001 s 578, Sch 2 paras 108(24), (25) with effect for corporation tax purposes as respects allowances and charges falling to be made for chargeable periods ending after 31 March 2001.

Defeased leasing

90—(1) The lessor under the finance lease is not entitled to capital allowances in respect of expenditure on the provision of the ship if—

(*a*) the lease, or

(*b*) any transaction or series of transactions of which the lease forms a part,

makes provision the effect of which is to remove the whole, or the greater part of, any non-compliance risk which, apart from that provision, would fall directly or indirectly on the lessor.

(2) For this purpose a ''non-compliance risk'' means a risk that a loss will be sustained by any person if payments under the lease are not made in accordance with its terms.

(3) For the purposes of this paragraph the lessor and any persons connected with him shall be treated as the same person.

(4) In this paragraph ''connected person'' has the meaning given by section 839 of the Taxes Act 1988.

Commentary—*Simon's Direct Tax Service* **D4.1413.**

Defeased leasing: excepted forms of security

91—(1) Paragraph 90 (defeased leasing) is subject to the following exceptions.

(2) It does not apply to the provision of security of any of the following kinds by the lessee, or a person connected with the lessee—

  (*a*) a mortgage of the ship;

  (*b*) security attaching—

    (i) to the ship's earnings, or

    (ii) to the proceeds of insurance policies on the ship;

  (*c*) security over rental rebates arising from the arm's length sale of the ship;

  (*d*) any other form of security relating to assets, sums or rights arising directly from the ordinary operation of the ship or from arm's length transactions involving the ship.

In this sub-paragraph "the ship" means the ship that is the subject of the lease.

(3) It does not apply to the provision of security by the lessee, or a person connected with the lessee, if the following conditions are met—

  (*a*) no deposit of money or other property by way of security is obtained by the lessor or any third party;

  (*b*) any payments under the security are limited to the amount of any rental payments under the lease in respect of which the lessee is in default.

(4) It does not apply to the provision of security by a third party where no security other than security of a kind mentioned in sub-paragraph (2)(*a*) to (*d*) is held by the third party or any person connected with the third party.

(5) It does not apply to the provision of security by a third party if the following conditions are met—

  (*a*) no deposit of money or other property by way of security is obtained by the lessor or any third party;

  (*b*) the security does not involve the assumption of any obligations of the lessee under the lease in return for a payment made (directly or indirectly) by the lessee or a person connected with him;

  (*c*) the security does not give rise to any payments to the lessor unless the lessee defaults on the rental payments under the lease;

  (*d*) any payments under the security are limited to the amount of the rental payments in default.

(6) For the purposes of this paragraph the lessor and any persons connected with him shall be treated as the same person.

(7) In this paragraph—

"connected person" has the meaning given by section 839 of the Taxes Act 1988; and

"third party" means a person not connected with either the lessor or the lessee.

Commentary—*Simon's Direct Tax Service* **D4.1413**.

Sale and lease-back arrangements

92—(1) The lessor under the finance lease is not entitled to capital allowances if the lease is part of sale and lease-back arrangements.

(2) For this purpose "sale and lease-back arrangements" means, subject to sub-paragraph (3), any arrangements that take the following form:

Step One

The ship is owned by a tonnage tax company and used for the purposes of its tonnage tax trade.

Step Two

A transaction is entered into, as a result of which (apart from this paragraph) capital allowances would become available to the lessor, under which—

  (*a*) the ship (or an interest in it) is sold, or

  (*b*) a person enters into a contract on the performance of which he will or may become the owner of the ship (or an interest in it), or

  (*c*) a person entitled to the benefit of any such contract assigns the benefit of it so far as it relates to the ship (or an interest in it).

Step Three

After the time of that transaction the ship is used for the purposes of a tonnage tax trade carried on—

  (*a*) by the original company, or

  (*b*) by another tonnage tax company that is a member of the same group,

without having been used since that time for the purposes of any other trade (except that of leasing).

(3) This paragraph does not apply if the ship is newly-constructed and the transaction mentioned in Step Two in sub-paragraph (2) is effected not more than four months after the first occasion on which the ship is brought into use by any person for any purpose.

(4) A person is regarded for the purposes of this paragraph as owning a ship if it is treated as [owned by him for the purposes of Part 2 of the Capital Allowances Act 2001][1].

Amendments—[1] Words in sub.-para (4) substituted by CAA 2001 s 578, Sch 2 para 108(26) with effect for corporation tax purposes as respects allowances and charges falling to be made for chargeable periods ending after 31 March 2001.

Certificates required to support claim by finance lessor

93—(1) Any claim by the lessor under a finance lease for capital allowances in respect of expenditure on the provision of a qualifying ship must be accompanied by a certificate by the lessor and the lessee stating either—

(*a*) that the ship is not leased, directly or indirectly, to a company subject to tonnage tax, or

(*b*) that neither paragraph 90 (defeased leasing) nor paragraph 92 (sale and lease-back arrangements) applies in relation to the lease.

(2) If any matter so certified ceases to be the case, the lessor must give notice of that fact to the Inland Revenue.

(3) Any such notice must be given within three months after the end of the chargeable period in which the change takes place.

(4) *(Amends* TMA 1970 s 98 Table column 2).

Commentary—*Simon's Direct Tax Service* **D4.1413**.

Quantitative restrictions on allowances

94—(1) Where the lessor under the finance lease is entitled to capital allowances in respect of expenditure on the provision of the ship, the following provisions apply.

(2) There is no entitlement to any first-year allowance.

(3) The lessor is entitled—

(*a*) in respect of the first £40 million of the cost of providing the ship, to writing-down allowances at a rate of 25% per annum on the reducing balance, and

(*b*) in respect of the next £40 million, to writing-down allowances at a rate of 10% per annum on the reducing balance.

(4) The expenditure within each of those bands shall be allocated to separate pools and dealt with under [Part 2 of the Capital Allowances Act 2001][1] in the same way as expenditure allocated to a class pool.

These pools are referred to below as "the 25% pool" and "the 10% pool".

(5) If the cost of providing the ship exceeds £80 million, the lessor is not entitled to capital allowances in respect of the excess.

Commentary—*Simon's Direct Tax Service* **D4.1413**.
Amendments—[1] Words in sub-para (4) substituted by CAA 2001 s 578, Sch 2 para 108(27) with effect for corporation tax purposes as respects allowances and charges falling to be made for chargeable periods ending after 31 March 2001.

Quantitative restrictions: further provisions as to rate bands, limit and pooling

95—(1) The rate bands and limit in paragraph 94 (quantitative restrictions on allowances) apply separately in relation to each ship.

(2) The amounts specified in that paragraph apply in relation to the whole cost of providing the ship.

(3) If—

(*a*) the cost is shared by two or more persons, or

(*b*) a person acquires a part share in the ship,

that paragraph applies as if there were substituted in sub-paragraph (3)(*a*) and (*b*) and sub-paragraph (5) in relation to each person the proportion of the figure specified that his share of the cost bears to the whole cost.

(4) The pools referred to in sub-paragraph (4) of that paragraph are class pools of all expenditure of a lessor that falls to be allocated to a 25% or 10% pool in respect of ships leased by him.

Commentary—*Simon's Direct Tax Service* **D4.1413**.

Quantitative restrictions: meaning of "cost of providing ship"

96—(1) For the purposes of paragraph 94 (quantitative restrictions on allowances) the cost of providing the ship means the total cost of providing it in a state ready to be brought into use for the purposes for which it is normally to be used.

This includes the cost of any accessories or additional equipment, or fitting out, necessary for the operation of the ship for those purposes.

(2) The cost of providing the ship shall be determined without regard to the provisions of [the Capital Allowances Act 2001][1] as to—

(*a*) when expenditure is treated as incurred, or

(*b*) when expenditure may be brought into account as qualifying expenditure.

(3) Further capital expenditure by the lessor on the ship shall be added to the original cost of providing the ship to determine—

(*a*) whether the lessor is entitled to capital allowances in respect of the further expenditure, and
(*b*) if he is, the rate of writing-down allowances to which he is entitled.

References to the cost of providing the ship shall accordingly be read as including any such further expenditure.

(4) The amounts to be taken into account under this paragraph are limited to the amounts that would otherwise have been qualifying expenditure for the purposes of capital allowances.

Commentary—*Simon's Direct Tax Service* **D4.1413**.
Amendments—¹ Words in sub-para (2) substituted by CAA 2001 s 578, Sch 2 para 108(28) with effect for corporation tax purposes as respects allowances and charges falling to be made for chargeable periods ending after 31 March 2001.

Quantitative restrictions: treatment of disposal proceeds

97—(1) The following provisions apply where—
(*a*) there is a disposal of a ship in relation to which paragraph 94 applies to restrict the capital allowances available, and
(*b*) a disposal value falls to be brought into account.

The reference in paragraph (*a*) to a disposal of ship includes a disposal of a part of a ship, or of an interest in a ship or a part of a ship.

(2) The disposal value is first allocated between the 25% pool and the 10% pool in the same proportions as the cost of providing the ship was allocated to those pools.

(3) If the amount allocated to the 25% pool exceeds the amount of qualifying expenditure remaining in that pool, any excess shall be taken to the 10% pool.

(4) A balancing charge arises only if the amount taken to the 10% pool exceeds the amount of qualifying expenditure remaining in that pool.

Commentary—*Simon's Direct Tax Service* **D4.1413**.

Quantitative restrictions: change of circumstances bringing case within restrictions

98—(1) The provisions of this paragraph apply where—
(*a*) the lessor under a finance lease has been entitled to capital allowances in circumstances in which paragraph 94 (quantitative restrictions on allowances) did not apply, and
(*b*) a change of circumstances brings the case within paragraph 89(1) so that the restrictions in paragraph 94 do apply.

(2) In this paragraph—
"the relevant period" means the period beginning—
(*a*) with the beginning of the accounting period of the lessor in which there occurs the change of circumstances in relation to which this paragraph applies, or
(*b*) if since the beginning of that period there has been a change of circumstances in relation to which paragraph 99 applied (change taking case out of restrictions), with the time of that change (or if there has been more than one such change, the last of them),
and ending with the time of the change of circumstances in relation to which this paragraph applies; and
"the lessor's normal pool" means the lessor's pool that contains the qualifying expenditure relating to the ship at the beginning of the relevant period.

(3) At the beginning of the relevant period an amount ("amount A") equal to—
(*a*) the tax written down value of the ship as at that time, or
(*b*) if less, the amount of unrelieved qualifying expenditure in the lessor's normal pool at that time,
shall be brought into account as a disposal value in the lessor's normal pool.

(4) At the same time an amount of qualifying expenditure equal to amount A shall be taken to a separate single-asset pool ("the temporary pool").

(5) Any qualifying expenditure or other items relating to the ship that would otherwise have been brought into account in the lessor's normal pool in the relevant period shall instead be brought into account in the temporary pool.

(6) At the end of the relevant period, the temporary pool shall be closed as if the ship had been disposed of by the lessor for an amount equal to its tax written down value at that time ("amount B"), and any resulting balancing allowance or balancing charge shall be given effect.

(7) The lessor shall be treated as if he had incurred qualifying expenditure equal to amount B on the provision of the ship for the purposes of the lessee's tonnage tax trade immediately after the end of the relevant period.

(8) There shall be allocated to the lessor's 25% and 10% pools the same proportions of amount B as the proportions of the actual cost of providing the ship that would have been so allocated if the case had been within paragraph 89(1) at all material times.

Commentary—*Simon's Direct Tax Service* **D4.1413**.

Quantitative restrictions: change of circumstances taking case out of restrictions

99—(1) The provisions of this paragraph apply where—

(a) the lessor under a finance lease has been entitled to capital allowances in circumstances in which paragraph 94 (quantitative restrictions on allowances) applied, and

(b) a change of circumstances takes the case out of paragraph 89(1) so that the restrictions in paragraph 94 no longer apply.

(2) When the change of circumstances occurs a disposal value shall be brought into account by the lessor equal to the tax written down value of the ship as at that time.

The provisions of paragraph 97 (treatment of disposal proceeds) apply as regards the allocation of that amount to the lessor's 25% and 10% pools.

(3) The lessor shall be treated as if he had incurred qualifying expenditure on the provision of the ship for the purposes of the lessee's non-tonnage tax trade immediately after the change of circumstances occurs.

(4) The amount of that expenditure shall be taken to be the whole of the expenditure on the ship that would have qualified for capital allowances if paragraph 94 had never applied, written down at 25% per annum on the reducing balance for the period beginning with the time when it was actually incurred and ending when the change of circumstances occurs.

Commentary—*Simon's Direct Tax Service* **D4.1413**.

Determination of tax written down value, etc

100—(1) This paragraph supplements paragraphs 98 and 99.

(2) The "tax written down value" of the ship at any time means what would be the amount of unrelieved qualifying expenditure at that time determined on the following assumptions—

(a) that the qualifying expenditure relating to the ship had been held in a single asset pool, and

(b) that there had been made to the lessor—

(i) the first-year allowance (if any) that was actually made to him,

(ii) any first-year allowance falling to be made to him that was postponed under [section 130 of the Capital Allowances Act 2001][1], and

(iii) the maximum amount of any writing-down allowances that, on the preceding assumptions, could have been made.

(3) The references in paragraph 98(3)(b) and sub-paragraph (2) above to the amount of "unrelieved qualifying expenditure" are to [the unrelieved qualifying expenditure that would otherwise have been carried forward under Chapter 5 of Part 2 of the Capital Allowances Act 2001][1].

(4) For the purpose of determining that amount at a time other than the beginning or end of an accounting period of the lessor, it shall be assumed that an accounting period of the lessor began or ended at that time.

Commentary—*Simon's Direct Tax Service* **D4.1413**.
Amendments—[1] Words in sub-paras (2)(b)(ii), (3) substituted by CAA 2001 s 578, Sch 2 paras 108(29), (30) with effect for corporation tax purposes as respects allowances and charges falling to be made for chargeable periods ending after 31 March 2001.

Quantitative restrictions: power to alter amounts by regulations

101—(1) The Inland Revenue may by regulations alter the amounts for the time being specified in sub-paragraph (3)(a) and (b) and sub-paragraph (5) of paragraph 94 (quantitative restrictions on allowances).

(2) The regulations may contain such incidental, supplementary and transitional provisions as appear to the Inland Revenue to be appropriate.

Exclusion of leases entered into on or before 23rd December 1999

102 The provisions of this Part do not apply in relation to a finance lease entered into on or before 23rd December 1999.

Commentary—*Simon's Direct Tax Service* **D4.1413**.

PART XI
SPECIAL RULES FOR OFFSHORE ACTIVITIES
Introduction

103—(1) This Part of this Schedule sets out special rules that apply where a qualifying ship operated by a tonnage tax company is engaged in offshore activities.

(2) The rules in this Part of this Schedule do not apply in an accounting period unless the total number of days in that period on which qualifying ships operated by that company are engaged in offshore activities exceeds 30.

Meaning of "offshore activities"

104—(1) In this Part of this Schedule "offshore activities" means activities in connection with the exploration or exploitation of so much of the seabed or subsoil or their natural resources as is situated in the UK sector of the continental shelf.

(2) The "UK sector of the continental shelf" means—

(*a*) any area designated by Order in Council under section 1(7) of the Continental Shelf Act 1964, and

(*b*) any waters within the seaward limits of the territorial sea of the United Kingdom.

Commentary—*Simon's Direct Tax Service* **D4.1414**.

Vessels to which special provisions do not apply

105—(1) The provisions of this Part of this Schedule do not apply to—

(*a*) offshore supply vessels,

(*b*) tugs,

(*c*) anchor-handling vessels, or

(*d*) tankers.

(2) The Treasury may make provision by order excluding other kinds of vessel from the application of the provisions of this Part of this Schedule.

Commentary—*Simon's Direct Tax Service* **D4.1414**.

Treatment of periods of inactivity

106 A period between contracts when a qualifying ship is not working shall not be taken to be a period during which the ship is engaged in offshore activities unless—

(*a*) the period of inactivity is specifically related to a forthcoming offshore activity, and

(*b*) it is impractical for the vessel to undertake other work in the meantime.

Commentary—*Simon's Direct Tax Service* **D4.1414**.

Profits from offshore activities to be computed according to ordinary rules

107—(1) The profits of a tonnage tax company from a qualifying ship in respect of periods during which the ship is engaged in offshore activities (its "offshore profits") are computed and charged to tax in accordance with ordinary corporation tax principles as if they were not part of the company's relevant shipping profits.

(2) Accordingly, the number of days in an accounting period during which a qualifying ship is so engaged shall be left out of account for the purposes of paragraph 4 (calculation of tonnage tax profits by reference to daily profit).

Commentary—*Simon's Direct Tax Service* **D4.1414**.

Application of ring fence provisions

108—(1) The provisions of Part VII (the ring fence: general provisions) apply in relation to a company's offshore activities as if they were not tonnage tax activities.

(2) The provisions of this Schedule apply in relation to a company's offshore profits as they apply to profits other than relevant shipping profits.

Commentary—*Simon's Direct Tax Service* **D4.1414**.

Chargeable gains from assets used for offshore activities

109 A period during which an asset is used for the purposes of offshore activities is treated for the purposes of paragraph 65 (chargeable gains on disposal of tonnage tax asset) as if it were a period during which the asset was not a tonnage tax asset.

Commentary—*Simon's Direct Tax Service* **D4.1414**.

Capital allowances: general

110—(1) A tonnage tax company may claim capital allowances for capital expenditure incurred in providing plant or machinery for the purposes of its offshore activities.

(2) In such a case [Part 2 of the Capital Allowances Act 2001 applies][1] as if—

(*a*) an asset used for the purposes of the company's offshore activities were provided by the company for those purposes on the first occasion after entry into tonnage tax on which it is brought into use for those purposes, and

(*b*) an amount of capital expenditure (the "notional qualifying expenditure") had been incurred at that time on its provision.

(3) The amount of the notional qualifying expenditure is given by paragraph 112 (existing assets) or paragraph 113 (new assets).

(4) Where an asset to which this paragraph applies ceases permanently to be used for the purposes of the company's offshore activities, it is treated for the purposes of [Part 2 of the Capital Allowances Act 2001][1] as it applies by virtue of this paragraph as if it had been disposed of at market value.

This does not apply if a disposal value is required to be brought into account under [section 61(1)][1] of that Act apart from this sub-paragraph.

Commentary—*Simon's Direct Tax Service* **D4.1414**.
Amendments—[1] Words in sub-paras (2), (4) substituted by CAA 2001 s 578, Sch 2 paras 108(31), (32) with effect for corporation tax purposes as respects allowances and charges falling to be made for chargeable periods ending after 31 March 2001.

Capital allowances: proportionate reduction of allowances

111—(1) This paragraph applies where in an accounting period of the company an asset to which paragraph 110 applies is used for the purposes of the company's offshore activities on some only of the days in the period.

(2) The amount of any writing-down allowance for that period in respect of expenditure incurred on the provision of the asset is restricted to the relevant proportion of the full allowance.

(3) Any writing-down allowance for a subsequent accounting period of the company in respect of such expenditure shall be calculated as if an allowance had been made of an amount equal to the full allowance, whether or not that amount (or any amount) was in fact claimed.

(4) For the purposes of this paragraph the full allowance means the allowance (if any) that would have been available apart from this paragraph.

(5) For the purposes of this paragraph the relevant proportion of the full allowance is given by:

$$\frac{OSD}{APD}$$

where—

OSD is the number of days in the accounting period on which the asset was used for the purposes of the company's offshore activities; and
APD is the number of days in that period.

Commentary—*Simon's Direct Tax Service* **D4.1414**.

Capital allowances: notional qualifying expenditure: existing assets

112—(1) This paragraph applies to determine the amount of notional qualifying expenditure for the purposes of paragraph 110 where the company was entitled before entry into tonnage tax to capital allowances in respect of expenditure on providing the asset.

(2) If the asset was brought into use for the purposes of the company's offshore activities immediately on entry into tonnage tax, the notional qualifying expenditure is equal to any unrelieved qualifying expenditure attributable to the asset.

[(3) In this paragraph "unrelieved qualifying expenditure" means the unrelieved qualifying expenditure that would otherwise have been carried forward under Chapter 5 of Part 2 of the Capital Allowances Act 2001.][1]

(4) The amount of unrelieved qualifying expenditure attributable to plant or machinery in a class pool, or the main pool, is the proportion of the whole given by:

$$\frac{AV}{PV}$$

where:

AV is the market value of the asset concerned immediately before entry into tonnage tax, and
PV is the aggregate market value at that time of all the assets in the pool.

(5) References in this paragraph to unrelieved qualifying expenditure include qualifying expenditure to the extent to which it is unrelieved by virtue of notice having been given under [section 130 of the Capital Allowances Act 2001 (notice postponing first-year or writing-down allowance).][1]

(6) If the asset was not brought into use for the purposes of the company's offshore activities immediately on entry into tonnage tax, the notional qualifying expenditure is the amount given by sub-paragraph (2) but written down in respect of the period between the company's entry into tonnage tax and the asset being brought into use for those purposes.

(7) The Inland Revenue shall make provision by regulations as to the basis on which the writing down mentioned in sub-paragraph (6) is to be done.

The regulations may make different provision for different descriptions of asset.

Commentary—*Simon's Direct Tax Service* **D4.1414**.
Amendments—[1] Words in sub-para (3) substituted, words substituted for sub-paras (5)(*a*), (*b*), by CAA 2001 s 578, Sch 2 paras 108(33), (34) with effect for corporation tax purposes as respects allowances and charges falling to be made for chargeable periods ending after 31 March 2001.

Capital allowances: notional qualifying expenditure: new assets

113—(1) This paragraph applies to determine the amount of notional qualifying expenditure for the purposes of paragraph 110 where the company was not entitled before entry into tonnage tax to capital allowances in respect of expenditure on providing the asset.

(2) If the asset was brought into use for the purposes of the company's offshore activities immediately on being acquired by the company, the notional qualifying expenditure is equal to the amount that would fall to be brought into account as qualifying expenditure under [Part 2 of the Capital Allowances Act 2001][1] apart from this Schedule.

(3) If the asset was not brought into use for the purposes of the company's offshore activities immediately on being acquired by the company, the notional qualifying expenditure is the amount referred to in sub-paragraph (2) written down in respect of the period between its acquisition by the company and its being brought into use for those purposes.

(4) The Inland Revenue shall make provision by regulations as to the basis on which the writing down mentioned in sub-paragraph (3) is to be done.

The regulations may make different provision for different descriptions of asset.

Commentary—*Simon's Direct Tax Service* **D4.1414**.
Amendments—[1] Words in sub-para (2) substituted by CAA 2001 s 578, Sch 2 para 108(35) with effect for corporation tax purposes as respects allowances and charges falling to be made for chargeable periods ending after 31 March 2001.

The training requirement

114—(1) The fact that a qualifying ship is used for the purposes of offshore activities does not affect the training requirement but an allowance is made under this paragraph.

(2) The amount of the allowance in an accounting period is equal to the aggregate of—

(a) the cash equivalent of the training provided that would not have had to be provided, and
(b) any payments in lieu of training made that would not have had to be made,

if the days on which the ship was engaged in offshore activities had been days on which it was not engaged in tonnage tax activities.

For the purposes of paragraph (a) the cash equivalent of training shall be calculated by reference to the current rate of payments in lieu of training.

(3) The amount of the allowance may be deducted by the company in computing the amount of corporation tax payable for that accounting period, so far as that is attributable to offshore activities.

(4) If in any accounting period the company is unable to deduct the full amount of—

(a) any allowance to which it is entitled under this paragraph for that period, and
(b) any amount brought forward under this sub-paragraph,

the balance may be carried forward and set against the amount of corporation tax payable in the next accounting period, so far as that is attributable to offshore activities.

(5) No deduction may be made by a company in computing its profits from offshore activities in respect of expenditure incurred in meeting the training requirement.

Commentary—*Simon's Direct Tax Service* **D4.1414**.

Interpretation

115 Expressions used in this Part of this Schedule that are defined for the purposes of Part VIII or IX of this Schedule have the same meaning in this Part.

PART XII
GROUPS, MERGERS AND RELATED MATTERS
Meaning of "group" and "member of group"

116 In this Schedule a "group" means—

(a) all the companies controlled by an individual, or
(b) where a company that is not controlled by another person controls one or more other companies, that company and all the companies controlled by it.

References to membership of a group shall be construed accordingly.

Commentary—*Simon's Direct Tax Service* **D4.1415**.

Companies treated as controlled by an individual

117—(1) For the purposes of this Schedule an individual is treated as controlling any company that is controlled—

(a) by him alone, or
(b) by him together with one or more associates of his, or
(c) subject to sub-paragraph (2), by any associate of his, with or without any other such associates.

(2) An individual shall not be treated as controlling a company by virtue of sub-paragraph (1)(*c*) if he does not have any significant influence over the affairs of the company in question.

Commentary—*Simon's Direct Tax Service* **D4.1416**.

Meaning of "control"

118—(1) In this Schedule "control", in relation to a company, means the power of a person to secure—

(*a*) by means of the holding of shares or the possession of voting power in or in relation to that or any other company, or

(*b*) by virtue of any powers conferred by the articles of association or other document regulating that or any other company,

that the affairs of the company are conducted in accordance with his wishes.

(2) For the purposes of this paragraph there shall be attributed to a person—

(*a*) any rights or powers which another person holds on his behalf or may be required to exercise at his direction or on his behalf,

(*b*) any rights or powers—

(i) of a company of which he has, or he and his associates have, control, or

(ii) of any two or more such companies, and

(*c*) any rights or powers of any associate of his, or of any two or more associates of his.

(3) The references in paragraphs (*b*) and (*c*) of sub-paragraph (2) to rights or powers of a company or associate include rights or powers attributed to the company or associate under paragraph (*a*) of that sub-paragraph.

(4) The references in paragraphs (*b*) and (*c*) of sub-paragraph (2) to rights or powers of an associate do not include rights or powers attributed to the associate under those paragraphs.

Commentary—*Simon's Direct Tax Service* **D4.1417**.

Company not to be treated as member of more than one group

119—(1) For the purposes of this Schedule a company may not, at the same time, be a member—

(*a*) of a tonnage tax group and a qualifying non-tonnage tax group, or

(*b*) of more than one tonnage tax group.

(2) If the rules in paragraphs 116 to 118 would produce that result in relation to a company, the following rules apply.

(3) As between a tonnage tax group and a qualifying non-tonnage tax group, the company shall be treated as a member of the tonnage tax group and not of the non-tonnage tax group.

(4) As between two tonnage tax groups, the company shall be treated as a member of the group whose tonnage tax election was made first and not of the other tonnage tax group.

(5) In the case of group elections made at the same time, the company may choose which election it joins in.

It is treated for the purposes of this Schedule as a member of the group in respect of which that election is made and not of any other tonnage tax group.

Commentary—*Simon's Direct Tax Service* **D4.1419**.

Arrangements for dealing with group matters

120—(1) The Inland Revenue may enter into arrangements with the qualifying companies in a group for one of those companies to deal on behalf of the group in relation to matters arising under this Schedule that may conveniently be dealt with on a group basis.

(2) Any such arrangements—

(*a*) may make provision in relation to cases where companies become or cease to be members of a group;

(*b*) may make provision for or in connection with the termination of the arrangements; and

(*c*) may make such supplementary, incidental, consequential or transitional provision as is necessary or expedient for the purposes of the arrangements.

(3) Any such arrangements do not affect—

(*a*) any requirement under this Schedule that an election be made jointly by all the qualifying companies in the group; or

(*b*) any liability under this Schedule or any other provision of the Tax Acts of a company to which the arrangements relate.

(4) The Secretary of State may also make such arrangements in relation to matters arising under this Schedule in relation to which he has functions.

Meaning of "merger" and "demerger"

121—(1) In this Schedule—

"merger" means a transaction by which one or more companies become members of a group, and "demerger" means a transaction by which one or more companies cease to be members of a group.

(2) References to a merger to which a group is a party include any merger affecting a member of the group.

Merger: between tonnage tax groups or companies

122—(1) This paragraph applies where there is a merger—

(*a*) between two or more tonnage tax groups,

(*b*) between one or more tonnage tax groups and one or more tonnage tax companies, or

(*c*) between two or more tonnage tax companies.

(2) In all those cases the group resulting from the merger is a tonnage tax group as if a group election had been made.

(3) That deemed election continues in force, subject to the provisions of this Schedule—

(*a*) if there is a dominant party to the merger, until that party's tonnage tax election would have expired;

(*b*) if there is no dominant party, until whichever of the existing tonnage tax elections had the longest period left to run would have expired.

Commentary—*Simon's Direct Tax Service* **D4.1415**.

Merger: tonnage tax group or company and qualifying non-tonnage tax group or company

123—(1) This paragraph applies where there is a merger between a tonnage tax group or company ("T") and a qualifying non-tonnage tax group or company ("QNT").

(2) If T is the dominant party, the group resulting from the merger is a tonnage tax group as if a group election had been made.

That deemed election continues in force, subject to the provisions of this Schedule, until T's election would have expired.

(3) If QNT is the dominant party, T's tonnage tax election ceases to be in force as from the date of the merger.

(4) If there is no dominant party—

(*a*) the group resulting from the merger may elect that T shall be treated as the dominant party (with the result that sub-paragraph (2) applies), and

(*b*) if it does not do so, T's tonnage tax election ceases to be in force as from the date of the merger.

(5) Any election under sub-paragraph (4)(*a*) must be made—

(*a*) jointly by all the qualifying companies in the group resulting from the merger,

(*b*) by notice to the Inland Revenue,

(*c*) within twelve months of the merger.

Commentary—*Simon's Direct Tax Service* **D4.1415**.

Merger: tonnage tax group or company and non-qualifying group or company

124—(1) This paragraph applies where there is a merger between a tonnage tax group or company ("T") and a non-qualifying group or company.

(2) In that case the group resulting from the merger is a tonnage tax group by virtue of T's election.

Merger: non-qualifying group or company and qualifying non-tonnage tax group or company

125—(1) This paragraph applies where there is a merger between a non-qualifying group or company ("NQ") and a qualifying non-tonnage tax group or company.

(2) In that case, if NQ is the dominant party the group resulting from the merger may make a tonnage tax election having effect as from the date of the merger.

(3) Any such election must be made—

(*a*) jointly by all the qualifying companies in the group resulting from the merger,

(*b*) by notice to the Inland Revenue,

(*c*) within twelve months of the merger.

Commentary—*Simon's Direct Tax Service* **D4.1415**.

Meaning of "dominant party" in relation to merger

126—(1) This paragraph explains what is meant by the references in this Schedule to the "dominant party" in relation to a merger.

(2) The "dominant party" is determined as follows—

(a) if the turnover generated by the relevant activities of one of the parties to the merger is more than twice that of the other, that one is the dominant party;

(b) if not, there is no dominant party.

(3) The relevant activities of a party to a merger are—

(a) for the purposes of—

(i) paragraph 122 (merger between tonnage tax groups or companies), or

(ii) paragraph 123 (merger between tonnage tax group or company and qualifying non-tonnage tax group or company),

the tonnage tax activities of that party;

(b) for the purposes of paragraph 125 (merger between non-qualifying group or company and qualifying non-tonnage tax group or company), all the activities of that party.

(4) The basis on which (and the periods by reference to which) the turnover from relevant activities is to be determined for the purposes of those paragraphs shall be such as may be agreed between the parties and the Inland Revenue.

(5) In default of such agreement—

(a) the Inland Revenue shall decide, and

(b) an appeal lies to the Special Commissioners against their decision.

(6) Notice of appeal must be given to the Inland Revenue within 30 days of their decision being notified to the parties.

Commentary—*Simon's Direct Tax Service* **D4.1415**.

Demerger: single company

127—(1) This paragraph applies where a tonnage tax company ceases to be a member of a tonnage tax group and does not become a member of another group.

(2) In that case—

(a) the company in question remains a tonnage tax company as if a single company election had been made, and

(b) that deemed election continues in force, subject to the provisions of this Schedule, until the group election would have expired.

(3) If two or more members of the previous group remain, and any of them is a qualifying company, the group consisting of those companies is a tonnage tax group by virtue of the previous group election.

Commentary—*Simon's Direct Tax Service* **D4.1415**.

Demerger: group

128—(1) This paragraph applies where a tonnage tax group splits into two or more groups.

(2) In that case each new group that contains a qualifying company that was a tonnage tax company before the demerger is a tonnage tax group as if a group election had been made.

(3) That deemed election continues in force, subject to the provisions of this Schedule, until the group election would have expired.

Commentary—*Simon's Direct Tax Service* **D4.1415**.

Duty to notify Inland Revenue of group changes

129—(1) A tonnage tax company that becomes or ceases to be a member of a group, or of a particular group, must give notice to the Inland Revenue of that fact.

(2) The notice must be given within the period of twelve months beginning with the date on which the company became or ceased to be a member of the group.

(3) (*Amends* TMA 1970 s 98 Table column 2).

Commentary—*Simon's Direct Tax Service* **D4.1415**.

PART XIII
APPLICATION OF PROVISIONS TO PARTNERSHIPS
Introduction

130—(1) The Inland Revenue may make provision by regulations as to the application of this Schedule in relation to activities carried on by a company in partnership.

(2) Nothing in the following provisions of this Part of this Schedule shall be read as restricting the generality of this power.

Calculation of partnership profits

131 The regulations may provide that—

(a) for the purpose of calculating the profits of a partner which is a tonnage tax company, the profits of the partnership shall be calculated as if the partnership were a tonnage tax company, and

(b) for the purpose of calculating the profits of a partner which is not a tonnage tax company, the profits of the partnership shall be calculated as if the partnership were not a tonnage tax company.

Commentary—*Simon's Direct Tax Service* **D4.1416**.

Qualifying partnerships

132—(1) The regulations may provide that activities carried on by a company in partnership are not to be regarded as qualifying activities of that company unless the partnership is a qualifying partnership.

"Qualifying activities" here means core qualifying activities, qualifying secondary activities or qualifying incidental activities.

(2) Subject to any provision made by the regulations, a "qualifying partnership" means a partnership that if it were a company would meet the requirements in paragraph 16(1) (qualifying companies).

Commentary—*Simon's Direct Tax Service* **D4.1416**.

Ships owned by or chartered to partners

133 The regulations may provide that a ship which is not partnership property but which—

(a) is owned by or chartered to a member (or two or more members) of a partnership, and

(b) is a ship in relation to which activities of the partnership business are carried on,

shall be treated as if it were owned by or chartered to every member of the partnership and as if everything done by or to any of the partners in relation to it had been done by or to all the partners.

Commentary—*Simon's Direct Tax Service* **D4.1416**.

Transactions not at arm's length

134 The regulations may provide that for the purposes of paragraphs 58 and 59 (transactions not at arm's length) the partnership shall be treated—

(a) as an entity separate and distinct from the persons that are its members, and

(b) as if it were a tonnage tax company.

Adjustments for capital allowance purposes

135 The regulations may provide that where a partner leaves tonnage tax, such adjustments shall be made for capital allowance purposes, in relation to that partner and all or any of the other partners, with respect to—

(a) the amount of qualifying expenditure under [Part 2 of the Capital Allowances Act 2001 (plant and machinery allowances)][1], and

(b) the amount of [the residue of qualifying expenditure under Part 3 of that Act (industrial buildings allowances)][1],

as may be specified in the regulations.

Amendments—[1] Words substituted by CAA 2001 s 578, Sch 2 para 108(36) with effect for corporation tax purposes as respects allowances and charges falling to be made for chargeable periods ending after 31 March 2001.

General

136 Regulations under this Part of this Schedule—

(a) may make different provision for different cases, and

(b) may contain such supplementary, incidental and transitional provision as appears to the Inland Revenue to be appropriate.

PART XIV

WITHDRAWAL OF RELIEF ETC ON COMPANY LEAVING TONNAGE TAX

Introduction

137—(1) This Part of this Schedule applies where a company ceases to be a tonnage tax company.

(2) The provisions of paragraphs 138 and 139 (exit charges: chargeable gains and balancing charges) apply where a company ceases to be a tonnage tax company—

(a) on ceasing to be a qualifying company for reasons relating wholly or mainly to tax, or

(b) under paragraph 42 (exclusion from tonnage tax where tax avoidance arrangements entered into).

(3) Paragraph 140 (ten year disqualification from re-entry into tonnage tax) applies in every case where a company ceases to be a tonnage tax company otherwise than on the expiry of a tonnage tax election.

Commentary—*Simon's Direct Tax Service* **D4.1417**.

Exit charge: chargeable gains

138—(1) Paragraph 65(1)(*a*) (chargeable gain: disposal of tonnage tax assets) has effect in relation to gains (but not losses) on all relevant disposals as if the company had never been a tonnage tax company.

(2) For this purpose a "relevant disposal" means a disposal—

(*a*) on or after the day on which the company ceases to be a tonnage tax company, or

(*b*) at any time during the period of six years immediately preceding that day when the company was a tonnage tax company.

(3) Where sub-paragraph (1) operates to increase the amount of the chargeable gain on a disposal made at a time within the period mentioned in sub-paragraph (2)(*b*), the gain is treated to the extent of the increase—

(*a*) as arising immediately before the company ceased to be a tonnage tax company, and

(*b*) as not being relevant shipping profits of the company.

(4) No relief, deduction or set-off of any description is allowed against the amount of that increase or the corporation tax on that amount.

Commentary—*Simon's Direct Tax Service* **D4.1417**.

Exit charge: balancing charges

139—(1) This paragraph applies if in a relevant accounting period during which the company was a tonnage tax company it was liable to a balancing charge in relation to which paragraph 78 (phasing-out of balancing charges) applied to reduce the amount of the charge.

(2) For this purpose a "relevant accounting period" means an accounting period ending not more than six years before the day on which the company ceased to be a tonnage tax company.

(3) The company is treated as having received an additional amount of profits chargeable to corporation tax equal to the aggregate of the amounts by which those balancing charges were reduced.

(4) Those additional profits are treated—

(*a*) as arising immediately before the company ceased to be a tonnage tax company, and

(*b*) as not being relevant shipping profits of the company.

(5) No relief, deduction or set-off of any description is allowed against those profits or against corporation tax on them.

Commentary—*Simon's Direct Tax Service* **D4.1417**.

Ten year disqualification from re-entry into tonnage tax

140—(1) A company election made by a former tonnage tax company is ineffective if made before the end of the period of ten years beginning with the date on which the company ceased to be a tonnage tax company.

(2) A group election that—

(*a*) is made in respect of a group whose members include a former tonnage tax company, and

(*b*) would result in that company becoming a tonnage tax company,

is ineffective if made before the end of the period of ten years beginning with the date on which that company ceased to be a tonnage tax company.

(3) Sub-paragraphs (1) and (2) do not prevent a company becoming a tonnage tax company under and in accordance with the rules in Part XII of this Schedule (groups, mergers and related matters).

(4) In this paragraph "former tonnage tax company" means a company that is not a tonnage tax company but has previously been a tonnage tax company.

Commentary—*Simon's Direct Tax Service* **D4.1417**.

Second or subsequent application of this Part

141 Where this Part of this Schedule applies on a second or subsequent occasion on which a company ceases to be a tonnage tax company (whether or not this Part applied on any of the previous occasions)—

(*a*) the references to the company ceasing to be a tonnage tax company shall be read as references to the last occasion on which it did so, and

(*b*) the references to the period during which the company was a tonnage tax company do not include any period before its most recent entry into tonnage tax.

PART XV
SUPPLEMENTARY PROVISIONS

Meaning of "ship"

142 In this Schedule "ship" means any vessel used in navigation, and includes a hovercraft.

Meaning of "on bareboat charter terms"

143 In this Schedule a charter "on bareboat charter terms" means a hiring of a ship for a stipulated period on terms which give the charterer possession and control of the ship, including the right to appoint the master and crew.

Meaning of "associate"

144—(1) In this Schedule "associate", in relation to an individual, means—

(a) a relative of that individual;
(b) a partner of that individual;
(c) the trustee or trustees of any settlement in relation to which—

(i) that individual, or
(ii) any relative (whether living or dead) of that individual,

is or was a settlor;

(d) where that individual is interested in any shares or obligations of a company that are subject to a trust, the trustee or trustees of the settlement concerned;
(e) where that individual is interested in any shares or obligations of a company that are part of the estate of a deceased person, the personal representatives of the deceased.

(2) In sub-paragraph (1)(a) and (c)(ii) "relative" means husband or wife, parent or remoter forebear, child or remoter issue, or brother or sister.

Section 831(4) of the Taxes Act 1988 applies for the purposes of this paragraph as it applies for the purposes of that Act.

(3) In sub-paragraph (1)(c) and (d) "settlement" and "settlor" have the same meaning as in Chapter IA of Part XV of the Taxes Act 1988 (see section 660G(1) and (2) of that Act).

Exercise of functions conferred on "the Inland Revenue"

145—(1) Any power to make regulations conferred by this Schedule on "the Inland Revenue" is exercisable only by the Board.

(2) Subject to that, references in this Schedule to "the Inland Revenue" are to any officer of the Board.

Meaning of "company" and related expressions

146 In this Schedule—

"company" means a body corporate or unincorporated association, but does not include a partnership;
"controlled foreign company" has the same meaning as in Chapter IV of Part XVII of the Taxes Act 1988 (tax avoidance: controlled foreign companies);
"single company" means a company that is not a member of a group.

Index of defined expressions

147 In this Schedule the following expressions are defined or otherwise explained by the provisions indicated:

group election	paragraph 7(1)(*b*)
initial period	paragraph 10(1) (and see paragraph 11(2))
Inland Revenue	paragraph 145
leaving (or entering) tonnage tax	paragraph 2(2)
member of group	paragraph 116
merger	paragraph 121(1)
minimum training obligation	paragraph 24
offshore activities (in Part XI)	paragraph 104
offshore profits (in Part XI)	paragraph 107(1)
payments in lieu of training	paragraph 29
pooling and related expressions (in Parts IX, X and XI)	paragraph 88(2) and (3)
operating (a ship)	paragraph 18
qualifying activity and qualifying expenditure (in Parts IX, X and XI)	paragraph 88(1)
qualifying company	paragraph 16(1) (and see paragraph 17)
qualifying group	paragraph 16(2)
qualifying incidental activities	paragraph 48
qualifying secondary activities	paragraph 47
qualifying ship	paragraphs 19 to 22
relevant shipping income	paragraph 44(2)
relevant shipping profits	paragraph 44(1) (and see paragraph 108(2))
renewal election	paragraph 15(1)
the 75% limit (on chartered-in tonnage)	paragraph 37
ship	paragraph 142
single company	paragraph 146
subject to tonnage tax	paragraph 2(2)
tonnage	paragraph 6(1)
tonnage tax	paragraph 1(1)
tonnage tax activities	paragraph 45 (and see paragraph 108(1))
tonnage tax asset (in Parts VIII and XI)	paragraph 64
tonnage tax company	paragraph 2(1)
tonnage tax election	paragraph 1(2) (and see Part II)
tonnage tax group	paragraph 2(1)
tonnage tax pool (in Part IX)	paragraph 69
tonnage tax profits	paragraphs 3 to 5 (and see Part XI)
tonnage tax trade	paragraph 53(1)
training commitment	paragraph 25 (and see paragraphs 27(4) and (5) and 28(2))

SCHEDULE 23

TAX TREATMENT OF AMOUNTS RELATING TO ACQUISITION ETC OF CERTAIN RIGHTS

Section 87

Commentary—*Simon's Direct Tax Service* **B3.1203**.
Revenue Interpretation RI 223—Guidance on the interpretation of FA 2000 Sch 23 in relation to indefeasible rights to use.

Rights to which this Schedule applies

1 This Schedule applies to—

(a) licences granted under section 1 of the Wireless Telegraph Act 1949 in accordance with regulations made under section 3 of the Wireless Telegraphy Act 1998 (bidding for licences), and
(b) indefeasible rights to use a telecommunications cable system (''IRUs''),

and to any right derived, directly or indirectly, from a right within paragraph (a) or (b).

Tax treatment of expenditure on acquisition and receipts from disposal

2—(1) Amounts that may in accordance with [generally accepted accounting practice][1] be taken into account in determining profit or loss for accounting purposes in respect of—

(a) expenditure on the acquisition of a right to which this section applies, or
(b) receipts from the disposal of any such right,

shall be treated as items of a revenue nature for tax purposes provided they are so taken into account in any relevant statutory accounts of the taxpayer.

(2) The reference in sub-paragraph (1) to the acquisition of a right to which this Schedule applies includes—

(a) the extension of rights attached to such a right, and

(*b*) in relation to a right subject to a derivative right, the cancellation or restriction of rights attached to the derivative right.

(3) The reference in sub-paragraph (1) to the disposal of a right to which this Schedule applies includes—

(*a*) the cancellation or restriction of rights attached to such a right, and

(*b*) the granting of a derivative right or the extension of rights attached to a derivative right.

Revenue Interpretation RI 223—Meaning of "taken into account".
Amendments—¹ Words substituted for the words "normal accounting practice" by FA 2002 s 103(4)(*f*) with effect from 24 July 2002.

Tax treatment of amounts arising from revaluation

3—(1) There shall also be taken into account for tax purposes as an item of a revenue nature any amount in respect of the revaluation of a right to which this Schedule applies that, in accordance with [generally accepted accounting practice]¹, falls to be taken into account for accounting purposes.

(2) This paragraph applies whether or not the item—

(*a*) may be so taken into account in determining profit or loss, or

(*b*) is so taken into account in any relevant statutory accounts of the taxpayer.

(3) An item taken into account for tax purposes under this paragraph shall be so taken into account as a credit or debit for the period of account in which it is recognised for accounting purposes in accordance with [generally accepted accounting practice]¹.

Amendments—¹ Words substituted for the words "normal accounting practice" by FA 2002 s 103(4)(*f*) with effect from 24 July 2002.

Tax treatment must accord with accounting approach in relevant group accounts

4—(1) If the taxpayer is a member of a group of companies for which consolidated group accounts are required to be prepared, the accounting approach adopted by the taxpayer for tax purposes in respect of items within paragraph 2 or 3 must not be more cautious than that adopted in the group accounts.

(2) The "accounting approach" means the accounting policies used in preparing the accounts and the methods of applying those policies.

(3) Where consolidated group accounts are required to be prepared for more than one group of which the taxpayer is a member, this paragraph applies in relation to each of them.

(4) In this paragraph—

"consolidated group accounts" means group accounts that satisfy the requirements of—

(*a*) section 227 of the Companies Act 1985, or

(*b*) in Northern Ireland, Article 235 of the Companies (Northern Ireland) Order 1986,

or the corresponding requirements of the law of a country outside the United Kingdom; and "group of companies" means a group as defined in—

(*a*) section 262(1) of the Companies Act 1985, or

(*b*) in Northern Ireland, Article 270(1) of the Companies (Northern Ireland) Order 1986,

or the corresponding provisions of the law of a country outside the United Kingdom.

Revenue Interpretation RI 223—Accounting approach in relevant group accounts.

Interpretation

5 In this Schedule—

...¹

...¹

"for tax purposes" means for the purposes of calculating the amount of any profits chargeable to income tax or corporation tax.

Revenue Interpretation RI 223—Non-traders can claim relief for IRUs against the relevant income stream from exploiting the right.
Amendments—¹ Definitions of "normal accounting practice" and "statutory accounts" repealed by FA 2002 s 141, Sch 40 Pt 3(16) with effect from 24 July 2002. The definitions previously read as follows—

" 'normal accounting practice' means normal accounting practice with respect to the statutory accounts of companies incorporated in a part of the United Kingdom;

'statutory accounts' means accounts that are required by law to be prepared and which meet the requirements of—

(*a*) section 226 of the Companies Act 1985, or
(*b*) in Northern Ireland, Article 234 of the Companies (Northern Ireland) Order 1986,
or the corresponding requirements of the law of a country outside the United Kingdom; and".

Transitional provision in relation to IRUs

6—(1) This Schedule does not apply to IRUs acquired before 21st March 2000.

(2) This Schedule does not apply to an IRU by virtue of its being acquired on or after that date, directly or indirectly, from an associate or an associated company if the associate or associated company acquired the IRU before that date.

For this purpose—

"associate" has the meaning given by section 417(3) and (4) of the Taxes Act 1988; and "associated company"—

(*a*) in relation to another company, has the meaning given by section 416(1) of that Act, and

(*a*) in relation to an individual, means a company of which that individual has control within the meaning of subsections (2) to (6) of that section.

Revenue Interpretation RI 223—Guidance on determining the date of acquisition.

SCHEDULE 24

NEW SCHEDULE 4A TO THE TAXATION OF CHARGEABLE GAINS ACT 1992

Section 91(2)

Note—This Schedule sets out TCGA 1992 Sch 4A as inserted by FA 2000 s 91(2).
Commentary—*Simon's Direct Tax Service* **C4.206, 301**.

SCHEDULE 25

NEW SCHEDULE 4B TO THE TAXATION OF CHARGEABLE GAINS ACT 1992

Section 92(2)

Note—This Schedule sets out TCGA 1992 Sch 4B as inserted by FA 2000 s 92(2).
Commentary—*Simon's Direct Tax Service* **C4.206, 301**.

SCHEDULE 26

TRANSFERS OF VALUE: ATTRIBUTION OF GAINS TO BENEFICIARIES

Section 92(4)

Commentary—*Simon's Direct Tax Service* C4.206, 301.

PART I

NEW SCHEDULE 4C TO THE TAXATION OF CHARGEABLE GAINS ACT 1992

1 (This Part sets out TCGA 1992 Sch 4C as inserted by FA 2000 s 92(4).

PART II

CONSEQUENTIAL AMENDMENTS

Taxation of Chargeable Gains Act 1992 (c.12)

2 (*Adds* TCGA 1992 s 90(5).

3 (*Amends* TCGA 1992 s 96(1), (2)).

4 (*Amends* TCGA 1992 s 97).

5 (*Adds* TCGA 1992 s 98(3)).

Taxes Act 1988

6 (*Amends* TA 1988 s 740(6)).

SCHEDULE 27

GROUP RELIEF IN CASE OF NON-RESIDENT COMPANIES ETC

Section 97

Commentary—*Simon's Direct Tax Service* D2.623.

PART I
AMENDMENTS OF CHAPTER IV OF PART X
OF THE TAXES ACT 1988
Availability of relief

1 (*Inserts* TA 1988 s 402(3A), (3B)).

2 (*Amends* TA 1988 s 413(2), (5)).

Limits on amount of relief

3 (*Amends* TA 1988 s 403A(10)).

4 (*Inserts* TA 1988 ss 403D, 403E).

Amendments of Schedule 18 to the Taxes Act 1988

5—(1) Schedule 18 to that Act (group relief: equity holders and profits or assets available for distribution) is amended as follows.

(2) (*Amends* TA 1988 Sch 18 para 1(3)(*d*), (5)(*c*)).

(3) (*Inserts* TA 1988 Sch 18 para 2(1A)).

(4) (*Inserts* TA 1988 Sch 18 para 4(5)).

(5) (*Inserts* TA 1988 Sch 18 para 5F).

(6) (*Amends* TA 1988 Sch 18 para 6).

Commencement

6—(1) Nothing in this Part of this Schedule has effect in relation to any determination whether the qualifying conditions for the purposes of section 403A(9) of the Taxes Act 1988 were met at any time before 1st April 2000.

(2) Nothing in section 403E of the Taxes Act 1988 (inserted by paragraph 4 above) has effect in relation to the determination of the amount available for surrender—

    (*a*) for an accounting period ending before 1st April 2000, or

    (*b*) for an accounting period beginning before 1st April 2000 and ending on or after that date if or to the extent that the loss or other amount is attributable to the part of the period falling before that date.

Any apportionment necessary for the purposes of paragraph (*b*) shall be made on a time basis except where that would work in an unjust or unreasonable manner in relation to any person, in which case it shall be made in such manner as may be just and reasonable.

(3) Paragraph 5 above has effect in relation to the application of Schedule 18 of the Taxes Act 1988, for any purpose, in relation to times on or after (but not before) 1st April 2000.

(4) Subject to the above provisions of this paragraph, this Part of this Schedule has effect in relation to accounting periods ending on or after 1st April 2000.

PART II
CONSEQUENTIAL AMENDMENTS
Section 76 of the Taxes Act 1988

7 (*Amends* TA 1988 s 76(1)(*aa*)).

Section 434A of the Taxes Act 1988

8 (*Amends* TA 1988 s 434A(2))

Section 502 of the Taxes Act 1988

9 (*Amends* TA 1988 s 502)

Schedule 24 to the Taxes Act 1988

10 (*Renumbers* TA 1988 Sch 24 para 5 as sub-para (1) and *adds* TA 1988 Sch 24 para 5(2)).

Schedule 18 to the Finance Act 1998

11 (*Inserts* FA 1998 Sch 18 para 68(3), (4)).

Commencement

12—(1) Paragraphs 7, 8, 10 and 11 have effect in relation to accounting periods ending on or after 1st April 2000.

(2) Paragraph 9 has effect wherever the enactment amended by that paragraph falls to be construed, so far as it applies provisions of Chapter IV of Part X of the Taxes Act 1988, as applying those provisions as amended by Part I of this Schedule.

SCHEDULE 28

RECOVERY OF TAX PAYABLE BY NON-RESIDENT COMPANY

Section 98

Commentary—*Simon's Direct Tax Service* **D2.642**.

Introduction

1 This Schedule applies where—

(*a*) an amount of corporation tax has been assessed on a company ("the taxpayer company") for an accounting period,

(*b*) the whole or any part of that amount is unpaid at the end of the period of six months after the time when it became payable, and

(*c*) that company is not resident in the United Kingdom.

Companies that may be required to pay unpaid tax

2—(1) The following companies may, by notice under this Schedule, be required to pay the unpaid tax—

(*a*) any company which was, at any time in the relevant period, a member of the same group of companies as the taxpayer company;

(*b*) any company which, at any time in the relevant period, was a member of a consortium which at that time owned the taxpayer company;

(*c*) any company which, at any time in the relevant period, was a member of the same group of companies as a company which at that time was a member of a consortium owning the taxpayer company.

(2) In this Schedule "the relevant period", in relation to an amount of unpaid corporation tax for an accounting period of the taxpayer company, means the period—

(*a*) beginning with whichever is the later of—

(i) twelve months before the start of that accounting period, and

(ii) 1st April 2000; and

(*b*) ending when the unpaid tax first became payable.

(3) Two companies shall be regarded as members of the same group of companies—

(*a*) for the purposes of sub-paragraph (1)(*a*), whenever one is the 51% subsidiary of the other or both are 51% subsidiaries of a third company;

(*b*) for the purposes of sub-paragraph (1)(*c*), whenever one would be treated as a member of the same group of companies as the other for the purposes of Chapter IV of Part X of the Taxes Act 1988 (group relief).

(4) For the purposes of this Schedule—

(*a*) a company shall be treated as a member of a consortium at any time when it would fall to be so treated for the purposes of Chapter IV of Part X of the Taxes Act 1988 (group relief); and

(*b*) references to a company being owned by a consortium shall be construed in the same way as any such references falling for the purposes of that Chapter to be construed in accordance with section 413(6)(*b*) of the Taxes Act 1988.

Notice requiring payment of unpaid tax

3—(1) The Board may serve a notice on any company within paragraph 2(1) requiring it, within 30 days of the service of the notice, to pay—

(*a*) the amount of the unpaid tax, or

(*b*) in a consortium case, the appropriate proportion of that amount (see paragraph 5).

(2) The notice must state—

(*a*) the amount of corporation tax assessed on the taxpayer company for the accounting period in question that remains unpaid,

(*b*) the date when it first became payable, and

(*c*) the amount required to be paid by the company on which the notice is served.

(3) The notice has effect—

(*a*) for the purposes of the recovery from that company of the amount required to be paid and of interest on that amount, and

(*b*) for the purposes of appeals,

as if it were a notice of assessment and that amount were an amount of tax due from that company.

(4) (*Amends* TMA 1970 s 87A(3)).

Time limit for giving notice

4—(1) Any notice under this Schedule must be served before the end of the period of three years beginning with the date on which the liability of the taxpayer company to corporation tax for the accounting period in question is finally determined.

(2) Where the unpaid tax is charged in consequence of a determination under paragraph 36 or 37 of Schedule 18 to the Finance Act 1998 (determination where no return delivered or return incomplete), that date shall be taken to be the date on which the determination is made.

(3) Where the unpaid tax is charged in a self-assessment, including a self-assessment that supersedes a determination (see paragraph 40 of Schedule 18 to the Finance Act 1998), that date shall be taken to be the latest of—

(*a*) the last date on which notice of enquiry may be given into the return containing the self-assessment;

(*b*) if notice of enquiry is given, 30 days after the enquiry is completed;

(*c*) if more than one notice of enquiry is given, 30 days after the last notice of completion;

(*d*) if after such an enquiry the Inland Revenue amend the return, 30 days after notice of the amendment is issued;

(*e*) if an appeal is brought against such an amendment, 30 days after the appeal is finally determined.

(4) If the unpaid tax is charged in a discovery assessment, that date shall be taken to be—

(*a*) where there is no appeal against the assessment, the date when the tax becomes due and payable;

(*b*) where there is such an appeal, the date on which the appeal is finally determined.

Limit on amount payable in consortium case

5—(1) In a consortium case, the amount that the company may be required to pay by notice under this Schedule is limited to the proportion of the unpaid tax corresponding—

(*a*) in the case of a company falling only within paragraph 2(1)(*b*), to the share which that company has had in the consortium for the relevant period;

(*b*) in the case of a company falling only within paragraph 2(1)(*c*), to the share which companies that have been members of the same group of companies as that company have had in the consortium for the relevant period;

(*c*) in the case of a company falling within paragraph 2(1)(*b*) and (*c*), to whichever is the greater of the amounts given by paragraphs (*a*) and (*b*) above.

(2) A ''consortium case'' means a case where the company falls within paragraph 2(1)(*b*) or (*c*) (or both), but does not fall within paragraph 2(1)(*a*).

(3) A member's share in a consortium, in relation to the relevant period, is whichever is the lowest in that period of the following percentages—

(*a*) the percentage of the ordinary share capital of the taxpayer company which is beneficially owned by that member;

(*b*) the percentage to which that member is beneficially entitled of any profits available for distribution to equity holders of the taxpayer company;

(*c*) the percentage to which that member would be beneficially entitled of any assets of the taxpayer company available for distribution to its equity holders on a winding-up.

If any of those percentages has fluctuated in the relevant period, the average percentage over the period shall be taken.

(4) Schedule 18 to the Taxes Act 1988 (equity holders and profits or assets available for distribution) applies for the purposes of sub-paragraph (3) above as it applies for the purposes of section 403C of that Act.

Supplementary provisions

6—(1) In this Schedule ''company'' means any body corporate.

(2) A company that has paid an amount in pursuance of a notice under this Schedule may recover that amount from the taxpayer company.

(3) A payment in pursuance of a notice under this Schedule is not allowed as a deduction in computing income or profits for any tax purposes.

SCHEDULE 29

CHARGEABLE GAINS: NON-RESIDENT COMPANIES AND GROUPS ETC

Section 102

Commentary—*Simon's Direct Tax Service* **D2.657, 658**.

PART I

APPLICATION OF TAXATION OF CHARGEABLE GAINS ACT 1992

Main amendments

1—(1) (*Repeals* TCGA s 170(2)(*a*), (9)(*b*)).

(2) The above amendments (referred to in this Schedule as ''the main amendments'') have effect in accordance with the following provisions of this Schedule.

Transfers within a group

2—(1) Section 171 of the Taxation of Chargeable Gains Act 1992 (transfers within a group: general provisions) is amended as follows.

(2) (*Substitutes* TCGA 1992 s 171(1), (1A) for sub-s (1)).

(3) (*Amends* TCGA 1992 s 171(2)).

(4) (*Amends* TCGA 1992 s 171(3)).

(5) (*Adds* TCGA 1992 s 171(6)).

(6) The above amendments, and the main amendments so far as they apply for the purposes of section 171, have effect in relation to disposals on or after 1st April 2000.

Transfer of United Kingdom branch or agency

3—(1) (*Repeals* TCGA 1992 s 172).

(2) The above amendment has effect in relation to disposals on or after 1st April 2000.

De-grouping charge

4—(1) Section 179 of the Taxation of Chargeable Gains Act 1992 (company ceasing to be member of group) is amended as follows.

(2) (*Substitutes* TCGA 1992 s 179(1), (1A) for sub-s (1)).

(3) (*Amends* TCGA 1992 s 179(2A)).

(4) (*Amends* TCGA 1992 s 179(2B), (2C), (2D), (3), (10)(*c*) and (13)).

(5) (*Repeals* TCGA 1992 s 179(11), (12)).

(6) The amendments made by sub-paragraphs (2) to (4) above, and the main amendments so far as they apply for the purposes of section 179, have effect in relation to assets acquired on or after 1st April 2000.

(7) The amendments made by sub-paragraph (5) above have effect in relation to gains accruing on or after 1st April 2000.

Reconstruction or amalgamation involving transfer of business

5—(1) Section 139 of the Taxation of Chargeable Gains Act 1992 (reconstruction or amalgamation involving transfer of business) is amended as follows.

(2) (*Substitutes* TCGA 1992 s 139(1)(*b*)).

(3) (*Inserts* TCGA 1992 s 139(1A)).

(4) The above amendments have effect in relation to disposals made on or after 1st April 2000.

Deemed disposal on non-resident ceasing to carry on trade in United Kingdom through branch or agency

6—(1) Section 25 of the Taxation of Chargeable Gains Act 1992 (non-residents: deemed disposals) is amended as follows.

(2) (*Inserts* TCGA 1992 s 25(3A)).

(3) (*Repeals* TCGA 1992 s 25(4)).

(4) The amendment in sub-paragraph (2) above has effect in relation to cases where section 139 or, as the case may be, section 171 has effect as amended by this Schedule.

(5) The amendment in sub-paragraph (3) above has effect in relation to cases where section 139 has effect as amended by this Schedule.

Restriction on set-off of pre-entry losses

7—(1) In Schedule 7A to the Taxation of Chargeable Gains Act 1992 (restriction on set-off of pre-entry losses), paragraph 1 (application and construction of Schedule) is amended as follows.

(2) (*Amends* TCGA 1992 Sch 7A para 1(3)).

(3) (*Inserts* TCGA 1992 Sch 7A para 1(3A)).

(4) (*Amends* TCGA 1992 Sch 7A para 1(4)(*a*)).

(5) (*Amends* TCGA 1992 Sch 7A para 1(5)).

(6) The above amendments, and the main amendments so far as they apply for the purposes of Schedule 7A, have effect in relation to the amount to be included in respect of chargeable gains in a company's total profits for any accounting period ending on or after 21st March 2000.

(7) Any question whether a company was, in relation to times before 21st March 2000, a member of a group shall be determined by reference to the position under the Taxation of Chargeable Gains Act 1992 as it stood before the main amendments.

(8) Any question whether a company was, in relation to times before 6th April 1992, a member of a group shall be determined by reference to the position under the Capital Gains Tax Act 1979.

(9) Where—

(a) immediately before the time when the main amendments have effect in relation to a company in accordance with sub-paragraph (6), the company was not a member of a group of companies for the purposes of section 170 of the Taxation of Chargeable Gains Act 1992 (as it stood before the main amendments), and

(b) immediately after that time, the company is a member of a group of companies for the purposes of that section (as amended by the main amendments),

Schedule 7A to that Act shall not have effect in relation to any losses accruing to the company before that time or any chargeable assets (within the meaning of paragraph 1(3A) of that Schedule) held by it immediately before that time.

Restrictions on setting losses against pre-entry gains

8—(1) The main amendments have effect for the purposes of Schedule 7AA to the Taxation of Chargeable Gains Act 1992 (restrictions on setting losses against pre-entry gains) in relation to accounting periods ending on or after 21st March 2000.

(2) Any question whether a company was, in relation to times before 21st March 2000, a member of a group shall be determined by reference to the position under the Taxation of Chargeable Gains Act 1992 as it stood before the main amendments.

Recovery of unpaid tax

9—(1) (*Substitutes* TCGA 1992 s 190 for ss 190, 191).

(2) (*Amends* TMA 1970 s 87A(3)).

(3) The above amendments, and the main amendments so far as they apply for the purposes of section 190 (as substituted by sub-paragraph (1) above), have effect in relation to gains accruing on or after 1st April 2000.

(4) Any question whether a company was a member of a group during the period of twelve months ending when such a gain accrued shall be determined in accordance with section 170 as amended by the main amendments.

Replacement of business assets by members of group

10—(1) Section 175 of the Taxation of Chargeable Gains Act 1992 is amended as follows.

(2) (*Amends* TCGA 1992 s 175(1)).

(3) (*Inserts* TCGA 1992 s 175(1A)).

(4) (*Inserts* TCGA 1992 s 175(2A)(ba)).

(5) (*Inserts* TCGA 1992 s 175(2AA)).

(6) (*Substitutes* TCGA 1992 s 175(3)).

(7) The above amendments, and the main amendments so far as they apply for the purposes of section 175, have effect in relation to cases in which—

(a) either the disposal or acquisition is on or after 1st April 2000, or

(b) both the disposal and acquisition are on or after that date.

(8) In a case falling within paragraph (a) of sub-paragraph (7) above, any question whether a company was, at the time of the acquisition or disposal corresponding to the disposal or acquisition referred to in that paragraph, a member of a group shall be determined in accordance with section 170 of the Taxation of Chargeable Gains Act 1992 as amended by the main amendments.

Transfers of assets within a group: trading stock

11—(1) (*Substitutes* TCGA 1992 s 173).

(2) The above amendment, and the main amendments so far as they apply for the purposes of section 173 (as substituted by sub-paragraph (1) above), have effect in relation to acquisitions and disposals on or after 1st April 2000.

Restriction of losses by reference to capital allowances

12—(1) (*Adds* TCGA 1992 s 41(8)).

(2) The above amendment has effect in relation to cases where the disposal first referred to in section 41(8) (as inserted by sub-paragraph (1) above) is on or after 1st April 2000.

Assets held on 6th April 1965: disposal outside group

13—(1) Section 174 of the Taxation of Chargeable Gains Act 1992 is amended as follows.

(2) (*Amends* TCGA 1992 s 174(4)).

(3) (*Repeals* TCGA 1992 s 174(5)).

(4) The above amendments, and the main amendments so far as they apply for the purposes of section 174, have effect in relation to acquisitions on or after 1st April 2000.

(5) Any question whether a company was, in relation to times before 1st April 2000, a member of a group shall be determined in accordance with section 170 of the Taxation of Chargeable Gains Act 1992 as it stood before the main amendments.

PART II
MINOR AND CONSEQUENTIAL AMENDMENTS
Section 97 of the Inheritance Tax Act 1984

14 The main amendments have effect for the purposes of section 97 of the Inheritance Tax Act 1984 (transfer of asset within a group of companies) in relation to disposals on or after 1st April 2000.

Section 132 of the Finance Act 1988

15—(1) (*Amends* FA 1988 s 132(6)).

(2) The above amendment, and the main amendments so far as they apply for the purposes of section 132, have effect in relation to cases in which the migrating company ceases to be resident in the United Kingdom on or after 1st April 2000.

(3) Any question whether a company was a member of a group during the period of twelve months ending when the migrating company ceased to be so resident shall be determined in accordance with section 170 of the Taxation of Chargeable Gains Act 1992 as amended by the main amendments.

Section 14 of the Taxation of Chargeable Gains Act 1992

16—(1) Section 14 of the Taxation of Chargeable Gains Act 1992 (non-resident groups of companies) is amended as follows.

(2) (*Substitutes* TCGA 1992 s 14(2)).

(3) (*Amends* TCGA 1992 s 14(3)).

(4) (*Amends* TCGA 1992 s 14(4)).

(5) The above amendments, and the main amendments so far as they apply for the purposes of section 14, have effect in cases in which section 41, 171, 173, 174(4), 175(1) or 179, as the case may be, have effect as amended by this Schedule.

Section 31A of the Taxation of Chargeable Gains Act 1992

17—(1) Section 31A of the Taxation of Chargeable Gains Act 1992 (asset-holding company leaving a group of companies) is amended as follows.

(2) (*Amends* TCGA 1992 s 31A(9)(*b*)).

(3) (*Inserts* TCGA 1992 s 31A(11)).

(4) The above amendments, and the main amendments so far as they apply for the purposes of sections 30 to 34 of that Act, have effect in relation to disposals on or after 1st April 2000.

Section 106 of the Taxation of Chargeable Gains Act 1992

18—(1) Section 106 of the Taxation of Chargeable Gains Act 1992 (disposal of shares and securities within prescribed period of acquisition) is amended as follows.

(2) (*Substitutes* TCGA 1992 s 106(2)–(2D) for sub-s 2).

(3) (*Amends* TCGA 1992 s 106(10)).

(4) The above amendments, and the main amendments so far as they apply for the purposes of section 106, have effect in relation to cases in which the prescribed period before the disposal (within the meaning of that section) begins on or after 1st April 2000.

Section 116 of the Taxation of Chargeable Gains Act 1992

19—(1) (*Amends* TCGA 1992 s 116(11)).

(2) The above amendment has effect in accordance with paragraph 3(2).

Section 117A of the Taxation of Chargeable Gains Act 1992

20—*(1) (Amends TCGA 1992 s 117A(8)(a)).*

(2) The above amendment has effect in accordance with paragraph 3(2).

Amendment—Repealed by FA 2002 s 141, Sch 40 Pt 3(10) with effect for accounting periods beginning after 30 September 2002.

Section 117B of the Taxation of Chargeable Gains Act 1992

21—*(1) (Amends TCGA 1992 s 117B(6)(a)).*

(2) The above amendment has effect in accordance with paragraph 3(2).

Amendment—Repealed by FA 2002 s 141, Sch 40 Pt 3(10) with effect for accounting periods beginning after 30 September 2002.

Section 138A of the Taxation of Chargeable Gains Act 1992

22 The main amendments have effect for the purposes of section 138A of the Taxation of Chargeable Gains Act 1992 (use of earn-out rights for exchange of securities) in relation to rights conferred on or after 1st April 2000.

Section 140 of the Taxation of Chargeable Gains Act 1992

23—(1) (*Amends* TCGA 1992 s 140(6)(*b*)).

(2) The above amendment has effect in relation to disposals on or after 1st April 2000.

Section 176 of the Taxation of Chargeable Gains Act 1992

24—(1) (*Amends* TCGA 1992 s 176(7)(*b*) and *repeals* TCGA 1992 s 176(7)(*c*)).

(2) The above amendment, and the main amendments so far as they apply for the purposes of section 176, have effect in relation to cases in which the depreciatory transaction (within the meaning of section 176) is on or after 1st April 2000.

Section 177 of the Taxation of Chargeable Gains Act 1992

25—(1) (*Amends* TCGA 1992 s 177(2)).

(2) The above amendment, and the main amendments so far as they apply for the purposes of section 177, have effect in relation to disposals on or after 1st April 2000.

Section 178 of the Taxation of Chargeable Gains Act 1992

26 (*Repeals* TCGA 1992 s 178)

Section 180 of the Taxation of Chargeable Gains Act 1992

27 (*Repeals* TCGA 1992 s 180).

Section 181 of the Taxation of Chargeable Gains Act 1992

28—(1) In section 181 of the Taxation of Chargeable Gains Act 1992 (exemption from de-grouping charge in the case of certain mergers)—

(*a*) (*Amends* TCGA 1992 s 181(1)).
(*b*) (*Repeals* TCGA 1992 s 181(5)).

(2) The amendment made by sub-paragraph (1)(*b*) above, and the main amendments so far as they apply for the purposes of section 181, have effect in relation to cases in which the company ceases to be a member of a group on or after 1st April 2000.

Section 192 of the Taxation of Chargeable Gains Act 1992

29 (*Amends* TCGA 1992 s 192(3)).

Section 211 of the Taxation of Chargeable Gains Act 1992

30—(1) Section 211 of the Taxation of Chargeable Gains Act 1992 (transfer of long term business of an insurance company) shall be amended as follows.

(2) (*Amends* TCGA s 211(2)).

(3) (*Inserts* TCGA 1992 s 211(2A)).

(4) (*Repeals* TCGA 1992 s 211(3)).

(5) The above amendments have effect in accordance with paragraph 5(4).

Section 216 of the Taxation of Chargeable Gains Act 1992

31 The main amendments have effect for the purposes of section 216 of the Taxation of Chargeable Gains Act 1992 (assets transferred from building society to company) in relation to transfers on or after 1st April 2000.

Section 217C of the Taxation of Chargeable Gains Act 1992

32—(1) (*Substitutes* TCGA 1992 s 217C(2)).

(2) The above amendment has effect in relation to cases in which the disposal by the incorporated society is on or after 1st April 2000.

Section 228 of the Taxation of Chargeable Gains Act 1992

33 The main amendments have effect for the purposes of section 228 of the Taxation of Chargeable Gains Act 1992 (conditions for roll-over relief: supplementary) in relation to disposals on or after 1st April 2000.

Section 253 of the Taxation of Chargeable Gains Act 1992

34 The main amendments have effect for the purposes of section 253 of the Taxation of Chargeable Gains Act 1992 (relief for loans to traders)—

(*a*) in relation to loans made on or after 1st April 2000;
(*b*) in relation to guarantees given on or after that date.

Section 276 of the Taxation of Chargeable Gains Act 1992

35—(1) (*Substitutes* TCGA 1992 s 276(8)–(10) for sub-s (8)).

(2) The above amendment has effect in cases in which section 41, 171, 173, 174(4), 179 or 181, as the case may be, has effect as amended by this Schedule.

Schedule A1 to the Taxation of Chargeable Gains Act 1992

36 The main amendments have effect for the purposes of paragraph 11 of Schedule A1 to the Taxation of Chargeable Gains Act 1992 (rules for application of taper relief) in relation to any determination whether, at any time on or after 1st April 2000, a company is a 51 per cent subsidiary of another company.

Schedule 2 to the Taxation of Chargeable Gains Act 1992

37 The main amendments have effect for the purposes of paragraph 5 of Schedule 2 to the Taxation of Chargeable Gains Act 1992 (disposals of assets held on 6th April 1965) in relation to any determination whether, at any time on or after 1st April 2000, a company is a member, or the principal company, of a group of companies.

Schedule 3 to the Taxation of Chargeable Gains Act 1992

38 The main amendments have effect for the purposes of paragraphs 8 and 9 of Schedule 3 to the Taxation of Chargeable Gains Act 1992 (disposals of assets held on 31st March 1982: supplementary provisions) in relation to any determination whether, at any time on or after 1st April 2000, a company is a member, or the principal company, of a group of companies.

Schedule 7B to the Taxation of Chargeable Gains Act 1992

39—(1) Schedule 7B to the Taxation of Chargeable Gains Act 1992 (modification of that Act in relation to overseas life insurance companies) is amended as follows.

(2) (*Inserts* TCGA 1992 Sch 7B paras 6A, 6B).

(3) (*Amends* TCGA 1992 Sch 7B para 9).

(4) (*Adds* TCGA 1992 Sch 7B para 15).

(5) The amendment made by sub-paragraph (2) above has effect in relation to cases where section 171 or, as the case may be, section 175 has effect as amended by this Schedule.

(6) The amendment made by sub-paragraph (3) above has effect in relation to cases where section 190 has effect as amended by this Schedule.

(7) The amendment made by sub-paragraph (4) above has effect in relation to cases where Schedule 7A has effect as amended by this Schedule.

Schedule 7C to the Taxation of Chargeable Gains Act 1992

40 The main amendments have effect for the purposes of Schedule 7C to the Taxation of Chargeable Gains Act 1992 (which is inserted by virtue of section 48 of this Act).

Section 136 of the Finance Act 1993

41—*(1) (Substitutes FA 1993 s 136(12)(d)).*

(2) The above amendment, and the main amendments so far as they apply for the purposes of section 136, have effect in relation to accrual periods beginning on or after 1st April 2000.

Amendment—Repealed by FA 2002 s 141, Sch 40 Pt 3(10) with effect for accounting periods beginning after 30 September 2002.

Section 136A of the Finance Act 1993

42—*(1) (Substitutes FA 1993 s 136A(10)(d)).*

(2) The above amendment, and the main amendments so far as they apply for the purposes of section 136A, have effect in relation to accrual periods beginning on or after 1st April 2000.

Amendment—Repealed by FA 2002 s 141, Sch 40 Pt 3(10) with effect for accounting periods beginning after 30 September 2002.

Schedule 17 to the Finance Act 1993

43—*(1) (Amends FA 1993 Sch 17 para 7(2)(b)).*

(2) The above amendment has effect in accordance with paragraph 3(2) above.

Amendment—Repealed by FA 2002 s 141, Sch 40 Pt 3(10) with effect for accounting periods beginning after 30 September 2002.

Schedule 9 to the Finance Act 1996

44—(1) Schedule 9 to the Finance Act 1996 (computational provisions in relation to loan relationships) is amended as follows.

(2) (*Substitutes* FA 1996 Sch 9 para (3)(*a*), (*b*)).

(3) (*Substitutes* FA 1996 Sch 9 para 11(5)).

(4) (*Substitutes* FA 1996 Sch 9 para 12(1)(*a*), (*b*)).

(5) The above amendments, and the main amendments so far as they apply for the purposes of paragraphs 11 and 12 of Schedule 9 to the Finance Act 1996, have effect in relation to transactions entered into, or series of transactions begun, on or after 1st April 2000.

Schedule 15 to the Finance Act 1996

45—(1) (*Amends* FA 1996 Sch 15 para 8(2)).

(2) The above amendment has effect in accordance with paragraph 3(2) above.

PART III
TRANSITIONAL PROVISIONS

46—(1) For the purposes of this paragraph—

(*a*) references to a company which was a member of an old group are references to it being, immediately before the time when the main amendments have effect in accordance with the preceding provisions of this Schedule, a member of a group for the purposes of section 170 of the Taxation of Chargeable Gains Act 1992 (as it stood before the main amendments), and

(*b*) references to a company which is a member of a new group are references to it being, immediately after that time, a member of a group for the purposes of that section (as amended by the main amendments).

(2) Where the same two or more companies were members of an old group and are members of a new group, those groups shall be regarded as the same group for the purposes of the provisions amended by this Schedule in relation to which the main amendments have effect.

(3) Sub-paragraph (2) above applies irrespective of whether the new group includes companies which were not members of the old group.

(4) Sub-paragraph (5) below applies in relation to a company which—

(*a*) was a member of an old group, but

(*b*) is not a member of a new group by reason only that—

   (i) the principal company of the old group is not the principal company of the new group, and

   (ii) the company in question is not an effective 51 per cent subsidiary of the principal company of the new group.

(5) For the purposes of the provisions amended by this Schedule in relation to which the main amendments have effect, section 170(3)(b) of the Taxation of Chargeable Gains Act 1992 shall not apply in relation to the company for so long as it remains an effective 51 per cent subsidiary of the company which was the principal company of the old group.

(6) Expressions used in this paragraph and in section 170 of the Taxation of Chargeable Gains Act 1992 shall be construed for the purposes of this paragraph in accordance with that section.

Commentary—*Simon's Direct Tax Service* **D2.651**.

[De-grouping charge: deferral until company leaves new group

47—(1) This paragraph has effect for the purposes of section 179 of the Taxation of Chargeable Gains Act 1992 as that section has effect in relation to assets acquired before 1st April 2000 ("old section 179").

(2) Where—

(a) a company would (apart from this paragraph) fall to be regarded for the purposes of old section 179 as ceasing to be a member of an old group at any time, but

(b) immediately before that time, it is also a member of a new group for the purposes of new section 179,

the company shall not be regarded for the purposes of old section 179 as ceasing to be a member of the old group unless or until it also ceases to be a member of the new group for the purposes of new section 179.

(3) Sub-paragraph (2) above does not prevent the company from being or becoming a member of another old group at any time.

(4) Where a company ceases to be a member of a new group on any occasion, it shall not by virtue of sub-paragraph (2) above be treated for the purposes of old section 179 as if it had on that occasion ceased to be a member of the same old group more than once.

(5) For the purposes of this paragraph—

(a) references to a company being a member of an old group are references to its being, for the purposes of old section 179, a member of a group of companies within the meaning given by old section 170;

(b) references to a company being a member of a new group are references to its being, for the purposes of new section 179, a member of a group of companies within the meaning given by new section 170; and

(c) references to a company ceasing to be a member of an old group or a new group shall be construed in accordance with paragraph (a) or (b) above, as the case may be.

(6) Where, for the purposes of sub-paragraph (2)(b) above, a company is not a member of a new group by reason only that—

(a) the principal company of the old group is not the principal company of the new group, and

(b) the company in question is not an effective 51 per cent subsidiary of the principal company of the new group,

subsection (3)(b) of new section 170 shall not apply in relation to the company for the purposes of this paragraph for so long as it remains an effective 51 per cent subsidiary of the company which was the principal company of the old group.

(7) In this paragraph—

(a) "new section 179" means section 179 of the Taxation of Chargeable Gains Act 1992 as it has effect in relation to assets acquired on or after 1st April 2000;

(b) "new section 170" means section 170 of that Act, as amended by the main amendments;

(c) "old section 170" means section 170 of the Taxation of Chargeable Gains Act 1992, as it stands before the main amendments.

(8) Expressions used in this paragraph and in section 170 of the Taxation of Chargeable Gains Act 1992 shall be construed in accordance with that section.][1]

Commentary—*Simon's Direct Tax Service* **D2.661**.
Revenue Internal Guidance—Capital Gains Manual CG 45406–45407 (operation of this section).
Amendments—[1] This paragraph inserted by FA 2001 s 79 and deemed to have been enacted as part of FA 2000 Sch 29.

SCHEDULE 30

DOUBLE TAXATION RELIEF

Section 103

Commentary—*Simon's Direct Tax Service* **F1.117**.

Power to make treaty provision for matching credit for tax spared in foreign country

1—(1) (*Repeals* TA 1988 s 788(5)(*b*)).

(2) This paragraph comes into force on 1st April 2000.

Matching credit for tax spared below immediate overseas subsidiary: treaty relief

2—(1) (*Amends* TA 1988 s 788(5)).

(2) This paragraph has effect in relation to any claim for credit in respect of underlying tax in relation to a dividend paid on or after 21st March 2000 by a company resident outside the United Kingdom to a company resident in the United Kingdom.

Matching credit for tax spared below immediate overseas subsidiary: unilateral relief

3—(1) Amend section 790 of the Taxes Act 1988 (unilateral relief) as follows.

(2) (*Amends* TA 1988 s 790(3)).

(3) (*Inserts* TA 1988 s 790(10A)–(10C)).

(4) This paragraph has effect in relation to any claim for credit, under any arrangements, in respect of underlying tax in relation to a dividend paid on or after 21st March 2000 by a company resident outside the United Kingdom to a company resident in the United Kingdom.

Relief for persons resident outside the UK who have branches or agencies in the UK

4—(1) Amend section 790 of the Taxes Act 1988 (unilateral relief) in accordance with sub-paragraphs (2) and (3).

(2) (*Amends* TA 1988 s 790(6)).

(3) (*Inserts* TA 1988 s 6A).

(4) Amend section 794 of the Taxes Act 1988 (requirement as to residence) in accordance with sub-paragraphs (5) and (6).

(5) (*Inserts* TA 1988 s 794(2)(*bb*)).

(6) (*Repeals* TA 1988 s 794(2)(*c*)).

(7) Amend section 801 of the Taxes Act 1988 (dividends paid between related companies: relief for UK and third country taxes) in accordance with sub-paragraphs (8) and (9).

(8) (*Amends* TA 1988 s 801(1)).

(9) (*Inserts* TA 1988 s 801(1A)).

(10) Amend section 801A of the Taxes Act 1988 (restriction of relief for underlying tax) in accordance with sub-paragraphs (11) and (12).

(11) (*Amends* TA 1988 s 801A(1)(*a*)).

(12) (*Amends* TA 1988 s 801A(2), (7), and (11)).

(13) In Schedule 19AC to the Taxes Act 1988 (modification of Act in relation to overseas life insurance companies) amend paragraph 13 (which notionally inserts certain provisions into section 794) as follows—

    (*a*) (*Repeals* TA 1988 Sch 19AC para 13(1)).
    (*b*) (*Amends* TA 1988 Sch 19AC para 13(2)).
    (*c*) (*Repeals* sub-s (3) as notionally inserted by TA 1988 Sch 19AC para 13(2)).
    (*d*) (*Amends* sub-s (4) as notionally inserted by TA 1988 Sch 19AC para 13(2)).

(14) The amendments made by this paragraph have effect in relation to [chargeable periods][1] ending on or after 21st March 2000.

Amendment—[1] Words in sub-para (14) substituted by FA 2001 s 81, Sch 27 para 7 and the paragraph above deemed to have been originally enacted as so amended, with the effect that the amendments made by this paragraph have effect for chargeable periods (not accounting periods) ending after 20 March 2000.

No double relief etc

5—(1) (*Inserts* TA 1988 s 793A).

(2) Subsections (1) and (2) of the section inserted by sub-paragraph (1) have effect in relation to claims for credit made on or after 21st March 2000.

(3) Subsection (3) of the section inserted by sub-paragraph (1) has effect in relation to arrangements made on or after 21st March 2000.

Limits on credit: minimisation of the foreign tax

6—(1) (*Inserts* TA 1988 s 795A).

(2) This paragraph has effect in relation to claims for credit made on or after 21st March 2000.

Foreign tax on amounts underlying non-trading credits

7—(1) Amend section 797A of the Taxes Act 1988 (foreign tax on interest brought into account as a non-trading credit) as follows.

(2) (*Amends* TA 1988 s 797A(1)).

(3) (*Amends* headnote to TA 1988 s 797A).

(4) The amendments made by this paragraph have effect in relation to accounting periods ending on or after 21st March 2000.

Restriction of relief for underlying tax

8—(1) Amend section 799 of the Taxes Act 1988 (computation of underlying tax) as follows.

(2) (*Amends* TA 1988 s 799(1)).

(3) (*Inserts* TA 1988 s 799(1A)).

(4) In subsection (3) (profits by reference to which underlying tax to be taken into account is calculated)—

    (*a*) (*Amends* TA 1988 s 799(3)(*a*)).
    (*b*) (*Repeals* TA 1988 s 799(*b*)).
    (*c*) (*Amends* TA 1988 s 799(*c*)).

(5) This paragraph has effect in relation to any claim for an allowance by way of credit made on or after 31st March 2001 in respect of a dividend paid by a company resident outside the United Kingdom to a company resident in the United Kingdom, unless the dividend was paid before that date.

(6) In determining, for the purpose of any such claim made on or after that date, the underlying tax of any such third, fourth or successive company as is mentioned in section 801(2) or (3) of the Taxes Act 1988, this paragraph shall be deemed to have had effect at the time the dividend paid by that company was paid.

Computation of underlying tax: the relevant profits

9—(1) Amend section 799 of the Taxes Act 1988 as follows.

(2) (*Inserts* TA 1988 s 799(5)–(7)).

(3) This paragraph has effect in relation to any claim for credit, under any arrangements, in respect of underlying tax in relation to a dividend paid on or after 21st March 2000 by a company resident outside the United Kingdom to a company resident in the United Kingdom.

Dividends paid between related companies but not covered by arrangements

10—(1) (*Repeals* TA 1988 s 800).

(2) This paragraph has effect in relation to dividends paid on or after 1st April 2000.

Restriction of relief for underlying tax: dividends paid between related companies

11—(1) Amend section 801 of the Taxes Act 1988 as follows.

(2) (*Inserts* TA 1988 s 801(2A)).

(3) This paragraph has effect in relation to any claim for an allowance by way of credit made on or after 31st March 2001 in respect of a dividend paid by a company resident outside the United Kingdom to a company resident in the United Kingdom, unless the dividend was paid before that date.

(4) In determining, for the purpose of any such claim made on or after that date, the underlying tax of any such third, fourth or successive company as is mentioned in section 801(2) or (3) of the Taxes Act 1988, this paragraph shall be deemed to have had effect at the time the dividend paid by that company was paid.

Dividends paid out of transferred profits

12—(1) (*Inserts* TA 1988 s 801B).

(2) This paragraph has effect in relation to any claim for credit, under any arrangements, in respect of underlying tax in relation to a dividend paid on or after 21st March 2000 by a company resident outside the United Kingdom to a company resident in the United Kingdom.

Separate streaming of dividend so far as representing an ADP dividend of a CFC

13—(1) (*Inserts* TA 1988 s 801C)

(2) This paragraph has effect in relation to any claim for an allowance by way of credit made on or after 31st March 2001 in respect of a dividend paid by a company resident outside the United Kingdom to a company resident in the United Kingdom, unless the dividend was paid before that date.

(3) In determining, for the purpose of any such claim made on or after that date, the underlying tax of any such third, fourth or successive company as is mentioned in section 801(2) or (3) of the Taxes Act 1988, this paragraph shall be deemed to have had effect at the time the dividend paid by that company was paid.

UK insurance companies trading overseas: repeal of section 802

14—(1) (*Repeals* TA 1988 s 802).

(2) This paragraph has effect in relation to accounting periods beginning on or after 1st April 2000.

Underlying tax: foreign taxation of group as a single entity

15—(1) (*Inserts* TA 1988 s 803A).

(2) This paragraph has effect in relation to any claim for credit, under any arrangements, in respect of underlying tax in relation to a dividend paid on or after 21st March 2000 by a company resident outside the United Kingdom to a company resident in the United Kingdom.

Life assurance companies with overseas branches etc: restriction of credit

16—(1) Amend section 804A of the Taxes Act 1988 (overseas life assurance business: restriction of credit) as follows.

(2) (*Substitutes* TA 1988 s 804A(1)–(1B) for sub-s (1)).

(3) (*Amends* TA 1988 s 804A(3)).

(4) (*Amends* S TA 1988 s 804A(5)).

(5) (*Amends* headnote to TA 1988 s 804A).

(6) This paragraph has effect in relation to accounting periods beginning on or after 1st April 2000.

Allocation of foreign tax to different categories of insurance business

17—(1) (*Inserts* TA 1988 s 804B).

(2) This paragraph has effect in relation to accounting periods beginning on or after 1st April 2000.

Allocation of expenses etc in a computation under Case I of Schedule D

18—(1) (*Inserts* TA 1988 ss 804C–804E).

(2) (*Amends* FA 1989 s 82(1)(*a*)).

(3) (*Amends* TA 1988 ss 436(3)(*a*), 439B(3)(*a*), and 441(4)(*a*)).

(4) This paragraph has effect in relation to periods of account beginning on or after 1st April 2000.

Interpretation of sections 804A to 804E

19—(1) (*Inserts* TA 1988 s 804F).

(2) The section inserted by sub-paragraph (1)—

(*a*) so far as relating to sections 804A and 804B, has effect in relation to accounting periods beginning on or after 1st April 2000; and

(*b*) so far as relating to sections 804C to 804E, has effect in relation to periods of account beginning on or after 1st April 2000.

Time limits for claims for credit relief

20—(1) Amend section 806 of the Taxes Act 1988 as follows.

(2) (*Substitutes* TA 1988 s 806(1)).

(3) This paragraph has effect in relation to claims for credit made on or after 21st March 2000.

Foreign dividends: onshore pooling and utilisation of certain unrelieved foreign tax

21—(1) (*Inserts* TA 1988 ss 806A–806H, 806J)

(2) The amendments made by sub-paragraph (1) have effect in relation to—

(*a*) dividends arising on or after 31st March 2001, and

(*b*) foreign tax in respect of such dividends,

(and accordingly the single related dividend or the single unrelated dividend which falls to be treated under those amendments as arising in any accounting period of a company shall not include any dividend arising on or before 30th March 2001).

Application of foreign dividend provisions to branches or agencies in the UK of persons resident elsewhere

22—(1) (*Inserts* TA 1988 s 806K).

(2) The amendment made by sub-paragraph (1) has effect in relation to—

(*a*) dividends arising on or after 31st March 2001, and

(*b*) foreign tax in respect of such dividends,

(and accordingly the single related dividend or single unrelated dividend which by virtue of that amendment falls to be treated as arising in any chargeable period shall not include any dividend arising on or before 30th March 2001).

Unrelieved foreign tax: profits of overseas branch or agency

23—(1) (*Inserts* TA 1988 ss 806L, 806M).

(2) The amendment made by sub-paragraph (1) has effect in relation to unrelieved foreign tax arising in any accounting period ending on or after 1st April 2000.

(3) No such tax shall be treated by virtue of that amendment as foreign tax in respect of income arising in any accounting period ended on or before 31st March 2000.

Foreign tax on amounts underlying non-trading credits

24—(1) Amend section 807A of the Taxes Act 1988 (disposals and acquisitions of company loan relationships) as follows.

(2) (*Amends* TA 1988 s 807A(2)).

(3) (*Amended* TA 1988 s 807A(7); *repealed by* FA 2002 s 141, Sch 40 Pt 3(13) with effect for accounting periods beginning after 30 September 2002.).

(4) This paragraph has effect in relation to accounting periods ending on or after 21st March 2000.

Royalties: special relationship

25—(1) (*Inserts* TA 1988 s 808B).

(2) This paragraph has effect in relation to royalties (as defined in the arrangements) payable on or after the day on which this Act is passed.

Postponement of capital allowances to obtain double taxation relief

26—(1) (*Repeals* TA 1988 s 810).

(2) This paragraph has effect in relation to claims made on or after 1st April 2000.

Time limits where reduction under s811 rendered excessive or insufficient

27—(1) Amend section 811 of the Taxes Act 1988 (deduction for foreign tax where no credit allowable) as follows.

(2) (*Inserts* TA 1988 s 811(4)–(10)).

(3) This paragraph has effect in relation to adjustments made on or after 21st March 2000.

Mutual agreement procedure

28—(1) (*Inserts* TA 1988 s 815AA).

(2) Subsections (1) to (3) of the section inserted by sub-paragraph (1) have effect where the solution or mutual agreement is reached or made on or after the day on which this Act is passed.

(3) Subsection (6) (and subsection (4) so far as relating to subsection (6)) of that section has effect in relation to the first presentation of a case on or after the day on which this Act is passed.

Restriction of interest on repayment of tax resulting from carry back of relievable tax

29—(1) Amend section 826 of the Taxes Act 1988 as follows.

(2) (*Inserts* TA 1988 s 826(7BB), (7BC)).

(3) (*Amends* TA 1988 s 826(7D)).

(4) (*Amends* TA 1988 s 826(7E)).

Time limits where deduction under s 278 of the 1992 Act rendered excessive or insufficient

30—(1) Amend section 278 of the Taxation of Chargeable Gains Act 1992 as follows.

(2) (*Renumbers* TCGA 1992 s 278 as sub-s (1)).

(3) (*Adds* TCGA 1992 s 278(2)–(7)).

(4) This paragraph has effect in relation to adjustments made on or after 21st March 2000.

SCHEDULE 31

CONTROLLED FOREIGN COMPANIES

Section 104

Commentary—*Simon's Direct Tax Service* D4.1201.

Introductory

1 Amend Chapter IV of Part XVII of the Taxes Act 1988 as follows.

Conditions for company to be controlled foreign company

2—(1) Amend section 747 as follows.

(2) (*Inserts* TA 1988 s 747(1A)).

Designer rate tax provisions: deemed lower level of taxation

3 (*Inserts* TA 1988 s 750A).

"Control" and the two "40 per cent" tests

4—(1) (*Inserts* TA 1988 s 755D).

(2) In consequence of sub-paragraph (1), in section 756(3) (application of provisions of Part XI)—

(*a*) (*Repeals* TA 1988 s 756(3)(*a*)).

(*b*) (*Amends* TA 1988 s 756(3)).

Exempt activities: wholesale, distributive, financial or service business

5—(1) In Part II of Schedule 25 (exempt activities) amend paragraph 6 as follows.

(2) (*Amends* TA 1988 Sch 25 para 6(2)(*b*)).

(3) (*Inserts* TA 1988 Sch 25 para 6(2A)).

Local holding companies

6—(1) In Part II of Schedule 25 (exempt activities) amend paragraph 6 as follows.

(2) (*Amends* TA 1988 Sch 25 para 6(3)).

Other holding companies

7—(1) In Part II of Schedule 25 (exempt activities) amend paragraph 6 as follows.

(2) (*Amends* TA 1988 Sch 25 para 6(4)).

(3) (*Inserts* TA 1988 Sch 25 para 6(4ZA)).

(4) (*Amends* TA 1988 Sch 25 para 6(4A)).

(5) (*Inserts* TA 1988 Sch 25 para 6(4AA)).

(6) (*Amends* TA 1988 Sch 25 para 6(4B)).

(7) (*Inserts* TA 1988 Sch 25 para 6(4BB)).

(8) (*Amends* TA 1988 Sch 25 para 6(5) and *inserts* TA 1988 Sch 25 para 6(5ZA)).

(9) (*Inserts* TA 1988 Sch 25 para 6(5ZB)).

(10) (*Inserts* TA 1988 Sch 25 para 6(5B)).

(11) (*Amends* TA 1988 Sch 25 para 6(6)).

Businesses to which requirement as to derivation of receipts applies

8—(1) In Part II of Schedule 25 (exempt activities) amend paragraph 11 as follows.

(2) (*Amends* TA 1988 Sch 25 para 11(1)).

Commencement

9—(1) Paragraph 2 has effect on and after 21st March 2000.

(2) Paragraph 3 has effect in relation to any accounting period of a company resident outside the United Kingdom which begins on or after 6th October 1999.

(3) Paragraph 4 has effect—

(*a*) for the purpose of determining whether at any time on or after 21st March 2000 a company resident outside the United Kingdom is to be regarded for the purposes of Chapter IV of Part XVII of the Taxes Act 1988 as controlled by persons resident in the United Kingdom; and

(*b*) for any accounting period of a company resident outside the United Kingdom which begins on or after 21st March 2000.

(4) Paragraphs 5 to 8 have effect in relation to any accounting period of a controlled foreign company which begins on or after 21st March 2000.

(5) In this paragraph "accounting period" and "controlled foreign company" have the same meaning as they have in Chapter IV of Part XVII of the Taxes Act 1988.

SCHEDULE 38

REGULATIONS FOR PROVIDING INCENTIVES FOR ELECTRONIC COMMUNICATIONS

Section 143(1)

Commentary—*Simon's Direct Tax Service* **A3.101; E1.806D**.

Introduction

1—(1) Regulations may be made in accordance with this Schedule for providing incentives to use electronic communications—

(*a*) for the purposes mentioned in section 132(1) of the Finance Act 1999 (power to provide for use of electronic communications for delivery of information and making of payments), or

(*b*) for any other communications with the tax authorities or in connection with taxation matters.

(2) The power to make regulations under this Schedule is conferred—

(*a*) on the Commissioners of Inland Revenue in relation to matters which are under their care and management, and

(*b*) on the Commissioners of Customs and Excise in relation to matters which are under their care and management.

Kinds of incentive

2—(1) The incentives shall be of such description as may be provided for in the regulations.

(2) They may, in particular, take the form of—

(*a*) discounts;

(*b*) the allowing of additional time to comply with any obligations under tax legislation (including obligations relating to the payment of tax or other amounts); or

(*c*) the facility to deliver information or make payments at more convenient intervals.

Commentary—*Simon's Direct Tax Service* **E1.806D**.

Conditions of entitlement

3—(1) The regulations may make provision as to the conditions of entitlement to an incentive.

(2) They may, in particular, make entitlement conditional—

(*a*) on the use of electronic communications for all communications or payments (or all communications and payments of a specified description) with, to or from the tax authority concerned, and

(*b*) on the use of specified means of electronic communication or payment acceptable to the tax authority concerned.

(3) The regulations may make provision for an appeal against a decision that the conditions of entitlement are not met.

Commentary—*Simon's Direct Tax Service* **E1.806D**.

Withdrawal of entitlement

4—(1) The regulations may make provision for the withdrawal of an incentive in specified circumstances.

(2) If they do, they may make provision—

(*a*) for giving notice of the withdrawal;

(*b*) for an appeal; and

(*c*) for the recovery of an amount not exceeding the value of the incentive.

(3) The regulations may provide that specified enactments relating to assessments, appeals and recovery of tax are to apply, with such adaptations as may be specified, in relation to the withdrawal of an incentive.

Commentary—*Simon's Direct Tax Service* **E1.806D**.

Power to authorise provision by directions

5 The regulations may authorise the making of any such provision as is mentioned in paragraph 3 or 4 by means of a specific or general direction given by the Commissioners of Inland Revenue or the Commissioners of Customs and Excise.

Commentary—*Simon's Direct Tax Service* **E1.806D**.

Power to provide for penalties

6—(1) The regulations may provide for contravention of, or failure to comply with, a specified provision of any such regulations to attract a penalty of a specified amount not exceeding £1,000.

(2) If they do, they may provide that specified enactments relating to penalties imposed in relation to any taxation matter (including enactments relating to assessments, review and appeals) are to apply, with or without modifications, in relation to penalties under the regulations.

Commentary—*Simon's Direct Tax Service* **E1.806D**.

General supplementary provisions

7—(1) Power to make provision by regulations under this Schedule includes power—

(*a*) to make different provision for different cases; and
(*b*) to make such incidental, supplemental, consequential and transitional provision in connection with any provision contained in any such regulations as the persons exercising the power think fit.

(2) The power to make regulations under this Schedule is exercisable by statutory instrument subject to annulment in pursuance of a resolution of the House of Commons.

Commentary—*Simon's Direct Tax Service* **E1.806D**.

Interpretation

8—(1) In this Schedule—

"discount" includes payment;
"electronic communications" includes any communications by means of a telecommunication system (within the meaning of the Telecommunications Act 1984);
"legislation" means any enactment, Community legislation or subordinate legislation;
"payment" includes a repayment;
"subordinate legislation" has the same meaning as in the Interpretation Act 1978;
"taxation matter" means any of the matters under the care and management of the Commissioners of Inland Revenue or the Commissioners of Customs and Excise;
"tax authorities" means—

(*a*) the Commissioners of Inland Revenue or the Commissioners of Customs and Excise,
(*b*) any officer of either body of Commissioners; or
(*c*) any other person who for the purposes of electronic communications is acting under the authority of either body of Commissioners;

"tax legislation" means legislation relating to any taxation matter.

(2) References in this Schedule to the delivery of information have the same meaning as in section 132 of the Finance Act 1999.

SCHEDULE 39

NEW SCHEDULE 1AA TO THE TAXES MANAGEMENT ACT 1970

Section 149(2)

Commentary—*Simon's Direct Tax Service* **A3.151**.

The Schedule inserted after Schedule 1 to the Taxes Management Act 1970 is as follows:

"Schedule 1AA

ORDERS FOR PRODUCTION OF DOCUMENTS

Introduction

1 The provisions of this Schedule supplement section 20BA.

Authorised officer of the Board

2—(1) In section 20BA(1) an 'authorised officer of the Board' means an officer of the Board authorised by the Board for the purposes of that section.

(2) The Board may make provision by regulations as to—

(*a*) the procedures for approving in any particular case the decision to apply for an order under that section, and
(*b*) the descriptions of officer by whom such approval may be given.

Notice of application for order

3—(1) A person is entitled—

    (*a*) to notice of the intention to apply for an order against him under section 20BA, and

    (*b*) to appear and be heard at the hearing of the application,

unless the appropriate judicial authority is satisfied that this would seriously prejudice the investigation of the offence.

(2) The Board may make provision by regulations as to the notice to be given, the contents of the notice and the manner of giving it.

Obligations of person given notice of application

4—(1) A person who has been given notice of intention to apply for an order under section 20BA(4) shall not—

    (*a*) conceal, destroy, alter or dispose of any document to which the application relates, or

    (*b*) disclose to any other person information or any other matter likely to prejudice the investigation of the offence to which the application relates.

This is subject to the following qualifications.

(2) Sub-paragraph (1)(*a*) does not prevent anything being done—

    (*a*) with the leave of the appropriate judicial authority,

    (*b*) with the written permission of an officer of the Board,

    (*c*) after the application has been dismissed or abandoned, or

    (*d*) after any order made on the application has been complied with.

(3) Sub-paragraph (1)(*b*) does not prevent a professional legal adviser from disclosing any information or other matter—

    (*a*) to, or to a representative of, a client of his in connection with the giving by the adviser of legal advice to the client; or

    (*b*) to any person—

        (i) in contemplation of, or in connection with, legal proceedings; and

        (ii) for the purpose of those proceedings.

This sub-paragraph does not apply in relation to any information or other matter which is disclosed with a view to furthering a criminal purpose.

(4) A person who fails to comply with the obligation in sub-paragraph (1)(*a*) or (*b*) above may be dealt with as if he had failed to comply with an order under section 20BA.

Exception of items subject to legal privilege

5—(1) Section 20BA does not apply to items subject to legal privilege.

(2) For this purpose ''items subject to legal privilege'' means—

    (*a*) communications between a professional legal adviser and his client or any person representing his client made in connection with the giving of legal advice to the client;

    (*b*) communications between a professional legal adviser and his client or any person representing his client or between such an adviser or his client or any such representative and any other person made in connection with or in contemplation of legal proceedings and for the purposes of such proceedings; and

    (*c*) items enclosed with or referred to in such communications and made—

        (i) in connection with the giving of legal advice; or

        (ii) in connection with or in contemplation of legal proceedings and for the purposes of such proceedings,

    when they are in the possession of a person who is entitled to possession of them.

(3) Items held with the intention of furthering a criminal purpose are not subject to legal privilege.

Resolution of disputes as to legal privilege

6—(1) The Board may make provision by regulations for the resolution of disputes as to whether a document, or part of a document, is an item subject to legal privilege.

(2) The regulations may, in particular, make provision as to—

    (*a*) the custody of the document whilst its status is being decided;

    (*b*) the appointment of an independent, legally qualified person to decide the matter;

    (*c*) the procedures to be followed; and

    (*d*) who is to meet the costs of the proceedings.

Complying with an order

7—(1) The Board may make provision by regulations as to how a person is to comply with an order under section 20BA.

(2) The regulations may, in particular, make provision as to—

    (*a*) the officer of the Board to whom the documents are to be produced,

    (*b*) the address to which the documents are to be taken or sent, and

    (*c*) the circumstances in which sending the documents by post complies with the order.

(3) Where an order under section 20BA applies to a document in electronic or magnetic form, the order shall be taken to require the person to deliver the information recorded in the document in a form in which it is visible and legible.

Procedure where documents are delivered

8—(1) The provisions of section 20CC(3) to (9) apply in relation to a document delivered to an officer of the Board in accordance with an order under section 20BA as they apply to a thing removed by an officer of the Board as mentioned in subsection (1) of section 20CC.

(2) In section 20CC(9) as applied by sub-paragraph (1) above the reference to the warrant concerned shall be read as a reference to the order concerned.

Sanction for failure to comply with order

9—(1) If a person fails to comply with an order made under section 20BA, he may be dealt with as if he had committed a contempt of the court.

(2) For this purpose "the court" means—

    (*a*) in relation to an order made by a Circuit judge, the Crown Court;

    (*b*) in relation to an order made by a sheriff, a sheriff court;

    (*c*) in relation to an order made by a county court judge, a county court in Northern Ireland.

Notice of order etc

10 The Board may make provision by regulations as to the circumstances in which notice of an order under section 20BA, or of an application for such an order, is to be treated as having been given.

General provisions about regulations

11 Regulations under this Schedule—

    (*a*) may contain such incidental, supplementary and transitional provision as appears to the Board to be appropriate, and

    (*b*) shall be made by statutory instrument which shall be subject to annulment in pursuance of a resolution of either House of Parliament.''.

SCHEDULE 40

REPEALS

Section 156

PART II

INCOME TAX, CORPORATION TAX AND CAPITAL GAINS TAX

(1) GIVING TO CHARITY

Chapter	Short title	Extent of repeal
1988 c. 1.	The Income and Corporation Taxes Act 1988.	In section 202, in subsection (6), the words "must not be paid by the employee under a covenant", and subsection (7). In section 339, subsections (2), (3), (3A), (3F), (6), (7) and (8) and, in subsection (9), the words "in subsections (1) to (4) above includes". In section 347A, subsections (2)(*b*), (7) and (8). In section 505(6), the words "and, for this purpose, all covenanted payments to charity (within the meaning of section 347A(7)) shall be treated as a single item".
1989 c. 26.	The Finance Act 1989.	Section 59.

Chapter	Short title	Extent of repeal
1990 c. 29.	The Finance Act 1990.	In section 25, in subsection (2), paragraphs (c) and (g) and, in subsection (12), paragraphs (b) and (e) and the word "and" immediately preceding paragraph (e).
1998 c. 36.	The Finance Act 1998.	In section 48, subsections (3), (6) and (7).

1 The repeals in section 202 of the Taxes Act 1988 have effect in accordance with section 38(7) of this Act.

2 The repeals in section 339 of the Taxes Act 1988 have effect in accordance with section 40(11) of this Act.

3 The repeals in sections 347A and 505 of the Taxes Act 1988 and the repeal of section 59 of the Finance Act 1989 have effect in accordance with section 41(9) of this Act.

4 The repeals in section 25 of the Finance Act 1990 have effect in accordance with section 39(10) of this Act.

(2) BENEFITS IN KINDS: DEREGULATORY AMENDMENTS

Chapter	Short title	Extent of repeal
1988 c. 1.	The Income and Corporation Taxes Act 1988.	Section 155(2).
		Section 160(1C).
		Section 161(1A) and (1B).
1994 c. 9.	The Finance Act 1994.	Section 88(5).

These repeals have effect in accordance with section 57(2) of this Act.

(3) CARS AVAILABLE FOR PRIVATE USE

Chapter	Short title	Extent of repeal
1996 c. 8.	The Finance Act 1996.	In Schedule 20, paragraph 40.
1999 c. 16.	The Finance Act 1999.	Section 47.

These repeals have effect in accordance with section 59 of this Act.

(4) OCCUPATIONAL AND PERSONAL PENSION SCHEMES

Chapter	Short title	Extent of repeal
1988 c. 1.	The Income and Corporation Taxes Act 1988.	In section 611(3), the words "retirement benefits" in both places where they occur. Section 630(3). Section 633(2). In section 638(4), the words "the aggregate of", paragraph (b) and the word "and" immediately preceding it. Section 641. Section 642. In section 645(3), the word "and" immediately preceding paragraph (c). Section 646(7). Section 660A(7).
1996 c. 8.	The Finance Act 1996.	In Schedule 21, paragraph 18.

1 The repeal of section 633(2) of the Taxes Act 1988 has effect in accordance with paragraph 9 of Schedule 13 to this Act.

2 The repeals in section 638(4) of that Act have effect in relation to contributions paid in the year 2001–02 and subsequent years of assessment.

3 The repeals of section 641 of that Act and paragraph 18 of Schedule 21 to the Finance Act 1996 have effect in accordance with paragraph 17 of Schedule 13 to this Act.

4 The repeal of section 642 of the Taxes Act 1988 has effect in accordance with paragraph 19 of Schedule 13 to this Act.

5 The repeal of section 646(7) of that Act has effect for the year 2001–02 and subsequent years of assessment.

6 The repeal of section 660A(7) of that Act has effect for the year 2001–02 and subsequent years of assessment.

(5) ENTERPRISE INVESTMENT SCHEME AND VENTURE CAPITAL TRUSTS

Chapter	Short title	Extent of repeal
1988 c. 1.	The Income and Corporation Taxes Act 1988.	Section 293(6)(*b*) and the word "and" immediately preceding it. Section 299B(7). In section 312(1), the definition of "the seven year period".
1992 c. 12.	The Taxation of Chargeable Gains Act 1992.	In Schedule 5B, in paragraph 19(1)— (*a*) the definition of "the five year period"; (*b*) the definition of "the seven year period".
1994 c. 9.	The Finance Act 1994.	In Schedule 15, paragraph 10(*c*).

1 The repeal in section 293(6) of the Taxes Act 1988 has effect in accordance with paragraph 12 of Schedule 17 to this Act.

2 The repeal in the Finance Act 1994 has effect in accordance with paragraph 13(2) of that Schedule.

3 The repeal in section 299B of the Taxes Act 1988 has effect in accordance with paragraph 14 of that Schedule.

4 The other repeals have effect in accordance with paragraph 8 of that Schedule.

(6) TAPER RELIEF FOR BUSINESS ASSETS

Chapter	Short title	Extent of repeal
1992 c. 12.	The Taxation of Chargeable Gains Act 1992.	In Schedule A1, in paragraph 22(1), the definitions of "full-time working officer or employee" and "qualifying office or employment".

These repeals have effect in accordance with section 67(7) of this Act.

(7) MEANING OF "RESEARCH AND DEVELOPMENT"

Chapter	Short title	Extent of repeal
1990 c. 1.	The Capital Allowances Act 1990.	Section 136. In section 139(1)(*d*)— (*a*) in the opening words, the words "or a class of trades"; (*b*) in sub-paragraphs (i) and (ii), the words "or, as the case may be, of trades of that class". Section 139(3).

These repeals have effect in accordance with section 68(2) of this Act.

(8) CAPITAL ALLOWANCES

Chapter	Short title	Extent of repeal
1990 c. 1.	The Capital Allowances Act 1990.	In section 41, in subsection (1), paragraphs (*b*) and (*c*) and the word "or" at the end of paragraph (*a*) and, in subsection (4), paragraph (*a*) and, in paragraph (*b*), the words from "or within (1)(*b*) or (*c*)" to "subsection (1)(*c*)" and the words "or subsection (1)(*b*) or (*c*)". Section 53(1)(*bb*).
1994 c. 9.	The Finance Act 1994.	In section 118, subsections (1) to (5) and (7) to (9).

1 The repeals in section 41 of the Capital Allowances Act 1990 have effect in accordance with section 74(1) of this Act.

2 The repeal in section 53 of that Act has effect in accordance with section 75(6)(*a*) of this Act.

3 The repeals in section 118 of the Finance Act 1994 have effect in accordance with section 73(2) of this Act.

(9) CONTRIBUTIONS TO LOCAL ENTERPRISE AGENCIES, ETC

Chapter	Short title	Extent of repeal
1988 c. 1.	The Income and Corporation Taxes Act 1988.	In section 79(11), the words "and before 1st April 2000". In section 79A— (*a*) in subsection (5)(*b*), the references to the Scottish Development Agency and the Highlands and Islands Development Board; (*b*) in subsection (7), the words "and before 1st April 2000".
1994 c. 9.	The Finance Act 1994.	Section 145(1).

(10) CAPITAL GAINS TAX: GIFTS AND TRUSTS

Chapter	Short title	Extent of repeal
1992 c. 12.	The Taxation of Chargeable Gains Act 1992.	In Schedule 10, paragraph 14(42).
1996 c. 8.	The Finance Act 1996.	In Schedule 38, paragraph 10(2)(*c*) and (*f*).

1 The repeal in Schedule 10 to the Taxation of Chargeable Gains Act 1992 has effect in accordance with section 92(5) of this Act.

2 The repeals in Schedule 38 to the Finance Act 1996 have effect in relation to disposals made on or after 9th November 1999.

(11) GROUPS AND GROUP RELIEF

Chapter	Short title	Extent of repeal
1970 c. 9.	The Taxes Management Act 1970.	In section 87A(3), the word "or" preceding "paragraph 75A(2)".
1988 c. 1.	The Income and Corporation Taxes Act 1988.	In section 402(4), the words from "if the share in the consortium" to "is nil or". In section 413— (*a*) in subsection (5), the words from the beginning to "Kingdom; and", paragraph (*c*) and the word "or" immediately preceding it; (*b*) subsections (8) and (9).
1992 c. 12.	The Taxation of Chargeable Gains Act 1992.	In section 170(8), the words ", or subsections (7) to (9),". In section 228(10)(*b*), the words "to (9)".

Chapter	Short title	Extent of repeal
1992 c. 48.	The Finance (No.2) Act 1992.	In Schedule 6, paragraph 3.
1998 c. 36.	The Finance Act 1998.	Section 81.

1 The repeal in section 87A(3) of the Taxes Management Act 1970 has effect in accordance with section 98(2) of this Act.

2 The repeal in section 402(4) of the Taxes Act 1988, the repeal of section 413(8) and (9) of that Act, the repeals in the Taxation of Chargeable Gains Act 1992 and the repeal of section 81 of the Finance Act 1998 have effect in accordance with section 100(5) of this Act.

3 The repeals in section 413(5) of the Taxes Act 1988 and the repeal in Schedule 6 to the Finance (No.2) Act 1992 have effect in accordance with paragraph 6 of Schedule 27 to this Act.

(12) GROUPS OF COMPANIES: CHARGEABLE GAINS

Chapter	Short title	Extent of repeal
1970 c. 9.	The Taxes Management Act 1970.	In section 87A(3), the words "or 179(11)".
1988 c. 39.	The Finance Act 1988.	In section 132(6), in the definition of group, the words "references to residence in the United Kingdom were omitted and".
1992 c. 12.	The Taxation of Chargeable Gains Act 1992.	In section 14(4)(b), the words "without subsections (2)(a), (9) and (12) to (14)". Section 25(4). In section 30(2)(b), the words "178 or". In section 31(7)(b), the words "178 or". In section 35(3)(d)(i), the words "172,". In section 170— (a) subsection (2)(a); (b) in subsection (9)(b), the words "(although resident in the United Kingdom)". Section 172. Section 174(1) to (3) and (5). In section 176(7), paragraph (c) and the word "and" immediately preceding it. Section 178. Section 179(11) and (12). Section 180. Section 181(5). In section 192(4), the words "178 or". In section 197(2)(b), the words "178(3) or". In section 211— (a) in subsection (2), the words "Subject to subsection (3) below" and paragraph (b) and the word "or" immediately following it; (b) subsection (3). In section 216(2)(b), (3) and (4), the words "178 or". In Schedule 4— (a) in paragraph 4(2), the words "178(3), 179(3)"; (b) paragraph 4(3); (c) paragraph 9(1)(a). In Schedule 7B, paragraph 7.
1992 c. 48.	The Finance (No.2) Act 1992.	Section 25(1).
1993 c. 34.	The Finance Act 1993.	Section 90.

1 The repeal in the Finance Act 1988 has effect in accordance with paragraph 15 of Schedule 29 to this Act.

2 The repeal in section 14 of the Taxation of Chargeable Gains Act 1992 has effect in accordance with paragraph 16 of that Schedule.

3 The repeal in section 25 of that Act has effect in accordance with paragraph 6(5) of that Schedule.

4 The repeals in section 170 of that Act have effect in accordance with paragraph 1 of that Schedule.

5 The repeal of section 172 of that Act, and the repeals in section 35 of and Schedule 7B to that Act, have effect in accordance with paragraph 3 of Schedule 29 to this Act.

6 In section 174 of that Act—

    (*a*) the repeal of subsections (1) to (3) has effect in accordance with paragraph 12 of that Schedule; and

    (*b*) the repeal of subsection (5) has effect in accordance with paragraph 13 of that Schedule.

7 The repeals in section 176 of that Act have effect in accordance with paragraph 24 of that Schedule.

8 The repeals in section 87A(3) of the Taxes Management Act 1970 and in section 179 of the Taxation of Chargeable Gains Act 1992 have effect in accordance with paragraph 4(7) of that Schedule.

9 The repeal in section 181 of the Taxation of Chargeable Gains Act 1992 has effect in accordance with paragraph 28 of that Schedule.

10 The repeals in section 211 of that Act, and the repeal of section 90 of the Finance Act 1993, have effect in accordance with paragraph 30 of that Schedule.

11 The repeal in section 25 of the Finance (No.2) Act 1992 has effect in accordance with paragraph 4(6) of that Schedule.

(13) DOUBLE TAXATION RELIEF

Chapter	Short title	Extent of repeal
1970 c. 9.	The Taxes Management Act 1970.	In section 42(7)(*a*), the words "810".
1988 c. 1.	The Income and Corporation Taxes Act 1988.	In section 750(3)(*b*), the words "other than section 810". In section 788(5), in the second sentence, paragraph (*b*) and the word "and" preceding it. Section 794(2)(*c*). Section 799(3)(*b*). Section 800. Section 802. Section 810. In Schedule 19AC, in paragraph 13, sub-paragraph (1) and, in sub-paragraph (2), the subsection (3) which is treated as inserted into section 794 of the Act.
1989 c. 26.	The Finance Act 1989.	In section 82(1)(*a*), the words "or foreign tax".

These repeals have effect in accordance with Schedule 30 to this Act.

(14) CONTROLLED FOREIGN COMPANIES

Chapter	Short title	Extent of repeal
1988 c. 1.	The Income and Corporation Taxes Act 1988.	In section 756(3), paragraph (*a*) and the words following paragraph (*b*). In Schedule 25, in paragraph 11(1), the word "and" immediately preceding paragraph (*g*).

These repeals have effect in accordance with paragraph 9 of Schedule 31 to this Act.

(15) INTERNATIONAL MATTERS

Chapter	Short title	Extent of repeal
1993 c. 34.	The Finance Act 1993.	In section 149, in subsections (4) and (5), the words "the asset or contract was held, or the liability was owed, by the company solely for trading purposes and". Section 164(6) and (7).

These repeals have effect in accordance with section 106(17) of this Act.

(16) INSURANCE

Chapter	Short title	Extent of repeal
1988 c. 1.	The Income and Corporation Taxes Act 1988.	In section 431(2), the definition of "investment reserve". In Schedule 19AC, paragraph 7(3)(*c*).
1993 c. 34.	The Finance Act 1993.	Section 177.
1994 c. 9.	The Finance Act 1994.	Section 224.

1 The repeals in the Taxes Act 1988 have effect in accordance with section 109(10) of this Act.

2 The other repeals have effect in accordance with section 107(12)(*c*) of this Act.

(17) PAYMENTS UNDER DEDUCTION OF TAX

Chapter	Short title	Extent of repeal
1970 c. 9.	The Taxes Management Act 1970.	In columns 1 and 2 of the Table in section 98— (*a*) the words "regulations under section 118D, 118F, 118G, 118H or 118I"; and (*b*) the words "regulations under section 124(3)".
1988 c. 1.	The Income and Corporation Taxes Act 1988.	In Part IV, Chapter VIIA. Section 124. In section 348(3), the words "or to any payment which is a relevant payment for the purposes of Chapter VIIA of Part IV". In section 349— (*a*) in subsection (1), the words "or to any payment which is a relevant payment for the purposes of Chapter VIIA of Part IV"; (*b*) in subsection (3), paragraph (*e*). Section 468M(4)(*b*). Section 482(11)(*a*). In section 582A(1), the words "and section 118B(4)". Section 841A. In Schedule 23A— (*a*) in paragraph 1(1), in the definition of "overseas securities", paragraph (*b*) and the word "and" preceding it; (*b*) in paragraph 1(1), in the definition of "UK securities", the words "quoted Eurobonds (as defined by section 124) held in a recognised clearing system or"; (*c*) paragraph 4(8).
1989 c. 26.	The Finance Act 1989.	In section 178(2)(*m*), the reference to section 118F of the Taxes Act 1988.
1996 c. 8.	The Finance Act 1996.	In Schedule 7, paragraph 28. Schedule 29. In Schedule 38, paragraph 6(2)(*a*) and (3).
1997 c. 58.	The Finance (No.2) Act 1997.	Section 38.

1 The repeal of Chapter VIIA of Part IV of the Taxes Act 1988, and related repeals, have effect in accordance with section 111(6)(*a*) of this Act.

2 The repeal of section 124 of that Act, and related appeals, have effect in accordance with section 111(6)(*b*) of this Act.

3 The repeal of section 482(11)(*a*) of that Act has effect in accordance with section 111(6)(*c*) of this Act.

(18) TAX TREATMENT OF EXPENDITURE ON PRODUCTION OR ACQUISITION OF FILMS

Chapter	Short title	Extent of repeal
1992 c. 48.	The Finance (No.2) Act 1992.	In section 43(3), paragraph (b) and the word "or" preceding it.

This repeal has effect in accordance with section 113(6) of this Act.

PART V

INFORMATION POWERS

Chapter	Short title	Extent of repeal
1970 c. 9.	The Taxes Management Act 1970.	In section 17, subsections (4B) and (4C).
1988 c. 1.	The Income and Corporation Taxes Act 1988.	In section 18, subsections (3) and (3AA). Section 482A.

These repeals have effect in relation to amounts paid, credited or received on or after 6th April 2001.

TRANSPORT ACT 2000

(2000 Chapter 38)

ARRANGEMENT OF SECTIONS

PART V

MISCELLANEOUS AND SUPPLEMENTARY

Supplementary

An Act to make provision about transport.   [30th November 2000]

PART V

MISCELLANEOUS AND SUPPLEMENTARY

Supplementary

275 Commencement

(1) Subject as follows, the preceding provisions of this Act come into force in accordance with provision made by the Secretary of State by order made by statutory instrument; and different provision may be made for different purposes.

(2) The power conferred by subsection (1) is exercisable as respects Wales by the National Assembly for Wales (and not the Secretary of State) in relation to Parts II and III (and the repeals relating to Part II).

(3) An order making provision for the coming into force of section 151—

(a) shall provide for it to come into force on 1st April in any year, and

(b) shall be made at least three months before the day on which it is to come into force.

(4) Section 231 (and Schedule 24), section 253 (and Schedule 28) and section 269 come into force on the day on which this Act is passed.

(5) In section 245, subsections (1) and (3) to (5), and subsections (2) and (8) so far as relating to subsections (3) to (5), shall be treated as having come into force on 10th May 2000.

276 Transitionals and savings

(1) The Secretary of State may by order made by statutory instrument make any transitional provisions or savings which he considers appropriate in connection with the coming into force of any provision of this Act.

(2) The power conferred by subsection (1) is exercisable as respects Wales by the National Assembly for Wales (and not the Secretary of State) in relation to Parts II and III (and the repeals relating to Part II).

277 Power to make amendments

(1) The Secretary of State may, in consequence of any provision of this Act or of any instrument made under it, by order made by statutory instrument make such amendments (including repeals or revocations) as appear to him to be appropriate in—

(a) any Act (whether public general or local) passed, or

(b) any subordinate legislation (within the meaning of the Interpretation Act 1978) made,

before that provision comes into force.

(2) The power conferred by subsection (1) is exercisable as respects Wales by the National Assembly for Wales (and not the Secretary of State) in relation to Parts II and III and any instruments made under them.

(3) No order shall be made under subsection (1) by the Secretary of State unless a draft of the order containing it has been laid before, and approved by resolution of, each House of Parliament.

278 Financial provision

(1) There shall be paid out of money provided by Parliament—

(a) any expenditure incurred by any Minister of the Crown or government department under or by virtue of this Act (apart from any expenditure to be met from the National Loans Fund), and

(b) any increase attributable to this Act in the sums payable out of money so provided under any other enactment.

(2) There shall be issued to the Secretary of State by the Treasury out of the National Loans Fund any sums required by him for—

(a) making loans under section 52 to a transferee, or

(b) making loans to the Strategic Rail Authority.

(3) There shall be paid into the National Loans Fund any repayment of, or payment of interest on, loans—

(a) made under section 52 by the Secretary of State to a transferee, or

(b) made by the Secretary of State to the Strategic Rail Authority.

(4) The assets of the National Loans Fund shall be reduced by an amount corresponding to such liability as the Secretary of State extinguishes by order under section 57.

(5) There shall be paid into the Consolidated Fund any sums received by any Minister of the Crown or government department under or by virtue of this Act (apart from any sums required to be paid into the National Loans Fund).

279 Extent

(1) Parts II and III, and the repeals relating to those Parts, and sections 255 and 256, 265, 267 and 268 and 270 and 271, and the repeals in Part V(2) of Schedule 31, extend only to England and Wales.

(2) Subject as follows, Part IV, sections 257 to 260 (and Schedule 29), sections 261 to 263 (and Schedule 30) and sections 264, 266 and 269, and Part V(1) of Schedule 31, extend only to England and Wales and Scotland.

(3) The amendments made by Parts I and IV, and the repeals and revocations relating to those Parts, have the same extent as the enactments to which they relate (except where it is otherwise provided).

(4) Sections 247 and 250, paragraph 14 of Schedule 14 and Schedule 26 extend to England and Wales, Scotland and Northern Ireland.

280 Short title

This Act may be cited as the Transport Act 2000.

SCHEDULES

SCHEDULE 7

TRANSFER SCHEMES: TAX

Section 64

Note—This Schedule was brought into force on 1 February 2001 by virtue of SI 2001/57 art 3.

Interpretation

1 In this Schedule—

"the 1988 Act" means the Income and Corporation Taxes Act 1988;

"the 1990 Act" means the Capital Allowances Act 1990;

"the 1992 Act" means the Taxation of Chargeable Gains Act 1992;

"relevant transfer" means a transfer of property, rights or liabilities under a transfer scheme;

"transferee" in relation to a relevant transfer means the person to whom the property, rights or liabilities are transferred;

"transferor" in relation to a relevant transfer means the person from whom the property, rights or liabilities are transferred.

Chargeable gains: general

2—(1) For the purposes of the 1992 Act a disposal constituted by a relevant transfer is to be taken (in relation to the transferee as well as the transferor) to be for a consideration such that no gain or loss accrues to the transferor.

(2) Sub-paragraph (1) has effect subject to the following provisions of this Schedule.

(3) (*Amends* TCGA 1992 s 35(3)(*d*)).

(4) Section 171(1) of the 1992 Act (provision in relation to disposal of assets from one member of a group of companies to another member of the group) does not apply if the disposal in question is constituted by a relevant transfer.

(5) Expressions used in this paragraph and in the 1992 Act have the same meanings in this paragraph as in that Act.

Chargeable gains: securities

3—(1) This paragraph applies if—

(*a*) assets are transferred to a company under a transfer scheme,

(*b*) in consequence the Secretary of State gives a direction under section 49 above, and

(*c*) the company issues securities in accordance with the direction.

(2) For the purposes of the 1992 Act the person to whom the securities are issued is to be treated as acquiring them for a consideration—

(*a*) provided by him wholly and exclusively for the securities, and

(*b*) equal to the market value of the assets transferred to the company under the scheme.

(3) This paragraph applies whether or not the person to whom the securities are issued is the person transferring the assets under the scheme.

(4) Expressions used in this paragraph and in the 1992 Act have the same meanings in this paragraph as in that Act.

4—(1) This paragraph applies if—

(*a*) the Secretary of State gives a direction under section 57 above requiring the CAA to release a company from liability in respect of debts,

(*b*) in connection with the direction the Secretary of State gives a direction or directions under section 58 above, and

(*c*) securities are issued in accordance with the direction or directions under section 58.

(2) Sub-paragraph (3) applies if the direction under section 58 requires securities to be issued to one person only or the directions under that section (taken together) require securities to be issued to one person only; and sub-paragraph (4) applies in any other case.

(3) For the purposes of the 1992 Act the person to whom the securities are issued is to be treated as acquiring them for a consideration—

(*a*) provided by him wholly and exclusively for the securities, and (*b*) equal to the amount of the liability affected by the release required by the direction under section 57.

(4) For the purposes of the 1992 Act a person to whom any of the securities are issued is to be treated as acquiring them for a consideration—

(*a*) provided by him wholly and exclusively for the securities, and

(*b*) equal to such part as is just and reasonable of the amount of the liability affected by the release required by the direction under section 57.

(5) This paragraph applies whether or not the person to whom the securities are issued, or any person to whom any of the securities are issued, is a person transferring anything under the transfer scheme in connection with which the direction under section 57 is given.

(6) Expressions used in this paragraph and in the 1992 Act have the same meanings in this paragraph as in that Act.

Chargeable gains: value shifting

5 Nothing in this Chapter and nothing done under it is to be regarded as a scheme or arrangement for the purposes of section 30 of the 1992 Act (tax-free benefits).

Chargeable gains: roll-over relief

6—(1) This paragraph applies if—

(*a*) but for section 154 of the 1992 Act (depreciating assets) a held-over gain would have been carried forward to a depreciating asset,

(*b*) the asset is the subject of a relevant transfer, and

(*c*) the Secretary of State is not the transferee under the relevant transfer.

(2) Section 154 is to have effect as if the gain had accrued to, and the claim for it to be held over had been made by, the transferee and as if the transferor's acquisition of the depreciating asset had been the transferee's acquisition of it.

(3) Expressions used in this paragraph and in section 154 have the same meanings in this paragraph as in that section.

Chargeable gains: restriction of losses

7—(1) If there has been a relevant transfer of an asset section 174(1) of the 1992 Act (which applies section 41 to cases where assets have been acquired without gain or loss) is to have effect as if the asset had been transferred to the transferee, and acquired by him, in relevant circumstances.

(2) This paragraph is not to prejudice paragraph 2.

(3) Expressions used in this paragraph and in section 174(1) of the 1992 Act have the same meanings in this paragraph as in section 174(1).

Chargeable gains: groups

8—(1) Sub-paragraph (2) applies if a company (the degrouped company)—

(*a*) acquired an asset from another company at any time when both were members of the same group of companies (the old group),

(*b*) ceases by virtue of a relevant transfer to be a member of the old group, and

(*c*) becomes by virtue of the transfer a member of another group of companies (the new group).

(2) Section 179 of the 1992 Act (company ceasing to be member of group) is not to treat the degrouped company as having by virtue of the transfer sold and immediately reacquired the asset.

(3) Sub-paragraph (4) applies if—

(*a*) sub-paragraph (2) applies to an asset, and

(*b*) the degrouped company ceases to be a member of the new group.

(4) On the company so ceasing section 179 of the 1992 Act is to have effect as if the degrouped company and the company from which it acquired the asset had been members of the new group at the time of acquisition.

(5) But sub-paragraph (4) does not apply if—

(*a*) at the time when the degrouped company ceases to be a member of the new group the company from which it acquired the asset also ceases to be a member of the new group,

(*b*) the companies are associated companies immediately before and immediately after that time, and

(*c*) the companies were associated companies at the time of acquisition.

(6) Expressions used in this paragraph and in section 179 of the 1992 Act have the same meanings in this paragraph as in that section.

9—(1) Sub-paragraph (3) applies if—

(*a*) a company (the degrouped company) ceases by virtue of a relevant transfer to be a member of a group of companies (the old group), (*b*) it becomes by virtue of the transfer a member of another group of companies (the new group),

(*c*) it ceases to be a member of the new group, and

(*d*) the condition in sub-paragraph (2) is satisfied.

(2) The condition is that—

(*a*) the degrouped company acquired an asset under a relevant transfer at a time falling before it ceases to be a member of the new group, and

(*b*) at the time of acquisition the degrouped company and the transferor were not members of the new group.

(3) On the degrouped company ceasing to be a member of the new group section 179 of the 1992 Act is to have effect as if the degrouped company and the transferor had been members of the new group at the time of acquisition.

(4) But sub-paragraph (3) does not apply if—

(*a*) at the time when the degrouped company ceases to be a member of the new group the transferor also ceases to be a member of the new group,

(*b*) the companies are associated companies immediately before and immediately after that time, and

(*c*) the companies were associated companies at the time of acquisition.

(5) Paragraph 8(4) and sub-paragraph (3) above may apply on the same occasion; but if paragraph 8(4) applies to an asset on a given occasion sub-paragraph (3) above does not apply to that asset on that occasion.

(6) Expressions used in this paragraph and in section 179 of the 1992 Act have the same meanings in this paragraph as in that section.

10—(1) Sub-paragraph (4) applies if—

(*a*) a company ceases by virtue of a relevant transfer to be a member of a group of companies (the old group),

(*b*) it becomes by virtue of the transfer a member of another group of companies (the new group),

(*c*) a company falling within sub-paragraph (2) (the degrouped company) ceases to be a member of the new group, and

(*d*) the condition in sub-paragraph (3) is satisfied.

(2) A company falls within this sub-paragraph if immediately before it ceases to be a member of the new group it is a subsidiary of—

(*a*) the company referred to in sub-paragraph (1)(*a*), or

(*b*) the principal company of the new group (if that company differs from the company referred to in sub-paragraph (1)(*a*)).

(3) The condition is that—

(*a*) the degrouped company acquired an asset under a relevant transfer at a time falling before it ceases to be a member of the new group, and

(*b*) at the time of acquisition the degrouped company and the transferor were not members of the new group.

(4) On the degrouped company ceasing to be a member of the new group section 179 of the 1992 Act is to have effect as if the degrouped company and the transferor had been members of the new group at the time of acquisition.

(5) But sub-paragraph (4) does not apply if—

(*a*) at the time when the degrouped company ceases to be a member of the new group the transferor also ceases to be a member of the new group,

(*b*) the companies are associated companies immediately before and immediately after that time, and

(*c*) the companies were associated companies at the time of acquisition.

(6) Expressions used in this paragraph and in section 179 of the 1992 Act have the same meanings in this paragraph as in that section.

Capital allowances

11—(1) This paragraph applies if—

(*a*) property which is plant or machinery is the subject of a relevant transfer,

(*b*) section 343 of the 1988 Act (company reconstructions without a change of ownership) does not apply in relation to the transfer, and

(*c*) the transfer scheme concerned contains provision for the disposal value of the property to be taken for the purposes of the Capital Allowances Acts to be of an amount specified in or determined in accordance with the scheme.

(2) For the purposes of the Capital Allowances Acts—

(*a*) the provision mentioned in sub-paragraph (1)(*c*) is to have effect (instead of section 26(1) or 59 of the 1990 Act) for determining an amount as the disposal value of the property or the price at which a fixture is to be treated as sold;

(b) the transferee is to be taken to have incurred expenditure of that amount on the provision of the property;

(c) in the case of a fixture, the expenditure which falls to be treated as incurred by the transferee is to be taken for the purposes of section 54 of the 1990 Act to be incurred by the giving of a consideration consisting in a capital sum of that amount.

(3) A provision mentioned in sub-paragraph (1)(c) for the determination of an amount may include provision—

(a) for a determination to be made by the Secretary of State in a manner described in the scheme;

(b) for a determination to be made by reference to factors so described or to the opinion of a person so described;

(c) for a determination to be capable of being modified (on one or more occasions) in a manner and in circumstances so described.

(4) The Treasury's consent is required for the making or modification of a determination under a provision mentioned in sub-paragraph (1)(c).

(5) The transferee's consent is also required for such a modification after the relevant transfer takes effect.

(6) If there is a determination or a modification of a determination under a provision mentioned in sub-paragraph (1)(c) all necessary adjustments—

(a) must be made by making assessments or by repayment or discharge of tax, and

(b) must be made notwithstanding any limitation on the time within which assessments may be made.

(7) In this paragraph "the Capital Allowances Acts" has the same meaning as in the Tax Acts and "fixture" has the same meaning as in Chapter VI of Part II of the 1990 Act.

Transfers of trading stock

12—(1) This paragraph applies if—

(a) under a relevant transfer trading stock of the transferor is transferred to the transferee, and

(b) the stock falls, immediately after the time when the transfer takes effect, to be treated as trading stock of the transferee.

(2) Sub-paragraphs (3) and (4) have effect in computing the profits or gains of the relevant trades for the purposes of the Corporation Tax Acts; and the relevant trades are—

(a) the trade in relation to which the stock is trading stock immediately before the time when the transfer takes effect, and

(b) the trade in relation to which it is trading stock after that time.

(3) The stock must be taken—

(a) to have been disposed of by the transferor in the course of the trade carried on by the transferor,

(b) to have been acquired by the transferee in the course of the trade carried on by the transferee, and

(c) subject to that, to have been disposed of and acquired at the time when the transfer takes effect.

(4) The stock must be valued for the purposes of each of the relevant trades as if the disposal and acquisition had been for a consideration which in relation to the transferor would have resulted in neither a profit nor a loss being brought into account in respect of the disposal in the accounting period of the transferor which ends with, or is current at, the time when the transfer takes effect.

(5) In this paragraph "trading stock" has the same meaning as in section 100 of the 1988 Act.

Trading losses: transfer of trade

13—(1) This paragraph applies if a transfer scheme provides for a relevant transfer as a result of which the transferor ceases to carry on a trade and the transferee begins to carry it on.

(2) A transferor treated as ceasing to carry on a trade for the purposes of section 343 of the 1988 Act (company reconstructions without a change of ownership) is to be so treated for the purposes of this paragraph.

(3) A transferee treated as beginning to carry on a trade for the purposes of that section is to be so treated for the purposes of this paragraph.

(4) Sub-paragraph (5) applies if the transfer will result in the transferee being entitled to relief for an amount in respect of the trade under section 393(1) of the 1988 Act (trading losses) by virtue of section 343(3).

(5) In such a case the scheme may provide that the amount is to be treated as such amount (the replacement amount) as is specified in or determined in accordance with the scheme.

(6) Sub-paragraph (7) applies if the trade concerned is in fact part of a trade of the transferor and the transferor is entitled to relief for an amount under section 393(1) in respect of the part retained.

(7) In such a case the scheme may provide that the amount is to be treated as such amount (the replacement amount) as is specified in or determined in accordance with the scheme.

(8) A provision under sub-paragraph (5) or (7) must be such that the replacement amount is not greater than the amount it replaces; and the replacement amount may be nil.

(9) When the scheme comes into force a provision made under sub-paragraph (5) or (7) is to have effect for the purposes of arriving at the amount of relief concerned.

Trading losses: change in ownership

14—(1) This paragraph applies if under a relevant transfer all the issued share capital of a company (the transferred company) is transferred from the CAA to—

(a) the Secretary of State, or

(b) a company whose shares are all held by the Secretary of State when the transfer takes effect.

(2) For the purposes of section 768 of the 1988 Act (disallowance of trading losses on change in company's ownership) the transfer is not to be taken to result in a change in the ownership of—

(a) the transferred company, or

(b) a company which is a wholly owned subsidiary of the transferred company when the transfer takes effect.

Leased assets

15—(1) This paragraph applies for the purposes of section 781 of the 1988 Act (assets leased to traders and others) if the interest of the lessor or the lessee under a lease, or any other interest in an asset, is transferred to a person under a relevant transfer.

(2) The transfer is to be treated as made without any capital sum having been obtained in respect of the interest by the transferor or the transferee; and this is so notwithstanding section 783(4) of that Act.

Securities

16—(1) This paragraph applies if securities are issued by a company in pursuance of a direction of the Secretary of State under section 49 or 58 above.

(2) A share issued by the company is to be treated for the purposes of the Corporation Tax Acts as if it had been issued wholly in consideration of a subscription paid to the company of an amount equal to the nominal value of the share.

(3) A debenture issued by the company is to be treated for the purposes of the Corporation Tax Acts as if it had been issued—

(a) wholly in consideration of a loan made to the company of an amount equal to the principal sum payable under the debenture, and

(b) wholly and exclusively for the purposes of the trade carried on by the company.

(4) If a debenture issued by the company includes provision for the payment of a sum expressed as interest in respect of a period falling wholly or partly before the issue of the debenture, a payment made in pursuance of the provision in respect of the period is to be treated for the purposes of the Corporation Tax Acts as if the debenture had been issued at the commencement of the period and (accordingly) as interest on the principal sum payable under the debenture.

(5) This paragraph has effect subject to paragraphs 3, 4 and 17.

17—(1) This paragraph applies if—

(a) securities are issued to a company in pursuance of a direction of the Secretary of State under section 49 or 58 above, and

(b) by virtue of any such security the company has a loan relationship for the purposes of the Corporation Tax Acts.

(2) For the purposes of Chapter II of Part IV of the Finance Act 1996 (loan relationships) the company is to be taken to have acquired its rights under the security wholly in consideration of a loan made by it to the issuing company of an amount equal to the principal sum payable under the security.

(3) Expressions used in this paragraph and in Chapter II of Part IV of the Finance Act 1996 have the same meanings in this paragraph as in that Chapter.

Stamp duty

18 (See the *Orange Tax Handbook*.)

Stamp duty reserve tax

19 (See the *Orange Tax Handbook*.)

Agreements

20—(1) Sub-paragraph (2) applies if the effect of—

(a) an agreement made under paragraph 9 or 11 of Schedule 6, (*b*) an instrument executed under paragraph 9 of Schedule 6, or

(*c*) an agreement treated as made under paragraph 10 of Schedule 6,

is to modify the effect of a transfer scheme.

(2) This Schedule, the 1988 Act, the 1990 Act and the 1992 Act are to have effect as if—

(*a*) the scheme had been made as modified, and

(*b*) anything done by or in relation to the preceding holder had (so far as relating to the property, rights or liabilities affected by the modification) been done by or in relation to the subsequent holder.

(3) Sub-paragraph (4) applies to a disposal of an asset if the disposal—

(*a*) is effected in pursuance of an agreement made or treated as made under paragraph 9 or 10 of Schedule 6 or is effected by an instrument executed under paragraph 9 of that Schedule, and

(*b*) is the grant of a lease of land or the creation of other rights and liabilities over land.

(4) For the purposes of the 1992 Act the disposal is to be taken (in relation to the person to whom it is made as well as the person making it) to be for a consideration such that no gain or loss accrues to the person making it.

(5) Section 171(1) of the 1992 Act (provision in relation to disposal of assets from one member of a group of companies to another member of the group) does not apply if sub-paragraph (4) applies to the disposal in question.

(6) References in this paragraph to an agreement or instrument include references to the agreement or instrument as varied in accordance with a direction under paragraph 19(4) of Schedule 6.

(7) For the purposes of sub-paragraph (2) the preceding holder is the person who without the modification—

(*a*) became (under the transfer scheme concerned) entitled or subject to the property, rights or liabilities affected by the modification, or

(*b*) remained (despite the transfer scheme concerned) entitled or subject to the property, rights or liabilities affected by the modification,

as the case may be.

(8) For the purposes of sub-paragraph (2) the subsequent holder is the person who (in consequence of the modification) becomes, or resumes being, entitled or subject to the property, rights or liabilities affected by the modification.

SCHEDULE 26

TRANSFERS: TAX

Section 250

Note—This Schedule was brought into force on 15 January 2001 by virtue of SI 2000/3376 art 2.

PART I

INTERPRETATION

1—(1) In this Schedule—

"the 1988 Act" means the Income and Corporation Taxes Act 1988,

...[1]

"the 1992 Act" means the Taxation of Chargeable Gains Act 1992,

["the Capital Allowances Act" means the Capital Allowances Act 2001 and includes, where the context admits, enactments which under the 1988 Act are to be treated as contained in the Capital Allowances Act 2001,][1]

"fixture" has the same meaning as in [Chapter 14 of Part 2 of the Capital Allowances Act][1],

"franchise company" means any body corporate which is, or is to be, the franchisee or the franchise operator under a franchise agreement, and

"qualifying transfer" means a transfer which is a relevant transfer for the purposes of any of Parts II to VI of this Schedule.

(2) So far as it relates to corporation tax, this Schedule is to be construed as one with the Corporation Tax Acts.

(3) So far as it relates to capital allowances, this Schedule is to be construed as one with [the Capital Allowances Act][1].

Amendments—[1] In sub-para (1), definition of "the 1990 Act" repealed, definition of "Capital Allowances Act" substituted for definition of "Capital Allowances Acts", definition of "fixture" amended, and in sub-para (3), words substituted, by CAA 2001 ss 578, 580, Sch 2 paras 109(1), (2), Sch 4 with effect for corporation tax purposes as respects allowances and charges falling to be made for chargeable periods ending after 31 March 2001.

PART II
TRANSFERS TO SRA FROM FRANCHISING DIRECTOR, SECRETARY OF STATE AND REGULATOR
Interpretation

2 In this Part of this Schedule—

"relevant transfer" means a transfer of property, rights or liabilities by virtue of—

    (*a*) section 215,

    (*b*) a scheme under paragraph 1 of Schedule 15, or

    (*c*) a scheme under paragraph 31 of Schedule 17,

"transferee", in relation to a relevant transfer, means the Authority, and

"transferor", in relation to a relevant transfer, means the person from whom the property, rights or liabilities are transferred.

Chargeable gains: no gain no loss

3 For the purposes of the 1992 Act a disposal by virtue of provision made under paragraph 34(*a*) of Schedule 17 is to be taken to be for a consideration such that no gain or loss accrues to the person making the disposal.

Chargeable gains: disposal of debts

4—(1) Sub-paragraph (2) applies if in the case of a relevant transfer—

    (*a*) a debt owed to the transferor is transferred to the transferee, and

    (*b*) the transferor would, apart from this paragraph, be the original creditor in relation to that debt for the purposes of section 251 of the 1992 Act (disposal of debts).

(2) The 1992 Act is to have effect as if the transferee (and not the transferor) were the original creditor for those purposes.

Capital allowances for plant and machinery

5—(1) This paragraph applies in relation to property if—

    (*a*) the property is plant or machinery to which a relevant transfer relates,

    (*b*) the property would have been treated for the purposes of [the Capital Allowances Act][1] (had the transferor incurred expenditure qualifying for allowances under [Part 2 of that Act][1] on the provision of the property) as disposed of by the transferor to the transferee on the transfer taking effect, and

    (*c*) the relevant order or scheme contains provision for the transferee to be taken for the purposes of [that Act][1] to have incurred capital expenditure of an amount specified in or determined in accordance with the order or scheme on the provision of the property.

(2) For the purposes of [the Capital Allowances Act][1]—

    (*a*) the transferee is to be taken to have incurred capital expenditure of that amount on the provision of the property for the purposes for which it is used by the transferee on and after the taking effect of the transfer,

    (*b*) the property is to be taken as belonging to the transferee in consequence of the transferee having incurred that expenditure, and

    (*c*) in the case of a fixture, the expenditure which falls to be treated as incurred by the transferee is to be taken for the purposes of [sections 181(1) and 182(1) of that Act][1] to be incurred by the giving of a consideration consisting in a capital sum of that amount.

(3) In sub-paragraph (1)(*c*) "the relevant order or scheme" means—

    (*a*) in the case of a transfer by virtue of section 215, an order made by the Secretary of State by statutory instrument, or

    (*b*) in the case of a transfer by virtue of a scheme under paragraph 1 of Schedule 15 or paragraph 31 of Schedule 17, the scheme concerned.

(4) A provision mentioned in sub-paragraph (1)(*c*) for the determination of an amount may include provision—

    (*a*) for a determination to be made by the Secretary of State in a manner described in the order or scheme,

    (*b*) for a determination to be made by reference to factors so described or to the opinion of a person so described, and

    (*c*) for a determination to be capable of being modified (on one or more occasions) in a manner and in circumstances so described.

(5) The Treasury's consent is required for the making or modification of a determination under a provision mentioned in sub-paragraph (1)(*c*).

(6) The transferee's consent is also required for such a modification after the relevant transfer takes effect.

(7) If there is a determination or a modification of a determination under a provision mentioned in sub-paragraph (1)(*c*) all necessary adjustments—

    (*a*) must be made by making assessments or by repayment or discharge of tax, and

    (*b*) must be made despite any limitation on the time within which assessments may be made.

Amendments—¹ Words in sub-paras (1), (2) substituted by CAA 2001 s 578, Sch 2 paras 109(3)–(5) with effect for income tax purposes, as respects allowances and charges falling to be made for chargeable periods ending after 5 April 2001, and for corporation tax purposes as respects allowances and charges falling to be made for chargeable periods ending after 31 March 2001.

Capital allowances for plant and machinery: connected persons

6 For the purposes of [Part 2 of the Capital Allowances Act]¹ references in that Part to a transaction (however described) between connected persons within the meaning of section 839 of the 1988 Act are not to include references to a relevant transfer.

Amendments—¹ Words substituted by CAA 2001 s 578, Sch 2 paras 109(6) with effect for income tax purposes, as respects allowances and charges falling to be made for chargeable periods ending after 5 April 2001, and for corporation tax purposes as respects allowances and charges falling to be made for chargeable periods ending after 31 March 2001.

Loan relationships

7—(1) Sub-paragraph (2) applies if as a result of a relevant transfer the transferee replaces, or (if the transferor had been a company) would have replaced, the transferor as a party to a loan relationship.

(2) Chapter II of Part IV of the Finance Act 1996 is to have effect in relation to the time when the relevant transfer takes effect and any later time as if—

    (*a*) the transferee had been a party to the loan relationship at the time the transferor became, or (if the transferor had been a company) would have become, a party to the loan relationship and at all times since that time, and

    (*b*) the loan relationship to which the transferee is a party after the time the transfer takes effect is the same loan relationship as that to which, by virtue of paragraph (*a*), it is treated as having been a party before that time.

(3) For the purposes of sub-paragraph (2) the transferor (and accordingly the transferee) is to be taken to have accounted for the loan relationship in accordance with an authorised accounting method corresponding to that in accordance with which the transferee accounts for the loan relationship in the accounting period in which the transfer takes effect.

(4) Expressions used in this paragraph and in Chapter II of Part IV of the Finance Act 1996 have the same meanings in this paragraph as in that Chapter.

PART III
TRANSFERS FROM BR TO SRA

Interpretation

8 In this Part of this Schedule—

    "relevant transfer" means a transfer of property, rights or liabilities by virtue of—

        (*a*) paragraph 11 of Schedule 18, or

        (*b*) a scheme under paragraph 1 of Schedule 19,

    "transferee", in relation to a relevant transfer, means the Authority, and

    "transferor", in relation to a relevant transfer, means the Board.

Chargeable gains: general

9 For the purposes of the 1992 Act a disposal—

    (*a*) constituted by a relevant transfer, or

    (*b*) by virtue of provision made under paragraph 4 of Schedule 19,

is to be taken (in relation to the person to whom the disposal is made as well as the person making the disposal) to be for a consideration such that no gain or loss accrues to the person making the disposal.

Chargeable gains: restriction of losses

10—(1) If there has been a disposal of an asset—

    (*a*) constituted by a relevant transfer, or

    (*b*) by virtue of provision made under paragraph 4 of Schedule 19,

subsection (8) of section 41 of the 1992 Act (which applies that section to cases where assets have been acquired without gain or loss) is to have effect as if the asset had been disposed of and acquired in circumstances mentioned in that subsection.

(2) This paragraph is not to prejudice paragraph 9.

Chargeable gains: groups

11—(1) Sub-paragraph (2) applies if a company (''the degrouped company'')—

(a) acquired an asset from another company at any time when both were members of the same group of companies (''the old group''), and
(b) ceases by virtue of a relevant transfer to be a member of the old group.

(2) Section 179 of the 1992 Act (company ceasing to be member of group) is not to treat the degrouped company as having by virtue of the transfer sold and immediately reacquired the asset.

(3) If sub-paragraph (2) applies to an asset, that section is to have effect on and after the first subsequent occasion on which the degrouped company ceases to be a member of a group of companies (''the new group''), otherwise than by virtue of a qualifying transfer, as if the degrouped company and the company from which it acquired the asset had been members of the new group at the time of acquisition.

(4) If, disregarding any preparatory transactions, a company would be regarded for the purposes of section 179 of the 1992 Act (and, accordingly, of this paragraph) as ceasing to be a member of a group of companies by virtue of a qualifying transfer, it is to be regarded for those purposes as so doing by virtue of the qualifying transfer and not by virtue of any preparatory transactions.

(5) In this paragraph ''preparatory transaction'' means anything done under or by virtue of this Part of this Act for the purpose of initiating, advancing or facilitating the qualifying transfer in question.

(6) Expressions used in this paragraph and in section 179 of the 1992 Act have the same meanings in this paragraph as in that section.

Chargeable gains: disposal of debts

12—(1) Sub-paragraph (2) applies if in the case of a relevant transfer—

(a) a debt owed to the transferor is transferred to the transferee, and
(b) the transferor would, apart from this paragraph, be the original creditor in relation to that debt for the purposes of section 251 of the 1992 Act (disposal of debts).

(2) The 1992 Act is to have effect as if the transferee (and not the transferor) were the original creditor for those purposes.

Continuity in relation to capital allowances etc where trade transferred

13—(1) If, apart from this paragraph—

(a) the transferor would be treated for the purposes of the Corporation Tax Acts as having ceased, by virtue of a relevant transfer taking effect, to carry on any trade, and
(b) the transferee would be treated as having begun, on that transfer taking effect, to carry it on,

the trade is not to be treated as permanently discontinued, nor a new trade as set up, for the purposes of the allowances and charges provided for by [the Capital Allowances Act]¹, but sub-paragraphs (2) to (4) are to apply.

(2) Subject to sub-paragraphs (3) and (4), in a case falling within sub-paragraph (1)—

(a) there are to be made to or on the transferee in accordance with [the Capital Allowances Act]¹ all such allowances and charges as would, if the transferor had continued to carry on the trade, have fallen to be made to or on the transferor, and
(b) the amount of any such allowance or charge is to be computed as if—

(i) the transferee had been carrying on the trade since the transferor began to do so, and
(ii) everything done to or by the transferor had been done to or by the transferee (but so that the relevant transfer itself, so far as it relates to any assets in use for the purpose of the trade, shall not be treated as giving rise to any such allowance or charge).

(3) For the purposes of the Corporation Tax Acts, only such amounts (if any) as may be specified in or determined in accordance with an order made by the Secretary of State by statutory instrument are to be allocated to the transferee in respect of expenditure by reference to which capital allowances may be made by virtue of sub-paragraph (2) in relation to anything to which the transfer relates.

(4) Sub-paragraph (2) is to affect the amounts falling to be taken into account in relation to the transferor as expenditure by reference to which capital allowances may be made only so far as necessary to give effect to a reduction of any such amount by a sum equal to so much of that amount as is allocated to the transferee as mentioned in sub-paragraph (3).

(5) An order under sub-paragraph (3) may include provision—

(a) for a determination to be made by the Secretary of State in a manner described in the order,
(b) for a determination to be made by reference to factors so described or to the opinion of a person so described, and
(c) for a determination to be capable of being modified (on one or more occasions) in a manner and in circumstances so described.

(6) The Treasury's consent is required for the making or modification of a determination of any such amount as is mentioned in sub-paragraph (3).

(7) The transferee's consent is also required for such a modification after the relevant transfer takes effect.

(8) In determining whether sub-paragraph (1) has effect in relation to a relevant transfer in a case where—

    (*a*) the transferor continues to carry on any trade or part of a trade after the transfer takes effect, or

    (*b*) the transferee was carrying on any trade before the transfer takes effect,

the trade or part of a trade which is continued, or was being carried on, shall for the purposes of that sub-paragraph be treated in relation to any trade or part of a trade which is transferred by virtue of the transfer as a separate trade and shall accordingly be disregarded.

(9) If there is a determination or a modification of a determination for any purposes of this paragraph, all necessary adjustments—

    (*a*) must be made by making assessments or by repayment or discharge of tax, and

    (*b*) must be made despite any limitation on the time within which assessments may be made.

Amendments—¹ Words in sub-paras (1), (2)(*a*) substituted by CAA 2001 s 578, Sch 2 paras 109(7) with effect for income tax purposes, as respects allowances and charges falling to be made for chargeable periods ending after 5 April 2001, and for corporation tax purposes as respects allowances and charges falling to be made for chargeable periods ending after 31 March 2001.

Capital allowances for plant and machinery

14—(1) This paragraph applies in relation to property if—

    (*a*) the property is plant or machinery to which a relevant transfer relates,

    (*b*) paragraph 13 does not apply in relation to the transfer of the property to the transferee,

    (*c*) the property would be treated for the purposes of [the Capital Allowances Act]¹ as disposed of by the transferor to the transferee on the transfer taking effect, and

    (*d*) the scheme concerned contains provision for the disposal value of the property to be taken for the purposes of [that Act]¹ to be of an amount specified in or determined in accordance with the scheme.

(2) For the purposes of [the Capital Allowances Act]¹—

    (*a*) the provision mentioned in sub-paragraph (1)(*d*) is to have effect (instead of [section 61(2) to (4), 72(3) to (5), 171, 196 or 423 of that Act]¹) for determining an amount as the disposal value of the property or the price at which a fixture is to be treated as sold,

    (*b*) the transferee is to be taken to have incurred capital expenditure of that amount on the provision of the property for the purposes for which it is used by the transferee on and after the taking effect of the transfer,

    (*c*) the property is to be taken as belonging to the transferee in consequence of the transferee having incurred that expenditure, and

    (*d*) in the case of a fixture, the expenditure which falls to be treated as incurred by the transferee is to be taken for the purposes of [sections 181(1) and 182(1) of that Act]¹ to be incurred by the giving of a consideration consisting in a capital sum of that amount.

(3) A provision mentioned in sub-paragraph (1)(*d*) for the determination of an amount may include provision—

    (*a*) for a determination to be made by the Secretary of State in a manner described in the scheme,

    (*b*) for a determination to be made by reference to factors so described or to the opinion of a person so described, and

    (*c*) for a determination to be capable of being modified (on one or more occasions) in a manner and in circumstances so described.

(4) The Treasury's consent is required for the making or modification of a determination under a provision mentioned in sub-paragraph (1)(*d*).

(5) The transferee's consent is also required for such a modification after the relevant transfer takes effect.

(6) If there is a determination or a modification of a determination under a provision mentioned in sub-paragraph (1)(*d*) all necessary adjustments—

    (*a*) must be made by making assessments or by repayment or discharge of tax, and

    (*b*) must be made despite any limitation on the time within which assessments may be made.

Amendments—¹ Words in sub-paras (1), (2) substituted by CAA 2001 s 578, Sch 2 paras 109(8)–(10) with effect for income tax purposes, as respects allowances and charges falling to be made for chargeable periods ending after 5 April 2001, and for corporation tax purposes as respects allowances and charges falling to be made for chargeable periods ending after 31 March 2001.

Capital allowances for plant and machinery: connected persons

15 For the purposes of [Part 2 of the Capital Allowances Act]¹references in that Part to a transaction (however described) between connected persons within the meaning of section 839 of the 1988 Act are not to include references to a relevant transfer.

Amendments—[1] Words substituted by CAA 2001 s 578, Sch 2 para 109(11) with effect for income tax purposes, as respects allowances and charges falling to be made for chargeable periods ending after 5 April 2001, and for corporation tax purposes as respects allowances and charges falling to be made for chargeable periods ending after 31 March 2001.

Leased assets

16—(1) Sub-paragraphs (2) and (3) apply for the purposes of section 781 of the 1988 Act (assets leased to traders and others) if the interest of the lessor or the lessee under a lease, or any other interest in an asset, is transferred to a person under a relevant transfer.

(2) The transfer is to be treated as made without any capital sum having been obtained in respect of the interest by the transferor; and this is so despite section 783(4) of that Act.

(3) If the interest is an interest under a lease, payments made by the transferor under the lease before the transfer takes effect are to be treated as if they had been made under that lease by the transferee.

(4) Sub-paragraph (5) applies for the purposes of section 781 of the 1988 Act if a lease, or any other interest in an asset, is granted by virtue of provision made under paragraph 4 of Schedule 19.

(5) The grant is to be treated as made without any capital sum having been obtained in respect of the lease, or interest, by the grantor; and this is so despite section 783(4) of that Act.

(6) No charge is to arise under section 781(1) of the 1988 Act by virtue of section 783(2) of that Act in a case where the capital sum mentioned in section 781(1)(*b*)(i) or (ii) of that Act is or forms part of the consideration obtained (or treated by section 783(4) of that Act as obtained) by the transferor on a disposal by virtue of a relevant transfer of securities of a subsidiary of the transferor.

(7) Expressions used in this paragraph and in sections 781 to 785 of the 1988 Act have the same meanings in this paragraph as in those sections.

Loan relationships

17—(1) Sub-paragraph (2) applies if, as a result of a relevant transfer, the transferee replaces the transferor as a party to a loan relationship.

(2) Chapter II of Part IV of the Finance Act 1996 is to have effect in relation to the time when the relevant transfer takes effect and any later time as if—

(*a*) the transferee had been a party to the loan relationship at the time the transferor became a party to the loan relationship and at all times since that time, and
(*b*) the loan relationship to which the transferee is a party after the time the transfer takes effect is the same loan relationship as that to which, by virtue of paragraph (*a*), it is treated as having been a party before that time.

(3) Expressions used in this paragraph and in Chapter II of Part IV of the Finance Act 1996 have the same meanings in this paragraph as in that Chapter.

Charge to tax under Case I of Schedule D

18—(1) This paragraph applies for the purpose of computing the profits or losses of the transferor and the transferee under Case I of Schedule D in respect of any trade or part of a trade transferred by a relevant transfer in relation to the time when the transfer takes effect and any later time.

(2) The trade or part of a trade transferred is to be treated as having been, at the time of its commencement and at all times since that time, a separate trade carried on by the transferee.

(3) The trade carried on by the transferee after the time the transfer takes effect is to be treated as the same trade as that which, by virtue of sub-paragraph (2), it is treated as having carried on before that time.

(4) This paragraph is subject to paragraphs 13 and 17.

PART IV
TRANSFERS TO SECRETARY OF STATE FROM SRA AND BR
Interpretation

19 In this Part of this Schedule—

"relevant transfer" means a transfer of property, rights or liabilities by virtue of—

(*a*) a scheme under paragraph 1 of Schedule 21 under which the property, rights or liabilities are transferred to the Secretary of State, or
(*b*) a scheme under paragraph 1 of Schedule 25,

"transferee", in relation to a relevant transfer, means the Secretary of State, and
"transferor", in relation to a relevant transfer, means the person from whom the property, rights or liabilities are transferred.

Chargeable gains: groups

20—(1) Sub-paragraph (2) applies if a company (''the degrouped company'')—

(a) acquired an asset from another company at any time when both were members of the same group of companies (''the old group''), and

(b) ceases by virtue of a relevant transfer to be a member of the old group.

(2) Section 179 of the 1992 Act (company ceasing to be member of group) is not to treat the degrouped company as having by virtue of the transfer sold and immediately reacquired the asset.

(3) If, disregarding any preparatory transactions, a company would be regarded for the purposes of section 179 of the 1992 Act (and, accordingly, of this paragraph) as ceasing to be a member of a group of companies by virtue of a relevant transfer, it is to be regarded for those purposes as so doing by virtue of the relevant transfer and not by virtue of any preparatory transactions.

(4) In this paragraph ''preparatory transaction'' means anything done under or by virtue of this Part of this Act for the purpose of initiating, advancing or facilitating the relevant transfer in question.

(5) Expressions used in this paragraph and in section 179 of the 1992 Act have the same meanings in this paragraph as in that section.

Capital allowances: actual consideration to be the disposal value

21—(1) Sub-paragraphs (2) to (4) apply for the purposes of [Part 3 of the Capital Allowances Act][1], and the other provisions of that Act which are relevant to that Part, if there is a disposal by virtue of a relevant transfer of the relevant interest in—

(a) an industrial building or structure, or

(b) a qualifying hotel or a commercial building or structure.

(2) The disposal is to be treated as a sale of that relevant interest.

(3) The sale moneys in respect of that sale are to be taken—

(a) if a capital sum is received by the transferor or a person connected with the transferor by way of consideration or compensation in respect of the disposal, to be an amount equal to that capital sum, or

(b) if no such capital sum is received, to be nil.

(4) [Sections 567 to 570 of that Act (sales treated as being for alternative amount)][1] are not to have effect in relation to that sale.

(5) Sub-paragraph (6) applies for determining, in the case of [plant or machinery][1] which is treated for the purposes of [the Capital Allowances Act][1] as disposed of by virtue of a relevant transfer, the amount which (in consequence of that disposal) is to be brought into account as the disposal value of that [plant or machinery][1] for the purposes of [section 60 of that Act (meaning of ''disposal value'' and ''disposal event'')][1].

(6) The amount is, subject to [section 62 of that Act (general limit on amount of disposal value)][1] to be taken—

(a) if a capital sum is received by the transferor or a person connected with the transferor by way of consideration or compensation in respect of the disposal, to be an amount equal to that capital sum, or

(b) if no such capital sum is received, to be nil.

(7) Sub-paragraph (8) applies if, in consequence of a disposal by virtue of a relevant transfer, [a person is treated by section 188 of the Capital Allowances Act as ceasing to own a fixture][1] at any time.

(8) The amount which, in consequence of that disposal, is to be brought into account as the disposal value of the fixture for the purposes of [section 60 of the Capital Allowances Act is, subject to section 62 of that Act][1], to be taken—

(a) if a capital sum is received by the transferor or a person connected with the transferor by way of consideration or compensation in respect of the disposal, to be an amount equal to that portion of that capital sum which falls (or, if the person to whom the disposal is made were entitled to an allowance, would fall) to be treated for the purposes of [Part 2 of that Act][1] as expenditure incurred by that person on the provision of the fixture, or

(b) if no such capital sum is received, to be nil.

(9) Sub-paragraphs (3), (6) and (8) have effect despite any other provision of [the Capital Allowances Act][1].

Amendments—[1] Words in sub-paras (1), (4)–(9) substituted by CAA 2001 s 578, Sch 2 paras 109(12)–(18) with effect for income tax purposes, as respects allowances and charges falling to be made for chargeable periods ending after 5 April 2001, and for corporation tax purposes as respects allowances and charges falling to be made for chargeable periods ending after 31 March 2001.

Leased assets

22—(1) Sub-paragraphs (2) and (3) apply for the purposes of section 781 of the 1988 Act (assets leased to traders and others) if the interest of the lessor or the lessee under a lease, or any other interest in an asset, is transferred to a person under a relevant transfer.

(2) The transfer is to be treated as made without any capital sum having been obtained in respect of the interest by the transferor; and this is so despite section 783(4) of that Act.

(3) If the interest is an interest under a lease, payments made by the transferor under the lease before the transfer takes effect are to be treated as if they had been made under that lease by the transferee.

(4) Sub-paragraph (5) applies for the purposes of section 781 of the 1988 Act if a lease, or any other interest in an asset, is granted by the transferor by virtue of provision made under paragraph 5 of Schedule 21 or paragraph 4 of Schedule 25.

(5) The grant is to be treated as made without any capital sum having been obtained in respect of the lease, or interest, by the transferor; and this is so despite section 783(4) of that Act.

(6) No charge is to arise under section 781(1) of the 1988 Act by virtue of section 783(2) of that Act in a case where the capital sum mentioned in section 781(1)(*b*)(i) or (ii) of that Act is or forms part of the consideration obtained (or treated by section 783(4) of that Act as obtained) by the transferor on a disposal by virtue of a relevant transfer of securities of a subsidiary of the transferor.

(7) Expressions used in this paragraph and in sections 781 to 785 of the 1988 Act have the same meanings in this paragraph as in those sections.

PART V

TRANSFERS FROM SRA TO FRANCHISE COMPANY

Interpretation

23 In this Part of this Schedule—

    "relevant transfer" means a transfer of property, rights or liabilities by virtue of a scheme under paragraph 1 of Schedule 21 under which the property, rights or liabilities are transferred to a franchise company,

    "transferee", in relation to a relevant transfer, means the franchise company to whom the property, rights or liabilities are transferred, and

    "transferor", in relation to a relevant transfer, means the person from whom the property, rights or liabilities are transferred.

Chargeable gains: disposals not to be treated as made at market value

24—(1) Section 17 of the 1992 Act (disposals and acquisitions treated as made at market value) is not to have effect in relation to—

    (*a*) a disposal constituted by a relevant transfer or a disposal by virtue of provision made under paragraph 5 of Schedule 21, or

    (*b*) the acquisition made by the person to whom the disposal is made.

(2) But sub-paragraph (1) does not apply—

    (*a*) if the person making the disposal is connected with the person making the acquisition, or

    (*b*) in the case of a disposal by virtue of provision made under paragraph 5 of Schedule 21, if the disposal is made by or to a person other than the transferor or the transferee.

(3) If sub-paragraph (1) applies to the disposal of an asset, the disposal is to be taken (in relation to the person making the acquisition as well as the person making the disposal) to be—

    (*a*) in a case where consideration in money or money's worth is given by the person making the acquisition or on his behalf in respect of the vesting of the asset in him, for a consideration equal to the amount or value of that consideration, or

    (*b*) in a case where no such consideration is given, for a consideration of nil.

Chargeable gains: groups

25—(1) Sub-paragraph (2) applies if a company ("the degrouped company")—

    (*a*) acquired an asset from another company at any time when both were members of the same group of companies ("the old group"), and

    (*b*) ceases by virtue of a relevant transfer to be a member of the old group.

(2) Section 179 of the 1992 Act (company ceasing to be member of group) is not to treat the degrouped company as having by virtue of the transfer sold and immediately reacquired the asset.

(3) If sub-paragraph (2) applies to an asset, that section is to have effect on and after the first subsequent occasion on which the degrouped company ceases to be a member of a group of companies ("the new group"), otherwise than by virtue of a qualifying transfer, as if the degrouped company and the company from which it acquired the asset had been members of the new group at the time of acquisition.

(4) If, disregarding any preparatory transactions, a company would be regarded for the purposes of section 179 of the 1992 Act (and, accordingly, of this paragraph) as ceasing to be a member of a group of companies by virtue of a qualifying transfer, it is to be regarded for those purposes as so doing by virtue of the qualifying transfer and not by virtue of any preparatory transactions.

(5) In this paragraph "preparatory transaction" means anything done under or by virtue of this Part of this Act for the purpose of initiating, advancing or facilitating the qualifying transfer in question.

(6) Expressions used in this paragraph and in section 179 of the 1992 Act have the same meanings in this paragraph as in that section.

Chargeable gains: disposal of debts

26—(1) Sub-paragraph (2) applies if in the case of a relevant transfer—

(*a*) a debt owed to the transferor is transferred to the transferee, and

(*b*) the transferor would, apart from this paragraph, be the original creditor in relation to that debt for the purposes of section 251 of the 1992 Act (disposal of debts).

(2) The 1992 Act is to have effect as if the transferee (and not the transferor) were the original creditor for those purposes.

Capital allowances: actual consideration to be the disposal value

27—(1) Sub-paragraphs (2) to (4) apply for the purposes of [Part 3 of the Capital Allowances Act][1], and the other provisions of that Act which are relevant to that Part, if there is a disposal by virtue of a relevant transfer of the relevant interest in—

(*a*) an industrial building or structure, or

(*b*) a qualifying hotel or a commercial building or structure.

(2) The disposal is to be treated as a sale of that relevant interest.

(3) The sale moneys in respect of that sale are to be taken—

(*a*) if a capital sum is received by the transferor or a person connected with the transferor by way of consideration or compensation in respect of the disposal, to be an amount equal to that capital sum, or

(*b*) if no such capital sum is received, to be nil.

(4) [Sections 567 to 570 of that Act (sales treated as being for alternative amount)][1] are not to have effect in relation to that sale.

(5) Sub-paragraph (6) applies for determining, in the case of [plant or machinery][1] which is treated for the purposes of [the Capital Allowances Act][1] as disposed of by virtue of a relevant transfer, the amount which (in consequence of that disposal) is to be brought into account as the disposal value of that [plant or machinery][1] for the purposes of [section 60 of that Act (meaning of "disposal value" and "disposal event")][1].

(6) The amount is, subject to [section 62 of that Act (general limit on amount of disposal value)][1] to be taken—

(*a*) if a capital sum is received by the transferor or a person connected with the transferor by way of consideration or compensation in respect of the disposal, to be an amount equal to that capital sum, or

(*b*) if no such capital sum is received, to be nil.

(7) Sub-paragraph (8) applies if, in consequence of a disposal by virtue of a relevant transfer, [a person is treated by section 188 of the Capital Allowances Act as ceasing to own a fixture][1] at any time.

(8) The amount which, in consequence of that disposal, is to be brought into account as the disposal value of the fixture for the purposes of [section 60 of the Capital Allowances Act is, subject to section 62 of that Act][1], to be taken—

(*a*) if a capital sum is received by the transferor or a person connected with the transferor by way of consideration or compensation in respect of the disposal, to be an amount equal to that portion of that capital sum which falls (or, if the person to whom the disposal is made were entitled to an allowance, would fall) to be treated for the purposes of [Part 2 of that Act][1] as expenditure incurred by that person on the provision of the fixture, or

(*b*) if no such capital sum is received, to be nil.

(9) Sub-paragraphs (3), (6) and (8) have effect despite any other provision of [the Capital Allowances Act][1].

Amendments—[1] Words in sub-paras (1), (4)–(9) substituted by CAA 2001 s 578, Sch 2 paras 109(19)–(25) with effect for income tax purposes, as respects allowances and charges falling to be made for chargeable periods ending after 5 April 2001, and for corporation tax purposes as respects allowances and charges falling to be made for chargeable periods ending after 31 March 2001.

Leased assets

28—(1) Sub-paragraphs (2) and (3) apply for the purposes of section 781 of the 1988 Act (assets leased to traders and others) if the interest of the lessor or the lessee under a lease, or any other interest in an asset, is transferred to a person under a relevant transfer.

(2) The transfer is to be treated as made without any capital sum having been obtained in respect of the interest by the transferor; and this is so despite section 783(4) of that Act.

(3) If the interest is an interest under a lease, payments made by the transferor under the lease before the transfer takes effect are to be treated as if they had been made under that lease by the transferee.

(4) Sub-paragraph (5) applies for the purposes of section 781 of the 1988 Act if a lease, or any other interest in an asset, is granted by the transferor by virtue of provision made under paragraph 5 of Schedule 21.

(5) The grant is to be treated as made without any capital sum having been obtained in respect of the lease, or interest, by the transferor; and this is so despite section 783(4) of that Act.

(6) No charge is to arise under section 781(1) of the 1988 Act by virtue of section 783(2) of that Act in a case where the capital sum mentioned in section 781(1)(*b*)(i) or (ii) of that Act is or forms part of the consideration obtained (or treated by section 783(4) of that Act as obtained) by the transferor on a disposal by virtue of a relevant transfer of securities of a subsidiary of the transferor.

(7) Expressions used in this paragraph and in sections 781 to 785 of the 1988 Act have the same meanings in this paragraph as in those sections.

Loan relationships

29—(1) Sub-paragraph (2) applies if, as a result of a relevant transfer, the transferee replaces the transferor as a party to a loan relationship.

(2) Chapter II of Part IV of the Finance Act 1996 is to have effect in relation to the time when the relevant transfer takes effect and any later time as if—

(*a*) the transferee had been a party to the loan relationship at the time the transferor became a party to the loan relationship and at all times since that time, and
(*b*) the loan relationship to which the transferee is a party after the time the transfer takes effect is the same loan relationship as that to which, by virtue of paragraph (*a*), it is treated as having been a party before that time.

(3) Expressions used in this paragraph and in Chapter II of Part IV of the Finance Act 1996 have the same meanings in this paragraph as in that Chapter.

PART VI
TRANSFERS OF FRANCHISE ASSETS
Interpretation

30 In this Part of this Schedule—

"relevant transfer" means a transfer of property, rights or liabilities by virtue of a scheme under paragraph 2 of Schedule 21 under which the property, rights or liabilities are transferred from a person which is, or has been, a franchise company,
"transferee", in relation to a relevant transfer, means the person to whom the property, rights or liabilities are transferred, and
"transferor", in relation to a relevant transfer, means the person from whom the property, rights or liabilities are transferred.

Chargeable gains: disposals not to be treated as made at market value

31—(1) Section 17 of the 1992 Act (disposals and acquisitions treated as made at market value) is not to have effect in relation to—

(*a*) a disposal constituted by a relevant transfer or a disposal by virtue of provision made under paragraph 5 of Schedule 21, or
(*b*) the acquisition made by the person to whom the disposal is made.

(2) But sub-paragraph (1) does not apply—

(*a*) if the person making the disposal is connected with the person making the acquisition, or
(*b*) in the case of a disposal by virtue of provision made under paragraph 5 of Schedule 21, if the disposal is made by or to a person other than the transferor or the transferee.

(3) If sub-paragraph (1) applies to the disposal of an asset, the disposal is to be taken (in relation to the person making the acquisition as well as the person making the disposal) to be—

(*a*) in a case where consideration in money or money's worth is given by the person making the acquisition or on his behalf in respect of the vesting of the asset in him, for a consideration equal to the amount or value of that consideration, or
(*b*) in a case where no such consideration is given, for a consideration of nil.

Chargeable gains: groups

32—(1) Sub-paragraph (2) applies if a company ("the degrouped company")—

(*a*) acquired an asset from another company at any time when both were members of the same group of companies ("the old group"), and
(*b*) ceases by virtue of a relevant transfer to be a member of the old group.

(2) Section 179 of the 1992 Act (company ceasing to be member of group) is not to treat the degrouped company as having by virtue of the transfer sold and immediately reacquired the asset.

(3) If sub-paragraph (2) applies to an asset, that section is to have effect on and after the first subsequent occasion on which the degrouped company ceases to be a member of a group of companies ("the new group"), otherwise than by virtue of a qualifying transfer, as if the degrouped company and the company from which it acquired the asset had been members of the new group at the time of acquisition.

(4) If, disregarding any preparatory transactions, a company would be regarded for the purposes of section 179 of the 1992 Act (and, accordingly, of this paragraph) as ceasing to be a member of a group of companies by virtue of a qualifying transfer, it is to be regarded for those purposes as so doing by virtue of the qualifying transfer and not by virtue of any preparatory transactions.

(5) In this paragraph "preparatory transaction" means anything done under or by virtue of this Part of this Act for the purpose of initiating, advancing or facilitating the qualifying transfer in question.

(6) Expressions used in this paragraph and in section 179 of the 1992 Act have the same meanings in this paragraph as in that section.

Chargeable gains: disposal of debts

33—(1) Sub-paragraph (2) applies if in the case of a relevant transfer—

　　(*a*) a debt owed to the transferor is transferred to the transferee, and
　　(*b*) the transferor would, apart from this paragraph, be the original creditor in relation to that debt for the purposes of section 251 of the 1992 Act (disposal of debts).

(2) The 1992 Act is to have effect as if the transferee (and not the transferor) were the original creditor for those purposes.

Capital allowances: actual consideration to be the disposal value

34—(1) Sub-paragraphs (2) to (5) apply for the purposes of [Part 3 of the Capital Allowances Act][1], and the other provisions of that Act which are relevant to that Part, if there is a disposal by virtue of a relevant transfer of the relevant interest in—

　　(*a*) an industrial building or structure, or
　　(*b*) a qualifying hotel or a commercial building or structure.

(2) The disposal is to be treated as a sale of that relevant interest.

(3) The sale moneys in respect of that sale are to be taken—

　　(*a*) if a capital sum is received by the transferor or a person connected with the transferor by way of consideration or compensation in respect of the disposal, to be an amount equal to that capital sum, or
　　(*b*) if no such capital sum is received, to be nil.

(4) The sale moneys in respect of that sale are to be taken, as respects the transferee only, to include in addition an amount equal to any capital sum received by a person other than the transferor or a person connected with the transferor by way of consideration or compensation in respect of the acquisition of the relevant interest by the transferee.

(5) [Sections 567 to 570 of that Act (sales treated as being for alternative amount)][1] are not to have effect in relation to that sale.

(6) Sub-paragraph (7) applies for determining, in the case of [plant or machinery][1] which is treated for the purposes of [the Capital Allowances Act][1] as disposed of by virtue of a relevant transfer, the amount which (in consequence of that disposal) is to be brought into account as the disposal value of that [plant or machinery][1] for the purposes of [sections 60 of that Act (meaning of "disposal value" and "disposal event")][1].

(7) The amount is, subject to [section 62 of that Act (general limit on amount of disposal value)][1] to be taken—

　　(*a*) if a capital sum is received by the transferor or a person connected with the transferor by way of consideration or compensation in respect of the disposal, to be an amount equal to that capital sum, or
　　(*b*) if no such capital sum is received, to be nil.

(8) Sub-paragraph (9) applies if, in consequence of a disposal by virtue of a relevant transfer, [a person is treated by section 188 of the Capital Allowances Act as ceasing to own a fixture][1] at any time.

(9) The amount which, in consequence of that disposal, is to be brought into account as the disposal value of the fixture for the purposes of [section 60 of the Capital Allowances Act is, subject to section 62 of that Act][1], to be taken—

　　(*a*) if a capital sum is received by the transferor or a person connected with the transferor by way of consideration or compensation in respect of the disposal, to be an amount equal to that portion of that capital sum which falls (or, if the person to whom the disposal is made were entitled to an allowance, would fall) to be treated for the purposes of [Part 2 of that Act][1] as expenditure incurred by that person on the provision of the fixture, or (*b*) if no such capital sum is received, to be nil.

(10) Sub-paragraphs (3), (4), (7) and (9) have effect despite any other provision of [the Capital Allowances Act][1].

Amendments—[1] Words in sub-paras (1), (5)–(10) substituted by CAA 2001 s 578, Sch 2 paras 109(26)–(32) with effect for income tax purposes, as respects allowances and charges falling to be made for chargeable periods ending after 5 April 2001, and for corporation tax purposes as respects allowances and charges falling to be made for chargeable periods ending after 31 March 2001.

Loan relationships

35—(1) Paragraph 11 of Schedule 9 to the Finance Act 1996 is not to have effect in a case where, as a result of a relevant transfer, the transferee replaces the transferor as a party to a loan relationship.

(2) Expressions used in this paragraph and in Chapter II of Part IV of the Finance Act 1996 have the same meanings in this paragraph as in that Chapter.

PART VII
OTHER PROVISIONS CONCERNING TRANSFERS
Chargeable gains: value shifting

36 Nothing in this Part of this Act and nothing done under it is to be regarded as a scheme or arrangement for the purposes of section 30 of the 1992 Act (tax-free benefits).

Chargeable gains: consequential amendment

37 (*amends* TCGA 1992 s 35(3)(*d*)).

Group relief

38 The existence of the powers of the Secretary of State or the Authority under this Part of this Act is not to be regarded (and nothing else in that Part is to be regarded) as—

(*a*) constituting arrangements falling within section 410(1) or (2) of the 1988 Act (arrangements for transfer of company to another group or consortium), or

(*b*) constituting option arrangements for the purposes of paragraph 5B of Schedule 18 to the 1988 Act.

Modifications of transfer schemes

39—(1) Sub-paragraph (2) applies if—

(*a*) the effect of a scheme under paragraph 1 of Schedule 15, paragraph 31 of Schedule 17, paragraph 1 of Schedule 19 or paragraph 1 of Schedule 25 is modified by an order made by the Secretary of State, or

(*b*) the effect of a scheme under paragraph 1 of Schedule 21 under which the property, rights or liabilities are transferred to the Secretary of State or a franchise company is modified by an agreement made under paragraph 15 of that Schedule.

(2) The Corporation Tax Acts (including this Schedule) are to have effect as if—

(*a*) the scheme had been made as modified, and

(*b*) anything done by or in relation to the preceding holder had (so far as relating to the property, rights or liabilities affected by the modification) been done by or in relation to the subsequent holder.

(3) For the purposes of sub-paragraph (2) the preceding holder is the person who without the modification—

(*a*) became (under the scheme concerned) entitled or subject to the property, rights or liabilities affected by the modification, or

(*b*) remained (despite the scheme concerned) entitled or subject to the property, rights or liabilities affected by the modification,

as the case may be.

(4) For the purposes of sub-paragraph (2) the subsequent holder is the person who (in consequence of the modification) becomes, or resumes being, entitled or subject to the property, rights or liabilities affected by the modification.

Stamp duty and stamp duty reserve tax

40 (See the *Orange Tax Handbook*.)

CAPITAL ALLOWANCES ACT 2001

(2001 Chapter 2)

ARRANGEMENT OF SECTIONS

PART 1
INTRODUCTION

CHAPTER 1
CAPITAL ALLOWANCES: GENERAL

CHAPTER 2
EXCLUSION OF DOUBLE RELIEF

PART 2
PLANT AND MACHINERY ALLOWANCES

CHAPTER 1
INTRODUCTION

CHAPTER 2
QUALIFYING ACTIVITIES

CHAPTER 3
QUALIFYING EXPENDITURE

Buildings, structures and land

Demolition costs

Expenditure on thermal insulation, safety measures, etc

CHAPTER 10

LONG-LIFE ASSETS

Long-life asset expenditure

Expenditure excluded from being long-life asset expenditure

Rules applying to long-life asset expenditure

Anti-avoidance provisions

CHAPTER 11

OVERSEAS LEASING

Basic terms

Certain expenditure to be pooled

Allowances reduced or, in certain cases, prohibited

Recovery of excess allowances

Recovery of allowances given in cases where prohibition applies

Application of Chapter in relation to joint lessees

Duties to supply information

Qualifying purposes

CHAPTER 14

FIXTURES

Introduction

CHAPTER 15

ASSET PROVIDED OR USED ONLY PARTLY FOR QUALIFYING ACTIVITY

CHAPTER 16

PARTIAL DEPRECIATION SUBSIDIES

CHAPTER 17

ANTI-AVOIDANCE

Relevant transactions

Restrictions on allowances

Finance leases

Sale and finance leasebacks

Sale and leaseback or sale and finance leaseback: election for special treatment

Miscellaneous and supplementary

CHAPTER 20
SUPPLEMENTARY PROVISIONS
Partnerships and successions

Miscellaneous

PART 3
INDUSTRIAL BUILDINGS ALLOWANCES

CHAPTER 1
INTRODUCTION

CHAPTER 2
INDUSTRIAL BUILDINGS
Buildings in use for the purposes of a qualifying trade

Qualifying hotels and sports pavilions

Commercial buildings (enterprise zones)

Supplementary provisions

CHAPTER 3
THE RELEVANT INTEREST IN THE BUILDING

CHAPTER 4
QUALIFYING EXPENDITURE
Introduction

CHAPTER 2
QUALIFYING EXPENDITURE

CHAPTER 3
QUALIFYING BUILDINGS AND QUALIFYING FLATS

CHAPTER 4 THE RELEVANT INTEREST IN THE FLAT

CHAPTER 5 INITIAL ALLOWANCES

CHAPTER 6 WRITING-DOWN ALLOWANCES

CHAPTER 7 BALANCING ADJUSTMENTS

CHAPTER 8
WRITING OFF QUALIFYING EXPENDITURE

CHAPTER 9
SUPPLEMENTARY PROVISIONS

PART 5
MINERAL EXTRACTION ALLOWANCES

CHAPTER 1
INTRODUCTION

CHAPTER 2
QUALIFYING EXPENDITURE ON MINERAL EXPLORATION AND ACCESS

CHAPTER 3

QUALIFYING EXPENDITURE ON ACQUIRING A MINERAL ASSET

CHAPTER 4

QUALIFYING EXPENDITURE: SECOND-HAND ASSETS

Assets reflecting expenditure on mineral exploration and access

Qualifying expenditure on assets limited by reference to historic costs

CHAPTER 5

OTHER KINDS OF QUALIFYING EXPENDITURE

CHAPTER 5

FIRST YEAR QUALIFYING EXPENDITURE

CHAPTER 6

ALLOWANCES AND CHARGES

First year allowances

Writing-down and balancing allowances and balancing charges

Unrelieved qualifying expenditure

Disposal values

Cases in which a person is entitled to a balancing allowance

PART 8
PATENT ALLOWANCES

CHAPTER 1
INTRODUCTION

CHAPTER 2
QUALIFYING EXPENDITURE

CHAPTER 3
ALLOWANCES AND CHARGES

CHAPTER 4
GIVING EFFECT TO ALLOWANCES AND CHARGES

CHAPTER 5
SUPPLEMENTARY PROVISIONS

PART 9
DREDGING ALLOWANCES

Qualifying expenditure on dredging, etc

Writing-down and balancing allowances

Giving effect to allowances

PART 10
ASSURED TENANCY ALLOWANCES

CHAPTER 1
INTRODUCTION

CHAPTER 2
THE RELEVANT INTEREST
Introduction

The relevant interest in the building

The relevant interest in the dwelling-house

CHAPTER 3
QUALIFYING EXPENDITURE

CHAPTER 4
QUALIFYING DWELLING-HOUSES

CHAPTER 5
WRITING-DOWN ALLOWANCES
Entitlement to and calculation of writing-down allowances

Interpretation

CHAPTER 6
BALANCING ADJUSTMENTS
General

Calculation of balancing adjustments

CAA 2001

CHAPTER 7

WRITING OFF QUALIFYING EXPENDITURE ATTRIBUTABLE TO DWELLING-HOUSE

CHAPTER 8

SUPPLEMENTARY PROVISIONS

PART 11

CONTRIBUTIONS

CHAPTER 1

EXCLUSION OF EXPENDITURE MET BY CONTRIBUTIONS

Rules excluding contributions

Exceptions to the general rule excluding contributions

CHAPTER 2

CONTRIBUTION ALLOWANCES

Contribution allowances under Parts 2 to 5

Effect of transfers of C's trade on contribution allowances under Parts 3, 4 and 5

Contribution allowances under Part 9

CAA 2001

CHAPTER 6
FINAL PROVISIONS
General interpretation

Amendments, repeals, citation etc

SCHEDULES

An Act to restate, with minor changes, certain enactments relating to capital allowances.

[22 March 2001]

PART 1
INTRODUCTION

CHAPTER 1
CAPITAL ALLOWANCES: GENERAL

Commentary—*Simon's Direct Tax Service* **Division B2.1.**

1 Capital allowances

(1) This Act provides for allowances in respect of capital expenditure (and for charges in connection with those allowances).

(2) The allowances for which this Act provides are those under—

     (*a*) Part 2 (plant and machinery allowances);
     (*b*) Part 3 (industrial buildings allowances);
     (*c*) Part 4 (agricultural buildings allowances);
     [(*ca*) Part 4A (flat conversion allowances);][1]
     (*d*) Part 5 (mineral extraction allowances);
     (*e*) Part 6 (research and development allowances);
     (*f*) Part 7 (know-how allowances);
     (*g*) Part 8 (patent allowances);
     (*h*) Part 9 (dredging allowances);
     (*i*) Part 10 (assured tenancy allowances).

(3) This Act also provides for allowances in respect of contributions to expenditure incurred on plant or machinery, industrial buildings or agricultural buildings, for the purposes of a mineral extraction trade or on dredging (see Part 11).

Commentary—*Simon's Direct Tax Service* **B2.101.**
Amendment—[1] Sub-s (2)(*ca*) inserted by FA 2001 s 67, Sch 19 Pt II para 1 with effect for expenditure incurred after 10 May 2001.

2 General means of giving effect to capital allowances

(1) Allowances and charges are to be given effect—

     (*a*) for income tax purposes, in calculating income for a chargeable period, and
     (*b*) for corporation tax purposes, in calculating profits for a chargeable period.

(2) For the meaning of "chargeable period", see section 6.

(3) Subsection (1) needs to be read with the following provisions about giving effect to allowances and charges—

sections 247 to 262 (plant and machinery allowances);
sections 352 to 355 (industrial buildings allowances);
sections 391 and 392 (agricultural buildings allowances);
[section 393T (flat conversion allowances)][1]
section 432 (mineral extraction allowances);
section 450 (research and development allowances);
section 463 (know-how allowances);
sections 478 to 480 (patent allowances);
section 489 (dredging allowances);
section 529 (assured tenancy allowances).

(4) In subsection (1)(b) "profits" has the same meaning as in section 6 of ICTA.

Commentary—*Simon's Direct Tax Service* **B2.106A**.
Former enactments—Sub-s (1): CAA 1990, ss 137(1), 140(1), (5), 144(1), (3), 161(2) ("chargeable period").
Sub-s (4): TA 1988 s 834(2).
Amendment—[1] Words in sub-s (3) inserted by FA 2001 s 67, Sch 19 Pt II para 2 with effect for expenditure incurred after 10 May 2001.

3 Claims for capital allowances

(1) No allowance is to be made under this Act unless a claim for it is made.

(2) The claim must be included in a tax return.

(3) In this Act "tax return" means—

(a) for income tax purposes, a return required to be made under TMA 1970, and
(b) for corporation tax purposes, a company tax return required to be made under Schedule 18 to FA 1998 (company tax returns, assessments and related matters).

(4) Subsection (2) does not apply for income tax purposes to a claim for an allowance under—

(a) section 258 (claim for allowance in respect of special leasing of plant or machinery),
(b) section 355 (claim to carry back balance of allowance in respect of buildings for miners etc),
or
(c) section 479 (claim for patent allowance in respect of non-trading expenditure),

which is instead subject to section 42 of TMA 1970 (procedure for making claims and claims not included in returns).

(5) Subsection (2) does not apply for corporation tax purposes to a claim for an allowance under—

(a) section 260(3)(b) (claim to carry back allowance in respect of special leasing of plant or machinery), or
(b) section 355 (claim to carry back balance of allowance in respect of buildings for miners etc),

which is instead subject to paragraphs 54 to 60 of Schedule 18 to FA 1998 (general provisions as to claims).

(6) This section is subject to section 42(6) and (7) of TMA 1970 (special provisions relating to partnerships).

Commentary—*Simon's Direct Tax Service* **B2.107A**.
Former enactments—Sub-s (1): *Ellis v BP Oil Northern Ireland Refinery Ltd* (CA) 59 TC 474, [1987] STC 52.
Sub-s (2): CAA 1990 s 140(3); FA 1998 Sch 18 para 79(1).
Sub-s (3): CAA 1990 ss 38F(5), 51(2) ("return"), ss 76B(8), 140(3), 147(3); FA 1998 Sch 18 paras 3(1), 79(1).
Sub-s (4): TA 1988 s 528(2); CAA 1990 s 17(3), s 141(1), (5).
Revenue Internal Guidance—Capital allowances manual CA 11130 (Where a business is carried on in partnership it is the partnership which claims the capital allowances and not the individual partners).

4 Capital expenditure

(1) In this Act "capital expenditure" and "capital sums" are used in the sense given in this section.

(2) "Capital expenditure" and "capital sums" do not include, in relation to a person incurring the expenditure or paying the sums—

(a) any expenditure or sum that may be deducted in calculating the profits or gains of a trade, profession or vocation or property business carried on by the person, or
(b) any expenditure or sum that may be deducted in calculating the emoluments of an employment or office held by the person.

(3) "Capital expenditure" and "capital sums" do not include, in relation to a recipient of the expenditure or sums—

(a) any amounts that are to be added in calculating the profits or gains of a trade, profession or vocation or property business carried on by the recipient, or
(b) any amounts that are emoluments of an employment or office held by the recipient.

(4) "Capital expenditure" and "capital sums" do not include, in relation to—

(a) a person incurring the expenditure or paying the sums, or (*b*) a recipient of the expenditure or sums,

any expenditure or sum in the case of which a deduction of income tax falls or may fall to be made under section 348 or 349(1) of ICTA (annual payments).

(5) Subsection (4) does not apply to any expenditure or sum in the case of which a deduction of income tax falls or may fall to be so made as a result of section 524(3)(*b*) of ICTA (receipts from sale of patent rights by person not resident in the UK).

Commentary—*Simon's Direct Tax Service* **B2.103**.
Former enactments—Sub-s (1): CAA 1990 s 159(1).
Sub-ss (2), (3): CAA 1990 s 159(1), (1A), s 161(2A).
Sub-s (4): CAA 1990 s 159(1).
Sub-s (5): TA 1988 s 532(4).
Revenue Internal Guidance—Capital allowances manual CA 11530 (If expenditure on the provision or construction of an asset was revenue expenditure and the asset is later permanently appropriated to fixed assets, the expenditure which qualifies for WDAs is the original expenditure incurred and not the market value of the asset at the time of the appropriation).
Modifications—CAA 2001 Sch 3 para 9 (modification of sub-ss (2), (3) above in relation to expenditure incurred or sums paid or received before 26 November 1996).

5 When capital expenditure is incurred

(1) For the purposes of this Act, the general rule is that an amount of capital expenditure is to be treated as incurred as soon as there is an unconditional obligation to pay it.

(2) The general rule applies even if the whole or a part of the expenditure is not required to be paid until a later date.

(3) There are the following exceptions to the general rule.

(4) If under an agreement—

(*a*) the capital expenditure is expenditure on the provision of an asset,
(*b*) an unconditional obligation to pay an amount of the expenditure comes into being as a result of the giving of a certificate or any other event,
(*c*) the giving of the certificate, or other event, occurs within the period of one month after the end of a chargeable period, and
(*d*) at or before the end of that chargeable period, the asset has become the property of, or is otherwise under the agreement attributed to, the person subject to the unconditional obligation to pay,

the expenditure is to be treated as incurred immediately before the end of that chargeable period.

(5) If under an agreement an amount of capital expenditure is not required to be paid until a date more than 4 months after the unconditional obligation to pay has come into being, the amount is to be treated as incurred on that date.

(6) If under an agreement—

(*a*) there is an unconditional obligation to pay an amount of capital expenditure on a date earlier than accords with normal commercial usage, and
(*b*) the sole or main benefit which might have been expected to be obtained thereby is that the amount would be treated, under the general rule, as incurred in an earlier chargeable period,

the amount is to be treated as incurred on the date on or before which it is required to be paid.

(7) This section—

(*a*) is subject to any provision of this Act which has the effect that expenditure is to be treated as incurred on a date later than would result from the application of this section, and
(*b*) does not apply to expenditure treated as incurred as a result of a person incurring an additional VAT liability.

Commentary—*Simon's Direct Tax Service* **B2.104**.
Former enactments—Sub-ss (1)–(3): CAA 1990 s 159(3).
Sub-s (4): CAA 1990 s 159(4).
Sub-s (5): CAA 1990 s 159(5).
Sub-s (6): CAA 1990 s 159(6).
Sub-s (7): CAA 1990 s 159(2), (7).
Revenue Internal Guidance—Capital allowances manual CA 11800 (sub-s (1) above: when date of delivering of goods is the relevant date).
CA 11800 (examples of sub-s (5)).
CA 11800 (milestone contracts).
CA 11800 (example showing operation of sub-s (6)).
CA 11800 (sub-s (6) above applied only where the amounts involved are substantial).
CA 11800 ("retentions" under contract: obligation to pay does not arise until condition giving rise to retention is satisfied).

6 Meaning of "chargeable period"

(1) In this Act "chargeable period" means—

(*a*) for income tax purposes, a period of account, or
(*b*) for corporation tax purposes, an accounting period of a company.

(2) "Period of account" means—

(*a*) in the case of a person entitled to an allowance or liable to a charge in calculating the profits of his trade, profession or vocation, a period for which accounts are drawn up for the purposes of the trade, profession or vocation, and

(*b*) in the case of any other person entitled to an allowance or liable to a charge, a tax year.

(3) Subsection (2)(*a*) is subject to subsections (4) to (6).

(4) If—

(*a*) two periods of account overlap, or

(*b*) one period of account includes another, the period common to both is to be treated as part of the first period of account only.

(5) If there is a gap between two periods of account, the gap is to be treated as part of the first period of account.

(6) If a period of account would (apart from this subsection) be longer than 18 months, that period must be treated as divided into separate periods of account—

(*a*) the first beginning with the start date of the original period, and

(*b*) each subsequent one beginning with an anniversary of that date, so as to ensure that none of the periods of account is longer than 12 months.

Commentary—*Simon's Direct Tax Service* **B2.102**.
Former enactments—Sub-s (1): CAA 1990 s 161(2) ("chargeable period").
Sub-s (2): CAA 1990 s 160(2), (5).
Sub-s (3): CAA 1990 s 160(2).
Sub-s (4): CAA 1990 s 160(3), (6).
Sub-s (5): CAA 1990 s 160(3).
Sub-s (6): CAA 1990 s 160(4).

CHAPTER 2
EXCLUSION OF DOUBLE RELIEF

7 No double allowances

(1) If an allowance is made under any Part of this Act to a person in respect of capital expenditure, no allowance is to be made to him under any other Part in respect of—

(*a*) that expenditure, or

(*b*) the provision of any asset to which that expenditure related.

(2) This section does not apply in relation to Parts 7 and 8 (know-how and patent allowances).

Commentary—*Simon's Direct Tax Service* **B2.114**.
Former enactments—Sub-s (1): CAA 1990 s 147(1), (2).
Sub-s (2): CAA 1990 s 147(1), (2).
Revenue Internal Guidance—Capital allowances manual CA 31800 (where expenditure qualifies for more than one type of allowance the taxpayer may choose which claim to make; other claims are then precluded).
Definition—"Capital expenditure", ss 4, 10(1).

8 No double relief through pooling under Part 2 (plant and machinery allowances)

(1) Subsection (2) applies if, under Part 2—

(*a*) any capital expenditure has been allocated to a pool, and

(*b*) an allowance or charge has been made to or on any person in respect of the pool.

(2) The person to or on whom the allowance or charge has been made is not entitled to an allowance under any Part other than Part 2 in respect of—

(*a*) the expenditure allocated to the pool, or

(*b*) the provision of any asset to which the allocated expenditure related.

(3) Subsection (4) applies if under any Part other than Part 2 an allowance has been made to a person in respect of any capital expenditure.

(4) The person to whom the allowance has been made is not entitled to allocate to any pool—

(*a*) that expenditure, or

(*b*) any expenditure on the provision of any asset to which the expenditure mentioned in paragraph (*a*) related.

(5) This section does not apply in relation to Parts 7 and 8 (know-how and patent allowances).

Commentary—*Simon's Direct Tax Service* **B2.114**.
Former enactments—Sub-ss (1), (2): CAA 1990 s 147(2).
Sub-ss (2), (3): CAA 1990 s 147(1).
Sub-s (5): CAA 1990 s 147(1), (2).
Definitions—"Capital expenditure", ss 4, 10(1).

9 Interaction between fixtures claims and other claims

(1) A person is not entitled to make a fixtures claim in respect of any capital expenditure relating to an asset if—

(*a*) any person entitled to do so has at any previous time claimed an allowance under any Part other than Part 2, and

(*b*) the claim was for an allowance in respect of capital expenditure relating, in whole or part, to the asset.

(2) Subsection (1) does not prevent a person making a fixtures claim in respect of capital expenditure if—

(*a*) the only previous claim was under Part 3 or 6 (industrial buildings and research and development allowances), and

(*b*) section 186(2) or 187(2) (limit on amount of expenditure that may be taken into account) applies to that expenditure.

(3) If a person entitled to do so has made a fixtures claim in respect of capital expenditure relating to an asset, no one is entitled to an allowance on a later claim under any Part other than Part 2 in respect of any capital expenditure relating to the asset.

(4) A person makes a fixtures claim in respect of expenditure if he makes a claim (in the sense given in section 202(3)) under Chapter 14 of Part 2 in respect of the expenditure as expenditure on the provision of a fixture.

Commentary—*Simon's Direct Tax Service* **B2.114**.
Former enactments—Sub-s (1): CAA 1990 s 147(2A).
Sub-s (2): CAA 1990 s 147(2B).
Sub-s (3): CAA 1990 s 147(2C).
Sub-s (4): CAA 1990 s 147(2D).
Definitions—"Capital expenditure", ss 4, 10(1).
Modification—CAA 2001 Sch 3 para 10 (this section does not apply for expenditure incurred before 24 July 1996).

10 Interpretation

(1) In this Chapter "capital expenditure" includes any contribution to capital expenditure.

(2) For the purposes of this Chapter—

(*a*) expenditure relates to an asset only if it relates to its provision, and

(*b*) the provision of an asset includes its construction or acquisition.

Commentary—*Simon's Direct Tax Service* **B2.114**.
Former enactments—Sub-s (1): CAA 1990 s 147(3).
Sub-s (2): CAA 1990 s 147(1), (2), (2A), (2C), (3).

PART 2

PLANT AND MACHINERY ALLOWANCES

Cross reference—See FA 2001 s 59(4) (withdrawal of capital allowances in respect of employees' vehicles immediately before 6 April 2002).
Modifications—CAA 2001 Sch 3 para 54 (where—

(*a*) at the beginning of the tax year 1990–91 machinery consisting of a mechanically propelled road vehicle was provided by a person for use in the performance of the duties of an office or employment held by him, and

(*b*) the machinery was also provided by him at the end of the tax year 1989–90 for use in the performance of the duties of that office or employment but without that provision being necessary,
this Part has effect as if the person had incurred capital expenditure on the provision of the machinery for the purposes of the office or employment in the tax year 1990–91—

(*a*) the amount of that expenditure being taken as the price which the machinery would have fetched if sold in the open market on 6th April 1990, and

(*b*) the person being treated as owning the machinery as a result of his having incurred that expenditure).
CAA 2001 Sch 3 para 55 (this Part does not apply to capital expenditure—

(*a*) which was not eligible expenditure within the meaning of FA 1976 s 39 (which brought expenditure previously not within Chapter I of Part III of FA 1971 within that Chapter but with certain exceptions), and

(*b*) which was incurred in a chargeable period ending before 6 April 1976).

CHAPTER 1

INTRODUCTION

Commentary—*Simon's Direct Tax Service* **Division B2.3**.

11 General conditions as to availability of plant and machinery allowances

(1) Allowances are available under this Part if a person carries on a qualifying activity and incurs qualifying expenditure.

(2) "Qualifying activity" has the meaning given by Chapter 2.

(3) Allowances under this Part must be calculated separately for each qualifying activity which a person carries on.

(4) The general rule is that expenditure is qualifying expenditure if—

(*a*) it is capital expenditure on the provision of plant or machinery wholly or partly for the purposes of the qualifying activity carried on by the person incurring the expenditure, and (*b*) the person incurring the expenditure owns the plant or machinery as a result of incurring it.

(5) But the general rule is affected by other provisions of this Act, and in particular by Chapter 3.

Commentary—*Simon's Direct Tax Service* **B2.303**.
Former enactments—Sub-s (4): CAA 1990 ss 22(1), 24(1), 79(1), (2).
Revenue Internal Guidance—Capital allowances manual CA 20070 (professional fees only qualify as expenditure on the provision of plant or machinery if they relate directly to the acquisition, transport or installaition of the plant or machinery).
CA 21100–21160 (meaning of ''machinery or plant'': survey of case law).
CA 27100 (assets provided for directors or employees: capital allowances are not normally restricted unless there is a ''blatant incongruity'' between the asset provided and the business requirements).
Definition—''Capital expenditure'', s 4.
Modification—CAA 2001 Sch 3 para 54 (vehicles provided by employees in 1990–91: see modification note at the start of this Part).
CAA 2001 Sch 3 para 55 (certain expenditure incurred before 6 April 1976: see modification note at the start of this Part).

12 Expenditure incurred before qualifying activity carried on

For the purposes of this Part, expenditure incurred for the purposes of a qualifying activity by a person about to carry on the activity is to be treated as if it had been incurred by him on the first day on which he carries on the activity.

Commentary—*Simon's Direct Tax Service* **B2.303**.
Former enactments—CAA 1990 s 83(2).
Modifications—CAA 2001 Sch 3 para 54 (vehicles provided by employees in 1990–91: see modification note at the start of this Part).
CAA 2001 Sch 3 para 55 (certain expenditure incurred before 6 April 1976: see modification note at the start of this Part).

13 Use for qualifying activity of plant or machinery provided for other purposes

(1) This section applies if a person—

(*a*) brings plant or machinery into use for the purposes of a qualifying activity carried on by him, and

(*b*) on the date when he does so, owns the plant or machinery as a result of having incurred capital expenditure (''actual expenditure'') on its provision for purposes other than those of that qualifying activity.

(2) The person is to be treated—

(*a*) as having incurred capital expenditure (''notional expenditure'') on the provision of the plant or machinery for the purposes of the qualifying activity on the date on which it is brought into use for those purposes, and

(*b*) as owning the plant or machinery as a result as having incurred that expenditure.

(3) Subject to subsection (4), the amount of the notional expenditure is the market value of the plant or machinery on the date when it is brought into use for the purposes of the qualifying activity.

(4) If the market value is greater than the actual expenditure, the amount of the notional expenditure is the amount of the actual expenditure, less any amount required to be deducted under subsection (5).

(5) The amount to be deducted is any amount that under section 218 or 224 would have been left out of account in determining the person's available qualifying expenditure if the actual expenditure had been incurred on the provision of the plant or machinery for the purposes of the qualifying activity.

(6) The question whether the provision of the plant or machinery is to be treated as wholly or only partly for the purposes of the qualifying activity is to be determined according to whether the use referred to in subsection (1)(*a*) is wholly or only partly for those purposes.

(7) This section is subject to section 161 (pre-trading expenditure on mineral exploration and access).

Commentary—*Simon's Direct Tax Service* **B2.303**.
Former enactments—Sub-s (1): CAA 1990 s 81(1).
Sub-ss (2), (3): CAA 1990 s 81(1), (1A)(*b*).
Sub-s (4): CAA 1990 s 81(2AA).
Sub-s (5): CAA 1990 s 81(2AB).
Sub-s (6): CAA 1990 s 81(2).
Sub-s (7): CAA 1990 s 81(1), (1A).
Definitions—''Available qualifying expenditure'', s 57; ''capital expenditure'', s 4.
Modifications—CAA 2001 Sch 3 para 11 (sub-ss (4), (5) above do not apply if the plant or machinery was brought into use before 21 March 2000).
CAA 2001 Sch 3 para 54 (vehicles provided by employees in 1990–91: see modification note at the start of this Part).
CAA 2001 Sch 3 para 55 (certain expenditure incurred before 6 April 1976: see modification note at the start of this Part).

14 Use for qualifying activity of plant or machinery which is a gift

(1) This section applies if a person—

(*a*) is the owner of plant or machinery as a result of a gift, and

(*b*) brings the plant or machinery into use for the purposes of a qualifying activity carried on by him.

(2) The person is to be treated—

(*a*) as having incurred capital expenditure on the provision of the plant or machinery for the purposes of the qualifying activity on the date on which it is brought into use for those purposes, and

(*b*) as owning the plant or machinery as a result of having incurred that expenditure.

(3) The amount of that capital expenditure is to be treated as being the market value of the plant or machinery on the date when it was brought into use for the purposes of the qualifying activity.

(4) The question whether the provision of the plant or machinery is to be treated as wholly or only partly for the purposes of the qualifying activity is to be determined according to whether the use referred to in subsection (1)(*b*) is wholly or only partly for those purposes.

(5) This section is subject to section 161 (pre-trading expenditure on mineral exploration and access).

Commentary—*Simon's Direct Tax Service* **B2.303**.
Former enactments—Sub-s (1): CAA 1990 s 81(1).
Sub-ss (2), (3): CAA 1990 s 81(1), (1A)(*b*).
Sub-s (4): CAA 1990 s 81(2).
Sub-s (5): CAA 1990 s 81(1), (1A).
Definition—"Capital expenditure", s 4.
Modifications—CAA 2001 Sch 3 para 12 (the section above applies with the insertion of sub-s (1A) if the plant or machinery was brought into use before 27 July 1989. Sub-s (1A) as inserted to read as follows—

"(1A) This section does not apply unless the donor was required by section 24(6) of CAA 1990 to bring into account for the purposes there mentioned a disposal value equal to the price which the plant or machinery would have fetched if sold in the open market at the time of the gift.").
CAA 2001 Sch 3 para 54 (vehicles provided by employees in 1990–91: see modification note at the start of this Part).
CAA 2001 Sch 3 para 55 (certain expenditure incurred before 6 April 1976: see modification note at the start of this Part).

CHAPTER 2
QUALIFYING ACTIVITIES

15 Qualifying activities

(1) Each of the following is a qualifying activity for the purposes of this Part—

(*a*) a trade,
(*b*) an ordinary Schedule A business,
(*c*) a furnished holiday lettings business,
(*d*) an overseas property business,
(*e*) a profession or vocation,
(*f*) a concern listed in section 55(2) of ICTA (mines, transport undertakings etc),
(*g*) the management of an investment company,
(*h*) special leasing of plant or machinery, and
(*i*) an employment or office,

but to the extent only that the profits or gains from the activity are, or (if there were any) would be, chargeable to tax.

(2) Subsection (1) is subject to the following provisions of this Part.

(3) This section, in so far as it provides for—

(*a*) an ordinary Schedule A business,
(*b*) an overseas property business, or
(*c*) special leasing of plant or machinery,

to be a qualifying activity, needs to be read with section 35 (expenditure on plant or machinery for use in a dwelling-house not qualifying expenditure in certain cases).

(4) Also, subsection (1)(*i*) needs to be read with sections 36 (restriction on qualifying expenditure in case of employment or office) and 80 (vehicles provided for purposes of employment or office).

Commentary—*Simon's Direct Tax Service* B2.304.
Former enactments—Sub-s (1)(*a*): CAA 1990 s 22(1)(*a*), s 24(1)(*a*).
Sub-s (1)(*b*): CAA 1990 s 28A(1).
Sub-s (1)(*c*): CAA 1990 s 29(1).
Sub-s (1)(*d*): CAA 1990 s 28A(1), s 161(2A).
Sub-s (1)(*e*): CAA 1990 s 27(1).
Sub-s (1)(*f*): change in law.
Sub-s (1)(*g*): CAA 1990 s 28(1).
Sub-s (1)(*h*): CAA 1990 s 61(1).
Sub-s (1)(*i*): CAA 1990 s 27(1).
Sub-s (1) final para: CAA 1990 s 83(2A).
Sub-s (3): CAA 1990 s 28A(3), s 61(2), s 161(2A).
Sub-s (4): CAA 1990 s 27(1).
Revenue Internal Guidance—Capital allowances manual CA 20040 (background to "special leasing").
Definitions—"Furnished holiday lettings business", s 17; "investment company", TA 1988 s 130; "ordinary Schedule A business", s 16.
Modifications—CAA 2001 Sch 3 para 54 (vehicles provided by employees in 1990–91: see modification note at the start of this Part).
CAA 2001 Sch 3 para 55 (certain expenditure incurred before 6 April 1976: see modification note at the start of this Part).

16 Ordinary Schedule A businesses

In this Part "ordinary Schedule A business" means a Schedule A business except in so far as it is a furnished holiday lettings business.

Commentary—*Simon's Direct Tax Service* **B2.304**.
Former enactments—CAA 1990 s 28A(1), s 29(1).
Definition—"Furnished holiday lettings business", s 17.
Modifications—CAA 2001 Sch 3 para 54 (vehicles provided by employees in 1990–91: see modification note at the start of this Part).
CAA 2001 Sch 3 para 55 (certain expenditure incurred before 6 April 1976: see modification note at the start of this Part).

17 Furnished holiday lettings businesses

(1) In this Part "furnished holiday lettings business" means a Schedule A business in so far as it consists of the commercial letting of furnished holiday accommodation in the United Kingdom.

(2) All commercial lettings of furnished holiday accommodation made by a particular person or partnership or body of persons are to be treated as one qualifying activity.

(3) "Commercial letting of furnished holiday accommodation" has the meaning given by section 504 of ICTA.

(4) If there is a letting of accommodation only part of which is holiday accommodation, such apportionments are to be made for the purposes of this section as are just and reasonable.

Commentary—*Simon's Direct Tax Service* **B2.304**.
Former enactments—Sub-s (1): CAA 1990 s 29(1).
Sub-s (2): TA 1988 s 503(1)(*b*); CAA 1990 s 29(2).
Sub-s (3): CAA 1990 s 29(2).
Sub-s (4): CAA 1990 s 29(3).
Definition—"Body of persons", TA 1988 s 832(1).
Modifications—CAA 2001 Sch 3 para 54 (vehicles provided by employees in 1990–91: see modifications note at the start of this Part).
CAA 2001 Sch 3 para 55 (certain expenditure incurred before 6 April 1976: see modification note at the start of this Part).

18 Management of investment companies

(1) For the purposes of this Part, the management of an investment company consists of pursuing those purposes expenditure on which would be treated as expenses of management within section 75 of ICTA.

(2) In this Part "investment company" has the meaning given by section 130 of ICTA.

Commentary—*Simon's Direct Tax Service* **B2.304**.
Former enactments—Sub-s (1): CAA 1990 s 28(4).
Sub-s (2): CAA 1990 s 28(1).
Definition—"Investment company", TA 1988 s 130.
Modifications—CAA 2001 Sch 3 para 54 (vehicles provided by employees in 1990–91: see modification note at the start of this Part).
CAA 2001 Sch 3 para 55 (certain expenditure incurred before 6 April 1976: see modification note at the start of this Part).

19 Special leasing of plant or machinery

(1) In this Part "special leasing", in relation to plant or machinery, means hiring out the plant or machinery otherwise than in the course of any other qualifying activity (and references to a lessor or lessee in the context of special leasing are to be read accordingly).

(2) A qualifying activity consisting of special leasing of plant or machinery begins when the plant or machinery is first hired out in the circumstances given in subsection (1).

(3) A qualifying activity consisting of special leasing of plant or machinery is permanently discontinued if the lessor permanently ceases to hire out the plant or machinery otherwise than in the course of any other qualifying activity.

(4) A person who has more than one item of plant or machinery that is the subject of special leasing has a separate qualifying activity in relation to each item.

(5) If a company carrying on any life assurance business—

    (*a*) hires out plant or machinery which is an investment asset (as defined by section 545(2)), and
    (*b*) does not do so in the course of a property business,

the company is to be treated for the purposes of subsection (1) as hiring out the plant or machinery otherwise than in the course of a qualifying activity.

Commentary—*Simon's Direct Tax Service* B2.304.
Former enactments—Sub-s (1): CAA 1990 s 61(1).
Sub-s (2): CAA 1990 s 61(1).
Sub-s (3): change in law.
Sub-s (4): CAA 1990 s 61(1).
Sub-s (5): TA 1988 s 434E(1), (2).
Definitions—"Life assurance business", s 544(5), TA 1988 s 431(2).
Modifications—CAA 2001 Sch 3 para 54 (vehicles provided by employees in 1990–91: see modification note at the start of this Part).
CAA 2001 Sch 3 para 55 (certain expenditure incurred before 6 April 1976: see modification note at the start of this Part).

CAA 2001

20 Employments and offices

(1) In section 15(1)(*i*) "employment" does not include an employment the performance of the duties of which is treated as the carrying on of a trade under section 314 of ICTA (divers and diving supervisors in the North Sea etc).

(2) Subsection (3) applies if the emoluments for any duties of an employment or office do not fall within Case I or II of Schedule E.

(3) This Part applies in relation to—

(*a*) those emoluments, or

(*b*) any other emoluments of the employment or office,

as if the performance of the duties did not belong to that employment or office.

Commentary—*Simon's Direct Tax Service* **B2.304**.
Former enactments—Sub-s (1): TA 1988 s 314(1); CAA 1990 s 27(1).
Sub-ss (2), (3): TA 1988 s 198(2).
Modifications—CAA 2001 Sch 3 para 54 (vehicles provided by employees in 1990–91: see modification note at the start of this Part).
CAA 2001 Sch 3 para 55 (certain expenditure incurred before 6 April 1976: see modification note at the start of this Part).

CHAPTER 3
QUALIFYING EXPENDITURE
Buildings, structures and land

21 Buildings

(1) For the purposes of this Act, expenditure on the provision of plant or machinery does not include expenditure on the provision of a building.

(2) The provision of a building includes its construction or acquisition.

(3) In this section, "building" includes an asset which—

(*a*) is incorporated in the building,

(*b*) although not incorporated in the building (whether because the asset is moveable or for any other reason), is in the building and is of a kind normally incorporated in a building, or

(*c*) is in, or connected with, the building and is in list A.

LIST A

ASSETS TREATED AS BUILDINGS

1. Walls, floors, ceilings, doors, gates, shutters, windows and stairs.
2. Mains services, and systems, for water, electricity and gas.
3. Waste disposal systems.
4. Sewerage and drainage systems.
5. Shafts or other structures in which lifts, hoists, escalators and moving walkways are installed.
6. Fire safety systems.

(4) This section is subject to section 23.

Commentary—*Simon's Direct Tax Service* B2.308.
Former enactments—Sub-s (1): CAA 1990 Sch AA1 para 1(1).
Sub-s (2): CAA 1990 Sch AA1 para 5(1).
Sub-s (3): CAA 1990 Sch AA1 para 1(2), (4), Table, column 1.
Revenue Internal Guidance—Capital Allowances Manual CA 22010 (summary of this section).
CA 22070 (raised floors).
CA 22080 (suspended ceiling).
CA 22090 (glasshouses).
Modifications—CAA 2001 Sch 3 para 13 (ss 21–24 do not apply in relation to expenditure—

(*a*) incurred before 30 November 1993;

(*b*) incurred before 6 April 1996 in pursuance of a contract entered into before 30 November 1993; or

(*c*) incurred before 6 April 1996 in pursuance of a contract entered into on or after 30 November 1993 for the purpose of securing that obligations under a contract entered into before 30 November 1993 are complied with).
CAA 2001 Sch 3 para 54 (vehicles provided by employees in 1990–91: see modification note at the start of this Part).
CAA 2001 Sch 3 para 55 (certain expenditure incurred before 6 April 1976: see modification note at the start of this Part).

22 Structures, assets and works

(1) For the purposes of this Act, expenditure on the provision of plant or machinery does not include expenditure on—

(*a*) the provision of a structure or other asset in list B, or

(*b*) any works involving the alteration of land.

LIST B

EXCLUDED STRUCTURES AND OTHER ASSETS

1. A tunnel, bridge, viaduct, aqueduct, embankment or cutting.
2. A way, hard standing (such as a pavement), road, railway, tramway, a park for vehicles or containers, or an airstrip or runway.
3. An inland navigation, including a canal or basin or a navigable river.

4. A dam, reservoir or barrage, including any sluices, gates, generators and other equipment associated with the dam, reservoir or barrage.

5. A dock, harbour, wharf, pier, marina or jetty or any other structure in or at which vessels may be kept, or merchandise or passengers may be shipped or unshipped.

6. A dike, sea wall, weir or drainage ditch.

7. Any structure not within items 1 to 6 other than—

(*a*) a structure (but not a building) within Chapter 2 of Part 3 (meaning of "industrial building"),

(*b*) a structure in use for the purposes of an undertaking for the extraction, production, processing or distribution of gas, and

(*c*) a structure in use for the purposes of a trade which consists in the provision of telecommunication, television or radio services.

(2) The provision of a structure or other asset includes its construction or acquisition.

(3) In this section—

(*a*) "structure" means a fixed structure of any kind, other than a building (as defined by section 21(3)), and

(*b*) "land" does not include buildings or other structures, but otherwise has the meaning given in Schedule 1 to the Interpretation Act 1978.

(4) This section is subject to section 23.

Commentary—*Simon's Direct Tax Service* B2.308.
Former enactments—Sub-s (1): CAA 1990 Sch AA1 para 2(1), (2), (4), Table 2, Column 1, notes 1 and 2.
Sub-s (2): CAA 1990 Sch AA1 para 5(1).
Sub-s (3): CAA 1990 Sch AA1 para 5(1), (3).
Revenue Internal Guidance—Capital allowances manual CA 220505 (other structures).
Modifications—CAA 2001 Sch 3 para 13 (ss 21–24 do not apply in relation to expenditure—

(*a*) incurred before 30 November 1993;
(*b*) incurred before 6 April 1996 in pursuance of a contract entered into before 30 November 1993; or
(*c*) incurred before 6 April 1996 in pursuance of a contract entered into on or after 30 November 1993 for the purpose of securing that obligations under a contract entered into before 30 November 1993 are complied with).
CAA 2001 Sch 3 para 54 (vehicles provided by employees in 1990–91: see modification note at the start of this Part).
CAA 2001 Sch 3 para 55 (certain expenditure incurred before 6 April 1976: see modification note at the start of this Part).

23 Expenditure unaffected by sections 21 and 22

(1) Sections 21 and 22 do not apply to any expenditure to which any of the provisions listed in subsection (2) applies.

(2) The provisions are—

section 28 (thermal insulation of industrial buildings);
section 29 (fire safety);
section 30 (safety at designated sports grounds);
section 31 (safety at regulated stands at sports grounds);
section 32 (safety at other sports grounds);
section 33 (personal security);
section 71 (software and rights to software);
section 40D of F(No 2)A 1992 (election relating to tax treatment of films expenditure).

(3) Sections 21 and 22 also do not affect the question whether expenditure on any item described in list C is, for the purposes of this Act, expenditure on the provision of plant or machinery.

(4) But items 1 to 16 of list C do not include any asset whose principal purpose is to insulate or enclose the interior of a building or to provide an interior wall, floor or ceiling which (in each case) is intended to remain permanently in place.

LIST C

EXPENDITURE UNAFFECTED BY SECTIONS 21 AND 22

1. Machinery (including devices for providing motive power) not within any other item in this list.

2. Electrical systems (including lighting systems) and cold water, gas and sewerage systems provided mainly—

(*a*) to meet the particular requirements of the qualifying activity, or

(*b*) to serve particular plant or machinery used for the purposes of the qualifying activity.

3. Space or water heating systems; powered systems of ventilation, air cooling or air purification; and any floor or ceiling comprised in such systems.

4. Manufacturing or processing equipment; storage equipment (including cold rooms); display equipment; and counters, checkouts and similar equipment.

5. Cookers, washing machines, dishwashers, refrigerators and similar equipment; washbasins, sinks, baths, showers, sanitary ware and similar equipment; and furniture and furnishings.

6. Lifts, hoists, escalators and moving walkways.

7. Sound insulation provided mainly to meet the particular requirements of the qualifying activity.

8. Computer, telecommunication and surveillance systems (including their wiring or other links).

9. Refrigeration or cooling equipment.

10. Fire alarm systems; sprinkler and other equipment for extinguishing or containing fires.

11. Burglar alarm systems.
12. Strong rooms in bank or building society premises; safes.
13. Partition walls, where moveable and intended to be moved in the course of the qualifying activity.
14. Decorative assets provided for the enjoyment of the public in hotel, restaurant or similar trades.
15. Advertising hoardings; signs, displays and similar assets.
16. Swimming pools (including diving boards, slides and structures on which such boards or slides are mounted).
17. Any glasshouse constructed so that the required environment (namely, air, heat, light, irrigation and temperature) for the growing of plants is provided automatically by means of devices forming an integral part of its structure.
18. Cold stores.
19. Caravans provided mainly for holiday lettings.
20. Buildings provided for testing aircraft engines run within the buildings.
21. Moveable buildings intended to be moved in the course of the qualifying activity.
22. The alteration of land for the purpose only of installing plant or machinery.
23. The provision of dry docks.
24. The provision of any jetty or similar structure provided mainly to carry plant or machinery.
25. The provision of pipelines or underground ducts or tunnels with a primary purpose of carrying utility conduits.
26. The provision of towers to support floodlights.
27. The provision of—
   (a) any reservoir incorporated into a water treatment works, or
   (b) any service reservoir of treated water for supply within any housing estate or other particular locality.
28. The provision of—
   (a) silos provided for temporary storage, or
   (b) storage tanks.
29. The provision of slurry pits or silage clamps.
30. The provision of fish tanks or fish ponds.
31. The provision of rails, sleepers and ballast for a railway or tramway.
32. The provision of structures and other assets for providing the setting for any ride at an amusement park or exhibition.
33. The provision of fixed zoo cages.

(5) In item 19 of list C, "caravan" includes, in relation to a holiday caravan site, anything that is treated as a caravan for the purposes of—
   (a) the Caravan Sites and Control of Development Act 1960, or
   (b) the Caravans Act (Northern Ireland) 1963.

Commentary—*Simon's Direct Tax Service* B2.307, 308.
Former enactments—Sub-ss (1), (2): CAA 1990 Sch AA1 para 4.
Sub-s (3): CAA 1990 Sch AA1 paras 1(3), 2(3); change to law.
Sub-s (4): CAA 1990 Sch AA1 para 1(4), Table 1, note 1.
List C: CAA 1990 Sch AA1 para 1(3), (4), Table 1, Column 2, note 2, para 2(4), Table 2, column 2, para 5(2).
Sub-s (5): Concession ESC B50.
Revenue Internal Guidance—Capital allowances manual CA 22030 (items in List C must qualify as plant under normal rules in order to qualify for capital allowances).
Modifications—CAA 2001 Sch 3 para 13 (ss 21–24 do not apply in relation to expenditure—
   (a) incurred before 30 November 1993;
   (b) incurred before 6 April 1996 in pursuance of a contract entered into before 30 November 1993; or
   (c) incurred before 6 April 1996 in pursuance of a contract entered into on or after 30 November 1993 for the purpose of securing that obligations under a contract entered into before 30 November 1993 are complied with).
CAA 2001 Sch 3 para 54 (vehicles provided by employees in 1990–91: see modification note at the start of this Part).
CAA 2001 Sch 3 para 55 (certain expenditure incurred before 6 April 1976: see modification note at the start of this Part).

24 Interests in land

(1) For the purposes of this Act, expenditure on the provision of plant or machinery does not include expenditure on the acquisition of an interest in land.

(2) In this section "land" does not include—
   (a) buildings or other structures, or
   (b) any asset which is so installed or otherwise fixed to any description of land as to become, in law, part of the land,
but otherwise has the meaning given in Schedule 1 to the Interpretation Act 1978.

(3) Subject to subsection (2), "interest in land" has the meaning given by section 175 (definitions in connection with provisions about fixtures).

Commentary—*Simon's Direct Tax Service* B2.306.
Former enactments—Sub-s (1): CAA 1990 Sch AA1 para 3(1).
Sub-s (2): CAA 1990 Sch AA1 paras 3(2), 5(3).
Sub-s (3): CAA 1990 Sch AA1 para 5(3).
Modifications—CAA 2001 Sch 3 para 13 (ss 21–24 do not apply in relation to expenditure—

(*a*) incurred before 30 November 1993;
(*b*) incurred before 6 April 1996 in pursuance of a contract entered into before 30 November 1993; or
(*c*) incurred before 6 April 1996 in pursuance of a contract entered into on or after 30 November 1993 for the purpose of securing that obligations under a contract entered into before 30 November 1993 are complied with).

CAA 2001 Sch 3 para 54 (vehicles provided by employees in 1990–91: see modification note at the start of this Part).
CAA 2001 Sch 3 para 55 (certain expenditure incurred before 6 April 1976: see modification note at the start of this Part).

25 Building alterations connected with installation of plant or machinery

If a person carrying on a qualifying activity incurs capital expenditure on alterations to an existing building incidental to the installation of plant or machinery for the purposes of the qualifying activity, this Part applies as if—

(*a*) the expenditure were expenditure on the provision of the plant or machinery, and
(*b*) the works representing the expenditure formed part of the plant or machinery.

Commentary—*Simon's Direct Tax Service* **B2.305**.
Former enactments—CAA 1990 s 66.
Definition—''Capital expenditure'', s 4.
Modifications—CAA 2001 Sch 3 para 54 (vehicles provided by employees in 1990–91: see modification note at the start of this Part).
CAA 2001 Sch 3 para 55 (certain expenditure incurred before 6 April 1976: see modification note at the start of this Part).

Demolition costs

26 Demolition costs

(1) This section applies if—

(*a*) plant or machinery is demolished, and
(*b*) the last use of the plant or machinery was for the purposes of a qualifying activity.

(2) If the person carrying on the qualifying activity replaces the plant or machinery with other plant or machinery then, for the purposes of this Part, the net cost of the demolition to that person is treated as expenditure incurred on the provision of the other plant or machinery.

(3) If the person carrying on the qualifying activity does not replace the plant or machinery, the net cost of the demolition to that person is allocated to the appropriate pool for the chargeable period in which the demolition takes place.

(4) In subsection (3)—

''the appropriate pool'' means the pool to which the expenditure on the demolished plant or machinery has been or would be allocated in accordance with this Part, and
''the net cost of the demolition'' means the amount, if any, by which the cost of the demolition exceeds any money received for the remains of the plant or machinery.

(5) Subsection (3) is subject to section 164(4) (abandonment expenditure before cessation of ring fence trade: election for special allowance).

Commentary—*Simon's Direct Tax Service* B2.309.
Former enactments—Sub-s (1): CAA 1990 s 62(1); change in law.
Sub-s (2): CAA 1990 s 62(1)(*a*).
Sub-s (3): CAA 1990 s 62(1)(*b*).
Sub-s (4): CAA 1990 s 62(2).
Sub-s (5): CAA 1990 s 62(1).
Definition—''Chargeable period'', s 6.
Modifications—CAA 2001 Sch 3 para 54 (vehicles provided by employees in 1990–91: see modification note at the start of this Part).
CAA 2001 Sch 3 para 55 (certain expenditure incurred before 6 April 1976: see modification note at the start of this Part).

Expenditure on thermal insulation, safety measures, etc

27 Application of Part to thermal insulation, safety measures, etc

(1) Subsection (2) has effect in relation to expenditure if—

(*a*) it is expenditure to which any of sections 28 to 33 applies, and
(*b*) an allowance under Part 2 or a deduction in respect of the expenditure could not, in the absence of this section, be made in calculating the income from the qualifying activity in question.

(2) This Part (including in particular section 11(4)) applies as if—

(*a*) the expenditure were capital expenditure on the provision of plant or machinery for the purposes of the qualifying activity in question, and
(*b*) the person who incurred the expenditure owned plant or machinery as a result of incurring it.

Commentary—*Simon's Direct Tax Service* **B2.310**.
Former enactments—Sub-s (1): CAA 1990 s 69(1)(*b*), (2), s 70(1), (2), s 71(1)(*c*), (*d*), s 161(3); change in the law.
Sub-s (2): CAA 1990 s 67(1), s 69(1), s 70(1), s 70(2), s 71(2).
Definition—''Capital expenditure'', s 4.
Modifications—CAA 2001 Sch 3 para 54 (vehicles provided by employees in 1990–91: see modification note at the start of this Part).
CAA 2001 Sch 3 para 55 (certain expenditure incurred before 6 April 1976: see modification note at the start of this Part).

28 Thermal insulation of industrial buildings

(1) This section applies to expenditure if a person carrying on a qualifying activity consisting of a trade has incurred it in adding insulation against loss of heat to an industrial building occupied by him for the purposes of the trade.

(2) This section also applies to expenditure if a person carrying on a qualifying activity consisting of an ordinary Schedule A business [or an overseas property business][1] has incurred it in adding insulation against loss of heat to an industrial building let by him in the course of the business.

(3) "Industrial building" means a building or structure which is in use for the purposes of a qualifying trade (within the meaning of Chapter 2 of Part 3).

Commentary—*Simon's Direct Tax Service* **B2.310**.
Former enactments—Sub-s (1): CAA 1990 s 67(1).
Sub-s (2): CAA 1990 s 67(4A).
Sub-s (3): CAA 1990 s 67(4).
Revenue Internal Guidance—Capital allowances manual CA 22220 (sub-s (1) covers expenditure on roof lining, double glazing, draught exclusion and cavity wall filling).
Definition—"Ordinary Schedule A business", s 16.
Modifications—CAA 2001 Sch 3 para 54 (vehicles provided by employees in 1990–91: see modification note at the start of this Part).
CAA 2001 Sch 3 para 55 (certain expenditure incurred before 6 April 1976: see modification note at the start of this Part).
Amendment—[1] Words inserted by FA 2001 s 69, Sch 21 para 1 with effect as respects allowances and charges falling to be made for chargeable periods ending after 5 April 2001 (for income tax purposes) or 31 March 2001 (for corporation tax purposes).

29 Fire safety

(1) This section applies to expenditure if a person carrying on a qualifying activity has incurred it in taking required fire precautions in respect of premises which he uses for the purposes of the qualifying activity.

(2) A person takes required fire precautions in respect of premises if—
  (a) he has been served with a notice under section 5(4) of the Fire Precautions Act 1971 specifying steps to be taken in respect of the premises, and
  (b) he takes the steps specified in the notice.

(3) A person also takes required fire precautions in respect of premises if—
  (a) he has not been served with a notice by the fire authority under section 5(4) of the 1971 Act, but has been sent or given a document by or on behalf of the fire authority that specifies steps that might have been specified in respect of the premises in such a notice, and
  (b) he takes the steps specified in the document.

(4) A person also takes required fire precautions in respect of premises if—
  (a) he has been served with a prohibition notice under section 10 of the 1971 Act in respect of the premises specifying matters giving rise to a risk of a kind mentioned in subsection (2) of that section, and
  (b) he takes steps to remedy the matters specified in the prohibition notice.

(5) This section has effect in relation to Northern Ireland subject to the modifications in subsection (6).

(6) The modifications are—
  (a) for the references to section 5(4) of the 1971 Act substitute references to Article 26(4) of the Fire Services (Northern Ireland) Order 1984,
  (b) for the reference to section 10 of the 1971 Act substitute a reference to Article 33 of the 1984 Order, and
  (c) for the references to a fire authority substitute references to the Fire Authority for Northern Ireland.

Commentary—*Simon's Direct Tax Service* **B2.310**.
Former enactments—Sub-s (1): CAA 1990 s 69(1), (2).
Sub-s (2): CAA 1990 s 69(1).
Sub-s (3): CAA 1990 s 69(2).
Sub-s (4): CAA 1990 s 69(2), IA 1978 s 17(2).
Sub-ss (5), (6): ESC B16.
Modifications—CAA 2001 Sch 3 para 54 (vehicles provided by employees in 1990–91: see modification note at the start of this Part).
CAA 2001 Sch 3 para 55 (certain expenditure incurred before 6 April 1976: see modification note at the start of this Part).

30 Safety at designated sports grounds

(1) This section applies to expenditure if a person carrying on a qualifying activity has incurred it in taking required safety precautions in respect of a sports ground which is—
  (a) designated under section 1 of the Safety of Sports Grounds Act 1975 as requiring a safety certificate, and
  (b) used by him for the purposes of the qualifying activity.

(2) A person takes required safety precautions in respect of the sports ground if—
  (a) a safety certificate has been issued under the 1975 Act for the sports ground, and
  (b) he takes steps necessary for compliance with the terms and conditions of the safety certificate.

(3)　A person also takes required safety precautions in respect of the sports ground if—

(*a*)　he has been sent or given a document by or on behalf of the local authority for the area in which the sports ground is situated,

(*b*)　the document specifies steps which, if taken, would—

(i)　be taken into account by the local authority in deciding what terms and conditions to include in a safety certificate to be issued under the 1975 Act for the sports ground, or

(ii)　lead to the amendment or replacement of a safety certificate issued or to be issued under the 1975 Act for the sports ground, and

(*c*)　he takes the steps specified in the document.

Commentary—*Simon's Direct Tax Service* **B2.310**.
Former enactments—Sub-s (1): CAA 1990 s 70(1), (3), (5).
Sub-s (2): CAA 1990 s 70(1), (5).
Revenue Internal Guidance—Capital allowances manual CA 22240 (provision of seats and seat covers is not within this section, but expenditure is likely to qualify as expenditure on plant; expenditure on construction of police control room will qualify).
Modifications—CAA 2001 Sch 3 para 54 (vehicles provided by employees in 1990–91: see modification note at the start of this Part).
CAA 2001 Sch 3 para 55 (certain expenditure incurred before 6 April 1976: see modification note at the start of this Part).

31 Safety at regulated stands at sports grounds

(1)　This section applies to expenditure if a person carrying on a qualifying activity has incurred it in taking required safety precautions in respect of a stand at a sports ground—

(*a*)　the use of which requires a safety certificate under Part III of the Fire Safety and Safety of Places of Sport Act 1987, and

(*b*)　which he uses for the purposes of the qualifying activity.

(2)　A person takes required safety precautions in respect of the stand at the sports ground if—

(*a*)　a safety certificate has been issued under the 1987 Act for the stand, and

(*b*)　he takes steps necessary for compliance with the terms and conditions of the safety certificate.

(3)　A person also takes required safety precautions in respect of the stand at the sports ground if—

(*a*)　he has been sent or given a document by or on behalf of the local authority for the area in which the sports ground is situated,

(*b*)　the document specifies steps which, if taken, would—

(i)　be taken into account by the local authority in deciding what terms and conditions to include in a safety certificate to be issued under the 1987 Act for the stand, or

(ii)　lead to the amendment or replacement of a safety certificate issued or to be issued under the 1987 Act for the stand, and

(*c*)　he takes the steps specified in the document.

Commentary—*Simon's Direct Tax Service* **B2.310**.
Former enactments—Sub-s (1): CAA 1990 s 70(1), (5).
Sub-s (2): CAA 1990 s 70(1), (5).
Sub-s (3): CAA 1990 s 70(1), (5).
Modifications—CAA 2001 Sch 3 para 54 (vehicles provided by employees in 1990–91: see modification note at the start of this Part).
CAA 2001 Sch 3 para 55 (certain expenditure incurred before 6 April 1976: see modification note at the start of this Part).

32 Safety at other sports grounds

(1)　This section applies to expenditure if a person carrying on a qualifying activity has incurred it in taking required safety precautions in respect of a sports ground—

(*a*)　which is of a kind described in section 1(1) of the Safety of Sports Grounds Act 1975 but in respect of which no designation order under that section is in force at the time when he takes those precautions, and

(*b*)　which he uses for the purposes of the qualifying activity,

and the expenditure is not incurred in respect of a sports ground stand which is within section 31(1)(*a*).

(2)　A person takes required safety precautions in respect of the sports ground if he takes steps which the relevant local authority certify would have fallen within section 30(2) or (3) if—

(*a*)　a designation order under section 1 of the 1975 Act had then been in force, and

(*b*)　a safety certificate had then been issued or applied for under the 1975 Act.

(3)　Any provision of regulations made under section 6(1)(*b*) of the 1975 Act (power of local authorities to charge fees) applies, with the necessary modifications, to the issue of a certificate for the purposes of subsection (2) as it applies to the issue of a safety certificate.

(4)　In subsection (2)—

(*a*)　"the relevant local authority" means the local authority for the area in which the sports ground is situated, and

(*b*)　"local authority" has the same meaning as in the 1975 Act.

Commentary—*Simon's Direct Tax Service* **B2.310**.
Former enactments—Sub-ss (1), (2): CAA 1990 s 70(2), (5).

Sub-s (3): CAA 1990 s 70(4).
Sub-s (4): CAA 1990 s 70(2), (5).
Modifications—CAA 2001 Sch 3 para 54 (vehicles provided by employees in 1990–91: see modification note at the start of this Part).
CAA 2001 Sch 3 para 55 (certain expenditure incurred before 6 April 1976: see modification note at the start of this Part).

33 Personal security

(1) This section applies to expenditure if—

    (*a*) it is incurred by an individual or partnership of individuals in connection with the provision for, or for use by, the individual, or any of the individuals, of a security asset,

    (*b*) the individual or partnership is carrying on a relevant qualifying activity, and

    (*c*) the special threat conditions are met.

(2) The special threat conditions are that—

    (*a*) the asset is provided or used to meet a threat which—

        (i) is a special threat to the individual's personal physical security, and

        (ii) arises wholly or mainly because of the relevant qualifying activity, and

    (*b*) the person incurring the expenditure—

        (i) has the sole object of meeting that threat in incurring that expenditure, and

        (ii) intends the asset to be used solely to improve personal physical security.

(3) If—

    (*a*) the person incurring the expenditure intends the asset to be used solely to improve personal physical security, but

    (*b*) there is another use which is incidental to improving personal physical security,

that other use is ignored for the purposes of this section.

(4) The fact that an asset improves the personal physical security of any member of the family or household of the individual concerned, as well as that of the individual, does not prevent this section from applying.

(5) If—

    (*a*) the asset is not intended to be used solely to improve personal physical security, but the expenditure incurred on it would otherwise be expenditure to which this section applies, and

    (*b*) the person incurring the expenditure intends the asset to be used partly to improve personal physical security,

this section applies only to the proportion of the expenditure attributable to the intended use to improve personal physical security.

(6) In this section "security asset" means an asset which improves personal security; and here "asset"—

    (*a*) does not include—

        (i) a car, ship or aircraft, or

        (ii) a dwelling or grounds appurtenant to a dwelling, but

    (*b*) subject to paragraph (*a*), includes equipment, a structure (such as a wall) and an asset which becomes fixed to land.

(7) Section 81 (extended meaning of "car") does not apply in relation to subsection (6)(*a*).

(8) In this section "relevant qualifying activity" means a qualifying activity consisting of—

    (*a*) a trade,

    (*b*) an ordinary Schedule A business,

    (*c*) a furnished holiday lettings business,

    (*d*) an overseas property business, or

    (*e*) a profession or vocation.

Commentary—*Simon's Direct Tax Service* B2.310.
Former enactments—Sub-s (1): CAA 1990 s 71(1).
Sub-s (2): CAA 1990 s 71(3), (4).
Sub-s (3): CAA 1990 s 72(2).
Sub-s (4): CAA 1990 s 73(3).
Sub-s (5): CAA 1990 s 71(5), (6).
Sub-s (6): CAA 1990 s 72(1), (4).
Sub-s (8): CAA 1990 s 28A(1), s 29(1), s 71(1), s 161(2A).
Revenue Internal Guidance—Capital allowances manual CA 22270 (interpretation of this section).
CA 22270 (meaning of "dwelling" and "grounds appurtenant to a dwelling")
Definitions—"Furnished holiday lettings business", s 17; "ordinary Schedule A business", s 16.
Modifications—CAA 2001 Sch 3 para 54 (vehicles provided by employees in 1990–91: see modification note at the start of this Part).
CAA 2001 Sch 3 para 55 (certain expenditure incurred before 6 April 1976: see modification note at the start of this Part).

Exclusion of certain types of expenditure

34 Expenditure by MPs and others on accommodation

(1) Expenditure is not qualifying expenditure if it is incurred by—

    (*a*) a member of the House of Commons,

    (*b*) a member of the Scottish Parliament,

    (*c*) a member of the National Assembly for Wales, or

    (*d*) a member of the Northern Ireland Assembly,

in or in connection with the provision or use of residential or overnight accommodation for the purpose given in subsection (2).

(2) The purpose is enabling the member to perform the duties of a member of the body in or about—

    (*a*) the place where the body sits, or

    (*b*) the constituency or region for which the member has been returned.

Commentary—*Simon's Direct Tax Service* **B2.311**.
Former enactments—Sub-ss (1), (2): CAA 1990 s 74.
Modifications—CAA 2001 Sch 3 para 54 (vehicles provided by employees in 1990–91: see modification note at the start of this Part).
CAA 2001 Sch 3 para 55 (certain expenditure incurred before 6 April 1976: see modification note at the start of this Part).

35 Expenditure on plant or machinery for use in dwelling-house not qualifying expenditure in certain cases

(1) This section applies if a person is carrying on a qualifying activity consisting of—

    (*a*) an ordinary Schedule A business,

    (*b*) an overseas property business, or

    (*c*) special leasing of plant or machinery.

(2) The person's expenditure is not qualifying expenditure if it is incurred in providing plant or machinery for use in a dwelling-house.

(3) If plant or machinery is provided partly for use in a dwelling-house and partly for other purposes, such apportionment of the expenditure incurred in providing that plant or machinery is to be made for the purposes of subsection (2) as is just and reasonable.

Commentary—*Simon's Direct Tax Service* **B2.311**.
Former enactments—Sub-ss (1), (2): CAA 1990 s 28A(3), s 61(2), s 161(2A).
Sub-s (3): CAA 1990 s 28A(4).
Revenue Internal Guidance—Capital allowances manual CA 23060 (in sub-s (2), a flat used as a residence is a dwelling-house, but a block of flats is not a single dwelling-house).
Definitions—''Dwelling-house'', s 531(1); ''ordinary Schedule A business'', s 16; ''special leasing'', s 19.
Modifications—CAA 2001 Sch 3 para 54 (vehicles provided by employees in 1990–91: see modification note at the start of this Part).
CAA 2001 Sch 3 para 55 (certain expenditure incurred before 6 April 1976: see modification note at the start of this Part).

[36 Restriction on qualifying expenditure in case of employment or office

(1) Where the qualifying activity consists of an employment or office—

    (*a*) expenditure on the provision of a mechanically propelled road vehicle, or a cycle, is not qualifying expenditure, and

    (*b*) other expenditure is qualifying expenditure only if the plant or machinery is necessarily provided for use in the performance of the duties of the employment or office.

(2) In this section ''cycle'' has the meaning given by section 192(1) of the Road Traffic Act 1988.][1]

Commentary—*Simon's Direct Tax Service* **B2.311**.
Former enactments—Sub-s (2): CAA 1990 s 27(2).
Modifications—CAA 2001 Sch 3 para 54 (vehicles provided by employees in 1990–91: see modification note at the start of this Part).
CAA 2001 Sch 3 para 55 (certain expenditure incurred before 6 April 1976: see modification note at the start of this Part).
Amendments—[1] Section substituted by FA 2001 s 59(1), (3) with effect for expenditure incurred after 5 April 2002.

37 Exclusion where sums payable in respect of depreciation

(1) Expenditure incurred by a person in providing plant or machinery for the purposes of a qualifying activity is not qualifying expenditure if it appears—

    (*a*) that during the period during which the plant or machinery will be used for the purposes of the qualifying activity sums are, or are to be, payable to that person directly or indirectly, and

    (*b*) that those sums are in respect of, or take account of, the whole of the depreciation of the plant or machinery resulting from its use for those purposes.

(2) Subsection (1) does not apply if the sums fall to be taken into account as income of the person or in calculating the profits of a qualifying activity carried on by him.

Commentary—*Simon's Direct Tax Service* **B2.311**.
Former enactments—Sub-ss (1), (2): CAA 1990 s 80(1).
Modifications—CAA 2001 Sch 3 para 54 (vehicles provided by employees in 1990–91: see modification note at the start of this Part).
CAA 2001 Sch 3 para 55 (certain expenditure incurred before 6 April 1976: see modification note at the start of this Part).

CAA 2001

38 Production animals etc

Expenditure is not qualifying expenditure if it is incurred on—

(a) animals or other creatures to which Schedule 5 to ICTA (treatment of farm animals etc for purposes of Case I of Schedule D) applies, or

(b) shares in such animals or creatures.

Commentary—*Simon's Direct Tax Service* B2.311.
Former enactments—CAA 1990 s 82(2).
Modifications—CAA 2001 Sch 3 para 54 (vehicles provided by employees in 1990–91: see modification note at the start of this Part).
CAA 2001 Sch 3 para 55 (certain expenditure incurred before 6 April 1976: see modification note at the start of this Part).

CHAPTER 4
FIRST-YEAR QUALIFYING EXPENDITURE
General

39 First-year allowances available for certain types of qualifying expenditure only

A first-year allowance is not available unless the qualifying expenditure is first-year qualifying expenditure under—

section 40	expenditure incurred for Northern Ireland purposes by small or medium-sized enterprises,
section 44	expenditure incurred by small or medium-sized enterprises, ...[2]
section 45	ICT expenditure incurred by small enterprises...[6]
section 45A	expenditure on energy-saving plant or machinery.][1]
[section 45D	expenditure on cars with low CO_2 emissions,][3]
[section 45E	expenditure on plant or machinery for gas refuelling station][4] [or
section 45F	section 45F expenditure on plant and machinery for use wholly in a ring fence trade.][5]

Commentary—*Simon's Direct Tax Service* B2.320.
Former enactments—CAA 1990 s 22(1).
Modifications—CAA 2001 Sch 3 para 54 (vehicles provided by employees in 1990–91: see modification note at the start of this Part).
CAA 2001 Sch 3 para 55 (certain expenditure incurred before 6 April 1976: see modification note at the start of this Part).
Amendment—[1] Words inserted by FA 2001 s 65, Sch 17 para 1 with effect as respects allowances and charges falling to be made for chargeable periods ending after 5 April 2001 (for income tax purposes) or 31 March 2001 (for corporation tax purposes).
[2] Word "or" repealed by FA 2001 s 110, Sch 33 Pt II(4) with effect as respects allowances and charges falling to be made for chargeable periods ending after 5 April 2001 (for income tax purposes) or 31 March 2001 (for corporation tax purposes).
[3] Words inserted by FA 2002 s 59, Sch 19 paras 1, 2 with effect for expenditure incurred after 16 April 2002.
[4] Words inserted by FA 2002 s 61, Sch 20 paras 1, 2 with effect for expenditure incurred after 16 April 2002.
[5] Words inserted by FA 2002 s 63, Sch 21 paras 1, 2 with effect for expenditure incurred after 16 April 2002.
[6] Word "or" repealed by FA 2002 s 141, Sch 40 Pt 3(7) with effect for expenditure incurred after 16 April 2002.

Types of expenditure which may qualify for first-year allowances

40 Expenditure incurred for Northern Ireland purposes by small or medium-sized enterprises

(1) Expenditure is first-year qualifying expenditure if—

(a) it is incurred on or before 11th May 2002,

(b) it is incurred by a small or medium-sized enterprise,

(c) it is incurred on the provision of plant or machinery for use primarily in Northern Ireland, and

(d) it is not excluded by—

(i) section 41 (miscellaneous exclusions from this section),

(ii) section 42 (plant or machinery partly for use outside Northern Ireland), or

(iii) section 46 (general exclusions).

(2) This section is subject to section 43 (effect of plant or machinery subsequently being primarily for use outside Northern Ireland).

Commentary—*Simon's Direct Tax Service* B2.321.
Former enactments—Sub-s (1): CAA 1990 s 22(3CA), (3CB).
Sub-s (2): CAA 1990 s 22(3CA).
Modifications—CAA 2001 Sch 3 para 50 (the section above does not apply for the purposes of CAA 2001 s 236(1)(a) if the expenditure was incurred before 12 May 1998).
CAA 2001 Sch 3 para 54 (vehicles provided by employees in 1990–91: see modification note at the start of this Part).
CAA 2001 Sch 3 para 55 (certain expenditure incurred before 6 April 1976: see modification note at the start of this Part).

41 Miscellaneous exclusions from section 40 (expenditure for Northern Ireland purposes etc)

(1) Expenditure is not first-year qualifying expenditure under section 40 if—

(a) it is long-life asset expenditure,

(b) it is expenditure on the provision of an aircraft or hovercraft, or

(c) it is expenditure on the provision of a goods vehicle for the purposes of a trade which consists primarily of the conveyance of goods.

(2) Expenditure is not first-year qualifying expenditure under section 40 if it is incurred on the provision of plant or machinery for use primarily in—

(*a*) agriculture, fishing or fish farming, or

(*b*) any relevant activity carried out in relation to agricultural produce, fish or any fish product for the purpose of bringing it to market,

unless it is authorised for the purposes of this section by the Department of Agriculture and Rural Development in Northern Ireland.

(3) An authorisation given by the Department—

(*a*) may be given either generally or specially, and

(*b*) may in any case be absolute or conditional;

and, if the authorisation is given generally, it may be modified by the Department.

(4) An authorisation is given specially if it is given so as to apply only to a specified item of expenditure or a specified person; otherwise, it is given generally.

(5) In this section—

[''agricultural produce'' has the same meaning as in section 6 of the European Communities Act 1972 (c 68),

''agriculture'' has the same meaning as in the Agriculture Act 1947 (c 48),][1]

''fish'' includes shellfish,

''fish farming'' means the intensive rearing, on a commercial basis, of fish intended for human consumption,

''fishing'' means a trade, or part of a trade, which consists of the catching or taking of fish,

''goods vehicle'' has the same meaning as in the Road Traffic (Northern Ireland) Order 1995,

''hovercraft'' has the same meaning as in the Hovercraft Act 1968, and

''relevant activity'' means transportation, storage, preparation, processing or packaging.

Commentary—*Simon's Direct Tax Service* **B2.321**.
Former enactments—Sub-s (1): CAA 1990 s 22(3CC).
Sub-s (2): CAA 1990 s 22(3CC), (3CD); Departments (Northern Ireland) Order, SI 1999/283, art 3, Sch 1.
Sub-ss (3), (4): CAA 1990 s 22(3CE).
Sub-s (5): CAA 1990 s 22(3CD) (''relevant activity''), (10).
Modifications—CAA 2001 Sch 3 para 54 (vehicles provided by employees in 1990–91: see modification note at the start of this Part).
CAA 2001 Sch 3 para 55 (certain expenditure incurred before 6 April 1976: see modification note at the start of this Part).
Amendments—[1] Definition of ''agricultural produce'' and ''agriculture'' substituted by the Intervention Board for Agricultural Produce (Abolition) Regulations, SI 2001/3686 reg 6(20) with effect from 15 November 2001.

42 Exclusion of plant or machinery partly for use outside Northern Ireland

(1) Expenditure on plant or machinery is not first-year qualifying expenditure under section 40 if—

(*a*) at the time when it is incurred, the person incurring it intends the plant or machinery to be used partly outside Northern Ireland, and

(*b*) the main benefit, or one of the main benefits, which could reasonably be expected to arise from the relevant arrangements is the obtaining of a first-year allowance, or a greater first-year allowance, in respect of the part of the expenditure that is attributable to that intended use outside Northern Ireland.

(2) For the purposes of subsection (1)—

(*a*) ''the relevant arrangements'' means—

(i) the transaction under which the expenditure is incurred, and

(ii) any scheme or arrangements of which that transaction forms part, and

(*b*) the part of the expenditure that is attributable under subsection (1)(*b*) is to be determined on a just and reasonable basis.

Commentary—*Simon's Direct Tax Service* **B2.321**.
Former enactments—Sub-s (1): CAA 1990 s 22(6D), (6E) (''the intended outside use'').
Sub-s (2): CAA 1990 s 22(6E).
Modifications—CAA 2001 Sch 3 para 54 (vehicles provided by employees in 1990–91: see modification note at the start of this Part).
CAA 2001 Sch 3 para 55 (certain expenditure incurred before 6 April 1976: see modification note at the start of this Part).

43 Effect of plant or machinery subsequently being primarily for use outside Northern Ireland

(1) Expenditure on the provision of plant or machinery is to be treated as never having been first-year qualifying expenditure under section 40 if, at any relevant time—

(*a*) the primary use to which the plant or machinery is put is a use outside Northern Ireland, or

(*b*) the plant or machinery is held for use otherwise than primarily in Northern Ireland.

(2) In subsection (1) ''relevant time'' means a time which—

(*a*) falls within the relevant period, and

(*b*) is a time when the plant or machinery is owned by—

(i) the person who incurred the expenditure, or

(ii) a person who is, or at any time in that period has been, connected with that person.

(3) ''The relevant period'' means—

(a) if the expenditure concerned exceeds £3.5 million, the period of 5 years beginning with the date of the incurring of that expenditure;

(b) in any other case, the period of 2 years beginning with that date.

(4) All such assessments and adjustments of assessments are to be made as are necessary to give effect to subsection (1).

(5) If a person who has made a return becomes aware that, after making it, anything in it has become incorrect because of the operation of this section, he must give notice to the Inland Revenue specifying how the return needs to be amended.

(6) The notice must be given within 3 months beginning with the day on which the person first became aware that anything in the return had become incorrect because of the operation of this section.

Commentary—*Simon's Direct Tax Service* **B2.321**.
Former enactments—Sub-s (1): CAA 1990 s 22B(1).
Sub-s (2): CAA 1990 s 22B(2).
Sub-s (3): CAA 1990 s 22B(2A).
Sub-s (4): CAA 1990 s 22B(3).
Sub-ss (5), (6): CAA 1990 s 22B(4).
Modifications—CAA 2001 Sch 3 para 54 (vehicles provided by employees in 1990–91: see modification note at the start of this Part).
CAA 2001 Sch 3 para 55 (certain expenditure incurred before 6 April 1976: see modification note at the start of this Part).

44 Expenditure incurred by small or medium-sized enterprises

(1) Expenditure is first-year qualifying expenditure if—

(a) it is incurred by a small or medium-sized enterprise, and

(b) it is not excluded by subsection (2) or section 46 (general exclusions).

(2) Long-life asset expenditure is not first-year qualifying expenditure under subsection (1).

Commentary—*Simon's Direct Tax Service* **B2.322**.
Former enactments—Sub-ss (1), (2): CAA 1990 s 22(3D).
Modifications—CAA 2001 Sch 3 para 50 (the section above does not apply for the purposes of CAA 2001 s 236(1)(a) if the expenditure was incurred before 2 July 1998).
CAA 2001 Sch 3 para 54 (vehicles provided by employees in 1990–91: see modification note at the start of this Part).
CAA 2001 Sch 3 para 55 (certain expenditure incurred before 6 April 1976: see modification note at the start of this Part).

45 ICT expenditure incurred by small enterprises

(1) Expenditure is first-year qualifying expenditure if—

(a) it is incurred on or before 31st March 2003,

(b) it is incurred by a small enterprise,

(c) it is expenditure on information and communications technology, and

(d) it is not excluded by section 46 (general exclusions).

(2) ''Expenditure on information and communications technology'' means expenditure on items within any of the following classes.

Class A. Computers and associated equipment
This class covers—

(a) computers,

(b) peripheral devices designed to be used by being connected to or inserted in a computer,

(c) equipment (including cabling) for use primarily to provide a data connection between—

(i) one computer and another, or

(ii) a computer and a data communications network, and

(d) dedicated electrical systems for computers.

For this purpose ''computer'' does not include computerised control or management systems or other systems that are part of a larger system whose principal function is not processing or storing information.

Class B. Other qualifying equipment
This class covers—

(a) wireless application protocol telephones,

(b) third generation mobile telephones,

(c) devices designed to be used by being connected to a television set and capable of receiving and transmitting information from and to data networks, and

(d) other devices—

(i) substantially similar to those within paragraphs (a), (b) and (c), and

(ii) capable of receiving and transmitting information from and to data networks.

This is subject to any order under subsection (3).

Class C. Software
This class covers the right to use or otherwise deal with software for the purposes of any equipment within Class A or B.

(3) The Treasury may make provision by order—

    (a) further defining the kinds of equipment within Class B, or

    (b) adding further kinds of equipment to that class.

Commentary—*Simon's Direct Tax Service* **B2.323**.
Former enactments—Sub-s (1): CAA 1990 s 22(3E).
Sub-s (2): CAA 1990 s 22(3F), (3G).
Sub-s (3): CAA 1990 s 22(3H).
Modifications—CAA 2001 Sch 3 para 14 (the section above does not apply in relation to expenditure incurred before 1 April 2000).
CAA 2001 Sch 3 para 50 (the section above does not apply for the purposes of CAA 2001 s 236(1)(a) if the expenditure was incurred before 1 April 2000).
CAA 2001 Sch 3 para 54 (vehicles provided by employees in 1990–91: see modification note at the start of this Part).
CAA 2001 Sch 3 para 55 (certain expenditure incurred before 6 April 1976: see modification note at the start of this Part).

[45A Expenditure on energy-saving plant or machinery

(1) Expenditure is first-year qualifying expenditure if—

    (a) it is expenditure on energy-saving plant or machinery that is unused and not second-hand,

    (b) it is incurred on or after 1st April 2001, and

    (c) it is not excluded by section 46 (general exclusions).

(2) Energy-saving plant or machinery means plant or machinery in relation to which the following conditions are met—

    (a) when the expenditure is incurred, or

    (b) when the contract for the provision of the plant or machinery is entered into.

(3) The conditions are that the plant or machinery—

    (a) is of a description specified by Treasury order, and

    (b) meets the energy-saving criteria specified by Treasury order for plant or machinery of that description.

(4) Any such order may make provision by reference to any technology list, or product list, issued by the Secretary of State (whether before or after the coming into force of this section).][1]

Commentary—*Simon's Direct Tax Service* **B2.324**.
Cross reference—See FA 2001 Sch 17 para 6 (transitional provisions which broadly permit expenditure incurred from 1 April 2001 to qualify for even though it is incurred before the making of the Treasury order referred to in sub-s (3) above).
See Capital Allowances (Energy-saving Plant and Machinery) Order, SI 2001/2541 art 3 (description of energy-saving plant and machinery).
Amendment—[1] This section inserted by FA 2001 s 65, Sch 17 para 2 with effect as respects allowances and charges falling to be made for chargeable periods ending after 5 April 2001 (for income tax purposes) or 31 March 2001 (for corporation tax purposes).

[45B Certification of energy-saving plant and machinery

(1) The Treasury may by order provide that, in such cases as may be specified in the order, no section 45A allowance may be made unless a relevant certificate of energy efficiency is in force.

A ''section 45A allowance'' means a first-year allowance in respect of expenditure that is first-year qualifying expenditure under section 45A.

(2) A certificate of energy efficiency is one certifying that—

    (a) particular plant or machinery, or

    (b) plant or machinery constructed to a particular design,

meets the energy-saving criteria specified in relation to that description of plant or machinery by order under section 45A.

(3) A relevant certificate of energy efficiency means one issued—

    (a) by the Secretary of State or a person authorised by the Secretary of State;

    (b) in the case of plant or machinery used or for use in Scotland, by the Scottish Ministers or a person authorised by them;

    (c) in the case of plant or machinery used or for use in Wales, by the National Assembly for Wales or a person authorised by it;

    (d) in the case of plant or machinery used or for use in Northern Ireland, by the Department of Enterprise, Trade and Investment in Northern Ireland or a person authorised by it.

(4) If a certificate of energy efficiency is revoked—

    (a) the certificate is to be treated for the purposes of this section as if it had never been issued, and

    (b) all such assessments and adjustments of assessments are to be made as are necessary as a result of the revocation.

(5) If a person who has made a tax return becomes aware that, as a result of the revocation of a certificate of energy efficiency after the return was made, the return has become incorrect, he must give notice to the Inland Revenue specifying how the return needs to be amended.

CAA 2001

(6) The notice must be given within 3 months beginning with the day on which the person first became aware that anything in the tax return had become incorrect because of the revocation of the certificate.][1]

Commentary—*Simon's Direct Tax Service* **B2.324**.
Cross reference—See Capital Allowances (Energy-saving Plant and Machinery) Order, SI 2001/2541 art 4 (certification of energy-saving plant and machinery).
Amendment—[1] This section inserted by FA 2001 s 65, Sch 17 para 2 with effect as respects allowances and charges falling to be made for chargeable periods ending after 5 April 2001 (for income tax purposes) or 31 March 2001 (for corporation tax purposes).

[45C Energy-saving components of plant or machinery

(1) This section applies for the purpose of apportioning expenditure incurred on plant or machinery if one or more components of the plant or machinery (but not all of it) is of a description specified by Treasury order under section 45A(3).

(2) If—

(a) only one of the components is of such a description, and

(b) an amount is specified by the order in respect of that component,

the part of the expenditure that is section 45A expenditure must not exceed that amount.

(3) If—

(a) more than one of the components is of such a description, and

(b) an amount is specified by the order in respect of each of those components,

the part of the expenditure that is section 45A expenditure must not exceed the total of those amounts.

(4) If the expenditure is treated under this Act as incurred in instalments, the proportion of each instalment that is section 45A expenditure is the same as the proportion of the whole of the expenditure that is section 45A expenditure.

(5) If this section applies, the expenditure is not apportioned under section 562(3) (apportionment where property sold with other property).

(6) In this section ''section 45A expenditure'' means expenditure that is first-year qualifying expenditure under section 45A.][1]

Commentary—*Simon's Direct Tax Service* **B2.324**.
Cross reference—See Capital Allowances (Energy-saving Plant and Machinery) Order, SI 2001/2541 art 5 (energy-saving components of plant or machinery).
Amendment—[1] This section inserted by FA 2001 s 65, Sch 17 para 2 with effect as respects allowances and charges falling to be made for chargeable periods ending after 5 April 2001 (for income tax purposes) or 31 March 2001 (for corporation tax purposes).

[45D Expenditure on cars with low carbon dioxide emissions

(1) Expenditure is first-year qualifying expenditure if—

(a) it is incurred in the period beginning with 17th April 2002 and ending with 31st March 2008,

(b) it is expenditure on a car which is first registered on or after 17th April 2002 and which is unused and not second-hand,

(c) the car—

(i) is an electrically-propelled car, or

(ii) is a car with low CO_2 emissions, and

(d) the expenditure is not excluded by section 46 (general exclusions).

(2) For the purposes of this section a car with low CO_2 emissions is a car which satisfies the conditions in subsections (3) and (4).

(3) The first condition is that, when the car is first registered, it is so registered on the basis of an EC certificate of conformity, or a UK approval certificate, that specifies—

(a) in the case of a car other than a bi-fuel car, a CO_2 emissions figure in terms of grams per kilometre driven, or

(b) in the case of a bi-fuel car, separate CO_2 emissions figures in terms of grams per kilometre driven for different fuels.

(4) The second condition is that the applicable CO_2 emissions figure in the case of the car does not exceed 120 grams per kilometre driven.

(5) For the purposes of subsection (4) the applicable CO_2 emissions figure in the case of a car other than a bi-fuel car is—

(a) where the EC certificate of conformity or UK approval certificate specifies only one CO_2 emissions figure, that figure, and

(b) where the certificate specifies more than one CO_2 emissions figure, the figure specified as the CO_2 emissions (combined) figure.

(6) For the purposes of subsection (4) the applicable CO_2 emissions figure in the case of a bi-fuel car is—

(a) where the EC certificate of conformity or UK approval certificate specifies more than one CO_2 emissions figure in relation to each fuel, the lowest CO_2 emissions (combined) figure specified, and

(b) in any other case, the lowest CO_2 figure specified by the certificate.

(7) The Treasury may by order amend the amount from time to time specified in subsection (4).

(8) In this section any reference to a car—

(a) includes a reference to a mechanically propelled road vehicle of a type commonly used as a hackney carriage, but

(b) does not include a reference to a motorcycle.

(9) For the purposes of this section, a car is an electrically-propelled car only if—

(a) it is propelled solely by electrical power, and

(b) that power is derived from—

(i) a source external to the vehicle, or

(ii) an electrical storage battery which is not connected to any source of power when the vehicle is in motion.

(10) In this section—

"bi-fuel car" means a car which is capable of being propelled by—

(a) petrol and road fuel gas, or

(b) diesel and road fuel gas;

"car" has the meaning given by section 81 (extended meaning of "car");

"diesel" means any diesel fuel within the definition in Article 2 of Directive 98/70/EC of the European Parliament and of the Council;

"EC certificate of conformity" means a certificate of conformity issued by a manufacturer under any provision of the law of a Member State implementing Article 6 of Council Directive 70/156/EEC, as amended;

"petrol" has the meaning given by Article 2 of Directive 98/70/ EC of the European Parliament and of the Council;

"road fuel gas" has the same meaning as in section 168AB of ICTA;

"UK approval certificate" means a certificate issued under—

(a) section 58(1) or (4) of the Road Traffic Act 1988, or

(b) Article 31A(4) or (5) of the Road Traffic (Northern Ireland) Order 1981][1]

Amendments—[1] Section inserted by FA 2002 s 59, Sch 19 paras 1, 3 with effect for expenditure incurred after 16 April 2002.

[45E Expenditure on plant or machinery for gas refuelling station

(1) Expenditure is first-year qualifying expenditure if—

(a) it is incurred in the period beginning with 17th April 2002 and ending with 31st March 2008,

(b) it is expenditure on plant or machinery for a gas refuelling station where the plant or machinery is unused and not second-hand, and

(c) it is not excluded by section 46 (general exclusions).

(2) For the purposes of this section expenditure on plant or machinery for a gas refuelling station is expenditure on plant or machinery installed at a gas refuelling station for use solely for or in connection with refuelling vehicles with natural gas or hydrogen fuel.

(3) For the purposes of subsection (2) the plant or machinery which is for use for or in connection with refuelling vehicles with natural gas or hydrogen fuel includes—

(a) any storage tank for natural gas or hydrogen fuel,

(b) any compressor, pump, control or meter used for or in connection with refuelling vehicles with natural gas or hydrogen fuel, and

(c) any equipment for dispensing natural gas or hydrogen fuel to the fuel tank of a vehicle.

(4) For the purposes of this section—

"gas refuelling station" means any premises, or that part of any premises, where vehicles are refuelled with natural gas or hydrogen fuel;

"hydrogen fuel" means a fuel consisting of gaseous or cryogenic liquid hydrogen which is used for propelling vehicles; and

"vehicle" means a mechanically propelled road vehicle.][1]

Amendments—[1] Section inserted by FA 2002 s 61, Sch 20 paras 1, 3 with effect for expenditure incurred after 16 April 2002.

[45F Expenditure on plant and machinery for use wholly in a ring fence trade

(1) Expenditure is first-year qualifying expenditure if—

(a) it is incurred on or after 17th April 2002,

(b) it is incurred by a company,

(c) it is incurred on the provision of plant or machinery for use wholly for the purposes of a ring fence trade, and

(d) it is not excluded by section 46 (general exclusions).

(2) This section is subject to section 45G (plant or machinery used for less than five years in a ring fence trade).

(3) In this section ''ring fence trade'' means a ring fence trade in respect of which tax is chargeable under section 501A of the Taxes Act 1988 (supplementary charge in respect of ring fence trades).][1]

Amendments—[1] Section inserted by FA 2002 s 63, Sch 21 paras 1, 3 with effect for expenditure incurred after 16 April 2002.

[45G Plant or machinery used for less than five years in a ring fence trade

(1) Expenditure incurred by a company on the provision of plant or machinery is to be treated as never having been first-year qualifying expenditure under section 45F if the plant or machinery—

(a) is at no time in the relevant period used in a ring fence trade carried on by the company or a company connected with it, or

(b) is at any time in the relevant period used for a purpose other than that of a ring fence trade carried on by the company or a company connected with it.

(2) For the purposes of this section ''the relevant period'' means whichever of the following periods, beginning with the incurring of the expenditure, first ends, namely—

(a) the period ending with the fifth anniversary of the incurring of the expenditure, or

(b) the period ending with the day preceding the first occasion on which the plant or machinery, after becoming owned by the company which incurred the expenditure, is not owned by a company which is either that company or a company connected with it.

(3) All such assessments and adjustments of assessments are to be made as are necessary to give effect to subsection (1).

(4) If a person who has made a return becomes aware that, after making it, anything in it has become incorrect because of the operation of this section, he must give notice to the Inland Revenue specifying how the return needs to be amended.

(5) The notice must be given within 3 months beginning with the day on which the person first became aware that anything in the return had become incorrect because of the operation of this section.

(6) In this section ''ring fence trade'' has the same meaning as in section 45F.][1]

Amendments—[1] Section inserted by FA 2002 s 63, Sch 21 paras 1, 4 with effect for expenditure incurred after 16 April 2002.

46 General exclusions applying to sections 40, 44 and 45

(1) Expenditure within any of the general exclusions in subsection (2) is not first-year qualifying expenditure under—

section 40   (expenditure incurred for Northern Ireland purposes by small or medium-sized enterprises),

section 44   (expenditure incurred by small or medium-sized enterprises), ...[2]

section 45   (ICT expenditure incurred by small enterprises)...[7]

section 45A   (expenditure on energy-saving plant or machinery).][1]

[section 45D   (expenditure on cars with low CO_2 emissions),][3]

[section 45E   (expenditure on plant or machinery for gas refuelling station)][4][, or

section 45F   (expenditure on plant and machinery for use wholly in a ring fence trade).][6]

(2) The general exclusions are—

General exclusion 1
The expenditure is incurred in the chargeable period in which the qualifying activity is permanently discontinued.

General exclusion 2
The expenditure is incurred on the provision of a car (as defined by section 81).

General exclusion 3
The expenditure is of the kind described in section 94 (ships).

General exclusion 4
The expenditure is of the kind described in section 95 (railway assets).

General exclusion 5
The expenditure would be long-life asset expenditure but for paragraph 20 of Schedule 3 (transitional provisions).

General exclusion 6
The expenditure is on the provision of plant or machinery for leasing (whether in the course of a trade or otherwise).
For this purpose, the letting of a ship on charter, or of any other asset on hire, is to be regarded as leasing (whether or not it would otherwise be so regarded).

General exclusion 7
The circumstances of the incurring of the expenditure are that—

(*a*) the provision of the plant or machinery on which the expenditure is incurred is connected with a change in the nature or conduct of a trade or business carried on by a person other than the person incurring the expenditure, and

(*b*) the obtaining of a first-year allowance is the main benefit, or one of the main benefits, which could reasonably be expected to arise from the making of the change.

General exclusion 8

Either of the following sections applies—

section 13 (use for qualifying activity of plant or machinery provided for other purposes);
section 14 (use for qualifying activity of plant or machinery which is a gift).

This is subject to section 161 (pre-trading expenditure on mineral exploration and access).

[(3) Subsection (1) is subject to the following provisions of this section.][3]

[(4) General exclusion 2 does not prevent expenditure being first-year qualifying expenditure under section 45D.][3]

[(5) General exclusion 6 does not prevent expenditure being first-year qualifying expenditure under section 45A, 45D or 45E.][5]

Commentary—*Simon's Direct Tax Service* **B2.325**.
Former enactments—Sub-s (2): CAA 1990 22(6B), (6C), s 38B(2)–(4), s 50(2), s 81(1).
Definition—"Chargeable period", s 6.
Modifications—CAA 2001 Sch 3 para 54 (vehicles provided by employees in 1990–91: see modification note at the start of this Part).
CAA 2001 Sch 3 para 55 (certain expenditure incurred before 6 April 1976: see modification note at the start of this Part).
Amendment—[1] Words inserted by FA 2001 s 65, Sch 17 para 3 with effect as respects allowances and charges falling to be made for chargeable periods ending after 5 April 2001 (for income tax purposes) or 31 March 2001 (for corporation tax purposes).
[2] Word "or" repealed by FA 2001 s 110, Sch 33 Pt II(4) with effect as respects allowances and charges falling to be made for chargeable periods ending after 5 April 2001 (for income tax purposes) or 31 March 2001 (for corporation tax purposes).
[3] Words in sub-s (1) inserted, and sub-ss (3), (4) inserted, by FA 2002 s 59, Sch 19 paras 1, 4 with effect for expenditure incurred after 16 April 2002.
[4] Words in sub-s (1) inserted by FA 2002 s 61, Sch 20 paras 1, 4 with effect for expenditure incurred after 16 April 2002.
[5] Sub-s (5) added by FA 2002 s 62 with effect for expenditure incurred after 16 April 2002.
[6] Words in sub-s (1) inserted by FA 2002 s 63, Sch 21 paras 1, 5 with effect for expenditure incurred after 16 April 2002.
[7] Word "or" repealed by FA 2002 s 141, Sch 40 Pt 3(7) with effect for expenditure incurred after 16 April 2002.

Expenditure of small or medium-sized enterprises

47 Expenditure of small or medium-sized enterprises: companies

(1) Use this section to decide whether expenditure incurred by a company is, for the purposes of this Chapter, incurred by—

(*a*) a small or medium-sized enterprise, or
(*b*) a small enterprise.

(2) The expenditure is incurred by a small or medium-sized enterprise if the company—

(*a*) qualifies (or is treated as qualifying) as small or medium-sized under the relevant companies legislation in relation to the financial year of the company in which the expenditure is incurred, and
(*b*) is not a member of a large group at the time when the expenditure is incurred.

(3) The expenditure is incurred by a small enterprise if the company—

(*a*) qualifies (or is treated as qualifying) as small under the relevant companies legislation in relation to the financial year of the company in which the expenditure is incurred, and
(*b*) is not a member of a large or medium-sized group at the time when the expenditure is incurred.

(4) Except in the case of a company formed and registered in Northern Ireland—

(*a*) "the relevant companies legislation" means section 247 of the Companies Act 1985, and
(*b*) "financial year" has the same meaning as in Part VII of the 1985 Act.

(5) In the case of such a company—

(*a*) "the relevant companies legislation" means Article 255 of the Companies (Northern Ireland) Order 1986, and
(*b*) "financial year" has the same meaning as in Part VIII of the 1986 Order.

(6) "Company" means—

(*a*) a company, or an overseas company, within the meaning of the 1985 Act, or
(*b*) a company, or a Part XXIII company, within the meaning of the 1986 Order.

Commentary—*Simon's Direct Tax Service* **B2.326**.
Former enactments—Sub-s (1): CAA 1990 ss 22A(1), 22AA(1).
Sub-s (2): CAA 1990 s 22A(1), (7).
Sub-s (3): CAA 1990 s 22AA (1), (7).
Sub-ss (4), (5): CAA 1990 ss 22A(6), (7), 22AA(6), (7).
Sub-s (6): CAA 1990 ss 22A(6), 22AA(6).
Modifications—CAA 2001 Sch 3 para 54 (vehicles provided by employees in 1990–91: see modification note at the start of this Part).
CAA 2001 Sch 3 para 55 (certain expenditure incurred before 6 April 1976: see modification note at the start of this Part).

48 Expenditure of small or medium-sized enterprises: businesses

(1) Use this section to decide whether expenditure incurred by a business is, for the purposes of this Chapter, incurred by—

    (*a*) a small or medium-sized enterprise, or

    (*b*) a small enterprise.

(2) In this section ''business'' means—

    (*a*) an individual,

    (*b*) a partnership of which all the members are individuals,

    (*c*) a registered friendly society within the meaning of Chapter II of Part XII of ICTA, or

    (*d*) a body corporate which is not a company but is within the charge to corporation tax.

(3) The expenditure is incurred by a small or medium-sized enterprise if—

    (*a*) the expenditure is incurred for the purposes of a qualifying activity carried on by the business, and

    (*b*) the business passes the hypothetical company test, in relation to that expenditure, as a small or medium-sized company.

(4) The expenditure is incurred by a small enterprise if—

    (*a*) the expenditure is incurred for the purposes of a qualifying activity carried on by the business, and

    (*b*) the business passes the hypothetical company test, in relation to that expenditure, as a small company.

(5) To apply the hypothetical company test, assume that—

    (*a*) the qualifying activity is carried on by a company (''the hypothetical company''),

    (*b*) every trade, business, profession or vocation carried on by the business is carried on by the business as part of that activity,

    (*c*) the financial years of the hypothetical company coincide with the chargeable periods of the business, and

    (*d*) accounts of the hypothetical company for any relevant chargeable period have been duly drawn up as if that period were a financial year of the company.

(6) The business passes the hypothetical company test as a small or medium-sized company in relation to the expenditure in question if, on the assumptions in subsection (5), the company would qualify (or be treated as qualifying) as small or medium-sized under the relevant companies legislation in relation to the financial year in which the expenditure is assumed to be incurred.

(7) The business passes the hypothetical company test as a small company in relation to the expenditure in question if, on the assumptions in subsection (5), the company would qualify (or be treated as qualifying) as small under the relevant companies legislation in relation to the financial year in which the expenditure is assumed to be incurred.

(8) Except in the case of a business carrying on a qualifying activity wholly or mainly in Northern Ireland—

    (*a*) ''the relevant companies legislation'' means section 247 of the Companies Act 1985, and

    (*b*) ''financial year'' has the same meaning as in Part VII of that Act;

and the reference in subsection (5)(*d*) to accounts being duly drawn up is to their being drawn up in accordance with that Act.

(9) In the case of such a business—

    (*a*) ''the relevant companies legislation'' means Article 255 of the Companies (Northern Ireland) Order 1986, and

    (*b*) ''financial year'' has the same meaning as in Part VIII of that Order;

and the reference in subsection (5)(*d*) to accounts being duly drawn up is to their being drawn up in accordance with that Order.

Commentary—*Simon's Direct Tax Service* B2.326.
Former enactments—Sub-s (1): CAA 1990 ss 22A(2), 22AA(2).
Sub-s (2): CAA 1990 ss 22A(6), 22AA(6).
Sub-s (3): CAA 1990 s 22A(2).
Sub-s (4): CAA 1990 s .22AA(2).
Sub-s (5): CAA 1990 ss 22A(2), (3), 22AA(2), (3).
Sub-s (6): CAA 1990 s 22A(2).
Sub-s (7): CAA 1990 s 22AA(2).
Sub-ss (8), (9): CAA 1990 s 22A(3), (6), (7), s 22AA(3), (6), (7); change in law.
Definition—''Chargeable period'', s 6.
Modifications—CAA 2001 Sch 3 para 54 (vehicles provided by employees in 1990–91: see modification note at the start of this Part).
CAA 2001 Sch 3 para 55 (certain expenditure incurred before 6 April 1976: see modification note at the start of this Part).

49 Whether company is a member of a large or medium-sized group

(1) Use this section to decide whether, for the purposes of section 47, a company is—

    (*a*) a member of a large group, or

    (*b*) a member of a large or medium-sized group.

(2) Subject to subsection (4), a company is a member of a large group at the time when any expenditure is incurred if—

(a) it is at that time the parent undertaking of a group which does not qualify as small or medium-sized in relation to the financial year of the parent undertaking in which that time falls, or

(b) it is at that time a subsidiary undertaking in relation to the parent undertaking of such a group.

(3) Subject to subsection (4), a company is a member of a large or medium-sized group at the time when any expenditure is incurred if—

(a) it is at that time the parent undertaking of a group which does not qualify as small in relation to the financial year of the parent undertaking in which that time falls, or

(b) it is at that time a subsidiary undertaking in relation to the parent undertaking of such a group.

(4) If, at the time when any expenditure is incurred by a company, any arrangements exist which are such that, had effect been given to them immediately before that time, the company or a successor of the company—

(a) would, at that time, have been a member of a large group, or

(b) would, at that time, have been a member of a large or medium-sized group,

the company incurring the expenditure is to be treated as a member of a large group or (as the case may be) a large or medium-sized group at that time.

(5) For the purposes of subsections (2) and (3), the question whether—

(a) a group qualifies as small or medium-sized, or

(b) a group qualifies as small,

is to be decided by reference to the relevant companies legislation (but reading references in that legislation to a parent company as references to a parent undertaking).

(6) In subsection (5) "the relevant companies legislation" means—

(a) except in the case of a company formed and registered in Northern Ireland, section 249 of the Companies Act 1985;

(b) in the case of such a company, Article 257 of the Companies (Northern Ireland) Order 1986.

(7) For the purposes of subsection (4) a company is the successor of another if—

(a) it carries on a trade which, in whole or in part, the other company has ceased to carry on, and

(b) the circumstances are such that section 343 of ICTA (company reconstructions without a change of ownership) applies in relation to the two companies as the predecessor and the successor within the meaning of that section,

and "arrangements" means arrangements of any kind (whether or not in writing or legally enforceable).

(8) In this section "financial year", "group", "parent undertaking" and "subsidiary undertaking" have the same meaning as in—

(a) except in the case of a company formed and registered in Northern Ireland, Part VII of the 1985 Act;

(b) in the case of such a company, Part VIII of the 1986 Order.

Commentary—*Simon's Direct Tax Service* **B2.326**.
Former enactments—Sub-s (2): CAA 1990 s 22A(4).
Sub-s (3): CAA 1990 s 22AA(4).
Sub-s (4): CAA 1990 ss 22A(5), 22AA(5).
Sub-ss (5), (6): CAA 1990 ss 22A(8), 22AA(8).
Sub-s (7): CAA 1990 ss 22A(6), (9), 22AA(6), (9).
Sub-s (8): CAA 1990 ss 22A(6), 22AA(6).
Modifications—CAA 2001 Sch 3 para 49 (modification of sub-paras (2), (5) in relation to any expenditure incurred before 12 May 1998, and for the purpose of determining whether expenditure incurred under a contract entered into before that date is first-year qualifying expenditure under CAA 2001 s 44, or whether expenditure is first-year qualifying expenditure under CAA 2001 Sch 3 para 46 or 48).
CAA 2001 Sch 3 para 54 (vehicles provided by employees in 1990–91: see modification note at the start of this Part).
CAA 2001 Sch 3 para 55 (certain expenditure incurred before 6 April 1976: see modification note at the start of this Part).

Supplementary

50 Time when expenditure is incurred

In determining whether expenditure is first-year qualifying expenditure under this Chapter, any effect of section 12 on the time at which it is to be treated as incurred is to be disregarded.

Commentary—*Simon's Direct Tax Service* **B2.320**.
Former enactments—CAA 1990 s 22(3B), (3C), (3CB), (3D), (3E).
Revenue Internal Guidance—Capital allowances manual CA 11750 (expenditure incurred in foreign currency: date of translation into sterling).
Modifications—CAA 2001 Sch 3 para 54 (vehicles provided by employees in 1990–91: see modification note at the start of this Part).
CAA 2001 Sch 3 para 55 (certain expenditure incurred before 6 April 1976: see modification note at the start of this Part).

51 Disclosure of information between UK tax authorities

(1) No obligation as to secrecy or other restriction on the disclosure of information imposed by statute or otherwise prevents—

(a) the Inland Revenue from disclosing information, for the purpose given in subsection (2), to the Department of Agriculture and Rural Development in Northern Ireland ("the Department") or an authorised officer of the Department, or

(b) the Department or an authorised officer of the Department from disclosing information for that purpose to the Inland Revenue.

(2) The purpose is assisting—

(a) the Board of Inland Revenue, in carrying out its functions relating to allowances made because of section 40 (expenditure incurred for Northern Ireland purposes by small or medium-sized enterprises), or

(b) the Department, in carrying out its functions under this Chapter.

(3) Information obtained as a result of a disclosure authorised by this section must not be disclosed except—

(a) to the Inland Revenue, the Department or an authorised officer of the Department, or

(b) for the purposes of any proceedings connected with a matter in relation to which the Board of Inland Revenue or the Department carry out the functions mentioned in subsection (2)(a) or (b).

Commentary—*Simon's Direct Tax Service* **B2.320**.
Former enactments—Sub-s (1): CAA 1990 s 22C(1); Departments (Northern Ireland) Order, SI 1999/283, art 3, Sch 1.
Sub-s (2): CAA 1990 s 22C(1).
Sub-s (3): CAA 1990 s 22C(2).
Modifications—CAA 2001 Sch 3 para 54 (vehicles provided by employees in 1990–91: see modification note at the start of this Part).
CAA 2001 Sch 3 para 55 (certain expenditure incurred before 6 April 1976: see modification note at the start of this Part).

CHAPTER 5
ALLOWANCES AND CHARGES
First-year allowances

52 First-year allowances

(1) A person is entitled to a first-year allowance in respect of first-year qualifying expenditure if—

(a) the expenditure is incurred in a chargeable period to which this Act applies, and

(b) the person owns the plant or machinery at some time during that chargeable period.

(2) Any first-year allowance is made for the chargeable period in which the first-year qualifying expenditure is incurred.

(3) The amount of the allowance is a percentage of the first-year qualifying expenditure in respect of which the allowance is made, as shown in the Table—

TABLE
AMOUNT OF FIRST-YEAR ALLOWANCES

Type of first-year qualifying expenditure	Amount
Expenditure qualifying under section 40 (expenditure incurred for Northern Ireland purposes by small or medium-sized enterprises)	100%
Expenditure qualifying under section 44 (expenditure incurred by small or medium-sized enterprises)	40%
Expenditure qualifying under section 45 (ICT expenditure incurred by small enterprises)	100%
[Expenditure qualifying under section 45A (expenditure on energy-saving plant or machinery)	100%][1]
[Expenditure qualifying under section 45D (expenditure on cars with low CO_2 emissions)	100%][2]
[Expenditure qualifying under section 45E (expenditure on plant or machinery for gas refuelling station)	100%][3]
[Expenditure qualifying under section 45F (expenditure on plant and machinery for use wholly in a ring fence trade) which is long-life asset expenditure	24%][4]
[Expenditure qualifying under section 45F (expenditure on plant and machinery for use wholly in a ring fence trade) other than long-life asset expenditure	100%][4].

(4) A person who is entitled to a first-year allowance may claim the allowance in respect of the whole or a part of the first-year qualifying expenditure.

(5) Subsection (1) needs to be read with section 236 (first-year allowances in respect of additional VAT liabilities) and is subject to—

section 205 (reduction of first-year allowance if plant or machinery provided partly for purposes other than those of qualifying activity),

section 210 (reduction of first-year allowance if it appears that a partial depreciation subsidy is or will be payable), and

sections 217, 223 and 241 (anti-avoidance: no first-year allowance in certain cases).

Commentary—*Simon's Direct Tax Service* **B2.330**.
Definitions—"Chargeable period", s 6; "partial depreciation subsidy", s 209.
Modifications—CAA 2001 Sch 3 para 54 (vehicles provided by employees in 1990–91: see modification note at the start of this Part).
CAA 2001 Sch 3 para 55 (certain expenditure incurred before 6 April 1976: see modification note at the start of this Part).
Amendment—[1] Words inserted by FA 2001 s 65, Sch 17 para 4 with effect as respects allowances and charges falling to be made for chargeable periods ending after 5 April 2001 (for income tax purposes) or 31 March 2001 (for corporation tax purposes).
[2] Words inserted by FA 2002 s 59, Sch 19 paras 1, 5 with effect for expenditure incurred after 16 April 2002.
[3] Words inserted by FA 2002 s 61, Sch 20 paras 1, 5 with effect for expenditure incurred after 16 April 2002.
[4] Words inserted by FA 2002 s 63, Sch 21 paras 1, 6 with effect for expenditure incurred after 16 April 2002.

Pooling

53 Pooling of qualifying expenditure

(1) Qualifying expenditure has to be pooled for the purpose of determining a person's entitlement to writing-down allowances and balancing allowances and liability to balancing charges.

(2) If a person carries on more than one qualifying activity, expenditure relating to the different activities must not be allocated to the same pool.

Commentary—*Simon's Direct Tax Service* **B2.331**.
Modifications—CAA 2001 Sch 3 para 54 (vehicles provided by employees in 1990–91: see modification note at the start of this Part).
CAA 2001 Sch 3 para 55 (certain expenditure incurred before 6 April 1976: see modification note at the start of this Part).

54 The different kinds of pools

(1) There are single asset pools, class pools and the main pool.

(2) A single asset pool may not contain expenditure relating to more than one asset.

(3) The following provide for qualifying expenditure to be allocated to a single asset pool—
    section 74 (car above the cost threshold);
    section 86 (short-life asset);
    section 127 (ship);
    section 206 (plant or machinery provided or used partly for purposes other than those of qualifying activity);
    section 211 (payment of partial depreciation subsidy);
    section 538 (contribution allowances: plant and machinery).

(4) A class pool is a pool which may contain expenditure relating to more than one asset.

(5) The following provide for qualifying expenditure to be allocated to a class pool—
    section 101 (long-life assets);
    section 107 (overseas leasing).

(6) Qualifying expenditure may be allocated to the main pool only if it does not fall to be allocated to a single asset pool or a class pool.

Commentary—*Simon's Direct Tax Service* **B2.331**.
Modifications—CAA 2001 Sch 3 para 54 (vehicles provided by employees in 1990–91: see modification note at the start of this Part).
CAA 2001 Sch 3 para 55 (certain expenditure incurred before 6 April 1976: see modification note at the start of this Part).

Writing-down and balancing allowances and balancing charges

55 Determination of entitlement or liability

(1) Whether a person is entitled to a writing-down allowance or a balancing allowance, or liable to a balancing charge, for a chargeable period is determined separately for each pool of qualifying expenditure and depends on—
    (*a*) the available qualifying expenditure in that pool for that period ("AQE"), and
    (*b*) the total of any disposal receipts to be brought into account in that pool for that period ("TDR").

(2) If AQE exceeds TDR, the person is entitled to a writing-down allowance or a balancing allowance for the period.

(3) If TDR exceeds AQE, the person is liable to a balancing charge for the period.

(4) The entitlement under subsection (2) is to a writing-down allowance except for the final chargeable period when it is to a balancing allowance.

(5) The final chargeable period is given by section 65.

(6) Subsection (2) is subject to section 110(1) (overseas leasing: allowances prohibited in certain cases).

Commentary—*Simon's Direct Tax Service* **B2.332**.
Former enactments—Sub-ss (1), (2): CAA 1990 24(2).
Sub-s (3): CAA 1990 s 24(5).
Sub-s (4): CAA 1990 s 24(2).
Definitions—"Available qualifying expenditure", s 57; "chargeable period", s 6; "disposal receipt" s 60(1).

Modifications—CAA 2001 Sch 3 para 54 (vehicles provided by employees in 1990–91: see modification note at the start of this Part).
CAA 2001 Sch 3 para 55 (certain expenditure incurred before 6 April 1976: see modification note at the start of this Part).

56 Amount of allowances and charges

(1) The amount of the writing-down allowance to which a person is entitled for a chargeable period is 25% of the amount by which AQE exceeds TDR.

(2) Subsection (1) is subject to—

   (a) section 102 (long-life asset expenditure: 6%), and

   (b) section 109 (overseas leasing: 10%).

(3) If the chargeable period is more or less than a year, the amount is proportionately increased or reduced.

(4) If the qualifying activity has been carried on for part only of the chargeable period, the amount is proportionately reduced.

(5) A person claiming a writing-down allowance may require the allowance to be reduced to a specified amount.

(6) The amount of the balancing charge to which a person is liable for a chargeable period is the amount by which TDR exceeds AQE.

(7) The amount of the balancing allowance to which a person is entitled for the final chargeable period is the amount by which AQE exceeds TDR.

Commentary—*Simon's Direct Tax Service* B2.332.
Former enactments—Sub-s (1): CAA 1990 s 24(2)(a).
Sub-ss (3), (4): CAA 1990 s 24(2)(a)(ii).
Sub-s (5): CAA 1990 s 24(3).
Sub-s (6): CAA 1990 s 24(5).
Sub-s (7): CAA 1990 s 24(2)(b).
Definitions—"Chargeable period", s 6; "final chargeable period", s 65.
Modifications—CAA 2001 Sch 3 para 54 (vehicles provided by employees in 1990–91: see modification note at the start of this Part).
CAA 2001 Sch 3 para 55 (certain expenditure incurred before 6 April 1976: see modification note at the start of this Part).

Available qualifying expenditure

57 Available qualifying expenditure

(1) The general rule is that a person's available qualifying expenditure in a pool for a chargeable period consists of—

   (a) any qualifying expenditure allocated to the pool for that period in accordance with section 58, and

   (b) any unrelieved qualifying expenditure carried forward in the pool from the previous chargeable period under section 59.

(2) A person's available qualifying expenditure in a pool for a chargeable period also includes any amount allocated to the pool for that period under—

   section 26(3) (net costs of demolition);

   section 86(2) or 87(2) (allocation of expenditure in short-life asset pool);

   section 111(3) (overseas leasing: standard recovery mechanism);

   section 129(1), 132(2), 133(3) or 137 (provisions relating to operation of single ship pool and deferment of balancing charges in respect of ships);

   [section 161C(2) (decommissioning expenditure incurred by person carrying on trade of oil extraction);][1]

   section 165(3) (abandonment expenditure incurred after cessation of ring fence trade);

   section 206(3) (plant or machinery used partly for purposes other than those of the qualifying activity);

   section 211(4) (partial depreciation subsidy paid).

(3) A person's available qualifying expenditure does not include any expenditure excluded by—

   section 8(4) or 9(1) (rules against double relief);

   section 166(2) (transfers of interests in oil fields: anti-avoidance);

   section 185(2), 186(2) or 187(2) (restrictions where other claims made in respect of fixture);

   section 218(1), 224(1), 228(2), 242(2), or 243(2) (general anti-avoidance provisions).

(4) Subsection (1) is also subject to section 220 (allocation to chargeable periods of expenditure incurred on plant or machinery for leasing under finance lease).

Commentary—*Simon's Direct Tax Service* B2.333.
Former enactments—Sub-s (1): CAA 1990 25(1).
Definitions—"Chargeable period", s 6; "unrelieved qualifying expenditure", s 59.
Modifications—CAA 2001 Sch 3 para 54 (vehicles provided by employees in 1990–91: see modification note at the start of this Part).
CAA 2001 Sch 3 para 55 (certain expenditure incurred before 6 April 1976: see modification note at the start of this Part).
Amendment—[1] Words inserted by FA 2001 s 68, Sch 20 Pt II paras 5, 9 with effect for—

   (a) expenditure incurred after 6 August 2000 and in a relevant chargeable period; or

   (b) expenditure incurred before 7 August 2000, if the expenditure is incurred in a relevant chargeable period and is either—

(i) decommissioning expenditure on UK infrastructure and is incurred in connection with an abandonment programme approved after 6 August 2000; or
(ii) decommissioning expenditure, is not decommissioning expenditure on UK infrastruture, and is incurred in connection with a decommissioning activity that takes place after 6 August 2000.
For these purposes, "relevant chargeable period" is a chargeable period ending after 5 April 2001 (for income tax purposes) or 31 March 2001 (for corporation tax purposes). "Decommissioning expenditure" and "decommissioning expenditure on UK infrastructure" have the same meaning as in CAA 2001 ss 161C, 161D. "Decommissioning activity" means an activity mentioned in CAA 2001 s 161B(1)(*a*)–(*c*).

58 Initial allocation of qualifying expenditure to pools

(1) The following rules apply to the allocation of a person's qualifying expenditure to the appropriate pool.

(2) An amount of qualifying expenditure is not to be allocated to a pool for a chargeable period if that amount has been taken into account in determining the person's available qualifying expenditure for an earlier chargeable period.

(3) Qualifying expenditure is not to be allocated to a pool for a chargeable period before that in which the expenditure is incurred.

(4) Qualifying expenditure is not to be allocated to a pool for a chargeable period unless the person owns the plant or machinery at some time in that period.

(5) If a first-year allowance is made in respect of an amount of first-year qualifying expenditure—
(*a*) subject to subsection (6), none of that amount is to be allocated to a pool for the chargeable period in which the expenditure is incurred, and
(*b*) the amount that may be allocated to a pool for any chargeable period is limited to the balance left after deducting the first-year allowance.

(6) If—
(*a*) a first-year allowance is made in respect of an amount of first-year qualifying expenditure,
(*b*) a disposal event occurs in respect of the plant or machinery in any chargeable period, and
(*c*) none of the balance left after deducting the first-year allowance has been allocated to a pool for an earlier chargeable period,
the balance (or some of it) must be allocated to a pool for the chargeable period in which the disposal event occurs.

(7) Subsection (6) applies even if the balance is nil (because of a 100% first-year allowance).

(8) "The appropriate pool" means whichever pool is applicable under the provisions of this Part apart from this section.

Commentary—*Simon's Direct Tax Service* B2.333.
Former enactments—Sub-ss (2), (3): CAA 1990 s 25(1).
Sub-s (4): FA 1994 s 118(6).
Sub-s (5): CAA 1990 s 25(1), (3), (4).
Sub-s (6): CAA 1990 s 24(6), (8), s 25(5).
Revenue Internal Guidance—Capital allowances manual CA 23010–23080 (meaning of "qualifying expenditure" with examples).
Definitions—"Available qualifying expenditure", s 57; "chargeable period", s 6; "disposal event", s 60(2).
Modifications—CAA 2001 Sch 3 para 54 (vehicles provided by employees in 1990–91: see modification note at the start of this Part).
CAA 2001 Sch 3 para 55 (certain expenditure incurred before 6 April 1976: see modification note at the start of this Part).

59 Unrelieved qualifying expenditure

(1) A person has unrelieved qualifying expenditure to carry forward from a chargeable period if for that period AQE exceeds TDR.

(2) The amount of the unrelieved qualifying expenditure is—
(*a*) the excess less the writing-down allowance made for the period, or
(*b*) if no writing-down allowance is claimed for the period, the excess.

(3) No amount may be carried forward as unrelieved qualifying expenditure from the final chargeable period.

Commentary—*Simon's Direct Tax Service* B2.333.
Former enactments—Sub-ss (1), (2): CAA 1990 s 25(1)(*b*).
Sub-s (3): CAA 1990 s 24(1).
Definitions—"Chargeable period", s 6; "final chargeable period", s 65.
Modifications—CAA 2001 Sch 3 para 54 (vehicles provided by employees in 1990–91: see modification note at the start of this Part).
CAA 2001 Sch 3 para 55 (certain expenditure incurred before 6 April 1976: see modification note at the start of this Part).

Disposal events and disposal values: general

60 Meaning of "disposal receipt" and "disposal event"

(1) In this Part "disposal receipt" means a disposal value that a person is required to bring into account in accordance with—
(*a*) sections 61, 62 and 63 (disposal events, disposal values and the general limit on the amount of a disposal value),

(*b*) any of the provisions of this Part listed in section 66, or

(*c*) paragraph 11 of Schedule 12 to FA 1997 (finance lease or loan: receipt of major lump sum) or any other enactment,

when read with sections 64 and 264(3) (cases in which no disposal value need be brought into account).

(2) In this Part "disposal event" means any event of a kind that requires a disposal value to be brought into account under this Part (whether under section 61(1) or otherwise).

(3) If—

(*a*) qualifying expenditure has been allocated to a pool, and

(*b*) more than one disposal event occurs in respect of the plant or machinery,

a disposal value is required to be brought into account in the pool in connection with the first event only.

(4) In subsection (3) "disposal event" does not include a disposal event arising under—

section 72 (computer software),

sections 140 and 143 (attribution of deferred balancing charge), or

section 238(2) (additional VAT rebates).

Commentary—*Simon's Direct Tax Service* **B2.334**.
Former enactments—Sub-s (3): CAA 1990 s 24(6); change in law.
Modifications—CAA 2001 Sch 3 para 54 (vehicles provided by employees in 1990–91: see modification note at the start of this Part).
CAA 2001 Sch 3 para 55 (certain expenditure incurred before 6 April 1976: see modification note at the start of this Part).

61 Disposal events and disposal values

(1) A person who has incurred qualifying expenditure is required to bring the disposal value of the plant or machinery into account for the chargeable period in which—

(*a*) the person ceases to own the plant or machinery;

(*b*) the person loses possession of the plant or machinery in circumstances where it is reasonable to assume that the loss is permanent;

(*c*) the plant or machinery has been in use for mineral exploration and access and the person abandons it at the site where it was in use for that purpose;

(*d*) the plant or machinery ceases to exist as such (as a result of destruction, dismantling or otherwise);

(*e*) the plant or machinery begins to be used wholly or partly for purposes other than those of the qualifying activity;

(*f*) the qualifying activity is permanently discontinued.

(2) The disposal value to be brought into account depends on the disposal event, as shown in the Table—

TABLE
DISPOSAL VALUES: GENERAL

1. Disposal event	2. Disposal value
1. Sale of the plant or machinery, except in a case where item 2 applies.	The net proceeds of the sale, together with— (*a*) any insurance money received in respect of the plant or machinery as a result of an event affecting the price obtainable on the sale, and (*b*) any other compensation of any description so received, so far as it consists of capital sums.
2. Sale of the plant or machinery where— (*a*) the sale is at less than market value, (*b*) there is no charge to tax under Schedule E, and (*c*) the condition in subsection (4) is met by the buyer.	The market value of the plant or machinery at the time of the sale.
3. Demolition or destruction of the plant or machinery.	The net amount received for the remains of the plant or machinery, together with— (*a*) any insurance money received in respect of the demolition or destruction, and (*b*) any other compensation of any description so received, so far as it consists of capital sums.
4. Permanent loss of the plant or machinery otherwise than as a result of its demolition or destruction.	Any insurance money received in respect of the loss and, so far as it consists of capital sums, any other compensation of any description so received.

1. Disposal event	2. Disposal value
5. Abandonment of the plant or machinery which has been in use for mineral exploration and access at the site where it was in use for that purpose.	Any insurance money received in respect of the abandonment and, so far as it consists of capital sums, any other compensation of any description so received.
6. Permanent discontinuance of the qualifying activity followed by the occurrence of an event within any of items 1 to 5.	The disposal value for the item in question.
7. Any event not falling within any of items 1 to 6.	The market value of the plant or machinery at the time of the event.

(3) The amounts referred to in column 2 of the Table are those received by the person required to bring the disposal value into account.

(4) The condition referred to in item 2 of the Table is met by the buyer if—

    (*a*) the buyer's expenditure on the acquisition of the plant or machinery cannot be qualifying expenditure under this Part or Part 6 (research and development allowances), or

    (*b*) the buyer is a dual resident investing company which is connected with the seller.

(5) In this section "mineral exploration and access" has the same meaning as in Chapter 13 (provisions affecting the mining and oil industries) and Part 5 (mineral extraction allowances).

Commentary—*Simon's Direct Tax Service* **B2.334**.
Former enactments—Sub-s (1): CAA 1990 s 24(6).
Sub-s (2): CAA 1990 ss 24(6), 26(1).
Table, item 1: CAA 1990 s 26(1)(*a*).
Table, item 2: CAA 1990 s 26(1)(*b*).
Table, item 3: CAA 1990 s 26(1)(*c*).
Table, item 4: CAA 1990 s 26(1)(*d*).
Table, item 5: change in law.
Table, item 6: CAA 1990 s 26(1)(*e*).
Table, item 7: CAA 1990 s 26(1)(*f*).
Sub-s (3): CAA 1990 s 26(1).
Sub-s (4): CAA 1990 s 26(1)(*b*).
Revenue Internal Guidance—Inspector's manual IM 2363 (decommissioning grants for fishing vessels are brought into account under this section).
Definitions—"Capital sum", s 4; "chargeable period", s 6; "disposal event", s 60(2); "dual resident investing company", s 577(1), TA 1988 s 404.
Modifications—CAA 2001 Sch 3 para 54 (vehicles provided by employees in 1990–91: see modification note at the start of this Part).
CAA 2001 Sch 3 para 55 (certain expenditure incurred before 6 April 1976: see modification note at the start of this Part).

62 General limit on amount of disposal value

(1) The amount of any disposal value required to be brought into account by a person in respect of any plant or machinery is limited to the qualifying expenditure incurred by the person on its provision.

(2) Subsection (3) applies if a person who is required to bring a disposal value into account has acquired the plant or machinery as a result of a transaction which was, or a series of transactions each of which was, between connected persons.

(3) The amount of the disposal value is limited to the amount of the qualifying expenditure on the provision of the plant or machinery incurred by whichever party to the transaction, or to any of the transactions, incurred the greatest such expenditure.

(4) This section is subject to section 239 (limit on disposal value where additional VAT rebate or rebates has or have been made in respect of original expenditure).

Commentary—*Simon's Direct Tax Service* **B2.334**.
Former enactments—Sub-s (1): CAA 1990 s 26(2).
Sub-s (2): CAA 1990 s 26(3).
Sub-s (3): CAA 1990 s 26(2), (3); change in law.
Modifications—CAA 2001 Sch 3 para 54 (vehicles provided by employees in 1990–91: see modification note at the start of this Part).
CAA 2001 Sch 3 para 55 (certain expenditure incurred before 6 April 1976: see modification note at the start of this Part).

63 Cases in which disposal value is nil

(1) If a person disposes of plant or machinery by way of gift in circumstances such that there is a charge to tax under Schedule E, the disposal value of the plant or machinery is nil.

(2) If a person carrying on a relevant qualifying activity makes a gift of plant or machinery used in the course of the activity—

    (*a*) to a charity within the meaning of section 506 of ICTA (charities: qualifying and non-qualifying expenditure),

    (*b*) to a body listed in section 507(1) of ICTA (various heritage bodies and museums), or

    (*c*) for the purposes of a designated educational establishment within the meaning of section 84 of ICTA (gifts to educational establishments), the disposal value of the plant or machinery is nil.

(3) In subsection (2) "relevant qualifying activity" means a qualifying activity consisting of—

    (*a*) a trade,

    (*b*) an ordinary Schedule A business,

    (*c*) a furnished holiday lettings business,

    (*d*) an overseas property business, or

    (*e*) a profession or vocation.

(4) Subsection (2) needs to be read with sections 83A(4) and 84(4) of ICTA (which provide for a charge to tax if subsection (2) applies in circumstances in which the donor or a connected person receives a benefit attributable to the gift).

(5) If expenditure is treated under section 27(2) (expenditure on thermal insulation, safety measures, etc) as having been incurred on plant or machinery, the disposal value of the plant or machinery is nil.

Commentary—*Simon's Direct Tax Service* **B2.334**.
Former enactments—Sub-s (1): CAA 1990 s 24(6); change in law.
Sub-s (2): TA 1988 s 83A(1), (2), (3)(*b*), s 84(1), (3)(*b*); change in law.
Sub-s (3): TA 1988 s 21A(1), s 65A(5), s 70A(5), s 83A(1), s 84(1).
Sub-s (5): CAA 1990 s 67(1), s 69(1), s 70(1), s 71(2).
Definitions—"Furnished holiday lettings business", s 17; "ordinary Schedule A business", s 16.
Cross-references—See FA 2002 Sch 18 para 9(3) (relief for donors in relation to community amateur sports clubs; sub-s (2) above has effect as if a registered club were a charity).
Modifications—CAA 2001 Sch 3 para 54 (vehicles provided by employees in 1990–91: see modification note at the start of this Part).
CAA 2001 Sch 3 para 55 (certain expenditure incurred before 6 April 1976: see modification note at the start of this Part).

64 Case in which no disposal value need be brought into account

(1) A person is not required to bring a disposal value into account in a pool for a chargeable period in respect of plant or machinery if none of the qualifying expenditure is or has been taken into account in a claim in determining the person's available qualifying expenditure in the pool for that or any previous chargeable period.

(2) Subsection (3) applies if—

    (*a*) a person ("C") has incurred qualifying expenditure on plant or machinery,

    (*b*) C acquired the plant or machinery as a result of a transaction which was, or a series of transactions each of which was, between connected persons,

    (*c*) any connected person (apart from C) who was a party to the transaction, or one of the series of transactions, is or has been required to bring a disposal value into account as a result of the transaction,

    (*d*) a disposal event ("the relevant disposal event") occurs in respect of the plant or machinery at a time when it is owned by C, and

    (*e*) none of C's qualifying expenditure is or has been taken into account in a claim in determining C's available qualifying expenditure for the chargeable period in which the relevant disposal event occurs or any previous chargeable period.

(3) If this subsection applies—

    (*a*) subsection (1) does not apply in relation to the relevant disposal event, and

    (*b*) C's qualifying expenditure is to be treated as allocated to the appropriate pool for the chargeable period in which the relevant disposal event occurs.

(4) In subsection (3)—

    (*a*) "qualifying expenditure" means, if a first-year allowance has been made to C, the amount (including a nil amount) remaining after deducting the allowance, and

    (*b*) "the appropriate pool" means whichever pool is applicable in relation to C under the provisions of this Part.

(5) A person takes expenditure into account in a claim if he takes it into account—

    (*a*) in a tax return;

    (*b*) by giving notice of an amendment of a tax return;

    (*c*) in any other claim under this Part.

Commentary—*Simon's Direct Tax Service* **B2.334**.
Former enactments—Sub-s (1): CAA 1990 s 24(6); change in law.
Sub-s (2): CAA 1990 s 24(6), s 26(3); change in law.
Sub-s (3): change in law.
Definitions—"Available qualifying expenditure", s 57; "chargeable period", s 6; "disposal event", s 60(2).
Modifications—CAA 2001 Sch 3 para 54 (vehicles provided by employees in 1990–91: see modification note at the start of this Part).
CAA 2001 Sch 3 para 55 (certain expenditure incurred before 6 April 1976: see modification note at the start of this Part).

The final chargeable period

65 The final chargeable period

(1) The final chargeable period for—

    (*a*) the main pool, or

(*b*) a long-life asset pool,

is the chargeable period in which the qualifying activity is permanently discontinued.

(2) The final chargeable period for a single asset pool is the first chargeable period in which any disposal event given in section 61(1) occurs.

(3) Subsection (2) is subject to—

sections 77(1) and 206(4) (no final chargeable period merely because plant or machinery begins to be used partly for purposes other than those of qualifying activity);
sections 86(2) and 87(2) (ending of short-life asset pool at four-year cut-off without final chargeable period);
section 132(2) (no final chargeable period for single ship pool).

(4) The final chargeable period for a class pool under section 107 (overseas leasing) is the chargeable period at the end of which the circumstances are such that there can be no more disposal receipts in any subsequent chargeable period.

Commentary—*Simon's Direct Tax Service* **B2.335**.
Former enactments—Sub-s (1): CAA 1990 s 24(2), s 38E(2), s 61(1); change in law.
Sub-s (2): CAA 1990 s 24(6), s 31(2), s 34(2), s 37(3), s 79(4), s 80(5).
Sub-s (4): CAA 1990 s 41(4).
Definitions—"Disposal event", s 60(2); "chargeable period", s 6; "disposal receipt" s 60(1).
Modifications—CAA 2001 Sch 3 para 54 (vehicles provided by employees in 1990–91: see modification note at the start of this Part).
CAA 2001 Sch 3 para 55 (certain expenditure incurred before 6 April 1976: see modification note at the start of this Part).

List of provisions outside this Chapter about disposal values

66 List of provisions outside this Chapter about disposal values

The provisions of this Part referred to in section 60(1)(*b*) are—

section 68	hire-purchase etc: disposal value on cessation of notional ownership
sections 72 and 73	grant of new software right: disposal value
section 79	cars: disposal value in avoidance cases
sections 88 and 89	short-life assets: disposal at under-value or to connected person
section 104	long-life assets: avoidance cases
sections 108, 111 and 114	overseas leasing: disposal values in various cases
sections 132 and 143	ships: ship used for overseas leasing etc; attribution of amount where balancing charge deferred
section 171	oil production sharing contracts: disposal values on cessation of ownership
sections 196 and 197	fixtures: disposal values on cessation of notional ownership and in avoidance cases
section 208	effect of significant reduction in use of plant or machinery for purposes of qualifying activity
section 211	effect of payment of partial depreciation subsidy
section 222	anti-avoidance: limit on disposal value
section 229	hire-purchase: disposal values in finance leasing and anti-avoidance cases
sections 238 and 239	additional VAT rebates

CHAPTER 6
HIRE-PURCHASE ETC AND PLANT OR MACHINERY PROVIDED BY LESSEE

Hire-purchase and similar contracts

67 Plant or machinery treated as owned by person entitled to benefit of contract, etc

(1) This section applies if—

(*a*) a person carrying on a qualifying activity incurs capital expenditure on the provision of plant or machinery for the purposes of the qualifying activity, and
(*b*) the expenditure is incurred under a contract providing that the person shall or may become the owner of the plant or machinery on the performance of the contract.

(2) The plant or machinery is to be treated for the purposes of this Part as owned by the person (and not by any other person) at any time when he is entitled to the benefit of the contract so far as it relates to the plant or machinery.

(3) At the time when the plant or machinery is brought into use for the purposes of the qualifying activity, the person is to be treated for the purposes of this Part as having incurred all capital expenditure in respect of the plant or machinery to be incurred by him under the contract after that time.

(4) If a person—

(*a*) is treated under subsection (2) as owning plant or machinery, (*b*) ceases to be entitled to the benefit of the contract in question so far as it relates to that plant or machinery, and

(*c*) does not then in fact become the owner of the plant or machinery,

the person is to be treated as ceasing to own the plant or machinery at the time when he ceases to be entitled to the benefit of the contract.

(5) This section is subject to section 69 (hire-purchase and fixtures) and subsection (3) is subject to section 229 (anti-avoidance).

Commentary—*Simon's Direct Tax Service* **B2.340**.
Former enactments—Sub-s (1): CAA 1990 s 60(1).
Sub-s (2): CAA 1990 s 60(1)(*a*).
Sub-s (3): CAA 1990 s 60(1)(*b*).
Sub-s (4): CAA 1990 s 60(2)(*a*).
Sub-s (5): CAA 1990 s 60(4).
Revenue Internal Guidance—Capital allowances manual CA 23310 (operation of this para and worked example).
Definition—"Capital expenditure", s 4.
Modifications—CAA 2001 Sch 3 para 15 (words in brackets in sub-s (2) omitted if the contract under which the expenditure was incurred was entered into before 27 July 1989).
CAA 2001 Sch 3 para 54 (vehicles provided by employees in 1990–91: see modification note at the start of this Part).
CAA 2001 Sch 3 para 55 (certain expenditure incurred before 6 April 1976: see modification note at the start of this Part).

68 Disposal value on cessation of notional ownership

(1) This section applies if a person—

(*a*) is treated under section 67(4) as ceasing to own plant or machinery, and

(*b*) is required to bring a disposal value into account as a result.

(2) If the plant or machinery has been brought into use for the purposes of the qualifying activity before the person ceases to own the plant or machinery, the disposal value is the total of—

(*a*) any relevant capital sums, and

(*b*) any capital expenditure treated under section 67(3) as having been incurred when the plant or machinery was brought into use but which has not in fact been incurred.

(3) If the plant or machinery has not been brought into use for the purposes of the qualifying activity before the person ceases to own the plant or machinery, the disposal value is the total of any relevant capital sums.

(4) "Relevant capital sums" means capital sums that the person receives or is entitled to receive by way of consideration, compensation, damages or insurance money in respect of—

(*a*) his rights under the contract, or

(*b*) the plant or machinery.

(5) This section is subject to section 229 (anti-avoidance).

Commentary—*Simon's Direct Tax Service* **B2.340**.
Former enactments—Sub-ss (1), (2): CAA 1990 s 60(2).
Sub-s (3): Change in law.
Sub-s (4): CAA 1990 s 60(2).
Revenue Internal Guidance—Capital allowances manual CA 23330 (worked example).
Definitions—"Capital expenditure", "capital sum", s 4.
Modifications—CAA 2001 Sch 3 para 54 (vehicles provided by employees in 1990–91: see modification note at the start of this Part).
CAA 2001 Sch 3 para 55 (certain expenditure incurred before 6 April 1976: see modification note at the start of this Part).

69 Hire-purchase etc and fixtures

(1) Section 67 does not—

(*a*) apply to expenditure incurred on plant or machinery which is a fixture, or

(*b*) prevent Chapter 14 (fixtures) applying in relation to expenditure on plant or machinery incurred under such a contract as is mentioned in section 67(1)(*b*).

(2) If—

(*a*) a person is treated under section 67(2) as owning plant or machinery,

(*b*) the plant or machinery becomes a fixture, and

(*c*) the person is not treated under Chapter 14 as being the owner of the plant or machinery,

the person is to be treated for the purposes of this Part as ceasing to own the plant or machinery at the time when it becomes a fixture.

(3) In this section "fixture" has the meaning given by section 173(1).

Commentary—*Simon's Direct Tax Service* **B2.340**.
Former enactments—Sub-s (1): CAA 1990 s 60A(1).
Sub-s (2): CAA 1990 s 60A(2).
Sub-s (3): CAA 1990 s 60A(3).
Modifications—CAA 2001 Sch 3 para 16 (sub- s (2) does not apply if the plant or machinery became a fixture before 28 July 2000).
CAA 2001 Sch 3 para 54 (vehicles provided by employees in 1990–91: see modification note at the start of this Part).
CAA 2001 Sch 3 para 55 (certain expenditure incurred before 6 April 1976: see modification note at the start of this Part).

Plant or machinery provided by lessee

70 Plant or machinery provided by lessee

(1) This section applies if—

  (*a*) under the terms of a lease, a lessee is required to provide plant or machinery,

  (*b*) the lessee incurs capital expenditure on the provision of that plant or machinery for the purposes of a qualifying activity which the lessee carries on,

  (*c*) the plant or machinery is not so installed or otherwise fixed in or to a building or any other description of land as to become, in law, part of that building or other land, and

  (*d*) the lessee does not own the plant or machinery.

(2) The lessee—

  (*a*) is to be treated as being the owner of the plant or machinery, as a result of incurring the capital expenditure, for so long as it continues to be used for the purposes of the qualifying activity, but

  (*b*) is not required to bring a disposal value into account because the lease ends.

(3) Subsection (4) applies if—

  (*a*) the plant or machinery continues to be used for the purposes of the lessee's qualifying activity until the lease ends,

  (*b*) the lessor holds the lease in the course of a qualifying activity, and

  (*c*) on or after the ending of the lease, a disposal event occurs in respect of the plant or machinery at a time when the lessor owns the plant or machinery as a result of the requirement under the terms of the lease.

(4) The lessor is required to bring a disposal value into account in the appropriate pool for the chargeable period in which the disposal event occurs.

(5) "The appropriate pool" means the pool which would be applicable under this Part in relation to the lessor's qualifying activity if—

  (*a*) the expenditure incurred by the lessee had been qualifying expenditure incurred by the lessor, and

  (*b*) that qualifying expenditure were being allocated to a pool for the chargeable period in which the disposal event occurs.

(6) In this section "lease" includes—

  (*a*) an agreement for a lease if the term to be covered by the lease has begun, and

  (*b*) any tenancy,

but does not include a mortgage (and "lessee" and "lessor" are to be read accordingly).

Commentary—*Simon's Direct Tax Service* **B2.340**.
Former enactments—Sub-s (1): CAA 1990 s 61(4).
Sub-s (2): CAA 1990 s 61(4); change in law.
Sub-ss (3)–(5): CAA 1990 s 24(6), (8), s 61(4); change in law.
Sub-s (6): CAA 1990 s 61(8).
Revenue Internal Guidance—Capital allowances manual CA 22250 (provision of seats and seat covers is not within this section, but expenditure is likely to qualify as expenditure on plant; expenditure on construction of police control room will qualify).
Definitions—"Capital expenditure", s 4; "chargeable period", s 6; "disposal event", s 60(2).
Modifications—CAA 2001 Sch 3 para 17 (paras (*c*) and (*d*) in sub-s (1) do not apply in relation to leases entered into before 12 July 1984, or on or after that date under an agreement made before that date).
CAA 2001 Sch 3 para 54 (vehicles provided by employees in 1990–91: see modification note at the start of this Part).
CAA 2001 Sch 3 para 55 (certain expenditure incurred before 6 April 1976: see modification note at the start of this Part).

CHAPTER 7
COMPUTER SOFTWARE

71 Software and rights to software

(1) For the purposes of this Part computer software is treated as plant (whether or not it would constitute plant apart from this section).

(2) If a person carrying on a qualifying activity incurs capital expenditure in acquiring, for the purposes of the qualifying activity, a right to use or otherwise deal with computer software, this Part applies as if—

  (*a*) the right and the software to which it relates were plant,

  (*b*) the plant were provided for the purposes of the qualifying activity, and

  (*c*) so long as the person is entitled to the right, the person owned the plant as a result of incurring the capital expenditure.

Commentary—*Simon's Direct Tax Service* **B2.341**.
Former enactments—Sub-s (1): CAA 1990 s 67A(2).
Sub-s (2): CAA 1990 s 67A(1).
Revenue Internal Guidance—Capital allowances manual CA 23410 (meaning of "computer software")
Definition—"Capital expenditure", s 4.
Modifications—CAA 2001 Sch 3 para 18 (the section above does not apply in relation to expenditure incurred before 10 March 1992).
CAA 2001 Sch 3 para 54 (vehicles provided by employees in 1990–91: see modification note at the start of this Part).
CAA 2001 Sch 3 para 55 (certain expenditure incurred before 6 April 1976: see modification note at the start of this Part).

72 Disposal values

(1) This section applies if a person—

    (*a*) has incurred qualifying expenditure on the provision of plant consisting of computer software or the right to use or otherwise deal with computer software, and

    (*b*) grants to another a right to use or otherwise deal with the whole or part of the computer software in circumstances in which the consideration for the grant—

        (i) consists of a capital sum, or

        (ii) would consist of a capital sum if the consideration were in money.

(2) The person is required to bring a disposal value into account unless—

    (*a*) while the person owned the computer software or the right to use or otherwise deal with the computer software, and

    (*b*) before the grant of the right referred to in subsection (1)(*b*),

there has been a disposal event falling within section 61(1)(*e*) (use for purposes other than those of the qualifying activity) or 61(1)(*f*) (permanent discontinuance of the qualifying activity).

(3) The disposal value to be brought into account under this section depends on the circumstances of the grant of the right, as shown in the Table—

TABLE

DISPOSAL VALUES: GRANT OF SOFTWARE RIGHT

1. Circumstances of grant	*2. Disposal value*
1. The grant is for a consideration not consisting entirely of money.	The market value of the right granted at the time of the grant.

2.   The grant is made where—
    (*a*) it is for no consideration or at less than market value,
    (*b*) there is no charge to tax under Schedule E, and
    (*b*) the condition in subsection (5) is met by the grantee.
	The market value of the right granted at the time of the grant.

3. The grant is made in circumstances other than those given in item 1 or 2.	The net consideration in money received in respect of the grant, together with—
	    (*a*) any insurance money received in respect of the computer software as a result of an event affecting the consideration obtainable on the grant, and
	    (*b*) any other compensation of any description so received, so far as it consists of capital sums.

(4) The amounts referred to in column 2 of the Table are those received by the person required to bring the disposal value into account.

(5) The condition referred to in item 2 of the Table is met by the grantee if—

    (*a*) the grantee's expenditure on the acquisition of the plant cannot be qualifying expenditure under this Part or Part 6 (research and development allowances), or

    (*b*) the grantee is a dual resident investing company which is connected with the grantor.

Commentary—*Simon's Direct Tax Service* B2.341.
Former enactments—Sub-ss (1), (2): CAA 1990 s 24(6A).
Table, item 1: CAA 1990 s 26(1)(*ea*).
Table, item 2: CAA 1990 s 26(1)(*eb*).
Table, item 3: CAA 1990 s 26(1)(*ec*).
Sub-s (4): CAA 1990 s 26(1)(*ec*).
Sub-s (5): CAA 1990 s 26(1)(*eb*).
Definitions—"Capital sum", s 4; "disposal event", s 60(2); "dual resident investing company", s 577(1), TA 1988 s 404.
Modifications—CAA 2001 Sch 3 para 54 (vehicles provided by employees in 1990–91: see modification note at the start of this Part).
CAA 2001 Sch 3 para 55 (certain expenditure incurred before 6 April 1976: see modification note at the start of this Part).

73 Limit on disposal values

(1) This section applies if a person is required to bring into account a disposal value in respect of—

    (*a*) computer software, or

    (*b*) the right to use or otherwise deal with computer software.

(2) For the purpose only of—

    (*a*) determining whether the limit on the disposal value under section 62 is exceeded, and

    (*b*) reducing the amount of that disposal value so that the limit is not exceeded,

the disposal value is to be taken to be increased by the amount given in subsection (3).

(3) The amount is the total of any disposal values which, in respect of that person and that plant, fall or have fallen to be brought into account under section 72.

Commentary—*Simon's Direct Tax Service* **B2.341**.
Former enactments—Sub-ss (1)–(3): CAA 1990 s 26(2), (2AA).
Modifications—CAA 2001 Sch 3 para 54 (vehicles provided by employees in 1990–91: see modification note at the start of this Part).
CAA 2001 Sch 3 para 55 (certain expenditure incurred before 6 April 1976: see modification note at the start of this Part).

CHAPTER 8
CARS, ETC
Cars above the cost threshold

74 Single asset pool

(1) Qualifying expenditure incurred on the provision of a car to which this section applies, if allocated to a pool, must be allocated to a single asset pool.

(2) This section applies to a car if—

    (*a*) the car is not a qualifying hire car (as defined by section 82), ...[2]

    (*b*) the capital expenditure incurred on its provision for the purposes of the qualifying activity exceeds £12,000[, and

    (*c*) the qualifying expenditure incurred on the provision of the car is not first-year qualifying expenditure under section 45D (expenditure on cars with low CO_2 emissions)][1]

(3) In this Chapter "car" has the meaning given by section 81 (extended meaning of "car").

(4) The Treasury may by order increase or further increase the sums of money specified in subsection (2) and in sections 75 and 76.

Commentary—*Simon's Direct Tax Service* **B2.342**.
Former enactments—Sub-ss (1), (2): CAA 1990 s 34(1), s 35(1).
Sub-s (3): CAA 1990 s 36(1).
Sub-s (4): CAA 1990 s 36(5).
Definitions—"Capital expenditure", s 4; "car", s 81.
Modifications—CAA 2001 Sch 3 para 19 (sub-s (2) applies with the substitution of "£8,000" for "£12,000" in relation to expenditure incurred or treated as incurred before 11 March 1992, or incurred under a contract entered into before that date).
CAA 2001 Sch 3 para 54 (vehicles provided by employees in 1990–91: see modification note at the start of this Part).
CAA 2001 Sch 3 para 55 (certain expenditure incurred before 6 April 1976: see modification note at the start of this Part).
Amendments—[1] Sub-s (2)(*c*) added by FA 2002 s 59, Sch 19 paras 1, 6 with effect for expenditure incurred after 16 April 2002.
[2] Word "and" repealed by FA 2002 s 141, Sch 40 Pt 3(7) with effect for expenditure incurred after 16 April 2002.

75 General limit on amount of writing-down allowance

(1) The amount of the writing-down allowance to be made to a person for a chargeable period in respect of qualifying expenditure incurred on the provision of a car to which section 74 applies must not exceed £3,000.

(2) The limit under subsection (1) is proportionately increased or reduced if the chargeable period is more or less than a year.

(3) The amount of the writing-down allowance may be further limited under—

    section 76 (expenditure met by another person),
    section 77 (effect of use partly for other purposes), or
    section 78 (effect of partial depreciation subsidy).

Commentary—*Simon's Direct Tax Service* **B2.342**.
Former enactments—Sub-ss (1), (2): CAA 1990 s 34(3)(*a*).
Definitions—"Car", s 81; "chargeable period", s 6.
Modifications—CAA 2001 Sch 3 para 19 (sub-s (1) applies with the substitution of "£2,000" for "£3,000" in relation to expenditure incurred or treated as incurred before 11 March 1992, or incurred under a contract entered into before that date).
CAA 2001 Sch 3 para 54 (vehicles provided by employees in 1990–91: see modification note at the start of this Part).
CAA 2001 Sch 3 para 55 (certain expenditure incurred before 6 April 1976: see modification note at the start of this Part).

76 Limit where part of expenditure met by another person

(1) Subsection (2) applies if, as a result of section 532 (general rule excluding contributions), only part of the capital expenditure incurred on the provision of a car to which section 74 applies is treated as incurred by a person.

(2) The amount of the writing-down allowance to be made to that person for a chargeable period in respect of the qualifying expenditure on the car must not exceed—

$$£3,000 \times \frac{E - X}{E}$$

where—

    E is the amount of capital expenditure incurred on the provision of the car, and
    X is the amount of the expenditure excluded by section 532.

(3) Subsection (4) applies if—

(*a*) capital expenditure exceeding £12,000 is incurred on the provision of a car to which section 74 applies, and

(*b*) a person ("the contributor") is entitled to writing-down allowances as a result of section 538 (contribution allowances for plant and machinery).

(4) The amount of the writing-down allowance to be made to the contributor for a chargeable period in respect of his contribution to the expenditure on the car must not exceed—

$$£3,000 \times \frac{C}{E}$$

where—

E is the amount of capital expenditure incurred on the provision of the car, and

C is the amount of the contribution.

(5) The limit under subsection (2) or (4) is proportionately increased or reduced if the chargeable period is more or less than a year.

Commentary—*Simon's Direct Tax Service* **B2.342**.
Former enactments—Sub-ss (1), (2): CAA 1990 s 34(3).
Sub-ss (3), (4): CAA 1990 s 35(1).
Sub-s (5): CAA 1990 s 34(3), 35(1).
Definitions—"Capital expenditure", s 4; "car", s 81; "chargeable period", s 6.
Modifications—CAA 2001 Sch 3 para 19 (sub-s (3) applies with the substitution of "£8,000" for "£12,000", and sub-ss (2), (4) apply with the substitution of "£2,000" for "£3,000" in relation to expenditure incurred or treated as incurred before 11 March 1992, or incurred under a contract entered into before that date).
CAA 2001 Sch 3 para 54 (vehicles provided by employees in 1990–91: see modification note at the start of this Part).
CAA 2001 Sch 3 para 55 (certain expenditure incurred before 6 April 1976: see modification note at the start of this Part).

77 Car used partly for purposes other than those of qualifying activity

(1) In the case of a single asset pool under section 74 there is no final chargeable period or disposal event merely because the car begins to be used partly for purposes other than those of the qualifying activity.

(2) For any chargeable period in which the car is used partly for purposes other than those of the qualifying activity—

(*a*) any writing-down allowance or balancing allowance to which the person is entitled, or

(*b*) any balancing charge to which the person is liable,

must be reduced to an amount which is just and reasonable having regard to the relevant circumstances.

(3) The relevant circumstances include, in particular, the extent to which the car is used in that chargeable period for purposes other than those of the qualifying activity.

(4) In calculating under section 59 the amount of unrelieved qualifying expenditure carried forward, a reduction of a writing-down allowance under this section is to be disregarded.

(5) If this section applies, Chapter 15 (plant or machinery provided or used partly for purposes other than those of the qualifying activity) does not apply.

Commentary—*Simon's Direct Tax Service* **B2.342**.
Former enactments—Sub-s (1): CAA 1990 s 34(5).
Sub-ss (2), (3): CAA 1990 s 34(5).
Sub-s (5): CAA 1990 s 34(5).
Revenue Internal Guidance—Capital allowances manual CA 23530 (example showing "just and reasonable" basis under sub-s (2)).
CA 23530 (a personal choice restriction may be made where there is a "blatant incongruity" between the type of car and the size and nature of the business).
Definitions—"Car", s 81; "chargeable period", s 6; "disposal event", s 60(2); "final chargeable period", s 65.
Modifications—CAA 2001 Sch 3 para 54 (vehicles provided by employees in 1990–91: see modification note at the start of this Part).
CAA 2001 Sch 3 para 55 (certain expenditure incurred before 6 April 1976: see modification note at the start of this Part).

78 Effect of partial depreciation subsidy

(1) This section applies if—

(*a*) a car to which section 74 applies is in use for the purposes of the qualifying activity,

(*b*) there is paid to the person carrying on that activity a sum in respect of, or which takes account of, part of the depreciation of the car resulting from that use, and

(*c*) the sum does not fall to be taken into account as income of that person or in calculating the profits of any qualifying activity carried on by him.

(2) The amount of—

(*a*) any writing-down allowance or balancing allowance to which the person is entitled, or

(*b*) any balancing charge to which the person is liable,

must be reduced to an amount which is just and reasonable having regard to the relevant circumstances.

(3) In calculating under section 59 the amount of unrelieved qualifying expenditure carried forward, a reduction of a writing-down allowance under subsection (2) is to be disregarded.

(4) This section has effect for the chargeable period in which any such sum as is mentioned in subsection (1)(*b*) is first paid and for any subsequent chargeable period.

(5) If this section applies, Chapter 16 (partial depreciation subsidies) does not apply.

Commentary—*Simon's Direct Tax Service* **B2.342**.
Former enactments—Sub-ss (1), (2): CAA 1990 s 34(5).
Sub-ss (4), (5): CAA 1990 s 34(5).
Definitions—"Car", s 81; "chargeable period", s 6; "partial depreciation subsidy", s 209.
Modifications—CAA 2001 Sch 3 para 54 (vehicles provided by employees in 1990–91: see modification note at the start of this Part).
CAA 2001 Sch 3 para 55 (certain expenditure incurred before 6 April 1976: see modification note at the start of this Part).

79 Cases where Chapter 17 (anti-avoidance) applies

(1) This section applies if—

(*a*) a disposal value is required to be brought into account under section 61, and
(*b*) the disposal event is that the person concerned ceases to own a car to which section 74 applies because of—

(i) a sale, or
(ii) the performance of a contract,

which is a relevant transaction for the purposes of Chapter 17 (anti-avoidance).

(2) The disposal value to be brought into account is—

(*a*) the market value of the car at the time of the event referred to in subsection (1), or
(*b*) if less, the capital expenditure incurred, or treated as incurred, on the provision of the car by the person disposing of it.

(3) The person acquiring the car is to be treated as having incurred capital expenditure on its provision of an amount equal to the disposal value required to be brought into account under subsection (2).

Commentary—*Simon's Direct Tax Service* B2.342.
Former enactments—Sub-s (1): CAA 1990 s 34(4).
Sub-s (2): CAA 1990 s 34(4).
Sub-s (3): CAA 1990 s 34(4).
Definitions—"Capital expenditure", s 4; "car", s 81; "disposal event", s 60(2).
Modifications—CAA 2001 Sch 3 para 54 (vehicles provided by employees in 1990–91: see modification note at the start of this Part).
CAA 2001 Sch 3 para 55 (certain expenditure incurred before 6 April 1976: see modification note at the start of this Part).

Vehicles provided for purposes of employment or office

80 Vehicles provided for purposes of employment or office

(1) This section applies if a person who is carrying on a qualifying activity consisting of an employment or office ("the employee")—

(a) incurs capital expenditure on the provision of a mechanically propelled road vehicle or a cycle, and
(b) owns the vehicle or cycle as a result of incurring that expenditure.

(2) References in this Part to qualifying expenditure include the employee's expenditure on the provision of the vehicle or cycle if it is provided partly for use in—

(a) the performance of the duties of the employment or office, or
(b) the kind of travelling in respect of which expenses would be deductible as qualifying travelling expenses under section 198 of ICTA.

(3) The amount of any balancing allowance to which the employee is entitled for the final chargeable period is—

$$(AQE - TDR) \times \frac{A}{B}$$

where—

AQE is the available qualifying expenditure in the pool for that period,
TDR is the total of any disposal receipts to be brought into account in that pool for that period,
A is the number of chargeable periods in the case of which the employee—

(a) has carried on the qualifying activity and owned the vehicle or cycle, and
(b) has claimed an allowance falling to be made to him by reference to expenditure incurred on the provision of the vehicle or cycle, and

B is the number of chargeable periods in the case of which the employee—

(a) has carried on the qualifying activity and owned the vehicle or cycle, and
(b) has been entitled to an allowance by reference to expenditure incurred on the provision of the vehicle or cycle.

(4) In this section "cycle" has the meaning given by section 192(1) of the Road Traffic Act 1988.[1]

Commentary—*Simon's Direct Tax Service* **B2.342**.
Former enactments—Sub-s (1): CAA 1990 s 27(2B), (2C).

Sub-s (2): CAA 1990 s 27(2A); change in law.
Sub-s (3): CAA 1990 s 27(2D), (2E).
Sub-s (4): CAA 1990 s 27(2B).
Definitions—"Available qualifying expenditure", s 57; "capital expenditure", s 4; "chargeable period", s 6; "disposal receipt" s 60(1); "final chargeable period", s 65.
Modifications—CAA 2001 Sch 3 para 54 (vehicles provided by employees in 1990–91: see modification note at the start of this Part).
CAA 2001 Sch 3 para 55 (certain expenditure incurred before 6 April 1976: see modification note at the start of this Part).
Amendments—[1] Section repealed by FA 2001 ss 59(2), (3), 110, Sch 33 Pt II(1) with effect for expenditure incurred after 5 April 2002.

Interpretation

81 Extended meaning of "car"

In this Part "car" means a mechanically propelled road vehicle other than one—

(a) of a construction primarily suited for the conveyance of goods or burden of any description, or

(b) of a type not commonly used as a private vehicle and unsuitable for such use.

References to a car accordingly include a motor cycle.

Commentary—*Simon's Direct Tax Service* **B2.342**.
Former enactments—CAA 1990 s 36(1).
Revenue Internal Guidance—Capital allowances manual CA 23510 (list of vehicles that do not qualify for allowance).
Modifications—CAA 2001 Sch 3 para 54 (vehicles provided by employees in 1990–91: see modification note at the start of this Part).
CAA 2001 Sch 3 para 55 (certain expenditure incurred before 6 April 1976: see modification note at the start of this Part).

82 Qualifying hire cars

(1) For the purposes of this Part a car is a qualifying hire car if—

(a) it is provided wholly or mainly for hire to, or the carriage of, members of the public in the ordinary course of a trade, and

(b) the case is within subsection (2), (3) or (4).

(2) The first case is where the following conditions are met—

(a) the number of consecutive days for which the car is on hire to, or used for the carriage of, the same person will normally be less than 30, and

(b) the total number of days for which it is on hire to, or used for the carriage of, the same person in any period of 12 months will normally be less than 90.

(3) The second case is where the car is provided for hire to a person who will himself use it—

(a) wholly or mainly for hire to, or for the carriage of, members of the public in the ordinary course of a trade, and

(b) in a way that meets the conditions in subsection (2).

(4) The third case is where the car is provided wholly or mainly for the use of a person in receipt of—

(a) a disability living allowance under—

(i) the Social Security Contributions and Benefits Act 1992, or

(ii) the Social Security Contributions and Benefits (Northern Ireland) Act 1992,

because of entitlement to the mobility component,

(b) a mobility supplement under a scheme made under the Personal Injuries (Emergency Provisions) Act 1939,

(c) a mobility supplement under an Order in Council made under section 12 of the Social Security (Miscellaneous Provisions) Act 1977, or

(d) any payment appearing to the Treasury to be of a similar kind and specified by them by order.

(5) For the purposes of subsection (2) persons who are connected with each other are to be treated as the same person.

Commentary—*Simon's Direct Tax Service* **B2.342**.
Former enactments—Sub-s (1): CAA 1990 s 36(1)(c).
Sub-s (2): CAA 1990 s 36(2)(a).
Sub-s (3): CAA 1990 s 36(2)(b).
Sub-s (4): CAA 1990 ss 22(6), 36(4).
Sub-s (5): CAA 1990 s 36(3).
Definition—"Car", s 81.
Modifications—CAA 2001 Sch 3 para 54 (vehicles provided by employees in 1990–91: see modification note at the start of this Part).
CAA 2001 Sch 3 para 55 (certain expenditure incurred before 6 April 1976: see modification note at the start of this Part).

CHAPTER 9

SHORT-LIFE ASSETS

83 Meaning of "short-life asset"

Plant or machinery in respect of which qualifying expenditure has been incurred is a short-life asset if—

(*a*) its treatment as a short-life asset is not ruled out by section 84, and
(*b*) the person incurring the expenditure elects for the plant or machinery to be treated as a short-life asset.

Commentary—*Simon's Direct Tax Service* **B2.343**.
Former enactments—CAA 1990 s 37(1).
Modifications—CAA 2001 Sch 3 para 54 (vehicles provided by employees in 1990–91: see modification note at the start of this Part).
CAA 2001 Sch 3 para 55 (certain expenditure incurred before 6 April 1976: see modification note at the start of this Part).

84 Cases in which short-life asset treatment is ruled out

Treatment of plant or machinery as a short-life asset is ruled out in any of the cases listed in column 1 of the Table, unless an exception listed in column 2 applies.

TABLE

SHORT-LIFE ASSET TREATMENT

1. Short-life asset treatment ruled out	2. Exception (if any)

1. The expenditure is treated as incurred for the purposes of a qualifying activity under—
   (*a*) section 13 (use for qualifying activity of plant or machinery provided for other purposes), or
   (*b*) section 14 (use for qualifying activity of plant or machinery which is a gift).	

2. The plant or machinery is the subject of special leasing (as defined by section 19).	
3. The plant or machinery is a car (as defined by section 81).	The car is within section 82(4) (cars hired out to persons receiving disability allowances etc).
4. The expenditure is long-life asset expenditure (see Chapter 10).	
5. The plant or machinery is provided for leasing.	The plant or machinery is a car which is within section 82(4) (cars hired out to persons receiving disability allowances etc). The plant or machinery will be used within the designated period (as defined by section 106) for a qualifying purpose (as defined by sections 122 to 125).
6. Section 109 provides only a 10% writing-down allowance in respect of expenditure on the plant or machinery.	
7. The plant or machinery is leased to two or more persons jointly in circumstances such that section 116 applies.	
8. The plant or machinery is a ship.	
9. The expenditure was incurred partly for the purposes of a qualifying activity and partly for other purposes (see Chapter 15).	
10. The expenditure is required to be allocated to a single asset pool under section 211 (partial depreciation subsidy).	

Commentary—*Simon's Direct Tax Service* **B2.343**.
Former enactments—CAA 1990 s 37(1)(*ba*).
Definition—''Short-life asset'', s 83.
Modifications—CAA 2001 Sch 3 para 54 (vehicles provided by employees in 1990–91: see modification note at the start of this Part).
CAA 2001 Sch 3 para 55 (certain expenditure incurred before 6 April 1976: see modification note at the start of this Part).

85 Election for short-life asset treatment: procedure

(1) An election under section 83 must specify—

   (*a*) the plant or machinery which is the subject of the election,
   (*b*) the qualifying expenditure incurred in respect of it, and
   (*c*) the date on which the expenditure was incurred.

(2) An election under section 83 must be made by notice given to the Inland Revenue—

   (*a*) for income tax purposes, on or before the normal time limit for amending a tax return for the tax year in which the relevant chargeable period ends;

(*b*) for corporation tax purposes, no later than 2 years after the end of the relevant chargeable period.

(3) "The relevant chargeable period" means—

(*a*) the chargeable period in which the qualifying expenditure was incurred, or

(*b*) if the qualifying expenditure was incurred in different chargeable periods, the first chargeable period in which any of the qualifying expenditure was incurred.

(4) An election under section 83 is irrevocable.

(5) All such assessments and adjustments of assessments are to be made as are necessary to give effect to the election.

Commentary—*Simon's Direct Tax Service* **B2.343**.
Former enactments—Sub-s (1): CAA 1990 s 37(1)(*c*), (2).
Sub-ss (2), (3): CAA 1990 s 37(2), (2A).
Sub-s (4): CAA 1990 s 37(2).
Sub-s (5): CAA 1990 s 37(4).
Revenue Internal Guidance—Capital allowances manual CA 23640 (procedure where separate identification of assets impossible).
Definitions—"Chargeable period", s 6; "normal time limit for amending a tax return", s 577(1); "short-life asset", s 83.
Modifications—CAA 2001 Sch 3 para 54 (vehicles provided by employees in 1990–91: see modification note at the start of this Part).
CAA 2001 Sch 3 para 55 (certain expenditure incurred before 6 April 1976: see modification note at the start of this Part).

86 Short-life asset pool

(1) Qualifying expenditure in respect of a short-life asset, if allocated to a pool, must be allocated to a single asset pool (a "short-life asset pool").

(2) If the final chargeable period for the short-life asset pool has not occurred before the four-year cut-off—

(*a*) the pool ends at the four-year cut-off without a final chargeable period,

(*b*) the available qualifying expenditure in the pool is allocated to the main pool for the first chargeable period ending after the four-year cut-off, and

(*c*) the asset ceases to be a short-life asset.

(3) In this Chapter "the four-year cut-off" means the fourth anniversary of the end of—

(*a*) the chargeable period in which the qualifying expenditure was incurred on the provision of the short-life asset, or

(*b*) if the qualifying expenditure was incurred in different chargeable periods, the first chargeable period in which any of the qualifying expenditure was incurred.

(4) For the purposes of subsection (2), the final chargeable period occurs before the four-year cut-off only if it ends on or before it.

Commentary—*Simon's Direct Tax Service* **B2.343**.
Former enactments—Sub-s (1): CAA 1990 s 37(3).
Sub-ss (2)–(4): CAA 1990 s 37(5).
Definitions—"Available qualifying expenditure", s 57; "chargeable period", s 6; "final chargeable period", s 65; "short-life asset", s 83.
Modifications—CAA 2001 Sch 3 para 54 (vehicles provided by employees in 1990–91: see modification note at the start of this Part).
CAA 2001 Sch 3 para 55 (certain expenditure incurred before 6 April 1976: see modification note at the start of this Part).

87 Short-life assets provided for leasing

(1) This section applies if—

(*a*) plant or machinery is a short-life asset on the basis that it has been provided for leasing but will be used within the designated period for a qualifying purpose (see item 5 of the Table in section 84),

(*b*) in a chargeable period ending on or before the four-year cut-off, the short-life asset begins to be used otherwise than for a qualifying purpose, and

(*c*) the time when it begins to be so used falls within the first 4 years of the designated period.

(2) If this section applies—

(*a*) the short-life asset pool ends without a final chargeable period,

(*b*) the available qualifying expenditure in the pool is allocated to the main pool for the chargeable period in which the asset begins to be used otherwise than for a qualifying purpose, and

(*c*) the asset ceases to be a short-life asset.

Commentary—*Simon's Direct Tax Service* **B2.343**.
Former enactments—Sub-s (1): CAA 1990 s 37(6).
Sub-s (2): CAA 1990 ss 37(6), 40(4).
Definitions—"Available qualifying expenditure", s 57; "chargeable period", s 6; "final chargeable period", s 65; "four-year cut-off", s 86(3); "short-life asset", s 83.
Modifications—CAA 2001 Sch 3 para 54 (vehicles provided by employees in 1990–91: see modification note at the start of this Part).
CAA 2001 Sch 3 para 55 (certain expenditure incurred before 6 April 1976: see modification note at the start of this Part).

88 Sales at under-value

If—

  (a) a short-life asset is disposed of at less than market value,

  (b) the disposal is not one in respect of which an election is made under section 89(6), and

  (c) there is no charge to tax under Schedule E,

the disposal value to be brought into account for the purposes of Chapter 5 is the market value of the asset.

Commentary—*Simon's Direct Tax Service* **B2.343**.
Former enactments—CAA 1990 ss 26(1)(b), 37(10).
Definition—''Short-life asset'', s 83.
Modifications—CAA 2001 Sch 3 para 54 (vehicles provided by employees in 1990–91: see modification note at the start of this Part).
CAA 2001 Sch 3 para 55 (certain expenditure incurred before 6 April 1976: see modification note at the start of this Part).

89 Disposal to connected person

(1) This section applies if, at any time before the four-year cut-off, a person (''the transferor'') disposes of a short-life asset to a connected person.

(2) Subject to subsection (6)—

  (a) the transferor is to be treated as having sold the short-life asset to the connected person for an amount equal to the available qualifying expenditure in the short-life asset pool for the chargeable period in which the disposal occurs, and

  (b) the connected person is to be treated as having incurred qualifying expenditure of the same amount in buying the short-life asset.

(3) Subject to subsection (6)—

  (a) sections 217 and 218 (restrictions on first-year and other allowances in the case of certain transactions between connected persons, to obtain a tax advantage etc), and

  (b) sections 222 to 225 (further restrictions in the case of sale and finance leaseback),

do not apply to the disposal.

(4) Immediately after the disposal of the short-life asset, the connected person is to be taken to have made an election under section 83 (so that the plant or machinery is a short-life asset in his hands).

(5) In relation to the connected person, ''the four-year cut-off'' means the date that would have been the four-year cut-off in relation to the transferor.

(6) Subsections (2) and (3) apply in relation to a disposal only if—

  (a) the transferor, and

  (b) the connected person,

elect that they should apply.

(7) An election under subsection (6) must be made by notice given to the Inland Revenue no later than 2 years after the end of the chargeable period in which the disposal occurred.

Commentary—*Simon's Direct Tax Service* **B2.343**.
Former enactments—Sub-ss (1)–(5): CAA 1990 s 37(8).
Sub-ss (6), (7): CAA 1990 s 37(9).
Definitions—''Available qualifying expenditure'', s 57; ''chargeable period'', s 6; ''four-year cut-off'', s 86(3); ''short-life asset'', s 83.
Modifications—CAA 2001 Sch 3 para 54 (vehicles provided by employees in 1990–91: see modification note at the start of this Part).
CAA 2001 Sch 3 para 55 (certain expenditure incurred before 6 April 1976: see modification note at the start of this Part).

CHAPTER 10
LONG-LIFE ASSETS

Commentary—*Simon's Direct Tax Service* B2.344.
Revenue Interpretation RI 241—(Modern printing equipment: application of long-life asset rules to equipment used in the printing industry).
Modifications—CAA 2001 Sch 3 para 20 (this Chapter modified with the effect that—

  (1) The Chapter does not apply in relation to any expenditure incurred—
    (a) before 26 November 1996, or
    (b) before 1 January 2001 in pursuance of a contract entered into before 26 November 1996.
  (2) The Chapter does not apply in relation to expenditure incurred by any person (''the purchaser'') on the acquisition of a long-life asset from another (''the seller'') if—
    (a) the seller has made a Part 2 claim in respect of expenditure incurred on the provision of the asset (''the seller's expenditure''),
    (b) the claim is one which the seller was entitled to make,
    (c) the seller's expenditure did not fall to be treated as long-life asset expenditure for the purposes of the claim, and
    (d) the seller's expenditure would have been so treated if one or more of the assumptions specified in (3) below were made.
  (3) The assumptions are that—
    (a) expenditure falling within (1) above is not prevented by that sub-paragraph from being long-life asset expenditure,
    (b) the seller's expenditure was not prevented by (2) above from being long-life asset expenditure, and
    (c) This Chapter or any provision corresponding to it applied for chargeable periods ending before 26 November 1996.

The reference in (1) above to expenditure incurred in pursuance of a contract entered into before 26 November 1996 does not, in the case of a contract varied at any time on or after that date, include a reference to any expenditure incurred under the contract that exceeds the expenditure that would have been incurred if the contract had not been varied.

Expressions used in this paragraph and in this Chapter have the same meaning in this paragraph as in this Chapter; and in particular references in this paragraph to a "Part 2 claim" are to be read in accordance with CAA 2001 s 103(3)).

Long-life asset expenditure

90 Long-life asset expenditure

"Long-life asset expenditure" means qualifying expenditure—

(a) incurred on the provision of a long-life asset for the purposes of a qualifying activity, and

(b) not excluded from being long-life asset expenditure by any of sections 93 to 100.

Commentary—*Simon's Direct Tax Service* **B2.344**.
Former enactments—CAA 1990 s 38A(1).
Modifications—CAA 2001 Sch 3 para 20 (see modification note at the start of this Chapter).
CAA 2001 Sch 3 para 54 (vehicles provided by employees in 1990–91: see modification note at the start of this Part).
CAA 2001 Sch 3 para 55 (certain expenditure incurred before 6 April 1976: see modification note at the start of this Part).

91 Meaning of "long-life asset"

(1) For the purposes of this Chapter "long-life asset" means plant or machinery which—

(a) if new, can reasonably be expected to have a useful economic life of at least 25 years, and

(b) if not new, could reasonably have been expected when new to have a useful economic life of at least 25 years.

(2) "New" means unused and not second-hand.

(3) The useful economic life of plant or machinery is the period—

(a) beginning when it is first brought into use by any person for any purpose, and

(b) ending when it is no longer used or likely to be used by anyone for any purpose as a fixed asset of a business.

Commentary—*Simon's Direct Tax Service* **B2.344**.
Former enactments—Sub-s (1): CAA 1990 s 38A(2).
Sub-s (2): CAA 1990 s 83(1) ("new").
Sub-s (3): CAA 1990 s 38A(3).
Revenue Internal Guidance—Capital allowances manual CA 23720 (asset is considered as a whole).
CA 23720 (useful economic life—link with accounting treatment).
Modifications—CAA 2001 Sch 3 para 20 (see modification note at the start of this Chapter).
CAA 2001 Sch 3 para 54 (vehicles provided by employees in 1990–91: see modification note at the start of this Part).
CAA 2001 Sch 3 para 55 (certain expenditure incurred before 6 April 1976: see modification note at the start of this Part).

92 Application of Chapter to part of expenditure

(1) If, under any of the following provisions of this Chapter, this Chapter applies to part only of the capital expenditure on plant and machinery—

(a) the part to which this Chapter applies, and

(b) the part to which it does not,

are to be treated for the purposes of this Act as expenditure on separate items of plant or machinery.

(2) For the purposes of subsection (1), all such apportionments are to be made as are just and reasonable.

Commentary—*Simon's Direct Tax Service* **B2.344**.
Former enactments—Sub-s (1): CAA 1990 s 38A(4).
Sub-s (2): CAA 1990 s 38A(5).
Definition—"Capital expenditure", s 4.
Modifications—CAA 2001 Sch 3 para 20 (see modification note at the start of this Chapter).
CAA 2001 Sch 3 para 54 (vehicles provided by employees in 1990–91: see modification note at the start of this Part).
CAA 2001 Sch 3 para 55 (certain expenditure incurred before 6 April 1976: see modification note at the start of this Part).

Expenditure excluded from being long-life asset expenditure

93 Fixtures etc

(1) Expenditure is not long-life asset expenditure if it is incurred on the provision of plant or machinery which is a fixture in, or is provided for use in, any building used wholly or mainly—

(a) as a dwelling-house, hotel, office, retail shop or showroom, or

(b) for purposes ancillary to the use referred to in paragraph (a).

(2) In this section—

"fixture" has the meaning given by section 173(1);

"retail shop" includes any premises of a similar character where a retail trade or business, including repair work, is carried on.

Commentary—*Simon's Direct Tax Service* **B2.344**.
Former enactments—Sub-s (1): CAA 1990 s 38B(1).
Sub-s (2): CAA 1990 s 38B(5).
Definitions—"Dwelling-house", s 531(1), "long-life asset", s 91; "long-life asset expenditure", s 90.
Modifications—CAA 2001 Sch 3 para 20 (see modification note at the start of this Chapter).

CAA 2001 Sch 3 para 54 (vehicles provided by employees in 1990–91: see modification note at the start of this Part).
CAA 2001 Sch 3 para 55 (certain expenditure incurred before 6 April 1976: see modification note at the start of this Part).

94 Ships

(1) Expenditure is not long-life asset expenditure if—

    (*a*) it is incurred before 1st January 2011 on the provision of a ship of a sea-going kind, and
    (*b*) each of the conditions in subsection (2) is met.

(2) The conditions are that—

    (*a*) the ship is not an offshore installation,
    (*b*) the ship would not be an offshore installation if the activity for the carrying on of which it is, or is to be, established or maintained were carried on in or under controlled waters, and
    (*c*) the primary use to which ships of the same kind are put by their owners (or, if their use is made available to others, those others) is a use otherwise than for sport or recreation.

(3) "Offshore installation" and "controlled waters" have the same meaning as in the Mineral Workings (Offshore Installations) Act 1971.

Commentary—*Simon's Direct Tax Service* B2.344.
Former enactments—Sub-ss (1)–(3): CAA 1990 s 38B(3); "long-life asset", s 91; "long-life asset expenditure", s 90.
Modifications—CAA 2001 Sch 3 para 20 (see modification note at the start of this Chapter).
CAA 2001 Sch 3 para 54 (vehicles provided by employees in 1990–91: see modification note at the start of this Part).
CAA 2001 Sch 3 para 55 (certain expenditure incurred before 6 April 1976: see modification note at the start of this Part).

95 Railway assets

(1) Expenditure is not long-life asset expenditure if it is incurred before 1st January 2011 on the provision of a railway asset used by any person wholly and exclusively for the purposes of a railway business.

(2) "Railway asset" means—

    (*a*) a locomotive, tram or other vehicle, or a carriage, wagon or other rolling stock designed or adapted for use on a railway;
    (*b*) anything which is, or is to be, comprised in any railway station, railway track or light maintenance depot or any apparatus which is, or is to be, installed in association with such a station, track or depot.

(3) "Railway business" means a business so far as carried on to provide a service to the public for carrying goods or passengers by means of a railway in the United Kingdom or the Channel Tunnel.

(4) For the purposes of subsection (1), a railway asset of a kind described in subsection (2)(*a*) is not to be treated as used otherwise than wholly and exclusively for the purposes of a railway business merely because it is used to carry goods or passengers—

    (*a*) from places inside the United Kingdom to places outside the United Kingdom, or
    (*b*) from places outside the United Kingdom to places inside the United Kingdom.

(5) In subsections (2) and (3), "railway" has the same meaning as in section 81(2) of the 1993 Act ("railway" includes tramways and other modes of guided transport).

(6) In this section—

    "the 1993 Act" means the Railways Act 1993;
    "goods" has the same meaning as in Part I of the 1993 Act;
    "railway station" and "railway track" include—

        (*a*) anything included in the definitions of "station" and "track" in section 83 of the 1993 Act, and
        (*b*) anything else that would be included if in section 83 "railway" had the meaning given in section 81(2) of the 1993 Act;

    "light maintenance depot" means—

        (*a*) any light maintenance depot within the meaning of Part I of the 1993 Act, and
        (*b*) any land or other property which is the equivalent of such a depot in relation to anything which is a railway only when "railway" has the meaning given by section 81(2) of the 1993 Act.

Commentary—*Simon's Direct Tax Service* B2.344.
Former enactments—Sub-s (1): CAA 1990 s 38B(4).
Sub-s (2): CAA 1990 s 38B(5).
Sub-s (3): CAA 1990 s 38B(5).
Sub-s (4): CAA 1990 s 38B(6).
Sub-s (5): CAA 1990 s 38B(5)
Sub-s (6): CAA 1990 s 38B(5).
Definitions—"Long-life asset", s 91; "long-life asset expenditure", s 90.
Modifications—CAA 2001 Sch 3 para 20 (see modification note at the start of this Chapter).
CAA 2001 Sch 3 para 54 (vehicles provided by employees in 1990–91: see modification note at the start of this Part).
CAA 2001 Sch 3 para 55 (certain expenditure incurred before 6 April 1976: see modification note at the start of this Part).

96 Cars

Expenditure is not long-life asset expenditure if it is incurred on the provision of a car (as defined by section 81).

Commentary—*Simon's Direct Tax Service* **B2.344**.
Former enactments—CAA 1990 s 38B(2).
Definition—"Long-life asset expenditure", s 90.
Modifications—CAA 2001 Sch 3 para 20 (see modification note at the start of this Chapter).
CAA 2001 Sch 3 para 54 (vehicles provided by employees in 1990–91: see modification note at the start of this Part).
CAA 2001 Sch 3 para 55 (certain expenditure incurred before 6 April 1976: see modification note at the start of this Part).

97 Expenditure within the relevant monetary limit: general

Expenditure is not long-life asset expenditure if it is—

(a) expenditure to which the monetary limits apply, and
(b) incurred in a chargeable period for which the relevant monetary limit is not exceeded.

Commentary—*Simon's Direct Tax Service* **B2.344**.
Former enactments—CAA 1990 ss 38C(1), 38D(1).
Definitions—"Chargeable period", s 6; "long-life asset", s 91; "long-life asset expenditure", s 90.
Modifications—CAA 2001 Sch 3 para 20 (see modification note at the start of this Chapter).
CAA 2001 Sch 3 para 54 (vehicles provided by employees in 1990–91: see modification note at the start of this Part).
CAA 2001 Sch 3 para 55 (certain expenditure incurred before 6 April 1976: see modification note at the start of this Part).

98 Expenditure to which the monetary limits apply

(1) The monetary limits apply to expenditure incurred by an individual for a chargeable period if—

(a) the expenditure was incurred by him for the purposes of a qualifying activity carried on by him,
(b) the whole of his time is substantially devoted in that period to the carrying on of that qualifying activity, and
(c) the expenditure is not within subsection (4).

(2) The monetary limits apply to expenditure incurred by a partnership for a chargeable period if—

(a) all of the members of the partnership are individuals,
(b) the expenditure was incurred by the partnership for the purposes of a qualifying activity carried on by it,
(c) at all times throughout that period at least half the partners for the time being devote the whole or a substantial part of their time to the carrying on of that qualifying activity, and
(d) the expenditure is not within subsection (4).

(3) The monetary limits apply for the purposes of corporation tax to any expenditure incurred by a company for a chargeable period other than expenditure within subsection (4).

(4) Expenditure is within this subsection if it is—

(a) incurred on the provision of a share in plant or machinery,
(b) treated as a result of section 538 (contribution allowances: plant and machinery) as incurred on the provision of plant or machinery, or
(c) incurred on the provision of plant or machinery for leasing (whether or not the leasing is in the course of a trade).

Commentary—*Simon's Direct Tax Service* **B2.344**.
Former enactments—Sub-s (1): CAA 1990 s 38C(2), (3); change in law.
Sub-s (2): CAA 1990 s 38C(1), (2), (4).
Sub-s (3): CAA 1990 s 38D(1).
Sub-s (4): CAA 1990 ss 38C(5), 38D(7).
Revenue Internal Guidance—Capital allowances manual CA 23740 (operation of the limit).
Definition—"Chargeable period", s 6.
Modifications—CAA 2001 Sch 3 para 20 (see modification note at the start of this Chapter).
CAA 2001 Sch 3 para 54 (vehicles provided by employees in 1990–91: see modification note at the start of this Part).
CAA 2001 Sch 3 para 55 (certain expenditure incurred before 6 April 1976: see modification note at the start of this Part).

99 The monetary limit

(1) The monetary limit in the case of a chargeable period of 12 months is £100,000.

(2) If, in the case of an individual or partnership, the chargeable period is longer or shorter than 12 months, the monetary limit is the amount given by a proportional increase or reduction of £100,000.

(3) If, in the case of a company, the chargeable period is shorter than 12 months, the monetary limit is the amount given by a proportional reduction of £100,000.

(4) If, in a chargeable period, a company has one or more associated companies, the monetary limit for that period is—

$$\frac{L}{N+1}$$

where—

L is the monetary limit applicable under subsection (1) or (3), and
N is the number of the associated companies.

(5) Section 13(4) and (5) of ICTA (companies which count as associated companies for the purposes of section 13(3)) applies for the purposes of subsection (4).

Commentary—*Simon's Direct Tax Service* B2.344.
Former enactments—Sub-s (1): CAA 1990 ss 38C(6), 38D(3).
Sub-s (2): CAA 1990 s 38C(7).
Sub-s (3): CAA 1990 s 38D(4).
Sub-s (4): CAA 1990 s 38D(5).
Sub-s (5): CAA 1990 s 38D(6).
Definition—"Chargeable period", s 6.
Modifications—CAA 2001 Sch 3 para 20 (see modification note at the start of this Chapter).
CAA 2001 Sch 3 para 54 (vehicles provided by employees in 1990–91: see modification note at the start of this Part).
CAA 2001 Sch 3 para 55 (certain expenditure incurred before 6 April 1976: see modification note at the start of this Part).

100 Exceeding the monetary limit

(1) The monetary limit for a chargeable period is exceeded if the total expenditure in that period that meets the conditions in subsection (2) exceeds that limit.

(2) The conditions are that the expenditure—

  (*a*) is long-life asset expenditure, or would be long-life asset expenditure in the absence of section 97 (expenditure within monetary limit), and
  (*b*) is expenditure to which the monetary limits apply.

(3) Subsection (4) applies if, in the case of any contract for the provision of plant or machinery, the capital expenditure which is (or is to be) incurred under the contract is (or may fall to be) treated for the purposes of this Act as incurred in different chargeable periods.

(4) All of the expenditure falling to be incurred under the contract on the provision of the plant or machinery is to be treated for the purposes of this section as incurred in the first chargeable period in which any of the expenditure is incurred.

Commentary—*Simon's Direct Tax Service* **B2.344**.
Former enactments—Sub-ss (1), (2): CAA 1990 ss 38C(1), (2), 38D(1), (2).
Sub-ss (3), (4): CAA 1990 s 38C(8), 38D(7).
Revenue Internal Guidance—Capital allowances manual CA 23740 (worked example).
Definitions—"Capital expenditure", s 4; "chargeable period", s 6; "long-life asset", s 91; "long-life asset expenditure", s 90.
Modifications—CAA 2001 Sch 3 para 20 (see modification note at the start of this Chapter).
CAA 2001 Sch 3 para 54 (vehicles provided by employees in 1990–91: see modification note at the start of this Part).
CAA 2001 Sch 3 para 55 (certain expenditure incurred before 6 April 1976: see modification note at the start of this Part).

Rules applying to long-life asset expenditure

101 Long-life asset pool

(1) Long-life asset expenditure to which this section applies, if allocated to a pool, must be allocated to a class pool ("the long-life asset pool").

(2) This section applies to long-life asset expenditure if—

  (*a*) it is incurred on the provision of long-life assets wholly and exclusively for the purposes of a qualifying activity, and
  (*b*) it is not expenditure which is required to be allocated to a single asset pool.

Commentary—*Simon's Direct Tax Service* B2.344.
Former enactments—Sub-s (1): CAA 1990 s 38E(2), (5).
Sub-s (2): CAA 1990 s 38E(1), (6).
Definitions—"Long-life asset", s 91; "long-life asset expenditure", s 90.
Modifications—CAA 2001 Sch 3 para 20 (see modification note at the start of this Chapter).
CAA 2001 Sch 3 para 54 (vehicles provided by employees in 1990–91: see modification note at the start of this Part).
CAA 2001 Sch 3 para 55 (certain expenditure incurred before 6 April 1976: see modification note at the start of this Part).

102 Writing-down allowances at 6%

(1) The amount of the writing-down allowance to which a person is entitled for a chargeable period in respect of expenditure which is long-life asset expenditure is 6% of the amount by which AQE exceeds TDR (see Chapter 5).

(2) Subsection (1) applies even if the long-life asset expenditure is in a single asset pool.

(3) In the case of expenditure which is within section 107(2)(*a*) and (*b*) (overseas leasing which is not protected leasing), this section is subject to sections 110, 114 and 115 (allowances prohibited in certain cases etc).

(4) Subsections (3) and (4) of section 56 (proportionate increases or reductions in amount in certain cases) apply for the purposes of subsection (1) of this section as they apply for the purposes of subsection (1) of that section.

Commentary—*Simon's Direct Tax Service* B2.344.
Former enactments—Sub-s (1): CAA 1990 s 38F(1).
Sub-s (2): CAA 1990 s 38F(2).
Sub-s (3): CAA 1990 s 38F(6).
Sub-s (4): CAA 1990 s 24(2)(*a*)(ii), s 38F(1).
Definitions—"Chargeable period", s 6; "long-life asset", s 91; "long-life asset expenditure", s 90.
Modifications—CAA 2001 Sch 3 para 20 (see modification note at the start of this Chapter).

CAA 2001 Sch 3 para 54 (vehicles provided by employees in 1990–91: see modification note at the start of this Part).
CAA 2001 Sch 3 para 55 (certain expenditure incurred before 6 April 1976: see modification note at the start of this Part).

Anti-avoidance provisions

103 Later claims

(1) Subsection (2) applies if—

(a) a person entitled to do so has made a Part 2 claim in respect of expenditure incurred on the provision of plant or machinery, and

(b) the expenditure fell to be treated as long-life asset expenditure for the purposes of the claim.

(2) If—

(a) at any time after making the Part 2 claim, that claimant or another person makes a Part 2 claim in respect of any qualifying expenditure incurred at any time (including a time before the incurring of the expenditure to which the earlier claim relates) on the provision of the same plant or machinery, and

(b) the expenditure to which the later claim relates—

(i) would not (but for this subsection) be treated for the purposes of the later claim as long-life asset expenditure, and

(ii) is not prevented from being long-life asset expenditure by any of sections 93 to 96,

this Part has effect in relation to the later claim as if the expenditure to which it relates were long-life asset expenditure.

(3) A person makes a Part 2 claim in respect of any expenditure if he—

(a) makes a tax return in which the expenditure is taken into account in determining his available qualifying expenditure for the purposes of this Part;

(b) gives notice of an amendment of a tax return which provides for the expenditure to be so taken into account;

(c) makes a claim in any other way for the expenditure to be so taken into account.

Commentary—*Simon's Direct Tax Service* **B2.344**.
Former enactments—Sub-ss (1), (2): CAA 1990 s 38F(3).
Sub-s (3): CAA 1990 s 38F(4).
Revenue Internal Guidance—Capital allowances manual CA 23750 (worked example).
Definitions—"Available qualifying expenditure", s 57; "long-life asset", s 91; "long-life asset expenditure", s 90.
Modifications—CAA 2001 Sch 3 para 20 (see modification note at the start of this Chapter).
CAA 2001 Sch 3 para 54 (vehicles provided by employees in 1990–91: see modification note at the start of this Part).
CAA 2001 Sch 3 para 55 (certain expenditure incurred before 6 April 1976: see modification note at the start of this Part).

104 Disposal value of long-life assets

(1) This section applies if—

(a) section 102 (writing-down allowances at 6%) has had effect in relation to any long-life asset expenditure incurred by a person ("the taxpayer"),

(b) any disposal event occurs in relation to the long-life asset,

(c) the disposal value to be brought into account by the taxpayer would (but for this section) be less than the notional written-down value of the long-life asset, and

(d) the disposal event is part of, or occurs as a result of, a scheme or arrangement the main purpose or one of the main purposes of which is the obtaining by the taxpayer of a tax advantage under this Part.

(2) The disposal value that the taxpayer must bring into account is the notional written-down value of the long-life asset.

(3) The notional written-down value is—

$$QE - A$$

where—

QE is the taxpayer's expenditure on the plant or machinery that is qualifying expenditure, and
A is the total of all allowances which could have been made to the taxpayer in respect of that expenditure if—

(a) that expenditure had been the only expenditure that had ever been taken into account in determining his available qualifying expenditure,

(b) that expenditure had not been prevented by the application of a monetary limit from being long-life asset expenditure, and

(c) all allowances had been made in full.

Commentary—*Simon's Direct Tax Service* **B2.344**.
Former enactments—Sub-ss (1), (2): CAA 1990 s 38G(1).
Sub-s (3): CAA 1990 s 38G(2), (3).
Revenue Internal Guidance—Capital allowances manual CA 23770 (worked example).
Definitions—"Available qualifying expenditure", s 57; "disposal event", s 60(2); "long-life asset", s 91; "long-life asset expenditure", s 90.
Modifications—CAA 2001 Sch 3 para 20 (see modification note at the start of this Chapter).
CAA 2001 Sch 3 para 54 (vehicles provided by employees in 1990–91: see modification note at the start of this Part).
CAA 2001 Sch 3 para 55 (certain expenditure incurred before 6 April 1976: see modification note at the start of this Part).

CHAPTER 11

OVERSEAS LEASING

Basic terms

105 "Leasing", "overseas leasing" etc

(1) In this Chapter—

(*a*) "leasing" includes letting a ship or aircraft on charter or letting any other asset on hire, and

(*b*) references to a lease include a sub-lease (and references to a lessor or lessee are to be read accordingly).

(2) Plant or machinery is used for overseas leasing if it is used for the purpose of being leased to a person who—

(*a*) is not resident in the United Kingdom, and

(*b*) does not use the plant or machinery exclusively for earning profits chargeable to tax.

(3) In this Chapter "profits chargeable to tax"—

(*a*) includes profits chargeable under section 830(4) of ICTA (profits from exploration and exploitation of the seabed etc), but

(*b*) excludes profits arising to a person who, under double taxation arrangements, is afforded or is entitled to claim any relief from the tax chargeable on those profits.

(4) "Double taxation arrangements" means arrangements specified in an Order in Council making any such provisions as are referred to in section 788 of ICTA.

(5) "Protected leasing" of plant or machinery means—

(*a*) short-term leasing of the plant or machinery (as defined in section 121), or

(*b*) if the plant or machinery is a ship, aircraft or transport container, the use of the ship, aircraft or transport container for a qualifying purpose under section 123 or 124 (letting on charter to UK resident etc).

(6) In this Chapter "qualifying activity" includes (subject to any provision to the contrary) any activity listed in section 15(1) even if any profits or gains from it are not chargeable to tax.

Commentary—*Simon's Direct Tax Service* **B2.345**.
Former enactments—Sub-s (1): CAA 1990 s 50(1), (2).
Sub-s (2): CAA 1990 s 42(1).
Sub-s (3): CAA 1990 ss 42(1), 50(3A).
Sub-s (4): CAA 1990 ss 42(1), 50(3A).
Sub-s (5): CAA 1990 s 50(3) ("permitted leasing").
Sub-s (6): CAA 1990 s 83(2A).
Revenue Internal Guidance—Capital allowances manual CA 24010 (meaning of "lease", "head lessor" and "end lessee").
CA 24010 (where there is a chain of leases, sub-s (2) is applied to the end lease).
CA 24100 (sub-s (5) – summary of conditions related to "protected leasing").
Modifications—CAA 2001 Sch 3 para 21 (sub-s (2) applies with the substitution of para (*b*) in relation to the use of plant or machinery for leasing under a lease entered into before 16 March 1993. Para (*b*) as substituted to read as follows—

"(*b*) does not use the plant or machinery for the purposes of a qualifying activity carried on there or for earning profits chargeable to tax by virtue of section 830(4) of ICTA, ".
CAA 2001 Sch 3 para 54 (vehicles provided by employees in 1990–91: see modification note at the start of this Part).
CAA 2001 Sch 3 para 55 (certain expenditure incurred before 6 April 1976: see modification note at the start of this Part).

106 The designated period

(1) Subject to subsection (2), the designated period, in relation to expenditure incurred by a person on the provision of plant or machinery, is the period of 10 years beginning with the date on which he first brought the plant or machinery into use.

(2) If the person who incurred the expenditure ceases to own the plant or machinery before the end of the 10 year period, the designated period ends on the date when he ceases to own it.

(3) For the purposes of subsection (2), a person is to be treated as continuing to own plant or machinery so long as it is owned by a person who—

(*a*) is connected with him, or

(*b*) acquired it from him as a result of one or more disposals on the occasion of which, or each of which, the qualifying activity carried on by the person making the disposal was treated as continuing under one of the relevant provisions of ICTA.

(4) "The relevant provisions of ICTA" means section 113(2) or 114(1) (effect of change in persons carrying on a trade etc).

Commentary—*Simon's Direct Tax Service* **B2.345**.
Former enactments—Sub-ss (1), (2): CAA 1990 ss 40(4), 50(3) ("the requisite period").
Sub-ss (3), (4): CAA 1990 s 40(5).
Modifications—CAA 2001 Sch 3 para 54 (vehicles provided by employees in 1990–91: see modification note at the start of this Part).
CAA 2001 Sch 3 para 55 (certain expenditure incurred before 6 April 1976: see modification note at the start of this Part).

Certain expenditure to be pooled

107 The overseas leasing pool

(1) Qualifying expenditure to which this section applies, if allocated to a pool, must be allocated to a class pool ("the overseas leasing pool").

(2) This section applies to qualifying expenditure if—

    (a) it is incurred on the provision of plant or machinery for leasing,

    (b) the plant or machinery is at any time in the designated period used for overseas leasing which is not protected leasing, and

    (c) the expenditure is not—

        (i) long-life asset expenditure, or

        (ii) expenditure that is required to be allocated to a single asset pool.

Commentary—*Simon's Direct Tax Service* **B2.346**.
Former enactments—Sub-s (1): CAA 1990 s 41(2).
Sub-s (2): CAA 1990 s 41(1), (6).
Modifications—CAA 2001 Sch 3 para 54 (vehicles provided by employees in 1990–91: see modification note at the start of this Part).
CAA 2001 Sch 3 para 55 (certain expenditure incurred before 6 April 1976: see modification note at the start of this Part).

108 Effect of disposal to connected person on overseas leasing pool

(1) This section applies if—

    (a) a person who has incurred qualifying expenditure which has been allocated to an overseas leasing pool disposes of the plant or machinery to a connected person,

    (b) the disposal is not an occasion on which the qualifying activity is treated as continuing under any of the relevant provisions of ICTA, and

    (c) a disposal value is required to be brought into account on that occasion under this Part.

(2) The disposal value to be brought into account is—

    (a) the market value of the plant or machinery at the time of the disposal, or

    (b) if less, the qualifying expenditure incurred by the person disposing of the plant or machinery.

(3) The person acquiring the plant or machinery is to be treated for the purposes of this Part as having incurred expenditure on its provision of an amount equal to the disposal value given by subsection (2).

(4) "The relevant provisions of ICTA" means section 113(2), 114(1) or 343(2) (effect of change in persons carrying on a trade etc or of company reconstruction).

Commentary—*Simon's Direct Tax Service* **B2.346**.
Former enactments—Sub-ss (1)–(4): CAA 1990 s 41(5).
Modifications—CAA 2001 Sch 3 para 54 (vehicles provided by employees in 1990–91: see modification note at the start of this Part).
CAA 2001 Sch 3 para 55 (certain expenditure incurred before 6 April 1976: see modification note at the start of this Part).

Allowances reduced or, in certain cases, prohibited

109 Writing-down allowances at 10%

(1) The amount of the writing-down allowance to which a person is entitled for a chargeable period in respect of expenditure to which this section applies is 10% of the amount by which AQE exceeds TDR (see Chapter 5).

(2) This section applies to expenditure incurred on the provision of plant or machinery for leasing if—

    (a) the plant or machinery is at any time in the designated period used for overseas leasing which is not protected leasing, and

    (b) the expenditure is not long-life asset expenditure.

(3) Subsection (2) applies to expenditure even if the expenditure is in a single asset pool.

(4) Subsections (3) and (4) of section 56 (proportionate increases or reductions in amount in certain cases) apply for the purposes of subsection (1) of this section as they apply for the purposes of subsection (1) of that section.

Commentary—*Simon's Direct Tax Service* **B2.346**.
Former enactments—Sub-s (1): CAA 1990 s 42(2).
Sub-s (2): CAA 1990 s 42(1), (2).
Sub-s (3): CAA 1990 s 42(2); change in law.
Sub-s (4): CAA 1990 s 24(2)(a)(ii), s 42(2).
Definition—"Chargeable period", s 6.
Modifications—CAA 2001 Sch 3 para 54 (vehicles provided by employees in 1990–91: see modification note at the start of this Part).
CAA 2001 Sch 3 para 55 (certain expenditure incurred before 6 April 1976: see modification note at the start of this Part).

110 Cases where allowances are prohibited

(1) A person is not entitled to any writing-down or balancing allowances in respect of qualifying expenditure which is within subsection (2).

(2) Expenditure is within this subsection if—

    (*a*) it is incurred on the provision of plant or machinery for leasing,

    (*b*) the plant or machinery is at any time in the designated period used for overseas leasing which is not protected leasing,

    (*c*) the plant or machinery is used otherwise than for a qualifying purpose (see sections 122 to 125), and

    (*d*) the lease is within any of the items in the list below.

LIST

LEASES IN RELATION TO WHICH ALLOWANCES ARE PROHIBITED

    1. The lease is expressed to be for a period of more than 13 years.

    2. The lease, or a separate agreement, provides for—

        (*a*) extending or renewing the lease, or

        (*b*) the grant of a new lease,

making it possible for the plant or machinery to be leased for a period of more than 13 years.

    3. There is a period of more than one year between the dates on which any two consecutive payments become due under the lease.

    4. Any payments are due under the lease or a collateral agreement other than periodical payments.

    5. If payments due under the lease or a collateral agreement are expressed as monthly amounts due over a period, any payment due for that period is not the same as any of the others.

But, for this purpose, ignore variations made under the terms of the lease which are attributable to changes in—

        (*a*) the rate of corporation tax or income tax,

        (*b*) the rate of capital allowances,

        (*c*) any rate of interest where the changes are linked to changes in the rate of interest applicable to inter-bank loans, or

        (*d*) the premiums charged for insurance of any description by a person who is not connected with the lessor or the lessee.

    6. The lessor or a person connected with the lessor will, or may in certain circumstances, become entitled at any time to receive from the lessee or any other person a payment, other than a payment of insurance money, which is—

        (*a*) of an amount determined before the expiry of the lease, and

        (*b*) referable to a value of the plant or machinery at or after the expiry of the lease.

For this purpose, it does not matter whether the payment relates to a disposal of the plant or machinery.

(3) In items 4 and 5 of the list ''collateral agreement'' means an agreement which might reasonably be construed as being collateral to the lease.

Commentary—*Simon's Direct Tax Service* **B2.346**.
Former enactments—Sub-ss (1)–(3): CAA 1990 s 42(3).
Modifications—CAA 2001 Sch 3 para 54 (vehicles provided by employees in 1990–91: see modification note at the start of this Part).
CAA 2001 Sch 3 para 55 (certain expenditure incurred before 6 April 1976: see modification note at the start of this Part).

Recovery of excess allowances

111 Excess allowances: standard recovery mechanism

(1) If—

    (*a*) expenditure incurred by a person in providing plant or machinery has qualified for a first-year allowance or a normal writing-down allowance, and

    (*b*) at any time in the designated period, the plant or machinery is used for overseas leasing which is not protected leasing,

the following provisions of this section have effect in relation to the person who is the owner of the plant or machinery when it is first so used.

(2) For the chargeable period in which the plant or machinery is first used as described in subsection (1)(*b*), the owner is—

    (*a*) liable to a balancing charge of an amount given by subsection (4), and

    (*b*) required to bring into account a disposal value of an amount given by that subsection.

(3) For the chargeable period following that in which the plant or machinery is first used as described in subsection (1)(*b*), an amount given by subsection (4) is to be allocated to whatever pool is appropriate for plant or machinery which is of that description and is provided for leasing and used for overseas leasing.

(4) The amounts are—

The balancing charge

The amount, if any, by which F + N exceeds T, where—

    F is the amount of any first-year allowance made in respect of the qualifying expenditure referred to in subsection (1)(*a*) (''E''),

N is the total of any normal writing-down allowances made in respect of E for the relevant chargeable periods, and

T is the total of the allowances that could have been made for the relevant chargeable periods if no first-year allowance or normal writing-down allowances had been or could have been made.

The disposal value
The amount, if any, by which E exceeds $(F + N)$, where E, F and N have the meaning given in relation to the amount of the balancing charge.

The amount to be allocated to the pool
The aggregate of the balancing charge and the disposal value.

(5) For the purpose of calculating N, the normal writing-down allowances that were made in respect of expenditure on an item of plant or machinery are to be determined as if that item were the only item of plant or machinery in relation to which Chapter 5 had effect.

(6) "The relevant chargeable periods" means the chargeable period in which the qualifying expenditure was incurred and any subsequent chargeable period up to and including the one in which the plant or machinery was first used as described in subsection $(1)(b)$.

Commentary—*Simon's Direct Tax Service* **B2.347**.
Former enactments—Sub-s (1): CAA 1990 s 46(1), (8).
Sub-s (2): CAA 1990 s 46(1)–(3).
Sub-s (3): CAA 1990 s 46(1).
Sub-s (4): CAA 1990 s 46(1)–(3), (8).
Sub-s (5): CAA 1990 s 46(4).
Sub-s (6): CAA 1990 s 46(2).
Revenue Internal Guidance—Capital allowances manual CA 24210 (effect of the recovery of excess relief).
CA 242106 (worked example illustrating sub-s (5)).
Definition—"Chargeable period", s 6.
Modifications—CAA 2001 Sch 3 para 54 (vehicles provided by employees in 1990–91: see modification note at the start of this Part).
CAA 2001 Sch 3 para 55 (certain expenditure incurred before 6 April 1976: see modification note at the start of this Part).

112 Excess allowances: connected persons

(1) Section 111 applies with the modifications in subsections (2) to (4) in a case in which—

(a) the owner acquired the plant or machinery as a result of a transaction between connected persons (or a series of transactions each of which was between connected persons),

(b) none of the relevant provisions of ICTA under which the qualifying activity might have been treated as continuing has applied in respect of the transaction (or transactions), and

(c) any of the connected persons is a person to whom—

(i) a first-year allowance or a normal writing-down allowance has been made in respect of expenditure on the provision of the plant or machinery, or

(ii) a balancing allowance has been made in respect of such expenditure without a first-year allowance or normal writing-down allowance having been claimed.

(2) For the purposes of section 111(2) and (3)—

E is the amount of the expenditure in respect of which an allowance within subsection $(1)(c)$ has been made,

F is the amount of any first-year allowance within subsection $(1)(c)$, and

N is the amount of any normal writing-down allowance or balancing allowance within subsection $(1)(c)$.

(3) For the purposes of section 111(2) and (3), any consideration paid or received on a disposal of the plant or machinery between the connected persons is to be disregarded.

(4) If a balancing allowance or a balancing charge has been made in respect of any of the transactions, the amount representing $F + N$ is to be adjusted in a just and reasonable manner.

(5) "The relevant provisions of ICTA" means section 113(2), 114(1) or 343(2) (effect of change in persons carrying on a trade etc or of company reconstruction).

Commentary—*Simon's Direct Tax Service* **B2.347**.
Former enactments—Sub-s (1): CAA 1990 s 46(5), (6), (8).
Sub-s (2): CAA 1990 s 46(5), (8).
Sub-ss (3)–(5): CAA 1990 s 46(5).
Modifications—CAA 2001 Sch 3 para 54 (vehicles provided by employees in 1990–91: see modification note at the start of this Part).
CAA 2001 Sch 3 para 55 (certain expenditure incurred before 6 April 1976: see modification note at the start of this Part).

113 Excess allowances: special provision for ships

(1) If the plant or machinery referred to in section 111 is a ship—

(a) no allowance is to be made in respect of the ship under section 131(3) (postponed allowances) for the first chargeable period of overseas use or any subsequent chargeable period,

(b) nothing in section 132(2) (disposal events and single ship pool) restricts the operation of section 111, and (*c*) the amount of any first-year or writing-down allowance in respect of the ship which has been postponed under section 130 and not made is to be allocated to a long-life asset pool or an overseas leasing pool for the chargeable period following the first chargeable period of overseas use.

(2) "The first chargeable period of overseas use" means the chargeable period in which the plant or machinery is first used for overseas leasing which is not protected leasing.

Commentary—*Simon's Direct Tax Service* **B2.347**.
Former enactments—Sub-s (1): CAA 1990 s 46(7), (8).
Sub-s (2): CAA 1990 s 46(8).
Definition—"Chargeable period", s 6.
Modifications—CAA 2001 Sch 3 para 54 (vehicles provided by employees in 1990–91: see modification note at the start of this Part).
CAA 2001 Sch 3 para 55 (certain expenditure incurred before 6 April 1976: see modification note at the start of this Part).

Recovery of allowances given in cases where prohibition applies

114 Prohibited allowances: standard recovery mechanism

(1) If—

(*a*) a first-year allowance, a writing-down allowance or a balancing allowance has been made in respect of expenditure incurred in providing plant or machinery, and

(*b*) at any time in the designated period, an event occurs such that the expenditure is brought within section 110(2) (cases where allowances are prohibited),

the following provisions have effect in relation to the person owning the plant or machinery immediately before that event.

(2) For the chargeable period in which the event occurs, the owner is—

(*a*) liable to a balancing charge of an amount equal to A – R, and

(*b*) required to bring into account a disposal value of an amount equal to E – (A – R).

(3) For the purposes of subsection (2)—

A is the amount of any allowances within subsection (1)(*a*),

R is any amount previously recovered under section 111 or 112 (recovery of excess allowances), and

E is the amount of the expenditure referred to in subsection (1)(*a*).

(4) For the purpose of calculating A, the amount of the allowances made in respect of expenditure on an item of plant or machinery is to be determined as if that item were the only item of plant or machinery in relation to which Chapter 5 had effect.

Commentary—*Simon's Direct Tax Service* **B2.347**.
Former enactments—Sub-s (1): CAA 1990 s 42(4), (9).
Sub-s (2): CAA 1990 s 42(4).
Sub-s (3): CAA 1990 s 42(4), (9).
Sub-s (4): CAA 1990 s 42(5).
Definition—"Chargeable period", s 6.
Modifications—CAA 2001 Sch 3 para 54 (vehicles provided by employees in 1990–91: see modification note at the start of this Part).
CAA 2001 Sch 3 para 55 (certain expenditure incurred before 6 April 1976: see modification note at the start of this Part).

115 Prohibited allowances: connected persons

(1) Section 114 applies with the modifications in subsection (2) in a case in which—

(*a*) an amount falls to be treated as a balancing charge under that section,

(*b*) the person on whom the balancing charge is to be imposed acquired the plant or machinery in question as a result of a transaction between connected persons (or a series of transactions each of which was between connected persons),

(*c*) none of the relevant provisions of ICTA under which the qualifying activity might have been treated as continuing has applied in respect of the transaction (or transactions), and

(*d*) a first-year allowance, a writing-down allowance or a balancing allowance in respect of expenditure on the provision of that plant or machinery has been made to any of those persons.

(2) For the purpose of calculating the balancing charge—

(*a*) A is the amount of any allowances within subsection (1)(*d*),

(*b*) any consideration paid or received on a disposal of the plant or machinery between the connected persons is to be disregarded, and

(*c*) if a balancing allowance or a balancing charge has been made in respect of any of the transactions, A is to be adjusted in a just and reasonable manner.

(3) "The relevant provisions of ICTA" means section 113(2), 114(1) or 343(2) (effect of change in persons carrying on a trade etc or of company reconstruction).

Commentary—*Simon's Direct Tax Service* **B2.347**.
Former enactments—Sub-s (1): CAA 1990 s 42(6).
Sub-s (2): CAA 1990 s 42(7).
Sub-s (3): CAA 1990 s 42(6).
Modifications—CAA 2001 Sch 3 para 54 (vehicles provided by employees in 1990–91: see modification note at the start of this Part).
CAA 2001 Sch 3 para 55 (certain expenditure incurred before 6 April 1976: see modification note at the start of this Part).

CAA 2001

Application of Chapter in relation to joint lessees

116 Mitigation of regime

(1) This section applies if—

    (*a*) plant or machinery is leased to two or more persons jointly,

    (*b*) at least one of them is a person who—

        (i) is not resident in the United Kingdom, and

        (ii) does not use the plant or machinery exclusively for earning profits chargeable to tax, and

    (*c*) the leasing is not protected leasing.

(2) Subsection (3) applies if, at any time when the plant or machinery is leased as described in subsection (1), the lessees use the plant or machinery for the purposes of a qualifying activity or activities but not for leasing.

(3) The expenditure on the provision of the plant or machinery is to be treated as not subject to sections 107, 109 and 110 if, and to the extent to which, it appears that the profits of the qualifying activity or activities will be chargeable to tax throughout—

    (*a*) the designated period, or

    (*b*) if shorter, the period of the lease.

(4) Subsection (5) applies if, under subsection (3), part of the expenditure is treated as not subject to section 107, 109 or 110.

(5) Whether or not the plant or machinery continues to be leased as described in subsection (1), Chapters 5 (allowances and charges) and 10 (long-life assets) and this Chapter have effect as if—

    (*a*) the part of the expenditure that is not subject to section 107, 109 or 110 were expenditure on the provision of a separate item of plant or machinery, and

    (*b*) the rest were expenditure which has been incurred on the provision of another item of plant or machinery (and which is subject to those sections).

(6) All such apportionments are to be made as are necessary as a result of subsection (5).

Commentary—*Simon's Direct Tax Service* **B2.348**.
Former enactments—Sub-s (1): CAA 1990 s 43(1).
Sub-ss (2), (3): CAA 1990 s 43(2).
Sub-ss (4)–(6): CAA 1990 s 43(3).
Revenue Internal Guidance—Capital allowances manual CA 24400 (examples illustrating effect of this section).
Modifications—CAA 2001 Sch 3 para 54 (vehicles provided by employees in 1990–91: see modification note at the start of this Part).
CAA 2001 Sch 3 para 55 (certain expenditure incurred before 6 April 1976: see modification note at the start of this Part).

117 Recovery of allowances in case of joint lessees

(1) If—

    (*a*) expenditure is incurred on the provision of plant or machinery which is leased as described in section 116(1),

    (*b*) the whole or a part of the expenditure has qualified for a normal writing-down allowance under section 116(3),

    (*c*) at any time in the designated period while the plant or machinery is so leased, no lessee uses the plant or machinery for the purposes of a qualifying activity or activities the profits of which are chargeable to tax, and

    (*d*) section 114 (recovery of prohibited allowances) does not apply at that time and has not applied at any earlier time,

sections 111 and 112 (recovery of excess allowances) apply as if the plant or machinery or (as the case may be) the separate item of plant or machinery referred to in section 116(5)(*a*) had at that time begun to be used for overseas leasing which is not protected leasing.

(2) If—

    (*a*) the whole or a part of any expenditure has qualified for—

        (i) a normal writing-down allowance otherwise than as a result of section 116(3), or

        (ii) a first-year allowance,

    (*b*) subsequently, but during the designated period, the plant or machinery is leased as described in section 116(1),

    (*c*) at any time in the designated period while the plant or machinery is so leased, no lessee uses the plant or machinery for the purposes of a qualifying activity or activities the profits of which are chargeable to tax, and

    (*d*) section 114 (recovery of prohibited allowances) does not apply at that time and has not applied at any earlier time,

sections 111 and 112 (recovery of excess allowances) apply as if the plant or machinery (and not any separate item of plant or machinery referred to in section 116(5)(*a*)) had at that time begun to be used for overseas leasing which is not protected leasing.

(3) Subsections (4) and (5) apply if—

(*a*) expenditure is incurred on the provision of plant or machinery which is leased as described in section 116(1),

(*b*) the whole or a part of the expenditure has qualified for a normal writing-down allowance under section 116(3),

(*c*) at the end of the designated period, the plant or machinery is leased as described in section 116(1) but subsection (1) has not had effect, and

(*d*) it appears that the extent to which the plant or machinery has been used for the purposes of a qualifying activity or activities the profits of which are chargeable to tax is less than the extent of such use taken into account in determining the amount of the expenditure which qualified for a normal writing-down allowance.

(4) Sections 111 and 112 (recovery of excess allowances) apply as if—

(*a*) a part of the expenditure corresponding to the reduction in the extent of use referred to in subsection (3)(*d*) were expenditure on the provision of a separate item of plant or machinery, and

(*b*) the separate item of plant or machinery had been used, on the last day of the designated period, for overseas leasing which is not protected leasing.

(5) Any disposal value subsequently brought into account under this Part in respect of the plant or machinery must be apportioned by reference to the extent of its use (determined at the end of the designated period) for the purposes of a qualifying activity or activities the profits of which are chargeable to tax.

(6) If an apportionment is made under subsection (5), section 116(6) does not apply.

Commentary—*Simon's Direct Tax Service* B2.348.
Former enactments—Sub-s (1): CAA 1990 s 44(1), (2).
Sub-s (2): CAA 1990 s 44(3), (5).
Sub-ss (3)–(6): CAA 1990 s 44(4).
Revenue Internal Guidance—Capital allowances manual CA 24400 (example illustrating effect of this section).
Modifications—CAA 2001 Sch 3 para 22 (modification of sub-ss (1), (3)–(5) if—

(*a*) the expenditure has been incurred on the provision of plant and machinery which is leased as described in CAA 2001 s 116(1),

(*b*) the whole or part of the expenditure has qualified for the first year allowance under CAA 1990 s 43(4) or CAA 2001 Sch 3 para 47(7)).

CAA 2001 Sch 3 para 54 (vehicles provided by employees in 1990–91: see modification note at the start of this Part).
CAA 2001 Sch 3 para 55 (certain expenditure incurred before 6 April 1976: see modification note at the start of this Part).

Duties to supply information

118 Certificate relating to protected leasing

(1) If—

(*a*) expenditure is incurred on the provision of plant or machinery, and

(*b*) before the expenditure has qualified for a normal writing-down allowance, the plant or machinery is used for overseas leasing which is protected leasing,

a claim for a writing-down allowance which takes account of that expenditure must be accompanied by a certificate.

(2) The certificate must specify—

(*a*) the description of protected leasing,

(*b*) the person to whom the plant or machinery has been leased, and

(*c*) if the certificate is given by reference to a chargeable period, all the items of plant or machinery (if more than one) relevant to that period.

(3) Subsection (1) applies, for the purposes of claims to first-year allowances, as if the references to a normal writing-down allowance and to a writing-down allowance included a first-year allowance.

(4) But nothing in subsection (3) prevents subsection (1) from continuing to apply if the use for protected leasing occurs after the expenditure has qualified for one allowance and before it qualifies for another.

Commentary—*Simon's Direct Tax Service* **B2.349**.
Former enactments—Sub-s (1): CAA 1990 s 48(1).
Sub-s (2): CAA 1990 s 48(1), (4).
Sub-ss (3), (4): CAA 1990 s 48(7).
Revenue Internal Guidance—Capital allowances manual CA 24100 (general explanation of protected leasing).
Definition—''Chargeable period'', s 6.
Modifications—CAA 2001 Sch 3 para 54 (vehicles provided by employees in 1990–91: see modification note at the start of this Part).
CAA 2001 Sch 3 para 55 (certain expenditure incurred before 6 April 1976: see modification note at the start of this Part).

119 Notice of change of use of plant or machinery

(1) If—

(*a*) any expenditure on plant or machinery has qualified for a first-year allowance or a normal writing-down allowance, and

(*b*) the plant or machinery is subsequently used at any time in the designated period for overseas leasing which is not protected leasing,

the person who then owns the plant or machinery must give notice of the fact to the Inland Revenue.

CAA 2001

(2) The notice must specify—

(a) the person who is not resident in the United Kingdom to whom the plant or machinery has been leased, and

(b) if the notice is given by reference to a chargeable period, all the items of plant or machinery (if more than one) relevant to that period.

(3) The notice must be given—

(a) no later than 3 months after the end of the chargeable period in which the plant or machinery is first used for overseas leasing which is not protected leasing, or

(b) if at the end of the 3 months the person required to give the notice does not know and cannot reasonably be expected to know that the plant or machinery is being so used, within 30 days of coming to know of it.

Commentary—*Simon's Direct Tax Service* **B2.349**.
Former enactments—Sub-s (1): CAA 1990 s 48(2), (7).
Sub-s (2): CAA 1990 s 48(4).
Sub-s (3): CAA 1990 s 48(3), (6).
Definition—"Chargeable period", s 6.
Modifications—CAA 2001 Sch 3 para 54 (vehicles provided by employees in 1990–91: see modification note at the start of this Part).
CAA 2001 Sch 3 para 55 (certain expenditure incurred before 6 April 1976: see modification note at the start of this Part).

120 Notice and joint lessees

(1) If expenditure is incurred on the provision of plant or machinery which is leased as described in section 116(1) (joint lessees: mitigation of regime), the lessor must give notice to the Inland Revenue.

(2) A notice under subsection (1) must specify—

(a) the names and addresses of the persons to whom the asset is jointly leased,

(b) the part of the expenditure properly attributable to each of them, and

(c) which of them (so far as the lessor knows) is resident in the United Kingdom.

(3) If circumstances occur such that section 117(1) or (2) (recovery of allowances) applies, the person who is then the lessor must give notice of the fact to the Inland Revenue.

(4) A notice under subsection (3) must specify—

(a) any of the joint lessees who is not resident in the United Kingdom to whom the plant or machinery has been leased, and

(b) if it is given by reference to a chargeable period, all the items of plant or machinery (if more than one) relevant to that period.

(5) A notice under this section must be given—

(a) no later than 3 months after the end of the chargeable period in which the plant or machinery is first leased as described in section 116(1) or (as the case may be) in which the circumstances referred to in subsection (3) occur, or

(b) if at the end of the 3 months the person required to give the notice does not know and cannot reasonably be expected to know that the plant or machinery is being so used, within 30 days of coming to know of it.

Commentary—*Simon's Direct Tax Service* **B2.349**.
Former enactments—Sub-ss (1), (2): CAA 1990 s 48(5).
Sub-s (3): CAA 1990 ss 44(2), 48(2), (3).
Sub-s (4): IA 1978 s 20(2); CAA 1990 ss 44(2), (3), s 48(2), (4).
Sub-s (5): IA 1978 s 20(2); CAA 1990 s 44(2), (3), s 48(2), (3), (5), (6).
Definition—"Chargeable period", s 6.
Modifications—CAA 2001 Sch 3 para 54 (vehicles provided by employees in 1990–91: see modification note at the start of this Part).
CAA 2001 Sch 3 para 55 (certain expenditure incurred before 6 April 1976: see modification note at the start of this Part).

Qualifying purposes

121 Meaning of "short-term leasing"

(1) Leasing of plant or machinery is short-term leasing if—

(a) the number of consecutive days for which it is leased to the same person will normally be less than 30, and

(b) the total number of days for which it is leased to that person in any period of 12 months will normally be less than 90.

(2) Leasing of plant or machinery is also short-term leasing if—

(a) the number of consecutive days for which the plant or machinery is leased to the same person will not normally exceed 365, and

(b) the total length of the periods for which it is leased in any consecutive period of 4 years within the designated period to lessees in circumstances not falling within section 125(4) (other qualifying purposes: non-leasing use) will not exceed 2 years.

(3) If any plant or machinery is leased as a number of items which—

(a) form part of a group of items of the same or a similar description, and

(b) are not separately identifiable,

all items in the group may be treated as used for short-term leasing if substantially the whole of the items in the group are so used.

(4) For the purposes of subsections (1) and (2) persons who are connected with each other are to be treated as the same person.

Commentary—*Simon's Direct Tax Service* B2.345.
Former enactments—Sub-s (1): CAA 1990 s 40(1).
Sub-s (2): CAA 1990 s 40(1), (2).
Sub-ss (3), (4): CAA 1990 s 40(3).
Revenue Internal Guidance—Capital allowances manual CA 24100 (general explantion of short-term leasing).
Modifications—CAA 2001 Sch 3 para 54 (vehicles provided by employees in 1990–91: see modification note at the start of this Part).
CAA 2001 Sch 3 para 55 (certain expenditure incurred before 6 April 1976: see modification note at the start of this Part).

122 Short-term leasing by buyer, lessee, etc

(1) Plant or machinery is used for a qualifying purpose at any time when any of the persons listed in subsection (2) uses it for short-term leasing (as defined by section 121).

(2) The persons are—

(a) the person ("X") who incurred expenditure on the provision of the plant or machinery;
(b) a person who is connected with X;
(c) a person who acquired the plant or machinery from X as a result of—

(i) a disposal on the occasion of which, or
(ii) two or more disposals on the occasion of each of which,

the qualifying activity carried on by the person making the disposal was treated as continuing under one of the relevant provisions of ICTA;
(d) a person to whom the plant or machinery is leased and who is resident in the United Kingdom;
(e) a person to whom the plant or machinery is leased, who is carrying on a qualifying activity in the United Kingdom and who uses the plant or machinery for the short-term leasing in the course of that activity.

(3) "The relevant provisions of ICTA" means section 113(2) or 114(1) (effect of change in persons carrying on a trade etc).

Commentary—*Simon's Direct Tax Service* B2.345.
Former enactments—Sub-s (1): CAA 1990 s 39(1), (3), (4).
Sub-s (2): CAA 1990 s 39(1), (3), (4), (10), s 40(5).
Sub-s (3): CAA 1990 s 40(5).
Modifications—CAA 2001 Sch 3 para 54 (vehicles provided by employees in 1990–91: see modification note at the start of this Part).
CAA 2001 Sch 3 para 55 (certain expenditure incurred before 6 April 1976: see modification note at the start of this Part).

123 Ships and aircraft

(1) A ship is used for a qualifying purpose at any time when it is let on charter in the course of a trade which consists of or includes operating ships by a person who is—

(a) resident in the United Kingdom or carries on the trade there, and
(b) responsible for navigating and managing the ship throughout the period of the charter and for defraying—

(i) all expenses in connection with the ship throughout that period, or
(ii) substantially all such expenses other than those directly incidental to a particular voyage or to the employment of the ship during that period.

(2) Subsection (1) applies, with the necessary modifications, in relation to aircraft as it applies in relation to ships.

(3) For the purposes of subsection (1)(b) a person is responsible for something if he—

(a) is responsible as principal, or
(b) appoints another person to be responsible in his place.

(4) Subsections (1) and (2) do not apply if the main object, or one of the main objects—

(a) of the letting of the ship or aircraft on charter,
(b) of a series of transactions of which the letting of the ship or aircraft on charter was one, or
(c) of any of the transactions in such a series,

was to obtain a writing-down allowance determined without regard to section 109 (writing-down allowances at 10%) in respect of expenditure incurred by any person on the provision of the ship or aircraft.

Commentary—*Simon's Direct Tax Service* B2.345.
Former enactments—Sub-s (1): CAA 1990 s 39(6).
Sub-s (2): CAA 1990 s 39(7).
Sub-s (3): CAA 1990 s 39(6).
Sub-s (4): CAA 1990 s 39(8).
Revenue Internal Guidance—Capital allowances manual CA 24120 (situation in which the "main object" provisions are likely to apply).
Modifications—CAA 2001 Sch 3 para 23 (sub-ss (1), (2) above do not apply if the main object (or one of the main objects)—
(a) of the letting of the ship or aircraft on charter,

(b) of a series of transactions of which the letting of the ship or aircraft on charter was one, or

(c) of any of the transactions in such a series,

was to obtain a first-year allowance in respect of expenditure which was first-year qualifying expenditure under CAA 2001 Sch 15 para 47 (concerning expenditure incurred 1992–93) and was incurred by any person on the provision of the ship or aircraft).

CAA 2001 Sch 3 para 54 (vehicles provided by employees in 1990–91: see modification note at the start of this Part).

CAA 2001 Sch 3 para 55 (certain expenditure incurred before 6 April 1976: see modification note at the start of this Part).

124 Transport containers

(1) A transport container is used for a qualifying purpose at any time when it is leased in the course of a trade which is carried on by a person who—

(a) is resident in the United Kingdom, or

(b) carries on the trade there,

and either of the conditions given below is met.

(2) The first condition is that—

(a) the person's trade consists of or includes the operation of ships or aircraft, and

(b) the container is at other times used by that person in connection with the operation of the ships or aircraft.

(3) The second condition is that the container is leased under a succession of leases to different persons who are not, or most of whom are not, connected with each other.

Commentary—*Simon's Direct Tax Service* **B2.345**.

Former enactments—Sub-ss (1)–(3): CAA 1990 s 39(9).

Modifications—CAA 2001 Sch 3 para 54 (vehicles provided by employees in 1990–91: see modification note at the start of this Part).

CAA 2001 Sch 3 para 55 (certain expenditure incurred before 6 April 1976: see modification note at the start of this Part).

125 Other qualifying purposes

(1) Plant or machinery is used for a qualifying purpose at any time when subsection (2) or (4) applies.

(2) This subsection applies if any of the persons listed in subsection (3) uses the plant or machinery for the purpose of a qualifying activity without leasing it.

(3) The persons are—

(a) the person (''X'') who incurred expenditure on the provision of the plant or machinery;

(b) a person who is connected with X;

(c) a person who acquired the plant or machinery from X as a result of—

(i) a disposal on the occasion of which, or

(ii) two or more disposals on the occasion of each of which,

the qualifying activity carried on by the person making the disposal was treated as continuing under one of the relevant provisions of ICTA.

(4) This subsection applies if—

(a) a lessee uses the plant or machinery for the purposes of a qualifying activity without leasing it, and

(b) if he had incurred expenditure on the provision of the plant or machinery at that time, the expenditure would have fallen to be included, in whole or in part, in his available qualifying expenditure for a chargeable period.

(5) ''The relevant provisions of ICTA'' means section 113(2) or 114(1) (effect of change in persons carrying on a trade etc).

Commentary—*Simon's Direct Tax Service* **B2.345**.

Former enactments—Sub-s (1): CAA 1990 s 39(1).

Sub-s (2): CAA 1990 s 39(5).

Sub-s (3): CAA 1990 s 39(5), (10), s 40(5).

Sub-s (4): CAA 1990 s 39(2).

Sub-s (5): CAA 1990 s 40(5).

Revenue Internal Guidance—Capital allowances manual CA 24110 (in a chain of leases, the test under sub-s (4) is applied to the end lessee).

Definitions—''Available qualifying expenditure'', s 57; ''chargeable period'', s 6.

Modifications—CAA 2001 Sch 3 para 54 (vehicles provided by employees in 1990–91: see modification note at the start of this Part).

CAA 2001 Sch 3 para 55 (certain expenditure incurred before 6 April 1976: see modification note at the start of this Part).

Minor definitions

126 Minor definitions

(1) In this Chapter ''normal writing-down allowance'' means a writing-down allowance of an amount determined without regard to sections 102 and 109 (reduced rates).

(2) In this Chapter any reference, in relation to any person, to expenditure having qualified for a normal writing-down allowance is to—

(a) the expenditure, or part of it, having fallen to be included in that person's available qualifying expenditure for any chargeable period, and

(b) that available qualifying expenditure being expenditure which is not subject to section 102 or 109.

(3) Any reference in this Chapter to a person's expenditure having qualified for a first-year allowance is to such an allowance having fallen to be made in respect of the whole or any part of the expenditure.

Former enactments—Sub-s (1): CAA 1990 s 50(3).
Sub-s (2): CAA 1990 s 50(4).
Sub-s (3): CAA 1990 s 50(4A).
Definitions—"Available qualifying expenditure", s 57; "chargeable period", s 6.
Modifications—CAA 2001 Sch 3 para 54 (vehicles provided by employees in 1990–91: see modification note at the start of this Part).
CAA 2001 Sch 3 para 55 (certain expenditure incurred before 6 April 1976: see modification note at the start of this Part).

CHAPTER 12
SHIPS
Pooling and postponement of allowances

127 Single ship pool

(1) Qualifying expenditure incurred on the provision of a ship for the purposes of a qualifying activity, if allocated to a pool, must be allocated to a single asset pool (a "single ship pool").

(2) Subsection (1) is subject to the exceptions given in section 128 and any election under section 129 to use the appropriate non-ship pool.

(3) In this Chapter "the appropriate non-ship pool", in relation to a ship, means the pool to which the expenditure incurred on the provision of the ship would be allocated, or would have been allocated, apart from this Chapter.

Commentary—*Simon's Direct Tax Service* B2.350.
Former enactments—Sub-ss (1), (2): CAA 1990 s 31(1), (2).
Revenue Internal Guidance—Capital allowances manual CA 25100 (meaning of "ship").
Modifications—CAA 2001 Sch 3 para 54 (vehicles provided by employees in 1990–91: see modification note at the start of this Part).
CAA 2001 Sch 3 para 55 (certain expenditure incurred before 6 April 1976: see modification note at the start of this Part).

128 Expenditure which is not to be allocated to single ship pool

(1) The expenditure is not to be allocated to a single ship pool if the ship is provided for leasing unless—

(a) the ship is not used for overseas leasing at any time in the designated period, or if it is, is used only for protected leasing, and
(b) it appears that the ship will be used for a qualifying purpose in the designated period and will not be used for any other purpose at any time in that period.

(2) The expenditure is not to be allocated to a single ship pool if the qualifying activity for the purposes of which the ship is provided is special leasing of plant or machinery.

(3) In subsection (1) "leasing", "overseas leasing", "protected leasing", "qualifying purpose" and "designated period" have the same meaning as in Chapter 11 (overseas leasing).

Commentary—*Simon's Direct Tax Service* B2.350.
Former enactments—Sub-ss (1), (2): CAA 1990 s 31(1).
Sub-s (3): CAA 1990 s 31(11).
Definition—"Special leasing", s 19.
Modifications—CAA 2001 Sch 3 para 54 (vehicles provided by employees in 1990–91: see modification note at the start of this Part).
CAA 2001 Sch 3 para 55 (certain expenditure incurred before 6 April 1976: see modification note at the start of this Part).

129 Election to use the appropriate non-ship pool

(1) A person who has incurred qualifying expenditure on the provision of a ship may, by an election made for a chargeable period, allocate to the appropriate non-ship pool—

(a) all or a part of any qualifying expenditure that would otherwise be allocated to a single ship pool, or
(b) all or a part of the available qualifying expenditure in a single ship pool.

(2) An election under this section must be made by notice given to the Inland Revenue—

(a) for income tax purposes, on or before the normal time limit for amending a tax return for the tax year in which the relevant chargeable period ends;
(b) for corporation tax purposes, no later than 2 years after the end of the relevant chargeable period.

(3) "The relevant chargeable period" means the chargeable period for which the election is made.

Commentary—*Simon's Direct Tax Service* B2.350.
Former enactments—Sub-s (1): CAA 1990 s 33(1), (3)–(5); change in law.
Sub-ss (2), (3): CAA 1990 s 33(5A).
Revenue Internal Guidance—Capital allowances manual CA 25150 (explanation with a worked example).
Definitions—"Available qualifying expenditure", s 57; "chargeable period", s 6; "normal time limit for amending a tax return", s 577(1).

Modifications—CAA 2001 Sch 3 para 54 (vehicles provided by employees in 1990–91: see modification note at the start of this Part).
CAA 2001 Sch 3 para 55 (certain expenditure incurred before 6 April 1976: see modification note at the start of this Part).

130 Notice postponing first-year or writing-down allowance

(1) A person who is entitled to a first-year allowance for a chargeable period in respect of qualifying expenditure on the provision of a ship may, by notice, postpone all or part of the allowance.

(2) A person who is entitled to a writing-down allowance for a chargeable period in respect of qualifying expenditure allocated to a single ship pool may, by notice, postpone all or part of the allowance.

(3) A notice under this section must specify the amount postponed.

(4) A notice under this section must be given to the Inland Revenue—

(*a*) for income tax purposes, on or before the normal time limit for amending a tax return for the tax year in which the relevant chargeable period ends;
(*b*) for corporation tax purposes, no later than 2 years after the end of the relevant chargeable period.

(5) "The relevant chargeable period" means the chargeable period for which the person is entitled to the allowance.

(6) If a person entitled to a first-year allowance in respect of qualifying expenditure on the provision of a ship claims the allowance in respect of part of the expenditure, subsection (1) applies to the allowance claimed.

(7) If a person entitled to a writing-down allowance in respect of qualifying expenditure allocated to a single ship pool requires the allowance to be reduced to a specified amount, subsection (2) applies to the allowance as so reduced.

Commentary—*Simon's Direct Tax Service* **B2.350**.
Former enactments—Sub-s (1): CAA 1990 s 30(1).
Sub-s (2): CAA 1990 s 30(1), (3).
Sub-s (3): CAA 1990 ss 30(1), 31(3).
Sub-ss (4), (5): CAA 1990 s 30(1), (1A), s 31(3), (3A).
Sub-s (6): CAA 1990 s 30(5).
Sub-s (7): CAA 1990 s 31(6).
Revenue Internal Guidance—Capital allowances manual CA 25200 (worked example).
Definitions—"Chargeable period", s 6; "normal time limit for amending a tax return", s 577(1).
Modifications—CAA 2001 Sch 3 para 54 (vehicles provided by employees in 1990–91: see modification note at the start of this Part).
CAA 2001 Sch 3 para 55 (certain expenditure incurred before 6 April 1976: see modification note at the start of this Part).

131 Effect of postponement

(1) If a person gives notice in respect of a chargeable period under section 130—

(*a*) the allowance is withheld or withdrawn to the extent that it is postponed, but
(*b*) sections 57 to 59 (calculation of available qualifying expenditure) apply as if the allowance had been made to the person without any postponement.

(2) On making a claim, the person is entitled to have all or part of a postponed first-year allowance made to him as a first-year allowance for one or more subsequent chargeable periods in which he is carrying on the qualifying activity.

(3) On making a claim, the person is entitled to have all or part of a postponed writing-down allowance made to him as a writing-down allowance for one or more subsequent chargeable periods in which he is carrying on the qualifying activity.

(4) The total amount of any first-year allowances made under subsection (2) or writing-down allowances made under subsection (3) must not exceed the amount of the postponed allowance in question.

(5) A writing-down allowance made under subsection (3) is ignored for the purposes of section 59 (unrelieved qualifying expenditure).

(6) The fact that a postponed writing-down allowance is claimed for a chargeable period does not affect entitlement to, or the amount of, any other writing-down allowance to which the person is otherwise entitled for that chargeable period.

(7) A postponed allowance is not, merely because of the postponement, included in the reference in section 403ZB(2) of ICTA (group relief) to an allowance or amount carried forward from an earlier period.

Commentary—*Simon's Direct Tax Service* **B2.350**.
Former enactments—Sub-s (1): CAA 1990 ss 30(2), 31(4).
Sub-s (2): CAA 1990 s 30(2).
Sub-s (3): CAA 1990 s 31(4).
Sub-s (4): CAA 1990 ss 30(2), 31(4).
Sub-s (6): CAA 1990 s 31(5).
Sub-s (7): CAA 1990 ss 30(4), 31(10).
Definitions—"Available qualifying expenditure", s 57; "chargeable period", s 6.

Modifications—CAA 2001 Sch 3 para 54 (vehicles provided by employees in 1990–91: see modification note at the start of this Part).
CAA 2001 Sch 3 para 55 (certain expenditure incurred before 6 April 1976: see modification note at the start of this Part).

132 Disposal events and single ship pool

(1) A person is required to bring a disposal value into account in a single ship pool if the ship—

    (*a*) is provided for leasing, and

    (*b*) begins to be used otherwise than for a qualifying purpose within the first 4 years of the designated period.

(2) If any disposal event (including one under subsection (1)) occurs in relation to a single ship pool—

    (*a*) the available qualifying expenditure in the single ship pool is allocated, for the chargeable period in which the event occurs, to the appropriate non-ship pool,

    (*b*) the disposal value must be brought into account as a disposal value for that chargeable period in the appropriate non-ship pool, and

    (*c*) the single ship pool ends without a final chargeable period and without any liability to a balancing charge arising.

(3) Subsections (1) and (2) apply even if, as a result of an election under section 129, some of the qualifying expenditure on the provision of the ship has been allocated to the appropriate non-ship pool.

(4) In subsection (1) "leasing", "qualifying purpose" and "designated period" have the same meaning as in Chapter 11 (overseas leasing).

Commentary—*Simon's Direct Tax Service* **B2.350**.
Former enactments—Sub-s (1): CAA 1990 ss 31(2), 40(4).
Sub-s (2): CAA 1990 ss 24(6), (8), 31(7).
Sub-s (3): CAA 1990 ss 31(7), 33(5).
Sub-s (4): CAA 1990 s 31(11).
Definitions—"Available qualifying expenditure", s 57; "chargeable period", s 6; "disposal event", s 60(2); "final chargeable period", s 65.
Modifications—CAA 2001 Sch 3 para 54 (vehicles provided by employees in 1990–91: see modification note at the start of this Part).
CAA 2001 Sch 3 para 55 (certain expenditure incurred before 6 April 1976: see modification note at the start of this Part).

133 Ship not used

(1) This section applies if—

    (*a*) a person has incurred qualifying expenditure on the provision of a ship for the purposes of a qualifying activity, and

    (*b*) the ship ceases to be owned by the person without having been brought into use for the purposes of the qualifying activity.

(2) Any writing-down allowances that have previously been made in respect of qualifying expenditure in the single ship pool (or which have been postponed) must be withdrawn.

(3) The amount of any writing-down allowances withdrawn under subsection (2) is allocated, for the chargeable period in which the person ceases to own the ship, to the appropriate non-ship pool.

(4) Any adjustments required by this section are in addition to any adjustments required under section 132 (disposal events and single ship pool).

Commentary—*Simon's Direct Tax Service* **B2.350**.
Former enactments—Sub-s (1): CAA 1990 ss 31(1), 32(1).
Sub-ss (2)–(4): CAA 1990 s 32(1).
Definition—"Chargeable period", s 6.
Modifications—CAA 2001 Sch 3 para 54 (vehicles provided by employees in 1990–91: see modification note at the start of this Part).
CAA 2001 Sch 3 para 55 (certain expenditure incurred before 6 April 1976: see modification note at the start of this Part).

Deferment of balancing charges

134 Deferment of balancing charges: introduction

(1) Sections 135 to 156 enable a balancing charge that arises when there is a disposal event in respect of a ship to be deferred and attributed to qualifying expenditure on another ship.

(2) In this Chapter "the deferment rules" means sections 135 to 156.

Commentary—*Simon's Direct Tax Service* **B2.351**.

135 Claim for deferment

(1) A person ("the shipowner") who is liable to a balancing charge for a chargeable period may claim deferment of all or part of the charge if—

    (*a*) in the chargeable period there is a disposal event ("the relevant disposal event") in respect of a ship ("the old ship"),

    (*b*) the old ship—

        (i) was provided for the purposes of a qualifying activity carried on by the shipowner, and

     (ii) was owned by the shipowner at some time in the chargeable period, and

  (c) the conditions in section 136 are met.

(2) The amount which may be deferred is subject to the limit in section 138.

(3) For income tax purposes, a claim for deferment must be made on or before the normal time limit for amending a tax return for the tax year in which the relevant chargeable period ends.

(4) ''The relevant chargeable period'' means the chargeable period for which the shipowner is liable to the balancing charge.

(5) For corporation tax purposes, Part IX of Schedule 18 to FA 1998 applies in relation to the making of a claim for deferment as it applies in relation to the making of a claim for an allowance.

Commentary—*Simon's Direct Tax Service* **B2.351**.
Former enactments—Sub-s (1): CAA 1990 s 33A(1), (2).
Sub-s (2): CAA 1990 s 33A(2).
Sub-ss (3), (4): CAA 1990 s 33F(2).
Sub-s (5): CAA 1990 s 33F(1).
Definitions—''Chargeable period'', s 6; ''disposal event'', s 60(2); ''normal time limit for amending a tax return'', s 577(1).
Modifications—CAA 2001 Sch 3 para 54 (vehicles provided by employees in 1990–91: see modification note at the start of this Part).
CAA 2001 Sch 3 para 55 (certain expenditure incurred before 6 April 1976: see modification note at the start of this Part).

136 Further conditions for deferment

The conditions referred to in section 135(1)(c) are that—

  (a) the relevant disposal event is of a kind mentioned in section 61(1)(a) to (d) (cessation of ownership, loss, abandonment, destruction etc of ship),

  (b) the old ship was a qualifying ship immediately before the relevant disposal event,

  (c) the shipowner has not incurred a loss in respect of the qualifying activity for the chargeable period for which he is liable to the balancing charge, and

  (d) no amount in respect of the old ship has been allocated to—

     (i) the overseas leasing pool,

     (ii) a single asset pool under section 206 (plant or machinery provided or used partly for purposes other than those of the qualifying activity),

     (iii) a single asset pool under section 211 (payment of partial depreciation subsidy), or

     (iv) a pool for a qualifying activity consisting of special leasing.

Commentary—*Simon's Direct Tax Service* **B2.351**.
Former enactments—CAA 1990 s 33A(1), (7).
Revenue Internal Guidance—Capital allowances manual CA 25400 (general explanation of this section).
Definitions—''Chargeable period'', s 6; ''disposal event'', s 60(2); ''special leasing'', s 19.
Modifications—CAA 2001 Sch 3 para 54 (vehicles provided by employees in 1990–91: see modification note at the start of this Part).
CAA 2001 Sch 3 para 55 (certain expenditure incurred before 6 April 1976: see modification note at the start of this Part).

137 Effect of deferment

A claim for deferment is given effect by allocating the amount deferred, for the chargeable period in respect of which the claim is made, to the appropriate non-ship pool.

Commentary—*Simon's Direct Tax Service* **B2.351**.
Former enactments—CAA 1990 s 33A(2).
Definition—''Chargeable period'', s 6.
Modifications—CAA 2001 Sch 3 para 54 (vehicles provided by employees in 1990–91: see modification note at the start of this Part).
CAA 2001 Sch 3 para 55 (certain expenditure incurred before 6 April 1976: see modification note at the start of this Part).

138 Limit on amount deferred

(1) The amount deferred must not exceed the smallest of the following amounts—

  (a) the amount of any balancing charge which, if the claim for deferment had not been made, would have been made for the chargeable period for which deferment is claimed in the appropriate non-ship pool;

  (b) the amount given by section 139 (amount taken into account in respect of the old ship);

  (c) the amount which is, or is expected to be, the amount of expenditure on new shipping incurred—

     (i) by the shipowner or, if the shipowner is a company, by another company which is a member of the same group at the time when the expenditure is incurred, and

     (ii) within the period of 6 years beginning with the relevant disposal event;

  (d) the amount of the shipowner's profits or income from the qualifying activity for the chargeable period for which deferment is claimed.

(2) In determining profits or income for the purposes of subsection (1)(d)—

  (a) any other amounts deferred under section 135 are to be taken into account, and

  (b) any amounts brought forward under section 385 or 393 of ICTA (losses) are to be disregarded.

Commentary—*Simon's Direct Tax Service* **B2.351**.
Former enactments—Sub-s (1): CAA 1990 s 33A(2), (3), (6); change in law.

Sub-s (2): CAA 1990 s 33A(3).
Definitions—"Chargeable period", s 6; "disposal event", s 60(2).
Modifications—CAA 2001 Sch 3 para 54 (vehicles provided by employees in 1990–91: see modification note at the start of this Part).
CAA 2001 Sch 3 para 55 (certain expenditure incurred before 6 April 1976: see modification note at the start of this Part).

139 Amount taken into account in respect of old ship

(1) The amount taken into account in respect of the old ship for the purposes of section 138(1)(b) is—

    (a) amount A, if no election has been made under section 129 (election to use appropriate non-ship pool) in respect of any of the qualifying expenditure incurred on the provision of the ship, or

    (b) amount B, in any other case.

(2) Amount A is the amount which falls to be brought into account as a disposal value in the appropriate non-ship pool under section 132(2)(b) as a result of the relevant disposal event, less the available qualifying expenditure allocated to the appropriate non-ship pool under section 132(2)(a).

(3) Amount B is—

$$DV - (QE - WDA - FYA)$$

where—

    DV is the amount of the disposal value required to be brought into account in respect of the old ship,
    QE is all the qualifying expenditure incurred in respect of the old ship,
    WDA is the maximum amount of any writing-down allowances which (on the assumptions in subsection (4)) could have been made in respect of that qualifying expenditure for chargeable periods up to (but not including) the one in respect of which the claim for deferment is made, and
    FYA is the total of any first-year allowances actually made or postponed in respect of the old ship.

(4) The assumptions are that—

    (a) all the qualifying expenditure in respect of the old ship is (and has always been) allocated to the appropriate non-ship pool, and

    (b) no other qualifying expenditure has been allocated to that pool.

(5) If an election is made under section 129 (election to use appropriate non-ship pool) after the determination under this section of the amount taken into account in respect of the old ship, the amount is, and is treated as always having been, amount B and not amount A.

Commentary—*Simon's Direct Tax Service* **B2.351**.
Former enactments—Sub-s (1): CAA 1990 s 33B(1), (2).
Sub-s (2): CAA 1990 s 33B(1).
Sub-s (3): CAA 1990 s 33B(2), (3).
Sub-s (4): CAA 1990 s 33B(3).
Sub-s (5): CAA 1990 s 33B(4).
Definitions—"Available qualifying expenditure", s 57; "chargeable period", s 6; "disposal event", s 60(2).
Modifications—CAA 2001 Sch 3 para 54 (vehicles provided by employees in 1990–91: see modification note at the start of this Part).
CAA 2001 Sch 3 para 55 (certain expenditure incurred before 6 April 1976: see modification note at the start of this Part).

Attribution of deferred amounts

140 Notice attributing deferred amounts to new expenditure

(1) The shipowner may, by notice to the Inland Revenue, attribute all or part of an amount deferred under section 135 to expenditure on new shipping.

(2) An amount attributed under this section is attributed to an equal amount of the expenditure on new shipping.

(3) Subsection (1) is subject to subsections (4) and (5) and section 141 (deferred amounts attributed to earlier expenditure first).

(4) Subsection (1) applies only if the expenditure on new shipping is incurred—

    (a) by the shipowner or, if the shipowner is a company, by another company which is a member of the same group at the time when the expenditure is incurred, and

    (b) within the period of 6 years beginning with the relevant disposal event.

(5) An amount may be attributed to expenditure on new shipping only to the extent that amounts have not already been attributed to it under this section.

(6) A notice given in respect of expenditure incurred by another company does not have effect unless the other company joins the shipowner in giving it.

Commentary—*Simon's Direct Tax Service* **B2.352**.
Former enactments—Sub-ss (1)–(3): CAA 1990 s 33A(5).
Sub-s (4): CAA 1990 s 33A(5), (8).
Sub-s (5): CAA 1990 s 33A(5).
Sub-s (6): CAA 1990 s 33A(5A).
Definition—"Disposal event", s 60(2).
Modifications—CAA 2001 Sch 3 para 54 (vehicles provided by employees in 1990–91: see modification note at the start of this Part).
CAA 2001 Sch 3 para 55 (certain expenditure incurred before 6 April 1976: see modification note at the start of this Part).

141 Deferred amounts attributed to earlier expenditure first

(1) No part of an amount deferred under section 135 is to be attributed to the whole or a part of any expenditure on new shipping (''the current expenditure'') if there is other expenditure (''the earlier expenditure'') which—

(a) was incurred before the current expenditure but at the same time as or after the relevant disposal event,

(b) was incurred by the shipowner or, if the shipowner is a company, by another company which was a member of the same group at the time the earlier expenditure was incurred, and

(c) is expenditure on new shipping, or would be treated as such but for an election under section 129 (election to use appropriate non-ship pool),

unless the condition in subsection (2) is met in relation to the earlier expenditure.

(2) The condition is that—

(a) amounts have been attributed to all the earlier expenditure under section 140, and

(b) the attributions have been made in the case of the amount deferred and any other amounts deferred under section 135 as a result of disposal events occurring at the same time as or before the relevant disposal event.

Commentary—*Simon's Direct Tax Service* **B2.352**.
Former enactments—Sub-s (1): CAA 1990 s 33D(6).
Sub-s (2): CAA 1990 s 33D(6); change in law.
Revenue Internal Guidance—Capital allowances manual CA 25500 (worked examples).
Definition—''Disposal event'', s 60(2).
Modifications—CAA 2001 Sch 3 para 54 (vehicles provided by employees in 1990–91: see modification note at the start of this Part).
CAA 2001 Sch 3 para 55 (certain expenditure incurred before 6 April 1976: see modification note at the start of this Part).

142 Variation of attribution

(1) The shipowner may, by notice, vary an attribution under section 140 (notice attributing deferred amounts to new expenditure).

(2) The notice must be given to the Inland Revenue on or before the time limit for the shipowner to make a claim for deferment in respect of the relevant chargeable period.

(3) For the time limit for making a claim for deferment, see section 135(3) to (5).

(4) For the purposes of subsection (2), it is to be assumed that—

(a) the shipowner is liable to a balancing charge for the relevant chargeable period, and

(b) a claim for deferment of that balancing charge can be made for the relevant chargeable period.

(5) ''The relevant chargeable period'' means the earliest chargeable period in which expenditure to which the variation relates is incurred.

(6) If the person to whose expenditure the notice relates is not the shipowner, a notice under subsection (1) does not have effect unless the person joins the shipowner in giving it.

Commentary—*Simon's Direct Tax Service* **B2.352**.
Former enactments—Sub-ss (1)–(5): CAA 1990 s 33F(4).
Sub-s (6): CAA 1990 s 33F(4A).
Definition—''Chargeable period'', s 6.
Modifications—CAA 2001 Sch 3 para 54 (vehicles provided by employees in 1990–91: see modification note at the start of this Part).
CAA 2001 Sch 3 para 55 (certain expenditure incurred before 6 April 1976: see modification note at the start of this Part).

143 Effect of attribution

(1) This section applies if a notice is given under section 140 attributing an amount to expenditure on new shipping.

(2) The amount must be brought into account as a disposal value—

(a) for the chargeable period in which the expenditure is incurred, and

(b) in the single ship pool to which the expenditure is allocated.

Commentary—*Simon's Direct Tax Service* **B2.352**.
Former enactments—CAA 1990 s 33C(1), (2).
Definition—''Chargeable period'', s 6.
Modifications—CAA 2001 Sch 3 para 54 (vehicles provided by employees in 1990–91: see modification note at the start of this Part).
CAA 2001 Sch 3 para 55 (certain expenditure incurred before 6 April 1976: see modification note at the start of this Part).

144 Amounts which cease to be attributable

(1) This section applies if—

(a) an amount has been deferred under section 135, and

(b) circumstances arise in which any part of the amount ceases (otherwise than by being attributed) to be attributable.

(2) The shipowner is assumed not to have been entitled to defer so much of the amount as ceases to be attributable.

(3) For the purposes of this section an amount is attributable if it may be attributed to expenditure on new shipping in accordance with section 140.

Commentary—*Simon's Direct Tax Service* **B2.352**.
Former enactments—CAA 1990 s 33A(4).
Modifications—CAA 2001 Sch 3 para 54 (vehicles provided by employees in 1990–91: see modification note at the start of this Part).
CAA 2001 Sch 3 para 55 (certain expenditure incurred before 6 April 1976: see modification note at the start of this Part).

145 Requirement to notify where no entitlement to defer amounts

(1) This section applies if—

    (*a*) an amount has been deferred under section 135, and
    (*b*) circumstances arise that require the shipowner to be treated as if he was not entitled to defer all or part of the amount.

(2) The shipowner must give notice of the fact to the Inland Revenue, specifying the circumstances.

(3) The notice must be given no later than 3 months after the end of the chargeable period in which the circumstances first arise.

(4) An assessment to tax chargeable as a result of the circumstances may be made at any time in the period which—

    (*a*) begins when those circumstances arise, and
    (*b*) ends 12 months after the shipowner gives notice of them to the Inland Revenue.

(5) Subsection (4) applies in spite of any limitation on the time for making assessments.

Commentary—*Simon's Direct Tax Service* **B2.352**.
Former enactments—Sub-ss (1)–(3): CAA 1990 s 33F(5).
Sub-ss (4), (5): CAA 1990 s 33F(6).
Definition—''Chargeable period'', s 6.
Modifications—CAA 2001 Sch 3 para 54 (vehicles provided by employees in 1990–91: see modification note at the start of this Part).
CAA 2001 Sch 3 para 55 (certain expenditure incurred before 6 April 1976: see modification note at the start of this Part).

Expenditure on new shipping

146 Basic meaning of expenditure on new shipping

(1) For the purposes of the deferment rules, expenditure on the provision of a ship is expenditure on new shipping if the conditions in subsection (3) are met.

(2) Subsection (1) is subject to sections 147 to 150.

(3) The conditions are that—

    (*a*) the expenditure is qualifying expenditure incurred by a person wholly and exclusively for the purposes of a qualifying activity carried on by him,
    (*b*) when the expenditure is incurred, it appears that the ship will—

       (i) be brought into use for the purposes of the qualifying activity as a qualifying ship, and
       (ii) continue to be a qualifying ship for at least 3 years after that, and

    (*c*) the expenditure is allocated to a single ship pool.

Commentary—*Simon's Direct Tax Service* **B2.353**.
Former enactments—CAA 1990 s 33D(1).
Modifications—CAA 2001 Sch 3 para 54 (vehicles provided by employees in 1990–91: see modification note at the start of this Part).
CAA 2001 Sch 3 para 55 (certain expenditure incurred before 6 April 1976: see modification note at the start of this Part).

147 Exclusions: ship previously owned

(1) Expenditure on the provision of a ship is not expenditure on new shipping if the person who incurred the expenditure—

    (*a*) has already owned the ship in the period of 6 years ending with the time when he first owns it as a result of incurring the expenditure, or
    (*b*) was connected at a material time with a person who owned the ship at any time during that period.

(2) For this purpose a material time is—

    (*a*) the time when the expenditure was incurred, or
    (*b*) any earlier time in the 6 year period beginning with the relevant disposal event.

Commentary—*Simon's Direct Tax Service* **B2.353**.
Former enactments—Sub-s (1): CAA 1990 s 33D(4).
Sub-s (2): CAA 1990 s 33D(5).
Definition—''Disposal event'', s 60(2).
Modifications—CAA 2001 Sch 3 para 54 (vehicles provided by employees in 1990–91: see modification note at the start of this Part).
CAA 2001 Sch 3 para 55 (certain expenditure incurred before 6 April 1976: see modification note at the start of this Part).

148 Exclusions: object to secure deferment

Expenditure on the provision of a ship is not expenditure on new shipping if the object, or one of the main objects, of—

(a) the transaction by which the ship was provided for the purposes of a qualifying activity carried on by the person who incurred the expenditure,

(b) any series of transactions of which that transaction was one, or

(c) any transaction in such a series,

was to secure the deferment of a balancing charge under section 135.

Commentary—*Simon's Direct Tax Service* **B2.353**.
Former enactments—CAA 1990 s 33D(4).
Modifications—CAA 2001 Sch 3 para 54 (vehicles provided by employees in 1990–91: see modification note at the start of this Part).
CAA 2001 Sch 3 para 55 (certain expenditure incurred before 6 April 1976: see modification note at the start of this Part).

149 Exclusions: later events

(1) Expenditure on the provision of a ship is not, and is treated as never having been, expenditure on new shipping if—

(a) at a time during the period mentioned in subsection (2), the ship is not a qualifying ship,

(b) the expenditure is allocated to a pool as a result of an election under section 129 (election to use appropriate non-ship pool), or

(c) section 107 applies in relation to the expenditure (overseas leasing).

(2) The period referred to in subsection (1)(a) is—

(a) the period of 3 years beginning with the time when the ship is first brought into use for the purposes of a qualifying activity carried on—

(i) by the person (''A'') who incurred the expenditure, or

(ii) if earlier, by a person connected with A, or

(b) if shorter, the period beginning with that time and ending when neither A nor a person connected with A owns the ship.

Commentary—*Simon's Direct Tax Service* **B2.353**.
Former enactments—Sub-s (1): CAA 1990 s 33D(2), (3).
Sub-s (2): CAA 1990 s 33D(2).
Modifications—CAA 2001 Sch 3 para 54 (vehicles provided by employees in 1990–91: see modification note at the start of this Part).
CAA 2001 Sch 3 para 55 (certain expenditure incurred before 6 April 1976: see modification note at the start of this Part).

150 Exclusions where expenditure not incurred by shipowner

(1) Expenditure on the provision of a ship is not, and is treated as never having been, expenditure on new shipping if—

(a) it is incurred by a company which is a member of the same group as the shipowner at the time when the expenditure is incurred, and

(b) subsection (2) or (4) applies.

(2) This subsection applies (subject to subsection (3)) if—

(a) the ship ceases to be owned by the company before it has been brought into use for the purposes of a qualifying activity carried on by the company, or

(b) a disposal event occurs in respect of the ship within 3 years of its first being brought into use for the purposes of a qualifying activity carried on by the company.

(3) But subsection (2) does not apply if the event which would otherwise result in that subsection applying is, or is the result of, the total loss of the ship or irreparable damage to it.

(4) This subsection applies if—

(a) after the expenditure is incurred, there is a time when the company and the shipowner are not members of the same group, and

(b) if the ship is brought into use for the purposes of a qualifying activity carried on by the company, that time is within 3 years of the ship first being so brought into use.

(5) A time falling after the total loss of the ship or irreparable damage to it is to be disregarded for the purposes of subsection (4).

(6) In this section ''irreparable damage'', in relation to a ship, means damage that puts it in a condition in which it is impossible, or not commercially worthwhile, to undertake the repairs required for restoring it to its previous use.

Commentary—*Simon's Direct Tax Service* **B2.353**.
Former enactments—Sub-s (1): CAA 1990 ss 33A(8), 33D(2A).
Sub-s (2): CAA 1990 s 33D(2A).
Sub-s (3): CAA 1990 s 33D(2B).
Sub-s (4): CAA 1990 s 33D(2A).
Sub-ss (5), (6): CAA 1990 s 33D(2B).
Definition—''Disposal event'', s 60(2).

Modifications—CAA 2001 Sch 3 para 54 (vehicles provided by employees in 1990–91: see modification note at the start of this Part).
CAA 2001 Sch 3 para 55 (certain expenditure incurred before 6 April 1976: see modification note at the start of this Part).

Qualifying ships

151 Basic meaning of qualifying ship

(1) For the purposes of the deferment rules, a ship is a qualifying ship if it is—

(*a*) of a sea-going kind, and

(*b*) registered as a ship with a gross tonnage of 100 tons or more in a register of shipping established and maintained under the law of any country or territory.

(2) This is subject to sections 152 to 154.

Commentary—*Simon's Direct Tax Service* B2.353.
Former enactments—CAA 1990 s 33E(1).
Modifications—CAA 2001 Sch 3 para 54 (vehicles provided by employees in 1990–91: see modification note at the start of this Part).
CAA 2001 Sch 3 para 55 (certain expenditure incurred before 6 April 1976: see modification note at the start of this Part).

152 Ships under 100 tons

(1) This section applies if the relevant disposal event is, or results from—

(*a*) the total loss of the old ship, or

(*b*) damage to the old ship that puts it in a condition in which it is impossible, or not commercially worthwhile, to undertake the repairs required for restoring it to its previous use.

(2) A registered ship may be a qualifying ship for the purposes of—

(*a*) section 136(*b*) (further conditions for deferment), or

(*b*) sections 146(3)(*b*) and 149(1)(*a*) (expenditure on new shipping),

even if it is not registered as a ship with a gross tonnage of 100 tons or more.

(3) In subsection (2) "registered ship" means a ship registered in a register of shipping established and maintained under the law of any country or territory.

Commentary—*Simon's Direct Tax Service* B2.353.
Former enactments—CAA 1990 s 33E(2).
Definition—"Disposal event", s 60(2).
Modifications—CAA 2001 Sch 3 para 54 (vehicles provided by employees in 1990–91: see modification note at the start of this Part).
CAA 2001 Sch 3 para 55 (certain expenditure incurred before 6 April 1976: see modification note at the start of this Part).

153 Ships which are not qualifying ships

(1) A ship is not a qualifying ship if the primary use to which ships of the same kind as that ship are put—

(*a*) by the persons who own them, or

(*b*) by others to whom they are made available,

is use for sport or recreation.

(2) A ship is not a qualifying ship at any time when—

(*a*) it is an offshore installation, or

(*b*) it would be such an installation if the activity for which it is to be established or maintained were carried on in or under controlled waters.

(3) "Offshore installation" and "controlled waters" have the same meaning as in the Mineral Workings (Offshore Installations) Act 1971.

Commentary—*Simon's Direct Tax Service* B2.353.
Former enactments—Sub-s (1): CAA 1990 s 33E(3).
Sub-ss (2), (3): CAA 1990 s 33E(4).
Modifications—CAA 2001 Sch 3 para 54 (vehicles provided by employees in 1990–91: see modification note at the start of this Part).
CAA 2001 Sch 3 para 55 (certain expenditure incurred before 6 April 1976: see modification note at the start of this Part).

154 Further registration requirement

(1) If—

(*a*) a person ("A") has incurred expenditure on the provision of a ship, and

(*b*) there is a time in the qualifying period, but more than 3 months after the beginning of that period, when the ship is not registered in a relevant register,

the ship is not a qualifying ship after that time.

(2) The qualifying period is—

(*a*) the period of 3 years beginning with the time when the ship is first brought into use for the purposes of a qualifying activity carried on—

(i) by A, or

(ii) if earlier, by a person connected with A, or

(b) if shorter, the period beginning with that time and ending when neither A nor a person connected with A owns the ship.

(3) In determining the qualifying period for the old ship, a qualifying activity carried on at any time by a person (''B'') is taken to be carried on at that time by a person connected with A if—

(a) it is subsequently carried on by A or a person connected with A, and
(b) the only changes in the persons carrying it on between the time that B does so and the time that A or a person connected with A does so are changes in respect of which, under section 113(2) or 343(2) of ICTA, the qualifying activity is not treated as having been discontinued.

(4) In this section ''relevant register'' means a register of shipping established and maintained—

(a) under the laws of any part of the British Islands, or
(b) under the laws of any country or territory which, at a time in the qualifying period for the ship, is an EEA State or a colony.

(5) ''EEA State'' means a State which is a contracting party to the Agreement on the European Economic Area signed at Oporto on 2nd May 1992 as adjusted by the Protocol signed at Brussels on 17th March 1993 (except that for the period before the Agreement came into force in relation to Liechtenstein it does not include the State of Liechtenstein).

Commentary—*Simon's Direct Tax Service* B2.353.
Former enactments—Sub-s (1): CAA 1990 s 33E(5), (9).
Sub-s (2): CAA 1990 s 33E(6), (9).
Sub-s (3): CAA 1990 s 33E(8), (9).
Sub-ss (4), (5): CAA 1990 s 33E(7).
Modifications—CAA 2001 Sch 3 para 24 (the section above does not apply in the case of a ship that was brought into use before 20 July 1994 for the purposes of a qualifying activity carried on by the person incurring the expenditure on the provision of the ship or a person connected with him).
CAA 2001 Sch 3 para 54 (vehicles provided by employees in 1990–91: see modification note at the start of this Part).
CAA 2001 Sch 3 para 55 (certain expenditure incurred before 6 April 1976: see modification note at the start of this Part).

Deferment of balancing charges: supplementary provisions

155 Change in the persons carrying on the qualifying activity

(1) This section applies if—

(a) a person is carrying on the qualifying activity previously carried on by the shipowner, and
(b) the only changes in the persons carrying on the qualifying activity since the shipowner carried it on are changes in respect of which, under section 113(2) or 343(2) of ICTA, it is not treated as having been discontinued.

(2) For the purposes of the deferment rules—

(a) expenditure incurred by a person mentioned in subsection (1)(a) for the purposes of the qualifying activity is to be treated as incurred by the shipowner, and
(b) in relation to the giving of any notice, a reference to the shipowner is to be read as a reference to the person carrying on the qualifying activity when the notice is given or is required to be given.

Commentary—*Simon's Direct Tax Service* B2.352.
Former enactments—Sub-s (1): CAA 1990 ss 33D(7), 33F(7).
Sub-s (2): CAA 1990 ss 33D(7), 33F(7); change in law.
Modifications—CAA 2001 Sch 3 para 54 (vehicles provided by employees in 1990–91: see modification note at the start of this Part).
CAA 2001 Sch 3 para 55 (certain expenditure incurred before 6 April 1976: see modification note at the start of this Part).

156 Connected persons

(1) For the purposes of the deferment rules a person (''B'') is connected with another person (''A'') at any time if, at that time—

(a) B is connected (in the sense given in section 839 of ICTA) with A,
(b) B is carrying on a qualifying activity previously carried on by A and the condition in subsection (2) is met, or
(c) B is connected (in the sense given in section 839 of ICTA) with a person who is carrying on a qualifying activity previously carried on by A and the condition in subsection (2) is met.

(2) The condition is that the only changes in the persons carrying on the qualifying activity since A carried it on are changes in respect of which, under section 113(2) or 343(2) of ICTA, the qualifying activity is not treated as having been discontinued.

(3) If expenditure is incurred by a person who is not the shipowner, the persons connected with him at any time include any person connected with the shipowner at that time as a result of subsection (1).

Commentary—*Simon's Direct Tax Service* B2.353.
Former enactments—CAA 1990 ss 33D(8), 33E(8).
Modifications—CAA 2001 Sch 3 para 54 (vehicles provided by employees in 1990–91: see modification note at the start of this Part).
CAA 2001 Sch 3 para 55 (certain expenditure incurred before 6 April 1976: see modification note at the start of this Part).

Further provisions

157 Adjustment of assessments etc

(1) All such assessments and adjustments of assessments are to be made as are necessary to give effect to this Chapter.

(2) Subsection (1) does not apply for the purposes of section 145 (see instead section 145(4) and (5)).

Commentary—*Simon's Direct Tax Service* B2.353.
Former enactments—Sub-s (1): CAA 1990 ss 30(3), 31(9), 33F(6).
Sub-s (2): CAA 1990 s 33F(6).
Modifications—CAA 2001 Sch 3 para 54 (vehicles provided by employees in 1990–91: see modification note at the start of this Part).
CAA 2001 Sch 3 para 55 (certain expenditure incurred before 6 April 1976: see modification note at the start of this Part).

158 Members of same group

For the purposes of this Chapter two companies are members of the same group at any time if they would be treated as members of the same group of companies at that time for the purposes of Chapter IV of Part X of ICTA (group relief).

Commentary—*Simon's Direct Tax Service* B2.353.
Former enactments—CAA 1990 ss 33A(8), 33D(2A).
Modifications—CAA 2001 Sch 3 para 54 (vehicles provided by employees in 1990–91: see modification note at the start of this Part).
CAA 2001 Sch 3 para 55 (certain expenditure incurred before 6 April 1976: see modification note at the start of this Part).

CHAPTER 13
PROVISIONS AFFECTING MINING AND OIL INDUSTRIES

Expenditure connected with mineral extraction trades

159 Meaning of "mineral extraction trade" etc

In this Chapter—
"mineral extraction trade", and
"mineral exploration and access",
have the same meaning as in Part 5 (mineral extraction allowances).

Commentary—*Simon's Direct Tax Service* B2.354.
Former enactments—CAA 1990 s 83(1).
Modifications—CAA 2001 Sch 3 para 54 (vehicles provided by employees in 1990–91: see modification note at the start of this Part).
CAA 2001 Sch 3 para 55 (certain expenditure incurred before 6 April 1976: see modification note at the start of this Part).

160 Expenditure treated as incurred for purposes of mineral extraction trade

For the purposes of this Part, expenditure incurred by a person—
(a) on the provision of plant or machinery for mineral exploration and access, and
(b) in connection with a mineral extraction trade carried on by him,
is to be treated as incurred for the purposes of that trade.

Commentary—*Simon's Direct Tax Service* B2.354.
Former enactments—CAA 1990 s 83(6).
Modifications—CAA 2001 Sch 3 para 54 (vehicles provided by employees in 1990–91: see modification note at the start of this Part).
CAA 2001 Sch 3 para 55 (certain expenditure incurred before 6 April 1976: see modification note at the start of this Part).

161 Pre-trading expenditure on mineral exploration and access

(1) This section applies if a person—
(a) incurs pre-trading expenditure on the provision of plant or machinery for the purposes of mineral exploration and access, and
(b) owns the plant or machinery on the first day of trading.
But this is subject to subsection (5).

(2) The person is to be treated for the purposes of this Part as if he had—
(a) sold the plant or machinery immediately before the first day of trading, and
(b) on that first day incurred capital expenditure on the provision of the plant or machinery for the purposes of the trade.

(3) The amount of the capital expenditure that the person is to be treated as having incurred is an amount equal to—
(a) the pre-trading expenditure, or
(b) if there has been an actual sale and re-acquisition before the first day of trading, the amount last incurred on the provision of the plant or machinery.

(4) In this section—

    (*a*) "pre-trading expenditure" means capital expenditure incurred before the day on which a person begins to carry on a mineral extraction trade, and

    (*b*) "the first day of trading", in relation to a person's pre-trading expenditure, means the day on which that person begins to carry on the mineral extraction trade.

(5) This section does not apply if the plant or machinery on which the pre-trading expenditure was incurred is sold, demolished, destroyed or abandoned before the first day of trading (but see section 402 (mineral extraction allowances: pre-trading expenditure on plant or machinery)).

Commentary—*Simon's Direct Tax Service* **B2.354**.
Former enactments—Sub-ss (1)–(3): CAA 1990 s 63(1).
Sub-s (4): CAA 1990 s 63(1); change in law.
Sub-s (5): CAA 1990 s 63(1).
Definition—"Capital expenditure", s 4.
Modifications—CAA 2001 Sch 3 para 25 (the section above does not apply in relation to pre-trading expenditure incurred before 1 April 1986; and cessation at source of mineral exploration and access before the first day of trading).
CAA 2001 Sch 3 para 54 (vehicles provided by employees in 1990–91: see modification note at the start of this Part).
CAA 2001 Sch 3 para 55 (certain expenditure incurred before 6 April 1976: see modification note at the start of this Part).

[Expenditure connected with reuse etc of offshore oil infrastructure

161A Meaning of "offshore infrastructure"

(1) In sections 161C and 161D "offshore infrastructure" means—

    (*a*) an offshore installation within the meaning given by section 44 of the Petroleum Act 1998 or a part of such an installation, or

    (*b*) something that would be, or would be a part of, an offshore installation within that meaning if in subsection (3) of that section "relevant waters" meant waters in a foreign sector of the continental shelf and other foreign tidal waters, or

    (*c*) a pipeline within the meaning of section 26 of that Act, or a part of such a pipeline, that is in, under or over waters in—

        (i) the territorial sea adjacent to the United Kingdom, or

        (ii) an area designated under section 1(7) of the Continental Shelf Act 1964, or

    (*d*) a pipeline within the meaning of section 26 of the Petroleum Act 1998, or a part of such a pipeline, that is in, under or over waters in a foreign sector of the continental shelf.

(2) In subsection (1)(*b*) and (*d*)—

    "foreign sector of the continental shelf" means an area within which rights are exercisable with respect to the sea bed and subsoil and their natural resources by a country or territory outside the United Kingdom;

    "foreign tidal waters" means tidal waters in an area within which rights are exercisable with respect to the bed and subsoil of the body of water in question and their natural resources by a country or territory outside the United Kingdom.][1]

Commentary—*Simon's Direct Tax Service* **D4.1011**.
Amendment—[1] Section inserted by FA 2001 s 68, Sch 20 Pt paras 5, 9 with effect for—
  (*a*) expenditure incurred after 6 August 2000 and in a relevant chargeable period; or
  (*b*) expenditure incurred before 7 August 2000, if the expenditure is incurred in a relevant chargeable period and is either—
    (i) decommissioning expenditure on UK infrastructure and is incurred in connection with an abandonment programme approved after 6 August 2000; or
    (ii) decommissioning expenditure, is not decommissioning expenditure on UK infrastructure, and is incurred in connection with a decommissioning activity that takes place after 6 August 2000.
For these purposes, "relevant chargeable period" is a chargeable period ending after 5 April 2001 (for income tax purposes) or 31 March 2001 (for corporation tax purposes). "Decommissioning expenditure" and "decommissioning expenditure on UK infrastructure" have the same meaning as in CAA 2001 ss 161C, 161D. "Decommissioning activity" means an activity mentioned in CAA 2001 s 161B(1)(*a*)–(*c*).

[161B Meaning of "decommissioning expenditure"

(1) In sections 161C and 161D "decommissioning expenditure" means expenditure in connection with—

    (*a*) preserving plant or machinery pending its reuse or demolition,

    (*b*) preparing plant or machinery for reuse, or

    (*c*) arranging for the reuse of plant or machinery.

(2) It is immaterial for the purposes of subsection (1)(*a*) whether the plant or machinery is reused, is demolished or is partly reused and partly demolished.

(3) It is immaterial for the purposes of subsection (1)(*b*) and (*c*) whether the plant or machinery is in fact reused.][1]

Commentary—*Simon's Direct Tax Service* **D4.1011**.
Amendment—[1] Section inserted by FA 2001 s 68, Sch 20 Pt paras 5, 9 with effect for—
  (*a*) expenditure incurred after 6 August 2000 and in a relevant chargeable period; or
  (*b*) expenditure incurred before 7 August 2000, if the expenditure is incurred in a relevant chargeable period and is either—
    (i) decommissioning expenditure on UK infrastructure and is incurred in connection with an abandonment programme approved after 6 August 2000; or

(ii) decommissioning expenditure, is not decommissioning expenditure on UK infrastructure, and is incurred in connection with a decommissioning activity that takes place after 6 August 2000.

For these purposes, "relevant chargeable period" is a chargeable period ending after 5 April 2001 (for income tax purposes) or 31 March 2001 (for corporation tax purposes). "Decommissioning expenditure" and "decommissioning expenditure on UK infrastructure" have the same meaning as in CAA 2001 ss 161C, 161D. "Decommissioning activity" means an activity mentioned in CAA 2001 s 161B(1)(*a*)–(*c*).

[161C Expenditure related to reuse etc qualifies for writing-down allowances

(1) This section applies where—

    (*a*) a person carrying on a trade of oil extraction incurs decommissioning expenditure, and

    (*b*) the plant or machinery concerned—

        (i) has been brought into use for the purposes of the trade, and

        (ii) is, or was when last in use for those purposes, offshore infrastructure.

(2) The decommissioning expenditure is allocated to the appropriate pool for the chargeable period in which it is incurred.

(3) Subsection (2) is subject to sections 161D and 164(4).

(4) In subsection (2) "the appropriate pool" means the pool to which the expenditure on the plant or machinery concerned has been or would be allocated in accordance with this Part.][1]

Commentary—*Simon's Direct Tax Service* **D4.1011**.
Amendment—[1] Section inserted by FA 2001 s 68, Sch 20 paras 5, 9 with effect for—

    (*a*) expenditure incurred after 6 August 2000 and in a relevant chargeable period; or

    (*b*) expenditure incurred before 7 August 2000, if the expenditure is incurred in a relevant chargeable period and is either—

        (i) decommissioning expenditure on UK infrastructure and is incurred in connection with an abandonment programme approved after 6 August 2000; or

        (ii) decommissioning expenditure, is not decommissioning expenditure on UK infrastructure, and is incurred in connection with a decommissioning activity that takes place after 6 August 2000.

For these purposes, "relevant chargeable period" is a chargeable period ending after 5 April 2001 (for income tax purposes) or 31 March 2001 (for corporation tax purposes). "Decommissioning expenditure" and "decommissioning expenditure on UK infrastructure" have the same meaning as in CAA 2001 ss 161C, 161D. "Decommissioning activity" means an activity mentioned in CAA 2001 s 161B(1)(*a*)–(*c*).

[161D Exceptions to section 161C(2)

(1) Subsection (2) of section 161C does not apply to decommissioning expenditure on UK infrastructure unless it is incurred in connection with measures taken, wholly or substantially, in order to comply with—

    (*a*) an abandonment programme within the meaning given by section 29 of the Petroleum Act 1998, or

    (*b*) any condition to which the approval of such a programme is subject.

(2) Subsection (2) of section 161C does not apply to expenditure in respect of which an allowance or deduction could be made apart from that subsection in taxing, or computing, the person's income for any tax purpose.

(3) For the purposes of subsection (1), decommissioning expenditure is "on UK infrastructure" if the plant or machinery concerned—

    (*a*) is offshore infrastructure within section 161A(1)(*a*) or (*c*), or

    (*b*) is not offshore infrastructure but was offshore infrastructure within section 161A(1)(*a*) or (*c*) when last in use for the purposes of the trade.][1]

Commentary—*Simon's Direct Tax Service* **D4.1011**.
Amendment—[1] Section inserted by FA 2001 s 68, Sch 20 paras 5, 9 with effect for—

    (*a*) expenditure incurred after 6 August 2000 and in a relevant chargeable period; or

    (*b*) expenditure incurred before 7 August 2000, if the expenditure is incurred in a relevant chargeable period and is either—

        (i) decommissioning expenditure on UK infrastructure and is incurred in connection with an abandonment programme approved after 6 August 2000; or

        (ii) decommissioning expenditure, is not decommissioning expenditure on UK infrastructure, and is incurred in connection with a decommissioning activity that takes place after 6 August 2000.

For these purposes, "relevant chargeable period" is a chargeable period ending after 5 April 2001 (for income tax purposes) or 31 March 2001 (for corporation tax purposes). "Decommissioning expenditure" and "decommissioning expenditure on UK infrastructure" have the same meaning as in CAA 2001 ss 161C, 161D. "Decommissioning activity" means an activity mentioned in CAA 2001 s 161B(1)(*a*)–(*c*).

Provisions relating to ring fence trades

162 Ring fence trade a separate qualifying activity

(1) If a person carries on a ring fence trade, it is a separate qualifying activity for the purposes of this Part.

(2) In this Chapter "ring fence trade" means activities which—

    (*a*) fall within any of paragraphs (*a*) to (*c*) of section 492(1) of ICTA (oil extraction activities, the acquisition, enjoyment or exploitation of oil rights, etc), and

    (*b*) constitute a separate trade (whether as a result of section 492(1) of ICTA or otherwise).

Commentary—*Simon's Direct Tax Service* **B2.354**.
Former enactments—Sub-s (1): TA 1988 s 492(1).
Sub-s (2): CAA 1990 ss 62A(2), 62B(5).
Revenue Internal Guidance—Oil Taxation Office Ring Fence CT manual OTRF 5.23, 5.24 (oil companies: treatment of consumable stores and inventories).
Modifications—CAA 2001 Sch 3 para 54 (vehicles provided by employees in 1990–91: see modification note at the start of this Part).
CAA 2001 Sch 3 para 55 (certain expenditure incurred before 6 April 1976: see modification note at the start of this Part).

163 Meaning of "abandonment expenditure"

(1) In sections 164 and 165 "abandonment expenditure" means expenditure which meets the requirements in subsections (2) to (4).

(2) The expenditure must have been incurred—

(a) for the purposes of, or in connection with, the closing down of an oil field or of any part of an oil field, and

(b) on [decommissioning][1] plant or machinery—

(i) which has been brought into use for the purposes of a ring fence trade, and

(ii) which is, or forms part of, an offshore installation or a submarine pipeline [or which, when last in use for the purposes of a ring-fence trade, was, or formed part of, such an installation or pipeline][1].

(3) The [decommissioning][1] of the plant or machinery must be carried out, wholly or substantially, to comply with—

(a) an abandonment programme, or

(b) any condition to which the approval of an abandonment programme is subject.

(4) The plant or machinery must not be replaced.

[(4A) In this section "decommissioning", in relation to any plant or machinery, means—

(a) demolishing the plant or machinery,

(b) preserving the plant or machinery pending its reuse or demolition,

(c) preparing the plant or machinery for reuse, or

(d) arranging for the reuse of the plant or machinery.

(4B) In determining whether expenditure is incurred on preserving plant or machinery pending its reuse or demolition, it is immaterial whether the plant or machinery is reused, is demolished or is partly reused and partly demolished.

(4C) In determining whether expenditure is incurred on preparing plant or machinery for reuse, or on arranging for the reuse of plant or machinery, it is immaterial whether the plant or machinery is in fact reused.][1]

(5) In this section—

(a) "oil field" has the same meaning as in Part I of OTA 1975, and

(b) "abandonment programme", "offshore installation" and "submarine pipeline" have the same meaning as in Part IV of the Petroleum Act 1998.

Commentary—*Simon's Direct Tax Service* **B2.354**.
Former enactments—Sub-ss (1), (2): CAA 1990 s 62A(1).
Sub-s (3): CAA 1990 s 62A(3).
Sub-s (4): CAA 1990 ss 62(1)(b), 62A(1).
Sub-s (5): CAA 1990 s 62A(1), (3).
Revenue Internal Guidance—Oil Taxation Office ring fence CT manual OTRF 5.1–5.16 (background to, and detailed explanation of, this section).
Definition—"Ring fence trade", s 162(2).
Modifications—CAA 2001 Sch 3 para 54 (vehicles provided by employees in 1990–91: see modification note at the start of this Part).
CAA 2001 Sch 3 para 55 (certain expenditure incurred before 6 April 1976: see modification note at the start of this Part).
Amendments—[1] In sub-s (2)(b) word "decommissioning" substituted for words "the demolition of", in sub-s (2)(b)(ii) words inserted, in sub-s (3) word "decommissioning" substituted for word "demolition", and sub-ss (4A)–(4C) inserted by FA 2001 s 68, Sch 20 paras 6, 9 with effect for—
(a) expenditure incurred after 6 August 2000, and in a relevant chargeable period; or
(b) expenditure incurred before 7 August 2000, if the expenditure is incurred in a relevant chargeable period and is incurred in connection with an abandonment programme approved after 6 August 2000.
For these purposes, "relevant chargeable period" is a chargeable period ending after 5 April 2001 (for income tax purposes) or 31 March 2001 (for corporation tax purposes).

164 Abandonment expenditure incurred before cessation of ring fence trade

(1) If a person carrying on a ring fence trade incurs abandonment expenditure, [and the plant or machinery concerned has been brought into use for the purposes of that trade,][1] he may elect to have a special allowance made to him.

(2) The election—

(a) must be made by notice to the Inland Revenue no later than 2 years after the end of the chargeable period in which the abandonment expenditure is incurred, and

(b) is irrevocable.

(3) The election must specify—

(*a*) the abandonment expenditure to which it relates, and

[(*b*) where the plant or machinery concerned has been or is to be demolished, any amounts received for its remains.][2]

(4) If a person makes an election under this section—

(*a*) he is entitled to a special allowance ...[2] for the chargeable period in which the abandonment expenditure is incurred, and

[(*b*) neither of sections 26(3) and 161C(2) (net cost of demolition where plant or machinery not replaced, or cost of preparing for reuse, added to existing pool) applies.][2]

[(5) The amount of the special allowance for a chargeable period is equal to so much of the abandonment expenditure to which the election relates as is incurred in that period.

(6) If plant or machinery is demolished, the total of any special allowances in respect of expenditure on decommissioning the plant or machinery is reduced by any amount received for the remains of the plant or machinery.

Here ''decommissioning'' has the meaning given by section 163(4A).

(7) Effect is given to subsection (6) by setting the amount (until wholly utilised)—

first, against any special allowance for the chargeable period in which the amount is received (as previously reduced in giving effect to subsection (6));

second, against special allowances for earlier chargeable periods (as so reduced and taking later such periods before earlier ones); and

third, against special allowances for later chargeable periods (as so reduced and taking earlier such periods before later ones).][2]

Commentary—*Simon's Direct Tax Service* **B2.354**.
Former enactments—Sub-s (1): CAA 1990 s 62A(4).
Sub-ss (2), (3): CAA 1990 s 62A(5).
Sub-ss (4), (5): CAA 1990 s 62A(4).
Definitions—''Chargeable period'', s 6; ''ring fence trade'', s 162(2).
Modifications—CAA 2001 Sch 3 para 26 (the section above does not apply if the chargeable period in which the abandonment expenditure was incurred ended before 1 July 1991).
CAA 2001 Sch 3 para 54 (vehicles provided by employees in 1990–91: see modification note at the start of this Part).
CAA 2001 Sch 3 para 55 (certain expenditure incurred before 6 April 1976: see modification note at the start of this Part).
Amendments—[1] Words in sub-s (1) inserted by FA 2001 s 68, Sch 20 paras 7(2), 9(9) and deemed always to have had effect.
[2] Sub-s (3)(*b*) substituted, words in sub-s (4)(*a*) repealed, sub-s (4)(*b*) substituted, and sub-ss (5)–(7) substituted for sub-s (5) by FA 2001 ss 68, 110, Sch 20 Pt II paras 7, 9, Sch 33 Pt II(5) with effect for—

(*a*) expenditure incurred after 6 August 2000, and in a relevant chargeable period; or
(*b*) expenditure incurred before 7 August 2000, if the expenditure is incurred in a relevant chargeable period and is incurred in connection with an abandonment programme approved after 6 August 2000.
For these purposes, ''relevant chargeable period'' is a chargeable period ending after 5 April 2001 (for income tax purposes) or 31 March 2001 (for corporation tax purposes).
Previously, sub-ss (3)–(5) read as follows—

''(3) The election must specify—

(*a*) the abandonment expenditure to which it relates, and
(*b*) any amounts received for the remains of the plant or machinery in question.

(4) If a person makes an election under this section—

(*a*) he is entitled to a special allowance, of an amount equal to the net abandonment cost, for the chargeable period in which the abandonment expenditure is incurred, and
(*b*) section 26(3) (net cost of demolition added to existing pool where plant or machinery not replaced) does not apply.

(5) ''The net abandonment cost'' means the amount by which the abandonment expenditure to which the election relates exceeds any amounts received for the remains of the plant or machinery.''

165 Abandonment expenditure within 3 years of ceasing ring fence trade

(1) This section applies if—

(*a*) a person (''the former trader'') has ceased to carry on a ring fence trade,
(*b*) the former trader incurs abandonment expenditure ...[1] within the post-cessation period, and
(*c*) the abandonment expenditure is not otherwise deductible in calculating the income of the former trader for any tax purpose.

(2) ''The post-cessation period'' means the period of 3 years immediately following the last day on which the former trader carried on the ring fence trade.

(3) If this section applies—

(*a*) an amount equal to the relevant abandonment cost is allocated to the appropriate pool for the chargeable period in which the former trader ceased to carry on the ring fence trade, and
(*b*) [where any of the abandonment expenditure was incurred on the demolition of plant or machinery,][2] any amount received within the post-cessation period for the remains of the plant or machinery does not constitute income of the former trader for any tax purpose.

(4) In subsection (3)—

''the appropriate pool'' means the pool to which the expenditure on the demolished plant or machinery has been allocated, and

''the relevant abandonment cost'' means the amount by which the abandonment expenditure exceeds any amounts received within the post-cessation period for the remains of [any plant or machinery on whose demolition any of the abandonment expenditure was incurred][2].

(5) All such adjustments, by discharge or repayment of tax or otherwise, are to be made as are necessary to give effect to this section.

Commentary—*Simon's Direct Tax Service* **B2.354**.
Former enactments—Sub-ss (1), (2): CAA 1990 s 62B(1).
Sub-s (3): CAA 1990 s 62B(2), (3).
Sub-s (4): CAA 1990 s 62B(2).
Sub-s (5): CAA 1990 s 62B(4).
Definitions—''Chargeable period'', s 6; ''ring fence trade'', s 162(2).
Modifications—CAA 2001 Sch 3 para 27 (the section above does not apply if the abandonment expenditure was incurred before 1 July 1991).
CAA 2001 Sch 3 para 54 (vehicles provided by employees in 1990–91: see modification note at the start of this Part).
CAA 2001 Sch 3 para 55 (certain expenditure incurred before 6 April 1976: see modification note at the start of this Part).
Amendments—¹ Words in sub-s (1) repealed by FA 2001 ss 68, 110, Sch 20 paras 8(2), 9(9), Sch 33 Pt II(5), and deemed always to have had effect.
² Words in sub-s (3)(*b*) inserted, and words in sub-s (4) substituted for words ''the plant or machinery'' by FA 2001 s 68, Sch 20 Pt II paras 8, 9 with effect for—
(*a*) expenditure incurred after 6 August 2000, and in a relevant chargeable period; or
(*b*) expenditure incurred before 7 August 2000, if the expenditure is incurred in a relevant chargeable period and is incurred in connection with an abandonment programme approved after 6 August 2000.
For these purposes, ''relevant chargeable period'' is a chargeable period ending after 5 April 2001 (for income tax purposes) or 31 March 2001 (for corporation tax purposes).

Transfers of interests in oil fields: anti-avoidance

166 Transfers of interests in oil fields: anti-avoidance

(1) This section applies if—

(*a*) there is, for the purposes of Schedule 17 to FA 1980, a transfer by a participator in an oil field of the whole or part of his interest in the field, and
(*b*) as part of the transfer, the old participator disposes of, and the new participator acquires—

(i) plant or machinery used, or expected to be used, in connection with the field, or
(ii) a share in such plant or machinery.

(2) The amount, if any, by which the new participator's expenditure exceeds the old participator's disposal value is to be left out of account in determining the new participator's available qualifying expenditure.

(3) In subsection (2)—

(*a*) ''the new participator's expenditure'' means the expenditure incurred by the new participator on the acquisition of the plant or machinery, and
(*b*) ''the old participator's disposal value'' means the disposal value to be brought into account by the old participator as a result of the disposal of the plant or machinery to the new participator.

(4) In this section—

(*a*) ''oil field'' and ''participator'' have the same meaning as in Part I of OTA 1975,
(*b*) ''the old participator'' means the participator whose interest in the oil field is wholly or partly transferred, and
(*c*) ''the new participator'' means the person to whom the interest in the oil field is transferred.

(5) Nothing in this section affects the operation of Chapter 17 (anti-avoidance).

Commentary—*Simon's Direct Tax Service* **B2.354**.
Former enactments—Sub-s (1): CAA 1990 s 64(1).
Sub-ss (2), (3): CAA 1990 s 64(2).
Sub-s (4): CAA 1990 s 64(3).
Sub-s (5): CAA 1990 s 64(4).
Revenue Internal Guidance—Oil Taxation Office ring fence CT manual OTRF 5.19 (interpretation of this section).
Definition—''Available qualifying expenditure'', s 57.
Modifications—CAA 2001 Sch 3 para 54 (vehicles provided by employees in 1990–91: see modification note at the start of this Part).
CAA 2001 Sch 3 para 55 (certain expenditure incurred before 6 April 1976: see modification note at the start of this Part).

Oil production sharing contracts

167 Oil production sharing contracts

(1) Sections 168 to 170 apply if—

(*a*) a person (''the contractor'') is entitled to an interest in a contract made with, or with the authorised representative of, the government of a country or territory in which oil is or may be produced, and
(*b*) the contract provides (among other things) for any plant or machinery of a description specified in the contract which—

(i) is provided by the contractor, and
(ii) has an oil-related use under the contract,

to be transferred (immediately or later) to the government or representative.

(2) For the purposes of this section and sections 168 to 170, plant or machinery has an oil-related use if it is used—

(*a*) to explore for, win access to or extract oil,

(*b*) for the initial storage or treatment of oil, or

(*c*) for other purposes ancillary to the extraction of oil.

(3) In this section and sections 168 to 170 ''oil'' has the meaning given by section 556(3).

Commentary—*Simon's Direct Tax Service* **B2.354**.
Former enactments—Sub-s (1): CAA 1990 s 64A(1)(*a*), (*b*), (3), (5).
Sub-s (2): CAA 1990 s 64A(11).
Sub-s (3): CAA 1990 s 64A(12).
Modifications—CAA 2001 Sch 3 para 28 (ss 167–171 do not apply if expenditure incurred before 21 March 2000; or treated as incurred by virtue of CAA 2001 s 13 and the conditions mentioned in sub-s (1) of that section were fulfilled before that date).
CAA 2001 Sch 3 para 54 (vehicles provided by employees in 1990–91: see modification note at the start of this Part).
CAA 2001 Sch 3 para 55 (certain expenditure incurred before 6 April 1976: see modification note at the start of this Part).

168 Expenditure on plant or machinery incurred by contractor

(1) This section applies if—

(*a*) the contractor incurs capital expenditure on the provision of plant or machinery of a description specified in the contract,

(*b*) the plant or machinery is to have an oil-related use under the contract, for the purposes of a trade of oil extraction carried on by the contractor,

(*c*) the amount of the expenditure is commensurate with the value of the contractor's interest under the contract, and

(*d*) the plant or machinery is transferred to the government or representative in accordance with the contract.

(2) Despite the transfer, the plant or machinery is to be treated for the purposes of this Part as owned by the contractor (and not by any other person) until—

(*a*) it ceases to be owned by the government or representative, or

(*b*) it ceases to be used, or held for use, by any person under the contract.

This is subject to section 170(2).

Commentary—*Simon's Direct Tax Service* **B2.354**.
Former enactments—Sub-s (1): CAA 1990 ss 64A(1)(*c*), (*d*), (*e*), 83(2A).
Sub-s (2): CAA 1990 s 64A(2).
Definition—''Capital expenditure'', s 4.
Modifications—CAA 2001 Sch 3 para 28 (ss 167–171 do not apply if expenditure incurred before 21 March 2000; or treated as incurred by virtue of CAA 2001 s 13 and the conditions mentioned in sub-s (1) of that section were fulfilled before that date).
CAA 2001 Sch 3 para 54 (vehicles provided by employees in 1990–91: see modification note at the start of this Part).
CAA 2001 Sch 3 para 55 (certain expenditure incurred before 6 April 1976: see modification note at the start of this Part).

169 Expenditure on plant or machinery incurred by participator

(1) This section applies if—

(*a*) a person (''the participator'') acquires an interest in the contract from—

    (i) the contractor, or

    (ii) another person who has acquired it (directly or indirectly) from the contractor,

(*b*) the participator incurs capital expenditure on the provision of plant or machinery,

(*c*) the plant or machinery is to have an oil-related use under the contract, for the purposes of a trade of oil extraction carried on by the participator,

(*d*) the amount of the expenditure is commensurate with the value of the participator's interest under the contract, and

(*e*) the plant or machinery is transferred to the government or representative in accordance with the contract.

(2) Despite the transfer, the plant or machinery is to be treated for the purposes of this Part as owned by the participator (and not by any other person) until—

(*a*) it ceases to be owned by the government or representative, or

(*b*) it ceases to be used, or held for use, by any person under the contract.

This is subject to section 170(2).

Commentary—*Simon's Direct Tax Service* **B2.354**.
Former enactments—Sub-s (1): CAA 1990 ss 64A(3), 83(2A).
Sub-s (2): CAA 1990 s 64A(4).
Definition—''Capital expenditure'', s 4.
Modifications—CAA 2001 Sch 3 para 28 (ss 167–171 do not apply if expenditure incurred before 21 March 2000; or treated as incurred by virtue of CAA 2001 s 13 and the conditions mentioned in sub-s (1) of that section were fulfilled before that date).
CAA 2001 Sch 3 para 54 (vehicles provided by employees in 1990–91: see modification note at the start of this Part).
CAA 2001 Sch 3 para 55 (certain expenditure incurred before 6 April 1976: see modification note at the start of this Part).

170 Participator's expenditure attributable to plant or machinery

(1) This section applies if—

(*a*) a person (''the relevant participator'') acquires an interest in the contract from—

    (i) the contractor, or

    (ii) another person who has acquired it (directly or indirectly) from the contractor, and (*b*) some of the expenditure incurred by the relevant participator to acquire the interest in the contract is attributable to plant or machinery which—

  (i) is treated by section 168 as owned by the contractor, or

  (ii) is treated by section 169 or subsection (2) as owned by another person (''the other participator'').

(2) The plant or machinery is to be treated for the purposes of this Part as owned by the relevant participator (and not by any other person) until—

  (*a*) it ceases to be owned by the government or representative, or

  (*b*) it ceases to be used, or held for use, by any person under the contract.

This is subject to a later application of this subsection.

(3) The person who, until subsection (2) applies, is treated as owning the plant or machinery is to be treated for the purposes of this Part as if he had disposed of it for a consideration equal to the relevant participator's expenditure attributable to it.

(4) The relevant participator is to be treated for the purposes of this Part as if—

  (*a*) he had incurred capital expenditure of an amount given by subsection (5), and

  (*b*) he owned the plant or machinery (in accordance with subsection (2)) as a result of having incurred that expenditure.

(5) The amount of that expenditure is—

  (*a*) the amount of the relevant participator's expenditure attributable to the plant or machinery, or

  (*b*) if less, the disposal value to be brought into account by the contractor or the other participator as a result of subsection (3).

(6) The expenditure attributable to plant or machinery for the purposes of this section is to be determined having regard to what is just and reasonable in the circumstances.

Commentary—*Simon's Direct Tax Service* **B2.354**.
Former enactments—Sub-s (1): CAA 1990 s 64A(5).
Sub-s (2): CAA 1990 s 64A(6).
Sub-s (3): CAA 1990 s 64A(7).
Sub-s (4): CAA 1990 s 64A(8).
Sub-s (5): CAA 1990 s 64A(8), (9).
Sub-s (6): CAA 1990 s 64A(10).
Definition—''Capital expenditure'', s 4.
Modifications—CAA 2001 Sch 3 para 28 (ss 167–171 do not apply if expenditure incurred before 21 March 2000; or treated as incurred by virtue of CAA 2001 s 13 and the conditions mentioned in sub-s (1) of that section were fulfilled before that date).
CAA 2001 Sch 3 para 54 (vehicles provided by employees in 1990–91: see modification note at the start of this Part).
CAA 2001 Sch 3 para 55 (certain expenditure incurred before 6 April 1976: see modification note at the start of this Part).

171 Disposal values on cessation of ownership

(1) This section applies if a person treated as owning plant or machinery under section 168(2), 169(2) or 170(2) ceases to be treated as owning it solely as a result of one of those provisions.

(2) If the person receives capital compensation, the disposal value to be brought into account is the amount of the compensation.

(3) If the person does not receive capital compensation, the disposal value to be brought into account is nil.

Commentary—*Simon's Direct Tax Service* **B2.354**.
Former enactments—Sub-s (1): CAA 1990 s 26(1)(*ef*)(*eg*).
Sub-s (2): CAA 1990 s 26(1)(*ef*).
Sub-s (3): CAA 1990 s 26(1)(*eg*).
Modifications—CAA 2001 Sch 3 para 28 (ss 167–171 do not apply if expenditure incurred before 21 March 2000; or treated as incurred by virtue of CAA 2001 s 13 and the conditions mentioned in sub-s (1) of that section were fulfilled before that date).
CAA 2001 Sch 3 para 54 (vehicles provided by employees in 1990–91: see modification note at the start of this Part).
CAA 2001 Sch 3 para 55 (certain expenditure incurred before 6 April 1976: see modification note at the start of this Part).

CHAPTER 14
FIXTURES
Introduction

172 Scope of Chapter etc

(1) This Chapter applies to determine entitlement to allowances under this Part in respect of expenditure on plant or machinery that is, or becomes, a fixture.

(2) For the purposes of this Part, ownership of plant or machinery that is, or becomes, a fixture is determined under this Chapter.

(3) The provisions of this Chapter that treat a person as being the owner of a fixture (see sections 176 to 184 and 193 to [195B][1]) are subject to the provisions of this Chapter which treat a person as ceasing to be the owner of a fixture (see sections 188 to [192A][1]).

(4) References in this Chapter to a person being treated—

  (*a*) as the owner of plant or machinery, or

  (*b*) as ceasing to be the owner of plant or machinery,

are to be read as references to the person being so treated for the purposes of this Part.

(5) This Chapter does not affect any entitlement a person has to an allowance as a result of section 538 (contribution allowances for plant and machinery).

Commentary—*Simon's Direct Tax Service* B2.355.
Former enactments—Sub-ss (1), (2): CAA 1990 s 51(1); change in law.
Sub-s (3): CAA 1990 ss 52(1), 53(1), 54(1), 55(1), 56.
Sub-s (4): CAA 1990 ss 52(1), (2), 53(1), (3), 54(1), 55(1), 56, 56A(2)(*c*), 56B(1)(*a*), 56C(1)(*d*), 57(2), (5)–(7), 58(1)–(4).
Sub-s (5): CAA 1990 s 51(8).
Modifications—CAA 2001 Sch 3 para 54 (vehicles provided by employees in 1990–91: see modification note at the start of this Part).
CAA 2001 Sch 3 para 55 (certain expenditure incurred before 6 April 1976: see modification note at the start of this Part).
Amendment—' ''195B'' substituted for ''195'', and ''192A'' substituted for ''192'' by FA 2001 s 66, Sch 18 para 1 with effect for expenditure incurred after 31 March 2001, and as respects allowances and charges falling to be made for chargeable periods ending after 5 April 2001 (for income tax purposes) or 31 March 2001 (for corporation tax purposes).

173 Meaning of "fixture" and "relevant land"

(1) In this Chapter "fixture"—

    (*a*) means plant or machinery that is so installed or otherwise fixed in or to a building or other description of land as to become, in law, part of that building or other land, and

    (*b*) includes any boiler or water-filled radiator installed in a building as part of a space or water heating system.

(2) In this Chapter "relevant land", in relation to a fixture means—

    (*a*) the building or other description of land of which the fixture becomes part, or

    (*b*) in the case of a boiler or water-filled radiator which is a fixture as a result of subsection (1)(*b*), the building in which it is installed as part of a space or water heating system.

Commentary—*Simon's Direct Tax Service* B2.355.
Former enactments—Sub-s (1): CAA 1990 s 51(2), (2A).
Sub-s (2): CAA 1990 s 51(2), (2A).
Revenue Internal Guidance—Capital allowances manual CA 26025 (meaning of ''fixture'').
Modifications—CAA 2001 Sch 3 para 54 (vehicles provided by employees in 1990–91: see modification note at the start of this Part).
CAA 2001 Sch 3 para 55 (certain expenditure incurred before 6 April 1976: see modification note at the start of this Part).

174 Meaning of "equipment lease" and "lease"

(1) In this Chapter "equipment lease" means—

    (*a*) an agreement entered into in the circumstances given in subsection (2), or

    (*b*) a lease entered into under or as a result of such an agreement.

(2) The circumstances are that—

    (*a*) a person incurs capital expenditure on the provision of plant or machinery for leasing,

    (*b*) an agreement is entered into for the lease, directly or indirectly from that person, of the plant or machinery to another person,

    (*c*) the plant or machinery becomes a fixture, and

    (*d*) the agreement is not an agreement for the plant or machinery to be leased as part of the relevant land.

(3) In this Chapter—

''equipment lessor'' means the person from whom (directly or indirectly) the equipment lease provides for the plant or machinery to be leased, and

''equipment lessee'' means the person to whom the equipment lease provides for the plant or machinery to be leased.

(4) Except in the context of leasing plant or machinery, any reference in this Chapter to a lease is to—

    (*a*) any leasehold estate in or, in Scotland, lease of, the land (whether in the nature of a head-lease, sub-lease or under-lease), or

    (*b*) any agreement to acquire such an estate or, in Scotland, lease;

and, in relation to such an agreement, ''grant'' is to be read accordingly.

Commentary—*Simon's Direct Tax Service* B2.355.
Former enactments—Sub-s (1): CAA 1990 s 51(2), 53(4).
Sub-s (2): CAA 1990 s 53(1).
Sub-s (3): CAA 1990 s 52(1), 53(1).
Sub-s (4): CAA 1990 s 51(2), (3).
Definition—''Capital expenditure'', s 4.
Modifications—CAA 2001 Sch 3 para 54 (vehicles provided by employees in 1990–91: see modification note at the start of this Part).
CAA 2001 Sch 3 para 55 (certain expenditure incurred before 6 April 1976: see modification note at the start of this Part).

175 Meaning of "interest in land", etc

(1) In this Chapter "interest in land" means—

    (*a*) the fee simple estate in the land or an agreement to acquire such an estate,

    (*b*) in relation to Scotland, the interest of the owner or an agreement to acquire such an interest,

    (*c*) a lease,

(*d*) an easement or servitude or an agreement to acquire an easement or servitude, and

(*e*) a licence to occupy land.

(2) If an interest in land is—

(*a*) conveyed or assigned by way of security, and

(*b*) subject to a right of redemption,

the person with the right of redemption is treated for the purposes of this Chapter as having that interest, and not the creditor.

Commentary—*Simon's Direct Tax Service* **B2.356**.
Former enactments—Sub-s (1): CAA 1990 s 51(2), (3).
Sub-s (2): CAA 1990 s 51(4).
Revenue Internal Guidance—Capital allowances manual CA 26150 (joint interests).
Modifications—CAA 2001 Sch 3 para 29 (if Abolition of Feudal Tenure etc (Scotland) Act 2000 Sch 12 para 51 has not come into force before the commencement of the section above, sub-s (1) above has effect until the appointed day as if para (*b*) is substituted to read as follows—

"(*b*) in Scotland, the estate or interest of the proprietor of the *dominium utile* (or, in the case of property other than feudal property, of the owner) and any agreement to acquire such an estate or interest,".
The appointed day means such day as may be appointed by the Scottish Ministers under Abolition of Feudal Tenure etc (Scotland) Act 2000 s 71 for the coming into force of the Act).
CAA 2001 Sch 3 para 54 (vehicles provided by employees in 1990–91: see modification note at the start of this Part).
CAA 2001 Sch 3 para 55 (certain expenditure incurred before 6 April 1976: see modification note at the start of this Part).

[175A Meaning of "energy services agreement"

(1) In this Chapter "energy services agreement" means an agreement entered into by an energy services provider ("the energy services provider") and another person ("the client") that makes provision, with a view to saving energy or using energy more efficiently, for—

(*a*) the design of plant or machinery, or one or more systems incorporating plant or machinery,

(*b*) obtaining and installing the plant or machinery,

(*c*) the operation of the plant or machinery,

(*d*) the maintenance of the plant or machinery, and

(*e*) the amount of any payments in respect of the operation of the plant or machinery to be linked (wholly or in part) to energy savings or increases in energy efficiency resulting from the provision or operation of the plant or machinery.

(2) In this Chapter "energy services provider" means a person carrying on a qualifying activity consisting wholly or mainly in the provision of energy management services.]¹

Commentary—*Simon's Direct Tax Service* **B2.356**.
Amendment—¹ Section inserted by FA 2001 s 66, Sch 18 para 2 with effect for expenditure incurred after 31 March 2001, and as respects allowances and charges falling to be made for chargeable periods ending after 5 April 2001 (for income tax purposes) or 31 March 2001 (for corporation tax purposes).

Persons who are treated as owners of fixtures

176 Person with interest in relevant land having fixture for purposes of qualifying activity

(1) If—

(*a*) a person incurs capital expenditure on the provision of plant or machinery for the purposes of a qualifying activity carried on by him,

(*b*) the plant or machinery becomes a fixture, and

(*c*) that person has an interest in the relevant land at the time the plant or machinery becomes a fixture,

that person is to be treated, on and after that time, as the owner of the fixture as a result of incurring the expenditure.

(2) If there are two or more persons with different interests in the relevant land who would be treated as the owner of the same fixture as a result of subsection (1), one interest only is taken into account under that subsection.

(3) The interest to be taken into account is given by the following rules—

Rule 1
If one of the interests is an easement or servitude or any agreement to acquire an easement or servitude, that interest is the interest to be taken into account.

Rule 2
If Rule 1 does not apply, but one of the interests is a licence to occupy land, that interest is the interest to be taken into account.

Rule 3
In any other case—

(*a*) except in Scotland, the interest to be taken into account is the interest which is not in reversion (at law or in equity and whether directly or indirectly) on any other interest in the relevant land which is held by any of the persons referred to in subsection (2), and

(*b*) in Scotland, the interest to be taken into account is the interest of whichever of the persons referred to in subsection (2) has, or last had, the right of use of the relevant land.

(4) Subsection (1) is subject to [sections 177(4) and 180A(4)]¹.

Commentary—*Simon's Direct Tax Service* **B2.356**.
Former enactments—Sub-s (1): CAA 1990 s 52(1).
Sub-ss (2), (3): CAA 1990 s 52(2).
Sub-s (4): CAA 1990 s 52(1).
Revenue Internal Guidance—Capital allowances manual CA 26150 (examples illustrating effects of this section).
Definition—"Capital expenditure", s 4.
Modifications—CAA 2001 Sch 3 para 54 (vehicles provided by employees in 1990–91: see modification note at the start of this Part).
CAA 2001 Sch 3 para 55 (certain expenditure incurred before 6 April 1976: see modification note at the start of this Part).
Amendment—¹ Words "sections 177(4) and 180A(4)" substituted for words "section 177(4)" by FA 2001 s 66, Sch 18 para 3 with effect for expenditure incurred after 31 March 2001, and as respects allowances and charges falling to be made for chargeable periods ending after 5 April 2001 (for income tax purposes) or 31 March 2001 (for corporation tax purposes).

177 Equipment lessors

(1) If—

  (a) the conditions in—

    (i) section 178 (equipment lessee has qualifying activity etc),

    (ii) section 179 (equipment lessor has right to sever fixture that is not part of building), or

    (iii) section 180 (equipment lease is part of affordable warmth programme),

  are met in relation to an equipment lease,

  (b) the equipment lessor and the equipment lessee are not connected persons, and

  (c) they elect that this section should apply,

the equipment lessor is to be treated, on and after the relevant time, as the owner of the fixture as a result of incurring the capital expenditure on the provision of the plant or machinery that is the subject of the equipment lease.

(2) The relevant time for the purposes of subsection (1) is (unless subsection (3) applies) the time when the equipment lessor incurs the expenditure.

(3) If—

  (a) the conditions in section 178 are met in relation to an equipment lease (but the conditions in sections 179 and 180 are not), and

  (b) the equipment lessor incurs the capital expenditure before the equipment lessee begins to carry on the qualifying activity,

the relevant time is the time when the equipment lessee begins to carry on the qualifying activity.

(4) If an election is made under this section, the equipment lessee is not to be treated under section 176 as the owner of the fixture.

(5) An election under this section must be made by notice to the Inland Revenue—

  (a) for income tax purposes, on or before the normal time limit for amending a tax return for the tax year in which the relevant chargeable period ends;

  (b) for corporation tax purposes, no later than 2 years after the end of the relevant chargeable period.

(6) "The relevant chargeable period" means the chargeable period in which the capital expenditure was incurred.

Commentary—*Simon's Direct Tax Service* **B2.356**.
Former enactments—Sub-s (1): CAA 1990 s 53(1), (1B), (1D), (2).
Sub-s (2): CAA 1990 s 53(1), (1B), (1D).
Sub-s (3): CAA 1990 s 53(1A).
Sub-s (4): CAA 1990 s 53(3).
Sub-s (5): CAA 1990 s 53(2), (2A).
Sub-s (6): CAA 1990 s 53(2A).
Revenue Internal Guidance—Capital allowances manual CA 26200 (explanation of this section).
Definitions—"Capital expenditure", s 4; "chargeable period", s 6; "normal time limit for amending a tax return", s 577(1).
Modifications—CAA 2001 Sch 3 para 30 (sub-s (1)(a)(i) does not apply if agreement for the lease of the plant or machinery was entered into before 19 March 1997).
CAA 2001 Sch 3 para 54 (vehicles provided by employees in 1990–91: see modification note at the start of this Part).
CAA 2001 Sch 3 para 55 (certain expenditure incurred before 6 April 1976: see modification note at the start of this Part).

178 Equipment lessee has qualifying activity etc

The conditions referred to in section 177(1)(a)(i) are that—

  (a) the equipment lease is for the lease of the plant or machinery for the purposes of a qualifying activity which is, or is to be, carried on by the equipment lessee,

  (b) if the equipment lessee had incurred the capital expenditure incurred by the equipment lessor on the provision of the plant or machinery that is the subject of the equipment lease, he would, as a result of section 176, have been entitled to an allowance in respect of it, and

  (c) the equipment lease is not for the lease of the plant or machinery for use in a dwelling-house.

Commentary—*Simon's Direct Tax Service* **B2.356**.
Former enactments—CAA 1990 s 53(1).
Definitions—"Capital expenditure", s 4; "dwelling-house", s 531(1).
Modifications—CAA 2001 Sch 3 para 31 (para (a) modified with the omission of the words "which is or is to be", and the addition of the word "and" at the end of that paragraph, if the agreement for the lease of the plant or machinery was entered into before 19 March 1997.
If the expenditure was incurred before 24 July 1996, para (c) does not apply, and para (b) to be substituted as follows—

"(*b*) if the equipment lessee had incurred the capital expenditure incurred by the equipment lessor on the provision of the plant or machinery, he would, by virtue of section 176, be treated as the owner of the fixture as a result of incurring the expenditure").
CAA 2001 Sch 3 para 54 (vehicles provided by employees in 1990–91: see modification note at the start of this Part).
CAA 2001 Sch 3 para 55 (certain expenditure incurred before 6 April 1976: see modification note at the start of this Part).

179 Equipment lessor has right to sever fixture that is not part of building

(1) The conditions referred to in section 177(1)(*a*)(ii) are that—

(*a*) the plant or machinery becomes a fixture by being fixed to land that is neither a building nor part of a building,

(*b*) the equipment lessee has an interest in the land when taking possession of the plant or machinery under the equipment lease,

(*c*) under the terms of the equipment lease, the equipment lessor is entitled to sever the plant or machinery, at the end of the period for which it is leased, from the land to which it is fixed at that time,

(*d*) under the terms of the equipment lease, the equipment lessor will own the plant or machinery on its severance in accordance with the equipment lease,

(*e*) the nature of the plant or machinery and the way in which it is fixed to land are such that its use on one set of premises does not, to any material extent, prevent it from being used, once severed, for the same purposes on a different set of premises,

(*f*) the equipment lease is one which under [generally accepted accounting practice][1] falls (or would fall) to be treated in the accounts of the equipment lessor as an operating lease, and

(*g*) the equipment lease is not for the lease of the plant or machinery for use in a dwelling-house.

(2) ...[2]

Commentary—*Simon's Direct Tax Service* **B2.356**.
Former enactments—Sub-s (1): CAA 1990 s 53(1B), (1C).
Sub-s (2): CAA 1990 s 53(1C).
Definition—"Dwelling-house", s 531(1).
Modifications—CAA 2001 Sch 3 para 32 (sub-s (1) above does not apply if agreement for the lease of the plant or machinery was entered into before 19 March 1997.
If the expenditure of the equipment lessor was incurred before 24 July 1996, the word "and" should be added at the end of sub-s (1)(*e*), and sub (1)(*g*) and the word "and" immediately before it should be omitted).
CAA 2001 Sch 3 para 54 (vehicles provided by employees in 1990–91: see modification note at the start of this Part).
CAA 2001 Sch 3 para 55 (certain expenditure incurred before 6 April 1976: see modification note at the start of this Part).
Amendments—[1] Words substituted for the words "normal accountancy practice" by FA 2002 s 103(4)(*g*) with effect from 24 July 2002.
[2] Sub-s (2) repealed by FA 2002 s 141, Sch 40 Pt 3(16) with effect from 24 July 2002. Sub-s (2) previously read as follows—
"(2) For the purposes of applying subsection (1)(*f*), the equipment lessor is to be treated as being a company incorporated in a part of the United Kingdom.".

180 Equipment lease is part of affordable warmth programme

(1) The conditions referred to in section 177(1)(*a*)(iii) are that—

(*a*) the plant or machinery which is the subject of the equipment lease consists of a boiler, heat exchanger, radiator or heating control that is installed in a building as part of a space or water heating system,

(*b*) the expenditure of the equipment lessor is incurred before 1st January 2008, and

(*c*) the equipment lease is approved for the purposes of this section as entered into as part of the affordable warmth programme.

(2) The approval mentioned in subsection (1)(*c*) may be given, with the consent of the Treasury—

(*a*) by the Secretary of State;

(*b*) in the case of buildings in Scotland, by the Scottish Ministers;

(*c*) in the case of buildings in Wales, by the National Assembly for Wales;

(*d*) in the case of buildings in Northern Ireland, by the Department for Social Development in Northern Ireland.

(3) If an approval is withdrawn, it is to be treated for the purposes of subsection (1)(*c*) as never having had effect.

Commentary—*Simon's Direct Tax Service* **B2.356**.
Former enactments—Sub-s (1): CAA 1990 s 53(1D), (1E).
Sub-s (2): CAA 1990 s 53(1F).
Sub-s (3): CAA 1990 s 53(1G).
Modifications—CAA 2001 Sch 3 para 33 (the section above does not apply if the expenditure of the equipment lessor was incurred before 28 July 2000).
CAA 2001 Sch 3 para 54 (vehicles provided by employees in 1990–91: see modification note at the start of this Part).
CAA 2001 Sch 3 para 55 (certain expenditure incurred before 6 April 1976: see modification note at the start of this Part).

[180A Energy services providers

(1) If—

(*a*) an energy services agreement is entered into,

(*b*) the energy services provider incurs capital expenditure under the agreement on the provision of plant or machinery,

(*c*) the plant or machinery becomes a fixture,

   (*d*) at the time the plant or machinery becomes a fixture—

      (i) the client has an interest in the relevant land, and

      (ii) the energy services provider does not,

   (*e*) the plant or machinery—

      (i) is not provided for leasing, and

      (ii) is not provided for use in a dwelling-house,

   (*f*) the operation of the plant or machinery is carried out wholly or substantially by the energy services provider or a person connected with him,

   (*g*) the energy services provider and the client are not connected persons, and

   (*h*) they elect that this section should apply,

the energy services provider is to be treated, on and after the time at which he incurs the expenditure, as the owner of the fixture as a result of incurring the expenditure.

(2) But if the client would not have been entitled to a section 176 allowance in respect of the expenditure if he had incurred it, subsection (1) does not apply unless the plant or machinery belongs to a class of plant or machinery specified by Treasury order.

(3) In subsection (2) a "section 176 allowance" means an allowance to which a person is entitled as a result of section 176.

(4) If an election is made under this section, the client is not to be treated under section 176 as the owner of the fixture.

(5) An election under this section must be made by notice to the Inland Revenue—

   (*a*) for income tax purposes, on or before the normal time limit for amending a tax return for the tax year in which the relevant chargeable period ends;

   (*b*) for corporation tax purposes, no later than 2 years after the end of the relevant chargeable period.

(6) The "relevant chargeable period" means the chargeable period in which the capital expenditure was incurred.][1]

Commentary—*Simon's Direct Tax Service* **B2.356**.
Cross reference—See Capital Allowances (Energy-saving Plant and Machinery) Order, SI 2001/2541 art 3 (description of energy-saving plant and machinery).
Amendment—[1] Section inserted by FA 2001 s 66, Sch 18 para 4 with effect for expenditure incurred after 31 March 2001, and as respects allowances and charges falling to be made for chargeable periods ending after 5 April 2001 (for income tax purposes) or 31 March 2001 (for corporation tax purposes).

181 Purchaser of land giving consideration for fixture

(1) If—

   (*a*) after any plant or machinery has become a fixture, a person ("the purchaser") acquires an interest in the relevant land,

   (*b*) that interest was in existence before the purchaser's acquisition of it, and

   (*c*) the consideration which the purchaser gives for the interest is or includes a capital sum that, in whole or in part, falls to be treated for the purposes of this Part as expenditure on the provision of the fixture,

the purchaser is to be treated, on and after the time of the acquisition, as the owner of the fixture as a result of incurring that expenditure.

[(2) Subsection (1) does not apply, and is to be treated as never having applied, if, immediately after the time of the acquisition, a person has a prior right in relation to the fixture.][2]

(3) For the purposes of [subsection (2), a person][2] has a prior right in relation to the fixture if he—

   (*a*) is treated as the owner of the fixture immediately before the time referred to in [subsection (2)][2] as a result of incurring expenditure on the provision of the fixture,

   (*b*) is not so treated as a result of section 538 (contribution allowances for plant and machinery),

   (*c*) is entitled to an allowance in respect of that expenditure, and

   (*d*) makes or has made a claim in respect of that expenditure.

(4) Subsection (1) is subject to [sections 182 and 182A][1].

Commentary—*Simon's Direct Tax Service* **B2.356**.
Former enactments—Sub-s (1): CAA 1990 s 54(1).
Sub-s (2): CAA 1990 s 56A(1), (2).
Sub-s (3): CAA 1990 s 56A(2), (3).
Sub-s (4): CAA 1990 s 54(2).
Revenue Internal Guidance—Capital allowances manual CA 26250 (example illustrating effect of this section).
Definition—"Capital sum", s 4.
Modifications—CAA 2001 Sch 3 para 34 (the word "and" at the end of sub-s (1)(*b*) to be omitted, and sub-s (1)(*bb*) to be inserted if the purchaser acquired the interest in the relevant land before 24 July 1996. Sub-s (1)(*bb*) to read as follows—

   "(*bb*) at the time of the purchaser's acquisition of the interest, either no person has previously become entitled to an allowance in respect of any capital expenditure incurred on the provision of the fixture or, if any person has become so entitled, that person has been or is required to bring the disposal value of the fixture into account under Chapter 5, and").
CAA 2001 Sch 3 para 54 (vehicles provided by employees in 1990–91: see modification note at the start of this Part).
CAA 2001 Sch 3 para 55 (certain expenditure incurred before 6 April 1976: see modification note at the start of this Part).

Amendment—[1] Words "sections 182 and 182A" substituted for words "section 182" by FA 2001 s 66, Sch 18 para 5 with effect for expenditure incurred after 31 March 2001, and as respects allowances and charges falling to be made for chargeable periods ending after 5 April 2001 (for income tax purposes) or 31 March 2001 (for corporation tax purposes).
[2] Sub-s (2), and words in sub-s (3), substituted by FA 2001 s 69, Sch 21 para 2(1), (2) with effect as respects allowances and charges falling to be made for chargeable periods ending after 5 April 2001 (for income tax purposes) or 31 March 2001 (for corporation tax purposes).

182 Purchaser of land discharging obligations of equipment lessee

(1) If—

 (a) after any plant or machinery has become a fixture, a person ("the purchaser") acquires an interest in the relevant land,

 (b) that interest was in existence before the purchaser's acquisition of it,

 (c) before that acquisition, the plant or machinery was let under an equipment lease, and

 (d) in connection with that acquisition, the purchaser pays a capital sum to discharge the obligations of the equipment lessee under the equipment lease,

the purchaser is to be treated, on and after the time of the acquisition, as the owner of the fixture as a result of incurring expenditure, consisting of that capital sum, on the provision of the fixture.

[(2) Subsection (1) does not apply, and is to be treated as never having applied, if, immediately after the time of the acquisition, a person has a prior right in relation to the fixture.

(3) Section 181(3) (test for whether person has a prior right) applies for the purposes of subsection (2).][1]

Commentary—*Simon's Direct Tax Service* **B2.356.**
Former enactments—Sub-s (1): CAA 1990 s 54(1), (2).
Sub-s (2): CAA 1990 s 56A(1), (2).
Sub-s (3): CAA 1990 s 56A(2), (3).
Revenue Internal Guidance—Capital allowances manual CA 26300 (example illustrating this section).
Definition—"Capital sum", s 4.
Modifications—CAA 2001 Sch 3 para 35 (the word "and" at the end of sub-s (1)(c) to be omitted; and sub-s (1)(cc) to be inserted if the purchaser acquired the interest in the relevant land before 24 July 1996. Sub-s (1)(cc) to read as follows—
"(cc) at the time of the purchaser's acquisition of the interest, either no person has previously become entitled to an allowance in respect of any capital expenditure incurred on the provision of the fixture or, if any person has become so entitled, that person has been or is required to bring the disposal value of the fixture into account under Chapter 5, and").
CAA 2001 Sch 3 para 54 (vehicles provided by employees in 1990–91: see modification note at the start of this Part).
CAA 2001 Sch 3 para 55 (certain expenditure incurred before 6 April 1976: see modification note at the start of this Part).
Amendments—[1] Sub-ss (2), (3) substituted by FA 2001 s 69, Sch 21 para 2(3) with effect as respects allowances and charges falling to be made for chargeable periods ending after 5 April 2001 (for income tax purposes) or 31 March 2001 (for corporation tax purposes).

[182A Purchaser of land discharging obligations of client under energy services agreement

(1) If—

 (a) after any plant or machinery has become a fixture, a person ("the purchaser") acquires an interest in the relevant land,

 (b) that interest was in existence before the purchaser's acquisition of it,

 (c) before that acquisition, the plant or machinery was provided under an energy services agreement, and

 (d) in connection with that acquisition, the purchaser pays a capital sum to discharge the obligations of the client under the energy services agreement,

the purchaser is to be treated, on and after the time of the acquisition, as the owner of the fixture as a result of incurring expenditure, consisting of that capital sum, on the provision of the fixture.

(2) Subsection (1) does not apply, and is to be treated as never having applied, if, immediately after the time of the acquisition, a person has a prior right in relation to the fixture.

(3) Section 181(3) (test for whether person has a prior right) applies for the purposes of subsection (2)][1]

Commentary—*Simon's Direct Tax Service* **B2.356**.
Amendment—[1] Section inserted by FA 2001 s 66, Sch 18 para 6 with effect for expenditure incurred after 31 March 2001, and as respects allowances and charges falling to be made for chargeable periods ending after 5 April 2001 (for income tax purposes) or 31 March 2001 (for corporation tax purposes).

183 Incoming lessee where lessor entitled to allowances

(1) If—

 (a) after any plant or machinery has become a fixture, a person ("the lessor") who has an interest in the relevant land grants a lease,

 (b) the lessor is entitled to an allowance in respect of the fixture for the chargeable period in which the lease is granted or would be if he were within the charge to tax,

 (c) the consideration which the lessee gives for the lease is or includes a capital sum that, in whole or in part, falls to be treated for the purposes of this Part as expenditure on the provision of the fixture,

 (d) the lessor and the lessee are not connected persons, and

 (e) the lessor and the lessee make an election under this section, the lessee is to be treated, on and after the time when the lease is granted, as the owner of the fixture as a result of incurring that expenditure.

(2) An election under this section must be made by notice to the Inland Revenue within 2 years after the date on which the lease takes effect.

Commentary—*Simon's Direct Tax Service* **B2.356**.
Former enactments—Sub-s (1): CAA 1990 s 55(1), (2), (4).
Sub-s (2): CAA 1990 s 55(3).
Definitions—"Capital sum", s 4; "chargeable period", s 6.
Modifications—CAA 2001 Sch 3 para 36 (sub-s (3) to be inserted if the person who had the interest in the relevant land granted the lease before 24 July 1996. Sub-s (3) to read as follows—

"(3) No election may be made under this section if it appears that the sole or main benefit that may be expected to accrue to the lessor from the grant of the lease and the making of an election is the obtaining of an allowance or deduction or a greater allowance or deduction or the avoidance or reduction of a charge under this Part.").

CAA 2001 Sch 3 para 54 (vehicles provided by employees in 1990–91: see modification note at the start of this Part).
CAA 2001 Sch 3 para 55 (certain expenditure incurred before 6 April 1976: see modification note at the start of this Part).

184 Incoming lessee where lessor not entitled to allowances

(1) If—

    (a) after any plant or machinery has become a fixture, a person ("the lessor") who has an interest in the relevant land grants a lease,

    (b) the lessor is not within section 183(1)(b),

    (c) before the lease is granted, the fixture has not been used for the purposes of a qualifying activity carried on by the lessor or any person connected with the lessor, and

    (d) the consideration which the lessee gives for the lease is or includes a capital sum that, in whole or in part, falls to be treated for the purposes of this Part as expenditure on the provision of the fixture,

the lessee is to be treated, on and after the time when the lease is granted, as the owner of the fixture as a result of incurring that expenditure.

[(2) Subsection (1) does not apply, and is to be treated as never having applied, if, immediately after the time when the lease is granted, a person has a prior right in relation to the fixture.

(3) Section 181(3) (test for whether person has a prior right) applies for the purposes of subsection (2).][1]

Commentary—*Simon's Direct Tax Service* **B2.356**.
Former enactments—Sub-s (1): CAA 1990 s 56.
Sub-s (2): CAA 1990 s 56A(1), (2).
Sub-s (3): CAA 1990 s 56A(2), (3).
Definition—"Capital sum", s 4.
Modifications—CAA 2001 Sch 3 para 37 (the word "and" at the end of sub-s (1)(c) above to be omitted, and sub-s (1)(cc) to be inserted if the person who had the interest in the relevant land granted the lease before 24 July 1996. Sub-s (1)(cc) to read as follows—

"(cc) at the time of the grant of the lease, no person has previously become entitled to an allowance in respect of any capital expenditure incurred on the provision of the fixture, and").

CAA 2001 Sch 3 para 54 (vehicles provided by employees in 1990–91: see modification note at the start of this Part).
CAA 2001 Sch 3 para 55 (certain expenditure incurred before 6 April 1976: see modification note at the start of this Part).
Amendments—[1] Sub-ss (2), (3) substituted by FA 2001 s 69, Sch 21 para 2(4) with effect as respects allowances and charges falling to be made for chargeable periods ending after 5 April 2001 (for income tax purposes) or 31 March 2001 (for corporation tax purposes).

Restrictions on amount of qualifying expenditure

185 Fixture on which a plant and machinery allowance has been claimed

(1) This section applies if—

    (a) a person ("the current owner") is treated as the owner of a fixture as a result of incurring capital expenditure ("new expenditure") on its provision,

    (b) the plant or machinery is treated as having been owned at a relevant earlier time by any person ("the past owner") as a result of incurring other expenditure,

    (c) the plant or machinery is within paragraph (b) otherwise than as a result of section 538 (contribution allowances for plant and machinery), and

    (d) the past owner is or has been required to bring the disposal value of the plant or machinery into account (as a result of having made a claim in respect of that other expenditure).

(2) If the new expenditure exceeds the maximum allowable amount, the excess—

    (a) is to be left out of account in determining the current owner's qualifying expenditure, or

    (b) if the new expenditure has already been taken into account for this purpose, is to be treated as expenditure that should never have been taken into account.

(3) The maximum allowable amount is—

$$D + I$$

where—

    D is the disposal value of the plant or machinery which the past owner has been or is required to bring into account, and

I is any of the new expenditure that is treated under section 25 (building alterations in connection with installation) as expenditure on the provision of the plant or machinery.

(4) If more than one disposal event has occurred requiring the past owner to bring the disposal value of the plant or machinery into account, the maximum allowable amount is calculated by reference only to the most recent of those events.

(5) For the purposes of this section, the current owner and the past owner may be the same person.

(6) In subsection (1)(*b*) "relevant earlier time" means (subject to subsection (7)) any time before the earliest time when the current owner is treated as owning the plant or machinery as a result of incurring the new expenditure.

(7) If, before the earliest time when the current owner is treated as owning the plant or machinery as a result of incurring the new expenditure—

    (*a*) any person has ceased to own the plant or machinery as a result of a sale,

    (*b*) the sale was not a sale of the plant or machinery as a fixture, and

    (*c*) the buyer and seller were not connected persons at the time of the sale,

the relevant earlier time does not include any time before the seller ceased to own the plant or machinery.

Commentary—*Simon's Direct Tax Service* **B2.357**.
Former enactments—Sub-s (1): CAA 1990 s 56B(1), (2).
Sub-s (2): CAA 1990 s 56B(1).
Sub-s (3): CAA 1990 s 56B(4)
Sub-s (4): CAA 1990 s 56B(5).
Sub-s (5): CAA 1990 s 56B(3).
Sub-s (6): CAA 1990 s 56B(6).
Sub-s (7): CAA 1990 s 56B(6), (7).
Revenue Internal Guidance—Capital allowances manual CA 26400 (it is the responsibility of the taxpayer to obtain and provide details of the prior claimant and the disposal value).
Definitions—"Capital expenditure", s 4; "disposal event", s 60(2).
Modifications—CAA 2001 Sch 3 para 38 (the section above does not apply if the disposal event which required the disposal value to be brought into account as mentioned in sub-s (1)(*d*) above occurred before 24 July 1996).
CAA 2001 Sch 3 para 54 (vehicles provided by employees in 1990–91: see modification note at the start of this Part).
CAA 2001 Sch 3 para 55 (certain expenditure incurred before 6 April 1976: see modification note at the start of this Part).

186 Fixture on which an industrial buildings allowance has been made

(1) This section applies if—

    (*a*) a person ("the past owner") has at any time claimed an allowance to which he is entitled under Part 3 (industrial buildings allowances) in respect of expenditure which was or included expenditure on the provision of plant or machinery,

    (*b*) the past owner has transferred the interest which is the relevant interest for the purposes of Part 3, and

    (*c*) the current owner of the plant or machinery makes a claim in respect of expenditure ("new expenditure") incurred—

        (i) on the provision of the plant or machinery, and

        (ii) at a time when it is a fixture in the building.

(2) If the new expenditure exceeds the maximum allowable amount, the excess is to be left out of account in determining the current owner's qualifying expenditure.

(3) The maximum allowable amount is—

$$\frac{F}{T} \times R$$

where—

F is the part of the consideration for the transfer by the past owner that is attributable to the fixture,
T is the total consideration for that transfer, and
R is the residue of qualifying expenditure attributable to the relevant interest immediately after that transfer, calculated on the assumption that the transfer was a sale of the relevant interest.

(4) For the purposes of this section the current owner of the plant or machinery is—

    (*a*) the person to whom the past owner transferred the relevant interest, or

    (*b*) any person who is subsequently treated as the owner of the plant or machinery.

(5) In this section "building" and "residue of qualifying expenditure" have the same meaning as in Part 3.

Commentary—*Simon's Direct Tax Service* **B2.358**.
Former enactments—Sub-ss (1), (2): CAA 1990 s 56C(1).
Sub-s (3): CAA 1990 s 56C(2), (3).
Sub-s (4): CAA 1990 s 56C(1).
Sub-s (5): CAA 1990 s 56C(4).
Modifications—CAA 2001 Sch 3 para 39 (the section above does not apply if the time mentioned in sub-s (1)(*c*)(ii) is before 24 July 1996).
CAA 2001 Sch 3 para 54 (vehicles provided by employees in 1990–91: see modification note at the start of this Part).
CAA 2001 Sch 3 para 55 (certain expenditure incurred before 6 April 1976: see modification note at the start of this Part).

187 Fixture on which a research and development allowance has been made

(1) This section applies if—

(a) a person has at any time claimed an allowance to which he is entitled under Part 6 (research and development allowances) in respect of qualifying expenditure under that Part (''Part 6 expenditure''),

(b) an asset representing the whole or part of the Part 6 expenditure (''the Part 6 asset'') has ceased to be owned by that person (''the past owner''),

(c) the Part 6 asset was or included plant or machinery, and

(d) the current owner makes a claim under this Part in respect of expenditure (''new expenditure'') incurred—

(i) on the provision of the plant or machinery, and

(ii) at a time when it is a fixture.

(2) If the new expenditure exceeds the maximum allowable amount, the excess is to be left out of account in determining the current owner's qualifying expenditure.

(3) The maximum allowable amount is—

$$\frac{F}{T} \times A$$

where—

F is the part of the consideration for the disposal of the Part 6 asset by the past owner that is attributable to the fixture,

T is the total consideration for that disposal, and

A is an amount equal to whichever is the smaller of—

(a) the disposal value of the Part 6 asset when the past owner ceased to own it, and

(b) so much of the Part 6 expenditure as related to the provision of the Part 6 asset.

(4) For the purposes of this section the current owner of the plant or machinery is—

(a) the person who acquired the Part 6 asset from the past owner, or

(b) any person who is subsequently treated as the owner of the plant or machinery.

Commentary—*Simon's Direct Tax Service* B2.358.
Former enactments—Sub-ss (1), (2): CAA 1990 s 56D(1).
Sub-s (3): CAA 1990 s 56D(2), (3).
Sub-s (4): CAA 1990 s 56D(1).
Modifications—CAA 2001 Sch 3 para 40 (the section above does not apply if the time mentioned in sub-s (1)(d)(ii) is before 24 July 1996).
CAA 2001 Sch 3 para 54 (vehicles provided by employees in 1990–91: see modification note at the start of this Part).
CAA 2001 Sch 3 para 55 (certain expenditure incurred before 6 April 1976: see modification note at the start of this Part).

Cessation of ownership of fixtures

188 Cessation of ownership when person ceases to have qualifying interest

(1) This section applies if a person is treated as the owner of a fixture under—

(a) section 176 (person with interest in land having fixture for purposes of qualifying activity),

(b) section 181 (purchaser of land giving consideration for fixture),

(c) section 182 (purchaser of land discharging obligations of equipment lessee),

[(ca) section 182A (purchaser of land discharging obligations of client under energy services agreement),][1]

(d) section 183 (incoming lessee where lessor entitled to allowances), or

(e) section 184 (incoming lessee where lessor not entitled to allowances).

(2) If the person ceases at any time to have the qualifying interest, he is to be treated as ceasing to be the owner of the fixture at that time.

(3) In this Chapter ''the qualifying interest'' means—

(a) if section 176, 181[, 182 or 182A][1] applies, the interest in the relevant land referred to in that section, and

(b) if section 183 or 184 applies, the lease referred to in that section.

(4) This section is subject to section 189.

Commentary—*Simon's Direct Tax Service* B2.357.
Former enactments—Sub-ss (1), (2): CAA 1990 s 57(2).
Sub-s (3): CAA 1990 s 57(3).
Sub-s (4): CAA 1990 s 57(2).
Revenue Internal Guidance—Capital allowances manual CA 26500 (examples illustrating definition of ''qualifying interest'' in sub-s (3)).
Modifications—CAA 2001 Sch 3 para 54 (vehicles provided by employees in 1990–91: see modification note at the start of this Part).
CAA 2001 Sch 3 para 55 (certain expenditure incurred before 6 April 1976: see modification note at the start of this Part).
Amendments—[1] Sub-s (1)(ca) inserted, and in sub-s (3)(a) words '', 182 or 182A'' substituted for words ''or 182'', by FA 2001 s 66, Sch 18 para 7 with effect for expenditure incurred after 31 March 2001, and as respects allowances and charges falling to be made for chargeable periods ending after 5 April 2001 (for income tax purposes) or 31 March 2001 (for corporation tax purposes).

CAA 2001

189 Identifying the qualifying interest in special cases

(1) If—

    (a) a person's qualifying interest is an agreement to acquire an interest in land, and

    (b) that interest is subsequently transferred or granted to that person,

the interest transferred or granted is to be treated as the qualifying interest.

(2) If a person's qualifying interest ceases to exist as a result of its being merged in another interest acquired by that person, that other interest is to be treated as the qualifying interest.

(3) If—

    (a) the qualifying interest is a lease, and

    (b) on its termination, a new lease of the relevant land (with or without other land) is granted to the lessee,

the new lease is to be treated as the qualifying interest.

(4) If—

    (a) the qualifying interest is a licence, and

    (b) on its termination, a new licence to occupy the relevant land (with or without other land) is granted to the licensee,

the new licence is to be treated as the qualifying interest.

(5) If—

    (a) the qualifying interest is a lease, and

    (b) with the consent of the lessor, the lessee remains in possession of the relevant land after the termination of the lease without a new lease being granted to him,

the qualifying interest is to be treated as continuing so long as the lessee remains in possession of the relevant land.

Commentary—*Simon's Direct Tax Service* **B2.357**.
Former enactments—Sub-s (1): CAA 1990 s 57(3).
Sub-ss (2)–(5): CAA 1990 s 57(4).
Modifications—CAA 2001 Sch 3 para 54 (vehicles provided by employees in 1990–91: see modification note at the start of this Part).
CAA 2001 Sch 3 para 55 (certain expenditure incurred before 6 April 1976: see modification note at the start of this Part).

190 Cessation of ownership of lessor where section 183 applies

(1) This section applies if a lessee is treated under section 183 (incoming lessee where lessor entitled to allowances) as the owner of a fixture.

(2) The lessor is to be treated as ceasing to be the owner of the fixture when the lessee begins to be treated as the owner.

Commentary—*Simon's Direct Tax Service* **B2.357**.
Former enactments—CAA 1990 s 57(5).
Modifications—CAA 2001 Sch 3 para 54 (vehicles provided by employees in 1990–91: see modification note at the start of this Part).
CAA 2001 Sch 3 para 55 (certain expenditure incurred before 6 April 1976: see modification note at the start of this Part).

191 Cessation of ownership on severance of fixture

If—

    (a) a person is treated as the owner of the fixture as a result of any provision of this Chapter,

    (b) the fixture is permanently severed from the relevant land (so that it ceases to be a fixture), and

    (c) once it is severed, it is not in fact owned by that person,

that person is to be treated as ceasing to be the owner of the fixture when it is severed.

Commentary—*Simon's Direct Tax Service* **B2.357**.
Former enactments—CAA 1990 s 57(7).
Modifications—CAA 2001 Sch 3 para 54 (vehicles provided by employees in 1990–91: see modification note at the start of this Part).
CAA 2001 Sch 3 para 55 (certain expenditure incurred before 6 April 1976: see modification note at the start of this Part).

192 Cessation of ownership of equipment lessor

(1) This section applies if an equipment lessor is treated under section 177 as the owner of a fixture.

(2) If—

    (a) the equipment lessor at any time assigns his rights under the equipment lease, or

    (b) the financial obligations of the equipment lessee under an equipment lease are at any time discharged (on the payment of a capital sum or otherwise),

the equipment lessor is to be treated as ceasing to be the owner of the fixture at that time (or, as the case may be, at the earliest of those times).

(3) The reference in subsection (2)(b) to the equipment lessee is, in a case where the financial obligations of the equipment lessee have become vested in another person (by assignment, operation of law or otherwise), a reference to the person in whom the obligations are vested when the capital sum is paid.

Commentary—*Simon's Direct Tax Service* **B2.357**.
Former enactments—Sub-ss (1), (2): CAA 1990 s 58(1).
Sub-s (3): CAA 1990 s 58(5).
Definitions—''Capital sum'', s 4.
Modifications—CAA 2001 Sch 3 para 54 (vehicles provided by employees in 1990–91: see modification note at the start of this Part).
CAA 2001 Sch 3 para 55 (certain expenditure incurred before 6 April 1976: see modification note at the start of this Part).

[192A Cessation of ownership of energy services provider

(1) This section applies if an energy services provider is treated under section 180A as the owner of a fixture.

(2) If—

    (*a*) the energy services provider at any time assigns his rights under the energy services agreement, or

    (*b*) the financial obligations of the client in respect of the fixture under an energy services agreement are at any time discharged (on the payment of a capital sum or otherwise),

the energy services provider is to be treated as ceasing to be the owner of the fixture at that time (or, as the case may be, the earliest of those times).

(3) The reference in subsection (2)(*b*) to the client is, in a case where the financial obligations of the client have become vested in another person (by assignment, operation of law or otherwise), a reference to the person in whom the obligations are vested when the capital sum is paid.]¹

Commentary—*Simon's Direct Tax Service* **B2.357**.
Amendment—¹ Section inserted by FA 2001 s 66, Sch 18 para 8 with effect for expenditure incurred after 31 March 2001, and as respects allowances and charges falling to be made for chargeable periods ending after 5 April 2001 (for income tax purposes) or 31 March 2001 (for corporation tax purposes).

Acquisition of ownership of fixture when another ceases to own it

193 Acquisition of ownership by lessor or licensor on termination of lease or licence

If, on the termination of a lease or licence, the outgoing lessee or licensee is treated under section 188 as ceasing to be the owner of a fixture, the lessor or licensor is to be treated, on and after the termination of the lease or licence, as the owner of the fixture.

Commentary—*Simon's Direct Tax Service* **B2.357**.
Former enactments—CAA 1990 s 57(6).
Modifications—CAA 2001 Sch 3 para 54 (vehicles provided by employees in 1990–91: see modification note at the start of this Part).
CAA 2001 Sch 3 para 55 (certain expenditure incurred before 6 April 1976: see modification note at the start of this Part).

194 Acquisition of ownership by assignee of equipment lessor

(1) If section 192(2)(*a*) applies (cessation of ownership of equipment lessor as a result of assignment), the assignee is to be treated, on and after the assignment—

    (*a*) as having incurred expenditure, consisting of the consideration given by him for the assignment, on the provision of the fixture, and

    (*b*) as being the owner of the fixture.

(2) For the purposes of section 192 (and subsection (1) and section 195) the assignee is to be treated as being an equipment lessor who owns the fixture under section 177.

Commentary—*Simon's Direct Tax Service* **B2.357**.
Former enactments—Sub-s (1): CAA 1990 s 58(2).
Sub-s (2): CAA 1990 s 58(3).
Revenue Internal Guidance—Capital allowances manual CA 26600 (example illustrating this section).
Modifications—CAA 2001 Sch 3 para 54 (vehicles provided by employees in 1990–91: see modification note at the start of this Part).
CAA 2001 Sch 3 para 55 (certain expenditure incurred before 6 April 1976: see modification note at the start of this Part).

195 Acquisition of ownership by equipment lessee

(1) If section 192(2)(*b*) applies (discharge of obligations of equipment lessee) because the equipment lessee has paid a capital sum, the equipment lessee is to be treated—

    (*a*) as having incurred expenditure, consisting of the capital sum, on the provision of the fixture, and

    (*b*) as being, on and after the time of payment, the owner of the fixture.

(2) Section 192(3) (assignee of equipment lessee) applies in relation to subsection (1).

Commentary—*Simon's Direct Tax Service* **B2.357**.
Former enactments—Sub-s (1): CAA 1990 s 58(4).
Sub-s (2): CAA 1990 s 58(5).
Revenue Internal Guidance—Capital allowances manual CA 26600 (example illustrating sub-s (2)).
Definition—''Capital sum'', s 4.
Modifications—CAA 2001 Sch 3 para 54 (vehicles provided by employees in 1990–91: see modification note at the start of this Part).
CAA 2001 Sch 3 para 55 (certain expenditure incurred before 6 April 1976: see modification note at the start of this Part).

[195A Acquisition of ownership by assignee of energy services provider

(1) If section 192A(2)(*a*) applies (cessation of ownership of energy services provider as a result of assignment), the assignee is to be treated, on and after the assignment—

(*a*) as having incurred expenditure, consisting of the consideration given by him for the assignment, on the provision of the fixture, and
(*b*) as being the owner of the fixture.

(2) For the purposes of section 192A (and subsection (1) and section 195B) the assignee is to be treated as being an energy services provider who owns the fixture under section 180A.]¹

Commentary—*Simon's Direct Tax Service* **B2.357**.
Amendment—¹ Section inserted by FA 2001 s 66, Sch 18 para 9 with effect for expenditure incurred after 31 March 2001, and as respects allowances and charges falling to be made for chargeable periods ending after 5 April 2001 (for income tax purposes) or 31 March 2001 (for corporation tax purposes).

[195B Acquisition of ownership by client

(1) If section 192A(2)(*b*) applies (discharge of obligations of client) because the client has paid a capital sum, the client is to be treated—

(*a*) as having incurred expenditure, consisting of the capital sum, on the provision of the fixture, and
(*b*) as being, on and after the time of payment, the owner of the fixture.

(2) Section 192A(3) (assignee of client) applies in relation to subsection (1).]¹

Commentary—*Simon's Direct Tax Service* **B2.357**.
Amendment—¹ Section inserted by FA 2001 s 66, Sch 18 para 9 with effect for expenditure incurred after 31 March 2001, and as respects allowances and charges falling to be made for chargeable periods ending after 5 April 2001 (for income tax purposes) or 31 March 2001 (for corporation tax purposes).

Disposal values

196 Disposal values in relation to fixtures: general

(1) The disposal value to be brought into account in relation to a fixture depends on the nature of the disposal event, as shown in the Table—

TABLE
DISPOSAL VALUES: FIXTURES

1. Disposal event	2. Disposal value
1. Cessation of ownership of the fixture under section 188 because of a sale of the qualifying interest except where item 2 applies.	The part of the sale price that— (*a*) falls to be treated for the purposes of this Part as expenditure incurred by the purchaser on the provision of the fixture, or (*b*) would fall to be so treated if the purchaser were entitled to an allowance.
2. Cessation of ownership of the fixture under section 188 because of a sale of the qualifying interest where— (*a*) the sale is at less than market value, and (*b*) the condition in subsection (2) is met by the purchaser.	The part of the price that would be treated for the purposes of this Part as expenditure by the purchaser on the provision of the fixture if— (*a*) the qualifying interest were sold at market value, (*b*) that sale took place immediately before the event which causes the former owner to be treated as ceasing to be the owner of the fixture, and (*c*) that event were disregarded in determining that market value.
3. Cessation of ownership of the fixture under section 188 where— (*a*) neither item 1 nor 2 applies, but (*b*) the qualifying interest continues in existence after that time or would so continue but for its becoming merged in another interest.	The disposal value given for item 2.
4. Cessation of ownership of the fixture under section 188 because of the expiry of the qualifying interest. In any other case, nil.	If the person receives a capital sum, by way of compensation or otherwise, by reference to the fixture, the amount of the capital sum.

1. Disposal event	2. Disposal value
5. Cessation of ownership of the fixture under section 190 because the lessee has become the owner under section 183.	The part of the capital sum given by the lessee for the lease referred to in section 183 that falls to be treated for the purposes of this Part as the lessee's expenditure on the provision of the fixture.
6. Cessation of ownership of the fixture under section 191 (severance).	The market value of the fixture at the time of the severance.
7. Cessation of ownership of the fixture because section 192(2)(a) (assignment of rights) applies.	The consideration given by the assignee for the assignment.
8. Cessation of ownership of the fixture because section 192(2)(b) (discharge of equipment lessee's obligations) applies on the payment of a capital sum.	The capital sum paid to discharge the financial obligations of the equipment lessee.
[8A. Cessation of ownership of the fixture because section 192A(2)(a) (assignment of rights) applies.	The consideration given by the assignee for the assignment.
8B. Cessation of ownership of the fixture because section 192A(2)(b) (discharge of client's obligations) applies on the payment of a capital sum.	The capital sum paid to discharge the financial obligations of the client.][1]
9. Permanent discontinuance of the qualifying activity followed by the sale of the qualifying interest.	The part of the sale price that— (a) falls to be treated as expenditure incurred by the purchaser on the provision of the fixture, or (b) would fall to be so treated if the purchaser were entitled to an allowance.
10. Permanent discontinuance of the qualifying activity followed by the demolition or destruction of the fixture.	The net amount received for the remains of the fixture, together with— (a) any insurance money received in respect of the demolition or destruction, and (b) any other compensation of any description so received, so far as it consists of capital sums.
11. Permanent discontinuance of the qualifying activity followed by the permanent loss of the fixture otherwise than as a result of its demolition or destruction.	Any insurance money received in respect of the loss and, so far as it consists of capital sums, any other compensation of any description so received.
12. The fixture begins to be used wholly or partly for purposes other than those of the qualifying activity.	The part of the price that would fall to be treated for the purposes of this Part as expenditure incurred by the purchaser on the provision of the fixture if the qualifying interest were sold at market value.

(2) The condition referred to in item 2 of the Table is met by the purchaser if—

    (a) the purchaser's expenditure on the provision of the fixture cannot be qualifying expenditure under this Part or Part 6 (research and development allowances), or

    (b) the purchaser is a dual resident investing company which is connected with the former owner.

(3) Items 1 and 5 of the Table are subject to sections 198 and 199 (election to fix apportionment on sale of qualifying interest or grant of lease).

(4) Section 192(3) (assignee of equipment lessee) applies in relation to item 8 of the Table.

[(4A) Section 192A(3) (assignee of client) applies in relation to item 8B of the Table.][1]

(5) Nothing in sections 188 to [192A][1] or this section prevents a disposal value having to be brought into account under Chapter 5 because of a disposal event not dealt with in these sections.

(6) This section is subject to section 197.

Commentary—*Simon's Direct Tax Service* **B2.357**.
Former enactments—Table, item 1: CAA 1990 s 59(1), (2).
Table, item 2: CAA 1990 s 59(1), (6).
Table, item 3: CAA 1990 s 59(1), (4), (5).
Table, item 4: CAA 1990 s 59(7).
Table, item 5: CAA 1990 s 59(1), (3).
Table, item 6: CAA 1990 s 26(1)(f).
Table, item 7: CAA 1990 s 58(2).
Table, item 8: CAA 1990 s 58(4).
Table, items 9–11: CAA 1990 s 59(8).
Table, item 12: CAA 1990 s 59(9).
Sub-s (2): CAA 1990 s 59(6).

Sub-s (3): CAA 1990 s 59(1).
Sub-s (4): CAA 1990 s 58(5).
Sub-s (5): CAA 1990 s 57(1).
Sub-s (6): CAA 1990 s 59(1).
Revenue Internal Guidance—Capital allowances manual CA 26700 (explanation of the section).
Definitions—"Capital sum", s 4; "disposal event", s 60(2); "dual resident investing company", s 577(1), TA 1988 s 404.
Modifications—CAA 2001 Sch 3 para 41 (sub-ss (6), (7) substituted for sub-s (6) above in relation to a fixture which a person is treated as ceasing to own before 24 July 1996. Sub-ss (6), (7) to read as follows—

"(6) If—

    (*a*) a person ("the former owner") is treated by virtue of section 188, 190 or 191 as ceasing to own a fixture,
    (*b*) another person incurs expenditure on the provision of the fixture, and
    (*c*) the former owner brings a disposal value into account under Chapter 5,

there is to be disregarded for the purposes of this Part so much (if any) of that expenditure as exceeds that disposal value.

(7) In relation to expenditure incurred before 27th July 1989, subsection (6) has effect with the substitution for the words following "the fixture" in paragraph (*b*) of the words "there is to be disregarded for the purposes of this Part so much (if any) of that expenditure as exceeds the disposal value which the former owner is required to bring into account under Chapter 5").
CAA 2001 Sch 3 para 54 (vehicles provided by employees in 1990–91: see modification note at the start of this Part).
CAA 2001 Sch 3 para 55 (certain expenditure incurred before 6 April 1976: see modification note at the start of this Part).
Amendments—¹ Words in Table in sub-s (1), and sub-s (4A), inserted, and in sub-s (5), word "192A" substituted for word "192", by FA 2001 s 66, Sch 18 para 10 with effect for expenditure incurred after 31 March 2001, and as respects allowances and charges falling to be made for chargeable periods ending after 5 April 2001 (for income tax purposes) or 31 March 2001 (for corporation tax purposes).

197 Disposal values in avoidance cases

(1) This section applies if—

    (*a*) a person ("the taxpayer") is treated under this Chapter as the owner of any plant or machinery as a result of incurring any expenditure,
    (*b*) any disposal event occurs in relation to the plant or machinery,
    (*c*) the disposal value to be brought into account by the taxpayer would (but for this section) be less than the notional written-down value of the plant or machinery, and
    (*d*) the disposal event is part of, or occurs as a result of, a scheme or arrangement the main purpose or one of the main purposes of which is the obtaining by the taxpayer of a tax advantage under this Part.

(2) The disposal value that the taxpayer must bring into account is the notional written-down value of the plant or machinery.

(3) The notional written-down value is—

$$QE - A$$

where—

QE is the taxpayer's expenditure on the plant or machinery that is qualifying expenditure,
A is the total of all allowances which could have been made to the taxpayer in respect of that expenditure if—

    (*a*) that expenditure had been the only expenditure that had ever been taken into account in determining his available qualifying expenditure, and
    (*b*) all allowances had been made in full.

Commentary—*Simon's Direct Tax Service* B2.358.
Former enactments—Sub-ss (1), (2): CAA 1990 s 59A(1).
Sub-s (3): CAA 1990 s 59A(2), (3).
Revenue Internal Guidance—Capital allowances manual CA 26750 (example illustrating sub-s (3)).
Definitions—"Available qualifying expenditure", s 57; "disposal event", s 60(2).
Modifications—CAA 2001 Sch 3 para 54 (vehicles provided by employees in 1990–91: see modification note at the start of this Part).
CAA 2001 Sch 3 para 55 (certain expenditure incurred before 6 April 1976: see modification note at the start of this Part).

Election to fix apportionment

198 Election to apportion sale price on sale of qualifying interest

(1) This section applies if the disposal value of a fixture is required to be brought into account in accordance with item 1 of the Table in section 196 (sale of qualifying interest at not less than market value, etc).

(2) The seller and the purchaser may jointly, by an election, fix the amount that is to be treated—

    (*a*) for the purposes of item 1 of the Table, and
    (*b*) for the other purposes of this Part,

as the part of the sale price that is expenditure incurred by the purchaser on the provision of the fixture.

(3) The amount fixed by the election must not exceed—

    (*a*) the amount of the capital expenditure which was treated as incurred by the seller on the provision of the fixture or of the plant or machinery which became the fixture, or
    (*b*) the actual sale price.

(4) If an election fixes the amount to be treated as the part of the sale price—

(*a*) the remaining amount (if any) of the sale price is to be treated for the purposes of this Act as expenditure attributable to the acquisition of the property which is not the fixture but is acquired for that amount, and

(*b*) if there is no remaining amount, the expenditure so attributable is to be treated for the purposes of this Act as nil.

(5) This section is subject to—

(*a*) sections 186 and 187 (fixtures on which industrial buildings allowance or research and development allowance has been made),

(*b*) section 197 (disposal values in avoidance cases), and

(*c*) sections 200 and 201 (further provisions about elections).

Commentary—*Simon's Direct Tax Service* **B2.357**.
Former enactments—Sub-s (1): CAA 1990 s 59B(1).
Sub-s (2): CAA 1990 s 59B(2).
Sub-s (3): CAA 1990 s 59B(3).
Sub-s (4): CAA 1990 s 59B(4).
Sub-s (5): CAA 1990 s 59B(2).
Revenue Internal Guidance—Capital allowances manual CA 26800 (District Valuer to be consulted on apportionment matters).
Definition—"Capital expenditure", s 4.
Modifications—CAA 2001 Sch 3 para 54 (vehicles provided by employees in 1990–91: see modification note at the start of this Part).
CAA 2001 Sch 3 para 55 (certain expenditure incurred before 6 April 1976: see modification note at the start of this Part).

199 Election to apportion capital sum given by lessee on grant of lease

(1) This section applies if the disposal value of a fixture is required to be brought into account in accordance with item 5 of the Table in section 196 (on acquisition of ownership by incoming lessee under section 183).

(2) The persons who are the lessor and the lessee for the purposes of section 183 may jointly, by an election, fix the amount that is to be treated—

(*a*) for the purposes of item 5 of the Table, and

(*b*) for the other purposes of this Part,

as the part of the capital sum that is expenditure incurred by the lessee on the provision of the fixture.

(3) The amount fixed by the election must not exceed—

(*a*) the amount of the capital expenditure which was treated as incurred by the lessor on the provision of the fixture or of the plant or machinery which became the fixture, or

(*b*) the actual capital sum.

(4) If an election fixes the amount to be treated as the part of the capital sum—

(*a*) the remaining amount (if any) of the capital sum is to be treated for the purposes of this Act as expenditure attributable to the acquisition of the property which is not the fixture but is acquired for that amount, and

(*b*) if there is no remaining amount, the expenditure so attributable is to be treated for the purposes of this Act as nil.

(5) This section is subject to—

(*a*) sections 186 and 187 (fixtures on which industrial buildings allowance or research and development allowance has been made),

(*b*) section 197 (disposal values in avoidance cases), and

(*c*) sections 200 and 201 (further provisions about elections).

Commentary—*Simon's Direct Tax Service* **B2.357**.
Former enactments—Sub-s (1): CAA 1990 s 59B(1).
Sub-s (2): CAA 1990 s 59B(2).
Sub-s (3): CAA 1990 s 59B(3).
Sub-s (4): CAA 1990 s 59B(4).
Sub-s (5): CAA 1990 s 59B(2).
Definitions—"Capital expenditure", s 4; "capital sum", s 4.
Modifications—CAA 2001 Sch 3 para 54 (vehicles provided by employees in 1990–91: see modification note at the start of this Part).
CAA 2001 Sch 3 para 55 (certain expenditure incurred before 6 April 1976: see modification note at the start of this Part).

200 Elections under sections 198 and 199: supplementary

(1) In this section and section 201, references to an election are to an election under section 198 or 199.

(2) An apportionment made by an election has effect in place of any apportionment that would otherwise be made under sections 562, 563 and 564(1) (apportionment and procedure for determining apportionment).

(3) An election is irrevocable.

(4) If, as a result of circumstances arising after the making of an election, the maximum amount which could be fixed by the election is reduced to an amount which is less than the amount specified in the election, the election is to be treated, for the purposes of this Act, as having specified the amount to which the maximum is reduced.

Commentary—*Simon's Direct Tax Service* **B2.357**.
Former enactments—Sub-s (2): CAA 1990 s 59B(5).
Sub-s (3): CAA 1990 s 59C(6).
Sub-s (4): CAA 1990 s 59C(3).
Modifications—CAA 2001 Sch 3 para 54 (vehicles provided by employees in 1990–91: see modification note at the start of this Part).
CAA 2001 Sch 3 para 55 (certain expenditure incurred before 6 April 1976: see modification note at the start of this Part).

201 Elections under sections 198 and 199: procedure

(1) An election must be made by notice to the Inland Revenue no later than 2 years after the date when—

(a) the purchaser acquires the qualifying interest, in the case of an election under section 198, or

(b) the lessee is granted the lease, in the case of an election under section 199.

(2) The amount fixed by an election must be quantified at the time when the election is made.

(3) The notice must state—

(a) the amount fixed by the election,

(b) the name of each of the persons making the election,

(c) information sufficient to identify the plant or machinery,

(d) information sufficient to identify the relevant land,

(e) particulars of—

(i) the interest acquired by the purchaser, in the case of an election under section 198, or

(ii) the lease granted to the lessee, in the case of an election under section 199, and

(f) the tax district references of each of the persons making the election.

(4) If a person—

(a) has joined in making an election, and

(b) subsequently makes a tax return for a period which is the first period for which he is making a tax return in which the election has an effect for tax purposes in his case,

a copy of the notice containing the election must accompany the return.

(5) The following provisions do not apply to the election—

(a) section 42 of, and Schedule 1A to, TMA 1970 (claims and elections for income tax purposes);

(b) paragraphs 54 to 60 of Schedule 18 to FA 1998 (claims and elections for corporation tax purposes).

(6) References in this section to a tax return, in the case of an election for the purposes of a trade, profession or business carried on by persons in partnership, are to be read, in relation to those persons, as references to a return under section 12AA of TMA 1970 (partnership returns).

Commentary—*Simon's Direct Tax Service* **B2.357**.
Former enactments—Sub-s (1): CAA 1990 s 59C(1), (4).
Sub-s (2): CAA 1990 s 59C(3).
Sub-s (3): CAA 1990 s 59C(2).
Sub-s (4): CAA 1990 ss 51(2) (''return''), 59C(5), (9) (''relevant period'').
Sub-s (5): CAA 1990 s 59C(7).
Sub-s (6): CAA 1990 s 59C(10).
Modifications—CAA 2001 Sch 3 para 54 (vehicles provided by employees in 1990–91: see modification note at the start of this Part).
CAA 2001 Sch 3 para 55 (certain expenditure incurred before 6 April 1976: see modification note at the start of this Part).

Further provisions

202 Interpretation

(1) Any reference in this Chapter to a person being entitled to an allowance in respect of expenditure on the provision of a fixture includes the person having a pool to which expenditure on the provision of the fixture has been allocated.

But this is subject to subsection (2).

(2) If—

(a) expenditure on the provision of the fixture has been allocated to a pool, and

(b) the person is required under section 61(1) to bring the disposal value of the fixture into account in the pool,

the person is not entitled to an allowance in respect of the expenditure allocated to that pool for any chargeable period after that in which the disposal event occurs.

(3) For the purposes of this Chapter, a person makes a claim in respect of expenditure if he—

(a) makes a claim for an allowance in respect of that expenditure,

(b) makes a tax return in which that expenditure is taken into account in determining his available qualifying expenditure for the purposes of this Part, or

(c) gives notice of an amendment of a tax return which provides for that expenditure to be so taken into account.

Commentary—*Simon's Direct Tax Service* **B2.355**.
Former enactments—Sub-ss (1), (2): CAA 1990 s 51(5).
Sub-s (3): CAA 1990 s 51(2) (''return''), (5A), s 147(2D).

Definitions—"Available qualifying expenditure", s 57; "chargeable period", s 6; "disposal event", s 60(2).
Modifications—CAA 2001 Sch 3 para 54 (vehicles provided by employees in 1990–91: see modification note at the start of this Part).
CAA 2001 Sch 3 para 55 (certain expenditure incurred before 6 April 1976: see modification note at the start of this Part).

203 Amendment of returns etc

(1) If a person who has made a tax return ("the taxpayer") becomes aware that, after making it, anything in it has become incorrect for any of the reasons given in subsection (2), the taxpayer must give notice to the Inland Revenue specifying how the return needs to be amended.

(2) The reasons are that—

(a) an approval given for the purposes of section 180 (affordable warmth programme) has been withdrawn;
(b) section 181(2), 182(2)[, 182A(2)][1] or 184(2) (another person has a prior right) applies in the taxpayer's case;
(c) section 185 (restriction on qualifying expenditure where another person has claimed an allowance) applies in the taxpayer's case;
(d) an election is made under section 198 or 199 (election to fix apportionment);
(e) section 200(4) (reduction in amount which can be fixed by an election) applies in the taxpayer's case.

(3) The notice must be given within 3 months beginning with the day on which the taxpayer first became aware that anything contained in the tax return had become incorrect for any of the reasons given in subsection (2).

(4) All such assessments and adjustments of assessments are to be made as are necessary to give effect to this Chapter.

Commentary—*Simon's Direct Tax Service* **B2.355, 357**.
Former enactments—Sub-s (1): CAA 1990 ss 51(2) ("return"), (6A), s 53(1H).
Sub-s (2): CAA 1990 ss 51(6A), 53(1H).
Sub-s (3): CAA 1990 ss 51(2) ("return"), (6A), 53(1H).
Sub-s (4): CAA 1990 ss 51(6), 53(1G).
Modifications—CAA 2001 Sch 3 para 54 (vehicles provided by employees in 1990–91: see modification note at the start of this Part).
CAA 2001 Sch 3 para 55 (certain expenditure incurred before 6 April 1976: see modification note at the start of this Part).
Amendment—[1] Word in sub-s (2)(b) inserted by FA 2001 s 66, Sch 18 para 11 with effect for expenditure incurred after 31 March 2001, and as respects allowances and charges falling to be made for chargeable periods ending after 5 April 2001 (for income tax purposes) or 31 March 2001 (for corporation tax purposes).

204 Appeals etc

(1) Subsections (2) and (3) apply if—

(a) any question arises as to whether any plant or machinery has become, in law, part of a building or other land, and
(b) that question is material to the tax liability (for whatever period) of two or more persons.

(2) The question is to be determined, for the purposes of the tax of all the persons concerned, by the Special Commissioners.

(3) The Special Commissioners must determine the question in the same way as an appeal, but all the persons concerned are entitled—

(a) to appear before and be heard by the Special Commissioners, or
(b) to make representations to them in writing.

(4) Subsections (5) and (6) apply if any question relating to an election under section 198 or 199 (apportionments) arises for determination by any body of Commissioners for the purposes of any proceedings before them.

(5) The Commissioners must determine the question separately from any other questions in those proceedings.

(6) Each of the persons who has joined in making the election is entitled—

(a) to appear before and be heard by the Commissioners, or
(b) to make representations to them in writing;

and the Commissioners' determination has effect as if made in an appeal to which each of those persons was a party.

Commentary—*Simon's Direct Tax Service* **B2.355, 357**.
Former enactments—Sub-ss (1)–(3): CAA 1990 s 51(7).
Sub-ss (4)–(6): CAA 1990 s 59C(8).
Modifications—CAA 2001 Sch 3 para 54 (vehicles provided by employees in 1990–91: see modification note at the start of this Part).
CAA 2001 Sch 3 para 55 (certain expenditure incurred before 6 April 1976: see modification note at the start of this Part).

CAA 2001

CHAPTER 15
ASSET PROVIDED OR USED ONLY PARTLY FOR QUALIFYING ACTIVITY

205 Reduction of first-year allowances

(1) If it appears that a person carrying on a qualifying activity has incurred expenditure on the provision of plant or machinery—

   (a) partly for the purposes of the qualifying activity, and

   (b) partly for other purposes,

any first-year allowance to which he is entitled in respect of the expenditure must be reduced to an amount which is just and reasonable having regard to the relevant circumstances.

(2) The relevant circumstances include, in particular, the extent to which it appears that the plant or machinery is likely to be used for purposes other than those of the qualifying activity in question.

(3) In calculating for the purposes of section 58 the balance left after deducting a first-year allowance, a reduction under subsection (1) is to be disregarded.

Commentary—*Simon's Direct Tax Service* **B2.359**.
Former enactments—Sub-ss (1), (2): CAA 1990 s 79(1).
Revenue Internal Guidance—Capital allowances manual CA 27005 (worked example illustrating "just and reasonable" basis under sub-s (1)).
CA 27100 (assets provided for directors or employees: capital allowances are not normally restricted unless there is a "blatant incongruity" between the asset provided and the business requirements).
Modifications—CAA 2001 Sch 3 para 54 (vehicles provided by employees in 1990–91: see modification note at the start of this Part).
CAA 2001 Sch 3 para 55 (certain expenditure incurred before 6 April 1976: see modification note at the start of this Part).

206 Single asset pool etc

(1) Qualifying expenditure to which this subsection applies, if allocated to a pool, must be allocated to a single asset pool.

(2) Subsection (1) applies to qualifying expenditure incurred by a person carrying on a qualifying activity—

   (a) partly for the purposes of the qualifying activity, and

   (b) partly for other purposes.

(3) If a person is required to bring a disposal value into account in a pool for a chargeable period because the plant or machinery begins to be used partly for purposes other than those of the qualifying activity, an amount equal to that disposal value is allocated (as expenditure on the plant or machinery) to a single asset pool for that chargeable period.

(4) In the case of a single asset pool under subsection (1), there is no final chargeable period or disposal event merely because the plant or machinery begins to be used partly for purposes other than those of the qualifying activity.

Commentary—*Simon's Direct Tax Service* **B2.359**.
Former enactments—Sub-ss (1), (2): CAA 1990 s 79(2).
Sub-s (3): CAA 1990 s 79(3).
Sub-s (4): CAA 1990 s 79(4).
Definitions—"Chargeable period", s 6; "disposal event", s 60(2); "final chargeable period", s 65.
Modifications—CAA 2001 Sch 3 para 54 (vehicles provided by employees in 1990–91: see modification note at the start of this Part).
CAA 2001 Sch 3 para 55 (certain expenditure incurred before 6 April 1976: see modification note at the start of this Part).

207 Reduction of allowances and charges on expenditure in single asset pool

(1) This section applies if a person's expenditure is in a single asset pool under section 206(1) or (3).

(2) The amount of—

   (a) any writing-down allowance or balancing allowance to which the person is entitled, or

   (b) any balancing charge to which the person is liable,

must be reduced to an amount which is just and reasonable having regard to the relevant circumstances.

(3) The relevant circumstances include, in particular, the extent to which it appears that the plant or machinery was used in the chargeable period in question for purposes other than those of the person's qualifying activity.

(4) In calculating under section 59 the amount of unrelieved qualifying expenditure carried forward, a reduction of a writing-down allowance under subsection (2) is to be disregarded.

(5) If a person entitled to a writing-down allowance for a chargeable period—

   (a) does not claim the allowance, or

   (b) claims less than the full amount of the allowance,

the unrelieved qualifying expenditure carried forward from the period is to be treated as not reduced or (as the case may be) only proportionately reduced.

Commentary—*Simon's Direct Tax Service* **B2.359**.

Former enactments—Sub-s (1): CAA 1990 s 79(2).
Sub-ss (2), (3): CAA 1990 s 79(5).
Sub-s (5): CAA 1990 s 79(6).
Definitions—"Chargeable period", s 6; "unrelieved qualifying expenditure", s 59.
Modifications—CAA 2001 Sch 3 para 54 (vehicles provided by employees in 1990–91: see modification note at the start of this Part).
CAA 2001 Sch 3 para 55 (certain expenditure incurred before 6 April 1976: see modification note at the start of this Part).

208 Effect of significant reduction in use for purposes of qualifying activity

(1) This section applies if—

    (*a*) expenditure is allocated to a single asset pool under this Chapter,
    (*b*) there is such a change of circumstances as would make it appropriate for any reduction falling to be made under section 207—

        (i) for the chargeable period in which the change takes place ("the relevant chargeable period"), or
        (ii) for any subsequent chargeable period,

    to represent a larger proportion of the amount reduced than would have been appropriate apart from the change,
    (*c*) no disposal value in respect of the plant or machinery would, apart from this section, fall to be brought into account for the relevant chargeable period, and
    (*d*) the market value of the plant or machinery at the end of the relevant chargeable period exceeds the available qualifying expenditure in that pool for that period by more than £1 million.

(2) If this section applies—

    (*a*) a disposal value is required to be brought into account in the single asset pool for the relevant chargeable period, and
    (*b*) section 206 applies as if, at the beginning of the following chargeable period, expenditure had been incurred on the provision of the plant or machinery of an amount equal to the disposal value brought into account as a result of paragraph (*a*).

Commentary—*Simon's Direct Tax Service* **B2.359**.
Former enactments—Sub-s (1): CAA 1990 s 79A(1).
Sub-s (2): CAA 1990 s 79A(2), (3).
Definitions—"Available qualifying expenditure", s 57; "chargeable period", s 6.
Modifications—CAA 2001 Sch 3 para 42 (the section above does not apply if the change of circumstances referred to in sub-s (1)(*b*) above occurs before 21 March 2000).
CAA 2001 Sch 3 para 54 (vehicles provided by employees in 1990–91: see modification note at the start of this Part).
CAA 2001 Sch 3 para 55 (certain expenditure incurred before 6 April 1976: see modification note at the start of this Part).

CHAPTER 16
PARTIAL DEPRECIATION SUBSIDIES

209 Meaning of "partial depreciation subsidy"

In this Chapter "partial depreciation subsidy" means a sum which—

    (*a*) is payable directly or indirectly to a person who has incurred qualifying expenditure for the purposes of a qualifying activity,
    (*b*) is in respect of, or takes account of, part of the depreciation of the plant or machinery resulting from its use for the purposes of that activity, and
    (*c*) does not fall to be taken into account as income of that person or in calculating the profits of any qualifying activity carried on by him.

Commentary—*Simon's Direct Tax Service* **B2.360**.
Former enactments—CAA 1990 s 80(1)–(3).
Modifications—CAA 2001 Sch 3 para 54 (vehicles provided by employees in 1990–91: see modification note at the start of this Part).
CAA 2001 Sch 3 para 55 (certain expenditure incurred before 6 April 1976: see modification note at the start of this Part).

210 Reduction of first-year allowances

(1) If—

    (*a*) a person has incurred qualifying expenditure for the purposes of a qualifying activity carried on by him, and
    (*b*) it appears that a partial depreciation subsidy is, or will be, payable to him in the period during which the plant or machinery will be used for the purposes of that qualifying activity,

the amount of any first-year allowance in respect of that expenditure must be reduced to an amount which is just and reasonable having regard to the relevant circumstances.

(2) In calculating for the purposes of section 58 the balance left after deducting a first-year allowance, a reduction under subsection (1) is to be disregarded.

Commentary—*Simon's Direct Tax Service* **B2.360**.
Former enactments—Sub-s (1): CAA 1990 s 80(2).
Definition—"Partial depreciation subsidy", s 209.

Modifications—CAA 2001 Sch 3 para 54 (vehicles provided by employees in 1990–91: see modification note at the start of this Part).
CAA 2001 Sch 3 para 55 (certain expenditure incurred before 6 April 1976: see modification note at the start of this Part).

211 Single asset pool etc

(1) Qualifying expenditure to which this subsection applies, if allocated to a pool, must be allocated to a single asset pool.

(2) Subsection (1) applies to qualifying expenditure if a partial depreciation subsidy relating to the plant or machinery has been paid to the person who incurred the expenditure.

(3) Subsection (4) applies if—

    (*a*) qualifying expenditure has been allocated to a pool, and

    (*b*) a partial depreciation subsidy relating to the plant or machinery is paid to that person.

(4) For the chargeable period in which the partial depreciation subsidy is paid—

    (*a*) the person is required to bring a disposal value into account in the pool referred to in subsection (3), and

    (*b*) an amount equal to the disposal value is allocated (as expenditure on the plant or machinery) to a single asset pool.

(5) If qualifying expenditure in respect of any plant or machinery is in a single asset pool under this section, there is no further allocation of that qualifying expenditure because a further partial depreciation subsidy is paid in respect of that plant or machinery.

Commentary—*Simon's Direct Tax Service* **B2.360**.
Former enactments—Sub-s (1): CAA 1990 s 80(5).
Sub-s (2): CAA 1990 s 80(3).
Sub-s (3): CAA 1990 s 80(4).
Sub-s (4): CAA 1990 s 80(5).
Sub-s (5): CAA 1990 s 80(7).
Definitions—"Chargeable period", s 6; "partial depreciation subsidy", s 209.
Modifications—CAA 2001 Sch 3 para 54 (vehicles provided by employees in 1990–91: see modification note at the start of this Part).
CAA 2001 Sch 3 para 55 (certain expenditure incurred before 6 April 1976: see modification note at the start of this Part).

212 Reduction of allowances and charges on expenditure in single asset pool

(1) This section applies if expenditure is in a single asset pool under section 211(1) or (4).

(2) The amount of—

    (*a*) any writing-down allowance or balancing allowance to which the person is entitled, or

    (*b*) any balancing charge to which the person is liable,

must be reduced to an amount which is just and reasonable having regard to the relevant circumstances.

(3) In calculating under section 59 the amount of unrelieved qualifying expenditure carried forward, a reduction of a writing-down allowance under subsection (2) is to be disregarded.

(4) If a person entitled to a writing-down allowance for a chargeable period—

    (*a*) does not claim the allowance, or

    (*b*) claims less than the full amount of the allowance,

the unrelieved qualifying expenditure carried forward from the period is to be treated as not reduced or (as the case may be) only proportionately reduced.

Commentary—*Simon's Direct Tax Service* **B2.360**.
Former enactments—Sub-s (1): CAA 1990 s 80(3).
Sub-s (2): CAA 1990 s 80(5)(*b*).
Sub-s (4): CAA 1990 s 80(6).
Definitions—"Chargeable period", s 6; "unrelieved qualifying expenditure", s 59.
Modifications—CAA 2001 Sch 3 para 54 (vehicles provided by employees in 1990–91: see modification note at the start of this Part).
CAA 2001 Sch 3 para 55 (certain expenditure incurred before 6 April 1976: see modification note at the start of this Part).

CHAPTER 17

ANTI-AVOIDANCE

Relevant transactions

213 Relevant transactions: sale, hire-purchase (etc) and assignment

(1) For the purposes of this Chapter, a person ("B") enters into a relevant transaction with another ("S") if—

    (*a*) S sells plant or machinery to B,

    (*b*) B enters into a contract with S providing that B shall or may become the owner of plant or machinery on the performance of the contract, or

    (*c*) S assigns to B the benefit of a contract providing that S shall or may become the owner of plant or machinery on the performance of the contract.

(2) For the purposes of this Chapter, references to B's expenditure under a relevant transaction are references—

(*a*) in the case of a sale within subsection (1)(*a*), to B's capital expenditure on the provision of the plant or machinery by purchase,

(*b*) in the case of a contract within subsection (1)(*b*), to B's capital expenditure under the contract so far as it relates to the plant or machinery, or

(*c*) in the case of an assignment within subsection (1)(*c*), to B's capital expenditure under the contract so far as it relates to the plant or machinery or is by way of consideration for the assignment.

(3) If—

(*a*) B is treated under section 14 (use for qualifying activity of plant or machinery which is a gift) as having incurred capital expenditure on the provision of plant or machinery, and

(*b*) the donor of the plant or machinery was S,

B is to be treated for the purposes of this Chapter as having incurred capital expenditure on the provision of the plant or machinery by purchasing it from S.

Commentary—*Simon's Direct Tax Service* **B2.365**.
Former enactments—Sub-ss (1), (2): CAA 1990 s 75(1)–(3).
Sub-s (3): CAA 1990 s 81(3).
Revenue Internal Guidance—Capital allowances manual CA 28200 (operation of this section).
Oil Taxation Office ring fence CT manual OTRF 5.17 (these rules apply in the usual way to the transfer of interests in oil fields, where plant is involved, if the conditions of the section are met; participators in a field are not, *per se*, connected persons).
Definition—''Capital expenditure'', s 4.
Modifications—CAA 2001 Sch 3 para 43 (sub-s (3) above does not apply if the plant or machinery was brought into use before 27 July 1989).
CAA 2001 Sch 3 para 54 (vehicles provided by employees in 1990–91: see modification note at the start of this Part).
CAA 2001 Sch 3 para 55 (certain expenditure incurred before 6 April 1976: see modification note at the start of this Part).

Restrictions on allowances

214 Connected persons

Allowances under this Part are restricted under sections 217 and 218 if—

(*a*) B enters into a relevant transaction with S, and

(*b*) B and S are connected with each other.

Commentary—*Simon's Direct Tax Service* **B2.366**.
Former enactments—CAA 1990 ss 75(1)–(3), 76(1).
Modifications—CAA 2001 Sch 3 para 54 (vehicles provided by employees in 1990–91: see modification note at the start of this Part).
CAA 2001 Sch 3 para 55 (certain expenditure incurred before 6 April 1976: see modification note at the start of this Part).

215 Transactions to obtain allowances

Allowances under this Part are restricted under sections 217 and 218 if—

(*a*) B enters into a relevant transaction with S, and

(*b*) it appears that the sole or main benefit which (but for this section) might have been expected to accrue to B or S, or to any other party, from—

    (i) the relevant transaction, or

    (ii) transactions of which the relevant transaction is one,

was obtaining an allowance under this Part.

Commentary—*Simon's Direct Tax Service* **B2.366**.
Former enactments—CAA 1990 s 75(1)–(3).
Modifications—CAA 2001 Sch 3 para 54 (vehicles provided by employees in 1990–91: see modification note at the start of this Part).
CAA 2001 Sch 3 para 55 (certain expenditure incurred before 6 April 1976: see modification note at the start of this Part).

216 Sale and leaseback, etc

(1) Allowances under this Part are restricted under sections 217 and 218 if—

(*a*) B enters into a relevant transaction with S, and

(*b*) the plant or machinery—

    (i) continues to be used for the purposes of a qualifying activity carried on by S, or

    (ii) is used after the date of the transaction for the purposes of a qualifying activity carried on by S or by a person (other than B) who is connected with S, without having been used since that date for the purposes of any other qualifying activity except that of leasing the plant or machinery.

(2) In this section—

''the date of the transaction'' means the date of the sale, the making of the contract or the assignment referred to in section 213(1)(*a*) to (*c*), and

''qualifying activity'' includes any activity listed in section 15(1) even if any profits or gains from it are not chargeable to tax.

Commentary—*Simon's Direct Tax Service* **B2.366**.

CAA 2001

Former enactments—Sub-s (1): CAA 1990 ss 75(1)–(3), 76(1).
Sub-s (2): CAA 1990 s 83(2A).
Modifications—CAA 2001 Sch 3 para 54 (vehicles provided by employees in 1990–91: see modification note at the start of this Part).
CAA 2001 Sch 3 para 55 (certain expenditure incurred before 6 April 1976: see modification note at the start of this Part).

217 No first-year allowance for B's expenditure

(1) If this section applies as a result of section 214, 215 or 216, a first-year allowance is not to be made in respect of B's expenditure under the relevant transaction.

(2) Any first-year allowance which is prohibited by subsection (1), but which has already been made, is to be withdrawn.

(3) If plant or machinery is the subject of a sale and finance leaseback (as defined in section 221) section 223 applies instead of this section.

Commentary—*Simon's Direct Tax Service* **B2.366**.
Former enactments—CAA 1990 s 75(1)–(3).
Modifications—CAA 2001 Sch 3 para 54 (vehicles provided by employees in 1990–91: see modification note at the start of this Part).
CAA 2001 Sch 3 para 55 (certain expenditure incurred before 6 April 1976: see modification note at the start of this Part).

218 Restriction on B's qualifying expenditure

(1) If this section applies as a result of section 214, 215 or 216, the amount, if any, by which B's expenditure under the relevant transaction exceeds D is to be left out of account in determining B's available qualifying expenditure.

D is defined in subsections (2) and (3).

(2) If S is required to bring a disposal value into account under this Part because of the relevant transaction, D is that disposal value.

(3) If S is not required to bring a disposal value into account under this Part because of the relevant transaction, D is whichever of the following is the smallest—

(a) the market value of the plant or machinery;
(b) if S incurred capital expenditure on the provision of the plant or machinery, the amount of that expenditure;
(c) if a person connected with S incurred capital expenditure on the provision of the plant or machinery, the amount of that expenditure.

(4) If plant or machinery is the subject of a sale and finance leaseback (as defined in section 221), section 224 or 225 applies instead of this section.

Commentary—*Simon's Direct Tax Service* **B2.366**.
Former enactments—Sub-ss (1), (2): CAA 1990 s 75(1)–(3).
Sub-s (3): CAA 1990 s 76(2), (4).
Sub-s (4): CAA 1990 ss 75(1)–(3), 76(7).
Definitions—"Available qualifying expenditure", s 57; "capital expenditure", s 4.
Modifications—CAA 2001 Sch 3 para 54 (vehicles provided by employees in 1990–91: see modification note at the start of this Part).
CAA 2001 Sch 3 para 55 (certain expenditure incurred before 6 April 1976: see modification note at the start of this Part).

Finance leases

219 Meaning of "finance lease"

(1) In this Chapter "finance lease" means any arrangements—

(a) which provide for plant or machinery to be leased or otherwise made available by a person ("the lessor") to another person ("the lessee"), and
(b) which, under [generally accepted accounting practice][1]—

(i) fall (or would fall) to be treated, in the accounts of the lessor or a person connected with the lessor, as a finance lease or a loan, or
(ii) are comprised in arrangements which fall (or would fall) to be so treated.

(2) ...[2]

(3) In this section "accounts", in relation to a company, includes any accounts which—

(a) relate to two or more companies of which that company is one, and
(b) are drawn up in accordance with—

(i) section 227 of the Companies Act 1985, or
(ii) Article 235 of the Companies (Northern Ireland) Order 1986.

Commentary—*Simon's Direct Tax Service* **B2.367**.
Former enactments—Sub-ss (1), (2): CAA 1990 s 82A(1), (2).
Sub-s (3): CAA 1990 s 82A(2).
Revenue Guidance—IR Tax Bulletin June 1998 p 539 (Capital Allowances on Finance Leases—explains how these rules are intended to operate).
Modifications—CAA 2001 Sch 3 para 54 (vehicles provided by employees in 1990–91: see modification note at the start of this Part).
CAA 2001 Sch 3 para 55 (certain expenditure incurred before 6 April 1976: see modification note at the start of this Part).

Amendments—¹ Words substituted for the words "normal accountancy practice" by FA 2002 s 103(4)(g) with effect from 24 July 2002.
² Sub-s (2) repealed by FA 2002 s 141, Sch 40 Pt 3(16) with effect from 24 July 2002. Sub-s (2) previously read as follows—

"(2) For the purpose of applying subsection (1)(b), the lessor and any person connected with the lessor are to be treated as being companies which are incorporated in a part of the United Kingdom.".

220 Allocation of expenditure to a chargeable period

(1) Subject to subsection (2), if a person incurs at any time in a chargeable period capital expenditure on the provision of plant or machinery for leasing under a finance lease—

(a) the part of the expenditure which is proportional to the part of that chargeable period falling before that time is not to be taken into account in determining that person's available qualifying expenditure for that period, but

(b) this does not prevent that part of the expenditure being taken into account in determining that person's available qualifying expenditure for any subsequent chargeable period.

(2) Subsection (1)(a) does not apply to a chargeable period if a disposal event occurs in that period in respect of the plant or machinery.

Commentary—*Simon's Direct Tax Service* B2.367.
Former enactments—Sub-s (1): CAA 1990 s 25(5A), (5C).
Sub-s (2): CAA 1990 ss 24(6), (8), 25(5B).
Definitions—"Available qualifying expenditure", s 57; "capital expenditure", s 4; "chargeable period", s 6; "disposal event", s 60(2).
Modifications—CAA 2001 Sch 3 para 44 (CAA 2001 ss 220, 229 do not apply in relation to expenditure incurred before 2 July 1997, or in the 12 months beginning with that date in pursuance of a contract entered into before that date).
CAA 2001 Sch 3 para 54 (vehicles provided by employees in 1990–91: see modification note at the start of this Part).
CAA 2001 Sch 3 para 55 (certain expenditure incurred before 6 April 1976: see modification note at the start of this Part).

Sale and finance leasebacks

221 Meaning of "sale and finance leaseback"

(1) For the purposes of this section and sections 222 to 228, plant or machinery is the subject of a sale and finance leaseback if—

(a) B enters into a relevant transaction with S,

(b) after the date of the transaction, the plant or machinery—

(i) continues to be used for the purposes of a qualifying activity carried on by S,

(ii) is used for the purposes of a qualifying activity carried on by S or by a person (other than B) who is connected with S, without having been used since that date for the purposes of any other qualifying activity except that of leasing the plant or machinery, or

(iii) is used for the purposes of a non-qualifying activity carried on by [S or by a person (other than B) who is connected with S]¹, without having been used since that date for the purposes of a qualifying activity except that of leasing the plant or machinery, and

(c) it is directly or indirectly as a consequence of having been leased under a finance lease that the plant or machinery is available to be so used after that date.

(2) In this section—

"the date of the transaction" means the date of the sale, the making of the contract or the assignment referred to in section 213(1)(a) to (c),

"non-qualifying activity" means any activity which is not a qualifying activity, and

"qualifying activity" includes any activity listed in section 15(1) even if any profits or gains from it are not chargeable to tax.

Commentary—*Simon's Direct Tax Service* B2.368.
Former enactments—Sub-s (1): CAA 1990 s 75(1)(b), (2)(b), (3)(b), s 76(1), s 76A(1), (2)(a), (b).
Sub-s (2): CAA 1990 s 76A(2)(b), (12) ("non-trading activities"), s 83(2A).
Modifications—CAA 2001 Sch 3 para 45 (CAA 2001 ss 221, 222, 224–226 do not apply in relation to expenditure incurred before 2 July 1998 if the relevant transaction is a purchase under a contract entered into before 2 July 1997; is itself a contract entered into before that date; or is an assignment made before that date, or in pursuance of a contract entered into before that date).
CAA 2001 Sch 3 para 54 (vehicles provided by employees in 1990–91: see modification note at the start of this Part).
CAA 2001 Sch 3 para 55 (certain expenditure incurred before 6 April 1976: see modification note at the start of this Part).
Amendments—¹ Words substituted by FA 2001 s 69, Sch 21 para 3 with effect as respects allowances and charges falling to be made for chargeable periods ending after 5 April 2001 (for income tax purposes) or 31 March 2001 (for corporation tax purposes).

222 Disposal value restricted

(1) If—

(a) plant or machinery is the subject of a sale and finance leaseback, and

(b) S is required to bring a disposal value into account under this Part because of the relevant transaction,

the disposal value is whichever of the amounts in subsection (2) is the smallest.

(2) The amounts are—

(a) the disposal value that S would be required to bring into account apart from subsection (1);

(b) the market value of the plant or machinery;

(*c*) if S incurred capital expenditure on the provision of the plant or machinery, the notional written-down value of that capital expenditure;

(*d*) if a person connected with S incurred capital expenditure on the provision of the plant or machinery, the notional written-down value of that capital expenditure.

(3) The notional written-down value is—

$$QE - A$$

where—

QE is the expenditure incurred by S, or the person connected with S, on the plant or machinery,

A is the total of all allowances which could have been made to S, or the person connected with S, in respect of that expenditure if—

(*a*) that expenditure had been qualifying expenditure,

(*b*) that expenditure had been the only expenditure that had ever been taken into account in determining his available qualifying expenditure,

(*c*) that expenditure had been treated as long-life asset expenditure only if it is in fact such expenditure, and

(*d*) all allowances had been made in full.

(4) This section does not apply if the finance lease or any transaction or series of transactions of which it forms a part makes provision such as is described in section 225(1) (sale and finance leasebacks: B's qualifying expenditure if lessor not bearing non-compliance risk).

Commentary—*Simon's Direct Tax Service* **B2.368**.
Former enactments—Sub-ss (1), (2): CAA 1990 s 76(2), 76A(2), (5), (9)(*a*).
Sub-s (3): CAA 1990 s 76A(9), (10).
Sub-s (4): CAA 1990 s 76A(6), (7)(*b*).
Definitions—"Available qualifying expenditure", s 57; "capital expenditure", s 4.
Modifications—CAA 2001 Sch 3 para 45 (CAA 2001 ss 221, 222, 224–226 do not apply in relation to expenditure incurred before 2 July 1998 if the relevant transaction is a purchase under a contract entered into before 2 July 1997; is itself a contract entered into before that date; or is an assignment made before that date, or in pursuance of a contract entered into before that date).
CAA 2001 Sch 3 para 54 (vehicles provided by employees in 1990–91: see modification note at the start of this Part).
CAA 2001 Sch 3 para 55 (certain expenditure incurred before 6 April 1976: see modification note at the start of this Part).

223 No first-year allowance for B's expenditure

(1) If plant or machinery is the subject of a sale and finance leaseback, a first-year allowance is not to be made in respect of B's expenditure under the relevant transaction.

(2) Any first-year allowance which is prohibited by subsection (1), but which has already been made, is to be withdrawn.

Commentary—*Simon's Direct Tax Service* **B2.368**.
Former enactments—CAA 1990 ss 75(1)–(3), 76(1), 76A(1).
Modifications—CAA 2001 Sch 3 para 54 (vehicles provided by employees in 1990–91: see modification note at the start of this Part).
CAA 2001 Sch 3 para 55 (certain expenditure incurred before 6 April 1976: see modification note at the start of this Part).

224 Restriction on B's qualifying expenditure

(1) If plant or machinery is the subject of a sale and finance leaseback the amount, if any, by which B's expenditure under the relevant transaction exceeds D is to be left out of account in determining B's available qualifying expenditure.

D is defined in subsections (2) and (3).

(2) If S is required to bring a disposal value into account under this Part because of the relevant transaction, D is that disposal value (determined in accordance with section 222).

(3) If S is not required to bring a disposal value into account under this Part because of the relevant transaction, D is whichever of the following is the smallest—

(*a*) the market value of the plant or machinery;

(*b*) if S incurred capital expenditure on the provision of the plant or machinery, the notional written-down value of that capital expenditure;

(*c*) if a person connected with S incurred capital expenditure on the provision of the plant or machinery, the notional written-down value of that capital expenditure.

(4) In this section "the notional written-down value", in relation to expenditure incurred by a person on the provision of plant or machinery, has the meaning given by section 222(3).

(5) This section does not apply if the finance lease or any transaction or series of transactions of which it forms a part makes provision such as is described in section 225(1).

Commentary—*Simon's Direct Tax Service* **B2.368**.
Former enactments—Sub-ss (1)–(3): CAA 1990 s 75(1)–(3), 76(2), s 76A(2), (5).
Sub-s (4): CAA 1990 s 76A(9), (10).
Sub-s (5): CAA 1990 s 76A(6), (7).
Definitions—"Available qualifying expenditure", s 57; "capital expenditure", s 4.
Modifications—CAA 2001 Sch 3 para 45 (CAA 2001 ss 221, 222, 224–226 do not apply in relation to expenditure incurred before 2 July 1998 if the relevant transaction is a purchase under a contract entered into before 2 July 1997; is itself a contract entered into before that date; or is an assignment made before that date, or in pursuance of a contract entered into before that date).

CAA 2001 Sch 3 para 54 (vehicles provided by employees in 1990–91: see modification note at the start of this Part).

CAA 2001 Sch 3 para 55 (certain expenditure incurred before 6 April 1976: see modification note at the start of this Part).

225 B's qualifying expenditure if lessor not bearing non-compliance risk

(1) This section applies if plant or machinery is the subject of a sale and finance leaseback, and the finance lease, or any transaction or series of transactions of which it forms a part, makes provision which—

(a) removes from the lessor the whole, or the greater part, of any risk, which would otherwise fall directly or indirectly on the lessor, of any person sustaining a loss if payments under the lease are not made in accordance with its terms, and

(b) does so otherwise than by means of guarantees from persons connected with the lessee.

(2) In such a case the following are not qualifying expenditure for the purposes of this Part—

(a) B's expenditure under the relevant transaction;

(b) if the lessor is a different person from B, the expenditure incurred by the lessor on the provision of the plant or machinery.

(3) For the purposes of determining whether this section applies, the lessor and the persons connected with the lessor are treated as the same person.

Commentary—*Simon's Direct Tax Service* **B2.368**.
Former enactments—Sub-s (1): CAA 1990 s 76A(6), (12) ("non-compliance risk").
Sub-s (2): CAA 1990 s 76A(7), (8).
Sub-s (3): CAA 1990 s 76A(6).
Modifications—CAA 2001 Sch 3 para 45 (CAA 2001 ss 221, 222, 224–226 do not apply in relation to expenditure incurred before 2 July 1998 if the relevant transaction is a purchase under a contract entered into before 2 July 1997; is itself a contract entered into before that date; or is an assignment made before that date, or in pursuance of a contract entered into before that date).
CAA 2001 Sch 3 para 54 (vehicles provided by employees in 1990–91: see modification note at the start of this Part).
CAA 2001 Sch 3 para 55 (certain expenditure incurred before 6 April 1976: see modification note at the start of this Part).

226 Qualifying expenditure limited in subsequent transactions

(1) Subsection (2) applies if—

(a) plant or machinery has been the subject of a sale and finance leaseback,

(b) S was required to bring a disposal value into account under this Part because of the relevant transaction,

(c) at any time after that event, a person ("P") becomes the owner of the plant or machinery as a result of incurring capital expenditure, and

(d) P's allowances are not restricted by any other provision of this Chapter.

(2) The amount of P's qualifying expenditure is limited to the sum of—

(a) the amount given by section 222 as the amount of S's disposal value, and

(b) so much of the actual amount of the expenditure as is treated as expenditure on the provision of plant or machinery under section 25 (building alterations connected with installation of plant or machinery).

Commentary—*Simon's Direct Tax Service* **B2.368**.
Former enactments—CAA 1990 s 76A(3), (4), (7).
Definition—"Capital expenditure", s 4.
Modifications—CAA 2001 Sch 3 para 45 (CAA 2001 ss 221, 222, 224–226 do not apply in relation to expenditure incurred before 2 July 1998 if the relevant transaction is a purchase under a contract entered into before 2 July 1997; is itself a contract entered into before that date; or is an assignment made before that date, or in pursuance of a contract entered into before that date).
CAA 2001 Sch 3 para 54 (vehicles provided by employees in 1990–91: see modification note at the start of this Part).
CAA 2001 Sch 3 para 55 (certain expenditure incurred before 6 April 1976: see modification note at the start of this Part).

Sale and leaseback or sale and finance leaseback: election for special treatment

227 Circumstances in which election may be made

(1) Section 228 applies if—

(a) B enters into a relevant transaction with S,

(b) the plant or machinery—

(i) is within section 216(1)(b) (sale and leaseback), or

(ii) is the subject of a sale and finance leaseback (see section 221),

(c) the conditions set out in subsection (2) are met, and

(d) B and S elect that section 228 should apply.

(2) The conditions are—

(a) that S incurred capital expenditure on the provision of the plant or machinery,

(b) that the plant or machinery was unused and not second-hand at or after the time when it was acquired by S,

(c) that the plant or machinery was acquired by S otherwise than as a result of a transaction to which section 217, 218, 223 or 224 applies,

(d) that the relevant transaction is effected not more than 4 months after the first occasion on which the plant or machinery is brought into use by any person for any purpose, and (*e*) that S has not—

    (i) made a claim for an allowance under this Act in respect of expenditure incurred on the provision of the plant or machinery,

    (ii) made a tax return in which such expenditure is taken into account in determining his available qualifying expenditure for the purposes of this Part, or

    (iii) given notice of any such amendment of a tax return as provides for such expenditure to be so taken into account.

(3) In subsection (2)(*b*) and (*c*), the references to the plant or machinery being acquired by S are, in a case where the relevant transaction between S and B falls within section 213(1)(*c*) (assignment), references to the making of the contract the benefit of which S assigns to B.

(4) An election under this section—

    (*a*) must be made by notice to the Inland Revenue no later than 2 years after the date of the transaction, and

    (*b*) is irrevocable.

(5) Nothing in—

    (*a*) section 42 of, or Schedule 1A to, TMA 1970 (claims and elections for income tax purposes), or

    (*b*) paragraphs 54 to 60 of Schedule 18 to FA 1998 (claims and elections for corporation tax purposes),

applies to such an election.

(6) In subsection (4) "the date of the transaction" means the date of the sale, the making of the contract or the assignment referred to in section 213(1)(*a*) to (*c*).

Commentary—*Simon's Direct Tax Service* **B2.369**.
Former enactments—Sub-s (1): CAA 1990 s 76B(1).
Sub-s (2): CAA 1990 s 76B(2), (6), (7), s 83(1) ("new").
Sub-s (3): CAA 1990 s 76B(7).
Sub-s (4): CAA 1990 s 76B(4), (5).
Sub-s (5): CAA 1990 s 76B(5).
Sub-s (6): CAA 1990 s 76B(6), (7).
Definitions—"Available qualifying expenditure", s 57; "capital expenditure", s 4.
Modifications—CAA 2001 Sch 3 para 54 (vehicles provided by employees in 1990–91: see modification note at the start of this Part).
CAA 2001 Sch 3 para 55 (certain expenditure incurred before 6 April 1976: see modification note at the start of this Part).

228 Effect of election: relaxation of restriction on B's qualifying expenditure, etc

(1) The effect of an election under section 227 in relation to B is that subsections (2) and (3) apply instead of section 218 or 224 (restriction on B's qualifying expenditure).

(2) The amount, if any, by which B's expenditure under the relevant transaction exceeds D is to be left out of account in determining B's available qualifying expenditure.

(3) D is whichever of the following is the smaller—

    (*a*) if S incurred capital expenditure on the provision of the plant or machinery, the amount of that expenditure;

    (*b*) if a person connected with S incurred capital expenditure on the provision of the plant or machinery, the amount of that expenditure.

(4) Nothing in subsections (1) to (3) prevents section 225 from applying.

(5) The effect of an election under section 227 in relation to S is—

    (*a*) that no allowance is to be made to S under this Act in respect of the capital expenditure on the provision of the plant or machinery, and

    (*b*) that the whole of that expenditure must be left out of account in determining the amount for any period of S's available qualifying expenditure for the purposes of this Part.

Commentary—*Simon's Direct Tax Service* **B2.369**.
Former enactments—Sub-ss (1)–(4): CAA 1990 s 76B(3)(*c*), (*d*).
Sub-s (5): CAA 1990 s 76B(3)(*a*), (*b*).
Definitions—"Available qualifying expenditure", s 57; "capital expenditure", s 4.
Modifications—CAA 2001 Sch 3 para 54 (vehicles provided by employees in 1990–91: see modification note at the start of this Part).
CAA 2001 Sch 3 para 55 (certain expenditure incurred before 6 April 1976: see modification note at the start of this Part).

Miscellaneous and supplementary

229 Hire-purchase etc

(1) This section applies if—

    (*a*) a person carrying on a qualifying activity incurs capital expenditure on the provision of plant or machinery for the purposes of the qualifying activity, and

    (*b*) the expenditure is incurred under a contract providing that the person shall or may become the owner of the plant or machinery on the performance of the contract.

(2) If—

(*a*) the person assigns the benefit of the contract to another before the plant or machinery is brought into use, and

(*b*) the circumstances are such that allowances to the assignee fall to be restricted under this Chapter,

section 68(3) (disposal value where person ceases to be entitled to benefit of contract before plant or machinery brought into use) does not apply.

(3) If the expenditure is incurred on the provision of plant or machinery for leasing under a finance lease—

(*a*) section 67(3) (expenditure due to be incurred under contract treated as incurred when plant or machinery brought into use), and

(*b*) section 68 (disposal values where person ceases to be entitled to benefit of contract),

do not apply.

(4) Subsection (5) applies if—

(*a*) a person is treated under section 67(4) as ceasing to own plant or machinery, and

(*b*) as a result of subsection (2) or (3), section 68(3) or (as the case may be) section 68 does not apply.

(5) If this subsection applies—

(*a*) the disposal value is the total of—

(i) any relevant capital sums, and

(ii) any capital expenditure that the person would have incurred if he had wholly performed the contract, but

(*b*) the person is to be treated, for the purpose only of bringing the disposal value into account, as having incurred the capital expenditure mentioned in paragraph (*a*)(ii) in the relevant chargeable period.

(6) "Relevant capital sums" means capital sums that the person receives or is entitled to receive by way of consideration, compensation, damages or insurance money in respect of—

(*a*) his rights under the contract, or

(*b*) the plant or machinery.

(7) The relevant chargeable period, for the purposes of subsection (5)(*b*), is the chargeable period in which the person is treated under section 67(4) as ceasing to own the plant or machinery.

Commentary—*Simon's Direct Tax Service* **B2.391**.
Former enactments—Sub-s (2): CAA 1990 s 25(6); change in law.
Sub-s (3): CAA 1990 s 60(2A).
Sub-ss (4)–(7): CAA 1990 s 25(6); change in law.
Definitions—"Capital expenditure", s 4; "capital sum", s 4; "chargeable period", s 6.
Modifications—CAA 2001 Sch 3 para 44 (CAA 2001 ss 220, 229 do not apply in relation to expenditure incurred before 2 July 1997, or in the 12 months beginning with that date in pursuance of a contract entered into before that date).
CAA 2001 Sch 3 para 54 (vehicles provided by employees in 1990–91: see modification note at the start of this Part).
CAA 2001 Sch 3 para 55 (certain expenditure incurred before 6 April 1976: see modification note at the start of this Part).

230 Exception for manufacturers and suppliers

(1) The restrictions in sections 217 and 218 do not apply in relation to any plant or machinery if—

(*a*) the relevant transaction is within section 213(1)(*a*) or (*b*), and

(*b*) the conditions in subsection (3) are met.

(2) The restrictions in sections 222 to 225 do not apply in relation to any plant or machinery if—

(*a*) the plant or machinery is the subject of a sale and finance leaseback which is within section 213(1)(*a*) or (*b*), and

(*b*) the conditions in subsection (3) are met.

(3) The conditions are that—

(*a*) the plant or machinery has never been used before the sale or the making of the contract,

(*b*) S's business, or part of S's business, is the manufacture or supply of plant or machinery of that class, and

(*c*) the sale is effected or the contract made in the ordinary course of that business.

Commentary—*Simon's Direct Tax Service* **B2.366**.
Former enactments—CAA 1990 s 76(5).
Modifications—CAA 2001 Sch 3 para 54 (vehicles provided by employees in 1990–91: see modification note at the start of this Part).
CAA 2001 Sch 3 para 55 (certain expenditure incurred before 6 April 1976: see modification note at the start of this Part).

231 Adjustments of assessments etc

All such assessments and adjustments of assessments are to be made as are necessary to give effect to this Chapter.

Former enactments—CAA 1990 s 75(5).
Modifications—CAA 2001 Sch 3 para 54 (vehicles provided by employees in 1990–91: see modification note at the start of this Part).
CAA 2001 Sch 3 para 55 (certain expenditure incurred before 6 April 1976: see modification note at the start of this Part).

CAA 2001

232 Meaning of connected person

(1) For the purposes of this Chapter one person is to be treated as connected with another if—

  (a) they would be treated as connected under section 839 of ICTA, or

  (b) they are to be treated as connected under subsection (2).

(2) If—

  (a) a public authority has at any time acquired plant or machinery from another public authority otherwise than by purchase, and

  (b) it is directly or indirectly as a consequence of having been leased under a finance lease that the plant or machinery is available for any use to which it is put,

the authority from whom the plant or machinery was acquired is to be treated, in relation to that plant or machinery, as connected with the acquiring authority and with every person connected with the acquiring authority.

(3) In subsection (2), "public authority" includes the Crown or any government or local authority.

(4) Subsection (2) does not apply in relation to section 219 (meaning of "finance lease").

Commentary—*Simon's Direct Tax Service* **B2.368**.
Former enactments—Sub-s (1): CAA 1990 ss 75(4), 76(6)(b), 76A(11).
Sub-s (2): CAA 1990 ss 76A(11), 82A(2).
Sub-s (3): CAA 1990 s 76A(12) ("public authority").
Sub-s (4): CAA 1990 s 76A(11).
Modifications—CAA 2001 Sch 3 para 54 (vehicles provided by employees in 1990–91: see modification note at the start of this Part).
CAA 2001 Sch 3 para 55 (certain expenditure incurred before 6 April 1976: see modification note at the start of this Part).

233 Additional VAT liabilities and rebates

This Chapter needs to be read with sections 241 to 245 (provision for cases where a person involved in a relevant transaction or a sale and finance leaseback incurs an additional VAT liability or receives an additional VAT rebate).

CHAPTER 18
ADDITIONAL VAT LIABILITIES AND REBATES
Introduction

234 Introduction

For the purposes of this Chapter—

  (a) "additional VAT liability" and "additional VAT rebate" have the meaning given by section 547,

  (b) the time when—

    (i) a person incurs an additional VAT liability, or

    (ii) an additional VAT rebate is made to a person,

  is given by section 548, and

  (c) the chargeable period in which an additional VAT liability or an additional VAT rebate accrues is given by section 549.

Commentary—*Simon's Direct Tax Service* **B2.375**.
Definitions—"Additional VAT liability", s 547(1); "additional VAT rebate", s 547(2); "chargeable period", s 6.
Modifications—CAA 2001 Sch 3 para 54 (vehicles provided by employees in 1990–91: see modification note at the start of this Part).
CAA 2001 Sch 3 para 55 (certain expenditure incurred before 6 April 1976: see modification note at the start of this Part).

Additional VAT liability

235 Additional VAT liability treated as qualifying expenditure

(1) This section applies if a person—

  (a) has incurred qualifying expenditure ("the original expenditure"), and

  (b) incurs an additional VAT liability in respect of the original expenditure at a time when the plant or machinery is provided for the purposes of the qualifying activity.

(2) The additional VAT liability is to be treated as qualifying expenditure—

  (a) which is incurred on the same plant or machinery as the original expenditure, and

  (b) which may be taken into account in determining the person's available qualifying expenditure for the chargeable period in which the additional VAT liability accrues.

Commentary—*Simon's Direct Tax Service* **B2.375**.
Former enactments—Sub-s (1): CAA 1990 s 24(1A).
Sub-s (2): CAA 1990 ss 24(1A), 159A(3).
Definitions—"Additional VAT liability", s 547(1); "available qualifying expenditure", s 57; "chargeable period", s 6.
Modifications—CAA 2001 Sch 3 para 54 (vehicles provided by employees in 1990–91: see modification note at the start of this Part).
CAA 2001 Sch 3 para 55 (certain expenditure incurred before 6 April 1976: see modification note at the start of this Part).

236 Additional VAT liability generates first-year allowance

(1) Subsection (2) applies if—

(*a*) the original expenditure was first-year qualifying expenditure, and

(*b*) the additional VAT liability is incurred at a time when the plant or machinery is provided for the purposes of the qualifying activity.

(2) The additional VAT liability is to be regarded for the purposes of this Part as first-year qualifying expenditure which—

(*a*) is incurred on the same plant or machinery and is the same type of first-year qualifying expenditure as the original expenditure, and

(*b*) entitles the person incurring the liability to a first-year allowance for the chargeable period in which the liability accrues.

(3) Subsections (3) and (4) of section 52 apply to first-year qualifying expenditure constituted by the additional VAT liability as they apply to other first-year qualifying expenditure.

(4) This section is subject to sections 237 and 241.

Commentary—*Simon's Direct Tax Service* **B2.375**.
Former enactments—Sub-s (1): CAA 1990 s 22(1A).
Sub-s (2): CAA 1990 ss 22(1B), 159A(3).
Sub-s (3): CAA 1990 s 22(1B).
Definitions—"Additional VAT liability", s 547(1); "chargeable period", s 6.
Modifications—CAA 2001 Sch 3 para 46 (for the purposes of sub-s(1)(*a*) above, first-year expenditure includes expenditure which is first-year expenditure under CAA 2001 Sch 3 paras 47 (expenditure incurred 1992–93) and 48 (expenditure by small or medium-sized enterprises 1997–1998)).
CAA 2001 Sch 3 para 54 (vehicles provided by employees in 1990–91: see modification note at the start of this Part).
CAA 2001 Sch 3 para 55 (certain expenditure incurred before 6 April 1976: see modification note at the start of this Part).

237 Exceptions to section 236

(1) An additional VAT liability is not first-year qualifying expenditure if at the time when the liability is incurred the plant or machinery is used for overseas leasing which is not protected leasing.

(2) An additional VAT liability is not first-year qualifying expenditure if, at the time when the liability is incurred, the original expenditure is treated under section 43 (plant or machinery subsequently primarily for use outside Northern Ireland) as expenditure which was never first-year qualifying expenditure.

Commentary—*Simon's Direct Tax Service* **B2.375**.
Former enactments—change in law.
Sub-s (1): CAA 1990 ss 22(6A), (6B), 46(2).
Sub-s (2): CAA 1990 s 22(3CA), 22B(1).
Definitions—"Additional VAT liability", s 547(1); "additional VAT rebate", s 547(2).
Modifications—CAA 2001 Sch 3 para 54 (vehicles provided by employees in 1990–91: see modification note at the start of this Part).
CAA 2001 Sch 3 para 55 (certain expenditure incurred before 6 April 1976: see modification note at the start of this Part).

Additional VAT rebate

238 Additional VAT rebate generates disposal value

(1) This section applies if—

(*a*) a person has incurred qualifying expenditure ("the original expenditure"),

(*b*) an additional VAT rebate is made to the person in respect of the original expenditure, and

(*c*) the person owns the plant or machinery on which the original expenditure was incurred at any time in the chargeable period in which the rebate is made.

(2) If (apart from this section) there would not be a disposal value to be brought into account in respect of the plant or machinery for the chargeable period in which the rebate accrues, the amount of the rebate must be brought into account as a disposal value for that chargeable period.

(3) If (apart from this section) there would be a disposal value to be brought into account in respect of the plant of machinery for the chargeable period in which the rebate accrues, the amount of the rebate must be brought into account as an addition to that disposal value.

Commentary—*Simon's Direct Tax Service* **B2.375**.
Former enactments—Sub-s (1): CAA 1990 s 24(7).
Sub-ss (2), (3): CAA 1990 s 24(7), 26(1)(*ee*), 159A(3).
Definitions—"Additional VAT rebate", s 547(2); "chargeable period", s 6.
Modifications—CAA 2001 Sch 3 para 54 (vehicles provided by employees in 1990–91: see modification note at the start of this Part).
CAA 2001 Sch 3 para 55 (certain expenditure incurred before 6 April 1976: see modification note at the start of this Part).

239 Limit on disposal value where additional VAT rebate

(1) Subsection (2) applies if—

(*a*) a person is required to bring a disposal value into account in respect of any plant or machinery, and

(*b*) any additional VAT rebate or rebates has or have been made to him in respect of the original expenditure.

CAA 2001

(2) The amount of the disposal value is limited to the amount of the original expenditure reduced by the total of any additional VAT rebates accruing in previous chargeable periods in respect of that expenditure.

But this is subject to subsections (3) to (6).

(3) Subsection (4) applies if the disposal value is required to be brought into account by section 238(2) (disposal value for additional VAT rebate on its own).

(4) The amount of the disposal value to be brought into account is limited to the amount of the original expenditure reduced by the amount of any disposal values brought into account in respect of the plant or machinery as a result of any earlier event.

(5) If—

(*a*) the person required to bring the disposal value into account has acquired the plant or machinery as a result of a transaction which was, or a series of transactions each of which was, between connected persons, and

(*b*) an additional VAT rebate has been made to any party to the transaction, or to any of the transactions,

the amount of the disposal value is limited to the greatest relevant expenditure of any of the parties.

(6) The relevant expenditure of a party is that party's qualifying expenditure on the provision of the plant or machinery, less any additional VAT rebate made to that party.

Commentary—*Simon's Direct Tax Service* **B2.375**.
Former enactments—Sub-s (2): CAA 1990 s 26(2).
Sub-ss (3), (4): CAA 1990 s 26(2A); change in law.
Sub-s (5): CAA 1990 s 26(2)–(4).
Sub-s (6): CAA 1990 s 26(2), (4).
Definition—''Additional VAT rebate'', s 547(2).
Modifications—CAA 2001 Sch 3 para 54 (vehicles provided by employees in 1990–91: see modification note at the start of this Part).
CAA 2001 Sch 3 para 55 (certain expenditure incurred before 6 April 1976: see modification note at the start of this Part).

Short-life assets: balancing allowance

240 Additional VAT liability

(1) This section applies if a person—

(*a*) was entitled to a balancing allowance for the final chargeable period for a short-life asset pool for a qualifying activity,

(*b*) has incurred, after the end of that period, an additional VAT liability in respect of the original expenditure on the provision of the short-life asset, and

(*c*) has not brought the liability into account in determining the amount of the balancing allowance.

(2) The person is entitled to a further balancing allowance, of an amount equal to the additional VAT liability, for the chargeable period of the qualifying activity in which the additional VAT liability accrues.

Commentary—*Simon's Direct Tax Service* **B2.376**.
Former enactments—Sub-s (1): CAA 1990 s 37(4A).
Sub-s (2): CAA 1990 ss 37(4A), 159A(3).
Definitions—''Additional VAT liability'', s 547(1); ''chargeable period'', s 6; ''final chargeable period'', s 65; ''short-life asset'', s 83.
Modifications—CAA 2001 Sch 3 para 54 (vehicles provided by employees in 1990–91: see modification note at the start of this Part).
CAA 2001 Sch 3 para 55 (certain expenditure incurred before 6 April 1976: see modification note at the start of this Part).

Anti-avoidance

241 No first-year allowance in respect of additional VAT liability

(1) This section applies if—

(*a*) one person (''B'') enters into a transaction with another person (''S'') which is a relevant transaction for the purposes of Chapter 17 (anti-avoidance), and

(*b*) a first-year allowance in respect of B's expenditure under the relevant transaction is prohibited by section 217(1) or 223(1).

(2) A first-year allowance is not to be made in respect of any additional VAT liability incurred by B in respect of his expenditure under the relevant transaction.

(3) Any first-year allowance which is prohibited by subsection (2), but which has already been made, is to be withdrawn.

Commentary—*Simon's Direct Tax Service* **B2.377**.
Former enactments—Sub-ss (1)–(3): CAA 1990 ss 75(1)–(3), 76(1), 76A(1).
Definition—''Additional VAT liability'', s 547(1).
Modifications—CAA 2001 Sch 3 para 54 (vehicles provided by employees in 1990–91: see modification note at the start of this Part).
CAA 2001 Sch 3 para 55 (certain expenditure incurred before 6 April 1976: see modification note at the start of this Part).

242 Restriction on B's qualifying expenditure: general

(1) This section applies instead of section 218 (restriction on B's qualifying expenditure in case other than sale and finance leaseback) if—

    (*a*) apart from this subsection, section 218 would apply, and

    (*b*) an additional VAT liability has been incurred by, or an additional rebate has been made to, any of the persons mentioned in that section.

(2) The amount, if any, by which E exceeds D is to be left out of account in determining B's available qualifying expenditure.

E and D are defined in subsections (3) to (6).

(3) Except where subsection (6) applies, E is the sum of—

    (*a*) B's expenditure under the relevant transaction, and

    (*b*) any additional VAT liability incurred by B in respect of that expenditure.

(4) If S is required to bring a disposal value into account under this Part because of the relevant transaction, D is that disposal value.

(5) If S is not required to bring a disposal value into account under this Part because of the relevant transaction, D is whichever of the following is the smallest—

    (*a*) the market value of the plant or machinery;

    (*b*) if S incurred capital expenditure on the provision of the plant or machinery, the amount of that expenditure—

        (i) increased by the amount of any additional VAT liability incurred by S in respect of that expenditure, and

        (ii) reduced by the amount of any additional VAT rebate made to S in respect of that expenditure;

    (*c*) if a person connected with S incurred capital expenditure on the provision of the plant or machinery, the amount of that expenditure—

        (i) increased by the amount of any additional VAT liability incurred by that person in respect of that expenditure, and

        (ii) reduced by the amount of any additional VAT rebate made to that person in respect of that expenditure.

(6) If—

    (*a*) S is not required to bring a disposal value into account under this Part because of the relevant transaction,

    (*b*) the smallest amount under subsection (5) is the market value of the plant or machinery, and

    (*c*) that value is determined inclusive of value added tax,

E is the amount of B's expenditure under the relevant transaction.

Commentary—*Simon's Direct Tax Service* **B2.377**.
Former enactments—Sub-ss (1)–(4): CAA 1990 s 75(1)–(3).
Sub-s (5): CAA 1990 s 76(2), (2B), (4).
Sub-s (6): CAA 1990 s 76(2A), (4).
Definitions—"Additional VAT liability", s 547(1); "additional VAT rebate", s 547(2); "available qualifying expenditure", s 57; "capital expenditure", s 4.
Modifications—CAA 2001 Sch 3 para 54 (vehicles provided by employees in 1990–91: see modification note at the start of this Part).
CAA 2001 Sch 3 para 55 (certain expenditure incurred before 6 April 1976: see modification note at the start of this Part).

243 Restriction on B's qualifying expenditure: sale and finance leaseback

(1) This section applies instead of section 224 (restriction on B's qualifying expenditure in case of sale and finance leaseback) if—

    (*a*) apart from this subsection, section 224 would apply, and

    (*b*) an additional VAT liability has been incurred by B.

(2) The amount, if any, by which E exceeds D is to be left out of account in determining B's available qualifying expenditure.

E and D are defined in subsections (3) to (7).

(3) Except where subsection (7) applies, E is the sum of—

    (*a*) B's expenditure under the relevant transaction, and

    (*b*) any additional VAT liability incurred by B in respect of that expenditure.

(4) If S is required to bring a disposal value into account under this Part because of the relevant transaction, D is that disposal value (determined in accordance with section 222).

(5) If S is not required to bring a disposal value into account under this Part because of the relevant transaction, D is whichever of the following is the smallest—

    (*a*) the market value of the plant or machinery;

    (*b*) if S incurred capital expenditure on the provision of the plant or machinery, the notional written-down value of that capital expenditure;

(c) if a person connected with S incurred capital expenditure on the provision of the plant or machinery, the notional written-down value of that capital expenditure.

(6) In this section "the notional written-down value", in relation to expenditure incurred by a person on the provision of plant or machinery, has the meaning given by section 222(3).

(7) If—

(a) S is not required to bring a disposal value into account under this Part because of the relevant transaction,

(b) the smallest amount under subsection (5) is the market value of the plant or machinery, and

(c) that value is determined inclusive of value added tax,

E is the amount of B's expenditure under the relevant transaction.

Commentary—*Simon's Direct Tax Service* **B2.377**.
Former enactments—Sub-ss (1)–(5): CAA 1990 ss 75(1)–(3), 76A(2), (5).
Sub-s (6): CAA 1990 s 76A(9), (10).
Sub-s (7): CAA 1990 s 76(2A), (4).
Definitions—"Additional VAT liability", s 547(1); "available qualifying expenditure", s 57; "capital expenditure", s 4.
Modifications—CAA 2001 Sch 3 para 51 (sub-s (7) above does not apply in relation to expenditure incurred before 2 July 1998 if the relevant transaction is a purchase under a contract entered into before 2 July 1997; is itself a contract entered into before that date; or is an assignment made before that date, or in pursuance of a contract entered into before that date).
CAA 2001 Sch 3 para 54 (vehicles provided by employees in 1990–91: see modification note at the start of this Part).
CAA 2001 Sch 3 para 55 (certain expenditure incurred before 6 April 1976: see modification note at the start of this Part).

244 B's qualifying expenditure if lessor not bearing non-compliance risk

An additional VAT liability is not qualifying expenditure for the purposes of this Part if—

(a) section 225 (restriction on B's qualifying expenditure if lessor not bearing compliance risk) applies, and

(b) the additional VAT liability is incurred—

(i) by B, in respect of the expenditure referred to in section 225(2)(a), or

(ii) by the lessor, in respect of the expenditure referred to in section 225(2)(b).

Commentary—*Simon's Direct Tax Service* **B2.377**.
Former enactments—CAA 1990 76A(6)–(8).
Definition—"Additional VAT liability", s 547(1).
Modifications—CAA 2001 Sch 3 para 51 (the section above does not apply in relation to expenditure incurred before 2 July 1998 if the relevant transaction is a purchase under a contract entered into before 2 July 1997; is itself a contract entered into before that date; or is an assignment made before that date, or in pursuance of a contract entered into before that date).
CAA 2001 Sch 3 para 54 (vehicles provided by employees in 1990–91: see modification note at the start of this Part).
CAA 2001 Sch 3 para 55 (certain expenditure incurred before 6 April 1976: see modification note at the start of this Part).

245 Effect of election under section 227 on additional VAT liability

(1) This section applies if—

(a) an election is made under section 227 (sale and leaseback or sale and finance leaseback: election for special treatment), and

(b) an additional VAT liability is incurred by S in respect of the capital expenditure incurred on the provision of the plant or machinery to which the election relates.

(2) The effect of the election is—

(a) that no allowance is to be made to S under this Act in respect of the additional VAT liability, and

(b) that the additional VAT liability must be left out of account in determining S's available qualifying expenditure for any period.

Commentary—*Simon's Direct Tax Service* **B2.377**.
Former enactments—CAA 1990 s 76B(3)(a), (b).
Definitions—"Additional VAT liability", s 547(1); "available qualifying expenditure", s 57; "capital expenditure", s 4.
Modifications—CAA 2001 Sch 3 para 54 (vehicles provided by employees in 1990–91: see modification note at the start of this Part).
CAA 2001 Sch 3 para 55 (certain expenditure incurred before 6 April 1976: see modification note at the start of this Part).

246 Miscellaneous

(1) All such assessments and adjustments of assessments are to be made as are necessary to give effect to sections 241 to 245.

(2) Section 232 (meaning of connected person) applies for the purposes of sections 242 and 243.

Commentary—*Simon's Direct Tax Service* **B2.377**.
Former enactments—Sub-s (1): CAA 1990 s 75(5).
Sub-s (2): CAA 1990 s 76A(11).
Modifications—CAA 2001 Sch 3 para 54 (vehicles provided by employees in 1990–91: see modification note at the start of this Part).
CAA 2001 Sch 3 para 55 (certain expenditure incurred before 6 April 1976: see modification note at the start of this Part).

CHAPTER 19
GIVING EFFECT TO ALLOWANCES AND CHARGES
Trades

247 Trades

If the qualifying activity of a person who is entitled or liable to an allowance or charge for a chargeable period is a trade, the allowance or charge is to be given effect in calculating the profits of that person's trade, by treating—

(a) the allowance as an expense of the trade, and
(b) the charge as a receipt of the trade.

Commentary—*Simon's Direct Tax Service* B2.380.
Former enactments—CAA 1990 ss 73(1), 140(2), 144(2), 161(2) ("chargeable period"), s 161(5).
Definition—"Chargeable period", s 6.
Modifications—CAA 2001 Sch 3 para 54 (vehicles provided by employees in 1990–91: see modification note at the start of this Part).
CAA 2001 Sch 3 para 55 (certain expenditure incurred before 6 April 1976: see modification note at the start of this Part).

Property businesses

248 Ordinary Schedule A businesses

If the qualifying activity of a person who is entitled or liable to an allowance or charge for a chargeable period is an ordinary Schedule A business, the allowance or charge is to be given effect in calculating the profits of that business, by treating—

(a) the allowance as an expense of that business, and
(b) the charge as a receipt of that business.

Commentary—*Simon's Direct Tax Service* B2.381.
Former enactments—CAA 1990 s 28A(1).
Definitions—"Chargeable period", s 6; "ordinary Schedule A business", s 16.
Modifications—CAA 2001 Sch 3 para 54 (vehicles provided by employees in 1990–91: see modification note at the start of this Part).
CAA 2001 Sch 3 para 55 (certain expenditure incurred before 6 April 1976: see modification note at the start of this Part).

249 Furnished holiday lettings businesses

(1) If the qualifying activity of a person who is entitled or liable to an allowance or charge for a chargeable period is a furnished holiday lettings business, the allowance or charge is to be given effect in calculating the profits of that business, by treating—

(a) the allowance as an expense of that business, and
(b) the charge as a receipt of that business.

(2) Section 503 of ICTA (letting of furnished holiday accommodation treated as trade for purposes of loss relief rules, etc) applies to profits calculated in accordance with subsection (1).

Commentary—*Simon's Direct Tax Service* B2.381.
Former enactments—Sub-s (1): CAA 1990 s 29(1).
Sub-s (2): CAA 1990 s 29(2).
Definitions—"Chargeable period", s 6; "furnished holiday lettings business", s 17.
Modifications—CAA 2001 Sch 3 para 54 (vehicles provided by employees in 1990–91: see modification note at the start of this Part).
CAA 2001 Sch 3 para 55 (certain expenditure incurred before 6 April 1976: see modification note at the start of this Part).

250 Overseas property businesses

If the qualifying activity of a person who is entitled or liable to an allowance or charge for a chargeable period is an overseas property business, the allowance or charge is to be given effect in calculating the profits of that business, by treating—

(a) the allowance as an expense of that business, and
(b) the charge as a receipt of that business.

Commentary—*Simon's Direct Tax Service* B2.381.
Former enactments—CAA 1990 ss 28A(1), 161(2A).
Definition—"Chargeable period", s 6.
Modifications—CAA 2001 Sch 3 para 54 (vehicles provided by employees in 1990–91: see modification note at the start of this Part).
CAA 2001 Sch 3 para 55 (certain expenditure incurred before 6 April 1976: see modification note at the start of this Part).

Activities analogous to trades

251 Professions and vocations

If the qualifying activity of a person who is entitled or liable to an allowance or charge for a chargeable period is carrying on a profession or vocation, the allowance or charge is to be given effect in calculating the profits or gains of that person's profession or vocation, by treating—

(a) the allowance as an expense of the profession or vocation, and
(b) the charge as a receipt of the profession or vocation.

Commentary—*Simon's Direct Tax Service* B2.382.
Former enactments—CAA 1990 ss 27(1), 140(4).
Definition—''Chargeable period'', s 6.
Modifications—CAA 2001 Sch 3 para 54 (vehicles provided by employees in 1990–91: see modification note at the start of this Part).
CAA 2001 Sch 3 para 55 (certain expenditure incurred before 6 April 1976: see modification note at the start of this Part).

252 Mines, transport undertakings etc

If the qualifying activity of a person who is entitled or liable to an allowance or charge for a chargeable period is a concern listed in section 55(2) of ICTA (mines, transport undertakings etc) the allowance or charge is to be given effect in calculating the profits of the concern under Case I of Schedule D, by treating—

(*a*) the allowance as an expense of the concern, and
(*b*) the charge as a receipt of the concern.

Commentary—*Simon's Direct Tax Service* B2.382.
Former enactments—Change in law.
Definition—''Chargeable period'', s 6.
Modifications—CAA 2001 Sch 3 para 54 (vehicles provided by employees in 1990–91: see modification note at the start of this Part).
CAA 2001 Sch 3 para 55 (certain expenditure incurred before 6 April 1976: see modification note at the start of this Part).

Investment companies

253 Investment companies

(1) This section applies if the qualifying activity of a person entitled to an allowance or liable to a charge for a chargeable period is the management of an investment company.

(2) The allowance is, as far as possible, to be given effect by deducting the amount of the allowance from any income for the period of the business; and section 75(4) of ICTA (addition of allowances to company's expenses of management) applies only in so far as it cannot be given effect in this way.

(3) The charge is to be given effect by treating the amount of the charge as income of the business.

(4) Except as provided by subsections (2) and (3), the Corporation Tax Acts apply in relation to the allowance or charge as if they were required to be given effect in calculating the profits of that person's trade for the purposes of Case I of Schedule D.

(5) Corresponding allowances or charges in the case of the same plant or machinery are not to be made under this Part both under this section and in another way.

(6) Expenditure to which this section applies is not to be taken into account otherwise than under this Part or as provided by section 75(4) of ICTA.

(7) This section is subject to sections 768B(8) and 768C(11) of ICTA.

Commentary—*Simon's Direct Tax Service* B2.383.
Former enactments—Sub-s (1): CAA 1990 s 28(1).
Sub-s (2): CAA 1990 s 28(2).
Sub-s (3): CAA 1990 s 28(2).
Sub-s (4): CAA 1990 s 28(3).
Sub-s (5): CAA 1990 s 28(5).
Sub-s (6): CAA 1990 s 28(6).
Definitions—''Investment company'', TA 1988 s 130; ''the Corporation Tax Acts'', TA 1988 s 831(1).
Modifications—CAA 2001 Sch 3 para 54 (vehicles provided by employees in 1990–91: see modification note at the start of this Part).
CAA 2001 Sch 3 para 55 (certain expenditure incurred before 6 April 1976: see modification note at the start of this Part).

Life assurance business

254 Introductory

(1) Sections 255 and 256 apply if a company which is carrying on any life assurance business is entitled or liable to any allowances or charges for a chargeable period in respect of plant or machinery consisting of a management asset.

(2) In this Chapter ''management asset'' has the same meaning as in Chapter 1 of Part 12 (life assurance business).

Commentary—*Simon's Direct Tax Service* D4.506.
Former enactments—Sub-s (1): TA 1988 s 434D(1).
Definitions—''Life assurance business'', s 544(5), TA 1988 s 431(2).
Modifications—CAA 2001 Sch 3 para 54 (vehicles provided by employees in 1990–91: see modification note at the start of this Part).
CAA 2001 Sch 3 para 55 (certain expenditure incurred before 6 April 1976: see modification note at the start of this Part).

255 Apportionment of allowances and charges

(1) Except where subsection (3) applies, the allowances or charges must be apportioned between the different categories of life assurance business carried on by the company, using the formula—

$$A \times \frac{B}{C}$$

where—

A is the amount of the allowance or charge,

B is the mean of the opening and closing liabilities of the category of life assurance concerned, and

C is the mean of the opening and closing liabilities of all the categories of life assurance business carried on by the company.

(2) In its application to an overseas life insurance company, subsection (1) has effect as if the references to liabilities were only to such liabilities as are attributable to the branch or agency in the United Kingdom through which the company carries on the business concerned.

(3) If—

(a) the company is charged to tax under section 441 of ICTA in respect of its overseas life assurance business, and

(b) the management asset in respect of which it is entitled to an allowance or liable to a charge for a chargeable period is provided outside the United Kingdom for use for the management of that business,

the allowance or charge must be allocated (without any apportionment) to that business.

Commentary—*Simon's Direct Tax Service* **D4.506**.
Former enactments—Sub-s (1): TA 1988 s 434D(4).
Sub-s (2): TA 1988 Sch 19AC para 9C.
Sub-s (3): TA 1988 s 434D(3).
Definitions—"Life assurance business", s 544(5), TA 1988 s 431(2).
Modifications—CAA 2001 Sch 3 para 54 (vehicles provided by employees in 1990–91: see modification note at the start of this Part).
CAA 2001 Sch 3 para 55 (certain expenditure incurred before 6 April 1976: see modification note at the start of this Part).

256 Different giving effect rules for different categories of business

(1) Subsection (2) applies if a company—

(a) carries on basic life assurance and general annuity business, and

(b) does not fall to be charged to tax in accordance with the provisions applicable to Case I of Schedule D in respect of the profits of that business.

(2) If this subsection applies—

(a) any allowances (or parts of allowances) to which the company is entitled in respect of the basic life assurance and general annuity business are to be given effect by treating them as additional expenses of management within section 76 of ICTA, and

(b) any charges (or parts of charges) to which the company is liable in respect of that business are to be given effect by treating the amount of the charges (or parts of charges) as income under Case VI of Schedule D for the chargeable period in question.

(3) Subsection (4) applies if, for a chargeable period, a company is charged to tax under—

(a) section 436 of ICTA (pension business and ISA business),

(b) section 439B of ICTA (life reinsurance business), or

(c) section 441 of ICTA (overseas life assurance business).

(4) If this subsection applies, then, for the purpose of calculating the profit under Case VI of Schedule D for the chargeable period in question—

(a) any allowances (or parts of allowances) to which the company is entitled in respect of any particular category of business are to be given effect by treating them as an expense of that category of business, and

(b) any charges (or parts of charges) to which the company is liable in respect of any particular category of business are to be given effect by treating them as receipts of that category of business.

Commentary—*Simon's Direct Tax Service* **D4.506**.
Former enactments—Sub-s (1): TA 1988 s 434D(6).
Sub-s (2): TA 1988 s 434D(6).
Sub-s (3): TA 1988 s 434D(3), (5).
Sub-s (4): TA 1988 s 434D(3), (5).
Definition—"Chargeable period", s 6.
Modifications—CAA 2001 Sch 3 para 54 (vehicles provided by employees in 1990–91: see modification note at the start of this Part).
CAA 2001 Sch 3 para 55 (certain expenditure incurred before 6 April 1976: see modification note at the start of this Part).
Friendly Societies (Modification of the Corporation Tax Acts) Regulations, SI 1997/473 reg 53C (modification to limit capital allowances on management assets of the life assurance business of friendly societies to that part of their basic life assurance and general annuity business that is taxable).

257 Supplementary

(1) Allowances and charges to which sections 255 and 256 apply are not to be given effect otherwise than in accordance with those sections.

(2) Subsection (1) does not prevent any allowance which is to be given effect under those sections from being taken into account in any calculation for the purposes of—

(a) section 89 of FA 1989 (calculation of "policy holders' share of profits"), or

(b) section 76(2) of ICTA (calculation for purposes of complying with restriction on amount of deductible management expenses).

(3) Expressions that are used—

(a) in sections 255 and 256, and

(b) in Chapter I of Part XII of ICTA (insurance companies and capital redemption business),

have the same meaning in those sections as in that Chapter.

Commentary—*Simon's Direct Tax Service* D4.506.
Former enactments—Sub-s (1): TA 1988 s 434D(8).
Sub-s (2): TA 1988 s 434D(8).
Modifications—CAA 2001 Sch 3 para 54 (vehicles provided by employees in 1990–91: see modification note at the start of this Part).
CAA 2001 Sch 3 para 55 (certain expenditure incurred before 6 April 1976: see modification note at the start of this Part).

Special leasing of plant or machinery

258 Special leasing: income tax

(1) This section applies for income tax purposes if the qualifying activity of a person entitled or liable to an allowance or charge for a chargeable period ("the current tax year") is special leasing of plant or machinery.

(2) Subject to subsection (3), the allowance is to be given effect by deducting it from the person's income for the current tax year from any qualifying activity the person has of special leasing of plant or machinery.

(3) If the plant or machinery leased under the special leasing was not used for the whole or any part of the current tax year for the purposes of a qualifying activity carried on by the lessee—

(a) the allowance, or

(b) a proportionate part of it,

is to be given effect by deducting the allowance, or the part of the allowance, from the person's income for the current tax year from that special leasing only.

(4) Any charge is to be given effect by treating the charge as income to be taxed under Case VI of Schedule D.

(5) If the amount to be deducted from a description of income specified in subsection (2) or (3) exceeds the person's income of that description for the current tax year, the excess must be deducted from the person's income of the same description for the next tax year, and so on for subsequent tax years.

(6) For the purposes of this section, income from special leasing of plant or machinery includes any charge treated as income under subsection (4).

(7) In this section, references to deducting an allowance (or a part of an allowance) from income include setting it off against income.

Commentary—*Simon's Direct Tax Service* B2.385.
Former enactments—Sub-s (1): CAA 1990 s 141(1).
Sub-s (2): CAA 1990 ss 73(2), 141(2).
Sub-s (3): CAA 1990 ss 27(1), 28(1), 28A(1), 29(1), 73(3), 141(2), 161(2A).
Sub-s (4): CAA 1990 s 73(2).
Sub-s (5): CAA 1990 s 141(2).
Sub-s (6): CAA 1990 s 83(1) ("income").
Sub-s (7): CAA 1990 s 141(2).
Revenue Internal Guidance—Capital allowances manual CA 29450 (explanation of sub-s (3) with example).
CA 29450 (treatment of company lessors under sub-s (3)).
Definition—"Special leasing", s 19.
Modifications—CAA 2001 Sch 3 para 54 (vehicles provided by employees in 1990–91: see modification note at the start of this Part).
CAA 2001 Sch 3 para 55 (certain expenditure incurred before 6 April 1976: see modification note at the start of this Part).

259 Special leasing: corporation tax (general)

(1) This section applies for corporation tax purposes if the qualifying activity of a company entitled or liable to an allowance or charge for a chargeable period ("the current accounting period") is special leasing of plant or machinery.

(2) Subject to subsection (3), the allowance is to be given effect by deducting it from the company's income for the current accounting period from any qualifying activity it has of special leasing of plant or machinery.

(3) If the plant or machinery leased under the special leasing was not used for the whole or any part of the current accounting period for the purposes of a qualifying activity carried on by the lessee—

(a) the allowance, or

(b) a proportionate part of it,

is to be given effect by deducting the allowance, or the part of the allowance, from the company's income for the current accounting period from that special leasing only.

(4) Any charge is to be given effect by treating the charge as income from special leasing of plant or machinery.

Commentary—*Simon's Direct Tax Service* **B2.385.**
Former enactments—Sub-s (1): CAA 1990 s 145(1).
Sub-s (2): CAA 1990 ss 73(2), 145(1).
Sub-s (3): CAA 1990 ss 27(1), 28(1), 28A(1), 29(1), 73(3), 145(1), 161(2A).
Sub-s (4): CAA 1990 s 73(2).
Definition—"Special leasing", s 19.
Modifications—CAA 2001 Sch 3 para 54 (vehicles provided by employees in 1990–91: see modification note at the start of this Part).
CAA 2001 Sch 3 para 55 (certain expenditure incurred before 6 April 1976: see modification note at the start of this Part).

260 Special leasing: corporation tax (excess allowance)

(1) This section applies if the amount to be deducted from a description of income specified in section 259(2) or (3) exceeds the company's income of that description for the current accounting period.

(2) Subject to subsections (3) to (6), the excess must (if the company remains within the charge to tax) be deducted from the company's income of the same description for the next accounting period (and so on for subsequent accounting periods).

(3) The company may, on making a claim, require the excess to be deducted from any profits—

    (a) of the current accounting period, and
    (b) if the company was then within the charge to tax, of any previous accounting period ending within the carry-back period.

(4) The carry-back period is a period which—

    (a) is of the same length as the current accounting period, and
    (b) ends at the start of the current accounting period.

(5) If the preceding accounting period began before the start of the carry-back period, the total amount of deductions that may be made from the profits of the preceding accounting period under—

    (a) subsection (3), and
    (b) any corresponding provision of the Corporation Tax Acts relating to losses,

must not exceed a part of those profits proportionate to the part of the period falling within the carry-back period.

(6) A claim under subsection (3) must be made no later than 2 years after the end of the current accounting period.

(7) If the deduction of the allowance (or of part of it) was subject to the restriction in section 259(3)—

    (a) subsections (3) to (6), and
    (b) section 403 of ICTA (group relief),

do not apply in relation to the allowance (or part of it).

(8) In this section "profits" has the same meaning as in section 6 of ICTA (charge to corporation tax etc).

Commentary—*Simon's Direct Tax Service* **B2.385.**
Former enactments—Sub-s (1): CAA 1990 s 145(2).
Sub-s (2): CAA 1990 s 145(2).
Sub-s (3): CAA 1990 s 145(3).
Sub-s (4): CAA 1990 s 145(4).
Sub-s (5): CAA 1990 s 145(4).
Sub-s (6): CAA 1990 s 145(5).
Sub-s (7): CAA 1990 s 61(5).
Sub-s (8): TA 1988 s 834(2).
Revenue Internal Guidance—Capital allowances manual CA 29450 (example of set off claim).
Definition—"The Corporation Tax Acts", TA 1988 s 831(1).
Modifications—CAA 2001 Sch 3 para 54 (vehicles provided by employees in 1990–91: see modification note at the start of this Part).
CAA 2001 Sch 3 para 55 (certain expenditure incurred before 6 April 1976: see modification note at the start of this Part).

261 Special leasing: life assurance business

In the case of a company which is carrying on any life assurance business—

    (a) subsections (3) to (6) of section 260, and
    (b) section 403 of ICTA (group relief),

do not apply in relation to an allowance to which the company is entitled under section 19 (special leasing of plant or machinery).

Former enactments—TA 1988 s 434E(6).
Definitions—"Life assurance business", s 544(5), TA 1988 s 431(2).
Modifications—CAA 2001 Sch 3 para 54 (vehicles provided by employees in 1990–91: see modification note at the start of this Part).
CAA 2001 Sch 3 para 55 (certain expenditure incurred before 6 April 1976: see modification note at the start of this Part).

Employments and offices

262 Employments and offices

If the qualifying activity of a person who is entitled or liable to an allowance or charge for a chargeable period is an employment or office, the allowance or charge is to be given effect, by treating—

(a) the allowance as an amount to be deducted from the emoluments of the employment or office, and

(b) the charge as an emolument of the employment or office.

Commentary—*Simon's Direct Tax Service* **B2.386**.
Former enactments—CAA 1990 ss 27(1), 140(4).
Definition—"Chargeable period", s 6.
Modifications—CAA 2001 Sch 3 para 54 (vehicles provided by employees in 1990–91: see modification note at the start of this Part).
CAA 2001 Sch 3 para 55 (certain expenditure incurred before 6 April 1976: see modification note at the start of this Part).

CHAPTER 20
SUPPLEMENTARY PROVISIONS
Partnerships and successions

263 Qualifying activities carried on in partnership

(1) This section applies if—

(a) a qualifying activity has been set up and is at any time carried on in partnership,

(b) there has been a change in the persons engaged in carrying on the qualifying activity, and

[(c) the change does not result in the qualifying activity being treated as permanently discontinued under section 113(1) or 337(1) of ICTA (changes in persons carrying on a trade etc and effect of company ceasing to trade etc).][1]

(2) In this section—

"the present partners" means the person or persons for the time being carrying on the qualifying activity,

"the partners at the time of the event" means the person or persons carrying on the qualifying activity at the time of the event in question,

"predecessors"—

(a) in relation to the present partners, means their predecessors in carrying on the qualifying activity, and

(b) in relation to the partners at the time of the event, means their predecessors in carrying on the qualifying activity, and

"qualifying activity"—

(a) does not include an employment or office, but

(b) includes any other activity listed in section 15(1) even if any profits or gains from it are not chargeable to tax.

(3) Any first-year allowance or writing-down allowance under this Part is to be made to the present partners.

(4) The amount of any allowance arising under subsection (3) is to be calculated as if—

(a) the present partners had at all times been carrying on the qualifying activity, and

(b) everything done to or by their predecessors in carrying on the qualifying activity had been done to or by the present partners.

(5) If any event occurs which gives rise or may give rise to a balancing allowance or a balancing charge under this Part, the allowance or charge is to be made to or on the partners at the time of the event.

(6) The amount of any allowance or charge arising under subsection (5) is to be calculated as if—

(a) the partners at the time of the event had at all times been carrying on the qualifying activity, and

(b) everything done to or by their predecessors in carrying on the qualifying activity had been done to or by the partners at the time of the event.

Commentary—*Simon's Direct Tax Service* **B2.390**.
Former enactments—Sub-s (1): CAA 1990 s 78(3), (4).
Sub-s (2): CAA 1990 ss 78(3)–(5), 83(2A).
Sub-ss (3), (4): CAA 1990 s 78(3).
Sub-ss (5), (6): CAA 1990 s 78(4).
Modifications—CAA 2001 Sch 3 para 54 (vehicles provided by employees in 1990–91: see modification note at the start of this Part).
CAA 2001 Sch 3 para 55 (certain expenditure incurred before 6 April 1976: see modification note at the start of this Part).
Amendments—[1] Sub-s (1)(c) substituted by FA 2001 s 69, Sch 21 para 4 with effect as respects allowances and charges falling to be made for chargeable periods ending after 5 April 2001 (for income tax purposes) or 31 March 2001 (for corporation tax purposes).

264 Partnership using property of a partner

(1) Subsection (2) applies if—

    (a) a qualifying activity is carried on in partnership,

    (b) plant or machinery is used for the purposes of the qualifying activity, and

    (c) the plant or machinery is owned by one or more of the partners but is not partnership property.

(2) The same allowances, deductions and charges are to be made under this Part in respect of the plant or machinery as would fall to be made if—

    (a) the plant or machinery had at all material times been owned by all the partners and been partnership property, and

    (b) everything done by or to any of the partners in relation to that plant or machinery had been done by or to all the partners.

(3) The disposal value of plant or machinery is not required to be brought into account if—

    (a) the plant or machinery is used for the purposes of a qualifying activity carried on in partnership,

    (b) a sale or gift of the plant or machinery is made by one or more of the partners to one or more of the partners, and

    (c) the plant or machinery continues to be used after the sale or gift for the purposes of the qualifying activity.

(4) The references in this section to use for the purposes of a qualifying activity do not include use—

    (a) as a result of a letting by the partner or partners in question to the partnership, or

    (b) in consideration of the making to the partner or partners in question of any payment which may be deducted in calculating the profits of the qualifying activity.

Commentary—*Simon's Direct Tax Service* **B2.390**.
Former enactments—Sub-ss (1), (2): CAA 1990 s 65(1).
Sub-s (3): CAA 1990 s 65(2).
Sub-s (4): CAA 1990 s 65(3).
Modifications—CAA 2001 Sch 3 para 54 (vehicles provided by employees in 1990–91: see modification note at the start of this Part).
CAA 2001 Sch 3 para 55 (certain expenditure incurred before 6 April 1976: see modification note at the start of this Part).

265 Successions: general

(1) This section applies if—

    (a) a person (''the successor'') succeeds to a qualifying activity which until that time was carried on by another person (''the predecessor''), and

    (b) the qualifying activity is treated as discontinued under section 113(1) or 337(1) of ICTA (changes in persons carrying on a trade, and special rules for corporation tax).

(2) Relevant property is to be treated for the purposes of this Part as if—

    (a) it had been sold to the successor when the succession takes place, and

    (b) the net proceeds of the sale were the market value of the property.

(3) ''Relevant property'' means any property which—

    (a) immediately before the succession, was owned by the predecessor and was either in use or provided and available for use for the purposes of the discontinued qualifying activity, and

    (b) immediately after the succession, and without being sold, is either in use or provided and available for use for the purposes of the new qualifying activity.

(4) No entitlement to a first-year allowance arises under this section.

(5) In this section ''qualifying activity''—

    (a) does not include an employment or office, but

    (b) includes any other activity listed in section 15(1) even if any profits or gains from it are not chargeable to tax.

Commentary—*Simon's Direct Tax Service* **B2.390**.
Former enactments—Sub-ss (1), (2): CAA 1990 s 78(1).
Sub-s (3): CAA 1990 s 78(1); change in law.
Sub-s (4): CAA 1990 s 78(1).
Sub-s (5): CAA 1990 ss 78(5), 83(2A).
Modifications—CAA 2001 Sch 3 para 54 (vehicles provided by employees in 1990–91: see modification note at the start of this Part).
CAA 2001 Sch 3 para 55 (certain expenditure incurred before 6 April 1976: see modification note at the start of this Part).

266 Election where predecessor and successor are connected persons

(1) This section applies if a person (''the successor'') succeeds to a qualifying activity which was until that time carried on by another person (''the predecessor'') and—

    (a) the two persons are connected with each other,

    (b) each of them is within the charge to tax on the profits of the qualifying activity, and

    (c) the successor is not a dual resident investing company.

(2) If this section applies, the predecessor and the successor may jointly elect for the provisions of section 267 to have effect.

(3) The election may be made whether or not any plant or machinery has actually been sold or transferred.

(4) The election must be made by notice to the Inland Revenue within 2 years after the date on which the succession takes effect.

(5) For the purposes of this section, the predecessor and the successor are connected with each other if any of the following conditions is met—

(a) they would be treated as connected persons under section 839 of ICTA;
(b) one of them is a partnership and the other has the right to a share in that partnership;
(c) one of them is a body corporate and the other has control over that body;
(d) both of them are partnerships and another person has the right to a share in both of them;
(e) both of them are bodies corporate, or one of them is a partnership and the other is a body corporate, and (in either case) another person has control over both of them.

(6) In subsection (5) any reference to a right to a share in a partnership is to be read as a reference to a right to a share of the assets or income of the partnership.

(7) Sections 104, 108 and 265 (disposal value of long-life assets, effect of disposal to connected person on overseas leasing pool and general provisions about successions) do not apply if an election is made under this section.

(8) This section does not apply if section 561 applies (transfer of UK trade to a company in another member State).

Commentary—*Simon's Direct Tax Service* **B2.390**.
Former enactments—Sub-s (1): CAA 1990 s 77(3).
Sub-s (2): CAA 1990 s 77(3).
Sub-s (3): CAA 1990 s 77(4)(a).
Sub-s (4): CAA 1990 s 77(3).
Sub-s (5): CAA 1990 s 77(5).
Sub-s (6): CAA 1990 s 77(6).
Sub-s (7): CAA 1990 s 77(8).
Sub-s (8): CAA 1990 s 152B(10).
Revenue Internal Guidance—Capital allowances manual CA 29040 (explanation of this section: the provisions do not apply where the qualifying activity is special leasing).
Definition—"Dual resident investing company", s 577(1), TA 1988 s 404.
Modifications—CAA 2001 Sch 3 para 52 (sub-s (7) above does not apply if the succession occurred before 27 July 1989).
CAA 2001 Sch 3 para 54 (vehicles provided by employees in 1990–91: see modification note at the start of this Part).
CAA 2001 Sch 3 para 55 (certain expenditure incurred before 6 April 1976: see modification note at the start of this Part).

267 Effect of election

(1) If an election is made under section 266, the following provisions have effect.

(2) For the purposes of making allowances and charges under this Part, relevant plant or machinery is treated as sold by the predecessor to the successor—

(a) when the succession takes place, and
(b) at a price which gives rise to neither a balancing allowance nor a balancing charge.

(3) "Relevant plant or machinery" means any plant or machinery which—

(a) immediately before the succession, was owned by the predecessor, and was either in use or provided and available for use for the purposes of the qualifying activity, and
(b) immediately after the succession, is owned by the successor, and is either in use or provided and available for use for the purposes of the qualifying activity.

(4) Allowances and charges are to be made under this Part to or on the successor as if everything done to or by the predecessor had been done to or by the successor.

(5) All such assessments and adjustments of assessments are to be made as are necessary to give effect to the election.

Commentary—*Simon's Direct Tax Service* **B2.390**.
Former enactments—Sub-s (1): CAA 1990 s 77(4).
Sub-s (2): CAA 1990 s 77(4)(a); change in law.
Sub-s (3): CAA 1990 s 77(4)(a); change in law.
Sub-s (4): CAA 1990 s 77(4)(b).
Sub-s (5): CAA 1990 s 77(7).
Modifications—CAA 2001 Sch 3 para 54 (vehicles provided by employees in 1990–91: see modification note at the start of this Part).
CAA 2001 Sch 3 para 55 (certain expenditure incurred before 6 April 1976: see modification note at the start of this Part).

268 Successions by beneficiaries

(1) This section applies if—

(a) a person succeeds to a qualifying activity as a beneficiary under the will or on the intestacy of a deceased person who carried on the qualifying activity,
(b) the qualifying activity is treated as discontinued under section 113(1) of ICTA (changes in persons carrying on a trade etc), and
(c) the beneficiary elects by notice to the Inland Revenue for this section to apply.

(2) In relation to the succession and any previous succession occurring on or after the death of the deceased, relevant plant or machinery is treated as if it had been sold to the beneficiary when the succession takes place.

(3) The net proceeds of the sale are treated as being the lesser of—

(a) the market value of the plant or machinery, and
(b) the unrelieved qualifying expenditure which would have been taken into account in calculating the amount of a balancing allowance for the appropriate chargeable period if the disposal value of the plant or machinery had been nil.

"Appropriate chargeable period" means the chargeable period in which the deceased person's qualifying activity was permanently discontinued.

(4) "Relevant plant or machinery" means plant or machinery which—

(a) was previously owned by the deceased,
(b) passes to the beneficiary with the qualifying activity, and
(c) is either used or provided and available for use by the beneficiary for the purposes of the qualifying activity.

(5) Subsections (6) and (7) apply if the beneficiary is required to bring a disposal value into account in respect of relevant plant or machinery.

(6) The provisions limiting the amount of the disposal value of property, that is—

(a) section 62 (limit on disposal value: general), and
(b) section 239 (limit on disposal value where additional VAT rebate),

apply in relation to the beneficiary to limit the disposal value by reference to expenditure incurred by the deceased or additional VAT rebates made to the deceased.

(7) Section 73 (limit on disposal value: software and rights to software) applies as if the previous disposal values to be taken into account in determining whether the limit under those provisions is exceeded were those of the deceased.

(8) In this section "qualifying activity"—

(a) does not include an employment or office, but
(b) includes any other activity listed in section 15(1) even if any profits or gains from it are not chargeable to tax.

Commentary—*Simon's Direct Tax Service* B2.390.
Former enactments—Sub-s (1): CAA 1990 s 78(1), (2).
Sub-ss (2)–(4): CAA 1990 s 78(2).
Sub-ss (5)–(7): CAA 1990 s 78(2A).
Sub-s (8): CAA 1990 ss 78(5), 83(2A).
Revenue Internal Guidance—Capital allowances manual CA 29060 (surviving spouse succeeding to deceased's business: unrelieved capital allowances of deceased cannot be used by survivor).
Definitions—"Additional VAT rebate", s 547(2); "unrelieved qualifying expenditure", s 59.
Modifications—CAA 2001 Sch 3 para 53 (sub-ss (6), (7) above do not apply if the election under this section was made before 6 April 1990).
CAA 2001 Sch 3 para 54 (vehicles provided by employees in 1990–91: see modification note at the start of this Part).
CAA 2001 Sch 3 para 55 (certain expenditure incurred before 6 April 1976: see modification note at the start of this Part).

Miscellaneous

269 Use of plant or machinery for business entertainment

(1) If—

(a) a person carrying on a qualifying activity, or
(b) an employee of that person,

provides business entertainment in connection with that activity, the use of plant or machinery for providing the entertainment is to be treated as use for purposes other than those of that activity.

(2) For the purposes of this section—

(a) "entertainment" includes hospitality of any kind, and
(b) the use of an asset for providing entertainment includes the use of an asset for providing anything incidental to the entertainment.

(3) "Business entertainment" does not include anything provided by a person for employees unless its provision for them is incidental to its provision for others.

(4) "Business entertainment" does not include the use of plant or machinery for the provision of anything by a person if—

(a) it is a function of that person's qualifying activity to provide it, and
(b) it is provided by that person in the ordinary course of that qualifying activity—

(i) for payment, or
(ii) free of charge with the object of advertising to the public generally.

(5) For the purposes of this section—

(a) directors of a company, or
(b) persons engaged in the management of a company,

are to be regarded as employed by the company.

CAA 2001

Commentary—*Simon's Direct Tax Service* B2.305.
Former enactments—Sub-s (1): TA 1988 s 577(1)(c), (5), (7)(b), (c).
Sub-s (2): TA 1988 s 577(5), (7)(a).
Sub-s (3): TA 1988 s 577(5), (7)(c).
Sub-s (4): TA 1988 s 577(10).
Sub-s (5): TA 1988 s 577(7)(c).
Modifications—CAA 2001 Sch 3 para 54 (vehicles provided by employees in 1990–91: see modification note at the start of this
Part).
CAA 2001 Sch 3 para 55 (certain expenditure incurred before 6 April 1976: see modification note at the start of this Part).

270 Shares in plant or machinery

(1) This Part applies in relation to a share in plant or machinery as it applies (under section 571) in relation to a part of plant or machinery.

(2) For the purposes of this Part, a share in plant or machinery is treated as used for the purposes of a qualifying activity so long as, and only so long as, the plant or machinery is used for the purposes of the qualifying activity.

Commentary—*Simon's Direct Tax Service* B2.305.
Former enactments—CAA 1990 s 83(4).
Modifications—CAA 2001 Sch 3 para 54 (vehicles provided by employees in 1990–91: see modification note at the start of this
Part).
CAA 2001 Sch 3 para 55 (certain expenditure incurred before 6 April 1976: see modification note at the start of this Part).

PART 3
INDUSTRIAL BUILDINGS ALLOWANCES

Commentary—*Simon's Direct Tax Service* **Division B2.2**.
Modifications—CAA 2001 Sch 3 para 79 (where CAA 1990 s 21(9) (expenditure on preparatory work on land where building
used before 6 April 1956) applied to any expenditure immediately before the commencement of CAA 2001 Part 3, so that
CAA 1990 Part I (industrial buildings and structures) except for CAA 1990 s 1 (initial allowances) applied to part of the
expenditure separately from the remainder, Part 3 of this Act, except for Chapter 5, similarly applies to the part of the
expenditure separately from the remainder).

CHAPTER 1
INTRODUCTION

271 Industrial buildings allowances

(1) Allowances are available under this Part if—

  (a) expenditure has been incurred on the construction of a building or structure,
  (b) the building or structure is (or, in the case of an initial allowance, is to be)—

    (i) in use for the purposes of a qualifying trade,
    (ii) a qualifying hotel,
    (iii) a qualifying sports pavilion, or
    (iv) in relation to qualifying enterprise zone expenditure, a commercial building or structure, and

  (c) the expenditure incurred on the construction of the building or structure, or other expenditure, is qualifying expenditure.

(2) In the rest of this Part—

  (a) "building" is short for "building or structure", and
  (b) "industrial building" means, subject to Chapter 2 (which defines terms used in subsection (1)(b) etc), a building or structure which is within subsection (1)(b).

(3) Allowances under this Part are made to the person who for the time being has the relevant interest in the building (see Chapter 3) in relation to the qualifying expenditure (see Chapter 4).

Commentary—*Simon's Direct Tax Service* B2.201, 203, 205, 206, 206A.
Former enactments—Sub-s (1): CAA 1990 ss 1(1), (2), 3(1), 6(1), 7(1),14, 18(1).
Sub-s (3): CAA 1990 ss 1(1), 3(1), 10(1), (3), 10A(2), (9), 10B(2), (8).
Revenue Internal Guidance—Capital allowances manual CA 31050 (meaning of "building").
CA 31110 (meaning of and "structure").
CA 32000 (meaning of "industrial building").
Modification—CAA 2001 Sch 3 para 79 (expenditure on preparatory work on land where building used before 6 April 1956: see
modification note at the start of this Part).

272 Expenditure on the construction of a building

(1) For the purposes of this Part, expenditure on the construction of a building does not include expenditure on the acquisition of land or rights in or over land.

(2) This Part has effect in relation to capital expenditure incurred by a person on repairs to a part of a building as if it were capital expenditure on the construction of that part of the building for the first time.

(3) For the purposes of subsection (2), expenditure incurred for the purposes of a trade on repairs to a building is to be treated as capital expenditure if it is not expenditure that would be allowed to be deducted in calculating the profits of the trade for tax purposes.

Commentary—*Simon's Direct Tax Service* **B2.222**.
Former enactments—Sub-s (1): CAA 1990 s 21(1).
Sub-ss (2), (3): CAA 1990 s 12.
Revenue Internal Guidance—Capital allowances manual, CA 31400 (summaries of allowable expenditure incurred in the construction or buying of a building and expenditure that does not qualify).
CA 37150 (Revenue approach to cases where expenditure is incurred long after an enterprise zone has ended but under a contract entered into before zone designation ceased).
Definition—"Capital expenditure", s 4.
Modification—CAA 2001 Sch 3 para 79 (expenditure on preparatory work on land where building used before 6 April 1956: see modification note at the start of this Part).

273 Preparation of sites for plant or machinery

(1) Subsection (2) applies if—

(a) capital expenditure is or has been incurred in preparing, cutting, tunnelling or levelling land for the purposes of preparing the land as a site for the installation of plant or machinery, and
(b) no allowance could (apart from this section) be made in respect of that expenditure under this Part or Part 2 (plant and machinery allowances).

(2) This Part has effect in relation to the expenditure as if—

(a) the purpose of incurring the expenditure were to prepare the land as a site for the construction of a building, and
(b) the installed plant or machinery were a building.

Commentary—*Simon's Direct Tax Service* **B2.222**.
Former enactment—Sub-ss (1), (2): CAA 1990 s 13.
Definition—"Capital expenditure", s 4.
Modification—CAA 2001 Sch 3 para 79 (expenditure on preparatory work on land where building used before 6 April 1956: see modification note at the start of this Part).

CHAPTER 2
INDUSTRIAL BUILDINGS

Buildings in use for the purposes of a qualifying trade

274 Trades and undertakings which are "qualifying trades"

(1) "Qualifying trade" means—

(a) a trade of a kind described in Table A, or
(b) an undertaking of a kind described in Table B, if the undertaking is carried on by way of trade.

TABLE A
TRADES WHICH ARE "QUALIFYING TRADES"

1.	*Manufacturing*	A trade consisting of manufacturing goods or materials.
2.	*Processing*	A trade consisting of subjecting goods or materials to a process. This includes (subject to section 276(3)) maintaining or repairing goods or materials.
3.	*Storage*	A trade consisting of storing goods or materials— (a) which are to be used in the manufacture of other goods or materials, (b) which are to be subjected, in the course of a trade, to a process, (c) which, having been manufactured or produced or subjected, in the course of a trade, to a process, have not yet been delivered to any purchaser, or (d) on their arrival in the United Kingdom from a place outside the United Kingdom.
4.	*Agricultural contracting*	A trade consisting of— (a) ploughing or cultivating land occupied by another, (b) carrying out any other agricultural operation on land occupied by another, or (c) threshing another's crops. For this purpose "crops" includes vegetable produce.
5.	*Working foreign plantations*	A trade consisting of working land outside the United Kingdom used for— (a) growing and harvesting crops, (b) husbandry, or (c) forestry.

For this purpose "crops" includes vegetable produce and "harvesting crops" includes the collection of vegetable produce (however effected).

6. *Fishing*   A trade consisting of catching or taking fish or shellfish.

7. *Mineral extraction* A trade consisting of working a source of mineral deposits. "Mineral deposits" includes any natural deposits capable of being lifted or extracted from the earth, and for this purpose geothermal energy is to be treated as a natural deposit. "Source of mineral deposits" includes a mine, an oil well and a source of geothermal energy.

TABLE B

UNDERTAKINGS WHICH ARE "QUALIFYING TRADES" IF CARRIED ON BY WAY OF TRADE

1. *Electricity*   An undertaking for the generation, transformation, conversion, transmission or distribution of electrical energy.

2. *Water*   An undertaking for the supply of water for public consumption.

3. *Hydraulic power*   An undertaking for the supply of hydraulic power.

4. *Sewerage*   An undertaking for the provision of sewerage services within the meaning of the Water Industry Act 1991.

5. *Transport*   A transport undertaking.

6. *Highway undertak-*   A highway undertaking, that is, so much of any undertaking relating to the
    ings   design, building, financing and operation of roads as is carried on—
                          (a) for the purposes of, or
                          (b) in connection with,
                          the exploitation of highway concessions.

7. *Tunnels*   A tunnel undertaking.

8. *Bridges*   A bridge undertaking.

9. *Inland navigation*   An inland navigation undertaking.

10. *Docks*   A dock undertaking.
                          A dock includes—
                          (a) any harbour, and
                          (b) any wharf, pier, jetty or other works in or at which vessels can ship or unship merchandise or passengers,
                          other than a pier or jetty primarily used for recreation.

(2) Item 6 of Table B needs to be read with Chapter 9 (application of this Part to highway undertakings).

Commentary—*Simon's Direct Tax Service* **B2.203**.
Former enactments—Sub-s (1): CAA 1990 s 18(1), (9).
Table A, item 1: CAA 1990 s 18(1)(e).
Table A, item 2: CAA 1990 s 18(1)(e), (3).
Table A, item 3: CAA 1990 s 18(1)(f).
Table A, item 4: CAA 1990 s 18(1)(h).
Table A, item 5: CAA 1990 s 18(1)(g), (9), (10).
Table A, item 6: CAA 1990 s 18(1)(j).
Table A, item 7: CAA 1990 ss 18(1)(g), 161(2).
Table B, item 1: CAA 1990 s 18(1)(b), (9).
Table B, item 2: CAA 1990 s 18(1)(b), (9).
Table B, item 3: CAA 1990 s 18(1)(b), (9).
Table B, item 4: CAA 1990 s 18(1)(b), (9).
Table B, item 5: CAA 1990 s 18(1)(b).
Table B, item 6: CAA 1990 ss 18(1)(da), 21(5AA).
Table B, item 7: CAA 1990 s 18(1)(c).
Table B, item 8: CAA 1990 s 18(1)(d).
Table B, item 9: CAA 1990 s 18(1)(b).
Table B, item 10: CAA 1990 s 18(1)(b), (9).
Revenue Internal Guidance—Capital allowances manual, CA 32205 (general definitions of "qualifying trades")
CA 32210, 32212 (meaning of "goods or materials").
CA 32211 (cold stores are industrial buildings: some qualify for plant and machinery allowances – in those cases a choice can be made of which allowance to claim).
CA 32213 (meaning of "subjection to a process").
CA 32217 (application to television companies, recording companies and radio studios).
CA 32221 (vehicle repair workshops: whether industrial buildings).
CA 32224 (Revenue interpretation of the various storage trades).
CA 32225 (meaning of "agricultural contracting").

CA 32226 (meaning of "foreign plantation").
CA 32228 (meaning of "mineral extraction")
CA 32230 (meaning of "transport undertaking").
CA 32232 (meaning of "dock undertaking").
Modifications—CAA 2001 Sch 3 para 56 (Table B, item 8 above does not apply in relation to expenditure treated as incurred before the end of the tax year 1956–57).
CAA 2001 Sch 3 para 72(*a*) (for the purposes of CAA 2001 s 336, a building is not treated as having been an industrial building under Table A, item 5(*b*) or (*c*) above in relation to any tax year before 1953–54).
CAA 2001 Sch 3 para 72(*b*) (for the purposes of CAA 2001 s 336, a building is not treated as having been an industrial building under Table B, item 7 above in relation to any tax year before 1952–53).
CAA 2001 Sch 3 para 79 (expenditure on preparatory work on land where building used before 6 April 1956: see modification note at the start of this Part).

275 Building used for welfare of workers
A building is in use for the purposes of a qualifying trade if it is—

(*a*) provided by the person carrying on the qualifying trade for the welfare of workers employed in that qualifying trade, and
(*b*) in use for the welfare of such workers.

Commentary—*Simon's Direct Tax Service* B2.212.
Former enactment—CAA 1990 s 18(1).
Revenue Internal Guidance—Capital allowances manual CA 32320 (summary of situation where there is an excepted use exclusion or the building is used by both workers and office staff and/or management).
Definition—"Qualifying trade", s 274.
Modification—CAA 2001 Sch 3 para 79 (expenditure on preparatory work on land where building used before 6 April 1956: see modification note at the start of this Part).

276 Parts of trades and undertakings
(1) Sections 274 and 275 apply in relation to part of a trade or undertaking as they apply in relation to a trade or undertaking.

But this is subject to subsections (2) and (3).

(2) If—

(*a*) a building is in use for the purpose of a trade or undertaking, and
(*b*) part only of the trade or undertaking is a qualifying trade,

the building is in use for the purposes of the qualifying trade only if it is in use for the purposes of that part of the trade or undertaking.

(3) Maintaining or repairing goods or materials is not a qualifying trade if—

(*a*) the goods or materials are employed in a trade or undertaking,
(*b*) the maintenance or repair is carried out by the person employing the goods or materials, and
(*c*) the trade or undertaking is not itself a qualifying trade.

Commentary—*Simon's Direct Tax Service* **B2.207, 209**.
Former enactments—Sub-ss (1), (2): CAA 1990 s 18(2).
Sub-s (3): CAA 1990 s 18(3).
Revenue Internal Guidance—Capital allowances manual CA 32300 (where only part of a trade is a qualifying trade it should be a siginificant, separate and identifiable part of the trade carried on).
Definition—"Qualifying trade", s 274.
Modification—CAA 2001 Sch 3 para 79 (expenditure on preparatory work on land where building used before 6 April 1956: see modification note at the start of this Part).

277 Exclusion of dwelling-houses, retail shops, showrooms, hotels and offices etc
(1) A building is not in use for the purposes of a qualifying trade if it is in use as, or as part of, or for any purpose ancillary to the purposes of—

(*a*) a dwelling-house;
(*b*) a retail shop, or premises of a similar character where a retail trade or business (including repair work) is carried on;
(*c*) a showroom;
(*d*) a hotel;
(*e*) an office.

(2) Subsection (3) is about buildings constructed for occupation by, or for the welfare of persons employed—

(*a*) on, or in connection with, working land outside the United Kingdom which is used as described in item 5 of Table A in section 274 (foreign plantations), or
(*b*) at, or in connection with, working a source of mineral deposits as defined in item 7 of Table A (mineral extraction).

(3) Subsection (1) does not apply to a building which this subsection is about if the building—

(*a*) is likely to be of little or no value to the person carrying on the trade when the land or source is no longer worked, or
(*b*) will cease to be owned by that person on the ending of a foreign concession under which the land or source is worked.

CAA 2001

(4) "Foreign concession" means a right or privilege granted by the government of, or any municipality or other authority in, a territory outside the United Kingdom.

(5) Subsection (1) is subject to section 283 (non-industrial part of building disregarded).

Commentary—*Simon's Direct Tax Service* **B2.211, 212**.
Former enactments—Sub-s (1): CAA 1990 s 18(4), (9).
Sub-s (2): CAA 1990 s 18(5), (9), (10).
Sub-s (3): CAA 1990 s 18(5).
Sub-s (4): CAA 1990 s 161(2).
Sub-s (5): CAA 1990 s 18(4).
Revenue Internal Guidance—Capital allowances manual CA 32311 (meaning of "retail shop" and shop).
CA 32312 (meaning of office).
CA 32313 (meaning of "ancillary").
Definition—"Qualifying trade", s 274.
Modification—CAA 2001 Sch 3 para 79 (expenditure on preparatory work on land where building used before 6 April 1956: see modification note at the start of this Part).

278 Building used by more than one licensee

A building used by more than one licensee of the same person is not in use for the purposes of a qualifying trade unless each licensee uses it, or the part to which the licence relates, for the purposes of a qualifying trade.

Commentary—*Simon's Direct Tax Service* **B2.203**.
Former enactment—CAA 1990 s 18(6).
Revenue Internal Guidance—Capital allowances manual CA 32350 (operation of this section).
Definition—"Qualifying trade", s 274.
Modifications—CAA 2001 Sch 3 para 57 (the section above does not apply in relation to a licence granted before 10 March 1982).
CAA 2001 Sch 3 para 79 (expenditure on preparatory work on land where building used before 6 April 1956: see modification note at the start of this Part).

Qualifying hotels and sports pavilions

279 Qualifying hotels

(1) A hotel is a qualifying hotel if the following conditions are met—

(a) the accommodation in the hotel is in a building of a permanent nature,

(b) the hotel is open for at least 4 months during April to October, and

(c) when the hotel is open during April to October—

(i) it has 10 or more letting bedrooms,

(ii) the sleeping accommodation it offers consists wholly or mainly of letting bedrooms, and

(iii) the services provided for guests normally include the provision of breakfast and an evening meal, the making of beds and the cleaning of rooms.

(2) Whether a hotel meets the conditions in subsection (1)(b) and (c) at any time in a chargeable period is to be determined by reference to the period given under subsections (3) to (5) ("the reference period").

(3) If the hotel was in use for the purposes of a trade carried on by—

(a) the person claiming the allowance, or

(b) a lessee occupying the hotel under a lease to which the relevant interest is reversionary,

throughout the 12 month period ending with the last day of the chargeable period, the reference period is that 12 month period.

(4) If the hotel was first used for the purposes of a trade carried on as described in subsection (3) after the beginning of the 12 month period referred to there, the reference period is the 12 month period beginning with the date on which it was first so used.

(5) If a hotel does not qualify under subsection (3) because it had fewer than 10 letting bedrooms until too late a date, the reference period is the 12 month period beginning with the date when it had 10 or more letting bedrooms.

(6) A hotel is not to be treated as meeting the conditions in subsection (1)(b) and (c) at any time in a chargeable period after it has ceased altogether to be used.

(7) A building (whether or not on the same site as any other part of the hotel) which is—

(a) provided by the person carrying on the trade for the welfare of workers employed in the hotel, and

(b) in use for the welfare of such workers,

is to be treated for the purposes of this section as part of the hotel.

(8) If a qualifying hotel is carried on by an individual (alone or in partnership), accommodation which, when the hotel is open during April to October, is normally used as a dwelling by—

(a) that individual, or

(b) a member of his family or household,

is to be treated for the purposes of this section as not being part of the hotel.

(9) In this section—

"building" does not include a structure, and

"letting bedroom" means a private bedroom available for letting to the public generally and not normally in the same occupation for more than one month.

Commentary—*Simon's Direct Tax Service* **B2.252, 253**.
Former enactments—Sub-s (1): CAA 1990 s 19(1), (2).
Sub-ss (2)–(4): CAA 1990 s 19(3).
Sub-s (5): CAA 1990 s 19(4).
Sub-s (6): CAA 1990 s 19(3).
Sub-s (7): CAA 1990 s 19(5).
Sub-s (8): CAA 1990 s 19(5), (2).
Sub-s (9): CAA 1990 s 19(1), (2).
Revenue Internal Guidance—Capital allowances manual CA 32401 (construction expenditure incurred before 12 April 1978—see also Sch 3 para 58).
CA 32402 (staff accommodation and proprietors' accommodation).
Modifications—CAA 2001 Sch 3 para 58 (the section above does not apply in relation to expenditure on the construction of the building incurred before 12 April 1978.
For the purposes of sub-s (1) above, expenditure is not to be treated as having been incurred after the date on which it was in fact incurred by reason only of CAA 1990 s 10(1)).
CAA 2001 Sch 3 para 79 (expenditure on preparatory work on land where building used before 6 April 1956: see modification note at the start of this Part).

280 Qualifying sports pavilions

A building is a qualifying sports pavilion if it is—

(a) occupied by a person carrying on a trade, and
(b) used as a sports pavilion for the welfare of all or any of the workers employed in that trade.

Commentary—*Simon's Direct Tax Service* **B2.212**.
Former enactment—CAA 1990 s 14.
Modification—CAA 2001 Sch 3 para 79 (expenditure on preparatory work on land where building used before 6 April 1956: see modification note at the start of this Part).

Commercial buildings (enterprise zones)

281 Commercial buildings (enterprise zones)

For the purposes of this Part as it applies in relation to qualifying enterprise zone expenditure, "commercial building" means a building which is used—

(a) for the purposes of a trade, profession or vocation, or
(b) as an office or offices (whether or not for the purposes of a trade, profession or vocation),

and which is not in use as, or as part of, a dwelling-house.

Commentary—*Simon's Direct Tax Service* **B2.262**.
Former enactments—CAA 1990 ss 6(1), 21(5).
Revenue Internal Guidance—Capital allowances manual CA 37200 (meaning of "commercial building").
Modification—CAA 2001 Sch 3 para 79 (expenditure on preparatory work on land where building used before 6 April 1956: see modification note at the start of this Part).

Supplementary provisions

282 Buildings outside the United Kingdom

A building outside the United Kingdom which is in use for the purposes of a trade is not an industrial building at any time when the profits of the trade are not assessable in accordance with the rules applicable to Case I of Schedule D.

Commentary—*Simon's Direct Tax Service* **B2.252**.
Former enactments—CAA 1990 s 18(13), (14).
Modification—CAA 2001 Sch 3 para 79 (expenditure on preparatory work on land where building used before 6 April 1956: see modification note at the start of this Part).

283 Non-industrial part of building disregarded

(1) This section applies if, apart from this section, but taking into account section 571 (parts of buildings etc)—

(a) part of a building would be an industrial building, and
(b) part ("the non-industrial part") would not.

(2) If the qualifying expenditure relating to the non-industrial part is no more than 25% of the qualifying expenditure relating to the whole of the building, the whole of the building is an industrial building.

Commentary—*Simon's Direct Tax Service* **B2.252**.
Former enactments—CAA 1990 s 18(7), (14).
Revenue Internal Guidance—Capital allowances manual CA 32700 (in applying the 25 per cent rule total capital expenditure incurred on the construction of the building, whenever incurred, and compared with total capital expenditure on non-qualifying parts).
CA 32700 (expenditure on non-qualifying parts of a building incurred before 16 March 1983 qualified if it was less than 10 per cent of the total construction expenditure).
CA 32700 (building used for qualifying and non-qualifying purposes: allowance is due if qualifying expenditure relating to non-qualifying part is less than 25% of total qualifying expenditre on whole building).
Modifications—CAA 2001 Sch 3 para 59 (sub-s (2) above applies with the substitution of "10%" for "25%" in relation to expenditure incurred before 16 March 1983).

CAA 2001 Sch 3 para 79 (expenditure on preparatory work on land where building used before 6 April 1956: see modification note at the start of this Part).

284 Roads on industrial estates etc

(1) A road on an industrial estate is an industrial building if the estate consists wholly or mainly of buildings that are treated under this Part as industrial buildings.

(2) For the purposes of this Part as it applies in relation to qualifying enterprise zone expenditure, ''industrial estate'' includes an area (such as a business park) which consists wholly or mainly of commercial buildings.

Commentary—*Simon's Direct Tax Service* **B2.222**.
Former enactments—Sub-s (1): CAA 1990 s 18(8).
Sub-s (2): change in law.
Modification—CAA 2001 Sch 3 para 79 (expenditure on preparatory work on land where building used before 6 April 1956: see modification note at the start of this Part).

285 Cessation of use and temporary disuse of building

For the purposes of this Part—

(a) a building is not to be regarded as ceasing altogether to be used merely because it falls temporarily out of use, and

(b) if a building is an industrial building immediately before a period of temporary disuse, it is to be treated as being an industrial building during the period of temporary disuse.

Commentary—*Simon's Direct Tax Service* **B2.236, 339**.
Former enactments—Sub-ss (1), (2): CAA 1990 ss 6(1), 7(1), 15(1).
Revenue Internal Guidance—Capital allowances manual CA 32800 (meaning of temporary disuse).
Modification—CAA 2001 Sch 3 para 79 (expenditure on preparatory work on land where building used before 6 April 1956: see modification note at the start of this Part).

CHAPTER 3
THE RELEVANT INTEREST IN THE BUILDING

286 General rule as to what is the relevant interest

(1) The relevant interest in relation to any qualifying expenditure is the interest in the building to which the person who incurred the expenditure on the construction of the building was entitled when the expenditure was incurred.

(2) Subsection (1) is subject to the following provisions of this Chapter and to sections 342 (highway undertakings) and 359 (provisions applying on termination of lease).

(3) If—

(a) the person who incurred the expenditure on the construction of the building was entitled to more than one interest in the building when the expenditure was incurred, and

(b) one of those interests was reversionary on all the others,

the reversionary interest is the relevant interest.

Commentary—*Simon's Direct Tax Service* **B2.221**.
Former enactments—Sub-ss (1), (2): CAA 1990 s 20(1).
Sub-s (3): CAA 1990 s 20(2).
Modification—CAA 2001 Sch 3 para 79 (expenditure on preparatory work on land where building used before 6 April 1956: see modification note at the start of this Part).

287 Interest acquired on completion of construction

For the purposes of determining the relevant interest, a person who—

(a) incurs expenditure on the construction of a building, and

(b) is entitled to an interest in the building on or as a result of the completion of the construction,

is treated as having had that interest when the expenditure was incurred.

Commentary—*Simon's Direct Tax Service* **B2.221**.
Former enactment—CAA 1990 s 21(2).
Definition—''Expenditure on the construction of a building'', s 272.
Modification—CAA 2001 Sch 3 para 79 (expenditure on preparatory work on land where building used before 6 April 1956: see modification note at the start of this Part).

288 Effect of creation of subordinate interest

(1) An interest does not cease to be the relevant interest merely because of the creation of a lease or other interest to which that interest is subject.

(2) This is subject to any election under section 290.

Commentary—*Simon's Direct Tax Service* **B2.221, 225, 239**.
Former enactments—Sub-s (1): CAA 1990 s 20(3).
Sub-s (2): CAA 1990 s 11(5).
Modification—CAA 2001 Sch 3 para 79 (expenditure on preparatory work on land where building used before 6 April 1956: see modification note at the start of this Part).

289 Merger of leasehold interest

If the relevant interest is a leasehold interest which is extinguished on—

    (a) being surrendered, or

    (b) the person entitled to the interest acquiring the interest which is reversionary on it,

the interest into which the leasehold interest merges becomes the relevant interest when the leasehold interest is extinguished.

Commentary—*Simon's Direct Tax Service* **B2.221, 239**.
Former enactments—CAA 1990 s 20(3).
Modification—CAA 2001 Sch 3 para 79 (expenditure on preparatory work on land where building used before 6 April 1956: see modification note at the start of this Part).

290 Election to treat grant of lease exceeding 50 years as sale

(1) Subsection (2) applies if—

    (a) expenditure has been incurred on the construction of a building,

    (b) a lease of the building is granted out of the interest which is the relevant interest in relation to the expenditure,

    (c) the duration of the lease exceeds 50 years, and

    (d) the lessor and the lessee elect for subsection (2) to apply.

(2) This Part applies as if—

    (a) the grant of the lease were a sale of the relevant interest by the lessor to the lessee at the time when the lease takes effect,

    (b) any capital sum paid by the lessee in consideration for the grant of the lease were the purchase price on the sale, and

    (c) the interest out of which the lease was granted had at that time ceased to be, and the interest granted by the lease had at that time become, the relevant interest.

(3) The election has effect in relation to all the expenditure—

    (a) in relation to which the interest out of which the lease is granted is the relevant interest, and

    (b) which relates to the building (or buildings) that is (or are) the subject of the lease.

Commentary—*Simon's Direct Tax Service* **B2.225**.
Former enactments—Sub-s (1): CAA 1990 s 11(1), (4).
Sub-s (2): CAA 1990 s 11(1).
Sub-s (3): CAA 1990 s 11(2).
Revenue Internal Guidance—Capital allowances manual CA 33100 (explanation with worked example).
Definition—''Capital sum'', s 4.
Modification—CAA 2001 Sch 3 para 79 (expenditure on preparatory work on land where building used before 6 April 1956: see modification note at the start of this Part).

291 Supplementary provisions with respect to elections

(1) No election may be made under section 290 by a lessor and lessee who are connected persons unless—

    (a) the lessor is a body discharging statutory functions, and

    (b) the lessee is a company of which it has control.

(2) No election may be made under section 290 if it appears that the sole or main benefit which may be expected to accrue to the lessor from the grant of the lease and the making of an election is obtaining a balancing allowance.

(3) Whether the duration of a lease exceeds 50 years is to be determined—

    (a) in accordance with section 38(1) to (4) and (6) of ICTA, and

    (b) without regard to section 359(3) (new lease granted as a result of the exercise of an option treated as continuation of old lease).

(4) An election under section 290 must be made by notice to the Inland Revenue within 2 years after the date on which the lease takes effect.

(5) All such adjustments, by discharge or repayment of tax or otherwise, are to be made as are necessary to give effect to the election.

Commentary—*Simon's Direct Tax Service* **B2.225**.
Former enactments—Sub-ss (1), (2): CAA 1990 s 11(6).
Sub-s (3): CAA 1990 s 11(4).
Sub-ss (4), (5): CAA 1990 s 11(3).
Modification—CAA 2001 Sch 3 para 79 (expenditure on preparatory work on land where building used before 6 April 1956: see modification note at the start of this Part).

CHAPTER 4
QUALIFYING EXPENDITURE

Introduction

292 Meaning of ''qualifying expenditure''

In this Part ''qualifying expenditure'' means expenditure which is qualifying expenditure under—

section 294	capital expenditure on construction of a building
section 295	purchase of unused building where developer not involved
section 296	purchase of building which has been sold unused by developer
section 301	qualifying expenditure on sale within 2 years of first use where all of expenditure is qualifying enterprise zone expenditure
section 303	qualifying expenditure on sale within 2 years of first use where part of expenditure is qualifying enterprise zone expenditure.

Commentary—*Simon's Direct Tax Service* **B2.222**.

293 Meaning of references to carrying on a trade as a developer

For the purposes of this Chapter—

(a) a developer is a person who carries on a trade which consists in whole or in part in the construction of buildings with a view to their sale, and

(b) an interest in a building is sold by the developer in the course of the development trade if the developer sells it in the course of the trade or (as the case may be) that part of the trade that consists in the construction of buildings with a view to their sale.

Commentary—*Simon's Direct Tax Service* **B2.223**.
Former enactments—CAA 1990 ss 10(3), (4), 10A(9).
Modification—CAA 2001 Sch 3 para 79 (expenditure on preparatory work on land where building used before 6 April 1956: see modification note at the start of this Part).

Qualifying expenditure

294 Capital expenditure on construction of a building

If—

(a) capital expenditure is incurred on the construction of a building, and

(b) the relevant interest in the building has not been sold or, if it has been sold, it has been sold only after the first use of the building,

the capital expenditure is qualifying expenditure.

Commentary—*Simon's Direct Tax Service* **B2.222**.
Former enactments—CAA 1990 ss 1(1), 3(1), 6(1), 10(1)(a), 10A(1), (2)(a).
Definition—"Capital expenditure", s 4.
Modification—CAA 2001 Sch 3 para 79 (expenditure on preparatory work on land where building used before 6 April 1956: see modification note at the start of this Part).

295 Purchase of unused building where developer not involved

(1) This section applies if—

(a) expenditure is incurred on the construction of a building,

(b) the relevant interest in the building is sold before the building is first used,

(c) a capital sum is paid by the purchaser for the relevant interest, and

(d) section 296 (purchase of building which has been sold unused by developer) does not apply.

(2) The lesser of—

(a) the capital sum paid by the purchaser for the relevant interest, and

(b) the expenditure incurred on the construction of the building,

is qualifying expenditure.

(3) The qualifying expenditure is to be treated as incurred by the purchaser when the capital sum became payable.

(4) If the relevant interest is sold more than once before the building is first used, subsection (2) has effect only in relation to the last of those sales.

Commentary—*Simon's Direct Tax Service* **B2.223, 263A**.
Former enactments—Sub-s (1): CAA 1990 ss 10(1), (3), 10A(1), (9).
Sub-ss (2), (3): CAA 1990 ss 10(1), 10A(2).
Sub-s (4): CAA 1990 ss 10(2), 10A(8).
Revenue Internal Guidance—Capital allowances manual CA 33520 (explanation with worked example).
Definition—"Capital sum", s 4.
Modification—CAA 2001 Sch 3 para 79 (expenditure on preparatory work on land where building used before 6 April 1956: see modification note at the start of this Part).

296 Purchase of building which has been sold unused by developer

(1) This section applies if—

(a) expenditure is incurred by a developer on the construction of a building, and

(b) the relevant interest in the building is sold by the developer in the course of the development trade before the building is first used.

(2) If—

(a) the sale of the relevant interest by the developer was the only sale of that interest before the building is used, and (*b*) a capital sum is paid by the purchaser for the relevant interest,

the capital sum is qualifying expenditure.

(3) If—

(*a*) the sale by the developer was not the only sale before the building is used, and

(*b*) a capital sum is paid by the purchaser for the relevant interest on the last sale,

the lesser of that capital sum and the price paid for the relevant interest on its sale by the developer is qualifying expenditure.

(4) The qualifying expenditure is to be treated as incurred by the purchaser when the capital sum referred to in subsection (2)(*b*) or (3)(*b*) became payable.

Commentary—*Simon's Direct Tax Service* **B2.223**.
Former enactments—Sub-s (1): CAA 1990 ss 10., 10A(9).
Sub-ss (2), (3): CAA 1990 ss 10(1), (3), 10A(2), (9).
Sub-s (4): CAA 1990 ss 10(1), 10A(2).
Revenue Internal Guidance—Capital allowances manual CA 33520 (explanation with worked example).
Definition—"Capital sum", s 4.
Modification—CAA 2001 Sch 3 para 79 (expenditure on preparatory work on land where building used before 6 April 1956: see modification note at the start of this Part).

297 Purchase of used building from developer

(1) This section applies if—

(*a*) expenditure is incurred by a developer on the construction of a building, and

(*b*) the relevant interest is sold by the developer in the course of the development trade after the building has been used.

(2) This Part has effect in relation to the person to whom the relevant interest is sold as if—

(*a*) the expenditure on the construction of the building had been qualifying expenditure,

(*b*) all appropriate writing-down allowances had been made to the developer, and

(*c*) any appropriate balancing adjustment had been made on the occasion of the sale.

(3) This section is subject to sections 301 and 303 (purchase of building in enterprise zone within 2 years of first use).

Commentary—*Simon's Direct Tax Service* **B2.224**.
Former enactments—Sub-s (1): CAA 1990 s 10(4).
Sub-s (2): CAA 1990 s 10(5).
Sub-s (3): CAA 1990 s 10(4).
Revenue Internal Guidance—Capital allowances manual CA 33530 (application of this section).
Definitions—"Balancing adjustment", s 314; "enterprise zone", s 298.
Modifications—CAA 2001 Sch 3 para 60 (the section above does not apply if the purchase price on the sale by the developer in sub-s (1)(*b*) above became payable before 27 July 1989).
CAA 2001 Sch 3 para 79 (expenditure on preparatory work on land where building used before 6 April 1956: see modification note at the start of this Part).

Qualifying enterprise zone expenditure

298 The time limit for qualifying enterprise zone expenditure

(1) For the purposes of sections 299 to 304, the time limit for expenditure on the construction of a building on a site in an enterprise zone is—

(*a*) 10 years after the site was first included in the zone, or

(*b*) if the expenditure is incurred under a contract entered into within those 10 years, 20 years after the site was first included in the zone.

(2) In those sections "EZ building" is short for "building on a site in an enterprise zone".

(3) In this Part "enterprise zone" means an area designated as such by an order—

(*a*) made by the Secretary of State[, the Scottish Ministers or the National Assembly for Wales][1] under powers conferred by Schedule 32 to the Local Government, Planning and Land Act 1980, or

(*b*) in Northern Ireland, made by the Department of the Environment under Article 7 of the Enterprise Zones (Northern Ireland) Order 1981.

Commentary—*Simon's Direct Tax Service* **B2.261, 262**.
Former enactments—Sub-s (1): CAA 1990 ss 1(1), (11), 6(1), (4A), 10A(1), (7), (10), 10B(1), (9), (10).
Sub-s (3): CAA 1990 s 21(4).
Revenue Internal Guidance—Capital allowances manual CA 37150 (application of this section).
Definition—"Expenditure on the construction of a building", s 272.
Modification—CAA 2001 Sch 3 para 79 (expenditure on preparatory work on land where building used before 6 April 1956: see modification note at the start of this Part).
Amendments—[1] Words inserted by FA 2001 s 69, Sch 21 para 5 with effect as respects allowances and charges falling to be made for chargeable periods ending after 5 April 2001 (for income tax purposes) or 31 March 2001 (for corporation tax purposes).

299 Application of section 294

If—

(*a*) capital expenditure is incurred on the construction of an EZ building, and (*b*) the expenditure is incurred within the time limit,

the qualifying expenditure given by section 294 is qualifying enterprise zone expenditure.

Commentary—*Simon's Direct Tax Service* **B2.262**.
Former enactments—CAA 1990 ss 1(1), 6(1).
Definitions—"Capital expenditure", s 4; "enterprise zone", s 298.
Modification—CAA 2001 Sch 3 para 79 (expenditure on preparatory work on land where building used before 6 April 1956: see modification note at the start of this Part).

300 Application of sections 295 and 296

If—

(*a*) expenditure is incurred on the construction of an EZ building, and
(*b*) all the expenditure is incurred within the time limit,

any qualifying expenditure given by sections 295 and 296 in relation to that expenditure is qualifying enterprise zone expenditure.

Commentary—*Simon's Direct Tax Service* **B2.263A**.
Former enactments—CAA 1990 s 10A(1), (2), (8), (9).
Definition—"Enterprise zone", s 298.
Modifications—CAA 2001 Sch 3 para 61 (CAA 2001 ss 300, 302 do not apply where the purchase price payable on the sale of the relevant interest in the building before it was used, or if there was more than one such sale before the building was used, the purchase price payable on the last of those sales, became payable before 16 December 1991).
CAA 2001 Sch 3 para 79 (expenditure on preparatory work on land where building used before 6 April 1956: see modification note at the start of this Part).

301 Purchase of building within 2 years of first use

(1) This section applies if—

(*a*) expenditure is incurred on the construction of an EZ building,
(*b*) all the expenditure is incurred within the time limit,
(*c*) the relevant interest in the building is sold—

   (i) after the building has been used, but
   (ii) within the period of 2 years beginning with the date on which the building was first used, and

(*d*) that sale ("the relevant sale") is the first sale in that period after the building has been used.

(2) If this section applies—

(*a*) any balancing adjustment which falls to be made on the occasion of the relevant sale is to be made, and
(*b*) the residue of qualifying expenditure immediately after the relevant sale is to be disregarded for the purposes of this Part.

(3) If a capital sum is paid by the purchaser for the relevant interest on the relevant sale—

(*a*) the purchaser is to be treated as having incurred qualifying expenditure that is qualifying enterprise zone expenditure of an amount given in subsection (4), (6) or (7), and
(*b*) in relation to that qualifying enterprise zone expenditure, this Part applies as if the building had not been used before the date of the relevant sale.

(4) Unless subsection (6) or (7) applies, the amount of the qualifying enterprise zone expenditure is the lesser of—

(*a*) the capital sum paid by the purchaser for the relevant interest on the relevant sale, and
(*b*) the expenditure incurred on the construction of the building.

(5) Subsections (6) and (7) apply if—

(*a*) the expenditure incurred on the construction of the EZ building was incurred by a developer, and
(*b*) the relevant interest in the building has been sold by the developer in the course of the development trade.

(6) If the sale by the developer is the relevant sale, the amount of the qualifying enterprise zone expenditure is the capital sum paid by the purchaser for the relevant interest on that sale.

(7) If the sale by the developer is not the relevant sale, the amount of the qualifying enterprise zone expenditure is the lesser of—

(*a*) the capital sum paid by the purchaser for the relevant interest on the relevant sale, and
(*b*) the price paid for the relevant interest on its sale by the developer.

(8) The qualifying expenditure is to be treated as incurred when the capital sum on the relevant sale became payable.

Commentary—*Simon's Direct Tax Service* **B2.263B**.
Former enactments—Sub-s (1): CAA 1990 s 10B(1).
Sub-s (2): CAA 1990 s 10B(2).
Sub-s (3): CAA 1990 ss 1(1), 3(1), 6(1), 10B(2).
Sub-s (4): CAA 1990 s 10B(4), (5).
Sub-ss (5)–(7): CAA 1990 s 10B(8).
Sub-s (8): CAA 1990 s 10B(2)(*c*).

Revenue Internal Guidance—Capital allowances manual CA 37375 (a person who is the first one to buy a used building in an enterprise zone within two years of first use is treated as buying an unused building).
Definitions—"Capital sum", s 4; "enterprise zone", s 298.
Modifications—CAA 2001 Sch 3 para 62 (CAA 2001 ss 301, 303 and 304 do not apply in relation to buildings first used before 16 December 1991).
CAA 2001 Sch 3 para 63 (modification of sub-s (1)(*c*), (*d*) if—

(*a*) the relevant interest in a building was sold on a date falling after the end of the period of two years beginning with the date on which the building or structure was first used; and
(*b*) that period ended, and the date on which the relevant interest was transferred fell, within the period beginning with 13 January 1994 and ending with 31 August 1994.
CAA 2001 Sch 3 para 79 (expenditure on preparatory work on land where building used before 6 April 1956: see modification note at the start of this Part).

Part of expenditure within time limit for qualifying enterprise zone expenditure

302 Qualifying enterprise zone expenditure where section 295 or 296 applies

(1) This section applies if—
  (*a*) expenditure is incurred on the construction of an EZ building,
  (*b*) only a part of the expenditure is incurred within the time limit, and
  (*c*) the circumstances are as described in—
    (i) section 295(1) (purchase of unused building where developer not involved), or
    (ii) section 296(1) (purchase of building which has been sold unused by developer).

(2) Only a part of the qualifying expenditure given by section 295(2) or 296(2) or (3) (as the case may be) is qualifying enterprise zone expenditure.

(3) The part of the qualifying expenditure that is qualifying enterprise zone expenditure is—

$$QE \times \frac{E}{T}$$

where—
QE is the qualifying expenditure,
E is the part of the expenditure on the construction of the EZ building that is incurred within the time limit, and
T is the total expenditure on the construction of the building.

Commentary—*Simon's Direct Tax Service* B2.263A.
Former enactments—Sub-s (1): CAA 1990 s 10A(1), (9).
Sub-s (2): CAA 1990 s 10A(3), (6).
Sub-s (3): CAA 1990 s 10A(4), (5).
Revenue Internal Guidance—Capital allowances manual CA 37450 (explanation with worked example).
Definition—"Enterprise zone", s 298.
Modifications—CAA 2001 Sch 3 para 61 (CAA 2001 ss 300, 302 do not apply where the purchase price payable on the sale of the relevant interest in the building before it was used, or if there was more than one such sale before the building was used, the purchase price payable on the last of those sales, became payable before 16 December 1991).
CAA 2001 Sch 3 para 63 (modification of sub-s (1)(*c*), (*d*) if—

(*a*) the relevant interest in a building was sold on a date falling after the end of the period of two years beginning with the date on which the building or structure was first used; and
(*b*) that period ended, and the date on which the relevant interest was transferred fell, within the period beginning with 13 January 1994 and ending with 31 August 1994.
CAA 2001 Sch 3 para 79 (expenditure on preparatory work on land where building used before 6 April 1956: see modification note at the start of this Part).

303 Purchase of building within 2 years of first use

(1) This section applies if—
  (*a*) expenditure is incurred on the construction of an EZ building,
  (*b*) only a part of the expenditure is incurred within the time limit,
  (*c*) the relevant interest in the building is sold—
    (i) after the building has been used, but
    (ii) within the period of 2 years beginning with the date on which the building was first used, and
  (*d*) that sale ("the relevant sale") is the first sale in that period after the building has been used.

(2) If this section applies—
  (*a*) any balancing adjustment which falls to be made on the occasion of the relevant sale is to be made, and
  (*b*) the residue of qualifying expenditure immediately after the relevant sale is to be disregarded for the purposes of this Part.

(3) If a capital sum is paid by the purchaser for the relevant interest on the relevant sale—
  (*a*) the purchaser is to be treated as having incurred qualifying expenditure—
    (i) part of which is qualifying enterprise zone expenditure ("Z"), and
    (ii) part of which is not ("N"), and
  (*b*) in relation to that qualifying expenditure, this Part applies as if the building had not been used before the date of the relevant sale.

(4) Unless section 304 (cases where developer involved) applies—

$$Z - L \times \frac{E}{T}$$

and

$$N = L - Z$$

where—

L is the lesser of—

    (a) the capital sum paid for the relevant interest on the relevant sale, and
    (b) the expenditure incurred on the construction of the building,

E is the part of the expenditure on the construction of the EZ building that is incurred within the time limit, and
T is the total expenditure on the construction of the building.

(5) Any qualifying expenditure arising under this section or section 304 is to be treated as incurred when the capital sum on the relevant sale became payable.

Commentary—*Simon's Direct Tax Service* **B2.263B**.
Former enactments—Sub-s (1): CAA 1990 s 10B(1).
Sub-s (2): CAA 1990 s 10B(2).
Sub-s (3): CAA 1990 ss 1(1), 3(1), 6(1), 10B(2), (3).
Sub-s (4): CAA 1990 s 10B(4), (5), (6), (7), (8).
Sub-s (5): CAA 1990 s 10B(2).
Definitions—''Balancing adjustment'', s 314; ''capital sum'', s 4; ''enterprise zone'', s 298.
Modifications—CAA 2001 Sch 3 para 62 (CAA 2001 ss 301, 303 and 304 do not apply in relation to buildings first used before 16 December 1991).
CAA 2001 Sch 3 para 63 (modification of sub-s (1)(c), (d)).
CAA 2001 Sch 3 para 79 (expenditure on preparatory work on land where building used before 6 April 1956: see modification note at the start of this Part).

304 Application of section 303 where developer involved

(1) This section applies if section 303 applies but—

    (a) the expenditure on the construction of the building was incurred by a developer, and
    (b) the relevant interest in the building has been sold by the developer in the course of the development trade;

and in this section Z, N, E and T have the same meaning as in section 303.

(2) If the sale by the developer is the relevant sale—

$$Z = C \times \frac{E}{T}$$

and

$$N = L - L \times \frac{E}{T}$$

where—

C is the capital sum paid for the relevant interest by the purchaser, and
L is the lesser of—

    (a) the capital sum paid for the relevant interest on the relevant sale, and
    (b) the expenditure incurred on the construction of the building.

(3) If the sale by the developer is not the relevant sale—

$$Z = D \times \frac{E}{T}$$

and

$$N = D - Z$$

where D is the lesser of—

    (a) the price paid for the relevant interest on its sale by the developer, and
    (b) the capital sum paid for the relevant interest on the relevant sale.

Commentary—*Simon's Direct Tax Service* **B2.263B**.
Former enactment—Sub-ss (1)–(3): CAA 1990 s 10B(8).
Definition—''Capital sum'', s 4.
Modification—CAA 2001 Sch 3 para 62 (CAA 2001 ss 301, 303 and 304 do not apply in relation to buildings first used before 16 December 1991).
CAA 2001 Sch 3 para 79 (expenditure on preparatory work on land where building used before 6 April 1956: see modification note at the start of this Part).

CHAPTER 5
INITIAL ALLOWANCES

305 Initial allowances for qualifying enterprise zone expenditure

(1) A person who has incurred qualifying enterprise zone expenditure is entitled to an initial allowance in respect of the expenditure if the building on which the expenditure is incurred is to be an industrial building—

    (*a*) occupied by that person or a qualifying lessee, or

    (*b*) used by a qualifying licensee.

(2) In this section—

    "qualifying lessee" means a lessee under a lease to which the relevant interest is reversionary, and

    "qualifying licensee" means a licensee of—

       (*a*) the person incurring the qualifying expenditure, or

       (*b*) a lessee of the person incurring the qualifying expenditure.

Commentary—*Simon's Direct Tax Service* **B2.232**.
Former enactments—Sub-s (1): CAA 1990 s 1(1), (4).
Sub-s (2): CAA 1990 s 1(3), (4).
Revenue Internal Guidance—Capital allowances manual CA 34050 (explanation of this section).
Definition—"Enterprise zone", s 298.
Modification—CAA 2001 Sch 3 para 64 (sub-s (1)(*b*) above does not apply in relation to a licence granted before 10 March 1982).

306 Amount of initial allowance and period for which allowance made

(1) The amount of the initial allowance is 100% of the qualifying enterprise zone expenditure.

(2) A person claiming an initial allowance under this section may require the allowance to be reduced to a specified amount.

(3) The initial allowance is made for the chargeable period in which the qualifying expenditure is incurred.

(4) For the purposes of subsection (3), expenditure incurred for the purposes of a trade, profession or vocation by a person about to carry it on is to be treated as if it had been incurred on the first day on which the person carries on the trade, profession or vocation.

Commentary—*Simon's Direct Tax Service* **B2.232, 261, 264**.
Former enactments—Sub-s (1): CAA 1990 s 1(1).
Sub-s (2): CAA 1990 s 1(5).
Sub-s (3): CAA 1990 s 1(1), 161(2).
Sub-s (4): CAA 1990 s 1(10). Change in law.

307 Building not industrial building when first used etc

(1) No initial allowance is to be made under section 305 if, when the building is first used, it is not an industrial building.

(2) An initial allowance which has been made in respect of a building which is to be an industrial building is to be withdrawn if, when the building is first used, it is not an industrial building.

(3) An initial allowance which has been made in respect of a building which has not been used is to be withdrawn if the person to whom the allowance was made sells the relevant interest before the building is first used.

(4) All such assessments and adjustments of assessments are to be made as are necessary to give effect to this section.

Commentary—*Simon's Direct Tax Service* B2.232.
Former enactments—Sub-ss (1), (2): CAA 1990 s 1(6).
Sub-s (3): CAA 1990 ss 10(1)(*a*), 10A(2)(*a*).
Sub-s (4): CAA 1990 s 1(6).

308 Grants affecting entitlement to initial allowances

(1) No initial allowance is to be made in respect of expenditure to the extent that it is taken into account for the purposes of a relevant grant or relevant payment made towards that expenditure.

(2) A grant or payment is relevant if it is—

    (*a*) a grant made under section 32, 34 or 56(1) of the Transport Act 1968,

    (*b*) a payment made under section 56(2) of the Transport Act 1968, or

    (*c*) a grant made under section 101 of the Greater London Authority Act 1999,

which is declared by the Treasury by order to be relevant for the purposes of the withholding of initial allowances.

(3) If a relevant grant or relevant payment towards the expenditure is made after the making of an initial allowance, the allowance is to be withdrawn to that extent.

(4) If the amount of the grant or payment is repaid by the grantee to the grantor, in whole or in part, the grant or payment is treated, to that extent, as never having been made.

(5) All such assessments and adjustments of assessments are to be made as are necessary to give effect to subsection (3) or (4).

(6) Any such assessment or adjustment is not out of time if it is made within 3 years of the end of the chargeable period in which the grant, payment or repayment was made.

Commentary—*Simon's Direct Tax Service* **B2.264**.
Former enactments—Sub-ss (1), (2): CAA 1990 s 1(7).
Sub-ss (3), (4): CAA 1990 s 1(8).
Sub-ss (5), (6): CAA 1990 s 1(9).
Modification—CAA 2001 Sch 3 para 65 (sub-s (2)(*c*) above applies as if the reference to a grant under the Greater London Authority Act 1999 s 101 included a reference to a grant under the London Regional Transport Act 1984 s 12 or the Transport (London) Act 1969 s 3).

CHAPTER 6
WRITING-DOWN ALLOWANCES

309 Entitlement to writing-down allowance

(1) A person is entitled to a writing-down allowance for a chargeable period if—

    (*a*) qualifying expenditure has been incurred on a building,

    (*b*) at the end of that chargeable period, the person is entitled to the relevant interest in the building in relation to that expenditure, and

    (*c*) at the end of that chargeable period, the building is an industrial building.

(2) A person claiming a writing-down allowance may require the allowance to be reduced to a specified amount.

Commentary—*Simon's Direct Tax Service* **B2.234**.
Former enactments—Sub-s (1): CAA 1990 s 3(1).
Sub-s (2): change in law.
Modification—CAA 2001 Sch 3 para 79 (expenditure on preparatory work on land where building used before 6 April 1956: see modification note at the start of this Part).

310 Basic rule for calculating amount of allowance

(1) The basic rule is that the writing-down allowance for a chargeable period is—

    (*a*) in the case of qualifying enterprise zone expenditure, 25% of the expenditure, and

    (*b*) in the case of other qualifying expenditure, 4% of the expenditure.

(2) The allowance is proportionately increased or reduced if the chargeable period is more or less than a year.

(3) This basic rule does not apply if section 311 applies.

Commentary—*Simon's Direct Tax Service* **B2.231, 254**.
Former enactments—Sub-s (1): CAA 1990 ss 3(2), 6(2).
Sub-s (2): CAA 1990 s 3(2).
Revenue Internal Guidance—Capital allowances manual CA 31205, 34510 (operation of this section).
Definition—"Enterprise zone", s 298.
Modifications—CAA 2001 Sch 3 para 66 (sub-s (1)(*b*) above applies with the substitution of "2%" for "4%" in relation to expenditure incurred before 6 November 1962).
CAA 2001 Sch 3 para 79 (expenditure on preparatory work on land where building used before 6 April 1956: see modification note at the start of this Part).

311 Calculation of allowance after sale of relevant interest

(1) If a relevant event occurs, the writing-down allowance for any chargeable period ending after the event is—

$$\text{RQE} \times \frac{A}{B}$$

where—

    RQE is the amount of the residue of qualifying expenditure immediately after the event,

    A is the length of the chargeable period, and

    B is the length of the period from the date of the event to the end of the period of 25 years beginning with the day on which the building was first used.

(2) On any later relevant event, the writing-down allowance is further adjusted in accordance with this section.

(3) "Relevant event" means—

    (*a*) a sale of the relevant interest in the building which is a balancing event to which section 314 applies, or

    (*b*) an event which is a relevant event for the purposes of this section under section 347 or 349 (additional VAT liabilities and rebates).

Commentary—*Simon's Direct Tax Service* **B2.234, 239**.
Former enactments—Sub-ss (1)–(3): CAA 1990 s 3(2B), (2C), (3).
Revenue Internal Guidance—Capital allowances manual CA 31205, 34510 (operation of this section).
Definitions—"Enterprise zone", s 298; "residue of qualifying expenditure", s 313.

Modifications—CAA 2001 Sch 3 para 67 (sub-s (1) above applies with the substitution (in the definition of "B") of "50 years" for "25 years" in relation to expenditure incurred before 6 November 1962).
CAA 2001 Sch 3 para 79 (expenditure on preparatory work on land where building used before 6 April 1956: see modification note at the start of this Part).

312 Allowance limited to residue of qualifying expenditure

(1) The amount of the writing-down allowance for a chargeable period is limited to the residue of qualifying expenditure.

(2) For this purpose the residue is ascertained immediately before writing off the writing-down allowance at the end of the chargeable period.

Commentary—*Simon's Direct Tax Service* **B2.234, 239**.
Former enactment—Sub-ss (1), (2): CAA 1990 s 3(4).
Modification—CAA 2001 Sch 3 para 79 (expenditure on preparatory work on land where building used before 6 April 1956: see modification note at the start of this Part).

313 Meaning of "the residue of qualifying expenditure"

The residue of qualifying expenditure is the qualifying expenditure that has not yet been written off in accordance with Chapter 8.

Commentary—*Simon's Direct Tax Service* **B2.235**.
Former enactment—CAA 1990 s 8(1).
Modification—CAA 2001 Sch 3 para 79 (expenditure on preparatory work on land where building used before 6 April 1956: see modification note at the start of this Part).

CHAPTER 7
BALANCING ADJUSTMENTS
General

314 When balancing adjustments are made

(1) A balancing adjustment is made if—
　(a) qualifying expenditure has been incurred on a building, and
　(b) a balancing event occurs while the building is an industrial building or after it has ceased to be an industrial building.

(2) A balancing adjustment is either a balancing allowance or a balancing charge and is made for the chargeable period in which the balancing event occurs.

(3) A balancing allowance or balancing charge is made to or on the person entitled to the relevant interest in the building immediately before the balancing event.

(4) No balancing adjustment is made if the balancing event occurs more than 25 years after the building was first used.

(5) If more than one balancing event within section 315(1) occurs during a period when the building is not an industrial building, a balancing adjustment is made only on the first of them.

Commentary—*Simon's Direct Tax Service* **B2.237**.
Former enactments—Sub-ss (1)–(3): CAA 1990 ss 4(1), 161(2) ("chargeable period").
Sub-s (4), (5): CAA 1990 s 4(2).
Revenue Internal Guidance—Capital allowances manual CA 35050 (operation of this section).
Definition—"Balancing event", s 315.
Modifications—CAA 2001 Sch 3 para 68 (sub-s (4) above applies with the substitution of "50 years" for "25 years" in relation to qualifying expenditure incurred before 6 November 1962).
CAA 2001 Sch 3 para 79 (expenditure on preparatory work on land where building used before 6 April 1956: see modification note at the start of this Part).

315 Main balancing events

(1) The following are balancing events for the purposes of this Part—
　(a) the relevant interest in the building is sold;
　(b) if the relevant interest is a lease, the lease ends otherwise than on the person entitled to it acquiring the interest reversionary on it;
　(c) the building is demolished or destroyed;
　(d) the building ceases altogether to be used (without being demolished or destroyed);
　(e) if the relevant interest depends on the duration of a foreign concession, the concession ends.

(2) "Foreign concession" means a right or privilege granted by the government of, or any municipality or other authority in, a territory outside the United Kingdom.

(3) Other balancing events are provided for by—
　section 328 (realisation of capital value where site of building is in enterprise zone);
　section 343 (ending of highway concession);
　section 350 (additional VAT rebates and balancing adjustments);
and a balancing event under this section may also occur as a result of section 317 (hotel not qualifying hotel for 2 years).

Commentary—*Simon's Direct Tax Service* **B2.237**.
Former enactments—Sub-s (1): CAA 1990 s 4(1).
Sub-s (2): CAA 1990 s 161(2) ("foreign concession").
Revenue Internal Guidance—Capital allowances manual CA 35050 (application of this section).
CA 35050 (meaning of "ceases altogether to be used").
Definition—"Balancing adjustment", s 314.
Modification—CAA 2001 Sch 3 para 79 (expenditure on preparatory work on land where building used before 6 April 1956: see modification note at the start of this Part).

316 Proceeds from main balancing events

(1) References in this Part to the proceeds from a balancing event within section 315(1) are to the amounts received or receivable in connection with the event, as shown in the Table—

TABLE
BALANCING EVENTS AND PROCEEDS

1. Balancing event	2. Proceeds from event
1. The sale of the relevant interest.	The net proceeds of the sale.
2. The demolition or destruction of the building.	The net amount received for the remains of the building, together with— (a) any insurance money received in respect of the demolition or destruction, and (b) any other compensation of any description so received, so far as it consists of capital sums.
3. The building ceases altogether to be used.	Any compensation of any description received in respect of the event, so far as it consists of capital sums.
4. A foreign concession ends.	Any compensation payable in respect of the relevant interest.

(2) The amounts referred to in column 2 of the Table are those received or receivable by the person whose entitlement to a balancing allowance or liability to a balancing charge is in question.

Commentary—*Simon's Direct Tax Service* **B2.237**.
Former enactments—Sub-ss (1), (2): CAA 1990 s 156(a)–(d).
Definition—"Balancing event", s 315.
Modification—CAA 2001 Sch 3 para 79 (expenditure on preparatory work on land where building used before 6 April 1956: see modification note at the start of this Part).

317 Balancing event where hotel not qualifying hotel for 2 years

(1) This section applies if—
  (a) a building ceases to be a qualifying hotel otherwise than on the occurrence of a balancing event which is within section 315(1), and
  (b) after the building ceases to be a qualifying hotel, a period of 2 years elapses—
    (i) in which it is not a qualifying hotel, and
    (ii) without the occurrence of a balancing event.

(2) This Part has effect as if—
  (a) the relevant interest in the building had been sold at the end of the 2 year period, and
  (b) the net proceeds of the sale were equal to the market value of that interest.

(3) Subsection (2) does not affect section 285 (building treated as industrial building during period of temporary disuse).

(4) But a building is not to be treated under section 285(b) as continuing to be a qualifying hotel for more than 2 years after the end of the chargeable period in which it falls temporarily out of use.

(5) This section does not apply to qualifying enterprise zone expenditure.

Commentary—*Simon's Direct Tax Service* **B2.251, 253, 254**.
Former enactments—Sub-ss (1), (2): CAA 1990 s 7(1).
Sub-ss (3), (4): CAA 1990 s 7(2).
Sub-s (5): CAA 1990 s 6(3).
Definitions—"Balancing event", s 315; "qualifying hotel", s 279.
Modification—CAA 2001 Sch 3 para 79 (expenditure on preparatory work on land where building used before 6 April 1956: see modification note at the start of this Part).

Calculation of balancing adjustments

318 Building an industrial building etc throughout

(1) This section provides for balancing adjustments where the building was—
  (a) an industrial building, or
  (b) used for research and development,
for the whole of the relevant period of ownership.

(2) A balancing allowance is made if—

(*a*) there are no proceeds from the balancing event, or
(*b*) the proceeds from the balancing event are less than the residue of qualifying expenditure immediately before the event.

(3) The amount of the balancing allowance is the amount of—

(*a*) the residue (if there are no proceeds);
(*b*) the difference (if the proceeds are less than the residue).

(4) A balancing charge is made if the proceeds from the balancing event are more than the residue, if any, of qualifying expenditure immediately before the event.

(5) The amount of the balancing charge is the amount of—

(*a*) the difference, or
(*b*) the proceeds (if the residue is nil).

Commentary—*Simon's Direct Tax Service* **B2.237**.
Former enactments—Sub-s (1): CAA 1990 s 4(5).
Sub-ss (2), (3): CAA 1990 s 4(3).
Sub-ss (4), (5): CAA 1990 s 4(4).
Definitions—''Balancing adjustment'', s 314; ''balancing event'', s 315; ''residue of qualifying expenditure'', s 313.
Modification—CAA 2001 Sch 3 para 79 (expenditure on preparatory work on land where building used before 6 April 1956: see modification note at the start of this Part).

319 Building not an industrial building etc throughout

(1) This section provides for balancing adjustments where the building was not—

(*a*) an industrial building, or
(*b*) used for research and development,

for a part of the relevant period of ownership.

(2) A balancing allowance is made if—

(*a*) there are no proceeds from the balancing event or the proceeds are less than the starting expenditure, and
(*b*) the net allowances made are less than the adjusted net cost of the building.

(3) The amount of the balancing allowance is the amount of the difference between the adjusted net cost of the building and the net allowances made.

(4) A balancing charge is made if the proceeds from the balancing event are equal to or more than the starting expenditure.

(5) The amount of the balancing charge is an amount equal to the net allowances made.

(6) A balancing charge is also made if—

(*a*) there are no proceeds from the balancing event or the proceeds are less than the starting expenditure, and
(*b*) the net allowances made are more than the adjusted net cost of the building.

(7) The amount of the balancing charge is the amount of the difference between the net allowances made and the adjusted net cost of the building.

Commentary—*Simon's Direct Tax Service* **B2.238**.
Former enactments—Sub-s (1): CAA 1990 s 4(5).
Sub-ss (2), (3): CAA 1990 s 4(7).
Sub-ss (4), (5): CAA 1990 s 4(6).
Sub-ss (6), (7): CAA 1990 s 4(7).
Revenue Internal Guidance—Capital allowances manual CA 35100 (explanation with worked example).
Definitions—''Adjusted net cost'', s 323; ''balancing adjustment'', s 314; ''balancing event'', s 315.
Modification—CAA 2001 Sch 3 para 79 (expenditure on preparatory work on land where building used before 6 April 1956: see modification note at the start of this Part).

320 Overall limit on balancing charge

The amount of a balancing charge made on a person must not exceed the amount of the net allowances made.

Commentary—*Simon's Direct Tax Service* **B2.239**.
Former enactment—CAA 1990 s 4(10).
Modification—CAA 2001 Sch 3 para 79 (expenditure on preparatory work on land where building used before 6 April 1956: see modification note at the start of this Part).

Meaning of ''the relevant period of ownership'' etc

321 The relevant period of ownership

The relevant period of ownership is the period beginning—

(*a*) with the day on which the building was first used for any purpose, or
(*b*) if the relevant interest has been sold after that day, with the day following that on which the sale (or the last such sale) occurred,

and ending with the day on which the balancing event occurs.

CAA 2001

Commentary—*Simon's Direct Tax Service* **B2.238**.
Former enactment—CAA 1990 s 4(9) (''the relevant period'').
Definition—''Balancing event'', s 315.
Modification—CAA 2001 Sch 3 para 79 (expenditure on preparatory work on land where building used before 6 April 1956: see modification note at the start of this Part).

322 Starting expenditure

(1) This section gives the starting expenditure for the purposes of this Chapter.

(2) If the person to or on whom the balancing allowance or balancing charge falls to be made is the person who incurred the qualifying expenditure, that expenditure is the starting expenditure.

(3) Otherwise, the starting expenditure is the residue of qualifying expenditure at the beginning of the relevant period of ownership.

(4) If section 340 (treatment of demolition costs) applies, the starting expenditure is increased by an amount equal to the net cost of the demolition.

Commentary—*Simon's Direct Tax Service* **B2.238**.
Former enactment—Sub-ss (1)–(4): CAA 1990 s 4(9) (''the capital expenditure'').
Definitions—''Capital expenditure'', s 4; ''residue of qualifying expenditure'', s 313.
Modification—CAA 2001 Sch 3 para 79 (expenditure on preparatory work on land where building used before 6 April 1956: see modification note at the start of this Part).

323 Adjusted net cost

The amount of the adjusted net cost is—

$$(S - P) \times \frac{I}{R}$$

where—

S is the starting expenditure,
P is the amount of any proceeds from the balancing event,
I is the number of days in the relevant period of ownership on which the building was an industrial building or used for research and development, and
R is the number of days in the whole of the relevant period of ownership.

Commentary—*Simon's Direct Tax Service* **B2.238**.
Former enactment—CAA 1990 s 4(9) (''the adjusted net cost'').
Definition—''Balancing event'', s 315.
Modification—CAA 2001 Sch 3 para 79 (expenditure on preparatory work on land where building used before 6 April 1956: see modification note at the start of this Part).

324 Net allowances

For the purposes of this Chapter, the amount of the net allowances made, in relation to any qualifying expenditure, is—

$$(I + WDA + RDA) - B$$

where—

I is the amount of any initial allowances made to the person in relation to that qualifying expenditure,
WDA is the amount of any writing-down allowances made to the person for chargeable periods ending on or before the date of the balancing event giving rise to the balancing adjustment,
RDA is the amount of any allowances under Part 6 (research and development allowances) made to the person for such chargeable periods, and
B is the amount of any balancing charges made on the person for such chargeable periods.

Commentary—*Simon's Direct Tax Service* **B2.238**.
Former enactment—CAA 1990 s 4(10).
Definitions—''Balancing adjustment'', s 314; ''balancing event'', s 315.
Modifications—CAA 2001 Sch 3 para 69 (the section above applies in relation to a mills, factories or exceptional depreciation allowance as it applies in relation to an allowance of any kind mentioned in that section).
CAA 2001 Sch 3 para 79 (expenditure on preparatory work on land where building used before 6 April 1956: see modification note at the start of this Part).

Balancing allowances restricted where sale subject to subordinate interest

325 Balancing allowances restricted where sale subject to subordinate interest

(1) This section applies if—

   (*a*) the relevant interest in a building is sold subject to a subordinate interest,

   (*b*) the person entitled to the relevant interest immediately before the sale (''the former owner'') would, apart from this section, be entitled to a balancing allowance under this Chapter as a result of the sale, and

   (*c*) condition A or B is met.

(2) Condition A is that—

   (*a*) the former owner,

(b) the person who acquires the relevant interest, and
(c) the person to whom the subordinate interest was granted,

or any two of them, are connected persons.

(3) Condition B is that it appears that the sole or main benefit which might have been expected to accrue to the parties or any of them from the sale or the grant, or transactions including the sale or grant, was the obtaining of an allowance under this Part.

(4) For the purpose of deciding what balancing adjustment is to be made in a case to which this section applies, the net proceeds to the former owner of the sale are to be increased—

(a) by an amount equal to any premium receivable by him for the grant of the subordinate interest, and
(b) if no rent, or no commercial rent, is payable in respect of the subordinate interest, by the amount by which the proceeds would have been greater if a commercial rent had been payable and the relevant interest had been sold in the open market.

(5) But the net proceeds of the sale are not to be treated as being greater than the amount which secures that no balancing allowance is made.

(6) If the terms on which a subordinate interest is granted are varied before the sale of the relevant interest—

(a) any capital consideration for the variation is to be treated for the purposes of this section as a premium for the grant of the interest, and
(b) the question whether any, and if so what, rent is payable in respect of the interest is to be determined by reference to the terms in force immediately before the sale.

(7) If this section applies in relation to a sale to deny or reduce a balancing allowance, the residue of qualifying expenditure immediately after the sale is nevertheless calculated as if the balancing allowance had been made or not reduced.

Commentary—*Simon's Direct Tax Service* **B2.243**.
Former enactments—Sub-ss (1)–(3): CAA 1990 s 5(1).
Sub-ss (4), (5): CAA 1990 s 5(2).
Sub-s (6): CAA 1990 s 5(5).
Sub-s (7): CAA 1990 s 5(3).
Revenue Internal Guidance—Capital allowances manual CA 35300 (background and worked examples).
Definitions—"Balancing adjustment", s 314; "residue of qualifying expenditure", s 313.
Modification—CAA 2001 Sch 3 para 79 (expenditure on preparatory work on land where building used before 6 April 1956: see modification note at the start of this Part).

326 Interpretation of section 325

(1) In section 325—

"commercial rent" means such rent as may reasonably be expected to have been required in respect of the subordinate interest (having regard to any premium payable for the grant of the interest) if the transaction had been at arm's length;
"premium" includes any capital consideration, except so much of any sum as corresponds to an amount of rent or profits falling to be calculated by reference to that sum under section 34 of ICTA;
"subordinate interest" means an interest in or right over the building, whether granted by the former owner or anyone else.

(2) In section 325 and this section—

"capital consideration" means consideration which consists of a capital sum or would be a capital sum if it had consisted of a money payment, and
"rent" includes any consideration which is not capital consideration.

Commentary—*Simon's Direct Tax Service* **B2.243**.
Former enactment—CAA 1990 s 5(4).
Definition—"Capital sum", s 4.
Modification—CAA 2001 Sch 3 para 79 (expenditure on preparatory work on land where building used before 6 April 1956: see modification note at the start of this Part).

Qualifying enterprise zone expenditure: effect of realising capital value

327 Capital value provisions: application of provisions

Sections 328 to 331 apply only if expenditure on the construction of a building has been incurred—

(a) at a time—
  (i) when the site of the building was wholly or mainly in an enterprise zone, and
  (ii) which was not more than 10 years after the site was first included in the zone, or

(b) under a contract entered into at such a time.

Commentary—*Simon's Direct Tax Service* **B2.264A**.
Former enactment—FA 1994 s 120(7), (8).
Revenue Internal Guidance—Capital allowances manual CA 37705–37760 (realisation of capital value from buildings in enterprise zones).
Definition—"Expenditure on the construction of a building", s 272.

Modification—CAA 2001 Sch 3 para 79 (expenditure on preparatory work on land where building used before 6 April 1956: see modification note at the start of this Part).

328 Balancing adjustment on realisation of capital value

(1) There is a balancing event if, while the building is an industrial building or after it has ceased to be one, any capital value is realised.

(2) No balancing allowance is to be made because of a balancing event under this section.

(3) The amount of capital value realised is to be treated as the proceeds from the balancing event.

(4) If a balancing event under this section occurs—

(a) section 319 (balancing adjustment where building not an industrial building etc throughout) has effect as if, immediately after the balancing event, the starting expenditure were reduced by the amount of capital value realised, and

(b) if the net proceeds of a sale of the relevant interest fall to be increased under section 325(4) (balancing allowances restricted where sale subject to subordinate interest), those proceeds as so increased are reduced by the amount of any capital value realised before the sale.

(5) Capital value is realised if an amount of capital value is paid which is attributable to an interest in land ("the subordinate interest") to which the relevant interest in the building is or will be subject.

(6) The capital value is realised on the making of the payment.

(7) The amount of capital value realised is the amount of capital value that is attributable to the subordinate interest under section 329.

Commentary—*Simon's Direct Tax Service* **B2.264, 264A**.
Former enactments—Sub-s (1): CAA 1990 s 4(1).
Sub-ss (2), (3): CAA 1990 s 4(9A).
Sub-s (4): CAA 1990 ss 4(9A), 5(2A).
Sub-ss (5)–(7): CAA 1990 s 4A(1).
Revenue Internal Guidance—Capital allowances manual CA 37710 (application of this section).
Definition—"Balancing adjustment", s 314.
Modifications—CAA 2001 Sch 3 para 71 (CAA 2001 ss 328–331 do not apply if the capital expenditure referred to in CAA 2001 s 327 was incurred under a contract entered into before 13 January 1994, which was not a conditional contract which became unconditional on or after 26 February 1994).
CAA 2001 Sch 3 para 79 (expenditure on preparatory work on land where building used before 6 April 1956: see modification note at the start of this Part).

329 Capital value that is attributable to subordinate interest

(1) Capital value is attributable to the subordinate interest if it is paid—

(a) in consideration of the grant of the subordinate interest,

(b) instead of any rent payable by the person entitled to the subordinate interest,

(c) in consideration of the assignment of such rent, or

(d) in consideration of—

(i) the surrender of the subordinate interest, or

(ii) the variation or waiver of any of the terms on which it was granted.

(2) If—

(a) no premium is given in consideration of the grant of the subordinate interest or any premium so given is less than the commercial premium, and

(b) no commercial rent is payable in respect of the subordinate interest,

capital value is attributable under subsection (1)(a) as if the commercial premium had been paid on and in consideration of the grant of the subordinate interest.

(3) If any value given instead of any rent payable by the person entitled to the subordinate interest is less than the commercial amount, capital value is attributable under subsection (1)(b) as if the commercial amount had been paid.

(4) If—

(a) any rent payable in respect of the subordinate interest is assigned, but

(b) no value is given in consideration of the assignment or any value so given is less than the commercial amount,

capital value is attributable under subsection (1)(c) as if the commercial amount had been given on and in consideration of the assignment.

(5) If—

(a) the subordinate interest is surrendered, or any of the terms on which the subordinate interest was granted are varied or waived, but

(b) no value is given in consideration of the surrender, variation or waiver or any value so given is less than the commercial amount,

capital value is attributable under subsection (1)(d) as if the commercial amount had been given on and in consideration of the surrender, variation or waiver.

(6) Capital value is not attributable to the subordinate interest if it is paid in consideration of the grant of a lease to which an election under section 290 (treating grant of lease exceeding 50 years as sale) applies.

Commentary—*Simon's Direct Tax Service* **B2.264A**.
Former enactments—Sub-s (1): CAA 1990 s 4A(2).
Sub-s (2): CAA 1990 s 4A(4).
Sub-s (3): CAA 1990 s 4A(6).
Sub-ss (4), (5): CAA 1990 s 4A(5).
Sub-s (6): CAA 1990 s 4A(8).
Modifications—CAA 2001 Sch 3 para 71 (CAA 2001 ss 328–331 do not apply if the capital expenditure referred to in CAA 2001 s 327 was incurred under a contract entered into before 13 January 1994, which was not a conditional contract which became unconditional on or after 26 February 1994).
CAA 2001 Sch 3 para 79 (expenditure on preparatory work on land where building used before 6 April 1956: see modification note at the start of this Part).

330 Exception for payments more than 7 years after agreement

(1) Capital value is not realised for the purposes of section 328 if the payment is made more than 7 years after—

    (*a*) the agreement under which the qualifying expenditure was incurred was entered into, or
    (*b*) if that agreement was conditional, the time when the agreement became unconditional.

(2) If an agreement is made to pay in respect of any event an amount of capital value which would be attributable to the subordinate interest, and—

    (*a*) the agreement is made, or if conditional becomes unconditional, before the end of the period of 7 years referred to in subsection (1), and
    (*b*) the event occurs, or any payment in consideration of the event is made, after the end of that period,

the event or payment is treated for the purposes of subsection (1) as occurring or made before the end of the 7 years.

(3) Subsection (1) does not apply if arrangements—

    (*a*) under which the person entitled to the relevant interest acquired it, or
    (*b*) which were made in connection with its acquisition,

include provision which requires, or makes substantially more likely, any of the events set out in subsection (4).

(4) The events are—

    (*a*) the subsequent sale of the relevant interest;
    (*b*) the subsequent grant of an interest in land out of the relevant interest;
    (*c*) any other event on which capital value attributable to the subordinate interest would be paid or treated as paid.

Commentary—*Simon's Direct Tax Service* **B2.264A**.
Former enactments—Sub-s (1): CAA 1990 s 4A(1).
Sub-s (2): CAA 1990 s 4A(11).
Sub-ss (3), (4): CAA 1990 s 4A(7).
Modifications—CAA 2001 Sch 3 para 71 (CAA 2001 ss 328–331 do not apply if the capital expenditure referred to in CAA 2001 s 327 was incurred under a contract entered into before 13 January 1994, which was not a conditional contract which became unconditional on or after 26 February 1994).
CAA 2001 Sch 3 para 79 (expenditure on preparatory work on land where building used before 6 April 1956: see modification note at the start of this Part).

331 Capital value provisions: interpretation

(1) ''Capital value'' means any capital sum—

    (*a*) including what would have been a capital sum if it had been a money payment (and references to payment are to be read accordingly), but
    (*b*) excluding so much of any sum as corresponds to an amount of rent or profits calculated by reference to that sum under section 34 of ICTA (premiums etc treated as rent).

(2) ''Interest in land'' means—

    (*a*) a leasehold estate in the land, whether in the nature of a head lease, sub-lease or under-lease;
    (*b*) an easement or servitude;
    (*c*) a licence to occupy land.

(3) References to granting an interest in land include agreeing to grant any such interest.

(4) In section 329—

''commercial amount'' means the amount that would have been given if the transaction had been at arm's length,

''commercial premium'' means the premium that would have been given if the transaction had been at arm's length, and

''commercial rent'' means such rent as may reasonably be expected to have been required in respect of the subordinate interest (having regard to any premium paid in consideration of the grant of the interest) if the transaction had been at arm's length.

(5) In the application of section 329 to Scotland, references to assignment are to be read as references to assignation.

Commentary—*Simon's Direct Tax Service* **B2.264A**.
Former enactments—Sub-s (1): CAA 1990 4A(3).

Sub-ss (2), (3): CAA 1990 s 4A(9).
Sub-s (4): CAA 1990 s 4A(4)–(6), (10).
Sub-s (5): CAA 1990 s 4A(13).
Revenue Internal Guidance—Capital allowances manual CA 37730 (meaning of "interest in land", "commercial amount", "commercial premium" and "commercial rent").
Definition—"Capital sum", s 4.
Modifications—CAA 2001 Sch 3 para 71 (CAA 2001 ss 328–331 do not apply if the capital expenditure referred to in CAA 2001 s 327 was incurred under a contract entered into before 13 January 1994, which was not a conditional contract which became unconditional on or after 26 February 1994).
CAA 2001 Sch 3 para 79 (expenditure on preparatory work on land where building used before 6 April 1956: see modification note at the start of this Part).

CHAPTER 8
WRITING OFF QUALIFYING EXPENDITURE

332 Introduction

For the purposes of this Part qualifying expenditure is written off to the extent and at the times specified in this Chapter.

Commentary—*Simon's Direct Tax Service* **B2.235**.
Former enactment—CAA 1990 s 8(1); change in law.
Modification—CAA 2001 Sch 3 para 79 (expenditure on preparatory work on land where building used before 6 April 1956: see modification note at the start of this Part).

333 Writing off initial allowances

If an initial allowance is made in respect of the qualifying expenditure, the amount of the allowance is written off at the time when the building is first used.

Commentary—*Simon's Direct Tax Service* **B2.235**.
Former enactment—CAA 1990 s 8(2).
Modification—CAA 2001 Sch 3 para 79 (expenditure on preparatory work on land where building used before 6 April 1956: see modification note at the start of this Part).

334 Writing off writing-down allowances

(1) If a writing-down allowance is made in respect of the qualifying expenditure, the amount of the allowance is written off at the end of the chargeable period for which the allowance is made.

(2) If a balancing event occurs at the end of the chargeable period referred to in subsection (1), the amount written off under that subsection is to be taken into account in calculating the residue of qualifying expenditure immediately before the event to determine what balancing adjustment (if any) is to be made.

Commentary—*Simon's Direct Tax Service* **B2.235**.
Former enactments—Sub-s (1): CAA 1990 s 8(3).
Sub-s (2): CAA 1990 s 8(4).
Definitions—"Balancing adjustment", s 314; "balancing event", s 315; "residue of qualifying expenditure", s 313.
Modification—CAA 2001 Sch 3 para 79 (expenditure on preparatory work on land where building used before 6 April 1956: see modification note at the start of this Part).

335 Writing off research and development allowances

(1) If an allowance under Part 6 (research and development allowances) is made in respect of the qualifying expenditure, the amount of the allowance is written off at the end of the chargeable period for which the allowance is made.

(2) If a balancing event occurs at the end of the chargeable period referred to in subsection (1), the amount written off under that subsection is to be taken into account in calculating the residue of qualifying expenditure immediately before that event to determine what balancing adjustment (if any) is to be made.

Commentary—*Simon's Direct Tax Service* **B2.235, 239**.
Former enactments—Sub-s (1): CAA 1990 s 8(5); change in law.
Sub-s (2): CAA 1990 s 8(6).
Definitions—"Balancing adjustment", s 314; "balancing event", s 315; "residue of qualifying expenditure", s 313.
Modification—CAA 2001 Sch 3 para 79 (expenditure on preparatory work on land where building used before 6 April 1956: see modification note at the start of this Part).

336 Writing off expenditure when building not an industrial building

(1) This section applies if for any period or periods between—
  (a) the time when the building was first used for any purpose, and
  (b) the time when the residue of qualifying expenditure falls to be ascertained,
the building was not an industrial building.

(2) An amount equal to the notional writing-down allowances for the period or periods is written off at the time when the residue falls to be ascertained.

(3) The notional writing-down allowances are the allowances that would have been made for the period or periods in question (if the building had remained an industrial building), at such rate or rates as would have been appropriate having regard to any relevant sale.

(4) In subsection (3) "relevant sale" means a sale of the relevant interest as a result of which a balancing adjustment falls to be made under section 314.

Commentary—*Simon's Direct Tax Service* **B2.235, 238**.
Former enactment—CAA 1990 s 8(7).
Definitions—"Balancing adjustment", s 314; "residue of qualifying expenditure", s 313.
Modifications—CAA 2001 Sch 3 para 72 (see modification notes for CAA 2001 s 274).
CAA 2001 Sch 3 para 79 (expenditure on preparatory work on land where building used before 6 April 1956: see modification note at the start of this Part).

337 Writing off or increase of expenditure where balancing adjustment made

(1) This section applies if the relevant interest in the building is sold.

(2) If a balancing allowance is made, the amount by which the residue of qualifying expenditure before the sale exceeds the net proceeds of the sale is written off at the time of the sale.

(3) If a balancing charge is made, the amount of the residue of qualifying expenditure is increased at the time of the sale by the amount of the charge.

(4) But if the balancing charge is made under section 319(6) (difference between net allowances made and adjusted net cost), the residue of qualifying expenditure immediately after the sale is limited to the net proceeds of the sale.

Commentary—*Simon's Direct Tax Service* **B2.235**.
Former enactments—Sub-s (1): CAA 1990 s 8(9)–(11).
Sub-s (2): CAA 1990 s 8(9).
Sub-s (3): CAA 1990 s 8(10).
Sub-s (4): CAA 1990 s 8(11).
Definitions—"Balancing adjustment", s 314; "residue of qualifying expenditure", s 313.
Modification—CAA 2001 Sch 3 para 79 (expenditure on preparatory work on land where building used before 6 April 1956: see modification note at the start of this Part).

338 Writing off capital value which has been realised

If a balancing event within section 328 occurs (realisation of capital value), an amount equal to any capital value realised is written off at the time of the event.

Commentary—*Simon's Direct Tax Service* **B2.264A**.
Former enactment—CAA 1990 s 8(12B).
Modification—CAA 2001 Sch 3 para 79 (expenditure on preparatory work on land where building used before 6 April 1956: see modification note at the start of this Part).

339 Crown or other person not within the charge to tax entitled to the relevant interest

(1) This section applies if at any time—

  (a) the Crown, or
  (b) a person who is not within the charge to tax,

("A") is entitled to the relevant interest in a building.

(2) Sections 333 to 338 (writing off qualifying expenditure) have effect as if all writing-down allowances and balancing adjustments had been made as could have been made if—

  (a) a person ("B") who—
    (i) is not the Crown,
    (ii) is within the charge to tax, and
    (iii) is not a company,
  had been entitled to the relevant interest, and
  (b) the other assumptions in subsection (3) had been made.

(3) The assumptions are that—

  (a) while A was entitled to the relevant interest, all things which were done in relation to the building—
    (i) by or to A, or
    (ii) by or to a person using the building under the authority of A,
  were done by or to B for the purposes of, and in the course of, a trade carried on by B,
  (b) any sale of the relevant interest in the building by or on behalf of A was made in connection with the termination of the trade carried on by B, and
  (c) B's periods of account for that trade had, in the case of each tax year, ended immediately before the beginning of the next tax year.

Commentary—*Simon's Direct Tax Service* **B2.235**.
Former enactments—Sub-ss (1), (2): CAA 1990 s 8(13), (14).
Sub-s (3): CAA 1990 s 8(13), (14).
Definition—"Balancing adjustment", s 314.
Modifications—CAA 2001 Sch 3 para 73 (the section above does not apply by virtue of sub-s (1)(b) above if the interest was sold before 29 July 1998).

CAA 2001 Sch 3 para 79 (expenditure on preparatory work on land where building used before 6 April 1956: see modification note at the start of this Part).

340 Treatment of demolition costs

(1) This section applies if—

(a) a building is demolished, and

(b) the person to or on whom any balancing allowance or balancing charge is or might be made is the person incurring the cost of the demolition.

(2) The net cost of the demolition is added to the residue of qualifying expenditure immediately before the demolition.

(3) "The net cost of the demolition" means the amount, if any, by which the cost of the demolition exceeds any money received for the remains of the property.

(4) If this section applies, neither the cost of the demolition nor the net cost of the demolition is treated for the purposes of any Part of this Act other than Part 10 (assured tenancy allowances) as expenditure on any other property replacing the property demolished.

Commentary—*Simon's Direct Tax Service* B2.227, 239.
Former enactment—CAA 1990 s 8(12).
Definition—"Residue of qualifying expenditure", s 313.
Modification—CAA 2001 Sch 3 para 79 (expenditure on preparatory work on land where building used before 6 April 1956: see modification note at the start of this Part).

CHAPTER 9
HIGHWAY UNDERTAKINGS

341 Carrying on of highway undertakings

(1) For the purposes of this Part the carrying on of a highway undertaking is to be treated as the carrying on of an undertaking by way of trade; and accordingly references in this Part (except sections 274 and 276) to a trade include a highway undertaking.

(2) For the purposes of this Part a person carrying on a highway undertaking is to be treated as occupying, for the purposes of the undertaking, any road in relation to which it is carried on.

(3) In this Chapter "highway undertaking" has the meaning given in item 6 of Table B in section 274.

(4) In that item and this Chapter "highway concession", in relation to a road, means—

(a) a right to receive sums from [the relevant authority][1] because the road is or will be used by the general public, or

(b) if the road is a toll road, the right to charge tolls in respect of the road.

[(5) In subsection (4) "the relevant authority" means—

(a) the Secretary of State,

(b) the Scottish Ministers,

(c) the National Assembly for Wales, or

(d) the Department for Regional Development in Northern Ireland.][1]

Commentary—*Simon's Direct Tax Service* B2.206A.
Former enactments—Sub-s (1): CAA 1990 s 21(5A).
Sub-s (2): CAA 1990 s 21(5B).
Sub-s (4): CAA 1990 s 21(5AA).
Modifications—CAA 2001 Sch 3 para 74 (CAA 2001 ss 341(4)(a), 343 and 344 do not apply in relation to expenditure incurred before 6 April 1995).
CAA 2001 Sch 3 para 79 (expenditure on preparatory work on land where building used before 6 April 1956: see modification note at the start of this Part).
Amendments—[1] Words in sub-s (4) substituted, and sub-s (5) inserted, by FA 2001 s 69, Sch 21 para 6 with effect as respects allowances and charges falling to be made for chargeable periods ending after 5 April 2001 (for income tax purposes) or 31 March 2001 (for corporation tax purposes).

342 The relevant interest

(1) For the purposes of Chapter 3 (the relevant interest in the building) as it applies to expenditure incurred on the construction of a road, a highway concession is not to be treated as an interest in the road.

(2) But if the person who incurred the expenditure on the construction of the road—

(a) was not entitled to an interest in the road when he incurred the expenditure, but

(b) was at that time entitled to a highway concession in respect of the road,

the highway concession is to be treated as the relevant interest in relation to that expenditure.

(3) Any question as to what is the relevant interest is to be determined on the assumption that, if section 344 (renewed or new concession treated as extension of earlier concession) applies, the renewed or new concession is a continuation of the earlier concession.

Commentary—*Simon's Direct Tax Service* B2.206A, 237.
Former enactments—Sub-s (1): CAA 1990 s 20(5).
Sub-s (2): CAA 1990 s 20(6).

Sub-s (3): CAA 1990 s 4(2AB).
Definition—''Highway concession'', s 341(4).
Modification—CAA 2001 Sch 3 para 79 (expenditure on preparatory work on land where building used before 6 April 1956: see modification note at the start of this Part).

343 Balancing adjustment on ending of concession

(1) If—

    (a) the relevant interest is a highway concession, and

    (b) the concession is brought to or comes to an end without being treated as extended under section 344,

the ending of the concession is a balancing event.

(2) The proceeds from such a balancing event are—

    (a) any insurance money received by the person entitled to the highway concession in respect of any qualifying expenditure, and

    (b) other compensation so received so far as it consists of capital sums.

Commentary—*Simon's Direct Tax Service* **B2.206A, 237**.
Former enactments—Sub-s (1): CAA 1990 s 4(1), (2AA).
Sub-s (2): CAA 1990 s 156.
Definitions—''Balancing adjustment'', s 314; ''highway concession'', s 341(4).
Modifications—CAA 2001 Sch 3 para 74 (CAA 2001 ss 341(4)(a), 343 and 344 do not apply in relation to expenditure incurred before 6 April 1995).
CAA 2001 Sch 3 para 79 (expenditure on preparatory work on land where building used before 6 April 1956: see modification note at the start of this Part).

344 Cases where highway concession is to be treated as extended

(1) A highway concession in respect of a road is to be treated as extended if—

    (a) the person entitled to the concession takes up a renewed concession in respect of the whole or a part of the road, or

    (b) that person or a person connected with him takes up a new concession in respect of—

        (i) the whole or a part of the road, or

        (ii) a road that includes the whole or a part of the road.

(2) But the concession is to be treated as extended only—

    (a) to the extent that the concession which has in fact ended, and the renewed or new concession, relate to the same road, and

    (b) for the period of the renewed or new concession.

(3) A person takes up a renewed or new concession if he is afforded, whether or not under legally enforceable arrangements, an opportunity to be granted the renewed or new concession and takes advantage of the opportunity.

(4) For the purposes of subsection (3) it does not matter whether the renewed or new concession is on the same terms as the previous concession or on modified terms.

(5) If—

    (a) a highway concession is treated as extended under this section, and

    (b) the period of the extension is different in relation to different parts of the road in relation to which the concession has been granted,

such apportionments are to be made for the purposes of section 343 as are just and reasonable.

Commentary—*Simon's Direct Tax Service* **B2.206A, 237**.
Former enactments—Sub-ss (1)–(4): CAA 1990 s 4(2AB).
Sub-s (5): CAA 1990 s 4(2AA).
Definition—''Highway concession'', s 341(4).
Modifications—CAA 2001 Sch 3 para 74 (CAA 2001 ss 341(4)(a), 343 and 344 do not apply in relation to expenditure incurred before 6 April 1995).
CAA 2001 Sch 3 para 79 (expenditure on preparatory work on land where building used before 6 April 1956: see modification note at the start of this Part).

CHAPTER 10
ADDITIONAL VAT LIABILITIES AND REBATES
Introduction

345 Introduction

For the purposes of this Chapter—

    (a) ''additional VAT liability'' and ''additional VAT rebate'' have the meaning given by section 547,

    (b) the time when—

        (i) a person incurs an additional VAT liability, or

        (ii) an additional VAT rebate is made to a person,

    is given by section 548, and

(*c*) the chargeable period in which, and the time when, an additional VAT liability or an additional VAT rebate accrues are given by section 549.

Commentary—*Simon's Direct Tax Service* **B2.262**.
Revenue Internal Guidance—Capital allowances manual CA 39050 (background to the capital goods scheme adjustments).

Additional VAT liabilities

346 Additional VAT liabilities and initial allowances

(1) This section applies if—

(*a*) a person was entitled to an initial allowance in respect of qualifying enterprise zone expenditure,

(*b*) the person entitled to the relevant interest in relation to that expenditure incurs an additional VAT liability in respect of that expenditure,

(*c*) the additional VAT liability is incurred at a time when the building is, or is to be, an industrial building—

    (i) occupied by the person entitled to the relevant interest or a qualifying lessee, or

    (ii) used by a qualifying licensee, and

(*d*) the additional VAT liability is incurred not more than 10 years after the site of the building was first included in the enterprise zone.

(2) If this section applies, the person entitled to the relevant interest is entitled to an initial allowance on the amount of the additional VAT liability.

(3) The amount of the initial allowance is 100% of the amount of the additional VAT liability.

(4) A person claiming an initial allowance under this section may require the allowance to be reduced to a specified amount.

(5) The allowance is made for the chargeable period in which the additional VAT liability accrues.

(6) The persons mentioned in subsection (1)(*a*) and (*b*) need not be the same.

Commentary—*Simon's Direct Tax Service* **B2.262**.
Former enactments—Sub-ss (1)–(3): CAA 1990 s 1(1A).
Sub-s (4): CAA 1990 s 1(5).
Sub-s (5): CAA 1990 ss 1(1A), 159A(3).
Definition—''Additional VAT liability'', s 547(1).
Modification—CAA 2001 Sch 3 para 79 (expenditure on preparatory work on land where building used before 6 April 1956: see modification note at the start of this Part).

347 Additional VAT liabilities and writing-down allowances

(1) This section applies if the person entitled to the relevant interest in relation to qualifying expenditure incurs an additional VAT liability in respect of that expenditure.

(2) If this section applies—

(*a*) the additional VAT liability is treated as qualifying expenditure, and

(*b*) the amount of the residue of qualifying expenditure is accordingly increased at the time when the liability accrues by the amount of the liability.

(3) The incurring of the additional VAT liability is a relevant event for the purposes of section 311 (calculation of writing-down allowances) that is to be treated as occurring at the time when the liability accrues.

Commentary—*Simon's Direct Tax Service* **B2.234**.
Former enactments—Sub-s (1): CAA 1990 s 3(2A).
Sub-s (2): CAA 1990 ss 3(2A), 159A(3).
Sub-s (3): CAA 1990 ss 3(2B), 159A(3).
Revenue Internal Guidance—Capital allowances manual CA 39200 (explanation with worked example).
Definitions—''Additional VAT liability'', s 547(1); ''residue of qualifying expenditure'', s 313.
Modification—CAA 2001 Sch 3 para 79 (expenditure on preparatory work on land where building used before 6 April 1956: see modification note at the start of this Part).

348 Additional VAT liabilities and writing off initial allowances

If an initial allowance is made in respect of an additional VAT liability incurred after the building is first used, the amount of the allowance is written off at the time when the liability accrues.

Commentary—*Simon's Direct Tax Service* **B2.235**.
Former enactments—CAA 1990 ss 8(2), 159A(3).
Definition—''Additional VAT liability'', s 547(1).
Modification—CAA 2001 Sch 3 para 79 (expenditure on preparatory work on land where building used before 6 April 1956: see modification note at the start of this Part).

Additional VAT rebates

349 Additional VAT rebates and writing-down allowances

(1) This section applies if—

(*a*) an additional VAT rebate is made in respect of qualifying expenditure to the person entitled to the relevant interest in relation to that qualifying expenditure, and (*b*) immediately before the rebate accrues, the residue of that qualifying expenditure is equal to, or greater than, the amount of the rebate.

(2) The making of the additional VAT rebate is a relevant event for the purposes of section 311 (calculation of writing-down allowances) that is to be treated as occurring at the time when the rebate accrues.

Commentary—*Simon's Direct Tax Service* **B2.234**.
Former enactments—Sub-s (1): CAA 1990 s 3(2C).
Sub-s (2): CAA 1990 ss 3(2C), 159A(3).
Former enactments—CAA 1990 ss 8(2), 159A(3).
Definition—"Additional VAT rebate", s 547(2).
Modification—CAA 2001 Sch 3 para 79 (expenditure on preparatory work on land where building used before 6 April 1956: see modification note at the start of this Part).

350 Additional VAT rebates and balancing adjustments

(1) If an additional VAT rebate is made in respect of qualifying expenditure to the person entitled to the relevant interest in relation to that qualifying expenditure—

(*a*) the making of the rebate is a balancing event for the purposes of this Part, but
(*b*) the making of balancing adjustments as a result of the event is subject to subsections (2) and (3).

(2) No balancing allowance is to be made as a result of the event.

(3) A balancing charge is not to be made as a result of the event unless—

(*a*) the amount of the additional VAT rebate is more than the amount of the residue of qualifying expenditure immediately before the time when the rebate accrues, or
(*b*) there is no such residue.

(4) The amount of the balancing charge is—

(*a*) the amount of the difference, or
(*b*) the amount of the rebate (if there is no residue).

(5) If a balancing charge is made under this section, the starting expenditure is reduced by the amount of that charge in a case where section 322(2) applies (person subject to balancing adjustment is the person who incurred the qualifying expenditure).

Commentary—*Simon's Direct Tax Service* **B2.234**.
Former enactments—Sub-s (1): CAA 1990 4(1).
Sub-s (2): CAA 1990 ss 4(2A), 159A(3).
Sub-s (3): CAA 1990 s 4(2A).
Sub-s (4): CAA 1990 s 4(2A).
Sub-s (5): CAA 1990 s 4(9) ("the capital expenditure").
Definitions—"Additional VAT rebate", s 547(2); "balancing adjustment", s 314; "residue of qualifying expenditure", s 313.
Modification—CAA 2001 Sch 3 para 79 (expenditure on preparatory work on land where building used before 6 April 1956: see modification note at the start of this Part).

351 Additional VAT rebates and writing off qualifying expenditure

If an additional VAT rebate is made in respect of qualifying expenditure, an amount equal to the rebate is written off at the time when the rebate accrues.

Commentary—*Simon's Direct Tax Service* **B2.235**.
Former enactment—CAA 1990 ss 8(12A), 159A(3).
Definition—"Additional VAT rebate", s 547(2).
Modification—CAA 2001 Sch 3 para 79 (expenditure on preparatory work on land where building used before 6 April 1956: see modification note at the start of this Part).

CHAPTER 11
GIVING EFFECT TO ALLOWANCES AND CHARGES

352 Trades

(1) An allowance or charge to which a person is entitled or liable under this Part is to be given effect in calculating the profits of that person's trade, by treating—

(*a*) the allowance as an expense of the trade, and
(*b*) the charge as a receipt of the trade.

(2) In the case of a person who—

(*a*) is entitled to an allowance or liable to a charge in respect of a commercial building, and
(*b*) occupies the building in the course of a profession or vocation,

the references in subsection (1) to a trade are to be read as references to the profession or vocation.

(3) Subsection (1) is subject to the following provisions of this Chapter.

Commentary—*Simon's Direct Tax Service* **B2.241**.
Former enactments—Sub-s (1): CAA 1990 ss 9(1), 140(2), 144(2), 161(5).
Sub-s (2): CAA 1990 ss 140(6), 144(4).
Sub-s (3): change in law.
Modification—CAA 2001 Sch 3 para 79 (expenditure on preparatory work on land where building used before 6 April 1956: see modification note at the start of this Part).

353 Lessors and licensors

(1) This section applies if—

(a) a person is entitled or liable to an allowance or charge for a chargeable period (''the relevant period''), but

(b) his interest in the building in question is or was subject to a lease or a licence at the relevant time.

(2) If the person's interest in the building is an asset of a Schedule A business carried on by him at any time in the relevant period, the allowance or charge is to be given effect in calculating the profits of that business for the relevant period, by treating—

(a) the allowance as an expense of that business, and

(b) the charge as a receipt of that business.

(3) If the person's interest in the building is an asset of an overseas property business carried on by him at any time in the relevant period, the allowance or charge is to be given effect in calculating the profits of the overseas property business for the relevant period, by treating—

(a) the allowance as an expense of that business, and

(b) the charge as a receipt of that business.

(4) If the person's interest in the building is not an asset of any property business carried on by him at any time in the relevant period, the allowance or charge is to be given effect by treating him as if he had been carrying on a Schedule A business in that period and as if—

(a) the allowance were an expense of that business, and

(b) the charge were a receipt of that business.

(5) In subsection (1) ''the relevant time'' means—

(a) in relation to an initial allowance, the time when the expenditure was incurred or any subsequent time before the building is used for any purpose;

(b) in relation to a writing-down allowance, the end of the relevant period;

(c) in relation to a balancing allowance or balancing charge, the time immediately before the event giving rise to the allowance or charge.

Commentary—*Simon's Direct Tax Service* **B2.241**.
Former enactments—Sub-s (1): CAA 1990 s 9(2), (4).
Sub-s (2): CAA 1990 s 9(1), (2).
Sub-s (3): CAA 1990 ss 9(1), (2), 161(2A).
Sub-s (4): CAA 1990 s 9(1), (2).
Sub-s (5): CAA 1990 s 9(3).
Definitions—''Overseas property business'', TA 1988 ss 64A(4), 70A(4), 832(1); ''property business'', s 577(1).
Modification—CAA 2001 Sch 3 para 79 (expenditure on preparatory work on land where building used before 6 April 1956: see modification note at the start of this Part).

354 Buildings temporarily out of use

(1) This section applies if a person is entitled to an allowance or liable to a charge for a chargeable period during which the building is treated as an industrial building under section 285 (building still industrial building despite temporary disuse).

(2) If, when the building was last in use as an industrial building—

(a) it was in use for the purposes of a trade which has since been permanently discontinued, or

(b) the relevant interest in the building was subject to a lease or a licence which has since come to an end,

section 353(4) applies to the person as if the relevant interest were subject to a lease or licence at the relevant time.

(3) If—

(a) the person is liable to a balancing charge, and

(b) when the building was last in use as an industrial building, it was in use as an industrial building for the purposes of a trade which was carried on by the person but which has since been permanently discontinued,

the same deductions may be made from the amount of the balancing charge as may be made under section 105 of ICTA (deductions allowed in case of post-cessation receipts) from an amount chargeable to tax under section 103 or 104(1) of ICTA.

(4) Subsection (3) does not affect the making of any deduction allowed under any other provision of the Tax Acts.

(5) For the purposes of this section the permanent discontinuance of a trade does not include an event treated as a permanent discontinuance under section 113(1) or 337(1) of ICTA (change in persons carrying on a trade etc and effect of company ceasing to trade etc).

(6) In this section ''trade'', in relation to a commercial building, includes a profession or vocation.

Commentary—*Simon's Direct Tax Service* **B2.236**.
Former enactments—Sub-s (1): CAA 1990 s 15ZA(1), (2), (5).
Sub-s (2): CAA 1990 s 15ZA(2), (5).
Sub-ss (3), (4): CAA 1990 s 15ZA(3).
Sub-s (5): CAA 1990 s 15ZA(4).

Sub-s (6): change in law.
Modification—CAA 2001 Sch 3 para 79 (expenditure on preparatory work on land where building used before 6 April 1956: see modification note at the start of this Part).

355 Buildings for miners etc: carry-back of balancing allowances

(1) This section applies if—

(*a*) a trade consists of or includes the working of a source of mineral deposits (within the meaning of item 7 of Table A in section 274),

(*b*) a balancing allowance falls to be made under this Part for the last chargeable period in which the trade is carried on,

(*c*) the event giving rise to the allowance is—

(i) the source of mineral deposits ceasing to be worked, or

(ii) the coming to an end of a foreign concession,

(*d*) the allowance is made for expenditure on a building which was constructed for occupation by, or for the welfare of, persons employed at or in connection with the working of the source of mineral deposits, and

(*e*) full effect cannot be given to the allowance because there are insufficient profits for that chargeable period.

(2) If this section applies, the person entitled to the allowance may claim that the balance of the allowance is to be given for the last preceding chargeable period, and so on for other preceding chargeable periods.

(3) But allowances are not to be given under subsection (2) for chargeable periods amounting in total to more than 5 years; but a proportionately reduced allowance may be given for a chargeable period of which part is required to make up the 5 years.

(4) In counting the 5 years, include any period for which an allowance might be made but cannot be given effect because there are insufficient profits.

(5) If this section applies to a company, no allowance may be given under this section so as to create or increase a loss in any accounting period.

(6) If this section applies to a company and a claim is made both under this section and under section 393A(1) of ICTA (relief for company trading losses)—

(*a*) effect is to be given to the claim under that section before this section is applied, and

(*b*) for the purposes of giving effect to the claim under that section, the allowance for which the claim under this section is made is to be disregarded.

Commentary—*Simon's Direct Tax Service* **B2.241**.
Former enactments—Sub-ss (1)–(4): CAA 1990 s 17(1).
Sub-ss (5), (6): CAA 1990 s 17(2).
Sub-s (7): CAA 1990 s .
Modification—CAA 2001 Sch 3 para 79 (expenditure on preparatory work on land where building used before 6 April 1956: see modification note at the start of this Part).

CHAPTER 12
SUPPLEMENTARY PROVISIONS

356 Apportionment of sums partly referable to non-qualifying assets

(1) If the sum paid for the sale of the relevant interest in a building is attributable—

(*a*) partly to assets representing expenditure for which an allowance can be made under this Part, and

(*b*) partly to assets representing other expenditure,

only so much of the sum as on a just and reasonable apportionment is attributable to the assets referred to in paragraph (*a*) is to be taken into account for the purposes of this Part.

(2) Subsection (1) applies to other proceeds from a balancing event in respect of a building as it applies to a sum given for the sale of the relevant interest in the building.

(3) Subsection (1) does not affect any other provision of this Act requiring an apportionment of the proceeds of a balancing event.

Commentary—*Simon's Direct Tax Service* **B2.223, 239**.
Former enactment—CAA 1990 s 21(3); change in law.
Definition—''Balancing event'', s 315.
Modification—CAA 2001 Sch 3 para 79 (expenditure on preparatory work on land where building used before 6 April 1956: see modification note at the start of this Part).

357 Arrangements having an artificial effect on pricing

(1) If—

(*a*) the relevant interest in a building is sold,

(*b*) related arrangements have been entered into, at or before the time when the sale price is fixed, which had the effect at that time of enhancing the value of the relevant interest, and

(c) the arrangements contain a provision which has an artificial effect on pricing (see subsection (4)),

the sum paid on the sale of the relevant interest is to be treated for the purposes of arriving at qualifying expenditure as reduced to what it would have been if the arrangements had not contained the provision having that artificial effect.

(2) If—

(a) qualifying expenditure is equal to a price paid on a sale of the relevant interest in a building,

(b) related arrangements have been entered into, at or before the time when the sale price is fixed, which had the effect at that time of enhancing the value of the relevant interest, and

(c) the arrangements contain a provision which has an artificial effect on pricing,

the proceeds from any balancing event subsequently occurring in relation to the building are to be treated for the purposes of this Part as reduced to what they would have been if the arrangements had not contained the provision having that artificial effect.

(3) ''Related arrangements'' means arrangements between two or more persons which relate—

(a) to an interest in or right over the building, or

(b) to other arrangements made with respect to such an interest or right;

and for this purpose it is immaterial whether the interest or right in question is granted by the person entitled to the relevant interest or another person.

(4) Arrangements contain a provision having an artificial effect on pricing to the extent that they go beyond what could reasonably have been regarded as required in comparable commercial transactions by the market conditions prevailing when the arrangements were entered into.

(5) ''Comparable commercial transactions'' means transactions—

(a) involving interests in or rights over buildings of the same kind as (or of a similar kind to) the building to which the arrangements relate, and

(b) made by persons dealing with each other at arm's length in the open market.

Commentary—*Simon's Direct Tax Service* **B2.224A**.
Former enactments—Sub-ss (1), (2): CAA 1990 s 10D(1)–(3), (5).
Sub-s (3): CAA 1990 s 10D(3).
Sub-ss (4), (5): CAA 1990 s 10D(4).
Revenue Internal Guidance—Capital allowances manual CA 39600 (background to this section).
Definition—''Balancing event'', s 315.
Modifications—CAA 2001 Sch 3 para 78 (the section above does not apply if the sale price fixed as mentioned in sub ss (1), (2) above became payable before 29 November 1994; or was fixed by a contract entered into before 29 November 1994 and became payable before 6 April 1995).
CAA 2001 Sch 3 para 79 (expenditure on preparatory work on land where building used before 6 April 1956: see modification note at the start of this Part).

358 Requisitioned land

(1) This section applies in relation to any period (''period of requisition'') for which compensation—

(a) is payable, or

(b) but for any agreement would be payable,

under section 2(1)(a) of the Compensation (Defence) Act 1939.

(2) This Part has effect in relation to the period of requisition as if the Crown had been in possession of the land for that period under a lease.

(3) If a person carrying on a trade is authorised by the Crown to occupy the land (or part of it) during the whole or a part of the period of requisition, this Part has effect as if the Crown had granted a sub-lease of the land (or that part of it) to the occupier.

(4) If subsection (2) or (3) applies, references in this Part to—

(a) the surrender of a leasehold interest,

(b) a leasehold interest being extinguished on the person entitled to it acquiring the interest which is reversionary on it, or

(c) the merger of a leasehold interest,

apply (with the necessary modifications) in relation to the lease under subsection (2) or the sub-lease under subsection (3).

(5) If the person who (subject to the rights of the Crown) is entitled to possession of the land pays any sum to—

(a) the Crown, or

(b) if subsection (3) applies, the occupier,

in respect of a building constructed on the land during the period of requisition, the sum is to be treated for the purposes of this Part as paid in consideration of the surrender of the lease or sub-lease (as the case may be).

Commentary—*Simon's Direct Tax Service* **B2.226**.
Former enactments—Sub-s (1): CAA 1990 s 16(1), (3).
Sub-s (2): CAA 1990 s 16(1).
Sub-s (3): CAA 1990 s 16(2).
Sub-ss (4), (5): CAA 1990 s 10D(4).

Modification—CAA 2001 Sch 3 para 79 (expenditure on preparatory work on land where building used before 6 April 1956: see modification note at the start of this Part).

359 Provisions applying on termination of lease

(1) This section applies for the purposes of this Part if a lease is terminated.

(2) If, with the consent of the lessor, the lessee of a building remains in possession of the building after the termination without a new lease being granted to him the lease is treated as continuing so long as the lessee remains in possession.

(3) If on the termination a new lease is granted to the lessee as a result of the exercise of an option available to him under the terms of the first lease, the second lease is treated as a continuation of the first.

(4) If on the termination the lessor pays a sum to the lessee in respect of a building comprised in the lease, the lease is treated as if it had come to an end by surrender in consideration of the payment.

(5) If on the termination—

    (*a*) another lease is granted to a different lessee, and

    (*b*) in connection with the transaction that lessee pays a sum to the person who was the lessee under the first lease,

the two leases are to be treated as if they were the same lease which had been assigned by the lessee under the first lease to the lessee under the second lease in consideration of the payment.

Commentary—*Simon's Direct Tax Service* **B2.225**.
Former enactments—Sub-s (1): CAA 1990 s 16(4)–(7).
Sub-s (2): CAA 1990 s 16(4).
Sub-s (3): CAA 1990 s 16(5).
Sub-s (4): CAA 1990 s 16(6).
Sub-s (5): CAA 1990 s 16(7).
Modification—CAA 2001 Sch 3 para 79 (expenditure on preparatory work on land where building used before 6 April 1956: see modification note at the start of this Part).

360 Meaning of "lease" etc

(1) In this Part "lease" includes—

    (*a*) an agreement for a lease if the term to be covered by the lease has begun, and

    (*b*) any tenancy,

but does not include a mortgage (and "lessee", "lessor" and "leasehold interest" are to be read accordingly).

(2) In the application of this Part to Scotland—

    (*a*) "leasehold interest" (or "leasehold estate") means the interest of a tenant in property subject to a lease, and

    (*b*) any reference to an interest which is reversionary on a leasehold interest or on a lease is to be read as a reference to the interest of the landlord in the property subject to the leasehold interest or lease.

Commentary—*Simon's Direct Tax Service* **B2.225**.
Former enactments—Sub-s (1): CAA 1990 s 161(2).
Sub-s (2): CAA 1990 ss 4A(13), 162.
Modification—CAA 2001 Sch 3 para 79 (expenditure on preparatory work on land where building used before 6 April 1956: see modification note at the start of this Part).

PART 4
AGRICULTURAL BUILDINGS ALLOWANCES

Commentary—*Simon's Direct Tax Service* **Division B2.5**.
Modifications—CAA 2001 Sch 3 para 82 (references in this Part to qualifying expenditure do not include—

    (*a*) expenditure incurred before 1 April 1986; or

    (*b*) payments made before 1 April 1987 under a contract entered into before 14 March 1984).

CAA 2001 Sch 3 para 83 (where it is provided under this Part that writing-down allowances are to be made in respect of any expenditure during a writing-down period of any specified length, if allowances were made under FA 1965 Sch 14 para 27(2)—

    (*a*) for income tax purposes, for either of the tax years 1964–65 and 1965–66, and

    (*b*) for accounting periods of a company falling wholly or partly within either of those years,

the periods for which allowances were made are added together in calculating the writing-down period, even though (according to the calendar) the same time is counted twice.)

CHAPTER 1
INTRODUCTION

361 Agricultural buildings allowances

(1) Allowances are available under this Part if—

    (*a*) capital expenditure has been incurred on the construction of a building (such as a farmhouse, farm building or cottage) or on the construction of fences or other works,

(b) the expenditure was incurred—

  (i) by a person having a freehold or leasehold interest in land in the United Kingdom occupied wholly or mainly for the purposes of husbandry, and

  (ii) for the purposes of husbandry on that land, and

(c) the expenditure, or other expenditure, is qualifying expenditure.

(2) In this Part—

(a) "agricultural building" means a building, fence or other works referred to in subsection (1)(a), and

(b) "the related agricultural land" means the land referred to in subsection (1)(b).

(3) Allowances under this Part are made to the person who for the time being has the relevant interest (see Chapter 2) in relation to the qualifying expenditure (see Chapter 3).

Commentary—*Simon's Direct Tax Service* B2.502.
Former enactments—Sub-s (1): CAA 1990 ss 123, 124(1), 125(1), 133(1)("agricultural lane"); change in law.
Revenue Internal Guidance—Capital allowances manual, CA 40100 (meaning of "farmhouse", "cottage" and "other works": farm shop may qualify for an allowance).
Definitions—"Capital expenditure", s 4; "husbandry", s 362.
Modification—CAA 2001 Sch 3 para 82 (exclusion of expenditure incurred before 1 April 1986: see modification note at the start of this Part).

362 Meaning of "husbandry"

(1) In this Part "husbandry" includes—

(a) any method of intensive rearing of livestock or fish on a commercial basis for the production of food for human consumption, and

(b) the cultivation of short rotation coppice.

(2) "Short rotation coppice" has the meaning given by section 154(3) of FA 1995 (meaning for general tax purposes: tree species planted at high density where stems harvested at intervals of less than 10 years).

Commentary—*Simon's Direct Tax Service* B2.502.
Former enactments—Sub-s (1): CAA 1990 s 133(1); FA 1995 s 154(1).
Sub-s (2): FA 1995 s 154(1)–(3).

363 Expenditure on the construction of a building

For the purposes of this Part, expenditure on the construction of a building does not include expenditure incurred on the acquisition of land or rights in or over land.

Commentary—*Simon's Direct Tax Service* B2.503.
Former enactment—CAA 1990 s 133(6).

CHAPTER 2
THE RELEVANT INTEREST

364 General rule as to what is the relevant interest

(1) The relevant interest in relation to any qualifying expenditure is the freehold or leasehold interest in the related agricultural land to which the person who incurred the expenditure on the construction of the agricultural building was entitled when the expenditure was incurred.

(2) Subsection (1) is subject to the following provisions of this Chapter.

(3) If, when the expenditure was incurred—

(a) the person was entitled to freehold and leasehold interests or to more than one leasehold interest in the related agricultural land, and

(b) one of those interests was reversionary on all the others,

the reversionary interest is the relevant interest.

Commentary—*Simon's Direct Tax Service* B2.506.
Former enactments—Sub-ss (1), (2): CAA 1990 s 125(1), (2).
Sub-s (3): CAA 1990 s 125(1), (3).
Definitions—"Agricultural building", s 361(2)(a); "related agricultural land", s 361(2)(b).
Modification—CAA 2001 Sch 3 para 82 (exclusion of expenditure incurred before 1 April 1986: see modification note at the start of this Part).

365 Effect of creation of subordinate lease

An interest does not cease to be the relevant interest merely because of the creation of a lease or other interest to which that interest is subject.

Commentary—*Simon's Direct Tax Service* B2.506.
Former enactment—CAA 1990 s 125(4).

366 Interest conveyed or assigned by way of security

If an interest in land is—

(a) conveyed or assigned by way of security, and
(b) subject to a right of redemption,

the person with the right of redemption is treated for the purposes of this Part as having that interest, and not the creditor.

Commentary—*Simon's Direct Tax Service* **B2.506**.
Former enactment—CAA 1990 s 133(4).

367 Merger of leasehold interest

(1) If the relevant interest is a leasehold interest which is extinguished on—

(a) being surrendered, or
(b) the person entitled to it acquiring the interest which is reversionary on it,

the interest into which the leasehold interest merges becomes the relevant interest when the leasehold interest is extinguished.

(2) If the person who owns the interest into which the leasehold interest is merged is not the same as the person who owned the leasehold interest, the relevant interest is to be treated for the purposes of this Part as acquired by the owner of the interest into which the leasehold interest is merged.

(3) Subsection (1) does not apply if a new lease of the whole or a part of the related agricultural land is granted to take effect on the extinguishment of the former leasehold interest.

Commentary—*Simon's Direct Tax Service* **B2.506, 509**.
Former enactments—Sub-s (1): CAA 1990 s 125(4).
Sub-s (2): CAA 1990 s 126(4).
Sub-s (3): CAA 1990 s 125(4).
Definition—''Related agricultural land'', s 361(2)(*b*).

368 Provisions applying on ending of lease

(1) This section applies if—

(a) a lease which is the relevant interest comes to an end, and
(b) section 367(1) does not apply.

(2) If a new lease of the whole or a part of the related agricultural land is granted to the same lessee, the lessee is to be treated as continuing to have the same relevant interest in the whole of the related agricultural land.

(3) If—

(a) a new lease of the whole or a part of the related agricultural land is granted to a different lessee, and
(b) that lessee (''the incoming lessee'') makes a payment to the outgoing lessee in respect of assets representing the qualifying expenditure,

the incoming lessee is to be treated as acquiring the relevant interest in the whole of the related agricultural land.

(4) In any other case, the former lease and the interest of the lessor under it are to be treated as the same interest; and so the relevant interest in the whole of the related agricultural land is to be treated as acquired by the lessor.

Commentary—*Simon's Direct Tax Service* **B2.509, 511**.
Former enactments—Sub-s (1): CAA 1990 s 126(5).
Sub-ss (2), (3): CAA 1990 s 126(5); change in law.
Sub-s (4): CAA 1990 s 126(5).
Definition—''Related agricultural land'', s 361(2)(*b*).
Modification—CAA 2001 Sch 3 para 82 (exclusion of expenditure incurred before 1 April 1986: see modification note at the start of this Part).

CHAPTER 3
QUALIFYING EXPENDITURE

369 Capital expenditure on construction of agricultural building

(1) If—

(a) capital expenditure has been incurred on the construction of an agricultural building,
(b) the expenditure was incurred for the purposes of husbandry as mentioned in section 361, and
(c) the relevant interest has not been sold or, if it has been sold, has been sold only after the first use of the building,

the capital expenditure is qualifying expenditure.

(2) Subsections (3) and (4) apply if the capital expenditure has been incurred on the construction of a farmhouse.

(3) If the accommodation and amenities of the farmhouse are proportionate to the nature and extent of the farm, only one third of the capital expenditure is to be taken into account under subsection (1).

(4) If they are disproportionate, only such part of the expenditure as is just and reasonable (and not exceeding one third) is to be taken into account under subsection (1).

(5) If—

    (*a*) the capital expenditure is incurred on the construction of any agricultural building other than a farmhouse, and

    (*b*) the building is to be used partly for the purposes of husbandry on the related agricultural land and partly for other purposes,

only such part of the expenditure as, on a just and reasonable apportionment, is referable to use for the purposes of husbandry is to be taken into account under subsection (1).

Commentary—*Simon's Direct Tax Service* **B2.503**.
Former enactments—Sub-ss (1)–(3): CAA 1990 ss 123, 124(1).
Sub-ss (4), (5): CAA 1990 s 124(1); change in law.
Revenue Internal Guidance—Capital allowances manual, CA 40200 (qualifying expenditure: worked examples).
Definitions—"Agricultural building", s 361(2)(*a*); "capital expenditure", s 4; related agricultural land", s 361(2)(*b*).
Modification—CAA 2001 Sch 3 para 82 (exclusion of expenditure incurred before 1 April 1986: see modification note at the start of this Part).

370 Purchase of relevant interest before first use of agricultural building

(1) This section applies if—

    (*a*) capital expenditure has been incurred on the construction of an agricultural building,

    (*b*) the expenditure was incurred for the purposes of husbandry as mentioned in section 361,

    (*c*) the relevant interest is sold before the building is first used, and

    (*d*) a capital sum is paid by the purchaser for the relevant interest.

(2) The lesser of—

    (*a*) the capital expenditure incurred on the construction of the agricultural building, and

    (*b*) the capital sum paid by the purchaser,

is qualifying expenditure.

(3) For the purposes of subsections (1) and (2)—

    (*a*) capital expenditure incurred on the construction of the agricultural building does not include any amount excluded from being taken into account under section 369(3) to (5), and

    (*b*) the capital sum paid by the purchaser for the relevant interest does not include any amount which, on a just and reasonable apportionment, is attributable to assets representing expenditure in respect of which an allowance cannot be made under this Part.

(4) Subsection (3)(*b*) does not affect sections 562, 563 and 564(1) (apportionment and procedure for determining apportionment).

(5) The qualifying expenditure is to be treated as incurred when the capital sum became payable.

(6) If the relevant interest is sold more than once before the building is first used, subsection (2) has effect only in relation to the last of those sales.

Commentary—*Simon's Direct Tax Service* **B2.508**.
Former enactments—Sub-s (1): CAA 1990 ss 123, 127(1), (3A); change in law.
Sub-s (2): CAA 1990 s 127(2)–(3B).
Sub-s (3): CAA 1990 ss 127(3A), 133(7); change in law.
Sub-s (4): CAA 1990 s 133(7).
Sub-s (5): CAA 1990 s 127(2).
Sub-s (6): CAA 1990 s 127(4).
Revenue Internal Guidance—Capital allowances manual, CA 40300 (worked examples).
Definitions—"Agricultural building", s 361(2)(*a*); "capital expenditure", s 4; "capital sum", s 4.
Modification—CAA 2001 Sch 3 para 82 (exclusion of expenditure incurred before 1 April 1986: see modification note at the start of this Part).

371 Different relevant interests in different parts of the related agricultural land

If a person is entitled to different relevant interests in different parts of the related agricultural land—

    (*a*) the expenditure is to be apportioned between those parts on a just and reasonable basis, and

    (*b*) this Part applies as if the person had incurred the expenditure apportioned to each part separately.

Commentary—*Simon's Direct Tax Service* **B2.508**.

CHAPTER 4
WRITING-DOWN ALLOWANCES

372 Entitlement to writing-down allowance

(1) A person is entitled to a writing-down allowance for a chargeable period if—

    (*a*) qualifying expenditure has been incurred,

(*b*) at any time during that chargeable period he is entitled to the relevant interest in relation to the qualifying expenditure, and

(*c*) that time falls within the writing-down period.

(2) The writing-down period, in relation to qualifying expenditure incurred by a person, is 25 years beginning with the first day of the chargeable period of that person in which the qualifying expenditure was incurred.

(3) A person claiming a writing-down allowance may require the allowance to be reduced to a specified amount.

Commentary—*Simon's Direct Tax Service* **B2.507**.
Former enactments—Sub-s (1): CAA 1990 ss 123, 126(1).
Sub-s (2): CAA 1990 s 123.
Sub-s (3): change in law.
Modifications—CAA 2001 Sch 3 para 82 (exclusion of expenditure incurred before 1 April 1986: see modification note at the start of this Part).
CAA 2001 Sch 3 para 83 (the writing-down period: see modification note at the start of this Part).

373 Basic rule for calculating amount of allowance

(1) The basic rule is that the writing-down allowance for a chargeable period is 4% of the qualifying expenditure.

(2) The allowance is proportionately increased or reduced if the chargeable period is more or less than a year.

Commentary—*Simon's Direct Tax Service* **B2.507**.
Former enactments—Sub-s (1): CAA 1990 s 123.
Sub-s (2): CAA 1990 s 146(2).
Modifications—CAA 2001 Sch 3 para 82 (exclusion of expenditure incurred before 1 April 1986: see modification note at the start of this Part).
CAA 2001 Sch 3 para 83 (the writing-down period: see modification note at the start of this Part).

374 First use of building not for purposes of husbandry, etc

(1) No writing-down allowance is to be made under section 372 if, when the agricultural building is first used, it is not used for the purposes of husbandry.

(2) Any writing-down allowance which has been made in respect of an agricultural building which has not been used is to be withdrawn if—

(*a*) when the building is first used, it is not used for the purposes of husbandry, or

(*b*) the person to whom the allowance was made sells the relevant interest before the building is first used.

(3) All such assessments and adjustments of assessments are to be made as are necessary to give effect to this section.

Commentary—*Simon's Direct Tax Service* **B2.507**.
Former enactments—Sub-s (1): CAA 1990 s 124(2).
Sub-s (2): CAA 1990 ss 124(2), 127(1), (2).
Sub-s (3): CAA 1990 ss 124(2), 127(2).
Definitions—''Agricultural building'', s 361(2)(*a*); ''husbandry'', s 362.
Modification—CAA 2001 Sch 3 para 83 (the writing-down period: see modification note at the start of this Part).

375 Effect of acquisition of relevant interest after first use of building

(1) This section applies if—

(*a*) a person (''the former owner'') would be entitled to an allowance under this Part in respect of any expenditure if he continued to be the owner of the relevant interest, and

(*b*) another person (''the new owner'') acquires the relevant interest in the whole or a part of the related agricultural land.

(2) For the purposes of subsection (1)(*b*), it is immaterial whether the relevant interest is acquired by transfer, by operation of law or otherwise.

(3) The former owner—

(*a*) is not entitled to an allowance for any chargeable period after that in which the acquisition occurs, and

(*b*) if the acquisition occurs during a chargeable period, is entitled only to an appropriate part of any writing-down allowance for that period.

(4) The new owner—

(*a*) is entitled to allowances for the chargeable period in which the acquisition occurs and for subsequent chargeable periods falling wholly or partly within the writing-down period, and

(*b*) if the acquisition occurs during a chargeable period, is entitled only to an appropriate part of any writing-down allowance for that period.

(5) If the new owner acquires the relevant interest in part only of the related agricultural land, subsections (3) and (4) apply to so much only of the allowance as is properly referable to that part of the agricultural land as if it were a separate allowance.

Commentary—*Simon's Direct Tax Service* B2.509.
Former enactments—Sub-ss (1), (2): CAA 1990 s 126(1).
Sub-s (3): CAA 1990 s 126(1), (2).
Sub-s (4): CAA 1990 ss 126(1), (2), 146(2).
Sub-s (5): CAA 1990 s 126(3).
Revenue Internal Guidance—Capital allowances manual, CA 41100 (worked example).
Definitions—"Related agricultural land", s 361(2)(*b*); "writing-down period", s 372(2).
Modification—CAA 2001 Sch 3 para 83 (the writing-down period: see modification note at the start of this Part).

376 Calculation of allowance after acquisition

(1) This section applies if—

(*a*) section 375 applies, and

(*b*) the acquisition is a balancing event under section 381 (as a result of an election made in accordance with section 382).

(2) The writing-down allowance for a chargeable period ending after the event is—

$$\text{RQE} \times \frac{A}{B}$$

where—

RQE is the residue of qualifying expenditure immediately after the event,

A is the length of the chargeable period, and

B is the length of the period from the date of the event to the end of the writing-down period.

(3) On any later acquisition that is a balancing event under section 381, the writing-down allowance is further adjusted in accordance with this section.

(4) The residue of qualifying expenditure immediately after a balancing event is calculated as mentioned in section 386, taking into account any balancing adjustment falling to be made on the event.

(5) For this purpose, any balancing allowance on that or any previous balancing event which is reduced or denied under section 389 (sale subject to subordinate interest) is to be treated as having been made in full.

(6) The allowance is proportionately reduced if the person entitled to the allowance is not entitled to the relevant interest in relation to the expenditure in question during part of the chargeable period.

Commentary—*Simon's Direct Tax Service* B2.510.
Former enactments—Sub-s (1): CAA 1990 s 129(1), (3).
Sub-s (2): CAA 1990 s 129(3).
Sub-s (4): CAA 1990 s 129(3).
Sub-s (5): CAA 1990 s 130(3).
Sub-s (6): CAA 1990 s 126(2).
Definitions—"Balancing adjustment", s 380; "writing-down period", s 372(2).
Modifications—CAA 2001 Sch 3 para 82 (exclusion of expenditure incurred before 1 April 1986: see modification note at the start of this Part).
CAA 2001 Sch 3 para 83 (the writing-down period: see modification note at the start of this Part).

377 Chargeable period when balancing adjustment made

A person is not entitled to a writing-down allowance for a chargeable period in which a balancing allowance or balancing charge is made to or on him in respect of the qualifying expenditure.

Commentary—*Simon's Direct Tax Service* B2.510.
Former enactment—CAA 1990 s 128(1).
Definition—"Balancing adjustment", s 380.
Modifications—CAA 2001 Sch 3 para 82 (exclusion of expenditure incurred before 1 April 1986: see modification note at the start of this Part).
CAA 2001 Sch 3 para 83 (the writing-down period: see modification note at the start of this Part).

378 Allowance limited to residue of qualifying expenditure

(1) The amount of a writing-down allowance for a chargeable period is limited to the residue of qualifying expenditure immediately before it is made or would, apart from this section, be made.

(2) The residue of qualifying expenditure is calculated in accordance with section 386.

Commentary—*Simon's Direct Tax Service* B2.507.
Former enactments—Sub-s (1): CAA 1990 s 146(1), (3).
Modifications—CAA 2001 Sch 3 para 82 (exclusion of expenditure incurred before 1 April 1986: see modification note at the start of this Part).
CAA 2001 Sch 3 para 83 (the writing-down period: see modification note at the start of this Part).

379 Final writing-down allowance

(1) In this section "the final writing-down allowance" means the writing-down allowance which is made—

(*a*) to the person who is entitled to the relevant interest when the writing-down period ends, and

(*b*) for the chargeable period in which it ends.

(2) If the final writing-down allowance would, apart from this section, be less than the amount of the residue of qualifying expenditure immediately before it is made, the allowance is increased to that amount.

(3) When determining the residue of qualifying expenditure under section 386 for the purposes of subsection (2), assume that all such writing-down allowances have been made to the persons who have been entitled to the relevant interest during the writing-down period as could have been made if each of them—

(*a*) had been entitled to allowances, and

(*b*) had claimed allowances in full.

Commentary—*Simon's Direct Tax Service* B2.509.
Former enactment—CAA 1990 s 126(6).
Definitions—"Residue of qualifying expenditure", s 386; "writing-down period", s 372(2).
Modifications—CAA 2001 Sch 3 para 82 (exclusion of expenditure incurred before 1 April 1986: see modification note at the start of this Part).
CAA 2001 Sch 3 para 83 (the writing-down period: see modification note at the start of this Part).

CHAPTER 5

BALANCING ADJUSTMENTS

General

380 When balancing adjustments are made

(1) A balancing adjustment is made if—

(*a*) qualifying expenditure has been incurred, and

(*b*) a balancing event occurs in a chargeable period for which a person would (apart from this section) be entitled to a writing-down allowance.

(2) A balancing adjustment is either a balancing allowance or a balancing charge and is made for the chargeable period in which the balancing event occurs.

(3) A balancing allowance or balancing charge is made to or on the person entitled to the relevant interest in relation to the qualifying expenditure immediately before the balancing event.

Commentary—*Simon's Direct Tax Service* B2.510.
Former enactment—CAA 1990 s 128(1).
Definition—"Balancing event", s 381.
Modification—CAA 2001 Sch 3 para 82 (exclusion of expenditure incurred before 1 April 1986: see modification note at the start of this Part).

381 Balancing events (on making an election)

(1) Any event described in subsection (2) is a balancing event, but only if an election is made in accordance with section 382 for it to be treated as such.

(2) The events are—

(*a*) the relevant interest is acquired as mentioned in section 375;

(*b*) the agricultural building is demolished or destroyed;

(*c*) the agricultural building ceases altogether to be used (without being demolished or destroyed).

Commentary—*Simon's Direct Tax Service* B2.510.
Former enactments—Sub-s (1): CAA 1990 129(1), (2).
Sub-s (2): CAA 1990 s 129(1); change in law.
Revenue Internal Guidance—Capital allowances manual, CA 41200 (operation of this section).
Definition—"Agricultural building", s 361(2)(*a*).

382 Requirements as to elections

(1) An election relating to an event within section 381(2)(*a*) must be made jointly by the former owner and the new owner.

(2) No election relating to such an event may be made if it appears that the sole or main benefit which might have been expected to accrue to the parties, or any of them, from—

(*a*) the acquisition, or

(*b*) transactions of which the acquisition is one,

is the obtaining of an allowance, or a greater allowance, under this Part.

(3) In determining for the purposes of subsection (2) what benefit might have been expected to accrue, sections 568 and 573 (sales treated as being for alternative amount) are to be disregarded.

(4) An election relating to an event within section 381(2)(*b*) or (*c*) must be made by the person entitled to the relevant interest immediately before the event.

(5) No election relating to any event may be made if any person by whom the election is to be made is not within the charge to tax.

(6) The election must be made by notice given to the Inland Revenue—

(*a*) for income tax purposes, on or before the normal time limit for amending a tax return for the tax year in which the relevant chargeable period ends;

(b) for corporation tax purposes, no later than 2 years after the end of the relevant chargeable period.

(7) "The relevant chargeable period" means the chargeable period in which the event in question occurs.

Commentary—*Simon's Direct Tax Service* **B2.510**.
Former enactments—Sub-s (1): CAA 1990 129(4).
Sub-ss (2), (3): CAA 1990 s 129(5).
Sub-s (4): CAA 1990 s 129(4).
Sub-s (5): CAA 1990 s 129(5).
Sub-ss (6), (7): CAA 1990 s 129(2).

383 Proceeds from balancing events

(1) References in this Part to the proceeds from a balancing event are to the amounts received or receivable in connection with the event, as shown in the Table—

TABLE

BALANCING EVENTS AND PROCEEDS

1. Balancing event	2. Proceeds from event
1. The sale of the relevant interest.	The net proceeds of the sale.
2. The acquisition of the relevant interest under section 368(3) (ending of lease where incoming lessee makes payment to outgoing lessee).	The net amount of the payment to the outgoing lessee.
3. The demolition or destruction of the agricultural building.	The net amount received for the remains of the building, together with— (a) any insurance money received in respect of the demolition or destruction, and (b) any other compensation of any description so received, so far as it consists of capital sums.
4. The agricultural building ceases altogether to be used.	Any compensation of any description received in respect of the event, so far as it consists of capital sums.

(2) The amounts referred to in column 2 of the Table are those received or receivable by the person whose entitlement to a balancing allowance or liability to a balancing charge is in question.

Commentary—*Simon's Direct Tax Service* **B2.510**.
Former enactments—Sub-s (1): CAA 1990 ss 128(2), 156; change in law.
Sub-s (2): CAA 1990 s 156.
Definitions—"Balancing event", s 381; "capital sum", s 4.

384 Exclusion of proportion of proceeds

(1) The amounts referred to in column 2 of the Table in section 383 do not include any amount which, on a just and reasonable apportionment, is attributable to assets representing expenditure in respect of which an allowance cannot be made under this Part.

(2) If the qualifying expenditure in respect of which the balancing adjustment is made was restricted as a result of—

(a) subsection (3) or (4) of section 369 (restrictions on expenditure on farmhouse), or
(b) subsection (5) of that section (restriction on expenditure on buildings to be used partly for purposes other than husbandry),

a corresponding proportion only of the amounts referred to in the Table in section 383 is to be treated as proceeds from the balancing event.

(3) Subsection (1) does not affect sections 562, 563 and 564(1) (apportionment and procedure for determining apportionment).

Commentary—*Simon's Direct Tax Service* **B2.510**.
Former enactments—Sub-s (1): CAA 1990 s 133(7); change in law.
Sub-s (2): CAA 1990 s 128(3).
Sub-s (3): CAA 1990 s 133(7).
Definitions—"Balancing adjustment", s 380; "balancing event", s 381; "husbandry", s 362.
Modification—CAA 2001 Sch 3 para 82 (exclusion of expenditure incurred before 1 April 1986: see modification note at the start of this Part).

Calculation of balancing adjustments

385 Calculation of balancing adjustment

(1) A balancing allowance is made if—

(a) there are no proceeds from the balancing event, or
(b) the proceeds from the balancing event are less than the residue of qualifying expenditure immediately before the event.

(2) The amount of the balancing allowance is the amount of—

  (*a*) the residue (if there are no proceeds);

  (*b*) the difference (if the proceeds are less than the residue).

(3) A balancing charge is made if the proceeds from the balancing event are more than the residue of qualifying expenditure immediately before the event.

(4) The amount of the balancing charge is the amount of the difference.

Commentary—*Simon's Direct Tax Service* **B2.510**.
Former enactments—Sub-ss (1), (2): CAA 1990 s 128(4).
Sub-ss (3), (4): CAA 1990 s 128(5).
Revenue Internal Guidance—Capital allowances manual, CA 41200 (operation of this section).
Definitions—"Balancing adjustment", s 380; "balancing event", s 381; "residue of qualifying expenditure", s 386.
Modification—CAA 2001 Sch 3 para 82 (exclusion of expenditure incurred before 1 April 1986: see modification note at the start of this Part).

386 The residue of qualifying expenditure

The residue of qualifying expenditure at any time is—

$$QE + B - A$$

where—

  QE is the amount of qualifying expenditure,

  B is the total amount of balancing charges previously made under this Part in respect of the expenditure, and

  A is the total amount of any allowances (including balancing allowances) previously made under this Part in respect of that expenditure (whether to the same or to different persons).

Commentary—*Simon's Direct Tax Service* **B2.510**.
Former enactment—CAA 1990 s 128(2); change in law.
Modification—CAA 2001 Sch 3 para 82 (exclusion of expenditure incurred before 1 April 1986: see modification note at the start of this Part).

387 Overall limit on balancing charge

The amount of a balancing charge made on a person in respect of any qualifying expenditure must not exceed the total allowances made under this Part to the person in respect of the expenditure for chargeable periods ending before that in which the balancing event occurs.

Commentary—*Simon's Direct Tax Service* **B2.510**.
Former enactment—CAA 1990 s 128(6); change in law.
Definition—"Balancing event", s 381.
Modifications—CAA 2001 Sch 3 para 80 (for the purposes of this section, an allowance is treated as having been made to a woman in relation to any qualifying expenditure if—

  (*a*) it was made to her husband for a chargeable period ending before 6 April 1990 in respect of an interest of hers which was the relevant interest in relation to that expenditure,

  (*b*) a balancing event occurs on or after that date, and

  (*c*) she is entitled to all or part of the proceeds from that balancing event).
CAA 2001 Sch 3 para 82 (exclusion of expenditure incurred before 1 April 1986: see modification note at the start of this Part).

388 Acquisition of relevant interest in part of land, etc

(1) This section applies if a balancing event relates to—

  (*a*) the acquisition of the relevant interest in part only of the related agricultural land in which the interest subsisted when the qualifying expenditure was incurred, or

  (*b*) only part of the agricultural building.

(2) Entitlement or liability to, and the amount of, the balancing adjustment, are determined by reference to the part of the qualifying expenditure that is properly attributable to the part of the related agricultural land or (as the case may be) the part of the agricultural building.

(3) Section 377 (no writing-down allowance for qualifying expenditure for the chargeable period in which a balancing adjustment is made) applies to the part of the qualifying expenditure referred to in subsection (2).

Commentary—*Simon's Direct Tax Service* **B2.510**.
Former enactment—CAA 1990 s 128(7).
Definitions—"Agricultural building", s 361(2)(*a*); "balancing adjustment", s 380; "balancing event", s 381; "related agricultural land", s 361(2)(*b*).
Modification—CAA 2001 Sch 3 para 82 (exclusion of expenditure incurred before 1 April 1986: see modification note at the start of this Part).

389 Balancing allowances restricted where sale subject to subordinate interest etc

(1) This section applies if—

  (*a*) the relevant interest is sold subject to a subordinate interest,

  (*b*) the person entitled to the relevant interest immediately before the sale ("the former owner") would, apart from this section, be entitled to a balancing allowance under this Chapter as a result of the sale, and

  (*c*) condition A or B is met.

(2) Condition A is that—

    (*a*) the former owner,

    (*b*) the person who acquires the relevant interest, and

    (*c*) the person to whom the subordinate interest was granted,

or any two of them, are connected persons.

(3) Condition B is that it appears that the sole or main benefit which might have been expected to accrue to the parties or any of them from the sale or the grant, or transactions including the sale or grant, was the obtaining of an allowance under this Part.

(4) For the purpose of deciding what balancing adjustment is to be made in a case to which this section applies, the net proceeds to the former owner of the sale are to be increased—

    (*a*) by an amount equal to any premium receivable by him for the grant of the subordinate interest, and

    (*b*) if no rent, or no commercial rent, is payable in respect of the subordinate interest, by the amount by which the proceeds would have been greater if a commercial rent had been payable and the relevant interest had been sold in the open market.

(5) But the net proceeds of the sale are not to be treated as being greater than the amount which secures that no balancing allowance is made.

(6) If the terms on which a subordinate interest is granted are varied before the sale of the relevant interest—

    (*a*) any capital consideration for the variation is to be treated for the purposes of this section as a premium for the grant of the interest, and

    (*b*) the question whether any, and if so what, rent is payable in respect of the interest is to be determined by reference to the terms in force immediately before the sale.

(7) If this section applies in relation to a sale to deny or reduce a balancing allowance, the residue of qualifying expenditure immediately after the sale is nevertheless calculated as if the balancing allowance had been made or not reduced.

Commentary—*Simon's Direct Tax Service* **B2.511**.
Former enactments—Sub-ss (1)–(3): CAA 1990 s 130(1).
Sub-ss (4), (5): CAA 1990 s 130(2).
Sub-s (6): CAA 1990 s 130(5).
Sub-s (7): CAA 1990 s 130(3).
Revenue Internal Guidance—Capital allowances manual, CA 41400 (worked example).
Definitions—"Balancing adjustment", s 380; "residue of qualifying expenditure", s 386.
Modification—CAA 2001 Sch 3 para 82 (exclusion of expenditure incurred before 1 April 1986: see modification note at the start of this Part).

390 Interpretation of section 389

(1) In section 389—

    "commercial rent" means such rent as may reasonably be expected to have been required in respect of the subordinate interest (having regard to any premium payable for the grant of the interest) if the transaction had been at arm's length;

    "premium" includes any capital consideration, except so much of any sum as corresponds to an amount of rent or profits falling to be calculated by reference to that sum under section 34 of ICTA;

    "subordinate interest" means an interest in or right over the related agricultural land, whether granted by the former owner or anyone else.

(2) In section 389 and this section—

    "capital consideration" means consideration which consists of a capital sum or would be a capital sum if it had consisted of a money payment, and

    "rent" includes any consideration which is not capital consideration.

Commentary—*Simon's Direct Tax Service* **B2.511**.
Former enactment—CAA 1990 s 130(4).
Definitions—"Capital sum", s 4; "related agricultural land", s 361(2)(*b*).

CHAPTER 6
SUPPLEMENTARY PROVISIONS
Giving effect to allowances and charges

391 Trades

An allowance or charge to which a person is entitled or liable under this Part is to be given effect in calculating the profits of that person's trade, by treating—

    (*a*) the allowance as an expense of the trade, and

    (*b*) the charge as a receipt of the trade.

Commentary—*Simon's Direct Tax Service* **B2.513**.
Former enactments—CAA 1990 s 132(1), 140(2), 144(2), 161(5).

392 Schedule A businesses

(1) This section applies if a person who is entitled or liable to an allowance or charge for a chargeable period was not carrying on a trade in that period.

(2) If the person was carrying on a Schedule A business at any time in that period, the allowance or charge is to be given effect in calculating the profits of that business, by treating—

    (*a*) the allowance as an expense of that business, and

    (*b*) the charge as a receipt of that business.

(3) If the person was not carrying on a Schedule A business at any time in that period, the allowance or charge is to be given effect by treating him as if he had been carrying on such a business in that period and as if—

    (*a*) the allowance were an expense of that business, and

    (*b*) the charge were a receipt of that business.

Commentary—*Simon's Direct Tax Service* **B2.513**.
Former enactments—CAA 1990 s 132(2), 140(2), 144(2), 161(5).

Meaning of "freehold interest", "lease" etc

393 Meaning of "freehold interest", "lease", etc

(1) In this Part "freehold interest in land" means—

    (*a*) the fee simple estate in the land, or

    (*b*) in relation to Scotland, the interest of the owner.

(2) In this Part "freehold interest in land" also includes—

    (*a*) an agreement to acquire the fee simple estate in the land, or

    (*b*) in relation to Scotland, an agreement to acquire the interest of the owner.

(3) In this Part "lease" includes—

    (*a*) an agreement for a lease if the term to be covered by the lease has begun, and

    (*b*) any tenancy,

but does not include a mortgage (and "lessee", "lessor" and "leasehold interest" are to be read accordingly).

(4) In the application of this Part to Scotland—

    (*a*) "leasehold interest" means the interest of a tenant in property subject to a lease, and

    (*b*) any reference to an interest which is reversionary on a leasehold interest or on a lease is to be read as a reference to the interest of the landlord in the property subject to the leasehold interest or lease.

Commentary—*Simon's Direct Tax Service* **B2.506**.
Former enactments—Sub-ss (1), (2): CAA 1990 s 125(1); Abolition of Feudal Tenure etc (Scotland) Act 2000, Sch 12, para 51.
Sub-s (3): CAA 1990 s 161(2) ("lease").
Sub-s (4): CAA 1990 s 162.
Modifications—CAA 2001 Sch 3 para 81(2) (if Abolition of Feudal Tenure etc (Scotland) Act 2000 Sch 12 para 51 has not come into force before the commencement of CAA 2001 Part 4, sub-s (1) above has effect until the appointed day as if para (*b*) is substituted to read as follows—

    "(*b*) in relation to Scotland, the estate or interest of the proprietor of the *dominium utile* (or, in the case of property other than feudal property, of the owner);").
CAA 2001 Sch 3 para 81(3) (sub-s (2) has effect until the appointed day as if sub-s (2)(*b*) were substituted as follows—

    "(*b*) in relation to Scotland, an agreement to acquire the estate or interest mentioned in subsection (1)(*b*);").

[PART 4A

FLAT CONVERSION ALLOWANCES][1]

Commentary—*Simon's Direct Tax Service* **Division B2.10**.
Amendment—[1] This Part inserted by FA 2001 s 67, Sch 19 Pt I with effect for expenditure incurred after 10 May 2001.

[CHAPTER 1

INTRODUCTION

393A Flat conversion allowances

(1) Allowances are available under this Part if a person incurs qualifying expenditure in respect of a flat.

(2) Allowances under this Part are made to the person who—

    (*a*) incurred the expenditure, and

    (*b*) has the relevant interest in the flat.

(3) In this Part "flat" means a dwelling which—

    (*a*) is a separate set of premises (whether or not on the same floor),

    (*b*) forms part of a building, and

(*c*) is divided horizontally from another part of the building.

(4) In this Part "dwelling" means a building or part of a building occupied or intended to be occupied as a separate dwelling.]¹

Commentary—*Simon's Direct Tax Service* **B2.1002**.
Amendment—¹ This section inserted by FA 2001 s 67, Sch 19 Pt I with effect for expenditure incurred after 10 May 2001.

[CHAPTER 2
QUALIFYING EXPENDITURE

393B Meaning of "qualifying expenditure"

(1) In this Part "qualifying expenditure" means capital expenditure incurred on, or in connection with—

(*a*) the conversion of part of a qualifying building into a qualifying flat,

(*b*) the renovation of a flat in a qualifying building if the flat is, or will be, a qualifying flat, or

(*c*) repairs to a qualifying building, to the extent that the repairs are incidental to expenditure within paragraph (*a*) or (*b*).

(2) Expenditure within subsection (1)(*a*) or (*b*) is not qualifying expenditure unless the part of the building, or the flat, in respect of which the expenditure is incurred—

(*a*) was unused, or

(*b*) was used only for storage,

throughout the period of one year ending immediately before the date on which the conversion or renovation work began.

(3) Expenditure is not qualifying expenditure if it is incurred on or in connection with—

(*a*) the acquisition of land or rights in or over land,

(*b*) the extension of a qualifying building (except to the extent required for the purpose of providing a means of getting to or from a qualifying flat),

(*c*) the development of land adjoining or adjacent to a qualifying building, or

(*d*) the provision of furnishings or chattels.

(4) For the purposes of this section, expenditure incurred on repairs to a building is to be treated as capital expenditure if it is not expenditure that would be allowed to be deducted in calculating the profits of a Schedule A business for tax purposes.

(5) Treasury regulations may make further provision as to expenditure which is, or is not, qualifying expenditure.]¹

Commentary—*Simon's Direct Tax Service* **B2.1003**.
Amendment—¹ This section inserted by FA 2001 s 67, Sch 19 Pt I with effect for expenditure incurred after 10 May 2001.

[CHAPTER 3
QUALIFYING BUILDINGS AND QUALIFYING FLATS

393C Meaning of "qualifying building"

(1) In this Part "qualifying building" means a building in respect of which the following requirements are met—

(*a*) all or most of the ground floor of the building must be authorised for business use,

(*b*) it must appear that, when the building was constructed, the storeys above the ground floor were for use primarily as one or more dwellings,

(*c*) the building must not have more than 4 storeys above the ground floor, and

(*d*) the construction of the building must have been completed before 1st January 1980.

(2) In subsection (1)(*a*) "authorised for business use" means—

(*a*) in the case of a building in England or Wales, authorised for use within class A1, A2, A3, B1 or D1(*a*) specified in the Schedule to the Town and Country Planning (Use Classes) Order 1987;

(*b*) in the case of a building in Scotland—

(i) authorised for use within class 1, 2, 3 or 4 specified in the Schedule to the Town and Country Planning (Use Classes) (Scotland) Order 1997,

(ii) authorised for a use specified in Article 3(5)(*j*) of that Order, or

(iii) authorised for use for the provision of medical or health services other than from premises attached to the residence of the consultant or practitioner;

(*c*) in the case of a building in Northern Ireland—

(i) authorised for use within class 1, 2, 3, 4 or 15(*a*) specified in the Schedule to the Planning (Use Classes) Order (Northern Ireland) 1989, or

(ii) authorised for a use specified in Article 3(5)(*b*), (*c*) or (*h*) of that Order.

(3) The attic storey does not count for the purposes of subsection (1)(*c*) unless it is or has been in use as a dwelling or part of a dwelling.

(4) The requirement in subsection (1)(*d*) is met even if the building has been extended on or after 1st January 1980, provided any extension was completed on or before 31st December 2000.

(5) Treasury regulations may make further provision as to the circumstances in which a building is, or is not, a qualifying building.]¹

Commentary—*Simon's Direct Tax Service* **B2.1004**.
Amendment—¹ This section inserted by FA 2001 s 67, Sch 19 Pt I with effect for expenditure incurred after 10 May 2001.

[393D Meaning of "qualifying flat"

(1) In this Part "qualifying flat" means a flat in respect of which the following requirements are met—

 (*a*) the flat must be in a qualifying building,
 (*b*) the flat must be suitable for letting as a dwelling,
 (*c*) the flat must be held for the purpose of short-term letting,
 (*d*) it must be possible to gain access to the flat without using the part of the ground floor of the building that is authorised for business use (as defined in section 393C(2)),
 (*e*) the flat must not have more than 4 rooms,
 (*f*) the flat must not be a high value flat,
 (*g*) the flat must not be (or have been) created or renovated as part of a scheme involving the creation or renovation of one or more high value flats, and
 (*h*) the flat must not be let to a person connected with the person who incurred the expenditure on its conversion or renovation.

(2) In subsection (1)(*c*) "short-term letting" means letting as a dwelling on a lease for a term (or, in Scotland, period) of not more than 5 years.

(3) For the purposes of subsection (1)(*e*), the following are ignored in determining the number of rooms in a flat—

 (*a*) any kitchen or bathroom, and
 (*b*) any closet, cloakroom or hallway not exceeding 5 square metres in area.

(4) For the purposes of this Part, if a flat is a qualifying flat immediately before a period when it is temporarily unsuitable for letting as a dwelling, it is to be treated as being a qualifying flat during that period.

(5) Treasury regulations may make further provision as to the circumstances in which a flat is, or is not, a qualifying flat.]¹

Commentary—*Simon's Direct Tax Service* **B2.1005**.
Amendment—¹ This section inserted by FA 2001 s 67, Sch 19 Pt I with effect for expenditure incurred after 10 May 2001.

[393E High value flats

(1) For the purposes of section 393D(1) a flat is a high value flat if the notional rent exceeds the relevant limit set out in the Table in subsection (5).

(2) The "notional rent" means the rent that could reasonably be expected for the flat on the relevant date, on the assumption that, on that date—

 (*a*) the conversion or renovation has been completed,
 (*b*) the flat is let furnished,
 (*c*) the lease does not require the tenant to pay a premium or make any other payments to the landlord or a person connected with the landlord,
 (*d*) the tenant is not connected with the person incurring the expenditure on the conversion or renovation of the flat, and
 (*e*) in the case of a flat in England or Wales or Scotland, the flat is let on a shorthold tenancy.

(3) The "relevant date" means the date on which expenditure on—

 (*a*) the conversion of part of the building into the flat, or
 (*b*) (as the case may be) the renovation of the flat,

is first incurred.

(4) "Shorthold tenancy" means—

 (*a*) in the case of a flat in England or Wales, an assured shorthold tenancy;
 (*b*) in the case of a flat in Scotland, a short assured tenancy.

(5) The limit for the notional rent is as shown in the Table—

TABLE

Number of rooms in flat		Flats in Greater London	Flats elsewhere
1	1 or 2 rooms	£350 per week	£150 per week
2	3 rooms	£425 per week	£225 per week
3	4 rooms	£480 per week	£300 per week

(6) Treasury regulations may make provision amending the notional rent limits in the Table in subsection (5).

(7) Section 393D(3) (determination of number of rooms in flat) applies for the purposes of this section.][1]

Commentary—*Simon's Direct Tax Service* B2.1005.
Amendment—[1] This section inserted by FA 2001 s 67, Sch 19 Pt I with effect for expenditure incurred after 10 May 2001.

[CHAPTER 4
THE RELEVANT INTEREST IN THE FLAT

393F General rule as to what is the relevant interest

(1) The relevant interest in a flat in relation to any qualifying expenditure is the interest in the flat to which the person who incurred the expenditure was entitled when it was incurred.

(2) Subsection (1) is subject to the following provisions of this Chapter and to section 393V (provisions applying on termination of lease).

(3) If—

(a) the person who incurred the qualifying expenditure was entitled to more than one interest in the flat when the expenditure was incurred, and
(b) one of those interests was reversionary on all the others,

the reversionary interest is the relevant interest in the flat.

(4) An interest does not cease to be the relevant interest merely because of the creation of a lease or other interest to which that interest is subject.

(5) If—

(a) the relevant interest is a leasehold interest, and
(b) that interest is extinguished on the person entitled to it acquiring the interest which is reversionary on it,

the interest into which the leasehold interest merges becomes the relevant interest when the leasehold interest is extinguished.][1]

Commentary—*Simon's Direct Tax Service* B2.1006.
Amendment—[1] This section inserted by FA 2001 s 67, Sch 19 Pt I with effect for expenditure incurred after 10 May 2001.

[393G Interest acquired on completion of conversion

For the purposes of determining the relevant interest in a flat, a person who—

(a) incurs expenditure on the conversion of part of a building into the flat, and
(b) is entitled to an interest in the flat on or as a result of the completion of the conversion,

is treated as having had that interest when the expenditure was incurred.][1]

Commentary—*Simon's Direct Tax Service* B2.1006.
Amendment—[1] This section inserted by FA 2001 s 67, Sch 19 Pt I with effect for expenditure incurred after 10 May 2001.

[CHAPTER 5
INITIAL ALLOWANCES

393H Initial allowances

(1) A person who has incurred qualifying expenditure in respect of a flat is entitled to an initial allowance in respect of the expenditure.

(2) The amount of the initial allowance is 100% of the qualifying expenditure.

(3) A person claiming an initial allowance under this section may require the allowance to be reduced to a specified amount.

(4) The initial allowance is made for the chargeable period in which the qualifying expenditure is incurred.][1]

Commentary—*Simon's Direct Tax Service* B2.1010.
Amendment—[1] This section inserted by FA 2001 s 67, Sch 19 Pt I with effect for expenditure incurred after 10 May 2001.

[393I Flat not qualifying flat or relevant interest sold before flat first let

(1) No initial allowance is to be made under section 393H if, at the relevant time, the flat is not a qualifying flat.

(2) An initial allowance which has been made in respect of a flat which is to be a qualifying flat is to be withdrawn if—

(a) the flat is not a qualifying flat at the relevant time, or
(b) the person to whom the allowance was made has sold the relevant interest in the flat before the relevant time.

(3) All such assessments and adjustments of assessments are to be made as are necessary to give effect to this section.

(4) In this section ''the relevant time'' means the time when the flat is first suitable for letting as a dwelling.]¹

Commentary—*Simon's Direct Tax Service* **B2.1010**.
Amendment—¹ This section inserted by FA 2001 s 67, Sch 19 Pt I with effect for expenditure incurred after 10 May 2001.

[CHAPTER 6
WRITING-DOWN ALLOWANCES

393J Entitlement to writing-down allowances

(1) A person is entitled to a writing-down allowance for a chargeable period if he has incurred qualifying expenditure in respect of a flat and, at the end of the chargeable period—

    (*a*) the person is entitled to the relevant interest in the flat,
    (*b*) the person has not granted a long lease of the flat out of the relevant interest in consideration of the payment of a capital sum, and
    (*c*) the flat is a qualifying flat.

(2) In subsection (1)(*b*) ''long lease'' means a lease the duration of which exceeds 50 years.

(3) Whether the duration of a lease exceeds 50 years is to be determined—

    (*a*) in accordance with section 38(1) to (4) and (6) of ICTA, and
    (*b*) without regard to section 393V(3) (new lease granted as a result of the exercise of an option treated as continuation of old lease).

(4) A person claiming a writing-down allowance may require the allowance to be reduced to a specified amount.]¹

Commentary—*Simon's Direct Tax Service* **B2.1011**.
Amendment—¹ This section inserted by FA 2001 s 67, Sch 19 Pt I with effect for expenditure incurred after 10 May 2001.

[393K Amount of allowance

(1) The writing-down allowance for a chargeable period is 25% of the qualifying expenditure.

(2) The allowance is proportionately increased or reduced if the chargeable period is more or less than a year.

(3) The amount of the writing-down allowance for a chargeable period is limited to the residue of qualifying expenditure.

(4) For this purpose the residue is ascertained immediately before writing off the writing-down allowance at the end of the chargeable period.]¹

Commentary—*Simon's Direct Tax Service* **B2.1011**.
Amendment—¹ This section inserted by FA 2001 s 67, Sch 19 Pt I with effect for expenditure incurred after 10 May 2001.

[393L Meaning of ''the residue of qualifying expenditure''

The residue of qualifying expenditure is the qualifying expenditure that has not yet been written off in accordance with Chapter 8.]¹

Commentary—*Simon's Direct Tax Service* **B2.1011**.
Amendment—¹ This section inserted by FA 2001 s 67, Sch 19 Pt I with effect for expenditure incurred after 10 May 2001.

[CHAPTER 7
BALANCING ADJUSTMENTS

393M When balancing adjustments are made

(1) A balancing adjustment is made if—

    (*a*) qualifying expenditure has been incurred in respect of a flat, and
    (*b*) a balancing event occurs.

(2) A balancing adjustment is either a balancing allowance or a balancing charge and is made for the chargeable period in which the balancing event occurs.

(3) A balancing allowance or balancing charge is made to or on the person who incurred the qualifying expenditure.

(4) No balancing adjustment is made if the balancing event occurs more than 7 years after the time when the flat was first suitable for letting as a dwelling.

(5) If more than one balancing event occurs, a balancing adjustment is made only on the first of them.]¹

Commentary—*Simon's Direct Tax Service* **B2.1012**.
Amendment—¹ This section inserted by FA 2001 s 67, Sch 19 Pt I with effect for expenditure incurred after 10 May 2001.

CAA 2001

[393N Balancing events

(1) The following are balancing events for the purposes of this Part—

(*a*) the relevant interest in the flat is sold;

(*b*) a long lease of the flat is granted out of the relevant interest in consideration of the payment of a capital sum;

(*c*) if the relevant interest is a lease, the lease ends otherwise than on the person entitled to it acquiring the interest reversionary on it;

(*d*) the person who incurred the qualifying expenditure dies;

(*e*) the flat is demolished or destroyed;

(*f*) the flat ceases to be a qualifying flat (without being demolished or destroyed).

(2) Section 393J(2) and (3) (meaning of ''long lease'') apply for the purposes of subsection (1)(*b*).]¹

Commentary—*Simon's Direct Tax Service* **B2.1012**.
Amendment—¹ This section inserted by FA 2001 s 67, Sch 19 Pt I with effect for expenditure incurred after 10 May 2001.

[393O Proceeds from balancing events

(1) References in this Part to the proceeds from a balancing event are to the amounts received or receivable in connection with the event, as shown in the Table—

TABLE

BALANCING EVENTS AND PROCEEDS

1 Balancing event	2 Proceeds from event
1. The sale of the relevant interest.	The net proceeds of the sale.
2. The grant of a long lease out of the relevant interest.	If the capital sum paid in consideration of the grant is less than the commercial premium, the commercial premium. In any other case, the capital sum paid in consideration of the grant.
3. The coming to an end of a lease, where a person entitled to the lease and a person entitled to any superior interest are connected persons.	The market value of the relevant interest in the flat at the time of the event.
4. The death of the person who incurred the qualifying expenditure.	The residue of qualifying expenditure immediately before the death.
5. The demolition or destruction of the flat.	The net amount received for the remains of the flat, together with— (*a*) any insurance money received in respect of the demolition or destruction, and (*b*) any other compensation of any description so received, so far as it consists of capital sums.
6. The flat ceases to be a qualifying flat.	The market value of the relevant interest in the flat at the time of the event.

(2) The amounts referred to in column 2 of the Table are those received or receivable by the person who incurred the qualifying expenditure.

(3) In Item 2 of the Table ''the commercial premium'' means the premium that would have been given if the transaction had been at arm's length.]¹

Commentary—*Simon's Direct Tax Service* **B2.1012**.
Amendment—¹ This section inserted by FA 2001 s 67, Sch 19 Pt I with effect for expenditure incurred after 10 May 2001.

[393P Calculation of balancing adjustments

(1) A balancing allowance is made if—

(*a*) there are no proceeds from the balancing event, or

(*b*) the proceeds from the balancing event are less than the residue of qualifying expenditure immediately before the event.

(2) The amount of the balancing allowance is the amount of—

(*a*) the residue (if there are no proceeds);

(*b*) the difference (if the proceeds are less than the residue).

(3) A balancing charge is made if the proceeds from the balancing event are more than the residue, if any, of qualifying expenditure immediately before the event.

(4) The amount of the balancing charge is the amount of—

(*a*) the difference, or

(*b*) the proceeds (if the residue is nil).

(5) The amount of a balancing charge made on a person must not exceed the total amount of—

(*a*) any initial allowances made to the person in respect of the expenditure, and
(*b*) any writing-down allowances made to the person in respect of the expenditure for chargeable periods ending on or before the date of the balancing event giving rise to the balancing adjustment.]¹

Commentary—*Simon's Direct Tax Service* **B2.1012**.
Amendment—¹ This section inserted by FA 2001 s 67, Sch 19 Pt I with effect for expenditure incurred after 10 May 2001.

[CHAPTER 8
WRITING OFF QUALIFYING EXPENDITURE

393Q Introduction

For the purposes of this Part qualifying expenditure is written off to the extent and at the times specified in this Chapter.]¹

Commentary—*Simon's Direct Tax Service* **B2.1015**.
Amendment—¹ This section inserted by FA 2001 s 67, Sch 19 Pt I with effect for expenditure incurred after 10 May 2001.

[393R Writing off initial allowances and writing-down allowances

(1) If an initial allowance is made in respect of the qualifying expenditure, the amount of the allowance is written off at the time when the flat is first suitable for letting as a dwelling.

(2) If a writing-down allowance is made in respect of the qualifying expenditure, the amount of the allowance is written off at the end of the chargeable period for which the allowance is made.

(3) If a balancing event occurs at the end of the chargeable period referred to in subsection (2), the amount written off under that subsection is to be taken into account in calculating the residue of qualifying expenditure immediately before the event to determine what balancing adjustment (if any) is to be made.]¹

Commentary—*Simon's Direct Tax Service* **B2.1015**.
Amendment—¹ This section inserted by FA 2001 s 67, Sch 19 Pt I with effect for expenditure incurred after 10 May 2001.

[393S Treatment of demolition costs

(1) This section applies if—
(*a*) a qualifying flat is demolished, and
(*b*) the person who incurred the qualifying expenditure incurs the cost of the demolition.

(2) The net cost of the demolition is added to the residue of qualifying expenditure immediately before the demolition.

(3) "The net cost of the demolition" means the amount, if any, by which the cost of the demolition exceeds any money received for the remains of the flat.

(4) If this section applies, neither the cost of the demolition nor the net cost of the demolition is treated for the purposes of any Part of this Act as expenditure on any other property replacing the flat demolished.]¹

Commentary—*Simon's Direct Tax Service* **B2.1015**.
Amendment—¹ This section inserted by FA 2001 s 67, Sch 19 Pt I with effect for expenditure incurred after 10 May 2001.

[CHAPTER 9
SUPPLEMENTARY PROVISIONS

393T Giving effect to allowances and charges

(1) This section applies if a person is entitled or liable under this Part to an allowance or charge for a chargeable period.

(2) If the person's interest in the flat is an asset of a Schedule A business carried on by him at any time in that period, the allowance or charge is to be given effect in calculating the profits of that business for that period, by treating—
(*a*) the allowance as an expense of that business, and
(*b*) the charge as a receipt of that business.

(3) If the person's interest in the flat is not an asset of a Schedule A business carried on by him at any time in that period, the allowance or charge is to be given effect by treating him as if he had been carrying on a Schedule A business in that period and as if—
(*a*) the allowance were an expense of that business, and
(*b*) the charge were a receipt of that business.]¹

Commentary—*Simon's Direct Tax Service* **B2.1016**.
Amendment—¹ This section inserted by FA 2001 s 67, Sch 19 Pt I with effect for expenditure incurred after 10 May 2001.

[393U Apportionment of sums partly referable to non-qualifying assets

(1) If the sum paid for the sale of the relevant interest in a flat is attributable—

(*a*) partly to assets representing expenditure for which an allowance can be made under this Part, and

(*b*) partly to assets representing other expenditure,

only so much of the sum as on a just and reasonable apportionment is attributable to the assets referred to in paragraph (*a*) is to be taken into account for the purposes of this Part.

(2) Subsection (1) applies to other proceeds from a balancing event in respect of a flat as it applies to a sum given for the sale of the relevant interest in the flat.

(3) Subsection (1) does not affect any other provision of this Act requiring an apportionment of the proceeds of a balancing event.][1]

Commentary—*Simon's Direct Tax Service* **B2.1017**.
Amendment—[1] This section inserted by FA 2001 s 67, Sch 19 Pt I with effect for expenditure incurred after 10 May 2001.

[393V Provisions applying on termination of lease

(1) This section applies for the purposes of this Part if a lease is terminated.

(2) If, with the consent of the lessor, the lessee of a flat remains in possession of the flat after the termination without a new lease being granted to him the lease is treated as continuing so long as the lessee remains in possession.

(3) If on the termination a new lease is granted to the lessee as a result of the exercise of an option available to him under the terms of the first lease, the second lease is treated as a continuation of the first.

(4) If on the termination the lessor pays a sum to the lessee in respect of a flat comprised in the lease, the lease is treated as if it had come to an end by surrender in consideration of the payment.

(5) If on the termination—

(*a*) another lease is granted to a different lessee, and

(*b*) in connection with the transaction that lessee pays a sum to the person who was the lessee under the first lease,

the two leases are to be treated as if they were the same lease which had been assigned by the lessee under the first lease to the lessee under the second lease in consideration of the payment.][1]

Commentary—*Simon's Direct Tax Service* **B2.1006**.
Amendment—[1] This section inserted by FA 2001 s 67, Sch 19 Pt I with effect for expenditure incurred after 10 May 2001.

[393W Meaning of "lease" etc

(1) In this Part "lease" includes—

(*a*) an agreement for a lease if the term to be covered by the lease has begun, and

(*b*) any tenancy,

but does not include a mortgage (and "lessee", "lessor" and "leasehold interest" are to be read accordingly).

(2) In the application of this Part to Scotland—

(*a*) "leasehold interest" (or "leasehold estate") means the interest of a tenant in property subject to a lease, and

(*b*) any reference to an interest which is reversionary on a leasehold interest or on a lease is to be read as a reference to the interest of the landlord in the property subject to the leasehold interest or lease.][1]

Commentary—*Simon's Direct Tax Service* **B2.1006**.
Amendment—[1] This section inserted by FA 2001 s 67, Sch 19 Pt I with effect for expenditure incurred after 10 May 2001.

PART 5

MINERAL EXTRACTION ALLOWANCES

Commentary—*Simon's Direct Tax Service* **Division B2.4**.
Modifications—CAA 2001 Sch 3 para 88 (this Part does not apply in relation to expenditure incurred before 1 April 1986 ("old expenditure") except as provided by the following provisions.
For the purposes of this Part—

(*a*) expenditure which by virtue of any provision of CAA 1990 s 119 (read with any provision of FA 1986 Sch 14) was treated immediately before the coming into force of this Act as expenditure incurred on 1 April 1986 for any purpose or purposes is to continue to be so treated;
(*b*) any allowances treated as having been made under FA 1986 Sch 13 is to continue to be so treated;
(*c*) any amount treated as qualifying expenditure for the purposes of FA 1986 Sch 13 is to continue to be so treated; and
(*d*) in relation to any expenditure to which FA 1986 Sch 14 para 6(4)(*a*) applied, CAA 2001 s 424 does not apply (so that no deduction is to be made from the amount of any disposal receipt by reference to the undeveloped market value of the land in question).
In the case of expenditure incurred in the acquisition of a mineral asset, nothing in para (3)(*c*) above affects the time as at which under CAA 2001 s 404 the undeveloped market value of an interest is to be determined.
In a case where—

(*a*) by virtue of any provision of this paragraph, the whole or any part of the outstanding balance (within the meaning of FA 1986 Sch 14 para 1) of an item of old expenditure is treated for the purposes of this Part as qualifying expenditure, and

(*b*) a balancing charge falls to be made under Chapter 6 of this Part in respect of the expenditure,

then, in determining the amount on which that charge falls to be made, CAA 2001 s 418(4) has effect (subject to CAA 2001 Sch 3 para 88(6)) as if CAA 2001 s 418(*b*) included a reference to allowances made in respect of the item under CAA 1968 Part I Chapter III.

Where the qualifying expenditure in respect of which a balancing charge falls to be made represents part only of the outstanding balance of an item of old expenditure, the reference in CAA 2001 Sch 3 para 88(5) to allowances made in respect of that item is to be construed as a reference to such part of those allowances as it is just and reasonable to apportion to that part of the balance (having regard to any apportionment made under FA 1986 Sch 14 para 3(2)).

CAA 2001 Sch 3 para 91 (where—

(*a*) a person (''the transferor'') disposes of any interest in an oil licence to another (''the transferee'') during the transitional period,

(*b*) part of the value of the interest is attributable to allowable exploration expenditure incurred by the transferor, and

(*c*) an election is made in accordance with this paragraph specifying an amount as the amount to be treated as so attributable,

then, for the purposes of this Part, the amount of any expenditure incurred—

(*a*) by the transferee in acquiring the interest from the transferor, or

(*b*) by any person subsequently acquiring the interest (or an interest deriving from the interest),

which is taken to be attributable to expenditure incurred, before the disposal to the transferee, on mineral exploration and access is the lesser of the amount specified in the election and the amount which, apart from CAA 2001 Sch 3 para 91(3), would be taken to be so attributable.

CHAPTER 1
INTRODUCTION

394 Mineral extraction allowances

(1) Allowances are available under this Part if a person carries on a mineral extraction trade and incurs qualifying expenditure.

(2) In this Part ''mineral extraction trade'' means a trade which consists of, or includes, the working of a source of mineral deposits.

(3) In this Part ''mineral deposits'' includes any natural deposits capable of being lifted or extracted from the earth, and for this purpose geothermal energy is to be treated as a natural deposit.

(4) Any reference in this Part to mineral deposits is to mineral deposits of a wasting nature.

(5) In this Part ''source of mineral deposits'' includes a mine, an oil well and a source of geothermal energy.

Commentary—*Simon's Direct Tax Service* **B2.401, 405.**
Former enactments—Sub-ss (1): CAA 1990 s 98(1), 105(1), 109(1).
Sub-s (2): CAA 1990 s 121(1) (''trade of mineral extraction'').
Sub-s (3): CAA 1990 s 161(2).
Sub-s (4): CAA 1990 s 121(2).
Sub-s (5): CAA 1990 s 121(1).
Modifications—CAA 2001 Sch 3 para 88 (expenditure incurred before 1 April 1986: see modification note at the start of this Part).
CAA 2001 Sch 3 para 91 (disposal of oil licences: see modification note at the start of this Part).

395 Qualifying expenditure

(1) In this Part ''qualifying expenditure'' means—

(*a*) expenditure on mineral exploration and access which is qualifying expenditure under Chapter 2,

(*b*) expenditure on acquiring a mineral asset which is qualifying expenditure under Chapter 3,

(*c*) expenditure which is treated as qualifying expenditure on mineral exploration and access under section 407(5) or 408(2), and

(*d*) expenditure which is qualifying expenditure under Chapter 5 (expenditure on works likely to become valueless and post-trading restoration expenditure).

But this is subject to subsections (2) and (3).

(2) Expenditure is not qualifying expenditure if it is excluded from being qualifying expenditure by section 399.

(3) Chapter 4 contains provisions limiting in certain cases the amount of expenditure which is qualifying expenditure.

Commentary—*Simon's Direct Tax Service* **B2.406.**
Former enactments—Sub-s (1): CAA 1990 s 105(1).
Sub-s (2): CAA 1990 s 105(1).
Sub-s (3): CAA 1990 s 105(3).
Definitions—''Mineral asset'', s 397; ''mineral exploration and access'', s 396.
Modifications—CAA 2001 Sch 3 para 88 (expenditure incurred before 1 April 1986: see modification note at the start of this Part).
CAA 2001 Sch 3 para 91 (disposal of oil licences: see modification note at the start of this Part).

396 Meaning of ''mineral exploration and access''

(1) In this Part ''mineral exploration and access'' means—

(*a*) searching for or discovering and testing the mineral deposits of a source, or

(*b*) winning access to such deposits.

(2) Expenditure on seeking planning permission necessary to enable—

    (*a*) mineral exploration and access to be undertaken at any place, or
    (*b*) any mineral deposits to be worked,

is treated as expenditure on mineral exploration and access if planning permission is not granted.

(3) "Seeking planning permission" includes pursuing an appeal against a refusal to grant planning permission.

Commentary—*Simon's Direct Tax Service* **B2.405, 406**.
Former enactments—Sub-s (1): CAA 1990 121(1).
Sub-ss (2), (3): CAA 1990 s 105(6).
Revenue Internal Guidance—Capital allowances manual, CA 50230 (meaning of "access" and "works").
Definition—"Mineral deposits", s 394(3).
Modifications—CAA 2001 Sch 3 para 88 (expenditure incurred before 1 April 1986: see modification note at the start of this Part).
CAA 2001 Sch 3 para 91 (disposal of oil licences: see modification note at the start of this Part).

397 Meaning of "mineral asset"

In this Part "mineral asset" means—

    (*a*) any mineral deposits or land comprising mineral deposits, or
    (*b*) any interest in or right over such deposits or land.

Commentary—*Simon's Direct Tax Service* **B2.405**.
Former enactment—CAA 1990 s 121(1).
Revenue Internal Guidance—Capital allowances manual CA 50220 (expenditure on non-mineral bearing land acquired to give access to adjacent mineral deposits is not qualifying expenditure).
Definition—"Mineral deposits", s 394(3).
Modifications—CAA 2001 Sch 3 para 88 (expenditure incurred before 1 April 1986: see modification note at the start of this Part).
CAA 2001 Sch 3 para 91 (disposal of oil licences: see modification note at the start of this Part).

398 Relationship between main types of qualifying expenditure

Subject to Chapter 4, expenditure on—

    (*a*) the acquisition of, or of rights over, the site of a source of mineral deposits, or
    (*b*) the acquisition of, or of rights over, mineral deposits,

is to be treated as expenditure on acquiring a mineral asset and not as expenditure on mineral exploration and access.

Commentary—*Simon's Direct Tax Service* **B2.406**.
Former enactment—CAA 1990 s 105(7).
Definitions—"Mineral asset", s 397; "mineral exploration and access", s 396; "mineral deposits", s 394(3); "source of mineral deposits", s 394(5).
Modifications—CAA 2001 Sch 3 para 88 (expenditure incurred before 1 April 1986: see modification note at the start of this Part).
CAA 2001 Sch 3 para 91 (disposal of oil licences: see modification note at the start of this Part).

399 Expenditure excluded from being qualifying expenditure

(1) Expenditure on the provision of plant or machinery is not qualifying expenditure except as provided by section 402 (pre-trading expenditure on plant or machinery).

(2) Expenditure on works constructed wholly or mainly for subjecting the raw product of a source to any process is not qualifying expenditure, unless the process is designed for preparing the raw product for use as such.

(3) Expenditure on buildings or structures provided for occupation by, or for the welfare of, workers is not qualifying expenditure except as provided by section 415.

(4) Expenditure on a building is not qualifying expenditure if the whole of the building was constructed for use as an office.

(5) Subsection (6) applies if part of a building or structure has been constructed for use as an office.

(6) The expenditure on the office part is not qualifying expenditure if it was more than 10% of the capital expenditure incurred on the construction of the whole.

Commentary—*Simon's Direct Tax Service* **B2.406**.
Former enactments—Sub-s (1): CAA 1990 105(4).
Sub-ss (2)–(6): CAA 1990 s 105(5).
Definition—"Capital expenditure", s 4.
Modifications—CAA 2001 Sch 3 para 88 (expenditure incurred before 1 April 1986: see modification note at the start of this Part).
CAA 2001 Sch 3 para 91 (disposal of oil licences: see modification note at the start of this Part).

CHAPTER 2

QUALIFYING EXPENDITURE ON MINERAL EXPLORATION AND ACCESS

400 Qualifying expenditure on mineral exploration and access

(1) Expenditure on mineral exploration and access is qualifying expenditure if—

    (*a*) it is capital expenditure, and

    (*b*) it is incurred for the purposes of a mineral extraction trade.

(2) Expenditure on mineral exploration and access incurred by a person in connection with a mineral extraction trade which that person carries on then or subsequently is to be treated as incurred for the purposes of that trade.

(3) But pre-trading expenditure on mineral exploration and access is qualifying expenditure only to the extent provided by—

    section 401 (pre-trading exploration expenditure), or

    section 402 (pre-trading expenditure on plant or machinery).

(4) Any pre-trading expenditure that is qualifying expenditure under either of those sections is to be treated as incurred on the first day of trading.

(5) In this Chapter—

    (*a*) ''pre-trading expenditure'' means capital expenditure incurred before the day on which a person begins to carry on a mineral extraction trade, and

    (*b*) ''the first day of trading'', in relation to a person's pre-trading expenditure, means the day on which that person begins to carry on the mineral extraction trade.

Commentary—*Simon's Direct Tax Service* **B2.406, 407**.
Former enactments—Sub-s (1): CAA 1990 ss 98(1), 105(1); change in law.
Sub-s (2): CAA 1990 s 102.
Sub-s (3): CAA 1990 s 105(2).
Sub-s (4): CAA 1990 ss 106(2), 107(3), 120(2).
Definitions—''Capital expenditure'', s 4; ''mineral exploration and access'', s 396; ''mineral extraction trade'', s 394(2).
Modifications—CAA 2001 Sch 3 para 88 (expenditure incurred before 1 April 1986: see modification note at the start of this Part).
CAA 2001 Sch 3 para 91 (disposal of oil licences: see modification note at the start of this Part).

401 Pre-trading exploration expenditure

(1) This section applies if—

    (*a*) a person incurs pre-trading expenditure on mineral exploration and access at a source, and

    (*b*) the expenditure is not incurred on the provision of plant or machinery.

(2) The amount of the expenditure (''pre-trading exploration expenditure'') that is qualifying expenditure depends on whether mineral exploration and access is continuing at the source on the first day of trading.

(3) If it is, so much of the pre-trading exploration expenditure as exceeds any relevant receipts is qualifying expenditure.

(4) If it is not, only so much of the pre-trading exploration expenditure as—

    (*a*) was incurred within 6 years ending on the first day of trading, and

    (*b*) exceeds any relevant receipts,

is qualifying expenditure.

(5) ''Relevant receipts'' means capital sums received—

    (*a*) by the person incurring the pre-trading exploration expenditure referred to in subsection (3) or (4), and

    (*b*) before the first day of trading,

so far as they are reasonably attributable to that expenditure.

Commentary—*Simon's Direct Tax Service* **B2.407**.
Former enactments—Sub-s (1): CAA 1990 s 107(1).
Sub-s (2): CAA 1990 s 107(2), (3), (5).
Sub-s (3): CAA 1990 s 107(2).
Sub-s (4): CAA 1990 s 107(3).
Sub-s (5): CAA 1990 s 107(4).
Definitions—''Capital sum'', s 4; ''mineral exploration and access'', s 396.
Modifications—CAA 2001 Sch 3 para 88 (CAA 2001 ss 401, 402 apply to expenditure incurred before 1 April 1986 (''old expenditure'') if—

    (*a*) that expenditure was incurred on mineral exploration and access,

    (*b*) immediately before 1 April 1986, no allowance had been made under Chapter III of Part I of CAA 1968 in respect of it, and

    (*c*) after that day and before mineral exploration and access ceases at the source in question, the person by whom the expenditure was incurred began or begins to carry on a trade of mineral extraction.

''Source'' has the same meaning as it had in FA 1986 Sch 14.
Expenditure incurred before 1 April 1986: see modification note at the start of this Part).
CAA 2001 Sch 3 para 91 (disposal of oil licences: see modification note at the start of this Part).

402 Pre-trading expenditure on plant or machinery

(1) This section applies if—

(*a*) a person incurs pre-trading expenditure on the provision of plant or machinery for mineral exploration and access,

(*b*) the plant or machinery was used in connection with mineral exploration and access at a source, and

(*c*) before the first day of trading, the plant or machinery is sold, demolished, destroyed or abandoned.

(2) The amount of the expenditure ("pre-trading expenditure on plant or machinery") that is qualifying expenditure depends on whether mineral exploration and access is continuing at the source on the first day of trading.

(3) If it is, so much of the pre-trading expenditure on plant or machinery as exceeds any relevant receipts is qualifying expenditure.

(4) If it is not, only so much of the pre-trading expenditure on plant or machinery as—

(*a*) was incurred within 6 years ending on the first day of trading, and

(*b*) exceeds any relevant receipts,

is qualifying expenditure.

(5) "Relevant receipts" means—

(*a*) if the plant or machinery is sold, the net proceeds to the person of the sale;

(*b*) if the plant or machinery is demolished or destroyed, the net amount received by the person for the remains of the plant or machinery, together with—

(i) any insurance money received by him in respect of the demolition or destruction, and

(ii) any other compensation of any description so received, so far as it consists of capital sums;

(*c*) if the plant or machinery is abandoned—

(i) any insurance money received by the person in respect of the abandonment, and

(ii) any other compensation of any description so received, so far as it consists of capital sums.

Commentary—*Simon's Direct Tax Service* **B2.407**.
Former enactments—Sub-s (1): CAA 1990 106(1), (4).
Sub-s (2): CAA 1990 s 106(4).
Sub-s (3): CAA 1990 s 106(2), (3).
Sub-s (4): CAA 1990 s 106(3), (4).
Sub-s (5): CAA 1990 ss 106(3), 156; change in law.
Definitions—"Capital sum", s 4; "mineral exploration and access", s 396.
Modifications—CAA 2001 Sch 3 para 88 (CAA 2001 ss 401, 402 apply to expenditure incurred before 1 April 1986 ("old expenditure") if—

(*a*) that expenditure was incurred on mineral exploration and access,

(*b*) immediately before 1 April 1986, no allowance had been made under Chapter III of Part I of CAA 1968 in respect of it, and

(*c*) after that day and before mineral exploration and access ceases at the source in question, the person by whom the expenditure was incurred began or begins to carry on a trade of mineral extraction.

"Source" has the same meaning as it had in FA 1986 Sch 14.
Expenditure incurred before 1 April 1986: see modification note at the start of this Part).
CAA 2001 Sch 3 para 91 (disposal of oil licences: see modification note at the start of this Part).

CHAPTER 3

QUALIFYING EXPENDITURE ON ACQUIRING A MINERAL ASSET

403 Qualifying expenditure on acquiring a mineral asset

(1) Expenditure on acquiring a mineral asset is qualifying expenditure if—

(*a*) it is capital expenditure, and

(*b*) it is incurred for the purposes of a mineral extraction trade.

(2) Subsection (1) is subject to—

section 404 (exclusion of undeveloped market value of land), and

section 406 (reduction where premium relief previously allowed).

(3) In this Chapter "the buyer", in relation to the acquisition of a mineral asset, means the person acquiring it.

Commentary—*Simon's Direct Tax Service* **B2.406, 410**.
Former enactments—Sub-s (1): CAA 1990 ss 98(1), 105(1); change in law.
Sub-s (2): CAA 1990 s 105(3).
Definitions—"Capital expenditure", s 4; "mineral asset", s 397; "mineral extraction trade", s 394(2).
Modifications—CAA 2001 Sch 3 para 88 (expenditure incurred before 1 April 1986: see modification note at the start of this Part).
CAA 2001 Sch 3 para 91 (disposal of oil licences: see modification note at the start of this Part).

404 Exclusion of undeveloped market value of land

(1) If the mineral asset is an interest in land, so much of the buyer's expenditure on acquiring the asset as is equal to the undeveloped market value of the interest is not qualifying expenditure.

(2) "The undeveloped market value of the interest" means the amount that, at the time of the acquisition, the interest might reasonably be expected to fetch on a sale in the open market on the assumptions in subsection (3).

(3) The assumptions are that—

(a) there is no source of mineral deposits on or in the land, and
(b) it will only ever be lawful to carry out existing permitted development.

(4) Development is existing permitted development if at the time of the acquisition—

(a) it has been, or had begun to be, lawfully carried out, or
(b) it could be lawfully carried out under planning permission granted by a general development order.

(5) In applying subsection (4) in relation to land outside the United Kingdom—

(a) whether, at the time of the acquisition, development has been, or had begun to be, lawfully carried out is to be determined according to the law of the territory in which the land is situated, and
(b) whether, at that time, development could be lawfully carried out under planning permission granted by a general development order is to be determined as if the land were in England.

(6) References in this section to the time of acquisition are not affected by section 434 (expenditure incurred before trade carried on).

(7) This section does not apply to the buyer's expenditure if an election under section 569 (election to treat sale as being for alternative amount) is made in relation to the acquisition.

Commentary—*Simon's Direct Tax Service* **B2.410**.
Former enactments—Sub-s (1): CAA 1990 s 110(1).
Sub-ss (2)–(4): CAA 1990 s 110(2).
Sub-s (5): CAA 1990 s 110(3); change in law.
Sub-s (6): CAA 1990 s 110(6).
Revenue Internal Guidance—Capital allowances manual CA 50340–50360 (procedures involving District Valuer re-ascertainment of undeveloped market value).
Definitions—"General development order", s 436; "mineral asset", s 397; "mineral deposits", s 394(3); "source of mineral deposits", s 394(5).
Modifications—CAA 2001 Sch 3 para 88 (expenditure incurred before 1 April 1986: see modification note at the start of this Part).
CAA 2001 Sch 3 para 91 (disposal of oil licences: see modification note at the start of this Part).

405 Qualifying expenditure where buildings or structures cease to be used

(1) This section applies if—

(a) section 404 (exclusion of undeveloped market value of land) applies to limit the buyer's qualifying expenditure on acquiring the mineral asset,
(b) the undeveloped market value of the interest in land includes the value of any buildings or structures on the land, and
(c) at the time of the acquisition, or at any later time, the buildings or structures permanently cease to be used for any purpose.

(2) The buyer is to be treated—

(a) as having incurred qualifying expenditure, on acquiring a mineral asset, of an amount equal to the unrelieved value of the buildings or structures, and
(b) as having incurred it when the buildings or structures permanently cease to be used for any purpose.

(3) The unrelieved value of the buildings or structures is—

$$V - (A - B)$$

where—

V is the value of the buildings or structures at the date of the acquisition (disregarding any value properly attributable to the land on which they stand),
A is the amount of any allowances made to the buyer under the provisions of this Act other than Part 10 (assured tenancy allowances) in respect of—

(a) the buildings or structures, or
(b) assets in the buildings or structures, and

B is the amount of any balancing charges made on the buyer under those provisions in respect of those buildings or structures or assets in them.

(4) References in this section to the time of acquisition are not affected by section 434 (time when expenditure incurred).

Commentary—*Simon's Direct Tax Service* **B2.410**.
Former enactments—Sub-ss (1), (2): CAA 1990 s 110(4).
Sub-s (3): CAA 1990 s 110(5).
Sub-s (4): CAA 1990 s 110(6).

Definition—"Mineral asset", s 397.
Modifications—CAA 2001 Sch 3 para 84 (in sub-s (3) above, "A" does not include, in cases where the buildings or structures have permanently ceased to be used for any purpose before 27 July 1989, the amount of any agricultural buildings allowances).
CAA 2001 Sch 3 para 88 (expenditure incurred before 1 April 1986: see modification note at the start of this Part).
CAA 2001 Sch 3 para 91 (disposal of oil licences: see modification note at the start of this Part).

406 Reduction where premium relief previously allowed

(1) This section applies if—

(a) the mineral asset is or includes an interest in land, and
(b) for chargeable periods previous to the chargeable period for which the buyer first becomes entitled to an allowance under this Part in respect of the expenditure on acquiring the mineral asset, deductions are made under section 87 of ICTA (deductions in calculating trading profits where premiums etc taxable).

(2) The amount of the expenditure on the acquisition of the mineral asset that is qualifying expenditure is reduced by—

$$D \times \frac{E}{T}$$

where—

D is the total of the deductions made under section 87 of ICTA in the earlier chargeable periods mentioned in subsection (1)(b),
E is the amount of the capital expenditure on the acquisition of the interest in land that would have been qualifying expenditure if the buyer had been entitled to allowances under this Part in those earlier periods, and
T is the total amount of the capital expenditure on the acquisition of the interest in land.

Commentary—*Simon's Direct Tax Service* B2.410.
Former enactment—CAA 1990 s 111.
Definitions—"Capital expenditure", s 4; "mineral asset", s 397.
Modifications—CAA 2001 Sch 3 para 88 (expenditure incurred before 1 April 1986: see modification note at the start of this Part).
CAA 2001 Sch 3 para 91 (disposal of oil licences: see modification note at the start of this Part).

CHAPTER 4

QUALIFYING EXPENDITURE: SECOND-HAND ASSETS

Assets reflecting expenditure on mineral exploration and access

407 Acquisition of mineral asset owned by previous trader

(1) This section applies if—

(a) a person carrying on a mineral extraction trade ("the buyer") incurs capital expenditure on acquiring a mineral asset ("asset X") for the purposes of that trade, and
(b) the conditions in subsection (3) are met.

(2) In this section "the buyer's expenditure" means the expenditure referred to in subsection (1)(a), less any amount which, under section 404 (exclusion of undeveloped market value of land), is not qualifying expenditure on the acquisition of the mineral asset.

(3) The conditions are that—

(a) expenditure was previously incurred on acquiring asset X or bringing it into existence by—
(i) the person from whom the buyer acquired asset X, or
(ii) an earlier owner of asset X,
in connection with a mineral extraction trade carried on by the person incurring that expenditure,
(b) part of the value of asset X is properly attributable to expenditure ("E1") on mineral exploration and access by the previous trader, and
(c) it is just and reasonable to attribute part of the buyer's expenditure ("E2") to that part of the value of asset X.

(4) In arriving at E1, any expenditure that is or has been deducted in calculating, for tax purposes, the profits of a trade carried on by the previous trader must be excluded.

(5) If this section applies—

(a) so much of the buyer's expenditure as is equal to the lesser of E1 and E2 is to be treated as qualifying expenditure on mineral exploration and access, and
(b) the buyer's expenditure on acquiring the mineral asset is reduced by the same amount.

(6) "The previous trader" means—

(a) the person incurring the expenditure mentioned in subsection (3)(a), or
(b) if there has been more than one such person, the last before the buyer acquired asset X.

(7) In this section references to asset X include—

(a) two or more assets which together make up asset X, and
(b) one asset from which, or two or more assets from the combination of which, asset X is derived.

Commentary—*Simon's Direct Tax Service* **B2.411**.
Former enactments—Sub-s (1): CAA 1990 113(1); change in law.
Sub-s (2): CAA 1990 ss 114(1), 115(3).
Sub-s (3): CAA 1990 ss 113(3), 115(1), (2).
Sub-s (4): CAA 1990 s 115(2A).
Sub-s (5): CAA 1990 s 115(2).
Sub-s (6): CAA 1990 ss 113(4), 115(3).
Sub-s (7): CAA 1990 ss 113(5), 115(3).
Definitions—''Capital expenditure'', s 4; ''mineral asset'', s 397; ''mineral exploration and access'', s 396; ''mineral extraction trade'', s 394(2).
Modifications—CAA 2001 Sch 3 para 85 (sub-s (4) above does not apply in relation to claims made before 26 November 1996).
CAA 2001 Sch 3 para 87(1), (2) (CAA 2001 ss 407, 410, and 411 do not apply if asset X is a mineral asset situated in the United Kingdom, and the capital expenditure incurred by the buyer consists of the payment of sums under a contract entered into by him before 16 July 1985).
CAA 2001 Sch 3 para 87(3) (CAA 2001 ss 407, 411 apply in relation to a case where asset X is a mineral asset situated in the United Kingdom, as if the references to an earlier owner of the asset did not include a person who has not owned the asset at any time after 31 March 1986).
CAA 2001 Sch 3 para 88 (expenditure incurred before 1 April 1986: see modification note at the start of this Part).
CAA 2001 Sch 3 para 91 (disposal of oil licences: see modification note at the start of this Part).

408 Acquisition of oil licence from non-trader

(1) This section applies if—

    (a) a person carrying on a mineral extraction trade (''the buyer'') incurs capital expenditure on acquiring an interest in an oil licence for the purposes of that trade,
    (b) the person from whom the interest was acquired (''the seller'') disposed of the interest without having carried on a mineral extraction trade,
    (c) part of the value of the interest is attributable to expenditure (''E1'') on mineral exploration and access by the seller, and
    (d) it is just and reasonable to attribute part of the buyer's expenditure (''E2'') to that part of the value of the interest.

(2) If this section applies—

    (a) so much of the buyer's expenditure as is equal to the lesser of E1 and E2 is to be treated as qualifying expenditure on mineral exploration and access, and
    (b) the buyer's expenditure on acquiring the interest in the oil licence is reduced by an amount equal to E2.

(3) In this section ''oil licence'' and ''interest in an oil licence'' have the same meaning as in Chapter 3 of Part 12.

Commentary—*Simon's Direct Tax Service* **B2.413**.
Former enactments—Sub-s (1): CAA 1990 ss 118(1), 138A(1)–(3); change in law.
Sub-s (2): CAA 1990 ss 118(2), 138A(1), (2).
Sub-s (3): CAA 1990 ss 118(2), 138A(4).
Definitions—''Capital expenditure'', s 4; ''mineral exploration and access'', s 396; ''mineral extraction trade'', s 394(2).
Modifications—CAA 2001 Sch 3 para 86 (the section above does not apply to acquisitions occurring before 13 September 1995).
CAA 2001 Sch 3 para 88 (expenditure incurred before 1 April 1986: see modification note at the start of this Part).
CAA 2001 Sch 3 para 91 (disposal of oil licences: see modification note at the start of this Part).

409 Acquisition of other assets from non-traders

(1) This section applies if—

    (a) a person carrying on a mineral extraction trade (''the buyer'') incurs capital expenditure on acquiring any assets for the purposes of that trade,
    (b) the person from whom the assets were acquired (''the seller'') disposed of the assets without having carried on a mineral extraction trade,
    (c) the assets represent expenditure on mineral exploration and access incurred by the seller, and
    (d) section 408 (acquisition of oil licence from non-trader) does not apply in relation to the acquisition.

(2) If this section applies, the buyer's expenditure is qualifying expenditure only to the extent that it does not exceed the amount of the seller's expenditure on mineral exploration and access that is represented by the assets.

(3) The references in this section to assets representing expenditure on mineral exploration and access include any results obtained from any search, exploration or inquiry on which the expenditure was incurred.

Commentary—*Simon's Direct Tax Service* **B2.412**.
Former enactments—Sub-ss (1), (2): CAA 1990 s 118(1); change in law.
Sub-s (3): CAA 1990 s 121(3).
Definitions—''Capital expenditure'', s 4; ''mineral exploration and access'', s 396; ''mineral extraction trade'', s 394(2).
Modifications—CAA 2001 Sch 3 para 88 (expenditure incurred before 1 April 1986: see modification note at the start of this Part).
CAA 2001 Sch 3 para 91 (disposal of oil licences: see modification note at the start of this Part).

Qualifying expenditure on assets limited by reference to historic costs

410 UK oil licence: limit is original licence payment

(1) This section applies if a person carrying on a mineral extraction trade ("the buyer") incurs capital expenditure on acquiring a mineral asset which is a UK oil licence, or an interest in such a licence, for the purposes of that trade.

(2) If this section applies, the buyer's expenditure is qualifying expenditure only to the extent that it does not exceed—

    (*a*) the original licence payment, or

    (*b*) if the mineral asset is an interest in a UK oil licence, such part of the original licence payment as it is just and reasonable to attribute to the interest.

(3) In this section "the original licence payment" means the amount paid to the relevant authority for the purpose of obtaining the licence by the person to whom the licence was granted.

(4) This section does not affect any expenditure that is treated as qualifying expenditure on mineral exploration and access under—

    section 407(5) (acquisition of mineral asset owned by previous trader), or

    section 408(2) (acquisition of oil licence from non-trader).

(5) In this section "UK oil licence" and "the relevant authority" have the same meaning as in Chapter 3 of Part 12.

Commentary—*Simon's Direct Tax Service* **B2.413**.
Former enactments—Sub-s (1): CAA 1990 116(1).
Sub-s (2): CAA 1990 s 116(1), (3).
Sub-s (3): CAA 1990 s 116(3).
Definitions—"Capital expenditure", s 4; "mineral asset", s 397; "mineral exploration and access", s 396; "mineral extraction trade", s 394(2); "UK oil licence", s 552(2).
Modifications—CAA 2001 Sch 3 para 87(1), (2) (CAA 2001 ss 407, 410, and 411 do not apply if asset X is a mineral asset situated in the United Kingdom, and the capital expenditure incurred by the buyer consists of the payment of sums under a contract entered into by him before 16 July 1985.
CAA 2001 Sch 3 para 88 (expenditure incurred before 1 April 1986: see modification note at the start of this Part).
CAA 2001 Sch 3 para 91 (disposal of oil licences: see modification note at the start of this Part).

411 Assets generally: limit is residue of previous trader's qualifying expenditure

(1) This section applies if—

    (*a*) a person carrying on a mineral extraction trade ("the buyer") incurs capital expenditure on acquiring an asset ("asset X") for the purposes of that trade, and

    (*b*) expenditure was previously incurred on acquiring asset X or bringing it into existence by—

        (i) the person from whom the buyer acquired asset X, or

        (ii) an earlier owner of asset X,

in connection with a mineral extraction trade carried on by the person incurring that expenditure.

(2) In this section "the buyer's expenditure" means the expenditure referred to in subsection (1)(*a*) less any amount which, under section 404 (exclusion of undeveloped market value of land), is not qualifying expenditure on the acquisition of the mineral asset.

(3) If this section applies, the buyer's expenditure is qualifying expenditure only to the extent that it does not exceed the residue of the previous trader's qualifying expenditure.

(4) The residue of the previous trader's qualifying expenditure is—

$$QE - (A - B)$$

where—

    QE is so much of the expenditure incurred by the previous trader on the acquisition or bringing into existence of asset X as constitutes qualifying expenditure for the purposes of this Part,

    A is the total of any allowances made under this Part in respect of the previous trader's qualifying expenditure, and

    B is the total of any balancing charges made under this Part in respect of the previous trader's qualifying expenditure.

(5) "The previous trader" means—

    (*a*) the person incurring the expenditure mentioned in subsection (1)(*b*), or

    (*b*) if there has been more than one such person, the last before the buyer acquired asset X.

(6) In this section references to asset X include—

    (*a*) two or more assets which together make up asset X, and

    (*b*) one asset from which, or two or more assets from the combination of which, asset X is derived.

(7) For the purposes of subsection (4), if the previous trader incurred expenditure on the acquisition or bringing into existence of one or more assets from which asset X is derived, QE is so much of that expenditure as—

    (*a*) was qualifying expenditure for the purposes of this Part, and

    (*b*) is just and reasonable to attribute to asset X;

and a similar apportionment is to be made to arrive at A and B.

(8) This section does not affect any expenditure that is treated as qualifying expenditure on mineral exploration and access under—

    section 407(5) (acquisition of mineral asset owned by previous trader), or

    section 408(2) (acquisition of oil licence from non-trader).

Commentary—*Simon's Direct Tax Service* **B2.411**.
Former enactments—Sub-s (1): CAA 1990 s 113(1), (3).
Sub-s (2): CAA 1990 s 114(1).
Sub-s (3): CAA 1990 s 114(2), (3).
Sub-s (4): CAA 1990 s 114(4), (6).
Sub-s (5): CAA 1990 s 113(4), 114(6).
Sub-s (6): CAA 1990 s 113(5), 114(6).
Sub-s (7): CAA 1990 s 113(6), 114(5).
Revenue Internal Guidance—Capital allowances manual CA 50610 (operation of this section).
Definitions—''Capital expenditure'', s 4; ''mineral asset'', s 397; ''mineral exploration and access'', s 396; ''mineral extraction trade'', s 394(2).
Modifications—CAA 2001 Sch 3 para 87(1), (2) (CAA 2001 ss 407, 410, and 411 do not apply if asset X is a mineral asset situated in the United Kingdom, and the capital expenditure incurred by the buyer consists of the payment of sums under a contract entered into by him before 16 July 1985).
CAA 2001 Sch 3 para 87(3) (CAA 2001 ss 407, 411 apply in relation to a case where asset X is a mineral asset situated in the United Kingdom, as if the references to an earlier owner of the asset did not include a person who has not owned the asset at any time after 31 March 1986).
CAA 2001 Sch 3 para 88 (expenditure incurred before 1 April 1986: see modification note at the start of this Part).
CAA 2001 Sch 3 para 91 (disposal of oil licences: see modification note at the start of this Part).

412 Transfers of mineral assets within group: limit is initial group expenditure

(1) Subject to section 413, this section applies if—

    (a) a company (''the buyer'') incurs capital expenditure on acquiring a mineral asset (''asset X'') from another company (''the seller''), and

    (b) the seller is a group company in relation to the buyer at the time of the acquisition.

(2) The buyer's expenditure on acquiring asset X is to be left out of account for the purposes of this Part to the extent that it exceeds—

    (a) the capital expenditure incurred by the seller on acquiring asset X, or

    (b) if asset X is an interest or right granted by the seller in a mineral asset acquired by the seller (''asset Y''), so much of the capital expenditure incurred by the seller on asset Y as on a just and reasonable apportionment is referable to asset X.

(3) If there is a sequence of acquisitions within subsection (1), apply subsection (2) in the same sequence (starting with the first acquisition in the sequence).

(4) Subsections (5) to (7) apply if—

    (a) the buyer is carrying on a mineral extraction trade, and

    (b) the asset is an interest in land.

(5) Section 404 (exclusion of undeveloped market value of land) applies to the buyer as if the time of the buyer's acquisition of the interest in land were—

    (a) the time of the seller's acquisition of the interest, or

    (b) if there is a sequence of acquisitions within subsection (1), the time when the interest was acquired by the company which is the seller in the first acquisition in the sequence.

(6) Subject to subsection (7), section 405 (qualifying expenditure where buildings or structures cease to be used) applies to the buyer as if the time of the buyer's acquisition of the interest in land were the time of the seller's acquisition of the interest.

(7) If there is a sequence of acquisitions within subsection (1), section 405 applies as if—

    (a) the time of the acquisition were the time when the interest was acquired by the company which is the seller in the first acquisition in the sequence, but

    (b) the allowances and balancing charges to be taken into account in calculating (under section 405(3)) the unrelieved value of the buildings or structures included any allowances or charges made to or on any seller in the sequence.

Commentary—*Simon's Direct Tax Service* **B2.414**.
Former enactments—Sub-s (1): CAA 1990 117(1).
Sub-s (2): CAA 1990 s 117(3), (4); change in law.
Sub-ss (4)–(6): CAA 1990 s 117(5).
Sub-s (7): CAA 1990 s 117(5), (6).
Definitions—''Capital expenditure'', s 4; ''mineral asset'', s 397; ''mineral extraction trade'', s 394(2).
Modifications—CAA 2001 Sch 3 para 88 (expenditure incurred before 1 April 1986: see modification note at the start of this Part).
CAA 2001 Sch 3 para 91 (disposal of oil licences: see modification note at the start of this Part).

413 Transfers of mineral assets within group: supplementary

(1) For the purposes of section 412, a company is a group company in relation to another company if—

    (a) it controls, or is controlled by, the other company, or

    (b) both companies are under the control of another person.

(2) Section 412 does not apply if—

(*a*) section 410 (UK oil licences: limit is original licence payment) applies to the acquisition, or

(*b*) the acquisition is a sale in respect of which an election is made under section 569 (election to treat sale as being for an alternative amount).

(3) Section 412 applies regardless of section 568 (sales between connected persons etc, or to obtain tax advantage, treated as at market value).

(4) Section 412 does not affect any expenditure that is treated as qualifying expenditure on mineral exploration and access under—

section 407(5) (acquisition of mineral asset owned by previous trader), or

section 408(2) (acquisition of oil licence from non-trader).

Commentary—*Simon's Direct Tax Service* **B2.414**.
Former enactments—Sub-s (1): CAA 1990 s 117(1).
Sub-ss (2), (3): CAA 1990 s 117(2).
Definitions—"Mineral asset", s 397; "mineral exploration and access", s 396; "UK oil licence", s 552(2).
Modifications—CAA 2001 Sch 3 para 88 (expenditure incurred before 1 April 1986: see modification note at the start of this Part).
CAA 2001 Sch 3 para 91 (disposal of oil licences: see modification note at the start of this Part).

CHAPTER 5
OTHER KINDS OF QUALIFYING EXPENDITURE

414 Expenditure on works likely to become valueless

(1) Expenditure is qualifying expenditure if—

(*a*) it is capital expenditure on constructing works in connection with the working of a source of mineral deposits,

(*b*) it is incurred for the purposes of a mineral extraction trade, and

(*c*) the works—

(i) are likely to be of little or no value, when the source is no longer worked, to the last person working the source, or

(ii) if the source is worked under a foreign concession, are likely to become valueless, when the concession ends, to the last person working the source under the concession.

(2) For the purposes of subsection (1), expenditure on constructing works does not include expenditure on acquiring the site of the works or any right in or over the site.

(3) In subsection (1)(*c*) "foreign concession" means a right or privilege granted by the government of, or any municipality or other authority in, a territory outside the United Kingdom.

Commentary—*Simon's Direct Tax Service* **B2.406**.
Former enactments—Sub-ss (1): CAA 1990 ss 98(1), 105(1); change in law.
Sub-s (2): CAA 1990 s 105(5).
Sub-s (3): CAA 1990 s 161(2).
Definitions—"Capital expenditure", s 4; "mineral extraction trade", s 394(2); "mineral deposits", s 394(3); "source of mineral deposits", s 394(5).
Modifications—CAA 2001 Sch 3 para 88 (expenditure incurred before 1 April 1986: see modification note at the start of this Part).
CAA 2001 Sch 3 para 91 (disposal of oil licences: see modification note at the start of this Part).

415 Contribution to buildings or works for benefit of employees abroad

(1) Subject to subsection (3), expenditure is qualifying expenditure if—

(*a*) it is incurred by a person carrying on a mineral extraction trade outside the United Kingdom and for the purposes of that trade,

(*b*) it is a contribution consisting of a capital sum to the cost of buildings or works to which this section applies, and

(*c*) the buildings or works are likely to be of little or no value, when the source is no longer worked, to the last person working the source.

(2) The buildings or works to which this section applies are—

(*a*) buildings to be occupied by persons employed at or in connection with the working of a source outside the United Kingdom;

(*b*) works for the supply of water, gas or electricity wholly or mainly to buildings occupied or to be occupied by persons so employed;

(*c*) works to be used to provide other services or facilities wholly or mainly for the welfare of persons so employed or their dependants.

(3) Expenditure is not qualifying expenditure if the person making the contribution—

(*a*) acquires an asset as a result of the expenditure, or

(*b*) is entitled to an allowance for the expenditure under any other provision of the Tax Acts.

Commentary—*Simon's Direct Tax Service* **B2.408**.
Former enactments—Sub-s (1): IA 1978 s 6(*c*); CAA 1990 s 108(1), (2).
Sub-s (2): CAA 1990 s 108(1).
Sub-s (3): IA 1978 s 6(*c*); CAA 1990 s 108(3).
Definition—"Mineral extraction trade", s 394(2).

Modifications—CAA 2001 Sch 3 para 88 (expenditure incurred before 1 April 1986: see modification note at the start of this Part).
CAA 2001 Sch 3 para 91 (disposal of oil licences: see modification note at the start of this Part).

416 Expenditure on restoration within 3 years of ceasing to trade

(1) If—

    (*a*) a person who has ceased to carry on a mineral extraction trade incurs expenditure on the restoration of a relevant site, and

    (*b*) the expenditure is incurred within 3 years from the last day of trading and meets the further conditions in subsection (3),

the net cost of the restoration is qualifying expenditure.

(2) The qualifying expenditure is treated as incurred on the last day of trading.

(3) The further conditions are that the expenditure—

    (*a*) has not been deducted in calculating for tax purposes the profits of any trade carried on by that person, and

    (*b*) would have been—

        (i) deductible in calculating the profits of the trade, or

        (ii) capable of being qualifying expenditure under this Chapter,

if the expenditure had been incurred while the trade was being carried on.

(4) If any expenditure incurred by a person is qualifying expenditure under this section—

    (*a*) the whole of the expenditure on the restoration (not just the net cost) is not deductible in calculating the person's income for any tax purposes, and

    (*b*) none of the amounts subtracted to produce the net cost is to be treated as the person's income for any tax purposes.

(5) "Restoration" includes—

    (*a*) landscaping,

    (*b*) in relation to land in the United Kingdom, the carrying out of any works required as a condition of granting planning permission for development consisting of the winning and working of minerals, and

    (*c*) in relation to land outside the United Kingdom, the carrying out of any works required by any equivalent condition imposed under the law of the territory in which the land is situated.

(6) A "relevant site" means—

    (*a*) the site of a source to the working of which the mineral extraction trade related, or

    (*b*) land used in connection with working such a source.

(7) "The net cost of the restoration" means the expenditure incurred on the restoration less any amounts—

    (*a*) received within 3 years from the last day of trading, and

    (*b*) attributable to the restoration of the relevant site (for instance, amounts for spoil or other assets removed from the site or for tipping rights).

(8) All such adjustments are to be made, by way of discharge or repayment of tax or otherwise, as are necessary to give effect to this section.

Commentary—*Simon's Direct Tax Service* **B2.409**.
Former enactments—Sub-ss (1)–(3): CAA 1990 109(1).
Sub-s (4): CAA 1990 s 109(5).
Sub-s (5): CAA 1990 s 109(3).
Sub-s (6): CAA 1990 s 109(1), (2).
Sub-s (7): CAA 1990 s 109(4).
Sub-s (8): CAA 1990 s 109(6).
Definition—"Mineral extraction trade", s 394(2).
Modifications—CAA 2001 Sch 3 para 88 (expenditure incurred before 1 April 1986: see modification note at the start of this Part).
CAA 2001 Sch 3 para 91 (disposal of oil licences: see modification note at the start of this Part).

[CHAPTER 5A

FIRST-YEAR QUALIFYING EXPENDITURE][1]

Amendments—[1] This Chapter inserted by FA 2002 s 63, Sch 21 paras 8, 9 with effect for expenditure incurred after 16 April 2002.

[General

416A First-year allowances available for certain types of qualifying expenditure

A first-year allowance is not available unless the qualifying expenditure is first-year qualifying expenditure under section 416B (expenditure incurred wholly for purposes of a ring fence trade).][1]

Amendments—[1] This section inserted by FA 2002 s 63, Sch 21 paras 8, 9 with effect for expenditure incurred after 16 April 2002.

[Types of expenditure which may qualify for first-year allowances

416B Expenditure incurred by company for purposes of a ring fence trade

(1) Expenditure is first-year qualifying expenditure if—

    (*a*) it is incurred on or after 17th April 2002,

    (*b*) it is incurred by a company,

    (*c*) it is incurred wholly for the purposes of a ring fence trade, and

    (*d*) it is not excluded by—

        (i) subsection (2) (acquisition of mineral asset), or

        (ii) subsection (3) (acquisition of asset representing expenditure of connected company).

(2) Expenditure is not first-year qualifying expenditure under this section if it is expenditure on acquiring a mineral asset.

(3) Expenditure is not first-year qualifying expenditure under this section if it is expenditure incurred by a company on the acquisition of an asset representing expenditure incurred by a company connected with that company.

(4) To the extent that references in this section to an asset representing expenditure incurred by a company include a reference to an asset representing expenditure on mineral exploration and access, they also include a reference to any results obtained from any search, exploration or inquiry on which any such expenditure was incurred.

(5) In this section ''ring fence trade'' means a ring fence trade in respect of which tax is chargeable under section 501A of the Taxes Act 1988 (supplementary charge in respect of ring fence trades).][1]

Amendments—[1] This section inserted by FA 2002 s 63, Sch 21 paras 8, 9 with effect for expenditure incurred after 16 April 2002.

[Supplementary

416C Time when expenditure is incurred

(1) In determining whether expenditure is first-year qualifying expenditure under this Chapter, any effect of the provisions specified in subsection (2) on the time at which the expenditure is to be treated as incurred is to be disregarded.

(2) The provisions are—

    (*a*) section 400(4) (which treats certain pre-trading expenditure as incurred on the first day of trading), and

(*b*) section 434 (which treats certain other expenditure incurred for the purposes of a trade about to be carried on as incurred on that day).][1]

Amendments—[1] This section inserted by FA 2002 s 63, Sch 21 paras 8, 9 with effect for expenditure incurred after 16 April 2002.

CHAPTER 6
ALLOWANCES AND CHARGES
[First-year allowances

416D First-year allowances

(1) A person is entitled to a first-year allowance in respect of first-year qualifying expenditure if the expenditure is incurred in a chargeable period to which this Act applies.

(2) Any first-year allowance is made for the chargeable period in which the first-year qualifying expenditure is incurred.

(3) The amount of the allowance is a percentage of the first-year qualifying expenditure in respect of which the allowance is made, as shown in the Table—

TABLE
AMOUNT OF FIRST-YEAR ALLOWANCES

Type of first-year qualifying expenditure	*Amount*
Expenditure qualifying under section 416B (expenditure incurred wholly for the purposes of a ring fence trade)	100%

(4) A person who is entitled to a first-year allowance may claim the allowance in respect of the whole or a part of the first-year qualifying expenditure.

(5) This section is subject to section 416E (artificially inflated claims for first-year allowances).][1]

Amendments—[1] This section inserted by FA 2002 s 63, Sch 21 para 10 with effect for expenditure incurred after 16 April 2002.

[416E Artificially inflated claims for first-year allowances.

(1) To the extent that a transaction is attributable to arrangements entered into wholly or mainly for a disqualifying purpose, it shall be disregarded in determining for a chargeable period the amount of any first-year allowance to which a person is entitled.

(2) For the purposes of this section, arrangements are entered into wholly or mainly for a "disqualifying purpose" if their main object, or one of their main objects, is to enable a person to obtain—

    (*a*) a first-year allowance to which he would not otherwise be entitled, or

    (*b*) a first-year allowance of a greater amount than that to which he would otherwise be entitled.

(3) In this section "arrangements" includes any scheme, agreement or understanding, whether or not legally enforceable.]¹

Amendments—¹ This section inserted by FA 2002 s 63, Sch 21 para 11 with effect for expenditure incurred after 16 April 2002.

Writing-down and balancing allowances and balancing charges

417 Determination of entitlement or liability

(1) Whether a person who has incurred qualifying expenditure is entitled to a writing-down allowance or a balancing allowance, or liable to a balancing charge, for a chargeable period depends on—

    (*a*) how much of the expenditure is unrelieved qualifying expenditure for that period ("UQE"), and

    (*b*) the total of any disposal receipts to be brought into account for that period ("TDR") by reference to the expenditure.

(2) If UQE exceeds TDR, the person is entitled to a writing-down allowance or a balancing allowance for the period.

(3) If TDR exceeds UQE, the person is liable to a balancing charge for the period.

(4) The entitlement under subsection (2) is to a writing-down allowance except in cases for which sections 426 to 431 provide for the entitlement to be to a balancing allowance.

Commentary—*Simon's Direct Tax Service* **B2.420**.
Former enactments—Sub-s (1): CAA 1990 ss 98(2), (3), 100(1).
Sub-s (2): CAA 1990 s 98(2), (3).
Sub-s (3): CAA 1990 s 100(1).
Definitions—"Disposal receipt", s 420; "unrelieved qualifying expenditure", s 419.
Modifications—CAA 2001 Sch 3 para 88 (expenditure incurred before 1 April 1986: see modification note at the start of this Part).
CAA 2001 Sch 3 para 91 (disposal of oil licences: see modification note at the start of this Part).

418 Amount of allowances and charges

(1) The amount of the writing-down allowance to which a person is entitled for any chargeable period in respect of qualifying expenditure is—

    (*a*) in the case of qualifying expenditure on the acquisition of a mineral asset, 10% of the amount by which UQE exceeds TDR;

    (*b*) in the case of other qualifying expenditure, 25% of the amount by which UQE exceeds TDR.

(2) If the chargeable period is more or less than a year, the amount of the writing-down allowance is proportionately increased or reduced.

(3) If the mineral extraction trade has been carried on for part only of the chargeable period, the amount of the writing-down allowance is proportionately reduced.

(4) The amount of the balancing charge to which a person is liable for a chargeable period in respect of qualifying expenditure is—

    (*a*) the amount by which TDR exceeds UQE, or

    (*b*) if less, the allowances for earlier chargeable periods in respect of the expenditure less the total of any balancing charges for those periods in respect of the expenditure.

[Where a person is liable to a balancing charge in respect of first-year qualifying expenditure for the chargeable period in which he incurred the expenditure, any first-year allowance made in respect of the expenditure shall be treated for the purposes of paragraph (*b*) as if it were an allowance for an earlier chargeable period.]¹

(5) The amount of the balancing allowance to which a person is entitled for a chargeable period in respect of qualifying expenditure is the amount by which UQE exceeds TDR.

(6) A person claiming a writing-down allowance or a balancing allowance may require the allowance to be reduced to a specified amount.

Commentary—*Simon's Direct Tax Service* **B2.420**.
Former enactments—Sub-s (1): CAA 1990 s 98(5).
Sub-ss (2), (3): CAA 1990 s 98(6).
Sub-s (4): CAA 1990 s 100(2), (3).
Sub-s (5): CAA 1990 s 98(4).
Sub-s (6): change in law.
Definitions—"Disposal receipt", s 420; "mineral asset", s 397; "mineral extraction trade", s 394(2).

CAA 2001

Modification—CAA 2001 Sch 3 para 88 (In a case where—

(*a*) by virtue of any provision of CAA 2001 Sch 3 para 88(5), the whole or any part of the outstanding balance (within the meaning of FA 1986 Sch 14 para 1) of an item of old expenditure is treated for the purposes of CAA 2001 Part 5 as qualifying expenditure, and

(*b*) a balancing charge falls to be made under CAA 2001 Part 5 Chapter 6 in respect of the expenditure,

then, in determining the amount on which that charge falls to be made, sub-s (4) above has effect (subject to CAA 2001 Sch 3 para 88(6) as if sub-s (4)(*b*) above included a reference to allowances made in respect of the item under CAA 1968 Part I Chapter III.

Expenditure incurred before 1 April 1986: see modification note at the start of this Part.

CAA 2001 Sch 3 para 91 (disposal of oil licences: see modification note at the start of this Part).

Amendments—¹ Words in sub-s (4) inserted by FA 2002 s 63, Sch 21 para 12 with effect for expenditure incurred after 16 April 2002.

Unrelieved qualifying expenditure

419 Unrelieved qualifying expenditure

(1) A person's unrelieved qualifying expenditure for the chargeable period in which the qualifying expenditure is incurred is

[(*a*) the whole of it, unless the expenditure is first-year qualifying expenditure, or

(*b*) if the expenditure is first-year qualifying expenditure, none of it,

but paragraph (*b*) is subject to subsections (3) to (5).]¹.

(2) A person's unrelieved qualifying expenditure for a chargeable period after that in which the qualifying expenditure is incurred is the amount, if any, by which it exceeds the aggregate of—

(*a*) the allowances made in respect of the expenditure for earlier chargeable periods, and

(*b*) the total of any disposal receipts for earlier chargeable periods.

[(3) If, in the case of expenditure which is first-year qualifying expenditure, a disposal receipt falls to be brought into account for the chargeable period in which the expenditure is incurred (''the initial period''), subsection (4) below applies.]¹

[(4) Where this subsection applies, the unrelieved balance of the expenditure shall be taken to be unrelieved qualifying expenditure for the initial period, but only for the purpose specified in subsection (5).]¹

[(5) The purpose is that of determining in accordance with sections 417 and 418—

(*a*) any question whether the person who incurred the expenditure—

(i) is entitled to a balancing allowance for the initial period, or

(ii) is liable to a balancing charge for that period, and

(*b*) if so, the amount of that balancing allowance or balancing charge.]¹

[(6) In this section ''the unrelieved balance of the expenditure'' means so much of the first-year qualifying expenditure in question as remains after deducting the amount of any first-year allowance given in respect of the whole or any part of that expenditure.]¹

Commentary—*Simon's Direct Tax Service* **B2.420**.

Former enactments—CAA 1990 s 98(2), (3).

Definition—''Disposal receipt'', s 420.

Modifications—CAA 2001 Sch 3 para 88 (expenditure incurred before 1 April 1986: see modification note at the start of this Part).

CAA 2001 Sch 3 para 91 (disposal of oil licences: see modification note at the start of this Part).

Amendments—¹ Words in sub-s (1) substituted for the words ''the whole of it'', and sub-ss (3)–(6) inserted, by FA 2002 s 63, Sch 21 para 13 with effect for expenditure incurred after 16 April 2002.

Disposal values

420 Meaning of "disposal receipt"

In sections 417 to 419 ''disposal receipt'' means a disposal value that a person is required to bring into account in accordance with—

(*a*) sections 421 to 425, or

(*b*) paragraph 11 of Schedule 12 to FA 1997 (finance lease or loan: receipt of major lump sum) or any other enactment.

Commentary—*Simon's Direct Tax Service* B2.420.

421 Disposal of, or ceasing to use, asset

(1) This section applies if—

(*a*) a person has incurred qualifying expenditure on providing assets (including the construction of works), and

(*b*) any of those assets—

(i) is disposed of, or

(ii) permanently ceases to be used by him for the purposes of a mineral extraction trade (whether because of the discontinuance of the trade or for any other reason).

(2) The person is required to bring the disposal value of the asset into account for the chargeable period in which the disposal or cessation occurs.

Commentary—*Simon's Direct Tax Service* **B2.420**.
Former enactment—CAA 1990 s 99(1).
Definition—''Mineral extraction trade'', s 394(2).
Modifications—CAA 2001 Sch 3 para 88 (expenditure incurred before 1 April 1986: see modification note at the start of this Part).
CAA 2001 Sch 3 para 91 (disposal of oil licences: see modification note at the start of this Part).

422 Use of asset otherwise than for permitted development etc

(1) This section applies if—

    (*a*) a person has acquired a mineral asset,

    (*b*) at any time after the acquisition, the asset begins to be used (by him or another person) in a way which constitutes development, and

    (*c*) the development is not—

        (i) existing permitted development, or

        (ii) development for the purposes of a mineral extraction trade carried on by the person.

(2) The person is required to bring the disposal value of the mineral asset into account for the chargeable period in which the use begins.

(3) Development is existing permitted development if at the time of the acquisition—

    (*a*) it has been, or had begun to be, lawfully carried out, or

    (*b*) it could be lawfully carried out under planning permission granted by a general development order.

(4) In applying subsection (3) in relation to land outside the United Kingdom—

    (*a*) whether, at the time of the acquisition, development has been, or had begun to be, lawfully carried out is to be determined according to the law of the territory in which the land is situated, and

    (*b*) whether, at that time, development could be lawfully carried out under planning permission granted by a general development order is to be determined as if the land were in England.

Commentary—*Simon's Direct Tax Service* **B2.420**.
Former enactments—Sub-ss (1), (2): CAA 1990 s 99(1), (2).
Sub-s (3): CAA 1990 s 99(2).
Sub-s (4): CAA 1990 ss 99(2), 110(3); change in law.
Definitions—''General development order'', s 436; ''mineral asset'', s 397; ''mineral extraction trade'', s 394(2).
Modifications—CAA 2001 Sch 3 para 88 (expenditure incurred before 1 April 1986: see modification note at the start of this Part).
CAA 2001 Sch 3 para 91 (disposal of oil licences: see modification note at the start of this Part).

423 Sections 421 and 422: amount of disposal value to be brought into account

(1) The disposal value to be brought into account under section 421 or 422 depends on the event requiring it to be brought into account, as shown in the Table—

TABLE

DISPOSAL VALUE FOR SECTIONS 421 AND 422

1. Event	2. Disposal value
1. Sale of the asset, except in a case where item 2 applies.	The net proceeds of the sale, together with— (*a*) any insurance money received in respect of the asset as a result of an event affecting the price obtainable on the sale, and (*b*) any other compensation of any description so received, so far as it consists of capital sums.
2. Sale of the asset where— (*a*) the sale is at less than market value, (*b*) there is no charge to tax under Schedule E, and (*c*) the condition in subsection (3) is met by the buyer.	The market value of the asset at the time of the sale.
3. Demolition or destruction of the asset.	The net amount received for the remains of the asset, together with— (*a*) any insurance money received in respect of the demolition or destruction, and (*b*) any other compensation of any description so received, so far as it consists of capital sums.

1. Event	2. Disposal value
4. Permanent loss of the asset otherwise than as a result of its demolition or destruction.	Any insurance money received in respect of the loss and, so far as it consists of capital sums, any other compensation of any description so received.
5. Permanent discontinuance of the trade followed by the occurrence of an event within any of items 1 to 4.	The disposal value for the item in question.
6. Any event not falling within any of items 1 to 5.	The market value of the asset at the time of the event.

(2) The amounts referred to in column 2 of the Table are those received by the person required to bring the disposal value into account.

(3) The condition referred to in item 2 of the Table is met by the buyer if—

(a) the buyer's expenditure on the acquisition of the asset cannot be qualifying expenditure under Part 2 or 6 (plant and machinery and research and development allowances), or

(b) the buyer is a dual resident investing company which is connected with the seller.

Commentary—*Simon's Direct Tax Service* **B2.420**.
Former enactments—Sub-s (1): CAA 1990 ss 26(1), 99(3).
Table, item 1: CAA 1990 s 26(1)(*a*).
Table, item 2: CAA 1990 s 26(1)(*a*).
Table, item 3: CAA 1990 s 26(1)(*c*).
Table, item 4: CAA 1990 s 26(1)(*d*).
Table, item 5: CAA 1990 s 26(1)(*e*).
Table, item 6: CAA 1990 s 26(1)(*f*).
Sub-s (2): CAA 1990 s 26(1).
Sub-s (3): CAA 1990 s 26(1)(*b*).
Definitions—''Capital sum'', s 4; ''dual resident investing company'', s 577(1), TA 1988 s 404.
Modifications—CAA 2001 Sch 3 para 88 (expenditure incurred before 1 April 1986: see modification note at the start of this Part).
CAA 2001 Sch 3 para 91 (disposal of oil licences: see modification note at the start of this Part).

424 Disposal value restricted in case of interest in land

(1) If the asset in relation to which a disposal value is required to be brought into account under section 421 or 422 is an interest in land, the disposal value is restricted by excluding the undeveloped market value of the interest.

(2) ''The undeveloped market value of the interest'' means the amount that, at the time of the disposal, the interest might reasonably be expected to fetch on a sale in the open market on the assumptions in subsection (3).

(3) The assumptions are that—

(a) there is no source of mineral deposits on or in the land, and

(b) it will only ever be lawful to carry out existing permitted development.

(4) Development is existing permitted development if at the time of the disposal—

(a) it has been, or had begun to be, lawfully carried out, or

(b) it could be lawfully carried out under planning permission granted by a general development order.

(5) In applying subsection (4) in relation to land outside the United Kingdom—

(a) whether, at the time of the disposal, development has been, or had begun to be, lawfully carried out is to be determined according to the law of the territory in which the land is situated, and

(b) whether, at that time, development could be lawfully carried out under planning permission granted by a general development order is to be determined as if the land were in England.

Commentary—*Simon's Direct Tax Service* **B2.420**.
Former enactments—Sub-s (1): CAA 1990 ss 99(3), 112(1).
Sub-s (2): CAA 1990 ss 110(2), 112(1), (2).
Sub-ss (3), (4): CAA 1990 s 110(2), 112(2).
Sub-s (5): CAA 1990 ss 110(3), 112(2); change in law.
Definitions—''General development order'', s 436; ''mineral deposits'', s 394(3); ''source of mineral deposits'', s 394(5).
Modifications—CAA 2001 Sch 3 para 88 (for the purposes of CAA 2001 Part 4, in relation to any expenditure to which FA 1986 Sch 14 para 6(4)(*a*) applied, the above section does not apply (so that no deduction is to be made from the amount of any disposal receipt by reference to the undeveloped market value of the land in question).
Expenditure incurred before 1 April 1986: see modification note at the start of this Part).
CAA 2001 Sch 3 para 91 (disposal of oil licences: see modification note at the start of this Part).

425 Receipt of capital sum

(1) This section applies if a person—

(a) has incurred qualifying expenditure, and

(b) receives a capital sum which, in whole or in part, it is reasonable to attribute to that expenditure.

(2) The person is required to bring into account as a disposal value for the chargeable period in which the capital sum is received so much of the capital sum as is reasonably attributable to the qualifying expenditure.

(3) This section does not apply if the capital sum falls to be brought into account under section 421 or 422.

Commentary—*Simon's Direct Tax Service* **B2.420**.
Former enactment—CAA 1990 s 99(4).
Definition—"Capital sum", s 4.
Modifications—CAA 2001 Sch 3 para 88 (expenditure incurred before 1 April 1986: see modification note at the start of this Part).
CAA 2001 Sch 3 para 91 (disposal of oil licences: see modification note at the start of this Part).

Cases in which a person is entitled to a balancing allowance

426 Pre-trading expenditure

A person's entitlement to an allowance for a chargeable period is to a balancing allowance if—

   (a) the expenditure is qualifying expenditure under—

      (i) section 401(4) (pre-trading exploration expenditure where exploration etc has ceased before first day of trading), or
      (ii) section 402 (pre-trading expenditure on plant or machinery), and

   (b) the first day of trading occurs in that chargeable period.

Commentary—*Simon's Direct Tax Service* **B2.421**.
Former enactment—CAA 1990 s 101(5).
Modifications—CAA 2001 Sch 3 para 88 (expenditure incurred before 1 April 1986: see modification note at the start of this Part).
CAA 2001 Sch 3 para 91 (disposal of oil licences: see modification note at the start of this Part).

427 Giving up exploration, search or inquiry

A person's entitlement to an allowance for a chargeable period is to a balancing allowance if—

   (a) the qualifying expenditure is expenditure on mineral exploration and access,
   (b) he gives up the exploration, search or inquiry to which the expenditure related in that chargeable period, and
   (c) he does not then or later carry on a mineral extraction trade which consists of or includes the working of mineral deposits to which the expenditure related.

Commentary—*Simon's Direct Tax Service* **B2.421**.
Former enactment—CAA 1990 s 101(6).
Definitions—"Mineral exploration and access", s 396; "mineral extraction trade", s 394(2); "mineral deposits", s 394(3).
Modifications—CAA 2001 Sch 3 para 88 (expenditure incurred before 1 April 1986: see modification note at the start of this Part).
CAA 2001 Sch 3 para 91 (disposal of oil licences: see modification note at the start of this Part).

428 Ceasing to work mineral deposits

(1) A person's entitlement to an allowance for a chargeable period is to a balancing allowance if—

   (a) in that chargeable period he permanently ceases to work particular mineral deposits, and
   (b) the qualifying expenditure is expenditure incurred—

      (i) on mineral exploration and access relating solely to those deposits, or
      (ii) on acquiring a mineral asset consisting of those deposits or part of them.

(2) If the person carrying on the mineral extraction trade is entitled to two or more mineral assets which at any time were—

   (a) comprised in a single mineral asset, or
   (b) otherwise derived from a single mineral asset,

subsection (1) does not apply until such time as the person permanently ceases to work the deposits comprised in all the mineral assets concerned taken together.

(3) For the purposes of subsection (2), if a mineral asset relates to, but does not actually consist of, mineral deposits, the deposits to which the asset relates are to be treated as comprised in the asset.

Commentary—*Simon's Direct Tax Service* **B2.421**.
Former enactments—Sub-s (1): CAA 1990 s 101(2).
Sub-ss (2), (3): CAA 1990 s 101(3).
Definitions—"Mineral asset", s 397; "mineral exploration and access", s 396; "mineral extraction trade", s 394(2); "mineral deposits", s 394(3).
Modifications—CAA 2001 Sch 3 para 88 (expenditure incurred before 1 April 1986: see modification note at the start of this Part).
CAA 2001 Sch 3 para 91 (disposal of oil licences: see modification note at the start of this Part).

CAA 2001

429 Buildings etc for benefit of employees abroad ceasing to be used

A person's entitlement to an allowance for a chargeable period is to a balancing allowance if—

(a) the expenditure is qualifying expenditure under section 415 (contributions to buildings or works for benefit of employees abroad), and

(b) in that chargeable period the buildings or works permanently cease to be used for the purposes of or in connection with the mineral extraction trade.

Commentary—*Simon's Direct Tax Service* **B2.421**.
Former enactment—CAA 1990 s 101(7).
Definition—"Mineral extraction trade", s 394(2).
Modifications—CAA 2001 Sch 3 para 88 (expenditure incurred before 1 April 1986: see modification note at the start of this Part).
CAA 2001 Sch 3 para 91 (disposal of oil licences: see modification note at the start of this Part).

430 Disposal of asset, etc

(1) A person's entitlement to an allowance for a chargeable period is to a balancing allowance if—

(a) the qualifying expenditure was incurred on the provision of any assets, and

(b) in that chargeable period any of those assets—

(i) is disposed of, or

(ii) otherwise permanently ceases to be used by him for the purposes of the mineral extraction trade.

(2) A person's entitlement to an allowance for a chargeable period is to a balancing allowance if any of the following events occurs in that chargeable period in relation to assets representing the qualifying expenditure—

(a) the person loses possession of the assets in circumstances where it is reasonable to assume that the loss is permanent;

(b) the assets cease to exist as such (as a result of destruction, dismantling or otherwise);

(c) the assets begin to be used wholly or partly for purposes other than those of the mineral extraction trade carried on by the person.

Commentary—*Simon's Direct Tax Service* **B2.421**.
Former enactments—Sub-s (1): CAA 1990 ss 99(1), 101(4).
Sub-s (2): CAA 1990 s 101(8).
Definition—"Mineral extraction trade", s 394(2).
Modifications—CAA 2001 Sch 3 para 88 (expenditure incurred before 1 April 1986: see modification note at the start of this Part).
CAA 2001 Sch 3 para 91 (disposal of oil licences: see modification note at the start of this Part).

431 Discontinuance of trade

A person's entitlement to an allowance for a chargeable period is to a balancing allowance if in that chargeable period the mineral extraction trade is permanently discontinued.

Commentary—*Simon's Direct Tax Service* **B2.421**.
Former enactments—CAA 1990 s 101(1), 161(2) ("chargeable event related to").
Definition—"Mineral extraction trade", s 394(2).
Modifications—CAA 2001 Sch 3 para 88 (expenditure incurred before 1 April 1986: see modification note at the start of this Part).
CAA 2001 Sch 3 para 91 (disposal of oil licences: see modification note at the start of this Part).

CHAPTER 7
SUPPLEMENTARY PROVISIONS

432 Giving effect to allowances and charges

An allowance or charge to which a person is entitled or liable under this Part is to be given effect in calculating the profits of that person's mineral extraction trade, by treating—

(a) the allowance as an expense of the trade, and

(b) the charge as a receipt of the trade.

Commentary—*Simon's Direct Tax Service* **B2.423**.
Former enactments—CAA 1990 ss 104, 140(2), 144(2), 161(2) ("chargeable period"), s 161(5).
Definition—"Mineral extraction trade", s 394(2).
Modifications—CAA 2001 Sch 3 para 88 (expenditure incurred before 1 April 1986: see modification note at the start of this Part).
CAA 2001 Sch 3 para 91 (disposal of oil licences: see modification note at the start of this Part).

433 Treatment of demolition costs

(1) The net cost to a person of demolishing an asset which represents qualifying expenditure is added to that qualifying expenditure in determining the amount of any balancing allowance or balancing charge for the chargeable period in which the demolition occurs.

(2) "The net cost of the demolition" means the amount, if any, by which the cost of the demolition exceeds any money received for the remains of the asset.

(3) If this section applies, the net cost of the demolition is not treated as expenditure incurred on any other asset which replaces the demolished asset.

Commentary—*Simon's Direct Tax Service* **B2.424**.
Former enactments—Sub-s (1): CAA 1990 s 103(1), 161(2) ("chargeable period related to").
Sub-s (2): CAA 1990 s 103(3).
Sub-s (3): CAA 1990 s 103(2).
Modifications—CAA 2001 Sch 3 para 88 (expenditure incurred before 1 April 1986: see modification note at the start of this Part).
CAA 2001 Sch 3 para 91 (disposal of oil licences: see modification note at the start of this Part).

434 Time when expenditure incurred

(1) For the purposes of this Part, expenditure incurred for the purposes of a mineral extraction trade by a person about to carry it on is treated as incurred by that person on the first day on which that person does carry it on.

(2) Subsection (1) does not apply to pre-trading expenditure on mineral exploration and access (for which specific provision is made by section 400(4)).

Commentary—*Simon's Direct Tax Service* **B2.405**.
Former enactment—CAA 1990 s 120(1).
Definitions—"Mineral exploration and access", s 396; "mineral extraction trade", s 394(2).
Modifications—CAA 2001 Sch 3 para 88 (expenditure incurred before 1 April 1986: see modification note at the start of this Part).
CAA 2001 Sch 3 para 91 (disposal of oil licences: see modification note at the start of this Part).

435 Shares in assets

(1) This Part applies in relation to a share in an asset as it applies (under section 571) in relation to a part of an asset.

(2) For the purposes of those provisions, a share in an asset is treated as used for the purposes of a trade so long as, and only so long as, the asset is used for the purposes of the trade.

Commentary—*Simon's Direct Tax Service* **B2.406**.
Former enactment—CAA 1990 s 121(5).
Modifications—CAA 2001 Sch 3 para 88 (expenditure incurred before 1 April 1986: see modification note at the start of this Part).
CAA 2001 Sch 3 para 91 (disposal of oil licences: see modification note at the start of this Part).

436 Meaning of "development" etc

(1) In this Part—
    "development",
    "development order",
    "general development order", and
    "planning permission",
have the meaning given by the relevant planning enactment.

(2) "The relevant planning enactment" means—
    (*a*) in relation to land in England or Wales, section 336(1) of the Town and Country Planning Act 1990;
    (*b*) in relation to land in Scotland, section 277(1) of the Town and Country Planning (Scotland) Act 1997;
    (*c*) in relation to land in Northern Ireland, Article 2(2) of the Planning (Northern Ireland) Order 1991.

Commentary—*Simon's Direct Tax Service* **B2.405**.
Former enactments—Sub-s (1): CAA 1990 s 121(1).
Sub-s (2): CAA 1990 s 121(1).
Modifications—CAA 2001 Sch 3 para 88 (expenditure incurred before 1 April 1986: see modification note at the start of this Part).
CAA 2001 Sch 3 para 91 (disposal of oil licences: see modification note at the start of this Part).

PART 6

RESEARCH AND DEVELOPMENT ALLOWANCES

Commentary—*Simon's Direct Tax Service* **Division B2.7**.

CHAPTER 1
INTRODUCTION

437 Research and development allowances

(1) Allowances are available under this Part if a person incurs qualifying expenditure on research and development.

(2) In this Part "research and development"—

CAA 2001

(*a*) has the meaning given by section 837A of ICTA (activities falling to be treated as research and development under [generally accepted accounting practice][1], subject to regulations), and

(*b*) includes oil and gas exploration and appraisal.

Commentary—*Simon's Direct Tax Service* **B2.701**.
Former enactment—Sub-s (2): CAA 1990 139(1).
Revenue Internal Guidance—Capital allowances manual CA 60200 (meaning of "research" and "development").
Amendments—[1] Words substituted for the words "normal accountancy practice" by FA 2002 s 103(4)(*g*) with effect from 24 July 2002.

438 Expenditure on research and development

(1) Expenditure on research and development includes all expenditure incurred for—

(*a*) carrying out research and development, or

(*b*) providing facilities for carrying out research and development.

(2) But it does not include expenditure incurred in the acquisition of—

(*a*) rights in research and development, or

(*b*) rights arising out of research and development.

(3) Nor does it include expenditure on the provision of a dwelling.

(4) But if—

(*a*) part of a building consists of a dwelling and the rest of the building is used for research and development, and

(*b*) no more than 25% of the capital expenditure referable to the construction or acquisition of the whole building is referable to the construction or acquisition of the dwelling,

the whole of the building is to be treated as used for research and development.

(5) For the purposes of subsection (4)(*b*), the expenditure referable to the construction or acquisition of the building is to be apportioned in a just and reasonable manner.

(6) Any additional VAT liability or rebate (as to which see Chapter 4) is to be disregarded in applying subsection (4)(*b*).

Commentary—*Simon's Direct Tax Service* **B2.702**.
Former enactments—Sub-ss (1), (2): CAA 1990 s 139(1).
Sub-ss (3)–(6): CAA 1990 s 137(3); change in law.

CHAPTER 2
QUALIFYING EXPENDITURE

439 Qualifying expenditure

(1) In this Part "qualifying expenditure" means capital expenditure incurred by a person on research and development directly undertaken by him or on his behalf if—

(*a*) he is carrying on a trade when the expenditure is incurred and the research and development relates to that trade, or

(*b*) after incurring the expenditure he sets up and commences a trade connected with the research and development.

(2) The same expenditure may not be taken into account as qualifying expenditure in relation to more than one trade.

(3) The trade by reference to which expenditure is qualifying expenditure is referred to in this Part as "the relevant trade" in relation to that expenditure.

(4) If capital expenditure is partly within subsection (1) and partly not, the expenditure is to be apportioned in a just and reasonable manner.

(5) References in this Chapter to research and development related to a trade include—

(*a*) research and development which may lead to or facilitate an extension of that trade, and

(*b*) research and development of a medical nature which has a special relation to the welfare of workers employed in that trade.

Commentary—*Simon's Direct Tax Service* **B2.703**.
Former enactments—Sub-s (1): CAA 1990 s 137(1).
Sub-s (2): CAA 1990 s 139(2).
Sub-s (4): CAA 1990 s 137(4); change in law.
Sub-s (5): CAA 1990 s 139(1).
Revenue Internal Guidance—Capital allowances manual CA 60400 (application of this section).
Simon's Tax Cases—*Salt v Buckley (Insp of Taxes)* [2001] STC (SCD) 262*.
Definition—"Capital expenditure", s 4.
Modification—CAA 2001 Sch 3 para 89 (sub-s (4) above does not apply to expenditure incurred before 27 July 1989).

440 Excluded expenditure: land

(1) Expenditure on the acquisition of land, or rights in or over land, is not qualifying expenditure.

(2) But that does not prevent such expenditure from being qualifying expenditure so far as it is referable to the acquisition of—

(*a*) a building or structure already constructed on the land,

(*b*) rights in or over such a building or structure, or

(*c*) plant or machinery which forms part of such a building or structure.

(3) For the purposes of subsection (2), the expenditure is to be apportioned in a just and reasonable manner.

Commentary—*Simon's Direct Tax Service* **B2.703**.
Former enactment—CAA 1990 137(2); change in law.

CHAPTER 3
ALLOWANCES AND CHARGES

Modification—CAA 2001 Sch 3 para 91 (where—

(*a*) a person ("the transferor") disposes of any interest in an oil licence to another ("the transferee") during the transitional period,

(*b*) part of the value of the interest is attributable to allowable exploration expenditure incurred by the transferor, and

(*c*) an election is made in accordance with this paragraph specifying an amount as the amount to be treated as so attributable, this Chapter has effect in relation to the disposal as if—

(*a*) the disposal were a disposal by which an asset representing the allowable exploration expenditure ceases to belong to the transferor, and

(*b*) the disposal value of that asset were an amount equal to the amount specified in the election).

441 Allowances

(1) A person who incurs qualifying expenditure is entitled to an allowance in respect of that expenditure for the relevant chargeable period equal to—

(*a*) the amount of the qualifying expenditure, or

(*b*) if a disposal value is required to be brought into account for that period in respect of that expenditure, the amount (if any) by which that expenditure exceeds the disposal value.

(2) The relevant chargeable period is—

(*a*) the chargeable period in which the expenditure is incurred, or

(*b*) if the expenditure was incurred before the chargeable period in which the relevant trade is set up and commenced, that chargeable period.

(3) A person claiming an allowance under this section may require the allowance to be reduced to a specified amount.

Commentary—*Simon's Direct Tax Service* **B2.702**.
Former enactments—Sub-s (1): CAA 1990 ss 137(1), 138(2); change in law.
Sub-s (2): CAA 1990 s 137(5).
Sub-s (3): change in law.
Definition—"Relevant trade", s 439(3).
Modification—CAA 2001 Sch 3 para 91 (disposal of oil licences: see modification note at the start of this Chapter).

442 Balancing charges

(1) This section applies if—

(*a*) an allowance is made to a person for a chargeable period in respect of qualifying expenditure, and

(*b*) the person is required to bring a disposal value into account for a later chargeable period in respect of that expenditure.

(2) The person is liable to a balancing charge for the later chargeable period in respect of the qualifying expenditure.

(3) The amount of the balancing charge is—

(*a*) the amount (if any) by which the disposal value to be brought into account for the period exceeds any unclaimed allowance, or

(*b*) if less, the allowance made in respect of the qualifying expenditure.

(4) "Unclaimed allowance" means any part of the allowance to which the person was entitled in respect of the qualifying expenditure but which has not been claimed.

(5) This section is to be read with section 449 (effect on balancing charges of additional VAT rebates in earlier chargeable periods).

Commentary—*Simon's Direct Tax Service* **B2.704**.
Former enactments—Sub-s (1): CAA 1990 138(1), (2); change in law.
Sub-ss (2), (3): CAA 1990 s 138(2), (2A); change in law.
Sub-s (4): change in law.
Modification—CAA 2001 Sch 3 para 91 (disposal of oil licences: see modification note at the start of this Chapter).

443 Disposal values and disposal events

(1) A person is required to bring a disposal value into account in respect of qualifying expenditure incurred by him if—

(*a*) he ceases to own an asset representing the expenditure, or (*b*) an asset representing the expenditure is demolished or destroyed at a time when he owns the asset.

(2) Subsection (1) is to be read with section 555 (disposal of oil licence with exploitation value).

(3) But a person is not required to bring a disposal value into account under subsection (1) if the disposal event gives rise to a balancing charge under Part 2 or 3 (plant and machinery allowances and industrial buildings allowances).

(4) The disposal value to be brought into account under subsection (1) depends on the disposal event, as shown in the Table—

TABLE

DISPOSAL VALUES

1. Disposal event	2. Disposal value
1. Sale of the asset at not less than market value.	The net proceeds of the sale.
2. Demolition or destruction of the asset.	The net amount received for the remains of the asset, together with— (*a*) any insurance money received in respect of the demolition or destruction, and (*b*) any other compensation of any description so received, so far as it consists of capital sums.
3. Any event not falling within item 1 or 2.	The market value of the asset at the time of the event.

(5) Subsection (4) is subject to—

   section 445 (costs of demolition),
   section 553 (nil value in case of disposal of oil licence relating to undeveloped area), and
   section 555 (disposal of oil licence with exploitation value).

(6) A person is also required to bring a disposal value into account by section 448 (additional VAT rebate generates disposal value).

(7) In this Chapter "disposal event" means an event of a kind that requires a disposal value to be brought into account under subsection (1).

Commentary—*Simon's Direct Tax Service* B2.704.
Former enactments—Sub-s (1): CAA 1990 s 138(1), (5).
Sub-s (2): CAA 1990 s 138A(1).
Sub-s (3): CAA 1990 s 138(6).
Sub-s (4): CAA 1990 s 138(4), (5); change in law.
Sub-s (5): CAA 1990 ss 138(5), 138A(1).
Sub-s (6): CAA 1990 s 138(3A).
Sub-s (7): CAA 1990 s 138(1).
Modification—CAA 2001 Sch 3 para 91 (disposal of oil licences: see modification note at the start of this Chapter).

444 Disposal events: chargeable period for which disposal value is to be brought into account

(1) The chargeable period for which a disposal value is to be brought into account under section 443(1) in respect of qualifying expenditure is given by this section.

(2) Subsection (3) applies if the disposal event occurs in or after the chargeable period for which the allowance in respect of the expenditure is made.

(3) The disposal value is to be brought into account for—

(*a*) the chargeable period in which the event occurs, or
(*b*) if the event occurs after the chargeable period in which the relevant trade is permanently discontinued, that chargeable period.

(4) If the disposal event occurs before the chargeable period for which the allowance in respect of the expenditure is made, the disposal value is to be brought into account for that chargeable period.

Commentary—*Simon's Direct Tax Service* B2.704.
Former enactments—Sub-s (2), (3): CAA 1990 s 138(2); change in law.
Sub-s (4): change in law.
Definition—"Relevant trade", s 439(3).
Modification—CAA 2001 Sch 3 para 91 (disposal of oil licences: see modification note at the start of this Chapter).

445 Costs of demolition

(1) This section applies if—

(*a*) an asset representing qualifying expenditure incurred by a person is demolished at a time when the person owns the asset, and
(*b*) the person incurred costs of demolition.

(2) The disposal value which the person is required to bring into account in respect of the qualifying expenditure is to be reduced by the cost to the person of the demolition.

(3) If the amount of the disposal value is reduced to nil (or less than nil) under subsection (2), the person is not required to bring a disposal value into account.

(4) If—

    (a) the cost to the person of the demolition exceeds the disposal value, and

    (b) before its demolition the asset had not begun to be used for purposes other than research and development related to the relevant trade,

the person is to be treated as incurring qualifying expenditure equal to the excess.

(5) That qualifying expenditure is to be treated as incurred—

    (a) when the demolition occurs, or

    (b) if that is on or after the date on which the relevant trade is permanently discontinued, immediately before the discontinuance.

(6) If this section applies, the cost to the person of the demolition is not to be treated for the purposes of this Act as expenditure on any property that replaces the demolished asset.

Commentary—*Simon's Direct Tax Service* **B2.704**.
Former enactments—Sub-s (1): CAA 1990 s 138(5); change in law.
Sub-s (2): CAA 1990 s 138(5).
Sub-ss (4), (5): CAA 1990 s 138(5).
Sub-s (6): CAA 1990 s 139(5).
Definition—"Relevant trade", s 439(3).
Modification—CAA 2001 Sch 3 para 91 (disposal of oil licences: see modification note at the start of this Chapter).

CHAPTER 4
ADDITIONAL VAT LIABILITIES AND REBATES

446 Introduction

For the purposes of this Chapter—

    (a) "additional VAT liability" and "additional VAT rebate" have the meaning given by section 547,

    (b) the time when—

        (i) a person incurs an additional VAT liability, or

        (ii) an additional VAT rebate is made to a person,

    is given by section 548, and

    (c) the chargeable period in which, and the time when, an additional VAT liability or an additional VAT rebate accrues are given by section 549.

Commentary—*Simon's Direct Tax Service* **B2.703**.
Definitions—"Additional VAT liability", s 547(1); "additional VAT rebate", s 547(2); "chargeable period", s 6(1).

447 Additional VAT liability treated as additional expenditure etc

(1) If a person—

    (a) has incurred qualifying expenditure ("the original expenditure"), and

    (b) incurs an additional VAT liability in respect of that expenditure,

the liability is to be treated as capital expenditure incurred on the same research and development as the original expenditure.

(2) But subsection (1) does not apply if by the time the liability is incurred—

    (a) the person who incurred the original expenditure has ceased to own the asset representing that expenditure, or

    (b) that asset has been demolished or destroyed.

(3) Any allowance arising as a result of this section is available for—

    (a) the chargeable period in which the liability accrues, or

    (b) if the liability accrued before the chargeable period in which the relevant trade is set up and commenced, that chargeable period,

rather than for the relevant chargeable period specified in section 441(2).

Commentary—*Simon's Direct Tax Service* **B2.703, 704, 706**.
Former enactments—Sub-s (1): CAA 1990 s 137(1A).
Sub-s (2): CAA 1990 s 137(1A), 138(1).
Sub-s (3): CAA 1990 ss 137(5), 159A(3).
Definitions—"Additional VAT liability", s 547(1); "capital expenditure", s 4; "relevant trade", s 439(3).

448 Additional VAT rebate generates disposal value

(1) This section applies if—

    (a) a person has incurred qualifying expenditure, and

    (b) an additional VAT rebate is made to the person in respect of that expenditure.

(2) But this section does not apply if by the time the rebate is made—

    (a) the person has ceased to own the asset representing that expenditure, or

(b) that asset has been demolished or destroyed.

(3) And this section does not apply if the rebate falls to be brought into account for the purpose of making allowances and charges under Part 2 or 3 (plant and machinery allowances and industrial buildings allowances).

(4) The person must bring the amount of the rebate into account—

(a) as a disposal value in respect of the qualifying expenditure for the appropriate chargeable period, or

(b) if the person would have to bring a disposal value into account under section 443(1) in respect of that expenditure for that chargeable period, as an addition to that disposal value.

(5) ''Appropriate chargeable period'' means—

(a) the chargeable period in which the rebate accrues, or

(b) if the rebate accrued before the chargeable period in which the relevant trade is set up and commenced, that chargeable period.

Commentary—*Simon's Direct Tax Service* B2.704.
Former enactments—Sub-ss (1), (2): CAA 1990 s 138(3A).
Sub-ss (3)–(5): CAA 1990 s 138(3A); change in law.
Definitions—''Additional VAT rebate'', s 547(2); ''relevant trade'', s 439(3).

449 Effect on balancing charges of additional VAT rebates in earlier chargeable periods

(1) Section 442 (balancing charges) has effect subject to this section if—

(a) an allowance is made to a person for a chargeable period (''the original period'') in respect of qualifying expenditure,

(b) the person is required to bring a disposal value into account for a later chargeable period in respect of that expenditure, and

(c) the person has been required by section 448(4)(a) to bring one or more disposal values (''VAT disposal values'') into account in respect of that expenditure for one or more chargeable periods after the original period but before the later chargeable period.

(2) In relation to the later chargeable period, subsection (3)(a) of section 442 applies as if the unclaimed allowance were reduced by—

$$DV - BC$$

where—

DV is the total amount of the VAT disposal values, and

BC is the total amount of any balancing charges to which the person is liable under that section as a result of bringing into account the VAT disposal values.

(3) In relation to the later chargeable period, subsection (3)(b) of section 442 applies as if the allowance made in respect of the qualifying expenditure were reduced by BC.

Commentary—*Simon's Direct Tax Service* B2.704.
Former enactments—Sub-s (1): CAA 1990 s 138(1), (2), (2A).
Sub-s (2): CAA 1990 s 138(2A); change in law.
Sub-s (3): CAA 1990 s 138(2A).
Definition—''Additional VAT rebate'', s 547(2).

CHAPTER 5
SUPPLEMENTARY PROVISIONS

450 Giving effect to allowances and charges

An allowance or charge to which a person is entitled or liable under this Part for a chargeable period is to be given effect in calculating the profits of the relevant trade, by treating—

(a) the allowance as an expense of the trade, and

(b) the charge as a receipt of the trade.

Commentary—*Simon's Direct Tax Service* B2.706.
Former enactments—CAA 1990 ss 137(1), 140(2), (5), 144(2), (3), 161(2) (''chargeable period''), s 161(5).

451 Sales: time of cessation of ownership

Any reference in this Part to the time when a person ceases to own an asset is to be read, in the case of a sale, as a reference to whichever is the earlier of—

(a) the time of completion, and

(b) the time when possession is given.

Commentary—*Simon's Direct Tax Service* B2.704.
Former enactment—CAA 1990 139(4).
Definition—''Relevant trade'', s 439(3).

PART 7
KNOW-HOW ALLOWANCES

CHAPTER 1
INTRODUCTION

Commentary—*Simon's Direct Tax Service* **B2.615–716**.

452 Know-how allowances

(1) Allowances are available under this Part if a person incurs qualifying expenditure on the acquisition of know-how.

(2) In this Part "know-how" means any industrial information or techniques likely to assist in—

    (*a*) manufacturing or processing goods or materials,

    (*b*) working a source of mineral deposits (including searching for, discovering or testing mineral deposits or obtaining access to them), or

    (*c*) carrying out any agricultural, forestry or fishing operations.

(3) In subsection (2)(*b*)—

    (*a*) "mineral deposits" includes any natural deposits capable of being lifted or extracted from the earth and for this purpose geothermal energy is to be treated as a natural deposit, and

    (*b*) "source of mineral deposits" includes a mine, an oil well and a source of geothermal energy.

Commentary—*Simon's Direct Tax Service* **B2.615**.
Former enactments—Sub-s (2): TA 1988 s 533(7).
Sub-s (3): TA 1988 ss 532(1), 533(7); CAA 1990 s 161(2).
Revenue Internal Guidance—Capital allowances manual CA 70030 (exclusion of commercial know-how).

453 Know-how as property

(1) Know-how is to be treated as property for the purposes of this Act.

(2) References in this Act to the purchase or sale of property include the acquisition or disposal of know-how.

Commentary—*Simon's Direct Tax Service* **B2.615**.
Former enactment—TA 1988 532(5).

CHAPTER 2
QUALIFYING EXPENDITURE

454 Qualifying expenditure

(1) In this Part "qualifying expenditure" means, subject to section 455, capital expenditure incurred on the acquisition of know-how by a person if—

    (*a*) the person is carrying on a trade at the time of the acquisition and the know-how is acquired for use in that trade,

    (*b*) the person acquires the know-how and subsequently sets up and commences a trade in which it is used,

    (*c*) the person acquires the know-how together with the trade or part of a trade in which it was used and the parties to the acquisition make an election under section 531(3)(*a*) of ICTA (consideration for know-how on disposal of trade to be treated as payment for goodwill unless parties otherwise elect), or

    (*d*) the person acquires the know-how together with the trade or part of a trade in which it was used and the trade in question was, before the acquisition, carried on wholly outside the United Kingdom.

(2) The same expenditure may not be taken into account as qualifying expenditure in relation to more than one trade.

(3) Qualifying expenditure incurred before the setting up and commencement of the relevant trade is to be treated for the purposes of this Part as incurred when the trade is set up and commenced.

(4) "Relevant trade" means the trade by reference to which expenditure is qualifying expenditure.

Commentary—*Simon's Direct Tax Service* **B2.615**.
Former enactments—Sub-s (1): TA 1988 s 530(1), 531(3).
Sub-s (2): TA 1988 s 530(1).
Sub-ss (3), (4): TA 1988 s 530(7).
Definition—"Capital expenditure", s 4.

455 Excluded expenditure

(1) Expenditure on the acquisition of know-how is not qualifying expenditure to the extent that it is otherwise deducted for tax purposes.

(2) Expenditure on the acquisition of know-how is not qualifying expenditure if—

(a) the buyer is a body of persons over whom the seller has control,

(b) the seller is a body of persons over whom the buyer has control, or

(c) the buyer and the seller are both bodies of persons and another person has control over both of them.

(3) In subsection (2) "body of persons" includes a partnership.

(4) Expenditure on the acquisition of know-how is not qualifying expenditure if it is treated as a payment for goodwill under section 531(2) of ICTA (consideration for know-how on disposal of trade to be treated as payment for goodwill, unless parties otherwise elect etc).

Commentary—*Simon's Direct Tax Service* **B2.615**.
Former enactments—Sub-s (1): TA 1988 s 530(1).
Sub-ss (2), (3): TA 1988 s 531(7).
Sub-s (4): TA 1988 s 531(2).

CHAPTER 3
ALLOWANCES AND CHARGES

456 Pooling of expenditure

(1) Qualifying expenditure has to be pooled for the purpose of determining a person's entitlement to writing-down allowances and balancing allowances and liability to balancing charges.

(2) There is a separate pool for each trade in respect of which the person has qualifying expenditure.

Commentary—*Simon's Direct Tax Service* **B2.616**.
Former enactment—TA 1988 s 530(2), (3).

457 Determination of entitlement or liability

(1) Whether a person is entitled to a writing-down allowance or a balancing allowance, or liable to a balancing charge, for a chargeable period is determined separately for each pool of qualifying expenditure and depends on—

(a) the available qualifying expenditure in that pool for that period ("AQE"), and

(b) the total of any disposal values to be brought into account in that pool for that period ("TDV").

(2) If AQE exceeds TDV, the person is entitled to a writing-down allowance or a balancing allowance for the period.

(3) If TDV exceeds AQE, the person is liable to a balancing charge for the period.

(4) The entitlement under subsection (2) is to a writing-down allowance except for the final chargeable period when it is to a balancing allowance.

(5) The final chargeable period is the chargeable period in which the trade is permanently discontinued.

Commentary—*Simon's Direct Tax Service* **B2.616**.
Former enactments—Sub-s (1): TA 1988 s 530(2), (3).
Sub-s (2): TA 1988 s 530(2).
Sub-s (3): TA 1988 s 530(3).
Sub-ss (4), (5): TA 1988 s 530(2).
Definition—"Available qualifying expenditure", s 459.

458 Amount of allowances and charges

(1) The amount of the writing-down allowance to which a person is entitled for a chargeable period is 25% of the amount by which AQE exceeds TDV.

(2) If the chargeable period is more or less than a year, the amount is proportionately increased or reduced.

(3) If the trade has been carried on for part only of the chargeable period, the amount is proportionately reduced.

(4) A person claiming a writing-down allowance may require the allowance to be reduced to a specified amount.

(5) The amount of the balancing charge to which a person is liable for a chargeable period is the amount by which TDV exceeds AQE.

(6) The amount of the balancing allowance to which a person is entitled for the final chargeable period is the amount by which AQE exceeds TDV.

Commentary—*Simon's Direct Tax Service* **B2.616**.
Former enactments—Sub-ss (1)–(3): TA 1988 s 530(2).
Sub-s (4): change in law
Sub-s (5): TA 1988 s 530(3).
Sub-s (6): TA 1988 s 530(2).
Definition—"Final chargeable period", s 457(5).

459 Available qualifying expenditure

A person's available qualifying expenditure in a pool for a chargeable period consists of—

(*a*) any qualifying expenditure allocated to the pool for that period in accordance with section 460, and

(*b*) any unrelieved qualifying expenditure carried forward in the pool from the previous chargeable period under section 461.

Commentary—*Simon's Direct Tax Service* B2.616.
Former enactment—TA 1988 s 530(4).

460 Allocation of qualifying expenditure to pools

(1) The following rules apply to the allocation of a person's qualifying expenditure to a pool.

(2) An amount of qualifying expenditure is not to be allocated to the pool for a chargeable period if that amount has been taken into account in determining the person's available qualifying expenditure for an earlier chargeable period.

(3) Qualifying expenditure is not to be allocated to the pool for a chargeable period before that in which the expenditure is incurred.

Commentary—*Simon's Direct Tax Service* B2.616.
Former enactment—Sub-ss (2), (3): TA 1988 s 530(4); change in law.
Definition—"Available qualifying expenditure", s 459.

461 Unrelieved qualifying expenditure

(1) A person has unrelieved qualifying expenditure to carry forward from a chargeable period if for that period AQE exceeds TDV.

(2) The amount of the unrelieved qualifying expenditure is—

(*a*) the excess less the writing-down allowance made for the period, or

(*b*) if no writing-down allowance is claimed for the period, the excess.

(3) No amount may be carried forward as unrelieved qualifying expenditure from the final chargeable period.

Commentary—*Simon's Direct Tax Service* B2.616.
Former enactment—Sub-ss (1), (2): TA 1988 s 530(4).
Definition—"Final chargeable period", s 457(5).

462 Disposal values

(1) A person is required to bring a disposal value into account for the chargeable period in which he sells know-how on which he has incurred qualifying expenditure.

(2) The disposal value to be brought into account is the net proceeds of the sale, so far as they consist of capital sums.

(3) But no disposal value need be brought into account if the consideration received for the sale is treated as a payment for goodwill under section 531(2) of ICTA (consideration for know-how on disposal of trade to be treated as payment for goodwill, unless parties otherwise elect).

Commentary—*Simon's Direct Tax Service* B2.616.
Former enactments—Sub-s (1): TA 1988 s 530(5).
Sub-s (2): TA 1988 s 530(5); change in law.
Sub-s (3): TA 1988 s 531(2).
Revenue Internal Guidance—Capital allowances manual CA 72000–72200 (whether receipts capital or income).
Definition—"Capital sum", s 4.

463 Giving effect to allowances and charges

An allowance or charge to which a person is entitled or liable under this Part for a chargeable period is to be given effect in calculating the profits of the trade, by treating—

(*a*) the allowance as an expense of the trade, and

(*b*) the charge as a receipt of the trade.

Commentary—*Simon's Direct Tax Service* B2.616.
Former enactments—TA 1988 s 532(1); CAA 1990 ss 140(2), 144(2), 161(2) ("chargeable period"), (5).

PART 8

PATENT ALLOWANCES

CHAPTER 1

INTRODUCTION

Commentary—*Simon's Direct Tax Service* B2.602–609.

464 Patent allowances

(1) Allowances are available under this Part if a person incurs qualifying expenditure on the purchase of patent rights.

(2) In this Part "patent rights" means the right to do or authorise the doing of anything which would, but for that right, be an infringement of a patent.

Commentary—*Simon's Direct Tax Service* **B2.601, 602**.
Former enactment—Sub-s (2): TA 1988 s 533(1).

465 Future patent rights

(1) References in this Part to expenditure incurred on the purchase of patent rights include expenditure incurred on obtaining a right to acquire future patent rights.

(2) If a person—

    (*a*) incurs expenditure on obtaining a right to acquire future patent rights, and
    (*b*) subsequently acquires those rights,

the expenditure is to be treated as having been expenditure on the purchase of those rights.

(3) "A right to acquire future patent rights" means a right to acquire in the future patent rights relating to an invention in respect of which the patent has not yet been granted.

(4) References in this Part to the proceeds of a sale of patent rights include a sum received from a person which is treated under this section as expenditure incurred by him on the purchase of patent rights.

Commentary—*Simon's Direct Tax Service* **B2.602**.
Former enactments—Sub-ss (1)–(3): TA 1988 533(5).
Sub-s (4): TA 1988 s 533(6).
Definition—"Patent rights", s 464(2).

466 Grant of licences

(1) The acquisition of a licence in respect of a patent is to be treated as the purchase of patent rights.

(2) The grant of a licence in respect of a patent is to be treated as a sale of part of patent rights.

(3) But the grant by a person entitled to patent rights of an exclusive licence is to be treated as a sale of the whole of those rights.

(4) "Exclusive licence" means a licence to exercise those rights to the exclusion of the grantor and all other persons for the period remaining until the rights come to an end.

Commentary—*Simon's Direct Tax Service* **B2.602**.
Former enactments—Sub-s (1), (2): TA 1988 s 533(2).
Sub-ss (3), (4): TA 1988 s 533(3).
Definition—"Patent rights", s 464(2).

CHAPTER 2
QUALIFYING EXPENDITURE

467 Qualifying expenditure

Expenditure is qualifying expenditure only if it is—

    (*a*) qualifying trade expenditure, or
    (*b*) qualifying non-trade expenditure.

Commentary—*Simon's Direct Tax Service* **B2.602**.
Definitions—"Qualifying trade expenditure", s 468(1); "qualifying non-trade expenditure", s 469.

468 Qualifying trade expenditure

(1) "Qualifying trade expenditure" means capital expenditure incurred by a person on the purchase of patent rights for the purposes of a trade within the charge to tax carried on by the person.

(2) The same expenditure may not be taken into account as qualifying trade expenditure in relation to more than one trade.

(3) Expenditure incurred for the purposes of a trade by a person about to carry on the trade is to be treated as if it had been incurred by him on the first day on which he carries on the trade.

(4) But subsection (3) does not apply if the person has before that day sold all the rights on the purchase of which the expenditure was incurred.

Commentary—*Simon's Direct Tax Service* **B2.602**.
Former enactments—Sub-s (1): TA 1988 ss 520(1), (2), 528(1), 532(1); CAA 1990 s 161(3).
Sub-s (2): TA 1988 s 520(1).
Sub-ss (3), (4): TA 1988 s 520(3).
Definitions—"Capital expenditure", s 4; "patent rights", s 464(2).

469 Qualifying non-trade expenditure

"Qualifying non-trade expenditure" means capital expenditure incurred by a person on the purchase of patent rights if—

    (a) any income receivable by the person in respect of the rights would be liable to tax, and

    (b) the expenditure is not qualifying trade expenditure.

Commentary—*Simon's Direct Tax Service* **B2.602**.
Former enactment—TA 1988 s 520(2).
Definitions—"Capital expenditure", s 4; "patent rights", s 464(2); "qualifying trade expenditure", s 468.

CHAPTER 3
ALLOWANCES AND CHARGES

470 Pooling of expenditure

(1) Qualifying expenditure has to be pooled for the purpose of determining a person's entitlement to writing-down allowances and balancing allowances and liability to balancing charges.

(2) There is a separate pool—

    (a) for each trade in respect of which the person has qualifying trade expenditure, and

    (b) for all of the person's qualifying non-trade expenditure.

Commentary—*Simon's Direct Tax Service* **B2.603**.
Former enactment—TA 1988 s 520(4), (6).
Definitions—"Patent rights", s 464(2); "qualifying non-trade expenditure", s 469; "qualifying trade expenditure", s 468.

471 Determination of entitlement or liability

(1) Whether a person is entitled to a writing-down allowance or a balancing allowance, or liable to a balancing charge, for a chargeable period is determined separately for each pool of qualifying expenditure and depends on—

    (a) the available qualifying expenditure in that pool for that period ("AQE"), and

    (b) the total of any disposal receipts to be brought into account in that pool for that period ("TDR").

(2) If AQE exceeds TDR, the person is entitled to a writing-down allowance or a balancing allowance for the period.

(3) If TDR exceeds AQE, the person is liable to a balancing charge for the period.

(4) The entitlement under subsection (2) is to a writing-down allowance except for the final chargeable period when it is to a balancing allowance.

(5) The final chargeable period for a pool to which qualifying trade expenditure has been allocated is the chargeable period in which the trade is permanently discontinued.

(6) The final chargeable period for a pool to which qualifying non-trade expenditure has been allocated is the chargeable period in which the last of the patent rights on which the person has incurred qualifying non-trade expenditure—

    (a) comes to an end without any of those rights being revived, or

    (b) is wholly disposed of.

Commentary—*Simon's Direct Tax Service* **B2.603, 604**.
Former enactments—Sub-s (1): TA 1988 s 520(4), (6).
Sub-s (2): TA 1988 s 520(4).
Sub-s (3): TA 1988 s 520(6).
Sub-ss (4), (5): TA 1988 s 520(4).
Sub-s (6): TA 1988 s 520(4), (5); change in law.
Definitions—"Available qualifying expenditure", s 473; "patent rights", s 464(2); "qualifying non-trade expenditure", s 469; "qualifying trade expenditure", s 468.

472 Amount of allowances and charges

(1) The amount of the writing-down allowance to which a person is entitled for a chargeable period is 25% of the amount by which AQE exceeds TDR.

(2) If the chargeable period is more or less than a year, the amount is proportionately increased or reduced.

(3) If in the case of qualifying trade expenditure the trade has been carried on for part only of the chargeable period, the amount is proportionately reduced.

(4) A person claiming a writing-down allowance may require the allowance to be reduced to a specified amount.

(5) The amount of the balancing charge to which a person is liable for a chargeable period is the amount by which TDR exceeds AQE.

(6) The amount of the balancing allowance to which a person is entitled for the final chargeable period is the amount by which AQE exceeds TDR.

Commentary—*Simon's Direct Tax Service* **B2.603, 604**.
Former enactments—Sub-ss (1)–(3): TA 1988 s 520(4).

Sub-s (4): change in law.
Sub-s (5): TA 1988 s 520(6).
Sub-s (6): TA 1988 s 520(4).
Definitions—''Final chargeable period'', s 471(5), (6); ''qualifying trade expenditure'', s 468.

473 Available qualifying expenditure

A person's available qualifying expenditure in a pool for a chargeable period consists of—

(*a*) any qualifying expenditure allocated to the pool for that period in accordance with section 474, and

(*b*) any unrelieved qualifying expenditure carried forward in the pool from the previous chargeable period under section 475.

Commentary—*Simon's Direct Tax Service* **B2.603, 604**.
Former enactment—TA 1988 s 521(1).
Definition—''Unrelieved qualifying expenditure'', s 475.

474 Allocation of qualifying expenditure to pools

(1) The following rules apply to the allocation of a person's qualifying expenditure to a pool.

(2) An amount of qualifying expenditure is not to be allocated to the pool for a chargeable period if that amount has been taken into account in determining the person's available qualifying expenditure for an earlier chargeable period.

(3) Qualifying expenditure is not to be allocated to the pool for a chargeable period before that in which the expenditure is incurred.

(4) Qualifying expenditure incurred on patent rights is not to be allocated to the pool for a chargeable period if in any earlier period those rights—

(*a*) have come to an end without any of them having been revived, or

(*b*) have been wholly disposed of.

Commentary—*Simon's Direct Tax Service* **B2.603**.
Former enactments—Sub-ss (2)–(4): TA 1988 ss 520(2), 521(1), 528(1); change in law.
Definitions—''Available qualifying expenditure'', s 473; ''patent rights'', s 464(2).

475 Unrelieved qualifying expenditure

(1) A person has unrelieved qualifying expenditure to carry forward from a chargeable period if for that period AQE exceeds TDR.

(2) The amount of the unrelieved qualifying expenditure is—

(*a*) the excess less the writing-down allowance made for the period, or

(*b*) if no writing-down allowance is claimed for the period, the excess.

(3) No amount may be carried forward as unrelieved qualifying expenditure from the final chargeable period.

Commentary—*Simon's Direct Tax Service* **B2.603**.
Former enactment—Sub-ss (1), (2): TA 1988 s 521(1).
Definition—''Final chargeable period'', s 471(5), (6).

476 Disposal value of patent rights

(1) In this Chapter ''disposal receipt'' means a disposal value that a person is required to bring into account in accordance with—

(*a*) this section, or

(*b*) paragraph 11 of Schedule 12 to FA 1997 (finance lease or loan: receipt of major lump sum) or any other enactment.

(2) A person is required to bring a disposal value into account for the chargeable period in which he sells the whole or a part of any patent rights on which he has incurred qualifying expenditure.

(3) Subject to section 477, the disposal value to be brought into account is the net proceeds of the sale, so far as they consist of capital sums.

Commentary—*Simon's Direct Tax Service* **B2.603**.
Former enactments—Sub-s (2): TA 1988 s 521(2).
Sub-s (3): TA 1988 s 521(2); change in law.
Definitions—''Capital sum'', s 4; ''patent rights'', s 464(2).

477 Limit on amount of disposal value

(1) The amount of any disposal value, or the total amount of any disposal values, required to be brought into account by a person—

(*a*) on the sale of the whole of any patent rights, or

(*b*) on one or more sales of part of any patent rights,

is limited to the capital expenditure incurred by the person on purchasing the rights.

(2) But subsection (3) applies if the person acquired the rights as a result of—

(*a*) a transaction which was between connected persons, or

(*b*) a series of transactions each of which was between connected persons.

(3) That amount, or total amount, is limited to the capital expenditure on purchasing the rights incurred by whichever party to the transaction, or to any of the transactions, incurred the greatest such expenditure.

Commentary—*Simon's Direct Tax Service* **B2.603, 607**.
Former enactments—Sub-s (1): TA 1988 s 521(3).
Sub-ss (2), (3): TA 1988 s 521(4).
Revenue Internal Guidance—Capital allowances manual CA 75110, 75120 (worked examples).
Definitions—''Capital expenditure'', s 4; ''patent rights'', s 464(2).

CHAPTER 4
GIVING EFFECT TO ALLOWANCES AND CHARGES

478 Persons having qualifying trade expenditure

An allowance or charge to which a person is entitled or liable under this Part for a chargeable period in respect of qualifying trade expenditure is to be given effect in calculating the profits of the trade, by treating—

(*a*) the allowance as an expense of the trade, and

(*b*) the charge as a receipt of the trade.

Commentary—*Simon's Direct Tax Service* **B2.608**.
Former enactments—TA 1988 ss 528(1), 532(1); CAA 1990 ss 140(2), 144(2), 161(2) (''chargeable period''), (5).
Definition—''Qualifying trade expenditure'', s 468.

479 Persons having qualifying non-trade expenditure: income tax

(1) This section applies for income tax purposes if a person is entitled or liable under this Part to an allowance or charge for a chargeable period (''the current tax year'') in respect of qualifying non-trade expenditure.

(2) An allowance is to be given effect by deducting it from or setting it off against the person's income from patents for the current tax year.

(3) If the amount to be deducted from or set off against the person's income from patents for that tax year exceeds the amount of that income, the excess must be deducted from or set off against the person's income from patents for the next tax year, and so on for subsequent tax years.

(4) A charge is to be given effect by treating the charge as income to be taxed under Case VI of Schedule D.

Commentary—*Simon's Direct Tax Service* **B2.608**.
Former enactments—Sub-s (1): TA 1988 s 528(2), (4).
Sub-ss (2), (3): TA 1988 s 528(2).
Sub-s (4): TA 1988 s 528(4).
Definitions—''Income from patents'', s 483, Sch 3 para 101(5); ''qualifying non-trade expenditure'', s 469.

480 Persons having qualifying non-trade expenditure: corporation tax

(1) This section applies for corporation tax purposes if a company is entitled or liable under this Part to an allowance or charge for a chargeable period (''the current accounting period'') in respect of qualifying non-trade expenditure.

(2) An allowance is to be given effect by deducting it from the company's income from patents for the current accounting period.

(3) If the amount to be deducted from the company's income from patents for that period exceeds the amount of that income, the excess must (if the company remains within the charge to tax) be deducted from its income from patents for the next accounting period, and so on for subsequent accounting periods.

(4) A charge is to be given effect by treating the charge as income of the company from patents.

Commentary—*Simon's Direct Tax Service* **B2.608**.
Former enactments—Sub-s (1): TA 1988 s 528(3), (4).
Sub-ss (2), (3): TA 1988 s 528(3).
Sub-s (4): TA 1988 s 528(4).
Definitions—''Income from patents'', s 483, Sch 3 para 101(5); ''qualifying non-trade expenditure'', s 469.

CHAPTER 5
SUPPLEMENTARY PROVISIONS

481 Anti-avoidance: limit on qualifying expenditure

(1) In the two cases given below, the amount (if any) by which the capital expenditure incurred by a person (''the buyer'') on the purchase of patent rights exceeds the relevant limit is to be left out of account in determining the buyer's qualifying expenditure.

(2) The first case is where the buyer and the seller are connected with each other.

(3) The second case is where it appears that the sole or main benefit which (but for this section) might have been expected to accrue to the parties from—

   (a) the sale, or

   (b) transactions of which the sale is one,

was obtaining an allowance under this Part.

(4) If the seller is required to bring a disposal value into account under this Part because of the sale, the relevant limit is that disposal value.

(5) If subsection (4) does not apply but the seller—

   (a) receives a capital sum on the sale, and

   (b) is chargeable to tax in respect of that sum in accordance with section 524 of ICTA,

the relevant limit is that sum.

(6) If neither subsection (4) nor subsection (5) applies, the relevant limit is whichever of the following is the smallest—

   (a) the market value of the rights;

   (b) if the seller incurred capital expenditure on acquiring the rights, the amount of that expenditure;

   (c) if a person connected with the seller incurred capital expenditure on acquiring the rights, the amount of that expenditure.

Commentary—*Simon's Direct Tax Service* **B2.607.**
Former enactments—Sub-ss (1)–(3): TA 1988 s 521(5).
Sub-ss (4)–(6): TA 1988 s 521(6).
Definitions—"Capital expenditure", s 4; "capital sum", s 4; "patent rights", s 464(2).
Modification—CAA 2001 Sch 3 para 102 (the section above does not apply to expenditure incurred before 1 April 1986, and sub-ss (5), (6) above do not apply to expenditure incurred before 27 July 1989).

482 Sums paid for Crown use etc treated as paid under licence

(1) This section applies if an invention which is the subject of a patent is used by or for the services of—

   (a) the Crown under sections 55 to 59 of the Patents Act 1977, or

   (b) the government of a country outside the United Kingdom under corresponding provisions of the law of that country.

(2) The use is to be treated as having taken place under a licence.

(3) Sums paid in respect of the use are to be treated as having been paid under a licence.

Former enactment—TA 1988 s 533(4).

483 Meaning of "income from patents"

For the purposes of this Part a person's "income from patents" means—

   (a) royalties or other sums paid in respect of the use of a patent,

   (b) balancing charges to which the person is liable under this Part, and

   (c) amounts on which tax is payable under section 524 or 525 of ICTA (taxation of receipts from sale of patent rights).

Commentary—*Simon's Direct Tax Service* **B2.608.**
Former enactment—TA 1988 s 533(1).
Definition—"Patent rights", s 464(2).

PART 9
DREDGING ALLOWANCES

Commentary—*Simon's Direct Tax Service* **Division B2.8.**
Modification—CAA 2001 Sch 3 (1) para 105 (where it is provided under this Part that writing-down allowances are to be made in respect of any expenditure during a writing-down period of any specified length, if allowances were made under FA 1965 Sch 14 para 27(2)—

   (a) for income tax purposes, for either of the tax years 1964–65 and 1965–66, and

   (b) for accounting periods of a company falling wholly or partly within either of those years,

the periods for which allowances were made are added together in calculating the writing-down period, even though (according to the calendar) the same time is counted twice.

Qualifying expenditure on dredging, etc

484 Dredging allowances

(1) Allowances are available under this Part if a person carries on a qualifying trade and qualifying expenditure has been incurred on dredging.

(2) In this Part "qualifying trade" means a trade or undertaking the whole or part of which—

   (a) consists of the maintenance or improvement of the navigation of a harbour, estuary or waterway, or

(*b*) is of a kind listed in Table A or B in section 274 (meaning of qualifying trade for purposes of industrial buildings allowances).

(3) "Dredging" does not include anything done otherwise than in the interests of navigation.

(4) Subject to subsection (3), "dredging" includes—

(*a*) the removal of anything forming part of, or projecting from the bed of, the sea or any inland water—

(i) by whatever means it is removed, and
(ii) even if, at the time of removal, it is wholly or partly above water, and

(*b*) the widening of an inland waterway.

Commentary—*Simon's Direct Tax Service* **B2.802, 803**.
Former enactments—Sub-s (2): CAA 1990 s 135(1).
Sub-ss (3), (4): CAA 1990 s 135(3).
Revenue Internal Guidance—Capital allowances manual CA 80200 (meaning of "dredging").

485 Qualifying expenditure

(1) Expenditure on dredging is qualifying expenditure if—

(*a*) it is capital expenditure,
(*b*) it is incurred for the purposes of a qualifying trade by the person carrying on the trade, and
(*c*) if the person does not carry on a qualifying trade within section 484(2)(*a*), the dredging is for the benefit of vessels coming to, leaving or using a dock or other premises occupied by the person for the purposes of the qualifying trade.

(2) If capital expenditure is incurred—

(*a*) partly for the purposes of a qualifying trade, and
(*b*) partly for other purposes,

the qualifying expenditure is the part of the capital expenditure that, on a just and reasonable apportionment, is referable to the purposes of the qualifying trade.

(3) If part only of a trade or undertaking is within section 484(2), subsection (2) of this section applies as if—

(*a*) the part which is within section 484(2), and
(*b*) the part which is not,

were separate trades.

Commentary—*Simon's Direct Tax Service* **B2.803**.
Former enactments—Sub-s (1): CAA 1990 s 134(1).
Sub-s (2): CAA 1990 s 134(6); change in law.
Sub-s (3): CAA 1990 s 135(1).
Definitions—"Capital expenditure", s 4; "qualifying trade", s 484(2).

486 Pre-trading expenditure of qualifying trades, etc

(1) If a person incurs capital expenditure with a view to carrying on a trade or a part of a trade, this Part applies as if the expenditure were incurred by the person on the first day on which the trade or part of the trade is carried on.

(2) If a person incurs capital expenditure—

(*a*) in connection with a dock or other premises, and
(*b*) with a view to occupying the dock or premises for the purposes of a qualifying trade which is not a qualifying trade within section 484(2)(*a*),

this Part applies as if the expenditure were incurred by the person when he first occupies the dock or premises for the purposes of the qualifying trade.

Commentary—*Simon's Direct Tax Service* **B2.804**.
Former enactments—Sub-s (1): CAA 1990 ss 134(7), 135(2); change in law.
Sub-s (2): CAA 1990 ss 134(7), 135(2).
Definitions—"Capital expenditure", s 4; "qualifying trade", s 484(2).

Writing-down and balancing allowances

487 Writing-down allowances

(1) A person is entitled to a writing-down allowance for a chargeable period if—

(*a*) qualifying expenditure has been incurred on dredging,
(*b*) at any time during the chargeable period, the person is carrying on the qualifying trade for the purposes of which the qualifying expenditure was incurred, and
(*c*) that time falls within the writing-down period.

(2) The writing-down period, in relation to qualifying expenditure incurred by a person, is 25 years beginning with the first day of the chargeable period of that person in which the qualifying expenditure was incurred.

(3) The amount of the writing-down allowance is 4% of the qualifying expenditure.

(4) The allowance is proportionately increased or reduced if the chargeable period is more or less than a year.

(5) The total amount of any writing-down allowances made in respect of any qualifying expenditure, whether to the same or different persons, must not exceed the amount of the expenditure.

(6) A person claiming a writing-down allowance may require the allowance to be reduced to a specified amount.

(7) A person is not entitled to a writing-down allowance for the chargeable period in which a balancing allowance is made to him in respect of the qualifying expenditure.

Commentary—*Simon's Direct Tax Service* **B2.801, 802**.
Former enactments—Sub-ss (1)–(3): CAA 1990 s 134(1).
Sub-s (4): CAA 1990 s 146(1), (2).
Sub-s (5): CAA 1990 s 146(3).
Sub-s (6): change in law.
Definition—"Qualifying trade", s 484(2).
Modifications—CAA 2001 Sch 3 para 103(1) (sub-s (2) applies with the substitution of "50 years" for "25 years" in relation to expenditure incurred before 6 November 1962).
CAA 2001 Sch 3 para 103(2) (sub-s (3) applies with the substitution of "2%" for "4%" in relation to expenditure incurred before 6 November 1962).
CAA 2001 Sch 3 (the writing-down period: see modification note at the start of this Part).

488 Balancing allowances

(1) A person is entitled to a balancing allowance for a chargeable period if—

  (*a*) qualifying expenditure has been incurred on dredging,
  (*b*) in that chargeable period, the qualifying trade for the purposes of which the expenditure was incurred has been—

    (i) permanently discontinued, or
    (ii) sold,

  (*c*) the person is the last person carrying on the qualifying trade before its discontinuance or sale, and
  (*d*) the amount of the expenditure exceeds the amount of the allowances previously made in respect of it, whether to the same or different persons.

(2) The amount of the balancing allowance is the amount of the difference.

(3) For the purposes of subsection (1)—

  (*a*) the permanent discontinuance of a trade does not include an event treated as a permanent discontinuance under section 113(1) or 337(1) of ICTA (change in persons carrying on a trade etc and effect of company ceasing to trade etc), and
  (*b*) a sale does not include a sale which is within subsection (4) or (5).

(4) A sale is within this subsection if any of the following conditions is met—

  (*a*) the buyer is a body of persons over whom the seller has control;
  (*b*) the seller is a body of persons over whom the buyer has control;
  (*c*) both the seller and the buyer are bodies of persons and another person has control over both of them;
  (*d*) the seller and the buyer are connected persons.

In this subsection "body of persons" includes a partnership.

(5) A sale is within this subsection if it appears that the sole or main benefit which might be expected to accrue to the parties, or any of them, from—

  (*a*) the sale, or
  (*b*) transactions of which the sale is one,

is the obtaining of a tax advantage under any of the provisions of this Act apart from Part 2 (plant and machinery allowances).

Commentary—*Simon's Direct Tax Service* **B2.805**.
Former enactments—Sub-s (1): CAA 1990 ss 134(2), 134(4).
Sub-s (2): CAA 1990 s 134(2).
Sub-ss (3)–(5): CAA 1990 s 134(4).
Definition—"Qualifying trade", s 484(2).
Modifications—CAA 2001 Sch 3 para 104 (in sub-s (1)(*d*) above, the reference to allowances previously made in respect of the expenditure includes any initial allowance made in respect of it under FA 1956 s 17 or CAA 1968 s 67, and except in relation to initial allowances, is to be construed as if FA 1956 s 17 had always had effect (instead of having effect only for chargeable periods after the year 1955–56)).

Giving effect to allowances

489 Giving effect to allowances

An allowance to which a person is entitled under this Part is to be given effect in calculating the profits of that person's trade, by treating the allowance as an expense of the trade.

Commentary—*Simon's Direct Tax Service* **B2.807**.
Former enactments—CAA 1990 ss 134(5), 140(2), 144(2), 161(2) ("chargeable period"), (5).

PART 10
ASSURED TENANCY ALLOWANCES

Commentary—*Simon's Direct Tax Service* **Division B2.9**.

CHAPTER 1
INTRODUCTION

490 Assured tenancy allowances

(1) Allowances are available under this Part if qualifying expenditure has been incurred on a building which consists of or includes a qualifying dwelling-house.

(2) A dwelling-house is not a qualifying dwelling-house unless—

    (*a*) it is let on a tenancy which is for the time being an assured tenancy, or

    (*b*) it has been let on an assured tenancy and the conditions in subsection (4) are met.

(3) ''Assured tenancy'' means—

    (*a*) an assured tenancy within the meaning of section 56 of the Housing Act 1980, or

    (*b*) an assured tenancy (but not an assured shorthold tenancy) for the purposes of the Housing Act 1988.

(4) The conditions referred to in subsection (2)(*b*) are that—

    (*a*) the dwelling-house is for the time being subject to a regulated tenancy or a housing association tenancy, and

    (*b*) the landlord under the tenancy is an approved body or was an approved body but has ceased to be such for any reason.

(5) In subsection (4) ''regulated tenancy'' and ''housing association tenancy'' have the same meaning as in the Rent Act 1977.

(6) Further requirements that have to be met for a dwelling-house to be a qualifying dwelling-house are given in sections 504 and 505; and subsection (2) is subject to section 506(2)(*b*) (temporary disuse of dwelling-house ignored).

Commentary—*Simon's Direct Tax Service* **B2.902, 903**.
Former enactments—Sub-s (1): CAA 1990 s 84(1).
Sub-s (2): CAA 1990 s 86(1), (2).
Sub-s (3): CAA 1990 s 97(1) (''assured tenancy'').
Sub-s (4): CAA 1990 s 86(2).
Sub-s (5): CAA 1990 s 86(4).
Revenue Internal Guidance—Capital allowances manual CA 85200 (background to assured tenancy scheme).
Definition—''Approved body'', s 492.

491 Allowances available in relation to old expenditure only

(1) Allowances under this Part are not available unless—

    (*a*) the qualifying expenditure was incurred after 9th March 1982 and before 1st April 1992, and

    (*b*) if the tenancy is an assured tenancy for the purposes of the Housing Act 1988, expenditure has been incurred which is within subsection (2) or (3).

(2) Expenditure is within this subsection if it was incurred by—

    (*a*) a company which was an approved body on 15th March 1988, or

    (*b*) a person who sold the relevant interest in the building, before any of the dwelling-houses comprised in it were used, to a company which was an approved body on 15th March 1988,

and either it was incurred before 15th March 1988 or it consists of the payment of sums under a contract entered into before that date.

(3) Expenditure is within this subsection if it was incurred by a company which—

    (*a*) was an approved body on 15th March 1988, and

    (*b*) bought or contracted to buy the relevant interest in the building before that date.

Commentary—*Simon's Direct Tax Service* **B2.902**.
Former enactments—Sub-s (1): CAA 1990 ss 84(1), (2), 96(3).
Sub-ss (2), (3): CAA 1990 s 84(1), (3).
Definition—''Approved body'', s 492; ''assured tenancy'', s 490(3).

492 Meaning of ''approved body''

In this Part ''approved body'' has the meaning given in section 56(4) of the Housing Act 1980.

Commentary—*Simon's Direct Tax Service* **B2.902**.
Former enactment—CAA 1990 s 97(1).
Revenue Internal Guidance—Capital allowances manual CA 85350 (''approved body'' is one of a description specified in an order made by the Secretary of State).

493 Expenditure on the construction of a building

(1) For the purposes of this Part, expenditure on the construction of a building does not include expenditure on the acquisition of land or rights in or over land.

(2) This Part has effect in relation to capital expenditure incurred by a person on repairs to a part of a building as if it were capital expenditure on the construction of that part of the building for the first time.

Commentary—*Simon's Direct Tax Service* **B2.902**.
Former enactments—Sub-s (1): CAA 1990 s 97(2).
Sub-s (2): CAA 1990 s 93(1).

CHAPTER 2
THE RELEVANT INTEREST
Introduction

494 Introduction

This Chapter identifies, in a case where a person has incurred expenditure on the construction of a building which is to be or include a qualifying dwelling-house—

    (a) the relevant interest in the building, and
    (b) the relevant interest in a dwelling-house comprised in the building.

Commentary—*Simon's Direct Tax Service* B2.904.

The relevant interest in the building

495 General rule as to what is the relevant interest in the building

(1) The relevant interest in the building is the interest in the building to which the person who incurred the expenditure on the construction of the building was entitled when the expenditure was incurred.

(2) Subsection (1) is subject to the following provisions of this Chapter.

(3) If—

    (a) the person who incurred the expenditure on the construction of the building was entitled to more than one interest in the building when the expenditure was incurred, and
    (b) one of those interests was reversionary on all the others,

the reversionary interest is the relevant interest.

Commentary—*Simon's Direct Tax Service* **B2.904**.
Former enactments—Sub-ss (1), (2): CAA 1990 s 95(1).
Sub-s (3): CAA 1990 s 95(2).

496 Interest acquired on completion of construction

For the purpose of determining the relevant interest, a person who—

    (a) incurs expenditure on the construction of a building, and
    (b) is entitled to an interest in the building on or as a result of the completion of the construction,

is treated as having had that interest when the expenditure was incurred.

Commentary—*Simon's Direct Tax Service* **B2.904**.
Former enactment—CAA 1990 s 97(3). Change in law.

497 Effect of creation of subordinate interest

An interest does not cease to be the relevant interest merely because of the creation of a lease or other interest to which that interest is subject.

Commentary—*Simon's Direct Tax Service* **B2.904**.
Former enactment—CAA 1990 s 95(3).

498 Merger of leasehold interest

If the relevant interest is a leasehold interest which is extinguished on—

    (a) being surrendered, or
    (b) the person entitled to it acquiring the interest which is reversionary on it,

the interest into which the leasehold interest merges becomes the relevant interest when the leasehold interest is extinguished.

Commentary—*Simon's Direct Tax Service* **B2.904**.
Former enactment—CAA 1990 s 95(3).

499 Provisions applying on termination of lease

(1) This section applies if the relevant interest in relation to expenditure on the construction of a building is a lease.

(2) If, with the consent of the lessor, the lessee of a building remains in possession after the termination of the lease without a new lease being granted to him, the lease is treated as continuing as long as the lessee remains in possession.

(3) If on the termination of the lease a new lease is granted to the lessee as a result of the exercise of an option available to him under the terms of the first lease, the second lease is treated as a continuation of the first.

(4) If on the termination of the lease the lessor pays a sum to the lessee in respect of a building comprised in the lease, the lease is treated as if it had come to an end by surrender in consideration of the payment.

(5) If on the termination of the lease—

(a) a new lease is granted to a different lessee, and
(b) in connection with the transaction that lessee makes a payment to the former lessee,

the two leases are treated as if they were the same lease which had been assigned by the former lessee to the new lessee in consideration of the payment.

Commentary—*Simon's Direct Tax Service* **B2.909**.
Former enactments—Sub-s (1): CAA 1990 s 94(1).
Sub-s (2): CAA 1990 s 94(2).
Sub-s (3): CAA 1990 s 94(3).
Sub-s (4): CAA 1990 s 94(4).
Sub-s (5): CAA 1990 s 94(5).

The relevant interest in the dwelling-house

500 The relevant interest in the dwelling-house

The relevant interest in a dwelling-house comprised in a building is the relevant interest in the building, to the extent that it subsists in the dwelling-house.

Commentary—*Simon's Direct Tax Service* B2.904.
Former enactment—CAA 1990 s 95(1).

CHAPTER 3
QUALIFYING EXPENDITURE

501 Capital expenditure on construction

If—

(a) capital expenditure has been incurred on the construction of a building which was to be or include a qualifying dwelling-house, and
(b) the relevant interest in the building has not been sold or, if it has been sold, it has been sold only after the first use of the building,

the capital expenditure is qualifying expenditure.

Commentary—*Simon's Direct Tax Service* B2.902.
Former enactment—CAA 1990 ss 85(1), (2), 87(1).
Definition—"Capital expenditure", s 4.

502 Purchase of unused dwelling-house where developer not involved

(1) This section applies if—

(a) expenditure has been incurred on the construction of a building which was to be or include a qualifying dwelling-house,
(b) the relevant interest was sold before the first use of any dwelling-house comprised in the building,
(c) a capital sum was paid by the purchaser for the relevant interest, and
(d) section 503 (purchase of dwelling-house sold unused by developer) does not apply.

(2) The lesser of—

(a) the capital sum paid by the purchaser for the relevant interest, and
(b) the expenditure incurred on the construction of the building,

is qualifying expenditure.

(3) The qualifying expenditure is to be treated as having been incurred when the capital sum became payable.

(4) If the relevant interest was sold more than once before the first use of any dwelling-house comprised in the building, subsection (2) has effect only in relation to the last of those sales.

Commentary—*Simon's Direct Tax Service* B2.902.
Former enactments—Sub-s (1): CAA 1990 s 91(1).
Sub-ss (2), (3): CAA 1990 s 91(1).
Sub-s (4): CAA 1990 s 91(2).
Definitions—"Capital sum", s 4; "qualifying dwelling-house", s 490(2).

503 Purchase of dwelling-house sold unused by developer

(1) This section applies if—

　(a) expenditure has been incurred by a developer on the construction of a building which was to be or include a qualifying dwelling-house, and

　(b) the relevant interest was sold by the developer in the course of the development trade before the first use of any dwelling-house comprised in the building.

(2) If—

　(a) the sale of the relevant interest by the developer was the only sale of that interest before the first use of any dwelling-house comprised in the building, and

　(b) a capital sum was paid by the purchaser for the relevant interest,

the capital sum is qualifying expenditure.

(3) If—

　(a) the sale by the developer was not the only sale before the first use of any dwelling-house comprised in the building, and

　(b) a capital sum was paid by the purchaser for the relevant interest on the last sale,

the lesser of that capital sum and the price paid for the relevant interest on its sale by the developer is qualifying expenditure.

(4) The qualifying expenditure is treated as having been incurred when the capital sum referred to in subsection (2)(b) or (3)(b) became payable.

(5) For the purposes of this section—

　(a) a developer is a person who carries on a trade which consists in whole or in part in the construction of buildings with a view to their sale, and

　(b) an interest in a building is sold by the developer in the course of the development trade if the developer sells it in the course of the trade or (as the case may be) that part of the trade that consists in the construction of buildings with a view to their sale.

Commentary—*Simon's Direct Tax Service* **B2.902**.
Former enactments—Sub-s (1): CAA 1990 s 91(1)., (3).
Sub-ss (2), (3): CAA 1990 s 91(1), (3).
Sub-s (4): CAA 1990 s 91(2), (3).
Sub-s (5): CAA 1990 s 91(3).
Definitions—"Capital sum", s 4; "qualifying dwelling-house", s 490(2).

CHAPTER 4
QUALIFYING DWELLING-HOUSES

504 Requirements relating to the landlord

(1) A dwelling-house is a qualifying dwelling-house only if the landlord is—

　(a) a company, and

　(b) the person who—

　　(i) incurred the qualifying expenditure on the building in which the dwelling-house is comprised, or

　　(ii) is for the time being entitled to the relevant interest in the dwelling-house.

(2) The requirement that the landlord must be a company does not apply in relation to expenditure incurred—

　(a) before 5th May 1983, or

　(b) on or after that date pursuant to a contract entered into before that date,

unless a person other than a company became entitled to the relevant interest on or after that date.

Commentary—*Simon's Direct Tax Service* **B2.903**.
Former enactments—Sub-s (1): CAA 1990 s 86(3).
Sub-s (2): CAA 1990 s 86(5).
Definition—"Qualifying dwelling-house", s 490(2).

505 Qualifying dwelling-houses: exclusions

(1) A dwelling-house is not a qualifying dwelling-house if any of the exclusions given below apply

Exclusion 1
The landlord under the tenancy is—

　(a) a housing association which is approved for the purposes of section 488 of ICTA, or

　(b) a self-build society within the meaning of the Housing Associations Act 1985.

Exclusion 2
The landlord and the tenant are connected persons.

Exclusion 3
The tenant is a director of a company which is or is connected with the landlord.

Exclusion 4
The landlord is a close company and the tenant is, for the purposes of Part XI of ICTA—

(*a*) a participator in that company, or

(*b*) an associate of such a participator.

Exclusion 5

The tenancy is entered into as part of a mutual arrangement for avoidance.

(2) In exclusion 5, a "mutual arrangement for avoidance" means an arrangement—

(*a*) between the landlords (or owners) of different dwelling-houses, and

(*b*) under which one landlord takes a person as a tenant in circumstances in which, if that person was the tenant of a dwelling-house let by the other landlord, that dwelling-house would not be a qualifying dwelling-house because of exclusion 2, 3 or 4.

Commentary—*Simon's Direct Tax Service* **B2.903**.
Former enactment—Sub-ss (1), (2): CAA 1990 s 86(3).
Definition—"Qualifying dwelling-house", s 490(2).

506 Dwelling-house ceasing to be qualifying dwelling-house

(1) If a dwelling-house ceases to be a qualifying dwelling-house otherwise than on a sale of the relevant interest in the dwelling-house, this Part has effect as if—

(*a*) the relevant interest in the dwelling-house had been sold at that time, and

(*b*) the net proceeds of the sale were equal to the market value of that interest at that time.

(2) For the purposes of this Part—

(*a*) a dwelling-house is not to be regarded as ceasing altogether to be used merely because it falls temporarily out of use, and

(*b*) if, immediately before any period of temporary disuse, a dwelling-house is a qualifying dwelling-house, it is to be regarded as continuing to be a qualifying dwelling-house during the period of temporary disuse.

Commentary—*Simon's Direct Tax Service* **B2.903**.
Former enactments—Sub-s (1): CAA 1990 s 89(1).
Sub-s (2): CAA 1990 s 89(2).
Definition—"Qualifying dwelling-house", s 490(2).

CHAPTER 5

WRITING-DOWN ALLOWANCES

Entitlement to and calculation of writing-down allowances

507 Entitlement to writing-down allowance

(1) A person is entitled to a writing-down allowance for a chargeable period if—

(*a*) qualifying expenditure has been incurred on a building,

(*b*) that person is or has been an approved body,

(*c*) at the end of that chargeable period the person is entitled to the relevant interest in the building, and

(*d*) at the end of that chargeable period, the building is or includes a qualifying dwelling-house or two or more qualifying dwellinghouses.

(2) A person claiming a writing-down allowance may require the allowance to be reduced to a specified amount.

Commentary—*Simon's Direct Tax Service* **B2.906**.
Former enactment—Sub-s (1): CAA 1990 s 85(1).
Sub-s (2): change in law.
Definitions—"Approved body", s 492; "chargeable period", s 6; "qualifying dwelling-house", s 490(2).

508 Basic rule for calculating amount of allowance

(1) The basic rule is that the writing-down allowance for a chargeable period is 4% of the qualifying expenditure attributable to the dwelling-house or (as the case may be) each dwelling-house falling within section 507(1)(*d*).

(2) The allowance is proportionately increased or reduced if the chargeable period is more or less than a year.

(3) The basic rule does not apply if section 509 applies.

Commentary—*Simon's Direct Tax Service* **B2.906**.
Former enactment—Sub-ss (1), (2): CAA 1990 s 85(2).
Definition—"Chargeable period", s 6.

509 Calculation of allowance after sale of relevant interest

(1) This section applies if—

(*a*) the relevant interest in a qualifying dwelling-house is sold, and

(*b*) a balancing adjustment falls to be made under section 513 as a result of the sale.

(2) If this section applies, the writing-down allowance for any chargeable period ending after the sale is—

$$RQE \times \frac{A}{B}$$

where—

RQE is the amount of the residue of qualifying expenditure attributable to the dwelling-house immediately after the sale,
A is the length of the chargeable period, and
B is the length of the period from the date of the sale to the end of the period of 25 years beginning with the day on which the dwelling-house was first used.

(3) On any later such sale, the writing-down allowance is further adjusted in accordance with this section.

Commentary—*Simon's Direct Tax Service* **B2.906.**
Former enactments—Sub-s (1): CAA 1990 s 85(3).
Sub-s (2): CAA 1990 s 85(3).
Sub-s (3): CAA 1990 s 85(3).
Definitions—"Chargeable period", s 6; "qualifying dwelling-house", s 490(2).

510 Allowance limited to residue of qualifying expenditure attributable to dwelling-house

(1) The amount of the writing-down allowance for a chargeable period in respect of a dwelling-house is limited to the residue of qualifying expenditure attributable to it.

(2) For this purpose the residue is ascertained immediately before writing off the writing-down allowance at the end of the chargeable period.

Commentary—*Simon's Direct Tax Service* **B2.906.**
Former enactment—Sub-ss (1), (2): CAA 1990 s 85(4).
Definition—"Chargeable period", s 6.

Interpretation

511 Qualifying expenditure attributable to dwelling-house

(1) If the building concerned consists of a single qualifying dwelling-house, then, subject to the relevant limit, the whole of the qualifying expenditure is attributable to the dwelling-house.

(2) If the qualifying dwelling-house forms part of a building, the qualifying expenditure attributable to the dwelling-house is, subject to the relevant limit, the total of—

(a) the part of the qualifying expenditure properly attributable to that dwelling-house, and
(b) if there are common parts of the building, such part of the qualifying expenditure on those common parts—

(i) as it is just and reasonable to attribute to that dwelling-house, and
(ii) as does not exceed 10% of the part referred to in paragraph (a).

(3) In this section "the relevant limit" means—

(a) £60,000, if the dwelling-house is in Greater London, and
(b) £40,000, if the dwelling-house is elsewhere.

(4) In subsection (2) "common parts", in relation to a building, means common parts of the building which—

(a) are not intended to be in separate occupation (whether for domestic, commercial or other purposes), but
(b) are intended to be of benefit to some or all of the qualifying dwellinghouses included in the building.

(5) For the purposes of subsection (2), the qualifying expenditure on any common parts of a building is so much of the expenditure on the construction of the building as it is just and reasonable to attribute to those parts.

Commentary—*Simon's Direct Tax Service* **B2.902.**
Former enactments—Sub-ss (1)–(3): CAA 1990 s 96(1).
Sub-ss (4), (5): CAA 1990 s 96(2).
Revenue Internal Guidance—Capital allowances manual CA 85450 (application of this section).
Definition—"Qualifying dwelling-house", s 490(2).

512 Residue of qualifying expenditure attributable to dwelling-house

(1) The residue of qualifying expenditure attributable to a dwelling-house is the qualifying expenditure attributable to that dwelling-house that has not yet been written off in accordance with Chapter 7.

(2) Subsection (1) is subject to section 528 (treatment of demolition costs).

Commentary—*Simon's Direct Tax Service* **B2.907.**
Former enactment—Sub-s (1): CAA 1990 s 90(1).

CHAPTER 6
BALANCING ADJUSTMENTS
General

513 When balancing adjustments are made

(1) A balancing adjustment is made if—

(*a*) qualifying expenditure has been incurred on a building, and

(*b*) a balancing event occurs in relation to a dwelling-house comprised in the building while it is a qualifying dwelling-house.

(2) A balancing adjustment is either a balancing allowance or a balancing charge and is made for the chargeable period in which the balancing event occurs.

(3) A balancing allowance or balancing charge is made to or on the person entitled to the relevant interest in the dwelling-house immediately before the balancing event.

(4) No balancing adjustment is made if the balancing event occurs more than 25 years after the dwelling-house was first used.

Commentary—*Simon's Direct Tax Service* **B2.908**.
Former enactments—Sub-ss (1)–(3): CAA 1990 s 87(1).
Sub-s (4): CAA 1990 s 87(2).
Definition—''Chargeable period'', s 6; ''qualifying dwelling-house'', s 490(2).

514 Balancing events

The following are balancing events in relation to a qualifying dwelling-house—

(*a*) the relevant interest in the dwelling-house is sold;

(*b*) if the relevant interest in the dwelling-house is a lease, the lease ends otherwise than on the person entitled to it acquiring the interest reversionary on it;

(*c*) the dwelling-house is demolished or destroyed;

(*d*) the dwelling-house ceases altogether to be used (without being demolished or destroyed).

Commentary—*Simon's Direct Tax Service* **B2.908**.
Former enactments—CAA 1990 ss 87(1), 150(4).
Definition—''Qualifying dwelling-house'', s 490(2).

515 Proceeds from balancing events

(1) References in this Part to the proceeds from a balancing event are to the amounts received or receivable in connection with the event, as shown in the Table—

TABLE
BALANCING EVENTS AND PROCEEDS

1. Balancing event	2. Proceeds from event
1. The sale of the relevant interest.	The net proceeds of the sale.
2. The demolition or destruction of the dwelling-house.	The net amount received for the remains of the dwelling-house, together with— (*a*) any insurance money received in respect of the demolition or destruction, and (*b*) any other compensation of any description so received, so far as it consists of capital sums.
3. The dwelling-house ceases altogether to be used.	Any compensation of any description received in respect of the event, so far it consists of capital sums.

(2) The amounts referred to in column 2 of the Table are those received or receivable by the person whose entitlement to a balancing allowance or liability to a balancing charge is in question.

Commentary—*Simon's Direct Tax Service* **B2.908**.
Former enactment—Sub-ss (1), (2): CAA 1990 s 156.
Definition—''Capital sum'', s 4.

Calculation of balancing adjustments

516 Dwelling-house a qualifying dwelling-house throughout

(1) This section provides for balancing adjustments in cases where the dwelling-house was a qualifying dwelling-house for the whole of the relevant period of ownership.

(2) A balancing allowance is made if—

(*a*) there are no proceeds from the balancing event, or

(*b*) the proceeds from the balancing event are less than the residue of qualifying expenditure attributable to the dwelling-house immediately before the event.

(3) The amount of the balancing allowance is the amount of—

 (*a*) the residue (if there are no proceeds);

 (*b*) the difference (if the proceeds are less than the residue).

(4) A balancing charge is made if the proceeds from the balancing event are more than the residue of qualifying expenditure attributable to the dwelling-house immediately before the event.

(5) The amount of the balancing charge is the amount of the difference.

Commentary—*Simon's Direct Tax Service* **B2.908**.
Former enactments—Sub-s (1): CAA 1990 s 88(1).
Sub-ss (2), (3): CAA 1990 s 87(3).
Sub-ss (4), (5): CAA 1990 s 87(4).
Definition—"Qualifying dwelling-house", s 490(2).

517 Dwelling-house not a qualifying dwelling-house throughout

(1) This section provides for balancing adjustments where the building was not a qualifying dwelling-house for a part of the relevant period of ownership.

(2) A balancing allowance is made if—

 (*a*) the proceeds from the balancing event are less than the starting expenditure attributable to the dwelling-house, and

 (*b*) the total amount of the relevant allowances in respect of that expenditure is less than the adjusted net cost of the dwelling-house.

(3) The amount of the balancing allowance is the amount of the difference between the adjusted net cost of the dwelling-house and the total amount of the relevant allowances.

(4) A balancing charge is made if the proceeds from the balancing event are equal to or more than the starting expenditure attributable to the dwelling-house.

(5) The amount of the balancing charge is equal to the total amount of the relevant allowances.

(6) A balancing charge is also made if—

 (*a*) the proceeds from the balancing event are less than the starting expenditure attributable to the dwelling-house, and

 (*b*) the total amount of the relevant allowances in respect of that expenditure is more than the adjusted net cost in relation to the dwelling-house.

(7) The amount of the balancing charge is the amount of the difference between the total amount of those allowances and the adjusted net cost.

(8) "The relevant allowances" means—

 (*a*) any initial allowance under paragraph 1 of Schedule 12 to FA 1982, and

 (*b*) any writing-down allowance made for a chargeable period ending on or before the date of the balancing event in question.

Commentary—*Simon's Direct Tax Service* **B2.908**.
Former enactments—Sub-s (1): CAA 1990 s 88(1).
Sub-ss (2), (3): CAA 1990 s 88(3).
Sub-ss (4), (5): CAA 1990 s 88(2).
Sub-ss (6), (7): CAA 1990 s 88(3).
Sub-s (8): CAA 1990 s 88(5) "the allowances given".
Definition—"Adjusted net cost", s 522; "chargeable period", s 6; "qualifying dwelling-house", s 490(2).

518 Overall limit on balancing charge

(1) The amount of a balancing charge made on a person in respect of any qualifying expenditure attributable to a dwelling-house must not exceed the total amount of the relevant allowances made to that person.

(2) "The relevant allowances" has the meaning given by section 517(8).

Commentary—*Simon's Direct Tax Service* **B2.908**.
Former enactment—Sub-ss (1), (2): CAA 1990 s 87(6).

519 Recovery of old initial allowances made on incorrect assumptions

(1) This section applies if—

 (*a*) an initial allowance has been made under paragraph 1 of Schedule 12 to FA 1982 in respect of expenditure relating to a dwelling-house, and

 (*b*) when the dwelling-house comes to be used, it is not a qualifying dwelling-house.

(2) All such assessments and adjustments of assessments are to be made as are necessary to secure that, despite the repeal of Schedule 12 to FA 1982, effect is given to the prohibition in paragraph 1(3) of that Schedule (on the making of initial allowances in respect of dwelling-houses which are not qualifying dwelling-houses).

Commentary—*Simon's Direct Tax Service* **B2.908**.
Former enactments—Sub-s (1): CAA 1990 s 87(7), (8).
Sub-s (2): CAA 1990 s 87(7).
Definition—"Qualifying dwelling-house", s 490(2).

Meaning of "the relevant period of ownership" etc

520 The relevant period of ownership

The relevant period of ownership is the period beginning—

(a) with the day on which the dwelling-house was first used for any purpose, or

(b) if the relevant interest in the dwelling-house has been sold after that day, with the day following that on which the sale (or the last such sale) occurred,

and ending with the day on which the balancing event occurs.

Commentary—*Simon's Direct Tax Service* **B2.908**.
Former enactment—CAA 1990 s 88(5) ("the relevant period").

521 Starting expenditure

(1) This section gives the starting expenditure attributable to a dwelling-house for the purposes of section 517.

(2) If the person to or on whom the balancing allowance or balancing charge falls to be made is the person who incurred the qualifying expenditure attributable to the dwelling-house, that expenditure is the starting expenditure.

(3) Otherwise, the starting expenditure is the residue of qualifying expenditure attributable to the dwelling-house at the beginning of the relevant period of ownership.

(4) If section 528 (treatment of demolition costs) applies, the starting expenditure is increased by an amount equal to the net cost of the demolition.

Commentary—*Simon's Direct Tax Service* **B2.908**.
Former enactment—CAA 1990 s 88(5) ("the capital expenditure").

522 Adjusted net cost

The amount of the adjusted net cost in relation to a dwelling-house is—

$$(S - P) \times \frac{I}{R}$$

where—

S is the starting expenditure attributable to the dwelling-house,
P is the amount of any proceeds from the balancing event,
I is the number of days in the relevant period of ownership on which the dwelling-house was a qualifying dwelling-house, and
R is the number of days in the whole of the relevant period of ownership.

Commentary—*Simon's Direct Tax Service* **B2.908**.
Former enactment—CAA 1990 s 88(5) ("adjusted net cost").
Definition—"Qualifying dwelling-house", s 490(2).

CHAPTER 7
WRITING OFF QUALIFYING EXPENDITURE ATTRIBUTABLE TO DWELLING-HOUSE

523 Introduction

For the purposes of this Part qualifying expenditure attributable to a dwelling-house is written off to the extent and at the times specified in this Chapter.

Commentary—*Simon's Direct Tax Service* **B2.908**.
Former enactment—CAA 1990 s 90(1).

524 Writing off initial allowances

If an initial allowance was made under paragraph 1 of Schedule 12 to FA 1982 in respect of a qualifying dwelling-house, the amount of the allowance is written off at the time of the first use of the dwelling-house.

Commentary—*Simon's Direct Tax Service* **B2.908**.
Former enactment—CAA 1990 s 90(2).
Definition—"Qualifying dwelling-house", s 490(2).

525 Writing off writing-down allowances

(1) If a writing-down allowance is made in respect of qualifying expenditure attributable to a dwelling-house, the amount of the allowance is written off at the end of the chargeable period for which the allowance is made.

(2) If a balancing event occurs at the end of a chargeable period, the amount written off under subsection (1) is to be taken into account in calculating the residue of qualifying expenditure immediately before the event to determine what balancing adjustment (if any) is to be made.

Commentary—*Simon's Direct Tax Service* **B2.908**.
Former enactments—Sub-s (1): CAA 1990 s 90(3).
Sub-s (2): CAA 1990 s 90(4).
Definition—''Chargeable period'', s 6.

526 Writing off expenditure for periods when building not used as qualifying dwelling-house

(1) This section applies if for any period or periods between—

    (*a*) the time when the whole or a part of the building was first used for any purpose, and

    (*b*) the time when the residue of qualifying expenditure attributable to a dwelling-house falls to be ascertained,

the building or part has not been a qualifying dwelling-house.

(2) An amount equal to the notional writing-down allowances for the period or periods is written off at the time when the residue falls to be ascertained.

(3) The notional writing-down allowances are the allowances that would have been made for the period or periods in question (if the building or part had remained a qualifying dwelling-house), at such rate or rates as would have been appropriate, having regard to any relevant sale.

(4) In subsection (3) ''relevant sale'' means a sale of the relevant interest as a result of which a balancing adjustment falls to be made under section 513.

Commentary—*Simon's Direct Tax Service* **B2.908**.
Former enactment—Sub-ss (1)–(4): CAA 1990 s 90(5).
Definition—''Qualifying dwelling-house'', s 490(2).

527 Writing off or increase of expenditure where balancing adjustment made

(1) This section applies if the relevant interest in the dwelling-house is sold.

(2) If a balancing allowance is made, the amount by which the residue of qualifying expenditure attributable to the dwelling-house before the balancing event exceeds the net proceeds from the event is written off at the time of the event.

(3) If a balancing charge is made, the amount of the residue of qualifying expenditure attributable to the dwelling-house is increased at the time of the balancing event by the amount of the charge.

(4) But if the balancing charge is made under section 517(6) (difference between relevant allowances and adjusted net cost), the residue of qualifying expenditure attributable to the dwelling-house immediately after the balancing event is limited to the net proceeds from the event.

Commentary—*Simon's Direct Tax Service* **B2.908**.
Former enactments—Sub-s (1): CAA 1990 s 90(6).
Sub-s (3): CAA 1990 s 90(7).
Sub-s (4): CAA 1990 s 90(8).

528 Treatment of demolition costs

(1) This section applies if—

    (*a*) a dwelling-house is demolished, and

    (*b*) the person to or on whom any balancing allowance or balancing charge is or might be made is the person incurring the cost of the demolition.

(2) The net cost of the demolition is added to the residue of qualifying expenditure attributable to the qualifying dwelling-house immediately before the demolition.

(3) ''The net cost of the demolition'' means the amount, if any, by which the cost of the demolition exceeds any money received for the remains of the property.

(4) If this section applies, the net cost of the demolition is not treated for the purposes of this Part as expenditure on any other property replacing the property demolished.

Commentary—*Simon's Direct Tax Service* **B2.908**.
Former enactment—Sub-ss (1)–(4): CAA 1990 s 90(9).
Definition—''Qualifying dwelling-house'', s 490(2).

CHAPTER 8
SUPPLEMENTARY PROVISIONS

529 Giving effect to allowances and charges

(1) If a person who is entitled or liable to an allowance or charge for a chargeable period was carrying on a Schedule A business at any time in that period, the allowance or charge is to be given effect in calculating the profits of that business, by treating—

    (*a*) the allowance as an expense of that business, and

    (*b*) the charge as a receipt of that business.

(2) If a person who is entitled or liable to an allowance or charge for a chargeable period was not carrying on a Schedule A business at any time in that period, the allowance or charge is to be given effect by treating him as if he had been carrying on such a business in that period and as if—

(*a*) the allowance were an expense of that business, and
(*b*) the charge were a receipt of that business.

Commentary—*Simon's Direct Tax Service* **B2.910**.
Former enactments—CAA 1990 ss 92, 140(2), 144(2), 161(5).
Definition—''Chargeable period'', s 6.

530 Apportionment of sums partly referable to non-qualifying assets

(1) If the sum paid for the sale of the relevant interest in a building is attributable—

(*a*) partly to assets representing expenditure for which an allowance can be made under this Part, and
(*b*) partly to assets representing other expenditure,

only so much of the sum paid as on a just and reasonable apportionment is attributable to the assets referred to in paragraph (*a*) is to be taken into account for the purposes of this Part.

(2) Subsection (1) applies to other proceeds from a balancing event in respect of a building as it applies to a sum given for the sale of the relevant interest in the building.

(3) Subsection (1) does not affect any other provision of this Part requiring an apportionment of the proceeds of a balancing event.

Commentary—*Simon's Direct Tax Service* **B2.908**.
Former enactment—Sub-ss (1)–(3): CAA 1990 s 97(4).

531 Meaning of ''dwelling-house'', ''lease'' etc

(1) In this Part ''dwelling-house'' has the same meaning as in the Rent Act 1977.

(2) In this Part ''lease'' includes—

(*a*) an agreement for a lease if the term to be covered by the lease has begun, and
(*b*) any tenancy,

but does not include a mortgage (and ''lessee'', ''lessor'' and ''leasehold interest'' are to be read accordingly).

(3) In the application of this Part to Scotland—

(*a*) ''leasehold interest'' means the interest of a tenant in property subject to a lease, and
(*b*) any reference to an interest which is reversionary on a leasehold interest or on a lease is to be read as a reference to the interest of the landlord in the property subject to the leasehold interest or lease.

Commentary—*Simon's Direct Tax Service* **B2.903**.
Former enactments—Sub-s (1): CAA 1990 s 97(1).
Sub-s (2): CAA 1990 s 161(2).
Sub-s (3): CAA 1990 s 162
Revenue Internal Guidance—Capital allowances manual CA 85400 (''dwelling house'' includes a maisonette or flat).

PART 11
CONTRIBUTIONS

CHAPTER 1
EXCLUSION OF EXPENDITURE MET BY CONTRIBUTIONS
Rules excluding contributions

532 The general rule excluding contributions

(1) For the purposes of this Act, the general rule is that a person (''R'') is to be regarded as not having incurred expenditure to the extent that it has been, or is to be, met (directly or indirectly) by—

(*a*) a public body, or
(*b*) a person other than R.

(2) In this Chapter ''public body'' means the Crown or any government or public or local authority (whether in the United Kingdom or elsewhere).

(3) The general rule does not apply for the purposes of Part 9 (dredging allowances).

(4) The general rule is subject to the exceptions in sections 534 to 536.

Commentary—*Simon's Direct Tax Service* **B2.111**.
Former enactments—Sub-s (1): TA 1988 s 532(1), CAA 1990 s 153(1).
Sub-s (2): CAA 1990 s 134(8), 153(1).
Sub-s (3): CAA 1990 s 153(4).

533 Exclusion of contributions to dredging

(1) For the purposes of Part 9, a person (''D'') who has incurred expenditure is to be regarded as not having incurred it for the purposes of a trade carried on or to be carried on by D to the extent that it has been, or is to be, met (directly or indirectly) by—

(*a*) a public body, or

(*b*) capital sums contributed by another person for purposes other than those of D's trade.

(2) Subsection (1) is not subject to the exceptions in sections 534 to 536.

Commentary—*Simon's Direct Tax Service* **B2.806**.
Former enactments—Sub-s (1): CAA 1990 s 134(8).
Definition—''Capital sum'', s 4.

Exceptions to the general rule excluding contributions

534 Northern Ireland regional development grants

(1) A person is to be regarded as having incurred expenditure (despite section 532(1)) to the extent that it is met (directly or indirectly) by a grant—

(*a*) made under Northern Ireland legislation, and

(*b*) declared by the Treasury by order to correspond to a grant under Part II of the Industrial Development Act 1982.

(2) Subject to subsection (3), the grant is to be treated as not falling within subsection (1) if, by virtue of paragraph 8 of Schedule 3 to OTA 1975, expenditure which has been or is to be met by the grant is not to be regarded for any of the purposes of Part I of OTA 1975 as having been incurred by any person.

(3) If only a proportion of the expenditure which has been or is to be met by the grant is expenditure which, if it were not so met, would be allowable under section 3 or 4 of OTA 1975, only a corresponding proportion of the grant is to be treated as not falling within subsection (1).

Commentary—*Simon's Direct Tax Service* **B2.111**.
Former enactments—Sub-s (1): TA 1988 s 532(1), CAA 1990 s 153(1).
Sub-s (2): FA 1982 s 137(2).
Sub-s (3): FA 1982 s 137(3).
Modifications—CAA 2001 Sch 3 para 106(1) (sub-s (1) applies as if a grant falling within that subsection included—

(*a*) a grant made under Part II of the Industrial Development Act 1982 on an application made before 1 April 1988;

(*b*) a grant made under Part I of the Industry Act 1972, or a grant made under Northern Ireland legislation and declared by the Treasury to correspond to a grant under that Part).

CAA 2001 Sch 3 para 106(2) (sub-s (2) does not apply in relation to expenditure incurred, or grants paid, before 10 March 1982).

535 Insurance or compensation money

A person is to be regarded as having incurred expenditure (despite section 532(1)) to the extent that it is met (directly or indirectly) by—

(*a*) insurance money, or

(*b*) other compensation money,

payable in respect of an asset which has been destroyed, demolished or put out of use.

Commentary—*Simon's Direct Tax Service* **B2.111**.
Former enactments—TA 1988 s 532(1), CAA 1990 s 153(2). Change in law.

536 Contributions not made by public bodies and not eligible for tax relief

(1) A person (''R'') is to be regarded as having incurred expenditure (despite section 532(1)) to the extent that the requirements in subsections (2) and (3) are satisfied in relation to the expenditure.

(2) The first requirement is that the person meeting R's expenditure (''C'') is not a public body.

(3) The second requirement is that—

(*a*) no allowance can be made under Chapter 2 in respect of C's expenditure, and

(*b*) the expenditure is not allowed to be deducted in calculating the profits of a trade or relevant activity carried on by C.

(4) When determining for the purposes of subsection (3)(*a*) whether an allowance can be made under Chapter 2, assume that C is within the charge to tax.

(5) In subsection (3)(*b*) ''relevant activity'' means—

(*a*) for the purposes of Part 2—

(i) an ordinary Schedule A business;

(ii) a furnished holiday lettings business;

(iii) an overseas property business;

(iv) a profession or vocation;

(v) any concern listed in section 55(2) of ICTA (mines, transport undertakings etc);

(vi) the management of an investment company;

(*b*) for other purposes, a profession or vocation.

Commentary—*Simon's Direct Tax Service* **B2.111**.
Former enactments—Sub-ss (1)–(3): TA 1988 s 532(1), CAA 1990 s 153(2).
Sub-s (4): TA 1988 s 532(1), CAA 1990 s 153(3).
Sub-s (5): TA 1988 s 532(1), CAA 1990 s 153(2). Change in law.
Definitions—''Overseas property business'', s 65A(4), 70A(4), TA 1988 s 832(1); ''ordinary Schedule A business'', s 16.
Modifications—CAA 2001 Sch 3 para 107 (sub-s (3)(*b*) does not apply in relation to contributions made before 27 July 1989).
CAA 2001 Sch 3 para 108 (in sub-s (5) as it applies for the purposes of CAA 2001 s 537(2), sub-s (5)(*a*)(iv), (*b*) do not apply in relation to contributions made before 27 July 1989).

CHAPTER 2

CONTRIBUTION ALLOWANCES

Contribution allowances under [Parts 2 to 4 and 5][1]

537 Conditions for contribution allowances under [Parts 2 to 4 and 5][1]

(1) This section gives general conditions for making contribution allowances under [Parts 2 to 4 and 5][1].

(2) The general conditions are that—

(*a*) a person (''C'') has contributed a capital sum to expenditure on the provision of an asset,
(*b*) the expenditure would (ignoring section 532(1))—

(i) have been regarded as wholly incurred by another person (''R''), and
(ii) if R is not a public body, have entitled R to allowances under Part 2, 3, 4 or 5 or to allocate the expenditure to a pool under Part 2, and

(*c*) C and R are not connected persons.

(3) In this section ''public body'' means the Crown or any public or local authority in the United Kingdom.

(4) In this Chapter ''relevant activity'' has the meaning given by section 536(5).

Commentary—*Simon's Direct Tax Service* **B2.112**.
Former enactments—Sub-ss (1)–(3): CAA 1990 s 154(1)–(4).
Sub-s (4): CAA 1990 s 154(5). Change in law.
Definition—''Capital sum'', s 4.
Modification—CAA 2001 Sch 3 para 109 (sub-s 2(*b*)(ii) applies in relation to contributions made before 6 April 1990 with the omission of ''or to allocate the expenditure to a pool under Part 2'').
Amendment—[1] Words in section heading and preceding sub-heading, and in sub-s (1), substituted for words ''Parts 2 to 5'' by FA 2001 s 67, Sch 19 Pt II para 3 with effect for expenditure incurred after 10 May 2001.

538 Plant and machinery

(1) This section is about contribution allowances under Part 2 and applies if—

(*a*) the general conditions for contribution allowances are met, and
(*b*) C's contribution is made for the purposes of a trade or relevant activity carried on, or to be carried on, by C.

(2) C is to be treated for the purposes of allowances under Part 2 as if—

(*a*) the contribution were expenditure incurred by C on the provision, for the purposes of C's trade or relevant activity, of the asset provided by means of C's contribution,
(*b*) C owned the asset as a result of incurring that expenditure at any time when R owns it or is treated under Part 2 as owning it, and
(*c*) the asset were at all material times in use for the purposes of C's trade or relevant activity.

(3) Expenditure treated as incurred under subsection (2)(*a*), if allocated to any pool, must be allocated to a single asset pool.

(4) Subsections (5) and (6) apply for the purposes of contribution allowances under Part 2 if the whole or a part of the trade or relevant activity for the purposes of which C's contribution was made is transferred.

(5) If the whole of the trade or relevant activity is transferred, writing-down allowances for chargeable periods ending after the date of the transfer are to be made to the transferee instead of to the transferor.

(6) If a part of the trade or relevant activity is transferred, writing-down allowances for chargeable periods ending after the date of the transfer are to be made to the transferee instead of to the transferor to the extent that they are properly referable to the part transferred.

Commentary—*Simon's Direct Tax Service* **B2.112, 305**.
Former enactments—Sub-s (1): CAA 1990 s 154(1), (2).
Sub-s (2): CAA 1990 ss 154(1), (2), 155(2).
Sub-s (3): CAA 1990 s 155(6). Change in law.
Sub-ss (4)–(6): CAA 1990 s 155(3).
Definition—''Chargeable period'', s 6.

539 Industrial buildings

(1) This section is about contribution allowances under Part 3 and applies if—

(*a*) the general conditions for contribution allowances are met, and (*b*) C's contribution is made for the purposes of a trade or relevant activity carried on, or to be carried on—

  (i) by C, or

  (ii) by a tenant of land in which C has an interest.

(2) C is to be treated for the purposes of allowances under Part 3 as if—

(*a*) the contribution were expenditure incurred by C on the provision, for the purposes of the trade or relevant activity, of an asset similar to that provided by means of C's contribution, and

(*b*) the asset were at all material times in use for the purposes of the trade or relevant activity.

(3) Subsection (4) applies if—

(*a*) C's contribution was made for the purposes of a trade or relevant activity carried on, or to be carried on, by a tenant of land in which C had an interest, and

(*b*) C was entitled to allowances as a result of subsection (2).

(4) A person is entitled to a writing-down allowance for a chargeable period if at the end of the period the person is entitled to the interest held by C when the contribution was made.

(5) For the purposes of subsection (4), the provisions of Part 3 relating to the relevant interest apply (with any necessary modifications) in relation to the contribution made for the purposes of the trade or relevant activity carried on, or to be carried on, by the tenant as they apply in relation to expenditure incurred on the construction of an industrial building.

(6) Section 311 (calculation of writing-down allowance after sale of relevant interest) does not apply in relation to writing-down allowances to be made in respect of contributions.

Commentary—*Simon's Direct Tax Service* **B2.112, 232.**
Former enactments—Sub-s (1): CAA 1990 s 154(1).
Sub-s (2): CAA 1990 ss 154(1), 155(2).
Sub-ss (3)–(5): CAA 1990 s 155(4).
Sub-s (6): CAA 1990 s 155(5).
Definition—"Chargeable period", s 6.

540 Agricultural buildings

(1) This section is about contribution allowances under Part 4 and applies if—

(*a*) the general conditions for contribution allowances are met, and

(*b*) C's contribution is made for the purposes of a trade or relevant activity carried on, or to be carried on—

  (i) by C, or

  (ii) by a tenant of land in which C has a interest.

(2) C is to be treated for the purposes of allowances under Part 4 as if—

(*a*) the contribution were expenditure incurred by C on the provision, for the purposes of the trade or relevant activity, of an asset similar to that provided by means of C's contribution, and

(*b*) the asset were at all material times in use for the purposes of the trade or relevant activity.

(3) Subsection (4) applies if—

(*a*) C's contribution was made for the purposes of a trade or relevant activity carried on, or to be carried on, by a tenant of land in which C had an interest, and

(*b*) C was entitled to allowances as a result of subsection (2).

(4) A person is entitled to a writing-down allowance for a chargeable period if at the end of the period the person is entitled to the interest held by C when the contribution was made.

(5) For the purposes of subsection (4), the provisions of Part 4 relating to the relevant interest apply (with any necessary modifications) in relation to the contribution made for the purposes of the trade or relevant activity carried on, or to be carried on, by the tenant as they apply in relation to expenditure incurred on the construction of an agricultural building.

Commentary—*Simon's Direct Tax Service* **B2.112, 503.**
Former enactments—Sub-s (1): CAA 1990 s 154(1).
Sub-s (2): CAA 1990 s 154(1), 155(2).
Sub-ss (3)–(5): CAA 1990 s 155(4).
Definition—"Chargeable period", s 6.

541 Mineral extraction

(1) This section is about contribution allowances under Part 5 and applies if—

(*a*) the general conditions for contribution allowances are met, and

(*b*) C's contribution is made for the purposes of a trade carried on, or to be carried on, by C.

(2) C is to be treated for the purposes of allowances under Part 5 as if—

(*a*) the contribution were expenditure incurred by C on the provision, for the purposes of C's trade, of an asset similar to that provided by means of C's contribution, and

(*b*) the asset were at all material times in use for the purposes of C's trade.

Commentary—*Simon's Direct Tax Service* **B2.112.**
Former enactments—Sub-s (1): CAA 1990 s 154(1).
Sub-s (2): CAA 1990 s 154(1), 155(2).

Effect of transfers of C's trade on contribution allowances under Parts 3, 4 and 5

542 Transfer of C's trade or relevant activity

(1) Subsections (2) and (3) apply for the purposes of contribution allowances under [Parts 3, 4 and 5][1] if—

    (*a*) C's contribution was made for the purposes of C's trade or relevant activity, and

    (*b*) the whole or a part of the trade or relevant activity is subsequently transferred.

(2) If the whole of the trade or relevant activity is transferred, writing-down allowances for chargeable periods ending after the date of the transfer are to be made to the transferee instead of to the transferor.

(3) If a part of the trade or relevant activity is transferred, writing-down allowances for chargeable periods ending after the date of the transfer are to be made to the transferee instead of to the transferor to the extent that they are properly referable to the part transferred.

Commentary—*Simon's Direct Tax Service* B2.112.
Former enactment—Sub-ss (1)–(3): CAA 1990 s 155(3).
Definition—"Chargeable period", s 6.
Modification—CAA 2001 Sch 3 para 110 (this section does not apply in relation to contributions made before 27 July 1989. CAA 2001 ss 368, 375 and 379 to apply instead with the necessary modifications).
Amendment—[1] Words in sub-s (1) substituted for words "Parts 3 to 5" by FA 2001 s 67, Sch 19 Pt II para 4 with effect for expenditure incurred after 10 May 2001.

Contribution allowances under Part 9

543 Contribution allowances under Part 9

A person who contributes a capital sum to expenditure incurred by another person on dredging is to be regarded for the purposes of Part 9 as incurring capital expenditure on that dredging.

Commentary—*Simon's Direct Tax Service* B2.112, 806.
Former enactment—CAA 1990 s 134(8).
Definitions—"Capital expenditure", s 4; "capital sum", s 4.

PART 12
SUPPLEMENTARY PROVISIONS

CHAPTER 1
LIFE ASSURANCE BUSINESS

Commentary—*Simon's Direct Tax Service* D4.504, 506.

544 Management assets

(1) No allowances are to be given or charges imposed in respect of management assets of any life assurance business carried on by a company except under Part 2 (plant and machinery allowances).

(2) An asset is a management asset of any life assurance business carried on by a company if it is provided for use, or used, for the management of that business of that company.

(3) The management of any life assurance business consists of pursuing those purposes expenditure on which would, on the assumption below, be treated as expenses of management under section 75 of ICTA as applied by 76 of ICTA.

(4) The assumption is that section 76(1)(*d*) (exclusion from expenses of management of expenses referable to pension business, ISA business, life reinsurance business and overseas life assurance business) is disregarded.

(5) In this Act "life assurance business" has the meaning given by section 431(2) of ICTA.

Former enactments—Sub-s (1): TA 1988 s 434D(2).
Sub-s (2): TA 1988 s 434D(1).
Sub-s (3): TA 1988 s 434D(7).
Definition—"Life assurance business", s 544(5), TA 1988 S 431(2).

545 Investment assets

(1) This section applies if a company which is carrying on any life assurance business holds an asset for purposes other than the management of that business.

(2) "Investment asset" means an asset that is within subsection (1).

[(3) Any allowance under this Act in respect of an investment asset shall be treated as referable to the category or categories of business to which income arising from the asset is or would be referable.

If income so arising is or would be referable to more than one category of business, the allowance shall be apportioned in accordance with sections 432ZA to 432E, or section 438B, of ICTA in the same way as the income.][1]

(4) If the company is charged to tax in respect of its life assurance business under Case I of Schedule D, no allowance in respect of an investment asset is to be taken into account in calculating the company's profits from that business.

(5) If the company is charged to tax under—

     (a) section 436 of ICTA (pension business and ISA business),

     (b) section 439B of ICTA (life reinsurance business), or

     (c) section 441 of ICTA (overseas life assurance business),

no allowance in respect of an investment asset is to be taken into account in calculating the company's profits from the category of life assurance business in question.

Former enactments—Sub-s (1): TA 1988 s 434E(1). Change in law.
Sub-s (2): TA 1988 s 434E(1).
Sub-s (3): TA 1988 s 434E(4).
Sub-ss (4), (5): TA 1988 s 434E(5).
Definition—"Life assurance business", s 544(5), TA 1988 S 431(2).
Amendments—¹ Sub-s (3) substituted by FA 2001 s 76, Sch 25 para 7 with effect from 6 April 2001.

CHAPTER 2
ADDITIONAL VAT LIABILITIES AND REBATES: INTERPRETATION, ETC

546 Introduction

This Chapter has effect for the interpretation of, and for otherwise supplementing—

     (a) Chapter 18 of Part 2 (plant and machinery allowances: additional VAT liabilities and rebates),

     (b) Chapter 10 of Part 3 (industrial buildings allowances: additional VAT liabilities and rebates), and

     (c) Chapter 4 of Part 6 (research and development allowances: additional VAT liabilities and rebates).

547 "Additional VAT liability" and "additional VAT rebate"

(1) "Additional VAT liability" means an amount which a person becomes liable to pay by way of adjustment under the VAT capital items legislation in respect of input tax.

(2) "Additional VAT rebate" means an amount which a person becomes entitled to deduct by way of adjustment under the VAT capital items legislation in respect of input tax.

Commentary—*Simon's Direct Tax Service* **B2.103**.
Former enactment—Sub-ss (1), (6): CAA 1990 s 159A(6).

548 Time when additional VAT liability or rebate is incurred or made

(1) The time when a person incurs an additional VAT liability or an additional VAT rebate is made to a person is the last day of the period—

     (a) which is one of the periods making up the VAT period of adjustment applicable to the asset in question under the VAT capital items legislation, and

     (b) in which the increase or decrease in use giving rise to the liability or rebate occurs.

(2) "VAT period of adjustment" means a period specified under the VAT capital items legislation by reference to which adjustments are made in respect of input tax.

Commentary—*Simon's Direct Tax Service* **B2.104**.
Former enactments—Sub-s (1): CAA 1990 s 159A(1), (2).
Sub-s (2): CAA 1990 s 159A(1), (2), (6).
Definitions—"Additional VAT liability", s 547(1); "additional VAT rebate", s 547(2).

549 Chargeable period in which, and time when, additional VAT liability or rebate accrues

(1) The chargeable period in which, and the time when, an additional VAT liability or additional VAT rebate accrues is set out in the Table.

TABLE
ACCRUAL OF VAT LIABILITIES AND REBATES

Circumstances	Chargeable period	Time of accrual
The liability or rebate is accounted for in a VAT return.	The chargeable period which includes the last day of the period to which the VAT return relates.	The last day of the period to which the VAT return relates.
The Commissioners of Customs and Excise assess the liability or rebate as due before a VAT return is made.	The chargeable period which includes the day on which the assessment is made.	The day on which the assessment is made.

Circumstances	Chargeable period	Time of accrual
The relevant activity is permanently discontinued before the liability or rebate is accounted for in a VAT return or assessed by the Commissioners.	The chargeable period in which the relevant activity is permanently discontinued.	The last day of the chargeable period in which the relevant activity is permanently discontinued.

(2) In the Table—

  (*a*) "VAT return" means a return made to the Commissioners of Customs and Excise for the purposes of value added tax, and

  (*b*) "the relevant activity" means the trade or, in relation to Part 2, the qualifying activity to which the additional VAT liability or additional VAT rebate relates.

Commentary—*Simon's Direct Tax Service* **B2.104**.
Former enactments—Sub-s (1): CAA 1990 s 159A(3), (4).
Sub-s (2): CAA 1990 s 159A(4), (7).
Definitions—"Additional VAT liability", s 547(1); "additional VAT rebate", s 547(2); "chargeable period", s 6.

550 Apportionment of additional VAT liabilities and rebates

(1) This section applies if—

  (*a*) any provision of this Act requires an allowance or charge to which a person is entitled or liable in respect of any qualifying expenditure to be determined by reference to—

    (i) a proportion only of that expenditure, or

    (ii) a proportion only of what that allowance or charge would have been apart from that provision, and

  (*b*) the person incurs an additional VAT liability or an additional VAT rebate is made to the person in respect of that expenditure.

(2) The additional VAT liability or rebate is subject to the same apportionment as the original expenditure, allowance or charge.

Commentary—*Simon's Direct Tax Service* **B2.110**.
Former enactment—CAA 1990 s 159A(5).
Definitions—"Additional VAT liability", s 547(1); "additional VAT rebate", s 547(2).

551 Supplementary

(1) In this Chapter, "the VAT capital items legislation" means any Act or instrument (whenever passed or made) providing for the proportion of input tax on an asset of a specified description which may be deducted by a person from his output tax to be adjusted from time to time as a result of—

  (*a*) an increase, or

  (*b*) a decrease,

in the extent to which the asset is used by him for making taxable supplies (or taxable supplies of a specified class or description) during a specified period.

(2) In this Chapter "the VAT capital items legislation" also includes any other Act or instrument (whenever passed or made) which provides for Article 20(2) to (4) of the Sixth VAT Directive to be given effect.

(3) "The Sixth VAT Directive" means the Sixth Directive of the Council of the European Communities on Value Added Tax, dated 17th May 1977.

(4) In this Chapter "input tax", "output tax" and "taxable supply" have the same meaning as in VATA 1994.

Commentary—*Simon's Direct Tax Service* **B2.104**.
Former enactment—Sub-ss (1)–(4): CAA 1990 s 159A(6).

CHAPTER 3
DISPOSALS OF OIL LICENCES: PROVISIONS RELATING TO PARTS 5 AND 6

Commentary—*Simon's Direct Tax Service* **B2.413, D4.1025**.

Introduction

552 Meaning of "oil licence" and "interest in an oil licence"

(1) In this Chapter "oil licence" means a UK oil licence or a foreign oil concession.

(2) In this Chapter "UK oil licence" means a licence under—

  (*a*) Part I of the Petroleum Act 1998 ("the 1998 Act"), or

  (*b*) the Petroleum (Production) Act (Northern Ireland) 1964 ("the 1964 Act"), authorising the winning of oil.

(3) In this Chapter "foreign oil concession" means any right which—

(*a*) is a right to search for or win oil that exists in its natural condition in a place to which neither the 1998 Act nor the 1964 Act applies, and

(*b*) is conferred or exercisable (whether or not under a licence) in relation to a particular area.

(4) In this Chapter "interest in an oil licence" includes, if there is an agreement which—

(*a*) relates to oil from the whole or a part of the licensed area, and

(*b*) was made before the extraction of the oil to which it relates,

any entitlement under the agreement to, or to a share of, that oil or the proceeds of its sale.

Former enactments—Sub-s (1): CAA 1990 s 138A(4).
Sub-s (2): Oil Taxation Act 1975 s 12(1), CAA 1990 ss 118A(4), 138A(4), TCGA 1992 s 196(5).
Sub-ss (3), (4): CAA 1990 ss 118A(4), 138A(4), TCGA 1992 s 196(5).

Oil licences relating to undeveloped areas

553 Consideration to be treated as nil

(1) This section applies if—

(*a*) there is a material disposal of an oil licence which, at the time of the disposal, relates to an undeveloped area, and

(*b*) any of the consideration for the disposal consists of—

(i) another oil licence, or an interest in another oil licence, which at that time relates to an undeveloped area, or

(ii) an obligation to undertake exploration work or appraisal work in an area which is or forms part of the licensed area in relation to the licence disposed of.

(2) The value of the consideration within subsection (1)(*b*) is to be treated as nil for the purposes of—

(*a*) Part 5 (mineral extraction allowances),

(*b*) Part 6 (research and development allowances), and

(*c*) section 555 (disposal of oil licence with exploitation value).

(3) A "material disposal" of an oil licence means any disposal (including a part disposal and a disposal of an interest in an oil licence) other than a disposal in relation to which section 568 or 569 (sales treated as being for alternative amount) has effect.

(4) If—

(*a*) the material disposal is part of a larger transaction under which one party makes to another material disposals of two or more licences, and

(*b*) at the time of disposal, each of those licences relates to an undeveloped area,

the licensed area for the purposes of subsection (1)(*b*) is the totality of the licensed areas in relation to those licences.

(5) In relation to a material disposal of a licence under which the buyer acquires an interest in the licence only so far as it relates to part of the licensed area, any reference in this section and section 554 to the licensed area is to be read as a reference only to that part of the licensed area to which the buyer's acquisition relates.

(6) In subsection (1)(*b*)—

"exploration work", in relation to an area, means work carried out for the purpose of searching for oil anywhere in that area, and

"appraisal work", in relation to an area, means work carried out for the purpose of ascertaining—

(*a*) the extent or characteristics of any oil-bearing area the whole or part of which lies in that area, or

(*b*) what the reserves of oil of any such oil-bearing area are.

Former enactments—Sub-s (1): CAA 1990 s 118A(1).
Sub-s (2): CAA 1990 s 118A(1).
Sub-s (3): CAA 1990 s 118A(2), TCGA 1992 s 196(5A).
Sub-s (4): CAA 1990 s 118A(3).
Sub-s (5): CAA 1990 s 118A(4), TCGA 1992 s 196(4).
Sub-s (6): CAA 1990 s 118A(4), TCGA 1992 s 196(6).
Definition—"Oil licence", s 552(1).

554 Circumstances in which oil licence relates to undeveloped area

(1) A UK oil licence relates to an undeveloped area if—

(*a*) no consent for development has been granted to the licensee for any part of the licensed area by the relevant authority, and

(*b*) no programme of development has been served on the licensee or approved for any part of the licensed area by the relevant authority.

(2) A foreign oil concession relates to an undeveloped area if—

(*a*) no development has actually taken place in any part of the licensed area, and

(*b*) no condition for the carrying out of development anywhere in that area has been satisfied—

(i) by the grant of any consent by the authorities of a country or territory exercising jurisdiction in relation to the area, or

(ii) by the approval or service on the licensee, by any such authorities, of any programme of development.

(3) Subsections (4) and (5) of section 36 of FA 1983 (meaning of development) apply for the purposes of subsections (1) and (2).

(4) In subsection (1) "licensee" means—

(*a*) the person entitled to the benefit of the licence or, if two or more persons are entitled to the benefit, each of those persons, and

(*b*) a person who has rights under an agreement which is—

(i) approved by the Board of Inland Revenue, and

(ii) certified by the relevant authority to confer on that person rights which are the same as, or similar to, those conferred by a licence.

(5) In subsection (2) "licensee" means the person with the concession or any person having an interest in it.

Former enactments—Sub-s (1): CAA 1990 s 138A(1), (2).
Sub-s (2): CAA 1990 s 118A(4), TCGA 1992 s 196(1A).
Sub-s (3): CAA 1990 s 118A(4), TCGA 1992s 196(3).
Sub-s (4): OTA 1975 s 12(1), CAA 1990 s 118A(4), TCGA 1992 s 196(5).
Sub-s (5): CAA 1990 s 118A(4), TCGA 1992 s 196(5).
Definition—"Oil licence", s 552(1).

Disposal of oil licence with exploitation value

555 Disposal of oil licence with exploitation value

(1) This section applies if—

(*a*) a person ("the seller") disposes of an interest in an oil licence to another ("the buyer"), and

(*b*) part of the value of the interest is attributable to allowable exploration expenditure incurred by the seller.

(2) For the purposes of Part 6 (research and development allowances) the disposal is to be treated as a disposal by which the seller ceases to own an asset representing the allowable exploration expenditure to which that part of the value of the interest is attributable.

(3) Part 6 applies as if the disposal value to be brought into account were equal to so much of the buyer's expenditure on acquiring the interest as it is just and reasonable to attribute to that part of the value of the interest.

(4) In this section "allowable exploration expenditure" means expenditure which—

(*a*) is incurred on mineral exploration and access within the meaning of Part 5 (mineral extraction allowances), and

(*b*) is qualifying expenditure for the purposes of Part 6.

Commentary—*Simon's Direct Tax Service* **B2.413**.
Former enactments—Sub-ss (1), (2): CAA 1990 s 138A(1), (2).
Sub-s (3): CAA 1990 s 138A(2).
Sub-s (4): CAA 1990 s 138A(3).
Definition—"Oil licence", s 552(1).

Minor definitions

556 Minor definitions

(1) In this Chapter "licensed area" means (subject to section 553(4) and (5))—

(*a*) in relation to a UK oil licence, the area to which the licence applies, and

(*b*) in relation to a foreign oil concession, the area in relation to which the right to search for or win oil is conferred or exercisable under the concession.

(2) In this Chapter "the relevant authority", in relation to a UK oil licence means—

(*a*) in the case of a licence under Part I of the 1998 Act, the Secretary of State, and

(*b*) in the case of a licence under the 1964 Act, the Department of Enterprise, Trade and Investment in Northern Ireland.

(3) In this Chapter "oil"—

(*a*) in relation to a UK oil licence, means any substance won or capable of being won under the authority of a licence granted under Part I of the 1998 Act or the 1964 Act, other than methane gas won in the course of operations for making and keeping mines safe, and

(*b*) in relation to a foreign oil concession, means any petroleum (as defined by section 1 of the 1998 Act).

Commentary—*Simon's Direct Tax Service* **B2.413**.
Former enactments—Sub-s (1): CAA 1990 s 118A(4), TCGA 1992 s 196(5).
Sub-s (2): OTA 1975 s 12(1), CAA 1990 s 118A(4), TCGA 1992 s 196(1), Departments (Northern Ireland) Order 1999, SI 1999/283 (NI 1) art 3, Sch 1.
Sub-s (3): OTA 1975 s 1(1), CAA 1990 ss 64A(12), 118A(4), 138A(4), TCGA 1992 s 196(5).
Definition—"Oil licence", s 552(1).

CHAPTER 4
PARTNERSHIPS, SUCCESSIONS AND TRANSFERS

557 Application of sections 558 and 559

Sections 558 (effect of partnership changes) and 559 (effect of successions) apply for the purposes of this Act other than—

    (*a*) Part 2 (plant and machinery allowances),

    (*b*) Part 6 (research and development allowances), and

    (*c*) Part 10 (assured tenancy allowances).

Commentary—*Simon's Direct Tax Service* **B2.109**.
Former enactments—CAA 1990 s 152(1), (3).

558 Effect of partnership changes

(1) This section applies if—

    (*a*) a relevant activity has been set up and is at any time carried on in partnership,

    (*b*) there has been a change in the persons engaged in carrying on the relevant activity, and

    [(*c*) the change does not result in the relevant activity being treated as permanently discontinued under section 113(1) or 337(1) of ICTA (changes in persons carrying on a trade etc and effect of company ceasing to trade etc).][1]

(2) In this section—

    ''the present partners'' means the person or persons for the time being carrying on the relevant activity, and

    ''predecessors'', in relation to the present partners, means their predecessors in carrying on the relevant activity.

(3) Any allowance or charge is to be made to or on the present partners.

(4) The amount of any allowance or charge arising under subsection (3) is to be calculated as if—

    (*a*) the present partners had at all times been carrying on the relevant activity, and

    (*b*) everything done to or by their predecessors in carrying on the relevant activity had been done to or by the present partners.

(5) In this section ''relevant activity'' means a trade, property business, profession or vocation.

Commentary—*Simon's Direct Tax Service* **B2.109**.
Former enactments—Sub-ss (1)–(4): CAA 1990 s 152(3).
Sub-s (5): Change in law.
Amendments—[1] Sub-s (1)(*c*) substituted by FA 2001 s 69, Sch 21 para 4 with effect as respects allowances and charges falling to be made for chargeable periods ending after 5 April 2001 (for income tax purposes) or 31 March 2001 (for corporation tax purposes).

559 Effect of successions

(1) This section applies if—

    (*a*) a person (''the successor'') succeeds to a relevant activity which until that time was carried on by another person (''the predecessor''), and

    (*b*) the relevant activity is treated as discontinued under section 113(1) or 337(1) of ICTA (change in persons carrying on a trade etc and effect of company ceasing to trade etc).

(2) The property in question is to be treated as if—

    (*a*) it had been sold to the successor when the succession takes place, and

    (*b*) the net proceeds of the sale were the market value of the property.

(3) The property in question is any property which—

    (*a*) immediately before the succession, was in use for the purposes of the discontinued relevant activity, and

    (*b*) immediately after the succession, and without being sold, is in use for the purposes of the new relevant activity.

(4) No entitlement to an initial allowance arises under this section.

(5) In this section ''relevant activity'' means a trade, property business, profession or vocation.

Commentary—*Simon's Direct Tax Service* **B2.109**.
Former enactments—Sub-ss (1)–(3): CAA 1990 s 152(1).
Sub-s (4): CAA 1990 s 152(2).
Sub-s (5): CAA 1990 s 152(1). Change in law.

560 Transfer of insurance company business

(1) This section applies if—

    (*a*) assets are transferred as part of, or in connection with, the transfer of the whole or part of the business of an insurance company to another company,

    (*b*) the transfer is—

(i) in accordance with [an insurance business transfer scheme to transfer business which consists of the effecting or carrying out of contracts of long-term insurance, or][1]

(ii) a qualifying overseas transfer within the meaning of paragraph 4A of Schedule 19AC to ICTA (overseas life insurance companies).

(2) But this section does not apply in relation to any asset transferred to a non-resident company unless the asset will fall to be treated, immediately after the transfer, as an asset which is held for the purposes of the whole or a part of so much of any business carried on by the non-resident company as is carried on through a branch or agency in the United Kingdom.

(3) This section also does not apply if section 561 applies (transfer of a UK trade to a company in another member State).

(4) If this section applies—

(a) any allowances and charges that would have been made to or on the transferor are to be made instead to or on the transferee, and

(b) the amount of any such allowance or charge is to be calculated as if everything done to or by the transferor had been done to or by the transferee,

but no sale or transfer of assets made to the transferee by the transferor is to be treated as giving rise to any such allowance or charge.

(5) In this section—

(a) "insurance company" has the same meaning as in Chapter I of Part XII of ICTA, ...[1]

[(b) "insurance business transfer scheme" means a scheme falling within section 105 of the Financial Services and Markets Act 2000 (c 8), including an excluded scheme falling within Case 2, 3 or 4 of subsection (3) of that section,

(c) "contracts of long-term insurance" means contracts which fall within Part II of Schedule 1 to the Financial Services and Markets Act 2000 (Regulated Activities) Order 2001 (SI 2001/544), and

(d) "non-resident company" means a company resident outside the United Kingdom.][1]

Commentary—*Simon's Direct Tax Service* **D4.528.**
Former enactments—Sub-s (1): CAA 1990 s 152A(1).
Sub-s (2): CAA 1990 s 152A(1A).
Sub-s (3): CAA 1990 s 152B(10).
Sub-s (4): CAA 1990 s 152A(2).
Sub-s (5): CAA 1990 s 152A(1B).
Modifications—CAA 2001 Sch 3 para 111 (sub-s (1) substituted, and sub-s (2) omitted, in relation to transfers sanctioned or authorised before 1 July 1994. Sub-s (1) as substituted to read as follows—

"(1) This section applies if assets are transferred as part of, or in connection with, a transfer of the whole or part of the long term business of an insurance company to another company in accordance with a scheme sanctioned by a court under section 49 of the Insurance Companies Act 1982.").
Friendly Societies (Modification of the Corporation Tax Acts) Regulations, SI 1997/473 reg 53D (modification of this section in respect of specified transactions occurring during chargeable periods ending after 31 March 2001).
Amendments—[1] Words in sub-s (1)(b)(i) substituted; and in sub-s (5), word in para (a) repealed, and paras (b)–(d) substituted for original para (b), by the Financial Services and Markets Act 2000 (Consequential Amendments) (Taxes) Order, SI 2001/3629 art 108 with effect from 1 December 2001 (immediately after the coming into force of the Financial Services and Markets Act 2000 ss 411, 432(1), Sch 20). SI 2001/3629 art 108 has effect for any transfer under a scheme falling within the Financial Services and Markets Act 2000 s 105, including an excluded scheme falling within Case 2, 3 or 4 of the Financial Services and Markets Act 2000 s 105(3).

561 Transfer of a UK trade to a company in another member State

(1) This section applies if—

(a) a qualifying company resident in one member State ("company A") transfers the whole or a part of a trade carried on by it in the United Kingdom to a qualifying company resident in another member State ("company B"),

(b) section 140A of TCGA 1992 (transfer of assets treated as no-gain no-loss disposal etc) applies in relation to the transfer, and

(c) immediately after the transfer company B—

(i) is resident in the United Kingdom, or

(ii) carries on in the United Kingdom through a branch or agency a trade which consists of, or includes, the trade or the part of the trade transferred.

(2) If this section applies—

(a) the transfer itself does not give rise to any allowances or charges under this Act, and

(b) in relation to assets included in the transfer, anything done to or by company A before the transfer is to be treated after the transfer as having been done to or by company B.

(3) If, for the purposes of subsection (2)(b), expenditure falls to be apportioned between assets included in the transfer and other assets, the apportionment is to be made in a just and reasonable manner.

(4) In this section "qualifying company" means a body incorporated under the law of a member State.

(5) If this section applies, section 343(2) of ICTA does not apply (effect of company reconstruction without change of ownership).

Commentary—*Simon's Direct Tax Service* **B2.116**.
Former enactments—Sub-s (1): CAA 1990 s 152B(1)–(3), TCGA 1992 s 140A(1).
Sub-s (2): CAA 1990 s 152B(4)–(6).
Sub-s (3): CAA 1990 s 152B(7).
Sub-s (4): TCGA 1992 s 140A(7).
Sub-s (5): CAA 1990 s 152B(10).
Revenue Internal Guidance—Capital allowances manual CA 15560 (application and operation of this section).

CHAPTER 5

MISCELLANEOUS

Apportionment

562 Apportionment where property sold together

(1) Any reference in this Act to the sale of property includes the sale of that property together with any other property.

(2) For the purposes of subsection (1), all property sold as a result of one bargain is to be treated as sold together even though—

(*a*) separate prices are, or purport to be, agreed for separate items of that property, or

(*b*) there are, or purport to be, separate sales of separate items of that property.

(3) If an item of property is sold together with other property, then, for the purposes of this Act—

(*a*) the net proceeds of the sale of that item are to be treated as being so much of the net proceeds of sale of all the property as, on a just and reasonable apportionment, is attributable to that item, and

(*b*) the expenditure incurred on the provision or purchase of that item is to be treated as being so much of the consideration given for all the property as, on a just and reasonable apportionment, is attributable to that item.

(4) This section applies, with the necessary modifications, to other proceeds (consisting of insurance money or other compensation) as it applies in relation to the net proceeds of a sale.

(5) This section applies in relation to Part 5 as if expenditure on the provision or purchase of an item of property included expenditure on the acquisition of—

(*a*) a mineral asset (as defined by section 397), or

(*b*) land outside the United Kingdom.

Commentary—*Simon's Direct Tax Service* **B2.110**.
Former enactments—Sub-s (1): CAA 1990 s 150(1).
Sub-s (2): CAA 1990 s 150(2).
Sub-s (3): CAA 1990 s 150(1). Change in law.
Sub-s (4): CAA 1990 s 150(3).
Sub-s (5): CAA 1990 s 150(5).
Revenue Internal Guidance—Capital allowances manual CA 12100–12400 (general application of this section).
CA 12100 (Revenue will not challenge amount apportioned to qualifying assets as too low unless they consider that something else is overvalued, assuming arm's length transaction).
CA 12300 (information required by District Valuer)

Procedure for determining certain questions

563 Procedure for determining certain questions affecting two or more persons

(1) This section applies in relation to the determination of a question if—

(*a*) at the time when the question falls to be determined, it appears that the determination is material to the liability to tax (for whatever period) of two or more persons, and

(*b*) section 564 provides for this section to apply.

(2) The Commissioners who are to determine the question, for the purposes of the tax of all the persons concerned, are given in subsections (3) to (5).

(3) If—

(*a*) the same body of General Commissioners has jurisdiction with respect to all the persons concerned, and

(*b*) those persons do not agree that the determination is to be made by the Special Commissioners, the determination is to be made by that body of General Commissioners.

(4) If—

(*a*) different bodies of General Commissioners have jurisdiction with respect to the persons concerned, and

(*b*) those persons do not agree that the determination is to be made by the Special Commissioners, the determination is to be made by such of those bodies of General Commissioners as the Board of Inland Revenue may direct.

(5) In any other case, the determination is to be made by the Special Commissioners.

(6) The Commissioners must determine the question in the same way as an appeal, but all the persons concerned are entitled—

(*a*) to appear before and be heard by the Commissioners, or
(*b*) to make representations to them in writing.

Commentary—*Simon's Direct Tax Service* **B2.110**.
Former enactments—Sub-s (1): TA 1988 s 532(1), CAA 1990 s 151(1).
Sub-ss (2)–(6): CAA 1990 s 151(1).
Revenue Internal Guidance—Capital allowance manual CA 12500 (inspectors will attend the hearing even if the dispute is between two taxpayers).
CA 12500 (the Commissioners' decision is final).
CA 12500 (the Commissioners' decision applies only in relation to capital allowances).

564 Questions to which procedure in section 563 applies

(1) Section 563 applies in relation to the determination for the purposes of any of Parts 3 to 11 or this Part of any question about the way in which a sum is to be apportioned.

(2) Section 563 applies in relation to any determination of the market value of property for the purposes of—

(*a*) any provision of Part 2 (plant and machinery allowances),
(*b*) section 423 (mineral extraction allowances: amount of disposal value to be brought into account),
(*c*) section 559 (effect of successions),
(*d*) section 568 or 569 (sales treated as being for alternative amount), or
(*e*) section 573 (transfers treated as sales).

(3) Section 563 applies in relation to any determination of the amount of any sums paid or proceeds for the purposes of section 357 (industrial buildings allowances: arrangements having an artificial effect on pricing).

(4) If section 561 (transfer of a UK trade to a company in another member State) applies, section 563 applies—

(*a*) for the purposes of the tax of both company A and company B referred to in that section, and
(*b*) in relation to the determination of any question of apportionment of expenditure under section 561(3).

Commentary—*Simon's Direct Tax Service* **B2.110**.
Former enactments—Sub-s (1): CAA 1990 s 151(1).
Sub-s (2): CAA 1990 s 151(2).
Sub-s (3): CAA 1990 s 151(1A).
Sub-s (4): CAA 1990 s 152B(8), (9). Change in law.

Tax agreements for income tax purposes

565 Tax agreements for income tax purposes

(1) This section applies if—

(*a*) a person is entitled to an allowance for income tax purposes,
(*b*) that person enters into a tax agreement with the Inland Revenue for the tax year in which the allowance would be given effect, and
(*c*) no assessment giving effect to the allowance is made for that tax year.

(2) In this section "tax agreement" means an agreement in writing as to the extent to which the allowance in question is to be given effect for the tax year in question.

(3) If this section applies, the allowance is to be treated as if it had been given effect under an assessment—

(*a*) for the tax year for which the tax agreement is made, and
(*b*) to the extent set out in the tax agreement.

(4) A tax agreement may relate to any method by which allowances are given effect under this Act.

Commentary—*Simon's Direct Tax Service* **B2.106A**.
Former enactments—Sub-ss (1), (2): CAA 1990 s 143(1).
Sub-s (3): CAA 1990 s 143(1).
Sub-s (4): CAA 1990 s 149.

Companies not resident in the United Kingdom

566 Companies not resident in the United Kingdom

(1) This section applies if a company not resident in the United Kingdom is—

(*a*) within the charge to corporation tax in respect of one source of income, and
(*b*) within the charge to income tax in respect of another source.

(2) Allowances related to any source of income are to be given effect against income chargeable to the same tax as is chargeable on income from that source.

Commentary—*Simon's Direct Tax Service* **B2.106A**.
Former enactments—CAA 1990 s 149.

Sales treated as being for alternative amount

567 Sales treated as being for alternative amount: introductory

(1) Sections 568 to 570 apply for the purposes of Parts 3, 4[, 4A][1], 5, 6 and 10.

(2) For the purposes of sections 568 to 570, the control test is met if—

(a) the buyer is a body of persons over whom the seller has control,

(b) the seller is a body of persons over whom the buyer has control,

(c) both the seller and the buyer are bodies of persons and another person has control over both of them, or

(d) the seller and the buyer are connected persons.

(3) In subsection (2) "body of persons" includes a partnership.

(4) For the purposes of sections 568 to 570, the tax advantage test is met if it appears that the sole or main benefit which might be expected to accrue from—

(a) the sale, or

(b) transactions of which the sale is one,

is the obtaining of a tax advantage by all or any of the parties under any provision of this Act except Part 2.

(5) Sections 568 to 570 do not apply if section 561 applies (transfer of a UK trade to a company in another member State).

Commentary—*Simon's Direct Tax Service* B2.108.
Former enactments—Sub-s (1): TA 1988 s 532(1), (2), (5), CAA 1990 s 157(1), (4), (5).
Sub-s (2): CAA 1990 s 157(1).
Sub-s (3): CAA 1990 s 157(2).
Sub-s (4): CAA 1990 s 157(1).
Sub-s (5): CAA 1990 s 152B(10).
Revenue Internal Guidance—Capital allowances manual CA 13100 (control test: background).
Amendment—[1] Word in sub-s (1) inserted by FA 2001 s 67, Sch 19 Pt II para 5 with effect for expenditure incurred after 10 May 2001.

568 Sales treated as being at market value

(1) A sale of property that is not at market value is treated as being at market value if—

(a) the control test is met, or

(b) the tax advantage test is met.

(2) This section is subject to any election under section 569.

Commentary—*Simon's Direct Tax Service* B2.108.
Former enactments—Sub-s (1): CAA 1990 s 157(1), (4).
Sub-s (2): CAA 1990 s 157(4).

569 Election to treat sale as being for alternative amount

(1) The parties to a sale of property that is not for the alternative amount may elect for the sale to be treated as being for the alternative amount if—

(a) the control test is met or section 573 applies (transfers treated as sales), and

(b) the tax advantage test is not met.

(2) Subsection (1) is subject to section 570.

(3) The alternative amount is the lower of market value and—

(a) if the sale is relevant for the purposes of Part 3 or 10, the residue of the qualifying expenditure immediately before the sale;

(b) if the sale is relevant for the purposes of Part 5, the unrelieved qualifying expenditure immediately before the sale;

(c) if the sale is relevant for the purposes of Part 6—

(i) in a case where an allowance under Part 6 is given for the expenditure represented by the asset sold, nil;

(ii) in any other case, the qualifying expenditure represented by the asset sold.

(4) In subsection (3) "residue of qualifying expenditure", "unrelieved qualifying expenditure" and "qualifying expenditure" have the same meaning as in the Part for the purposes of which the sale is relevant.

(5) If the sale—

(a) is relevant for the purposes of Part 3 or 10, and

(b) is treated as being for the residue of the qualifying expenditure immediately before the sale,

no balancing adjustment is to be made as a result of the sale under section 319 (building not an industrial building, etc throughout) or 517 (building not a qualifying dwelling-house throughout).

(6) If, after the date of the sale, an event occurs as a result of which a balancing charge would have fallen to be made on the seller if—

(a) he had continued to own the property, and

(*b*) he had done all such things, and been allowed all such allowances, as were done by or allowed to the buyer,

the balancing charge is to be made on the buyer.

(7) All such assessments and adjustments of assessments are to be made as are necessary to give effect to the election.

(8) For the purposes of this section and section 570, a sale is relevant for the purposes of a Part if it is of property of a kind that is relevant for deciding whether an allowance or charge is made under that Part.

Commentary—*Simon's Direct Tax Service* **B2.108**.
Former enactments—Sub-ss (1), (2): CAA 1990 s 158(1).
Sub-s (3): CAA 1990 s 158(1), (2).
Sub-s (4): CAA 1990 s 158(2).
Sub-s (5): CAA 1990 s 4(8), 88(4).
Sub-s (6): CAA 1990 s 158(1).
Sub-s (7): CAA 1990 s 158(4).
Modification—CAA 2001 Sch 3 para 112 (sub-s (3)(*a*) substituted in relation to a transfer before 16 March 1993; a transfer pursuant to a contract entered into before that date; and a transfer pursuant to a contract entered into for the purpose of securing that obligations under a contract entered into before that date are complied with. Sub-s (3)(*a*) as substituted to read as follows—
"(*a*) any of the parties is not resident in the United Kingdom at the time of the transfer and the circumstances are not at that time such that a relevant allowance or charge falls or might fall to be made to or on that party as a result of the transfer;'').

570 Elections: supplementary

(1) Section 569(1)[1] does not apply to a sale that is relevant for the purposes of Part 4 [or 4A][1].

(2) No election under section 569 may be made if—
    (*a*) the circumstances of the sale or the parties to it mean that a relevant allowance or charge will not be capable of falling to be made, or
    (*b*) the buyer is a dual resident investing company.

(3) In subsection (2)(*a*) ''relevant allowance or charge'' means an allowance or charge under Part 3, 5, 6, 9 or 10 which (ignoring the circumstances mentioned in subsection (2)(*a*)) would or might fall to be made, as a result of the sale, to or on any of the parties to it.

(4) If the sale is relevant for the purposes of Part 10, no election under section 569 may be made unless, at the time of the sale or any earlier time, both the seller and the buyer are or have been approved bodies (as defined in section 492).

(5) An election under section 569 must be made by notice to the Inland Revenue not later than 2 years after the sale.

Commentary—*Simon's Direct Tax Service* **B2.108**.
Former enactments—Sub-s (1): CAA 1990 s 158(5).
Sub-ss (2)–(4): CAA 1990 s 158(3).
Sub-s (5): CAA 1990 s 158(1).
Revenue Internal Guidance—Capital allowances manual CA 13200 (background to this section).
Definition—''Dual resident investing company'', s 77(1), TA 1988 s 404.
Amendment—[1] Words in sub-s (1) inserted by FA 2001 s 67, Sch 19 Pt II para 6 with effect for expenditure incurred after 10 May 2001.

CHAPTER 6
FINAL PROVISIONS
General interpretation

571 Application of Act to parts of assets

(1) In this Act references to an asset of any kind (including a building or structure, plant or machinery or works) include a part of an asset.

(2) But subsection (1) does not apply if the context otherwise requires.

Former enactments—Sub-s (1): CAA 1990 s 161(1), (7).
Sub-s (2): CAA 1990 s 161(7).

572 References to sale of property and time of sale

(1) In this Act references to the sale of property include—
    (*a*) the exchange of property, and
    (*b*) the surrender for valuable consideration of a leasehold interest (or, in Scotland, the interest of the tenant in property subject to a lease).

(2) For the purposes of subsection (1), any provision of this Act referring to a sale has effect with the necessary modifications, including, in particular, those in subsection (3).

(3) The modifications are that—
    (*a*) references to the net proceeds of sale and to the price include the consideration for the exchange or surrender, and

(*b*) references to capital sums included in the net proceeds of sale or paid on a sale include so much of the consideration for the exchange or surrender as would have been a capital sum if it had been a money payment.

(4) Any reference in this Act (except in Part 6) to the time of any sale is to be read as a reference to whichever is the earlier of—

(*a*) the time of completion, and
(*b*) the time when possession is given.

Commentary—*Simon's Direct Tax Service* **B2.108**.
Former enactments—Sub-s (1): CAA 1990 ss 150(4), 162.
Sub-ss (2), (3): CAA 1990 s 150(4).
Sub-s (4): CAA 1990 s 161(8).
Definition—"Capital sum", s 4.

573 Transfers treated as sales

(1) This section applies for the purposes of Parts 3, 4[, 4A][1] and 10 and other provisions of this Act relevant to those Parts if—

(*a*) there is a transfer of the interest which is the relevant interest for the purposes of the Part in question, and
(*b*) the transfer is not a sale.

(2) The transfer is treated as a sale of the relevant interest.

(3) The sale is treated as being at market value, subject to any election under section 569 (election to treat sale as being for alternative amount).

(4) This section does not apply if section 561 applies (transfer of a UK trade to a company resident in another member State).

Commentary—*Simon's Direct Tax Service* **B2.108A**.
Former enactments—Sub-ss (1), (2): CAA 1990 ss 21(6), 87(5), 133(8).
Sub-s (3): CAA 1990 ss 21(6), (7), 87(5), 133(8), (9), 157(4).
Sub-s (4): CAA 1990 s 152B(10).
Amendment—[1] Word in sub-s (1) inserted by FA 2001 s 67, Sch 19 Pt II para 7 with effect for expenditure incurred after 10 May 2001.

574 Meaning of "control"

(1) In this Act "control" is used in the sense given in this section.

(2) In relation to a body corporate ("company A"), "control" means the power of a person ("P") to secure—

(*a*) by means of the holding of shares or the possession of voting power in relation to that or any other body corporate, or
(*b*) as a result of any powers conferred by the articles of association or other document regulating that or any other body corporate,

that the affairs of company A are conducted in accordance with P's wishes.

(3) In relation to a partnership, "control" means the right to a share of more than half of the assets, or of more than one half of the income, of the partnership.

Commentary—*Simon's Direct Tax Service* **B2.108**.
Former enactment—CAA 1990 s 161(2).

575 Connected persons

(1) Section 839 of ICTA (how to tell whether persons are connected) applies for the purposes of this Act.

(2) Subsection (1) is subject to—

(*a*) section 156 (connected persons for purposes of deferring balancing charges in respect of ships),
(*b*) section 232 (connected persons for purposes of Chapter 17 of Part 2—anti-avoidance),
(*c*) section 246(2) (connected persons where additional VAT liability is incurred in anti-avoidance case), and
(*d*) section 266(5) (elections where predecessor and successor are connected persons),

(which give "connected person" an extended meaning).

Commentary—*Simon's Direct Tax Service* **B2.108**.
Former enactments—Sub-s (1): TA 1988 ss 24(1), 38(1)(*c*), 521(4), (7), CAA 1990 ss 4(2AB), 5(1)(*c*), 11(6)(*a*), 22(6A)(*b*)(iii), 22B(2)(*b*), 26(1)(*b*), (*eb*)(i), (3), 36(3), 37(8), 50(6), 53(2), 55(4)(*a*), 56(*d*), 56B(7)(*b*), 86(3), 130(1)(*c*)(i), 154(3), 157(1)(*a*).
Definition—"Additional VAT liability", s 547(1).

576 Meaning of "the Inland Revenue" etc

(1) Subject to subsection (2), in this Act "the Inland Revenue" means any officer of the Board of Inland Revenue.

(2) In section 51(1) and (3)(*a*) (disclosure by or to Inland Revenue of information relating to first-year allowances in Northern Ireland cases) "the Inland Revenue" means the Board of Inland Revenue or any officer of the Board.

(3) In this Act "the Board of Inland Revenue" means the Commissioners of Inland Revenue (as to which, see in particular the Inland Revenue Regulation Act 1890).

Former enactments—Sub-ss (1), (2): Change in law.
Sub-s (3): CAA 1990 s 161(2).

577 Other definitions

(1) In this Act—

"dual resident investing company" has the same meaning as in section 404 of ICTA (limitation of group relief in relation to certain dual resident companies);
"market value", in relation to any asset, means the price the asset would fetch in the open market;
"the normal time limit for amending a tax return", in relation to a tax year, means the first anniversary of the 31st January following the tax year;
"notice" means a notice in writing;
"property business" means a Schedule A business or an overseas property business;
"tax return" has the meaning given by section 3(3);
"tax year" means, in relation to income tax, a year for which any Act provides for income tax to be charged;
"the tax year 2001–02" means the tax year beginning on 6th April 2001 (and any corresponding expression in which two years are similarly mentioned is to be read in the same way).

(2) Any reference to the setting up, commencement or permanent discontinuance of—

(*a*) a trade,
(*b*) a property business,
(*c*) a profession, or
(*d*) a vocation,

includes, except where the contrary is expressly provided, the occurring of an event which, under any provision of the Income Tax Acts or Corporation Tax Acts, is to be treated as equivalent to the setting up, commencement or permanent discontinuance of a trade, property business, profession or vocation.

(3) Any reference in this Act to an allowance made includes an allowance which would be made but for an insufficiency of profits, or other income, against which to make it.

(4) For the purposes of this Act a person obtains a tax advantage if he—

(*a*) obtains an allowance or a greater allowance, or
(*b*) avoids a charge or secures the reduction of a charge.

(5) In Schedule 1—

(*a*) Part 1 gives the meaning of abbreviated references in this Act to Acts about tax, and
(*b*) Part 2 lists where expressions used in this Act are defined or otherwise explained.

Former enactments—Sub-s (1): "dual resident investing company" CAA 1990 s 161(2),
"market value" TA 1988 ss 521(6), CAA 1990 ss 7(1)(*a*), 21(6), 26(1)(*b*), (*f*), 34(4)(*a*), 37(10), 41(5)(*a*), 59(5), (6), (9), 76(2)(*a*), 78(1), 81(1), 138(4), 152(1), 157(4), 158(1),
"notice" CAA 1990 s 161(2),
"the normal time limit for amending a tax return" CAA 1990 ss 30(1A), 31(3A), 33(5A), 33F(2), 37(2A), 53(2A), 68(9AA), 129(2).
Sub-s (2): CAA 1990 s 161(6). Change in law.
Sub-s (3): CAA 1990 ss 38G(4), 59A(4), 129(5), 157(1)(*b*).
Definition—"Overseas property business", s 65A(4), 70A(4), TA 1988 s 832(1).

Amendments, repeals, citation etc

578 Consequential amendments

Schedule 2 contains consequential amendments.

579 Commencement and transitional provisions and savings

(1) This Act has effect—

(*a*) for income tax purposes, as respects allowances and charges falling to be made for chargeable periods ending on or after 6th April 2001, and
(*b*) for corporation tax purposes, as respects allowances and charges falling to be made for chargeable periods ending on or after 1st April 2001.

(2) References in this Act to a chargeable period to which this Act applies are to the chargeable periods given in subsection (1).

(3) Subsection (1) is subject to Schedule 3, which contains transitional provisions and savings.

Commentary—*Simon's Direct Tax Service* **B2.101B**.

580 Repeals

Schedule 4 contains repeals.

581 Citation

This Act may be cited as the Capital Allowances Act 2001.

SCHEDULES

SCHEDULE 1

ABBREVIATIONS AND DEFINED EXPRESSIONS

Section 577

PART 1

ABBREVIATIONS

FA 1937	The Finance Act 1937 (c 54)
FA 1941	The Finance Act 1941 (c 30)
FA 1956	The Finance Act 1956 (c 54)
FA 1965	The Finance Act 1965 (c 25)
CAA 1968	The Capital Allowances Act 1968 (c 3)
TMA 1970	The Taxes Management Act 1970 (c 9)
FA 1971	The Finance Act 1971 (c 68)
OTA 1975	The Oil Taxation Act 1975 (c 22)
FA 1976	The Finance Act 1976 (c 40)
FA 1982	The Finance Act 1982 (c 39)
FA 1983	The Finance Act 1983 (c 28)
FA 1986	The Finance Act 1986 (c 41)
ICTA	The Income and Corporation Taxes Act 1988 (c 1)
FA 1989	The Finance Act 1989 (c 26)
CAA 1990	The Capital Allowances Act 1990 (c 1)
TCGA 1992	The Taxation of Chargeable Gains Act 1992 (c 12)
F(No 2)A 1992	The Finance (No 2) Act 1992 (c 48)
VATA 1994	The Value Added Tax Act 1994 (c 23)
FA 1995	The Finance Act 1995 (c 4)
FA 1997	The Finance Act 1997 (c 16)
FA 1998	The Finance Act 1998 (c 36)

PART 2

DEFINED EXPRESSIONS

accounting period	section 12 of ICTA
additional VAT liability	section 547(1)
additional VAT rebate	section 547(2)
adjusted net cost (in Chapter 7 of Part 3)	section 323
adjusted net cost (in Chapter 6 of Part 10)	section 522
agricultural building	section 361(2)(a)
approved body (in Part 10)	section 492
assured tenancy	section 490(3)
available qualifying expenditure (in Part 2)	section 57
available qualifying expenditure (in Part 7)	section 459
available qualifying expenditure (in Part 8)	section 473
balancing adjustment (in Part 3)	section 314
balancing adjustment (in Part 4)	section 380
[balancing adjustment (in Part 4A)	section 393M][1]
balancing adjustment (in Part 10)	section 513
balancing event (in Part 3)	section 315
balancing event (in Part 4)	section 381
[balancing event (in Part 4A)	section 393N][1]

balancing event (in Part 10)	section 514
body of persons	section 832(1) of ICTA
the Board of Inland Revenue	section 576(3)
building (in Part 3—includes structure)	section 271(1)
capital expenditure	section 4 and (in Chapter 2 of Part 1) section 10(1)
capital sum	section 4
car (in Part 2)	section 81
chargeable period	section 6
commercial building (in Part 3, in relation to qualifying enterprise zone expenditure)	section 281
connected persons (general meaning)	section 575(1)
connected persons (special extended meaning for certain purposes)	sections 156, 232, 246(2) and 266(5)
control	section 574
the Corporation Tax Acts	section 831(1) of ICTA
developer, carrying on a trade as (in Chapter 4 of Part 3)	section 293
development and development order (in Part 5)	section 436
disposal event (in Part 2)	section 60(2)
disposal event (in Chapter 3 of Part 6)	section 443(7)
disposal receipt (in Part 2)	section 60
disposal receipt (in Part 5)	section 420
disposal receipt (in Chapter 3 of Part 8)	section 476(1)
dredging	section 484(3), (4)
dual resident investing company	section 577(1) and section 404 of ICTA
[dwelling (in Part 4A)	section 393A(4)][1]
dwelling-house	section 531(1)
enterprise zone (in Part 3)	section 298(3)
expenditure on the construction of a building (in Part 3)	section 272
expenditure on the construction of a building (in Part 4)	section 363
expenditure on the construction of a building (in Part 10)	section 493
final chargeable period (in Part 2)	section 65
final chargeable period (in Part 7)	section 457(5)
final chargeable period (in Part 8)	section 471(5) and (6)
first-year qualifying expenditure	Chapter 4 of Part 2
fixture (in Part 2)	section 173(1)
[flat (in Part 4A)	section 393A(3)][1]
four-year cut-off (in Chapter 9 of Part 2)	section 86(3)
furnished holiday lettings business (in Part 2)	section 17
general development order (in Part 5)	section 436
highway concession (in Chapter 9 of Part 3)	section 341(4)
husbandry (in Part 4)	section 362
income from patents (in Part 8)	section 483 and paragraph 101(5) of Schedule 3
industrial building	section 271(2) and Chapter 2 of Part 3
the Inland Revenue	section 576
interest in an oil licence (in Chapter 3 of Part 12)	section 552(4)
investment company	section 130 of ICTA
investment asset (in relation to life assurance business)	section 545(2)
know-how (in Part 7)	section 452(2)
lease and related expressions (in Part 3)	section 360
lease and related expressions (in Part 4)	section 393
[lease and related expressions (in Part 4A)	section 393W][1]
lease and related expressions (in Part 10)	section 531
life assurance business	section 544(5) and section 431(2) of ICTA
long-life asset (in Chapter 10 of Part 2)	section 91
long-life asset expenditure (in Chapter 10 of Part 2)	section 90
market value	section 577(1)
mineral asset (in Part 5)	section 397
mineral exploration and access (in Part 5)	section 396
mineral extraction trade (in Part 5)	section 394(2)

unrelieved qualifying expenditure (in Part 8)	section 475
within the charge to tax	section 832(1) of ICTA
writing-down period (in Part 4)	section 372(2)
writing-down period (in Part 9)	section 487(2)

Amendments— ¹ Words inserted by FA 2001 s 67, Sch 19 Pt II para 8 with effect for expenditure incurred after 10 May 2001.

SCHEDULE 2

CONSEQUENTIAL AMENDMENTS

Section 578

THE TAXES MANAGEMENT ACT 1970 (C 9)

Section 42 (procedure for making claims etc)

1 In subsection (7), for paragraphs (*c*) and (*d*) substitute—

"(*c*) sections 3, 83, 89, 129, 131, 135, 177, 183, 266, 268, 290, 355, 381 and 569 of the Capital Allowances Act; and

(*d*) sections 40B(5), 40D, 41 and 42 of the Finance (No 2) Act 1992.''

Section 57 (regulations about appeals)

2 For subsection (3)(*b*) substitute—

"(*b*) provisions corresponding to section 563 of the Capital Allowances Act (determination of apportionment affecting tax liability of two or more persons), and''.

Section 58 (proceedings in tax cases in Northern Ireland)

3 In subsection (3)(*b*), for "section 151 of the Capital Allowances Act 1990 (proceedings to which more than one taxpayer is a party)'' substitute "section 563 of the Capital Allowances Act (determination of apportionment affecting tax liability of two or more persons)''.

Section 98 (special returns, etc)

4—(1) In the Table, in column 1, omit "Sections 23(4) and 49(4) of the Capital Allowances Act 1990''.

(2) In the Table, in column 2, for "Sections 22B(4), 23(2), 33F(5), 48, 49(2), 51(6A) and 53(1H) of the Capital Allowances Act 1990'' substitute "Sections 43(5) and (6), 118 to 120, 145(2) and (3) and 203 of the Capital Allowances Act''.

Schedule 3 (rules for assigning proceedings to General Commissioners)

5 In paragraph 10, for "section 151 of the Capital Allowances Act 1990'' substitute "section 563 of the Capital Allowances Act''.

THE FINANCE ACT 1982 (C 39)

Section 137 (expenditure met by regional development plans to be disregarded for certain purposes)

6 Omit subsections (2), (3), (6) and (7).

THE LONDON REGIONAL TRANSPORT ACT 1984 (C 32)

Schedule 5 (transitional provisions and savings)

7 In paragraph 5, omit paragraph (*b*) and the word "and'' before it.

THE FILMS ACT 1985 (C 21)

Section 6 (certification of films as British films)

8 In subsection (1), for "section 68 of the Capital Allowances Act 1990 (expenditure on production and acquisition of films etc)'' substitute "section 40D of the Finance (No 2) Act 1992 (election relating to tax treatment of films expenditure)''.

Schedule 1 (certification of films as British films)

9—(1) In paragraph 2(1), for "section 68 of the Capital Allowances Act 1990'' substitute "section 40D of the Finance (No 2) Act 1992''.

(2) In paragraph 3(1), for "section 68 of the Capital Allowances Act 1990" substitute "section 40D of the Finance (No 2) Act 1992".

THE TRUSTEE SAVINGS BANKS ACT 1985 (C 58)
Schedule 2 (taxation)

10 In paragraph 1—

(a) in sub-paragraph (1), for "the Capital Allowances Act 1990" substitute "the Capital Allowances Act 2001", and

(b) in sub-paragraph (2), for "those Acts" substitute "that Act".

THE INCOME AND CORPORATION TAXES ACT 1988 (C 1)
Section 43C (transfer of rent: exceptions, etc)

11 In subsection (2)(a), for "the Capital Allowances Acts" substitute "the Capital Allowances Act (including enactments which under this Act are to be treated as contained in that Act)".

Section 43E (interposed lease: exceptions, etc)

12 In subsection (3)(a), for "the Capital Allowances Acts" substitute "the Capital Allowances Act (including enactments which under this Act are to be treated as contained in that Act)".

Section 65A (Case V income from land outside UK: income tax)

13 In subsection (7), omit "and section 29 of the 1990 Act (provisions relating to furnished holiday accommodation)".

Section 70A (Case V income from land outside UK: corporation tax)

14 In subsection (6), omit "and section 29 of the 1990 Act (provisions relating to furnished holiday accommodation)".

Section 75 (expenses of management: investment companies)

15 In subsection (4), for the words from "section 28 of the 1990 Act (capital allowances for investment companies)" to the end of the subsection substitute "section 15(1)(g) of the Capital Allowances Act (plant and machinery allowances) so far as effect cannot be given to them under section 253(2) of that Act".

Section 83A (gifts in kind to charities, etc)

16—(1) In subsection (2), omit paragraph (b) and the word "or" before it.

(2) In subsection (3), omit paragraph (b) and the word "and" before it.

(3) In subsection (4)(a) after "subsection (3) above" insert "or section 63(2) of the Capital Allowances Act".

Section 84 (gifts to educational establishments)

17—(1) In subsection (1)—

(a) in paragraph (a), for "machinery or plant" substitute "plant or machinery", and

(b) omit paragraph (b) and the word "or" before it.

(2) In subsection (2)—

(a) for "qualifies as machinery or plant" substitute "qualifies as plant or machinery", and

(b) for "Part II of the 1990 Act as machinery or plant" substitute "Part 2 of the Capital Allowances Act as plant or machinery".

(3) In subsection (3), omit paragraph (b) and the word "and" before it.

(4) In subsection (4)(a), after "subsection (3) above" insert "or section 63(2) of the Capital Allowances Act".

Section 87 (taxable premiums etc)

18 In subsection (7), for "Part IV of the 1990 Act in respect of expenditure falling within section 105(1)(b) of that Act (mineral depletion)" substitute "Part 5 of the Capital Allowances Act in respect of expenditure falling within section 403 (mineral asset expenditure)".

Section 91 (cemeteries)

19 For subsection (9) substitute—

"(9) Section 532 of the Capital Allowances Act (general rule excluding contributions) shall apply for the purposes of this section as it applies for the purposes of that Act."

Section 91C (mineral exploration and access)

20 In paragraph (*a*), for "section 121(1) of the Capital Allowances Act 1990" substitute "section 396(1) of the Capital Allowances Act".

Section 116 (arrangements for transferring relief)

21 In subsection (4), for paragraph (*b*) substitute—

"(*b*) any allowance to be given effect under Part 2 of the Capital Allowances Act in respect of a special leasing of plant or machinery were an allowance to be given effect in calculating the profits of that trade."

Section 117 (restriction on relief: individuals)

22—(1) In subsection (1), omit—

(*a*) "or allowed" (in each place),
(*b*) "or section 141 of the 1990 Act", and
(*c*) paragraph (*b*) and the word "or" before it.

(2) In subsection (2), in the definition of "the aggregate amount", omit—

(*a*) "or allowed",
(*b*) "or section 141 of the 1990 Act", and
(*c*) paragraph (*b*) and the word "or" before it.

(3) In relation to any chargeable period to which this Act applies, the repeals made by sub-paragraph (2) are not to exclude from an individual's aggregate amount for the purposes of section 117 of ICTA any amounts included in the individual's aggregate amount at any time before the chargeable periods to which this Act applies.

Section 118 (restriction on relief: companies)

23—(1) In subsection (1), omit—

(*a*) "or allowed" (in each place),
(*b*) "or section 145 of the 1990 Act", and
(*c*) paragraph (*b*) and the word "or" before it.

(2) In subsection (2), in the definition of "the aggregate amount", omit—

(*a*) "or allowed",
(*b*) "or section 145 of the 1990 Act", and
(*c*) paragraph (*b*) and the word "or" before it.

(3) In relation to any chargeable period to which this Act applies, the repeals made by sub-paragraph (2) are not to exclude from a company's aggregate amount for the purposes of section 118 of ICTA any amounts included in the company's aggregate amount at any time before the chargeable periods to which this Act applies.

Section 197C (definition of mileage profit)

24 In subsection (5), for "which, by virtue of Part II of the Capital Allowances Act 1990 falls to be made to the employee" substitute "to which, under Part 2 of the Capital Allowances Act (plant and machinery allowances), the employee is entitled".

Section 198 (relief for necessary expenses)

25 In subsection (2), omit "and Part II of the 1990 Act (capital allowances in respect of machinery and plant)".

Section 343 (company reconstructions without a change of ownership)

26 In subsection (2), for "the Capital Allowances Acts" substitute "the Capital Allowances Act (including enactments which under this Act are to be treated as contained in that Act)".

Section 359 (loan to buy machinery or plant)

27—(1) In subsection (1)—

(*a*) for "section 44 of the 1968 Act" substitute "section 264 of the Capital Allowances Act",
(*b*) for "any year of assessment in respect of machinery or plant" substitute "any period of account in respect of plant or machinery",
(*c*) for "the basis period (as defined in section 72 of that Act) for that year" substitute "that period of account",
(*d*) for "that machinery or plant" substitute "that plant or machinery", and
(*e*) for "the year of assessment" substitute "the period of account".

(2) In subsection (3)—

(*a*) in paragraph (*a*), for "Part II of the 1990 Act" substitute "Part 2 of the Capital Allowances Act" and for "machinery or plant" substitute "plant or machinery", and

(*b*) in paragraph (*b*), for "machinery or plant" substitute "plant or machinery".

Section 379A (Schedule A losses)

28 In subsection (2)(*a*), for "the 1990 Act" substitute "the Capital Allowances Act".

Section 384 (restrictions on right of set-off)

29—(1) In subsection (6), for "under Chapter I of Part III of the Finance Act 1971 in respect of expenditure incurred on the provision of machinery or plant" substitute "under Part 2 of the Capital Allowances Act in respect of expenditure incurred on the provision of plant or machinery".

(2) In subsection (10), omit the words following paragraph (*b*) and after that subsection insert—

"(11) Expressions used in subsections (6) to (8) and in Part 2 of the Capital Allowances Act have same meaning in those subsections as in that Part; and those subsections are without prejudice to section 384A."

New section 384A (restriction of set-off of plant and machinery allowances)

30 After section 384 insert—

"384A Restriction of set-off of allowances against general income

(1) Relief shall not be given to an individual under sections 380 and 381 by reference to a first-year allowance under Part 2 of the Capital Allowances Act (plant and machinery allowances) in the circumstances specified in subsection (2) or (4) below.

(2) The circumstances are that the allowance is in respect of expenditure incurred on the provision of plant or machinery for leasing in the course of a qualifying activity and—

(*a*) at the time when the expenditure was incurred, the qualifying activity was carried on by the individual in question in partnership with a company (with or without other partners), or

(*b*) a scheme has been effected or arrangements have been made (whether before or after that time) with a view to the qualifying activity being so carried on by that individual.

(3) For the purposes of subsection (2) above letting a ship on charter shall be regarded as leasing it if, apart from this subsection, it would not be so regarded.

(4) The circumstances are that the allowance is made in connection with—

(*a*) a qualifying activity which at the time when the expenditure was incurred was carried on by the individual in partnership or which has subsequently been carried on by him in partnership or transferred to a person who was connected with him, or

(*b*) an asset which after that time has been transferred by the individual to a person who was connected with him or, at a price lower than its market value, to any other person,

and the condition in subsection (5) below is met.

(5) The condition is that a scheme has been effected or arrangements have been made (whether before or after the time referred to in subsection (4) above) such that the sole or main benefit that might be expected to accrue to the individual from the transaction under which the expenditure was incurred was the obtaining of a reduction in tax liability by means of relief under sections 380 and 381.

(6) Where relief has been given in circumstances in which subsection (1) applies it shall be withdrawn by the making of an assessment under Case VI of Schedule D.

(7) Section 839 (how to tell whether persons are connected) applies for the purposes of subsection (4) above.

(8) Expressions used in this section and in Part 2 of the Capital Allowances Act have the same meaning as in that Part."

Former enactment—CAA 1990 s 142.

Section 389 (supplementary provisions relating to carry-back of terminal losses)

31 In subsection (2)—

(*a*) for "Part IV of the 1990 Act" substitute "Part 5 of the Capital Allowances Act",

(*b*) for "section 17(1) of the 1990 Act" substitute "section 355 of that Act", and

(*c*) for "section 17(1)" (in both places) substitute "section 355".

Section 393A (losses: set off against profits of the same, or an earlier, accounting period)

32—(1) In subsection (2C)(*b*), for "section 62A of the 1990 Act (demolition costs relating to offshore machinery or plant)" substitute "section 164 of the Capital Allowances Act (abandonment expenditure incurred before cessation of ring fence trade)".

(2) Omit subsections (5) and (6).

(3) In subsection (11)—

(*a*) in paragraph (*a*), for "section 62B of the 1990 Act (post-cessation abandonment expenditure related to offshore machinery or plant)" substitute "section 165 of the Capital Allowances Act (abandonment expenditure within 3 years of ceasing ring fence trade)", and
(*b*) in paragraph (*b*), for "section 109 of that Act (restoration expenditure incurred after cessation of trade of mineral extraction)" substitute "section 416 of that Act (expenditure on restoration within 3 years of ceasing to trade)" and for "the last day on which it carried on the trade" substitute "the last day of trading".

(4) In subsection (12), for "section 62A of the 1990 Act" substitute "section 162 of the Capital Allowances Act".

Section 395 (leasing contracts and company reconstructions)

33 In subsection (1)—

(*a*) in paragraph (*a*), for "machinery or plant" substitute "plant or machinery", and
(*b*) in paragraph (*c*), for "within the meaning of Part II of the 1990 Act" substitute "within the meaning of Part 2 of the Capital Allowances Act".

Section 397 (restriction of relief in case of farming and market gardening)

34—(1) In subsection (5)—

(*a*) omit the definition of "basis year", and
(*b*) in the definition of "chargeable period" omit the words from "or any basis period" to the end of the definition.

(2) Omit subsection (6).

(3) In subsection (7), for the words from "but so that" to the end of the subsection substitute "but disregarding—

(*a*) any allowance or charge under the Capital Allowances Act (including enactments which under this Act are to be treated as contained in that Act); and
(*b*) any provision of that Act requiring allowances and charges to be treated as expenses and receipts of the trade".

Section 400 (write-off of government investment)

35—(1) In subsection (2)(*c*), for "section 145(2) of the 1990 Act" substitute "section 260(2) of the Capital Allowances Act".

(2) In subsection (4), for "section 145(3) of the 1990 Act" substitute "section 260(3) of the Capital Allowances Act".

(3) In subsection (6), for "section 153 of the 1990 Act" substitute "section 532 or 536 of the Capital Allowances Act".

Section 403ZB (amounts eligible for group relief: excess capital allowances)

36 In subsection (1), for the words from "the surrender period" to the end of the subsection substitute "for the surrender period to the extent that they are to be given effect under section 260 of the Capital Allowances Act (special leasing: excess allowance)."

Section 407 (relationship between group relief and other relief)

37—(1) In subsection (1)(*b*), for "section 145(3) of the 1990 Act" substitute "section 260(3) of the Capital Allowances Act".

(2) In subsection (2)(*b*), for "section 145(3) of the 1990 Act" substitute "section 260(3) of the Capital Allowances Act".

Section 411 (exclusion of double allowance)

38 In subsection (10)—

(*a*) omit "Without prejudice to the provisions of section 161(5) of the 1990 Act", and
(*b*) for "that Act, except Parts III and VII" substitute "the Capital Allowances Act, except Parts 6 and 10".

Sections 434D and 434E (capital allowances: management assets; investment assets)

39 Omit sections 434D and 434E.

Section 487 (credit unions)

40 In subsection (4), for "section 306 of the 1970 Act (capital allowances)" substitute "Part 2 of the Capital Allowances Act (plant and machinery allowances)".

Section 492 (treatment of oil extraction activities etc for tax purposes)

41—(1) In subsection (5), for "section 141 of the 1990 Act" substitute "section 258 of the Capital Allowances Act".

(2) In subsection (6), for "section 145 of the 1990 Act" substitute "section 259 or 260 of the Capital Allowances Act".

(3) In subsection (7), for "section 145(1) of the 1990 Act" substitute "section 259 of the Capital Allowances Act".

Section 495 (regional development grants)

42—(1) In subsection (1), for "Part I, II or VII of the 1990 Act (capital allowances relating to industrial buildings, machinery or plant and research and development)" substitute "Part 2, 3 or 6 of the Capital Allowances Act (capital allowances relating to plant and machinery, industrial buildings or research and development)".

(2) In subsection (3), for "Part I, II or VII of the 1990 Act" substitute "Part 2, 3 or 6 of the Capital Allowances Act".

(3) In subsection (7), in the definition of "regional development grant" for the words from "means" to the end substitute "means a grant falling within section 534(1) of the Capital Allowances Act".

Section 518 (harbour reorganisation schemes)

43 In subsection (4), for "the provisions of the Capital Allowances Acts" substitute "the Capital Allowances Act (including enactments which under this Act are to be treated as contained in that Act)".

Sections 520 to 523 (patents)

44 Omit sections 520 to 523.

Section 525 (capital sums: death, winding up or partnership change)

45 In subsection (3), for "section 152 of the 1990 Act (succession to trades)" substitute "section 559 of the Capital Allowances Act (effect of successions)".

Section 528 (patents: manner of making allowances and charges)

46—(1) Omit subsection (1).

(2) In subsections (2) and (3), for "section 520, 522, 523 or 526 as those provisions apply" (in each place) substitute "section 526 as that provision applies".

(3) After subsection (3) insert—

"(3A) In this section references to a person's or a company's income from patents are references to that income after any allowance has been deducted from or set off against it under section 479 or 480 of the Capital Allowances Act."

(4) Omit subsection (4).

Section 530 (disposal of know-how)

47 Omit section 530.

Section 531 (disposal of know-how: supplementary provisions)

48—(1) In subsection (1), for "as disposal value under section 530(5)" substitute "as a disposal value under section 462 of the Capital Allowances Act".

(2) In subsection (3), omit the words following paragraph (*b*).

(3) In subsection (4), for "as disposal value under section 530(5)" substitute "as a disposal value under section 462 of the Capital Allowances Act".

(4) In subsection (7), omit "and section 530(1) and (6)".

Section 532 (application of 1990 Act)

49 For section 532 substitute—

"532 Application of Capital Allowances Act

The Tax Acts have effect as if sections 524 to 529 and 531, this section and section 533 were contained in the Capital Allowances Act."

Section 533 (interpretation of sections 520 to 532)

50—(1) In each of subsections (1) to (5), for "sections 520 to 532" substitute "sections 524 to 529".

(2) In subsection (1)—

(a) in paragraph (b) of the definition of "income from patents", omit "520(6), 523(3)," and after "525" insert "or section 472(5) of, or paragraph 100 of Schedule 3 to, the Capital Allowances Act", and

(b) omit the definition of "the commencement of the patent".

(3) In subsection (7), for "sections 530 and 531" substitute "section 531".

Section 577 (business entertaining expenses)

51—(1) In subsection (1)—

(a) at the end of paragraph (a) insert "and", and

(b) omit paragraph (c) and the word "and" before it.

(2) In subsection (7)(a), omit ", or to the use of an asset for," (in both places).

(3) In subsection (10), omit ", or any claim for capital allowances in respect of the use of an asset for,".

New sections 578A and 578B (expenditure on car hire)

52 After section 578 insert—

"578A Expenditure on car hire

(1) This section provides for a reduction in the amounts—

(a) allowable as deductions in computing profits chargeable to tax under Case I or II of Schedule D,

(b) which can be included as expenses of management of an investment company (as defined by section 130), or

(c) allowable as deductions from emoluments chargeable to tax under Schedule E,

for expenditure on the hiring of a car to which this section applies.

(2) This section applies to the hiring of a car—

(a) which is not a qualifying hire car, and

(b) the retail price of which when new exceeds £12,000.

"Car" and "qualifying hire car" are defined by section 578B.

(3) The amount which would, apart from this section, be allowable or capable of being included must be reduced by multiplying it by the fraction—

$$\frac{£12,000 + P}{2P}$$

where P is the retail price of the car when new.

(4) If an amount has been reduced under subsection (3) and subsequently—

(a) there is a rebate (however described) of the rentals, or

(b) there occurs in connection with the rentals a transaction that falls within section 94 (debts deducted and subsequently released),

the amount otherwise taxable in respect of the rebate or transaction must be reduced by multiplying it by the fraction in subsection (3) above.

578B Expenditure on car hire: supplementary

(1) In section 578A "car" means a mechanically propelled road vehicle other than one—

(a) of a construction primarily suited for the conveyance of goods or burden of any description, or

(b) of a type not commonly used as a private vehicle and unsuitable for such use.

References to a car accordingly include a motor cycle.

(2) For the purposes of section 578A, a car is a qualifying hire car if—

(a) it is hired under a hire-purchase agreement (within the meaning of section 784(6)) under which there is an option to purchase exercisable on the payment of a sum equal to not more than 1 per cent. of the retail price of the car when new, or

(b) it is a qualifying hire car for the purposes of Part 2 of the Capital Allowances Act (under section 82 of that Act).

(3) In section 578A and this section "new" means unused and not second-hand.

(4) The power under section 74(4) of the Capital Allowances Act to increase or further increase the sums of money specified in Chapter 8 of Part 2 of that Act includes the power to increase or further increase the sum of money specified in section 578A(2)(b) or (3)."

Former enactment—CAA 1990 s 35(2)–(4).

Simon's Tax Cases—CAA 1990 s 35(2), *Lloyds UDT Finance Ltd v Chartered Finance Trust Holdings plc and others (Britax International GmbH and another, Pt 20 defendants)* [2001] STC 1652.

Section 623 (retirement annuities: relevant earnings)

53 In subsection (5), for "any of the Capital Allowances Acts" substitute "the Capital Allowances Act (including enactments which under this Act are to be treated as contained in that Act)".

Section 646 (meaning of "net relevant earnings")

54 In subsection (3), for "the 1990 Act (including enactments which under this Act are to be treated as contained in the 1990 Act)" substitute "the Capital Allowances Act (including enactments which under this Act are to be treated as contained in that Act)".

Section 768 (change in ownership of company: disallowance of trading losses)

55 In subsection (6), for "section 161(6) of the 1990 Act" substitute "section 577(3) of the Capital Allowances Act".

Section 768B (change in ownership of investment company: deductions generally)

56 In subsection (8), for "section 28 of the 1990 Act" substitute "section 253 of the Capital Allowances Act".

Section 781 (assets leased to traders and others)

57 In subsection (9), for "section 60(2) of the 1990 Act" substitute "section 68 of the Capital Allowances Act".

Section 828 (orders and regulations made by the Treasury or the Board)

58 In subsection (4), for "section 22(6)(*d*) or 36(4)(*d*) of the 1990 Act" substitute "section 82(4)(*d*) of the Capital Allowances Act".

Section 831 (interpretation of Act)

59 Section 831(3) continues to have effect with the addition of the definition of "the 1990 Act" (an amendment originally made by paragraph 8(35) of Schedule 1 to the Capital Allowances Act 1990).

Section 832 (interpretation of the Tax Acts)

60 In subsection (1)—

(*a*) in the definition of "capital allowance", for "the Capital Allowances Acts" substitute "the Capital Allowances Act (including enactments which under this Act are to be treated as contained in that Act)", and
(*b*) for the definition of "the Capital Allowances Acts" substitute—

""the Capital Allowances Act" means the Capital Allowances Act 2001;".

Section 834 (interpretation of the Corporation Tax Acts)

61 In subsection (2), omit "and also for sections 144 and 145 of the 1990 Act".

Section 835 ("total income" in the Income Tax Acts)

62 In subsection (8), for paragraph (*c*) substitute—

"(*c*) any allowance given effect under section 258 or 479 of the Capital Allowances Act;".

Schedule 18 (group relief)

63 In paragraph 1(6)—

(*a*) in paragraph (*b*)(i) and (ii), for "Part II of the 1990 Act" substitute "Part 2 of the Capital Allowances Act" and for "machinery or plant" substitute "plant or machinery", and
(*b*) in paragraph (*b*)(iii), for "section 137 of the 1990 Act" substitute "Chapter 3 of Part 6 of the Capital Allowances Act" and for "Part VII" substitute "Part 6".

Schedule 19AC (modification of Act in relation to overseas life insurance companies)

64—(1) Omit paragraph 9C (application of section 434D(4) in relation to overseas life insurance company).

(2) In paragraph 10B(2A) (modification of section 440 in relation to overseas life insurance company), in the inserted subsection (4AA), for "Section 81 of the 1990 Act (as it has effect by virtue of section 83(2A) of that Act)" substitute "Section 13 of the Capital Allowances Act (use for qualifying activity of plant or machinery provided for other purposes)".

Schedule 21 (tax relief in connection with schemes for rationalising industry and other redundancy schemes)

65 In paragraph 6(1)(*a*), for "Part I or II of the 1990 Act in taxing the trade" substitute "Part 2 or 3 of the Capital Allowances Act in calculating the profits of a trade".

Schedule 24 (assumptions for calculating chargeable profits, creditable tax and corresponding United Kingdom tax of foreign companies)

66—(1) In paragraph 10(1)—

(*a*) for "machinery or plant for the purposes of its trade, that machinery or plant shall be assumed, for the purposes of Part II of the 1990 Act" substitute "plant or machinery for the purposes of its trade, that plant or machinery shall be assumed, for the purposes of Part 2 of the Capital Allowances Act", and

(*b*) for "section 81 of that Act (expenditure treated as equivalent to market value at the time the machinery or plant is brought into use)" substitute "section 13 of that Act (use for qualifying activity of plant or machinery provided for other purposes)".

(2) In paragraph 10(2), for "Part II of the 1990 Act" substitute "Part 2 of the Capital Allowances Act".

(3) In paragraph 11A—

(*a*) at the end of the heading insert "and expenditure on car hire", and

(*b*) in sub-paragraph (4) for "section 34, 35 or 96 of the 1990 Act" substitute "section 578A or 578B or section 74(2), 75(1), 76(2), (3) or (4) or 511(3) of the Capital Allowances Act".

Schedule 28A (change in ownership of investment company: deductions)

67—(1) In paragraph 6(*d*), for "section 28 of the 1990 Act" substitute "section 253 of the Capital Allowances Act".

(2) In paragraph 13(1)(*e*), for "section 28 of the 1990 Act" substitute "section 253 of the Capital Allowances Act".

Schedule 28AA (provision not at arm's length)

68 In paragraph 13(*a*), for "the 1990 Act" substitute "the Capital Allowances Act".

THE FINANCE ACT 1988 (C 39)

Schedule 12 (building societies: change of status)

69 In paragraph 3(1), for "the Capital Allowances Act 1990 (capital allowances)" substitute "the Capital Allowances Act 2001".

THE FINANCE ACT 1989 (C 26)

Section 86 (spreading of relief for acquisition expenses)

70 In subsection (5A), for "by virtue of section 434D(6)(*a*) of the Taxes Act (capital allowances in respect of expenditure on management assets)" substitute "under section 256(2)(*a*) of the Capital Allowances Act (giving effect to capital allowances referable to basic life assurance and general annuity business of company carrying on life assurance business)".

THE ELECTRICITY ACT 1989 (C 29)

Schedule 11 (taxation provisions)

71—(1) For paragraph 5(3) substitute—

"(3) Section 291(1) of the Capital Allowances Act 2001 (supplementary provisions with respect to elections) shall not prevent the application of section 290 of that Act (election to treat grant of lease exceeding 50 years as sale) where the lease is a lease to which this sub-paragraph applies."

(2) In paragraph 5(4)(*a*), for "section 44 of the Finance Act 1971 or section 24 of the 1990 Act" substitute "Chapter 5 of Part 2 of the Capital Allowances Act 2001".

(3) In paragraph 5(4)(*b*), for the words from "section 44" to "Chapter VI of Part II of the 1990 Act" substitute "Chapters 5 and 14 of Part 2 of the Capital Allowances Act 2001".

(4) For paragraph 5(5) substitute—

"(5) In sub-paragraph (4) above "the transferor" means the transferor under the transfer scheme in question and expressions which are used in Chapter 14 of Part 2 of the Capital Allowances Act 2001 have the same meanings as in that Chapter; and in construing that sub-paragraph section 511(2) of the 1988 Act shall be disregarded."

THE FINANCE ACT 1990 (C 29)

Section 126 (pools payments for football ground improvements)

72 In subsection (4), for "Section 153 of the Capital Allowances Act 1990" substitute "Section 532 of the Capital Allowances Act 2001".

THE FINANCE ACT 1991 (C 31)

Section 65 (reimbursement by defaulter in respect of certain abandonment expenditure)

73 In subsection (8), for "section 153 of the Capital Allowances Act 1990 (subsidies, contributions, etc)" substitute "section 532 of the Capital Allowances Act (the general rule excluding contributions)".

Section 78 (sharing of transmission facilities)

74—(1) In subsection (4)—

    (a) for "Capital Allowances Act 1990" substitute "Capital Allowances Act ";

    (b) for "machinery or plant" (in each place) substitute "plant or machinery"; and

    (c) for "section 24 of that Act" substitute "section 60 of that Act".

(2) In subsection (5) for "machinery or plant" (in both places) substitute "plant or machinery".

THE SOCIAL SECURITY CONTRIBUTIONS AND BENEFITS ACT 1992 (C 4)

Schedule 2 (levy of Class 4 contributions with income tax)

75—(1) In paragraph 1, omit paragraph (b).

(2) In paragraph 2, omit the words from "subject to deduction" to the end.

THE SOCIAL SECURITY CONTRIBUTIONS AND BENEFITS (NORTHERN IRELAND) ACT 1992 (C 7)

Schedule 2 (levy of Class 4 contributions with income tax)

76—(1) In paragraph 1, omit paragraph (b).

(2) In paragraph 2, omit the words from "subject to deduction" to the end.

THE TAXATION OF CHARGEABLE GAINS ACT 1992 (C 12)

Section 37 (consideration chargeable to tax on income)

77 In subsection (2), for paragraphs (a) and (b) substitute—

    "(a) taken into account in the making of a balancing charge under the Capital Allowances Act but excluding Part 10 of that Act,

    (b) brought into account as the disposal value of plant or machinery under Part 2 of that Act, or

    (c) brought into account as the disposal value of an asset representing qualifying expenditure under Part 6 of that Act."

Section 41 (restriction of losses by reference to capital allowances etc)

78—(1) In subsection (3), for paragraphs (a) and (b) substitute—

    "(a) by a transfer by way of sale in relation to which an election under section 569 of the Capital Allowances Act was made, or

    (b) by a transfer to which section 268 of that Act applies,".

(2) In subsection (4), for paragraph (a) substitute—

    "(a) any allowance under the Capital Allowances Act,".

(3) In subsection (7)—

    (a) for "machinery or plant" (in each place) substitute "plant or machinery",

    (b) for "Part II of the 1990 Act, and neither section 79 (assets used only partly for trade purposes) nor section 80 (wear and tear subsidies) of that Act" substitute "Part 2 of the Capital Allowances Act, and neither Chapter 15 (assets provided or used only partly for qualifying activity) nor Chapter 16 (partial depreciation subsidies) of that Part", and

    (c) for "capital expenditure" substitute "qualifying expenditure".

Section 195 (allowance of certain drilling expenditure)

79—(1) In subsection (2), for paragraphs (*b*) and (*c*) substitute:

"(*b*) either it is expenditure in respect of which the person was entitled to an allowance under section 441 of the Capital Allowances Act (research and development allowances) for a relevant chargeable period which began before the date of the disposal or it would have been such expenditure if the trading condition had been fulfilled, and

(*c*) on the disposal, section 443 of that Act (disposal values) applies in relation to the expenditure or would apply if the trading condition had been fulfilled (and the expenditure had accordingly been qualifying expenditure under Part 6 of that Act)."

(2) In subsection (3)—

(*a*) for "section 137 of the 1990 Act" substitute "section 441 of the Capital Allowances Act", and

(*b*) omit the definition of "basis year" and the word "and" before it.

(3) In subsection (4), for "trading receipt" substitute "disposal value" and for paragraphs (*a*) and (*b*) substitute—

"(*a*) is required to be brought into account under section 443 of the Capital Allowances Act; or

(*b*) would be required to be so brought into account if the trading condition had been fulfilled (and the expenditure had accordingly been qualifying expenditure under Part 6 of that Act)."

(4) Omit subsection (5).

(5) In subsection (6)—

(*a*) for "which had not in fact been allowed or become allowable" substitute "in respect of which the person had not in fact been entitled to an allowance",

(*b*) for "section 137 of the 1990 Act" substitute "section 441 of the Capital Allowances Act", and

(*c*) omit paragraph (*b*) and the word "and" before it.

(6) In subsection (8), for "Part VII of the Capital Allowances Act 1990 (allowances for research and development expenditure)" substitute "Part 6 of the Capital Allowances Act (research and development allowances)".

Section 288 (interpretation)

80 In subsection (1), omit the definition of "the 1990 Act" and after the definition of "building society" insert—

""the Capital Allowances Act" means the Capital Allowances Act 2001;".

Schedule 3 (assets held on 31st March 1982)

81 In paragraph 7(8), for "section 121 of the 1990 Act" substitute "section 394 of the Capital Allowances Act".

THE FINANCE (NO 2) ACT 1992 (C 48)

New sections 40A to 40D (films)

82 Before section 41 insert—

"40A Revenue nature of expenditure on master versions of films

(1) Expenditure incurred on the production or acquisition of a master version of a film is to be regarded for the purposes of the Tax Acts as expenditure of a revenue nature unless an election under section 40D below has effect with respect to it.

(2) If expenditure on the master version of a film is regarded as expenditure of a revenue nature under subsection (1) above, sums received from the disposal of the master version are to be regarded for the purposes of the Tax Acts as receipts of a revenue nature (if they would not be so regarded apart from this subsection).

(3) For the purposes of subsection (2) above sums received from the disposal of a master version of a film include—

(*a*) sums received from the disposal of any interest or right in or over the master version, including an interest or right created by the disposal, and

(*b*) insurance, compensation or similar money derived from the master version.

(4) In this section—

(*a*) "expenditure of a revenue nature" means expenditure which, if it were incurred in the course of a trade the profits of which are chargeable to tax under Case I of Schedule D, would be taken into account for the purpose of computing the profits or losses of the trade, and

(*b*) "receipts of a revenue nature" means receipts which, if they were receipts of such a trade, would be taken into account for that purpose.

(5) For the purposes of this section and sections 40B to 40D below, a "master version" of a film means a master negative, master tape or master audio disc of the film and includes any rights in the film (or its soundtrack) that are held or acquired with the master negative, master tape or master audio disc.

40B Allocation of expenditure to periods

(1) In computing the profits or gains accruing to any person from a trade or business which consists of or includes the exploitation of master versions of films, expenditure which is—

    (*a*) incurred on the production or acquisition of a master version of a film, and

    (*b*) expenditure of a revenue nature (whether as a result of section 40A above or otherwise),

must be allocated to relevant periods in accordance with this section.

(2) Subsection (1) above does not apply if an election under section 40D below has effect with respect to the expenditure.

(3) In this section "relevant period" means—

    (*a*) a period for which the accounts of the trade or business concerned are made up, or

    (*b*) if no accounts of the trade or business concerned are made up for a period—

        (i) if the profits or gains accrue to a company within the charge to corporation tax, the accounting period of the company;

        (ii) in any other case, the period the profits or gains of which are taken into account in assessing the income of the trade or business for a year of assessment.

(4) The amount of expenditure falling within subsection (1) above which falls to be allocated to any relevant period is so much as is just and reasonable, having regard to—

    (*a*) the amount of that expenditure which remains unallocated at the beginning of that period,

    (*b*) the proportion which the estimated value of the master version of the film which is realised in that period (whether by way of income or otherwise) bears to the aggregate of the value so realised and the estimated remaining value of the master version at the end of that period, and

    (*c*) the need to bring the whole of the expenditure falling within subsection (1) above into account over the time during which the value of the master version is expected to be realised.

(5) In addition to any expenditure which is allocated to a relevant period in accordance with subsection (4) above, if a claim is made, there must also be allocated to that period so much of the unallocated expenditure as is specified in the claim and does not exceed the difference between—

    (*a*) the amount allocated to that period in accordance with subsection (4) above, and

    (*b*) the value of the master version of the film which is realised in that period (whether by way of income or otherwise).

(6) A claim under subsection (5) above must be made—

    (*a*) for the purposes of income tax, on or before the first anniversary of the 31st January next following the year of assessment in which ends the relevant period mentioned in that subsection;

    (*b*) for the purposes of corporation tax, not later than two years after the end of the relevant period to which the claim relates.

(7) In subsection (5) above "the unallocated expenditure", in relation to a relevant period, is any expenditure falling within subsection (1) above—

    (*a*) which does not fall to be allocated to that period in accordance with subsection (4) above, and

    (*b*) which has not been allocated to any earlier relevant period in accordance with subsection (4) or (5) above.

40C Cases where section 40B does not apply

(1) To the extent that a deduction has been made in respect of any expenditure for a relevant period under section 42 below—

    (*a*) that expenditure must not be allocated under section 40B above, and

    (*b*) no other expenditure incurred on the production or acquisition of the master version of the film is to be allocated under section 40B above to the relevant period.

(2) Section 40B above does not apply to the profits of a trade in which the master version of the film constitutes trading stock, as defined by section 100(2) of the Taxes Act 1988.

40D Election for sections 40A and 40B not to apply

(1) Sections 40A and 40B above do not apply to expenditure—

    (*a*) in relation to which an election is made under this section, and

    (*b*) which meets the conditions in subsection (2) below.

(2) The conditions are that—

    (*a*) the expenditure is incurred—

(i) by a person who carries on a trade or business which consists of or includes the exploitation of master versions of films, and

(ii) on the production or acquisition of a master version of a film,

(b) the master version is certified by the Secretary of State under paragraph 3 of Schedule 1 to the Films Act 1985 as a qualifying film, tape or disc for the purposes of this section, and

(c) the value of the master version is expected to be realisable over a period of not less than two years.

(3) An election under this section—

(a) must relate to all expenditure incurred (or to be incurred) on the production or acquisition of the master version in question,

(b) must be made by giving notice to the Inland Revenue, in such form as the Board of Inland Revenue may determine, and

(c) is irrevocable.

(4) Notice under subsection (3)(b) above must be given—

(a) for the purposes of income tax, on or before the first anniversary of the 31st January next following the year of assessment in which ends the relevant period in which the master version of the film is completed;

(b) for the purposes of corporation tax, not later than two years after the end of the relevant period in which the master version of the film is completed.

(5) In subsection (4) above "relevant period" has the same meaning as in section 40B above.

(6) For the purposes of subsection (4) above, the master version of a film is completed—

(a) at the time when it is first in a form in which it can reasonably be regarded as ready for copies of it to be made and distributed for presentation to the public, or

(b) if the expenditure in question was incurred on the acquisition of the master version and it was acquired after the time mentioned in paragraph (a) above, at the time it was acquired.

(7) An election may not be made under this section in relation to expenditure on a master version of a film if a claim has been made in respect of any of that expenditure under section 41 or 42 below."

Former enactment—CAA 1990 s 68(1)–(10).

Section 41 (relief for preliminary expenditure)

83 In subsection (1)(c), for "section 68(9) of the 1990 Act" substitute "section 40D above".

Section 42 (relief for production or acquisition expenditure)

84—(1) In subsection (1)(b)—

(a) for "subsections (3) to (6) of section 68 of the 1990 Act" substitute "section 40B above", and

(b) for "subsection (9) of that section" substitute "section 40D above".

(2) In subsection (4)(c), for "section 68(3) to (6) of the 1990 Act, section" substitute "section 40B or".

(3) In subsection (7), for "section 68(3) to (6) of the 1990 Act" substitute "section 40B above".

Section 43 (interpretation of sections 41 and 42)

85 In subsection (1)—

(a) for "41 and 42" substitute "40A to 42",

(b) for "section 68(10) of the 1990 Act" substitute "section 40A(4) above",

(c) for "section 68 of the 1990 Act", in each place where it occurs, substitute "section 40D above",

(d) for "section 68(3) of the 1990 Act" substitute "section 40B(3) above", and

(e) omit the definition of "the 1990 Act".

Schedule 10 (furnished accommodation)

86—(1) In paragraph 9(3)—

(a) for "section 24 of the Capital Allowances Act 1990" substitute "section 55 of the Capital Allowances Act ", and

(b) for "machinery and plant" substitute "plant or machinery".

(2) In paragraph 9(5)—

(a) for "section 24 of the Capital Allowances Act 1990" substitute "section 55 of the Capital Allowances Act ", and

(b) for "machinery and plant" substitute "plant or machinery".

(3) In paragraph 11(6)—

(*a*) for "section 24 of the Capital Allowances Act 1990" substitute "section 55 of the Capital Allowances Act ", and

(*b*) for "machinery and plant" substitute "plant or machinery".

Schedule 17 (Northern Ireland electricity)

87—(1) In paragraph 5(4)—

(*a*) for "section 11 of the Capital Allowances Act 1990 (long leases)" substitute "section 290 of the Capital Allowances Act 2001 (election to treat grant of lease exceeding 50 years as sale)",

(*b*) for "long lease within the meaning" substitute "lease which satisfies the condition in subsection (1)(*c*) ",

(*c*) in paragraph (*a*), for "section 8" substitute "Chapter 8 of Part 3",

(*d*) in paragraph (*b*), for "section 11(6)(*a*)" substitute "section 291(1)",

(*e*) for "sections 157 and 158" substitute "sections 567 to 570", and

(*f*) for "section 11" substitute "section 290".

(2) In paragraph 5(5)—

(*a*) for "paragraphs (*a*) and (*b*) of subsection (1) of section 55 of the Capital Allowances Act 1990 (expenditure incurred by incoming lessee: transfer of allowances)" substitute "section 183(1)(*a*) and (*b*) of the Capital Allowances Act (incoming lessee where lessor entitled to allowances)",

(*b*) in paragraph (*a*) for "Part II of that Act" substitute "Part 2 of that Act",

(*c*) after that paragraph insert "and", and

(*d*) omit paragraph (*c*) and the word "and" before it.

(3) In paragraph 6(1), for "section 11 of the Capital Allowances Act 1990" substitute "section 290 of the Capital Allowances Act 2001".

(4) In paragraph 6(4), for "section 55 of the Capital Allowances Act 1990" substitute "section 183 of the Capital Allowances Act 2001".

THE FINANCE ACT 1993 (C 34)

Section 92 (the basic rule: sterling to be used)

88 In subsection (2)—

(*a*) for "section 28 or 61(1) of the Capital Allowances Act 1990", substitute "section 19 or 253 of the Capital Allowances Act", and

(*b*) for "section 28 or 61(1) of that Act" substitute "section 19 or 253 of that Act".

Section 93 (use of currency other than sterling)

89 In subsection (5), for "section 22B, 34, 35, 38C, 38D or 79A of the Capital Allowances Act 1990" substitute "section 578A(2) or (3) of the Taxes Act 1988 or section 43(3), 74(2), 75(1), 76(2), (3) or (4), 99(1), (2) or (3) or 208(1) of the Capital Allowances Act".

THE AGRICULTURE ACT 1993 (C 37)

Schedule 2 (provisions relating to carrying out approved schemes or reorganisation)

90 In paragraph 19(4) and (5)(*b*), for "the Capital Allowances Act 1990" substitute "the Capital Allowances Act 2001".

THE FINANCE ACT 1994 (C 9)

Schedule 24 (provisions relating to the Railways Act 1993)

91—(1) In paragraph 1(1)—

(*a*) omit the definition of "the Allowances Act",

(*b*) after the definition of "the Board" insert—

""the Capital Allowances Act" means the Capital Allowances Act 2001 and includes, where the context admits, enactments which under the Taxes Act 1988 are to be treated as contained in the Capital Allowances Act 2001;", and

(*c*) in the definition of "fixture", for "Chapter VI of Part II of the Allowances Act" substitute "Chapter 14 of Part 2 of the Capital Allowances Act".

(2) In paragraph 1(4)(*c*), for "the Capital Allowances Acts" substitute "the Capital Allowances Act".

(3) In paragraph 20(1) and (2)(*a*), for "the Capital Allowances Acts" substitute "the Capital Allowances Act".

(4) In paragraph 20(8), for "section 77 of the Allowances Act (successions to trades: connected persons)" substitute "sections 266 and 267 of the Capital Allowances Act (election where predecessor and successor are connected persons)".

(5) In paragraph 21(1), for "the Capital Allowances Acts" substitute "the Capital Allowances Act".

(6) In paragraph 21(2)—

(a) in paragraph (a), for "subsection (6) of section 21 of the Allowances Act (transfer of industrial buildings or structures to be deemed to be sale at market price)" substitute "section 573 of the Capital Allowances Act (transfers treated as sales) as it applies for the purposes of Part 3 of that Act",

(b) in paragraph (b), for "that subsection" substitute "that section" and for "the Capital Allowances Acts" substitute "that Act", and

(c) for "by virtue of that subsection or any other provision of those Acts), sections 157 and 158 of the Allowances Act" substitute "under that section or any other provision of the Capital Allowances Act), sections 567 to 570 of that Act".

(7) In paragraph 21(3)—

(a) for "the Capital Allowances Acts" substitute "the Capital Allowances Act",

(b) for "those Acts" substitute "that Act",

(c) in paragraph (a), for "section 26(1) or 59 of the Allowances Act" substitute "section 61(2) to (4), 72(3) to (5), 171, 196 or 423 of the Capital Allowances Act", and

(d) in paragraph (c), for "section 54" substitute "sections 181(1) and 182(1)".

(8) In paragraph 22(2)—

(a) for "building or structure" (in both places) substitute "building",

(b) for "Part I of the Allowances Act" substitute "Part 3 of the Capital Allowances Act", and

(c) for "sections 157 and 158" substitute "sections 567 to 570".

(9) In paragraph 22(3)—

(a) for "machinery or plant" (in the first and second places) substitute "plant or machinery",

(b) for "section 24 of the Allowances Act (balancing adjustments) shall, subject to section 26(2) and (3) of that Act (disposal value of machinery or plant not to exceed capital expenditure incurred on its provision)" substitute "section 55 of the Capital Allowances Act (determination of entitlement or liability) shall, subject to section 62 of that Act (general limit on amount of disposal value)", and

(c) for "the Capital Allowances Acts" substitute "the Capital Allowances Act".

(10) In paragraph 22(4)—

(a) for "section 57(2) of the Allowances Act" substitute "section 188 of the Capital Allowances Act",

(b) for "section 24 of that Act shall, subject to section 26(2) and (3)" substitute "section 55 of that Act shall, subject to section 62",

(c) in paragraph (a), for "Part II" substitute "Part 2 ", and

(d) for "the Capital Allowances Acts" substitute "the Capital Allowances Act".

Schedule 25 (Northern Ireland Airports Limited)

92—(1) In paragraph 5(2), for "the 1990 Act" (in both places) substitute "the Capital Allowances Act 2001".

(2) In paragraph 5(3)—

(a) omit the definition of "the 1990 Act",

(b) for "section 4 of the 1990 Act" substitute "Chapter 7 of Part 3 of the Capital Allowances Act 2001", and

(c) for "section 20 of the 1990 Act" substitute "Chapter 3 of Part 3 of the Capital Allowances Act 2001".

THE COAL INDUSTRY ACT 1994 (C 21)

Schedule 4 (taxation provisions)

93—(1) In paragraph 1(2)—

(a) after the definition of "the 1988 Act" insert—

""the Capital Allowances Act" includes, where the context admits, enactments which under the 1988 Act are to be treated as contained in the Capital Allowances Act,", and

(b) in the definition of "fixture", for "Chapter VI of Part II of the 1990 Act" substitute "Chapter 14 of Part 2 of the Capital Allowances Act".

(2) In paragraph 19(1) and (2), for "the Capital Allowances Acts" substitute "the Capital Allowances Act".

(3) In paragraph 19(3)(b) and (4)(b), for "section 145(2) of the 1990 Act" substitute "section 260 of the Capital Allowances Act".

(4) In paragraph 20(1), for "the Capital Allowances Acts" substitute "the Capital Allowances Act".

(5) In paragraph 20(2)—

(*a*) in paragraph (*a*), for "subsection (6) of section 21 of the 1990 Act (transfer of industrial buildings or structures to be deemed to be sale at market price)" substitute "section 573 of the Capital Allowances Act (transfers treated as sales) as it applies for the purposes of Part 3 of that Act",

(*b*) in paragraph (*b*), for "that subsection (6)" substitute "that section" and for "the Capital Allowances Acts" substitute "that Act",

(*c*) for "that subsection" substitute "that section", and

(*d*) for "those Acts), sections 157 and 158 of the 1990 Act" substitute "that Act), sections 567 to 570 of that Act".

(6) In paragraph 20(3)—

(*a*) for "the Capital Allowances Acts" substitute "the Capital Allowances Act",

(*b*) for "those Acts" substitute "that Act",

(*c*) in paragraph (*a*), for "section 26(1) or 59 of the 1990 Act" substitute "section 61(2) to (4), 72(3) to (5), 171, 196 or 423 of the Capital Allowances Act", and

(*d*) in paragraph (*c*), for "section 54" substitute "sections 181(1) and 182(1)".

(7) In paragraph 20(4), for "under section 99 of the 1990 Act (disposal receipts in relation to mineral extraction allowances)" substitute "in accordance with sections 421 to 425 of the Capital Allowances Act (mineral extraction allowances: disposal receipts)".

(8) In paragraph 20(5)—

(*a*) in paragraph (*a*), for "Part V of the 1990 Act (agricultural buildings etc)" substitute "Part 4 of the Capital Allowances Act (agricultural buildings allowances)" and for "section 129(2)" substitute "section 382",

(*b*) in paragraph (*b*), for "the Capital Allowances Acts" substitute "that Act", and

(*c*) for "section 128(2) of that Act (calculation of balancing allowance or charge)" substitute "section 385 of the Capital Allowances Act (calculation of balancing adjustment)".

(9) In paragraph 20(6)—

(*a*) in paragraph (*a*), for "relevant event for the purposes of section 138 of the 1990 Act (assets representing allowable scientific research expenditure ceasing to belong to traders)" substitute "disposal event for the purposes of Chapter 3 of Part 6 of the Capital Allowances Act (research and development allowances: allowances and charges)",

(*b*) in paragraph (*b*), for "subsection (2) of that section" substitute "that Chapter", and

(*c*) for "that section" substitute "that Chapter".

(10) In paragraph 20(7)—

(*a*) for "the 1990 Act" substitute "the Capital Allowances Act", and

(*b*) for "section 157(1)(*a*)" substitute "section 568(1)(*a*)".

(11) In paragraph 21(2), for "the Capital Allowances Acts" substitute "the Capital Allowances Act".

(12) In paragraph 21(3)—

(*a*) for "Chapter VI of Part II of the 1990 Act" substitute "Chapter 14 of Part 2 of the Capital Allowances Act",

(*b*) for "the Capital Allowances Acts" substitute "the Capital Allowances Act",

(*c*) for "they did" substitute "it did", and

(*d*) for "those Acts" substitute "that Act".

(13) In paragraph 21(4)—

(*a*) for "section 61 of the 1990 Act" substitute "section 70 of the Capital Allowances Act",

(*b*) for "the Capital Allowances Acts" substitute "the Capital Allowances Act",

(*c*) for "machinery or plant" (in each place) substitute "plant or machinery".

(14) In paragraph 22, for "Part II of the 1990 Act" substitute "Part 2 of the Capital Allowances Act".

THE ATOMIC ENERGY AUTHORITY ACT 1995 (C 37)

Schedule 3 (taxation provisions)

94—(1) In paragraph 14(1), for the definition of "the Capital Allowances Acts" substitute—

"'the Capital Allowances Act' means the Capital Allowances Act 2001 and includes, where the context admits, enactments which under the 1988 Act are to be treated as contained in the Capital Allowances Act 2001."

(2) In paragraph 14(3), for "Capital Allowances Acts" substitute "Capital Allowances Act".

(3) For paragraph 15 substitute—

"Industrial buildings

15 Where any transfer effected by a transfer scheme is a relevant event for the purposes of section 311 of the Capital Allowances Act, the Secretary of State may for the purposes of that section by order make provision specifying the values to be assigned to RQE and B in relation to that event."

(4) In paragraph 16—

(*a*) for the heading substitute "Plant and machinery", and

(*b*) for "Part II of the Capital Allowances Act 1990 (capital allowances in respect of machinery and plant)" substitute "Part 2 of the Capital Allowances Act (plant and machinery allowances)".

(5) For paragraph 17 substitute—

"Research and development

17—(1) For the purposes of Part 6 of the Capital Allowances Act (research and development allowances) a successor company in which an asset representing allowable research and development expenditure is vested in accordance with a transfer scheme shall be treated as having incurred, on the date on which the transfer scheme comes into force, capital expenditure of the prescribed amount on the research and development in question; and that research and development shall be taken to have been directly undertaken by the successor company or on its behalf.

(2) In sub-paragraph (1) above "allowable research and development expenditure" means capital expenditure incurred by the Authority on research and development directly undertaken by the Authority or on their behalf.

(3) In this paragraph—

"asset" includes part of an asset;

"research and development" has the same meaning as in Part 6 of the Capital Allowances Act;

and references to expenditure incurred on research and development shall be construed in accordance with section 438 of that Act."

(6) In paragraph 18(1), for "section 520 of the 1988 Act (allowances for expenditure on purchase of patent rights)" substitute "section 468 of the Capital Allowances Act (qualifying trade expenditure)".

(7) In paragraph 18(2), for "section 533 of the 1988 Act" substitute "section 464(2) of the Capital Allowances Act".

(8) In paragraph 19(1), for "section 530 of the 1988 Act (disposal of know-how)" substitute "section 454 of the Capital Allowances Act (qualifying expenditure)".

(9) In paragraph 19(2), after "Subsections (2) and (7) of section 531 of the 1988 Act (provisions supplementary to section 530)" insert "and subsections (2) and (3) of section 455 of the Capital Allowances Act (excluded expenditure)".

(10) In paragraph 19(3), for "section 533(7) of the 1988 Act" substitute "section 452(2) of the Capital Allowances Act".

(11) In paragraph 20, for "Part II of the Capital Allowances Act 1990 (machinery and plant)" substitute "Parts 2, 7 and 8 of the Capital Allowances Act (plant and machinery, know-how and patents)".

(12) In paragraph 22, for "Capital Allowances Acts" substitute "Capital Allowances Act".

THE FINANCE ACT 1996 (C 8)

Section 151 (benefits under pilot schemes)

95 In subsection (2), for "section 153 of the Capital Allowances Act 1990 (subsidies etc)" substitute "section 532 of the Capital Allowances Act (exclusion of expenditure met by contributions)".

Schedule 8 (loan relationships)

96 In paragraph 3(6)(*c*)(i), for "section 28 of the Capital Allowances Act 1990 (machinery and plant of investment companies)" substitute "Part 2 of the Capital Allowances Act (plant and machinery allowances)".

THE BROADCASTING ACT 1996 (C 55)

Schedule 7 (transfer schemes relating to BBC transmission network: taxation provisions)

97—(1) in paragraph 1(1), omit the definition of "the Allowances Act" and for the definition of "the Capital Allowances Acts" substitute—

""the Capital Allowances Act" means the Capital Allowances Act 2001 and includes, where the context admits, enactments which under the Taxes Act 1988 are to be treated as contained in the Capital Allowances Act 2001."

(2) In paragraph 1(3)(*b*), for "the Capital Allowances Acts" substitute "the Capital Allowances Act".

(3) In paragraph 12(3)—

    (a) for "the Capital Allowances Acts" substitute "the Capital Allowances Act", and

    (b) for "those Acts" substitute "that Act".

(4) In paragraph 13(1)—

    (a) in the heading, omit "and structures", and

    (b) for "Part I of the Allowances Act (industrial buildings and structures)" substitute "Part 3 of the Capital Allowances Act (industrial buildings allowances)".

(5) In paragraph 13(2), for "Part I of the Allowances Act" substitute "Part 3 of the Capital Allowances Act".

(6) In paragraph 14(1)—

    (a) in the heading, for "machinery and plant" substitute "plant and machinery", and

    (b) for "Part II of the Allowances Act (capital allowances in respect of machinery and plant)" substitute "Part 2 of the Capital Allowances Act (plant and machinery allowances)".

(7) In paragraph 15(2)—

    (a) for "paragraphs (a) and (b) of subsection (1) of section 55 of the Allowances Act (expenditure incurred by incoming lessee: transfer of allowances)" substitute "section 183(1)(a) and (b) of the Capital Allowances Act (incoming lessee where lessor entitled to allowances)",

    (b) for "Part II" substitute "Part 2", and

    (c) for "subsection (4)(a)" substitute "subsection (1)(d)".

(8) In paragraph 15(3)—

    (a) for "paragraphs (a), (c) and (d) of section 56 of the Allowances Act (expenditure incurred by incoming lessee: lessor not entitled to allowances)" substitute "section 184(1)(a) to (c) of the Capital Allowances Act (incoming lessee where lessor not entitled to allowances)", and

    (b) for "Part II" substitute "Part 2".

(9) In paragraph 16, for "Part II of the Allowances Act (machinery and plant)" substitute "Part 2 of the Capital Allowances Act (plant and machinery allowances)".

(10) For paragraph 17 substitute—

"Capital allowances: agricultural buildings allowances

17—(1) This paragraph applies where there is a relevant transfer of property which is the relevant interest in relation to any expenditure for which the BBC would be entitled to an allowance (other than a balancing allowance) under Part 4 of the Capital Allowances Act (agricultural buildings allowances).

(2) Where this paragraph applies, then, as respects the transferee—

    (a) his acquisition of the relevant interest shall be treated for the purposes of Part 4 of the Capital Allowances Act as a balancing event within subsection (2)(a) of section 381 (regardless of the lack of any election); and

    (b) section 376(2) shall apply as if—

        (i) the value to be assigned to RQE (residue of qualifying expenditure immediately after event) were the prescribed amount; and

        (ii) the value to be assigned to B (remaining writing-down period) were such as the Secretary of state may by order specify.

(3) This paragraph shall not have effect in relation to any property if paragraph 12(3) has effect in relation to it."

THE FINANCE ACT 1997 (C 16)

Schedule 12 (leasing arrangements: finance leases and loans)

98—(1) For paragraph 11(3)(a) to (c) substitute—

    "(a) Part 2 of the Capital Allowances Act (plant and machinery allowances),

    (b) Part 5 of that Act (mineral extraction allowances), or

    (c) Part 8 of that Act (patent allowances)".

(2) In paragraph 11(8), for "the Capital Allowances Acts" substitute "the Capital Allowances Act" and omit "or its basis period".

(3) For paragraph 11(9)(a) and (b) substitute "section 40B(1) or 42 of the Finance (No 2) Act 1992 (expenditure in connection with films etc),".

(4) In paragraph 11(10), for "under section 68(8) of the Capital Allowances Act 1990" substitute "under section 40A(2) of the Finance (No 2) Act 1992".

(5) In paragraph 11(13), for "section 154 of the Capital Allowances Act 1990" substitute "sections 537 to 542 of the Capital Allowances Act".

(6) For paragraph 11(14) substitute—

    "(14) In sub-paragraph (8) above—

"the Capital Allowances Act" includes enactments which under the Taxes Act 1988 are to be treated as contained in the Capital Allowances Act;

"chargeable period" has the meaning given by section 6 of the Capital Allowances Act.".

(7) Omit paragraph 11(15).

THE FINANCE (NO 2) ACT 1997 (C 58)
Section 48 (films: relief for production or acquisition expenditure)

99—(1) In subsection (1), for "section 68(3) to (6) of the 1990 Act, section" substitute "section 40B or".

(2) For subsection (9) substitute—

"(9) Subsections (1) to (5) of section 5 of the Capital Allowances Act 2001 (when capital expenditure is incurred) apply for determining when for the purposes of this section any expenditure is incurred as they apply for determining when for the purposes of that Act any capital expenditure is incurred, but as if, in subsection (6) of that section, "at an earlier time" were substituted for "in an earlier chargeable period".".

THE FINANCE ACT 1998 (C 36)
Section 117 (company tax returns, assessments and related matters)

100—(1) In subsection (1), at the end of paragraph (*b*), insert "and".

(2) For subsection (1)(*d*) and the word "and" before it substitute—

"and also make provision in relation to claims for allowances under the Capital Allowances Act."

Section 118 (claims for income tax purposes)

101 In subsection (5)(*b*), for "the Capital Allowances Act 1990" substitute "the Capital Allowances Act".

Schedule 6 (adjustment on change of accounting basis)

102 *In paragraph 4(4), for "the Capital Allowances Act 1990" substitute "the Capital Allowances Act".*

Amendment—This paragraph repealed by FA 2002 s 141, Sch 40 Pt 3(8) with effect in accordance with FA 2002 s 64(6), Sch 22 paras 16, 17.

Schedule 18 (company tax returns, assessments and related matters)

103—(1) For paragraph 78 (application of Part IX of the Schedule) substitute—

"78 This Part of this Schedule applies to claims for allowances under the Capital Allowances Act which—

(*a*) are made for corporation tax purposes, and

(*b*) are required under section 3 of that Act to be included in a tax return."

(2) For paragraph 79(1) (claim to be included in company tax return) substitute—

"79—(1) A claim for capital allowances must be included in the claimant company's company tax return for the accounting period for which the claim is made."

THE FINANCE ACT 1999 (C 16)
Schedule 6 (tax treatment of receipts by way of reverse premium)

104 In paragraph 5, for "section 153 of the Capital Allowances Act 1990 (subsidies, contributions, etc)" substitute "section 532 of the Capital Allowances Act (the general rule excluding contributions)".

THE GREATER LONDON AUTHORITY ACT 1999 (C 29)
Schedule 33 (taxation)

105—(1) In paragraph 4(3), for "the Capital Allowances Acts" substitute "the Capital Allowances Act 2001".

(2) In paragraph 4(8), for "section 77 of the Capital Allowances Act 1990 (successions to trades: connected persons)" substitute "section 266 of the Capital Allowances Act 2001 (election where predecessor and successor are connected persons)".

(3) For paragraph 4(9) substitute—

''(9) Except as provided by this paragraph, a qualifying transfer in relation to which this paragraph applies shall be taken for the purposes of the Capital Allowances Act 2001 not to give rise to—

(*a*) any writing-down allowances, balancing allowances or balancing charges under Chapter 5 of Part 2 of that Act (plant and machinery allowances and charges),

(*b*) any disposal value being treated as received for the purposes of that Chapter,

(*c*) any qualifying expenditure being treated as incurred for the purposes of that Chapter, or

(*d*) any writing-down allowances, balancing allowances or balancing charges under Part 3 of that Act (industrial buildings allowances).

(10) In this paragraph and paragraph 10 below ''the Capital Allowances Act 2001'' includes, where the context admits, enactments which under the Taxes Act 1988 are to be treated as contained in the Capital Allowances Act 2001.''

(4) In paragraph 10(3), for ''the Capital Allowances Acts'' substitute ''the Capital Allowances Act 2001''.

(5) In paragraph 10(9), for ''section 77 of the Capital Allowances Act 1990 (successions to trades: connected persons)'' substitute ''section 266 of the Capital Allowances Act 2001 (election where predecessor and successor are connected persons)''.

(6) For paragraph 10(10) substitute—

''(10) Except as provided by this paragraph, a relevant transfer in relation to which this paragraph applies shall be taken for the purposes of the Capital Allowances Act 2001 not to give rise to—

(*a*) any writing-down allowances, balancing allowances or balancing charges under Chapter 5 of Part 2 of that Act (plant and machinery allowances and charges),

(*b*) any disposal value being treated as received for the purposes of that Chapter,

(*c*) any qualifying expenditure being treated as incurred for the purposes of that Chapter, or

(*d*) any writing-down allowances, balancing allowances or balancing charges under Part 3 of that Act (industrial buildings allowances).''

(7) In paragraph 11(2)—

(*a*) for ''Part I of the Capital Allowances Act 1990'' substitute ''Part 3 of the Capital Allowances Act 2001'', and

(*b*) for ''Chapter VI of Part II'' substitute ''Chapter 14 of Part 2''.

(8) In paragraph 11(4)—

(*a*) for ''Part I of the Capital Allowances Act 1990'' substitute ''Part 3 of the Capital Allowances Act 2001'',

(*b*) for ''Chapter VI of Part II of the Capital Allowances Act 1990'' substitute ''Chapter 14 of Part 2 of the Capital Allowances Act 2001'', and

(*c*) for ''section 51(3)'' substitute ''section 175(1)''.

(9) In paragraph 12(1)—

(*a*) omit paragraph (*a*),

(*b*) for ''section 52(2)'' substitute ''section 176(2) or (3)'', and

(*c*) for ''section 60'' substitute ''sections 67 and 68.''

(10) In paragraph 12(2)—

(*a*) for ''Part II of the Capital Allowances Act 1990'' substitute ''Part 2 of the Capital Allowances Act 2001'', and

(*b*) for ''section 26(1)(*f*)'' substitute ''item 7 in the Table in section 61(2)''.

THE FINANCE ACT 2000 (C 17)

Section 105 (corporation tax: use of currencies other than sterling)

106 In subsection (3), for ''any of the items referred to in section 25(1) of the Capital Allowances Act 1990 which fall to be taken into account'' substitute ''any amount falls to be taken into account under Chapter 5 of Part 2 of the Capital Allowances Act as available qualifying expenditure''.

Schedule 12 (provision of services through an intermediary)

107 In paragraph 7, in the paragraph headed ''Step Four'', for ''section 27 of the Capital Allowances Act 1990 (plant and machinery: extension of allowances to employments etc)'' substitute ''Part 2 of the Capital Allowances Act ''.

Schedule 22 (tonnage tax)

108—(1) In paragraph 41(4), for ''section 82A of the Capital Allowances Act 1990'' substitute ''section 219 of the Capital Allowances Act 2001''.

(2) For paragraph 69(2) substitute—

''(2) In this paragraph ''unrelieved qualifying expenditure'' has the same meaning as in Chapter 5 of Part 2 of the Capital Allowances Act 2001.''

(3) In paragraph 69(4), for paragraphs (*a*) and (*b*) substitute "section 130 of the Capital Allowances Act 2001 (notice postponing first-year or writing-down allowance)".

(4) For paragraph 70(2) substitute—

"(2) Sections 61(1)(*e*), 206(3) and 207 of the Capital Allowances Act 2001 (effect of use partly for qualifying activity and partly for other purposes) apply as follows—

(*a*) references to a qualifying activity shall be read as not including references to the tonnage tax trade, and

(*b*) references to purposes other than those of a qualifying activity shall be read as including references to the purposes of the tonnage tax trade."

(5) In paragraph 72(1), for "sections 33A to 33F of the Capital Allowances Act 1990" substitute "sections 135 to 156 of the Capital Allowances Act 2001".

(6) For paragraph 73(2) substitute—

"(2) Sections 206(1), (2) and (4) and 207 of the Capital Allowances Act 2001 (operation of single asset pool for mixed use assets) apply as follows—

(*a*) references to a qualifying activity shall be read as not including references to the tonnage tax trade, and

(*b*) references to purposes other than those of a qualifying activity shall be read as including references to the purposes of the tonnage tax trade."

(7) For paragraph 75(2) and (3) substitute—

"(2) If the asset was acquired before entry into tonnage tax, section 61(1)(*e*) of the Capital Allowances Act 2001 applies (disposal event if plant or machinery begins to be used wholly or partly for purposes other than those of the qualifying activity), but reading the reference in that provision to the qualifying activity as a reference to the tonnage tax trade.

(3) If the asset was acquired after entry into tonnage tax and begins to be used wholly or partly for the purposes of a qualifying activity carried on by the company, section 13 of the Capital Allowances Act 2001 (use for qualifying activity of plant or machinery provided for other purposes) applies as follows—

(*a*) references to purposes which were not those of any qualifying activity shall be read as including references to the purposes of the tonnage tax trade, and

(*b*) references to the qualifying activity carried on by him shall be read as not including references to the tonnage tax trade."

(8) For paragraph 76(2) substitute—

"(2) Sections 61(1)(*e*), 206(3) and 207 of the Capital Allowances Act 2001 (effect of use partly for qualifying activity and partly for other purposes) apply as follows—

(*a*) references to a qualifying activity shall be read as not including references to the tonnage tax trade, and

(*b*) references to purposes other than those of a qualifying activity shall be read as including references to the purposes of the tonnage tax trade."

(9) In paragraph 77(2), for "Part II of the Capital Allowances Act 1990" substitute "Part 2 of the Capital Allowances Act 2001" and for "references in that Part of that Act to a trade" substitute "references in that Part of that Act to a qualifying activity".

(10) In paragraph 80(2), for "section 24(6)(*c*)(i) to (iii) of the Capital Allowances Act 1990" substitute "section 61(1)(*a*) to (*d*) of the Capital Allowances Act 2001".

(11) In paragraph 80(4), for "Sections 33A to 33F of the Capital Allowances Act 1990" substitute "Sections 135 to 156 of the Capital Allowances Act 2001".

(12) For paragraph 82 substitute—

"**82** If any identifiable part of a building or structure is used for the purposes of a company's tonnage tax trade, that part is treated for the purposes of Part 3 of the Capital Allowances Act 2001 as used otherwise than as an industrial building."

(13) In paragraph 83(1), for "disposal event occurs in relation to an industrial building or structure" substitute "balancing event occurs in relation to an industrial building".

(14) For the first sentence of paragraph 83(2) substitute—

"(2) A "balancing event" means an event by reason of which the company is required by Part 3 of the Capital Allowances Act 2001 to bring into account any proceeds."

(15) For paragraph 83(3)(*a*) substitute—

"(*a*) the proceeds to be brought into account in respect of the industrial building are limited to the market value of the relevant interest when the company entered tonnage tax; and".

(16) In paragraph 84(1), omit "or structure".

(17) In paragraph 84(2), for "The provisions of section 8(1) to (12) of the Capital Allowances Act 1990 (writing off of expenditure and meaning of "residue of expenditure) substitute "Section 313 and Chapter 8 of Part 3 of the Capital Allowances Act 2001 (meaning of "residue of qualifying expenditure" and writing off qualifying expenditure)".

(18) In paragraph 85(1), for "Part II of the Capital Allowances Act 1990 (plant and machinery)" substitute "Part 2 of the Capital Allowances Act 2001 (plant and machinery allowances)".

(19) In paragraph 86(1), for "Part I of the Capital Allowances Act 1990 (industrial buildings)" substitute "Part 3 of the Capital Allowances Act 2001 (industrial buildings allowances)".

(20) For paragraph 87(1)(b) substitute—

"(b) the expenditure shall be disregarded for the purposes of calculating the person's entitlement to a writing-down allowance or balancing allowance or liability to a balancing charge."

(21) In paragraph 88(1), for the definitions of "capital allowance" and "qualifying activity" substitute—

""capital allowance" means any allowance under the Capital Allowances Act 2001;
"qualifying activity" means any activity in respect of which a person may be entitled to a capital allowance;".

(22) For paragraph 88(2) and (3) substitute—

"(2) In this Part of this Schedule any reference to pooling or to single asset pools, class pools or the main pool shall be construed in accordance with sections 53 and 54 of the Capital Allowances Act 2001."

(23) In paragraph 88(4), for "the Capital Allowances Act 1990" substitute "the Capital Allowances Act 2001".

(24) In paragraph 89(1), for "Part II of the Capital Allowances Act 1990" substitute "Part 2 of the Capital Allowances Act 2001".

(25) In paragraph 89(2), for "section 82A of the 1990 Act" substitute "section 219 of that Act".

(26) In paragraph 92(4), for "belonging to him for the purposes of Part II of the Capital Allowances Act 1990" substitute "owned by him for the purposes of Part 2 of the Capital Allowances Act 2001".

(27) In paragraph 94(4), for "Part II of the Capital Allowances Act 1990" substitute "Part 2 of the Capital Allowances Act 2001".

(28) In paragraph 96(2), for "the Capital Allowances Act 1990" substitute "the Capital Allowances Act 2001".

(29) In paragraph 100(2)(b)(ii), for "section 30(1)(a) or (c) of the Capital Allowances Act 1990" substitute "section 130 of the Capital Allowances Act 2001".

(30) In paragraph 100(3), for "the balance that would otherwise have been carried forward under Part II of the Capital Allowances Act 1990" substitute "the unrelieved qualifying expenditure that would otherwise have been carried forward under Chapter 5 of Part 2 of the Capital Allowances Act 2001".

(31) In paragraph 110(2), for "the provisions of Part II of the Capital Allowances Act 1990 apply" substitute "Part 2 of the Capital Allowances Act 2001 applies".

(32) In paragraph 110(4)—

(a) for "Part II of the Capital Allowances Act 1990" substitute "Part 2 of the Capital Allowances Act 2001", and
(b) for "section 24(6)(c)" substitute "section 61(1)".

(33) For paragraph 112(3) substitute—

"(3) In this paragraph "unrelieved qualifying expenditure" means the unrelieved qualifying expenditure that would otherwise have been carried forward under Chapter 5 of Part 2 of the Capital Allowances Act 2001."

(34) In paragraph 112(5), for paragraphs (a) and (b) substitute "section 130 of the Capital Allowances Act 2001 (notice postponing first-year or writing-down allowance)".

(35) In paragraph 113(2), for "Part II of the Capital Allowances Act 1990" substitute "Part 2 of the Capital Allowances Act 2001".

(36) In paragraph 135—

(a) for "Part II of the Capital Allowances Act 1990 (plant and machinery)" substitute "Part 2 of the Capital Allowances Act 2001 (plant and machinery allowances)", and
(b) for "unrelieved qualifying expenditure under Part I of that Act (industrial buildings)" substitute "the residue of qualifying expenditure under Part 3 of that Act (industrial buildings allowances)".

THE TRANSPORT ACT 2000 (C 38)

Schedule 26 (transfers: tax)

109—(1) In paragraph 1(1)—

(a) omit the definition of "the 1990 Act",
(b) for the definition of "the Capital Allowances Acts" substitute—

""the Capital Allowances Act'' means the Capital Allowances Act 2001 and includes, where the context admits, enactments which under the 1988 Act are to be treated as contained in the Capital Allowances Act 2001,'', and

(c) in the definition of "fixture", for "Chapter VI of Part II of the 1990 Act" substitute "Chapter 14 of Part 2 of the Capital Allowances Act".

(2) In paragraph 1(3), for "the Capital Allowances Acts" substitute "the Capital Allowances Act".

(3) In paragraph 5(1)(b), for "the Capital Allowances Acts" substitute "the Capital Allowances Act" and for "Part II of the 1990 Act" substitute "Part 2 of that Act".

(4) In paragraph 5(1)(c), for "those Acts" substitute "that Act".

(5) In paragraph 5(2)—

(a) for "those Acts" substitute "the Capital Allowances Act", and
(b) for "section 54 of the 1990 Act" substitute "sections 181(1) and 182(1) of that Act".

(6) In paragraph 6, for "Part II of the 1990 Act" substitute "Part 2 of the Capital Allowances Act".

(7) In paragraph 13(1) and (2)(a), for "the Capital Allowances Acts" substitute "the Capital Allowances Act".

(8) In paragraph 14(1)(c), for "the Capital Allowances Acts" substitute "the Capital Allowances Act".

(9) In paragraph 14(1)(d), for "those Acts" substitute "that Act".

(10) In paragraph 14(2)—

(a) for "those Acts" substitute "the Capital Allowances Act",
(b) in paragraph (a), for "section 26(1) or 59 of the 1990 Act" substitute "section 61(2) to (4), 72(3) to (5), 171, 196 or 423 of that Act", and
(c) in paragraph (d), for "section 54 of the 1990 Act" substitute "sections 181(1) and 182(1) of that Act".

(11) In paragraph 15, for "Part II of the 1990 Act" substitute "Part 2 of the Capital Allowances Act".

(12) In paragraph 21(1), for "Part I of the 1990 Act" substitute "Part 3 of the Capital Allowances Act".

(13) In paragraph 21(4), for "Sections 157 and 158 of that Act (sales between connected persons or without change of control)" substitute "Sections 567 to 570 of that Act (sales treated as being for alternative amount)".

(14) In paragraph 21(5)—

(a) for "machinery or plant" (in both places) substitute "plant or machinery",
(b) for "the Capital Allowances Acts" substitute "the Capital Allowances Act", and
(c) for "section 24 of the 1990 Act (balancing adjustments)" substitute "section 60 of that Act (meaning of "disposal value" and "disposal event")".

(15) In paragraph 21(6), for "section 26(2) and (3) of that Act (disposal value of machinery or plant not to exceed capital expenditure incurred on its provision)" substitute "section 62 of that Act (general limit on amount of disposal value)".

(16) In paragraph 21(7), for "a fixture is treated by section 57(2) of the 1990 Act as ceasing to belong to a person" substitute "a person is treated by section 188 of the Capital Allowances Act as ceasing to own a fixture".

(17) In paragraph 21(8)—

(a) for "section 24 of that Act is, subject to section 26(2) and (3) of that Act" substitute "section 60 of the Capital Allowances Act is, subject to section 62 of that Act", and
(b) for "Part II of that Act" substitute "Part 2 of that Act".

(18) In paragraph 21(9), for "the Capital Allowances Acts" substitute "the Capital Allowances Act".

(19) In paragraph 27(1), for "Part I of the 1990 Act" substitute "Part 3 of the Capital Allowances Act".

(20) In paragraph 27(4), for "Sections 157 and 158 of that Act (sales between connected persons or without change of control)" substitute "Sections 567 to 570 of that Act (sales treated as being for alternative amount)".

(21) In paragraph 27(5)—

(a) for "machinery or plant", in both places where it occurs, substitute "plant or machinery",
(b) for "the Capital Allowances Acts" substitute "the Capital Allowances Act", and
(c) for "section 24 of the 1990 Act (balancing adjustments)" substitute "section 60 of that Act (meaning of "disposal value" and "disposal event")".

(22) In paragraph 27(6), for "section 26(2) and (3) of that Act (disposal value of machinery or plant not to exceed capital expenditure incurred on its provision)" substitute "section 62 of that Act (general limit on amount of disposal value)".

(23) In paragraph 27(7), for ''a fixture is treated by section 57(2) of the 1990 Act as ceasing to belong to a person'' substitute ''a person is treated by section 188 of the Capital Allowances Act as ceasing to own a fixture''.

(24) In paragraph 27(8)—

    (a) for ''section 24 of that Act is, subject to section 26(2) and (3) of that Act'' substitute ''section 60 of the Capital Allowances Act is, subject to section 62 of that Act'', and

    (b) for ''Part II of that Act'' substitute ''Part 2 of that Act''

(25) In paragraph 27(9), for ''the Capital Allowances Acts'' substitute ''the Capital Allowances Act''.

(26) In paragraph 34(1), for ''Part I of the 1990 Act'' substitute ''Part 3 of the Capital Allowances Act''.

(27) In paragraph 34(5), for ''Sections 157 and 158 of that Act (sales between connected persons or without change of control)'' substitute ''Sections 567 to 570 of that Act (sales treated as being for alternative amount)''.

(28) In paragraph 34(6)—

    (a) for ''machinery or plant'' (in both places) substitute ''plant or machinery'',

    (b) for ''the Capital Allowances Acts'' substitute ''the Capital Allowances Act'', and

    (c) for ''section 24 of the 1990 Act (balancing adjustments)'' substitute ''sections 60 of that Act (meaning of ''disposal value'' and ''disposal event'')''.

(29) In paragraph 34(7), for ''section 26(2) and (3) of that Act (disposal value of machinery or plant not to exceed capital expenditure incurred on its provision)'' substitute ''section 62 of that Act (general limit on amount of disposal value)''.

(30) In paragraph 34(8), for ''a fixture is treated by section 57(2) of the 1990 Act as ceasing to belong to a person'' substitute ''a person is treated by section 188 of the Capital Allowances Act as ceasing to own a fixture''.

(31) In paragraph 34(9)—

    (a) for ''section 24 of that Act is, subject to section 26(2) and (3) of that Act'' substitute ''section 60 of the Capital Allowances Act is, subject to section 62 of that Act'', and

    (b) for ''Part II of that Act'' substitute ''Part 2 of that Act''.

(32) In paragraph 34(10), for ''the Capital Allowances Acts'' substitute ''the Capital Allowances Act''.

SCHEDULE 3

TRANSITIONALS AND SAVINGS

Section 579

PART 1

CONTINUITY OF THE LAW

Commentary—*Simon's Direct Tax Service* B2.101B.

1 The repeal of provisions and their enactment in a rewritten form in this Act does not affect the continuity of the law.

2 Paragraph 1—

    (a) does not apply to any change in the law effected by this Act, and

    (b) is subject to paragraph 8.

3 Any subordinate legislation or other thing which—

    (a) has been made or done, or has effect as if made or done, under or for the purposes of a repealed provision, and

    (b) is in force or effective immediately before the commencement of the corresponding rewritten provision,

has effect after that commencement as if made or done under or for the purposes of the rewritten provision.

4 Any reference (express or implied) in any enactment, instrument or document to—

    (a) a rewritten provision, or

    (b) things done or falling to be done under or for the purposes of a rewritten provision,

is to be read as including, in relation to times, circumstances or purposes in relation to which any corresponding repealed provision had effect, a reference to the repealed provision or (as the case may be) things done or falling to be done under or for the purposes of the repealed provision.

5 Any reference (express or implied) in any enactment, instrument or document to—

    (a) a repealed provision, or

    (b) things done or falling to be done under or for the purposes of a repealed provision, is to be read as including, in relation to times, circumstances or purposes in relation to which any corresponding rewritten provision has effect, a reference to the rewritten provision or (as the case may be) things done or falling to be done under or for the purposes of the rewritten provision.

6 Paragraphs 1 to 5 have effect instead of section 17(2) of the Interpretation Act 1978 (but are without prejudice to any other provision of that Act).

7 Paragraphs 4 and 5 apply only in so far as the context permits.

PART 2
CHANGES IN THE LAW

Commentary—*Simon's Direct Tax Service* **B2.101B**.**8**—(1) This paragraph applies where, in the case of any person—

(*a*) a thing is done or an event occurs before the relevant date, and
(*b*) by reason of a change in the law effected by this Act, the tax consequences of that thing or event for a relevant chargeable period are different from what they would otherwise have been.

(2) If that person so elects, this Act has effect in relation to that period with such modifications as may be necessary to secure that those consequences are the same as they would have been without the change in the law.

(3) If this paragraph applies in the case of two or more persons in relation to the same thing or event, an election made under sub-paragraph (2) by any one of those persons is of no effect unless a corresponding election is made by the other or each of the others.

(4) An election under sub-paragraph (2) must be made by notice given to the Inland Revenue—

(*a*) for income tax purposes, within the normal time limit for amending a tax return for the tax year in which the chargeable period ends;
(*b*) for corporation tax purposes, no later than 2 years after the end of the chargeable period.

(5) In this paragraph—

"relevant chargeable period" means—

(*a*) in relation to a change effected by section 536(5)(*a*) or 537(4), the earliest chargeable period for which the tax consequences of the thing or event are different from what they would otherwise have been;
(*b*) in relation to any other change, a chargeable period which begins before and ends on or after the relevant date;

"the relevant date" means 6th April 2001 for income tax purposes and 1st April 2001 for corporation tax purposes.

PART 3
GENERAL
Capital expenditure

9 Subsections (2) and (3) of section 4 apply with the omission of the words "or property business" in relation to expenditure incurred or sums paid or received before 26th November 1996.

Former enactment—FA 1997 Sch 15 para 9(2).

Exclusion of double relief

10 Section 9 does not apply in relation to expenditure incurred before 24th July 1996.

Former enactment—FA 1997 Sch 16 para 7(3).

PART 4
PLANT AND MACHINERY ALLOWANCES

INTRODUCTION
Use for qualifying activity of plant or machinery provided for other purposes

11 Subsections (4) and (5) of section 13 do not apply if the plant or machinery was brought into use before 21st March 2000.

Former enactment—FA 2000 s 75(6)(*c*).

Use for qualifying activity of plant or machinery which is a gift

12 Section 14 applies with the insertion after subsection (1) of—

"(1A) This section does not apply unless the donor was required by section 24(6) of CAA 1990 to bring into account for the purposes there mentioned a disposal value equal to the price which the plant or machinery would have fetched if sold in the open market at the time of the gift.",

if the plant or machinery was brought into use before 27th July 1989.

Former enactment—CAA 1990 s 81(4).

QUALIFYING EXPENDITURE

Buildings, structures and land

13 Sections 21 to 24 do not apply in relation to expenditure—

(a) incurred before 30th November 1993;
(b) incurred before 6th April 1996 in pursuance of a contract entered into before 30th November 1993; or
(c) incurred before 6th April 1996 in pursuance of a contract entered into on or after 30th November 1993 for the purpose of securing that obligations under a contract entered into before 30th November 1993 are complied with.

Former enactment—FA 1994 s 117(2).

FIRST-YEAR QUALIFYING EXPENDITURE

ICT expenditure incurred by small companies

14 Section 45 does not apply in relation to expenditure incurred before 1st April 2000.

Former enactment—CAA 1990 s 22(3E).

HIRE-PURCHASE AND SIMILAR CONTRACTS

Plant or machinery acquired under hire purchase etc

15 Section 67(2) applies with the omission of the words in brackets if the contract under which the expenditure was incurred was entered into before 27th July 1989.

Former enactment—CAA 1990 s 60(3).

Plant or machinery on hire purchase etc: fixtures

16 Section 69(2) does not apply if the plant or machinery became a fixture before 28th July 2000.

Former enactment—FA 2000 s 80(3)(b).

Plant or machinery provided by lessee

17 In section 70(1), paragraphs (c) and (d) do not apply if the lease was entered into before 12th July 1984, or on or after that date under an agreement made before that date.

Former enactment—CAA 1990 s 61(4).

COMPUTER SOFTWARE

Software and rights to software

18 Section 71 does not apply to expenditure incurred before 10th March 1992.

Former enactment—F(No 2)A 1992 s 68(8).

CARS, ETC

Cars above the cost threshold

19 In relation to expenditure incurred or treated as incurred before 11th March 1992, or incurred under a contract entered into before that date—

(a) sections 74(2) and 76(3) apply with the substitution of "£8,000" for "£12,000"; and
(b) sections 75(1) and 76(2) and (4) apply with the substitution of "£2,000" for "£3,000".

Former enactment—F(No 2)A 1992 s 71(6), (7).

LONG-LIFE ASSETS
Long-life asset expenditure

20—(1) Chapter 10 of Part 2 does not apply to any expenditure incurred—

(a) before 26th November 1996, or

(b) before 1st January 2001 in pursuance of a contract entered into before 26th November 1996.

(2) Chapter 10 of Part 2 does not apply to expenditure incurred by any person (''the purchaser'') on the acquisition of a long-life asset from another (''the seller'') if—

(a) the seller has made a Part 2 claim in respect of expenditure incurred on the provision of the asset (''the seller's expenditure''),

(b) the claim is one which the seller was entitled to make,

(c) the seller's expenditure did not fall to be treated as long-life asset expenditure for the purposes of the claim, and

(d) the seller's expenditure would have been so treated if one or more of the assumptions specified in sub-paragraph (3) were made.

(3) The assumptions are that—

(a) expenditure falling within sub-paragraph (1) is not prevented by that sub-paragraph from being long-life asset expenditure,

(b) the seller's expenditure was not prevented by sub-paragraph (2) from being long-life asset expenditure, and

(c) Chapter 10 of Part 2 or any provision corresponding to it applied for chargeable periods ending before 26th November 1996.

(4) The reference in sub-paragraph (1) to expenditure incurred in pursuance of a contract entered into before 26th November 1996 does not, in the case of a contract varied at any time on or after that date, include a reference to any expenditure incurred under the contract that exceeds the expenditure that would have been incurred if the contract had not been varied.

(5) Expressions used in this paragraph and in Chapter 10 of Part 2 have the same meaning in this paragraph as in that Chapter; and in particular references in this paragraph to a ''Part 2 claim'' are to be read in accordance with section 103(3).

Former enactment—CAA 1990 s 38H.

OVERSEAS LEASING
Meaning of ''overseas leasing''

21 Section 105(2) applies with the substitution for paragraph (b) of—

''(b) does not use the plant or machinery for the purposes of a qualifying activity carried on there or for earning profits chargeable to tax by virtue of section 830(4) of ICTA, '',

in relation to the use of plant or machinery for leasing under a lease entered into before 16th March 1993.

Former enactment—FA 1993 s 116(4).

Recovery of first-year allowances in case of joint lessees

22—(1) Sub-paragraphs (2) and (3) apply if—

(a) expenditure has been incurred on the provision of plant or machinery which is leased as described in section 116(1),

(b) the whole or a part of the expenditure has qualified for a first-year allowance under—

(i) section 43(4) of CAA 1990, or

(ii) paragraph 47(7).

(2) Section 117(1) applies as if the reference in paragraph (b) to expenditure qualifying for a normal writing-down allowance under section 116(3) included a reference to expenditure qualifying for the first-year allowance.

(3) Subsections (3) to (5) of section 117 apply as if the reference in section 117(3)(b) to expenditure qualifying for a normal writing-down allowance under section 116(3) included a reference to expenditure qualifying for the first-year allowance.

Former enactment—CAA 1990 s 44(5).

Letting ships or aircraft to obtain old first-year allowance not a qualifying purpose

23 Subsections (1) and (2) of section 123 do not apply if the main object, or one of the main objects—

(a) of the letting of the ship or aircraft on charter,

(b) of a series of transactions of which the letting of the ship or aircraft on charter was one, or

(c) of any of the transactions in such a series,

was to obtain a first-year allowance in respect of expenditure which was first-year qualifying expenditure under paragraph 47 and was incurred by any person on the provision of the ship or aircraft.

Former enactment—CAA 1990 s 39(8)(*b*).

SHIPS: DEFERMENTS ETC

Further registration requirement

24 Section 154 does not apply in the case of a ship that was brought into use before 20th July 1994 for the purposes of a qualifying activity carried on by the person incurring the expenditure on the provision of the ship or a person connected with him.

Former enactment—CAA 1990 s 33E(5).

MINING AND OIL INDUSTRIES

Pre-trading expenditure on mineral exploration and access

25 Section 161 does not apply if—

(*a*) the person incurred the pre-trading expenditure before 1st April 1986; and
(*b*) before the first day of trading, the mineral exploration and access at the source in question had ceased.

Former enactment—CAA 1990 s 63(2).

Abandonment expenditure incurred before cessation of ring fence trade

26 Section 164 does not apply if the chargeable period in which the abandonment expenditure was incurred ended before 1st July 1991.

Former enactment—CAA 1990 s 62A(6); FA 1990 s 60.

Abandonment expenditure incurred after cessation of ring fence trade

27 Section 165 does not apply if the abandonment expenditure was incurred before 1st July 1991.

Former enactment—CAA 1990 s 62B(1)(*b*); FA 1990 s 60.

Oil production sharing contracts

28 Sections 167 to 171 do not apply if —

(*a*) the expenditure was incurred before 21st March 2000; or
(*b*) the expenditure is treated as incurred by virtue of section 13 and the conditions mentioned in subsection (1) of that section were fulfilled before that date.

Former enactment—FA 2000 s 81(3).

FIXTURES

Meaning of "interest in land" for purposes of Chapter 14 of Part 2 (fixtures)

29—(1) Sub-paragraph (2) applies if paragraph 51 of Schedule 12 to the Abolition of Feudal Tenure etc (Scotland) Act 2000 has not come into force before the commencement of section 175.

(2) Section 175(1) has effect until the appointed day as if for paragraph (*b*) there were substituted—

"(*b*) in Scotland, the estate or interest of the proprietor of the *dominium utile* (or, in the case of property other than feudal property, of the owner) and any agreement to acquire such an estate or interest,".

(3) In sub-paragraph (2) "the appointed day" means such day as may be appointed by the Scottish Ministers under section 71 of the Abolition of Feudal Tenure etc (Scotland) Act 2000 for the coming into force of the Act.

Former enactment—CAA 1990 s 51(3)(*b*).

Equipment lessors

30 Section 177(1)(*a*)(i) does not apply if the agreement for the lease of the plant or machinery was entered into before 19th March 1997.

Former enactment—FA 1997 Sch 16 para 3(6).

Equipment lessee has qualifying activity etc

31 Section 178 applies—

(*a*) if the agreement for the lease of the plant or machinery was entered into before 19th March 1997, with the omission of the words "which is or is to be" in paragraph (*a*) and the addition of the word "and" at the end of that paragraph; and

(*b*) if that expenditure was incurred before 24th July 1996, with the omission of paragraph (*c*) and the substitution for paragraph (*b*) of—

"(*b*) if the equipment lessee had incurred the capital expenditure incurred by the equipment lessor on the provision of the plant or machinery, he would, by virtue of section 176, be treated as the owner of the fixture as a result of incurring the expenditure".

Former enactment—FA 1997 Sch 16 para 3(6), (7).

Equipment lessor has right to sever fixture that is not part of building

32 Section 179(1) does not apply if the agreement for the lease of the plant or machinery was entered into before 19th March 1997 and applies with—

(*a*) the addition at the end of paragraph (*e*) of the word "and", and

(*b*) the omission of paragraph (*g*) and the word "and" immediately before it,

if the expenditure of the equipment lessor was incurred before 24th July 1996.

Former enactment—FA 1997 Sch 16 para 3(6), (7).

Equipment lease is part of affordable warmth programme

33 Section 180 does not apply if the expenditure of the equipment lessor was incurred before 28th July 2000.

Former enactment—FA 2000 s 79(3).

Purchaser of land giving consideration for fixture

34 Section 181 applies with—

(*a*) the omission of the word "and" at the end of paragraph (*b*) of subsection (1); and

(*b*) the insertion after that paragraph of—

"(*bb*) at the time of the purchaser's acquisition of the interest, either no person has previously become entitled to an allowance in respect of any capital expenditure incurred on the provision of the fixture or, if any person has become so entitled, that person has been or is required to bring the disposal value of the fixture into account under Chapter 5, and",

if the purchaser acquired the interest in the relevant land before 24th July 1996.

Former enactment—FA 1997 Sch 16 para 4(5), Sch 18 Pt VI(12) Note 2.

Purchaser of land discharging obligations of equipment lessee

35 Section 182 applies with—

(*a*) the omission of the word "and" at the end of paragraph (*c*) of subsection (1); and

(*b*) the insertion after that paragraph of—

"(*cc*) at the time of the purchaser's acquisition of the interest, either no person has previously become entitled to an allowance in respect of any capital expenditure incurred on the provision of the fixture or, if any person has become so entitled, that person has been or is required to bring the disposal value of the fixture into account under Chapter 5, and",

if the purchaser acquired the interest in the relevant land before 24th July 1996.

Former enactment—FA 1997 Sch 16 para 4(5), Sch 18 Pt VI(12) Note 2.

Incoming lessee where lessor entitled to allowances

36 Section 183 applies with the insertion after subsection (2) of—

"(3) No election may be made under this section if it appears that the sole or main benefit that may be expected to accrue to the lessor from the grant of the lease and the making of an election is the obtaining of an allowance or deduction or a greater allowance or deduction or the avoidance or reduction of a charge under this Part.",

if the person who had the interest in the relevant land granted the lease before 24th July 1996.

Former enactment—FA 1997 Sch 18 Pt VI(12) Note 3.

Incoming lessee where lessor not entitled to allowances

37 Section 184 applies with—

(*a*) the omission of the word "and" at the end of paragraph (*c*) of subsection (1); and

(*b*) the insertion after that paragraph of—

"(*cc*) at the time of the grant of the lease, no person has previously become entitled to an allowance in respect of any capital expenditure incurred on the provision of the fixture, and",

if the person who had the interest in the relevant land granted the lease before 24th July 1996.

Former enactment—FA 1997 Sch 16 para 4(6), Sch 18 Pt VI(12) Note 3.

Fixture on which a plant and machinery allowance has been claimed

38 Section 185 does not apply if the disposal event which required the disposal value to be brought into account as mentioned in subsection (1)(*d*) occurred before 24th July 1996.

Former enactment—CAA 1990 s 56B(2)(*c*).

Fixture on which industrial buildings allowance has been made

39 Section 186 does not apply if the time mentioned in subsection (1)(*c*)(ii) is before 24th July 1996.

Former enactment—CAA 1990 s 56C(1)(*e*).

Fixture on which research and development allowance has been made

40 Section 187 does not apply if the time mentioned in subsection (1)(*d*)(ii) is before 24th July 1996.

Former enactment—CAA 1990 s 56D(1)(*e*).

Disposal value in relation to fixtures: general

41 In relation to a fixture which a person is treated as ceasing to own before 24th July 1996, section 196 applies with the substitution for subsection (6) of—

"(6) If—

(*a*) a person ("the former owner") is treated by virtue of section 188, 190 or 191 as ceasing to own a fixture,

(*b*) another person incurs expenditure on the provision of the fixture, and

(*c*) the former owner brings a disposal value into account under Chapter 5,

there is to be disregarded for the purposes of this Part so much (if any) of that expenditure as exceeds that disposal value.

(7) In relation to expenditure incurred before 27th July 1989, subsection (6) has effect with the substitution for the words following "the fixture" in paragraph (*b*) of the words "there is to be disregarded for the purposes of this Part so much (if any) of that expenditure as exceeds the disposal value which the former owner is required to bring into account under Chapter 5".

Former enactment—CAA 1990 s 59(11); FA 1997 Sch 18 Pt VI(12) Note 3.

ASSETS PROVIDED OR USED ONLY PARTLY FOR QUALIFYING ACTIVITY

Effect of significant reduction in use for purposes of qualifying activity

42 Section 208 does not apply if the change of circumstances referred to in subsection (1)(*b*) of that section occurs before 21st March 2000.

Former enactment—FA 2000 s 75(6)(*b*).

ANTI-AVOIDANCE

Relevant transactions: sale, hire-purchase (etc) and assignment

43 Section 213(3) does not apply if the plant or machinery was brought into use before 27th July 1989.

Former enactment—CAA 1990 s 81(4).

Hire purchase etc and finance leases

44 Sections 220 and 229 do not apply in relation to expenditure incurred before 2nd July 1997, or in the 12 months beginning with that date in pursuance of a contract entered into before that date.

Former enactment—F(No 2) 1997 ss 44(5), 45(2).

Sale and finance leasebacks

45 Sections 221, 222 and 224 to 226 do not apply in relation to expenditure incurred before 2nd July 1998 if the relevant transaction—

(*a*) is a purchase under a contract entered into before 2nd July 1997;

(*b*) is itself a contract entered into before that date; or (*c*) is an assignment made before that date, or in pursuance of a contract entered into before that date.

Former enactment—F(No 2)A 1997 s 46(3).

ADDITIONAL VAT LIABILITIES AND REBATES

Expenditure which is first-year qualifying expenditure: general

46—(1) For the purposes of section 236(1)(*a*) (entitlement to first-year allowance in respect of additional VAT liability where original expenditure was first-year qualifying expenditure), first-year qualifying expenditure includes expenditure which is first-year qualifying expenditure under paragraph 47 or 48.

(2) A first-year allowance under this paragraph is made for the chargeable period in which the additional VAT liability accrues.

(3) The amount of such an allowance is a percentage of the additional VAT liability in respect of which the allowance is made, as shown in the Table—

TABLE

AMOUNT OF FIRST-YEAR ALLOWANCES
(PRE-COMMENCEMENT ORIGINAL EXPENDITURE)

Type of original first-year qualifying expenditure	Amount
Expenditure qualifying under paragraph 47 (expenditure incurred 1992–93).	40%
Expenditure qualifying under paragraph 48 (expenditure incurred 1997–98 by small or medium-sized enterprises) which is not long-life asset expenditure.	50%
Expenditure qualifying under paragraph 48 (expenditure incurred 1997–98 by small or medium-sized enterprises) which is long-life asset expenditure.	12%

Former enactments—Sub-para (1): CAA 1990 s 22(3B), (3C).
Sub-para (2): CAA 1990 s 159A(3).
Sub-para (3): CAA 1990 s 22(1).

Expenditure incurred 1992–93

47—(1) Expenditure is first-year qualifying expenditure under this paragraph if—

(*a*) it was incurred in the period beginning with 1st November 1992 and ending with 31st October 1993, and

(*b*) it is not excluded by sub-paragraphs (3) to (8).

(2) In determining whether expenditure is first-year qualifying expenditure under this paragraph, any effect of section 12 on the time at which it is to be treated as incurred is to be disregarded.

(3) Expenditure is not first-year qualifying expenditure under this paragraph if it was incurred—

(*a*) in the chargeable period in which there was a permanent discontinuance of the qualifying activity, or

(*b*) on the provision of a car other than a qualifying hire car (as defined by section 82).

(4) Expenditure on the provision of plant or machinery for leasing is not first-year qualifying expenditure under this paragraph if it appears that the expenditure is of the kind described in section 109(2) or 110(2) (expenditure on plant or machinery which is used for overseas leasing etc).

(5) Expenditure on the provision of plant or machinery for leasing is not first-year qualifying expenditure under this paragraph if—

(*a*) the expenditure was incurred on or after 14th April 1993,

(*b*) the person to whom the plant or machinery is to be or is leased, or a person who is connected with that person, used the plant or machinery for any purpose at any time before its provision for leasing, and

(*c*) the expenditure does not fall within any of the categories of expenditure on plant or machinery for leasing given in sub-paragraph (6).

(6) The categories referred to in sub-paragraph (5)(*c*) are as follows.

Category 1. Expenditure on leasing qualifying by reference to Chapter 11 of Part 2 (overseas leasing)

It appears that the plant or machinery—

(*a*) will be used for a qualifying purpose (as defined by sections 122 to 125) in the designated period (as defined by section 106), and

(*b*) will not be used for any other purpose at any time in that period.

Category 2. Enterprise zones

The circumstances of the incurring of the expenditure are that—

    (*a*) the expenditure is incurred on the provision of plant or machinery which is to be an integral part of a building or structure, and

    (*b*) expenditure incurred at that time on the construction of the building or structure would be qualifying enterprise zone expenditure to which Chapter 5 of Part 3 (initial allowances for qualifying enterprise zone expenditure) would apply.

Category 3. Fixtures

The circumstances of the incurring of the expenditure are that—

    (*a*) expenditure is incurred on the provision of plant or machinery which is fixed to land or a building,

    (*b*) the person who incurs it is the lessor of the land or building, and

    (*c*) a transfer of the person's interest in the land or building would operate to transfer that person's interest in the plant or machinery.

Category 4. Cars hired out to the disabled etc

The expenditure is incurred on the provision of a car which is within section 82(4) (cars hired out to persons receiving disability allowances etc).

(7) Sub-paragraph (4) does not prevent expenditure being first-year qualifying expenditure, if it appears that—

    (*a*) the plant or machinery will be leased as described in section 116(1), and

    (*b*) the circumstances are such that section 116(3) will require the whole or any part of the expenditure to be treated as not subject to section 107, 109 or 110.

(8) Any first-year allowance under sub-paragraph (7) (when read with section 236) is to be made on the same basis and subject to the same apportionments (if any) as would be applicable in the case of a writing-down allowance under section 116(5).

Former enactments—Sub-paras (1), (2): CAA 1990 s 22(3B).
Sub-paras (3)–(5): CAA 1990 s 22(6A).
Sub-para (6): CAA 1990 s 22(4)(*c*), (5), (6), (11).

Expenditure by small or medium-sized enterprises, 1997–98

48—(1) Expenditure is first-year qualifying expenditure under this paragraph if—

    (*a*) it was incurred in the period beginning with 2nd July 1997 and ending with 1st July 1998;

    (*b*) it was incurred by a small or medium-sized enterprise; and

    (*c*) it is not excluded by sub-paragraph (3).

(2) In determining whether expenditure is first-year qualifying expenditure under this paragraph, any effect of section 12 on the time at which it is to be treated as incurred is to be disregarded.

(3) Expenditure is not first-year qualifying expenditure under this paragraph if it is within any of the general exclusions given in section 46(2).

(4) In this paragraph, "small or medium-sized enterprise" is to be read in accordance with sections 47 to 49, read with paragraph 50.

Former enactments—Sub-paras (1)–(3): CAA 1990 s 22(3C).
Sub-para (4): CAA 1990 s 22(6B), (6C).

Whether a company is a member of large or medium-sized group

49—(1) This paragraph applies in relation to any expenditure incurred before 12th May 1998, and for the purpose of determining—

    (*a*) whether expenditure incurred under a contract entered into before that date is first-year qualifying expenditure under section 44, or

    (*b*) whether expenditure is first-year qualifying expenditure under paragraph 46 or 48.

(2) Section 49 applies with the substitution in subsection (2) of "parent company" for "parent undertaking" and the omission of the words in brackets in subsection (5).

(3) In section 49 as it so applies "parent company"—

    (*a*) except in the case of a company formed and registered in Northern Ireland, has the same meaning as in Part VII of the Companies Act 1985;

    (*b*) in the case of such a company, has the same meaning as in Part VIII of the Companies (Northern Ireland) Order 1986 (SI 1986/1032 (NI 6)).

Former enactment—FA 1998 s 85(10).

Expenditure which is not first-year qualifying expenditure

50 For the purposes of section 236(1)(*a*)—

(*a*) section 40 (expenditure for Northern Ireland purposes by small or medium-sized enterprises) does not apply if the expenditure was incurred before 12th May 1998;

(*b*) section 44 (expenditure by small or medium-sized enterprises) does not apply if the expenditure was incurred before 2nd July 1998;

(*c*) section 45 (ICT expenditure by small enterprises) does not apply if the expenditure was incurred before 1st April 2000.

Former enactment—CAA 1990 s 22(3CB), (3D), (3E).

Anti-avoidance

51 Sections 243(7) and 244 do not apply in relation to expenditure incurred before 2nd July 1998 if the relevant transaction—

(*a*) is a purchase under a contract entered into before 2nd July 1997;

(*b*) is itself a contract entered into before that date; or

(*c*) is an assignment made before that date, or in pursuance of a contract entered into before that date.

Former enactment—F(No 2)A 1997 s 46(3).

SUPPLEMENTARY PROVISIONS

Successions by beneficiaries

52 Section 266(7) does not apply if the succession occurred before 27th July 1989.

Former enactment—CAA 1990 s 77(8).

53 Subsections (6) and (7) of section 268 do not apply if the election under that section was made before 6th April 1990.

Former enactment—FA 1990 Sch 13 para 3(2).

GENERAL

Vehicles provided by employees in 1990–91

54—(1) This paragraph applies if—

(*a*) at the beginning of the tax year 1990–91 machinery consisting of a mechanically propelled road vehicle was provided by a person for use in the performance of the duties of an office or employment held by him, and

(*b*) the machinery was also provided by him at the end of the tax year 1989–90 for use in the performance of the duties of that office or employment but without that provision being necessary.

(2) Part 2 of this Act has effect as if the person had incurred capital expenditure on the provision of the machinery for the purposes of the office or employment in the tax year 1990–91—

(*a*) the amount of that expenditure being taken as the price which the machinery would have fetched if sold in the open market on 6th April 1990, and

(*b*) the person being treated as owning the machinery as a result of his having incurred that expenditure.

Former enactment—FA 1990 s 87(3).

Certain expenditure incurred before 6th April 1976

55 Part 2 of this Act does not apply to capital expenditure—

(*a*) which was not eligible expenditure within the meaning of section 39 of FA 1976 (which brought expenditure previously not within Chapter I of Part III of FA 1971 within that Chapter but with certain exceptions), and

(*b*) which was incurred in a chargeable period ending before 6th April 1976.

Former enactment—CAA 1990 s 82(1).

PART 5
INDUSTRIAL BUILDINGS ALLOWANCES

INDUSTRIAL BUILDINGS
Bridge undertakings

56 In section 274, item 8 of Table B (bridge undertakings) does not apply if the expenditure was treated as incurred before the end of the tax year 1956–57.

Former enactment—CAA 1990 s 18(12).

Building used by more than one licensee

57 Section 278 does not apply if the licence was granted before 10th March 1982.

Former enactment—CAA 1990 s 18(6).

Qualifying hotels

58—(1) Section 279 does not apply if the expenditure on the construction of the building was incurred before 12th April 1978.

(2) Expenditure is not to be treated for the purposes of sub-paragraph (1) as having been incurred after the date on which it was in fact incurred by reason only of section 10(1) of CAA 1990.

Former enactment—CAA 1990 s 19(6).

Non-industrial part of building disregarded

59 Section 283(2) applies with the substitution of "10%" for "25%" if the expenditure was incurred before 16th March 1983.

Former enactment—CAA 1990 s 18(7).

QUALIFYING EXPENDITURE
Purchase of used building from developer

60 Section 297 does not apply if the purchase price on the sale by the developer mentioned in subsection (1)(*b*) of that section became payable before 27th July 1989.

Former enactment—CAA 1990 s 10(4)(*c*).

Qualifying enterprise zone expenditure

61 Sections 300 and 302 do not apply if—

(*a*) the purchase price payable on the sale of the relevant interest in the building before it was used, or

(*b*) if there was more than one such sale before the building was used, the purchase price payable on the last of those sales,

became payable before 16th December 1991.

Former enactment—F(No 2)A 1992 Sch 13 para 14.

62 Sections 301, 303 and 304 do not apply in relation to buildings first used before 16th December 1991.

Former enactment—F(No 2)A 1992 Sch 13 para 15.

63 If—

(*a*) the relevant interest in a building was sold on a date falling after the end of the period of two years beginning with the date on which the building or structure was first used; and

(*b*) that period ended, and the date on which the relevant interest was transferred fell, within the period beginning with 13th January 1994 and ending with 31st August 1994,

paragraphs (*c*) and (*d*) of sections 301(1) and 303(1) apply as if the period there referred to were the period beginning with the date on which the building or structure was first used and ending with 31st August 1994.

Former enactment—FA 1994 s 121(1).

INITIAL ALLOWANCES

Building occupied by qualifying licensee

64 Section 305(1)(*b*) does not apply if the licence was granted before 10th March 1982.

Former enactment—CAA 1990 s 1(4).

Grants affecting entitlement to initial allowances

65 Section 308(2)(*c*) applies as if the reference to a grant under section 101 of the Greater London Authority Act 1999 (c 29) included a reference to a grant under section 12 of the London Regional Transport Act 1984 (c 32) or section 3 of the Transport (London) Act 1969 (c 35).

Former enactment—CAA 1990 s 1(7)(*b*).

WRITING-DOWN ALLOWANCES

Basic rule for calculating amount of allowance

66 Section 310(1)(*b*) applies with the substitution of ''2%'' for ''4%'' in the case of expenditure incurred before 6th November 1962.

Former enactment—CAA 1990 s 3(2).

Calculation of amount after relevant event

67 Section 311(1) applies with the substitution (in the definition of ''B'') of ''50 years'' for ''25 years'' in the case of expenditure incurred before 6th November 1962.

Former enactment—CAA 1990 s 3(3).

BALANCING ADJUSTMENTS

When balancing adjustments are made

68 Section 314(4) applies with the substitution of ''50 years'' for ''25 years'' if the qualifying expenditure was incurred before 6th November 1962.

Former enactment—CAA 1990 s 4(2).

Net allowance given

69—(1) Section 324 applies in relation to a mills, factories or exceptional depreciation allowance as it applies in relation to an allowance of any kind mentioned in that section.

(2) In sub-paragraph (1) ''mills, factories or exceptional depreciation allowance'', in relation to any building or structure, means—

    (*a*) any allowance granted for a tax year under section 15 of FA 1937 in respect of it or premises of which it forms part, including any amount which under that section was to be allowed as a deduction in computing profits or gains for that year, and

    (*b*) any allowance granted under section 19 of FA 1941 in respect of it or premises of which it forms part.

(3) Where such an allowance as is mentioned in sub-paragraph (2) was granted in respect of premises which include several buildings or structures—

    (*a*) the whole amount of the allowance is to be apportioned between the buildings and structures, and

    (*b*) only that part of the allowance which is apportioned to the building or structure in question is to be taken into account.

Former enactment—CAA 1990 s 4(10) and (12).

70 For the purposes of section 324 an allowance is treated as having been made to a woman in relation to any qualifying expenditure if—

    (*a*) it was made to her husband for a chargeable period ending before 6th April 1990 in respect of an interest of hers which was the relevant interest in relation to that expenditure,

    (*b*) a balancing event occurs on or after that date, and

    (*c*) she is entitled to all or part of the proceeds from that balancing event.

Former enactment—CAA 1990 s 4(11).

Balancing adjustment on realisation of capital value

71 Sections 328 to 331 do not apply if the capital expenditure referred to in section 327 was incurred under a contract which—

    (*a*) was entered into before 13th January 1994, and

(*b*) was not a conditional contract which became unconditional on or after 26th February 1994.

Former enactment—FA 1994 s 120(7), (8).

WRITING OFF QUALIFYING EXPENDITURE

Writing off qualifying expenditure when building not an industrial building

72 For the purposes of section 336 a building is not treated as having been an industrial building—

(*a*) under item 5(*b*) or (*c*) or 6 of Table A in section 274 (working foreign plantations or fishing) for any tax year before 1953–54, or

(*b*) under item 7 of Table B in section 274 (tunnel undertakings) for any tax year before 1952–53.

Former enactment—CAA 1990 s 8(8).

Crown or other person not within the charge to tax entitled to the relevant interest

73 Section 339 does not apply by virtue of subsection (1)(*b*) if the interest was sold before 29th July 1988.

Former enactment—CAA 1990 s 8(14).

HIGHWAY UNDERTAKINGS

Special provisions relating to highway concessions

74 Sections 341(4)(*a*), 343 and 344 do not apply in relation to expenditure incurred before 6th April 1995.

Former enactment—FA 1995 s 99(10).

ADDITIONAL VAT LIABILITIES AND REBATES

Additional VAT liabilities and initial allowances: 1992–93 cases

75—(1) This paragraph applies if—

(*a*) a person was entitled to an initial allowance in respect of 1992–93 qualifying expenditure,

(*b*) the person entitled to the relevant interest in relation to that expenditure incurs an additional VAT liability in respect of that expenditure, and

(*c*) the additional VAT liability is incurred at a time when the building is, or is to be, an industrial building—

(i) occupied for the purposes of a trade carried on by the person entitled to the relevant interest or a qualifying lessee, or

(ii) used for the purposes of trade carried on by a qualifying licensee.

(2) If this paragraph applies, the person entitled to the relevant interest is entitled to an initial allowance on the amount of the additional VAT liability.

(3) The amount of the initial allowance is 20% of the additional VAT liability.

(4) The allowance is made for the chargeable period in which the additional VAT liability accrues.

(5) The persons mentioned in sub-paragraph (1)(*a*) and (*b*) need not be the same.

(6) In this paragraph "qualifying lessee" and "qualifying licensee" have the same meaning as in section 305.

Former enactments—CAA 1990 ss 1(1A), 2A(1)(*a*)(i), (ii), (4), (5)(*b*).

Additional VAT liabilities and initial allowances: further case

76—(1) This paragraph applies if—

(*a*) a person was entitled to an initial allowance in respect of qualifying enterprise zone expenditure, and

(*b*) the person entitled to the relevant interest in relation to that expenditure incurs an additional VAT liability in respect of that expenditure,

but there is no entitlement to an initial allowance under section 346 because the condition in subsection (1)(*d*) of that section is not met.

(2) If in such a case—

(*a*) the conditions in paragraph 74(1) are met except for the condition that the original entitlement to an initial allowance was in respect of 1992–93 qualifying expenditure, and

(*b*) some or all of the qualifying enterprise zone expenditure would have been 1992–93 qualifying expenditure but for paragraph 76(2),

the person entitled to the relevant interest is entitled to an initial allowance under paragraph 74(3) on the appropriate part or on all of the additional VAT liability (as the case may be).

(3) The allowance is made for the chargeable period in which the additional VAT liability accrues.

Former enactments—CAA 1990 ss 1(1A), 2A(1)(*a*)(i), (ii), (4), (5)(*b*).

1992–93 qualifying expenditure

77—(1) "1992–93 qualifying expenditure" means expenditure which is—

(a) qualifying expenditure which is within section 294 and is 1992–93 construction expenditure, or

(b) the 1992–93 element of qualifying expenditure which is within section 295 or 296.

(2) Qualifying enterprise zone expenditure is not to be taken into account as 1992–93 qualifying expenditure for the purposes of sub-paragraph (1).

(3) Expenditure is 1992–93 construction expenditure if it was incurred on the construction of a building under a contract which was entered into—

(a) in the period beginning with 1st November 1992 and ending with 31st October 1993, or

(b) for the purpose of securing compliance with obligations under a contract entered into in that period,

and which was not entered into for the purpose of securing compliance with obligations under a contract entered into before 1st November 1992.

(4) The 1992–93 element of qualifying expenditure within section 295 or 296 is—

$$QE \times \frac{E}{T}$$

where—

QE is the amount of qualifying expenditure,

E is the amount of 1992–93 construction expenditure, and

T is the amount of expenditure on the construction of the building.

(5) If the expenditure on the construction of the building was incurred by a person carrying on a trade as a developer who—

(a) was entitled to the relevant interest in the building before 1st November 1992, and

(b) sold that interest in the course of that trade under a contract entered into in the period beginning with 1st November 1992 and ending with 31st October 1993,

the 1992–93 construction expenditure for the purposes of sub-paragraph (4) includes any expenditure on the construction of the building incurred under a contract entered into before 1st November 1993 or for the purpose of securing compliance with obligations under such a contract.

Former enactments—CAA 1990 ss 2A, 10C.
Revenue Internal Guidance—Capital allowances manual CA 270–275 (meaning of "expenditure incurred under contracts")

SUPPLEMENTARY PROVISIONS
Arrangements having an artificial effect on pricing

78 Section 357 does not apply if the sale price fixed as mentioned in subsections (1) and (2)—

(a) became payable before 29th November 1994; or

(b) was fixed by a contract entered into before 29th November 1994 and became payable before 6th April 1995.

Former enactment—FA 1995 s 100(3).

GENERAL
Expenditure on preparatory work on land where building used before 6th April 1956

79—(1) Sub-paragraph (2) applies where section 21(9) of CAA 1990 (expenditure on preparatory work on land where building used before 6th April 1956) applied to any expenditure immediately before the commencement of Part 3 of this Act, so that Part I of that Act (industrial buildings and structures) except for section 1 (initial allowances) applied to part of the expenditure separately from the remainder.

(2) Where this sub-paragraph applies, Part 3 of this Act, except for Chapter 5, similarly applies to the part of the expenditure separately from the remainder.

Former enactment—CAA 1990 s 21(9).

PART 6
AGRICULTURAL BUILDINGS ALLOWANCES
Overall limit on balancing charge

80 For the purposes of section 387 an allowance is treated as having been made to a woman in relation to any qualifying expenditure if—

(a) it was made to her husband for a chargeable period ending before 6th April 1990 in respect of an interest of hers which was the relevant interest in relation to that expenditure,

CAA 2001

(*b*) a balancing event occurs on or after that date, and

(*c*) she is entitled to all or part of the proceeds from that balancing event.

Former enactment—CAA 1990 s 128(8).

Meaning of "freehold interest in land" for purposes of Part 4

81—(1) Sub-paragraphs (2) and (3) apply if paragraph 51 of Schedule 12 to the Abolition of Feudal Tenure etc (Scotland) Act 2000 has not come into force before the commencement of Part 4 of this Act.

(2) Section 393(1) has effect until the appointed day as if for paragraph (*b*) there were substituted—

"(*b*) in relation to Scotland, the estate or interest of the proprietor of the *dominium utile* (or, in the case of property other than feudal property, of the owner);".

(3) Section 393(2) has effect until the appointed day as if for paragraph (*b*) there were substituted—

"(*b*) in relation to Scotland, an agreement to acquire the estate or interest mentioned in subsection (1)(*b*);".

(4) In sub-paragraphs (2) and (3) "the appointed day" means such day as may be appointed by the Scottish Ministers under section 71 of the Abolition of Feudal Tenure etc (Scotland) Act 2000 for the coming into force of the Act.

Former enactment—CAA 1990 s 125(1)(*b*).

Exclusion of expenditure incurred before 1st April 1986

82 References in Part 4 of this Act to qualifying expenditure do not include—

(*a*) expenditure incurred before 1st April 1986; or

(*b*) payments made before 1st April 1987 under a contract entered into before 14th March 1984.

Former enactments—CAA 1990 ss 123, 133(3).

The writing-down period

83—(1) This paragraph applies where it is provided under Part 4 that writing-down allowances are to be made in respect of any expenditure during a writing-down period of any specified length.

(2) If allowances were made under paragraph 27(2) of Schedule 14 to FA 1965—

(*a*) for income tax purposes, for either of the tax years 1964–65 and 1965–66, and

(*b*) for accounting periods of a company falling wholly or partly within either of those years,

the periods for which allowances were made are added together in calculating the writing-down period, even though (according to the calendar) the same time is counted twice.

Former enactment—CAA 1990 s 146(4).

PART 7

MINERAL EXTRACTION ALLOWANCES

QUALIFYING EXPENDITURE ON ACQUIRING A MINERAL ASSET

Qualifying expenditure where buildings or structures cease to be used

84 In section 405(3) "A" does not include, in cases where the buildings or structures have permanently ceased to be used for any purpose before 27th July 1989, the amount of any agricultural buildings allowances.

Former enactment—CAA 1990 s 110(5).

QUALIFYING EXPENDITURE: SECOND-HAND ASSETS

Claims before 26th November 1996 in respect of acquisition of mineral asset owned by previous trader

85 Section 407(4) does not apply in relation to claims made before 26th November 1996.

Former enactment—CAA 1990 s 115(2A); FA 1997 s 66(2), (5).

Acquisition of oil licence from non-trader before 13th September 1995

86 Section 408 does not apply to acquisitions occurring before 13th September 1995.

Former enactment—FA 1996 s 180(4).

Restrictions on qualifying expenditure in case of UK oil licence and certain other assets inapplicable for expenditure pre-16th July 1985

87—(1) The sections listed in sub-paragraph (2) do not apply if—

(*a*) asset X is a mineral asset situated in the United Kingdom, and

(*b*) the capital expenditure incurred by the buyer consists of the payment of sums under a contract entered into by him before 16th July 1985.

(2) The sections are—

(*a*) section 407 (acquisition of mineral asset owned by previous trader),

(*b*) section 410 (UK oil licence: qualifying expenditure limited by reference to original licence payment), and

(*c*) section 411 (assets generally: qualifying expenditure limited by reference to previous trader's unrelieved qualifying expenditure).

(3) Sections 407 and 411 apply, in relation to a case where asset X is a mineral asset situated in the United Kingdom, as if the references to an earlier owner of the asset did not include a person who has not owned the asset at any time after 31st March 1986.

(4) In the case of a mineral asset which consists of or includes an interest in or right over mineral deposits or land, the asset is not to be regarded for the purposes of this paragraph as situated in the United Kingdom unless the deposits or land are or is so situated.

(5) Expressions used in this paragraph and Chapter 4 of Part 5 have the same meaning in this paragraph as they have in that Chapter.

Former enactments—CAA 1990 ss 113(2), (3), 121(2).

Expenditure incurred pre-1st April 1986

88—(1) Part 5 of this Act does not apply in relation to expenditure incurred before 1st April 1986 ("old expenditure") except as provided by the following provisions of this paragraph.

(2) Sections 401 and 402 apply to old expenditure if—

(*a*) that expenditure was incurred on mineral exploration and access,

(*b*) immediately before 1st April 1986, no allowance had been made under Chapter III of Part I of CAA 1968 in respect of it, and

(*c*) after that day and before mineral exploration and access ceases at the source in question, the person by whom the expenditure was incurred began or begins to carry on a trade of mineral extraction.

In this sub-paragraph "source" has the same meaning as it had in Schedule 14 to FA 1986.

(3) For the purposes of Part 5—

(*a*) expenditure which by virtue of any provision of section 119 of CAA 1990 (read with any provision of Schedule 14 to FA 1986) was treated immediately before the coming into force of this Act as expenditure incurred on 1st April 1986 for any purpose or purposes is to continue to be so treated;

(*b*) any allowances treated as having been made under Schedule 13 to FA 1986 is to continue to be so treated;

(*c*) any amount treated as qualifying expenditure for the purposes of that Schedule is to continue to be so treated; and

(*d*) in relation to any expenditure to which paragraph 6(4)(*a*) of Schedule 14 to FA 1986 applied, section 424 does not apply (so that no deduction is to be made from the amount of any disposal receipt by reference to the undeveloped market value of the land in question).

(4) In the case of expenditure incurred in the acquisition of a mineral asset, nothing in sub-paragraph (3)(*c*) affects the time as at which under section 404 the undeveloped market value of an interest is to be determined.

(5) In a case where—

(*a*) by virtue of any provision of this paragraph, the whole or any part of the outstanding balance (within the meaning of paragraph 1 of Schedule 14 to FA 1986) of an item of old expenditure is treated for the purposes of Part 5 as qualifying expenditure, and

(*b*) a balancing charge falls to be made under Chapter 6 of that Part in respect of the expenditure,

then, in determining the amount on which that charge falls to be made, subsection (4) of section 418 has effect (subject to sub-paragraph (6)) as if paragraph (*b*) of that subsection included a reference to allowances made in respect of the item under Chapter III of Part I of CAA 1968.

(6) Where the qualifying expenditure in respect of which a balancing charge falls to be made represents part only of the outstanding balance of an item of old expenditure, the reference in sub-paragraph (5) to allowances made in respect of that item is to be construed as a reference to such part of those allowances as it is just and reasonable to apportion to that part of the balance (having regard to any apportionment made under paragraph 3(2) of Schedule 14 to FA 1986).

Former enactment—CAA 1990 s 119.

PART 8
RESEARCH AND DEVELOPMENT ALLOWANCES
Expenditure incurred partly on research and development

89 Section 439(4) does not apply to expenditure incurred before 27th July 1989.

Former enactment—CAA 1990 s 137(4).

References to research and development in relation to new trades

90—(1) Where—

(*a*) a trade is set up and commenced in the year of assessment 1999–00, and

(*b*) its first period of account ends after 6th April 2001,

Part 6 of this Act has effect in relation to that year as if references to research and development were references to scientific research.

(2) In this paragraph "scientific research" means any activities in the fields of natural or applied science for the extension of knowledge.

Disposal of oil licences

91—(1) Sub-paragraphs (2) and (3) apply where—

(*a*) a person ("the transferor") disposes of any interest in an oil licence to another ("the transferee") during the transitional period,

(*b*) part of the value of the interest is attributable to allowable exploration expenditure incurred by the transferor, and

(*c*) an election is made in accordance with this paragraph specifying an amount as the amount to be treated as so attributable.

(2) Chapter 3 of Part 6 has effect in relation to the disposal as if—

(*a*) the disposal were a disposal by which an asset representing the allowable exploration expenditure ceases to belong to the transferor, and

(*b*) the disposal value of that asset were an amount equal to the amount specified in the election.

(3) For the purposes of Part 5 of this Act, the amount of any expenditure incurred—

(*a*) by the transferee in acquiring the interest from the transferor, or

(*b*) by any person subsequently acquiring the interest (or an interest deriving from the interest),

which is taken to be attributable to expenditure incurred, before the disposal to the transferee, on mineral exploration and access is the lesser of the amount specified in the election and the amount which, apart from this sub-paragraph, would be taken to be so attributable.

(4) An election—

(*a*) must be made by notice to the Board of Inland Revenue given by the transferor, and

(*b*) subject to sub-paragraph (5), does not have effect unless a copy of it is served on the transferee and the transferee consents to it.

(5) If the Special Commissioners are satisfied—

(*a*) that the disposal was made under or in pursuance of an agreement entered into by the transferor and the transferee on the mutual understanding that a quantified (or quantifiable) part of the value of the interest disposed of was attributable to allowable exploration expenditure, and

(*b*) that the part quantified in accordance with that understanding and the amount specified in the election are the same,

they may dispense with the need for the transferee to consent to the election.

(6) Any question falling to be determined by the Special Commissioners under sub-paragraph (5) is to be determined by them in the same way as an appeal; but both the transferor and the transferee are entitled to appear and be heard by those Commissioners or to make representations to them in writing.

(7) Subject to sub-paragraph (8), an election may specify any amount, including a nil amount, as the amount to be treated as mentioned in sub-paragraph (1)(*c*).

(8) Where—

(*a*) a return has been made for a chargeable period of the transferor, and

(*b*) the return includes, at the time when it is made, an amount which, disregarding the provisions of this paragraph, would be treated under Chapter 3 of Part 6 as a trading receipt accruing in that period,

the election must not specify an amount less than the amount included in the return unless the Board of Inland Revenue agrees the lesser amount in question.

(9) An election made in accordance with this paragraph—

(*a*) is irrevocable, and

(*b*) may not be varied after it is made.

(10) For the purposes of this paragraph a disposal is a disposal made during the transitional period if it is one made—

(*a*) before 13th September 1995, or

(*b*) on or after that date in pursuance of any obligation to make the disposal which, immediately before that date, was an unconditional obligation.

(11) For the purposes of sub-paragraph (10), the fact that a third party who is not connected with the transferor or the transferee may, by exercising any right or withholding any permission, prevent the fulfilment of an obligation does not prevent the obligation from being treated as unconditional.

(12) In sub-paragraph (11) the reference to a third party is a reference to any person, body, government or public authority, whether within or outside the United Kingdom.

(13) In this paragraph—

"allowable exploration expenditure" has the same meaning as in section 555;

"mineral exploration and access" has the same meaning as in Part 5.

(14) All such assessments and adjustments of assessments are to be made as are necessary to give effect to this paragraph.

Former enactment—CAA 1990 s 138B.

PART 9
PATENT ALLOWANCES

EXPENDITURE INCURRED BEFORE 1ST APRIL 1986
Scope of paragraphs 93 to 101

92—(1) Paragraphs 93 to 101 apply to capital expenditure incurred by a person before 1st April 1986 on the purchase of patent rights.

(2) Chapters 2 to 4 of Part 8 do not apply to such expenditure, except for certain provisions which are specifically applied by paragraph 101.

Former enactments—TA 1988 ss 522(1), 523(1)–(3).

Qualifying expenditure and unrelieved qualifying expenditure

93—(1) In this paragraph and paragraphs 94 to 101, "qualifying expenditure" means capital expenditure incurred before 1st April 1986 on the purchase of patent rights.

(2) The result of Steps 1 to 3 is the unrelieved qualifying expenditure for a chargeable period.

Step 1

Take an item of qualifying expenditure.

Step 2

Subtract any writing-down allowances made in respect of that expenditure for earlier chargeable periods.

Step 3

If the person who incurred the expenditure sold any part of the patent rights before the beginning of the chargeable period, subtract the net proceeds of sale (so far as they consist of capital sums).

Former enactment—TA 1988 s 523(5).

Entitlement to writing-down allowances

94—(1) A writing-down allowance is made for a chargeable period in respect of an item of qualifying expenditure if—

(*a*) the chargeable period falls wholly or partly within the writing-down period for that expenditure (as determined in accordance with paragraph 95),

(*b*) paragraph 97 does not prohibit writing-down allowances for that period, and

(*c*) either—

(i) the trade use condition is met for that period, or

(ii) any income receivable by that person in respect of the patent rights in that period would be liable to tax.

(2) The trade use condition is that—

(*a*) the person is carrying on in the chargeable period a trade which is within the charge to tax, and

(*b*) at any time in the chargeable period the patent rights, or other rights out of which they were granted, were, or were to be, used for the purposes of the trade.

(3) The total writing-down allowances made in respect of an item of qualifying expenditure (whether to the same or to different persons) must not exceed the amount of that expenditure.

Former enactments—Sub-paras (1), (2): TA 1988 ss 522(2), 528(1).
Sub-para (3): TA 1988 s 522(7); CA 1990 s 146(3).

The writing-down period

95—(1) The writing-down period for an item of qualifying expenditure—

    (*a*) begins at the beginning of the chargeable period in respect of which the expenditure is incurred, and

    (*b*) is of a length determined in accordance with the Table, which shows the basic rule, and the rules which apply instead of the basic rule in the cases described in items 2 and 3.

TABLE
LENGTH OF WRITING-DOWN PERIODS FOR QUALIFYING EXPENDITURE

Rule	Length of writing-down period
1. Basic rule.	17 years.
2. Patent rights are purchased for a specified period.	Whichever is shorter— (a) 17 years; (b) the number of years comprised within the specified period.
3. Patent rights begin one complete year or more after the commencement of the patent, and item 2 does not apply.	17 years, less the number of complete years which, when the rights began, have elapsed since the commencement of the patent; or if 17 complete years have so elapsed, one year.

(2) For the purpose of determining the writing-down period, expenditure incurred for the purposes of a trade by a person about to carry on the trade is treated as if incurred on the first day on which that person carries on that trade, unless that person has by then sold all the rights on which the expenditure was incurred.

(3) "The commencement of the patent", means, in relation to a patent, the date as from which the patent rights become effective.

Former enactments—TA 1988 ss 522(1), (3)–(7), 533(1).

Calculation of writing-down allowances

96—(1) The basic rule for calculating a writing-down allowance for an item of qualifying expenditure is—

$$E \times \frac{C}{W}$$

where—

E is the amount of the qualifying expenditure;

C is the length of the part of the chargeable period falling within the writing-down period;

W is the length of the writing-down period.

(2) The basic rule is subject to the rules about—

    (*a*) cessation of writing-down allowances (paragraph 97), and

    (*b*) reduced writing-down allowances (paragraph 98).

Former enactments—Sub-para (1): TA 1988 s 522(1), (7); CAA 1990 s 146(2).

End of writing-down allowances

97—(1) No writing-down allowance is to be made to a person for a chargeable period in respect of qualifying expenditure incurred on the purchase of patent rights if any of the following occur in that period—

    (*a*) the patent rights come to an end without being subsequently revived,

    (*b*) the person sells all of those rights, or so much of them as that person still owned at the beginning of the chargeable period, or

    (*c*) the person sells part of those rights, and the net proceeds of sale for that period (so far as they consist of capital sums) are not less than the amount of the unrelieved qualifying expenditure for that period.

(2) If a writing-down allowance in respect of qualifying expenditure is prohibited by sub-paragraph (1) for a chargeable period, no writing-down allowance is to be made in respect of that expenditure for any subsequent chargeable period.

Former enactment—TA 1988 s 523(1).

Reduced writing-down allowance

98—(1) If a person sells part of any patent rights in a chargeable period, and for that period U is greater than N, the writing-down allowance for that period is—

$$\frac{U - N}{Y}$$

where—

U is the unrelieved qualifying expenditure for the chargeable period,

N is the net proceeds of any sales of the patent rights which take place in the chargeable period (so far as those proceeds consist of capital sums), and

Y is the number of complete years of the writing-down period remaining at the beginning of the chargeable period.

(2) If an amount is calculated under sub-paragraph (1) for a chargeable period, that amount is also the amount of the writing-down allowance for subsequent chargeable periods until another sale in a period for which U is greater than N causes a fresh calculation to be made under sub-paragraph (1).

(3) If a chargeable period is more or less than a year, an allowance calculated under sub-paragraph (1) or (2) is proportionately increased or reduced.

Former enactment—TA 1988 s 523(4); change in law.

Balancing allowance on sale or expiry of patent rights

99—(1) A person is entitled to a balancing allowance for a chargeable period in respect of qualifying expenditure if there is unrelieved qualifying expenditure for that period and any of the following occur in that period—

(*a*) the patent rights come to an end without subsequently being revived, or
(*b*) the person sells all of those rights, or so much of them as that person still owned at the beginning of the period.

This is subject to sub-paragraph (2).

(2) The person is not entitled to a balancing allowance unless—

(*a*) a writing-down allowance has been given in respect of the expenditure, or
(*b*) a writing-down allowance could, but for the rights coming to an end or being sold, have been given in respect of the expenditure.

(3) The amount of the balancing allowance is—

(*a*) in the case of a sale, equal to the unrelieved qualifying expenditure for the chargeable period, less the net proceeds of sales taking place in the chargeable period (so far as they consist of capital sums), and
(*b*) in any other case, equal to the unrelieved qualifying expenditure for the chargeable period.

Former enactment—TA 1988 s 523(2), (6)(*a*).

Balancing charges

100—(1) A balancing charge is made on a person for a chargeable period in respect of qualifying expenditure if in that period—

(*a*) the person sells some or all of the patent rights, and
(*b*) the net proceeds of sale (so far as they consist of capital sums) from the sales in that period exceed any unrelieved qualifying expenditure for that period.

The charge is calculated in accordance with sub-paragraphs (2) to (5).

(2) If there is no unrelieved qualifying expenditure, the amount of the balancing charge is equal to the net proceeds of sale (so far as they consist of capital sums).

This is subject to sub-paragraphs (4) and (5).

(3) If there is some unrelieved qualifying expenditure, the amount of the balancing charge is equal to the amount by which the net proceeds of sale (so far as they consist of capital sums) exceed the unrelieved qualifying expenditure.

This is subject to sub-paragraphs (4) and (5).

(4) The total amount of the first balancing charge must not exceed the total writing-down allowances actually given in respect of the expenditure.

(5) The total amount on which a second or further balancing charge is made must not exceed the total writing-down allowances actually made in respect of the expenditure, less the amount of any earlier charge.

Former enactments—Sub-paras (1)–(3): TA 1988 523(3).
Sub-paras (4), (5): TA 1988 s 523(6)(*b*).

Giving effect to allowances and charges

101—(1) Sub-paragraph (2) applies if—

(*a*) a person is entitled to a writing-down allowance or a balancing allowance or liable to a balancing charge in respect of qualifying expenditure, and

(*b*) the trade use condition is met.

(2) The allowance or charge is to be given effect in calculating the profits of that person's trade, by treating—

(*a*) the allowance as an expense of the trade, and

(*b*) the charge as a receipt of the trade.

(3) Sub-paragraph (4) applies if—

(*a*) a person is entitled to a writing-down allowance or a balancing allowance or liable to a balancing charge in respect of qualifying expenditure, and

(*b*) the trade use condition is not met.

(4) Sections 479 and 480 apply in relation to giving effect to the allowance or charge referred to in sub-paragraph (3) as they apply in relation to giving effect to an allowance or charge under Chapter 3 of Part 8 in respect of qualifying non-trade expenditure.

(5) For the purposes of Part 8 a person's "income from patents" includes balancing charges to which the person is liable in respect of qualifying expenditure.

Former enactments—TA 1988 ss 528(1)–(4), 532(1), 533(1); CAA 1990 ss 140(2), 144(2), 161(2) ("chargeable period"), (5).

SUPPLEMENTARY PROVISIONS

Limit on qualifying expenditure

102 Section 481 does not apply to expenditure incurred before 1st April 1986, and subsections (5) and (6) of that section do not apply to expenditure incurred before 27th July 1989.

Former enactment—FA 1989 Sch 13 para 27.

PART 10
DREDGING ALLOWANCES
Writing-down allowances

103—(1) Section 487(2) applies with the substitution of "50 years" for "25 years" in the case of expenditure incurred before 6th November 1962.

(2) Section 487(3) applies with the substitution of "2%" for "4%" in the case of expenditure incurred before 6th November 1962.

Former enactment—CAA 1990 s 134(1).

Balancing allowances

104 The reference in section 488(1)(*d*) to allowances previously made in respect of the expenditure—

(*a*) includes any initial allowance made in respect of it under section 17 of FA 1956 or section 67 of CAA 1968, and

(*b*) except in relation to initial allowances, is to be construed as if section 17 of FA 1956 had always had effect (instead of having effect only for chargeable periods after the year 1955–56).

Former enactment—CAA 1990 s 134(3).

The writing-down period

105—(1) This paragraph applies where it is provided under Part 9 that writing-down allowances are to be made in respect of any expenditure during a writing-down period of any specified length.

(2) If allowances were made under paragraph 27(2) of Schedule 14 to the Finance Act 1965—

(*a*) for income tax purposes, for either of the tax years 1964–65 and 1965–66, and

(*b*) for accounting periods of a company falling wholly or partly within either of those years,

the periods for which allowances were made are added together in calculating the writing-down period, even though (according to the calendar) the same time is counted twice.

Former enactment—CAA 1990 s 146(4).

PART 11

CONTRIBUTIONS

Regional development grants

106—(1) Section 534(1) applies as if a grant falling within that subsection included—

(*a*) a grant made under Part II of the Industrial Development Act 1982 (c 52) on an application made before 1st April 1988;

(*b*) a grant made under Part I of the Industry Act 1972 (c 63), or a grant made under Northern Ireland legislation and declared by the Treasury to correspond to a grant under that Part.

(2) Section 534(2) does not apply if the expenditure was incurred, or the grant was paid, before 10th March 1982.

Former enactments—CAA 1990 s 153(1); FA 1982 s 137(7).

Contributions not made by public bodies and not eligible for tax relief

107 Section 536 applies with the omission of subsection (3)(*b*) in relation to contributions made before 27th July 1989.

Former enactment—CAA 1990 s 153(5).

Conditions for allowances

108 In section 536(5), as it applies for the purposes of section 537(2), paragraphs (*a*)(iv) and (*b*) do not apply in relation to contributions made before 27th July 1989.

Former enactment—CAA 1990 s 154(5)(*a*).

109 Section 538(2)(*b*)(ii) applies in relation to contributions made before 6th April 1990 with the omission of ''or to allocate the expenditure to a pool under Part 2''.

Former enactment—FA 1990 Sch 13 para 5(2).

Agricultural buildings

110 Sections 368, 375 and 379 apply with the necessary modifications, instead of section 542, in relation to contributions made before 27th July 1989.

Former enactment—CAA 1990 s 155(7).

PART 12

SUPPLEMENTAL

Transfer of insurance company business

111 Section 560 applies with—

(*a*) the substitution for subsection (1) of—

''(1) This section applies if assets are transferred as part of, or in connection with, a transfer of the whole or part of the long term business of an insurance company to another company in accordance with a scheme sanctioned by a court under section 49 of the Insurance Companies Act 1982.''; and

(*b*) the omission of subsection (2), in relation to transfers sanctioned or authorised before 1st July 1994.

Former enactment—FA 1995 s 53(2).

Election regarding sale consideration

112—(1) In relation to a transfer to which this paragraph applies, section 569(3) applies with the substitution for paragraph (*a*) of—

''(*a*) any of the parties is not resident in the United Kingdom at the time of the transfer and the circumstances are not at that time such that a relevant allowance or charge falls or might fall to be made to or on that party as a result of the transfer;''.

(2) This paragraph applies to—

(*a*) a transfer before 16th March 1993;

(*b*) a transfer in pursuance of a contract entered into before that date; and

(*c*) a transfer in pursuance of a contract entered into for the purpose of securing that obligations under a contract entered into before that date are complied with.

Former enactment—FA 1993 s 117(5).

CAA 2001

PART 13

OTHER ENACTMENTS

113—(1) Subsections (2) and (3) of section 578A of ICTA (expenditure on car hire) apply with the substitution of "£8,000" for "£12,000" in relation to expenditure incurred under a contract entered into before 11th March 1992.

(2) Subsection (4) of that section does not apply in relation to rebates made or transactions occurring before 29th April 1996.

Former enactment—Sub-para (1): F(No 2)A 1992 s 71(8).
Sub-para (2): FA 1996 Sch 39 para 1(4).

114 Paragraph 18A of Schedule 30 to ICTA (transitional provisions and savings) continues to have effect in relation to any relief to which it applied before the commencement of this Act despite the repeal by this Act of paragraph 8(43) of Schedule 1 to CAA 1990.

Former enactment—CAA 1990 Sch 1 para 8(43).

115 The repeals made by CAA 1990 do not have effect in relation to capital expenditure—

(a) which was not eligible expenditure within the meaning of section 39 of FA 1976 (which brought expenditure previously not within Chapter I of Part III of FA 1971 within that Chapter but with certain exceptions), and

(b) which was incurred in a chargeable period ending before 6th April 1976.

Former enactment—CAA 1990 s 82(1).

116—(1) Sections 40A to 40D of F(No 2)A 1992 (films) apply with the necessary modifications in relation to—

(a) expenditure on the production of a film—

(i) completed before 21st March 2000, or

(ii) completed on or after that date, if the first day of principal photography is before that date, unless the person incurring the expenditure elects that those modifications should not apply;

(b) expenditure on the acquisition of a film, tape or disc incurred before 6th April 2000.

(2) The necessary modifications are—

(a) the substitution for section 40A(1) of—

"(1) Expenditure which—

(a) is incurred on the production or acquisition of a film, tape or disc, and

(b) would, apart from this subsection, constitute capital expenditure on the provision of plant or machinery for the purposes of Part 2 of the Capital Allowances Act,

is to be regarded for the purposes of the Tax Acts as expenditure of a revenue nature unless an election under section 40D below has effect with respect to it.";

(b) in section 40A(2), the substitution of "the production or acquisition of a film, tape or disc" for "the master version of a film" and of "of the film, tape or disc" for "of the master version";

(c) in section 40A(3), the substitution of "film, tape or disc" for "master version of a film" and of "the film, tape or disc" for "the master version" (in both places);

(d) the substitution for section 40A(5) of—

"(5) In this section and sections 40B to 40D below—

(a) any reference to a film is a reference to an original master negative of the film and its soundtrack, if any;

(b) any reference to a tape is a reference to an original master film tape or original master audio tape; and

(c) any reference to a disc is a reference to an original master film disc or original master audio disc;

and any reference to the acquisition of a film, tape or disc includes a reference to the acquisition of any description of rights in a film, tape or disc.";

(e) in section 40B(1), the substitution of "films, tapes or discs" for "master versions of films" and of "film, tape or disc" for "master version of a film";

(f) in section 40B(4), the substitution of "film, tape or disc" for "master version of the film" and of "film, tape or disc" for "master version";

(g) in section 40B(5), the substitution of "film, tape or disc" for "master version of the film";

(h) in section 40C(1), the substitution of "film, tape or disc" for "master version of the film";

(i) in section 40C(2), the substitution of "film, tape or disc" for "master version of the film";

(j) in section 40D(2), the substitution of "films, tapes or discs" for "master versions of films", of "film, tape or disc" for "master version of a film" and of "the film, tape or disc" for "the master version" (in both places);

(k) in section 40D(3), the substitution of "film, tape or disc" for "master version";

(l) in section 40D(4), the substitution of "film, tape or disc" for "master version of the film" (in both places);

(*m*) in section 40D(6), the substitution of "a film, tape or disc" for "the master version of a film" and of "of the film, tape or disc" for "of the master version"; and

(*n*) in section 40D(7), the substitution of "film, tape or disc" for "master version of a film".

(3) An election under sub-paragraph (1)(*a*) is irrevocable.

(4) For the purposes of sub-paragraph (1)(*a*) a film is completed at the time when it is first in a form in which it can reasonably be regarded as ready for copies of it to be made and distributed for presentation to the general public.

(5) In sub-paragraph (1)(*b*)—

(*a*) "film" means an original master negative of the film and its soundtrack, if any;

(*b*) "tape" means an original master film tape or original master audio tape; and

(*c*) "disc" means an original master film disc or original master audio disc;

and the acquisition of a film, tape or disc includes the acquisition of any description of rights in a film, tape or disc.

Former enactment—FA 2000 s 113(5), (6).

117 Section 40D of F(No 2)A 1992 (election relating to tax treatment of films expenditure) applies with the omission of—

(*a*) paragraph (*a*) of subsection (1); and

(*b*) subsections (3) to (7),

if the film, tape or disc of the film was completed before 10th March 1992.

Former enactment—F(No 2)A 1992 s 69(5).

SCHEDULE 4

REPEALS

Section 580

Short title and chapter	Extent of repeal
Taxes Management Act 1970 (c 9)	In section 98 in column 1 of the Table the words "Sections 23(4) and 49(4) of the Capital Allowances Act 1990".
Finance Act 1982 (c 39)	Section 137(2), (3), (6) and (7).
London Regional Transport Act 1984 (c 32)	In Schedule 5, paragraph 5(b) and the word "and" before it.
Income and Corporation Taxes Act 1988 (c 1)	In sections 65A(7) and 70A(6) the words "and section 29 of the 1990 Act (provisions relating to furnished holiday accommodation)".
	In section 83A, in subsection (2), paragraph (b) and the word "or" before it and in subsection (3), paragraph (b) and the word "and" before it.
	In section 84, in subsection (1), paragraph (b) and the word "or" before it and in subsection (3), paragraph (b) and the word "and" before it.
	In section 117, in subsection (1), the words "or allowed" (in each place), "or section 141 of the 1990 Act", paragraph (b) and the word "or" before it, and, in subsection (2), in the definition of "the aggregate amount", the words "or allowed", "or section 141 of the 1990 Act", paragraph (b) and the word "or" before it.
	In section 118, in subsection (1) the words "or allowed" (in each place), "or section 145 of the 1990 Act", paragraph (b) and the word "or" before it, and, in subsection (2), in the definition of "the aggregate amount", the words "or allowed", "or section 145 of the 1990 Act", and paragraph (b) and the word "or" before it.
	In section 198(2), the words "and Part II of the 1990 Act (capital allowances in respect of machinery and plant)".
	In section 384(10), the words following paragraph (b).
	Section 393A(5) and (6).

Short title and chapter	Extent of repeal
	In section 397, in subsection (5), the definition of "basis year" and, in the definition of "chargeable period", the words from "or any basis period" to the end of the definition; and subsection (6).
	In section 411(10) the words "Without prejudice to the provisions of section 161(5) of the 1990 Act".
	Sections 434D and 434E.
	Sections 520 to 523.
	Section 528(1) and (4).
	Section 530.
	In section 531, in subsection (3), the words following paragraph (b) and in subsection (7) the words "and section 530(1) and (6)".
	In section 533(1), in paragraph (b) of the definition of "income from patents", the words "520(6), 523(3)," and the definition of "the commencement of the patent".
	In section 577, in subsection (1), paragraph (c) and the word "and" before it, in subsection (7)(a) the words ", or to the use of an asset for," (in both places) and in subsection (10) the words ", or any claim for capital allowances in respect of the use of an asset for,".
	In section 834(2), the words "and also for sections 144 and 145 of the 1990 Act".
	In Schedule 19AC, paragraph 9C.
Finance Act 1989 (c 26)	Section 121.
	In Schedule 13, paragraph 27.
Capital Allowances Act 1990 (c 1)	The whole Act.
Finance Act 1990 (c 29)	Sections 60, 87 and 103.
	In Schedule 7, paragraph 9.
	In Schedule 9, paragraph 5.
	In Schedule 13, paragraphs 1 to 6.
	Schedule 17.
Finance Act 1991 (c 31)	Sections 59 to 61.
	Schedule 14.
	In Schedule 15, paragraph 28.
Disability Living Allowance and Disability Working Allowance Act 1991 (c 21)	In Schedule 2, paragraphs 20 and 21.
Water (Consolidation) (Consequential Provisions) Act 1991 (c 60)	In Schedule 1, paragraph 53.
Social Security Contributions and Benefits Act 1992 (c 4)	In Schedule 2, paragraph 1(b) and, in paragraph 2, the words from "subject to deduction" to the end.
Social Security (Consequential Provisions) Act 1992 (c 6)	In Schedule 2, paragraph 109.
Social Security Contributions and Benefits (Northern Ireland) Act 1992 (c 7)	In Schedule 2, paragraph 1(b) and, in paragraph 2, the words from "subject to deduction" to the end.
Social Security (Consequential Provisions) (Northern Ireland) Act 1992 (c 9)	In Schedule 2, paragraph 38.
Taxation of Chargeable Gains Act 1992 (c 12)	In section 195, in subsection (3), the words from "and "basis year"" to the end, subsection (5) and in subsection (6), paragraph (b) and the word "and" before it.
	In section 288(1), the definition of "the 1990 Act".
	In Schedule 10, paragraph 21.

Short title and chapter	Extent of repeal
Finance (No 2) Act 1992 (c 48)	In section 43(1), the definition of "the 1990 Act".
	Sections 67 to 71.
	Schedule 13.
	In Schedule 17, in paragraph 5(5), paragraph (c) and the word "and" before it.
Finance Act 1993 (c 34)	Sections 113 to 117.
	Schedules 12 and 13.
Finance Act 1994 (c 9)	Sections 117, 118(6)(a), 119(1), 120 and 121.
	Sections 211(1) and 212 to 213.
	Section 214(4) to (6).
	In Schedule 24, in paragraph 1(1), the definition of "the Allowances Act".
	In Schedule 25, in paragraph 5(3), the definition of "the 1990 Act".
Value Added Tax Act 1994 (c 23)	In Schedule 14, paragraph 11.
Finance Act 1995 (c 4)	Sections 94 to 101.
	In Schedule 8, paragraphs 23(1) and 24.
	In Schedule 9, paragraph 3.
Finance Act 1996 (c 8)	Sections 135(3) to (5), 179 and 180.
	In Schedule 20, paragraph 44.
	In Schedule 21, paragraphs 26 to 34.
	Schedule 35.
	In Schedule 39, paragraph 1(1), (3) and (4).
Broadcasting Act 1996 (c 55)	In Schedule 7, in paragraph 1(1), the definition of "the Allowances Act" and in paragraph 13(1), in the heading the words "and structures".
Planning (Consequential Provisions) (Scotland) Act 1997 (c 11)	In Schedule 2, paragraph 45.
Finance Act 1997 (c 16).	Sections 66(2) and (5), 84 and 86.
	In Schedule 12, in paragraph 11, in sub-paragraph (8) the words "or its basis period" and sub-paragraph (15).
	Schedule 14.
	In Schedule 15, paragraphs 3, 4, 5(3), 7, 8 and (9)(2).
	Schedule 16.
Finance (No 2) Act 1997 (c 58)	Sections 42 to 47.
Social Security Act 1998 (c 14)	Section 59(2).
Petroleum Act 1998 (c 17).	In Schedule 4, paragraph 27.
Finance Act 1998 (c 36)	Sections 83 to 85.
	In Schedule 5, paragraphs 40 and 47 to 61.
	In Schedule 7, in paragraph 1 the word "528(1)(a)" and paragraph 4.
Finance Act 1999 (c 16).	Sections 50(2), 77 and 78.
	In Schedule 5, paragraph 2(3).
	In Schedule 11, paragraphs 4 to 8.
Greater London Authority Act 1999 (c 29).	In Schedule 33, paragraph 12(1)(a).
Finance Act 2000 (c 17).	Sections 70 to 72.
	Section 75(1) to (3), (5) and (6)(b) and (c).
	Section 76(1).
	Section 77.
	Section 79.
	Sections 80 and 81.
	Section 113.
	In Schedule 19, paragraphs 7 to 11.
	In Schedule 22, in paragraph 84(1) the words "or structure".
Transport Act 2000 (c 38).	In Schedule 26, in paragraph 1(1), the definition of "the 1990 Act".

Short title and chapter	Extent of repeal
Finance (No.2) Act 1992 (c. 48).	In section 65(1), the definition of "the 1990 Act".
Finance Act 1993 (c.34).	Sections 67 to 74. Schedule 13. In Schedule 12, in paragraph 5(5), paragraph (a) and the word "and" before it.
Finance Act 1994 (c.9).	Sections 113 to 117. Schedules 12 and 13. Sections 117, 118(10a), 119(1), 120 and 121. Sections 211(1) and 212 to 219. Section 214(4)(b), (c). In Schedule 22A, in paragraph 1(1), the definition of "the Allowances Act". In Schedule 25, in paragraph 5(2), the definition of "the 1990 Act".
Value Added Tax Act 1994 (c. 23).	In Schedule 14, paragraph 11.
Finance Act 1995 (c.4).	Sections 94 to 101. In Schedule 8, paragraphs 23(1) and 24. In Schedule 9, paragraph 3.
Finance Act 1996 (c.8).	Sections 135(1) to (7), 179 and 180. In Schedule 20, paragraph 44. In Schedule 21, paragraphs 2c to 34. Schedule 35. In Schedule 39, paragraph 1(1), (3) and (4).
Broadcasting Act 1996 (c.55).	In Schedule 7, in paragraph 1(1), the definition of "the Allowances Act", and in paragraph 13(1), in the heading, the words "and charities".
Planning (Consequential Provisions) (Scotland) Act 1997 (c.11).	In Schedule 2, paragraph 45.
Finance Act 1997 (c.16).	Sections 80(2) and (3), 84 and 86. In Schedule 12, in paragraph 11, in sub-paragraph (8) the words "for its basic period", and sub-paragraph (10). Schedule 14. In Schedule 15, paragraphs 1, 4, 5(b), 7, 8 and 9, (12). Schedule 16.
Finance (No.2) Act 1997 (c.58).	Sections 42 to 47.
Social Security Act 1998 (c.14).	Section 59(2).
Petroleum Act 1998 (c.17), Finance Act 1998 (c.36).	In Schedule 4, paragraph 27. Sections 28 to 35. In Schedule 5, paragraphs 48 and 47 to 61. In Schedule 7, in paragraph 1 the word "28 May", and paragraph 8.
Finance Act 1999 (c.16).	Sections 50, 52, 77 and 78. In Schedule 4, paragraph 2(3). In Schedule 11, paragraphs 4 to 8.
Greater London Authority Act 1999 (c.29).	In Schedule 33, paragraph 1.2(1)(a).
Finance Act 2000 (c.17).	Sections 70 to 72. Section 75(1)(a), (3), (5) and (6)(b) and (c). Section 78(1). Section 97. Section 79. Sections 80 and 81. Section 113. In Schedule 19, paragraphs 7 to 11. In Schedule 22, in paragraph 84(1) the words "or structure". In Schedule 20, in paragraph 1(1), the definition of "the 1990 Act".
Transport Act 2000 (c.38),	

FINANCE ACT 2001

(2001 Chapter 9)

ARRANGEMENT OF SECTIONS

PART 3

INCOME TAX, CORPORATION TAX AND CAPITAL GAINS TAX

CHAPTER 1
CHARGE AND RATES

Income tax

Corporation tax

CHAPTER 2
OTHER PROVISIONS

Employment

Enterprise incentives

Capital allowances

Other relieving provisions

Pension funds

Limited liability partnerships

Schedule 24—Creative artists: relief for fluctuating profits
        Part 1—New Schedule 4A to the Taxes Act 1988
        Part 2—Consequential amendments
Schedule 25—Limited liability partnerships: investment LLPs and property investment LLPs
Schedule 26—Capital gains tax: taper relief: business assets
Schedule 27—Double taxation relief
Schedule 28—Life policies, life annuities and capital redemption policies
        Part 1—Assignment or surrender of part of the rights
        Part 2—Provision of information by insurers etc
Schedule 29—Amendments to machinery of self-assessment
        Part 1—Amendment or correction of return
        Part 2—Enquiries into returns
        Part 3—Referral of questions during enquiry
        Part 4—Procedure on completion of enquiry
        Part 5—Minor and consequential amendments
Schedule 33—Repeals

An Act to grant certain duties, to alter other duties, and to amend the law relating to the National Debt and the Public Revenue, and to make further provision in connection with Finance.

[11 May 2001]

PART 3
INCOME TAX, CORPORATION TAX AND CAPITAL GAINS TAX

CHAPTER 1
CHARGE AND RATES
Income tax

50 Charge and rates for 2001–02

Income tax shall be charged for the year 2001–02, and for that year—

    (*a*) the starting rate shall be 10%,
    (*b*) the basic rate shall be 22%, and
    (*c*) the higher rate shall be 40%.

Commentary—*Simon's Direct Tax Service* **E1.102.**

51 Starting rate limit for 2001–02

(1) For the year 2001–02 the amount specified in section 1(2)(*aa*) of the Taxes Act 1988 (the starting rate limit) shall be £1,880.

(2) Accordingly, section 1(4) of that Act (indexation), so far as it relates to the amount so specified, does not apply for that year.

Commentary—*Simon's Direct Tax Service* **E1.102.**

52 Children's tax credit: amount for 2001–02 and subsequent years

(1) (*amends* TA 1988 s 257AA(2)).

(2) This section has effect for the year 2001–02 and subsequent years of assessment.

Commentary—*Simon's Direct Tax Service* **E2.502.**

53 Children's tax credit: baby rate

(1)–(3) (*insert* TA 1988 s 257AA(2A), (3A), (4A)).

(4) In section 257C(1) and (3) of the Taxes Act 1988 (indexation) for ''257AA(2)'' substitute ''257AA(2) and (2A)''.

(5) Schedule 13B to the Taxes Act 1988 (children's tax credit: provisions applicable where child lives with more than one adult in a year of assessment) is amended in accordance with Schedule 11 to this Act.

(6) Subsections (1) to (3) and (5) above have effect for the year 2002–03 and subsequent years of assessment.

(7) Subsection (4) above has effect for the purposes of the application of section 257AA of the Taxes Act 1988 for the year 2003–04 and subsequent years of assessment.

Commentary—*Simon's Direct Tax Service* **E2.502.**

Corporation tax

54 Charge and main rate for financial year 2002

Corporation tax shall be charged for the financial year 2002 at the rate of 30%.

Commentary—*Simon's Direct Tax Service* **D2.108.**

55 Small companies' rate and fraction for financial year 2001

For the financial year 2001—

    (*a*) the small companies' rate shall be 20%, and

    (*b*) the fraction mentioned in section 13(2) of the Taxes Act 1988 (marginal relief for small companies) shall be one fortieth.

Commentary—*Simon's Direct Tax Service* **D2.109.**

56 Corporation tax starting rate and fraction for financial year 2001

For the financial year 2001—

    (*a*) the corporation tax starting rate shall be 10%, and

    (*b*) the fraction mentioned in section 13AA(3) of the Taxes Act 1988 (marginal relief for small companies) shall be one fortieth.

Commentary—*Simon's Direct Tax Service* **D2.109A.**

CHAPTER 2
OTHER PROVISIONS

Employment

57 Mileage allowances: exemptions and relief

(1) (*inserts* TA 1988 ss 197AD–197AH).

(2) (*inserts* TA 1988 Sch 12AA).

(3) The consequential amendments in Part 2 of Schedule 12 to this Act have effect.

(4) This section has effect for the year 2002–03 and subsequent years of assessment.

Commentary—*Simon's Direct Tax Service* **E4.705.**

58 Mileage allowances: nil liability notices

(1) This section applies if—

    (*a*) mileage allowance payments are made to an employee or office-holder in respect of the use of a vehicle that is not a company vehicle, or

    (*b*) mileage allowance relief is available in respect of the use by an employee or office-holder of a vehicle.

(2) A nil liability notice in force immediately before 6th April 2002 shall cease to have effect in relation to—

    (*a*) payments made, or

    (*b*) benefits, facilities, non-cash vouchers, credit-tokens or cash vouchers provided,

in respect of expenses incurred in connection with the use of the vehicle by the employee or office-holder for business travel.

(3) In subsection (2) "nil liability notice" means a notice under—

    (*a*) section 144(1) of the Taxes Act 1988 (notice of nil liability in respect of non-cash vouchers, credit-tokens or cash vouchers), or

    (*b*) section 166(1) of that Act (notice of nil liability in respect of payments, benefits or facilities).

(4) In this section—

"business travel" has the meaning given by paragraph 2 of Schedule 12AA to the Taxes Act 1988;

"company vehicle" has the meaning given by paragraph 6 of Schedule 12AA to that Act; and

"mileage allowance payments" has the meaning given by section 197AD(2) of that Act.

Commentary—*Simon's Direct Tax Service* **E4.651, E4.705.**

59 Employees' vehicles: withdrawal of capital allowances

(1) (substitutes CAA 2001 s 36).

(2) (*repeals* CAA 2001 s 80).

(3) The above amendments apply to expenditure incurred on or after 6th April 2002.

(4) Where immediately before 6th April 2002—

(*a*) expenditure incurred by an employee on the provision of a mechanically propelled road vehicle, or a cycle, was qualifying expenditure for the purposes of Part 2 of the Capital Allowances Act 2001, and

(*b*) the employee is treated for the purposes of that Part as owning an asset as a result of that expenditure having been incurred,

the employee shall be treated for the purposes of that Part of that Act as if he had ceased to own the asset at that time.

(5) In subsection (4)—

"employee" includes an office-holder; and

"cycle" has the meaning given by section 192(1) of the Road Traffic Act 1988.

Commentary—*Simon's Direct Tax Service* **E4.711.**

60 Exemption for works bus services: extension to minibuses

(1) Section 197AA of the Taxes Act 1988 (works bus services: exemption from charge on benefits) is amended as follows.

(2)–(5), (6) (*amend* TA 1988 s 197AA(1)–(3), (6), *insert* sub-s (9)).

(7) This section has effect for the year 2002–03 and subsequent years of assessment.

Commentary—*Simon's Direct Tax Service* **E4.612.**

61 Employee share ownership plans

The provisions relating to employee share ownership plans are amended in accordance with Schedule 13 to this Act.

Commentary—*Simon's Direct Tax Service* **E4.528.**

Enterprise incentives

62 Enterprise management incentives

Schedule 14 to this Act (which amends Schedule 14 to the Finance Act 2000 (enterprise management incentives)) has effect.

Commentary—*Simon's Direct Tax Service* **E4.543.**

63 Enterprise investment scheme

Schedule 15 to this Act (which makes amendments relating to the enterprise investment scheme) has effect.

Commentary—*Simon's Direct Tax Service* **E3.102.**

64 Venture capital

(1) Schedule 16 to this Act has effect.

(2) In that Schedule—

Part 1 makes amendments relating to venture capital trusts; and

Part 2 makes amendments relating to the corporate venturing scheme.

Commentary—*Simon's Direct Tax Service* **E3.602, E3.629.**

Capital allowances

65 Energy-saving plant and machinery

Schedule 17 to this Act (first-year allowances in respect of expenditure on energy-saving plant and machinery) has effect—

(*a*) for income tax purposes, as respects allowances and charges falling to be made for chargeable periods ending on or after 6th April 2001, and

(*b*) for corporation tax purposes, as respects allowances and charges falling to be made for chargeable periods ending on or after 1st April 2001.

Commentary—*Simon's Direct Tax Service* **B2.301, B2.321.**

66 Fixtures provided in connection with energy management services

(1) Schedule 18 to this Act (fixtures provided in connection with provision of energy management services) has effect in relation to expenditure incurred on or after 1st April 2001.

(2) The Schedule has effect—

(*a*) for income tax purposes, as respects allowances and charges falling to be made for chargeable periods ending on or after 6th April 2001, and

(*b*) for corporation tax purposes, as respects allowances and charges falling to be made for chargeable periods ending on or after 1st April 2001.

Commentary—*Simon's Direct Tax Service* **B2.350, B2.351.**

67 Conversion of parts of business premises into flats

Schedule 19 to this Act (capital allowances in respect of expenditure on the conversion of parts of business premises into flats) has effect in relation to expenditure incurred on or after the day on which this Act is passed.

Commentary—*Simon's Direct Tax Service* **B2.101.**

68 Decommissioning of offshore oil infrastructure

Schedule 20 to this Act (capital allowances in respect of expenditure incurred on decommissioning offshore infrastructure) has effect.

Commentary—*Simon's Direct Tax Service* **B2.337, D4.1010.**

69 Minor amendments

(1) Schedule 21 (which makes minor amendments to the Capital Allowances Act 2001) has effect.

(2) The amendments made by the Schedule have effect—

(*a*) for income tax purposes, as respects allowances and charges falling to be made for chargeable periods ending on or after 6th April 2001, and

(*b*) for corporation tax purposes, as respects allowances and charges falling to be made for chargeable periods ending on or after 1st April 2001.

Commentary—*Simon's Direct Tax Service* **B2.109, B2.206A, B2.262, B2.302.**

Other relieving provisions

70 Relief for expenditure on remediation of contaminated land

(1) Schedule 22 to this Act (tax relief for expenditure on land remediation) has effect for accounting periods ending on or after 1st April 2001.

(2) In that Schedule—

Part 1 provides for a deduction for certain capital expenditure in computing the profits of a Schedule A business or the profits of a trade for the purposes of Case I of Schedule D,

Part 2 provides for entitlement to relief,

Part 3 provides for the manner of giving effect to the relief,

Part 4 makes special provision for companies carrying on life assurance business, and

Part 5 contains supplementary provisions.

(3) Schedule 23 to this Act (which contains consequential amendments) has effect accordingly.

Commentary—*Simon's Direct Tax Service* **D2.201, D2.1401.**

71 Creative artists: relief for fluctuating profits

(1) (*Inserts* TA 1988 s 95A).

(2) (*Inserts* TA 1988 Sch 4A).

(3) (*Repeals* TA 1988 ss 534, 535, 537A, 538 with effect for payments actually receivable after 5 April 2001).

(4) Part 2 of Schedule 24 to this Act contains amendments consequential on the preceding provisions of this section.

Commentary—*Simon's Direct Tax Service* **B3.816, B3.833.**

72 Expenditure on film production etc

(*Amends* F(No 2)A 1997 s 48(2)(*a*)).

Commentary—*Simon's Direct Tax Service* **B3.1307.**

73 Deductions for business gifts: yearly limit

(1) Section 577 of the Taxes Act 1988 (prohibition on deduction of expenses in providing business entertainment or gifts) is amended as follows.

(2) (*Amends* TA 1988 s 577(8)(*b*)).

(3) (*Amends* TA 1988 s 577(8A)).

(4) This section applies in relation to the year 2001–02 and subsequent years of assessment or, in the case of companies, in relation to accounting periods beginning on or after 1st April 2001.

Commentary—*Simon's Direct Tax Service* **B3.1438, E4.704.**

Pension funds

74 Payments to employers out of pension funds

(1) Section 601 of the Taxes Act 1988 (charge on payment to employer out of funds held for purposes of exempt approved scheme) is amended as follows.

(2) (*Amends* TA 1988 s 601(2)).

(3) (*Inserts* TA 1988 s 601(2A)).

(4) This section applies to payments made to employers after the passing of this Act.

Commentary—*Simon's Direct Tax Service* **E7.238.**

Limited liability partnerships

75 Limited liability partnerships: general

(1) (*Substitutes* TA 1988 s 118ZA).

(2) (*Substitutes* TCGA 1992 s 59A).

(3) (*Inserts* TCGA 1992 s 169A).

(4) (*Amends* TCGA 1992 s 170(9)(*b*)).

(5) Subsection (3) above shall be deemed to have come into force on 3rd May 2001 and applies where section 59A(1) of the Taxation of Chargeable Gains Act 1992 ceased or ceases to apply as mentioned in section 169A of that Act (as inserted by that subsection) on or after that date.

(6) The other provisions of this section shall be deemed to have come into force on 6th April 2001.

Commentary—*Simon's Direct Tax Service* **C1.207, C3.201, E5.305.**

76 Limited liability partnerships: investment LLPs and property investment LLPs

(1) Schedule 25 to this Act has effect with respect to limited liability partnerships whose business consists wholly or mainly in the making of investments.

(2) The provisions of that Schedule shall be deemed to have come into force on 6th April 2001.

Commentary—*Simon's Direct Tax Service* **E5.305.**

Chargeable gains

77 Notional transfers within a group

(1) Section 171A of the Taxation of Chargeable Gains Act 1992 (notional transfers within a group) shall be deemed to have been enacted with the following amendments.

(2), (3) (*Amend* TCGA 1992 s 171A(2)–(4)).

Commentary—*Simon's Direct Tax Service* **D2.652A.**

78 Taper relief: assets qualifying as business assets

(1) Schedule A1 to the Taxation of Chargeable Gains Act 1992 (application of taper relief) shall have effect with the amendments specified in Schedule 26 to this Act.

(2) Those amendments shall have effect, and be deemed always to have had effect, as if they had been included among the amendments made by section 67 of the Finance Act 2000.

Commentary—*Simon's Direct Tax Service* **C2.1423, C2.1428.**

79 De-grouping charge: transitional relief

(*Inserts* FA 2000 Sch 29 para 47).

Commentary—*Simon's Direct Tax Service* **D2.661.**

80 Attribution of gains of non-resident companies

(1) Section 13 of the Taxation of Chargeable Gains Act 1992 (attribution of gains to members of non-resident companies) is amended as follows.

(2) (*Amends* TCGA 1992 s 13(4)).

(3) (*Substitutes* TCGA 1992 s 13(5)(*b*)).

(4) (*Substitutes* TCGA 1992 s 13(5A), (5B) for s (5A)).

(5) (*Inserts* TCGA 1992 s 13(10B)).

(6) This section applies to chargeable gains accruing as mentioned in section 13(1) of the Taxation of Chargeable Gains Act 1992 on or after 7th March 2001.

Commentary—*Simon's Direct Tax Service* **D2.316.**

International matters

81 Double taxation relief

Schedule 27 to this Act (double taxation relief) has effect.

Commentary—*Simon's Direct Tax Service* **F1.117, F1.122, F1.134.**

82 Controlled foreign companies: acceptable distribution policy

(1) Part I of Schedule 25 to the Taxes Act 1988 (acceptable distribution policy) is amended as follows.

(2) (*Amends* TA 1988 Sch 25 para 2).

(3) (*Inserts* TA 1988 Sch 25 para 2B).

(4)–(6) (*Amend* TA 1988 Sch 25 para 4).

(7) (*Inserts* TA 1988 Sch 25 para 4A).

(8) This section applies to dividends paid on or after 7th March 2001 by a controlled foreign company for any accounting period of that controlled foreign company which ends on or after that date.

(9) In this section "accounting period" and "controlled foreign company" have the same meaning as they have in Chapter IV of Part XVII of the Taxes Act 1988.

Commentary—*Simon's Direct Tax Service* **D4.1220.**

Miscellaneous

83 Life policies, life annuity contracts and capital redemption policies

(1) Schedule 28 to this Act (which makes amendments relating to Chapter II of Part XIII of the Taxes Act 1988) has effect.

(2) The amendments made by Part 1 of that Schedule (which relate to the assignment or surrender of part of, or a share in, the rights conferred by a policy or contract) have effect, in the case of any policy or contract, in relation to any year (within the meaning given by section 546(4) of the Taxes Act 1988) beginning on or after 6th April 2001.

(3) The amendments made by Part 2 of that Schedule (which relate to the provision by insurers etc of information relating to chargeable events happening in connection with a policy or contract) have effect in relation to chargeable events happening on or after 6th April 2002.

Commentary—*Simon's Direct Tax Service* **E3.501, E3.503.**

84 Exclusion of deductions for deemed manufactured payments

(1) Section 736B of the Taxes Act 1988 (deemed manufactured payments in case of stock lending arrangements) is amended as follows.

(2) (*Amends* TA 1988 s 736B(2)).

(3) (*Inserts* TA 1988 s 736B(2A)).

(4) This section applies to payments treated under section 736B as made on or after 3rd October 2000.

Commentary—*Simon's Direct Tax Service* **A7.716, A7.802.**

85 Deduction of tax: payments between companies etc

(1) (*Inserts* TA 1988 s 349A–349D).

(2) (*Inserts* TMA 1970 s 98(4A)–(4C)).

(3) (*Inserts* TA 1988 s 338(4)(*aa*)).

(4) Subsections (1) to (3) apply to payments made on or after 1st April 2001.

(5) Sections 247 and 248 of the Taxes Act 1988 (companies within a group may elect for section 349 not to apply to payments between them) shall cease to have effect.

(6) Subsection (5) applies in relation to payments made after the day on which this Act is passed.

Commentary—*Simon's Direct Tax Service* **A3.402.**

86 Profits for purposes of small companies' relief

(1) Section 13 of the Taxes Act 1988 (small companies' relief) is amended in accordance with subsections (2) to (4).

(2) (*Amends* TA 1988 s 13(7)).

(3) (*Inserts* TA 1988 s 13(7A)).

(4) (*Substitutes* TA 1988 s 13(8AA)).

(5) (*Inserts* TA 1988 s 13ZA).

(6) The amendments made by this section apply for the purposes of accounting periods ending on or after 1st April 2001.

Commentary—*Simon's Direct Tax Service* A3.402, D2.109.

87 Tax deductions and credits: end of provisional repayment regime

(1) The provisions of section 438A of, and Schedule 19AB to, the Taxes Act 1988 (provisional repayments in respect of tax borne by deduction and tax credits) shall cease to have effect as follows.

(2) Those provisions shall not apply in relation to income tax borne by deduction from payments received after 30th September 2001.

(3) For the purposes of the following provisions (as they apply in relation to tax credits)—

   (*a*) section 121 of the Finance Act 1993 (application of Schedule 19AB to tax exempt business of friendly societies) and any regulations under that section, and
   (*b*) any regulations under section 333B of the Taxes Act 1988 (individual savings account business etc of insurance companies and friendly societies),

that Schedule shall be deemed to continue to apply in relation to pension business of insurance companies as it would do so apart from subsection (2).

(4) The power to make regulations under each of the sections referred to in subsection (3) includes power to set out the text of that Schedule as applied by regulations under that section.

(5) The provisions of section 438A of, and Schedule 19AB to, the Taxes Act 1988 shall not apply in relation to tax credits in respect of distributions made on or after 6th April 2004.

Commentary—*Simon's Direct Tax Service* A3.402, A7.1126, D4.534.

General

88 Amendments to the machinery of self-assessment

(1) Schedule 29 to this Act (amendments to the machinery of self-assessment) has effect.

(2) In that Schedule—

   Part 1 makes provision about the amendment or correction of returns,
   Part 2 makes provision about enquiries into returns,
   Part 3 makes provision for the referral of questions to the Special Commissioners during an enquiry,
   Part 4 makes provision about the procedure on completion of an enquiry, and
   Part 5 contains minor and consequential amendments.

(3) Except as otherwise provided, the amendments in that Schedule have effect as from the passing of this Act in relation to returns—

   (*a*) whether made before or after the passing of this Act, and
   (*b*) whether relating to periods before or after the passing of this Act.

Commentary—*Simon's Direct Tax Service* E1.802.

89 Recovery proceedings: minor amendments

(1) (*Amends* TMA 1970 ss 66(1), 67(1)).

(2) (*Substitutes* TMA 1970 s 69).

(3) (*Amends* TMA 1970 s 70(2)(*a*)).

Commentary—*Simon's Direct Tax Service* E1.824.

90 Repayment supplements: claim for relief involving two or more years

(1) Section 824 of the Taxes Act 1988 (repayment supplements) is amended as follows.

(2) (*Inserts* TA 1988 s 824(2C)).

(3) (*Inserts* TA 1988 s 824(3)(*ab*)).

(4) This section applies in relation to repayments made after the passing of this Act.

Commentary—*Simon's Direct Tax Service* E1.827.

91 Power to revise excessive penalties

(1) (*Amends* TMA 1970 s 100(6)).

(2) This section applies in relation to penalties determined at any time whether before or after the passing of this Act.

Commentary—*Simon's Direct Tax Service* E1.826.

PART 5
MISCELLANEOUS AND SUPPLEMENTARY PROVISIONS
Miscellaneous

107 Interest on unpaid tax, etc: foot-and-mouth disease

(1) This section applies in any case where, in exercise of their powers of care and management, the Commissioners of Inland Revenue agree that, by reason of circumstances arising as a result of the outbreak of foot-and-mouth disease, the payment of tax by a person may be deferred.

For this purpose "tax" includes any amount chargeable by way of tax, or as a result of the non-payment of tax, in respect of which interest would, apart from this section, be chargeable.

(2) Where this section applies no interest on the amount deferred shall be chargeable in respect of the period—

   (*a*) beginning with 31st January 2001 or, if the Commissioners so direct in any case, any later date from which the agreement for deferred payment has effect, and
   (*b*) ending with the date on which the agreement for deferred payment ceases to have effect.

(3) An agreement for deferred payment ceases to have effect at the end of the period of deferment specified in the agreement, subject as follows.

An agreement for deferred payment shall be treated as not ceasing to have effect if, or to the extent that, the Commissioners agree (whether before or after the end of the period of deferment specified in the agreement) to extend that period by reason of circumstances arising as a result of the outbreak of foot-and-mouth disease.

(4) For the purposes of subsection (3) as it applies to an agreement for payment by instalments, the period of deferment in relation to each instalment ends with the date on or before which that instalment is to be paid.

But if any instalment is not paid by the agreed date and the Commissioners do not agree in accordance with that subsection to extend the period of deferment, the whole agreement shall be treated as ceasing to have effect on that date.

(5) This section shall cease to have effect on a date specified by the Treasury by order made by statutory instrument.

This is without prejudice to its continued operation in relation to an agreement for deferred payment made by the Commissioners before the specified date.

(6) This section applies—

   (*a*) whether the agreement for deferred payment was made before or after the passing of this Act, and
   (*b*) whether the agreement for deferred payment was made before or after the amount to which it relates became due and payable.

(7) If in any case the Commissioners are satisfied that, although no agreement for deferred payment such as is mentioned in subsection (1) was made, such an agreement could have been made, this section shall apply as if such an agreement had been made.

The terms of the notional agreement shall be assumed to be such as the Commissioners are satisfied would have been agreed in the circumstances.

Commentary—*Simon's Direct Tax Service* A3.1321, 1323.
Modifications—Social Security Contributions (Deferred Payments and Interest) Regulations, SI 2001/1818 (application of this section for the purposes of Class 1, Class 1A and Class 1B social security contributions.
In sub-s (1), after the words "of tax", where it first occurs, the words "or a relevant contribution" to be inserted; and the second paragraph of that sub-section to be substituted; in sub-s (2), "12th May 2001" to be substituted for "31st January 2001", and in sub-s (6)(*a*), "the coming into force of the Social Security Contributions (Deferred Payments and Interest) Regulations 2001" to be substituted for "the passing of this Act". The substituted text in sub-s (1) to read as follows—

"For this purpose—

'relevant contribution' means a Class 1 contribution, a Class 1A contribution or a Class 1B contribution, within the meaning of section 1(2) of the Social Security Contributions and Benefits Act 1992, or, in the case of a contribution payable in Northern Ireland, section 1(2) of the Social Security Contributions and Benefits (Northern Ireland) Act 1992, in respect of which interest would apart from this section be chargeable; and
'tax' includes any amount chargeable by way of tax, or as a result of the non-payment of tax, in respect of which interest would apart from this section be chargeable.").

108 Trading funds

(1) Section 2C of the Government Trading Funds Act 1973 (limits on borrowing and public dividend capital) is amended as follows.

(2) In subsection (3) (upper limit on aggregate of borrowing etc maxima of trading funds), for "£2,000 million" substitute "£8,000 million".

(3) In subsection (4) (power to increase limit in subsection (3) but not above £4,000 million), for "£4,000 million" substitute "£10,000 million".

Supplementary

109 Interpretation

In this Act "the Taxes Act 1988" means the Income and Corporation Taxes Act 1988.

110 Repeals and revocations

(1) The enactments mentioned in Schedule 33 to this Act (which include provisions that are spent or of no practical utility) are repealed or revoked to the extent specified.

(2) The repeals and revocations specified in that Schedule have effect subject to the commencement provisions and savings contained or referred to in the notes set out in that Schedule.

111 Short title

This Act may be cited as the Finance Act 2001.

SCHEDULES

SCHEDULE 11

CHILDREN'S TAX CREDIT: BABY RATE: SUPPLEMENTARY

Section 53

Commentary—*Simon's Direct Tax Service* **E2.502.**

Introduction

1 Schedule 13B to the Taxes Act 1988 (children's tax credit: provisions applicable where child lives with more than one adult in a year of assessment) is amended as follows.

Child living with married or unmarried couple

2 (*amends* TA 1988 Sch 13B para 3).

Election that credit should go to lower-earning partner

3 (*amends* TA 1988 Sch 13B para 5).

Child living with more than one adult: other cases

4 (*amends* TA 1988 Sch 13B para 6).

Combined cases

5 (*amends* TA 1988 Sch 13B para 7).

Change of circumstances

6 (*amends* TA 1988 Sch 13B para 8).

SCHEDULE 12

MILEAGE ALLOWANCES

Section 57

Commentary—*Simon's Direct Tax Service* **E4.705.**

PART 1

NEW SCHEDULE 12AA TO THE TAXES ACT 1988

(*inserts* TA 1988 Sch 12AA).

PART 2

CONSEQUENTIAL AMENDMENTS

The Taxes Act 1988

1–15 (*amend* TA 1988 ss 153, 163, 167, 168, 192, 198, 200A, 200C, 200F, 332, 578A, 589, 589B, 646, Sch 12 para 1A).

Finance Act 2000 (c. 17)

16 (*amends* FA 2000 Sch 12 para 11(4)).

SCHEDULE 13

EMPLOYEE SHARE OWNERSHIP PLANS: AMENDMENTS

Section 61

Commentary—*Simon's Direct Tax Service* **E4.528.**

Introductory

1 Schedule 8 to the Finance Act 2000 (employee share ownership plans) is amended in accordance with this Schedule.

The employment requirement

2—(1) (*amends* FA 2000 Sch 8 para 14).

(2) This paragraph has effect in relation to awards of shares (within the meaning of Schedule 8 to the Finance Act 2000) made after the passing of this Act.

Meaning of "salary"

3—(1) (*Amends* FA 2000 Sch 8 para 48).

(2) This paragraph has effect in relation to any award of partnership shares (within the meaning of Schedule 8 to the Finance Act 2000) in relation to which the eligibility time falls after the passing of this Act.

(3) For this purpose "the eligibility time" means the time at which an individual, in order to participate in the award, is required, in accordance with paragraph 13(1)(*b*) of that Schedule, to be eligible to so participate.

No charge to tax on award of shares, etc

4—(1) (*Adds* FA 2000 Sch 8 para 78(3)).

(2) This paragraph has effect for the year 2001–02 and subsequent years of assessment.

Charge on disposal of beneficial interest during holding period

5—(1) (*Repeals* FA 2000 Sch 8 para 82(2)).

(2) This amendment shall be deemed always to have had effect.

Charge on distributions in respect of unappropriated shares

6—(1) (*Amends* FA 2000 Sch 8 para 88(3), (4)).

(2) This paragraph has effect in relation to any shares acquired by the trustees of an employee share ownership plan after the passing of this Act.

(3) For the purposes of sub-paragraph (2), "the trustees of an employee share ownership plan" means the body of persons established in accordance with paragraph 68 of Schedule 8 to the Finance Act 2000.

Dividend shares ceasing to be subject to plan: tax credit

7—(1) (*Amends* FA 2000 Sch 8 para 93(2)).

(2) This amendment shall be deemed always to have had effect.

Gains accruing to trustees

8—(1) (*Amends* FA 2000 Sch 8 para 98(2), (3)).

(2) This paragraph has effect in relation to any shares acquired by the trustees of an employee share ownership plan after the passing of this Act.

(3) For the purposes of sub-paragraph (2), "the trustees of an employee share ownership plan" means the body of persons established in accordance with paragraph 68 of Schedule 8 to the Finance Act 2000.

SCHEDULE 14

ENTERPRISE MANAGEMENT INCENTIVES: AMENDMENTS

Commentary—*Simon's Direct Tax Service* **E4.543.**

Section 62

1 Schedule 14 to the Finance Act 2000 (enterprise management incentives) is amended in accordance with this Schedule.

Period of notice

2 (*Amends* FA 2000 Sch 14 para 2).

3 (*Amends* FA 2000 Sch 14 para 4(4)).

General requirements to be met by option

4 (*Substitutes* FA 2000 Sch 14 para 8(*c*))

Purpose of granting option

5 (*Amends* FA 2000 Sch 14 para 9).

Value of options in respect of a company's shares

6 (*Substitutes* FA 2000 Sch 14 para 11).

Income tax: option to acquire shares at less than market value

7 (*Substitutes* FA 2000 Sch 14 para 45(2)–(4)).

Income tax: option to acquire shares at nil cost

8 (*Substitutes* FA 2000 Sch 14 para 46(2)).

Disqualifying events: alteration of share capital

9 (*Substitutes* FA 2000 Sch 14 para 47(1)(*e*)).

10—(1) Paragraph 49 (disqualifying events: alterations of share capital) is amended as follows.

(2) (*amends* FA 2000 Sch 14 para 49(1)).

(3) (*substitutes* FA 2000 Sch 14 para 49(2)).

Income tax charge arising on disqualifying event

11—(1) Paragraph 53 (effect of disqualifying event) is amended as follows.

(2) (*substitutes* FA 2000 Sch 14 para 53(2)–(2D)).

(3) (*amends* FA 2000 Sch 14 para 53(3)).

Qualifying requirements for replacement option

12 (*amends* FA 2000 Sch 14 para 63).

Commencement

13—(1) The amendments made by paragraphs 2 to 6 and 12 have effect in relation to any right to acquire shares granted after the passing of this Act.

(2) The amendments made by paragraphs 7, 8 and 11 have effect in relation to any right to acquire shares exercised after the passing of this Act.

(3) The amendments made by paragraphs 9 and 10 have effect in relation to any alteration made to the share capital of a company after the passing of this Act.

SCHEDULE 15

ENTERPRISE INVESTMENT SCHEME: AMENDMENTS

Section 63

Commentary—*Simon's Direct Tax Service* **E3.102.**

PART 1

INCOME TAX RELIEF

Introductory

1 Chapter III of Part VII of the Taxes Act 1988 is amended in accordance with this Part.

Oil activities

2 (*amends* TA 1988 s 289).

3 (*amends* TA 1988 s 289A(7)).

4 (*amends* TA 1988 s 293(3B)(*b*)).

5 (*amends* TA 1988 s 297).

Requirement as to the money raised

6 In section 289 (eligibility for relief)—

  (*a*) (*substitutes* TA 1988 s 289(*c*), (*d*)).

  (*b*) (*amends* TA 1988 s 289(3).

7 (*amends* TA 1988 s 307).

8 (*amends* TA 1988 s 310).

Repayment supplements

9—(1) (*amends* TA 1988 s 289A).

(2) The amendment made by this paragraph has effect in relation to repayments of tax on or after 7th March 2001.

Designated period

10 (*substitutes* TA 1988 s 291(1)(*b*)).

11 (*amends* TA 1988 s 291A(1)(*a*)).

Unquoted company requirement

12 (*inserts* TA 1988 s 293(1A), (1B), (2)).

13 (*amends* TA 1988 s 312(1E)).

Royalties and licence fees

14—(1) In relation to shares issued on or after 6th April 2000, section 293 (qualifying companies) has effect, and shall be deemed always to have had effect, with the following amendment.

(2) (*amends* TA 1988 s 293(3C)).

Value received by individual etc

15—(1), (2) (*amend* TA 1988 s 300(1), (1A)).

(3), (4) (*insert* TA 1988 s 300(1AA), (1B), (1BA)–(1BC)).

(5) (*amends* TA 1988 s 300(1C)).

(6) (*amends* TA 1988 s 300(4)(*a*), (5)).

16 (*inserts* TA 1988 s 300A).

17 (*amends* TA 1988 s 301(4A), (5)).

18 (*inserts* TA 1988 s 301A).

Repayment of share capital

19 (*amends* TA 1988 s 303).

20 (*inserts* TA 1988 s 303AA).

21 (*substitutes* TA 1988 s 303A(2), *repeals* TA 1988 s 303A(8) and *amends* TA 1988 s 303A(9)).

Claims

22—(1) (*substitutes* TA 1988 s 306(1)(*a*)).

(2) The amendment made by this paragraph has effect in relation to shares issued on or after 6th April 2001.

Information

23—(1) (*amends* TA 1988 s 310(1)).

(2) (*amends* TA 1988 s 310(2)).

(3) (*inserts* TA 1988 s 310(2A)).

(4) (*amends* TA 1988 s 310(4)).

(5) The amendments made by this paragraph have effect in relation to events occurring on or after 7th March 2001.

Interpretation

24 (*amends* TA 1988 s 312(1)).

PART 2

POSTPONEMENT OF CHARGEABLE GAIN ON REINVESTMENT

Introductory

25 Schedule 5B to the Taxation of Chargeable Gains Act 1992 is amended in accordance with this Part.

Requirement as to the money raised

26 (*amends* TCGA 1992 Sch 5B para 1(2)).

27—(1) (*amends* TCGA 1992 Sch 5B para 1A(4)).

(2) (*inserts* TCGA 1992 Sch 5B para 1A(4A)).

28 (*inserts* TCGA 1992 Sch 5B para 16(4A)).

Designated period

29 (*amends* TCGA 1992 Sch 5B para 3(1)).

Value received by investor

30—(1), (2) (*amend* TCGA 1992 Sch 5B para 13(1)).

(3) (*inserts* TCGA 1992 Sch 5B para 13(1A), (1B)).

(4) (*repeals* TCGA 1992 Sch 5B para 13(4)).

(5) (*amends* TCGA 1992 Sch 5B para 13(10)).

(6) (*adds* TCGA 1992 Sch 5B para 13(12)).

31 (*inserts* TCGA 1992 Sch 5B para 13A–13C).

Value received by persons other than the investor

32 (*amends* TCGA 1992 Sch 5B para 14(1), (3), (7)).

Certain receipts to be disregarded

33 (*inserts* TCGA 1992 Sch 5B para 14AA).

34 (*substitutes* **TCGA 1992 Sch 5B para 14A(2)**, *repeals* **sub-para (7)**, and *amends* **sub-para (8)**).

Information

35—(1)–(4) (*amend* TCGA 1992 Sch 5B para 16(1)(a), *insert* sub-para (2A), (3A), *amend* sub-para (5).

(5) The amendments made by this paragraph have effect in relation to events occurring on or after 7th March 2001.

Trustees: anti-avoidance

36 (*amends* TCGA 1992 Sch 5B para 18(1), (2)(*a*), *inserts* sub-para (2)(*ab*)).

Interpretation

37 (*amends* TCGA 1992 Sch 5B para 19(1)).

PART 3

MISCELLANEOUS AND GENERAL

Loss relief

38—(1) Section 576 of the Taxes Act 1988 (supplementary provisions relating to relief for losses on shares in trading companies) is amended as follows.

(2) (*amends* sub-s 576(4)).

(3) (*inserts* sub-s (4A)(*ab*), and *amends* sub-s(4A)(*b*)).

(4) The amendment made by sub-paragraph (3)(*b*) has effect in relation to shares issued on or after 6th April 2001.

(5) The other amendments made by this paragraph have effect—

    (*a*) in relation to shares issued on or after 7th March 2001, and (*b*) in relation to shares issued after 5th April 1998 but before 7th March 2001, in respect of any part of the relevant period which falls on or after 7th March 2001.

(6) For the purposes of sub-paragraph (5)(*b*) ''relevant period'' has the meaning given in section 576(5) of the Taxes Act 1988.

Penalties in connection with returns etc

39—(1) (*amends* TMA 1970 s 98 Table Column 2).

(2) This paragraph has effect in relation to shares issued on or after 6th April 2001, for claims for relief under Chapter III of Part VII of the Taxes Act 1988 made for the year 2000–01 or any later year of assessment.

Commencement

40—(1) Except where provision is made to the contrary, the amendments made by this Schedule have effect in accordance with the following provisions of this paragraph.

(2) The amendments made by paragraphs 2 to 8, 10 to 14, 24, 26 to 29 and 37 have effect—

(*a*) in relation to shares issued on or after 7th March 2001, and
(*b*) in respect of the application of Chapter III of Part VII of the Taxes Act 1988 and Schedule 5B to the Taxation of Chargeable Gains Act 1992 on or after 7th March 2001 in relation to shares—

(i) that were issued after 31st December 1993 but before 7th March 2001, and
(ii) to which income tax relief or deferral relief was attributable immediately before 7th March 2001.

(3) The amendments made by paragraphs 15 to 21, 30 to 34 and 36 have effect—

(*a*) in relation to shares issued on or after 7th March 2001, and
(*b*) in relation to shares issued before that date, in respect of the application of the provisions mentioned in sub-paragraph (2)(*b*) in relation to—

(i) value received (within the meaning of section 300 of the Taxes Act 1988 or paragraph 13 of Schedule 5B to the Taxation of Chargeable Gains Act 1992), and
(ii) repayments made,

on or after that date.

(4) For the purposes of this paragraph—

''deferral relief'' has the same meaning as in Schedule 5B to the Taxation of Chargeable Gains Act 1992 (enterprise investment scheme: reinvestment);
''income tax relief'' means relief under Chapter III of Part VII of the Taxes Act 1988 (enterprise investment scheme); and
''repayment'' means a repayment, redemption, repurchase or payment mentioned in section 303(1) of the Taxes Act 1988 or paragraph 14(1) of Schedule 5B to the Taxation of Chargeable Gains Act 1992.

SCHEDULE 16

VENTURE CAPITAL

Section 64

Commentary—*Simon's Direct Tax Service* **E3.602, E3.629.**

PART 1

VENTURE CAPITAL TRUSTS

Meaning of ''qualifying holdings''

1—(1) (*amends* TA 1988 Sch 28B para 3(8)(*a*)).

(2) The amendment made by this paragraph has effect, and shall be deemed always to have had effect, for the purpose of determining whether shares or securities issued on or after 6th April 2000 are, for the purposes of section 842AA of the Taxes Act 1988 (venture capital trusts), to be regarded as comprised in a company's qualifying holdings.

2—(1) (*substitutes* TA 1988 Sch 28B para 6(1), (2) (2AA) for paras (1), (2)).

(2) The amendment made by this paragraph has effect for the purpose of determining whether shares or securities held by the trust company (within the meaning of Schedule 28B to the Taxes Act 1988) on or after 7th March 2001 are, for the purposes of that Schedule, to be regarded as comprised in that company's qualifying holdings.

Income tax relief: repayment supplements

3—(1) (*repeals* TA 1988 Sch 15B para 1(7)).

(2) The amendment made by this paragraph has effect in relation to repayments of tax on or after 7th March 2001.

PART 2
CORPORATE VENTURING SCHEME

Introductory

4 Schedule 15 to the Finance Act 2000 (corporate venturing scheme) is amended in accordance with this Part.

Money raised by issue of shares

5—(1), (2) (*substitute* para 36(1)–(1C) for sub-para (1), and *amend* sub-para (5)).

(3) The amendments made by this paragraph have effect—

(*a*) in relation to shares issued on or after 7th March 2001, and

(*b*) in respect of the application of Schedule 15 to the Finance Act 2000 (corporate venturing scheme) on or after 7th March 2001 in relation to shares—

(i) that were issued after 31st March 2000 but before 7th March 2001, and

(ii) to which investment relief (within the meaning of that Schedule) was attributable immediately before 7th March 2001.

Receipt of replacement value

6—(1)–(5) (*amend* para 54(1)(c), *insert* sub-para (2A), *substitute* sub-para (3)(*a*), (*b*) for sub-para (3)(*a*)–(*c*), *insert* sub-para (3A), and *substitute* sub-para (4)).

(6) The amendment made by sub-paragraph (1) shall be deemed always to have had effect.

(7) Subject to that, the amendments made by this paragraph have effect—

(*a*) in relation to shares issued on or after 7th March 2001, and

(*b*) in relation to shares issued after 31st March 2000 but before 7th March 2001, in respect of value received (within the meaning of paragraph 49 of Schedule 15 to the Finance Act 2000) on or after 7th March 2001.

7—(1) (*adds* para 55(5)).

(2) The amendment made by this paragraph shall be deemed always to have had effect.

Value received by other persons

8—(1) (*amends* para 56(3)).

(2) The amendment made by this paragraph has effect—

(*a*) in relation to shares issued on or after 7th March 2001, and

(*b*) in respect of shares issued after 31st March 2000 but before 7th March 2001, in relation to any repayment (within the meaning of paragraph 57(2) of Schedule 15 to the Finance Act 2000) made on or after 7th March 2001.

Insignificant repayments disregarded

9—(1) (*amends* para 57(1)).

(2) (*amends* para 57(3)).

(3) The amendment made by sub-paragraph (1) has effect—

(*a*) in relation to shares issued on or after 7th March 2001, and

(*b*) in respect of shares issued after 31st March 2000 but before 7th March 2001, in relation to repayments (within the meaning of paragraph 57(2) of Schedule 15 to the Finance Act 2000) made on or after 7th March 2001.

(4) The amendment made by sub-paragraph (2) shall be deemed always to have had effect.

SCHEDULE 17

CAPITAL ALLOWANCES: ENERGY-SAVING PLANT AND MACHINERY

Section 65

Commentary—*Simon's Direct Tax Service* B2.301, B2.321.

1 (*amends* CAA 2001 s 39).

2 (*inserts* CAA 2001 ss 45A–45C)).

3 (*amends* CAA 2001 s 46(1)).

4 (***amends* CAA 2001 s 52(3)).**

5 (*amends* TMA 1970 s 98 Table Column 2).

6—(1) For the purposes of section 45A(2) of the Capital Allowances Act 2001, if—

(*a*) expenditure on plant or machinery is incurred, or a contract for the provision of plant or machinery is entered into, before the first order is made under section 45A(3) of that Act; and

(*b*) if that order had been made before the relevant time, the conditions in section 45A(3) of that Act would have been met,

those conditions shall be treated as if they were met at the relevant time.

(2) In sub-paragraph (1) "the relevant time" means the time when the expenditure was incurred or (as the case may be) the contract was entered into.

SCHEDULE 18

CAPITAL ALLOWANCES: FIXTURES PROVIDED IN CONNECTION WITH ENERGY MANAGEMENT SERVICES

Section 66

Commentary—*Simon's Direct Tax Service* **B2.350, B2.351.**

1 (*amends* CAA 2001 s 172(3)).

2 (***inserts* CAA 2001 s 175A).**

3 (***amends* CAA 2001 s 176(4)).**

4 (*inserts* CAA 2001 s 180A).

5 (*amends* CAA 2001 s 181(4)).

6 (*inserts* CAA 2001 s 182A).

7—(1) Section 188 of that Act (cessation of ownership when person ceases to have qualifying interest) is amended as follows.

(2), (3) (*insert* CAA 2001 s 188(1)(*ca*), and *amend* sub-s (3)(*a*)).

8 (***inserts* CAA 2001 s 192A).**

9 (*inserts* CAA 2001 ss 195A, 195B).

10—(1) Section 196 of that Act (disposal values in relation to fixtures) is amended as follows.

(2)–(4) (*amend* CAA 2001 s 196(1), *insert* sub-s (4A) and *amend* sub-s (5)).

11 (*amends* CAA 2001 s 203(2)(*b*)).

SCHEDULE 19

CAPITAL ALLOWANCES: CONVERSION OF PARTS OF BUSINESS PREMISES INTO FLATS

Section 67

Commentary—*Simon's Direct Tax Service* **B2.101.**

PART 1

NEW PART 4A OF THE CAPITAL ALLOWANCES ACT 2001

(*inserts* CAA 2001 Pt 4A (ss 393A–393W)).

PART 2

CONSEQUENTIAL AMENDMENTS

1 (***inserts* CAA 2001 s 1(2)(*ca*)).**

2 (*amends* CAA 2001 s 2(3)).

3 (*amends* CAA 2001 s 537(1)).

4 (*amends* CAA 2001 s 542(1)).

5 (***amends* CAA 2001 s 567(1)).**

6 (***amends* CAA 2001 s 570(1)).**

7 (*amends* CAA 2001 s 573(1)).

8—(1) Part 2 of Schedule 1 to that Act (list of defined expressions) is amended as follows.

(2), (3) (*amend* CAA 2001 Sch 1 Pt 2).

SCHEDULE 20

CAPITAL ALLOWANCES: OFFSHORE OIL INFRASTRUCTURE

Section 68

Commentary—*Simon's Direct Tax Service* **B2.337, D4.1010.**

PART 1

CHARGEABLE PERIODS ENDING BEFORE 1ST OR 6TH APRIL 2001

Writing-down allowances: infrastructure from UK or non-UK oil fields

1 In Chapter VII of Part II of the Capital Allowances Act 1990 (machinery and plant: miscellaneous expenditure), after section 62 insert—

"62AA Reuse etc of offshore oil infrastructure

(1) This section applies where—

(a) a person carrying on a trade of oil extraction incurs decommissioning expenditure, and
(b) the machinery or plant concerned—

(i) has been brought into use for the purposes of the trade, and
(ii) is, or was when last in use for those purposes, offshore infrastructure.

(2) In this section—

"decommissioning expenditure" has the meaning given by section 62AB;
"offshore infrastructure" has the meaning given by section 62AC.

(3) The person's qualifying expenditure for the chargeable period in which the decommissioning expenditure is incurred is treated for the purposes of sections 24 and 25 as increased by the amount of the decommissioning expenditure.

(4) Subsection (3) above is subject to subsections (5) and (6) below and section 62A(4A).

(5) Subsection (3) above does not apply to decommissioning expenditure on UK infrastructure unless it is incurred in connection with measures taken, wholly or substantially, in order to comply with—

(a) an abandonment programme within the meaning given by section 29 of the Petroleum Act 1998, or
(b) any condition to which the approval of such a programme is subject.

(6) Subsection (3) above does not apply to expenditure in respect of which an allowance or deduction could be made apart from that subsection in taxing, or computing, the person's income for any purpose of income tax or corporation tax.

(7) For the purposes of subsection (5) above, decommissioning expenditure is "on UK infrastructure" if the machinery or plant concerned—

(a) is offshore infrastructure within section 62AC(1)(a) or (c), or
(b) is not offshore infrastructure but was offshore infrastructure within section 62AC(1)(a) or
(c) when last in use for the purposes of the trade.

62AB Meaning of "decommissioning expenditure" in section 62AA

(1) In section 62AA "decommissioning expenditure" means expenditure in connection with—

(a) preserving machinery or plant pending its reuse or demolition,
(b) preparing machinery or plant for reuse,
(c) arranging for the reuse of machinery or plant, or
(d) demolishing machinery or plant.

(2) It is immaterial for the purposes of subsection (1)(a) above whether the machinery or plant is reused, is demolished or is partly reused and partly demolished.

(3) It is immaterial for the purposes of subsection (1)(b) and (c) above whether the machinery or plant is in fact reused.

62AC Meaning of "offshore infrastructure" in section 62AA

(1) In section 62AA "offshore infrastructure" means—

(a) an offshore installation within the meaning given by section 44 of the Petroleum Act 1998 or a part of such an installation, or
(b) something that would be, or would be a part of, an offshore installation within that meaning if in subsection (3) of that section "relevant waters" meant waters in a foreign sector of the continental shelf and other foreign tidal waters, or
(c) a pipeline within the meaning of section 26 of that Act, or a part of such a pipeline, that is in, under or over waters in—

(i) the territorial sea adjacent to the United Kingdom, or
(ii) an area designated under section 1(7) of the Continental Shelf Act 1964, or

(*d*) a pipeline within the meaning of section 26 of the Petroleum Act 1998, or a part of such a pipeline, that is in, under or over waters in a foreign sector of the continental shelf.

(2) In subsection (1)(*b*) and (*d*) above—

"foreign sector of the continental shelf" means an area within which rights are exercisable with respect to the sea bed and subsoil and their natural resources by a country or territory outside the United Kingdom;

"foreign tidal waters" means tidal waters in an area within which rights are exercisable with respect to the bed and subsoil of the body of water in question and their natural resources by a country or territory outside the United Kingdom.".

Ring fence trades: special allowance for pre-cessation abandonment expenditure

2—(1) Section 62A of the Capital Allowances Act 1990 (special allowance for costs of demolition of offshore machinery or plant) is amended as follows.

(2) In subsection (1) (section applies to expenditure that would otherwise fall within section 62(1)(*b*)), after "section 62(1)(*b*)" insert "or 62AA(3)".

(3) In subsection (1)(*c*)—

(*a*) for "the demolition of" substitute "decommissioning"; and

(*b*) after "which is or forms part of" insert ", or when last in use for the purposes of the trade was or formed part of,".

(4) In subsection (3)(*a*), for "demolition" (in both places) substitute "decommissioning".

(5) After subsection (3) insert—

"(3A) In this section "decommissioning", in relation to any machinery or plant, means—

(*a*) demolishing the machinery or plant,

(*b*) preserving the machinery or plant pending its reuse or demolition,

(*c*) preparing the machinery or plant for reuse, or

(*d*) arranging for the reuse of the machinery or plant.

(3B) For the purposes of this section—

(*a*) in determining whether expenditure is incurred on preserving machinery or plant pending its reuse or demolition, it is immaterial whether the machinery or plant is reused, is demolished or is partly reused and partly demolished; and

(*b*) in determining whether expenditure is incurred on preparing machinery or plant for reuse, or on arranging for the reuse of machinery or plant, it is immaterial whether the machinery or plant is in fact reused.".

(6) For subsection (4) (entitlement to special allowance) substitute—

"(4) If the person incurring any abandonment expenditure so elects, for the chargeable period in which that expenditure is incurred there shall be made to that person an allowance equal to so much of the abandonment expenditure to which the election relates as is incurred in that period.

(4A) If a person makes such an election, neither of sections 62(1)(*b*) and 62AA(3) applies.

(4B) If machinery or plant is demolished, the total of any allowances under subsection (4) above in respect of expenditure on the decommissioning of the machinery or plant is reduced by the amount of any moneys received for the remains of the machinery or plant.

(4C) Effect is given to subsection (4B) above by setting the amount (until wholly utilised)—

first, against any allowance under subsection (4) above for the chargeable period in which the amount is received (as previously reduced in giving effect to subsection (4B));

second, against allowances under that subsection for earlier chargeable periods (as so reduced and taking later such periods before earlier ones); and

third, against allowances under that subsection for later chargeable periods (as so reduced and taking earlier such periods before later ones).".

(7) In subsection (5)(*a*) (election must specify amounts received for remains), for "subsection (4)(*a*)" substitute "subsection (4B)".

(8) In the sidenote, for "demolition" substitute "decommissioning".

Ring fence trades: allowances for post-cessation expenditure

3—(1) Section 62B of the Capital Allowances Act 1990 (abandonment expenditure incurred within 3 years of ceasing ring fence trade) is amended as follows.

(2) In subsection (1)(*b*) (section applies where expenditure incurred within 3 years of ceasing trade), for "the demolition of" substitute "decommissioning".

(3) In subsection (1)(*c*) (section applies where expenditure would have been abandonment expenditure under section 62A if incurred earlier), for "demolition" substitute "decommissioning".

(4) In subsection (2) (expenditure net of receipts for remains is eligible for allowances), for "the machinery or plant referred to in that paragraph" substitute "any of the machinery or plant referred to in that paragraph on whose demolition any of the post-cessation expenditure was incurred".

Commencement of Part 1

4—(1) The amendments made by this Part of this Schedule apply to expenditure that is incurred—

(a) on or after 7th August 2000, and

(b) in a relevant chargeable period.

(2) The amendments made by paragraph 1 also apply to expenditure incurred before 7th August 2000 if the expenditure—

(a) is incurred in a relevant chargeable period, and

(b) is within sub-paragraph (3) or (4).

(3) Expenditure is within this sub-paragraph if—

(a) it is decommissioning expenditure on UK infrastructure, and

(b) it is incurred in connection with an abandonment programme approved on or after 7th August 2000.

(4) Expenditure is within this sub-paragraph if—

(a) it is decommissioning expenditure,

(b) it is not decommissioning expenditure on UK infrastructure, and

(c) it is incurred in connection with a decommissioning activity that takes place on or after 7th August 2000.

(5) The amendments made by paragraphs 2 and 3 also apply to expenditure incurred before 7th August 2000 if the expenditure—

(a) is incurred in a relevant chargeable period, and

(b) is incurred in connection with an abandonment programme approved on or after 7th August 2000.

(6) In sub-paragraphs (3) and (4), "decommissioning expenditure" and "decommissioning expenditure on UK infrastructure" have the same meaning as in the section 62AA inserted by paragraph 1.

(7) In sub-paragraph (4)(c) "decommissioning activity" means an activity mentioned in any of paragraphs (a) to (d) of the section 62AB(1) inserted by paragraph 1.

(8) In this paragraph "relevant chargeable period" means—

(a) for income tax purposes, a chargeable period ending before 6th April 2001, and

(b) for corporation tax purposes, a chargeable period ending before 1st April 2001.

PART 2

CHARGEABLE PERIODS ENDING ON OR AFTER 1ST OR 6TH APRIL 2001

Writing-down allowances: infrastructure from UK or non-UK oil fields

5 (*inserts* CAA 2001 s 161A–161D and *amends* s 57(2)).

Ring fence trades: meaning of "abandonment expenditure"

6 (*amends* CAA 2001 s 163).

Ring fence trades: special allowance for pre-cessation expenditure

7—(1) Section 164 of the Capital Allowances Act 2001 (abandonment expenditure incurred before cessation of ring fence trade) is amended as follows.

(2)–(6) (*amend* CAA 2001 s 164(1), (3), (4), and *substitute* sub-ss (5)–(7) for sub-s (5)).

Ring fence trades: allowances for post-cessation expenditure

8—(1) Section 165 of the Capital Allowances Act 2001 (abandonment expenditure incurred within 3 years of ceasing ring fence trade) is amended as follows.

(2)–(4) (*amend* CAA 2001 s 165(1), (3), (4)).

Commencement of Part 2

9—(1) The amendments made by this Part of this Schedule (but see sub-paragraph (9)) apply to expenditure that is incurred—

(a) on or after 7th August 2000, and

(b) in a relevant chargeable period.

(2) The amendments made by paragraph 5 also apply to expenditure incurred before 7th August 2000 if the expenditure—

(a) is incurred in a relevant chargeable period, and

(b) is within sub-paragraph (3) or (4).

(3) Expenditure is within this sub-paragraph if—

(a) it is decommissioning expenditure on UK infrastructure, and

(b) it is incurred in connection with an abandonment programme approved on or after 7th August 2000.

(4) Expenditure is within this sub-paragraph if—

(a) it is decommissioning expenditure,

(b) it is not decommissioning expenditure on UK infrastructure, and

(c) it is incurred in connection with a decommissioning activity that takes place on or after 7th August 2000.

(5) The amendments made by paragraphs 6 to 8 (but see sub-paragraph (9)) also apply to expenditure incurred before 7th August 2000 if the expenditure—

(a) is incurred in a relevant chargeable period, and

(b) is incurred in connection with an abandonment programme approved on or after 7th August 2000.

(6) In sub-paragraphs (3) and (4), "decommissioning expenditure" and "decommissioning expenditure on UK infrastructure" have the same meaning as in the sections 161C and 161D inserted by paragraph 5.

(7) In sub-paragraph (4)(c) "decommissioning activity" means an activity mentioned in any of paragraphs (a) to (c) of the section 161B(1) inserted by paragraph 5.

(8) In this paragraph "relevant chargeable period" means—

(a) for income tax purposes, a chargeable period ending on or after 6th April 2001, and

(b) for corporation tax purposes, a chargeable period ending on or after 1st April 2001.

(9) Sub-paragraphs (1) to (8) do not apply to the amendments made by paragraphs 7(2) and 8(2).

Those amendments shall be deemed always to have had effect.

SCHEDULE 21

CAPITAL ALLOWANCES: MINOR AMENDMENTS

Section 69

Commentary—*Simon's Direct Tax Service* **B2.109, B2.206A, B2.262, B2.302.**

Thermal insulation of industrial buildings

1 (*amends* CAA 2001 s 28(2)).

Fixtures: purchasers of land and incoming lessees

2—(1), (2) (*amend* CAA 2001 s 181).

(3) (*substitutes* CAA 2001 s 182(2), (3)).

(4) (*substitutes* CAA 2001 s 184(2), (3)).

Meaning of "sale and finance leaseback"

3 (*amends* CAA 2001 s 221).

Effect of partnership changes

4—(1) (*substitutes* CAA 2001 s 263(1)(c)).

(2) (*substitutes* CAA 2001 s 558(1)(c)).

Enterprise zones

5 (*amends* CAA 2001 s 298(3)).

Highway concessions

6—(1), (2) (*amend* CAA 2001 s 341(4) and *add* sub-s (5)).

SCHEDULE 22

REMEDIATION OF CONTAMINATED LAND

Section 70

Commentary—*Simon's Direct Tax Service* **Division D2.14.**

PART 1

DEDUCTION FOR CAPITAL EXPENDITURE

Deduction for capital expenditure

1—(1) This paragraph applies if—

(a) land in the United Kingdom is, or has been, acquired by a company for the purposes of a trade carried on by the company,

(b) at the time of acquisition all or part of the land is or was in a contaminated state (see paragraph 3), and

(c) the company incurs capital expenditure which is qualifying land remediation expenditure in respect of the land (see paragraph 2).

(2) For the purposes of corporation tax such capital expenditure as is qualifying land remediation expenditure shall (if the company so elects) be allowed as a deduction in computing the profits of the trade for the accounting period in which that expenditure is incurred.

(3) For the purposes of sub-paragraph (2) any capital expenditure incurred for the purposes of a trade by a company about to carry it on shall be treated as if it had been incurred by that company on the first day on which it does carry it on and in the course of doing so.

(4) Sub-paragraph (2) shall not apply to so much of the qualifying land remediation expenditure as—

(a) represents expenditure which has been allowed as a deduction in computing the profits arising from the trade for any accounting period preceding the period in which the expenditure is incurred, or

(b) represents capital expenditure in respect of which an allowance has been, or may be, made under the enactments relating to capital allowances.

(5) A company is not entitled to a deduction under this paragraph in respect of expenditure on land all or part of which is in a contaminated state, if the land is in that state wholly or partly as a result of any thing done or omitted to be done at any time by the company or a person with a relevant connection to the company.

(6) An election under this paragraph must specify the accounting period in respect of which it is made.

(7) The election must be made by notice in writing to the Inland Revenue.

(8) The notice must be given before the end of the period of two years beginning with the end of the company's accounting period to which the election relates.

Commentary—*Simon's Direct Tax Service* **D2.1402.**

Qualifying land remediation expenditure

2—(1) For the purposes of this Schedule "qualifying land remediation expenditure" of a company means expenditure of the company that meets the conditions in sub-paragraphs (2) to (6).

(2) The first condition is that it is expenditure on land all or part of which is in a contaminated state (see paragraph 3).

(3) The second condition is that the expenditure is expenditure on relevant land remediation directly undertaken by the company or on its behalf (see paragraph 4).

(4) The third condition is that the expenditure is incurred—

(a) on employee costs (see paragraph 5), or

(b) on materials (see paragraph 6),

or is qualifying expenditure on sub-contracted land remediation (see paragraphs 9 to 11).

(5) The fourth condition is that the expenditure would not have been incurred had the land not been in a contaminated state (see paragraph 7).

(6) The fifth condition is that the expenditure is not subsidised (see paragraph 8).

Commentary—*Simon's Direct Tax Service* **D2.1403.**

Land in a contaminated state

3—(1) For the purposes of this Schedule land is in a contaminated state if, and only if, it is in such a condition, by reason of substances in, on or under the land, that—

(a) harm is being caused or there is a possibility of harm being caused; or

(b) pollution of controlled waters is being, or is likely to be, caused.

(2) For the purposes of this Schedule, a nuclear site is not land in a contaminated state.

(3) In this paragraph a "nuclear site" means—

(a) any site in respect of which a nuclear site licence is for the time being in force, or

(b) any site in respect of which, after the revocation or surrender of a nuclear site licence, the period of responsibility of the licensee has not yet come to an end;

and "nuclear site licence", "licensee" and "period of responsibility" have the same meaning as in the Nuclear Installations Act 1965.

Commentary—*Simon's Direct Tax Service* **D2.1403.**

Relevant land remediation

4—(1) For the purposes of this Schedule relevant land remediation, in relation to land acquired by a company, means—

(*a*) activities falling within sub-paragraph (2), and

(*b*) if there are such activities, preparatory activity falling within sub-paragraph (4) which satisfies the condition in sub-paragraph (5).

(2) The activities referred to in sub-paragraph (1)(*a*) are the doing of any works, the carrying out of any operations or the taking of any steps in relation to—

(*a*) the land in question,

(*b*) any controlled waters affected by that land, or

(*c*) any land adjoining or adjacent to that land,

for the purpose described in sub-paragraph (3).

(3) The purpose referred to in sub-paragraph (2) is that of—

(*a*) preventing or minimising, or remedying or mitigating the effects of, any harm, or any pollution of controlled waters, by reason of which the land is in a contaminated state; or

(*b*) restoring the land or waters to their former state.

(4) The preparatory activity referred to in sub-paragraph (1)(*b*) is the doing of anything for the purpose of assessing the condition of—

(*a*) the land in question,

(*b*) any controlled waters affected by that land, or

(*c*) any land adjoining or adjacent to that land.

(5) Preparatory activity satisfies the condition referred to in sub-paragraph (1)(*b*) if it is activity connected to such activities falling within sub-paragraph (2) as are undertaken by the company (whether directly or on its behalf).

(6) For the purposes of this paragraph, controlled waters are "affected by" land in a contaminated state if (and only if) the land in question is in such a condition, by reason of substances in, on or under the land, that pollution of those waters is being, or is likely to be, caused.

Commentary—*Simon's Direct Tax Service* **D2.1403.**

Employee costs

5—(1) For the purposes of this Schedule the employee costs of a company are—

(*a*) the emoluments paid by the company to directors or employees of the company, including all salaries, wages, perquisites and profits whatsoever other than benefits in kind;

(*b*) the secondary Class 1 national insurance contributions paid by the company; and

(*c*) the contributions paid by the company to any pension fund (within the meaning of section 231A(4) of the Taxes Act 1988) operated for the benefit of directors or employees of the company.

(2) The employee costs of a company attributable to relevant land remediation are those paid to, or in respect of, directors or employees directly and actively engaged in that relevant land remediation.

(3) In the case of a director or employee partly engaged directly and actively in relevant land remediation the following rules apply—

(*a*) if the time he spends so engaged is less than 20% of his total working time, none of the employee costs relating to him are treated as attributable to relevant land remediation;

(*b*) if the time he spends so engaged is more than 80% of his total working time, the whole of the employee costs relating to him are treated as attributable to relevant land remediation;

(*c*) in any other case, an appropriate proportion of the employee costs relating to him are treated as attributable to relevant land remediation.

(4) For the purpose of sub-paragraphs (2) and (3) persons who provide services, such as secretarial or administrative services, in support of activities carried on by others, are not, by virtue of providing those services, to be treated as themselves directly and actively engaged in those activities.

Commentary—*Simon's Direct Tax Service* **D2.1403.**

Expenditure on materials

6 For the purposes of this Schedule expenditure on materials is attributable to relevant land remediation if the materials are employed directly in that relevant land remediation.

Commentary—*Simon's Direct Tax Service* **D2.1403.**

Expenditure incurred because of contamination

7—(1) Without prejudice to the generality of paragraph 2(5), this paragraph has effect for the purpose of determining whether expenditure would or would not have been incurred had not all or part of the land been in a contaminated state.

(2) If expenditure on the land is increased by reason only that the land is in a contaminated state, the amount by which such expenditure is increased shall be considered to be expenditure satisfying the condition in paragraph 2(5).

(3) If any works are done, operations are carried out or steps are taken mainly for the purpose described in paragraph 4(3), expenditure on such works, operations or steps shall be taken to satisfy the condition in paragraph 2(5).

Commentary—*Simon's Direct Tax Service* **D2.1403.**

Subsidised expenditure

8—(1) For the purposes of this Schedule a company's expenditure is treated as subsidised to the extent that—

(*a*) a grant or subsidy is obtained in respect of the expenditure; or
(*b*) it is otherwise met directly or indirectly by any person other than the company.

(2) For the purposes of this Schedule a grant, subsidy or payment that is not allocated to particular expenditure shall be allocated to expenditure of the recipient in such manner as is just and reasonable.

Qualifying expenditure on sub-contracted land remediation

9—(1) The provisions of paragraphs 10 and 11 have effect for determining the amount of the qualifying expenditure of a company ("the company") on sub-contracted land remediation.

(2) For the purposes of this Schedule the company incurs expenditure on sub-contracted land remediation if it makes a payment (a "sub-contractor payment") to another person ("the sub-contractor") in respect of relevant land remediation contracted out by the company to that person.

Commentary—*Simon's Direct Tax Service* **D2.1404.**

Treatment of expenditure where company and sub-contractor are connected persons

10—(1) Where—

(*a*) the company and the sub-contractor are connected persons, and
(*b*) in accordance with [generally accepted accounting practice][1]—

(i) the whole of the sub-contractor payment has been brought into account in determining the sub-contractor's profit or loss for a relevant period, and
(ii) all of the sub-contractor's relevant expenditure has been so brought into account,

the whole of the payment (up to the amount of the sub-contractor's relevant expenditure) is qualifying expenditure on sub-contracted land remediation.

(2) In sub-paragraph (1)—

(*a*) references to the "relevant expenditure" of the sub-contractor are to expenditure that—

(i) is incurred by the sub-contractor in carrying on, on behalf of the company, the activities to which the sub-contractor payment relates,
(ii) is not of a capital nature,
(iii) is incurred on employee costs or materials, and
(iv) is not subsidised;

(*b*) a "relevant period" means a period—

(i) for which accounts are drawn up for the sub-contractor, and
(ii) that ends not more than twelve months after the end of the company's period of account in which the sub-contractor payment is, in accordance with [generally accepted accounting practice][1], brought into account in determining the company's profit or loss.

(3) Paragraph 5 (employee costs) and paragraph 8 (subsidised expenditure) apply for the purposes of determining whether the sub-contractor's expenditure meets the requirements of sub-paragraph (2)(*a*)(iii) and (iv).

For this purpose the references in those paragraphs to a company shall be read as references to the sub-contractor.

(4) Any apportionment of expenditure of the company or the sub-contractor necessary for the purposes of this paragraph shall be made on a just and reasonable basis.

Commentary—*Simon's Direct Tax Service* **D2.1404.**
Amendments—[1] Words substituted for the words "normal accounting practice" by FA 2002 s 103(4)(*h*) with effect from 24 July 2002.

Treatment of sub-contractor payment in other cases

11 Where—

(*a*) the company makes a sub-contractor payment, and
(*b*) paragraph 10 (treatment of expenditure where company and sub-contractor are connected) does not apply,

the whole of the amount of the sub-contractor payment is treated as qualifying expenditure on sub-contracted land remediation.

Commentary—*Simon's Direct Tax Service* **D2.1404.**

PART 2

ENTITLEMENT TO LAND REMEDIATION RELIEF

Entitlement to relief

12—(1) This paragraph applies if—

    (*a*) land in the United Kingdom is, or has been, acquired by a company for the purposes of a Schedule A business or a trade carried on by the company,

    (*b*) at the time of acquisition all or part of the land is or was in a contaminated state, and

    (*c*) the company incurs qualifying land remediation expenditure in respect of the land.

(2) A company is entitled to land remediation relief for an accounting period if the company's qualifying land remediation expenditure is deductible in that period.

(3) The company's qualifying land remediation expenditure is deductible in that period if it is allowable as a deduction in computing for tax purposes the profits for that period of a Schedule A business or a trade carried on by the company.

(4) A company is not entitled to land remediation relief in respect of expenditure on land all or part of which is in a contaminated state, if the land is in that state wholly or partly as a result of any thing done or omitted to be done at any time by the company or a person with a relevant connection to the company.

Commentary—*Simon's Direct Tax Service* **D2.1410.**

PART 3

MANNER OF GIVING EFFECT TO RELIEF

Deduction in computing profits of Schedule A business or trade

13 Where—

    (*a*) a company is entitled to land remediation relief for an accounting period,

    (*b*) it is carrying on a Schedule A business or a trade in that period, and

    (*c*) it has qualifying land remediation expenditure that is allowable as a deduction in computing for tax purposes the profits of the Schedule A business or the trade for that period,

it may (on making a claim) treat that qualifying land remediation expenditure as if it were an amount equal to 150% of the actual amount.

Commentary—*Simon's Direct Tax Service* **D2.1411.**

Entitlement to land remediation tax credit

14—(1) A company may claim a land remediation tax credit if in an accounting period it has a "qualifying land remediation loss".

(2) A company has a "qualifying land remediation loss" for this purpose if in an accounting period—

    (*a*) paragraph 13 applies, and

    (*b*) the company incurs a Schedule A loss or a trading loss in that period in the Schedule A business or the trade referred to in paragraph 13(*b*).

(3) The amount of the qualifying land remediation loss is equal to the lesser of—

    (*a*) 150% of the related qualifying land remediation expenditure, and

    (*b*) so much of the company's Schedule A loss or trading loss as is unrelieved.

(4) For this purpose the amount of a Schedule A loss or trading loss that is "unrelieved" is the amount of that loss reduced by the amount of—

    (*a*) any relief that was or could have been obtained by the company making a claim under section 392A(1) or 393A(1)(*a*) of the Taxes Act 1988 to set the loss against profits of whatever description of the same accounting period,

    (*b*) any other relief obtained by the company in respect of the loss, including relief under section 393A(1)(*b*) of that Act (losses set against profits of an earlier accounting period), and

    (*c*) any loss surrendered under section 403(1) of that Act (surrender of relief to group or consortium members).

(5) No account shall be taken for this purpose of—

    (*a*) any Schedule A losses or trading losses brought forward from an earlier accounting period under section 392A(2) or 393(1) of the Taxes Act 1988, or

    (*b*) any trading losses carried back from a later accounting period under section 393A(1)(*b*) of that Act.

(6) Sub-paragraphs (7) to (9) apply for the purpose of determining the amount of a Schedule A loss that is "unrelieved" in an accounting period in a case where the Schedule A loss is a loss treated under section 432AB(3) of the Taxes Act 1988 as an amount of expenses of management under section 76 of that Act.

(7) If in that accounting period no amount falls to be carried forward to a succeeding accounting period under section 75(3) of the Taxes Act 1988 (carrying forward expenses of management and charges on income where such expenses and charges exceed amount of profits from which deductible), no amount of the Schedule A loss is unrelieved.

(8) If in that accounting period an amount falls to be carried forward to a succeeding accounting period under section 75(3) of that Act, the amount of the Schedule A loss that is unrelieved is equal to the lesser of—

    (*a*) the amount of the Schedule A loss, and
    (*b*) the amount which so falls to be carried forward.

(9) In determining for the purposes of sub-paragraphs (7) and (8) whether there is an amount which falls to be carried forward under section 75(3) of the Taxes Act 1988, there shall be disregarded any amounts brought forward from an earlier accounting period and treated as expenses of management for the period in question by virtue of—

    (*a*) a previous application of section 75(3) of that Act, or
    (*b*) paragraph 4(4) of Schedule 11 to the Finance Act 1996 (loan relationships deficit carried forward and treated as expenses of management).

(10) If—

    (*a*) the company is an insurance company, and
    (*b*) it is treated under section 432AA of the Taxes Act 1988 as carrying on more than one Schedule A business,

references in this paragraph to a Schedule A loss shall be construed in accordance with section 432AB(4) or (6) of that Act (aggregation of losses where an insurance company is treated under section 432AA as having more than one Schedule A business).

Commentary—*Simon's Direct Tax Service* **D2.1412.**

Amount of land remediation tax credit

15—(1) The amount of the land remediation tax credit to which a company is entitled for an accounting period is an amount equal to 16% of the amount of the qualifying land remediation loss for the period.

(2) The Treasury may by order substitute for the percentage for the time being specified in sub-paragraph (1) such other percentage as they think fit.

(3) An order under sub-paragraph (2) may make such incidental, supplemental, consequential or transitional provision as the Treasury think fit.

Commentary—*Simon's Direct Tax Service* **D2.1412.**

Payment in respect of land remediation tax credit

16—(1) Where—

    (*a*) the company is entitled to a land remediation tax credit for an accounting period, and
    (*b*) makes a claim,

the Inland Revenue shall pay to the company the amount of the credit.

(2) An amount payable in respect of—

    (*a*) a land remediation tax credit, or
    (*b*) interest on a land remediation tax credit under section 826 of the Taxes Act 1988,

may be applied in discharging any liability of the company's to pay corporation tax, and to the extent that it is so applied the Inland Revenue's obligation under sub-paragraph (1) is discharged.

(3) Where the company's company tax return for the accounting period is enquired into by the Inland Revenue, no payment in respect of a land remediation tax credit for that period need be made before the Inland Revenue's enquiries are completed (see paragraph 32 of Schedule 18 to the Finance Act 1998).

In those circumstances the Inland Revenue may make a payment on a provisional basis of such amount as they think fit.

(4) No payment need be made in respect of a land remediation tax credit for an accounting period before the company has paid to the Inland Revenue any amount that it is required to pay for payment periods ending in that accounting period—

    (*a*) under the PAYE regulations, or
    (*b*) in respect of Class 1 national insurance contributions.

(5) In this paragraph—

"PAYE regulations" means regulations under section 203 of the Taxes Act 1988;

"payment period" means a period which ends on the 5th day of a month and for which the company is liable to account for income tax and national insurance contributions to the Inland Revenue.

Commentary—*Simon's Direct Tax Service* **D2.1413.**

Restriction on losses carried forward

17—(1) For the purposes of section 392A of the Taxes Act 1988 (relief of Schedule A losses against future Schedule A losses), a company's Schedule A loss for a period in which it claims a land remediation tax credit is treated as reduced by the amount of the loss surrendered.

(2) For the purposes of section 393 of the Taxes Act 1988 (relief of trading losses against future trading profits), a company's trading loss for a period for which it claims a land remediation tax credit is treated as reduced by the amount of the loss surrendered.

(3) Sub-paragraph (4) applies if in an accounting period—

(a) a company's Schedule A loss is a loss treated under section 432AB(3) of the Taxes Act 1988 as an amount of expenses of management under section 76 of that Act,

(b) an amount falls to be carried forward to a succeeding accounting period under section 75(3) of that Act (carrying forward expenses of management and charges on income where such expenses and charges exceed amount of profits from which deductible), and

(c) the company claims a land remediation tax credit for the accounting period.

(4) Where this sub-paragraph applies, the amount which falls to be carried forward to a succeeding accounting period under section 75(3) of the Taxes Act 1988 is treated as reduced by the amount of the loss surrendered.

(5) For the purposes of this paragraph the amount of the loss surrendered is—

(a) where the maximum amount of land remediation tax credit was claimed, the whole of the qualifying land remediation loss for that period;

(b) where less than the maximum amount was claimed, a corresponding proportion of the qualifying land remediation loss for that period.

The "maximum amount" here means the amount specified in paragraph 15(1).

Commentary—*Simon's Direct Tax Service* **D2.1413.**

Tax credit not income

18 A payment in respect of a land remediation tax credit is not income of the company for any tax purpose.

Commentary—*Simon's Direct Tax Service* **D2.1413.**

Certain qualifying land remediation expenditure excluded for purposes of capital gains

19 If in an accounting period—

(a) a company has a qualifying land remediation loss, and

(b) by virtue of that qualifying land remediation loss, a payment is made to the company in respect of a land remediation tax credit,

the related qualifying land remediation expenditure shall be treated as if it were expenditure excluded for the purposes of capital gains tax under section 39 of the Taxation of Chargeable Gains Act 1992.

Commentary—*Simon's Direct Tax Service* **D2.1413.**

PART 4
SPECIAL PROVISION FOR LIFE ASSURANCE BUSINESS
Limitation on relief

20 Where for any accounting period the profits arising to an insurance company from its life assurance business, or from any category of its life assurance business, fall to be computed in accordance with the provisions of the Taxes Act 1988 applicable to Case I of Schedule D, no deduction for capital expenditure under paragraph 1 and no land remediation relief under paragraph 12 shall be allowable.

Commentary—*Simon's Direct Tax Service* **D2.1420.**

Provision in respect of "I minus E" basis

21 Paragraphs 22 to 28 apply where for any accounting period the profits arising to an insurance company from its life assurance business fall to be computed otherwise than in accordance with the provisions of the Taxes Act 1988 applicable to Case I of Schedule D.

Commentary—*Simon's Direct Tax Service* **D2.1420.**

Entitlement to relief: "I minus E" basis

22—(1) Sub-paragraph (2) applies if—

(*a*) land in the United Kingdom is a management asset of a company,

(*b*) at the time of acquisition by the company all or part of the land is or was in a contaminated state, and

(*c*) in any accounting period, the company incurs qualifying expenditure in respect of the land.

(2) Where this sub-paragraph applies, the company is entitled to relief for that accounting period in respect of its qualifying expenditure.

(3) For the purposes of this paragraph, the amount of a company's qualifying expenditure in an accounting period is the amount of its qualifying land remediation expenditure in that period reduced by the amount (if any) which by virtue of section 76(1)(*d*) of the Taxes Act 1988 is not to be treated as expenses of management.

(4) A company is not entitled to relief under this paragraph in respect of expenditure on land all or part of which is in a contaminated state, if the land is in that state wholly or partly as a result of any thing done or omitted to be done at any time by the company or a person with a relevant connection to the company.

(5) For the purposes of this paragraph, land is a management asset of a company if it is—

(*a*) an asset provided for use or used for the management of life assurance business carried on by the company, or

(*b*) an asset in respect of which expenditure is being incurred with a view to such use by the company.

Commentary—*Simon's Direct Tax Service* **D2.1420.**

Giving effect to relief: enhanced expenses of management

23—(1) If a company is entitled to relief under paragraph 22 for an accounting period in respect of its qualifying expenditure, sub-paragraph (2) shall apply for the purposes of section 76 of the Taxes Act 1988 (computing profits of company carrying on life assurance business: deduction of expenses of management etc).

(2) Where this sub-paragraph applies, the company may (on making a claim) treat an amount equal to 150% of the actual amount of the qualifying expenditure (as determined in accordance with paragraph 22(3)) as part of its expenses of management for that period.

Commentary—*Simon's Direct Tax Service* **D2.1420, 1421.**

Entitlement to life assurance company tax credit

24—(1) A company may claim a life assurance company tax credit under this paragraph if in an accounting period it has a "qualifying loss".

(2) A company has a "qualifying loss" for this purpose if in an accounting period—

(*a*) the company is entitled to relief under paragraph 22, and

(*b*) an amount falls to be carried forward to a succeeding accounting period under section 75(3) of the Taxes Act 1988 (carrying forward expenses of management and charges on income where such expenses and charges exceed amount of profits from which deductible).

(3) In determining for the purposes of sub-paragraph (2)(*b*) whether there is an amount which falls to be carried forward under section 75(3) of that Act, there shall be disregarded any amounts brought forward from an earlier accounting period and treated as expenses of management for the period in question by virtue of—

(*a*) a previous application of section 75(3) of that Act, or

(*b*) paragraph 4(4) of Schedule 11 to the Finance Act 1996 (loan relationships deficit carried forward and treated as expenses of management).

(4) The amount of the qualifying loss is equal to the lesser of—

(*a*) 150% of the related qualifying expenditure, and

(*b*) such amount as is determined in accordance with sub-paragraph (3) to be an amount which falls to be carried forward as described in sub-paragraph (2)(*b*).

Commentary—*Simon's Direct Tax Service* **D2.1420, 1421.**

Amount of life assurance company tax credit

25—(1) The amount of the life assurance company tax credit to which a company is entitled for an accounting period is equal to 16% of the amount of the qualifying loss for the period.

(2) The Treasury may by order substitute for the percentage for the time being specified in sub-paragraph (1) such other percentage as they think fit.

(3) An order under sub-paragraph (2) may make such incidental, supplemental, consequential or transitional provision as the Treasury think fit.

Commentary—*Simon's Direct Tax Service* **D2.1420, 1421.**

Payment in respect of life assurance company tax credit, etc

26 Paragraph 16 (payment) and paragraph 18 (tax credit not to be treated as income) shall have effect in relation to life assurance company tax credits with the substitution for each reference to a land remediation tax credit of a reference to a life assurance company tax credit.

Commentary—*Simon's Direct Tax Service* **D2.1420, 1421.**

Restriction on carrying forward expenses of management

27—(1) For the purposes of subsection (3) of section 75 of the Taxes Act 1988 (carrying forward expenses of management and charges on income where they exceed amount of profits from which deductible), the amount which may be carried forward under that subsection for a period in which the company claims a life assurance company tax credit is treated as reduced by the amount of the expenses of management surrendered.

(2) For the purposes of sub-paragraph (1) the amount of the expenses of management surrendered is—

(a) where the maximum amount of life assurance company tax credit was claimed, the whole of the qualifying loss for that period;
(b) where less than the maximum amount was claimed, a corresponding proportion of the qualifying loss for that period.

The "maximum amount" here means the amount specified in paragraph 25(1).

Commentary—*Simon's Direct Tax Service* **D2.1420, 1421.**

Certain qualifying expenditure excluded for purposes of capital gains

28 If in an accounting period—

(a) a company has a qualifying loss, and
(b) by virtue of that qualifying loss, a payment is made to the company in respect of a life assurance company tax credit,

the related qualifying expenditure shall be treated as if it were expenditure excluded for the purposes of capital gains tax under section 39 of the Taxation of Chargeable Gains Act 1992.

Commentary—*Simon's Direct Tax Service* **D2.1420, 1421.**

PART 5
SUPPLEMENTARY PROVISIONS
Artificially inflated claims for deduction, relief or tax credit

29—(1) To the extent that a transaction is attributable to arrangements entered into wholly or mainly for a disqualifying purpose, it shall be disregarded in determining for an accounting period the amount of—

(a) any deduction for capital expenditure which is allowed under paragraph 1,
(b) any land remediation relief to which a company is entitled under paragraph 12,
(c) any land remediation tax credit to which a company is entitled under paragraph 14,
(d) any relief to which a company carrying on life assurance business is entitled under paragraph 22, and
(e) any life assurance company tax credit to which such a company is entitled under paragraph 24.

(2) Arrangements are entered into wholly or mainly for a "disqualifying purpose" if their main object, or one of their main objects, is to enable a company to obtain—

(a) a deduction for capital expenditure which would not otherwise be allowed or of a greater amount than that which would otherwise be allowed;
(b) land remediation relief to which the company would not otherwise be entitled or of a greater amount than that to which it would otherwise be entitled;
(c) a land remediation tax credit to which it would not otherwise be entitled or of a greater amount than that to which it would otherwise be entitled;
(d) relief under paragraph 22 to which it would not otherwise be entitled or of a greater amount than that to which it would otherwise be entitled; or
(e) a life assurance company tax credit to which it would not otherwise be entitled or of a greater amount than that to which it would otherwise be entitled.

(3) In this paragraph "arrangements" includes any scheme, agreement or understanding, whether or not legally enforceable.

Commentary—*Simon's Direct Tax Service* **D2.1415.**

Funding of tax credits

30 Section 10 of the Exchequer and Audit Departments Act 1866 (gross revenues to be paid to Exchequer) shall be construed as allowing the Commissioners of Inland Revenue to deduct payments for or in respect of—

(*a*) land remediation tax credits, and

(*b*) life assurance company tax credits,

before causing the gross revenues of their department to be paid to the accounts mentioned in that section.

Interpretation

31—(1) In this Schedule—

"harm" means—

(*a*) harm to the health of living organisms,

(*b*) interference with the ecological systems of which any living organisms form part,

(*c*) offence to the senses of human beings, or

(*d*) damage to property;

"the Inland Revenue" means any officer of the Board;

"insurance company" has the same meaning as it has in Chapter I of Part XII of the Taxes Act 1988;

"land" means any estate, interest or rights in or over land;

"life assurance business" has the same meaning as it has in Chapter I of Part XII of the Taxes Act 1988;

"national insurance contributions" means contributions under Part I of the Social Security Contributions and Benefits Act 1992 or Part I of the Social Security Contributions and Benefits (Northern Ireland) Act 1992;

"pollution of controlled waters" means the entry into controlled waters of any poisonous, noxious or polluting matter or any solid waste matter;

"qualifying loss" has the meaning given in paragraph 24;

"qualifying land remediation loss" has the meaning given in paragraph 14;

"Schedule A loss" has the meaning given by section 392A of the Taxes Act 1988; and

"substance" means any natural or artificial substance, whether in solid or liquid form or in the form of a gas or vapour.

(2) In this Schedule "controlled waters"—

(*a*) in relation to England and Wales, has the same meaning as in Part III of the Water Resources Act 1991;

(*b*) in relation to Scotland, has the same meaning as in section 30A of the Control of Pollution Act 1974;

(*c*) in relation to Northern Ireland, means water in waterways and underground strata (as defined in Article 2(2) of the Water (Northern Ireland) Order 1999).

(3) For the purposes of this Schedule, a person has a relevant connection to a company in a case where the company's land is in a contaminated state wholly or partly as a result of any thing done or omitted to be done by the person if—

(*a*) he is or was connected to the company when any such thing is or was done, or omitted to be done, by him,

(*b*) he is or was connected to the company at the time when the land in question is or was acquired by the company, or

(*c*) he is or was connected to the company at any time when relevant land remediation is or was undertaken by the company (whether directly or on its behalf).

(4) Section 839 of the Taxes Act 1988 (connected persons) applies for the purposes of this Schedule.

Commentary—*Simon's Direct Tax Service* **D2.1403, 1410.**

Transitional provisions

32—(1) This Schedule does not apply to expenditure incurred before the day on which this Act is passed.

(2) For this purpose no account shall be taken of section 401 of the Taxes Act 1988 (earlier expenditure treated as incurred when Schedule A business or trading begins).

SCHEDULE 23

LAND REMEDIATION: CONSEQUENTIAL AMENDMENTS

Section 70

Commentary—*Simon's Direct Tax Service* **D2.201.**

Computation under Schedule A

1 (*adds* TA 1988 s 21A(5)).

Computation of profits of insurance companies

2 (*inserts* TA 1988 s 76(7B)).

Interest

3—(1) Section 826 of the Taxes Act 1988 (interest on tax overpaid) is amended as follows.

(2)–(5) (*insert* TA 1988 s 826(1)(*e*), (3B) and *amend* sub-ss (8A), (8BA)).

Claim must be made in tax return

4 (*adds* FA 1998 Sch 18 para 10(2A)).

Recovery of excessive tax credit

5 (*amends* FA 1998 Sch 18 para 52(2), (5)).

Claims relating to remediation of contaminated land

6 (*inserts* FA 1998 Sch 18 Pt IXB (paras 83G–83L)).

SCHEDULE 24

CREATIVE ARTISTS: RELIEF FOR FLUCTUATING PROFITS

Section 71

Commentary—*Simon's Direct Tax Service* **B3.816, B3.833.**

PART 1
NEW SCHEDULE 4A TO THE TAXES ACT 1988

1 (*inserts* TA 1988 Sch 4A).

PART 2
CONSEQUENTIAL AMENDMENTS

2—(1) (*substitutes* TMA 1970 s 46C(3)(*d*)).

(2) This paragraph applies in relation to claims made in respect of payments actually receivable on or after 6th April 2001.

3—(1) (*substitutes* TMA 1970 Sch 1B para 1(2), (3)).

(2) This paragraph applies for the year 2001–01 and subsequent years of assessment.

4—(1) (*amends* TA 1988 s 537).

(2) This paragraph applies in relation to payments actually receivable on or after 6th April 2001.

SCHEDULE 25

LIMITED LIABILITY PARTNERSHIPS: INVESTMENT LLPS AND PROPERTY INVESTMENT LLPS

Section 76

Commentary—*Simon's Direct Tax Service* **E5.305.**

Meaning of "investment LLP" and "property investment LLP"

1—(1) (*inserts* TA 1988 s 842B).

(2) (*amends* TA 1988 s 832(1)).

(3) (*amends* TA 1988 s 288(1)).

Pension funds, &c: exclusion of exemptions from tax in case of income from property investment LLPs

2 (*inserts* TA 1988 s 659E).

Pension funds, &c: exclusion of exemption from trusts rate in case of income from property investment LLPs

3—(1) Section 686 of the Taxes Act 1988 (accumulation and discretionary trusts: special rates of tax) is amended as follows.

(2), (3) (*amend* TA 1988 s 686(2)(*c*) and *insert* sub-s (6A)).

Pension funds, &c: exclusion of exemptions in case of gains from property investment LLPs

4 (*adds* TCGA 1992 s 271(12)).

Insurance companies: treatment of income or gains arising from property investment LLP

5 (*inserts* **TA 1988 ss 438B, 438C**).

Insurance companies: double taxation relief

6 (*amends* TA 1988 s 804B(2), (4)).

Insurance companies: capital allowances

7 (*substitutes* CAA 2001 s 545(3)).

Friendly societies: exclusion of exemptions from tax

8—(1) (*inserts* TA 1988 s 460(2)(*cb*)).

(2) (*inserts* TA 1988 s 461(3A)).

(3) (*inserts* TA 1988 s 461B(2A)).

Exclusion of relief on loans to buy into investment LLP

9 (*amends* TA 1988 s 362(2)).

SCHEDULE 26
CAPITAL GAINS TAX: TAPER RELIEF: BUSINESS ASSETS
Section 78

Commentary—*Simon's Direct Tax Service* **C2.1423, C2.1428.**

Introductory

1 Schedule A1 to the Taxation of Chargeable Gains Act 1992 (application of taper relief) is amended as follows.

Conditions for assets other than shares to qualify as business assets

2 (*amends* TCGA 1992 Sch A1 para 5(3)(*a*)).

Companies which are qualifying companies

3 (*inserts* TCGA 1992 Sch A1 para 6(1A), (2A) and *adds* sub-paras (4)–(7)).

Meaning of "material interest"

4 (*inserts* TCGA 1992 Sch A1 para 6A).

Interpretation of Schedule A1

5 (*amends* TCGA 1992 Sch A1 para 22).

Qualifying shareholdings in joint venture companies

6 (*repeals* TCGA 1992 Sch A1 para 23(8)).

Joint enterprise companies: relevant connection

7 (*inserts* TCGA 1992 Sch A1 para 24).

SCHEDULE 27

DOUBLE TAXATION RELIEF

Section 81

Commentary—*Simon's Direct Tax Service* **F1.117, F1.122, F1.134.**

Computation of income subject to foreign tax

1—(1) Section 795 of the Taxes Act 1988 is amended as follows.

(2), (3) (*amend* TA 1988 s 795(2)(*b*) and *insert* sub-s (3A)).

(4) This paragraph has effect in relation to dividends paid on or after 31st March 2001 by a company resident outside the United Kingdom to a company resident in the United Kingdom (whenever any such dividend as is mentioned in section 801(2) or (3) of the Taxes Act 1988 was paid).

Restriction of relief for underlying tax

2—(1) Section 799 of the Taxes Act 1988 (computation of underlying tax) is amended as follows.

(2), (3) (*insert* TA 1988 s 799(1A), (1B)).

(4) This paragraph has effect in relation to any claim for an allowance by way of credit made on or after 31st March 2001 in respect of a dividend paid by a company resident outside the United Kingdom to a company resident in the United Kingdom, unless the dividend was paid before that date.

(5) In determining, for the purpose of any such claim made on or after that date, the underlying tax of any such third, fourth or successive company as is mentioned in section 801(2) or (3) of the Taxes Act 1988, this paragraph shall be taken to have had effect at the time the dividend paid by that company was paid.

Credit for underlying tax: UK company related through overseas company

3—(1) Section 801 of the Taxes Act 1988 (dividends paid between related companies: relief for UK and third country taxes) is amended as follows.

(2), (3) (*amend* TA 1988 s 801(2) and *insert* sub-ss (4A)–(4D))

(4) This paragraph has effect in relation to any claim for an allowance by way of credit made on or after 31st March 2001 in respect of a dividend paid by a company resident outside the United Kingdom to a company resident in the United Kingdom, unless the dividend was paid before that date.

(5) In determining, for the purpose of any such claim made on or after that date, the underlying tax of any such third, fourth or successive company as is mentioned in section 801(2) or (3) of the Taxes Act 1988, this paragraph shall be taken to have had effect at the time the dividend paid by that company was paid.

Dividends that give rise to eligible unrelieved foreign tax

4—(1) Section 806A of the Taxes Act 1988 (eligible unrelieved foreign tax) is amended as follows.

(2) (*amends* TA 1988 s 806A(5)).

(3) The amendment made by this paragraph has effect in relation to—

    (*a*) dividends arising on or after 31st March 2001 to companies resident in the United Kingdom from companies resident outside the United Kingdom, and
    (*b*) foreign tax in respect of such dividends,

(whenever the dividend mentioned in the amendment was paid).

The amounts that are eligible unrelieved foreign tax

5—(1) Section 806B (determination of the amounts that are eligible unrelieved foreign tax) is amended as follows.

(2), (3) (*substitute* TA 1988 806B(3)–(6) and *amend* sub-s (9)).

(4) The amendments made by this paragraph have effect in relation to—

    (*a*) dividends arising on or after 31st March 2001 to companies resident in the United Kingdom from companies resident outside the United Kingdom, and
    (*b*) foreign tax in respect of such dividends,

(whenever any such dividend as is mentioned in section 801(2) or (3) of the Taxes Act 1988 was paid).

Underlying tax excluded from claim not to be allowed under section 811

6—(1) Section 811 of the Taxes Act 1988 (deduction for foreign tax where no credit allowable) is amended as follows.

(2) (*amends* TA 1988 s 811(2)).

(3) This paragraph has effect in relation to income arising on or after 31st March 2001.

Relief for non-resident persons with branches or agencies in the UK

7—(1) The amendments made by paragraph 4 of Schedule 30 to the Finance Act 2000 shall have effect, and be taken always to have had effect, in accordance with the following provisions of this paragraph.

(2) (*amends* FA 2000 Sch 30 para 4).

(3) That paragraph shall be taken to have been originally enacted as so amended.

SCHEDULE 28

LIFE POLICIES, LIFE ANNUITIES AND CAPITAL REDEMPTION POLICIES

Section 83

Commentary—*Simon's Direct Tax Service* **E3.501, E3.503.**

PART 1

ASSIGNMENT OR SURRENDER OF PART OF THE RIGHTS

Introductory

1 Chapter II of Part XIII of the Taxes Act 1988 is amended in accordance with the following provisions of this Part of this Schedule.

Interpretation

2 (*inserts* TA 1988 s 539(3A)).

Life policies: chargeable events

3 (*amends* TA 1988 s 540(1)).

Life policies: computation of gain

4 (*amends* TA 1988 s 541(1), (4)).

Life annuity contracts: chargeable events

5 (*amends* TA 1988 s 542(1)(*c*), (3)).

Life annuity contracts: computation of gain

6 (*amends* TA 1988 s 543(1)).

Capital redemption policies: chargeable events

7 (*amends* TA 1988 s 545(1)(*d*)).

The value of a part or share assigned

8—(1) Section 546 (calculation of certain amounts for the purposes of sections 540, 542 and 545) is amended as follows.

(2), (3) (*amend* TA 1988 s 546(1) and *add* sub-s (6)).

Assignments etc involving co-ownership

9 (*inserts* TA 1988 s 546A).

Charging tax in respect of certain section 546 excesses

10 (*inserts* TA 1988 ss 546B–546D).

Method of charging gain to tax

11—(1) Section 547 is amended as follows.

(2)–(6) (*amend* TA 1988 s 547(1), (5A) and (7), *insert* sub-s (1A), and *substitute* sub-s (4)).

Method of charging gain to tax: multiple interests

12 (*substitutes* TA 1988 s 547A(2)).

Corresponding deficiency relief

13 (*amends* TA 1988 s 549(1)).

Relief where gain charged at higher rate

14 (*inserts* TA 1988 s 550(5A)).

Right of individual to recover tax from trustees

15 (*amends* TA 1988 s 551(1)(*b*)).

Right of company to recover tax from trustees

16 (*amends* TA 1988 s 551A(1)(*b*)).

Non-resident policies and off-shore capital redemption policies

17—(1) Section 553 is amended as follows.

(2)–(4) (*amend* TA 1988 s 553(3), (6) and (10)).

PART 2
PROVISION OF INFORMATION BY INSURERS ETC

Information: duty of insurers

18 (*substitutes* TA 1988 ss 552, 552ZA for s 552).

Duties of overseas insurers' tax representatives

19 (*substitutes* TA 1988 s 552B(2)).

Penalties

20 In section 98 of the Taxes Management Act 1970, in the second column of the Table—

(*a*) for the entry "section 552(1) to (4);" substitute "section 552;"; and

(*b*) for the entry "regulations under section 552(4A)" substitute "regulations under section 552ZA(6);".

SCHEDULE 29

AMENDMENTS TO MACHINERY OF SELF-ASSESSMENT

Section 88

Commentary—*Simon's Direct Tax Service* **E1.802.**

PART 1
AMENDMENT OR CORRECTION OF RETURN

Assessment by Revenue treated as included in return

1 (*amends* TMA 1970 and *inserts* sub-s (3A)).

Power to amend or correct personal or trustee return

2 (*repeals* TMA 1970 s 9(4)–(6) and *inserts* TMA 1970 ss 9ZA, 9ZB).

Power to amend or correct partnership return

3 (*repeals* TMA 1970 s 12AB(2)–(4), *amends* sub-s (5) and *inserts* TMA 1970 ss 12ABA, 12ABB).

PART 2
ENQUIRIES INTO RETURNS

Enquiry into personal or trustee return

4—(1) (*substitutes* TMA 1970 ss 9A–9D for s 9A).

(2) (*amends* TMA 1970 s 9A(2)(*a*) as it applies for returns for years of assessment before the year 2001–02).

Enquiry into partnership return

5—(1) (*substitutes* TMA 1970 ss 12AC–12AE for TMA 1970 s 12AC).

(2) (*amends* TMA 1970 s 12AC(2)(*a*) as substituted above, as it applies in relation to returns for years of assessment before the year 2001–02).

PART 3

REFERRAL OF QUESTIONS DURING ENQUIRY

Enquiry into personal, trustee or partnership return

6—(1) (*inserts* TMA 1970 Pt IIIA (ss 28ZA–28ZE)).

(2) This paragraph applies—

(*a*) where the notice of enquiry is given after the passing of this Act, or
(*b*) where the enquiry is in progress immediately before the passing of this Act.

For the purposes of paragraph (*b*) an enquiry is in progress until the officer's enquiries fall to be treated as completed under section 28A(5) or, as the case may be, section 28B(5) of the Taxes Management Act 1970 (as those provisions had effect apart from this Schedule).

Enquiry into company tax return

7—(1) (*inserts* FA 1998 Sch 18 paras 31A–31D).

(2) This paragraph applies in relation to an enquiry under Part IV of Schedule 18 to the Finance Act 1998—

(*a*) in relation to which notice of enquiry is given after the passing of this Act, or
(*b*) which is in progress (within the meaning of paragraph 31(5) of that Schedule) immediately before the passing of this Act.

PART 4

PROCEDURE ON COMPLETION OF ENQUIRY

Procedure on completion of enquiry into personal or trustee return

8—(1) (*substitutes* TMA 1970 s 28A).

(2) This paragraph applies—

(*a*) where the notice of enquiry is given after the passing of this Act, or
(*b*) where the enquiry is in progress immediately before the passing of this Act.

For the purposes of paragraph (*b*) an enquiry is in progress until the officer's enquiries fall to be treated as completed under section 28A(5) of the Taxes Management Act 1970 (as that provision had effect apart from this Schedule).

Procedure on completion of enquiry into partnership return

9—(1) (*substitutes* TMA 1970 s 28B).

(2) This paragraph applies—

(*a*) where the notice of enquiry is given after the passing of this Act, or
(*b*) where the enquiry is in progress immediately before the passing of this Act.

For the purposes of paragraph (*b*) an enquiry is in progress until the officer's enquiries fall to be treated as completed under section 28B(5) of the Taxes Management Act 1970 (as that provision had effect apart from this Schedule).

Procedure on completion of enquiry into claims, &c not included in returns

10—(1) (*substitutes* TMA 1970 Sch 1A para 7).

(3) This paragraph applies—

(*a*) where the notice of enquiry is given after the passing of this Act, or
(*b*) where the enquiry is in progress immediately before the passing of this Act.

For the purposes of paragraph (*b*) an enquiry is in progress until the officer's enquiries fall to be treated as completed under paragraph 7(4) of Schedule 1A to the Taxes Management Act 1970 (as that provision had effect apart from this Schedule).

PART 5

MINOR AND CONSEQUENTIAL AMENDMENTS

Appeals

11—(1) (*substitutes* TMA 1970 ss 31–31D for TMA 1970 s 31).

(2) This paragraph applies in relation to—

(*a*) amendments of a self-assessment under section 9C of the Taxes Management Act 1970 as inserted by paragraph 4 of this Schedule,

(*b*) closure notices issued under section 28A(1) or 28B(1) of that Act as substituted by paragraphs 8 and 9 of this Schedule,

(*c*) amendments of partnership returns under section 30B(1) of that Act where notice of the amendment is issued after the passing of this Act, and

(*d*) assessments to tax which are not self-assessments where the notice of the assessment is issued after the passing of this Act.

12—(1) Schedule 1A to the Taxes Management Act 1970 (claims etc not included in returns) is amended as follows.

(2)–(7) (*amend* TMA 1970 Sch 1A paras 9 and 10).

(8) This paragraph applies in relation to closure notices issued under paragraph 7 of Schedule 1A to the Taxes Management Act 1970 as substituted by paragraph 10 of this Schedule.

13—(1) Part XI of Schedule 18 to the Finance Act 1998 (company tax returns: supplementary provisions) is amended as follows.

(2) (*inserts* FA 1998 Sch 18 para 93(2A)).

Due date for payment after amendment or correction of return

14 (*amends* TMA 1970 s 59B).

15 (*inserts* TMA 1970 Sch 3ZA).

16—(1) Paragraphs 14 and 15 above apply where the relevant day is, or is after, the day on which this Act is passed.

(2) In sub-paragraph (1) the "relevant day" means the first day of the period of 30 days specified in the relevant provision of Schedule 3ZA to the Taxes Management Act 1970 (as inserted by paragraph 15 above).

Effect of return on recovery proceedings

17—(1) (*amends* TMA 1970 s 28C(4)).

(2) (*amends* FA 1998 Sch 18 para 40(4)).

(3) This paragraph applies in relation to proceedings begun after the passing of this Act.

Other amendments of the Taxes Management Act 1970

18 (*amends* TMA 1970 s 12AA(10A)).

19 (*amends* TMA 1970 s 12AB(1)).

20 (*amends* TMA 1970 s 12B(1)).

21 (*amends* TMA 1970 s 19A).

22 (*amends* TMA 1970 s 29(7).

23 (*amends* TMA 1970 s 30(5)(*b*)).

24 (*amends* TMA 1970 s 30B).

25 (*amends* TMA 1970 s 33A).

26 (*amends* TMA 1970 s 42(6)(*a*)).

27 (*amends* TMA 1970 s 46B(2)).

28 (*amends* TMA 1970 s 46C).

29 (*amends* TMA 1970 s 46D(2)).

30 (*amends* TMA 1970 s 50).

31 (*amends* TMA 1970 s 55).

32 (*amends* TMA 1970 s 95A(1)).

33 (*amends* TMA 1970 s 118(1)).

34—(1) Schedule 1A to the Taxes Management Act 1970 (claims etc not included in returns) is amended as follows.

(2) (*amends* TMA 1970 Sch 1A para 2A(2)).

(3) (*amends* TMA 1970 Sch 1A para 4(3)).

(4), (5) (*amend* TMA 1970 Sch 1A para 8(1), (2)).

Consequential amendments of other enactments

35 (*amends* TA 1988 s 379A(3), Sch 28AA para 6(7)).

36 (*amends* FA 1993 Sch 19 paras 4, 7).

37 (*amends* FA 1995 Sch 22 paras 11, 12).

38 (*amends* FA 1998 ss 110, 111, Sch 18 para 27).

39 (*amends* SSC(TF)A 1999 s 12(5)).

40 In Article 11(5) of the Social Security Contributions (Transfer of Functions, etc) (Northern Ireland) Order 1999 (application of section 31(5A) to (5E) of the 1970 Act in relation to elections under Article 11(4))—

(*a*) for ''(5A) to (5E) of section 31'' substitute ''(2) to (7) of section 31D'', and
(*b*) for ''subsection (4) of that section'' substitute ''subsection (1) of that section''.

SCHEDULE 33

REPEALS

Section 110

Note—The repeals made under this Schedule are already in effect and have therefore been omitted.

CRIMINAL JUSTICE AND POLICE ACT 2001

(2001 Chapter 16)

ARRANGEMENT OF SECTIONS

PART 2

POWERS OF SEIZURE

Additional powers of seizure

PART 5
POLICE ORGANISATION
Minor and consequential amendments

PART 6
MISCELLANEOUS AND SUPPLEMENTAL

Supplemental

SCHEDULES:

An Act to make provision for combating crime and disorder; to make provision about the disclosure of information relating to criminal matters and about powers of search and seizure; to amend the Police and Criminal Evidence Act 1984, the Police and Criminal Evidence (Northern Ireland) Order 1989 and the Terrorism Act 2000; to make provision about the police, the National Criminal Intelligence Service and the National Crime Squad; to make provision about the powers of the courts in relation to criminal matters; and for connected purposes.

[11 May 2001]

PART 2
POWERS OF SEIZURE
Additional powers of seizure

50 Additional powers of seizure from premises

(1) Where—

(a) a person who is lawfully on any premises finds anything on those premises that he has reasonable grounds for believing may be or may contain something for which he is authorised to search on those premises,

(b) a power of seizure to which this section applies or the power conferred by subsection (2) would entitle him, if he found it, to seize whatever it is that he has grounds for believing that thing to be or to contain, and

(c) in all the circumstances, it is not reasonably practicable for it to be determined, on those premises—

     (i) whether what he has found is something that he is entitled to seize, or

     (ii) the extent to which what he has found contains something that he is entitled to seize,

that person's powers of seizure shall include power under this section to seize so much of what he has found as it is necessary to remove from the premises to enable that to be determined.

(2) Where—

(a) a person who is lawfully on any premises finds anything on those premises ("the seizable property") which he would be entitled to seize but for its being comprised in something else that he has (apart from this subsection) no power to seize,

(b) the power under which that person would have power to seize the seizable property is a power to which this section applies, and

(c) in all the circumstances it is not reasonably practicable for the seizable property to be separated, on those premises, from that in which it is comprised,

that person's powers of seizure shall include power under this section to seize both the seizable property and that from which it is not reasonably practicable to separate it.

(3) The factors to be taken into account in considering, for the purposes of this section, whether or not it is reasonably practicable on particular premises for something to be determined, or for something to be separated from something else, shall be confined to the following—

(*a*) how long it would take to carry out the determination or separation on those premises;

(*b*) the number of persons that would be required to carry out that determination or separation on those premises within a reasonable period;

(*c*) whether the determination or separation would (or would if carried out on those premises) involve damage to property;

(*d*) the apparatus or equipment that it would be necessary or appropriate to use for the carrying out of the determination or separation; and

(*e*) in the case of separation, whether the separation—

(i) would be likely, or

(ii) if carried out by the only means that are reasonably practicable on those premises, would be likely,

to prejudice the use of some or all of the separated seizable property for a purpose for which something seized under the power in question is capable of being used.

(4) Section 19(6) of the 1984 Act and Article 21(6) of the Police and Criminal Evidence (Northern Ireland) Order 1989 (SI 1989/1341 (NI 12)) (powers of seizure not to include power to seize anything that a person has reasonable grounds for believing is legally privileged) shall not apply to the power of seizure conferred by subsection (2).

(5) This section applies to each of the powers of seizure specified in Part 1 of Schedule 1.

(6) Without prejudice to any power conferred by this section to take a copy of any document, nothing in this section, so far as it has effect by reference to the power to take copies of documents under section 28(2)(*b*) of the Competition Act 1998 (c. 41), shall be taken to confer any power to seize any document.

51 Additional powers of seizure from the person

(1) Where—

(*a*) a person carrying out a lawful search of any person finds something that he has reasonable grounds for believing may be or may contain something for which he is authorised to search,

(*b*) a power of seizure to which this section applies or the power conferred by subsection (2) would entitle him, if he found it, to seize whatever it is that he has grounds for believing that thing to be or to contain, and

(*c*) in all the circumstances it is not reasonably practicable for it to be determined, at the time and place of the search—

(i) whether what he has found is something that he is entitled to seize, or

(ii) the extent to which what he has found contains something that he is entitled to seize,

that person's powers of seizure shall include power under this section to seize so much of what he has found as it is necessary to remove from that place to enable that to be determined.

(2) Where—

(*a*) a person carrying out a lawful search of any person finds something (''the seizable property'') which he would be entitled to seize but for its being comprised in something else that he has (apart from this subsection) no power to seize,

(*b*) the power under which that person would have power to seize the seizable property is a power to which this section applies, and

(*c*) in all the circumstances it is not reasonably practicable for the seizable property to be separated, at the time and place of the search, from that in which it is comprised,

that person's powers of seizure shall include power under this section to seize both the seizable property and that from which it is not reasonably practicable to separate it.

(3) The factors to be taken into account in considering, for the purposes of this section, whether or not it is reasonably practicable, at the time and place of a search, for something to be determined, or for something to be separated from something else, shall be confined to the following—

(*a*) how long it would take to carry out the determination or separation at that time and place;

(*b*) the number of persons that would be required to carry out that determination or separation at that time and place within a reasonable period;

(*c*) whether the determination or separation would (or would if carried out at that time and place) involve damage to property;

(*d*) the apparatus or equipment that it would be necessary or appropriate to use for the carrying out of the determination or separation; and

(*e*) in the case of separation, whether the separation—

(i) would be likely, or

(ii) if carried out by the only means that are reasonably practicable at that time and place, would be likely,

to prejudice the use of some or all of the separated seizable property for a purpose for which something seized under the power in question is capable of being used.

(4) Section 19(6) of the 1984 Act and Article 21(6) of the Police and Criminal Evidence (Northern Ireland) Order 1989 (SI 1989/1341 (NI 12)) (powers of seizure not to include power to seize anything a person has reasonable grounds for believing is legally privileged) shall not apply to the power of seizure conferred by subsection (2).

(5) This section applies to each of the powers of seizure specified in Part 2 of Schedule 1.

52 Notice of exercise of power under s. 50 or 51

(1) Where a person exercises a power of seizure conferred by section 50, it shall (subject to subsections (2) and (3)) be his duty, on doing so, to give to the occupier of the premises a written notice—

(a) specifying what has been seized in reliance on the powers conferred by that section;

(b) specifying the grounds on which those powers have been exercised;

(c) setting out the effect of sections 59 to 61;

(d) specifying the name and address of the person to whom notice of an application under section 59(2) to the appropriate judicial authority in respect of any of the seized property must be given; and

(e) specifying the name and address of the person to whom an application may be made to be allowed to attend the initial examination required by any arrangements made for the purposes of section 53(2).

(2) Where it appears to the person exercising on any premises a power of seizure conferred by section 50—

(a) that the occupier of the premises is not present on the premises at the time of the exercise of the power, but

(b) that there is some other person present on the premises who is in charge of the premises,

subsection (1) of this section shall have effect as if it required the notice under that subsection to be given to that other person.

(3) Where it appears to the person exercising a power of seizure conferred by section 50 that there is no one present on the premises to whom he may give a notice for the purposes of complying with subsection (1) of this section, he shall, before leaving the premises, instead of complying with that subsection, attach a notice such as is mentioned in that subsection in a prominent place to the premises.

(4) Where a person exercises a power of seizure conferred by section 51 it shall be his duty, on doing so, to give a written notice to the person from whom the seizure is made—

(a) specifying what has been seized in reliance on the powers conferred by that section;

(b) specifying the grounds on which those powers have been exercised;

(c) setting out the effect of sections 59 to 61;

(d) specifying the name and address of the person to whom notice of any application under section 59(2) to the appropriate judicial authority in respect of any of the seized property must be given; and

(e) specifying the name and address of the person to whom an application may be made to be allowed to attend the initial examination required by any arrangements made for the purposes of section 53(2).

(5) The Secretary of State may by regulations made by statutory instrument, after consultation with the Scottish Ministers, provide that a person who exercises a power of seizure conferred by section 50 shall be required to give a notice such as is mentioned in subsection (1) of this section to any person, or send it to any place, described in the regulations.

(6) Regulations under subsection (5) may make different provision for different cases.

(7) A statutory instrument containing regulations under subsection (5) shall be subject to annulment in pursuance of a resolution of either House of Parliament.

Return or retention of seized property

53 Examination and return of property seized under s. 50 or 51

(1) This section applies where anything has been seized under a power conferred by section 50 or 51.

(2) It shall be the duty of the person for the time being in possession of the seized property in consequence of the exercise of that power to secure that there are arrangements in force which (subject to section 61) ensure—

(a) that an initial examination of the property is carried out as soon as reasonably practicable after the seizure;

(b) that that examination is confined to whatever is necessary for determining how much of the property falls within subsection (3);

(c) that anything which is found, on that examination, not to fall within subsection (3) is separated from the rest of the seized property and is returned as soon as reasonably practicable after the examination of an the seized property has been completed; and (*d*) that, until the initial examination of all the seized property has been completed and anything which does not fall within subsection (3) has been returned, the seized property is kept separate from anything seized under any other power.

(3) The seized property falls within this subsection to the extent only—

(*a*) that it is property for which the person seizing it had power to search when he made the seizure but is not property the return of which is required by section 54;

(*b*) that it is property the retention of which is authorised by section 56; or

(*c*) that it is something which, in all the circumstances, it will not be reasonably practicable, following the examination, to separate from property falling within paragraph (*a*) or (*b*).

(4) In determining for the purposes of this section the earliest practicable time for the carrying out of an initial examination of the seized property, due regard shall be had to the desirability of allowing the person from whom it was seized, or a person with an interest in that property, an opportunity of being present or (if he chooses) of being represented at the examination.

(5) In this section, references to whether or not it is reasonably practicable to separate part of the seized property from the rest of it are references to whether or not it is reasonably practicable to do so without prejudicing the use of the rest of that property, or a part of it, for purposes for which (disregarding the part to be separated) the use of the whole or of a part of the rest of the property, if retained, would be lawful.

54 Obligation to return items subject to legal privilege

(1) If, at any time after a seizure of anything has been made in exercise of a power of seizure to which this section applies—

(*a*) it appears to the person for the time being having possession of the seized property in consequence of the seizure that the property—

(i) is an item subject to legal privilege, or

(ii) has such an item comprised in it,

and

(*b*) in a case where the item is comprised in something else which has been lawfully seized, it is not comprised in property falling within subsection (2),

it shall be the duty of that person to secure that the item is returned as soon as reasonably practicable after the seizure.

(2) Property in which an item subject to legal privilege is comprised falls within this subsection if—

(*a*) the whole or a part of the rest of the property is property falling within subsection (3) or property the retention of which is authorised by section 56; and

(*b*) in all the circumstances, it is not reasonably practicable for that item to be separated from the rest of that property (or, as the case may be, from that part of it) without prejudicing the use of the rest of that property, or that part of it, for purposes for which (disregarding that item) its use, if retained, would be lawful.

(3) Property falls within this subsection to the extent that it is property for which the person seizing it had power to search when he made the seizure, but is not property which is required to be returned under this section or section 55.

(4) This section applies—

(*a*) to the powers of seizure conferred by sections 50 and 51;

(*b*) to each of the powers of seizure specified in Parts 1 and 2 of Schedule 1; and

(*c*) to any power of seizure (not falling within paragraph (*a*) or (*b*)) conferred on a constable by or under any enactment, including an enactment passed after this Act.

55 Obligation to return excluded and special procedure material

(1) If, at any time after a seizure of anything has been made in exercise of a power to which this section applies—

(*a*) it appears to the person for the time being having possession of the seized property in consequence of the seizure that the property—

(i) is excluded material or special procedure material, or

(ii) has any excluded material or any special procedure material comprised in it,

(*b*) its retention is not authorised by section 56, and

(*c*) in a case where the material is comprised in something else which has been lawfully seized, it is not comprised in property falling within subsection (2) or (3),

it shall be the duty of that person to secure that the item is returned as soon as reasonably practicable after the seizure.

(2) Property in which any excluded material or special procedure material is comprised falls within this subsection if—

(*a*) the whole or a part of the rest of the property is property for which the person seizing it had power to search when he made the seizure but is not property the return of which is required by this section or section 54; and (*b*) in all the circumstances, it is not reasonably practicable for that material to be separated from the rest of that property (or, as the case may be, from that part of it) without prejudicing the use of the rest of that property, or that part of it, for purposes for which (disregarding that material) its use, if retained, would be lawful.

(3) Property in which any excluded material or special procedure material is comprised falls within this subsection if—

(*a*) the whole or a part of the rest of the property is property the retention of which is authorised by section 56; and

(*b*) in all the circumstances, it is not reasonably practicable for that material to be separated from the rest of that property (or, as the case may be, from that part of it) without prejudicing the use of the rest of that property, or that part of it, for purposes for which (disregarding that material) its use, if retained, would be lawful.

(4) This section applies (subject to subsection (5)) to each of the powers of seizure specified in Part 3 of Schedule 1.

(5) In its application to the powers of seizure conferred by—

(*a*) section 931(5) of the Criminal justice Act 1988 (c. 33),

(*b*) section 56(5) of the Drug Trafficking Act 1994 (c. 37), and

(*c*) Article 51(5) of the Proceeds of Crime (Northern Ireland) Order 1996 (SI 1996/1299 (NI 6)),

this section shall have effect with the omission of every reference to special procedure material.

(6) In this section, except in its application to—

(*a*) the power of seizure conferred by section 8(2) of the 1984 Act,

(*b*) the power of seizure conferred by Article 10(2) of the Police and Criminal Evidence (Northern Ireland) Order 1989 (SI 1989/1341 (NI 12)),

(*c*) each of the powers of seizure conferred by the provisions of paragraphs 1 and 3 of Schedule 5 to the Terrorism Act 2000 (c. 11), and

(*d*) the power of seizure conferred by paragraphs 15 and 19 of Schedule 5 to that Act of 2000, so far only as the power in question is conferred by reference to paragraph 1 of that Schedule,

"special procedure material" means special procedure material consisting of documents or records other than documents.

56 Property seized by constables etc

(1) The retention of—

(*a*) property seized on any premises by a constable who was lawfully on the premises,

(*b*) property seized on any premises by a relevant person who was on the premises accompanied by a constable, and

(*c*) property seized by a constable carrying out a lawful search of any person,

is authorised by this section if the property falls within subsection (2) or (3).

(2) Property falls within this subsection to the extent that there are reasonable grounds for believing—

(*a*) that it is property obtained in consequence of the commission of an offence; and

(*b*) that it is necessary for it to be retained in order to prevent its being concealed, lost, damaged, altered or destroyed.

(3) Property falls within this subsection to the extent that there are reasonable grounds for believing—

(*a*) that it is evidence in relation to any offence; and

(*b*) that it is necessary for it to be retained in order to prevent its being concealed, lost, altered or destroyed.

(4) Nothing in this section authorises the retention (except in pursuance of section 54(2)) of anything at any time when its return is required by section 54.

(5) In subsection (1)(*b*) the reference to a relevant person's being on any premises accompanied by a constable is a reference only to a person who was so on the premises under the authority of—

(*a*) a warrant under section 448 of the Companies Act 1985 (c. 6) authorising him to exercise together with a constable the powers conferred by subsection (3) of that section;

(*b*) a warrant under Article 441 of the Companies (Northern Ireland) Order 1986 (SI 1986/1032 (NI 6)) authorising him to exercise together with a constable the powers conferred by paragraph (3) of that Article;

(*c*) a warrant under section 199 of the Financial Services Act 1986 (c. 60) authorising him to exercise together with a constable the powers conferred by subsection (3) of that section;

(*d*) a warrant under section 43 of the Banking Act 1987 (c. 22) authorising him to exercise together with a constable the powers conferred by subsection (2) of that section; or

(*e*) a warrant under section 44A of the Insurance Companies Act 1982 (c. 50) authorising him to exercise together with a constable the powers conferred by subsection (3) of that section.

57 Retention of seized items

(1) This section has effect in relation to the following provisions (which are about the retention of items which have been seized and are referred to in this section as "the relevant provisions")—

(a) section 22 of the 1984 Act;
(b) Article 24 of the Police and Criminal Evidence (Northern Ireland) Order 1989 (SI 1989/1341 (NI 12));
(c) section 20CC(3) of the Taxes Management Act 1970 (c. 9);
(d) paragraph 4 of Schedule 9 to the Weights and Measures (Northern Ireland) Order 1981 (SI 1981/231 (NI 10));
(e) section 44A(6) of the Insurance Companies Act 1982;
(f) section 448(6) of the Companies Act 1985 (c. 6);
(g) paragraph 4 of Schedule 8 to the Weights and Measures Act 1985 (c. 72);
(h) section 199(5) of the Financial Services Act 1986;
(i) Article 441(6) of the Companies (Northern Ireland) Order 1986;
(j) section 43(4) of the Banking Act 1987;
(k) section 40(4) of the Human Fertilisation and Embryology Act 1990 (c. 37);
(l) section 5(4) of the Knives Act 1997 (c. 21);
(m) paragraph 7(2) of Schedule 9 to the Data Protection Act 1998 (c. 29);
(n) section 28(7) of the Competition Act 1998 (c. 41);
(o) section 176(8) of the Financial Services and Markets Act 2000 (c. 8);
(p) paragraph 7(2) of Schedule 3 to the Freedom of Information Act 2000 (c. 36).

(2) The relevant provisions shall apply in relation to any property seized in exercise of a power conferred by section 50 or 51 as if the property had been seized under the power of seizure by reference to which the power under that section was exercised in relation to that property.

(3) Nothing in any of sections 53 to 56 authorises the retention of any property at any time when its retention would not (apart from the provisions of this Part) be authorised by the relevant provisions.

(4) Nothing in any of the relevant provisions authorises the retention of anything after an obligation to return it has arisen under this Part.

58 Person to whom seized property is to be returned

(1) Where—
  (a) anything has been seized in exercise of any power of seizure, and
  (b) there is an obligation under this Part for the whole or any part of the seized property to be returned,
the obligation to return it shall (subject to the following provisions of this section) be an obligation to return it to the person from whom it was seized.

(2) Where—
  (a) any person is obliged under this Part to return anything that has been seized to the person from whom it was seized, and
  (b) the person under that obligation is satisfied that some other person has a better right to that thing than the person from whom it was seized,
his duty to return it shall, instead, be a duty to return it to that other person or, as the case may be, to the person appearing to him to have the best right to the thing in question.

(3) Where different persons claim to be entitled to the return of anything that is required to be returned under this Part, that thing may be retained for as long as is reasonably necessary for the determination in accordance with subsection (2) of the person to whom it must be returned.

(4) References in this Part to the person from whom something has been seized, in relation to a case in which the power of seizure was exercisable by reason of that thing's having been found on any premises, are references to the occupier of the premises at the time of the seizure.

(5) References in this section to the occupier of any premises at the time of a seizure, in relation to a case in which—
  (a) a notice in connection with the entry or search of the premises in question, or with the seizure, was given to a person appearing in the occupier's absence to be in charge of the premises, and
  (b) it is practicable, for the purpose of returning something that has been seized, to identify that person but not to identify the occupier of the premises,
are references to that person.

Remedies and safeguards

59 Application to the appropriate judicial authority

(1) This section applies where anything has been seized in exercise, or purported exercise, of a relevant power of seizure.

(2) Any person with a relevant interest in the seized property may apply to the appropriate judicial authority, on one or more of the grounds mentioned in subsection (3), for the return of the whole or a part of the seized property.

(3) Those grounds are—
  (a) that there was no power to make the seizure;

(b) that the seized property is or contains an item subject to legal privilege that is not comprised in property falling within section 54(2);

(c) that the seized property is or contains any excluded material or special procedure material which—

(i) has been seized under a power to which section 55 applies;
(ii) is not comprised in property falling within section 55(2) or (3); and
(iii) is not property the retention of which is authorised by section 56;

(d) that the seized property is or contains something seized under section 50 or 51 which does not fall within section 53(3);

and subsections (5) and (6) of section 55 shall apply for the purposes of paragraph (c) as they apply for the purposes of that section.

(4) Subject to subsection (6), the appropriate judicial authority, on an application under subsection (2), shall—

(a) if satisfied as to any of the matters mentioned in subsection (3), order the return of so much of the seized property as is property in relation to which the authority is so satisfied; and

(b) to the extent that that authority is not so satisfied, dismiss the application.

(5) The appropriate judicial authority—

(a) on an application under subsection (2),

(b) on an application made by the person for the time being having possession of anything in consequence of its seizure under a relevant power of seizure, or

(c) on an application made—

(i) by a person with a relevant interest in anything seized under section 50 or 51, and
(ii) on the grounds that the requirements of section 53(2) have not been or are not being complied with,

may give such directions as the authority thinks fit as to the examination, retention, separation or return of the whole or any part of the seized property.

(6) On any application under this section, the appropriate judicial authority may authorise the retention of any property which—

(a) has been seized in exercise, or purported exercise, of a relevant power of seizure, and

(b) would otherwise fall to be returned,

if that authority is satisfied that the retention of the property is justified on grounds falling within subsection (7).

(7) Those grounds are that (if the property were returned) it would immediately become appropriate—

(a) to issue, on the application of the person who is in possession of the property at the time of the application under this section, a warrant in pursuance of which, or of the exercise of which, it would be lawful to seize the property; or

(b) to make an order under—

(i) paragraph 4 of Schedule 1 to the 1984 Act,
(ii) paragraph 4 of Schedule 1 to the Police and Criminal Evidence (Northern Ireland) Order 1989 (SI 1989/1341 (NI 12)),
(iii) section 20BA of the Taxes Management Act 1970 (c. 9), or
(iv) paragraph 5 of Schedule 5 to the Terrorism Act 2000 (c. 11), under which the property would fall to be delivered up or produced to the person mentioned in paragraph (a).

(8) Where any property which has been seized in exercise, or purported exercise, of a relevant power of seizure has parts (''part A'' and ''part B'') comprised in it such that—

(a) it would be inappropriate, if the property were returned, to take any action such as is mentioned in subsection (7) in relation to part A,

(b) it would (or would but for the facts mentioned in paragraph (a)) be appropriate, if the property were returned, to take such action in relation to part B, and

(c) in all the circumstances, it is not reasonably practicable to separate part A from part B without prejudicing the use of part B for purposes for which it is lawful to use property seized under the power in question,

the facts mentioned in paragraph (a) shall not be taken into account by the appropriate judicial authority in deciding whether the retention of the property is justified on grounds falling within subsection (7).

(9) If a person fails to comply with any order or direction made or given by a judge of the Crown Court in exercise of any jurisdiction under this section—

(a) the authority may deal with him as if he had committed a contempt of the Crown Court; and

(b) any enactment relating to contempt of the Crown Court shall have effect in relation to the failure as if it were such a contempt.

(10) The relevant powers of seizure for the purposes of this section are—

(a) the powers of seizure conferred by sections 50 and 51;

(b) each of the powers of seizure specified in Parts 1 and 2 of Schedule 1; and (*c*) any power of seizure (not falling within paragraph (*a*) or (*b*)) conferred on a constable by or under any enactment, including an enactment passed after this Act.

(11) References in this section to a person with a relevant interest in seized property are references to—

(*a*) the person from whom it was seized;
(*b*) any person with an interest in the property; or
(*c*) any person, not falling within paragraph (*a*) or (*b*), who had custody or control of the property immediately before the seizure.

(12) For the purposes of subsection (11)(*b*), the persons who have an interest in seized property shall, in the case of property which is or contains an item subject to legal privilege, be taken to include the person in whose favour that privilege is conferred.

60 Cases where duty to secure arises

(1) Where property has been seized in exercise, or purported exercise, of any power of seizure conferred by section 50 or 51, a duty to secure arises under section 61 in relation to the seized property if—

(*a*) a person entitled to do so makes an application under section 59 for the return of the property;
(*b*) in relation to England, Wales and Northern Ireland, at least one of the conditions set out in subsections (2) and (3) is satisfied;
(*c*) in relation to Scotland, the condition set out in subsection (2) is satisfied; and
(*d*) notice of the application is given to a relevant person.

(2) The first condition is that the application is made on the grounds that the seized property is or contains an item subject to legal privilege that is not comprised in property falling within section 54(2).

(3) The second condition is that—

(*a*) the seized property was seized by a person who had, or purported to have, power under this Part to seize it by virtue only of one or more of the powers specified in subsection (6); and
(*b*) the application—

(i) is made on the ground that the seized property is or contains something which does not fall within section 53(3); and
(ii) states that the seized property is or contains special procedure material or excluded material.

(4) In relation to property seized by a person who had. or purported to have, power under this Part to seize it by virtue only of one or more of the powers of seizure conferred by—

(*a*) section 93I(5) of the Criminal Justice Act 1988 (c. 33),
(*b*) section 56(5) of the Drug Trafficking Act 1994 (c. 37), or
(*c*) Article 51(5) of the Proceeds of Crime (Northern Ireland) Order 1996 (SI 1996/1299 (NI 6)),

the second condition is satisfied only if the application states that the seized property is or contains excluded material.

(5) In relation to property seized by a person who had, or purported to have, power under this Part to seize it by virtue only of one or more of the powers of seizure specified in Part 3 of Schedule 1 but not by virtue of—

(*a*) the power of seizure conferred by section 8(2) of the 1984 Act,
(*b*) the power of seizure conferred by Article 10(2) of the Police and Criminal Evidence (Northern Ireland) Order 1989 (SI 1989/1341 (NI 12)),
(*c*) either of the powers of seizure conferred by paragraphs 1 and 3 of Schedule 5 to the Terrorism Act 2000 (c. 11), or
(*d*) either of the powers of seizure conferred by paragraphs 15 and 19 of Schedule 5 to that Act of 2000 so far as they are conferred by reference to paragraph 1 of that Schedule,

the second condition is satisfied only if the application states that the seized property is or contains excluded material or special procedure material consisting of documents or records other than documents.

(6) The powers mentioned in subsection (3) are—

(*a*) the powers of seizure specified in Part 3 of Schedule 1;
(*b*) the powers of seizure conferred by the provisions of Parts 2 and 3 of the 1984 Act (except section 8(2) of that Act);
(*c*) the powers of seizure conferred by the provisions of Parts 3 and 4 of the Police and Criminal Evidence (Northern Ireland) Order 1989 (except Article 10(2) of that Order);
(*d*) the powers of seizure conferred by the provisions of paragraph 11 of Schedule 5 to the Terrorism Act 2000; and
(*e*) the powers of seizure conferred by the provisions of paragraphs 15 and 19 of that Schedule so far as they are conferred by reference to paragraph 11 of that Schedule.

(7) In this section "a relevant person" means any one of the following—

(*a*) the person who made the seizure;

(*b*) the person for the time being having possession, in consequence of the seizure, of the seized property;

(*c*) the person named for the purposes of subsection (1)(*d*) or (4)(*d*) of section 52 in any notice given under that section with respect to the seizure.

61 The duty to secure

(1) The duty to secure that arises under this section is a duty of the person for the time being having possession, in consequence of the seizure, of the seized property to secure that arrangements are in force that ensure that the seized property (without being returned) is not, at any time after the giving of the notice of the application under section 60(1), either—

(*a*) examined or copied, or

(*b*) put to any use to which its seizure would, apart from this subsection, entitle it to be put,

except with the consent of the applicant or in accordance with the directions of the appropriate judicial authority.

(2) Subsection (1) shall not have effect in relation to any time after the withdrawal of the application to which the notice relates.

(3) Nothing in any arrangements for the purposes of this section shall be taken to prevent the giving of a notice under section 49 of the Regulation of Investigatory Powers Act 2000 (c. 23) (notices for the disclosure of material protected by encryption etc) in respect of any information contained in the seized material; but subsection (1) of this section shall apply to anything disclosed for the purpose of complying with such a notice as it applies to the seized material in which the information in question is contained.

(4) Subsection (9) of section 59 shall apply in relation to any jurisdiction conferred on the appropriate judicial authority by this section as it applies in relation to the jurisdiction conferred by that section.

62 Use of inextricably linked property

(1) This section applies to property, other than property which is for the time being required to be secured in pursuance of section 61, if—

(*a*) it has been seized under any power conferred by section 50 or 51 or specified in Part 1 or 2 of Schedule 1, and

(*b*) it is inextricably linked property.

(2) Subject to subsection (3), it shall be the duty of the person for the time being having possession, in consequence of the seizure, of the inextricably linked property to ensure that arrangements are in force which secure that that property (without being returned) is not at any time, except with the consent of the person from whom it was seized, either—

(*a*) examined or copied, or

(*b*) put to any other use.

(3) Subsection (2) does not require that arrangements under that subsection should prevent inextricably linked property from being put to any use falling within subsection (4).

(4) A use falls within this subsection to the extent that it is use which is necessary for facilitating the use, in any investigation or proceedings, of property in which the inextricably linked property is comprised.

(5) Property is inextricably linked property for the purposes of this section if it falls within any of subsections (6) to (8).

(6) Property falls within this subsection if—

(*a*) it has been seized under a power conferred by section 50 or 51; and

(*b*) but for subsection (3)(*c*) of section 53, arrangements under subsection (2) of that section in relation to the property would be required to ensure the return of the property as mentioned in subsection (2)(*c*) of that section.

(7) Property falls within this subsection if—

(*a*) it has been seized under a power to which section 54 applies; and

(*b*) but for paragraph (*b*) of subsection (1) of that section, the person for the time being having possession of the property would be under a duty to secure its return as mentioned in that subsection.

(8) Property falls within this subsection if—

(*a*) it has been seized under a power of seizure to which section 55 applies; and

(*b*) but for paragraph (*c*) of subsection (1) of that section, the person for the time being having possession of the property would be under a duty to secure its return as mentioned in that subsection.

Construction of Part 2

63 Copies

(1) Subject to subsection (3)—

 (*a*) in this Part, "seize" includes "take a copy of", and cognate expressions shall be construed accordingly;

 (*b*) this Part shall apply as if any copy taken under any power to which any provision of this Part applies were the original of that of which it is a copy; and

 (*c*) for the purposes of this Part, except sections 50 and 51, the powers mentioned in subsection (2) (which are powers to obtain hard copies etc of information which is stored in electronic form) shall be treated as powers of seizure, and references to seizure and to seized property shall be construed accordingly.

(2) The powers mentioned in subsection (1)(*c*) are any powers which are conferred by—

 (*a*) section 19(4) or 20 of the 1984 Act;

 (*b*) Article 21(4) or 22 of the Police and Criminal Evidence (Northern Ireland) Order 1989 (SI 1989/1341 (NI 12));

 (*c*) section 46(3) of the Firearms Act 1968 (c. 27);

 (*d*) section 43(5)(*aa*) of the Gaming Act 1968 (c. 65);

 (*e*) section 20C(3A) of the Taxes Management Act 1970 (c. 9);

 (*f*) section 32(6)(*b*) of the Food Safety Act 1990 (c. 16);

 (*g*) Article 34(6)(*b*) of the Food Safety (Northern Ireland) Order 1991 (SI 1991/762 (NI 7));

 (*h*) section 28(2)(*f*) of the Competition Act 1998 (c. 41); or

 (*i*) section 8(2)(*c*) of the Nuclear Safeguards Act 2000 (c. 5).

(3) Subsection (1) does not apply to section 50(6) or 57.

64 Meaning of "appropriate judicial authority"

(1) Subject to subsection (2), in this Part "appropriate judicial authority" means—

 (*a*) in relation to England and Wales and Northern Ireland, a judge of the Crown Court;

 (*b*) in relation to Scotland, a sheriff.

(2) In this Part "appropriate judicial authority", in relation to the seizure of items under any power mentioned in subsection (3) and in relation to items seized under any such power, means—

 (*a*) in relation to England and Wales and Northern Ireland, the High Court;

 (*b*) in relation to Scotland, the Court of Session.

(3) Those powers are—

 (*a*) the powers of seizure conferred by—

  (i) section 448(3) of the Companies Act 1985 (c. 6);

  (ii) Article 441(3) of the Companies (Northern Ireland) Order 1986 (SI 1986/1032 (NI 6)); and

  (iii) section 28(2) of the Competition Act 1998; and

 (*b*) any power of seizure conferred by section 50, so far as that power is exercisable by reference to any power mentioned in paragraph (*a*).

65 Meaning of "legal privilege"

(1) Subject to the following provisions of this section, references in this Part to an item subject to legal privilege shall be construed—

 (*a*) for the purposes of the application of this Part to England and Wales, in accordance with section 10 of the 1984 Act (meaning of "legal privilege");

 (*b*) for the purposes of the application of this Part to Scotland, in accordance with section 33 of the Criminal Law (Consolidation) (Scotland) Act 1995 (c. 39) (interpretation); and

 (*c*) for the purposes of the application of this Part to Northern Ireland, in accordance with Article 12 of the Police and Criminal Evidence (Northern Ireland) Order 1989 (meaning of "legal privilege").

(2) In relation to property which has been seized in exercise, or purported exercise, of—

 (*a*) the power of seizure conferred by section 28(2) of the Competition Act 1998, or

 (*b*) so much of any power of seizure conferred by section 50 as is exercisable by reference to that power,

references in this Part to an item subject to legal privilege shall be read as references to a privileged communication within the meaning of section 30 of that Act.

(3) In relation to property which has been seized in exercise, or purported exercise, of—

 (*a*) the power of seizure conferred by section 20C of the Taxes Management Act 1970 (c. 9), or

 (*b*) so much of any power of seizure conferred by section 50 as is exercisable by reference to that power,

references in this Part to an item subject to legal privilege shall be construed in accordance with section 20C(4A) of that Act.

(4) An item which is, or is comprised in, property which has been seized in exercise, or purported exercise, of the power of seizure conferred by section 448(3) of the Companies Act 1985 (c. 6) shall be taken for the purposes of this Part to be an item subject to legal privilege if, and only if, the seizure of that item was in contravention of section 452(2) of that Act (privileged information).

(5) An item which is, or is comprised in, property which has been seized in exercise, or purported exercise, of the power of seizure conferred by Article 441(3) of the Companies (Northern Ireland) Order 1986 (SI 1986/1032 (NI 6)) shall be taken for the purposes of this Part to be an item subject to legal privilege if, and only if, the seizure of that item was in contravention of Article 445(2) of that Order (privileged information).

(6) An item which is, or is comprised in, property which has been seized in exercise, or purported exercise, of the power of seizure conferred by sub-paragraph (2) of paragraph 3 of Schedule 2 to the Timeshare Act 1992 (c. 35) shall be taken for the purposes of this Part to be an item subject to legal privilege if, and only if, the seizure of that item was in contravention of sub-paragraph (4) of that paragraph (privileged documents).

(7) An item which is, or is comprised in, property which has been seized in exercise, or purported exercise, of the power of seizure conferred by paragraph 1 of Schedule 9 to the Data Protection Act 1998 (c. 29) shall be taken for the purposes of this Part to be an item subject to legal privilege if, and only if, the seizure of that item was in contravention of paragraph 9 of that Schedule (privileged communications).

(8) An item which is, or is comprised in, property which has been seized in exercise, or purported exercise, of the power of seizure conferred by paragraph 1 of Schedule 3 to the Freedom of Information Act 2000 (c. 36) shall be taken for the purposes of this Part to be an item subject to legal privilege if, and only if, the seizure of that item was in contravention of paragraph 9 of that Schedule (privileged communications).

(9) An item which is, or is comprised in, property which has been seized in exercise, or purported exercise, of so much of any power of seizure conferred by section 50 as is exercisable by reference to a power of seizure conferred by—

  (a) section 448(3) of the Companies Act 1985,
  (b) Article 441(3) of the Companies (Northern Ireland) Order 1986,
  (c) paragraph 3(2) of Schedule 2 to the Timeshare Act 1992,
  (d) paragraph 1 of Schedule 9 to the Data Protection Act 1998, or
  (e) paragraph 1 of Schedule 3 to the Freedom of Information Act 2000;

shall be taken for the purposes of this Part to be an item subject to legal privilege if, and only if, the item would have been taken for the purposes of this Part to be an item subject to legal privilege had it been seized under the power of seizure by reference to which the power conferred by section 50 was exercised.

66 General interpretation of Part 2

(1) In this Part—

  "appropriate judicial authority" has the meaning given by section 64;
  "documents" includes information recorded in any form;
  "item subject to legal privilege" shall be construed in accordance with section 65;
  "premises" includes any vehicle, stall or moveable structure (including an offshore installation) and any other place whatever, whether or not occupied as land;
  "offshore installation" has the same meaning as in the Mineral Workings (Offshore Installations) Act 1971 (c. 61);
  "return", in relation to seized property, shall be construed in accordance with section 58, and cognate expressions shall be construed accordingly;
  "seize", and cognate expressions, shall be construed in accordance with section 63(1) and subsection (5) below;
  "seized property" in relation to any exercise of a power of seizure, means (subject to subsection (5)) anything seized in exercise of that power; and
  "vehicle" includes any vessel, aircraft or hovercraft.

(2) In this Part references, in relation to a time when seized property is in any person's possession in consequence of a seizure ("the relevant time"), to something for which the person making the seizure had power to search shall be construed—

  (a) where the seizure was made on the occasion of a search carried out on the authority of a warrant, as including anything of the description of things the presence or suspected presence of which provided grounds for the issue of the warrant;
  (b) where the property was seized in the course of a search on the occasion of which it would have been lawful for the person carrying out the search to seize anything which on that occasion was believed by him to be, or appeared to him to be, of a particular description, as including—

    (i) anything which at the relevant time is believed by the person in possession of the seized property, or (as the case may be) appears to him, to be of that description; and
    (ii) anything which is in fact of that description;

(*c*) where the property was seized in the course of a search on the occasion of which it would have been lawful for the person carrying out the search to seize anything which there were on that occasion reasonable grounds for believing was of a particular description, as including—

    (i) anything which there are at the relevant time reasonable grounds for believing is of that description; and

    (ii) anything which is in fact of that description;

(*d*) where the property was seized in the course of a search to which neither paragraph (*b*) nor paragraph (*c*) applies, as including anything which is of a description of things which, on the occasion of the search, it would have been lawful for the person carrying it out to seize otherwise than under section 50 and 51; and

(*e*) where the property was seized on the occasion of a search authorised under section 82 of the Terrorism Act 2000 (c. 11) (seizure of items suspected to have been, or to be intended to be, used in commission of certain offences), as including anything—

    (i) which is or has been, or is or was intended to be, used in the commission of an offence such as is mentioned in subsection (3)(*a*) or (*b*) of that section; or

    (ii) which at the relevant time the person who is in possession of the seized property reasonably suspects is something falling within sub-paragraph (*i*).

(3) For the purpose of determining in accordance with subsection (2), in relation to any time, whether or to what extent property seized on the occasion of a search authorised under section 9 of the Official Secrets Act 1911 (c. 28) (seizure of evidence of offences under that Act having been or being about to be committed) is something for which the person making the seizure had power to search, subsection (1) of that section shall be construed—

(*a*) as if the reference in that subsection to evidence of an offence under that Act being about to be committed were a reference to evidence of such an offence having been, at the time of the seizure, about to be committed; and

(*b*) as if the reference in that subsection to reasonable ground for suspecting that such an offence is about to be committed were a reference to reasonable ground for suspecting that at the time of the seizure such an offence was about to be committed.

(4) References in subsection (2) to a search include references to any activities authorised by virtue of any of the following—

(*a*) section 28(1) of the Trade Descriptions Act 1968 (c. 29) (power to enter premises and to inspect and seize goods and documents);

(*b*) section 29(1) of the Fair Trading Act 1973 (c. 41) (power to enter premises and to inspect and seize goods and documents);

(*c*) paragraph 9 of the Schedule to the Prices Act 1974 (c. 24) (powers of entry and inspection);

(*d*) section 162(1) of the Consumer Credit Act 1974 (c. 39) (powers of entry and inspection);

(*e*) section 11(1) of the Estate Agents Act 1979 (c. 38) (powers of entry and inspection);

(*f*) Schedule 9 to the Weights and Measures (Northern Ireland) Order 1981 (SI 1981/231 (NI 10));

(*g*) section 79 of, or Schedule 8 to, the Weights and Measures Act 1985 (c. 72) (powers of entry and inspection etc);

(*h*) section 29 of the Consumer Protection Act 1987 (c. 43) (powers of search etc);

(*i*) Article 22 of the Consumer Protection (Northern Ireland) Order 1987 (SI 1987/2049 (NI 20));

(*j*) section 32(5) of the Food Safety Act 1990 (c. 16) (power to inspect records relating to a food business);

(*k*) paragraph 3 of the Schedule to the Property Misdescriptions Act 1991 (c. 29) (powers of seizure etc);

(*l*) Article 33(6) of the Food Safety (Northern Ireland) Order 1991 (SI 1991/762 (NI 7));

(*m*) paragraph 3 of Schedule 2 to the Timeshare Act 1992 (c. 35) (powers of officers of enforcement authority).

(5) References in this Part to a power of seizure include references to each of the powers to take possession of items under—

(*a*) section 44A(3) of the Insurance Companies Act 1982 (c. 50);

(*b*) section 448(3) of the Companies Act 1985 (c. 6);

(*c*) section 199(3) of the Financial Services Act 1986 (c. 60);

(*d*) Article 441(3) of the Companies (Northern Ireland) Order 1986 (SI 1986/1032 (NI 6));

(*e*) section 43(2) of the Banking Act 1987 (c. 22);

(*f*) section 2(5) of the Criminal Justice Act 1987 (c. 38);

(*g*) section 40(2) of the Human Fertilisation and Embryology Act 1990 (c. 37);

(*h*) section 28(2)(*c*) of the Competition Act 1998 (c. 41); and

(*i*) section 176(5) of the Financial Services and Markets Act 2000 (c. 8);

and references in this Part to seizure and to seized property shall be construed accordingly.

(6) In this Part, so far as it applies to England and Wales—

(*a*) references to excluded material shall be construed in accordance with section 11 of the 1984 Act (meaning of "excluded material"); and

(*b*) references to special procedure material shall be construed in accordance with section 14 of that Act (meaning of "special procedure material").

(7) In this Part, so far as it applies to Northern Ireland—

    (*a*) references to excluded material shall be construed in accordance with Article 13 of the Police and Criminal Evidence (Northern Ireland) Order 1989 (SI 1989/1341 (NI 12)) (meaning of "excluded material"); and

    (*b*) references to special procedure material shall be construed in accordance with Article 16 of that Order (meaning of "special procedure material").

(8) References in this Part to any item or material being comprised in other property include references to its being mixed with that other property.

(9) In this Part "enactment" includes an enactment contained in Northern Ireland legislation.

Supplemental provisions of Part 2

67 Application to customs officers

The powers conferred by section 114(2) of the 1984 Act and Article 85(1) of the Police and Criminal Evidence (Northern Ireland) Order 1989 (application of provisions relating to police officers to customs officers) shall have effect in relation to the provisions of this Part as they have effect in relation to the provisions of that Act or, as the case may be, that Order.

68 Application to Scotland

(1) In the application of this Part to Scotland—

    (*a*) subsection (4) of section 54 and subsection (10) of section 59 shall each have effect with the omission of paragraph (*c*) of that subsection;

    (*b*) section 55 and subsection (3)(*c*) of section 59 shall be omitted; and

    (*c*) Schedule 1 shall have effect as if the powers specified in that Schedule did not include any power of seizure under any enactment mentioned in that Schedule, so far as it is exercisable in Scotland by a constable, except a power conferred by an enactment mentioned in subsection (2).

(2) Those enactments are—

    (*a*) section 43(5) of the Gaming Act 1968 (c. 65);

    (*b*) section 44A(3) of the Insurance Companies Act 1982 (c. 50);

    (*c*) section 448(3) of the Companies Act 1985 (c. 6);

    (*d*) section 199(3) of the Financial Services Act 1986 (c. 60);

    (*e*) section 43(2) of the Banking Act 1987 (c. 22); and

    (*f*) section 176(5) of the Financial Services and Markets Act 2000 (c. 8).

69 Application to powers designated by order

(1) The Secretary of State may by order—

    (*a*) provide for any power designated by the order to be added to those specified in Schedule 1 or section 63(2);

    (*b*) make any modification of the provisions of this Part which the Secretary of State considers appropriate in consequence of any provision made by virtue of paragraph (*a*);

    (*c*) make any modification of any enactment making provision in relation to seizures, or things seized, under a power designated by an order under this subsection which the Secretary of State considers appropriate in consequence of any provision made by virtue of that paragraph.

(2) Where the power designated by the order made under subsection (1) is a power conferred in relation to Scotland, the Secretary of State shall consult the Scottish Ministers before making the order.

(3) The power to make an order under subsection (1) shall be exercisable by statutory instrument; and no such order shall be made unless a draft of it has been laid before Parliament and approved by a resolution of each House.

(4) In this section "modification" includes any exclusion, extension or application.

70 Consequential applications and amendments of enactments

Schedule 2 (which applies enactments in relation to provision made by this Part and contains minor and consequential amendments) shall have effect.

PART 5
POLICE ORGANISATION
Minor and consequential amendments

128 Amendments relating to NCIS and NCS

(1) Schedule 6 to this Act (which makes minor and consequential amendments relating to this Part) shall have effect.

Note—Words omitted from this section are not relevant to this Handbook.

PART 6

MISCELLANEOUS AND SUPPLEMENTAL

Supplemental

136 General interpretation

In this Act—

"the 1984 Act" means the Police and Criminal Evidence Act 1984 (c. 60);

"the 1996 Act" means the Police Act 1996 (c. 16); and

"the 1997 Act" means the Police Act 1997 (c. 50).

137 Repeals

The enactments and instruments mentioned in Schedule 7 (which include spent provisions) are hereby repealed or (as the case may be) revoked to the extent specified in the third column of that Schedule.

138 Short title, commencement and extent

(1) This Act may be cited as the Criminal Justice and Police Act 2001.

(2) The provisions of this Act, other than this section and sections 42 and 43, 81 to 85, 109, 116(7) and 119(7), shall come into force on such day as the Secretary of State may by order made by statutory instrument appoint; and different days may be appointed under this subsection for different purposes.

(3) An order under subsection (2) may contain such savings as the Secretary of State thinks fit.

(4) Section 85 comes into force at the end of the period of two months beginning with the day on which this Act is passed.

(5) Subject to subsections (6) to (12), this Act extends to England and Wales only.

(6) The following provisions of this Act extend to the United Kingdom—

    (*a*) sections 33 to 38;

    (*b*) Part 2;

    (*c*) section 86(1) and (2);

    (*d*) Part 5 so far as it relates to the National Criminal Intelligence Service;

    (*e*) section 127; and

    (*f*) section 136 and this section.

(7) Except in so far as it contains provision relating to the matters mentioned in section 745(1) of the Companies Act 1985 (c. 6) (companies registered or incorporated in Northern Ireland or outside Great Britain), section 45 extends to Great Britain only.

(8) Section 126 extends to Great Britain only.

(9) Sections 29, 39 to 41, 72, 75, 84 and 134 extend to England and Wales and Northern Ireland only.

(10) Section 83 extends to Northern Ireland only.

(11) Section 86(3) has the same extent as section 27 of the Petty Sessions (Ireland) Act 1851 (c. 93).

(12) An amendment, repeal or revocation contained in Schedule 4, 6 or 7 has the same extent as the enactment or instrument to which it relates.

SCHEDULES

SCHEDULE 1

POWERS OF SEIZURE

Sections 50, 51 & 55

PART 1

POWERS TO WHICH SECTION 50 APPLIES

Taxes Management Act 1970 (c. 9)

13 The power of seizure conferred by section 20C of the Taxes Management Act 1970 (seizure of evidence of offences involving serious fraud).

. . .

SCHEDULE 2

APPLICATIONS AND MINOR AND CONSEQUENTIAL AMENDMENTS

Section 70

PART 1
APPLICATION OF ENACTMENTS

. . .

Disclosure of information

11 Any provision which—

(*a*) restricts the disclosure, or permits the disclosure only for limited purposes or in limited circumstances, of information obtained through the exercise of a power of seizure specified in Part 1 or 2 of Schedule 1, or

(*b*) confers power to make provision which does either or both of those things,

shall apply in relation to information obtained under section 50 or 51 in reliance on the power in question as it applies in relation to information obtained through the exercise of that power.

Interpretation

12 For the purposes of this Part of this Schedule, an item is seized, or information is obtained, under section 50 or 51 in reliance on a power of seizure if the item is seized, or the information obtained, in exercise of so much of any power conferred by that section as is exercisable by reference to that power of seizure.

PART 2
MINOR AND CONSEQUENTIAL AMENDMENTS

13—(1) In each of the provisions mentioned in sub-paragraph (2) (which confer powers to require the production of information contained in a computer in a visible and legible form)—

(*a*) for "contained in a computer" there shall be substituted "stored in any electronic form"; and

(*b*) after "in which it is visible and legible" there shall be inserted "or from which it can readily be produced in a visible and legible form".

(2) Those provisions are—

. . .

(*d*) section 20C(3A) of the Taxes Management Act 1970 (c. 9);

. . .

Note—Words omitted from this Schedule are not relevant to this Handbook.

SCHEDULE 6

MINOR AND CONSEQUENTIAL AMENDMENTS RELATING TO NCIS AND NCS

Section 128

PART 3
MISCELLANEOUS OTHER ENACTMENTS

. . .

Income and Corporation Taxes Act 1988 (c. 1)

71 In section 842A of the Income and Corporation Taxes Act 1988 (meaning of "local authority" in the Tax Acts), in subsection (1)—

(*a*) in paragraph (*a*) the words "or the Service Authority for the National Criminal Intelligence Service or the Service Authority for the National Crime Squad" shall be omitted; and

(*b*) in both paragraphs (*b*) and (*c*) the words "or the Service Authority for the National Criminal Intelligence Service" shall be omitted.

. . .

Note—Words omitted from this Schedule are not relevant to this Handbook.

SCHEDULE 7

REPEALS AND REVOCATIONS

Section 137

PART 5

NCIS AND NCS

The Income and Corporation Taxes Act 1988 (c. 1).	In section 842A(1)—
	(a) in paragraph (a), the words ", or the Service Authority for the National Criminal Intelligence Service or the Service Authority for the National Crime Squad"; and
	(b) in both paragraphs (b) and (c), the words "or the Service Authority for the National Criminal Intelligence Service".

. . .

Note—Words omitted from this Schedule are not relevant to this Handbook.

ANTI-TERRORISM, CRIME AND SECURITY ACT 2001

(2001 Chapter 24)

ARRANGEMENT OF SECTIONS

PART 3

DISCLOSURE OF INFORMATION

PART 14

SUPPLEMENTAL

SCHEDULES

An Act to amend the Terrorism Act 2000; to make further provision about terrorism and security; ...; and for connected purposes.   [14th December 2001]

PART 3

DISCLOSURE OF INFORMATION

17 Extension of existing disclosure powers

(1) This section applies to the provisions listed in Schedule 4, so far as they authorise the disclosure of information.

(2) Each of the provisions to which this section applies shall have effect, in relation to the disclosure of information by or on behalf of a public authority, as if the purposes for which the disclosure of information is authorised by that provision included each of the following—

(a) the purposes of any criminal investigation whatever which is being or may be carried out, whether in the United Kingdom or elsewhere;

(*b*) the purposes of any criminal proceedings whatever which have been or may be initiated, whether in the United Kingdom or elsewhere;

(*c*) the purposes of the initiation or bringing to an end of any such investigation or proceedings;

(*d*) the purpose of facilitating a determination of whether any such investigation or proceedings should be initiated or brought to an end.

(3) The Treasury may by order made by statutory instrument add any provision contained in any subordinate legislation to the provisions to which this section applies.

(4) The Treasury shall not make an order under subsection (3) unless a draft of it has been laid before Parliament and approved by a resolution of each House.

(5) No disclosure of information shall be made by virtue of this section unless the public authority by which the disclosure is made is satisfied that the making of the disclosure is proportionate to what is sought to be achieved by it.

(6) Nothing in this section shall be taken to prejudice any power to disclose information which exists apart from this section.

(7) The information that may be disclosed by virtue of this section includes information obtained before the commencement of this section.

18 Restriction on disclosure of information for overseas purposes

(1) Subject to subsections (2) and (3), the Secretary of State may give a direction which—

(*a*) specifies any overseas proceedings or any description of overseas proceedings; and

(*b*) prohibits the making of any relevant disclosure for the purposes of those proceedings or, as the case may be, of proceedings of that description.

(2) In subsection (1) the reference, in relation to a direction, to a relevant disclosure is a reference to a disclosure authorised by any of the provisions to which section 17 applies which—

(*a*) is made for a purpose mentioned in subsection (2)(*a*) to (*d*) of that section; and

(*b*) is a disclosure of any such information as is described in the direction.

(3) The Secretary of State shall not give a direction under this section unless it appears to him that the overseas proceedings in question, or that overseas proceedings of the description in question, relate or would relate—

(*a*) to a matter in respect of which it would be more appropriate for any jurisdiction or investigation to be exercised or carried out by a court or other authority of the United Kingdom, or of a particular part of the United Kingdom;

(*b*) to a matter in respect of which it would be more appropriate for any jurisdiction or investigation to be exercised or carried out by a court or other authority of a third country; or

(*c*) to a matter that would fall within paragraph (*a*) or (*b*)—

(i) if it were appropriate for there to be any exercise of jurisdiction or investigation at all; and

(ii) if (where one does not exist) a court or other authority with the necessary jurisdiction or functions existed in the United Kingdom, in the part of the United Kingdom in question or, as the case may be, in the third country in question.

(4) A direction under this section shall not have the effect of prohibiting—

(*a*) the making of any disclosure by a Minister of the Crown or by the Treasury; or

(*b*) the making of any disclosure in pursuance of a Community obligation.

(5) A direction under this section—

(*a*) may prohibit the making of disclosures absolutely or in such cases, or subject to such conditions as to consent or otherwise, as may be specified in it; and

(*b*) must be published or otherwise issued by the Secretary of State in such manner as he considers appropriate for bringing it to the attention of persons likely to be affected by it.

(6) A person who, knowing of any direction under this section, discloses any information in contravention of that direction shall be guilty of an offence and liable—

(*a*) on conviction on indictment, to imprisonment for a term not exceeding two years or to a fine or to both;

(*b*) on summary conviction, to imprisonment for a term not exceeding three months or to a fine not exceeding the statutory maximum or to both.

(7) The following are overseas proceedings for the purposes of this section—

(*a*) criminal proceedings which are taking place, or will or may take place, in a country or territory outside the United Kingdom;

(*b*) a criminal investigation which is being, or will or may be, conducted by an authority of any such country or territory.

(8) References in this section, in relation to any proceedings or investigation, to a third country are references to any country or territory outside the United Kingdom which is not the country or territory where the proceedings are taking place, or will or may take place or, as the case may be, is not the country or territory of the authority which is conducting the investigation, or which will or may conduct it.

(9) In this section "court" includes a tribunal of any description.

19 Disclosure of information held by revenue departments

(1) This section applies to information which is held by or on behalf of the Commissioners of Inland Revenue or by or on behalf of the Commissioners of Customs and Excise, including information obtained before the coming into force of this section.

(2) No obligation of secrecy imposed by statute or otherwise prevents the disclosure, in accordance with the following provisions of this section, of information to which this section applies if the disclosure is made—

(*a*) for the purpose of facilitating the carrying out by any of the intelligence services of any of that service's functions;

(*b*) for the purposes of any criminal investigation whatever which is being or may be carried out, whether in the United Kingdom or elsewhere;

(*c*) for the purposes of any criminal proceedings whatever which have been or may be initiated, whether in the United Kingdom or elsewhere;

(*d*) for the purposes of the initiation or bringing to an end of any such investigation or proceedings; or

(*e*) for the purpose of facilitating a determination of whether any such investigation or proceedings should be initiated or brought to an end.

(3) No disclosure of information to which this section applies shall be made by virtue of this section unless the person by whom the disclosure is made is satisfied that the making of the disclosure is proportionate to what is sought to be achieved by it.

(4) Information to which this section applies shall not be disclosed by virtue of this section except by the Commissioners by or on whose behalf it is held or with their authority.

(5) Information obtained by means of a disclosure authorised by subsection (2) shall not be further disclosed except—

(*a*) for a purpose mentioned in that subsection; and

(*b*) with the consent of the Commissioners by whom or with whose authority it was initially disclosed;

and information so obtained otherwise than by or on behalf of any of the intelligence services shall not be further disclosed (with or without such consent) to any of those services, or to any person acting on behalf of any of those services, except for a purpose mentioned in paragraphs (*b*) to (*e*) of that subsection.

(6) A consent for the purposes of subsection (5) may be given either in relation to a particular disclosure or in relation to disclosures made in such circumstances as may be specified or described in the consent.

(7) Nothing in this section authorises the making of any disclosure which is prohibited by any provision of the Data Protection Act 1998.

(8) References in this section to information which is held on behalf of the Commissioners of Inland Revenue or of the Commissioners of Customs and Excise include references to information which—

(*a*) is held by a person who provides services to the Commissioners of Inland Revenue or, as the case may be, to the Commissioners of Customs and Excise; and

(*b*) is held by that person in connection with the provision of those services.

(9) In this section "intelligence service" has the same meaning as in the Regulation of Investigatory Powers Act 2000.

(10) Nothing in this section shall be taken to prejudice any power to disclose information which exists apart from this section.

20 Interpretation of Part 3

(1) In this Part—

"criminal investigation" means an investigation of any criminal conduct, including an investigation of alleged or suspected criminal conduct and an investigation of whether criminal conduct has taken place;

"information" includes—

(*a*) documents; and

(*b*) in relation to a disclosure authorised by a provision to which section 17 applies, anything that falls to be treated as information for the purposes of that provision;

"public authority" has the same meaning as in section 6 of the Human Rights Act 1998; and

"subordinate legislation" has the same meaning as in the Interpretation Act 1978.

(2) Proceedings outside the United Kingdom shall not be taken to be criminal proceedings for the purposes of this Part unless the conduct with which the defendant in those proceedings is charged is criminal conduct or conduct which, to a substantial extent, consists of criminal conduct.

(3) In this section—

"conduct" includes acts, omissions and statements; and

"criminal conduct" means any conduct which—

(*a*) constitutes one or more criminal offences under the law of a part of the United Kingdom; or

(*b*) is, or corresponds to, conduct which, if it all took place in a particular part of the United Kingdom, would constitute one or more offences under the law of that part of the United Kingdom.

PART 14
SUPPLEMENTAL

127 Commencement

(1) Except as provided in subsections (2) to (4), this Act comes into force on such day as the Secretary of State may appoint by order.

(2) The following provisions come into force on the day on which this Act is passed—

(*a*) Parts 2 to 6,

(*b*)–(*h*) ...

(*i*) this Part, except section 125 and Schedule 8 so far as they relate to the entries—

(i) in Part 1 of Schedule 8,

(ii) in Part 5 of Schedule 8, in respect of the Nuclear Installations Act 1965,

(iii) in Part 6 of Schedule 8, in respect of the British Transport Commission Act 1962 and the Ministry of Defence Police Act 1987, so far as those entries extend to Scotland,

(iv) in Part 7 of Schedule 8, in respect of Schedule 5 to the Terrorism Act 2000.

(3), (4) ...

(5) Different days may be appointed for different provisions and for different purposes.

(6) An order under this section—

(*a*) must be made by statutory instrument, and

(*b*) may contain incidental, supplemental, consequential or transitional provision.

Note—Sub-ss (2)(*b*)–(*h*), (3), (4) are outside the scope of this work.

129 Short title

This Act may be cited as the Anti-terrorism, Crime and Security Act 2001.

SCHEDULES

SCHEDULE 4

EXTENSION OF EXISTING DISCLOSURE POWERS

Section 17

PART 1
ENACTMENTS TO WHICH SECTION 17 APPLIES

...

49 Finance Act 2000

Paragraph 34(3) of Schedule 22 to the Finance Act 2000.

...

Note—Provisions omitted are outside the scope of this work.

FINANCE ACT 2002

(2002 Chapter 23)

ARRANGEMENT OF SECTIONS

PART 2

VALUE ADDED TAX

PART 3

INCOME TAX, CORPORATION TAX AND CAPITAL GAINS TAX

CHAPTER 1

CHARGE AND RATE BANDS

Income tax

Corporation tax

CHAPTER 2

OTHER PROVISIONS

Employment income and related matters

Chargeable gains

New reliefs

FA 2002

Capital allowances and related matters

Computation of profits

Financial instruments

Loan relationships

Foreign exchange gains and losses, loan relationships and currency

Loan relationships and other money debts

Derivative contracts

Intangible fixed assets

Insurance

International matters

Supplementary charge in respect of ring fence trades

Deduction of tax

An Act to grant certain duties, to alter other duties, and to amend the law relating to the National Debt and the Public Revenue, and to make further provision in connection with finance.

[24 July 2002]

PART 3
INCOME TAX, CORPORATION TAX AND CAPITAL GAINS TAX

CHAPTER 1
CHARGE AND RATE BANDS

Income tax

26 Charge and rates for 2002–03

Income tax shall be charged for the year 2002–03, and for that year—

    (*a*) the starting rate shall be 10%;

    (*b*) the basic rate shall be 22%;

    (*c*) the higher rate shall be 40%.

Commentary—*Simon's Direct Tax Service* **E4.911.**

27 Indexed rate bands for 2002–03: PAYE deductions etc

For the year 2002–03, the following provisions of the Taxes Act 1988 shall have effect as if "17th June" were substituted for "17th May"—

    (*a*) section 1(5A) (which provides that statutory inflation-linked changes to income tax rate bands for a year of assessment do not require changes to be made to PAYE deductions or repayments until 18th May in that year);

    (*b*) section 257C(2A) (which makes corresponding provision in relation to personal allowances etc) as it has effect for the application of—

        (i) section 257AA(2) of that Act (children's tax credit), and

        (ii) section 265 of that Act (blind person's allowance).

Commentary—*Simon's Direct Tax Service* **E4.911.**

28 Personal allowance for 2003–04 for those aged under 65

(1) For the year 2003–04 the amount specified in section 257(1) of the Taxes Act 1988 (personal allowance for those aged under 65) shall be taken to be £4,615.

(2) Accordingly, section 257C(1) of that Act (indexation), so far as it relates to the amount so specified, does not apply for that year.

Commentary—*Simon's Direct Tax Service* **E2.302.**

29 Personal allowances for 2003–04 for those aged 65 or over

(1) For the year 2003–04—

    (*a*) the amount specified in section 257(2) of the Taxes Act 1988 (personal allowance for those aged between 65 and 74) shall be taken to be £6,610;

    (*b*) the amount specified in section 257(3) of that Act (personal allowance for those aged 75 or over) shall be taken to be the indexed amount plus £240.

In paragraph (*b*) "the indexed amount" means the amount that would apply by virtue of section 257C(1) of that Act (indexation).

(2) Accordingly, section 257C(1), so far as it relates to the amounts specified in section 257(2) and (3), does not apply for that year (except as it applies for the purposes of subsection (1)(*b*) above).

Commentary—*Simon's Direct Tax Service* **E2.302.**

Corporation tax

30 Charge and main rate for financial year 2003

Corporation tax shall be charged for the financial year 2003 at the rate of 30%.

Commentary—*Simon's Direct Tax Service* **D2.108.**

31 Small companies' rate and fraction for financial year 2002

For the financial year 2002—

    (*a*) the small companies' rate shall be 19%, and

    (*b*) the fraction mentioned in section 13(2) of the Taxes Act 1988 (marginal relief for small companies) shall be 11/400ths.

Commentary—*Simon's Direct Tax Service* **D2.109, 109A.**

32 Corporation tax starting rate and fraction for financial year 2002

For the financial year 2002—

(*a*) the corporation tax starting rate shall be 0%, and

(*b*) the fraction mentioned in section 13AA(3) of the Taxes Act 1988 (marginal relief for small companies) shall be 19/400ths.

Commentary—*Simon's Direct Tax Service* **D2.109, 109A.**

CHAPTER 2

OTHER PROVISIONS

Employment income and related matters

33 Employer-subsidised public transport bus services

(1) In Part 5 of the Taxes Act 1988 (provisions relating to the Schedule E charge), section 197AB (exclusion of tax charge in respect of support by employer for certain transport services) is amended as follows.

(2) In subsection (2) (main definitions), in the definition of "qualifying journey" after "means" insert "the whole or part of".

(3) For subsection (3) (conditions of exemption) substitute—

"(3) Except in the case of a local bus service, the exemption conferred by this section is subject to the condition that the terms on which the service is available to the employees mentioned in subsection (1) must not be more favourable than those available to other passengers.

(3A) The exemption conferred by this section is in every case subject to the condition that the service must be available generally to employees of the employer (or each employer) concerned.".

(4) In subsection (4) (minor definitions), at the appropriate place insert—

""local bus service" means a local service as defined by section 2 of the Transport Act 1985;".

(5) After that subsection insert—

"(5) If under this section there is no charge to tax under section 154 (or there would be no charge if the employee were in employment to which Chapter 2 of Part 5 applied), there is no charge to tax under section 141 (non-cash vouchers) in respect of a voucher evidencing the employee's entitlement to use the service.".

(6) This section has effect for the year 2002–03 and subsequent years of assessment.

Commentary—*Simon's Direct Tax Service* **E4.612.**

34 Car fuel: calculation of cash equivalent of benefit

(1) In Part 5 of the Taxes Act 1988 (provisions relating to the Schedule E charge), section 158 (benefits in kind: car fuel) is amended as follows.

(2) For subsections (2) to (2B) (calculation of cash equivalent) substitute—

"(2) Subject to the following provisions of this section, the cash equivalent of that benefit is the appropriate percentage of £14,400.

The "appropriate percentage" means the appropriate percentage determined under Schedule 6 for the purpose of calculating the cash equivalent of the benefit of the car for which the fuel is provided.".

(3) In subsection (4) (power to substitute different amounts by Treasury order), for "a different Table for any of the Tables in subsection (2) above" substitute "a different amount for that specified in subsection (2) above".

(4) For subsection (5) (proportionate reduction where car unavailable for part of the year) substitute—

"(5) The cash equivalent of the benefit in any year is proportionately reduced (see subsection (8) below) if the car for which the fuel is provided is unavailable (within the meaning of Schedule 6) for any part of the year.".

(5) After subsection (6) (nil cash equivalent where fuel provided on terms that employee meets cost of private use or fuel is made available only for business travel) insert—

"(6A) The cash equivalent of the benefit in any year is proportionately reduced (see subsection (8) below) if for any part of that year—

(*a*) the facility for the provision of fuel as mentioned in subsection (1) above is not available, or

(*b*) the employee is required to make good to the person providing the fuel the whole of the expense incurred by him in connection with the provision of the fuel for his private use and he does so, or

(*c*) the fuel is made available only for business travel.

(6B) The fact that any of the conditions specified in subsection (6A) above is met for part of a year shall be disregarded if there is a time later in that year when any of those conditions is not met.''.

(6) At the end of the section add—

''(8) Where the cash equivalent falls to be proportionately reduced under subsection (5) or (6A) above (or under both those subsections), the reduced amount is given by:

$$CE \times \frac{365-D}{365}$$

where—

CE is the amount of the cash equivalent before any reduction; and
D is the total number of days in the year on which either the car is unavailable or one or more of the conditions in subsection (6A) above is met.''.

(7) After that subsection add—

''(9) References in this section to fuel do not include any facility or means for supplying electrical energy for an electrically propelled vehicle.''.

(8) This section has effect for the year 2003–04 and subsequent years of assessment.

Commentary—*Simon's Direct Tax Service* E4.629.

35 Statutory paternity pay and statutory adoption pay

In section 150 of the Taxes Act 1988 (allowances and payments charged to income tax under Schedule E), after paragraph (*d*) insert—

''(*e*) payments of statutory paternity pay or statutory adoption pay under Part 12ZA or 12ZB of the Social Security Contributions and Benefits Act 1992 or, in Northern Ireland, under any corresponding legislation in force there.''.

Commentary—*Simon's Direct Tax Service* E1.111.

36 Exemption of minor benefits: application to non-cash vouchers

(1) In section 155ZB of the Taxes Act 1988 (power to provide for exemption of minor benefits), after subsection (2) add—

''(3) If by virtue of regulations under this section there is no charge to tax under section 154 in respect of a benefit (or there would be no charge if the employee were in employment to which Chapter 2 of Part 5 applied), there is no charge to tax under section 141 (non-cash vouchers) in respect of a voucher evidencing the employee's entitlement to the benefit.''.

(2) This section has effect for the year 2002–03 and subsequent years of assessment.

Commentary—*Simon's Direct Tax Service* E4.432.

37 Minor amendments to Schedule E charge

(1) Schedule 6 to this Act (which makes a number of minor changes to the Schedule E charge to income tax) has effect.

(2) The amendments made by that Schedule have effect for the year 2002–03 and subsequent years of assessment.

38 Provision of services through an intermediary: minor amendments

(1) Schedule 12 to the Finance Act 2000 (c 17) (provision of services through an intermediary) is amended as follows.

(2) In Part 2 (the deemed Schedule E payment), after paragraph 7 insert—

''*Reimbursed expenses*

7A—(1) The reference in Step Three of the calculation in paragraph 7 to expenses met by the intermediary includes expenses met by the worker and reimbursed by the intermediary.

(2) Where the intermediary is a partnership and the worker is a member of the partnership, expenses met by the worker for and on behalf of the intermediary shall be treated for the purposes of sub-paragraph (1) as expenses met by the worker and reimbursed by the intermediary.

Treatment of mileage allowances

7B—(1) Where—

(*a*) the intermediary provides a vehicle for the worker, and
(*b*) the worker would have been entitled to an amount of mileage allowance relief for a tax year in respect of the use of the vehicle if the worker had been employed by the client and the vehicle had not been a company vehicle (within the meaning of paragraph 6 of Schedule 12AA to the Taxes Act 1988),

Step Three of the calculation in paragraph 7 has effect as if that amount were an amount of expenses deductible under that Step.

(2) Where—

    (*a*) the intermediary is a partnership,

    (*b*) the worker is a member of the partnership, and

    (*c*) the worker provides a vehicle for the purposes of the business of the partnership,

then for the purposes of sub-paragraph (1) the vehicle shall be regarded as provided by the intermediary for the worker.

(3) Where the worker receives payments from the intermediary that are exempt from income tax under Schedule E by virtue of section 197AD or 197AE of the Taxes Act 1988 (mileage allowance payments and passenger payments), Step Seven of the calculation in paragraph 7 has effect as if the worker were chargeable to income tax under Schedule E in respect of the payments.''.

(3) In Part 3 (supplementary provisions), in paragraph 12(2) (date of deemed payment where intermediary is a company), after ''relevant events'' insert—

    ''(*za*) the company ceasing to trade;''.

(4) In that Part, in paragraph 18(3) (restriction on expenses deductible in calculating profits of partnership intermediary), for paragraph (*a*) substitute—

    ''(*a*) the amount that, in calculating the deemed Schedule E payment, is deducted under Step Three of the calculation in paragraph 7, and''.

(5) This section has effect for the year 2002–03 and subsequent years of assessment.

Commentary—*Simon's Direct Tax Service* E4.1013, 1019.

39 Employee share ownership plans: minor amendments

(1) Schedule 8 to the Finance Act 2000 (c 17) (employee share ownership plans) is amended as follows.

(2) In paragraph 94 (PAYE: shares ceasing to be subject to plan), for '', subsection (3) of section 203F of the Taxes Act 1988 (PAYE: tradeable assets)'' substitute—

    ''(*a*) section 203F of the Taxes Act 1988 (PAYE: readily convertible assets) shall have effect as if the participant were being provided with assessable income in the form of those shares—

        (i) at the time the shares cease to be subject to the plan, and

        (ii) in respect of the relevant employment in which the participant is employed at that time (or, if he is not employed in relevant employment at that time, the relevant employment in which he was last employed before that time), and

    (*b*) subsection (3) of that section''.

(3) In paragraph 95 (PAYE: shares ceasing to be subject to plan), in sub-paragraph (6), for the words from ''a company'' to ''to whom'' substitute ''the company which employs the participant in relevant employment at the time when the shares cease to be subject to the plan (or, if the participant is not employed in relevant employment at that time, the company which last employed him in relevant employment before that time), provided that that company is one to whom''.

(4) In paragraph 96 (PAYE: capital receipts), in sub-paragraph (2), for the words from ''the company'' to ''to whom'' substitute ''the company which employs the participant in relevant employment at the time the trustees receive the sum of money referred to in sub-paragraph (1) (or, if the participant is not employed in relevant employment at that time, the company which last employed him in relevant employment before that time), provided that that company is one to whom''.

(5) In paragraph 127 (jointly owned companies), at the end insert—

    ''(4) A company controlled by a jointly owned company may not—

        (*a*) be a participating company in more than one group plan, or

        (*b*) if the jointly owned company or any other company controlled by it is a participating company in a group plan, be a participating company in a different group plan.''.

(6) In paragraph 128(2) (meaning of ''readily convertible asset''), after ''this Schedule'' insert ''(and that section in its application in relation to shares which cease to be subject to a plan)''.

(7) This section has effect for the year 2002–03 and subsequent years of assessment.

(8) However, nothing in subsection (5) prevents a company continuing to be a participating company in a group plan in which it was a participating company immediately before the day on which this Act is passed (and for the purposes of this subsection ''participating company'' and ''group plan'' have the same meaning as in Schedule 8 to the Finance Act 2000 (c 17)).

Commentary—*Simon's Direct Tax Service* E4.538.

40 Treatment of deductions from payments to sub-contractors

(1) In Chapter 4 of Part 13 of the Taxes Act 1988 (sub-contractors in the construction industry), after section 559 (deductions on account of tax etc from payments to certain sub-contractors) insert—

"559A Treatment of sums deducted under s 559

(1) A sum deducted under section 559 from a payment made by a contractor—

  (*a*) shall be paid to the Board, and

  (*b*) shall be treated for the purposes of income tax or, as the case may be, corporation tax as not diminishing the amount of the payment.

(2) If the sub-contractor is not a company a sum deducted under section 559 and paid to the Board shall be treated as being income tax paid in respect of the sub-contractor's relevant profits.

If the sum is more than sufficient to discharge his liability to income tax in respect of those profits, so much of the excess as is required to discharge any liability of his for Class 4 contributions shall be treated as being Class 4 contributions paid in respect of those profits.

(3) If the sub-contractor is a company—

  (*a*) a sum deducted under section 559 and paid to the Board shall be treated, in accordance with regulations, as paid on account of any relevant liabilities of the sub-contractor;

  (*b*) regulations shall provide for the sum to be applied in discharging relevant liabilities of the year of assessment in which the deduction is made;

  (*c*) if the amount is more than sufficient to discharge the sub-contractor's relevant liabilities, the excess may be treated, in accordance with the regulations, as being corporation tax paid in respect of the sub-contractor's relevant profits; and

  (*d*) regulations shall provide for the repayment to the sub-contractor of any amount not required for the purposes mentioned in paragraphs (*b*) and (*c*).

(4) For the purposes of subsection (3) the "relevant liabilities" of a sub-contractor are any liabilities of the sub-contractor, whether arising before or after the deduction is made, to make a payment to a collector of inland revenue in pursuance of an obligation as an employer or contractor.

(5) In this section—

  (*a*) "the sub-contractor" means the person for whose labour (or for whose employees' or officers' labour) the payment is made;

  (*b*) references to the sub-contractor's "relevant profits" are to the profits from the trade, profession or vocation carried on by him in the course of which the payment was received;

  (*c*) "Class 4 contributions" means Class 4 contributions within the meaning of the Social Security Contributions and Benefits Act 1992 (c 4) or the Social Security Contributions and Benefits (Northern Ireland) Act 1992 (c 7).

(6) References in this section to regulations are to regulations made by the Board.

(7) Regulations under this section—

  (*a*) may contain such supplementary, incidental or consequential provision as appears to the Board to be appropriate, and

  (*b*) may make different provision for different cases.".

(2) In section 829 of the Taxes Act 1988 (application of Income Tax Acts to public departments), after subsection (2) insert—

"(2A) Subsections (1) and (2) above have effect in relation to Chapter 4 of Part 13 of this Act (sub-contractors in the construction industry) as if the whole of any deduction required to be made under section 559 were in all cases a deduction of income tax.".

(3) In section 59D of the Taxes Management Act 1970 (c 9) (payment of corporation tax), in subsection (4)(*d*) (amounts treated as corporation tax previously paid), for "under section 559" substitute "by virtue of regulations under 559A".

(4) This section has effect in relation to deductions made under section 559 of the Taxes Act 1988 on or after 6th April 2002.

Regulations under section 559A of that Act, inserted by this section, may be made so as to have effect in relation to any such deductions made on or after that date.

Commentary—*Simon's Direct Tax Service* **E4.529.**

41 Parliamentary visits to EU candidate countries: tax treatment of members' expenses

(1) This section amends—

  (*a*) section 200 of the Taxes Act 1988 (which treats allowances paid to a Member of Parliament in respect of, among other things, expenses of visiting the national parliament of another member State as not being income for tax purposes), and

  (*b*) section 200ZA of that Act (which makes corresponding provision in relation to members of the Scottish Parliament, the National Assembly for Wales and the Northern Ireland Assembly).

(2) In subsection (3)(*b*) of section 200, and in paragraph (*b*) of the definition of "EU travel expenses" in subsection (3) of section 200ZA, after "of another member State" insert "or of a candidate country".

(3) After subsectioin (3) of each section insert—

''(4) In subsection (3) above 'candidate country' means Bulgaria, Cyprus, the Czech Republic, Estonia, Hungary, Latvia, Lithuania, Malta, Poland, Romania, the Slovak Republic, Slovenia or Turkey.

(5) The Treasury shall by order made by statutory instrument make such amendments to the definition in subsection (4) above as are necessary to secure that the countries listed are those that are from time to time candidates for membership of the European Union.''.

[ISOE

(4) This section applies in relation to sums paid on or after 1st April 2002.

Chargeable gains

42 Reallocation within group of gain or loss accruing under section 179

(1) After section 179 of the Taxation of Chargeable Gains Act 1992 (c 12) (company ceasing to be member of group) insert—

''179A Reallocation within group of gain or loss accruing under section 179

(1) This section applies where—

    (a) a company (''company A'') is treated by virtue of section 179(3) or (6) as having sold and immediately reacquired an asset at market value, and

    (b) a chargeable gain or an allowable loss accrues to the company on the deemed sale.

(2) In this section ''time of accrual'' means—

    (a) in a case where section 179(3) applies, the time at which, by virtue of section 179(4), the gain or loss referred to in subsection (1) above is treated as accruing to company A;

    (b) in a case where section 179(6) applies, the latest time at which the company satisfies the conditions in section 179(7).

(3) If—

    (a) a joint election under this section is made by company A and a company (''company C'') that was a member of the relevant group at the time of accrual, and

    (b) the conditions in subsections (6) to (8) below are all met,

the chargeable gain or allowable loss accruing on the deemed sale, or such part of it as may be specified in the election, shall be treated as accruing not to company A but to company C.

(4) In subsection (3) above ''the relevant group'' means—

    (a) in a case where section 179(3) applies, the group of which company A was a member at the time of accrual;

    (b) in a case where section 179(6) applies, the second group referred to in section 179(5).

(5) Where two or more elections are made each specifying a part of the same gain or loss, the total amount specified may not exceed the whole of that gain or loss.

(6) The first condition is that, at the time of accrual, company C—

    (a) was resident in the United Kingdom, or

    (b) owned assets that were chargeable assets in relation to it.

(7) The second condition is that neither company A nor company C was at that time a qualifying friendly society within the meaning given by section 171(5)).

(8) The third condition is that company C was not at that time an investment trust, a venture capital trust or a dual resident investing company.

(9) A gain or loss treated by virtue of this section as accruing to a company that is not resident in the United Kingdom shall be treated as accruing in respect of a chargeable asset held by that company.

(10) An election under this section must be made—

    (a) by notice to an officer of the Board;

    (b) no later than two years after the end of the accounting period of company A in which the time of accrual fell.

(11) Any payment by company A to company C, or by company C to company A, in pursuance of an agreement between them in connection with the election—

    (a) shall not be taken into account in computing profits or losses of either company for corporation tax purposes, and

    (b) shall not for any purposes of the Corporation Tax Acts be regarded as a distribution or a charge on income,

provided it does not exceed the amount of the chargeable gain or allowable loss that is treated as, as a result of the election, as accruing to company C.

(12) For the purposes of this section an asset is a ''chargeable asset'' in relation to a company at a particular time if any gain accruing to the company on a disposal of the asset by the company at that time would be a chargeable gain and would by virtue of section 10(3) form part of its chargeable profits for corporation tax purposes.''.

(2) In Schedule 7B to that Act (modification of Act in relation to overseas life insurance companies), immediately before paragraph 8 insert—

"7A In section 179A(12), the words "section 11(2)(*b*), (*c*) or (*d*) of the Taxes Act" shall be treated as substituted for "section 10(3)"".".

(3) In section 97(1) of the Inheritance Tax Act 1984 (c 51) (transfers within group, etc)—

(*a*) after sub-paragraph (ii) of paragraph (*a*) insert "or—

(iii) an election under section 179A of that Act as a result of which a chargeable gain is treated as accruing to the transferor company instead of to another member of the group, or an allowable loss is treated as accruing to another member of the group instead of to the transferor company,";

(*b*) in paragraph (*aa*) for "the deemed transfer" substitute "the election".

(4) This section applies—

(*a*) in relation to a case where a company is treated by virtue of section 179(3) of the Taxation of Chargeable Gains Act 1992 (c 12) as having sold and immediately reacquired an asset, where the company's ceasing to be a member of the group in question happens on or after 1st April 2002;

(*b*) in relation to a case where a company is so treated by virtue of section 179(6) of that Act, where the relevant time (within the meaning of that subsection) is on or after that date.

Commentary—*Simon's Direct Tax Service* **D2.661.**

43 Roll-over of degrouping charge on business assets

(1) After section 179A of the Taxation of Chargeable Gains Act 1992 (c 12) (inserted by section 42 above) insert—

"179B Roll-over of degrouping charge on business assets

(1) Where a company is treated by virtue of section 179(3) or (6) as having sold and immediately reacquired an asset at market value, relief under section 152 or 153 (roll-over relief on replacement of business assets) is available in accordance with this section in relation to any gain accruing to the company on the deemed sale.

(2) For this purpose, sections 152 and 153 and the other enactments specified in Schedule 7AB apply with the modifications set out in that Schedule.

(3) Where there has been an election under section 179A, any claim for relief available in accordance with this section must be made by company C rather than company A.

(4) For this purpose, the enactments modified by Schedule 7AB have effect as if—

(*a*) references to company A, except those in sections 152(1)(*a*) and (1B), 153(1B), 153A(5), 159(1), 175 and 198(1), were to company C;

(*b*) the references to "that company" in section 159(1) and "the company" in section 185(3)(*b*) were to company C;

(*c*) the reference to "that trade" in section 198(1) were to a ring fence trade carried on by company C.

(5) Where there has been an election under section 179A in respect of part only of the chargeable gain accruing on the deemed sale of an asset, the enactments modified by Schedule 7AB and subsections (3) and (4) above apply as if the deemed sale had been of a separate asset representing a corresponding part of the asset; and any necessary apportionments shall be made accordingly.

(6) A reference in this section to company A or to company C is to the company referred to as such in section 179A.".

(2) After Schedule 7AA to the 1992 Act insert the Schedule 7AB set out in Schedule 7 to this Act.

(3) In section 86(2) of the Finance Act 1993 (c 34) (roll-over relief: power to amend section 155 of the 1992 Act by order), at the end add—

"Any such order may make such consequential amendments of Schedule 7AB as appear to the Treasury to be appropriate.".

(4) This section applies—

(*a*) in relation to a case where a company is treated by virtue of section 179(3) of the 1992 Act as having sold and immediately reacquired an asset, where the company's ceasing to be a member of the group in question happens on or after 1st April 2002;

(*b*) in relation to a case where a company is so treated by virtue of section 179(6) of that Act, where the relevant time (within the meaning of that subsection) is on or after that date.

Commentary—*Simon's Direct Tax Service* **D2.661, 658.**

44 Exemptions for disposals by companies with substantial shareholding

(1) In Chapter 1 of Part 6 of the Taxation of Chargeable Gains Act 1992 (c 12) (provisions relating to chargeable gains of companies), after section 192 insert—

"Disposals by companies with substantial shareholding

192A Exemptions for gains or losses on disposal of shares etc

Schedule 7AC (exemptions for disposal of shares etc by companies with substantial shareholding) has effect.''.

(2) Schedule 8 to this Act (exemptions for disposals by companies with substantial shareholding) has effect.

In that Schedule—

     Part 1 contains Schedule 7AC to be inserted after Schedule 7AB to the Taxation of Chargeable Gains Act 1992 (c 12) (inserted by Schedule 7 to this Act); and
     Part 2 contains consequential amendments.

(3) This section and Schedule 8 to this Act apply in relation to disposals on or after 1st April 2002.

(4) Paragraph 38 of the Schedule 7AC inserted by that Schedule (degrouping: time when deemed sale and reacquisition treated as taking place) has effect where the time of degrouping or relevant time (as defined for the purposes of that paragraph) is on or after that date.

(5) The amendment made by paragraph 2 of Schedule 8 to this Act has effect where the company in question ceases to be a member of the group in question on or after that date.

Commentary—*Simon's Direct Tax Service* **D2.301.**

45 Share exchanges and company reconstructions

(1) Schedule 9 to this Act (chargeable gains: share exchanges and company reconstructions) has effect.

(2) In that Schedule—

     Part 1 provides for the replacement of sections 135 and 136 of the Taxation of Chargeable Gains Act 1992;
     Part 2 makes consequential amendments; and
     Part 3 provides for commencement.

Commentary—*Simon's Direct Tax Service* **C2.726, 727.**

46 Taper relief: holding period for business assets

(1) In the table in section 2A(5) of the Taxation of Chargeable Gains Act 1992 (c 12) (calculation of taper relief), for the first two columns (under the heading "Gains on disposals of business assets") substitute—

Number of whole years in qualifying holding period	Percentage of gain chargeable
1	50
2 or more	25

(2) This section applies to disposals on or after 6th April 2002.

Commentary—*Simon's Direct Tax Service* **C2.1402.**

47 Taper relief: minor amendments

Schedule 10 to this Act contains minor amendments relating to taper relief under the Taxation of Chargeable Gains Act 1992 (c 12).

Commentary—*Simon's Direct Tax Service* **C2.1414.**

48 Use of trading losses against chargeable gains

(1) In section 72 of the Finance Act 1991 (c 31) (use of trading losses against chargeable gains), in subsection (4) (which has the effect that the maximum amount of trading loss that may be so used is calculated by reference to the amount of chargeable gains after taper relief) for "disregarding section 3(1)" substitute "disregarding sections 2A (taper relief) and 3(1) (annual exempt amount)''.

(2) The amendment in subsection (1) has effect in relation to claims under that section in respect of trading losses sustained in the year 2004–05 or subsequent years of assessment, subject to the following provisions.

(3) A person making a claim under section 72 of that Act in respect of a trading loss sustained in the year 2002–03 may elect that, for the purposes of the claim, the amendment made by subsection (1) above shall have effect—

     (a) in relation to the chargeable gains accruing to him in the year 2001–02,
     (b) in relation to the chargeable gains accruing to him in the year 2002–03, or
     (c) in relation to the chargeable gains accruing to him in the year 2001–02 and the year 2002–03.

(4) A person making a claim under that section in respect of a trading loss sustained in the year 2003–04 may elect that, for the purposes of the claim, the amendment made by subsection (1) above shall have effect—

    (*a*) in relation to the chargeable gains accruing to him in the year 2002–03,

    (*b*) in relation to the chargeable gains accruing to him in the year 2003–04, or

    (*c*) in relation to the chargeable gains accruing to him in the year 2002–03 and the year 2003–04.

(5) An election under subsection (3) or (4) must be made—

    (*a*) in writing,

    (*b*) to an officer of the Board,

    (*c*) within the time for making a claim under section 72 of the Finance Act 1991 (c 31) in respect of a trading loss sustained in the year 2002–03 or, as the case may be, the year 2003–04,

and must specify the year or years of assessment in relation to the chargeable gains of which it is made.

Commentary—*Simon's Direct Tax Service* **C2.1403, E1.603.**

49 Election to forgo roll-over relief on transfer of business

(1) After section 162 of the Taxation of Chargeable Gains Act 1992 (c 12) (roll-over relief on transfer of business) insert—

> **"162A Election for section 162 not to apply**
>
> (1) Section 162 shall not apply where the transferor makes an election under this section.
>
> (2) An election under this section must be made by a notice given to an officer of the Board no later than the relevant date.
>
> (3) Except where subsection (4) below applies, the relevant date is the second anniversary of the 31st January next following the year of assessment in which the transfer of the business took place.
>
> (4) Where, by the end of the year of assessment following the one in which the transfer of the business took place, the transferor has disposed of all the new assets, the relevant date is the first anniversary of the 31st January next following the year of assessment in which the transfer of the business took place.
>
> (5) For the purposes of subsection (4) above—
>
>   (*a*) a disposal of any of the new assets by the transferor shall be disregarded if it falls within section 58(1) (transfers between husband and wife); but
>
>   (*b*) where a disposal of any assets to a person is disregarded by virtue of paragraph (*a*) above, a subsequent disposal by that person of any of those assets (other than a disposal to the transferor) shall be regarded as a disposal by the transferor.
>
> (6) All such adjustments shall be made, whether by way of discharge or repayment of tax, the making of assessments or otherwise, as are required to give effect to an election under this section.
>
> (7) Where, immediately before it was transferred, the business was owned by two or more persons—
>
>   (*a*) each of them has a separate entitlement to make an election under this section;
>
>   (*b*) an election made by a person by virtue of paragraph (*a*) above shall apply only to—
>
>   (i) the share of the amount of the gain on the old assets, and
>
>   (ii) the share of the new assets,
>
>   that is attributable to that person for the purposes of this Act.
>
> (8) The reference in subsection (7) above to ownership by two or more persons includes, in Scotland as well as elsewhere in the United Kingdom, a reference to ownership by a partnership consisting of two or more persons.
>
> (9) Expressions used in this section and in section 162 have the same meaning in this section as in that one.
>
> But references in this section to new assets also include any shares or debentures that are treated by virtue of one or more applications of section 127 (including that section as applied by virtue of any enactment relating to chargeable gains) as the same asset as the new assets.".

(2) This section applies in relation to a transfer of a business on or after 6th April 2002.

Commentary—*Simon's Direct Tax Service* **C3.401.**

50 Shares acquired on same day: election for alternative treatment

(1) After section 105 of the Taxation of Chargeable Gains Act 1992 (c 12) (disposal on or before day of acquisition of shares and other unidentified assets) insert—

"105A Shares acquired on same day: election for alternative treatment

(1) Subsection (2) below applies where an individual—

   (a) acquires shares ("the relevant shares") of the same class, on the same day and in the same capacity, and

   (b) some of the relevant shares ("the approved-scheme shares") are shares acquired by him as a result of—

      (i) the exercise of a qualifying option within the meaning of paragraph 1(1) of Schedule 14 to the Finance Act 2000 (enterprise management incentives) in circumstances where paragraph 44, 45 or 46 of that Schedule (exercise of option to acquire shares) applies, or

      (ii) the exercise of an option to which subsection (1) of section 185 of the Taxes Act (approved share option schemes) applies in circumstances where paragraphs (a) and (b) of subsection (3) of that section apply.

(2) Where the individual first makes a disposal of any of the relevant shares, he may elect for subsections (3) to (5) below to have effect in relation to that disposal and all subsequent disposals of any of those shares.

(3) In circumstances where section 105 applies, that section shall have effect as if—

   (a) paragraph (a) of subsection (1) of that section required the approved-scheme shares to be treated as acquired by the individual by a single transaction separate from the remainder of the relevant shares (which shall also be treated by virtue of that paragraph as acquired by the individual by a single transaction), and

   (b) subsection (1) of that section required the approved-scheme shares to be treated as disposed of after the remainder of the relevant shares.

(4) If the relevant shares include shares to which relief under Chapter 3 of Part 7 of the Taxes Act or deferral relief (within the meaning of Schedule 5B to this Act) is attributable—

   (a) paragraph 4(4) of that Schedule has effect as if it required the approved-scheme shares falling within paragraph (a), (b), (c) or (d) of that provision to be treated as disposed of after the remainder of the relevant shares falling within the paragraph in question, and

   (b) section 299 of the Taxes Act has effect for the purposes of section 150A(4) below as if it required—

      (i) the approved-scheme shares falling within paragraph (a), (b), (c) or (d) of subsection (6A) of section 299 of that Act to be treated as disposed of after the remainder of the relevant shares falling within the paragraph in question, and

      (ii) the approved-scheme shares to which subsection (6B) of that section applies to be treated as disposed of after the remainder of the relevant shares to which that subsection applies.

(5) Where section 127 applies in relation to any of the relevant shares ("the reorganisation shares"), that section shall apply separately to such of those shares as are approved-scheme shares and to the remainder of the reorganisation shares (so that those approved-scheme shares and the remainder of the reorganisation shares are treated as comprised in separate holdings of original shares and identified with separate new holdings).

(6) In subsection (5)—

   (a) the reference to section 127 includes a reference to that section as it is applied by virtue of any enactment relating to chargeable gains, and

   (b) "original shares" and "new holding" have the same meaning as in section 127 or (as the case may be) that section as applied by virtue of the enactment in question.

(7) For the purposes of subsection (1) above—

   (a) any shares to which relief under Chapter 3 of Part 7 of the Taxes Act is attributable and which were transferred to an individual as mentioned in section 304 of that Act, and

   (b) any shares to which deferral relief (within the meaning of Schedule 5B to this Act), but not relief under that Chapter, is attributable and which were acquired by an individual on a disposal to which section 58 above applies,

shall be treated as acquired by the individual on the day on which they were issued.

(8) In this section the references to Chapter 3 of Part 7, section 299 and section 304 of the Taxes Act shall be read as references to those provisions as they apply to shares issued after 31st December 1993 (enterprise investment scheme).

105B Provision supplementary to section 105A

(1) The provisions of section 105A have effect in the case of any disposal notwithstanding that some or all of the securities disposed of are otherwise identified—

   (a) by the disposal, or

   (b) by a transfer or delivery giving effect to it.

(2) An election must be made, by a notice given to an officer of the Board, on or before the first anniversary of the 31st January next following the year of assessment in which the individual first makes a disposal of any of the relevant shares.

(3) Where—

    (*a*) an election is made in respect of the relevant shares, and

    (*b*) any shares ("the other shares") acquired by the individual on the same day and in the same capacity as the relevant shares cease to be treated under section 104(4) as shares of a different class from the relevant shares,

the election shall have effect in respect of the other shares from the time they cease to be so treated.

(4) In determining for the purposes of section 105A(2) and subsection (2) above whether the individual has made a disposal of any of the relevant shares, sections 122(1) and 128(3) shall be disregarded.

(5) No election may be made in respect of ordinary shares in a venture capital trust.

For this purpose "ordinary shares" has the meaning given in section 151A(7).

(6) For the purposes of section 105A, shares in a company shall not be treated as being of the same class unless they are so treated by the practice of a recognised stock exchange, or would be so treated if dealt with on that recognised stock exchange.

(7) In section 105A(2) to (5) and subsections (2) to (4) above, any reference to the relevant shares or to the approved-scheme shares includes a reference to the securities (if any) directly or indirectly derived from the shares in question by virtue of one or more applications of section 127 (including that section as applied by virtue of any enactment relating to chargeable gains).

(8) In this section—

    "the approved-scheme shares" has the same meaning as in section 105A;

    "election" means an election under that section;

    "the relevant shares" has the same meaning as in that section; and

    "securities" has the meaning given in section 104(3);

and in subsection (4) the reference to section 128(3) includes a reference to that provision as it is applied by virtue of any enactment relating to chargeable gains.".

(2) The amendment made by subsection (1) has effect in relation to shares acquired by an individual on or after 6th April 2002.

(3) For this purpose—

    (*a*) any shares to which relief under Chapter 3 of Part 7 of the Taxes Act 1988 is attributable and which were transferred to an individual as mentioned in section 304 of that Act, and

    (*b*) any shares to which deferral relief (within the meaning of Schedule 5B to the Taxation of Chargeable Gains Act 1992 (c 12)), but not relief under that Chapter, is attributable and which were acquired by an individual on a disposal to which section 58 of that Act applies,

shall be treated as acquired by the individual on the day on which they were issued.

(4) In subsection (3)(*a*), the references to Chapter 3 of Part 7 and section 304 of the Taxes Act 1988 shall be read as references to those provisions as they apply to shares issued after 31st December 1993 (enterprise investment scheme).

Commentary—*Simon's Direct Tax Service* **C2.701A.**

51 Deduction of personal losses from gains treated as accruing to settlors

Schedule 11 to this Act (deduction of personal losses from gains treated as accruing to settlors) has effect.

Commentary—*Simon's Direct Tax Service* **C4.390.**

52 Capital gains tax: variation of dispositions taking effect on death

(1) In section 62(7) of the Taxation of Chargeable Gains Act 1992 (c 12) (election to treat subsequent variation of dispositions taking effect on death as if effected by deceased) for the words from "unless" to the end of the subsection substitute "unless the instrument contains a statement by the persons making the instrument to the effect that they intend the subsection to apply to the variation.".

(2) This section applies in relation to instruments made on or after 1st August 2002.

Commentary—*Simon's Direct Tax Service* **C1.206, I4.411, 421, 434, 444.**

New reliefs

53 Tax relief for expenditure on research and development

(1) Schedule 12 to this Act has effect for accounting periods ending on or after 1st April 2002.

(2) In that Schedule—

Part 1 makes provision about tax relief for large companies on expenditure on research and development;

Part 2 makes provision about tax relief for small companies on expenditure on research and development that is sub-contracted to them;

Parts 3 to 6 make provision about the form of the relief, special provision about insurance companies and supplementary and general provision.

Commentary—*Simon's Direct Tax Service* **D2.1201, 1202, 1209, 1210.**

54 Tax relief for expenditure on vaccine research etc

(1) Schedule 13 to this Act (which makes provision for tax relief for companies' expenditure on vaccine research etc) has effect.

(2) Schedule 14 to this Act (which makes provision consequential on Schedule 13) has effect.

Commentary—*Simon's Direct Tax Service* **D2.1201, 1209.**

55 Gifts of medical supplies and equipment

(1) This section applies where, for humanitarian purposes, a company makes a gift from trading stock of medical supplies, or medical equipment, for human use.

(2) For the purposes of the Tax Acts, no amount shall be required to be brought into account as a trading receipt of the company in consequence of the making of the gift.

(3) Any costs of transportation, delivery or distribution incurred by the company in making the gift may be deducted in computing for the purposes of corporation tax the profits of the company's trade for the accounting period in which the costs are incurred.

(4) In any case where—

(*a*) relief is given under subsection (2) in respect of the making of a gift and any benefit received in any accounting period by the company or any connected person is in any way attributable to the making of that gift, or
(*b*) relief is given under subsection (3) and any benefit so received is in any way attributable to the company's incurring of the costs referred to in that subsection,

the company shall in respect of that period be charged to corporation tax under Case I of Schedule D or, if the company is not chargeable to corporation tax under that Case for that period, under Case VI of Schedule D on an amount equal to the amount of that benefit.

(5) Section 839 of the Taxes Act 1988 (connected persons) applies for the purposes of subsection (4).

(6) The Treasury may by order provide that this section is not to have effect in relation to medical supplies or medical equipment of such descriptions as may be specified in the order.

(7) This section has effect in relation to gifts made on or after 1 April 2002.

Commentary—*Simon's Direct Tax Service* **D2.231.**

56 R&D tax relief for small and medium-sized enterprises: minor and consequential amendments

Schedule 15 to this Act (which makes minor amendments to Schedule 20 to the Finance Act 2000 (tax relief for R&D expenditure of small and medium-sized enterprises), including amendments consequential on Schedules 12 and 13 to this Act) has effect for accounting periods ending on or after 1st April 2002.

57 Community investment tax relief

(1) Schedule 16 to this Act (community investment tax relief) has effect.

(2) Schedule 17 to this Act (which makes provision consequential on the introduction of community investment tax relief) has effect.

(3) Schedules 16 and 17 shall come into force on such day as the Treasury may by order appoint.

(4) On and after that day—

(*a*) Schedule 16 shall have effect in relation to—

(i) investments made on or after such day as the Treasury may so appoint, being a day not earlier than 17th April 2002, and
(ii) claims made on or after such day as the Treasury may so appoint; and

(*b*) paragraphs 2 to 4 of Schedule 17 shall have effect for years of assessment ending on or after the day appointed under paragraph (*a*)(i), and
(*c*) paragraph 5 of that Schedule shall have effect for accounting periods ending on or after that day.

Commentary—*Simon's Direct Tax Service* **E3.101.**

58 Relief for community amateur sports clubs

(1) Schedule 18 to this Act (relief for community amateur sports clubs) has effect.

(2) Parts 1, 5 and 6 of that Schedule shall be deemed to have come into force on 1st April 2002.

Accordingly, an application under that Schedule by a club to be registered as a community amateur sports club may be granted with effect from that date or any subsequent date before the passing of this Act.

(3) Parts 2 and 4 of that Schedule have effect in relation to accounting periods ending on or after 1st April 2002.

(4) Part 3 of that Schedule has effect in relation to gifts made on or after 6th April 2002.

Commentary—*Simon's Direct Tax Service* B3.240.

Capital allowances and related matters

59 Cars with low carbon dioxide emissions

Schedule 19 to this Act (first-year allowances in respect of expenditure on cars with low CO_2 emissions and exemption from single asset pool rules) has effect in relation to expenditure incurred on or after 17th April 2002.

Commentary—*Simon's Direct Tax Service* B2.324, 330, 342.

60 Expense of hiring cars with low carbon dioxide emissions

(1) In section 578A of the Taxes Act (expenditure on car hire) after subsection (2) (cars to which section 578A applies) insert—

"(2A) This section does not apply to the hiring of a car, other than a motorcycle, if—

(a) it is an electrically-propelled car, or

(b) it is a car with low CO_2 emissions.

(2B) In subsection (2A) above—

"car" has the meaning given by section 578B;

"car with low CO_2 emissions" has the meaning given by section 45D of the Capital Allowances Act 2001 (c 2) (expenditure on cars with low CO_2 emissions to be first-year qualifying expenditure);

"electrically-propelled car" has the meaning given by that section.".

(2) The amendment made by this section has effect in relation to expenditure—

(a) which is incurred on or after 17th April 2002 on the hiring of a car which is first registered on or after that date, and

(b) which is incurred on the hiring of a car, for a period of hire which begins on or before 31st March 2008, under a contract entered into on or before 31st March 2008.

Commentary—*Simon's Direct Tax Service* B2.324, 330, 342.

61 Plant or machinery for gas refuelling station: first-year allowances

Schedule 20 to this Act (first-year allowances in respect of expenditure on plant or machinery for gas refuelling station) has effect in relation to expenditure incurred on or after 17th April 2002.

Commentary—*Simon's Direct Tax Service* B2.324, 330, 342.

62 Expenditure on green technologies: leasing

(1) In section 46 of the Capital Allowances Act 2001 (c 2) (general exclusions affecting first-year qualifying expenditure) after subsection (4) (which is inserted by Schedule 19) insert—

"(5) General exclusion 6 does not prevent expenditure being first-year qualifying expenditure under section 45A, 45D or 45E.".

(2) The amendment made by this section has effect in relation to expenditure incurred on or after 17th April 2002.

Commentary—*Simon's Direct Tax Service* B2.324, 330, 342.

63 First-year allowances for expenditure wholly for a ring fence trade

(1) Schedule 21 to this Act shall have effect.

(2) In that Schedule—

(a) Part 1 makes provision for and in connection with first-year allowances under Part 2 of the Capital Allowances Act 2001 in respect of expenditure incurred by a company on the provision of plant or machinery for use wholly for the purposes of a ring fence trade chargeable to tax under section 501A of the Taxes Act 1988 (inserted by section 91 of this Act); and

(b) Part 2 makes provision for and in connection with first-year allowances under Part 5 of that Act (mineral extraction allowances) in respect of expenditure incurred by a company wholly for the purposes of such a trade.

(3) The amendments made by that Schedule have effect in relation to expenditure incurred on or after 17th April 2002.

Commentary—*Simon's Direct Tax Service* D4.1002, 1010.

Computation of profits

64 Adjustment on change of basis

(1) The provisions of Schedule 22 to this Act have effect as to the adjustment or adjustments to be made for tax purposes where—

    (*a*) there is, from one period of account to the next of a trade, profession or vocation, a change of basis in computing profits for the purposes of Case I or II of Schedule D,

    (*b*) the old basis accorded with the law or practice applicable in relation to the period of account before the change, and

    (*c*) the new basis accords with the law and practice applicable in relation to the period of account after the change.

For the purposes of paragraphs (*b*) and (*c*) the practice applicable in any case means the accepted practice in cases of that description as to how profits should be computed for the purposes of Case I or II of Schedule D.

(2) A ''change of basis'' means—

    (*a*) a relevant change of accounting approach, or

    (*b*) a change in the tax adjustments applied.

(3) A ''relevant change of accounting approach'' means a change of accounting principle or practice that, in accordance with generally accepted accounting practice, gives rise to a prior period adjustment.

(4) A ''tax adjustment'' means any such adjustment as is mentioned in section 42(1) of the Finance Act 1998 (c 36) (adjustments required or authorised by law in computing profits for tax purposes).

(5) A ''change in the tax adjustments applied''—

    (*a*) does not include a change made in order to comply with amending legislation not applicable to the previous period of account, but

    (*b*) includes a change resulting from a change of view as to what is required or authorised by law, or as to whether any adjustment is so required or authorised.

(6) The provisions of this section and Schedule 22 to this Act have effect in place of the provisions of section 44 of, and Schedule 6 to, the Finance Act 1998 (c 36).

Commentary—*Simon's Direct Tax Service* **B4.212–215.**

65 Postponement of change to mark to market in certain cases

(1) This section applies in relation to the computation in accordance with the provisions of Case I of Schedule D of the profits of the insurance business, other than life assurance business, of—

    (*a*) an insurance company,

    (*b*) a corporate member of Lloyd's, or

    (*c*) a controlled foreign company.

(2) For periods of account to which this section applies nothing in—

    (*a*) section 70 of the Taxes Act 1988 (assessment to corporation tax on full amount of profits, etc), or

    (*b*) section 42 of the Finance Act 1998 (c 36) (computation of profits to be on basis giving true and fair view),

prevents the company from computing the profits of that business on a realisation basis rather than a mark to market basis.

A ''realisation basis'' means not recognising a profit or loss on an asset until it is realised, and a ''mark to market basis'' means bringing assets into account in each period of account at a fair value.

(3) Subject to subsection (4), this section applies in relation to any period of account that—

    (*a*) began before 1st August 2001, and

    (*b*) ends before 31st July 2002.

(4) This section does not apply if—

    (*a*) an earlier period of account beginning on or after 1st January 2001 ended with an accounting date different from that with which the previous period of account ended,

    (*b*) the change of accounting date was notified—

        (i) to the registrar of companies, or

        (ii) in the case of a company established under the law of a country or territory outside the United Kingdom, to the corresponding authority of that country or territory,

on or after 17th April 2002, and

    (*c*) the purpose, or one of the purposes, for which the change was made was so that a subsequent period of account would be one to which section 64 above applies (computation of profits: adjustment on change of basis).

(5) In this section—

''controlled foreign company'' has the same meaning as in Chapter 4 of Part 17 of the Taxes Act 1988; and "corporate member of Lloyd's" means a corporate member as defined in section 230(1) of the Finance Act 1994 (c 9).

Commentary—*Simon's Direct Tax Service* **D4.540**.

66 Election to continue postponement of mark to market

(1) Where section 65 (postponement of change to mark to market in certain cases) applies in relation to a period of account, the company may elect that it shall continue to apply in relation to subsequent periods of account as regards assets held by it on 1st January 2002.

Any such election must be made within twelve months after the end of the accounting period of the company current on that date.

(2) An insurance company that carries on both long-term business and business other than long-term business may make an election under this section limited to assets held by the company otherwise than in the company's long-term insurance fund.

(3) For the purpose of determining whether an election under this section applies to an asset in a case where—

(*a*) assets are realised by the company in an accounting period beginning on or after 1st January 2002,

(*b*) the assets are of such a kind that the particular assets realised are not readily identifiable,

(*c*) the realisation does not exhaust the company's holding, and

(*d*) some but not all of the company's holding was acquired after 1st January 2002,

assets realised shall be identified with assets acquired on the same basis as that used by the company for accounting purposes, unless the basis used by the company is "last in, first out" in which case assets realised shall be identified with assets acquired on or before 1st January 2002 in priority to assets acquired after that day.

(4) Where a company has made an election under this section and—

(*a*) an asset in relation to which the election has effect is transferred to another company ("the transferee company") in pursuance of a transfer scheme, and

(*b*) immediately after the transfer either—

(i) the transferee company is resident in the United Kingdom, or

(ii) the asset is held for the purposes of a business carried on by the transferee company in the United Kingdom through a branch or agency,

this section applies as if the transferee company had made an election under this section in relation to that asset.

(5) In this section—

"insurance business" means business that consists of the effecting or carrying out of contracts of insurance and for the purposes of this definition "contract of insurance" has the meaning given in Article 3(1) of the Financial Services and Markets Act 2000 (Regulated Activities) Order 2001 (SI 2001/544);

"insurance company", "long-term business" and "long-term insurance fund" have the same meaning as in Chapter 1 of Part 12 of the Taxes Act 1988 (see section 431(2) of that Act);

"transfer scheme" means—

(*a*) a scheme under section 105 of the Financial Services and Markets Act 2000 (c 8), including an excluded scheme falling within Case 2, 3 or 4 of subsection (3) of that section, or

(*b*) a qualifying overseas transfer scheme.

(6) A "qualifying overseas transfer scheme" means—

(*a*) so much of a transfer of the whole or part of the business of an overseas life insurance company carried on through a branch or agency in the United Kingdom as takes place in accordance with an authorisation granted outside the United Kingdom for the purposes of Article 11 of the third life insurance directive, or

(*b*) so much of a transfer of the whole or part of the business of an insurance company other than an overseas life insurance company as takes place in accordance with an authorisation granted outside the United Kingdom for the purposes of Article 12 of the third non-life insurance directive.

(7) In subsection (6)—

"overseas life insurance company" has the same meaning as in Chapter 2 of Part 12 of the Taxes Act 1988 (see section 431(2) of that Act);

"the third life insurance directive" means Council Directive 92/96/EEC on the co-ordination of laws, regulations and administrative provisions relating to direct life assurance and amending Directive 79/267/EEC and 990/96/EEC; and

"the third non-life insurance directive" means Council Directive 92/49/ EEC on the co-ordination of laws, regulations and administrative provisions relating to direct insurance other than life assurance and amending Directives 73/239/EEC and 88/357/EEC.

Commentary—*Simon's Direct Tax Service* **D4.540**.

67 Mark to market: miscellaneous amendments

(1) In section 473 of the Taxes Act 1988 (roll-over of securities held as circulating capital)—

(*a*) in the opening words of subsection (2), omit '', if the securities were not such as are mentioned in subsection (1)(*b*) above'';

(*b*) in subsection (2)(*a*), and in subsection (7), for ''would result'' substitute ''results''; and

(*c*) in subsection (2)(*b*) for ''would be'' substitute ''is''.

(2) After subsection (2) of that section insert—

''(2A) This section does not apply to securities in respect of which unrealised profits or losses, calculated by reference to the fair value of the securities at the end of a period of account, are taken into account in the period of account in which the transaction mentioned in subsection (2) above occurs.

(2B) Subsection (2A) above shall be disregarded in determining for the purposes of section 66 of the Finance Act 2002 (election to continue postponement of mark to market) whether an asset was held by a person on 1st January 2002.''.

(3) In section 81 of the Finance Act 1999 (c 16) (acquisitions disregarded under insurance companies concession), at the end add—

''(13) If the relevant company changes from—

(*a*) not recognising a profit or loss on an asset until it is realised, to

(*b*) bringing assets into account in each period of account at a fair value,

then, in calculating the amount of any adjustment required under Schedule 22 to the Finance Act 2002 (calculation of adjustment on change of basis), the amount to be taken into account as the cost of the asset in relation to a period of account before the change is the cost of the previous acquisition.''.

(4) The provisions of this section come into force as follows—

(*a*) the amendments in subsections (1) and (2) apply in relation to periods of account ending on or after 1st August 2001;

(*b*) the amendment in subsection (3) applies wherever an adjustment falls to be made under Schedule 22 to the Finance Act 2002 (see Part 5 of that Schedule).

Commentary—*Simon's Direct Tax Service* **D4.540.**

68 Expenditure involving crime

(1) In section 577A(1) of the Taxes Act 1988 (no deduction to be made for expenditure incurred in making a payment the making of which constitutes a criminal offence)—

(*a*) after ''incurred'' insert ''(*a*)'', and

(*b*) at the end insert '', or

(*b*) in making a payment outside the United Kingdom where the making of a corresponding payment in any part of the United Kingdom would constitute a criminal offence there.''.

(2) This section applies in relation to expenditure incurred on or after 1st April 2002.

Commentary—*Simon's Direct Tax Service* **B3.1202.**

Financial instruments

69 Qualifying contracts for unallowable purposes

(1) After section 168 of the Finance Act 1994 (c 9) insert—

''168A Qualifying contracts for unallowable purposes

(1) Where in any accounting period a qualifying contract to which a company is party has an unallowable purpose, any amounts which for that period fall, in the case of the company, to be brought into account for the purposes of section 155 above as part of amount B shall (subject to subsection (2) below) not include so much of the amounts given by the accounting method used as respects the contract as, on a just and reasonable apportionment, is referable to the unallowable purpose.

(2) The total of any amounts which by virtue of subsection (1) above are not to be brought into account in the accounting period as part of amount B may not exceed the maximum amount.

(3) For the purposes of subsection (2) above, the maximum amount, in relation to the accounting period, is—

(a) if in the accounting period amount B exceeds amount A, the amount by which amount B exceeds amount A; and

(b) if in the accounting period amount A exceeds or equals amount B, nil.

(4) For the purposes of subsection (3) above, amount A and amount B shall be determined in relation to the qualifying contract in accordance with section 155 above and, in so determining amount B, so much of any amount as is referable to the unallowable purpose of the contract shall (notwithstanding subsection (1) above) be brought into account.

(5) For the purposes of this section a qualifying contract to which a company is party shall be taken to have an unallowable purpose in an accounting period where the purposes for which, at times during that period, the company is party to the contract include a purpose ("the unallowable purpose") which is not amongst the business or other commercial purposes of the company.

(6) For the purposes of this section the business and other commercial purposes of a company do not include the purposes of any part of its activities in respect of which it is not within the charge to corporation tax.

(7) For the purposes of this section, where one of the purposes for which a company is party to a qualifying contract at any time is a tax avoidance purpose, that purpose shall be taken to be a business or other commercial purpose of the company only where it is not the main purpose, or one of the main purposes, for which the company is party to the contract at that time.

(8) The reference in subsection (7) above to a tax avoidance purpose is a reference to any purpose that consists in securing a tax advantage (whether for the company or any other person).

(9) In this section "tax advantage" has the same meaning as in Chapter 1 of Part 17 of the Taxes Act 1988 (tax avoidance).".

(2) Subject to subsection (3), this section has effect for accounting periods ending on or after 26th July 2001 in relation to any qualifying contract to which a company is party, unless the company has ceased to be a party to the contract before that date.

(3) Where such an accounting period begins before 26th July 2001, there shall not be included in the amounts, which by virtue of section 168A(1) of the Finance Act 1994 (c 9) (as it has effect subject to section 168A(2) (maximum amount)) are not to be brought into account, such part of those amounts as, on a just and reasonable apportionment, is attributable to the part of the accounting period which falls before 26th July 2001.

(4) For the purposes of subsection (3), section 168A(3) shall have effect for the purposes of determining the maximum amount in section 168A(2) as if the references in section 168A(3) to amount A and amount B were references to such part of amount A or amount B as, on a just and reasonable apportionment, is attributable to the part of the accounting period which falls after 25th July 2001.

Commentary—*Simon's Direct Tax Service* **D2.1010.**
Amendment—This section repealed by FA 2002 s 141, Sch 40 Pt 3(13) with effect for accounting periods beginning after 30 September 2002.

70 Forward premiums and discounts under currency contracts

(1) In section 153 of the Finance Act 1994 (c 9) (qualifying payments), for subsections (4) and (5) (premiums and discounts) substitute—

"(5) For the purposes of this Chapter, in the case of any qualifying contract which is a currency contract,—

(a) the amount of any forward discount arising under the contract to a qualifying company shall be treated as a qualifying payment received by the company; and
(b) the amount of any forward premium arising under the contract from a qualifying company shall be treated as a qualifying payment made by the company.

(6) The amounts of any forward discounts and premiums arising under a contract to a qualifying company shall be determined for the purposes of subsection (5) above—

(a) in accordance with subsections (7) to (9) below in the case of a currency contract which provides for a rate of exchange between the reporting currency and another currency, and
(b) in accordance with subsection (10) below in the case of a currency contract which provides for a rate of exchange between two currencies, neither of which is the reporting currency.

(7) For the purposes of subsection (5)(a) above, the cases where a forward discount arises under a currency contract to a company are those cases where—

(a) the acquisition spot price exceeds the acquisition contract price, or
(b) the sale contract price exceeds the sale spot price;

and the amount of the forward discount is the amount of the excess mentioned in paragraph (a) or (b) above, as the case may be.

(8) For the purposes of subsection (5)(b) above, the cases where a forward premium arises under a currency contract from a company are those cases where—

(a) the acquisition contract price exceeds the acquisition spot price, or
(b) the sale spot price exceeds the sale contract price;

and the amount of the forward premium is the amount of the excess mentioned in paragraph (a) or (b) above, as the case may be.

(9) In subsections (7) and (8) above—

"the acquisition contract price" means the amount of any currency (other than the reporting currency) to be acquired under the contract by the company, expressed in the reporting currency, using the rate of exchange determined by the terms of the contract;

"the acquisition spot price" means the amount of any currency (other than the reporting currency) to be acquired under the contract by the company, expressed in the reporting currency, using such rate of exchange for the date on which the company becomes entitled to rights and subject to duties under the contract as is used for the purposes of the company's accounts (as defined in section 156(6) below);

"the sale contract price" means the amount of any currency (other than the reporting currency) to be disposed of under the contract by the company, expressed in the reporting currency, using the rate of exchange determined by the terms of the contract;

"the sale spot price" means the amount of any currency (other than the reporting currency) to be disposed of under the contract by the company, expressed in the reporting currency, using such rate of exchange for the date on which the company becomes entitled to rights and subject to duties under the contract as is used for the purposes of the company's accounts (as defined in section 156(6) below).

(10) Where this subsection has effect in accordance with subsection (6)(b) above, the amounts of any forward premiums and discounts arising under the contract are the amounts which, in accordance with generally accepted accounting practice, are brought into account in the same way as any forward premiums and discounts which fall to be determined in accordance with subsections (7) and (8) above.

(11) Subsection (5) above is subject to subsection (12) below.

(12) Where a qualifying company is using, as respects a qualifying contract which is a currency contract, a basis of accounting which conforms to generally accepted accounting practice and—

(a) an amount which would, but for this subsection, fall to be treated as a qualifying payment by virtue of subsection (5) above is brought into account by the company, in accordance with that basis of accounting, as a qualifying payment made or received by the company but otherwise than by virtue of being a forward premium or discount, or

(b) that basis of accounting is such that no forward premiums or discounts are treated as arising under a qualifying contract,

subsection (5) above shall not have effect in relation to that amount or, as the case may be, in relation to that contract.

(13) In this section "the reporting currency" means sterling, unless the case is one where section 93 of the Finance Act 1993 (c 34) (use of foreign currency) applies, in which case it means the currency which is the relevant foreign currency for the purposes of that section.".

(2) This section has effect for accounting periods ending on or after 26th July 2001 in relation to any currency contract to which a company is party, unless the company has ceased to be a party to the contract before that date.

Commentary—*Simon's Direct Tax Service* **D2.1021.**
Amendment—This section repealed by FA 2002 s 141, Sch 40 Pt 3(13) with effect for accounting periods beginning after 30 September 2002.

Loan relationships

71 Accounting method where rate of interest etc is reset

(1) After section 88 of the Finance Act 1996 (c 8) insert—

"88A Accounting method where rate of interest is reset

(1) This section applies where—

(a) the conditions in subsections (2) and (3) below are satisfied in relation to an asset representing a creditor relationship of a company; and

(b) the object, or one of the main objects, of the company entering into or becoming a party to the creditor relationship was the securing, whether for itself or any other person, of a tax advantage (within the meaning of Chapter 1 of Part 17 of the Taxes Act 1988).

(2) The first condition is that there is or has at any time been a change in—

(a) the rate of interest payable in the case of the asset;

(b) the amount payable to discharge the debt; or

(c) the time at which any payments under the asset (whether of interest or otherwise) fall due.

(3) The second condition is that the difference between—

(a) the fair value of the asset immediately after the change, and

(b) the issue price of the asset,

is equal to at least 5 per cent of the issue price of the asset.

(4) On and after the day on which the conditions in subsections (2) and (3) above become satisfied in the case of an asset, the only accounting method authorised for the purposes of this Chapter for use by any company as respects a creditor relationship represented by the asset shall be an authorised mark to market basis of accounting.

(5) Where section 90 below applies in consequence of subsection (4) above, no debit shall be brought into account under subsection (2)(c) or (3)(b) of that section.

(6) In determining the fair value of an asset for any purpose of this section it shall be assumed that all amounts payable by the debtor will be paid in full as they fall due.''.

(2) This section has effect on and after the relevant day.

(3) Where an authorised mark to market basis of accounting—

(*a*) is required by virtue of this section to be used on and after the relevant day as respects a creditor relationship of a company, but

(*b*) was not being used immediately before that day as respects the relationship,

the asset representing the relationship shall be treated for the purposes of Chapter 2 of Part 4 of the Finance Act 1996 as having been acquired by the company for the asset's fair value (as determined for the purposes of section 88A of that Act) on the relevant day.

(4) For the purposes of this section ''the relevant day'' is—

(*a*) 19th December 2001, in a case where section 88A of that Act applies by reason of a change in the rate of interest payable in the case of the asset in question; or

(*b*) 24th April 2002, in any other case.

Commentary—*Simon's Direct Tax Service* D2.1110.

72 Convertible securities etc: loan relationships

(1) Section 92 of the Finance Act 1996 (c 8) (convertible securities etc) is amended as follows.

(2) Amend subsection (1) (the assets to which section 92 applies) in accordance with subsections (3) to (9).

(3) In paragraph (*b*) (which requires the asset to carry rights to acquire any shares in a company) for ''any shares in a company'' substitute ''shares in a company''.

(4) After paragraph (*b*) insert—

''(*bb*) the only shares that may be so acquired under any such provision are shares which, at the time when the asset comes or came into existence are or were, and at all times since have been,—

(i) qualifying ordinary shares in one or more companies, or

(ii) mandatorily convertible preference shares in one or more companies;''.

(5) In paragraph (*c*) (extent to which shares may be acquired under that provision not to be determined using specified cash value) for ''that provision'', where first occurring, substitute ''any such provision''.

(6) In paragraph (*d*) (asset not to be a relevant discounted security within the meaning of Schedule 13 to the Finance Act 1996) after ''Act'' insert ''or an excluded indexed security within the meaning of that Schedule''.

(7) After paragraph (*d*) insert—

''(*dd*) the rights attached to the asset do not include provision by virtue of which the company may require a person other than the issuing company to acquire the asset for an amount which would, if payable on redemption, be an amount involving a deep gain for the purposes of paragraph 3 of that Schedule;''.

(8) In paragraph (*e*) (more than negligible likelihood of the right to acquire shares being exercised to significant extent)—

(*a*) for ''the right'' substitute ''the rights'', and

(*b*) omit ''and''.

(9) After paragraph (*e*) insert—

''(*ee*) the rights to acquire shares in a company (whether by conversion or exchange or otherwise) are such that exercising them to their full extent would result in the replacement of the asset—

(i) wholly by shares, or

(ii) in a case where exercising the rights to acquire shares to their full extent would not confer an entitlement to a whole number of shares, wholly by shares and a cash adjustment in respect of the fraction of a share so arising,

and the ending of the creditor relationship; and''.

(10) After subsection (1) insert—

''(1A) In subsection (1) above—

''the issuing company'' means the company that brought into existence the asset mentioned in subsection (1) above;

''mandatorily convertible preference shares'' means shares (other than qualifying ordinary shares) which are issued upon terms that stipulate that, by a time no more than 24 hours after their acquisition by a person who immediately before that acquisition had the creditor relationship represented by those shares, they must be converted into or exchanged for qualifying ordinary shares;

''qualifying ordinary shares'' means shares in a company which satisfy the conditions in subsections (1B) and (1C) below.

(1B) The first condition is that the shares are shares representing some or all of the issued share capital (by whatever name called) of the company, other than—

    (a) capital the holders of which have a right to a dividend at a fixed rate but have no other right to share in the profits of the company, or

    (b) capital the holders of which have no right to a dividend of any description nor any other right to share in the profits of the company.

(1C) The second condition is that the shares are—

    (a) shares which are listed on a recognised stock exchange, or

    (b) shares in a company which is a trading company or a holding company;

and for this purpose ''trading company'' and ''holding company'' have the meaning given by paragraph 22(1) of Schedule A1 to the Taxation of Chargeable Gains Act 1992 (c 12).''.

(11) After subsection (1C) insert—

''(1D) For the purposes of subsection (1)(*ee*)(ii) above, the amount which may be paid by way of a cash adjustment may not exceed five per cent of the value of the relevant shares at the relevant time; and for these purposes—

    (a) ''the relevant shares'' means the shares which would be acquired by exercising the rights attached to the asset to their full extent, and

    (b) ''the relevant time'' means the time at which the rights to acquire those shares are exercised.''.

(12) In consequence of the amendments made by this section and sections 73 and 74, the sidenote becomes ''Convertible securities etc: creditor relationships''.

(13) The amendments made by this section do not have effect for the purpose of determining, in relation to such part of an accounting period as falls before 26th July 2001, whether an asset is, or has ceased to be, an asset to which section 92 of the Finance Act 1996 (c 8) applies.

(14) Subsection (15) has effect where—

    (a) an asset is, immediately before 26th July 2001, an asset to which section 92 of the Finance Act 1996 (c 8) applies, but

    (b) on that date, by virtue only of the amendments of that section made by this section, the asset ceases to be an asset to which that section applies.

(15) Where this subsection has effect, the asset shall be taken to have ceased immediately before 26th July 2001 to be an asset to which section 92 of the Finance Act 1996 (c 8) applies and, accordingly, any deemed disposal and reacquisition under subsection (7) of that section shall be treated as having taken place immediately before that date.

(16) Subject to subsections (13) to (15), the amendments made by this section have effect for accounting periods ending on or after 26th July 2001 in relation to any asset representing a creditor relationship of a company, unless the creditor relationship in question is one to which the company ceased to be a party before that date.

Commentary—*Simon's Direct Tax Service* D2.1126.

73 Convertible securities etc: issuing company not to be connected company

(1) In section 92 of the Finance Act 1996 (convertible securities etc) after subsection (1D) (which is inserted by section 72) insert—

''(1E) This section does not apply to an asset representing a creditor relationship of a company if, for the accounting period in which the asset comes into existence, there is a connection between the company and the company which is the issuing company in relation to that asset.

(1F) If, in the case of an asset representing a creditor relationship of a company, the company and the company which is the issuing company in relation to that asset become companies between which, for any accounting period, there is a connection—

    (a) the asset shall cease to be an asset to which this section applies, and

    (b) it shall be treated, for the purposes of subsection (7)(a) below, as having ceased to be such an asset at the time when the circumstances giving rise to that connection arose.

(1G) Section 87(3) above (connection between a company and another person for an accounting period) applies for the purposes of subsections (1E) and (1F) above.''.

(2) The amendments made by this section do not have effect for the purpose of determining, in relation to such part of an accounting period as falls before 19th December 2001, whether an asset is, or has ceased to be, an asset to which section 92 of the Finance Act 1996 applies.

(3) Subsection (4) has effect where—

    (a) an asset is, immediately before 19th December 2001, an asset to which section 92 of the Finance Act 1996 applies, but

    (b) on that date, by virtue only of the amendments of that section made by this section, the asset ceases to be an asset to which that section applies.

(4) Where this subsection has effect, the asset shall be taken to have ceased immediately before 19th December 2001 to be an asset to which section 92 of the Finance Act 1996 (c 8) applies and,

accordingly, any deemed disposal and reacquisition under subsection (7) of that section shall be treated as having taken place immediately before that date.

(5) Subject to subsections (2) to (4), the amendments made by this section have effect for accounting periods ending on or after 19th December 2001 in relation to any asset representing a creditor relationship of a company—

(*a*) unless the creditor relationship in question is one to which the company ceased to be a party before that date, or

(*b*) unless, as regards the company holding the asset representing the creditor relationship immediately before 19th December 2001 ("the creditor company") and the company which brought that asset into existence ("the issuing company"), the first or the second condition is satisfied.

(6) The first condition is that, during any period before 19th December 2001 when the creditor company was holding the asset, there was an accounting period in which there was no connection between the creditor company and the issuing company.

(7) The second condition is that immediately before 19th December 2001—

(*a*) the creditor company was not a 100 per cent subsidiary of the issuing company,

(*b*) the issuing company was not a 100 per cent subsidiary of the creditor company, and

(*c*) the creditor company and the issuing company were not 100 per cent subsidiaries of the same company.

(8) Section 87(3) of the Finance Act 1996 (c 8) (connection between a company and another person for an accounting period) applies for the purposes of subsection (6).

(9) In its application for the purposes of subsection (7), section 838 of the Taxes Act 1988 (meaning of "subsidiaries" for the purposes of the Tax Acts) has effect as if in subsection (1)(*b*) of that section—

(*a*) "a 100 per cent subsidiary" were substituted for "a 75 per cent subsidiary", and

(*b*) "not less than 100 per cent" were substituted for "not less than 75 per cent".

Commentary—*Simon's Direct Tax Service* **D2.1126.**

74 Convertible securities etc: debtor relationships

(1) After section 92 of the Finance Act 1996 insert—

"92A Convertible securities etc: debtor relationships

(1) This section applies to a liability if—

(*a*) the liability represents a debtor relationship of a company ("the debtor company"); and

(*b*) the rights attached to the asset that represents the corresponding creditor relationship include provision by virtue of which a person is or may become entitled to acquire (whether by conversion or exchange or otherwise)—

(i) any shares in the debtor company, or

(ii) any shares in another company.

(2) The debits falling for any accounting period to be brought into account for the purposes of this Chapter in respect of a debtor relationship represented by a liability to which this section applies shall not include debits in relation to any of the amounts falling within subsection (3) below.

(3) The amounts are—

(*a*) any amounts payable by the debtor company in respect of, or in connection with, any such acquisition of shares as is described in subsection (1)(*b*)(ii) above, but not any amounts to which subsection (4) below applies; and

(*b*) any charges or expenses incurred by the debtor company as described in paragraph (*b*), (*c*) or (*d*) of section 84(3) above, where the related transaction in question relates to, or is connected with, the acquisition of shares by another person (whether by conversion or exchange or otherwise) as described in subsection (1)(*b*) above.

(4) This subsection applies to amounts payable by the debtor company, as described in subsection (3)(*a*) above, in respect of the debtor relationship in a case where—

(*a*) the debtor company is carrying on a banking business or a business consisting wholly or partly in dealing in securities, and

(*b*) it entered into the debtor relationship in the ordinary course of that business.

(5) For the purposes of subsection (4) above "securities" has the same meaning as in section 473 of the Taxes Act.

(6) Subject to subsection (7) below, only an authorised accruals basis of accounting shall be used for ascertaining the amounts which fall to be taken into account as described in subsection (2) above.

(7) The requirement in subsection (6) above to use an authorised accruals basis of accounting does not apply in the case of a debtor relationship where—

    (*a*) the debtor company is carrying on a banking business or a business consisting wholly or partly in dealing in securities, and

    (*b*) it entered into the debtor relationship in the ordinary course of that business.''.

(2) The amendments made by this section have effect—

    (*a*) in relation to any amounts falling within section 92A(3)(*a*), where those amounts fall to be paid after 25th July 2001, and

    (*b*) in relation to any charges or expenses falling within section 92A(3)(*b*), where those charges or expenses accrue after 25th July 2001.

Commentary—*Simon's Direct Tax Service* **D2.1126.**

75 Asset-linked loan relationships

(1) Section 93 of the Finance Act 1996 (c 8) (relationships linked to the value of chargeable assets) is amended as follows.

(2) In subsection (1) (application of section and exclusion of cases where dealing in loan relationships is part of a trade)—

    (*a*) for ''unless it is one'' substitute ''unless—

        (*a*) in a case where the loan relationship is a creditor relationship, the asset representing the loan relationship is one''; and

    (*b*) at the end of that subsection insert—

        ''(*b*) in a case where the loan relationship is a debtor relationship, the liability representing the loan relationship is a liability entered into by the company in the course of activities forming an integral part of a trade carried on by the company; or

        (*c*) the loan relationship is one to which section 93A below applies.''.

(3) In subsection (10) (meaning of chargeable asset) for the words from ''if'' to the end substitute—

    ''the asset is—

        (*a*) an estate or interest in land (wherever situated), or

        (*b*) qualifying ordinary shares which are listed on a recognised stock exchange.''.

(4) Subsection (11) (assumptions applying to determine if disposal is chargeable gain for the purposes of subsection (10)) shall cease to have effect.

(5) After subsection (12) insert—

    ''(12A) In subsection (10)(*b*) above ''qualifying ordinary shares'', in relation to a company, means shares representing some or all of the issued share capital (by whatever name called) of the company, other than—

        (*a*) capital the holders of which have a right to a dividend at a fixed rate but have no other right to share in the profits of the company, or

        (*b*) capital the holders of which have no right to a dividend of any description nor any other right to share in the profits of the company.''.

(6) Subsection (13) (which makes provision in respect of certain indices which, in consequence of the amendment made by subsection (3) above, cannot be indices of chargeable assets) shall cease to have effect.

(7) At the end of the section add—

    ''(14) This section is supplemented by section 93B below.''.

(8) The amendments made by this section do not have effect for the purpose of determining, in relation to such part of an accounting period as falls before 26th July 2001, whether a loan relationship is, or has ceased to be, a loan relationship to which section 93 of the Finance Act 1996 (c 8) applies.

(9) Subject to subsection (8), the amendments made by this section have effect for accounting periods ending on or after 26th July 2001 in relation to any loan relationship of a company, unless the loan relationship in question is one to which the company ceased to be a party before that date.

Commentary—*Simon's Direct Tax Service* **D2.1127.**

76 Asset-linked loan relationships involving guaranteed returns

(1) After section 93 of the Finance Act 1996 (c 8) insert—

''93A Relationships linked to the value of chargeable assets: guaranteed returns

    (1) This section applies to a loan relationship which is a creditor relationship of a company if—

        (*a*) that loan relationship and one or more other transactions are associated transactions designed to produce a guaranteed return;

        (*b*) any such other transaction is a disposal of futures or options; and

        (*c*) the guaranteed return comprises the return consisting of the amount that must be paid to discharge the money debt arising in connection with that loan relationship taken together with the return from any one or more of the disposals of futures or options.

(2) For the purposes of this section a loan relationship of a company and one or more disposals of futures or options are transactions designed to produce a guaranteed return if, taking the transactions together, it would be reasonable to assume, from considering—

(*a*) the likely effect of the transactions,

(*b*) the circumstances in which the transactions are entered into, or in which any of them is entered into, or

(*c*) the matters in both of paragraphs (*a*) and (*b*),

that the main purpose of the transactions, or one of their main purposes, is or was the production of a guaranteed return from the loan relationship and any one or more of the disposals.

(3) For the purposes of this section a guaranteed return is produced from the loan relationship and any one or more of the disposals of futures or options wherever (taking all the transactions together) risks from fluctuations in the underlying subject matter are so eliminated or reduced as to produce a return from the transactions—

(*a*) the amount of which is not, to any significant extent, attributable (otherwise than incidentally) to any such fluctuations; and

(*b*) which equates, in substance, to the return on an investment of money at interest.

(4) For the purposes of subsection (3) above the cases where risks from fluctuations in the underlying subject matter are eliminated or reduced shall be deemed to include any case where the main reason, or one of the main reasons, for the choice of that subject matter is—

(*a*) that there appears to be no risk that that subject matter will fluctuate; or

(*b*) that the risk that it will fluctuate appears to be insignificant.

(5) In this section—

(*a*) the references, in relation to a loan relationship, to the underlying subject matter are references to the value of chargeable assets of a particular description to which that relationship is linked;

(*b*) the references, in relation to a disposal of futures or options, to the underlying subject matter are references to or to the value of the commodities, currencies, shares, stock or securities, interest rates, indices or other matters to which, or to the value of which, those futures or options are referable.

(6) Subsection (5)(*a*) above is to be construed in accordance with section 93 above.

(7) For the purposes of this section—

(*a*) references to the disposal of futures or options are to be construed in accordance with paragraphs 4 and 4A of Schedule 5AA to the Taxes Act 1988;

(*b*) references to the return from one or more disposals of futures or options are to be construed in accordance with paragraph 5 of that Schedule; and

(*c*) references to associated transactions are to be construed in accordance with paragraph 6 of that Schedule.''.

(2) The amendment made by this section has effect for accounting periods ending on or after 26th July 2001 in relation to any loan relationship of a company, unless the loan relationship in question is one to which the company ceased to be a party before that date.

Commentary—*Simon's Direct Tax Service* **D2.1127.**

77 Loan relationships ceasing to be within section 93 of the Finance Act 1996

(1) After section 93A of the Finance Act 1996 (c 8) (which is inserted by section 76) insert—

"93B Loan relationships ceasing to be within section 93

(1) Where a loan relationship of a company—

(*a*) ceases at any time to be a loan relationship to which section 93 above applies, but

(*b*) does not cease at that time to be a loan relationship of that company,

subsection (2) below shall have effect in relation to the asset representing that relationship.

(2) Where this subsection has effect in relation to an asset representing a loan relationship of a company, the company shall be deemed for the purposes of the Taxation of Chargeable Gains Act 1992 (c 12) and this Chapter—

(*a*) to have disposed of the asset for the relevant consideration immediately before the time when the loan relationship ceases to be one to which section 93 above applies, and

(*b*) to have re-acquired it for the relevant consideration immediately after that time.

(3) Any deemed disposal and re-acquisition of an asset under subsection (2) above shall be treated for the purposes of the Taxation of Chargeable Gains Act 1992 as a transaction in the case of which—

(*a*) sections 127 to 130 of that Act would apply, apart from the provisions of section 116 of that Act, by virtue of any provision of Chapter 2 of Part 4 of that Act;

(*b*) the asset in question represents both the original shares and the new holding for the purposes of those sections;

(*c*) the market value of the asset at the time of the transaction is an amount equal to the relevant consideration.

(4) Subject to subsection (5) below, in subsections (2) and (3) above "the relevant consideration", in relation to an asset, means the amount that would have been taken, in accordance with the relevant accounting method, to be the value of the asset at the time of its deemed disposal if that method had been applied to the asset for tax purposes at all times until then.

(5) Section 93(5) above shall not apply in the case of a deemed disposal and re-acquisition under subsection (2) above; but the amount of the relevant consideration in such a case shall be treated for the purposes of the Taxation of Chargeable Gains Act 1992 (c 12) as reduced by so much (if any) of the amount mentioned in subsection (4) above as is referable to interest which—

(*a*) is not paid or payable to the company before the time of the deemed disposal; but

(*b*) is interest falling to be brought into account under section 93(2) and (3) above as having accrued before that time.

(6) In subsection (4) above "the relevant accounting method", in relation to an asset representing a loan relationship of a company, means the accounting method which, for the accounting period of that company in which the deemed re-acquisition takes place, is used as respects that asset and the part of that accounting period beginning with the deemed re-acquisition.

(7) This section shall be construed as one with section 93 above.''.

(2) The amendment made by this section does not have effect in relation to a loan relationship which, before 26th July 2001, ceased to be a loan relationship to which section 93 of the Finance Act 1996 (c 8) (as it has effect by virtue of section 75(8) above) applies.

(3) Subject to subsection (2), the amendment made by this section has effect for accounting periods ending on or after 26th July 2001 in relation to any loan relationship of a company, unless the loan relationship in question is one to which the company ceased to be a party before that date.

Commentary—*Simon's Direct Tax Service* D2.1127.

78 Guaranteed returns on transactions involving futures and options

(1) Schedule 5AA to the Taxes Act 1988 (guaranteed returns on transactions in futures and options) is amended as follows.

(2) In paragraph 2 (transactions to which Schedule applies) at the end insert—

"(3) This Schedule also applies to a transaction if it is one of the disposals of futures or options to which section 93A of the Finance Act 1996 (loan relationships linked to the value of chargeable assets designed to produce guaranteed returns when taken together with disposals of options and futures) refers.''.

(3) In paragraph 4 (meaning of disposals of futures or options) after sub-paragraph (4) insert—

"(4A) Where this paragraph has effect in relation to one of the associated transactions to which section 93A of the Finance Act 1996 (c 8) refers, sub-paragraph (4) shall have effect as if for paragraph (a) of that sub-paragraph there were substituted—

"(a) any one of the associated transactions to which section 93A of the Finance Act 1996 refers is the grant of an option,''.''.

(4) In paragraph 4A (futures running to delivery and options exercised) after sub-paragraph (10) insert—

"(10A) Where this paragraph has effect in relation to one of the associated transactions to which section 93A of the Finance Act 1996 refers—

(a) sub-paragraph (1)(a) shall have effect as if for "two or more related transactions" there were substituted "two or more of the associated transactions to which section 93A of the Finance Act 1996 refers", and

(b) sub-paragraph (1)(c) shall have effect as if for "the other transaction, or one of the other transactions," there were substituted "one of the other transactions''.''.

(5) In paragraph 6 (meaning of related transactions) after sub-paragraph (3) insert—

"(3A) Where this paragraph has effect in relation to one of the associated transactions to which section 93A of the Finance Act 1996 refers—

(a) sub-paragraph (1) shall have effect as if for "two or more transactions are related" there were substituted "two or more transactions are associated transactions to which section 93A of the Finance Act 1996 refers", and

(b) sub-paragraph (2) shall have effect as if for "related transactions" there were substituted "associated transactions to which that section refers''.''.

(6) This section has effect for accounting periods ending on or after 26th July 2001 in relation to profits and gains realised, and losses sustained, on or after that date.

Amendment—This section repealed by FA 2002 ss 83(1)(*b*), (3), 141, Sch 27 paras 24, 25, Sch 40 Pt 3(13) with effect for accounting periods beginning after 30 September 2002.

Foreign exchange gains and losses, loan relationships and currency

79 Forex and exchange gains and losses from loan relationships etc

(1) The following provisions shall cease to have effect—

   (*a*) paragraph 4 of Schedule 9 to the Finance Act 1996 (c 8) (which excludes foreign exchange gains and losses from the computation of credits and debits under the loan relationships legislation); and

   (*b*) in consequence, sections 125 to 169 of the Finance Act 1993 (c 34) (taxation of foreign exchange gains and losses).

(2) Schedule 23 to this Act (which makes provision in relation to exchange gains and losses from loan relationships etc) shall have effect.

(3) The amendments made by subsection (1) and by Parts 1 and 2 of Schedule 23 have effect in relation to accounting periods beginning on or after 1st October 2002.

Commentary—*Simon's Direct Tax Service* **D2.901, 1102, 1105.**

80 Corporation tax: currency

(1) Schedule 24 to this Act (which makes provision in relation to corporation tax and currency) shall have effect.

(2) This section has effect in relation to accounting periods beginning on or after 1st October 2002.

Commentary—*Simon's Direct Tax Service* **D2.910–912.**

81 Transitional provision

(1) The Treasury may by regulations make such transitional or consequential provision, or such savings (with or without modifications), as they may from time to time consider appropriate in consequence of, or otherwise in connection with, any provision of section 79 or 80 or Schedule 23 or 24 (or any repeal consequential on any such provision).

(2) The power conferred by subsection (1) includes power—

   (*a*) to make different provision for different cases or different purposes;

   (*b*) to amend any statutory instrument; and

   (*c*) to make incidental or supplementary provision.

(3) The provision that may be made by virtue of subsection (1) or (2) includes provision for or in connection with bringing amounts into account—

   (*a*) for the purposes of the Taxation of Chargeable Gains Act 1992 (c 12), as if they were chargeable gains or allowable losses; or

   (*b*) for the purposes of Chapter 2 of Part 4 of the Finance Act 1996 (c 8), as if they were credits or debits in respect of a loan relationship or a related transaction of the company concerned.

(4) Nothing in any provision of Schedule 23 or 24 shall prejudice the operation of this section.

(5) Nothing in this section or in Schedule 23 or 24 limits the operation of section 16 or 17 of the Interpretation Act 1978 (c 30) (effect of repeals).

Regulations—See the Exchange Gains and Losses (Transitional Provisions and Savings) Regulations, SI 2002/1969.

Loan relationships and other money debts

82 Loan relationships: general amendments

(1) Schedule 25 to this Act (which makes provision in relation to loan relationships) shall have effect.

(2) The amendments made by Parts 1 and 2 of that Schedule have effect in relation to accounting periods beginning on or after 1st October 2002.

Commentary—*Simon's Direct Tax Service* **D2.1118, 1119, 1121.**

Derivative contracts

83 Derivative contracts

(1) The following shall have effect—

   (*a*) Schedule 26 to this Act (which makes provision for the taxation of derivative contracts);

   (*b*) Schedule 27 to this Act (which makes minor and consequential amendments relating to the taxation of derivative contracts); and

   (*c*) Schedule 28 to this Act (which contains transitional provisions etc in connection with the coming into force of this section and Schedules 26 and 27).

(2) Sections 147 to 175 and 177 of the Finance Act 1994 (c 9) (which make provision for the taxation of interest rate and currency contracts) shall cease to have effect.

(3) This section has effect in relation to accounting periods beginning on or after 1st October 2002.

(4) Subsection (3) is subject to any specific provision of Schedule 28.

Commentary—*Simon's Direct Tax Service* **D2.1010.**

Intangible fixed assets

84 Gains and losses from intangible fixed assets of company

(1) Schedule 29 to this Act has effect with respect to gains and losses from a company's intangible fixed assets.

(2) Schedule 30 to this Act contains consequential amendments.

Commentary—*Simon's Direct Tax Service* **B3.801.**

Insurance

85 Gains of insurance company from venture capital investment partnership

(1) In Chapter 3 of Part 6 of the Taxation of Chargeable Gains Act 1992 (c 12) (insurance), after section 211 insert—

> **"211A Gains of insurance company from venture capital investment partnership**
>
> Schedule 7AD to this Act has effect with respect to the gains of an insurance company from a venture capital investment partnership.".

(2) After Schedule 7AC to that Act (inserted by Part 1 of Schedule 8 to this Act) insert the Schedule 7AD set out in Schedule 31 to this Act.

Commentary—*Simon's Direct Tax Service* **C3.203.**

86 Lloyd's underwriters

(1) Schedule 32 to this Act (which makes provision about the taxation of Lloyd's underwriters) has effect.

(2) The amendments in that Schedule have effect in relation to quota share contracts (within the meaning of section 178 of the Finance Act 1993 (c 34) or section 225 of the Finance Act 1994) entered into on or after 17th April 2002.

Commentary—*Simon's Direct Tax Service* **E5.614.**

87 Life policies etc: chargeable events

(1) Chapter 2 of Part 13 of the Taxes Act 1988 (life policies, life annuities and capital redemption policies) is amended in accordance with the following provisions of this section.

(2) Section 541 (computation of gain in case of life policy or, as applied by section 545, capital redemption policy) is amended as follows.

(3) In subsection (1)(c) (amounts and values to be brought into account in computing gain on an assignment) before "of any previously assigned share in the rights conferred by the policy" insert ", subject to subsection (3A) below,".

(4) After subsection (3) (assignments between connected persons) insert—

> "(3A) The amount or value of such a previously assigned share as is mentioned in paragraph (c) of subsection (1) above falls to be brought into account for the purposes of that paragraph only where that share was so assigned—
>
> > (a) in a year (as defined in section 546(4)) beginning on or before 5th April 2001; or
> >
> > (b) for money or money's worth in a year (as so defined) beginning on or after 6th April 2001.".

(5) Section 543 (life annuity contracts: computation of gain) is amended as follows.

(6) In subsection (1)(b) (amounts and values to be brought into account in computing gain on an assignment) before "of any previously assigned share in the rights conferred by the contract" insert ", subject to subsection (2A) below,".

(7) After subsection (2) (which applies section 541(3): assignments between connected persons) insert—

> "(2A) The amount or value of such a previously assigned share as is mentioned in paragraph (b) of subsection (1) above falls to be brought into account for the purposes of that paragraph only where that share was so assigned—
>
> > (a) in a year (as defined in section 546(4)) beginning on or before 5th April 2001; or
> >
> > (b) for money or money's worth in a year (as so defined) beginning on or after 6th April 2001.".

(8) Section 546B (special provision in respect of certain section 546 excesses) is amended as follows.

(9) In subsection (1) (application of section) after paragraph (b) add—

> "This subsection is subject to subsection (1A) below.".

(10) After subsection (1) insert—

> "(1A) In the case of a policy which is a qualifying policy (whether or not the premiums under the policy are eligible for relief under section 266) this section applies only if—

    (*a*) the section 546 excess occurs within the time described in section 540(1)(*b*)(i); or

    (*b*) the policy has been converted into a paid-up policy within that time.''.

(11) The amendments made by subsections (2) to (7) have effect in relation to any assignment on or after 6th April 2002 of the rights conferred by a policy or contract.

(12) The amendments made by subsections (8) to (10) have effect and shall be taken always to have had effect, in relation to any policy, in relation to any year (as defined in section 546(4) of the Taxes Act 1988) beginning on or after 6th April 2001.

Commentary—*Simon's Direct Tax Service* E3.505–507, 509.

International matters

88 Extension of power to give effect to double taxation arrangements

(1) In section 788(1) of the Taxes Act 1988 (relief by agreement with other countries: power to give effect to arrangements), for ''made with the government of any territory'' substitute ''made in relation to any territory''.

(2) The following amendments are consequential on that above—

    (*a*) in sections 788(7)(*a*), 790(3), (5)(*b*), (10A)(*d*) and (10C), 792(1) and (3), 793A(1)(*a*) and (3), 795A(1)(*b*), 812(2), 815AA(1) and 815C(1) of the Taxes Act 1988, for ''with the government of'' substitute ''in relation to'';

    (*b*) in the headings (or sidenotes) to sections 788 and 815C of the Taxes Act 1988, for ''countries'' substitute ''territories'';

    (*c*) in section 816(1) of the Taxes Act 1988, for ''government'' substitute ''authorities'';

    (*d*) in section 816(2) of the Taxes Act 1988, for ''government with'' substitute ''authorities of the territory in relation to'';

    (*e*) in section 816(2ZA) of the Taxes Act 1988, for ''government with'' substitute ''authorities of the territory in relation to'', for ''is bound'' substitute ''are bound'' and for ''has undertaken'' substitute ''have undertaken'';

    (*f*) in sections 277(1) (twice) and (3) and 278(1) of the Taxation of Chargeable Gains Act 1992 (c 12), for ''country'' substitute ''territory''.

(3) This section applies on and after the date on which this Act is passed in relation to arrangements made before that date (as well as in relation to arrangements made on or after that date).

Commentary—*Simon's Direct Tax Service* F1.111.

89 Controlled foreign companies: territorial exclusions from s 748 exemptions

(1) In section 748 of the Taxes Act 1988 (controlled foreign companies: cases where no apportionment falls to be made under section 747(3)) after subsection (5) insert—

    ''(6) This section is subject to section 748A.''.

(2) After section 748 of the Taxes Act 1988 insert—

''748A Territorial exclusions from exemption under section 748.

    (1) Nothing in section 748 prevents an apportionment under section 747(3) falling to be made as regards an accounting period of a controlled foreign company if the company—

        (*a*) is a company incorporated in a territory to which this section applies as respects that accounting period; or

        (*b*) is at any time in that accounting period liable to tax in such a territory by reason of domicile, residence or place of management; or

        (*c*) at any time in that accounting period carries on business through a branch or agency in such a territory.

    (2) The condition in subsection (1)(*c*) above is not satisfied as regards an accounting period of a controlled foreign company if the business carried on by the company in that period through branches or agencies in territories to which this section applies, taken as a whole, is only a minimal part of the whole of the business carried on by the company in that period.

    (3) The territories to which this section applies as respects an accounting period of a controlled foreign company are those specified as such in regulations made by the Treasury.

    (4) Regulations under subsection (3) above—

        (*a*) may make different provision for different cases or with respect to different territories; and

        (*b*) may contain such incidental, supplemental, consequential or transitional provision as the Treasury may think fit.

    (5) A statutory instrument containing regulations under subsection (3) above shall not be made unless a draft of the instrument has been laid before, and approved by a resolution of, the House of Commons.''.

(3) This section has effect in relation to accounting periods of controlled foreign companies beginning on or after the day on which this Act is passed.

(4) In this section "accounting period" and "controlled foreign company" have the same meaning as in Chapter 4 of Part 17 of the Taxes Act 1988.

Commentary—*Simon's Direct Tax Service* **D4.1230.**

90 Controlled foreign companies and treaty non-resident companies

(1) In section 747 of the Taxes Act 1988 (imputation of chargeable profits and creditable tax of controlled foreign companies), after subsection (1A) insert—

"(1B) In determining, for the purposes of any provision of this Chapter except subsection (1)(*a*) above, whether a company is a person resident in the United Kingdom, section 249 of the Finance Act 1994 (under which a company is treated as non-resident if it is so treated for double taxation relief purposes) shall be disregarded.".

(2) Subsection (1)—

    (*a*) shall be deemed to have come into force on 1st April 2002, and
    (*b*) does not apply to a company that—

        (i) by virtue of section 249 of the Finance Act 1994 (c 9) was treated as resident outside the United Kingdom, and not resident in the United Kingdom, immediately before that date, and
        (ii) has not subsequently ceased to be so treated.

Supplementary charge in respect of ring fence trades

Commentary—*Simon's Direct Tax Service* **D4.1202.**

91 Supplementary charge in respect of ring fence trades

After section 501 of the Taxes Act 1988 insert—

"501A Supplementary charge in respect of ring fence trades

(1) Where in any accounting period beginning on or after 17th April 2002 a company carries on a ring fence trade, a sum equal to 10 per cent of its adjusted ring fence profits for that period shall be charged on the company as if it were an amount of corporation tax chargeable on the company.

(2) A company's adjusted ring fence profits for an accounting period are the amount which, on the assumption mentioned in subsection (3) below, would be determined for that period (in accordance with this Chapter) as the profits of the company's ring fence trade chargeable to corporation tax.

(3) The assumption is that financing costs are left out of account in computing—

    (*a*) the amount of the profits or loss of any ring fence trade of the company's for each accounting period beginning on or after 17th April 2002; and
    (*b*) where for any such period the whole or part of any loss relief is surrendered to the company in accordance with section 492(8), the amount of that relief or, as the case may be, that part.

(4) For the purposes of this section, "financing costs" means the costs of debt finance.

(5) In calculating the costs of debt finance for an accounting period the matters to be taken into account include—

    (*a*) any costs giving rise to debits in respect of debtor relationships of the company under Chapter 2 of Part 4 of the Finance Act 1996 (loan relationships);
    (*b*) any exchange gain or loss, within the meaning of Chapter 2 of Part 2 of the Finance Act 1993, in relation to debt finance;
    (*c*) any trading profit or loss, under Chapter 2 of Part 4 of the Finance Act 1994 (interest rate and currency contracts), in relation to debt finance;
    (*d*) the financing cost implicit in a payment under a finance lease; and
    (*e*) any other costs arising from what would be considered in accordance with generally accepted accounting practice to be a financing transaction.

(6) Where an amount representing the whole or part of a payment falling to be made by a company—

    (*a*) falls (or would fall) to be treated as a finance charge under a finance lease for the purposes of accounts relating to that company and one or more other companies and prepared in accordance with generally accepted accounting practice, but
    (*b*) is not so treated in the accounts of the company,

the amount shall be treated for the purposes of this section as financing costs falling within subsection (5)(*d*) above.

(7) If—

    (*a*) in computing the adjusted ring fence profits of a company for an accounting period, an amount falls to be left out of account by virtue of subsection (5)(*d*) above, but
    (*b*) the whole or any part of that amount is repaid,

the repayment shall also be left out of account in computing the adjusted ring fence profits of the company for any accounting period.

(8) In this section "finance lease" means any arrangements—

(*a*) which provide for an asset to be leased or otherwise made available by a person to another person ("the lessee"), and

(*b*) which, under generally accepted accounting practice,—

(i) fall (or would fall) to be treated, in the accounts of the lessee or a person connected with the lessee, as a finance lease or a loan, or

(ii) are comprised in arrangements which fall (or would fall) to be so treated.

(9) For the purposes of applying subsection (8)(*b*) above, the lessee and any person connected with the lessee are to be treated as being companies which are incorporated in a part of the United Kingdom.

(10) In this section "accounts", in relation to a company, includes any accounts which—

(*a*) relate to two or more companies of which that company is one, and

(*b*) are drawn up in accordance with—

(i) section 227 of the Companies Act 1985, or

(ii) Article 235 of the Companies (Northern Ireland) Order 1986.".

Commentary—*Simon's Direct Tax Service* **D4.1002, 1010.**

92 Assessment, recovery and postponement of supplementary charge

(1) After section 501A of the Taxes Act 1988 insert—

"501B Assessment, recovery and postponement of supplementary charge

(1) Subject to subsection (3) below, the provisions of section 501A(1) relating to the charging of a sum as if it were an amount of corporation tax shall be taken as applying, subject to the provisions of the Taxes Acts, and to any necessary modifications, all enactments applying generally to corporation tax, including—

(*a*) those relating to returns of information and the supply of accounts, statements and reports;

(*b*) those relating to the assessing, collecting and receiving of corporation tax;

(*c*) those conferring or regulating a right of appeal; and

(*d*) those concerning administration, penalties, interest on unpaid tax and priority of tax in cases of insolvency under the law of any part of the United Kingdom.

(2) Accordingly (but without prejudice to subsection (1) above) the Management Act shall have effect as if any reference to corporation tax included a reference to a sum chargeable under section 501A(1) as if it were an amount of corporation tax.

(3) In any regulations made under section 32 of the Finance Act 1998 (as at 17th April 2002, the Corporation Tax (Treatment of Unrelieved Surplus Advance Corporation Tax) Regulations 1999)—

(*a*) references to corporation tax do not include a reference to a sum chargeable on a company under section 501A(1) as if it were corporation tax; and

(*b*) references to profits charged to corporation tax do not include a reference to adjusted ring fence profits, within the meaning of section 501A(1).

(4) In this section "the Taxes Acts" has the same meaning as in the Management Act.".

(2) In section 59E of the Taxes Management Act 1970 (c 9) (further provision as to when corporation tax is due and payable) in subsection (11) (extension of references in the section to corporation tax) after paragraph (*b*) add—

"(*c*) to any sum chargeable on a company under section 501A(1) of the principal Act (supplementary charge in respect of ring fence trades) as if it were an amount of corporation tax chargeable on the company".

(3) In Schedule 18 to the Finance Act 1998 (c 36) (company tax returns: assessments and related matters) in paragraph 1 (meaning of "tax") in the second sentence (amounts assessable or chargeable as if they were corporation tax) for the word "and" immediately preceding the paragraph beginning "section 747(4)(*a*)" substitute the following paragraph—

"section 501A(1) of that Act (supplementary charge in respect of ring fence trades), and".

(4) In paragraph 8 of that Schedule (calculation of tax payable) after paragraph number 1 of the third step insert—

"1A Any sum chargeable under section 501A(1) of that Act (supplementary charge in respect of ring fence trades).".

(5) Regulation 3 of the Instalment Payment Regulations (large companies) is amended as follows.

(6) In paragraph (1) (which, subject to paragraphs (2) and (3), defines a large company) for "paragraphs (2) and (3)," substitute "paragraphs (2) to (3A),".

(7) After paragraph (3) insert—

"(3A) Any question whether a company is, or is not, a large company as respects an accounting period beginning on or after 17th April 2002 shall, so far as not falling to be determined by reference to the company's total liability, be determined as it would have been determined apart from section 501A of the Taxes Act (supplementary charge in respect of ring fence trades).''.

(8) The amendment by this section of any provision contained in regulations shall not be taken to have prejudiced any power to make further regulations revoking or amending that provision, whether in relation to the same or any other chargeable periods.

(9) In this section ''the Instalment Payment Regulations'' means the Corporation Tax (Instalment Payments) Regulations 1998 (SI 1998/3175).

Commentary—*Simon's Direct Tax Service* **D4.1002, 1010.**

93 Supplementary charge: transitional provisions

(1) In the case of a straddling period, that is to say, an accounting period which begins before 17th April 2002 and ends on or after that date—

    (*a*) sections 501A and 501B of the Taxes Act 1988 (which are inserted by sections 91 and 92) shall apply as if so much of the straddling period as falls before 17th April 2002, and so much of that period as falls on or after that date, were separate accounting periods; and

    (*b*) all necessary apportionments between the two separate accounting periods shall be made in proportion to the number of days in those periods.

(2) In the case of a straddling period, the Instalment Payment Regulations shall apply separately—

    (*a*) in relation to any tax chargeable on the company under section 501A(1) of the Taxes Act 1988; and

    (*b*) in relation to any other tax chargeable on the company.

(3) In their application by virtue of paragraph (*a*) of subsection (2), the Instalment Payment Regulations shall have effect in relation to the tax mentioned in that paragraph as if—

    (*a*) the deemed accounting period treated under subsection (1)(*a*) as beginning on 17th April 2002 were an accounting period for the purposes of those Regulations; and

    (*b*) that tax were chargeable for that period.

(4) Any reference in the Instalment Payment Regulations to the total liability of a company shall accordingly be construed—

    (*a*) in their application by virtue of paragraph (*a*) of subsection (2), as a reference to the tax mentioned in that paragraph; and

    (*b*) in their application by virtue of paragraph (*b*) of that subsection, as a reference to the amount that would be the company's total liability for the straddling period if the tax mentioned in paragraph (*a*) of that subsection were left out of account.

(5) For the purposes of the Instalment Payment Regulations—

    (*a*) a company shall be regarded as a large company as respects the deemed accounting period under subsection (3)(*a*) if, and only if, it is a large company for those purposes as respects the straddling period; and

    (*b*) any question whether a company is a large company as respects the straddling period shall be determined as it would have been determined apart from section 501A of the Taxes Act 1988.

(6) In this section ''the Instalment Payment Regulations'' has the same meaning as in section 92.

Commentary—*Simon's Direct Tax Service* **D4.1002, 1010.**

Deduction of tax

94 Deduction of tax: payments to exempt bodies etc

(1) In section 349A of the Taxes Act 1988 (exceptions to requirement to deduct tax from certain payments made by a company)—

    (*a*) in subsection (1)—

        (i) after ''by a company'' insert ''or a local authority'', and

        (ii) after ''the company'' insert ''or authority''.

    (*b*) in subsection (6)—

        (i) after ''section'' insert ''(*a*)'', and

        (ii) at the end insert '', and

    (*b*) a payment by a partnership is treated as made by a local authority if any member of the partnership is a local authority''.

(2) In section 349B of that Act (section 349A(1): conditions to be met), after subsection (2) insert—

    ''(3) The third of those conditions is that the payment is made to—

        (*a*) a local authority;

        (*b*) a health service body within the meaning of section 519A(2);

        (*c*) a public office or department of the Crown to which section 829(1) applies;

        (*d*) a charity (within the meaning of section 506(1));

        (*e*) a body for the time being mentioned in section 507(1) (bodies that are allowed the same exemption from tax as charities the whole income of which is applied to charitable purposes);

(*f*) an Association of a description specified in section 508 (scientific research organisations);

(*g*) the United Kingdom Atomic Energy Authority;

(*h*) the National Radiological Protection Board;

(*i*) the administrator (within the meaning of section 611AA) of a scheme entitled to exemption under section 592(2) or 608(2)(*a*) (exempt approved schemes and former approved superannuation funds);

(*j*) the trustees of a scheme entitled to exemption under section 613(4) (Parliamentary pension funds);

(*k*) the persons entitled to receive the income of a fund entitled to exemption under section 614(3) (certain colonial, etc pension funds);

(*l*) the trustees or other persons having the management of a fund entitled to exemption under section 620(6) (retirement annuity trust schemes); or

(*m*) a person holding investments or deposits for the purposes of a scheme entitled to exemption under section 643(2) (approved personal pension schemes).

(4) The fourth of those conditions is that—

(*a*) the person to whom the payment is made is, or is the nominee of, the plan manager of a plan,

(*b*) an individual investing under the plan is entitled to exemption by virtue of regulations under section 333 (personal equity plans and individual savings accounts), and

(*c*) the plan manager receives the payment in respect of investments under the plan.

(5) The fifth of those conditions is that—

(*a*) the person to whom the payment is made is a society or institution with whom tax-exempt special savings accounts (within the meaning of section 326A) may be held, and

(*b*) the society or institution receives the payment in respect of investments held for the purposes of such accounts.

(6) The sixth of those conditions is that the person beneficially entitled to the income in respect of which the payment is made is a partnership each member of which is—

(*a*) a person or body mentioned in subsection (3) above, or

(*b*) a person or body mentioned in subsection (7) below.

(7) The persons and bodies referred to in subsection (6)(*b*) above are—

(*a*) a company resident in the United Kingdom;

(*b*) a company that—

(i) is not resident in the United Kingdom,

(ii) carries on a trade there through a branch or agency, and

(iii) is required to bring into account, in computing its chargeable profits (within the meaning of section 11(2)), the whole of any share of that payment that falls to it by reason of sections 114 and 115;

(*c*) the European Investment Fund.

(8) The Treasury may by order amend—

(*a*) subsection (3) above;

(*b*) subsection (7) above;

so as to add to, restrict or otherwise alter the persons and bodies falling within that subsection.''.

(3) In section 349C (directions disapplying section 349A(1))—

(*a*) in subsection (1)—

(i) after ''a company'' insert ''or local authority'', and

(ii) after ''the company'' insert ''or authority'',

(*b*) in subsection (2) for ''neither'' substitute ''none'', and

(*c*) for subsection (4) substitute—

''(4) In this section—

''company'' includes a partnership of which any member is a company; and

''local authority'' includes a partnership of which any member is a local authority.''.

(4) In section 349D (section 349A(1): consequences of reasonable but incorrect belief)—

(*a*) in subsection (1)—

(i) in paragraph (*a*) after ''company'' insert ''or local authority'',

(ii) in paragraphs (*b*) and (*c*) after ''company'' insert ''or authority'', and

(iii) in paragraph (*d*) for ''neither'' substitute ''none'', and

(*b*) for subsection (2) substitute—

''(2) In this section—

''company'' includes a partnership of which any member is a company; and

''local authority'' includes a partnership of which any member is a local authority.''.

(5) In section 98 of the Taxes Management Act 1970 (c 9) (special returns, etc), in subsection (4B)—

(*a*) in paragraph (*a*), after ''a company'' insert ''or local authority'',

(*b*) in paragraph (*b*)—

(i) after "the company" insert "or authority", and
(ii) for "either", in each place, substitute "one",

(*c*) in paragraph (*c*), after "the company" insert "or authority", and
(*d*) in paragraph (*d*), for "neither" substitute "none".

(6) In that section, for subsection (4C) substitute—

"(4C) In subsection (4B) above—

'company' includes a partnership of which any member is a company; and
'local authority' includes a partnership of which any member is a local authority.".

(7) The amendments made by this section apply for the purposes of payments made on or after 1st October 2002.

Commentary—Simon's Direct Tax Service **A3.426.**

95 Deduction of tax by persons dealing in financial instruments

(1) Section 349 of the Taxes Act 1988 (payment of annual interest etc) is amended as follows.

(2) In subsection (3) (cases where obligation to make interest payments net of tax does not apply), at the end insert "or

(i) in the case of a person who is authorised for the purposes of the Financial Services and Markets Act 2000 and whose business consists wholly or mainly of dealing in financial instruments as principal, to interest paid by that person in the ordinary course of his business.".

(3) After subsection (4) insert—

"(5) For the purposes of subsection (3)(i) above, a financial instrument includes—

(*a*) any money,
(*b*) any shares or securities,
(*c*) an option, future or contract for differences if, but only if, its underlying subject-matter is (or is primarily) a financial instrument, or financial instruments, and
(*d*) an instrument the underlying subject-matter of which is (or is primarily) creditworthiness.

(6) For the purposes of subsection (5) above, the "underlying" subject-matter of an instrument the effect of which depends on an index or factor is the matter by reference to which the index or factor is determined.".

(4) This section applies in relation to the payment of interest on or after 1st October 2002.

Commentary—Simon's Direct Tax Service **A3.426.**

96 Cross-border royalties

(1) After section 349D of the Taxes Act 1988 insert—

"349E Deductions under section 349(1): payment of royalties overseas

(1) Where—

(*a*) a company makes a payment of a royalty to which section 349(1) applies, and
(*b*) the company reasonably believes that, at the time the payment is made, the payee is entitled to relief in respect of the payment under any arrangements under section 788 (double taxation relief),

the company may, if it thinks fit, calculate the sum to be deducted from the payment under section 349(1) by reference to the rate of income tax appropriate to the payee pursuant to the arrangements.

(2) But, where the payee is not at that time entitled to such relief, section 350 and Schedule 16 shall have effect as if subsection (1) above never applied in relation to the payment.

(3) Where the Board are not satisfied that the payee will be entitled to such relief in respect of one or more payments to be made by a company, they may direct the company that subsection (1) above is not to apply to the payment or payments.

(4) A direction under subsection (3) above may be varied or revoked by a subsequent such direction.

(5) In this section—

"payee", in relation to a payment, means the person beneficially entitled to the income in respect of which the payment is made; and
"royalty" includes—

(*a*) any payment received as a consideration for the use of, or the right to use, any copyright, patent, trade mark, design, process or information, or
(*b*) any proceeds of sale of all or any part of any patent rights.

(6) Paragraph 3(1) of Schedule 18 to the Finance Act 1998 (c 36) (requirement to make return in respect of information relevant to application of Corporation Tax Acts) has effect as if the reference to the Corporation Tax Acts included a reference to this section.

(7) Paragraph 20 of that Schedule (penalties for incorrect returns), in its application to an error relating to information required in a return by virtue of subsection (6) above, has effect as if—

    (*a*) the reference in sub-paragraph (1) to a tax-related penalty were a reference to an amount not exceeding £3000, and

    (*b*) sub-paragraphs (2) and (3) were omitted.''.

(2) In section 350(1A) of that Act, at the end insert ''(or, where the payment is one to which subsection (1) of section 349E applies, the rate referred to in that subsection)''.

(3) In section 98 of the Taxes Management Act 1970 (c 9) (special returns etc)—

    (*a*) in subsection (4A)(*b*), after ''subsection (4B)'' insert ''or (4D)'', and

    (*b*) after subsection (4C) insert—

''(4D) A payment is within this subsection if—

    (*a*) it is a payment to which section 349(1) of the principal Act (requirement to deduct tax) applies,

    (*b*) it is made by a company which, purporting to rely on section 349E(1) of that Act (power for companies to take account of double taxation treaty relief when paying royalties), deducts less tax from the payment than required by section 349(1) of that Act, and

    (*c*) at the time the payment is made the payee (within the meaning of section 349E of that Act) is not entitled to relief in respect of the payment under any arrangements under section 788 of that Act (double taxation relief) and the company—

        (i) does not believe that it is entitled to such relief, or

        (ii) if it does so believe, cannot reasonably do so.''.

(4) This section applies in relation to payments made on or after 1st October 2002.

Commentary—*Simon's Direct Tax Service* A3.426.

Charitable giving

97 Gifts of real property to charity

(1) In section 587B of the Taxes Act 1988 (gifts of shares and securities to charities) in subsection (9), in the definition of ''qualifying investment'', omit the word ''and'' immediately preceding paragraph (*d*) and at the end of that paragraph insert

    ''; and

    (*e*) a qualifying interest in land''.

(2) After that subsection insert—

''(9A) In this section a ''qualifying interest in land'' means—

    (*a*) a freehold interest in land, or

    (*b*) a leasehold interest in land which is a term of years absolute,

where the land in question is in the United Kingdom.

This subsection is subject to subsections (9B) to (9D) below.

(9B) Where a person makes a disposal to a charity of—

    (*a*) the whole of his beneficial interest in such freehold or leasehold interest in land as is described in subsection (9A)(*a*) or (*b*) above, and

    (*b*) any easement, servitude, right or privilege so far as benefiting that land,

the disposal falling within paragraph (*b*) above is to be regarded for the purposes of this section as a disposal by the person of the whole of his beneficial interest in a qualifying interest in land.

(9C) Where a person who has a freehold or leasehold interest in land in the United Kingdom grants a lease for a term of years absolute (or, in the case of land in Scotland, grants a lease) to a charity of the whole or part of that land, the grant of that lease is to be regarded for the purposes of this section as a disposal by the person of the whole of the beneficial interest in the leasehold interest so granted.

(9D) For the purposes of subsection (9A) above, an agreement to acquire a freehold interest and an agreement for a lease are not qualifying interests in land.

(9E) In the application of this section to Scotland—

    (*a*) references to a freehold interest in land are references to the interest of the owner,

    (*b*) references to a leasehold interest in land which is a term of years absolute are references to a tenant's right over or interest in a property subject to a lease, and

    (*c*) references to an agreement for a lease do not include references to missives of let that constitute an actual lease.''.

(3) After subsection (11) of that section insert—

''(12) This section is supplemented by section 587C below.''.

(4) In consequence of the amendments made by subsections (1) to (3), the sidenote of section 587B becomes ''Gifts of shares, securities and real property to charities etc''.

(5) After section 587B of the Taxes Act 1988 insert—

"587C Supplementary provision for gifts of real property

(1) This section applies for the purposes of section 587B where a qualifying investment is a qualifying interest in land.

(2) Where two or more persons—

(a) are jointly beneficially entitled to the qualifying interest in land, or

(b) are, taken together, beneficially entitled in common to the qualifying interest in land,

section 587B applies only if each of those persons disposes of the whole of his beneficial interest in the qualifying interest in land to the charity.

(3) Relief under section 587B shall be available to each of the persons referred to in subsection (2) above, but the amount that may be allowed as respects any of them shall be only such share of the relevant amount as they may agree in the case of that person.

(4) No person may make a claim for a relief under subsection (2) of section 587B unless he has received a certificate given by or on behalf of the charity.

(5) The certificate must—

(a) specify the description of the qualifying interest in land which is the subject of the disposal,

(b) specify the date of the disposal, and

(c) contain a statement that the charity has acquired the qualifying interest in land.

(6) If, in the case of a disposal of a qualifying interest in land, a disqualifying event occurs at any time in the relevant period, the person (or each of the persons) who made the disposal to the charity shall be treated as never having been entitled to relief under section 587B in respect of the disposal.

(7) All such assessments and adjustments of assessments are to be made as are necessary to give effect to subsection (6) above.

(8) For the purposes of subsection (6) above a disqualifying event occurs if the person (or any one of the persons) who made the disposal or any person connected with him (or any one of them)—

(a) becomes entitled to an interest or right in relation to all or part of the land to which the disposal relates, or

(b) becomes party to an arrangement under which he enjoys some right in relation to all or part of that land,

otherwise than for full consideration in money or money's worth.

(9) A disqualifying event does not occur, for the purposes of subsection (6) above, if a person becomes entitled to an interest or right as mentioned in subsection (8)(a) above as a result of a disposition of property on death, whether the disposition is effected by will, under the law relating to intestacy or otherwise.

(10) For the purposes of subsection (6) above the relevant period is the period beginning with the date of the disposal of the qualifying interest in land and ending with—

(a) in the case of an individual, the fifth anniversary of the 31st January next following the end of the year of assessment in which the disposal was made, and

(b) in the case of a company, the sixth anniversary of the end of the accounting period in which the disposal was made.

(11) Section 839 (connected persons) applies for the purposes of this section.

(12) This section shall be construed as one with section 587B.".

(6) This section has effect in relation to any disposal of a qualifying interest in land to a charity where the disposal is made—

(a) in the case of a disposal to the charity by an individual, on or after 6th April 2002, or

(b) in the case of a disposal to the charity by a company, on or after 1st April 2002.

(7) Subsection (9E)(a) of section 587B of the Taxes Act 1988 has effect until the appointed day as if for "the interest of the owner" there were substituted "the estate or interest of the proprietor of the *dominium utile* (or, in the case of property other than feudal property, of the owner)".

(8) For the purposes of subsection (7) "the appointed day" means such day as may be appointed by the Scottish Ministers under section 71 of the Abolition of Feudal Tenure etc (Scotland) Act 2000 for the purposes of the Act.

Commentary—*Simon's Direct Tax Service* E1.501.

98 Gift aid: election to be treated as if gift made in previous tax year

(1) A person ("the donor") who makes a gift that is a qualifying donation within section 25 of the Finance Act 1990 (c 29) (gift aid) may elect to be treated for the purposes of that section as if the gift were a qualifying donation made by him in the previous year of assessment.

(2) Any such election must be made by notice in writing to an officer of the Inland Revenue—

(*a*) on or before the date on which the donor delivers his return for the previous year of assessment under section 8 of the Taxes Management Act 1970 (c 9) (personal return), and

(*b*) not later than the 31st January next following the end of that year.

(3) No such election may be made unless in the previous year the grossed up amount of the gift would, if made in that year, be payable out of profits or gains brought into charge to income tax or capital gains tax.

(4) The effect of an election under this section is that the provisions of section 25(6) to (9A) of the Finance Act 1990 (c 29) have effect in relation to the donor as if the gift were a qualifying donation made in the previous year of assessment.

(5) An election under this section does not affect the position of the recipient of the gift.

The reference in section 25(10) of the Finance Act 1990 to the relevant year of assessment shall be construed accordingly as a reference to the year of assessment in which the gift is actually made.

(6) This section has effect in relation to gifts made on or after 6th April 2003.

Commentary—*Simon's Direct Tax Service* **E1.504A.**

Films

99 Restriction of relief to films genuinely intended for theatrical release

(1) Relief under the following provisions is available only for a film that is genuinely intended for theatrical release—

(*a*) section 40D of the Finance (No 2) Act 1992 (c 48) (election to claim capital allowances for production or acquisition expenditure);

(*b*) section 41 of that Act (relief for pre-production expenditure);

(*c*) section 42 of that Act (three year write-off for production or acquisition expenditure);

(*d*) section 48 of the Finance (No 2) Act 1997 (c 58) (relief for expenditure on production or acquisition of film with total production expenditure of £15 million or less).

(2) For the purposes of subsection (1)—

(*a*) the relevant intention is the intention at the time the film is completed of the person then entitled to determine how the film is to be exploited;

(*b*) "theatrical release" means exhibition to the paying public at the commercial cinema;

(*c*) a film is not regarded as genuinely intended for theatrical release unless it is intended that a significant proportion of the earnings from the film should be obtained by such exhibition.

(3) Subject to the following provisions, this section applies to any film—

(*a*) completed on or after 17th April 2002, or

(*b*) completed before 1st January 2002 but not certified by the Secretary of State before 17th April 2002.

unless an application for certification was received by the Secretary of State before 17th April 2002.

References in this subsection to certification are to certification of the master version of the film under Schedule 1 to the Films Act 1985 (c 21) as a qualifying film, tape or disc.

(4) This section does not apply to a film completed on or after 17th April 2002 if—

(*a*) it is a drama with an average production expenditure per hour of running time of the completed film greater than £500,000, and

(*b*) it was commissioned on or before 17th April 2002 and the first day of principal photography was on or before 30th June 2002.

(5) For the purposes of subsection (4) "drama" does not include—

(*a*) anything in the nature of—

(i) an advertisement or promotional film,

(ii) a discussion programme, news or current affairs programme, quiz show, panel show, variety show or similar entertainment, or

(iii) a training film, or

(*b*) a film of a live event or of a theatrical or artistic performance given otherwise than for the purpose of being filmed;

but it includes a documentary involving the dramatic reconstruction of events if the dramatic content forms 50% or more of the running time.

(6) For the purposes of this section—

(*a*) a film is completed at the time when it is first in a form in which it can reasonably be regarded as ready for copies of it to be made and distributed for presentation to the general public;

(*b*) the production expenditure on a film means the total of all expenditure on the production of the film, whenever incurred and whether or not incurred by the person claiming relief; and

(*c*) subsections (6A) and (7) of section 48 of the Finance (No. 2) Act 1997 (c 58) (production expenditure: exclusion of deferments and treatment of transactions not at arm's length) apply as they apply for the purposes of that section.

Commentary—*Simon's Direct Tax Service* **B3.1307B.**

100 Exclusion of deferments from production expenditure

(1) Section 48 of the Finance (No 2) Act 1997 (c 58) (relief for expenditure on production or acquisition of qualifying film with total production expenditure of £15 million or less) is amended as follows.

(2) In subsection (6) (meaning of "total production expenditure"), for "subject to subsection (7)" substitute "subject to subsections (6A) and (7)".

(3) After that subsection insert—

"(6A) For the purposes of this section the production expenditure on a film shall be taken not to include any amount that at the time the film is completed—

(a) has not been paid, and

(b) is not the subject of an unconditional obligation to pay within four months after the date of completion.".

(4) This section applies to films completed on or after 17th April 2002.

For this purpose a film is completed at the time when it is first in a form in which it can reasonably be regarded as ready for copies of it to be made and distributed for presentation to the general public.

Commentary—*Simon's Direct Tax Service* **B3.1307B.**

101 Restriction of relief for successive acquisitions of the same film

(1) Relief under section 48 of the Finance (No 2) Act 1997 (relief for expenditure on production or acquisition of film with total production expenditure of £15 million or less) in respect of acquisition expenditure is available only in relation to an acquisition—

(a) by the producer, or

(b) directly from the producer,

and not in relation to any subsequent acquisition (or in relation to any acquisition within paragraph (a) or (b) other than the first).

(2) For this purpose—

(a) "acquisition expenditure" means expenditure to which subsection (3) of section 42 of the Finance (No 2) Act 1992 (c 48) applies (relief for acquisition expenditure);

(b) "acquisition" means acquisition of the master negative of a film, or any master tape or master disc of a film, within the meaning of that section; and

(c) "the producer" means the person who commissions the making of the film and is entitled to control its exploitation.

(3) This section applies to acquisition expenditure incurred on or after 30th June 2002.

For this purpose when expenditure is incurred shall be determined as for the purposes of section 48 of the Finance (No 2) Act 1997 (c 58) see subsection (9) of that section).

Commentary—*Simon's Direct Tax Service* **B3.1307B.**

Miscellaneous

102 Distributions: reasonable commercial return for use of principal secured

(1) In section 209 of the Taxes Act 1988 (meaning of "distribution") after subsection (3A) insert—

"(3AA) If, in the case of any security issued by a company, the amount of new consideration received by the company for the issue of the security exceeds the amount of the principal secured by the security—

(a) the amount of the principal so secured shall be treated for the purposes of paragraph (d) of subsection (2) above as increased to the amount of the new consideration so received; and

(b) subsection (3A) above, so far as relating to that paragraph, shall not have effect in relation to the security;

but this subsection is subject to sections 209A and 209B.".

(2) After that section insert—

"209A Section 209(3AA): link to shares of company or associated company

(1) Subsection (3AA) of section 209 does not apply in relation to a security issued by a company (the "issuing company") if the security is one which to a significant extent reflects dividends or other distributions in respect of, or fluctuations in the value of, shares in one or more companies each of which is—

(a) the issuing company; or

(b) an associated company of the issuing company;

but this subsection is subject to the following provisions of this section.

(2) Subsection (1) above does not prevent subsection (3AA) of section 209 above from applying in relation to a security if—

(a) the issuing company is a bank or securities house;

(b) the security is issued by the issuing company in the ordinary course of its business; and (*c*) the security reflects dividends or other distributions in respect of, or fluctuations in the value of, shares in companies falling within paragraph (*a*) or (*b*) of subsection (1) above by reason only that the security reflects fluctuations in a qualifying index.

(3) In subsection (2)(*c*) above "qualifying index" means an index whose underlying subject matter includes both—

> (*a*) shares in one or more companies falling within paragraph (*a*) or (*b*) of subsection (1) above, and
>
> (*b*) shares in one or more companies falling within neither of those paragraphs,

and which is an index such that the shares falling within paragraph (*b*) above represent a significant proportion of the market value of the underlying subject matter of the index.

(4) In this section—

> "bank" has the meaning given by section 840A;
> "securities house" means any person—
>
> > (*a*) who is authorised for the purposes of the Financial Services and Markets Act 2000; and
> >
> > (*b*) whose business consists wholly or mainly of dealing in financial instruments as principal;
>
> and in paragraph (*b*) above "financial instrument" has the meaning given by section 349(5) and (6).

(5) For the purposes of this section a company is an "associated company" of another at any time if at that time one has control of the other or both are under the control of the same person or persons.

(6) For the purposes of subsection (5) above, "control", in relation to a company, means the power of a person to secure—

> (*a*) by means of the holding of shares or the possession of voting power in or in relation to the company or any other company, or
>
> (*b*) by virtue of any powers conferred by the articles of association or other document regulating the company or any other company,

that the affairs of the company are conducted in accordance with his wishes.

(7) There shall be left out of account for the purposes of subsection (6) above—

> (*a*) any shares held by a company, and
>
> (*b*) any voting power or other powers arising from shares held by a company,

if a profit on a sale of the shares would be treated as a trading receipt of a trade carried on by the company and the shares are not, within the meaning of Chapter 1 of Part 12, assets of an insurance company's long-term insurance fund (see section 431(2)).

209B Section 209(3AA): hedging arrangements

(1) Subsection (3AA) of section 209 does not at any time apply in relation to a security issued by a company (the "issuing company") if at that time, or any earlier time on or after 17th April 2002, there are or have been any hedging arrangements that relate to some or all of the company's liabilities under the security.

(2) Subsection (1) above does not prevent subsection (3AA) of section 209 from applying in relation to a security at any time if—

> (*a*) conditions 1 to 4 below are satisfied in relation to any such hedging arrangements at that time; and
>
> (*b*) at all earlier times on or after 17th April 2002 when there have been hedging arrangements that relate to some or all of the company's liabilities under the security, conditions 1 to 4 below were satisfied in relation to those hedging arrangements.

(3) Where subsection (3AA) of section 209 at any time ceases to apply in relation to a security by virtue of this section, subsection (2)(*d*) of that section shall have effect in relation to the security as from that time as it would have had effect if subsection (3AA) had never applied in relation to the security.

(4) Condition 1 is that the hedging arrangements do not constitute, include, or form part of, any scheme or arrangement the purpose or one of the main purposes of which is the avoidance of tax or stamp duty.

(5) Condition 2 is that the hedging arrangements are such that, where for the purposes of corporation tax a deduction in respect of the security falls to be made at any time by the issuing company, then at that time, or within a reasonable time before or after it, any amounts intended under the hedging arrangements to offset some or all of that deduction arise—

> (*a*) to the issuing company; or
>
> (*b*) to a company which is a member of the same group of companies as the issuing company.

(6) Condition 3 is that the whole of every amount arising as mentioned in subsection (5) above is brought into charge to corporation tax—

(*a*) by a company falling within paragraph (*a*) or (*b*) of that subsection, or

(*b*) by two or more companies, taken together, each of which falls within paragraph (*a*) or (*b*) of that subsection.

(7) Condition 4 is that for the purposes of corporation tax any deductions in respect of expenses of establishing or administering the hedging arrangements are reasonable, in proportion to the amounts required to be brought into charge to corporation tax by subsection (6) above.

(8) For the purposes of this section "hedging arrangements", in relation to a security, means any scheme or arrangement for the purpose, or for purposes which include the purpose, of securing that an amount of income or gain accrues, or is received or receivable, whether directly or indirectly, which is intended to offset some or all of the amounts which fall to be brought into account, in accordance with generally accepted accounting practice, in respect of amounts accruing or falling to be paid in accordance with the terms of the security.

(9) Any reference in this section to two companies being members of the same group of companies is a reference to their being members of the same group of companies for the purposes of Chapter 4 of Part 10 of this Act (group relief).".

(3) This section has effect in relation to interest and other distributions out of assets of a company in respect of securities of the company where the interest is paid, or the distribution is made, on or after 17th April 2002.

Commentary—*Simon's Direct Tax Service* **D1.122.**

103 References to accounting practice and periods of account

(1) In section 832(1) of the Taxes Act 1988 (interpretation of the Tax Acts), at the appropriate places insert—

    ""generally accepted accounting practice" has the meaning given by section 836A;";

    ""for accounting purposes" means for the purposes of accounts drawn up in accordance with generally accepted accounting practice;"; and

    ""period of account"—

        (*a*) in relation to a person, means any period for which the person draws up accounts, and

        (*b*) in relation to a trade, profession, vocation or other business means any period for which accounts of the business are drawn up;".

(2) After section 836 of that Act insert—

"836A Generally accepted accounting practice

(1) In the Tax Acts, unless the context otherwise requires, "generally accepted accounting practice"—

    (*a*) means generally accepted accounting practice with respect to accounts of UK companies that are intended to give a true and fair view, and

    (*b*) has the same meaning in relation to—

        (i) individuals,

        (ii) entities other than companies, and

        (iii) companies that are not UK companies,

as it has in relation to UK companies.

(2) In subsection (1) "UK companies" means companies incorporated or formed under the law of a part of the United Kingdom.".

(3) In section 288(1) of the Taxation of Chargeable Gains Act 1992 (interpretation), at the appropriate place insert—

    ""period of account" has the meaning given by section 832(1) of the Taxes Act;".

(4) In the following provisions for "normal accounting practice" or "normal accountancy practice", wherever occurring, substitute "generally accepted accounting practice"—

    (*a*) in the Taxes Act 1988, sections 43A(1), 297(5B), 494AA(2), 798B(1) and 837A(2), and in Schedule 28B, paragraph 4(6B);

    (*b*) in the Finance Act 1993 (c 34), sections 93(2), 150(6)(*c*) and (11)(*c*), 154(11)(*c*), (12)(*d*), (13)(*b*), (13A)(*d*) and (13B)(*d*), 155(7), (11)(*d*) and (12)(*b*), 156(2)(*e*) and (4)(*b*) and 159(1)(*b*);

    (*c*) in the Finance Act 1994 (c 9), section 156(3)(*a*) and (4)(*a*);

    (*d*) in the Finance Act 1996 (c 8), sections 84(2)(*b*) and 85(2)(*a*), in Schedule 9, paragraph 14(1) and (2) and in Schedule 10, paragraph 1(3)(*a*) and (4);

    (*e*) in the Finance Act 1997 (c 16), in Schedule 12, paragraphs 1(1)(*c*) and (2)(*a*), 3(1) and (2), 4(5), 6(1)(*a*), 15(1)(*c*) and (2), 22, 28(5) and 30(1);

    (*f*) in the Finance Act 2000 (c 17), in Schedule 14, paragraph 22(4), in Schedule 15, paragraph 29(4), in Schedule 20, paragraphs 6(1), 10(1)(*b*) and (2)(*b*)(ii) and 25(1), and in Schedule 23, paragraphs 2(1), 3(1) and (3) and 5;

    (*g*) in the Capital Allowances Act 2001 (c 2), sections 179(1)(*f*), 219(1) and 437;

    (*h*) in the Finance Act 2001 (c 9), in Schedule 22, paragraphs 10(1)(*b*) and (2)(*b*)(ii).

(5) In section 42(1) of the Finance Act 1998 (c 36) (computation of profits of trade, profession or vocation), for ''on an accounting basis which gives a true and fair view'' substitute ''in accordance with generally accepted accounting practice''.

(6) The amendments made by subsections (1) to (3) above have effect for the purposes of provisions of this Act using the expressions mentioned (including provisions inserted by amendment in other enactments) whenever those provisions are expressed to have effect or to come, or to have come, into force. This is without prejudice to the general effect of those amendments.

Commentary—*Simon's Direct Tax Service* **A1.152.**

104 Discounted securities etc

(1) Schedule 13 to the Finance Act 1996 (discounted securities: income tax provisions) is amended as follows.

(2) After paragraph 3 (meaning of ''relevant discounted security'') insert—

> *''Issue price etc of securities issued in accordance with qualifying earn-out right*

3A—(1) This paragraph applies where a security is issued to a person in accordance with the terms of a qualifying earn-out right.

(2) In any such case the issue price of the security shall be taken for the purposes of this Schedule to be the sum of—

> (*a*) the market value, immediately before the issue of the security, of the right to be issued with the security in accordance with the terms of the qualifying earn-out right, and
> (*b*) any amount payable for the issue of the security in accordance with those terms,

and any reference in this Schedule to the amount paid by the person in respect of his acquisition of the security shall be taken as a reference to that sum.

(3) For the purposes of this paragraph a ''qualifying earn-out right'' is so much of any right conferred on a person as—

> (*a*) constitutes the whole or any part of the consideration for the transfer by him of shares in or debentures of a company or for the transfer of the whole or part of a business or interest in a business carried on by him or by him and others in partnership;
> (*b*) consists in either a right to be issued with securities of another company or a right which is capable of being discharged in accordance with its terms by the issue of such securities; and
> (*c*) is such that the value of the consideration mentioned in paragraph (*a*) above is unascertainable at the time when the right is conferred.''.

(3) After paragraph 9 (other transactions deemed to be at market value) insert—

> *''Securities issued to connected person etc at price in excess of market value: transfer to connected person*

9A—(1) Where a relevant discounted security is transferred by a person (''the relevant person'') to a person connected with him and—

> (*a*) the occasion of the relevant person's acquisition of the security was its issue to him,
> (*b*) the relevant person was, at the time of issue, connected with the issuer or the conditions in sub-paragraph (2) below are satisfied, and
> (*c*) the amount paid by the relevant person in respect of his acquisition of the security exceeds the market value of the security at the time of issue,

the relevant person shall be taken for the purposes of this Schedule not to sustain a loss from the discount on the relevant discounted security.

(2) The conditions mentioned in sub-paragraph (1)(*b*) above are that—

> (*a*) the security is a security issued by a close company;
> (*b*) at the time of issue, the relevant person was not connected with the company;
> (*c*) securities of the same kind as that issued to him were also issued to other persons; and
> (*d*) he and some or all of those other persons, taken together, controlled the company.

(3) In sub-paragraph (2)(*d*) above, ''control'' shall be construed in accordance with section 416 of the Taxes Act 1988.

(4) For the purposes of this section, section 414 of the Taxes Act 1988 (meaning of ''close company'' in the Tax Acts) shall have effect with the omission of subsection (1)(*a*) (exclusion of companies not resident in the United Kingdom).

(5) Section 839 of the Taxes Act 1988 (connected persons) shall apply for the purposes of this paragraph.''.

(4) Schedule 13 to the Finance Act 1996 (c 8) shall have effect, and be deemed always to have had effect, with the amendment made by subsection (2).

(5) The amendment made by subsection (3) has effect in relation to transfers on and after 26th March 2002.

Commentary—*Simon's Direct Tax Service* **A7.602.**

105 Financial trading stock

(1) In section 100 of the Taxes Act 1988 (valuation of trading stock at discontinuance of trade) in subsection (1B), omit paragraph (a) (which relates to stock consisting of certain debts and is superseded by Chapter 2 of Part 4 of the Finance Act 1996 (c 8) (loan relationships)).

(2) In Schedule 12 to the Finance Act 1988 (c 39) (building societies: change of status)—

(a) in paragraph 1 (which provides that paragraphs 2 to 7 apply where there is a transfer of the whole of a building society's business to a successor company in accordance with section 97 etc of the Building Societies Act 1986 (c 53)) for "2" substitute "3"; and

(b) omit paragraph 2 (which relates to gilt-edged securities and other financial trading stock and is superseded by Chapter 2 of Part 4 of the Finance Act 1996).

Commentary—*Simon's Direct Tax Service* **B3.1016.**

106 Valuation of trading stock on transfer of trade

(1) In section 100 of the Taxes Act 1988 (valuation of trading stock at discontinuance of trade), after subsection (2) insert—

"(3) Where trading stock falling to be valued under paragraph (a) of subsection (1) above is sold or transferred together with other assets, so much of the amount realised on the sale or, as the case may be, of the value of the consideration given for the transfer as on a just and reasonable apportionment is properly attributable to each asset shall be treated for the purposes of this section as the amount realised on the sale or, as the case may be, the value of the consideration given for the transfer, of that asset.".

(2) Subsection (1) applies where the sale or transfer in question takes place after the passing of this Act.

Commentary—*Simon's Direct Tax Service* **B3.1016.**

107 Banks etc in compulsory liquidation

(1) Schedule 12 to the Finance (No 2) Act 1992 (c 48) is amended is follows.

(2) In paragraph 3 (taxation of certain receipts under Case VI of Schedule D) omit paragraph (c) of sub-paragraph (3) (which has become unnecessary because no interest or dividends any longer fall within it).

(3) At the end of paragraph 3, insert—

"(5) This paragraph and paragraph 4 below have effect for the purposes of corporation tax notwithstanding anything in section 80(5) of the Finance Act 1996 (matters to be brought into account in the case of loan relationships only under Chapter 2 of Part 4 of that Act).".

(4) In paragraph 4 (relief from tax) omit sub-paragraph (3) (which provides for deductions from sums excluded from paragraph 3(2) by paragraph 3(3)(c)).

(5) The amendments made by this section have effect in relation to accounting periods beginning on or after 1st October 2002.

Commentary—*Simon's Direct Tax Service* **D4.1121.**

108 Manufactured dividends and interest

(1) Schedule 23A to the Taxes Act 1988 (manufactured dividends and interest) is amended as follows.

(2) In paragraph 2A (manufactured dividends on UK equities: deductibility of manufactured payment in case of manufacturer) at the end of sub-paragraph (1) (amount paid to be deductible against total income) insert ", subject to sub-paragraph (1A) below".

(3) After that sub-paragraph insert—

"(1A) An amount shall be allowable under sub-paragraph (1) above as a deduction against total income only to the extent that—

(a) the dividend manufacturer receives the dividend on the equities which is represented by the manufactured dividend, or receives a payment which is representative of that dividend, and is chargeable to income tax on the dividend or other payment so received;

(b) the dividend manufacturer is treated under section 730A (repos) as receiving a payment of interest in respect of the equities and is chargeable to income tax on that payment; or

(c) a chargeable gain accrues to the dividend manufacturer as a result of a transaction whose nature is such as to give rise to the payment of a manufactured dividend by him,

but the amount allowable by virtue of paragraph (c) above is limited to so much of the chargeable gain as does not exceed the manufactured dividend paid as a result of the transaction.

(1B) Where an amount is allowable under sub-paragraph (1) above by reference to the whole or any part of—

(a) a dividend or other payment falling within paragraph (a) of sub-paragraph (1A) above,

(b) a payment of interest which a person is treated as receiving, as mentioned in paragraph (b) of that sub-paragraph, or

(c) a chargeable gain falling within paragraph (c) of that sub-paragraph,

(the "utilised portion" of the dividend, other payment or chargeable gain) no other amount shall be allowable under sub-paragraph (1) above by reference to all or any of the utilised portion of the dividend, other payment or chargeable gain.".

(4) In paragraph 3 (manufactured interest on UK securities) in sub-paragraph (2) (tax treatment of interest manufacturer) in paragraph (c) (amount allowable as a deduction) at the end add ", but only to the extent that—

      (i) it would be so allowable if it were interest, or

      (ii) so far as not falling within sub-paragraph (i) above, it falls within sub-paragraph (2A) below".

(5) After that sub-paragraph insert—

"(2A) An amount of manufactured interest falls within this sub-paragraph if and to the extent that the interest manufacturer—

(a) receives the periodical payment of interest on the securities which is represented by the manufactured interest, or receives a payment which is representative of that periodical payment of interest, and is chargeable to income tax on the periodical payment or representative payment so received;

(b) is treated under section 713(2)(a) or (3)(b) (accrued income scheme) as entitled to a sum in respect of a transfer of the securities and is chargeable to income tax on that sum; or

(c) is treated under section 730A (repos) as receiving a payment of interest in respect of the securities and is chargeable to income tax on that payment.

(2B) Where an amount is allowable under sub-paragraph (2)(c) above by reference to the whole or any part of—

(a) a periodical payment of interest, or a payment representative of such a payment, falling within paragraph (a) of sub-paragraph (2A) above,

(b) a sum falling within paragraph (b) of that sub-paragraph, or

(c) a payment of interest which a person is treated as receiving, as mentioned in paragraph (c) of that sub-paragraph,

(the "utilised portion" of the interest, sum or other payment) no other amount shall be allowable under sub-paragraph (2)(c) above by reference to all or any of the utilised portion of the interest, sum or other payment.".

(6) The amendments made by subsections (2) and (3) have effect in relation to manufactured dividends paid on or after 17th April 2002.

(7) The amendments made by subsections (4) and (5) have effect in relation to manufactured interest paid on or after 17th April 2002.

Commentary—*Simon's Direct Tax Service* A7.807, 811.

109 Venture capital trusts

(1) Schedule 33 to this Act has effect.

(2) In that Schedule—

Part 1 enables regulations to make provision for cases where a venture capital trust is being wound up,

Part 2 enables regulations to make provision for cases where there is a merger of two or more venture capital trusts,

Part 3 enables regulations to make provision about the time allowed for venture capital trusts to invest money raised from issues (other than initial issues) of ordinary share capital, and

Part 4 contains supplementary provisions.

Commentary—*Simon's Direct Tax Service* E3.635.

PART 6

MISCELLANEOUS AND SUPPLEMENTARY PROVISIONS

Recovery of taxes etc due in other member States

134 Recovery of taxes etc due in other member States

(1) Schedule 39 to this Act has effect with respect to the recovery in the United Kingdom of amounts in respect of which a request for enforcement has been made in accordance with the Mutual Assistance Recovery Directive by an authority in another member State.

(2) The "Mutual Assistance Recovery Directive" means Council Directive 76/308/EEC, as amended by Council Directive 2001/44/EC.

(3) No obligation of secrecy imposed by statute or otherwise precludes a tax authority in the United Kingdom—

    (a) from disclosing information to another tax authority in the United Kingdom in connection with a request for enforcement made by the competent authority of another member State;

    (b) from disclosing information that is required to be disclosed to the competent authority of another member State by virtue of the Mutual Assistance Recovery Directive;

    (c) from disclosing information for the purposes of a request made by the tax authority under that Directive for the enforcement in another member State of an amount claimed by the authority in the United Kingdom.

(4) In subsection (3) "tax authority in the United Kingdom" means—

    (a) the Commissioners of Customs and Excise,

    (b) the Commissioners of Inland Revenue, or

    (c) in relation to agricultural levies of the European Community within the meaning of section 6 of the European Communities Act 1972 (c 72), any relevant Minister within the meaning of that section.

(5) Subsection (3)(a) does not apply in relation to disclosure by the Commissioners of Inland Revenue to a relevant Minister.

(6) The Treasury may by regulations make such provision as appears to them appropriate for the purpose of giving effect to any future amendments of the Mutual Assistance Recovery Directive.

The regulations may amend, replace or repeal any of the provisions of subsections (1) to (4) above or of Schedule 39.

(7) Regulations under subsection (6) shall be made by statutory instrument which shall be subject to annulment in pursuance of a resolution of the House of Commons.

Mandatory e-filing

135 Mandatory e-filing

(1) The Commissioners of Inland Revenue ("the Commissioners") may make regulations requiring the use of electronic communications for the delivery by specified persons of specified information required or authorised to be delivered by or under legislation relating to a taxation matter.

(2) Regulations under this section may make provision—

    (a) as to the electronic form to be taken by information delivered to the Inland Revenue using electronic communications;

    (b) requiring persons to prepare and keep records of information delivered to Inland Revenue by means of electronic communications;

    (c) for the production of the contents of records kept in accordance with the regulations;

    (d) as to conditions that must be complied with in connection with the use of electronic communications for the delivery of information;

    (e) for treating information as not having been delivered unless conditions imposed by any of the regulations are satisfied;

    (f) for determining the time at which and person by whom information is to be taken to have been delivered;

    (g) for authenticating whatever is delivered.

(3) Regulations under this section may also make provision (which may include provision for the application of conclusive or other presumptions) as to the manner of proving for any purpose—

    (a) whether any use of electronic communications is to be taken as having resulted in the delivery of information;

    (b) the time of delivery of any information for the delivery of which electronic communications have been used;

    (c) the person by whom information delivered by means of electronic communications was delivered;

    (d) the contents of anything so delivered;

    (e) the contents of any records;

    (f) any other matter for which provision may be made by regulations under this section.

(4) Regulations under this section may—

    (a) allow any authorisation or requirement for which the regulations may provide to be given or imposed by means of a specific or general direction given by the Commissioners;

    (b) provide that the conditions of any such authorisation or requirement are to be taken to be satisfied only where the Inland Revenue are satisfied as to specified matters;

    (c) allow a person to refuse to accept delivery of information in an electronic form or by means of electronic communications except in such circumstances as may be specified in or determined under the regulations;

    (d) allow or require use to be made of intermediaries in connection with—

        (i) the delivery of information by means of electronic communications; or

        (ii) the authentication or security of anything transmitted by any such means.

(5) Regulations under this section may contain provision—

    (a) requiring the Inland Revenue to notify persons appearing to them to be, or to have become, a person of a specified description and accordingly required to use electronic communications for any purpose in accordance with the regulations,

    (b) enabling a person so notified to have the question whether he is a person of such a description determined in the same way as an appeal.

(6) Regulations under this section may provide—

    (a) that information delivered by means of electronic communications must meet standards of accuracy and completeness set by specific or general directions given by the Commissioners, and

    (b) that failure to meet those standards may be treated—

        (i) as a failure to deliver the information, or

        (ii) as a failure to comply with the requirements of the regulations.

(7) The power to make provision by regulations under this section includes power—

    (a) to provide for a contravention of, or any failure to comply with, the regulations to attract a penalty of a specified amount not exceeding £3,000;

    (b) to provide that specified enactments relating to penalties imposed for the purposes of any taxation matter (including enactments relating to assessments, review and appeal) apply, with or without modifications, in relation to penalties under the regulations;

    (c) to make different provision for different cases;

    (d) to make such incidental, supplemental, consequential and transitional provision in connection with any provision contained in any of the regulations as the Commissioners think fit.

(8) References in this section to the delivery of information include references to any of the following (however referred to)—

    (a) the production or furnishing to a person of any information, account, record or document;

    (b) the giving, making, issue or surrender to, or service on, any person of any notice, notification, statement, declaration, certificate or direction;

    (c) the imposition on any person of any requirement or the issue to any person of any request;

    (d) the making of any return, claim, election or application;

    (e) the amendment or withdrawal of anything mentioned in paragraphs (a) to (d) above.

(9) Regulations under this section shall be made by statutory instrument subject to annulment in pursuance of a resolution of the House of Commons.

(10) In this section—

"the Inland Revenue" means—

    (a) the Commissioners,

    (b) any officer of the Commissioners, or

    (c) any other person who for the purposes of electronic communications is acting under the authority of the Commissioners;

"legislation" means any enactment, Community legislation or subordinate legislation;

"specified" means specified by or under regulations under this section;

"subordinate legislation" has the same meaning as in the Interpretation Act 1978 (c 30);

"taxation matter" means a taxation matter within the care and management of the Commissioners.

136 Use of electronic communications under other provisions

(1) Any power to make subordinate legislation for or in connection with the delivery of information conferred in relation to a taxation matter on—

    (a) the Commissioners of Inland Revenue, or

    (b) the Treasury,

includes power to make any such provision in relation to the delivery of that information as could be made in exercise of the power conferred by section 135.

(2) Provision made in exercise of the powers conferred by section 135 or subsection (1) above has effect notwithstanding so much of any enactment or subordinate legislation as would otherwise—

    (a) allow information to be delivered otherwise than by means of electronic communications, or

    (b) preclude the use of an intermediary in connection with its delivery.

(3) Expressions used in this section and section 135 have the same meaning in this section as in that section.

(4) Nothing in this section shall be read as restricting the generality of the power conferred by section 135.

Registers of UK gilts

138 Authority of Bank of England to discharge functions in place of Bank of Ireland

(1) The Bank of England has authority, in the event of the Bank of Ireland ceasing to perform any of its functions in relation to United Kingdom government stock, to discharge any of the Bank of Ireland's functions in relation to such stock in place of the Bank of Ireland.

(2) The enactments relating to United Kingdom government stock have effect in relation to anything done in the circumstances mentioned in subsection (1) for the purposes of discharging any such functions—

(a) as if any reference to the Bank of Ireland were a reference to the Bank of England, and
(b) as if any reference to an officer of the Bank of Ireland were a reference to the corresponding officer of the Bank of England.

(3) In particular, sections 59 and 66 of the National Debt Act 1870 (c 71) (provisions protecting the Bank and its officers from liability) apply to the Bank of England and to officers of that Bank in relation to anything done in the circumstances mentioned in subsection (1) above for the purposes of discharging any functions of the Bank of Ireland in relation to United Kingdom government stock.

(4) In this section—

"enactment" includes an enactment contained in subordinate legislation within the meaning of the Interpretation Act 1978 (c 30);
"United Kingdom government stock" means stock or bonds of any of the descriptions included in Part 1 of Schedule 11 to the Finance Act 1942 (c 21) (whether on or after the passing of this Act).

(5) This section shall be deemed always to have had effect.

139 Closure of UK gilts registers kept in Ireland

(1) The Treasury may by order made by statutory instrument provide—

(a) that no further stock or bonds may be registered in either of the Irish gilts registers on or after such day as the order may appoint ("the appointed day"), and
(b) for the transfer to the English gilts register of the entries subsisting in each of those registers at the beginning of the appointed day.

(2) The power conferred by subsection (1)(b) includes power to make provision in relation to stock and bonds which were not registered in either of the Irish gilts registers on the appointed day, but which should have been.

(3) An order under this section may contain such consequential, incidental, supplementary and transitional provision as appears to the Treasury to be necessary or expedient, including provision amending, repealing or revoking any enactment.

(4) In subsection (3) "enactment" means any enactment contained in—

(a) an Act, whenever passed, or
(b) an instrument, whenever made, under an Act, whenever passed.

(5) In this section—

"the English gilts register" is the register required to be kept at the office of the Chief Registrar of the Bank of England under section 47 of the Finance Act 1942 (c 21) (registration of government stock); and
"the Irish gilts registers" are—

(a) the register required to be kept in Belfast under that section, and
(b) the register required to he kept in Dublin under that section.

(6) A statutory instrument containing an order under this section is subject to annulment in pursuance of a resolution of the House of Commons.

140 Administration of UK gilts

(1) In section 47 of the Finance Act 1942 (transfer and registration of government stock)—

(a) for subsection (1)(b) (power to provide for the keeping of stock and bond registers by the Banks of England and Ireland) substitute—

"(b) for the administration of such stock and bonds (including the registration of holders) by such one or more persons as the Treasury may appoint in accordance with the regulations and the closure of any register;", and

(b) after subsection (1E) insert—

"(1EA) Persons appointed in accordance with regulations under subsection (1)(b) shall be appointed on such terms (including terms as to the making of payments by the Treasury) as the Treasury consider appropriate, and the persons who may be so appointed include the Bank of England.".

(2) The Treasury may by order made by statutory instrument make such consequential, incidental, supplementary and transitional provision as appears to the Treasury to be necessary or expedient in consequence of the amendments made by subsection (1), including provision amending, repealing or revoking any enactment.

(3) In subsection (2) "enactment" means any enactment contained in—

(a) an Act, whenever passed, or
(b) an instrument, whenever made, under an Act, whenever passed.

(4) A statutory instrument containing an order under subsection (2) is subject to annulment in pursuance of a resolution of the House of Commons.

(5) Sums payable by the Treasury by virtue of section 47(1EA) of the Finance Act 1942 (c 21) (as inserted by subsection (1) above) shall be met out of the National Loans Fund with recourse to the Consolidated Fund.

(6) This section shall come into force on such day as the Treasury may by order made by statutory instrument appoint.

Supplementary

141 Repeals

(1) The enactments mentioned in Schedule 40 to this Act (which include provisions that are spent or of no practical utility) are repealed to the extent specified.

(2) The repeals specified in that Schedule have effect subject to the commencement provisions and savings contained or referred to in the notes set out in that Schedule.

142 Interpretation

In this Act "the Taxes Act 1988" means the Income and Corporation Taxes Act 1988 (c 1).

143 Short title

This Act may be cited as the Finance Act 2002.

SCHEDULES

SCHEDULE 6

MINOR AMENDMENTS TO SCHEDULE E CHARGE

Section 37

Commentary—*Simon's Direct Tax Service* **E4.514.**

Share options

1 In section 135 of the Taxes Act 1988 (gains by directors and employees from share options), for subsection (5)(*a*) substitute—

"(*a*) the amount so charged shall be deducted from any amount which is chargeable under subsection (1) above by reference to the gain realised by the exercise, assignment or release of that right; and".

Credit-tokens and non-cash vouchers

2 In section 144 of the Taxes Act 1988 (supplementary provisions relating to vouchers and credit-tokens), after subsection (4) insert—

"(4A) Section 142(1) has effect as if—

(*a*) use of a credit-token by a relation of an employee were use of the token by the employee, and

(*b*) money, goods or services obtained by a relation of an employee by use of a credit-token were money, goods or services obtained by the employee by the employee's use of the token.".

3 In each of the following provisions of the Taxes Act 1988—

(*a*) section 157 (cars available for private use),

(*b*) section 159AA (vans available for private use), and

(*c*) section 159AC (heavier commercial vehicles available for private use),

in subsection (3)(*b*) after "him" insert "or a relation of his (within the meaning of section 144)".

Taxation of benefit where income received free of tax

4 In section 144A(1) of the Taxes Act 1988 (payments etc received free of tax), for the words from "income of the employee" to the end substitute "emoluments of the employment and charged to income tax under Schedule E for the tax year in which the date mentioned in paragraph (*c*) above falls".

Benefits in connection with termination of employment or change in duties or emoluments

5 In section 148 of the Taxes Act 1988 (payments and other benefits in connection with termination of employment, etc), for subsection (2) substitute—

"(2) For the purposes of this section "benefit" includes anything which, disregarding any exemption—

    (*a*) would be an emolument of the employment, or
    (*b*) would be chargeable to tax as an emolument of the employment,

if received for the performance of the duties of the employment.

(2A) But subsection (1) does not apply—

    (*a*) to any payment or other benefit received in connection with any change in the duties of, or emoluments from, a person's employment to the extent that it is a benefit which, if received for the performance of the duties of the employment, would fall within paragraph 1(1) of Schedule 11A, or
    (*b*) to any payment or other benefit received in connection with the termination of a person's employment—

        (i) that is a benefit which, if received for the performance of the duties of the employment, would fall within section 155(1) or (5), 155AA, 156A, 157(3), 159AA(3), 159AC(3), 200B(2)(*b*), 200E(2)(*b*), 588(1), 589A or 643(1), or
        (ii) to the extent that it is a benefit which, if so received, would not be included in the emoluments of that person by virtue of section 200D(1) or 200J(2).".

Priority between charges under sections 148 and 595 of the Taxes Act 1988

6 In section 595 of the Taxes Act 1988 (charge to tax in respect of certain sums paid by employer etc), in subsection (1)(*a*) after "if" insert "(disregarding section 148) it is".

SCHEDULE 7

CHARGEABLE GAINS: ROLL-OVER OF DEGROUPING CHARGE: MODIFICATION OF ENACTMENTS

Section 43

Commentary—*Simon's Direct Tax Service* **D2.661.**

The following Schedule is inserted after Schedule 7AA to the Taxation of Chargeable Gains Act 1992 (c 12)—

"SCHEDULE 7AB

ROLL-OVER OF DEGROUPING CHARGE: MODIFICATION OF ENACTMENTS

Introductory

1—(1)This Schedule sets out how sections 152 and 153 and other related enactments are modified for the purposes of section 179B (roll-over of degrouping charge on business assets).

(2) In the enactments as so modified—

"company A" and "company B" have the same meanings as in section 179;
"relevant asset" means the asset mentioned in section 179B(1);
"deemed sale" means the sale of the relevant asset that is treated as taking place by virtue of section 179(3) or (6);
"deemed sale consideration" means the amount for which company A is treated as having sold the relevant asset;
"time of accrual" means—

    (*a*) in a case where section 179(3) applies, the time at which, by virtue of section 179(4), the gain or loss accruing on the deemed sale is treated as accruing to company A;
    (*b*) in a case where section 179(6) applies, the latest time at which the company satisfies the conditions in section 179(7).

Section 152

2—(1) For subsection (1) of section 152 (roll-over relief) substitute—

"(1) If—

    (*a*) company B was carrying on a trade at the time when it disposed of the relevant asset to company A,
    (*b*) the relevant asset was used, and used only, for the purposes of that trade throughout the period when it was owned by company B,

(c) an amount that is not less than the deemed sale consideration is applied by company A in acquiring other assets, or an interest in other assets (''the new assets''),

(d) on acquisition the new assets are taken into use, and used only, for the purposes of a trade carried on by company A,

(e) both the relevant asset and the new assets are within the classes of assets listed in section 155, and

(f) company A makes a claim as respects the amount applied as mentioned in paragraph (c),

company A shall be treated for the purposes of this Act as if the deemed sale consideration were (if otherwise of a greater amount) reduced to such amount as would secure that neither a gain nor a loss accrues to the company in respect of the deemed sale.

(1A) Where subsection (1) applies, company A shall be treated for the purposes of this Act as if the amount or value of the consideration for the acquisition of, or of the interest in, the new assets were reduced by the same amount as the amount of the reduction under that subsection.

(1B) Subsection (1) does not affect the value at which company A is treated by virtue of section 179 as having reacquired the relevant asset.

(1C) Subsection (1A) does not affect the treatment for the purposes of this Act of the other party to the transaction involving the new assets.''.

(2) In subsection (2) of that section (application of subsection (1) where old assets held on 6th April 1965)—

(a) for ''subsection (1)(a)'' substitute ''subsection (1)'';

(b) for ''subsection (1)(b)'' substitute ''subsection (1A)''.

(3) In subsection (3) of that section (reinvestment period), for ''after the disposal of, or of the interest in, the old assets'' substitute ''after the time of accrual''.

(4) In subsection (5) of that section (new assets must be acquired for purposes of trade), for ''the trade'' substitute ''the trade carried on by company A''.

(5) In subsection (6) of that section (apportionment where part of building etc not used for purposes of trade), omit ''or disposal'' and insert at the end ''or of the deemed sale consideration''.

(6) After that subsection insert—

''(6A) In subsection (6) ''period of ownership'', in relation to the relevant asset, means the period during which the asset was owned by company B.''.

(7) In subsection (7) of that section (apportionment where old assets not used for purposes of trade throughout period of ownership)—

(a) for the words from the beginning to ''period of ownership'' substitute ''If the relevant asset was not used for the purposes of the trade carried on by company B throughout the period during which it was owned by that company'';

(b) for the words from ''or disposal'' to the end substitute ''of the asset or of the deemed sale consideration''.

(8) In subsection (9) of that section (''period of ownership'' does not include period before 31st March 1982), for ''''period of ownership'' does not'' substitute ''the references to the period during which the relevant asset was owned by company B do not''.

(9) In subsection (11) of that section (apportionment of consideration for assets not all of which are subject of claim), omit ''or disposal'' and insert at the end ''; and similarly in relation to the deemed sale consideration''.

Section 153

3 For subsection (1) of section 153 (assets only partly replaced) substitute—

''(1) If—

(a) an amount that is less than the deemed sale consideration is applied by company A in acquiring other assets, or an interest in other assets (''the new assets''),

(b) the difference between the deemed sale consideration and the amount so applied (''the shortfall'') is less than the amount of the gain (whether all chargeable gain or not) accruing on the deemed sale,

(c) the conditions in paragraphs (a), (b), (d) and (e) of section 152(1) are satisfied, and

(d) company A makes a claim as respects the amount applied as mentioned in paragraph (a) above,

company A shall be treated for the purposes of this Act as if the amount of the gain accruing as mentioned in paragraph (b) above were reduced to the same amount as the shortfall (with a proportionate reduction, if not all of that gain is chargeable gain, in the amount of the chargeable gain).

(1A) Where subsection (1) applies, company A shall be treated for the purposes of this Act as if the amount or value of the consideration for the acquisition of, or of the interest in, the new assets were reduced by the amount by which the gain is reduced (or as the case may be the amount by which the chargeable gain is proportionately reduced) under that subsection.

(1B) Subsection (1) does not affect the value at which company A is treated by virtue of section 179 as having reacquired the relevant asset.

(1C) Subsection (1A) does not affect the treatment for the purposes of this Act of the other party to the transaction involving the new assets.''.

Section 153A

4—(1) In subsection (1) of section 153A (provisional application of sections 152 and 153)—

 (*a*) for the words from ''a person'' to ''takes place'' substitute ''company A declares, in its return for the chargeable period in which the time of accrual falls'';
 (*b*) for ''the trade'' substitute ''a trade carried on by company A'';
 (*c*) for ''the whole or any specified part of the consideration'' substitute ''an amount equal to the deemed sale consideration or any specified part of that amount''.

In subsection (5) of that section (meaning of ''relevant day''), for paragraphs (*a*) and (*b*) substitute ''the fourth anniversary of the last day of the accounting period of company A in which the time of accrual falls''.

Section 155

5 In section 155 (relevant classes of assets), in Head A of Class 1, after paragraph 2 insert—

 ''In Head A ''the trade'' means—

  (*a*) for the purposes of determining whether the relevant asset is within this head, the trade carried on by company B;
  (*b*) for the purposes of determining whether the new assets are within this head, the trade carried on by company A.''.

Section 159

6—(1) In subsection (1) of section 159 (new assets must be chargeable assets), for the words from ''in the case of a person'' to the second ''in relation to him'' substitute ''if the relevant asset (or, as the case may be, the property mentioned in section 179(3)(*b*)) is a chargeable asset in relation to company A at the time of accrual, unless the new assets are chargeable assets in relation to that company''.

(2) In subsection (2) of that section (subsection (1) not to apply where new assets acquired by UK resident after disposal of old ones)—

 (*a*) for paragraph (*a*) substitute—
 ''(*a*) company A acquires the new assets after the time of accrual, and'';
 (*b*) in paragraph (*b*) for ''the person'' substitute ''that company''.

(3) In subsection (3) of that section (subsection (2) not to apply in certain cases where new assets acquired by dual resident), for ''the person'' substitute ''company A''.

(4) In subsection (6) of that section (definitions)—

 (*a*) in paragraph (*a*) for ''''the old assets'' and ''the new assets'' have the same meanings'' substitute ''''the new assets'' has the same meaning'';
 (*b*) omit paragraph (*b*).

(5) Omit subsection (7) of that section (acquisitions before 14th March 1989).

Section 175

7—(1) In subsection (2) of section 175 (single-trade rule for group members not to apply in case of dual resident investing company)—

 (*a*) for ''the consideration for the disposal of the old assets'' substitute ''the amount of the deemed sale consideration'';
 (*b*) for ''''the old assets'' and ''the new assets'' have the same meanings'' substitute ''''the new assets'' has the same meaning''.

(2) In subsection (2A) of that section (claim by two group members to be treated as same person for roll-over purposes), for paragraph (*a*) substitute—

 ''(*a*) company A is a member of a group of companies at the time of accrual,''.

(3) In subsection (2AA) of that section (conditions for claim under subsection (2A))—

 (*a*) in paragraph (*a*) for the words from the beginning to ''chargeable assets'' substitute ''that company A is resident in the United Kingdom at the time of accrual, or the relevant asset (or, as the case may be, the property mentioned in section 179(3)(*b*)) is a chargeable asset'';
 (*b*) in paragraph (*b*) for ''the assets'' substitute ''the new assets (within the meaning of section 152)''.

(4) Immediately before subsection (2B) of that section (roll-over relief for group member not itself carrying on trade) insert—

 ''(2AB) Section 152 or 153 shall apply where—

(*a*) company B was not carrying on a trade at the time when it disposed of the relevant asset to company A, but was a member of a group of companies at that time, and

(*b*) immediately before that time the relevant asset was used, and used only, for the purposes of the trade which (in accordance with subsection (1) above) is treated as carried on by the members of the group which carried on a trade,

as if company B had been carrying on that trade.''.

(5) In subsection (2B) of that section—

(*a*) omit paragraph (*a*);

(*b*) in paragraph (*b*), for ''those purposes'' substitute ''the purposes of the trade which (in accordance with subsection (1) above) is treated as carried on by the members of the group which carry on a trade''.

(6) Omit subsection (4) of that section (acquisitions before 20th March 1990).

Section 185

8—(1) In subsection (3) of section 185 (no roll-over relief in certain cases where company acquires new assets after becoming non-resident)—

(*a*) omit it ''the company''

(*b*) for paragraph (*a*) substitute—

''(*a*) the time of accrual falls before the relevant time; and'';

(*c*) insert ''the company'' at the beginning of paragraph (*b*).

(2) In subsection (5) of that section (definitions), in paragraph (*c*) for ''''the old assets'' and ''the new assets'' have the same meanings'' substitute ''''the new assets'' has the same meaning''.

Section 198

9—(1) For subsection (1) of section 198 (replacement of business assets used in connection with oil fields) substitute—

''(1) If at the time of accrual the relevant asset (or, as the case may be, the property mentioned in section 179(3)(*b*)) was used by company A for the purposes of a ring fence trade carried on by it, section 152 or 153 shall not apply unless the new assets are on acquisition taken into use, and used only, for the purposes of that trade.''.

(2) In subsection (3) of that section (new asset conclusively presumed to be depreciating asset), for ''in relation to any of the consideration on a material disposal'' substitute ''in a case falling within subsection (1) above''.

(3) In subsection (5) of that section (definitions), omit paragraph (*a*).

Schedule 22 to the Finance Act 2000

10 In sub-paragraph (2) of paragraph 67 of Schedule 22 to the Finance Act 2000 (c 17) (no roll-over relief for tonnage tax assets)—

(*a*) after ''the disposal'', in the first and third places, insert ''or deemed sale'';

(*b*) in paragraph (*a*) after ''Asset No 1'' insert ''or, as the case may be, the deemed sale consideration''.''.

SCHEDULE 8

CHARGEABLE GAINS: EXEMPTIONS IN CASE OF SUBSTANTIAL SHAREHOLDING

Section 44(2)

PART 1

NEW SCHEDULE 7AC TO THE TAXATION OF CHARGEABLE GAINS ACT 1992

Commentary—*Simon's Direct Tax Service* D2.301.

1 The following Schedule is inserted after Schedule 7AB to the Taxation of Chargeable Gains Act 1992 (c 12)—

''SCHEDULE 7AC

EXEMPTIONS FOR DISPOSALS BY COMPANIES WITH SUBSTANTIAL SHAREHOLDING

PART 1

THE EXEMPTIONS

The main exemption

1—(1) A gain accruing to a company (''the investing company'') on a disposal of shares or an interest in shares in another company (''the company invested in'') is not a chargeable gain if the requirements of this Schedule are met.

(2) The requirements are set out in—

Part 2 (the substantial shareholding requirement), and
Part 3 (requirements to be met in relation to the investing company and the company invested in).

(3) The exemption conferred by this paragraph does not apply in the circumstances specified in paragraph 5 or the cases specified in paragraph 6.

Subsidiary exemption: disposal of asset related to shares where main exemption conditions met

2—(1) A gain accruing to a company (''company A'') on a disposal of an asset related to shares in another company (''company B'') is not a chargeable gain if either of the following conditions is met.

(2) The first condition is that—

(*a*) immediately before the disposal company A holds shares or an interest in shares in company B, and
(*b*) any gain accruing to company A on a disposal at that time of the shares or interest would, by virtue of paragraph 1, not be a chargeable gain.

(3) The second condition is that—

(*a*) immediately before the disposal company A does not hold shares or an interest in shares in company B but is a member of a group and another member of that group does hold shares or an interest in shares in company B, and
(*b*) if company A, rather than that other company, held the shares or interest, any gain accruing to company A on a disposal at that time of the shares or interest would, by virtue of paragraph 1, not be a chargeable gain.

(4) Where assets of a company are vested in a liquidator under section 145 of the Insolvency Act 1986 (c 45) or Article 123 of the Insolvency (Northern Ireland) Order 1989 or otherwise, this paragraph applies as if the assets were vested in, and the acts of the liquidator in relation to the assets were the acts of, the company (acquisitions from or disposals to him by the company being disregarded accordingly).

(5) The exemption conferred by this paragraph does not apply in the circumstances specified in paragraph 5 or the cases specified in paragraph 6.

Subsidiary exemption: disposal of shares or related asset where main exemption conditions previously met

3—(1) A gain accruing to a company (''company A'') on a disposal of shares, or an interest in shares or an asset related to shares, in another company (''company B'') is not a chargeable gain if the following conditions are met.

(2) The conditions are—

(*a*) that at the time of the disposal company A meets the requirement in paragraph 7 (the substantial shareholding requirement) in relation to company B;
(*b*) that a chargeable gain or allowable loss would, apart from this paragraph, accrue to company A on the disposal (but see sub-paragraph (3) below);
(*c*) that at the time of the disposal—

(i) company A is resident in the United Kingdom, or
(ii) any chargeable gain accruing to company A on the disposal would, by virtue of section 10(3), form part of that company's chargeable profits for corporation tax purposes;

(*d*) that there was a time within the period of two years ending with the disposal (''the relevant period'') when, if—

(i) company A, or
(ii) a company that at any time in the relevant period was a member of the same group as company A,

had disposed of shares or an interest in shares in company B that it then held, a gain accruing would, by virtue of paragraph 1, not have been a chargeable gain; and

    (*e*) that, if at the time of the disposal the requirements of paragraph 19 (requirements relating to company invested in) are not met in relation to company B, there was a time within the relevant period when company B was controlled by—

        (i) company A, or

        (ii) company A together with any persons connected with it, or

        (iii) a company that at any time in the relevant period was a member of the same group as company A, or

        (iv) any such company together with any persons connected with it.

(3) Sub-paragraph (1) does not apply if—

    (*a*) the condition in sub-paragraph (2)(*b*) is met but would not be met but for a failure to meet the requirement in paragraph 18(1)(*b*) (requirement as to investing company to be met immediately after the disposal), and

    (*b*) the failure to meet that requirement is not due to—

        (i) the fact that company A has been wound up or dissolved, or

        (ii) where the winding up or dissolution takes place as soon as is reasonably practicable in the circumstances, the fact that company A is about to be wound up or dissolved.

(4) In determining for the purpose of sub-paragraph (2)(*d*) whether a gain accruing on the hypothetical disposal referred to would have been a chargeable gain, the requirements of paragraph 18(1)(*b*) and of paragraph 19(1)(*b*) (requirement as to company invested in to be met immediately after the disposal) shall be assumed to be met.

(5) Where—

    (*a*) immediately before the disposal company B holds an asset,

    (*b*) the expenditure allowable in computing any gain or loss on that asset, were it to be disposed of by company B immediately before that disposal, would fall to be reduced because of a claim to relief under section 165 (gifts relief) in relation to an earlier disposal, and

    (*c*) that earlier disposal took place within the relevant period,

sub-paragraph (1) does not prevent a gain accruing to company A on the disposal from being a chargeable gain but any loss so accruing is not an allowable loss.

(6) Where assets of company B are vested in a liquidator under section 145 of the Insolvency Act 1986 or Article 123 of the Insolvency (Northern Ireland) Order 1989 or otherwise, sub-paragraph (5)(*a*) applies as if the assets were vested in the company.

(7) In determining "the relevant period" for the purposes of sub-paragraph (2)(*d*) or (*e*) or sub-paragraph (5)(*c*), section 28 (time of disposal under contract) applies with the omission of subsection (2) (postponement of time of disposal in case of conditional contract).

(8) The exemption conferred by this paragraph does not apply in the circumstances specified in paragraph 5 or the cases specified in paragraph 6.

Application of exemptions in priority to provisions deeming there to be no disposal etc

4—(1) For the purposes of determining whether an exemption conferred by this Schedule applies, the question whether there is a disposal shall be determined without regard to—

    (*a*) section 116(10) (reorganisation, conversion of securities, etc treated as not involving disposal),

    (*b*) section 127 (share reorganisations etc treated as not involving disposal), or

    (*c*) section 192(2)(*a*) (distribution not treated as capital distribution).

(2) Sub-paragraph (1) does not apply to a disposal of shares if the effect of its applying would be that relief attributable to the shares under Schedule 15 to the Finance Act 2000 (corporate venturing scheme) would be withdrawn or reduced under paragraph 46 of that Schedule (withdrawal or reduction of investment relief on disposal of shares).

(3) Where or to the extent that an exemption conferred by this Schedule does apply—

    (*a*) the provisions mentioned in sub-paragraph (1)(*a*) and (*b*) do not apply in relation to the disposal, and

    (*b*) the provision mentioned in sub-paragraph (1)(*c*) does not apply in relation to the subject matter of the disposal.

(4) Where section 127 is disapplied by sub-paragraph (3)(*a*) in a case in which that section would otherwise have applied in relation to the disposal by virtue of paragraph 84 of Schedule 15 to the Finance Act 2000 (corporate venturing scheme: share exchanges), paragraph 85 of that Schedule (attribution of relief to new shares) does not apply.

(5) In this paragraph any reference to section 127 includes a reference to that provision as applied by any enactment relating to corporation tax.

Circumstances in which exemptions do not apply

5—(1) Where in pursuance of arrangements to which this paragraph applies—

    (*a*) an untaxed gain accrues to a company ("company A") on a disposal of shares, or an interest in shares or an asset related to shares, in another company ("company B"), and (*b*) before the accrual of that gain—

(i) company A acquired control of company B, or the same person or persons acquired control of both companies, or

(ii) there was a significant change of trading activities affecting company B at a time when it was controlled by company A, or when both companies were controlled by the same person or persons,

none of the exemptions in this Schedule applies to the disposal.

(2) This paragraph applies to arrangements from which the sole or main benefit that (but for this paragraph) could be expected to arise is that the gain on the disposal would, by virtue of this Schedule, not be a chargeable gain.

(3) For the purposes of sub-paragraph (1)(*a*) a gain is "untaxed" if the gain, or all of it but a part that is not substantial, represents profits that have not been brought into account (in the United Kingdom or elsewhere) for the purposes of tax on profits for a period ending on or before the date of the disposal.

(4) The reference in sub-paragraph (3) to profits being brought into account for the purposes of tax on profits includes a reference to the case where—

(*a*) an amount in respect of those profits is apportioned to a company resident in the United Kingdom by virtue of subsection (3) of section 747 of the Taxes Act 1988 (imputation of chargeable profits etc of controlled foreign companies), and

(*b*) a sum is chargeable on that company in respect of that amount by virtue of subsection (4) of that section for an accounting period of that company ending on or before the date of disposal.

(5) For the purposes of sub-paragraph (1)(*b*)(ii) there is a "significant change of trading activities affecting company B" if—

(*a*) there is a major change in the nature or conduct of a trade carried on by company B or a 51% subsidiary of company B, or

(*b*) there is a major change in the scale of the activities of a trade carried on by company B or a 51% subsidiary of company B, or

(*c*) company B or a 51% subsidiary of company B begins to carry on a trade.

(6) In this paragraph—

"arrangements" includes any scheme, agreement or understanding, whether or not legally enforceable;

"major change in the nature or conduct of a trade" has the same meaning as in section 768 of the Taxes Act (change of ownership of company: disallowance of trading losses);

"profits" means income or gains (including unrealised income or gains).

Other cases excluded from exemptions

6—(1) The exemptions conferred by this Schedule do not apply—

(*a*) to a disposal that by virtue of any enactment relating to chargeable gains is deemed to be for a consideration such that no gain or loss accrues to the person making the disposal,

(*b*) to a disposal a gain on which would, by virtue of any enactment not contained in this Schedule, not be a chargeable gain, or

(*c*) to a deemed disposal under section 440(1) or (2) of the Taxes Act (deemed disposal on transfer of asset of insurance company from one category to another).

(2) The hypothetical disposal referred to in paragraph 2(2)(*b*) or (3)(*b*) or paragraph 3(2)(*d*) shall be assumed not to be a disposal within sub-paragraph (1)(*a*), (*b*) or (*c*) above.

PART 2
THE SUBSTANTIAL SHAREHOLDING REQUIREMENT
The requirement

7 The investing company must have held a substantial shareholding in the company invested in throughout a twelve-month period beginning not more than two years before the day on which the disposal takes place.

Meaning of "substantial shareholding"

8—(1) For the purposes of this Schedule a company holds a "substantial shareholding" in another company if it holds shares or interests in shares in that company by virtue of which—

(*a*) it holds not less than 10% of the company's ordinary share capital,

(*b*) it is beneficially entitled to not less than 10% of the profits available for distribution to equity holders of the company, and

(*c*) it would be beneficially entitled on a winding up to not less than 10% of the assets of the company available for distribution to equity holders.

This is without prejudice to what is meant by "substantial" where the word appears in other contexts.

(2) Schedule 18 to the Taxes Act 1988 (meaning of equity holder and determination of profits or assets available for distribution) applies for the purposes of sub-paragraph (1).

(3) In that Schedule as it applies for those purposes—

(a) for any reference to sections 403C and 413(7) of that Act, or either of those provisions, substitute a reference to sub-paragraph (1) above;

(b) omit the words in paragraph 1(4) from ''but'' to the end;

(c) omit paragraph 5(3) and paragraphs 5B to 5F; and

(d) omit paragraph 7(1)(b).

Aggregation of holdings of group companies

9—(1) For the purposes of paragraph 7 (the substantial shareholding requirement) a company that is a member of a group is treated—

(a) as holding any shares or interest in shares held by any other company in the group, and

(b) as having the same entitlement as any such company to any rights enjoyed by virtue of holding shares or an interest in shares.

(2) Sub-paragraph (1) is subject to paragraph 17(4) (exclusion of aggregation in case of assets of long-term insurance fund of insurance company).

Effect of earlier no-gain/no-loss transfer

10—(1) For the purposes of this Part the period for which a company has held shares is treated as extended by any earlier period during which the shares concerned, or shares from which they are derived, were held—

(a) by a company from which the shares concerned were transferred to the first-mentioned company on a no-gain/no-loss transfer, or

(b) by a company from which the shares concerned, or shares from which they are derived, were transferred on a previous no-gain/no-loss transfer—

   (i) to a company within paragraph (a), or

   (ii) to another company within this paragraph.

(2) For the purposes of sub-paragraph (1)—

(a) a ''no-gain/no-loss transfer'' means a disposal and corresponding acquisition that by virtue of any enactment relating to chargeable gains are deemed to be for a consideration such that no gain or loss accrues to the person making the disposal;

(b) a transfer shall be treated as if it had been a no-gain/no-loss transfer if it is a transfer to which subsection (1) of section 171 (transfers within a group) would apply but for subsection (3) of that section.

(3) Where sub-paragraph (1) applies to extend the period for which a company (''company A'') is treated as having held any shares, that company shall be treated for the purposes of this Part as having had at any time the same entitlement—

(a) to shares, and

(b) to any rights enjoyed by virtue of holding shares,

as the company (''company B'') that at that time held the shares concerned or, as the case may be, the shares from which they are derived.

(4) The shares and rights to be so attributed to company A include any holding or entitlement attributed at that time to company B under paragraph 9 (aggregation of holdings of group companies).

(5) In this paragraph, except in paragraphs (a) to (c) of sub-paragraph (6), ''shares'' includes an interest in shares.

(6) For the purposes of this paragraph shares are ''derived'' from other shares only where—

(a) a company becomes a co-owner of shares previously owned by it alone, or vice versa,

(b) a company's interest in shares as co-owner changes (without the company ceasing to be a co-owner),

(c) one holding of shares is treated by virtue of section 127 as the same asset as another, or

(d) there is a sequence of two or more of the occurrences mentioned in paragraphs (a) to (c).

The reference in paragraph (c) to section 127 includes a reference to that provision as applied by any enactment relating to corporation tax.

Effect of deemed disposal and reacquisition

11—(1) For the purposes of this Part a company is not regarded as having held shares throughout a period if, at any time during that period, there is a deemed disposal and reacquisition of—

(a) the shares concerned, or

(b) shares, or an interest in shares, from which those shares are derived.

(2) For the purposes of this Part a company is not regarded as having held an interest in shares throughout a period if, at any time during that period, there is a deemed disposal and reacquisition of—

(a) the interest concerned, or

(b) shares, or an interest in shares, from which that interest is derived.

(3) In this paragraph—

"deemed disposal and reacquisition" means a disposal and immediate reacquisition treated as taking place under any enactment relating to corporation tax;

"derived" has the same meaning as in paragraph 10.

Effect of repurchase agreement

12—(1) This paragraph applies where—

(a) a company that holds shares in another company transfers the shares under a repurchase agreement, and

(b) by virtue of section 263A(1) (agreements for sale and repurchase of securities) the disposal is disregarded for the purposes of the enactments relating to chargeable gains.

(2) During the period of the repurchase agreement—

(a) the original owner shall be treated for the purposes of this Part as continuing to hold the shares transferred and accordingly as retaining his entitlement to any rights attached to them, and

(b) the interim holder shall be treated for those purposes as not holding the shares transferred and as not becoming entitled to any such rights.

This is subject to the following qualification.

(3) If at any time before the end of the period of the repurchase agreement the original owner, or another member of the same group as the original owner, becomes the holder—

(a) of any of the shares transferred, or

(b) of any shares directly or indirectly representing any of the shares transferred,

sub-paragraph (2) does not apply after that time in relation to those shares or, as the case may be, in relation to the shares represented by those shares.

(4) In this paragraph a "repurchase agreement" means an agreement under which—

(a) a person ("the original owner") transfers shares to another person ("the interim holder") under an agreement to sell them, and

(b) the original owner or a person connected with him is required to buy them back either—

(i) in pursuance of an obligation to do so imposed by that agreement or by any related agreement, or

(ii) in consequence of the exercise of an option acquired under that agreement or any related agreement.

For the purposes of paragraph (b) agreements are related if they are entered into in pursuance of the same arrangements (regardless of the date on which either agreement is entered into).

(5) Any reference in this paragraph to the period of a repurchase agreement is to the period beginning with the transfer of the shares by the original owner to the interim holder and ending with the repurchase of the shares in pursuance of the agreement.

Effect of stock lending arrangements

13—(1) This paragraph applies where—

(a) a company that holds shares in another company transfers the shares under a stock lending arrangement, and

(b) by virtue of section 263B(2) (stock lending arrangements) the disposal is disregarded for the purposes of the enactments relating to chargeable gains.

(2) During the period of the stock lending arrangement—

(a) the lender shall be treated for the purposes of this Part as continuing to hold the shares transferred and accordingly as retaining his entitlement to any rights attached to them, and

(b) the borrower shall be treated for those purposes as not holding the shares transferred and as not becoming entitled to any such rights.

This is subject to the following qualification.

(3) If at any time before the end of the period of the stock lending arrangement the lender, or another member of the same group as the lender, becomes the holder—

(a) of any of the shares transferred, or

(b) of any shares directly or indirectly representing any of the shares transferred,

sub-paragraph (2) does not apply after that time in relation to those shares or, as the case may be, in relation to the shares represented by those shares.

(4) In this paragraph a "stock lending arrangement" means arrangements between two persons ("the borrower" and "the lender") under which—

(a) the lender transfers shares to the borrower otherwise than by way of sale, and

(b) a requirement is imposed on the borrower to transfer those shares back to the lender otherwise than by way of sale.

(5) Any reference in this paragraph to the period of a stock lending arrangement is to the period beginning with the transfer of the shares by the lender to the borrower and ending—

(*a*) with the transfer of the shares back to the lender in pursuance of the arrangement, or

(*b*) when it becomes apparent that the requirement for the borrower to make a transfer back to the lender will not be complied with.

(6) The following provisions apply for the purposes of this paragraph as they apply for the purposes of section 263B—

(*a*) subsections (5) and (6) of that section (references to transfer back of securities to include transfer of other securities of the same description);

(*b*) section 263C (references to transfer back of securities to include payment in respect of redemption).

Effect in relation to company invested in of earlier company reconstruction etc

14—(1) This paragraph applies where shares in one company ("company X")—

(*a*) are exchanged (or deemed to be exchanged) for shares in another company ("company Y"), or

(*b*) are deemed to be exchanged by virtue of section 136 for shares in company X and shares in another company ("company Y"),

in circumstances such that, under section 127 as that section applies by virtue of section 135 or 136, the original shares and the new holding are treated as the same asset.

(2) Where company Y—

(*a*) is the company invested in, and is accordingly the company by reference to which the requirement of paragraph 7 (the substantial shareholding requirement) falls to be met, or

(*b*) is a company by reference to which, by virtue of this paragraph, that requirement may be met, or

(*c*) is a company by reference to which, by virtue of paragraph 15 (effect of earlier demerger) that requirement may be met,

that requirement may instead be met, in relation to times before the exchange (or deemed exchange), by reference to company X.

(3) If in any case that requirement can be met by virtue of this paragraph (or by virtue of this paragraph together with paragraph 15), it shall be treated as met.

(4) In sub-paragraph (1) "original shares" and "new holding" shall be construed in accordance with sections 126, 127, 135 and 136.

Effect in relation to company invested in of earlier demerger

15—(1) This paragraph applies where shares in one company ("the subsidiary") are transferred by another company ("the parent company") on a demerger.

(2) Where the subsidiary—

(*a*) is the company invested in, and is accordingly the company by reference to which the requirement of paragraph 7 (the substantial shareholding requirement) falls to be met, or

(*b*) is a company by reference to which, by virtue of this paragraph, that requirement may be met, or

(*c*) is a company by reference to which, by virtue of paragraph 14 (effect of earlier company reconstruction etc), that requirement may be met,

that requirement may instead be met, in relation to times before the transfer, by reference to the parent company.

(3) If in any case that requirement can be met by virtue of this paragraph (or by virtue of this paragraph together with paragraph 14), it shall be treated as met.

(4) In this paragraph a "transfer of shares on a demerger" means a transfer such that, by virtue of section 192(2)(*b*), sections 126 to 130 apply as if the parent company and the subsidiary were the same company and the transfer were a reorganisation of that company's share capital not involving a disposal or acquisition.

Effect of investing company's liquidation

16 Where assets of the investing company, or of a company that is a member of the same group as the investing company, are vested in a liquidator under section 145 of the Insolvency Act 1986 or Article 123 of the Insolvency (Northern Ireland) Order 1989 or otherwise, this Part applies as if the assets were vested in, and the acts of the liquidator in relation to the assets were the acts of, the company (acquisitions from or disposals to him by the company being disregarded accordingly).

Special rules for assets of insurance company's long-term insurance fund

17—(1) In the following two cases paragraph 8(1) (meaning of substantial shareholding) has effect as if, in paragraphs (*a*), (*b*) and (*c*), "30%" were substituted for "10%".

(2) The first case is where the investing company is an insurance company and the disposal is of an asset of its long-term insurance fund.

(3) The second case is where—

(*a*) the investing company is a 51% subsidiary of an insurance company, and

(*b*) the insurance company holds as an asset of its long-term insurance fund shares or an interest in shares—

(i) in the investing company, or

(ii) in another company through which it owns shares in the investing company.

The reference in paragraph (*b*)(ii) to owning shares through another company has the same meaning as in section 838 of the Taxes Act (subsidiaries).

(4) Where the investing company is a member of a group that includes an insurance company, paragraph 9 (aggregation of holdings of group companies) does not apply in relation to shares or an interest in shares held by the insurance company as assets of its long-term insurance fund.

(5) In this paragraph "insurance company" and "long-term insurance fund" have the meanings given by section 431(2) of the Taxes Act.

PART 3

REQUIREMENTS TO BE MET IN RELATION TO INVESTING COMPANY AND COMPANY INVESTED IN

Requirements relating to the investing company

18—(1) The investing company must—

(*a*) have been a sole trading company or a member of a qualifying group throughout the period ("the qualifying period")—

(i) beginning with the start of the latest twelve-month period by reference to which the requirement of paragraph 7 (the substantial shareholding requirement) is met, and

(ii) ending with the time of the disposal, and

(*b*) be a sole trading company or a member of a qualifying group immediately after the time of the disposal.

(2) For this purpose a "qualifying group" means—

(*a*) a trading group, or

(*b*) a group that would be a trading group if the activities of any group member that is not established for profit were disregarded to the extent that they are carried on otherwise than for profit.

In determining whether a company is established for profit, no account shall be taken of any object or power of the company that is only incidental to its main objects.

(3) The requirement in sub-paragraph (1)(*a*) is met if the investing company was a sole trading company for some of the qualifying period and a member of a qualifying group for the remainder of that period.

(4) The requirement in sub-paragraph (1)(*a*) is treated as met if at the time of the disposal—

(*a*) the investing company is a member of a group, and

(*b*) there is another member of the group in relation to which that requirement would have been met if—

(i) the subject matter of the disposal had been transferred to it immediately before the disposal in circumstances in which section 171(1) (transfers within a group) applied, and

(ii) it had made the disposal.

(5) If the disposal is by virtue of section 28(1) or (2) (asset disposed of under contract) treated as made at a time before the asset is conveyed or transferred, the requirements in sub-paragraph (1)(*a*) and (*b*) must also be complied with as they would have effect if the references in those provisions and sub-paragraph (4) to the time of the disposal were to the time of the conveyance or transfer.

(6) In this paragraph a "sole trading company" means a trading company that is not a member of a group.

Requirements relating to the company invested in

19—(1) The company invested in must—

(*a*) have been a qualifying company throughout the period—

(i) beginning with the start of the latest twelve-month period by reference to which the requirement of paragraph 7 (the substantial shareholding requirement) is met, and

(ii) ending with the time of the disposal, and

(*b*) be a qualifying company immediately after the time of the disposal.

(2) For this purpose a "qualifying company" means a trading company or the holding company of a trading group or a trading subgroup.

(3) If the disposal is by virtue of section 28(1) or (2) (asset disposed of under contract) treated as made at a time before the asset is conveyed or transferred, the requirements in sub-paragraph (1)(*a*) and (*b*) must also be complied with as they would have effect if the references there to the time of the disposal were to the time of the conveyance or transfer.

Meaning of "trading company"

20—(1) In this Schedule "trading company" means a company carrying on trading activities whose activities do not include to a substantial extent activities other than trading activities.

(2) For the purposes of sub-paragraph (1) "trading activities" means activities carried on by the company—

(*a*) in the course of, or for the purposes of, a trade being carried on by it,
(*b*) for the purposes of a trade that it is preparing to carry on,
(*c*) with a view to its acquiring or starting to carry on a trade, or
(*d*) with a view to its acquiring a significant interest in the share capital of another company that—

(i) is a trading company or the holding company of a trading group or trading subgroup, and
(ii) if the acquiring company is a member of a group, is not a member of that group.

(3) Activities do not qualify as trading activities under sub-paragraph (2)(*c*) or (*d*) unless the acquisition is made, or (as the case may be) the company starts to carry on the trade, as soon as is reasonably practicable in the circumstances.

(4) The reference in sub-paragraph (2)(*d*) to the acquisition of a significant interest in the share capital of another company is to an acquisition of ordinary share capital in the other company—

(*a*) such as would make that company a 51% subsidiary of the acquiring company, or
(*b*) such as would give the acquiring company a qualifying shareholding in a joint venture company without making the two companies members of the same group.

Meaning of "trading group"

21—(1) In this Schedule "trading group" means a group—

(*a*) one or more of whose members carry on trading activities, and
(*b*) the activities of whose members, taken together, do not include to a substantial extent activities other than trading activities.

(2) For the purposes of sub-paragraph (1) "trading activities" means activities carried on by a member of the group—

(*a*) in the course of, or for the purposes of, a trade being carried on by any member of the group,
(*b*) for the purposes of a trade that any member of the group is preparing to carry on,
(*c*) with a view to any member of the group acquiring or starting to carry on a trade, or
(*d*) with a view to any member of the group acquiring a significant interest in the share capital of another company that—

(i) is a trading company or the holding company of a trading group or trading subgroup, and
(ii) is not a member of the same group as the acquiring company.

(3) Activities do not qualify as trading activities under sub-paragraph (2)(*c*) or (*d*) unless the acquisition is made, or (as the case may be) the group member in question starts to carry on the trade, as soon as is reasonably practicable in the circumstances.

(4) The reference in sub-paragraph (2)(*d*) to the acquisition of a significant interest in the share capital of another company is to an acquisition of ordinary share capital in the other company—

(*a*) such as would make that company a member of the same group as the acquiring company, or
(*b*) such as would give the acquiring company a qualifying shareholding in a joint venture company without making the joint venture company a member of the same group as the acquiring company.

(5) For the purposes of this paragraph the activities of the members of the group shall be treated as one business (with the result that activities are disregarded to the extent that they are intra-group activities).

Meaning of "trading subgroup"

22—(1) In this Schedule "trading subgroup" means a subgroup—

(*a*) one or more of whose members carry on trading activities, and
(*b*) the activities of whose members, taken together, do not include to a substantial extent activities other than trading activities.

(2) For the purposes of sub-paragraph (1) "trading activities" means activities carried on by a member of the subgroup—

(*a*) in the course of, or for the purposes of, a trade being carried on by any member of the subgroup,
(*b*) for the purposes of a trade that any member of the subgroup is preparing to carry on,
(*c*) with a view to any member of the subgroup acquiring or starting to carry on a trade, or

(*d*) with a view to any member of the subgroup acquiring a significant interest in the share capital of another company that—

    (i) is a trading company or the holding company of a trading group or trading subgroup, and
    (ii) is not a member of the same group as the acquiring company.

(3) Activities do not qualify as trading activities under sub-paragraph (2)(*c*) or (*d*) unless the acquisition is made, or (as the case may be) the subgroup member in question starts to carry on the trade, as soon as is reasonably practicable in the circumstances.

(4) The reference in sub-paragraph (2)(*d*) to the acquisition of a significant interest in the share capital of another company is to an acquisition of ordinary share capital in the other company—

    (*a*) such as would make that company a member of the same subgroup as the acquiring company, or
    (*b*) such as would give the acquiring company a qualifying shareholding in a joint venture company without making the two companies members of the same group.

(5) For the purposes of this paragraph the activities of the members of the subgroup shall be treated as one business (with the result that activities are disregarded to the extent that they are intra-subgroup activities).

Treatment of holdings in joint venture companies

23—(1) This paragraph applies where a company ("the company") has a qualifying shareholding in a joint venture company.

(2) In determining whether the company is a trading company—

    (*a*) its holding of shares in the joint venture company shall be disregarded, and
    (*b*) it shall be treated as carrying on an appropriate proportion—

        (i) of the activities of the joint venture company, or
        (ii) where the joint venture company is a holding company, of the activities of that company and its 51% subsidiaries.

This sub-paragraph does not apply if the company is a member of a group and the joint venture company is a member of the same group.

(3) In determining whether the company is a member of a trading group or the holding company of a trading group—

    (*a*) every holding of shares in the joint venture company by a member of the group having a qualifying shareholding in that company shall be disregarded, and
    (*b*) each member of the group having a qualifying shareholding in the joint venture company shall be treated as carrying on an appropriate proportion—

        (i) of the activities of the joint venture company, or
        (ii) where the joint venture company is a holding company, of the activities of that company and its 51% subsidiaries.

This sub-paragraph does not apply if the joint venture company is a member of the group.

(4) In determining whether the company is the holding company of a trading subgroup—

    (*a*) every holding of shares in the joint venture company by the company and any of its 51% subsidiaries having a qualifying shareholding in the joint venture company shall be disregarded, and
    (*b*) the company and each of its 51% subsidiaries having a qualifying shareholding in the joint venture company shall be treated as carrying on an appropriate proportion—

        (i) of the activities of the joint venture company, or
        (ii) where the joint venture company is a holding company, of the activities of that company and its 51% subsidiaries.

This sub-paragraph does not apply if the joint venture company is a member of the same group as the company.

(5) In sub-paragraphs (2)(*b*), (3)(*b*) and (4)(*b*) "an appropriate proportion" means a proportion corresponding to the percentage of the ordinary share capital of the joint venture company held by the company concerned.

(6) In this paragraph "shares", in relation to a joint venture company, includes securities of that company or an interest in shares in or securities of that company.

(7) For the purposes of this paragraph the activities of a joint venture company that is a holding company and its 51% subsidiaries shall be treated as a single business (so that activities are disregarded to the extent that they are intra-group activities or, as the case may be, intra-subgroup, activities).

Meaning of "joint venture company" and "qualifying shareholding"

24—(1) For the purposes of this Schedule a company is a "joint venture company" if, and only if—

    (*a*) it is a trading company or the holding company of a trading group or trading subgroup, and (*b*) there are five or fewer persons who between them hold 75% or more of its ordinary share capital.

In determining whether there are five or fewer such persons as are mentioned in paragraph (*b*), the members of a group are treated as if they were a single company.

(2) For the purposes of this Schedule—

(*a*) a company that is not a member of a group has a "qualifying shareholding" in a joint venture company if, and only if, it holds shares or an interest in shares in the joint venture company by virtue of which it holds 10% or more of that company's ordinary share capital;

(*b*) a company that is a member of a group has a "qualifying shareholding" in a joint venture company if, and only if—

(i) it holds ordinary share capital of the joint venture company, and

(ii) the members of the group between them hold 10% or more of the ordinary share capital of that company.

Effect in relation to company invested in of earlier company reconstruction, demerger etc

25 The provisions of—

(*a*) paragraph 14 (effect of earlier company reconstruction etc), and

(*b*) paragraph 15 (effect of earlier demerger),

have effect in relation to the requirements of paragraph 19 (requirements in relation to company invested in) as they have effect in relation to the requirement of paragraph 7 (the substantial shareholding requirement).

PART 4

INTERPRETATION

Meaning of "company", "group" and related expressions

26—(1) In this Schedule—

(*a*) "company" has the meaning given by section 170(9); and

(*b*) references to a group, or to membership of a group, shall be construed in accordance with the provisions of section 170 read as if "51 per cent" were substituted for "75 per cent".

(2) References in this Schedule to a "subgroup" are to companies that would form a group but for the fact that one of them is a 51% subsidiary of another company.

(3) In this Schedule "holding company"—

(*a*) in relation to a group, means the company described in section 170 as the principal company of the group;

(*b*) in relation to a subgroup, means a company that would be the holding company of a group but for being a 51% subsidiary of another company.

(4) In this Schedule "51% subsidiary" has the meaning given by section 838 of the Taxes Act.

In applying that section for the purposes of this Schedule, any share capital of a registered industrial and provident society shall be treated as ordinary share capital.

(5) References in this Schedule to a "group" or "subsidiary" shall be construed with any necessary modifications where applied to a company incorporated under the law of a country or territory outside the United Kingdom.

Meaning of "trade"

27 In this Schedule "trade" means anything that—

(*a*) is a trade, profession or vocation, within the meaning of the Income Tax Acts, and

(*b*) is conducted on a commercial basis with a view to the realisation of profits.

Meaning of "twelve-month period"

28 For the purposes of this Schedule a "twelve-month period" means a period ending with the day before the first anniversary of the day with which, or in the course of which, the period began.

Meaning of "interest in shares"

29—(1) References in this Schedule to an interest in shares are to an interest as a co-owner of shares.

(2) It does not matter whether the shares are owned jointly or in common, or whether the interests of the co-owners are equal.

Meaning of "asset related to shares"

30—(1) This paragraph explains what is meant by an asset related to shares in a company.

(2) An asset is related to shares in a company if it is—

(*a*) an option to acquire or dispose of shares or an interest in shares in that company, or
(*b*) a security to which are attached rights by virtue of which the holder is or may become entitled to acquire or dispose of (whether by conversion or exchange or otherwise)—

   (i) shares or an interest in shares in that company, or
   (ii) an option to acquire or dispose of shares or an interest in shares in that company, or
   (iii) another security falling within this paragraph, or

(*c*) an option to acquire or dispose of any security within paragraph (*b*) or an interest in any such security, or
(*d*) an interest in, or option over, any such option or security as is mentioned in paragraph (*a*), (*b*) or (*c*), or
(*e*) any interest in, or option over, any such interest or option as is mentioned in paragraph (*d*) or this paragraph.

(3) In determining whether a security is within sub-paragraph (2)(*b*), no account shall be taken—

(*a*) of any rights attached to the security other than rights relating, directly or indirectly, to shares of the company in question, or
(*b*) of rights as regards which, at the time the security came into existence, there was no more than a negligible likelihood that they would in due course be exercised to a significant extent.

(4) The references in this paragraph to an interest in a security or option have a meaning corresponding to that given by paragraph 29 in relation to an interest in shares.

Index of defined expressions

31 In this Schedule the expressions listed below are defined or otherwise explained by the provisions indicated:

PART 5
CONSEQUENTIAL PROVISIONS
Meaning of "chargeable shares" or "chargeable asset"

32 Any exemption conferred by this Schedule shall be disregarded in determining whether shares are "chargeable shares", or an asset is a "chargeable asset", for the purposes of any enactment relating to corporation tax or capital gains tax.

Negligible value claims

33—(1) This paragraph applies where—

(*a*) a company makes a claim under section 24(2) (assets of negligible value) in relation to shares held by it, and
(*b*) by virtue of this Schedule any loss accruing to the company on a disposal of the shares at the time of the claim would not be an allowable loss.

(2) Where this paragraph applies the company may not exercise the option under section 24(2) to specify a time earlier than the time of the claim as the time when the shares are treated as sold and reacquired by virtue of that subsection.

(3) This paragraph applies to—

(*a*) an interest in shares in a company, or
(*b*) an asset related to shares in a company,

as it applies to shares in that company.

Reorganisations etc: deemed accrual of chargeable gain or allowable loss held over on earlier transaction

34—(1) The exemptions conferred by this Schedule do not apply to or affect a chargeable gain or allowable loss deemed to accrue on a disposal by virtue of section 116(10)(*b*) (reorganisations, conversions and reconstructions: deemed accrual of gain or loss held over on earlier transaction).

(2) Sub-paragraph (1) does not apply where the relevant earlier transaction was a deemed disposal and reacquisition under section 92(7) of the Finance Act 1996 (convertible securities etc).

Recovery of charge postponed on transfer of assets to non-resident company

35—(1) This paragraph applies where—

(*a*) a company disposes of an asset in circumstances falling within section 140(4) (recovery of charge postponed on transfer of assets to non-resident company), and
(*b*) by virtue of this Schedule any gain accruing to the company on the disposal would not be a chargeable gain.

(2) Where this paragraph applies the amount by which the consideration received on the disposal would be treated as increased by virtue of section 140(4) shall instead be treated as accruing to the company, at the time of the disposal, as a chargeable gain to which this Schedule does not apply.

(3) Any reference in section 140 to an amount being brought or taken into account under or in accordance with subsection (4) of that section includes a reference to an amount being treated, by virtue of sub-paragraph (2) above, as accruing as a chargeable gain.

Appropriation of asset to trading stock

36—(1) Where—

(*a*) an asset acquired by a company otherwise than as trading stock of a trade carried on by it is appropriated by the company for the purposes of the trade as trading stock (whether on the commencement of the trade or otherwise), and
(*b*) if the company had then sold the asset for its market value, a chargeable gain or allowable loss would have accrued to the company but for an exemption conferred by this Schedule,

the company is treated for the purposes of the enactments relating to chargeable gains as if it had thereby disposed of the asset for its market value.

(2) Section 173 (transfers within a group: trading stock) applies in relation to this paragraph as it applies in relation to section 161 (appropriations to and from stock).

Recovery of held-over gain on claim for gifts relief

37—(1) This paragraph applies where—

(*a*) a company disposes of an asset,
(*b*) the expenditure allowable in computing a gain or loss on that disposal falls to be reduced because of a claim for relief under section 165 (gifts relief) in relation to an earlier disposal, and
(*c*) by virtue of this Schedule any gain accruing to the company on the disposal mentioned in paragraph (*a*) would not be a chargeable gain.

(2) Where this paragraph applies the amount of the held-over gain, or an appropriate proportion of it, shall be treated as accruing to the company, at the time of the disposal mentioned in sub-paragraph (1)(*a*), as a chargeable gain to which this Schedule does not apply.

(3) An "appropriate proportion" means a proportion determined on a just and reasonable basis having regard to the subject matter of the disposal mentioned in sub-paragraph (1)(*a*) and the subject matter of the earlier disposal that was the subject of the claim for relief under section 165.

In this paragraph "held-over gain" has the same meaning as in section 165.

Degrouping: time when deemed sale and reacquisition treated as taking place

38—(1) Where—

(*a*) a company, as a result of ceasing at any time ("the time of degrouping") to be a member of a group, is treated by section 179(3) as having sold and immediately reacquired an asset, and
(*b*) if the company owning the asset at the time of degrouping had disposed of it immediately before that time, any gain accruing on the disposal would by virtue of this Schedule not have been a chargeable gain,

section 179(3) shall have effect as if it provided for the deemed sale and reacquisition to be treated as taking place immediately before the time of degrouping.

(2) Where—

(*a*) a company, as a result of ceasing at any time ("the relevant time") to satisfy the conditions in section 179(7), is treated by section 179(6) as having sold and immediately reacquired an asset, and

(*b*) if the company owning the asset at the relevant time had disposed of it immediately before that time, any gain accruing on the disposal would by virtue of this Schedule not have been a chargeable gain,

section 179(6) shall have effect as if it provided for the deemed sale and reacquisition to be treated as taking place immediately before the relevant time.

(3) Any reference in this paragraph to a disposal or other event taking place immediately before the time of degrouping or the relevant time is to its taking place immediately before that time but on the same day.

Effect of FOREX matching regulations

39—(1) No gain or loss shall be treated as arising under the FOREX matching regulations on a disposal on which by virtue of this Schedule any gain would not be a chargeable gain.

(2) The "FOREX matching regulations" means any regulations made under Schedule 15 to the Finance Act 1993 (exchange gains and losses: alternative method of calculation).".

PART 2
CONSEQUENTIAL AMENDMENTS
Degrouping: time of accrual of chargeable gain or allowable loss

2 In section 179(4) of the Taxation of Chargeable Gains Act 1992 (c 12) (deemed sale and reacquisition on company ceasing to be member of group: time when chargeable gain or allowable loss treated as accruing), for "which, apart from this subsection, would accrue" substitute "accruing".

Treatment of furnished holiday lettings

3—(1) Section 241 of the Taxation of Chargeable Gains Act 1992 (furnished holiday lettings) is amended as follows.

(2) In subsection (3) (commercial letting of furnished holiday accommodation to be treated as trade for certain purposes), for the opening words substitute—

"Subject to subsections (4) to (8) below, for the purposes of the provisions mentioned in subsection (3A) below—".

(3) After that subsection insert—

"(3A) The provisions referred to in subsection (3) above are—

sections 152 to 157 (roll-over relief on replacement of business asset),
section 165 (gifts relief),
section 253 (relief for loans to traders),
Schedule A1 (taper relief),
Schedule 6 (retirement relief etc), and
Schedule 7AC (exemptions for disposals by companies with substantial shareholding).".

(4) In subsection (4) for "sections mentioned in subsection (3)" substitute "provisions mentioned in subsection (3A)".

Overseas life insurance companies

4 In Schedule 7B of the Taxation of Chargeable Gains Act 1992 (c 12) (modification of Act in relation to overseas life insurance companies), after paragraph 15 add—

"16 In Schedule 7AC, in paragraph 3(2)(*c*)(ii), the words "section 11(2)(*b*), (*c*) or (*d*) of the Taxes Act" shall be treated as substituted for the words "section 10(3)".".

Corporate venturing scheme

5 In Schedule 15 to the Finance Act 2000 (c 17) (the corporate venturing scheme), in paragraphs 84(1) and 85(1) after "(see paragraph 83" insert "and paragraph 4 of Schedule 7AC to the Taxation of Chargeable Gains Act 1992".

SCHEDULE 9

CHARGEABLE GAINS: SHARE EXCHANGES AND COMPANY
RECONSTRUCTIONS

Section 45

Commentary—*Simon's Direct Tax Service* **D2.726, 727.**

PART 1

PROVISIONS REPLACING SECTIONS 135 AND 136 OF THE TAXATION
OF CHARGEABLE GAINS ACT 1992

Share exchanges

1 For section 135 of the Taxation of Chargeable Gains Act 1992 (exchange of securities for those in another company) substitute—

"135 Exchange of securities for those in another company

(1) This section applies in the following circumstances where a company ("company B") issues shares or debentures to a person in exchange for shares in or debentures of another company ("company A").

(2) The circumstances are:

Case 1

Where company B holds, or in consequence of the exchange will hold, more than 25% of the ordinary share capital of company A.

Case 2

Where company B issues the shares or debentures in exchange for shares as the result of a general offer—

(c) made to members of company A or any class of them (with or without exceptions for persons connected with company B), and
(d) made in the first instance on a condition such that if it were satisfied company B would have control of company A.

Case 3

Where company B holds, or in consequence of the exchange will hold, the greater part of the voting power in company A.

(3) Where this section applies, sections 127 to 131 (share reorganisations etc) apply with the necessary adaptations as if company A and company B were the same company and the exchange were a reorganisation of its share capital.

(4) In this section "ordinary share capital" has the meaning given by section 832(1) of the Taxes Act and also includes—

(a) in relation to a unit trust scheme, any rights that are treated by section 99(1)(b) of this Act (application of Act to unit trust schemes) as shares in a company, and
(b) in relation to a company that has no share capital, any interests in the company possessed by members of the company.

(5) This section applies in relation to a company that has no share capital as if references to shares in or debentures of the company included any interests in the company possessed by members of the company.

(6) This section has effect subject to section 137(1) (exchange must be for bona fide commercial reasons and not part of tax avoidance scheme).".

Scheme of reconstruction involving issue of securities

2 For section 136 of the Taxation of Chargeable Gains Act 1992 (c 12) (reconstruction or amalgamation involving issue of securities) substitute—

"136 Scheme of reconstruction involving issue of securities

(1) This section applies where—

(a) an arrangement between a company ("company A") and—

(i) the persons holding shares in or debentures of the company, or
(ii) where there are different classes of shares in or debentures of the company, the persons holding any class of those shares or debentures,

is entered into for the purposes of, or in connection with, a scheme of reconstruction, and
(b) under the arrangement—

(i) another company (''company B'') issues shares or debentures to those persons in respect of and in proportion to (or as nearly as may be in proportion to) their relevant holdings in company A, and

(ii) the shares in or debentures of company A comprised in relevant holdings are retained by those persons or are cancelled or otherwise extinguished.

(2) Where this section applies—

(a) those persons are treated as exchanging their relevant holdings in company A for the shares or debentures held by them in consequence of the arrangement, and

(b) sections 127 to 131 (share reorganisations etc) apply with the necessary adaptations as if company A and company B were the same company and the exchange were a reorganisation of its share capital.

For this purpose shares in or debentures of company A comprised in relevant holdings that are retained are treated as if they had been cancelled and replaced by a new issue.

(3) Where a reorganisation of the share capital of company A is carried out for the purposes of the scheme of reconstruction, the provisions of subsections (1) and (2) apply in relation to the position after the reorganisation.

(4) In this section—

(a) ''scheme of reconstruction'' has the meaning given by Schedule 5AA to this Act;

(b) references to ''relevant holdings'' of shares in or debentures of company A are—

(i) where there is only one class of shares in or debentures of the company, to holdings of shares in or debentures of the company, and

(ii) where there are different classes of shares in or debentures of the company, to holdings of a class of shares or debentures that is involved in the scheme of reconstruction (within the meaning of paragraph 2 of Schedule 5AA);

(c) references to shares or debentures being retained include their being retained with altered rights or in an altered form, whether as the result of reduction, consolidation, division or otherwise; and

(d) any reference to a reorganisation of a company's share capital is to a reorganisation within the meaning of section 126.

(5) This section applies in relation to a company that has no share capital as if references to shares in or debentures of the company included any interests in the company possessed by members of the company.

(6) This section has effect subject to section 137(1) (scheme of reconstruction must be for bona fide commercial reasons and not part of tax avoidance scheme).''.

Meaning of ''scheme of reconstruction''

3 After Schedule 5A to the Taxation of Chargeable Gains Act 1992 insert—

''SCHEDULE 5AA

MEANING OF ''SCHEME OF RECONSTRUCTION''

Introductory

1 In section 136 ''scheme of reconstruction'' means a scheme of merger, division or other restructuring that meets the first and second, and either the third or the fourth, of the following conditions.

First condition: issue of ordinary share capital

2 The first condition is that the scheme involves the issue of ordinary share capital of a company (''the successor company'') or of more than one company (''the successor companies'')—

(a) to holders of ordinary share capital of another company (''the original company'') or, where there are different classes of ordinary share capital of that company, to holders of one or more classes of ordinary share capital of that company (the classes ''involved in the scheme of reconstruction''), or

(b) to holders of ordinary share capital of more than one other company (''the original companies'') or, where there are different classes of ordinary share capital of one or more of the original company or companies, to holders of ordinary share capital of any of those companies or of one or more classes of ordinary share capital of any of those companies (the classes ''involved in the scheme of reconstruction''),

and does not involve the issue of ordinary share capital of the successor company, or (as the case may be) any of the successor companies, to anyone else.

Second condition: equal entitlement to new shares

3—(1) The second condition is that under the scheme the entitlement of any person to acquire ordinary share capital of the successor company or companies by virtue of holding relevant shares, or relevant shares of any class, is the same as that of any other person holding such shares or shares of that class.

(2) For this purpose "relevant shares" means shares comprised—

(*a*) where there is one original company, in the ordinary share capital of that company or, as the case may be, in the ordinary share capital of that company of a class involved in the scheme of reconstruction;

(*b*) where there is more than one original company, in the ordinary share capital of any of those companies or, as the case may be, in the ordinary share capital of any of those companies of a class involved in the scheme of reconstruction.

Third condition: continuity of business

4—(1) The third condition is that the effect of the restructuring is—

(*a*) where there is one original company, that the business or substantially the whole of the business carried on by the company is carried on—

(i) by a successor company which is not the original company, or

(ii) by two or more successor companies (which may include the original company);

(*b*) where there is more than one original company, that all or part of the business or businesses carried on by one or more of the original companies is carried on by a different company, and the whole or substantially the whole of the businesses carried on by the original companies are carried on—

(i) where there is one successor company, by that company (which may be one of the original companies), or

(ii) where there are two or more successor companies, by those companies (which may be the same as the original companies or include any of those companies).

(2) The reference in sub-paragraph (1)(*a*)(ii) or (*b*)(ii) to the whole or substantially the whole of a business, or businesses, being carried on by two or more companies includes the case where the activities of those companies taken together embrace the whole or substantially the whole of the business, or businesses, in question.

(3) For the purposes of this paragraph a business carried on by a company that is under the control of another company is treated as carried on by the controlling company as well as by the controlled company.

Section 840 of the Taxes Act (meaning of "control") applies for the purposes of this sub-paragraph.

(4) For the purposes of this paragraph the holding and management of assets that are retained by the original company, or any of the original companies, for the purpose of making a capital distribution in respect of shares in the company shall be disregarded.

In this sub-paragraph "capital distribution" has the same meaning as in section 122.

Fourth condition: compromise or arrangement with members

5 The fourth condition is that—

(*a*) the scheme is carried out in pursuance of a compromise or arrangement—

(i) under section 425 of the Companies Act 1985 or Article 418 of the Companies (Northern Ireland) Order 1966, or

(ii) under any corresponding provision of the law of a country or territory outside the United Kingdom, and

(*b*) no part of the business of the original company, or of any of the original companies, is transferred under the scheme to any other person.

Preliminary reorganisation of share capital to be disregarded

6 Where a reorganisation of the share capital of the original company, or of any of the original companies, is carried out for the purposes of the scheme of reconstruction, the provisions of the first and second conditions apply in relation to the position after the reorganisation.

Subsequent issue of shares or debentures to be disregarded

7 An issue of shares in or debentures of the successor company, or any of the successor companies, after the latest date on which any ordinary share capital of the successor company, or any of them, is issued—

(*a*) in consideration of the transfer of any business, or part of a business, under the scheme, or

(*b*) in pursuance of the compromise or arrangement mentioned in paragraph 5(*a*),

shall be disregarded for the purposes of the first and second conditions.

Interpretation

8—(1) In this Schedule "ordinary share capital" has the meaning given by section 832(1) of the Taxes Act and also includes—

    (*a*) in relation to a unit trust scheme, any rights that are treated by section 99(1)(*b*) of this Act (application of Act to unit trust schemes) as shares in a company, and

    (*b*) in relation to a company that has no share capital, any interests in the company possessed by members of the company.

(2) Any reference in this Schedule to a reorganisation of a company's share capital is to a reorganisation within the meaning of section 126.".

PART 2
CONSEQUENTIAL AMENDMENTS
Taxes Act 1988

4—(1) The Taxes Act 1988 is amended as follows.

(2) In section 299 (disposal of shares)—

    (*a*) in subsection (6D), as that section applies to shares issued after 31st December 1993 (enterprise investment scheme), and

    (*b*) in subsection (4C), as that section applies to shares issued before 1st January 1994 (business expansion scheme),

for "(whether or not by virtue of section 135(3) of that Act)" substitute "(including a case where that section applies by virtue of any enactment relating to chargeable gains)", and for the words from "shall be construed" to the end substitute "have the same meaning as in section 127 of the 1992 Act (or, as the case may be, that section as applied by virtue of the enactment concerned)".

(3) In section 312(3) (interpretation of Chapter 3 of Part 7: references to disposal of shares), for "136(1)" substitute "136".

(4) In section 473(6) (conversion etc of securities held as circulating capital), for "136(3)" substitute "135(5), 136(5)".

(5) In section 757 (disposal of material interests in non-qualifying offshore funds), for subsections (5) and (6) substitute—

    "(5) Section 135 of the 1992 Act (exchange of securities for those in another company treated as not involving a disposal) does not apply for the purposes of this Chapter if the company that is company A for the purposes of that section is or was at a material time a non-qualifying offshore fund and the company that is company B for those purposes is not such a fund.

In a case where that section would apply apart from this subsection, the exchange in question (of shares, debentures or other interests in or of an entity that is or was at a material time a non-qualifying offshore fund) shall for the purposes of this Chapter constitute a disposal of interests in the offshore fund for a consideration equal to their market value at the time of the exchange.

(6) Section 136 of the 1992 Act (scheme of reconstruction involving issue of securities treated as exchange not involving disposal) does not apply for the purposes of this Chapter so as to require persons to be treated as exchanging shares, debentures or other interests in or of an entity that is or was at a material time a non-qualifying offshore fund for assets that do not constitute interests in such a fund.

In a case where that section would apply apart from this subsection, the deemed exchange in question (of shares, debentures or other interests in or of an entity that is or was at a material time a non-qualifying offshore fund) shall for the purposes of this Chapter constitute a disposal of interests in the offshore fund for a consideration equal to their market value at the time of the deemed exchange.".

(6) In section 758(6) (offshore funds operating equalisation arrangements: events treated as disposal), for the words from "section 135" to the end substitute "any provision of Chapter 2 of Part 4 of that Act".

(7) In section 842 (investment trusts), at the end of subsection (4) add "and "scheme of reconstruction" has the same meaning as in section 136 of that Act".

Taxation of Chargeable Gains Act 1992

5—(1) The Taxation of Chargeable Gains Act 1992 (c 12) is amended as follows.

(2) In section 31 (distributions within a group followed by a disposal of shares), for subsection (6)(*b*) substitute—

    "(*b*) an exchange, or deemed exchange, of shares in or debentures of a company held by company A for shares in or debentures of another company, being a company associated with company A immediately after the transaction, that is treated by virtue of section 135 or 136 as a reorganisation of share capital within the meaning of section 126 to which sections 127 to 131 apply with the necessary adaptations, or".

(3) In section 34 (transactions treated as a reorganisation of capital)—

(a) in subsections (1)(a), (1A), (1B) and (1C)(a) for "sections 127 and 135(3)" substitute "section 135 or 136";

(b) in the closing words of subsection (1) for "section 135(3)" substitute "section 135 or 136"; and

(c) in subsection (2) for the words from the beginning to "and in those subsections" substitute "In subsections (1) to (1C)" (the words omitted being unnecessary).

(4) In section 102 (collective investment schemes with property divided into separate parts), in subsection (3)(b) after "135" insert "or 136".

(5) In section 137 (restriction on application of sections 135 and 136)—

(a) in subsection (1), for ", reconstruction or amalgamation" substitute "or scheme of reconstruction"; and

(b) in subsection (6), for "section 136(3)" substitute "section 135(5), 136(5)".

(6) In section 138(1) (procedure for clearance in advance), for ", reconstruction or amalgamation" substitute "or scheme of reconstruction".

(7) In section 139 (reconstruction involving transfer of business), for subsection (9) substitute—

"(9) In this section "scheme of reconstruction" has the same meaning as in section 136.".

(8) In section 147 (quoted options treated as part of new holdings)—

(a) in subsection (1) for "or amalgamation" substitute ", exchange or scheme of reconstruction"; and

(b) in subsection (2) at the end insert "and "scheme of reconstruction" has the same meaning as in section 136".

(9) In section 151B (venture capital trusts: supplementary), in subsection (8) for paragraph (c) substitute—

"(c) a reference to the exchanged holding is, in relation to section 135 or 136, to the shares in the company referred to in that section as company A.".

(10) In section 171(3) (transfers within a group) for "by virtue of sections 127 and 135" substitute "by section 127 as it applies by virtue of section 135".

(11) In section 211(2)(a) (transfer of long term business of insurance company), after "scheme of reconstruction" insert "within the meaning of that section".

(12) In section 251 (debts: general provisions)—

(a) in subsection (2) for "132 and 135" substitute "132, 135 and 136";

(b) in subsection (3)—

(i) for "132 and 135" substitute "132, 135 and 136", and

(ii) for "either section 132 or 135" substitute "section 132, 135 or 136";

(c) in subsection (6)(b) for the words from "unaffected" to the end substitute "to which section 135 applies and which is unaffected by section 137(1)".

(13) In Schedule A1 (taper relief), in paragraph 18(1)(b) (special rules for assets acquired in the reconstruction of mutual businesses etc) for "subsection (3)" substitute "subsection (2)(a)".

(14) In Schedule 6 (retirement relief: supplementary provisions), in paragraph 2(2) for "section 135(3)" substitute "section 135 or 136".

Finance Act 2000

6—(1) Schedule 15 to the Finance Act 2000 (c 17) (corporate venturing scheme) is amended as follows.

(2) In paragraph 71 (tax avoidance), in sub-paragraph (1)(b)(ii) for "reconstructions and amalgamations" substitute "schemes of reconstruction".

(3) In paragraph 82(1) (company reconstructions and amalgamations), in the closing words for "company reconstructions and amalgamations" substitute "share exchanges and company reconstructions".

(4) In paragraph 93(7) (identification of shares on a disposal: cases to which section 127 applies)—

(a) for "(whether or not by virtue of section 135(3) of that Act)" substitute "(including a case where that section applies by virtue of any enactment relating to chargeable gains)"; and

(b) for the words from "shall be construed" to the end substitute "have the same meaning as in section 127 of the 1992 Act (or, as the case may be, that section as applied by virtue of the enactment concerned)".

(5) In paragraph 96 (meaning of "disposal")—

(a) in sub-paragraph (2)(a) for "section 136(1)" substitute "section 136";

(b) in sub-paragraph (2)(b) for "sections 135 and 136 of that Act to bona fide reconstructions and amalgamations" substitute "section 136 of that Act to bona fide schemes of reconstruction".

PART 3
COMMENCEMENT
General commencement date

7—(1) Subject to paragraph 8, the provisions of this Schedule have effect in relation to shares or debentures issued on or after 17th April 2002 ("the commencement date").

(2) The reference in sub-paragraph (1) to shares or debentures includes any interests falling to be treated as shares or debentures for the purposes of section 135 or 136 of the Taxation of Chargeable Gains Act 1992 (c 12) as substituted by this Schedule.

Commencement provision for certain consequential amendments

8—(1) Paragraph 4(2), (3) and (5) and paragraph 6(2), (4) and (5) have effect in relation to disposals on or after the commencement date.

(2) Paragraph 4(4) has effect in relation to transactions to which section 473 of the Taxes Act 1988 applies occurring on or after the commencement date.

(3) Paragraph 4(6) has effect in relation to events occurring on or after the commencement date.

(4) Paragraph 4(7) has effect in relation to shares and securities (within the meaning of section 842 of the Taxes Act 1988) issued on or after the commencement date.

SCHEDULE 10

CHARGEABLE GAINS: TAPER RELIEF: MINOR AMENDMENTS

Section 47

Commentary—*Simon's Direct Tax Service* **C2.1414.**

Introduction

1 Schedule A1 to the Taxation of Chargeable Gains Act 1992 (c 12) (taper relief) is amended as follows.

Periods of share ownership that do not count because of change of activity by company

2 Paragraph 11 (periods of share ownership not to count where there is a change of activity by the company) shall cease to have effect in relation to disposals on or after 17th April 2002.

Periods of share ownership not to count where company is not active

3—(1) After that paragraph insert—

"Periods of share ownership not to count if company is not active

11A—(1) Where there is a disposal of an asset consisting of shares in a company, any period after 5th April 1998 during which the asset consisted of shares in a company that—

    (*a*) was a close company, and
    (*b*) was not active,

shall not count for the purposes of taper relief.

(2) Subject to the following provisions of this paragraph, a company is regarded as active at any time when—

    (*a*) it is carrying on a business of any description,
    (*b*) it is preparing to carry on a business of any description, or
    (*c*) it or another person is winding up the affairs of a business of any description that it has ceased to carry on.

(3) In sub-paragraph (2) above—

    (*a*) references to a business include a business that is not conducted on a commercial basis or with a view to the realisation of a profit, and
    (*b*) references to carrying on a business include holding assets and managing them.

(4) For the purposes of this paragraph a company is not regarded as active by reason only of its doing all or any of the following—

    (*a*) holding money (in any currency) in cash or on deposit;
    (*b*) holding other assets whose total value is insignificant;
    (*c*) holding shares in or debentures of a company that is not active;
    (*d*) making loans to an associated company or to a participator or an associate of a participator;
    (*e*) carrying out administrative functions in order to comply with requirements of the Companies Act 1985 or the Companies (Northern Ireland) Order 1986 or other regulatory requirements.

(5) Notwithstanding anything in sub-paragraphs (2) to (4) above a company shall be treated as active for the purposes of this paragraph if—

    (*a*) it is the holding company of a group of companies that contains at least one active company, or

    (*b*) it has a qualifying shareholding in a joint venture company or is the holding company of a group of companies any member of which has a qualifying shareholding in a joint venture company.

(6) In this paragraph "associated company" has the meaning given by section 416 of the Taxes Act and "participator" and "associate" have the meaning given by section 417 of that Act.

(7) Any reference in this paragraph to shares in or debentures of a company includes an interest in, or option in respect of, shares in or debentures of a company.".

(2) The amendment made by sub-paragraph (1) has effect in relation to disposals on or after 17th April 2002.

Meaning of "holding company"

4—(1) In paragraph 22(1) (interpretation) for the definition of "holding company" substitute—

    ""holding company" means a company that has one or more 51% subsidiaries;".

(2) In paragraph 23 (provisions as to holdings in joint venture companies), omit the following provisions—

    (*a*) the final sentence of sub-paragraph (4);

    (*b*) sub-paragraph (5);

    (*c*) in sub-paragraph (7), the words ", (5)(*b*)".

(3) The amendments in this paragraph apply to disposals on or after 17th April 2002 and as they so apply have effect in relation to periods of ownership on or after that date.

Meaning of "interest in shares"

5—(1) In paragraph 22(1) (interpretation), at the appropriate place insert—

    ""interest in shares" means an interest as a co-owner (whether the shares are owned jointly or in common, and whether or not the interests of the co-owners are equal), and "interest in debentures", in relation to any debentures, has a corresponding meaning;".

(2) The amendment in sub-paragraph (1) applies to disposals on or after 17th April 2002 and as it so applies has effect in relation to periods of ownership on or after that date.

Meaning of "joint venture company" and "qualifying shareholding"

6—(1) In paragraph 22(1) (interpretation), at the appropriate places insert—

    ""joint venture company" has the meaning given by paragraph 23(2) below;";

    ""qualifying shareholding", in relation to a joint venture company, has the meaning given by paragraph 23(3) below;".

(2) In paragraph 23(2) and (3) for "this paragraph" substitute "this Schedule".

(3) The amendments in this paragraph have effect in relation to disposals on or after 17th April 2002.

Meaning of "ordinary share capital"

7—(1) In paragraph 22(1) (interpretation) at the appropriate place insert—

    ""ordinary share capital" has the meaning given by section 832(1) of the Taxes Act;".

(2) Omit paragraphs 23(10) and 24(6).

(3) The amendments in this paragraph apply to disposals on or after 17th April 2002.

Debentures to be treated as shares

8—(1) In paragraph 22(1) (interpretation), in the definition of "shares" for "includes any securities of that company" substitute—

    "includes—

        (*a*) any securities of that company, and

        (*b*) any debentures of that company that are deemed, by virtue of section 251(6), to be securities for the purposes of that section".

(2) The amendment made by sub-paragraph (1) applies in relation to disposals on or after 6th April 2001 (so that assets disposed of on or after that date that are treated as shares by virtue of that sub-paragraph shall be treated as having been shares in relation to all times relevant for the purposes of Schedule A1).

This is subject to the following provisions.

(3) In relation to any time before 17th April 2002, the amendment made by sub-paragraph (1) does not apply to the references to shares in the following provisions of that Schedule—

   (*a*) paragraph 5 (conditions for assets other than shares to qualify as business assets);
   (*b*) paragraph 6A (meaning of "material interest" for purposes of paragraph 6);
   (*c*) paragraph 11 (periods of share ownership not to count where there is a change of activity by the company), except sub-paragraph (6);
   (*d*) paragraph 11A (periods of share ownership not to count if company is not active);
   (*e*) paragraph 12 (periods of share ownership not to count in a case of value-shifting);
   (*f*) the definition of "unlisted company" in paragraph 22(1).

(4) The amendment made by sub-paragraph (1) does not apply to the references to shares in paragraph 18(1) of that Schedule (special rules for assets acquired in the reconstruction of mutual businesses etc) in so far as they relate to shares issued before 17th April 2002.

Meaning of "trading company"

9—(1) In paragraph 22(1) (interpretation), for the definition of "trading company" substitute—

     ""trading company" has the meaning given by paragraph 22A below;".

(2) After that paragraph insert—

"Meaning of "trading company"

22A—(1) In this Schedule "trading company" means a company carrying on trading activities whose activities do not include to a substantial extent activities other than trading activities.

(2) For the purposes of sub-paragraph (1) above "trading activities" means activities carried on by the company—

   (*a*) in the course of, or for the purposes of, a trade being carried on by it,
   (*b*) for the purposes of a trade that it is preparing to carry on,
   (*c*) with a view to its acquiring or starting to carry on a trade, or
   (*d*) with a view to its acquiring a significant interest in the share capital of another company that—

      (i) is a trading company or the holding company of a trading group, and
      (ii) if the acquiring company is a member of a group of companies, is not a member of that group.

(3) Activities do not qualify as trading activities under sub-paragraph (2)(*c*) or (*d*) above unless the acquisition is made, or (as the case may be) the company starts to carry on the trade, as soon as is reasonably practicable in the circumstances.

(4) The reference in sub-paragraph (2)(*d*) above to the acquisition of a significant interest in the share capital of another company is to an acquisition of ordinary share capital in the other company—

   (*a*) such as would make that company a 51% subsidiary of the acquiring company, or
   (*b*) such as would give the acquiring company a qualifying shareholding in a joint venture company without making the two companies members of the same group of companies.".

(3) The amendments in this paragraph apply to disposals on or after 17th April 2002 and as they so apply have effect in relation to periods of ownership on or after that date.

Meaning of "trading group"

10—(1) In paragraph 22(1) (interpretation), for the definition of "trading group" substitute—

     ""trading group" has the meaning given by paragraph 22B below;".

(2) After paragraph 22A (inserted by paragraph 9 above) insert—

"Meaning of "trading group"

22B—(1) In this Schedule "trading group" means a group of companies—

   (*a*) one or more of whose members carry on trading activities, and
   (*b*) the activities of whose members, taken together, do not include to a substantial extent activities other than trading activities.

(2) For the purposes of sub-paragraph (1) above "trading activities" means activities carried on by a member of the group—

   (*a*) in the course of, or for the purposes of, a trade being carried on by any member of the group,
   (*b*) for the purposes of a trade that any member of the group is preparing to carry on,
   (*c*) with a view to any member of the group acquiring or starting to carry on a trade, or
   (*d*) with a view to any member of the group acquiring a significant interest in the share capital of another company that—

      (i) is a trading company or the holding company of a trading group, and
      (ii) is not a member of the same group of companies as the acquiring company.

(3) Activities do not qualify as trading activities under sub-paragraph (2)(*c*) or (*d*) above unless the acquisition is made, or (as the case may be) the group member in question starts to carry on the trade, as soon as is reasonably practicable in the circumstances.

(4) The reference in sub-paragraph (2)(*d*) above to the acquisition of a significant interest in the share capital of another company is to an acquisition of ordinary share capital in the other company—

(*a*) such as would make that company a member of the same group of companies as the acquiring company, or

(*b*) such as would give the acquiring company a qualifying shareholding in a joint venture company without making the joint venture companies a member of the same group of companies as the acquiring company.

(5) For the purposes of this paragraph the activities of the members of the group shall be treated as one business (with the result that activities are disregarded to the extent that they are intra-group activities).''.

(3) The amendments in this paragraph apply to disposals on or after 17th April 2002 and as they so apply have effect in relation to periods of ownership on or after that date.

Joint venture companies

11—(1) Paragraph 23 (qualifying shareholding in joint venture companies) is amended as follows.

(2) In sub-paragraph (2)(*b*) (meaning of ''joint venture company'': requirement that 75% of ordinary share capital held by not more than five companies), for ''companies'' substitute ''persons''.

(3) In sub-paragraph (3)(*a*) and (*b*) (meaning of ''qualifying shareholding'': holding of more than 30% of ordinary share capital), for ''more than 30%'' substitute ''10% or more''.

(4) After sub-paragraph (7) insert—

''(7A) For the purposes of this paragraph the activities of a joint venture company that is a holding company and its 51% subsidiaries shall be treated as a single business (so that activities are disregarded to the extent that they are intra-group activities).''.

(5) The amendments in this paragraph apply to disposals on or after 17th April 2002 and as they so apply have effect in relation to periods of ownership on or after that date.

Joint enterprise companies

12—(1) Paragraph 24 (joint enterprise companies: relevant connection) is amended as follows.

(2) In sub-paragraph (2) (meaning of ''joint enterprise company'': requirement that 75% of ordinary share capital held by not more than five companies), for ''companies'' substitute ''persons''.

(3) In sub-paragraph (4)(*a*) and (*b*) (meaning of ''qualifying shareholding'': holding of more than 30% of ordinary share capital), for ''more than 30%'' substitute ''10% or more''.

(4) The amendments in this paragraph apply to disposals on or after 17th April 2002 and as they so apply have effect in relation to periods of ownership on or after that date.

SCHEDULE 11

CHARGEABLE GAINS: DEDUCTION OF PERSONAL LOSSES FROM GAINS TREATED AS ACCRUING TO SETTLORS

Section 51

Commentary—*Simon's Direct Tax Service* **C4.390.**

Introduction

1 The Taxation of Chargeable Gains Act 1992 (c 12) is amended in accordance with paragraphs 2 to 6.

Section 2

2—(1) Section 2 (persons and gains chargeable to capital gains tax, and allowable losses) is amended as follows.

(2) In subsection (5) (computation of tax in cases where gains treated as accruing to settlor etc in respect of trust gains), for the word ''and'' at the end of paragraph (*a*) substitute—

''(*aa*) every amount which is treated by virtue of sections 77 and 86 as an amount of chargeable gains accruing to the person in question for that year, reduced as follows—

(i) first, by making the deductions for which subsection (2) provides in respect of any allowable losses accruing to that person;

(ii) then, where taper relief would be deductible by the trustees of the settlement in question but for section 77(1)(*b*)(i) or 86(1)(*e*)(ii), by applying reductions in respect of taper relief under section 2A at the rates that would be applicable in the case of the trustees;

and''.

(3) In paragraph (*b*) of that subsection, omit ''77, 86,''.

(4) After that subsection insert—

''(6) Allowable losses must (notwithstanding section 2A(6)) be deducted under paragraph (*a*)(i) of subsection (5) above before any may be deducted under paragraph (*aa*)(i) of that subsection.

(7) Where in any year of assessment—

(*a*) there are amounts treated as accruing to a person by virtue of section 77 or 86,

(*b*) two or more of those amounts, or elements of them—

(i) relate to different settlements, and

(ii) attract taper relief (by virtue of subsection (5)(*aa*)(ii) above) at the same rate, or are not eligible for taper relief, and

(*c*) losses are deductible from the amounts or elements mentioned in paragraph (*b*) above (''the equal-tapered amounts'') but are not enough to exhaust them all,

the deduction applicable to each of the equal-tapered amounts shall be the appropriate proportion of the aggregate of those losses.

The ''appropriate proportion'' is that given by dividing the equal-tapered amount in question by the total of the equal-tapered amounts.

(8) The references to section 86 in subsection (5)(*aa*) above (in the opening words) and subsection (7)(*a*) above include references to that section read with section 10A.''.

Section 77

3 In section 77 (charge on settlor with interest in settlement), in subsection (1)(*b*) (amount by reference to which settlor is charged), for the words from ''would'' to the end substitute—

''would be chargeable to tax for the year in respect of those gains if—

(i) the gains were not eligible for taper relief, but section 2(2) applied as if they were (so that the order of deducting losses provided for by section 2A(6) applied), and

(ii) section 3 were disregarded,

and''.

Section 86

4 In section 86 (attribution of gains to settlors with interest in non-resident or dual resident settlements), in subsection (1)(*e*) (amount by reference to which settlor is charged), for the words from ''if'' to the end substitute ''if—

(i) the assumption as to residence specified in subsection (3) below were made, and

(ii) any chargeable gains on the disposals were not eligible for taper relief, but section 2(2) applied as if they were (so that the order of deducting losses provided for by section 2A(6) applied);''.

Section 86A

5—(1) Section 86A (attribution of gains to settlor in section 10A cases) is amended as follows.

(2) In subsection (2) (reduction in amounts attributed to settlor in accordance with section 10A by reference to chargeable amounts paid to beneficiaries during his period of non-residence)—

(*a*) in paragraph (*a*), for ''the amount falling within section 86(1)(*e*)'' substitute ''the tapered section 86(1)(*e*) amount'';

(*b*) in paragraph (*b*), for ''the amounts falling within section 86(1)(*e*)'' substitute ''the tapered section 86(1)(*e*) amounts''.

(3) After that subsection insert—

''(2A) In subsection (2) above ''tapered section 86(1)(*e*) amount'' means an amount falling within section 86(1)(*e*) as it would apply with the omission of sub-paragraph (ii).

(2B) Where subsection (2) above has effect to reduce an amount that is treated by virtue of section 86 as accruing to the settlor for a year of assessment—

(*a*) the reduced amount shall be treated as falling within paragraph (*b*) of section 2(5) and not paragraph (*aa*);

(*b*) section 86(1)(*e*) shall have effect in relation to that amount with the omission of sub-paragraph (ii).''.

(4) In subsection (7) (reduction in gains available for attribution to beneficiaries by amounts attributed to settlor in accordance with section 10A), for the words from ''the amount or'' to ''so attributed'' substitute ''the tapered section 10A amount''.

(5) After that subsection insert—

"(7A) In subsection (7) above "the tapered section 10A amount" means the amount, or aggregate of the amounts, falling to be attributed as mentioned in that subsection, minus the total amount of any taper relief that would be deductible from that amount or aggregate by the trustees of the settlement but for section 86(1)(e)(ii).

Where section 86A(2) has effect to reduce that amount or aggregate, the words from "minus" to "section 86(1)(e)(ii)" above do not apply.".

Section 87

6—(1) Section 87 of that Act (attribution of gains to beneficiaries) is amended as follows.

(2) In subsection (3) (reduction in gains available for attribution to beneficiaries by amounts attributed to settlor under section 86), for the words from "reduced by the amount" to the end substitute "reduced by the tapered section 86(4) amount".

(3) After that subsection insert—

"(3A) In subsection (3) above "the tapered section 86(4) amount" means the amount, or aggregate of the amounts, treated as accruing as mentioned in subsection (3)(a) above, minus the total amount of any taper relief that would be deductible from that amount or aggregate by the trustees of the settlement but for section 86(1)(e)(ii).".

Commencement

7 This Schedule applies in relation to chargeable gains treated as accruing to a person by virtue of section 77 or 86 (read, where appropriate, with section 10A) of the Taxation of Chargeable Gains Act 1992 (c 12) in the year 2003–04 and subsequent years of assessment.

Election for Schedule to apply for years earlier than 2003–04

8—(1) This Schedule also applies, if the person so elects, in relation to chargeable gains so accruing to a person in any of the years of assessment 2000–01, 2001–02 and 2002–03.

(2) An election under this paragraph—

(a) must be made by a notice given to an officer of the Board no later than 31st January 2005;

(b) where chargeable gains are treated as accruing in respect of two or more settlements, may be restricted to those treated as accruing in respect of the settlement or settlements specified in the election.

(3) All such adjustments shall be made, whether by way of discharge or repayment of tax, the making of assessments or otherwise, as are required to give effect to an election under this paragraph.

(4) Where—

(a) a person makes an election under this paragraph for any one or more of the years of assessment 2000–01, 2001–02 and 2002–03, and

(b) the effect of the election, or (as the case may be) both or all of them taken together, is to increase the total amount of tax that the person is entitled to recover from the trustees of a particular settlement for those three years under section 78(1)(a) of the Taxation of Chargeable Gains Act 1992 or paragraph 6 of Schedule 5 to that Act,

the trustees of that settlement must join in the election, or (as the case may be) each of them that has that effect or contributes to it.

SCHEDULE 12

TAX RELIEF FOR EXPENDITURE ON RESEARCH AND DEVELOPMENT

Section 53

Commentary—*Simon's Direct Tax Service* **D2.1201, 1202, 1209, 1210.**

PART 1

ENTITLEMENT TO RELIEF FOR R&D EXPENDITURE: LARGE COMPANIES

Entitlement to relief under this Part

1—(1) A company (in this Part referred to as "the company") is entitled to tax relief under this Part for an accounting period if—

(a) it is a large company throughout that period, and

(b) its qualifying R&D expenditure for that period is not less than—

(i) £25,000, if the accounting period is a period of 12 months, or

(ii) such amount as bears to £25,000 the same proportion as the accounting period bears to 12 months.

(2) For the purposes of this paragraph the company's qualifying R&D expenditure is "for an accounting period" if it is deductible in computing for tax purposes the profits for that period of a trade carried on by the company (including expenditure that is so deductible by virtue of section 401 of the Taxes Act 1988).

Meaning of "large company" and "small or medium-sized enterprise"

2—(1) For the purposes of this Schedule—

(a) "large company" means a company that does not qualify as a small or medium-sized enterprise; and

(b) "small or medium-sized enterprise" means a small or medium-sized enterprise as defined in Commission Recommendation 96/280/EC of 3rd April 1996.

(2) The Treasury may by order amend sub-paragraph (1)(b) so as to substitute another definition of "small or medium-sized enterprise" for the definition that is for the time being effective for the purposes of this Schedule.

Qualifying R&D expenditure

3 For the purposes of this Schedule the company's "qualifying R&D expenditure" is—

(a) its qualifying expenditure on direct research and development (see paragraph 4),

(b) its qualifying expenditure on sub-contracted research and development (see paragraph 5), and

(c) its qualifying expenditure on contributions to independent research and development (see paragraph 6).

Qualifying expenditure on direct research and development

4—(1) The company's qualifying expenditure on direct research and development is expenditure incurred by it where the following conditions are satisfied.

(2) The first condition is that the expenditure is incurred on research and development directly undertaken by the company.

(3) The second condition is that the expenditure is incurred—

(a) on staffing costs, or

(b) on consumable stores.

(4) The third condition is that the expenditure is attributable to relevant research and development in relation to the company.

(5) The fourth condition is that the expenditure is not of a capital nature.

(6) The fifth condition is that, if the expenditure is incurred in carrying on activities contracted out to the company, they are contracted out—

(a) by a large company, or

(b) by any person otherwise than in the course of a trade, profession or vocation the profits of which are chargeable to tax under Case I or II of Schedule D.

Expenditure on research and development directly undertaken on company's behalf

5—(1) The company's qualifying expenditure on sub-contracted research and development is expenditure incurred by it where the following conditions are satisfied.

(2) The first condition is that the expenditure is incurred in making payments to—

(a) a qualifying body,

(b) an individual, or

(c) a partnership, each member of which is an individual,

in respect of research and development contracted out by the company to the body, individual or partnership concerned ("the sub-contracted R&D").

(3) The second condition is that the sub-contracted research and development is directly undertaken on behalf of the company by the body, individual or partnership concerned.

(4) The third condition is that the expenditure is attributable to relevant research and development in relation to the company.

(5) The fourth condition is that the expenditure is not of a capital nature.

(6) The fifth condition is that, if the sub-contracted R&D is itself contracted out to the company, it is contracted out—

(a) by a large company, or

(b) by any person otherwise than in the course of a trade, profession or vocation the profits of which are chargeable to tax under Case I or II of Schedule D.

Qualifying expenditure on contributions to independent research and development

6—(1) The company's qualifying expenditure on contributions to independent research and development is expenditure incurred by it where the following conditions are satisfied.

(2) The first condition is that the expenditure is incurred in making payments to—

    (*a*) a qualifying body,

    (*b*) an individual, or

    (*c*) a partnership, each member of which is an individual,

for the purpose of funding research and development carried on by the body, individual or partnership concerned (''the funded R&D'').

(3) The second condition is that the funded R&D is relevant research and development in relation to the company.

(4) The third condition is that the funded R&D is not contracted out to the qualifying body, individual or partnership concerned by another person.

(5) The fourth condition is that—

    (*a*) if the payment is made to an individual, the company is not connected with the individual when the payment is made, and

    (*b*) if the payment is made to a partnership (other than a qualifying body), the company is not connected with any member of the partnership when the payment is made.

PART 2

ENTITLEMENT TO RELIEF FOR R&D EXPENDITURE: WORK SUBCONTRACTED TO SMALL OR MEDIUM-SIZED ENTERPRISE

Entitlement to relief under this Part

7—(1) A company (''the SME'') is entitled to tax relief under this Part for an accounting period if—

    (*a*) it qualifies as a small or medium-sized enterprise in that period, and

    (*b*) its aggregate R&D expenditure for that period is not less than—

        (i) £25,000, if the accounting period is a period of 12 months, or

        (ii) such amount as bears to £25,000 the same proportion as the accounting period bears to 12 months.

(2) In this paragraph ''aggregate R&D expenditure'' of the SME means the aggregate of—

    (*a*) its qualifying sub-contracted R&D expenditure (see paragraph 8), and

    (*b*) its qualifying R&D expenditure within the meaning of Schedule 20 to the Finance Act 2000 (c 17) (tax relief for R&D expenditure of small and medium-sized enterprises).

(3) For this purpose the SME's aggregate R&D expenditure is ''for an accounting period'' if it is deductible in computing for tax purposes the profits for that period of a trade carried on by the SME (including expenditure that is so deductible by virtue of section 401 of the Taxes Act 1988).

(4) Any relief to which a company is entitled under this Part for an accounting period is in addition to any relief to which it may be entitled under Schedule 20 to the Finance Act 2000 (c 17).

Qualifying sub-contracted R&D expenditure

8 For the purposes of this Schedule, the SME's ''qualifying sub-contracted R&D expenditure'' is the expenditure incurred by the SME on research and development that is contracted out to it where—

    (*a*) that research and development is contracted out to the SME—

        (i) by a large company, or

        (ii) by any person otherwise than in the course of carrying on a trade, profession or vocation the profits of which are chargeable to tax under Case I or II of Schedule D; and

    (*b*) the conditions of either paragraph 9 or paragraph 10 are satisfied.

Expenditure on research and development directly undertaken by the SME

9—(1) The first condition of this paragraph is that the expenditure is incurred on research and development directly undertaken by the SME.

(2) The second condition is that the expenditure is incurred—

    (*a*) on staffing costs, or

    (*b*) on consumable stores.

(3) The third condition is that the expenditure is attributable to relevant research and development in relation to the SME.

(4) The fourth condition is that the expenditure is not of a capital nature.

Expenditure on research and development directly undertaken on SME's behalf

10—(1) The first condition of this paragraph is that the expenditure is incurred in making payments to—

    (*a*) a qualifying body,

    (*b*) an individual, or

    (*c*) a partnership, each member of which is an individual,

in respect of research and development contracted out by the SME to the body, individual or partnership concerned.

(2) The second condition is that the research and development is directly undertaken on behalf of the SME by the body, individual or partnership concerned.

(3) The third condition is that the expenditure is attributable to relevant research and development in relation to the SME.

(4) The fourth condition is that the expenditure is not of a capital nature.

PART 3
THE RELIEF
Deduction in computing profits of trade

11—(1) This paragraph applies where a company is entitled to relief under Part 1 or 2 of this Schedule for an accounting period.

(2) In so far as the company's qualifying expenditure for that period is deductible in computing for tax purposes the profits for that period of a trade carried on by the company, it is entitled (on making a claim) to an additional deduction in computing the profits of the trade for that period of an amount equal to 25% of the qualifying expenditure.

(3) In sub-paragraph (2) "qualifying expenditure" means—

   (a) in the case of relief under Part 1, qualifying R&D expenditure (see paragraph 3), and
   (b) in the case of the relief under Part 2, qualifying sub-contracted R&D expenditure (see paragraph 8).

PART 4
SPECIAL PROVISION FOR GIVING RELIEF TO INSURANCE COMPANIES
Treated as large companies

12 Where, in an accounting period, an insurance company (within the meaning of Chapter 1 of Part 12 of the Taxes Act 1988)—

   (a) carries on life assurance business, and
   (b) qualifies as a small or medium-sized enterprise

Parts 1 to 3 of this Schedule apply to that company as if it did not qualify as such an enterprise in that period.

Entitlement to relief in respect of "I minus E" basis

13—(1) This paragraph applies where for any accounting period the profits arising to a company from its life assurance business are not charged to corporation tax under Case I of Schedule D.

(2) The provisions of Part 3 which allow a deduction in calculating the profits of a trade apply in relation to the company to treat amounts as disbursed as expenses of management.

(3) Where by virtue of section 436, 439B or 441 of the Taxes Act 1988—

   (a) any profits arising to the company from any category of life assurance business are treated as income chargeable under Case VI of Schedule D, and
   (b) the profits of that part of that business are computed in accordance with the provisions of that Act applicable to Case I of that Schedule,

Part 3 of this Schedule has effect as if the references to the trade carried on by the company were references to that part of that business (and sub-paragraph (2) does not apply in relation to that part).

(4) Subject to sub-paragraph (3), the provisions of Part 3 do not apply to allow any deduction in any computation of the profits of the company's life assurance business made in accordance with the provisions of the Taxes Act 1988 applicable to Case I of Schedule D.

PART 5
SUPPLEMENTARY PROVISIONS
Research and development expenditure of group companies

14—(1) Sub-paragraph (2) applies where—

   (a) a company ("A") incurs expenditure on making a payment to another company ("B") in respect of activities contracted out by A to B,
   (b) the expenditure incurred on the payment is research and development expenditure of A, and
   (c) A and B are members of the same group at the time the payment is made.

(2) For the purposes of this Schedule—

(*a*) any of the activities contracted out by A to B and directly undertaken by B shall be treated (to the extent it would not otherwise be the case) as research and development directly undertaken by B, and

(*b*) where B makes a payment to a third party ("C") in respect of any of those activities that are contracted out by B to C and directly undertaken by C, those activities shall be treated (to the extent that it would not otherwise be the case) as research and development contracted out by B to C.

(3) For the purposes of this paragraph A and B are members of the same group if they are members of the same group of companies for the purposes of Chapter 4 of Part 10 of the Taxes Act 1988 (group relief).

Refunds of contributions to independent research and development etc

15—(1) This paragraph applies where a company receives a payment refunding the whole or any part of—

(*a*) any qualifying expenditure on sub-contracted research and development (see paragraph 5),

(*b*) any qualifying expenditure on contributions to independent research and development (see paragraph 6), or

(*c*) any expenditure which is qualifying sub-contracted R&D expenditure by virtue of paragraph 10,

in respect of which it obtains relief under this Schedule.

(2) The appropriate amount shall be treated as income of the company chargeable to tax under Case I of Schedule D for the accounting period in which the payment is made.

(3) Where, by virtue of paragraph 13(3) (profits of life assurance business chargeable to tax under Case VI of Schedule D), the relief obtained in respect of the contribution or expenditure concerned is a deduction in computing for tax purposes the profits of a part of the life assurance business of the company—

(*a*) sub-paragraph (2) does not apply, and

(*b*) the appropriate amount shall be treated as income referrable to that part which is chargeable to tax under Case VI of Schedule D for the accounting period in which the payment is made.

(4) For this purpose "the appropriate amount" means 25% of the payment.

Artificially inflated claims for deduction

16—(1) To the extent that a transaction is attributable to arrangements entered into wholly or mainly for a disqualifying purpose, it shall be disregarded in determining for an accounting period the amount of any relief to which a company is entitled under this Schedule.

(2) Arrangements are entered into wholly or mainly for a "disqualifying purpose" if their main object, or one of their main objects, is to enable a company to obtain relief under this Schedule to which it would not otherwise be entitled or of a greater amount than that to which it would otherwise be entitled.

(3) In this paragraph "arrangements" includes any scheme, agreement or understanding, whether or not legally enforceable.

PART 6
GENERAL PROVISIONS

Meaning of "relevant research and development", "staffing costs" and "consumable stores"

17 The following provisions of Schedule 20 to the Finance Act 2000 (c 17) (tax relief for R&D expenditure of small and medium-sized enterprises) apply for the purposes of this Schedule as they apply for the purposes of that Schedule—

(*a*) paragraph 4 (relevant research and development);

(*b*) paragraph 5 (staffing costs); and

(*c*) paragraph 6 (expenditure on consumable stores).

Meaning of "qualifying body"

18—(1) For the purposes of this Schedule "qualifying body" means—

(*a*) a charity (within the meaning of section 506(1) of the Taxes Act 1988);

(*b*) an institution of higher education;

(*c*) an Association of a description specified in section 508 of the Taxes Act 1988 (scientific research organisations);

(*d*) a health service body within the meaning of section 519A(2) of that Act; or

(*e*) any other body prescribed, or of a description prescribed, by the Treasury, by order, for the purposes of this Schedule.

(2) In sub-paragraph (1)(*b*), "institution of higher education" means—

(*a*) an institution within the higher education sector within the meaning of the Further and Higher Education Act 1992 (c 13);

(*b*) an institution within the higher education sector within the meaning of Part 2 of the Further and Higher Education (Scotland) Act 1992 (c 37) or a central institution within the meaning of the Education (Scotland) Act 1980 (c 44); or

(*c*) a higher education institution within the meaning of Article 30(3) of the Education and Libraries (Northern Ireland) Order 1993 (1993/ 2810 (NI 12)).

(3) An order under this paragraph shall have effect in relation to such accounting periods or expenditure as may be specified in the order (which may include accounting periods beginning, or expenditure incurred, before the time the order is made).

Other definitions etc

19—(1) In this Schedule—

"life assurance business" has the meaning given in section 431(2) of the Taxes Act 1988;

"research and development" has the meaning given by section 837A of the Taxes Act 1988.

(2) Section 839 of the Taxes Act 1988 (connected persons) applies for the purposes of this Schedule.

Transitional provision

20—(1) This Schedule does not apply to expenditure incurred before 1st April 2002. For this purpose no account shall be taken of section 401 of the Taxes Act 1988 (pre-trading expenditure treated as incurred when trading begins).

(2) Paragraphs 1(1) and 7(1) (requirement of minimum amount of qualifying expenditure in an accounting period) apply to an accounting period beginning before and ending after that date as if so much of the period as falls on or after that date were a separate accounting period.

SCHEDULE 13

TAX RELIEF FOR EXPENDITURE ON VACCINE RESEARCH ETC

Section 54

Commentary—*Simon's Direct Tax Service* **D2.1201, 1209.**

PART 1

ENTITLEMENT TO RELIEF

Entitlement to relief under this Schedule

1—(1) A company is entitled to relief under this Schedule for an accounting period if the company's qualifying expenditure for that period (see paragraph 2) is not less than—

(*a*) £25,000, if the accounting period is a period of 12 months, or

(*b*) such amount as bears to £25,000 the same proportion as the accounting period bears to 12 months.

(2) Relief under this Schedule in respect of any expenditure is in addition to any relief in respect of that expenditure under Schedule 20 to the Finance Act 2000 (c 17) or Schedule 12 to this Act (tax relief for expenditure on research and development).

Qualifying expenditure

2—(1) For the purposes of this Schedule "qualifying expenditure" means—

(*a*) qualifying expenditure on direct research and development (see paragraphs 3 to 5),

(*b*) qualifying expenditure on sub-contracted research and development (see paragraphs 6 to 11), or

(*c*) qualifying expenditure on contributions to independent research and development (see paragraph 12).

(2) The qualifying expenditure of a company "for an accounting period" is determined as follows.

(3) The qualifying expenditure on direct or sub-contracted research and development for an accounting period is—

(*a*) in the case of company that qualifies as a small or medium-sized enterprise in that period, qualifying expenditure that—

  (i) is deductible in computing for tax purposes the profits for that period of a trade carried on by the company, or

  (ii) would have been so deductible had the company, at the time the expenditure was incurred, been carrying on a trade consisting of the activities in respect of which it was incurred,

(disregarding for this purpose section 401 of the Taxes Act 1988 (pre-trading expenditure treated as incurred when trading begins));

(*b*) in the case of a company that does not qualify as a small or medium-sized enterprise in that period, qualifying expenditure that is deductible in computing for tax purposes the profits for that period of a trade carried on by the company (including expenditure that is so deductible by virtue of section 401 of the Taxes Act 1988).

(4) The qualifying expenditure on contributions to independent research and development for an accounting period is the expenditure that is incurred on contributions paid in that period.

Qualifying expenditure on direct research and development

3—(1) Qualifying expenditure of a company on direct research and development is expenditure incurred by the company that satisfies the following conditions.

(2) The first condition is that the expenditure is on qualifying R&D activity (see paragraph 4) directly undertaken by the company.

(3) The second condition is that the qualifying R&D activity on which the expenditure is incurred is relevant research and development in relation to the company.

(4) The third condition is that the expenditure is not of a capital nature.

(5) The fourth condition is that the expenditure is incurred—

(*a*) on staffing costs, or

(*b*) on consumable stores.

(6) The fifth condition is that the expenditure is not incurred by the company in carrying on activities the carrying on of which is contracted out to the company by any person.

(7) The sixth condition is that the expenditure is not subsidised.

Qualifying R&D activity

4—(1) For the purposes of this Schedule "qualifying R&D activity" means research and development relating to—

(*a*) vaccines or medicines for the prevention or treatment of tuberculosis,

(*b*) vaccines or medicines for the prevention or treatment of malaria,

(*c*) vaccines for the prevention of infection by human immunodeficiency virus, or

(*d*) vaccines or medicines for the prevention of the onset, or for the treatment, of acquired immune deficiency syndrome resulting from infection by human immunodeficiency virus in prescribed clades only.

(2) For the purposes of sub-paragraph (1) "prescribed clade" means clade A, C, D or E or such other clade or clades as the Treasury may by regulations prescribe.

(3) The Treasury may make provision by regulations further defining the purposes referred to in sub-paragraph (1)(*a*), (*b*), (*c*) or (*d*).

(4) In sub-paragraph (1) references to vaccines or medicines are to vaccines or medicines for use in humans.

Meaning of "relevant R&D", "small or medium-sized enterprise", "staffing costs", "consumable stores" and "subsidised".

5—(1) For the purposes of this Schedule "relevant research and development", in relation to a company, means research and development—

(*a*) related to a trade carried on by the company, or

(*b*) from which it is intended that a trade to be carried on by the company will be derived.

(2) For the purposes of this Schedule research and development related to a trade carried on by the company includes research and development which may lead to or facilitate an extension of that trade.

(3) The following provisions of Schedule 20 to the Finance Act 2000 (c 17) (tax relief for R&D expenditure of small and medium-sized companies) apply for the purposes of this Schedule as they apply for the purposes of that Schedule—

(*a*) paragraph 2 (meaning of "small or medium-sized enterprise");

(*b*) paragraph 5 (staffing costs);

(*c*) paragraph 6 (expenditure on consumable stores); and

(*d*) paragraph 8 (subsidised expenditure),

except that in their application for the purposes of this Schedule, references in that Schedule to relevant research and development shall be construed in accordance with sub-paragraphs (1) and (2) above.

Qualifying expenditure on sub-contracted research and development

6—(1) Paragraphs 7 to 11 make provision for determining the qualifying expenditure of a company on sub-contracted research and development.

This is subject to sub-paragraph (3).

(2) For the purposes of those paragraphs a company ("the principal") incurs expenditure on sub-contracted research and development if it makes a payment (a "sub-contractor payment") to another person ("the sub-contractor") in respect of research and development contracted out by the company to that person.

(3) Where the sub-contractor is—

   (a) a charity (within the meaning of section 506(1) of the Taxes Act 1988),

   (b) a university, or

   (c) an Association of a description specified in section 508 of that Act (scientific research organisations),

paragraphs 7(1) and 8 to 11 do not apply and expenditure of the principal on sub-contracted expenditure is qualifying expenditure if it satisfies the conditions of paragraph 7(2) to (6).

Conditions that must be satisfied by qualifying expenditure on sub-contracted research and development

7—(1) Expenditure of a company on sub-contracted research and development is not qualifying expenditure unless it satisfies the following conditions.

(2) The first condition is that the expenditure is on research and development directly undertaken on behalf of the company by the sub-contractor.

(3) The second condition is that the expenditure is on qualifying R&D activity (see paragraph 4).

(4) The third condition is that the R&D activity in respect of which the expenditure is incurred is relevant research and development in relation to the company.

(5) The fourth condition is that the expenditure is not of a capital nature.

(6) The fifth condition is that the expenditure is not subsidised.

Treatment of sub-contractor payment where principal and sub-contractor are connected persons

8—(1) Where the principal and the sub-contractor are connected persons and in accordance with generally accepted accounting practice—

   (a) the whole of the sub-contractor payment has been brought into account in determining the sub-contractor's profit or loss for a relevant period, and

   (b) all of the sub-contractor's relevant expenditure has been so brought into account,

the whole of the payment (up to the amount of the sub-contractor's relevant expenditure) is qualifying expenditure on sub-contracted research and development.

This is subject to paragraph 7 (conditions that must be satisfied by qualifying expenditure on sub-contracted R&D).

(2) In sub-paragraph (1)—

   (a) "relevant expenditure" has the meaning given by paragraph 9, and

   (b) "relevant period" means a period—

      (i) for which accounts are drawn up by the sub-contractor, and

      (ii) that ends not more than twelve months after the end of the principal's period of account in which the sub-contractor payment is, in accordance with generally accepted accounting practice, brought into account in determining the principal's profit or loss.

(3) Any apportionment of expenditure of the principal or the sub-contractor necessary for the purposes of this paragraph shall be made on a just and reasonable basis.

Relevant expenditure of the sub-contractor

9—(1) For the purposes of paragraph 8 the "relevant expenditure" of the sub-contractor is expenditure that—

   (a) is incurred by the sub-contractor in carrying on, on behalf of the principal, the activities to which the sub-contractor payment relates, and

   (b) satisfies the following conditions.

(2) The first condition is that the expenditure is not of a capital nature as regards the sub-contractor.

(3) The second condition is that the expenditure is incurred—

   (a) on staffing costs, or

   (b) on consumable stores.

In applying (by virtue of paragraph 5 above) paragraph 5 of Schedule 20 to the Finance Act 2000 (c 17) (meaning of "staffing costs") for the purposes of this sub-paragraph, the references to the company shall be read as references to the sub-contractor.

(4) The third condition is that the expenditure is not subsidised.

In applying (by virtue of paragraph 5 above) paragraph 8 of that Schedule (subsidised expenditure) for the purposes of this paragraph, the references to the company shall be read as references to the sub-contractor.

Election for connected persons treatment

10—(1) The principal and the sub-contractor may in any case jointly elect that paragraph 8 (treatment of sub-contractor payment where principal and sub-contractor are connected) shall apply to sub-contractor payments made by the principal to the sub-contractor.

(2) Any such election must be made in relation to all sub-contractor payments paid under the same contract or other arrangement.

(3) The election must be made by notice in writing given to the Inland Revenue.

(4) The notice must be given not later than two years after the end of the company's accounting period in which the contract or other arrangement is entered into.

(5) An election under this paragraph, once made, is irrevocable.

Treatment of sub-contractor payment in other cases

11 Where the principal makes a sub-contractor payment and—

 (a) the principal and the sub-contractor are not connected persons, and
 (b) no election is made under paragraph 10 (election for connected persons treatment),

65% of the amount of the sub-contractor payment is treated as qualifying expenditure on sub-contracted research and development.

This is subject to paragraph 7 (conditions that must be satisfied by qualifying expenditure on sub-contracted R&D).

Qualifying expenditure on contributions to independent research and development

12—(1) Expenditure of a company on contributions to independent research and development is qualifying expenditure where the following conditions are satisfied.

(2) The first condition is that the expenditure must be incurred on payments made to—

 (a) a charity (within the meaning of section 506(1) of the Taxes Act 1988),
 (b) a university, or
 (c) an Association of a description specified in section 508 of that Act (scientific research organisations),

for the purpose of funding qualifying R&D activity carried on by the body in question.

(3) The second condition is that the R&D activity must be research and development related to a trade carried on by the company.

PART 2

MANNER OF GIVING EFFECT TO RELIEF: SMALL AND MEDIUM-SIZED COMPANIES

Application of this Part

13 This Part provides for how relief under this Schedule for an accounting period is to be given in the case of a company that qualifies as a small or medium-sized company in that period.

Deduction in computing profits of trade

14—(1) Where a company—

 (a) is entitled to relief under this Schedule for an accounting period in respect of any qualifying expenditure, and
 (b) is carrying on a trade in that period,

it may (on making a claim) make the appropriate deduction in computing the profits of the trade for that period.

(2) For this purpose the appropriate deduction is—

 (a) 50% of so much of the qualifying expenditure as is expenditure in respect of which the company is also entitled to relief under Schedule 20 to the Finance Act 2000 (c 17), and
 (b) 150% of so much of the qualifying expenditure as is not expenditure in respect of which the company is also entitled to relief under that Schedule.

(3) This paragraph is without prejudice to any other deduction in respect of the qualifying expenditure.

Alternative treatment of pre-trading expenditure: deemed trading loss

15—(1) Where a company—

 (a) is entitled to relief under this Schedule for an accounting period in respect of any qualifying expenditure, and
 (b) is not carrying on a trade in that period,

it may elect to be treated as if it had incurred a trading loss in that accounting period.

(2) The amount of the trading loss is—

(a) 50% of so much of the qualifying expenditure as is expenditure in respect of which the company is also entitled to relief under Schedule 20 to the Finance Act 2000 (c 17), and

(b) 150% of so much of the qualifying expenditure as is not expenditure in respect of which the company is also entitled to relief under that Schedule.

(3) Section 401 of the Taxes Act 1988 (relief for pre-trading expenditure) does not apply to qualifying expenditure in respect of which an election is made under this paragraph.

(4) An election under this paragraph must—

(a) specify the accounting period in respect of which it is made, and

(b) be made by notice in writing to the Inland Revenue given not later than two years after the end of the accounting period to which the election relates.

(5) Where a company is treated under this paragraph as incurring a trading loss in an accounting period, the trading loss may not be set off against profits of a preceding accounting period under section 393A(1)(b) of the Taxes Act 1988 unless the company in entitled to tax relief under this paragraph for that earlier period.

(6) Where a company is treated under this paragraph as incurring a trading loss in an accounting period and the company begins, in that accounting period or a later accounting period, to carry on a trade derived from the research and development in relation to which the tax relief in question was obtained under this paragraph, then—

(a) subject to paragraph 19 (restriction on losses carried forward), and

(b) to the extent that—

(i) the company has not obtained relief in respect of the trading loss under any other provision, and

(ii) the loss has not been surrendered under section 403(1) of the Taxes Act 1988 (surrender of relief to group or consortium members),

the loss shall be treated as if it were a loss of that trade brought forward under section 393 of that Act (relief of trading losses against future trading profits).

Entitlement to tax credit

16—(1) A company may claim a tax credit for an accounting period in which it has a surrenderable loss.

(2) A company has a "surrenderable loss" for an accounting period—

(a) if paragraph 14 applies and the company incurs a trading loss in that period in the trade mentioned in sub-paragraph (1)(b) of that paragraph;

(b) if paragraph 15 applies and the company is treated under that paragraph as incurring a trading loss.

(3) The amount of the surrenderable loss is equal to the lower of—

(a) so much of the trading loss referred to in sub-paragraph (2) above as is unrelieved, and

(b) the total amount deductible under paragraph 14 or, as the case may be, the total deemed trading loss under paragraph 15.

(4) For this purpose the amount of a trading loss that is "unrelieved" means the amount of that loss reduced by—

(a) any relief that was or could have been obtained by the company making a claim under section 393A(1)(a) of the Taxes Act 1988 to set the loss against profits of whatever description of the same accounting period,

(b) any other relief obtained by the company in respect of the loss, including relief under section 393A(1)(b) of that Act (losses set against profits of an earlier accounting period),

(c) any loss surrendered under section 403(1) of that Act (surrender of relief to group or consortium members), or

(d) any loss surrendered under paragraph 15 of Schedule 20 to the Finance Act 2000 (c 17) (entitlement to R&D tax credit).

(5) No account shall be taken for this purpose of any losses—

(a) brought forward from an earlier accounting period under section 393(1) of the Taxes Act 1988, or

(b) carried back from a later accounting period under section 393A(1)(b) of that Act.

Amount of credit

17—(1) The amount of the tax credit to which a company is entitled for an accounting period is 16% of the surrenderable loss for the period, subject to the following limit.

(2) The limit is that the total of the tax credits to which the company is entitled for an accounting period under this Schedule and under Schedule 20 to the Finance Act 2000 may not exceed the total of the company's PAYE and NICs liabilities for payment periods ending in that accounting period.

(3) The Treasury may by order substitute for the percentage for the time being specified in sub-paragraph (1) such other percentage as they think fit.

(4) An order under sub-paragraph (3) may make such incidental, supplementary, consequential and transitional provision as the Treasury think fit.

(5) Paragraph 17 of Schedule 20 to the Finance Act 2000 (calculation of total amount of company's PAYE and NICs liabilities for a payment period) applies for the purposes of this paragraph as it applies for the purposes of paragraph 16 of that Schedule.

Payment in respect of tax credit

18—(1) Where—

    (*a*) a company is entitled to a tax credit under this Schedule for an accounting period, and
    (*b*) makes a claim,

the Inland Revenue shall pay to the company the amount of the credit.

(2) An amount payable in respect of—

    (*a*) a tax credit under this Schedule, or
    (*b*) interest on a tax credit under this Schedule under section 826 of the Taxes Act 1988,

may be applied in discharging any liability of the company to pay corporation tax, and to the extent that it is so applied the Inland Revenue's obligation under sub-paragraph (1) is discharged.

(3) Where the company's company tax return for the accounting period is enquired into by the Inland Revenue, no payment in respect of a tax credit under this Schedule for that period need be made before the Inland Revenue's enquiries are completed (see paragraph 32 of Schedule 18 to the Finance Act 1998 (c 36)).

In those circumstances the Inland Revenue may make a payment on a provisional basis of such amount as they think fit.

(4) No payment need be made in respect of a tax credit under this Schedule for an accounting period before the company has paid to the Inland Revenue any amount that it is required to pay for payment periods ending in that accounting period—

    (*a*) under the PAYE regulations, or
    (*b*) in respect of Class 1 national insurance contributions.

Restriction on losses carried forward

19—(1) For the purposes of section 393 of the Taxes Act 1988 (relief of trading losses against future trading profits), a company's trading loss for a period for which it claims a tax credit under this Schedule is treated as reduced by the amount of the loss surrendered.

(2) The amount of the loss surrendered is—

    (*a*) where the maximum amount of tax credit was claimed, the whole of the surrenderable loss for that period, and
    (*b*) where less than the maximum amount was claimed, a corresponding proportion of the surrenderable loss for that period.

The "maximum amount" here means the amount specified in paragraph 17(1).

Payment in respect of tax credit not income

20 A payment in respect of a tax credit under this Schedule is not income of the company for tax purposes.

PART 3

MANNER OF GIVING EFFECT TO RELIEF: LARGE COMPANIES

Deduction in computing profits of trade

21—(1) This paragraph applies where a company that does not qualify as a small or medium-sized enterprise in an accounting period is entitled to relief under this Schedule for that period.

(2) In so far as the company's qualifying expenditure for that period is deductible in computing for tax purposes the profits for that period of a trade carried on by the company, it is entitled (on making a claim) to an additional deduction in computing the profits of the trade for that period of an amount equal to 50% of the qualifying expenditure.

(3) In so far as the company's qualifying expenditure for that period is not so deductible, it may (on making a claim) treat 150% of that qualifying expenditure as if it were so deductible.

(4) This paragraph is without prejudice to any other deduction in respect of the qualifying expenditure.

PART 4

SPECIAL PROVISION FOR GIVING RELIEF TO INSURANCE COMPANIES

Treated as large companies

22 Where, in an accounting period, an insurance company (within the meaning of Chapter 1 of Part 12 of the Taxes Act 1988)—

(a) carries on life assurance business, and

(b) qualifies as a small or medium-sized enterprise,

Parts 2 and 3 of this Schedule apply to that company as if it did not qualify as such an enterprise in that period.

Entitlement to relief in respect of "I minus E" basis

23—(1) This paragraph applies where for any accounting period the profits arising to a company from its life assurance business are not charged to corporation tax under Case I of Schedule D.

(2) The provisions of Part 3 which allow a deduction in calculating the profits of a trade apply in relation to the company to treat amounts as disbursed as expenses of management.

(3) Where by virtue of section 436, 439B or 441 of the Taxes Act 1988—

(a) any profits arising to the company from any category of life assurance business are treated as income chargeable under Case VI of Schedule D, and

(b) the profits of that part of that business are computed in accordance with the provisions of that Act applicable to Case I of that Schedule,

Part 3 of this Schedule has effect as if the references to the trade carried on by the company were references to that part of that business (and sub-paragraph (2) does not apply in relation to that part).

(4) Subject to sub-paragraph (3), the provisions of Part 3 do not apply to allow any deduction in any computation of the profits of the company's life assurance business made in accordance with the provisions of the Taxes Act 1988 applicable to Case I of Schedule D.

PART 5

SUPPLEMENTARY PROVISIONS

Artificially inflated claims for deduction or tax credit

24—(1) To the extent that a transaction is attributable to arrangements entered into wholly or mainly for a disqualifying purpose, it shall be disregarded in determining for an accounting period the amount of—

(a) any relief to which a company is entitled under paragraph 14, 15 or 21, and

(b) any tax credit to which a company is entitled under this Schedule.

(2) Arrangements are entered into wholly or mainly for a "disqualifying purpose" if their main object, or one of their main objects, is to enable a company to obtain—

(a) relief under paragraph 14, 15 or 21 to which it would not otherwise be entitled or of a greater amount than that to which it would otherwise be entitled; or

(b) a tax credit under this Schedule to which it would not otherwise be entitled or of a greater amount than that to which it would otherwise be entitled.

(3) In this paragraph "arrangements" includes any scheme, agreement or understanding, whether or not legally enforceable.

Refunds of contributions to independent research and development

25—(1) This paragraph applies where a company receives a payment refunding the whole or any part of—

(a) any qualifying expenditure on sub-contracted research and development to which paragraph 6(3) applies (research sub-contracted to charities, universities and scientific research organisations), or

(b) any qualifying expenditure on contributions to independent research and development (see paragraph 12),

in respect of which it obtains relief under this Schedule.

(2) The appropriate amount shall be treated as income of the company chargeable to tax under Case I of Schedule D for the accounting period in which the payment is made.

(3) Where, by virtue paragraph 23(3) (profits of life assurance business chargeable to tax under Case VI of Schedule D), the relief obtained in respect of the contribution or expenditure concerned is a deduction in computing for tax purposes the profits of a part of the life assurance business of the company—

(a) sub-paragraph (2) does not apply, and

(b) the appropriate amount shall be treated as income referrable to that part which is chargeable to tax under Case VI of Schedule D for the accounting period in which the payment is made.

(4) For this purpose "the appropriate amount" means—

(a) where the company qualifies as a small or medium-sized enterprise in the accounting period in which it obtains the relief—

(i) if it is entitled to relief under Schedule 20 to the Finance Act 2000 (c 17) in respect of the qualifying expenditure refunded, 50% of the payment, and

(ii) in any other case, 150% of the payment; and

(b) where the company does not so qualify—

(i) if the relief falls within paragraph 21(2) (relief for qualifying expenditure deductible in computing profits for tax purposes), 50% of the payment, and

(ii) in any other case, 150% of the payment.

Funding of tax credits

26 Section 10 of the Exchequer and Audit Departments Act 1866 (c 39) (gross revenues to be paid to Exchequer) shall be construed as allowing the Commissioners of Inland Revenue to deduct payments for or in respect of tax credits under this Schedule before causing the gross revenues of their department to be paid to the account mentioned in that section.

Interpretation

27—(1) In this Schedule—

"the Inland Revenue" means any officer of the Board;

"life assurance business" has the meaning given in section 431(2) of the Taxes Act 1988;

"national insurance contributions" means contributions under Part 1 of the Social Security Contributions and Benefits Act 1992 (c 4) or Part 1 of the Social Security Contributions and Benefits (Northern Ireland) Act 1992 (c 7);

"PAYE regulations" means regulations under section 203 of the Taxes Act 1988;

"payment period" has the meaning given in paragraph 17(2) of Schedule 20 to the Finance Act 2000;

"research and development" has the meaning given by section 837A of the Taxes Act 1988;

"surrenderable loss" has the meaning given in paragraph 16(2).

(2) Section 839 of the Taxes Act 1988 (connected persons) applies for the purposes of this Schedule.

(3) For the purposes of this Schedule a company not within the charge to corporation tax that incurs qualifying expenditure is treated as having such accounting periods as it would have—

(a) if it carried on a trade consisting of the qualifying R&D activity on which the expenditure is incurred, and

(b) if it had started to carry on that trade when it started to carry on that activity.

Commencement and transitional provision

28—(1) This Schedule applies only to expenditure incurred on or after such day (being a day not earlier than 1st April 2002) as the Treasury may by order appoint.

(2) For the purposes of determining the expenditure incurred on or after that day no account shall be taken of section 401 of the Taxes Act 1988 (pre-trading expenditure treated as incurred when trading begins).

(3) Paragraph 1(1) (requirement of minimum amount of qualifying expenditure in an accounting period) applies to an accounting period beginning before and ending on or after that day as if so much of the period as falls on or after that date were a separate accounting period.

SCHEDULE 14

TAX CREDITS UNDER SCHEDULE 13: CONSEQUENTIAL AMENDMENTS

Section 54

Commentary—*Simon's Direct Tax Service* D2.1201, 1209.

Interest

1—(1) Section 826 of the Taxes Act 1988 (interest on tax overpaid) is amended as follows.

(2) In subsection (1) (payments which carry interest) after paragraph (d) insert—

"(da) a payment of a tax credit falls to be made to a company under Schedule 13 to the Finance Act 2002 in respect of an accounting period, or".

(3) After subsection (3A) (material date for repayments of R&D tax credit) insert—

"(3AA) In relation to a payment of tax credit falling within subsection (1)(da) above, the material date is whichever is the later of—

(a) the filing date for the company's company tax return for the accounting period for which the tax credit is claimed, and (*b*) the date on which the company tax return or amended company tax return containing the claim for payment of the tax credit is delivered to the Inland Revenue.

For this purpose "the filing date", in relation to a company tax return, has the same meaning as in Schedule 18 to the Finance Act 1998.".

(4) In subsection (8A) (recovery of overpaid interest)—

(*a*) in paragraph (*a*) for "or (*d*)" substitute "(*d*), (*da*)", and

(*b*) in paragraph (*b*)(ii) after "R&D tax credit" insert ", tax credit under Schedule 13 to the Finance Act 2002".

(5) In subsection (8BA) (cases where there is a change in the amount of the R&D tax credit etc) after "R&D tax credit" (in both places) insert ", tax credit under Schedule 13 to the Finance Act 2002".

Claim must be made in tax return

2 In Schedule 18 to the Finance Act 1998 (c 36) (company tax returns, assessments and related matters), in paragraph 10 (other claims and elections to be included in return), at the end insert—

"(3) A claim to which Part 9C of this Schedule applies (claims for tax credits under Schedule 13 to the Finance Act 2002) can only be made by being included in a company tax return (see paragraph 83N).".

Recovery of excessive tax credits

3 In paragraph 52 of that Schedule (recovery of excessive repayments, etc)—

(*a*) in sub-paragraph (2) (excessive repayments to which paragraphs 41 to 48 apply), after paragraph (*bb*) insert—

"(*bc*) tax credit under Schedule 13 to the Finance Act 2002,",

(*b*) in sub-paragraph (5) (connection of assessment for excessive payment to an accounting period), after paragraph (*ac*) insert—

"(*ad*) an amount of tax credit under Schedule 13 to the Finance Act 2002 paid to a company for an accounting period,", and

(*c*) at the end of that sub-paragraph, after "(*ac*)" insert ", (*ad*)".

Claims for tax credits

4 After Part 9B of that Schedule insert—

"PART 9C
CLAIMS FOR TAX CREDIT UNDER SCHEDULE 13 TO THE FINANCE ACT 2002
Introduction

83M This Part of this Schedule applies to claims for tax credits under Schedule 13 to the Finance Act 2002 (vaccine research etc).

Claim to be included in company tax return

83N—(1) A claim to which this Part of this Schedule applies must be made by being included in the claimant company's company tax return for the accounting period for which the claim is made.

(2) It may be included in the return originally made or by amendment.

Content of claim

83O A claim to which this Part of this Schedule applies must specify the amount of the relief claimed, which must be an amount quantified at the time the claim is made.

Amendment or withdrawal of claim

83P A claim to which this Part of this Schedule applies may be amended or withdrawn by the claimant company only by amending its company tax return.

Time limit for claims

83Q—(1) A claim to which this Part of this Schedule applies may be made, amended or withdrawn at any time up to the first anniversary of the filing date for the company tax return of the claimant company for the accounting period for which the claim is made.

(2) The claim may be made, amended or withdrawn at a later date if the Inland Revenue allow it.

Penalty

83R—(1) The company is liable to a penalty where it—

(a) fraudulently or negligently makes a claim to which this Part of this Schedule applies which is incorrect, or

(b) discovers that such a claim made by it (neither fraudulently nor negligently) is incorrect and does not remedy the error without unreasonable delay.

(2) The penalty is an amount not exceeding the excess credit claimed, that is, the difference between—

(a) the amount of the credit to which the company is entitled under Schedule 13 to the Finance Act 2002 for the accounting period to which the claim relates, and

(b) the amount of such credit claimed by the company for that period.''.

Commencement

5 This Schedule has effect in relation to tax credits payable under Schedule 13 in respect of expenditure incurred on or after such day as the Treasury may appoint under paragraph 28 of that Schedule.

SCHEDULE 15

R&D TAX RELIEF FOR SMALL AND MEDIUM-SIZED ENTERPRISES: MINOR AND CONSEQUENTIAL AMENDMENTS

Section 56

Commentary—*Simon's Direct Tax Service* **D2.1201.**

1 Schedule 20 to the Finance Act 2000 (c 17) (R&D tax relief for small and medium-sized enterprises) is amended as follows.

2—(1) In paragraph 1 (entitlement to R&D tax relief)—

(a) in sub-paragraph (1)(b) (requirement that qualifying R&D expenditure is not less than £25,000), for ''the company's qualifying R&D expenditure (see paragraph 3)'' substitute ''the aggregate of its qualifying R&D expenditure (see paragraph 3) and its qualifying sub-contracted R&D expenditure (within the meaning of paragraph 8 of Schedule 12 to the Finance Act 2002)'';

(b) after sub-paragraph (3) insert—

''(3A) For the purposes of sub-paragraph (1)(b) a company's qualifying sub-contracted R&D expenditure (within the meaning of paragraph 8 of Schedule 12 to the Finance Act 2002) is deductible in an accounting period if it is allowable as a deduction in computing for tax purposes the profits for that period of a trade carried on by the company.''.

(2) This paragraph does not apply in relation to a company's qualifying sub-contracted R&D expenditure (within the meaning of paragraph 8 of Schedule 12 to this Act) incurred before 1st April 2002.

For this purpose no account shall be taken of section 401 of the Taxes Act 1988 (pre-trading expenditure treated as incurred when trading begins).

3 In paragraph 5 (staffing costs)—

(a) in sub-paragraph (1)(c) omit ''(within the meaning of section 231A(4) of the Taxes Act 1988)'', and

(b) after sub-paragraph (1) insert—

''(1A) In sub-paragraph (1)(c) ''pension fund'' means any scheme, fund or other arrangements established and maintained (whether in the United Kingdom or elsewhere) for the purpose of providing pensions, retirement annuities, allowances, lump sums, gratuities or other superannuation benefits (with or without subsidiary benefits).

In this sub-paragraph ''scheme'' includes any deed, agreement or series of agreements.''.

4 In paragraph 8 (subsidised expenditure), for the second sentence of sub-paragraph (2) substitute—

''For this purpose the following are not State aids—

(a) R&D tax relief and R&D tax credits;

(b) tax relief under Schedule 12 to the Finance Act 2002 (tax relief for expenditure on research and development);

(c) tax relief and tax credits under Schedule 13 to that Act (tax relief for expenditure on vaccine research etc).''

5 In paragraph 12 (treatment of sub-contractor payments where principal and sub-contractor unconnected), for paragraph (b) substitute—

''(b) the company and the sub-contractor are not connected persons, and

(c) no election is made under paragraph 11,''.

SCHEDULE 16

COMMUNITY INVESTMENT TAX RELIEF

Section 57

Commentary—*Simon's Direct Tax Service* **D2.1301, E3.101.**

PART 1

INTRODUCTION

Eligibility for tax relief

1—(1) An individual or company (''the investor'') that makes an investment (''the investment'') in a body is eligible for relief in respect of the investment if—

(a) that body is accredited as a community development finance institution under this Schedule at the time the investment is made (see Part 2);

(b) the investment is a qualifying investment (see Part 3); and

(c) the general conditions of Part 4 are satisfied.

(2) In this Schedule references to ''the CDFI'' are to the body in which the investment is made.

Meaning of ''investment''

2—(1) For the purposes of this Schedule, a person makes an investment in a body at any time when—

(a) he makes a loan (whether secured or unsecured) to the body, or

(b) an issue of securities of or shares in the body, for which he has subscribed, is made to him

(2) For the purposes of sub-paragraph (1)(a)—

(a) a person does not make a loan to a body where—

(i) the body uses overdraft facilities provided by that person, or

(ii) that person subscribes for or otherwise acquires securities of the body;

(b) where the loan agreement authorises the body to draw down amounts of the loan over a period of time, the loan is treated as made at the time when the first amount is drawn down.

Meaning of ''the five year period''

3 In this Schedule ''the five year period'' means the period of five years beginning with the day the investment is made (''the investment date'').

PART 2

ACCREDITED COMMUNITY DEVELOPMENT FINANCE INSTITUTIONS

Application and criteria for accreditation

4—(1) Applications for accreditation as a community development finance institution must be made to the Secretary of State in such form and manner as he may specify.

(2) The Secretary of State shall accredit a body if, and only if, he is satisfied—

(a) that the body's principal objective is to provide (directly or indirectly)—

(i) finance, or

(ii) finance and access to business advice,

for enterprises for disadvantaged communities, and

(b) that the body satisfies such other criteria as may be specified in regulations made by the Treasury.

(3) For the purposes of this paragraph ''enterprises for disadvantaged communities'' include—

(a) enterprises located in disadvantaged areas, and

(b) enterprises owned or operated by, or designed to serve, members of disadvantaged groups.

(4) The criteria mentioned in paragraph (b) of sub-paragraph (2) may include criteria relating to the enterprises to which the body provides or proposes to provide finance or access to business advice.

(5) Regulations under that paragraph may—

(a) make the provision mentioned in that paragraph by reference to any material published by, or on behalf of, the Secretary of State (whether before or after the coming into force of this paragraph), and

(b) make different provision for different cases or circumstances or in relation to different areas.

(6) Without prejudice to the generality of sub-paragraph (5)(b), those regulations may, in particular, make different provision in the case of bodies whose principal objective in providing finance as mentioned in sub-paragraph (2)(a) is to invest directly in enterprises that use the money raised for the purposes of the business of the enterprise in cases where—

(a) that business does not include the provision of finance for other enterprises, or (*b*) if it includes any such provision, the nature and extent of that provision satisfies such conditions as the Treasury may, by regulations, prescribe.

(7) Where the Secretary of State accredits a body of the kind mentioned in sub-paragraph (6), he shall specify in the accreditation that the body is accredited as a retail community development finance institution.

Terms and conditions of accreditation

5—(1) An accreditation under this Schedule shall—

    (*a*) be made on—

        (i) such terms as regulations may require, and

        (ii) such other terms as the Secretary of State considers appropriate, and

    (*b*) be made conditional upon compliance with—

        (i) such requirements as regulations may require, and

        (ii) such other requirements as the Secretary of State considers appropriate.

(2) The requirements that may be imposed by virtue of sub-paragraph (1)(*b*) include requirements relating to the provision of information.

(3) Regulations may—

    (*a*) make provision for appeals to the Special Commissioners against refusals to grant accreditation under this Schedule;

    (*b*) make provision about the consequences of a failure to comply with any requirement of an accreditation, including—

        (i) provision for the withdrawal of the accreditation with effect from the time of the failure or a later time; and

        (ii) provision for the imposition of penalties;

    (*c*) make provision for the making of decisions by the Secretary of State as to any matter required to be decided for the purposes of the regulations;

    (*d*) make different provision for different cases or circumstances or in relation to different areas; and

    (*e*) make such incidental, supplemental, transitional and consequential provision as appears to the Treasury to be necessary or expedient.

(4) In this paragraph "regulations" means regulations made by the Treasury.

Delegation of Secretary of State's functions

6 The Secretary of State may delegate any functions conferred on him by or under this Part.

Period of accreditation

7—(1) An accreditation has effect for a period of three years beginning on such day as may be specified in the accreditation, being a day which is no earlier than—

    (*a*) if the body is not accredited under this Schedule at the time the application is made, the day the accreditation is granted, and

    (*b*) if the body is so accredited, the time the body's current accreditation expires.

This is subject to sub-paragraphs (2) and (3).

(2) Where the application for an accreditation is made before 6th April 2003, the accreditation may specify that it is to have effect for a period—

    (*a*) beginning on 17th April 2002 or such later day as may be specified in the accreditation, and

    (*b*) ending immediately before the third anniversary of the day the accreditation is granted.

(3) Where the body is accredited at the time the application is made and it makes a request under this sub-paragraph, the new accreditation may specify that the existing accreditation is to be treated for the purposes of this Schedule (including sub-paragraph (1)(*b*) above) as expiring immediately before the grant of the new accreditation (if it would otherwise expire at a later time).

(4) This paragraph has effect subject to paragraph 5(3)(*b*) (power to provide for the withdrawal of accreditation).

PART 3
QUALIFYING INVESTMENTS

Introduction

8 For the purposes of this Schedule the investment is a "qualifying investment" in the CDFI if—

    (*a*) the investment consists of—

        (i) a loan in relation to which the conditions of paragraph 9 are satisfied,

        (ii) securities in relation to which the conditions of paragraph 10 are satisfied, or

        (iii) shares in relation to which the conditions of paragraph 11 are satisfied;

(*b*) the investor receives from the CDFI a valid tax relief certificate in relation to the investment (see paragraph 12); and

(*c*) the requirements of paragraph 13 are met in relation to pre-arranged protection against risks.

Conditions to be satisfied in relation to loans

9—(1) The first condition of this paragraph is that either—

(*a*) the CDFI receives from the investor, on the investment date, the full amount of the loan, or

(*b*) if the loan agreement authorises the CDFI to draw down amounts of the loan over a period of time, the end of that period is not later than 18 months after the investment date.

(2) The second condition is that the loan must not carry any present or future right to be converted into or exchanged for a loan which is, or securities, shares, or other rights which are, redeemable within the five year period.

(3) The third condition is that the loan must not have been made on terms that allow any person to require—

(*a*) the repayment during the first two years of the five year period of any of the loan capital advanced in those two years,

(*b*) the repayment during the third year of that period of more than 25% of the loan capital outstanding at the end of those two years,

(*c*) the repayment before the end of the fourth year of that period of more than 50% of that loan capital, or

(*d*) the repayment before the end of that period of more than 75% of that loan capital.

(4) For the purposes of sub-paragraph (3), any requirement arising as a consequence of a failure of the CDFI to fulfil any obligation of the loan agreement shall be disregarded if that obligation—

(*a*) is imposed by reason only of the commercial risks to which the investor is exposed as lender under that agreement, and

(*b*) is no more likely to be breached than any obligation that might reasonably have been agreed in respect of the loan in the absence of this Schedule.

(5) The Treasury may by order substitute for any percentage for the time being specified in sub-paragraph (3) such other percentage as they think fit; and any such substitution shall have effect in relation to loans made by a person on or after such date as may be specified in the order.

Conditions to be satisfied in relation to securities

10—(1) The first condition of this paragraph is that the securities must be—

(*a*) subscribed for wholly in cash, and

(*b*) fully paid for on the investment date.

(2) The second condition is that the securities must not carry—

(*a*) any present or future right to be redeemed within the five year period, or

(*b*) any present or future right to be converted into or exchanged for a loan which is, or securities, shares or other rights which are, redeemable within that period.

Conditions to be satisfied in relation to shares

11—(1) The first condition of this paragraph is that the shares must be—

(*a*) subscribed for wholly in cash, and

(*b*) fully paid up on the investment date.

Shares are not fully paid up for the purposes of paragraph (*b*) if there is any undertaking to pay cash to the CDFI at a future date in connection with the acquisition of the shares.

(2) The second condition is that the shares must not carry—

(*a*) any present or future right to be redeemed during the five year period, or

(*b*) any present or future right to be converted into or exchanged for a loan which is, or securities, shares or other rights which are, redeemable within that period.

Tax relief certificates

12—(1) For the purposes of this Schedule a "tax relief certificate" means a certificate issued by the CDFI in respect of the investment, which is in such form as the Board may specify.

(2) The CDFI must not, in relation to an accreditation period—

(*a*) if it is accredited for that period as a retail community development finance institution (see paragraph 4(7)), issue tax relief certificates in respect of investments made in the CDFI in that period with an aggregate value exceeding £10 million, and

(*b*) in any other case, issue tax relief certificates in respect of investments made in the CDFI in that period with an aggregate value exceeding £20 million.

(3) For the purposes of sub-paragraph (2) the value of an investment made in the CDFI is—

(*a*) if the investment consists of a loan—

(i) the amount of the loan, or

(ii) where the loan agreement authorises the CDFI to draw down amounts of the loan over a period of time, the amount committed under the loan agreement; and

(*b*) if the investment consists of securities or shares, the amount subscribed for them.

(4) The Treasury may, by order, substitute for any amount for the time being specified in sub-paragraph (2) such other amount as they think fit.

(5) Any such substitution shall have effect in relation to such accreditation periods as may be specified in the order; and those periods may, if the substitution increases the amount for the time being specified in sub-paragraph (2), include periods beginning before the order takes effect.

(6) Any tax relief certificate issued wholly or partly in contravention of sub-paragraph (2) is invalid.

(7) A body is liable to a penalty not exceeding £3000 if it issues a tax relief certificate which is made fraudulently or negligently.

Pre-arranged protection against risks

13—(1) Any arrangements—

(*a*) under which the investment is made, or

(*b*) made, before the investor makes the investment, in relation to or in connection with the making of the investment,

must not include arrangements (''excluded arrangements'') the main purpose of which, or one of the main purposes of which, is (by means of any insurance, indemnity or guarantee or otherwise) to provide partial or complete protection for the investor against what would otherwise be the risks attached to making the investment.

(2) For the purposes of sub-paragraph (1), excluded arrangements do not include any arrangements which are confined to the provision for the investor of any such protection against those risks as might reasonably be expected to be provided for commercial reasons if the investment were made in the course of a business of banking.

(3) For the purposes of this paragraph ''arrangements'' includes any scheme, agreement or understanding, whether or not legally enforceable.

PART 4

GENERAL CONDITIONS

No control of CDFI by investor

14—(1) The investor must not control the CDFI at any time during the five year period.

(2) In this paragraph references to the investor include any person connected with the investor.

(3) Where the CDFI is a body corporate, the question whether the investor controls the CDFI shall, for the purposes of this paragraph, be determined in accordance with section 840 of the Taxes Act 1988.

This is subject to sub-paragraph (6).

(4) In any other case, the investor shall be treated, for those purposes, as having control of the CDFI if he has power to secure—

(*a*) by means of the possession of voting power in the CDFI, or

(*b*) by virtue of any powers conferred by the constitution of, or any other document regulating, the CDFI,

that the affairs of the body are conducted in accordance with his wishes. This is subject to sub-paragraphs (5) and (6).

(5) Where the CDFI is a partnership and the investor is a member of that partnership, for the purposes of determining in accordance with this paragraph whether the investor controls the CDFI the other members of that partnership shall not, by virtue of their membership of the CDFI, be treated as partners of the investor.

(6) In determining whether the investor controls the CDFI there shall be attributed to the investor (to the extent that it would not otherwise be the case)—

(*a*) any rights or powers that the investor is entitled to acquire at a future date or will, at a future date, become entitled to acquire, and

(*b*) any rights or powers which another person holds on behalf of the investor or may be required to exercise, by direction, on his behalf.

Beneficial ownership

15—(1) The investor must be the sole beneficial owner of the investment when it is made.

(2) Where the investment consists of a loan, the person beneficially entitled to repayment of the loan shall be treated as the beneficial owner of the loan for the purposes of this Schedule.

Investor must not be accredited

16 The investor must not be accredited as a community development finance institution under this Schedule (see Part 2) on the investment date.

No acquisition of share in partnership

17—(1) Where the CDFI is a partnership, the investment must not consist of or include any amount of capital contributed by the investor on becoming a member of the partnership.

(2) For this purpose, the amount of capital contributed by the investor on becoming a member of the partnership includes any amount which—

    (*a*) purports to be provided by the investor by way of loan capital, and

    (*b*) is accounted for as partners' capital in the accounts of the partnership.

No tax avoidance purpose

18 The investment must not be made as part of a scheme or arrangement the main purpose of which, or one of the main purposes of which, is the avoidance of tax.

PART 5
FORM OF RELIEF
Individual investors

19—(1) This paragraph applies where the investor is—

    (*a*) an individual, and

    (*b*) eligible for relief in respect of the investment (see paragraph 1(1)).

(2) Where the investor makes a claim in respect of a loan, securities or shares for a relevant tax year in accordance with this Part, the amount of his liability for that year to income tax on his total income shall be reduced by the smaller of—

    (*a*) 5% of the invested amount in respect of that loan or those securities or shares for the year, and

    (*b*) the amount which reduces his liability to zero.

(3) For this purpose the "relevant" tax years are—

    (*a*) the tax year in which the investment date falls, and

    (*b*) each of the four subsequent tax years.

(4) The investor is entitled to make a claim for relief for a relevant tax year if—

    (*a*) it appears to him that the conditions for the relief are for the time being satisfied, and

    (*b*) he has received a tax relief certificate (see paragraph 12) relating to the investment from the CDFI,

but no claim may be made before the end of the tax year to which it relates.

(5) Sub-paragraph (4) is subject to the following provisions—

    (*a*) paragraph 22 (loans: no claim after disposal or excessive repayments or receipts of value);

    (*b*) paragraph 23 (securities or shares: no claim after disposal or excessive receipts of value);

    (*c*) paragraph 24 (loss of accreditation by CDFI).

(6) In determining for the purposes of sub-paragraph (2) the amount of income tax to which the investor would be liable apart from this paragraph, no account shall be taken of—

    (*a*) any income tax reduction under Chapter 1 of Part 7 of the Taxes Act 1988 or under section 347B of that Act;

    (*b*) any income tax reduction under section 353(1A) of that Act;

    (*c*) any relief by way of a reduction of liability to tax which is given in accordance with any arrangements having effect by virtue of section 788, or by way or a credit under section 790(1), of that Act;

    (*d*) any tax at the basic rate on so much of that person's income as is income the income tax on which he is entitled to charge against any other person or to deduct, retain or satisfy out of any payment.

Company investors

20—(1) This paragraph applies where the investor is—

    (*a*) a company, and

    (*b*) eligible for relief in respect of the investment (see paragraph 1(1)).

(2) Where the investor makes a claim for a relevant accounting period in respect of a loan, securities or shares in accordance with this Part, the amount of its liability for corporation tax for that period shall be reduced by the smaller of—

    (*a*) 5% of the invested amount in respect of that loan or those securities or shares for the period, and

    (*b*) the amount which reduces the investor's liability to zero.

(3) For this purpose the "relevant" accounting periods are—

  (*a*) the accounting period in which the investment date falls, and
  (*b*) each of the accounting periods in which the subsequent four anniversaries of that date fall.

(4) The investor is entitled to make a claim for relief for a relevant accounting period if—

  (*a*) it appears to the investor that the conditions for the relief are for the time being satisfied, and
  (*b*) it has received a tax relief certificate (see paragraph 12) relating to the investment from the CDFI,

but no claim may be made before the end of the accounting period to which it relates.

(5) Sub-paragraph (4) is subject to the following provisions—

  (*a*) paragraph 22 (loans: no claim after disposal or excessive repayments or receipts of value);
  (*b*) paragraph 23 (securities or shares: no claim after disposal or excessive receipts of value);
  (*c*) paragraph 24 (loss of accreditation by CDFI);
  (*d*) paragraph 25 (accreditation of the investor).

Determination of "the invested amount"

21—(1) This paragraph applies for the purpose of determining "the invested amount" in respect of any loan, securities or shares comprised in the investment.

This is subject to paragraphs 31(2) and 38 (which adjust "the invested amount" in certain cases where value is received).

(2) In the case of a loan, the invested amount is—

  (*a*) for the tax year or accounting period in which the investment date falls, the average capital balance for the first year of the five year period;
  (*b*) for the tax year or accounting period in which the first anniversary of the investment date falls, the average capital balance for the second year of the five year period;
  (*c*) for any subsequent tax year or accounting period—

    (i) the average capital balance for the period of one year beginning with the anniversary of the investment date falling in the tax year or accounting period concerned, or
    (ii) if less, the average capital balance for the period of six months beginning eighteen months after the investment date.

(3) In the case of securities or shares, the invested amount for a tax year or accounting period is the amount subscribed by the investor for the securities or shares.

(4) For the purposes of this paragraph, the average capital balance of the loan for a period is the mean of the daily balances of capital outstanding during the period.

Loans: no claim after disposal or excessive repayments or receipts of value

22—(1) Where the investment consists of a loan, no claim may be made in respect of a tax year or accounting period if—

  (*a*) the investor disposes of the whole or any part of the loan before the qualifying date relating to that year or period,
  (*b*) at any time after the investment is made but before that qualifying date, the amount of the capital outstanding on the loan is reduced to nil, or
  (*c*) before that qualifying date, paragraphs (*a*) and (*b*) of paragraph 30(1) (repayments of loan in five year period exceeding permitted limits) apply in relation to the investment (whether by virtue of paragraph 31 (receipts of value treated as repayments) or otherwise).

For the purposes of paragraph (*a*) any repayment of the loan is to be disregarded.

(2) For the purposes of this paragraph the qualifying date relating to a tax year or accounting period is the anniversary of the investment date next occurring after the end of that year or period.

Securities or shares: no claim after disposal or excessive receipts of value

23—(1) Where the investment consists of securities or shares, a claim made in respect of a tax year or accounting period must relate only to those securities or shares held by the investor, as sole beneficial owner, continuously throughout the period—

  (*a*) beginning when the investment is made, and
  (*b*) ending immediately before the qualifying date relating to the tax year or accounting period.

(2) No claim for relief may be made in relation to a tax year or accounting period if before the qualifying date relating to that year or period paragraphs (*a*) to (*d*) of paragraph 32(1) (receipts of value in five year period exceeding permitted limits) apply in relation to the investment or any part of it.

(3) For the purposes of this paragraph, the qualifying date relating to a tax year or accounting period is the anniversary of the investment date next occurring after the end of that year or period.

Loss of accreditation by the CDFI

24—(1) Where the CDFI ceases to be accredited under Part 2 with effect from a time ("the relevant time") within the five year period, no claim for relief relating to the investment may be made by the investor—

(a) for the relevant tax year or accounting period, or

(b) for any later tax year or accounting period.

(2) For the purposes of sub-paragraph (1) the relevant tax year or accounting period is—

(a) where the relevant time falls within the first year of the five year period, the tax year or accounting period in which the investment date fell, and

(b) in any other case, the year or period in which fell the last anniversary of that date before the relevant time (or, if the relevant time itself falls on an anniversary of the investment date, the year or period in which that anniversary falls).

Accreditation of the investor

25—(1) Where the investor is a company and becomes accredited with effect from a time ("the relevant time") within the five year period, no claim for relief relating to the investment may be made by the investor for the relevant accounting period or any later period.

(2) For the purposes of sub-paragraph (1) the relevant accounting period is—

(a) where the relevant time falls within the first year of the five year period, the accounting period in which the investment date fell, and

(b) in any other case, the period in which fell the last anniversary of that date before the relevant time (or, if the relevant time itself falls on an anniversary of the investment date, the period in which that anniversary falls).

Attribution

26—(1) In this Schedule—

(a) references to the relief attributable to any loan, securities or shares in respect of a tax year shall be read as references to the reduction made in the investor's liability to income tax for that year that is attributed to that loan, or those securities or shares, in accordance with this paragraph, and

(b) references to the relief attributable to any loan, securities or shares in respect of an accounting period shall be read as references to the reduction made in the investor's liability to corporation tax for that period that is attributed to that loan, or those securities or shares, in accordance with this paragraph.

This is subject to the provisions of Part 6 for the withdrawal or reduction of relief.

(2) Where the investor's liability to income or corporation tax is reduced for a tax year or accounting period under this Part, then—

(a) where the reduction is obtained by reason of one loan, or securities or shares comprised in one issue, the amount of the tax reduction shall be attributed to that loan or those securities or shares, and

(b) where the reduction is obtained by reason of a loan or loans, securities or shares comprised in two or more investments, the reduction—

(i) shall be apportioned between the loan or loans, securities or shares in each of those investments in the same proportions as the invested amounts in respect of the loan or loans, securities or shares for the year or period, and

(ii) shall be attributed to that loan or those loans, securities or shares accordingly.

(3) Where under this paragraph an amount of any reduction of income tax or corporation tax is attributed to any securities in the same issue, a proportionate part of that amount shall be attributed to each security.

(4) Where under this paragraph an amount of any reduction of income tax or corporation tax is attributed to any shares in the same issue, a proportionate part of that amount shall be attributed to each of those shares.

(5) If corresponding bonus shares are issued to the investor in respect of any shares ("the original shares") comprised in the investment that have been continuously held by the investor, as sole beneficial owner, from the time they were issued until the issue of the bonus shares—

(a) a proportionate part of any amount attributed to the original shares, in respect of a tax year or accounting period, immediately before the bonus shares are issued shall be attributed to each of the shares in the holding comprising the original shares and the bonus shares, in respect of that year or period, and

(b) after the issue of the bonus shares, this Schedule shall apply as if—

(i) the original issue had included the bonus shares, and

(ii) the bonus shares had been held by the investor, as sole beneficial owner, continuously from the time the original shares were issued until the bonus shares were issued.

(6) In sub-paragraph (5)—

"corresponding bonus shares" means bonus shares that are in the same company, of the same class, and carry the same rights as the original shares; and

"original issue" means the issue of shares forming the investment.

(7) If relief attributable to a loan or any securities or shares falls to be withdrawn under Part 6, the relief attributable to that loan or each of those securities or shares shall be reduced to nil.

(8) If relief attributable to any securities or shares falls to be reduced under that Part by any amount, the relief attributable to each of those securities or shares shall be reduced by a proportionate part of that amount.

PART 6
WITHDRAWAL OF RELIEF
Manner of withdrawal of relief

27—(1) This paragraph applies where any relief has been obtained which—

(a) is subsequently found not to have been due, or

(b) falls to be withdrawn or reduced under this Part.

(2) Where the investor is an individual, the relief shall be withdrawn or reduced by making an assessment to income tax under Case VI of Schedule D for the tax year for which the relief was obtained.

(3) No assessment shall be made under sub-paragraph (2) in respect of an individual by reason of any event occurring after his death.

(4) Where the investor is a company, the relief shall be withdrawn or reduced by making an assessment to corporation tax under Case VI of Schedule D for the accounting period for which the relief was obtained.

Disposal of loan during five year period

28—(1) Where the investment consists of a loan, if within the five year period—

(a) the investor disposes of the whole of the investment, otherwise than by way of a permitted disposal, or

(b) the investor disposes of a part of the investment,

any relief attributable to the investment in respect of any tax year or accounting period must be withdrawn.

(2) For the purposes of this paragraph—

(a) a disposal is "permitted" if—

(i) it is by way of a distribution in the course of dissolving or winding up the CDFI,

(ii) it is a disposal within section 24(1) of the 1992 Act (entire loss, destruction, dissipation or extinction of asset),

(iii) it is a deemed disposal under section 24(2) of that Act (claim that value of asset has become negligible), or

(iv) it is made after the CDFI has ceased to be accredited under this Schedule, and

(b) a full or partial repayment of the loan shall not be treated as giving rise to a disposal.

Disposal of shares or securities during five year period

29—(1) This paragraph applies where the investment consists of securities or shares and—

(a) the investor disposes of the whole or any part of the investment ("the former investment") within the five year period,

(b) the CDFI has not ceased to be accredited before the disposal, and

(c) the disposal does not arise by virtue of an event within paragraph 35(1)(a) (repayment, redemption or repurchase of securities or shares included in the investment).

(2) If the disposal is not a qualifying disposal, any relief attributable to the former investment in respect of any tax year or accounting period must be withdrawn.

(3) If the disposal is a qualifying disposal, any relief attributable to the former investment for a tax year or accounting period must—

(a) if it is greater than an amount equal to 5% of the amount or value of the consideration (if any) which the investor receives for the former investment, be reduced by that amount, and

(b) in any other case, be withdrawn.

(4) For the purposes of this paragraph "qualifying disposal" means a disposal that is—

(a) by way of a bargain made at arm's length for full consideration, or

(b) a permitted disposal (within the meaning of paragraph 28).

(5) Where for any tax year or accounting period—

(a) the amount of relief attributable to the former investment ("A") is less than (*b*) the amount (''B'') which is equal to 5% of the invested amount in respect of the former investment for that year or period,

sub-paragraph (3)(*a*) shall have effect in relation to that year or period as if the amount or value referred to in that sub-paragraph were reduced by multiplying it by the fraction—

$$\frac{A}{B}$$

(6) Where the amount of relief attributable to the former investment in respect of a tax year or accounting period has been reduced before the relief was obtained, the amount of relief attributable to that investment shall be deemed for the purposes of sub-paragraph (5) to be the amount of the relief that would have been attributable had no such reduction been made before the relief was obtained.

(7) Sub-paragraph (6) does not apply to a reduction by virtue of paragraph 26(5) (attribution of relief where there is a corresponding issue of bonus shares).

Repayments of loan capital

30—(1) Where the investment consists of a loan, if—

(*a*) the average capital balance of the loan for the third, fourth or final year of the five year period is less than the permitted balance for the year in question, and
(*b*) the difference between those balances is not an amount of insignificant value,

any relief attributable to the investment in respect of any tax year or accounting period must be withdrawn.

(2) For the purposes of this paragraph—

''the average capital balance'' of the loan for a period is the mean of the daily balances of capital outstanding during that period, disregarding any non-standard repayments of the loan made in that period or at any earlier time;
''the permitted balance'' of the loan is—

(*a*) for the third year of the five year period, 75% of the average capital balance for the period of six months beginning 18 months after the investment date,
(*b*) for the fourth year of that period, 50% of that balance, and
(*c*) for the final year of that period, 25% of that balance.

(3) For the purposes of sub-paragraph (2), a repayment of the loan is a non-standard repayment if it is made—

(*a*) at the choice or discretion of the CDFI and not as a direct or indirect consequence of any obligation provided for under the terms of the loan agreement, or
(*b*) as a consequence of the failure of the CDFI to fulfil any obligation of the loan agreement which—

(i) is imposed by reason only of the commercial risks to which the investor is exposed as lender under that agreement, and
(ii) is no more likely to be breached than any obligation that might reasonably have been agreed in respect of the loan in the absence of this Schedule.

(4) For the purposes of this paragraph ''an amount of insignificant value'' means an amount which—

(*a*) does not exceed £1,000, or
(*b*) if it exceeds that amount, is insignificant in relation to the average capital balance of the loan for the year of the five year period in question.

Value received treated as repayment of loan

31—(1) This paragraph applies where the investment consists of a loan and the investor receives any value (other than insignificant value) from the CDFI during the period of restriction.

(2) The investor shall be treated for the purposes of—

(*a*) paragraph 21 (determination of ''invested amount''), and
(*b*) paragraph 30 (repayments of loan capital),

as having received a repayment of the loan of an amount equal to the amount of the value received.

(3) For those purposes the repayment shall be treated as made—

(*a*) where the value was received in the first or second year of the period of restriction, at the beginning of that second year, and
(*b*) where the value was received in a later year of that period, at the beginning of the year in question.

(4) For the purposes of paragraph 30 the repayment shall be treated as a repayment other than a non-standard repayment (within the meaning of that paragraph).

(5) For the purposes of this paragraph the investor receives insignificant value where he receives an amount of insignificant value; and for this purpose ''an amount of insignificant value'' means an amount which—

(*a*) does not exceed £1,000, or

(*b*) if it exceeds that amount, is insignificant in relation to the average capital balance of the loan for the year of the period of restriction in which the value is received.

(6) For the purposes of sub-paragraph (5)(*b*)—

(*a*) "the average capital balance" of the loan for a year is the mean of the daily balances of capital outstanding during the year (disregarding the receipt of value in question), and

(*b*) any value received in the first year of the period of restriction shall be treated as received at the beginning of the second year of that period.

(7) This paragraph is subject to paragraph 37 (value received where there is more than one investment).

(8) Value received shall be disregarded, for the purposes of this paragraph, to the extent to which relief attributable to any loan, securities or shares in respect of any one or more tax years or accounting periods has already been reduced or withdrawn on its account.

Value received by investor where the investment consists of securities or shares

32—(1) Where the investment consists of securities or shares and—

(*a*) the investor receives any value (other than insignificant value) from the CDFI during the period of restriction,

(*b*) the investment or a part of it is held by the investor at the time the value is received and has been held by him, as sole beneficial owner, continuously since the investment was made ("the continuing investment"),

(*c*) the receipt is wholly or partly in excess of the permitted level of receipts in respect of the continuing investment, and

(*d*) the amount of that excess ("the excess") is not an amount of insignificant value,

any relief attributable to the continuing investment in respect of any tax year or accounting period must be withdrawn.

(2) For the purposes of sub-paragraph (1) the permitted level of receipts is exceeded where—

(*a*) any amount of value is received by the investor (disregarding any amounts of insignificant value) in the first three years of the period of restriction, or

(*b*) the aggregate amount of value received by the investor (disregarding any amounts of insignificant value)—

    (i) before the beginning of the fifth year of that period, exceeds 25% of the invested capital;

    (ii) before the beginning of the final year of that period, exceeds 50% of the invested capital;

    (iii) before the end of that period, exceeds 75% of the invested capital.

(3) In this paragraph—

"the invested capital", in relation to the continuing investment, means the amount subscribed for the securities or shares concerned;

"an amount of insignificant value" means an amount of value which—

    (*a*) does not exceed £1,000, or

    (*b*) if it exceeds that amount, is insignificant in relation to the amount subscribed by the investor for the securities or shares comprising the continuing investment;

and for the purposes of sub-paragraph (1) the investor receives insignificant value where he receives an amount of insignificant value.

(4) This paragraph is subject to paragraph 37 (value received where there is more than one investment).

(5) Value received shall be disregarded, for the purposes of this paragraph, to the extent to which relief attributable to any loan, securities or shares in respect of any one or more tax years or accounting periods has already been reduced or withdrawn on its account.

Meaning of "period of restriction"

33 In this Part "the period of restriction" in relation to the investment is the period of six years beginning one year before the investment date.

Aggregation of receipts of insignificant value

34—(1) Where—

(*a*) value is received ("the relevant receipt") by the investor from the CDFI at any time during the period of restriction relating to the investment,

(*b*) the investor has received from the CDFI one or more receipts of insignificant value at a time or times during that period but not later than the time of the relevant receipt, and

(*c*) the aggregate amount of the value of the receipts within paragraph (*a*) and (*b*) is not an amount of insignificant value,

the investor shall be treated for the purposes of this Schedule as if the relevant receipt had been a receipt of an amount of value equal to that aggregate amount.

For this purpose a receipt does not fall within paragraph (*b*) if the whole or any part of it has previously been aggregated under this sub-paragraph.

(2) For the purposes of this paragraph ''an amount of insignificant value'' means an amount of value which—

    (*a*) does not exceed £1,000, or

    (*b*) if it exceeds that amount, is insignificant in relation to the relevant amount.

(3) Where the investment consists of a loan, the relevant amount for the purposes of sub-paragraph (2) is—

    (*a*) if the relevant receipt is received in the first or second year of the period of restriction, the average capital balance of the loan for the second year of that period, and

    (*b*) if the relevant receipt is received in a later year, the average capital balance of the loan for the year in question.

(4) For the purposes of sub-paragraph (3)—

    (*a*) the average capital balance of the loan for a year is the mean of the daily balances of capital outstanding during the year, and

    (*b*) the relevant receipt and any receipts within sub-paragraph (1)(*b*) shall be disregarded when calculating the average capital balance for the year in question.

(5) Where the investment consists of securities or shares, the relevant amount for the purposes of sub-paragraph (2) is—

    (*a*) if the relevant receipt is received in the first year of the period of restriction, the amount subscribed for the securities or shares, and

    (*b*) in any other case, the amount subscribed for such of the securities or shares as—

        (i) are held by the investor at the time the relevant receipt is received, and

        (ii) have been held by him, as sole beneficial owner, continuously since the investment was made.

When value is received

35—(1) For the purposes of this Part the investor receives value from the CDFI at any time when the CDFI—

    (*a*) repays, redeems or repurchases any securities or shares included in the investment;

    (*b*) releases or waives any liability of the investor to the CDFI or discharges, or undertakes to discharge, any liability of the investor to a third person;

    (*c*) makes a loan or advance to the investor which has not been repaid in full before the investment is made;

    (*d*) provides a benefit or facility for—

        (i) the investor or any associates of the investor, or

        (ii) if the investor is a company, directors or employees of the investor or any of their associates;

    (*e*) disposes of an asset to the investor for no consideration or for a consideration which is or the value of which is less than the market value of the asset;

    (*f*) acquires an asset from the investor for a consideration which is or the value of which is more than the market value of the asset; or

    (*g*) makes a payment to the investor other than a qualifying payment.

(2) For the purposes of sub-paragraph (1)(*b*) the CDFI shall be treated as having released or waived a liability if the liability is not discharged within 12 months of the time when it ought to have been discharged.

(3) For the purposes of sub-paragraph (1)(*c*) there shall be treated as if it were a loan made by the CDFI to the investor—

    (*a*) the amount of any debt incurred by the investor to the CDFI (other than an ordinary trade debt), and

    (*b*) the amount of any debt due from the investor to a third person which has been assigned to the CDFI.

(4) For the purposes of this paragraph—

    (*a*) references to a debt or liability do not, in relation to a person, include references to any debt or liability which would be discharged by the making by that person of a qualifying payment;

    (*b*) references to a benefit or facility do not include references to any benefit or facility provided in circumstances such that, if a payment had been made of an amount equal to its value, that payment would have been a qualifying payment; and

    (*c*) any reference to a payment or disposal to a person includes a reference to a payment or disposal made to that person indirectly or to his order or for his benefit.

In paragraphs (*a*) to (*c*) references to ''a person'' include references to any person who, at any time in the period of restriction in question, is connected with that person, whether or not he is so connected at the material time.

(5) In this paragraph—

''qualifying payment'' means—

(*a*) any payment by any person for any goods, services or facilities provided by the investor (in the course of his trade or otherwise) which is reasonable in relation to the market value of those goods, services or facilities;

(*b*) the payment by any person of any interest which represents no more than a reasonable commercial return on money lent to that person;

(*c*) the payment by any company of any dividend or other distribution which does not exceed a normal return on any investment in shares in or securities of that company;

(*d*) any payment for the acquisition of an asset which does not exceed its market value;

(*e*) the payment by any person, as rent for any property occupied by the person, of an amount not exceeding a reasonable and commercial rent for the property; and

(*f*) a payment in discharge of an ordinary trade debt; and

''ordinary trade debt'' means any debt for goods or services supplied in the ordinary course of a trade or business where any credit given—

(*a*) does not exceed six months, and

(*b*) is not longer than that normally given to customers of the person carrying on the trade or business.

The amount of value received

36 For the purposes of this Part the amount of the value received is—

(*a*) in a case within paragraph 35(1)(*a*), the amount received by the investor;

(*b*) in a case within paragraph 35(1)(*b*), the amount of the liability;

(*c*) in a case within paragraph 35(1)(*c*)—

(i) the amount of the loan or advance, less

(ii) the amount of any repayment made before the investment is made;

(*d*) in a case within paragraph 35(1)(*d*)—

(i) the cost to the CDFI of providing the benefit or facility, less

(ii) any consideration given for it by the investor or any associate of his;

(*e*) in a case within paragraph 35(1)(*e*) or (*f*), the difference between the market value of the asset and the consideration (if any) received for it; and

(*f*) in a case within paragraph 35(1)(*g*), the amount of the payment.

Value received where there is more than one investment

37—(1) This paragraph applies where—

(*a*) the investor makes two or more investments in the CDFI (being investments in relation to which the investor is eligible for and claims relief), and

(*b*) the investor receives value (other than value within paragraph 35(1)(*a*)) which falls within the periods of restriction relating to two or more of those investments.

(2) Where this paragraph applies, paragraphs 31, 32, 34 and 38 have effect in relation to each investment referred to in sub-paragraph (1)(*b*) as if the amount of the value received were reduced by multiplying it by the fraction—

$$\frac{A}{B}$$

(3) For this purpose—

(*a*) A is the appropriate amount in respect of the investment in question, and

(*b*) B is the aggregate of that amount and the appropriate amount or amounts in respect of the other investment or investments.

(4) Where the investment consists of a loan, the appropriate amount for the purposes of sub-paragraph (3) is—

(*a*) if the value is received in the first or second year of the period of restriction, the average capital balance of the loan for the second year of that period, and

(*b*) if the value is received in a later year, the average capital balance of the loan for the year in question.

(5) For the purposes of sub-paragraph (4)—

(*a*) the average capital balance of the loan for a year is the mean of the daily balances of capital outstanding during the year, and

(*b*) the receipt of value shall be disregarded when calculating the average capital balance for the year in question.

(6) Where the investment consists of securities or shares, the appropriate amount for the purposes of sub-paragraph (3) is—

(*a*) if the value is received in the first year of the period of restriction, the amount subscribed for the securities or shares, and

(*b*) in any other case, the amount subscribed for such of the securities or shares as—

(i) are held by the investor at the time the value is received, and

(ii) have been held by him, as sole beneficial owner, continuously since the investment was made.

Effect of receipt of value on future claims for relief

38—(1) This paragraph applies where the investment consists of securities or shares and—

(a) the investor receives any value (other than insignificant value) from the CDFI during the period of restriction, and

(b) the investment or a part of it is held by the investor at the time the value is received and has been held by him, as sole beneficial owner, continuously since the investment was made ("the continuing investment"),

but no relief attributable to the continuing investment is withdrawn under paragraph 32 as a result of the receipt.

(2) For the purposes of calculating any relief in respect of any securities or shares included in the continuing investment for any relevant tax year or accounting period, the amount subscribed for the securities or shares comprising the continuing investment shall be treated as reduced by the amount of the value received.

(3) For this purpose the "relevant" tax years or accounting periods are—

(a) any tax year or accounting period ending on or after the anniversary of the investment date immediately preceding the receipt of value, or

(b) if the value was received on an anniversary of the investment date, any tax year or accounting period ending on or after that anniversary.

(4) For the purposes of this paragraph the investor receives insignificant value where he receives an amount of insignificant value; and for these purposes "an amount of insignificant value" means an amount of value which—

(a) does not exceed £1,000, or

(b) if it exceeds that amount, is insignificant in relation to the amount subscribed by the investor for the securities or shares comprising the continuing investment.

Receipts of value by and from connected persons

39 In paragraphs 31 to 38 references to the investor or the CDFI include references to any person who at any time in the period of restriction relating to the investment is connected with the investor or, as the case may be, CDFI, whether or not he is connected at the material time.

PART 7

RESTRUCTURING OF CDFI

Rights issues etc

40—(1) Where—

(a) the investor holds shares ("the existing holding") in the CDFI which are of the same class and held in the same capacity,

(b) there is by virtue of such an allotment as is mentioned in section 126(2)(a) of the 1992 Act (an allotment of shares or debentures in respect of and in proportion to an original holding), other than an allotment of corresponding bonus shares, a reorganisation affecting the existing holding,

(c) immediately following the reorganisation, relief is attributable to the shares comprised in the existing holding or the shares or debentures allotted in respect of those shares, in respect of one or more tax years or accounting periods, and

(d) if relief is attributable to the shares comprised in the existing holding at that time, those shares have been held by the investor continuously from the time they were issued until the reorganisation,

sections 127 to 130 of that Act (treatment of share capital following a reorganisation) shall not apply in relation to the existing holding.

(2) Subsection (10) of section 116 of that Act (reorganisations, conversions and reconstructions) shall not apply in any case where the old asset consists of shares held (in the same capacity) by the investor—

(a) that have been held by the investor continuously from the time they were issued until the relevant transaction, and

(b) to which relief is attributable immediately before that transaction.

In this sub-paragraph "old asset" and "the relevant transaction" have the meanings given in section 116 of that Act.

(3) For the purposes of sub-paragraph (1)—

"corresponding bonus shares" means bonus shares that—

(a) are issued in respect of shares comprised in the existing holding, and

(b) are of the same class, and carry the same rights as, those shares;

"reorganisation" has the meaning given in section 126 of that Act.

(4) The following provisions of the 1992 Act have effect subject to this paragraph—

section 116 (reorganisations, conversions and reconstructions);
Chapter 2 of Part 4 (reorganisation of share capital, conversion of securities etc).

Company reconstructions etc

41—(1) Where—

(a) the investor holds shares in or debentures of a company ("company A"),

(b) there is a reconstruction or amalgamation affecting that holding ("the existing holding"),

(c) immediately before the reconstruction or amalgamation, relief is attributable to the shares or debentures comprised in the existing holding in respect of one or more tax years or accounting periods, and

(d) the shares or debentures comprised in the existing holding have been held by the investor continuously from the time they were issued until the reconstruction or amalgamation,

sections 135 and 136 of the 1992 Act (share exchanges and company reconstructions) shall not apply in respect of the existing holding.

(2) Sub-paragraph (1)(a) applies only where the shares or debentures are held by the investor in the same capacity.

(3) For the purposes of sub-paragraph (1) a "reconstruction or amalgamation" means an issue by a company of shares in or debentures of that company in exchange for or in respect of shares in or debentures of company A.

(4) The following provisions of the 1992 Act have effect subject to this paragraph—

section 116 (reorganisations, conversions and reconstructions);
Chapter 2 of Part 4 (reorganisation of share capital, conversion of securities etc).

PART 8

SUPPLEMENTARY AND GENERAL

Information to be provided by the investor

42—(1) Where—

(a) the investor has obtained relief in respect of the investment, and

(b) an event occurs by reason of which relief attributable to the investment for any tax year or accounting period falls to be withdrawn or reduced by virtue of paragraph 28, 29, 30 or 32,

the investor must give the Inland Revenue a notice containing particulars of the event.

(2) Where sub-paragraph (1) requires the giving of a notice, then, subject to sub-paragraph (3) the investor must give the notice not later than—

(a) if the investor is an individual, 31st January next following the tax year in which the event occurred, and

(b) if the investor is a company, the end of the period of 12 months beginning with the end of the accounting period in which the event occurred.

(3) Where—

(a) the investor is required to give a notice by virtue of the receipt of value by a person connected with the investor (see paragraph 39), and

(b) the end of the period of 60 days beginning when the investor comes to know of that event is later than the final notice date under subparagraph (2),

the notice must be given within that 60 day period.

(4) In this paragraph "the Inland Revenue" means any officer of the Board.

Disclosure

43—(1) No obligation as to secrecy or other restriction on the disclosure of information imposed by statute or otherwise prevents the disclosure of information—

(a) by the Secretary of State to the Inland Revenue for the purpose of assisting the Inland Revenue to discharge their functions under the Tax Acts so far as relating to matters arising under this Schedule, or

(b) by the Inland Revenue to the Secretary of State for the purpose of assisting the Secretary of State to discharge his functions under this Schedule.

(2) Information obtained by such disclosure shall not be further disclosed except for the purposes of legal proceedings arising out of the functions referred to.

(3) In this paragraph "the Inland Revenue" means any officer of the Board.

Nominees

44—(1) For the purposes of this Schedule—

   (a) loans made by or to, or disposed of by, a nominee for a person shall be treated as made by or to, or disposed of by, that person;

   (b) securities or shares subscribed for by, issued to, acquired or held by or disposed of by a nominee for a person shall be treated as subscribed for by, issued to, acquired or held by or disposed of by that person.

(2) For the purposes of sub-paragraph (1) references to things done by or to a nominee for a person include things done by or to a bare trustee for a person.

Application for postponement of tax pending appeal

45 No application shall be made under section 55(3) or (4) of the Taxes Management Act 1970 (c 9) (application for postponement of payment of tax pending appeal) on the ground that a person is eligible for relief unless a claim for the relief has been duly made by the person under Part 5 of this Schedule.

Meaning of "issue of securities or shares"

46—(1) In this Schedule—

   (a) references (however expressed) to an issue of securities of any body are to such securities of that body as carry the same rights and are issued under the same terms and on the same day, and

   (b) references (however expressed) to an issue of shares in any body are to such shares in that body as are of the same class and issued on the same day.

(2) In this Schedule references (however expressed) to an issue of securities of or shares in a body to a person are references to such of the securities or shares in an issue of securities of or shares in that body as are issued to that person in one capacity.

Identification of securities or shares on a disposal

47—(1) In any case where—

   (a) the investor disposes of part of a holding of securities or shares ("the holding"), and

   (b) the holding includes securities or shares to which relief is attributable in respect of one or more tax years or accounting periods that have been held continuously by the investor from the time they were issued until the disposal,

this paragraph applies for the purpose of identifying the securities or shares disposed of.

(2) For the purposes of this paragraph "holding" means—

   (a) any number of securities of a company carrying the same rights and issued under the same terms held by the investor in the same capacity, growing or diminishing as securities carrying those rights and issued under those terms are acquired or disposed of, or

   (b) any number of shares in a company of the same class held by the investor in the same capacity, growing or diminishing as shares of that class are acquired or disposed of.

(3) Where securities or shares included in the holding have been acquired by the investor on different days, then, for the purposes of capital gains tax or corporation tax on chargeable gains and of this Schedule, any disposal by the investor of any of those securities or shares shall be treated as relating to those acquired on an earlier day rather than to those acquired on a later day.

(4) Where securities or shares included in the holding have been acquired by the investor on the same day, then, for the purposes of capital gains tax or corporation tax on chargeable gains and of this Schedule, if there is a disposal by the investor of any of those securities or shares, any securities or shares—

   (a) to which relief is attributable, and

   (b) which have been held by the investor continuously from the time they were issued until the time of disposal,

shall be treated as disposed of after any other securities or shares included in the holding which were acquired by the investor on that day.

(5) Chapter 1 of Part 4 of the 1992 Act (share pooling, etc) shall have effect subject to this paragraph.

(6) Sections 104 to 107 of that Act (which make provision for the purposes of capital gains tax and corporation tax on chargeable gains for the identification of securities and shares on a disposal) shall not apply to securities or shares to which relief is attributable.

(7) In a case to which section 127 of that Act (equation of original shares and new holding) applies, shares comprised in the new holding shall be treated for the purposes of sub-paragraphs (3) and (4) as acquired when the original shares were acquired.

(8) In sub-paragraph (7)—

    (*a*) the reference to section 127 includes a reference to that section as it is applied by virtue of any enactment relating to chargeable gains, and

    (*b*) "original shares" and "new holding" have the same meaning as in section 127 or (as the case may be) that section as applied by virtue of the enactment in question.

Meaning of "disposal"

48—(1) Subject to sub-paragraph (2), in this Schedule "disposal" shall be construed in accordance with the 1992 Act, and cognate expressions shall be construed accordingly.

(2) An investor shall be treated for the purposes of this Schedule, and for the purposes of capital gains tax or corporation tax on chargeable gains, as disposing of any securities or shares which but for paragraph 41 he—

    (*a*) would be treated as exchanging for other securities or shares by virtue of section 136 of the 1992 Act, or

    (*b*) would be so treated but for section 137(1) of the 1992 Act (which restricts section 136 of that Act to bona fide reconstructions).

Construction of references to investment being "held continuously"

49—(1) This paragraph applies where for the purposes of this Schedule it falls to be determined whether the investor has held the investment (or any part of it) continuously throughout any period.

(2) The investor shall not be treated as having held the investment (or any part of it) continuously throughout a period if—

    (*a*) he is deemed, under any provision of the 1992 Act, to have disposed of and immediately reacquired the investment (or part) at any time during the period, or

    (*b*) he is treated as having disposed of the investment (or part) at any such time, by virtue of paragraph 48(2).

Meaning of "associate"

50—(1) In this Schedule "associate", in relation to a person, means—

    (*a*) any relative or partner of that person,

    (*b*) the trustee or trustees of any settlement in relation to which that person, or any relative of his (living or dead), is or was a settlor, and

    (*c*) where that person is interested in any shares or obligations of a company which are subject to any trust or are part of the estate of a deceased person—

        (i) the trustee or trustees of the settlement concerned or, as the case may be, the personal representatives of the deceased, and

        (ii) if that person is a company, any other company interested in those shares or obligations.

(2) In sub-paragraph (1)(*a*) and (*b*) "relative" means husband or wife, parent or remoter forebear or child or remoter issue.

(3) In sub-paragraph (1)(*b*) "settlor" and "settlement" have the same meaning as in Chapter 1A of Part 15 of the Taxes Act 1988 (see section 660G(1) and (2)).

Minor definitions etc

51—(1) In this Schedule—

    "the Board" means the Commissioners of Inland Revenue;

    "body" includes an unincorporated association;

    "relief" means relief under Part 5 of this Schedule;

    "tax year" means a year of assessment;

    "the 1992 Act" means the Taxation of Chargeable Gains Act 1992 (c 12).

(2) For the purposes of this Schedule shares in a company shall not be treated as being of the same class unless they would be so treated if dealt with on the Stock Exchange.

(3) Section 839 of the Taxes Act 1988 (connected persons) applies for the purposes of this Schedule.

(4) For the purposes of this Schedule the market value at any time of any asset is the price which it might reasonably be expected to fetch on a sale at that time in the open market free from any interest or right which exists by way of security in or over it.

(5) In this Schedule—

    (*a*) references to relief obtained by the investor in respect of any investment (or part of an investment) include references to relief obtained by the investor in respect of that investment (or part) at any time after the investor has disposed of it, and (*b*) references to the withdrawal or reduction of relief obtained by the investor in respect of the investment (or any part of it) include references to the withdrawal or reduction of relief obtained in respect of that investment (or part) at any such time.

(6) In the case of any condition that cannot be satisfied until a future date—

(*a*) references in this Schedule to a condition being satisfied for the time being are to nothing having occurred to prevent its being satisfied, and
(*b*) references to its continuing to be satisfied are to nothing occurring to prevent its being satisfied.

Index of defined expressions

52 In this Schedule the following expressions are defined or otherwise explained by the provisions indicated:

associate	paragraph 50
the Board	paragraph 51(1)
body	paragraph 51(1)
the CDFI	paragraph 1(2)
disposal	paragraph 48
the five year period	paragraph 3
held continuously (in relation to securities or shares)	paragraph 49
the invested amount	paragraph 21
the investment	paragraph 1
the investment date	paragraph 3
the investor	paragraph 1
issue of securities or shares	paragraph 46
owner (in relation to a loan)	paragraph 15(2)
the 1992 Act	paragraph 51(1)
period of restriction	paragraph 33
relief	paragraph 51(1)
tax relief certificate	paragraph 12

SCHEDULE 17

COMMUNITY INVESTMENT TAX RELIEF: CONSEQUENTIAL AMENDMENTS

Section 57

Commentary—*Simon's Direct Tax Service* **D2.1301, E3.101.**

1 In section 98 of the Taxes Management Act 1970 (c 9), in the second column of the Table, after the final entry insert—

"paragraph 42 of Schedule 16 to the Finance Act 2002".

2 In section 289A of the Taxes Act 1988 (form of relief under enterprise investment scheme), after subsection (5)(*c*) insert—

"(*ca*) any income tax reduction under paragraph 19(2) of Schedule 16 to the Finance Act 2002 (community investment tax relief),".

3 In Schedule 15B to that Act (venture capital trusts: relief from income tax), after paragraph 1(6)(*d*) insert—

"(*da*) any income tax reduction under paragraph 19(2) of Schedule 16 to the Finance Act 2002 (community investment tax relief),".

4 In section 25 of the Finance Act 1990 (c 29) (donations to charity by individuals), in subsection (7) omit "and" at the end of paragraph (*b*) and at the end of paragraph (*c*) insert

"and
(*d*) paragraph 19(6)(*d*) of Schedule 16 to the Finance Act 2002.".

5 In Schedule 18 to the Finance Act 1998 (c 36) (company tax returns, assessments and related matters), in paragraph 8 (calculation of tax payable), after paragraph 1A of the second step of the calculation in sub-paragraph (1) insert—

"1B. Any relief under Part 5 of Schedule 16 to the Finance Act 2002 (community investment tax relief).".

SCHEDULE 18

RELIEF FOR COMMUNITY AMATEUR SPORTS CLUBS

Section 58

Commentary—*Simon's Direct Tax Service* **B3.240, E1.504.**

PART 1

CLUBS ENTITLED TO BE REGISTERED

The requirements

1 A club is entitled to be registered as a community amateur sports club if it is, and is required by its constitution to be, a club that—

    (*a*) is open to the whole community,

    (*b*) is organised on an amateur basis, and

    (*c*) has as its main purpose the provision of facilities for, and promotion of participation in, one or more eligible sports.

In this Schedule ''registered club'' means a club that is so registered.

Open to the whole community

2—(1) A club is open to the whole community if—

    (*a*) membership of the club is open to all without discrimination,

    (*b*) the facilities of the club are available to members without discrimination, and

    (*c*) any fees are set at a level that does not pose a significant obstacle to membership or use of the club's facilities.

(2) For the purposes of sub-paragraph (1) ''discrimination'' includes indirect discrimination and includes, in particular—

    (*a*) discrimination on grounds of ethnicity, nationality, sexual orientation, religion or beliefs;

    (*b*) discrimination on grounds of sex, age or disability, except as a necessary consequence of the requirements of a particular sport.

(3) This paragraph does not prevent a club from having different classes of membership depending on—

    (*a*) the age of the member;

    (*b*) whether the member is a student;

    (*c*) whether the member is waged or unwaged;

    (*d*) whether the member is a playing or a non-playing member;

    (*e*) how far from the club the member lives;

    (*f*) any restriction on the days or times when the member has access to the club's facilities.

Organised on an amateur basis

3—(1) A club is organised on an amateur basis if—

    (*a*) it is non-profit making,

    (*b*) it provides for members and their guests only the ordinary benefits of an amateur sports club, and

    (*c*) its constitution provides for any net assets on the dissolution of the club to be applied for approved sporting or charitable purposes.

(2) A club is ''non-profit making'' if its constitution requires any surplus income or gains to be reinvested in the club and does not permit any distribution of club assets, in cash or in kind, to members or third parties.

This does not prevent donations by the club to charities or to other clubs that are registered as community amateur sports clubs.

(3) The ordinary benefits of an amateur sports club are—

    (*a*) provision of sporting facilities;

    (*b*) reasonable provision and maintenance of club-owned sports equipment;

    (*c*) provision of suitably qualified coaches;

    (*d*) provision, or reimbursement of the costs, of coaching courses;

    (*e*) provision of insurance cover;

    (*f*) provision of medical treatment;

    (*g*) reimbursement of reasonable travel expenses incurred by players and officials travelling to away matches;

    (*h*) reasonable provision of post-match refreshments for players and match officials;

    (*i*) sale or supply of food or drink as a social adjunct to the sporting purposes of the club.

(4) Sub-paragraph (3) does not prevent a club from—

(a) entering into an agreement with a member for the supply to the club of goods or services, or
(b) employing and paying remuneration to staff who are also members of the club,

provided the terms are approved by the governing body of the club without the member concerned being present and are agreed with the member on an arm's length basis.

(5) In relation to the application of the net assets on the dissolution of the club, "approved sporting or charitable purposes" means such of the following as may be approved by the members of the club in general meeting or by the members of the governing body of the club—

(a) the purposes of the governing body of an eligible sport for the purposes of which the club existed, for use in related community sport;
(b) the purposes of another club that is registered as a community amateur sports club;
(c) the purposes of a charity.

PART 2

EXEMPTIONS FOR REGISTERED CLUBS

Exemption for trading income

4—(1) Where—

(a) a club is a registered club throughout an accounting period,
(b) its trading income for that period (before deduction of any expenses) does not exceed £15,000,
(c) the whole of that income is applied for qualifying purposes, and
(d) the club makes a claim under this paragraph to the Inland Revenue, it shall be exempt from corporation tax on that income.

(2) In relation to an accounting period that is shorter than 12 months, subparagraph (1)(b) has effect as if the amount specified there were proportionately reduced.

(3) Where a club is a registered club for only part of an accounting period, subparagraph (1) has effect as if—

(a) that part were a separate accounting period;
(b) the club's trading income for that part were the proportionately reduced amount of its trading income for the actual accounting period.

(4) In this paragraph "trading income" means income that (apart from this paragraph) is chargeable under Case I of Schedule D.

Exemption for interest and gift aid income

5—(1) Where—

(a) a club is a registered club throughout an accounting period,
(b) the whole of its interest income and gift aid income for that period is applied for qualifying purposes, and
(c) the club makes a claim under this paragraph to the Inland Revenue,

it shall be exempt from corporation tax on that income.

(2) Where a club is a registered club for only part of an accounting period, subparagraph (1) has effect as if—

(a) that part were a separate accounting period;
(b) the club's interest income for that part were the proportionately reduced amount of its interest income for the actual accounting period.

(3) In this paragraph—

(a) "interest income", in relation to a club, means interest on which (apart from this paragraph) the club is chargeable to tax under paragraph (a) of Case III of Schedule D (as set out in section 18(3A) of the Taxes Act 1988);
(b) "gift aid income", in relation to a club, means gifts to the club that are treated as annual payments by section 25(10) of the Finance Act 1990 (c 29) (gift aid) as it applies by virtue of paragraph 9(1) below.

Exemption for property income

6—(1) Where—

(a) a club is a registered club throughout an accounting period,
(b) its property income for that period (before deduction of any expenses) does not exceed £10,000,
(c) the whole of that income is applied for qualifying purposes, and
(d) the club makes a claim under this paragraph to the Inland Revenue, it shall be exempt from corporation tax on that income.

(2) In relation to an accounting period that is shorter than 12 months, subparagraph (1)(b) has effect as if the amount specified there were proportionately reduced.

(3) Where a club is a registered club for only part of an accounting period, subparagraph (1) has effect as if—

(a) that part were a separate accounting period;

(b) the club's property income for that part were the proportionately reduced amount of its property income for the actual accounting period.

(4) In this paragraph "property income" means income that (apart from this paragraph) is chargeable to tax under Schedule A.

Exemption for chargeable gains

7 A gain accruing to a registered club shall not be a chargeable gain if—

(a) the whole of the gain is applied for qualifying purposes, and

(b) the club makes a claim under this paragraph to the Inland Revenue.

Exemption reduced where club incurs non-qualifying expenditure

8—(1) This paragraph applies where—

(a) any of a club's income or gains for an accounting period are exempted from tax under this Part (or would be so exempted but for this paragraph), and

(b) in that accounting period the club incurs expenditure for non-qualifying purposes.

(2) In this paragraph—

A is the total amount of income and gains mentioned in subparagraph (1)(a);

N is the amount of the expenditure mentioned in sub-paragraph (1)(b);

T is the aggregate of—

(a) the club's income (whether taxable or not, and before deduction of any expenses) for the accounting period, and

(b) the club's gains that are chargeable gains, together with those that would be chargeable but for paragraph 7, for that period.

(3) Where N is less than T, the total amount of income and gains for the accounting period exempted under this Part is reduced to—

$$A-\left(A\times\frac{N}{T}\right)$$

(4) Where N is equal to T, the total amount of income and gains for the accounting period exempted under this Part is reduced to nil.

(5) Where N is greater than T—

(a) the total amount of income and gains for the accounting period exempted under this Part is reduced to nil, and

(b) the surplus amount is carried back to previous accounting periods (taking later ones before earlier ones) and deducted from the amounts exempted under this Part for those periods, until it is exhausted.

In paragraph (b) "the surplus amount" means—

$$\left(A\times\frac{N}{T}\right)-A$$

(6) The reference in paragraph (b) of sub-paragraph (5) to previous accounting periods is to accounting periods ending not more than six years before the end of the accounting period mentioned in paragraph (a) of that subparagraph.

(7) To the extent that an amount exempted under this Part has been reduced under sub-paragraph (3), (4) or (5) in respect of expenditure incurred for non-qualifying purposes in a particular accounting period, it may not be reduced again under sub-paragraph (5) in respect of expenditure so incurred in a later accounting period.

(8) All such adjustments shall be made, whether by way of assessment or otherwise, as may be required in consequence of sub-paragraph (5).

(9) Where by virtue of this paragraph there is an amount of a registered club's income and gains for which relief under this Part is not available, the club may, by notice to the Inland Revenue, specify which items of the income and gains are, in whole or in part, to be attributed to that amount.

If, within 30 days of being required to do so by the Inland Revenue, a registered club does not give notice under this sub-paragraph, the items of its income and gains that are to be attributed to the amount in question shall be such as the Inland Revenue may determine.

PART 3
RELIEFS FOR DONORS

9—(1) Section 25 of the Finance Act 1990 (c 29) (gift aid) has effect as if a registered club were a charity.

For the purposes of that section as so applied, membership fees are not gifts.

(2) Section 23 of the Inheritance Tax Act 1984 (c 51) (gifts to charities) has effect as if—

(*a*) a registered club were a charity;
(*b*) in subsection (5) of that section (no exemption where property may become applicable for purposes that are not charitable etc), for the words from "other than charitable purposes" to the end there were substituted "other than—

(*a*) the purposes of the club in question;
(*b*) the purposes of another club that is registered as a community amateur sports club;
(*c*) the purposes of the governing body of an eligible sport (within the meaning of Schedule 18 to the Finance Act 2002) for the purposes of which the club in question exists; or
(*d*) the purposes of a charity.".

(3) The following enactments also have effect as if a registered club were a charity—

(*a*) section 83A of the Taxes Act (gifts in kind to charities etc);
(*b*) section 257 of the Taxation of Chargeable Gains Act 1992 (c 12) (gifts to charities etc);
(*c*) section 63(2) of the Capital Allowances Act (gifts of plant or machinery to charities etc).

PART 4

CHARGEABLE GAINS: PROPERTY CEASING TO BE HELD FOR QUALIFYING PURPOSES

10—(1) This paragraph applies where a club holds property and, without disposing of it—

(*a*) ceases to be a registered club, or
(*b*) ceases to hold the property for qualifying purposes.

(2) Where this paragraph applies—

(*a*) the club shall be treated for the purposes of the Taxation of Chargeable Gains Act 1992 as having disposed of, and immediately reacquired, the property at the time of the cessation for a consideration equal to its market value at that time;
(*b*) any gain accruing on the deemed disposal shall be treated for the purposes of paragraph 7 as not accruing to a registered club;
(*c*) if and so far as any of the property represents, directly or indirectly, the consideration for the disposal of assets by the club, any gain accruing on that disposal shall be treated for the purposes of paragraph 7 as not having accrued to a registered club.

(3) An assessment in respect of a chargeable gain accruing by virtue of subparagraph (2) may be made at any time not more than three years after the end of the accounting period in which the club ceases to be a registered club or (as the case may be) to hold the property for qualifying purposes.

PART 5

REGISTRATION

Registration and termination

11—(1) A club that applies to the Inland Revenue to be registered as a community amateur sports club shall be so registered if the Inland Revenue are satisfied that it is entitled to be.

(2) The Inland Revenue may register a club with effect from such date as they may specify (which may be before the date of the application).

(3) If it appears to the Inland Revenue that a registered club is not, or is no longer, entitled to be registered, they may terminate the club's registration with effect from such date as they may specify (which may be before the date of the decision to terminate the registration).

(4) Where the Inland Revenue—

(*a*) register a club,
(*b*) refuse a club's application for registration, or
(*c*) terminate a club's registration,

they shall notify the club accordingly.

(5) The Inland Revenue may publish the names and addresses of registered clubs.

Information etc

12 A club that makes an application to be registered must—

(*a*) provide the Inland Revenue with such information relating to the application as they may reasonably require;
(*b*) if required to do so by the Inland Revenue, produce for inspection by them any books, documents or other records in the club's possession, or under its control, that contain such information.

Appeals

13—(1) An appeal to the General Commissioners may be brought against a decision of the Inland Revenue under paragraph 11.

(2) Notice of an appeal under this paragraph must be given—

    (*a*) in writing,

    (*b*) within 30 days of the date of the notification under paragraph 11(4),

    (*c*) to the Inland Revenue.

(3) The notice of appeal must specify the grounds of appeal.

(4) On the hearing of the appeal the Commissioners may allow the appellant to put forward grounds not specified in the notice, and take them into consideration, if satisfied that the omission was not wilful or unreasonable.

(5) Where the appeal is against a refusal to register a club, or against a decision to register it with effect from a particular date, the Commissioners (if they do not dismiss the appeal) may either—

    (*a*) direct that the club be registered with effect from a specified date, or

    (*b*) remit the matter to the Inland Revenue for reconsideration.

(6) Where the appeal is against a decision to terminate the registration of a club, or to do so with effect from a particular date, the Commissioners (if they do not dismiss the appeal) may either—

    (*a*) rescind the termination,

    (*b*) direct that the termination have effect from a specified date, or

    (*c*) remit the matter to the Inland Revenue for reconsideration.

(7) The provisions of the Taxes Management Act 1970 (c 9) relating to appeals under the Taxes Acts shall apply to an appeal under this paragraph as they apply to those appeals.

PART 6

INTERPRETATION

"Eligible sport"

14—(1) For the purposes of this Schedule "eligible sport" means a sport that is designated for those purposes by Treasury order.

A sport may be so designated by reference to its appearing in a list maintained by a body specified in the order.

(2) An order under this paragraph shall be made by statutory instrument which shall be subject to annulment in pursuance of a resolution of the House of Commons.

Regulations—See the Relief for Community Amateur Sports Clubs (Designation) Order, SI 2002/1966.

"Inland Revenue"

15—(1) Subject to sub-paragraph (2), references in this Schedule to the Inland Revenue are to any officer of the Board.

(2) References to the Inland Revenue in paragraphs 11 and 13(1), (5) and (6) are to the Board.

Other expressions

16 In this Schedule—

    (*a*) "dispose", "disposal", "gain" and "chargeable gain" shall be construed in accordance with the Taxation of Chargeable Gains Act 1992 (c 12);

    (*b*) "for qualifying purposes" means for the purposes of providing facilities for, and promoting participation in, one or more eligible sports, and "for non-qualifying purposes" shall be construed accordingly.

SCHEDULE 19

CAPITAL ALLOWANCES: CARS WITH LOW CARBON DIOXIDE EMISSIONS

Section 59

Commentary—*Simon's Direct Tax Service* **B2.324, 330, 342.**

Introductory

1 The Capital Allowances Act 2001 (c 2) is amended as follows.

Types of expenditure for which first-year allowances available

2 In section 39, after the entry relating to section 45A add'',

section 45D expenditure on cars with low CO_2 emissions,''.

First-year qualifying expenditure: car with low carbon dioxide emissions

3 After section 45C insert—

"45D Expenditure on cars with low carbon dioxide emissions

(1) Expenditure is first-year qualifying expenditure if—

    (a) it is incurred in the period beginning with 17th April 2002 and ending with 31st March 2008,

    (b) it is expenditure on a car which is first registered on or after 17th April 2002 and which is unused and not second-hand,

    (c) the car—

        (i) is an electrically-propelled car, or

        (ii) is a car with low CO_2 emissions, and

    (d) the expenditure is not excluded by section 46 (general exclusions).

(2) For the purposes of this section a car with low CO_2 emissions is a car which satisfies the conditions in subsections (3) and (4).

(3) The first condition is that, when the car is first registered, it is so registered on the basis of an EC certificate of conformity, or a UK approval certificate, that specifies—

    (a) in the case of a car other than a bi-fuel car, a CO_2 emissions figure in terms of grams per kilometre driven, or

    (b) in the case of a bi-fuel car, separate CO_2 emissions figures in terms of grams per kilometre driven for different fuels.

(4) The second condition is that the applicable CO_2 emissions figure in the case of the car does not exceed 120 grams per kilometre driven.

(5) For the purposes of subsection (4) the applicable CO_2 emissions figure in the case of a car other than a bi-fuel car is—

    (a) where the EC certificate of conformity or UK approval certificate specifies only one CO_2 emissions figure, that figure, and

    (b) where the certificate specifies more than one CO_2 emissions figure, the figure specified as the CO_2 emissions (combined) figure.

(6) For the purposes of subsection (4) the applicable CO_2 emissions figure in the case of a bi-fuel car is—

    (a) where the EC certificate of conformity or UK approval certificate specifies more than one CO_2 emissions figure in relation to each fuel, the lowest CO_2 emissions (combined) figure specified, and

    (b) in any other case, the lowest CO_2 figure specified by the certificate.

(7) The Treasury may by order amend the amount from time to time specified in subsection (4).

(8) In this section any reference to a car—

    (a) includes a reference to a mechanically propelled road vehicle of a type commonly used as a hackney carriage, but

    (b) does not include a reference to a motorcycle.

(9) For the purposes of this section, a car is an electrically-propelled car only if—

    (a) it is propelled solely by electrical power, and

    (b) that power is derived from—

        (i) a source external to the vehicle, or

        (ii) an electrical storage battery which is not connected to any source of power when the vehicle is in motion.

(10) In this section—

    "bi-fuel car" means a car which is capable of being propelled by—

        (a) petrol and road fuel gas, or

        (b) diesel and road fuel gas;

    "car" has the meaning given by section 81 (extended meaning of "car");

    "diesel" means any diesel fuel within the definition in Article 2 of Directive 98/70/EC of the European Parliament and of the Council;

    "EC certificate of conformity" means a certificate of conformity issued by a manufacturer under any provision of the law of a member State implementing Article 6 of Council Directive 70/156/EEC, as amended;

    "petrol" has the meaning given by Article 2 of Directive 98/70/ EC of the European Parliament and of the Council;

    "road fuel gas" has the same meaning as in section 168AB of ICTA;

    "UK approval certificate" means a certificate issued under—

        (a) section 58(1) or (4) of the Road Traffic Act 1988, or

        (b) Article 31A(4) or (5) of the Road Traffic (Northern Ireland) Order 1981.".

General exclusions affecting first-year qualifying expenditure

4—(1) Section 46 is amended as follows.

(2) In subsection (1) (expenditure which is subject to the general exclusions) after the entry relating to section 45A add ",

section 45D (expenditure on cars with low CO_2 emissions),".

(3) After subsection (2) (general exclusions listed for the purposes of subsection (1)) insert—

"(3) Subsection (1) is subject to the following provisions of this section.

(4) General exclusion 2 does not prevent expenditure being first-year qualifying expenditure under section 45D.".

Amount of first-year allowances

5 In section 52(3), in the Table, after the entry relating to expenditure qualifying under section 45A add—

"Expenditure qualifying under section 45D (expenditure on cars with low CO_2 emissions)	100%".

Single asset pool in relation to cars above cost threshold

6 In section 74, in subsection (2) (cars to which section 74 applies) after paragraph (*b*) insert

", and
(*c*) the qualifying expenditure incurred on the provision of the car is not first-year qualifying expenditure under section 45D (expenditure on cars with low CO_2 emissions)".

SCHEDULE 20

CAPITAL ALLOWANCES: PLANT OR MACHINERY FOR GAS REFUELLING STATION

Section 61

Commentary—*Simon's Direct Tax Service* **B2.324, 330, 342.**

Introductory

1 The Capital Allowances Act 2001 (c 2) is amended as follows.

Types of expenditure for which first-year allowances available

2 In section 39, after the entry relating to section 45D (which is inserted by Schedule 19 to this Act) add—

"section 45E expenditure on plant or machinery for gas refuelling station".

First-year qualifying expenditure: plant or machinery for gas refuelling station

3 After section 45D (which is added by Schedule 19 to this Act) insert—

"45E Expenditure on plant or machinery for gas refuelling station

(1) Expenditure is first-year qualifying expenditure if—

(*a*) it is incurred in the period beginning with 17th April 2002 and ending with 31st March 2008,

(*b*) it is expenditure on plant or machinery for a gas refuelling station where the plant or machinery is unused and not second-hand, and

(*c*) it is not excluded by section 46 (general exclusions).

(2) For the purposes of this section expenditure on plant or machinery for a gas refuelling station is expenditure on plant or machinery installed at a gas refuelling station for use solely for or in connection with refuelling vehicles with natural gas or hydrogen fuel.

(3) For the purposes of subsection (2) the plant or machinery which is for use for or in connection with refuelling vehicles with natural gas or hydrogen fuel includes—

(*a*) any storage tank for natural gas or hydrogen fuel,

(*b*) any compressor, pump, control or meter used for or in connection with refuelling vehicles with natural gas or hydrogen fuel, and

(*c*) any equipment for dispensing natural gas or hydrogen fuel to the fuel tank of a vehicle.

(4) For the purposes of this section—

"gas refuelling station" means any premises, or that part of any premises, where vehicles are refuelled with natural gas or hydrogen fuel;

"hydrogen fuel" means a fuel consisting of gaseous or cryogenic liquid hydrogen which is used for propelling vehicles; and

"vehicle" means a mechanically propelled road vehicle.".

General exclusions affecting first-year qualifying expenditure

4 In section 46, in subsection (1) (expenditure which is subject to the general exclusions) after the entry relating to section 45D (which is added by Schedule 19 to this Act) add—

"section 45E (expenditure on plant or machinery for gas refuelling station)".

Amount of first-year allowance

5 In section 52(3), in the Table, after the entry relating to expenditure qualifying under section 45D (which is added by Schedule 19 to this Act) add—

"Expenditure qualifying under section 45E (expenditure on plant or machinery for gas refuelling station)	100%".

SCHEDULE 21

FIRST-YEAR ALLOWANCES FOR EXPENDITURE WHOLLY FOR A RING FENCE TRADE

Section 63

Commentary—*Simon's Direct Tax Service* **D4.1002.**

PART 1

PLANT AND MACHINERY

Introductory

1 Part 2 of the Capital Allowances Act 2001 (c 2) (plant and machinery allowances) is amended as follows.

Types of expenditure for which first-year allowances available

2 In section 39, after the entry relating to section 45E (which is added by Schedule 20 to this Act) add ", or

section 45F expenditure on plant and machinery for use wholly in a ring fence trade.".

First-year qualifying expenditure: plant and machinery for use wholly in a ring fence trade

3 After section 45E (which is inserted by Schedule 20 to this Act) insert—

"45F Expenditure on plant and machinery for use wholly in a ring fence trade

(1) Expenditure is first-year qualifying expenditure if—

    (*a*) it is incurred on or after 17th April 2002,

    (*b*) it is incurred by a company,

    (*c*) it is incurred on the provision of plant or machinery for use wholly for the purposes of a ring fence trade, and

    (*d*) it is not excluded by section 46 (general exclusions).

(2) This section is subject to section 45G (plant or machinery used for less than five years in a ring fence trade).

(3) In this section "ring fence trade" means a ring fence trade in respect of which tax is chargeable under section 501A of the Taxes Act 1988 (supplementary charge in respect of ring fence trades).".

Plant or machinery used for less than five years in a ring fence trade

4 After section 45F insert—

"45G Plant or machinery used for less than five years in a ring fence trade

(1) Expenditure incurred by a company on the provision of plant or machinery is to be treated as never having been first-year qualifying expenditure under section 45F if the plant or machinery—

    (*a*) is at no time in the relevant period used in a ring fence trade carried on by the company or a company connected with it, or

    (*b*) is at any time in the relevant period used for a purpose other than that of a ring fence trade carried on by the company or a company connected with it.

(2) For the purposes of this section "the relevant period" means whichever of the following periods, beginning with the incurring of the expenditure, first ends, namely—

(*a*) the period ending with the fifth anniversary of the incurring of the expenditure, or

(*b*) the period ending with the day preceding the first occasion on which the plant or machinery, after becoming owned by the company which incurred the expenditure, is not owned by a company which is either that company or a company connected with it.

(3) All such assessments and adjustments of assessments are to be made as are necessary to give effect to subsection (1).

(4) If a person who has made a return becomes aware that, after making it, anything in it has become incorrect because of the operation of this section, he must give notice to the Inland Revenue specifying how the return needs to be amended.

(5) The notice must be given within 3 months beginning with the day on which the person first became aware that anything in the return had become incorrect because of the operation of this section.

(6) In this section "ring fence trade" has the same meaning as in section 45F.".

General exclusions affecting first-year qualifying expenditure

5 In section 46, in subsection (1) (expenditure which is subject to the general exclusions) after the entry relating to section 45E (which is added by Schedule 20 to this Act) add ", or

section 45F (expenditure on plant and machinery for use wholly in a ring fence trade).".

Amount of first-year allowances

6 In section 52(3), in the Table, after the entry relating to expenditure qualifying under section 45E (which is added by Schedule 20 to this Act) add—

"Expenditure qualifying under section 45F (expenditure on plant and machinery for use wholly in a ring fence trade) which is long-life asset expenditure	24%
Expenditure qualifying under section 45F (expenditure on plant and machinery for use wholly in a ring fence trade) other than long-life asset expenditure	100%".

Penalty for failure to provide information etc

7—(1) The Taxes Management Act 1970 (c 9) is amended as follows.

(2) In the second column of the Table in section 98, in the entry relating to requirements imposed by provisions of the Capital Allowances Act, after "45B(5) and (6)," insert "45G(4) and (5),".

PART 2
MINERAL EXTRACTION ALLOWANCES
Introductory

8 Part 5 of the Capital Allowances Act 2001 (c 2) (mineral extraction allowances) is amended as follows.

First-year qualifying expenditure

9 After section 416, insert the following Chapter—

"CHAPTER 5A
FIRST-YEAR QUALIFYING EXPENDITURE
General

416A First-year allowances available for certain types of qualifying expenditure

A first-year allowance is not available unless the qualifying expenditure is first-year qualifying expenditure under section 416B (expenditure incurred wholly for purposes of a ring fence trade).

Types of expenditure which may qualify for first-year allowances

416B Expenditure incurred by company for purposes of a ring fence trade

(1) Expenditure is first-year qualifying expenditure if—

(*a*) it is incurred on or after 17th April 2002,

(*b*) it is incurred by a company,

(*c*) it is incurred wholly for the purposes of a ring fence trade, and

(*d*) it is not excluded by—

(i) subsection (2) (acquisition of mineral asset), or

(ii) subsection (3) (acquisition of asset representing expenditure of connected company).

(2) Expenditure is not first-year qualifying expenditure under this section if it is expenditure on acquiring a mineral asset.

(3) Expenditure is not first-year qualifying expenditure under this section if it is expenditure incurred by a company on the acquisition of an asset representing expenditure incurred by a company connected with that company.

(4) To the extent that references in this section to an asset representing expenditure incurred by a company include a reference to an asset representing expenditure on mineral exploration and access, they also include a reference to any results obtained from any search, exploration or inquiry on which any such expenditure was incurred.

(5) In this section "ring fence trade" means a ring fence trade in respect of which tax is chargeable under section 501A of the Taxes Act 1988 (supplementary charge in respect of ring fence trades).

Supplementary

416C Time when expenditure is incurred

(1) In determining whether expenditure is first-year qualifying expenditure under this Chapter, any effect of the provisions specified in subsection (2) on the time at which the expenditure is to be treated as incurred is to be disregarded.

(2) The provisions are—

(a) section 400(4) (which treats certain pre-trading expenditure as incurred on the first day of trading), and

(b) section 434 (which treats certain other expenditure incurred for the purposes of a trade about to be carried on as incurred on that day).".

First-year allowances

10 At the beginning of Chapter 6 (allowances and charges) insert—

"First-year allowances

416D First-year allowances

(1) A person is entitled to a first-year allowance in respect of first-year qualifying expenditure if the expenditure is incurred in a chargeable period to which this Act applies.

(2) Any first-year allowance is made for the chargeable period in which the first-year qualifying expenditure is incurred.

(3) The amount of the allowance is a percentage of the first-year qualifying expenditure in respect of which the allowance is made, as shown in the Table—

TABLE
AMOUNT OF FIRST-YEAR ALLOWANCES

Type of first-year qualifying expenditure	Amount
Expenditure qualifying under section 416B (expenditure incurred wholly for the purposes of a ring fence trade)	100%

(4) A person who is entitled to a first-year allowance may claim the allowance in respect of the whole or a part of the first-year qualifying expenditure.

(5) This section is subject to section 416E (artificially inflated claims for first-year allowances).".

Artificially inflated claims for first-year allowances

11 After section 416D insert—

"416E Artificially inflated claims for first-year allowances.

(1) To the extent that a transaction is attributable to arrangements entered into wholly or mainly for a disqualifying purpose, it shall be disregarded in determining for a chargeable period the amount of any first-year allowance to which a person is entitled.

(2) For the purposes of this section, arrangements are entered into wholly or mainly for a "disqualifying purpose" if their main object, or one of their main objects, is to enable a person to obtain—

(a) a first-year allowance to which he would not otherwise be entitled, or

(b) a first-year allowance of a greater amount than that to which he would otherwise be entitled.

(3) In this section "arrangements" includes any scheme, agreement or understanding, whether or not legally enforceable.".

Amount of allowances and charges: balancing charge for period in which expenditure incurred

12—(1) Section 418 is amended as follows.

(2) In subsection (4) (amount of balancing charge) after paragraph (*b*) insert the following as a second sentence—

"Where a person is liable to a balancing charge in respect of first-year qualifying expenditure for the chargeable period in which he incurred the expenditure, any first-year allowance made in respect of the expenditure shall be treated for the purposes of paragraph (*b*) as if it were an allowance for an earlier chargeable period.".

Unrelieved qualifying expenditure: effect of first-year qualifying expenditure

13—(1) Section 419 is amended as follows.

(2) In subsection (1) (amount of qualifying expenditure which is unrelieved qualifying expenditure for the chargeable period in which the expenditure is incurred) for "the whole of it" substitute—

"(*a*) the whole of it, unless the expenditure is first-year qualifying expenditure, or
(*b*) if the expenditure is first-year qualifying expenditure, none of it,

but paragraph (*b*) is subject to subsections (3) to (5).".

(3) After subsection (2) insert—

"(3) If, in the case of expenditure which is first-year qualifying expenditure, a disposal receipt falls to be brought into account for the chargeable period in which the expenditure is incurred ("the initial period"), subsection (4) below applies.

(4) Where this subsection applies, the unrelieved balance of the expenditure shall be taken to be unrelieved qualifying expenditure for the initial period, but only for the purpose specified in subsection (5).

(5) The purpose is that of determining in accordance with sections 417 and 418—

(*a*) any question whether the person who incurred the expenditure—

(i) is entitled to a balancing allowance for the initial period, or
(ii) is liable to a balancing charge for that period, and

(*b*) if so, the amount of that balancing allowance or balancing charge.

(6) In this section "the unrelieved balance of the expenditure" means so much of the first-year qualifying expenditure in question as remains after deducting the amount of any first-year allowance given in respect of the whole or any part of that expenditure.".

SCHEDULE 22

COMPUTATION OF PROFITS: ADJUSTMENT ON CHANGE OF BASIS

Section 64

Commentary—*Simon's Direct Tax Service* **B4.212, 215.**

PART 1
INTRODUCTION
General scheme

1—(1) Where there is a change of basis within section 64, one or more adjustments shall be made in accordance with this Schedule.

(2) Any such adjustment shall be calculated and given effect in accordance with the provisions of Part 2 of this Schedule (general rules), subject to the provisions of Part 3 of this Schedule (special rules for certain cases).

(3) Part 4 of this Schedule contains supplementary provisions and Part 5 provides for commencement.

PART 2
GENERAL RULES
Calculation of adjustment

2 The amount of the adjustment is calculated as follows:

First step

Add together any amounts representing the extent to which, comparing the two bases, profits were understated (or losses overstated) on the old basis:

1. Receipts which on the new basis would have been brought into account in computing the profits of a period of account before the change of basis, to the extent that they were not so brought into account.

2. Expenses which on the new basis fall to be brought into account in computing the profits of a period of account after the change, to the extent that they were brought into account in computing the profits of a period of account before the change of basis.

3. Deductions in respect of opening trading stock or opening work in progress in the first period of account on the new basis, to the extent that they—

(*a*) are not matched by credits in respect of closing trading stock or closing work in progress in the last period of account before the change, or

(*b*) are calculated on a different basis that if used to calculate those credits would have given a higher figure.

4. Amounts recognised for accounting purposes in respect of depreciation in the last period of account before the change, to the extent that they were not the subject of an adjustment for tax purposes, where such an adjustment would be required on the new basis.

Second step

Then deduct any amounts representing the extent to which, comparing the two bases, profits were overstated (or losses understated) on the old basis:

1. Receipts which were brought into account in a period of account before the change, to the extent that they would not have been so brought into account if the profits had been computed on the new basis.

2. Expenses which were not brought into account in computing the profits of a period of account before the change, to the extent that they—

(*a*) would have been brought into account for a period of account before the change if the profits had been computed on the new basis, and

(*b*) would have been brought into account for a period of account after the change if the profits had continued to be computed on the old basis.

3. Credits in respect of closing trading stock or closing work in progress in the last period of account before the change of basis, to the extent that they—

(*a*) are not matched by deductions in respect of opening trading stock or opening work in progress in the first period of account on the new basis, or

(*b*) are calculated on a different basis that if used to calculate those deductions would have given a lower figure.

An amount so deducted may not be deducted again in computing the profits of a period of account.

Meaning of items being brought into account

3—(1) The references in paragraph 2 to items being brought into account in a period of account before the change of basis are to their being brought into account—

(*a*) in computing the profits of the same trade, profession or vocation, and

(*b*) in accordance with the law or practice then applicable.

(2) For the purposes of sub-paragraph (1)(*a*) a trade, profession or vocation is not regarded as the same if section 113(1) or 337(1) of the Taxes Act 1988 applies (deemed discontinuance on change of persons carrying on trade, profession or vocation).

(3) For the purposes of sub-paragraph (1)(*b*) the practice applicable in any case means the accepted practice in cases of that description as to how profits should be computed for the purposes of Case I or II of Schedule D.

Giving effect to positive adjustment

4—(1) If the amount of the adjustment is positive, it is chargeable to tax.

(2) An amount so chargeable to income tax—

(*a*) is treated as income arising on the last day of the first period of account for which the new basis is adopted;

(*b*) is chargeable under Case VI of Schedule D;

(*c*) in the case of an individual whose income from the trade, profession or vocation in question is—

(i) relevant earnings within section 623(2)(*c*) or 644(2)(*c*) of the Taxes Act 1988, or

(ii) earned income within section 833(4)(*c*) of that Act,

is similarly relevant earnings or earned income for the tax year in which it is charged to tax; and

(*d*) is treated for the purposes of Chapters 1 and 2 of Part 10 of the Taxes Act 1988 (loss relief) as profits of the trade, profession or vocation for the chargeable period for which it is charged to tax.

(3) An amount so chargeable to corporation tax is treated as a receipt of the trade, profession or vocation arising on the last day of the first period of account for which the new basis is adopted.

Giving effect to negative adjustment

5—(1) If the amount of the adjustment is negative, it is allowed as a deduction in computing profits.

(2) An amount so allowed as a deduction in computing profits is treated as an expense of the trade, profession or vocation arising on the last day of the first period of account for which the new basis is adopted.

PART 3
SPECIAL RULES FOR CERTAIN CASES

No adjustment for certain expenses previously brought into account

6—(1) This paragraph applies where as a result of a change of basis expenses brought into account before the change on the old basis would on the new basis be brought into account over more than one period of account after the change.

(2) In such a case—

    (*a*) no adjustment shall be made under this Schedule, and

    (*b*) the expenses may not be deducted in computing the profits of the trade, profession or vocation for any period of account after the change.

Cases where adjustment not required until asset realised or written off

7—(1) This paragraph applies where there is a change of basis resulting from a tax adjustment affecting the calculation of—

    (*a*) any amount brought into account—

        (i) in respect of closing trading stock or work in progress in the last period of account before the change of basis, or

        (ii) in respect of opening trading stock or work in progress in the first period of account on the new basis, or

    (*b*) any amount brought into account in respect of depreciation.

(2) The adjustment required by paragraph 2 in such a case shall be brought into account only when the asset to which it relates is realised or written off.

Change from realisation basis to mark to market

8—(1) This paragraph applies where there is a change of basis from—

    (*a*) not recognising a profit or loss on an asset until the asset is realised, to

    (*b*) bringing assets into account in each period of account at a fair value.

(2) To the extent that in such a case—

    (*a*) a receipt within item 1 of the First step in paragraph 2 represents the fair value of an asset that is trading stock (within the meaning of section 100 of the Taxes Act 1988), or

    (*b*) an expense within item 2 of that step relates to such an asset,

any resulting adjustment shall not be given effect until the period of account in which the value of the asset in question is realised.

This is subject to any election under paragraph 9.

Election for spreading where paragraph 8 applies

9—(1) Where paragraph 8 applies the person who is chargeable to tax in respect of any adjustment charge may elect that the adjustment charge shall be spread over six periods of account in accordance with the following provisions.

(2) The election must be made—

    (*a*) by notice in writing,

    (*b*) to an officer of the Board,

    (*c*) within the time allowed.

(3) The time allowed is—

    (*a*) for income tax purposes, up to and including the 31st January following the tax year in which the change of basis occurs;

    (*b*) for corporation tax purposes, within twelve months of the end of the first accounting period to which the new basis applies.

(4) If an election is made, then, in each of the six periods of account beginning with the first period to which the new basis applies an amount equal to one-sixth of the amount of the adjustment charge is treated as arising and chargeable to tax.

(5) If before the whole of the adjustment charge has been charged to tax the trade, profession or vocation is permanently discontinued, the whole of the amount so far as not previously brought into charge to tax is treated as arising and chargeable to tax immediately before the discontinuance.

Application of paragraphs 8 and 9 in case of transfer of insurance business

10—(1) This paragraph applies where—

(*a*) an asset to which paragraph 8 or 9 applies is transferred from one insurance company to another in pursuance of a transfer scheme, and

(*b*) immediately after the transfer either—

(i) the transferee company is resident in the United Kingdom, or

(ii) the asset is held for the purposes of a business carried on by the transferee company in the United Kingdom through a branch or agency.

(2) The asset shall not be regarded for the purposes of paragraph 8 as having been realised by the transferor by reason of its being transferred in pursuance of the transfer scheme.

(3) If the transfer is of the entire business of the transferor, the transferee is responsible under paragraph 8 or 9 for bringing into account any amount required to be brought into account after the transfer.

(4) In this paragraph—

"insurance company" has the same meaning as in Chapter 2 of Part 12 of the Taxes Act 1988 (see section 431(2) of that Act); and

"transfer scheme" means—

(*a*) a scheme under section 105 of the Financial Services and Markets Act 2000 (c 8), including an excluded scheme falling within Case 2, 3 or 4 of subsection (3) of that section, or

(*b*) a qualifying overseas transfer scheme.

(5) A "qualifying overseas transfer scheme" means—

(*a*) so much of a transfer of the whole of part of the business of an overseas life insurance company carried on through a branch or agency in the United Kingdom as takes place in accordance with an authorisation granted outside the United Kingdom for the purposes of Article 11 of the third life insurance directive, or

(*b*) so much of a transfer of the whole of part of the business of an insurance company other than an overseas life insurance company as takes place in accordance with an authorisation granted outside the United Kingdom for the purposes of Article 12 of the third non-life insurance directive.

(6) In sub-paragraph (5)—

"overseas life insurance company" has the same meaning as in Chapter 2 of Part 12 of the Taxes Act 1988 (see section 431(2) of that Act);

"the third life insurance directive" means Council Directive 92/96/EEC on the co-ordination of law regulations and administrative provisions relating to direct life assurance and amending Directive 79/267/EEC and 990/96/EEC; and

"the third non-life insurance directive" means Council Directive 92/49/EEC on the co-ordination of laws, regulations and administrative provisions relating to direct insurance other than life assurance and amending Directives 73/239/EEC and 88/357/EEC.

Spreading of adjustment charge on ending of exemption for barristers and advocates

11—(1) This paragraph applies where an individual makes a change of basis—

(*a*) on ceasing to take advantage of the exemption given by section 43 of the Finance Act 1998 (c 36) (barristers and advocates in early years of practice), or

(*b*) on that exemption coming to an end.

(2) Where this paragraph applies any adjustment charge is spread over ten tax years, as follows.

(3) In each of the nine tax years beginning with that in which the whole amount would otherwise be chargeable to tax, an amount equal to whichever is the less of—

(*a*) one-tenth of the amount of the adjustment charge, and

(*b*) 10% of the profits of the profession for that tax year,

is treated as arising and chargeable to tax.

For the purposes of paragraph (*b*) the profits of the profession means the profits as computed for the purposes of Case II of Schedule D, leaving out of account any allowances or charges under the Capital Allowances Act 2001 (c 2).

(4) In the tenth tax year the balance of the adjustment charge is treated as arising and chargeable to tax.

(5) If before the whole of the adjustment charge has been charged to tax the profession is permanently discontinued, the preceding provisions of this paragraph continue to apply, but with the omission of the alternative limit in sub-paragraph (3)(*b*) by reference to profits of the profession.

(6) This paragraph has effect subject to any election under paragraph 12.

Election to accelerate payment of adjustment charge under paragraph 11

12—(1) A person who under paragraph 11 is chargeable to tax for a tax year on an amount representing part of an adjustment charge may elect that the amount treated as income arising in that tax year should be increased.

(2) The election must be made—

    (a) by notice in writing,
    (b) to an officer of the Board,
    (c) on or before the 31st January following the tax year in question.

(3) The election must specify the amount to be treated as income arising in the tax year, which may be any amount up to the whole of the adjustment charge so far as not previously charged to tax.

(4) Where an election has been made, paragraph 11 applies in relation to any subsequent tax year as if the original amount of the adjustment charge were reduced by the additional amount treated as arising in the year for which the election was made.

PART 4
SUPPLEMENTARY PROVISIONS

Application of provisions to partnerships

13—(1) In the case of a trade, profession or vocation carried on in partnership, the amount of any adjustment under this Schedule shall be computed—

    (a) for income tax purposes, as if the partnership were an individual resident in the United Kingdom, and
    (b) for corporation tax purposes, as if the partnership were a company resident in the United Kingdom.

(2) Subject to the following provisions of this paragraph—

    (a) each partner's share of any amount chargeable to tax under this Schedule shall be determined according to the profit-sharing arrangements for the twelve months ending immediately before the date on which the new basis was adopted; and
    (b) any election under this Schedule must be made jointly by all the persons who have been members of the partnership in that twelve month period.

(3) If paragraph 11 applies (spreading of adjustment charge in certain cases), then, subject to sub-paragraph (4) below, each partner's share of the amount chargeable in any tax year shall be determined—

    (a) for the first tax year, according to the profit-sharing arrangements for the twelve months ending immediately before the date on which the new basis was adopted, and
    (b) for any subsequent tax year, according to the profit-sharing arrangements for the twelve months immediately preceding the anniversary in that year of that date.

(4) If paragraph 11(5) applies (effect of discontinuance of profession), then—

    (a) each partner's share of any amount chargeable on or after the discontinuance is determined as follows—

        (i) if the discontinuance occurs on the date on which the new basis was adopted, according to the profit-sharing arrangements for the twelve months ending immediately before that date;
        (ii) if the discontinuance occurs after that date but before the first anniversary of that date, according to the profit-sharing arrangements for the period between that date and the date of discontinuance;
        (iii) if the discontinuance occurs after the first anniversary of the date on which the new basis was adopted, according to the profit-sharing arrangements for the period between the immediately preceding anniversary of that date and the date of discontinuance; and

    (b) any election under paragraph 12 after the discontinuance must be made by each former partner separately.

(5) For the purposes of this paragraph—

    (a) "profit-sharing arrangements" means the rights of the partners to share in the profits of the trade, profession or vocation for the period in question; and
    (b) references to the date on which a new basis was adopted are to the first day of the first period of account for which the new basis was adopted.

(6) The provisions of section 111 of the Taxes Act 1988 (general provisions as to taxation of partnerships), except subsection (1) (partnership not to be treated as separate entity), do not apply to the extent that the preceding provisions of this paragraph apply.

Liability of personal representatives in case of death of person chargeable

14 In the case of the death of a person who, if he had not died, would have been chargeable to tax under this Schedule on an amount representing part of an adjustment charge—

(*a*) the tax which would have been so chargeable shall be assessed and charged on his personal representatives and shall be a debt due from and payable out of his estate, and

(*b*) his personal representatives may make any election under this Schedule that he might have made.

Interpretation

15 In this Schedule—

"adjustment charge" means a charge under Part 2 of this Schedule; and

"tax year" means a year of assessment.

PART 5
COMMENCEMENT
General rule

16 The provisions of this Schedule apply to a change of basis taking effect in a period of account ending on or after 1st August 2001.

Application of provisions to certain earlier changes of basis

17—(1) So far as they relate to a change of basis within—

(*a*) paragraph 6 (no adjustment for certain expenses previously brought into account), or

(*b*) paragraph 8 (change from realisation basis to mark to market),

the provisions of this Schedule apply to a change of basis taking effect in a period of account ending before 1st August 2001 if a relevant return is delivered or voluntarily amended by the taxpayer on or after that date.

(2) For the purposes of sub-paragraph (1) a "relevant return" means—

(*a*) a return under section 8 or 8A of the Taxes Management Act 1970 (c 9) (personal or trustee return),

(*b*) a partnership return, or

(*c*) a company tax return,

for the period in which the change of basis took effect or a subsequent period of account ending before 1st August 2001.

(3) The reference in sub-paragraph (1) to the voluntary amendment of such a return is to—

(*a*) an amendment under section 9ZA or 12ABA of the Taxes Management Act 1970 (amendment of personal, trustee or partnership return by taxpayer), or

(*b*) an amendment of a company tax return by the company otherwise than in response to a closure notice.

(4) An adjustment that would be required by virtue of this paragraph to be given effect in a period of account ending before 1st August 2001 shall be given effect in the first period of account ending on or after that date.

Period in which change of basis takes effect

18 The references in paragraphs 16 and 17 to the period of account in which a change of basis takes effect are to the first period of account in which the new basis is adopted.

SCHEDULE 23

EXCHANGE GAINS AND LOSSES FROM LOAN RELATIONSHIPS ETC

Section 79

Commentary—*Simon's Direct Tax Service* D2.1102.

PART 1

AMENDMENTS OF THE FINANCE ACT 1996
Introductory

1 Chapter 2 of Part 4 of the Finance Act 1996 (c 8) (loan relationships) is amended in accordance with the following provisions of this Part.

Meaning of "related transaction"

2—(1) Section 84 (debits and credits brought into account) is amended as follows.

(2) In subsection (5) (meaning of "related transaction" in the section) for "In this section" substitute "In this Chapter".

(3) In subsection (6) (disposals and acquisitions for the purposes of the section) for "for the purposes of this section" substitute "for the purposes of subsection (5) above".

Exchange gains and losses from loan relationships etc

3 After section 84 (debits and credits brought into account) insert—

"84A Exchange gains and losses from loan relationships

(1) The reference in section 84(1)(*a*) above to the profits, gains and losses arising to a company from its loan relationships and related transactions includes a reference to exchange gains and losses arising to the company from its loan relationships.

(2) Subsection (1) above is subject to the following provisions of this section.

(3) Subsection (1) above does not have effect in relation to—

(*a*) so much of an exchange gain or loss arising to a company in relation to an asset representing a loan relationship of the company as falls within subsection (4) below; or
(*b*) so much of an exchange gain or loss arising to a company in relation to a liability representing a loan relationship of the company as falls within subsection (5) below; or
(*c*) so much of any exchange gain or loss arising to a company as results from any translation from one currency to another pursuant to section 93A(4) of the Finance Act 1993 of the profit or loss of part of the company's business and falls within subsection (4) below; or
(*d*) so much of an exchange gain or loss arising to a company in relation to an asset or liability representing a loan relationship of the company as falls within a description prescribed for the purpose in regulations made by the Treasury.

(4) For the purposes of subsection (3)(*a*) or (*c*) above, an exchange gain or loss falls within this subsection to the extent that, in accordance with generally accepted accounting practice, an amount representing the whole or part of it is carried to or sustained by a reserve maintained by the company.

(5) For the purposes of subsection (3)(*b*) above, an exchange gain or loss falls within this subsection to the extent that, in accordance with generally accepted accounting practice, an amount representing the whole or part of it—

(*a*) is carried to or sustained by a reserve maintained by the company; and
(*b*) is set off by or against an amount falling within subsection (6) below.

(6) An amount falls within this subsection if—

(*a*) it represents the whole or part of an exchange gain or loss arising to the company in relation to any asset of the company; and
(*b*) in accordance with generally accepted accounting practice it is carried to or sustained by the reserve mentioned in subsection (5)(*a*) above.

(7) Where by virtue of subsection (3) above subsection (1) above does not have effect in relation to an amount representing the whole or part of an exchange gain or loss, section 84(2)(*b*) above shall not have effect in relation to that amount (but this subsection is subject to regulations under subsection (8) below).

(8) The Treasury may by regulations make provision for or in connection with bringing into account in prescribed circumstances amounts in relation to which subsection (1) above does not, by virtue of subsection (3) above, have effect.

(9) The reference in subsection (8) above to bringing amounts into account is a reference to bringing amounts into account—

(*a*) for the purposes of this Chapter, as credits or debits in respect of the loan relationships of the company concerned; or
(*b*) for the purposes of the Taxation of Chargeable Gains Act 1992.

(10) Any power to make regulations under this section includes power to make different provision for different cases.".

Authorised accounting methods

4—(1) Section 85 is amended as follows.

(2) In subsection (2) (accounting methods authorised only if the conditions in the paragraphs of the subsection are satisfied) after paragraph (*b*) insert—

"(*bb*) it contains proper provision for determining exchange gains and losses from loan relationships for accounting periods; and".

(3) In paragraph (*c*) of that subsection (accruals basis not to give debits by reference to valuation at different times of asset representing loan relationship) after "(other than" insert "provision in respect of exchange losses or".

Convertible securities etc: exchange gains and losses

5—(1) Section 92 (convertible securities etc: creditor relationships) is amended as follows.

(2) In subsection (2) (which, in the case of securities to which the section applies, confines the amounts to be brought into account under the Chapter to interest) after "confined to" insert "(*a*)" and at the end of the subsection add

> "; and
>
> (*b*) amounts relating to exchange gains or losses".

(3) After subsection (5) (consideration for purposes of Taxation of Chargeable Gains Act 1992 (c 12) to be adjusted by excluding certain amounts relating to interest brought into account under subsections (2) and (3)) insert—

> "(5A) For the purposes of that Act the amount or value of the consideration for any disposal of the asset—
>
> > (*a*) shall be increased by the addition of any relevant exchange losses, determined in accordance with subsection (5C) below; and
> >
> > (*b*) shall (after giving effect to any such increase) be reduced (but not below nil) by the deduction of any relevant exchange gains, determined in accordance with that subsection.
>
> (5B) In subsection (5C) below—
>
> > "relevant accounting period" means any accounting period beginning on or after 1st October 2002; and
> >
> > "the relevant condition" is that the asset in question is an asset to which this section applies and is held by the company making the disposal.
>
> (5C) For the purposes of subsection (5A) above, relevant exchange gains or, as the case may be, losses in the case of any asset are—
>
> > (*a*) the amount of any exchange gains or, as the case may be, losses brought into account under subsections (2) and (3) above in respect of the asset, by the company making the disposal, for a relevant accounting period throughout which the relevant condition is satisfied; and
> >
> > (*b*) for any relevant accounting period not falling within paragraph (*a*) above in which the relevant condition is at some time satisfied, an amount which, on a just and reasonable apportionment, represents so much of the amount of any exchange gains or, as the case may be, losses brought into account under subsections (2) and (3) above in respect of the asset, by the company making the disposal, for that period as is referable to the part of the period for which the relevant condition is satisfied.
>
> (5D) Where—
>
> > (*a*) the amount of the relevant exchange gains falling to be deducted under subsection (5A)(*b*) above, exceeds
> >
> > (*b*) the amount required to reduce the amount or value of the consideration to nil,
>
> the excess shall be treated for the purposes of section 38(1)(*c*) of the Taxation of Chargeable Gains Act 1992 as incidental costs of making the disposal of the asset.".

(4) In subsection (6)—

> (*a*) in the opening words (construction of references to disposal in subsection (5)) for "subsection (5)" substitute "subsections (5) and (5A)"; and
>
> (*b*) in paragraph (*b*) (disposals within the meaning of the Taxation of Chargeable Gains Act 1992 but for section 127 or 116(10)) omit "127 or".

(5) In subsection (9) (which, subject to subsection (10), gives the meaning of "the relevant consideration") for "subsection (10)" substitute "subsections (10) and (10A)".

(6) After subsection (10) (which disapplies subsection (5) in the case of a deemed disposal and re-acquisition under subsection (7) but makes corresponding provision) insert—

> "(10A) Subsection (5A) above shall not apply in the case of a deemed disposal and re-acquisition under subsection (7) above; but in any such case the amount of the relevant consideration, after any reduction under subsection (10) above, shall be treated for the purposes of the Taxation of Chargeable Gains Act 1992 as further adjusted by making the same additions and deductions (and for the purposes of both the disposal and the re-acquisition) as would fall to be made under subsection (5A) above if it were the consideration for an actual disposal and that subsection also applied in relation to the corresponding acquisition.".

Extension of s. 100 to exchange gains and losses and to items other than money debts

6 For section 100 (interest on judgments, imputed interest, etc) substitute—

> **"100 Interest, and exchange gains and losses, on debts etc not arising from the lending of money**
>
> (1) For the purposes of the Corporation Tax Acts, a company has a relationship to which this section applies in any case where—

(*a*) the company stands, or has stood, in the position of a creditor or debtor as respects a money debt;

(*b*) the money debt is not one which arose from a transaction for the lending of money (so that, in consequence of section 81(1)(*b*) above, there is no loan relationship); and

(*c*) the money debt is one—

    (i) on which interest is payable to or by the company; or

    (ii) in relation to which exchange gains or losses arise to the company;

and references to a relationship to which this section applies, and to a company's being party to such a relationship, shall be construed accordingly.

(2) Where a company has a relationship to which this section applies—

(*a*) this Chapter shall have effect in relation to the interest payable under, or the exchange gains or losses arising to the company from, the relationship as it has effect in relation to interest payable under, or (as the case may be) exchange gains or losses arising to the company from, a loan relationship to which the company is a party; but

(*b*) the only credits or debits to be brought into account for the purposes of this Chapter in respect of the relationship are those relating to the interest or (as the case may be) to the exchange gains or losses;

and, subject to paragraph (*b*) above, references in the Corporation Tax Acts to a loan relationship accordingly include a reference to a relationship to which this section applies.

(3) References in this section to interest payable on a money debt include a reference to any amount which, in pursuance of Schedule 28AA to the Taxes Act 1988 (provision not at arm's length), falls to be treated as—

(*a*) interest on a money debt; or

(*b*) interest on an amount which is treated as a money debt;

and references in the other provisions of this section to a money debt accordingly include a reference to the amount on which that amount so falls to be treated as interest.

(4) Except as provided by subsection (7) below, any question whether debits or credits falling to be brought into account by virtue of this section in relation to a company—

(*a*) are to be brought into account under section 82(2) above, or

(*b*) are to be treated as non-trading debits or non-trading credits,

shall be determined in accordance with subsection (5) below (in the case of interest) or subsection (6) below (in the case of an exchange gain or loss).

(5) In the case of interest, any such question shall be determined according to the extent (if any) to which the interest—

(*a*) is paid for the purposes of a trade carried on by the company;

(*b*) is received in the course of activities forming an integral part of such a trade; or

(*c*) in the case of deemed interest, would be deemed to be so paid or received.

(6) In the case of an exchange gain or loss, any such question shall be determined according to the extent (if any) to which the money debt—

(*a*) is owed by the company for the purposes of a trade carried on by the company; or

(*b*) is held in the course of activities forming an integral part of such a trade.

(7) Any debits or credits which—

(*a*) relate to interest payable under the Tax Acts, and

(*b*) fall to be brought into account by virtue of this section in relation to any company,

are to be treated as non-trading debits or credits.

(8) To the extent that debits or credits fall to be brought into account by a company under section 82(2) above in the case of a relationship to which this section applies, the company shall be regarded for the purposes of the Corporation Tax Acts as being party to the relationship for the purposes of a trade carried on by the company.

(9) No exchange gains or losses shall be taken to arise for the purposes of this section if the money debt in question—

(*a*) is an amount of tax,

(*b*) is an amount of tax payable under the law of a territory outside the United Kingdom, or

(*c*) is an amount which would, but for any statutory provision or rule of law to the contrary other than section 74(1)(*f*) or (*g*) of the Taxes Act 1988, be deductible as an expense in computing profits in accordance with Case I of Schedule D or as an expense of management within section 75 of the Taxes Act 1988,

except to the extent that, in the case of a money debt falling within paragraph (*b*) above, a reduction in respect of the tax there mentioned falls to be made under section 811 of the Taxes Act 1988 (double taxation relief: deduction for foreign tax where no credit allowable).

(10) For the purposes of this section so far as relating to exchange gains and losses, each of the following shall be treated as a money debt owed to a company—

(*a*) any currency held by the company;

(*b*) in the case of a company carrying on insurance business, any deferred acquisition costs, within the meaning of Assets item G.II in the Balance Sheet Format set out after paragraph 9 of Schedule 9A to Companies Act 1985 (form and content of accounts of insurance companies and groups) as read with note (17) of the Notes on the Balance Sheet Format (which follow immediately after that format).

(11) For the purposes of this section so far as relating to exchange gains and losses, each of the following shall be treated as a money debt owed by a company—

(*a*) any provision made by the company for the purposes of its statutory accounts in respect of a liability to which the company may become subject;
(*b*) in the case of a company carrying on insurance business—

(i) any provision made by the company for unearned premiums, within the meaning of Liabilities item C.1 in the Balance Sheet Format set out after paragraph 9 of Schedule 9A to Companies Act 1985, as read with note (20) of the Notes on the Balance Sheet Format (which follow immediately after that format);
(ii) any provision for unexpired risks, as defined in paragraph 81(1) of that Schedule.

(12) A provision does not fall within paragraph (*a*) of subsection (11) above unless—

(*a*) the duty to settle the liability in question would (if the company were to become subject to it) be owed for the purposes of a trade, a Schedule A business or an overseas property business (within the meaning of section 70A of the Taxes Act 1988); and
(*b*) the provision falls to be taken into account (apart from this Chapter) in computing the profits or losses of the trade, Schedule A business or overseas property business for corporation tax purposes.

(13) This section has effect subject to the provisions of Schedules 9 and 11 to this Act.''.

Interpretation

7—(1) Section 103 is amended as follows.

(2) In subsection (1) (definitions) insert each of the following definitions at the appropriate place—

''''exchange gain'' and ''exchange loss'' shall be construed in accordance with subsections (1A) and (1B) below;'';
''''related transaction'' shall be construed in accordance with section 84 above (see subsections (5) and (6) of that section);''.

(3) After subsection (1) insert—

''(1A) References in this Chapter to exchange gains or exchange losses, in the case of any company, are references respectively to—

(*a*) profits or gains, or
(*b*) losses,

which arise as a result of comparing at different times the expression in one currency of the whole or some part of the valuation put by the company in another currency on an asset or liability of the company.

If the result of such a comparison is that neither an exchange gain nor an exchange loss arises, then for the purposes of this Chapter an exchange gain of nil shall be taken to arise in the case of that comparison.

(1B) Any reference in this Chapter to an exchange gain or loss from a loan relationship of a company is a reference to an exchange gain or loss arising to a company in relation to an asset or liability representing a loan relationship of the company.''.

Bad debt etc: cases where departure allowed from assumption of prompt payment in full

8—(1) Paragraph 5 of Schedule 9 is amended as follows.

(2) After sub-paragraph (1) (departure from assumption of full and prompt payment of debt allowed only to extent debt is bad debt etc) insert—

''(1A) Such a departure shall be made only where the first and second conditions (set out in sub-paragraphs (2) and (2A) below) are satisfied.''.

(3) In sub-paragraph (2) (requirement for appropriate adjustments in form of credits where bad debt etc is paid or departure otherwise ceases to be allowed) for ''Such a departure shall be made only where'' substitute ''The first condition is that''.

(4) After sub-paragraph (2) insert—

''(2A) The second condition is that, in determining the credits and debits to be brought into account in respect of exchange gains and losses, the accounting arrangements allowing the departure require a debt—

(*a*) to be left out of account, to the extent that such a departure is allowed; and
(*b*) to be taken into account again, to the extent that it is represented by credits brought into account under subparagraph (2) above.''.

Bad debts etc where parties have a connection

9—(1) Paragraph 6 of Schedule 9 is amended as follows.

(2) In sub-paragraph (3) (assumption that debts will be paid in full to be applied as if no departure authorised by virtue of paragraph 5 except as provided by sub-paragraph (4)) for "paragraph 5" substitute "paragraph 5(1)".

(3) At the end of the paragraph add—

"(8) Nothing in this paragraph affects the debits or credits to be brought into account for the purposes of this Chapter in respect of exchange gains or losses arising from a debt.".

Transactions not at arm's length

10—(1) Paragraph 11 of Schedule 9 is amended as follows.

(2) In sub-paragraph (1), for "Subject to sub-paragraphs (2) and (3) below," substitute "Subject to sub-paragraphs (2) to (3A) below,".

(3) After sub-paragraph (3) insert—

"(3A) Sub-paragraph (1) above shall not apply to any exchange gains or losses.".

Exchange gains and losses where loan not on arm's length terms

11 After paragraph 11 of Schedule 9 insert the following paragraph—

"Exchange gains and losses where loan not on arm's length terms

11A—(1) Where a company has a debtor relationship in an accounting period and in the case of that accounting period—

(a) the whole of any interest or other distribution out of the assets of the company in respect of securities of the company that represent the relationship falls by virtue of section 209(2)(*da*) or (*e*)(vii) of the Taxes Act 1988 to be regarded as a distribution for the purposes of the Corporation Tax Acts, or

(b) the profits and losses of the company fall by virtue of Schedule 28AA to that Act (provision not at arm's length) to be computed for tax purposes as if the loan had not been made,

any exchange gains or losses which arise in that accounting period in respect of a liability representing the debtor relationship shall be left out of account in determining the debits or credits to be brought into account for the purposes of this Chapter.

(2) Where a company has a debtor relationship in an accounting period and in the case of that accounting period—

(a) part of any interest or other distribution out of the assets of the company in respect of securities of the company that represent the relationship falls by virtue of section 209(2)(*da*) or (*e*)(vii) of the Taxes Act 1988 to be regarded as a distribution for the purposes of the Corporation Tax Acts, or

(b) the profits and losses of the company fall by virtue of Schedule 28AA to that Act to be computed for tax purposes as if the loan had in part not been made,

the proportionate part of any exchange gains or losses which arise in that accounting period in respect of a liability representing the debtor relationship shall be left out of account in determining the debits or credits to be brought into account for the purposes of this Chapter.

(3) In sub-paragraph (2) above, the "proportionate part" of an exchange gain or loss is that part which bears to the whole the proportion which—

(a) in a case falling within paragraph (a) of that sub-paragraph, the part of the interest or other distribution out of assets that falls to be regarded as a distribution for the purposes of the Corporation Tax Acts bears to the whole of that interest or other distribution out of assets; or

(b) in a case falling within paragraph (b) of that sub-paragraph, the part of the loan that falls to be treated as if it had not been made bears to the whole of the loan.

(4) Where—

(a) a company has a creditor relationship in an accounting period,

(b) the transaction giving rise to the loan is such that it would not have been entered into at all if the parties had been dealing at arm's length, and

(c) there is no corresponding debtor relationship such that there would, or would apart from section 84A(2) to (10) of this Act, fall to be brought into account for the purposes of this Chapter, in respect of exchange gains or losses from that debtor relationship, debits or (as the case may be) credits corresponding to, and of the same amount as, the credits or debits that would (apart from this paragraph) fall to be brought into account for the purposes of this Chapter in respect of exchange gains or losses from the creditor relationship,

any exchange gains or losses which arise in that accounting period in respect of an asset representing the creditor relationship shall be left out of account in determining the debits or credits to be brought into account for the purposes of this Chapter.

(5) Where—

    (a) a company has a creditor relationship in an accounting period,

    (b) the circumstances are such that, had the parties to the transaction giving rise to the loan been dealing at arm's length, the terms would have been the same, except that the amount of the loan would have been an amount (referred to in sub-paragraph (6) below as "the adjusted amount") greater than nil but less than its actual amount, and

    (c) there is no such corresponding debtor relationship as satisfies, in relation to that creditor relationship, the condition set out in sub-paragraph (4)(c) above,

sub-paragraph (4) above shall not apply, but the excess portion of any exchange gain or loss which arises in the accounting period in respect of an asset representing the creditor relationship shall be left out of account in determining the debits or credits to be brought into account for the purposes of this Chapter.

(6) In sub-paragraph (5) above, the "excess portion" of an exchange gain or loss is so much of the gain or loss as remains after subtracting that part which bears to the whole the proportion which the adjusted amount bears to the amount of the loan.".

Continuity of treatment: groups etc

12 In paragraph 12 of Schedule 9, for sub-paragraph (8) (which applies sub-paragraphs (4) and (5) of paragraph 11 of the Schedule) substitute—

    "(8) Sub-paragraph (5) of paragraph 11 above has effect for the purposes of this paragraph as it has effect for the purposes of that paragraph.".

Loan relationships for unallowable purposes

13 In paragraph 13 of Schedule 9, for sub-paragraph (1) (which disallows debits attributable to unallowable purposes)—

    (a) for "the debits", where first occurring, substitute the following paragraphs—

        "(a) the debits, and

        (b) the credits in respect of exchange gains,"; and

    (b) after "the debits", where next occurring, insert "or credits (as the case may be)".

Life assurance business

14—(1) Paragraph 1 of Schedule 11 is amended as follows.

(2) Before sub-paragraph (2) (effect on debits and credits of applying I minus E basis to profits and gains from loan relationships of insurance companies referable to life assurance business) insert—

    "(1B) In applying the I minus E basis for any accounting period in respect of any life assurance business carried on by an insurance company, no exchange gains or losses shall be taken to arise for the purposes of section 100 of this Act except to the extent that the money debt for the purposes of that section—

    (a) arises as a result of an amount of income or expenses which falls to be taken into account in applying the I minus E basis not being paid when it is due and payable; or

    (b) is one that is treated as a money debt for the purposes of that section by virtue of subsection (11)(a) of that section in accordance with subsection (12) of that section by reference to a Schedule A business or an overseas property business.

This sub-paragraph has effect notwithstanding sub-paragraph (1) above."

Special provisions for insurers: apportionments

15 In paragraph 3A of Schedule 11 (cases where money debt of insurance company is represented by a liability of the long term business fund) in sub-paragraph (1)—

    (a) in paragraph (a), for "money debt" substitute "loan relationship"; and

    (b) in paragraph (b), omit "debt or".

Savings and transitional provisions in the Finance Act 1996

16 In Schedule 15 (savings and transitional provisions) omit paragraphs 22 to 24.

PART 2

AMENDMENTS OF OTHER LEGISLATION

The Income and Corporation Taxes Act 1988

Charges on income

17—(1) Section 494 of the Taxes Act 1988 is amended in accordance with the following provisions of this paragraph.

(2) Subsection (2) (debits not to be brought into account in a manner which results in the reduction of what would otherwise be the company's ring fence profits, except as provided in the subsequent paragraphs) is amended as follows.

(3) In paragraph (*c*) (debits in respect of a deemed loan relationship)—

    (*a*) for "a loan relationship deemed to exist for the purposes of section 100 of that Act," substitute "a relationship to which section 100 of that Act applies,";

    (*b*) after "to the extent that" insert "(i)"; and

    (*c*) after "above;" insert

        "or

            (ii) the exchange loss arising from that relationship is in respect of a money debt on which the interest payable (if any) is, or would be, such expenditure;

      as the case may be;".

(4) In paragraph (*d*) (debits in respect of debtor relationship which is creditor relationship of associated company)—

    (*a*) for "in the case of debits" substitute "in the case of a net debit for an accounting period"; and

    (*b*) for "the debit", in both places where occurring, substitute "the net debit".

(5) In the second sentence of that subsection (interpretation) for "any loan relationship deemed to exist for the purposes of section 100 of that Act" substitute "any relationship to which section 100 of that Act applies".

(6) After the second sentence insert the following as a third sentence—

    "For the purposes of paragraph (*d*) above, the net debit for an accounting period in respect of a debtor relationship of a company is the amount if any by which—

        (i) the aggregate of the debits for the period in respect of the relationship, exceeds

        (ii) the credits in respect of exchange gains arising from the relationship for the period.".

(7) After subsection (2) insert—

    "(2ZA) Credits in respect of exchange gains from a company's loan relationships shall not be brought into account for the purposes of Chapter 2 of Part 4 of the Finance Act 1996 in respect of any loan relationship of a company in any manner that results in an increase of what would otherwise be the company's ring fence profits, except to the extent that, if the credit had been a debit in respect of an exchange loss from the relationship, it would have been brought into account by virtue of any of paragraphs (*a*) to (*c*) of subsection (2) above.".

(8) In subsection (2A) (debits prevented from reducing ring fence profits by subsection (2) to be brought into account for purposes of Chapter 2 of Part 4 of Finance Act 1996 (c 8) as non-trading debits)—

    (*a*) after "Where any debit" insert "or credit";

    (*b*) in paragraph (*b*)—

        (i) after "in accordance with subsection (2)" insert "or (2ZA)"; and

        (ii) after "reduction" insert "or, as the case may be, increase"; and

    (*c*) in the closing words—

        (i) after "that debit" insert "or credit"; and

        (ii) after "non-trading debit" insert "or, as the case may be, non-trading credit".

(9) After subsection (2A) insert—

    "(2B) Where, in accordance with subsection (2) above, any proportion (including the whole) of a net debit, within the meaning of paragraph (*d*) of that subsection, cannot be brought into account in a manner that results in any reduction of what would otherwise be the company's ring fence profits, subsection (2A) above shall apply—

        (*a*) separately in relation to that proportion of each of the debits and each of the credits brought into account in determining the amount of the net debit, and

        (*b*) on the assumption that that proportion of each of those debits and credits falls within paragraph (*b*) of that subsection.".

Supplementary charge in respect of ring fence trades

18—(1) In section 501A of the Taxes Act 1988, subsection (5) (computation of financing costs) is amended as follows.

(2) In paragraph (*a*) (costs giving rise to debits in respect of debtor relationships) after "(loan relationships)" insert ", other than debits in respect of exchange losses from such relationships (see section 103(1A) and (1B) of that Act)".

(3) For paragraph (*b*) (exchange gain or loss, within the meaning of Chapter 2 of Part 2 of the Finance Act 1993 (c 34), in relation to debt finance) substitute—

    "(*b*) any exchange gain or loss from a debtor relationship, within the meaning of that Chapter (see section 103(1A) and (1B) of that Act), in relation to debt finance;".

Controlled foreign companies

19 In section 747A of the Taxes Act 1988 (controlled foreign companies: special rule for computing chargeable profits) in subsection (9), for paragraph (*b*) (which defines "the appointed day" as such day as may be appointed under section 165(7)(*b*) of the Finance Act 1993) substitute—

"(*b*) "the appointed day" is 23rd March 1995.".

Double taxation relief

20—(1) Section 798B of the Taxes Act 1988 (adjustments of interest and dividends for spared tax etc) is amended as follows.

(2) In subsection (5) (meaning of "qualifying losses") for paragraph (*a*) (exchange losses under Finance Act 1993) substitute—

"(*a*) exchange losses falling to be brought into account as debits for the purposes of Chapter 2 of Part 4 of the Finance Act 1996 (loan relationships); and".

Provision not at arm's length: foreign exchange gains and losses

21—(1) In Schedule 28AA to the Taxes Act 1988 (provision not at arm's length) paragraph 8 (foreign exchange gains and losses etc) is amended as follows.

(2) In sub-paragraph (1) (exceptions)—

(*a*) for "Subject to sub-paragraph (2)" substitute "Subject to sub-paragraph (3)"; and
(*b*) for paragraph (*a*) (which relates to Chapter 2 of Part 2 of the Finance Act 1993) substitute—

"(*a*) Chapter 2 of Part 4 of the Finance Act 1996 (loan relationships) in respect of exchange gains or losses from loan relationships (as defined in section 103(1A) and (1B) of that Act), or".

(3) For sub-paragraph (2) (saving for certain provisions of sections 136 and 136A of the Finance Act 1993 (c 34) (application of arm's length test)) substitute—

"(3) Sub-paragraph (1) above shall not affect so much of paragraph 11A of Schedule 9 to the Finance Act 1996 (loan relationships: exchange gains or losses where loan not on arm's length terms) as has effect by reference to whether profits or losses fall to be computed by virtue of this Schedule as if the whole or any part of a loan had not been made.".

The Finance Act 1995

Miscellaneous amendments

22—(1) The Finance Act 1995 (c 4) is amended as follows.

(2) Omit section 131 (which made transitional provision in relation to exchange gains and losses and which is spent).

(3) In Part 2 of Schedule 24 (amendments of certain enactments) in paragraph 7 (commencement on day appointed under section 165(7)(*b*) of Finance Act 1993) for the words following "come into force on" substitute "23rd March 1995".

The Finance Act 2000

Tonnage tax

23—(1) Schedule 22 to the Finance Act 2000 (c 17) is amended as follows.

(2) In paragraph 50 (relevant shipping income: certain interests etc) in sub-paragraph (2) (income to which paragraph 50 applies) at the end of paragraph (*a*) insert "and".

(3) In paragraph 63 (meaning of "finance costs") in sub-paragraph (2)(*c*) (exchange gain or loss) for "within the meaning of Chapter II of Part II of the Finance Act 1993" substitute "within the meaning given by section 103(1A) of the Finance Act 1996".

The Finance Act 2002

Intangible fixed assets: assets entirely excluded: financial assets

24—(1) Schedule 29 to the Finance Act 2002 (gains and losses of a company from intangible fixed assets) is amended as follows.

(2) In paragraph 75 (assets entirely excluded: financial assets) in sub-paragraph (3) for paragraph (*a*) (money debts) substitute—

"(*a*) loan relationships;".

PART 3

TRANSITIONAL PROVISIONS ETC

Anti-avoidance: change of accounting period

25—(1) This paragraph applies where—

(a) a company changes its accounting date so that it has an accounting period which begins on or after 1st October 2001 but ends before 30th September 2002; and

(b) the change of accounting date is or was made for the purpose, or for purposes which include the purpose, specified in sub-paragraph (2).

(2) The purpose is that of securing, in the case of any subsequent accounting period beginning before 1st October 2002,—

(a) that where an amount, or a bigger amount, would have fallen to be brought into account as a credit under Chapter 2 of Part 4 of the Finance Act 1996 (c 8) if the other provisions of this Schedule had had effect in relation to the period, no amount, or a smaller amount, falls to be brought into account in accordance with section 128 or 130 of the Finance Act 1993; or

(b) that where no amount, or a smaller amount, would have fallen to be brought into account as a debit under that Chapter if the other provisions of this Schedule had had effect in relation to the period, an amount, or a bigger amount, falls to be brought into account in accordance with section 128 or 130 of the Finance Act 1993.

(3) Where this paragraph applies, the other provisions of this Schedule shall have effect in relation to the subsequent accounting period mentioned in sub-paragraph (2) as if it were an accounting period beginning on or after 1st October 2002.

(4) In this paragraph, any reference to this Schedule includes a reference to—

(a) subsection (1) of section 79;

(b) the amendments made by Schedule 24, so far as relating to the amendments and other provisions made by or under this Schedule; and

(c) any repeal of any enactment which is consequential on any provision made by or under this Schedule.

Deferred foreign exchange gains

26—(1) The repeal of sections 139 to 143 of the Finance Act 1993 (foreign exchange gains and losses) does not prevent the making of a claim under section 139 of that Act (deferral of unrealised gains) by a company in respect of a gain accruing in an accrual period which begins with, or at any time in, the last accounting period of the company which begins before 1st October 2002; but any such claim shall have effect subject to the following provisions of this paragraph and (subject to regulations under section 81) regulations under Chapter 2 of Part 2 of that Act.

(2) Amounts which, but for the repeal of subsections (4) to (10) of section 140 of the Finance Act 1993, would fall to be treated by virtue of those subsections as exchange gains for an accrual period which consists of, or falls in, an accounting period beginning on or after 1st October 2002—

(a) shall be brought into account for that accounting period as if they were credits falling for the purposes of Chapter 2 of Part 4 of the Finance Act 1996 (c 8) to be brought into account in respect of the company's loan relationships;

(b) shall be treated for the purposes of that Chapter as non-trading credits, to the extent that they would, but for the repeal of subsections (5), (8) or (9) of section 140 of the Finance Act 1993 (c 34), have fallen to be treated by virtue of those subsections as non-trading exchange gains; and

(c) except as provided by paragraph (b), shall be brought into account under section 82(2) of the Finance Act 1996 (trading credits).

(3) Before the expiration of the period of 2 years following the end of its first accounting period beginning on or after 1st October 2002, a company may elect for any amounts that would otherwise fall to be brought into account for that accounting period in accordance with paragraph (a) of sub-paragraph (2) instead to be brought into account in accordance with that sub-paragraph, but—

(a) over the first 6 accounting periods of the company which begin on or after 1st October 2002; and

(b) in instalments of an equal amount for each such accounting period.

(4) If a company—

(a) makes an election under sub-paragraph (3), but

(b) ceases to be within the charge to corporation tax before six accounting periods of the company which begin on or after 1st October 2002 have elapsed,

any instalment under that sub-paragraph which does not fall to be brought into account for an earlier accounting period shall be brought into account for the accounting period in which the company ceases to be within the charge to corporation tax.

(5) The provision that may be made by regulations under subsection (8) of section 84A of the Finance Act 1996 includes provision for amounts which have been reduced to nil under regulations made under paragraph 4 of Schedule 15 to the Finance Act 1993 (alternative method of calculation) to be brought into account (as defined in subsection (9) of that section) for an accounting period beginning on or after 1st October 2002.

Cross reference—See the Exchange Gains and Losses (Bringing into Account Gains or Losses) Regulations, SI 2002/1970.

SCHEDULE 24

CORPORATION TAX: CURRENCY

Section 80

Commentary—*Simon's Direct Tax Service* **D2.910–912.**

The Finance Act 1993

Introductory

1 The Finance Act 1993 is amended as follows.

The basic rule: sterling to be used

2 In section 92(1) (which provides that the basic rule is subject to section 93) for "section 93" substitute "sections 93 and 93A".

Use of currency other than sterling: accounts as a whole etc in foreign currency

3—(1) Section 93 is amended as follows.

(2) In subsection (1) (application of section) for "either the first condition or the second condition" substitute "the condition in subsection (2) below".

(3) In subsection (2) (the first condition), for "The first condition is" substitute "The condition is".

(4) Omit subsection (3) (the second condition, which is superseded by the new section 93A inserted by paragraph 4).

(5) Omit subsection (6) (different parts carried on through different branches, which is superseded by the new section 93A).

(6) In subsection (7) (definitions) omit the definitions of—

    (*a*) "branch"; and
    (*b*) "the closing rate/net investment method".

(7) In subsection (7), in the definition of "the relevant foreign currency" for "the first condition" substitute "the condition in subsection (2) above".

(8) In consequence of the amendments made by this paragraph, the sidenote to the section becomes "Use of currency other than sterling: accounts as a whole etc in foreign currency.".

Use of currency other than sterling: accounts etc partly from statements in foreign currency

4 After section 93 insert—

"93A Use of other currency: accounts partly from statements in foreign currency

(1) This section applies where in an accounting period a company carries on a business and either the first condition or the second condition is fulfilled.

(2) The first condition is that—

    (*a*) the accounts of the company as a whole are prepared in sterling but, so far as relating to part of the business, they are prepared, using the closing rate/net investment method, from financial statements and records prepared in a currency other than sterling; or
    (*b*) in the case of a company which is not resident in the United Kingdom, the company makes a return of accounts for its branch in the United Kingdom prepared in sterling but, so far as relating to part of the business, it is prepared, using that method, from financial statements and records prepared in a currency other than sterling.

(3) The second condition is that—

    (*a*) the accounts of the company as a whole are prepared in a currency other than sterling ("the first currency") in accordance with generally accepted accounting practice but, so far as relating to part of the business, they are prepared, using the closing rate/net investment method, from financial statements and records prepared in a currency ("the second currency") which is neither sterling nor the first currency; or
    (*b*) in the case of a company which is not resident in the United Kingdom, the company makes a return of accounts for its branch in the United Kingdom prepared in a currency other than sterling ("the first currency") in accordance with generally accepted accounting practice, but, so far as relating to part of the business, it is prepared, using the closing rate/net investment method, from financial statements and records prepared in a currency ("the second currency") which is neither sterling nor the first currency.

(4) The profits or losses of the part of the business for an accounting period shall for the purposes of corporation tax be found by—

    (*a*) taking the amount of all the profits and losses of the part of the business for the period computed and expressed in the relevant foreign currency; and

(b) taking—

(i) in a case where the first condition is fulfilled, the sterling equivalent, or

(ii) in a case where the second condition is fulfilled, the equivalent in the first currency,

of the amount found by applying paragraph (a) above.

(5) In a case where the second condition is fulfilled, effect shall be given to subsection (4) above before effect is given to section 93(4) above.

(6) In the application for the purposes of subsection (4)(a) above of—

(a) section 578A(2) or (3) of the Taxes Act 1988, or

(b) section 43(3), 74(2), 75(1), 76(2), (3) or (4), 99(1), (2) or (3) or 208(1) of the Capital Allowances Act,

it shall be assumed that any sterling amount mentioned in any of those sections is its equivalent expressed in the relevant foreign currency.

(7) Where for any accounting period—

(a) the accounts of the company, so far as relating to a part of its business, are prepared, using the closing rate/net investment method, from financial statements and records prepared in a currency which is not sterling and, where the second condition is fulfilled, is not the first currency, or

(b) in the case of a company which is not resident in the United Kingdom, its return of accounts for its branch in the United Kingdom, so far as relating to a part of the company's business, is prepared, using that method, from such financial statements and records,

then, if different such financial statements and records are prepared in different currencies, the company shall be treated for the purposes of this section as having a separate part of a separate business for each such different currency (and this section shall accordingly apply separately in relation to each such part).

(8) In this section, "part of a business" includes any collection of assets and liabilities.

(9) In this section, unless the context otherwise requires—

"accounts" has the same meaning as in section 93 above;

"the closing rate/net investment method" means the method so called as described under the title "Foreign currency translation" in the Statement of Standard Accounting Practice issued in April 1983 by the Institute of Chartered Accountants in England and Wales;

"losses" has the same meaning as in section 92 above, except that it does not include allowable losses within the meaning of the Taxation of Chargeable Gains Act 1992;

"profits" has the same meaning as in section 92 above, except that it does not include chargeable gains within the meaning of that Act;

"the relevant foreign currency" means the currency in which the financial statements and records mentioned in subsection (2) or, as the case may be, (3) above are prepared;

"return of accounts" has the same meaning as in section 93 above.".

Rules for ascertaining currency equivalents: general

5 For section 94, substitute—

"94AA Rules for ascertaining currency equivalents: general

(1) Where any receipt or expense, or the value of any asset, liability or derivative contract, of a company—

(a) is to be taken into account in making a computation under subsection (1) of section 92 above for an accounting period, and

(b) is denominated in a currency other than sterling,

it shall be translated into its sterling equivalent by reference to a rate determined in accordance with subsection (4) below.

(2) Where the amount of any receipt or expense, or the value of any asset, liability or derivative contract, of a company—

(a) falls to be brought into account for the purposes of the accounts mentioned in paragraph (a), or the return of accounts mentioned in paragraph (b), of subsection (2) of section 93 above,

(b) is denominated in a currency other than the relevant foreign currency, within the meaning of that section, and

(c) accordingly falls to be translated into the relevant foreign currency,

the amount or value shall for the purposes of that section be translated from the currency mentioned in paragraph (b) above into the relevant foreign currency by reference to a rate determined in accordance with subsection (4) below.

(3) Where, for any purpose of any provision of section 93A(4) or (6) above, any profit or loss denominated in one currency falls to be translated into its equivalent expressed in another currency, the translation shall be made by reference to a rate determined in accordance with subsection (4) below.

(4) The rate is—

(*a*) the rate used in the preparation of the accounts of the company for the accounting period in question, if that rate is an arm's length exchange rate for the relevant day, or

(*b*) in any other case, the London closing exchange rate for the relevant day.

(5) The reference in subsection (4)(*a*) above to the exchange rate used in the preparation of the accounts of the company includes a reference to any exchange rate implied by a derivative contract whose underlying subject matter is currency.

(6) Nothing in this section affects the operation of Chapter 4 of Part 17 of the Taxes Act 1988 (controlled foreign companies).

(7) Nothing in paragraph 88 of Schedule 18 to the Finance Act 1998 (company tax returns, assessments and related matters) shall be taken to prevent an amount being translated under this section for an accounting period by reference to an exchange rate which was not the exchange rate used to translate that amount for the purposes of the Corporation Tax Acts for another accounting period (whether of the same or a different company).

(8) In this section—

"accounts" has the same meaning as in section 93 above;
"arm's length exchange rate" means such exchange rate as might reasonably be expected to be agreed between persons dealing at arm's length;
"derivative contract" shall be construed in accordance with Schedule 26 to the Finance Act 2002;
"the relevant day"—

(*a*) where the rate used in the preparation of the accounts is an exchange rate for a particular day, means that day; and

(*b*) where the rate used in the preparation of the accounts is an average rate for a number of days, means each of those days;

"underlying subject matter", in relation to a derivative contract, shall be construed in accordance with Schedule 26 to the Finance Act 2002.".

Rules for ascertaining sterling equivalent for section 93(4) or (5)

6 After section 94AA insert—

"94AB Rules for ascertaining sterling equivalent for section 93(4) or (5)

(1) Where the amount of any receipt or expense, or the value of any asset, liability or derivative contract, of a company falls to be translated into its sterling equivalent for the purposes of section 93(4) or (5) above, the translation shall be made by reference to a rate which is an arm's length exchange rate for the appropriate day.

(2) For the purposes of subsection (1) above, the "appropriate day" is the day the rate for which would have been used if the accounts, or return of accounts, of the company were translated into sterling in accordance with generally accepted accounting practice in relation to foreign currency translation.

(3) Nothing in this section affects the operation of Chapter 4 of Part 17 of the Taxes Act 1988 (controlled foreign companies).

(4) Nothing in paragraph 88 of Schedule 18 to the Finance Act 1998 (company tax returns, assessments and related matters) shall be taken to prevent an amount being translated under this section for an accounting period by reference to an exchange rate which was not the exchange rate used to translate that amount for the purposes of the Corporation Tax Acts for another accounting period (whether of the same or a different company).

(5) In this section—

"accounts" has the same meaning as in section 93 above;
"arm's length exchange rate" has the same meaning as in section 94AA;
"derivative contract" shall be construed in accordance with Schedule 26 to the Finance Act 2002.".

The Finance Act 1994

Lloyd's underwriters: corporations etc

7—(1) Section 226 of the Finance Act 1994 (c 9) (provisions which are not to apply to corporate members of Lloyd's) is amended as follows.

(2) Subsection (1) (which prevents sections 92 to 95 of the Finance Act 1993 (c 34) from applying) shall cease to have effect (and sections 92 to 94AB of that Act shall accordingly apply for the purposes of computing for the purposes of corporation tax the profits or losses of a corporate member's underwriting business).

SCHEDULE 25

LOAN RELATIONSHIPS

Section 82

Commentary—*Simon's Direct Tax Service* D2.1121, 1128, 1129.

PART 1

AMENDMENTS OF THE FINANCE ACT 1996

Introductory

1 Chapter 2 of Part 4 of the Finance Act 1996 (c 8) (loan relationships) is amended in accordance with the following provisions of this Part of this Schedule.

Meaning of "loan relationship" etc: method of settlement

2—(1) Section 81 is amended as follows.

(2) In subsection (2) (which defines a money debt as a debt which falls to be settled by the payment of money etc)—

    (a) for "which falls" substitute "which is, or has at any time been, one that falls, or that may at the option of the debtor or of the creditor fall,"; and

    (b) after paragraph (b) insert—

        "disregarding any other option exercisable by either party.".

Non-trading deficit on loan relationships

3—(1) Section 83 is amended as follows.

(2) In subsection (2) (ways in which relief may be given on a claim in respect of the whole or any part of the deficit) after "the deficit", where first occurring, insert "(to the extent that it is not surrendered as group relief by virtue of section 403 of the Taxes Act 1988)".

(3) At the end of paragraph (a) of that subsection (claim to set off against other profits of the period) insert "or".

(4) Paragraph (b) of that subsection (claim to treat as eligible for group relief) shall cease to have effect.

(5) Paragraph (d) of that subsection (claim to carry forward and set against non-trading profits of next accounting period) shall cease to have effect.

(6) For subsection (3) (any balance to be carried forward and treated as a deficit of the next accounting period) substitute—

    "(3A) So much of the deficit for the deficit period as is not—

        (a) surrendered as group relief by virtue of section 403 of the Taxes Act 1988, or

        (b) treated in any of the ways specified in subsection (2) above,

    shall be carried forward and set against non-trading profits of the company for succeeding accounting periods.".

(7) Subsection (4) (provisions relating to amount carried forward and treated as deficit for next accounting period, which becomes of no further utility) shall cease to have effect.

(8) In subsection (9) (which introduces Schedule 8) for "subsection (2) above" substitute "subsection (2)(a) or (c) above or where subsection (3A) above has effect)".

Debits and credits brought into account

4—(1) Section 84 is amended as follows.

(2) In subsection (2)(b) (which provides that the reference in subsection (1) to profits, gains and losses includes any which, in accordance with normal accountancy practice, are carried to or sustained by certain reserves) for "normal accountancy practice" substitute "generally accepted accounting practice".

(3) After subsection (4) insert—

    "(4A) Where—

        (a) different authorised accounting methods are used for the purposes of this Chapter as respects the same loan relationship for different parts of the same accounting period or for successive accounting periods, and

        (b) no debit or credit falls to be brought into account under subsection (2)(c) or (3)(b) of section 90 below in consequence of the change of method, but

        (c) an amount is brought into account for the purposes of the company's statutory accounts in respect of the change of method, that amount shall be taken for the purposes of this Chapter to be included among the sums in respect of which debits and credits fall to be brought into account for the purposes of this Chapter in accordance with subsection (1)(*a*) above.''.

Authorised accounting methods

5—(1) Section 85 is amended as follows.

(2) In subsection (2) (accounting methods authorised only if the conditions in the paragraphs of the subsection are satisfied) for paragraph (*a*) (conformity to normal accountancy practice) substitute—

    ''(*a*) subject to paragraphs (*b*) to (*c*) below, it is in conformity with generally accepted accounting practice to use that method in that case;''.

(3) In paragraph (*b*) of that subsection (provision for allocating payments under a loan relationship to accounting periods) after ''payments under a loan relationship'' insert '', or arising as a result of a related transaction,''.

Application of accounting methods

6—(1) Section 86 is amended as follows.

(2) In subsection (3) (method to be used where basis used in statutory accounts is, or equates to, an authorised accounting method) after paragraph (*b*) insert—

    ''but this subsection is subject to subsections (3A) and (3D) below.''.

(3) After subsection (3) insert—

    ''(3A) If, in the case of a company falling within subsection (8)(*c*) or (*d*) below, an authorised mark to market basis of accounting—

        (*a*) would be used as respects some or all of the company's loan relationships, were the company a UK company following generally accepted accounting practice, but
        (*b*) is not the basis of accounting used as respects those loan relationships in the company's statutory accounts,

the company may elect to use an authorised mark to market basis of accounting as its authorised accounting method for the purposes of this Chapter in relation to every loan relationship as respects which that basis would be used if the company were a UK company following generally accepted accounting practice.

    (3B) Any election under subsection (3A) above—

        (*a*) must be made before the expiration of the period of two years following the end of the company's first accounting period beginning on or after 1st October 2002 in which it is party to a loan relationship in relation to which such an election may be made;
        (*b*) has effect for that accounting period and all subsequent accounting periods of the company; and
        (*c*) is irrevocable.

    (3C) A company which makes an election under sub-paragraph (3A) above as respects its loan relationships shall be taken for the purposes of Schedule 26 to the Finance Act 2002 (derivative contracts) to have at the same time made an election under sub-paragraph (2) of paragraph 19 of that Schedule having effect—

        (*a*) for the accounting periods mentioned in subsection (3B)(*b*) above, and
        (*b*) as respects any derivative contracts to which the company is or may become party in any of those accounting periods,

and that election shall so have effect notwithstanding anything in paragraph (*a*) or (*b*) of sub-paragraph (3) of that paragraph.

    (3D) If, in the case of a company falling within subsection (8)(*c*) or (*d*) below which has not made an election under subsection (3A) above,—

        (*a*) an authorised mark to market basis of accounting would be used for an accounting period—

            (i) as respects some or all of the company's loan relationships, and
            (ii) as respects some or all of the company's derivative contracts,

    were the company a UK company following generally accepted accounting practice, and
        (*b*) that basis of accounting—

            (i) is used in the company's statutory accounts as respects those derivative contracts for that accounting period, but
            (ii) is not the basis of accounting used in those accounts as respects those loan relationships for that accounting period,

the company must for that accounting period use an authorised mark to market basis of accounting as its authorised accounting method for the purposes of this Chapter in relation to every loan relationship as respects which that basis would be used if the company were a UK company following generally accepted accounting practice.''.

FA 2002

(4) In subsection (4) (authorised accruals basis to be used where authorised accounting method not determined under subsection (3)) for "determined under subsection (3) above," substitute the following paragraphs—

"(*a*) a method determined under subsection (3) above,

(*b*) an authorised mark to market method in accordance with an election under subsection (3A) above, or

(*c*) an authorised mark to market method in accordance with subsection (3D) above,".

(5) In subsection (7) (meaning of "fair value") the words from ""fair value"" onwards become a separate definition and after that definition insert the following definition—

""UK company" means a company incorporated or formed under the law of a part of the United Kingdom.".

(6) In subsection (8) (meaning of "statutory accounts" in the section) for "In this section" substitute "In this Chapter".

Accounting method where parties have a connection

7—(1) Section 87 is amended as follows.

(2) In subsection (3) (meaning of connection between company and another person) in paragraph (*a*) (case where one company has had control of the other in an accounting period or in the two years preceding it)—

(*a*) omit ", or in the two years before the beginning of that period,"; and

(*b*) at the end of the paragraph, insert "or".

(3) In paragraph (*b*) of that subsection (case where both companies under control of same person in that period or those two years) omit ", or in those two years,".

(4) Omit paragraph (*c*) of that subsection (company was close company and other person was participator or associate of participator in that period or those two years).

(5) In subsection (5) (persons indirectly standing in position of creditor or debtor by reference to a series of loan relationships) after "series of loan relationships" insert "or money debts which would be loan relationships if a company directly stood in the position of creditor or debtor".

(6) After subsection (5) insert—

"(5A) Where a trade, profession or business is carried on by two or more persons in partnership ("the firm") and the firm stands in the position of a creditor or debtor as respects a money debt, any question—

(*a*) whether there is for the purposes of this Chapter a connection, within the meaning of this section, between any two companies for an accounting period in the case of a loan relationship, or

(*b*) to what extent any amount is to be treated under this Chapter in any particular way as a result of there being, or not being, such a connection,

shall be determined as if to the extent of his appropriate share each of the partners separately, instead of the firm, stood in the position of a creditor or, as the case may be, debtor as respects the money debt.

The reference in the words following paragraph (*b*) above to partners does not include a reference to the general partner of a limited partnership which is a collective investment scheme within the meaning of section 235 of the Financial Services and Markets Act 2000.

(5B) For the purposes of subsection (5A) above, a partner's "appropriate share" is the share that would be apportioned to him if an apportionment were made in the shares in which any profit or loss computed in accordance with subsection (1) of section 114 of the Taxes Act 1988 for the accounting period in question would be apportioned between the partners under subsection (2) of that section.".

(7) Omit subsections (6) to (8) (meaning of "control", "participator" and "associate").

Meaning of "control" in section 87

8 After section 87 insert—

"87A Meaning of "control" in section 87

(1) For the purposes of section 87 above, "control", in relation to a company, means the power of a person to secure—

(*a*) by means of the holding of shares or the possession of voting power in or in relation to the company or any other company, or

(*b*) by virtue of any powers conferred by the articles of association or other document regulating the company or any other company,

that the affairs of the company are conducted in accordance with his wishes.

(2) There shall be left out of account for the purposes of this section—

(*a*) any shares held by a company, and

(b) any voting power or other powers arising from shares held by a company,

if a profit on a sale of the shares would be treated as a trading receipt of a trade carried on by the company and the shares are not, within the meaning of Chapter 1 of Part 12 of the Taxes Act 1988, assets of an insurance company's long-term insurance fund (see section 431(2) of that Act).

(3) Where section 114 of the Taxes Act 1988 (partnerships involving companies: special rules for computing profits and losses) applies in relation to a partnership, any property, rights or powers held or exercisable for the purposes of the partnership shall be treated for the purposes of this section, as respects any time in an accounting period of the partnership, as if—

(a) the property, rights or powers had been apportioned between, and were held or exercisable by, the partners severally, and

(b) the apportionment had been in the shares in which the profit or loss of the accounting period of the partnership would be apportioned between the partners under subsection (2) of that section,

but taking the references in paragraphs (a) and (b) above to partners as not including a reference to the general partner of a limited partnership which is a collective investment scheme within the meaning of section 235 of the Financial Services and Markets Act 2000.''.

Inconsistent application of accounting methods

9 Section 89 (which has become unnecessary because, in accordance with generally accepted accounting practice, a similar adjustment falls to be recognised in the profit and loss account of the company and debits or credits accordingly fall to be brought into account pursuant to section 84(1) of the Finance Act 1996 (c 8)) shall cease to have effect.

Changes of accounting method

10—(1) Section 90 is amended as follows.

(2) In subsection (1) (application of section) after ''where'' insert ''(a)'' and at the end of the subsection add—

''(b) the change or method is in pursuance of a requirement of this Chapter as to the basis of accounting to be used for the purposes of this Chapter in the case of the loan relationship; and

(c) the case does not fall within subsection (1A) below''.

(3) After subsection (1) insert—

''(1A) The case falls within this subsection if, for the purposes of the company's statutory accounts, the different authorised accounting methods mentioned in subsection (1) above are also used as respects the loan relationship for the same parts of the same accounting period or, as the case may be, for the same successive accounting periods as are mentioned in subsection (1) above.''.

Payments subject to deduction of tax

11 Section 91 shall cease to have effect.

Indexed gilt-edged securities

12—(1) Section 94 is amended as follows.

(2) After subsection (3) (adjustment of opening value by reference to movement in retail prices index between earlier time and later time) insert—

''(3A) Where the authorised accounting method applied is an accruals basis of accounting, the amount which is the opening value shall be taken to be the amount of the value which (disregarding interest) accrued to the company under the loan relationship before the earlier time.''.

(3) In subsection (6) (the percentage increase or decrease in retail prices index) after paragraph (b) insert—

''except that where the earlier time falls at the beginning of an accounting period which begins with the first day of a month, the index for the previous month shall be used for the purposes of paragraph (a) above.''.

Manufactured interest

13—(1) Section 97 is amended as follows.

(2) In subsection (1) (application of section)—

(a) for ''This section applies where—'' substitute ''For the purposes of the Corporation Tax Acts, a company has a relationship to which this section applies in any case where—'';

(b) in paragraph (a), for ''any company'' substitute ''the company'';

(c) in paragraph (b), for ''that relationship'' substitute ''that loan relationship''; and

(d) after paragraph (b), add—

''and references to a relationship to which this section applies, and to a company's being party to such a relationship, shall be construed accordingly''.

(3) For subsection (2) (treatment of the manufactured interest) substitute—

 "(2) Where a company has a relationship to which this section applies—

 (a) this Chapter shall have effect in relation to the company and the manufactured interest under the relationship—

 (i) as it would have effect if the manufactured interest were interest payable on a loan by, or (as the case may be) to, the company and were accordingly interest under a loan relationship to which the company is a party, and

 (ii) where that company is the company to which the manufactured interest is payable, as if that relationship were the one under which the real interest is payable, but

 (b) the only credits or (subject to subsection (4A) below) debits to be brought into account for the purposes of this Chapter by virtue of this section in respect of a relationship are those relating to that interest,

and, subject to paragraphs (a)(ii) and (b) above, references in the Corporation Tax Acts to a loan relationship accordingly include a reference to a relationship to which this section applies.".

(4) After subsection (3) (trading and non-trading debits and credits) insert—

 "(3A) To the extent that debits or credits fall to be brought into account by a company under section 82(2) above in the case of a relationship to which this section applies, the company shall be regarded for the purposes of this Chapter as being party to the relationship for the purposes of a trade carried on by the company.".

(5) In subsection (4) (which applies the section to a deemed manufactured payment under section 737A(5) of the Taxes Act 1988 as if such a representative payment had in fact been made) before "737A(5)" insert "736B(2) or".

(6) After subsection (4) insert—

 "(4A) Where, for the purposes of section 736B of the Taxes Act 1988, a company is the borrower under a stock lending arrangement, then (pursuant to subsection (2A) of that section (which precludes deductions or group relief for the borrower)) no debits are to be brought into account for the purposes of this Chapter by that company in respect of the deemed representative payment under that section which is treated under subsection (4) above as if it had in fact been made.".

Interpretation: "shares" not to include building society shares

14 In section 103(1) (definitions) in the definition of "share", at the end insert "but does not include a share in a building society".

Interpretation: miscellaneous

15 In section 103(1) (definitions) insert the following definitions at the appropriate place—

 " "derivative contract" has the same meaning as in Schedule 26 to the Finance Act 2002;";

 " "statutory accounts" has the meaning given by section 86(8) above".

Provision continuing to be made on accruals basis after company ceases to be party

16 At the end of section 103 (interpretation) insert—

 "(6) Where—

 (a) a company ceases to be a party to a loan relationship in an accounting period (the "cessation period"),

 (b) profits, gains or losses arise to the company from the loan relationship or a related transaction in that accounting period, and

 (c) the credits or debits brought into account for the purposes of this Chapter for that accounting period do not include credits or debits which represent the whole of those profits, gains or losses,

credits or debits in respect of so much of those profits, gains or losses as are not represented by credits or debits brought into account for the cessation period shall continue to be brought into account under this Chapter over one or more subsequent accounting periods ("post-cessation periods") as in the case of a loan relationship to which the company is a party in those periods and subsections (7) and (8) below shall apply.

 (7) In any case falling within subsection (6) above, any question—

 (a) whether, in a post-cessation period, the company is to any extent a party to the loan relationship—

 (i) for the purposes of a trade carried on by it, or

 (ii) for any other particular purpose or purposes, or

 (b) whether, in a post-cessation period, the loan relationship is to any extent referable to a particular business, or a particular class, category or description of business, carried on by the company,

shall be determined by reference to the circumstances immediately before the company ceased to be a party to the loan relationship instead of the circumstances in the post-cessation period.

(8) In any case falling within subsection (6) above, any question—

(*a*) whether the loan relationship has to any extent a particular purpose in a post-cessation period, or

(*b*) whether there is a connection between the company and any other person for a post-cessation period,

shall be determined by reference to the circumstances in the cessation period instead of the circumstances in the post-cessation period.''.

Claims to treat deficit as eligible for group relief

17 In Schedule 8 (loan relationships: claims relating to deficits) paragraph 2 (claims under section 83(2)(*b*)) shall cease to have effect.

Claim to carry back deficit to previous accounting periods

18—(1) Paragraph 3 of Schedule 8 is amended as follows.

(2) In sub-paragraph (2)(*a*)(i) (which refers to a claim under section 83(2)(*a*) or (*b*)) for ''under subsection (2)(*a*) or (*b*)'' substitute ''under subsection (2)(*a*)''.

(3) In sub-paragraph (6)(*e*) (which refers to a claim under section 83(2)(*a*) or (*b*)) for ''under section 83(2)(*a*) or (*b*)'' substitute ''under section 83(2)(*a*)''.

Deficit carried forward and set against non-trading profits of succeeding accounting periods

19—(1) Paragraph 4 of Schedule 8 (claim to carry forward deficit to next accounting period) is amended as follows.

(2) For sub-paragraph (1) (application of paragraph) substitute—

''(1) This paragraph applies where, pursuant to section 83(3A) of this Act, any of the deficit for a deficit period is to be carried forward and set against non-trading profits for succeeding accounting periods.''.

(3) In sub-paragraph (2) (treatment of amount to which the claim relates) for ''The amount to which the claim relates'' substitute ''The amount carried forward from the deficit period, reduced by any amount claimed under sub-paragraph (3) below,''.

(4) Re-number sub-paragraph (3) (definition of ''non-trading profits'') as sub-paragraph (6) and before that sub-paragraph insert—

''(3) The company may make a claim for so much of the amount carried forward from the deficit period as may be specified in the claim to be excepted from being set against non-trading profits of the accounting period immediately following the deficit period.

(4) Any claim under sub-paragraph (3) above must be made before the expiration of the period of 2 years following the end of that accounting period.

(5) So much of the amount carried forward from the deficit period as—

(*a*) cannot be relieved under sub-paragraph (2) above against non-trading profits of the accounting period immediately following the deficit period, or

(*b*) is the subject of a claim under sub-paragraph (3) above in respect of that accounting period,

shall be treated for the purposes of this Chapter as if it were an amount of non-trading deficit on the company's loan relationships for that accounting period which, pursuant to section 83(3A) of this Act, falls to be carried forward and set against non-trading profits of succeeding accounting periods (and this paragraph shall apply accordingly).''.

(5) In consequence of the amendments made by this paragraph—

(*a*) the heading to that paragraph becomes ''*Carry forward of deficit to succeeding accounting periods*''; and

(*b*) in the title of the Schedule, ''Claims'' becomes ''Claims etc''.

Distributions

20 In Schedule 9 (loan relationships: special computational provisions) in paragraph 1, at the beginning insert ''(1)'' and at the end insert—

''(2) Nothing in section 80(5) of this Act prevents an amount which, by virtue of sub-paragraph (1) above, is not brought into account for the purposes of this Chapter from being brought into account for the purposes of corporation tax apart from this Chapter.''.

Life assurance policies and capital redemption policies

21 After paragraph 1 of Schedule 9 insert—

"Life assurance policies and capital redemption policies

1A—(1) The credits and debits to be brought into account for the purposes of this Chapter shall not include any credits or debits relating to—

    (*a*) a policy of life assurance; or

    (*b*) a capital redemption policy, within the meaning of Chapter 2 of Part 13 of the Taxes Act 1988.

(2) Nothing in section 80(5) of this Act prevents an amount which, by virtue of sub-paragraph (1) above, is not brought into account for the purposes of this Chapter from being brought into account for the purposes of corporation tax apart from this Chapter.''.

Late interest: further cases where paragraph 2 of Schedule 9 applies

22—(1) Paragraph 2 of Schedule 9 is amended as follows.

(2) In sub-paragraph (1) (application of paragraph) for the words following ''company'' substitute ''(''the debtor company'') in a case falling within any of sub-paragraphs (1A) to (1D) below.''.

(3) After sub-paragraph (1) insert—

''(1A) The first case is where there is, for the relevant accounting period, a connection (within the meaning of section 87 of this Act) between the debtor company and a person standing in the position of creditor as respects the loan relationship.

(1B) The second case is where there is a time in the relevant accounting period when the debtor company is a close company and a person standing in the position of a creditor as respects the loan relationship is—

    (*a*) a participator in the debtor company,

    (*b*) the associate of a person who is such a participator at that time, or

    (*c*) a company of which such a participator has control or in which such a participator has a major interest,

and the debt is not one that is owed to, or to persons acting for, a limited partnership which is a collective investment scheme within the meaning of section 235 of the Financial Services and Markets Act 2000.

(1C) The third case is where—

    (*a*) a person standing in the position of a creditor as respects the loan relationship is a company (''the creditor company''); and

    (*b*) there is a time in the relevant accounting period when the debtor company has a major interest in the creditor company or the creditor company has a major interest in the debtor company.

(1D) The fourth case is where the loan is one made by trustees of a retirement benefits scheme (as defined in section 611 of the Taxes Act 1988) and—

    (*a*) there is a time in the relevant accounting period when the debtor company is the employer of employees to whom the scheme relates; or

    (*b*) there is for the relevant accounting period a connection, within the meaning of section 87 of this Act, between the debtor company and such an employer; or

    (*c*) a company is such an employer and there is a time in the relevant accounting period when the debtor company has a major interest in that company or that company has a major interest in the debtor company.''.

(4) After sub-paragraph (2) insert—

''(3) References in this paragraph to a person who stands in the position of a creditor as respects a loan relationship include references to a person who indirectly stands in that position by reference to a series of loan relationships or money debts which would be loan relationships if a company directly stood in the position of creditor or debtor.

(4) Where this paragraph applies in relation to a debtor relationship by virtue of sub-paragraph (3) above, the reference to the corresponding creditor relationship in sub-paragraph (2)(*b*) above is a reference to the creditor relationship of the person who indirectly stands in the position of a creditor as respects the debtor relationship.

(5) For the purposes of this section, section 414 of the Taxes Act 1988 (meaning of ''close company'' in the Tax Acts) shall have effect with the omission of subsection (1)(*a*) (exclusion of companies not resident in the United Kingdom).

(6) In this paragraph—

    ''associate'' has the meaning given by section 417(3) and (4) of the Taxes Act 1988;

    ''control'' has the same meaning as in section 87 of this Act (see section 87A);

    ''participator'', in relation to a close company, means a person who, by virtue of section 417 of the Taxes Act 1988, is a participator in the company for the purposes of Part 11 of that Act, other than a person who is a participator for those purposes by virtue only of being a loan creditor of the company;

"the relevant accounting period" means the accounting period mentioned in sub-paragraph (2)(*a*) above.

(7) Paragraph 20 below (major interests) applies for the purposes of this paragraph.".

Bad debts and consortium relief

23 In Schedule 9, after paragraph 5 (bad debt etc) insert—

"Bad debts and consortium relief

5A—(1) This paragraph applies where the conditions in sub-paragraphs (2) and (3) below are satisfied.

(2) The first condition is that by virtue of paragraph 5 above a debit is or has been brought into account for the purposes of this Chapter for any group accounting period by—

(*a*) a company ("the member company") which is a member of a consortium by which a consortium company is owned; or

(*b*) a company (a "group member") which is a member of the same group of companies as the member company but is not itself a member of the consortium.

(3) The second condition is that the debit is or was in respect of a creditor relationship of the member company or group member and—

(*a*) the consortium company, or

(*b*) if that company is a holding company, a consortium company which is a subsidiary of that company,

is or, as the case may be, was the debtor ("the debtor consortium company").

(4) Any reference in this paragraph to a "relevant creditor relationship" is a reference to a creditor relationship (whether of the member company or a group member) which falls within sub-paragraph (3) above.

(5) For the purposes of this paragraph there is for any group accounting period a "relevant net debit" in relation to the relevant creditor relationships if—

(*a*) the total of the debits brought into account for that period by virtue of paragraph 5 above in respect of those relationships by—

(i) the member company, and

(ii) every group member,

exceeds

(*b*) the total of any related debt recovery credits so brought into account by those companies for that period in respect of those relationships,

and the amount of the relevant net debit is the amount of that excess.

(6) Where there is for any group accounting period a relevant net debit in relation to the relevant creditor relationships, the amount of the relevant net debit shall be reduced by so much of any amount which—

(*a*) may be surrendered as group relief by the debtor consortium company, and

(*b*) is claimed as group relief for that accounting period by the member company or any group member,

as does not exceed the amount of the relevant net debit.

(7) Where a relevant net debit falls to be reduced under sub-paragraph (6) above by any amount ("the relevant reduction"), each of the debits brought into account in determining the relevant net debit shall be reduced by an amount found by apportioning between those debits, in proportion to their respective amounts, the amount of the relevant reduction.

(8) For the purposes of this paragraph there is for any group accounting period a "surplus of related debt recovery credits" in relation to the relevant creditor relationships if—

(*a*) the total amount of any related debt recovery credits brought into account under paragraph 5 above for the period in respect of those relationships by—

(i) the member company, and

(ii) every group member,

exceeds

(*b*) the total of the debits brought into account for that period by virtue of paragraph 5 above in respect of those relationships by those companies.

(9) Where there is for any group accounting period a surplus of related debt recovery credits in relation to the relevant creditor relationships, each of the related debt recovery credits falling to be brought into account by virtue of paragraph 5(2) above in respect of those relationships shall be reduced (but not below nil) by the appropriate amount.

For the purposes of this sub-paragraph "the appropriate amount" is the amount found by apportioning between those related debt recovery credits, in proportion to their respective amounts, the cumulative net sub-paragraph (6) reduction for earlier group accounting periods in respect of the relevant creditor relationships.

(10) In this paragraph, for any group accounting period the cumulative net sub-paragraph (6) reduction for earlier group accounting periods in respect of the relevant creditor relationships is—

    (*a*) the total amount by which the relevant net debits in respect of those relationships for any previous group accounting periods have been reduced by virtue of sub-paragraph (6) above; less

    (*b*) so much of that total amount as has been previously apportioned under sub-paragraph (9) above.

(11) Any reference in this paragraph to a "relevant claim for group relief" is a reference to a claim by the member company or a group member for group relief in respect of an amount which may be surrendered as group relief by the debtor consortium company.

(12) Any relevant claim for group relief for a group accounting period shall be reduced by so much of the cumulative net amount of relevant net debits for earlier group accounting periods in respect of the relevant creditor relationships as does not exceed the total amount of the claim.

Where there are two or more such claims for the same group accounting period which in total exceed that cumulative net amount, each of them shall be reduced by an amount found by apportioning that cumulative net amount between them in proportion to their respective amounts.

(13) In this paragraph, for any group accounting period the cumulative net amount of relevant net debits for earlier group accounting periods in respect of the relevant creditor relationships is the total amount of the relevant net debits for those earlier periods in respect of those relationships, after any reductions falling to be made under this paragraph in the amounts of those relevant net debits.

(14) If there is for any group accounting period—

    (*a*) a relevant claim for group relief (as reduced by virtue of sub-paragraph (12) above, where applicable), and

    (*b*) no relevant net debit in respect of the relevant creditor relationships,

the claim (as so reduced) shall be carried forward and treated for the purposes of sub-paragraph (12) above as increasing any relevant claim for group relief made by the claimant company for its next accounting period (or, if there is no other relevant claim for group relief made by that company for that period, as the relevant claim for group relief by that company for that period).

(15) Where—

    (*a*) the debtor consortium company has brought an amount into account by virtue of paragraph 5(3) above for an accounting period in relation to a debtor relationship, and

    (*b*) the corresponding creditor relationship is a relevant creditor relationship,

an equal amount shall be treated for the purposes of this paragraph as not being a debit brought into account for that period under paragraph 5(1) in relation to the creditor relationship.

(16) Where section 403C of the Taxes Act 1988 (amount of relief in consortium cases) applies, effect shall be given to that section before effect is given to this paragraph.

(17) In this paragraph "group accounting period" means—

    (*a*) any accounting period of the member company beginning on or after 1st October 2002, or

    (*b*) any accounting period of a group member which begins on or after that date and corresponds to such an accounting period of the member company,

and any such accounting period of the member company and any such corresponding accounting periods of one or more group members shall be regarded for the purposes of this paragraph as being the same accounting period.

(18) For the purposes of this paragraph an accounting period of a group member corresponds to an accounting period of the member company if—

    (*a*) the two accounting periods coincide;

    (*b*) the accounting period of the member company includes more than half of the accounting period of the group member; or

    (*c*) the accounting period of the member company includes part of the accounting period of the group member, but the remainder of that period does not fall within any accounting period of the member company.

(19) In this paragraph—

    "consortium claim" means a claim for group relief made by virtue of section 402(3) of the Taxes Act 1988;

    "consortium company" means a company falling within any of paragraphs (*a*) to (*c*) of section 402(3) of the Taxes Act 1988 (surrender of relief between members of consortia);

    "cumulative net amount of relevant net debits" shall be construed in accordance with sub-paragraph (13);

    "cumulative net sub-paragraph (6) reduction" shall be construed in accordance with sub-paragraph (10) above;

    "debtor consortium company" shall be construed in accordance with sub-paragraph (3) above;

"group accounting period" shall be construed in accordance with sub-paragraphs (17) and (18) above;

"group member" shall be construed in accordance with sub-paragraph (2)(*b*) above;

"group relief" has the meaning given by section 402(1) of the Taxes Act 1988;

"holding company" means a company falling within section 402(3)(*c*) of the Taxes Act 1988;

"member", in relation to a consortium, has the same meaning as in Chapter 4 of Part 10 of the Taxes Act 1988 (group relief);

"member company" shall be construed in accordance with sub-paragraph (2)(*a*) above;

"related debt recovery credit", in relation to a group accounting period, means a credit falling to be brought into account for the purposes of this Chapter for that period by the member company or a group member by virtue of paragraph 5(2) above in connection with a bad debt owed by the debtor consortium company;

"relevant claim for group relief" shall be construed in accordance with sub-paragraph (11) above;

"relevant creditor relationship" shall be construed in accordance with sub-paragraph (4) above;

"relevant net debit" shall be construed in accordance with sub-paragraph (5) above;

"subsidiary", in relation to a company which is a holding company, means a company falling within section 402(3)(*b*) of the Taxes Act 1988 by reference to that holding company;

"surplus of related debt recovery credits" shall be construed in accordance with sub-paragraph (9) above;

"surrendering company" has the meaning given by section 402(1) of the Taxes Act 1988.

(20) Any reference in this paragraph to two companies being members of the same group of companies is a reference to their being members of the same group of companies for the purposes of Chapter 4 of Part 10 of this Act (group relief).

(21) Any reference in this paragraph to a company being owned by a consortium shall be construed in accordance with section 413(6) of the Taxes Act 1988.".

Bad debt etc where parties have a connection

24—(1) Paragraph 6 of Schedule 9 is amended as follows.

(2) In sub-paragraph (2) (credits and debits to be computed subject to sub-paragraphs (3) to (6)) after "sub-paragraphs (3) to (6)" insert "and paragraphs 6A and 6B".

(3) In sub-paragraph (3) (assumption that every amount will be paid in full to be applied, subject to any departure allowed by sub-paragraph (4)) after "sub-paragraph (4)" insert "or paragraph 6A or 6B".

Bad debt etc: parties having connection and creditor company in insolvent liquidation etc

25 After paragraph 6 of Schedule 9 insert—

"*Bad debt etc parties having connection and creditor in insolvent liquidation etc*

6A—(1) This paragraph applies in any case falling within paragraph 6(1) above where—

(*a*) the company which has the creditor relationship ("the creditor company") has gone into insolvent liquidation;

(*b*) an administration order is in force in relation to that company under Part 2 of the Insolvency Act 1986 or Part 3 of the Insolvency (Northern Ireland) Order 1989;

(*c*) an appointment of a provisional liquidator is in force in relation to that company under section 135 of that Act or Article 115 of that Order; or

(*d*) under the law of a country or territory outside the United Kingdom, an event has occurred, or circumstances exist, corresponding to any of those described in paragraphs (*a*) to (*c*) above.

(2) Where this paragraph applies, a departure from the assumption that every amount payable under the relationship will be paid in full shall be allowed in relation to any amount accruing to the creditor company under the relationship—

(*a*) in a case falling within paragraph (*a*) of sub-paragraph (1) above, at a time after the commencement of the winding up;

(*b*) in a case falling within paragraph (*b*) of that sub-paragraph, at a time when the administration order is in force;

(*c*) in a case falling within paragraph (*c*) of that sub-paragraph, at a time when the appointment of the provisional liquidator is in force; or

(*d*) in a case falling within paragraph (*d*) of that sub-paragraph, at a time corresponding to that described in paragraph (*a*), (*b*) or (*c*) above (as the case may be).

(3) For the purposes of this paragraph, a company goes into insolvent liquidation if it goes into liquidation, as defined in section 247(2) of the Insolvency Act 1986 or Article 6(2) of the Insolvency (Northern Ireland) Order 1989, at a time when its assets are insufficient for the payment of its debts and other liabilities and the expenses of the winding up.".

Bad debt etc: companies becoming connected

26 After paragraph 6A of Schedule 9 insert—

"Bad debt etc: companies becoming connected

6B—(1) Where—

(*a*) paragraph 6 above applies in relation to a creditor relationship of a company (the "creditor company") in the case of an accounting period, and

(*b*) another company (the "debtor company") stands in the position of a debtor as respects the money debt,

a departure from the assumption mentioned in paragraph 6(3) above shall be allowed in accordance with sub-paragraphs (2) to (4) or (5) to (7) below.

(2) A departure from the assumption mentioned in paragraph 6(3) above shall be allowed in the case of the creditor relationship if—

(*a*) a departure has been allowed under paragraph 5(1) above in respect of the creditor relationship for a previous accounting period for which there was no connection between the creditor company and the debtor company; and

(*b*) the first accounting period of the creditor company for which there is or was such a connection is an accounting period beginning on or after 1st October 2002.

(3) A departure shall be allowed under sub-paragraph (2) above to the extent only that the debits brought into account by the creditor company for the accounting period in respect of the relationship are not more than they would have been if it were assumed that the aggregate of the amounts payable in respect of the creditor relationship were equal to the pre-connection value of the asset representing the creditor relationship.

(4) The "pre-connection value" of the asset representing the creditor relationship is the value of that asset as shown in the accounts of the creditor company at the end of the accounting period immediately preceding the accounting period mentioned in sub-paragraph (2)(*b*) above.

(5) A departure from the assumption mentioned in paragraph 6(3) above shall be allowed for the accounting period in respect of the creditor relationship, if the conditions in sub-paragraph (6) below are satisfied.

(6) The conditions are that—

(*a*) the creditor company acquired its rights under the relationship by virtue of an arm's length transaction;

(*b*) for the accounting period in which it acquired those rights, there was no connection between the creditor company and the person from whom it acquired the asset; and

(*c*) there had been no such connection between the creditor company and the debtor company at any time in the period which—

(i) begins 4 years before the date on which the company acquired those rights; and

(ii) ends twelve months before that date.

(7) A departure shall be allowed under sub-paragraph (5) above to the extent only that the debits brought into account by the creditor company for the accounting period in respect of the relationship are not more than they would have been if—

(*a*) it were assumed that the aggregate of the amounts payable in respect of the relationship were equal to the price paid by the company to acquire its rights; and

(*b*) no departure were allowed from the assumption in paragraph (*a*) above.

(8) For the purposes of this paragraph, there is a connection between a company and another person at any time if at that time—

(*a*) the other person is a company and one of the companies has control of the other, or

(*b*) the other person is a company and both companies are under the control of the same person,

and there is a connection between a company and another person for an accounting period if there is a connection (within paragraph (*a*) or (*b*) above) between the company and the person at any time in that accounting period.

(9) For the purposes of sub-paragraph (8) above "control" has the meaning given for the purposes of section 87 by section 87A of this Act.".

Bad debt etc: departure not permitted by paragraph 6: subsequent cessation of connection

27 After paragraph 6B of Schedule 9 insert—

"Bad debt etc: departure not permitted by paragraph 6: cessation of connection

6C—(1) Where, in the case of a creditor relationship of a company,—

(*a*) a departure that would otherwise have been allowed under paragraph 5(1) above in respect of an amount is or was, by virtue of paragraph 6 above, not allowed in the case of an accounting period; and (*b*) there is a subsequent accounting period for which there is, within the meaning of section 87 of this Act, no connection between the company and any person standing in the position of a debtor as respects that debt,

sub-paragraphs (2) and (3) below shall apply.

(2) Where this sub-paragraph applies, no credit shall be required to be brought into account by virtue of paragraph 5(2) above in respect of an amount—

(*a*) for the first accounting period falling within sub-paragraph (1)(*b*) above, or

(*b*) for any subsequent such accounting period,

to the extent that the amount in question corresponds to the amount mentioned in sub-paragraph (1)(*a*) above.

(3) Where this sub-paragraph applies, no debit shall be brought into account in respect of an amount—

(*a*) for the first accounting period falling within sub-paragraph (1)(*b*) above, or

(*b*) for any subsequent such accounting period,

to the extent that the amount in question represents the amount mentioned in sub-paragraph (1)(*a*) above.''.

Imported losses etc

28 In paragraph 10 of Schedule 9 at the end insert—

''(5) Amounts which, by virtue of this paragraph, are not brought into account for the purposes of this Chapter as respects any matter are in consequence also amounts which, in accordance with section 80(5) of this Act, are not to be brought into account for the purposes of corporation tax as respects that matter apart from this Chapter.''.

Continuity of treatment: groups etc

29—(1) Paragraph 12 of Schedule 9 is amended as follows.

(2) After sub-paragraph (2) insert—

''(2A) This paragraph does not apply where the transferor company uses an authorised mark to market basis of accounting as respects the loan relationship, but in any such case—

(*a*) the amount to be brought into account by the transferee company in respect of the transaction, the result of the series of transactions, or the transfer must be the fair value of the asset, or of the rights under or interest in the asset, as at the date on which the transferee company becomes party to the loan relationship; and

(*b*) paragraph (*b*) of sub-paragraph (2) above shall have effect for the purposes of section 90 of this Act (changes of accounting method).''.

Loan relationships for unallowable purposes

30 In paragraph 13 of Schedule 9, after sub-paragraph (1) insert—

''(1A) Amounts which, by virtue of this paragraph, are not brought into account for the purposes of this Chapter as respects any matter are in consequence also amounts which, in accordance with section 80(5) of this Act, are not to be brought into account for the purposes of corporation tax as respects that matter apart from this Chapter.''.

Debits and credits treated as relating to capital expenditure

31—(1) Paragraph 14 of Schedule 9 is amended as follows.

(2) In sub-paragraphs (1) and (2), for ''normal accountancy practice'', in each place where occurring, substitute ''generally accepted accounting practice''.

(3) After sub-paragraph (2) add—

''(3) No debit may be brought into account by virtue of this paragraph if it is taken into account in arriving at the amount of expenditure in relation to which a debit may be given by Schedule 29 to the Finance Act 2002 (gains and losses of a company from intangible fixed assets).''.

Repo transactions and stock lending

32—(1) Paragraph 15 is amended as follows.

(2) After sub-paragraph (4) (equivalent rights) insert—

''(4A) In consequence of sub-paragraph (1) above—

(*a*) the person transferring the rights mentioned in sub-paragraph (3)(*a*) above does not, as a result of the transfer, fall to be regarded for the purposes of this Chapter as ceasing to be party to the loan relationship; and

(*b*) the person to whom those rights are transferred does not, as a result of the transfer, fall to be regarded for the purposes of this Chapter as being party to the loan relationship;

but nothing in sub-paragraph (1) or paragraph (*b*) above shall prevent any credit in respect of interest from being brought into account for the purposes of this Chapter by the person described in that paragraph.''.

(3) After sub-paragraph (6) (which provides that the paragraph is without prejudice to section 730A(2) and (6)) insert—

"(6A) Nothing in this paragraph affects section 807A(2A) of the Taxes Act 1988 (double taxation relief in the case of repo or stock lending agreement).''.

Discounted securities where companies have a connection

33—(1) Paragraph 17 of Schedule 9 is amended as follows.

(2) In sub-paragraph (1) (accounting periods to which the paragraph applies) for paragraph (b) substitute—

"(*b*) at any time in that period another company stands in the position of a creditor as respects that security;''.

(3) In sub-paragraph (5) (meaning of "connection" between companies) in paragraph (*a*) (one of the companies has had control of the other in the accounting period or the preceding two years)—

(*a*) omit ", or in the period of two years before the beginning of that period,''; and
(*b*) after "control of" insert ", or a major interest in,''.

(4) In paragraph (*b*) of that sub-paragraph (both companies under control of same person in that period or those two years) omit ", or in those two years,''.

(5) For sub-paragraph (8) (which defines what it is for the benefit of a security to be available to a company) substitute—

"(8) Any reference in this paragraph to a person who stands in the position of a creditor as respects a relevant discounted security includes a reference to a person who indirectly stands in that position by reference to a series of relevant discounted securities.

(8A) Where this paragraph applies by virtue of sub-paragraph (8) above, the reference to the corresponding creditor relationship in sub-paragraph (1)(d) above is a reference to the creditor relationship of the company which indirectly stands in the position of a creditor as respects the relevant discounted security.''.

(6) For sub-paragraph (9) (meaning of "control") substitute—

"(9) For the purposes of this paragraph "control", in relation to a company, has the same meaning as in section 87 of this Act (see section 87A).

(10) Paragraph 20 below (major interests) applies for the purposes of this paragraph.''.

Discounted securities of close companies

34—(1) Paragraph 18 of Schedule 9 is amended as follows.

(2) In sub-paragraph (1) (accounting periods to which the paragraph applies)—

(*a*) after "any accounting period" insert "("the relevant period")'';
(*b*) in paragraph (*a*), after "a close company" insert "("the issuing company")''; and
(*c*) omit the word "and" immediately preceding paragraph (*b*).

(3) In paragraph (*b*) of that sub-paragraph, for the words preceding sub-paragraph (i) (which relate to beneficial ownership at any time in or before the accounting period in question) substitute—

"(*b*) at any time in that period there is a person who stands in the position of a creditor as respects that security and who at that time is—''.

(4) At the end of paragraph (b) of that sub-paragraph add "; and

(*c*) the debt is not one that is owed to, or to persons acting for, a limited partnership which is a collective investment scheme within the meaning of section 235 of the Financial Services and Markets Act 2000.''.

(5) After sub-paragraph (1) insert—

"(1A) But for any such accounting period this paragraph shall not apply in relation to that debtor relationship if—

(*a*) at all times in the period when there is such a person as is described in sub-paragraph (1)(*b*) above, that person is a company; and
(*b*) credits representing the full amount of the discount that is referable to the period are brought into account for the purposes of this Chapter in respect of the corresponding creditor relationship.''.

(6) For sub-paragraph (2) (debits not to be brought into account by the issuing company for any accounting period before that in which the security is redeemed) substitute—

"(2) The debits falling in the case of the issuing company to be brought into account for the purposes of this Chapter in respect of the loan relationship shall be adjusted so that every debit relating to the amount of the discount that is referable to the relevant period ("the relevant debits") is brought into account for the accounting period in which the security is redeemed, instead of for the relevant period.

This sub-paragraph does not apply where the relevant period is the accounting period in which the security is redeemed.

(2A) Where at some (but not all) times in the relevant period there is such a person as is described in sub-paragraph (1)(*b*) above—

   (*a*) part only of the relevant debits shall be brought into account in accordance with sub-paragraph (2) above; and
   (*b*) that part is the part which bears to the whole of the relevant debits the proportion which the part of the relevant period for which there is such a person bears to the whole of that period.''.

(7) After sub-paragraph (2A) insert—

''(2B) References in this paragraph to the amount of the discount that is referable to an accounting period are references to the amount relating to the difference between—

   (*a*) the issue price of the security, and
   (*b*) the amount payable on redemption,

which (apart from sub-paragraphs (2) and (2A) above) would for that accounting period be brought into account for the purposes of this Chapter in the case of the issuing company.''.

(8) After sub-paragraph (2B) insert—

''(2C) Any reference in this paragraph to a person who stands in the position of a creditor as respects a relevant discounted security includes a reference to a person who indirectly stands in that position by reference to a series of relevant discounted securities.

(2D) Where this paragraph applies by virtue of sub-paragraph (2C) above, the reference to the corresponding creditor relationship in sub-paragraph (1A)(*c*) above is a reference to the creditor relationship of the person who indirectly stands in the position of a creditor as respects the relevant discounted security.''.

(9) After sub-paragraph (3) insert—

''(3A) For the purposes of this paragraph there is a connection between one company and another for an accounting period if—

   (*a*) there is a time in that period when one of the companies has had control of the other, or
   (*b*) there is a time in that period when both the companies have been under the control of the same person.

(3B) In this paragraph ''control'', in relation to a company, has the same meaning as in section 87 of this Act (see section 87A).''.

(10) In sub-paragraph (4) (definitions) omit the definition of ''control''.

(11) In that sub-paragraph, in the definition of ''participator''—

   (*a*) after ''''participator'''' insert '', in relation to a company,''; and
   (*b*) for the words from ''by virtue only'' to the end of the definition substitute ''by reason only that he is a loan creditor of the company.''.

Partnerships involving companies

35 In Schedule 9, after paragraph 18 insert—

''*Partnerships involving companies*

19—(1) This paragraph applies where—

   (*a*) a trade, profession or business is carried on by persons in partnership (''the firm'');
   (*b*) any of those persons is a company (a ''company partner''); and
   (*c*) a money debt is owed by or to the firm.

(2) In any such case—

   (*a*) in computing the profits and losses of the trade, profession or business for the purposes of corporation tax in accordance with section 114(1) of the Taxes Act 1988 (computation as if the partnership were a company) no debits or credits shall be brought into account under this Chapter in relation to the money debt or any loan relationship that would fall to be treated for the purposes of the computation as arising from the money debt; but
   (*b*) debits and credits shall be brought into account under this Chapter in relation to the money debt (and any loan relationship treated as arising from it) in accordance with the following provisions of this paragraph by each company partner for each of its accounting periods in which the conditions in sub-paragraph (1) above are satisfied.

(3) The debits and credits to be brought into account as mentioned in sub-paragraph (2)(*b*) above shall be determined separately in the case of each company partner.

(4) For the purpose of determining those debits and credits in the case of any particular company partner—

(*a*) the money debt owed by or to the firm shall be treated as if it were instead owed by or, as the case may be, to that company partner, for the purposes of the trade, profession or business which that company partner carries on,

(*b*) the money debt shall continue to be regarded as arising from a transaction for the lending of money if that is in fact the case (so that the company partner is treated as having a loan relationship), and

(*c*) anything done by or in relation to the firm in connection with the money debt shall be treated as done by or in relation to the company partner,

and debits and credits (the "gross debits and credits") shall be determined accordingly.

(5) The debits and credits to be brought into account under this Chapter pursuant to sub-paragraph (2)(*b*) above in the case of any particular company partner shall be that company partner's appropriate share of the gross debits and credits determined in accordance with sub-paragraph (4) above in the case of that company partner.

(6) For the purposes of sub-paragraph (5) above, the "appropriate share", in the case of a company partner, is the share that would be apportioned to that company partner if—

(*a*) the gross debits and credits determined in accordance with sub-paragraph (4) above in the case of that company partner fell to be apportioned between the partners; and

(*b*) the apportionment fell to be made in the shares in which any profit or loss computed in accordance with subsection (1) of section 114 of the Taxes Act 1988 would be apportioned between them under subsection (2) of that section.

(7) If, in a case where the money debt owed by or to the firm arises from a transaction for the lending of money, there is a time in an accounting period of any company at which—

(*a*) a person who is a company partner stands in relation to the debt in the position of a creditor (if it is owed by the firm) or a debtor (if it is owed to the firm) and accordingly has a creditor relationship or debtor relationship (as the case may be),

(*b*) that company partner, whether alone or taken together with one or more other company partners connected with it, controls the partnership, and

(*c*) that or any other company partner falls to be treated in accordance with sub-paragraph (4) above as if it had the debtor relationship or creditor relationship that corresponds to the creditor relationship or debtor relationship mentioned in paragraph (*a*) above,

sub-paragraph (8) below shall apply with respect to that accounting period, if it is an accounting period of a company partner mentioned in paragraph (*a*) or (*c*) above.

(8) Where this sub-paragraph applies, there shall be taken for the purposes of this Chapter to be a connection by virtue of section 87(3)(*a*) of this Act for the accounting period of the company partner mentioned in paragraph (*a*) of sub-paragraph (7) above, between that company partner and each company partner (including that company partner) that falls within paragraph (*c*) of that sub-paragraph.

(9) For the purposes of sub-paragraph (7) above, one company partner is connected with another at any time in an accounting period if at that or any other time in the accounting period one controls the other or both are under the control of the same person.

(10) The only accounting method authorised for use by a company partner in determining the debits and credits to be brought into account under this paragraph is an authorised accruals basis of accounting, but this sub-paragraph is subject to sub-paragraph (11) below.

(11) Where the company partner uses an authorised mark to market basis of accounting in relation to its interest in the partnership, the only accounting method authorised for use in determining the debits and credits to be brought into account under this paragraph by that company partner is an authorised mark to market basis of accounting, unless a provision of this Chapter requires the use of an authorised accruals basis of accounting.

(12) Subsection (3) of section 84A of this Act does not apply in relation to a company partner as respects the debits and credits to be brought into account by virtue of this paragraph except to the extent that, in the accounts of the firm, exchange gains and losses are carried to or sustained by a reserve in a manner corresponding to that described in that section in relation to a company.

(13) Where the firm holds a relevant discounted security, within the meaning of paragraph 17 above, each of the partners shall be treated for the purposes of this paragraph as beneficially entitled to that share of the security to which he would be entitled if all the partners were companies and such an apportionment as is described in sub-paragraph (6)(*b*) above were made.

(14) In this paragraph "control"—

(*a*) in relation to a company, has the same meaning as in section 87 of this Act (see section 87A); and

(*b*) in relation to a partnership, has the meaning given by section 840 of the Taxes Act 1988.".

Interpretation of Schedule 9: "major interest"

36 In Schedule 9, after paragraph 19 insert—

"Interpretation of references to major interests

20—(1) For the purposes of any provision which applies this paragraph, the cases where a company ("company A") has a major interest in another company ("company B") at any time are those cases where at that time—

> (*a*) company A and one other person, taken together, have control of company B; and
>
> (*b*) company A and the other person each have interests, rights and powers representing at least 40 per cent of the holdings, rights and powers in respect of which company A and the other person fall to be taken as having control of company B; and
>
> (*c*) company A, or a company connected with it, and the other person, or, if that person is a company, a company connected with it, both satisfy the first condition, or both satisfy the second condition, in sub-paragraph (2) below.

(2) A person—

> (*a*) satisfies the first condition if he stands in the position of a creditor in relation to a loan relationship as respects which company B stands in the position of a debtor; and
>
> (*b*) satisfies the second condition if he stands in the position of a debtor in relation to a loan relationship as respects which company B stands in the position of a creditor.

(3) The reference in sub-paragraph (1)(*b*) above to interests, rights and powers does not include interests, rights or powers arising from shares held by a company if—

> (*a*) a profit on a sale of the shares would be treated as a trading receipt of a trade carried on by the company; and
>
> (*b*) the shares are not, within the meaning of Chapter 1 of Part 12 of the Taxes Act 1988, assets of an insurance company's long-term insurance fund (see section 431(2) of that Act).

(4) For the purposes of sub-paragraph (1) above, any question—

> (*a*) whether two persons taken together have control of a company at any time, or
>
> (*b*) whether a person has at any time interests, rights and powers representing at least 40 per cent of the holdings, rights and powers in respect of a company,

shall be determined after attributing to any person which is a company all the interests, rights and powers of any company connected with it.

(5) Where section 114 of the Taxes Act 1988 (partnerships involving companies: special rules for computing profits and losses) applies in relation to a partnership, any property, rights or powers held or exercisable for the purposes of the partnership shall be treated for the purposes of this paragraph, as respects any time in an accounting period of the partnership, as if—

> (*a*) the property, rights or powers had been apportioned between, and were held or exercisable by, the partners severally, and
>
> (*b*) the apportionment had been in the shares in which the profit or loss of the accounting period of the partnership would be apportioned between the partners under subsection (2) of that section,

but taking the references in paragraphs (*a*) and (*b*) above to partners as not including a reference to the general partner of a limited partnership which is a collective investment scheme within the meaning of section 235 of the Financial Services and Markets Act 2000.

(6) Where a trade, profession or business is carried on by two or more persons in partnership ("the firm") and the firm stands in the position of a creditor or debtor as respects a money debt, any question—

> (*a*) whether a company has a major interest (within the meaning of this paragraph) in another company for an accounting period in the case of a loan relationship, or
>
> (*b*) to what extent any amount is to be treated under this Chapter in any particular way as a result of a company having, or (as the case may be) not having, such a major interest in another company,

shall be determined as if to the extent of his appropriate share each of the partners separately, instead of the firm, stood in the position of a creditor or, as the case may be, debtor as respects the money debt.

The reference in the words following paragraph (*b*) above to partners does not include a reference to the general partner of a limited partnership which is a collective investment scheme within the meaning of section 235 of the Financial Services and Markets Act 2000.

(7) For the purposes of sub-paragraph (6) above, a partner's "appropriate share" is the share that would be apportioned to him if an apportionment were made in the shares in which any profit or loss computed in accordance with subsection (1) of section 114 of the Taxes Act 1988 for the accounting period in question would be apportioned between the partners under subsection (2) of that section.

(8) For the purposes of this paragraph, a company is connected with another company if one controls the other or both are controlled by the same company.

(9) For the purposes of this paragraph, "control", in relation to a company, has the same meaning as in section 87 of this Act (see section 87A).

(10) Where two or more persons taken together have the power mentioned in subsection (1) of section 87A of this Act (as read with the other provisions of that section) they shall be taken for the purposes of sub-paragraph (1)(*a*) above to have control of the company in question.''.

Investment trusts and venture capital trusts: treatment of capital reserves

37—(1) Schedule 10 (collective investment schemes) is amended as follows.

(2) For paragraph 1 substitute—

''Investment trusts and venture capital trusts: capital reserves

1A—(1) Where any profits, gains or losses arising to an investment trust from a creditor relationship for an accounting period are carried to or sustained by a capital reserve in accordance with the Statement of Recommended Practice used for that accounting period, those profits, gains or losses must not be brought into account as credits or debits for the purposes of this Chapter, notwithstanding section 84(2)(*b*) of this Act.

(2) Where any profits, gains or losses arising to a venture capital trust from a creditor relationship for an accounting period—

    (*a*) are carried to or sustained by a capital reserve in accordance with the Statement of Recommended Practice used for the accounting period as if the venture capital trust were an investment trust, or

    (*b*) would be carried to or sustained by a capital reserve if the venture capital trust were an investment trust and were using that Statement of Recommended Practice,

those profits, gains or losses must not be brought into account as credits or debits for the purposes of this Chapter, notwithstanding section 84(2)(*b*) of this Act.

(3) For the purposes of this paragraph, the Statement of Recommended Practice used for an accounting period is—

    (*a*) in relation to an accounting period for which it is permitted to be used, the Statement of Recommended Practice relating to Investment Trust Companies, issued by the Association of Investment Trust Companies in December 1995, as from time to time modified, amended or revised, or

    (*b*) in relation to any accounting period for which it is permitted to be used, any subsequent Statement of Recommended Practice relating to investment trusts, as from time to time modified, amended or revised.''.

Authorised unit trusts and open-ended investment companies

38—(1) Schedule 10 (collective investment schemes) is amended as follows.

(2) For paragraph 2 (which makes special provision in relation to authorised unit trusts and is applied to open-ended investment companies by regulations under section 152 of the Finance Act 1995 (c 4)) and the heading immediately preceding it substitute—

''Authorised unit trusts

''**2A**—(1) Where any profits, gains or losses arising to an authorised unit trust from a creditor relationship in an accounting period are capital profits, gains or losses, those profits, gains or losses must not be brought into account as credits or debits for the purposes of this Chapter, notwithstanding section 84(2)(*b*) of this Act.

(2) For the purposes of this paragraph, capital profits, gains or losses arising from a creditor relationship in an accounting period are such profits, gains or losses arising from a creditor relationship as fall to be dealt with under—

    (*a*) the heading ''net gains/losses on investments during the period'', or

    (*b*) the heading ''other gains/losses'',

in the statement of total return for the accounting period.

(3) For the purposes of sub-paragraph (2) above, the statement of total return for an accounting period is the statement of total return which, in accordance with the Statement of Recommended Practice used for the accounting period, must be included in the accounts contained in the annual report of the authorised unit trust which deals with the accounting period.

(4) For the purposes of sub-paragraph (3) above, ''Statement of Recommended Practice'' means—

    (*a*) in relation to any accounting period for which it is required or permitted to be used, the Statement of Recommended Practice relating to Authorised Unit Trust Schemes issued by the Investment Management Regulatory Organisation Limited in January 1997, as from time to time modified, amended or revised; or

    (*b*) in relation to any accounting period for which it is required or permitted to be used, any subsequent Statement of Recommended Practice relating to authorised unit trust schemes, as from time to time modified, amended or revised.

(5) The Treasury may by order amend this paragraph so as to alter the definition of capital profits, gains or losses in consequence of the modification, amendment, revision or replacement of a Statement of Recommended Practice.

(6) The power to make an order under this paragraph includes power—

    (*a*) to make different provision for different cases; and

    (*b*) to make such consequential, supplementary, incidental or transitional provision, or savings, as appear to the Treasury to be necessary or expedient (including provision amending any enactment or any instrument made under any enactment).

Open-ended investment companies

2B—(1) Where any profits, gains or losses arising to an open-ended investment company from a creditor relationship in an accounting period are capital profits, gains or losses, those profits, gains or losses must not be brought into account as credits or debits for the purposes of this Chapter, notwithstanding section 84(2)(*b*) of this Act.

(2) For the purposes of this paragraph, capital profits, gains or losses arising from a creditor relationship in an accounting period are such profits, gains or losses arising from a creditor relationship as fall to be dealt with under—

    (*a*) the heading "net gains/losses on investments during the period", or

    (*b*) the heading "other gains/losses",

in the statement of total return for the accounting period.

(3) For the purposes of sub-paragraph (2) above, the statement of total return for an accounting period is the statement of total return which, in accordance with the Statement of Recommended Practice used for the accounting period, must be included in the accounts contained in the annual report of the open-ended investment company which deals with the accounting period.

(4) For the purposes of sub-paragraph (3) above, "Statement of Recommended Practice" means—

    (*a*) in relation to any accounting period for which it is required or permitted to be used, the Statement of Recommended Practice relating to Open-Ended Investment Companies issued by the Financial Services Authority in November 2000, as from time to time modified, amended or revised; or

    (*b*) in relation to any accounting period for which it is required or permitted to be used, any subsequent Statement of Recommended Practice relating to open-ended investment companies, as from time to time modified, amended or revised.

(5) The Treasury may by order amend this paragraph so as to alter the definition of capital profits, gains or losses in consequence of the modification, amendment, revision or replacement of a Statement of Recommended Practice.

(6) The power to make an order under this paragraph includes power—

    (*a*) to make different provision for different cases; and

    (*b*) to make such consequential, supplementary, incidental or transitional provision, or savings, as appear to the Treasury to be necessary or expedient (including provision amending any enactment or any instrument made under any enactment).".

Distributing offshore funds

39 For paragraph 3 of that Schedule substitute—

"**3**—(1) For the purposes of paragraph 5(1) of Schedule 27 to the Taxes Act 1988 (computation of UK equivalent profit), the assumptions to be made in determining what, for any period, would be the total profits of an offshore fund are to include the assumptions in sub-paragraphs (2) and (3) below.

(2) The first assumption is that the provisions of this Chapter so far as they relate to the creditor relationships of a company do not apply for the purposes of corporation tax in computing the profits or loss of an offshore fund.

(3) The second assumption is that for the purposes of corporation tax the profits and gains, and losses, that are to be taken to arise from the creditor relationships of an offshore fund are to be computed—

    (*a*) in accordance with the provisions applicable, in the case of unauthorised unit trusts, for the purposes of income tax; and

    (*b*) as if the provisions so applicable had effect in relation to an accounting period of an offshore fund as they have effect, in the case of unauthorised unit trusts, in relation to a year of assessment.

(4) In this paragraph "unauthorised unit trust" means the trustees of any unit trust scheme which is not an authorised unit trust but is a unit trust scheme for the purposes of section 469 of the Taxes Act 1988.".

Life assurance business

40—(1) In Schedule 11 (loan relationships: special provisions for insurers) Part 1 (insurance companies) is amended as follows.

(2) In paragraph 1 (I minus E basis) after sub-paragraph (1) (which provides that nothing in the Chapter prevents profits and gains from loan relationships of insurance companies referable to life assurance business from being included in profits and gains chargeable in accordance with the I minus E basis) insert—

"(1A) Where—

(a) the I minus E basis is applied for any accounting period in respect of any life assurance business carried on by an insurance company, and

(b) in that accounting period the insurance company is a party to a loan relationship which is to any extent referable to that business,

then, in applying the I minus E basis to that business, sections 92(1)(*f*), 93(1)(*a*) and (*b*) and 96(1)(b) of this Act shall be disregarded in relation to that loan relationship to that extent.".

Adjustments in the case of chargeable assets etc

41—(1) In Schedule 15 (loan relationships: savings and transitional provisions) paragraph 11 is amended as follows.

(2) After sub-paragraph (2) insert—

"(2A) If, in a case where the continuing loan relationship is a creditor relationship,—

(a) the company acquired its rights under the relationship on or before 31st March 1996 by virtue of an arm's length transaction,

(b) for the accounting period in which it acquired those rights—

(i) there was no connection (as defined in sub-paragraph (2C) below) between the company and the person from whom the company acquired the asset, but

(ii) there was such a connection between the company and a company standing in the position of a debtor as respects the money debt, and

(c) there had been no such connection between the companies mentioned in paragraph (*b*)(ii) above at any time in the period which—

(i) begins 4 years before the date on which the company acquired those rights, and

(ii) ends twelve months before that date,

this paragraph shall have effect as if the amount mentioned in sub-paragraph (2)(*b*) above were an amount equal to the greater of the amounts mentioned in sub-paragraph (2B) below.

(2B) Those amounts are—

(a) the fair value of the rights at the time when the company ceases to be a party to the loan relationship; and

(b) the fair value of the rights on 1st April 1996.

(2C) For the purposes of sub-paragraph (2A) above there is a connection between a company and another person at any time if at that time—

(a) the other person is a company and one of the companies has control of the other,

(b) the other person is a company and both companies are under the control of the same person, or

(c) the company is a close company and the other person is a participator in that company or the associate of a person who is such a participator,

and there is a connection between a company and another person for an accounting period if there is a connection (within paragraphs (*a*) to (*c*) above) between the company and the person at any time in that accounting period.

(2D) For the purposes of sub-paragraph (2C) above—

(a) subsections (2) to (6) of section 416 of the Taxes Act 1988 (meaning of control) shall apply as they apply for the purposes of Part 11 of that Act;

(b) subject to paragraph (*c*) below, "participator" and "associate" have the meaning given for the purposes of that Part by section 417 of that Act;

(c) a person shall not be regarded as a participator in relation to a company by reason only that he is a loan creditor of the company.".

Reduction of paragraph 11 credit where s.251(4) of 1992 Act prevents paragraph 8 loss

42 In Schedule 15, after paragraph 11 (other adjustments in the case of chargeable assets etc) insert—

"Reduction of para. 11 credit where s.251(4) of 1992 Act prevents para. 8 loss

11A—(1) This paragraph applies where, in the case of any asset representing in whole or in part a loan relationship of a company, an amount representing a deemed allowable loss would (apart from this paragraph) fall or have fallen to be brought into account in accordance with paragraph

8(3) above for an accounting period (whenever beginning or ending), but for section 251(4) of the 1992 Act (no allowable loss on disposal of debt acquired from connected person).

(2) Where this paragraph applies, the amount of any credit falling within sub-paragraph (3) below shall be treated for the purposes of this Chapter as reduced (but not below nil) by the amount described in sub-paragraph (1) above.

(3) A credit falls within this sub-paragraph if (apart from this paragraph)—

    (*a*) the credit falls to be given by virtue of paragraph 11(3)(*a*) above for an accounting period beginning on or after 1st October 2002; and

    (*b*) the loan relationship mentioned in paragraph 11(1)(*a*) above in the case of the credit is the same loan relationship as the one mentioned in sub-paragraph (1) above.''.

PART 2

AMENDMENTS OF OTHER ENACTMENTS

The Taxes Act 1988

Introductory

43 The Taxes Act 1988 is amended as follows.

Incidental costs of obtaining loan finance

44 In section 77(2)(*a*) (meaning of ''qualifying loan'' etc) omit sub-paragraph (ii) (interest deductible under section 338 against total profits).

Group relief

45 In section 403ZC (amounts eligible for group relief: non-trading deficit on loan relationships) omit subsection (2) (which refers to a claim under section 83(2) of the Finance Act 1996 (c 8)).

Apportionment of income and gains

46—(1) Section 432A is amended as follows.

(2) In subsection (9A)(*a*) (meaning of ''net value'') for ''money debt'' substitute ''loan relationship''.

(3) In subsection (9B) (definitions)—

    (*a*) in paragraph (*b*) of the definition of ''investment reserve'' for ''money debt'' substitute ''loan relationship''; and

    (*b*) omit the definition of ''money debt''.

Building society shares: regulations for deduction of tax

47—(1) Section 477A(3) (where regulations apply for any year of assessment, dividends or interest to be dealt with for the purposes of corporation tax as there described) is amended as follows.

(2) In paragraph (*a*) (liability to pay to be treated as a liability arising under a loan relationship) at the beginning insert ''to the extent that it would not otherwise fall to be so regarded,''.

(3) In paragraph (*aa*) (dividends or interest payable to company to be treated as payable in pursuance of right under loan relationship) after ''payable to a company,'' insert ''then, to the extent that they would not otherwise fall to be so regarded,''.

Building society shares: incidental costs of issuing qualifying shares

48 In section 477B, after subsection (1) (which allows deduction of such costs) insert—

''(1A) A deduction shall not be allowed by virtue of subsection (1) above to the extent that the costs in question fall to be brought into account as debits for the purposes of Chapter 2 of Part 4 of the Finance Act 1996 (loan relationships).''.

European Economic Interest Groupings

49—(1) Section 510A is amended as follows.

(2) In paragraph (*b*) of subsection (3) (charging tax in respect of gains) for ''gains'' substitute ''chargeable gains''.

(3) After that paragraph add

    '';

but paragraph (*a*) above is subject to subsection (6A) below.''.

(4) After subsection (6) (trade or profession carried on by grouping treated for tax on income and gains as carried on by a partnership) insert—

"(6A) Chapter 2 of Part 4 of the Finance Act 1996 (loan relationships) shall have effect in relation to a grouping as it has effect in relation to a partnership (see in particular section 87A of, and paragraphs 19 and 20 of Schedule 9 to, that Act).".

Funding bonds issued in respect of interest on certain debts

50 In section 582, after subsection (3) insert—

"(3A) Chapter 2 of Part 4 of the Finance Act 1996 has effect subject to and in accordance with this section, notwithstanding anything in section 80(5) of that Act (matters to be brought into account in the case of loan relationships only under Chapter 2 of Part 4 of that Act).".

Transfers of income arising from securities

51 In section 730, after subsection (2) insert—

"(2A) This section does not have effect for the purposes of Chapter 2 of Part 4 of the Finance Act 1996 (loan relationships).".

Treatment of price differential on sale and repurchase of securities

52—(1) Section 730A is amended as follows.

(2) After subsection (5) insert—

"(5A) For the purposes of the Corporation Tax Acts, a company has a relationship to which this section applies in any case where—

(*a*) the circumstances are as set out in subsection (1) above; and
(*b*) interest on a deemed loan is deemed by virtue of subsection (2) above to be paid by or to the company;

and references to a relationship to which this section applies, and to a company's being party to such a relationship, shall be construed accordingly.".

(3) For subsection (6) (application of Chapter 2 of Part 4 of the Finance Act 1996 (c 8) in relation to deemed interest) substitute—

"(6) Where a company has a relationship to which this section applies—

(*a*) Chapter 2 of Part 4 of the Finance Act 1996 (loan relationships) shall, as respects that company, have effect in relation to the interest deemed by virtue of subsection (2) above to be paid or received by the company under that relationship as it would have effect if it were interest under a loan relationship to which the company is a party,
(*b*) the debits and credits falling to be brought into account for the purposes of that Chapter so far as they relate to the deemed interest shall be those given by the use in relation to the deemed interest of an authorised accruals basis of accounting, and
(*c*) the only debits or credits to be brought into account for the purposes of that Chapter by virtue of this subsection in respect of a relationship are those relating to that deemed interest,

and, subject to paragraphs (*b*) and (*c*) above, references in the Corporation Tax Acts to a loan relationship accordingly include a reference to a relationship to which this section applies.".

(4) After subsection (6A) (trading or non-trading debits or credits) insert—

"(6B) To the extent that debits or credits fall to be brought into account by a company under section 82(2) above in the case of a relationship to which this section applies, the company shall be regarded for the purposes of Chapter 2 of Part 4 of the Finance Act 1996 as being party to the relationship for the purposes of a trade carried on by the company.".

Restriction of relief for payments of interest

53—(1) Section 787 is amended as follows.

(2) After subsection (1) insert—

"(1A) This section has effect in relation to Chapter 2 of Part 4 of the Finance Act 1996 (loan relationships) but taking the reference in subsection (1) above to giving relief to any person in respect of any payment of interest as including a reference to the bringing into account by any person in accordance with that Chapter of any debit in respect of interest (whether a payment or not); and other references in this section to relief shall be construed accordingly.".

(3) For subsection (3) (determination of question as to benefit that might be expected to accrue in a case where the relief is claimed by virtue of section 83(2)(*b*) of the Finance Act 1996 (c 8)) substitute—

"(3) Where the relief is claimed by virtue of section 403—

(*a*) in respect of a deficit to which section 83 of the Finance Act 1996 applies (non-trading deficit on loan relationships), or
(*b*) in respect of trading losses, in a case where in computing those losses debits in respect of loan relationships are treated under section 82(2)(*b*) of that Act as expenses of the trade which are deductible in computing the profits of the trade,

any question under this section as to what benefit might be expected to accrue from the transaction in question shall be determined by reference to the claimant company and the surrendering company taken together.''.

Limits on credit: corporation tax

54 In section 797, in subsection (3B) (amounts that must be allocated to trading profits) in paragraph (*b*) (claims under section 83(2)(*d*) of the Finance Act 1996) for ''a claim under subsection (2)(*d*) of'' substitute ''subsection (3A) of''.

Foreign tax on items giving rise to a non-trading credit

55—(1) Section 797A is amended as follows.

(2) In subsection (5) (which specifies certain amounts under section 83 of the Finance Act 1996 which are to be aggregated for the purposes of subsection (4))—

    (*a*) in paragraph (*a*)—

        (i) for ''(2)(*b*), (*c*) or (*d*)'' substitute ''(2)(*c*)''; and

        (ii) for the words from ''(group relief'' to ''deficits)'' substitute ''(deficit carried back and set against profits)'';

    (*b*) after paragraph (*a*) insert—

        ''(*aa*) so much of any non-trading deficit for that period as is surrendered as group relief by virtue of section 403 of the Taxes Act 1988; and''; and

    (*c*) in paragraph (*b*), for ''(3)'' substitute ''(3A)''.

(3) In subsection (6), for ''in pursuance of a claim under section 83(2)(*d*)'' substitute ''under section 83(3A)''.

Investment trusts

56—(1) Section 842 is amended as follows.

(2) In paragraph (*a*) of subsection (1) (income must be wholly or mainly eligible investment income)—

    (*a*) after ''the company's income'' insert ''(as determined in accordance with subsection (1AB) below)''; and

    (*b*) after ''eligible investment income'' insert ''(as so determined)''.

(3) In paragraph (*e*) of subsection (1) (company must not retain more than 15% of eligible investment income)—

    (*a*) for ''more than'' substitute ''an amount which is greater than''; and

    (*b*) after ''eligible investment income'' insert ''(determined in accordance with subsection (1AB) below)''.

(4) After subsection (1AA) insert—

    ''(1AB) In determining for the purposes of paragraph (*a*) or (*e*) of subsection (1) above (and accordingly of subsection (2A)(*b*) below)—

        (*a*) the amount of a company's income, or

        (*b*) the amount of income which a company derives from shares or securities,

    the amounts to be brought into account under Chapter 2 of Part 4 of the Finance Act 1996 in respect of the company's loan relationships shall be determined without reference to any debtor relationships of the company.''.

Venture capital trusts

57—(1) Section 842AA is amended as follows.

(2) In paragraph (*f*) of subsection (2) (company must not retain more than 15% of income derived from shares or securities) for ''more than'' substitute ''an amount which is greater than''.

(3) In section 842AA(11) (which applies provisions of section 842 to provisions of section 842AA)—

    (*a*) before paragraph (*a*) insert the following paragraph—

        ''(*za*) subsection (1AB) of that section shall apply in relation to subsection (2)(*a*) above as it applies in relation to subsection (1)(*a*) of that section;''; and

    (*b*) in paragraph (*b*) (which applies subsections (2A) to (2C) of section 842 to subsection (2)(*f*) of section 842AA) after ''subsections'' insert ''(1AB) and''.

Change in ownership of investment company

58—(1) Schedule 28A is amended as follows.

(2) In paragraph 6(*dc*) (amounts in issue for the purposes of section 768B: non-trading deficit carried forward under section 83(3) of the Finance Act 1996 (c 8)) for ''83(3)'' substitute ''83(3A)''.

(3) In paragraph 7(1)(*d*) (apportionment for section 768B in case of debits falling to be brought into account otherwise than on the assumption that interest does not accrue until paid) omit "and" immediately preceding sub-paragraph (iii) and at the end of that sub-paragraph insert

> ", and
>
>> "(iv) so falls to be brought into account without any adjustment under paragraph 17 or 18 of that Schedule (debit relating to amount of discount referable to the relevant accounting period to be brought into account instead for the accounting period in which the security is redeemed),".

(4) In paragraph 7(1)(*e*) (apportionment for section 768B in case of debits falling to be brought into account on the assumption that interest does not accrue until paid) omit "and" immediately preceding sub-paragraph (iii) and at the end of that sub-paragraph insert

> ", and
>
>> (iv) so falls to be brought into account with such an adjustment as is mentioned in paragraph (*d*)(iv) above,".

(5) Omit paragraph 7(2) (which relates to charges consisting of interest and which accordingly has no further application).

(6) In paragraph 11(1) (debits that fall within paragraph 11)—

> (*a*) for the word "and" immediately preceding paragraph (*c*) substitute the following paragraph—
>
>> "(*bb*) so falls to be brought into account with an adjustment under paragraph 17 or 18 of that Schedule (debit relating to amount of discount referable to the relevant accounting period to be brought into account instead for the accounting period in which the security is redeemed); and"; and
>
> (*b*) in paragraph (*c*) (accounting period in which the debit would have been brought into account, apart from the sub-paragraph mentioned in paragraph (*b*)) for "apart from the sub-paragraph" substitute "apart from paragraphs 2(2), 17 and 18 of that Schedule,".

(7) In paragraph 13(1)(*ec*) (amounts in issue for the purposes of section 768C: non-trading deficit carried forward under section 83(3) of the Finance Act 1996 (c 8)) for "83(3)" substitute "83(3A)".

(8) In paragraph 16(1)(*d*) (manner of apportionment in case of debits falling to be brought into account otherwise than on the assumption that interest does not accrue until paid) omit "and" immediately preceding sub-paragraph (iii) and at the end of that sub-paragraph insert

> ", and
>
>> (iv) so falls to be brought into account without any adjustment under paragraph 17 or 18 of that Schedule (debit relating to amount of discount referable to the relevant accounting period to be brought into account instead for the accounting period in which the security is redeemed),".

(9) In paragraph 16(1)(*e*) (manner of apportionment in case of debits falling to be brought into account on the assumption that interest does not accrue until paid) omit "and" immediately preceding sub-paragraph (iii) and at the end of that sub-paragraph insert

> ", and
>
>> (iv) so falls to be brought into account with such an adjustment as is mentioned in paragraph (*d*)(iv) above,".

(10) Omit paragraph 16(2) (which relates to charges consisting of interest and which accordingly has no further application).

The Finance Act 1988

Commercial woodlands

59—(1) Schedule 6 to the Finance Act 1988 (c 39) is amended as follows.

(2) In consequence of Chapter 2 of Part 4 of the Finance Act 1996 (c 8) (loan relationships) in paragraph 3 (abolition of Schedule D election etc) omit—

> (*a*) sub-paragraphs (3)(*a*), (4)(*a*) and (5)(*a*) and (*b*);
> (*b*) in sub-paragraph (5), in the words following paragraph (*c*), the word "group"; and
> (*c*) sub-paragraph (6).".

The Taxation of Chargeable Gains Act 1992

Interest charged to capital

60—(1) Section 40 of the Taxation of Chargeable Gains Act 1992 (c 12) is amended as follows.

(2) After subsection (3) add—

> "(4) In consequence of Chapter 2 of Part 4 of the Finance Act 1996 (loan relationships) this section does not have effect in relation to interest referable to an accounting period ending on or after 1st April 1996.".

PART 3
TRANSITIONAL PROVISIONS
Interpretation

61 In this Part of this Schedule—

"new accounting period" means an accounting period beginning on or after 1st October 2002;

"old accounting period" means an accounting period beginning before 1st October 2002.

Discounted securities where companies have a connection

62 Where—

(a) in consequence of the amendments made by paragraph 33 above, the condition in sub-paragraph (1)(c) of paragraph 17 of Schedule 9 to the Finance Act 1996 (connection between issuing company and other company) is satisfied as respects a new accounting period of the issuing company, but

(b) that condition would not have been satisfied had the accounting period been an old accounting period, and

(c) the debtor relationship in question is a debtor relationship of the issuing company on the first day of its first new accounting period,

that paragraph shall not have effect in relation to that debtor relationship.

Discounted securities of close companies

63—(1) This paragraph applies in any case where—

(a) by virtue of paragraph 18 of Schedule 9 to the Finance Act 1996 (c 8) an amount ("the deferred amount") is not brought into account by a company for the purposes of Chapter 2 of Part 4 of that Act in respect of a debtor relationship for an old accounting period; and

(b) the relevant discounted security concerned has not been redeemed before the beginning of the company's first new accounting period.

(2) As regards any new accounting period, paragraph 18(2) of that Schedule shall be taken to have had effect in relation to the old accounting period as if, instead of preventing the bringing of amounts into account for any accounting period before that in which the security is redeemed, it had provided for the deferred amount to be brought into account for the accounting period in which the security is redeemed instead of for the old accounting period.

Authorised unit trusts and open-ended investment companies

64—(1) Where—

(a) an amount of interest under a creditor relationship of an authorised unit trust or open-ended investment company is paid to the trust or company,

(b) the amount paid is not interest which, in the case of the trust or company, was brought into account for the purposes of corporation tax for an old accounting period,

(c) the amount paid is not interest in relation to which any credit falls (apart from under this sub-paragraph) to be brought into account for the purposes of Chapter 2 of Part 4 of the Finance Act 1996 (loan relationships) in the case of the trust or company, and

(d) the amount paid is not an amount of interest which, in relation to a transfer before the first new day, was unrealised interest within the meaning of section 716 of the Taxes Act 1988,

credits shall be brought into account for the purposes of Chapter 2 of Part 4 of the Finance Act 1996 in the case of the trust or company as if the amount paid were interest accruing, and becoming due and payable, at the time when it is paid.

(2) Where, apart from Chapter 2 of Part 4 of the Finance Act 1996, any authorised unit trust or open-ended investment company would be treated under subsection (2) or (4) of section 714 of the Taxes Act 1988 (treatment of deemed sums and reliefs under accrued income scheme)—

(a) as receiving any amount at the end of a period beginning before, and ending during, the trust or company's first new accounting period, or

(b) as entitled to any allowance or any amount in such a period,

that amount shall be brought into account as a non-trading credit or, as the case may be, a non-trading debit given for the purposes of Chapter 2 of Part 4 of the Finance Act 1996 for the trust or company's first new accounting period.

(3) Where—

(a) an authorised unit trust or open-ended investment company holds a relevant discounted security on the last old day,

(b) the security was not transferred or redeemed on that day, and

(c) there is an amount which, if the trust or company had made a transfer of that security on that day, by selling it for its adjusted closing value,—

(i) would have been charged under paragraph 1 of Schedule 13 to the Finance Act 1996 (c 8) to tax under Case III or IV of Schedule D, or

(ii) would have been eligible for relief from tax on a claim for the purposes of paragraph 2 of that Schedule,

that amount shall be brought into account as a non-trading credit, or (as the case may be) a non-trading debit, given for the purposes of Chapter 2 of Part 4 of that Act for the accounting period mentioned in sub-paragraph (4) below.

(4) That period is the accounting period in which falls whichever is the earliest of the following, that is to say,—

(a) the first day that falls after the last old day and is a day on which, under the terms on which the security was issued, the holder of the security is entitled to require it to be redeemed;

(b) the day on which the security is redeemed; or

(c) the day on which the trust or company makes a disposal of the security.

(5) For the purposes of sub-paragraph (3)(c), the "adjusted closing value" of a relevant discounted security held by the trust or company on the last old day is the amount which for the purposes of Chapter 2 of Part 4 of the Finance Act 1996 is the opening value, as at the first new day, of the trust or company's rights and liabilities under the relationship represented by that security.

(6) Sub-paragraph (7) of paragraph 5 of Schedule 15 to the Finance Act 1996 (determination of opening value where accruals basis of accounting is used) applies for the purposes of sub-paragraph (5) as it applies for the purposes of that paragraph, but—

(a) taking the reference to 1st April 1996 as a reference to the first new day; and

(b) applying paragraph 4 of that Schedule (determination of amounts treated as accruing on or after 1st April 1996) for these purposes with the same modification.

(7) In sub-paragraphs (3) to (6)—

"redeem" shall be construed in accordance with Schedule 13 to the Finance Act 1996 (discounted securities: income tax provisions);

"relevant discounted security" has the same meaning as in that Schedule;

"transfer" has the same meaning as in that Schedule.

(8) In this paragraph—

"creditor relationship" has the same meaning as in Chapter 2 of Part 4 of the Finance Act 1996;

"the first new day" means the first day of the trust or company's first new accounting period;

"the last old day" means the last day of the trust or company's last old accounting period;

"the trust or company" means the authorised unit trust or open-ended investment company in question.

SCHEDULE 26

DERIVATIVE CONTRACTS

Section 83

Commentary—*Simon's Direct Tax Service* **D2.1010.**

PART 1

INTRODUCTION

Profits arising from derivative contracts

1—(1) For the purposes of corporation tax all profits arising to a company from its derivative contracts shall be chargeable to tax as income in accordance with this Schedule.

(2) Except where otherwise indicated, the amounts to be brought into account in accordance with this Schedule in respect of any matter are the only amounts to be brought into account for the purposes of corporation tax in respect of that matter.

PART 2

DERIVATIVE CONTRACTS

Derivative contracts and relevant contracts

2—(1) For the purposes of the Corporation Tax Acts a company's derivative contracts are those of its relevant contracts which satisfy the following provisions of this Schedule.

(2) For the purposes of this Schedule a "relevant contract" is—

(a) an option,

(b) a future, or

(c) a contract for differences.

Contracts to satisfy accounting requirements etc

3—(1) A relevant contract is not a derivative contract for the purposes of this Schedule for any accounting period unless—

    (a) it is treated for accounting purposes as a derivative financial instrument,

    (b) in the case of a relevant contract falling within paragraph 6 or 7 which is not treated as described in paragraph (a), it is treated for accounting purposes as a financial asset, or

    (c) in the case of a relevant contract which is not treated as described in paragraph (a) or (b), it falls within sub-paragraph (2).

(2) A relevant contract falls within this sub-paragraph if—

    (a) its underlying subject matter is commodities, or

    (b) it is a contract for differences whose underlying subject matter is—

        (i) intangible fixed assets,

        (ii) weather conditions, or

        (iii) creditworthiness.

(3) For the purposes of sub-paragraph (1)(a), a relevant contract of a company is treated for accounting purposes as a derivative financial instrument for an accounting period if, for that accounting period, it is so treated for the purposes of the relevant accounting standard used by the company for that accounting period (or would be so treated if the company were a company which used the relevant accounting standard in respect of the relevant contract).

(4) For the purposes of sub-paragraph (1)(b), a relevant contract of a company is treated for accounting purposes as a financial asset for an accounting period if, for that accounting period, it is so treated for the purposes of the relevant accounting standard used by the company for that accounting period (or would be so treated if the company were a company which used the relevant accounting standard in respect of the relevant contract).

(5) For the purposes of sub-paragraphs (3) and (4), the ''relevant accounting standard'' used by a company for an accounting period is—

    (a) in relation to any accounting period for which it is required or permitted to be used by the company, Financial Reporting Standard 13 issued in September 1998 by the Accounting Standards Board, as it has effect for periods of account ending on 31st December 2002, or

    (b) in relation to any accounting period for which it is required or permitted to be used by the company, any subsequent accounting standard dealing with transactions which are derivative financial instruments or financial assets under Financial Reporting Standard 13, as from time to time amended.

Contracts excluded by virtue of their underlying subject matter

4—(1) A relevant contract is not a derivative contract for the purposes of this Schedule if its underlying subject matter consists wholly of any one or more of the excluded types of property or is treated as consisting wholly of such property.

(2) For the purposes of this paragraph as it relates to an option or future, the excluded types of property are—

    (a) land, whether situated in the United Kingdom or elsewhere;

    (b) tangible movable property, other than commodities which are tangible assets;

    (c) intangible fixed assets;

    (d) shares in a company;

    (e) rights of a unit holder under a unit trust scheme; and

    (f) any assets representing loan relationships to which either section 92 or 93 of the Finance Act 1996 (c 8) applies.

(3) For the purposes of this paragraph as it relates to a contract for differences, the excluded types of property are those falling within paragraphs (a), (b) and (d) to (f) of sub-paragraph (2).

(4) Paragraph 9 applies for the purpose of determining whether the underlying subject matter of a relevant contract is to be treated as consisting wholly of any one or more of the excluded types of property.

(5) This paragraph has effect subject to paragraphs 5 to 8 (which qualify the exclusion of relevant contracts by this paragraph).

Qualified exclusion: contract held by company for purposes of trade

5—(1) Paragraph 4 does not prevent a relevant contract to which this paragraph applies from being a derivative contract.

(2) This paragraph applies to a relevant contract of a company if—

    (a) it is entered into or acquired by the company for the purposes of a trade carried on by it, and

    (b) its underlying subject matter consists, or is treated as consisting, wholly of—

        (i) shares in a company,

        (ii) rights of a unit holder under a unit trust scheme, or

(iii) assets representing a loan relationship to which either section 92 or 93 of the Finance Act 1996 (c 8) applies.

(3) Paragraph 9 applies for the purpose of determining whether the underlying subject matter of a relevant contract is to be treated as consisting wholly of the property referred to in sub-paragraph (2)(*b*).

Qualified exclusion: contract producing guaranteed return

6—(1) Paragraph 4 does not prevent a relevant contract to which this paragraph applies from being a derivative contract.

(2) This paragraph applies to a relevant contract of a company if—

   (*a*) its underlying subject matter consists, or is treated as consisting, wholly of—

      (i) shares in a company,
      (ii) rights of a unit holder under a unit trust scheme, or
      (iii) assets representing a loan relationship to which either section 92 or 93 of the Finance Act 1996 applies, and

   (*b*) it satisfies the condition in sub-paragraph (3).

(3) The condition referred to in sub-paragraph (2)(*b*) is that—

   (*a*) the relevant contract is designed to produce a guaranteed return, or
   (*b*) the relevant contract and one or more of the following, namely—

      (i) one or more other relevant contracts, whose underlying subject matter consists wholly or partly of shares in a company, rights of a unit holder under a unit trust scheme or assets representing loan relationships to which either section 92 or 93 of the Finance Act 1996 applies, and which would be derivative contracts if the condition in this sub-paragraph were satisfied in relation to them,
      (ii) one or more assets representing loan relationships to which either section 92 or 93 of that Act applies, and
      (iii) one or more assets representing loan relationships to which section 93A of that Act applies,

are associated transactions designed to produce a guaranteed return.

(4) For the purposes of this paragraph—

   (*a*) the return on a relevant contract of a company comprises any amounts accruing to the company as respects the contract for any accounting period, and
   (*b*) the return on an asset representing a loan relationship of a company is the amount that must be paid to discharge the money debt arising in connection with that relationship.

(5) For the purposes of this paragraph the relevant contract in question is, or that contract and the other associated transactions are, designed to produce a guaranteed return if, as regards that contract, or as regards that contract and the other associated transactions taken together, it would be reasonable to assume, from considering—

   (*a*) the likely effect of that contract or of that contract and the other associated transactions,
   (*b*) the circumstances in which—

      (i) that contract is entered into or acquired, or
      (ii) the contract and the other associated transactions, or any of them, are entered into or acquired, or

   (*c*) the matters in both of paragraphs (*a*) and (*b*),

that the main purpose (or one of the main purposes) of that contract, or of that contract and the other associated transactions, is or was the production of a guaranteed return from that contract, or from that contract and any one or more of the other associated transactions.

(6) For the purposes of this paragraph a guaranteed return is produced from the relevant contract in question, or from that contract and any one or more of the other associated transactions, wherever (as regards that contract or as regards that contract and those transactions, taken together) risks from fluctuations in the underlying matter of that contract, or of that contract or any one or more of the other associated transactions, are so eliminated or reduced as to produce a return from that contract, or from that contract and any one or more of the other associated transactions, which equates, in substance, to the return on an investment of money at interest.

(7) For the purposes of sub-paragraph (6) the cases where risks from fluctuations in the underlying matter of the relevant contract in question, or of that contract or any one or more of the other associated transactions, are eliminated or reduced shall be deemed to include any case where the main reason, or one of the main reasons, for the choice of that underlying matter is—

   (*a*) that there appears to be no risk that it will fluctuate, or
   (*b*) that the risk that it will fluctuate appears to be insignificant.

(8) In this paragraph—

(*a*) the references, in relation to an asset representing a loan relationship to which section 92 of the Finance Act 1996 (c 8) applies, to the underlying matter are references to the value of shares in a company which may be acquired under that relationship;

(*b*) the references, in relation to an asset representing a loan relationship to which section 93 or 93A of the Finance Act 1996 applies, to the underlying matter are references to the value of chargeable assets of a particular description to which that relationship is linked;

(*c*) the references, in relation to a relevant contract, to fluctuations in the underlying matter are references to fluctuations determined by reference to its underlying subject matter.

(9) For the purposes of this paragraph a company is a connected company in relation to another company if, in the accounting period in question, there is a connection between the company and that other company; and whether there is a connection between those companies shall be determined in accordance with sections 87(3) and (4) and 87A of the Finance Act 1996 (c 8) (disregarding section 88 of that Act).

(10) Paragraph 9 applies for the purpose of determining whether the underlying subject matter of a relevant contract is to be treated as consisting wholly of the property referred to in sub-paragraph (2)(*a*).

Qualified exclusion: guaranteed amount payable on maturity

7—(1) Paragraph 4 does not prevent a relevant contract to which this paragraph applies from being a derivative contract.

(2) This paragraph applies to a relevant contract of a company if—

(*a*) its underlying subject matter consists, or is treated as consisting, wholly of—

(i) shares in a company,

(ii) rights of a unit holder under a unit trust scheme, or

(iii) assets representing a loan relationship to which either section 92 or 93 of the Finance Act 1996 applies, and

(*b*) it satisfies the condition in sub-paragraph (3).

(3) The condition referred to in sub-paragraph (2)(*b*) is that—

(*a*) the relevant contract is designed to secure that the relevant amount payable in respect of the relevant contract does not fall below the guaranteed amount, or

(*b*) the relevant contract and one or more of the following, namely—

(i) one or more other relevant contracts, whose underlying subject matter consists wholly or partly of shares in a company, rights of a unit holder under a unit trust scheme or assets representing loan relationships to which either section 92 or 93 of the Finance Act 1996 applies, and which would be derivative contracts if the condition in this sub-paragraph were satisfied in relation to them,

(ii) one or more assets representing loan relationships to which either section 92 or 93 of that Act applies, and

(iii) one or more assets representing loan relationships to which section 93A of that Act applies,

are associated transactions designed to secure that the relevant amount payable in respect of the associated transactions does not fall below the guaranteed amount.

(4) For the purposes of this paragraph the relevant contract in question is, or that contract and the other associated transactions are, designed to secure that the relevant amount payable in respect of that contract, or that contract and any one or more of the other associated transactions, does not fall below the guaranteed amount if, as regards that contract, or as regards that contract and the transactions, taken together, it would be reasonable to assume, from considering—

(*a*) the likely effect of that contract or of that contract and the other associated transactions,

(*b*) the circumstances in which—

(i) that contract is entered into or acquired, or

(ii) that contract and the other associated transactions, or any of them, are entered into or acquired, or

(*c*) the matters in both of paragraphs (*a*) and (*b*),

that the main purpose (or one of the main purposes) of that contract, or of that contract and the other associated transactions, is or was to secure that the relevant amount so payable does not fall below the guaranteed amount.

(5) For the purposes of this paragraph the guaranteed amount is—

(*a*) in a case where the relevant contract in question is designed as described in sub-paragraph (3)(*a*), 80% of the consideration paid or payable by the company for entering into, or acquiring, that contract, or

(*b*) in a case where the relevant contract in question and the other associated transactions are designed as described in sub-paragraph (3)(*b*), 80% of the consideration paid or payable by the company or a company which is a connected company in relation to that company for entering into, or acquiring, any one or more of the associated transactions.

(6) For the purposes of this paragraph the relevant amount payable is—

(a) in a case where the relevant contract in question is designed as described in sub-paragraph (3)(a), the amount payable, in money or money's worth, to any person on the maturity of that contract, or

(b) in a case where the relevant contract in question and the other associated transactions are designed as described in sub-paragraph (3)(b), the amount payable, in money or money's worth, to any person on the maturity of any one or more of the associated transactions.

(7) For the purposes of sub-paragraph (6) the amount payable on maturity is—

(a) in the case of a relevant contract, the amount payable on performance of the relevant contract, or

(b) in the case of an asset representing a loan relationship, the amount that must be paid to discharge the money debt arising in connection with that relationship.

(8) For the purposes of this paragraph a company is a connected company in relation to another company if, in the accounting period in question, there is a connection between the company and that other company; and whether there is a connection between those companies shall be determined in accordance with sections 87(3) and (4) and 87A of the Finance Act 1996 (c 8) (disregarding section 88 of that Act).

(9) Paragraph 9 applies for the purpose of determining whether the underlying subject matter of a relevant contract is to be treated as consisting wholly of the property referred to in sub-paragraph (2)(a).

(10) This paragraph has effect subject to paragraph 48 (which provides for a company to elect to treat a relevant contract falling within this paragraph as two assets).

Qualified exclusion: contract held by company to provide insurance benefits

8—(1) Paragraph 4 does not prevent a relevant contract to which this paragraph applies from being a derivative contract.

(2) This paragraph applies to a relevant contract of a company if—

(a) the company is a company carrying on long-term insurance business,

(b) the relevant contract is or was entered into or acquired by the company in order to provide such benefits as are described in sub-paragraph (3), and

(c) the underlying subject matter of the relevant contract consists, or is treated as consisting, wholly of—

(i) shares in a company,

(ii) rights of a unit holder under a unit trust scheme, or

(iii) assets representing a loan relationship to which either section 92 or 93 of the Finance Act 1996 (c 8) applies.

(3) The benefits referred to in sub-paragraph (2)(b) are benefits under policies of life insurance or capital redemption policies where—

(a) the terms of the policy or contract permit part of the rights conferred by the policy or contract to be surrendered by the holder of the policy or contract at intervals of one year or less, and

(b) the amount which may be paid on the surrender of such part of the rights conferred equates, in substance, to the return on an investment of money at interest.

(4) Paragraph 9 applies for the purpose of determining whether the underlying subject matter of a relevant contract is to be treated as consisting wholly of the property referred to in sub-paragraph (2)(c).

Underlying subject matter which is subordinate or of small value disregarded

9—(1) This paragraph applies in relation to a relevant contract which falls within any of sub-paragraphs (2) to (4).

(2) A relevant contract falls within this sub-paragraph if its underlying subject matter consists of—

(a) any one or more of the excluded types of property falling within paragraphs (a) to (f) of sub-paragraph (2) of paragraph 4 (or, in the case of a contract for differences, within paragraphs (a), (b) and (d) to (f) of that sub-paragraph), and

(b) other underlying subject matter which is—

(i) subordinate in relation to any of the property referred to in paragraph (a), or

(ii) of small value in comparison with the value of the underlying subject matter as a whole.

(3) A relevant contract falls within this sub-paragraph if its underlying subject matter consists of—

(a) any one or more of the excluded types of property falling within paragraphs (a) to (c) of sub-paragraph (2) of paragraph 4 (or, in the case of a contract for differences, within paragraphs (a) and (b) of that sub-paragraph), and

(b) other underlying subject matter which is—

(i) subordinate in relation to any of the property referred to in paragraph (a), or

(ii) of small value in comparison with the value of the underlying subject matter as a whole.

(4) A relevant contract falls within this sub-paragraph if its underlying subject matter consists of—

(*a*) any one or more of the excluded types of property falling within paragraphs (*d*) to (*f*) of sub-paragraph (2) of paragraph 4, and

(*b*) other underlying subject matter which is—

(i) subordinate in relation to any of the property referred to in paragraph (*a*), or

(ii) of small value in comparison with the value of the underlying subject matter as a whole.

(5) Where this paragraph applies in relation to a relevant contract, its underlying subject matter shall be treated for the purposes of this Schedule as if it consisted wholly of—

(*a*) in the case of a relevant contract falling within sub-paragraph (2), the excluded types of property referred to in paragraph (*a*) of that sub-paragraph,

(*b*) in the case of a relevant contract falling within sub-paragraph (3), the excluded types of property referred to in paragraph (*a*) of that sub-paragraph, or

(*c*) in the case of a relevant contract falling within sub-paragraph (4), the excluded types of property referred to in paragraph (*a*) of that sub-paragraph.

(6) For the purposes of this paragraph whether part of the underlying subject matter of a relevant contract of a company is subordinate or of small value is to be determined by reference to the time when the company enters into or acquires the relevant contract.

Associated transactions

10—(1) For the purposes of this Part of this Schedule two or more transactions are associated transactions if all of them are entered into or acquired in pursuance of the same scheme or arrangements.

(2) Nothing in this Part shall be construed as preventing transactions with different parties, or transactions with parties different from the parties to the scheme or arrangements in pursuance of which they are entered into or acquired, from being associated transactions.

(3) For the purposes of this paragraph the cases in which any two or more transactions are to be taken to be entered into or acquired in pursuance of the same scheme or arrangements shall include any case in which it would be reasonable to assume, from either or both of—

(*a*) the likely effect of the transactions, and

(*b*) the circumstances in which the transactions, or any of them, are entered into or acquired,

that neither of them or, as the case may be, none of them would have been entered into or acquired independently of the other or the others.

(4) In this paragraph "scheme or arrangements" includes schemes, arrangements and understandings of any kind, whether or not legally enforceable.

Meaning of "underlying subject matter"

11—(1) In this Part of this Schedule references to the underlying subject matter of a relevant contract are to be construed in accordance with this paragraph.

(2) The underlying subject matter of an option is—

(*a*) the property which would fall to be delivered if the option were exercised, or

(*b*) where the property which would so fall to be delivered is a derivative contract, the underlying subject matter of that derivative contract.

(3) The underlying subject matter of a future is—

(*a*) the property which, if the future were to run to delivery, would fall to be delivered at the date and price agreed when the contract is made, or

(*b*) where the property which would so fall to be delivered is a derivative contract, the underlying subject matter of that derivative contract.

(4) The underlying subject matter of a contract for differences is—

(*a*) where the contract for differences relates to fluctuations in the value or price of property described in the contract, the property so described, or

(*b*) where an index or factor is designated in the contract for differences, the matter by reference to which the index or factor is determined.

(5) In the case of a contract for differences, its underlying subject matter may include—

(*a*) interest rates;

(*b*) weather conditions;

(*c*) creditworthiness.

(6) Interest rates are not the underlying subject matter of a relevant contract in a case where, under the terms of that contract,—

(*a*) the date on which a party to that contract becomes subject to a duty to make a payment is a variable date, and

(*b*) the amount of that payment varies according to the date of payment,

and the terms of the relevant contract refer to an interest rate or rates for the purpose only of establishing that amount.

Definition of terms relating to derivative contracts

12—(1) This paragraph defines these expressions for the purposes of this Part of this Schedule—

   (a) a capital redemption policy;
   (b) a contract for differences;
   (c) a future;
   (d) intangible fixed assets;
   (e) an option;
   (f) shares in a company;
   (g) a warrant.

(2) A "capital redemption policy" is a contract effected in the course of capital redemption business (within the meaning of section 458 of the Taxes Act 1988).

(3) A "contract for differences" is a contract the purpose or pretended purpose of which is to make a profit or avoid a loss by reference to fluctuations in—

   (a) the value or price of property described in the contract, or
   (b) an index or other factor designated in the contract.

(4) For the purposes of sub-paragraph (3)(b) an index or factor may be determined by reference to any matter and, for those purposes, a numerical value may be attributed to any variation in a matter.

(5) None of the following is a contract for differences—

   (a) a future;
   (b) an option;
   (c) a contract of insurance;
   (d) a capital redemption policy;
   (e) a contract of indemnity;
   (f) a guarantee;
   (g) a warranty;
   (h) a loan relationship.

(6) A "future" is a contract for the sale of property under which delivery is to be made—

   (a) at a future date agreed when the contract is made, and
   (b) at a price so agreed.

(7) For the purposes of sub-paragraph (6)(b) a price is to be taken to be agreed when the contract is made—

   (a) notwithstanding that it is left to be determined by reference to the price at which a contract is to be entered into on a market or exchange or could be entered into at a time and place specified in the contract; or
   (b) in a case where the contract is expressed to be by reference to a standard lot and quality, notwithstanding that provision is made for a variation in the price to take account of any variation in quantity or quality on delivery.

(8) An "option" includes a warrant.

(9) A "warrant" is an instrument which entitles the holder to subscribe for shares in a company or assets representing a loan relationship of a company; and for these purposes it is immaterial whether the shares or assets to which the warrant relates exist or are identifiable.

(10) References to a future or option do not include references to a contract whose terms provide—

   (a) that, after setting off their obligations to each other under the contract, a cash payment is to be made by one party to the other in respect of the excess, if any, or
   (b) that each party is liable to make to the other party a cash payment in respect of all that party's obligations to the other under the contract,

and do not provide for the delivery of any property.

Nothing in this sub-paragraph has effect to exclude, from references to a future or option, references to a future or option whose underlying subject matter is currency.

(11) "Intangible fixed assets" has the same meaning as in Part 1 of Schedule 29 to this Act, but any asset excluded by Part 10 of that Schedule is not an intangible fixed asset for the purposes of this Part of this Schedule.

(12) "Share", in relation to a company, means any share in the company under which an entitlement to receive distributions may arise.

Power to amend paragraphs 2 to 12

13—(1) The Treasury may by order amend any of paragraphs 2 to 12.

(2) The provision that may be made by an order under this paragraph includes provision—

   (a) adding to, or varying, the descriptions of contract which are derivative contracts within paragraph 2 or removing any such description of contract, or
   (b) adding to, or varying, the descriptions of contracts which are excluded under paragraph 4 or removing any such description of contract.

(3) The provision that may be made under sub-paragraph (2)(*b*), in relation to contracts which are excluded under paragraph 4, includes provision adding to, or varying, the provisions which qualify the exclusion of contracts under that paragraph or removing any such qualifying provision.

(4) To the extent that an order under this paragraph includes provision—

(*a*) varying the requirements under paragraph (*a*) or (*b*) of sub-paragraph (1) of paragraph 3 as to the treatment of a contract for accounting purposes, or

(*b*) adding to, or varying, the descriptions of contracts which fall within sub-paragraph (2) of that paragraph,

it may provide for such variations to have effect in relation to accounting periods which end on or after the day on which the order comes into force (whenever beginning).

(5) The power to make an order under this paragraph includes power—

(*a*) to make different provision for different cases, and

(*b*) to make such consequential, supplementary, incidental or transitional provisions, or savings, as appear to the Treasury to be necessary or expedient (including provision amending any enactment or any instrument made under an enactment).

PART 3
METHOD OF TAXATION
Method of bringing amounts into account

14—(1) For the purposes of corporation tax the profits and losses arising from the derivative contracts of a company shall be computed in accordance with this paragraph using the credits and debits given for the accounting period in question by the following provisions of this Schedule.

(2) To the extent that, in any accounting period, a derivative contract of a company is one to which the company is party for the purposes of a trade carried on by it, the credits and debits given in respect of that contract for that period shall be treated (according to whether they are credits or debits) either—

(*a*) as receipts of that trade falling to be brought into account in computing the profits of that trade for that period; or

(*b*) as expenses of that trade which are deductible in computing those profits.

(3) Where for any accounting period there are, in respect of the derivative contracts of a company, credits and debits that are not brought into account under sub-paragraph (2), they shall be brought into account for that accounting period as if they were non-trading credits or non-trading debits falling to be brought into account for the purposes of Chapter 2 of Part 4 of the Finance Act 1996 (c 8) in respect of loan relationships of the company.

(4) Sub-paragraph (2), so far as it provides for any amount to be deductible as mentioned in paragraph (*b*) of that sub-paragraph, shall have effect notwithstanding anything in section 74 of the Taxes Act 1988 (allowable deductions).

Credits and debits brought into account

15—(1) The credits and debits to be brought into account in the case of any company in respect of its derivative contracts shall be the sums which, in accordance with an authorised accounting method and when taken together, fairly represent, for the accounting period in question—

(*a*) all profits and losses of the company which (disregarding any charges or expenses) arise to the company from its derivative contracts and related transactions; and

(*b*) all charges and expenses incurred by the company under or for the purposes of its derivative contracts and related transactions.

(2) The reference in sub-paragraph (1)(*a*) to the profits and losses arising to a company does not include a reference to any amounts required to be transferred to the company's share premium account.

(3) The reference in sub-paragraph (1)(*a*) to the profits and losses arising to a company includes—

(*a*) a reference to any profits or losses which, in accordance with generally accepted accounting practice, are carried to or sustained by any reserve maintained by the company, and

(*b*) a reference to any forward premiums or discounts which arise from a derivative contract whose underlying subject matter consists wholly or partly of currency and which, in accordance with generally accepted accounting practice, are brought into account as profits or losses.

(4) The reference in sub-paragraph (1)(*b*) to charges and expenses incurred for the purposes of a company's derivative contracts and related transactions does not include a reference to any charges or expenses other than those incurred directly—

(*a*) in bringing any of those contracts into existence;

(*b*) in entering into or giving effect to any of those transactions;

(*c*) in making payments under any of those contracts or in pursuance of any of those transactions; or (*d*) in taking steps for ensuring the receipt of payments under any of those contracts or in accordance with any of those transactions.

(5) Where—

  (*a*) any charges or expenses are incurred by a company for purposes connected—

    (i) with entering into a derivative contract or related transaction, or

    (ii) with giving effect to any obligation that might arise under a derivative contract or related transaction,

  (*b*) at the time when the charges or expenses are incurred, the contract or transaction is one into which the company may enter but has not entered, and

  (*c*) if that contract or transaction had been entered into by that company, the charges or expenses would be charges or expenses incurred as mentioned in sub-paragraph (4),

those charges or expenses shall be treated for the purposes of this Schedule as charges or expenses in relation to which debits may be brought into account in accordance with sub-paragraph (1)(*b*) to the same extent as if the contract or transaction had been entered into.

(6) Where—

  (*a*) different authorised accounting methods are used for the purposes of this Schedule as respects the same derivative contract for different parts of the same accounting period or for successive accounting periods, and

  (*b*) an amount is brought into account for the purposes of the company's statutory accounts in respect of the change of method,

that amount shall be taken for the purposes of this Schedule to be included among the sums in respect of which credits and debits fall to be brought into account for the purposes of this Schedule in accordance with sub-paragraph (1)(*a*).

(7) In this Schedule "related transaction", in relation to a derivative contract, means any disposal or acquisition (in whole or in part) of rights or liabilities under the derivative contract.

(8) The cases where there shall be taken for the purposes of sub-paragraph (7) to be a disposal or acquisition of rights or liabilities under a derivative contract shall include—

  (*a*) those where such rights or liabilities are transferred or extinguished by any sale, gift, surrender or release, and

  (*b*) those where the contract is discharged by performance in accordance with its terms.

(9) This paragraph has effect subject to paragraph 16.

Exchange gains and losses arising from derivative contracts

16—(1) The reference in paragraph 15(1)(*a*) to the profits and losses arising to a company from its derivative contracts and related transactions includes a reference to exchange gains and losses arising to the company from its derivative contracts.

(2) Sub-paragraph (1) is subject to the following provisions of this paragraph.

(3) Sub-paragraph (1) does not have effect in relation to—

  (*a*) so much of an exchange gain or loss arising to a company, in relation to a derivative contract whose underlying subject matter consists wholly or partly of currency, as falls within sub-paragraph (4),

  (*b*) so much of any exchange gain or loss arising to a company as results from any translation from one currency to another pursuant to section 93A(4) of the Finance Act 1993 (c 34) of the profit or loss of part of the company's business and falls within sub-paragraph (6), or

  (*c*) so much of an exchange gain or loss arising to a company, in relation to a derivative contract whose underlying subject matter consists wholly or partly of currency, as falls within a description prescribed for the purpose in regulations made by the Treasury.

(4) For the purposes of sub-paragraph (3)(*a*), an exchange gain or loss falls within this sub-paragraph to the extent that in accordance with generally accepted accounting practice an amount representing the whole or part of it—

  (*a*) is carried to or sustained by a reserve maintained by the company; and

  (*b*) is set off by or against an amount falling within sub-paragraph (5).

(5) An amount falls within this sub-paragraph if—

  (*a*) it represents the whole or part of an exchange gain or loss arising to the company in relation to any asset of the company; and

  (*b*) in accordance with generally accepted accounting practice it is carried to or sustained by the reserve mentioned in sub-paragraph (4).

(6) For the purposes of sub-paragraph (3)(*b*), an exchange gain or loss falls within this sub-paragraph to the extent that, in accordance with generally accepted accounting practice, an amount representing the whole or part of it is carried to or sustained by a reserve maintained by the company.

(7) Where, by virtue of sub-paragraph (3), sub-paragraph (1) does not have effect in relation to an amount representing the whole or part of an exchange gain or loss, paragraph 15(3) shall not have

effect in relation to that amount (but this sub-paragraph is subject to regulations under sub-paragraph (8)).

(8) The Treasury may by regulations make provision for or in connection with bringing into account in prescribed circumstances amounts in relation to which sub-paragraph (1) does not, by virtue of sub-paragraph (3), have effect.

(9) The reference in sub-paragraph (8) to bringing amounts into account is a reference to bringing amounts into account—

(*a*) for the purposes of this Schedule, as credits or debits arising to a company from its derivative contracts and related transactions; or

(*b*) for the purposes of the Taxation of Chargeable Gains Act 1992 (c 12).

(10) Any power to make regulations under this paragraph includes power to make different provision for different cases.

Regulations—See the Exchange Gains and Losses (Bringing into Account Gains or Losses) Regulations, SI 2002/1970.

PART 4
ACCOUNTING METHODS
Authorised accounting methods

17—(1) Subject to the following provisions of this Schedule, the alternative accounting methods that are authorised for the purposes of this Schedule are—

(*a*) an accruals basis of accounting; and

(*b*) a mark to market basis of accounting under which any derivative contract to which that basis is applied is brought into account in each accounting period at a fair value.

(2) An accounting method applied in any case shall be treated as authorised for the purposes of this Schedule only if—

(*a*) subject to paragraphs (*b*) to (*d*), it is in conformity with generally accepted accounting practice to use that method in that case;

(*b*) it contains proper provision for allocating payments under a derivative contract, or arising as a result of a related transaction, to accounting periods;

(*c*) it contains proper provision for determining exchange gains and losses from a derivative contract for accounting periods; and

(*d*) where it is an accruals basis of accounting, it does not contain any provision (other than provision in respect of exchange losses or provision comprised in authorised arrangements for bad debt) that gives debits by reference to the valuation at different times of any derivative contract.

(3) In the case of an accruals basis of accounting, proper provision for allocating payments under a derivative contract to accounting periods is provision which—

(*a*) allocates payments to the period to which they relate, without regard to the periods in which they are made or received or in which they become due and payable;

(*b*) includes provision which, where payments relate to two or more periods, apportions them on a just and reasonable basis between the different periods;

(*c*) assumes, subject to authorised arrangements for bad debt, that every amount payable to the company under the derivative contract will be paid in full as it becomes due;

(*d*) secures the making of the adjustments required in the case of the derivative contract by authorised arrangements for bad debt; and

(*e*) provides, subject to authorised arrangements for bad debt, that, where there is a release of any liability owed by the company under the derivative contract, the appropriate amount in respect of the release is credited to the company in the accounting period in which the release takes place.

(4) In the case of a mark to market basis of accounting, proper provision for allocating payments under a derivative contract to accounting periods is provision which allocates payments to the periods in which they become due and payable.

(5) In this paragraph the references to authorised arrangements for bad debt are references to accounting arrangements under which debits and credits are brought into account in conformity with the provisions of paragraph 22.

(6) In this paragraph "fair value", in relation to a derivative contract of a company, means the amount which, at the time as at which the value falls to be determined, is the amount that the company would obtain from or, as the case may be, would have to pay to an independent person for—

(*a*) the transfer of all the company's rights under the contract in respect of amounts which at that time are not yet due and payable; and

(*b*) the release of all the company's liabilities under the contract in respect of amounts which at that time are not yet due and payable.

Application of accounting methods

18—(1) This paragraph has effect, subject to the following provisions of this Schedule, for the determination of which of the alternative authorised accounting methods that are available by virtue of paragraph 17 is to be used as respects the derivative contracts of a company.

(2) Different methods may be used as respects different derivative contracts or, as respects the same derivative contract, for different accounting periods or different parts of the same accounting period.

(3) If a basis of accounting which is or equates with an authorised accounting method is used as respects any derivative contract of a company in a company's statutory accounts, then the method which is to be used for the purposes of this Schedule as respects that contract for the accounting period, or part of a period, for which that basis is used in those accounts shall be—

  (*a*) where the basis used in those accounts is an authorised accounting method, that method; and
  (*b*) where it is not, the authorised accounting method to which it equates;

but this sub-paragraph is subject to paragraphs 19 to 21.

(4) For any period or part of a period for which the authorised accounting method to be used as respects a derivative contract of a company is not—

  (*a*) the method determined under sub-paragraph (3),
  (*b*) an authorised mark to market basis of accounting in accordance with an election under paragraph 19, or
  (*c*) an authorised mark to market basis of accounting in accordance with paragraph 20 or 21,

an authorised accruals basis of accounting shall be used for the purposes of this Schedule as respects that derivative contract.

(5) For the purposes of this paragraph (but subject to sub-paragraph (6))—

  (*a*) a basis of accounting equates with an authorised accruals basis of accounting if it purports to allocate payments under a derivative contract to accounting periods according to when they are taken to accrue; and
  (*b*) a basis of accounting equates with an authorised mark to market basis of accounting if it purports in respect of a derivative contract—

    (i) to produce credits or debits computed by reference to the determination, as at different times in an accounting period, of a fair value; and
    (ii) to produce credits or debits relating to payments under that derivative contract according to when they become due and payable.

(6) An accounting method which purports to make any such allocation of payments under a derivative contract as is mentioned in sub-paragraph (5)(*a*) shall be taken for the purposes of this paragraph to equate with an authorised mark to market basis of accounting (rather than with an authorised accruals basis of accounting) if—

  (*a*) it purports to bring that derivative contract into account in each accounting period at a value which would be fair value if the valuation were made on the basis that any periodic payments falling to be made under the contract were to be disregarded to the extent that they have already accrued; and
  (*b*) the credits and debits produced in the case of that contract by that method (when it is properly applied) correspond, for all practical purposes, to the credits and debits produced in the case of that contract, and for the same accounting period, by an authorised mark to market basis of accounting.

Application of accounting methods: election to follow generally accepted accounting practice

19—(1) Sub-paragraph (2) has effect if, in the case of a company falling within paragraph 52(1)(*c*) or (*d*) (companies whose statutory accounts are accounts to which Part 1 of Schedule 21C or 21D to the Companies Act 1985 (c 6) applies or accounts falling to be drawn up in accordance with the requirements imposed under the law of the home state),—

  (*a*) an authorised mark to market basis of accounting would be used as respects some or all of the company's derivative contracts, were the company a UK company following generally accepted accounting practice, but
  (*b*) that is not the basis of accounting used as respects those derivative contracts in the company's statutory accounts.

(2) Where this sub-paragraph has effect in relation to a company, the company may elect to use an authorised mark to market basis of accounting as its authorised accounting method for the purposes of this Schedule in relation to every derivative contract as respects which that basis would be used were it a UK company following generally accepted accounting practice.

(3) Any election under sub-paragraph (2)—

  (*a*) must be made before the expiration of the period of two years following the end of the company's first accounting period beginning on or after 1st October 2002 in which it is party to a derivative contract in relation to which an election under sub-paragraph (2) may be made;
  (*b*) has effect for that accounting period and all subsequent accounting periods of the company; and
  (*c*) is irrevocable.

(4) A company which makes an election under sub-paragraph (2) as respects its derivative contracts shall be taken for the purposes of Chapter 2 of Part 4 of the Finance Act 1996 (c 8) to have at the same time made an election under section 86(3A) of that Act having effect—

(*a*) for the accounting periods mentioned in sub-paragraph (3)(*b*), and

(*b*) as respects any loan relationships to which the company is or may become party in any of those accounting periods,

and that election shall so have effect notwithstanding anything in paragraph (*a*) or (*b*) of subsection (3B) of that section.

Application of accounting methods: requirement to follow generally accepted accounting practice

20—(1) Sub-paragraph (2) has effect if, in the case of a company falling within paragraph 52(1)(*c*) or (*d*),—

(*a*) the company has not made an election under paragraph 19,

(*b*) an authorised mark to market basis of accounting would be used for an accounting period—

(i) as respects some or all of the company's derivative contracts, and

(ii) as respects some or all of its loan relationships,

were the company a UK company following generally accepted accounting practice, and

(*c*) that basis of accounting—

(i) is used in the company's statutory accounts as respects those loan relationships for that accounting period, but

(ii) is not the basis of accounting used in the company's statutory accounts as respects those derivative contracts for that accounting period.

(2) Where this sub-paragraph has effect in relation to any accounting period, the company must for that accounting period use an authorised mark to market basis of accounting as its authorised accounting method for the purposes of this Schedule in relation to every derivative contract as respects which that basis would be used were it a UK company following generally accepted accounting practice.

(3) Sub-paragraph (4) has effect where, in the case of a derivative contract of a company,—

(*a*) the company uses, as respects the contract, a basis of accounting other than an authorised mark to market basis of accounting for an accounting period (the "preceding period"), but

(*b*) by virtue of sub-paragraph (2), the company must for the succeeding accounting period (the "first mark to market period") use, as respects the contract, an authorised mark to market basis of accounting as its authorised accounting method for the purposes of this Schedule.

(4) Where this sub-paragraph has effect in relation to a derivative contract of a company, the company shall be deemed—

(*a*) to have disposed of the contract immediately before the end of the preceding period for a consideration of an amount equal to the fair value of the contract at that time, and

(*b*) to have reacquired it for the same consideration immediately after the beginning of the first mark to market period.

Basis of accounting for contracts falling within paragraph 6, 7 or 8

21—(1) This paragraph applies in relation to a contract which is a derivative contract for the purposes of this Schedule by virtue of—

(*a*) paragraph 6 (contracts producing a guaranteed return),

(*b*) paragraph 7 (contracts where guaranteed amount payable on maturity), or

(*c*) paragraph 8 (contracts to provide insurance benefits).

(2) Where this paragraph applies in relation to a derivative contract, the accounting method to be used as respects the derivative contract for an accounting period shall be an authorised mark to market basis of accounting.

PART 5

SPECIAL PROVISION FOR BAD DEBT ETC

Bad debt etc

22—(1) In determining the credits and debits to be brought into account in accordance with an accruals basis of accounting, a departure from the assumption in the case of the derivative contracts of a company that every amount payable under those contracts to the company will be paid in full as it becomes due shall be allowed to the extent only that—

(*a*) a debt is a bad debt;

(*b*) a doubtful debt is estimated to be bad; or

(*c*) a liability to pay any amount is released.

(2) Such a departure shall be made only where the accounting arrangements of the company satisfy sub-paragraphs (3) and (4).

(3) This sub-paragraph is satisfied if, the accounting arrangements allowing the departure also require appropriate adjustments, in the form of credits, to be made if the whole or any part of an

amount taken or estimated to represent an amount of bad debt is paid or otherwise ceases to be an amount in respect of which such a departure is allowed.

(4) This sub-paragraph is satisfied if, in determining any credits and debits to be brought into account in respect of exchange gains and losses arising from the company's derivative contracts, the accounting arrangements allowing the departure require an amount payable under a derivative contract—

(a) to be left out of account, to the extent that such a departure is allowed; and

(b) to be taken into account again, to the extent that it is represented by credits brought into account under sub-paragraph (3).

(5) Where—

(a) in the case of a derivative contract of a company, a liability owed by the company to pay an amount under the contract is released, and

(b) the release takes place in an accounting period for which an authorised accruals basis of accounting is used as respects the contract,

no credit in respect of the release shall be required to be brought into account in the case of the company if the release is part of a relevant arrangement or compromise (within the meaning given by section 74(2) of the Taxes Act 1988).

PART 6

SPECIAL COMPUTATIONAL PROVISIONS

Derivative contracts for unallowable purposes

23—(1) Where in any accounting period a derivative contract of a company has an unallowable purpose, this paragraph shall apply for the purpose of determining the credits and debits which fall, in the case of the company, to be brought into account for the purposes of this Schedule.

(2) Subject to sub-paragraph (4), the credits to be brought into account in the case of the derivative contract for the accounting period shall not include so much of the exchange credits given by the authorised accounting method used as respects the contract as, on a just and reasonable apportionment, is referable to the unallowable purpose.

(3) Subject to sub-paragraph (4), the debits to be brought into account in the case of the derivative contract for the accounting period shall not include so much of the debits given by the authorised accounting method used as respects the contract as, on a just and reasonable apportionment, is referable to the unallowable purpose.

(4) If, in the case of the derivative contract,—

(a) the amount of the debits referable to the unallowable purpose, in accordance with sub-paragraph (3), for that accounting period, exceeds

(b) the amount of the exchange credits referable to that purpose, in accordance with sub-paragraph (2), for that accounting period,

the difference between the amounts (the "net loss") may be brought into account as a debit to the extent permitted by sub-paragraph (5).

(5) An amount of accumulated net losses may be brought into account for an accounting period if, and to the extent that, there is for that period an amount of accumulated credits (other than exchange credits).

(6) For the purposes of sub-paragraph (5) the amount of accumulated net losses is, in relation to an accounting period,—

(a) the amount of any net loss arising, in the case of the derivative contract, for that accounting period or any earlier accounting period, in accordance with sub-paragraph (4), less

(b) the amount of any such net loss as was brought into account in accordance with sub-paragraph (5) in any earlier accounting period.

(7) For the purposes of sub-paragraph (5) the amount of accumulated credits (other than exchange credits) is, in relation to an accounting period,—

(a) the amount of any credits (other than exchange credits) arising, in the case of the derivative contract, for that accounting period or any earlier accounting period, less

(b) an amount equal to the amount of any net loss, arising in the case of the derivative contract, which was brought into account in accordance with sub-paragraph (5) in any earlier accounting period.

(8) Amounts which, by virtue of this paragraph, are not brought into account for the purposes of this Schedule as respects any matter are in consequence also amounts which, in accordance with paragraph 1(2), are not to be brought into account for the purposes of corporation tax as respects that matter apart from this Schedule.

(9) For the purposes of this paragraph, a credit is an exchange credit, in the case of a company, to the extent that it is attributable to any exchange gains arising to the company which, by virtue of

paragraph 16, are included in the reference to the profits arising to the company in paragraph 15(1)(*a*).

(10) This paragraph is supplemented by paragraph 24.

Derivative contracts for unallowable purposes: supplementary

24—(1) For the purposes of paragraph 23 a derivative contract to which a company is party shall be taken to have an unallowable purpose in an accounting period where the purposes for which, at times during that period, the company—

    (*a*) is party to the contract, or

    (*b*) enters into transactions which are related transactions by reference to that contract,

include a purpose ("the unallowable purpose") which is not amongst the business or other commercial purposes of the company.

(2) For the purposes of this paragraph the business and other commercial purposes of a company do not include the purposes of any part of its activities in respect of which it is not within the charge to corporation tax.

(3) For the purposes of this paragraph, where one of the purposes for which a company—

    (*a*) is party to a derivative contract at any time, or

    (*b*) enters into a transaction which is a related transaction by reference to any derivative contract of the company,

is a tax avoidance purpose, that purpose shall be taken to be a business or other commercial purpose of the company only where it is not the main purpose, or one of the main purposes, for which the company is party to the contract at that time or, as the case may be, for which the company enters into that transaction.

(4) The reference in sub-paragraph (3) to a tax avoidance purpose is a reference to any purpose that consists in securing a tax advantage (whether for the company or any other person).

(5) In this paragraph "tax advantage" has the same meaning as in Chapter 1 of Part 17 of the Taxes Act 1988 (tax avoidance).

Debits and credits treated as relating to capital expenditure

25—(1) This paragraph applies where any debit or credit given by an authorised accounting method for any accounting period in respect of a company's derivative contract is allowed by generally accepted accounting practice to be treated, in the accounts of the company, as an amount brought into account in determining the value of a fixed capital asset or project.

(2) Notwithstanding the application to it of the treatment allowed by generally accepted accounting practice, the debit or credit shall be brought into account for the purposes of corporation tax, for the accounting period for which it is given, in the same way as a debit or credit which, in accordance with generally accepted accounting practice, is brought into account in determining the company's profit or loss for that period.

(3) No debit may be brought into account by virtue of this paragraph if it is taken into account in arriving at the amount of expenditure in relation to which a debit may be given by Schedule 29 to this Act.

Transfers of value to connected companies

26—(1) This paragraph applies where—

    (*a*) as a result of the expiry of an option of a company which, until its expiry, was a derivative contract of the company, there is a transfer of value by the company ("the transferor") to a company which is a connected company in relation to it ("the transferee"), and

    (*b*) the transferee is not chargeable to corporation tax, in respect of the derivative contract, under or by virtue of this Schedule.

(2) In order to determine, for the purposes of sub-paragraph (1)(*a*), whether there is a transfer of value, it shall be assumed that—

    (*a*) if there had not been a connection between the transferor and the transferee, the option would not have expired, and

    (*b*) if there had not been such a connection, it would have been exercised on the date on which it expired.

(3) Where this paragraph applies in relation to the expiry of the option of the transferor, the transferor shall bring the appropriate amount into account in accordance with paragraph 15 for the appropriate accounting period as a credit in respect of the derivative contract.

(4) In sub-paragraph (3)—

    (*a*) the appropriate accounting period is the accounting period of the transferor in which the option expired, and

    (*b*) the appropriate amount is the amount (if any) paid by the transferor to the transferee for the grant of the option by the transferee.

(5) In this paragraph "option" has the same meaning as in paragraph 12, apart from sub-paragraph (10).

(6) For the purposes of this paragraph, a company is a connected company in relation to another company if, in the accounting period in question, there is a connection between the company and that other company; and whether there is a connection between those companies shall be determined in accordance with sections 87(3) and (4) and 87A of the Finance Act 1996 (c 8) (disregarding section 88 of that Act).

Exchange gains and losses where derivative contracts not on arm's length terms

27—(1) Sub-paragraph (2) applies where—

    (*a*) a company is party to a derivative contract in an accounting period,

    (*b*) as regards the derivative contract, an exchange gain or exchange loss arises to the company for the accounting period in question, and

    (*c*) the profits and losses of the company fall by virtue of Schedule 28AA to the Taxes Act 1988 (provision not at arm's length) to be computed for tax purposes as if the company were not party to the derivative contract.

(2) Where this sub-paragraph applies, any exchange gains and losses which arise to the company from the derivative contract for the accounting period in question shall be left out of account in determining the credits and debits which are, in the case of the company, to be brought into account for the purposes of this Schedule.

(3) Sub-paragraph (4) applies where—

    (*a*) a company is party to a derivative contract in an accounting period,

    (*b*) as regards the derivative contract an exchange gain or exchange loss arises to the company for the accounting period in question, and

    (*c*) the profits and losses of the company fall by virtue of Schedule 28AA to the Taxes Act 1988 to be computed for tax purposes as if the terms of the derivative contract were those that would have been agreed by the company and the other party to the derivative contract had they been dealing at arm's length.

(4) Where this sub-paragraph applies, the credits and debits which are, in the case of the company, to be brought into account for the purposes of this Schedule shall be determined on the assumption that, in the accounting period in question, the amount of any exchange gain or loss arising to the company from the derivative contract is the adjusted amount.

(5) In sub-paragraph (4) the "adjusted amount" is the amount of an exchange gain or loss (including an exchange gain of nil) which would have arisen from the derivative contract if the terms of the contract were those that would have been agreed by the company and the other party to the derivative contract had they been dealing at arm's length.

Transactions within groups

28—(1) This paragraph applies where, as a result of any transaction or series of transactions falling within sub-paragraph (2), one of the companies there referred to ("the transferee company") directly or indirectly replaces the other ("the transferor company") as a party to a derivative contract.

(2) The transactions or series of transactions referred to in sub-paragraph (1) are—

    (*a*) a related transaction between two companies that are—

        (i) members of the same group, and

        (ii) within the charge to corporation tax in respect of that transaction;

    (*b*) a series of transactions having the same effect as a related transaction between two companies each of which—

        (i) has been a member of the same group at any time in the course of that series of transactions, and

        (ii) is within the charge to corporation tax in respect of the related transaction;

    (*c*) a transfer between two companies of business consisting of the effecting or carrying out of contracts of long-term insurance which has effect under an insurance business transfer scheme; and

    (*d*) any transfer between two companies which is a qualifying overseas transfer within the meaning of paragraph 4A of Schedule 19AC to the Taxes Act 1988 (transfer of business of overseas life insurance company).

(3) The credits and debits to be brought into account for the purposes of this Schedule in the case of the two companies shall be determined as follows—

    (*a*) the transaction, or series of transactions, by virtue of which the replacement takes place shall be disregarded except for the purpose of identifying the company in whose case any credit or debit not relating to that transaction, or those transactions, is to be brought into account; and

    (*b*) the transferor company and the transferee company shall be deemed (except for that purpose) to be the same company.

(4) References in this paragraph to one company replacing another as a party to a derivative contract shall include references to a company becoming a party to any derivative contract which confers rights or imposes duties which are equivalent to any rights or duties of the other company under a derivative contract of which that other company has previously ceased to be a party.

(5) In this paragraph "insurance business transfer scheme" means a scheme falling within section 105 of the Financial Services and Markets Act 2000 (c 8), including an excluded scheme falling within Case 2, 3 or 4 of subsection (3) of that section.

(6) In this paragraph references to companies being members of the same group of companies shall be construed in accordance with section 170 of the Taxation of Chargeable Gains Act 1992 (c 12).

(7) This paragraph has effect subject to paragraphs 29 and 30.

Transactions within groups: exceptions relating to insurance

29—(1) Paragraph 28 does not apply by virtue of sub-paragraph (2)(*a*) or (*b*) of that paragraph in relation to any transfer of an asset, or of any rights or duties under or interest in an asset, where the asset was within one of the categories set out in section 440(4)(*a*) to (*e*) of the Taxes Act 1988 (assets held for certain categories of long term business) either immediately before the transfer or immediately afterwards.

(2) Paragraph 28 does not apply by virtue of sub-paragraph (2)(*c*) or (*d*) of that paragraph in relation to any transfer of an asset, or of any rights or duties under or interest in an asset, where—

    (*a*) the asset was an asset within one of the categories set out in section 440(4) of the Taxes Act 1988 immediately before the transfer, and
    (*b*) is not an asset within that category immediately afterwards.

(3) For the purposes of sub-paragraph (2) above, where one of the companies is an overseas life insurance company an asset shall be taken to be within the same category both immediately before the transfer and immediately afterwards if it—

    (*a*) was an asset within one category immediately before the transfer, and
    (*b*) is an asset within the corresponding category immediately afterwards.

(4) In this paragraph "overseas life insurance company" has the same meaning as in Chapter 1 of Part 12 of the Taxes Act 1988.

Transactions within groups: authorised mark to market basis of accounting

30 Paragraph 28 does not apply where the transferor company uses an authorised mark to market basis of accounting as respects the derivative contract in question, but in any such case the amount to be brought into account by the transferee company in respect of the transaction referred to in that paragraph, or in respect of the series of transactions there referred to, taken together, must be the fair value of the derivative contract as at the date of transfer to the transferee company.

Derivative contracts with non-residents

31—(1) This paragraph applies in relation to a company where, as a result of any transaction,—

    (*a*) the company and a non-resident both become party to a derivative contract,
    (*b*) the company becomes party to a derivative contract to which a non-resident is party, or
    (*c*) a non-resident becomes party to a derivative contract to which the company is party.

(2) For each accounting period for any part of which the company and the non-resident are both party to a derivative contract, the credits and debits which fall, in the case of the company, to be brought into account for the purposes of this Schedule as respects the derivative contract shall not include, in a case where that contract makes provision for notional interest payments, any relevant debit arising in relation to that contract.

(3) For the purposes of sub-paragraph (2) the amount of a relevant debit shall be computed by determining, as regards that accounting period, the amount (if any) by which—

    (*a*) the aggregate of any notional interest payments made by the company to the non-resident while the company and the non-resident are both party to the derivative contract, exceeds
    (*b*) the aggregate of any notional interest payments made by the non-resident to the company during that time.

(4) For the purposes of sub-paragraphs (2) and (3) a notional interest payment is any payment the amount of which falls to be determined (wholly or mainly) by applying to a notional principal amount specified in a derivative contract, for a period so specified, a rate the value of which at all times is the same as that of a rate of interest so specified.

(5) Sub-paragraph (2) shall not apply where the company is a bank, building society, financial trader or recognised clearing house and—

    (*a*) the company is party to the derivative contract solely for the purposes of a trade or part of a trade carried on by it in the United Kingdom, and
    (*b*) it is party to the derivative contract otherwise than as agent or nominee of another person.

(6) Sub-paragraph (2) shall not apply where—

(*a*) the non-resident is party to the derivative contract solely for the purposes of a trade or part of a trade carried on by him in the United Kingdom through a branch or agency, and

(*b*) he is party to the derivative contract otherwise than as agent or nominee of another person.

(7) Sub-paragraph (2) shall not apply where arrangements made in relation to the territory in which the non-resident is resident—

(*a*) have effect by virtue of section 788 of the Taxes Act 1988, and

(*b*) make provision, whether for relief or otherwise, in relation to interest (as defined in the arrangements).

(8) Where the non-resident is party to the contract as agent or nominee of another person, sub-paragraph (7) shall have effect as if the reference to the territory in which the non-resident is resident were a reference to the territory in which that other person is resident.

(9) In this paragraph—

"non-resident" means a person who is not resident in the United Kingdom;

"recognised clearing house" has the meaning given by section 285 of the Financial Services and Markets Act 2000 (c 8).

PART 7
COLLECTIVE INVESTMENT SCHEMES
Authorised unit trusts: capital profits and losses

32—(1) Where any profits or losses arising to an authorised unit trust from a derivative contract in an accounting period are capital profits or losses, they must not be brought into account as credits or debits for the purposes of this Schedule, notwithstanding paragraph 15.

(2) For the purposes of this paragraph, capital profits and losses arising from a derivative contract in an accounting period are such profits and losses arising from a derivative contract as fall to be dealt with under—

(*a*) the heading "net gains/losses on investments during the period", or

(*b*) the heading "other gains/losses",

in the statement of total return for the accounting period.

(3) For the purposes of sub-paragraph (2), the statement of total return for an accounting period is the statement of total return which, in accordance with the Statement of Recommended Practice used for the accounting period, must be included in the accounts contained in the annual report of the authorised unit trust which deals with the accounting period.

(4) For the purposes of sub-paragraph (3), the "Statement of Recommended Practice" used for an accounting period is—

(*a*) in relation to any accounting period for which it is required or permitted to be used, the Statement of Recommended Practice relating to Authorised Unit Trust Schemes issued by the Investment Management Regulatory Organisation Limited in January 1997, as from time to time modified, amended or revised, or

(*b*) in relation to any accounting period for which it is required or permitted to be used, any subsequent statement of recommended practice dealing with accounting requirements relating to authorised unit trust schemes, as from time to time modified, amended or revised.

Open-ended investment companies: capital profits and losses

33—(1) Where any profits or losses arising to an open-ended investment company from a derivative contract in an accounting period are capital profits or losses, they must not be brought into account as credits or debits for the purposes of this Schedule, notwithstanding paragraph 15.

(2) For the purposes of this paragraph, capital profits and losses arising from a derivative contract in an accounting period are such profits and losses arising from a derivative contract as fall to be dealt with under—

(*a*) the heading "net gains/losses on investments during the period", or

(*b*) the heading "other gains/losses",

in the statement of total return for the accounting period.

(3) For the purposes of sub-paragraph (2), the statement of total return for an accounting period is the statement of total return which, in accordance with the Statement of Recommended Practice used for the accounting period, must be included in the accounts contained in the annual report of the open-ended investment company which deals with the accounting period.

(4) For the purposes of sub-paragraph (3), the "Statement of Recommended Practice" used for an accounting period is—

(*a*) in relation to any accounting period for which it is required or permitted to be used, the Statement of Recommended Practice relating to Open-Ended Investment Companies issued by the Financial Services Authority in November 2000, as from time to time modified, amended or revised; or (*b*) in relation to any accounting period for which it is required or permitted to be used, any subsequent statement of recommended practice dealing with accounting requirements relating to open-ended investment companies issued by the Financial Services Authority, as from time to time modified, amended or revised.

Power to amend paragraphs 32 and 33

34—(1) The Treasury may by order amend paragraph 32 or 33 so as to alter the definition of capital profits or losses in consequence of the modification, amendment, revision or replacement of a Statement of Recommended Practice.

(2) The power to make an order under this paragraph includes power—

    (*a*) to make different provision for different cases, and

    (*b*) to make such consequential, supplementary, incidental or transitional provisions, or savings, as appear to the Treasury to be necessary or expedient (including provision amending any enactment or any instrument made under an enactment).

Distributing offshore funds

35—(1) For the purposes of paragraph 5(1) of Schedule 27 to the Taxes Act 1988 (computation of UK equivalent profit), the assumptions to be made in determining what, for any period, would be the total profits of an offshore fund are to include the assumptions in sub-paragraphs (2) and (3).

(2) The first assumption is that this Schedule does not apply for the purposes of corporation tax in computing the profits or loss of an offshore fund.

(3) The second assumption is that for the purposes of corporation tax the profits and losses that are to be taken to arise from the derivative contracts of an offshore fund are to be computed—

    (*a*) in accordance with the provisions applicable, in the case of unauthorised unit trusts, for the purposes of income tax; and

    (*b*) as if the provisions so applicable had effect in relation to an accounting period of an offshore fund as they have effect, in the case of unauthorised unit trusts, in relation to a year of assessment.

(4) In this paragraph ''unauthorised unit trust'' means the trustees of any unit trust scheme which is not an authorised unit trust but is a unit trust scheme for the purposes of section 469 of the Taxes Act 1988.

Contracts relating to holdings in unit trust schemes, open-ended investment companies and offshore funds

36—(1) This paragraph applies in relation to a relevant contract to which a company is party in an accounting period if—

    (*a*) it is not a derivative contract for the purposes of this Schedule, and

    (*b*) its underlying subject matter consists wholly or partly of a holding which is, in that period, a relevant holding.

(2) Where this paragraph applies in relation to a relevant contract of a company in an accounting period—

    (*a*) the Corporation Tax Acts shall have effect for that period (and any succeeding accounting period in which the relevant contract is a relevant contract of the company) as if the relevant contract were a derivative contract, and

    (*b*) the accounting method to be used as regards the relevant contract for that period (and any such succeeding period) shall be an authorised mark to market basis of accounting.

(3) For the purposes of this paragraph a person holds a relevant holding in an accounting period if, at any time in that period, he holds—

    (*a*) any rights under a unit trust scheme,

    (*b*) any shares in an open-ended investment company, or

    (*c*) any relevant interests in an offshore fund,

and there is a time in that period when that scheme, company or fund fails to satisfy the non-qualifying investments test.

(4) For the purposes of this paragraph—

    (*a*) ''a relevant interest in an offshore fund'' has the same meaning as in paragraph 7 of Schedule 10 to the Finance Act 1996 (c 8), and

    (*b*) a unit trust scheme, open-ended investment company or offshore fund fails to satisfy the non-qualifying investments test if it fails to satisfy the test in paragraph 8 of that Schedule.

Contract which becomes contract to which paragraph 36 applies

37—(1) This paragraph applies if the conditions in sub-paragraphs (2) and (3) are satisfied in relation to any relevant contract of a company.

(2) The first condition is that—

(*a*) the company is party to the relevant contract in two successive accounting periods (''the first and second accounting periods''), and

(*b*) paragraph 36 applies in relation to that relevant contract for the second accounting period but not the first.

(3) The second condition is that the relevant contract was, immediately before the beginning of the second accounting period, a chargeable asset.

(4) Where an opening valuation of the relevant contract falls to be made at the beginning of the second accounting period (for the purposes of bringing an amount into account for that period on a mark to market basis of accounting), the value of that contract at that time shall be taken for the purpose of the opening valuation to be equal to whatever, in relation to a disposal immediately before the end of the first accounting period, would have been taken to be the market value of that contract for the purposes of the Taxation of Chargeable Gains Act 1992 (c 12).

(5) When the company ceases to be a party to the relevant contract it shall bring into account, for the accounting period in which it ceased to be a party to that contract, the amount of any chargeable gain or allowable loss which would have been treated as accruing to the company on the assumption—

(*a*) that it had made a disposal of the asset immediately before the beginning of the second accounting period, and

(*b*) that the disposal had been for a consideration equal to the value (if any) given to the relevant contract in the accounts of the company at the end of the first accounting period.

(6) For the purposes of this paragraph an asset is a chargeable asset if any gain accruing on the disposal of the asset by the company would be a chargeable gain for the purposes of the Taxation of Chargeable Gains Act 1992 (and includes any obligations under futures contracts which, by virtue of section 143 of that Act, are regarded as assets to the disposal of which that Act applies).

Investment trusts and venture capital trusts: capital reserves

38—(1) Where any profits or losses arising to an investment trust from a derivative contract for an accounting period are carried to or sustained by a capital reserve in accordance with the Statement of Recommended Practice used for the accounting period, those profits and losses must not be brought into account as credits or debits for the purposes of this Schedule, notwithstanding paragraph 15.

(2) Where any profits or losses arising to a venture capital trust from a derivative contract for an accounting period—

(*a*) are carried to or sustained by a capital reserve in accordance with the Statement of Recommended Practice used for the accounting period as if the venture capital trust were an investment trust, or

(*b*) would be carried to or sustained by a capital reserve if the venture capital trust were an investment trust and were using that Statement of Recommended Practice,

those profits and losses must not be brought into account as credits or debits for the purposes of this Schedule, notwithstanding paragraph 15.

(3) For the purposes of this paragraph, the Statement of Recommended Practice used for an accounting period is—

(*a*) in relation to any accounting period for which it is permitted to be used, the Statement of Recommended Practice relating to Investment Trust Companies issued by the Association of Investment Trust Companies in December 1995, as from time to time modified, amended or revised, or

(*b*) in relation to any accounting period for which it is permitted to be used, any subsequent Statement of Recommended Practice relating to investment trusts, as from time to time modified, amended or revised.

Investment trusts: approval for purposes of section 842 of the Taxes Act 1988

39—(1) For the purpose of determining whether a company may be approved for the purposes of section 842 of the Taxes Act 1988 (investment trusts) for any accounting period, the excess of any relevant credits arising in that period over any relevant debits so arising shall be treated for the purposes of that section as income derived from shares or securities.

(2) For the purposes of this paragraph ''relevant credits'' and ''relevant debits'', in relation to an accounting period, are credits and debits which are brought into account in respect of that period by virtue of paragraph 14(3) as if they were non-trading credits and non-trading debits falling to be brought into account for the purposes of Chapter 2 of Part 4 of the Finance Act 1996 (c 8) in respect of loan relationships of the company.

Venture capital trusts: approval for purposes of section 842AA of the Taxes Act 1988

40—(1) For the purpose of determining whether a company may be approved for the purposes of section 842AA of the Taxes Act 1988 (venture capital trusts) for any accounting period, the excess of any relevant credits arising in that period over any relevant debits so arising shall be treated for the purposes of that section as income derived from shares or securities.

(2) For the purposes of this paragraph "relevant credits" and "relevant debits", in relation to an accounting period, are credits and debits which are brought into account in respect of that period by virtue of paragraph 14(3) as if they were non-trading credits and non-trading debits falling to be brought into account for the purposes of Chapter 2 of Part 4 of the Finance Act 1996 in respect of loan relationships of the company.

PART 8

INSURANCE AND MUTUAL TRADING COMPANIES

Application of Schedule to insurance and mutual trading companies

41—(1) This Schedule shall apply in relation to insurance and mutual trading companies as it applies in relation to other companies.

(2) Sub-paragraph (1) is subject to paragraphs 42 and 43.

Application of Part 1 of Schedule 11 of the Finance Act 1996

42—(1) Part 1 of Schedule 11 of the Finance Act 1996 (special provision with respect to loan relationships for insurance companies) shall have effect (subject to sub-paragraphs (2) to (4)) in relation to derivative contracts as it has effect in relation to loan relationships.

(2) Any provision of that Part of that Schedule which applies only to debtor relationships (within the meaning of Chapter 2 of Part 4 of that Act) shall not have effect in relation to derivative contracts for the purposes of sub-paragraph (1).

(3) That Part of that Schedule shall have effect in its application in relation to derivative contracts as if—

(a) references to Chapter 2 of Part 4 of the Finance Act 1996 were references to this Schedule;
(b) references to section 80(5) of that Act were references to paragraph 1(2) of this Schedule,
(c) references to section 82(2) of that Act were references to paragraph 14(2) of this Schedule, and
(d) references to credits and debits given in respect of a loan relationship by Chapter 2 of Part 4 of that Act were references, respectively, to the credits and debits given in respect of a derivative contract by this Schedule.

(4) In the application of that Part of that Schedule in the case of any contract of an insurance company—

(a) which is a derivative contract by virtue of paragraph 5, and
(b) to which the insurance company is party for the purposes of any life assurance business, or any category of life assurance business, carried on by it or partly for those purposes,

any credits or debits given in respect of the contract shall not, to the extent that they are referable to that business or any category of that business, be brought into account in accordance with that Schedule as it has effect by virtue of this paragraph (and accordingly the provisions applicable apart from this Schedule shall, to that extent, apply for the purposes of computing the profits of an insurance company for the purposes of corporation tax).

Non-life mutual business

43—(1) This paragraph applies in relation to any contract of a mutual trading company—

(a) which is a derivative contract by virtue of paragraph 5, and
(b) to which the mutual trading company is party, at any time in an accounting period, for the purposes of any non-life mutual business carried on by it or partly for those purposes.

(2) Where this paragraph applies in relation to a contract, this Schedule shall have effect in relation to the contract subject to sub-paragraph (3).

(3) To the extent that the credits or debits which, but for this sub-paragraph, fall to be brought into account in respect of the contract for that period are referable to any non-life mutual business they shall not be brought into account under this Schedule.

(4) The extent to which any credits or debits are referable to the purposes of any non-life mutual business or to other purposes shall be determined by apportioning those credits and debits on a just and reasonable basis.

PART 9

MISCELLANEOUS

Derivative contracts ceasing to be held for purposes of trade

44—(1) This paragraph applies where—

(a) a company is party to a relevant contract which is a derivative contract by virtue of paragraph 5 (contracts entered into or acquired by a company for the purposes of a trade carried on by it), and (*b*) the purposes for which the company entered into or acquired the relevant contract cease at any time (''the relevant time'') to be the company's purposes in relation to that relevant contract, but

(*c*) the company continues to be party to the relevant contract after the relevant time.

(2) Where this paragraph applies, the company shall be deemed—

(*a*) to have disposed of the relevant contract immediately before the relevant time for a consideration of an amount equal to the fair value of the contract at the relevant time, and

(*b*) to have reacquired it immediately after that time for the same consideration.

Contracts becoming held for purposes of trade

45—(1) This paragraph applies where a relevant contract of a company—

(*a*) whose underlying subject matter consists, or is treated as consisting, wholly of—

    (i) shares in a company,

    (ii) rights of a unit holder under a unit trust scheme, or

    (iii) assets representing a loan relationship to which either section 92 or 93 of the Finance Act 1996 (c 8) applies,

(*b*) which is a chargeable asset, and

(*c*) which was entered into or acquired by the company otherwise than for the purposes of a trade carried on by it,

is at any time appropriated by the company for the purposes of a trade carried on by it.

(2) Where this paragraph applies—

(*a*) section 161 of the Taxation of Chargeable Gains Act 1992 (c 12) (appropriations to and from stock) shall have effect in relation to the appropriation of that contract, but

(*b*) the company may not make an election under subsection (3) of that section in relation to that appropriation.

(3) For the purposes of this paragraph an asset is a chargeable asset if any gain accruing on the disposal of the asset by the company would be a chargeable gain for the purposes of the Taxation of Chargeable Gains Act 1992 (and includes any obligations under futures contracts which, by virtue of section 143 of that Act, are regarded as assets to the disposal of which that Act applies).

(4) Paragraph 9 applies for the purpose of determining whether the underlying subject matter of a relevant contract is to be treated as consisting wholly of the property referred to in sub-paragraph (1)(*a*).

Contracts where part of underlying subject matter of excluded type

46—(1) This paragraph applies to a relevant contract of a company—

(*a*) which is an option or future,

(*b*) which satisfies the requirements of paragraph 3 (accounting requirements etc), and

(*c*) whose underlying subject matter falls within sub-paragraph (2).

(2) The underlying subject matter of a relevant contract falls within this sub-paragraph if it consists of—

(*a*) any one or more of the excluded types of property falling within paragraphs (*a*) to (*f*) of sub-paragraph (2) of paragraph 4, and

(*b*) underlying subject matter other than that referred to in paragraph (*a*).

(3) Where this paragraph applies to a relevant contract of a company, it shall be treated for the purposes of the Corporation Tax Acts as if it were two separate contracts, namely—

(*a*) a relevant contract of the company whose underlying subject matter consists of the excluded types of property referred to in sub-paragraph (2)(*a*), and

(*b*) a relevant contract of the company whose underlying subject matter consists of the underlying subject matter referred to in sub-paragraph (2)(*b*).

(4) For the purposes of giving effect to sub-paragraph (3) all such apportionments as are just and reasonable shall be made.

(5) This paragraph does not apply to a relevant contract if it is determined in accordance with paragraph 9 that the underlying subject matter of the relevant contract in question is to be treated as consisting wholly of any one or more of the excluded types of property referred to in sub-paragraph (2)(*a*).

Contracts where underlying subject matter of different excluded types

47—(1) This paragraph applies to a relevant contract of a company—

(*a*) which is an option or future,

(*b*) which satisfies the requirements of paragraph 3 (accounting requirements etc), and

(*c*) whose underlying subject matter falls within sub-paragraph (2).

(2) The underlying subject matter of the relevant contract falls within this sub-paragraph if it consists, or is treated as consisting, wholly of—

(*a*) any one or more of the excluded types of property falling within paragraphs (*a*) to (*c*) of sub-paragraph (2) of paragraph 4, and

(*b*) any one or more of the excluded types of property falling within paragraphs (*d*) to (*f*) of that sub-paragraph.

(3) Where this paragraph applies to a relevant contract of a company, it shall be treated for the purposes of the Corporation Tax Acts as if it were two separate contracts, namely—

(*a*) a relevant contract of the company whose underlying subject matter consists of the excluded types of property referred to in sub-paragraph (2)(*a*), and

(*b*) a relevant contract of the company whose underlying subject matter consists of the excluded types of property referred to in sub-paragraph (2)(*b*).

(4) For the purposes of giving effect to sub-paragraph (3) all such apportionments as are just and reasonable shall be made.

(5) Paragraph 9 applies for the purpose of determining whether the underlying subject matter of a relevant contract is to be treated as consisting wholly of the excluded types of property referred to in paragraphs (*a*) and (*b*) of sub-paragraph (2).

(6) If a relevant contract of a company is one to which this paragraph applies in consequence of the application of paragraph 9 (as described in sub-paragraph (5)), any underlying subject matter of the contract which is subordinate or of small value and which is disregarded in accordance with that paragraph shall be apportioned in accordance with sub-paragraph (4). But if and so far as the underlying subject matter of a relevant contract is disregarded in accordance with paragraph 9 by reason of being subordinate in relation to such property as is referred to in paragraph (*a*) or, as the case may be, paragraph (*b*) of sub-paragraph (3), it shall be apportioned accordingly.

(7) This paragraph does not apply to a relevant contract if it is determined in accordance with paragraph 9 that the underlying subject matter of the relevant contract in question is to be treated as consisting wholly of—

(*a*) any one or more of the excluded types of property falling within paragraphs (*a*) to (*c*) of sub-paragraph (2) of paragraph 4, or

(*b*) any one or more of the excluded types of property falling within paragraphs (*d*) to (*f*) of that sub-paragraph.

Election to treat contract as two assets

48—(1) This paragraph applies to a relevant contract of a company if it would, but for an election under this paragraph, be a derivative contract to which paragraph 7 applies.

(2) Where this paragraph applies to a relevant contract of a company, the company may elect that its relevant contract shall be treated for the purposes of the Corporation Tax Acts as if it were—

(*a*) a creditor relationship of the company which is a relevant zero coupon bond, and

(*b*) an option of the company whose underlying subject matter is the same as the underlying subject matter of the relevant contract to which this paragraph applies.

(3) For the purposes of sub-paragraph (2) a relevant zero coupon bond is a zero coupon bond—

(*a*) issued at the time when the consideration for entering into, or acquiring, the relevant contract to which this paragraph applies was payable by the company,

(*b*) falling to be redeemed—

    (i) on the date on which that relevant contract falls to be performed, or

    (ii) in a case where that relevant contract may fall to be performed on more than one date, on the date which is the last of those dates, and

(*c*) issued at a price equal to the amount that would have been the market value of a zero coupon bond—

    (i) issued at that time,

    (ii) falling to be redeemed on that date or, as the case may be, on that last date, and

    (iii) producing, by the time of its redemption, an amount equal to the amount which is the guaranteed amount in relation to that relevant contract.

(4) The only accounting method authorised for the purposes of Chapter 2 of Part 4 of the Finance Act 1996 (c 8) for use by a company as respects a creditor relationship arising under sub-paragraph (2)(*a*) shall be an authorised mark to market basis of accounting.

(5) None of paragraphs 6 to 8 shall apply to an option arising under paragraph (2)(*b*).

(6) For the purposes of giving effect to sub-paragraph (2) all such apportionments as are just and reasonable shall be made.

(7) An election under sub-paragraph (2) in relation to a relevant contract—

(*a*) may only be made within the period of two years following the end of the company's first accounting period in which it is party to the relevant contract;

(*b*) has effect for that accounting period and all subsequent accounting periods of the company; and

(*c*) is irrevocable.

(8) For the purposes of this paragraph a ''zero coupon bond'' is a security—

(a) whose issue price is less than the amount payable on redemption, and

(b) which does not provide for any amount to be payable by way of interest.

(9) For the purposes of this paragraph "market value" has the same meaning as in the Taxation of Chargeable Gains Act 1992 (c 12).

Partnerships involving companies

49—(1) This paragraph applies where—

(a) a trade, profession or business is carried on by persons in partnership ("the firm");

(b) any of those persons is a company (a "company partner"); and

(c) the firm is party to a contract which is a derivative contract or would be a derivative contract if the firm were a company.

(2) In any such case—

(a) in computing the profits and losses of the trade, profession or business for the purposes of corporation tax in accordance with section 114(1) of the Taxes Act 1988 (computation as if the partnership were a company) no credits or debits shall be brought into account under this Schedule in respect of the contract; but

(b) credits and debits shall be brought into account under this Schedule in respect of the contract in accordance with the following provisions of this paragraph by each company partner for each of its accounting periods in which the conditions in sub-paragraph (1) are satisfied.

(3) The credits and debits to be brought into account as mentioned in sub-paragraph (2)(b) shall be determined separately in the case of each company partner.

(4) For the purpose of determining those credits and debits in the case of any particular company partner—

(a) the contract entered into or acquired by the firm shall be treated as if it were instead entered into or acquired by that company partner, for the purposes of the trade, profession or business which that company partner carries on,

(b) anything done by or in relation to the firm in connection with the contract shall be treated as done by or in relation to the company partner, and

(c) to the extent that any exchange gains or losses arising from the contract are carried to or sustained by a reserve maintained by the firm and are set off by or against another amount as described in paragraph 16(4), the exchange gains or losses shall to that extent be treated as carried to or sustained by such a reserve maintained by the company partner and set off by or against another amount,

and credits and debits (the "gross credits and debits") shall be determined accordingly.

(5) The credits and debits to be brought into account under this Schedule pursuant to sub-paragraph (2)(b) in the case of any particular company partner shall be that company partner's appropriate share of the gross credits and debits determined in accordance with sub-paragraph (4) in the case of that company partner.

(6) For the purposes of sub-paragraph (5), the "appropriate share", in the case of a company partner, is the share that would be apportioned to that company partner if—

(a) the gross credits and debits determined in accordance with sub-paragraph (4) in the case of that company partner fell to be apportioned between the partners; and

(b) the apportionment fell to be made in the shares in which any profit or loss computed in accordance with subsection (1) of section 114 of the Taxes Act 1988 would be apportioned between them under subsection (2) of that section.

Partnerships involving companies: application of accounting methods

50—(1) This paragraph has effect where, in accordance with paragraph 49, credits and debits in respect of a contract of a firm are to be brought into account under this Schedule by a company partner for any accounting period of that company partner.

(2) Where this paragraph has effect, paragraph 18 shall apply in relation to the contract, subject to sub-paragraph (3).

(3) Where as respects any accounting period or any part of an accounting period—

(a) the credits and debits in respect of the contract, which fall to be brought into account under this Schedule by the company partner in accordance with paragraph 49, are not brought into account by the company partner for the purposes of its statutory accounts, but

(b) the company partner brings its share in the profits or loss of the firm into account on a mark to market basis of accounting for the purposes of its statutory accounts,

the company partner must use in relation to that period or, as the case may be, that part of a period, an authorised mark to market basis of accounting in relation to the contract for the purposes of this Schedule.

(4) For the purposes of this paragraph "company partner" and "firm" have the same meanings as in paragraph 49.

Prevention of deduction of tax

51 Notwithstanding anything in section 349 of the Taxes Act 1988 or any other provision of the Tax Acts, where the profits and losses arising from a derivative contract of a company are computed in accordance with this Schedule, the company shall not be required, on making a payment under the contract, to deduct out of it any sum representing an amount of income tax on it.

PART 10

INTERPRETATION

Statutory accounts

52—(1) In this Schedule "statutory accounts", in relation to a company, means—

(a) any accounts relating to that company that are drawn up in accordance with any requirements of the Companies Act 1985 (c 6) or the Companies (Northern Ireland) Order 1986 (SI 1986/1032 (NI 6)) that apply in relation to that company;

(b) any accounts relating to that company that are drawn up in accordance with any requirements of regulations under section 70 of the Friendly Societies Act 1992 (c 40) that apply in relation to that company;

(c) any accounts relating to that company which are accounts to which Part 1 of Schedule 21C to the Companies Act 1985 or Part 1 of Schedule 21D to that Act applies;

(d) in the case of a company which—

    (i) is not subject to such requirements as are mentioned in paragraphs (a) or (b), and

    (ii) is a company in whose case there are no accounts for the period in question that fall within paragraph (c),

any accounts relating to the company drawn up in accordance with requirements imposed in relation to that company under the law of its home state; and

(e) in the case of a company which—

    (i) is not subject to any such requirements as are mentioned in paragraph (a), (b) or (d), and

    (ii) is a company in whose case there are no accounts for the period in question that fall within paragraph (c),

the accounts relating to the company that most closely correspond to the accounts which, in the case of a company formed and registered under the Companies Act 1985 (c 6), are required under that Act.

(2) For the purposes of sub-paragraph (1), the home State of a company is the country or territory under whose law the company is incorporated.

Derivative and relevant contracts of person

53—(1) For the purposes of this Schedule references to a relevant contract of a person are references to a relevant contract entered into or acquired by a person; and references to a person's being party to a relevant contract shall be construed accordingly.

(2) For the purposes of sub-paragraph (1), a relevant contract is acquired by a person if that person becomes entitled to the rights, and subject to the liabilities, under the relevant contract whether by assignment or otherwise.

(3) Where—

(a) a company ceases to be party to a derivative contract in an accounting period (the "cessation period"),

(b) profits or losses arise to the company from the derivative contract or a related transaction in the cessation period, and

(c) the credits or debits brought into account for the purposes of this Schedule for the cessation period do not include credits or debits which represent the whole of those profits or losses,

credits or debits in respect of so much of those profits or losses as are not represented by credits or debits brought into account for the cessation period shall continue to be brought into account under this Schedule over one or more subsequent accounting periods ("post-cessation periods") as in the case of a derivative contract to which the company is party in those periods and sub-paragraphs (4) and (5) shall apply.

(4) In any case falling within sub-paragraph (3), any question—

(a) whether, in a post-cessation period, the company is, or is to any extent, party to the contract for the purposes of a trade carried on by it, or

(b) whether, in a post-cessation period, the contract is to any extent referable to a particular business, or a particular class, category or description of business, carried on by the company,

shall be determined by reference to the circumstances immediately before the company ceased to be party to the contract instead of the circumstances in the post-cessation period.

(5) In any case falling within sub-paragraph (3), any question—

(a) whether the contract has to any extent a particular purpose in a post-cessation period, or

(b) whether there is a connection between the company and any other person for a post-cessation period,

shall be determined by reference to the circumstances in the cessation period instead of the circumstances in the post-cessation period.

(6) For the purposes of the Corporation Tax Acts references to a person's derivative contracts and to a person's being party to a derivative contract shall be construed accordingly.

General interpretation

54—(1) In this Schedule—

"authorised accounting method", "authorised accruals basis of accounting" and "authorised mark to market basis of accounting" shall be construed in accordance with paragraph 17;

"bank" means any of the following—

(a) the Bank of England;

(b) any person falling within section 840A(1)(b) of the Taxes Act 1988; and

(c) any firm falling within section 840A(1)(c) of that Act;

"contract for differences" shall be construed in accordance with paragraph 12;

"contract of insurance" has the meaning given by Article 3(1) of the Financial Services and Markets Act 2000 (Regulated Activities) Order 2001 (SI 2001/544);

"derivative contract" shall be construed in accordance with paragraph 2;

"exchange gain" and "exchange loss" shall be construed in accordance with sub-paragraphs (2) and (3);

"fair value" has the meaning given by paragraph 17;

"future" has the meaning given by paragraph 12;

"insurance company" means a company which effects or carries out contracts of insurance;

"intangible fixed assets" has the meaning given by paragraph 12;

"investment trust" is a company approved for the purposes of section 842 of the Taxes Act 1988 (investment trusts) for an accounting period;

"life assurance business" has the same meaning as in section 431 of the Taxes Act 1988;

"long-term insurance business" means business which consists of the effecting and carrying out of contracts which fall within Part II of Schedule 1 to the Financial Services and Markets Act 2000 (Regulated Activities) Order 2001 and "contract of long-term insurance" means any contract which falls within that Part of that Schedule;

"non-life mutual business" means any mutual trading, or any mutual insurance or other mutual business, which (in either case) is not life assurance business;

"option" has the meaning given by paragraph 12;

"related transaction" has the meaning given by paragraph 15;

"relevant contract" has the meaning given by paragraph 2;

"shares", in relation to a company, has (except in paragraphs 39 and 40) the meaning given by paragraph 12;

"statutory accounts" has the meaning given by paragraph 52;

"UK company" means a company incorporated or formed under the law of a part of the United Kingdom;

"underlying subject matter" has the meaning given by paragraph 11;

"warrant" has the meaning given by paragraph 12.

(2) References in this Schedule to exchange gains or exchange losses, in the case of any company, are references respectively to—

(a) profits or gains, or

(b) losses,

which arise as a result of comparing at different times the expression in one currency of the whole or some part of the valuation put by the company in another currency on an asset or liability of the company.

If the result of such a comparison is that neither an exchange gain nor an exchange loss arises, then for the purposes of this Schedule an exchange gain of nil shall be taken to arise in the case of that comparison.

(3) A reference to an exchange gain or loss from a company's derivative contract is a reference to an exchange gain or loss arising to a company in relation to a derivative contract of the company.

(4) In this Schedule "financial trader" means—

(a) any person who—

(i) falls within section 31(1)(a), (b) or (c) of the Financial Services and Markets Act 2000 (c 8), and

(ii) has permission under that Act to carry on one or more of the activities specified in Article 14 and, in so far as it applies to that Article, Article 64 of the Financial Services and Markets Act 2000 (Regulated Activities) Order 2001 (SI 2001/544); or

(b) any person not falling within paragraph (a) who is approved by the Board for the purposes of this paragraph.

SCHEDULE 27

DERIVATIVE CONTRACTS: MINOR AND CONSEQUENTIAL AMENDMENTS

Section 83

Commentary—*Simon's Direct Tax Service* **D2.1010.**

The Taxes Act 1988

1 The Taxes Act 1988 is amended as follows.

2 In section 15(1) (Schedule A), in paragraph 2(3) of Schedule A (profits of Schedule A business computed without regard to certain items), for the third indent (which relates to qualifying payments within Chapter 2 of Part 4 of the Finance Act 1994 (c 9)), substitute—

"—credits or debits within Schedule 26 to the Finance Act 2002 (derivative contracts).".

3—(1) In section 128 (gains arising in course of dealing in commodity and financial futures etc), in the first sentence—

(*a*) at the beginning insert "(1)",
(*b*) after "(1)", as so inserted, insert "For the purposes of income tax,", and
(*c*) for "apart from this section" substitute "apart from this subsection".

(2) At the end of the first sentence of that section (as amended by sub-paragraph (1)), insert—

"(2) For the purposes of corporation tax, any gain arising to any company in the course of dealing in financial futures or in qualifying options, which apart from this subsection would constitute profits or gains chargeable to tax under Schedule D otherwise than as the profits of a trade, shall not be chargeable to tax under Case V or VI of Schedule D.".

(3) At the beginning of the second sentence (and after subsection (2) as inserted by sub-paragraph (2)) insert "(3)".

4—(1) In section 399 (dealings in commodity futures etc: withdrawal of loss relief), in subsection (1) (losses, arising in course of dealing where gains would constitute non-trading profits or gains chargeable under Schedule D for the purposes of the Tax Acts, not to be allowable against profits or gains chargeable to tax under Schedule D)—

(*a*) for "section 128 above" substitute "section 128(1) above", and
(*b*) for "for the purposes of the Tax Acts" substitute "for the purposes of the Income Tax Acts".

(2) After subsection (1A) of that section insert—

"(1B) If, apart from section 143(1) of the 1992 Act or section 128(2) above, gains arising in the course of dealing in financial futures or in qualifying options would constitute, for the purposes of the Corporation Tax Acts, profits and gains chargeable to tax under Case V or VI of Schedule D, then any loss arising in the course of that dealing shall not be allowable against profits and gains which are chargeable to tax under Case V or VI of Schedule D.".

5 In section 440 (transfers between categories of assets held by insurance companies) after subsection (2A) (treatment of deemed disposal and re-acquisition of loan relationships) insert—

"(2B) Where under subsection (1) or (2) above there is a deemed disposal and re-acquisition of any derivative contract of a company, any authorised accounting method used as respects that contract for the purposes of Schedule 26 to the Finance Act 2002 shall be applied as respects that contract as if the contract that is deemed to be disposed of and the contract that is deemed to be re-acquired were different assets.".

6 Omit section 468AA (authorised unit trusts: futures and options).

7—(1) Section 468L (interest distributions) is amended as follows.

(2) In subsection (9) (meaning of "qualifying investments") after paragraph (*e*) insert—

"(*f*) derivative contracts whose underlying subject matter consists wholly of any one or more of the matters referred to in paragraphs (*a*) to (*e*) above;
(*g*) contracts for differences whose underlying subject matter consists wholly of interest rates or creditworthiness or both of those matters.".

(3) In subsection (11) (assumption as to investments of other authorised unit trust which are to be regarded as qualifying investments) after "within paragraphs (*a*) to (*c*)" insert ", (*f*) and (*g*)".

(4) After subsection (12G) insert—

"(12H) For the purposes of this section—

"contract for differences" has the same meaning as in paragraph 12 of Schedule 26 to the Finance Act 2002;
"derivative contract" means—

(*a*) a contract which is a derivative contract within the meaning of that Schedule, or
(*b*) a contract which is, in the accounting period in question, treated as if it were a derivative contract by virtue of paragraph 36 of that Schedule (contracts relating to holdings in unit trust schemes, open-ended investment companies and offshore funds);
"underlying subject matter" has the same meaning as in paragraph 11 of that Schedule.".

8 In section 501A (supplementary charge in respect of ring fence trades) in subsection (5) (computation of financing costs) for paragraph (*c*) (any trading profit or loss, under Chapter 2 of Part 4 of the Finance Act 1994 (c 9) (interest rate and currency contracts), in relation to debt finance) substitute—

> "(*c*) any credit or debit falling to be brought into account under Schedule 26 to the Finance Act 2002 (derivative contracts) in relation to debt finance;".

9 In section 768B (change in ownership of investment company: deductions generally)—

> (*a*) in subsection (10) (restriction of debits brought into account in respect of loan relationships) at end insert "(including debits so brought into account by virtue of paragraph 14(3) of Schedule 26 to the Finance Act 2002)", and
> (*b*) in subsection (13) (modified application of section 768) after "its loan relationships" insert "(or its derivative contracts by virtue of paragraph 14(3) of Schedule 26 to the Finance Act 2002)".

10 In section 768C (deductions: asset transferred within group) in subsection (9) (restriction of debits to be brought into account) at end insert "(including debits so brought into account by virtue of paragraph 14(3) of Schedule 26 to the Finance Act 2002)".

11 In section 798B (restriction of relief on certain interest and dividends: meaning of "financial expenditure"), in subsection (5) (meaning of "qualifying losses"), for paragraph (*b*) (losses brought into account for purposes of Chapter 2 of Part 4 of the Finance Act 1994) substitute—

> "(*b*) the amount (if any) by which debits brought into account in respect of a derivative contract for the purposes of Schedule 26 to the Finance Act 2002 (derivative contracts) exceed credits so brought into account;".

12—(1) Section 807A (disposals and acquisitions of company loan relationships with or without interest) is amended as follows.

(2) In subsection (2)(*b*)(ii) (foreign tax to be disregarded so far as attributable to qualifying payment within Chapter 2 of Part 4 of the Finance Act 1994 (c 9) relating to a time when a company is not party to a contract)—

> (*a*) for "relevant qualifying payment" substitute "relevant payment", and
> (*b*) for "the interest rate or currency contract concerned" substitute "the derivative contract concerned".

(3) In subsection (7) (definitions) insert the following definition at the appropriate place—

> ""relevant payment" means a payment the amount of which falls to be determined (wholly or mainly) by applying to a notional principal amount specified in a derivative contract, for a period so specified, a rate the value of which at all times is the same as that of a rate of interest so specified;".

(4) In that subsection, omit the definition of "relevant qualifying payment".

13 In section 834(1) (interpretation of the Corporation Tax Acts) insert the following definition at the appropriate place—

> ""derivative contract" has the same meaning as it has for the purpose of Schedule 26 to the Finance Act 2002;".

14—(1) Schedule 5AA (guaranteed returns on transactions in futures and options) is amended as follows.

(2) In paragraph 1 (profits and gains of transactions with guaranteed returns chargeable to tax under Schedule 5AA of the Taxes Act 1988)—

> (*a*) omit paragraphs (*b*) and (*c*) of sub-paragraph (2) (exceptions for profits and gains arising from a qualifying contract and profits and gains arising to an authorised unit trust),
> (*b*) omit sub-paragraph (3) (definitions of "qualifying company" and "qualifying contract"),
> (*c*) in sub-paragraph (5) (when in loss in transaction sustained for purposes of sections 392 and 396 of the Taxes Act 1988), omit "and 396",
> (*d*) in sub-paragraph (6) (specified amounts not to be brought into account for purposes of income tax, corporation tax or capital gains tax except under Schedule 5AA or section 392 or 396)—
>
> > (i) omit ", corporation tax", and
> > (ii) omit "or 396", and
>
> (*e*) omit sub-paragraph (7) (bringing receipts into account in any Case I computation made in respect of life insurance).

(3) In paragraph 2 (transactions to which Schedule 5AA applies) omit sub-paragraph (3) (application of Schedule to disposals of futures or options to which section 93A of the Finance Act 1996 (c 8) refers).

(4) In paragraph 4 (meaning of disposals of futures or options) omit sub-paragraph (4A) (application of paragraph to associated transactions to which section 93A of the Finance Act 1996 refers).

(5) In paragraph 4A (futures running to delivery and options exercised)—

> (*a*) in sub-paragraph (5)(*b*) (loss in deemed transaction brought into account for purposes of section 392 or 396 or the Taxes Act 1988 in accordance with paragraph 1(5) of Schedule 5AA), omit "or 396", and

(*b*) omit sub-paragraph (10A) (application of paragraph to associated transactions to which section 93A of the Finance Act 1996 (c 8) refers).

(6) In paragraph 6 (meaning of related transactions) omit sub-paragraph (3A) (application of paragraph to associated transactions to which section 93A of the Finance Act 1996 refers).

(7) Omit paragraph 9 (apportionment in the case of insurance companies).

15—(1) Schedule 28AA (provision not at arm's length) is amended as follows.

(2) In paragraph 8 (foreign exchange gains and losses and financial instruments), in sub-paragraph (1) (exceptions)—

    (*a*) after "sub-paragraph (3)" insert "and sub-paragraph (4)", and

    (*b*) for paragraph (*b*) (which relates to Chapter 2 of Part 4 of the Finance Act 1994 (c 9)) substitute—

        "(*b*) Schedule 26 to the Finance Act 2002 (derivative contracts) in respect of exchange gains and losses (as defined in paragraph 54 of that Schedule),".

(3) In that paragraph, after sub-paragraph (3) (which is inserted by Schedule 23 to this Act) insert—

    "(4) Sub-paragraph (1) above shall not affect so much of paragraph 27 of Schedule 26 to the Finance Act 2002 (derivative contracts: exchange gains or losses where derivative contract not on arm's length terms) as has effect by reference to whether profits or losses fall to be computed by virtue of this Schedule as if a company were not party to a derivative contract or as if the terms of the contract to which it is party were different.".

The Finance Act 1994

16 In section 226 (provisions of the Finance Act 1993 (c 34) and Finance Act 1994 which are not to apply in the case of Lloyd's underwriters) for subsection (3) (contracts and options in premium trust fund of corporate member not to be qualifying contracts for purposes of Chapter 2 of Part 4 of the Finance Act 1994) substitute—

    "(3) No relevant contract (within the meaning of Schedule 26 to the Finance Act 2002) forming part of a premium trust fund of a corporate member shall be a derivative contract.".

The Finance Act 1996

17 The Finance Act 1996 is amended as follows.

18—(1) Section 93A (loan relationships linked to the value of chargeable assets: guaranteed returns) is amended as follows.

(2) In subsection (1) (creditor relationships to which section applies)—

    (*a*) in paragraph (*a*) for "a disposal of futures or options" substitute "a derivative contract falling within paragraph 6 of Schedule 26 to the Finance Act 2002 ("an associated derivative contract")", and

    (*b*) in paragraph (*b*) for "the disposals of futures or options" substitute "the associated derivative contracts".

(3) In subsection (2) (transactions designed to produce guaranteed return)—

    (*a*) for "disposals of futures or options" substitute "associated derivative contracts", and

    (*b*) for "any one or more of the disposals" substitute "any one or more of the associated derivative contracts".

(4) In subsection (3) (production of a guaranteed return)—

    (*a*) for "any one or more of the disposals of futures or options" substitute "any one or more of the associated derivative contracts", and

    (*b*) omit paragraph (*a*).

(5) In subsection (5) (meaning of "underlying subject matter"), for paragraph (*b*) substitute—

    "(*b*) the references, in relation to an associated derivative contract, to the underlying subject matter are to be construed in accordance with paragraphs 6(2)(*a*) and 11 of Schedule 26 to the Finance Act 2002.".

(6) Omit subsection (7) (use of terms appearing in Schedule 5AA to the Taxes Act 1988).

19—(1) Section 101 (financial instruments) is amended as follows.

(2) In subsection (1) (Chapter 2 of Part 4 of Finance Act 1994 not to apply to profit and loss on certain financial instruments brought into account under Chapter 2 of Part 4 of Finance Act 1996)—

    (*a*) for "Chapter II of Part IV of the Finance Act 1994 (provisions relating to certain financial instruments)" substitute "Schedule 26 to the Finance Act 2002 (provisions relating to derivative contracts)",

    (*b*) for "in accordance with that Chapter" substitute "in accordance with that Schedule", and

    (*c*) for "a qualifying contract" substitute "a derivative contract".

(3) Omit subsections (2) to (6).

20—(1) Schedule 10 (loan relationships: collective investment schemes) is amended as follows.

(2) In paragraph 8 (non-qualifying investments test) in sub-paragraph (2) (meaning of "qualifying investments") after paragraph (*d*) insert—

"(*e*) derivative contracts whose underlying subject matter consists wholly of any one or more of the matters referred to in paragraphs (*a*) to (*d*) above;

(*f*) contracts for differences whose underlying subject matter consists wholly of interest rates or creditworthiness or both of those matters.".

(3) In that paragraph, in sub-paragraph (4) (relevant assumption in a case where a qualifying investment is a qualifying holding) after "within paragraphs (*a*) to (*c*)" insert ", (*e*) and (*f*)".

(4) In that paragraph, after sub-paragraph (7D) insert—

"(7E) For the purposes of this paragraph—

"contract for differences" has the same meaning as in paragraph 12 of Schedule 26 to the Finance Act 2002;

"derivative contract" means—

(*a*) contract which is a derivative contract within the meaning of that Schedule, or

(*b*) a contract which is, in the accounting period in question, treated as if it were a derivative contract by virtue of paragraph 36 of that Schedule (contracts relating to holdings in unit trust schemes, open-ended investment companies and offshore funds);

"underlying subject matter" has the same meaning as in paragraph 11 of that Schedule.".

21 Omit Schedule 12 (meaning of debt contract or option).

The Finance Act 2000

22 The Finance Act 2000 (c 17) is amended as follows.

23—(1) Schedule 22 (tonnage tax) is amended as follows.

(2) In paragraph 50 (income which, otherwise than under Schedule 22 to the Finance Act 2000, falls to be taken into account as trading income from trade consisting of tonnage tax activities) in sub-paragraph (2), for paragraph (*c*) substitute—

"(*c*) any credit falling to be brought into account under Schedule 26 to the Finance Act 2002 (derivative contracts).".

(3) In paragraph 63 (ring-fencing of accounting periods where company is tonnage tax company: meaning of "finance costs") in sub-paragraph (2), for paragraph (*b*) substitute—

"(*b*) any credit or debit falling to be brought into account under Schedule 26 to the Finance Act 2002 (derivative contracts), in relation to debt finance;".

The Finance Act 2002

24 The Finance Act 2002 is amended as follows.

25 Section 78 (which amends the provision made by Schedule 5AA of the Taxes Act 1988 as regards corporation tax in relation to guaranteed returns on transactions involving futures and options, provision as regards which is made in Schedule 26 in relation to accounting periods beginning on or after 1st October 2002) shall cease to have effect.

26 In Schedule 29 (taxation of intangible fixed assets) in paragraph 75 (which provides for the Schedule not to apply to financial assets) for sub-paragraph (3)(*b*) (financial assets to include qualifying contracts within Chapter 2 of Part 4 of the Finance Act 1994) substitute—

"(*b*) derivative contracts (see Part 2 of Schedule 26 to this Act),".

SCHEDULE 28

DERIVATIVE CONTRACTS: TRANSITIONAL PROVISIONS ETC

Section 83

Commentary—*Simon's Direct Tax Service* D2.1010.

Anti-avoidance: change of accounting period

1—(1) This paragraph applies where—

(*a*) a company changes its accounting date in such a way that an accounting period of the company, which begins on or after 1st October 2001, ends before 30th September 2002; and

(*b*) the change of accounting date is or was made for the purpose, or for purposes which include the purpose, specified in sub-paragraph (2).

(2) The purpose is that of securing, in the case of any subsequent accounting period beginning before 1st October 2002,—

(*a*) that where an amount, or a bigger amount, would have fallen to be brought into account as a credit under Schedule 26 if that Schedule had had effect in relation to the period, no amount, or a smaller amount, falls to be brought into account in accordance with section 159 or 160 of the Finance Act 1994 (c 9); or

(b) that where no amount, or a smaller amount, would have fallen to be brought into account as a debit under Schedule 26 if that Schedule had had effect in relation to the period, an amount, or a bigger amount, falls to be brought into account in accordance with section 159 or 160 of the Finance Act 1994.

(3) Where this paragraph applies, Schedule 26 shall have effect in relation to the subsequent accounting period mentioned in sub-paragraph (2) as if it were an accounting period beginning on or after 1st October 2002.

(4) For the purposes of this paragraph, references to Schedule 26 include references to—

    (a) section 83(2), and

    (b) any repeal of any enactment which is consequential on any provision made by or under that Schedule.

Qualifying contracts to which company ceases to be party before commencement day

2—(1) This paragraph applies if the conditions in sub-paragraphs (2) and (3) are satisfied in relation to any contract of a company.

(2) The first condition is that the company was a party to a qualifying contract (within the meaning of Chapter 2 of Part 4 of the Finance Act 1994) before its commencement day, but is not a party to it on that commencement day.

(3) The second condition is that, if the company had been a party to the contract on its commencement day, the contract would have been a derivative contract.

(4) To the extent that amounts have been brought into account in computing, in accordance with Chapter 2 of Part 4 of the Finance Act 1994, the profits or losses accruing to the company from the contract in an old period of the company, they shall not be brought into account again by the company as credits or debits given in respect of that contract for the first new period or any subsequent accounting period of the company by Schedule 26.

Qualifying contracts which become derivative contracts

3—(1) This paragraph applies if the conditions in sub-paragraphs (2) and (3) are satisfied in relation to any contract of a company.

(2) The first condition is that the company is a party to the contract immediately before and on its commencement day.

(3) The second condition is that the contract—

    (a) was a qualifying contract (within the meaning of Chapter 2 of Part 4 of the Finance Act 1994 (c 9)) immediately before the company's commencement day, and

    (b) as from that day is a derivative contract.

(4) If the sum of the amounts that would, on the assumptions in sub-paragraph (6)(a) and (b), have fallen to be brought into account as regards the contract in accordance with—

    (a) Chapter 2 of Part 2 of the Finance Act 1993 (c 34), or

    (b) Chapter 2 of Part 4 of the Finance Act 1994,

for the purposes of computing corporation tax for an old period of the company is different from the sum of the amounts that would, on the assumption in sub-paragraph (6)(c), have fallen to be brought into account as regards the contract in accordance with Schedule 26 for those purposes (if that Schedule had had effect in relation to that period), sub-paragraph (5) shall apply as regards the amount of that difference.

(5) Where this sub-paragraph applies, the amount of the difference shall be brought into account—

    (a) as a credit under Schedule 26 in the company's first new period, if a greater profit or smaller loss would have been brought into account for the old period under that Schedule, or

    (b) as a debit under that Schedule in the company's first new period, if a smaller profit or greater loss would have been brought into account for the old period under that Schedule.

(6) The assumptions referred to in sub-paragraph (4) are that—

    (a) section 137 of the Finance Act 1993,

    (b) sections 165 to 168A of the Finance Act 1994, and

    (c) paragraphs 23 to 31 of Schedule 26,

would not have had effect in the case of the contract.

Contracts which become derivative contracts: chargeable assets

4—(1) This paragraph applies if the conditions in sub-paragraphs (2) to (4) are satisfied in relation to any contract of a company.

(2) The first condition is that the company is a party to the contract immediately before and on its commencement day.

(3) The second condition is that the contract—

(*a*) was not a qualifying contract (within the meaning of Chapter 2 of Part 4 of the Finance Act 1994) immediately before the company's commencement day, but

(*b*) as from that day is a derivative contract.

(4) The third condition is that the contract was, immediately before the company's commencement day, a chargeable asset.

(5) Where this paragraph applies, the company shall, when it ceases to be a party to the contract, bring into account, for the accounting period in which it ceased to be a party to the contract, the amount of any chargeable gain or allowable loss which would have been treated as accruing to the company on the assumption—

(*a*) that it had made a disposal of the asset immediately before its commencement day, and

(*b*) that the disposal had been for a consideration equal to the value (if any) given to the contract in the accounts of the company at the end of the company's accounting period immediately before its first new period.

(6) Sub-paragraph (5) has effect subject to sub-paragraph (7).

(7) The company may elect that a debit representing the amount of any allowable loss, which under sub-paragraph (5) is to be brought into account for the accounting period in which it ceased to be a party to the contract, shall be brought into account for that accounting period as if it were a non-trading debit falling to be brought into account for the purposes of Chapter 2 of Part 4 of the Finance Act 1996 (c 8) in respect of a loan relationship of the company.

(8) An election under sub-paragraph (7) may only be made within the period of two years following the end of the accounting period in which the company ceased to be a party to the contract.

(9) For the purposes of this paragraph an asset is a chargeable asset if any gain accruing on the disposal of the asset by the company would be a chargeable gain for the purposes of the Taxation of Chargeable Gains Act 1992 (c 12) (and includes any obligations under futures contracts which, by virtue of section 143 of that Act, are regarded as assets to the disposal of which that Act applies).

(10) This paragraph has effect subject to paragraph 5.

Contracts: election to treat as two assets

5—(1) This paragraph applies if the conditions in sub-paragraphs (2) to (4) are satisfied in relation to any contract of a company.

(2) The first condition is that the company is a party to the contract immediately before and on its commencement day.

(3) The second condition is that the contract—

(*a*) was not a qualifying contract (within the meaning of Chapter 2 of Part 4 of the Finance Act 1994 (c 9)) immediately before the company's commencement day, but

(*b*) as from that day would, but for an election under sub-paragraph (5) of this paragraph, be a derivative contract to which paragraph 7 of Schedule 26 (contracts designed to secure guaranteed amount) applies.

(4) The third condition is that the contract was, immediately before the company's commencement day, a chargeable asset.

(5) Where this paragraph applies the company may elect that its contract shall be treated for the purposes of the Corporation Tax Acts as if it were—

(*a*) a creditor relationship of the company which is a zero coupon bond (within the meaning of paragraph 48 of Schedule 26), and

(*b*) an option of the company whose underlying subject matter is the same as the underlying subject matter of the contract to which this paragraph applies;

and sub-paragraphs (4) to (6) of that paragraph shall apply to a creditor relationship and an option arising under this sub-paragraph as they apply to a creditor relationship and an option arising under paragraph 48(2) of Schedule 26.

(6) An election under sub-paragraph (5) in relation to a contract—

(*a*) may only be made within the period of two years following the end of the company's first new period;

(*b*) has effect for the company's first new period and all subsequent accounting periods of the company; and

(*c*) is irrevocable.

(7) Where an election under sub-paragraph (5) has been made by a company in relation to a contract, the company shall, when it ceases to be a party to the contract, bring into account, for the accounting period in which it ceases to be a party to the contract, the amount of any chargeable gain or allowable loss which would have been treated as accruing to the company on the assumption—

(*a*) that it had made a disposal of the asset immediately before its commencement day, and

(*b*) that the disposal had been for a consideration equal to the value (if any) given to the contract in the accounts of the company at the end of the company's accounting period immediately before its first new period.

(8) Sub-paragraph (7) has effect subject to sub-paragraph (9).

(9) The company may elect that a debit representing the amount of any allowable loss, which under sub-paragraph (7) is to be brought into account for the accounting period in which it ceases to be a party to the contract, shall be brought into account for that accounting period as if it were a non-trading debit falling to be brought into account for the purposes of Chapter 2 of Part 4 of the Finance Act 1996 (c 8) in respect of a loan relationship of the company.

(10) An election under sub-paragraph (9) may only be made within the period of two years following the end of the accounting period in which the company ceases to be a party to the contract.

(11) For the purposes of this paragraph references to an asset being a chargeable asset shall be construed in accordance with paragraph 4(9).

(12) In this paragraph ''option'' and ''underlying subject matter'' have the same meanings as in Schedule 26.

Contracts which become derivative contracts: contracts within Schedule 5AA to the Taxes Act 1988

6—(1) This paragraph applies if the conditions in sub-paragraphs (2) to (5) are satisfied in relation to any contract of a company.

(2) The first condition is that the company is a party to the contract immediately before and on its commencement day.

(3) The second condition is that the contract—

    (*a*) was not a qualifying contract (within the meaning of Chapter 2 of Part 4 of the Finance Act 1994 (c 9)) immediately before the company's commencement day, but
    (*b*) as from that day is a derivative contract.

(4) The third condition is that the contract was, immediately before the company's commencement day, a transaction to which Schedule 5AA to the Taxes Act 1988 applied.

(5) The fourth condition is that, on or after the company's commencement day, a relevant event occurs.

(6) For the purposes of this paragraph a relevant event is an event which would, if Schedule 5AA to the Taxes Act 1988 had continued to apply to the contract for the purposes of corporation tax, have given rise to an amount of profits falling to be charged under that Schedule.

(7) A credit representing that amount of profits (''a relevant credit'') shall be brought into account by virtue of paragraph 14(3) of Schedule 26 for the accounting period in which the relevant event occurs as if it were a non-trading credit falling to be brought into account for the purposes of Chapter 2 of Part 4 of the Finance Act 1996 (c 8) in respect of a loan relationship of the company.

(8) The amount of the relevant credit is the sum of—

    (*a*) the amount of profits which would have been chargeable under Schedule 5AA to the Taxes Act 1988 if it had continued to apply to the contract, and
    (*b*) the amount of any debits given by Schedule 26 in respect of the contract for the first new period and any subsequent accounting period ending with the accounting period in which the relevant event occurred,

less the amount of any credits given by Schedule 26 in respect of the contract for those accounting periods.

Interpretation

7 For the purposes of this Schedule—

    (*a*) a company's commencement day is the first day of its first accounting period to begin on or after 1st October 2002,
    (*b*) a company's first new period is its first accounting period to begin on or after that date, and
    (*c*) an old period of the company is any accounting period of the company ending before the first day of its first new period.

SCHEDULE 29

GAINS AND LOSSES OF A COMPANY FROM INTANGIBLE FIXED ASSETS

Section 84(1)

Commentary—*Simon's Direct Tax Service* **B3.801.**

PART 1

INTRODUCTION

Gains and losses in respect of intangible fixed assets

1—(1) A company's gains in respect of intangible fixed assets are chargeable to corporation tax as income in accordance with this Schedule.

(2) This Schedule also has effect for determining how a company's losses in respect of intangible fixed assets are brought into account for the purposes of corporation tax.

(3) Except where otherwise indicated, the amounts to be brought into account in accordance with this Schedule in respect of any matter are the only amounts to be brought into account for the purposes of corporation tax in respect of that matter.

Intangible assets

2—(1) In this Schedule "intangible asset" has the meaning it has for accounting purposes.

(2) References in this Schedule to an intangible asset include, in particular, any intellectual property. For this purpose "intellectual property" means—

  (a) any patent, trade mark, registered design, copyright or design right, plant breeders' rights or rights under section 7 of the Plant Varieties Act 1997 (c 66),

  (b) any right under the law of a country or territory outside the United Kingdom corresponding to, or similar to, a right within paragraph (a),

  (c) any information or technique not protected by a right within paragraph (a) or (b) but having industrial, commercial or other economic value, or

  (d) any licence or other right in respect of anything within paragraph (a), (b) or (c).

(3) This paragraph is subject to Part 10 (excluded assets).

Intangible fixed assets

3—(1) In this Schedule an "intangible fixed asset", in relation to a company, means an intangible asset acquired or created by the company for use on a continuing basis in the course of the company's activities.

(2) References in this Schedule to an intangible fixed asset include an option or other right—

  (a) to acquire an intangible asset that if acquired would be a fixed asset, or

  (b) to dispose of an intangible fixed asset.

(3) Unless otherwise indicated, the provisions of this Schedule apply to an intangible fixed asset whether or not it is capitalised in the company's accounts.

(4) This paragraph is subject to any such provision of regulations under paragraph 104 (finance leasing etc) as is mentioned in sub-paragraph (2)(a) of that paragraph (assets to be treated as intangible fixed assets of finance lessor).

Goodwill

4—(1) Except as otherwise indicated, the provisions of this Schedule apply to goodwill as to an intangible fixed asset.

(2) In this Schedule "goodwill" has the meaning it has for accounting purposes.

Company not drawing up correct accounts

5—(1) If a company does not draw up accounts in accordance with generally accepted accounting practice ("correct accounts")—

  (a) the provisions of this Schedule apply as if correct accounts had been drawn up, and

  (b) the amounts referred to in this Schedule as being recognised for accounting purposes are those that would have been recognised if correct accounts had been drawn up.

(2) If a company draws up accounts that rely to any extent on amounts derived from an earlier period of account for which the company did not draw up correct accounts, the amounts referred to in this Schedule as being recognised for accounting purposes in the later period are those that would have been recognised if correct accounts had been drawn up for the earlier period.

(3) The provisions of this paragraph apply where the company does not draw up accounts at all as well as where it draws up accounts that are not correct.

Reference to consolidated group accounts

6—(1) In determining whether a company's accounts are correct, reference may be made to any view as to—

  (a) the useful life of an asset, or

  (b) the economic value of an asset,

taken for the purposes of consolidated group accounts prepared for any group of companies of which the company is a member.

(2) In sub-paragraph (1)—

  "consolidated group accounts" means group accounts that satisfy the requirements of—

    (a) section 227 of the Companies Act 1985 (c 6), or

    (b) in Northern Ireland, Article 235 of the Companies (Northern Ireland) Order 1986 (SI 1986/1032 (NI 6)), or the corresponding requirements of the law of a country outside the United Kingdom; and ''group of companies'' means a group as defined in—

   (a) section 262(1) of that Act, or
   (b) in Northern Ireland, Article 270(1) of that Order,

or the corresponding provision of the law of a country outside the United Kingdom.

(3) This paragraph does not apply if or to the extent that the consolidated group accounts are prepared—

   (a) in accordance with the requirements of the law of a country outside the United Kingdom, and
   (b) on a basis that, in relation to the matters mentioned in sub-paragraph (1), substantially diverges from generally accepted accounting practice.

PART 2
DEBITS IN RESPECT ON INTANGIBLE FIXED ASSETS
Introduction

7—(1) This Part provides for debits to be brought into account by a company for tax purposes in respect of—

   (a) expenditure on an intangible fixed asset that is written off for accounting purposes as it is incurred (see paragraph 8);
   (b) writing down the capitalised cost of an intangible fixed asset—

      (i) on an accounting basis (see paragraph 9), or
      (ii) on a fixed-rate basis (see paragraphs 10 and 11); and

   (c) the reversal of a previous accounting gain in respect of an intangible fixed asset (see paragraph 12).

(2) This Part does not apply in relation to amounts brought into account in connection with the realisation of an intangible fixed asset (see Part 4).

Expenditure written off as it is incurred

8—(1) Where in a period of account expenditure on an intangible fixed asset is recognised in a company's profit and loss account, a corresponding debit shall be brought into account for tax purposes.

(2) Subject to any adjustment required for tax purposes, the amount of the debit recognised for tax purposes is the same as the amount of the loss recognised by the company for accounting purposes.

(3) Nothing in—

section 74(1)(m) or (p) of the Taxes Act 1988 (annual payments and patent royalties not to be deducted in computing profits under Case I or II of Schedule D), or
section 817(1)(b) of that Act (annual payments not to be deducted in arriving at the amount of profits or gains for tax purposes),

has effect to prevent a debit being brought into account for tax purposes by a company in accordance with this paragraph (and given effect accordingly under Part 6).

(4) This paragraph does not apply to a loss that represents previously capitalised expenditure.

Writing down on accounting basis

9—(1) Where in a period of account a loss is recognised in the company's profit and loss account in respect of capitalised expenditure on an intangible fixed asset—

   (a) by way of amortisation, or
   (b) as a result of an impairment review,

a corresponding debit shall be brought into account for tax purposes.

(2) The reference in sub-paragraph (1) to an ''impairment review'' does not include the valuation of an asset for the purpose of determining the amount of expenditure to be capitalised in the first place.

(3) The amount of the debit for tax purposes in respect of expenditure on an asset is, in the period of account in which the expenditure is capitalised:

$$\text{Accounting Loss} \times \frac{\text{Tax Cost}}{\text{Accounting Cost}}$$

where—

Accounting Loss is the amount of the loss recognised for accounting purposes,
Tax Cost is the amount of expenditure on the asset that is recognised for tax purposes, and
Accounting Cost is the amount capitalised in respect of expenditure on the asset.

(4) Subject to any adjustment required for tax purposes, the amount of the expenditure on the asset that is recognised for tax purposes is the same as the amount of expenditure on the asset capitalised by the company.

FA 2002

(5) The amount of the debit for tax purposes in respect of expenditure on an asset is, in a subsequent period of account:

$$\text{Accounting Loss} \times \frac{\text{Tax Value}}{\text{Accounting Value}}$$

where—

Accounting Loss is the amount of the loss recognised for accounting purposes,
Tax Value is the tax written down value of the asset immediately before the amortisation charge is made or, as the case may be, the impairment loss is recognised for accounting purposes, and
Accounting Value is the value of the asset recognised for accounting purposes immediately before the amortisation charge or, as the case may be, the impairment review.

(6) In this paragraph ''capitalised'' means capitalised for accounting purposes.

Writing down at fixed rate: election for fixed-rate basis

10—(1) A company may elect to write down the cost of an intangible fixed asset for tax purposes at a fixed rate.

(2) An election to that effect may be made whether or not the asset is written down for accounting purposes.

(3) An election under this paragraph must be made—

    (a) in writing,
    (b) to the Inland Revenue,
    (c) no later than two years after the end of the accounting period in which the asset is created or acquired by the company making the election.

(4) An election under this paragraph in relation to an asset has effect in relation to all expenditure on the asset that is capitalised for accounting purposes.

(5) An election under this paragraph is irrevocable.

(6) Paragraph 9 (writing down on accounting basis) does not apply to an asset in respect of which an election is made under this paragraph.

Writing down at fixed rate: calculation

11—(1) Where an election is made for writing down at a fixed rate, a debit equal to—

    (a) 4% of the cost of the asset, or
    (b) if less, the balance of the tax written down value,

shall be brought into account for tax purposes in each accounting period beginning with that in which the relevant expenditure is incurred.

(2) If the accounting period is less than 12 months, the amount mentioned in sub-paragraph (1)(a) above shall be proportionately reduced.

(3) The cost of the asset means the cost recognised for tax purposes.

(4) Subject to any adjustment required for tax purposes, the cost of the asset recognised for tax purposes is the same as the amount capitalised for accounting purposes in respect of expenditure on the asset.

(5) After a part realisation of the asset the reference in sub-paragraph (1)(a) to the cost of the asset shall be read as a reference to—

    (a) the cost recognised for tax purposes in respect of the value of the asset recognised for accounting purposes immediately after the part realisation, and
    (b) the cost so recognised of any subsequent expenditure on the asset that is capitalised for accounting purposes.

(6) On a further part realisation, sub-paragraph (5) applies again.

Reversal of previous accounting gain

12—(1) Where in a period of account a loss is recognised in the company's profit and loss account reversing (in whole or in part) a gain recognised in a previous period of account in respect of which a credit was brought into account for tax purposes under Part 3 (credits in respect of intangible fixed assets), a corresponding debit shall be brought into account for tax purposes.

(2) The amount of the debit to be brought into account for tax purposes is:

$$\text{Accounting Loss} \times \frac{\text{Previous Credit}}{\text{Accounting Gain}}$$

where—

Accounting Loss is the amount of the loss recognised for accounting purposes,
Accounting Gain is the amount of the gain that is (in whole or in part) reversed, and
Previous Credit is the amount of the credit previously brought into account for tax purposes in respect of the gain.

(3) References in this paragraph to the recognition of a loss reversing a gain recognised in a previous period of account do not include a loss recognised by way of amortisation, or as a result of an impairment review, of an asset that has previously been the subject of a revaluation within the meaning of paragraph 15.

PART 3
CREDITS IN RESPECT OF INTANGIBLE FIXED ASSETS
Introduction

13—(1) This Part provides for credits to be brought into account by a company for tax purposes in respect of—

    (*a*) receipts in respect of intangible fixed assets that are recognised in the profit and loss account as they accrue (see paragraph 14),

    (*b*) revaluation of an intangible fixed asset (see paragraph 15),

    (*c*) credits recognised for accounting purposes in respect of negative goodwill (see paragraph 16), and

    (*d*) the reversal of previous accounting debits in respect of an intangible fixed asset (see paragraph 17).

(2) This Part does not apply in relation to amounts brought into account in connection with the realisation of an intangible fixed asset within the meaning of Part 4.

Receipts recognised as they accrue

14—(1) Where in a period of account a gain representing a receipt in respect of an intangible fixed asset is recognised in the company's profit and loss account, a corresponding credit shall be brought into account for tax purposes.

(2) Subject to any adjustment required for tax purposes, the amount of the credit recognised for tax purposes under this paragraph is the same as the amount of the gain recognised by the company for accounting purposes.

Revaluation

15—(1) Where in a period of account the accounting value of an intangible fixed asset is increased on a revaluation, a credit shall be brought into account for tax purposes.

(2) The amount of the credit for tax purposes is—

    (*a*) the amount corresponding for tax purposes to the increase in value (see sub-paragraph (3)), or

    (*b*) if less, the net aggregate amount of relevant tax debits previously brought into account (see sub-paragraph (4)).

(3) The amount corresponding for tax purposes to the increase in value is:

$$\text{Accounting Adjustment} \times \frac{\text{Tax Value}}{\text{Accounting Value}}$$

where—

    Accounting Adjustment is the amount of the increase in the accounting value of the asset,

    Tax Value is the tax written down value of the asset immediately before the revaluation, and

    Accounting Value is the accounting value of the asset by reference to which the revaluation is carried out.

(4) The net aggregate amount of relevant tax debits previously brought into account is:

Previous Debits – Previous Credits

where—

    Previous Debits is the total amount of debits previously brought into account for tax purposes in respect of the asset under paragraph 9 (writing down on accounting basis), and

    Previous Credits is the total amount of any credits previously brought into account for tax purposes in respect of the asset under this paragraph.

(5) For the purposes of this paragraph a "revaluation" includes—

    (*a*) the valuation of an asset for which a value is shown in the company's balance sheet but which has not previously been the subject of a valuation, and

    (*b*) the restoration of past losses.

(6) This paragraph does not apply to an asset in respect of which an election has been made under paragraph 10 (election for writing down at fixed rate).

Negative goodwill

16—(1) Where in a period of account a gain is recognised in the company's profit and loss account in respect of negative goodwill arising on an acquisition of a business, a corresponding credit shall be brought into account for tax purposes.

(2) The amount of the credit is so much of the gain recognised for accounting purposes as, on a just and reasonable apportionment, is attributable to intangible fixed assets.

Reversal of previous accounting loss

17—(1) Where in a period of account a gain is recognised in the company's profit and loss account reversing (in whole or in part) a loss recognised in a previous period of account in respect of which a debit was brought into account for tax purposes under Part 2 (debits in respect of intangible fixed assets), a corresponding credit shall be brought into account for tax purposes.

(2) The amount of the credit to be brought into account for tax purposes is:

$$\text{Accounting Gain} \times \frac{\text{Tax Debit}}{\text{Accounting Loss}}$$

where—

Accounting Gain is the amount of the gain recognised for accounting purposes,
Accounting Loss is the amount of the loss that is reversed (in whole or in part), and
Tax Debit is the amount of the tax debit brought into account in respect of the loss.

(3) This paragraph does not apply to a gain on a revaluation within the meaning of paragraph 15.

PART 4
REALISATION OF INTANGIBLE FIXED ASSETS

Introduction

18 This Part provides for credits or debits to be brought into account for tax purposes on the realisation by a company of an intangible fixed asset.

Meaning of "realisation"

19—(1) References in this Schedule to the realisation of an intangible fixed asset are to a transaction resulting, in accordance with generally accepted accounting practice—

(*a*) in the asset ceasing to be recognised in the company's balance sheet, or
(*b*) in a reduction in the accounting value of the asset.

For this purpose a "transaction" includes any event giving rise to a gain recognised for accounting purposes.

(2) In relation to an intangible fixed asset that has no balance sheet value (or no longer has a balance sheet value), sub-paragraph (1) applies as if it did have a balance sheet value.

(3) References in this Schedule to a "part realisation" are to a realisation falling within sub-paragraph (1)(*b*).

Realisation of asset written down for tax purposes

20—(1) This paragraph applies where there is a realisation of an intangible fixed asset in respect of which debits have been brought into account for tax purposes—

(*a*) under paragraph 9 (writing down on accounting basis), or
(*b*) under paragraphs 10 and 11 (writing down at fixed rate).

(2) Where this paragraph applies—

(*a*) if the proceeds of realisation exceed the tax written down value of the asset, a credit equal to the excess shall be brought into account for tax purposes;
(*b*) if the proceeds of realisation are less than the tax written down value of the asset, a debit equal to the shortfall shall be brought into account for tax purposes; and
(*c*) if there are no proceeds of realisation, a debit equal to the tax written down value shall be brought into account for tax purposes.

(3) References in this paragraph to the tax written down value of an asset are to its tax written down value immediately before the realisation.

Realisation of asset shown in balance sheet and not written down for tax purposes

21—(1) This paragraph applies where there is a realisation of an intangible fixed asset for which a value is shown in the company's balance sheet but which is not within paragraph 20 (asset written down for tax purposes).

(2) Where this paragraph applies—

(*a*) if the proceeds of realisation exceed the cost of the asset, a credit equal to the excess shall be brought into account for tax purposes;
(*b*) if the proceeds of realisation are less than the cost of the asset, a debit equal to the shortfall shall be brought into account for tax purposes; and
(*c*) if there are no proceeds of realisation, a debit equal to the cost of the asset shall be brought into account for tax purposes.

(3) The cost of the asset means the cost recognised for tax purposes.

(4) Subject to any adjustment required for tax purposes, the cost of the asset recognised for tax purposes is the same as the amount of expenditure on the asset capitalised by the company for accounting purposes.

(5) After a part realisation of the asset the references in sub-paragraph (2)(*a*), (*b*) and (*c*) to the cost of the asset shall be read as a reference to—

    (*a*) the cost recognised for tax purposes in respect of the value of the asset recognised for accounting purposes immediately after the part realisation, and

    (*b*) the cost so recognised of any subsequent expenditure on the asset that is capitalised for accounting purposes.

(6) On a further part realisation, sub-paragraph (5) applies again.

Apportionment in case of part realisation

22—(1) In the case of a part realisation the reference in paragraph 20 to the tax written down value of the asset, or, as the case may be, the reference in paragraph 21 to the cost of the asset, shall be read as references to the appropriate proportion of that amount.

(2) That proportion is given by:

$$\frac{\text{Reduction in Accounting Value}}{\text{Previous Accounting Value}}$$

where—

    Reduction in Accounting Value is the difference between the accounting value immediately before the realisation compared with that immediately after the realisation; and
    Previous Accounting Value is the accounting value immediately before the realisation.

Realisation of asset not shown in balance sheet

23—(1) This paragraph applies where there is a realisation of an intangible fixed asset in relation to which neither paragraph 20 (asset written down for tax purposes) nor paragraph 21 (asset shown in balance sheet but not written down) applies.

(2) Where this paragraph applies, a credit equal to any proceeds of realisation shall be brought into account for tax purposes.

Meaning of "proceeds of realisation"

24—(1) In this Schedule the "proceeds of realisation" of an asset means the amount recognised for accounting purposes as the proceeds of realisation, reduced by the amount so recognised as incidental costs of realisation.

(2) The amounts referred to in sub-paragraph (1) are subject to any adjustment required for tax purposes.

Relief in case of reinvestment

25 The preceding provisions of this Part have effect subject to Part 7 (relief in case of reinvestment).

Abortive expenditure on realisation

26—(1) Where in a period of account—

    (*a*) a loss is recognised in the company's profit and loss account in respect of expenditure by the company for the purposes of a transaction that would constitute a realisation of an intangible fixed asset, but

    (*b*) the transaction does not proceed to completion,

a corresponding debit shall be brought into account for tax purposes.

(2) Subject to any adjustment required for tax purposes, the amount of the debit recognised for tax purposes is the same as the amount of the loss recognised by the company for accounting purposes.

PART 5

CALCULATION OF TAX WRITTEN DOWN VALUE

Asset written down on accounting basis

27—(1) For the purposes of this Schedule the tax written down value of an intangible fixed asset to which paragraph 9 applies (writing down on accounting basis) is given by:

Tax Cost – Debits + Credits

where—

    Tax Cost is the cost of the asset recognised for tax purposes;

Debits is the total amount of the debits previously brought into account for tax purposes in respect of the asset under paragraph 9; and

Credits is the total amount of any credits previously brought into account for tax purposes in respect of the asset under paragraph 15 (revaluation).

(2) Subject to any adjustment required for tax purposes, the cost of the asset recognised for tax purposes is the same as the amount of the expenditure on the asset that is capitalised for accounting purposes.

(3) This paragraph has effect subject to paragraph 29 in the case of an asset that has been the subject of a part realisation.

Asset written down at fixed rate

28—(1) For the purposes of this Schedule the tax written down value of an intangible fixed asset in respect of which an election has been made under paragraph 10 (election for writing down at fixed rate) is given by:

$$\text{Tax Cost} - \text{Debits}$$

where—

Tax Cost is the cost of the asset recognised for tax purposes; and

Debits is the total amount of the debits previously brought into account for tax purposes in respect of the asset under paragraph 11 (writing down on fixed-rate basis: calculation).

(2) Subject to any adjustment required for tax purposes, the cost of the asset recognised for tax purposes is the same as the amount of the expenditure on the asset that is capitalised for accounting purposes.

(3) This paragraph has effect subject to paragraph 29 in the case of an asset that has been the subject of a part realisation.

Effect of part realisation of asset

29—(1) The tax written down value of an intangible asset that has been the subject of a part realisation is determined as follows.

(2) The tax written down value of the asset immediately after the part realisation is given by:

$$\text{Previous Tax Value} \times \frac{\text{New Accounting Value}}{\text{Previous Accounting Value}}$$

where—

Previous Tax Value is the tax written down value of the asset immediately before the part realisation;

New Accounting Value is the accounting value of the asset immediately after the part realisation; and

Previous Accounting Value is the accounting value immediately before the part realisation.

(3) Subsequently, the tax written down value of the asset is determined in accordance with paragraph 27 or 28—

(*a*) taking the cost of the asset recognised for tax purposes to be the tax written down value given by sub-paragraph (2) above together with the cost recognised for tax purposes of subsequent expenditure on the asset that is capitalised for accounting purposes; and

(*b*) taking account only of debits and credits brought into account for tax purposes after the part realisation.

(4) On a further part realisation, the preceding provisions of this paragraph apply again.

PART 6
HOW CREDITS AND DEBITS ARE GIVEN EFFECT

Introduction

30—(1) Credits and debits to be brought into account for tax purposes under this Schedule are given effect in accordance with this Part.

(2) Credits and debits in respect of assets held for the purposes mentioned in—

(*a*) paragraph 31 (assets held for purposes of trade), or

(*b*) paragraph 32 (assets held for purposes of property business) or

(*c*) paragraph 33 (assets held for purposes of certain concerns taxed under Case I of Schedule D),

are given effect in accordance with the paragraph in question.

(3) Other credits and debits (''non-trading credits and debits'') are given effect in accordance with paragraphs 34 and 35.

(4) Any apportionment necessary where an asset is held for purposes falling within more than one of the provisions mentioned above shall be made on a just and reasonable basis.

(5) The provisions mentioned in this paragraph have effect subject to paragraph 36 (special provisions relating to insurance companies).

Asset held for purposes of trade

31 Credits and debits to be brought into account in any accounting period in respect of an asset held by the company for the purposes of a trade carried on by it in that period are given effect by treating—

    (a) credits as receipts of the trade, and
    (b) debits as expenses of the trade,

in calculating the profits of the trade for tax purposes.

Asset held for purposes of property business

32—(1) Credits and debits to be brought into account in any accounting period in respect of an asset held by the company for the purposes of a property business carried on by it in that period are given effect by treating—

    (a) credits as receipts of the business, and
    (b) debits as expenses of the business,

in computing the profits of the business for tax purposes.

(2) A "property business" means—

    (a) an ordinary Schedule A business,
    (b) a furnished holiday lettings business, or
    (c) an overseas property business.

(3) In this paragraph —

    "ordinary Schedule A business" means a Schedule A business except in so far as it is a furnished holiday lettings business; and
    "furnished holiday lettings business" means a Schedule A business in so far as it consists of the commercial letting of furnished holiday accommodation (as defined in section 504 of the Taxes Act 1988) in the United Kingdom.

(4) Section 503 of the Taxes Act 1988 (letting of furnished holiday accommodation treated as separate, single trade) applies for the purposes of this Schedule.

Assets held for purposes of mines, transport undertakings, etc

33 Credits and debits to be brought into account in any accounting period in respect of an asset held by the company for the purposes of a concern listed in section 55(2) of the Taxes Act 1988 (mines, transport undertakings, etc) that is carried on by the company in that period are given effect by treating—

    (a) credits as receipts of the concern, and
    (b) debits as expenses of the concern,

in computing the profits of the concern under Case 1 of Schedule D.

Non-trading credits and debits

34—(1) Where, or to the extent that, in an accounting period, there are—

    (a) credits in respect of intangible fixed assets that are not within any of paragraphs 31 to 33 ("non-trading credits"), or
    (b) debits in respect of intangible fixed assets that are not within any of those paragraphs ("non-trading debits"),

the company's aggregate non-trading gain or loss on intangible fixed assets must be calculated.

(2) There is a non-trading gain on intangible fixed assets if—

    (a) there are only non-trading credits, or
    (b) there are both non-trading credits and non-trading debits and the aggregate of the former exceeds the aggregate of the latter.

The amount of the non-trading gain is the aggregate amount of the credits or, as the case may be, the amount of the excess.

(3) There is a non-trading loss on intangible fixed assets if—

    (a) there are only non-trading debits, or
    (b) there are both non-trading credits and non-trading debits and the aggregate of the latter exceeds the aggregate of the former.

The amount of the non-trading loss is the aggregate amount of the debits or, as the case may be, the amount of the excess.

(4) A non-trading gain on intangible fixed assets is chargeable to tax under Case VI of Schedule D.

(5) A non-trading loss on intangible fixed assets is given effect in accordance with the following paragraph.

Claim to set non-trading loss against total profits

35—(1) A company that has a non-trading loss on intangible fixed assets for an accounting period may claim to have the whole or part of the loss set off against the company's total profits for that period.

(2) Any such claim must be made not later than the end of the period of two years immediately following the end of the accounting period to which it relates, or within such further period as the Inland Revenue may allow.

(3) To the extent that the loss is not—

    (a) set off against total profits on a claim under sub-paragraph (1), or
    (b) surrendered by way of group relief (see section 403 of the Taxes Act 1988),

it is carried forward to the next accounting period of the company and treated as if it were a non-trading debit of that period.

Special provisions relating to insurance companies

36—(1) Nothing in this Schedule shall be read as preventing profits and gains arising from intangible fixed assets of an insurance company from being included, where—

    (a) the assets are referable to life assurance business carried on by the company, and
    (b) the I minus E basis is applied in relation to that business,

in profits and gains on which the company is chargeable to tax in accordance with that basis.

(2) Where for any accounting period the I minus E basis is applied in relation to life assurance business carried on by an insurance company, the effect of applying that basis is that credits or debits falling to be brought into account under this Schedule in respect of intangible fixed assets of the company referable to that business—

    (a) are not brought into account as mentioned in paragraph 31 (assets held for purposes of trade), but
    (b) subject to the following provisions of this paragraph, are instead brought into account under paragraph 34 as non-trading credits or, as the case may be, non-trading debits.

(3) Where an insurance company carries on basic life assurance and general annuity business—

    (a) a separate computation of the credits and debits referable to that business shall be made under paragraph 34 (non-trading credits and debits),
    (b) any resulting non-trading gain in respect of intangible assets is chargeable to tax as mentioned in sub-paragraph (4) of that paragraph, and
    (c) any resulting non-trading loss in respect of intangible assets is treated as additional expenses of management within section 76 of the Taxes Act 1988.

(4) References in any enactment to the computation of any profits of an insurance company in accordance with the provisions of the Taxes Act 1988 applicable to Case I of Schedule D have effect as if those provisions included the provisions of this Schedule, but only to the extent that they relate to the bringing into account of debits in respect of royalties.

(5) Where an insurance company carries on life assurance business or any category of life assurance business—

    (a) the credits and debits under this Schedule referable to that business or category of business, other than debits in respect of royalties, shall be disregarded for the purposes of any computations falling to be made in relation to that business or category of business in accordance with the provisions applicable to Case I of Schedule D, and
    (b) accordingly, the amounts to be brought into account in any such computations shall be determined under the provisions applicable apart from this Schedule.

(6) In this paragraph "the I minus E basis" means the basis commonly so called under which a company carrying on life assurance business is charged to tax on that business otherwise than under Case I of Schedule D.

PART 7

ROLL-OVER RELIEF IN CASE OF REALISATION AND REINVESTMENT

The relief

37—(1) This Part provides for relief where a company realises an intangible fixed asset (the "old asset") and incurs expenditure on other intangible fixed assets ("other assets").

(2) A company is entitled to relief under this Part only if—

    (a) the conditions in paragraph 38 are met in relation to the old asset and its realisation,
    (b) the conditions in paragraph 39 are met in relation to the expenditure on other assets, and
    (c) the company claims the relief in accordance with paragraph 40.

Conditions to be met in relation to the old asset and its realisation

38—(1) The following conditions must be met in relation to the old asset and its realisation—

   (*a*) the asset must have been a chargeable intangible asset of the company throughout the period during which it was held by the company; and

   (*b*) the proceeds of realisation of the asset must exceed—

      (i) the cost of the asset, or

      (ii) in the case of a part realisation, the appropriate proportion of the cost of the asset, or

      (iii) in the case of the realisation of an asset that has been the subject of a part realisation, the adjusted cost of the asset.

(2) If the asset was a chargeable intangible asset of the company—

   (*a*) at the time of its realisation, and

   (*b*) for a substantial part of, but not throughout, the period during which it was held by the company,

a part of the asset representing the time for which it was a chargeable intangible asset shall be treated for the purposes of this Part as if it were a separate asset in relation to which the condition in sub-paragraph (1) (*a*) was wholly met.

Any apportionment necessary for this purpose shall be made on a just and reasonable basis.

(3) In sub-paragraph (1)(*b*) ''the cost of the asset'' means the total of the capitalised expenditure on the asset recognised for tax purposes.

For the calculation of the appropriate proportion or adjusted cost, see paragraph 42.

(4) The condition in sub-paragraph (1)(*b*) is necessarily met if the asset has no cost as defined above.

Conditions to be met in relation to the expenditure on other assets

39—(1) The following conditions must be met in relation to the expenditure on other assets—

   (*a*) the expenditure must be incurred in the period—

      (i) beginning twelve months before the date of realisation of the old asset or at such earlier time as the Inland Revenue may by notice allow, and

      (ii) ending three years after the date of realisation of the old asset or at such later time as the Inland Revenue may by notice allow;

   (*b*) the expenditure must be capitalised by the company for accounting purposes; and

   (*c*) the assets on which the expenditure is incurred must be chargeable intangible assets in relation to the company immediately after the expenditure is incurred.

(2) For the purposes of this paragraph expenditure is regarded as incurred when it is recognised for accounting purposes.

Claim for relief

40 A claim by a company for relief under this Part must specify—

   (*a*) the old assets to which the claim relates, and

   (*b*) in relation to each old asset—

      (i) the expenditure on other assets by reference to which relief is claimed, and

      (ii) the amount of the relief claimed.

How the relief is given: general

41—(1) A company that is entitled to, and claims, relief under this Part is treated for the purposes of this Schedule as if—

   (*a*) the proceeds of realisation of the old asset, and

   (*b*) the cost recognised for tax purposes of acquiring the other assets, were each reduced by the amount available for relief.

(2) If the amount of qualifying expenditure on other assets is equal to or greater than the proceeds of realisation of the old asset, the amount available for relief is the amount by which the proceeds of realisation exceed the cost of the old asset.

(3) If the amount of qualifying expenditure on other assets is less than the proceeds of realisation of the old asset, the amount available for relief is the amount (if any) by which the qualifying expenditure on other assets exceeds the cost of the old asset.

(4) In this paragraph—

   (*a*) ''qualifying expenditure'' means expenditure in relation to which the conditions in paragraph 39 are met;

   (*b*) ''the cost of the old asset'' means the total of the capitalised expenditure on the asset recognised for tax purposes;

   (*c*) the references to the cost of the old asset shall be read—

      (i) in the case of a part realisation, as references to the appropriate proportion of the cost, and

(ii) in the case of the realisation of an asset that has been the subject of a part realisation, as references to the adjusted cost.

For the calculation of the appropriate proportion and the adjusted cost, see paragraph 42.

(5) The relief does not affect the treatment for any purpose of the Taxes Acts of any other party to any transaction involved in the realisation of the old asset or the expenditure on the other assets.

Determination of appropriate proportion or adjusted cost

42—(1) Any reference in paragraph 38 or 41 to the appropriate proportion of the cost of the old asset in the case of a part realisation is to the proportion given by:

$$\frac{\text{Reduction in Accounting Value}}{\text{Previous Accounting Value}}$$

where—

Reduction in Accounting Value is the difference between the accounting value immediately before the part realisation compared with that immediately after the part realisation; and

Previous Accounting Value is the accounting value immediately before the part realisation.

(2) In the case of an asset that has previously been the subject of a part realisation the reference in sub-paragraph (1) to the cost of the old asset shall be read as a reference to the adjusted cost.

(3) Any reference in paragraph 38 or 41, or sub-paragraph (2) above, to the adjusted cost in the case where the old asset has previously been the subject of a part realisation is to the amount given by deducting from the cost of the old asset the total of the amounts given by sub-paragraphs (1) and (2) above in relation to earlier part realisations.

Declaration of provisional entitlement to relief

43—(1) A company realising an intangible fixed asset may make a declaration of provisional entitlement to relief under this Part.

(2) A declaration of provisional entitlement is a declaration by the company, in its company tax return for the accounting period in which the realisation takes place, that the company—

(*a*) has realised an intangible fixed asset,

(*b*) proposes to meet the conditions for relief under this Part, and

(*c*) is accordingly provisionally entitled to relief of a specified amount.

(3) While the declaration continues in force, this Part applies as if the conditions for relief under this Part were met.

(4) A declaration of provisional entitlement ceases to have effect if, or to the extent that—

(*a*) it is withdrawn, or

(*b*) it is superseded by a claim for relief under this Part.

(5) So far as not previously withdrawn or superseded, a declaration of provisional entitlement ceases to have effect four years after the end of the accounting period in which the realisation took place.

(6) On a declaration of provisional entitlement ceasing to have effect, in whole or in part, all necessary adjustments shall be made, by assessment or otherwise.

This applies notwithstanding any limitation on the time within which assessments or amendments may be made.

Realisation and reacquisition

44 This Part applies where a company realises an asset and subsequently reacquires it as if what is reacquired were a different asset from that previously realised.

Deemed realisations and deemed acquisitions to be disregarded

45—(1) This Part does not apply in relation to a deemed realisation of an asset except as provided by—

(*a*) paragraph 65 (application of roll-over relief in relation to deemed realisation as a result of degrouping), or

(*b*) paragraph 67 (application of roll-over relief in relation to reallocated degrouping charge).

(2) No account shall be taken for the purposes of this Part of any deemed reacquisition.

PART 8

GROUPS OF COMPANIES

Introduction

46—(1) This Part has effect for the purposes of this Schedule to determine whether companies form a group and, where they do, which is the principal company of the group.

(2) In this Part references to a company apply only to—

(*a*) a company within the meaning of the Companies Act 1985 (c 6) or the Companies (Northern Ireland) Order 1986 (SI 1986/1032 (NI 6));

(*b*) a company (other than a limited liability partnership) constituted under any other Act or by a Royal Charter or letters patent;

(*c*) a company formed under the law of a country or territory outside the United Kingdom;

(*d*) a registered industrial and provident society within the meaning of section 486 of the Taxes Act 1988;

(*e*) an incorporated friendly society within the meaning of the Friendly Societies Act 1992 (c 40); or

(*f*) a building society.

(3) In this Schedule the expressions "group" and "subsidiary" shall be construed with any necessary modifications where applied to a company formed under the law of a country outside the United Kingdom.

General rule: a company and its 75% subsidiaries form a group

47—(1) A company ("the principal company of the group") and all its 75% subsidiaries form a group, and if any of those subsidiaries have 75% subsidiaries the group includes them and their 75% subsidiaries, and so on.

(2) Sub-paragraph (1) has effect subject to the following provisions of this Part.

Membership of group restricted to effective 51% subsidiaries of principal company

48 A group of companies does not include any company (other than the principal company of the group) that is not an effective 51% subsidiary of the principal company of the group.

Principal company cannot be 75% subsidiary of another company

49—(1) A company cannot be the principal company of a group if it is itself a 75% subsidiary of another company.

(2) Notwithstanding sub-paragraph (1), where—

(*a*) a company ("the subsidiary") is a 75% subsidiary of another company, and

(*b*) those companies are prevented from being members of the same group by paragraph 48 (the effective 51% subsidiary requirement),

the subsidiary may, if the requirements of paragraphs 47 and 48 are met, itself be the principal company of another group, unless this enables a further company to be the principal company of a group of which the subsidiary would be a member.

Company cannot be member of more than one group

50—(1) A company cannot be a member of more than one group.

(2) If a company would otherwise be a member of two or more groups, the group of which it is a member is determined by applying the following rules (applying the rules successively in the order shown until an answer is obtained).

(3) In the following provisions the principal company of each group is referred to as the "head of a group".

(4) The first rule is that the company is a member of the group of which it would be a member if, in applying paragraph 48 (the effective 51% subsidiary requirement), there were left out of account—

(*a*) any amount to which a head of a group is beneficially entitled of any profits available for distribution to equity holders of a head of another group, or

(*b*) any amount to which a head of a group would be beneficially entitled of any assets of a head of another group available for distribution to its equity holders on a winding up.

(5) The second rule is that the company is a member of the group the head of which is beneficially entitled to a percentage of the profits available for distribution to equity holders of the company that is greater than the percentage of those profits to which any other head of a group is so entitled.

(6) The third rule is that the company is a member of the group the head of which would be beneficially entitled to a percentage of any assets of the company available for distribution to its equity holders on a winding up that is greater than the percentage of those assets to which any other head of a group would be so entitled.

(7) The fourth rule is that the company is a member of the group the head of which owns directly or indirectly a percentage of the company's ordinary share capital that is greater than the percentage of that capital owned directly or indirectly by any other head of a group.

The provisions of section 838(2) to (10) of the Taxes Act 1988 apply for the interpretation of this sub-paragraph as they apply for the interpretation of subsection (1)(*a*) of that section (definition of "51% subsidiary").

Continuity of identity of group

51—(1) For the purposes of this Schedule—

(a) a group of companies remains the same group of companies so long as the same company is the principal company of the group, and

(b) if the principal company of a group becomes a member of another group, the first group and the other group shall be regarded as the same (and the question whether a company has ceased to be a member of a group shall be determined accordingly).

(2) For the purposes of this Schedule the passing of a resolution or the making of an order, or any other act, for the winding up of a member of a group is not regarded as the occasion of that or any other company ceasing to be a member of the group.

Meaning of "effective 51% subsidiary"

52 For the purposes of this Schedule a company ("the subsidiary") is an effective 51% subsidiary of another company ("the parent") if, and only if, the parent—

(a) is beneficially entitled to more than 50% of any profits available for distribution to equity holders of the subsidiary, and

(b) would be beneficially entitled to more than 50% of any assets of the subsidiary available for distribution to its equity holders on a winding up.

Meaning of equity holder and profits or assets available for distribution

53—(1) Schedule 18 to the Taxes Act 1988 (meaning of equity holder and determination of profits or assets available for distribution) applies for the purposes of paragraphs 50 and 52.

(2) In that Schedule as it applies for the purposes of those paragraphs—

(a) for any reference to sections 403C and 413(7) of that Act, or either of those provisions, substitute a reference to those paragraphs;

(b) omit the words in paragraph 1(4) from "but" to the end;

(c) omit paragraph 5(3) and paragraphs 5B to 5F; and

(d) omit paragraph 7(1)(b).

Supplementary provisions

54—(1) In applying for the purposes of this Part the definition of "75% subsidiary" in section 838 of the Taxes Act 1988, any share capital of a registered industrial and provident society shall be treated as ordinary share capital.

(2) The provisions of section 170(12) to (14) of the Taxation of Chargeable Gains Act 1992 (c 12) (application to certain statutory bodies of provisions relating to groups of companies) apply for the purposes of this Part as they apply for the purposes of sections 171 to 181 of that Act.

PART 9
APPLICATION OF PROVISIONS TO GROUPS OF COMPANIES

Transfers within a group

55—(1) Where—

(a) an intangible fixed asset is transferred from one company ("the transferor") to another company ("the transferee") at a time when both companies are members of the same group, and

(b) the asset is a chargeable intangible asset in relation to the transferor immediately before the transfer and in relation to the transferee immediately after the transfer,

the transfer of the asset is treated for the purposes of this Schedule as tax-neutral (see paragraph 139).

(2) Sub-paragraph (1) does not apply—

(a) if the transferor or transferee is a qualifying society within the meaning of section 461A of the Taxes Act 1988 (incorporated friendly societies entitled to exemption from tax), or

(b) if the transferee is a dual resident investing company within the meaning of section 404 of that Act (limitation of group relief).

Roll-over relief on reinvestment: application to group member

56—(1) The following provisions have effect as regards the application of Part 7 (roll-over relief in case of realisation and reinvestment) in relation to a company that is a member of a group.

(2) That Part applies where—

(a) the realisation of the old asset is by a company that, at the time of the realisation, is a member of a group,

(b) the expenditure on other assets is by another company that, at the time the expenditure is incurred—

    (i) is a member of the same group as the company mentioned in paragraph (*a*), and
    (ii) is not a dual resident investing company,

(*c*) the other assets are chargeable intangible assets in relation to the company mentioned in paragraph (*b*) immediately after the expenditure is incurred, and
(*d*) the claim is made by both companies,

as if both companies were the same person.

(3) That Part does not apply if the expenditure on other assets is expenditure on the acquisition of assets acquired from another member of the same group by a tax-neutral transfer.

(4) Expressions used in this paragraph that are defined for the purposes of Part 7 have the same meaning in this paragraph.

Roll-over relief on reinvestment: acquisition of group company treated as equivalent to acquisition of underlying assets

57—(1) Where a company ("company A") acquires a controlling interest in another company ("company B") and intangible fixed assets ("underlying assets") are held—

(*a*) by company B, or
(*b*) by one or more other companies that were not in the same group as company A before its acquisition of a controlling interest in company B but as a result of that acquisition are in the same group as company A immediately after the acquisition,

Part 7 (roll-over relief in case of realisation and reinvestment) has effect in accordance with the following provisions.

(2) The expenditure by company A on the acquisition of a controlling interest in company B is treated as expenditure on acquiring the underlying assets.

(3) The amount of expenditure that is treated as incurred by company A on acquiring the underlying assets is taken to be—

(*a*) the tax written down value of the underlying assets immediately before the acquisition, or
(*b*) if less, the amount or value of the consideration for the acquisition by company A of the controlling interest in company B.

(4) The requirement that the assets be chargeable intangible assets in relation to company A immediately after the expenditure is incurred on acquiring them is treated as met in relation to the underlying assets if they are chargeable intangible assets in relation to the company by which they are held immediately after the acquisition by company A of a controlling interest in company B.

(5) The tax written down value of the underlying assets in the hands of the company by which they are held shall be reduced by the amount available for relief, and if—

(*a*) there is more than one underlying asset, and
(*b*) the amount of expenditure on other assets that is treated as incurred exceeds the amount available for relief,

the company by which the underlying assets are held may decide how the amount available for relief is to be allocated in reducing the tax written down values of the assets.

If there is more than one such company, they may agree between them how that amount is to be allocated.

(6) A claim for relief under Part 7 made by virtue of this paragraph must be made jointly by company A and the company or companies holding the underlying assets concerned.

(7) For the purposes of this paragraph company A acquires a controlling interest in company B if the two companies are not in the same group and there is an acquisition by company A of shares in company B such that those two companies are in the same group immediately after the acquisition.

(8) Expressions used in this paragraph that are defined for the purposes of Part 7 have the same meaning in this paragraph.

Company ceasing to be member of group ("degrouping")

58—(1) This paragraph applies where—

(*a*) a company ("the transferor") that is a member of a group ("the group") transfers an intangible fixed asset ("the relevant asset") to another company ("the transferee"),
(*b*) the relevant asset is a chargeable intangible asset in relation to the transferor immediately before the transfer and in relation to the transferee immediately after the transfer, and
(*c*) the transferee—
    (i) having been a member of the group at the time of the transfer, or
    (ii) having subsequently become a member of the group,

ceases to be a member of the group after the transfer and before the end of the period of six years after the date of the transfer.

(2) If, when the transferee ceases to be a member of the group, the relevant asset is held by the transferee or an associated company also leaving the group, this Schedule has effect as if the

transferee, immediately after the transfer of the relevant asset to it, had realised the asset for its market value at that time and immediately reacquired the asset at that value.

(3) The adjustments required to be made in consequence of sub-paragraph (2), by the transferee or a company to which the relevant asset has been subsequently transferred, in relation to the period between—

(a) the transfer of the relevant asset to the transferee, and

(b) the transferee ceasing to be a member of the group,

shall be made by bringing the aggregate net credit or debit into account as if it had arisen immediately before the transferee ceased to be a member of the group.

(4) For the purposes of Part 6 (how credits and debits are given effect) credits or debits brought into account by virtue of this paragraph take their character from the purposes for which the relevant asset was held by the transferee immediately after the transfer.

Provided that, in a case where—

(a) the asset was then held by the transferee for the purposes of a trade, business or concern within paragraph 31, 32 or 33, and

(b) the transferee ceased to carry on that trade, business or concern before it ceased to be a member of the group,

any credit or debit brought into account by virtue of this paragraph in respect of the asset shall be treated for the purposes of Part 6 as a non-trading credit or debit.

(5) This paragraph has effect subject to—

paragraph 59 (associated companies leaving group at the same time),

paragraph 60 (principal company becoming member of another group),

paragraph 61 (company ceasing to be member of group by reason of exempt distribution), and

paragraph 62 (merger carried out for bona fide commercial reasons).

Degrouping: associated companies leaving group at the same time

59—(1) Where two or more associated companies cease to be members of a group at the same time, paragraph 58 does not have effect in relation to a transfer from one to another of those companies.

(2) But where—

(a) a company ("the transferee") that has ceased to be a member of a group of companies ("the first group") acquired an asset from another company ("the transferor") which was a member of that group at the time of the transfer,

(b) sub-paragraph (1) applies in relation to the transferee's ceasing to be a member of the first group so that paragraph 58 does not have effect,

(c) the transferee subsequently ceases to be a member of another group of companies ("the second group"), and

(d) there is a relevant connection between the two groups (see sub-paragraph (3)),

paragraph 58 has effect in relation to the transferee's ceasing to be a member of the second group as if it were the second group of which both companies had been members at the time of the transfer.

(3) For the purposes of sub-paragraph (2) there is a relevant connection between the first group and the second group if, at the time when the transferee ceases to be a member of the second group, the company which is the principal company of that group is under the control of—

(a) the company that is the principal company of the first group or, if that group no longer exists, was the principal company of that group when the transferee ceased to be a member of it; or

(b) any person or persons who control the company mentioned in paragraph (a) or who have had it under their control at any time in the period since the transferee ceased to be a member of the first group; or

(c) any person or persons who have, at any time in that period, had under their control either—

(i) a company that would have been a person falling within paragraph (b) if it had continued to exist, or

(ii) a company that would have been a person falling within this paragraph (whether by reference to a company that would have been a person falling within paragraph (b) or by reference to a company or series of companies falling within this provision).

(4) The provisions of section 416(2) to (6) of the Taxes Act 1988 (meaning of control) have effect for the purposes of sub-paragraph (3) as they have effect for the purposes of Part 11 of that Act.

But a person carrying on a business of banking shall not be regarded for those purposes as having control of a company by reason only of having, or of the consequences of having exercised, any rights in respect of loan capital or debt issued or incurred by the company for money lent by that person to the company in the ordinary course of that business.

Degrouping: principal company becoming member of another group

60—(1) Paragraph 58 does not apply where a company ceases to be a member of a group by reason only of the fact that the principal company of the group becomes a member of another group ("the second group").

(2) But if, in a case where paragraph 58 would have applied but for sub-paragraph (1) above, after the transfer and before the end of the period of six years after the date of the transfer—

(*a*) the transferee ceases to satisfy the condition that it is both a 75% subsidiary and an effective 51% subsidiary of one or more members of the second group ("the qualifying condition"), and

(*b*) at the time at which the transferee ceases to satisfy that condition, the relevant asset is held by the transferee or another company in the same group,

this Schedule has effect as if the transferee, immediately after the transfer to it of the relevant asset, had realised the asset for its market value at that time and immediately reacquired the asset at that value.

(3) The adjustments required to be made in consequence of sub-paragraph (2), by the transferee or a company to which the relevant asset has been subsequently transferred, in relation to the period between—

(*a*) the transfer of the relevant asset to the transferee, and

(*b*) the transferee ceasing to satisfy the qualifying condition,

shall be made by bringing the aggregate net credit or debit into account as if it had arisen immediately before the transferee ceased to satisfy the qualifying condition.

(4) For the purposes of Part 6 (how credits and debits are given effect) credits or debits brought into account by virtue of this paragraph take their character from the purposes for which the relevant asset was held by the transferee immediately after the transfer.

Provided that, in a case where—

(*a*) the asset was then held by the transferee for the purposes of a trade, business or concern within paragraph 31, 32 or 33, and

(*b*) the transferee ceased to carry on that trade, business or concern before it ceased to satisfy the qualifying condition,

any credit or debit brought into account by virtue of this paragraph in respect of the asset shall be treated for the purposes of Part 6 as a non-trading credit or debit.

(5) This paragraph is subject to paragraph 62 (merger carried out for bona fide commercial reasons).

Degrouping: company ceasing to be member of group by reason of exempt distribution

61—(1) Paragraphs 58 and 60 do not apply in a case where a company ceases to be a member of a group by reason only of an exempt distribution, unless there is a chargeable payment within five years after the making of the exempt distribution.

(2) If within five years after the making of the exempt distribution there is a chargeable payment, all such adjustments as may be required, by way of assessment, amendment of returns or otherwise, may be made within the period of three years after the making of the chargeable payment.

This applies notwithstanding any time limit on the making of an assessment or the amendment of a return.

(3) In this paragraph—

"exempt distribution" means a distribution that is exempt by virtue of section 213(2) of the Taxes Act 1988; and

"chargeable payment" has the meaning given in section 214(2) of that Act.

(4) In determining for the purposes of this paragraph whether one company is a 75% subsidiary of another, the other company—

(*a*) shall be treated as not being the owner of any share capital that it owns directly in a body corporate if a profit on a sale of the shares would be treated as a trading receipt of its trade, and

(*b*) shall be treated as not being the owner of any share capital that it owns indirectly and which is owned directly by a body corporate for which a profit on the sale of the shares would be a trading receipt.

Degrouping: merger carried out for bona fide commercial reasons

62—(1) Paragraphs 58 to 61 do not apply where—

(*a*) the transferee ceases to be a member of a group of companies ("the group") as part of a merger, and

(*b*) the merger is carried out for bona fide commercial reasons and the avoidance of liability to tax is not the main or one of the main purposes of the merger.

(2) For this purpose a "merger" means an arrangement (which in this paragraph includes a series of arrangements) whereby—

(*a*) one or more companies ("the acquiring company" or, as the case may be, "the acquiring companies") none of which is a member of the group acquires or acquire, otherwise than with a view to their disposal, one or more interests in the whole or part of the business which, before the arrangement took effect, was carried on by the transferee, and

(*b*) one or more members of the group acquires or acquire, otherwise than with a view to their disposal, one or more interests in the whole or part of the business or each of the businesses which, before the arrangement took effect, was carried on either by the acquiring company or acquiring companies or by a company at least 90% of the ordinary share capital of which was then beneficially owned by two or more of the acquiring companies,

and in respect of which the conditions in sub-paragraph (4) below are fulfilled.

(3) For the purposes of sub-paragraph (2) a member of a group of companies shall be treated as carrying on as one business the activities of that group.

(4) The conditions referred to in sub-paragraph (2) are—

(*a*) that not less than 25% by value of each of the interests acquired as mentioned in sub-paragraph (2)(*a*) and (*b*) consists of a holding of ordinary share capital, and the remainder of the interest, or as the case may be of each of the interests, acquired as mentioned in sub-paragraph (2)(*b*) consists of a holding of share capital (of any description) or debentures or both; and

(*b*) that the value or, as the case may be, the aggregate value of the interest or interests acquired as mentioned in sub-paragraph (2)(*a*) is substantially the same as the value or, as the case may be, the aggregate value of the interest or interests acquired as mentioned in sub-paragraph (2)(*b*); and

(*c*) that the consideration for the acquisition of the interest or interests acquired by the acquiring company or acquiring companies as mentioned in sub-paragraph (2)(*a*), disregarding any part of that consideration which is small by comparison with the total, either consists of, or is applied in the acquisition of, or consists partly of and as to the balance is applied in the acquisition of, the interest or interests acquired by members of the group as mentioned in sub-paragraph (2)(*b*).

(5) For the purposes of sub-paragraph (4) the value of an interest shall be determined as at the date of its acquisition.

Degrouping: group member ceasing to exist

63 References in paragraphs 58 to 61 (degrouping) to a company ceasing to be a member of a group do not include cases where a company ceases to be a member of a group in consequence of another member of the group ceasing to exist.

Degrouping: supplementary provisions

64 For the purposes of paragraphs 58 to 61 (degrouping)—

(*a*) two or more companies are associated if, by themselves, they would form a group of companies; and

(*b*) an asset acquired by a company is treated as the same as an asset owned at a later time by that company or an associated company if the value of the second asset is derived in whole or in part from the first asset.

Degrouping: application of roll-over relief in relation to degrouping charge

65—(1) Part 7 (roll-over relief in case of reinvestment) applies with the following modifications where a company is treated as having realised an asset by virtue of paragraph 58 or 60 (degrouping)—

(*a*) in paragraph 38 (conditions to be met in relation to the old asset), for the references to the old asset being a chargeable intangible asset in relation to the company substitute a reference to its being a chargeable intangible asset in relation to the transferor;

(*b*) in paragraph 39(1) (conditions to be met in relation to expenditure on other assets), for the references to the date of realisation of the old asset substitute references to—

(i) in a case within paragraph 58, the date on which the transferee ceased to be a member of the group, and

(ii) in a case within paragraph 60, the date on which the transferee ceased to satisfy the qualifying condition;

(*c*) references to the proceeds of realisation shall be read as references to the amount for which the transferee is treated as having realised the asset.

(2) A reduction of the deemed realisation proceeds as a result of a claim for relief under Part 7 does not affect the value at which the company is deemed to have reacquired the asset.

(3) In this paragraph "the transferee" and "the transferor" have the same meaning as in paragraph 58.

Reallocation of degrouping charge within group

66—(1) This paragraph applies where a chargeable realisation gain accrues to a company ("company X") under paragraph 58 or 60 in respect of an asset.

(2) For the purposes of this paragraph—

(*a*) "the relevant time" is—

(i) in a case within paragraph 58, immediately before company X ceases to be a member of the group;

(ii) in a case within paragraph 60, immediately before company X ceases to satisfy the qualifying condition;

(b) "the relevant group" is—

   (i) in a case within paragraph 58, the group of which company X was a member at the relevant time;

   (ii) in a case within paragraph 60, the second group (within the meaning of that paragraph).

(3) Company X and a company that was a member of the relevant group at the relevant time ("company Y") may jointly elect that the gain, or such part of it as may be specified in the election, shall be treated as accruing to company Y and not to company X.

(4) An election to that effect may be made only if the following two conditions are met.

(5) The first condition is that at the relevant time company Y—

   (a) was resident in the United Kingdom, or

   (b) carried on a trade in the United Kingdom through a branch or agency and was not by virtue of arrangements under Part 18 of the Taxes Act 1988 (double taxation relief) exempt from corporation tax in respect of the profits or gains of that branch or agency.

(6) The second condition is that company Y was not at the relevant time—

   (a) a qualifying society within the meaning of section 461A of the Taxes Act 1988 (incorporated friendly societies entitled to exemption from tax), or

   (b) a dual resident investing company within the meaning of section 404 of that Act (limitation of group relief).

(7) An election under this paragraph must be made—

   (a) by notice in writing to the Inland Revenue,

   (b) not later than two years after the end of the accounting period of company X in which the relevant time falls.

(8) The effect of the election is that the gain, or the part specified in the election, is treated—

   (a) as if it had accrued to company Y at the relevant time as a non-trading credit for the purposes of Part 6 (how credits and debits are given effect), and

   (b) where company Y is not resident in the United Kingdom at the relevant time, as if it had accrued in respect of an asset held for the purposes of a branch or agency of the company in the United Kingdom.

Application of roll-over relief in relation to reallocated degrouping charge

67—(1) Where an election has been made under paragraph 66, this paragraph applies for the purpose of enabling company Y to make a claim under Part 7 (roll-over relief on reinvestment).

(2) For that purpose—

   (a) Part 7 applies as if the deemed realisation of the asset had been by company Y and not company X,

   (b) the conditions in paragraph 38 (conditions to be met in relation to the old asset) are treated as met in relation to the asset if they would have been met if there had been no election and company X had made the claim, and

   (c) the proceeds of realisation and the cost of the old asset recognised for tax purposes are what they would have been if there had been no election and company X had made the claim.

(3) Where the election relates to part only of the gain on the deemed realisation of an asset, Part 7 and this paragraph apply as if the deemed realisation had been of a separate asset representing a corresponding part of the asset, and any necessary apportionments shall be made accordingly.

Recovery of degrouping charge from another group company or controlling director

68—(1) This paragraph applies where—

   (a) a company ("the taxpayer company") is liable to a degrouping charge,

   (b) an amount of corporation tax has been assessed on the company for the relevant accounting period, and

   (c) the whole or part of that amount is unpaid at the end of the period of six months after the time when it became payable.

(2) The following persons may be required, by notice under paragraph 69, to pay the amount of corporation tax referable to the degrouping charge or, if less, the amount of the unpaid tax—

   (a) if the taxpayer company was a member of a group at the relevant time—

      (i) a company that was at that time the principal company of the group, and

      (ii) any other company that at any time in the period of twelve months ending with the relevant time was a member of that group and owned the relevant asset or any part of it;

   (b) if at the relevant time the taxpayer company is not resident in the United Kingdom but carries on a trade in the United Kingdom through a branch or agency, any person who is, or during the period of twelve months ending with that time was, a controlling director of the taxpayer company or of a company that has, or within that period had, control of the taxpayer company.

(3) For the purposes of this paragraph—

(a) the relevant accounting period is the accounting period in which the degrouping charge falls to be brought into account by the taxpayer company;

(b) the relevant time is—

(i) in a case within paragraph 58, when the taxpayer company ceased to be a member of the group;

(ii) in a case within paragraph 60, when the taxpayer company ceased to satisfy the qualifying condition;

(iii) where there has been an election under paragraph 66 (reallocation of degrouping charge within group), the time that would have been the relevant time under sub-paragraph (i) or (ii) if there had been no such election;

(c) the relevant asset is the asset in respect of which the degrouping charge arises.

(4) The amount of corporation tax referable to a degrouping charge is the difference between—

(a) the tax in fact payable for the relevant accounting period, and

(b) the tax that would have been payable for that period in the absence of the degrouping charge.

(5) References in this paragraph to a degrouping charge are to—

(a) a credit required to be brought into account under paragraph 58(3) or 60(3), or

(b) where there has been an election under paragraph 66 (reallocation of degrouping charge within group), a credit required to be brought into account as a result of the election.

(6) In this paragraph—

"director", in relation to a company, has the meaning given by section 168(8) of the Taxes Act 1988 (read with subsection (9) of that section) and includes any person falling within section 417(5) of that Act (read with subsection (6) of that section);

"controlling director", in relation to a company, means a director of the company who has control of it (construing control in accordance with section 416 of the Taxes Act 1988); and

"group" and "principal company" have the meaning that would be given by Part 8 of this Schedule if in that Part for references to 75% subsidiaries there were substituted references to 51% subsidiaries.

Recovery of degrouping charge from another group company or controlling director: procedure etc

69—(1) The Inland Revenue may serve a notice on a person within paragraph 68(2) requiring him, within 30 days of the service of the notice, to pay—

(a) the amount of the tax referable to the degrouping charge, or

(b) if less, the amount that remains unpaid of the corporation tax payable by the taxpayer company for the relevant accounting period.

(2) The notice must state—

(a) the amount of the tax referable to the degrouping charge,

(b) the amount of corporation tax assessed on the taxpayer company for the relevant accounting period that remains unpaid and the date when it first become payable, and

(c) the amount required to be paid by the person on whom the notice is served.

(3) The notice has effect—

(a) for the purposes of the recovery from that person of the amount required to be paid and of interest on that amount, and

(b) for the purposes of appeals,

as if it were a notice of assessment and that amount were an amount of tax due from that person.

(4) In section 87A(3) of the Taxes Management Act 1970 (c 9) (date from which interest runs in the case of an assessment of a company's tax on another person), for "or Schedule 28 to the Finance Act 2000" substitute ", Schedule 28 to the Finance Act 2000 or paragraph 69 of Schedule 29 to the Finance Act 2002".

(5) A person who has paid an amount in pursuance of a notice under this paragraph may recover that amount from the taxpayer company.

(6) A payment in pursuance of a notice under this paragraph is not allowed as a deduction in computing any income, profits or losses for any tax purposes.

Recovery of degrouping charge from another group company or controlling director: time limit

70—(1) Any notice under paragraph 69 must be served before the end of the period of three years beginning with the date on which the liability of the taxpayer company to corporation tax for the relevant accounting period is finally determined.

(2) Where the unpaid tax is charged in consequence of a determination under paragraph 36 or 37 of Schedule 18 to the Finance Act 1998 (c 36) (determination where no return delivered or return incomplete), the date mentioned in sub-paragraph (1) shall be taken to be the date on which the determination was made.

(3) Where the unpaid tax is charged in a self-assessment, including a self-assessment that supersedes a determination (see paragraph 40 of Schedule 18 to the Finance Act 1998), the date mentioned in sub-paragraph (1) shall be taken to be the latest of—

(a) the last date on which notice of enquiry may be given into the return containing the self-assessment;

(b) if notice of enquiry is given, 30 days after the enquiry is completed;

(c) if more than one notice of enquiry is given, 30 days after the last notice of completion;

(d) if after such an enquiry the Inland Revenue amend the return, 30 days after notice of the amendment is issued;

(e) if an appeal is brought against such an amendment, 30 days after the appeal is finally determined.

(4) If the unpaid tax is charged in a discovery assessment (see paragraph 41 of Schedule 18 to the Finance Act 1998), the date mentioned in sub-paragraph (1) shall be taken to be—

(a) where there is no appeal against the assessment, the date when the tax becomes due and payable;

(b) where there is such an appeal, the date on which the appeal is finally determined.

Payments between group members in respect of reliefs

71—(1) This paragraph applies to payments—

(a) for group roll-over relief, or

(b) for the reallocation of a degrouping charge.

(2) A payment for group roll-over relief means a payment made—

(a) in connection with a claim for relief under Part 7 (roll-over relief in case of realisation and reinvestment) made by virtue of—

    (i) paragraph 56 (realisation by one group company and reinvestment by another), or

    (ii) paragraph 57 (acquisition of group company treated as equivalent to acquisition of underlying assets),

(b) by the company whose proceeds of realisation are reduced as a result of the claim,

(c) to a company whose acquisition costs are reduced (in a case within paragraph 56) or the tax written-down value of whose assets is reduced (in a case within paragraph 57) as a result of the claim,

(d) in pursuance of an agreement between those companies in connection with the claim.

(3) A payment for the reallocation of a degrouping charge means a payment made—

(a) in connection with an election under paragraph 66 (reallocation of degrouping charge within group),

(b) by the company to which the chargeable realisation gain accrues to the company to which as a result of the election the whole or part of that gain is treated as accruing,

(c) in pursuance of an agreement between those companies in connection with the election.

(4) A payment to which this paragraph applies—

(a) shall not be taken into account in computing profits or losses of either company for corporation tax purposes, and

(b) shall not for any of the purposes of the Corporation Tax Acts be regarded as a distribution or a charge on income,

provided it does not exceed the amount of the relief.

(5) For this purpose the amount of the relief is—

(a) in the case of a payment in connection with a claim for relief under paragraph 56, the amount of the reduction as a result of the claim in the acquisition costs of the company to which the payment is made;

(b) in the case of a payment in connection with a claim for relief under paragraph 57, the amount of the reduction as a result of the claim in the tax-written down value of the assets of the company to which the payment is made;

(c) in the case of a payment in connection with an election under paragraph 66, the amount treated as a result of the election as accruing to the company to which the payment is made.

PART 10
EXCLUDED ASSETS
Introduction

72—(1) This Part provides for the exclusion from this Schedule of certain assets. Where or to the extent that an asset of any description is so excluded, an option or other right to acquire or dispose of an asset of that description is similarly excluded.

(2) This Part provides for three kinds of exclusion—

(a) assets within paragraphs 73 to 77 are entirely excluded from this Schedule;

(b) assets within paragraphs 78 to 81 are excluded from the provisions of this Schedule except as regards royalties;

(*c*) assets within paragraph 82 or 83 are excluded from the provisions of this Schedule to the extent specified in the paragraph concerned.

(3) Where by virtue of any of those paragraphs an asset is excluded to the extent that—

(*a*) it represents certain rights, or
(*b*) it is an asset of a certain description, or
(*c*) it is held for certain purposes, or
(*d*) it represents expenditure of a certain kind,

the provisions of this Schedule apply as if there were a separate asset representing so much of the asset as is not so excluded.

(4) The other provisions of the Corporation Tax Acts have effect as if there were a separate asset representing so much of the asset as is excluded.

(5) Any apportionment necessary for the purposes of sub-paragraphs (3) and (4) shall be made on a just and reasonable basis.

Assets entirely excluded: rights over tangible assets

73 This Schedule does not apply to an intangible fixed asset to the extent that it represents—

(*a*) rights enjoyed by virtue of an estate, interest or right in or over land, or
(*b*) rights in relation to tangible movable property.

Assets entirely excluded: oil licences

74—(1) This Schedule does not apply to an oil licence or an interest in an oil licence.

(2) In sub-paragraph (1) an "oil licence" means a UK oil licence or a foreign oil concession.

(3) In this paragraph—

"UK oil licence" means a licence under—

(*a*) Part I of the Petroleum Act 1998 (c 17) ("the 1998 Act"), or
(*b*) the Petroleum Production (Northern Ireland) Act 1964 (c 28 (NI)) ("the 1964 Act"),

authorising the winning of oil; and
"foreign oil concession" means any right that—

(*a*) is a right to search for or win oil that exists in its natural condition in a place to which neither the 1998 Act nor the 1964 Act applies, and
(*b*) is conferred or exercisable (whether or not under a licence) in relation to a particular area.

(4) In sub-paragraph (1) "interest in an oil licence" includes, if there is an agreement that—

(*a*) relates to oil from the whole or a part of the licensed area, and
(*b*) was made before the extraction of the oil to which it relates,

any entitlement under the agreement to, or to a share of, that oil or the proceeds of its sale.

(5) In sub-paragraph (4)(*a*) "licensed area" means—

(*a*) in relation to a UK oil licence, the area to which the licence applies, and
(*b*) in relation to a foreign oil concession, the area in relation to which the right to search for or win oil is conferred or exercisable under the concession.

(6) In this paragraph "oil"—

(*a*) in relation to a UK oil licence, means any substance won or capable of being won under the authority of a licence granted under Part 1 of the 1998 Act or the 1964 Act, other than methane gas won in the course of making and keeping mines safe, and
(*b*) in relation to a foreign oil concession, means any petroleum (as defined by section 1 of the 1998 Act).

Assets entirely excluded: financial assets

75—(1) This Schedule does not apply to financial assets.

(2) "Financial asset" here has the meaning it has for accounting purposes.

(3) The expression includes—

[(*a*) loan relationships;][1]
[(*b*) derivative contracts (see Part 2 of Schedule 26 to this Act),][2]
(*c*) contracts or policies of insurance or capital redemption policies, and
(*d*) rights under a collective investment scheme within the meaning of the Financial Services and Markets Act 2000 (c 8) (see section 235 of that Act).

Amendments—[1] Sub-para (3)(*a*) substituted by FA 2002 s 79, Sch 23 para 24 with effect for accounting periods beginning after 30 September 2002. Sub-para (3)(*a*) previously read as follows—

"(*a*) money debts within the meaning of Chapter 2 of Part 4 of the Finance Act 1996 (c 8) (loan relationships) (see section 81(2) of that Act),".
[2] Sub-para (3)(*b*) substituted by FA 2002 s 83(1)(*b*), Sch 27 paras 24, 26 with effect for accounting periods beginning after 30 September 2002. Sub-para (3)(*b*) previously read as follows—

"(*b*) qualifying contracts within Chapter 2 of Part 4 of the Finance Act 1994 (c 9) (financial instruments) (see sections 147 to 148 of that Act),".

Assets entirely excluded: rights in companies, trusts, etc

76—(1) This Schedule does not apply to an asset to the extent that it represents—

(*a*) shares or other rights in relation to the profits, governance or winding up of a company,

(*b*) rights under a trust, or

(*c*) the interest of a partner in a partnership.

(2) Sub-paragraph (1)(*b*) does not apply to rights that for accounting purposes fall to be treated as representing an interest in trust property that is an intangible fixed asset to which this Schedule applies.

(3) Sub-paragraph (1)(*c*) does not apply to an interest that for accounting purposes falls to be treated as representing an interest in partnership property that is an intangible fixed asset to which this Schedule applies.

Assets entirely excluded: non-commercial purposes etc

77 This Schedule does not apply to an intangible fixed asset to the extent that it is held—

(*a*) for a purpose that is not a business or other commercial purpose of the company, or

(*b*) for the purpose of activities in respect of which the company is not within the charge to corporation tax.

Assets excluded except as regards royalties: life assurance business

78—(1) Except as regards royalties, this Schedule does not apply to an intangible fixed asset to the extent that it is held by an insurance company for the purposes of its life assurance business.

(2) Sub-paragraph (1) does not apply to computer software.

Assets excluded except as regards royalties: mutual trade or business

79—(1) Except as regards royalties, this Schedule does not apply to an intangible fixed asset to the extent that it is held for the purposes of any mutual trade or business.

(2) Sub-paragraph (1) does not apply to life assurance business.

Assets excluded except as regards royalties: films and sound recordings

80—(1) Except as regards royalties, this Schedule does not apply to an intangible fixed asset held by a company to the extent that it represents expenditure by the company on the production or acquisition of a master version of a film or sound recording.

(2) For this purpose ''master version''—

(*a*) in relation to a film has the meaning given by section 40A(5) of the Finance (No 2) Act 1992 (c 48) (revenue nature of expenditure on master version of films); and

(*b*) in relation to a sound recording means a master tape or master audio disc of the recording.

Assets excluded except as regards royalties: computer software treated as part of cost of related hardware

81 Except as regards royalties, this Schedule does not apply to an intangible fixed asset held by a company to the extent that it represents expenditure by the company on computer software that falls to be treated for accounting purposes as part of the costs of the related hardware.

Assets excluded to extent specified: research and development

82—(1) This paragraph applies to an intangible fixed asset held by a company to the extent that it represents expenditure by the company on research and development.

(2) The following provisions of this Schedule do not apply to such an asset—

(*a*) Part 2 (debits in respect of intangible fixed assets) does not apply, except for paragraph 12 (debit on reversal of previous accounting gain) so far as it relates to credits previously brought into account under paragraph 14 (receipts recognised as they accrue);

(*b*) Part 3 (credits in respect of intangible fixed assets) does not apply, except for paragraph 14.

(3) Part 4 (debits and credits on realisation of intangible fixed asset) applies as if the cost of the asset did not include any expenditure on research and development.

(4) In this paragraph ''research and development'' has the meaning given by section 837A of the Taxes Act 1988 and includes oil and gas exploration and appraisal.

Assets excluded to extent specified: election to exclude capital expenditure on computer software

83—(1) This paragraph applies to an intangible fixed asset held by a company to the extent that it represents capital expenditure by the company on computer software in respect of which the company has made an election under this paragraph.

(2) An insurance company that carries on life assurance business may also make an election under this paragraph in respect of so much of any capital expenditure on computer software as is not referable to its basic life assurance and general annuity business.

(3) The effect of an election under this paragraph is as follows—

(a) Part 2 does not apply to the asset, except for paragraph 12 (debit on reversal of previous accounting gain) so far as it relates to credits previously brought into account under paragraph 14 (receipts recognised as they accrue);

(b) Part 3 does not apply to the asset, except for paragraph 14;

(c) Part 4 (debits and credits on realisation of intangible fixed asset) applies as if the cost of the asset did not include any expenditure in respect of which an election under this paragraph has been made;

(d) a credit shall be brought into account under this Schedule in respect of the asset only to the extent that the receipts to which the credit relates do not fall to be taken into account in computing disposal values under section 72 of the Capital Allowances Act 2001 (c 2).

(4) Any election under this paragraph must specify the expenditure to which it relates, and must be made—

(a) in writing,

(b) to the Inland Revenue,

(c) not more than two years after the end of the accounting period in which the expenditure was incurred.

(5) An election under this paragraph is irrevocable.

(6) The references in this paragraph—

(a) to capital expenditure, and

(b) to the time when such expenditure is incurred,

have the same meaning as if this paragraph were contained in the Capital Allowances Act 2001.

PART 11
TRANSFER OF BUSINESS OR TRADE
Company reconstruction involving transfer of business

84—(1) This paragraph applies where—

(a) a scheme of reconstruction involves the transfer of the whole or part of the business of one company ("the transferor") to another company ("the transferee"), and

(b) the transferor receives no part of the consideration for the transfer (otherwise than by the transferee taking over the whole or part of the liabilities of the business).

For this purpose "scheme of reconstruction" has the same meaning as in section 136 of the Taxation of Chargeable Gains Act 1992 (c 12).

(2) If the assets included in the transfer include intangible fixed assets that are chargeable intangible assets in relation to the transferor immediately before the transfer and in relation to the transferee immediately after the transfer, the transfer of those assets is treated for the purposes of this Schedule as tax-neutral (see paragraph 140).

(3) If a transfer falls within sub-paragraph (1) and also within paragraph 55 (transfers within a group), that paragraph applies and this paragraph does not.

(4) This paragraph does not apply if the transferor or the transferee is—

(a) a qualifying society within the meaning of section 461A of the Taxes Act 1988 (incorporated friendly societies entitled to exemption from tax), or

(b) a dual resident investing company within the meaning of section 404 of that Act (limitation of group relief).

(5) This paragraph applies only if the reconstruction—

(a) is effected for bona fide commercial reasons, and

(b) does not form part of a scheme or arrangements of which the main purpose, or one of the main purposes, is avoidance of liability to corporation tax, capital gains tax or income tax.

(6) The requirements of sub-paragraph (5) are treated as met where, before the transfer, the Inland Revenue have, on the application of the transferee, notified that company that they are satisfied that the requirements of that sub-paragraph will be met.

For the procedure on such an application, see paragraph 88.

Transfer of UK trade between companies resident in different EU member States

85—(1) This paragraph applies where—

(a) an EU company resident in one member State ("the transferor") transfers the whole or part of a trade carried on by it in the United Kingdom to an EU company resident in another member State ("the transferee"),

(b) the transfer is wholly in exchange for securities issued by the transferee to the transferor, and (*c*) a claim is made under this paragraph by the transferor and the transferee.

(2) If the transfer includes intangible fixed assets that are chargeable intangible assets in relation to the transferor immediately before the transfer and in relation to the transferee immediately after the transfer, the transfer of those assets is treated for the purposes of this Schedule as tax-neutral (see paragraph 140).

(3) For the purposes of this paragraph a company is regarded as resident in a member State if it is within a charge to tax under the law of the State because it is regarded as resident for the purposes of the charge.

For this purpose a company is treated as not within a charge to tax under the law of a member State if it falls to be regarded for the purposes of any double taxation relief arrangements to which the State is a party as resident in a territory which is not within any of the member States.

(4) This paragraph applies only if the transfer of the trade or part—

    (*a*) is effected for bona fide commercial reasons, and
    (*b*) does not form part of a scheme or arrangements of which the main purpose, or one of the main purposes, is avoidance of liability to corporation tax, capital gains tax or income tax.

(5) The requirements of sub-paragraph (4) are treated as met where, before the transfer, the Inland Revenue have, on the application of the transferor and the transferee, notified those companies that they are satisfied that the requirements of that sub-paragraph will be met.

For the procedure on such an application, see paragraph 88.

(6) In this paragraph—

    (*a*) ''EU company'' means a body incorporated under the law of a member State; and
    (*b*) ''securities'' includes shares.

Postponement of charge on transfer of assets to non-resident company.

86—(1) This paragraph applies where—

    (*a*) a company resident in the United Kingdom and carrying on a trade outside the United Kingdom through a branch or agency (''the transferor'') transfers that trade, or part of it, together with the whole assets of the company used for the purposes of the trade or part (or together with the whole of those assets other than cash) to a company not resident in the United Kingdom (''the transferee''),
    (*b*) the trade or part is so transferred wholly or partly in exchange for securities consisting of shares, or of shares and loan stock, issued by the transferee to the transferor, and
    (*c*) the shares so issued, either alone or taken together with any other shares in the transferee already held by the transferor, amount in all to not less than one quarter of the ordinary share capital of the transferee.

(2) If the transfer includes intangible fixed assets that are chargeable intangible assets in relation to the transferor immediately before the transfer (''relevant assets''), the transferor may claim that this Schedule shall have effect in accordance with the following provisions.

(3) If the proceeds of realisation of a relevant asset exceed the cost of the asset recognised for tax purposes, the proceeds of realisation are treated as reduced—

    (*a*) if the securities are the whole consideration for the transfer, by the amount of the excess, and
    (*b*) if the securities are not the whole of that consideration, by the appropriate proportion of the excess.

For this purpose ''the appropriate proportion'' means the proportion that the market value of the securities at the time of the transfer bears to the market value of the whole of the consideration at that time.

(4) If at any time after the transfer the transferor realises the whole or part of the securities held by it immediately before that time, the transferor shall bring into account for tax purposes a credit equal to the whole or the appropriate proportion of the aggregate deferred gain.

For this purpose—

    ''the appropriate proportion'' means the proportion that the market value of the part of the securities disposed of bears to the market value of the securities held immediately before the disposal; and
    ''the aggregate deferred gain'' means the aggregate of the amounts by which the proceeds of realisation of relevant assets were reduced under sub-paragraph (3), so far as not already taken into account under this sub-paragraph or sub-paragraph (5).

(5) If at any time within six years after the transfer the transferee realises any of the relevant assets held by it immediately before that time, the transferor shall bring into account for tax purposes a credit equal to the whole or the appropriate proportion of the aggregate deferred gain.

For this purpose—

    ''the appropriate proportion'' means the proportion that the deferred gain attributable to the relevant assets realised bears to the deferred gain attributable to the relevant assets held immediately before the time of the realisation;

"the aggregate deferred gain" means the aggregate of the amounts by which the proceeds of realisation of relevant assets were reduced under sub-paragraph (3), so far as not already taken into account under this sub-paragraph or sub-paragraph (4); and

"the deferred gain attributable to" any relevant assets means the aggregate of the amounts by which the proceeds of realisation of those assets were reduced under sub-paragraph (3).

(6) There shall be disregarded—

(a) for the purposes of sub-paragraph (4), any disposal within section 171 of the Taxation of Chargeable Gains Act 1992 (c 12) (transfers within a group); and

(b) for the purposes of sub-paragraph (5), any transfer by one member of a group (within the meaning of Part 8 of this Schedule) to another.

(7) Where a person acquires securities or an asset on a disposal disregarded under sub-paragraph (6) (and without there having been a previous disposal not so disregarded), a subsequent disposal of the securities or asset by that person shall be treated as a disposal by the transferor or, as the case may be, the transferee.

(8) This paragraph applies only if the transfer of the trade or part—

(a) is effected for bona fide commercial reasons, and

(b) does not form part of a scheme or arrangements of which the main purpose, or one of the main purposes, is avoidance of liability to corporation tax, capital gains tax or income tax.

(9) The requirements of sub-paragraph (8) are treated as met where, before the transfer, the Inland Revenue have, on the application of the transferor, notified that company that they are satisfied that the requirements of that sub-paragraph will be met.

For the procedure on such an application, see paragraph 88.

(10) No claim may be made under this paragraph as regards a transfer in relation to which a claim is made under paragraph 87 (transfer of non-UK trade).

Transfer of non-UK trade

87—(1) This paragraph applies where—

(a) an EU company resident in the United Kingdom ("the transferor") transfers to an EU company resident in another member State ("the transferee") the whole or part of a trade that, immediately before the time of the transfer, the transferor carried on in a member State other than the United Kingdom ("the other member State") through a branch or agency,

(b) the transfer—

(i) includes the whole of the assets of the transferor used for the purposes of the trade or part (or the whole of those assets other than cash), and

(ii) is wholly or partly in exchange for securities issued by the transferee to the transferor,

(c) the transfer includes intangible fixed assets—

(i) that are chargeable intangible assets in relation to the transferor immediately before the transfer, and

(ii) in the case of one or more of which the proceeds of realisation exceed the cost recognised for tax purposes, and

(d) the transferor makes a claim under this paragraph.

(2) Where tax would have been chargeable under the law of the other member State in respect of the transfer of those assets but for the Mergers Directive, Part 18 of the Taxes Act 1988 (double taxation relief), including any arrangements having effect by virtue of section 788 of that Act (bilateral relief), shall apply as if the amount of tax, calculated on the required basis, that would have been payable under that law in respect of the transfer of those assets but for that Directive, were tax payable under that law.

(3) For this purpose "the required basis" is that—

(a) so far as permitted under the law of the other member State, any losses arising on the transfer are set against any gains so arising, and

(b) any relief available to the transferor under that law has been duly claimed.

(4) In this paragraph—

"EU company" means a body incorporated under the law of a member State;

"the Mergers Directive" means the Directive of the Council of the European Communities dated 23rd July 1990 on the common system of taxation applicable to mergers, divisions, transfers of assets and exchanges of shares concerning companies of different member States (No 90/434/EEC);

"securities" includes shares.

(5) For the purposes of this paragraph a company is regarded as resident in another member State if it is within a charge to tax under the law of the State because it is regarded as resident for the purposes of the charge.

For this purpose a company shall be treated as not within a charge to tax under the law of a member State if it falls to be regarded for the purposes of any double taxation relief arrangements to which the State is a party as resident in a territory which is not within any of the member States.

(6) No claim may be made under this paragraph as regards a transfer in relation to which a claim is made under paragraph 86 (postponement of charge on transfer of assets to non-resident company).

(7) This paragraph applies only if the transfer of the trade or part—

(*a*) is effected for bona fide commercial reasons, and

(*b*) does not form part of a scheme or arrangements of which the main purpose, or one of the main purposes, is avoidance of liability to corporation tax, capital gains tax or income tax.

(8) The requirements of sub-paragraph (7) are treated as met where, before the transfer, the Inland Revenue have, on the application of the transferor, notified that company that they are satisfied that the requirements of that sub-paragraph will be met.

For the procedure on such an application, see paragraph 88.

Procedure on application for clearance

88—(1) This paragraph applies in relation to an application under paragraph 84(6), 85(5), 86((9) or 87(8).

(2) The application must be in writing and must contain particulars of the operations that are to be effected.

(3) The Inland Revenue may, within 30 days of the receipt of the application or of any further particulars previously required under this sub-paragraph, by notice require the applicant to furnish further particulars for the purpose of enabling the Inland Revenue to make their decision.

If any such notice is not complied with within 30 days or such longer period as the Inland Revenue may allow, the Inland Revenue need not proceed further on the application.

(4) The Inland Revenue shall notify their decision to the applicant within 30 days of receiving the application or, if they give a notice under sub-paragraph (3), within 30 days of the notice being complied with.

(5) If the Inland Revenue notify the applicant that they are not satisfied as mentioned in paragraph 84(6), 85(5), 86(9) or 87(8) or do not notify their decision to the applicant within the time required by sub-paragraph (4), the applicant may within 30 days of the notification or of that time require the Inland Revenue to transmit the application, together with any notice given and further particulars furnished under sub-paragraph (3), to the Special Commissioners.

In that event any notification by the Special Commissioners shall have effect for the purposes of paragraph 84(6), 85(5), 86(9) or 87(8) as if it were a notification by the Inland Revenue.

(6) If any particulars furnished under this paragraph do not fully and accurately disclose all facts and considerations material for the decision of the Inland Revenue or the Special Commissioners, any resulting notification by the Inland Revenue or the Commissioners is void.

Transfer of life assurance business

89—(1) This paragraph applies where there is—

(*a*) a transfer between two companies of business consisting of the effecting or carrying out of contracts of long-term insurance which has effect under an insurance business transfer scheme, or

(*b*) a transfer between two companies that is a qualifying overseas transfer within the meaning of paragraph 4A of Schedule 19AC to the Taxes Act 1988 (transfer of business of overseas life insurance company),

and the assets included in the transfer include intangible fixed assets that are chargeable intangible assets in relation to the transferor company immediately before the transfer and in relation to the successor company immediately after the transfer.

(2) Where this paragraph applies the transfer of those assets is treated for the purposes of this Schedule as tax-neutral (see paragraph 140).

(3) In this paragraph—

"contracts of long-term insurance" means contracts that fall within Part 2 of Schedule 1 to the Finance Services and Markets Act (Regulated Activities) Order 2001 (SI 2001/544); and

"insurance business transfer scheme" means a scheme falling within section 105 of the Financial Services and Markets Act 2000 (c 8) or an excluded scheme falling within Case 2, 3 or 4 of subsection (3) of that section.

Transfer of business of building society to company

90—(1) Where—

(*a*) there is a transfer of the whole of a building society's business to a company ("the successor company") in accordance with section 97 and the other applicable provisions of the Building Societies Act 1986 (c 53), and

(*b*) the assets included in the transfer include intangible fixed assets that are chargeable intangible assets in relation to the society immediately before the transfer and in relation to the successor company immediately after the transfer, the transfer of those assets is treated for the purposes of this Schedule as tax-neutral (see paragraph 140).

(2) If because of the transfer a company ceases to be a member of the same group as the society, that event shall not cause paragraph 58 or 60 (deemed realisation and reacquisition) to have effect as respects any asset acquired by the company from the society or any other member of the same group.

(3) Where the society and the successor company are members of the same group at the time of the transfer but later cease to be so, that later event shall not cause paragraph 58 or 60 to have effect as respects—

(a) any asset acquired by the successor company on or before the transfer from the society or any other member of the same group, or

(b) any asset acquired from the society or any other member of the same group by a company other than the successor company that is a member of the same group at the time of the transfer.

(4) Where a company which is a member of the same group as the society at the time of the transfer—

(a) ceases to be a member of that group and becomes a member of the same group as the successor company, and

(b) subsequently ceases to be a member of that group,

paragraph 58 has effect on that later event as respects any asset to which this sub-paragraph applies that is acquired by the company otherwise than from the successor company as if it had been acquired from the successor company.

(5) Sub-paragraph (4) applies to any asset acquired by the company from the society, or from another company which is a member of the same group at the time of the transfer, when the company and the society, or the company, the society and the other company, were members of the same group.

(6) Sub-paragraph (4) does not apply where—

(a) the company which acquired the asset is a 75% subsidiary of the company from which it was acquired, or vice versa, and

(b) those companies cease simultaneously to be members of the same group as the successor company but continue to be members of the same group as one another.

Amalgamation of or transfer of engagements by certain societies

91—(1) Where—

(a) there is an amalgamation of two or more societies to which this paragraph applies or a transfer of engagements from one such society to another, and

(b) in the course of or as part of the amalgamation or transfer of engagements, there are transferred from one society (''the transferor'') to another (''the transferee'') intangible fixed assets that are chargeable intangible assets in relation to the transferor immediately before the transfer and in relation to the transferee immediately after the transfer,

the transfer of those assets is treated for the purposes of this Schedule as tax-neutral (see paragraph 140).

(2) The societies to which this paragraph applies are—

(a) a building society,

(b) a registered industrial and provident society within the meaning of section 486 of the Taxes Act 1988, and

(c) a co-operative association in relation to which subsections (1) and (8) of that section have effect as they have effect in relation to a registered industrial and provident society.

PART 12
TRANSACTIONS BETWEEN RELATED PARTIES
Transfer between company and related party treated as being at market value

92—(1) Where there is a transfer of an intangible asset from a company to a related party or to a company from a related party and, in either case, the asset is a chargeable intangible asset—

(a) in relation to the transferor immediately before the transfer, or

(b) in relation to the transferee immediately after the transfer,

the transfer is treated for all purposes of the Taxes Acts (as regards both the transferor and the transferee) as being at market value.

This is subject to the following two exceptions.

(2) The first exception is where the consideration for the transfer—

(a) falls to be adjusted for tax purposes under Schedule 28AA to the Taxes Act 1988 (provision not at arm's length), or

(b) falls within that Schedule without falling to be so adjusted.

(3) For the purposes of sub-paragraph (2)(*b*) the consideration for a transfer falls within Schedule 28AA to the Taxes Act 1988 without falling to be adjusted under that Schedule in a case where—

    (*a*) the conditions in paragraph 1(1) of that Schedule are met,

    (*b*) the actual provision does not differ from the arm's length provision, and

    (*c*) if the actual provision had differed from the arm's length provision in such a way as to confer a potential advantage in relation to United Kingdom taxation as defined in paragraph 5(1) of that Schedule, paragraph 5(2) of that Schedule would not have applied (under which there is taken to be no such potential advantage if certain conditions are met).

(4) The second exception is where any provision of this Schedule applies so as to make the transfer tax-neutral.

(5) In sub-paragraph (1) ''market value'' means the price the asset might reasonably be expected to fetch on a sale in the open market.

Exclusion of roll-over relief in case of part realisation involving related party

93 Part 7 (roll-over relief in case of reinvestment) does not apply in relation to the part realisation by a company of an intangible fixed asset if a person who is a related party in relation to the company acquires an interest of any description—

    (*a*) in that asset, or

    (*b*) in an asset whose value is derived in whole or in part from that asset, as a result of, or in connection with, the part realisation.

Delayed payment of royalty payable by company to related party

94—(1) This paragraph applies where a royalty is payable by a company to or for the benefit of a related party.

(2) If—

    (*a*) the royalty is not paid in full within the period of twelve months after the end of the period of account in which a debit in respect of it is recognised by the company for accounting purposes, and

    (*b*) credits representing the full amount of the royalty are not brought into account under this Schedule in any accounting period by the person to whom it is payable,

the royalty shall be brought into account for the purposes of this Schedule only when it is paid.

Meaning of ''related party''

95—(1) For the purposes of this Schedule a person (''P'') is a ''related party'' in relation to a company (''C'') in the following cases:

Case One

P is a company and either—

    (*a*) P has control of, or holds a major interest in, C, or

    (*b*) C has control of, or holds a major interest in, P.

Case Two

P is a company and P and C are both under the control of the same person (but see sub-paragraph (2)).

Case Three

C is a close company and P is—

    (*a*) a participator in C, or

    (*b*) an associate of a participator in C.

(2) Case Two does not apply if the person controlling both P and C is – the Crown,

    a Minister of the Crown or a government department,
    the Scottish Ministers,
    the National Assembly for Wales,
    a Minister within the meaning of the Northern Ireland Act 1998 (c 47) or a Northern Ireland department,
    a foreign sovereign power, or
    an international organisation.

Meaning of ''control'' and ''major interest''

96—(1) For the purposes of this Part ''control'', in relation to a company, is the power of a person to secure—

(*a*) by means of the holding of shares or the possession of voting power in or in relation to the company or any other company, or

(*b*) by virtue of any powers conferred by the articles of association or other document regulating the company or any other company,

that the affairs of the company are conducted in accordance with his wishes.

(2) For the purposes of this Part, a person has a "major interest" in a company if—

(*a*) he and one other person together have control of that company, and

(*b*) the rights and powers by means of which they have such control represent, in the case of each of them, at least 40% of the total.

The reference in paragraph (*a*) to two persons together having control of a company is to two persons who, taken together, have the power mentioned in sub-paragraph (1).

(3) Paragraphs 97 to 99 (rights and powers to be taken into account) apply in relation to the determination for the purposes of this Part whether a person has control of, or a major interest in, a company.

Rights and powers to be taken into account: general

97—(1) There shall be attributed to each relevant person—

(*a*) rights and powers that he is entitled to acquire at a future date or will, at a future date, become entitled to acquire;

(*b*) rights and powers of other persons, to the extent that they are required, or may be required, to be exercised in any one or more of the following ways—

(i) on his behalf;
(ii) under his direction;
(iii) for his benefit;

(*c*) rights and powers of a person connected with him;

(*d*) rights and powers that would be attributed to a person connected with him if that person were a relevant person.

(2) Sub-paragraph (1)(*b*) does not apply, in a case where a loan has been made by one person to another, to rights and powers conferred in relation to property of the borrower by the terms of any security relating to the loan.

(3) In sub-paragraphs (1)(*b*) to (*d*), the references to a person's rights and powers include rights or powers that he is entitled to acquire at a future date or will, at a future date, become entitled to acquire.

(4) In this paragraph a "relevant person" means a person whose rights or powers are relevant to the determination of the question whether a person has control of or a major interest in a company.

Rights and powers to be taken into account: rights and powers held jointly

98—(1) References in this Part of this Schedule—

(*a*) to rights and powers of a person, or

(*b*) to rights and powers that a person is or will become entitled to acquire,

include rights or powers that are exercisable by that person, or when acquired will be exercisable by him, only jointly with one or more other persons.

(2) Sub-paragraph (1) has effect subject to paragraph 99 (partnerships).

Rights and powers to be taken into account: partnerships

99—(1) The rights and powers of a person as a member of a partnership shall be disregarded unless he has control of or a major interest in the partnership.

(2) Whether a person has control of or a major interest in a partnership shall be determined in accordance with paragraphs 96 to 98 as in relation to a company.

For this purpose references in those paragraphs to any other company shall be read as including any other partnership.

Meaning of "participator" and "associate"

100—(1) In this Part "participator", in relation to a close company, has the meaning it has for the purposes of Part 11 of the Taxes Act 1988 (close companies) (see section 417(1) of that Act), except that it does not include a person by reason only of his being a loan creditor of the company within the meaning of that Part (see section 417((7) to (9) of that Act).

(2) In this Part "associate", in relation to a participator in a close company, has the meaning given by section 417(3) of that Act.

Connected persons

101—(1) This paragraph explains what is meant in this Part when a person is referred to as being connected with another person.

Any provision that one person is connected with another means that they are connected with one another.

(2) A person is connected with an individual if that person is the individual's wife or husband, or is a relative, or the wife or husband or a relative, of the individual or of the individual's wife or husband.

For the purposes of this sub-paragraph "relative" means brother, sister, ancestor or lineal descendant.

(3) A person in his capacity as trustee of a settlement is connected with—

(a) any individual who in relation to the settlement is a settlor,

(b) any person who is connected with such an individual, and

(c) any body corporate that is connected with that settlement.

For the purposes of this sub-paragraph "settlement" and "settlor" have the same meaning as in Chapter 1A of Part 15 of the Taxes Act 1988 (settlements: liability of settlor) (see section 660G(1) and (2) of that Act).

(4) For the purposes of sub-paragraph (3) above a body corporate is connected with a settlement if—

(a) it is a close company (or only not a close company because it is not resident in the United Kingdom) and the participators include the trustees of the settlement, or

(b) it is controlled by a company falling within paragraph (a) above.

(5) A person is connected with a company if they are related parties within Case One or Case Two in paragraph 95(1) above.

(6) For the purposes of sub-paragraph (5) above and for the purposes of paragraph 95 as it applies for the purposes of that sub-paragraph—

(a) "company" includes any body corporate or unincorporated association, but does not include a partnership; and

(b) a unit trust scheme shall be treated as if it were a company and as if the rights of the unit holders were shares in the company.

PART 13

SUPPLEMENTARY PROVISIONS

Treatment of grants and other contributions to expenditure

102—(1) This paragraph applies where a grant or other payment is intended by the payer to meet, directly or indirectly, expenditure of a company on an intangible fixed asset.

(2) A gain recognised in the company's profit and loss account in respect of the grant or other payment is treated for the purposes of paragraph 14 (receipts recognised as they accrue) as a gain representing a receipt in respect of the intangible fixed asset.

(3) This paragraph does not apply to a grant within paragraph 103 (grants to be left out of account for tax purposes).

Grants to be left out of account for tax purposes

103—(1) This paragraph applies to—

(a) grants under Part 2 of the Industrial Development Act 1982 (c 52) (regional development grants); and

(b) grants made under Northern Ireland legislation and declared by the Treasury by order to correspond to a grant under that Part.

These are referred to below in this paragraph as "exempt grants".

(2) Any gain recognised in the company's profit and loss account in respect of an exempt grant shall be disregarded for the purposes of this Schedule.

(3) Where as a result of an exempt grant being brought into account by a company there is a reduction—

(a) in the amount of a loss recognised in the company's profit and loss account, or

(b) in the amount of expenditure on an intangible fixed asset that is capitalised for accounting purposes,

the amount of the reduction shall be added back for the purposes of this Schedule.

Finance leasing etc

104—(1) The Treasury may make provision by regulations as to the application of this Schedule in relation to a company that is the finance lessor of an intangible asset that is the subject of a finance lease.

(2) The regulations may provide—

(*a*) that, notwithstanding that the asset is accounted for by the finance lessor as a financial asset, this Schedule shall apply as if the asset were an intangible fixed asset of the lessor and not a financial asset;

(*b*) that this Schedule shall apply as if the amount at which the asset is recognised in the finance lessor's balance sheet were capitalised expenditure on an intangible fixed asset, but that—

(i) no election may be made under paragraph 10 (election for writing down on fixed rate basis) in respect of that amount; and

(ii) that amount is not to be treated as capitalised expenditure for the purposes of paragraph 39(1)(*b*) (roll-over relief in case of realisation and reinvestment: conditions to be met in relation to expenditure on other assets);

(*c*) that where an asset formerly recognised by the lessor for accounting purposes as an intangible fixed asset becomes subject to a finance lease (and accordingly comes to be accounted for as a financial asset) the value of the asset so created is recognised as realisation proceeds of the intangible fixed asset on the change of accounting treatment;

(*d*) that assets partially excluded from this Schedule by paragraph 78 to 81 (assets excluded except as regards royalties) are entirely excluded from this Schedule as regards the finance lessor if they are subject to a finance lease and are accounted for by the lessor as financial assets;

(*e*) for excluding from the regulations assets used by the finance lessee for the purposes of a trade or business in respect of which he is within the charge to income tax;

(*f*) that an intangible asset counts as an existing asset in the hands of the finance lessor if the finance lessee—

(i) is a company for whom the asset was the whole or part of an existing asset, or

(ii) a person who is a related party in relation to such a company.

(3) The regulations may contain such consequential, supplementary, incidental and transitional provision, including provision modifying the operation of other provisions of the Corporation Tax Acts, as appears to the Treasury to be appropriate.

(4) References in this paragraph to a finance lease—

(*a*) have the meaning they have for accounting purposes, and

(*b*) include hire-purchase, conditional sale or other arrangements if they are of a similar character to a finance lease.

(5) References to the finance lessor or finance lessee have a corresponding meaning.

(6) Regulations under this paragraph may be made so as to have effect from 1st April 2002.

Regulations—See the Corporation Tax (Finance Leasing of Intangible Assets) Regulations, SI 2002/1967.

Assets acquired or realised together

105—(1) Any reference in this Schedule to the acquisition or realisation of an asset includes the acquisition or realisation of that asset together with other assets.

(2) For the purposes of this Schedule assets acquired or realised as a result of one bargain are treated as acquired or realised together even though—

(*a*) separate prices are, or purport to be, agreed for separate assets, or

(*b*) there are, or purport to be, separate acquisitions or realisations of separate assets.

(3) Where assets are acquired together—

(*a*) any values allocated to particular assets by the company in accordance with generally accepted accounting practice shall be accepted for the purposes of this Schedule;

(*b*) if no such values are allocated by the company, so much of the expenditure as on a just and reasonable apportionment is properly attributable to each asset shall be treated for the purposes of this Schedule as referable to that asset.

(4) Where assets are realised together, so much of the proceeds of realisation as on a just and reasonable apportionment is properly attributable to each asset shall be treated for the purposes of this Schedule as proceeds of the realisation of that asset.

Deemed market value acquisition: adjustment of amounts in case of nil accounting value

106—(1) This paragraph applies where a company is treated for the purposes of this Schedule as acquiring an asset at market value but the accounting value of the asset transferred, in the hands of the transferee, is nil.

(2) Where this paragraph applies—

(*a*) any reference in this Schedule to—

(i) the cost of the asset recognised for accounting purposes,

(ii) the accounting value of the asset, or

(iii) the amount of any loss recognised for accounting purposes in respect of capitalised expenditure on the asset,

shall be read as references to the cost, value or loss that would have been recognised if the asset had been acquired at market value; and

(*b*) any revaluation of the asset (as defined in paragraph 15) shall be disregarded.

Treatment of fungible assets

107—(1) For the purposes of this Schedule fungible assets of the same kind held by the same person in the same capacity shall be treated as indistinguishable parts of a single asset, growing or diminishing as additional assets of the same kind are created or acquired or some of the assets are realised.

(2) In this Schedule ''fungible assets'' here means assets of a nature to be dealt in without identifying the particular assets involved.

Asset ceasing to be chargeable intangible asset: deemed realisation at market value

108—(1) Where an asset ceases to be a chargeable intangible asset in relation to a company—

(a) on the company ceasing to be resident in the United Kingdom, or
(b) in the case of a company that is not resident in the United Kingdom, in any circumstances not involving the realisation of the asset by the company, or
(c) on the asset beginning to be held for the purposes of a mutual trade or business,

this Schedule has effect as if the company had, immediately before the asset ceased to be a chargeable intangible asset in relation to it, realised the asset for its market value at that time and immediately reacquired it at that value.

(2) Sub-paragraph (1) has effect subject to paragraph 109 (postponement of gain in certain cases).

Asset ceasing to be chargeable intangible asset: postponement of gain in certain cases

109—(1) Where—

(a) paragraph 108 (asset ceasing to be chargeable asset: deemed realisation at market value) applies by reason of a company (''company A'') ceasing to be resident in the United Kingdom,
(b) immediately before company A ceases to be resident in the United Kingdom the asset is held by it for the purposes of a trade carried on by it outside the United Kingdom through a branch or agency,
(c) the proceeds of the deemed realisation of the asset exceed the original cost of the asset recognised for tax purposes,
(d) immediately after company A ceases to be resident in the United Kingdom it is a 75% subsidiary of another company (''company B'') that is resident in the United Kingdom, and
(e) company A and company B so elect by notice given to the Inland Revenue not later than two years after the date when company A ceased to be resident in the United Kingdom,

this Schedule has effect as if the proceeds of the deemed realisation of the asset were reduced by the amount of the excess referred to in paragraph (c). The amount of the reduction is referred to below in this paragraph as ''the postponed gain''.

(2) If company A subsequently realises the asset before the end of the period of six years after the date on which the company ceased to be resident in the United Kingdom, company B shall bring into account for tax purposes a credit equal to the postponed gain or, in the case of a part realisation, the appropriate proportion of the postponed gain.

The appropriate proportion is given by:

$$\frac{\text{Old Value} - \text{New Value}}{\text{Old Value}}$$

where—

Old Value is the market value of the asset immediately before the part realisation, and
New Value is the market value of the asset immediately after the part realisation.

(3) Sub-paragraph (2) does not apply—

(a) to the extent that the postponed gain has already been brought into account on a previous part realisation, or
(b) if the postponed gain has already been brought into account under sub-paragraph (4).

(4) If at any time after company A ceases to be resident in the United Kingdom—

(a) it ceases to be a 75% subsidiary of company B on the disposal by that company of ordinary shares of company A, or
(b) after it has ceased to be such a subsidiary otherwise than on such a disposal, company B disposes of such shares, or
(c) company B ceases to be resident in the United Kingdom,

company B shall bring into account for tax purposes a credit equal to the postponed gain.

This sub-paragraph does not apply if, or to the extent that, the postponed gain has already been brought into account under sub-paragraph (2).

(5) Any credit falling to be brought into account under sub-paragraph (4)(c) shall be brought into account immediately before company B ceases to be resident in the United Kingdom.

(6) A credit brought into account by company B under this paragraph is treated as a non-trading credit for the purposes of Part 6 (how debits and credits are given effect).

Asset becoming chargeable intangible asset

110—(1) This paragraph applies where an asset becomes a chargeable intangible asset in relation to a company—

(a) on the company becoming resident in the United Kingdom, or

(b) in the case of a company that is not resident in the United Kingdom, on beginning to be held for the purposes of a trade carried on by it in the United Kingdom through a branch or agency, or

(c) on the asset ceasing to be held for the purposes of a mutual trade or business.

(2) Where this paragraph applies this Schedule has effect as if the company had acquired the asset, immediately after it became a chargeable intangible asset in relation to the company, for its accounting value at that time.

Tax avoidance arrangements to be disregarded

111—(1) Tax avoidance arrangements shall be disregarded in determining—

(a) whether debits are to be brought into account under paragraph 9 (writing down on accounting basis) or the amount of such debits, or

(b) whether a credit is to be brought into account under Part 4 (realisation) or the amount of any such credit.

(2) Arrangements are "tax avoidance arrangements" if their main object or one of their main objects is to enable a company—

(a) to obtain a debit under paragraph 9 to which it would not otherwise be entitled or of a greater amount than that to which it would otherwise be entitled, or

(b) to avoid having to bring a credit into account under Part 4 or to reduce the amount of any such credit.

(3) In this paragraph—

"arrangements" includes any scheme, agreement or understanding, whether or not legally enforceable; and

"brought into account" means brought into account for tax purposes.

Debits not allowed in respect of expenditure not generally deductible for tax purposes

112—(1) No debit may be brought into account for tax purposes under this Schedule in respect of expenditure that is not generally deductible for tax purposes.

(2) Expenditure is "not generally deductible for tax purposes" if, or to the extent that, revenue expenditure of that description incurred for the purposes of a trade would be non-deductible by virtue of—

(a) section 577 of the Taxes Act 1988 (expenditure on business entertainment or gifts),

(b) section 577A of that Act (crime-related expenditure),

(c) section 578A of that Act (expenditure on expensive hired cars), or

(d) section 76(1) to (3) of the Finance Act 1989 (c 26) (expenditure on providing non-approved non-taxable retirement benefits).

Delayed payment of emoluments

113—(1) Where—

(a) a debit in respect of emoluments is recognised by a company for accounting purposes, and

(b) the emoluments are not paid until after the end of the period of nine months beginning with the end of the period of account in which the debit is recognised,

the emoluments shall be brought into account for the purposes of this Schedule only when they are paid.

(2) For the purposes of this paragraph—

(a) "emoluments" means emoluments allocated either—

(i) in respect of particular offices or employments (or both), or

(ii) generally in respect of offices or employments (or both); and

(b) emoluments are paid when they are treated as received (applying the rules in section 202B of the Taxes Act 1988 as for the purposes of section 202A(1)(a) of that Act (receipts basis of assessment for Schedule E)).

(3) This paragraph applies to potential emoluments as it applies to emoluments.

For this purpose—

(a) potential emoluments are amounts or benefits reserved in the accounts of an employer, or held by an intermediary, with a view to their becoming emoluments, and

(b) potential emoluments are regarded as paid when they become emoluments that are paid.

(4) Any adjustment required by this paragraph of an accounting debit that is partly referable to an amount to which this paragraph applies and partly to other matters shall be made on a just and reasonable basis.

(5) If a calculation for tax purposes has to be made before the end of the period of nine months mentioned in sub-paragraph (1)(*b*) and emoluments have not been paid—

    (*a*) it shall be assumed for the purpose of making the calculation that they will not be paid before the end of that period, but

    (*b*) the calculation shall be adjusted if the emoluments are subsequently paid before the end of that period and a claim is made.

Any such claim to adjust a calculation must be made to the Inland Revenue before the end of the period of two years beginning with the end of the period of account concerned.

Delayed payment of pension contributions

114—(1) This paragraph applies where—

    (*a*) a debit in respect of pension contributions is recognised by a company for accounting purposes, and

    (*b*) the contributions are not paid until after the end of the period of account in which the debit is recognised.

(2) Where this paragraph applies, the contributions shall be brought into account for the purposes of this Schedule only when they are paid.

(3) For the purposes of this paragraph "pension contributions" means—

    (*a*) sums paid by an employer by way of contributions under a scheme to which section 592 of the Taxes Act 1988 applies (exempt approved schemes),

    (*b*) sums paid to the trustees of such a scheme that are treated for the purposes of that section as employer's contributions (see subsection (6A) of that section), or

    (*c*) expenses within section 76(5) or (6) of the Finance Act 1989 (c 26) (expenses of providing benefits under non-approved retirement benefit scheme).

(4) Any adjustment required by this paragraph of an accounting debit that is partly referable to an amount to which this paragraph applies and partly to other matters shall be made on a just and reasonable basis.

Bad debts etc

115—(1) For the purposes of this Schedule a debt shall be brought into account on the assumption that the amount payable will be paid in full when it becomes due, except to the extent that—

    (*a*) the debt is bad,

    (*b*) the debt is estimated to be bad, or

    (*c*) the debt is released as part of a statutory insolvency arrangement.

(2) In sub-paragraph (1)(*c*) a "statutory insolvency arrangement" means—

    (*a*) a voluntary arrangement that has taken effect under or by virtue of the Insolvency Act 1986 (c 45) or the Insolvency (Northern Ireland) Order 1989 (SI 1989/2405 (NI 19)), or

    (*b*) a compromise or arrangement that has taken effect under section 425 of the Companies Act 1985 (c 6) or Article 418 of the Companies (Northern Ireland) Order 1986 (SI 1986/1032 (NI 6)).

(3) Where a debt is released as mentioned in sub-paragraph (1)(*c*) any gain in respect of the release brought into account for accounting purposes by the debtor shall be disregarded for the purposes of this Schedule.

(4) Any other gain in respect of an unpaid debt in respect of an intangible fixed asset that is brought into account by the debtor for accounting purposes is treated for the purposes of paragraph 14 (receipts recognised as they accrue) as a gain in respect of an intangible fixed asset.

(5) Any adjustment required by this paragraph of an accounting gain or loss that is partly referable to an amount affected by this paragraph and partly to other matters shall be made on a just and reasonable basis.

Assumptions for computing chargeable profits of controlled foreign companies

116—(1) In computing the amount mentioned in section 747(6) of the Taxes Act 1988 (chargeable profits of controlled foreign company) the following assumptions shall be made for the purpose of applying the provisions of this Schedule.

(2) It shall be assumed that any intangible fixed asset acquired or created by the company before the beginning of the first accounting period—

    (*a*) in respect of which an apportionment under section 747(3) falls to be made, or

    (*b*) which is an ADP exempt period,

was acquired or created by the company at the beginning of that accounting period at a cost equal to its value recognised for accounting purposes at that time.

(3) Notwithstanding paragraph 4(1) of Schedule 24 of the Taxes Act 1988 (assumption that all available reliefs have been claimed), it shall be assumed that the company has not claimed any relief under Part 7 (roll-over relief in case of reinvestment) or made any provisional declaration of entitlement to such relief.

But this assumption does not apply, if notice is given in accordance with paragraph 4(2) of that Schedule requesting that it should not apply, to such claims, and to such extent, as may be specified in the notice.

(4) Expressions used in this paragraph that are defined for the purposes of Chapter 4 of Part 17 of the Taxes Act 1988 (controlled foreign companies) have the same meaning in this paragraph.

(5) The assumption in sub-paragraph (2) above does not affect the determination of the question whether this Schedule applies to an asset in accordance with paragraph 118 (application of Schedule to assets created or acquired after commencement).

PART 14
COMMENCEMENT AND TRANSITIONAL PROVISIONS
Commencement date

117—(1) The commencement date for the purposes of this Schedule is 1st April 2002.

(2) In this Part—

"after commencement" means on or after that date and "before commencement" means before that date; and

"the existing law" means the law as it was before commencement.

Application of Schedule to assets created or acquired after commencement

118—(1) Except as otherwise expressly provided, the provisions of this Schedule apply only to intangible fixed assets of a company ("the company") that—

(a) are created by the company after commencement, or

(b) are acquired by the company after commencement from a person who at the time of the acquisition is not a related party in relation to the company, or

(c) are acquired by the company after commencement from a person who at the time of the acquisition is a related party in relation to the company in the cases specified in sub-paragraph (2).

As to when assets are regarded as created or acquired, see paragraphs 120 to 125.

(2) The cases mentioned in sub-paragraph (1)(c) in which this Schedule applies to assets acquired by the company after commencement from a related party are—

(a) where the asset is acquired from a company in relation to which the asset was a chargeable intangible asset immediately before the acquisition;

(b) where the asset is acquired from a person ("the intermediary") who acquired the asset after commencement from a third person—

(i) who was not at the time of that acquisition a related party in relation to the intermediary or, where the intermediary was not a company, a company in relation to which the intermediary was a related party, and

(ii) who is not, at the time of the acquisition by the company, a related party in relation to the company;

(c) where the asset was created, whether by the person from whom it is acquired or any other person, after commencement.

(3) Intangible fixed assets to which, by virtue of sub-paragraph (1), this Schedule does not apply in the absence of express provision to that effect are referred to in this Schedule as "existing assets".

(4) Sub-paragraph (1) has effect subject to —

(a) paragraph 126 (application of Schedule to fungible assets), and

(b) paragraph 127 (certain assets acquired on transfer of a business treated as existing assets).

(5) The following paragraphs contain provision for the application of this Schedule in relation to certain existing assets—

paragraphs 128 and 129 (application of Schedule to certain existing assets);

paragraphs 130 to 132 (application of roll-over relief in relation to certain existing assets).

(6) Nothing in this paragraph shall be read as restricting the application of this Schedule in accordance with paragraph 119 (application of Schedule to royalties).

Application of Schedule to royalties

119—(1) This Schedule—

(a) applies to royalties recognised for accounting purposes after commencement, and

(b) does not apply to royalties recognised for accounting purposes before commencement,

subject to the following provisions.

(2) To the extent that royalties have been brought into account before commencement, they shall not be brought into account again under this Schedule after commencement.

(3) To the extent that royalties would have been brought into account before commencement if the provisions of this Schedule had been in force, and were not so brought into account, they shall be brought into account immediately after commencement.

(4) For the purposes of this paragraph an amount is "brought into account" if—

(a) it is brought into account for tax purposes, or
(b) it would have been so brought into account if the person concerned had been within the charge to corporation tax.

Assets regarded as created or acquired when expenditure incurred

120—(1) This paragraph has effect for the purposes of paragraph 118 (application of Schedule to assets created or acquired after commencement) and applies to all intangible assets except those to which paragraph 121 or 122 applies (certain internally-generated assets).

(2) An intangible asset to which this paragraph applies is regarded as created or acquired after commencement to the extent that expenditure on its creation or acquisition is incurred after commencement.

As to whether expenditure on the creation or acquisition of the asset was incurred after commencement, see paragraphs 123 to 125.

(3) If only part of the expenditure on the creation or acquisition of the asset is incurred after commencement—

(a) this Schedule has effect as if there were a separate asset representing the expenditure so incurred, and
(b) the enactments that apply where this Schedule does not apply have effect as if there were a separate asset representing the expenditure not so incurred.

Any apportionment necessary for this purpose shall be made on a just and reasonable basis.

Internally-generated goodwill: whether created before or after commencement

121 For the purposes of paragraph 118 (application of Schedule to assets created or acquired after commencement) internally-generated goodwill is regarded as created before (and not after) commencement if the business in question was carried on at any time before commencement by the company or a related party.

Certain other internally-generated assets: whether created before or after commencement

122—(1) This paragraph has effect for the purposes of paragraph 118 (application of Schedule to assets created or acquired after commencement) and applies to an internally-generated asset representing expenditure that under the existing law is not qualifying expenditure for the purposes of any allowance under the Capital Allowances Act 2001 (c 2) ("non-qualifying expenditure").

(2) If only part of the expenditure on the creation or acquisition of the asset is non-qualifying expenditure—

(a) this Schedule has effect as if there were separate assets representing the non-qualifying expenditure and the other expenditure, and
(b) if this Schedule does not apply to the former, the enactments that apply where this Schedule does not apply also have effect as if there were a separate asset representing the non-qualifying expenditure.

Any apportionment necessary for this purpose shall be made on a just and reasonable basis.

(3) An asset to which this paragraph applies is regarded for the purposes of paragraph 118 as created before (and not after) commencement if the asset in question was held at any time before commencement by the company or a related party.

Expenditure on acquisition treated as incurred when recognised for accounting purposes

123—(1) For the purposes of paragraph 120 (assets regarded as created or acquired when expenditure incurred) the general rule is that expenditure on the acquisition of an asset is treated as incurred when it is recognised for accounting purposes.

(2) This is subject to—

paragraph 124 (chargeable gains rules to be followed in certain cases), and
paragraph 125 (capital allowances rule to be followed in certain cases).

When expenditure treated as incurred: chargeable gains rule to be followed in certain cases

124 For the purposes of paragraph 120 (assets regarded as created or acquired when expenditure incurred) expenditure on the acquisition of the asset that—

(a) does not qualify for any form of tax relief against income under the existing law, and
(b) would be treated as incurred after commencement under the general rule in paragraph 123,

shall be treated as incurred before commencement if the asset is (or would be) treated as disposed of (and thus acquired) before commencement for the purposes of the Taxation of Chargeable Gains Act 1992 (c 12).

When expenditure treated as incurred: capital allowances general rule to be followed in certain cases

125—(1) For the purposes of paragraph 120 (assets regarded as created or acquired when expenditure incurred) expenditure on the creation or acquisition of an asset that under the existing law is qualifying expenditure for the purposes of any allowance under the Capital Allowances Act 2001 (c 2) is treated as incurred when an unconditional obligation to pay it comes into being.

(2) For this purpose there may be an unconditional obligation to pay although the whole or part of the expenditure is not required to be paid until a later date.

Application of Schedule to fungible assets

126—(1) The provisions of this paragraph have effect for the purposes of this Part in relation to assets to which paragraph 107 applies (treatment of fungible assets as single asset)

(2) Paragraph 107 applies as if—

    (*a*) existing assets, and

    (*b*) intangible fixed assets that are not existing assets, were assets of different kinds.

(3) Where paragraph 107 applies (by virtue of sub-paragraph (2) or otherwise)—

    (*a*) a single asset comprising existing assets is treated as itself being an existing asset, and

    (*b*) a single asset comprising intangible fixed assets that are not existing assets is treated as itself being an asset to which this Schedule applies.

(4) The realisation by a company of an intangible fixed asset that apart from sub-paragraph (2) would be regarded as part of a single asset comprising both existing assets and assets that are not existing assets shall be regarded as diminishing the single asset of the company comprising existing assets in priority to diminishing the single asset of the company comprising assets that are not existing assets.

(5) Intangible fixed assets acquired by a company that would not otherwise be regarded as existing assets shall be treated as existing assets to the extent that they are to be identified, in accordance with the following rules, with existing assets realised by the company.

(6) The rules are—

    (*a*) that assets acquired are to be identified with existing assets of the same kind realised by the company within the period beginning 30 days before and ending 30 days after the date of the acquisition;

    (*b*) that assets realised earlier are to be identified before assets realised later;

    (*c*) that assets acquired earlier are to be identified before assets acquired later.

The reference in paragraph (*a*) to assets "of the same kind" are to assets that are, or but for sub-paragraph (2) would be, treated by virtue of paragraph 107 as part of a single asset.

Certain assets acquired on transfer of business treated as existing assets

127—(1) This paragraph applies where—

    (*a*) an asset that is an existing asset in the hands of a company ("the transferor company") is transferred to another company ("the transferee company"), and

    (*b*) the transfer is one in relation to which—

        (i) section 139 of the Taxation of Chargeable Gains Act 1992 (c 12) (reconstruction or amalgamation involving transfer of business), or

        (ii) section 140A of that Act (transfer of UK trade to company resident in another member State),

applies with the effect that the transferor company is treated for the purposes of that Act as disposing of the asset for a consideration that secures that neither a gain nor a loss accrues to that company.

(2) Where this paragraph applies the asset shall be treated for the purposes of this Schedule as an existing asset in the hands of the transferee company.

(3) This paragraph does not apply where the transfer mentioned in sub-paragraph (1) occurred before 28th June 2002.

Application of Schedule to certain existing telecommunication rights

128—(1) This Schedule applies to an existing asset consisting of a licence or other right within Schedule 23 to the Finance Act 2000 (c 17) (certain telecommunication rights).

(2) This Schedule has effect in relation to the asset—

    (*a*) as regards amounts to be brought into account for tax purposes in accounting periods ending after commencement, and (*b*) as if amounts brought into account for tax purposes in earlier accounting periods under Schedule 23 to the Finance Act 2000 had been so brought into account under this Schedule.

(3) If the asset—

(*a*) was acquired before the beginning of the first accounting period to which this Schedule applies in relation to it, and

(*b*) is a chargeable intangible asset immediately after the beginning of that period,

it shall be treated for the purposes of Part 7 (roll-over relief on realisation and reinvestment) as if it had been a chargeable intangible asset at all material times between its acquisition and the beginning of that period.

(4) Schedule 23 to the Finance Act 2000 shall cease to have effect for the purposes of corporation tax as regards accounting periods ending after commencement.

Application of Schedule to existing Lloyd's syndicate capacity

129—(1) This Schedule applies to an existing asset consisting of the rights of a member of Lloyd's under a syndicate within the meaning of Chapter 5 of Part 4 of the Finance Act 1994 (c 9) (taxation of corporate members of Lloyd's).

(2) This Schedule has effect in relation to the asset as regards amounts to be brought into account for tax purposes in accounting periods ending after commencement.

(3) For the purposes of paragraph 9(5) (writing down on accounting basis: calculation of amount of debit for tax purposes) as it applies to the first accounting period to which this Schedule applies in relation to such an asset, the tax written down value of the asset shall be computed under paragraph 27 as if the debits to be deducted under that paragraph included all accounting losses previously recognised in respect of the asset, whether or not they gave rise to a deduction for tax purposes.

(4) If the asset—

(*a*) was acquired before the beginning of the first accounting period to which this Schedule applies in relation to it, and

(*b*) is a chargeable intangible asset immediately after the beginning of that period,

it shall be treated for the purposes of Part 7 (roll-over relief on realisation and reinvestment) as if it had been a chargeable intangible asset at all material times between its acquisition and the beginning of that period.

Roll-over relief: application in relation to disposal of existing asset after commencement

130—(1) This paragraph provides for the application of Part 7 (roll-over relief in case of reinvestment) where a company disposes of an existing asset after commencement.

References in this paragraph to the disposal of an asset have the same meaning as in the Taxation of Chargeable Gains Act 1992 (c 12).

(2) Part 7 applies in accordance with this paragraph with the following adaptations—

(*a*) for references to the realisation of the old asset substitute references to its disposal;

(*b*) for references to its being a chargeable intangible asset substitute references to its being a chargeable asset within the Taxation of Chargeable Gains Act 1992;

(*c*) for references to the proceeds of its realisation substitute references to the net proceeds of disposal under that Act; and

(*d*) for references to its cost recognised for tax purposes substitute references to the cost under that Act.

(3) For the purposes of sub-paragraph (2)(*b*) an asset is a chargeable asset within the Taxation of Chargeable Gains Act 1992 in relation to a company at any time if, were the asset to be disposed of at that time, any gain accruing to the company on the disposal would be a chargeable gain within the meaning of that Act, and either—

(*a*) at that time the company is resident or ordinarily resident in the United Kingdom, or

(*b*) the gain would form part of the company's chargeable profits for corporation tax purposes by virtue of section 10(3) of that Act,

unless the company (were it to dispose of the asset at that time) would fall to be regarded for the purposes of any double taxation relief arrangements as not liable in the United Kingdom to tax on any gain accruing to it on the disposal.

(4) For the purposes of sub-paragraph (2)(*c*) the net proceeds of disposal under the Taxation of Chargeable Gains Act 1992 (c 12) shall be taken to be the amount of value of the consideration for the disposal reduced by any incidental costs of making the disposal that would be allowable as a deduction under section 38(1)(*c*) of that Act.

(5) For the purposes of sub-paragraph (2)(*d*) the cost under the Taxation of Chargeable Gains Act 1992 shall be taken to be an amount equal to the difference between the net proceeds of disposal as defined in sub-paragraph (4) and the amount of the chargeable gain on the disposal.

(6) Paragraph 93 (exclusion of roll-over relief in case of part realisation involving related party) does not apply in a case where Part 7 applies by virtue of this paragraph.

(7) Where a company is entitled to relief under Part 7 by virtue of this paragraph, it is treated for the purposes of the Taxation of Chargeable Gains Act 1992 as if the consideration for the disposal of the old asset were reduced by the amount available for relief.

This does not affect the treatment for any purpose of the Taxes Acts of the other party to any transaction involved in the disposal of the old asset or the expenditure on other assets.

Roll-over relief: application in relation to degrouping charge on existing asset arising after commencement

131—(1) This paragraph provides for the application of Part 7 (roll-over relief in case of reinvestment) where—

(*a*) a company is treated by virtue of subsection (3) or (6) of section 179 of the Taxation of Chargeable Gains Act 1992 (degrouping charge) as having sold and reacquired an existing asset, and

(*b*) the time at which by virtue of subsection (4) or (8) of that section the gain is treated as accruing is after commencement.

(2) Part 7 applies in accordance with this paragraph with the adaptations specified in paragraph 129(2) and the following further adaptations (which correspond to those in paragraph 65)—

(*a*) in paragraph 38 (conditions to be met in relation to the old asset), for the references to the old asset being a chargeable intangible asset throughout the period during which it was held by the company substitute a reference to its being a chargeable asset within the Taxation of Chargeable Gains Act 1992 throughout the period during which it was held by the company referred to in section 179 of that Act as company B;

(*b*) in paragraph 39(1) (conditions to be met in relation to expenditure on the other assets), for the references to the date of realisation of the old asset substitute references to—

(i) in a case within subsection (3) of section 179 of that Act, the time at which the gain is treated as accruing under subsection (4) of that section, and

(ii) in a case within subsection (6) of that section, the time at which the gain is treated as accruing under subsection (8) of that section;

(*c*) references to the proceeds of realisation shall be read as references to the amount of the consideration for which the company is treated under that Act as having sold and reacquired the asset.

(3) Paragraph 129(3) (meaning of "chargeable asset") applies for the purposes of sub-paragraph (2)(*a*) of this paragraph.

(4) Paragraph 93 (exclusion of roll-over relief in case of part realisation involving related party) does not apply in a case where Part 7 applies by virtue of this paragraph.

(5) A company entitled to relief under Part 7 by virtue of this paragraph is treated for the purposes of the Taxation of Chargeable Gains Act 1992 (c 12) as if the consideration for the disposal of the old asset were reduced by the amount available for relief.

This does not affect the treatment for any purpose of the Taxes Acts of the other party to any transaction involved in the disposal of the old asset or the expenditure on other assets.

Roll-over relief: transitory interaction with relief on replacement of business asset

132—(1) In relation to the disposal after commencement of an asset that is both—

(*a*) an asset of a class specified in section 155 of the Taxation of Chargeable Gains Act 1992 (assets qualifying for roll-over relief on replacement of business asset), and

(*b*) an intangible fixed asset,

the period specified in section 152(3) of that Act (period within which new assets must be acquired) does not include, and may not be extended so as to include, any period after commencement.

(2) Subject to that, relief may be claimed in such a case either under Part 7 of this Schedule (roll-over relief on realisation and reinvestment) or under section 152 or 153 of the Taxation of Chargeable Gains Act 1992, or partly under Part 7 and partly under section 152 or 153.

(3) For the purposes of any such claim under section 152 or 153 any expenditure on other assets within the meaning of Part 7 shall be treated as if it were an amount applied as mentioned in section 152(1).

(4) For the purposes of any such claim under Part 7 any amount applied as mentioned in section 152(1) shall be treated as if it were expenditure incurred on other assets.

(5) Classes 4 to 7 in section 155 of the Taxation of Chargeable Gains Act 1992 (goodwill and various types of quota) shall cease to have effect for the purposes of corporation tax as regards the acquisition of new assets that are chargeable intangible assets.

(6) References in this paragraph to the disposal of an asset have the same meaning as in that Act.

PART 15

INTERPRETATION

References to expenditure on an asset

133—(1) References in this Schedule to expenditure on an asset are to any expenditure (including abortive expenditure)—

(a) for the purpose of acquiring or creating, or establishing title to, the asset, or

(b) by way of royalty in respect of the use of the asset, or

(c) for the purpose of maintaining, preserving or enhancing, or defending title to, the asset.

(2) No account shall be taken of capital expenditure on tangible assets in determining for the purposes of this Schedule the amount of expenditure on an intangible asset.

"Capital expenditure" here has the same meaning as in the Capital Allowances Act 2001 (c 2).

(3) Any necessary apportionment shall be made on a just and reasonable basis in a case where expenditure is incurred partly as mentioned in sub-paragraph (1) or (2) and partly otherwise.

References to amounts recognised in profit and loss account

134 References in this Schedule to an amount recognised in a company's profit and loss account for a period include—

(a) an amount recognised in a statement of total recognised gains and losses or other statement of items brought into account in computing the company's profits and losses for that period; and

(b) an amount that would have been so recognised if a profit and loss account or other such statement as is mentioned in paragraph (a) had been drawn up for that period in accordance with generally accepted accounting practice.

Meaning of "accounting value"

135 References in this Schedule to the "accounting value" of an asset are to the net book value (or carrying amount) of the asset recognised for accounting purposes.

Meaning of "adjustments required for tax purposes"

136 References in this Schedule to "adjustments required for tax purposes" are to any adjustment required—

(a) by Schedule 28AA to the Taxes Act 1988 (provision not at arm's length), or

(b) by any provision of this Schedule.

Meaning of "chargeable intangible asset" and "chargeable realisation gain"

137—(1) For the purposes of this Schedule—

(a) an asset is a "chargeable intangible asset" in relation to a company at any time if, were it to be realised by the company at that time, any gain on its realisation would be a chargeable realisation gain;

(b) there is a "chargeable realisation gain" if a gain on the realisation of an asset gives rise to a credit required to be brought into account for tax purposes under Part 4 (realisation of intangible fixed asset).

(2) For the purposes of sub-paragraph (1)—

(a) there is a gain on the realisation of an asset in any case if the circumstances are such that paragraph 20(2)(a), 21(2)(a) or 23(2) applies, and

(b) there shall be disregarded in determining whether there is such a gain—

(i) the availability of relief under Part 7 (roll-over relief on realisation and reinvestment), and

(ii) any provision of this Schedule under which a transfer of an asset is to be treated as tax-neutral.

Interpretation provisions relating to insurance companies

138—(1) In this Schedule "insurance company", "life assurance business", "long-term business", "long-term insurance fund" and "basic life assurance and general annuity business" have the same meaning as in Chapter 1 of Part 12 to the Taxes Act 1988 (see section 431(2) of that Act).

(2) Any question arising in the case of an intangible fixed asset held by an insurance company as to the extent to which—

(a) the asset is to be treated for the purposes of this Schedule as held for the purposes of any category of business carried on by the company, or

(b) credits or debits under this Schedule in respect of the asset are to be treated as referable to any such category of business,

shall be determined in accordance with section 432A of the Taxes Act 1988 as that section would apply (apart from this Schedule) in relation to income or gains from the asset.

(3) Any question arising as to the extent to which royalties payable by an insurance company are referable to any class of business carried on by the company shall be determined in accordance with section 432A of the Taxes Act 1988 as that section would apply if—

(*a*) the right in respect of the enjoyment or exercise of which the royalties are payable was an asset held by the company, and

(*b*) the royalties payable were income from that asset.

Meaning of "royalty"

139 In this Schedule "royalty" means a royalty in respect of the enjoyment or exercise of rights that constitute an intangible fixed asset.

Meaning of "tax-neutral transfer"

140—(1) This paragraph applies to a transfer of an asset that is, by virtue of any provision of this Schedule, to be treated as a "tax-neutral" transfer.

(2) Where this paragraph applies—

(*a*) the transfer is regarded for the purposes of this Schedule as not involving any realisation of the asset by the transferor or any acquisition of that asset by the transferee, and

(*b*) the transferee is treated for the purposes of this Schedule as having held the asset at all times when it was held by the transferor and as having done all such things in relation to the asset as were done by the transferor.

(3) This means, in particular—

(*a*) that the original cost of the asset in the hands of the transferor is treated as the original cost in the hands of the transferee, and

(*b*) that all such debits and credits in relation to the asset as have been brought into account for tax purposes by the transferor under this Schedule are treated as if they had been so brought into account by the transferee.

The reference in paragraph (*a*) to the cost of the asset is to the cost recognised for tax purposes.

Meaning of "the Inland Revenue"

141—(1) Functions under these provisions are functions of the Board—

paragraph 35(2) (relief against total profits: power to allow longer period for claim), paragraph 39(1)(*a*) (roll-over relief: power to allow longer reinvestment period),

paragraphs 84(5), 85(5), 86(9), 87(8) and 88 (transfers treated as tax-neutral, etc: clearance procedure).

These functions are within section 4A of the Inland Revenue Regulation Act 1890 (c 21) (functions of Board exercisable by officer acting with their authority).

(2) Subject to sub-paragraph (1), references in this Schedule to "the Inland Revenue" are to any officer of the Board.

(3) In this paragraph "the Board" means the Commissioners of Inland Revenue.

Meaning of "the Taxes Acts"

142 In this Schedule "the Taxes Acts" means the enactments relating to income tax, corporation tax or chargeable gains.

Index of defined expressions

143 The expressions listed below are defined or otherwise explained by the provisions indicated:

long-term business and long-term insurance fund	paragraph 138(1)
major interest (in Part 12)	paragraphs 96(2) and (3) and 97 to 99
non-trading credits or debits	paragraph 34(1)
non-trading gain (or loss) on intangible fixed assets	paragraph 34(2) or (3)
old asset (in Part 7)	paragraph 37(1)
other assets (in Part 7)	paragraph 37(1)
part realisation (of asset)	paragraph 19(3)
principal company (of group)	paragraph 47(1) and Part 8 generally
proceeds of realisation	paragraph 24
profit and loss account (amounts recognised in)	paragraph 134
realisation (of asset)	paragraph 19
related party	paragraph 95 to 101
royalty	paragraph 139
subsidiary (in relation to company formed outside UK)	paragraph 46(3)
the Taxes Acts	paragraph 142
tax-neutral transfer	paragraph 140
tax written down value	Part 5

SCHEDULE 30

GAINS AND LOSSES OF A COMPANY FROM INTANGIBLE FIXED ASSETS: CONSEQUENTIAL AMENDMENTS

Section 84(2)

Commentary—*Simon's Direct Tax Service* **B3.801.**

General provisions about deductions

1—(1) For sections 337 and 337A of the Taxes Act 1988 (corporation tax: general provisions about taxation of income) substitute—

"337 Company beginning or ceasing to carry on trade

(1) Where a company begins or ceases—

    (*a*) to carry on a trade, or
    (*b*) to be within the charge to corporation tax in respect of a trade, the company's income shall be computed as if that were the commencement or, as the case may be, the discontinuance of the trade, whether or not the trade is in fact commenced or discontinued.

(2) Subsection (1) applies to a Schedule A business or overseas property business as it applies to a trade.

337A Computation of company's profits or income: exclusion of general deductions

(1) For the purposes of corporation tax, subject to any provision of the Corporation Tax Acts expressly authorising a deduction—

    (*a*) a company's profits shall be computed without any deduction in respect of dividends or other distributions, and
    (*b*) a company's income from any source shall be computed without any deduction in respect of charges on income.

(2) In computing a company's income from any source for the purposes of corporation tax—

    (*a*) no deduction shall be made in respect of interest except in accordance with Chapter 2 of Part 4 of the Finance Act 1996 (loan relationships); and
    (*b*) no deduction shall be made in respect of losses from intangible fixed assets within Schedule 29 to the Finance Act 2002 except in accordance with that Schedule.''

(2) For section 338 of the Taxes Act 1988 (corporation tax: charges on income) substitute—

"338 Charges on income deducted from total profits

(1) Charges on income are allowed as deductions from a company's total profits in computing the corporation tax chargeable for an accounting period.

(2) They are deducted from the company's total profits for the period as reduced by any other relief from tax other than group relief.

(3) The amount of the deduction is limited to the amount that reduces the company's total profits for the period to nil.

(4) Except as otherwise provided, a deduction is allowed only in respect of payments made by the company in the accounting period concerned.

(5) The above provisions are subject to any express exceptions in the Corporation Tax Acts.

338A Meaning of "charges on income"

(1) This section defines what payments or other amounts are "charges on income" for the purposes of corporation tax.

This section has effect subject to any express exceptions in the Corporation Tax Acts.

(2) Subject to the following provisions of this section, the following (and only the following) are charges on income—

> (a) annuities or other annual payments that meet the conditions specified in section 338B;
> (b) qualifying donations within the meaning of section 339 (qualifying donations to charity);
> (c) amounts allowed as charges on income under section 587B(2)(a)(ii) (gifts of shares etc to charity).

(3) No payment that is deductible in computing profits or any description of profits for the purposes of corporation tax shall be treated as a charge on income.

(4) No payment shall be treated as a charge on income if (without being so deductible) it is—

> (a) an annuity payable by an insurance company, or
> (b) an annuity or other annual payment payable by a company wholly or partly in satisfaction of any claim under an insurance policy in relation to which the company is the insurer.

In paragraph (a) "insurance company" has the same meaning as in Chapter 1 of Part 12.

338B Charges on income: annuities or other annual payments

(1) An annuity or other annual payment is a charge on income if—

> (a) the requirements specified in subsection (2) are met, and
> (b) it is not excluded from being a charge on income for the purposes of corporation tax—
>> (i) by any of the following provisions of this section, or
>> (ii) by any other provision of the Corporation Tax Acts.

(2) The requirements are that the payment—

> (a) is made under a liability incurred for a valuable and sufficient consideration,
> (b) is not charged to capital,
> (c) is ultimately borne by the company, and
> (d) in the case of a company not resident in the United Kingdom, is incurred wholly and exclusively for the purposes of a trade which is or is to be carried on by it in the United Kingdom through a branch or agency.

(3) An annuity or other annual payment made to a person not resident in the United Kingdom shall be treated as a charge on income only if the following conditions are met.

(4) The conditions are that the company making the payment is resident in the United Kingdom and that either—

> (a) the company deducts tax from the payment in accordance with section 349, and accounts under Schedule 16 for the tax so deducted, or
> (b) the person beneficially entitled to the income in respect of which the payment is made is a company that is not resident in the United Kingdom but which carries on a trade in the United Kingdom through a branch or agency and the payment falls to be brought into account in computing the chargeable profits (within the meaning given by section 11(2) of that company, or
> (c) the payment is one payable out of income brought into charge to tax under Case V of Schedule D.

(5) An annuity or other annual payment is not a charge on income if—

> (a) it is payable in respect of the company's loan relationships, or
> (b) it is a royalty to which Schedule 29 to the Finance Act 2002 applies (intangible fixed assets).

(6) Nothing in this section prevents an annuity or other annual payment from being a charge on income if it is a qualifying donation (within the meaning of section 339).".

(3) In section 214(1) of the Taxes Act 1988 (chargeable payments connected with exempt distributions), in paragraph (c) (payments not to be treated as distributions for purposes of certain provisions) for "sections 337(2) and 338(2)(a)" substitute "section 337A(1)".

(4) In section 834(1) of the Taxes Act 1988 (interpretation of the Corporation Tax Acts), in the definition of "charges on income" for "338" substitute "338A".

(5) In Schedule 23A to the Taxes Act 1988 (manufactured dividends), in paragraph 4(2)(b) for "338(4)(a)" substitute "338B(4)(a)".

Surrender of non-trading loss by way of group relief

2—(1) In section 403 of the Taxes Act 1988 (amounts that may be surrendered by way of group relief)—

(*a*) in subsection (1)(*b*) (amounts that may be surrendered if available for group relief) for "or management expenses which are" substitute ", management expenses or a non-trading loss on intangible fixed assets";

(*b*) in subsection (3), in the first sentence (meaning of availability for group relief), for "and management expenses" substitute "management expenses and a non-trading loss on intangible fixed assets";

(*c*) in subsection (3), in the second sentence (order in which amounts treated as used), for "and finally management expenses" substitute ", management expenses and finally a non-trading loss on intangible fixed assets".

(2) In section 403ZD of the Taxes Act 1988 (further provisions as to amounts available for group relief), after subsection (5) insert—

"(6) A non-trading loss on intangible fixed assets means a non-trading loss on intangible fixed assets, within the meaning of Schedule 29 to the Finance Act 2002, for the surrender period.

It does not include so much of any such loss as is attributable to an amount being carried forward under paragraph 35(3) of that Schedule (amounts carried forward from earlier periods).".

Extension of charitable exemption to non-trading gains

3 In section 505(1) of the Taxes Act 1988 (charities: exemptions), in paragraph (*c*) (income charged under Schedule D) after sub-paragraph (*iib*) insert—

"(*iic*) from tax under Case VI of Schedule D in respect of non-trading gains on intangible fixed assets under Schedule 29 to the Finance Act 2002, and".

Change in ownership of company with unused non-trading loss

4—(1) Chapter 6 of Part 17 of the Taxes Act 1988 (tax avoidance: miscellaneous) is amended as follows.

(2) In section 768C, after subsection (12) add—

"(13) This section applies in relation to an asset to which Schedule 29 to the Finance Act 2002 applies (intangible fixed assets), with the following adaptations—

(*a*) for the reference to section 171(1) of the 1992 Act substitute a reference to paragraph 55 of that Schedule;

(*b*) for any reference to a chargeable gain under that Act substitute a reference to a chargeable realisation gain within the meaning of that Schedule that is a credit within paragraph 34(1)(*a*) of that Schedule (non-trading credits);

(*c*) for any reference to a disposal of the asset substitute a reference to its realisation within the meaning of that Schedule;

(*d*) for the reference to the relevant provisions of the 1992 Act substitute a reference to Part 6 of that Schedule.".

(3) After section 768D insert—

"768E Change in ownership of company with unused non-trading loss on intangible fixed assets

(1) Where there is a change in the ownership of an investment company and either—

(*a*) paragraph (*a*), (*b*) or (*c*) of section 768B(1) applies, or

(*b*) section 768C applies,

the following provisions have effect to prevent relief being given under paragraph 35 of Schedule 29 to the Finance Act 2002 by setting a non-trading loss on intangible fixed assets incurred by the company before the change of ownership against profits arising after the change.

(2) The accounting period in which the change of ownership occurs is treated for that purpose as two separate accounting periods, the first ending with the change and the second consisting of the remainder of the period.

(3) The profits or losses of the period in which the change occurs are apportioned to those two periods—

(*a*) where paragraph (*a*), (*b*) or (*c*) of section 768B(1) applies, in accordance with Parts 2 and 3 of Schedule 28A, or

(*b*) where section 768C applies, in accordance with Parts 5 and 6 of that Schedule,

unless in any case the specified method of apportionment would work unjustly or unreasonably in which case such other method shall be used as appears just and reasonable.

(4) Relief under paragraph 35 of Schedule 29 to the Finance Act 2002 against total profits of the same accounting period is available only in relation to each of those periods considered separately.

(5) A loss made in any accounting period beginning before the change of ownership may not be set off under paragraph 35(3) of Schedule 29 to the Finance Act 2002 against—

(a) in a case where paragraph (a), (b) or (c) of section 768B(1) applies, profits of an accounting period ending after the change of ownership;
(b) in a case where section 768C applies, so much of those profits as represents the relevant gain within the meaning of that section.

(6) Subsections (8) and (9) of section 768 (time limits for assessment; information powers) apply for the purposes of this section as they apply for the purposes of that section.

(7) In this section "investment company" has the same meaning as in Part 4.".

(4) In paragraph 6 of Schedule 28A to the Taxes Act 1988 (amounts in issue for purposes of section 768B), after paragraph (dd) insert—

"(de) the amount of any non-trading credits or debits in respect of intangible fixed assets that fall to be brought into account for that period under paragraph 34 of Schedule 29 to the Finance Act 2002;
(df) the amount of any non-trading loss on intangible fixed assets carried forward to that accounting period under paragraph 35(3) of that Schedule;".

(5) In paragraph 7 of that Schedule (apportionment for purposes of section 768B), after paragraph (f) insert—

"(g) in the case of any such credit or debit as is mentioned in paragraph 6(de), by apportioning to each accounting period the credits or debits that would fall to be brought into account in that period if it were a period of account for which accounts were drawn up in accordance with generally accepted accounting practice;
(h) in the case of any such loss as is mentioned in paragraph 6(df) above, by apportioning the whole amount of the loss to the first part of the accounting period being divided.".

(6) In paragraph 13(1) of that Schedule (amounts in issue for purposes of section 768C), after paragraph (ed) insert—

"(ee) the amount of any non-trading credits or debits in respect of intangible fixed assets that fall to be brought into account for that period under paragraph 34 of Schedule 29 to the Finance Act 2002;
(ef) the amount of any non-trading loss on intangible fixed assets carried forward to that accounting period under paragraph 35(3) of that Schedule;".

(7) In paragraph 16 of that Schedule (apportionment for purposes of section 768C), after paragraph (f) insert—

"(g) in the case of any such credit or debit as is mentioned in paragraph 13(ee), by apportioning to each accounting period the credits or debits that would fall to be brought into account in that period if it were a period of account for which accounts were drawn up in accordance with generally accepted accounting practice;
(h) in the case of any such loss as is mentioned in paragraph 13(ef), by apportioning the whole amount of the loss to the first part of the accounting period being divided.".

Double taxation relief

5—(1) Part 18 of the Taxes Act 1988 (double taxation relief) is amended as follows.

(2) In section 795 (computation of income subject to foreign tax), in subsection (4) (application of that section notwithstanding certain other provisions) after "notwithstanding anything in" insert " – (a)" and at the end insert –

", or
(b) paragraph 1(3) of Schedule 29 to the Finance Act 2002 (matters to be brought into account in respect of intangible fixed assets only under that Schedule).".

(3) In the heading to section 797A (foreign tax on items giving rise to a non-trading credit), at the end add ": loan relationships".

(4) After that section insert—

"797B Foreign tax on items giving rise to a non-trading credit: intangible fixed assets

(1) This section applies for the purposes of any arrangements where, in the case of a company—

(a) a non-trading credit relating to an item is brought into account for the purposes of Schedule 29 to the Finance Act 2002 (intangible fixed assets) for an accounting period ("the applicable accounting period"), and
(b) there is in respect of that item an amount of foreign tax for which, under the arrangements, credit is allowable against United Kingdom tax computed by reference to that item.

(2) It shall be assumed that tax chargeable under Case VI of Schedule D on the profits and gains arising for the applicable accounting period from the company's intangible fixed assets falls to be computed on the actual amount of its non-trading credits for that period, and without any deduction in respect of non-trading debits.

(3) Section 797(3) shall have effect as if—

(*a*) there were for the applicable accounting period an amount equal to the adjusted amount of the non-trading debits falling to be brought into account by being set against profits of the company for that period of any description, and

(*b*) different parts of that amount might be set against different profits.

(4) For this purpose the adjusted amount of a company's non-trading debits for an accounting period is given by:

Total Debits – Amount Carried Forward

where—

Total Debits is the aggregate amount of the company's non-trading debits for that accounting period under Schedule 29 to the Finance Act 2002 (intangible fixed assets), and

Amount Carried Forward is the amount (if any) carried forward to the next accounting period of the company under paragraph 35(3) of that Schedule (carry-forward of non-trading loss in respect of which no claim is made for it to be set against total profits of current period).''.

(5) In section 811 (deduction for foreign tax where no credit available), in subsection (3) (application of that section notwithstanding certain other provisions) after ''notwithstanding anything in'' insert ''—(*a*)'' and at the end insert—

'', or

(*b*) paragraph 1(3) of Schedule 29 to the Finance Act 2002 (matters to be brought into account in respect of intangible fixed assets only under that Schedule).''.

Value-shifting provisions

6—(1) After section 33 of the Taxation of Chargeable Gains Act 1992 (provisions supplementary to sections 30 to 32) insert—

''33A Modification of sections 30 to 33 in relation to chargeable intangible asset

(1) Sections 30 to 33 have effect in relation to a chargeable intangible asset subject to the following modifications.

In this section ''chargeable intangible asset'' has the same meaning as in Schedule 29 to the Finance Act 2002.

(2) Any reference in those sections—

(*a*) to a disposal or part disposal of the asset shall be read as a reference to its realisation or part realisation within the meaning of that Schedule (see paragraph 19 of that Schedule);

(*b*) to an disposal of the asset under section 171(1) shall be read as a reference to its transfer under paragraph 55 of that Schedule (transfers within a group);

(*c*) to a disposal of the asset under section 179 shall be read as a reference to its realisation under paragraph 58 or 60 of that Schedule (degrouping).

(3) In section 31(6), paragraph (*c*) shall not apply to a revaluation where the profit on the revaluation is wholly taken into account as a credit under that Schedule (see paragraph 15 of that Schedule).

(4) None of the conditions in section 31(9) shall be treated as satisfied if the asset with enhanced value is a chargeable intangible asset within the meaning of that Schedule.

(5) The reference in section 32(2)(*b*) to the cost of the underlying asset shall be read, in the case of a chargeable intangible asset, as a reference to the capitalised value of the asset recognised for accounting purposes.''.

SCHEDULE 31

GAINS OF INSURANCE COMPANY FROM VENTURE CAPITAL INVESTMENT PARTNERSHIP

Section 85

Commentary—*Simon's Direct Tax Service* **C3.203.**

The following Schedule is inserted after Schedule 7AC to the Taxation of Chargeable Gains Act 1992 (c 12)—

''SCHEDULE 7AD

GAINS OF INSURANCE COMPANY FROM VENTURE CAPITAL INVEST-MENT PARTNERSHIP

Introduction

1 This Schedule applies where the assets of the long-term insurance fund of an insurance company (''the company'') include assets held by the company as a limited partner in a venture capital investment partnership (''the partnership'').

Meaning of "venture capital investment partnership"

2—(1) A "venture capital investment partnership" means a partnership in relation to which the following conditions are met.

(2) The first condition is that the sole or main purpose of the partnership is to invest in unquoted shares or securities.

This condition shall not be regarded as met unless it appears from—

(*a*) the agreement constituting the partnership, or
(*b*) any prospectus issued to prospective partners,

that that is the sole or main purpose of the partnership.

(3) The second condition is that the partnership does not carry on a trade.

(4) The third condition is that not less than 90% of the book value of the partnership's investments is attributable to investments that are either—

(*a*) shares or securities that were unquoted at the time of their acquisition by the partnership, or
(*b*) shares that were quoted at the time of their acquisition by the partnership but which it was reasonable to believe would cease to be quoted within the next twelve months.

(5) For the purposes of the third condition—

(*a*) the following shall be disregarded—

(i) any holding of cash, including cash deposited in a bank account or similar account but not cash acquired wholly or partly for the purpose of realising a gain on its disposal;
(ii) any holding of quoted shares or securities acquired by the partnership in exchange for unquoted shares or securities;

(*b*) whether the 90% test is met shall be determined by reference to the values shown in the partnership's accounts at the end of a period of account of the partnership.

(6) Where a partnership ceases to meet the above conditions, the company shall be treated as if the partnership had continued to be a venture capital investment partnership until the end of the period of account of the partnership during which it ceased to meet the conditions.

(7) A partnership that ceases to meet those conditions cannot qualify again as a venture capital investment partnership.

For this purpose a partnership is treated as the same partnership notwithstanding a change in membership if any person who was a member before the change remains a member.

Interest in relevant assets of partnership treated as single asset

3—(1) Where this Schedule applies section 59 (partnerships) does not have effect to make the company chargeable on its share of gains accruing on each disposal of relevant assets of the partnership.

(2) Instead—

(*a*) the company's interest in relevant assets of the partnership is treated as a single asset ("the single asset") acquired by the company when it became a member of the partnership, and
(*b*) the following provisions of this Schedule have effect.

(3) For the purposes of this Schedule the "relevant assets" of the partnership are the shares and securities held by the partnership, other than qualifying corporate bonds.

(4) Nothing in this Schedule shall be read—

(*a*) as affecting the operation of section 59 in relation to partners who are not insurance companies carrying on long-term business or are not limited partners, or
(*b*) as imposing any liability on the partnership as such.

The cost of the single asset

4—(1) The company is treated as having given, wholly and exclusively for the acquisition of the single asset, consideration equal to the amount of capital contributed by it on becoming a member of the partnership.

(2) Any further amounts of capital contributed by it to the partnership are treated on a disposal of the single asset as expenditure incurred wholly and exclusively on the asset for the purpose of enhancing its value and reflected in its state or nature at the time of the disposal.

(3) Where the investments of the partnership include qualifying corporate bonds, the amount to be taken into account under sub-paragraph (1) or (2) is proportionately reduced.

(4) The reduction is made by applying to that amount the fraction:

$$\frac{A-B}{A}$$

where—

A is the book value of all shares and securities held by the partnership at the end of the period of account of the partnership in which the amount of capital in question is fully invested by the partnership, and

B is the book value of all qualifying corporate bonds held by the partnership at the end of that period of account,

(5) For the purposes of sub-paragraph (5) the "book value" means the value shown in the partnership's accounts at the end of the period of account.

Deemed disposal of single asset in case of distribution

5—(1) There is a disposal of the single asset on each occasion on which the company receives a distribution from the partnership that does not consist entirely of income or the proceeds of sale or redemption of assets that are not relevant assets.

(2) The disposal is taken to be for a consideration equal to the amount of the distribution or of so much of it as does not consist of income or the proceeds of sale or redemption of assets that are not relevant assets.

(3) Where—

(*a*) the partnership disposes of relevant assets on which a chargeable gain or allowable loss would accrue if they were held by the company alone, and

(*b*) no distribution of the proceeds of the disposal is made within twelve months of the disposal,

the company is treated as having received its share of the proceeds as a distribution at the end of the period of account of the partnership following that in which the disposal took place, or at the end of the period of six months after the date of the disposal, whichever is the later.

(4) The operation of sub-paragraph (3) is not affected by the partnership having ceased to be a venture capital investment partnership before the time at which the distribution is treated as received by the company.

(5) Where sub-paragraph (3) applies, any subsequent actual distribution of the proceeds is disregarded.

Apportionment in case of part disposal

6—(1) For the purposes of section 42 (apportionment of cost etc in case of part disposal) the market value of the property remaining undisposed of on a part disposal of the single asset shall be determined as follows.

(2) If there is no further disposal of that asset in the period of account in which the part disposal in question takes place, the market value of the property remaining undisposed of shall be taken to be equal to the company's share of the book value of the relevant assets of the partnership as shown in the partnership's accounts at the end of that period of account.

(3) If there is a further disposal of that asset in the period of account in which the part disposal in question takes place, or more than one, the market value of the property remaining undisposed of shall be taken to be equal to the sum of—

(*a*) the amount or value of the consideration on the further disposal or, as the case may be, the total amount or value of the consideration on the further disposals, and

(*b*) the amount (if any) of the company's share of the book value of the relevant assets of the partnership as shown in the partnership's accounts at the end of that period of account.

Disposal of partnership asset giving rise to offshore income gain

7—(1) Nothing in this Schedule shall be read as affecting the operation of Chapter 5 of Part 17 of the Taxes Act (offshore funds).

(2) Where an offshore income gain accrues to the company under that Chapter from the disposal of any relevant asset of the partnership, the amount of any distribution received or treated as received by the company from the partnership that represents the whole or part of the proceeds of disposal of that asset is treated for the purposes of this Schedule as reduced by the amount of the whole or a corresponding part of the offshore income gain.

Exclusion of negligible value claim

8 No claim may be made in respect of the single asset under section 24(2) (assets that have become of negligible value).

Investment in other venture capital investment partnerships

9—(1) For the purposes of paragraph 2 (meaning of "venture capital investment partnership") an investment by way of capital contribution to another venture capital investment partnership shall be treated as an investment in unquoted shares or securities.

(2) The Treasury may by regulations make provision, in place of but corresponding to that made by paragraphs 3 to 8, in relation to gains accruing on a disposal of relevant assets by such a partnership.

(3) The regulations may make provision for any period of account to which, in accordance with paragraphs 11 to 13, this Schedule applies.

Interpretation

10—(1) In this Schedule—

"insurance company", "long-term business" and "long-term insurance fund" have the same meaning as in Chapter 1 of Part 12 of the Taxes Act (see section 431(2) of that Act); "limited partner" means—

(a) a person carrying on a business as a limited partner in a partnership registered under the Limited Partnership Act 1907, or

(b) a person carrying on a business jointly with others who, under the law of a country or territory outside the United Kingdom, is not entitled to take part in the management of the business and is not liable beyond a certain limit for debts or obligations incurred for the purposes of the business;

"relevant assets" has the meaning given by paragraph 3(3);

"securities" has the same meaning as in section 132 and also includes any debentures;

"unquoted" and quoted", in relation to shares or securities, refer to listing on a recognised stock exchange.

(2) References in this Schedule to the partnership's accounts are to accounts drawn up in accordance with generally accepted accounting practice.

If no such accounts are drawn up, the references to the treatment of any matter, or the amounts shown, in the accounts of the partnership are to what would have appeared if accounts had been drawn up in accordance with generally accepted accounting practice.

(3) References in this Schedule to capital contributed to a limited partnership include amounts purporting to be provided by way of loan if—

(a) the loan carries no interest,

(b) all the limited partners are required to make such loans, and

(c) the loans are accounted for as partners' capital, or partners' equity, in the accounts of the partnership.

(4) For the purposes of this Schedule the assets of—

(a) a Scottish partnership, or

(b) a partnership under the law of any other country or territory under which assets of a partnership are regarded as held by or on behalf of the partnership as such,

shall be treated as held by the members of the partnership in the proportions in which they are entitled to share in the profits of the partnership.

References in this Schedule to the company's interest in, or share of, the partnership's assets shall be construed accordingly.

General commencement and transitional provisions

11—(1) Subject to paragraph 12 (election to remain outside Schedule), this Schedule applies—

(a) to periods of account of the partnership beginning on or after 1st January 2002, and

(b) to a period of account of the partnership beginning before that date and ending on or after it, unless the company elects that it shall not do so.

(2) Where the company became a member of the partnership before the beginning of the first period of account of the partnership to which this Schedule applies, the cost of the single asset at the beginning of that period of account shall be taken to be equal to the total of the relevant indexed base costs.

(3) For the purposes of sub-paragraph (2)—

(a) the "indexed base cost" means—

(i) in relation to a holding that by virtue of section 104 is to be treated as a single asset, what would be the indexed pool of expenditure within the meaning of section 110 if the holding were disposed of, and

(ii) in relation to any other asset, the amount of expenditure together with the indexation allowance that would be fall to be deducted if the asset were disposed of; and

(b) the "relevant indexed base costs" means the indexed base costs that would be taken into account in computing in accordance with section 59 the gain or loss of the company if all the shares and securities (other than qualifying corporate bonds) held by the partnership were disposed of on the last day of the company's accounting period immediately preceding its first accounting period beginning on or after 1st January 2002.

(4) No account shall be taken under this Schedule of a distribution by the partnership in a period of account to which this Schedule applies to the extent that it represents a chargeable gain accruing in an earlier period to which this Schedule does not apply.

Election to remain outside Schedule

12—(1) If the company—

  (*a*) became a member of the partnership before the beginning of the first period of account of the partnership to which this Schedule would otherwise apply, or

  (*b*) made its first contribution of capital to the partnership before 17th April 2002,

it may elect that the provisions of this Schedule shall not apply to it in relation to that partnership.

How and when election to be made

13 Any election under paragraph 10 or 11 must be made—

  (*a*) by notice to an officer of the Board,

  (*b*) not later than the end of the period of two years after the end of the company's first accounting period beginning on or after 1st January 2002.''.

SCHEDULE 32

LLOYD'S UNDERWRITERS

Section 86

Commentary—*Simon's Direct Tax Service* E5.614, 621.

Individuals

1 Chapter 3 of Part 2 of the Finance Act 1993 (c 34) (Lloyd's underwriters, etc) is amended as follows.

2 In section 178 (stop loss and quota share insurance), in subsection (1) (deductions), for paragraph (*c*) substitute—

  ''(*c*) where an amount is payable by him under a quota share contract—

    (i) so much of that amount as exceeds the amount of transferred losses that are declared on or before the date the contract takes effect (''the declared amount''), or

    (ii) if the contract does not take effect, the amount so payable under the contract.''

3 After subsection (3) of that section insert—

  ''(3A) Where the amount payable by a member under a quota share contract is less than the declared amount, the difference between the two amounts shall be treated as a trading receipt in computing the profits arising from the member's underwriting business in the year of assessment which corresponds to the underwriting year in which the contract takes effect.

  (3B) Where a member has entered a quota share contract, any amount paid by him to cover a cash call in respect of transferred losses that are not declared at the time the contract takes effect shall be treated—

    (*a*) for the purposes of subsection (1)(c)(i) and (3A) above, as an amount payable under the contract, and

    (*b*) for the purposes of section 172, as a payment made at the time the contract takes effect.''.

4 For subsection (4) of that section substitute—

  ''(4) For the purposes of this section—

    ''cash call'' has the same meaning as in Part 1 of Schedule 20 to this Act;

    ''quota share contract'' means any contract between a member and another person which—

      (*a*) is made in accordance with the rules or practice of Lloyd's, and

      (*b*) provides for that other person to take over any rights and liabilities of the member under any of the syndicates of which he is a member;

    and where the taking over of a member's rights and liabilities is conditional upon the occurrence of any event, the contract does not take effect until that event occurs; and

    ''transferred loss'', in relation to such a contract, means a loss for which that other person takes over liability under the contract (disregarding, in the case of a loss that has been declared at the time it is taken over, any part of it in respect of which the member has paid a cash call before that time).''.

5 In section 184(1) (interpretation), in the definition of ''stop-loss insurance'', after ''business'' insert '', except insurance taken out by entering a quota share contract (within the meaning of section 178 above)''.

Corporate bodies

6 Chapter 5 of Part 4 of the Finance Act 1994 (c 9) (Lloyd's underwriters: corporations etc) is amended as follows.

7 In section 225 (stop loss and quota share insurance), in subsection (1) (deductions), for paragraph (*b*) substitute—

> ''(*b*) where an amount is payable by it under a quota share contract—
>
>> (i) so much of that amount as exceeds the amount of transferred losses that are declared on or before the date the contract takes effect (''the declared amount''), or
>>
>> (ii) if the contract does not take effect, the amount so payable under the contract.''

8 After subsection (3) of that section insert—

> ''(3A) Where the amount payable by a corporate member under a quota share contract is less than the declared amount—
>
>> (*a*) if the underwriting year in which the contract takes effect falls within a single accounting period, the difference between the two amounts (''the surplus'') shall be treated as a trading receipt in computing the profits arising from the member's underwriting business for that period, and
>>
>> (*b*) if that underwriting year falls within two or more accounting periods, the apportioned part of the surplus shall be treated as a trading receipt in computing the profits arising from the member's underwriting business for each of those periods.
>
> (3B) Where a corporate member has entered a quota share contract, any amount paid by it to cover a cash call in respect of transferred losses that are not declared at the time the contract takes effect shall be treated for the purposes of subsections (1)(*b*)(i) and (3A) above, as an amount payable under the contract at that time.''.

9 For subsection (4) of that section substitute—

> ''(4) In this section—
>
>> ''apportioned part'', in relation to any insurance money or other amount, means a part apportioned under section 72 of the Taxes Act 1988;
>>
>> ''cash call'' means a request for funds which, in pursuance of a contract made in accordance with the rules and practices of Lloyd's, is made to a corporate member by the agent of a syndicate of which it is a member;
>>
>> ''quota share contract'' means any contract between a corporate member and another person which—
>>
>>> (*a*) is made in accordance with the rules or practice of Lloyd's; and
>>>
>>> (*b*) provides for that other person to take over any rights and liabilities of the member under any of the syndicates of which it is a member;
>>
>> and where the taking over of a member's rights and liabilities is conditional upon the occurrence of any event, the contract does not take effect until that event occurs; and
>>
>> ''transferred loss'', in relation to such a contract, means a loss for which that other person takes over liability under the contract (disregarding, in the case of a loss that has been declared at the time it is taken over, any part of it in respect of which the member has paid a cash call before that time).''.

10 In section 230(1) (interpretation), in the definition of ''stop-loss insurance'', after ''business'' insert ''except insurance taken out by entering a quota share contract (within the meaning of section 225 above)''.

SCHEDULE 33

VENTURE CAPITAL TRUSTS

Section 109

Commentary—*Simon's Direct Tax Service* **E3.635.**

PART 1

VENTURE CAPITAL TRUSTS: WINDING UP

Meaning of ''VCT-in-liquidation''

1—(1) In this Part of this Schedule ''VCT-in-liquidation'' means a company—

> (*a*) that is being wound up (whether or not under the law of a part of the United Kingdom and whether under the law of one, or more than one, territory),
>
> (*b*) that was a venture capital trust immediately before the commencement of its winding-up, and
>
> (*c*) whose winding up is for *bona fide* commercial reasons and is not part of a scheme or arrangement the main purpose of which, or one of the main purposes of which, is the avoidance of tax.

(2) Regulations may, for purposes of this Part of this Schedule, make provision as to when a company's winding up is to be treated as commencing or ending in a case where it is wound up otherwise than under the law of a part of the United Kingdom or otherwise than under the law of a single territory.

Power to treat VCT-in-liquidation as VCT

2—(1) Regulations may make provision for tax enactments specified by the regulations to have effect as if—

(a) a VCT-in-liquidation that is not a venture capital trust were, or were during any prescribed period of its winding-up, a venture capital trust;

(b) VCT approval withdrawn from a company—

(i) at any time during the period when it is a VCT-in-liquidation, or

(ii) at any time during a prescribed part of that period,

were withdrawn at a prescribed time (and not at the time at which it is actually withdrawn).

(2) In this paragraph ''prescribed'' means specified by, or determined under, regulations.

Power to treat conditions for VCT approval as fulfilled with respect to VCT-in-liquidation

3—(1) Regulations may make provision for conditions specified in section 842AA(2) of the Taxes Act 1988 (conditions for approval as a VCT) to be treated for purposes of section 842AA(2) and (3) of that Act as fulfilled, or as conditions that will be fulfilled, with respect to a VCT-in-liquidation.

(2) Provision under sub-paragraph (1) may be made so as to apply in relation to a VCT-in-liquidation—

(a) throughout its winding-up, or

(b) during prescribed periods of its winding-up.

(3) Regulations may, for purposes of tax enactments specified by the regulations, make provision for VCT approval to be treated as having been withdrawn, with effect as from a time specified by or determined under the regulations, from a VCT-in-liquidation from whom the Board would have power to withdraw such approval but for provision made under sub-paragraph (1).

Power to make provision about distributions by VCT-in-liquidation

4—(1) Regulations may make provision for tax enactments specified by the regulations—

(a) to apply in relation to distributions from a VCT-in-liquidation (including, in particular, distributions in the course of dissolving it or winding it up);

(b) not to apply in relation to such distributions;

(c) to apply in relation to such distributions with modifications specified by the regulations.

(2) Provision under sub-paragraph (1) may be made so as to apply in relation to distributions from a VCT-in-liquidation made—

(a) at any time during its winding-up, or

(b) during periods of its winding-up specified by, or determined under, regulations.

Power to facilitate disposals to VCT by VCT-in-liquidation

5—(1) Regulations may make provision authorised by sub-paragraph (2) for cases where shares in or securities of a company are acquired by a venture capital trust (''the trust company'') from a VCT-in-liquidation.

(2) The provision that may be made under sub-paragraph (1) for such a case is—

(a) provision for conditions specified in section 842AA(2) of the Taxes Act 1988 (conditions for approval as a VCT) to be treated for purposes of section 842AA(2) and (3) of that Act as fulfilled, or as conditions that will be fulfilled, with respect to the trust company in relation to periods ending after the acquisition;

(b) provision for the shares or securities acquired to be treated, at times after the acquisition when they are held by the trust company, as meeting requirements of Schedule 28B to the Taxes Act 1988 (provisions for determining whether shares or securities held by a venture capital trust form part of its qualifying holdings);

(c) provision for shares in the trust company issued in connection with the acquisition of the shares or securities from the VCT-in-liquidation and either—

(i) issued to a person who is a member of the VCT-in-liquidation, or

(ii) issued to the VCT-in-liquidation and distributed by it in the course of its winding-up or dissolution to a person who is one of its members,

to be treated, for purposes of Schedule 5C to the Taxation of Chargeable Gains Act 1992 (c 12), as representing shares in the VCT-in-liquidation held by that person.

(3) Provision under sub-paragraph (1) may be made so as to apply in relation to shares or securities acquired from a VCT-in-liquidation—

(a) at any time during its winding-up, or

(*b*) during periods of its winding-up specified by, or determined under, regulations.

(4) In this paragraph "securities" means any securities and includes any liability that is a security in relation to a company by reason of section 842AA(12)(*a*) of the Taxes Act 1988.

Provision in respect of periods before and after winding-up

6—(1) Any power under paragraphs 2 to 5 to make provision in relation to a VCT-in-liquidation includes power to make corresponding or similar provision in relation to—

(*a*) a company for whose winding up an application has been made to a court and which is not a VCT-in-liquidation but would be if, at the time that application was made, the court had ordered the company's winding-up to commence at that time;

(*b*) a company that has been a VCT-in-liquidation but is no longer a VCT-in-liquidation because it has been wound up.

(2) For the purposes of making provision in reliance on sub-paragraph (1), references in paragraphs 2 to 5 (however expressed) to a VCT-in-liquidation's winding-up, or to the commencement or ending of its winding-up, may be taken to be references to, or to the commencement or ending of, the extension period for a company to which sub-paragraph (1) applies.

(3) In this paragraph—

"the extension period"—

(*a*) in relation to a company to which sub-paragraph (1)(*a*) applies, means the period beginning with the making of the application and ending with the earlier of its final determination and the company becoming a company that is being wound up, and

(*b*) in relation to company to which sub-paragraph (1)(*b*) applies, means the period between the end of the company's winding-up and the company's dissolution;

"prescribed" means specified by, or determined under, regulations.

Part 1: supplementary provisions and interpretation

7—(1) Provision made by regulations under paragraphs 2 to 6 applies in cases, and subject to conditions, specified by regulations.

(2) Such provision may (but need not) be made so as to have effect in a particular case only for such period as may be specified by, or determined under, regulations.

(3) Such provision may be made in relation to any—

(*a*) VCT-in-liquidation, or

(*b*) company such as is mentioned in paragraph 6(1),

whose winding-up commences on or after 17th April 2002.

(4) In this Part of this Schedule "VCT approval" means approval for the purposes of section 842AA of the Taxes Act 1988 (approval as a VCT).

(5) References in this Part of this Schedule to things done by a VCT-in-liquidation include things done by a liquidator of a VCT-in-liquidation.

PART 2
VENTURE CAPITAL TRUSTS: MERGERS
Power to facilitate mergers of VCTs

8—(1) The Treasury may by regulations make provision authorised by paragraph 9 for cases where—

(*a*) there is a merger of two or more companies each of which is a venture capital trust immediately before the merger begins to be effected, and

(*b*) the merger is for *bona fide* commercial reasons and is not part of a scheme or arrangement the main purpose of which, or one of the main purposes of which, is the avoidance of tax.

(2) Provision made by regulations under sub-paragraph (1) applies—

(*a*) in cases, and

(*b*) subject to conditions (including conditions requiring approvals to be obtained),

specified by the regulations.

(3) Provision made by regulations under sub-paragraph (1) may apply in relation to any merger where the transactions for effecting the merger take place on or after 17th April 2002.

Provision that may be made by regulations under paragraph 8(1)

9—(1) The provision that may be made under paragraph 8(1) for a case where there is a merger of two or more companies ("the merging companies") is—

(*a*) provision for the successor company, or any of the merging companies, to be treated (whether at times before, during or after the merger) as a venture capital trust for purposes of tax enactments specified by regulations;

(*b*) provision for paragraph 3 of Schedule 15B to the Taxes Act 1988 (loss of relief on disposal of VCT shares within three years of their issue) not to apply in the case of disposals of shares in a merging company made in the course of effecting the merger;

(*c*) provision for such disposals not to be chargeable events for the purposes of Schedule 5C to the Taxation of Chargeable Gains Act 1992 (c 12) (VCTs: deferred charge on re-investment);

(*d*) provision for conditions specified in section 842AA(2) of the Taxes Act 1988 (conditions for approval as a VCT) to be treated (whether at times before, during or after the merger) for purposes of section 842AA(2) and (3) of that Act as fulfilled, or as conditions that will be fulfilled, with respect to the successor company or any of the merging companies;

(*e*) provision for shares in or securities of a company that are acquired (whether at times before, during or after the merger) by the successor company from a merging company to be treated, at times after the acquisition when they are held by the successor company, as meeting requirements of Schedule 28B to the Taxes Act 1988 (provisions for determining whether shares or securities held by a venture capital trust form part of its qualifying holdings);

(*f*) provision for tax enactments specified by regulations to apply, with or without adaptations, in relation to the merger or transactions taking place (whether before, during or after the merger) in connection with the merger;

(*g*) provision authorising disclosure for tax purposes connected with the merger—

     (i) by the Board or officers of the Board,

     (ii) to any of the merging companies or the successor company,

     (iii) of any information provided to the Board, or any officer of the Board, by or on behalf of any of the merging companies or the successor company.

(2) In this paragraph "securities" has the same meaning as in section 842AA of the Taxes Act 1988.

Meaning of "merger" and "successor company"

10—(1) For the purposes of this Part of this Schedule there is a merger of two or more companies ("the merging companies") if—

(*a*) shares in one of the merging companies ("company A") are issued to members of the other merging company or companies, and

(*b*) the shares issued to members of the other merging company or, in the case of each of the other merging companies, the shares issued to members of that other company, are issued—

     (i) in exchange for their shares in that other company, or

     (ii) by way of consideration for a transfer to company A of the whole or part of the business of that other company.

(2) For the purposes of this Part of this Schedule there is also a merger of two or more companies ("the merging companies") if—

(*a*) shares in a company ("company B") that is not one of the merging companies are issued to members of the merging companies, and

(*b*) in the case of each of the merging companies, the shares issued to members of that company are issued—

     (i) in exchange for their shares in that company, or

     (ii) by way of consideration for a transfer to company B of the whole or part of the business of that company.

(3) In this Part of this Schedule "the successor company"—

(*a*) in relation to a merger such as is described in sub-paragraph (1), means the company that fulfils the role of company A, and

(*b*) in relation to a merger such as is described in sub-paragraph (2), means the company that fulfils the role of company B.

PART 3

TIME ALLOWED FOR VCT TO INVEST MONEY RAISED BY FURTHER SHARE ISSUE

Power to disapply, or limit operation of, section 842AA(5B) of the Taxes Act 1988

11—(1) Regulations may make provision for section 842AA(5B) of the Taxes Act 1988 (use of money raised by VCTs further issue of shares disregarded during grace period)—

(*a*) not to apply, or to be treated as not having applied, in specified cases;

(*b*) to apply, or to be treated as having applied, in specified cases—

     (i) only to a specified extent;

     (ii) only if specified conditions (including conditions requiring approvals to be obtained) are satisfied.

(2) Provision made by regulations under sub-paragraph (1) may (but need not) be made so that, in any particular case, section 842AA(5B) of the Taxes Act 1988—

(*a*) does not apply, or is treated as not having applied, at prescribed times or with effect as from a prescribed time, or

(*b*) applies, or is treated as having applied, in accordance with provision made under sub-paragraph (1)(*b*) at prescribed times or with effect as from a prescribed time.

(3) Regulations under sub-paragraph (1) may make provision in relation to shares issued on or after 17th April 2002.

(4) In sub-paragraph (1) ''specified'' means specified by regulations and in sub-paragraph (2) ''prescribed'' means specified by, or determined under, regulations.

Withdrawal of VCT approval in cases for which provision made under paragraph 11

12—(1) Regulations may make provision for withdrawal of approval of a company for the purposes of section 842AA of the Taxes Act 1988 (venture capital trusts) to be treated—

(*a*) in a case where the withdrawal is by reference to a condition for approval that would have been, or would be, fulfilled but for provision made under paragraph 11, and

(*b*) for purposes of enactments specified by regulations,

as having taken effect as from a time specified in the notice of the withdrawal that is earlier than the time when the notice is given to the company.

(2) Provision made under sub-paragraph (1) has effect subject to the provisions of section 842AA(9) of the Taxes Act 1988 (retrospective effect of notices of withdrawal of VCT approval) as to the earliest time that may be specified by such a notice.

Consequential amendment in section 842AA(5A) of the Taxes Act 1988

13 In section 842AA(5A) of the Taxes Act 1988 (subsection (5B) applies where VCT makes further issue of shares), after ''Subsection (5B) below applies'' insert '', subject to any regulations under paragraph 11 of Schedule 33 to the Finance Act 2002,''.

PART 4
SUPPLEMENTARY

Extension of existing powers to give effect to VCT reliefs

14—(1) Section 73 of the Finance Act 1995 (c 4) (power to make regulations giving effect to VCT reliefs) shall have effect as if the reliefs mentioned in subsection (1) of that section included any relief arising by reason of regulations under Part 1 or 2 of this Schedule.

(2) The powers conferred by those Parts of this Schedule are additional to those that (whether or not by reason of sub-paragraph (1)) are conferred by that section.

Penalties for non-compliance with regulations under this Schedule

15 In each column of the Table in section 98 of the Taxes Management Act 1970 (c 9) (penalties for failure to furnish information etc), after the final entry insert ''Regulations under Schedule 33 to the Finance Act 2002.''.

Regulations under this Schedule: inclusion of supplementary etc provisions

16—(1) Regulations under this Schedule may—

(*a*) contain such administrative provisions (including provision for advance clearances and provision for the withdrawal of clearances) as appear to the Treasury to be necessary or expedient;

(*b*) authorise the Board to give notice to any person requiring him to provide such information, specified in the notice, as they may reasonably require in order to determine whether any conditions imposed by regulations under this Schedule are met;

(*c*) make different provision for different cases;

(*d*) include such supplementary, incidental and transitional provisions as appear to the Treasury to be appropriate;

(*e*) include provision having retrospective effect.

(2) Without prejudice to any specific provisions in this Schedule, a power conferred by any provision of this Schedule to make regulations includes power to provide for the Board, or an officer of the Board, to exercise a discretion in dealing with any matter.

Interpretation of Schedule

17 In this Schedule—

"company" includes any body corporate or unincorporated association but does not include a partnership, and shall be construed in accordance with section 99 of the Taxation of Chargeable Gains Act 1992 (c 12) (application of Act to unit trust schemes);

"regulations" means regulations made by the Treasury;

"shares" includes stock;

"tax enactments" means provisions of or made under—

    (*a*) the Tax Acts,
    (*b*) the Taxation of Chargeable Gains Act 1992 (c 12) or any other enactment relating to capital gains tax, or
    (*c*) the Taxes Management Act 1970 (c 9);

"venture capital trust" has the meaning given by section 842AA of the Taxes Act 1988.

SCHEDULE 39

RECOVERY OF TAXES ETC DUE IN OTHER MEMBER STATES

Section 134(1)

Introduction

1—(1) This Schedule applies where in accordance with the Mutual Assistance Recovery Directive an authority in another member State makes a request for the recovery in the United Kingdom of a sum claimed by that authority in that State.

(2) In this Schedule—

    (*a*) the "Mutual Assistance Recovery Directive" has the meaning given by section 134; and
    (*b*) the "foreign claim" means the claim in relation to which a request under that Directive is made as mentioned in sub-paragraph (1).

Enforcement of claims in the United Kingdom

2—(1) Subject to the following provisions of this Schedule—

    (*a*) such proceedings may be taken by or on behalf of the relevant UK authority to enforce the foreign claim, by way of legal proceedings, distress, diligence or otherwise, as might be taken to enforce a corresponding UK claim, and
    (*b*) any enactment or rule of law relating to a corresponding UK claim shall apply, with any necessary adaptations, in relation to the foreign claim.

(2) "The relevant UK authority" means—

    (*a*) in relation to matters corresponding to those within the care and management of the Commissioners of Customs and Excise, those Commissioners;
    (*b*) in relation to matters corresponding to those within the care and management of the Commissioners of Inland Revenue, those Commissioners;
    (*c*) in relation to agricultural levies of the European Community, the relevant Minister, that is—

        (i) in England, the Secretary of State,
        (ii) in Scotland, the Scottish Ministers,
        (iii) in Wales, the National Assembly for Wales, and
        (iv) in Northern Ireland, the Department of Agriculture and Rural Development.

(3) A "corresponding UK claim" means a claim in the United Kingdom corresponding to the foreign claim.

(4) The enactments referred to in sub-paragraph (1)(*b*) include, in particular, those relating to the recovery of penalties and of interest on unpaid amounts.

Power to make supplementary provision by regulations

3—(1) The Treasury may make provision by regulations—

    (*a*) as to what is a corresponding UK claim in relation to any description of foreign claim, and
    (*b*) as to such other procedural and other supplementary matters as appear to them appropriate for implementing the Mutual Assistance Recovery Directive.

(2) In relation to a case where there is no claim in the United Kingdom that is directly equivalent to a particular description of foreign claim, regulations under sub-paragraph (1)(*a*) may prescribe as the corresponding UK claim one that appears to the Treasury to be closest to an equivalent.

(3) The power conferred by sub-paragraph (1)(*b*) includes power to make any provision appearing to the Treasury to be appropriate to give effect to any Commission Directive laying down detailed rules for implementing the Mutual Assistance Recovery Directive.

(4) The relevant UK authority may make provision by regulations as to the application, non-application or adaptation in relation to foreign claims of any enactment or rule of law applicable to corresponding UK claims.

This is without prejudice to the application of any such enactment or rule in relation to foreign claims in circumstances not dealt with by regulations under this sub-paragraph.

(5) Regulations under this paragraph shall be made by statutory instrument which shall be subject to annulment in pursuance of a resolution of the House of Commons.

Proceedings on contested claims

4—(1) Except where permitted by virtue of regulations under paragraph 3(4) applying an enactment that permit such proceedings in the case of a corresponding UK claim, no proceedings under this Schedule shall be taken against a person if he shows that proceedings relevant to his liability on the foreign claim are pending, or are about to be instituted, before a court, tribunal or other competent body in the member State in question.

(2) For this purpose proceedings are pending so long as an appeal may be brought against any decision in the proceedings.

(3) Proceedings under this Schedule may be taken if the proceedings in the member State are not prosecuted or instituted with reasonable expedition.

Claims determined in taxpayer's favour

5—(1) No proceedings under this Schedule shall be taken against a person if a final decision on the foreign claim has been given in his favour by a court, tribunal or other competent body in the member State in question.

(2) For this purpose a final decision is one against which no appeal lies or against which an appeal lies within a period that has expired without an appeal having been brought.

(3) If he shows that such a decision has been given in respect of part of the claim no proceedings under this Schedule shall be taken in relation to that part.

Other supplementary provisions

6 For the purposes of proceedings under this Schedule—

(*a*) a request made by an authority in another member State shall be taken to be duly made in accordance with the Mutual Assistance Recovery Directive unless the contrary is proved, and

(*b*) except as mentioned in paragraph 5, no question may be raised as to a person's liability on the foreign claim.

SCHEDULE 40

REPEALS

Section 141

PART 3
INCOME TAX, CORPORATION TAX AND CAPITAL GAINS TAX

(1) DEDUCTIONS FROM PAYMENTS TO SUB-CONTRACTORS

Short title and chapter	Extent of repeal
Income and Corporation Taxes Act 1988 (c 1)	In section 559— (a) in subsection (4), the words from "and the sum so deducted" to the end; (b) subsections (5) and (5A); (c) in subsection (8).
Finance Act 1998 (c 36)	In Schedule 7, in paragraph 1 the words "559(4)(b) and (5) (twice)". In Schedule 8, paragraph 2(1).

These repeals have effect in accordance with section 40(4) of this Act.

(2) COMPANY RECONSTRUCTIONS

Short title and chapter	Extent of repeal
Income and Corporation Taxes Act 1988 (c 1)	In section 842(3)(c), the words "or amalgamation".
Taxation of Chargeable Gains Act 1992 (c 12)	In the heading before section 135, the words "and amalgamations".
	In section 139(1), in the heading, in subsection (1)(a) and in subsection (5) (twice), the words "or amalgamation".
	In section 211(2)—
	(a) in paragraph (a), and
	(b) in the closing words, the words "or amalgamation".
	In section 214C(2)(a) and (3), the words "or amalgamation".
Finance (No 2) Act 1992 (c 48)	Section 35(1).

These repeals have effect in accordance with paragraphs 7 and 8 of Schedule 9 to this Act.

(3) TAPER RELIEF

Short title and chapter	Extent of repeal
Taxation of Chargeable Gains Act 1992 (c 12)	In section 2A(8)(b)(ii), the words "11 or".
	In Schedule A1—
	(a) paragraph 11;
	(b) in paragraph 22(1), in the definition of "51 per cent subsidiary", the words "(except in paragraph 11 above)";
	(c) in paragraph 23, the final sentence of sub-paragraph (4), sub-paragraph (5), in sub-paragraph (7) the words ", (5)(b)" and sub-paragraphs (9) and (10);
	(d) paragraph 24(6).

These repeals have effect in accordance with paragraphs 2, 4 and 7 of Schedule 10 to this Act.

(4) GAINS TREATED AS ACCRUING TO SETTLORS

Short title and chapter	Extent of repeal
Taxation of Chargeable Gains Act 1992 (c 12)	In section 2(5)(b), the words "77, 86,".
	Section 77(6A).
	Section 86(4A).
	In section 86A(8), the words "or aggregate amount".
Finance Act 1998 (c 36)	In Schedule 21, paragraph 6(1) and (2).

These repeals have effect in accordance with paragraphs 7 and 8 of Schedule 11 to this Act.

(5) TAX RELIEF FOR RESEARCH AND DEVELOPMENT EXPENDITURE

Short title and chapter	Extent of repeal
Finance Act 2000 (c 17)	In Schedule 20—
	(a) in paragraph 5(1)(c), the words "(within the meaning of section 231A(4) of the Taxes Act 1988)";
	(b) in paragraph 12, the word "and" at the end of paragraph (a).

These repeals have effect for accounting periods ending on or after 1st April 2002.

(6) COMMUNITY INVESTMENT TAX CREDIT

Short title and chapter	Extent of repeal
Finance Act 1990 (c 29)	In section 25(7), the word "and" at the end of paragraph (b).

This repeal has effect in accordance with section 57(3) and (4)(b) of this Act.

(7) CARS WITH LOW CARBON DIOXIDE EMISSIONS

Short title and chapter	Extent of repeal
Capital Allowances Act 2001 (c 2)	In section 39, the word "or" preceding the words "section 45A". In section 46(1), the word "or" preceding the words "section 45A". In section 74(2), the word "and" preceding paragraph (b).

These repeals have effect in accordance with section 59 of this Act.

(8) COMPUTATION OF PROFITS

Short title and chapter	Extent of repeal
Income and Corporation Taxes Act 1988 (c 1)	In section 473(2), the words, ", if the securities were not such as are mentioned in subsection (1)(b) above".
Finance Act 1998	Section 44. Schedule 6.
Capital Allowances Act 2001 (c 2)	In Schedule 2, paragraph 102.

1 The repeal in section 473(2) of the Taxes Act 1988 has effect in accordance with section 67(4)(a) of this Act.

2 The other repeals have effect in accordance with section 64(6) of and paragraphs 16 and 17 of Schedule 22 to this Act.".

(9) ASSET-LINKED LOAN RELATIONSHIPS

Short title and chapter	Extent of repeal
Finance Act 1996 (c 8)	In section 92, in subsection (1)(e), the word "and". Section 93(11) and (13).

1 The repeal in section 92 of the Finance Act 1996 (c 8) has effect in accordance with section 72 of this Act.

2 The repeals in section 93 of that Act have effect in accordance with section 75 of this Act.

(10) FOREX AND EXCHANGE GAINS AND LOSSES FROM LOAN RELATIONSHIPS ETC

Short title and chapter	Extent of repeal
Income and Corporation Taxes Act 1988 (c 1)	In section 15(1), the second indent of paragraph 2(3) of Schedule A. Section 56(3A) to (3D). In Schedule 24, paragraphs 13 to 19. In Schedule 27, paragraph 5(2A)(a) so far as relating to sections 125 to 133 of the Finance Act 1993.
Taxation of Chargeable Gains Act 1992 (c 12)	In section 117(A1), the words "(subject to sections 117A and 117B below)". Sections 117A and 117B.
Finance Act 1993 (c 34)	Section 60. Sections 125 to 169. Schedules 15 to 17. In Schedule 18, paragraph 2.
Finance Act 1994 (c 9)	Sections 114 to 116. Section 226(2).
Finance Act 1995 (c 4)	Section 52(2).

Short title and chapter	Extent of repeal
	Section 131. In Schedule 24, paragraphs 1 to 3. In Schedule 25, paragraphs 6(5) and 7.

Finance Act 1996	In section 85(2), the word "and" at the end of paragraph (*b*).
	In section 92(6)(*b*), the words "127 or".
	In Schedule 9—
	  (a) paragraphs 4 and 11(4);
	  (b) in paragraph 13(6), the definition of "related transaction";
	  (c) in paragraph 15(1), the words "for the purposes of section 84 of this Act".
	In Schedule 11, in paragraph 3A(1)(*b*), the words "debt or".
	In Schedule 14, paragraphs 67 to 74.
	In Schedule 15, paragraphs 22 to 24.
	In Schedule 20, paragraphs 68 to 70.

Finance Act 1998 (c 36)	Section 108(3) and (4)(*a*).
	In section 109—
	  (a) subsections (1) and (2);
	  (b) subsection (4) so far as relating to those subsections;
	  (c) subsection (5) so far as relating to the enactments specified in paragraph (*a*) of it.
	Section 110(4)(*b*).
	Schedule 4, paragraph 7.

Finance Act 2000 (c 17)	Section 106. In Schedule 22, paragraph 50(2)(*b*). In Schedule 29, paragraphs 20, 21 and 41 to 43.

1 The repeal in Schedule 27 to the Taxes Act 1988 has effect for account periods beginning on or after 1st October 2002.

2 The other repeals have effect in accordance with section 78(3) of this Act and Schedule 23 to this Act.

(11) CORPORATION TAX: CURRENCY

Short title and chapter	Extent of repeal
Finance Act 1993 (c 34)	In section 93, subsections (3) and (6) and, in subsection (7), the definitions of "branch" and "closing rate/net investment method".
Finance Act 1994 (c 9)	Section 226(1).
Finance Act 1998	Section 163(3)(*b*) and (*c*).

These repeals have effect in accordance with section 80 of this Act and Schedule 24 to this Act.

(12) LOAN RELATIONSHIPS: GENERAL AMENDMENTS

Short title and chapter	Extent of repeal

Income and Corporation Taxes Act 1988 (c 1)	In section 77(2)(*a*), sub-paragraph (ii) and the preceding word "or".
	Section 403ZC(2).
	In section 432A(9B), the definition of "money debt".
	In section 797A, the second sentence in subsection (5) and in subsection (7).
	In Schedule 28A—
	  (a) in paragraph 7, in sub-paragraph (1)(*d*), the word "and" preceding sub-paragraph (iii), in sub-paragraph (1)(*e*), the word "and" preceding sub-paragraph (iii), and sub-paragraph (2);
	  (b) in paragraph 16, in sub-paragraph (1)(*d*), the word "and" preceding sub-paragraph (iii), in sub-paragraph (1)(*e*), the word "and" preceding sub-paragraph (iii), and sub-paragraph (2).

Short title and chapter	Extent of repeal
Finance Act 1988 (c 39)	In Schedule 6, in paragraph 3— (a) sub-paragraphs (3)(*a*), (4)(*a*) and (5)(*a*) and (*b*); (b) in sub-paragraph (5), in the words following paragraph (*c*), the word "group"; (c) sub-paragraph (6).
Finance Act 1996 (c 8)	In section 83— (a) in subsection (2), paragraphs (*b*) and (*d*) and the word "or" at the end of paragraph (*c*); (b) subsection (4); (c) in subsection (7), in paragraph (*a*), the word "(*b*)", and paragraph (*b*) and the preceding word "and". In section 87— (a) in subsection (3), in paragraph (*a*) the words "or in the two years before the beginning of that period", in paragraph (*b*) the words "or in those two years", and paragraph (*c*) and the preceding word "or"; (b) subsections (6) to (8). Section 89. Section 91. In Schedule 8, paragraph 2. In Schedule 9, in paragraph 17— (a) in sub-paragraph (5), in paragraph (*a*) the words "or in the period of two years before the beginning of that period" and in paragraph (*b*) the words "or in those two years"; (b) sub-paragraphs (6) and (7). In Schedule 9, in paragraph 18— (a) in sub-paragraph (1), the word "and" immediately preceding paragraph (*b*); (b) in sub-paragraph (4), the definition of "control".
Finance Act 1998 (c 36)	Section 82(1) and (2)(*c*) and (*e*).

These repeals have effect in accordance with section 82(2) of this Act.

(13) DERIVATIVE CONTRACTS

Short title and chapter	Extent of repeal
Income and Corporation Taxes Act 1988 (c 1)	Section 468AA. In section 807A(7), the definition of "relevant qualifying payment". In Schedule 5AA— (*a*) in paragraph 1, sub-paragraphs (2)(*b*) and (*c*) and (3), in sub-paragraph (5), the words "and 396", in sub-paragraph (6), the words ", corporation tax" and "or 396", and sub-paragraph (7); (*b*) paragraph 2(3); (*c*) paragraph 4(4A); (*d*) in paragraph 4A, in sub-paragraph (5)(*b*) the words "or 396", and sub-paragraph (10A); (*e*) paragraph 6(3A); (*f*) paragraph 9. In Schedule 27, paragraph 5(2A) so far as relating to sections 159 and 160 of, and paragraph 1 of Schedule 18 to, the Finance Act 1994.
Finance Act 1990 (c 29)	Section 81(1).
Finance Act 1994 (c 9)	Sections 147 to 175. Section 177. Schedule 18.

Short title and chapter	Extent of repeal
Finance Act 1995 (c 4)	Section 52(3).
	Section 132.
Finance Act 1996 (c 8)	Section 93A(3)(*a*) and (7).
	Section 101(2) to (6).
	Schedule 12.
	In Schedule 14, paragraphs 75 to 79.
	In Schedule 15, paragraph 25.
	In Schedule 20, paragraph 71.
Finance Act 1998 (c 36)	Section 99(2) and (3).
	In section 109—
	(*a*) subsection (3);
	(*b*) subsection (4) so far as relating to subsection (3);
	(*c*) subsection (5) so far as relating to the enactments specified in paragraph (*b*) of it.
Finance Act 2000 (c 17)	In Schedule 30, paragraph 24(3).
Finance Act 2002	Sections 69 and 70.
	Section 78.

1 The repeal in Schedule 27 to the Taxes Act 1988 has effect for account periods beginning on or after 1st October 2002.

2 The other repeals have effect in accordance with section 83(3) of this Act.

(14) DEDUCTION OF TAX: PAYMENTS TO EXEMPT BODIES ETC

Short title and chapter	Extent of repeal
Income and Corporation Taxes Act 1988 (c 1)	Section 349B(1)(b) and the word ''or'' preceding it.

This repeal has effect in accordance with section 93(7) of this Act.

(15) GIFTS OF REAL PROPERTY TO CHARITY

Short title and chapter	Extent of repeal
Income and Corporation Taxes Act 1988	In section 587B(9), the word ''and'' preceding paragraph (d).

This repeal has effect in accordance with section 97 of this Act.

(16) REFERENCES TO ACCOUNTING PRACTICE AND PERIODS OF ACCOUNT

Short title and chapter	Extent of repeal
Taxes Management Act 1970 (c 9)	In section 12AB(5), the definition of ''period of account''.
Income and Corporation Taxes Act 1988 (c 1)	Section 43A(2).
	Section 91A(8).
	Section 91B(11)(*e*) and the word ''and'' preceding it.
	In section 297(5B), the second sentence.
	Section 494AA(2)(*b*) and the word ''or'' preceding it.
	In section 560(2), the words from ''and in paragraph (f)'' to the end.
	In section 834(1), in the definition of ''accounting date'', the words from ''and ''period of account''' to the end.
	Section 837A(5).
	In section 842B(2), the second sentence.
	In Schedule 5, in paragraphs 2(6) and 6(4), the definitions of ''period of account''.
	In Schedule 28B, in paragraph 4(6B), the second sentence.
Finance Act 1988 (c 39)	In section 86(3), the definition of ''period of account''.
Finance Act 1989 (c 26)	In section 43(9), the definition of ''period of account''.

Short title and chapter	Extent of repeal
Taxation of Chargeable Gains Act 1992 (c 9)	In section 161(3A), the words from "and in paragraph (a)" to the end.
	In section 13(5B), the second sentence.
Finance Act 1997 (c 16)	In Schedule 12—
	(a) in paragraph 1(1)(*c*), the words ", in the case of companies incorporated in any part of the United Kingdom," and "for the purposes of the accounts of such companies";
	(b) in paragraph 4(5), the words ", if the recipient were a company incorporated in the United Kingdom,";
	(c) in paragraph 15(1)(*c*), the words ", in the case of companies incorporated in any part of the United Kingdom," and "for the purposes of the accounts of such companies";
	(d) paragraph 28(1) to (4).
Finance Act 1998 (c 36)	Section 45.
	In Schedule 18, in paragraph 14(2), the second sentence.
Finance Act 1999 (c 16)	In Schedule 6, paragraph 3(5).
Finance Act 2000 (c 17)	In Schedule 14, in paragraph 22(4), the second sentence.
	In Schedule 15, in paragraph 29(4), the second sentence.
	In Schedule 20, in paragraph 25(1), the definition of "normal accounting practice".
	In Schedule 23, in paragraph 5, the definitions of "normal accounting practice" and "statutory accounts".
Capital Allowances Act 2001 (c 2)	Section 179(2).
	Section 219(2).

(17) FINANCIAL TRADING STOCK

Short title and chapter	Extent of repeal
Income and Corporation Taxes Act 1988 (c 1)	Section 100(1B)(a).
Finance Act 1988 (c 39)	In Schedule 12, paragraph 2.

(18) BANKS ETC IN COMPULSORY LIQUIDATION

Short title and chapter	peal
Finance (No 2) Act 1992 (c 48)	In Schedule 12, paragraphs 3(3)(c) and 4(3).
Finance Act 1998 (c 36)	In Schedule 7, in paragraph 8, the words "3(3)(c) and".

These repeals have effect in accordance with section 107 of this Act.

PART 5
MISCELLANEOUS

RECOVERY OF TAX DUE IN OTHER MEMBER STATES

Short title and chapter	Extent of repeal
Finance Act 1977 (c 36)	Section 11.
Finance Act 1980 (c 48)	In section 17—
	(a) subsection (1);
	(b) in subsection (2A), the words "(1) and";
	(c) in subsection (3), the words from the beginning to "passing to this Act;".

INDEX

A

ACCIDENT INSURANCE POLICY
Revenue practice, SP 6/92

ACCOMMODATION
living—
  employee, provided for—
    additional charge on, cost over £75,000, TA 1988 s 146, PR 7/7/83
    Chevening House, exception for occupation of, TA 1988 s 147
    deemed director, PR 25/1/89, PR 11/5/89, PR 14/7/89
    employee earning £8,500 or more, exceptions for, TA 1988 ss 155(2), (3), 163
    general charge on, TA 1988 s 145
    multiple occupation during same period, ESC A90
    open market rental agreement, where charge based on, ESC A90
    priority of rules applying to, TA 1988 s 146A
    Revenue practice, PR 22/11/90
    Scotland, application to, ESC A56
    valuation, PR 19/4/90
  temporary residents in UK, application to—
    capital gains tax, TCGA 1992, s 9(4)
    income tax, TA 1988 s 336(3)

ACCOUNTANCY PRACTICE
tax computation, relationship with, PR/12/4/95, RI 231

ACCOUNTANT
papers of, power to call for, TMA 1970 ss 20A, 20B

ACCOUNTING PERIODS
beginning of, TA 1988 s 12(2), (6), (8)
charge to tax on, TA 1988 s 12(1)
commencement of business, TA 1988 s 12(4)
end of, TA 1988 s 12(3), (8)
insurance company, long term business, transfer of, TA 1988 s 12(7A)
meaning, TA 1988 s 12(2)–(8)
more than one trade, determination of, TA 1988 s 12(5), (5A)
retail co-operative societies, ESC C12
uncertainty of beginning or end, TA 1988 s 12(8)
winding up, effect on, TA 1988 s 12(7)

ACCRUED INCOME
inheritance tax on, relief from higher rate, TA 1988 s 699

ACCRUED INCOME SCHEME
accrued amount, meaning, TA 1988 s 713(4), (6), (7), (9)
associated companies, debts between, application to, FA 1993 s 63
death, TA 1988 s 721
deemed sum, tax charge on—
  exceptions from, TA 1988 s 715
  general rule, TA 1988 s 714(2), (6)
deep gain securities, not applicable to, FA 1989 Sch 11 para 17
double taxation relief, TA 1988 s 807

ACCRUED INCOME SCHEME—*continued*
European single currency provisions, SI 1998/3177 regs 31–35
foreign securities: delayed remittances, TA 1988 s 723
information, power to obtain, TA 1988 s 728
interest—
  accrued, transfer with or without, TA 1988 s 711(5), (6)
  default, TA 1988 s 718
  meaning, TA 1988 s 711(9)
  payment day, meaning, TA 1988 s 711(2)
  period, meaning, TA 1988 s 711(3), (4)
  unrealised, in default, TA 1988 s 719
  unrealised, transfer of, TA 1988 s 716
  variable rate, TA 1988 s 717
Lloyd's underwriter, premiums trust fund, trustees, TA 1988 s 720(3)
new issues of securities, TA 1988 s 726A
nominee, treatment of, TA 1988 s 720(1)
rebate amount, meaning, TA 1988 s 713(5), (6), (8), (9)
relief, procedure for—
  exceptions, TA 1988 s 715
  generally, TA 1988 s 714(3)–(5)
securities—
  identification of, for capital gains tax purposes, TCGA 1992 ss 106A, 108
  meaning, TA 1988 s 710(2)–(4), (7)–(9)
  sale and repurchase, TA 1988 s 727A
settlement day, meaning, TA 1988 s 712
stock lending, TA 1988 s 727
trading stock, TA 1988 s 722
transfer, meaning, TA 1988 s 710(5), (6)
transfer of assets abroad, application to, TA 1988 s 742(4)–(7)
transfer of securities, chargeable gain, computation of, TCGA 1992 s 119
transfer of securities with accrued interest—
  meaning, TA 1988 s 711(5), (6)
  transferee, relief for, TA 1988 s 713(2)(*b*)
  transferor, deemed sum to, TA 1988 s 713(2)(*a*)
transfer of securities without accrued interest—
  meaning, TA 1988 s 711(5), (6)
  transferee, deemed sum to, TA 1988 s 713(3)(*b*)
  transferor, relief for, TA 1988 s 713(3)(*a*)
trustee, application to, TA 1988 s 720(1), (2), (4)–(8)
unrealised interest—
  default, in, TA 1988 s 719
  transfer of, TA 1988 s 716
variable rate of securities, TA 1988 s 717

ACCUMULATION TRUST. *See* SETTLEMENTS

ADDITIONAL PERSONAL ALLOWANCE. *See* PERSONAL RELIEFS

ADDITIONAL VOLUNTARY CONTRIBUTIONS (AVCs). *See* OCCUPATIONAL PENSION SCHEMES

ADJUDICATION BY BOARD OF INLAND REVENUE. *See* BOARD OF INLAND REVENUE

BANK INTEREST. *See* INTEREST PAYABLE

BANKRUPTCY. *See* INSOLVENCY

BARE TRUSTEES
capital gains tax, treatment for, TCGA 1992 s 60

BARRISTERS
accounting, basis of, FA 1998 s 43

BASIC RATE. *See* RATES OF TAX

BENEFICIAL LOANS
advance for expenses, treatment of, SP 7/79
alternative method of calculation of benefit, TA 1988 Sch 7 para 5
bridging loan, treatment of, ESC A5(*b*)
commercial loans, exemption for, RI 85
director's overdrawn loan account with company, RD 3
eligible loan, meaning, TA 1988 Sch 7 para 19(1), (2)
employment, obtained by reason of, meaning, TA 1988 Sch 7 Pt 1
exceptions from charge, TA 1988 s 161
general provisions, TA 1988 s 160
home loan, meaning, TA 1988 Sch 7 para 19(1), (2)
interest eligible for relief, TA 1988 Sch 7 Pt III
normal method of calculation of benefit, TA 1988 Sch 7 para 4
official rate of interest, SI 1989/1297 reg 5, PR 25/1/00
ordinary commercial terms, on, TA 1988 s 161, Sch 7A
qualifying, treatment of, TA 1988 s 161A
replacement, TA 1988 s 160(3A), Sch 7 paras 2–4
restriction of relief to basic rate, TA 1988 Sch 7 Pt IV

BENEFICIARIES
income taxed at lower rate, TA 1988 s 698A, F(No 2)A 1997 s 33
Scottish trusts, application to, FA 1993 s 118
self-assessment, tax obligations, PR 20/1/97

BENEFITS
pilot schemes, under, taxation of—
benefit, meaning, FA 1996 s 151(6)
Earnings Top-up, exemption from income tax, SI 1996/2396
Government pilot scheme, meaning, FA 1996 s 151(3), (4)
Jobmatch pilot scheme, exemption for, ESC A90
orders, power to make, FA 1996 s 151(1), (2), (5), (7), (8)
training vouchers for Jobmatch pilot scheme, treatment of, ESC A90
taxable, rates for 2002–03, Misc VIII
taxation of—
jobfinder's grant, relief for, FA 1996 s 152
pilot schemes, under. *See* PILOT SCHEMES **ABOVE**

BENEFITS IN KIND. *See also* EMPLOYEE EARNING £8,500 OR MORE; REMOVAL EXPENSES AND BENEFITS
agricultural worker, board and lodging, ESC A60
apportionment of, PR 29/6/79
award scheme, taxed, SP 6/85
Christmas party or the like, ESC A70 para B
counselling services for redundant employees, exclusion of, TA 1988 ss 589A, 589B
disability, employment costs resulting from, SI 2002/1596
dispensations, TA 1988 s 166
duties of employment, used in performance of, TA 1988 s 155ZA
exemptions, Hansard 23/5/79

BENEFITS IN KIND—*continued*
generally, SP A15
higher cost housing area, payment towards, ESC A67
late night journeys, ESC A66
living accommodation—
charge to tax on, TA 1988 ss 145, 146
duties of employment, used in performance of, TA 1988 s 155ZA
employee earning £8,500 or more, exceptions for, TA 1988 ss 155(2), (3), 163
priority of rules, TA 1988 s 146A
Scotland, application to, ESC A56
luncheon vouchers, exclusion from tax charge, ESC A2
meals (canteen), provided for all staff, TA 1988 s 155(5); ESC A74
minor, exemption of, TA 1988 s 155ZB; SI 2002/205
minister of religion, TA 1988 s 332; ESC A61
occupational pension schemes, employer's contributions, TA 1988 ss 595, 596, 596A
part business and part private use, calculating cash equivalent, Tax Bulletin, Issue 49, October 2000
Pepper v Hart, Revenue Practice, PR 21/1/93
personal pension schemes—
employer's contributions, TA 1988 s 643
withdrawal of approval of approved arrangements, TCGA 1992 s 239B
public transport, disruption of, allowance for, ESC A58
qualifying training course, not chargeable to tax, TA 1988 s 588(1)
return of, requirement to make, by employer, TMA 1970 s 15(7)–(9)
severely disabled employee, home to work travel, ESC A59
small gift by third party, ESC A70 para A
sporting and recreational facilities, exclusion of, TA 1988 s 197G
suggestion scheme, not charged to tax under Schedule E, ESC A57
VAT, treatment of, SP A6, A7; PR 12/4/78
vouchers—
cash, TA 1988 s 143
credit tokens, TA 1988 s 143
dispensation, TA 1988 s 144(1), (2)
non-cash, TA 1988 s 141
transport, TA 1988 s 141(6), (7)
welfare counselling, SI 2000/2080

BEREAVEMENT ALLOWANCE, WIDOW'S. *See* PERSONAL RELIEFS

BETTERMENT LEVY
allowance for, TCGA 1992 Sch 11 para 17

BETTING
winnings—
exemption from capital gains tax, TCGA 1992 s 51(1)

BLACKMAIL. *See* CRIMINAL PAYMENTS

BLIND PERSON'S ALLOWANCE. *See* PERSONAL RELIEFS

BOARD OF INLAND REVENUE. *See also* COMMISSIONERS OF INLAND REVENUE
accountants, PR 4/02
accounts, IRRA 1890 s 13
appointment of, IRRA 1890 s 1
collectors and officers—
appointment of, IRRA 1890 s 4
character of, unlawful assumption of, IRRA 1890 s 12

COMMUNITY AMATEUR SPORTS CLUBS, RELIEF FOR
chargeable gains where property ceasing to be held for qualifying purpose, FA 2002 Sch 18 para 10
donors, for, FA 2002 Sch 18 para 9
eligible sport, meaning, FA 2002 Sch 18 para 14
exemptions, FA 2002 Sch 18 paras 4–8
registration—
  entitlement, FA 2002 Sch 18 paras 1–3
  Inland Revenue, by, FA 2002 Sch 18 paras 11–13

COMMUNITY INVESTMENT TAX RELIEF
accreditation of investor, FA 2002 Sch 16 para 25
accredited community development finance institutions, FA 2002 Sch 16 paras 4–7
  general conditions, FA 2002 Sch 16 paras 14–18
  loss of accreditation, FA 2002 Sch 16 para 26
  restructuring, FA 2002 Sch 16 paras 40, 41
associate, meaning, FA 2002 Sch 16 para 50
attribution, FA 2002 Sch 16 para 26
company investors, FA 2002 Sch 16 para 20
disclosure of information, FA 2002 Sch 16 para 43
eligibility for, FA 2002 Sch 16 para 1
five year period, FA 2002 Sch 16 para 3
general conditions, FA 2002 Sch 16 paras 14–18
information provided by investor, FA 2002 Sch 16 para 42
individual investors, FA 2002 Sch 16 para 19
invested amount, determination of, FA 2002 Sch 16 para 21
investment—
  held continuously, meaning, FA 2002 Sch 16 para 49
  meaning, FA 2002 Sch 16 para 2
loans, FA 2002 Sch 16 para 22
nominees, FA 2002 Sch 16 para 44
postponement of tax pending appeal, application for, FA 2002 Sch 16 para 45
qualifying investments, FA 2002 Sch 16 paras 8–13
securities or shares, FA 2002 Sch 16 paras 23, 46, 47
withdrawal, FA 2002 Sch 16 paras 27–39

COMPANIES
company officer, responsibility of, TMA 1970 s 108
company partnership—
  computation of profit and losses, TA 1988 ss 114, 115
  transfer of relief, arrangement for, TA 1988 s 116
connected, TCGA 1992 s 286
control of, TA 1988 s 840
dissolution, Companies Act 1985 s 652; ESC C16
dual resident, double taxation relief, SI 2001/1156
late return, penalties for, ESC B46
limited, supply of services through, Misc V
liquidation, in, tax on, TA 1988 s 342
meaning, TCGA 1992 s 288(1)
payments which are not distributions, income tax, overdue, interest on, TMA 1970 s 87
proper officer, meaning, TMA 1970 s 108(3)
resident, ceasing to be. *See* NON-RESIDENT COMPANIES
self-assessment—
  appointed day, FA 1998 s 117(5), Sch 18 para 96
  capital allowances, claims for, FA 1998 Sch 18 para 78
  claims and elections, FA 1998 Sch 18 para 54
  enquiry into company tax return, FA 1998 Sch 18 para 24
  excessive assessments or repayments, FA 1998 Sch 18 para 50
  filing date, FA 1998 Sch 18 para 14

COMPANIES—*continued*
self-assessment—*continued*
  fraud or negligence, penalty for, FA 1998 Sch 18 para 89
  generally, TMA 1970 s 28F; PR 25/9/96; FA 1998 Sch 18
  group relief, claims for, FA 1998 Sch 18 para 66
  no return delivered, where, TMA 1970 s 28D; FA 1998 para 17
  notice complied with in part, where, TMA 1970 s 28E
  penalties, FA 1998 Sch 18 paras 17–20
  records, duty to keep and preserve, FA 1998 Sch 18 para 21
  Revenue determinations and assessments, FA 1998 Sch 18 para 36
  Special Commissioners, appeal to, FA 1998 Sch 18 para 94
  special provisions, FA 1998 Sch 18 para 84
  tax payable, FA 1998 Sch 18 para 8
  tax returns and assessments, FA 1998 Sch 18
tax returns, FA 1998 Sch 18
UK tax, ceasing to be liable to—
  accounting period, end of, TA 1988 s 12(3)(*e*)
  deemed disposal of assets, TCGA 1992 s 186(1), (2)
  foreign assets, meaning, TCGA 1992 s 187(6)
  postponement of tax charge, TCGA 1992 s 187
  rollover relief, exclusion of, TCGA 1992 s 186(1), (3); FA 1994 s 236(9)

COMPENSATION AND DAMAGES
annuities, exemption from tax, TA 1988 ss 329A, 329B
capital gains tax, exemption from, TCGA 1992 s 51(2)
compensation fund application of provisions, FA 1975 Sch 5 para 21
Foreign Compensation Act 1950, payments under, ESC D50
Holocaust victims, bank accounts of, ESC A100
interest on, exemption from income tax, TA 1988 s 329
termination payment—
  charge to tax on, TA 1988 s 148, Sch 11 para 13
  disability, meaning, SP 10/81
  exclusions from charge, TA 1988 s 188; PR 26/6/73
  legal costs, treatment of, ESC A81; RI 61
  occupational pension scheme—
    contribution to, SP 2/81
    interaction with, SP 13/91
World War II claims, late compensation for, ESC F20

COMPOSITE RATE SCHEME
application of 1987–88 rate to 1988–89
relevant orders, F(No 2)A 1992 s 64

COMPULSORY ACQUISITION
compensation for, treatment as trading receipts—
  reimbursed removal expenses, SP 8/79
  temporary loss of profits, SP 8/79
tenant, by, application to, SP 13/93, RI 205

COMPUTATIONS
rounded to nearest £1,000 PR 18/8/93; SP 15/93

COMPUTER EQUIPMENT
limited exemption for, TA 1988 s 156A
software—
  capital allowances for, CAA 2001 s 71; RI 56
  disposal value of, CAA 2001 ss 72, 73
websites and servers, tax status, PR 11/4/00

COMPUTER RECORDS
investigation, power to call for, in, FA 1988 s 127

CORPORATION TAX—*continued*
notice of liability to, TMA 1970 s 10
ownership, change of—
postponed tax, TA 1988 s 767AA
recovery from other persons, TA 1988 ss 767A, 767B
participator in close company, loan to, liability to tax on, TMA 1970 s 109; TA 1988 s 419, 420
pay and file. *See* PAY AND FILE
payment of—
arrangements with group of companies, FA 1998 s 36
due and payable date, TMA 1970 s 59E; FA 1998 s 30
generally, TMA 1970 s 59D
penalty—
failure to make return, TMA 1970 s 94
incorrect return, TMA 1970 ss 96, 97
petroleum revenue tax, deduction for, TA 1988 s 500
rate of, FA 2002 s 30
reconstruction without change of ownership, TA 1988 ss 343, 344
return of profits for, TMA 1970 ss 11, 11AA, 11AC–11AE; F(No 2)A 1987 s 82; FA 1990 s 91
scheme of, TA 1970 s 243(4); TA 1988 s 8
self-assessment. *See under* SELF-ASSESSMENT
small companies' rate, FA 1997 s 59, FA 2000 s 36, FA 2002 s 31
small companies' relief, TA 1988 s 13; PR 10/3/83, PR 17/6/88
starting rate, TA 1988 s 13AA, FA 2002 s 32
tax returns, FA 1998 Sch 18
time for payment—
companies trading before 1965, TA 1970 s 244
generally, TA 1988 s 10
tonnage tax. *See* TONNAGE TAX
trade—
cessation of, TA 1988 s 337(1)
commencement of, TA 1988 s 337(1)
profits or losses of, computation of. *See* EXPENSES
currency—
equivalents, ascertaining, FA 1993 ss 94AA, 94AB
other than sterling, use of, FA 1993 ss 93, 93A, 95; SI 1994/3230
parts of trades, application to, FA 1993 s 95; SI 1994/3230
petroleum extraction companies, parts of trades, application to, FA 1993 s 94A
sterling to be used, FA 1993 s 92

COSTS
appeal hearing, power of Special Commissioners, TMA 1970 s 56C
legal costs—
termination payments (Schedule E), in connection with, ESC A81; RI 61

COUNSELLING
redundant employee, for, TA 1988 ss 589A, 589B

CREDIT UNION
charge to tax, TA 1988 s 487

CRIMINAL PAYMENTS
blackmail—
expenditure involving, disallowance of, TA 1988 s 577A(1A)
extortion, (Scotland), expenditure involving, disallowance of, TA 1988 s 577A(1A), (C)

CROWN
civil proceedings against—
in County Court, CPA 1947 s 15
in High Court, CPA 1947 s 13
in Sheriff Court (Scotland), CPA 1947 s 44
Northern Ireland, SI 1981/233
parties to, authorised Departments as, CPA 1947 s 17
removal of, CPA 1947 s 20
Rules, SI 1998/3132 RSC Order 77
service of documents, CPA 1947 s 18
venue, CPA 1947 s 19
debts, damages and costs, interest on, CPA 1947 s 24
discovery of documents, CPA 1947 s 28
documents, discovery of, CPA 1947 s 28
execution by, CPA 1947 s 26
extent of act, CPA 1947 s 52
High Court—
civil proceedings in, CPA 1947 s 13
summary applications to, CPA 1947 s 14
interpleader, CPA 1947 s 16
interpretation, CPA 1947 s 38
meaning, CPA 1947 s 38
Northern Ireland, application to, CPA 1947 s 53
parties to, CPA 1947 s 17
pending proceedings, saving for, CPA 1947 s 36
proceedings—
abolition, CPA 1947 s 13 Sch 1
civil proceedings, meaning, CPA 1947 s 23
costs, CPA 1947 s 24
County Court—
civil proceedings in, CPA 1947 s 15
rules, CPA 1947 s 35
courts other than High Court or County Courts, in, CPA 1947 s 43
references to, CPA 1947 s 23
relief—
generally, CPA 1947 s 21
interpleader, CPA 1947 s 16
right to sue, CPA 1947 ss 1, 23
rules of court, application of, CPA 1947 ss 35, 50
satisfaction of orders against, CPA 1947 s 25
savings, CPA 1947 s 35
Scotland, CPA 1947 ss 41–51
application of provisions, CPA 1947 s 41
crown—
documents in possession of—
recovery of, CPA 1947 s 47
satisfaction of orders against, CPA 1947 s 45
excluded provisions, CPA 1947 s 42
interpretation, CPA 1947 ss 43, 51
pending proceedings, CPA 1947 s 51
service of documents, CPA 1947 s 18
sheriff court, proceedings in, CPA 1947 s 44
statutory provisions, application of, CPA 1947 s 31
writs abolished, CPA 1947 s 33

CROWN SERVANTS
engaged overseas, exception from tax, ESC A25
foreign service allowance, exemption, TA 1988 s 319
salary, treatment of for pension purposes—
personal pension scheme, TA 1988 s 654
retirement annuity, TA 1988 s 629
tax, exemption from, ESC A25

CYCLE. *See also* FIXED PROFIT CAR SCHEME
parking facilities, provision of, FA 1999 s 49
provision of, TA 1988 s 197AC
safety equipment, provision of, TA 1988 s 197AC

D

DAMAGES. *See* COMPENSATION AND DAMAGES

DERIVATIVE CONTRACTS

accounting methods, FA 2002 Sch 26 paras 17–21
accounting requirements, satisfying, FA 2002 Sch 26 para 3
amendment of provisions, FA 2002 Sch 26 para 13
associated transactions, FA 2002 Sch 26 para 10
bad debts, provision for, FA 2002 Sch 26 para 22
capital expenditure, debits and credits relating to, FA 2002 Sch 26 para 25
collective investment schemes, FA 2002 Sch 26 paras 32–40
connected companies, transfers of value to, FA 2002 Sch 26 para 26
deduction of tax, prevention of, FA 2002 Sch 26 para 51
definitions, FA 2002 Sch 26 paras 12, 52–54
exchange gains and losses arising from, FA 2002 Sch 26 para 16—
   contract not on arm's length terms, FA 2002 Sch 26 para 27
excluded contracts, FA 2002 Sch 26 para 4
groups, transactions within, FA 2002 Sch 26 paras 28–30
insurance and mutual trading companies, FA 2002 Sch 26 paras 41–43
meaning, FA 2002 Sch 26 para 2
method of taxation, FA 2002 Sch 26 paras 14–16
non-residents, with, FA 2002 Sch 26 para 31
partnerships involving companies, FA 2002 Sch 26 paras 49, 50
profits arising from, FA 2002 Sch 26 para 1
purposes of trade—
   becoming held for, FA 2002 Sch 26 para 45
   ceasing to be held for, FA 2002 Sch 26 para 44
qualified exclusion from provisions, FA 2002 Sch 26 paras 5–8
relevant, references to, FA 2002 Sch 26 para 53
transitional provisions, FA 2002 Sch 26 para 28
two assets, election to treat as, FA 2002 Sch 26 para 48
unallowable purposes, FA 2002 Sch 26 paras 23, 24
underlying subject matter—
   different excluded types, of, FA 2002 Sch 26 para 47
   excluded contracts, FA 2002 Sch 26 para 4
   meaning, FA 2002 Sch 26 para 11
   part of excluded type, FA 2002 Sch 26 para 46
   subordinate or small value, FA 2002 Sch 26 para 9

DESIGN

registration fees, deduction for, TA 1988 s 83
rights, disposal of, spreading provisions, TA 1988 s 537A

DESIGNATED AREA

meaning, FA 1973 s 38(2)(e); TA 1988 ss 502(2)(a), 830(2)(c); TCGA 1992 s 276(2)(e)
oil taxation, purposes of, TA 1988 s 502(1)
territorial extension of tax charge, FA 1973 s 38(7) Sch 15

DEVELOPMENT LAND TAX

double taxation conventions, SP 4/84
negotiations on liability, SP 2/79

DIPLOMATIC IMMUNITY

consul and other officers—
   foreign state, in service of, in UK, exemption from tax, TA 1988 ss 321, 322

DIRECTORS

assets transferred by, to employers and others, ESC A85

DIRECTORS—*continued*

benefits legislation, application to, TA 1988 s 167(1)(a), (5)
business expansion scheme company, position of, in, TA 1988 s 291(3)
expenses, treatment of, as emoluments, TA 1988 s 153
fees received by—
   company, ESC A37 paras 2, 3
   partnership, ESC A37 para 1; SP A29
indemnity insurance. *See* EMPLOYEE LIABILITY AND INDEMNITY INSURANCE
meaning of, in relation to—
   benefits in kind, TA 1988 s 168(8)–(11)
   close company, TA 1988 s 417(5), (6)
   non-resident company, TCGA 1992 s 190
   occupational pension scheme, TA 1988 s 612(1)
   personal pension scheme, TA 1988 s 644(6)
   share options, TA 1988 s 136(5)
tax paid by employer, benefit in kind, TA 1988 s 164

DISABILITY PENSIONS

exemption from tax—
   excess over ordinary level, ESC A62
   generally, TA 1988 s 315

DISABLED PERSONS

car accessories, provision of, TA 1988 s 168A(11)
employment costs, treatment of, SI 2002/1596
vehicle maintenance grant for, exempt from tax, TA 1988 s 327

DISCONTINUANCE OF TRADE. *See* TRADE

DISCOUNT

taxation, SP 4/97

DISCOVERY

power to raise assessment following, TMA 1970 s 29(3); SP 8/91
requiring sanction of the Board, FA 1998 s 110

DISCRETIONARY TRUSTS

additional or applicable rate tax, liability to—
   distributions treated as income, TA 1988 s 686A
   income, on, TA 1988 s 686
   payments by, on, TA 1988 s 687—
      payments to companies under, TA 1988 s 687A, F(No 2)A 1997 s 27
      rate, PR 4/12/96, F(No 2)A 1997 s 32
non-resident, payments to, double taxation relief, SP 3/86
overseas income of, double taxation relief on, TA 1988 s 809; ESC B18
Schedule F trust rate, TA 1988 s 686(1A)
scheme for employees/directors to acquire shares, TA 1988 s 688

DISCS. *See* FILMS, TAPES AND DISCS

DISPENSATIONS. *See also* BENEFITS IN KIND

general provisions, TA 1988 s 116
vouchers, TA 1988 s 141(6), (7)

DISPOSALS

asset—
   capital sum derived from asset, TCGA 1992 s 22
   close company, shares in—
      assets transferred at under value, TCGA 1992 s 125
      shortfall, relief for, TCGA 1992 s 124
   compensation received, treatment of—
      asset held at 6 April 1965, TCGA 1992 Sch 2 para 23
      building, destroyed or irreparably damaged, TCGA 1992 s 23(6),(7)

DISPOSALS—*continued*
  asset—*continued*
    compensation received, treatment of—*continued*
      generally, TCGA 1992 s 23
      wasting asset, TCGA 1992 s 23(8)
    consideration charged to income tax, exclusion of, TCGA 1992 ss 37, 52(2), (3)
    contingent liability, treatment of, TCGA 1992 s 49
    deep discount security, TCGA 1992 s 118
    deferred consideration, TCGA 1992 s 48
    feu duty, capitalised value of, TCGA 1992 s 37(3)
    ground annual, capitalised value of, TCGA 1992 s 37(3)
    hire purchase, application to, TCGA 1992 s 27
    insurance money received, treatment of, TCGA 1992 s 23(3)–(5)
    land acquired under compulsory powers, TCGA 1992 s 245
    loss, destruction, etc, treatment of, TCGA 1992 s 24(1), (3)
    meaning, TCGA 1992 s 21(2)
    mortgage or charge on asset, TCGA 1992 s 26
    negligible value, asset becoming of, TCGA 1992 s 24(2), (3)
    non-resident, by, deemed, TCGA 1992 s 25
    rentcharge, capitalised value of, TCGA 1992 s 37(3)
    right to income, TCGA 1992 s 37(3)
    series of transactions, TCGA 1992 ss 19, 20
    time of—
      compulsory acquisition of land, TCGA 1992 s 246
      general rule, TCGA 1992 s 28

DISTRIBUTIONS. *See also* DIVIDENDS
  administration of estates, treatment of non-qualifying distributions, F(No 2)A 1997 s 21
  bonus issue—
    repayment of share capital, TA 1988 ss 210, 211; PR June 1968
    tax credits, effect on, F(No 2)A 1997 Sch 5
  close company, extended meaning of, TA 1988 s 418
  corporation tax, exclusion from charge to, TA 1988 s 208
  dealers, taxation of, TA 1988 s 95, F(No 2)A 1997 s 24
  demerger, exemption as, TA 1988 s 213
  dissolution of company (under Companies Act 1985 s 652), ESC C16
  equity notes, interest on, treated as, TA 1988 s 209(2)(*e*)(vii), (9)–(11); PR 15/2/93, PR 19/3/93
  exempt fund, by, F(No 2)A 1997 Sch 4(7)
  fixed-rate preference shares, F(No 2)A 1997 s 25
  hedging arrangments, security issued for, TA 1988 s 209B
  information, provision of, TA 1988 ss 234, 234A
  interest, excessive, excess treated as, TA 1988 s 209(2)(*d*)
  interest on securities, treated as—
    convertible securities on, TA 1988 s 209(2)(*e*)(ii)
    equity notes, TA 1988 s 209(2)(*e*)(vii)
    redeemable share capital, on, TA 1988 s 209(2)(*e*)(i)
    return dependent on results, TA 1988 s 209(2)(*e*)(iii)
    securities connected with shares in company, TA 1988 s 209(2)(*e*)(vi)
    75% subsidiary relationship, TA 1988 s 209(2), (8A)–(8F); FA 1995 s 87(8)
  interest paid, not treated as, TA 1988 s 212
  interest, treated as, new consideration, exclusion for, TA 1988 s 209(3)

DISTRIBUTIONS—*continued*
  interpretation, TA 1988 s 254
  loan or money society, treatment of, ESC C2
  lower rate, application of—
    company distributions, FA 1993 ss 77–79, Sch 6
    income from distributions, TA 1988 ss 1A, 4(1A)
  meaning, TA 1988 s 209; PR June 1970
  members, transfer to or from, benefit treated as, TA 1988 s 209(2)(*f*), (4)–(7)
  new consideration, other than, treated as, TA 1988 s 209(2)(*b*), (6)
  non-qualifying—
    relation to tax credit, TA 1988 s 233(2)
    return of, TA 1988 s 234(5)–(8), 253
  overseas life assurance fund, TA 1988 s 441A
  pension funds, withdrawal of tax credit, F(No 2) A 1997 s 19
  purchase of own shares, application to, TA 1988 s 229(3)
  qualifying, relation to tax credit, TA 1988 s 231, F(No 2)A 1997 Sch 5
  redeemable share capital issued other than for new consideration, TA 1988 s 209(2)(*c*), (*e*)(i), (8)
  repayment of share capital—
    bonus issue following, TA 1988 s 210
    matters treated as or not treated as, TA 1988 s 211
  shares of company or associated company, link to, TA 1988 s 209A
  stock dividend, not treated as, TA 1988 s 230
  stock dividend treated as income, F(No 2)A 1997 s 34, Sch 4 para 10
  tax credit accompanying, value of, PR 4/12/96
  tax credit restrictions, F(No 2) 1997 Sch 4

DIVERS
  charge to tax under Schedule D Case I, TA 1988 s 314

DIVIDEND STRIPPING
  associated companies, between, TCGA 1992 s 177

DIVIDENDS. *See also* DISTRIBUTIONS
  corporation tax, no deduction for, TA 1988 s 337(2)(*a*)
  distribution, treated as, TA 1988 s 209(2)(*a*)
  double taxation relief, regulations, SI 1973/317, SI 1999/3330, SI 2001/1156
  election for payment without accounting for ACT, PR December 1972
  public revenue—
    deduction of tax, TA 1988 ss 350, 350A
    meaning, TA 1988 s 349(4)
  tax credit accompanying, value of, PR 4/12/96
  Treasury etc, belonging to, meaning, TA 1988 s 49(3)

DOCTORS
  superannuation contributions, relief for, ESC A9

DOCUMENTS. *See also* INFORMATION
  delivery of, TMA 1970 s 115—
    orders for, SI 2000/2875
  entry to obtain, with warrant, TMA 1970 s 20C
  failure to produce, penalty for, TMA 1970 s 97AA
  falsification of, in investigation, TMA 1970 s 20BB
  investigation, power to call for, in—
    failure to produce documents, TMA 1970 s 97AA
    generally, TMA 1970 s 19A
    tax accountant's, TMA 1970 ss 20A, 20B
    taxpayer's and others', TMA 1970 ss 20, 20B
  meaning, TMA 1970 s 20D
  ownership of, guidance note, PR 23/2/90
  removal of, procedure, TMA 1970 s 20CC

DOCUMENTS—*continued*
service of, TMA 1970 s 115
warrant, entry by, to obtain, TMA 1970 s 20C

DOMICILE
change in law, PR 16/1/96
determination of, for Schedule E, TA 1988 s 207
person not, in UK, exemption from taxation of
interest on government stocks paid to, F(No
2)A 1931 s 22(1)(*b*); FA 1940 s 60(1)
person not, in UK, offshore income gains,
application of, to, TA 1988 s 762(5)

DONATIO MORTIS CAUSA
capital gains tax, exemption from, TCGA 1992
s 62(5)

DOUBLE TAXATION RELIEF
accrued income scheme, effect on, TA 1988 s 807
admissible and inadmissible taxes, PR 27/3/95
aggregated profits, treatment of, PR 1/02
Argentina, treaty with, SI 1997/1777
avoidance scheme or arrangement, TA 1988
s 801A(1), (6)–(8), (11)
capital gains tax, for purposes of, TCGA 1992
s 277; SP 6/88
chargeable gains, tax as, for purposes of, TA 1988
s 797; SP 6/88
co-operation between tax authorities, PR 2/3/78
Czechoslovakia, agreement with, states of, SP 5/93
deceased person's estate, non-resident, payments
to, SP 3/86
discretionary trust—
non-resident, payments to, SP 3/86
overseas income of, TA 1988 s 809; ESC B18
dividends—
branch or agency, application of rules to, TA
1988 s 806K
interest from overseas included in trading profits,
exclusion from exemption, TA 1988
s 808
overseas, claim for allowance relating to tax on,
TA 1988 s 803, SI 1999/3330
restriction on relief, TA 1988 s 798
spared tax, adjustment of dividends for, TA 1988
s 798A
transferred profits, paid from, TA 1988 s 801B
underlying tax on, SI 2001/1156
unrelieved foreign tax, TA 1988 ss 806A–806J
dual resident companies, SI 2001/1156
election against credit, TA 1988 s 805
foreign loan interest, bank, restriction of relief—
spared tax, adjustment of interest for, TA 1988
s 798A
tax credit relief, TA 1988 s 798; SI 1999/3330
underlying tax, TA 1988 s 803
foreign tax—
branches or agencies in UK, application of
provisions to, TA 1988 s 806C
deduction of from income, TA 1988 s 811
different categories of insurance business,
allocation to, TA 1988 s 804B
minimisation, TA 1988 s 795A
paid, adjustments to, RI 206
unrelieved—
claims, TA 1988 s 806G
dividends, on, TA 1988 s 806A
eligible amounts, TA 1988 s 806B
onshore pooling, TA 1988 s 806C
overseas branch or agency, profits of, TA
1988 ss 806L, 806M
qualifying dividends, TA 1988 s 806C
utilisation of, TA 1988 ss 806D, 806E
group—
aggregated profits, treatment of, PR 1/02
surrender of relievable tax within, SI 2001/1163

DOUBLE TAXATION RELIEF—*continued*
information, disclosure of, to foreign government,
TA 1988 ss 788(3), 816; TCGA 1992
s 277(4)
insurance company—
different categories of business, restriction of
credit, TA 1988 s 804B
expenses, allocation of, TA 1988 ss 804C–804E
interest brought into account as a non-trading
credit, TA 1988 s 797A
mutual agreement procedure, TA 1988 s 815AA
overseas life assurance business, restriction of
credit, TA 1988 s 804A
overseas resident, tax credit, calculation of, FA
1989 s 115
regulations, TA 1988 s 791; SI 1970/488, SI 1973/
317
related companies, dividends between—
UK and third country taxes, relief for, TA 1988
s 801
relief—
allowance of, TA 1988 s 793
Channel Islands, application to, TA 1988
s 794(2)(*a*)
Chile, additional tax in, RI 239
election against, TA 1988 s 805
income subject to foreign tax, computation of,
TA 1988 s 795
Isle of Man, application to, TA 1988 s 794(2)(*a*)
limits on credit—
corporation tax, TA 1988 s 797; PR 27/6/78
income tax, TA 1988 s 796
residence in UK, requirement as to, TA 1988
s 794(1)
restrictions, TA 1988 ss 798, 798A, 798B
Schedule E, application to, TA 1988 s 794(2)(*b*)
time limit for claim, TA 1988 s 806
unitary taxation, withdrawal of relief, where
imposed, TA 1988 ss 812–815
years of commencement, restriction for, TA
1988 s 804
relievable tax—
repayment, restriction of interest on, TA 1988
s 826
surrender of, TA 1988 s 806H
royalties and know-how payments from abroad,
ESC B8
South African secondary tax on companies, RI 125
spared tax, adjustment of interest for, TA 1988
s 798A
subsidiary company, meaning, TA 1988 s 792(2)
time limit for claim for credit relief, TA 1988 s 806
transitional provisions on introduction of current
year basis, FA 1994 Sch 20 paras 10–13
treaty relief—
current arrangements, TA 1988 s 788
former arrangements (old law), TA 1988 s 789
interest paid, procedure, RI 79
overseas resident, tax credit, calculation of, FA
1989 s 115
regulations, TA 1988 s 791; SI 1970/488, SI
1973/317
Turkey, compulsory fund surcharge in, RI 240
underlying tax—
computation of, TA 1988 s 799; PR 19/10/79
credit for, TA 1988 ss 806F, 806G
foreign group, taxation as single entity, TA 1988
s 803A
meaning, TA 1988 s 792(1)
relief for, SP 3/01
restriction of relief for, TA 1988 s 801A
split rate taxes, SP 3/01
trade investment in overseas company—
insurance company, ESC C1(b)
portfolio shareholder, ESC C1(a)
unilateral relief, TA 1988 s 790; SP 7/91, SP 12/93

DOUBLE TAXATION RELIEF—*continued*
  unitary taxation, withdrawal of relief, where imposed, TA 1988 ss 812–815; RI 102
  US/UK agreement—
    exchange of information, PR 2/3/78
    US government employees working in UK, PR 7/2/78
  USSR, agreement with, status of, SP 3/92
  years of commencement of income, restriction of credit, TA 1988 s 804
  Yugoslavia, agreement with, status of, SP 6/93

DREDGING
  allowances. *See* DREDGING ALLOWANCES
  contributions, exclusion of, CAA 2001 s 533
  meaning, CAA 2001 s 484(4)

DREDGING ALLOWANCES
  availability of, CAA 2001 s 484
  balancing allowances, entitlement to, CAA 2001 s 488
  contribution allowances, CAA 2001 s 543
  giving effect to, CAA 2001 s 489
  qualifying expenditure, meaning, CAA 2001 s 485
  qualifying trade—
    meaning, CAA 2001 s 484(2)
    pre-trading expenditure, CAA 2001 s 486
  writing-down, entitlement to, CAA 2001 s 487

DUAL RESIDENT COMPANIES
  group relief, application to, TA 1988 s 404
  non-resident, treatment as, FA 1994 ss 249–251

DUAL RESIDENTS
  rollover relief, application to, TCGA 1992 s 159
  settlement. *See* SETTLEMENTS

E

EASEMENTS
  meaning—
    mines, quarries, etc, TA 1988 s 119(3)
    wayleave, electric line, TA 1988 s 120(5)

EDUCATION AND TRAINING
  charitable status of school—
    temporary loss of, ESC D47
  employee, for, TA 1988 ss 588, 589
  expenses borne by employee, relief for, ESC A64
  New Deal 50plus, payments under FA 2000 s 84
  qualifying course for vocational training—
    phasing out, FA 1991 s 32(2), (2A)
    public financial assistance, provision of, SI 1992/734
  tax relief, PR 4/12/96
  training courses for business proprietors, expenditure on, RI 1

EDUCATIONAL ESTABLISHMENTS
  gifts to, deduction for—
    further and higher education establishments, designated—
      England and Wales, SI 1992/42 Sch Pt III
      Scotland, SI 1992/42 Sch Pt IV
    operation of relief, TA 1988 s 84
    schools, designated—
      England and Wales, SI 1992/42 Sch Pt I
      Scotland, SI 1992/42 Sch Pt II

ELECTRICITY BOARDS
  charge to tax on, TA 1988 s 511(1)–(3), (6)

ELECTRONIC COMMERCE
  websites and servers, tax status, PR 4/00

ELECTRONIC COMMUNICATIONS
  acceptance of, SI 1993/744 reg 2A

ELECTRONIC COMMUNICATIONS—*continued*
  delivery of information and payments, proof of, SI 1973/744 reg 2D
  incentives, power to provide, FA 2000 s 143, Sch 38
  mandatory e-filing, FA 2002 s 135
  other provisions, use under, FA 2002 s 136
  proof of content, SI 1993/744 reg 2B
  regulations facilitating use of, FA 1999 s 132, SI 2000/945
  sender or recipient of information, proof of identity, SI 1993/744 reg 2C
  student loans, notices concerning repayment, SI 2002/680 reg 2
  unauthorised means, use of, SI 1993/744 reg 2E
  use of, FA 1999 s 133

EMOLUMENTS
  for year where no employment held, TA 1988 s 19(1) para 4A
  received in UK, meaning, TA 1988 s 132(5)
  return or, requirement to make, by payer, TMA 1970 s 16
  work done abroad, for, SP A17

EMPLOYED EARNERS
  See NIC section of this publication.

EMPLOYEE EARNING £8,500 OR MORE
  beneficial loan. *See* BENEFICIAL LOANS
  benefit in kind—
    accommodation, living—
      additional charge on, cost over £75,000, TA 1988 s 146
      duties of employment, used in performing, TA 1988 s 155ZA
      expenses on, TA 1988 s 155(3), 163
      general charge on, TA 1988 s 145
      priority of rules applying to, TA 1988 s 146A
      Scotland, application to, ESC A56
    application to directors, TA 1988 ss 153(1), 167
    asset, annual value of, TA 1988 s 156(6), (7)
    asset transfer by employee, ESC A85
    asset, transfer to employee, TA 1988 s 156(3), (4)
    asset, use by employee, TA 1988 s 156(5)
  canteen meal, exception for, TA 1988 s 155(5)
  car—
    accessories—
      available after car first made available, TA 1988 s 168C
      disabled, revision for, TA 1988 s 16A(11)
      not included in list price, TA 1988 s 168B
      replacements, TA 1988 s 168E; SI 1994/777
    appropriate percentage, reduction of value, SI 2001/1123
    automatic, for disabled drivers, TA 1988 Sch 6 para 5A
    bi-fuel, TA 1988 Sch 6 para 5
    cap for expensive car, TA 1988 s 168G
    capital contributions, TA 1988 s 168D
    cash equivalent, TA 1988 Sch 6 paras 1–7
    classic cars, TA 1988 s 168F
    contribution by employee, TA 1988 Sch 6 para 7; RD 1
    diesel, TA 1988 Sch 6 para 5D
    discounts, TA 1988 Sch 6 para 5E
    electrically propelled, TA 1988 Sch 6 para 5G
    emission figures, with, TA 1988 Sch 6 paras 3, 4
    meaning, TA 1988 s 168(5), (6)
    no emission figures, with, TA 1988 Sch 6 para 5C
    periods when unavailable, TA 1988 Sch 6 para 6
    pooled, use of, TA 1988 s 159
    provision by employer, TA 1988 ss 155(1), 157, Sch 6

FIXTURES AND FITTINGS—*continued*
  apportionment, election to fix—*continued*
    irrevocable, being, CAA 2001 s 200(3)
    procedure, CAA 2001 s 201
    reduction of amount, CAA 2001 s 200(4)
    sale of qualifying interest, on, CAA 2001 s 198
  cessation of ownership—
    equipment lessor, of, CAA 2001 s 192
    incoming lessee entitled to allowances, where, CAA 2001 s 190
    person ceasing to have qualifying interest, CAA 2001 s 188
    qualifying interest, identification of, CAA 2001 s 189
    severance, on, CAA 2001 s 191
  claim, CAA 2001 s 202(3)
    other claims, interaction between, CAA 2001 s 9
  disposal values—
    avoidance cases, in, CAA 2001 s 197
    table of, CAA 2001 s 196
  election by lessor and lessee, RI 86
  energy management services, provision in connection with, FA 2001 s 66
  energy services agreement—
    meaning, CAA 2001 s 175A
    obligations of client, discharge by purchaser of land, CAA 2001 s 182A
  energy service providers, CAA 2001 s 180A
    assignee, acquisition of ownership by, CAA 2001 s 195A
    cessation of ownership, CAA 2001 s 192A
    client, acquisition of ownership by, CAA 2001 s 195B
  entitlement to allowance, CAA 2001 s 202(1), (2)
  equipment lease—
    affordable warmth programme, as part of, CAA 2001 s 180
    meaning, CAA 2001 s 174
  equipment lessee—
    acquisition of ownership by, CAA 2001 s 195
    meaning, CAA 2001 s 174(3)
    purchaser of land discharging obligations of, CAA 2001 s 182
    qualifying activity, for, CAA 2001 s 178
    severance, right of, CAA 2001 s 179
  equipment lessor—
    assignee, acquisition of ownership by, CAA 2001 s 194
    cessation of ownership of, CAA 2001 s 192
    meaning, CAA 2001 s 174(3)
    treatment of, CAA 2001 s 177
  interest in land—
    meaning, CAA 2001 s 175(1)
    person having interest in—
     energy service providers, CAA 2001 s 180A
     meaning, CAA 2001 s 175(2)
     qualifying activity, having fixture for purposes of, CAA 2001 s 176
  lease, meaning, CAA 2001 s 174(4)
  licence to occupy land, RI 217
  long-life assets, exclusion, CAA 2001 s 93
  machinery and plant. *See* MACHINERY AND PLANT
  meaning, CAA 2001 s 173(1)
  purchaser of land—
    consideration given by, CAA 2001 s 181
    energy services agreement, discharging obligations under, CAA 2001 s 182A
    obligations of equipment lessee, discharging obligations of, CAA 2001 s 182
  qualifying expenditure, restrictions on amount of—
    industrial buildings allowance made, where, CAA 2001 s 186
    plant and machinery allowance claimed, where, CAA 2001 s 185
    research and development allowance made, where, CAA 2001 s 187

FIXTURES AND FITTINGS—*continued*
  relevant land—
    incoming lessee, rights of—
     lessor entitled to allowances, where, CAA 2001 s 183
     lessor not entitled to allowances, where, CAA 2001 s 184
    meaning, CAA 2001 s 173(2)
  returns, amendment of, CAA 2001 s 203
  scope of provisions, CAA 2001 s 172
  acquisition of ownership—
    assignee of equipment lessor, by, CAA 2001 s 194
    equipment lessee, by, CAA 2001 s 195
  lease or licence, on termination of, CAA 2001 s 193

FLAT CONVERSION ALLOWANCES
  availability of, CAA 2001 s 393A
  balancing adjustments—
    balancing events, CAA 2001 s 393N
    proceeds from, CAA 2001 s 393G
    calculation of, CAA 2001 s 393P
    when made, CAA 2001 s 393M
  demolition costs, treatment of, CAA 2001 s 393S
  flat, meaning, CAA 2001 s 393A(3)
  giving effect to, CAA 2001 s 393T
  high value flats, CAA 2001 s 393E
  initial allowances, CAA 2001 s 393H
    flat not qualifying or relevant interest sold before first letting, CAA 2001 s 393I
    writing off, CAA 2001 s 393R
  lease, meaning, CAA 2001 s 393W
  non-qualifying assets, apportionment of sums partly referable to, CAA 2001 s 393U
  qualifying buildings, CAA 2001 s 393C
  qualifying expenditure—
    meaning, CAA 2001 s 393B
    writing off—
     demolition costs, treatment of, CAA 2001 s 393S
     initial allowances, CAA 2001 s 393R
     writing-down allowances, CAA 2001 s 393R
  qualifying flat, meaning, CAA 2001 s 393D
  relevant interest in flat—
    completion of conversion, acquired on, CAA 2001 s 393G
    general rule, CAA 2001 s 393F
  termination of lease, provisions applying on, CAA 2001 s 393V
  writing-down allowances—
    amount of, CAA 2001 s 393K
    entitlement to, CAA 2001 s 393J
    residue of qualifying expenditure, meaning, CAA 2001 s 393L
    writing off, CAA 2001 s 393R

FOOTBALL GROUND
  pools payments for improvements to, FA 1990 s 126

FOOTBALL POOLS
  athletic sports etc, payments in support of, FA 1991 s 121
  donation element, treatment of, SP C1
  football grounds, payments for improvements to, FA 1990 s 126
  pools payments—
    football ground improvements, for, FA 1990 s 126

FOOTBALL TRANSFER FEES
  tax treatment, FA 1999 s 63

FOREIGN COMPENSATION ACT 1950
  compensation under, ESC D50

FRIENDLY SOCIETIES—*continued*
  charge to corporation tax, TA 1988 s 463; F(No 2)A 1997 Sch 3
  commencement of new provisions, F(No 2)A 1992 Sch 9 para 22
  distributions—
    tax credit, F(No 2)A 1997 s 30(4), FA 1998 s 90
  exempt business—
    meaning, SI 1999/622 reg 2
    provisional repayments, SI 1999/622; SI 2001/3973
  gilt-edged securities, periodic accounting for tax on interest, SI 1999/624
  incorporated—
    assets transferred on incorporation, TA 1988 s 465A; TCGA 1992 ss 143A, 143B, 217A
    disposal of assets, capital allowances, effect of, TCGA 1992 s 217C
    qualifying, application of provisions relating to, TA 1988 s 461A–461C
    rights of members transferred, TCGA 1992 s 217B
  long term business, transfer of, PR 17/7/90
  meaning, TA 1988 s 466(2)
  members—
    maximum benefits, TA 1988 s 464
  provisional repayment of tax, SI 1998/3175 reg 15
  qualifying policies—
    application to, TA 1988 Sch 15 para 3
    transitional provisions, FA 1991 Sch 9 paras 4, 5
  registered—
    contracts made on or before 13 March 1984, FA 1984 s 73
    endowment business—
      exemption of, TA 1988 s 460
      meaning, TA 1988 s 466(1)
    life or endowment business—
      exemption of, TA 1988 s 460
      meaning, TA 1988 s 466(1)
      non-qualifying policy, effect of, TA 1988 s 462
      policy made before 20 March 1991, election for, TA 1988 s 462A
    other business, taxation of, general rules, TA 1988 s 461
    registered before 3 May 1966 (''old societies''), qualifying policies, provisions relating to, TA 1988 s 465
  self-assessment, society with non-annual actuarial investigations, TMA s 11AE
  unregistered, exemption of income and gains, TA 1988 s 459

FUEL. *See* CAR FUEL

FUNDED COMPANY
  meaning (equity notes), TA 1988 s 209(11)

FUNDING BONDS
  interest payable, issue in respect of, treatment of, TA 1988 s 582

FUNDS IN COURT
  capital gains tax, treatment for, TCGA 1992 s 61
  income on, treatment of, TA 1988 s 469A

FURNISHED HOLIDAY LETTINGS
  commercial, CAA 2001 s 17(3)
  plant and machinery, capital allowances on—business, meaning, CAA 2001 s 17
  rollover relief, not affected by longer lettings outside holiday period, RI 28
  trade, treatment as, TA 1988 ss 503, 504; TCGA 1992 s 241; CAA 2001 s 249(2); PR 17/8/84

FURNISHED LETTINGS
  rent a room, provisions for, F(No 2)A 1992 Sch 10
  Schedule A, charge under, TA 1988 s 15(1) para 4
  wear and tear allowance, ESC B47

FUTURES. *See* FINANCIAL FUTURES

FUTURES EXCHANGE
  recognition of, TCGA 1992 s 288(6), (7), Misc XI

G

GALLANTRY AWARDS
  annuities and pensions exempt from tax, TA 1988 s 317(*c*)
  decorations for valour, exempt from tax on chargeable gains, TCGA 1992 s 268

GAMBLING. *See* BETTING

GAS COUNCIL
  charge to tax on, TA 1988 s 511(7)

GENERAL ANNUITY BUSINESS
  insurance company, of, charge to tax, TA 1988 s 437
  old contracts, transitional relief for, FA 1991 Sch 7 para 16

GENERAL COMMISSIONERS
  appointment of, TMA 1970 s 2
  assigning proceedings to—
    capital gains tax proceedings, general rule for, TMA 1970 Sch 3 para 2
    corporation tax etc, TMA 1970 Sch 3 para 4
    directions by the Board, TMA 1970 Sch 3 paras 8, 9
    elections etc, procedure for making, TMA 1970 Sch 3 para 5
    generally, TMA 1970 Sch 3 paras 1, 10
    income tax proceedings, general rule for, TMA 1970 Sch 3 para 2
    partnerships, TMA 1970 Sch 3 para 7
    PAYE appeals, TMA 1970 Sch 3 para 3
    relevant place, meaning, TMA 1970 s 44(1), Sch 3 para 1
    taxpayer, meaning, TMA 1970 Sch 3 para 1
  change of name, proposed, F(No 2)A 1992 s 75(1)(*a*), (2), (3)
  clerk—
    appointment of, TMA 1970 s 3
    compensation for loss of office, FA 1972 s 130
    declaration on taking office, TMA 1970 s 6(2), Sch 1 Pt I
    indemnity, TMA 1970 s 3A
  costs, SI 2001/1304
  declaration of secrecy, TMA 1970 s 6(1)(*a*), Sch 1 Pt I
  divisions—
    in England and Wales, TMA 1970 s 2(2)
    in Northern Ireland, TMA 1970 s 2(2)
    in Scotland, TMA 1970 s 2(3), (4)
    local government areas, changes in, FA 1973 s 41
  indemnity, TMA 1970 s 3A
  jurisdiction—
    appeals on claims, in, TMA 1970 s 42, Sch 2
    assigning proceedings to. *See* ASSIGNING PROCEEDINGS TO
    generally, TMA 1970 ss 44, 46, 46A, Sch 3; SI 1994/1812
    right of election on appeal, TMA 1970 s 46
  legal proceedings, costs and expenses in, TMA 1970 s 2A
  Northern Ireland, for, FA 1988 s 134
  penalty proceedings before, TMA 1970 s 100C

HOUSING CORPORATION
  disposals of land by, TCGA 1992 ss 218, 219

HOUSING FOR WALES
  disposals of land by, TCGA 1992 ss 218, 219

HOUSING GRANTS
  exemption from tax, TA 1988 s 578

HOVERCRAFT
  rollover relief, TCGA 1992 s 155 Class 2

HUMAN RIGHTS
  Convention rights—
    articles, HRA 1998 Sch 1
    derogations, HRA 1998 ss 14, 16
    interpretation, HRA 1998 s 2
    judicial acts, HRA 1998 s 9
    legislation—
      declaration of incompatibility, HRA 1998 s 4
      interpretation compatible with, HRA 1998 s 3
      intervention by Crown, HRA 1998 s 5
      meaning, HRA 1998 s 21
      statements of compatibility, HRA 1998 s 19
    meaning, HRA 1998 s 1
    public authorities, acts of—
      interpretation compatible with, HRA 1998 s 6
      judicial remedies relating to, HRA 1998 s 8
      proceedings concerning, HRA 1998 s 7
    remedial action in relation to, HRA 1998 s 10
    remedial orders, HRA 1998 Sch 2
    reservations, HRA 1998 ss 15, 17
  existing, safeguard for, HRA 1998 s 11
  freedom of expression, HRA 1998 s 13

HUSBAND AND WIFE. *See also* MARRIAGE;
    MARRIED WOMAN
  asset held at 6 April 1965, TCGA 1992 Sch 2 para
    22
  business expansion scheme relief, TA 1988 s 304
  capital gains tax, application to, TCGA 1992 s 58;
    PR 21/11/90
  independent taxation, introduction of,
      consequential amendments, FA 1988 Sch 3;
      PR 8/1/90
  joint loan, treatment of, RI 15
  jointly held assets—
    declarations relating to, TA 1988 s 282B
    treatment of, TA 1988 s 282A
  living together, meaning, TA 1988 s 282
  maintenance payment. *See* MAINTENANCE
      PAYMENTS
  married couple's allowance, TA 1988
    ss 257A–257BB
  more than one wife, PR 16/2/78
  personal reliefs, transitional provisions, TA 1988
    ss 257D–257F
  private residence exemption—
    generally, TCGA 1992 s 222(6); ESC D3, ESC
      D6
    separated couple, SP D9
  property loan, interest on—
    MIRAS, application of, TA 1988 ss 373(7)
      376(2), (3)

I

INCAPACITATED PERSONS. *See also* MINOR
  capital gains tax charge, TMA 1970 s 77
  income tax charge, TMA 1970 s 72
  meaning, TMA 1970 s 118(1)

INCAPACITY BENEFIT
  PAYE operation of, SI 1993/744 regs 98A–H
  Schedule E charge, FA 1994 s 139

INCENTIVE AWARDS SCHEME
  treatment, SP 6/85

INCIDENTAL OVERNIGHT EXPENSES
  treatment of, TA 1988 s 200A

INCOME SUPPORT
  income tax treatment, TA 1988 ss 151, 152

INCOME TAX
  Acts—
    application from year to year, TA 1988 s 820
    government departments, application to, TA
      1988 s 829
    interpretation of, TA 1988 s 833
    meaning, TA 1988 s 831(1)(*b*)
    Scottish trusts, application to, FA 1993 s 118
  additional rate, discretionary trust, trustees'
      liability, TA 1988 ss 686, 687
  applicable rate, meaning, TA 1988 s 701(3A)
  application of rate limits, TA 1988 s 1(2)
  assessment to 5 April each year, TA 1988 s 2(2)
  basic rate—
    income charged at, TA 1988 s 1(2)(*a*), (3)
    limit, meaning, TA 1988 s 1(3)
    Scottish taxpayers, for, SA 1998 ss 73, 74
  charge to, TA 1988 s 1; FA 1997 s 54
  composite rate, SI 1985/1696
  company—
    income not liable to, TA 1988 s 6(2)
    payments by, treatment for tax purposes, TA
      1988 s 7
    repayment of tax, TA 1988 s 7
  discounted securities—
    abroad, assets transferred, FA 1996 Sch 13 para
      12
    accrued income scheme, FA 1996 Sch 13 para
      11
    charge to tax on realised profit, FA 1996 Sch 13
      para 1
    connected persons, transfers between, FA 1996
      Sch 13 para 8
    conversion, extinguishment by, FA 1996 Sch 13
      para 5
    deemed market value, transactions at, FA 1996
      Sch 13 para 9
    deep gain on redemption, FA 1996 Sch 13 para
      3(3)
    excluded indexed securities, FA 1996 Sch 13
      para 13
    extinguished by conversion, FA 1996 Sch 13
      para 5
    generally, FA 1996 Sch 13 paras 15, 16
    gilt strips, FA 1996 Sch 13 para 14
    income exempt, treatment of losses where, FA
      1996 Sch 13 para 7
    issue of securities in separate tranches, FA 1996
      Sch 13 para 10
    personal representatives, transfer by, FA 1996
      Sch 13 para 6(7), (8)
    realised losses on, relief for, FA 1996 Sch 13
      para 2
    relevant discounted security, meaning, FA 1996
      Sch 13 para 3
    transfer of security, meaning, FA 1996 Sch 13
      para 4
    trustees, transfer or redemption by, FA 1996 Sch
      13 para 6(1)–(6)
  Employment Zone programmes, exemption of
      payments under, FA 2000 s 85
  fractions of a pound, charge to, TA 1988 s 2(1)
  fraudulent evasion, offence of, FA 2000 s 144
  higher rate, charge to, TA 1988 s 1(2)(*b*)
  indexation of rate limits, TA 1988 s 1(4)–(6)
  indexed rate bands, FA 2002 s 27
  interest on overdue income tax, TMA 1970 s 86
    (new version)

INDUSTRIAL BUILDINGS ALLOWANCE—
continued
miners, buildings for, CAA 2001 s 355
net, amount of, CAA 2001 s 324
non-qualifying assets, apportionment of sums
    partly referable to, CAA 2001 s 356
part of building, application to, CAA 2001 s 283;
    PR 25/3/81; PR 20/12/83
qualifying expenditure—
    balancing adjustments, increase or writing off
        on, s 337
    construction, capital expenditure on, CAA 2001
        s 294
    enterprise zone—
        balancing adjustments. *See* balancing
            adjustments, *above*
        construction of building, capital expenditure
            on, CAA 2001 s 299
        initial allowances, CAA 2001 s 305
        part within time limit for, CAA 2001
            ss 301–303
        purchase of building within 2 years of first
            use, CAA 2001 ss 301, 303, 304
        time limit, CAA 2001 s 298
        unused buildings, purchase of, CAA 2001
            ss 300, 302
    meaning, CAA 2001 s 292
    residue, allowance limited to, CAA 2001 s 312
        meaning, CAA 2001 s 313
    unused building, purchase of—
        developer not involved, where, CAA 2001
            s 295
        developer, sale by, CAA 2001 s 296
    used building, purchase from developer, CAA
        2001 s 297
    writing off—
        additional VAT rebates, CAA 2001 s 351
        balancing adjustment made, where, CAA 2001
            s 337
        building not industrial, where, CAA 2001
            s 336
        demolition costs, CAA 2001 s 340
        extent and time of, CAA 2001 s 332
        initial allowances, CAA 2001 ss 333, 334
        realised capital value, of, CAA 2001 s 338
        relevant interest, Crown or person not within
            charge to tax entitled to, CAA 2001
            s 339
        research and development allowances, CAA
            2001 s 335
        writing-down allowances, CAA 2001 s 334
qualifying trades—
    meaning, CAA 2001 s 274
    parts of, CAA 2001 s 276
    table of, CAA 2001 s 274
requisitioned land, for, CAA 2001 s 358
small workshops, estate of, SP 4/80
storage of goods or materials, trade consisting of,
    RI 212
trades, giving effect to for, CAA 2001 s 352
writing-down—
    additional VAT liabilities, CAA 2001 s 347
    additional VAT rebates, CAA 2001 s 349
    calculation of—
        basic rule, CAA 2001 s 310
        sale of relevant interest, after, CAA 2001
            s 311
    entitlement to, CAA 2001 s 309
    residue of qualifying expenditure, limited to,
        CAA 2001 s 312
        meaning, CAA 2001 s 313
writing off, CAA 2001 s 334

INFANTS. *See* MINOR

INFORMATION
delay in using, arrears of tax given up where, ESC
    A19
disclosure of—
    double taxation agreements, under, TA 1988
        ss 788(2), 816; TCGA 1992 s 277(4)
    EC member states, tax authorities in, FA 1978
        s 77; TA 1988 s 816(2A); FA 1989
        s 182A; FA 1990 s 125
    offences, FA 1989 ss 182, 182A
    UK revenue departments, between, FA 1972
        s 127
international exchange of, TA 1988 s 815C

INHERITANCE TAX
acceptance of property in lieu, SP 6/87
accrued income, relief from higher rate tax on, TA
    1988 s 699, F(No 2)A 1997 s 34, Sch 4 para
    17
assets put into settlement, interaction with income
    tax, SP 1/82
capital transfer tax, change of name to, FA 1986
    s 100
death benefits under superannuation arrangements,
    SP 10/86
discretionary trusts, treatment of income, SP 8/86
funeral expenses, deduction for, SP 7/87
loan to pay, interest relief on, TA 1988 s 364
substitute forms, use of, SP 2/93
valuation for, application of, TCGA 1992 s 274

INITIAL ALLOWANCE. *See* CAPITAL
ALLOWANCES

INLAND REVENUE. *See* BOARD OF INLAND
REVENUE

INMARSAT. *See* INTERNATIONAL MARITIME
SATELLITE ORGANISATION

INMATES
return of, requirement to make, TMA 1970 s 14

INSOLVENCY
preferential debts—
    categories of, IA 1986 s 386, Sch 6
    company winding up, in, IA 1986 s 175
    relevant date, meaning, IA 1986 s 387
    taxation aspects, PR June 1990

INSPECTOR OF TAXES. *See also* BOARD OF
INLAND REVENUE
appointment of, IRRA 1890 s 4; TMA 1970 s 1(2),
    (2A), (2B)
declaration on appointment, TMA 1970 s 6(4), Sch
    1 Pt III
liaison with Head Office, PR 6/9/89
magistrates' courts, power to conduct proceedings
    in, IRRA 1890 s 27
obstruction of, IRRA 1890 s 11
proceedings begun by another inspector, power to
    continue, TMA 1970 s 1(3)
sheriffs' court, power to conduct proceedings in,
    IRRA 1890 s 27

INSURANCE COMPANIES
acquisitions disregarded under concession, FA
    1999 s 81
apportionment—
    1982 securities, treatment of, FA 1990 Sch 6
        para 12
    income and gains, TA 1988 s 432A
    income of non-participating funds, TA 1988
        ss 432C, 432D
    participating funds, TA 1988 s 432E; SI 1990/
        1541, F(No 2)A 1997 Sch 3 para 2

LOCAL AUTHORITY ASSOCIATIONS
exemption from—
  chargeable gain, charge to tax on, TCGA 1992
    s 271(3)
  income tax and corporation tax, TA 1988
    s 519(2)
meaning, TA 1988 s 519(3)

LOCAL ENTERPRISE AGENCIES
contributions to, deduction for, TA 1988 s 79

LOCAL GOVERNMENT RESIDUARY BODY
local authority, treatment as, TA 1988 s 842(2)(*b*)

LOCATION OF ASSETS
rules for determining, TCGA 1992 s 275

LOCUM TENENS
insurance policy to cover cost of, tax treatment of
  premiums paid under, PR 30/4/96

LODGERS
return of, requirement to make, TMA 1970 s 14

LONG-SERVICE AWARDS
tax on, exclusion of charge to, ESC A22

LORRY
road-user charge, FA 2002 s 137

LORRY DRIVERS
meals, relief for expenditure on, SP 16/80
self-employed, overnight subsistence for, RI 51

LOSS RELIEF FOR INCOME TAX
accounts basis—
  application of, ESC A87
anticipated claims, RI 234
carry forward, TA 1988 s 385
cessation of business—
  capital allowances brought forward, ESC A8
  terminal loss, carry back, TA 1988 ss 388, 389
commercial basis test, TA 1988 s 384
commodity futures, withdrawal of relief, TA 1988
  s 399
debts, transactions in, inclusion of interest, TA
  1988 s 398
deposits, transactions in, inclusion of interest, TA
  1988 s 398
early years of trading, carry back, TA 1988 s 381
farming and market gardening, restriction of relief,
  "hobby farming", TA 1988 s 397
financial futures, withdrawal of relief, TA 1988
  s 399
first year allowances, restriction on set-off, TA
  1988 s 384A
interest paid, trading loss, treatment as, TA 1988
  s 390
late claims, RI 96
loan relationship deficits, carry-back, FA 1996
  Schs 8, 11, F(No 2)A 1997 s 40
options, qualifying, withdrawal of relief, TA 1988
  s 399
Schedule D Case VI, TA 1988 s 392
terminal loss, carry back, TA 1988 ss 388, 389
trade carried on abroad, TA 1988 s 391
trade, profession or vocation, application to, TA
  1988 ss 380(1), 381(7), 384(10), 385(1)
trading loss, set off against general income—
  capital gains tax, set off against, FA 1991 s 72;
    RI 47
  carry-back against profits of previous three
    years, TA 1988 s 393A, F(No 2)A 1997
    s 39
  computation of, as for profits, TA 1988 s 382(4)
  current year of assessment, in, TA 1988 s 380(1)

LOSS RELIEF FOR INCOME TAX—*continued*
trading loss, set off against general income—
  continued
  early years of trading, three year carry back, TA
    1988 s 381
  following year of assessment, in, TA 1988
    s 380(2)
  preceding year of assessment, application to, FA
    1994 s 209(1)
  profession or vocation, application to, TA 1988
    s 380(1), 381(7), 383(12)(*b*), 384(10)
  transitional provisions for current year basis of
    assessment, RI 97

**LOSS RELIEF FOR INCOME TAX AND
CORPORATION TAX**
average loss, no deduction for excess, TA 1988
  s 74(1)(*k*)
commodity futures, withdrawal of relief, TA 1988
  s 399
debts, transactions in, inclusion of interest, TA
  1988 s 398
deposits, transactions in, inclusion of interest, TA
  1988 s 398
farming and market gardening, restriction of relief,
  "hobby farming", TA 1988 s 397
financial futures, withdrawal of relief, TA 1988
  s 399
options, withdrawal of relief, TA 1988 s 399

LOTTERY
donation element, treatment of, SP C1

LOWER RATE OF INCOME TAX. *See* RATES
OF TAX

LUMP SUM PAYMENTS. *See also* TERMINATION
PAYMENTS
retirement—
  closed or frozen pension schemes, changes after
    5 April 1980, ESC A33
  generally, TA 1988 s 190; SP 13/91

LUNCHEON VOUCHERS. *See* VOUCHERS

M

MACHINERY AND PLANT
abortive expenditure on, relief for, RI 10
anti-avoidance—
  assessments, adjustment of, CAA 2001 s 231
  connected person—
    meaning, CAA 2001 s 232
    transactions between, CAA 2001 s 214
  finance lease—
    allocation of expenditure to chargeable period,
      CAA 2001 s 220
    meaning, CAA 2001 s 219
  first-year allowances, restricted, CAA 2001 s 217
  hire purchase, CAA 2001 s 229
  manufacturers and suppliers, CAA 2001 s 230
  qualifying expenditure, restriction on, CAA 2001
    s 218
  relevant transactions, CAA 2001 s 213
  sale and finance leasebacks—
    disposal value, restriction on, CAA 2001 s 222
    first-year allowance not made, CAA 2001
      s 223
    meaning, CAA 2001 s 221
    non-compliance risk, lessor not bearing, CAA
      2001 s 225
    qualifying expenditure, restriction on, CAA
      2001 s 224
    special treatment, election for, CAA 2001
      ss 227, 228, 245
    subsequent transaction, qualifying expenditure
      limited in, CAA 2001 s 226
    VAT liabilities, additional, CAA 2001 s 243

MACHINERY AND PLANT—*continued*
- overseas leasing—*continued*
  - pool—*continued*
    - disposal to connected person, effect of, CAA 2001 s 108
    - prohibited allowances, CAA 2001 s 110
      - connected persons, CAA 2001 s 115
      - standard recovery mechanism, CAA 2001 s 114
    - protected leasing, certificate relating to, CAA 2001 s 118
    - qualifying purposes, CAA 2001 s 125
    - ships and aircraft, use of, CAA 2001 s 123
    - short-term—
      - meaning, CAA 2001 s 121
      - qualifying purpose, CAA 2001 s 122
    - transport containers, CAA 2001 s 124
    - use for, CAA 2001 s 105(2)
    - writing-down allowances, CAA 2001 s 109
  - painting, treatment as "plant", PR 31/12/79
  - partial depreciation subsidy—
    - first-year allowances, reduction of, CAA 2001 s 210
    - meaning, CAA 2001 s 209
    - single asset pool, assets in, CAA 2001 ss 211, 212
  - partnership—
    - amendment of claim, SP A26
    - qualifying activities, CAA 2001 s 263
    - successions, CAA 2001 s 265
      - beneficiaries, by, CAA 2001 s 268
      - predecessor and successor being connected persons, CAA 2001 ss 266, 267
    - using partner's own property, CAA 2001 s 264
  - pre-trading expenditure, CAA 2001 s 12
  - profession or vocation, application to, CAA 2001 s 251
  - qualifying activities—
    - asset provided or used partly for—
      - first-year allowances, reduction of, CAA 2001 s 205
      - significant reduction in use, effect of, CAA 2001 s 208
      - single asset pool, allocation to, CAA 2001 ss 206, 207
    - availability of allowances for, CAA 2001 s 11
    - employments and offices, CAA 2001 s 20
    - expenditure incurred before carrying on, CAA 2001 s 12
    - furnished holiday lettings business, CAA 2001 s 17
    - gift, use of, CAA 2001 s 14
    - investment companies, management of, CAA 2001 s 18
    - list of, CAA 2001 s 15
    - ordinary Schedule A business, CAA 2001 s 16
    - plant or machinery provided for other purposes, use of, CAA 2001 s 13
    - special leasing, CAA 2001 s 19
  - qualifying expenditure—
    - buildings, on, CAA 2001 s 21
    - demolition, on, CAA 2001 s 26
    - exclusions—
      - depreciation, CAA 2001 s 37
      - dwelling-house, plant or machinery for use in, CAA 2001 s 35
      - employment or office, for, CAA 2001 s 36; FA 2001 s 59
      - Members of Parliament, etc, accommodation for, CAA 2001 s 34
      - production animals, on, CAA 2001 s 38
    - existing building, alterations to, CAA 2001 s 25
    - fire safety, on, CAA 2001 s 29
    - first year—
      - information and communications technology, expenditure by small enterprises, CAA 2001 ss 45, 46

MACHINERY AND PLANT—*continued*
- qualifying expenditure—*continued*
  - first year—*continued*
    - large or medium-sized group, company as member of, CAA 2001 s 49
    - Northern Ireland, small or medium-sized enterprises in, CAA 2001 ss 40–43, 46
    - small or medium-sized enterprises, incurred by, CAA 2001 ss 44, 46–48
    - time when expenditure incurred, CAA 2001 s 50
    - types of expenditure for which available, CAA 2001 s 39
    - UK tax authorities, disclosure of information between, CAA 2001 s 51
  - interests in land, exclusion of expenditure on, CAA 2001 s 24
  - meaning, CAA 2001 s 11
  - personal security, on, CAA 2001 s 33
  - pooling—
    - available expenditure, CAA 2001 s 57
    - initial allocation, CAA 2001 s 58
    - purpose of, CAA 2001 s 53
    - types of pool, CAA 2001 s 54
  - safety at designated sports grounds, on, CAA 2001 ss 30–32
  - safety measures, on, CAA 2001 s 27
  - structures, assets and works, on, CAA 2001 s 22
  - thermal expenditure, on, CAA 2001 ss 27, 28
  - unaffected by provisions, CAA 2001 s 23
  - unrelieved, carrying forward, CAA 2001 s 59
  - renewals basis, change to capital allowances basis, ESC B1
  - ring fence trade, use in, CAA 2001 s 45F
    - less than five years, for, CAA 2001 s 45G
  - rollover relief, TCGA 1992 s 155 Class 1 Head B
  - shares in, CAA 2001 s 271
  - ships. *See* SHIPS
  - short-life assets—
    - additional VAT liability, CAA 2001 s 240
    - connected persons, disposal to, CAA 2001 s 89
    - leasing, provided for, CAA 2001 s 87
    - meaning, CAA 2001 s 83
    - pool, CAA 2001 s 86
    - treatment of, SP 1/86
      - election for, CAA 2001 s 85
      - ruled out, where, CAA 2001 s 84
    - undervalue, sales at, CAA 2001 s 88
  - special leasing, CAA 2001 s 19
    - corporation tax, CAA 2001 ss 259, 260
    - income tax, CAA 2001 s 258
    - life assurance business, CAA 2001 s 261
  - succession to trade—
    - ownership without change of, TA 1988 s 343(2)
  - thermal insulation, CAA 2001 s 28
  - VAT liabilities, additional—
    - anti-avoidance, CAA 2001 ss 233, 241
    - assessments and adjustments, CAA 2001 s 246
    - election for special treatment, effect of, CAA 2001 s 245
    - first-year allowance, generating, CAA 2001 s 236
      - anti-avoidance, CAA 2001 s 241
      - exceptions, CAA 2001 s 237
    - meaning, CAA 2001 s 234
    - qualifying expenditure, restriction on—
      - generally, CAA 2001 s 242
      - non-compliance risk, lessor not bearing, CAA 2001 s 244
      - sale and finance leaseback, CAA 2001 s 243
    - qualifying expenditure, treated as, CAA 2001s 235
    - short-life assets, s 240
  - VAT rebates, additional—
    - anti-avoidance, and, CAA 2001 ss 233, 241
    - disposal value—
      - generating, CAA 2001 s 238

MACHINERY AND PLANT—*continued*
  VAT rebates, additional—*continued*
    disposal value—*continued*
      limit on, CAA 2001 s 239
      meaning, CAA 2001s 234
    writing down allowance—
      amount of, CAA 2001 s 56
      disposal value of long-life assets, CAA 2001
        s 104
      entitlement, determination of, CAA 2001 s 5
      long-life assets, CAA 2001 s 102
  yacht, treatment of, PR 26/4/79

MAINTENANCE FUNDS FOR HISTORIC
    BUILDINGS
  higher rate less applicable rate tax, liability to, TA
    1988 s 694
  Schedule 4 direction, meaning, TA 1988 s 690
  settled and other property, treated as separate
    settlements, TA 1988 s 693
  settlor—
    not income of, TA 1988 s 691
    reimbursement of expenditure of, TA 1988 s 692

MAINTENANCE PAYMENTS
  child of the family, meaning, TA 1988 s 347B(7)
  court orders, under, retrospective dating, SP 6/81
  existing obligation—
    1989–90 onwards, effect of, FA 1988 s 38; RI
      100
    meaning, FA 1988 s 36(4)–(6)
  maintenance assessment under Child Support Act
    1991, TA 1988 s 347B(8)–(13)
  payer resident abroad, ESC A12
  qualifying—
    meaning, TA 1988 s 347B(1)
    treatment of, TA 1988 s 347B(2)–(5)
  relief for—
    concessionary relief, ESC A52
    restriction of, for 1994–95 et seq, FA 1994 s 79
  retrospective dating, SP 6/81
  school fees, payment of, SP 15/80

MANAGEMENT EXPENSES
  franked investment income, TA 1988 ss 242–244;
    RI 37
  insurance companies—
    general provisions, TA 1988 s 76
    regulatory levies, SI 1992/2744; ESC C21
  investment companies, TA 1988 s 75
  loan finance, incidental costs of, claim as, TA 1988
    s 77

MANUFACTURED DIVIDENDS AND
    INTEREST
  commencement, SI 1997/992, SI 1997/993
  company payments, TA 1988 Sch 16, SI 1997/992,
    SI 1997/993
  deemed payments, TA 1988 s 736B
  foreign income dividends—
    deductibility of payment in case of manufacturer,
      TA 1988 Sch 23A para 2A
    gilt-edged securities etc, TA 1988 Sch 23A para
      3A
    treatment, TA 1988 Sch 23A para 2
    UK securities, TA 1988 Sch 23A paras 3, 3A, SI
      1997/993
  general rules, TA 1988 Sch 23A; SI 1997/992, SI
    1997/993
  gilt-edged securities etc, interest representative of,
    TA 1988 Sch 23A para 3A
  liability for income tax, TA 1988 Sch 23A, SI
    1997/992
  overseas dividends—
    French indemnity payments, SI 1996/1826
    general provisions, TA 1988 Sch 23A para 4; SI
      1993/2004

MANUFACTURED DIVIDENDS AND
    INTEREST—*continued*
  overseas dividends—*continued*
    non-residents, payment to, SI 1993/1957
  pension funds, relief for, ESC C19
  regulations, scope of, TA 1988 Sch 23A para 8
  relief for, Regulations, SI 1995/3036
  sale and repurchase of securities: deemed
    manufactured payments, TA 1988
    ss 737A–737C
  stock lending arrangements, deemed manufactured
    payments, TA 1988 s 736B
  tax deducted, treatment of—
    company payments, accounting for tax on, SI
      1997/992, SI 1997/993
    general rules, TA 1988 s 737
  UK securities, TA 1988 Sch 23A paras 3, 3A, SI
    1997/992, SI 1997/993

MARKET GARDENING. *See* FARMING AND
    MARKET GARDENING

MARKET MAKERS
  circulating capital, securities held as, conversion of,
    TA 1988 s 473
  UK government securities, exclusion of interest on
    borrowed money, TA 1988 s 475

MARKET VALUE. *See also* VALUATION
  meaning, TCGA 1992 s 272
  quoted shares and securities—
    at 6 April 1965, TCGA 1992 Sch 11 para 6(2),
      (4)
    generally, TCGA 1992 s 273(3), (4), Sch 11 para
      7
  unit trust—
    at 6 April 1965, TCGA 1992 Sch 11 para 6(3)
    generally, TCGA 1992 s 272(5)
  shares, securities; previous no gain/no loss
    disposal, rebasing to 1982, SP 5/89; ESC
    D44

MARRIED COUPLE'S ALLOWANCE. *See*
    PERSONAL RELIEFS

MATERNITY PAY
  payments under, chargeable under Schedule E, TA
    1988 s 150
  statutory. *See* STATUTORY MATERNITY PAY
  taxation of, SP 1/78

MEANINGS. *See* WORDS AND PHRASES SECTION
    POST.

MEDICAL INSURANCE RELIEF
  approved benefits—
    approved treatments and associated services, SI
      1994/1518 para 6
    cash benefits, SI 1994/1518 para 7
    other rights, SI 1994/1518 para 8
  disentitlement, to SI 1994/1518 reg 3
  rate of relief, PR 4/12/96
  recovery of tax from payee, SI 1994/1518 regs 4, 5
  withdrawal of relief, F(No 2)A 1997 s 17

MEDICAL SUPPLIES AND EQUIPMENT
  humanitarian purposes, gifts for, FA 2002 s 55

MEMBER OF EUROPEAN PARLIAMENT
  cessation as member, resettlement grants on, TA
    1988 s 190(2)(c)

MEMBERS OF PARLIAMENT
  accommodation, expenditure on, TA 1988 s 198(4)
  dissolution, payments to, on, TA 1988 s 190(2)(a)
  expenses allowance, TA 1988 s 200

MEMBERS OF PARLIAMENT—*continued*
plant and machinery, disallowed expenditure, CAA 2001 s 34

MERGERS DIRECTIVE
non-UK trade, transfer of, TA 1988 s 815A
text of, 90/434/EEC
transfer of trade between EC companies, share exchange—
in UK, TCGA 1992 ss 140A, 140B
outside UK, TCGA 1992 ss 140C, 140D

MIGRATION OF COMPANIES. *See also* NON-RESIDENT COMPANIES
consent, TA 1988 s 765; RI 221
control, meaning, TA 1988 s 840
debenture, meaning, TA 1988 s 767(5)
director, meaning, TA 1988 s 767(5)
EC member states, movements of capital between, Capital Movements Directive—
implementation in UK, TA 1988 s 765A; SI 1990/1671; SP 2/92
text of, 88/361/EEC
funds (in relation to insurance company), meaning, TA 1988 s 767(5)
insurance company, meaning, TA 1988 s 767(5)
offences, TA 1988 s 766
outstanding tax, payment of—
arrangements for, FA 1988 s 130
liability of other persons for, FA 1988 s 132
penalties, FA 1988 s 131
procedure for, SP 2/90
share, meaning, TA 1988 s 767(5)
transfer, meaning, TA 1988 s 767(5)

MILEAGE ALLOWANCE. *See* FIXED PROFIT CAR SCHEME

MILK QUOTAS
permanent cuts, compensation for, RI 67
request to practitioners, RI 68
rollover relief, TCGA 1992 s 155 Class 5
superlevy, deduction for, RI 77

MINERAL EXPLORATION AND ACCESS
expenditure incurred on, deductibility, TA 1988 s 91C

MINERAL EXTRACTION
allowance. *See* MINERAL EXTRACTION ALLOWANCES
expenditure incurred for, CAA 2001 s 160
meaning, CAA 2001 s 396
pre-trading expenditure, CAA 2001 s 161

MINERAL EXTRACTION ALLOWANCES
availability of, CAA 2001 s 394
balancing allowance—
amount of, CAA 2001 s 418
ceasing to work mineral deposits, on, CAA 2001 s 428
discontinuance of trade, on, CAA 2001 s 431
disposal of asset, on, CAA 2001 s 430
employees abroad, ceasing to use buildings or works for benefit of, CAA 2001 s 429
entitlement to, CAA 2001 s 417
giving up exploration, search or inquiry, on, CAA 2001 s 427
pre-trading expenditure, for, CAA 2001 s 426
balancing charge—
amount of, CAA 2001 s 418
entitlement to, CAA 2001 s 417
contribution allowances, CAA 2001 s 541
demolition costs, treatment of, CAA 2001 s 433
development, meaning, CAA 2001 s 436
disposal receipt, meaning, CAA 2001 s 420

MINERAL EXTRACTION ALLOWANCES—*continued*
disposal values—
amount of, CAA 2001 s 423
capital sum, receipt of, CAA 2001 s 425
disposal of or ceasing to use asset, CAA 2001 s 421
disposal receipt, meaning, CAA 2001 s 420
interest in land, of, CAA 2001 s 424
permitted development, use of asset other than for, CAA 2001 s 422
first year, CAA 2001 ss 416A, 416C, 416D
artificially inflated claims, CAA 2001 s 416E
giving effect to, CAA 2001 s 432
mineral asset—
acquiring, qualifying expenditure—
buildings or structures ceasing to be used, CAA 2001 s 405
generally, CAA 2001 s 403
premium relief previously allowed, reduction on, CAA 2001 s 406
previous trader, owned by, CAA 2001 s 407
undeveloped market value of land, exclusion of, CAA 2001 s 404
group, transfer within, CAA 2001 ss 412, 413
meaning, CAA 2001 s 397
mineral exploration and access—
meaning, CAA 2001 s 396
qualifying expenditure—
nature of, CAA 2001 s 400
plant or machinery, pre-trading expenditure on, CAA 2001 s 402
pre-trading, CAA 2001 ss 401, 402
offshore oil infrastructure—
decommissioning expenditure, meaning, CAA 2001 s 161B
meaning, CAA 2001 s 161A
reuse of, CAA 2001 s 161D
qualifying expenditure—
employees abroad, contribution to buildings or works for benefit of, CAA 2001 s 415
excluded expenditure, CAA 2001 s 399
historic costs, limited by reference to—
assets generally, CAA 2001 s 411
group, transfers of mineral assets within, CAA 2001 ss 412, 413
UK oil licence, CAA 2001 s 410
main types of, relationship between, CAA 2001 s 398
meaning, CAA 2001 s 395
mineral asset, on acquiring—
buildings or structures ceasing to be used, CAA 2001 s 405
generally, CAA 2001 s 403
premium relief previously allowed, reduction on, CAA 2001 s 406
previous trader, owned by, CAA 2001 s 407
undeveloped market value of land, exclusion of, CAA 2001 s 404
mineral exploration and access, on—
nature of, CAA 2001 s 400
plant or machinery, pre-trading expenditure on, CAA 2001 s 402
pre-trading, CAA 2001 ss 401, 402
planning application, SP 4/78
restoration, on, CAA 2001 s 416
second-hand assets, on—
non-traders, acquired from, CAA 2001 s 409
oil licence, acquisition from non-trader, CAA 2001 s 408
previous trader, mineral asset owned by, CAA 2001 s 407
unrelieved, CAA 2001 s 419
works likely to become valueless, on, CAA 2001 s 414
relevant planning enactments, CAA 2001 s 436(2)

PAYE—*continued*

  regulations—*continued*

    tax-free emoluments, SI 1993/744 reg 22

    troncs, SI 1993/744 reg 5

    underpayments, collection of, SI 1993/744
      regs 101, 107, 108

  repayments of unemployment benefit etc, persons
    claiming, to, TA 1988 s 204

  settlement agreements, TA 1988 s 206A

  share options etc, gains from, TA 1988 s 203FB;
    FA 1998 s 67

  shares ceasing to be subject to plan, FA 2001 Sch 8
    para 94

  trading arrangements within, TA 1988
    ss 203F–203H; FA 1998 ss 64–66

  year end adjustments, informal, SP A11

PAYMENT OF TAX

  cheque, by, TMA 1970 s 70A; FA 1994 Sch 19
    para 22

  corporation tax, TMA 1970 s 59D; FA 1994 s 195

  electronic transfer, by, PR 1/4/93

  foot-and-mouth disease, relief in case of, FA 2001
    s 107

  income tax, on account of, TMA 1970 s 59A

  instalments, by, TA 1988 s 34(8); TCGA 1992
    s 280; PR 22/6/72

  payments made before passing of Finance Act,
    adjustments for—

    over-deductions, TA 1988 s 822

    under-deductions, TA 1988 s 821

PAYROLL GIVING SCHEME

  agency costs, contribution by employer to, TA
    1988 s 86A

  operation of scheme, TA 1988 s 202; FA 2000
    s 38; SI 1986/2211

PENALTIES

  accounts, incorrect—

    capital gains tax, TMA 1970 ss 95, 97

    corporation tax, TMA 1970 ss 96, 97

    income tax, TMA 1970 ss 95, 97

  appeal against determination, TMA 1970 s 100B

  award of, summary power of appeal
    Commissioners, TMA 1970 s 53

  certificate of non-liability to income tax, incorrect—

    provision fraudulently or negligently, TMA 1970
    s 99A(*a*)

    undertaking in, failure to comply with, TMA
    1970 s 99A(*b*)

  court, proceedings before—

    Court of Session (as Court of Exchequer), TMA
    1970 s 100D

    High Court, TMA 1970 s 100D

  criminal prosecution, interaction with, TMA 1970
    s 104; SP 2/88

  deduction of income tax, refusal to allow, TMA
    1970 s 106(1)

  documents, failure to produce, TMA 1970 s 97AA

  evidence of profits, in proceedings, TMA 1970
    s 101

  failure to make return, for—

    capital gains tax, TMA 1970 s 93

    corporation tax, TMA 1970 s 94

    income tax, TMA 1970 s 93

    partnership, TMA 1970 s 93A

  General Commissioners, proceedings before, TMA
    1970 s 100C

  incorrect return, assisting in preparation of, TMA
    1970 s 99

  incorrect return, for—

    capital gains tax, TMA 1970 ss 95, 97

    corporation tax, TMA 1970 ss 96, 97

    income tax, TMA 1970 ss 95, 97

    partnership, TMA 1970 s 95A(2)

  Inland Revenue fines, recovery of, IRRA 1890 s 36

PENALTIES—*continued*

  interest on, TMA 1970 s 103A

  landfill tax, treatment of, TA 1988 s 827(1C)

  late filing, automatic penalties, TMA 1970 s 98A;
    ESC B45; SP A14

  mitigation by Commissioners of Inland Revenue,
    IRRA 1890 s 35(1); TMA 1970 s 102

  recovery of, by Commissioners of Inland Revenue,
    IRRA 1890 s 36

  return for, failure to make—

    capital gains tax, TMA 1970 s 93

    corporation tax, TMA 1970 s 94

    income tax, TMA 1970 s 93

  return, incorrect—

    capital gains, TMA 1970 ss 95, 97

    corporation tax, TMA 1970 ss 96, 97

    income tax, TMA 1970 ss 95, 97

  Scotland, criminal liability for false statements to
    obtain allowances, TMA 1970 s 107

  Special Commissioners, proceedings before, TMA
    1970 s 100C

  special returns, application to, TMA 1970 s 98

  tax geared, two or more, for same tax, TMA 1970
    s 97A

  time limits, TMA 1970 s 103

  unpaid tax, surcharge on—

    capital gains tax, TMA 1970 s 59C

    income tax, TMA 1970 s 59C

  value added tax, treatment of, TA 1988 s 827(1)

PENSION BUSINESS

  insurance company—

    charge to tax, TA 1988 s 436

    exemption from tax, TA 1988 s 438

    repayment of tax credits and deducted tax, on
    account, procedure for, SI 1992/2326

  meaning, TA 1988 s 431B

PENSION FUNDS

  tax credit, withdrawal of entitlement, F(No 2)A
    1997 s 19

PENSION SCHEMES, UNAPPROVED

  benefits under, charge to tax, TA 1988 ss 596A,
    596B, 596C

  closed or frozen schemes, changes after 5 April
    1980, ESC A33

  expenses of, prohibition of deductions for, FA 1989
    s 76

PENSIONS. *See also* FOREIGN PENSIONS;
  OCCUPATIONAL PENSION SCHEMES; PENSION
  SCHEMES, UNAPPROVED; PERSONAL
  PENSION SCHEMES

  armed forces, PR 29/6/78

  disability, excess over ordinary level, exemption
    for, ESC A62

  divorce, sharing on, SI 2000/1085, PR April 2000

  foreign—

    1/10th relief, TA 1988 s 196

    charge to tax on, TA 1988 s 58

  taxable under Schedule E—

    generally, TA 1988 s 19(1) paras 2–4

    voluntary, TA 1988 s 133

PERMANENT HEALTH INSURANCE. *See*
  BENEFITS IN KIND

PERSONAL ALLOWANCE. *See* PERSONAL
  RELIEFS

PERSONAL EQUITY PLAN (PEP)

  allotment or non-allotment of shares in certain
    circumstances, SI 1989/469 reg 4(3)(*aa*),
    (3A)

  cash deposit, interest on, SI 1989/469 regs 27(2),
    18

RETURNS—*continued*
  companies—
    enquiries into, Revenue power to make—
      generally, TMA 1970 s 11AB
      insurance company with non-annual actuarial
        investigations, TMA 1970 s 11AD
      non-annual accounting of general insurance
        business, TMA 1970 s 11AC
    records to be kept, TMA 1970 s 12B
    requirement to make, TMA 1970 s 11; FA 1990
      s 91
    section 11 notice, TMA 1970 s 11(1)
    self-assessment, to include—
      friendly societies with non-annual actuarial
        investigations, TMA 1970 s 11AE
      generally, TMA 1970 ss 11AA
      non-annual accounting of general insurance
        business, TMA 1970 s 11AC
      non-annual actuarial investigations, insurance
        companies with, TMA 1970 s 11AD
  delay in rendering, interest and penalties, SP A14,
    SP 3/88, SP 6/89
  determination of tax where not delivered, TMA
    1970 s 28C
  electronic lodgement, TMA 1970 Sch 3A; SI 1997/
    57; SP 1/97
  enquiries—
    Revenue, power to make—
      company—
        friendly societies with non-annual actuarial
          investigations, TMA 1970 s 11AE
        generally, TMA 1970 s 11AB; FA 1994
          s 183
        insurance companies with non-annual
          actuarial investigations, TMA 1970
          s 11AD
        non-annual accounting of general insurance
          business, TMA 1970 s 11AC
      partnership, TMA 1970 s 12AC
      self-assessment, for purposes of, TMA 1970
        s 9A, SP 1/99
  European economic interest grouping (EEIG)—
    requirement to make, TMA 1970 s 12A
  failure to make—
    penalty for—
      capital gains tax, TMA 1970 s 93
      corporation tax, TMA 1970 s 94
      income tax, TMA 1970 s 93
      partnership return, TMA 1970 s 93A
  form of, prescribed by Commissioners of Inland
    Revenue, TMA 1970 s 113; PR 16/8/90
  late returns—
    interest charged, SP A14
    penalties for, ESC B46; SP A14
  loss, destruction or damage to, TMA 1970 s 112
  partnership—
    contents, TMA 1970 s 12AA(6), (7)
    enquiries into, Revenue power to make, TMA
      1970 s 12AC
    generally, TMA 1970 s 12AA
    records to be kept, TMA 1970 s 12B
    requirement to make, TMA 1970 ss 8, 12AA(2),
      (3)
    statement, to include, TMA 1970 s 12AB
  personal—
    records to be kept, TMA 1970 s 12B
    requirement to make, TMA 1970 s 8
    self-assessment, to include, TMA 1970 s 9
  records to be kept, TMA 1970 s 12B
  substitute forms, use of, SP 5/87
  total income, TA 1988 s 836
  trustees—
    enquiries into, Revenue power to make, FA 1994
      s 180
    records to be kept, TMA 1970 s 12B
    requirement to make, TMA 1970 s 8A
    self-assessment, to include, TMA 1970 s 9

RETURNS—*continued*
  trustees—*continued*
    wrong period, amendment of return made for,
      TMA 1970 ss 28AA, 28AB

REVERSE PREMIUM
  arrangements not at arm's length, FA 1999 Sch 6
    para 3
  capital allowances, receipts taken into account for,
    FA 1999 Sch 6 para 5
  connected persons, FA 1999 Sch 6 para 8
  insurance companies, special rules for, FA 1999
    Sch 6 para 4
  main residence, exclusion of transactions relating
    to, FA 1999 Sch 6 para 6
  sale and lease-back arrangement, exclusion of
    consideration under, FA 1999 Sch 6 para 7
  tax treatment, FA 1999 s 54, Sch 6

ROLLOVER RELIEF. *See* REPLACEMENT OF
  BUSINESS ASSETS

ROMAN CATHOLIC COMMUNITIES. *See*
  RELIGIOUS COMMUNITIES

ROYAL ULSTER CONSTABULARY. *See* ARMED
  FORCES

ROYALTIES
  basic rate, charge to, TA 1988 s 3(*b*)
  owner abroad, requirement to deduct tax, TA 1988
    s 536, 537B
  payment from abroad, double taxation relief on,
    ESC B8
  special relationship, TA 1988 s 808B

RULINGS
  post-transaction, PR 26/9/96
  pre-transaction, PR 26/9/96

S

SALE AND LEASEBACK
  consideration received, taxation of, TA 1988 s 780
  finance leases. *See* MACHINERY AND PLANT
  reliefs, limitation on, TA 1988 s 779

SALE AND REPURCHASE OF SECURITIES
  (''REPOS'')
  agreement in force—
    generally, TA 1988 s 731(2B)–(2F)
    meaning, TA 1988 s 731 (2D)
  deemed manufactured payments, TA 1988
    ss 737A–737E
  gilt interest payable gross—
    general provisions, TA 1988 s 51A
  price differential, treatment of, TA 1988 ss 730A,
    730B; TCGA 1992 s 263A

SATELLITES
  rollover relief, TCGA 1992 s 155 Class 3

SAVINGS
  lower rate, application of, to income from, TA 1988
    ss 1A, 4(1A)

**SAVINGS RELATED SHARE OPTION
  SCHEME.** *See* SHARE OPTION SCHEMES

SCHEDULE A
  agent, collection of tax from, TA 1988 s 23
  assignment, meaning of in Scotland, TA 1988
    s 24(5)
  business treated as trade, CAA 2001 s 15
  caravan, application to, TA 1988 s 15(1) para 3
  charge to tax—
    mutual business, TA 1988 s 21C

TRADE—*continued*
debt written-back, taxability of, RI 238
discontinuance, ESC C16
financial services levies and repayments, treatment
of, TA 1988 ss 76A, 76B
in UK, transfer between EC companies, share
exchange—
anti-avoidance, TCGA 1992 s 140B
relief, TCGA 1992 s 140A
nature or conduct of, major change in, together
with change in ownership—
meaning, SP 10/91
trading loss—
carry back, TA 1988 s 768A
carry forward, TA 1988 s 768
outside UK, transfer for shares—
between EC companies—
anti-avoidance, TCGA 1992 s 140D
relief, TCGA 1992 s 140C
other transfers, TCGA 1992 s 140

TRADE MARKS
registration fees—
deduction for, TA 1988 s 83

TRADE UNIONS
exemption of, TA 1988 s 467(1)–(3)
meaning, TA 1988 s 467(4)(*a*), (*ba*), (*c*)
provident benefits, expenses for purpose of, SP 6/
78, SP 1/84

TRADING EXPENDITURE
pre-trading—
incurred by another person, RI 32
revenue, TA 1988 s 401

TRADING LOSS. *See* LOSS RELIEF FOR INCOME
TAX

TRADING STOCK
appropriations—
from, TCGA 1992 s 161(2)
to, TCGA 1992 s 161(1), (3), (4)
provisions, use of formulae, RI 98
valuation of—
cessation of trade, on, TA 1988 ss 100, 102
motor dealers, RI 83

TRAINING AND ENTERPRISE COUNCILS
contributions to, deductibility for, TA 1988 s 79A

TRAINING COURSES. *See* EDUCATION AND
TRAINING

TRANSACTIONS IN SECURITIES
abnormal dividend, meaning, TA 1988 s 709(4)–(6)
appeals—
procedure for, TA 1988 s 705
tribunal, TMA 1970 s 6(1)(*c*), Sch 1 Pt I; TA
1988 s 706
clearance procedure, TA 1988 s 707; SP 3/80
directors' pension scheme, use of, RD 6
information, power to obtain, TA 1988 s 708
prescribed circumstances A–E, TA 1988 s 704
tax advantage—
cancellation of, procedure for, TA 1988 s 703
meaning, TA 1988 s 709(1)

TRANSFER OF ASSETS ABROAD
accrued income scheme, application to, TA 1988
s 742(4)–(7)
associated operation, meaning, TA 1988 s 742(1)
double charge to tax, prevention of, TA 1988 s 744
income tax, charge to, TA 1988 s 743, F(No 2)A
1997 s 34, Sch 4 para 20
information, power to obtain, TA 1988 s 745

TRANSFER OF ASSETS ABROAD—*continued*
Ireland, Republic of, persons resident in, TA 1988
s 746
non-resident company, treatment of, TA 1988
s 742(8)
non-transferor—
exemption from liability, TA 1988 s 741
liability of, general rules, TA 1988 s 740
prevention of avoidance—
exemption from provisions, TA 1988 s 741
general rules, TA 1988 s 739, RI 201

TRANSFER OF BUSINESS TO A COMPANY
group, transfer within, TCGA 1992 s 101A
in UK, transfer for shares between EC companies—
anti-avoidance, TCGA 1992 s 140B
EC Mergers Directive, 90/434/EEC—
chargeable gains, tax on, relief for, TCGA
1992 s 140A
outside UK, transfer for shares—
between EC companies—
anti-avoidance, TCGA 1992 s 140D
EC Mergers Directive, 90/434/EEC
relief, chargeable gains, tax on, TCGA 1992
s 140C
relief, double taxation, TA 1988 s 815A
not within EC Mergers Directive, TCGA s 140
rollover relief, TCGA 1992 s 162
election as to, TCGA 1992 s 162A
scheme of reconstruction or amalgamation,
treatment of TCGA 1992 s 139
transferee becoming investment trust, TCGA 1992
ss 101, 101A
venture capital trust, to, TCGA 1992, ss 101B,
101C

TRANSFER OF SECURITIES. *See* SHARES AND
SECURITIES

TRANSFER PRICING. *See* ASSOCIATED PERSONS

TRANSMISSION FACILITIES
sharing of—
capital allowances, treatment of, FA 1991 s 78
chargeable gains, relief for, TCGA 1992 s 267

TRANSPORT VOUCHERS
exclusion from tax charge, TA 1988 s 141(6)
meaning, TA 1988 s 141(7)

TRAVELLING EXPENSES
construction industry, site-based staff, allowances
for, ESC [13/2/81]
foreign travel—
board and lodging expenses, PR 1/11/76
double deduction, prevention of, TA 1988
s 194(9)
duties performed wholly outside UK, TA 1988
s 194(2)–(6)
employee's family, of, RI 237
non-domiciled persons, TA 1988 s 195
removal expenses and benefits, interaction with,
TA 1988 Sch 11A paras 12(4), 21(7), (8)
spouse or child, TA 1988 s 194(2)
travel to and from UK, TA 1988 s 194(3)–(8)
HM Forces on leave, facilities for, exemption from
tax on, TA 1988 s 197
ordinary commuting and private travel, exclusion—
area-based employee, TA 1988 Sch 12A para 7
generally, TA 1988 Sch 12A para 1
ordinary commuting, meaning, TA 1988 Sch
12A paras 2(1), 3
permanent workplace, TA 1988 Sch 12A
paras 4, 6
private travel, meaning, TA 1988 Sch 12A
paras 2(2), 3

WORDS AND PHRASES

Words in brackets indicate the context in which the word or phrase is used.

asset—*continued*
  (transfers abroad), TA 1988 s 742(9)
  transfers abroad, TA 1988 s 742(9)(*a*)
assigned contract (life annuity), TA 1988 s 544(2)
assigned policy, TA 1988 s 544(1)
assignment (Scotland), TA 1988 s 24(5)
associate—
  (close company), TA 1988 s 417(3)
  (community investment tax relief), FA 2002 Sch 16
    para 50
  (entrepreneurs relief), TCGA 1992 s 164N(1)
  (enterprise investment scheme), TA 1988 s 417(3),
    (4)
  (investment relief), FA 2000 Sch 15 para 99
  (services provided through intermediary), FA 2000
    Sch 12 para 19
  (tonnage tax), FA 2000 Sch 22 para 144
  (venture capital trust), TA 1988 Sch 28B para 5(5)
associated—
  company, TA 1988 ss 416(1), 502(3), 774(4)(*d*);
    FA 2000 Sch 8 para 126; ESC C9; SP C4
    para 2; PR 21/10/83
  disposals (retirement relief), TCGA 1992 s 164(7)
  operation, TA 1988 s 742(1)
  payment (revocable settlement), TA 1988 s 678(3)
  person (leasing), TA 1988 s 783(10)
  state, IA 1978 Sch 1
assurance undertaking, SI 1998/1870 reg 2(1)
assured tenancy—
  (capital allowances), CAA 2001 s 490(3)
  investing in housing, TA 1988 s 508B(7)
author, TA 1988 ss 534(7), 535(11)
authorised insurance company, TA 1988 s 630(1)
authorised unit trust, TA 1988 s 468(6), SI 1989/
    469 reg 2(1), SI 1998/1870 reg 2(1)(*b*), SI
    2001/117 reg 2(1)
authority exercising or having compulsory powers,
    TCGA 1992 s 243(5)
available accommodation, TA 1988 s 336(3),
    TCGA 1992 s 9(4)
averaging (farming and market gardening), TA
    1988 s 96
back-up officer, SI 2000/2129 reg 2
bank, TA 1988 s 840A
Bank of England, IA 1978 Sch 1
Bank of Ireland, IA 1978 Sch 1
banker, TA 1988 ss 45, 123(1)
banking business, ordinary course of, SP 12/91;
    SP 4/96
bareboat charter terms, FA 2000 Sch 22 para 143
base rate, SI 2000/2129 reg 2
base year, FA 1984 Sch 14 paras 4(2), 14(5)
basic life assurance business, TA 1988 s 431(2);
    FA 1989 s 84
basic rate commutable pension, TA 1988 Sch 23
    para 3(4)
basic rate lump sum, TA 1988 Sch 23 para 3(4)
basic rate non-commutable pension, TA 1988 Sch
    23 para 4(4)
basic valuation (exchange gains and losses), FA
    1993 s 159
basis year—
  (delayed overseas income), TA 1988 s 585(9)
beneficiary, SI 2000/2089 reg 2(1)
benefit officer, TA 1988 s 152(7)
benefits received (absolute interest), TA 1988
    s 697(3)
Board, the, TMA 1970 s 1(1); TA 1988 s 832(1);
    TCGA 1992 s 288(1); F(No 2)A 1997 s 3,
    Sch 2
body of persons, TMA 1970 s 118(1); TA 1988
    s 832(1)
bonus date (share option scheme), TA 1988 Sch
    9 para 17
bonus issue, F(No 2)A 1997 s 35, Sch 5 para 6
bonus share capital, TA 1988 s 251(1)
borrower (student loans), SI 2000/944 reg 2

branch or agency, TMA 1970 s 118(1); TA 1988
    s 834(1); TCGA 1992 s 10(6); PR 31/12/79
British citizen, SI 2000/2129 reg 2
British citizen from the Channel Islands or Isle
    of Man, SI 2000/2129 reg 2
British Islands, IA 1978 Sch 1
British possession, IA 1978 Sch 1
broker—
  (controlled foreign company), TA 1988 Sch 25
    para 9(2)
  (returns), TMA 1970 s 21(7)
building, CAA 2001 s 21
building regulations, IA 1978 Sch 1
building society, TA 1988 s 832(1); TCGA 1992
    s 288(1)
bus, SI 2002/205 reg 2
business—
  entertainment, TA 1988 s 577(5)
  establishment (controlled foreign company), TA
    1988 Sch 25 para 7(1)
  major change in the nature or conduct of, SP 10/91
  travel, TA 1988 s 168(5)(*c*), Sch 12AA para 2
calculation period, FA 1984 Sch 14 para 5(1)
capital allowance, TA 1988 s 832(1); TCGA 1992
    s 41(4)
capital amount, TA 1988 s 777(13)
capital consideration, CAA 2001 s 390(2)
capital distribution, TCGA 1992 s 122(5)(*b*)
capital expenditure—
  (capital allowances), CAA 2001 ss 4, 10
  (cemeteries), TA 1988 s 91(2), (8)
capital gains, TCGA 1992 s 1(1)
capital interest, TA 1988 Sch 25 para 11(4)
capital payment (beneficiary), TCGA 1992 s 97(1)
capital payment received, TCGA 1992 s 97(5)
capital redemption business, TA 1988 s 458(3)
capital redemption policy, TA 1988 s 539(3), FA
    2002 Sch 26 para 12(2)
capital sum—
  (capital allowances), CAA 2001 s 4
  (capital gains tax), TCGA 1992 s 22(3)
  (leased assets), TA 1988 s 785
  (revocable settlement), TA 1988 s 677(9)
capital value, CAA 2001 s 331(1)
car, TA 1988 s 168(5)(*a*), Sch 12AA para 3(2);
    CAA 2001 s 81
caravan, TA 1988 s 367(1)
care, TA 1988 s 155A(7)
carrying on a business of holding investments, RI
    229
cash equivalent (beneficial loan), TA 1988 Sch 7
    para 3
cash voucher, TA 1988 ss 143(3), 203F; SI 1994/
    1212 reg 3
central funds, IA 1978 Sch 1
certificate of deposit, TA 1988 ss 56(5), 56A
certificate of tax deposit, FA 1995 s 139
Chamber of Shipping, SI 2000/2129 reg 2
Channel Islands (tax credit relief), TA 1988
    s 794(2)(*a*)
charge on income, TA 1988 s 338(2)
charge on residue, TA 1988 ss 701(6), 702(*b*)
chargeable business asset, TCGA 1992 Sch 6
    paras 7(3),12(2); PR 17/10/78
chargeable company (leaving group), TCGA 1992
    Sch 6 para 12(2)
chargeable event—
  (capital redemption policy), TA 1988 s 545(1)
  (employee share ownership trust), FA 1989 s 69
  (life annuity contract), TA 1988 s 542(1)
  (life policy), TA 1988 s 540(1)
chargeable expense (non-cash voucher), TA 1988
    s 141(1)
chargeable gain, TCGA 1992 s 15(2)
chargeable intangible asset, FA 2002 Sch 29 para
    137
chargeable payment (demerger), TA 1988 s 214(1)

dealing, TA 1988 Sch 27 para 4(2)(*b*)
dealing in commodities, TA 1988 Sch 27 para 4(2)
death, disclaimer following, TCGA 1992 s 62(6), (8), (9)
debentures, TA 1988 s 767(5)
debt, SI 1998/3177 reg 2(1)
debt on a security, TCGA 1992 s 132(3)(*b*); PR June 1969
decommissioning expenditure, CAA 2001 161B
decoration for valour, TA 1988 s 317; TCGA 1992 s 268
deductible contributions (redundancy), TA 1988 Sch 21 para 1(1)
deed of arrangement, TCGA 1992 s 66(5)
deemed disposal (non-resident companies), TCGA 1992 ss 185–187
deemed sum (accrued income scheme), TA 1988 ss 714(2), (6), 715
default in interest (accrued income scheme), TA 1988 s 718
deferral relief, TCGA 1992 Sch 5B para 19(2)
deferred charges (gains before 31 March 1982), TCGA 1992 Sch 4
delayed remittances, TA 1988 s 585; TCGA 1992 s 279
Deltaplus limit, SI 1992/568 reg 5
demerger, TA 1988 s 218
dependent relative, TCGA 1992 s 226
dependent subsidiary, FA 1988 s 86
deposit—
  composite rate deposit, TA 1988 s 481(4)
  (deposit-taker), TA 1988 s 481(3)
  qualifying time deposit, TA 1988 s 482(6)
  relevant, TA 1988 s 481(4), (5)
deposit-taker, TA 1988 s 481(3)
depositary interest, SI 1989/469 reg 2(1); SI 2001/117 reg 2(1)
depreciating asset, TCGA 1992 s 154(7)
derivative, SI 1998/3177 reg 2(1)
designated area, FA 1973 s 38(2)(*e*); TA 1988 ss 502(2)(*a*), 830(2)(*c*); TCGA 1992 s 276(2)(*e*)
designated educational establishment, TA 1988 s 84(5)
detached national exports, ESC A84
development corporation, TA 1988 s 560(5)
development licence, TA 1988 s 312(1)
direction period (controlled foreign company), TA 1988 Sch 26 para 3(1)(*a*)
director—
  (benefits), TA 1988 s 168(8)
  (close company), TA 1988 s 417(5)
  (receipts basis assessment), TA 1988 s 202B(5), (6)
  (share options), TA 1988 s 136(5)
  (venture capital trust), TA 1988 Sch 28B para 5(5)
director's or higher-paid employment, TA 1988 s 167(1)
disabled person's trusts, TA 1988 s 715(8); TCGA 1992 Sch 1 para 1(1)
discontinuance—
  terminal loss, TA 1988 s 389(4)
  trade, profession or vocation, TA 1988 s 63
discovery, TMA 1970 s 29(3); SP 8/91
discretionary trust, SI 2000/2089 reg 2(1)
dispensation, TA 1988 ss 144(1), (2), 166
disposal—
  (capital gains tax), TCGA 1992 s 21(2)
  (community investment tax relief), FA 2002 Sch 16 para 48
  (deep discount securities), TA 1988 Sch 4 para 7
  (held-over gain), TCGA 1992 Sch 7 para 4(3)
  (offshore fund), TA 1988 s 757(2)
  equalisation element, involving, TA 1988 Sch 28 para 6(3)
  event, CAA 2001 s 60(2)
  part, TCGA 1992 Sch A1 para 22(4)

disposal—*continued*
  receipt, CAA 2001 ss 60(1), 420
  within marriage, TCGA 1992 Sch 5B para 19(3)(*b*)
distributable pool, TA 1988 Sch 8 para 1
distribution (corporation tax), TA 1988 ss 14(2), 209, 418(1)
distribution period (unit trust), TA 1988 ss 468(6), 469(6)
diver, TA 1988 s 314
dividend—
  (controlled foreign company), TA 1988 Sch 25 para 2(3)
  (Schedule C), TA 1988 s 45
  (Treasury, in name of), TA 1988 s 49(3)
dividend manufacturer, TA 1988 Sch 23A para 1
diving supervisor, TA 1988 s 314
documents, TMA 1970 ss 19A, 20D(3), 33A, CJPA 2001 s 66(1)
domestic premises, TA 1988 s 155A(7)
donatio mortis causa, TCGA 1992 s 62(5)
double taxation relief arrangements, TA 1988 s 788; TCGA 1992 s 288(1), CAA 2001 s 105(4)
dredging, CAA 2001 s 484(3)
dual resident, TCGA 1992 ss 159, 160; FA 1994 ss 249–251
dual resident company, SI 2001/1156 reg 2
due date (payment of tax), TMA 1970 s 59C(12)
dwelling-house, CAA 2001 s 531(1)
earned income, TA 1988 s 833(4)
earnings basis, TA 1988 s 110(3)
easement, TA 1988 s 119(3)
EC certificate of conformity, TA 1988 Sch 6 para 5B
EC type-approval certificate, TA 1988 Sch 6 para 5B
EEA Agreement, SI 1989/469 reg 2(1), SI 1998/1870 reg 2(1), SI 1999/881 reg 2, SI 2000/2129 reg 2; SI 2001/117 reg 2(1)
EEA State, SI 1989/469 reg 2(1), SI 1998/1870 reg 2(1), SI 2000/2129 reg 2(1); SI 2001/117 reg 2(1)
effective officer complement, SI 2000/2129 reg 2(1)
ejectment (Northern Ireland), TMA 1970 s 117
electricity board, TA 1988 s 511(6)
electronic communications, FA 1999 s 132 (10)
electronic lodgement, TMA 1970 Sch 3A
eligible beneficiary, TCGA 1992 Sch A1 paras 7, 20, 22(1)
eligible officer trainee, SI 2000/2129 reg 7
eligible person—
  qualifying distributions, TA 1988 s 231(3C)
  repos, TA 1988 s 51A
eligible shares—
  (enterprise investment scheme), TA 1988 s 289(7); TCGA 1992 Sch 5B para 19(3)(*a*)
  (entrepreneurs relief), TCGA 1992 s 164N(1)
eligible sport, FA 2002 Sch 18 para 14
employee—
  (assessment, collection etc), TA 1988 s 203L(1)
  benefit trust, TA 1988 s 360A(5), Sch 8 para 7(5)
  (company), TA 1988 s 612(1)
  (emoluments, return of), TMA 1970 s 15(13)
  (liabilities and indemnity insurance), TA 1988 s 201AA; FA 1995 s 92
  (profit-related pay), TA 1988 s 169(2)
  (returns), TMA 1970 s 15(11)(*a*)
  (travelling expenses), TA 1988 Sch 12A para 1(2)
  (share options), TA 1988 s 136(5)
employee's disposal (retirement relief), TCGA 1992 Sch 6 para 4(1)(*b*)
employee share ownership plan, FA 2000 Sch 8 para 1
employer, TA 1988 s 203L(1); SI 2001/117 reg 2(1)
employer's association, TA 1988 s 467(4)(*b*), (*bb*)

group scheme (share option), TA 1988 Sch 9
  para 1(3)
guarantee payment (oil taxation), FA 1991
  s 63(1)(a)
guarantor (oil taxation), FA 1991 s 62(5)(b)
harbour authority, TA 1988 s 518(10)
harbour reorganisation scheme, TA 1988 s 518(10)
harm, FA 2001 Sch 22 para 31(1)
health service body, TA 1988 s 519A
heavier commercial vehicle, TA 1988 s 159AC(4)
held over gain, TCGA 1992 s 154(1)(a)
herd, TA 1988 Sch 5 para 8(1)
High Commissioner, TA 1988 s 320(4)
High Court, IA 1978 Sch 1
High Level Stop Loss Fund (Lloyd's), FA 1993
  s 184(1)
highway concession, CAA 2001 s 341(4)
highway undertaking, CAA 2001 s 341(3)
hire-purchase agreement, TA 1988 s 784(6)
holding company, TCGA 1992 Sch 7AC para
  26(3)
  (controlled foreign company), TA 1988 Sch 25
    para 12(1)
  (group relief), TA 1988 ss 229(1), 413(3)
  (overseas life assurance business), SI 2000/2089
    reg 2(1)
  (retirement relief), TCGA 1992 Sch 6 para 1(2)
  (taper relief), TCGA 1992 Sch A1 para 22(1); RI
    228
holiday accommodation, TA 1988 s 504(2)
house-boat, TA 1988 s 367(1)
housing—
  association, TA 1988 s 560(5)
hovercraft, TCGA 1992 s 155 Class 2
husbandry, CAA 2001 s 362
IMO number, SI 2000/2129 reg 2
incapacitated person, TMA 1970 s 118(1)
incapacity benefit, FA 1994 s 139
incidental costs—
  (capital gains tax), TCGA 1992 s 38(1)(c), (4)
  (obtaining finance), TA 1988 ss 77(6), 477B(3)
incidental overnight expenses, TA 1988 s 200A
inclusive price (car), TA 1988 s 168(5)(e)
income—
  distributed, TA 1988 s 689A(1)(a)
  patents, from, TA 1988 s 533(1), CAA 2001 s 483
  relevant earnings, TA 1988 s 644(1)
  support, TA 1988 ss 151, 152
Income Tax Acts, IA 1978 Sch 1; TA 1988
  s 831(1)(b)
incoming company, TCGA 1992 Sch 3 para 9(2)
incorporated friendly society, SI 1998/1870 reg
  2(1)
independent accountant (profit-related pay), TA
  1988 s 184
independent agent (non-resident person), FA 1995
  Sch 23 paras 6, 7
indexation allowance, TCGA 1992 s 53(1)
individual pension account, SI 2001/117 reg 4
individual savings account business, SI 1998/1871
  reg 3
industrial and provident society, SI 1989/469 reg
  2(1)
industrial assurance business, TA 1988 s 832(1)
industrial building or structure, CAA 2001
  s 271(2)
industrial or provident society, TA 1988
  s 486(12), SI 1998/1870 reg 2(1)
infant, TMA 1970 ss 73, 77, 118(1)
information, ACSA 2001 s 20(1)
informers, IRRA 1890 s 32
IHT undertaking, TCGA 1992 s 258(9)
initial dividend, TA 1988 Sch 25 para 4(1)(a)
initial storage (oil), TA 1988 s 502(2)
Inland Revenue, IRRA 1890 s 39; TMA 1970
  s 1(1); CAA 2001 s 576
inspector, TMA 1970 s 118(1); TA 1988 s 832(1)

insurance business, FA 2002 s 66(5)
insurance business transfer scheme, CAA 2001
  s 560(5)
insurance company—
  (generally), TA 1988 ss 659B, 659C; FA 1995 s 60
  (migration), TA 1988 s 767(5)
insurance contract, TA 1988 Sch 25 para 11(7)
intangible asset, FA 2002 Sch 29 para 2
intangible fixed asset, FA 2002 Sch 29 para 3
intellectual property, FA 2000 Sch 20 para 7
interest, TMA 1970 s21(7), TA 1988 ss 711(9),
  736B, 798(3), 832(1), Sch 23A
interest in land, TCGA 1992 s 164H(3), CAA
  2001 ss 175(1), 331(2)
interest in oil licence, TCGA 1992 s 196(5), CAA
  2001 s 552(4)
interest in possession, PR 12/2/76
interest in shares, TCGA 1992 Sch 7AC para 29
interest payment day (securities), TA 1988
  s 711(2)
interest period (securities), TA 1988 s 711(3)
interim claim, TA 1988 s 369(9), Sch 14 para
  7(5); SI 1989/2387 reg 6
interim payments (friendly societies), TA 1988
  Sch 15 para 3(11)
investment—
  advice, FA 1996 s 148(6)
  business—
    (community relief), FA 2002 Sch 16 para 2
    (controlled foreign company), TA 1988 Sch 25
      para 9
  company, TA 1988 s 130; SI 2000/2089 reg 2(1)
  exchange, TA 1988 s 841(3); TCGA 1992 s 285
  limited liability partnership, TA 1988 s 842(1)
  manager, TMA 1970 s 97(2); ESC B40; SP 15/91;
    RI 29
  relief, FA 2000 Sch 15 para 1
  reserve, TA 1988 s 431(2)
  trust, TA 1988 s 842(1), SI 1989/469 reg 2(1)
  trust holding, TA 1988 s 842(3); TCGA 1992
    s 100(1)
investor—
  (enterprise investment scheme) TCGA 1992 Sch
    5B para 1(1)(a)
  (venture capital trust), TCGA 1992 Sch 5C para
    1(1)(a)
investor protection scheme, TA 1988 s 76(8)
irregular payment (PAYE settlement agreement),
  SP 5/96
issue of shares, FA 2000 Sch 15 para 98
issuing company (non-resident policy), TA 1988
  Sch 15 para 24(1)
job release scheme, TA 1988 ss 150(a), 191
joint venture company, TCGA 1992 Sch 7AC
  para 24
know-how, TA 1988 s 533(7), CAA 2001 s 452
  (2)
land, IA 1978 Sch 1; TCGA 1992 s 288(1), FA
  2001 Sch 22 para 3(1)
land in a contaminated state, FA 2001 Sch 22
  para 3
Land Clauses Acts, IA 1978 Sch 1
large caravan, TA 1988 s 367(1)
large company, FA 2001 Sch 12 para 2
lease—
  (asset), TA 1988 s 789
  (capital allowances), CAA 2001 ss 393W, 360(1),
    383(3), 531(2)
  (capital gains tax), TCGA 1992 Sch 8
  (Schedule A), TMA 1970 ss 19(3)(a), 90(1); TA
    1988 s 24(1)
leasehold interest (Scotland), CAA 2001 ss 393W,
  360(2), 393(4), 531(3)
leasing (machinery and plant), CAA 2001
  s 105(1)
legal privilege, CJPA 2001 s 65

net relevant earnings, TA 1988 ss 623(6), 646(7)
new—
  association (constituency), TCGA 1992 s 264
  consideration, TA 1988 s 254(1), TCGA 1992
    s 217(6)
  holding (pooling), TCGA 1992 ss 104(3), 126(1)
  non-resident policy, TA 1988 Sch 15 para 24(1)
  parliamentary constituency, TCGA 1992 s 264(1)
  society (friendly society), TA 1988 s 466(2)
nil payment notice, FA 2001 s 58(3)
nominee (CGT), TCGA 1992 s 60
non-basis period, TA 1988 s 804(8)
non-cash voucher, TA 1988 ss 141(7), 203G; SI
  1994/1212 reg 6
non-financial trade, FA 2000 Sch 15 para 11
non-financial trading group, FA 2000 Sch 15 para
  12
non-marketable securities, TCGA 1992 s 121
non-qualifying distribution, TA 1988 s 233(2)
non-qualifying offshore fund, TA 1988 s 760(1)
non-resident, TCGA 1992 Sch 5B para 19(1)
non-resident group, TCGA 1992 s 14(4)
non-resident trust, FA 1984 s 70, Sch 14
non-taxable consideration, TA 1988 s 704E(3)
non-trading income, TA 1988 Sch 25 para 12(6)
non-voting fixed-rate preference shares, TA 1988
  Sch 25 para 2(7)
normal accounting practice, TA 1988 s 43A(2)
normal commercial loan, TA 1988 Sch 18 para
  1(5)
normal writing down allowance, CAA 2001
  s 126(1)
Northern Ireland—
  licence, TA 1988 s 312(1)
  proceedings in, TMA 1970 s 58
notional winding-up, TA 1988 Sch 18 para 3(2)
nuclear site, FA 2001 Sch 22 para 3(3)
nursing home, TA 1988 s 298(5), Sch 28B para
  5(1)
obtained by reason of employment (loan), TA
  1988 Sch 7 Pt I
official agent (consular), TA 1988 s 321(3)
official rate of interest, TA 1988 s 160(5); SI
  1989/1297 reg 5
officer, IRRA 1890 s 39
offshore fund, TA 1988 s 759(1)
offshore income gain, TA 1988 s 763
offshore infrastructure, CAA 2001 s 161A
oil, TA 1988 s 502(1), CAA 2001 s 556 (3)
oil and gas exploration and appraisal, TA 1988
  s 837B
oil exploration, TCGA 1992 s 164N(1)
oil exploration or exploitation, TCGA 1992 Sch 3
  para 7
oil extraction activities, TA 1988 s 502(1)
oil licence, CAA 2001 s 552(1)
oil rights, TA 1988 s 502(1)
oil rig—
  (enterprise investment scheme), TA 1988 s 298(5)
  (entrepreneurs' relief), TCGA 1992 s 164N(1)
  (venture capital trust), TA 1988 Sch 28B para 5(1)
old society (friendly society), TA 1988 s 465(1)
one estate, land managed as, TA 1988 ss 26, 31
open-ended investment company, FA 1995 s 152,
  SI 1997/1154, SI 1998/1870 reg 2(2), SI
  2001/117 reg 2(1)
operative event (pooling), TCGA 1992 s 110(7)
ordinary commuting, TA 1988 Sch 12A para 2(1)
ordinary Schedule A business, CAA 2001 s 16
ordinary share, TA 1988 s 210(4); TCGA 1992
  s 126(1)
ordinary share capital, TA 1988 s 832(1); TCGA
  1992 s 228(9), Sch 5B para 19(1)
ordinary trade debt, TA 1988 s 301(5)
outgoing company—
  (capital gains), TCGA 1992 Sch 3 para 9(2)
out placement counselling, TA 1988 s 589A, B

outstanding capital, TA 1988 Sch 25 para
  11(4)(*e*)
overlap profits and losses (Sch D Cases I and II),
  TA 1988 s 63A
overseas—
  company, TA 1988 s 759(6)
  customer, TA 1970 s 577(6)
  dividend, TA 1988 Sch 23A para 1
  group, RI 221
  life insurance company, TA 1988 s 431(1)
  public revenue dividend, TA 1988 s 45
  securities, TA 1988 s 732(4), Sch 23A para 1
  State authority, TA 1988 s 88A(4)
  tax, TA 1988 s 804(8), Sch 23A para 1
  tax credit, TA 1988 Sch 23A para 1
  territory, TA 1988 s 615(7)
owned directly or indirectly, TA 1988 s 838(2)
owner of copyright, TA 1988 s 536(1)
parallel pooling, TCGA 1992 s 112
parallel trades, TA 1988 s 292
parent company, TA 1988 ss 173(3),
  293(3A)–(3F)
parental responsibility, TA 1988 s 155A(7)
part disposal (CGT), TCGA 1992 s 21(2)
partial depreciation subsidy, CAA 2001 s 209
participant (profit sharing scheme), TA 1988
  s 186(2)
participant's salary, TA 1988 s 187(5)
participating company (share option scheme), TA
  1988 Sch 9 para 1(4)
participator, TA 1988 s 417(1)
passenger transport undertaking, TA 1988 s 141(7)
patent rights, TA 1988 s 533(1), CAA 2001 s 464
pay (profit-related), TA 1988 s 169(1)
PAYE regulations, TA 1988 s 203L(3)
payment (redundancy scheme), TA 1988 Sch 21
  para 1(1)
payment day (accrued income scheme), TA 1988
  s 711(2)
payment for group relief, TA 1988 s 402(6)
payment not out of profits or gains brought into
  charge, TA 1988 s 350(2)
payment (PAYE), TA 1988 s 203A
pension, TA 1988 s 615(7)
pension business, TA 1988 s 431B
Pensions (Increase) Acts, TA 1988 s 615(7)
pension tax credit withdrawal, F(No 2)A 1997
  s 19
period of absence (dwelling-house), TCGA 1992
  s 223(7)
period of account—
  corporation tax, TMA 1970 ss 11(5), 12AB(5)
  election for herd basis, TA 1988 Sch 5 paras 2(6),
    6(4)
  insurance, FA 2000 s 107(7)
period of default (payment of tax), TMA 1970
  s 59C(12)
period of retention (profit sharing scheme), TA
  1988 Sch 10 para 2
periodical payment, TA 1988 s 347B(7)
periodical return (insurance company), TA 1988
  s 431(1)
permanent health insurance, ESC A26
permanent interest bearing share, TCGA 1992
  s 117(11)(*b*), (12)
permanent workplace, TA 1988 Sch 12A para 4
person—
  chargeable (redundancy scheme), TA 1988 Sch 21
    para 1(1)
personal company, TCGA 1992 Sch 6 para 1(2)
personal equity plan (PEP), TA 1988 s 331;
  TCGA 1992 s 151
personal injuries, TA 1988 s 329(4)
personal pension—
  arrangements, TA 1988 s 630
  scheme, TA 1988 s 630
  scheme administrator, TA 1988 ss 630, 638(1)

personal pension—*continued*
  unit trust, SI 2001/117 reg 2(1)
personal representative, TA 1988 s 701(4)
pilots' benefit fund, TA 1988 s 607(4)
plan investment, SI 1989/469 reg 2(1)
plan investor, SI 1989/469 reg 2(1)
plan manager, SI 1989/469 reg 2(1)
plan shares, FA 2000 Sch 8 para 130
pleasure craft—
  (enterprise investment scheme), TA 1988 s 298(5)
  (entrepreneurs' relief) TCGA 1992 s 164N(1)
  (venture capital trust), TA 1988 Sch 28B para 5(1)
policy holders' fraction, TA 1988 s 431(2)
policy (insurance), TA 1988 s 466(2), Sch 15
  para 14
political party, TCGA 1992 s 264(8)
pollution of controlled waters, FA 2001 Sch 22
  para 31(1)
pooled fund, SI 2000/2316 reg 2(1), SI 2001/117
  reg 2(1)
post-war credits, FA 1972 s 131
pre-direction period (controlled foreign
  companies), TA 1988 Sch 24 para 9(1)
preference dividend, TA 1988 s 832(1)
preference share—
  (bonus issue), TA 1988 s 210(4)
  (pooling), TCGA 1992 Sch 2 para 8(1)
premises—
  (controlled foreign companies), TA 1988 Sch 25
    para 7(2)
  (Schedule A), TA 1988 s 24(1)
  (seizure), CJPA 2001 s 66(1)
premium—
  (agricultural buildings), CAA 2001 s 390(1)
  (industrial buildings), CAA 2001 s 326(1)
  (lease), TA 1988 s 24(1), (3)
premiums trust fund (Lloyd's)—
  corporate members, FA 1994 s 220(1)
  individual members, TA 1988 s 457(1); FA 1993
    s 184(1)
prescribed assets, TCGA 1992 ss 159
prescribed period (shares etc), TCGA 1992
  s 106(10)
pre-transaction ruling, PR 26/9/96
previous owner, TA 1988 Sch 28 para 4(3)
primary dividend (controlled foreign companies),
  TA 1988 Sch 26 para 6(1)(c)
primary fund, TA 1988 Sch 27 para 6(1)(a)
primary legislation, HRA 1998 s 21
primary period (charity: non-qualifying
  expenditure), TA 1988 Sch 20 para 11(a)
principal, TA 1988 s 23(7)
principal Act, TMA 1970 s 118(1)
principal company, TA 1970 s 272(1)(c)
principal member (controlled foreign companies),
  TA 1988 Sch 25 para 15(2)
principal private residence—
  (CGT), TCGA 1992 s 222(5)
prior five years (loss hobby farming), TA 1988
  s 397(5)
prior period of loss, TA 1988 s 397(5)
private travel, TA 1988 Sch 12A para 2(2)
private use, TA 1988 ss 159AC(5), 168(5)(*f*),
  (5A)(*f*)
Privy Council, IA 1978 Sch 1
process, PR 25/3/81
product obtainable from the living animal, TA
  1988 Sch 5 para 8(3)
production herd, TA 1988 Sch 5 para 8(5)
profit-related—
  pay, TA 1988 s 169(1)
  pay scheme, TA 1988 s 169(1)
profit sharing scheme (approved), TA 1988 s 187
profits—
  (capital gains tax), TMA 1970 s 29(8)(b); TCGA
    1992 s 170(1)

profits—*continued*
  (corporation tax), TMA 1970 s 29(8)(c); TA 1988
    s 6(4)(a)
  (income tax), TMA 1970 s 29(8)(a)
  (profit-related pay), TA 1988 s 169(1)
profits available for distribution (purchase of own
  shares), TA 1988 s 221(7)
profits chargeable to tax, CAA 2001 s 105(3)
profits or assets available for distribution (group
  relief), TA 1988 Sch 18 para 1(1)
proper officer (company), TMA 1970 s 108(3)
property development, TA 1988 s 298(5), Sch
  28B para 5(1); TCGA 1992 s 164N(1)
property investment LLP, TA 1988 s 842B(1)
protected leasing, CAA 2001 s 105(5)
provident benefits (trade union), TA 1988 s 467(2)
public company (profit-related pay), TA 1988
  s 180(4)
public lending right, TA 1988 s 537
public transport road service, TA 1988
  s 197AB(2)
public revenue, TA 1988 s 45
public revenue dividend, TA 1988 s 45; TA 1988
  s 512(3)
purchase of own shares, TA 1988 s 219(1)
purchased life annuity, TA 1988 s 657(1)
qualifying—
  accounting period (election for herd basis), TA
    1988 Sch 5 paras 2(6), 6(4)
  award (criminal injuries), TA 1988 s 329C(1)
  beneficiary, FA 1985 s 70(3)(b)
  body, FA 2002 Sch 12 para 18
  borrower (MIRAS), TA 1988 s 376(1)
  buildings, CAA 2001 s 393C(1)
  business activity, TA 1988 s 289(2); TCGA 1992
    Sch 5B para 19(1)
  certificate of deposit (deposit-taker), TA 1988
    s 482(6)
  company, TA 1988 s 298(3); TCGA 1992 s 164G,
    Sch A1 paras 6, 22(1), Sch 5B para 19(1);
    PR 2/12/96
  contract, FA 2000 s 107(7)
  convertible securities, FA 1990 Sch 10
  corporate bond, TCGA 1992 s 117
  disposal (retirement relief), TCGA 1992 Sch 6 para
    4(1)
  distribution (ACT), TA 1988 s 14(2)
  EEA investment company, SI 2001/117 reg 2(1)
  exchange of shares, FA 2000 Sch 14 para 60
  expenditure—
    (dredging), CAA 2001 s 485 (1)
    (flat conversion), CAA 2001 s 393B
    (industrial buildings), CAA 2001 s 292
    (know-how allowances), CAA 2001 s 454(1)
    (mineral extraction allowances), CAA 2001
      s 395
    (patent allowances), CAA 2001 s 468
    (research and development allowances), CAA
      2001 s 439
    trade, CAA 2001 s 469
  film, F(No 2)A 1992 s 43
  flat, CAA 2001 s 393D
  fund (offshore), TA 1988 Sch 27 para 6(2)
  holding (venture capital trust), TA 1988 Sch 28B
  hotel, CAA 2001 s 279
  individual (enterprise investment scheme), TA
    1988 s 291
  interest, TA 1988 s 356D(1)
  investment—
    (enterprise investment scheme), TCGA 1992 Sch
      5B para 1(2), (4)
    (entrepreneurs' relief), TCGA 1992 s 164A(8)
    (venture capital trust), TCGA 1992 Sch 5C para
      1(2), (4)
  lender, TA 1988 s 376(4)–(6)
  loan (capital gains tax relief), TCGA 1992 s 253(1)
  maintenance payment, TA 1988 347B(1)